PRONUNCIATION KEY

a	a as in **at, bad**
ā	a as in **ape**, ai as in **pain**, ay as in **day**
ä	a as in **father, car**
e	e as in **end, pet**
ē	e as in **me**, ee as in **feet**, ea as in **meat**, ie as in **piece**, y as in **finally**
i	i as in **it, pig**
ī	i as in **ice, fine**, ie as in **lie**, y as in **my**
o	o as in **odd, hot**
ō	o as in **old**, oa as in **oat**, ow as in **low**, oe as in **toe**
ô	o as in **coffee, fork**, au as in **author**, aw as in **law**, a as in **all**
oo	oo as in **wood**, u as in **put**
o͞o	oo as in **fool**, ue as in **true**
oi	oi as in **oil**, oy as in **boy**
ou	ou as in **out**, ow as in **cow**
u	u as in **up, mud**, o as in **oven, love**
ur	ur as in **turn**, er as in **term**, ir as in **bird**, or as in **word**
yo͞o	u as in **use**, ue as in **cue**, ew as in **few**, eu as in **feud**
ə	a as in **ago**, e as in **taken**, i as in **pencil**, o as in **lemon**, u as in **helpful**
b	b as in **bat, above, job**
ch	ch as in **chin, such**, tch as in **hatch**
d	d as in **dear, soda, bad**
f	f as in **five, defend, leaf**, ff as in **off**
g	g as in **game, ago, fog**
h	h as in **hit, ahead**
hw	wh as in **white, which**
j	j as in **joke, enjoy**, g as in **gem**, dge as in **edge**
k	k as in **kit, baking, seek**, ck as in **tack**, c as in **cat**
l	l as in **lid, sailor, feel**, ll as in **ball, allow**
m	m as in **man, family, dream**
n	n as in **not, final, on**
ng	ng as in **singer, long**, n as in **sink**
p	p as in **pail, repair, soap**
r	r as in **ride, parent, four**
s	s as in **sat, aside, cats**, c as in **cent**, ss as in **pass**
sh	sh as in **shoe, wishing, fish**
t	t as in **tag, pretend, hat**
th	th as in **thin, ether, both**
t͟h	th as in **this, mother, smooth**
v	v as in **very, favor, salve**
w	w as in **wet, reward**
y	y as in **yes**
z	z as in **zoo, gazing**, zz as in **jazz**, s as in **rose, dogs**
zh	s as in **treasure**, z as in **azure**, ge as in **garage**

School
Dictionary

Macmillan

School

Dictionary

Macmillan

William D. Halsey / Editorial Director
Christopher G. Morris / Editor

Macmillan Publishing Co., Inc.
New York
Collier Macmillan Publishers
London

Photo Credits: (top to bottom and left to right; all details of original photographs)

Page 1086 New York Public Library Picture Collection; Buffalo Museum of Science; page 1087 International Museum of Photography at George Eastman House; Marconi Co. Ltd., Marconi House, Chelmsford, Essex; United Air Lines Photo; Smithsonian Institution, Washington, D.C.; United Press International; page 1092 © 1979 Smithsonian Institution; National Geographic Photographer George F. Mobley, Courtesy U.S. Capitol Historical Society (ptg. by John Vanderlyn); page 1093 © Candace Cochrane; Library of Congress; National Geographic Photographer George F. Mobley, Courtesy U.S. Capitol Historical Society (ptg. by Howard Chandler Christy); National Archives; Washington University Gallery of Art, St. Louis, Mo. (ptg. by Bingham); U.S. Naval Academy (ptg. by Thomas Birch); page 1094 Courtesy of the New York Historical Society (ptg. by John Hill); Pana-Vue Slides; Culver Service, First National Bank of St. Joseph, Mo. (ptg. by Edward J. Holsag); page 1095 Art In The U.S. Capitol (ptg. by Francis Bicknell Carpenter), Gift of Mrs. Elizabeth Thompson; ptg. by Stanley Arthurs; Union Pacific Railroad Museum Collection; Sophia Smith Collection, Smith College; Brown Brothers; page 1096 United Air Lines Photo; Ford Motor Company, News Dept., Dearborn, Mich.; U.S. Army Signal Corps; Wide World Photos; Publishers Photo Service; U.S. Army Photo; page 1097 United Nations; Westinghouse; NASA; IBM; EPA; page P10 United Press International, National Portrait Gallery, Smithsonian Institution, Washington, D.C.

For maps and diagrams contained in the Reference Section, acknowledgment is given to Donnelley Cartographic Services.

Grateful acknowledgment is given to the following authors and publishers for permission to adapt information in preparation of the world languages map contained in the Reference Section of this Book: H. Fullard and H. C. Darby, **Aldine University Atlas**, George Philip & Son Ltd., London, 1970; **Pergamon World Atlas**, 1968 Pergamon Press Ltd. and PWN-Polish Scientific Publishers, Poland; J. H. Greenberg, **The Languages of Africa**, Indiana University, Bloomington, 1966; E. A. Gregersen, Language in Africa: An Introductory Survey, Gordon and Breach Science Publishers, Inc., New York, 1977.

For photographs of the Presidents of the United States, acknowledgment is given to the White House Historical Association. Photographs by National Geographic Society.

Library of Congress Catalog Card Number 80-81023

ISBN 0-02-195310-4

Macmillan Publishing Co., Inc., 866 Third Avenue, New York, New York 10022
Collier Macmillan Canada Ltd.

Manufactured in the United States of America

9 8 7 6 5 4 3 2

CONTENTS

EDITORIAL STAFF

PREFACE

The **Macmillan School Dictionary** is a special book designed to help you learn about the English language and use it more effectively. This book makes the study of words a fascinating subject that comes to life. As you grow familiar with the dictionary, you will find it to be attractive, interesting, and easy to use.

The **Macmillan School Dictionary** contains 65,000 entry words and 95,000 meanings. The words have been carefully selected to meet your needs. Vocabulary has been drawn from various sources. The most important source is textbooks. The editors studied and selected vocabulary found in the current textbooks of all major publishers. A second important source is literature—the novels, short stories, essays, poems, and plays that you read. Another source is current magazines and newspapers. Finally, the dictionary includes the terms and expressions that occur frequently in everyday conversation.

In the **Macmillan School Dictionary,** every entry word is defined clearly. The most common words have the simplest definitions. More complex terms are defined in a more sophisticated manner. Besides providing definitions, the dictionary offers 37,000 examples of words in context. These examples give you a better understanding of how words are actually used in sentences. The dictionary also contains 1,500 illustrations that clarify and extend definitions.

Other kinds of information are also provided in the dictionary. Etymologies, or word histories, of many entry words are clearly explained. Thousands of idioms are identified and defined. Notes on usage give important information on points of grammar. In addition, the dictionary includes many language study essays for selected words. These essays discuss a wide range of topics relating to the English language.

The **Macmillan School Dictionary** contains many more special features. Near the front of the book, the **Guide to the Dictionary** explains how to use the dictionary and offers practical exercises. The **Practice Pages** at the end of the book provide additional exercises to develop your dictionary skills. Finally, a new reference section toward the back of the dictionary contains world maps, information on world languages, an overview of United States Presidents, a summary of important historical events, and charts showing metric and customary weights and measurements.

The **Macmillan School Dictionary** is a valuable reference book. By using it often, you will learn a great deal about words, and you will develop the ability to communicate more effectively with others.

The Editors

SAMPLE PAGE

Main entry

cache (kash) *n.* **1.** a hiding place, especially for provisions or treasure. **2.** something hidden or stored in such a place. —*v.t.,* **cached, cach·ing.** to hide or store in a cache.

Syllable division

ca·jol·er·y (kə jō′lər ē) *n. pl.,* **ca·jol·er·ies.** persuasion by flattery, soothing words, or false promises.

Pronunciation

Cal·ais (kal′ā) *n.* a port city on the northern coast of France. It is the continental European city closest to England.

Definition

cal·i·for·ni·um (kal′ə fôr′nē ə m) *n.* a man-made radioactive element first produced in 1950. Symbol: **Cf**

cal·la (kal′ə) *n.* any of several plants that bear tiny flowers on a spike inside a showy white or yellow spathe. Also, **calla lily.**

Variants

cam·o·mile (kam′ə mīl′) *also,* **cham·o·mile.** *n.* any of several strong-smelling plants found in temperate regions, having flowers that resemble the daisy. The flowers of certain species are dried and used to make tea.

Part of speech

can·dle·light (kand′əl līt′) *n.* **1.** the light given by a candle or candles. **2.** twilight; dusk; nightfall.

cap·size (kap′sīz, kap sīz′) *v.,* **cap·sized, cap·siz·ing.** —*v.t.* to cause to overturn: *Rough waves capsized the boat.* —*v.i.* to overturn: *The boat capsized in the hurricane.*

Inflected forms

car·go (kär′gō) *n.* *pl.,* **car·goes** or **car·gos.** the goods or merchandise carried by a ship, plane, or vehicle: *The freighter carried a cargo of rice.*

caus·al (kô′zəl) *adj.* of, indicating, or acting as a cause: *There is often a causal relationship between poor study habits and poor grades.* —**caus′al·ly,** *adv.*

Run-on entry

cen·taur (sen′tôr) *n.* *Greek Mythology.* one of a race of creatures having the head, arms, and torso of a man, and the body and legs of a horse.

Subject label

Usage labels

cheap·skate (chēp′skāt′) *n.* *Informal.* a stingy person.

chem·ist (kem′ist) *n.* **1.** a person who is a student of or expert in chemistry. **2.** *British.* another word for **druggist.**

civ·ics (siv′iks) *n., pl.* the study of the function, services, and purpose of a government and of the duties, rights, and privileges of citizenship. ▲ used with a singular verb.

Usage note

civil war **1.** a war between two sections or groups within a country. **2.** *Civil War.* in the United States, the war between the North and the South from 1861 to 1865.

Subentry

Illustration

clar·i·net (klar′ə net′) *n.* a musical instrument of the woodwind family, having a single-reed mouthpiece and played by means of finger holes and keys.

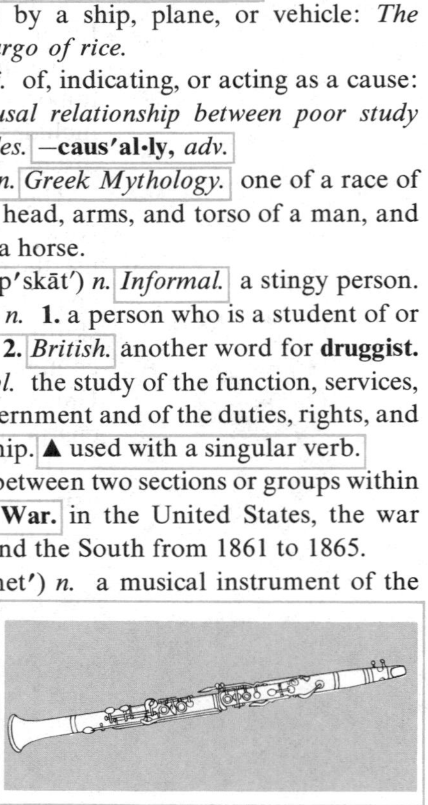

G8

clear·head·ed (klēr'hed'id) *adj.* not mentally confused; alert: *Although everyone around him panicked because of the fire, he remained clear-headed.* Illustrative sentence

clime (klīm) *n. Archaic.* country; region: *. . . that sweet golden clime where the traveler's journey is done* (William Blake). Quotation

clock·work (klok'wurk') *n.* a mechanism made up of gears, wheels, and springs, such as that which runs a clock or other mechanical device.

like clockwork. with great regularity, precision, and smoothness: *The robbers planned the holdup so well that it went like clockwork.* Idiom

com·et (kom'it) *n.* a bright heavenly body made up of ice, frozen gases, and dust particles, and having a long, visible tail that points away from the sun. A comet travels around the sun in an elliptical orbit. [Old French *comete,* going back to Greek *komētes* having long hair; referring to the fact that the tail of a comet looks like long strands of hair.] Etymology

●The name **Connecticut** comes from an Algonquian word meaning "beside the long tidal river" and indicated the area near what is now the Connecticut River. Settlers used the name for the river itself and later for nearby settlements, the colony, and eventually the state. Language note

connective tissue, tissue found throughout the body that serves to connect and support other tissues and organs. Compound entry

Cor·o·na·do, Fran·cis·co Vás·quez de (kôr' ə nä'dō; fran sis'kō väs'kes dā) 1500?–1544, Spanish explorer of southwestern North America. Biographical entry

Cos·ta Ri·ca (kos'tə rē'kə) a country in Central America, between Nicaragua and Panama. Capital, San José. Area, 19,575 sq. mi. Pop. (1971 est.), 1,790,000. —**Costa Rican.** Geographical entry

cot[1] (kot) *n.* a narrow bed, especially one made of canvas stretched on a folding frame. [Hindi *khat* bed, couch.]

cot[2] (kot) *n.* **1.** a small house; cottage. **2.** a small structure for shelter or protection, especially one for animals. [Old English *cot* cottage.] Homographs with superscript numbers

cu. in., cubic inch; cubic inches. Abbreviation

-cy *suffix* (used to form nouns) **1.** the quality, state, condition, or fact of being: *bankruptcy.* **2.** the office, position, or rank of: *captaincy.* Suffix

cy·clo·pe·di·a (sī'klə pē'dē ə) *also,* **cy·clo·pae·di·a.** *n.* another word for **encyclopedia.** Cross reference

GUIDE TO THE DICTIONARY

Using Your Dictionary

The purpose of the **Macmillan School Dictionary** is to serve as a reference source of information about words in the English language. The dictionary, however, is only a valuable tool if it is used correctly. Just as there is a proper way to use an encyclopedia or an atlas, there is also a proper way to use the dictionary.

The pages that follow explain how to use the **Macmillan School Dictionary.** These explanatory pages are divided into two parts. The first part tells about locating the different types of words in the dictionary. It explains how to use the guide words and alphabetical listings on each page. It also explains how to recognize and locate compound entries, inflected forms, plurals, and abbreviations. In addition, you will learn how to locate words even when you are unable to spell them.

The second part of the introduction discusses the additional information that the dictionary provides for each word. This section tells about the spelling, syllable division, and pronunciation of words. It discusses multiple meanings, special labels and terms, word usage, etymologies, and illustrations.

By reading the pages that follow, you will prepare yourself to use the **Macmillan School Dictionary** most effectively. You will be able to take fullest advantage of all the information that the dictionary provides.

MAIN ENTRIES AND HOW TO FIND THEM

The Main Entry

Think of your dictionary as a long list of words. Each word in the list is called a **main entry.** Main entries are printed in a heavy black type called **boldface type.** Look for main entries at the left-hand margin of each column.

Information about a main entry follows it in lighter type. The main entry, plus this information, make up what we call an **entry.** In the examples below, **bumblebee, bump, bumper, bumpkin, bumptious,** and **bumpy** are main entries.

bum·ble·bee (bum′bəl bē′) *n.* any of several species of thick-bodied, hairy bees closely related to honeybees. Bumblebees make a loud humming sound.

bump (bump) *v.i.* **1.** to strike or knock suddenly; collide: *The two cars bumped into each other.* **2.** to move with a bump or series of bumps: *The wagon bumped down the dirt road.* —*v.t.* to hit suddenly; knock against: *He bumped his knee on the chair.* —*n.* **1.** a heavy blow or jolt; thump: *The bump on his head knocked him out.* **2.** a swelling or lump: *Mike had a bump on his forehead from the blow.* **3.** any uneven part that rises above the surrounding surface: *a bump in a road.*

Bumblebee

bump·er (bum′pər) *n.* **1.** a heavy metal bar or strip attached to the front and rear ends of a car or truck to protect the body of the vehicle against damage or shock. **2.** a cup or glass filled to the brim, especially when drunk as a toast. —*adj.* very large or abundant: *a bumper crop of wheat.*

bump·kin (bump′kin) *n.* a simple or awkward fellow from the country.

bump·tious (bump′shəs) *adj.* unpleasantly bold or conceited. —**bump′tious·ly,** *adv.* —**bump′tious·ness,** *n.*

bump·y (bum′pē) *adj.,* **bump·i·er, bump·i·est. 1.** having bumps; full of bumps: *a bumpy piece of wood.* **2.** causing bumps or jolts: *a bumpy road.* –**bum′pi·ly,** *adv.* —**bump′i·ness,** *n.*

Bumper

Alphabetical Order

Main entries are arranged in alphabetical order. All the main entries that start with **a** are listed together at the beginning of the book. All the main entries that begin with **b** come next. Then come the **c** entries, and so on through **z**.

All the entries under each letter of the alphabet are arranged in alphabetical order, too, letter by letter. All the letters in the **a** section of your dictionary start with the same first letter. The second letter decides the order of words in the list:

already   arrive
a**m**   a**u**tomobile

The word **already** comes before **am** because **l** comes before **m** in the alphabet.

Sometimes the second or third letter or even the fourth letter is the same. Then you have to look at a letter even farther along in the word:

an**t**   anyone   anteater
an**x**ious   any**p**lace   ante**l**ope
an**y**   any**t**hing   ante**n**na

Groups of main entries starting with **b, c,** and other letters are alphabetized in exactly the same way.

TRY THIS 1

See how well you really know the alphabet. Arrange the words in each column so they are in correct alphabetical order.

1. claim	2. creak	3. computer
clue	crew	company
clean	credit	complete
cliff	creek	compound

4. Now arrange all the words in one longer list as they should appear in your dictionary.

Using Quarters of the Dictionary

Main entries are fairly easy to find in the **Macmillan School Dictionary** when you know alphabetical order and when you know how to spell the word you need. This section of the **Guide** will show you how to locate words quickly and easily.

Suppose you want to look up the word **sight.** You know that you have to look in the section of the dictionary with all the **s** words. But do you know how to open the book to the **s** section, or at least to a nearby letter? Would you find the **s** words nearer the front or nearer the back of your dictionary? Open the book to where you think **s** is. See whether you were correct.

Words beginning with **a** or **z** are easy. But the farther you get from the ends of the alphabet, the harder it is to decide just where to open your dictionary. Searching through the book wastes a lot of time, so it helps to have a plan. You need to have a good idea of where to find words beginning with each letter. Index tabs showing the first letter in each section are helpful, if your dictionary has them.

The middle of the alphabet comes between **m** and **n.** So you might think that the middle of the dictionary should come between **m** words and **n** words.

abcdefghijklm   /   nopqrstuvwxyz

Then try this. Divide 1064, the total number of entry pages in the **Macmillan School Dictionary,** by 2. Check to see what kind of main entries are on page 532. You will find that you are not at the exact middle of the alphabet. You are in the first half, among the **l** words. This is because letters of the alphabet don't all have the same number of entries.

TRY THIS 2

1. Look up the following letter sections. How many pages of entries does each one have?

   Q   D   A   M

   C   S   Z   X

2. Which two letters have the most entries?
3. Which two letters have the fewest entries?

Here is a suggestion to help you open your book quickly quite near the section you want. Think of your dictionary as being divided into four equal parts, or quarters. About one-fourth of the pages in the book are in each quarter. Here is how the letters of the alphabet group when the book is divided into quarters:

First Quarter: ABCD

Second Quarter: EFGHIJKL

Third Quarter: MNOPQR

Fourth Quarter: STUVWXYZ

Learn how these quarter divisions work. They can work like signposts that direct you to the part of the dictionary you want. To find the word **sight,** for example, think "**S** is in the fourth quarter. It comes just before **t,** so I must look three-quarters of the way through my dictionary." Try this. See if you can open your book to the **s** words.

TRY THIS 3

In which quarter would you find each of the following words?

1. car   2. pudding   3. gnu   4. kangaroo   5. water

Now see if you can open your dictionary to the letter section in which each appears.

Guide Words

You can open your dictionary fairly close to the letter section you want by using the quarter divisions. Here is an example. Suppose you are looking for **sight,** and you open to the **t** words instead of the **s** words. You know that **s** words come before **t** words, so you would just turn back a few pages. But, once you find the **s** words, what should your next step be?

Your **Macmillan School Dictionary** provides another kind of signpost to help you find the word you are looking for. You do not have to search through every page in the **s** section to find **sight.** Look at the top outer corner of each page. There you will find pairs of words:

shovelful/shrink   sidelong/sign   signal/sill

These pairs of words are **guide words.** The first guide word on a page tells you the *first* main entry that appears on the page. The other guide word tells you the *last* main entry that appears on the page. Look at the guide words **shovelful/shrink. Sight** cannot be on that page. **Sight** comes after **shrink** in alphabetical order, so you must look farther on. Next, look at the guide words **signal/sill. Sight** cannot be on this page either. **Sight** comes before **signal** in alphabetical order. You will find **sight** on the page with the guide words **sidelong/sign. Sight** comes between these two entries in alphabetical order. Once you find the right page by using the guide words, look through the main entries. Think about alphabetical order.

Now look in your dictionary for **sight.** Use the "quarters" plan and the guide words to find it quickly.

TRY THIS 4

Look up each of the following main entries in your dictionary. Write each word. Next to it write the guide words for the page.

1. dinner	2. panther	3. stork
4. crocodile	5. lion	6. lark
7. lizard	8. leopard	9. earthquake
10. turtle	11. tiger	12. roadrunner

Spelling Entries Correctly

If you can spell a main entry, you should be able to find it in the **Macmillan School Dictionary.** But finding a word that you do not know how to spell can be a problem. The *Table of English Spellings* can help.

Suppose you want to know something about the spice **cinnamon.** You decide to look up the word in the dictionary. Many people have trouble spelling **cinnamon.** What can you do if you do not know how to spell it? You might guess. **Cinnamon** begins with an **s** sound, so you might look for it first in the **s** section. You could try **sinamon, sinnamon,** or **sinnemin.** But you would not find the word you want.

Turn to the *Table of English Spellings* on pages G38-G39 of this **Guide.** The table matches the sounds of English with all the letters that can stand for the sounds. The first sound in **cinnamon** is **s,** so find this sound first. You will find several spellings for it: **s, c, ps, sc, sch, ss.** Make a list of these spellings. The short **i** is the next sound, so list the possible spellings for this sound. Then list the possible spellings for each sound in the rest of the word. Put the spellings together in different ways. Check the words you make in the dictionary. Since the most common spellings are given first and since you have already looked in the **s**'s, you should next look under the **c**'s. In this way, you will find the correct spelling.

TRY THIS 5

Use your dictionary to check the spellings of the words below. Some of the words are spelled correctly. Then use the Table of English Spellings to find the correct spelling of words spelled incorrectly. Write each word.

1. orkid
2. frajel
3. aker
4. strength
5. misterious
6. oficer
7. skeleton
8. reddish
9. vacant
10. alluminim
11. senery
12. fonograf

KINDS OF MAIN ENTRIES

Most of the main entries in this dictionary are single words, such as **bicycle, sight,** and **green.** You have already learned how these words are alphabetized. You have also learned how to find them easily. But some main entries are made up of more than one word, and others are only parts of words. Here are some of these other kinds of main entries.

Compound Entries

A **compound entry** is a phrase made up of two or more words. Compound entries are included in this dictionary because they have special meanings. For example, a **hot dog** is not a **dog** that is **hot**. A **spelling bee** is not a **bee** that knows how to **spell**.

Compound entries are alphabetized as if they were just one word with no spaces in between.

Find three compound entries below.

cloud	room
cloud chamber	room and board
cloudless	roomer
cloudy	rooming house

You will find some phrases that you cannot understand even though you understand every word in the phrase. There is a separate compound entry for phrases like these. You may know the meaning of the word **black** and the word **sheep**, but these meanings do not explain what a **black sheep** is. You must look up the separate main entry for **black sheep.**

> **black sheep,** a person who is regarded as a disgrace or discredit by the other members of the person's family or group.

Not all phrases are compound entries. Phrases such as **baseball glove** and **motor oil** are not shown as compound entries because you can easily understand what they mean by looking up each word. A **baseball glove** is a glove used in playing baseball, and **motor oil** is oil for a motor. So, if you are trying to understand a phrase that does not appear in the dictionary as a separate entry, look up each word. By taking the meanings of these words and putting them together, you will know what the phrase means.

TRY THIS 6

Copy the phrases below. Write "compound" next to the compound entries. Remember, a compound entry is a phrase that has a special meaning.

1. sweet potato	2. red tape
3. sweet candy	4. blue string
5. business office	6. cottage cheese
7. post office	8. toasted cheese
9. Little League	10. white cat
11. basketball league	12. white elephant
13. fried egg	14. acid test
15. nest egg	16. history test

Now look up the phrases. Which ones are entries in the dictionary? Did you guess right?

Abbreviations

Sometimes when you write, you shorten a word or phrase. Then, just a few letters stand for the whole word or phrase. For example, **Feb.** stands for **February,** and **jr.** stands for **junior.** These shortened forms of words are **abbreviations.**

Most abbreviations are followed by a period. This period shows that they are shortened forms. Abbreviations are alphabetized just as whole words are.

Find three abbreviations below:

Apr.	apse	astron.
apricot	apt.	astronaut
April	aptitude	astronautic
April Fool's Day	aptitude test	astronomer

Prefixes and Suffixes

Some main entries are not words at all. They are only prefixes and suffixes, or parts of words. A word part that is added to the end of a word is called a **suffix.** A word part that is added to the beginning of a word is called a **prefix.** You will find these prefixes and suffixes in the dictionary because they help to form words. Many of our words are formed by adding word parts to words. For example, if you add the suffix **-ness** to the word **cold,** you get a new word, **coldness.** If you add the prefix **un-** to the word **happy,** you get **unhappy.**

TRY THIS 7

1. Copy the words listed under the suffixes **-ness, -ly, -ment,** and **-er.** Then add the suffix to the words listed to make other words.

-ness	-ly	-ment	-er
careful	new	amaze	build
glad	sad	disappoint	jump
light	soft	improve	play
quick	year	measure	read

2. Now add the prefixes **un-, re-, pre-,** and **post-** to the words listed below each one. What words do you find?

un-	re-	pre-	post-
breakable	cycle	date	date
button	do	school	graduate
fasten	pay	view	script
grateful	spell	war	war

Prefixes and suffixes can be used to form a great many new words. You may sometimes come across words formed with prefixes and suffixes that you cannot find in your dictionary. You can figure out the meaning of such a word. Just look up the meaning of the prefix or suffix and the meaning of the basic word. For example, suppose that you read that a plant is "nonedible." This word does not appear in your dictionary, so you must look up its parts, **non-** and **edible.** They are entered in your dictionary.

  non- *prefix.* opposite of or lack of; not . . .

  ed·i·ble . . . *adj.* that can be eaten; fit to eat.

From these two entries, you can figure out what a "nonedible" plant is. It is a plant that cannot be eaten.

Geographical Entries

The main entry list also contains many names of countries, states, cities, lakes, mountains, and the like. These geographical entries are listed alphabetically under their actual names. Do not look for them under words such as *Mount, Cape,* or *Lake* that tell you what they are. For example, Mount Everest is listed in the **e's** as **Everest, Mount,** and Lake Superior is listed in the **s's** as **Superior, Lake.**

  Good Hope, Cape of a cape at the southernmost tip of Africa, on the Atlantic.

  Ve·su·vi·us, Mount (vi soo′vē əs) an active volcano in southern Italy, southeast of Naples. A major eruption occurred in A.D. 79, burying the ancient Roman city of Pompeii.

Biographical Entries

The names of many famous or important people appear as main entries in your dictionary. They are listed alphabetically by their last names. First names are not considered in alphabetizing. This means, for example, that Helen Keller is listed as **Keller, Helen,** and Paul Revere is listed as **Revere, Paul.**

  Ar·thur (är′thər) *n.* **1.** a legendary king of ancient Britain and the leader of the knights of the Round Table. The real King Arthur was probably a military chieftain who led the Britons against the Saxons early in the sixth century A.D. **2. Chester A.** 1830–1886, the twenty-first president of the United States, from 1881 to 1885.

  Night·in·gale, Florence (nīt′ən gāl′, nī′ting gāl′) 1820–1910, English nurse considered the founder of modern nursing.

Homographs

Many words in English are spelled in exactly the same way as other words. But they have different meanings and have come into our language in different ways. These words are called **homographs.**

Suppose you read this sentence in a story about olden times. "The knights put on their mail before the battle." You might find this sentence confusing if you think of **mail** as letters. That meaning of **mail** does not fit here. When you check your dictionary, you will find two main entries for **mail.** The meaning of the second entry fits the story.

> **mail**[1] . . . *n.* **1.** letters and packages sent or received by post. **2.** . . . [Old French *male* a bag, pouch; originally referring to the pouch in which letters were carried.]
> **mail**[2] . . . *n.* flexible armor for protecting the body, made of . . . rings of metal. . . . [Old French *maille*.]

In this dictionary, homographs are entered separately. They have a small number above and to the right of the main entry word. There may be two or more entries in such groups of homographs.

> **bow**[1] . . . *v.i.* **1.** to bend the head or upper part of the body forward in respect, submission, or greeting . . .
> **bow**[2] . . . *n.* **1.** a weapon for shooting arrows, consisting of a strip of flexible wood that is bent and held by a taut string connecting the two ends. **2.** a knot with two or more loops extending from it . . .
> **bow**[3] . . . *n.* **1.** the forward end of a boat, ship, or aircraft. **2.** the rower nearest the bow of a boat . . .

TRY THIS 8

How many kinds of entries can you identify? Match each entry on the left with the correct word or phrase on the right. Write each entry. Next to it, write the describing word or phrase.

1. anti-	one word entry
2. A.M.	compound entry
3. arm[1]	abbreviation
4. Audubon, John James	suffix
5. -ation	prefix
6. Azov, Sea of	geographical entry
7. apartment house	biographical entry
8. ax	homograph

Now rearrange the entries in alphabetical order.

Words that are *related to* main entries are often included in the information that follows the main entry. Such words are called **secondary entries.** They are printed in heavy black type that is slightly smaller than the type used for main entries.

Inflected Forms

In English, changes in the meaning of a word are often shown by changes in the form of the word. For example, to speak of more than one **country,** we change the word to **countries.** To show that an action happened in the past, we change the word **run** to **ran.** To explain how **long** one thing is when it is compared to other things, we say it is **longer** or the **longest.** These changed forms of a word are called **inflected forms.** The main word that is changed is called the **base word.** Four kinds of words can be inflected. They are nouns, adjectives and adverbs, and verbs.

Nouns

A **noun** is a word that names a person, place, thing, or idea. Base words, such as **girl, mountain, desk,** or **joy** name one person, place, thing, or idea. They are called **singular** nouns. When you want to name more than one, you use inflected forms of the nouns: **girls, mountains, desks, joys.** These are called **plural** nouns.

Most nouns form the plural by adding **-s** to the singular form. These nouns follow the regular pattern of the English language, so they are called **regular.** Regular plurals do not present any special problem in writing or speaking, so they are not entered. Nouns like **dog** and **king** do not have the plural forms as secondary, or inflected, entries.

Some nouns do not add the regular **-s** ending. The plural of **church** is **churches,** the plural of **jelly** is **jellies,** and the plural of **mouse** is **mice.** These plurals are *not* regular, so they are listed as secondary entries in your dictionary. They follow the abbreviation for noun, *n.*, and the abbreviation for plural, *pl.*

jel·ly . . . *n. pl.,* **jel·lies.**

TRY
THIS
9

Write the plural of the following nouns. Check your dictionary. Remember, if you don't find an inflected form listed for a noun, just add **-s** to make it plural.

1. wolf	2. moose	3. party
4. brother-in-law	5. bicycle	6. monkey
7. cupful	8. louse	9. house
10. fox	11. ox	12. deer

Adjectives and Adverbs

Adjectives are words that describe nouns or pronouns. **Adverbs** are words that describe verbs, adjectives, or other adverbs.

Adjectives and adverbs have two kinds of inflected forms. One gives the idea of "more." The other gives the idea of "most." Inflected forms that mean "more" are called **comparatives**. The comparative of **tall** is **taller**: Mary is **taller** (more tall) than Sue. The comparative of **fast** is **faster**: David runs **faster** (more fast) than John. Inflected forms that mean "most" are called **superlatives**. The words **tallest** (Ted is the **tallest** boy in the class.) and **fastest** (Joan reads the **fastest**.) are superlatives.

Most comparatives in English are formed by adding the ending **-er.** Most superlatives are formed by adding **-est.** Usually the spelling of the base word does not change. For example, **tall + -er** forms the comparative **taller. Fast + -est** forms the superlative **fastest.** These **-er** and **-est** forms are **regular.** They are not listed in the dictionary. Sometimes the spelling of a word changes when the comparative or superlative is formed. Then the inflected forms are entered in the dictionary.

> **hot** . . . hot·ter, hot·test.
> **hap·py** . . . hap·pi·er, hap·pi·est.

When the comparative and superlative of **hot** are formed, the **t** at the end is doubled. When the comparative and superlative of **happy** are formed, the **y** changes to **i.**

In a few cases, comparatives and superlatives are quite different from the root word. These forms are given in your dictionary.

> **bad** . . . worse, worst.
> **well** . . . bet·ter, best.

There is another way to show the idea of "more" or "most." Many words, especially long ones, sound awkward if you add **-er** or **-est.** You simply put the word **more** or **most** in front of the word. You say **more familiar,** not **familiarer.** You say **most valuable,** not **valuablest.** You can usually tell when to do this by thinking about how the words sound.

TRY
THIS
10

Write the comparative and superlative forms of the adjectives and adverbs below. Check with your dictionary. Remember, if you don't find inflected forms listed, just add **-er** and **-est.**

1. funny	2. old	3. small
4. sad	5. new	6. little
7. many	8. soon	9. big
10. few	11. late	12. large

Verbs

You remember that **verbs** are words that show action. Inflections are used to show when actions take place. If something is happening now, the present tense is used. For example: I **go** to school. We **grow** tomatoes in the backyard.

When you want a verb to show a time that is not the present, you use an inflected form. Your dictionary usually shows three inflected forms. They are the **past tense** (Last year I **grew** two inches.), the **past participle** (I have **grown** taller than Amy.), and the **present participle** (The corn has stopped **growing**.)

grow . . . grew, grown, grow·ing.

Sometimes the past tense and the past participle have the same form. (I **told** him to stop teasing me. I have **told** him to stop many times before.) Then, only one form is given for both of them. The present participle follows.

tell . . . told, tel·ling.

Most English verbs add **-ed** to form the past tense and the past participle. (He **painted** the boat. We have **painted** the walls.) They add **-ing** to form the present participle. (She is **painting** a picture.) These verbs are **regular.** Their inflected forms of regular verbs are not given in your dictionary.

If a verb does not follow the regular **-ed, -ing** pattern, the inflected forms are shown.

wade . . .wad·ed, wad·ing.
hur·ry . . . hur·ried, hur·ry·ing.
bring . . . brought, bring·ing.
go . . . went, gone, go·ing.

TRY THIS 11

Write the past tense, the past participle, and the present participle of each of the following verbs. Check with your dictionary. Remember, if you don't find inflected forms listed, just add **-ed** to form the past tense and past participle and **-ing** to form the present participle.

1. learn	2. find	3. add
4. run	5. lose	6. subtract
7. hit	8. put	9. multiply
10. take	11. push	12. divide

Derived Words

Earlier, when you read about the different kinds of main entries in your dictionary, you read about **suffixes.** You learned how suffixes can be added to base words to form new words. For example, when the suffix **-ly** is added to the base word **sad,** another word, **sadly,** is formed. The word **sadly** comes from, or is **derived** from, the word **sad.** So it is called a **derived word.** Derived words often appear as **run-on entries** in your dictionary. They are added, or "run-on," at the end of an entry.

> **sad** . . . *adj.,* **sad·der, sad·dest. 1.** feeling or showing unhap-
> piness, sorrow, or gloom. . . .—**sad·ly,** *adv.* —**sad·ness,** *n.*

The meaning of a derived word can usually be understood from the meaning of the base word plus the meaning of the suffix. The base word **row** means "to use oars to propel a boat." The suffix **-er** means "a person who carries out the action of a verb." So you know that a **rower** is "a person who uses oars to propel a boat." This derived word is not listed as a main entry. It is simply placed at the end of the entry for **row.**

> **row** . . . *v.i.* to use oars to propel a boat. —**row′er,** *n.*

Derived words have separate entries if they have special meanings or if the meaning is not simply the meaning of base word plus the meaning of suffix. For example, **racer** is a main entry. Its second meaning cannot be understood from the meaning of its base word **race** plus the meaning of **-er.**

> **rac·er** . . . *n.* **1.** a person or thing that races or takes part in a
> race, or is able to go very fast. **2.** any of a group of swift
> American snakes, especially the blacksnake.

When you want to find a derived word, look for it as a main entry first. If you do not find it, look for it as a run-on at the end of the entry for its base word. To find **slowly,** look under **slow.** To find **toughness,** look under **tough.**

TRY THIS 12

Find each derived word below in your dictionary. Write each word. Next to the word, write "run-on entry" or "main entry."

1. singer	2. skater	3. powerfully
4. nameless	5. primness	6. boiler
7. juiciness	8. loudly	9. sincerely
10. winglike	11. statement	12. researcher

Subentries

Sometimes a word is closely related to a main entry but is different in form. Then it may be a **subentry.** It may be the plural form of a singular entry. It may be the capitalized form of a main entry. It may be the small-letter form of a main entry that begins with a capital letter. It may be one word or more than one word.

> **lau·rel** . . . **1.** a medium-sized evergreen tree . . . **4. laurels.**
> an honor; distinction.

TRY THIS 13

Find the main entry for each subentry listed below. Write the main entry. Next to it, write the subentry.

1. beads
2. Derby
3. Revolutionary
4. the creeps
5. the Colonies
6. expenses
7. hades
8. sales
9. majors

Variant Spellings

Some words have more than one correct spelling; for example, **ax** and **axe.** In this dictionary, the more widely used spelling appears as the main entry. Other spellings are called **variant spellings.** They appear as secondary entries. The word *also* always comes before a variant spelling.

> **ax** . . . *also,* **axe.** . . .
> **dry·er** . . . *also,* **dri·er.** . . .

TRY THIS 14

Find one or more variant spellings for each of these words.

1. gasoline
2. rhyme
3. Romania
4. lollipop
5. theater
6. ameba
7. labeler
8. ketchup
9. grueling

Variant Terms

Sometimes two or more different words have exactly the same meaning. **Cougar, puma,** and **mountain lion,** or **geographical** and **geographic** are examples. The word that is used most is the main entry. The other words appear as secondary entries. They are called **variant terms** or **variant words.** A variant term appears at the end of an entry or at the end of a definition. The word "Also" always comes before a variant term.

> **cou·gar** . . . *n.* a tawny or grayish-brown wildcat of North, Central, and South America, having a small round head, long limbs, and a slender, muscular body. Also, **puma, mountain lion.**

ge·o·graph·i·cal . . . *adj.* of or relating to geography. Also, **ge·o·graph·ic** . . . .

pan·da . . . *n.* **1.** a bearlike animal native to the bamboo forests of southwestern China, having a shaggy white coat with black markings. Also, **giant panda. 2.** . . . .

Cross References

Full information about an entry is often given under another main entry. A **cross reference** in heavy black type shows you the main entry you must find to get all the information you want.

ar·che·ol·o·gy . . . another spelling of **archaeology.**
am·bus·cade . . . another word for **ambush.**
po·ta·to . . . **3.** see **sweet potato.**
For·mo·sa . . . another name for **Taiwan.**

TRY THIS 15

Look up the entries below in your dictionary. Write the cross reference for each word. Under that main entry you will find full information.

1. centre   2. angle worm   3. gaol
4. moving picture 5. possum   6. coco
7. armour   8. children   9. petrol
10. gym   11. Old Delhi   12. Rumania

Idioms

Another kind of secondary entry is the **idiom.** An idiom is a group of words whose meaning is different from the meanings of the separate words. The words **to break camp** do not mean to "smash up a tent and camping equipment." Instead, they mean "to pack up camping equipment."

Idioms are listed separately at the end of the main entry for their most important, or key, word. **To break camp** appears under **camp.**

TRY THIS 16

Look up each of the following main entries and read all the idioms listed. Select one idiom for each main entry and write a sentence using it.

1. go   2. ear[1]   3. bat[1]
4. hand   5. hook   6. head

WHAT THIS DICTIONARY TELLS ABOUT WORDS

You have learned about the kinds of words that can be found in the **Macmillan School Dictionary**—how to find them and how to spell them. Next you will find out what other kinds of information your dictionary gives about these words.

How to Divide Words

Syllable Division

When you are writing, you often need to divide words into smaller pieces, or **syllables.** Most main entries in your dictionary are divided into syllables by black dots.

> **in·for·ma·tion**
> **e·nough**
> **Al·a·bam·a**

Syllable divisions tell you where to divide a word that will not fit on one line. Suppose you are writing **information.** You discover that you must write part of the word on one line and the rest of it on the next line. You may break off **information** after **in-, infor-,** or **informa-.** Where you break it depends on how much space you have at the end of the line. Be sure to put a hyphen after the syllable to show that there is more to come. Never break up a word so that only one letter is left on a line. For example, do not divide **enough** after **e-** or **Alabama** after **Alabam-.** Many words in the dictionary are not divided by dots at all. Words like **awe, sweet,** and **bread** are not divided. This means that the word should not be broken up at all when you are writing.

> **TRY THIS 17**
>
> Divide each word into syllables. Write the words with the syllable divisions just as they appear in the main entries or secondary entries in your dictionary.
>
> | | | |
> |---|---|---|
> | 1. canoe | 2. comfortably | 3. chemical |
> | 4. elementary | 5. kindergarten | 6. houses |
> | 7. caterpillar | 8. chocolate | 9. barest |

How to Pronounce Words

Pronunciation

Your dictionary can be a great help when you want to know how to pronounce a new word. Suppose you read about **gneiss** (a kind of rock). You want to tell a friend about it, but you are not sure how to say the word.

Look up **gneiss** and find the pronunciation. It is shown in parentheses right after the main entry word.

gneiss (nīs)

Respelling

The pronunciation (nīs) is a **respelling** of **gneiss.** A main entry spelling often does not help you pronounce a word because the alphabet has 26 letters, but these letters can stand for 40 different sounds. A single letter may stand for different sounds. For example, **i** has one sound in **it,** another in **ice,** and another in **April.** The 40 different sounds of the alphabet can be spelled in about 250 different ways.

The first sound in **gneiss** can be spelled **n, gn, kn, nn,** or **pn.** So the way a word is spelled may not tell you how to say it. For this reason, the **Macmillan School Dictionary** respells words, using a special alphabet. These respellings help you match the sound of a word to its spelling.

The *Pronunciation Key* on page G40 and the page facing the front cover shows these respellings. Look at the left-hand column. Each letter symbol stands for only one sound. In the right-hand column are common words in which the sound is heard. The sample words help you understand the sound of the letter symbol.

You will find a shorter pronunciation key at the bottom of each right-hand page of the dictionary. It contains the most important sounds and the sounds that usually give the most trouble.

> at; āpe; cär; end; mē; it; īce; hot; ōld; fôrk; wood; fōōl; oil; out; up; turn; sing; thin; this; **hw** in white; **zh** in treasure. The symbol ə stands for the sound of **a** in about, **e** in taken, **i** in pencil, **o** in lemon, and **u** in circus.

To figure out the pronunciation of a word, go back and forth from the respelling to the pronunciation key. For example, the respelling for **gneiss** (nīs) begins with the **n** sound in **not.** It is followed by the **i** sound in **ice.** Then it ends with the **s** sound in **sat.** When you put these sounds together in the correct order, you will know how to pronounce **gneiss.**

TRY THIS 18

1. Write the respelling for each of these words. Think how each word is pronounced.

bough	slough[2]	tough
cough	rough	though
dough	sought	nought

2. How many sounds did you find for *-ough?*

Accent Marks

In long words pronunciations are divided into syllables. Then the syllables are separated by spaces. The syllables help you to figure out the word, piece by piece.

When you say a long word, you do not say each part of the word in exactly the same tone of voice. You say some syllables with more **stress,** or force, than others. When you say **private,** you put more stress or force on the first syllable. But when you say **provide,** you put more stress on the second syllable. An **accent mark** follows a syllable that is stressed.

> **pri·vate** (pri′vit)
> **pro·vide** (prə vīd′)

In some words more than one syllable is stressed. Usually one syllable receives more force than the others. We say this syllable receives **primary stress** and the other syllable receives **secondary stress.** Your dictionary shows primary stress with a heavy accent mark (′). It shows secondary stress with a lighter accent mark (′).

> **sub·way** (sub′wā′)
> **sub·sti·tute** (sub′stə tōōt′)
> **tail·gate** (tāl′gāt′)
> **tape·worm** (tāp′wurm′)

One-syllable words have no accent mark.

Schwa

The pronunciation key in this dictionary has only one symbol that is not an actual letter of the alphabet. That symbol is the **schwa.** It looks like an upside-down letter **e** (ə). The schwa can stand for any one of the five vowels when that vowel is not stressed. That is why the schwa is sometimes called the "unstressed vowel sound." Think of the way you say the vowel **a** in **ago, i** in **pencil,** or **o** in **lemon.** That is what schwa sounds like.

Pronunciation Syllables

The syllables of the pronunciation are not always the same as the syllables of the main entry. Syllables in the respelling are divided according to how a word is spoken, not according to how it is divided in writing.

> **lab·o·ra·to·ry** (lab′rə tôr′ē)
> **prac·ti·cal·ly** (prak′tik lē)
> **su·per·fi·cial** (sōō′pər fish′əl)
> **surf·cast·ing** (surf′kas′ting)

When you are writing and continue a word on the next line, use the syllable divisions of the main entry. When you want to know how to say a word, use the syllable divisions of the pronunciation.

Say these words aloud. Think about the way you stress the different syllables. Where should primary and secondary stress marks go in the pronunciation? Copy the pronunciations and add the stress marks.

1. **for·ty** (fôr tē)
2. **tel·e·phone** (tel ə fōn)
3. **be·gin** (bi gin)
4. **tem·per·a·ture** (tem pər ə chər)
5. **con·nect** (kə nekt)
6. **vol·ca·no** (vol kā nō)
7. **ho·tel** (hō tel)
8. **week·end** (wēk end)

Alternate Pronunciations

Different people say certain words in different ways. So some words have more than one pronunciation.

a·dult (ə dult′, ad′ult)
pa·ja·mas (pə jä′məz, pə jam′əz)

Usually the first pronunciation is the most common one, but sometimes other pronunciations are used just as often. Choose the pronunciation with which you feel comfortable. It will be quite acceptable. All of the pronunciations given in this dictionary are considered to be correct English.

How Words Are Classified

Parts of Speech

Words can be grouped, or classified, according to how they are used. When you talk about a word's use, or job, in a sentence, you are talking about its **part of speech**. This dictionary uses the eight parts of speech. They are **noun, pronoun, verb, adjective, adverb, preposition, conjunction,** and **interjection.** In addition verbs are divided into **transitive** and **intransitive.** Transitive verbs have a direct object. (Fred broke the glass.) Intransitive verbs do not have a direct object. (The dish broke when I dropped it.) The following abbreviations are used for the parts of speech.

n.	noun	**adj.**	adjective
pron.	pronoun	**adv.**	adverb
v.	verb	**prep.**	preposition
v.t.	transitive verb	**conj.**	conjunction
v.i.	intransitive verb	**interj.**	interjection

When a word has only one part of speech, the abbreviation for that part of speech follows the pronunciation.

how (hou) *adv.*
hug (hug) *v.t.*, **hugged, hug·ging.**

Sometimes a word is used as more than one part of speech. Then the abbreviation for each part of speech is listed before the meanings for that part of speech. A dash (—) comes before each different part-of-speech abbreviation to separate the groups of meanings.

> **mop** (mop) *n.* **1.** a cleaning device that has a bundle of coarse yarn, cloth, sponge, or other absorbent material fastened at the end of a long handle. **2.** . . . —*v.t.*, **mopped, mop·ping. 1.** to clean, dry, or wipe with a mop . . . **2.** . . .

When more than one part of speech is given, the first one is usually the one people use most often. The second one is the one people use next most often, and so on.

What Words Mean

Definitions

Your dictionary can help you in two important ways. It can help you to learn the meaning of new words, and it can help you to learn new meanings for words you already know.

You will find some words in your dictionary that have only one meaning, or **definition.**

> **flat·boat** (flat′bōt′) *n.* a large boat with a flat bottom and square ends, used for carrying freight on rivers or canals.

Multiple Meanings

Most words have more than one meaning. When a word has more than one meaning, the definitions are numbered within the entry. The most common meaning is placed first. The second most common meaning is placed second, and so on.

> **so·ci·e·ty** (sə sī′ ə tē) *n. pl.,* **so·ci·e·ties. 1.** human beings as a group; all people. **2.** a group of people forming a community and having common interests, traditions, and culture: *Our ancestors lived in an agricultural society.* **3.** a group of people gathered together or associated for a common purpose or interest: *John belongs to a literary society.* **4.** the wealthy or aristocratic members of a community; fashionable people as a group. **5.** companionship; company: *The family enjoyed his society and often invited him to dinner.* . . .

Suppose you read that "The young millionaire's party at the yacht club was attended by all of *society.*" Which of the above definitions of **society** would you choose?

Context

You were correct if you chose definition 4. The **context** helped you to choose the correct meaning. The context is a sentence in which a word is used. It makes the meaning of the word clear. In this case, definitions 1, 2, 3, and 5 do not fit the context as well as definition 4 does.

When you want to be very sure that you have chosen the right definition for a sentence, put the definition, or part of it, in place of the word in the context sentence. See if the sentence makes sense. If you use definition 4, your sentence would read "The young millionaire's party at the yacht club was attended by all of *the wealthy members of the community.*"

TRY THIS 20

Each underlined word below has only one part of speech, but it has more than one meaning. Look up the words in your dictionary. Write the word and the number of the definition that best fits the way the word is used in the sentence.

1. The antenna on Mr. North's roof blew away.
2. A good golfer handles a driver well.
3. Come listen to my new album.

For these underlined words, tell which part of speech and which definition best fits the way the word is used in the sentence.

4. Will you please sketch my dog?
5. I will skim the reference book for the information.
6. Mary blushed when she had to answer the question.

Illustrative Sentences and Phrases

At the end of many definitions in this dictionary, you will find **illustrative sentences** or **illustrative phrases.** They show how the entry word is actually used. From these examples, you can better understand the meaning of the word.

> **grat·i·fy** . . . **1.** to give pleasure or satisfaction to; please: *I was gratified by the news that my grandfather had recovered from his illness.*
> **haunt** . . . **2.** to come often to the mind of so as to trouble or bother: *Memories of the shipwreck haunted the old sailor.*
> **key** . . . **4.** something that leads to or is a way of getting something: *Hard work can sometimes be the key to success in business.*

How Words Are Used

The **Macmillan School Dictionary** uses special **labels** to give you extra information about many words and their definitions. Sometimes the word has only one definition, or the label goes with all the definitions. Then the label is placed near the beginning of the entry. When a label goes with only one definition of a word, it follows the definition number.

Subject Labels

Such labels as *Chemistry, Law, Sports,* and *Mathematics,* tell you what field of knowledge a word belongs to. They are **subject labels.**

> **Ar·gus** (är′gəs) *n. pl.,* **Ar·gus·es. 1.** *Greek Mythology.* a giant with a hundred eyes. . . .
>
> **balk** (bôk) *v.t.* **1.** to stop short and refuse to go on . . . **2.** *Baseball.* (of a pitcher) to make an illegal motion while pitching the ball with one or more runners on base.
>
> **al·ti·tude** (al′tə to͞od′, al′tə tyo͞od′) *n.* **1.** the elevation above any given point, especially above the earth's surface or sea level . . . **3.** *Geometry.* the perpendicular distance from the base of a figure to its highest point. **4.** *Astronomy.* the angle of elevation of a celestial body above the horizon.
>
> **Ju·no** (jo͞o′nō) *n. Roman Mythology.* the goddess who was the wife and sister of Jupiter and queen of the gods. She was also the protectress of women and marriage. In Greek mythology she was called Hera.

TRY THIS 21

Write the words below. Write the special field of knowledge that each word or definition belongs to. Check the labels in your dictionary.

1. tackle (noun 3)
2. ball (noun 6)
3. Gordian knot
4. equation (definition 1)
5. balance (noun 8)
6. life cycle
7. double time (definition 1)
8. pawn² (definition 1)
9. draft (noun 13)
10. Thor
11. green (noun 3)
12. family (noun 6)

Usage Labels

You cannot use all words and meanings for every situation. Some words that were common many years ago are rarely used today. Other words cannot be used in all forms of speaking and writing. Such words are given **usage labels** in your dictionary. These labels tell you when it is better to use other words instead. When a word or meaning does not have a usage label, you may use it in any kind of speech or writing

Archaic words or definitions are ones that were once often used, but they are no longer common. You will probably see them only when you read stories, plays, and poems that were written long ago. You would not want to use them in your own speech or writing. Archaic words are included in your dictionary to help you understand them when you find them in reading.

> **be·shrew** (bi shro͞o′) *v.t. Archaic.* to curse: *Beshrew me, if I would do such a wrong* (Shakespeare, *Othello*).

Informal words are often used in everyday speech. They are not found in formal writing, such as term papers, legal contracts, or scientific papers. For example, you would not use the same language when you talk on the telephone to a friend that you would use when you write a report for English class or for the school paper.

> **bag** (bag) *n.* **1.** a container made of paper, cloth, leather, . . .
> —*v.t.* **1.** to kill or capture (game) in hunting: *The hunter bagged three birds.* **2.** *Informal.* to seize or capture; trap: *The police officer bagged the thief.* . . .
> **to be left holding the bag.** *Informal.* to be left to take full blame or responsibility: *When my friend's ball broke our neighbor's window, he ran away and I was left holding the bag.*

Slang words and phrases are very informal. They can be used in even fewer situations than informal words and phrases. Slang words and phrases are usually colorful words. We pick them for special effect when we talk with family and friends. Slang words and phrases are not normally used in writing except in stories about people who use slang in everyday speech.

> **bang**[1] (bang) *n.* **1.** a loud, sudden, or explosive noise . . . **4.** *Slang.* a large amount of pleasure or excitement; thrill; kick: *My brother gets a bang out of riding on the roller coaster.*

The label *British* shows that a word, meaning, or spelling is common in Great Britain but is not widely used by Americans in their speech or writing.

> **lor·ry** (lôr′ē) . . . **2.** *British.* a truck.
> **col·our** (kul′ər) *British.* another spelling of **color.**
> **ar·mor** (är′mər) *also, British,* **ar·mour.**

TRY THIS 22

Look up each item below and tell whether it is **informal, slang, archaic,** or **British.** Write each word and its label.

1. centre	2. betimes
3. scary	4. gabby
5. crackpot	6. gaol
7. snooze	8. to mean business
9. shady (adjective - definition 3)	10. get-up
11. letup	12. bite (noun - definition 4)
13. mutt	14. beef (noun - definition 3)
15. petrol	16. to beef up
17. goon	18. lift (noun - definition 6)
19. on deck	20. dough (definition 3)

How to Choose Your Words

Usage Notes

Usage labels tell you special ways and situations in which words are used. **Usage notes** tell you how educated speakers and writers use words in current English. Usage notes are introduced by a dark triangle (▲).

> **ain't** (ānt) **1.** am not. **2.** is not; are not. **3.** has not; have not.
> ▲ **Ain't** is not considered to be good English by most people. Because of this, careful speakers try to avoid using *ain't*.

> **none** (nun) *pron.* . . . . ▲ In the past, **none** was used only or mainly with a singular verb: *None of his friends has ever been to Paris*. In current usage, **none** is also used with a plural verb: *None of the passengers were aware of the danger.* —*adv.* . . . .

Other kinds of usage notes explain the difference between words that are easily confused.

> ▲ **Adapt** and **adopt** have different meanings, but they are often confused because they are spelled and pronounced in somewhat the same way. **Adapt** means to change something so that it can be used for another purpose: *The writer adapted his novel for a television script*. **Adopt** means to take something for one's own: *The school adopted the name "Wildcats" as a nickname for its football team.*

> ▲ **Affect** and **effect** sound the same and have the same basic meaning, but they belong to different parts of speech and should not be confused. **Affect** is a verb: *Daily exercise will affect your health*. **Effect** is most commonly used as a noun: *Daily exercise will have a good effect on your health.*

Where Words Come From

Etymologies

It is interesting to know how certain words came to be part of our language. Brief histories of where many words come from are included in your dictionary. These histories are called **etymologies.** Etymologies are placed in brackets [ ] at the ends of entries.

> **pas·teur·ize** (pas'chə rīz')*v.t.*, **pas·teur·ized, pas·teur·iz·ing.** to heat (milk or other food) to a temperature high enough to destroy disease-producing bacteria and organisms that cause food spoilage. [From Louis *Pasteur,* who invented this process.] —**pas'teur·i·za'tion,** *n.*

> **ted·dy bear** (ted'ē) *also,* **Ted·dy bear.** a toy resembling a small bear, usually stuffed with soft material and covered with furlike fabric. [From *Teddy,* a nickname of President Theodore Roosevelt; from a cartoon in which he was shown sparing the life of a bear cub while hunting.]

How to Learn About Words from Pictures

Illustrations

Pictures can often add to the understanding of a word that you get from the definition. The following examples show how your knowledge of a word can be increased by an illustration.

Read the entries below without looking at the illustrations.

> **ear**[1] (ēr) *n.* **1.** the organ of the body by which people and animals hear. In mammals, the ear has three parts: the external ear, the middle ear, and the inner ear. **2.** . . .

> **trampoline** (tram′pə lēn′, tram′pə lēn′) *n.* a piece of gymnastic equipment consisting of canvas or net attached by springs to a metal frame on legs, used for acrobatic tumbling.

> **gob·let** (gob′lit) *n.* a drinking glass with a base and a stem.

> **jave·lin** (jav′lin) *n.* . . . a lightweight metal shaft that resembles a spear. It is thrown for distance in athletic contests.

How is the **ear** divided into parts? What is the shape of a **trampoline?** How does a **goblet** compare with a drinking glass in shape? How is a **javelin** thrown?

Now look at the illustrations. Can you give a more complete answer to these questions now?

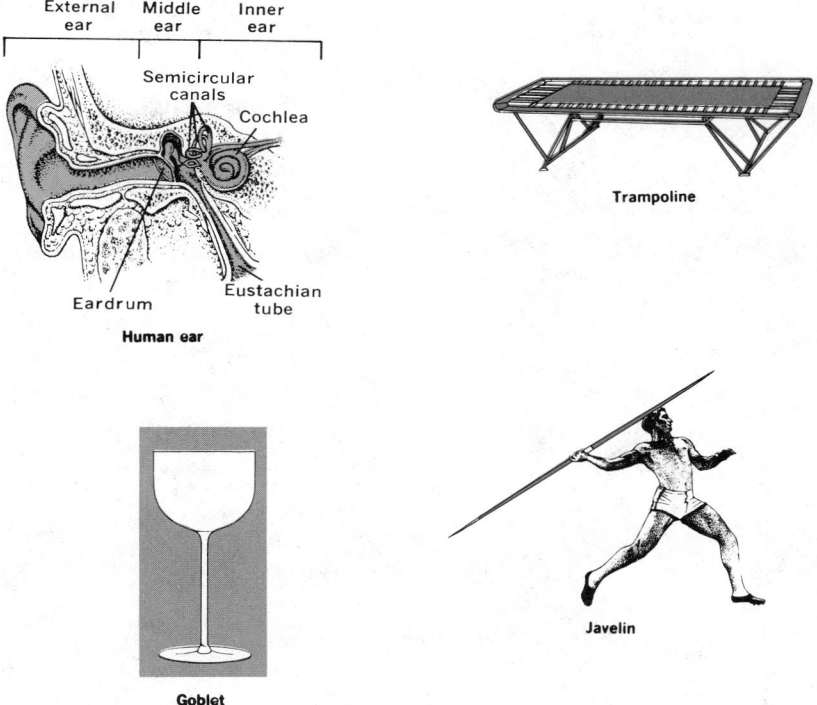

Human ear

Trampoline

Goblet

Javelin

How to Learn More About Language

Language Notes

You have now learned about many different kinds of information that you can find in the **Macmillan School Dictionary.** This dictionary also has a special kind of extra information. It is in the form of **language notes.** Language notes are short essays that tell you more about language than an ordinary dictionary entry tells you. Language notes are found throughout the dictionary below the entry words to which they are related.

Answer the questions below. Read the language notes for the words in parentheses.

1. In what year was the first English dictionary published? **(dictionary)**

2. What new word did Captain John Smith introduce into the English language? **(American English)**

3. What are the ten most commonly used words in English? **(frequency)**

4. How many words are there in the biggest dictionary ever made? **(Oxford)**

5. What word in English has the most different meanings? **(multiple)**

6. What king of England couldn't speak English? **(King's English)**

7. What did the famous dictionary maker Samuel Johnson say when asked why he had defined a word incorrectly? **(Johnson)**

8. How many different words did William Shakespeare use in his plays? **(vocabulary)**

9. What famous writer said that the word **fish** could just as well be spelled *ghoti?* **(spelling)**

10. Where does the name of your state come from? (Look up your own state's entry.)

A.D.	Anno Domini (after Christ)	pop.	population
adj.	adjective	prep.	preposition
adv.	adverb	pron.	pronoun
approx.	approximately	sing.	singular
B.C.	before Christ	sq. mi.	square miles
conj.	conjunction	St.	Saint
def.	definition	U.S.	United States
est.	estimated	v.	verb
interj.	interjection	v.i.	intransitive verb
n.	noun	v.t.	transitive verb
pl.	plural		

TABLE OF ENGLISH SPELLINGS

This table shows the different ways that sounds may be spelled in English. For each sound, the spellings are listed in the order they most frequently appear in

SOUND	SPELLING	EXAMPLE
a	a, au, ai	hand, laugh, plaid
ā	a, a-consonant-e, ai, ay, eigh, ea, ei, ey, au	paper, rate, rain, pay, eight, steak, veil, obey, gauge
b	b, bb	bit, rabbit
ch	ch, t, tch, ti, c	chin, nature, batch, mention, cello
d	d, dd, ed	dive, ladder, failed
e	e, ea, a, ai, ie, eo, u, ae, ay, ei, ue	met, weather, many, said, friend, jeopardy, bury, aesthetic, says, heifer, guess
ē	e, y, ee, ea, e-consonant-e, i-consonant-e, ie, ei, ey, ae, ay, oe, eo	he, city, bee, beach, cede, machine, field, deceive, key, Caesar, quay, amoeba, people
f	f, ph, ff, gh	fine, physical, off, laugh
g	g, gg, gue, gh	go, stagger, catalogue, ghost
h	h, wh	he, whom
hw	wh	wheel
i	i, i-consonant-e, a-consonant-e, y, ie, ui, ei, ee, e, ia, u, o	bit, give, damage, myth, sieve, build, counterfeit, been, pretty, carriage, busy, women
ī	i-consonant-e, i, y, igh, ie, ei, eigh, uy, ai, ey, ye, eye	fine, tiger, try, high, tie, stein, height, buy, aisle, geyser, dye, eye
j	g, j, dg, d, gg, di	magic, jump, ledger, graduate, exaggerate, soldier
k	c, k, ck, ch, cc, qu, q, cq, cu, que	cat, key, tack, chord, account, liquor, Iraq, acquaint, biscuit, bisque
l	l, ll	line, hall
m	m, mm, mb, mn	mine, hammer, climb, hymn
n	n, nn, kn, gn, pn	nice, funny, knee, gnome, pneumonia
ng	ng, n, ngue	sing, link, tongue
o	o, a	lock, watch
ō	o, o-consonant-e, oa, ow, ou, oe, oo, eau, oh, ew, au	so, bone, boat, know, soul, foe, brooch, beau, oh, sew, mauve

words. Use the table to help you locate words that you know how to pronounce but don't know how to spell.

SOUND	SPELLING	EXAMPLE
ô	o, a, au, aw, ough, augh, oa	order, fall, author, jaw, bought, caught, broad
oi	oi, oy, aw, uoy	foil, toy, lawyer, buoy
oo	u, oo, ou, o	full, look, should, wolf
o͞o	oo, u, o, u-consonant-e, ou, ew, ue, o-consonant-e, ui, eu, oe	tool, luminous, who, flute, soup, jewel, true, lose, fruit, maneuver, canoe
ou	ou, ow, ough	out, now, bough
p	p, pp	pill, happy
r	r, rr, wr, rh	ray, parrot, wrong, rhyme
s	s, c, ss, sc, st, ps, sch	song, city, mess, scene, listen, psychology, schism
sh	ti, sh, ci, ssi, si, ss, ch, s, sci, ce, sch	nation, shin, special, mission, expansion, tissue, machine, sugar, conscience, ocean, schist
t	t, tt, ed, pt, th	ten, bitter, topped, ptomaine, thyme
th	th	thin
t̲h̲	th	them, bathe
u	u, o, ou, o-consonant-e, oo, oe	sun, son, touch, come, flood, does
ur	er, or, ur, ir, yr, our, ear, err, eur, yrrh	fern, worst, turn, thirst, myrtle, courage, earth, err, amateur, myrrh
v	v, f	vine, of
w	w, u, o	we, queen, choir
y	i, y, j	onion, yes, hallelujah
yo͞o	u, u-consonant-e, ew, eu, ue, iew, eau, ieu, ueue	music, use, new, feud, cue, view, beautiful, adieu, queue
z	s, z, x, zz, ss	has, zoo, xylophone, fuzz, scissors
zh	si, s, g, z, zi	division, treasure, garage, azure, brazier
ə	o, a, i, e, ou, u, ai	lemon, ago, pencil, taken, furious, circus bargain

a	a as in **at, bad**
ā	a as in **ape**, ai as in **pain**, ay as in **day**
ä	a as in **father, car**
e	e as in **end, pet**
ē	e as in **me**, ee as in **feet**, ea as in **meat**, ie as in **piece**, y as in **finally**
i	i as in **it, pig**
ī	i as in **ice, fine**, ie as in **lie**, y as in **my**
o	o as in **odd, hot**
ō	o as in **old**, oa as in **oat**, ow as in **low**, oe as in **toe**
ô	o as in **coffee, fork**, au as in **author**, aw as in **law**, a as in **all**
oo	oo as in **wood**, u as in **put**
o͞o	oo as in **fool**, ue as in **true**
oi	oi as in **oil**, oy as in **boy**
ou	ou as in **out**, ow as in **cow**
u	u as in **up, mud**, o as in **oven, love**
ur	ur as in **turn**, er as in **term**, ir as in **bird**, or as in **word**
yo͞o	u as in **use**, ue as in **cue**, ew as in **few**, eu as in **feud**
ə	a as in **ago**, e as in **taken**, i as in **pencil**, o as in **lemon**, u as in **helpful**
b	b as in **bat, above, job**
ch	ch as in **chin, such**, tch as in **hatch**
d	d as in **dear, soda, bad**
f	f as in **five, defend, leaf**, ff as in **off**
g	g as in **game, ago, fog**
h	h as in **hit, ahead**
hw	wh as in **white, which**
j	j as in **joke, enjoy**, g as in **gem**, dge as in **edge**
k	k as in **kit, baking, seek**, ck as in **tack**, c as in **cat**
l	l as in **lid, sailor, feel**, ll as in **ball, allow**
m	m as in **man, family, dream**
n	n as in **not, final, on**
ng	ng as in **singer, long**, n as in **sink**
p	p as in **pail, repair, soap**
r	r as in **ride, parent, four**
s	s as in **sat, aside, cats**, c as in **cent**, ss as in **pass**
sh	sh as in **shoe, wishing, fish**
t	t as in **tag, pretend, hat**
th	th as in **thin, ether, both**
th	th as in **this, mother, smooth**
v	v as in **very, favor, salve**
w	w as in **wet, reward**
y	y as in **yes**
z	z as in **zoo, gazing**, zz as in **jazz**, s as in **rose, dogs**
zh	s as in **treasure**, z as in **seizure**, ge as in **garage**

1. **Semitic**	4. **Greek Ninth Century B.C.**
2. **Phoenician**	5. **Greek Eighth Century B.C.**
3. **Early Hebrew**	6. **English**

A is the first letter of the English alphabet. Since about 4000 years ago, the alphabet of every language that developed from ancient Semitic (**1**) has begun with a letter that looked like our modern capital **A**. In the Phoenician (**2**) and early Hebrew (**3**) alphabet, this letter was called *aleph,* meaning "ox." If you turn the letter **A** upside-down, you will see a design that looks like the head and horns of an ox. The Greeks borrowed *aleph,* reversed its design, and called it *alpha* (**4**). By the eighth century B.C., the Greeks were writing *alpha* (**5**) almost exactly the way we write the capital letter **A** today (**6**). Because it is the first letter of the alphabet, **A** is often used, as for marking schoolwork or for grading food, to show the first or highest quality or rank.

a, A (ā) *n. pl.,* **a's, A's. 1.** the first letter of the English alphabet. **2.** the shape of this letter. **3.** the first item in a series or group. **4.** the highest rating as a mark of excellence: *She got an A in history last year.* **5.** *Music.* the first and last notes of the scale of A major.

a¹ (ə; *stressed* ā) *indefinite article.* **1.** any: *A dog would love that bone.* **2.** one: *He won a hundred dollars.* **3.** one single: *There was not a person in sight.* **4.** one of a particular class or group: *The orange is a fruit.* **A** used before words that begin with a consonant sound: *a cat, a house, a youngster.* [Short for Old English *an* one.]

a² (ə; *stressed* ā) *prep.* to, in, or for each; per: *three times a year, two dollars a pound.* [Short for Old English *an* on, in, to.]

a- *prefix* in; on; to; at: *atop, aboard, afoot.*

a. 1. about. **2.** acre; acres. **3.** *Sports.* assist.

A 1. angstrom. **2.** argon. **3.** answer.

A-1 *also,* **A-one, A number 1.** *adj. Informal.* first-rate; first-class; excellent: *The athlete was in A-1 shape.* [From the rating *A-1* given in the *Register of British and Foreign Shipping* published by Lloyd's, a British insurance company, to ships in first-class condition.]

AA 1. Alcoholics Anonymous. **2.** antiaircraft.

AAA, American Automobile Association.

Aa·chen (ä′kən) *n.* a city in West Germany, west of the Rhine. It was once the capital of Charlemagne's empire. Pop. (1969 est.), 177,600. Also, *French,* **Aix-la-Chapelle.**

aard·vark (ärd′värk′) *n.* an animal having a long, sticky tongue and powerful claws, native to southern and east-central Africa. It feeds on ants and termites.

Aar·on (ar′ən) *n.* in the Old Testament, the elder brother of Moses and the first high priest of the Hebrews.

Aardvark

ab- *prefix* from; departing from; away from: *abnormal.*

A.B., Bachelor of Arts. Also, **B.A.**

ab·a·ca (ab′ə kä′) *n.* **1.** a large tropical plant bearing leaves from which Manila hemp is made. **2.** another word for **Manila hemp.**

a·back (ə bak′) *adv.* **taken aback.** suddenly surprised or startled: *I was taken aback by her angry reply to my question.*

ab·a·cus (ab′ə kəs) *n. pl.,* **ab·a·cus·es** or **ab·a·ci** (ab′ə sī′). a device consisting of a frame with balls or beads that slide back and forth in grooves or on wires, used especially for adding and subtracting. Abacuses have been used since ancient times and are still widely used in the Far East.

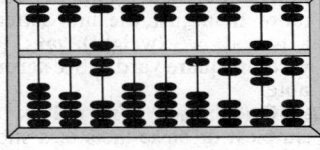
Abacus

A·ba·dan (ä′bä dän′) *n.* a city in southwestern Iran. Pop. (1966), 272,962.

a·baft (ə baft′) *prep.* in the stern or rear of a ship. —*adv.* at or toward the stern of a ship.

ab·a·lo·ne (ab′ə lō′nē) *n.* any of a group of sea animals that can be eaten, having an ear-shaped shell that is lined with mother-of-pearl and perforated along part of the outer rim.

a·ban·don (ə ban′dən) *v.t.* **1.** to go away from without intending to return; forsake completely; leave behind: *The sailors abandoned the sinking ship.* **2.** to give up (something) completely: *He abandoned all hope of making the football team.* **3.** to surrender (oneself) completely, as to an emotion or influence: *She abandoned herself to grief.* —*n.* complete surrender to one's impulses or emotions: *The lost child cried with abandon. The crowd*

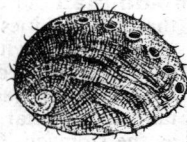
Abalone

cheered with abandon when the home team won. —**a·ban′-don·ment**, *n.*

a·ban·doned (ə ban′dənd) *adj.* **1.** left behind or alone; deserted; forsaken: *The boys spent the afternoon exploring an old abandoned house.* **2.** evil; wicked; immoral: *an abandoned life.*

a·base (ə bās′) *v.t.,* **a·based, a·bas·ing.** to lower in rank, position, or reputation; humiliate; humble: *The proud man refused to abase himself by begging.* —**a·base′ment**, *n.*

a·bash (ə bash′) *v.t.* to make embarrassed or ashamed; disconcert: *The boy was abashed by his error.*

a·bate (ə bāt′) *v.t., v.i.,* **a·bat·ed, a·bat·ing.** to make or become less in force, intensity, or amount: *The gale winds abated after several hours. Nothing could abate his rage over her insulting remarks.* —**a·bate′ment**, *n.*

ab·at·toir (ab′ə twär′) *n.* another word for **slaughter-house.**

ab·bé (ab′ā) *n. French.* a member of the clergy, especially a priest. ▲ used as a title of respect.

ab·bess (ab′is) *n. pl.,* **ab·bess·es.** a woman who is the head of a community of nuns.

ab·bey (ab′ē) *n. pl.,* **ab·beys. 1.** a monastery that is under the rule of an abbot. **2.** a convent that is under the rule of an abbess. **3.** a group of monks or nuns living in a monastery or convent. **4.** a church or other building that is or was part of an abbey.

ab·bot (ab′ət) *n.* a man who is the head of a community of monks.

abbr., abbreviation. Also, **abbrev.**

ab·bre·vi·ate (ə brē′vē āt′) *v.t.,* **ab·bre·vi·at·ed, ab·bre·vi·at·ing. 1.** to shorten (a word or phrase) so that one or more letters stand for the whole, such as *Feb.* for *February, pt.* for *pint,* or *G.B.* for *Great Britain.* **2.** to make shorter; shorten: *to abbreviate a speech.*

ab·bre·vi·a·tion (ə brē′vē ā′shən) *n.* **1.** one or more letters standing for the whole of a word or phrase. **2.** the act of abbreviating.

▲ Many **abbreviations** may be written either with or without periods. An abbreviation that is made up of the first letter of two or more words is often written without periods: *PTA* (Parent-Teacher Association), *UN* (United Nations), *mph* (miles per hour). An abbreviation that includes more than just the first letter of a word generally has a period: *wt.* (weight), *pres.* (president), *sq. yd.* (square yard or square yards). See **acronym** for an additional usage note.

ABC (ā′bē′sē′) *also,* **ABC's.** *n.* **1.** the alphabet. **2.** the simplest or basic facts of a subject: *to learn the ABC's of chemistry.*

ab·di·cate (ab′də kāt′) *v.,* **ab·di·cat·ed, ab·di·cat·ing.** —*v.t.* to give up or renounce formally (power, rights, or responsibility): *The aged king abdicated the throne in favor of his son.* —*v.i.* to give up or renounce power, rights, or responsibility, such as a throne: *King Edward VIII of Great Britain abdicated in 1936.* —**ab′di·ca′tion**, *n.* —**ab′di·ca′tor**, *n.*

ab·do·men (ab′də mən, ab dō′mən) *n.* **1.** the largest of the body cavities of man and other animals with backbones; belly. It is located between the chest and the pelvis and contains many vital organs, such as the stomach, the intestines, the kidneys, and the liver. **2.** the rear section of the body of an insect, spider, or crustacean.

Abdomen of an insect

ab·dom·i·nal (ab dom′ən əl) *adj.* of or relating to the abdomen: *abdominal pain, to have abdominal surgery.* —**ab·dom′i·nal·ly**, *adv.*

ab·duct (ab dukt′) *v.t.* to carry off (someone) unlawfully by force or trickery; kidnap: *The criminals abducted the child and held her for ransom.* —**ab·duc′tion**, *n.* —**ab·duc′tor**, *n.*

a·beam (ə bēm′) *adv.* **1.** alongside a ship, especially directly opposite the middle of a ship's side. **2.** at right angles to a ship's keel.

a·bed (ə bed′) *adv.* in bed: *He lay abed until late in the morning.*

A·bel (ā′bəl) *n.* in the Old Testament, the second son of Adam and Eve. He was murdered by his older brother Cain.

Ab·er·deen (ab′ər dēn′) *n.* a city on the eastern coast of central Scotland. Pop. (1971), 182,006.

Aberdeen Angus, any of a breed of beef cattle originating in Scotland and now raised in many parts of the world, having a stocky body, black hair, and no horns. Also, **Angus.**

ab·er·rant (ə ber′ənt, ab′ər ənt) *adj.* differing from what is usual, normal, or correct; abnormal: *The doctors noticed an aberrant pattern in the patient's heartbeat.*

ab·er·ra·tion (ab′ə rā′shən) *n.* **1.** a going away or differing from what is usual, normal, or correct: *His rudeness was an aberration of character; he is usually very polite.* **2.** a slight mental disorder. **3.** the failure of a lens or mirror to focus the light rays from an object at a single point, causing the formation of a blurred or otherwise imperfect image. **4.** an apparent change in the position of a heavenly body, caused by the movement of the earth that takes place between the time when light leaves the heavenly body and the time when it reaches the observer on earth.

a·bet (ə bet′) *v.t.,* **a·bet·ted, a·bet·ting.** to encourage or help, especially in wrongdoing: *She abetted the thief by refusing to tell the police of his whereabouts.* —**a·bet′ment**, *n.* —**a·bet′tor;** *also,* **a·bet′ter**, *n.*

a·bey·ance (ə bā′əns) *n.* a state of temporary inactivity or suspension: *Hold the decision in abeyance until we learn all the facts.*

ab·hor (ab hôr′) *v.t.,* **ab·horred, ab·hor·ring.** to feel disgust or hatred for; detest; loathe: *Joan abhorred all violence.* —**ab·hor′rer**, *n.*

ab·hor·rence (ab hôr′əns) *n.* **1.** a feeling of disgust or hatred: *He has an abhorrence of war.* **2.** something disgusting or loathsome.

ab·hor·rent (ab hôr′ənt) *adj.* causing disgust, hatred, or loathing; detestable: *Murder is an abhorrent crime.*

a·bide (ə bīd′) *v.,* **a·bode** or **a·bid·ed, a·bid·ing.** —*v.i.* **1.** to continue to live or dwell; reside: *to abide in the city.* **2.** to continue to exist; last; endure: *True courage will abide even in the worst of times.* **3.** to continue to stay; remain. —*v.t.* to put up with; bear patiently; tolerate: *The teacher could not abide rudeness in the classroom.* —**a·bid′er**, *n.*

   to abide by. a. to accept and obey: *You must abide by the rules of the game.* **b.** to live up to; carry out; fulfill: *John failed to abide by his promise.*

a·bid·ing (ə bī′ding) *adj.* continuing; lasting; enduring: *to have abiding faith in God.* —**a·bid′ing·ly**, *adv.*

Ab·i·djan (ab′i jän′) *n.* the capital of the Ivory Coast, a port city in the southeastern part of the country. Pop. (1970 est.), 460,000.

Ab·i·lene (ab′ə lēn′) *n.* a city in west-central Texas. Pop. (1970), 89,653.

a·bil·i·ty (ə bil′ə tē) *n. pl.,* **a·bil·i·ties. 1.** the power to do or act: *Man is the only creature that has the ability to speak.* **2.** talent or skill: *He showed great ability as a carpenter. Her abilities were evident in the high quality of her poetry.*

-ability *suffix* (used to form nouns) having the capability of being: *availability.*

ab·ject (ab′jekt, ab jekt′) *adj.* **1.** completely hopeless; miserable: *abject slavery.* **2.** low in character; base: *an abject liar.* —**ab′ject·ly,** *adv.* —**ab′ject·ness,** *n.*

ab·jure (ab joor′) *v.t.,* **ab·jured, ab·jur·ing.** to give up on oath; renounce: *He abjured his allegiance to the country of his birth.* —**ab′jur·a′tion,** *n.* —**ab·jur′er,** *n.*

ab·la·tion (ab lā′shən) *n.* a process in which a special protective coating on the nose cone of a spacecraft slowly melts away. It is caused by the heat produced when the spacecraft reenters the earth's atmosphere. As the coating melts away, excess heat is carried off so as to prevent damage to the main structure of the spacecraft.

ab·la·tive (ab′lə tiv) *n.* a grammatical case in Latin and certain other languages that indicates movement, direction, source, cause, and the like.

a·blaze (ə blāz′) *adj.* **1.** in flames; on fire: *The house was ablaze when the firemen arrived.* **2.** brilliantly lit; gleaming: *The Christmas tree was ablaze with colored lights.*

a·ble (ā′bəl) *adj.,* **a·bler, a·blest. 1.** having enough power, skill, or means to do something: *The child was able to read and write at an early age. An ostrich is not able to fly.* **2.** having or showing unusual ability, talent, or intelligence: *He is an able pianist.*

-able *suffix* **1.** (used to form adjectives from verbs) **a.** able to or capable of being: *eatable, tolerable.* **b.** worthy of being: *believable, laudable, commendable.* **c.** likely to: *perishable.* **2.** (used to form adjectives from nouns) **a.** worthy of or able to cause: *comfortable, objectionable.* **b.** tending toward: *peaceable.*

a·ble-bod·ied (ā′bəl bod′ēd) *adj.* having a strong, healthy body; capable of doing physical work.

able-bodied seaman, an experienced and skilled sailor in the merchant marine who has passed an examination on his ability as a seaman.

a·bloom (ə bloom′) *adj.* in bloom; flowering: *The lilacs are abloom.*

ab·lu·tion (ə bloo′shən) *also,* **ablutions.** *n.* a washing or cleansing of one's body or a part of it, especially as part of a religious ceremony.

a·bly (ā′blē) *adv.* in an able manner; skillfully: *Tom plays baseball ably.*

ab·ne·ga·tion (ab′nə gā′shən) *n.* the act of giving up one's rights, desires, or interests; self-denial.

ab·nor·mal (ab nôr′məl) *adj.* very different from what is normal, usual, or average; unusual: *This chilly weather is abnormal for July. It is abnormal for a person to be eight feet tall.* —**ab·nor′mal·ly,** *adv.*

ab·nor·mal·i·ty (ab′nôr mal′ə tē) *n. pl.,* **ab·nor·mal·i·ties. 1.** the state of being abnormal. **2.** something that is abnormal.

a·board (ə bôrd′) *adv.* in, on, or into a ship, train, airplane, or other vehicle: *That passenger came aboard in Chicago.* —*prep.* in, on, or into (a ship, train, airplane, or other vehicle): *The men loaded the cargo aboard the ship.*

all aboard. get in; get on. ▲ a call used to warn passengers that a ship, train, or other vehicle is about to depart.

a·bode (ə bōd′) *v.* a past tense and past participle of **abide.** —*n.* the place where one lives; dwelling; home.

a·bol·ish (ə bol′ish) *v.t.* to put an end to; do away with completely: *to abolish an unfair law.*

ab·o·li·tion (ab′ə lish′ən) *n.* **1.** the act of abolishing or the state of being abolished. **2.** *also,* **Abolition.** the abolishing of Negro slavery in the United States.

ab·o·li·tion·ist (ab′ə lish′ə nist) *n.* **1.** a person who is in favor of abolishing something. **2.** *also,* **Abolitionist.** a person who favored the abolition of Negro slavery in the United States before the Civil War.

A-bomb (ā′bom′) *n.* another word for **atomic bomb.**

a·bom·i·na·ble (ə bom′ə nə bəl) *adj.* **1.** very disgusting; hateful; loathsome; detestable: *The cruel dictator's treatment of his people was abominable.* **2.** very unpleasant, disagreeable, or distasteful: *He has abominable table manners.* —**a·bom′i·na·bly,** *adv.*

abominable snowman, a creature that supposedly lives in the Himalaya Mountains, often believed to resemble a bear, ape, or primitive man. There is no definite proof that it actually exists. Also, **yeti.**

a·bom·i·nate (ə bom′ə nāt′) *v.t.,* **a·bom·i·nat·ed, a·bom·i·nat·ing. 1.** to feel disgust, hatred, or loathing for; abhor; detest: *She abominates war.* **2.** to dislike strongly: *He abominates driving in heavy traffic.*

a·bom·i·na·tion (ə bom′ə nā′shən) *n.* **1.** something disgusting, hateful, or loathsome. **2.** a strong feeling of disgust, hatred, or loathing.

ab·o·rig·i·nal (ab′ə rij′ə nəl) *adj.* **1.** living or existing in a place from the earliest known time; native: *The Indians are the aboriginal people of America.* **2.** of or relating to aborigines: *The boomerang was originally an aboriginal weapon.* —*n.* an aboriginal person, plant, or animal.

ab·o·rig·i·ne (ab′ə rij′ə nē) *n.* **1.** one of the original or earliest known inhabitants of a country: *The aborigines of Australia are believed to be unrelated to any other group of people.* **2.** any of the original plants or animals of a region.

a·bort (ə bôrt′) *v.i.* **1.** to give birth to a fetus before it has developed enough to be able to live. **2.** to end something, such as a mission or project, before completion: *The pilots were given orders to abort because their plane developed engine trouble.* —*v.t.* **1.** to cause an abortion of. **2.** to end before completion: *to abort a space mission.*

a·bor·tion (ə bôr′shən) *n.* **1.** the birth of a fetus before it has developed enough to be able to live, especially when this is caused intentionally. **2.** something that fails to succeed, such as a mission or project.

a·bor·tion·ist (ə bôr′shə nist) *n.* a person who performs an abortion or abortions.

a·bor·tive (ə bôr′tiv) *adj.* **1.** failing to succeed; fruitless: *Until 1953 all attempts to climb Mount Everest were abortive.* **2.** *Medicine.* causing an abortion: *abortive drugs.* **3.** not fully formed or developed. —**a·bor′tive·ly,** *adv.* —**a·bor′tive·ness,** *n.*

a·bound (ə bound′) *v.i.* to exist in great quantity or large numbers; be plentiful: *Buffalo used to abound on the plains of North America.*

to abound with or **to abound in.** to be rich in; to be filled with: *The Amazon rain forest abounds with wild animals.*

a·bout (ə bout′) *prep.* **1.** in regard to; of; concerning: *We know about the plan. That book is about Abraham Lincoln.* **2.** connected with: *There is something strange about him.* **3.** on every side of; around: *A moat runs about the castle.* **4.** on the point of; ready. ▲ followed by an infinitive: *We are about to start on our trip.* **5.** around or over the parts of; here and there; in or on: *Wind scattered the leaves about the yard.* —*adv.* **1.** nearly; approximately: *There were about a thousand people in the crowd.* **2.** all but; almost: *We are about ready to go.* **3.** in several directions; all around: *to look about.* **4.** here and there; to and fro: *to wander about.* **5.** in or to the opposite direction: *Hearing her name called out, she turned about.* —*adj.* on the move;

at; āpe; cär; end; mē; it; īce; hot; ōld; fôrk; wood; fool; oil; out; up; turn; sing; thin; this; hw in white; zh in treasure. The symbol ə stands for the sound of **a** in about, **e** in taken, **i** in pencil, **o** in lemon, and **u** in circus.

astir: *He was up and about two days after he became ill.*

a·bout-face (ə bout′fās′) *n.* **1.** the act of turning around and facing in the opposite direction, as in a military drill. **2.** a change from one attitude of opinion to its opposite: *He has made an about-face in his political beliefs since he was a young man.* —*v.i.* **a·bout-faced, a·bout-fac·ing.** to turn and face in the opposite direction.

a·bove (ə buv′) *adv.* **1.** in, at, or to a higher place or position; overhead: *Stars glittered above.* **2.** in an earlier part of a book or other piece of writing: *See the examples given above.* —*prep.* **1.** over or higher than; rising beyond: *The building towered above the city. His voice was heard above the roar of the train.* **2.** superior to the influence of; not likely to stoop to: *She is above cheating on a test.* **3.** superior to in rank, position, or importance: *A captain is above a lieutenant in the army.* **4.** in preference to: *This above all, to thine own self be true* (Shakespeare, *Hamlet*). **5.** more than; over: *Anything above fifty dollars will be too expensive.* —*adj.* placed, written, or mentioned earlier: *the above explanation, the above example.* —*n.* something that is placed, written, or mentioned earlier.

a·bove-board (ə buv′bôrd′) *adv., adj.* without deception, dishonesty, or concealment: *All his dealings with us have been open and aboveboard.* [*Above + board;* from the idea that a person who plays cards with his hands *above* the *board,* or table, cannot cheat by changing cards under the table.]

ab·ra·ca·dab·ra (ab′rə kə dab′rə) *n.* **1.** a secret word that is supposed to have magic power. **2.** meaningless talk; gibberish.

a·brade (ə brād′) *v.t.,* **a·brad·ed, a·brad·ing.** to wear off or away by rubbing or scraping: *He abraded the skin on his knee when he fell on the sidewalk.*

A·bra·ham (ā′brə ham′, ā′brə həm) *n.* in the Old Testament, the ancestor of the Hebrew people.

a·bra·sion (ə brā′zhən) *n.* **1.** the act or process of wearing off or away by rubbing or scraping. **2.** a scraped area or spot: *He suffered abrasions on his face in the accident.*

a·bra·sive (ə brā′siv, ə brā′ziv) *n.* a substance used for cleaning, grinding, or polishing: *Sandpaper is an abrasive.* —*adj.* wearing away by rubbing or scraping; causing or capable of causing abrasion: *Sandpaper has an abrasive surface.*

a·breast (ə brest′) *adv., adj.* side by side and facing or moving in the same direction: *The troops marched two abreast.*

  abreast of or **abreast with.** up with: *A doctor must keep abreast of new developments in medical research.*

a·bridge (ə brij′) *v.t.,* **a·bridged, a·bridg·ing.** **1.** to shorten, especially by leaving out less important parts; condense: *to abridge a book.* **2.** to make less; lessen; restrict: *The king abridged the privileges of the nobles.*

a·bridg·ment (ə brij′mənt) *also,* **a·bridge·ment.** *n.* **1.** a shortened version of a book or other written work. **2.** the act of abridging or the state of being abridged: *The reporters protested that the new law was an abridgment of freedom of the press.*

a·broad (ə brôd′) *adv.* **1.** out of one's country; in or to a foreign land: *to travel abroad. He lived abroad for several years.* **2.** in circulation; current: *Rumors of victory were abroad.* **3.** over a large area; far and wide: *The good news spread abroad quickly.*

ab·ro·gate (ab′rə gāt′) *v.t.,* **ab·ro·gat·ed, ab·ro·gat·ing.** to put an end to by authority; abolish; annul: *to abrogate a law.* —**ab′ro·ga′tion,** *n.*

a·brupt (ə brupt′) *adj.* **1.** happening quickly or without warning; sudden; unexpected: *The bus made an abrupt stop in the middle of the highway.* **2.** impolite or blunt: *He has an abrupt manner of speaking.* **3.** steep: *The road makes*

an abrupt descent at the edge of town. —**a·brupt′ly,** *adv.* —**a·brupt′ness,** *n.*

Ab·sa·lom (ab′sə ləm) *n.* in the Old Testament, the favorite son of King David. He was killed after waging a war of rebellion against his father.

ab·scess (ab′ses) *n. pl.,* **ab·scess·es.** a collection of pus resulting from an infection in the tissues of some part of the body.

ab·scessed (ab′sest) *adj.* having an abscess: *an abscessed tooth.*

ab·scis·sa (ab sis′ə) *n. pl.,* **ab·scis·sas** or **ab·scis·sae** (ab-sis′ē). **1.** on a graph, the distance of a point from the vertical axis measured parallel to the horizontal axis, used to define the point in the Cartesian coordinate system. **2.** the line, number, or algebraic expression representing this distance.

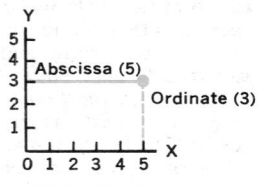

ab·scond (ab skond′) *v.i.* to go away secretly and conceal oneself, especially to avoid arrest: *The treasurer absconded with the company's funds.*

ab·sence (ab′səns) *n.* **1.** the state of being away or not being present: *His absence from work was caused by illness.* **2.** a period of being away: *The soldier came home after an absence of three years.* **3.** the state of being without; lack: *The absence of light in the room caused him to stumble against the table.*

ab·sent (*adj.,* ab′sənt; *v.,* ab sent′) *adj.* **1.** not in a certain place at a given time; not present; away: *She was absent from school because of illness.* **2.** not existing; lacking: *Gills are absent in an adult frog.* **3.** not showing any interest or attention; preoccupied: *She had an absent expression on her face.* —*v.t.* to take or keep (oneself) away: *He absented himself from the conference.* —**ab′sent·ly,** *adv.*

ab·sen·tee (ab′sən tē′) *n.* a person who is absent, as from work or school.

absentee ballot, a ballot that enables a voter who cannot be present at the polls to vote by mail.

ab·sen·tee·ism (ab′sən tē′iz′əm) *n.* habitual or repeated absence, as from work or school.

absentee landlord, a person who owns and rents land or buildings in a place in which he does not live.

ab·sent-mind·ed (ab′sənt mīn′did) *adj.* **1.** not alert to or aware of one's surroundings or actions; lost in thought; preoccupied: *She stared out the window in an absent-minded way.* **2.** likely to forget; forgetful: *The absent-minded man was always misplacing his personal belongings.* —**ab′sent-mind′ed·ly,** *adv.* —**ab′sent-mind′ed·ness,** *n.*

ab·sinthe (ab′sinth) *n.* a bitter, green liqueur with a licorice taste, flavored with wormwood and anise.

ab·so·lute (ab′sə lōōt′) *adj.* **1.** complete or perfect: *absolute purity.* **2.** free from all restrictions or limitations: *The king had absolute power over his subjects.* **3.** certain; positive: *We have absolute proof of his innocence.* —**ab′so·lute′ness,** *n.*

absolute alcohol, ethyl alcohol that is at least ninety-nine percent pure.

ab·so·lute·ly (ab′sə lōōt′lē, ab′sə lōōt′lē) *adv.* **1.** to the fullest extent or highest degree; completely: *The scenery was absolutely beautiful.* **2.** positively; definitely: *Are you absolutely sure of your answer?*

absolute temperature, temperature measured from absolute zero.

absolute value, the numerical value of a given number, whether the number is positive or negative. The absolute value of −2 is 2.

absolute zero, theoretically, the temperature at which

all motion of molecules in a substance would stop and it would have no heat whatsoever. Absolute zero is zero on the Kelvin temperature scale and is equal to −273.15 degrees centigrade, or −459.67 degrees Fahrenheit.

ab·so·lu·tion (ab′sə loo′shən) *n.* **1.** formal forgiveness of sins, especially by a priest. **2.** forgiveness of or freedom from obligation, guilt, or penalty.

ab·so·lut·ism (ab′sə loo tiz′əm) *n.* a system of government in which the power of the ruler is unlimited.

ab·solve (ab zolv′, ab solv′) *v.t.,* **ab·solved, ab·solv·ing.** **1.** to free from guilt or blame: *The thief's confession absolved the other man who had been suspected of the crime.* **2.** to set (someone) free, as from an obligation, duty, or responsibility. **3.** to forgive the sins of: *The priest absolved the man after he had confessed and done penance.* —**ab·solv′er,** *n.*

ab·sorb (ab sôrb′, ab zôrb′) *v.t.* **1.** to take in or soak up (liquid): *A sponge absorbs water.* **2.** to take up all the attention of; engross: *The fascinating book absorbed her.* **3.** to take in and make part of itself: *The Roman Empire absorbed many territories.* **4.** to take in (light, sound, or heat) without reflection or echo: *The walls of this building absorb sound.*

ab·sorbed (ab sôrbd′, ab zôrbd′) *adj.* very interested; preoccupied; rapt: *He was so absorbed in his book that he didn't hear me come into the room.*

ab·sorb·en·cy (ab sôr′bən sē, ab zôr′bən sē) *n.* the state of being absorbent.

ab·sorb·ent (ab sôr′bənt, ab zôr′bənt) *adj.* absorbing or capable of absorbing: *absorbent cotton.* —*n.* a material that absorbs: *Blotting paper is an absorbent.*

ab·sorb·ing (ab sôr′bing, ab zôr′bing) *adj.* very interesting; engrossing: *an absorbing film.* —**ab·sorb′ing·ly,** *adv.*

ab·sorp·tion (ab sôrp′shən, ab zôrp′shən) *n.* **1.** the act or process of absorbing: *Food passes from the intestines into the blood by means of absorption.* See **adsorption** for illustration. **2.** complete attention; engrossment.

ab·stain (ab stān′) *v.i.* **1.** to keep oneself from doing something; hold oneself back; refrain: *John abstains from eating certain foods when he's in training for the football team.* **2.** to choose not to vote: *In the United Nations voting, three neutral countries abstained.* —**ab·stain′er,** *n.*

ab·ste·mi·ous (ab stē′mē əs) *adj.* moderate or sparing, especially in the use of food and drink: *Since his illness my uncle has had to be more abstemious.* —**ab·ste′mi·ous·ly,** *adv.*

ab·sten·tion (ab sten′shən) *n.* **1.** the act or practice of abstaining: *an abstention from smoking cigarettes.* **2.** the act or fact of not voting: *There were eight votes in favor, six against, and three abstentions.*

ab·sti·nence (ab′stə nəns) *n.* the act or practice of doing without certain foods, drink, or pleasures, especially for religious reasons: *an abstinence from eating candy during Lent.*

ab·stract (*adj.,* ab′strakt, ab strakt′; *v., defs. 1, 3* abstrakt′, *def. 2* ab′strakt; *n.,* ab′strakt) *adj.* **1.** expressing a quality that can be thought of apart from any particular thing having that quality: *"Goodness" and "beauty" are abstract nouns.* **2.** not concerned with real or practical examples or instances; general: *abstract science.* **3.** relating to or designating a style of art that does not represent real objects directly, but uses lines, shapes, and colors to express emotions or ideas: *an abstract painting.* —*v.t.* **1.** to separate (a quality) from particular things having that quality: *to abstract the idea of coldness from all objects that are cold.* **2.** to make a brief account of (a book, speech, or the like); summarize. **3.** to take away; remove: *to abstract gold from ore.* —*n.* a summary of a book, speech,

or other work. —**ab·stract′ly,** *adv.* —**ab·stract′ness,** *n.*
in the abstract. without reference to particular examples or instances; in theory: *Wealthy people know poverty only in the abstract.*

ab·stract·ed (ab strak′tid) *adj.* lost in thought; preoccupied. —**ab·stract′ed·ly,** *adv.*

ab·strac·tion (ab strak′shən) *n.* **1.** the act or process of separating a quality from particular things having that quality. **2.** an idea formed in this way: *Heat, redness, love, and anger are abstractions.* **3.** an abstract work of art. **4.** the act of withdrawing or removing; separation.

ab·struse (ab stroos′) *adj.* hard to understand: *an abstruse poem, an abstruse scientific theory.* —**ab·struse′ly,** *adv.* —**ab·struse′ness,** *n.*

ab·surd (ab surd′, ab zurd′) *adj.* contrary to reason, common sense, or truth; ridiculous: *It is absurd to believe that the earth is flat.* —**ab·surd′ly,** *adv.* —**ab·surd′ness,** *n.*

ab·surd·i·ty (ab sur′də tē, ab zur′də tē) *n. pl.,* **ab·surdi·ties.** **1.** the state or quality of being absurd; foolishness. **2.** something absurd: *His theory about the origin of life was full of absurdities.*

a·bun·dance (ə bun′dəns) *n.* a quantity or amount that is more than enough; plentiful or overflowing supply: *The farmer had an abundance of food. The book contained an abundance of information.*

a·bun·dant (ə bun′dənt) *adj.* more than enough; plentiful: *The campers had an abundant supply of food.* —**a·bun′dant·ly,** *adv.*
  abundant in. having in great quantity: *The lake was abundant in fish.*

a·buse (*v.,* ə byooz′; *n.,* ə byoos′) *v.t.,* **a·bused, a·bus·ing.** **1.** to use improperly or wrongly; misuse: *The mayor abused his authority by giving all the important city jobs to his friends.* **2.** to hurt by treating wrongly; mistreat; injure: *The inmates of the prison camp were abused by the guards.* **3.** to attack with harsh or insulting language. —*n.* **1.** wrong or improper use; misuse: *a dictator's abuse of power.* **2.** cruel or rough treatment; injury: *During the trip over the mountains our car took much abuse.* **3.** a practice or custom that is unfair or that does harm. **4.** harsh or insulting language.

a·bu·sive (ə byoo′siv, ə byoo′ziv) *adj.* **1.** having or using harsh or insulting language: *an abusive political speech.* **2.** wrongly or improperly used; corrupt: *Putting the innocent man in jail was an abusive exercise of police power.* **3.** involving cruel or rough treatment; injurious: *Abusive handling ruined the camera.* —**a·bu′sive·ly,** *adv.* —**a·bu′sive·ness,** *n.*

a·but (ə but′) *v.i.,* **a·but·ted, a·but·ting.** to touch at one end or side; adjoin; border: *Our land abuts on the forest.*

a·but·ment (ə but′mənt) *n.* **1.** a structure on either end of an arch or bridge, used to support weight or resist pressure. **2.** something that abuts on something else.

a·bys·mal (ə biz′məl) *adj.* **1.** too deep or great to be measured; very deep; immeasurable: *an abysmal crevice in a glacier, abys-*

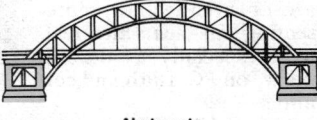

Abutments

at; āpe; cär; end; mē; it; īce; hot; ōld; fôrk;
wood; fool; oil; out; up; turn; sing; thin; **this**;
hw in white; zh in treasure. The symbol ə
stands for the sound of **a** in about, **e** in taken,
i in pencil, **o** in lemon, and **u** in circus.

mal sorrow at the death of a loved one. **2.** extremely poor or bad; wretched; miserable: *They lived under abysmal conditions in the slums.* —**a·bys′mal·ly,** *adv.*

a·byss (ə bis′) *n. pl.,* **a·byss·es. 1.** an immeasurably deep or bottomless pit or opening in the surface of the earth; chasm. **2.** anything too deep or great to be measured: *the abyss of outer space, to sink into an abyss of grief.*

Ab·ys·sin·i·a (ab′ə sin′ē ə) *n.* see **Ethiopia.** —**Ab′yssin′i·an,** *adj., n.*

Ac, the symbol for actinium.

AC, A.C., a.c., alternating current.

a·ca·cia (ə kā′shə) *n.* **1.** any of a group of trees or shrubs found in warm regions throughout the world, many of which bear delicate, fernlike leaves and clusters of white, yellow, or orange flowers. Some species yield useful products, such as gum arabic or tannic acid. **2.** any of several other trees, especially certain locust trees. **3.** another word for **gum arabic.**

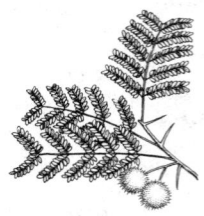

Acacia leaves and flowers

ac·a·dem·ic (ak′ə dem′ik) *adj.* **1.** of or relating to an academy, school, or college: *an academic degree, academic studies.* **2.** relating to liberal or general education, especially to studies that prepare a student for college: *He is taking an academic course in high school.* **3.** not practical; theoretical: *Whether a person can think without using words is an academic question.* Also, **ac·a·dem·i·cal** (ak′ə dem′i kəl). —**ac′a·dem′i·cal·ly,** *adv.*

academic freedom, the freedom of a teacher or student to teach, study, or discuss any subject without fear of interference.

a·cad·e·my (ə kad′ə mē) *n. pl.,* **a·cad·e·mies. 1.** a private high school. **2.** a school giving instruction or training in a particular field: *a military academy, an academy of music.* **3.** a society or institution for the encouragement and advancement of literature, science, or the arts. [French *académie* a place of learning, going back to Greek *Akādēmeia,* a grove near ancient Athens where Plato established a school, from *Akādēmos,* a hero in Greek legends who originally owned this grove.]

A·ca·di·a (ə kā′dē ə) *n.* a former French colony in eastern Canada, including most of what is now the Maritime Provinces. —**A·ca′di·an,** *adj., n.*

a·can·thus (ə kan′thəs) *n. pl.,* **a·can·thus·es** or **a·can·thi** (ə kan′thī). **1.** any of a group of plants native to the Mediterranean region, bearing large spiny leaves and clusters of white or colored flowers. **2.** a design in art or architecture representing an acanthus leaf, used especially as decorations on Corinthian columns.

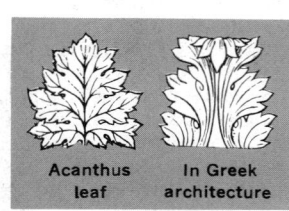

Acanthus leaf   **In Greek architecture**

Acanthus

a cap·pel·la (ä′ kə pel′ə) without instrumental accompaniment: *The choir sang a cappella.*

A·ca·pul·co (ak′ə pool′kō, ä′kä pool′kō) *n.* a resort city on the southwestern coast of Mexico. Pop. (1970), 174,378.

acc. 1. accusative. **2.** account.

ac·cede (ak sēd′) *v.i.,* **ac·ced·ed, ac·ced·ing. 1.** to give consent or approval; agree: *The judge acceded to the lawyer's request for a recess in the trial.* **2.** to gain control or possession of something, such as an office, title, or position: *Queen Elizabeth II acceded to the throne in 1952.*

accel., accelerando.

ac·ce·le·ran·do (ak sel′ə rän′dō) *adv., adj. Music.* gradually increasing in speed.

ac·cel·er·ate (ak sel′ə rāt′) *v.,* **ac·cel·er·at·ed, ac·cel·er·at·ing.** —*v.t.* **1.** to increase the speed of; cause to go faster: *to accelerate an automobile. Running up a flight of stairs accelerates a person's heartbeat.* **2.** to cause to happen sooner; hasten: *The bad weather accelerated our departure.* **3.** *Physics.* to change the speed or direction of (a moving body). —*v.i.* **1.** to increase in speed; go faster: *The car accelerated as it went down the hill.*

ac·cel·er·a·tion (ak sel′ə rā′shən) *n.* **1.** the act of accelerating or the state of being accelerated: *The hiring of twenty additional workers caused an acceleration in the rate of production.* **2.** *Physics.* **a.** a change in the speed or direction of a moving body. **b.** the rate of such a change per unit of time. The acceleration of a falling object is 32 feet per second per second.

ac·cel·er·a·tor (ak sel′ə rā′tər) *n.* **1.** a device for increasing the speed of a machine, especially the foot pedal that controls the speed of an automobile engine. **2.** *Physics.* any of various devices that accelerate subatomic particles to high speeds and high energies, such as a cyclotron or a synchrotron.

ac·cel·er·om·e·ter (ak sel′ə rom′ə tər) *n.* a device that is used to measure acceleration, as in an aircraft or spacecraft.

ac·cent (*n.,* ak′sent; *v.,* ak′sent, ak sent′) *n.* **1.** greater force or emphasis given to a particular syllable or word in speech. In the word *access,* the accent is on the first syllable; in the word *accept,* the accent is on the second syllable. **2.** a mark used in writing and printing to indicate a syllable that is spoken with greater force or emphasis. In this dictionary the mark ′ is used to show a strong or primary accent, and the mark ′ is used to show a weaker or secondary accent, as in the word *ac·cen·tu·ate* (aksen′chōō āt′). **3.** any of various marks used in certain languages to show how a particular letter is pronounced. In the word *consommé,* the accent over the *e* indicates that it is pronounced as (ā). **4.** a special manner of pronouncing words that is characteristic of a certain part of a country, or of a person speaking a language that is not his native one: *He has a Midwestern accent. My grandmother speaks English with a German accent.* **5.** stress or importance; emphasis: *a biology course with an accent on laboratory work.* **6.** stress on certain words or syllables marking the rhythm of a line of verse. **7.** *Music.* **a.** stress or emphasis given to certain notes or chords. **b.** a mark used to indicate this. —*v.t.* **1.** to pronounce (a syllable, word, or words) with particular stress or emphasis: *to accent the first syllable of the word "accident."* **2.** to mark with a written or printed accent. **3.** to stress or emphasize; accentuate.

accent mark, see **accent** *(defs. 2, 3).*

ac·cen·tu·ate (ak sen′chōō āt′) *v.t.,* **ac·cen·tu·at·ed, ac·cen·tu·at·ing. 1.** to increase the effect of; point up; emphasize; stress: *The boy's height accentuated his thinness.* **2.** to mark or pronounce with an accent. —**ac·cen′tu·a′tion,** *n.*

ac·cept (ak sept′) *v.t.* **1.** to agree to take (something offered): *to accept a present. He accepted the nomination of his party.* **2.** to receive with favor or approval: *The students quickly accepted their new teacher.* **3.** to agree or consent to: *The team accepted the referee's decision.* **4.** to answer yes to: *to accept an invitation, to accept an offer.* **5.** to adjust oneself to; submit to: *He refused to accept the fact that he had been defeated.* **6.** to receive or regard as true, satisfactory, or sufficient; believe in: *The scientist's theories were not accepted until long after his death.* **7.** to take upon oneself; assume; undertake: *He accepted the responsibility of feeding the dog.* —*v.i.* to take something offered.

ac·cept·a·ble (ak sep′tə bəl) *adj.* **1.** good enough to be accepted; satisfactory: *His report was acceptable, but not really outstanding.* **2.** pleasing, welcome, or agreeable: *Her plan for the picnic was acceptable to the whole group.* —**ac·cept′a·bil′i·ty,** *n.* —**ac·cept′a·bly,** *adv.*

ac·cept·ance (ak sep′təns) *n.* **1.** the act of taking something that is offered: *the acceptance of a present.* **2.** a favorable reception; approval: *The new product gained wide acceptance among the public.* **3.** a believing something to be true: *the acceptance of a scientific theory.*

ac·cess (ak′ses) *n. pl.,* **ac·cess·es. 1.** the right or permission to approach, enter, or use; admittance: *The foreign visitors were denied access to the guided missile base.* **2.** a way of approaching; means of approach: *The only access to the farm was a dirt road.*

ac·ces·si·ble (ak ses′ə bəl) *adj.* **1.** easy to reach, enter, or approach: *When the new highway is finished, the airport will be accessible from all directions.* **2.** able to be acquired; obtainable; attainable: *The information you want is not readily accessible.* —**ac·ces′si·bil′i·ty,** *n.* —**ac·ces′si·bly,** *adv.*

ac·ces·sion (ak sesh′ən) *n.* **1.** the act of coming into control or possession of something, such as an office, title, or position: *the accession of a new king to the throne.* **2.** an increase by the addition of something: *The library collection was enlarged by the accession of fifty new volumes.* **3.** something that is added: *The new books were a valuable accession.*

ac·ces·so·ry (ak ses′ər ē) *also,* **ac·ces·sa·ry.** *n. pl.,* **ac·ces·so·ries. 1.** something that is not necessary but adds to appearance or usefulness; extra thing that is helpful in a secondary way: *A radio or an air-conditioning unit are car accessories. Her gloves, hat, purse, and other accessories matched her dress very well.* **2.** a person who, without being present at the scene of a crime, helps another in committing the crime or in escaping from the law after the crime. —*adj.* contributing in a secondary way; additional; extra: *The listing of street addresses is an accessory function of a telephone directory.*

ac·ci·dent (ak′sə dənt) *n.* **1.** something that happens unexpectedly or without apparent cause or reason: *The discovery of an oil well on the farm was a happy accident.* **2.** an unfortunate event that is not expected or intended, usually causing harm or injury; mishap: *He suffered a broken leg in the traffic accident.* **3.** chance; fortune: *I found the missing watch completely by accident while cleaning out my desk.*

ac·ci·den·tal (ak′sə dent′əl) *adj.* happening by chance; unexpected; unintentional: *Columbus' discovery of America was accidental; he was searching for a route to India.* —*n. Music.* a sign, such as a flat, sharp, or natural, that does not appear in the key signature and changes the pitch of the note or notes it goes before.

ac·ci·den·tal·ly (ak′sə den′təl ē, ak′sə dent′lē) *adv.* by chance: *I met her accidentally on the bus.*

ac·claim (ə klām′) *v.t.* **1.** to greet or welcome with loud or enthusiastic approval; hail; applaud: *The crowd acclaimed the astronauts.* **2.** to announce or declare with strong approval: *The judges acclaimed her the winner.* —*n.* enthusiastic praise or welcome.

ac·cla·ma·tion (ak′lə mā′shən) *n.* **1.** an enthusiastic show of approval: *The victorious team was received with acclamation by its fans.* **2.** a vote by voice, especially an enthusiastic or unanimous vote of approval: *The motion was passed by acclamation.*

ac·cli·mate (ak′lə māt′, ə klī′mit) *v.,* **ac·cli·mat·ed, ac·cli·mat·ing.** —*v.t.* to adjust or adapt to a new place or situation, or to new surroundings: *Dave quickly acclimated himself to his new school.* —*v.i.* to become adjusted or

adapted to a new place or situation, or to new surroundings: *The fish acclimated easily to their new tank.* —**ac′cli·ma′tion,** *n.*

ac·cli·ma·tize (ə klī′mə tīz′) *v.t., v.i.,* **ac·cli·ma·tized, ac·cli·ma·tiz·ing.** to acclimate. —**ac·cli′ma·ti·za′tion,** *n.*

ac·co·lade (ak′ə lād′) *n.* **1.** something given as an award or honor: *The scientist received many accolades for his great discoveries.* **2.** the ceremony used in making someone a knight, usually a light tap on the shoulder with the flat side of a sword.

ac·com·mo·date (ə kom′ə dāt′) *v.,* **ac·com·mo·dat·ed, ac·com·mo·dat·ing.** —*v.t.* **1.** to have or make room for; hold: *This car can accommodate five passengers.* **2.** to furnish with a place to stay or sleep: *That motel can accommodate 200 guests.* **3.** to do a favor or service for; help; oblige: *When we asked for directions, the policeman accommodated us.* **4.** to make fit or suitable; adapt; adjust: *Accommodate yourself to the new situation.* —*v.i.* to come into adjustment; become adjusted: *The lens of the eye accommodates in order to see objects at different distances.*

ac·com·mo·dat·ing (ə kom′ə dā′ting) *adj.* ready or willing to help; helpful; obliging: *The accommodating policeman directed us to our exact destination.* —**ac·com′mo·dat′ing·ly,** *adv.*

ac·com·mo·da·tion (ə kom′ə dā′shən) *n.* **1.** the act of accommodating or the state of being accommodated; adjustment; adaptation. **2. accommodations.** a place to stay or sleep, often with food: *accommodations at a motel, tourist accommodations on an airplane.* **3.** aid, comfort, or convenience: *These rest areas are for the accommodation of travelers.* **4.** something that fills a need or is helpful, such as a loan. **5.** the automatic adjustment of the lens of the eye for seeing objects at different distances.

ac·com·pa·ni·ment (ə kum′pə ni mənt) *n.* **1.** a thing that goes along with something else: *We had turkey with stuffing and cranberry sauce as accompaniments.* **2.** a musical part that provides a background for a main part: *The girl sang with a piano accompaniment.*

ac·com·pa·nist (ə kum′pə nist) *n.* a person who performs a musical accompaniment.

ac·com·pa·ny (ə kum′pə nē) *v.t.,* **ac·com·pa·nied, ac·com·pa·ny·ing.** **1.** to go along or in company with; act as a companion or escort to: *I'll accompany you to the movie theater.* **2.** to be or happen in connection or combination with: *The slides that accompanied the lecture were very interesting.* **3.** to perform a musical accompaniment for or to: *He accompanied the violinist on the piano.*

ac·com·plice (ə kom′plis) *n.* a person who knowingly helps another in committing a crime or in other wrongdoing: *The driver of the car used in the escape was an accomplice of the bank robber.*

ac·com·plish (ə kom′plish) *v.t.* to succeed in completing or carrying out; perform: *The pilot accomplished his mission and returned to the base.*

ac·com·plished (ə kom′plisht) *adj.* **1.** successfully completed; done: *an accomplished task.* **2.** skilled; expert: *an accomplished drummer, an accomplished swimmer.*

ac·com·plish·ment (ə kom′plish mənt) *n.* **1.** the act of accomplishing or the state of being accomplished; completion: *The accomplishment of our goal will be very dif-*

at; āpe; cär; end; mē; it; īce; hot; ōld; fôrk; wood; fōōl; oil; out; up; turn; sing; thin; this; hw in white; zh in treasure. The symbol ə stands for the sound of a in about, e in taken, i in pencil, o in lemon, and u in circus.

ficult. **2.** something done successfully; achievement: *Man's first landing on the moon was a great accomplishment.* **3.** skill, art, or ability, especially one that is acquired through training: *Skiing is one of his many accomplishments.*

ac·cord (ə kôrd′) *n.* **1.** the state of being in agreement; harmony: *The decision was in accord with the wishes of the people.* **2.** an agreement between parties, especially one between nations. —*v.t.* to grant or give as earned or due; concede: *He was accorded praise for his achievements.* —*v.i.* to be in harmony or agreement: *Her opinions on politics accord with his.*

   of one's own accord or **on one's own accord.** by a person's own choice or will; voluntarily: *The boys cleaned their room of their own accord.*

ac·cord·ance (ə kôrd′əns) *n.* **1.** the state of being in agreement; harmony: *John acted in accordance with our wishes.* **2.** the act of according, granting, or giving.

ac·cord·ing (ə kôr′ding) *adj.* in harmony; agreeing.

   according to. a. in agreement with: *Everything went according to our plan.* **b.** in proportion to; in relation to: *Each man was paid according to the amount of work he did.* **c.** on the authority of; as stated by or in: *According to the weather reports, it will snow tomorrow.*

ac·cord·ing·ly (ə kôr′ding lē) *adv.* **1.** in a fitting or suitable manner: *The dance is informal, so dress accordingly.* **2.** consequently; therefore.

ac·cor·di·on (ə kôr′dē ən) *n.* a portable musical wind instrument with keys, metal reeds, and a bellows. It produces tones when the player squeezes or expands the bellows, forcing air through the reeds. —*adj.* resembling the folds of the bellows of an accordion: *a skirt with accordion pleats.*

Bellows

Piano keyboard

Button keyboard

Accordion

ac·cost (ə kôst′) *v.t.* to approach boldly and speak to: *The movie star was accosted by two boys who wanted his autograph.*

ac·count (ə kount′) *n.* **1.** a spoken or written statement; report; description: *The witness gave a detailed account of the accident. I read an account of the fire in the morning newspaper.* **2.** a statement of reasons, causes, or grounds; explanation: *Give us an account of your strange behavior.* **3.** a record or statement of business or financial dealings: *My mother keeps the household accounts.* **4.** a sum of money deposited with a bank; bank account. **5.** a firm or company that is a client or customer: *That advertising agency has two new accounts.* **6.** worth; importance: *a man of no account.* —*v.t.* to consider to be: *I account him an honest man.*

   on account. a. as partial payment of a larger amount. **b.** on credit: *He bought the television set on account.*

   on account of. a. because of: *The game was postponed on account of rain.* **b.** for the sake of; in consideration of.

   on no account. under no circumstances; never: *On no account should you leave the baby at home alone.*

   on one's account. for one's sake or benefit: *Don't leave the party early on my account.*

   to account for. a. to give a satisfactory explanation for: *How do you account for your lateness?* **b.** to be the reason for: *The heavy snowfall accounts for the large number of traffic accidents.* **c.** to be responsible for: *The delivery boy had to account for all the money he collected.*

   to call to account. a. to demand an explanation from: *The hostess called her guest to account for his rude behavior.* **b.** to scold; reprimand; rebuke.

   to give a good account of oneself. to behave or perform well.

   to take account of or **to take into account. a.** to take into consideration; allow for: *You must take into account the fact that he has been sick lately.* **b.** to take note of: *History will take account of his great leadership.*

ac·count·a·ble (ə koun′tə bəl) *adj.* **1.** liable to be called to account; responsible: *He must be held accountable for his actions.* **2.** capable of being explained: *Her rude reply was accountable; she had a bad headache.* —**ac·count′a·bil′i·ty,** *n.* —**ac·count′a·bly,** *adv.*

ac·count·ant (ə kount′ənt) *n.* a person whose job is recording, managing, or examining financial records or accounts, as for a business firm.

ac·count·ing (ə koun′ting) *n.* **1.** the system, practice, or occupation of recording, managing, or examining financial records or accounts. **2.** a formal report or statement, as of business dealings.

ac·cou·ter (ə kōō′tər) *v.t.* to furnish with clothing or equipment: *The soldiers were accoutered for desert warfare.*

ac·cou·ter·ments (ə kōō′tər mənts) *also,* **ac·cou·tre·ments.** *n., pl.* **1.** personal equipment or accessories: *She had a camera, a guidebook, and all the other accouterments of a tourist.* **2.** the equipment of a soldier other than his weapons and clothing.

ac·cou·tre (ə kōō′tər) *v.t.,* **ac·cou·tred, ac·cou·tring.** another spelling of **accouter.**

Ac·cra (ak′rə, ə krä′) *also,* **Ak·kra.** *n.* the capital and largest city of Ghana, on the southern coast of the country. Pop. (1970), 663,880.

ac·cred·it (ə kred′it) *v.t.* **1.** to consider to belong to; ascribe or attribute; credit: *Scientists accredit the discovery of the laws of motion to Isaac Newton.* **2.** to send or provide with official authority or credentials: *to accredit an ambassador.* **3.** to certify as meeting certain official standards or requirements: *to accredit a college.* **4.** to accept as true; believe.

ac·cre·tion (ə krē′shən) *n.* **1.** an increase in size by natural growth or by an outside addition. **2.** something that is added; outside addition.

ac·cru·al (ə krōō′əl) *n.* **1.** the act or process of accruing. **2.** an amount accrued.

ac·crue (ə krōō′) *v.i.,* **ac·crued, ac·cru·ing. 1.** to come as a result of natural growth or addition: *Many benefits accrued to the community from the construction of new housing.* **2.** to grow in amount; accumulate: *Interest on this savings account accrues from the day of deposit.*

acct., account; accountant.

ac·cu·mu·late (ə kyōō′myə lāt′) *v.,* **ac·cu·mu·lat·ed, ac·cu·mu·lat·ing.** —*v.t.* to gather or pile up (something); collect; amass: *He accumulated a large collection of books during his teaching career.* —*v.i.* to grow in size, quantity, or number; increase gradually: *A pile of papers had accumulated on his desk.*

ac·cu·mu·la·tion (ə kyōō′myə lā′shən) *n.* **1.** the act or process of accumulating: *The accumulation of much evidence against the defendant led to his conviction.* **2.** something that is accumulated or has accumulated; mass; collection: *an accumulation of dust in the corner of a room.*

ac·cu·ra·cy (ak′yər ə sē) *n.* freedom from errors or mistakes; correctness; exactness: *She did her work with accuracy.*

ac·cu·rate (ak′yər it) *adj.* **1.** making few or no errors or mistakes; exact; precise: *an accurate typist, an accurate watch.* **2.** without errors or mistakes; correct; truthful: *The early reports of the battle were not accurate.* —**ac′cu·rate·ly,** *adv.* —**ac′cu·rate·ness,** *n.*

ac·curs·ed (ə kur′sid, ə kurst′) *also,* **ac·curst** (ə kurst′). *adj.* **1.** under a curse; doomed; ill-fated. **2.** worthy of

8

curses; hateful: *an accursed tyrant.* —**ac·curs′ed·ly,** *adv.*
—**ac·curs′ed·ness,** *n.*

accus., accusative.

ac·cu·sa·tion (ak′yə zā′shən) *n.* **1.** a statement that a person has committed a crime or offense; charge of wrongdoing: *He denied the accusation that he had stolen the money.* **2.** the crime or offense charged. **3.** the act of accusing.

ac·cu·sa·tive (ə kyōō′zə tiv) *n.* **1.** a grammatical case in Latin, Greek, and certain other languages that shows the direct object of a verb or the object of certain prepositions. It corresponds to the objective case in English. **2.** a word or construction in this case. —*adj.* relating to this case.

ac·cuse (ə kyōōz′) *v.t.,* **ac·cused, ac·cus·ing. 1.** to charge with a crime or offense; bring charges against: *The police accused him of armed robbery.* **2.** to find at fault or in error; blame: *His teacher accused him of doing careless work.* —**ac·cus′er,** *n.*

ac·cused (ə kyōōzd′) *adj.* charged with a crime or offense. —*n.* a person or persons charged with a crime or offense, especially the defendant in a criminal case.

ac·cus·tom (ə kus′təm) *v.t.* to make familiar by use, custom, or habit: *His years as a politician had accustomed him to public speaking.*

ac·cus·tomed (ə kus′təmd) *adj.* usual; customary; habitual: *The dog lay in his accustomed place by the fire.*
   accustomed to. in the habit of; used to: *He is accustomed to sleeping late on Saturdays.*

ace (ās) *n.* **1.** a playing card having a single symbol of the suit it represents. **2.** a person who is an expert at something: *Karen is an ace at tennis.* **3.** a combat pilot who has shot down five or more enemy planes. **4.** in tennis and other racket games, a serve that the opponent fails to return. —*adj.* of the highest quality; expert: *Bob is an ace pitcher.*
   within an ace of. at the very point of; close to.

ac·et·an·i·lide (as′ə tan′əl īd′) *n.* a white crystalline compound that is used as a drug to relieve pain and reduce fever.

ac·e·tate (as′ə tāt′) *n.* **1.** a salt or ester of acetic acid. **2.** cellulose acetate or any of its products, especially a cellulose acetate fabric, fiber, or yarn.

a·ce·tic (ə sē′tik) *adj.* relating to or producing vinegar or acetic acid.

acetic acid, a colorless, liquid acid having a strong odor and a sour taste. It is the acid in vinegar and is widely used in the production of textile fibers, plastics, and drugs.

a·cet·y·lene (ə set′əl ēn′) *n.* a colorless, highly flammable gas that is widely used in combination with oxygen in the cutting and welding of metals.

a·ce·tyl·sal·i·cyl·ic acid (a sēt′əl sal′ə sil′ik) another name for **aspirin.**

ache (āk) *v.i.,* **ached, ach·ing. 1.** to have or be in pain, especially dull or continuous pain: *Her tooth ached all morning. His whole body ached after the rough football game.* **2.** *Informal.* to be eager; long; yearn: *The homesick soldier ached to return to his native land.* —*n.* continuous, usually dull, pain: *an ache in one's back.*

a·chieve (ə chēv′) *v.t.,* **a·chieved, a·chiev·ing. 1.** to carry out successfully; accomplish: *to achieve one's goals. He achieved all that he set out to do.* **2.** to succeed in gaining; attain: *to achieve fame, to achieve the rank of major.* —**a·chiev′er,** *n.*

a·chieve·ment (ə chēv′mənt) *n.* **1.** something achieved, especially by unusual effort or skill; accomplishment: *The invention of the telephone was a great achievement.* **2.** the act of achieving: *The army's achievement of its objective involved great loss of life.*

achievement test, a test measuring how much a person has learned in a particular subject over a certain period of time.

A·chil·les (ə kil′ēz) *n. Greek Legend.* a Greek warrior in the Trojan War. Achilles was killed by Paris, who wounded him in his heel, the only spot where he could be injured.

Achilles′ tendon, the tendon that joins the muscles of the calf to the bone of the heel.

ach·ro·mat·ic (ak′rə mat′ik) *adj.* refracting white light without separating it into the colors of the spectrum: *an achromatic lens.*

ac·id (as′id) *n.* any of a class of chemical compounds containing hydrogen and having a sour taste in a water solution. Acids react with bases to form salts and turn blue litmus paper red. —*adj.* **1.** of, relating to, or like an acid. **2.** sharp and biting to the taste; sour. **3.** sharp, as in tone or manner; ill-tempered; biting: *acid remarks.* —**ac′id·ly,** *adv.* —**ac′id·ness,** *n.*

Achilles' tendon

a·cid·ic (ə sid′ik) *adj.* containing or forming acid.

a·cid·i·fy (ə sid′ə fī′) *v.t., v.i.,* **a·cid·i·fied, a·cid·i·fy·ing.** to make acid or become acid.

a·cid·i·ty (ə sid′ə tē) *n. pl.,* **a·cid·i·ties. 1.** the quality or state of being acid; sourness; tartness. **2.** the degree of being acid.

acid test, something that tests the real quality, character, or worth of a person or thing: *This election will be the acid test of his ability as a politician.* [From the use of *acid* as a *test* for gold.]

ac·knowl·edge (ak nol′ij) *v.t.,* **ac·knowl·edged, ac·knowl·edg·ing. 1.** to admit the truth or fact of; concede: *He acknowledged his error.* **2.** to recognize the authority, rights, or claims of: *The tribe acknowledged him as their chief.* **3.** to show or express appreciation or gratitude for: *to acknowledge a gift by sending a note of thanks.* **4.** to show or make known that one has received or noticed (something): *She acknowledged the letter in a prompt reply.*

ac·knowl·edg·ment (ak nol′ij mənt) *also,* **ac·knowl·edge·ment.** *n.* **1.** the act of admitting or conceding: *an acknowledgment of one's mistakes.* **2.** recognition, as of authority, rights, or claims: *acknowledgment of a king's right to rule.* **3.** a thing given or done to show that one has received something: *Their letter was an acknowledgment of the shipment.* **4.** an expression of gratitude, recognition, or appreciation: *an acknowledgment of a gift.*

ac·me (ak′mē) *n.* the highest point; peak; zenith: *Winning the Nobel Prize was the acme of his career as a writer.*

ac·ne (ak′nē) *n.* a skin condition characterized by pimples or other blemishes on the face, back, or chest. It results from clogged and inflamed pores of the oil glands.

ac·o·lyte (ak′ə līt′) *n.* **1.** a person who helps a minister or priest at certain religious services; altar boy. **2.** any attendant or assistant; follower.

A·con·ca·gua (ak′ən kog′wə) *n.* a mountain in western Argentina, in the Andes. It is the highest peak in the Western Hemisphere.

ac·o·nite (ak′ə nīt′) *n.* **1.** any of a group of poisonous

at; āpe; cär; end; mē; it; īce; hot; ōld; fôrk;
wood; fōol; oil; out; up; turn; sing; thin; this;
hw in white; zh in treasure. The symbol ə
stands for the sound of **a** in about, **e** in taken,
i in pencil, **o** in lemon, and **u** in circus.

plants of the Northern Hemisphere, bearing blue, white, purple, or yellow hood-shaped flowers. Also, **wolfsbane, monkshood. 2.** a drug obtained from these plants, formerly used to relieve pain.

a·corn (ā′kôrn, ā′kərn) *n.* the nut of the oak tree.

a·cous·tic (ə kōōs′tik) *adj.* **1.** relating to the sense or organs of hearing, to sound, or to the science of sound: *An auditorium should have good acoustic qualities.* **2.** used to absorb and deaden sound: *acoustic tile.* Also, **a·cous·ti·cal** (ə kōōs′ti kəl). —**a·cous′ti·cal·ly,** *adv.*

a·cous·tics (ə kōōs′tiks) *n., pl.* **1.** the qualities of a room, theater, auditorium, or the like that determine how well sound is carried and heard in it. ▲ used with a plural verb. **2.** the science that deals with sound. ▲ used with a singular verb.

ac·quaint (ə kwānt′) *v.t.* **1.** to make familiar: *Acquaint yourself with the new rules.* **2.** to let know; inform: *Shall we acquaint him with our decision before going on?*

ac·quaint·ance (ə kwānt′əns) *n.* **1.** a person whom one knows, but who is not a close friend. **2.** a relationship between people who are not close friends; the state of being acquainted: *We had a brief acquaintance with them one summer.* **3.** knowledge of something, especially as a result of personal experience or contact; familiarity: *Long and careful study gave him a thorough acquaintance with Shakespeare's plays.*

to make someone's acquaintance. to get to know someone.

ac·quaint·ance·ship (ə kwān′tən ship′) *n.* the state of being acquainted.

ac·quaint·ed (ə kwān′tid) *adj.* **1.** known to one, or each other, but not close friends: *Are you two acquainted?* **2.** familiar: *I have been one acquainted with the night* (Robert Frost).

ac·qui·esce (ak′wē es′) *v.i.,* **ac·qui·esced, ac·qui·esc·ing.** to consent or agree by remaining silent or by not raising objections; submit quietly: *In 1938 France and England acquiesced to Germany's occupation of Czechoslovakia.*

ac·qui·es·cence (ak′wē es′əns) *n.* the act of acquiescing; agreement without protest: *The rebels overthrew the king with the acquiescence of the army.*

ac·qui·es·cent (ak′wē es′ənt) *adj.* consenting or agreeing without protest: *They were acquiescent to our plan.* —**ac′qui·es′cent·ly,** *adv.*

ac·quire (ə kwīr′) *v.t.,* **ac·quired, ac·quir·ing.** to come into possession of; gain or obtain as one's own: *to acquire wealth and property, to acquire an education, to acquire the ability to speak a foreign language.*

ac·quire·ment (ə kwīr′mənt) *n.* **1.** the act of acquiring: *the acquirement of wealth.* **2.** something acquired; attainment; accomplishment.

ac·qui·si·tion (ak′wə zish′ən) *n.* **1.** the act of acquiring: *The United States' acquisition of Alaska occurred in 1867.* **2.** something received or acquired: *The museum displayed its recent acquisitions.*

ac·quis·i·tive (ə kwiz′ə tiv) *adj.* eager or inclined to acquire things; grasping: *a greedy and acquisitive person.* —**ac·quis′i·tive·ly,** *adv.* —**ac·quis′i·tive·ness,** *n.*

ac·quit (ə kwit′) *v.t.,* **ac·quit·ted, ac·quit·ting. 1.** to free or clear from an accusation or charge of crime; declare not guilty; exonerate: *The jury acquitted him after a short trial.* **2.** to conduct (oneself); behave: *The team acquitted itself well in its first game.*

ac·quit·tal (ə kwit′əl) *n.* a setting free from a criminal charge, especially by a verdict of not guilty: *The jury voted for acquittal of the defendant.*

a·cre (ā′kər) *n.* **1.** a measure of land equal to 43,560 square feet, or 160 square rods. **2. acres.** lands; property.

a·cre·age (ā′kər ij) *n.* an area of land measured in acres: *How much acreage does that farmer own?*

ac·rid (ak′rid) *adj.* **1.** burning, biting, or irritating to the taste or smell: *the acrid smell of cigarette smoke.* **2.** biting or cutting in manner, temper, or tone: *The critic made acrid comments about the new play.* —**ac′rid·ly,** *adv.* —**ac′rid·ness,** *n.*

ac·ri·mo·ni·ous (ak′rə mō′nē əs) *adj.* bitter or sarcastic in temper, manner, or tone; caustic: *The book is an acrimonious attack on the present administration.* —**ac′ri·mo′ni·ous·ly,** *adv.* —**ac′ri·mo′ni·ous·ness,** *n.*

ac·ri·mo·ny (ak′rə mō′nē) *n.* sharpness or bitterness in temper, manner, or tone: *We were shocked at the acrimony of his remarks about his brother.*

ac·ro·bat (ak′rə bat′) *n.* a person skilled in performing feats or stunts requiring great physical strength, control, and agility, such as swinging on a trapeze or walking on a tightrope.

ac·ro·bat·ic (ak′rə bat′ik) *adj.* relating to or like an acrobat or acrobatics: *an acrobatic leap.* —**ac′ro·bat′i·cal·ly,** *adv.*

ac·ro·bat·ics (ak′rə bat′iks) *n., pl.* **1.** the stunts or skills of an acrobat. **2.** any display of great skill or agility: *The pianist performed musical acrobatics.*

ac·ro·nym (ak′rə nim′) *n.* a word formed by combining the first letters or syllables of a series of other words. *Radar* is an acronym for *r*adio *d*etecting *a*nd *r*anging.

▲ **Acronyms** are short forms of longer terms, as are **abbreviations.** Although there are no specific rules for determining which short forms become acronyms and which become abbreviations, there are certain differences between them. **Acronyms** are words and are therefore pronounced in the same way as other words. The word *scuba* is an acronym formed from *s*elf-*c*ontained *u*nderwater *b*reathing *a*pparatus. **Abbreviations** are not independent words and are not pronounced, but are spoken by naming the individual letters. *C.O.D.* is the abbreviation of *c*ash *o*n *d*elivery. Sometimes an abbreviation becomes an acronym. For example, the abbreviation *a.w.o.l.,* meaning *a*bsent *w*ithout *l*eave (from military duty), is now usually written as a word, *AWOL,* and pronounced (ā′wôl).

a·crop·o·lis (ə krop′ə lis) *n. pl.,* **a·crop·o·lis·es. 1.** a strongly fortified place in an ancient Greek city, usually built on the highest part. **2. Acropolis.** a fortified place on the highest hill in ancient Athens, famous for its temples and monuments.

a·cross (ə krôs′) *adv.* **1.** from one side to the other: *We came across in a boat.* **2.** on or to the other side: *We'll soon be across.* —*prep.* **1.** from one side of to the other; over: *He drove across the bridge.* **2.** on the other side of; beyond: *She lives in the house across the street.* **3.** in a direction so as to cross: *The cat walked across our path.*

to come across or **to run across.** to come into contact with or find unexpectedly: *I came across some old coins when I cleaned the attic.*

a·cros·tic (ə krôs′tik) *n.* a poem or other arrangement of words in which the first, last, or certain other letters in each line, taken in order, form a word or a phrase.

F ew plants grow when it is cold,
L ocked up in the ground's stronghold.
O ver them the snowflakes fall,
W inter white till April's call.
E arth wakes up, it's almost May,
R ain brings blossoms every day.

Acrostic

act (akt) *n.* **1.** something done; deed: *Saving the child was an act of bravery.* **2.** the process of doing something: *The burglars were caught in the act of opening the safe.* **3.** a formal decision or law, as of a legislature: *The United States can declare war only by an act of Congress.* **4.** one of the main divisions of a play or opera: *"Hamlet"* has five acts. **5.** a short performance that is usually one of several on a program: *The magician's act follows the intermission.* **6.** a show of false or insincere behavior; pretense: *Her crying was just an act.* —*v.i.* **1.** to do or perform something: *The doctor acted quickly to save the injured man.* **2.** to conduct oneself; behave: *He acted like a gentleman.* **3.** to be an actor; play a part: *She has acted in several recent films.* **4.** to have or produce an effect: *The drug acted quickly.* **5.** to pretend to be: *She acted calm, although she was very worried.* **6.** to serve or function: *He acted as chairman of the meeting.* —*v.t.* **1.** to behave in a manner that is suitable for: *Act your age.* **2.** to play the part of; perform: *He acts Romeo with great passion.* **3.** to pretend to be or behave like: *to act the fool.*

to act on or **to act upon.** to behave according to; follow: *Act on his orders.*

to act up. *Informal.* **a.** to behave mischievously or playfully: *The children were acting up again.* **b.** to cause trouble: *His stomach acted up after dinner.*

ACTH, a hormone that is produced by the pituitary gland and stimulates the adrenal gland to secrete its hormones. It can be obtained from the pituitary gland of hogs and other animals for use in the treatment of certain diseases, such as arthritis, rheumatic fever, and asthma.

act·ing (ak'ting) *adj.* temporarily performing the duties of another: *The council president served as the acting mayor.* —*n.* the act, art, or occupation of performing as an actor.

ac·tin·ic (ak tin'ik) *adj.* relating to or having actinism: *actinic rays.*

ac·tin·ism (ak'tə niz'əm) *n.* the property of ultraviolet rays, X rays, and other forms of radiant energy that enables them to produce chemical changes.

ac·tin·i·um (ak tin'ē əm) *n.* a rare, radioactive metallic element found in pitchblende and other uranium ores. Symbol: **Ac**

ac·tion (ak'shən) *n.* **1.** the process of acting or doing: *The action of throwing a ball involves many different muscles.* **2.** great energy or activity: *The general was a man of action.* **3.** a thing that is done; act; deed: *Actions speak louder than words.* **4. actions.** behavior; conduct: *We couldn't understand his strange actions at the party.* **5.** effect; influence: *The action of waves wears away rock.* **6.** a way of moving or operating: *a washing machine with gentle action.* **7.** a mechanism by which something operates: *the action of a rifle.* **8.** battle; combat: *He was wounded in action.* **9.** the events in a story, play, or the like. **10.** a lawsuit.

in action. in a state of activity; at work; in operation.

to take action. to become active; start to act: *The police took action immediately to find the criminal.*

ac·ti·vate (ak'tə vāt') *v.t.*, **ac·ti·vat·ed, ac·ti·vat·ing.** **1.** to cause to work or operate; put into action; make active: *Turning this switch activates the machine. The general activated a unit of soldiers who had been on reserve duty.* **2.** *Physics.* to make radioactive. **3.** *Chemistry.* to cause a reaction in; make more reactive. —**ac'ti·va'tion,** *n.*

ac·tive (ak'tiv) *adj.* **1.** full of action or movement; busy: *an active child.* **2.** energetic; lively; vigorous: *Judy has an active mind.* **3.** taking part in an action; participating: *Everyone must take an active part in decorating for the dance.* **4.** acting or capable of acting; working; functioning: *an active volcano.* **5.** *Grammar.* relating to or designating the voice of a verb whose subject is shown as performing the action expressed by the verb. In the sentences *Tom caught the ball* and *Sue bought a coat* the verbs *caught* and *bought* are in the active voice. —*n.* **1.** the active voice. **2.** a verb form in this voice. —**ac'tive·ly,** *adv.* —**ac'tive·ness,** *n.*

active duty, full-time military service.

ac·ti·vist (ak'tə vist) *n.* a person who believes in and actively supports a cause: *a civil rights activist.*

ac·tiv·i·ty (ak tiv'ə tē) *n. pl.,* **ac·tiv·i·ties.** **1.** the quality or state of being active; movement; action: *the activity of the mind.* **2.** brisk or vigorous action; energy; liveliness: *There was little activity in the quiet town.* **3.** a thing done or to be done: *Jane is involved in many school activities.*

act of God, an occurrence or event that is caused by the forces of nature and could not have been foreseen or prevented by humans, such as an earthquake.

ac·tor (ak'tər) *n.* **1.** a person who plays a role or performs, as in a play, motion picture, television program, or the like. **2.** a person who acts; doer.

ac·tress (ak'tris) *n. pl.,* **ac·tress·es.** a woman or girl who plays a role or performs, as in a play or motion picture.

Acts (akts) *n.* a book of the New Testament, thought to have been written by Saint Luke. Also, **Acts of the Apostles.**

ac·tu·al (ak'chōō əl) *adj.* in existence; existing; real: *The actual result differed from what we had expected.*

ac·tu·al·i·ty (ak'chōō al'ə tē) *n. pl.,* **ac·tu·al·i·ties.** **1.** the state or quality of being actual; reality. **2.** an actual condition or circumstance; fact.

ac·tu·al·ly (ak'chōō ə lē) *adv.* in fact; really.

ac·tu·ate (ak'chōō āt') *v.t.,* **ac·tu·at·ed, ac·tu·at·ing.** **1.** to put into action or motion: *A spring actuates the trap.* **2.** to incite or influence to act; motivate: *He was actuated by a desire for fame.* —**ac'tu·a'tion,** *n.* —**ac'tu·a'tor,** *n.*

a·cu·men (ə kyōō'mən) *n.* keenness of mind or judgment: *She shows great acumen as a businesswoman.*

ac·u·punc·ture (ak'yōō pungk'chər) *n.* the practice, originally Chinese, of inserting needles into various parts of the body in order to treat diseases or to serve as an anesthetic during surgery. [Latin *acus* needle + PUNCTURE.]

a·cute (ə kyōōt') *adj.* **1.** having or showing quickness and keenness in seeing and understanding: *an acute mind.* **2.** very sensitive; keen: *acute hearing.* **3.** sharp; intense: *acute pain.* **4.** (of a disease) developing and reaching a crisis quickly: *acute appendicitis.* **5.** very important; crucial: *The school has an acute need for additional funds.* **6.** high in pitch; shrill: *Dogs can hear acute sounds that people cannot hear.* —**a·cute'ly,** *adv.* —**a·cute'ness,** *n.*

acute accent, a mark used in certain languages to indicate the sound of a vowel, as in French *lycée,* or a difference in meaning, as in Spanish *quién.*

acute angle, an angle that is less than ninety degrees.

ad (ad) *n.* another word for **advertisement.**

ad- *prefix* used to express motion toward or nearness to: *adjoin.*

A.D., in the (given) year since the birth of Christ. ▲ used in expressing dates: *Nero became emperor of Rome in* A.D. *54.* [Abbreviation of *anno Domini.*]

ad·age (ad'ij) *n.* an old and familiar saying that is believed to be true; proverb. For example: *The early bird catches the worm.*

a·da·gio (ə dä'jō, ə dä'jē ō') *Music. adv.* slowly. —*adj.* slow. —*n. pl.,* **adagios.** **1.** a musical composition, movement, or part in adagio tempo. **2.** a ballet dance in slow tempo.

---

at; āpe; cär; end; mē; it; īce; hot; ōld; fôrk; wood; fōōl; oil; out; up; turn; sing; thin; **this;** hw in white; zh in treasure. The symbol ə stands for the sound of **a** in about, **e** in taken, **i** in pencil, **o** in lemon, and **u** in circus.

Ad·am (ad′əm) *n.* in the Old Testament, the first man. With his wife Eve, he began the human race.

ad·a·mant (ad′ə mənt, ad′ə mant′) *adj.* totally unyielding: *The judge was adamant in his refusal to change his decision.* —*n.* in old legends, a substance so hard that it could not be cut or broken. —**ad′a·mant·ly,** *adv.*

Ad·ams (ad′əmz) **1. John.** 1735–1826, the second president of the United States, from 1797 to 1801. **2. John Quin·cy** (kwin′sē). 1767–1848, his son; the sixth president of the United States, from 1825 to 1829. **3.** **Samuel.** 1722–1803, a patriot and leader in the American Revolution.

Adam's apple, a lump in the throat just below the chin, formed by the largest cartilage of the larynx. [From the belief that a piece of the *apple* from the tree of knowledge stuck in *Adam's* throat.]

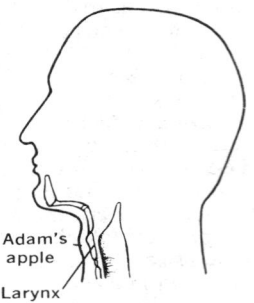

Adam's apple

Larynx

a·dapt (ə dapt′) *v.t.* **1.** to change to meet new requirements or to fit new uses; modify; alter: *The college professor had to adapt his teaching methods when he taught a grammar school class.* **2.** to adjust (oneself) to new conditions or surroundings. —*v.i.* to become adjusted: *That animal became extinct because it could not adapt to changes in its environment.*

▲ **Adapt** and **adopt** have different meanings, but they are often confused because they are spelled and pronounced in somewhat the same way. **Adapt** means to change something so that it can be used for another purpose: *The writer adapted his novel for a television script.* **Adopt** means to take something for one's own: *The school adopted the name "Wildcats" as a nickname for its football team.*

a·dapt·a·ble (ə dap′tə bəl) *adj.* **1.** capable of being adapted. **2.** capable of adapting. —**a·dapt′a·bil′i·ty,** *n.* —**a·dapt′a·ble·ness,** *n.*

ad·ap·ta·tion (ad′əp tā′shən) *n.* **1.** the act of adapting or the state of being adapted. **2.** a thing produced by adapting: *This story is an adaptation of an old folk tale.* **3.** a change in a plant or animal so that it is better suited to survive in its environment.

a·dapt·ed (ə dap′təd) *adj.* suited; fitted: *A frog's hind legs are well adapted for swimming.*

a·dapt·er (ə dap′tər) *n.* **1.** a person who adapts something. **2.** a device for modifying an apparatus for a new use. **3.** a device for connecting two pieces of equipment that would not otherwise operate together.

add (ad) *v.t.* **1.** to put (something) together with another or others of the same kind: *He added a new stamp to his collection.* **2.** to unite or combine with: *to add cream to coffee, to add a porch to a house.* **3.** to find the sum of: *to add a column of figures.* **4.** to say or write further: *Do you wish to add anything to what he has said?* —*v.i.* **1.** to find the sum of numbers; perform addition: *He learned to add before he learned to multiply.* **2.** to make or serve as an addition; contribute something more: *The balloons added to the party atmosphere. Don't add to our problems by complaining.*

    to add up. a. to equal an expected or desired total. **b.** to be meaningful or reasonable: *The facts don't add up in this case.*

    to add up to. to amount to: *Their actions added up to a deliberate violation of the rules.*

ad·dend (ad′end, ə dend′) *n.* any number or quantity that can be added to another. In the example $8 + 4 = 12$, 8 and 4 are the addends.

ad·den·dum (ə den′dəm) *n. pl.,* **ad·den·da** (ə den′də). something that is added; addition.

ad·der (ad′ər) *n.* **1.** a poisonous snake of northern Europe and Asia, having a brown skin with black markings. **2.** the hognose snake of North America. **3.** any of various snakes of Africa, especially the puff adder. [Middle English *naddre* a viper, from Old English *nædre.* The letter *n* was lost from the word because people hearing the phrase *a nadder* though it was *an adder.*]

ad·dict (*n.,* ad′ikt; *v.,* ə dikt′) *n.* **1.** a person who has a strong and constant need for a harmful substance, especially a narcotic drug: *a heroin addict.* **2.** a person who is strongly devoted to some activity or pleasure. —*v.t.* to cause (someone) to become an addict.

ad·dict·ed (ə dik′tid) *adj.* **1.** unable to do without some harmful substance: *to be addicted to drugs.* **2.** inclined by strong habit or preference: *to be addicted to watching television.*

ad·dic·tion (ə dik′shən) *n.* the condition of being addicted, especially complete dependence on a harmful drug.

ad·dic·tive (ə dik′tiv) *adj.* causing addiction: *Heroin is an addictive drug.*

adding machine, a machine consisting of a set of keys that, when struck, print numbers on a roll of paper. Adding machines can add, and some can also subtract, multiply, and divide.

Ad·dis Ab·a·ba (ad′is ab′ə bə) the capital and largest city of Ethiopia, in the central part of the country. Pop. (1968 est.), 684,100.

Ad·di·son, Joseph (ad′ə sən) 1672–1719, English writer.

ad·di·tion (ə dish′ən) *n.* **1.** the act or process of adding: *The addition of seasoning improved the flavor of the stew.* **2.** the process of finding the sum of two or more numbers. $9 + 2 + 5 = 16$ is an example of addition. **3.** something that is added: *They raised funds to build an addition to the museum.*

    in addition or **in addition to.** as well; also; besides: *In addition to being on the baseball team, he is also a member of the football team.*

ad·di·tion·al (ə dish′ən əl) *adj.* added; further: *He makes additional money by working nights.* —**ad·di′tion·al·ly,** *adv.*

ad·di·tive (ad′ə tiv) *n.* a substance added in small quantities to improve or change another substance or thing: *a gasoline additive, an additive put in a food to prevent spoiling.* —*adj.* relating to or involving addition.

additive identity, a number that, when added to another number, produces a sum equal to that other number. Zero is the additive identity, since $0 + 5 = 5$ and $\frac{3}{4} + 0 = \frac{3}{4}$.

additive inverse, either one of a pair of numbers whose sum is zero, such as 5 and –5 or $\frac{3}{4}$ and $-\frac{3}{4}$.

ad·dle (ad′əl) *v.,* **ad·dled, ad·dling.** *v.t.* **1.** to make confused. **2.** to cause (an egg) to become rotten. —*v.i.* to become addled.

ad·dress (*n.,* ə dres′, ad′res; *v.,* ə dres′) *n. pl.,* **ad·dress·es. 1.** a formal speech: *The President's address to the nation will be on television.* **2.** the place at which a person lives or an organization is located: *His address is 90 Pine Lane. That store's address is 545 Main Street.* **3.** the writing on a letter, package, or other item indicating where it is to be delivered. **4.** personal manner in conversation: *She has the poise and address of an experienced actress.* —*v.t.* **1.** to speak formally to: *to address a political convention.* **2.** to direct (writing or speech): *The judge addressed his remarks to the jury.* **3.** to direct (oneself) in speech or writing: *He addressed himself to the crowd.* **4.** to write the destination on (a letter, package, or other item to be delivered). **5.** to use proper form in speaking or writing to: *You should address the king as "Your Majesty."* **6.** to direct one's energies or attention; apply (oneself): *I'll address myself to the hardest job first.*

ad·dress·ee (ad′res ē′) *n.* a person to whom a letter, package, or other item is addressed.

ad·duce (ə dōōs′, ə dyōōs′) *v.t.*, **ad·duced, ad·duc·ing.** to present as proof, reason, or example: *The speaker adduced a great many facts to support his argument.*

Ad·e·laide (ad′əl ād′) *n.* a city in southern Australia. Pop. (1970 est.), 825,400.

A·den (ad′ən, äd′ən) *n.* **1.** a region on the southeastern coast of Southern Yemen, formerly a British protectorate. **2.** the capital of Southern Yemen. Pop. (1970 est.), 250,000. **3. Gulf of.** a western inlet of the Arabian Sea, between southern Arabia and eastern Africa.

A·de·nau·er, Konrad (ad′ən ou′ər; kon′rad) 1876–1967, German statesman.

ad·e·nine (ad′ən ēn′) *n.* a purine base that is an essential constituent of DNA and RNA.

ad·e·noi·dal (ad′ən oid′əl) *adj.* relating to the adenoids.

ad·e·noids (ad′ən oidz′) *n., pl.* the growths of glandular tissue in the upper part of the throat, behind the nose. If the adenoids become swollen, they may make breathing and speaking difficult.

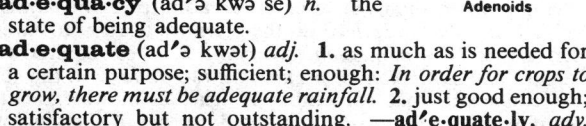

Adenoids

a·dept (*adj.*, ə dept′; *n.*, ad′ept) *adj.* highly skilled; expert; proficient: *He is adept at performing magic tricks.* —*n.* a person who is highly skilled; an expert. —**a·dept′ly,** *adv.* —**a·dept′ness,** *n.*

ad·e·qua·cy (ad′ə kwə sē) *n.* the state of being adequate.

ad·e·quate (ad′ə kwət) *adj.* **1.** as much as is needed for a certain purpose; sufficient; enough: *In order for crops to grow, there must be adequate rainfall.* **2.** just good enough; satisfactory but not outstanding. —**ad′e·quate·ly,** *adv.* —**ad′e·quate·ness,** *n.*

ad·here (ad hēr′) *v.i.*, **ad·hered, ad·her·ing. 1.** to stick or hold fast: *The gum adhered to his shoe.* **2.** to hold faithfully or firmly; remain attached or devoted; follow closely: *Despite the injury to the team's quarterback, the coach adhered to the original plan for the game.*

ad·her·ence (ad hēr′əns) *n.* **1.** the act or the state of adhering. **2.** firm attachment; faithful support: *adherence to a cause, adherence to a belief.*

ad·her·ent (ad hēr′ənt) *n.* a person who believes in or follows a cause, leader, organization, or the like; firm supporter; advocate: *He is an adherent of strict gun-control laws.* —*adj.* sticking or holding fast; adhering.

ad·he·sion (ad hē′zhən) *n.* **1.** the act or the state of sticking or holding fast. **2.** faithful attachment; adherence. **3.** the abnormal growing together of organs or parts that are normally separate.

ad·he·sive (ad hē′siv) *adj.* **1.** tending to stick or hold fast; clinging: *Paste and glue have adhesive properties.* **2.** having a sticky surface that will hold fast to something; gummed: *an adhesive label.* —*n.* **1.** an adhesive substance: *Glue is an adhesive.* **2.** see **adhesive tape.** —**ad·he′sive·ness,** *n.*

adhesive tape, a tape coated on one side with a sticky substance.

ad hoc (ad hok′) for a specific and limited purpose: *an ad hoc committee.* [Latin *ad hoc* literally, to this.]

a·dieu (ə dōō′, ə dyōō′) *interj.* good-by; farewell. —*n. pl.*, **a·dieus** or **a·dieux** (ə dōōz′, ə dyōōz′). good-by; farewell. [Old French *adieu.*]

ad in·fi·ni·tum (ad′ in′fə nī′təm) without limit; endlessly. [Latin *ad infinitum* literally, to the infinite.]

a·di·os (ä′dē ōs′) *interj.* good-by; farewell. —*n. pl.*, **a·di·os·es.** good-by; farewell. [Spanish *adiós.*]

ad·i·pose (ad′ə pōs′) *adj.* relating to animal fat; fatty: *adipose tissue.*

Ad·i·ron·dacks (ad′ə ron′daks) *n., pl.* a mountain range in northeastern New York. Also, **Adirondack Mountains.**

adj., adjective.

ad·ja·cent (ə jā′sənt) *adj.* lying next to or near; adjoining: *The barn is adjacent to the house.* —**ad·ja′cent·ly,** *adv.*

adjacent angle, in geometry, either of two angles having the same vertex and a common side.

ad·jec·ti·val (aj′ik tī′vəl) *adj.* **1.** of or relating to an adjective: *The suffixes "-ous" and "-ful" are adjectival endings.* **2.** functioning as an adjective. In the sentence "The freight handling office is closed," *freight handling* is an adjectival phrase. —**ad′jec·ti·val·ly,** *adv.*

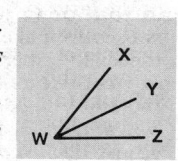

Adjacent angles
XWY and *YWZ* are
adjacent angles

ad·jec·tive (aj′ik tiv) *n.* a word that modifies a noun or pronoun. An adjective may describe the word it modifies (the *red* car, a *sad* boy, Bill is *tall*) or in some way limit the word (*his* bat, *many* books, *three* dogs). A word that can be used alone after a noun and the verb "seem" (The dog seems *hungry*) and after a noun and the verb "to be" (The baby is *asleep*) is an adjective. —*adj.* relating to or used as an adjective.

ad·join (ə join′) *v.t.* to be very close to or touch on; be next to: *The garage adjoins the house.* —*v.i.* to be close together or touching: *The two farms adjoin.*

ad·join·ing (ə joi′ning) *adj.* being next to; adjacent: *The school has an adjoining playground.*

ad·journ (ə jurn′) *v.t.* to put off to a later time; postpone; defer: *The chairman adjourned the meeting. The judge adjourned the court until the following week.* —*v.i.* **1.** to stop work or proceedings until a later time: *The Senate adjourned for the summer.* **2.** *Informal.* to go from one place to another: *Since we've finished eating, let's adjourn to the living room.*

ad·journ·ment (ə jurn′mənt) *n.* **1.** the act of adjourning or the state of being adjourned: *The chairman called for a vote on adjournment.* **2.** the time during which a group or formal body is not in session: *a month's adjournment of the court.*

ad·judge (ə juj′) *v.t.*, **ad·judged, ad·judg·ing. 1.** to decide or settle by law: *The defendant was adjudged guilty of the crime.* **2.** to award or grant by law: *The money was adjudged to the defendant.* **3.** to judge to be; deem; consider.

ad·ju·di·cate (ə jōō′də kāt′) *v.t.*, **ad·ju·di·cat·ed, ad·ju·di·cat·ing.** to consider and decide by law: *to adjudicate a case in civil court.* —**ad·ju′di·ca′tion,** *n.*

ad·junct (aj′ungkt) *n.* something added to another thing but not a necessary part of it; less important or secondary thing: *A dial indicating the correct day and month is an adjunct to a wristwatch.*

---

at; āpe; cär; end; mē; it; īce; hot; ōld; fôrk; wood; fōōl; oil; out; up; turn; sing; thin; **th**is; hw in white; zh in treasure. The symbol ə stands for the sound of **a** in about, **e** in taken, **i** in pencil, **o** in lemon, and **u** in circus.

ad·jure (ə joor') *v.t.,* **ad·jured, ad·jur·ing.** **1.** to order solemnly, especially under oath: *The judge adjured the witness to testify truthfully.* **2.** to urge seriously; request earnestly: *His friend adjured him to be careful.* **—ad′ju·ra′tion,** *n.*

ad·just (ə just') *v.t.* **1.** to change or arrange to fit a need or demand; make suitable: *to adjust the length of a skirt.* **2.** to move or arrange the parts of so as to put in proper working order; regulate: *to adjust the brakes of an automobile.* **3.** to bring into the proper state or condition; arrange satisfactorily; settle: *to adjust an insurance claim.* **—v.i.** to become accustomed; adapt oneself: *The old man found it hard to adjust to his new surroundings.* **—ad·just′a·ble,** *adj.*

ad·just·er (ə jus'tər) *also,* **ad·jus·tor.** *n.* **1.** a thing that is used to make an adjustment. **2.** a person who adjusts, especially a person who adjusts insurance claims.

ad·just·ment (ə just'mənt) *n.* **1.** the act of adjusting or the state of being adjusted: *a perfect adjustment of an instrument.* **2.** a method or device by which something is adjusted: *the adjustments on a microscope.* **3.** the process of determining or settling something: *the adjustment of an insurance claim.*

ad·ju·tant (aj'ə tənt) *n.* **1.** a military officer who acts as an administrative assistant to a commanding officer. **2.** an aide; assistant. **3.** see **adjutant stork.**

adjutant stork, a very large stork found in India and Africa. Also, **adjutant bird.** [Perhaps because the bird's stiff walk was thought to resemble the walk of a military officer.]

ad-lib (ad'lib') *v.,* **ad-libbed, ad-lib·bing.** **—v.t.** to make up on the spur of the moment; improvise: *to ad-lib a speech. The comedian ad-libbed several jokes.* **—v.i.** to do or say something without previous preparation: *The speaker lost his notes and had to ad-lib.* **—n.** an improvised remark, joke, song, or the like; something ad-libbed. **—adj.** made up on the spur of the moment; improvised: *an ad-lib remark.* **—adv.** in an improvised way. [Latin *ad libitum* literally, at one's pleasure.]

Adm., Admiral.

ad·min·is·ter (ad min'is tər) *v.t.* **1.** to control the operation of; manage; direct: *to administer a college, to administer a department of the government.* **2.** to give out; dispense; provide; supply: *to administer medicine. The Red Cross administers aid in disaster areas.* **3.** to give or offer formally: *The judge administered the oath to the witness.* **—v.i.** to be of service; contribute: *to administer to the well-being of the community.*

ad·min·is·trate (ad min'is trāt') *v.t., v.i.,* **ad·min·is·trat·ed, ad·min·is·trat·ing.** to administer.

ad·min·is·tra·tion (ad min'is trā'shən) *n.* **1.** the act or method of managing or directing a business, organization, government, or the like. **2.** a group of people having the power to manage or direct something: *a school administration.* **3.** the executive branch of a government. **4. the Administration.** the President of the United States, together with his cabinet and the other officials who make up the executive branch of the government. **5.** the period during which a chief executive holds office. **6.** the act of administering something: *the administration of an oath, the administration of justice.*

ad·min·is·tra·tive (ad min'is trā'tiv) *adj.* of or relating to administration or management: *A business executive must have administrative skill.* **—ad·min′is·tra′tive·ly,** *adv.*

ad·min·is·tra·tor (ad min'is trā'tər) *n.* **1.** a person who administers. **2.** a person appointed by a court of law to manage or settle the estate of a dead person.

ad·mi·ra·ble (ad'mər ə bəl) *adj.* deserving admiration; excellent: *admirable work. He achieved an admirable record as a senator.* **—ad′mi·ra·ble·ness,** *n.* **—ad′mi·ra·bly,** *adv.*

ad·mi·ral (ad'mər əl) *n.* **1.** a naval officer of the highest rank. **2.** in the U. S. Navy: **a.** an officer ranking above a vice admiral and below a fleet admiral. **b.** any other officer ranking above a captain. See **fleet admiral, rear admiral,** and **vice admiral.** **3.** either of two species of brightly colored butterflies.

ad·mi·ral·ty (ad'mər əl tē) *n.* *pl.,* **ad·mi·ral·ties.** **1.** the branch of law that deals with matters involving ships and shipping. **2. Admiralty.** the department of the British government that has charge of naval affairs.

ad·mi·ra·tion (ad'mə rā'shən) *n.* **1.** a feeling of high regard or esteem: *She earned the admiration of all who knew her.* **2.** the act of viewing something with appreciation and delight: *the admiration of a beautiful painting.*

ad·mire (ad mīr') *v.t.,* **ad·mired, ad·mir·ing.** **1.** to feel high regard or esteem for: *to admire a person's character. I admire his manner of dealing with people.* **2.** to regard with appreciation and delight: *to admire a painting, to admire a friend's new coat.* **—ad·mir′ing·ly,** *adv.*

ad·mir·er (ad mīr'ər) *n.* a person who admires: *The pretty girl had many admirers among the boys in her class.*

ad·mis·si·bil·i·ty (ad mis'ə bil'ə tē) *n.* the quality of being admissible: *The lawyer questioned the admissibility of the new evidence.*

ad·mis·si·ble (ad mis'ə bəl) *adj.* **1.** that can be allowed or properly considered; allowable: *an admissible argument. Illness is an admissible reason for absence from school.* **2.** that can be admitted: *Children are not admissible to that film.* **—ad·mis′si·bly,** *adv.*

ad·mis·sion (ad mish'ən) *n.* **1.** the act of granting or being granted the right to enter; an admitting: *the admission of students to college.* **2.** the privilege or right to enter or use: *to have admission to a club.* **3.** a fee required to enter: *The admission to this game is two dollars.* **4.** the act of conceding that something is true; acknowledgment; confession: *an admission of guilt.* **5.** the act of allowing or granting as valid or relevant: *the admission of an argument in debate.*

ad·mit (ad mit') *v.,* **ad·mit·ted, ad·mit·ting.** **—v.t.** **1.** to grant entrance to; allow to enter; let in: *The ushers admitted only one person at a time. John was admitted to the club last week.* **2.** to concede to be true; acknowledge; confess; grant: *to admit one's guilt. I'll admit you're right.* **3.** to recognize as valid or relevant: *to admit evidence in a trial.* **4.** to be the means of entrance for: *This pass will admit you to the show.* **5.** to have the room to hold; accommodate: *The auditorium admits 500 people.* **—v.i.** **1.** to allow the possibility: *His outrageous behavior admits of no apology.* **2.** to provide access; open: *That door admits to the engine room.*

ad·mit·tance (ad mit'əns) *n.* **1.** permission to enter; privilege of entrance: *Show your ticket to gain admittance to the theater.* **2.** the act of admitting or the state of being admitted.

ad·mit·ted·ly (ad mit'id lē) *adv.* by one's own admission or by common agreement: *I am admittedly a very poor swimmer.*

ad·mix (ad miks') *v.t., v.i.* to mix into something else; blend.

ad·mix·ture (ad miks'chər) *n.* **1.** something added in mixing. **2.** the act of mixing. **3.** something formed by mixing; mixture.

ad·mon·ish (ad mon'ish) *v.t.* **1.** to caution against some action; warn: *He was admonished not to cut class again.* **2.** to scold or rebuke mildly: *The lifeguard admonished them for running near the pool.* **—ad·mon′ish·ment,** *n.*

ad·mo·ni·tion (ad′mə nish′ən) *n.* **1.** the act of admonishing; warning. **2.** a mild reprimand.

ad·mon·i·to·ry (ad mon′ə tôr′ē) *adj.* cautioning; warning: *The police officer spoke to the motorist in an admonitory tone of voice.*

a·do (ə dōō′) *n.* fuss; bustle; difficulty.

a·do·be (ə dō′bē) *n.* **1.** a brick that has been dried in the sun, used as a building material. **2.** a building made of such bricks. **3.** the clay from which such bricks are made. —*adj.* constructed or made of adobe: *an adobe house.*

Adobe house

ad·o·les·cence (ad′əl es′əns) *n.* **1.** the period of life between childhood and adulthood; youth. **2.** the state of being adolescent.

ad·o·les·cent (ad′əl es′ənt) *n.* a person between childhood and adulthood, especially one between the ages of twelve and eighteen. —*adj.* of or relating to adolescence or an adolescent; youthful; immature: *adolescent behavior.*

A·don·is (ə don′is, ə dō′nis) *n.* **1.** *Greek Mythology.* a handsome youth who was loved by Aphrodite. **2.** any handsome young man.

a·dopt (ə dopt′) *v.t.* **1.** to take (a child of other parents) into one's family to be raised as one's own: *The young couple adopted the orphan girl.* **2.** to take and use as one's own: *The tune of a British song was adopted for "The Star-Spangled Banner."* **3.** to accept or approve, especially by formal vote: *The board adopted the proposal after much debate.* ▲ See **adapt** for usage note.

a·dop·tion (ə dop′shən) *n.* **1.** the act of adopting or the state of being adopted: *the adoption of a child.* **2.** acceptance or approval: *the adoption of a proposal.*

a·dop·tive (ə dop′tiv) *adj.* related by adoption: *Her adoptive parents were the only family she knew.*

a·dor·a·ble (ə dôr′ə bəl) *adj.* **1.** delightful; lovable; charming: *an adorable child.* **2.** worthy of adoration. —**a·dor′a·ble·ness,** *n.* —**a·dor′a·bly,** *adv.*

ad·o·ra·tion (ad′ə rā′shən) *n.* **1.** the act of honoring or worshiping as divine: *the adoration of Christ by the Magi.* **2.** deep love and devotion: *a mother's adoration of her children.*

a·dore (ə dôr′) *v.t.,* **a·dored, a·dor·ing. 1.** to have love and admiration for; idolize: *Her students adored her.* **2.** to honor as divine; worship. **3.** *Informal.* to have a great liking for: *I adore your new hat.* —**a·dor′er,** *n.* —**a·dor′ing·ly,** *adv.*

a·dorn (ə dôrn′) *v.t.* to add something beautiful to; make beautiful; ornament; decorate: *to adorn a room with flowers. Her face has adorned many magazine covers.* —**a·dorn′er,** *n.*

a·dorn·ment (ə dôrn′mənt) *n.* **1.** something that adorns; ornament; decoration: *She wore a garland of flowers as an adornment for her hair.* **2.** the act of adorning.

ad·re·nal (ə drēn′əl) *adj.* **1.** located near or on the kidneys. **2.** relating to or from the adrenal glands. —*n.* see **adrenal gland.**

adrenal gland, one of a pair of small glands above the kidneys. The adrenal glands secrete adrenalin and several other hormones. Also, **suprarenal gland.**

ad·ren·a·lin (ə dren′əl in) *also,* **ad·ren·a·line.** *n.* a hormone secreted by the adrenal glands, especially under conditions of excitement, danger, or stress. Adrenalin makes the heart beat faster, quickens the rate of breathing, and produces other changes that enable the body to deal more effectively with an emergency. Adrenalin can also be produced synthetically. Trademark: **Adrenalin.** Also, **epinephrine.**

A·dri·at·ic (ā′drē at′ik) *n.* a sea between Italy and Yugoslavia, an arm of the Mediterranean. Also, **Adriatic Sea.**

a·drift (ə drift′) *adv., adj.* **1.** moving with the current or wind; without being anchored or steered; floating freely: *The boys accidentally set the canoe adrift.* **2.** without direction or aim: *She was adrift in the city for a few weeks until she found a job.*

a·droit (ə droit′) *adj.* smoothly skillful; deft; clever: *Her adroit handling of the problem prevented a crisis.* —**a·droit′ly,** *adv.* —**a·droit′ness,** *n.*

ad·sorb (ad sôrb′, ad zôrb′) *v.t.* to retain (a gas, liquid, or dissolved substance) on the surface instead of absorbing it: *A window pane adsorbs moisture during a rainstorm.*

ad·sorp·tion (ad sôrp′shən, ad zôrp′shən) *n.* the process of adsorbing: *the adsorption of gases by a charcoal filter.*

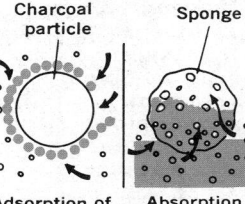
Charcoal particle   Sponge
Adsorption of gas molecules   Absorption of water
Adsorption

ad·u·la·tion (aj′ə lā′shən) *n.* lavish praise or flattery; too much praise: *The politician's speech was filled with adulation for his party's candidate.*

ad·u·la·to·ry (aj′ə lə tôr′ē) *adj.* lavishly praising or flattering: *an adulatory speech.*

a·dult (ə dult′, ad′ult) *n.* **1.** a grown man or woman; mature person. **2.** a plant or animal that has reached full growth. **3.** a person who is legally of age, usually a person more than twenty-one years old. —*adj.* **1.** having reached full size and strength; fully grown; mature: *an adult person, an adult wolf, an adult moth.* **2.** relating to or for adults: *adult education.*

a·dul·ter·ant (ə dul′tər ənt) *n.* a substance or element that adulterates something.

a·dul·ter·ate (ə dul′tə rāt′) *v.t.,* **a·dul·ter·at·ed, a·dul·ter·at·ing.** to lessen the quality of (something) by including in it inferior or inappropriate substances: *to adulterate milk with water. The writer felt that the addition of many new slang terms had adulterated the language.*

a·dul·ter·a·tion (ə dul′tə rā′shən) *n.* **1.** the process of adulterating. **2.** an adulterated substance or product: *Wine thinned with water is an adulteration.*

a·dul·ter·er (ə dul′tər ər) *n.* a person who commits adultery, especially a man.

a·dul·ter·ess (ə dul′tər is, ə dul′tris) *n. pl.,* **a·dul·ter·ess·es.** a woman who commits adultery.

a·dul·ter·ous (ə dul′tər əs) *adj.* **1.** guilty of adultery: *an adulterous person.* **2.** relating to adultery: *adulterous behavior.*

a·dul·ter·y (ə dul′tər ē) *n. pl.,* **a·dul·ter·ies.** unfaithfulness of a married man to his wife or a married woman to her husband by having sexual relations with another person.

a·dult·hood (ə dult′hood′) *n.* the state of being an adult.

adv. **1.** adverb. **2.** advertisement.

at; āpe; cär; end; mē; it; īce; hot; ōld; fôrk; wood; fōol; oil; out; up; turn; sing; thin; this; hw in white; zh in treasure. The symbol ə stands for the sound of a in about, e in taken, i in pencil, o in lemon, and u in circus.

ad·vance (ad vans′) v., **ad·vanced, ad·vanc·ing.** —v.t. **1.** to move (something) forward: *He advanced the hands on the clock to the correct time. The football team advanced the ball ten yards.* **2.** to help the progress of; further: *Charles Darwin's work advanced the science of biology.* **3.** to offer; propose: *to advance a theory.* **4.** to raise to a higher or more favorable position or rank. **5.** to make earlier, as a time, date, or event: *to advance a wedding from June 30 to June 12.* **6.a.** to pay (an amount) before due or promised. **b.** to lend: *The bank advanced him five hundred dollars.* —v.i. **1.** to move forward; proceed: *The army advanced to the gates of the city.* **2.** to move up in position, rank, or esteem; progress: *The young man advanced rapidly in his new job.* **3.** to increase in price, rate, or value: *Railroad stocks advanced two points.* —n. **1.** movement forward: *The troops made a steady advance.* **2.** progress; improvement: *The discovery of polio vaccine was an advance in medical knowledge.* **3.a.** a payment given before due: *He received an advance on his next month's salary.* **b.** a loan. **4. advances.** attempts to gain the friendship or approval of someone: *Her cold manner discouraged all advances.* —adj. **1.** situated in front: *an advance guard.* **2.** ahead of time: *advance information, advance notice, an advance showing of a film.*

ad·vanced (ad vanst′) adj. **1.** ahead of others; modern; progressive: *an advanced theory, advanced techniques of manufacturing.* **2.** past the beginning or elementary stage; not primary: *advanced algebra.* **3.** near the end in development or time: *a man of advanced age.*

ad·vance·ment (ad vans′mənt) n. **1.** progress or improvement: *scientific advancement.* **2.** a promotion to a higher rank or position: *This job has opportunities for advancement.* **3.** movement forward.

ad·van·tage (ad van′tij) n. **1.** a useful or helpful circumstance, factor, or event; something of benefit; asset: *The basketball player's height gave him a great advantage over shorter opponents.* **2.** benefit; gain: *More practice will be to your advantage.*
  to advantage. favorably or effectively: *to display a painting to advantage.*
  to take advantage of. a. to use profitably: *to take advantage of an opportunity.* **b.** to exploit unfairly: *He took advantage of his neighbor's generous nature and borrowed all his tools.*

ad·van·ta·geous (ad′vən tā′jəs) adj. giving an advantage or benefit; favorable; helpful: *Capturing his opponent's queen put him in a very advantageous position in the chess game.* —**ad′van·ta′geous·ly,** adv. —**ad′van·ta′geous·ness,** n.

ad·vent (ad′vent) n. **1.** a coming into being; arrival: *the advent of spring, the advent of old age.* **2. Advent. a.** the birth of Christ. **b.** a period of religious observance including the four Sundays before Christmas.

Ad·vent·ist (ad′ven tist) n. a member of a Christian denomination believing that the Second Coming of Christ will soon occur.

ad·ven·ti·tious (ad′ven tish′əs) adj. **1.** added by accident from outside; not inherent or essential. **2.** (of part of a plant or animal) appearing in an unusual or abnormal place, such as buds growing from the roots of a plant. —**ad′ven·ti′tious·ly,** adv. —**ad′ven·ti′tious·ness,** n.

ad·ven·ture (ad ven′chər) n. **1.** a difficult and dangerous undertaking in which risk is involved: *Columbus' voyage to the New World was a great adventure.* **2.** dangerous and exciting activity: *a spirit of adventure, a life filled with adventure.* **3.** a thrilling or unusual experience: *A day in the city was always an adventure for her.* —v., **ad·ven·tured, ad·ven·tur·ing.** —v.i. to have hazardous or thrilling experiences. —v.t. to risk; venture.

ad·ven·tur·er (ad ven′chər ər) n. **1.** a person who seeks or has adventures. **2.** a person who uses deceitful, dishonest methods to make money or to advance himself.

ad·ven·ture·some (ad ven′chər səm) adj. eager for adventure; adventurous.

ad·ven·tur·ess (ad ven′chər is) n. pl., **ad·ven·tur·ess·es.** a woman who schemes or uses her charms to obtain wealth or social position.

ad·ven·tur·ous (ad ven′chər əs) adj. **1.** eager for adventure; willing to encounter danger: *an adventurous knight.* **2.** full of danger; hazardous: *an adventurous voyage.* —**ad·ven′tur·ous·ly,** adv. —**ad·ven′tur·ous·ness,** n.

ad·verb (ad′vurb′) n. a word that modifies a verb, adjective, or another adverb. An adverb may indicate such ideas as manner (He walked *slowly*), time (She is *rarely* angry), place (The boat sailed *away*), or degree (I am *very* tired). Most adverbs are formed by adding the suffix *-ly* to an adjective or participle, such as "sad*ly*," "clever*ly*," or "excited*ly*."

ad·ver·bi·al (ad vur′bē əl) adj. **1.** of or relating to an adverb: *The suffix "-ly" is an adverbial ending.* **2.** functioning as an adverb. In the sentence "He ran as fast as he could," *as fast as he could* is an adverbial phrase. —**ad·ver′bi·al·ly,** adv.

ad·ver·sar·y (ad′vər ser′ē) n. pl., **ad·ver·sar·ies.** a person or group that is hostile toward or competing with another; opponent or enemy: *That district attorney is a dedicated adversary of organized crime.*

ad·verse (ad vurs′, ad′vurs) adj. **1.** unfavorable to one's interests or to what is desired: *adverse circumstances. The football game was played under adverse weather conditions.* **2.** antagonistic; hostile: *an adverse attitude, adverse criticism.* **3.** acting in an opposite or contrary direction, especially so as to hinder: *The ship met adverse winds.* —**ad·verse′ly,** adv. —**ad·verse′ness,** n.

ad·ver·si·ty (ad vur′sə tē) n. pl., **ad·ver·si·ties. 1.** a condition of misfortune, hardship, or suffering: *He showed courage in the face of adversity.* **2.** an instance of misfortune; unfavorable event: *She became successful despite many adversities.*

ad·vert (ad vurt′) v.i. to call attention: refer: *The candidate adverted to the accusations made by his opponent.*

ad·ver·tise (ad′vər tīz′) v., **ad·ver·tised, ad·ver·tis·ing.** —v.t. **1.** to make a public announcement describing the good qualities of (a product, service, cause, idea, or the like) in such a way as to make people want to buy it or support it: *to advertise a cough medicine, to advertise a new television series.* **2.** to make known publicly: *to advertise a political rally.* —v.i. **1.** to inquire about or seek something by public notice (with *for*): *She advertised for a babysitter in the local newspaper.* **2.** to present advertisements: *That company advertises frequently on national television.* —**ad′ver·tis′er,** n.

ad·ver·tise·ment (ad′vər tīz′mənt, əd vur′tiz mənt) n. a public announcement, usually printed or broadcast, especially one that promotes a product or service: *This magazine contains many advertisements for the new fall fashions in women's clothing.*

ad·ver·tis·ing (ad′vər tī′zing) n. **1.** the use of public announcements to promote the sale of a product or the success of something. **2.** the business of preparing and placing advertisements, especially in newspapers and magazines or on television or radio: *Her father works in advertising.* **3.** advertisements: *A newspaper earns most of its profit from advertising.*

ad·vice (əd vīs′) n. **1.** an opinion offered as guidance as to what course of action should be followed; counsel: *He asked his teacher for advice in choosing a college.* **2.** also, **advices.** information; news.

ad·vis·a·bil·i·ty (əd vī′zə bil′ə tē) *n.* the quality of being advisable: *He consulted his doctor on the advisability of following the new diet.*

ad·vis·a·ble (əd vī′zə bəl) *adj.* that would be good advice; worthy of being recommended; wise; sensible: *It is advisable to drive at a slower speed on wet roads.* —**ad·vis′a·bly,** *adv.*

ad·vise (əd vīz′) *v.,* **ad·vised, ad·vis·ing.** —*v.t.* **1.** to give advice to; counsel: *I advise you not to buy that coat. His lawyer advised him to cooperate with the authorities.* **2.** to suggest as a sound course; recommend: *I advise caution in dealing with him.* **3.** to notify; inform: *The letter advised her that she had been chosen for the position.* —*v.i.* **1.** to give advice: *I'll do as you advise.* **2.** to confer; discuss: *He advised with his staff before announcing his candidacy.*

ad·vis·ed·ly (əd vī′zid lē) *adv.* by design; deliberately: *I use the term "blackmail" advisedly.*

ad·vise·ment (əd vīz′mənt) *n.* serious consideration or consultation: *The manager took the workers' complaints under advisement.*

ad·vis·er (əd vī′zər) *also,* **ad·vi·sor.** *n.* **1.** a person who advises. **2.** a teacher or professor who is appointed to advise students about their studies, choice of career, and the like.

ad·vis·o·ry (əd vī′zər ē) *adj.* **1.** having the power to advise: *The mayor appointed an advisory panel.* **2.** giving advice: *an advisory report.*

ad·vo·ca·cy (ad′və kə sē) *n.* the act of advocating; support.

ad·vo·cate (*v.,* ad′və kāt′; *n.,* ad′və kit) *v.t.,* **ad·vo·cat·ed, ad·vo·cat·ing.** to plead in favor of; urge; support: *He advocates prison reform. The council advocated a change of policy.* —*n.* **1.** a person who publicly supports a cause or policy; supporter: *Martin Luther King was an advocate of nonviolence.* **2.** a person who pleads the cause of another, especially a lawyer.

advt., advertisement.

adz (adz) *also,* **adze.** *n.* a tool resembling an ax, used for trimming and shaping timber. It has a blade set at right angles to the handle and curving inward.

AEC, Atomic Energy Commission.

Ae·ge·an (i jē′ən) *n.* a sea between Greece and Turkey, an arm of the Mediterranean. Also, **Aegean Sea.**

ae·gis (ē′jis) *also,* **e·gis.** *n.* **1.** sponsorship or support: *The relief program was carried out under the aegis of the federal government.* **2.** protection; guard.

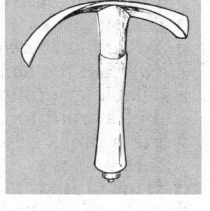

Adz

Ae·gis·thus (i jis′thəs) *n. Greek Legend.* the lover of Clytemnestra. See **Clytemnestra.**

Ae·ne·as (i nē′əs) *n. Greek and Roman Legend.* the Trojan warrior who was the hero of Virgil's *Aeneid* and whose descendants are said to have founded Rome.

Ae·ne·id (i nē′id) *n.* a Latin epic poem by Virgil, describing the adventures of Aeneas.

Ae·o·lus (ē′ə ləs) *n. Greek Mythology.* the god of the winds.

ae·on (ē′ən, ē′on) another spelling of **eon.**

aer·ate (er′āt) *v.t.,* **aer·at·ed, aer·at·ing. 1.** to mix with air: *to aerate drinking water.* **2.** to expose to air: *to aerate soil by plowing.* **3.** to charge or fill (a liquid) with gas: *Soda is aerated with carbon dioxide.* **4.** to expose to the chemical action of oxygen; oxygenate: *The blood is aerated in respiration.* —**aer·a′tion,** *n.* —**aer′a·tor,** *n.*

aer·i·al (er′ē əl) *adj.* **1.** of or in the air: *aerial acrobatics, an aerial ascent in a balloon.* **2.** like air; light and thin.

3. for, from, or relating to aircraft: *aerial photography.* **4.** growing in the air rather than in soil or water: *a tree with aerial roots.* —*n.* a radio or television antenna. —**aer′i·al·ly,** *adv.*

aer·i·a·list (er′ē ə list) *n.* a person who performs in the air, as on a trapeze or high wire.

ae·rie (er′ē, ēr′ē) *also,* **ey·rie, ey·ry.** *n.* **1.** a nest built high on a cliff or mountainside by an eagle, hawk, or other bird of prey. **2.** a building in a high, remote place.

aero- *combining form* of the air; air: *aerodynamics.*

aer·obe (er′ōb) *n.* a microorganism that requires oxygen for life.

aer·o·bic (e rō′bik) *adj.* **1.** living only in the presence of oxygen: *aerobic bacteria.* **2.** relating to or produced by microorganisms requiring oxygen.

aer·o·drome (er′ə drōm′) *n. British.* another word for **airdrome.**

aer·o·dy·nam·ics (er′ō dī nam′iks) *n., pl.* the branch of physics that deals with the laws of motion of air and other gases, and with the forces exerted by such gases on bodies moving in them. ▲ used with a singular verb.

aer·ol·o·gy (er ol′ə jē) *n.* the branch of meteorology that deals with the study of air, especially in the upper atmosphere.

aer·o·nau·tic (er′ə nô′tik) *adj.* of or relating to aeronautics. Also, **aer·o·nau·ti·cal** (er′ə nô′ti kəl). —**aer′o·nau′ti·cal·ly,** *adv.*

aer·o·nau·tics (er′ə nô′tiks) *n., pl.* **1.** the science or art of flight. **2.** the branch of engineering concerned with designing, making, and flying aircraft. ▲ used with a singular verb in both definitions.

aer·o·pause (er′ō pôz′) *n.* the region where outer space is considered to begin and where the atmosphere will not support aircraft.

aer·o·plane (er′ə plān′) *n. British.* another word for **airplane.**

aer·o·sol (er′ə sôl′) *n.* a mass of very fine solid or liquid particles suspended in a gas. Smoke, fog, and smog are aerosols.

aerosol bomb, a container from which a liquid sealed under pressure with a gas can be released in the form of a fine mist or spray, used for dispensing insecticide, paint, and other materials.

aer·o·space (er′ō spās′) *n.* the earth's atmosphere and outer space, considered as the region in which aircraft or spacecraft are operated. —*adj.* relating to aerospace and all aspects of human activity in or for this region: *aerospace medicine, the aerospace industry.*

Aes·chy·lus (es′kə ləs) 525–456 B.C., Greek writer of tragedies.

Ae·sop (ē′səp, ē′sop) 620?–560? B.C., Greek writer of fables.

aes·thete (es′thēt) *also,* **es·thete.** *n.* **1.** a person who is

Cap
Valve
Spring
Gas
Solution
Container

Aerosol bomb

particularly sensitive to and appreciative of art and beauty. **2.** a person who pretends to be sensitive to art and beauty.

aes·thet·ic (es thet′ik) *also,* **es·thet·ic.** *adj.* **1.** of or relating to art and beauty or to what is beautiful, especially as distinguished from what is useful or practical: *aesthetic values, to judge a building from an aesthetic point of view.* **2.** highly sensitive to or appreciative of art and beauty. **3.** of or relating to aesthetics.

aes·thet·i·cal·ly (es thet′ik lē) *also,* **es·thet·i·cal·ly.** *adv.* **1.** according to aesthetic standards. **2.** in an aesthetic manner: *The room was decorated aesthetically.*

aes·thet·ics (es thet′iks) *also,* **es·thet·ics.** *n., pl.* the branch of philosophy that studies beauty in art and nature. ▲ used with a singular verb.

AF, Air Force. Also, **A.F.**

a·far (ə fär′) *adv.* at or to a distance; far away.
from afar. from a distance.

af·fa·ble (af′ə bəl) *adj.* easy to approach and speak to; pleasant; friendly. —**af′fa·bil′i·ty,** *n.* —**af′fa·bly,** *adv.*

af·fair (ə fer′) *n.* **1.** a matter or business done or to be done: *Moving to a new home can be a difficult affair.* **2. affairs.** the practical matters with which a person or group is involved: *The affairs of his business left him little time to spend with his family.* **3.** a private or personal concern: *That's none of your affair.* **4.** a romantic relationship between two people, especially a brief or temporary one. **5.** a social gathering or party: *The wedding was a lovely affair.* **6.** *Informal.* a thing or object: *The first cake she baked was a sad affair.*

af·fect¹ (ə fekt′) *v.t.* **1.** to produce an effect in; act upon; influence: *That drug affects the nervous system. The long railroad strike affected the nation's economy.* **2.** to influence the emotions of; move: *The newspaper photographs of the flood victims affected us deeply.* [Latin *affectus,* the past participle of *afficere* to act upon.]

▲ **Affect** and **effect** sound the same and have the same basic meaning, but they belong to different parts of speech and should not be confused. **Affect** is a verb: *Daily exercise will affect your health.* **Effect** is most commonly used as a noun: *Daily exercise will have a good effect on your health.*

af·fect² (ə fekt′) *v.t.* **1.** to put on a false show of; pretend to have or feel; feign: *He affected boldness although he was really frightened.* **2.** to prefer to have, use, or wear; have a liking for: *She affects casual clothes.* [Latin *affectāre* to strive for, try to have.]

af·fec·ta·tion (af′ek tā′shən) *n.* an artificial manner of acting or speaking, usually to impress or deceive others: *an affectation of innocence. His interest in modern art is an affectation.*

af·fect·ed¹ (ə fek′tid) *adj.* **1.** acted upon or influenced: *The proposed highway was opposed by the affected homeowners.* **2.** influenced emotionally; moved. **3.** impaired; afflicted. [From *affect¹*.]

af·fect·ed² (ə fek′tid) *adj.* **1.** assumed for show; artificial: *affected behavior. He has an affected British accent.* **2.** assuming or displaying an artificial manner of acting or speaking: *an affected person.* [From *affect²*.] —**af·fect′ed′ly,** *adv.* —**af·fect′ed·ness,** *n.*

af·fect·ing (ə fek′ting) *adj.* emotionally moving; stirring: *The drama contained several affecting scenes.* —**af·fect′ing·ly,** *adv.*

af·fec·tion (ə fek′shən) *n.* **1.** tender feeling or fondness; warm attachment: *the affection of a dog for its master. She has a great affection for her family.* **2.** a disease or diseased condition.

af·fec·tion·ate (ə fek′shə nit) *adj.* full of, expressing, or displaying affection; loving; tender: *an affectionate smile, an affectionate message.* —**af·fec′tion·ate·ly,** *adv.*

af·fer·ent (af′ər ənt) *adj.* leading or conducting to a central organ or point: *afferent nerve fibers.*

af·fi·ance (ə fī′əns) *v.t.* **af·fi·anced, af·fi·anc·ing.** to pledge to be married; betroth: *Claire was affianced to Peter.*

af·fi·da·vit (af′ə dā′vit) *n.* a written declaration made by a person who swears under oath that it is true, usually before a judge or other recognized authority.

af·fil·i·ate (*v.,* ə fil′ē āt′; *n.,* ə fil′ē it) *v.,* **af·fil·i·at·ed, af·fil·i·at·ing.** —*v.t.* **1.** to join in close association; connect; unite: *The merger affiliates two large companies.* **2.** to associate (oneself) as a member or supporter: *He is not affiliated with any organized political party.* —*v.i.* to join or associate oneself. —*n.* **1.** an organization or group that is closely connected with a larger organization: *Our local television station is an affiliate of the national network.* **2.** a person who is affiliated; associate.

af·fil·i·a·tion (ə fil′ē ā′shən) *n.* the state of being affiliated; association; connection: *Our Boy Scout troop has an affiliation with the national organization.*

af·fin·i·ty (ə fin′ə tē) *n. pl.,* **af·fin·i·ties.** **1.** a natural attraction or liking: *The young couple had a great affinity for each other.* **2.** a close relation or similarity: *the affinity between the Spanish and Italian languages.* **3.** *Chemistry.* the force of attraction by which the atoms of certain elements unite with those of certain others to form compounds.

af·firm (ə furm′) *v.t.* **1.** to state positively; declare firmly: *The senator affirmed his innocence of the charges of corruption.* **2.** to give formal approval to; confirm; ratify: *The committee affirmed his nomination.*

af·fir·ma·tion (af′ər mā′shən) *n.* **1.** the act of stating positively; firm declaration. **2.** a confirmation; ratification, as of a legal decision.

af·firm·a·tive (ə fur′mə tiv) *adj.* stating that something is true or valid; saying "yes;" assenting: *He gave an affirmative reply to my question by nodding his head.* —*n.* **1.** a word or expression of assent or agreement, such as "yes." **2.** the side that argues in favor of the proposition in a debate. —**af·firm′a·tive·ly,** *adv.*
in the affirmative. in agreement; saying yes.

af·fix (*v.,* ə fiks′; *n.,* af′iks) *v.t.* **1.** to attach or fasten: *to affix stamps to an envelope.* **2.** to add at the end; append: *He affixed his name to the document.* —*n. pl.,* **af·fix·es.** a syllable or group of syllables added to the beginning or end of a word to change its meaning or to make another word; a prefix or suffix. The forms *anti-, pre-, -ment,* and *-ly* are affixes.

af·flict (ə flikt′) *v.t.* to cause great suffering and pain to; distress severely: *Susan was afflicted with poison ivy. God afflicted Job with disease and tragedy to test his faith.*

af·flic·tion (ə flik′shən) *n.* **1.** the state of being afflicted; misery; suffering. **2.** any cause of pain or suffering; misfortune: *Blindness is a severe affliction.*

af·flu·ence (af′lōō əns) *n.* **1.** a large amount of money, goods, or property; great material wealth. **2.** any abundant supply; profusion.

af·flu·ent (af′lōō ənt) *adj.* **1.** having much money, goods, or property; wealthy; prosperous; rich: *an affluent society.* **2.** in abundance; plentiful; profuse: *She received affluent praise for her poetry.* —**af′flu·ent·ly,** *adv.*

af·ford (ə fôrd′) *v.t.* **1.** to be able to bear the expense of; have the money for: *Can you afford a new coat?* **2.** to be able to spare or give: *I can't afford the time to help him.* **3.** to be able to do without harm. **4.** to yield or supply; give; provide: *The holiday afforded us a chance to rest.*

af·fray (ə frā′) *n.* a noisy brawl or quarrel; public disturbance.

af·fright (ə frīt′) *v.t. Archaic.* to frighten.

af·front (ə frunt′) *n.* an insulting act or remark, especially one that is open and deliberate: *Your rude comments about my home were an affront to me.* —*v.t.* to insult openly; offend deliberately: *The audience affronted the speaker by jeering loudly throughout his speech.* [Old French *afronter* to strike in the face.]

Af·ghan (af′gan, af′gən) *n.* **1.** a person who was born or is living in Afghanistan. **2.** a long-headed dog of a breed originally from Afghanistan, having a coat of long, silky, usually tan hair, large, drooping ears, and a long tail. **3. afghan.** a knitted or crocheted wool blanket or shawl, made in colored squares, stripes, or other patterns. —*adj.* of or relating to Afghanistan or its people.

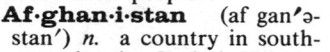

Afghan

Af·ghan·i·stan (af gan′ə stan′) *n.* a country in south-central Asia. Capital, Kabul. Area, 250,000 sq. mi. Pop. (1971 est.), 17,480,000.

a·fi·ci·o·na·do (ə fish′ē ə nä′dō, ə fē′sē ə nä′dō) *n. pl.*, **a·fi·ci·o·na·dos.** an enthusiastic supporter; devotee; fan: *an aficionado of bullfighting, an aficionado of the ballet.* [Spanish *aficionado,* from *aficionar* to inspire affection, going back to Latin *affectiō* feeling.]

a·field (ə fēld′) *adv.* **1.** off the correct or usual path or course: *His comments led the discussion far afield.* **2.** away from home; abroad. **3.** on, in, or to the field.

a·fire (ə fīr′) *adv., adj.* **1.** on fire: *to set a log afire. The old ship was afire.* **2.** as if on fire: *The crew was afire with a spirit of mutiny.*

a·flame (ə flām′) *adv., adj.* **1.** on fire; flaming; burning. **2.** as if on fire: *Her cheeks were aflame from the frosty air.*

AFL-CIO, the American Federation of Labor and the Congress of Industrial Organizations, a national organization of labor unions formed in 1955.

a·float (ə flōt′) *adv., adj.* **1.** floating on water: *That is the largest ship afloat.* **2.** on board ship; at sea. **3.** in circulation: *There are strange rumors afloat.* **4.** covered by water; flooded: *The deck was afloat.* **5.** out of difficulty, especially financial difficulty: *to keep a business afloat.*

a·flut·ter (ə flut′ər) *adv., adj.* **1.** fluttering: *The leaves were aflutter in the strong breeze.* **2.** nervously confused or agitated; excited: *The children were all aflutter as Christmas Eve drew nearer.*

a·foot (ə foot′) *adv., adj.* **1.** on foot; by walking: *We proceeded afoot.* **2.** in progress or motion; stirring: *There's an evil plot afoot.*

a·fore (ə fôr′) *adv., prep., conj.* another word for **before.**

a·fore·men·tioned (ə fôr′men′shənd) *adj.* mentioned before: *The aforementioned rules apply to all persons who use the playground.*

a·fore·said (ə fôr′sed′) *adj.* said or mentioned before.

a·fore·thought (ə fôr′thôt′) *adj.* planned beforehand; premeditated: *He committed the crime with malice aforethought.*

a·foul (ə foul′) *adv., adj.* in collision or entanglement; tangled; snarled: *a sailboat with its lines afoul.*

 to run afoul of. to become entangled with; get into trouble with: *His dishonest business activities caused him to run afoul of the law.*

Afr., Africa; African.

a·fraid (ə frād′) *adj.* **1.** feeling fear; frightened: *Are you afraid of snakes? He is afraid to fly in an airplane.* **2.** feeling unhappiness or regret; sorry: *I'm afraid I won't be able to meet you tonight.*

a·fresh (ə fresh′) *adv.* anew; again: *He started afresh after his first attempt had failed.*

Af·ri·ca (af′ri kə) *n.* a continent south of Europe, between the Atlantic and Indian oceans. Area, 11,677,000 sq. mi. Pop. (1971 est.), 354,000,000.

Af·ri·can (af′ri kən) *adj.* of or relating to Africa, its people, or their languages or culture. —*n.* a person who was born or is living in Africa.

Af·ri·kaans (af′ri käns′) *n.* one of the two official languages of South Africa. Afrikaans is a dialect of Dutch that developed from the language spoken by the seventeenth-century Dutch settlers.

Af·ri·ka·ner (af′ri kä′nər) *n.* a South African who is of European descent, especially one of Dutch descent.

Af·ro (af′rō) *n. pl.,* **Af·ros.** a hair style in which naturally wiry hair is worn in a high, rounded mass. [From *Africa,* because this style was first worn by African Negroes.]

Af·ro-A·mer·i·can (af′rō ə mer′i kən) *adj.* **1.** of or relating to American Negroes. **2.** relating to the culture of American Negroes, especially as influenced by African culture. —*n.* an American Negro.

aft (aft) *adv., adj.* at, near, or toward the rear of a ship or an aircraft.

af·ter (af′tər) *prep.* **1.** in or at the rear of; behind: *The boy walked after his father.* **2.** in pursuit or search of: *The hounds ran after the fox. The prospector set out after gold.* **3.** following in time; later than: *It is ten minutes after three o'clock. He arrived shortly after dark.* **4.** as a result of; because of: *After that remark, you'll have to apologize.* **5.** in spite of; regardless of: *After all we've said, he still won't change his mind.* **6.** concerning; about: *He inquired after your health.* **7.** in imitation of; in the style of: *a building designed after the Parthenon.* **8.** with a name like: *He was named after his uncle.* **9.** below in rank, order, or importance: *After the president, he has the highest salary in the company.* —*adv.* **1.** in the rear; behind: *"And Jill came tumbling after."* **2.** later; subsequently: *I arrived on Sunday, and he came two days after.* —*conj.* following the time that: *It happened after you left.* —*adj.* **1.** later; subsequent: *in after years.* **2.** toward the rear or stern of a ship.

af·ter·birth (af′tər burth′) *n.* the mass of matter expelled from the uterus after the birth of a child, consisting chiefly of the placenta.

af·ter·burn·er (af′tər bur′nər) *n.* a device that injects fuel into the hot exhaust of a jet engine, thereby creating additional thrust.

af·ter·deck (af′tər dek′) *n.* the deck at a ship's stern.

af·ter·ef·fect (af′tər i fekt′) *n.* an effect that occurs some time after its cause; delayed effect: *the aftereffects of a drug. Germany's economic depression of the 1920's was an aftereffect of World War I.*

af·ter·glow (af′tər glō′) *n.* **1.** a glow remaining after the light that caused it has gone, as in the western sky after sunset. **2.** a good feeling lingering after a pleasant experience.

af·ter·im·age (af′tər im′ij) *n.* an image that continues to be seen after the light that caused it is no longer there. If you look at a bright neon sign and then close your eyes, you will see an afterimage.

af·ter·life (af′tər līf′) *n.* life after death.

at; āpe; cär; end; mē; it; īce; hot; ōld; fôrk; wood; fōol; oil; out; up; turn; sing; thin; this; hw in white; zh in treasure. The symbol ə stands for the sound of **a** in about, **e** in taken, **i** in pencil, **o** in lemon, and **u** in circus.

af·ter·math (af′tər math′) *n.* a resulting situation; consequence or consequences: *the aftermath of a hurricane, the aftermath of an epidemic.* [*After* + earlier *math* a mowing. The original meaning was a second mowing of grass from land in the same season.]

af·ter·noon (af′tər nōōn′) *n.* the part of the day from noon until evening.

af·ter·taste (af′tər tāst′) *n.* a taste that remains after what caused it is gone: *The medicine left an unpleasant aftertaste.*

af·ter·thought (af′tər thôt′) *n.* a later or second thought or idea: *His name was added to the list as an afterthought.*

af·ter·ward (af′tər wərd) *also,* **af·ter·wards.** *adv.* at a later time; subsequently: *We swam for an hour, and afterward we rested.*

Ag, the symbol for silver. [Abbreviation of Latin *argentum* silver.]

a·gain (ə gen′) *adv.* **1.** once more; another time: *His first attempt failed, so he tried again.* **2.** on the other hand: *We might go, and again we might not.* **3.** moreover; besides; furthermore: *Again, we should consider the risks involved.* **4.** in or to a former position or state: *He ran to the corner and then back again.*

   again and again. many times; often.

   as much again. as much as the original amount.

   now and again. occasionally; sometimes: *We visit him now and again.*

a·gainst (ə genst′) *prep.* **1.** in opposition to: *He voted against the bill.* **2.** in the opposite direction to: *The salmon swam against the current.* **3.a.** in contact with: *She leaned her bicycle against a tree.* **b.** so as to strike or come into contact with: *He drove his fist against the wall.* **4.** as a protection or defense from; in preparation for: *to save against an emergency.* **5.** on a background of; in contrast with: *The painting shows a blue vase against a yellow wall.* **6.** as a charge upon: *He received an advance against next week's salary.*

Ag·a·mem·non (ag′ə mem′non) *n. Greek Legend.* a king of Mycenae who led the Greeks in the Trojan War.

a·gape (ə gāp′) *adj., adv.* with the mouth wide open, especially in wonder or disbelief: *He stared agape at the mysterious figure in the shadows.*

a·gar (ä′gär, ag′ər) *also,* **a·gar-a·gar** (ä′gär ä′gär, ag′ər ag′ər). *n.* **1.** a jellylike product obtained from certain seaweeds, used especially as a medium for growing bacteria in a laboratory. **2.** a medium for growing bacteria that contains agar.

Ag·as·siz, Louis (ag′ə sē) 1807–1873, U.S. zoologist and geologist, born in Switzerland.

ag·ate (ag′it) *n.* **1.** a semiprecious variety of quartz, usually having variously colored layers or bands. **2.** a playing marble that is made of or looks like agate.

a·ga·ve (ə gä′vē) *n.* any of a group of desert plants of the Western Hemisphere, having long flower stalks and thick, fleshy leaves. The most familiar is the century plant.

Polished agate
(def. 1)

age (āj) *n.* **1.** the length of time that a person, animal, or thing has existed: *Her age is ten years. He retired at the age of sixty-five.* **2.** a particular period or stage of life: *middle age.* **3.** the latter part of life; old age: *to be weary with age.* **4.** a particular period of history: *the atomic age, the age of mammals.* **5.** *also,* **ages.** *Informal.* a long time: *I haven't heard from her in ages.* —*v.,* **aged, ag·ing** *or* **age·ing.** —*v.t.* **1.** to cause to grow old; make old: *Years of ill health aged him prematurely.* **2.** to allow to mature or ripen with time: *to*

age wine, to age beef. —*v.i.* to become old or mature: *He has aged noticeably since his illness.*

   of age. having reached the age when full adult rights and responsibilities apply, usually twenty-one years.

-age *suffix* (used to form nouns) **1.** the act or process of: *breakage.* **2.** the condition or the state of: *wreckage.* **3.** a collection of: *wordage.* **4.** the amount of: *acreage.* **5.** the fee for or cost of: *postage.* **6.** a home or place of: *orphanage.* [Old French *-age,* from Late Latin *-āticum* related to.]

a·ged (*adj., def. 1* ā′jid; *defs. 2, 3* ājd; *n.,* ā′jid) *adj.* **1.** grown old; old: *She helped take care of her aged grandfather.* **2.** having the age of: *a boy aged three.* **3.** having a desired quality as the result of aging: *aged cheese.* —*n.* **the aged.** old people as a group: *medical care for the aged.*

age·less (āj′lis) *adj.* **1.** not growing old or showing signs of old age. **2.** never-ending; eternal: *the ageless majesty of the ocean.*

a·gen·cy (ā′jən sē) *n. pl.,* **a·gen·cies. 1.** a company or person that has the power to do business for others: *an insurance agency, an advertising agency, an employment agency.* **2.** the office or place of business of such a company or person. **3.** an administrative department of government. **4.** the means, action, or power by or through which a thing is done: *He was set free through the agency of his country's ambassador.*

a·gen·da (ə jen′də) *n.* a list of things to be done: *The reading of the minutes was the first item on the agenda of the meeting.* ▲ Originally, **agenda** was the plural form of *agendum.* Today *agenda* is usually considered a singular noun.

a·gent (ā′jənt) *n.* **1.** a person having the power to represent or act for another: *an insurance agent. The actor's agent represented him during the contract negotiations.* **2.** something that produces or is used to produce a certain effect: *Soap is a cleansing agent.* **3.** a member of a government agency, especially a law enforcement agency: *an agent of the FBI.*

a·gent pro·vo·ca·teur (ā′jənt prə vok′ə toor′) *n. pl.,* **a·gents pro·vo·ca·teurs** (ā′jənts prə vok′ə toor′). a person secretly placed in a organization or group to provoke illegal acts for which the group can then be blamed.

ag·er·a·tum (aj′ə rā′təm) *n.* any of various ornamental plants related to the sunflower, having clusters of blue, white, or pink flowers.

ag·glom·er·ate (*v.,* ə glom′ə rāt′; *n., adj.,* ə glom′ər it) *v.t., v.i.,* **ag·glom·er·at·ed, ag·glom·er·at·ing.** to gather in a mass or cluster. —*n.* **1.** a group of things gathered together in a mass or cluster. **2.** a rock formed of a mass of volcanic fragments fused together. —*adj.* gathered together in a mass or cluster: *an agglomerate whole.* —**ag·glom′er·a′tion,** *n.*

ag·glu·ti·nate (*v.,* ə glōōt′ən āt′; *adj.,* ə glōōt′ən it) *v.t., v.i.,* **ag·glu·ti·nat·ed, ag·glu·ti·nat·ing. 1.** to unite with or as if with glue; stick together. **2.** to clump together, as bacteria or blood cells. —*adj.* joined with or as if with glue.

ag·glu·ti·na·tion (ə glōōt′ən ā′shən) *n.* **1.** the process of sticking together or the state of being stuck together. **2.** a clumping together of bacteria or blood cells in the body due to the presence of an antibody. **3.** a collection of parts stuck together.

ag·glu·tin·in (ə glōōt′ən in) *n.* a substance that causes agglutination, such as an antibody.

ag·gran·dize (ə gran′dīz, ag′rən dīz′) *v.t.,* **ag·gran·dized, ag·gran·diz·ing.** to make greater, larger, or more important, as in power, wealth, or rank: *The king made an effort to aggrandize his empire.* —**ag·gran′dize·ment,** *n.* —**ag·gran′diz·er,** *n.*

ag·gra·vate (ag′rə vāt′) *v.t.*, **ag·gra·vat·ed, ag·gra·vat·ing. 1.** to make worse or more severe: *The chilly, damp weather aggravated his cold. Violence at the border aggravated the tension between the two countries.* **2.** to annoy; irritate: *His constant complaining aggravated her.* —**ag′gra·vat′ing·ly,** *adv.* —**ag′gra·va′tor,** *n.*

ag·gra·va·tion (ag′rə vā′shən) *n.* **1.** making worse or more severe: *the aggravation of a wound by infection.* **2.** annoyance; irritation: *The passengers expressed their aggravation at the delay.* **3.** something that aggravates.

ag·gre·gate (*adj., n.,* ag′rə git; *v.,* ag′rə gāt′) *adj.* composed of parts gathered together: *The aggregate number of marathon runners from all towns was 194.* —*n.* **1.** a whole composed of separate parts; mass or group of individual things: *Soil is an aggregate of many different minerals.* **2.** a sum total: *The aggregate of receipts from all sources was $1000.* —*v.t.,* **ag·gre·gat·ed, ag·gre·gat·ing. 1.** to collect or gather into a mass or group. **2.** to amount to; total. —**ag′gre·gate·ly,** *adv.* —**ag′gre·gate·ness,** *n.*
   in the aggregate. taken together; as a whole.

ag·gre·ga·tion (ag′rə gā′shən) *n.* **1.** the collecting of individual things into a single mass or whole. **2.** such a group or collection: *The variety show featured a large aggregation of talented performers.*

ag·gres·sion (ə gresh′ən) *n.* **1.** a hostile or unprovoked attack or assault: *A country that invades the territory of its neighbor is guilty of aggression.* **2.** the habit or policy of making assaults or attacks.

ag·gres·sive (ə gres′iv) *adj.* **1.** relating to or showing aggression: *a nation with an aggressive foreign policy.* **2.** forceful; bold: *an aggressive salesperson, an aggressive advertising campaign.* —**ag·gres′sive·ly,** *adv.* —**ag·gres′sive·ness,** *n.*

ag·gres·sor (ə gres′ər) *n.* a person, nation, or group that engages in aggression.

ag·grieve (ə grēv′) *v.t.,* **ag·grieved, ag·griev·ing.** to cause grief, trouble, or injury to; distress: *His family was aggrieved by his dishonest behavior.*

a·ghast (ə gast′) *adj.* filled with fear, shock, or amazement: *She was aghast at his suggestion that she help him cheat on the test.*

ag·ile (aj′əl) *adj.* **1.** able to move quickly and easily; nimble: *A deer is an agile animal.* **2.** able to think quickly: *Kate has an agile mind.* —**ag′ile·ly,** *adv.* —**ag′ile·ness,** *n.*

a·gil·i·ty (ə jil′ə tē) *n.* quickness and ease in motion or thought; nimbleness: *An acrobat must have great agility.*

Ag·in·court (aj′in kôrt′) *n.* a village in northern France, the site of an English victory over the French in 1415.

ag·i·tate (aj′ə tāt′) *v.,* **ag·i·tat·ed, ag·i·tat·ing.** —*v.t.* **1.** to move or shake roughly or irregularly; stir up: *The wind agitated the trees.* **2.** to move to and fro with a regular motion: *A washing machine agitates clothes.* **3.** to disturb the feelings of; stir up; perturb; excite: *The rude behavior of the members agitated the chairman.* —*v.i.* to seek to arouse public interest, especially in an effort to bring about change: *The students agitated for a greater role in school policy by picketing the dean's office.* —**ag′i·tat′ed·ly,** *adv.*

ag·i·ta·tion (aj′ə tā′shən) *n.* **1.** the act of agitating. **2.** the state of being emotionally upset or shaken. **3.** an effort to arouse public interest in some matter.

ag·i·ta·tor (aj′ə tā′tər) *n.* **1.** a person who seeks to arouse interest or support for a cause, especially a political one. **2.** a device for shaking or stirring.

a·gleam (ə glēm′) *adv., adj.* gleaming: *The lights of the Christmas tree were all agleam.*

a·glit·ter (ə glit′ər) *adv., adj.* glittering.

a·glow (ə glō′) *adv., adj.* glowing.

ag·nos·tic (ag nos′tik) *n.* a person who believes that nothing is known or can be known about the existence of God. —*adj.* relating to agnostics or their beliefs. ▲ See **atheist** for usage note.

ag·nos·ti·cism (ag nos′tə siz əm) *n.* the beliefs or practices of agnostics.

Ag·nus De·i (ag′nəs dā′ē) **1.** a prayer in the Mass starting with the words "Agnus Dei" or "Lamb of God." **2.** the music for this prayer. **3.** an image of a lamb representing Christ, especially one with a halo and the banner of the Cross. [Latin *Agnus Deī* Lamb of God.]

a·go (ə gō′) *adj.* before now; past: *He left ten minutes ago.* —*adv.* in the past: *Dinosaurs lived long ago.*

a·gog (ə gog′) *adj., adv.* in a state of excitement or eager expectation: *The crowd was agog as the game entered the final inning.*

ag·o·nize (ag′ə nīz′) *v.,* **ag·o·nized, ag·o·niz·ing.** —*v.i.* to feel great discomfort, anguish, or pain; suffer greatly: *We agonized over the terrible choice we were faced with.* —*v.t.* to cause to suffer great discomfort, anguish, or pain. —**ag′o·niz′ing·ly,** *adv.*

ag·o·ny (ag′ə nē) *n. pl.,* **ag·o·nies. 1.** great pain, suffering, or anguish of mind or body: *He was in agony from a toothache. She suffered agony at the death of her close friend.* **2.** violent movements of the body resembling a struggle, sometimes preceding death.

a·gou·ti (ə gōō′tē) *n. pl.,* **a·gou·tis** or **a·gou·ties.** a burrowing rodent found in the West Indies and Central and South America, related to the guinea pig. It is about the size of a rabbit.

A·gra (ä′grə) *n.* a city in north-central India, the site of the Taj Mahal. Pop. (1971 est.), 591,917.

Agouti

a·grar·i·an (ə grer′ē ən) *adj.* **1.** relating to farm land, its use, or its ownership: *Agrarian reformers believe that land should be distributed more fairly among farmers.* **2.** relating to farmers or farming interests; agricultural.

a·gree (ə grē′) *v.,* **a·greed, a·gree·ing.** —*v.i.* **1.** to have the same opinion or feeling; concur: *All the others wanted to go to the beach, but Jim didn't agree.* **2.** to consent: *He agreed to lend us the money.* **3.** to reach an understanding; come to terms: *The car dealer and my mother agreed on a price. The two sides finally agreed on the terms of the treaty.* **4.** to be in harmony; coincide: *Your description of the robbery does not agree with the official report.* **5.** *Grammar.* to correspond in case, number, gender, or person. In the sentence *These books are new,* the words *these* and *are* agree with the subject *books.* —*v.t.* to acknowledge or accept; admit; grant: *I agree that the delay was all my fault.*
   to agree with. to produce no ill effect in; be good or healthful for; suit: *Long plane trips usually do not agree with me.*

a·gree·a·ble (ə grē′ə bəl) *adj.* **1.** to one's liking; pleasant: *She has an agreeable personality.* **2.** willing to consent:

at; āpe; cär; end; mē; it; īce; hot; ōld; fôrk; wood; fōōl; oil; out; up; turn; sing; thin; this; hw in white; zh in treasure. The symbol ə stands for the sound of a in about, e in taken, i in pencil, o in lemon, and u in circus.

Are you agreeable to my suggestion? —**a·gree′a·ble·ness,** *n.* —**a·gree′a·bly,** *adv.*

a·gree·ment (ə grē′mənt) *n.* **1.** an understanding reached by two or more persons or groups, such as a treaty or contract: *a trade agreement between two nations. By agreement, neither of us ever mentioned the incident again.* **2.** the state of agreeing; harmony; accord: *My views on the subject are in agreement with his.* **3.** *Grammar.* the correspondence of words in case, number, gender, or person. The phrases *that coat* and *those men* are in agreement, but *this man* is not in agreement.

ag·ri·cul·tur·al (ag′rə kul′chər əl) *adj.* relating to farms or farming; of agriculture: *agricultural research, an agricultural college.* —**ag′ri·cul′tur·al·ly,** *adv.*

ag·ri·cul·tur·al·ist (ag′rə kul′chər ə list) *n.* another word for **agriculturist.**

ag·ri·cul·ture (ag′rə kul′chər) *n.* the science, art, or business of cultivating the soil, producing crops, and raising livestock; farming.

ag·ri·cul·tur·ist (ag′rə kul′chər ist) *n.* **1.** a farmer. **2.** an expert in the science of agriculture.

a·gron·o·mist (ə gron′ə mist) *n.* a student of or an expert in agronomy.

a·gron·o·my (ə gron′ə mē) *n.* the branch of scientific agriculture concerned with crop production, including the cultivation of farm land and conservation and improvement of soil.

a·ground (ə ground′) *adv., adj.* on or onto the bottom; stranded, as in shallow water: *He ran the boat aground on the sand bar.*

agt., agent.

a·gue (ā′gyōo) *n.* **1.** a malarial fever marked by regularly recurring cold, hot, and sweating stages. **2.** any fit of shivering; chill.

ah (ä) *interj.* used to show any of various feelings, such as pain, sorrow, joy, admiration, or surprise.

a·ha (ä hä′) *interj.* used to show any of various feelings, such as triumph, satisfaction, discovery, surprise, or scorn.

A·hab (ā′hab) king of Israel in the ninth century B.C. He was influenced by his wife, Jezebel, to become a worshiper of idols.

a·head (ə hed′) *adv.* **1.** in front: *He walked ahead of his friends. The American runner was now ahead.* **2.** forward; onward: *Go ahead with your plan.* **3.** toward the future; in advance: *to plan ahead. Set the clock ahead one hour.* **4.** having as a profit or advantage: *The home team is two goals ahead.*

> **to get ahead.** to advance one's position: *to get ahead in the business world.*

a·hem (ə hem′) *interj.* a sound made by clearing the throat, used especially to attract attention or to give warning.

Ah·med·a·bad (ä′məd ä bäd′) also, **Ah·mad·a·bad.** *n.* a city in west-central India. Pop. (1971), 1,588,378.

a·hoy (ə hoi′) *interj.* used as a greeting or to attract attention, especially by sailors in hailing another ship.

aid (ād) *v.t.* to give help or support to; assist: *He aided the scientist in his work. The local police aided the federal agents.* —*v.i.* to give help: *Two Boy Scouts aided in the rescue.* —*n.* **1.** help or support; assistance: *The old man walked with the aid of a cane.* **2.** a person or thing that is helpful: *He used the dictionary as an aid in writing his composition.*

aide (ād) *n.* **1.** a helper or assistant: *a nurse's aide, an aide to the President.* **2.** another word for **aide-de-camp.**

aide-de-camp (ād′də kamp′) *n. pl.,* **aides-de-camp.** a military officer who serves as an assistant to a superior officer, especially a general.

ai·grette (ā′gret, ā gret′) *n.* **1.** a plume or tuft of feathers, especially the feathers of the egret, worn as an ornament on hats and helmets. **2.** ornamental jewelry imitating such feathers.

ail (āl) *v.t.* to cause illness, trouble, or discomfort to: *What ails you?* —*v.i.* to be ill or indisposed: *He has been ailing for years.*

ai·lan·thus (ā lan′thəs) *n. pl.,* **ai·lan·thus·es.** a tree bearing featherlike leaves and clusters of small, greenish flowers.

ai·le·ron (ā′lə ron′) *n.* a movable section on the rear edge of an airplane wing, used to control movement of the plane in flight.

ail·ment (āl′mənt) *n.* an illness or affliction: *He is always complaining about his many ailments.*

Ailanthus

aim (ām) *v.t.* **1.** to point or direct (a weapon or blow) for the purpose of hitting a target: *to aim a rifle. The boxer aimed a punch at the other fighter's jaw.* **2.** to direct toward or intend for: *The new law is aimed at reducing traffic accidents.* —*v.i.* **1.** to point or direct a weapon or blow: *to aim at a target.* **2.** to have as a goal; intend: *He aims to become a professional baseball player.* —*n.* **1.** the act of pointing or directing a weapon or blow at a target. **2.** the ability to hit a target. **3.** a purpose; intention; goal: *Her aim is to become a doctor.*

aim·less (ām′lis) *adj.* without purpose or direction: *aimless wanderings, aimless remarks.* —**aim′less·ly,** *adv.* —**aim′less·ness,** *n.*

ain't (ānt) **1.** am not. **2.** is not; are not. **3.** has not; have not.

▲ **Ain't** is not considered to be good English by most people. Because of this, careful speakers try to avoid using *ain't.*

Ai·nu (ī′nōo) *n. pl.,* **Ai·nus** or **Ai·nu.** **1.** a member of an aboriginal race of northern Japan, having light skin and dark hair. **2.** the language of the Ainus, believed to be unrelated to any other known language.

air (er) *n.* **1.** the mixture of gases that surrounds and envelops the earth, forming its atmosphere. Air is invisible, odorless, and tasteless, and it consists chiefly of nitrogen and oxygen, with small amounts of argon, carbon dioxide, neon, and other gases. **2.** the open space above the earth; sky: *He threw the ball into the air.* **3.** a moving current of air; light wind. **4.** fresh air: *Please open the window and let in some air.* **5.** the impression, mood, or feeling given by a person or thing: *He has an air of mystery about him.* **6. airs.** haughty or affected manners assumed to impress others: *to put on airs.* **7.** a melody or tune. —*v.t.* **1.** to freshen, ventilate, or dry by exposing to air: *to air a room. He aired his winter clothing after taking it out of the trunk.* **2.** to bring to public notice; express publicly: *The workers aired their complaints.*

> **in the air.** going around; in circulation: *Rumors of a strike were in the air.*
> **off the air.** not broadcasting or being broadcast.
> **on the air.** broadcasting or being broadcast.
> **to clear the air.** to remove tension or disagreements, as through discussion.
> **to walk on air.** to be very happy.
> **up in the air.** unsettled; undecided: *The date of the concert is still up in the air.*

air base, a place from which military airplanes operate.

air bladder **1.** a sac filled with air or another gas, found in most fish. It aids in maintaining buoyancy in the water. **2.** any air-filled sac, as in a bird or plant.

air·borne (er'bôrn') *adj.* **1.** carried by the air: *airborne pollen.* **2.** transported by airplanes or gliders: *airborne artillery.* **3.** off the ground; in flight: *By midnight we were airborne.*

air brake, a brake that is operated by the action of compressed air against a piston or pistons, used especially in trains, trucks, and buses.

air coach, coach accommodations on an airplane.

air·con·di·tion (er'kən dish'ən) *v.t.* to provide with or ventilate by air conditioning: *to air-condition a room.*

air·con·di·tioned (er'kən dish'ənd) *adj.* having air conditioning.

air conditioner, a machine used for air conditioning.

air conditioning, a system for controlling the temperature, humidity, purity, and circulation of the air in an enclosed area, such as a building, room, or motor vehicle.

air·cool (er'kōōl') *v.t.* to reduce heat in by circulating air around or through: *to air-cool an automobile engine.*

air·craft (er'kraft') *n. pl.,* **air·craft.** any machine designed for flight in the air, including airplanes, airships, gliders, and balloons. An aircraft may be supported by the action of air against its wings or by buoyancy.

aircraft carrier, a warship that serves as a base for aircraft, having a large, flat deck designed so that airplanes can take off from and land on it.

air·drome (er'drōm') *n.* another word for **airport.**

air·drop (er'drop') *v.t.,* **air·dropped, air·drop·ping.** to drop (food, supplies, or personnel) by parachute from aircraft in flight. —*n.* the act of dropping something by parachute from aircraft in flight.

Aire·dale (er'dāl') *n.* the largest breed of terrier, having a wiry tan coat with dark markings on the back and shoulders.

air·field (er'fēld') *n.* **1.** the landing field of an airport. **2.** an airport, especially a small one.

air·foil (er'foil') *n.* **1.** any part, such as a wing, aileron, or rudder, designed to help lift or control an aircraft by regulating the flow of air over or around its surface. **2.** any body or surface that serves to control the direction of a flow of air.

Airedale

air force **1.** the branch of a country's armed forces in charge of aircraft and air warfare. **2. Air Force.** the air force of the United States.

air gun, a rifle or pistol using compressed air to propel its bullet or other charge.

air hammer, an automatic hammer driven by compressed air.

air hole **1.** a hole through which air is permitted to pass in or out. **2.** a natural opening in the ice on a river, pond, or the like.

air·i·ly (er'ə lē) *adv.* in an airy manner; lightly; gaily.

air·i·ness (er'ē nis) *n.* the quality or state of being airy.

air·ing (er'ing) *n.* **1.** exposure to air for the purpose of drying or freshening: *to give a blanket an airing.* **2.** exposure to public knowledge or discussion: *The students' grievances received a thorough airing at the council meeting.* **3.** a walk or ride in the open air.

air lane, a route used regularly by aircraft.

air·less (er'lis) *adj.* **1.** without air. **2.** without fresh air; stuffy. **3.** without any wind; still.

air letter **1.** a letter sent by air mail. **2.** a lightweight

sheet of paper designed to fold into the form of an envelope, used for writing a letter to be sent by air mail.

air·lift (er'lift') *n.* an emergency system of transporting people or supplies by aircraft when roads or other land approaches to a place are closed. —*v.t.* to transport (something) by airlift: *to airlift food to a town that is cut off by a blizzard.*

air·line (er'līn') *n.* **1.** a system and equipment for transporting people and goods by aircraft. **2.** a business organization owning and managing such a system. **3.** a route used by such a system.

air·lin·er (er'lī'nər) *n.* a large passenger airplane.

air lock, an airtight chamber in which air pressure can be varied, allowing passage between two places that do not have the same air pressures.

air·mail (er'māl') *also,* **air·mail.** *v.t.* to send by air mail. —*adj.* of or relating to air mail: *an air-mail letter.* —*adv.* by air mail: *Send this package air-mail.*

air mail **1.** mail carried by aircraft between cities. **2.** a system of transporting mail by aircraft.

air·man (er'mən) *n. pl.,* **air·men** (er'mən). **1.** a pilot or other member of the crew of an aircraft. **2.** an enlisted man in the U.S. Air Force.

air mass, a widespread body of air that has approximately the same temperature, humidity, and pressure throughout.

air mile, a unit of distance in air navigation, equal to approximately 6076 feet.

air·plane (er'plān') *n.* an aircraft that is heavier than air and has fixed wings, is supported in flight by the action of air against its wings, and is driven by an engine or engines.

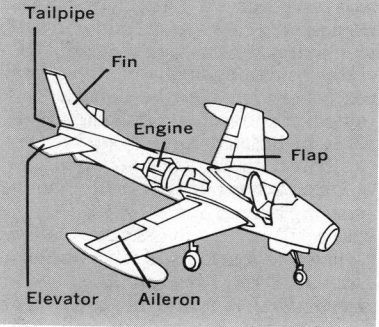

Airplane

air plant, a plant that grows on another plant for support; epiphyte.

air pocket, a downward current of air causing an airplane to drop suddenly.

air police, members of the Air Force assigned to police duties.

air·port (er'pôrt') *n.* an area equipped with facilities necessary for the landing, take-off, repair, and storage of aircraft and for the loading and discharge of passengers and cargo.

air pressure, the pressure exerted in all directions by the weight of the air; atmospheric pressure. Air pressure at sea level is 14.7 pounds per square inch.

air pump, a machine for compressing air in, or removing air from, a container, or for forcing air through pipes or other apparatus.

air raid, an attack by aircraft, especially the dropping

at; āpe; cär; end; mē; it; īce; hot; ōld; fôrk; wood; fōōl; oil; out; up; turn; sing; thin; this; hw in white; zh in treasure. The symbol ə stands for the sound of **a** in about, **e** in taken, **i** in pencil, **o** in lemon, and **u** in circus.

of bombs on populated or industrial areas by organized groups of airplanes.

air rifle, a rifle powered by compressed air, especially one that shoots BB's.

air sac, one of a number of membranous sacs of air in the body of a bird. Air sacs are connected with the lungs and aid in breathing.

air shaft, a passage to permit fresh air to flow into a mine, building, or the like.

air·ship (er′ship′) *n.* any lighter-than-air aircraft that is driven by a motor and that can be steered.

air·sick (er′sik′) *adj.* sick as a result of the motion of an aircraft. —**air′sick′ness,** *n.*

air·space (er′spās′) *n.* the space above some part of the earth, especially the space above a country, considered as subject to certain laws of that country.

air speed, the speed of an aircraft relative to the air through which it is moving rather than to the ground.

air·strip (er′strip′) *n.* a paved or cleared area where aircraft can land and take off.

air·tight (er′tīt′) *adj.* **1.** so tight as to prevent air or gas from entering or escaping. **2.** free of weak points that could easily be attacked, proved wrong, or criticized: *The prosecuting attorney presented an airtight case against the accused man.*

air-to-air (er′tōō er′) *adj.* launched from an aircraft and directed at an airborne target: *an air-to-air guided missile.*

air·waves (er′wāvz′) *n., pl.* radio or television broadcasting: *the highest-paid performer of the airwaves.*

air·way (er′wā′) *n.* **1.** a route for aircraft; air lane. **2.** a passage used to permit a flow of fresh air, as in a mine.

air·wor·thy (er′wur′thē) *adj.* (of an aircraft) in good or safe condition for flying. —**air′wor′thi·ness,** *n.*

air·y (er′ē) *adj.,* **air·i·er, air·i·est. 1.** light as air in appearance or movement; delicate or graceful: *an airy gown.* **2.** light-hearted; gay: *an airy tune.* **3.** open to the flow of air; breezy: *an airy apartment.* **4.** having no more substance than air does; unreal; imaginary: *an airy scheme for earning money.*

aisle (īl) *n.* **1.** a passageway between sections of seats in a place of assembly, such as a theater or stadium. **2.** any similar passageway: *an aisle between counters in a department store.* **3.** a side division of a church, set off from the main part by pillars or arches.

Aix-la-Cha·pelle (āks′lä shä pel′) *n.* the French name for **Aachen.**

a·jar¹ (ə jär′) *adj., adv.* partly open: *The door was left ajar.* [Middle English *on char* in the act of turning, from Old English *on cerre.*]

a·jar² (ə jär′) *adv., adj.* out of harmony; in disorder: *My nerves are all ajar since the accident.* [*At + jar².*]

A·jax (ā′jaks) *n. Greek Legend.* a Greek hero in the Trojan War, known for his great bravery.

a·kim·bo (ə kim′bō) *adj., adv.* with the hands on the hips and elbows out: *He stood with arms akimbo.*

a·kin (ə kin′) *adj.* **1.** belonging to the same family; related by blood: *His mother and my mother are akin.* **2.** similar in character or properties; of the same kind: *Love and friendship are akin.*

Ak·ron (ak′rən) *n.* a city in northeastern Ohio. Pop. (1970), 275,425.

-al¹ *suffix* (used to form adjectives from nouns) of, relating to, or characterized by: *medicinal, historical.* [Latin *-ālis.*]

-al² *suffix* (used to form nouns from verbs) the act, process, or result: *recital, denial, arrival.* [Latin *-ālia.*]

Al, the symbol for aluminum.

Ala., Alabama.

Al·a·bam·a (al′ə bam′ə) *n.* a state in the southeastern United States. Capital, Montgomery. Area, 51,609 sq. mi. Pop. (1970), 3,444,165. Abbreviation, **Ala.** —**Al′a·bam′an;** *also,* **Al′a·bam′i·an,** *adj., n.*

● The name **Alabama** comes from two Choctaw words meaning "thicket clearers" or "plant gatherers." Originally the name of a local tribe, the term was used later to indicate first the river near the tribal village, then the territory, and, finally, the state.

al·a·bas·ter (al′ə bas′tər) *n.* **1.** a smooth, whitish stone used especially in sculpture. Alabaster is a fine-grained, translucent variety of gypsum. **2.** a calcite of a semitranslucent, hard variety, often having bandlike markings. —*adj.* resembling alabaster; smooth, translucent, and pale: *a person with alabaster skin.*

a la carte (ä′ lə kärt′) *also,* **à la carte.** with a separate price for each item on the menu, rather than one price for a complete meal. [French *à la carte* literally, according to the menu.]

a·lack (ə lak′) *interj.* an exclamation expressing regret, dismay, or disappointment.

a·lac·ri·ty (ə lak′rə tē) *n.* **1.** eager willingness: *He accepted the offer with alacrity.* **2.** swiftness; liveliness: *to move with alacrity.*

a la king (ä′ lə king′) *also,* **à la king.** cooked in cream sauce with mushrooms and pimentos or green peppers: *chicken a la king.*

al·a·me·da (al′ə mē′də, al′ə mā′də) *n.* a shaded public walk lined with poplar or other trees.

Al·a·mo (al′ə mō′) *n.* a fortified mission in San Antonio, Texas, that was attacked and captured by Mexican troops in 1836. All of its defenders were killed.

a la mode (ä′ lə mōd′) *also,* **à la mode. 1.** served with ice cream: *apple pie a la mode.* **2.** braised with vegetables and served with a rich brown sauce: *beef a la mode.* **3.** in style; fashionable. [French *à la mode* literally, in the manner or fashion of.]

a·larm (ə lärm′) *n.* **1.** a sudden fear of danger: *The clap of thunder filled the child with alarm.* **2.** a warning of danger: *Give the alarm.* **3.** a device or signal that warns, rouses, or calls to action: *a burglar alarm.* —*v.t.* **1.** to cause to feel sudden fear: *Reports of an approaching storm alarmed the ship's passengers.* **2.** to warn of danger.

alarm clock, a clock that can be set to ring, buzz, or sound at any given time in order to wake up a person.

a·larm·ing (ə lär′ming) *adj.* causing fear and excitement; disturbing: *alarming news.* —**a·larm′ing·ly,** *adv.*

a·larm·ist (ə lär′mist) *n.* a person who is inclined to become alarmed or to alarm others needlessly or on slight grounds.

a·lar·um (ə lar′əm) *n. Archaic.* a call to action or to arms.

a·las (ə las′) *interj.* an exclamation expressing disappointment, sorrow, or regret.

Alas., Alaska.

A·las·ka (ə las′kə) *n.* the largest state of the United States, on the extreme northwestern peninsula of North America. Capital, Juneau. Area, 586,412 sq. mi. Pop. (1970), 302,173. Abbreviation, **Alas.** —**A·las′kan,** *adj., n.*

● **Alaska** comes from a word meaning "mainland" or "great land," which was used by the inhabitants of the Aleutian Islands to distinguish the Alaskan peninsula from their island homes. This name replaced "Russian America" when the United States purchased Alaska in 1867.

Alaskan malamute, a wolflike dog of a breed native to northwestern Alaska, having a thick, coarse coat and a large, bushy tail.

Alaskan malamute

alb (alb) *n.* a floor-length white linen robe with narrow sleeves, worn by Roman Catholic and some Anglican priests at the celebration of the Mass and other ceremonies.

al·ba·core (al′bə kôr′) *n. pl.,* **al·ba·cores** or **al·ba·core.** an important food and game fish that is related to the tuna. It is found mostly in warm seas and is distinguished from other tunas by its long pectoral fins.

Al·ba·ni·a (al bā′nē ə) *n.* a country in southeastern Europe, on the Balkan Peninsula. Capital, Tirana. Area, 11,100 sq. mi. Pop. (1971 est.), 2,226,000.

Al·ba·ni·an (al bā′nē ən) *n.* **1.** a person who was born or is living in Albania. **2.** the language of Albania. —*adj.* of or relating to Albania, its people, or their language.

Al·ba·ny (ôl′bə nē) *n.* the capital of New York, in the eastern part of the state. Pop. (1970), 114,873.

al·ba·tross (al′bə trôs′) *n. pl.,* **al·ba·tross·es.** any of various web-footed sea birds, found chiefly in the southern oceans, having a long, hooked beak. An albatross is capable of very long flights. One species has a wing span of up to eleven feet, the largest of any living bird.

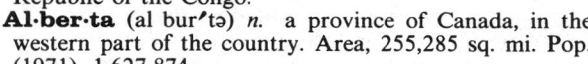

Albatross

al·be·it (ôl bē′it) *conj.* even though; although: *We had an enjoyable, albeit rather tiring, day at the zoo.*

Al·bert (al′bərt) *n.* **1. Prince.** 1819–1861, the husband of Queen Victoria of Great Britain. **2. Lake.** a lake in east-central Africa, on the border between Uganda and the Democratic Republic of the Congo.

Al·ber·ta (al bur′tə) *n.* a province of Canada, in the western part of the country. Area, 255,285 sq. mi. Pop. (1971) 1,627,874.

al·bi·nism (al′bə niz′əm) *n.* the state of being an albino.

al·bi·no (al bī′nō) *n. pl.,* **al·bi·nos. 1.** a person born with a lack of normal coloring, having pale, milky skin, very light hair, and pink eyes. **2.** any plant or animal with a lack of normal coloring.

Al·bi·on (al′bē ən) *n.* another name for **England. ▲** used chiefly in literature.

al·bum (al′bəm) *n.* **1.** a book with blank pages in which to keep collected items: *a stamp album, a photograph album.* **2.** a holder for phonograph records. **3.** a long-playing phonograph record, or a set of records sold as a unit.

al·bu·men (al byoō′mən) *n.* **1.** the white of an egg. **2.** another word for **albumin.**

al·bu·min (al byoō′min) *n.* a protein that dissolves in water and is found in the whites of eggs and other plant and animal tissues and fluids.

Al·bu·quer·que (al′bə kur′kē) *n.* the largest city of New Mexico, in the north-central part of the state. Pop. (1970), 243,751.

Al·ca·traz (al′kə traz′) *n.* an island in San Francisco Bay, the site of a former federal prison of the same name.

al·che·mist (al′kə mist) *n.* a person who studied or practiced alchemy.

al·che·my (al′kə mē) *n.* a system of chemistry practiced during the Middle Ages. It was chiefly concerned with attempts to turn common metals into gold and with the search for a substance that would prolong life and cure all diseases.

al·co·hol (al′kə hôl′) *n.* **1.** an odorless, flammable liquid that evaporates quickly and is produced synthetically or by fermenting grain, fruit, or other starchy or sugary substances. It is the substance in liquor that causes drunkenness and is used widely in the manufacture of drugs and other chemicals. Also, **ethyl alcohol, grain alcohol. 2.** any drink containing this liquid, such as gin or bourbon. **3.** *Chemistry.* any of a group of colorless, flammable, organic compounds, such as wood alcohol.

al·co·hol·ic (al′kə hô′lik) *adj.* **1.** of, containing, or caused by alcohol. **2.** suffering from alcoholism. —*n.* a person who suffers from alcoholism.

al·co·hol·ism (al′kə hô liz′əm) *n.* **1.** a chronic disease characterized by an uncontrollable urge to drink alcoholic beverages. **2.** a diseased condition of the body caused by the excessive or prolonged use of alcoholic beverages.

Al·cott, Louisa May (ôl′kət, ôl′kot) 1832–1888, U.S. author.

al·cove (al′kōv′) *n.* **1.** a small room or recess opening off a larger room. **2.** any closed-off space or area that is set back or apart: *an alcove in a garden.*

Al·deb·a·ran (al deb′ər ən) *n.* a giant red star, one of the brightest in the sky, and the brightest in the constellation Taurus.

Al·den, John (ôl′dən) 1599?–1687, Puritan settler in Plymouth Colony.

al·der (ôl′dər) *n.* any of a group of trees or shrubs growing in cool, moist regions of the Northern Hemisphere. Most alders have scaly bark and oval leaves.

Alder

al·der·man (ôl′dər mən) *n. pl.,* **al·der·men** (ôl′dər mən). a member of the governing body or council of a city or town, often representing a certain ward or district.

ale (āl) *n.* an alcoholic drink made from hops and malt. It is similar to beer, but heavier and more bitter.

a·lee (ə lē′) *adv., adj.* on or toward the lee side of a ship.

A·lep·po (ə lep′ō) *n.* a city in northwestern Syria. Pop. (1970), 639,361.

a·lert (ə lurt′) *adj.* **1.** keenly watchful: *An alert guard is needed for sentry duty.* **2.** quick to act or learn; lively; active: *Her work shows that she has an alert mind.* —*n.* **1.** a signal that warns of possible danger; alarm: *an air alert.* **2.** the length of time an alert lasts: *They hid in the cellar during the alert.* —*v.t.* **1.** to warn to be ready: *The coast guard alerted the town about the approaching hurricane.* **2.** to make aware of: *He alerted his friends to the fact that the water supply was running low.* —**a·lert′ly,** *adv.* —**a·lert′ness,** *n.*

on the alert. on the lookout; watchful: *He was on the alert for any sign of danger.*

at; āpe; cär; end; mē; it; īce; hot; ōld; fôrk; wood; fōōl; oil; out; up; turn; sing; thin; this; hw in white; zh in treasure. The symbol ə stands for the sound of a in about, e in taken, i in pencil, o in lemon, and u in circus.

A·leu·tian Islands (ə lōō′shən) a chain of islands in the northern Pacific Ocean, extending southwest from Alaska. The islands are part of the state of Alaska. Land area, 6391 sq. mi. Pop. (1970), 8057. Also, **Aleutians.**

ale·wife (āl′wīf′) *n. pl.,* **ale·wives** (āl′wīvz′). a small bony fish found along the Atlantic coast of the United States. It swims upstream in large numbers to spawn.

Al·ex·an·der the Great (al′ig zan′dər) 356–323 B.C., king of Macedonia from 336 to 323 B.C., and conqueror of an empire that extended from Egypt to India.

Al·ex·an·dri·a (al′ig zan′drē ə) *n.* **1.** a port city in northeastern Egypt, on the Mediterranean. It was the capital of Egypt in ancient times and was founded by Alexander the Great in 332 B.C. Pop. (1970 est.), 2,032,000. **2.** a city in northern Virginia, a suburb of Washington, D.C. Pop. (1970), 110,938.

Al·ex·an·dri·an (al′ig zan′drē ən) *adj.* **1.** of ancient Alexandria. **2.** of Alexander the Great or his reign.

al·fal·fa (al fal′fə) *n.* any of a group of plants resembling clover, many of which are widely grown as food for cattle and other livestock.

Al·fred the Great (al′-frid) 849–899, king of the West Saxons from 871 to 899.

al·fres·co (al fres′kō) *also,* **al fres·co.** *adv., adj.* in the open air; outdoors.

alg., algebra.

al·gae (al′jē) *n., pl. sing.,* **al·ga** (al′gə). a large group of plants that lack true roots and flowers, including scums formed in ponds and

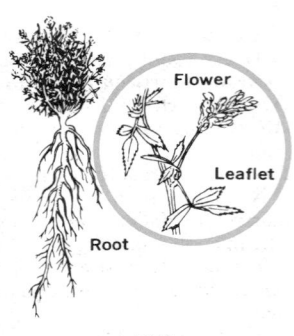

Flower

Leaflet

Root

Alfalfa

most kinds of seaweed. Algae range in size from microscopic, one-celled organisms to giant seaweeds and kelps. The best-known kinds have chlorophyll and are found in water.

al·ge·bra (al′jə brə) *n.* the branch of mathematics in which quantities and the relationships between them are shown by letters, numerals, and abstract symbols. For example: *If $2x + y = 7$, and $x = 3$, then $y = 1$.*

al·ge·bra·ic (al′jə brā′ik) *adj.* relating to or used in algebra: *$2x + y = 7$ is an algebraic equation.* Also, **al·ge·bra·i·cal** (al′jə brā′i kəl). —**al′ge·bra′i·cal·ly,** *adv.*

Al·ge·ri·a (al jēr′ē ə) *n.* a country in northern Africa, on the Mediterranean, formerly a French possession. Capital, Algiers. Area, 919,515 sq. mi. Pop. (1971 est.), 14,770,000. —**Al·ge′ri·an,** *adj.*

Al·giers (al jērz′) *n.* the capital of Algeria, a port on the Mediterranean. Pop. (1966), 943,142.

Al·gon·qui·an (al gong′kē ən, al gong′kwē ən) *n. pl.,* **Al·gon·qui·ans** or **Al·gon·qui·an. 1.** a family of North American Indian languages, including Cree, Delaware, Shawnee, Ojibwa, Blackfoot, and Cheyenne. **2.** a member of any tribe that spoke one of these languages. —*adj.* of or relating to this family of languages.

Al·gon·quin (al gong′kin, al gong′kwin) *n. pl.,* **Al·gon·quins** or **Al·gon·quin. 1.** a member of an Indian tribe that spoke an Algonquian language and lived along the Ottawa and St. Lawrence Rivers in southeastern Canada. **2.** the language spoken by this tribe.

al·go·rithm (al′gə rith′əm) *n.* a procedure for performing a mathematical operation.

Al·ham·bra (al ham′brə) *n.* a palace in Granada, Spain, built by Moorish princes in the thirteenth century.

a·li·as (ā′lē əs) *n. pl.,* **a·li·as·es.** another name by which a person calls himself, usually to hide his real identity; assumed name: *William H. Bonney's alias was Billy the Kid.* —*adv.* also known as; otherwise called: *Arnold Brown, alias Arthur Bell.*

al·i·bi (al′ə bī′) *n. pl.,* **al·i·bis. 1.** a claim or proof of having been somewhere else when a crime or other act was committed: *Part of the thief's plan was to establish an alibi ahead of time.* **2.** an excuse: *Do you have any alibi for not arriving on time?* —*v.i.,* **al·i·bied, al·i·bi·ing.** to offer an excuse: *His brother alibied for him.*

al·ien (āl′yən, ā′lē ən) *n.* a person who is not a citizen of the country in which he is living. —*adj.* **1.** of or belonging to another country or people; foreign. **2.** not familiar or natural; strange; unfamiliar: *an alien pattern of behavior.* **3.** not compatible; opposed: *Censorship of the press is alien to our democratic tradition.*

al·ien·ate (āl′yə nāt′, ā′lē ə nāt′) *v.t.,* **al·ien·at·ed, al·ien·at·ing. 1.** to cause (someone) to feel unfriendly, indifferent, or hostile: *His thoughtless conduct alienated the whole family.* **2.** to cause to be withdrawn or isolated: *Some young people feel alienated from society.* —**al′ien·a′tion,** *n.*

a·light[1] (ə līt′) *v.i.,* **a·light·ed** or **a·lit, a·light·ing. 1.** to step down from; get off: *The girl alighted from her pony.* **2.** to land from flight: *The bee alighted on the flower.* [Old English *ālīhtan* to remove weight from, descend.]
to alight on or **to alight upon.** to discover or come upon by chance: *to alight upon a rare stamp.*

a·light[2] (ə līt′) *adv., adj.* **1.** lighted up; aglow: *a church alight with candles. Her face was alight with joy.* **2.** on fire; burning. [Past participle of obsolete *alight* to light up, from Old English *alīhtan.*]

a·lign (ə līn′) *also,* **a·line.** *v.t.* **1.** to bring into line: *He aligned his golf club with the ball.* **2.** to ally (oneself) with others for a common cause: *In the voting the Republicans aligned themselves with the southern Democrats.* **3.** to adjust (the wheels of a vehicle) to their proper position. **4.** to adjust (the parts of a machine or device) for proper functioning. —*v.i.* to fall into line.

a·lign·ment (ə līn′mənt) *also,* **a·line·ment.** *n.* **1.** the act of aligning or the state of being aligned: *The wheels of the car are out of alignment.* **2.** a line or lines formed by aligning. **3.** the act or policy of allying with others.

a·like (ə līk′) *adv.* in the same way; similarly: *She and her twin sister often dress alike.* —*adj.* like one another; similar: *No two people have fingerprints that are alike.*

al·i·men·ta·ry (al′ə men′tər ē, al′ə ment′rē) *adj.* of or relating to food and nutrition.

alimentary canal, a continuous tube extending from the mouth to the anus, through which food passes as it is digested, then absorbed, and finally eliminated as waste matter.

al·i·mo·ny (al′ə mō′nē) *n.* a fixed sum of money that is regularly paid by a man under court order for his wife's support after they are divorced or while they are legally separated.

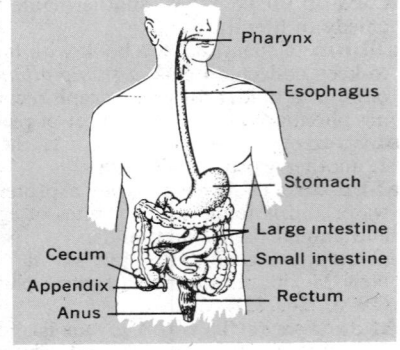

Pharynx

Esophagus

Stomach

Large intestine

Small intestine

Cecum

Appendix

Rectum

Anus

Alimentary canal

a·line (ə līn′) *v.t., v.i.,* **a·lined, a·lin·ing.** another spelling of **align.** —**a·line′ment,** *n.*

a·lit (ə lit′) a past tense and past participle of **alight**[1].

a·live (ə līv′) *adj.* **1.** having life; living: *If you don't put those flowers in water, they won't be alive much longer.* **2.** in force or operation; active: *She wanted to keep alive her children's belief in Santa Claus.* **3.** full of life; animated; lively: *My sister was alive with excitement the night of her first dance.* **4.** of all living: *Jack was the proudest boy alive the day he won the scholarship.* —**a·live′ness,** *n.*
 alive to. sensitive to; aware of: *A mother must be alive to all the needs of a newborn baby.*
 alive with. filled or swarming with: *The porch was alive with mosquitoes.*

al·ka·li (al′kə lī′) *n. pl.,* **al·ka·lis** or **al·ka·lies.** **1.** any of a group of strong bases that dissolve in water, or the salts formed when these bases react with acids. Ammonia and lye are common alkalis. **2.** any mineral salt that dissolves in water, or a mixture of such salts. Alkalis are found in soils, especially desert soil.

alkali metal, any of a group of soft, metallic elements. The alkali metals are lithium, sodium, potassium, rubidium, cesium, and francium.

al·ka·line (al′kə līn′) *adj.* of, like, or containing an alkali. —**al·ka·lin·i·ty** (al′kə lin′ə tē), *n.*

al·ka·line-earth metal (al′kə līn′urth′) any of a group of metallic elements. The alkaline-earth metals are beryllium, magnesium, calcium, strontium, barium, and radium.

al·ka·lize (al′kə līz′) *v.,* **al·ka·lized, al·ka·liz·ing.** —*v.t.* to make (something) alkaline. —*v.i.* to become alkaline.

al·ka·loid (al′kə loid′) *n.* any of a group of alkaline substances, including morphine, caffeine, and quinine. Alkaloids are obtained chiefly from certain plants and are widely used in medicine.

all (ôl) *adj.* **1.** the whole of: *I finished all the work you gave me. We ate all the ice cream.* **2.** the entire number of: *Delegates from all states attended the political convention.* **3.** the greatest possible: *The pilot returned to the base with all due speed.* **4.** any whatever: *The crisis has gone beyond all hope.* **5.** nothing but; only: *This is all nonsense.* —*n.* **1.** everything one has: *Charlie gave his all when he sprinted toward the finish line.* **2.** everything: *All is lost.* —*pron.* **1.** the whole quantity, amount, or number: *All of the cake is gone.* **2.** every one; each: *All answered yes.* —*adv.* **1.** wholly; completely; entirely: *Your figures are all wrong.* **2.** each; apiece: *The score at the half was seven all.*
 above all. before everything else; most of all: *Above all, a lifeguard must be a good swimmer.*
 after all. all things considered; despite everything: *Even though some people couldn't come, it was, after all, a good party.*
 all but. almost; nearly: *His business was all but ruined during the depression.*
 all in. *Informal.* exhausted; weary.
 all in all. everything considered; on the whole.
 all of. no less than: *He's all of sixty years old.*
 all out. *Informal.* with the greatest effort possible: *We went all out to help her.*
 all over. a. finished; ended. **b.** many places; everywhere: *We searched for the dog all over.* **c.** *Informal.* in every way; typically: *That's Henry all over.*
 at all. a. in any way: *He can't sing at all.* **b.** under any circumstances: *He refuses to drive at all.*
 for all or **for all that. a.** in spite of: *For all her kind words, she was still not to be trusted.* **b.** as far as: *For all we know, he's lying.*
 in all. altogether: *In all, about fifty people attended.*

Al·lah (al′ə, ä′lə) *n.* in the Muslim religion, God.

Al·la·ha·bad (al′ə hə bad′, ä′lə hä bäd′) *n.* a city in north-central India, on the Ganges. Pop. (1971), 491,702.

all-A·mer·i·can (ôl′ə mer′i kən) *adj.* **1.** typical of the United States: *an all-American girl.* **2.** selected as the best of its type in the United States: *an all-American football team.* —*n.* an all-American player or athlete: *He is an all-American in basketball.*

all-a·round (ôl′ə round′) *adj.* **1.** good at many things: *an all-around athlete.* **2.** good for many purposes: *an all-around education.* Also, **all-round.**

al·lay (ə lā′) *v.t.,* **al·layed, al·lay·ing.** **1.** to put to rest; quiet; calm: *The veterinarian allayed the child's fears about her sick dog.* **2.** to make less severe: *The ice pack allayed the pain in his ankle.*

all clear, a signal indicating that an air raid is over.

al·le·ga·tion (al′ə gā′shən) *n.* a statement or declaration, especially one made without proof.

al·lege (ə lej′) *v.t.,* **al·leged, al·leg·ing.** **1.** to state or declare, especially without proof: *He alleged his innocence before the court.* **2.** to give as an excuse, reason, or defense. —**al·lege′a·ble,** *adj.* —**al·leg′er,** *n.*

al·leged (ə lejd′) *adj.* declared or assumed to be so, but without proof; supposed: *The alleged murderer was later proven to be innocent.* —**al·leg·ed·ly** (ə lej′id lē), *adv.*

Al·le·ghe·ny (al′ə gā′nē) *n.* a river in western Pennsylvania and southwestern New York. It joins the Monongahela at Pittsburgh to form the Ohio River.

Allegheny Mountains, a mountain range extending from north-central Pennsylvania through western Maryland, eastern West Virginia, and western Virginia. It is part of the Appalachian mountain system. Also, **Alleghenies.**

al·le·giance (ə lē′jəns) *n.* **1.** loyalty to a government, country, or ruler: *to pledge allegiance to the United States.* **2.** loyalty or devotion to a person, cause, or thing: *The workers felt great allegiance to the president of their union.*

al·le·gor·i·cal (al′ə gôr′i kəl) *adj.* relating to or having an allegory: *an allegorical poem.* Also, **al·le·gor·ic** (al′ə gôr′ik). —**al′le·gor′i·cal·ly,** *adv.*

al·le·go·ry (al′ə gôr′ē) *n. pl.,* **al·le·go·ries.** a story that teaches a lesson or shows something about life by having the characters and events stand for ideas, people, or moral principles. Aesop's fables are examples of allegories.

al·le·gret·to (al′ə gret′ō) *Music. adj., adv.* slower than allegro, but rather lively. —*n. pl.,* **al·le·gret·tos.** a piece, movement, or passage in a rather lively tempo.

al·le·gro (ə lā′grō, ə leg′rō) *Music. adj., adv.* faster than allegretto but slower than presto; lively; fast. —*n. pl.,* **al·le·gros.** a piece, movement, or passage in a fast tempo.

al·le·lu·ia (al′ə lōō′yə) another word for **hallelujah.**

Al·len, E·than (al′ən; ē′thən) 1738–1789, American leader in the Revolutionary War.

Al·len·town (al′ən toun′) *n.* a city in southeastern Pennsylvania. Pop. (1970), 109,527.

al·ler·gen (al′ər jən) *n.* a substance that causes allergy.

al·ler·gen·ic (al′ər jen′ik) *adj.* causing allergy.

al·ler·gic (ə lur′jik) *adj.* **1.** of or caused by allergy: *A rash is sometimes an allergic reaction.* **2.** having an allergy: *She is allergic to chocolate.* **3.** *Informal.* having a strong dislike (with *to*): *Dennis is allergic to hard work.*

al·ler·gy (al′ər jē) *n. pl.,* **al·ler·gies.** an abnormal sensitivity of the body to a certain substance that is harmless

---

at; āpe; cär; end; mē; it; īce; hot; ōld; fôrk;
wood; fōōl; oil; out; up; turn; sing; thin; this;
hw in white; zh in treasure. The symbol ə
stands for the sound of a in about, e in taken,
i in pencil, o in lemon, and u in circus.

to most people, such as pollen, dust, animal hair, wool, or certain foods. Allergies result in reactions such as hives, rashes, sneezing, and asthma.

al·le·vi·ate (ə lē′vē āt′) *v.t.,* **al·le·vi·at·ed, al·le·vi·at·ing.** to make easier to bear; relieve; lessen: *The pill alleviated the pain of her headache.* —**al·le′vi·a′tion,** *n.*

al·ley¹ (al′ē) *n. pl.,* **al·leys. 1.** a narrow street or passageway, especially one at the rear of a row of buildings. **2.** see **bowling alley. 3.** a path or walk bordered by trees or shrubbery. [Old French *alee* a passage, walk.]
　up one's alley. *Slang.* to one's liking; suited to one's talents: *This job should be right up his alley.*

al·ley² (al′ē) *n. pl.,* **al·leys.** a large playing marble, used to shoot at other marbles. [Short for *alabaster,* of which the best marbles were originally made.]

al·ley·way (al′ē wā′) *n.* a narrow or short passageway between buildings.

All Fools' Day, another name for **April Fools' Day.**

All·hal·lows (ôl hal′ōz) *n.* another name for **All Saints' Day.**

al·li·ance (ə lī′əns) *n.* **1.** a formal agreement between two or more nations to cooperate closely, as in fighting a war or trading goods. **2.** any similar agreement in which persons or groups join together for a common cause: *Government and business formed an alliance to bolster the nation's weak economy.* **3.** the persons, nations, or groups taking part in such an agreement.

al·lied (ə līd′, al′īd) *adj.* **1.** united by treaty or agreement for a common purpose: *allied nations, allied labor unions.* **2.** related or similar: *Painting and sculpture are allied arts.* **3. Allied.** of or relating to the Allies.

Al·lies (al′īz, ə līz′) *n., pl.* **1.** the nations allied against the Axis in World War II, especially the United States, Great Britain, and the Soviet Union. **2.** the nations allied against the Central Powers in World War I, especially Great Britain, Russia, France, and the United States.

al·li·ga·tor (al′ə gā′tər) *n.* **1.** a large reptile with a thick, tough skin, similar to the crocodile but having a broader snout. **2.** leather made from the skin of an alligator. [Spanish *el lagarto* the lizard, from Latin *lacertus* a lizard.]

alligator pear, another term for **avocado.**

all-im·por·tant (ôl′ im·pôr′tənt) *adj.* very important; essential.

al·lit·er·a·tion (ə lit′ə·rā′shən) *n.* the repetition of the same initial letter, sound, or group of sounds in a series of words. For example: *She sells seashells by the seashore.*

Alligator

Crocodile

al·lit·er·a·tive (ə lit′ə rā′tiv) *adj.* of or characterized by alliteration: *an alliterative song.*

al·lo·cate (al′ə kāt′) *v.t.,* **al·lo·cat·ed, al·lo·cat·ing.** to set aside or divide for a specific purpose: *to allocate funds for public housing.* —**al′lo·ca′tion,** *n.*

al·lot (ə lot′) *v.t.,* **al·lot·ted, al·lot·ting.** to give out or assign as a share: *The teacher allotted five minutes to each question on the test.* —**al·lot′ment,** *n.*

al·lot·ro·py (ə lot′rə pē) *n.* the existence of a chemical element in two or more forms that have different structures.

all-out (ôl′ out′) *adj.* complete; total: *He made an all-out effort to win the race.*

all·o·ver (ôl′ō′vər) *adj.* covering the whole surface: *Her dress had an allover pattern of polka dots.*

al·low (ə lou′) *v.t.* **1.** to grant permission to or for; permit: *His father allows him to drive the car. Smoking is not allowed in this theater.* **2.** to let have; give: *She allows her daughter five dollars a week for lunch money.* **3.** to take into account or make provision for: *You must allow extra time for the trip because of the heavy traffic.* **4.** to accept as true or valid: *to allow a point in an argument.*
　to allow for. to make provision for: *He allowed for medical expenses in planning the household budget.*
　to allow of. to admit of; permit: *This problem allows of only one solution.*

al·low·a·ble (ə lou′ə bəl) *adj.* that can be allowed; not forbidden. —**al·low′a·bly,** *adv.*

al·low·ance (ə lou′əns) *n.* **1.** a quantity granted or set apart, especially a sum of money given regularly or for a particular purpose: *Billy gets an allowance of one dollar a week. The salesman receives a travel allowance.* **2.** a reduction in price given in return for something: *The salesman gave us an allowance of $600 on our old car when we traded it in for a new one.* **3.** the act of allowing or conceding; acceptance: *the court's allowance of a claim.*
　to make allowance for or **to make allowances for.** to take into consideration: *They made allowance for his inexperience and overlooked his mistakes.*

al·loy (*n.,* al′oi, ə loi′; *v.,* ə loi′) *n.* **1.** a metal formed by fusing two or more metals, or a metal and another substance: *Brass is an alloy of copper and zinc. Alloys tend to be harder, stronger, and more resistant to heat than the substances of which they are made.* **2.** a less valuable metal mixed with a more valuable one. **3.** something that lessens the purity or value of another thing. —*v.t.* **1.** to combine (two or more metals) so as to form an alloy. **2.** to make less pure or valuable by mixing: *His pleasure in eating the stolen pie was alloyed with guilt.*

all right 1. satisfactory; acceptable: *His work is all right. It's all right with me if you go.* **2.** safe; uninjured; well: *Are you all right?* **3.** yes; agreed: *All right, I'll do it.* **4.** satisfactorily: *He's doing all right.* **5.** without fail; certainly: *I'll be there, all right.* ▲ See **alright** for usage note.

all-round (ôl′ round′) another word for **all-around.**

All Saints' Day, a church festival celebrated in honor of all the saints. It falls on November 1. Also, **Allhallows, Hallowmas.**

All Souls' Day, in the Roman Catholic Church, a day of services and prayer for the souls in purgatory. It falls on November 2.

all·spice (ôl′spīs′) *n.* **1.** a spice made from dried and ground berries of the pimento tree. Its flavor resembles a blend of cinnamon, nutmeg, and cloves. **2.** the berry itself.

all-star (ôl′stär′) *adj.* made up of exceptional or star players or performers: *an all-star basketball team, a movie with an all-star cast.*

al·lude (ə lood′) *v.i.,* **al·lud·ed, al·lud·ing.** to refer to indirectly; mention casually or in passing: *Don't even allude to his poor play in yesterday's game.*

al·lure (ə loor′) *v.t.,* **al·lured, al·lur·ing.** to fascinate or attract with something tempting or desirable. —*n.* the power to allure; fascination; attractiveness: *the allure of traveling to faraway countries.* —**al·lur′er,** *n.*

al·lure·ment (ə loor′mənt) *n.* **1.** something that allures: *The scholarship offered him was a powerful allurement.* **2.** the power to allure: *the allurement of the sea.*

al·lur·ing (ə loor′ing) *adj.* very attractive or tempting: *She has an alluring smile.*

al·lu·sion (ə loo′zhən) *n.* a mention made indirectly or in passing: *This novel contains many allusions to the Bible and the works of Shakespeare.*

al·lu·vi·al (ə lōō′vē əl) *adj.* of, relating to, or composed of alluvium: *an alluvial deposit.* —*n.* alluvial material.

al·lu·vi·um (ə lōō′vē əm) *n. pl.,* **al·lu·vi·ums** or **al·lu·vi·a** (ə lōō′vē ə). mud, sand, or other material carried and deposited by a river or other flowing water.

al·ly (*v.,* ə lī′; *n.,* al′ī, ə lī′) *v.t.,* **al·lied, al·ly·ing.**
1. to unite or associate (oneself) for a common purpose: *The United States allied itself with England and Canada during World War II.* **2.** to connect by some similarity or common feature; relate. —*n. pl.,* **al·lies.** a person, nation, or group united with another for a common purpose: *France was an ally of the American colonies during the Revolutionary War.*

Al·ma-A·ta (äl′mä ä′tä) *n.* a city in the south-central Soviet Union. Pop. (1976 est.), 851,000.

al·ma ma·ter (äl′mə mä′tər) *also,* **Al·ma Ma·ter.**
1. the school, college, or university that a person has attended: *John F. Kennedy's alma mater was Harvard University.* **2.** the official song of a school, college, or university. [Latin *alma māter* nourishing mother.]

al·ma·nac (ôl′mə nak′) *n.* **1.** a reference book that is compiled every year, containing general information and important statistics on many different subjects. **2.** a book arranged by days, weeks, and months, containing facts and forecasts about the weather, the tides, and the rising and setting of the sun.

al·might·y (ôl mī′tē) *adj.* having limitless power; all-powerful. —*n.* **the Almighty.** God.

al·mond (ä′mənd, am′ənd) *n.* **1.** the edible, oval-shaped nut of a tree growing in warm regions. The sweet variety of almond is widely used in desserts, candy, and cooking. **2.** the tree that bears this fruit.

al·mond-eyed (ä′mənd īd′, am′ənd īd′) *adj.* having narrow, oval-shaped eyes.

al·mon·er (al′mə nər, ä′mə nər) *n.* a person who gives out alms as an official duty, as for a church or royal court.

al·most (ôl′mōst) *adv.* very nearly: *The skater almost fell on the ice, but he caught his balance just in time.*

alms (ämz) *n., pl.* money or gifts for the poor. ▲ used with a singular or plural verb.

alms·house (ämz′hous′) *n. pl.,* **alms·hous·es** (ämz′-hou′ziz). a home for people too poor to support themselves; poorhouse.

al·oe (al′ō) *n. pl.,* **al·oes.** **1.** any of a group of cactuslike plants found chiefly in tropical and southern Africa. Most aloes have thick, fleshy leaves with spiny edges and red or yellow flowers growing at the top of tall, leafless stalks. **2. aloes.** a bitter drug made from the juice of this plant's leaves. ▲ used with a singular verb. **3.** the century plant of North America.

a·loft (ə lôft′) *adv.* **1.** in or to a place far above the ground; high up. **2.** in or toward the rigging of a ship; far above the deck.

Aloe

a·lo·ha (ə lō′ə, ä lō′hä) *n., interj.*
1. greetings; hello. **2.** good-by; farewell. [Hawaiian *aloha* literally, love.]

a·lone (ə lōn′) *adj.* **1.** apart from anyone or anything else: *The orphan was all alone in the world.* **2.** excluding all other persons or things; only; solely: *The Supreme Court alone can declare a law unconstitutional.* —*adv.* without anyone or anything else: *My brother lives alone in his apartment.*
let alone. not to mention: *Wes can't even make toast, let alone cook an entire meal.*
to leave alone or **to let alone.** to leave undisturbed; not bother or interfere with: *He's in a bad mood, so leave him alone.*

to leave well enough alone or **to let well enough alone.** to be content with things the way they are.

a·long (ə lông′) *prep.* over the length of: *Flowers grew along the path. We walked along the highway.* —*adv.*
1. onward; forward: *The car moved along swiftly.* **2.** near or on one's person; with one: *She brought her umbrella along.*
all along. from the start: *He knew about the plan all along.*
along with. a. together with: *Let her go along with you to the market.* **b.** in addition to.
to get along. a. to manage successfully; get by. **b.** to be compatible; agree: *The children got along well together.* **c.** to go away; move on. **d.** to advance; progress: *The man was getting along in years.*

a·long·shore (ə lông′shôr′) *adv.* near, beside, or parallel to the shore.

a·long·side (ə lông′sīd′) *adv.* at, close to, or by the side: *They brought the rescue boat alongside.* —*prep.* by or at the side of; beside: *The car was parked alongside the curb.*
alongside of. side by side with; next to: *The soldiers stood at attention alongside of each other.*

a·loof (ə lōōf′) *adv.* at a distance in position or feeling; apart: *Their sister always remained aloof from the twins' quarrels.* —*adj.* not warm or friendly; reserved; distant: *The queen had an aloof manner toward her subjects.*
—**a·loof′ly,** *adv.* —**a·loof′ness,** *n.*

a·loud (ə loud′) *adv.* **1.** with the voice: *All the students will read their reports aloud to the class.* **2.** loudly: *He shouted aloud.*

alp (alp) *n.* a high mountain or mountain peak.

al·pac·a (al pak′ə) *n.* **1.** a South American animal closely related to the llama, raised in the Andes Mountains for its fine, silky wool. **2.** its wool. **3.** a silky, lightweight fabric woven from or containing this wool, used especially for coats and suits.

al·pen·horn (al′pən-hôrn′) *n.* a long, slightly curved, wooden horn, used by herdsmen in the Alps.

al·pen·stock (al′pən-stok′) *n.* a strong staff having an iron point, used in mountain climbing.

al·pha (al′fə) *n.* **1.** the first

Alpaca *(def. 1)*

letter of the Greek alphabet (A, α) corresponding to the English letter A, a. **2.** the first in a group or series; beginning.

alpha and omega, the beginning and the end; the first and the last. [From the names of the first and last letters of the Greek alphabet.]

al·pha·bet (al′fə bet′) *n.* **1.** a series of letters or characters used to write a language, arranged in their proper or customary order. **2.** any system of characters or symbols representing sounds or words: *In this dictionary pronunciation is shown by a phonetic alphabet.* [Latin *alphabētum*

at; āpe; cär; end; mē; it; īce; hot; ōld; fôrk; wood; fōōl; oil; out; up; turn; sing; thin; this; hw in white; zh in treasure. The symbol ə stands for the sound of a in about, e in taken, i in pencil, o in lemon, and u in circus.

the letters of a language, from Greek *alphabētos,* from *alpha* α and *bēta* β, the first two letters of the Greek alphabet.]

• The **alphabet** that we use today is one of about fifty alphabets used in the modern world. Although these alphabets may differ in the number and design of their letters, they are all based on the idea of using symbols to represent the sounds of language. The alphabet is one of man's greatest inventions because it enables us to record language in a form that can be seen and to store vast amounts of information.

The first alphabets appeared about 4000 years ago in what we now call the Middle East. These early alphabets, which included **ancient Semitic, early Hebrew,** and **early Phoenician,** were most probably based on ancient Egyptian picture writing, which is called *hieroglyphics.* All of these alphabets, which belong to a group called the **North Semitic** alphabets, contained 22 letters that were placed in a fixed order that could be memorized and recited. Each letter had a name, the first sound of the name being the sound that the letter represented. For example, the second letter of these alphabets was called *beth* which, like our second letter *B,* stood for a *b* sound. Unlike our modern alphabet, these ancient alphabets had no symbols for vowels. The North Semitic alphabets spread westward along the north coast of the Mediterranean, probably by way of the Phoenicians who were great seafarers and traders, and were the source of the **ancient Greek** alphabet. The names of the letters, such as *beth,* which became *beta,* were only slightly changed by the Greeks. For the most part, the shape of the North Semitic letters was also used. The Greeks added several new letters to stand for speech sounds that were not represented in the North Semitic alphabets. They also used some of the North Semitic letters to stand for vowel sounds which had not previously been represented. The Greek alphabet was the source of the **Etruscan** alphabet. The Etruscans, who settled north of Rome before the eighth century B.C., used the 22 North Semitic letters and four additional Greek letters in their alphabet. The shape and sound of the Etruscan letters were adopted, with only minor changes, in the **Latin** alphabet. In later years, certain Greek and Etruscan letters were dropped from the Latin alphabet and a new letter, *G,* was added. By about the first century A.D., the Latin alphabet consisted of 23 letters, lacking only the modern letters *W, U,* and *J,* that were to be added to certain Western alphabets during the Middle Ages. Our modern **English** alphabet is a direct descendant of the Latin alphabet.

al·pha·bet·i·cal (al′fə bet′i kəl) *adj.* **1.** in the order of the letters of the alphabet: *The words defined in a dictionary are listed in alphabetical order.* **2.** relating to or using an alphabet. Also, **al·pha·bet·ic** (al′fə bet′ik). —**al′pha·bet′i·cal·ly,** *adv.*

al·pha·bet·ize (al′fə bə tīz′) *v.t.,* **al·pha·bet·ized, al·pha·bet·iz·ing.** to arrange in alphabetical order: *His secretary alphabetized the list of names.* —**al·pha·bet·i·za·tion** (al′fə bet′ə zā′shən), *n.* —**al′pha·bet·i′zer,** *n.*

alpha particle, a positively charged particle that is identical to the nucleus of an atom of helium. It consists of two protons and two neutrons. Alpha particles are given off by certain radioactive substances.

alpha ray, a stream of alpha particles.

al·pine (al′pīn) *adj.* **1.** of, like, or situated in high mountains: *alpine flowers.* **2. Alpine.** of or relating to the Alps.

Alps (alps) *n., pl.* a mountain system in south-central Europe, extending in an arc from the Mediterranean coast near the French-Italian border to the Balkan Peninsula.

al·read·y (ôl red′ē) *adv.* **1.** before or by this time; previously: *He has already left. The job has already been done.* **2.** so soon: *Are you finished already?*

▲ The adverb **already** should not be confused with the two words **all ready. Already** means "previously" and "so soon." **All ready** means "completely ready": *Mary was all ready to go at eight o'clock.*

al·right (ôl rīt′) another spelling of **all right.** ▲ The form *alright* is not considered to be a correct spelling of the phrase **all right,** and careful writers avoid using it.

Al·sace (al sās′) *n.* a region and former province in eastern France.

Al·sace-Lor·raine (al′sās lô rān′) *n.* a region in eastern France, on the German and Swiss borders. It was part of Germany from 1871 to 1919 and from 1940 to 1945.

Al·sa·tian (al sā′shən) *n.* **1.** a person who was born or is living in Alsace. **2.** another name for **German shepherd.** —*adj.* of or relating to Alsace or its people.

al·so (ôl′sō) *adv.* in addition; as well; too: *He is a good swimmer and also plays tennis well.*

al·so-ran (ôl′sō ran′) *n. Informal.* **1.** a horse that fails to finish in first, second, or third place in a race. **2.** a person who loses in a competition, especially one who finishes far behind the winner.

Alta., Alberta.

Al·tai Mountains (al tī′, äl tī′) a mountain system of central Asia.

al·tar (ôl′tər) *n.* **1.** a raised structure or place where religious services are performed. **2.** in some Christian churches, the table where Communion services are held. **3.** a place where sacrifices are offered to a god.

altar boy, a boy or man who aids a priest during religious services, as during Mass.

al·tar·piece (ôl′tər pēs′) *n.* a decorative drapery or panel behind or above an altar.

al·ter (ôl′tər) *v.t.* **1.** to make different; change: *The tailor altered the dress to fit her.* **2.** to castrate or spay (an animal). —*v.i.* to become different; change: *His attitude toward his schoolwork has altered in the past year.* —**al′ter·a·ble,** *adj.* —**al′ter·a·bly,** *adv.*

al·ter·a·tion (ôl′tə rā′shən) *n.* **1.** the act of altering or the state of being altered: *The alterations on the coat will take at least one day.* **2.** the result of altering; change: *There's been an alteration in our plans.*

al·ter·ca·tion (ôl′tər kā′shən) *n.* a loud or angry dispute.

al·ter e·go (ôl′tər ē′gō) a constant companion or very close friend. [Latin *alter ego* literally, another I.]

al·ter·nate (*v.,* ôl′tər nāt′; *adj., n.,* ôl′tər nit) *v.,* **al·ter·nat·ed, al·ter·nat·ing.** —*v.i.* **1.** to take turns: *My brother and I alternate at washing the car.* **2.** to follow each other by turns; happen or appear in turn: *Red squares alternate with black ones on this checkerboard.* **3.** to pass back and forth from one condition, action, or place to another. —*v.t.* **1.** to do or perform by turns: *The entertainer alternated singing and dancing.* **2.** to cause to follow one another by turns. —*adj.* **1.** occurring or following by turns: *alternate layers of cake and icing.* **2.** every other: *I have piano lessons on alternate Mondays.* **3.** taking the place of another; substitute; alternative: *The club sent an alternate delegate to the convention.* —*n.* a person who takes the place of another; substitute. —**al′ter·nate·ly,** *adv.* —**al′ter·na′tion,** *n.*

alternate angles, two angles that are not adjacent to each other and are formed on opposite sides of a line that crosses two other lines.

alternating current, an electric current in which the electrons flow regularly first in one direction and then in the other.

al·ter·na·tive (ôl tur′nə tiv) *n.* **1.** a choice between two or more things: *In the story, the hero was faced with the alternative of betraying his men or being executed.* **2.** one of the things that may be chosen: *He realized that the alternative to death was dishonor.* **3.** other or remaining choice: *You have no alternative but to admit you were lying.* —*adj.* being or giving a choice between two or more things.

al·ter·na·tor (ôl′tər nā′tər) *n.* a generator that produces alternating electric current.

al·though (ôl thō′) *also,* **al·tho.** *conj.* in spite of the fact that; even though; though: *Although I ate a big dinner, I was very hungry soon afterward.*

al·tim·e·ter (al tim′ə tər, al′tə mē′tər) *n.* an instrument for measuring altitude above sea level or the ground, used chiefly in aircraft.

al·ti·tude (al′tə tōōd′, al′tə tyōōd′) *n.* **1.** the elevation above any given point, especially above the earth's surface or sea level: *He kept the plane at an altitude of 8000 feet.* **2. altitudes.** great heights; high places: *Frostbite is common in some mountain altitudes.* **3.** *Geometry.* the perpendicular distance from the base of a figure to its highest point. **4.** *Astronomy.* the angle of elevation of a celestial body above the horizon.

al·to (al′tō) *n. pl.,* **al·tos. 1.** the lowest female voice; contralto. **2.** the highest male voice; countertenor. **3.** a singer who has such a voice. **4.** a musical instrument that has a similar range. **5.** a musical part for such a voice or instrument. —*adj.* **1.** able to sing or play alto: *an alto voice, an alto recorder.* **2.** for an alto.

al·to·geth·er (ôl′tə geth′ər) *adv.* **1.** entirely; wholly; completely: *He missed the target altogether.* **2.** with everything included; in all: *There were twelve of us at the meeting altogether.* **3.** on the whole; everything considered: *Altogether, it was a good party.*

al·tru·ism (al′trōō iz′əm) *n.* an unselfish concern for the welfare of other people.

al·tru·ist (al′trōō ist) *n.* a person who is unselfishly concerned about the welfare of other people. —**al′tru·is′tic,** *adj.* —**al′tru·is′ti·cal·ly,** *adv.*

al·um (al′əm) *n.* any of a group of mineral salts, especially a salt of potassium and aluminum that is used in dyeing and tanning, in medicine, and in water purification.

a·lu·mi·num (ə lōō′mə nəm) *n.* a light, soft, silvery-white metallic element that is obtained from bauxite. Aluminum is the most abundant metal. It is an excellent conductor of heat and electricity, and is used in making machinery, appliances, building materials, transportation equipment, and many other products. Symbol: Al Also, *British,* **al·u·min·i·um** (al′yə min′ē əm).

a·lum·na (ə lum′nə) *n. pl.,* **a·lum·nae** (ə lum′nē). a female graduate or former student of a school, college, or university.

a·lum·nus (ə lum′nəs) *n. pl.,* **a·lum·ni** (ə lum′nī). a graduate or former student of a school, college, or university, especially a male graduate.

al·ve·o·lus (al vē′ə ləs) *n. pl.,* **al·ve·o·li** (al vē′ə lī′). **1.** a small cavity or pit in the body. **2.** a socket in the jawbone in which a tooth fits. **3.** one of the small air sacs of the lungs.

al·ways (ôl′wāz, ôl′wez) *adv.* **1.** at all times; on every occasion; all the time: *He is always kind to his friends. The weather is always cold at the North Pole.* **2.** throughout all time; forever: *I'll remember you*

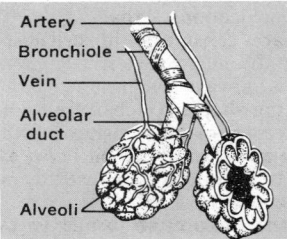
Artery
Bronchiole
Vein
Alveolar duct
Alveoli
Alveolus *(def. 3)*

always. **3.** *Informal.* in any case: *If there are no seats left, we can always stand.*

a·lys·sum (ə lis′əm) *n.* any of a group of low, branching plants of the mustard family, bearing clusters of small white or yellow flowers.

am (am, əm) the first person singular, present tense, of **be:** *I am going to the store.*

Am, the symbol for americium.

Am., America; American.

AM 1. a method of radio broadcasting by which a signal is transmitted over radio waves by altering the amplitude of the waves. **2.** a broadcasting system using this method. **3.** relating to or using an AM broadcasting system: *an AM radio, an AM station.* [Abbreviation of *amplitude modulation.*]

A.M. 1. the time from midnight to noon: *He gets up at 7 A.M.* Also, **a.m.** [Abbreviation of *ante meridiem.*] **2.** Master of Arts; M.A.

AMA, American Medical Association.

a·mal·gam (ə mal′gəm) *n.* **1.** an alloy of mercury with another metal or metals. Silver amalgam is used for filling teeth. **2.** any mixture or combination: *The population of New York City is an amalgam of many different nationalities.*

a·mal·ga·mate (ə mal′gə māt′) *v.,* **a·mal·ga·mat·ed, a·mal·ga·mat·ing.** —*v.t.* **1.** to unite so as to form a whole; merge: *The city decided to amalgamate several school districts into one.* **2.** to combine (a metal or metals) with mercury. —*v.i.* to unite together; combine; merge: *The two labor unions amalgamated.* —**a·mal′gam·a′tion,** *n.*

a·man·u·en·sis (ə man′yōō en′sis) *n. pl.,* **a·man·u·en·ses** (ə man′yōō en′sēz). a person employed to write down what another person says or to copy what another person has written.

am·a·ranth (am′ə ranth′) *n.* **1.** any of a group of weeds and garden plants, some of which are grown for their colorful leaves or showy flowers. **2.** an imaginary flower that never fades or wilts.

Am·a·ril·lo (am′ə ril′ō) *n.* a city in northwestern Texas. Pop. (1970), 127,010.

am·a·ryl·lis (am′ə ril′is) *n. pl.,* **am·a·ryl·lis·es.** any of a group of plants found chiefly in tropical America, bearing large, bright-colored, lilylike flowers.

a·mass (ə mas′) *v.t.* to collect (a great quantity); gather; accumulate: *The movie star amassed great wealth.*

am·a·teur (am′ə chər, am′ə tər) *n.* **1.** a person who does something as a pastime or for pleasure, rather than as a profession or for money: *Albert Einstein was a gifted amateur at the violin.* **2.** a person who does something without experience or professional skill: *The clear fingerprints left by the thief show that the crime was the work of an amateur.* **3.** an athlete who has never competed for money or earned money through his athletic skill. —*adj.* **1.** done by or relating to amateurs: *amateur sports.* **2.** being an amateur: *an amateur actor.* **3.** characteristic of amateurs; amateurish: *an amateur attempt at writing a novel.*

Amaryllis

at; āpe; cär; end; mē; it; īce; hot; ōld; fôrk; wood; fōōl; oil; out; up; turn; sing; thin; this; hw in white; zh in treasure. The symbol ə stands for the sound of a in about, e in taken, i in pencil, o in lemon, and u in circus.

am·a·teur·ish (am′ə choor′ish, am′ə toor′ish) *adj.* performed as though by an amateur; not expert: *an amateurish production of a play.* —**am′a·teur′ish·ly,** *adv.* —**am′a·teur′ish·ness,** *n.*

am·a·to·ry (am′ə tôr′ē) *adj.* relating to or expressing love: *an amatory letter.*

a·maze (ə māz′) *v.t.,* **a·mazed, a·maz·ing.** to overwhelm with wonder or surprise; astound: *The girl's skill at solving mathematical problems amazed all those who knew her.* —**a·maz·ed·ly** (ə mā′zid lē), *adv.*

a·maze·ment (ə māz′mənt) *n.* overwhelming wonder or surprise; astonishment.

a·maz·ing (ə mā′zing) *adj.* causing amazement; wonderful; astonishing: *an amazing sight, an amazing event.* —**a·maz′ing·ly,** *adv.*

Am·a·zon (am′ə zon′) *n.* **1.** the longest river in South America, flowing from the Andes across Brazil into the Atlantic. It carries the largest volume of water of any river in the world. **2.** *Greek Legend.* one of a race of female warriors, said to have lived near the Black Sea. **3.** *also,* **amazon.** any large or powerful woman.

Am·a·zo·ni·an (am′ə zō′nē ən) *adj.* **1.** of or relating to the Amazon River or the region it drains. **2.** *also,* **amazonian.** relating to or characteristic of an Amazon.

Amb., Ambassador.

am·bas·sa·dor (am bas′ə dər) *n.* **1.** a diplomat of the highest rank. Some ambassadors are sent as official representatives to a foreign country or government and live in that country. Other ambassadors are given special assignments to represent their country in the United Nations or another international body. **2.** any representative or messenger: *That musician is an ambassador of good will for her country.* —**am·bas·sa·dor·i·al** (am bas′ə dôr′ē əl), *adj.* —**am·bas′sa·dress,** *n.*

am·bas·sa·dor-at-large (am bas′ə dər at lärj′) *n. pl.,* **am·bas·sa·dors-at-large.** an ambassador assigned to no particular country or specific task.

am·bas·sa·dor·ship (am bas′ə dər ship′) *n.* the position, rank, or term of office of an ambassador.

am·ber (am′bər) *n.* **1.** a hard, translucent, yellowish-orange or yellowish-brown material used especially for jewelry, carvings, and electrical insulation. Amber is a fossil formed from the resin of pine trees that grew millions of years ago. **2.** the color of amber; yellowish orange or yellowish brown. —*adj.* **1.** made of amber. **2.** having the color amber.

am·ber·gris (am′bər grēs′, am′bər gris) *n.* a grayish, waxy substance formed in the intestines of sperm whales, used in making perfume.

am·bi·dex·trous (am′bi deks′trəs) *adj.* able to use both hands equally well: *He's ambidextrous enough to be able to write with either hand.* —**am′bi·dex′trous·ly,** *adv.* —**am′bi·dex′trous·ness,** *n.*

am·bi·ence (am′bē əns) *also,* **am·bi·ance.** *n.* surroundings and atmosphere. *The room had a cozy ambience.*

am·bi·gu·i·ty (am′bə gyōō′ə tē) *n. pl.,* **am·bi·gu·i·ties.** **1.** the condition of having more than one possible meaning; vagueness of purpose or meaning: *I don't know how he feels about that issue because of the ambiguity of his statements.* **2.** something that is unclear or vague, or that has more than one meaning.

am·big·u·ous (am big′yōō əs) *adj.* **1.** having more than one possible meaning. The sentence *Tom told Bill that his dog bit the mailman* is ambiguous because we cannot be sure from the word "his" whether the dog belongs to Tom or to Bill. **2.** unclear; vague: *an ambiguous attitude.* —**am·big′u·ous·ly,** *adv.* —**am·big′u·ous·ness,** *n.*

am·bi·tion (am bish′ən) *n.* **1.** a strong desire or drive to succeed or to achieve something: *a man of ambition. My*

sister has an ambition to become a doctor. **2.** the object of such a desire: *His ambition is to be captain of the football team.*

am·bi·tious (am bish′əs) *adj.* **1.** full of or showing ambition: *an ambitious politician.* **2.** strongly desirous; eager: *He is ambitious to win first prize in the contest.* **3.** requiring great ability or effort: *The governor proposed an ambitious program to end water pollution.* —**am·bi′tious·ly,** *adv.* —**am·bi′tious·ness,** *n.*

am·biv·a·lence (am biv′ə ləns) *n.* the quality or state of being ambivalent: *His ambivalence toward his studies showed in the fact that he often worked hard one day and then did nothing the next.*

am·biv·a·lent (am biv′ə lənt) *adj.* having or showing conflicting feelings about an object, person, or idea: *I'd like to take a trip, but I'm ambivalent because it will cost a lot of money.* —**am·biv′a·lent·ly,** *adv.*

am·ble (am′bəl) *v.i.,* **am·bled, am·bling.** **1.** to walk at a relaxed, leisurely pace: *We ambled through the store, looking at the items displayed on the counters.* **2.** (of a horse) to move at a slow, easy pace by lifting both legs on the same side together. —*n.* **1.** a slow, leisurely pace in walking. **2.** a leisurely stroll or walk: *We decided to take an amble down the boardwalk.* **3.** the ambling gait of a horse. —**am′bler,** *n.*

am·bro·sia (am brō′zhə) *n.* **1.** *Greek and Roman Mythology.* the food of the gods, capable of making anyone who ate it immortal. **2.** something particularly delicious or delightful to the taste or smell.

am·bro·sial (am brō′zhəl) *adj.* of or like ambrosia; particularly delicious or delightful.

am·bu·lance (am′byə ləns) *n.* a specially equipped vehicle that is used for carrying persons who are sick, injured, or wounded.

am·bu·la·to·ry (am′byə lə tôr′ē) *adj.* **1.** able to walk: *an ambulatory patient.* **2.** of or relating to walking: *ambulatory exercise.*

am·bus·cade (am′bəs kād′) *n., v.,* **am·bus·cad·ed, am·bus·cad·ing.** another word for **ambush.**

am·bush (am′boosh) *n. pl.,* **am·bush·es.** **1.** a surprise attack from a hidden position: *The patrol moved cautiously for fear of an enemy ambush.* **2.** a hidden position for surprise attack: *The bandits waited in ambush over the top of the hill.* —*v.t.* to make a surprise attack on from a hidden position: *The bandits ambushed the enemy troops.* —**am′bush·er,** *n.*

a·me·ba (ə mē′bə) *also,* **a·moe·ba.** *n. pl.,* **a·me·bas** or **a·me·bae** (ə mē′bē). an animal consisting of a single cell. An ameba is so small it can be seen only through a microscope. It moves and takes in food by sending out projections that are constantly in motion, so that it is always changing shape. Amebas are found in fresh or salt water, moist earth, or as parasites in other animals.

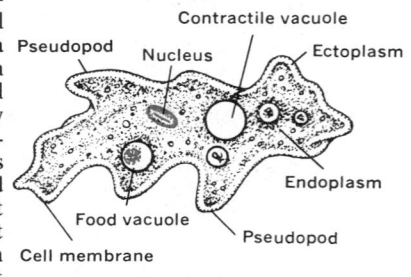

Ameba

a·me·bic (ə mē′bik) *also,* **a·moe·bic.** *adj.* **1.** of or relating to an ameba. **2.** caused by an ameba or amebas: *an amebic disease.*

a·mel·io·rate (ə mēl′yə rāt′) *v.,* **a·mel·io·rat·ed, a·mel·io·rat·ing.** —*v.t.* to make (something) better; improve: *The union wanted to ameliorate working conditions in the* *factory.* —*v.i.* to grow or become better. —**a·mel′io·ra′-tion,** *n.*

a·men (ā′men′, ä′men′) *interj.* may it be so; so be it. ▲ said after a prayer or after other statements to express agreement or approval. —*n.* an uttering of this word: *The congregation responded to the minister's statement with a hearty "Amen."*

A·men (ä′mən) *also,* **A·mon, Am·mon.** *n.* one of the gods worshiped in ancient Egypt.

a·me·na·ble (ə mē′nə bəl, ə men′ə bəl) *adj.* **1.** willing to accept or pay attention to; open to: *Our teacher is always amenable to suggestions for new projects.* **2.** liable to be called to account; answerable: *Citizens are amenable to the laws of their country.* —**a·me′na·bil′i·ty, a·me′na·ble-ness,** *n.* —**a·me′na·bly,** *adv.*

a·mend (ə mend′) *v.t.* **1.** to alter formally: *In 1865 the Constitution was amended to outlaw slavery.* **2.** to change for the better; improve; correct: *to amend the living conditions of the poor.*

a·mend·ment (ə mend′mənt) *n.* **1.** the act of amending or the state of being amended. **2.** the result of amending; a change. **3.** a formal change made by parliamentary or constitutional procedure: *Women were given the right to vote by an amendment to the Constitution.*

a·mends (ə mendz′) *n., pl.* **to make amends.** to make up for (loss, injury, or insult): *He tried to make amends for his rude behavior by sending a letter of apology.*

a·men·i·ty (ə men′ə tē) *n. pl.,* **a·men·i·ties. 1. amenities. a.** polite social actions or behavior, especially certain standard or accepted ones. **b.** agreeable features; pleasant qualities: *He enjoyed all the amenities of a happy home life.* **2.** pleasantness; agreeableness.

Amer., America; American.

A·mer·i·ca (ə mer′i kə) *n.* **1.** the United States. **2.** North America or South America. **3.** *also,* **the Americas.** North, Central, and South America considered as a whole; the Western Hemisphere.

●The name **America** comes from the Italian explorer *Amerigo* (which is *Americus* in Latin) Vespucci, who was mistakenly believed to have discovered the Western Hemisphere.

A·mer·i·can (ə mer′i kən) *adj.* **1.** of, relating to, or characteristic of the United States or its people: *the American flag.* **2.** of, relating to, or characteristic of the Americas or their people: *The coyote is an American animal.* —*n.* **1.** a person who was born or is living in the United States; a citizen of the United States. **2.** a person who was born or is living in the Americas.

A·mer·i·ca·na (ə mer′i kan′ə) *n., pl.* books, documents, and other materials that relate to American history or culture.

American cheese, any of several mild white or yellow cheddar or process cheeses.

American eagle, the North American bald eagle, the national emblem of the United States.

American English, the English language as spoken and written in the United States.

●**American English** began to develop as soon as the first colonists from England arrived in the New World. For example, the word *canoe,* which was not used in England, appears in a book written in 1608 by Captain John Smith. The colonists had to invent new words to describe the many things they found in America that were unfamiliar to them.

In colonial times, most writers and critics in both England and America thought that American English was inferior to British English. One eighteenth-century American writer stated that the most serious kind of grammatical error was to use an American word in place of a similar term used in Great Britain. Thomas Jefferson was criticized by several English writers for using the word *belittle.*

After the Revolutionary War, Americans wanted to be independent of British influence in language, just as they had become politically independent. So American English came to be considered completely acceptable in this country. Writers such as James Fenimore Cooper began to use American expressions in their books. Noah Webster published a dictionary that gave American rather than British spellings for words, such as *center* instead of *centre.*

In Great Britain, American English was still considered to be an "impure" form of the language. American words such as *lengthy, reliable, talented,* and *influential* were attacked as "vile" and "barbarous" by prominent English writers, although all these terms were derived from words commonly used in England. It was not until after the Civil War, when writers such as Mark Twain became popular in England, that American English really became accepted in Great Britain.

American Indian, see **Indian** (def. 1).

A·mer·i·can·ism (ə mer′i kə niz′əm) *n.* **1.** a word, phrase, or expression originating in the United States or found mainly in American English. *Hamburger, canyon, flunk,* and *OK* are Americanisms. **2.** a custom, trait, or belief peculiar to the United States. **3.** devotion to or support of the United States, its institutions, and its traditions.

A·mer·i·can·ize (ə mer′i kə nīz′) *v.t., v.i.,* **A·mer·i·can-ized, A·mer·i·can·iz·ing.** to make or become American, as in habits, customs, beliefs, or manners. —**A·mer′i·can-i·za′tion,** *n.*

American Legion, an organization of veterans of the U.S. armed forces of World Wars I and II, the Korean War, and the war in Vietnam, founded in 1919.

American plan, in hotels, a system of charging guests at a fixed rate that includes both room and meals.

American Revolution, a war fought from 1775 to 1783 between Great Britain and its American colonies, in which the colonies gained their independence. Also, **Revolutionary War.**

American Samoa, an island group in Samoa, administered by the United States. Capital, Pago Pago. Land area, 76 sq. mi. Pop. (1971 est.), 30,000.

am·er·i·ci·um (am′ə rish′ē əm) *n.* a radioactive metallic element having a silvery-white color, produced by the bombardment of uranium and plutonium by high-energy helium ions. Symbol: **Am**

A·mer·i·go Ves·puc·ci (ə mer′ə gō ves pōō′chē) see **Vespucci, Amerigo.**

Am·er·ind (am′ə rind′) *n.* an American Indian or an Eskimo. Also, **Am·er·in·di·an** (am′ə rin′dē ən).

am·e·thyst (am′ə thist) *n.* **1.** purple or violet quartz, used as a gem. **2.** a purple or violet color.

a·mi·a·ble (ā′mē ə bəl) *adj.* having a pleasing and kindly disposition; good-natured; friendly: *The amiable gentleman smiled when he was hit with a snowball.* —**a′mi·a·bil′i·ty,** *n.* —**a′mi·a·bly,** *adv.*

at; āpe; cär; end; mē; it; īce; hot; ōld; fôrk; wood; fōōl; oil; out; up; turn; sing; thin; **th**is; hw in white; zh in treasure. The symbol ə stands for the sound of **a** in about, **e** in taken, **i** in pencil, **o** in lemon, and **u** in circus.

33

am·i·ca·ble (am′ə kə bəl) *adj.* characterized by friendliness and good will; peaceable: *After an amicable discussion the dispute was settled.* —**am′i·ca·bil′i·ty,** *n.* —**am′·i·ca·bly,** *adv.*

a·mid (ə mid′) *prep.* in the middle or midst of; surrounded by; among: *The house stood amid a grove of pine trees.*

a·mid·ships (ə mid′ships′) *adv.* in or toward the middle of a ship.

a·midst (ə midst′) *prep.* another word for **amid**.

a·mi·go (ə mē′gō) *n. pl.,* **a·mi·gos.** friend. [Spanish *amigo* friend, from Latin *amícus.*]

a·mi·no acid (ə mē′nō, am′ə nō′) any of a group of organic acids composed of carbon, hydrogen, oxygen, and nitrogen. Amino acids are needed by organisms to make proteins.

Am·ish (ä′mish, am′ish) *n., pl.* a Protestant religious denomination, closely related to the Mennonites. It was founded in Switzerland in the seventeenth century. The Amish, most of whom live in the United States, follow simple customs and refuse to take oaths or perform military service. —*adj.* of, belonging to, or relating to this sect.

a·miss (ə mis′) *adj.* faulty; wrong; improper: *I knew that something was amiss from the worried look on her face.* —*adv.* not in the proper manner or order; improperly; wrongly.

to take amiss. to take offense at; resent.

am·i·ty (am′ə tē) *n. pl.,* **am·i·ties.** peaceful and friendly relations; friendship: *The conference succeeded in achieving amity between the two nations.*

Am·man (ä män′, a man′) *n.* the capital of Jordan, in the northwestern part of the country. Pop. (1977 est.), 711,900.

am·me·ter (am′mē′tər) *n.* an instrument used for measuring the strength of an electric current in amperes.

Am·mon (am′ən) *n.* another name for the god **Amen.**

am·mo·ni·a (ə mōn′yə) *n.* **1.** a colorless, gaseous compound of nitrogen and hydrogen having a highly pungent odor. Ammonia is

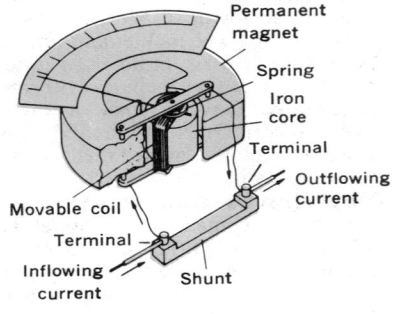

Ammeter

used especially in fertilizers and in the production of other chemicals. **2.** a solution of ammonia in water, used as a household cleaner.

am·mu·ni·tion (am′yə nish′ən) *n.* **1.** bullets, shells, and other projectiles for use in firearms and artillery. **2.** any type of explosive weapon, such as a grenade or bomb. **3.** anything used in attack or defense: *The scandal provided new ammunition for the senator's political opponents.*

am·ne·sia (am nē′zhə) *n.* partial or total loss of memory, especially as the result of brain injury, mental illness, disease, or shock.

am·nes·ty (am′nis tē) *n. pl.,* **am·nes·ties.** a general pardon given to prisoners, outlaws, or rebels who have committed offenses against a government: *At the end of the war the President granted amnesty to all men who had refused to serve in the army.*

am·ni·on (am′nē ən) *n. pl.,* **am·ni·ons** or **am·ni·a** (am′nē ə). a membrane that forms a fluid-filled sac surrounding the embryo in reptiles, birds, and mammals.

a·moe·ba (ə mē′bə) *n. pl.,* **a·moe·bas** or **a·moe·bae** (ə mē′bē). another spelling of **ameba**.

a·moe·bic (ə mē′bik) another spelling of **amebic**.

a·mok (ə muk′, ə mok′) another spelling of **amuck**.

A·mon (ä′mən) *n.* another name for the god **Amen**.

a·mong (ə mung′) *prep.* **1.** in the midst of; surrounded by: *The campers pitched their tent among the trees.* **2.** in the company of: *He lived among the poor.* **3.** in the number or class of: *He is considered the best among the young poets.* **4.** by, with, or through many or all of: *That candidate is popular among college students.* **5.** in shares for each of: *He divided the prize among the winners.* **6.** by the combined or joint action of: *Among us, we can raise the money.* ▲ See **between** for usage note.

a·mongst (ə mungst′) *prep.* another word for **among**.

a·mor·al (ā môr′əl, ā mor′əl) *adj.* not having or interested in moral standards; neither moral nor immoral: *Science is amoral.* —**a·mor·al·i·ty** (ā′mə ral′ə tē), *n.* —**a·mor′al·ly,** *adv.*

am·o·rous (am′ər əs) *adj.* **1.** inclined to love or to fall in love: *Don Juan's amorous disposition.* **2.** produced by or showing love: *an amorous glance.* **3.** of or relating to love. —**am′o·rous·ly,** *adv.* —**am′o·rous·ness,** *n.*

a·mor·phous (ə môr′fəs) *adj.* **1.** without definite form or shape; shapeless: *Groups of amorphous clouds floated across the sky.* **2.** of no particular kind or character; unorganized: *The people opposed to that policy are an amorphous group at present.* **3.** *Chemistry.* (of a solid) not formed of crystals: *Glass is amorphous.* —**a·mor′phous·ly,** *adv.* —**a·mor′phous·ness,** *n.*

am·or·tize (am′ər tīz′) *v.t.,* **am·or·tized, am·or·tiz·ing.** to pay (a debt) gradually, usually by making payments of equal amounts over a period of time. —**am′or·ti·za′·tion,** *n.*

A·mos (ā′məs) *n.* **1.** a Hebrew prophet and social reformer of the eighth century B.C. **2.** the book of the Old Testament containing his prophecies.

a·mount (ə mount′) *n.* **1.** numerical quantity; sum: *He paid the full amount of the bill.* **2.** any quantity: *We have a large amount of work to do. No amount of criticism could persuade him that he was wrong.* —*v.i.* **1.** to equal in number or quantity; add up: *The bill amounts to ten dollars.* **2.** to be equal in value, significance, or effect: *That remark amounts to a threat.* **3.** (of a person) to develop into; become: *He'll never amount to anything.*

▲ **Amount** and **number** both refer to a quantity. **Amount** is usually used when a quantity is considered as a whole and its separate units cannot be counted: *There is a great amount of information in books.* **Number** is usually used when the separate units that make up the quantity can be counted: *He read a large number of books during the past school year.*

a·mour (ə moor′) *n.* a love affair, especially a secret one.

amp. **1.** ampere; amperes. **2.** amperage.

am·per·age (am′pər ij) *n.* the strength of an electric current measured in amperes.

am·pere (am′pēr) *n.* the standard unit for measuring the strength of an electric current. It is equal to the amount of current produced by one volt acting through a resistance of one ohm. [From André Marie *Ampère,* 1775–1836, a French physicist.]

am·per·sand (am′pər sand′) *n.* the symbol (&) representing the word "and": *Smith & Company.*

am·phet·a·mine (am fet′ə mēn′, am fet′ə min) *n.* a colorless liquid compound, used as a drug to relieve colds and as a stimulant to the central nervous system. This drug should not be taken without medical supervision.

am·phib·i·an (am fib′ē ən) *n.* **1.** any of a class of cold-blooded animals with backbones, including frogs, toads, and salamanders, usually living in or near water and having moist, scaleless skin. Their eggs are usually laid in water or moist places and hatch into legless larvae with gills, which develop into adults with lungs and two pairs of legs. **2.** any animal or plant that lives both on land and in water, such as an alligator or a seal. **3.** an aircraft that is designed to take off from and land on either water or land; seaplane. **4.** a tank or other vehicle that can travel on both land and water. —*adj.* **1.** of, relating to, or characteristic of the class of amphibians. **2.** another word for **amphibious.**

am·phib·i·ous (am fib′ē əs) *adj.* **1.** capable of living both on land and in water. **2.** adapted or suitable for use on land or water: *an amphibious airplane.* **3.** carried out by the action of both land and naval forces: *an amphibious attack.*

am·phi·the·a·ter (am′fə thē′ə tər) *also,* **am·phi·the·a·tre.** *n.* **1.** an oval or circular structure with rising rows of seats around a central open space. **2.** a room having rising rows of seats arranged around a central area, such as a classroom or an operating room in a hospital. **3.** a level area of ground that is completely surrounded by rising slopes.

Amphitheater

am·pho·ra (am′fər ə) *n. pl.,* **am·pho·rae** (am′fər ē) or **am·pho·ras.** a two-handled jar or vase with a narrow neck, broad body, and tapering base. It was used by the ancient Greeks and Romans.

am·ple (am′pəl) *adj.,* **am·pler, am·plest. 1.** large in size or extent; roomy: *The car has an ample trunk.* **2.** more than enough; abundant: *We have ample time to finish the job.* **3.** enough; sufficient; adequate: *Joe earns ample money for his needs.* —**am′ple·ness,** *n.* —**am′ply,** *adv.*

am·pli·fi·ca·tion (am′plə fi kā′shən) *n.* **1.** the act of amplifying or the state of being amplified. **2.** something used to amplify; additional matter. **3.** an increase in the strength of an electronic signal.

am·pli·fi·er (am′plə fī′ər) *n.* **1.** a device for increasing the strength of an electronic signal. **2.** the part of a sound-reproduction system that contains such a device. **3.** a person or thing that amplifies.

am·pli·fy (am′plə fī′) *v.t.,* **am·pli·fied, am·pli·fy·ing. 1.** to add to or expand; enlarge on: *He amplified his statement by providing explanatory details.* **2.** to increase the strength of (an electronic signal).

am·pli·tude (am′plə tōōd′, am′plə tyōōd′) *n.* **1.** the state or quality of being ample; largeness; abundance; fullness. **2.** the distance that a vibrating body, such as a pendulum, moves in either direction from a central position. **3.** the highest strength reached by an alternating electric current during a complete cycle.

amplitude modulation, see **AM.**

am·pu·tate (am′pyə tāt′) *v.t.,* **am·pu·tat·ed, am·pu·tat·ing.** to cut off, especially to remove (a limb) by means of surgery: *Because of the seriousness of the infection, the doctor was forced to amputate the patient's leg below the knee.* —**am′pu·ta′tion,** *n.*

am·pu·tee (am′pyə tē′) *n.* a person who has had a limb amputated.

Am·ster·dam (am′stər dam′) *n.* the capital and largest

city of the Netherlands, in the west-central part of the country. Pop. (1971 est.), 820,406.

amt., amount.

a·muck (ə muk′) *also,* **a·mok** *adv.* **to run amuck.** to lose control of oneself and rush about wildly, especially with intent to attack or kill.

am·u·let (am′yə lit) *n.* an object worn as a protection against disease, bad luck, or evil; a charm.

A·mund·sen, Ro·ald (ä′mən sən; rō′äl) 1872–1928, the Norwegian explorer who discovered the South Pole in 1911.

a·muse (ə myōōz′) *v.t.,* **a·mused, a·mus·ing. 1.** to cause to laugh or smile; please the sense of humor of: *His jokes amused all of us.* **2.** to keep pleasantly busy or interested; entertain: *He amused himself by reading.*

a·mused (ə myōōzd′) *adj.* **1.** feeling happiness or enjoyment: *an amused audience.* **2.** showing happiness or enjoyment: *He had an amused glint in his eye.* —**a·mus·ed·ly** (ə myōō′zid lē), *adv.*

a·muse·ment (ə myōōz′mənt) *n.* **1.** the state of being amused; enjoyment. **2.** something that amuses or entertains.

amusement park, a park or other area containing various games, rides, and other forms of amusement, such as a Ferris wheel, merry-go-round, or roller coaster.

a·mus·ing (ə myōō′zing) *adj.* causing laughter, happiness, or enjoyment. —**a·mus′ing·ly,** *adv.*

an (an; *unstressed* ən) *indefinite article* the form of the word **a** used before words that begin with a vowel sound: *an apple, an hour.*

-an *suffix* **1.** (used to form nouns) **a.** a person who was born or is living in: *Mexican.* **b.** a person belonging to or associated with: *Republican, Lutheran.* **c.** a person skilled or expert in: *mathematician, magician.* **2.** (used to form adjectives) of, relating to, belonging to, or characteristic of: *Shakespearean, American.*

a·nach·ro·nism (ə nak′rə niz′əm) *n.* **1.** something or someone that is out of or past its proper time: *A suit of armor worn in battle today would be an anachronism.* **2.** the placement of something in a time to which it does not belong: *To speak of Shakespeare using a typewriter is an anachronism.*

a·nach·ro·nis·tic (ə nak′rə nis′tik) *adj.* containing or involving an anachronism. —**a·nach·ro·nis′ti·cal·ly,** *adv.*

an·a·con·da (an′ə kon′də) *n.* **1.** a very large snake that crushes its prey in its coils and is native to tropical South America. It feeds mostly on fish, water birds, and small animals. **2.** any large constrictor, such as the python or boa.

Anaconda

a·nae·mi·a (ə nē′mē ə) another spelling of **anemia.**

a·nae·mic (ə nē′mik) another spelling of **anemic.**

an·aer·obe (an er′ōb, an′ə rōb′) *n.* a microorganism that is able to live in a place where there is no free oxygen.

an·aer·o·bic (an′e rō′bik, an′ə rō′bik) *adj.* able to live or grow where there is no free oxygen.

an·aes·the·sia (an′is thē′zhə) another spelling of **anesthesia.**

an·aes·the·si·ol·o·gist (an′is thē′zē ol′ə jist) another spelling of **anesthesiologist.**

an·aes·the·si·ol·o·gy (an′is thē′zē ol′ə jē) another spelling of **anesthesiology.**

an·aes·thet·ic (an′is thet′ik) another spelling of **anesthetic.** —**an′aes·thet′i·cal·ly,** *adv.*

an·aes·the·tist (ə nes′thə tist) another spelling of **anesthetist.**

an·aes·the·tize (ə nes′thə tīz′) another spelling of **anesthetize.**

an·a·gram (an′ə gram′) *n.* **1.** a word or phrase made by changing the order of the letters of another word or phrase. The word *veil* is an anagram of the word *evil.* **2. anagrams.** a game in which the players form words by changing the order of letters or by adding letters.

An·a·heim (an′ə hīm′) *n.* a city in southwestern California. Pop. (1970), 166,701.

a·nal (ān′əl) *adj.* of, relating to, or near the anus.

an·al·ge·si·a (an′əl jē′zē ə) *n.* the relieving or removing of pain, especially without the loss of consciousness.

an·al·ge·sic (an′əl jē′zik) *adj.* relieving or removing pain: *an analgesic drug.* —*n.* a remedy that is used to relieve or remove pain: *Aspirin is one of the most common analgesics.*

an·a·log computer (an′əl ôg′, an′əl og′) also, **an·a·logue computer.** a computer in which numbers directly represent physical quantities, such as weight, length, temperature, or voltage. A slide rule is a simple form of analog computer.

a·nal·o·gous (ə nal′ə gəs) *adj.* alike or similar in certain ways; comparable: *The gills of a fish are analogous to the lungs of an animal.* —**a·nal′o·gous·ly,** *adv.*

a·nal·o·gy (ə nal′ə jē) *n. pl.,* **a·nal·o·gies. 1.** a likeness in certain ways between things that are otherwise unlike; partial similarity: *There is an analogy between the gills of a fish and the lungs of an animal.* **2.** any comparison or parallel: *The historian drew an analogy between the current war and one that took place in ancient times.*

●In language, the word **analogy** means "the process of changing or forming a word according to rules or general patterns." Analogy can help to simplify writing and speaking, but, because English spelling and pronunciation often do not follow rules and patterns, it can also lead to natural mistakes. A child or foreigner learning English will know the general rule that by adding an *-s* to the end of a noun, such as *hand* or *boy,* you form its plural. By forming the plural of *foot* or *child* according to analogy, this person would incorrectly write or say "foots" and "childs," instead of the correct *feet* and *children.* The only way to learn the correct spelling and pronunciation of English words is to learn the rules and patterns of our language and then to memorize the many words that are exceptions to the rules.

Analogy, which is really a "common sense" way of writing and speaking, has helped to remove some of these confusing, irregular words from our language. English, which has developed over the last 1500 years, used to have many more irregular words than it has now. An example of this is the plural of the noun *cow,* which originally was "kine." This was simplified to *cows* by analogy with the *-s* ending that English nouns normally have in the plural. The past tense of the verb *dive* has also been changed in this way, although the old form *dove* and the newer form *dived* are both used.

Analogy helps language to grow by allowing us to invent new words that are patterned after older ones. A word such as *finalize,* which has only recently come into our language, is the result of analogy. It is derived from the adjective *final,* and is based on a pattern that appears quite often in English, as in the words *civilize* and *familiarize,* which come from *civil* and *familiar.* Analogy also produces new words that come directly from older words. The word *skyjack,* which was invented in the late 1960's when airplane hijacking first became common, was formed by analogy with the older word *hijack.*

---

a·nal·y·sis (ə nal′ə sis) *n. pl.,* **a·nal·y·ses** (ə nal′ə sēz′). **1.** a method of finding out the nature of something by separating it into parts: *An analysis of the water from the river indicated that it was highly polluted. An analysis of his testimony shows that he did not tell the truth.* **2.** a statement of the results of such an examination. **3.** any careful and detailed examination: *This article gives an analysis of the recent election.* **4.** another word for **psychoanalysis.**

an·a·lyst (an′əl ist) *n.* **1.** a person who analyzes or is skilled in analysis: *He is an experienced political analyst.* **2.** another word for **psychoanalyst.**

an·a·lyt·i·cal (an′əl it′i kəl) *adj.* of, relating to, or using analysis: *She has an analytical mind.* Also, **an·a·lyt·ic** (an′əl it′ik). —**an′a·lyt′i·cal·ly,** *adv.*

analytic geometry, a branch of mathematics in which geometric figures are described and analyzed in terms of algebra and plotted in space by means of coordinates.

an·a·lyze (an′əl īz′) *v.t.,* **an·a·lyzed, an·a·lyz·ing. 1.** to find out the nature of (something) by separating it into parts: *to analyze a chemical solution.* **2.** to examine carefully and in detail: *The detective analyzed the evidence in the case.*

an·a·pest (an′ə pest′) *n.* **1.** in poetry, a metrical foot consisting of two unaccented or short syllables followed by an accented or long syllable. The line *And the sheen of their spears was like stars on the sea* (Lord Byron) contains four anapests. **2.** a line of verse made up of such feet.

an·ar·chic (an är′kik) *adj.* of, like, or causing anarchy. Also, **an·ar·chi·cal** (an är′ki kəl). —**an·ar′chi·cal·ly,** *adv.*

an·ar·chism (an′ər kiz′əm) *n.* the political theory that all forms of government and governmental restraint are morally wrong and must be abolished.

an·ar·chist (an′ər kist) *n.* **1.** a person who believes in or supports anarchy or anarchism. **2.** any person who promotes disorder or stirs up revolt. —**an′ar·chis′tic,** *adj.*

an·ar·chy (an′ər kē) *n.* **1.** the total absence of government and law. **2.** a state of complete disorder and confusion; chaos.

a·nath·e·ma (ə nath′ə mə) *n. pl.,* **a·nath·e·mas. 1.** in certain churches, the formal denunciation of a person or the condemnation of a practice or doctrine. **2.** any strong denunciation or curse. **3.** a person or thing that is cursed, denounced, or hated.

a·nath·e·ma·tize (ə nath′ə mə tīz′) *v.t.,* **a·nath·e·ma·tized, a·nath·e·ma·tiz·ing.** to pronounce an anathema against; denounce; curse.

An·a·to·li·a (an′ə tō′lē ə) *n.* another name for **Asia Minor.** —**An′a·to′li·an,** *adj., n.*

an·a·tom·i·cal (an′ə tom′i kəl) *adj.* of or relating to anatomy. Also, **an·a·tom·ic** (an′ə tom′ik). —**an′a·tom′i·cal·ly,** *adv.*

a·nat·o·mist (ə nat′ə mist) *n.* a person who is skilled in anatomy.

a·nat·o·mize (ə nat′ə mīz′) *v.t.,* **a·nat·o·mized, a·nat·o·miz·ing. 1.** to dissect (an animal or plant) in order to study the structure and relationships of its parts. **2.** to analyze (something) closely. —**a·nat′o·mi·za′tion,** *n.*

a·nat·o·my (ə nat′ə mē) *n. pl.*, **a·nat·o·mies. 1.** the branch of science that deals with the structure of animals or plants and the relationships of their parts. **2.** the structure of an animal or plant or any of its parts. **3.** the dissection of animals or plants in order to study their structure. **4.** a detailed examination; analysis: *the anatomy of a crime.*

-ance *suffix* **1.** (used to form nouns from verbs) **a.** the process or action of: *continuance, utterance.* **b.** the state, quality, or condition of: *resemblance, complaisance.* **c.** the result of an action: *contrivance.* **d.** an agent of: *conveyance.* **2.** (used to form nouns from adjectives ending in *-ant*) the state, quality, or condition of: *ignorance, brilliance, vigilance.*

an·ces·tor (an′ses·tər) *n.* **1.** a person from whom one is descended; forefather: *His ancestors came to this country from France.* **2.** something from which another thing is developed or descended: *The Wright brothers' plane is an ancestor of modern jet aircraft.*

an·ces·tral (an ses′trəl) *adj.* of, relating to, or inherited from ancestors: *an ancestral home, an ancestral trait.* —**an·ces′tral·ly,** *adv.*

an·ces·tress (an′ses′tris) *n. pl.*, **an·ces·tress·es.** a woman from whom a person is descended.

an·ces·try (an′ses′trē) *n. pl.*, **an·ces·tries. 1.** a person's line of family descent; lineage. **2.** ancestors as a group.

an·chor (ang′kər) *n.* **1.** a device for preventing a boat or ship from drifting. An anchor usually grips the bottom and is attached to the vessel by a chain or cable. **2.** any device that holds something in place. **3.** something that gives support or security: *Hope was his anchor.* —*v.t.* **1.** to hold (a boat or ship) in place by an anchor. **2.** to fasten in place; fix firmly: *Anchor the shelf to the wall.* —*v.i.* to lower the anchor overboard and remain held fast: *We anchored in the bay.*

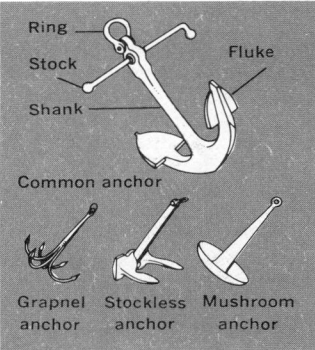

Ring
Stock
Fluke
Shank
Common anchor
Grapnel anchor
Stockless anchor
Mushroom anchor

at anchor. held fast by an anchor: *The ship was at anchor.*
to cast anchor or **to drop anchor.** to lower an anchor overboard.
to ride at anchor. to be held fast by an anchor.
to weigh anchor. to take up an anchor.

an·chor·age (ang′kər ij) *n.* **1.** a place for anchoring. **2.** something that fastens or holds securely: *The ropes were used as anchorage for the crates.*

An·chor·age (ang′kər ij) *n.* a port city in southern Alaska. It is the largest city in the state. Pop. (1970), 48,029.

an·cho·rite (ang′kə rīt′) *n.* a person who lives completely apart from society, especially for religious reasons; hermit.

an·chor·man (ang′kər man′) *n. pl.*, **an·chor·men** (ang′kər men′). **1.** the main announcer on a news broadcast. **2.** the last runner in a relay race. —**an′chor·wom′an,** *n.*

an·cho·vy (an′chō vē) *n. pl.*, **an·cho·vies.** any of various saltwater and freshwater fish, closely related to the herring. Anchovies are canned or made into a paste.

an·cient (ān′shənt) *adj.* **1.** of or relating to times long past, especially before the fall of the Western Roman Empire in A.D. 476: *Plato was an ancient philosopher.* **2.** of great age; very old: *Marriage is an ancient tradition.*

—*n.* **1.** a very old person. **2. the ancients.** civilized peoples of long ago, especially the ancient Greeks and Romans: *Slavery was a common practice among the ancients.* —**an′cient·ly,** *adv.* —**an′cient·ness,** *n.*

ancient history, history from the beginning of recorded events to the fall of the Western Roman Empire in A.D. 476.

an·cil·lar·y (an′sə ler′ē) *adj.* that helps or supports in a secondary way; supplementary; auxiliary: *In addition to a raise in salary, his new contract contains ancillary benefits.*

-ancy, another form of the suffix **-ance,** as in *vacancy.*

and (and; *unstressed* ənd, ən) *conj.* **1.** as well as; moreover: *He is big and strong. Susan and Jane came to visit me.* **2.** added to; plus: *Two and two make four.* **3.** as a result or consequence; then: *Treat him fairly and he'll be fair with you.* **4.** *Informal.* to: *Try and finish the work today.*

An·da·lu·sia (an′də lōō′zhə) *n.* a historic region of southern Spain, now divided into eight provinces. —**An′da·lu′sian,** *adj., n.*

an·dan·te (än dän′tā, an dan′tē) *Music. adv., adj.* slower than moderato but faster than adagio; moderately slow. —*n.* a composition, movement, or part in such a tempo.

An·de·an (an dē′ən, an′dē ən) *adj.* of or relating to the Andes.

An·der·sen, Hans Christian (an′dər sən; hanz) 1805–1875, Danish author of fairy tales.

An·der·son, Sherwood (an′dər sən) 1876–1941, U.S. novelist and short-story writer.

An·des (an′dēz) *n., pl.* the longest mountain system in the world, extending along the west coast of South America.

and·i·ron (and′ī′ərn) *n.* either of two metal supports for holding wood in a fireplace. Also, **firedog.**

and/or, both or either. ▲ **And/or** is used to show that either the word *and* or the word *or* may be used to connect two parts of a sentence, depending upon what is meant. *He hopes to play on the basketball team and/or the baseball team* means that he hopes to play on both of the teams or on either one of them.

Andirons

An·dor·ra (an dôr′ə) *n.* **1.** a country in southwestern Europe, between France and Spain. Area, 175 sq. mi. Pop. (1971), 20,550. **2.** the capital of this country. —**An·dor·ran** (an dôr′ən), *adj., n.*

An·dre·a del Sar·to (än drä′ə del sär′tō) 1486–1531, Italian painter.

An·drew, Saint (an′drōō) *n.* one of the Twelve Apostles of Jesus. He is the patron saint of Scotland.

An·dro·cles (an′drə klēz′) also, **An·dro·clus** (an′drə kləs). *n. Roman Legend.* a slave spared in the arena by a lion because he had once removed a thorn from its paw.

an·dro·gen (an′drə jən) *n.* any of various hormones

at; āpe; cär; end; mē; it; īce; hot; ōld; fôrk; wood; fōōl; oil; out; up; turn; sing; thin; **t**his; hw in white; zh in treasure. The symbol ə stands for the sound of **a** in about, **e** in taken, **i** in pencil, **o** in lemon, and **u** in circus.

that control and stimulate the development of masculine characteristics.

An·drom·a·che (an drom′ə kē) *n. Greek Legend.* the wife of Hector.

An·drom·e·da (an drom′ə də) *n.* **1.** *Greek Mythology.* an Ethiopian princess whom Perseus rescued from a sea monster and then took as his wife. **2.** a constellation in the northern sky, thought to resemble the shape of a woman with outstretched arms.

an·ec·do·tal (an′ik dōt′əl) *adj.* relating to or consisting of anecdotes: *an anecdotal magazine article.* —**an′ec·do′-tal·ly,** *adv.*

an·ec·dote (an′ik dōt′) *n.* a short account of some incident or event, especially one intended to amuse or illustrate: *The speaker related several anecdotes about George Washington.*

a·ne·mi·a (ə nē′mē ə) *also,* **a·nae·mi·a.** *n.* a condition in which the blood does not have enough hemoglobin or red corpuscles. It is characterized by paleness, weakness, and fatigue.

a·ne·mic (ə nē′mik) *also,* **a·nae·mic.** *adj.* **1.** relating to, having, or characteristic of anemia. **2.** lacking vitality or spirit.

an·e·mom·e·ter (an′ə mom′ə tər) *n.* an instrument for measuring the speed of the wind.

a·nem·o·ne (ə nem′ə nē) *n.* **1.** any of various plants having slender stems, lobed or notched leaves, and small white or colored flowers. Also, **windflower. 2.** see **sea anemone.**

a·nent (ə nent′) *prep.* in regard to; concerning; about.

aneroid barometer, a barometer in which the flexible top of a metal box containing a partial vacuum contracts and expands according to changes in air pressure. When the box contracts or expands, it moves a spring attached to a pointer that registers the change.

Anemometer

an·es·the·sia (an′is thē′zhə) *also,* **an·aes·the·sia.** *n.* a loss of sensation in the body, especially of the sense of pain.

an·es·the·si·ol·o·gist (an′is thē′zē ol′ə jist) *also,* **an·aes·the·si·ol·o·gist.** *n.* a physician who specializes in anesthesiology.

an·es·the·si·ol·o·gy (an′is thē′ze ol′ə jē) *also,* **an·aes·the·si·ol·o·gy.** *n.* the branch of medicine that deals with anesthesia.

an·es·thet·ic (an′is thet′ik) *also,* **an·aes·thet·ic.** *n.* a drug or other substance that causes anesthesia: *Ether is an anesthetic.* —*adj.* **1.** causing anesthesia. **2.** relating to anesthesia. —**an′es·thet′i·cal·ly,** *adv.*

a·nes·the·tist (ə nes′thə tist) *also,* **a·naes·the·tist.** *n.* a person who is trained and licensed to give anesthetics.

a·nes·the·tize (ə nes′thə tīz′) *also,* **a·naes·the·tize.** *v.t.,* **a·nes·the·tized, a·nes·the·tiz·ing.** to make insensible, especially to pain: *to anesthetize a patient before surgery.* —**a·nes′the·ti·za′tion,** *n.*

an·eu·rysm (an′yə riz′əm) *also,* **an·eu·rism.** *n.* a sac formed by the dilation of the wall of an artery weakened by disease, injury, or infection.

a·new (ə nōō′, ə nyōō′) *adv.* in a new or different way; over again: *to begin something anew.*

an·gel (ān′jəl) *n.* **1.** one of the group of immortal, spiritual beings who serve as the attendants and messengers of God. **2.** an attendant or guardian spirit: *Her good angel watched over her.* **3.** a person thought of as like an angel in goodness, beauty, or kindliness. **4.** *Informal.* a person who provides funds for something, especially a play or other theatrical production.

an·gel·fish (ān′jəl fish′) *n. pl.,* **an·gel·fish** or **an·gel·fish·es.** any of various colorful saltwater and freshwater fish which often have long, trailing strands on the outer edges of their fins.

Angelfish

an·gel·ic (an jel′ik) *adj.* **1.** like or characteristic of an angel; good, beautiful, and kindly: *The little girl had an angelic face.* **2.** of or relating to angels. Also, **an·gel·i·cal** (an jel′i kəl). —**an·gel′i·cal·ly,** *adv.*

An·ge·li·co, Fra (an jel′i kō′; frä) 1387–1455, Italian painter.

An·ge·lus (an′jə ləs) *also,* **an·ge·lus.** *n.* **1.** in the Roman Catholic Church, a prayer said in celebration of the Annunciation. **2.** a bell rung at morning, noon, and evening to announce the time for saying this prayer.

an·ger (ang′gər) *n.* a strong feeling of displeasure toward a person or thing that opposes, annoys, harms, or mistreats one; rage; wrath: *In an outburst of anger the girl threw a book at her brother.* —*v.t.* to make angry: *The student's rudeness angered the teacher.* —*v.i.* to become angry.

an·gi·o·sperm (an′jē ə spurm′) *n.* another word for **flowering plant.**

an·gle¹ (ang′gəl) *n.* **1.** the figure formed by two lines extending from the same point or by two planes extending from the same straight line. **2.** the space between these lines or planes. **3.** the amount of divergence between such lines or planes, measured in degrees: *The rocket was launched at a 90° angle to the ground.* **4.** a sharp corner: *an angle of a building.* **5.** a point of view; aspect: *We must consider the problem from every angle.* —*v.,* **an·gled, an·gling.** —*v.t.* to cause to move or turn at an angle: *to angle a billiard ball.* —*v.i.* to move or bend at an angle: *The road angles to the left.* [Latin *angulus* a corner.]

an·gle² (ang′gəl) *v.i.,* **an·gled, an·gling.** to fish with a hook and line. [Old English *angel* a fishhook.]
 to angle for. to use tricks or schemes to try to get something: *The young girl angled for compliments on her new dress.*

angle of incidence, the angle that a ray, as of light, striking a surface forms with a line perpendicular to that surface at the point of striking.

angle of reflection, the angle that a ray, as of light, reflected from a surface forms with a line perpendicular to that surface at the point of reflection.

an·gler (ang′glər) *n.* **1.** a person who fishes with a hook and line. **2.** see **anglerfish.**

an·gler·fish (ang′glər fish′) *n.* a saltwater fish having a large head, a wide mouth, and a rod extending from the head with which it lures its prey.

An·gles (ang′gəlz) *n., pl.* a Germanic tribe that settled in Britain in the fifth and sixth centuries.

an·gle·worm (ang′gəl wurm′) *n.* another word for **earthworm.**

An·gli·can (ang′gli kən) *adj.* of or relating to the Church of England or to any of the churches related to it. —*n.* a member of the Church of England or any of the churches related to it.

Obtuse angle (150°)
Acute angles
Right angle 90°
60°
30°

Types of angles

An·gli·can·ism (ang′gli kə niz′əm) *n.* the body of beliefs and practices of the Church of England.

An·gli·cize (ang′glə sīz′) *v.t.,* **An·gli·cized, An·gli·ciz·ing. 1.** to adopt (a foreign word or phrase) into English, sometimes with a slight change in pronunciation, form, or meaning. *Chauffeur* is a French word that has been Anglicized. **2.** to cause to adapt to or acquire English traits, institutions, or beliefs. —**An′gli·ci·za′tion,** *n.*

an·gling (ang′gling) *n.* the act or sport of fishing.

Anglo- *combining form* **1.** English: *Anglo-Norman.* **2.** English and: *Anglo-American.*

An·glo-A·mer·i·can (ang′glō ə mer′i kən) *adj.* **1.** English and American: *an Anglo-American trade agreement.* **2.** of or relating to Anglo-Americans. —*n.* an American of English birth or descent.

An·glo-French (ang′glō french′) *adj.* English and French. —*n.* see **Anglo-Norman** (*def. 2*).

An·glo-Nor·man (ang′glō nôr′mən) *n.* **1.** one of the Normans who settled in England after the Norman Conquest in 1066. **2.** a dialect of Old French brought into England by the Norman conquerers and spoken by the upper classes in England from the Norman Conquest through the fourteenth century. —*adj.* of or relating to the Anglo-Normans or their language.

An·glo-Sax·on (ang′glō sak′sən) *n.* **1.** a member or descendant of one of the Germanic tribes that invaded England in the fifth and sixth centuries. **2.** any Englishman of the period from the fifth century to the Norman Conquest in 1066. **3.** any person of English nationality or descent. **4.** the language of the Anglo-Saxons; Old English. —*adj.* of or relating to the Anglo-Saxons, their language, or their culture.

An·go·la (ang gō′lə) *n.* a country on the west coast of southern Africa, formerly Portuguese West Africa. Capital, Luanda. Area, 481,350 sq. mi. Pop. (1978 est.), 830,000.

An·go·ra (ang gôr′ə) *n.* **1.** another name for **Ankara. 2.a.** see **Angora cat. b.** see **Angora goat. c.** see **Angora rabbit. 3.** *also,* **angora. a.** another name for **mohair. b.** yarn or knitted fabric made from the hair of the Angora rabbit.

Angora cat, any domestic cat with long, silky hair.

Angora goat, a goat of a breed that originated in Asia Minor, raised for its long, silky hair, which is called mohair.

Angora rabbit, a domestic rabbit bred for its long, silky hair.

an·gos·tu·ra (ang′gəs toor′ə, ang′gəs tyoor′ə) *n.* the aromatic, bitter bark of certain South American trees, used especially for making a kind of bitters.

Angora goat

an·gry (ang′grē) *adj.,* **an·gri·er, an·gri·est. 1.** feeling or showing anger: *She gave him an angry look. He was angry with his brother for breaking his model plane.* **2.** threatening and raging, as if in anger: *an angry sea.* **3.** painfully inflamed: *an angry rash.* —**an′gri·ly,** *adv.* —**an′gri·ness,** *n.*

ang·strom (ang′strəm) *also,* **Ang·strom.** *n.* a unit of measurement equal to one-hundred-millionth of a centimeter, used to express the wavelength of light or other radiation. [From Anders J. *Ångström,* 1814–1874, a Swedish physicist.]

an·guish (ang′gwish) *n.* very great suffering of body or mind; agony: *We were in anguish over our classmate's tragic loss.*

an·guished (ang′gwisht) *adj.* having or showing anguish: *an anguished moan.*

an·gu·lar (ang′gyə lər) *adj.* **1.** having or forming an angle or angles; sharp-cornered: *an angular piece of rock.* **2.** measured by an angle: *angular distance.* **3.** having prominent bones; gaunt: *a man with an angular face.* —**an′gu·lar·ly,** *adv.*

an·gu·lar·i·ty (ang′gyə lar′ə tē) *n. pl.,* **an·gu·lar·i·ties. 1.** the quality or state of being angular. **2.** an angular part or form.

An·gus (ang′gəs) *n.* another word for **Aberdeen Angus.**

an·hy·dride (an hī′drīd) *n.* an oxide that forms an acid or base when it is added to water.

an·hy·drous (an hī′drəs) *adj.* (of a chemical compound) having no water, especially water of crystallization.

an·ile (an′īl) *adj.* like a doddering old woman; foolish; feeble-minded.

an·i·line (an′əl in) *also,* **an·i·lin.** *n.* an oily, poisonous liquid derived chiefly from nitrobenzene and used in making rubber, dyes, and drugs. —*adj.* made of, derived from, or relating to aniline.

aniline dye 1. any of a number of dyes made from aniline. **2.** any synthetic dye.

an·i·mad·ver·sion (an′ə mad′vur′zhən) *n.* **1.** an unfavorable remark. **2.** dislike; aversion.

an·i·mal (an′ə məl) *n.* **1.** any living being that is not a plant, such as a human being, a wolf, a bird, a fish, a snake, a fly, or a worm. An animal is distinguished from a plant by its ability to move about in its environment or move some parts of its body, by its inability to produce its own food by photosynthesis, and by the fact that it has sense organs. **2.** any animal except human beings; beast. **3.** any mammal, as distinguished from birds, reptiles, and the like: *Cows and whales are animals.* **4.** a person who acts like a beast; coarse, brutish person. —*adj.* of, relating to, or derived from animals: *animal fats, animal instincts.*

animal husbandry, the branch of agriculture dealing with the breeding, raising, and care of livestock.

an·i·mate (*v.,* an′ə māt′; *adj.,* an′ə mit) *v.t.,* **an·i·mat·ed, an·i·mat·ing. 1.** to give life, vividness, or interest to; enliven: *Delight animated her face.* **2.** to move to action; inspire; incite: *Love of his country animated his heroic actions.* —*adj.* having life; alive: *An animal is an animate being.*

an·i·mat·ed (an′ə mā′tid) *adj.* **1.** full of life, activity, or spirit; lively; vivacious: *The animated speaker easily held the attention of her audience.* **2.** made to move as if alive: *animated puppets.* —**an′i·mat′ed·ly,** *adv.*

animated cartoon, a motion picture consisting of a series of drawings, each of which shows a slight change from the drawing before it. When the drawings are photographed and projected in rapid succession, the figures seem to move.

an·i·ma·tion (an′ə mā′shən) *n.* **1.** liveliness; spirit: *The old sailor told the story with great animation.* **2.** the act of animating or the state of being animated. **3.** the process and technique of preparing animated cartoons.

at; āpe; cär; end; mē; it; īce; hot; ōld; fôrk; wood; fōōl; oil; out; up; turn; sing; thin; **this**; hw in white; zh in treasure. The symbol ə stands for the sound of **a** in about, **e** in taken, **i** in pencil, **o** in lemon, and **u** in circus.

a·ni·ma·to (ä′nə mä′tō) *Music. adj.* lively; animated. —*adv.* in a spirited, lively manner.

an·i·mism (an′ə miz′əm) *n.* the belief that inanimate things and forces, such as trees, rocks, and winds, have souls or spirits.

an·i·mos·i·ty (an′ə mos′ə tē) *n. pl.,* **an·i·mos·i·ties.** open hostility or hatred; enmity: *The deep animosity between the two nations led to war. The candidate felt great animosity toward his opponent.*

an·i·mus (an′ə məs) *n.* **1.** open hostility or hatred; enmity; animosity. **2.** an animating spirit or force.

an·i·on (an′ī′ən) *n.* a negatively-charged ion of an electrolyte, attracted to the anode in electrolysis.

an·ise (an′is) *n.* **1.** a plant related to parsley, widely cultivated in the Mediterranean region, India, and South America. **2.** another word for **aniseed.**

an·i·seed (an′i sēd′, an′is sēd′) *n.* the fragrant seed of the anise, having a spicy, licoricelike taste, used as a flavoring and in some medicines.

An·jou (an′jōō) *n.* a region and former province in western France, in the Loire valley.

An·ka·ra (ang′kər ə) *n.* the capital of Turkey, in the west-central part of the country. It was formerly known as Angora. Pop. (1970), 1,208,800.

an·kle (ang′kəl) *n.* **1.** the joint that connects the foot and the leg. **2.** the part of the leg that is located at and just above this joint.

an·kle·bone (ang′kəl bōn′) *n.* the bone of the ankle. Also, **talus.**

an·klet (ang′klit) *n.* **1.** a short sock reaching just above the ankle. **2.** an ornamental band or chain worn around the ankle.

an·nals (an′əlz) *n., pl.* **1.** written accounts of events recorded year by year. **2.** any historical record or chronicle; history: *the annals of crime, the annals of professional football.*

An·nam (ə nam′) *n.* a former French protectorate in Indochina, now part of Vietnam. —**An·nam·ese** (an′ə mēz′), *adj., n.*

An·nap·o·lis (ə nap′ə lis) *n.* the capital of Maryland, in the central part of the state. The United States Naval Academy is located there. Pop. (1970), 29,592.

An·na·pur·na (an′ə poor′nə) *n.* a mountain of the Himalayas, in west-central Nepal.

Ann Ar·bor (an′ är′bər) a city in southeastern Michigan. Pop. (1970), 99,797.

Anne (an) 1665–1714, the queen of Great Britain from 1702 to 1714.

an·neal (ə nēl′) *v.t.* **1.** to heat and then slowly cool (metal or glass) to make less brittle. **2.** to toughen or temper: *to anneal one's mind to endure hardships.*

an·ne·lid (an′əl id) *n.* any of various worms whose bodies are made up of ringlike segments, such as the earthworm.

an·nex (*v.,* ə neks′; *n.,* an′eks) *v.t.* to add or attach, as to something larger: *The king annexed the region to his kingdom.* —*n. pl.,* **an·nex·es.** a building used as an addition to another: *The school built an annex because of the increased enrollment.* —**an′nex·a′tion,** *n.*

Annelid

an·ni·hi·late (ə nī′ə lāt′) *v.t.,* **an·ni·hi·lat·ed, an·ni·hi·lat·ing.** to destroy totally; reduce to nothing: *The bombers annihilated the city.* —**an·ni′hi·la′tion,** *n.*

an·ni·ver·sa·ry (an′ə vur′sər ē) *n. pl.,* **an·ni·ver·sa·ries.** **1.** the yearly return of the date on which some important event occurred in an earlier year: *My grandparents recently celebrated their fiftieth wedding anniversary.* **2.** a celebra-

tion of the return of such an event. —*adj.* of or relating to an anniversary: *an anniversary gift.*

an·no Dom·i·ni (an′ō dom′i nī′) *Latin.* in the year of the Lord. Abbreviation, **A.D.** ▲ used to indicate dates occurring since the birth of Christ.

an·no·tate (an′ə tāt′) *v.t.,* **an·no·tat·ed, an·no·tat·ing.** to provide with critical or explanatory notes: *Many scholars have annotated the plays of Shakespeare.* —**an′no·ta′tor,** *n.*

an·no·ta·tion (an′ə tā′shən) *n.* **1.** a critical or explanatory note or comment. **2.** the act of annotating or the state of being annotated.

an·nounce (ə nouns′) *v.,* **an·nounced, an·nounc·ing.** —*v.t.* **1.** to make known publicly or officially; proclaim: *The principal announced that the school would be closed because of the blizzard.* **2.** to make known the approach, arrival, or presence of: *The conductor announced each station as the train stopped.* **3.** to make known; indicate: *Gathering clouds announced the coming storm.* **4.** to serve as the announcer for: *to announce a basketball game.* —*v.i.* to serve as a radio or television announcer.

an·nounce·ment (ə nouns′mənt) *n.* **1.** the act of announcing or the state of being announced. **2.** a public statement that makes something known: *The President will make an important announcement on television tonight.* **3.** a written or printed notice of an event: *a wedding announcement.*

an·nounc·er (ə noun′sər) *n.* **1.** a person on radio or television who introduces programs and performers, identifies the station, or presents advertisements, bulletins, or news items. **2.** any person who announces something.

an·noy (ə noi′) *v.t.* to be troublesome or irritating to; vex; bother: *His carelessness annoyed her. We were annoyed by the unnecessary delay.* —**an·noy′er,** *n.*

an·noy·ance (ə noi′əns) *n.* **1.** a person or thing that annoys; nuisance: *Her brother's constant teasing was a great annoyance to her.* **2.** the act of annoying or the state of being annoyed: *Her angry remark showed her annoyance at his actions.*

an·noy·ing (ə noi′ing) *adj.* troublesome; irritating; vexing: *an annoying delay.* —**an·noy′ing·ly,** *adv.*

an·nu·al (an′yōō əl) *adj.* **1.** relating to or measured by the year: *a child's annual growth, a person's annual salary.* **2.** happening or returning once a year; yearly: *That store has an annual sale of all its summer clothing.* **3.** done during a year: *The earth makes an annual course around the sun.* **4.** (of a plant) living or lasting for only one year or season: *Corn, wheat, and cucumbers are annual plants.* —*n.* **1.** a journal or other publication issued once a year. **2.** a plant that lives or lasts for only one year or season. —**an′nu·al·ly,** *adv.*

annual ring, any of the rings seen in the cross section of a tree trunk or other woody plant stem. Each ring represents a year's growth.

an·nu·i·ty (ə nōō′ə tē, ə nyōō′ə tē) *n. pl.,* **an·nu·i·ties.** **1.** a specified amount of money paid yearly or at other fixed intervals. **2.** the right to receive or obligation to pay such an amount of money. **3.** an investment, usually made with an insurance company, by which a fixed income is paid during

Annual rings

the investor's lifetime or for a certain number of years.

an·nul (ə nul′) *v.t.,* **an·nulled, an·nul·ling.** to do away with; declare invalid: *to annul a marriage.* —**an·nul′ment,** *n.*

an·nu·lar (an′yə lər) *adj.* relating to, made up of, or shaped like a ring or rings.

annular eclipse, a solar eclipse in which a portion of the sun is visible as a ring surrounding the dark body of the moon.

an·num (an′əm) *n. Latin.* a year.

an·nun·ci·a·tion (ə nun′sē ā′shən) *n.* **1. the Annunciation.** the announcement brought by the angel Gabriel to the Virgin Mary that she was to give birth to Christ. **2. Annunciation.** the church festival commemorating this announcement. It falls on March 25.

an·ode (an′ōd) *n.* **1.** an electrode through which electrons leave an electrical device or medium. When electricity is used to produce a chemical reaction, the positive electrode is the anode. When a chemical reaction is used to produce electricity, the negative electrode is the anode. **2.** in electrolysis, an electrode that has a comparative lack of electrons and is positively charged. Negatively charged ions are oxidized at the anode. **3.** in an electron tube, an electrode or plate that attracts electrons.

an·o·dyne (an′ə dīn′) *n.* **1.** a medicine that relieves pain; analgesic. **2.** anything that soothes or calms.

a·noint (ə noint′) *v.t.* **1.** to cover or smear with oil or an oily substance; apply ointment to. **2.** to put oil on as an act of consecration: *to anoint a king.* —**a·noint′ment,** *n.*

a·nom·a·lous (ə nom′ə ləs) *adj.* different from the usual or normal; irregular; abnormal. —**a·nom′a·lous·ly,** *adv.* —**a·nom′a·lous·ness,** *n.*

a·nom·a·ly (ə nom′ə lē) *n. pl.,* **a·nom·a·lies.** something different from the usual or normal; irregularity; abnormality: *Snow in Florida is an anomaly.*

a·non (ə non′) *adv. Archaic.* **1.** in a little while; soon. **2.** at another time; again.

   ever and anon. again and again; now and then.

anon., anonymous.

an·o·nym·i·ty (an′ə nim′ə tē) *n.* the condition of being anonymous: *He prefers to make contributions to charity in anonymity.*

a·non·y·mous (ə non′ə məs) *adj.* **1.** of unknown authorship or origin; without any name given: *an anonymous book, an anonymous telephone call.* **2.** not giving one's name; not known by name: *The author of the book on organized crime preferred to remain anonymous.* —**a·non′·y·mous·ly,** *adv.*

a·noph·e·les (ə nof′ə lēz′) *n. pl.,* **a·noph·e·les.** any mosquito that can transmit malaria to man by its bite.

an·oth·er (ə nuth′ər) *adj.* **1.** one more; an additional: *Do you want another soda?* **2.** different: *Let's try another place to eat today.* **3.** similar or the same in character or achievements: *That writer thinks he's another Shakespeare.* —*pron.* **1.** one more; an additional one: *He finished the sandwich and then ordered another.* **2.** a different person or thing: *That plan didn't work, so we'll use another.*

an·ox·i·a (an ok′sē ə) *n.* a condition in which the body cells fail to receive or to use enough oxygen.

ans., answer.

an·swer (an′sər) *n.* **1.** something spoken or written as a reply: *None of the students could give an answer to the teacher's question. Did you receive an answer to your letter?* **2.** something done in reply or return: *Further bombing was the enemy's answer to our peace offerings.* **3.** the solution to a problem: *To find the correct answer, multiply by two.* **4.** any solution or explanation: *His friend helped him find*

Anopheles

the answer to his troubles. —*v.t.* **1.** to speak or write in reply to: *She answered my letter.* **2.** to act in response to: *She ran to answer the telephone.* **3.** to be suitable or enough for; serve: *This money should answer your needs.* —*v.i.* **1.** to give an answer: *He answered in a loud and clear voice.* **2.** to be responsible or accountable: *He will have to answer for the missing funds.* **3.** to agree or conform: *He answers to the description of the thief.*

   to answer back. *Informal.* to reply rudely; talk back: *Bill answered back when his mother scolded him.*

an·swer·a·ble (an′sər ə bəl) *adj.* **1.** accountable; responsible: *The treasurer of the company is answerable for all financial records.* **2.** that can be answered.

ant (ant) *n.* any of a group of small insects related to bees and wasps. Ants are found in all temperate and tropical regions of the world. They live in colonies that may contain as few as several dozen individuals or as many as 1,500,000.

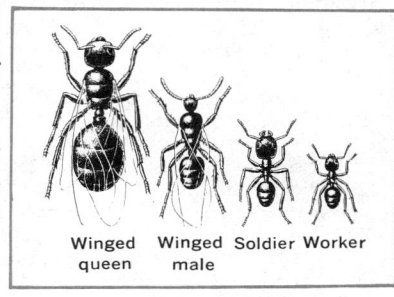

Winged queen Winged male Soldier Worker

Types of ants

-ant *suffix* **1.** (used to form adjectives) doing or being: *defiant, radiant.* **2.** (used to form nouns) a person or thing that does: *servant, lubricant.*

ant., antonym.

ant·ac·id (ant′as′id) *n.* a chemical substance that neutralizes acids, especially a remedy for stomach acidity. —*adj.* that can neutralize acids.

an·tag·o·nism (an tag′ə niz′əm) *n.* active opposition or strong feeling against; hostility: *The rival political groups felt great antagonism toward each other.*

an·tag·o·nist (an tag′ə nist) *n.* a person who opposes, fights, or competes with another; adversary.

an·tag·o·nis·tic (an tag′ə nis′tik) *adj.* acting or being in opposition; hostile. —**an·tag′o·nis′ti·cal·ly,** *adv.*

an·tag·o·nize (an tag′ə nīz′) *v.t.,* **an·tag·o·nized, an·tag·o·niz·ing.** to provoke dislike or hostility in; make unfriendly: *His nasty comments about her new dress antagonized her.*

ant·arc·tic (ant ärk′tik, ant är′tik) *adj.* of or relating to the South Pole or to the south polar regions. —*n.* **the Antarctic.** another name for **Antarctica.**

Ant·arc·ti·ca (ant ärk′ti kə, ant är′ti kə) *n.* an ice-covered continent surrounding the South Pole and lying mainly within the Antarctic Circle. Area, (approx.) 5,500,000 sq. mi.

Antarctic Circle also, **antarctic circle.** an imaginary line around the earth running parallel to the equator at 66°33′ south latitude, or about 1600 miles from the South Pole.

Antarctic Ocean, a body of water surrounding Antarctica, consisting of the southernmost parts of the Atlantic, Pacific, and Indian Oceans.

at; āpe; cär; end; mē; it; īce; hot; ōld; fôrk; wood; fōol; oil; out; up; turn; sing; thin; this; hw in white; zh in treasure. The symbol ə stands for the sound of **a** in about, **e** in taken, **i** in pencil, **o** in lemon, and **u** in circus.

ant bear, a gray anteater of tropical Central and South America. It is the largest kind of anteater.

an·te (an'tē) *n.* **1.** in poker, a stake that each player must pay before receiving a hand or drawing new cards. **2.** *Slang.* any amount required as a share. —*v.t., v.i.,* **an·ted** or **an·**

Ant bear

teed, an·te·ing. to pay an ante: *Each man anted a dime.*

ante- *prefix* **1.** previous in time; prior to: *antebellum.* **2.** before in position; in front of: *antechamber.*

ant·eat·er (ant'ē'tər) *n.* any of various toothless animals of tropical Central and South America that feed on ants and termites. They have long narrow heads, long, sticky tongues, and powerful front claws.

an·te·bel·lum (an'tē bel'əm) *adj.* before the war, especially before the American Civil War: *the antebellum South.*

an·te·ced·ent (an'tə sēd'ənt) *n.* **1.** a thing or event that occurs before another: *A drop in air pressure is often an antecedent to a storm.* **2.** *Grammar.* a noun or clause to which a pronoun refers. In the sentence *He bought a new hat, but left it on the bus,* the noun *hat* is the antecedent of the pronoun *it.* **3. antecedents. a.** the previous events or influences in a person's life. **b.** a person's ancestors. —*adj.* occurring or existing before; preceding; prior: *the conditions antecedent to the Industrial Revolution.* —**an'·te·ced'ent·ly,** *adv.*

an·te·cham·ber (an'tē chām'bər) *n.* another word for **anteroom.**

an·te·date (an'ti dāt') *v.t.,* **an·te·dat·ed, an·te·dat·ing. 1.** to be or happen earlier than; precede in time: *Propeller-driven planes antedated jet planes.* **2.** to give (something) a date earlier than the correct one: *to antedate a check.*

an·te·di·lu·vi·an (an'tē də lōō'vē ən) *adj.* **1.** of or relating to the period before the Biblical Flood. **2.** very old or old-fashioned: *antediluvian social attitudes.* —*n.* **1.** a person who lived before the Biblical Flood. **2.** a very old or old-fashioned person.

an·te·lope (ant'əl ōp') *n. pl.,* **an·te·lope** or **an·te·lopes. 1.** any of various cud-chewing animals that are closely related to goats, having unbranched horns and cloven hoofs. Antelopes are native to Africa and southern Asia. **2.** another name for **pronghorn.**

Antelope

an·te me·rid·i·em (an'tē mə rid'ē əm) between midnight and noon. Abbreviation, **A.M.** [Latin *ante merīdiem* before noon.]

an·ten·na (an ten'ə) *n. pl.,* **an·ten·nas** (*def. 1*) or **an·ten·nae** (an ten'ē) (*def. 2*). **1.** a metal structure, wire, or set of wires used to receive or transmit radio or television signals; aerial. **2.** one of a pair of jointed sense organs, or feelers, on the head of an insect or crustacean.

an·te·pe·nult (an'tē pē'nult) *n.* the third-to-last syllable in a word. In the word *port·fo·li·o,* the syllable *fo* is the antepenult.

an·te·ri·or (an tēr'ē ər) *adj.* **1.** at or toward the front or head; fore: *the anterior lobe of the brain.* **2.** earlier in time.

an·te·room (an'tē rōōm', an'tē room') *n.* a room serving as a waiting room or entrance to a larger or main room.

an·them (an'thəm) *n.* **1.** a song of gladness, praise, devotion, or patriotism: *"God Save the Queen" is the national anthem of Great Britain.* **2.** a piece of sacred choral music with words usually taken from a Biblical passage.

an·ther (an'thər) *n.* in a flower, the pollen-bearing part of the stamen.

ant hill, a mound of dirt or other material heaped up by ants around the entrance to their underground nest.

an·thol·o·gist (an thol'ə jist) *n.* a person who collects material for an anthology.

an·thol·o·gy (an thol'ə jē) *n. pl.,* **an·thol·o·gies.** a collection of varied written works or passages within a single book or set: *an anthology of French poetry.*

An·tho·ny, Susan B. (an'thə nē) 1820–1906, U.S. social reformer and leader of the women's suffrage movement.

an·thra·cite (an'thrə sīt') *n.* a very hard, glossy black coal with a high carbon content. It burns with a low, smokeless flame. Also, **hard coal.**

an·thrax (an'thraks) *n.* a highly infectious, usually fatal disease of animals, especially cows and sheep, that can be transmitted to man. It is caused by a bacterium.

an·thro·poid (an'thrə poid') *adj.* **1.** resembling man; manlike: *A gorilla is an anthropoid ape.* **2.** resembling an ape. —*n.* any ape that resembles man.

an·thro·pol·o·gist (an'thrə pol'ə gist) *n.* a student of or an expert in anthropology.

an·thro·pol·o·gy (an'thrə pol'ə jē) *n.* the science that deals with the physical, cultural, and social development of man, including his origin, evolution, behavior, and geographic distribution from prehistoric times to the present. —**an·thro·po·log·i·cal** (an'thrə pə loj'i kəl), *adj.* —**an'·thro·po·log'i·cal·ly,** *adv.*

anti- *prefix* **1.** opposed to; against: *antitrust, anticlerical.* **2.** expressing the opposite or reverse of: *anticlimax.* **3.** operating against; counteracting: *antifreeze, antiaircraft.*

an·ti·air·craft (an'tē er'kraft') *adj.* for use against aircraft in flight: *an antiaircraft missile.*

an·ti·bi·ot·ic (an'tē bī ot'ik) *n.* any of a group of substances, such as penicillin or streptomycin, produced by molds, bacteria, and other microorganisms. Antibiotics are used in medicine to kill or slow the growth of disease-causing bacteria, viruses, or fungi. —*adj.* of or relating to antibiotics.

an·ti·bod·y (an'ti bod'ē) *n. pl.,* **an·ti·bod·ies.** any of various proteins in the blood serum produced by the body as a normal function or in response to the presence of a harmful foreign substance. Antibodies neutralize or destroy germs and can give immunity against certain diseases.

an·tic (an'tik) *n.* a silly or comical action; caper; prank: *the antics of a clown, the antics of a puppy.* —*adj.* grotesque; bizarre; ludicrous: *A political party may be feared, respected, efficient, fierce . . . but if it is antic, it is hopeless* (Eugene Burdick).

An·ti·christ (an'ti krīst') *n.* **1.** in early Christian prophecy, the great enemy or opponent of Christ. **2.** *also,* **antichrist.** any opponent of Christ or Christianity.

an·tic·i·pate (an tis'ə pāt') *v.t.,* **an·tic·i·pat·ed, an·tic·i·pat·ing. 1.** to look forward to; expect: *I do not anticipate any trouble. We anticipate his arrival at four o'clock.* **2.** to foresee and deal with in advance: *He anticipated my objections to his idea.* **3.** to be before (another) in doing something; precede: *The Vikings are now believed to have anticipated Columbus in the discovery of America.* —**an·tic'i·pa'tor,** *n.*

an·tic·i·pa·tion (an tis'ə pā'shən) *n.* **1.** the act of anticipating or the state of being anticipated. **2.** a feeling of excited expectation.

an·ti·cler·i·cal (an′tē kler′i kəl) *adj.* opposed to the influence and activities of the church or clergy.

an·ti·cli·mac·tic (an′ti klī mak′tic) *adj.* of, having, or like an anticlimax. —**an′ti·cli·mac′ti·cal·ly,** *adv.*

an·ti·cli·max (an′ti klī′maks) *n. pl.,* **an·ti·cli·max·es.** **1.** an unexpected, sudden change from something important or dignified to something trivial or absurd. In the sentence *My house burned down, my wallet was stolen, and I didn't have time to eat lunch,* the phrase *and I didn't have time to eat lunch* is an anticlimax. **2.** anything that is much less important or interesting than what has come before it: *The long trip home was an anticlimax after our exciting visit to Paris.*

an·ti·cline (an′ti klīn′) *n.* a rock formation in which the layers slope downward from the crest in opposite directions.

an·ti·cy·clone (an′ti sī′-klōn) *n.* an atmospheric condition consisting of a mass of air currents rotating about a center of high barometric pressure.

an·ti·do·tal (an′ti dōt′əl) *adj.* of, like, or acting as an antidote.

an·ti·dote (an′ti dōt′) *n.* **1.** a medicine or other remedy to counteract the effects of a poison. **2.** any counteracting remedy: *An interesting book is an antidote to boredom.*

An·tie·tam (an tē′təm) *n.* a creek in northwestern Maryland, the site of one of the major battles of the Civil War.

an·ti·freeze (an′ti frēz′) *n.* any substance added to a liquid to lower its freezing point, especially an alcohol mixture added to the water in automobile radiators to prevent it from freezing in cold weather.

an·ti·gen (an′tə jən) *n.* a substance that causes the body to produce antibodies, such as a toxin or bacterium.

An·tig·o·ne (an tig′ə nē) *n. Greek Legend.* the daughter of Oedipus. She was condemned to death for giving her brother a proper burial against the command of Creon, her uncle.

An·ti·gua (an tē′gə, an tē′gwə) *n.* one of the Leeward Islands, in the West Indies. Capital, St. John's. Area, 108 sq. mi. Pop. (1971 est.), 60,000.

an·ti·his·ta·mine (an′ti his′tə mēn) *n.* any of several drugs that counteract the effect of histamine in the body. Antihistamines are used chiefly in the treatment of colds and such allergic reactions as hives, hayfever, and asthma.

an·ti·knock (an′tē nok′) *n.* a chemical substance that is added to gasoline to reduce knocking in an automobile engine.

An·til·les (an til′ēz) *n., pl.* the islands of the West Indies excluding the Bahamas, divided into the Greater Antilles and the Lesser Antilles.

an·ti·log·a·rithm (an′ti lô′gə rith′əm, an′ti log′ə-rith′əm) *n.* the number corresponding to a given logarithm. In the expression $2^3 = 8$, the logarithm is 3 and the antilogarithm is 8.

an·ti·ma·cas·sar (an′ti mə kas′ər) *n.* a small ornamental covering put over the back and arms of a chair.

an·ti·mat·ter (an′tē mat′ər) *n. Physics.* a theoretical form of matter consisting of antiparticles.

an·ti·mis·sile (an tē mis′əl) *adj.* designed or used for defense against ballistic and guided missiles.

an·ti·mo·ny (an′ti mō′nē) *n.* a crystalline metallic element with a silver or bluish-white luster, used chiefly in

Anticline
Cross section of stratified rock

alloys to increase the hardness and brittleness of other metals. Symbol: Sb

an·ti·neu·tron (an′tē nōō′tron, an′tē nyōō′tron) *n. Physics.* the antiparticle of the neutron.

An·ti·och (an′tē ok′) *n.* the capital of ancient Syria.

an·ti·par·ti·cle (an′tē pär′ti kəl) *n. Physics.* any of a group of subatomic particles, each of which corresponds to one of the particles that make up ordinary matter but has opposite magnetic properties to its corresponding particle and, in the case of charged particles, opposite charge. When a particle and its antiparticle collide, they destroy each other and their combined mass is changed into energy.

an·ti·pas·to (an′ti päs′tō) *n. pl.,* **an·ti·pas·tos.** an Italian dish served as an appetizer, consisting of small portions of various foods.

an·tip·a·thy (an tip′ə thē) *n. pl.,* **an·tip·a·thies.** **1.** a feeling of strong dislike; distaste; aversion: *He has an antipathy for any kind of violence.* **2.** a person or thing that arouses such dislike.

an·tip·o·dal (an tip′əd əl) *adj.* of or relating to antipodes; on opposite sides of the earth.

an·tip·o·des (an tip′ə dēz′) *n., pl.* **1.** two places on the earth's surface that are exactly opposite one another: *The North Pole and the South Pole are antipodes.* **2.** two opposite or contrary things: *Love and hate are antipodes.*

an·ti·pro·ton (an′tē prō′ton) *n. Physics.* the antiparticle of the proton.

an·ti·quar·i·an (an′tə kwer′ē ən) *adj.* of or relating to antiquities. —*n.* another word for **antiquary.**

an·ti·quar·y (an′tə kwer′ē) *n. pl.,* **an·ti·quar·ies.** a person who collects, studies, or deals in antiquities.

an·ti·quate (an′tə kwāt′) *v.t.,* **an·ti·quat·ed, an·ti·quat·ing.** to cause to become old-fashioned; make out-of-date.

an·ti·quat·ed (an′tə kwā′tid) *adj.* old-fashioned; out-of-date: *antiquated ideas, an antiquated style of dress.*

an·tique (an tēk′) *adj.* **1.** of, belonging to, or in the style of times long ago: *antique furniture, an antique watch.* **2.** of, belonging to, or in the style of ancient Greece or Rome: *an antique temple.* —*n.* **1.** something made very long ago. **2.** a work of art or craftsmanship that is valued for its age, especially one that is more than one hundred years old. —*v.t.,* **an·tiqued, an·ti·quing.** to make (something) appear old: *to antique a chair.*

an·tiq·ui·ty (an tik′wə tē) *n. pl.,* **an·tiq·ui·ties.** **1.** the early ages of history, especially the period before the Middle Ages. **2.** the people and cultures of ancient times. **3.** the quality of being ancient; great age: *a ring that is valued for its antiquity.* **4. antiquities.** objects belonging to or remaining from ancient times.

an·ti·Se·mit·ic (an′tē sə mit′ik) *adj.* prejudiced or discriminating against Jews.

an·ti·Sem·i·tism (an′tē sem′ə tiz′əm) *n.* prejudice or discrimination against Jews.

an·ti·sep·tic (an′ti sep′tik) *n.* a substance that kills or stops the growth of germs. Alcohol, iodine, and hydrogen peroxide are common antiseptics. —*adj.* **1.** preventing infection or decay by killing or stopping the growth of germs. **2.** free from germs; sterilized. —**an′ti·sep′ti·cal·ly,** *adv.*

at; āpe; cär; end; mē; it; īce; hot; ōld; fôrk; wood; fōōl; oil; out; up; turn; sing; thin; this; hw in white; zh in treasure. The symbol ə stands for the sound of **a** in about, **e** in taken, **i** in pencil, **o** in lemon, and **u** in circus.

an·ti·so·cial (an′tē sō′shəl) *adj.* **1.** not liking companionship or the society of others; unsociable: *an antisocial person.* **2.** opposed to the general good of society: *Murder is an antisocial act.* —**an′ti·so′cial·ly,** *adv.*

an·tith·e·sis (an tith′ə sis) *n. pl.,* **an·tith·e·ses** (an tith′-ə sēz′). **1.** the exact opposite: *Hope is the antithesis of despair.* **2.** opposition; contrast: *The antithesis of bravery and cowardice was the theme of the story.* **3.** the contrast of strongly opposed ideas in speech or writing. *"Ask not what your country can do for you—ask what you can do for your country"* (John F. Kennedy) is an example of antithesis.

an·ti·tox·in (an′ti tok′sin) *n.* **1.** an antibody formed in the body that provides protection against a specific poison released by invading bacteria. **2.** a serum containing such an antibody, obtained from the blood of horses or other animals that have been injected with a toxin.

an·ti·trades (an′ti trādz′) *n., pl.* winds that blow above, and in a direction opposite to, the trade winds.

an·ti·trust (an′tē trust′) *adj.* opposed to or regulating monopolies, trusts, or other business combinations or practices that hinder free trade and interfere with competition.

ant·ler (ant′lər) *n.* **1.** one of the branched horns of deer, elk, moose, and other related animals. Antlers are shed each year and replaced by new ones. **2.** any of the branches of such a horn.

ant lion, an insect whose larva feeds on ants and other wingless insects, which it catches by digging a pit into which the prey falls and is trapped.

Antlers

An·to·ny, Mark (an′tə nē) 83?–30 B.C., Roman general and political leader, a friend and military ally of Julius Caesar.

an·to·nym (an′tə nim′) *n.* a word that has the opposite meaning of another word. *Young* and *old, up* and *down,* and *east* and *west* are antonyms.

● An **antonym** is a word whose meaning is the exact opposite of the meaning of another word. A word that has exactly the same meaning as another word is called a **synonym.** Our language contains very few real synonyms because there is no need to have two or more words that stand for exactly the same thing. For example, the meaning of the word "happy" is very similar to the meaning of the words "cheerful" and "joyful." But each word has a shade of meaning that distinguishes it from the other two and keeps them from being true synonyms.

There are, however, many real antonyms in English because it is often necessary to express the opposite of the meaning of a word. When we want to express the opposite of "happy" we use the word "sad" which is its antonym.

Ant·werp (ant′wurp) *n.* the largest city in Belgium, a port in the northern part of the country. Pop. (1970 est.), 226,570.

A·nu·bis (ə nōō′bis, ə nyōō′bis) *n. Egyptian Mythology.* the son of Osiris and a god of the underworld, represented as a man with the head of a jackal.

A number 1, another term for A–1.

a·nus (ā′nəs) *n. pl.,* **a·nus·es.** an opening at the lower end of the alimentary canal, through which solid waste products pass from the body.

an·vil (an′vəl) *n.* **1.** an iron or steel block on which heat-softened metals are hammered into desired shapes. **2.** one of the three small bones of the middle ear, lying between the hammer and the stirrup and shaped like an anvil.

Anvil (*def.* 1)

anx·i·e·ty (ang zī′ə tē) *n. pl.,* **anx·i·e·ties. 1.** a feeling of fearful uneasiness or worry about what may happen: *The mother's anxiety became deeper as the hours passed and the missing child was not found.* **2.** something that causes this feeling: *Lack of money is one of his chief anxieties.* **3.** an earnest and eager desire: *His anxiety to please his new employer kept him working until late at night.*

anx·ious (angk′shəs, ang′shəs) *adj.* **1.** uneasy, worried, and fearful about what may happen: *The mother was always anxious about her children's safety when they were out after dark.* **2.** showing, causing, or resulting from anxiety: *an anxious look.* **3.** earnestly and eagerly desiring: *The boy was anxious to make friends at his new school.* —**anx′ious·ly,** *adv.* —**anx′ious·ness,** *n.*

an·y (en′ē) *adj.* **1.** one, no matter which; some, whatever kind: *Take any seat. Any information will help.* **2.** some, in whatever quantity or number: *Have you any apples?* **3.** every: *Any child can do this problem.* **4.** at all: *I haven't any change.* —*pron.* any one or ones; any quantity or number: *We haven't any left. He scored higher than any of the others.* —*adv.* to any extent or degree: *Stop before you go any farther.*

an·y·bod·y (en′ē bod′ē, en′ē bud′ē) *pron. pl.,* **an·y·bod·ies.** any person whatever; anyone: *Has anybody seen Jack?* —*n.* a person of importance: *Everybody who is anybody was at the party.* ▲ **Anybody** and **anyone** are both singular. In writing and formal speech, they are used with a singular pronoun: *Anyone who wants to tell the class about his hobby may speak tomorrow.* In conversation, they are often used with a plural pronoun: *If anybody asks for me, tell them* (rather than *him* or *her*) *I've gone home for the day.*

an·y·how (en′ē hou′) *adv.* **1.** in any case; at any rate; nevertheless: *I didn't really want to go anyhow. The movie was half over, but we went in anyhow.* **2.** in any way whatever.

an·y·one (en′ē wun′) *pron.* any person whatever; anybody. ▲ The pronoun **anyone** and the two words **any one** are spelled alike, but they do not mean the same thing. **Anyone** means "any person": *Anyone may attend the meeting.* **Any one** means "any of a group" and is followed by *of: Any one of these books will help you.* See **anybody** for an additional usage note.

an·y·place (en′ē plās′) *adv. Informal.* anywhere.

an·y·thing (en′ē thing′) *pron.* any thing whatever: *I'll do anything you say. I didn't have anything to eat all day.* —*adv.* to any extent; at all: *Frank isn't anything like his brother.*

anything but. by no means; not at all.

an·y·time (en′ē tīm′) *adv.* at any time: *You are free to leave anytime.*

an·y·way (en′ē wā′) *adv.* **1.** in any case; at any rate; nevertheless: *Anyway, I am glad it happened. It began to rain, but we finished the game anyway.* **2.** in any manner or way: *He did his homework just anyway.*

an·y·where (en′ē hwer′, en′ē wer′) *adv.* **1.** in, at, or to any place: *Just put it down anywhere.* **2.** *Informal.* to any extent; at all: *Did I come anywhere near the right answer?*

an·y·wise (en′ē wīz′) *adv.* in any way; to any degree; at all.

A-OK (ā′ō kā′) *also,* **A·o·kay.** *adj., adv., interj. Informal.* excellent; perfect.

A-one (ā′wun′) another word for **A-1.**

a·or·ta (ā ôr′tə) *n. pl.,* **a·or·tas** or **a·or·tae** (ā ôr′tē) the main artery of the body. It carries the blood from the left ventricle of the heart to all parts of the body except the lungs.

AP, Associated Press, a United States news agency that gathers and distributes news stories and pictures throughout the world.

a·pace (ə pās′) *adv.* swiftly; quickly; rapidly: *Great weeds do grow apace* (Shakespeare, *Richard III*).

A·pach·e (ə pach′ē) *n. pl.,* **A·pach·es** or **A·pach·e.** **1.** a member of an Indian tribe living in the southwestern United States. **2.** the language spoken by these people. —*adj.* of or relating to the Apaches, their language, or their culture.

a·pache (ə päsh′) *n.* a ruffian, gangster, or thug of Paris. [French *apache,* from *Apache.*]

a·part (ə pärt′) *adv.* **1.** away from one another; separated in space or time: *The houses are fifty feet apart. The two trains left three hours apart.* **2.** into two or more parts; in or to pieces: *He tore the book apart. The mechanic took the engine apart.* **3.** at a distance; aside: *He sat apart from the others.* **4.** as a separate consideration; independently: *Viewed apart, the matter becomes clearer.*
   apart from. other than; besides: *Apart from the poor acting of the leading man, the movie was very good.*

a·part·heid (ə pär′tīd, ə pärt′hāt′) *n.* racial segregation, especially as an official policy in South Africa.

a·part·ment (ə pärt′mənt) *n.* a room or set of rooms to live in, usually in a large building.

apartment house, a building divided into a number of apartments.

ap·a·thet·ic (ap′ə thet′ik) *adj.* having or showing little interest, concern, or desire to act; indifferent: *The apathetic student never paid attention in class.* —**ap′a·thet′i·cal·ly,** *adv.*

ap·a·thy (ap′ə thē) *n.* a lack of interest, concern, or desire to act; indifference: *He views current events with a great degree of apathy.*

ape (āp) *n.* **1.** any of several large, tailless monkeys that are somewhat similar to man in form and build and are able to stand or walk nearly erect, including the chimpanzee, gibbon, gorilla, and orangutan. **2.** any monkey. **3.** a person who imitates; mimic. —*v.t.,* **aped, ap·ing.** to imitate; mimic. —**ape′like′,** *adj.* —**ap′er,** *n.*

Ap·en·nines (ap′ə nīnz′) *n., pl.* a mountain system that extends along the length of the Italian peninsula.

ap·er·ture (ap′ər chər) *n.* **1.** a hole, gap, or other opening. **2.** an opening through which light passes into a camera or other optical instrument.

a·pex (ā′peks) *n. pl.,* **a·pex·es** or **ap·i·ces.** **1.** the highest point; tip: *the apex of a triangle, the apex of a mountain.* **2.** the highest achievement: *Hitting a home run in the World Series was the apex of his baseball career.*

a·pha·sia (ə fā′zhə) *n.* total or partial loss of the ability to use or understand spoken or written language. It is a symptom of brain disease or injury.

a·phe·li·on (ə fē′lē ən) *n. pl.,* **a·phe·li·ons** or **a·phe·li·a** (ə fē′lē ə) the point in the orbit of a planet or other heavenly body at which it is farthest away from the sun.

a·phid (ā′fid, af′id) *n.* any of a group of small insects that live by sucking juices from plants; plant louse.

aph·o·rism (af′ə riz′əm) *n.* a short statement expressing a general truth. For example: *A little learning is a dangerous thing* (Alexander Pope).

aph·ro·dis·i·ac (af′rə diz′ē ak′) *n.* a drug or food that arouses sexual desire. —*adj.* stimulating sexual desire.

Aph·ro·di·te (af′rə dī′tē) *n. Greek Mythology.* the goddess of love and beauty. In Roman mythology she was called Venus.

A·pi·a (ä pē′ə, ä′pē ä′) *n.* the capital of Western Samoa. Pop. (1971 est.), 30,593.

a·pi·ar·y (ā′pē er′ē) *n. pl.,* **a·pi·ar·ies.** a place where bees are kept; collection of beehives.

ap·i·ces (ap′ə sēz′, ā′pə sēz′) a plural of **apex.**

a·piece (ə pēs′) *adv.* for or to each one; each: *These candy bars are fifteen cents apiece. Give the boys two cookies apiece.*

ap·ish (ā′pish) *adj.* **1.** like an ape. **2.** stupidly or foolishly imitative. —**ap′ish·ly,** *adv.* —**ap′ish·ness,** *n.*

a·plomb (ə plom′, ə plum′) *n.* complete self-possession or self-confidence; poise: *He handled the difficult problem with aplomb.*

APO, Army Post Office.

a·poc·a·lypse (ə pok′ə lips′) *n.* **1.** a prophecy or revelation. **2. Apocalypse.** the last book of the New Testament. Also, **Revelation. 3.** the end of the world; doomsday.

A·poc·ry·pha (ə pok′rə fə) *n., pl.* **1.** fourteen books that form an appendix to the Old Testament in certain versions of the Bible. Eleven of these books are accepted by Roman Catholics, but none of the fourteen is regarded as authentic by Protestants and Jews. **2.** various early Christian writings of uncertain origin, rejected as part of the New Testament. **3. apocrypha.** writings or statements of doubtful authorship or authenticity.

a·poc·ry·phal (ə pok′rə fəl) *adj.* **1.** of doubtful authenticity; probably false: *The yarns that the old sailor told were mostly apocryphal.* **2. Apocryphal.** of or relating to the Apocrypha.

ap·o·gee (ap′ə jē) *n.* the point in the orbit of the moon or an artificial earth satellite at which it is farthest away from the earth.

Apogee

A·pol·lo (ə pol′ō) *n. pl.,* **A·pol·los. 1.** *Greek and Roman Mythology.* the god of manly beauty, poetry, music, prophecy, and healing. He was also considered to be the god of the sun and, as such, was god of light and truth. **2.** *also,* **apollo.** a very handsome young man.

a·pol·o·get·ic (ə pol′ə jet′ik) *adj.* making an apology; expressing regret: *He wrote an apologetic note to his hostess saying he was sorry he could not attend her party.* —**a·pol′o·get′i·cal·ly,** *adv.*

a·pol·o·gist (ə pol′ə jist) *n.* a person who speaks or writes in defense of another person or a cause, faith, or idea: *He is an apologist for Marxism.*

a·pol·o·gize (ə pol′ə jīz′) *v.i.,* **a·pol·o·gized, a·pol·o·giz·ing. 1.** to acknowledge and express regret for a fault, error, or offense: *He apologized to his teacher for being rude.* **2.** to speak or write in defense of another person or a cause, faith, or idea.

a·pol·o·gy (ə pol′ə jē) *n. pl.,* **a·pol·o·gies. 1.** an expression of regret for a fault, error, or offense: *Please accept my apology for being late.* **2.** something spoken or written in defense of a person, cause, or idea. **3.** a poor substitute; makeshift: *The old raft was a sad apology for a boat.*

ap·o·plec·tic (ap′ə plek′tik) *adj.* **1.** of, relating to, or causing apoplexy: *an apoplectic stroke.* **2.** suffering from apoplexy: *an apoplectic patient.* **3.** seemingly on the verge of having a stroke; violently excited: *He was apoplectic with rage.* —*n.* a person suffering from apoplexy. —**ap′o·plec′ti·cal·ly,** *adv.*

ap·o·plex·y (ap′ə plek′sē) *n.* a sudden weakness or paralysis, with or without loss of consciousness, caused by a rupture or blockage of blood vessels in the brain; stroke.

a·pos·ta·sy (ə pos′tə sē) *n. pl.,* **a·pos·ta·sies.** a desertion or renunciation of one's religion, cause, political party, or principles.

a·pos·tate (ə pos′tāt) *n.* a person who deserts or renounces his religion, cause, political party, or principles.

a·pos·tle (ə pos′əl) *n.* **1. Apostle.** an early disciple of Christ, especially one of the twelve originally chosen by Christ to preach His gospel. **2.** any early Christian leader or missionary. **3.** a leader or early advocate of any movement or cause: *an apostle of world disarmament.*

Apostles' Creed, a formal statement of Christian faith that affirms the apostolic teachings. It begins with the statement "I believe in God the Father Almighty."

ap·os·tol·ic (ap′əs tol′ik) *adj.* **1.** of or relating to the Apostles, their times, or their teachings. **2.** *also,* **Apostolic.** of or relating to the Pope; papal.

a·pos·tro·phe¹ (ə pos′trə fē) *n.* a punctuation mark (') used in the following ways: **1.** to indicate the omission of one or more letters in a word or phrase, as in *you're* for *you are,* or *e'er* for *ever.* **2.** to indicate the possessive case of nouns and indefinite pronouns, as in *Paul's desk, anyone's concern, the children's room.* **3.** to indicate the plural of letters and figures, as in *the three R's, five 6's.* [Latin *apostrophus* this punctuation mark.]

a·pos·tro·phe² (ə pos′trə fē) *n.* a figure of speech in which a thing or person, often absent or imaginary, is directly addressed as if present. For example: *Milton! thou should'st be living at this hour* (William Wordsworth). [Latin *apostrophē* this figure of speech, from Greek *apostrophē* turning away.]

apothecaries' measure, a system of liquid measure used in pharmacy.

apothecaries' weight, a system of weights used in pharmacy.

a·poth·e·car·y (ə poth′ə ker′ē) *n. pl.,* **a·poth·e·car·ies.** a person who prepares and sells drugs and medicines; druggist; pharmacist.

ap·o·thegm (ap′ə them′) *n.* a short, instructive saying; maxim. For example: *Live and let live.*

a·poth·e·o·sis (ə poth′ē ō′sis) *n. pl.,* **a·poth·e·o·ses** (ə poth′ē ō′sēz). **1.** the act of raising a human being to the rank of a god; deification. **2.** a glorified ideal; perfect example: *She was the very apotheosis of womanhood.*

app. 1. apparent; apparently. **2.** appendix. **3.** appointed.

Ap·pa·la·chi·an Mountains (ap′ə lā′chē ən) the principal mountain system in eastern North America, extending from southeastern Canada to north-central Alabama. Also, **Ap·pa·la·chi·ans** (ap′ə lā′chē ənz).

ap·pall (ə pôl′) *also,* **ap·pal.** *v.t.,* **ap·palled, ap·pall·ing.** to fill with horror or dismay; terrify or shock: *We were appalled by the news of the war.*

ap·pall·ing (ə pô′ling) *adj.* causing horror or dismay; shocking; dreadful. —**ap·pall′ing·ly,** *adv.*

ap·pa·ra·tus (ap′ə rat′əs, ap′ə rā′təs) *n. pl.,* **ap·pa·rat·us** or **ap·pa·rat·us·es. 1.** a device or mechanism used for a particular purpose: *an apparatus for breathing underwater.* **2.** an organized set of instruments, materials, or equipment designed for a particular use. **3.** a group of organs working together to perform a particular function: *The intestines are part of the digestive apparatus.*

ap·par·el (ə par′əl) *n.* clothing or garments; attire. —*v.t.,* **ap·par·eled, ap·par·el·ing;** *also, British,* **ap·par·elled, ap·par·el·ling.** to clothe; dress: *Robin Hood's band was appareled in green.*

ap·par·ent (ə par′ənt) *adj.* **1.** easily seen or understood; plainly visible; evident: *His black eye was apparent even though he wore dark glasses. It was apparent that he was lying.* **2.** appearing or seeming real or true, although not necessarily so: *The apparent size of a star in the sky is much smaller than its real size.* —**ap·par′ent·ly,** *adv.*

ap·pa·ri·tion (ap′ə rish′ən) *n.* **1.** a ghost; phantom. **2.** something strange, startling, or unexpected that comes suddenly into view.

ap·peal (ə pēl′) *n.* **1.** an earnest request or call, as for help or sympathy: *The prisoner made an appeal for mercy.* **2.** the power or ability to attract, charm, or interest: *Sports have a great appeal to many boys.* **3.** *Law.* **a.** the action of bringing a case before a higher court to be heard again. **b.** a request for this. —*v.i.* **1.** to make an earnest request: *The townspeople appealed to the governor for aid after the flood.* **2.** to be attractive, charming, or interesting: *This food doesn't appeal to me.* **3.** to address someone in an effort to gain support or acceptance: *The President appealed to the people for their support.* **4.** *Law.* to bring a case, or request that a case be brought, before a higher court to be heard again. —*v.t. Law.* to start proceedings for the appeal of (a case).

ap·peal·ing (ə pē′ling) *adj.* attractive, charming, or interesting. —**ap·peal′ing·ly,** *adv.*

ap·pear (ə pēr′) *v.i.* **1.** to come into view; become visible: *The snowy mountain peaks appeared in the distance.* **2.** to give the impression of being; seem: *He appeared interested, but was actually bored.* **3.** to be or become clear or plain to the mind: *It appears that you were mistaken.* **4.** to come or be presented before the public: *He has often appeared on the stage.* **5.** to come formally before an authoritative body: *He appeared as a witness at the trial.*

ap·pear·ance (ə pēr′əns) *n.* **1.** the act of appearing or coming into view: *the appearance of the sun above the horizon.* **2.** outward look or aspect: *The shabby appearance of his clothes made us think he was poor.* **3.** outward show: *In spite of his troubles, he gave the appearance of being happy.* **4.** the act of coming before the public: *This was his first appearance on the stage.* **5. appearances.** outward signs.

to keep up appearances. to maintain the outward signs of what is normal or proper.

to put in an appearance. to appear briefly; attend for a short time.

ap·pease (ə pēz′) *v.t.,* **ap·peased, ap·peas·ing. 1.** to cause to be satisfied: *to appease one's hunger.* **2.** to bring to a state of peace or quiet: *to appease someone's anger.* **3.** to pacify by giving in to demands or making concessions: *John appeased his parents by promising to study harder.* —**ap·peas′er,** *n.*

ap·pease·ment (ə pēz′mənt) *n.* **1.** the act of appeasing or the state of being appeased. **2.** a policy of trying to avoid war with an aggressive nation by giving in to its demands.

ap·pel·lant (ə pel′ənt) *n.* a person who appeals, especially to a higher court. —*adj.* of or relating to legal appeals; appellate.

ap·pel·late (ə pel′it) *adj.* **1.** relating to legal appeals. **2.** having the power to hear and rule on legal appeals: *an appellate court.*

ap·pel·la·tion (ap′ə lā′shən) *n.* **1.** a descriptive name or title: In *Catherine the Great,* the appellation of Catherine is *the Great.* **2.** the act of naming.

ap·pend (ə pend′) *v.t.* to add or attach as a subordinate or extra part: *The author appended explanatory notes at the end of the text.*

ap·pend·age (ə pen′dij) *n.* **1.** something appended; addition. **2.** a subordinate part attached to and extending from the main part of the body of a plant or animal. Legs, wings, branches, and horns are appendages.

ap·pen·dec·to·my (ap′ən dek′tə mē) *n. pl.,* **ap·pen·dec·to·mies.** removal of the appendix by means of surgery, especially because of appendicitis.

ap·pen·di·ci·tis (ə pen′də sī′tis) *n.* an inflammation of the appendix, especially when accompanied by swelling, severe abdominal pain, and the danger of a ruptured appendix.

ap·pen·dix (ə pen′diks) *n. pl.,* **ap·pen·dix·es** or **ap·pen·di·ces** (ə pen′də sēz′). **1.** a thin, saclike structure attached to the upper part of the large intestine. In man, it is two to three inches in length, is located in the lower right abdomen, and has no apparent function. Also, **vermiform appendix. 2.** any of various outgrowths or projections of bodily organs. **3.** a section of additional related material at the end of a book or other piece of writing: *This mathematics book has an appendix containing tables of logarithms.*

ap·per·tain (ap′ər tān′) *v.i.* to belong as a part; relate: *Many responsibilities appertain to the office of President of the United States.*

ap·pe·tite (ap′ə tīt′) *n.* **1.** a desire for food: *Growing boys usually have large appetites.* **2.** a natural or strong desire; craving: *Jim has an appetite for adventure and excitement.*

ap·pe·tiz·er (ap′ə tī′zər) *n.* food or drink served as a first course or before a meal, usually to stimulate the appetite.

ap·pe·tiz·ing (ap′ə tī′zing) *adj.* appealing to the appetite; savory: *Julia prepared an appetizing dinner.* —**ap′pe·tiz′ing·ly,** *adv.*

Ap·pi·an Way (ap′ē ən) an ancient Roman road, begun in 312 B.C., that extended from Rome to the Adriatic Sea. Part of it still exists today.

ap·plaud (ə plôd′) *v.t.* **1.** to show approval or enjoyment of by clapping the hands: *The audience applauded him when he finished his song.* **2.** to approve; praise: *The mayor's plan for reform was applauded by all the citizens.* —*v.i.* to show approval or enjoyment by clapping the hands: *The audience kept applauding long after the curtain came down.*

ap·plause (ə plôz′) *n.* **1.** a clapping of the hands to show approval or enjoyment: *Loud applause greeted the star's appearance on stage.* **2.** any show of approval or appreciation; praise: *His first novel received the applause of the critics.*

ap·ple (ap′əl) *n.* **1.** a roundish fruit with red, yellow, or green skin, and a firm, edible outer part surrounding a core with small seeds. **2.** any of numerous cultivated trees bearing this fruit.

   apple of one's eye. a person or thing that is most precious or dear.

apple butter, a thick, brown, spiced applesauce, used as a spread for bread.

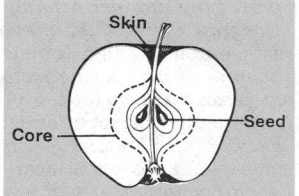
Cross section of an apple

ap·ple·jack (ap′əl jak′) *n.* a brandy made by distilling apple cider that has fermented.

ap·ple·sauce (ap′əl sôs′) *n.* a food consisting of apples sweetened and stewed to a pulp.

ap·pli·ance (ə plī′əns) *n.* a device, machine, or piece of equipment for a particular use, especially one for household use: *An electric iron, a toaster, a can opener, and a dishwasher are appliances.*

ap·pli·ca·ble (ap′lə kə bəl) *adj.* that can be applied; suitable; relevant: *That law is not applicable in this case.* —**ap′pli·ca·bil′i·ty,** *n.*

ap·pli·cant (ap′lə kənt) *n.* a person who asks or applies for something; candidate: *There were ten applicants for the job of principal.*

ap·pli·ca·tion (ap′lə kā′shən) *n.* **1.** the act of putting to use: *the application of scientific discoveries to the needs of industry.* **2.** the act of putting on: *the application of ointment to a burn.* **3.** something put on or applied: *This application will soothe the sore area.* **4.** a way of being applied or used: *This rule has many applications.* **5.** a request made personally or in writing: *The corporal's application for a transfer was denied.* **6.** a written form used in making such a request: *He filled out the application for admission to college.* **7.** close or careful attention: *application to one's studies.*

ap·pli·ca·tor (ap′lə kā′tər) *n.* a device for applying something, such as shoe polish, paint, or medicine.

ap·plied (ə plīd′) *adj.* used to solve practical problems; put to practical use: *applied science, applied mathematics.*

ap·pli·qué (ap′lə kā′) *n.* a design or decoration made of one material and then sewed or otherwise fastened to the background of another. —*adj.* decorated in this way. —*v.t.,* **ap·pli·quéd, ap·pli·qué·ing.** to decorate with or apply as appliqué.

ap·ply (ə plī′) *v.,* **ap·plied, ap·ply·ing.** —*v.t.* **1.** to put into use or practice; employ: *He applied force to pry open the locked door.* **2.** to bring into contact with; put on: *to apply paint to a wall.* **3.** to use (a word or statement) to refer to a particular person or thing: *His classmates applied the nickname "Red" to the boy because of the color of his hair.* **4.** to devote (oneself) fully: *He applied himself to his homework.* —*v.i.* **1.** to make a request; ask: *Janet applied for a scholarship to nursing school. Carl applied for a job as a salesman.* **2.** to be suitable or related: *The rule that nouns form their plural by adding "s" does not apply to the word "mouse."*

ap·point (ə point′) *v.t.* **1.** to name or select for an office or position: *We must appoint someone to be the temporary treasurer. Members of the Supreme Court are appointed by the President.* **2.** to arrange or decide on by agreement or authority; fix: *The judge appointed the trial date.* **3.** to furnish; equip. ▲ now used chiefly in combination in the past participle: *a well-appointed boat.*

ap·point·ee (ə poin′tē′) *n.* a person named to an office or position.

ap·poin·tive (ə poin′tiv) *adj.* relating to or filled by appointment rather than election: *The position of Secretary of State is an appointive office.*

ap·point·ment (ə point′mənt) *n.* **1.** the act of naming or selecting someone for an office or position: *The vacancy in the city council was filled by appointment.* **2.** an office or position so filled: *He accepted a high appointment in*

at; āpe; cär; end; mē; it; īce; hot; ōld; fôrk; wood; fŏŏl; oil; out; up; turn; sing; thin; this; hw in white; zh in treasure. The symbol ə stands for the sound of a in about, e in taken, i in pencil, o in lemon, and u in circus.

government. **3.** an arrangement to meet or see someone at a certain time and place; engagement: *I have a doctor's appointment at ten o'clock.* **4. appointments.** furnishings; equipment.

Ap·po·mat·tox (ap′ə mat′əks) *n.* a town in central Virginia where Robert E. Lee formally surrendered to U. S. Grant on April 9, 1865.

ap·por·tion (ə pôr′shən) *v.t.* to divide and give out proportionally or according to a rule or plan; distribute in portions: *They apportioned the money they raised at the fair to three charities.*

ap·por·tion·ment (ə pôr′shən mənt) *n.* **1.** the act of apportioning or the state of being apportioned; distribution according to a rule or plan. **2.** the distribution of seats in a legislative body to states or other areas, according to the population of those areas: *In the last apportionment of the House of Representatives, New York lost a few seats and California gained a few.*

ap·po·site (ap′ə zit) *adj.* well-suited; appropriate; pertinent: *an apposite remark.*

ap·po·si·tion (ap′ə zish′ən) *n. Grammar.* **1.** the placing of a noun or a noun phrase near another noun or noun phrase so that the second explains and has the same grammatical construction as the first. **2.** the relationship existing between such words. In the sentence *I read a book about Sir Christopher Wren, the architect,* the phrase *Sir Christopher Wren* and the phrase *the architect* are in apposition. —**ap′po·si′tion·al,** *adj.* —**ap′po·si′tion·al·ly,** *adv.*

ap·pos·i·tive (ə poz′ə tiv) *n.* a word, phrase, or clause that is in apposition. —*adj.* relating to or placed in apposition.

ap·prais·al (ə prā′zəl) *n.* **1.** the act of appraising or the state of being appraised. **2.** a price or value assigned in appraising; estimate.

ap·praise (ə prāz′) *v.t.,* **ap·praised, ap·prais·ing. 1.** to estimate the value of; fix a price for: *to appraise land, to appraise a diamond ring.* **2.** to estimate the quality or significance of; judge: *to appraise a situation, to appraise a man's character.* —**ap·prais′er,** *n.*

ap·pre·cia·ble (ə prē′shə bəl) *adj.* enough to be felt or noticed; perceptible: *His work has shown an appreciable improvement.* —**ap·pre′cia·bly,** *adv.*

ap·pre·ci·ate (ə prē′shē āt′) *v.,* **ap·pre·ci·at·ed, ap·pre·ci·at·ing.** —*v.t.* **1.** to recognize the value or quality of; value or regard highly: *Vincent Van Gogh's paintings were not appreciated by the public until after his death.* **2.** to be grateful for: *I appreciate your help.* **3.** to be aware of or sensitive to: *We appreciate the dangers involved in such an experiment.* **4.** to raise in value: *The repairs we made will appreciate our house.* —*v.i.* to rise in value: *The value of land has appreciated in that town.*

ap·pre·ci·a·tion (ə prē′shē ā′shən) *n.* **1.** the act of recognizing value or quality: *She has an appreciation of fine foods.* **2.** sensitive understanding: *to have a keen appreciation of the music of Mozart.* **3.** gratitude: *I express my deep appreciation for your help.* **4.** an increase in value.

ap·pre·cia·tive (ə prē′shə tiv, ə prē′shē ā′tiv) *adj.* feeling or showing appreciation: *The appreciative audience applauded loudly.* —**ap·pre′cia·tive·ly,** *adv.*

ap·pre·hend (ap′ri hend′) *v.t.* **1.** to seize and take into custody; arrest; capture: *The police apprehended the burglar.* **2.** to grasp with the mind; understand: *Do you fully apprehend the meaning of his words?* **3.** to look forward to with fear; dread: *The soldier apprehended his tour of combat duty.*

ap·pre·hen·sion (ap′ri hen′shən) *n.* **1.** a fear of what may happen: *The thought of going to the hospital filled me with apprehension.* **2.** arrest; capture: *the apprehension of a criminal.* **3.** understanding.

ap·pre·hen·sive (ap′ri hen′siv) *adj.* fearful about what may happen; uneasy; worried: *Are you apprehensive about today's test?* —**ap′pre·hen′sive·ly,** *adv.* —**ap′pre·hen′·sive·ness,** *n.*

ap·pren·tice (ə pren′tis) *n.* **1.** a person who works for a skilled worker in order to learn a trade or art. In earlier times, apprentices were bound by contract to work for their masters for a definite period of time in return for training. **2.** any learner or beginner. —*v.t.,* **ap·pren·ticed, ap·pren·tic·ing.** to take on or place as an apprentice.

ap·pren·tice·ship (ə pren′tis ship′) *n.* **1.** the condition of being an apprentice. **2.** the period of time during which a person works as an apprentice.

ap·prise (ə prīz′) *v.t.,* **ap·prised, ap·pris·ing.** to give notice to; inform: *The news bulletin apprised motorists of the hazardous driving conditions on the icy highways.*

ap·proach (ə prōch′) *v.i.* to come near: *The car approached swiftly. The hour of attack is approaching.* —*v.t.* **1.** to come near or close to, as in time, place, or quality: *It is approaching midnight.* **2.** to go to with a plan or request: *She approached her employer with the hope of getting a raise.* **3.** to deal with: *We should approach the problem from this angle.* —*n. pl.,* **ap·proach·es. 1.** the act of coming near: *the approach of spring.* **2.** a method of dealing with or doing something: *We must find a new approach to the pollution problem.* **3.** a way of reaching a place or person: *The only approach to the town was blocked by snow.*

ap·proach·a·ble (ə prō′chə bəl) *adj.* **1.** possible to approach; accessible: *The town was approachable from only one direction.* **2.** easy to approach or talk to; friendly: *an approachable person.* —**ap·proach′a·bil′i·ty,** *n.*

ap·pro·ba·tion (ap′rə bā′shən) *n.* expression of a favorable opinion; approval, acceptance, or praise: *The senate gave its approbation to the bill by passing it unanimously.*

ap·pro·pri·ate (*adj.,* ə prō′prē it; *v.,* ə prō′prē āt′) *adj.* suitable for an occasion; fitting; proper: *Is this dress appropriate for the party?* —*v.t.,* **ap·pro·pri·at·ed, ap·pro·pri·at·ing. 1.** to set apart for a particular use: *Congress appropriated funds to build a new guided missile system.* **2.** to take for oneself, especially without permission: *He appropriated his brother's baseball bat without asking.* —**ap·pro′pri·ate·ly,** *adv.* —**ap·pro′pri·ate·ness,** *n.*

ap·pro·pri·a·tion (ə prō′prē ā′shən) *n.* **1.** something appropriated, especially a sum of public money set aside for a particular use. **2.** the act of appropriating.

ap·prov·al (ə prōo′vəl) *n.* **1.** favorable opinion; acceptance: *The president's actions were looked on with approval by most people.* **2.** official consent; permission: *The magazine will not be able to reprint that article without the author's approval.*

on approval. for a customer to try or examine before deciding whether to buy: *These records will be sent to you on approval.*

ap·prove (ə prōov′) *v.,* **ap·proved, ap·prov·ing.** —*v.t.* **1.** to be favorable toward; think well of: *The teacher approved my summer reading list.* **2.** to consent to officially: *Congress approved the annual budget.* —*v.i.* to have or give a favorable opinion (often with *of*): *My mother doesn't approve of my playing football.* —**ap·prov′ing·ly,** *adv.*

ap·prox·i·mate (*adj.,* ə prok′sə mit; *v.,* ə prok′sə māt′) *adj.* nearly correct or exact: *The approximate value of this clock is fifty dollars.* —*v.t.,* **ap·prox·i·mat·ed, ap·prox·i·mat·ing. 1.** to come near or close to: *Your calculation approximates the actual width of the room.* **2.** to estimate: *Approximate the time it will take you to finish the job.* —**ap·prox′i·mate·ly,** *adv.*

ap·prox·i·ma·tion (ə prok′sə mā′shən) *n.* **1.** the act of approximating. **2.** something that is nearly correct, as an estimated amount; close estimate: *The figure 8,000,000 is an approximation of the population of New York City.*

ap·pur·te·nance (ə purt'ən əns) *n.* something that goes along with another more important thing; accessory: *He bought the farm with its machinery, tools, and other appurtenances.*

Apr., April.

a·pri·cot (ā'prə kot', ap'rə kot') *n.* **1.** an orange-colored fruit resembling a small peach. **2.** the tree this fruit grows on. **3.** a pale orange-yellow color. —*adj.* having the color apricot.

A·pril (ā'prəl) *n.* the fourth month of the year, having thirty days. [Latin *Aprīlis,* possibly from Greek *Aphrō,* short for *Aphroditē* the Greek goddess of love. This month was associated with love.]

Apricot leaves and fruit

April Fools' Day, a day when tricks and practical jokes are often played on people. It falls on April 1. Also, **All Fool's Day.**

a·pron (ā'prən) *n.* **1.** a garment worn over the front of the body to protect one's clothes. **2.** a hard-surfaced area in front of an airplane hangar or terminal. **3.** the part of a stage in front of the curtain.

ap·ro·pos (ap'rə pō') *adj.* suitable for an occasion; to the point; appropriate; fitting: *Your jokes are not apropos to our serious discussion.* —*adv.* at the right time; appropriately.

   apropos of. with regard to; in relation to: *My question is apropos of the letter you sent me.*

apse (aps) *n.* in a building, a semicircular recess with a domed or arched ceiling, especially one at the east end of a church.

apt (apt) *adj.* **1.** likely; inclined: *You're apt to have an accident if you don't drive more carefully.* **2.** appropriate; suitable: *an apt reply.* **3.** quick to learn: *He is an apt student in mathematics.* —**apt'ly,** *adv.* —**apt'ness,** *n.*

apt. *pl.,* **apts.** apartment.

ap·ti·tude (ap'tə tōōd', ap'tə tyōōd') *n.* **1.** a natural ability or talent: *Brian has an aptitude for learning languages.* **2.** quickness in learning or understanding: *a pupil of great aptitude.*

aptitude test, a test given to determine a person's ability to learn to do certain kinds of work or to acquire certain skills.

A·qa·ba, Gulf of (ä'kä bä') a gulf at the northeastern end of the Red Sea.

aq·ua·lung (ak'wə lung') *n.* a device for breathing underwater, having a valve that supplies air according to the needs of the diver. Trademark: **Aqua-Lung.**

aq·ua·ma·rine (ak'wə mə rēn') *n.* **1.** a transparent stone having a pale blue or bluish-green color, used as a gem. **2.** a bluish-green color. —*adj.* having the color aquamarine.

Aqualung

aq·ua·naut (ak'wə nôt') *n.* a person who is trained to live in an underwater chamber and to do scientific research and experiments relating to the ocean. [Latin *aqua* water + Greek *nautes* sailor, on the model of *astronaut.*]

aq·ua·plane (ak'wə plān') *n.* a board on which a person can stand and ride across the surface of the water while being towed by a motorboat. —*v.i.,* **aq·ua·planed, aq·ua·plan·ing.** to ride an aquaplane.

a·quar·i·um (ə kwer'ē əm) *n. pl.,* **a·quar·i·ums** or **a·quar·i·a** (ə kwer'ē ə). **1.** a tank, bowl, or similar container, partly of glass or other transparent material, in which living fish, water animals, and water plants are kept and observed. **2.** a building where collections of such animals and plants are exhibited or studied.

A·quar·i·us (ə kwer'ē əs) *n.* **1.** a constellation thought to resemble a man pouring water out of a vase. **2.** the eleventh sign of the zodiac.

a·quat·ic (ə kwat'ik, ə kwot'ik) *adj.* **1.** (of a plant or animal) growing or living in or on water. **2.** performed in or on water: *Swimming and skin diving are aquatic sports.*

aq·ue·duct (ak'wə dukt') *n.* **1.** a pipe or artificial channel for carrying water, especially over long distances. **2.** a structure supporting such a pipe or channel.

a·que·ous (ā'kwē əs, ak'wē əs) *adj.* of, like, or containing water; watery: *an aqueous solution.*

aqueous humor, in the eye, the clear, watery fluid filling the space between the cornea and the lens.

aq·ui·line (ak'wə līn, ak'wə lin) *adj.* **1.** curved like an eagle's beak: *an aquiline nose.* **2.** of or like an eagle.

A·qui·nas, Saint Thomas (ə kwī'nəs) 1225?–1274, Italian philosopher and theologian.

Ar, the symbol for argon.

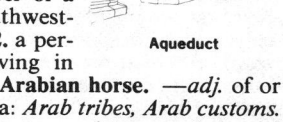
Aqueduct

Ar·ab (ar'əb) *n.* **1.** a member of a Semitic people inhabiting southwestern Asia and North Africa. **2.** a person who was born or is living in Arabia. **3.** another word for **Arabian horse.** —*adj.* of or relating to the Arabs or Arabia: *Arab tribes, Arab customs.*

ar·a·besque (ar'ə besk') *n.* **1.** an elaborate design of flowers, leaves, or other figures mixed together. **2.** a position in ballet in which the dancer stands on one leg with the other extended straight backward. —*adj.* relating to or done in the style of arabesque.

A·ra·bi·a (ə rā'bē ə) *n.* a large peninsula in southwestern Asia. Area, (approx.) 1,000,000 sq. mi.

A·ra·bi·an (ə rā'bē ən) *adj.* of or relating to Arabia or its people. —*n.* another word for **Arab.**

Arabesque *(def. 1)*

Arabian horse, any of a breed of horses native to Arabia, noted for their speed, grace, and intelligence.

Arabian Nights, a collection of stories of adventure and romance from Arabia, Persia, and India, dating from the tenth century.

Arabian Sea, the northwestern part of the Indian Ocean, between Arabia and India.

Ar·a·bic (ar'ə bik) *adj.* of or relating to the Arabs, their language, or their culture. —*n.* the Semitic language of the Arabs, spoken in most of the Middle East and North Africa.

at; āpe; cär; end; mē; it; īce; hot; ōld; fôrk; wood; fōōl; oil; out; up; turn; sing; thin; this; hw in white; zh in treasure. The symbol ə stands for the sound of **a** in about, **e** in taken, **i** in pencil, **o** in lemon, and **u** in circus.

Arabic numerals, the number symbols 1, 2, 3, 4, 5, 6, 7, 8, 9, and 0. This numbering system is believed to have been developed in India about 2000 years ago. The numerals are called *Arabic* because they were introduced to Western Europe by Arab scholars.

ar·a·ble (ar′ə bəl) *adj.* (of land) fit for plowing or cultivation.

a·rach·nid (ə rak′nid) *n.* any of a large group of animals having four pairs of legs, no wings or antennae, and a body divided into two parts. Spiders, mites, scorpions, and ticks are arachnids.

Ar·a·gon (ar′ə gon′) *n.* a historic region and former kingdom in northeastern Spain.

Ar·al Sea (ar′əl) an inland sea in the southwestern Soviet Union.

Ar·a·ma·ic (ar′ə mā′ik) *n.* an ancient Semitic language spoken throughout the Middle East in Biblical times. It was spoken by Jesus.

A·rap·a·ho (ə rap′ə hō) *n. pl.,* **A·rap·a·ho** or **A·rap·a·hos.** **1.** a member of a North American Indian tribe that lived in Wyoming and Colorado. **2.** the Algonquian language of this tribe. *—adj.* of or relating to the Arapaho, their language, or their culture.

ar·bi·ter (är′bə tər) *n.* **1.** a person chosen to settle a dispute; arbitrator. **2.** a person whose opinion or decision is final: *an arbiter of good manners, an arbiter of women's fashions.*

ar·bi·trar·y (är′bə trer′ē) *adj.* **1.** based on someone's personal opinion or will rather than on rule, law, or reason: *His decision was arbitrary and unfair.* **2.** relying only on personal judgment or will rather than on the guidance of rules or law; despotic: *an arbitrary ruler, arbitrary government.* **3.** based on whim or chance, rather than calculation: *an arbitrary choice.* **—ar′bi·trar′i·ly,** *adv.* **—ar′bi·trar′i·ness,** *n.*

ar·bi·trate (är′bə trāt′) *v.,* **ar·bi·trat·ed, ar·bi·trat·ing.** *—v.t.* **1.** to decide as an arbitrator; settle: *He arbitrated the differences between the two groups.* **2.** to submit to arbitration: *Neither the union nor the company would arbitrate their dispute.* *—v.i.* **1.** to act as an arbitrator. **2.** to submit a dispute to arbitration.

ar·bi·tra·tion (är′bə trā′shən) *n.* a method of settling a dispute in which an impartial person or group is called in to make the final decision: *Labor and management agreed to submit to arbitration in the contract negotiations.*

ar·bi·tra·tor (är′bə trā′tər) *n.* **1.** a person chosen by the parties in a dispute to settle or decide their differences. **2.** a person who has the power to make final decisions; arbiter: *The referee is the arbitrator in a football game.*

ar·bor (är′bər) *n.* an area covered and shaded by trees, shrubs, or a vine-covered trellis, especially such an area in a garden.

ar·bo·re·al (är bôr′ē əl) *adj.* **1.** of, like, or relating to trees. **2.** living in trees: *Squirrels are arboreal animals.*

ar·bo·re·tum (är′bə rē′təm) *n. pl.,* **ar·bo·re·tums** or **ar·bo·re·ta** (är′bə rē′tə). a garden where trees and shrubs are grown for study or exhibition.

ar·bor·vi·tae (är′bər vī′tē) *n.* any of various evergreen shrubs or trees having scalelike leaves. Many varieties are grown as ornamental trees or as hedges.

ar·bu·tus (är byōō′təs) *n. pl.,* **ar·bu·tus·es. 1.** a trailing evergreen plant found in North America, bearing fragrant pink or white flowers in early spring. **2.** any of various evergreen shrubs or trees related to the heath.

Arborvitae leaves

arc (ärk) *n.* **1.** a continuous curved line between any two points on a circle. **2.** any line curving in this way. **3.** a hot and bright electric current flowing in a curved path between two electrodes separated by a small space. *—v.i.,* **arced** or **arcked, arc·ing** or **arck·ing. 1.** to move in a curved line. **2.** to form an electric arc.

Arc, Joan of (ärk) see **Joan of Arc.**

ar·cade (är kād′) *n.* **1.** a passageway covered by an arched roof. **2.** any covered passageway, street, or area opening onto a street, especially one with shops along its sides. **3.** a row of arches with their supporting columns.

Arcade

Ar·ca·di·a (är kā′dē ə) *n.* **1.** a mountainous region of ancient Greece, noted for the simple and peaceful life of its people. **2.** *also,* **arcadia.** a place of ideal calm, pleasantness, and simplicity. **—Ar·ca′di·an,** *adj., n.*

Arc de Tri·omphe (ärk də trē ōnf′) an arch in Paris, built as a monument by Napoleon Bonaparte to celebrate the victories of his troops. Also, **Arch of Triumph.**

arch¹ (ärch) *n. pl.,* **arch·es. 1.** a curved structure that spans a space, usually made up of wedge-shaped blocks fitted together in a semicircle or similar shape. It is generally built to support the weight of material above it, but may be merely ornamental. **2.** a monument consisting of an arch or arches. **3.** a curved line or shape: *the arch of an eyebrow.* **4.** anything like an arch in shape or function. **5.** the raised, curved part of the foot between the ball and the heel: *Good shoes give support to the arches.* **6.** see **archway.** *—v.t.* **1.** to form (something) into an arch; curve: *The cat arched its back.* **2.** to cover or span with an arch: *A small bridge arched the stream.* *—v.i.* to have the form of an arch: *Two huge trees arched over the roof of the house.* [Old French *arche* a curved structure, from medieval Latin *arca,* from Latin *arcus* bow, arc.]

arch² (ärch) *adj.* **1.** sly; mischievous: *She looked back and gave him an arch smile.* **2.** chief; leading: *the arch criminal.* [From *arch-.*] **—arch′ly,** *adv.* **—arch′ness,** *n.*

arch- *prefix* chief; principal: *archbishop, archangel, archenemy.*

ar·chae·o·log·i·cal (är′kē ə loj′i kəl) *also,* **ar·che·o·log·i·cal.** *adj.* of or relating to archaeology. **—ar′chae·o·log′i·cal·ly,** *adv.*

ar·chae·ol·o·gist (är′kē ol′ə jist) *also,* **ar·che·ol·o·gist.** *n.* a student of or an expert in archaeology.

ar·chae·ol·o·gy (är′kē ol′ə jē) *also,* **ar·che·ol·o·gy.** *n.* the scientific study of the way man lived in the past. Archaeologists dig up the remains of ancient cities, towns, and tombs and then study the tools, weapons, pottery, monuments, and other things that they find.

ar·cha·ic (är kā′ik) *adj.* **1.** no longer in common use in speech or writing: *"Thou" and "thy" are archaic forms of "you" and "yours."* **2.** of an earlier time; out-of-date: *archaic customs.* **—ar·cha′i·cal·ly,** *adv.*

● In this dictionary, the term **Archaic** means that a word or meaning was once common in English, but is not used very often today. You might ask: "If a word isn't used in today's language, why put it in the dictionary at all?" The reason is that not all the words you read, either in or out of school, are modern words. For example, many words that are no longer used are found in the Bible or in the works of great writers of the past, such as William Shakespeare. You need to know the meanings of archaic words like *shalt, hast,* and *wouldst* when you read the plays of Shakespeare. Therefore we include such words in this dictionary.

ar·cha·ism (är′kē iz′əm) *n.* something archaic, especially an archaic word or phrase.

arch·an·gel (ärk′ān′jəl) *n.* an angel of the highest rank.

arch·bish·op (ärch′bish′əp) *n.* a bishop of the highest rank.

arch·di·o·cese (ärch′dī′ə sēz′, ärch′dī′ə sis) *n.* a church district consisting of several dioceses. An archdiocese is governed by an archbishop.

arch·duch·ess (ärch′duch′is) *n. pl.,* **arch·duch·ess·es.** **1.** the wife or widow of an archduke. **2.** a princess of the former royal family of Austria.

arch·duke (ärch′dōōk′, ärch′dyōōk′) *n.* a prince of the former royal family of Austria.

arched (ärcht) *adj.* **1.** having the form of an arch. **2.** covered with or having an arch or arches.

arch·en·e·my (ärch′en′ə mē) *n. pl.,* **arch·en·e·mies.** a chief or principal enemy.

ar·che·o·log·i·cal (är′kē ə log′i kəl) another spelling of **archaeological.**

ar·che·ol·o·gist (är′kē ol′ə jist) another spelling of **archaeologist.**

ar·che·ol·o·gy (är′kē ol′ə jē) another spelling of **archaeology.**

arch·er (är′chər) *n.* a person who shoots with a bow and arrow.

arch·er·y (är′chər ē) *n.* **1.** the practice, skill, or sport of shooting with a bow and arrow. **2.** a group or company of archers.

arch·e·type (är′kə tīp′) *n.* the original or ideal model or pattern from which all other things of the same type are developed or copied: *Alexander Graham Bell's invention is the archetype of all modern telephones.*

Ar·chi·me·des (är′kə mē′dēz) 287?–212 B.C., Greek mathematician, physicist, and inventor.

ar·chi·pel·a·go (är′kə pel′ə gō′) *n. pl.,* **ar·chi·pel·a·gos** or **ar·chi·pel·a·goes.** **1.** a large group of islands. **2.** a large body of water having many islands.

ar·chi·tect (är′kə tekt′) *n.* **1.** a person whose profession is to design, draw plans for, and supervise the construction of buildings or other structures. **2.** the creator, maker, or designer of anything: *James Madison and Benjamin Franklin were among the architects of the United States Constitution.*

ar·chi·tec·tur·al (är′kə tek′chər əl) *adj.* of, relating to, or characteristic of architecture. —**ar′chi·tec′tur·al·ly,** *adv.*

ar·chi·tec·ture (är′kə tek′chər) *n.* **1.** the science, art, or profession of designing, planning, and constructing buildings or other structures. **2.** a particular style or method of designing or constructing buildings: *modern architecture.* **3.** architectural work or works: *We saw some outstanding architecture on our trip to Rome.* **4.** the construction or design of anything: *the architecture of a motion picture or novel.*

ar·chi·trave (är′kə trāv′) *n.* in architecture, a beam resting directly on top of a column of a building.

ar·chives (är′kīvz) *n., pl.* **1.** public records, papers, or documents, as of a government or institution. **2.** the place where such records, papers, or documents are kept.

Arch of Triumph, another name for **Arc de Triomphe.**

arch·way (ärch′wā′) *n.* **1.** an entrance or passage under an arch. **2.** an arch over a passage.

arc lamp, a lamp in which high-intensity light is pro-

duced by an electric arc between two carbon electrodes surrounded by a gas. Also, **arc light.**

arc·tic (ärk′tik, är′tik) *adj.* **1.** of or relating to the North Pole or the north polar regions. **2.** extremely cold; frigid. —*n.* **1. the Arctic.** an ice-covered region surrounding the North Pole. **2. arctics.** warm, waterproof overshoes.

Arctic Circle also, **arctic circle.** an imaginary line around the earth running parallel to the equator at 66°33′ north latitude, or about 1600 miles from the North Pole.

Arctic Ocean, an ocean north of the Arctic Circle and surrounding the North Pole.

Arc·tu·rus (ärk toor′əs, ärk tyoor′əs) *n.* a giant orange star, one of the brightest in the sky and the brightest in the constellation Boötes.

ar·dent (ärd′ənt) *adj.* full of eagerness, enthusiasm, or passion: *He is an ardent supporter of the senator.* —**ar′dent·ly,** *adv.*

ar·dor (är′dər) *n.* great enthusiasm; strong passion: *He spoke with ardor in support of the proposal.*

ar·du·ous (är′jōō əs) *adj.* requiring great effort or energy; difficult; strenuous: *an arduous task.* —**ar′du·ous·ly,** *adv.* —**ar′du·ous·ness,** *n.*

are (är) **1.** the second person singular of **be:** *You are late.* **2.** the present plural of **be:** *We are glad you could join us.*

ar·e·a (er′ē ə) *n.* **1.** the amount of surface within a given set of limits, especially as measured in square units: *The area of our yard is 400 square feet.* **2.** a particular space, section, or region: *a slum area. That part of the country is a farming area.* **3.** a section set aside for a particular use: *a picnic area, the dining area of a house.* **4.** a field of interest or activity: *He has a good education in the area of science. I don't have much knowledge in that area.*

area code, a combination of three numbers that represents one of the geographic areas into which the United States and Canada are divided for the purpose of communication by telephone: *The area code for the state of Colorado is 303.* These numbers are dialed before the local number in calling from one area to another.

ar·e·a·way (er′ē ə wā′) *n.* **1.** a sunken space or passage in front of the windows or entrance of a cellar or basement. **2.** a passageway between buildings.

a·re·na (ə rē′nə) *n.* **1.** in ancient Rome, the central part of an amphitheater, used for contests involving gladiators or for other performances. **2.** any similar place used for public meetings or entertainment: *a boxing arena, a circus arena.* **3.** a scene or area of conflict or activity: *the arena of politics.* [Latin *arēna* sand. Sand was used to cover the ground of Roman amphitheaters.]

aren't (ärnt, är′ənt) **1.** are not: *These shoes aren't new.* **2.** am not. ▲ used in asking questions: *Aren't I allowed to come along?*

Ar·es (er′ēz) *n. Greek Mythology.* the god of war. In Roman mythology he was called Mars.

ar·gent (är′jənt) *adj. Archaic.* made of silver; silvery-white.

Ar·gen·ti·na (är′jən tē′nə) *n.* a country in southern South America. Capital, Buenos Aires. Area, 1,072,072 sq. mi. Pop. (1971 est.), 23,550,000.

Ar·gen·tine (är′jən tēn′, är′jən tīn′) *adj.* of or relating to Argentina or its people. —*n.* a person who was born

at; āpe; cär; end; mē; it; īce; hot; ōld; fôrk; wood; fōōl; oil; out; up; turn; sing; thin; this; hw in white; zh in treasure. The symbol ə stands for the sound of a in about, e in taken, i in pencil, o in lemon, and u in circus.

or is living in Argentina. Also, **Ar·gen·tin·e·an** (är′jən-tin′ē ən).

ar·gon (är′gon) *n.* a colorless, inert gaseous element that makes up about one percent of the earth's atmosphere. It is used especially in electric light bulbs. Symbol: Ar

Ar·go·naut (är′gə nôt′) *n. Greek Legend.* any of the men who sailed with Jason in search of the Golden Fleece.

ar·go·sy (är′gə sē) *n. pl.,* **ar·go·sies.** **1.** a large merchant ship. **2.** a fleet of such ships.

ar·got (är′gō, är′gət) *n.* the special language or slang used by a particular group or class, especially the secret language of thieves.

ar·gue (är′gyoō) *v.,* **ar·gued, ar·gu·ing.** —*v.i.* **1.** to have a disagreement or dispute: *My father and my uncle often argue about politics.* **2.** to give reasons for or against something: *He argued against the plan.* —*v.t.* **1.** to give reasons for or against; debate: *Let's not argue the matter.* **2.** to persuade (someone) by giving reasons: *His wife tried to argue him out of selling his car.* **3.** to try to establish (something) by giving reasons; maintain; contend: *to argue that someone is wrong.* **4.** to show; indicate: *Her accent argues that she was born in New York City.* —**ar′gu·a·ble,** *adj.* —**ar′gu·er,** *n.*

ar·gu·ment (är′gyə mənt) *n.* **1.** a discussion of a disputed subject; debate: *They had an argument over whose turn it was to wash the dishes.* **2.** a reason or reasons given to support or oppose something: *What are the arguments for accepting the proposal?* **3.** a process or line of reasoning: *I couldn't follow his argument.* **4.** a summary of the chief points of a book, poem, or other literary work.

ar·gu·men·ta·tion (är′gyə men tā′shən) *n.* **1.** the process of forming and giving reasons and of developing conclusions from them. **2.** argument; debate.

ar·gu·men·ta·tive (är′gyə men′tə tiv) *adj.* fond of arguing; quarrelsome. —**ar′gu·men′ta·tive·ly,** *adv.* —**ar′gu·men′ta·tive·ness,** *n.*

Ar·gus (är′gəs) *n. pl.,* **Ar·gus·es.** **1.** *Greek Mythology.* a giant with a hundred eyes. **2.** a very watchful or alert person.

ar·gyle (är′gīl) *also,* **Ar·gyle.** *n.* **1.** a diamond-shaped pattern of contrasting colors, used especially in knitting. **2.** a sock having this pattern. —*adj.* having this pattern.

a·ri·a (är′ē ə, er′ē ə) *n.* a musical composition for one voice with instrumental accompaniment, as in an opera.

Ar·i·ad·ne (ar′ē ad′nē) *n. Greek Legend.* the daughter of King Minos, who gave Theseus the ball of thread by which he found his way out of the labyrinth of the Minotaur.

ar·id (ar′id) *adj.* **1.** having little rainfall; dry; parched: *an arid wasteland.* **2.** uninteresting; lifeless: *an arid book.* —**a·rid·i·ty** (ə rid′ə tē), **ar′id·ness,** *n.* —**ar′id·ly,** *adv.*

Ar·i·el (er′ē əl) *n.* in Shakespeare's play *The Tempest,* an airy spirit who used magic to help Prospero.

Ar·ies (er′ēz) *n.* **1.** a constellation in the northern sky, thought to resemble a ram in shape. **2.** the first sign of the zodiac.

a·right (ə rīt′) *adv.* correctly; rightly: *Report me and my cause aright* (Shakespeare, *Hamlet*).

a·rise (ə rīz′) *v.i.,* **a·rose, a·ris·en, a·ris·ing.** **1.** to come into being; appear; originate: *Questions often arise as we read. They dealt with each problem as it arose.* **2.** to get up; stand up: *The audience arose and applauded the cast.* **3.** to move upward; rise; ascend: *Smoke arose from the chimney.*

ar·is·toc·ra·cy (ar′is tok′rə sē) *n. pl.,* **ar·is·toc·ra·cies.** **1.** a class of persons inheriting a high social position by birth; nobility. **2.** a government in which such a class has control. **3.** a government in which control is held by a privileged or superior class. **4.** any group of persons su-

perior or outstanding because of wealth, intelligence, or culture: *the intellectual aristocracy of a country.*

a·ris·to·crat (ə ris′tə krat′) *n.* **1.** a member of an aristocracy; nobleman or noblewoman. **2.** a person who has the attitudes associated with the aristocracy. **3.** a person who advocates government by the aristocracy.

a·ris·to·crat·ic (ə ris′tə krat′ik) *adj.* **1.** characteristic of or suiting an aristocrat: *an aristocratic manner, aristocratic attitudes.* **2.** of or belonging to the aristocracy: *an aristocratic family.* **3.** relating to or supporting government by aristocracy. —**a·ris′to·crat′i·cal·ly,** *adv.*

Ar·is·toph·a·nes (ar′is tof′ə nēz′) 448?–385 B.C., Greek writer of comic plays.

Ar·is·to·te·li·an (ar′is tə tē′lē ən, ə ris′tə tē′lē ən) *adj.* relating to or characteristic of Aristotle or his philosophy: *Aristotelian logic.* —*n.* a follower of Aristotle or his philosophy.

Ar·is·tot·le (ar′is tot′əl) 384–322 B.C., Greek philosopher and scientist.

a·rith·me·tic (*n.,* ə rith′mə tik′; *adj.,* ar′ith met′ik) *n.* **1.** the science and technique of computing with numbers. Arithmetic deals with four basic operations: addition, subtraction, multiplication, and division. **2.** an act of calculation using one or more of these operations: *You must have made a mistake in your arithmetic.* —*adj. also,* **ar·ith·met·i·cal** (ar′ith met′i cal). of, relating to, or according to the rules of arithmetic: *arithmetic calculations.* —**ar′ith·met′i·cal·ly,** *adv.*

a·rith·me·ti·cian (ə rith′mə tish′ən) *n.* a student of or an expert in arithmetic.

ar·ith·met·ic mean (ar′ith met′ik) a value that is obtained by dividing the sum of a set of quantities by the number of quantities; average. The arithmetic mean of 2, 4, 11, and 7 is 6.

ar·ith·met·ic progression (ar′ith met′ik) a series of numbers in which the difference between any two successive numbers is the same. 1, 3, 5, 7, 9 and 10, 17, 24, 31, 38 are arithmetic progressions.

Ariz., Arizona.

Ar·i·zo·na (ar′ə zō′nə) *n.* a state in the southwestern United States, bordering on Mexico. Capital, Phoenix. Area, 113,909 sq. mi. Pop. (1970), 1,772,482. Abbreviation, **Ariz.** —**Ar′i·zo′nan,** *adj., n.*

● **Arizona** comes from an Indian word meaning "little spring" or "place of the small spring" and originally referred to a very small area of present-day Arizona. With the discovery of silver, this region became famous and its name spread to include the surrounding territory.

---

ark (ärk) *n.* **1.** a large, flat-bottomed, clumsy boat. **2.** the ark built by Noah. **3.** see **Ark of the Covenant.**

Ark., Arkansas.

Ar·kan·sas (är′kən sô′; *def. 2 also* är kan′zəs) *n.* **1.** a state in the south-central United States. Capital, Little Rock. Area, 53,104 sq. mi. Pop. (1970), 1,923,295. Abbreviation, **Ark.** **2.** a river flowing from west-central Colorado into the Mississippi River. —**Ar·kan·san** (är-kan′zən), *adj., n.*

● **Arkansas** is the form that French explorers gave to a Siouan tribal name, which meant "downstream people." This name was transferred from the tribe to the river near the original Indian village, from there to the surrounding territory, and eventually to the state. The English version originally ended with a "w," the spelling closest to the French pronunciation, but the earlier French spelling with a final "s" was made official later.

Ark of the Covenant **1.** a sacred chest in which the ancient Hebrews kept the two stone tablets containing the Ten Commandments. **2.** a cabinet in a synagogue in which the scrolls of the Torah and other sacred books are kept.

Ark·wright, Sir Richard (ärk′rīt′) 1732–1792, English inventor and industrialist.

Ar·ling·ton (är′ling tən) *n.* **1.** one of the largest national cemeteries in the United States, in northwestern Virginia. **2.** a county in northern Virginia, a suburb of Washington, D.C. Pop. (1970), 174,284. **3.** a city in northeastern Texas. Pop. (1970), 90,643.

arm¹ (ärm) *n.* **1.** either of the two upper limbs of the human body, especially the part between the shoulder and the wrist. **2.** the forelimb of any animal. **3.** something used to support or cover the human arm: *the arm of a chair, the arm of a coat.* **4.** anything branching out from a larger body: *an arm of the sea, the arm of a phonograph.* **5.** a branch or part of an organization: *Congress is an arm of the government.* **6.** authority; power: *the arm of the law.* [Old English *earm* this part of the body.]
  at arm's length. on a formal or unfriendly basis; at a distance.
  with open arms. with an eager welcome; cordially.

arm² (ärm) *n.* **1.** any weapon, especially a firearm. See also **arms.** **2.** a combat branch of the armed forces: *the air arm of the Marine Corps.* —*v.t.* **1.** to provide with weapons: *to arm troops for war.* **2.** to provide with something that protects or strengthens: *The porcupine is armed with quills.* **3.** to prepare; equip: *College armed her with a good education.* **4.** to set or prepare to explode or detonate: *to arm a bomb, to arm a missile.* —*v.i.* to prepare for war or conflict, especially by equipping oneself with weapons: *The soldiers armed for battle.* [Old French *armer* to provide with weapons, from Latin *armāre*, from *arma* weapons.]

ar·ma·da (är mä′də) *n.* **1.** a large fleet of warships. **2. the Armada.** see **Spanish Armada.**

ar·ma·dil·lo (är′mə dil′ō) *n. pl.,* **ar·ma·dil·los.** any of several insect-eating, burrowing animals having an armorlike shell of bony plates, a long snout, strong, sharp claws, and a long tail. Armadillos are found in South America and parts of the southern United States. [Spanish *armadillo* literally, little armored creature; because of its armorlike shell.]

Armadillo

Ar·ma·ged·don (är′mə ged′ən) *n.* **1.** the site of the world's great and final battle between the forces of good and evil, as foretold in the Bible. **2.** any great and decisive battle.

ar·ma·ment (är′mə mənt) *n.* **1. armaments.** military forces, equipment, and supplies, especially considered as the entire military strength of a nation. **2.** *also,* **armaments.** the weapons with which a military unit, ship, or plane is equipped. **3.** the process of arming: *The country's armament took two months.*

ar·ma·ture (är′mə chər) *n.* **1.** a rotating part of an electric motor or dynamo, consisting of an iron core with coils of wire around it. **2.** a piece of soft iron placed across the poles of a magnet to preserve magnetic power. **3.** a vibrating iron part of an electric buzzer or relay. **4.** a part or organ of an animal or plant that functions as a protective covering, such as the shell of a turtle. **5.** any protective covering; armor. **6.** a framework used to support clay or other material that is being made into a sculpture.

arm·band (ärm′band′) *n.* a band worn around the upper part of the arm as a badge or symbol: *The dead man's family wore black armbands as a sign of mourning.*

arm·chair (ärm′cher′) *n.* a chair with supports at each side for one's arms or elbows. —*adj.* dealing with problems indirectly or without actual experience: *My uncle is an armchair detective, with a huge library of mystery novels.*

armed (ärmd) *adj.* **1.** having, bearing, or supported by arms or weapons: *armed troops, an armed conflict.* **2.** prepared; equipped: *He came to the meeting armed with facts and figures.* **3.** having an arm or arms. ▲ usually used in combination: *one-armed, long-armed.*

armed forces, all of the military forces of a nation, considered as a whole. The armed forces of the United States include the Army, Navy, Marines, Air Force, and Coast Guard.

Ar·me·ni·a (är mē′nē ə) *n.* **1.** a republic in the southwestern Soviet Union, bordering on Turkey and Iran. Official name: **Armenian Soviet Socialist Republic.** Area, 11,500 sq. mi. Pop. (1970), 2,492,000. **2.** an ancient country in northeastern Asia Minor, now a region consisting of Soviet Armenia and parts of eastern Turkey and northwestern Iran. —**Ar·me′ni·an,** *adj., n.*

arm·ful (ärm′fool′) *n. pl.,* **arm·fuls.** as much as one arm or both arms can hold: *an armful of packages.*

arm·hole (ärm′hōl′) *n.* an opening in a garment for the arm.

ar·mi·stice (är′mi stis) *n.* a temporary stop of fighting by mutual agreement; truce.

Armistice Day, see **Veterans Day.**

ar·mor (är′mər) *also, British,* **ar·mour.** *n.* **1.** a covering, as of metal, formerly worn to protect the body in battle. **2.** a protective metal covering used on tanks, warships, or other military vehicles and equipment. **3.** armored military vehicles. **4.** any protective covering, such as that of an armadillo. —*v.t.* to cover or furnish with armor. —**ar′mor·like′,** *adj.*

ar·mored (är′mərd) *also, British,* **ar·moured.** *adj.* **1.** protected by armor: *an armored ship.* **2.** equipped with armored vehicles: *armored troops.*

armored car, a vehicle covered with armor plate, often used to transport money or other valuable cargo.

Helmet

Beaver
Gorget

Breastplate

Gauntlet

Cuisse

Greave

Armor

ar·mor·er (är′mər ər) *also, British,* **ar·mour·er.** *n.* **1.** a person who makes or repairs armor. **2.** a military man or other person who has charge of firearms. **3.** a person or company that makes weapons.

ar·mo·ri·al (är môr′ē əl) *adj.* relating to heraldry.

armor plate, specially hardened steel used as a protective covering, as on a tank or warship.

at; āpe; cär; end; mē; it; īce; hot; ōld; fôrk; wood; fōōl; oil; out; up; turn; sing; thin; **this**; hw in white; zh in treasure. The symbol ə stands for the sound of **a** in about, **e** in taken, **i** in pencil, **o** in lemon, and **u** in circus.

ar·mor·y (är′mər ē) *n. pl.,* **ar·mor·ies. 1.** a building that is the headquarters and training center of a National Guard or other military reserve unit. **2.** a place where weapons are kept; arsenal. **3.** a place where weapons are manufactured.

ar·mour (är′mər) *British.* another spelling of **armor.**

arm·pit (ärm′pit′) *n.* the hollow under the arm at the shoulder.

arm·rest (ärm′rest′) *n.* a support for the arm or elbow, as on a chair.

arms (ärmz) *n., pl.* **1.** weapons, especially firearms: *The defeated troops laid down their arms.* **2.** see **coat of arms.**
  to bear arms. a. to possess or carry weapons: *The Bill of Rights gives each citizen the right to bear arms.* **b.** to serve in the armed forces.
  to take up arms. to prepare to fight.
  under arms. furnished with weapons; ready for war: *That country has over two million men under arms.*
  up in arms. ready to fight; hostile; indignant: *The residents were up in arms over the plan to build a highway through their property.*

Arm·strong, Neil (ärm′strông) 1930—, U.S. astronaut, the first man to set foot on the moon.

ar·my (är′mē) *n. pl.,* **ar·mies. 1.** a large, organized body of soldiers armed and trained for combat on land: *The ancient Romans had a powerful army.* **2.** *also,* **Army.** the branch of the military forces of a nation trained chiefly for land operations. In some countries it also includes the air force. **3.** in the U.S. Army, the largest military unit, consisting of two or more corps. **4.** a large body of persons organized for a common cause: *An army of protesting students marched to the White House.* **5.** any large group; multitude: *an army of ants, an army of motorists on their way to the beach.*

ar·ni·ca (är′ni kə) *n.* **1.** any of a group of plants bearing clusters of yellow flowers. **2.** a medicinal liquid made from the dried flowers and roots of this plant.

Ar·no (är′nō) *n.* a river in north-central Italy.

Ar·nold (är′nəld) **1. Benedict.** 1741–1801, U.S. general in the Revolutionary War who became a traitor. **2. Matthew.** 1822–1888, English poet, critic, and essayist.

a·ro·ma (ə rō′mə) *n.* a pleasant or agreeable odor; fragrance.

ar·o·mat·ic (ar′ə mat′ik) *adj.* having an aroma; fragrant. —**ar′o·mat′i·cal·ly,** *adv.*

a·rose (ə rōz′) the past tense of **arise:** *I arose at seven o'clock this morning.*

a·round (ə round′) *prep.* **1.** in a circle about: *She wore a belt around her waist.* **2.** along the circumference or outer edge of: *to walk around the block.* **3.** so as to surround or envelop: *Her arms were around the child.* **4.** on all sides of: *Around us lay the ruins of the burned building.* **5.** here and there in: *The tourists wandered around the city.* **6.** somewhere in or near: *Please stay around the house.* **7.** somewhat near, as in time or amount; about: *I'll meet you around six o'clock.* **8.** on another side of: *Her house is around the corner from mine.* —*adv.* **1.** in a circle or circular course: *The wheel spun around and around.* **2.** in circumference: *The pole measures two feet around.* **3.** on all sides; in various directions: *She looked around for a policeman.* **4.** here and there; about: *We spread the news around.* **5.** *Informal.* somewhere near: *Why not stay around for a few minutes?* **6.** to a particular place: *Come around again tomorrow.* **7.** in or to the opposite direction: *He spun around quickly.* ▲ See **round** for usage note.

a·rous·al (ə rou′zəl) *n.* the act of arousing or the state of being aroused.

a·rouse (ə rouz′) *v.t.,* **a·roused, a·rous·ing. 1.** to stir up;

excite: *His angry speech aroused the crowd.* **2.** to awaken: *His friend aroused him for breakfast.*

ar·peg·gio (är pej′ē ō′) *n. pl.,* **ar·peg·gi·os.** *Music.* **1.** the playing of the notes of a chord in succession. **2.** a chord played in this way.

ar·que·bus (är′kwə bəs) *n. pl.,* **ar·que·bus·es.** another spelling of **harquebus.**

ar·raign (ə rān′) *v.t.* to state formally the charge against (someone) before a judge, and record an answer to the charge. —**ar·raign′ment,** *n.*

ar·range (ə rānj′) *v.,* **ar·ranged, ar·rang·ing.** —*v.t.* **1.** to put in proper, convenient, or pleasing order: *to arrange a list of names in alphabetical order, to arrange the furniture in a room.* **2.** to help to bring about; prepare for; plan: *Who arranged the meeting?* **3.** to settle; determine: *to arrange the terms of payment of a debt.* **4.** to adapt (a musical composition) for instruments or voices for which it was not originally written. —*v.i.* **1.** to make plans or preparations: *Can you arrange to meet us tonight?* **2.** to come to an agreement: *I'll arrange with him about the tickets.* —**ar·rang′er,** *n.*

ar·range·ment (ə rānj′mənt) *n.* **1.** the act of putting in order or the state of being put in order: *The arrangement of the books took two hours.* **2.** the result of arranging or ordering; something arranged in a particular way: *a flower arrangement.* **3.** the style or manner in which something is ordered: *He drew a diagram showing the arrangement of electrons in an atom.* **4. arrangements.** plans; preparations: *to make arrangements for a dance.* **5.** settlement; adjustment: *The arrangement of the dispute pleased us all.* **6.a.** an adaptation of a musical composition for instruments or voices for which it was not originally written. **b.** any musical work so adapted.

ar·rant (ar′ənt) *adj.* out-and-out; downright: *an arrant fool.*

ar·ras (ar′əs) *n.* **1.** a type of tapestry with a rich design. **2.** any screen or wall hanging of tapestry. [From *Arras,* a city in northern France, where this tapestry was made.]

ar·ray (ə rā′) *n.* **1.** an orderly grouping or arrangement, as of troops for battle. **2.** a large, imposing collection; display: *an array of jewels.* **3.** persons or things on display or in order: *The movie features an array of famous stars.* **4.** clothing, especially fine clothing; attire: *She was dressed in rich array.* —*v.t.* **1.** to place in order: *to array troops.* **2.** to dress, especially in fine clothing; adorn: *She was arrayed like a queen.*

ar·rears (ə rērz′) *n., pl.* money that is due but has not been paid.
  in arrears. behind in payments, duties, or obligations.

ar·rest (ə rest′) *v.t.* **1.** to seize or take into custody by authority of the law: *The police arrested the criminal.* **2.** to stop; check: *to arrest the progress of a disease with drugs.* **3.** to catch and hold; engage: *This newspaper article arrested my attention.* —*n.* **1.** a seizure by authority of the law; the act of taking into custody: *There were ten arrests in the town yesterday.* **2.** the act of stopping; check.
  under arrest. held by authority of the law.

ar·rest·ing (ə res′ting) *adj.* holding the attention; striking.

ar·riv·al (ə rī′vəl) *n.* **1.** the act of arriving: *Reporters were awaiting the arrival of the President.* **2.** a person or thing that arrives or has arrived.

ar·rive (ə rīv′) *v.i.,* **ar·rived, ar·riv·ing. 1.** to reach a place by traveling: *We will arrive in Denver at midnight.* **2.** (of time) to be at hand; come: *The week of exams has arrived.* **3.** to become successful or famous: *After writing for years, he has finally arrived as a novelist.*
  to arrive at. to come to or reach: *We arrived at the decision after much discussion.*

ar·ri·ve·der·ci (ä′rē ve der′chē) *interj.* until we meet again; good-by for now. [Italian *arrivederci*.]

ar·ro·gance (ar′ə gəns) *n.* too much pride or confidence mixed with a lack of respect for other people; conceit; haughtiness.

ar·ro·gant (ar′ə gənt) *adj.* characterized by or showing too much pride and a lack of respect for other people; conceited and haughty: *an arrogant person, an arrogant attitude.* —**ar′ro·gant·ly,** *adv.*

ar·ro·gate (ar′ə gāt′) *v.t.,* **ar·ro·gat·ed, ar·ro·gat·ing.** to claim or seize without right: *The dictator arrogated powers that belonged to the people.* —**ar′ro·ga′tion,** *n.*

ar·row (ar′ō) *n.* **1.** a slender shaft, usually pointed at one end and having feathers at the other, made to be shot from a bow. **2.** a symbol in the shape of an arrow, used to indicate direction or position, as on a road sign. **3.** something like an arrow in shape or use: *An arrow of light shone through the window.*

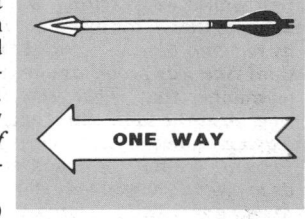

Arrows

ar·row·head (ar′ō hed′) *n.* the pointed tip or head of an arrow.

ar·row·root (ar′ō rōōt′, ar′ō root′) *n.* **1.** an easily digestible starch made from the roots of a tropical American plant, used as a thickening agent in cooking. **2.** the plant itself, widely grown in the West Indies and other tropical regions. It has long, pointed leaves and small, white flowers. [South American Indians used the *root* of this plant to absorb poison from *arrow* wounds.]

ar·roy·o (ə roi′ō) *n. pl.,* **ar·roy·os. 1.** a dry bed of a stream; gully. **2.** a small river or stream.

ar·se·nal (är′sə nəl) *n.* **1.** a place for storing or making arms and ammunition. **2.** a collection of firearms or other weapons. **3.** a store or collection: *He had an arsenal of facts and figures to support his argument.*

ar·se·nic (*n.,* är′sə nik; *adj.,* är sen′ik) *n.* **1.** a chemical element, usually in the form of silver-gray or blackish crystals with metallic luster, used especially in alloys and poisonous compounds. **2.** a white, tasteless, highly poisonous compound, used especially in rat, insect, and weed poisons. Symbol: **As**

ar·son (är′sən) *n.* the crime of deliberately setting fire to a building or other property.

ar·son·ist (är′sə nist) *n.* a person who commits arson.

art¹ (ärt) *n.* **1.** the creation or study of the beautiful or the meaningful, as in painting, music, literature, or drama. **2.** a particular activity carried on for the purpose of creating something beautiful or meaningful. Painting, sculpture, and literature are forms of art. **3.** the works produced by creative activity: *an exhibit of Indian art.* **4.** a special skill; knack: *He is a master of the art of saying things well.* **5.** a skilled craft or occupation: *the navigator's art, the art of diplomacy.* **6. the arts. a.** the different forms of creative activity thought of as a group. **b.** the branches of learning that are not sciences; liberal arts; humanities. **7.** a branch of learning or study: *He took a course in industrial arts.* **8.** human skill or effort, as distinguished from the work of nature. **9.** sly cleverness; cunning. [Old French *art* skill, from Latin *ars* skill.]

art² (ärt) *Archaic.* the second person singular, present indicative of **be:** *Thou art not for the fashion of these times* (Shakespeare). [Old English *eart* (thou) art.]

Ar·te·mis (är′tə mis) *n. Greek Mythology.* the goddess of the hunt and of the moon, and twin sister of Apollo. In Roman mythology she was called Diana.

ar·te·ri·al (är tēr′ē əl) *adj.* **1.** of, relating to, or like an artery or arteries. **2.** of, relating to, or designating the blood in the arteries. Arterial blood becomes bright red as a result of mixing with oxygen as it passes through the lungs.

ar·te·ri·ole (är tēr′ē ōl′) *n.* any of the very small blood vessels located at the ends of the arteries and serving to carry blood from the arteries to the capillaries.

ar·te·ri·o·scle·ro·sis (är tēr′ē ō skli rō′sis) *n.* a disease in which the walls of the arteries thicken and harden, thus making it difficult for the blood to circulate.

ar·ter·y (är′tər ē) *n. pl.,* **ar·ter·ies. 1.** one of the tubes carrying blood away from the heart to all parts of the body. **2.** a main road or channel, as of communication or transportation.

ar·te·sian well (är tē′zhən) a well from which water rises without pumping as a result of underground water pressure.

art·ful (ärt′fəl) *adj.* **1.** showing cunning or deceit; crafty: *The bank robbers had artful ways of avoiding capture by the police.* **2.** done with or showing art or skill: *The actor's performance was artful.* —**art′ful·ly,** *adv.* —**art′ful·ness,** *n.*

ar·thrit·ic (är thrit′ik) *adj.* of, relating to, or afflicted with arthritis. —*n.* a person who is afflicted with arthritis.

ar·thri·tis (är thrī′tis) *n.* a painful inflammation of a joint or joints of the body.

ar·thro·pod (är′thrə pod′) *n.* any of a group of animals without backbones, that have jointed legs and bodies, including insects, spiders, and crabs.

Ar·thur (är′thər) *n.* **1.** a legendary king of ancient Britain and the leader of the knights of the Round Table. The real King Arthur was probably a military chieftain who led the Britons against the Saxons early in the sixth century A.D. **2. Chester A.** 1830–1886, the twenty-first president of the United States, from 1881 to 1885.

Ar·thu·ri·an (är thoor′ē ən) *adj.* relating to King Arthur or to the legends about him and his knights.

ar·ti·choke (är′tə chōk′) *n.* **1.** a thistlelike plant belonging to the composite family. **2.** the yellowish-green flower head of this plant, cooked and eaten as a vegetable.

ar·ti·cle (är′ti kəl) *n.* **1.** a piece of writing on a particular subject, forming part of a larger publication, such as a newspaper, magazine, or encyclopedia: *The professor wrote an article on space exploration for the magazine.* **2.** a particular thing or object; item: *Several articles were stolen from the house. She bought some new articles of clothing.* **3.** a separate clause or section of a formal document, such as a treaty, constitution, or contract: *Article I of*

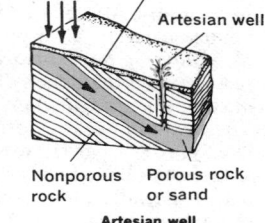

Rainfall Topsoil

Artesian well

Nonporous rock   Porous rock or sand

Artesian well

Artichoke

at; āpe; cär; end; mē; it; īce; hot; ōld; fôrk; wood; fōōl; oil; out; up; turn; sing; thin; this; hw in white; zh in treasure. The symbol ə stands for the sound of **a** in about, **e** in taken, **i** in pencil, **o** in lemon, and **u** in circus.

the U.S. Constitution deals with the powers of Congress. **4.** *Grammar.* any one of the words *a, an,* or *the,* used before a noun or noun phrase, as in *a house, an apple, the mayor. A* and *an* are indefinite articles and *the* is the definite article.

Articles of Confederation, the first constitution of the United States, adopted by the thirteen original colonies in 1781. It was replaced by the present Constitution in 1788.

ar·tic·u·late (*adj.,* är tik′yə lit; *v.,* är tik′yə lāt′) *adj.* **1.** spoken clearly in distinct syllables and words: *When the boy mumbled, what he said was not articulate enough to be understood.* **2.** able to speak: *The baby was not yet articulate.* **3.** able to express one's thoughts clearly and effectively: *The senator was an articulate spokesman for civil rights.* **4.** said or presented clearly and effectively: *The lawyer won the case because he made an articulate plea to the jury.* **5.** having joints; segmented: *an articulate animal.* —*v.,* **ar·tic·u·lat·ed, ar·tic·u·lat·ing.** —*v.t.* **1.** to pronounce clearly. **2.** to put into words; express effectively: *He found it hard to articulate his feelings toward her.* —*v.i.* **1.** to pronounce syllables and words clearly: *An actor must be able to articulate.* **2.** to form a joint or connection: *The bones of the arm articulate at the elbow.* —**ar·tic′u·late·ly,** *adv.* —**ar·tic′u·late·ness,** *n.* —**ar·tic′u·la′tion,** *n.*

ar·ti·fact (är′tə fakt′) *n.* anything made or changed by man, especially a tool, weapon, or other simple object used in ancient times.

ar·ti·fice (är′tə fis) *n.* **1.** a clever or cunning trick: *The prisoner escaped from jail by an artifice.* **2.** trickery; deception.

ar·tif·i·cer (är tif′ə sər) *n.* a skilled workman; craftsman.

ar·ti·fi·cial (är′tə fish′əl) *adj.* **1.** not natural; man-made: *A lamp gives artificial light.* **2.** made in imitation of something natural or real: *artificial flowers.* **3.** not sincere or genuine; affected: *artificial manners, an artificial show of sympathy.* —**ar′ti·fi′cial·ly,** *adv.*

ar·ti·fi·ci·al·i·ty (är′tə fish′ē al′ə tē) *n. pl.,* **ar·ti·fi·ci·al·i·ties. 1.** the quality of being artificial. **2.** something that is artificial.

artificial respiration, the forcing of air into and out of the lungs to restore normal breathing to a person who has stopped breathing or is having great difficulty in breathing.

ar·til·ler·y (är til′ər ē) *n.* **1.** large, heavy, mounted firearms, such as cannons, howitzers, and mortars. **2.** the part of an army that uses such firearms.

ar·til·ler·y·man (är til′ər ē mən) *n. pl.,* **ar·til·lery·men** (är til′ər ē mən). a soldier in the artillery.

ar·ti·san (är′tə zən) *n.* a person who is skilled in a particular craft; craftsman.

art·ist (är′tist) *n.* **1.** a person who is skilled in or whose work is one of the arts, especially a painter or sculptor. **2.** a skilled public performer: *Singers, dancers, and other artists performed on the television show.* **3.** a person who shows talent or skill in his work: *He is a real artist at planning a political campaign.*

ar·tis·tic (är tis′tik) *adj.* **1.** of or relating to art or artists. **2.** skillfully and tastefully done: *The dancer gave an artistic performance.* —**ar·tis′ti·cal·ly,** *adv.*

art·ist·ry (är′tis trē) *n.* artistic quality, methods, skill, or workmanship.

art·less (ärt′lis) *adj.* **1.** without trickery or deceit; sincere; naive: *the artless questions of a young child.* **2.** not artificial; simple; natural: *The dancer moved with artless grace.* **3.** lacking skill or knowledge; ignorant. —**art′less·ly,** *adv.* —**art′less·ness,** *n.*

ar·um (er′əm) *n.* **1.** any of a group of small plants that have a cluster of tiny flowers on a spike surrounded by a large, flowerlike leaf. **2.** any of several similar plants, such as the calla lily.

-ary *suffix* **1.** (used to form nouns) a person or thing connected with: *missionary, revolutionary.* **2.** (used to form adjectives) being or relating to: *secondary, honorary.*

Ar·y·an (er′ē ən, ar′ē ən) *n.* **1.** a member of a group of prehistoric wandering people who spoke an Indo-European language. **2.** a former name for the Indo-European family of languages. **3.** in the doctrine of the Nazi party: **a.** a member of the Nordic race, supposedly superior to other racial groups. **b.** any non-Jewish Caucasian. —*adj.* of or relating to Aryans.

as (az) *adv.* **1.** to the same amount or degree; equally: *The first movie was exciting, but the second was not as good.* **2.** for example; for instance: *I have dresses in several colors, as red and blue.* —*conj.* **1.** to the same degree or extent that: *She was proud as she could be.* **2.** in the same way or manner that: *That tribe lives as men did in the Stone Age.* **3.** at the same time that; while: *Bob arrived as we were leaving.* **4.** because; since: *As you are not ready, we will wait for you.* **5.** that the result is or was: *He was so insulting as to offend everyone.* **6.** though: *Late as it was, we decided to visit our friends.* —*prep.* in the manner or role of: *I speak as a friend.* —*pron.* **1.** that; which: *He goes to the same school as I do.* **2.** a fact that: *That book belongs to me, as you well know.*

> **as for** or **as to.** with respect to; concerning: *As for vacations, I prefer the beach to the country.*
>
> **as if** or **as though.** as it would be if: *The rude boy behaved as if he had no manners.*
>
> **as is.** in the present condition; just as it is: *The house will be sold as is.*
>
> **as of.** beginning at or on (a certain time or date): *As of January 6, my brother will be old enough to drive a car.*
>
> **as yet.** up to this time; so far: *Ed has not as yet finished his work.*

As, the symbol for arsenic.

as·a·fet·i·da (as′ə fet′ə də) *also,* **as·a·foet·i·da.** *n.* a brown gum resin that smells like garlic, obtained from the roots of various central Asian plants of the parsley family. It was formerly used in medicines.

as·bes·tos (as bes′təs, az bes′təs) *n.* any of several varieties of a grayish mineral whose fibers may be woven or pressed into material that does not burn, is resistant to heat and chemical action, and does not conduct electricity.

as·cend (ə send′) *v.i.* **1.** to move upward; rise: *The elevator ascended slowly.* **2.** to move upward to a higher condition, rank, or level: *He has ascended to the rank of general.* —*v.t.* **1.** to go up (something); climb: *to ascend a mountain.* **2.** to come to occupy; succeed to: *to ascend the throne.*

as·cen·dan·cy (ə sen′dən sē) *also,* **as·cen·den·cy.** *n.* the quality or state of having power or control; domination: *British ascendancy in Asia ended after World War II.*

as·cen·dant (ə sen′dənt) *also,* **as·cen·dent.** *adj.* **1.** moving upward; ascending; rising. **2.** superior; dominant: *an ascendant position in public life.* —*n.* a position of power or control.

> **in the ascendant.** in or coming to a dominant, influential, or superior position.

as·cen·sion (ə sen′shən) *n.* **1.** the act or process of ascending. **2. Ascension.** in the Bible, the passing of Christ from earth to heaven after His resurrection.

Ascension Day, the day on which Christ passed from earth to heaven, now celebrated annually on the fortieth day after Easter. Also, **Ascension Thursday.**

as·cent (ə sent′) *n.* **1.** a movement upward; rise: *the ascent of a balloon filled with helium.* **2.** the act of climbing or going up: *Snow made an ascent of the mountain impossible.* **3.** a place or way that one ascends; upward slope: *a steep ascent.* **4.** a movement upward in condition, rank, or level: *His fellow workers were surprised by his rapid ascent to the presidency of the company.*

as·cer·tain (as′ər tān′) *v.t.* to find out with certainty; determine: *Have you ascertained the identity of the person who wrote the letter?* **—as′cer·tain′a·ble,** *adj.* **—as′cer·tain′a·bly,** *adv.* **—as′cer·tain′ment,** *n.*

as·cet·ic (ə set′ik) *n.* a person who lives simply and denies himself any of the material comforts and pleasures of life, especially for religious reasons. **—***adj.* relating to or characteristic of ascetics or asceticism. **—as·cet′i·cal·ly,** *adv.*

as·cet·i·cism (ə set′ə siz′əm) *n.* the way of life of an ascetic; extreme self-denial.

a·scor·bic acid (ə skôr′bik) see **vitamin C.**

as·cot (as′kət, as′kot) *n.* a necktie or scarf worn with one end placed over the other. [From *Ascot,* a racetrack in England where this neckwear was fashionable.]

as·cribe (əs krīb′) *v.t.* **as·cribed, as·crib·ing. 1.** to regard (something) as coming from a particular cause or source: *They ascribed the accident to carelessness.* **2.** to think of (something) as belonging to: *to ascribe selfishness to other people.* **—as·crib′a·ble,** *adj.*

as·crip·tion (əs krip′shən) *n.* **1.** the act of ascribing. **2.** an expression or statement that ascribes.

Ascot

a·sep·tic (ə sep′tik, ā sep′tik) *adj.* free from disease-causing germs. **—a·sep′ti·cal·ly,** *adv.*

a·sex·u·al (ā sek′shōō əl) *adj. Biology.* **1.** without sex or distinct sexual organs. **2.** not involving the union of male and female germ cells. The cell division of amebas is a form of asexual reproduction. **—a·sex′u·al·ly,** *adv.*

As·gard (as′gärd) *n. Norse Mythology.* the home of the gods and of heroes killed in battle.

ash¹ (ash) *n.* **1.** a gray-white, powdery substance left after something has been burned. See also **ashes. 2.** fine particles of lava. [Old English *asce* this powdery substance.]

ash² (ash) *n. pl.,* **ash·es. 1.** any of a group of shade trees related to the olive, usually having winged seeds. **2.** the wood of any of these trees, used for timber. [Old English *æsc* this tree.]

a·shamed (ə shāmd′) *adj.* **1.** feeling shame, as when a person realizes that his actions or thoughts are foolish or improper: *John was ashamed that he had become angry over such a foolish thing.* **2.** unwilling through fear or shame: *He was ashamed to tell his family that he had failed the examination.* **—a·sham·ed·ly** (ə shā′mid lē), *adv.*

ash can, a can or similar receptacle for ashes or trash.

ash·en¹ (ash′ən) *adj.* **1.** ash-colored; pale. **2.** consisting of ashes. [*Ash¹* + *-en².*]

ash·en² (ash′ən) *adj.* made of the wood of the ash tree. [*Ash²* + *-en².*]

ash·es (ash′iz) *n., pl.* **1.** a gray-white powdery substance left after something has been burned. **2.** this substance together with partially burned material, as in a fireplace. **3.** the remains of a dead body after it has been cremated or has decayed. **4.** the remains of something that has been destroyed; ruins: *Their hopes were turned to ashes by the crushing defeat.*

a·shore (ə shôr′) *adv., adj.* **1.** on or to the shore. **2.** on land.

ash tray, a receptacle for tobacco ashes.

Ash Wednesday, the first day of Lent. It falls on the seventh Wednesday before Easter. [From the custom of placing *ashes* on the forehead as a symbol of repentance on this day.]

ash·y (ash′ē) *adj.,* **ash·i·er, ash·i·est. 1.** of, resembling, or covered with ashes. **2.** ash-colored; pale.

A·sia (ā′zhə) *n.* the largest continent, bounded on the west by the Ural and Caucasus Mountains, the Black, Mediterranean, and Red Seas, on the south by the Indian Ocean, and on the east by the Pacific Ocean. Area, (approx.) 17,124,000 sq. mi. Pop. (1971 est.), 2,104,000,000.

Asia Minor, a peninsula in western Asia, bounded by the Black and Mediterranean Seas. It includes most of the Asian part of Turkey. Area, 287,000 sq. mi.

A·sian (ā′zhən) *adj.* of or relating to Asia or its people. **—***n.* a person who was born or is living in Asia. ▲ See **Asiatic** for usage note.

Asian flu, a kind of influenza caused by a strain of virus first recognized in Asia in 1957.

A·si·at·ic (ā′zhē at′ik) *n., adj.* another word for **Asian.** ▲ **Asiatic** is now generally considered offensive; **Asian** is preferred.

a·side (ə sīd′) *adv.* **1.** on or to one side; out of the way; away: *Step aside, please.* **2.** out of consideration or use: *Mountain climbing is enjoyable if you can put aside your fear of heights.* **3.** in reserve; in keeping: *The librarian promised to keep that book aside for me.* **—***n.* a remark not intended to be heard by all those who are present, especially an actor's remark intended for the audience but not the other characters.
   aside from. a. apart from; independent of: *Your comment is aside from the argument.* **b.** except for: *I have done all the housework aside from washing the dishes.*

as·i·nine (as′ə nīn′) *adj.* stupid; silly. **—as′i·nine′ly,** *adv.*

as·i·nin·i·ty (as′ə nin′ə tē) *n. pl.,* **as·i·nin·i·ties. 1.** the quality of being asinine; silliness. **2.** something that is asinine, such as a remark.

ask (ask) *v.t.* **1.** to put a question about; inquire about: *We asked the way to town.* **2.** to put a question to; inquire of: *Ask the teacher if you're not sure what the word means.* **3.** to call for the answer to: *to ask a question.* **4.a.** to make a request of: *He asked a policeman for directions.* **b.** to make a request for: *to ask a favor.* **5.** to invite: *She asked twenty people to the party.* **6.** to set as a price; demand: *to ask a high price for an old car.* **7.** to require: *He asks too much from his workers.* **—***v.i.* **1.** to make inquiries: *Ted asked about you last week.* **2.** to make a request: *She asked for another piece of cake.*

a·skance (ə skans′) *adv.* with a side glance; sideways.
   to look askance at. to distrust or disapprove of; be suspicious of: *She looked askance at Jim's rude behavior.*

a·skew (ə skyōō′) *adv., adj.* on or to one side; out of the proper position: *The painting hung askew until she straightened it.*

a·slant (ə slant′) *adv.* in a slanting direction; on a slant. **—***adj.* slanting. **—***prep.* slantingly across or over.

a·sleep (ə slēp′) *adj.* **1.** in a state of sleep; sleeping: *The baby is asleep.* **2.** (of an arm, leg, or other body part) without feeling; numb: *His foot was asleep because he sat in the same position for so long.* **—***adv.* into a state of sleep: *Please wake me if I fall asleep.*

at; āpe; cär; end; mē; it; īce; hot; ōld; fôrk; wood; fōōl; oil; out; up; turn; sing; thin; **th**is; hw in white; zh in treasure. The symbol ə stands for the sound of **a** in about, **e** in taken, **i** in pencil, **o** in lemon, and **u** in circus.

asp (asp) *n.* **1.** a kind of cobra native to Egypt. It was worshiped by the ancient Egyptians and is said to have been used by Cleopatra to kill herself. **2.** any of several other poisonous snakes, especially a viper native to Europe.

as·par·a·gus (əs par′ə gəs) *n.* **1.** the young green or white spears of a plant of the lily family. It is cooked and eaten as a vegetable. The spears grow from underground stems and bear scalelike leaves at the tip. **2.** the plant itself. It is raised in most parts of the world.

ASPCA, American Society for the Prevention of Cruelty to Animals.

as·pect (as′pekt) *n.* **1.** any of the ways in which something can be viewed by the mind: *He didn't understand all the aspects of the problem. Looked at from this aspect, the situation doesn't seem as serious.* **2.** appearance; look: *the striking aspect of the mountains.* **3.** facial expression; countenance: *The minister was a dignified man of somber aspect.* **4.** the direction in which something faces; exposure: *This room has southern and western aspects.*

as·pen (as′pən) *n.* any of several poplar trees found in the Northern Hemisphere, bearing small, rounded leaves that tremble in the slightest breeze.

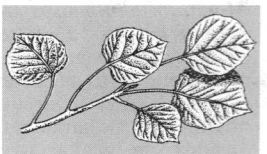
Aspen leaves

as·per·i·ty (as per′ə tē) *n. pl.,* **as·per·i·ties.** **1.** harshness of manner or temper; bitterness; severity: *She was so angry that she answered his question with great asperity.* **2.** hardship; difficulty: *The asperities of the frontier made life hard for the pioneers.*

as·per·sion (əs pur′zhən) *n.* **1.** a damaging or untrue statement; slander: *to cast aspersions on a person's good name.* **2.** the act of slandering; defaming.

as·phalt (as′fôlt) *n.* **1.** a brown or black tarlike substance, occurring in nature and also obtained as a byproduct of petroleum refining. **2.** a mixture of this substance with gravel or sand, used especially for paving roads. —*v.t.* to pave or cover with asphalt.

as·pho·del (as′fə del′) *n.* any of several plants of the lily family, having trumpet-shaped white or yellow flowers on a spike.

as·phyx·i·a (as fik′sē ə) *n.* a state of unconsciousness caused by a lack of oxygen and an increase of carbon dioxide in the blood and body tissues.

as·phyx·i·ate (as fik′sē āt′) *v.,* **as·phyx·i·at·ed, as·phyx·i·at·ing** —*v.t.* to cause to die or become unconscious because of lack of oxygen. —*v.i.* to die or become unconscious because of lack of oxygen. —**as·phyx′i·a′tion,** *n.*

as·pic (as′pik) *n.* a jelly made from meat, poultry, fish, or vegetable juices, chilled and often served as a molded salad dish.

as·pi·rant (as′pər ənt, əs pīr′ənt) *n.* a person who aspires to or seeks something, such as advancement, a high position, or honors.

as·pi·rate (*v.,* as′pə rāt′; *n., adj.,* as′pər it) *v.t.,* **as·pi·rat·ed, as·pi·rat·ing.** **1.** to begin the pronunciation of (a word or syllable) with a puff of breath or with an *h* sound. In the pronunciation of the word *when,* when the *wh* is aspirated, the word is pronounced *hwen.* **2.** to follow (the pronunciation of a consonant) with a puff of breath. The letters *p, t,* and *k* are aspirated when followed by a vowel, as in *palm, ton,* and *kid.* **3.** to remove (something) by means of suction. —*n.* **1.** the sound of the letter *h.* **2.** a consonant whose pronunciation is followed by a puff of breath. —*adj.* pronounced with an aspirate or followed by a puff of breath.

as·pi·ra·tion (as′pə rā′shən) *n.* **1.** a strong desire to attain a goal; high ambition: *She has aspirations to become a great writer.* **2.** the object of such desire or ambition: *Being a doctor is his aspiration.* **3.** the act of breathing; a breath. **4.** the pronunciation of an aspirate. **5.** the removal of something, such as a fluid or gas from a body cavity, by the use of suction.

as·pi·ra·tor (as′pə rā′tər) *n.* **1.** any machine or device that uses suction. **2.** a medical instrument that removes fluids and gases from a body cavity by the use of suction.

as·pire (əs pīr′) *v.i.,* **as·pired, as·pir·ing.** to seek ambitiously to attain something; aim: *The young soldier aspired after glory. The senator aspired to the Presidency.*

as·pi·rin (as′pər in) *n.* **1.** a white, crystalline substance derived from salicylic acid, used in tablet form as a medicine to relieve pain and fever. **2.** a tablet of aspirin.

ass (as) *n. pl.,* **ass·es.** **1.** a long-eared animal of the horse family; donkey. **2.** a stupid person; fool.

as·sa·gai (as′ə gī′) *also,* **as·se·gai.** *n. pl.,* **as·sa·gais.** a slender spear made of hard wood, used by some tribes of southern Africa.

as·sail (ə sāl′) *v.t.* **1.** to attack with physical violence. **2.** to attack vigorously with arguments or abuse: *The townspeople assailed the mayor for raising taxes.* —**as·sail′a·ble,** *adj.* —**as·sail′er,** *n.*

as·sail·ant (ə sā′lənt) *n.* a person who assails; attacker: *The police rescued the man from his assailant.*

as·sas·sin (ə sas′in) *n.* someone who murders an important or famous person, especially for political reasons.

as·sas·si·nate (ə sas′ə nāt′) *v.t.,* **as·sas·si·nat·ed, as·sas·si·nat·ing.** to murder (an important or famous person), especially for political reasons: *The police captured the man who assassinated the President.* —**as·sas′si·na′tion,** *n.* —**as·sas′si·na′tor,** *n.*

as·sault (ə sôlt′) *n.* **1.** a violent or vigorous attack: *The lies told about him were an assault on his honor.* **2.** *Law.* an unlawful attempt or threat to do physical violence to a person. —*v.t.* to make an assault on; attack: *The soldiers assaulted the enemy fort.*

assault and battery *Law.* the carrying out of a threat to commit violence against a person.

as·say (*v.,* ə sā′; *n.,* ə sā′, as′ā) *v.t.* **1.** to test (an ore, mineral, alloy, or the like) by chemical means to determine the nature or quality of its ingredients: *They assayed the ore to find out how much gold was in it.* **2.** to put to trial; test: *The candidate assayed his chances of winning before deciding to run.* **3.** to try to do; attempt: *to assay a difficult task.* —*n.* **1.** a chemical analysis of an ore, mineral, alloy, or the like, to determine the nature or quality of its ingredients. **2.** any substance so analyzed. —**as·say′er,** *n.*

as·se·gai (as′ə gī′) *n. pl.,* **as·se·gais.** another spelling of **assagai.**

as·sem·blage (ə sem′blij) *n.* **1.** a group of persons or things gathered together; collection: *The entire assemblage wished Susan a happy birthday.* **2.** the act of putting or fitting parts together to construct something: *the assemblage of a model plane.* **3.** the act of assembling or the state of being assembled.

as·sem·ble (ə sem′bəl) *v.,* **as·sem·bled, as·sem·bling.** —*v.t.* **1.** to gather or bring together; collect: *Bob assembled a large stamp collection.* **2.** to put or fit together: *to assemble cars in a factory. The parts of the bicycle had to be assembled before I could ride it.* —*v.i.* to meet or come together; convene: *A crowd assembled outside the theater.* —**as·sem′bler,** *n.*

as·sem·bly (ə sem′blē) *n. pl.,* **as·sem·blies.** **1.** a group of people gathered together for a common purpose. **2.** a body of lawmakers. **3.** **Assembly.** in certain states of the United States, the lower house of the legislature.

4. the act or process of fitting together parts to make a whole. **5.** a group of parts that fit or work together. **6.** the act of assembling or the state of being assembled.

assembly line, a line of workers and machines along which a product is moved to be assembled. Each worker or machine adds something to the product in turn until it is put together completely.

as·sem·bly·man (ə sem′blē mən) *n. pl.,* **as·sem·bly·men** (ə sem′blē mən). a member of a legislative assembly, especially of the lower house of a state legislature. —**as·sem′bly·wom′an,** *n.*

as·sent (ə sent′) *v.i.* to express agreement; concur: *Frank thought the plan was foolish and refused to assent to it.* —*n.* agreement; consent: *The principal gave his assent to our idea.*

as·sert (ə surt′) *v.t.* **1.** to state firmly and clearly; affirm: *The lawyer asserted that his client was not guilty.* **2.** to insist upon recognition of: *He asserted his rights by demanding to be treated fairly.* —**as·sert′er,** *n.*

to assert oneself. to put forward or defend one's own position or rights in a bold manner.

as·ser·tion (ə sur′shən) *n.* **1.** a positive statement; declaration: *His assertion was later proven to be false.* **2.** the act of putting forward or maintaining.

as·ser·tive (ə sur′tiv) *adj.* bold and forward in manner; asserting oneself; aggressive: *He is an assertive person and always wants his own way.* —**as·ser′tive·ly,** *adv.* —**as·ser′tive·ness,** *n.*

as·sess (ə ses′) *v.t.* **1.** to set the official value of (property) for taxation. **2.** to fix the amount of (a tax, fine, or damages): *The judge assessed a fine of fifty dollars.* **3.** to tax or charge (a person or property): *The club assesses each member five dollars for dues.* **4.** to evaluate: *The coach assessed the ability of each player who tried out for the team.*

as·sess·ment (ə ses′mənt) *n.* **1.** the act of assessing. **2.** the amount or value assessed. **3.** an estimation; evaluation: *What is your assessment of the situation?*

as·ses·sor (ə ses′ər) *n.* a person who assesses property for taxation.

as·set (as′et) *n.* **1.** something valuable or useful; advantage: *Being tall is a great asset for a basketball player.* **2. assets.** the property and resources of a business or person that have a cash value and can be used to pay the owner's debts.

as·sev·er·ate (ə sev′ə rāt′) *v.t.,* **as·sev·er·at·ed, as·sev·er·at·ing.** to declare solemnly or positively; affirm. —**as·sev′er·a′tion,** *n.*

as·si·du·i·ty (as′ə dōō′ə tē, as′ə dyōō′ə tē) *n.* constant or careful attention; diligence.

as·sid·u·ous (ə sij′ōō əs) *adj.* constantly attentive; diligent: *Karen is an assiduous student who always works very hard.* —**as·sid′u·ous·ly,** *adv.* —**as·sid′u·ous·ness,** *n.*

as·sign (ə sīn′) *v.t.* **1.** to give out; distribute; allot: *The teacher assigned a different science project to each student.* **2.** to select for a duty or office; appoint: *A new principal was assigned to the school.* **3.** to fix definitely; designate: *The president of the club assigned a date for the next meeting.* **4.** *Law.* to transfer (a right, property, or interest): *When the farmer couldn't pay his debts, he had to assign his land to his creditors.* —**as·sign′a·ble,** *adj.* —**as·sign′er,** *n.*

as·sign·ee (ə sī′nē′) *n.* a person to whom something is assigned, especially one to whom a right, property, or interest is legally transferred.

as·sign·ment (ə sīn′mənt) *n.* **1.** something that is assigned, such as a task or job: *Our homework assignment included ten multiplication problems. The reporter's assignment was to write a story about the election.* **2.** the act of assigning or the state of being assigned: *His assignment to*

the new position meant that he would have to move to Boston. **3.** *Law.* **a.** the transfer of a right, property, or interest. **b.** a document by which such a transfer is made.

as·sim·i·late (ə sim′ə lāt′) *v.,* **as·sim·i·lat·ed, as·sim·i·lat·ing** —*v.t.* **1.** to take in and make part of oneself: *He assimilated every fact he could learn about his favorite baseball team.* **2.** to absorb and convert into living tissue: *In the human body, food is assimilated in the small intestine.* **3.** to absorb (a social group) into a larger or more dominant culture: *The United States has assimilated the immigrants of many different nations.* —*v.i.* to be or become assimilated. —**as·sim′i·la′tor,** *n.*

as·sim·i·la·tion (ə sim′ə lā′shən) *n.* **1.** the act of assimilating or the state of being assimilated. **2.** a process in which a social group gradually takes on the characteristics of a larger or more dominant culture. **3.** the process by which digested food is absorbed and converted into living tissue. **4.** in language, a process in which a sound changes to become similar to another nearby sound. *Grandma* pronounced *gramma* is an example of assimilation.

As·si·si (ə sē′zē) *n.* a town in central Italy, noted as the birthplace of Saint Francis.

as·sist (ə sist′) *v.t.* to give help or aid to: *He assisted his father in cleaning out the garage.* —*v.i.* to help; aid: *He assisted in choosing the site for the new building.* —*n.* **1.** the act of helping; aid: *He got the job with an assist from his uncle.* **2.** in baseball, a throwing or handling of the ball that helps a teammate to put out a base runner. **3.** in ice hockey or basketball, a pass that helps a teammate to score a goal.

as·sist·ance (ə sis′təns) *n.* the act of assisting; aid or support: *His assistance was very valuable to us during the project.*

as·sist·ant (ə sis′tənt) *n.* a person who assists; helper; aide: *His assistant took charge of the office while he was away.* —*adj.* serving in a position under another person: *The assistant principal helps the principal in running the school.*

as·siz·es (ə sī′ziz) *n.,pl.* in England, court sessions held periodically in each county to try cases by jury.

assn., association.

assoc. 1. associate. **2.** association.

as·so·ci·ate (*v.,* ə sō′shē āt′, ə sō′sē āt′; *n., adj.,* ə sō′shē it, ə sō′sē it) *v.,* **as·so·ci·at·ed, as·so·ci·at·ing.** —*v.t.* **1.** to connect in one's mind: *Because the boy associated darkness with danger, he was afraid to turn out the light.* **2.** to join or connect (oneself) as a friend, companion, or partner: *He associated himself with the law firm.* **3.** to join together; combine; connect: *Happiness is often associated with freedom.* —*v.i.* **1.** to keep company as a friend, companion, or partner; be friendly: *He refused to associate with the man who had cheated him.* **2.** to form a union or combination; unite: *Hydrogen associates freely with oxygen.* —*n.* **1.** a person who is frequently in the company of another; companion; friend. **2.** a person who is connected with another or others in some business or action; partner; colleague. —*adj.* having secondary membership, status, or privileges: *an associate professor.*

Associated Press, see **AP.**

---

at; āpe; cär; end; mē; it; īce; hot; ōld; fôrk;
wood; fōōl; oil; out; up; turn; sing; thin; this;
hw in white; zh in treasure. The symbol ə
stands for the sound of **a** in about, **e** in taken,
i in pencil, **o** in lemon, and **u** in circus.

as·so·ci·a·tion (ə sō′sē ā′shən, ə sō′shē ā′shən) *n.*
1. an organized group of people with common interests;
society: *Our doctor was president of the local medical association.* **2.** the act of associating or the state of being
associated; relationship; connection. **3.** a connection made
in the mind between one thought or feeling and another:
the association between "red" and "blood." **4.** such a
thought or feeling: *This house has many happy associations
for me.*

as·so·ci·a·tive (ə sō′shē ā′tiv, ə sō′sē ā′tiv) *adj.*
1. relating to or resulting from association. **2.** *Mathematics.* relating to or designating a law stating that the sum
or product of two or more quantities will be the same
regardless of the way in which they are grouped. For example: (6 + 12) + 5 is the same as 6 + (12 + 5) and *a* x
(b x c) is the same as (a x b) x c.

as·so·nance (as′ə nəns) *n.* **1.** similarity or repetition of
sounds, as in poetry. **2.** a form of partial rhyme in which
the stressed vowel sounds are alike but the consonant
sounds are different, as in *same* and *take* or *labor* and
haven.

as·sort (ə sôrt′) *v.t.* to put into groups or categories; sort:
Assort these cards by color. —**as·sort′er,** *n.*

as·sort·ed (ə sôr′tid) *adj.* of various kinds: *a pound of
assorted cookies.*

as·sort·ment (ə sôrt′mənt) *n.* **1.** a collection of various
kinds of things: *an assortment of cheeses.* **2.** the act of
assorting or the state of being assorted.

asst., assistant.

as·suage (ə swāj′) *v.t.,* **as·suaged, as·suag·ing. 1.** to
make less severe; ease: *The drug assuaged the pain of his
broken arm.* **2.** to calm; pacify: *He is difficult to assuage
when he's angry.* **3.** to satisfy: *The meal assuaged her appetite.* —**as·suage′ment,** *n.*

as·sume (ə soōm′) *v.t.,* **as·sumed, as·sum·ing. 1.** to take
for granted as true; suppose as a fact: *I assume we'll arrive
on time if we leave now.* **2.** to take upon oneself; undertake:
He assumed responsibility for feeding the dog. **3.** to take
on; adopt: *to assume a new name.* **4.** to take for oneself;
seize: *The dictator assumed control of the country.* **5.** to
put on a show of; pretend: *He assumed indifference whenever her name was mentioned.*

as·sumed (ə soōmd′) *adj.* **1.** pretended; false: *an assumed name.* **2.** taken for granted as true: *That is an
assumed fact.*

as·sum·ing (ə soō′ming) *adj.* arrogant; bold.

as·sump·tion (ə sump′shən) *n.* **1.** the act of assuming
or the state of being assumed. **2.** something taken for
granted: *His assumption proved to be wrong.* **3. the Assumption. a.** the taking up into heaven of the body and
soul of the Virgin Mary after her death. **b.** a church festival celebrating this event. It falls on August 15.

as·sur·ance (ə shoor′əns) *n.* **1.** the act of assuring or the
state of being assured: *Because of her assurance that she
would be invited to the dance, she bought a new dress.*
2. a positive declaration intended to give confidence; guarantee: *We had his assurance that he would pay for the
damage.* **3.** freedom from doubt; certainty: *He had assurance of her loyalty.* **4.** self-confidence; aplomb. **5.** *British.*
another word for **insurance.**

as·sure (ə shoor′) *v.t.,* **as·sured, as·sur·ing. 1.** to state
positively to; tell positively: *I assure you that they will
come.* **2.** to make certain; guarantee: *Her hard work assured the success of the project.* **3.** to make certain; convince: *He assured us of his honesty.* **4.** to give confidence
to; reassure: *to assure a frightened child.* **5.** to make safe
or secure: *He assured his position in the firm.* **6.** to insure.

as·sured (ə shoord′) *adj.* **1.** made certain; guaranteed:
an assured victory. **2.** self-possessed; confident: *He spoke*
in his usual assured way. —**as·sur·ed·ly** (ə shoor′id lē,
ə shoord′lē), *adv.*

As·syr·i·a (ə sir′ē ə) *n.* an ancient empire in southwestern Asia. —**As·syr′i·an,** *adj., n.*

as·ta·tine (as′tə tēn′) *n.* a radioactive chemical element,
usually produced artificially from bismuth. It is one of the
halogens. Symbol: **At**

as·ter (as′tər) *n.* **1.** the daisylike flower of any of a large
group of plants that bloom in the
fall. **2.** a plant bearing such flowers. [Latin *aster* a star, from
Greek *astēr;* because the flower
was thought to be shaped like a
star.]

Asters

as·ter·isk (as′tə risk′) *n.* a
star-shaped mark (*) used in
printing or writing to point out a
reference or a footnote, or to show
that something is missing from the
text. —*v.t.* to mark with an asterisk.

a·stern (ə sturn′) *adv., adj.*
1. at or toward the rear of a ship.
2. behind a ship. **3.** backward.

as·ter·oid (as′tə roid′) *n.* any of thousands of small,
rocky bodies that revolve around the sun, chiefly between
the orbits of Mars and Jupiter. Also, **planetoid.**

asth·ma (az′mə) *n.* a chronic disease that is usually
caused by an allergic reaction. It is characterized by attacks of difficult breathing, wheezing, and coughing.

asth·mat·ic (az mat′ik) *adj.* relating to or having
asthma. —*n.* a person who has asthma.

a·stig·ma·tism (ə stig′mə tiz′əm) *n.* a defect in a lens,
especially the lens of the eye, in which light rays coming
from a single point are not focused at a single point. Astig-
matism causes blurred vision or unclear images. —**a·stig-
mat·ic** (as′tig mat′ik), *adj.*

a·stir (ə stur′) *adv., adj.* **1.** in motion; stirring; active.
2. out of bed.

as·ton·ish (əs ton′ish) *v.t.* to surprise greatly; amaze:
The news astonished him.

as·ton·ish·ing (əs ton′i shing) *adj.* causing astonishment; amazing. —**as·ton′ish·ing·ly,** *adv.*

as·ton·ish·ment (əs ton′ish mənt) *n.* **1.** surprise;
amazement: *He gazed in astonishment at the man he had
thought to be dead.* **2.** something that causes amazement
or surprise.

as·tound (əs tound′) *v.t.* to surprise or amaze greatly;
stun: *The announcement that she had won the raffle as-
tounded her.* —**as·tound′ing·ly,** *adv.*

a·strad·dle (ə strad′əl) *adv., adj., prep.* another word for
astride.

as·tra·khan (as′trə kən) *n.* **1.** the curly fur of young
lambs, originally from the region of Astrakhan. It is a
grade of karakul wool. **2.** a cloth woven to resemble this.

As·tra·khan (as′trə kən) *n.* a port city on the lower
Volga River, in the southwestern Soviet Union. Pop.
(1970), 410,000.

as·tral (as′trəl) *adj.* relating to or from the stars.

a·stray (ə strā′) *adj., adv.* off the right path or track: *The
cow went astray. His poor advice led her astray.*

a·stride (ə strīd′) *adj., adv.* with one leg on each side.
—*prep.* with one leg on each side of: *Jim sat astride the
fence.*

as·trin·gen·cy (əs trin′jən sē) *n.* the state of being astringent.

as·trin·gent (əs trin′jənt) *n.* a substance that shrinks
the tissues of the body. Astringents are used to stop the
flow of blood from a wound or cut. —*adj.* **1.** causing the

tissues of the body to shrink: *an astringent lotion.* **2.** stern, severe, or harsh. —**as·trin′gent·ly,** *adv.*

as·tro·gate (as′trə gāt′) *v.t., v.i.,* **as·tro·gat·ed, as·tro·gat·ing.** to navigate (a spacecraft) in outer space. —**as′tro·ga′tion,** *n.* —**as′tro·ga′tor,** *n.*

as·tro·labe (as′trə lāb′) *n.* an instrument formerly used for measuring the positions of the stars, planets, and other heavenly bodies. It has been replaced by the sextant.

as·trol·o·ger (əs trol′ə jər) *n.* a person who practices astrology.

as·trol·o·gy (əs trol′ə jē) *n.* the study of the influence that the stars and planets supposedly have on people and events, so as to predict the future. —**as·tro·log·i·cal** (as′trə loj′i kəl), *adj.* —**as′tro·log′i·cal·ly,** *adv.*

astron. **1.** astronomer. **2.** astronomical. **3.** astronomy.

as·tro·naut (as′trə nôt′) *n.* a person who is trained to fly in or navigate a spacecraft.

as·tro·naut·ics (as′trə nô′tiks) *n.,pl.* the science that deals with the design, construction, and operation of spacecraft. ▲ used with a singular verb. —**as·tro·naut·ic** (as′trə-nô′tik); *also,* **as′tro·naut′i·cal,** *adj.*

as·tron·o·mer (əs tron′ə mər) *n.* a student of or an expert in astronomy.

as·tro·nom·i·cal (as′trə nom′i kəl) *adj.* **1.** of or relating to astronomy. **2.** very great; unbelievably large: *The dealer set an astronomical price on the rare diamond.* Also, **as·tro·nom·ic** (as′trə nom′ik). —**as′tro·nom′i·cal·ly,** *adv.*

astronomical unit, a unit of length used to measure distances in astronomy. It is equal to the distance between the earth and the sun, or about 93 million miles.

astronomical year, another term for **solar year.**

as·tron·o·my (əs tron′ə mē) *n.* the science that deals with the planets, stars, and other heavenly bodies, including the study of their size, position, motion, and physical characteristics.

as·tro·phys·ics (as′trō fiz′iks) *n.,pl.* the branch of astronomy that deals with the physical and chemical nature of the stars, planets, and other heavenly bodies. ▲ used with a singular verb. —**as·tro·phys·i·cal** (as′trō fiz′i kəl), *adj.*

as·tute (əs tōōt′, əs tyōōt′) *adj.* having or showing a keen mind; shrewd: *an astute businessman, an astute essay.* —**as·tute′ly,** *adv.* —**as·tute′ness,** *n.*

A·sun·ción (ä sōōn syōn′) *n.* the capital and largest city of Paraguay, in the southwestern part of the country. Pop. (1968 est.), 365,000.

a·sun·der (ə sun′dər) *adv.* **1.** into pieces or separate parts: *The wall had been torn asunder by the blast.* **2.** apart from each other: *The wind scattered the leaves asunder.*

As·wan High Dam (as′wän) a large dam in southeastern Egypt, on the Nile.

a·sy·lum (ə sī′ləm) *n.* **1.** a place that provides care for helpless people, such as orphans or the insane. **2.** shelter or protection, such as that sought by a fugitive. Some countries grant asylum to political fugitives from other countries. **3.** a place that provides safety or protection, such as a church.

a·sym·met·ri·cal (ā′si met′ri kəl) *adj.* not symmetrical. Also, **a·sym·met·ric** (ā′si met′rik). —**a′sym·met′ri·cal·ly,** *adv.*

a·sym·me·try (ā sim′ə trē) *n.* a lack of symmetry.

at (at) *prep.* **1.** in, on, or by: *He stood at his mother's side. The race started at the top of the hill.* **2.** to or toward: *Look at this picture.* **3.** in a place, state,

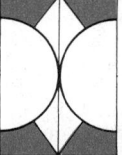 

Symmetrical   Asymmetrical

or condition of: *My brother is at home. The children are at play.* **4.** near or during the age or time of: *We ate at noon. He died at seventy.* **5.** because of: *She cried at the thought of leaving.* **6.** in the rate, order, or position of: *The train traveled at sixty miles per hour.* **7.** in the amount of; for: *The dress was sold at half price.* **8.** in the method or manner of: *The teams were chosen at random.* **9.** by way of; through: *He entered at the back door.*

At, the symbol for astatine.

at·a·vism (at′ə viz′əm) *n.* the reappearance, usually after several generations, of a physical trait of an ancestor.

a·tax·i·a (ə tak′sē ə) *n.* lack of coordination of the voluntary muscles. —**a·tax′ic,** *adj.*

ate (āt) the past tense of **eat.**

-ate *suffix* **1.** (used to form adjectives from nouns) relating to or having: *affectionate, collegiate.* **2.** (used to form certain verbs) **a.** to become: *evaporate.* **b.** to cause to become: *activate.* **c.** to combine or treat with: *chlorinate.* **3.** (used to form nouns) **a.** an office or function: *directorate, delegate.* **b.** the object or result of an action: *syndicate.*

at·el·ier (at′əl yā′) *n.* a workshop or studio, especially that of an artist.

a tem·po (ä tem′pō) *Music.* going back to the original tempo.

Ath·a·pas·can (ath′ə pas′kən) *n.* a family of languages spoken by various Indian tribes of northwestern Canada and Alaska and the western United States, including the Apache and Navaho languages. —*adj.* of or relating to this family of languages.

a·the·ism (ā′thē iz′əm) *n.* the belief that there is no God.

a·the·ist (ā′thē ist) *n.* a person who does not believe in the existence of God.

▲ **Atheist** is sometimes confused with **agnostic,** but they do not have the same meaning. An **atheist** believes that there is no God. An **agnostic** is not sure whether or not God exists.

a·the·is·tic (ā′thē is′tik) *adj.* of or relating to atheism or atheists.

A·the·na (ə thē′nə) *also,* **A·the·ne** (ə thē′nē). *n. Greek Mythology.* the goddess of wisdom and the arts and crafts. In Roman mythology she was called Minerva. Also, **Pallas Athena.**

A·the·ni·an (ə thē′nē ən) *adj.* of or relating to Athens, especially ancient Athens, its people, or their culture. —*n.* **1.** a person who was born or is living in Athens. **2.** a person who lived in ancient Athens.

Ath·ens (ath′ənz) *n.* the capital of Greece, in the eastern part of the country. It was the most important and powerful of the ancient Greek city-states. For centuries Athens was the leading cultural center of the Mediterranean area. Pop. (1971), 862,133.

a·thirst (ə thurst′) *adj.* **1.** having a strong desire; eager: *The warriors were athirst for battle.* **2.** thirsty.

ath·lete (ath′lēt) *n.* a person who has ability or training in sports, games, or other activities requiring physical strength, skill, and endurance.

athlete's foot, an infection of the foot, occurring most frequently between the toes. It is caused by a fungus and is highly contagious.

at; āpe; cär; end; mē; it; īce; hot; ōld; fôrk; wood; fōōl; oil; out; up; turn; sing; thin; **th**is; **hw** in white; **zh** in treasure. The symbol ə stands for the sound of **a** in about, **e** in taken, **i** in pencil, **o** in lemon, and **u** in circus.

ath·let·ic (ath let′ik) *adj.* **1.** relating to, like, or for an athlete or athletics: *athletic equipment, an athletic journal.* **2.** physically active and strong: *an athletic boy.* —**ath·let′i·cal·ly,** *adv.*

ath·let·ics (ath let′iks) *n., pl.* **1.** athletic games, sports, or activities. ▲ usually used with a plural verb. **2.** the practice or principles of athletic activities or physical training. ▲ used with a singular verb.

a·thwart (ə thwôrt′) *adv.* from side to side; crosswise. —*prep.* **1.** from side to side of; across. **2.** in opposition to; against. **3.** across the line or course of: *The tugboat was athwart the bow of the schooner.*

-ation *suffix* (used to form nouns) **1.** the action or process of: *education.* **2.** the condition or state of being: *isolation.* **3.** the result of: *information.*

-ative *suffix* (used to form adjectives) **1.** tending to: *talkative.* **2.** of or relating to: *authoritative.*

At·lan·ta (at lan′tə) *n.* the capital and largest city of Georgia, in the northwestern part of the state. Pop. (1970), 496,973.

At·lan·tic (at lan′tik) *n.* an ocean separating Europe and Africa from North America and South America. Also, **Atlantic Ocean.** —*adj.* **1.** of or relating to the Atlantic: *an Atlantic fish.* **2.** on, along, or near the coast of the Atlantic: *an Atlantic port.*

Atlantic City, a resort city on the eastern coast of southern New Jersey.

At·lan·tis (at lan′tis) *n.* a legendary island or continent in the Atlantic that supposedly sank into the sea.

At·las (at′ləs) *n. Greek Mythology.* a giant condemned by Zeus to hold the heavens on his shoulders forever.

at·las (at′ləs) *n.* a book of maps. [Pictures of *Atlas* holding up the heavens were formerly used to illustrate books of maps.]

Atlas Mountains, a mountain range in northwestern Africa, lying in Morocco and parts of Algeria and Tunisia.

at·mos·phere (at′məs fēr′) *n.* **1.** the mass of gases surrounding the earth or any other heavenly body. The earth's atmosphere is made up of air. **2.** the air in a particular place: *the stifling atmosphere of a crowded subway train.* **3.** a feeling or mood, as of a place: *the cheerful atmosphere of a party, a restaurant with a quiet atmosphere.* **4.** a unit of pressure equal to atmospheric pressure at sea level, or 14.69 pounds per square inch.

at·mos·pher·ic (at′məs fer′ik) *adj.* of, in, or relating to the atmosphere. —**at′mos·pher′i·cal·ly,** *adv.*

atmospheric pressure, the pressure produced by the weight of the earth's atmosphere. At sea level it is equal to 14.69 pounds per square inch.

at. no., atomic number.

at·oll (at′ôl, ə tôl′) *n.* a ring-shaped coral island or string of islands surrounding a lagoon.

at·om (at′əm) *n.* **1.** the smallest particle of a chemical element that has the chemical properties of that element. It is made up of a central nucleus containing protons and neutrons around which electrons travel in circular or elliptical paths. **2.** any very small particle; tiny bit: *There's not an atom of proof that he is guilty.* [Latin *atomus* smallest particle, from Greek *atomos* not able to be divided; from the former belief that an atom could not be divided or split.]

atom bomb, another term for **atomic bomb.**

a·tom·ic (ə tom′ik) *adj.* **1.** of or relating to an atom or atoms: *an atomic reaction.* **2.** using atomic energy: *a missile with an atomic warhead.* **3.** very small; minute. —**a·tom′i·cal·ly,** *adv.*

atomic age, the period in history characterized by the use of atomic energy; the present age.

atomic bomb, a nuclear bomb whose great force is pro-

duced from the energy released from the splitting of atoms of heavy elements, such as uranium or plutonium. Also, **atom bomb, A-bomb.**

atomic clock, an extremely accurate electric clock that is regulated by the movements within atoms or molecules.

atomic energy, another term for **nuclear energy.**

atomic mass, the mass of an atom, usually expressed in atomic mass units.

atomic mass unit, a unit of mass equal to one-twelfth of the mass of the most common kind of carbon atom.

atomic number, the number of protons in the nucleus of an atom of an element.

atomic pile, another term for **nuclear reactor.**

atomic reactor, another term for **nuclear reactor.**

atomic theory, the theory that all matter in the universe is composed of atoms.

atomic weight, the average weight of an atom of a chemical element, measured against the standard of an atom of carbon, whose weight is set at 12.

at·om·ize (at′ə mīz′) *v.t.,* **at·om·ized, at·om·iz·ing. 1.** to break up into atoms or very small particles. **2.** to make (a liquid) into a fine spray. —**at′om·i·za′tion,** *n.*

at·om·iz·er (at′ə mī′zər) *n.* a device that turns a liquid into a fine spray: *a perfume atomizer.*

Atomizer

atom smasher, see **accelerator** *(def. 2).*

a·ton·al (ā tōn′əl) *adj. Music.* having no key. —**a·to·nal·i·ty** (ā′tō nal′ə tē), *n.* —**a·ton′al·ly,** *adv.*

a·tone (ə tōn′) *v.i.,* **a·toned, a·ton·ing.** to make up, as for a wrong; make amends: *He atoned for his mistake by doing the work over.*

a·tone·ment (ə tōn′mənt) *n.* **1.** something done to make up for a wrong or injury; amends. **2. the Atonement.** the redemption of man through the life, sufferings, and death of Christ.

a·top (ə top′) *prep.* on the top of.

A·tre·us (ā′trē əs) *n. Greek Legend.* a king of Mycenae and the father of Agamemnon and Menelaus.

a·tri·um (ā′trē əm) *n. pl.,* **a·tri·a** (ā′trē ə) or **a·tri·ums. 1.** the main room or entrance hall of an ancient Roman house, having an opening in the roof. **2.** a chamber of the body, especially one of the auricles of the heart.

a·tro·cious (ə trō′shəs) *adj.* **1.** very cruel, brutal, or wicked: *an atrocious crime.* **2.** *Informal.* very bad; distasteful; offensive: *Her table manners are atrocious.* —**a·tro′cious·ly,** *adv.* —**a·tro′cious·ness,** *n.*

a·troc·i·ty (ə tros′ə tē) *n. pl.,* **a·troc·i·ties. 1.** something that is atrocious, as a cruel or brutal act: *Many atrocities were committed during the war.* **2.** the state or quality of being atrocious: *the atrocity of his crime.* **3.** *Informal.* something that is very bad: *That book is an atrocity.*

at·ro·phy (at′rə fē) *n.* **1.** a wasting away of the body or any of its parts: *A complete lack of physical activity can cause atrophy of the muscles.* **2.** any wasting away; decay: *the atrophy of the power of a great nation* —*v.,* **at·ro·phied, at·ro·phy·ing.** —*v.i.* to waste away: *The muscles in his broken leg atrophied while he was confined in bed.* —*v.t.* to cause to waste away.

at·ro·pine (at′rə pēn′) *n.* a poisonous drug made synthetically or obtained from belladonna and similar plants. It is used in medicine in very small doses to relieve spasms and to dilate the pupil of the eye.

at·tach (ə tach′) *v.t.* **1.** to fasten to or on; join; connect: *She attached a sign to the bulletin board.* **2.** to add at the end; affix; append: *He attached his signature to the contract.* **3.** to bind by ties of affection, gratitude, or loyalty: *He is attached to his family.* **4.** to consider (something) as belonging to; attribute: *The boy attached much importance to his father's advice.* **5.** to appoint or assign officially, usually on a temporary basis: *The training sergeant was attached to the battalion of recruits.* **6.** to take (property) by legal authority: *His creditors attached his salary to collect what he owed them.* —*v.i.* to belong; adhere: *A broad range of responsibilities attach to this job.* —**at·tach′a·ble,** *adj.*

at·ta·ché (at′ə shā′) *n.* a person who is assigned to a diplomatic staff, especially one who is a specialist in a particular field: *a military attaché.* [French *attaché,* from the past participle of *attacher* to attach.]

attaché case, a slim briefcase for carrying papers.

at·tach·ment (ə tach′mənt) *n.* **1.** the act of attaching or the state of being attached. **2.** affection; devotion: *The child showed strong attachment to his friends.* **3.** a part or device that is connected to a machine or implement for a special purpose: *The movie camera had an attachment for filming indoors.* **4.** a part that connects two things or holds them together; fastening. **5.** the act of taking property by legal authority.

at·tack (ə tak′) *v.t.* **1.** to set upon with force or arms; assault: *The soldiers attacked the fort.* **2.** to write or speak against: *The candidate attacked the governor's policies in his speech.* **3.** to start to work on vigorously: *He attacked the problem with enthusiasm.* **4.** to act on or affect harmfully: *A plant disease attacked the elms in our yard.* —*v.i.* to make an attack: *The enemy attacked without warning.* —*n.* **1.** the act of attacking: *The attack on the fort will begin at dawn.* **2.** a sudden onset, as of a disease: *an attack of asthma.* —**at·tack′er,** *n.*

at·tain (ə tān′) *v.t.* **1.** to achieve or gain (something) through work or effort: *Marie Curie attained fame by discovering radium.* **2.** to arrive at; reach: *Richard attained a height of six feet when he was fifteen.* —**at·tain′a·ble,** *adj.*

at·tain·der (ə tān′dər) *n.* the taking away of all civil rights from a person who has been sentenced to death or declared an outlaw.

at·tain·ment (ə tān′mənt) *n.* **1.** the act of attaining: *Jim's desire was the attainment of success.* **2.** something attained; accomplishment: *Albert Einstein was given a Nobel Prize for his attainments in physics.*

at·taint (ə tānt′) *v.t.* to take away all civil rights from (a person sentenced to death or outlawed).

at·tar (at′ər) *n.* the oil obtained from the petals of flowers, especially roses, used in making perfume.

at·tempt (ə tempt′) *v.t.* to make an effort to do (something); try: *Bob attempted to learn to ski.* —*n.* **1.** a putting forth of effort to do something: *They made an attempt to climb the mountain.* **2.** an assault or attack: *to make an attempt on a person's life.*

at·tend (ə tend′) *v.t.* **1.** to be present at: *to attend a meeting, to attend a play, to attend church.* **2.** to take care of or wait on: *The doctor attended the patient.* **3.** to be with (another) so as to provide service or companionship: *Two maids attended the queen.* **4.** to occur with or result from: *Fever attends many diseases.* —*v.i.* **1.** to be present: *She enjoys the theater, but she does not attend often.* **2.** to take care of: *The nurse attended to her patients. Please attend to this matter immediately.* **3.** to pay attention; give heed: *Attend to what the doctor tells you.*

at·ten·dance (ə ten′dəns) *n.* **1.** the act or the state of being present: *Her attendance at school was poor last year. A large crowd was in attendance.* **2.** the number of persons present: *The attendance at the concert was over 300.*

3. a record of persons present: *The teacher took attendance.* **4.** the act or the state of taking care of a person or thing: *In addition to the patient's own doctor, a specialist was in attendance.*

at·ten·dant (ə ten′dənt) *n.* **1.** a person who takes care of or waits on another: *an attendant at a parking lot.* **2.** a person who is with another so as to provide service or companionship: *an attendant of a king.* **3.** a person who is present. —*adj.* **1.** occurring at the same time or as a result; accompanying: *war and its attendant evils.* **2.** providing care or service: *an attendant nurse.*

at·ten·tion (ə ten′shən) *n.* **1.** the act or power of watching, listening, or fixing one's thoughts on something: *The speaker had our undivided attention.* **2.** careful thought; consideration: *This matter will receive my immediate attention.* **3. attentions.** acts of courtesy, thoughtfulness, or devotion. **4.** a military position in which a person stands erect, with his arms at his sides, his feet together, and his eyes straight ahead: *The soldiers stood at attention when the general entered the room.* —*interj.* a command to take this position.

at·ten·tive (ə ten′tiv) *adj.* **1.** paying attention: *an attentive audience.* **2.** courteous; considerate; thoughtful: *an attentive host.* —**at·ten′tive·ly,** *adv.* —**at·ten′tive·ness,** *n.*

at·ten·u·ate (ə ten′yo͞o āt′) *v.t.,* **at·ten·u·at·ed, at·ten·u·at·ing. 1.** to make thin or slender: *The boy attenuated the rubber band by stretching it.* **2.** to lessen or reduce; weaken: *The effect of the illness was attenuated by the drug.* —**at·ten′u·a′tion,** *n.*

at·test (ə test′) *v.t.* **1.** to bear witness to (something); declare to be true or genuine: *to attest a will. The witness attested the truth of the defendant's claims.* **2.** to be proof of; show clearly: *His high grades attest his good study habits.* —*v.i.* to bear witness: *to attest to the validity of a document.*

at·tic (at′ik) *n.* the space directly below the roof of a house or other building.

At·ti·ca (at′i kə) *n.* a region and province in east-central Greece. Athens is its chief city and capital.

At·ti·la (at′əl ə, ə til′ə) A.D. 406?–453, the king of the Huns from about 433 until 453.

at·tire (ə tīr′) *v.t.,* **at·tired, at·tir·ing.** to dress, especially in fine or costly garments: *The girl was attired in her best clothes.* —*n.* clothes; apparel: *elegant attire.*

at·ti·tude (at′ə to͞od′, at′ə tyo͞od′) *n.* **1.** a manner of thinking, acting, or feeling: *He has a good attitude toward his work.* **2.** a position of the body that suggests an emotion or condition: *She stood at the window in an attitude of watchfulness.* **3.** the position of an aircraft or spacecraft in relation to some point of reference, such as the earth.

at·tor·ney (ə tur′nē) *n. pl.,* **at·tor·neys. 1.** a lawyer. **2.** a person who has been given the right to act in another person's place, especially in a legal matter.

attorney at law *pl.,* **attorneys at law.** a lawyer.

attorney general *pl.,* **attorneys general** or **attorney generals.** the chief law officer of a national or state government.

at·tract (ə trakt′) *v.t.* **1.** to be appealing to; draw the attention or interest of; fascinate: *The scenery in these mountains attracts many tourists.* **2.** to draw to oneself or

at; āpe; cär; end; mē; it; īce; hot; ōld; fôrk;
wood; fo͞ol; oil; out; up; turn; sing; thin; **th**is;
hw in white; zh in treasure. The symbol ə
stands for the sound of **a** in about, **e** in taken,
i in pencil, **o** in lemon, and **u** in circus.

itself by physical force: *The north pole of one magnet attracts the south pole of another magnet.* —**at·trac′er;** also, **at·trac′tor,** *n.*

at·trac·tion (ə trak′shən) *n.* **1.** the act or power of attracting: *the attraction of a magnet.* **2.** a person or thing that attracts: *The magician was the main attraction at the children's party.*

at·trac·tive (ə trak′tiv) *adj.* **1.** having an appealing quality; pleasing: *an attractive dress. Mary is an attractive person.* **2.** having the power of attracting: *Gravity is an attractive force.* —**at·trac′tive·ly,** *adv.* —**at·trac′tive·ness,** *n.*

at·trib·ute (*v.,* ə trib′yōōt; *n.,* at′rə byōōt′) *v.t.,* **at·trib·ut·ed, at·trib·ut·ing.** to consider (something) as belonging to, produced by, or resulting from: *Harry attributed his good health to eating properly. The scholar attributed the painting to Rembrandt.* —*n.* **1.** something that is thought of as belonging to a person or thing, such as a quality or characteristic: *One of Frank's attributes is friendliness.* **2.** an object thought of as a symbol, as of a god: *A hunter's bow was one of the attributes of the goddess Diana.* —**at·trib′ut·a·ble,** *adj.* —**at′tri·bu′tion,** *n.*

at·trib·u·tive (ə trib′yə tiv) *adj.* relating to an adjective, or a noun used as an adjective, that comes before and modifies a noun. In the phrase *school bus,* the noun *school* is an attributive word. —*n.* an attributive word. In the phrase *green jacket, green* is an attributive. —**at·trib′u·tive·ly,** *adv.*

at·tri·tion (ə trish′ən) *n.* **1.** a wearing away by friction. **2.** a gradual wearing down or weakening: *a war of attrition.*

at·tune (ə tōōn′, ə tyōōn′) *v.t.,* **at·tuned, at·tun·ing.** to bring into harmony or accord: *His mind was soon attuned to the peace and quiet of country life.*

atty., attorney.

a·typ·i·cal (ā tip′i kəl) *adj.* not typical: *A bird that cannot fly is atypical.* —**a·typ′i·cal·ly,** *adv.*

Au, the symbol for gold. [Abbreviation of Latin *aurum.*]

au·burn (ô′bərn) *n.* a reddish-brown color. —*adj.* having the color auburn; reddish-brown.

Auck·land (ôk′lənd) *n.* a port city in northern New Zealand. Pop. (1970 est.), 152,300.

auc·tion (ôk′shən) *n.* a public sale at which articles or property are sold to the highest bidder. —*v.t.* to sell at an auction: *He auctioned his collection of paintings.*

auc·tion·eer (ôk′shə nēr′) *n.* a person who conducts sales by auction.

au·da·cious (ô dā′shəs) *adj.* **1.** not showing any fear; recklessly bold: *The audacious explorer went alone into the jungle.* **2.** not showing respect; impudent: *Her audacious behavior shocked us.* —**au·da′cious·ly,** *adv.* —**au·da′cious·ness,** *n.*

au·dac·i·ty (ô das′ə tē) *n.* **1.** boldness or courage; daring. **2.** shameless boldness; impudence.

au·di·ble (ô′də bəl) *adj.* loud enough to be heard: *The radio was barely audible after Jim turned down the volume.* —**au′di·bil′i·ty,** *n.* —**au′di·bly,** *adv.*

au·di·ence (ô′dē əns) *n.* **1.** a group of people gathered to hear and see something, such as a play. **2.** a group of people who give attention to something: *That television program has a large audience.* **3.** people who appreciate and support something: *Hockey has a growing audience in this country.* **4.** a formal meeting with a person of rank or position: *an audience with the Pope.* **5.** an opportunity to be heard; hearing: *an audience with a committee.*

au·di·o (ô′dē ō′) *adj.* **1.** of or relating to sound. **2.** of or relating to the reproduction, transmission, or reception of sound. —*n.* the audio part of television.

audio frequency, any frequency at which a sound

wave can be heard by a person with normal hearing, ranging from about 15 cycles to 20,000 cycles per second.

au·di·om·e·ter (ô′dē om′ə tər) *n.* an instrument that produces controlled sounds, used for testing a person's hearing.

au·di·o·vis·u·al (ô′dē ō vizh′ōō əl) *adj.* **1.** of or relating to hearing and sight. **2.** relating to or using such teaching materials as films, recordings, television, and photographs.

au·dit (ô′dit) *v.t.* **1.** to examine (financial accounts and records) to make sure they are correct. **2.** to attend (a college course) as a listener, without receiving credit for attendance. —*v.i.* to examine financial accounts and records. —*n.* **1.** an examination of financial accounts and records. **2.** a statement of the financial accounts and records that have been examined.

au·di·tion (ô dish′ən) *n.* a short performance that tests the abilities of a singer, musician, actor, or other performer. —*v.t.* to give an audition to (a performer): *The director auditioned three actors for the part.* —*v.i.* to perform in an audition: *Eighteen actors auditioned for the leading role.*

au·di·tor (ô′də tər) *n.* **1.** a person who audits financial accounts and records. **2.** a hearer; listener.

au·di·to·ri·um (ô′də tôr′ē əm) *n. pl.,* **au·di·to·ri·ums.** **1.** a large room in a church, school, theater, or other building for public gatherings. **2.** a building used for public gatherings.

au·di·to·ry (ô′də tôr′ē) *adj.* of or relating to hearing.

auditory nerve, the nerve carrying impulses from the inner ear to the brain.

Au·du·bon, John James (ô′də bon′) 1785–1851, American artist and naturalist, noted for his paintings of birds.

auf Wie·der·seh·en (ouf vē′dər zā′ən) *German.* until we meet again; good-by for now.

Aug., August.

au·ger (ô′gər) *n.* a tool or drill for boring holes in wood or in the earth.

aught¹ (ôt) *also,* **ought.** *n.* anything; any part. —*adv.* in any way; at all. [Old English *āwiht* anything.]

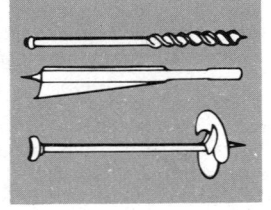

Augers

aught² (ôt) *also,* **ought.** *n.* **1.** zero. **2.** nothing; naught. [Earlier *naught,* from Old English *nāwiht. A naught* was incorrectly written as *an aught.*]

aug·ment (ôg ment′) *v.t.* to make greater; increase; enlarge: *He augmented his art collection by buying two new paintings.* —*v.i.* to become greater; increase; grow. —**aug·ment′a·ble,** *adj.* —**aug′men·ta′tion,** *n.*

au grat·in (ō grat′ən, ō grät′ən) covered with bread crumbs and grated cheese and baked or grilled until brown. [French *au gratin.*]

Augs·burg (ôgz′bərg) *n.* a city in southern West Germany. Pop. (1969 est.), 214,400.

au·gur (ô′gər) *n.* **1.** any of a group of priests of ancient Rome who predicted future events from signs or omens. **2.** any fortuneteller; soothsayer. —*v.t.* **1.** to predict (something) from signs or omens. **2.** to be a sign or omen of; given promise of. —*v.i.* to predict from signs or omens.

  to augur ill. to be a bad sign or omen: *The quarterback's injury augurs ill for our chances of winning the championship.*

  to augur well. to be a good sign or omen.

au·gu·ry (ô′gyər ē) *n. pl.,* **au·gu·ries.** **1.** the art or practice of predicting future events from signs or omens. **2.** a sign or omen.

au·gust (ô gust′) *adj.* **1.** inspiring awe, reverence, or admiration; magnificent; majestic; imposing: *the august Capitol building in Washington.* **2.** dignified; eminent: *an august assembly.* —**au·gust′ly,** *adv.* —**au·gust′ness,** *n.*

Au·gust (ô′gəst) *n.* the eighth month of the year, having thirty-one days. [Old English *August,* from Latin *Augustus.* This month was named for *Augustus,* the first emperor of Rome.]

Au·gus·ta (ô gus′tə) *n.* the capital of Maine, in the southern part of the state. Pop. (1970), 21,945.

Au·gus·tine, Saint (ô′gəs tēn′, ô gus′tin) A.D. 354–430, Christian theologian, the most important of the early church fathers.

Au·gus·tus (ô gus′təs) 63 B.C.–A.D. 14, the first emperor of Rome, from 27 B.C. to A.D. 14.

au jus (ō jōōs′) *French.* (of meat) served with the gravy that forms naturally from the juices of the meat while it is cooking: *roast beef au jus.*

auk (ôk) *n.* any of several diving birds found in arctic waters, having webbed feet, short wings, and black and white feathers.

au lait (ō lā′) *French.* with milk.

auld lang syne (ōld′ lang zīn′) the days of long ago; the good old days. [Scottish *auld lang syne* literally, old long ago.]

aunt (ant, änt) *n.* **1.** the sister of one's father or mother. **2.** the wife of one's uncle.

Auk

au·ra (ôr′ə) *n. pl.,* **au·ras.** the distinctive character or atmosphere arising from and surrounding a person or thing: *There's an aura of mystery about him. There was an aura of peace in the cathedral.*

au·ral (ôr′əl) *adj.* of or relating to the ear or to the sense of hearing. —**au′ral·ly,** *adv.*

Au·re·li·us (ô rē′lē əs) see **Marcus Aurelius.**

au·re·ole (ôr′ē ōl′) *n.* **1.** in art, a circle of light surrounding the head of a sacred person. **2.** a bright area around the sun or moon, especially when seen through fog.

Au·re·o·my·cin (ôr′ē ō mī′sin) *n. Trademark.* an antibiotic drug used against certain infections caused by bacteria and viruses.

au re·voir (ō rə vwär′) *French.* until we meet again; good-by.

au·ri·cle (ôr′i kəl) *n.* **1.** either of the two upper chambers or cavities of the heart. The auricles receive blood from the veins and send it to the ventricles. **2.** the external ear.

au·ric·u·lar (ô rik′yə lər) *adj.* **1.** of or relating to the ear or to the sense of hearing. **2.** of or relating to an auricle of the heart.

au·rochs (ôr′oks) *n. pl.,* **au·rochs.** an extinct wild ox of Europe, believed to be the direct ancestor of modern domestic cattle.

Au·ro·ra (ə rôr′ə) *n.* **1.** *Roman Mythology.* the goddess of the dawn. **2. aurora.** shining bands or streamers of light appearing in the night sky.

Aurochs

au·ro·ra aus·tra·lis (ə-rôr′ə ôs trā′lis) the auro-ra seen in the Southern Hemisphere. Also, **southern lights.**

au·ro·ra bo·re·al·is (ə rôr′ə bôr′ē al′is) the aurora seen in the Northern Hemisphere. Also, **northern lights.**

aus·pic·es (ôs′pə siz) *n., pl.* **1.** signs or omens, especially those that indicate success. **2.** support or guidance; pa-tronage: *The tour was conducted under the auspices of the school board.* [Latin *auspicium* a prediction made from watching birds.]

aus·pi·cious (ôs pish′əs) *adj.* showing promise of success; favorable: *The football team's victory was an auspicious beginning for the season.* —**aus·pi′cious·ly,** *adv.* —**aus·pi′cious·ness,** *n.*

Aus·ten, Jane (ôs′tən) 1775–1817, English novelist.

aus·tere (ôs tēr′) *adj.* **1.** severe or stern, as in manner or appearance: *He was an austere old man who rarely smiled.* **2.** severely simple; unadorned: *The austere room contained only a chair and table.* **3.** lacking comforts or pleasures; frugal or harsh: *the austere life of the early pioneers.* —**aus·tere′ly,** *adv.* —**aus·tere′ness,** *n.*

aus·ter·i·ty (ôs ter′ə tē) *n. pl.,* **aus·ter·i·ties. 1.** the quality or condition of being austere. **2.** *also,* **austerities.** austere and self-denying behavior or practices: *the austerities of a monastery.*

Austin (ôs′tin) *n.* the capital of Texas, in the south-central part of the state. Pop. (1970), 251,808.

Aus·tral·a·sia (ôs′trə lā′zhə) *n.* Australia, New Zealand, New Guinea, New Britain, and other smaller islands of the southwestern Pacific. —**Aus′tral·a′sian,** *adj., n.*

Aus·tra·lia (ôs trāl′yə) *n.* **1.** a continent southeast of Asia, between the Indian and Pacific oceans. It is the smallest of the continents. Area, 2,941,526 sq. mi. Pop. (1971), 12,338,587. **2.** a country including this continent and the island of Tasmania. Capital, Canberra. Area, 2,967,909 sq. mi. Pop. (1971), 12,728,461.

Aus·tra·lian (ôs trāl′yən) *adj.* of or relating to Australia, its people, their language, or their culture. —*n.* **1.** a person who was born or is living in Australia. **2.** one of the people native to Australia; Australian aborigine. **3.** any of the languages spoken by the aborigines of Australia.

Australian ballot, a ballot containing the names of all candidates in an election. It is marked in secrecy by the voter. It was first used in Australia.

Aus·tri·a (ôs′trē ə) *n.* a country in central Europe. Capital, Vienna. Area 32,374 sq. mi. Pop. (1971), 7,456,745. —**Aus′tri·an,** *adj., n.*

au·then·tic (ô then′tik) *adj.* **1.** that can be accepted as true; reliable; trustworthy: *The eyewitness gave an authentic account of the accident.* **2.** being what it appears or claims to be; genuine; real: *The boys found an authentic Indian arrowhead.* —**au·then′ti·cal·ly,** *adv.*

au·then·ti·cate (ô then′tə kāt′) *v.t.,* **au·then·ti·cat·ed, au·then·ti·cat·ing.** to show to be authentic: *The lawyer authenticated the signature by comparing it with one in a letter.* —**au·then′ti·ca′tion,** *n.*

au·then·tic·i·ty (ô′then tis′ə tē) *n.* the state or quality of being authentic: *The art critic questioned the authenticity of the painting.*

au·thor (ô′thər) *n.* **1.** the writer of a book, story, play, poem, or other written work: *Charles Dickens was the author of many novels.* **2.** a person who originates or begins something; creator: *He was the author of the plan.* —*v.t.* to be the author of: *to author a book.*

au·thor·i·tar·i·an (ə thôr′ə ter′ē ən) *adj.* in favor of total obedience to authority and opposed to individual

at; āpe; cär; end; mē; it; īce; hot; ōld; fôrk; wood; fōōl; oil; out; up; turn; sing; thin; this; hw in white; zh in treasure. The symbol ə stands for the sound of a in about, e in taken, i in pencil, o in lemon, and u in circus.

freedom: *The dictator set up an authoritarian government.* —*n.* an authoritarian person. —**au·thor'i·tar'i·an·ism,** *n.*

au·thor·i·ta·tive (ə thôr'ə tā'tiv) *adj.* **1.** worthy of acceptance or belief; reliable: *The reporter got the story from an authoritative source.* **2.** coming from or having authority: *The mayor made an authoritative statement.* **3.** showing authority: *The army officer had an authoritative manner.* —**au·thor'i·ta'tive·ly,** *adv.* —**au·thor'i·ta'tive·ness,** *n.*

au·thor·i·ty (ə thôr'ə tē) *n. pl.,* **au·thor·i·ties. 1.** the power or right to act, command, enforce obedience, or make decisions: *The dictator had absolute authority. The captain had authority over the men on his ship.* **2.** a person or group having such a right or power: *Report this incident to the authorities. He works for the city's housing authority.* **3.** a trustworthy source of information or advice: *The encyclopedia is an authority on many subjects.* **4.** an expert on a particular subject: *That professor is an authority on the life of Lincoln.*

au·thor·i·za·tion (ô'thər i zā'shən) *n.* **1.** the act of authorizing. **2.** legal right or power: *The writer gave the magazine authorization to publish his story.*

au·thor·ize (ô'thə rīz') *v.t.,* **au·thor·ized, au·thor·iz·ing. 1.** to give authority to: *He was authorized by the president of the company to sign the contract.* **2.** to approve officially: *The mayor authorized the appointment of a new police chief.*

au·thor·ized (ô'thə rīzd') *adj.* having authority: *an authorized agent.*

Authorized Version, the King James Version of the Bible, published in England in 1611.

au·thor·ship (ô'thər ship') *n.* the origin or source of a written work: *This book is of unknown authorship.*

au·to (ô'tō) *n. pl.,* **au·tos.** see **automobile.**

au·to·bi·og·ra·phy (ô'tə bī og'rə fē) *n. pl.,* **au·to·bi·og·ra·phies.** the story of a person's own life written by himself. —**au·to·bi·og·ra·pher** (ô'tə bī og'rə fər), *n.* —**au·to·bi·o·graph·ic** (ô'tə bī'ə graf'ic); also, **au'to·bi'o·graph'i·cal,** *adj.* —**au'to·bi'o·graph'i·cal·ly,** *adv.*

au·toc·ra·cy (ô tok'rə sē) *n. pl.,* **au·toc·ra·cies. 1.** a form of government in which one person holds absolute power. **2.** a country ruled by an autocrat.

au·to·crat (ô'tə krat') *n.* **1.** a ruler who has absolute power. **2.** a person who is arrogant and domineering toward other people.

au·to·crat·ic (ô'tə krat'ik) *adj.* of or like an autocrat or an autocracy: *The company's president was an autocratic man.* —**au'to·crat'i·cal·ly,** *adv.*

au·to·graph (ô'tə graf') *n.* **1.** a person's own signature. **2.** something written in a person's own handwriting. —*v.t.* **1.** to write one's signature in or on: *The writer autographed a copy of her book for me.* **2.** to write in one's own handwriting. —**au'to·graph'ic;** also, **au'to·graph'i·cal,** *adj.*

au·to·mat (ô'tə mat') *n.* a cafeteria in which food is obtained from small compartments whose doors open when the proper coins are put in the slots.

au·to·mate (ô'tə māt') *v.t.,* **au·to·mat·ed, au·to·mat·ing.** to convert to or operate by automation: *to automate the printing of a newspaper.*

au·to·mat·ic (ô'tə mat'ik) *adj.* **1.** acting, moving, or operating by itself: *We have an automatic washing machine.* **2.** done without a person's control: *Breathing is an automatic action of the body during sleep.* **3.** (of a firearm) capable of firing and reloading continuously until the trigger is released: *an automatic rifle.* —*n.* an automatic firearm. —**au'to·mat'i·cal·ly,** *adv.*

au·to·ma·tion (ô'tə mā'shən) *n.* the development and use of machines or systems of machines that are self-

operating or are operated by other machines rather than by people.

au·tom·a·ton (ô tom'ə ton') *n.* **1.** a machine that acts, moves, or operates by itself. **2.** a person whose behavior is mechanical.

au·to·mo·bile (ô'tə mə bēl') *n.* a passenger vehicle usually having four wheels and driven by an engine powered by gasoline; car. —*adj.* of or for automobiles.

au·to·mo·tive (ô'tə mō'tiv) *adj.* **1.** of, relating to, or for an automobile or automobiles: *automotive engineering, the automotive industry.* **2.** self-propelled; self-moving.

au·to·nom·ic (ô'tə nom'ik) *adj.* of or relating to the autonomic nervous system.

autonomic nervous system, the part of the nervous system that controls and regulates the involuntary actions of the body, such as the beating of the heart.

au·ton·o·mous (ô ton'ə məs) *adj.* free from outside rule or control; self-governing; independent: *The United States is an autonomous country.* —**au·ton'o·mous·ly,** *adv.*

au·ton·o·my (ô ton'ə mē) *n. pl.,* **au·ton·o·mies.** the quality, condition, or right of being autonomous; self-government.

au·top·sy (ô'top'sē) *n. pl.,* **au·top·sies.** a medical examination of a dead body, especially in order to find the cause of death; post-mortem.

au·tumn (ô'təm) *n.* the season of the year coming between summer and winter; fall. —*adj.* relating to or characteristic of autumn.

au·tum·nal (ô tum'nəl) *adj.* relating to or characteristic of autumn: *apples and other autumnal fruit.*

autumnal equinox, the equinox that takes place on or about September 23. It marks the beginning of autumn in the Northern Hemisphere.

aux·il·ia·ry (ôg zil'yər ē, ôg zil'ər ē) *adj.* **1.** giving aid or support; helping: *The sailboat has an auxiliary engine.* **2.** additional; supplementary: *auxiliary policemen.* —*n. pl.,* **aux·il·ia·ries. 1.** something that is attached to give aid or support. **2.** a group that is a subsidiary of a larger group: *The men's civic club has a ladies' auxiliary.* **3.** see **auxiliary verb. 4. auxiliaries.** foreign troops in the service of a nation at war.

auxiliary verb, a verb used before the main verb in a verb phrase to express the tense, mood, or voice of the main verb. In the sentence *They will go,* the word *will* is an auxiliary verb.

av. 1. avenue. **2.** average. **3.** avoirdupois.

A.V., Authorized Version.

a·vail (ə vāl') *v.t.* to be of advantage or worth to: *My help will not avail you now.* —*v.i.* to be of use or value; help. —*n.* use; help; advantage: *His efforts were of no avail.*
  to avail oneself of, to take advantage of; make use of: *Bruce availed himself of the books in the library.*

a·vail·a·bil·i·ty (ə vā'lə bil'ə tē) *n. pl.,* **a·vail·a·bil·i·ties.** the state or quality of being available.

a·vail·a·ble (ə vā'lə bəl) *adj.* **1.** that can be had; obtainable: *This dress is available in all sizes.* **2.** that can be used: *The telephone is now available.* —**a·vail'a·bly,** *adv.*

av·a·lanche (av'ə lanch') *n.* **1.** the swift, sudden fall of a mass of snow, ice, earth, or rocks down a mountain slope. **2.** anything like an avalanche: *Tom was overwhelmed by an avalanche of work.*

a·vant-garde (ə vänt'gärd') *n.* a group of people who use or experiment with new, daring, or extreme styles or ideas, especially in the arts. —*adj.* new, daring, or extreme in styles or ideas: *an avant-garde movie.* [French *avant-garde* literally, advance guard.]

av·a·rice (av'ər is) *n.* an intense desire to acquire money and keep it; greed for wealth or possessions.

av·a·ri·cious (av'ə rish'əs) *adj.* greedy for wealth or possessions: *The avaricious merchant charged an unfair price for his goods.* —**av·a·ri′cious·ly,** *adv.* —**av·a·ri′cious·ness,** *n.*

a·vast (ə vast′) *interj.* stop; stay; cease. ▲ used as a command on board a ship.

a·vaunt (ə vônt′) *interj. Archaic.* go away; begone.

ave., avenue.

A·ve Ma·ri·a (ä′vä mə rē′ə) *n.* a Roman Catholic prayer to the Virgin Mary. Also, **Hail Mary.**

a·venge (ə venj′) *v.t.,* **a·venged, a·veng·ing.** to get revenge for: *The young man swore to avenge his father's murder.* —**a·veng′er,** *n.*

av·e·nue (av′ə nyoo′, av′ə noo′) *n.* **1.** a street or thoroughfare, especially a wide one. **2.** a road or walk lined with trees. **3.** a way of reaching or accomplishing something: *Hard work is an avenue to success.*

a·ver (ə vur′) *v.t.,* **a·verred, a·ver·ring.** to declare positively; assert: *He averred that he had not cheated.*

av·er·age (av′rij, av′ər ij) *n.* **1.** a number found by dividing the sum of two or more quantities by the number of quantities: *The average of 2, 4, 6, and 8 is 5.* **2.** the typical, ordinary, or usual amount or kind: *This year's rainfall came close to the average.* —*adj.* **1.** found by figuring an average: *the average yield of a crop, the average speed of a car.* **2.** usual; typical; ordinary: *a man of average height, an average American.* —*v.,* **av·er·aged, av·er·ag·ing.** —*v.t.* **1.** to find the average of: *Jim averaged his bowling scores.* **2.** to do, have, or amount to as an average: *That basketball player averages 20 points per game.* —*v.i.* to be or amount to an average.

on the average. considered from the basis of an average: *On the average, it rains more in Boston than it does in Phoenix.*

a·verse (ə vurs′) *adj.* strongly opposed; unwilling (with *to*): *Jane was averse to doing homework.* —**a·verse′ly,** *adv.* —**a·verse′ness,** *n.*

a·ver·sion (ə vur′zhən) *n.* **1.** a strong opposition or dislike; antipathy: *Beth has an aversion to insects.* **2.** a cause of dislike or opposition: *Spiders are Helen's chief aversion.*

a·vert (ə vurt′) *v.t.* **1.** to turn away or aside: *Jim averted his eyes from the glare of the sun.* **2.** to prevent; avoid: *Hank narrowly averted a crash by slamming on the car's brakes.* —**a·vert′i·ble,** *adj.*

a·vi·ar·y (ā′vē er′ē) *n. pl.,* **a·vi·ar·ies.** a large cage, building, or enclosure for birds.

a·vi·a·tion (ā′vē ā′shən, av′ē ā′shən) *n.* **1.** the science or art of flying in heavier-than-air aircraft. **2.** the production and design of heavier-than-air aircraft.

a·vi·a·tor (ā′vē ā′tər, av′ē ā′tər) *n.* a person who flies an airplane or other heavier-than-air aircraft.

av·id (av′id) *adj.* **1.** very eager or enthusiastic: *an avid sports fan, an avid reader of mystery stories.* **2.** having a great desire; greedy: *to be avid for wealth.* —**av′id·ly,** *adv.* —**av′id·ness,** *n.*

a·vid·i·ty (ə vid′ə tē) *n.* great eagerness or greed.

av·o·ca·do (av′ə kä′dō) *n. pl.,* **av·o·ca·dos.** **1.** a pear-shaped tropical fruit having a buttery texture and a nutty flavor, eaten raw in salads, desserts, and other dishes. Also, **alligator pear.** **2.** the tree bearing this fruit.

Halved avocado

av·o·ca·tion (av′ə kā′shən) *n.* an interest or pastime that a person has in addition to his regular occupation; hobby: *Our family doctor's avocation is collecting antique clocks.* —**av′o·ca′tion·al,** *adj.*

a·void (ə void′) *v.t.* to keep away from; shun; evade: *He tried his best to avoid trouble.* —**a·void′a·ble,** *adj.* —**a·void′a·bly,** *adv.*

a·void·ance (ə void′əns) *n.* the act of avoiding something: *The avoidance of war is one of the goals of the United Nations.*

a·voir·du·pois (av′ər də poiz′) *n.* see **avoirdupois weight.**

avoirdupois weight, a system of weights based on a pound that contains sixteen ounces. It is used in the United States, Great Britain, and Canada for weighing all goods except drugs and precious metals.

A·von (ā′von, av′ən) *n.* a river in central England. It flows past Stratford, the birthplace of Shakespeare.

a·vouch (ə vouch′) *v.t.* **1.** to declare positively; assert; affirm. **2.** to vouch for; guarantee.

a·vow (ə vou′) *v.t.* to declare frankly or openly; admit; acknowledge: *He avowed his failure without hesitation.*

a·vow·al (ə vou′əl) *n.* a frank or open declaration, admission, or acknowledgment: *an avowal of one's true feelings.*

a·vowed (ə voud′) *adj.* openly declared or acknowledged: *an avowed enemy.* —**a·vow·ed·ly** (ə vou′id lē, ə voud′lē), *adv.*

a·wait (ə wāt′) *v.t.* **1.** to wait for; anticipate: *She had long awaited the day of the party.* **2.** to be ready or in store for: *Many surprises await him in his new career.*

a·wake (ə wāk′) *v.,* **a·woke** or **a·waked, a·wak·ing.** —*v.t.* **1.** to rouse from sleep; wake. **2.** to make active; stir up or excite: *The witness' startling testimony awoke new interest in the case.* —*v.i.* **1.** to cease to sleep: *I awoke at dawn.* **2.** to become active or aroused: *People are now awaking to the need for conservation of natural resources.* —*adj.* **1.** not asleep: *He lay awake worrying about how he was going to pay the rent.* **2.** alert; aware: *He was awake to the risks involved in the plan.*

a·wak·en (ə wā′kən) *v.t., v.i.* to awake; wake up: *The barking dog awakened him. The film awakened memories of her trip to Paris.*

a·wak·en·ing (ə wā′kə ning) *n.* **1.** the act of waking. **2.** an awareness; realization. —*adj.* arousing; growing; increasing: *As he grew older, Tom had an awakening sense of loyalty to his family.*

a·ward (ə wôrd′) *v.t.* **1.** to give after careful consideration, especially as deserved or due: *The soldier was awarded a medal for bravery. The judges awarded Carol first prize for her essay.* **2.** to grant by judicial decision: *The jury awarded damages to the plaintiff.* —*n.* **1.** something that is awarded: *He received many awards for his paintings.* **2.** a decision or finding, as of a judge or arbitrator.

a·ware (ə wer′) *adj.* knowing or realizing; conscious: *The king was aware of the plot against him.* —**a·ware′ness,** *n.*

a·wash (ə wôsh′, ə wosh′) *adv., adj.* covered with or washed over by water: *The decks of the ship were awash during the storm.*

a·way (ə wā′) *adv.* **1.** from this or that place; off: *The ship sailed away into the sunset.* **2.** at a distance: *They stood several feet away from us.* **3.** in another place; absent: *He was away from his desk.* **4.** in another direction; aside: *He turned away from us to hide his tears.* **5.** from or out of

at; āpe; cär; end; mē; it; īce; hot; ōld; fôrk; wood; fool; oil; out; up; turn; sing; thin; this; hw in white; zh in treasure. The symbol ə stands for the sound of **a** in about, **e** in taken, **i** in pencil, **o** in lemon, and **u** in circus.

one's possession or use: *Throw away that old coat.* **6.** at or to an end; out of existence: *The old plant withered away.* **7.** without interruption; continuously: *She worked away at her typewriter.* **8.** without hesitation or delay; directly: *Fire away!* —*v.t.* **1.** distant; far: *The school is three miles away.* **2.** absent; gone: *My brother has been away for two weeks.*

 away with. take (someone or something) away: *Away with this man!*

 to do away with. a. to put an end or stop to; get rid of: *The new club president did away with all the old rules.* **b.** to kill.

awe (ô) *n.* great wonder combined with fear or reverence: *We stood in awe of the king.* —*v.t.*, **awed, aw·ing.** to inspire or fill with awe: *We were awed by the fury of the storm.*

a·weigh (ə wā′) *adj.* (of an anchor) raised clear of the bottom.

awe·some (ô′səm) *adj.* **1.** inspiring awe: *The dinosaur was an awesome creature.* **2.** showing awe: *an awesome look.* —**awe′some·ly,** *adv.* —**awe′some·ness,** *n.*

awe-struck (ô′struk′) *adj.* filled with awe. Also, **awe-strick·en** (ô′strik′ən).

aw·ful (ô′fəl) *adj.* **1.** causing fear, dread, or awe; terrible: *an awful disaster.* **2.** *Informal.* very bad, distasteful, or ugly: *awful handwriting.* **3.** *Informal.* very large; great: *That's an awful lot of money.* —*adv. Informal.* extremely; terribly: *I'm awful glad to see you.* —**aw′ful·ness,** *n.*

aw·ful·ly (ô′fə lē, ôf′lē) *adv.* **1.** dreadfully; terribly. **2.** *Informal.* very; extremely: *It's awfully nice to see you again.*

a·while (ə hwīl′) *adv.* for a short time: *After the long walk, they sat down and rested awhile.*

awk·ward (ôk′wərd) *adj.* **1.** lacking ease, skill, or grace in movement or bearing: *The dancer gave an awkward performance.* **2.** difficult or embarrassing: *Inviting two girls to the same dance placed Al in an awkward situation.* **3.** difficult to use, manage, or handle: *The large cabinet was an awkward piece of furniture to move.* —**awk′ward·ly,** *adv.* —**awk′ward·ness,** *n.*

awl (ôl) *n.* a pointed tool used for making small holes and for working designs into the surface of leather or wood.

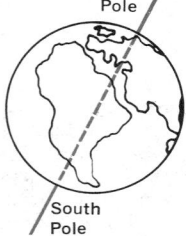

Awl

aw·ning (ô′ning) *n.* a rooflike cover of canvas or other material, as over a door or window, used as a shelter from the sun or rain.

a·woke (ə wōk′) the past tense and past participle of **awake.**

AWOL (ā′wôl′) *adv., adj.* absent from one's military post or duties without official leave. [*A*(bsent) *W*(ith)*O*(ut) *L*(eave).]

a·wry (ə rī′) *adv., adj.* **1.** twisted or turned to one side; askew. **2.** off the right course; wrong; amiss.

ax (aks) *also,* **axe.** *n. pl.,* **ax·es.** a tool consisting of a metal blade attached to a handle, used especially for cutting down trees and chopping wood. —*v.t.* to chop or cut with an ax.

axe (aks) *n., v.t.,* **axed, ax·ing.** another spelling of **ax.**

ax·es[1] (ak′sēz) the plural of **axis.**

ax·es[2] (ak′siz) the plural of **ax.**

ax·i·al (ak′sē əl) *adj.* of, relating to, or forming an axis.

ax·il (ak′sil) *n.* the upper angle formed where a leafstalk or stem joins the stem on which it grows.

ax·i·om (ak′sē əm) *n.* **1.** a statement or principle accepted as true without proof; self-evident or universally accepted truth. For example: *The shortest distance between two points is a straight line.* **2.** an established principle, rule, or law.

ax·i·o·mat·ic (ak′se ə mat′ik) *adj.* of, relating to, or like an axiom; self-evident: *It is axiomatic that night follows day.* —**ax′i·o·mat′i·cal·ly,** *adv.*

ax·is (ak′sis) *n. pl.,* **ax·es. 1.** a real or imaginary straight line around which an object or body, such as the earth, rotates or seems to rotate. **2.** a straight, central line around which the parts of a plane or solid figure are symmetrically arranged. **3.** another word for **number line. 4. the Axis.** the World War II alliance between Germany, Italy, and, later, Japan and other nations.

ax·le (ak′səl) *n.* a shaft or bar on which a wheel or pair of wheels turns.

ax·le·tree (ak′səl trē′) *n.* a fixed axle connecting a pair of wheels, as on a cart or wagon. Each end of the axletree has a spindle or bearings on which the wheel turns.

North Pole

South Pole

Earth's axis

ax·on (ak′son) *also,* **ax·one** (ak′sōn). *n.* a long, slender extension of a nerve cell that carries impulses away from the body of the cell.

aye (ī) *also,* **ay.** *n.* an affirmative vote or voter. —*adv.* yes; yea.

Ayr·shire (er′shər) *n.* one of a breed of hardy, long-horned dairy cattle that may be white, red, or brown, or any combination of these colors.

a·za·lea (ə zāl′yə) *n.* any of a group of shrubs related to the rhododendron, bearing clusters of funnel-shaped flowers.

A·zores (ə zôrz′, ā′zôrz) *n., pl.* an island group in the North Atlantic, west of and belonging to Portugal. Land area, 894 sq. mi. Pop. (1968 est.), 603,000.

A·zov, Sea of (ä zôf′) a northern arm of the Black Sea, in the western Soviet Union.

Az·tec (az′tek) *n.* **1.** a member of a large group of Indian tribes having a well-developed civilization and controlling an empire in central Mexico at the time of the Spanish conquest in 1519. **2.** another word for **Nahuatl.** —*adj.* of or relating to the Aztecs, their language, or their culture. —**Az′tec·an,** *adj.*

az·ure (azh′ər) *n.* a clear sky-blue color. —*adj.* having the color azure; sky-blue.

at; āpe; cär; end; mē; it; īce; hot; ōld; fôrk; wood; fōōl; oil; out; up; turn; sing; thin; **th**is; **hw** in white; **zh** in treasure. The symbol ə stands for the sound of **a** in about, **e** in taken, **i** in pencil, **o** in lemon, and **u** in circus.

B

Egyptian Hieroglyphics ⌷⌷	**5. Greek Ninth Century B.C.** я
2. Semitic ⊣ 𝙮 ◁	**6. Greek Classical Capitals** Β
3. Phoenician ⊰	**7. Latin Fourth Century B.C. Capitals** Β
4. Early Hebrew ⊰	**8. English** Β

B is the second letter of the English alphabet. An Egyptian hieroglyphic **(1)** which stood for "house," was probably the earliest ancestor of our modern letter **B.** A modified form of this symbol was used as the second letter of the ancient Semitic alphabet **(2).** In the Phoenician **(3)** and early Hebrew **(4)** alphabets, this letter was called *beth,* meaning "house." The Greeks borrowed *beth* and called it *beta.* The English word "alphabet" comes from a combination of *alpha* and *beta,* the first two letters of the Greek alphabet. By about 2800 years ago, the Greeks were writing *beta* **(5)** very much like a modern capital letter **B** that has been turned around. Several hundred years later, the Greeks reversed *beta* **(6),** and it was in this form that it was borrowed and used in the Latin alphabet **(7).** From Roman times until the present **(8),** there have been almost no changes in the way that the capital letter **B** is written.

b, B (bē) *n. pl.,* **b's, B's. 1.** the second letter of the English alphabet. **2.** the second item in a series or group. **3.** *Music.* the first and last notes of the scale of B major.

B, the symbol for boron.

b. 1. born. **2.** book. **3.** base. **4.** bass.

B. 1. British. **2.** Bible. **3.** Bay.

Ba, the symbol for barium.

B.A., Bachelor of Arts. Also, **A.B.**

baa (bä) *n.* the sound that is made by a sheep; bleat. —*v.i.,* **baaed, baa·ing.** to make such a sound; bleat.

Ba·al (bā'əl) *n. pl.,* **Ba·al·im** (bā'ə lim). **1.** the chief god of the ancient Semites, especially the Canaanites and Phoenicians. He was worshiped under different names in various communities. **2.** a false god; idol.

Baal·bek (bäl'bek, bāl'bek) *n.* a town in northeastern Lebanon, the site of several ancient temples.

Bab·bitt metal (bab'it) any of various alloys having a lead or tin base and smaller amounts of antimony or copper, used to reduce friction, as in bearings. [From the American inventor Isaac *Babbitt,* 1799–1862.]

bab·ble (bab'əl) *v.,* **bab·bled, bab·bling.** —*v.i.* **1.** to make sounds that are unclear or meaningless: *The baby gurgled and babbled.* **2.** to talk foolishly or too much; chatter. **3.** to make a continuous murmuring sound: *The brook babbled.* —*v.t.* **1.** to say in an unclear or meaningless way: *The feverish man kept babbling his wife's name until he fell asleep.* **2.** to utter foolishly: *She babbled all kinds of gossip.* —*n.* **1.** unclear or meaningless sounds or talk. **2.** a continuous murmuring sound. —**bab'bler,** *n.*

babe (bāb) *n.* **1.** a baby or young child. **2.** a naive, inexperienced, or helpless person.

Ba·bel (bā'bəl, bab'əl) *n.* **1.** in the Old Testament, Babylon. **2. Tower of Babel.** in the Old Testament, a tower begun in Babel by the descendants of Noah in order to reach heaven. God kept them from finishing the tower by changing their language into many different languages so that they could not understand each other. **3.** *also,* **babel.** a confused mixture of many voices or languages.

ba·boon (ba boon') *n.* a large African monkey that has a long, doglike face, cheek pouches for storing food, front and back legs of almost the same length, and usually a short tail.

ba·bush·ka (bə boosh'kə) *n.* a woman's kerchief, often made or folded in the shape of a triangle, worn over the head and tied under the chin.

ba·by (bā'bē) *n. pl.,* **ba·bies. 1.** a newborn or very young child. **2.** the youngest member of a family or group. **3.** a person who behaves like a child; childish person. **4.** a newborn or very young animal. —*adj.* **1.** for a baby: *a baby blanket.* **2.** of or like a baby; childish: *a baby face.* **3.** newborn or very young: *a baby rabbit.* —*v.t.,* **ba·bied, ba·by·ing.** to treat like a baby; pamper; coddle: *The mother babied the sick child.*

Baboon

baby carriage, a small, four-wheeled carriage for a baby, usually with a folding top.

ba·by·hood (bā'bē hood') *n.* **1.** the state of being a baby. **2.** the time during which a person is a baby.

ba·by·ish (bā'bē ish) *adj.* like a baby; childish. —**ba'by·ish·ly,** *adv.* —**ba'by·ish·ness,** *n.*

Bab·y·lon (bab'ə lən) *n.* the capital of Babylonia, on the Euphrates River.

Bab·y·lo·ni·a (bab'ə lō'nē ə) *n.* an ancient empire in Mesopotamia that flourished from about 1900 B.C. until 538 B.C., when it was conquered by the Persians.

Bab·y·lo·ni·an (bab'ə lō'nē ən) *adj.* of or relating to Babylon or Babylonia. —*n.* **1.** a person who lived in Babylonia. **2.** the Semitic language of Babylonia.

ba·by's-breath (bā'bēz breth') *n.* a plant bearing thick clusters of tiny white or pink flowers.

ba·by-sit (bā'bē sit') *v.i.,* **ba·by-sat** (bā'bē sat'), **ba·by-sit·ting.** to take care of a young child or children while the parents are away temporarily. —**ba'by-sit'ter,** *n.*

bac·ca·lau·re·ate (bak'ə lôr'ē it) *n.* **1.** another word for **bachelor's degree. 2.** a sermon or address delivered to a graduating class at commencement.

Bac·chus (bak'əs) *n. Roman Mythology.* the god of wine. In Greek mythology he was called Dionysus.

Bach, Jo·hann Se·bas·tian (bäk; yō'hän sə bas'-chən) 1685–1750, German composer and organist.

bach·e·lor (bach'ə lər) *n.* a man who has not married.

Bachelor of Arts, a bachelor's degree in the liberal arts or social sciences.

Bachelor of Science, a bachelor's degree in science or mathematics.

bach·e·lor's-but·ton (bach'ə lerz but'ən) *n.* **1.** a plant bearing many slender branching stems and showy flowers. **2.** any of several plants with button-shaped flowers.

bachelor's degree, an undergraduate degree given by a college or university to a person who has completed a four-year program or its equivalent. Also, **baccalaureate.**

ba·cil·lus (bə sil'əs) *n. pl.,* **ba·cil·li** (bə sil'ī). **1.** any bacterium shaped like a rod or cylinder, especially one that forms spores. **2.** any bacterium.

back (bak) *n.* **1.** the rear part of the human body, from the neck to the end of the spine. **2.** the upper part of the body of an animal corresponding to the human back. **3.** the spinal column; backbone: *He fell and injured his back.* **4.** the part opposite to or farthest from the front; rear part: *the back of a closet. He sat in the back of the classroom.* **5.** the other side; reverse: *Mr. Jones signed his name on the back of the check.* **6.** the part of an object that protects or supports the human back: *the back of a chair, the back of a bench.* **7.a.** a player whose regular position is behind that of players in the front line, as in football. **b.** the position occupied by such a player. —*v.t.* **1.** to support or help: *Are you going to back Frank for election as class president?* **2.** to cause to move backward: *Jane backed the car into the garage.* **3.** to provide with a backing; strengthen at the back: *to back a picture with cardboard.* —*v.i.* to move backward: *The frightened girl backed away from the growling dog.* —*adj.* **1.** at or in the rear: *a back door.* **2.** belonging to the past; not current: *a back copy of a magazine.* **3.** in a backward direction; reversed: *a back somersault.* —*adv.* **1.** at, to, or toward the rear; backward: *Please step back so that I may pass.* **2.** in, to, or toward a former place or position: *Put the box back on the shelf.* **3.** in, to, or toward a former condition or state: *My cold has come back.* **4.** in or into the past: *The earthquake happened back in 1906.* **5.** in reply or return: *Don't hit him back.* **6.** in check; under control: *The dam held back the floodwaters.*

  back and forth. first in one direction and then in the other; to and fro.

  back of. *Informal.* behind.

  behind one's back. without a person's knowledge or approval; in secret: *He pretends to be her friend, but he constantly criticizes her behind her back.*

  to back out or **to back out of.** to withdraw from or fail to keep a promise, agreement, or the like.

  to go back on. *Informal.* to refuse to keep a pledge or promise.

  to turn one's back on. to ignore, neglect, or abandon: *Jack never turned his back on me when I needed help.*

back·ache (bak'āk') *n.* an ache or pain in one's back.

back·bite (bak'bīt') *v.i.,* **back·bit** (bak'bit'), **back·bit·ten** (bak'bit'ən), **back·bit·ing.** to say mean or unfriendly things about someone who is not present. —**back'bit'er,** *n.*

back·board (bak'bôrd') *n.* **1.** a board forming or supporting the back of something. **2.** in basketball, the raised, upright board to which the basket is attached.

back·bone (bak'bōn') *n.* **1.** the spinal column; spine. **2.** the strongest or most important part: *Brave men formed the backbone of the first settlements in the West.* **3.** strength of character or firmness of will: *It took backbone for Larry to stand up for his beliefs.*

back·break·ing (bak'brā'king) *adj.* calling for great strength or effort; physically exhausting: *Moving the piano upstairs was backbreaking work.*

back·drop (bak'drop') *n.* a curtain hung at the back of a stage, often painted to represent a scene.

back·er (bak'ər) *n.* a person who supports another person or an undertaking, especially by providing money.

back·field (bak'fēld') *n. Football.* **1.** the four players whose regular positions are behind the linemen; the quarterback, two halfbacks, and the fullback. **2.** the area behind the linemen.

back·fire (bak'fīr') *n.* **1.** an improper explosion in a gasoline engine, causing a loud noise. A backfire occurs when fuel is ignited at the wrong time during the engine's cycle, or when it is ignited outside the engine's cylinders. **2.** a fire built to stop an advancing forest or prairie fire by burning off an area in its path. —*v.i.,* **back·fired, back·fir·ing. 1.** to have a backfire: *The truck backfired as it switched into gear.* **2.** to bring about results that are opposite to those hoped for or expected: *The businessman's plan to make money backfired, and he became bankrupt.*

back·gam·mon (bak'gam'ən) *n.* a game for two people played on a special board with dice and fifteen pieces for each player. The throw of the dice determines how many places the pieces move.

back·ground (bak'ground') *n.* **1.** the part of a picture or scene that is, or appears to be, furthest from the viewer's eye: *The artist painted a waterfall in the background of the picture.* **2.** a surface around or behind objects or designs: *The kitchen wallpaper has yellow tulips on a white background.* **3.** past events or facts that help to explain some later event or situation: *the background of World War II.* **4.** a person's past experience and education: *He does not have the right kind of background for the job.*

background music, music that accompanies the speech or action in a play, motion picture, or broadcast.

back·hand (bak'hand') *n.* **1.** a stroke in tennis and other games, made with the arm drawn across the body and the back of the hand turned outward. **2.** handwriting that slants toward the left. —*adj.* backhanded. —*adv.* with a backhand stroke.

back·hand·ed (bak'han'did) *adj.* **1.** done or made with the back of the hand, or with the back of the hand turned outward: *a backhanded tennis stroke.* **2.** slanting to the left: *backhanded handwriting.* **3.** not direct or straightforward: *The statement "Although he is sloppy and disorganized, his work is fairly good" is a backhanded compliment.* —**back'hand'ed·ly,** *adv.* —**back'hand'ed·ness,** *n.*

back·ing (bak'ing) *n.* **1.** approval or assistance; support: *The students tried to get the backing of the principal for a new gymnasium.* **2.** supporters or backers as a group. **3.** something used to support, form, or strengthen a back: *The picture has a cardboard backing.*

back·lash (bak'lash') *n. pl.,* **back·lash·es.** a strong feeling or an action that comes as a reaction to some force or event: *The rise in crime caused a backlash against prison reforms.*

B

back·log (bak′lôg′, bak′log′) *n.* **1.** reserve supply: *a backlog of business experience.* **2.** a large amount of unfinished work: *a backlog of orders to fill.* **3.** a large log at the back of a fireplace to keep the fire going.

back·pack (bak′pak″) *n.* a pack for camping supplies supported by a metal frame and carried on the back. —*v.i.* to go hiking or camping using a backpack. —**back′-pack′er,** *n.*

back·rest (bak′rest′) *n.* a support for the back.

back seat, a seat to the rear.

to take a back seat to. *Informal.* to occupy a less important position than someone or something else: *The older man disliked having to take a back seat to the new, younger employees.*

back-seat driver (bak′sēt′) *Informal.* a person who offers unwanted advice, especially in a passenger car.

back·side (bak′sīd′) *n.* the rump; buttocks.

back·slide (bak′slīd′) *v.i.,* **back·slid** (bak′slīd′), **back-slid** or **back·slid·den** (bak′slid′ən), **back·slid·ing.** to return to former or undesirable habits or practices. —**back′-slid′er,** *n.*

back·spin (bak′spin′) *n.* a backward spin on a ball that is moving forward.

back·stage (bak′stāj′) *adj.* relating to, located, or happening in the area of a theater behind the stage. —*adv.* in, to, or toward the backstage area of a theater.

back·stop (bak′stop′) *n.* **1.** a fence, screen, or wall used in sports to stop the ball from going too far beyond the playing area. **2.** a player who stops the ball, especially the catcher in baseball.

back·stroke (bak′strōk′) *n.* a stroke in swimming made while lying on the back. The swimmer moves his or her arms alternately up and back into the water while kicking his or her feet rapidly.

back talk *Informal.* a reply that is rude or disrespectful.

back·track (bak′trak′) *v.i.* **1.** to return by the same route or path; retrace one's course: *The group backtracked on the trail so that they wouldn't get lost in the woods.* **2.** to take an opposite position or stand: *The frightened boy backtracked on his earlier account of the accident.*

back·ward (bak′wərd) *adv.* also, **back·wards. 1.** toward the back; to the rear: *She threw the ball backward.* **2.** with the back first: *He was walking backward and fell.* **3.** opposite to the usual or right way; in reverse: *He tried to recite the alphabet backward.* **4.** toward or into the past. *Look backward in time and imagine life in 1800.* **5.** toward a worse state or condition. —*adj.* **1.** directed or turned toward the back or rear: *a backward glance, backward movement.* **2.** behind in growth or development: *a backward area.* **3.** done with the back foremost. **4.** shy; bashful. —**back′ward·ly,** *adv.* —**back′ward·ness,** *n.*

▲ Both **backward** and **backwards** may be used as adverbs: *The car rolled backward (or backwards) in the parking lot.* Only **backward** may be used as an adjective: *The swimmer performed a backward dive* (not *a backwards dive*).

back·wash (bak′wôsh′, bak′wosh′) *n.* **1.** water moved backward by the force of an object moving through it. **2.** a backward current of air from an airplane propeller. **3.** the aftereffect of an event or condition.

back·wa·ter (bak′wô′tər) *n.* **1.** water turned or held back by an obstruction, tide, or opposing current. **2.** a place or condition thought of as dull or backward. —*adj.* dull or backward: *a backwater town.*

back·woods (bak′woodz′) *n., pl.* heavily wooded or thinly settled areas that are far from cities or towns.

back·woods·man (bak′woodz′mən) *n. pl.,* **back·woods·men** (bak′woodz′mən). a person who lives in or comes from the backwoods.

back·yard (bak′yärd′) *n.* a yard behind a house or other building. —*adj.* of or in a backyard: *a backyard fence.*

ba·con (bā′kən) *n.* salted and smoked meat from the back and sides of a hog.

Ba·con, Francis (bā′kən) 1561–1626, English essayist, statesman, and philosopher.

bac·te·ri·a (bak tēr′ē ə) *n., pl. sing.,* **bac·te·ri·um.** one-celled organisms that are so small that they can be seen only through a microscope. Bacteria are found in air, soil, and water, and in and on all plants and animals. Some kinds of bacteria cause diseases. Others are useful to man, as in the processing of cheeses.

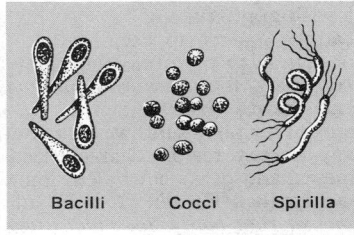

Bacilli   Cocci   Spirilla

Bacteria

bac·te·ri·al (bak tēr′ē əl) *adj.* relating to or produced by bacteria: *a bacterial stomach infection.*

bac·te·ri·ol·o·gist (bak tēr′ē ol′ə jist) *n.* a student of or an expert in bacteriology.

bac·te·ri·ol·o·gy (bak tēr′ē ol′ə jē) *n.* the science that deals with bacteria.

bac·te·ri·um (bak tēr′ē əm) the singular of **bacteria.**

Bac·tri·an camel (bak′trē ən) a two-humped camel of central Asia.

bad (bad) *adj.,* **worse, worst. 1.** having little quality or worth; below standard; poor: *That employee's work is bad.* **2.** evil; wicked; immoral: *His friends are a bad influence on him.* **3.** severe or violent: *a bad storm, a bad fall, a bad cough.* **4.** having errors; incorrect; faulty: *bad spelling.* **5.** not pleasant; disagreeable: *a bad smell, bad weather.* **6.** having a harmful effect; damaging: *Polluted air is bad for your lungs.* **7.** distressing; unfavorable; unfortunate: *We were sorry to hear the bad news that Jack had been in an accident.* **8.** regretful; sorry; distressed: *He felt bad about causing so much trouble.* **9.** in poor health. **10.** rotten or spoiled: *Milk turns bad if it is not kept cool.* —*n.* something that is bad: *The good outweighed the bad in his character.* —*adv. Informal.* badly. —**bad′ness,** *n.*

not bad or **not half bad.** fairly good; acceptable.

to be in bad. *Informal.* to be in disfavor: *I'm in bad with my mother because I was late for dinner.*

▲ At one time, the adjective **bad,** not the adverb **badly,** was used in sentences with linking verbs such as *look, smell,* and *feel: Mary looked bad during her illness.* Today, the adverb *badly* is sometimes used in conversation in place of *bad,* especially with the word *feel: I feel badly about having to miss your party.*

bad blood, hatred or hostility: *There has always been bad blood between the two families.*

bade (bad, bād) a past tense of **bid.**

Ba·den-Pow·ell, Sir Robert (bād′ən pō′əl) 1857–1941, British general who founded the Boy Scout movement.

badge (baj) *n.* an emblem or mark worn to show rank, membership, or achievement: *a sheriff's badge.*

at; āpe; cär; end; mē; it; īce; hot; ōld; fôrk; wood; fōol; oil; out; up; turn; sing; thin; <u>th</u>is; hw in white; zh in treasure. The symbol ə stands for the sound of **a** in about, **e** in taken, **i** in pencil, **o** in lemon, and **u** in circus.

badg·er (baj′ər) *n.* **1.** any of a group of animals having a heavy body, short legs, long claws, and a short, thick tail. Badgers live in holes in the ground, which they have burrowed, and they usually feed at night. **2.** the yellowish-gray fur of a badger. —*v.t.* to keep on annoying or tormenting; pester: *The district attorney badgered the witness with questions.*

Badger

Bad·lands (bad′landz′) *n., pl.* **1.** a barren, heavily eroded region in southwestern South Dakota. **2. badlands.** any barren region characterized by numerous ridges, mesas, and peaks cut by erosion.

bad·ly (bad′lē) *adv.* **1.** in a bad manner: *The engine of the car runs badly. Joe's plans turned out badly.* **2.** *Informal.* very much: *He needs new shoes badly.* ▲ See usage note under **bad.**

bad·min·ton (bad′min′tən) *n.* a game similar to tennis, in which a shuttlecock is hit back and forth over a high net with light rackets. [From *Badminton,* an English duke's estate where the game was introduced.]

bad-tem·pered (bad′tem′pərd) *adj.* cross or quarrelsome; irritable.

Baf·fin Bay (baf′in) an inlet of the Atlantic Ocean, west of Greenland and east of Baffin Island.

Baffin Island, a large Canadian island west of Greenland, at the mouth of Hudson Bay. Area, approx. 200,000 sq. mi.

baf·fle (baf′əl) *v.t.,* **baf·fled, baf·fling. 1.** to bewilder or puzzle greatly; confuse; perplex: *The magician's escape from a locked box baffled the audience. Complicated crossword puzzles often baffle me.* **2.** to control or hold back the progress or flow of. —*n.* a wall or screen for controlling or changing the flow of fluids or sound waves: *a baffle on a loudspeaker.* —**baf′fle·ment,** *n.* —**baf′fler,** *n.*

bag (bag) *n.* **1.** a container made of paper, cloth, leather, or other flexible material: *a shopping bag, a mail bag.* **2.** the amount that a bag can hold: *I ate a bag of popcorn at the movie.* **3.** something like a bag in shape: *This sweater has bags at the elbows.* **4.** a purse; handbag. **5.** a suitcase or satchel; valise: *Have you packed your bags yet?* **6.** the amount of game killed or captured in hunting. **7.** a base in baseball. —*v.,* **bagged, bag·ging.** —*v.t.* **1.** to kill or capture (game) in hunting: *The hunter bagged three birds.* **2.** *Informal.* to seize or capture; trap: *The police officer bagged the thief.* **3.** to put into a bag: *The cashier bagged my apples.* —*v.i.* to hang loosely; sag: *His slacks bagged at the knees.* —**bag′like′,** *adj.*

to be left holding the bag. *Informal.* to be left to take full blame or responsibility: *When my friend's ball broke our neighbor's window, he ran away and I was left holding the bag.*

bag·a·telle (bag′ə tel′) *n.* something of little value or importance; trifle.

Bag·dad (bag′dad) another spelling of **Baghdad.**

ba·gel (bā′gəl) *n.* a doughnut-shaped roll made of yeast dough, cooked in simmering water and then baked.

bag·gage (bag′ij) *n.* **1.** suitcases, bags, and other belongings that a person takes with him or her when traveling; luggage. **2.** portable equipment and supplies of an army, such as tents, bedding, and cooking utensils.

bag·gy (bag′ē) *adj.,* **bag·gi·er, bag·gi·est.** hanging loosely; bulging: *baggy trousers.* —**bag′gi·ness,** *n.*

Bagh·dad (bag′dad) *also,* **Bag·dad.** *n.* the capital of Iraq, in the east-central part of the country, on the Tigris River. Pop. (1970 est.), 1,300,000.

bag·pipe (bag′pīp′) *also,* **bag·pipes.** *n.* a shrill-toned musical instrument, used especially in Scotland, consisting of a leather windbag from which air is forced through several pipes.

Bagpipe

bah (bä) *interj.* an exclamation of contempt or disbelief.

Ba·ha·mas (bə hä′məz) *n.* an island country in the West Indies, southeast of Florida. Land area, 4404 sq. mi. Pop. (1978 est.), 219,000. Capital, Nassau. Also, **Bahama Islands.** —**Ba·ham·i·an** (bə hā′mē ən, bə hä′mē ən) *adj., n.*

Bah·rain (bä rān′) *also,* **Bah·rein.** an island country, a sheikdom, in the Persian Gulf. Capital, Manama. Land area, 240 sq. mi. Pop. (1978 est.), 276,000.

bail[1] (bāl) *n.* **1.** money given to a court to obtain the temporary release of a person under arrest and to guarantee his appearance for trial at a specified time. **2.** a person or persons providing bail. —*v.t.* to obtain the temporary release of (a person under arrest) by providing bail (often with *out*). [Old French *bail* custody.]

to go bail or **to stand bail.** to supply bail.

to bail out. a. to supply bail for. **b.** to help (a person) in a financial crisis or other emergency: *Whenever he's out of money he comes to me to bail him out.*

bail[2] (bāl) *n.* the curved handle of a kettle, pail, or similar container. [Probably of Scandinavian origin.]

bail[3] (bāl) *v.t.* **1.** to remove (water) from a boat with a pail or similar container. **2.** to clear (a boat) of water with a pail or similar container (often with *out*): *to bail out a boat.* —*v.i.* to bail water: *We bailed desperately for an hour, but the boat sank anyway.* [French *baille* bucket.]

to bail out. to parachute from an aircraft, especially in an emergency.

bail·iff (bā′lif) *n.* **1.** a court officer who guards the prisoners and the jurors and keeps order in a courtroom. **2.** an assistant to a sheriff. **3.** in England, a person who manages an estate for the owner; steward.

bail·i·wick (bā′lə wik′) *n.* **1.** the office, jurisdiction, or district of a bailiff. **2.** a field in which a person has special or superior knowledge, interest, or authority: *American history is his bailiwick.*

bails·man (bālz′mən) *n. pl.,* **bails·men** (bālz′mən). a person who gives bail or serves as security for another.

bairn (bern) *n. Scottish.* a son or daughter; child.

bait (bāt) *n.* **1.** food or any other lure used to attract fish or other animals so that they may be caught: *The fisherman used worms as bait.* **2.** anything that tempts or attracts: *Money was the bait that attracted her to the job.* —*v.t.* **1.** to place food or any other lure on or in: *We baited the trap for the mice with cheese.* **2.** to torment or annoy, especially with insulting remarks; harass: *Sometimes children bait each other by calling silly names.* **3.** to set dogs upon (an animal) for sport: *In the Middle Ages people used to bait bears.*

baize (bāz) *n.* a thick woolen fabric with a long nap, used especially for curtains and table covers.

Ba·ja California (bä′hə) another name for **Lower California.**

bake (bāk) *v.,* **baked, bak·ing.** —*v.t.* **1.** to cook (food) by dry indirect heat, especially in an oven: *to bake a cake.* **2.** to dry or harden by heating: *The potter baked the bowls in a kiln.* —*v.i.* **1.** to cook food by baking. **2.** to become baked: *The potatoes baked slowly.*

bak·er (bā′kər) *n.* a person who makes and sells bread and other baked goods.

baker's dozen, a dozen plus one; thirteen. [From a former custom among *bakers* of adding an extra roll to each *dozen* as protection against the penalties for giving too few.]

bak·er·y (bā′kər ē) *n. pl.,* **bak·er·ies.** a place where bread and other baked goods are made or sold.

bak·ing (bā′king) *n.* **1.** the act of baking. **2.** the amount or batch baked at one time.

baking powder, a powder used in baking to make dough or batter rise.

baking soda, another term for **sodium bicarbonate.**

Ba·ku (bä kōō′) *n.* a port city in the southwestern Soviet Union, on the west coast of the Caspian Sea. Pop. (1971 est.), 870,000.

bal., balance.

bal·ance (bal′əns) *n.* **1.** an equality between opposing forces or elements: *There is a balance between good and evil in his nature.* **2.** the ability to keep one's body in a steady, upright position: *The tightrope walker lost his balance and fell into the net.* **3.** a pleasing or harmonious arrangement of parts: *There was a good balance between light and dark colors in the painting.* **4.** an instrument for weighing, especially an instrument consisting of a horizontal bar having a pan hung from either end, that pivots on a central point as weights are placed in the pans. **5.** the part that is left over; remainder: *I will finish the balance of my homework later.* **6.** something that counterbalances or offsets something else: *His generosity is a good balance for his brother's stinginess.* **7.** mental or emotional steadiness; sound mental condition: *The captain maintained his balance during the emergency.* **8.** *Bookkeeping.* **a.** an equality between the debit and credit sides of an account. **b.** the difference between the debit and credit sides of an account. **9.** see **balance wheel.** —*v.,* **bal·anced, bal·anc·ing.** —*v.t.* **1.** to put or keep in a steady state, condition, or position: *The waiter balanced the tray of dishes on his hand.* **2.** to compare or estimate the value, weight, or importance of: *The jury balanced the testimony of the two witnesses in deciding the case.* **3.** to make up for; offset. **4.** to place or keep in proportion; equalize: *Mother and I can't balance the seesaw unless my brother sits on my side.* **5.** to be equal or in proportion to: *The white balances the black in the wallpaper.* **6.** *Bookkeeping.* **a.** to find the difference between the debit and credit sides of (an account). **b.** to make the debit and credit sides of (an account) equal. **c.** to settle (an account) by paying the amount due. —*v.i.* **1.** to be in or come into a steady state, condition, or position: *The acrobat balanced on the wire.* **2.** to be equal: *His income and his expenses balanced this month.* **3.** *Bookkeeping.* (of an account) to have the debit and credit sides equal to each other: *Her checking account doesn't balance.*

    in the balance. uncertain or undecided: *The decision on the new gym will hang in the balance until after the school board meets.*

balance of payments, the difference between the total payments made by one country to all foreign countries and their total payments to that country.

balance of power, equal economic or military power among nations or groups of nations. It is maintained to prevent domination by any one nation or group of nations.

balance of trade, the difference in value between the exports and imports of a nation.

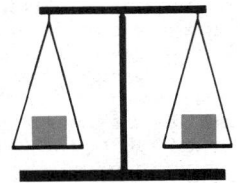

Balance

balance wheel, a wheel that regulates the mechanism and rate of motion, as of the hands of a watch or clock.

Bal·bo·a, Vas·co de (bal bō′ə; väs′kō dä) 1475?–1517, the Spanish explorer who discovered the Pacific Ocean.

bal·brig·gan (bal brig′ən) *n.* a knitted cotton cloth, used especially for hosiery or underwear. [From *Balbriggan,* an Irish town where it was first made.]

bal·co·ny (bal′kə nē) *n. pl.,* **bal·co·nies.** **1.** a platform projecting from the wall of a building and enclosed by a low wall or railing. **2.** a projecting upper floor with seats in a theater, auditorium, church, or other place of assembly.

bald (bôld) *adj.* **1.** having little or no hair on the head. **2.** without usual or natural covering: *a bald mountain peak.* **3.** not disguised; simple: *the bald truth.* **4.** (of animals) having white on the face or head: *a bald horse.* —*v.i.* to lose one's hair; become bald: *He is balding rapidly.* —**bald′ness,** *n.*

Balcony

bald eagle, a large eagle of North America that is brown with a white head, neck, and tail. It is the national symbol of the United States. Also, **American eagle.**

bal·der·dash (bôl′dər dash′) *n., interj.* nonsense; foolishness.

bal·dric (bôl′drik) *n.* a belt, often richly ornamented, worn over one shoulder and across the chest, used to hold a sword or bugle.

bale (bāl) *n.* a large bundle of bulky goods compressed, tightly tied, or otherwise prepared for shipping or storage: *a bale of hay.* —*v.t.,* **baled, bal·ing.** to make into a bale or bales: *to bale cotton.* —**bal′er,** *n.*

Bal·e·ar·ic Islands (bal′ē ar′ik) a Spanish island group in the western Mediterranean. Land area, 1936 sq. mi. Pop. (1970), 532,946.

ba·leen (bə lēn′) *n.* another word for **whalebone.**

bale·ful (bāl′fəl) *adj.* full of evil or danger; sinister: *The old man gave the boys a baleful look when he found them playing in his yard.* —**bale′ful·ly,** *adv.* —**bale′ful·ness,** *n.*

Ba·li (bä′lē) *n.* an island in Indonesia, east of Java. Area, 2905 sq. mi. Pop. (1961 est.), 1,775,000.

Ba·li·nese (bä′lə nēz′) *n. pl.,* **Ba·li·nese.** **1.** a person who was born or is living in Bali. **2.** the language of Bali. —*adj.* of or relating to Bali, its people, their language, or their culture.

balk (bôk) *v.i.* **1.** to stop short and refuse to go on or act (often with *at*): *The horse balked when he approached the fence. I balked at the thought of going to the party alone.* **2.** *Baseball.* (of a pitcher) to make an illegal motion while pitching the ball with one or more runners on base. —*v.t.* to keep from going on; hinder: *Mother balked our plans to go camping.* —*n.* **1.** something that hinders or obstructs. **2.** *Baseball.* an act of balking.

Bal·kan (bôl′kən) *adj.* of or relating to the Balkan Peninsula, the Balkan States, or the Balkan Mountains. —*n.* **the Balkans.** the Balkan States.

---

at; āpe; cär; end; mē; it; īce; hot; ōld; fôrk; wood; fōōl; oil; out; up; turn; sing; thin; this; hw in white; zh in treasure. The symbol ə stands for the sound of **a** in about, **e** in taken, **i** in pencil, **o** in lemon, and **u** in circus.

Balkan Mountains, a mountain range on the Balkan Peninsula, extending across the north-central part of Bulgaria.

Balkan Peninsula, a peninsula in southeastern Europe, bordered by the Black and Aegean Seas on the east and the Adriatic Sea on the west.

Balkan States, the countries on the Balkan Peninsula, including Yugoslavia, Romania, Bulgaria, Albania, and Greece. Also, **the Balkans.**

balk·y (bô′kē) *adj.,* **balk·i·er, balk·i·est.** given to balking; stubborn: *a balky horse.*

ball¹ (bôl) *n.* **1.** any round body; globe: *Bill rolled his kite string into a ball.* **2.** a round or roundish object used in various sports and games, such as baseball, tennis, or golf. **3.** any game played with such an object, especially baseball. **4.** a ball put into motion or play in a specified manner: *a high ball, a curve ball.* **5.** a rounded, protruding part of something: *the ball of the foot.* **6.** *Baseball.* a pitch that fails to pass over home plate in the area between the batter's knees and shoulders and that is not swung at by him. **7.** a solid, usually round, projectile that is larger than shot and is fired from a cannon or other firearm. —*v.t.* to form, wind, or gather into a ball or balls: *to ball yarn.* [Old Norse *böllr* ball, globe.] —**ball′like′,** *adj.*

ball² (bôl) *n.* **1.** a large, formal dance. **2.** *Slang.* a very enjoyable time: *We had a ball at the Christmas party.* [Old French *bal* a dance, from *baler* to dance.]

bal·lad (bal′əd) *n.* **1.** a sentimental or romantic song of two or more verses, each sung to the same melody. **2.** a poem or song that tells a story, written in simple verse and short stanzas. Ballads of popular origin were usually changed as they were passed along by word of mouth through the years.

ball-and-sock·et joint (bôl′ən sok′it) a joint, as that of the hip or shoulder, formed by a ball or knob in a socket, permitting limited rotary movement in every direction.

bal·last (bal′əst) *n.* **1.** a heavy material such as sand, placed in a ship to steady it or in a balloon to control its altitude. **2.** anything that gives steadiness, especially to a person: *Jane's common sense was a ballast to the family in times of crisis.* **3.** gravel or crushed rock used as a bed for the ties of a railroad. —*v.t.* to fill, provide, or steady with ballast: *to ballast a ship.*

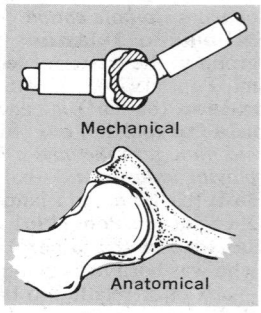

Mechanical

Anatomical

Ball-and-socket joints

ball bearing **1.** a bearing consisting of a number of metal balls on which the moving parts of a machine turn. **2.** any of these metal balls.

bal·le·ri·na (bal′ə rē′nə) *n.* a woman or girl ballet dancer.

bal·let (ba lā′, bal′ā) *n.* **1.** a form of dancing, usually set to music, that combines formal steps and positions in continuous, flowing movement. **2.** a theatrical presentation in which a story or theme is presented by such dancing. **3.** a group or company of dancers who perform in such a presentation.

bal·lis·tic (bə lis′tik) *adj.* of, relating to, or used in ballistics.

ballistic missile, a self-propelled missile that is controlled as it rises, but is a free-falling object in its descent.

bal·lis·tics (bə lis′tiks) *n., pl.* the science that deals with the motion of projectiles, such as bombs or bullets, and the conditions that affect their motion.

bal·loon (bə lōōn′) *n.* **1.** a rubber bag, often brightly colored, that is filled with air or gas and used as a toy or decoration. **2.** an airtight bag made of tough, light material, filled with a gas that is lighter than air and designed to rise and float in the atmosphere. A basket or container is often attached to its bottom for carrying scientific instruments or passengers. —*v.i.* to swell out or expand like a balloon: *The parachute ballooned as soon as the jumper pulled the cord.*

bal·lot (bal′ət) *n.* **1.** a written or printed form used to cast a secret vote. **2.** the total number of votes cast in an election: *The ballot was recorded after the polls closed.* **3.** the system of secret voting by ballots or voting machines. **4.** the list of candidates running in an election: *There were six names on the ballot.* —*v.i.* to cast a ballot or ballots; vote. [Italian *ballotta* little ball, a form of *balla* ball; from the ancient Greek method of voting by using small white balls to indicate approval and small black balls to indicate disapproval.]

ballot box, a box into which ballots are put.

ball park, a stadium for playing baseball.

ball·play·er (bôl′plā′ər) *n.* a person who plays any of various games in which a ball is used, especially one who plays baseball.

ball-point pen (bôl′point′) a pen whose point is a small metal ball that rolls the ink from a cartridge onto the writing surface.

ball·room (bôl′rōōm′, bôl′room′) *n.* a large room for dances or other social gatherings.

bal·ly·hoo (bal′ē hōō′) *Informal. n. pl.,* **bal·ly·hoos.** **1.** exaggerated or sensational advertising or publicity. **2.** a noisy uproar; clamor. —*v.t.,* **bal·ly·hooed, bal·ly·hoo·ing.** to advertise or promote (someone or something) with ballyhoo. [Said to be named after *Ballyhooly,* an Irish village famous for its noisy quarrels.]

balm (bäm) *n.* **1.** a fragrant oily or gummy resin obtained from certain trees or shrubs, often used as a salve; balsam. **2.** any fragrant ointment or oil that heals or soothes. **3.** anything that heals or soothes: *Sleep was a balm to his troubled mind.*

balm·y (bä′mē) *adj.,* **balm·i·er, balm·i·est.** **1.** mild and soothing: *balmy spring weather.* **2.** fragrant. —**balm′i·ly,** *adv.* —**balm′i·ness,** *n.*

ba·lo·ney (bə lō′nē) *n.* **1.** another spelling of **bologna.** **2.** *Slang.* nonsense; foolishness.

bal·sa (bôl′sə) *n.* **1.** a strong, lightweight wood used especially for making airplane or boat models and in rafts and floats. **2.** any of a group of tropical American trees from which this wood is obtained.

bal·sam (bôl′səm) *n.* **1.** any of a group of fragrant, oily or gummy resins obtained from certain trees or shrubs, used in cough drops, candies, and medicine, in products for the hair, and in making a soothing salve. **2.** a tree yielding such resins, as the balsam fir. **3.** a bushy plant that is widely cultivated for its showy flowers.

balsam fir **1.** a North American evergreen tree of the pine family. **2.** the wood of this tree, used especially to make boxes, crates, and paper pulp.

Bal·tic (bôl′tik) *n.* an inland sea in northern Europe, bordered by Germany and Poland on the south, Denmark and Sweden on the west, and Finland and the Soviet Union on the east. Also, **Baltic Sea.** —*adj.* of or relating to the Baltic or the Baltic States.

Baltic States, Estonia, Latvia, and Lithuania.

Bal·ti·more (bôl′tə môr′) *n.* the largest city in Maryland, on the Chesapeake Bay. Pop. (1970), 905,759.

Baltimore oriole, a North American songbird closely related to the meadowlark and blackbird. The male has brilliant markings of orange and black.

B

bal·us·ter (bal′əs tər) *n.* one of the small posts that support the railing of a staircase, parapet, or similar structure.

bal·us·trade (bal′əs trād′) *n.* a row of balusters and the handrail they support, as on a staircase.

Baluster   Balustrade

Ba·ma·ko (bä′mä kō′) *n.* the capital and the largest city of Mali, in the southwestern part of the country. Pop. (1969 est.), 189,200.

bam·bi·no (bam bē′nō) *n. pl.,* **bam·bi·ni** (bam bē′nē) or **bam·bi·nos.** **1.** a baby or child. **2.** a figure of the baby Jesus. [Italian *bambino* baby.]

bam·boo (bam bōō′) *n. pl.,* **bam·boos.** **1.** the hollow, jointed, woody stems of any of a large group of plants of the grass family, used to make furniture, window shades, canes, and fishing poles. **2.** a plant bearing these stems, having slender branches and sword-shaped leaves. Some bamboo plants may reach a height of 120 feet.

bam·boo·zle (bam bōō′zəl) *v.t.,* **bam·boo·zled, bam·boo·zling.** *Informal.* to deceive or cheat by tricking or confusing: *The sly salesman bamboozled us into buying the worthless car.*

Bamboo trees

ban (ban) *v.t.,* **banned, ban·ning.** to forbid officially; prohibit: *The management banned smoking in the theater.* —*n.* **1.** the official or formal forbidding of something: *The treaty placed a ban on the testing of nuclear weapons.* **2.** an official condemnation by church authorities.

ba·nal (bān′əl, bə nal′) *adj.* dull or boring from having been used or said very often; trite; commonplace: *The guests' banal comments about how big she had grown began to tire the child.* —**ba′nal·ly,** *adv.*

ba·nal·i·ty (bā nal′ə tē, bə nal′ə tē) *n. pl.,* **ba·nal·i·ties.** **1.** a banal remark or idea: *His conversation is full of remarks about the weather and other banalities.* **2.** the quality of being banal.

ba·nan·a (bə nan′ə) *n.* **1.** a narrow, slightly curved fruit having a sweet, creamy flesh and yellow or red skin. **2.** the treelike plant bearing this fruit, having a high, thick stalk and large, deep green leaves. It is found in nearly all tropical regions of the world.

Ba·na·ras (bə när′əs) another spelling of **Benares.**

band¹ (band) *n.* **1.** a group of persons or animals: *a band of thieves, a band of gorillas.* **2.** a group of musicians organized to play together, especially on wind and percussion instruments: *a marching band, a dance band.* —*v.i.* to unite in a group: *The citizens banded together to oppose the new highway.* —*v.t.* to unite (persons or things) in a group: *The residents banded themselves together to clean up the block.* [French *bande* band, troop.]

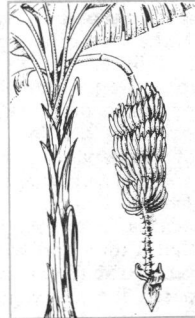
Banana plant

band² (band) *n.* **1.** a flat strip of material used for trimming or binding: *She wore a red band in her hair. There were iron bands around the barrel to strengthen it.* **2.** a strip of another color or material; stripe; bar: *The barber*

pole had bands of white and red around it. **3.** a particular range of wavelengths or frequencies in radio broadcasting. —*v.t.* to mark or provide with a band or bands: *He banded the leg of the pigeon for identification.* [Old French *bande* bond, tie; of Germanic origin.]

band·age (ban′dij) *n.* a strip of cloth or other material used in covering or binding a wound or injury. —*v.t.,* **band·aged, band·ag·ing.** to bind or cover with a bandage.

band-aid (band′ād′) *n.* a small bandage made of gauze and tape, with adhesive on one side to stick to the skin. Trademark: **Band-Aid.**

ban·dan·na (ban dan′ə) *also,* **ban·dan·a.** *n.* a large handkerchief, often brightly colored or patterned: *The rodeo rider wore a bandanna around his neck.*

band·box (band′boks′) *n. pl.,* **band·box·es.** a box of cardboard or other light material used for holding hats, collars, and other articles.

ban·deau (ban dō′) *n. pl.,* **ban·deaux** (ban dōz′) or **ban·deaus.** a narrow band, especially one worn about the hair.

ban·di·coot (ban′də kōōt′) *n.* **1.** a large rat of India and Ceylon, that may grow to over a foot in length and often damages gardens and rice fields. **2.** any of a group of small animals native to Australia and neighboring islands, having a pouch for their young, large hind feet, and slender forefeet with long, sharp claws.

Bandicoot

ban·dit (ban′dit) *n. pl.,* **ban·dits** or **ban·dit·ti** (ban dit′ē). a robber or outlaw.

ban·dit·ry (ban′də trē) *n.* the work of bandits; robbing and plundering.

band·mas·ter (band′mas′tər) *n.* the conductor of a musical band.

ban·do·leer (ban′də lēr′) *also,* **ban·do·lier.** *n.* a broad belt worn over the shoulder and across the chest, with loops or small pockets used for carrying ammunition and other small articles.

band saw, a saw consisting of an endless saw-toothed steel belt running over and driven by pulleys.

band·stand (band′stand′) *n.* a platform for musical concerts, often having a roof when situated outdoors.

Ban·dung (bän′dōōng) *n.* a city in Indonesia, in western Java. Pop. (1961), 972,566.

band·wag·on (band′wag′ən) *n.* a decorated wagon that carries a musical band in a parade or similar procession. **on the bandwagon** or **aboard the bandwagon.** *Informal.* on the successful or popular side: *The candidate's victory in the primary was so impressive that everyone climbed on the bandwagon.*

ban·dy (ban′dē) *v.t.,* **ban·died, ban·dy·ing.** **1.** to give and take; exchange: *The two boys pretended they were boxing and playfully bandied blows.* **2.** to throw or knock back and forth: *to bandy a ball over a net.* —*adj.* (of legs) bent or curved outward; bowed.

ban·dy-leg·ged (ban′dē leg′id) *adj.* with the legs bent or curved outward; bowlegged.

bane (bān) *n.* a cause of death, ruin, or injury: *Drought and blight were the bane of the farmers.*

at; āpe; cär; end; mē; it; īce; hot; ōld; fôrk; wood; fōōl; oil; out; up; turn; sing; thin; **this**; hw in white; zh in treasure. The symbol ə stands for the sound of **a** in about, **e** in taken, **i** in pencil, **o** in lemon, and **u** in circus.

bane·ber·ry (bān′ber′ē) *n. pl.,* **bane·ber·ries. 1.** a plant bearing clusters of small white flowers and white or red berries. **2.** the poisonous berry of this plant.

bane·ful (bān′fəl) *adj.* causing death, ruin, or injury: *a baneful influence.* —**bane′ful·ly,** *adv.* —**bane′ful·ness,** *n.*

bang¹ (bang) *n.* **1.** a loud, sudden, or explosive noise: *The door shut with a bang.* **2.** a heavy, noisy blow; thump; whack: *I fell and gave my head a good bang on the floor.* **3.** *Informal.* a sudden burst of energy or activity: *The race started off with a bang.* **4.** *Slang.* a large amount of pleasure or excitement; thrill; kick: *My brother gets a bang out of riding on the roller coaster.* —*v.t.* **1.** to strike or hit (something) noisily or violently: *My sled banged the tree, but I was not hurt.* **2.** to make a loud noise by slamming (something): *I banged the window shut.* —*v.i.* **1.** to make a loud, sudden, or explosive noise: *The shutters banged in the wind.* **2.** to strike or bump noisily or violently: *Charlie banged into the chair as he looked for the light switch in the dark.* —*adv. Informal.* suddenly and violently: *The baseball player ran bang into the fence as she tried to catch the ball.* [Of Scandinavian origin.]
   to bang up. to do damage to (something): *The driver banged up his car badly in the crash.*

bang² (bang) *n. usually,* **bangs.** hair worn over or across the forehead. —*v.t.* to cut (hair) short and straight across the forehead. [Of uncertain origin.]

Ban·ga·lore (bang′gə lôr′) *n.* a city in southern India. Pop. (1976 est.), 1,540,741.

Bang·kok (bang′kok) *n.* the capital, largest city, and chief port of Thailand, in the south-central part of the country. Pop. (1972 est.), 3,133,834.

Ban·gla·desh (bang′glə desh′, bäng′glə desh′) *also,* **Ban·gla Desh.** *n.* a country located north of the Bay of Bengal and east of India. It was formerly the province of **East Pakistan.** Capital, Dacca. Area, 54,501 sq. mi. Pop. (1974), 71,479,071.

ban·gle (bang′gəl) *n.* a circular band worn as an ornament around the wrist, arm, or ankle.

Ban·gui (bäng′gē) *n.* the capital of the Central African Republic, in the southwestern part of the country. Pop. (1971 est.), 187,000.

bang-up (bang′up′) *adj. Slang.* exceptionally good; excellent: *Matthew did a bang-up job of waxing the car.*

ban·ian (ban′yən) another spelling of **banyan.**

ban·ish (ban′ish) *v.t.* **1.** to punish by forcing to leave a country: *The king was deposed and banished from the country.* **2.** to send or drive away: *His captors warned him to banish all thoughts of trying to escape.* —**ban′ishment,** *n.*

ban·is·ter (ban′is tər) *n.* a handrail and its upright supports along the edge of a staircase or other raised structure.

Ban·jer·ma·sin (bän′jər mä′sin) *n.* a port city in Indonesia, on the southern coast of Borneo. Pop. (1971), 281,673

ban·jo (ban′jō) *n. pl.,* **ban·jos** or **ban·joes.** a stringed musical instrument, usually having five strings, with a long neck and a round body.

Ban·jul (bän′jool) *n.* the capital of Gambia, in the western part of the country. Pop. (1978), 45,600.

bank¹ (bangk) *n.* **1.** a long pile or mound: *The bulldozer dug up a bank of dirt.* **2.** the rising ground bordering a body of water. **3.** a steep slope: *The mountain road has a bank to the left around the bend.* **4.** a rise in the sea floor or bed of a river over which the water is shallow. **5.** a tilt to one side made by an airplane in turning. —*v.t.* **1.** to border with a bank;

Banjo

raise a bank around: *They banked the river with sandbags to hold back the water in case of a flood.* **2.** to form into a bank; pile: *The plow banked the snow along the side of the street.* **3.** to cover (a fire) with ashes, earth, or fuel so that it will burn slowly: *The workers banked the fire before closing time at the steel factory.* **4.** to slope so that the outer edge is higher: *The tractors banked the sides of the road.* **5.** to tilt (an airplane) when making a turn so that one wing is higher than the other. —*v.i.* **1.** to lie or form in banks: *Fallen leaves banked on the lawn.* **2.** to tilt an airplane when turning: *The pilot banked sharply to the left.* [Of Scandinavian origin.]

bank² (bangk) *n.* **1.** a place of business that safeguards, lends, exchanges, and issues money and carries on a number of other financial dealings. **2.** a small closed container, often with a slot, into which money may be placed for saving. **3.** any reserve supply, as of blood. **4.** a place that stores such a supply. —*v.t.* to deposit in a bank: *I banked twenty dollars this week.* —*v.i.* to do business with a bank: *We bank downtown.* [Italian *banca* bench or counter (of a banker or moneychanger); of Germanic origin.]
   to bank on or **to bank upon.** *Informal.* to depend on; be sure about: *You can bank on his going, so buy him a ticket.*

bank³ (bangk) *n.* **1.** a group of objects arranged in a line or in rows: *a bank of spotlights.* **2.a.** a bench for rowers in a galley. **b.** a row or tier of oars. **3.** a row of keys on an organ. —*v.t.* to arrange in a bank. [Old French *banc* bench, from Late Latin *bancus.*]

bank account, money deposited in a bank under the name of a person, that can be withdrawn by him or her.

bank·book (bangk′book′) *n.* a book held by a person, in which the deposits, withdrawals, and balance relating to his or her bank account are shown. Also, **passbook.**

bank·er (bang′kər) *n.* a person who helps manage a bank.

bank·ing (bang′king) *n.* the business carried on by a bank; business of managing a bank.

bank note, a piece of paper issued by a bank that can be exchanged for or used as money.

bank·rupt (bangk′rupt′) *n.* a person who is declared unable to pay his or her debts by a court of law, and whose property is divided among the people to whom he or she owes money. —*adj.* **1.** unable to pay one's debts. **2.** without a certain quality or thing; lacking. —*v.t.* to make bankrupt: *Heavy debts and bad management bankrupted his company.*

bank·rupt·cy (bangk′rupt′sē) *n. pl.,* **bank·rupt·cies. 1.** the state of being bankrupt; financial ruin. **2.** total ruin or failure.

ban·ner (ban′ər) *n.* **1.** a piece of cloth with some emblem or motto on it: *Marchers in the parade carried colorful banners.* **2.** a flag. **3.** a headline extending across the top of a newspaper page. —*adj.* leading or outstanding: *Winning the league championship made it a banner year for our football team.*

banns (banz) *n., pl.* a public announcement in church that a man and woman are to be married.

ban·quet (bang′kwit) *n.* **1.** a large, elaborate meal prepared for many guests or for a special occasion; feast. **2.** a formal or ceremonial dinner, often followed by speeches: *a banquet for a political candidate.* —*v.t.* to entertain at a banquet: *The embassy banqueted the visiting ambassador.* —*v.i.* to attend a banquet.

ban·quette (bang ket′) *n.* an upholstered bench, as along a wall in a restaurant.

ban·shee (ban′shē) *also,* **ban·shie.** *n.* in Irish and Scottish folklore, a female spirit who is supposed to wail when there will soon be a death in the family.

B

ban·tam (ban′təm) *n.* **1.** *also,* **Bantam.** a small chicken of any of various breeds. Some of the males are known for their fighting ability. **2.** a small person who is cocky or quarrelsome. —*adj.* small. [From *Bantam,* a city in Java, from which such chickens were supposedly imported.]

ban·tam·weight (ban′təm wāt′) *n.* an athlete competing in the next-to-lowest weight class in boxing or wrestling or the lowest weight class in weight lifting.

ban·ter (ban′tər) *n.* good-natured, playful teasing or joking: *There was much banter among the teammates after the game.* —*v.i.* to exchange good-natured, playful remarks.

Ban·tu (ban′tōō) *n. pl.,* **Ban·tu** or **Ban·tus.** **1.** a member of any of numerous Negroid tribes in central and southern Africa. **2.** any of the languages spoken by these tribes. —*adj.* of or relating to the Bantu or their languages.

ban·yan (ban′yən) *also,* **ban·ian.** *n.* any of several large trees of Asia, whose branches send down roots that enter the ground and develop into new trunks. One tree will often cover a large area of ground.

Banyan

ban·zai (bän′zī′) *interj.* a Japanese battle cry, cheer, or greeting. [Japanese *banzai* literally, may you live ten thousand years.]

ba·o·bab (bā′ō bab′) *n.* a tree found mostly in tropical Africa, having a broad trunk, thick spreading branches, and a fruit resembling a gourd. The fibers of its bark are used for making rope.

bap·tism (bap′tiz′əm) *n.* **1.** a religious ceremony of pouring or sprinkling water on a person or dipping him in water, as a sign of admission into a Christian church. **2.** any new and often difficult experience or trial: *She had her baptism as a teacher yesterday.*

bap·tis·mal (bap tiz′məl) *adj.* of or relating to baptism.

Bap·tist (bap′tist) *n.* **1.** a member of a Protestant church that baptizes believers by dipping them completely in water. **2. the Baptist.** John the Baptist. —*adj.* of or relating to the Baptists, their doctrines, or their practices.

bap·tis·tery (bap′tis trē) *n. pl.,* **bap·tis·ter·ies.** a part of a church, or a separate building, in which baptism is performed.

bap·tis·try (bap′tis trē) *n. pl.,* **bap·tis·tries.** another spelling of **baptistery.**

bap·tize (bap tīz′, bap′tīz) *v.t.,* **bap·tized, bap·tiz·ing.** **1.** to ceremonially admit (a person) into a Christian church by dipping in water or pouring or sprinkling water upon. **2.** to give a name to; christen: *We baptized our baby Elizabeth.* **3.** to cleanse or purify in spirit. —**bap·tiz′er,** *n.*

bar (bär) *n.* **1.** a piece of metal, wood, or other material, longer than it is wide or thick, used as a barrier, fastening, lever, or support: *The prison cell had bars across the window.* **2.** an oblong piece of solid material: *a bar of soap, a bar of gold.* **3.** anything that hinders or blocks progress; obstacle; barrier: *Lack of education can be a bar to business success.* **4.** a bank of sand or other material blocking navigation or the flow of water, as at the mouth of a river. **5.** a stripe or band: *The football jersey had bars of red and gold on it.* **6.a.** a counter where food or drinks, especially alcoholic drinks, are served. **b.** a place containing such a counter. **7.a.** the profession

Bar (def. 9)

of a lawyer: *He was admitted to the bar after he passed his examinations.* **b.** lawyers as a group. **8.** a court of law. **9.** *Music.* **a.** a vertical line placed on a staff to mark the division between two measures. **b.** a unit of music contained between two such lines; measure. **c.** two parallel vertical lines marking the end of a section or composition. Also, **double bar.** —*v.t.,* **barred, bar·ring.** **1.** to fasten with a bar: *Bar the door.* **2.** to hinder or block: *Armed guards barred the way into the building.* **3.** to prevent; prohibit: *Smoking was barred in the hospital halls.* **4.** to keep out; exclude: *Boys younger than eight were barred from the club.* **5.** to mark or provide with bars. —*prep.* except; excluding: *Bob thinks that this is the best bowling alley in town, bar none.*

Ba·rab·bas (bə rab′əs) *n.* in the New Testament, the prisoner who was released instead of Jesus when Pilate asked the crowd which of the two should be spared.

barb (bärb) *n.* **1.** a point or hook extending backward from the tip: *The barb of the fishhook hooked onto the fish's mouth. My sleeve ripped on the barbs of the wire fence.* **2.** something that hurts, especially an unkind remark. —*v.t.* to furnish with a barb or barbs: *to barb an arrow.*

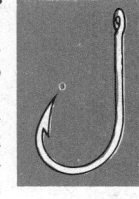
Barb

Bar·ba·dos (bär bā′dōz) *n.* an island nation in the Lesser Antilles, the easternmost island of the West Indies. Capital, Bridgetown. Area, 166 sq. mi. Pop. (1971 est.), 240,000.

bar·bar·i·an (bär ber′ē ən) *n.* **1.** a person who belongs to a primitive people, group, or tribe. **2.** a crude, coarse, or brutal person. **3.** a person who lacks understanding or appreciation of literature or the arts. **4.** in ancient or medieval times, a foreigner, especially one who was not Greek, Roman, or Christian and therefore considered to be uncivilized. —*adj.* **1.** characteristic of or like a barbarian; uncivilized; savage: *barbarian customs.* **2.** foreign; alien.

bar·bar·ic (bär bar′ik) *adj.* **1.** of, relating to, or characteristic of barbarians; uncivilized; savage: *barbaric tribes, barbaric rites.* **2.** crude or wild in style or manner: *barbaric art.*

bar·ba·rism (bär′bə riz′əm) *n.* **1.** a primitive or uncivilized condition: *Cave men lived in barbarism for centuries.* **2.** an act, custom, or quality characteristic of such a condition: *Beating a child is a barbarism.* **3.** a word or phrase that is not approved or accepted in the usage of a language. *Drownded* is a barbarism for *drowned.*

bar·bar·i·ty (bär bar′ə tē) *n. pl.,* **bar·bar·i·ties.** **1.** savage or brutal cruelty. **2.** an act of savage or brutal cruelty.

bar·ba·rize (bär′bə rīz′) *v.t., v.i.,* **bar·ba·rized, bar·ba·riz·ing.** to make or become barbarous: *Brutal treatment and long imprisonment barbarized the men.*

bar·ba·rous (bär′bər əs) *adj.* **1.** not civilized; primitive: *In ancient times barbarous tribes inhabited many parts of the world.* **2.** brutally harsh or cruel: *barbarous living conditions in the slums of a large city.* **3.** crude; coarse: *His behavior is barbarous.* **4.** relating to or using words or phrases not in accepted use. [Latin *barbaricus* foreign, uncivilized, from Greek *barbarikos,* from *barbaros* foreign.

at; āpe; cär; end; mē; it; īce; hot; ōld; fôrk; wood; fōōl; oil; out; up; turn; sing; thin; this; hw in white; zh in treasure. The symbol ə stands for the sound of **a** in about, **e** in taken, **i** in pencil, **o** in lemon, and **u** in circus.

To the ancient Greeks foreign languages sounded as if they were made up of nonsense syllables, like "bar-bar." Therefore, a person who spoke a foreign language was called *barbaros.*] **—bar′ba·rous·ly,** *adv.* **—bar′ba·rous·ness,** *n.*

Bar·ba·ry (bär′bər ē) *n.* a region in North Africa, including Libya, Tunisia, Algeria, and Morocco.

Barbary Coast, the Mediterranean coast of the Barbary States.

Barbary States, Morocco, Algeria, Tunisia, and the region of Tripoli when under Turkish control, used as a refuge by pirates from the sixteenth to the early nineteenth century.

bar·be·cue (bär′bə kyōō′) *n.* **1.** a gathering, usually outdoors, at which meat is roasted over an open fire. **2.** a spit, grill, or pit used for roasting meat. **3.** a whole animal or other meat roasted over an open fire, especially with a highly seasoned sauce. **—v.t.,** **bar·be·cued, bar·be·cu·ing.** to cook (meat) over an open fire or by direct heat, especially with a highly seasoned sauce.

barbed (bärbd) *adj.* **1.** having a barb or barbs: *We used barbed fishhooks to catch the trout.* **2.** sharp or sarcastic; cutting: *Her barbed remarks hurt his feelings.*

barbed wire, a wire or set of twisted wires to which barbs are attached at short intervals, used for fences.

bar·bel (bär′bəl) *n.* **1.** a threadlike growth hanging from the mouths of certain fish, used as feelers. **2.** any of various freshwater fish having such feelers.

bar·bell (bär′bel′) *n.* a bar with one or more weights at both ends, used for exercise and in weight lifting.

bar·ber (bär′bər) *n.* a person whose business is cutting hair and shaving or trimming beards. **—v.t.** to trim or cut the hair or beard of (someone).

Barbels

bar·ber·ry (bär′ber′ē) *n. pl.,* **bar·ber·ries.** **1.** any of a group of shrubs having small thorns, fragrant yellow flowers, and sour red or purple berries. **2.** the berry itself.

bar·ber·shop (bär′bər shop′) *n.* a barber's place of business.

bar·bi·can (bär′bi kən) *n.* a tower or other fortification at a bridge or gate leading into a castle or city.

bar·bi·tu·rate (bär bich′ər it, bär bich′ə rāt′) *n.* any of a group of drugs used chiefly for bringing on sleep and as tranquilizers. Barbiturates are often habit-forming.

bar·ca·role (bär′kə rōl′) *also,* **bar·ca·rolle.** *n.* **1.** a song sung by Venetian gondoliers. **2.** music having the style and rhythm of this song.

Bar·ce·lo·na (bär′sə lō′nə) *n.* a port city in northeastern Spain. Pop. (1970), 1,741,979.

bard (bärd) *n.* **1.** in ancient times, a person who composed and sang poems about heroes and heroic deeds. **2.** any poet. **3. the Bard.** William Shakespeare.

bare¹ (ber) *adj.,* **bar·er, bar·est.** **1.** without covering or clothing; naked: *In winter the trees are bare. If you walk on this wooden floor with bare feet, you may get splinters.* **2.** without contents, furnishings, or decoration; empty: *The cupboard was bare. There were no pictures to brighten the bare walls.* **3.** without disguise or adornment; plain: *The bare facts are that the money is missing and one of our employees took it.* **4.** just enough; mere: *The old man could afford only the bare necessities of life.* **—v.t.,** **bared, bar·ing.** to make bare; uncover; expose: *The dog bared his fangs. The poet bared his deepest feelings in his work.* [Old English *bær* without covering.] **—bare′ness,** *n.*

   to lay bare. to open to view; uncover; expose: *The lawyer laid bare the witness's motives at the trial.*

bare² (ber) *Archaic.* a past tense of **bear¹.**

bare·back (ber′bak′) *adj.* on the unsaddled back of a horse or other animal: *a bareback rider.* **—adv.** without a saddle: *to ride bareback.*

bare·faced (ber′fāst′) *adj.* without concealment or embarrassment; shameless; open: *a barefaced lie.*

bare·foot (ber′foot′) *adj., adv.* with the feet bare: *a barefoot boy, to walk barefoot on the beach.* Also, **bare·foot·ed** (ber′foot′id).

bare·hand·ed (ber′han′did) *adv.* **1.** with the hands uncovered: *They boxed barehanded.* **2.** without tools, weapons, or other means: *The old man claimed that he had once killed a wolf barehanded.* **—adj.** with the hands bare: *The boy made a barehanded catch.*

bare·head·ed (ber′hed′id) *adj., adv.* with the head uncovered.

bare·leg·ged (ber′leg′id) *adj., adv.* with the legs bare.

bare·ly (ber′lē) *adv.* **1.** hardly; scarcely: *There was barely enough food to go around.* **2.** in a bare way; poorly: *The whole family lived in one barely furnished room.*

Bar·ents Sea (bar′ənts) a part of the Arctic Ocean north of Norway and the Soviet Union.

bar·gain (bär′gin) *n.* **1.** something bought or offered at a low price; something worth more than the price paid for it: *At only twenty dollars this bicycle is a bargain.* **2.** an agreement on the terms of a business deal or other arrangement: *My brother and I made a bargain that I would wash the dishes if he would dry them.* **3.** the terms of such an agreement: *The salesman drove a hard bargain and charged us more than we thought he would.* **—v.i.** to discuss or argue over the terms of a bargain: *The salesman and the customer bargained before they agreed on a price for the car.*

   in the bargain or **into the bargain.** in addition; besides: *He damaged the other car, and wrecked his own in the bargain.*

   to bargain for or **to bargain on.** to be prepared for; count on; expect: *Cleaning out the attic was more work than I bargained for.*

   to strike a bargain. to reach an agreement.

barge (bärj) *n.* **1.** a flat-bottomed boat for carrying freight on rivers, canals, and other inland waterways: *a coal barge.* **2.** a large boat, often highly decorated, used for recreation, pageants, or formal ceremonies. **—v.,** **barged, barg·ing.** **—v.i.** **1.** to move clumsily and abruptly: *He barged out of the room, knocking over a chair in his hurry.* **2.** *Informal.* to enter or force oneself rudely or heedlessly: *to barge into a meeting, to barge in on a conversation.* **—v.t.** to transport (freight) by barge.

bar graph, a graph in which different quantities are represented by rectangles of different lengths.

bar·i·tone (bar′ə tōn′) *n.* **1.** a male voice that is lower than tenor and higher than bass. **2.** a singer who has such a voice. **3.** a musical instrument that has a similar range. **4.** a musical part for such a voice or instrument. **—adj.** **1.** able to sing or play the baritone: *a baritone voice, a baritone saxophone.* **2.** for the baritone.

bar·i·um (bar′ē əm) *n.* a soft, silver-white metallic element, used especially in alloys and paints. Symbol: **Ba**

bark¹ (bärk) *n.* the outer covering of the branches, stems, trunks, and roots of trees and other woody plants. **—v.t.** **1.** to strip the bark off of. **2.** to rub the skin off of; scrape: *to bark one's shins.* [Of Scandinavian origin.]

bark² (bärk) *n.* **1.** the sharp, abrupt cry made by a dog. **2.** a cry or sound like this: *the bark of a seal, the bark of a gun.* **—v.i.** **1.** to make this sound: *The dog barked when the robber entered the house.* **2.** to speak loudly and sharply: *The teacher barked at us when we slammed the door.* **—v.t.** to speak in a loud, sharp tone: *The sergeant barked orders at the soldiers.* [Old English *beorcan* to bark.]

bark³ (bärk) *also,* **barque.** *n.* **1.** a ship with three or more masts, all square-rigged except for the aftermost one, which is fore-and-aft-rigged. **2.** *Archaic.* a sailing ship, especially a small one. [Middle French *barque* small ship, from Italian *barca* boat, from Late Latin *barca.*]

Bark³ *(def. 1)*

bar·keep·er (bär′kē′pər) *n.* a person who owns, manages, or tends a bar where alcoholic liquors are served. Also, **bar·keep** (bär′kēp′).

bar·ken·tine (bär′kən tēn′) *also,* **bar·quen·tine.** *n.* a ship with three or more masts, the foremast square-rigged and the other masts fore-and-aft-rigged.

bark·er (bär′kər) *n.* **1.** an animal, especially a dog that makes a barking sound. **2.** a person who stands outside a show, as at a carnival, and urges customers to go in by lively, loud talking.

bar·ley (bär′lē) *n.* **1.** the grain of a hollow-stemmed plant of the grass family. It is used mainly as animal feed, but is often made into malt and used for flavoring cereals and beverages, such as beer. **2.** the plant bearing this grain, having short, spear-shaped leaves.

bar magnet, a magnet shaped like a bar.

bar·maid (bär′mād′) *n.* a woman who serves customers in a bar.

bar·man (bär′mən) *n. pl.,* **bar·men** (bär′mən). a man who serves customers in a bar; bartender.

bar mitz·vah (bär mits′və) **1.** a ceremony held for a Jewish boy when he becomes thirteen, marking his assumption of religious responsibilities. **2.** a boy for whom this ceremony is held. [Hebrew *bar mitzvāh* literally, son of the commandment.]

barn (bärn) *n.* a building for storing hay, grain, and other farm produce, and for housing farming equipment and cows and other livestock.

bar·na·cle (bär′nə kəl) *n.* any of various small shellfish that attach themselves to underwater objects, such as ship bottoms, rocks, and wharves.

barn dance 1. a party, usually held in a barn, at which square dances or other folk dances are done. **2.** a folk dance resembling a slow polka.

Rock barnacles

Goose barnacle

barn·storm (bärn′stôrm′) *v.i.* **1.** to tour rural or outlying areas, making brief stops, as to give campaign speeches or lectures or to present plays: *The presidential candidate barnstormed through five states.* **2.** to tour rural or outlying areas as a stunt flier or pilot. —*v.t.* to tour (an area) in such a manner: *The senator barnstormed the Southwest.* —**barn′storm′er,** *n.*

barn swallow, a swallow that has a long, forked tail and usually builds mud nests in chimneys or on the rafters inside barns.

Bar·num, P(hineas) T(aylor) (bär′nəm) 1810–1891, U.S. showman.

barn·yard (bärn′yärd′) *n.* a yard surrounding or next to a barn.

bar·o·gram (bär′ə gram′) *n.* a record traced by a barograph.

bar·o·graph (bär′ə graf′) *n.* an aneroid barometer that automatically records its readings.

ba·rom·e·ter (bə rom′ə tər) *n.* **1.** an instrument for measuring atmospheric pressure, used in weather forecasting and to determine height above sea level. **2.** anything that indicates changes: *The stock market is a barometer of business activity.*

bar·o·met·ric (bar′ə met′rik) *adj.* of or indicated by a barometer: *barometric pressure.* Also, **bar·o·met·ri·cal** (bar′ə met′ri-kəl). —**bar′o·met′ri·cal·ly,** *adv.*

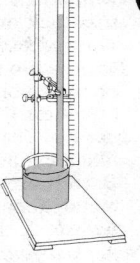
Barometer

bar·on (bar′ən) *n.* **1.** a British nobleman of the lowest rank. **2.** a nobleman of certain European countries or of Japan, having a similar rank. **3.** in the Middle Ages, a lord who held lands as a vassal of a king or other high-ranking nobleman. **4.** a person who has great power or influence, especially in business or industry: *an oil baron, a cattle baron.*

bar·on·ess (bar′ə nis) *n. pl.,* **bar·on·ess·es. 1.** the wife or widow of a baron. **2.** a noblewoman holding the rank of baron in her own right, as by inheritance.

bar·on·et (bar′ə nit) *n.* a member of the lowest hereditary order of honor in Great Britain. Although a baronet is not a nobleman, he is addressed as *Sir,* and may write *Bart.* after his name. For example: *Sir James Jones, Bart.*

ba·ro·ni·al (bə rō′nē əl) *adj.* **1.** of or relating to a baron or a barony. **2.** suiting a baron; stately; magnificent: *a baronial mansion, baronial splendor.*

bar·o·ny (bar′ə nē) *n. pl.,* **bar·o·nies. 1.** the land held by a baron. **2.** the rank or title of a baron.

ba·roque (bə rōk′) *adj.* **1.** characteristic of or resembling a very ornate style of art and architecture that is marked by the use of curved rather than straight lines. **2.** characteristic of or resembling a very ornate style of music that is marked by strong, complex rhythms. **3.** showy or ornate in an extreme or grotesque way. **4.** (of pearls) irregular in shape. —*n.* the baroque style, or a period when such a style was popular. [French *baroque* this style, from Italian *barocco,* probably from Federigo *Barocci,* 1528–1612, an Italian painter who painted in this style.]

ba·rouche (bə rōōsh′) *n.* a large four-wheeled carriage with two double seats facing each other.

barque (bärk) another spelling of **bark³.**

bar·quen·tine (bär′kən tēn′) another spelling of **barkentine.**

bar·racks (bar′əks) *n., pl.* **1.** a building or set of buildings for housing soldiers or other military personnel. **2.** any plain, usually temporary housing for many people.

bar·ra·cu·da (bar′ə kōō′də) *n. pl.,* **bar·ra·cu·das** or **bar·ra·cu·da.** any of a group of ferocious fish found in warm seas throughout the world, having a long and narrow body, a large mouth, and sharp teeth. Barracudas have been known to attack swimmers.

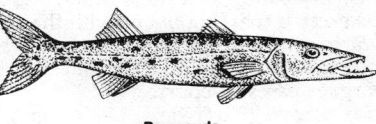
Barracuda

at; āpe; cär; end; mē; it; īce; hot; ōld; fôrk; wood; fōōl; oil; out; up; turn; sing; thin; **th**is; hw in white; zh in treasure. The symbol ə stands for the sound of **a** in about, **e** in taken, **i** in pencil, **o** in lemon, and **u** in circus.

bar·rage (bə räzh′) *n.* **1.** a heavy amount of fire from artillery or other guns: *The barrage from the enemy mortars kept the men pinned down in the trenches.* **2.** any large or overwhelming amount: *The reporters met the President with a barrage of questions.* —*v.t.,* **bar·raged, bar·rag·ing.** to attack or confront with a barrage: *The movie star was barraged with requests for her autograph.*

Bar·ran·quil·la (bär′räng kē′yä) *n.* the chief seaport of Colombia, in the northern part of the country. Pop. (1969 est.), 816,700.

bar·rel (bar′əl) *n.* **1.** a large wooden container shaped like a cylinder, having bulging sides and round, flat ends. Barrels are usually made up of boards bound together by metal hoops. **2.** any container resembling this: *a trash barrel.* **3.** the amount that a barrel can hold: *The family packed four barrels of dishes when they moved.* **4.** any of various measures of weight or quantity. The standard U.S. barrel for liquids holds 31½ gallons. **5.** the tube-shaped part of a gun through which the bullet or shell is shot. **6.** any part shaped like a cylinder or tube: *the barrel of a fountain pen.* **7.** *Informal.* a large quantity: *a barrel of fun, a barrel of money.* —*v.,* **bar·reled, bar·rel·ing;** *also, British,* **bar·relled, bar·rel·ling.** —*v.t.* to put or pack in barrels. —*v.i. Informal.* to move rapidly: *Steve barreled in through the front door when he heard the phone ringing.*

barrel organ, another term for **hand organ.**

bar·ren (bar′ən) *adj.* **1.** having little or no plant life; not productive: *barren soil.* **2.** not able to produce offspring: *a barren woman, a barren fruit tree.* **3.** not leading to any results or gain: *The barren talks with the union failed to prevent a strike.* **4.** without interest, charm, or hopefulness; empty; dreary: *The future seemed barren for the old woman until her stolen money was recovered.* —*n. also,* **barrens.** an area of barren land. —**bar′ren·ness,** *n.*

bar·rette (bə ret′) *n.* a clasp or clip, often in the shape of a bar, for holding the hair in place.

bar·ri·cade (bar′ə kād′) *n.* **1.** a hastily made barrier for defense: *The rebels built barricades against the approaching army.* **2.** any barrier that blocks passage: *The police barricades kept the crowds back.* —*v.t.,* **bar·ri·cad·ed, bar·ri·cad·ing.** to block; obstruct: *Fallen trees barricaded the road.*

Bar·rie, Sir James M. (bar′ē) 1860–1937, Scottish playwright and novelist.

bar·ri·er (bar′ē ər) *n.* **1.** something that blocks the way: *A mountain barrier sealed off the valley.* **2.** something that restricts or hinders: *The country's lack of industry was a barrier to economic growth.* **3.** something that divides or keeps apart: *The difference in language was a barrier between the people of the two nations.*

barrier reef, a coral reef that is parallel to the shoreline, usually acting as a breakwater.

bar·ring (bär′ing) *prep.* with the exception of; except for: *Barring delays, we will arrive on Wednesday.*

bar·ris·ter (bar′is tər) *n.* in Great Britain, a lawyer who argues cases in court.

bar·room (bär′rōōm′, bär′room′) *n.* a room or place having a bar where alcoholic drinks are sold.

bar·row¹ (bar′ō) *n.* **1.** see **wheelbarrow.** [Old English *bearwe* wheelbarrow.]

bar·row² (bar′ō) *n.* a mound of earth or stones marking an ancient grave. [Old English *beorg* hill, mound.]

Bar·row, Point (bar′ō) *n.* a small Alaskan peninsula that is the northernmost point of the United States.

bar sinister, a diagonal stripe on a coat of arms, falsely supposed to indicate illegitimate birth.

Bart., Baronet.

bar·tend·er (bär′ten′dər) *n.* a person who makes and serves alcoholic drinks at a bar.

bar·ter (bär′tər) *v.t.* to trade (goods for other goods) without using money: *The early settlers bartered seed for animal skins with the Indians.* —*v.i.* to barter goods. —*n.* **1.** the act or practice of bartering: *Among these tribes trade is carried on by barter.* **2.** something bartered.

Bar·thol·o·mew, Saint (bär thol′ə myōō′) one of the twelve apostles.

Bart·lett pear (bärt′lit) a large, yellow, juicy pear. [From Enoch *Bartlett,* a merchant who popularized it in the United States.]

Bar·tók, Be·la (bär′tok; bā′lə) 1881–1945, Hungarian composer and pianist.

Bar·ton, Clara (bärt′ən) 1821–1912, the founder of the American Red Cross.

ba·sal (bā′səl) *adj.* of or at the base; forming the base; fundamental; basic.

basal metabolism, the amount of energy used up by an animal or plant when it is completely at rest. Basal metabolism is measured by the rate of oxygen used up and heat given off.

ba·salt (bə sôlt′) *n.* a dark, usually fine-grained volcanic rock.

bas·cule bridge (bas′kyōōl) a drawbridge hinged at the bank so that it may be raised to allow ships to pass under it.

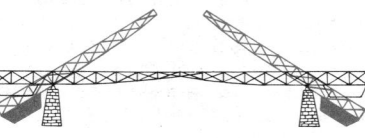
Bascule bridge

base¹ (bās) *n. pl.,* **bas·es.** **1.** the part on which a thing rests or stands: *The base of the statue was a marble block.* **2.** the underlying part that supports something; foundation: *That political party has a broad base among the working people.* **3.** the lowest part; bottom: *The base of the mountain is surrounded by thick jungle.* **4.** the chief or essential part of a thing; main element: *This paint has an oil base.* **5.** a military area and facilities where supplies are kept or from which operations are started: *an air force base, a missile base.* **6.** any center or starting point of activity: *the base of a mountain climbing expedition.* **7.** a station, goal, or safety area in certain games. **8.** any of the four corners of a baseball diamond. **9.** *Chemistry.* a compound that reacts with an acid to form a salt. A base has bitter taste in a water solution and turns red litmus paper blue. **10.** *Mathematics.* **a.** the number in a numerical system that marks the point in counting when a new digit is added at the left and counting begins again. Simple arithmetic is usually done in the decimal system, whose base is 10. According to this system, the numeral 40 represents 4 times the base of 10. Computers use the binary system, whose base is 2. According to this system, the numeral 10 represents 1 times the base of 2. **b.** a line or plane in a geometrical figure on which it is thought to rest: *the base of a triangle.* —*v.t.,* **based, bas·ing.** **1.** to place on a basis or foundation: *to base a house on concrete. Alice always tries to base her opinions on the facts. This movie is based on a popular novel.* **2.** to locate; station: *These troops have been based in Europe for two years.* [Latin *basis* foundation, pedestal, from Greek *basis* step, pedestal.]

off base. *Informal.* not accurate; mistaken: *Your guess was really off base.*

base² (bās) *adj.,* **bas·er, bas·est.** **1.** having or showing a lack of decency or bravery; morally low; dishonorable: *Abandoning his men during the battle was a base act.* **2.** menial; degrading: *base labor.* **3.** low in value in comparison to something else: *Iron is a base metal.* [Old French *bas* low, from Late Latin *bassus* low, short.] —**base′ly,** *adv.* —**base′ness,** *n.*

base·ball (bās′bôl′) *n.* **1.** a game played with a ball and bat between two teams of nine players each, on a field having four bases that form a diamond. A player of the team at bat tries to hit the ball and reach base without being put out. To score a run, the player must reach home base by way of first, second, and third bases. Each team is allowed three outs per inning, and a game consists of nine innings. **2.** the hard, rawhide-covered ball used in this game.

base·board (bās′bôrd′) *n.* a strip of board, molding, or similar material at the bottom of a wall, for covering the line where the wall meets the floor.

base·born (bās′bôrn′) *adj.* **1.** of humble birth or origin. **2.** born out of wedlock; illegitimate.

base hit, the hitting of a pitched baseball in a way that allows the batter to get on base without benefit of an opponent's error and without forcing out a runner already on base.

Ba·sel (bä′zəl) *n.* a city in northwestern Switzerland, on the Rhine. Pop. (1973 est.), 202,000.

base·less (bās′lis) *adj.* having no basis in fact: *The story was just a baseless rumor.*

base line **1.** a line serving as a base. **2.** *Baseball.* an area within which a base runner must stay while running from one base to another. **3.** a line marking the boundary of the playing area in certain other sports, such as tennis or basketball.

base·man (bās′mən) *n. pl.,* **base·men** (bās′mən). a baseball player stationed near first, second, or third base. ▲ used only in the compounds *first baseman, second baseman,* and *third baseman.*

base·ment (bās′mənt) *n.* the lowest story of a building, below or partly below the ground.

ba·sen·ji (bə sen′jē) *n.* a short-haired dog of a breed that originated in central Africa, usually having a reddish-brown or black coat with white markings. It does not bark, but makes a sound similar to a chuckle or a whine.

base runner *Baseball.* a member of the team at bat who is on base or trying to reach a base.

bas·es¹ (bā′siz) the plural of **base¹.**

ba·ses² (bā′sēz) the plural of **ba·sis.**

bash (bash) *Informal. v.t.* to strike with a smashing blow: *The force from the collision bashed in the side of the car.* —*n. pl.,* **bash·es.** such a blow.

bash·ful (bash′fəl) *adj.* easily embarrassed; very shy: *The little boy was bashful in front of strangers.* —**bash′·ful·ly,** *adv.* —**bash′ful·ness,** *n.*

ba·sic (bā′sik) *adj.* **1.** of, at, or forming the base; fundamental: *Food is a basic human need. The basic difference between his bicycle and mine is that mine uses gears.* **2.** *Chemistry.* **a.** of or containing a base. **b.** alkaline. —*n. usually,* **basics.** something that is basic: *First, learn the basics of cooking; then you can try to cook fancy dishes later.*

ba·si·cal·ly (bā″si kə lē, bā′sik lē) *adv.* for the most part; fundamentally: *I know you don't trust him, but basically he's an honest person.*

bas·il (baz′əl, bā′zəl) *n.* **1.** a sweet-smelling plant of the mint family whose leaves are used for seasoning food. **2.** the leaves themselves.

ba·sil·i·ca (bə sil′i kə) *n.* **1.** a public building in ancient Rome, usually a rectangular hall with rows of columns on either side and a broad central aisle ending in a semicircular area. Basilicas were used chiefly as courtrooms and for

Basenji

public meeting places. **2.** an early Christian church built on the model of the Roman building.

bas·i·lisk (bas′ə lisk′) *n.* **1.** a mythical monster resembling a lizard, whose breath and gaze were said to be deadly. **2.** a tropical American lizard related to the iguana, having a crest along the back, a tail that it can raise or lower, and a sac on the head that it can inflate with air.

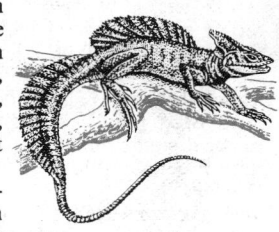

Basilisk

ba·sin (bā′sin) *n.* **1.** a shallow, round container with sloping sides, used especially for holding liquids. **2.** the amount that such a container will hold. **3.** a bowl or sink for washing, as in a bathroom. **4.** the entire region drained by a river and its tributaries: *the Nile basin.* **5.** an enclosed place containing water: *The harbor has a boat basin.*

ba·sis (bā′sis) *n. pl.,* **ba·ses.** **1.** a fundamental part on which a thing rests or depends; foundation; support: *the basis for a belief. What is the basis for your accusation against him?* **2.** the main part or chief ingredient: *The basis of this sauce is chicken broth.*

bask (bask) *v.i.* **1.** to lie and enjoy a pleasant warmth: *The cat basked in the sun.* **2.** to take pleasure: *He basked in his friends' words of praise.*

bas·ket (bas′kit) *n.* **1.** a container made by weaving together twigs, rushes, straw, cane, strips of wood, or the like, and usually having a handle or handles: *a clothes basket.* **2.** something resembling a basket in shape or use: *a wire basket on the handlebars of a bicycle.* **3.** the amount that a basket will hold: *a basket of pears.* **4.** in basketball: **a.** a metal hoop having a circular net open at the bottom hanging from it, through which the ball is thrown in order to score. **b.** a goal scored by tossing the ball through the basket.

bas·ket·ball (bas′kit bôl′) *n.* **1.** a game played with a large, round, air-filled ball on a rectangular court between two teams of five players each. To score, a player must toss the ball through a raised basket at the opponent's end of the court. **2.** the ball used in this game.

bas·ket·ry (bas′ki trē) *n.* **1.** the art of weaving baskets. **2.** baskets as a group.

basket weave, a loose weave in cloth made by interlacing two or more threads at the same time. It resembles the weave in a basket.

bas mitz·vah (bäs mits′və) see **bat mitzvah.**

Basque (bask) *n.* **1.** a member of a people living in the Pyrenees in southwestern France and northern Spain. **2.** the language of the Basque people, apparently having no relation to any other known language. — *adj.* of or relating to the Basques or their language.

bas-re·lief (bä′ri lēf′, bas′ri lēf′) *n.* a carving or sculpture on a flat surface, such as a wall or door, in which the figures stand out only slightly from the background. Also, **low relief.**

bass¹ (bās) *n. pl.,* **bass·es.** **1.** the lowest adult male voice. **2.** a singer who has such a voice. **3.** a musical instrument that has a similar range. **4.** a musical part for such a voice

at; āpe; cär; end; mē; it; īce; hot; ōld; fôrk; wood; fŏŏl; oil; out; up; turn; sing; thin; this; hw in white; zh in treasure. The symbol ə stands for the sound of **a** in about, e in taken, i in pencil, o in lemon, and u in circus.

or instrument. —*adj.* **1.** able to sing or play the bass: *a bass voice, a bass clarinet.* **2.** for the bass. [A form of *base²*; influenced in spelling by Italian *basso* low.]

bass² (bas) *n. pl.,* **bass·es** or **bass.** any of various freshwater or saltwater food and game fish of North America. [A form of dialectal English *barse* perch, from Old English *bærs.*]

bass³ (bas) *n.* **1.** basswood. **2.** bast. [A form of *bast.*]

bass clef (bās) a clef placed on the fourth line of a musical staff, indicating that this line corresponds to the note F below middle C. Also, **F clef.** See **clef** for illustration.

bass drum (bās) the largest type of drum. It gives off a deep, booming sound and is usually held so that both sides can be struck.

bas·set (bas′it) *n.* a short-legged dog with a long body and drooping ears.

bass horn (bās) another term for **tuba.**

bas·si·net (bas′ə net′) *n.* a basket used as a baby's cradle, often on legs and with a hood at one end.

bas·so (bas′ō) *n. pl.,* **bas·sos.** a bass singer, voice, or part.

bas·soon (bə sōōn′) *n.* a wind instrument with a low range. It consists of a long, doubled wooden tube and a curved metal mouthpiece which contains a double reed.

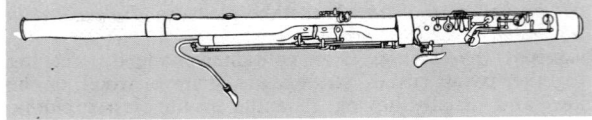

Bassoon

bass vi·ol (bās′vī′əl) the largest and deepest-toned stringed instrument, shaped like a violin and played either with a bow or by hand. Also, **double bass, contrabass.**

bass·wood (bas′wood′) *n.* **1.** a linden tree that grows in North America. **2.** its soft, light wood, widely used in cabinetmaking.

bast (bast) *n.* **1.** the strong, flexible fibers obtained from the inner bark of certain trees and from the stems or leaves of certain plants, used especially in making cloth, rope, and heavy paper. **2.** another word for **phloem.**

bas·tard (bas′tərd) *n.* a child born to parents who are not married to each other.

baste¹ (bāst) *v.t.,* **bast·ed, bast·ing.** to apply melted butter, gravy, fat, or other liquid to (food) while cooking: *She used a large spoon to baste the turkey.* [Of uncertain origin.]

baste² (bāst) *v.t.,* **bast·ed, bast·ing.** to sew temporarily with long, loose stitches that are usually pulled out after the final sewing: *to baste a hem.* [Old French *bastir* to sew loosely; of Germanic origin.]

baste³ (bāst) *v.t.,* **bast·ed, bast·ing.** *Informal.* to beat soundly; thrash. [Old Norse *beysta* to beat.]

Bas·tille (bas tēl′) *n.* a fortress in Paris used as a prison before the French Revolution. Its destruction by the people on July 14, 1789, was one of the opening acts of the revolution. The anniversary of this date, **Bastille Day,** is celebrated as a national holiday in France.

bas·ti·na·do (bas′tə nā′dō) *n. pl.,* **bas·ti·na·does. 1.** a blow or beating with a stick, especially on the soles of the feet. **2.** a stick; cudgel.

bas·tion (bas′chən) *n.* **1.** a part of a rampart or fortification projecting from the main part, that allows the defenders a wider firing range. **2.** any fortified or firmly established place or position; stronghold: *That country is a bastion of freedom.*

Ba·su·to·land (bə sōō′tō land′) *n.* see **Lesotho.**

bat¹ (bat) *n.* **1.** a wooden stick or club, especially one used

for hitting the ball in baseball and other games. **2.** the right or turn to bat. **3.** a hard blow. **4.** *Slang.* a spree; binge. —*v.,* **bat·ted, bat·ting.** —*v.i.* **1.** to use a bat in baseball and other games. **2.** to take a turn at bat: *Our team bats next.* —*v.t.* **1.** to hit with a bat: *to bat a ball.* **2.** to have a batting average of (a certain figure): *He batted .319 for the season.* [Old English *batt* cudgel, club.]

at bat. in the act or position of batting.

right off the bat. *Informal.* at once; immediately: *I knew the answer right off the bat.*

to go to bat for. *Informal.* to defend; support: *He went to bat for me when I was in trouble.*

bat² (bat) *n.* a small animal with a furry body like that of a mouse and wings of thin skin stretched over a framework of elongated bones. Bats are active at night and are the only mammals that can fly. Many species use a kind of natural radar by which the echo of their cries indicates the size and position of an object.

Bat²

bat³ (bat) *v.t.,* **bat·ted, bat·ting.** *Informal.* to flutter; wink: *to bat one's eyelashes.* [Old French *batre* to beat, from Latin *battuere* to beat.]

not bat an eye or **not bat an eyelash.** to fail to show any emotion or surprise.

Ba·taan (bə tan′) *n.* a peninsula in the Philippines, west of Manila, where U.S. troops surrendered to the Japanese in 1942.

batch (bach) *n. pl.,* **batch·es. 1.** a number of persons or things taken together; group: *The teacher has just finished grading a batch of papers.* **2.** a quantity of material prepared at one time or needed for one operation: *a batch of dough, a batch of cement.* **3.** an amount baked at one time: *a batch of sugar cookies.*

bate (bāt) *v.t., v.i.,* **bat·ed, bat·ing.** *Archaic.* to diminish or lessen; abate.

with bated breath. with breath checked or held because of wonder, fear, or excitement: *The crowd waited for the astronauts' landing with bated breath.*

ba·teau (ba tō′) *n. pl.,* **ba·teaux** (ba tōz′). any of various lightweight, flat-bottomed boats used chiefly in the United States and Canada.

bath (bath) *n. pl.,* **baths** (ba<u>th</u>z, baths). **1.** a washing or dipping of something, especially the body, in water or other liquid: *John gave the dog a bath.* **2.** the water or other liquid used for bathing: *His bath was too hot.* **3.** a container for such liquid, as a bathtub: *Clean out the bath when you're done.* **4.** a room equipped for bathing; bathroom. **5.** *also,* **baths.** a set of rooms or a building used for bathing: *the public baths of the ancient Romans.* **6.** a solution or other preparation in which something is washed or dipped for chemical treatment: *an acid bath.*

bathe (bā<u>th</u>) *v.,* **bathed, bath·ing.** —*v.i.* **1.** to take a bath: *She bathes each evening before going to bed.* **2.** to go into a body of water to swim or to cool oneself; go swimming: *to bathe in the ocean.* —*v.t.* **1.** to give a bath to: *to bathe a baby.* **2.** to wash or moisten with water or other liquid to cleanse, soothe, or heal: *to bathe the eyes, to bathe a wound.* **3.** to make wet; moisten: *Sweat bathed his forehead.* **4.** to cover or envelop as if with liquid: *He turned a switch and the room was bathed in light.* —**bath′er,** *n.*

bath·house (bath′hous′) *n. pl.,* **bath·hous·es** (bath′hou′ziz). **1.** a building equipped for bathing. **2.** a building having dressing rooms for swimmers.

bathing suit, a garment worn while swimming.

ba·thos (bā′thŏs) *n.* a sudden and ridiculous descent from the elevated to the commonplace in speech or writing. For example: *The senator pledged to oppose war, fight poverty, and name a new state flower.*

bath·robe (bath′rōb′) *n.* a loose, coatlike garment worn before and after bathing or for lounging.

bath·room (bath′rōōm′, bath′room′) *n.* a room usually having a toilet, sink, and bathtub or shower.

Bath·she·ba (bath shē′bə) *n.* in the Old Testament, the wife of King David and mother of King Solomon.

bath·tub (bath′tŭb′) *n.* a tub in which to bathe, now usually one permanently fixed in a bathroom and having faucets and a drain.

Bath·urst (bath′ərst) *n.* the former capital of Gambia, now known as Banjul.

bath·y·scaph (bath′i skaf′) *also,* **bath·y·scaphe** (bath′i-skāf′). *n.* a craft for deep-sea exploration, consisting of a thick-walled steel sphere suspended beneath a large hull. The crew and scientific instruments are carried in the sphere and the hull is filled with gasoline, which makes it buoyant. A bathyscaph has electric motors that enable it to move horizontally.

bath·y·sphere (bath′i sfēr′) *n.* a hollow, watertight steel globe that has observation windows, used for under-sea exploration. A bathysphere is suspended by cables from a surface vessel and cannot move independently.

ba·tik (bə tēk′) *n.* **1.** a method of hand printing colored designs on cloth by putting a wax coating on those parts that are not to be dyed. **2.** cloth decorated by this method. [Javanese *'mbatik* wax painting.]

ba·tiste (bə tēst′) *n.* any of several fine, soft, sheer fabrics.

bat mitz·vah (bät mits′və) **1.** a ceremony held for a Jewish girl when she becomes thirteen, marking her assumption of religious responsibilities. **2.** a girl for whom this ceremony is held. Also, **bas mitzvah.**

ba·ton (bə tŏn′) *n.* **1.** a wand used by a conductor to direct the performance of an orchestra or band. **2.** a rod with a knob at one or both ends, carried by a drum major or majorette and twirled in a showy manner. **3.** a short staff or truncheon used as a symbol of office, command, or authority: *a field marshal's baton.* **4.** a short stick that is handed from one runner to the next in a relay race.

Bat·on Rouge (bat′ən rōōzh′) the capital of Louisiana, in the south-central part of the state, on the Mississippi. Pop. (1970), 165,963.

ba·tra·chi·an (bə trā′kē ən) *n.* a tailless amphibian, such as a frog or toad.

bats·man (bats′mən) *n. pl.,* **bats·men** (bats′mən). a batter in cricket.

bat·tal·ion (bə tal′yən) *n.* **1.** a military unit made up of two or more companies or batteries and a headquarters and forming part of a brigade or regiment. **2.** any large group of persons or things; host: *Battalions of volunteers searched for the lost child.*

bat·ten[1] (bat′ən) *n.* **1.** a piece of sawed timber used especially for flooring. **2.** a light strip of wood used in building, especially to cover or reinforce a joint between boards. **3.** a long, narrow strip of wood or metal used for various purposes on a ship, especially to fasten a tarpaulin over a hatch. —*v.t.* to fasten, furnish, or strengthen with battens: *The crew battened down the hatches of the ship as the storm was about to break.* [A form of *baton.*]

bat·ten[2] (bat′ən) *Archaic. v.i.* to grow fat by feeding well; thrive, as cattle. —*v.t.* to make fat. [Old Norse *batna* to get better.]

bat·ter[1] (bat′ər) *v.t.* **1.** to strike or beat with heavy, repeated blows: *High winds battered the ship. The boxer battered his opponent.* **2.** to break or damage by rough treatment: *a battered old car.* —*v.i.* to strike or beat

heavily and repeatedly; pound; hammer: *The firemen battered away at the door of the burning house.* [From *bat*[1] + *-er*[3].]

bat·ter[2] (bat′ər) *n.* a thin mixture of flour, liquid, and other ingredients beaten together for use in cooking: *pancake batter.* [Probably from *batter*[1].]

bat·ter[3] (bat′ər) *n.* a player who is batting or whose turn it is to bat in baseball, softball, or cricket. [*Bat*[1] + *-er*[1].]

battering ram **1.** a heavy beam used in ancient warfare for battering down walls or gates. It often had an iron ram's head at the end. **2.** any heavy beam, log, or bar used to knock down a door or wall.

bat·ter·y (bat′ər ē) *n. pl.,* **bat·ter·ies.** **1.** a group of two or more electric cells that can produce electric current by means of chemical action. Batteries provide the electricity for flashlights, portable radios, hearing aids, and automobiles. **2.** any group of similar or related things used or thought of as a unit: *A battery of bright lights shone on the stage.* **3.** a set of two or more heavy guns or other weapons used as a unit. **4.** the basic unit of artillery, corresponding to a company or infantry. **5.** *Law.* the unlawful beating or touching of another person. **6.** *Baseball.* a team's pitcher and catcher, considered as a unit.

bat·ting (bat′ing) *n.* **1.** the act or manner of using a bat, especially in a game. **2.** cotton or wool fibers that have been pressed into sheets or layers, used especially in bandaging wounds or as padding for upholstery or quilts.

batting average, a mathematical average indicating the batting ability of a baseball player, obtained by dividing the number of hits the player has made by the number of times the player has officially batted. A player who has batted 500 times and has 150 hits has a batting average of .300.

bat·tle (bat′əl) *n.* **1.** a fight between opposing armed forces on land, at sea, or in the air: *A decisive battle of the Civil War was fought at Gettysburg.* **2.** fighting; warfare; combat: *to die in battle.* **3.** any fight or contest; conflict; struggle: *Life in the Arctic is a constant battle against the elements. There was a battle for the championship between the two teams.* —*v.,* **bat·tled, bat·tling.** —*v.i.* to fight or struggle: *The armies battled for three days. The two players battled for possession of the ball.* —*v.t.* to fight or struggle against: *The ship battled the high waves.* —**bat′tler,** *n.*

bat·tle·ax (bat′əl aks′) *also,* **bat·tle·axe.** *n. pl.,* **bat·tle·ax·es.** a heavy, wide-bladed ax, formerly used as a weapon in war.

battle cry **1.** a shout or cry of troops in battle; war cry. **2.** a motto or slogan used in any contest or conflict: *"Down with poverty" was the political party's battle cry.*

bat·tle·dore (bat′əl dôr′) *n.* a small racket used in the game of battledore and shuttlecock.

battledore and shuttlecock, an ancient game from which the modern game of badminton was developed.

bat·tle·field (bat′əl fēld′) *n.* a place where a battle is fought or was once fought.

bat·tle·front (bat′əl frunt′) *n.* a place where a battle is being fought; front.

bat·tle·ground (bat′əl ground′) *n.* a battlefield.

bat·tle·ment (bat′əl mənt) *n.* **1.** a low wall formerly built along the top of a fort or tower, having a series of

at; āpe; cär; end; mē; it; īce; hot; ōld; fôrk; wood; fōōl; oil; out; up; turn; sing; thin; **th**is; **hw** in white; **zh** in treasure. The symbol ə stands for the sound of **a** in about, **e** in taken, **i** in pencil, **o** in lemon, and **u** in circus.

openings through which soldiers could shoot at the enemy. **2.** a similar wall built for decoration.

battle royal **1.** a fight or struggle involving many people; riot: *The police and the protesters had quite a battle royal.* **2.** a loud, heated argument: *The discussion between the umpire and the players soon became a battle royal.*

bat·tle·ship (bat′əl ship′) *n.* a large warship having the most powerful guns and the heaviest armor of any naval vessel.

bat·ty (bat′ē) *adj.,* **bat·ti·er, bat·ti·est.** *Slang.* crazy.

bau·ble (bô′bəl) *n.* a showy, worthless trinket; trifle: *She spends her money on cheap bracelets and other baubles.*

Bau·de·laire, Charles (bōd′əl er′) 1821–1867, French poet.

baux·ite (bôk′sīt) *n.* a claylike substance made up of several different minerals. It is the chief ore of aluminum. [French *bauxite,* from Les *Baux,* a town in southeastern France where it was first found.]

Ba·var·i·a (bə ver′ē ə) *n.* the largest state of West Germany, in the southeastern part of the country. At various times in history it was a separate duchy, kingdom, and republic. Area, 27,239 sq. mi. Pop. (1969 est.), 10,568,900. —**Ba·var′i·an,** *adj., n.*

bawd·y (bô′dē) *adj.,* **bawd·i·er, bawd·i·est.** indecent or lewd; obscene. —**bawd′i·ly,** *adv.* —**bawd′i·ness,** *n.*

bawl (bôl) *v.i.* **1.** to weep or sob loudly; wail: *The child bawled when his mother left him.* **2.** to shout or yell; bellow. —*v.t.* to call out noisily; shout: *The sergeant bawled his orders to the soldiers.* —*n.* a loud shout or outcry: *a bawl of anger.*

to bawl out. *Informal.* to scold or reprimand severely: *The boss bawled them out for coming in late.*

bay¹ (bā) *n.* an arm of a sea or lake extending into the land; broad inlet. A bay is usually smaller than a gulf and is widest at its mouth. [Old French *baie* inlet, from Spanish *bahia;* possibly of Iberian origin.]

bay² (bā) *n.* **1.** a space or section of a wall or building between two columns, beams, pillars, or the like. **2.** an outward projection in a wall containing a window or set of windows. **3.** see **bay window. 4.** a compartment or area in an aircraft that is used for a particular purpose: *a cargo bay.* [Old French *baée* opening, from *baer* to stand open.]

bay³ (bā) *n.* **1.** a deep, long barking or howling of a dog: *We heard the bay of hounds chasing a rabbit.* **2.** the position of a cornered animal or person forced to turn and face pursuers: *The big lion had turned at bay* (Ernest Hemingway). **3.** the position of an animal or person being held or kept off: *The bronco kept the cowboys at bay.* —*v.i.* to bark with a deep, long howl: *The campers heard a wolf baying at the moon.* [Old French *(a)bai* barking, from *(a)baiier* to bark.]

bay⁴ (bā) *n.* **1.** any of various evergreen trees or shrubs having stiff, smooth leaves and small berries; laurel. **2.** any of various shrubs or trees resembling the laurel. [Old French *baie* berry, from Latin *bāca.*]

bay⁵ (bā) *n.* **1.** a reddish-brown color. **2.** a horse or other animal of this color. —*adj.* having the color bay; reddish-brown. [Old French *bai* bay-colored, from Latin *badius.*]

bay·ber·ry (bā′ber′ē) *n. pl.,* **bay·ber·ries. 1.** a North American shrub having fragrant leaves and pale-blue berries coated with wax. **2.** the small, round berry itself, used for making scented soaps and fragrant candles. **3.** a tropi-

Bay² *(def. 1)*

cal American tree having large leathery leaves that yield a fragrant oil used in making bay rum.

bay leaf, the dried, spicy leaf of the laurel, used as a seasoning in cooking.

bay·o·net (bā′ə net′) *n.* a large knife or dagger that can be attached to the muzzle of a rifle and used for stabbing or slashing in hand-to-hand fighting. —*v.t.,* **bay·o·net·ed, bay·o·net·ing.** to stab or slash with a bayonet.

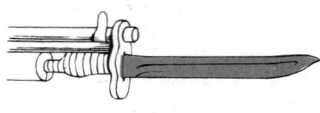

Bayonet

[French *baïonnette,* from *Bayonne,* a French city where bayonets were first made.]

bay·ou (bī′ōō, bī′ō) *n. pl.,* **bay·ous.** a marshy, sluggish, sometimes stagnant inlet or outlet of a river, lake, or gulf, especially in the southern United States. [French *bayou,* from Choctaw *bayuk* stream.]

bay rum, a fragrant liquid used in cosmetics and medicines, originally made from the leaves of the bayberry tree, but now prepared from a mixture of certain oils, alcohol, and water.

bay window, a window or set of windows projecting outward from the wall of a building and forming an alcove or recess in the room within.

ba·zaar (bə zär′) *also,* **ba·zar.** *n.* **1.** a sale of various things for some special purpose: *a charity bazaar.* **2.** a place for the sale of various kinds of goods. **3.** in Middle Eastern and Far Eastern countries, a marketplace or street lined with shops or stalls.

ba·zoo·ka (bə zōō′kə) *n.* a portable tube-shaped weapon for firing rockets at tanks. [From its resemblance to the *bazooka,* a long, slender musical instrument invented and named by the American comedian Bob Burns, 1890–1956.]

BB *pl.,* **BB's.** a very small lead shot, about ⅕ of an inch in diameter, used especially in a type of air rifle.

BBC, British Broadcasting Corporation.

BB gun, an air rifle that uses BB's.

bbl. *pl.,* **bbls.** barrel.

B.C. before Christ. ▲ used in expressing dates: *Aristotle was born in 384 B.C.*

bd. 1. board. **2.** bond.

bd. ft., board foot or board feet.

bdl., bundle.

be (bē) *v.i.,* **been, be·ing.** Present tense: *sing.,* first person, **am;** second, **are;** third, **is;** *pl.,* **are.** Past tense: *sing.,* first person, **was;** second, **were;** third, **was;** *pl.,* **were. 1.** to have reality; exist or live: *To be or not to be* (Shakespeare, *Hamlet*). *There are many who admire him.* **2.** to take place; happen; occur: *The wedding was last month.* **3.** to occupy a place, position, or situation: *Your coat is on the chair. He is in debt.* **4.** to remain or continue as before: *Let me be; don't bother me.* **Be** is also used: **a.** to join the subject of a sentence to a word or words that tell something about it: *The car is blue. She is a teacher. Let x be 10. The work is done.* **b.** to form a question or command: *Is your brother home? Be still!* **c.** with the present participle of another verb to show continuous action: *He is studying for a history test. I was standing near him when he fell.* **d.** with the past participle of a transitive verb to form the passive: *He was injured in the game. She was chosen for the award.* **e.** to show that something is expected to happen: *He is to join us later. You are not to reveal what I tell you.*

Be, the symbol for beryllium.

be- *prefix* **1.** throughout; all around; all over: *besiege, be-*

Bazooka

sprinkle. **2.** about: *bemoan.* **3.** make; cause to be: *betroth, bedazzle.* **4.** furnish with: *bejewel,- bespeckled.*

beach (bēch) *n. pl.,* **beach·es.** the gently sloping shore of an ocean or other body of water, especially that part covered by sand or pebbles. —*v.t.* to run or haul (a boat) onto a beach.

beach·comb·er (bēch′kō′mər) *n.* **1.** a vagrant or loafer who lives on the seashore. **2.** a long wave that rolls in from the ocean and onto the beach.

beach·head (bēch′hed′) *n.* **1.** an area on an enemy shore first seized and held by invading troops. **2.** an advance position or foothold: *The vaccine developed by Jonas Salk established a beachhead in the fight against polio.*

bea·con (bē′kən) *n.* **1.** a guiding or warning signal, especially a light or fire. **2.** a lighthouse, buoy, or other object placed so as to guide or warn ships. **3.** anything that warns, signals, or guides.

bead (bēd) *n.* **1.** a small, usually round ball or piece of glass, wood, metal, or other material, having a hole through it so that it can be strung on a thread or wire with other objects of the same kind. **2. beads. a.** a necklace of beads. **b.** a rosary. **3.** any small, roundish body: *Beads of sweat formed on his brow.* **4.** a small, metal knob on the muzzle of a gun to aim by. —*v.t.* to furnish or decorate with beads or beading: *The dressmaker beaded the dress.* —*v.i.* to collect in beads or drops: *Water beaded on the side of the glass.* —**bead′like′,** *adj.*

  to draw a bead on. to take careful aim at.

  to tell one's beads or **to say one's beads.** to say prayers with a rosary.

bead·ing (bē′ding) *n.* **1.** decorative work made of beads. **2.** material consisting of or decorated with beads. **3.** lace or embroidered trimming having openwork through which ribbon may be run.

bea·dle (bēd′əl) *n.* in the Church of England, a minor parish official having such duties as ushering and keeping order during services.

bead·work (bēd′wurk′) *n.* decorative work made of beads.

bead·y (bē′dē) *adj.,* **bead·i·er, bead·i·est.** small, round, and glittering: *The bird had beady eyes.*

bea·gle (bē′gəl) *n.* a smooth-coated dog having short legs, drooping ears, and usually white, tan, and black markings, used in hunting rabbits. [Possibly from Old French *bee-*

Beagle

gueule noisy person; literally, open throat, going back to Late Latin *badāre* to gape + *gula* throat; said to refer to the loud bark of this breed.]

beak (bēk) *n.* **1.** the horny, projecting mouth part of a bird; bill. **2.** a similar projecting part in other animals, such as the horny jaws of turtles. **3.** something resembling a bird's beak, such as the spout of a pitcher. **4.** a pointed projection at the prow of an ancient warship, used to ram or pierce enemy ships. —**beak′-like′,** *adj.*

beak·er (bē′kər) *n.* **1.** a large, open container of glass or other material, often having a lip for pouring, used especially in laboratories. **2.** a large drinking cup or goblet with a wide mouth. **3.** the contents of a beaker.

Beaks

beam (bēm) *n.* **1.** a long, heavy piece of wood, steel, or other material, used in building: *Many beams were needed for the barn's frame.* **2.** one of the heavy pieces of timber serving as a horizontal support in a ship. **3.** the widest part of a ship. **4.** a ray or shaft, as of light: *The beams of the searchlight were like columns in the night sky.* **5.** a continuous radio signal transmitted in one direction, to guide aircraft or ships. **6.** a suggestion or hint; gleam: *a beam of hope.* —*v.t.* **1.** to send out in beams or rays. **2.** to direct or transmit (a broadcast or radio signal) in a certain direction: *That radio program is beamed to our troops overseas.* —*v.i.* **1.** to shine brightly; radiate: *The sun beamed down.* **2.** to smile radiantly or joyfully: *The actress beamed as she accepted the award.*

  off the beam. a. not following the course indicated by a radio beam. **b.** *Informal.* wrong; incorrect.

  on the beam. a. following the course indicated by a radio beam. **b.** *Informal.* right; correct.

beam·ing (bē′ming) *adj.* bright; shining; radiant: *a beaming smile, a beaming face.* —**beam′ing·ly,** *adv.*

bean (bēn) *n.* **1.** a smooth seed of any of various plants, eaten as a vegetable, such as the string bean, lima bean, and kidney bean. **2.** the long, narrow pod containing such seeds. The pods of some varieties are cooked and eaten with the seed still inside. **3.** any of the plants that produce these seeds and pods.

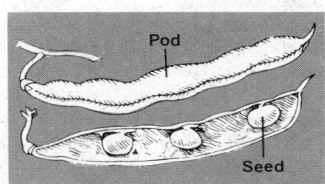

Bean (string bean)

4. a similar seed of any of various unrelated plants: *a coffee bean.* —**bean′like′,** *adj.*

bean·bag (bēn′bag′) *n.* a small cloth bag filled with beans and used in certain games.

bean·ie (bē′nē) *n.* a small cap without a brim.

bean·stalk (bēn′stôk′) *n.* the main stem of a bean plant.

bear¹ (ber) *v.,* **bore, borne** or **born, bear·ing.** —*v.t.* **1.** to hold up; support: *Beams bear the weight of the roof.* **2.** to carry; transport: *to bear gifts.* **3.** to have as a feature or characteristic: *The letter bears his signature.* **4.** to give birth to: *to bear a child.* **5.** to bring forth; produce: *The apple tree bore fruit.* **6.** to hold in the mind or emotions: *I bear no grudge against you.* **7.** to carry or behave (oneself): *She bears herself nobly.* **8.** to put up with; endure or tolerate: *I can't bear his rudeness.* **9.** to accept or acknowledge; assume: *to bear the blame, to bear the expense.* —*v.i.* **1.** to lean or press; weigh: *The burden of his grief bore heavily upon him.* **2.** to lie or move in a particular direction: *Bear left at the intersection to reach the town.* **3.** to bring forth young or fruit: *The pear tree did not bear this year.* [Old English *beran* to carry, support.]

  to bear down. a. to press or weigh down: *The heavy bundle bore him down.* **b.** to make a strong effort: *The runner bore down as he neared the finish line.*

  to bear down on or **to bear down upon. a.** to make a great effort towards: *He bore down on the task at hand.* **b.** to put pressure on; press hard: *He bore down on the pencil and broke the point.* **c.** to approach rapidly.

at; āpe; cär; end; mē; it; īce; hot; ōld; fôrk; wood; fool; oil; out; up; turn; sing; thin; this; hw in white; zh in treasure. The symbol ə stands for the sound of **a** in about, **e** in taken, **i** in pencil, **o** in lemon, and **u** in circus.

to bear on or **to bear upon.** to be relevant to; relate to: *This evidence bears on the crime.*

to bear out. to confirm or support; prove to be right: *The facts bear out my story.*

to bear up. to support a weight or strain; endure: *The fabric bore up well during testing.*

to bear with. to be patient or tolerant toward: *Bear with my faults.*

bear² (ber) *n.* **1.** a large, heavy animal with coarse, thick fur, powerful legs and claws, and a short, stumpy tail, such as the grizzly bear, polar bear, black bear, or brown bear. Bears are the largest meat-eating animals, and are found in North and South America, Asia, Europe, and the Arctic. **2.** a rough, rude, or surly person. **3.** a person who believes that prices on the stock market are going to fall, especially one who sells stock with the hope of buying it back later at a lower price. [Old English *bera* this animal.] —**bear′like′,** *adj.*

bear·a·ble (ber′ə bəl) *adj.* that can be borne or endured; tolerable: *The amusing comments of his friend made the boring movie bearable.* —**bear′a·bly,** *adv.*

bear·bait·ing (ber′bā′ting) *n.* the former sport of setting dogs to attack a chained bear.

beard (bērd) *n.* **1.** a growth of hair on the cheeks, chin, and throat of a man. **2.** any growth resembling a beard, such as the hair on the chin of a goat, the bristles near the beak of certain birds, or the hairlike tuft on the head of a stalk of wheat. —*v.t.* to face or defy boldly (an opponent or difficulty): *to beard a lion in his den.*

beard·ed (bēr′did) *adj.* having a beard.

beard·less (bērd′lis) *adj.* **1.** having no beard. **2.** young or inexperienced.

bear·er (ber′ər) *n.* **1.** a person or thing that carries, supports, or brings: *a flag bearer, a bearer of good news.* **2.** a person who holds or presents a check or other order for payment of money.

bear·ing (ber′ing) *n.* **1.** a way of carrying or behaving oneself: *The tall woman had a regal bearing.* **2.** connection or relation in thought: *Your comments have no bearing on the matter we are discussing.* **3.** position or direction in relation to another point or to the points of the compass. **4. bearings.** knowledge or understanding of one's position or direction: *The pilot lost his bearings in the storm and landed at the wrong airfield.* **5.** a part of a machine that holds or supports a moving part and allows it to move with less friction. **6.** the act or power of producing or bringing forth: *That fruit tree is past bearing.*

bear·ish (ber′ish) *adj.* **1.** rough or rude; surly. **2.** expecting a decline in the price of stocks. —**bear′ish·ly,** *adv.* —**bear′ish·ness,** *n.*

bear·skin (ber′skin′) *n.* **1.** the skin of a bear. **2.** a coat, rug, or robe made from this skin. **3.** a tall, black fur cap, such as that worn by some soldiers or drum majors.

beast (bēst) *n.* **1.** any animal other than man, especially a large four-footed animal. **2.** a person who is coarse, brutal, or cruel.

beast·ly (bēst′lē) *adj.,* **beast·li·er, beast·li·est. 1.** brutal or coarse; like a beast. **2.** *Informal.* disagreeable; nasty: *We have had beastly weather this summer.* —*adv. Informal.* very: *It's beastly hot today.* —**beast′li·ness,** *n.*

beast of burden, an animal used for carrying or pulling loads.

beat (bēt) *v.,* **beat, beat·en** or **beat, beat·ing.** —*v.t.* **1.** to strike or hit again and again; pound: *to beat a drum. The angry man beat the table with his fists.* **2.** to defeat or outdo: *I beat him at checkers. The runner beat his own record.* **3.** to flap repeatedly: *The bird beat its wings against the cage.* **4.** to shape or flatten by hammering: *to beat gold into thin sheets.* **5.** to stir or mix vigorously: *to beat egg*

whites. **6.** to mark or measure (time or rhythm), as with a baton, by tapping the foot, or by waving the hand. **7.** to hunt through in order to find a person or thing: *The men beat the brush for the quail.* **8.** to make (a path) by repeated walking: *to beat a trail through the woods.* **9.** *Informal.* to bewilder or baffle: *It beats me how she gets such high marks without studying.* —*v.i.* **1.** to strike or pound repeatedly: *The waves beat against the shore.* **2.** to throb: *The heart beats rhythmically.* **3.** to make a sound when struck: *The drums beat in time to the march.* **4.** to sail against the wind in a zigzag course: *The boat beat along the coast.* —*n.* **1.** a stroke or blow, especially one made again and again: *the beat of a drum.* **2.** a throb: *the beat of the heart.* **3.** a regular or customary course or round: *a policeman's beat. That reporter's beat is city hall.* **4.** *Music.* **a.** the basic unit of time or accent. **b.** a movement used to show this, as with a baton or the hand. —*adj. Informal.* very tired; exhausted.

to beat around the bush. *Informal.* to approach a matter in a roundabout way; avoid coming to the point.

to beat back or **to beat off.** to drive back by force: *The soldiers beat back the attacking forces.*

to beat down. to force (a seller) to lower his price.

to beat it. *Slang.* to leave hurriedly.

to beat up. *Informal.* to give a beating to; thrash.

beat·en (bēt′ən) *v.* a past participle of **beat.** —*adj.* **1.** formed or shaped by blows; hammered: *The necklace was made of beaten gold.* **2.** worn by use; commonly used: *The travelers went off the beaten path and discovered new and interesting places.* **3.** thwarted or vanquished; defeated: *He emerged from the failure a beaten man.* **4.** mixed by vigorous stirring: *Add a beaten egg to the batter.*

beat·er (bē′tər) *n.* **1.** a device or appliance used for beating: *The cook used an electric beater to mix the ingredients.* **2.** a person who drives game out from hiding for a hunter. **3.** a person who beats.

be·a·tif·ic (bē′ə tif′ik) *adj.* bringing or showing great happiness or blessedness; blissful: *The mother looked at her baby with a beatific smile.* —**be′a·tif′i·cal·ly,** *adv.*

be·at·i·fi·ca·tion (bē at′ə fi kā′shən) *n.* **1.** the act of beatifying or state of being beatified. **2.** in the Roman Catholic Church, declaration by the Pope that a deceased person is one of the blessed in heaven and is entitled to public honor. It is one of the steps toward canonization.

be·at·i·fy (bē at′ə fī′) *v.t.,* **be·at·i·fied, be·at·i·fy·ing. 1.** to make extremely happy. **2.** in the Roman Catholic Church, to declare the beatification of.

beat·ing (bē′ting) *n.* **1.** the act of a person or thing that beats. **2.** a series of forceful blows; thrashing: *The smaller boy got a beating from the bully.* **3.** a throbbing: *The beating of her heart became faster when she was frightened.* **4.** a severe loss or defeat: *They gave our team quite a beating.* **5.** rough treatment: *The car took a beating on those old roads.*

be·at·i·tude (bē at′ə tōōd′, bē at′ə tyōōd′) *n.* **1.** great happiness or blessedness; bliss. **2. the Beatitudes.** in the New Testament, the pronouncements made by Jesus in the Sermon on the Mount blessing those who have particular virtues. Each begins with the words "Blessed are."

beat·nik (bēt′nik) *n.* a person of the 1950's who rebelled against the values of middle-class society and was characterized by unconventional clothing and speech.

beau (bō) *n. pl.,* **beaux** or **beaus** (bōz). **1.** a sweetheart or boyfriend of a girl or woman. **2.** a man who cares too much about his clothes and appearance; dandy.

Beau Brum·mell (bō′ brum′əl) a fop; dandy. [From George Bryan (*Beau*) Brummell, 1778–1840, a leader of English society and men's fashion.]

Beau·fort Scale (bō′fərt) a scale of wind velocities, ranging from zero for speeds of less than one mile per hour (calm) to seventeen for speeds above seventy-five miles per hour (hurricane). [From Sir Francis *Beaufort,* 1774–1857, a British admiral who introduced it.]

Beaufort Sea, an arm of the Arctic Ocean, bordering northern Alaska and northwestern Canada.

Beau·mont (bō′mont) *n.* a port city in southeastern Texas. Pop. (1970), 115,919.

Beau·re·gard, Pi·erre G. T. (bō′rə gärd′; pē er′) 1818–1893, Confederate general in the Civil War.

beau·te·ous (byōo′tē əs) *adj.* beautiful. —**beau′te·ous·ly,** *adv.*

beau·ti·cian (byōo tish′ən) *n.* a person who works in a beauty parlor, especially a hairdresser.

beau·ti·ful (byōo′ti fəl) *adj.* having qualities that please the senses or mind; full of beauty: *The smell of the roses is beautiful. Beth has beautiful long hair. Beethoven composed beautiful music.* —**beau′ti·ful·ly,** *adv.* —**beau′ti·ful·ness,** *n.*

beau·ti·fy (byōo′tə fī′) *v.t.,* **beau·ti·fied, beau·ti·fy·ing.** to make beautiful; add beauty to. —**beau′ti·fi·ca′tion,** *n.* —**beau′ti·fi′er,** *n.*

beau·ty (byōo′tē) *n. pl.,* **beau·ties. 1.** a quality or combination of qualities that please the senses or mind: *We were amazed by the beauty of the countryside.* **2.** a person or thing that is beautiful: *That yacht is a beauty.* **3.** an outstanding or very pleasing feature or part: *The beauty of this recipe is that it's so easy to prepare.*

beauty mark, a mole or other small mark on the skin.

beauty parlor, a place where hairdressing, manicuring, and other beauty treatments for women are given. Also, **beauty salon, beauty shop.**

beaux (bōz) a plural of **beau.**

bea·ver[1] (bē′vər) *n.* **1.** an animal having a stocky body, soft grayish-brown fur, and a broad, flat tail and webbed hind feet that help it to swim. It builds its den in or on the banks of shallow streams and builds a dam of branches, stones, and mud to protect this den. **2.** the fur of this animal. **3.** a man's top hat, originally made of beaver fur. [Old English *beofer.*] —**bea′ver·like′,** *adj.*

Beaver

bea·ver[2] (bē′vər) *n.* a movable piece of armor attached to a helmet in order to protect the mouth and chin. [Old French *baviere* this piece of armor, bib. It was thought to resemble a child's bib.]

bea·ver·board (bē′vər bôrd′) *n.* a thin, stiff material made of compressed wood fibers, used for partitions, ceilings, and temporary structures. Trademark: **Beaverboard.**

be·calmed (bi kämd′) *adj.* kept motionless by lack of wind: *The sailboat was becalmed in the bay.*

be·came (bi kām′) the past tense of **become.**

be·cause (bi kôz′, bi kuz′) *conj.* due to the fact that; since: *Tom was cold because he forgot to wear his sweater.*
  because of. by reason of; on account of: *I went swimming because of the heat.*

Bech·u·a·na·land (bech′ōo ä′nə land′) *n.* see **Botswana.**

beck (bek) *Archaic. n.* a nod or other gesture given as a call or command. —*v.t., v.i.* to beckon.
  at one's beck and call. subject to one's slightest wish; ready to do one's bidding: *The assistant had to be at his employer's beck and call.*

Beck·et, Saint Thomas à (bek′it) 1118?–1170, English religious leader, archbishop of Canterbury.

Beck·ett, Samuel (bek′it) 1906—, Irish writer, living mostly in France.

beck·on (bek′ən) *v.t.* **1.** to signal, summon, or direct (someone) by a sign or gesture: *She beckoned me to come closer.* **2.** to be inviting to; attract: *The smell of bread beckoned the hungry boy.* —*v.i.* **1.** to signal or summon: *He beckoned to the waiter to bring him a menu.* **2.** to attract.

be·cloud (bi kloud′) *v.t.* to hide or obscure: *Angry arguments beclouded the real issue that was dividing the two sides.*

be·come (bi kum′) *v.,* **be·came, be·come, be·com·ing.** —*v.i.* to come to be; grow to be: *The tired child became cranky. Tadpoles become frogs.* —*v.t.* **1.** to look well on; suit: *A blue shirt becomes your brother.* **2.** to be suitable or appropriate for: *Such impolite behavior does not become you.*
  to become of. to happen to: *What has become of my umbrella?*

be·com·ing (bi kum′ing) *adj.* **1.** looking well on; flattering: *The color green is becoming to you.* **2.** suitable; appropriate: *The lieutenant was punished for conduct not becoming to an officer.* —**be·com′ing·ly,** *adv.*

bed (bed) *n.* **1.** a piece of furniture for sleeping or resting, usually consisting of a mattress and springs and a supporting framework. **2.** any place or thing used for sleeping or resting: *A pillow was the kitten's bed.* **3.** something resembling a bed in shape or function: *a bed of leaves.* **4.** the use of a bed for the night; lodging. **5.** a piece of ground used for planting: *She planted beds of roses and tulips in her garden.* **6.** the ground at the bottom of a body of water: *The stream had a bed of sand and pebbles.* **7.** a part or surface serving as a foundation or support: *The road was built on a bed of gravel.* **8.** a layer; stratum: *The workmen drilled through beds of sand and clay.* —*v.,* **bed·ded, bed·ding.** —*v.t.* **1.** to provide with a place to sleep: *The farmer bedded his mules in the barn.* **2.** to put or take to bed: *The mother was busy getting her sleepy baby bedded.* **3.** to set or plant in the ground: *She bedded her rose bushes by the front door.* —*v.i.* to go to bed.
  to bed down. a. to provide with a place to sleep: *to bed down cattle.* **b.** to go to bed; sleep.

be·daub (bi dôb′) *v.t.* to smear with something that is dirty.

be·daz·zle (bi daz′əl) *v.t.,* **be·daz·zled, be·daz·zling.** to bewilder or confuse greatly; overwhelm: *The tourist was bedazzled by the big city.*

bed·bug (bed′bug′) *n.* a small, wingless, bloodsucking insect that often infests beds and upholstery.

bed·cham·ber (bed′chām′bər) *n.* another word for **bedroom.**

bed·clothes (bed′klōz′, bed′klōthz′) *n., pl.* coverings used on a bed, such as sheets and blankets.

bed·ding (bed′ing) *n.* **1.** bedclothes: *I changed the bedding and sent some sheets to the laundry.* **2.** materials for a bed: *He used straw for the oxen's bedding.* **3.** a bottom

Bedbug

at; āpe; cär; end; mē; it; īce; hot; ōld; fôrk; wood; fōōl; oil; out; up; turn; sing; thin; this; hw in white; zh in treasure. The symbol ə stands for the sound of **a** in about, **e** in taken, **i** in pencil, **o** in lemon, and **u** in circus.

layer; foundation: *The workmen laid down a bedding of gravel for the road.*

Bede, Saint (bēd) 673?—735?, English historian.

be·deck (bi dek') *v.t.* to adorn: *The Christmas tree was bedecked with ornaments.*

be·dev·il (bi dev'əl) *v.t.,* **be·dev·iled, be·dev·il·ing;** *also,* British, **be·dev·illed, be·dev·il·ling. 1.** to worry or harass; plague; torment: *The businessman was bedeviled by lack of money and many debts.* **2.** *Archaic.* to bewitch. —**be·dev'il·ment,** *n.*

be·dew (bi dōō', bi dyōō') *v.t. Archaic.* to moisten with or as with dew: *The raindrops bedewed the window.*

bed·fast (bed'fast') *adj.* bedridden.

bed·fel·low (bed'fel'ō) *n.* **1.** a person who shares a bed with another. **2.** a companion or ally; associate: *Misery acquaints a man with strange bedfellows* (Shakespeare, *The Tempest*).

be·dim (bi dim') *v.t.,* **be·dimmed, be·dim·ming.** to make dim; obscure.

be·di·zen (bi dī'zən, bi diz'ən) *v.t. Archaic.* to dress or adorn gaudily.

bed·lam (bed'ləm) *n.* **1.** a scene of wild uproar and confusion: *It was bedlam at the department store during the sale.* **2.** *Archaic.* an insane asylum. [A form of *Bethlehem* in the name *Hospital of St. Mary of Bethlehem,* an insane asylum in London.]

Bed·ou·in (bed'ōō in) *n.* **1.** a member of a large group of wandering Arab tribes who live in the desert regions of North Africa and the Middle East. **2.** any wanderer or nomad. —*adj.* of, relating to, or like the Bedouins.

bed·pan (bed'pan') *n.* a pan used as a toilet by a person who is confined to bed.

bed·post (bed'pōst') *n.* one of the vertical supports at the corners of certain beds.

be·drag·gled (bi drag'əld) *adj.* wet, dirty, and limp: *The stray kitten was hungry and bedraggled.*

bed·rid·den (bed'rid'ən) *adj.* confined to bed: *Measles kept him bedridden for weeks.*

bed·rock (bed'rok') *n.* **1.** the solid rock that lies under the soil and other loose materials of the earth's surface. **2.** a foundation; basis: *The scientist's theory was formed on a bedrock of careful research.* **3.** the lowest point or level; bottom.

bed·roll (bed'rōl') *n.* a sleeping bag, blankets, or other bedding that can be rolled up and carried, usually used for sleeping outdoors.

bed·room (bed'rōōm', bed'room') *n.* a room for sleeping.

bed·side (bed'sīd') *n.* the side of a bed, especially of a sick person: *Robert hurried to his friend's bedside.*

bed·sore (bed'sôr') *n.* a sore caused by prolonged pressure against a bed. People who are bedridden for long periods of time often get bedsores.

bed·spread (bed'spred') *n.* a covering placed on a bed for decoration or protection.

bed·stead (bed'sted') *n.* a framework that supports the springs and mattress of a bed.

bed·time (bed'tīm') *n.* the time for going to bed: *The child's bedtime is usually seven o'clock.*

bee (bē) *n.* **1.** any of a group of winged, often stinging, insects that have a thick, hairy body and feed on nectar and pollen. Bees are related to wasps and ants. Some bees, such as the honeybee, live in colonies, or hives, of many thousands and are often raised for the honey and beeswax they make. **2.** a gathering or meeting combining work, pleasure, and, often, competition: *a spelling bee, a quilting bee.*

bee·bread (bē'bred') *n.* a mixture of pollen and honey or nectar, made by bees to feed their larvae or young.

beech (bēch) *n. pl.,* **beech·es. 1.** any of a group of trees found in cooler regions of the Northern Hemisphere, having light-gray bark and small nuts that may be eaten. **2.** the wood of this tree.

beech·nut (bēch'nut') *n.* the nut of the beech tree, used to make cooking oil and flavorings.

beef (bēf) *n. pl.,* **beeves** *(def. 2)* or **beefs** *(def. 3).* **1.** the meat of a full-grown steer, cow, or bull. **2.** a full-grown steer, cow, or bull that is raised for meat. **3.** *Slang.* a complaint. —*v.i. Slang.* to complain: *Jane beefed about having to wash the dishes.*

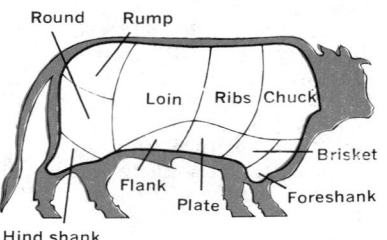

Cuts of beef

Round, Rump, Loin, Ribs, Chuck, Brisket, Foreshank, Plate, Flank, Hind shank

to beef up. *Informal.* to add force or vigor to; strengthen: *The candidate beefed up his campaign by making more speeches.*

beef cattle, cattle raised for meat.

beef·steak (bēf'stāk') *n.* a slice of beef for broiling or frying.

beef·y (bē'fē) *adj.,* **beef·i·er, beef·i·est.** strong and muscular; brawny: *The football player was tall and beefy.* —**beef'i·ness,** *n.*

bee·hive (bē'hīv') *n.* **1.** a natural or man-made hive for a colony of bees. **2.** a busy, crowded place: *The store was a beehive of activity during the sale.*

bee·keep·er (bē'kē'pər) *n.* a person who raises bees.

bee·line (bē'līn') *n.* a direct line or course, as the course a bee follows to its hive.

to make a beeline for or **to make a beeline to.** to go directly to: *The little boy made a beeline for the cake.*

Be·el·ze·bub (bē el'zə bub') *n.* the Devil; Satan.

been (bin) the past participle of **be.**

beer (bēr) *n.* an alcoholic drink usually made from malt and hops.

bees·wax (bēz'waks') *n.* the yellow wax secreted by honeybees to make their honeycombs. Beeswax is used in candles, cosmetics, floorwax, and other products.

beet (bēt) *n.* **1.** the fleshy root of any of a group of leafy plants, especially the common red beet, which is cooked and eaten as a vegetable. **2.** the plant bearing this root, having leaves that may be eaten cooked or raw. **3.** see **sugar beet.** —**beet'like',** *adj.*

Bee·tho·ven, Lud·wig van (bā'tō'vən; lōōd'wig vän) 1770–1827, German composer.

bee·tle¹ (bēt'əl) *n.* **1.** any insect having biting mouth parts and hard, sheathlike front wings that, when folded back, cover the thin, delicate hind wings. **2.** any insect resembling a beetle. [Old English *bitela* beetle, literally, biting insect, from *bītan* to bite.]

bee·tle² (bēt'əl) *n.* a heavy hammering tool, usually having a wooden head, used for driving wedges, pounding paving stones, and similar purposes. —*v.t.,* **bee·tled, bee·tling.** to pound with a beetle. [Old English *bīetel* hammer, from *bēatan* to beat.]

bee·tle³ (bēt'əl) *v.i.,* **bee·tled, bee·tling.** to stick out; jut out: *The cliffs beetled over the shore.* —*adj.* (of eyebrows) sticking out. [From *beetle-browed.*]

Beet

bee·tle-browed (bēt'əl broud') *adj.* **1.** having eyebrows that stick out. **2.** scowling; frowning.

beet sugar, sugar obtained from the sugar beet.

beeves (bēvz) a plural of **beef.**

be·fall (bi fôl′) *v.,* **be·fell** (bi fel′), **be·fall·en, be·fall·ing.** —*v.t.* to happen to: *The old man told us about the awful misfortune that befell him.* —*v.i.* to come to pass; happen.

be·fit (bi fit′) *v.t.,* **be·fit·ted, be·fit·ting.** to be suitable or appropriate for: *The general expects to be treated with the dignity that befits his rank.*

be·fit·ting (bi fit′ing) *adj.* suitable; fitting; proper. —**be·fit′ting·ly,** *adv.*

be·fog (bi fôg′, bi fog′) *v.t.,* **be·fogged, be·fog·ging. 1.** to surround with fog: *Mist befogged the skyline.* **2.** to confuse: *The candidate befogged the campaign issues.*

be·fore (bi fôr′) *prep.* **1.** in front of; ahead of: *She stood before me in line at the cafeteria.* **2.** earlier than: *Bill arrived before dinner.* **3.** rather than: *The soldier chose death before surrender.* **4.** in the presence or sight of: *The shy girl was afraid to appear before strangers.* **5.** in an earlier or more important position than: *A comes before B. The mother put the welfare of her child before all else.* **6.** under the consideration of: *We must deal with the problem before us.* —*adv.* **1.** in front; in advance; ahead: *Several soldiers went before to scout.* **2.** at an earlier time; previously: *He has been to my house before.* **3.** earlier; sooner: *I will telephone you at six o'clock, not before.* —*conj.* **1.** previous to the time when: *He spoke to me before he left.* **2.** rather than; sooner than: *I would starve before I would beg.*

be·fore·hand (bi fôr′hand′) *adv., adj.* ahead of time; in advance: *Dad found out beforehand what time the train left.*

be·foul (bi foul′) *v.t.* to make dirty or foul; soil: *Oil had befouled the beach.*

be·friend (bi frend′) *v.t.* to act as a friend to; assist: *to befriend a stranger.*

be·fud·dle (bi fud′əl) *v.t.,* **be·fud·dled, be·fud·dling.** to confuse or bewilder completely: *The complicated instructions befuddled him.*

beg (beg) *v.,* **begged, beg·ging.** —*v.t.* **1.** to ask for as charity: *to beg food and clothes.* **2.** to ask for earnestly or humbly: *Joe begged me to help him.* —*v.i.* **1.** to ask alms or charity: *The old man begged for a meal.* **2.** to ask earnestly or humbly: *He begged for mercy.*

to beg off. to ask to be excused from a promise: *He said he would go, but then begged off.*

be·gan (bi gan′) the past tense of **begin.**

be·get (bi get′) *v.t.,* **be·got** or (*archaic*) **be·gat** (bi gat′), **be·got·ten** or **be·got, be·get·ting. 1.** to sire; father: *Abraham begat Issac.* **2.** to give rise to; produce: *Jealousy begets hatred.* —**be·get′ter,** *n.*

beg·gar (beg′ər) *n.* **1.** a person who asks for charity, especially a person who does so for a living. **2.** a very poor person; pauper. **3.** a fellow; rascal. —*v.t.* **1.** to make very poor. **2.** to outdo; surpass: *That man's wealth beggars description.*

beg·gar·ly (beg′ər lē) *adj.* poor; inadequate: *He wore a torn, beggarly coat.* —**beg′gar·li·ness,** *n.*

beg·gar·y (beg′ər ē) *n.* **1.** extreme poverty. **2.** beggars as a group.

be·gin (bi gin′) *v.,* **be·gan, be·gun, be·gin·ning.** —*v.i.* **1.** to do or be the first part of something; start: *When the little boy fell down, he began to cry.* **2.** to come into being; arise: *The epidemic began last month.* —*v.t.* **1.** to do the first part of; start to do: *They began their homework.* **2.** to bring into being; originate: *Teenagers began the current fashion of having long hair.*

be·gin·ner (bi gin′ər) *n.* **1.** a person who is just beginning to do or learn something: *Paul skates well for a beginner.* **2.** a person who begins or originates something.

be·gin·ning (bi gin′ing) *n.* **1.** the first part: *The beginning of the movie was dull.* **2.** the time at which something

begins: *A gun signaled the beginning of the race.* **3.** the act of starting: *He made a good beginning on his homework.* **4.** a first cause; source; origin: *The beginning of their quarrel is unknown.* **5.** *also,* **beginnings.** the first or basic stage: *The book was about the beginnings of the United States of America.*

be·gone (bi gôn′, bi gon′) *v.i. Archaic.* to go away; depart. ▲ usually used as a command.

be·gon·ia (bi gōn′yə) *n.* **1.** the large flower of certain tropical plants. The flowers may be white, yellow, red, purple, or pink. **2.** the plant bearing this flower.

be·got (bi got′) the past tense and a past participle of **beget.**

be·got·ten (bi got′ən) a past participle of **beget.**

be·grime (bi grīm′) *v.t.,* **be·grimed, be·grim·ing.** to make grimy; soil: *Mud begrimed the boy's face.*

be·grudge (bi gruj′) *v.t.,* **be·grudged, be·grudg·ing. 1.** to envy (someone) the possession or pleasure of: *Don't begrudge him his good fortune.* **2.** to give or allow reluctantly: *He begrudged the beggar a few pennies.* —**be·grudg′ing·ly,** *adv.*

be·guile (bi gīl′) *v.t.,* **be·guiled, be·guil·ing. 1.** to trick by guile; mislead; deceive: *The swindler's friendly manner beguiled us into trusting him.* **2.** to amuse or delight; charm: *Mother's bedtime stories beguiled the children.* **3.** to pass (time) pleasantly. —**be·guile′ment,** *n.* —**be·guil′er,** *n.*

be·gun (bi gun′) the past participle of **begin.**

be·half (bi haf′) *n.* **1. in behalf of** or **on behalf of. a.** in the interest of; for the benefit of: *A fair was planned in behalf of the orphanage.* **b.** in the name of: *The minister accepted the contribution on behalf of his congregation.* **2. in one's behalf** or **on one's behalf.** in the interest or aid of: *The lawyer spoke in behalf of his client.*

be·have (bi hāv′) *v.,* **be·haved, be·hav·ing.** —*v.i.* **1.** to act in a particular way: *The little boy behaved bravely when he fell down.* **2.** to act properly: *Did the students behave when the teacher was gone?* —*v.t.* to act, especially in a proper way: *Keep quiet and behave yourself.*

be·hav·ior (bi hāv′yər) *also, British,* **be·hav·iour.** *n.* **1.** a manner of behaving or acting; conduct: *His behavior was disgraceful.* **2.** the manner in which something acts under given circumstances: *The scientist studied the behavior of coal under pressure.*

be·head (bi hed′) *v.t.* to cut off the head of; decapitate.

be·held (bi held′) the past tense and past participle of **behold.**

be·he·moth (bi hē′məth) *n.* **1.** in the Bible, an enormous animal that may have been the hippopotamus. **2.** any creature or thing of enormous size or power.

be·hest (bi hest′) *n.* order; command; bidding: *The teacher acted at the principal's behest.*

be·hind (bi hīnd′) *prep.* **1.** at or toward the back of; in the rear of: *I sat behind a very tall man.* **2.** at or on the farther side of; beyond: *The path runs behind those hedges.* **3.** later than; after: *Our train came ten minutes behind the first one.* **4.** less advanced than; inferior to: *She was behind her friends in her schoolwork.* **5.** hidden by: *Fear lay behind her show of bravery.* **6.** causing or helping to cause: *What was the reason behind his actions?* **7.** in support of; sup-

at; āpe; cär; end; mē; it; īce; hot; ōld; fôrk; wood; fŏŏl; oil; out; up; turn; sing; thin; **th**is; **hw** in white; **zh** in treasure. The symbol ə stands for the sound of **a** in about, **e** in taken, **i** in pencil, **o** in lemon, and **u** in circus.

porting; backing: *The senators are fully behind the President's plan.* **8.** remaining after: *Leave your cares behind you.* —*adv.* **1.** in a place or condition departed from: *She remained behind after her friends left.* **2.** at or toward the back; in the rear: *I went first; Luis walked behind.* **3.** not on time; slow: *They are behind in their work.* **4.** not up to date; overdue: *He fell behind in his payments.*

be·hind·hand (bi hīnd′hand′) *adv., adj.* behind; late: *Tom is always behindhand with his homework.*

be·hold (bi hōld′) *v.t.,* **be·held, be·hold·ing.** to look at; gaze upon; see: *The travelers beheld a beautiful valley.* —*interj.* look; see. —**be·hold′er,** *n.*

be·hold·en (bi hōld′ən) *adj.* obligated; indebted: *I am beholden to you for your helpful advice.*

be·hoove (bi hōōv′) *v.t.,* **be·hooved, be·hoov·ing.** to be necessary, right, or good for: *It behooves you to be honest.*

beige (bāzh) *n.* a pale-brown or grayish-tan color. —*adj.* having the color beige.

Bei·jing (bā′jing′) another spelling of Peking.

be·ing (bē′ing) *n.* **1.** existence; life: *Those mountains came into being millions of years ago.* **2.** a creature: *a supernatural being.*

Bei·rut (bā rōōt′) *n.* the capital, largest city, and chief port of Lebanon, in the west-central part of the country, on the Mediterranean. Pop. (1970 est.), 484,870.

be·jew·el (bi jōō′əl) *v.t.,* **be·jew·eled, be·jew·el·ing;** *also, British,* **be·jew·elled, be·jew·el·ling.** to ornament with jewels: *Ancients bejeweled their statues.*

bel (bel) *n. Physics.* a unit for measuring the loudness of sounds. One bel is equal to ten decibels. [From Alexander Graham *Bell.*]

be·la·bor (bi lā′bər) *also, British,* **be·la·bour.** *v.t.* **1.** to beat soundly; thrash. **2.** to attack with words: *She belabored her friend for being late.* **3.** to deal with (something) for too long a time: *The speaker belabored the point long after the audience had lost interest.*

be·lat·ed (bi lā′tid) *adj.* delayed; late: *a belated birthday present, a belated arrival at a party.* —**be·lat′ed·ly,** *adv.* —**be·lat′ed·ness,** *n.*

be·lay (bi lā′) *v.t.,* **be·layed, be·lay·ing.** *Nautical.* **1.** to fasten (a rope) by winding it around a belaying pin, cleat, or similar object. **2.** *Informal.* to stop; hold. ▲ used chiefly as a command.

belaying pin *Nautical.* a removable pin around which ropes can be fastened.

belch (belch) *v.i.* **1.** to let out gas noisily from the stomach through the mouth. **2.** to throw out its contents violently: *Flames belched from the windows of the burning house.* —*v.t.* to throw out violently or suddenly: *The chimney belched smoke and sparks.* —*n. pl.,* **belch·es.** the act of belching.

bel·dam (bel′dəm) *also,* **bel·dame** (bel′dəm, bel′dām′). *n.* an ugly old woman; hag.

be·lea·guer (bi lē′gər) *v.t.* **1.** to surround or shut in with troops; besiege: *The soldiers beleaguered the castle.* **2.** to surround or harass; beset: *Creditors constantly beleaguered him. The reporters beleaguered the mayor with questions.*

Belaying pins

Be·lém (bə lem′) *n.* a port city in northeastern Brazil. Pop. (1975 est.), 565,097.

Bel·fast (bel′fast) *n.* the capital, largest city, and chief port of Northern Ireland, on the eastern coast of the country. Pop. (1978 est.), 354,400.

bel·fry (bel′frē) *n. pl.,* **bel·fries. 1.** a bell tower, especially one attached to a church or other structure. **2.** the part of a steeple or tower in which a bell or bells are hung.

Bel·gian (bel′jən) *n.* a person who was born or is living in Belgium. —*adj.* of or relating to Belgium, its people, or their culture.

Belgian Congo, a former Belgian colony in central Africa, now the Republic of Zaire. See **Zaire.**

Belgian hare, a reddish-brown domestic rabbit.

Bel·gium (bel′jəm) *n.* a country in northwestern Europe, on the North Sea. Capital, Brussels. Area, 11,779 sq. mi. Pop. (1977 est.), 9,837,413.

Bel·grade (bel′grād) *n.* the capital, largest city, and major port of Yugoslavia, in the eastern part of the country. Pop. (1976 est.), 770,140.

Belfry

Be·li·al (bē′lē əl, bēl′yəl) *n.* in the New Testament, the Devil.

be·lie (bi lī′) *v.t.,* **be·lied, be·ly·ing. 1.** to give a false idea of; disguise: *His smile belies his sadness.* **2.** to show to be false; contradict: *Evidence belied the guilty charge and proved him innocent.* **3.** to fail to come up to.

be·lief (bi lēf′) *n.* **1.** acceptance of the truth or reality of: *He has a belief in life on other planets.* **2.** something that is believed; opinion; conviction: *We must defend our belief that all men are created equal.* **3.** confidence, especially in another person; faith; trust. ▲ See **faith** for usage note.

be·lieve (bi lēv′) *v.,* **be·lieved, be·liev·ing.** —*v.t.* **1.** to accept as true or real: *I believe your story.* **2.** to think (somebody) is telling the truth: *The team believed the coach when she said they would win.* **3.** to have the opinion; think; suppose: *I believe Jean went out shopping.* —*v.i.* to have faith or trust: *to believe in God.* —**be·liev′a·ble,** *adj.* —**be·liev′er,** *n.*

to make believe. to imagine; pretend: *Joe and Bill made believe that they were cowboys.*

be·lit·tle (bi lit′əl) *v.t.,* **be·lit·tled, be·lit·tling.** to cause to seem small or less important; disparage: *The loser of the race belittled the winner's success because he was jealous.*

Be·lize (be lēz′) *n.* a country on the northeastern coast of Central America, on the Caribbean, formerly British Honduras. Capital, Belmopan. Area, 8,867 sq. mi. Pop. (1974 est.), 130,000.

bell (bel) *n.* **1.** a hollow instrument, usually cup-shaped and made of metal, that makes a ringing sound when struck by a clapper, hammer, or similar object. **2.** a sound made by a bell. **3.** something that is like a bell in shape or use, such as a doorbell or the flared lower end of a trumpet. **4.** *Nautical.* **a.** a stroke of a bell that is rung aboard ship to mark each half hour during the watches, which begin at 4:00, 8:00, and 12:00. One bell signals the end of the first half hour of a watch, and an additional bell is struck for every half hour that follows, so that eight bells signal the end of each four-hour watch. **b.** a half-hour interval that is marked by these bells. —*v.t.* **1.** to put a bell on: *We belled our cat so that birds could hear him and fly away to safety.* **2.** to cause to flare out like a bell.

Bell, Alexander Gra·ham (bel; grā′əm) 1847–1922, American inventor of the telephone, born in Scotland.

bel·la·don·na (bel′ə don′ə) *n.* **1.** a plant of Europe and Asia, having poisonous black berries. Also, **deadly nightshade. 2.** a drug made from this plant; atropine.

B

bell·bot·tom (bel′bot′əm) *also,* **bell·bot·tomed,** *adj.* (of trousers) gradually flaring from below the knee to the bottom of each leg.

bell·bot·toms (bel′bot′əmz) *n., pl.* bell-bottom trousers.

bell·boy (bel′boi′) *n.* a person employed in a hotel to carry luggage, attend to guests, and run errands.

bell buoy, a buoy having a bell that is rung by the motion of the waves.

belle (bel) *n.* **1.** a beautiful woman or girl. **2.** the most beautiful, popular, or admired woman or girl: *She was the belle of the ball.*

Bel·ler·o·phon (bə ler′ə fon′) *n. Greek Legend.* the hero who killed the monster Chimera with the help of the winged horse Pegasus.

bell·hop (bel′hop′) *n. Informal.* bellboy.

bel·li·cose (bel′ə kōs′) *adj.* showing a willingness or eagerness to fight; warlike: *a bellicose nation.* —**bel·li·cos·i·ty** (bel′ə kos′ə tē), *n.*

bel·lig·er·ence (bə lij′ər əns) *n.* **1.** the state or quality of being belligerent: *The bully's belligerence frightened the boy.* **2.** fighting; warfare.

bel·lig·er·en·cy (bə lij′ər ən sē) *n.* **1.** the state of being at war. **2.** belligerence.

bel·lig·er·ent (bə lij′ər ənt) *adj.* **1.** eager or willing to fight; hostile: *It was the belligerent boy who started the fight.* **2.** engaged in warfare; at war: *belligerent countries.* —*n.* a country or person engaged in warfare or fighting. —**bel·lig·er·ent·ly,** *adv.*

bell jar, a bell-shaped glass container, used especially in laboratories to cover objects, to contain gases, or to create a vacuum.

bel·low (bel′ō) *v.i.* **1.** to make a loud, deep sound: *The bull bellowed and roared.* **2.** to cry out in a loud, deep voice: *The injured man bellowed with pain.* —*v.t.* to utter (words or sounds) loudly and deeply. —*n.* **1.** a loud, deep sound: *the bellow of a bull, the bellow of a foghorn.* **2.** any loud, deep outcry.

bel·lows (bel′ōz) *n., pl.* **1.** a device for producing a strong air current, used for such purposes as making a fire burn faster or sounding a musical instrument. A bellows consists of an air chamber that can be expanded to draw air into it and contracted to force air out. **2.** anything that is like a bellows, such as the collapsible connection between the lens and the body of a folding camera.

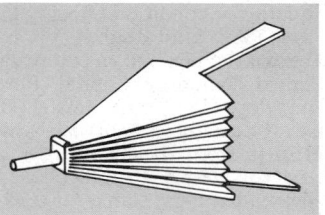

Bellows

bell·weth·er (bel′weth′ər) *n.* **1.** a male sheep that leads the flock, usually having a bell around its neck. **2.** a person or thing that leads or marks a trend: *The state of Maine is often thought of as a bellwether in Presidential elections.*

bel·ly (bel′ē) *n. pl.,* **bel·lies. 1.** the front part of the human body between the chest and pelvis; abdomen. **2.** the underside of the body of an animal. **3.** the stomach. **4.** the inside or interior of something: *The belly of the ship was filled with cargo.* **5.** a curved or bulging surface or part: *The belly of a bottle holds more liquid than the neck.* **6.** the front or under surface of anything: *The airplane landed on its*

Bell-bottoms

belly. —*v.,* **bel·lied, bel·ly·ing.** —*v.i.* to swell or billow out; bulge: *The ship's sails bellied out.* —*v.t.* to cause (something) to swell or billow out.

bel·ly·ache (bel′ē āk′) *n.* a pain in the abdomen, especially in the stomach. —*v.i.,* **bel·ly·ached, bel·ly·ach·ing.** *Slang.* to complain peevishly; grumble: *Pete bellyached about having to wash the car.* —**bel′ly·ach·er,** *n.*

bel·ly·band (bel′ē band′) *n.* a strap that forms part of a harness and goes under an animal's belly.

bel·ly·but·ton (bel′ē but′ən) *n. Informal.* the navel.

Bel·mo·pan (bel mō′pän) *n.* the capital of Belize, in the north-central part of the country. Pop. (1971), 5,000.

Be·lo Ho·ri·zon·te (bel′ō hôr′ə zon′tē) a city in southeastern Brazil. Pop. (1970), 1,235,001.

be·long (bi lông′) *v.i.* to have a proper place; be suitable or right: *The lamp belongs on that table.*

to belong to. a. to be the property of: *This book belongs to me.* **b.** to be a part of; be connected with: *This vest belongs to my blue suit.* **c.** to be a member of.

be·long·ings (bi lông′ingz) *n., pl.* personal property; possessions: *We packed our belongings before we moved.*

be·lov·ed (bi luv′id, bi luvd′) *adj.* much loved. —*n.* a person who is dearly loved.

be·low (bi lō′) *adv.* **1.** in or to a lower place: *From the roof we could see cars in the street below.* **2.** on or to a lower floor or deck: *The sailors stowed the cargo below.* **3.** in a later part of a book or other piece of writing: *A detailed diagram of the model airplane is given below.* —*prep.* **1.** in a lower place or position than: *The hem of her dress was below the knee.* **2.** lower in rank, degree, or amount than; less than: *It is five degrees below zero today. The dress was on sale for five dollars below the original price.* **3.** unworthy of; beneath: *It is below her to be dishonest.*

belt (belt) *n.* **1.** a strip or band of leather or other material worn around the waist. Belts are used as a support for clothing, tools, or weapons or as an ornament. **2.** any strip or band: *A belt of highways surrounded the city.* **3.** a region or zone having distinctive characteristics: *We saw mile after mile of farms when we drove through the wheat belt.* **4.** *Mechanics.* **a.** an endless flexible band that passes around two or more wheels or pulleys, used to transmit power or motion from one to the other. **b.** see **conveyor belt. 5.** *Informal.* a strong or powerful blow. —*v.t.* **1.** to encircle or fasten with a belt: *to belt a skirt.* **2.** to beat or strike with a belt or strap. **3.** *Informal.* to strike forcefully: *The batter belted the ball into the bleachers.*

below the belt. a. in boxing, below the waist. **b.** unfair; unfairly: *The politician felt that criticism of his family was below the belt.*

to tighten one's belt. to live in a more thrifty way.

belt·ing (bel′ting) *n.* **1.** material used for belts. **2.** *Informal.* a beating; thrashing.

be·lu·ga (bə lōō′gə) *n.* **1.** a freshwater sturgeon of the Black Sea, Caspian Sea, and Volga River, whose eggs are eaten as caviar. **2.** a white whale living in the shallow coastal waters of Arctic seas.

be·moan (bi mōn′) *v.t.* to grieve over; lament: *The prisoner bemoaned his fate.*

be·mused (bi myōōzd′) *adj.* **1.** lost in thought; preoccupied. **2.** confused; bewildered.

at; āpe; cär; end; mē; it; īce; hot; ōld; fôrk; wood; fōōl; oil; out; up; turn; sing; thin; **th**is; hw in white; zh in treasure. The symbol ə stands for the sound of **a** in about, **e** in taken, **i** in pencil, **o** in lemon, and **u** in circus.

Be·na·res (bə när'is) *also,* **Ba·na·ras.** *n.* a city in northeastern India. It is a holy city of the Hindu religion. Official name: **Varanasi.** Pop. (1976 est.), 583,856.

bench (bench) *n. pl.,* **bench·es. 1.** a long, often backless seat. **2.** a sturdy worktable, especially one used by an artisan: *The cobbler mended shoes at his bench.* **3.a.** a seat for judges in a court of law. **b.** the office or position of a judge: *She was appointed to the bench.* **c.** a judge or judges who preside in a court of law. —*v.t.* to keep (a player) from playing in a game or games: *The coach benched him for the rest of the season.*
on the bench. a. serving as a judge in a court of law. **b.** *Sports.* (of a player) not playing in the game: *The substitute was on the bench until the captain was hurt.*

bench mark, a surveyor's mark made on a rock or other permanent object whose elevation is known, used as a starting point or as a guide for measuring other elevations.

bend (bend) *v.,* **bent, bend·ing.** —*v.t.* **1.** to change the shape of (something), especially by making it crooked or curved: *to bend a wire hanger, to bend one's knees.* **2.** to cause to yield; make submissive: *She could not bend the child to her will.* **3.** to direct or turn, as in a particular direction: *The hikers bent their steps toward home. He bent all his energies toward building up his business.* —*v.i.* **1.** to become curved or crooked: *The branch bent under the weight of its fruit.* **2.** to take a stooping position; bow: *Steve bent over to tie his shoe.* **3.** to turn in a particular direction: *The river bends westward.* **4.** to give in; submit; yield: *She bent to her parents' wishes.* —*n.* **1.** a thing that is curved or bent; crook: *a bend in a river.* **2.** any of several knots used to join two ropes or to fasten a rope to something else. **3. the bends.** a painful condition caused by nitrogen gas bubbles in the body; caisson disease. It is caused by a rapid decrease in pressure of air or water on the body, such as when a deep-sea diver rises to the surface of the water too quickly.
to bend over backward or **to bend over backwards.** to make a great effort; do one's best: *Susan bent over backward to help her friend.*

be·neath (bi nēth') *prep.* **1.** lower than; below: *We stood beneath the stars.* **2.** directly under; underneath: *After the boat trip I was glad to feel the earth beneath my feet.* **3.** not fitting the dignity of; unworthy of: *Telling a lie is beneath him.* —*adv.* below; underneath.

Ben·e·dict, Saint (ben'ə dikt') 480?–550?, Italian monk, founder of the Benedictine order.

Ben·e·dic·tine (*n.,* ben'ə dik'tin; *adj.,* ben'ə dik'tēn) *n.* a monk or nun belonging to the order founded by Saint Benedict in the sixth century. —*adj.* of or relating to Saint Benedict or his religious order.

ben·e·dic·tion (ben'ə dik'shən) *n.* a blessing, especially one given at the close of a religious service.

ben·e·fac·tion (ben'ə fak'shən) *n.* a charitable gift, especially of money.

ben·e·fac·tor (ben'ə fak'tər) *n.* a person who gives help or financial aid; patron: *The young man's benefactor paid for his college education.* —**ben'e·fac'tress,** *n.*

ben·e·fice (ben'ə fis) *n.* a church office, especially that of a rector or vicar, and the income that comes with it.

be·nef·i·cence (bə nef'ə səns) *n.* **1.** the act of doing good; kindness or generosity. **2.** a charitable gift or act.

be·nef·i·cent (bə nef'ə sənt) *adj.* doing or causing good; being charitable. —**be·nef'i·cent·ly,** *adv.*

ben·e·fi·cial (ben'ə fish'əl) *adj.* having a good effect; advantageous; helpful: *Some insects are beneficial to plants.* —**ben'e·fi'cial·ly,** *adv.*

ben·e·fi·ci·ar·y (ben'ə fish'ē er'ē) *n. pl.,* **ben·e·fi·ci·ar·ies. 1.** a person who receives anything as a benefit: *He was the beneficiary of a generous scholarship.* **2.** a person

named to receive the money or property from a will, trust, or insurance policy.

ben·e·fit (ben'ə fit) *n.* **1.** something that helps or betters a person or thing; advantage: *Knowing how to speak French was of great benefit when she visited Paris.* **2.** money or other services given by an insurance company, government agency, or other institution, as to sick, disabled, or aged persons: *Health insurance benefits helped pay for her operation.* **3.** a social or theatrical event held to raise money for some charity or cause. —*v.t.* to be useful or helpful to: *Rain will benefit the crops.* —*v.i.* to gain or profit; receive help: *We can all benefit from the teacher's knowledge.*

Ben·e·lux (ben'ə luks') *n.* the economic union of Belgium, the Netherlands, and Luxembourg.

Be·nét, Stephen Vincent (bə nā') 1899–1943, U.S. writer.

be·nev·o·lence (bə nev'ə ləns) *n.* **1.** the desire to do good; kindliness; generosity: *Mr. Martin's benevolence was shown by his many hours of work with handicapped children.* **2.** an act of kindness; charitable gift.

be·nev·o·lent (bə nev'ə lənt) *adj.* doing or desiring to do good; kindly; generous: *The benevolent man donated much money to charity.* —**be·nev'o·lent·ly,** *adv.*

Ben·gal (beng'gôl) *n.* **1.** a former province and historic region of northeastern India, divided between India and Pakistan in 1947. The part that formerly belonged to Pakistan is now the country of Bangladesh. **2. Bay of.** a part of the Indian Ocean between Burma and India.

Ben·ga·lese (ben'gə lēz') *adj.* of or relating to Bengal or its people. —*n. pl.,* **Ben·ga·lese.** a person who was born or is living in Bengal.

Ben·gha·zi (ben gä'zē) *also,* **Ben·ga·si.** *n.* one of the two capitals of Libya, a port city in the northeastern part of the country. Pop. (1970 est.), 170,000.

be·night·ed (bi nī'tid) *adj.* **1.** mentally or morally ignorant: *The benighted man was full of superstitions.* **2.** overtaken by darkness or night: *A blanket whiteness of benighted snow* (Robert Frost).

be·nign (bi nīn') *adj.* **1.** kindly or gentle in nature: *My grandfather is a benign old man.* **2.** favorable; beneficial: *the benign climate of a tropical island.* **3.** not malignant: *The benign tumor caused no damage to her health.*

be·nig·nant (bi nig'nənt) *adj.* **1.** kindly toward others: *a benignant ruler.* **2.** favorable; beneficial. —**be·nig'nan·cy,** *n.* —**be·nig'nant·ly,** *adv.*

be·nig·ni·ty (bi nig'nə tē) *n. pl.,* **be·nig·ni·ties. 1.** the quality or condition of being kindly toward others; kindliness. **2.** a kind deed.

Benin (be nēn') *n.* a country in western Africa, formerly called Dahomey. Capital, Porto-Novo. Area, 44,713 sq. mi. Pop. (1978 est.), 3,340,000.

ben·i·son (ben'ə zən) *n.* a blessing.

Ben·ja·min (ben'jə min) *n.* **1.** in the Old Testament, the youngest son of Jacob. **2.** the tribe of Israel that is descended from him.

bent (bent) *v.* the past tense and past participle of **bend.** —*adj.* **1.** crooked or curved: *a bent wire.* **2.** firmly determined; set: *Harry was bent on going camping.* —*n.* a leaning or ability: *Susan has a natural bent for sports.*

be·numb (bi num') *v.t.* to make numb.

Ben·ze·drine (ben'zə drēn') *n. Trademark.* a drug used as a stimulant, especially to help a person stay awake.

ben·zene (ben'zēn) *n.* a colorless liquid that catches fire easily. It is obtained mainly from coal tar and is used as a solvent and in the manufacture of chemicals. Also, **benzol.**

ben·zine (ben'zēn) *n.* a colorless liquid that catches fire easily. It is obtained by distilling petroleum and is used as a solvent and as a motor fuel.

ben·zo·ic acid (ben zō′ik) a colorless or white acid found in certain plants and also made synthetically. It is used in dyes, cosmetics, and medicine.

ben·zo·in (ben′zō in) *n.* a fragrant resin obtained from a tree found in southeast Asia, used in medicine and perfume.

ben·zol (ben′zôl) *n.* another word for **benzene**.

be·queath (bi kwēth′, bi kwēth′) *v.t.* **1.** to give or leave (property) by will: *Mr. Jones bequeathed his money to his niece.* **2.** to hand down: *Our forefathers bequeathed a heritage of freedom to us.*

be·quest (bi kwest′) *n.* **1.** something bequeathed; legacy: *Mr. Smith's will contained a bequest of one thousand dollars for each of his grandchildren.* **2.** the act of bequeathing.

be·rate (bi rāt′) *v.t.,* **be·rat·ed, be·rat·ing.** to find fault with sharply; scold severely: *His father berated him for hitting his brother.*

Ber·ber (bur′bər) *n.* **1.** a member of a people living in North Africa, especially in Morocco and Algeria. **2.** the language spoken by the Berbers. —*adj.* of or relating to the Berbers or their language.

be·reave (bi rēv′) *v.t.,* **be·reaved** or **be·reft, be·reav·ing.** to make forlorn and alone, usually as the result of the death of a loved one: *The children were bereaved by the death of their dog.*

be·reave·ment (bi rēv′mənt) *n.* the condition of being made forlorn and alone, usually as a result of the death of a loved one.

be·reft (bi reft′) *v.* a past tense of **bereave.** —*adj.* deprived: *The fire in his apartment left him bereft of all his belongings.*

be·ret (bə rā′) *n.* a soft, round cap, usually without a brim.

berg (burg) *n.* see **iceberg.**

ber·i·ber·i (ber′ē ber′ē) *n.* a disease affecting the heart, muscles, and nervous system, caused by a lack of vitamin B_1.

Ber·ing Sea (bēr′ing, ber′ing) the northernmost part of the Pacific Ocean, between Siberia and Alaska.

Bering Strait, a narrow waterway connecting the Bering Sea with the Arctic Ocean.

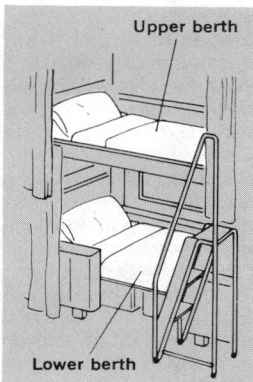
Beret

Berke·ley (burk′lē) *n.* a city in western California, on the eastern shore of San Francisco Bay. Pop. (1970), 116, 716.

ber·ke·li·um (bər kē′lē əm) *n.* a radioactive element made from such elements as americium. Symbol: **Bk** [From *Berkeley,* California, where this element was first isolated.]

ber·lin (bər lin′, bur′lin) *n.* a closed, four-wheeled carriage with a raised front seat for the driver.

Ber·lin (bər lin′) *n.* the former capital of Germany, now divided into West Berlin and East Berlin.

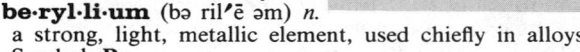
Berlin

Ber·mu·da (bər- myōō′də) *n.* a group of British islands in the Atlantic Ocean, about 600 miles east of North Carolina. Land area, 21 sq. mi. Pop. (1975 est.), 60,000.

Bermuda shorts, shorts reaching almost to the knees. Also, **Ber·mu·das** (bər myōō′dəz). [From *Bermuda,* where American tourists had tailors make shorts for them

that were patterned after the shorts worn by British soldiers stationed there.]

Bern (burn) *also,* **Berne.** *n.* the capital of Switzerland, in the west-central part of the country. Pop. (1977), 146,800.

ber·ry (ber′ē) *n. pl.,* **ber·ries.** **1.** any small, pulpy fruit with many seeds, such as the raspberry or strawberry. **2.** any fleshy fruit with a skin around it, usually containing many seeds, such as the tomato, grape, or cranberry. —**ber′ry·like′,** *adj.*

ber·serk (bər surk′, bər zurk′) *adj.* in a wild or violent rage. —*adv.* into a wild or violent rage: *The bull went berserk when it saw the red cape.*

berth (burth) *n.* **1.** a bed or bunk on a train or ship. **2.** a place for a ship to anchor or dock. **3.** a job or position: *He has a berth on the starting team in football.* —*v.t.* **1.** to bring (a ship) into a berth. **2.** to provide with a berth. —*v.i.* to come into a berth: *The ship berthed in the harbor.*

to give a wide berth to. to keep away from; avoid: *We give a wide berth to our neighbor's unfriendly dog.*

ber·yl (ber′əl) *n.* a hard mineral found in various colors, especially green or greenish blue. Emeralds and aquamarines are varieties of beryl.

be·ryl·li·um (bə ril′ē əm) *n.* a strong, light, metallic element, used chiefly in alloys. Symbol: **Be**

be·seech (bi sēch′) *v.t.,* **be·sought** or **be·seeched, be·seech·ing.** to ask (someone) earnestly; implore; beg: *I beseech you, help us before it is too late.* —**be·seech′ing·ly,** *adv.*

be·seem (bi sēm′) *v.t.* to be suitable or fitting for; suit.

be·set (bi set′) *v.t.,* **be·set, be·set·ting.** **1.** to attack from all sides; harass: *Many problems beset the new teacher.* **2.** to hem in; surround: *Enemy troops beset the camp under cover of night.*

be·set·ting (bi set′ing) *adj.* constantly attacking; always present: *The youth's besetting problem was his lack of self-confidence.*

be·shrew (bi shrōō′) *v.t. Archaic.* to curse: *Beshrew me, if I would do such a wrong* (Shakespeare, *Othello*).

be·side (bi sīd′) *prep.* **1.** at or by the side of; near: *Sit beside me.* **2.** in comparison with: *My book seems short beside the one you are reading.* **3.** in addition to; besides. **4.** apart from; not connected with: *What he said was quite beside the point.* —*adv.* besides.

beside oneself. out of one's senses: *She was beside herself with anger over the insult.*

be·sides (bi sīdz′) *adv.* **1.** moreover; furthermore: *I don't want to go; besides, it's too late.* **2.** in addition; also: *Ruth has a pet cat and dog, and a pony besides.* —*prep.* also, **beside.** in addition to; other than: *Besides you, no one else is coming to lunch.*

be·siege (bi sēj′) *v.t.,* **be·sieged, be·sieg·ing.** **1.** to sur-

Upper berth
Lower berth

at; āpe; cär; end; mē; it; īce; hot; ōld; fôrk; wood; fōōl; oil; out; up; turn; sing; thin; this; hw in white; zh in treasure. The symbol ə stands for the sound of a in about, e in taken, i in pencil, o in lemon, and u in circus.

round with armed forces in order to capture; lay siege to: *Soldiers besieged the fort.* **2.** to crowd around: *Autograph seekers besieged the famous singer.* **3.** to overwhelm or harass: *The store manager was besieged with complaints.* —**be·sieg′er**, *n.*

be·smear (bi smēr′) *v.t.* to smear over; soil.

be·smirch (bi smurch′) *v.t.* to make dirty; soil: *to besmirch a person's reputation.*

be·sought (bi sôt′) a past tense and a past participle of **beseech.**

be·spake (bi spāk′) *Archaic.* a past tense of **bespeak.**

be·span·gle (bi spang′gəl) *v.t.,* **be·span·gled, be·spangling.** to decorate or cover with spangles.

be·spat·ter (bi spat′ər) *v.t.* to spatter, as with mud; soil; sully.

be·speak (bi spēk′) *v.t.,* **be·spoke** or *(archaic)* **be·spake, be·spo·ken** or **be·spoke, be·speak·ing. 1.** to give evidence of; show: *Charles' expensive clothes bespeak great wealth.* **2.** to arrange for in advance; order; reserve.

be·spec·ta·cled (bi spek′tə kəld) *adj.* wearing eyeglasses.

be·spoke (bi spōk′) a past tense and a past participle of **bespeak.**

be·spo·ken (bi spō′kən) a past participle of **bespeak.**

be·sprin·kle (bi spring′kəl) *v.t.,* **be·sprin·kled, be·sprinkling.** to sprinkle over; scatter over.

Bes·se·mer process (bes′ə mər) a method of making steel in which a blast of air is blown through molten iron to remove carbon and impurities. [From Sir Henry *Bessemer,* 1813–1898, an English inventor who developed it.]

best (best) *adj.* superlative of **good. 1.** of the highest quality; superior to all others: *Jerry is the best speller in the class.* **2.** most desirable or suitable: *What is the best way to get home from here?* **3.** largest: *The trip took the best part of the day.* —*adv.* superlative of **well¹. 1.** in the most excellent way; most successfully: *I work best when I work by myself.* **2.** in the highest degree; most fully: *I like this dress best.* —*n.* **1.** something of the highest quality or excellence: *Do your best on the test.* **2.** a person or persons with the highest reputation or greatest ability: *That outfielder is the best on the team.* —*v.t.* to outdo; defeat: *Jim bested Carl at wrestling.*

  at best. under the most favorable circumstances; at most: *Billy may earn, at best, sixty dollars a month delivering newspapers.*

  had best. would be wise to; ought to: *You had best get home before midnight.*

  to get the best of or **to have the best of.** to defeat: *Harry got the best of John in the chess game.*

  to make the best of. to do as well as possible with: *We made the best of the tiresome bus ride.*

bes·tial (bes′chəl) *adj.* having the qualities of a beast; savage; brutish. —**bes′tial·ly,** *adv.*

bes·ti·al·i·ty (bes′chē al′ə tē) *n. pl.,* **bes·ti·al·i·ties. 1.** the quality, character, or nature of a beast. **2.** a bestial act.

be·stir (bi stur′) *v.t.,* **be·stirred, be·stir·ring.** to rouse to action or activity: *Tom hated to bestir himself early in the morning.*

best man, the chief attendant of the bridegroom at a wedding.

be·stow (bi stō′) *v.t.* to present (something) as a gift; give; confer: *The school bestowed honors on the bright student.* —**be·stow′al,** *n.*

be·strew (bi strōō′) *v.t.,* **be·strewed, be·strewed** or **be·strewn, be·strew·ing. 1.** to scatter over (a surface): *The children bestrewed the floor with toys.* **2.** to scatter (things) around: *The careless boy bestrewed candy wrappers on the sidewalk.*

be·stride (bi strīd′) *v.t.,* **be·strode** (bi strōd′) or **be·strid** (be strid′), **be·strid·den** (be strid′ən) or **be·strid, be·striding.** to sit on or stand over (something) with one leg on each side; straddle.

best seller, a book that sells in very large quantities.

bet (bet) *n.* **1.** an agreement or promise to give or pay something to another person if he is right about something and you are wrong; wager: *I made a bet for a dime that our team would win.* **2.** the amount of money or the thing risked in a bet: *His bet was a quarter against my fifty cents.* **3.** something on which such an agreement is made: *That horse is a good bet.* —*v.,* **bet** or **bet·ted, bet·ting.** —*v.t.* **1.** to agree to give or pay (something) in a bet. **2.** to say confidently: *I bet she will be late.* —*v.i.* to make a bet: *Yesterday we bet on a horse that lost.*

be·ta (bā′tə, bē′tə) *n.* the second letter of the Greek alphabet (B,β).

be·take (bi tāk′) *v.t.,* **be·took, be·tak·en, be·tak·ing.** to cause to go: *The boy betook himself to the store.*

beta particle, an electron ejected from the atomic nucleus of an element that is radioactive.

beta ray, a stream of beta particles.

be·ta·tron (bā′tə tron′) *n.* a device in which electrons are accelerated to high speeds by a varying magnetic field.

be·tel (bēt′əl) *n.* a climbing pepper plant found in Asia.

Be·tel·geuse (bēt′əl jōōz′) *n.* a giant red star that is the brightest star in the constellation Orion.

bête noire (bāt′nwär′) a person or thing that is particularly dreaded or disliked; bugbear. [French *bête noire,* literally, black beast.]

Beth·a·ny (beth′ə nē) *n.* an ancient village in Palestine, east of Jerusalem.

Beth·el (beth′əl) *n.* an ancient town in Palestine, near Jerusalem.

be·think (bi thingk′) *v.t.,* **be·thought** (bi thôt′), **be·think·ing.** to remind (oneself): *The old man bethought himself of his younger days.*

Beth·le·hem (beth′lə hem′) *n.* an ancient town near Jerusalem, in what is now western Jordan. It was the birthplace of Jesus Christ.

be·tide (bi tīd′) *v.t., v.i.,* **be·tid·ed, be·tid·ing.** to happen (to); befall.

be·times (bi tīmz′) *adv. Archaic.* in good time; early.

be·to·ken (bi tō′kən) *v.t.* to be a sign or token of: *The gift betokens his affection for her.*

be·took (bi tŏŏk′) the past tense of **betake.**

be·tray (bi trā′) *v.t.* **1.** to aid the enemy of; be a traitor to: *He betrayed his country.* **2.** to be unfaithful or false to: *Carol never betrayed her friend's trust.* **3.** to make known: *The traitor betrayed the secret plans to the enemy.* **4.** to show: *The child's eyes betrayed her fear.* —**be·tray′al,** *n.* —**be·tray′er,** *n.*

be·troth (bi trōth′, bi trôth′) *v.t.* to promise to give in marriage: *Mr. Jones betrothed his daughter to the young lawyer.* —**be·troth′al,** *n.*

be·trothed (bi trōthd′, bi trôtht′) *n.* a person who is engaged to be married. —*adj.* engaged to be married.

bet·ter¹ (bet′ər) *adj.* comparative of **good. 1.** of higher quality or excellence: *I think this is a better movie than the last one I saw.* **2.** more suitable or desirable: *Copper is a better conductor of heat than iron.* **3.** improved in health: *My sister is much better today.* **4.** larger; greater: *She spends the better part of her salary on clothes.* —*adv.* comparative of **well¹. 1.** in a more excellent way: *Cactuses grow better in a hot, dry climate.* **2.** to a higher degree; more: *The trip took better than two hours.* —*n.* **1.** something better: *Which is the better of the two books?* **2.** also, **betters.** a person's superior, as in position or power: *Jim listened to his betters.* —*v.t.* **1.** to make better; improve: *You can* *better yourself by studying harder.* **2.** to outdo; surpass: *The runner bettered his former record.* [Old English *betera* better, comparative of good.]

   better off. in a better position or condition: *We'd be better off staying right here until the rain stops.*

   had better. would be wise to; ought to: *He had better start studying if he wants to pass the test.*

   to get the better of or **to have the better of.** to defeat.

   to think better of. to think again and more wisely of: *Marcia thought better of sending the letter after rereading it.*

bet·ter² (bet′ər) *also,* **bet·tor.** *n.* a person who bets. [*Bet* + -*er*¹.]

bet·ter·ment (bet′ər mənt) *n.* the act of bettering or the state of being bettered; improvement.

be·tween (bi twēn′) *prep.* **1.** in the space, time, or range separating: *Put the table between the two chairs. Fran rarely eats between meals.* **2.** joining; connecting: *There is a bridge between the island and the mainland.* **3.** involving: *a discussion between students and teachers.* **4.** by the joint action of: *Between them, the two boys can mow the lawn in an hour.* **5.** one or the other of: *Mary had to choose between the two dresses.* —*adv.* in the space, time, or range separating: *There are two houses with a vacant lot between.*

   between you and me. in confidence: *This secret is between you and me.*

   in between. in a middle position: *The apartment has two rooms with a hall in between.*

   ▲ **Between** and **among** should not be confused. **Between** is usually used for two persons or things and **among** is usually used for three or more: *The pie was divided between the two boys. The four girls talked among themselves.* **Between** is also used with three or more when each item is considered separately: *The teacher explained the difference between ducks, geese, and swans.*

be·twixt (bi twikst′) *prep., adv.* between.

   betwixt and between. in a middle position.

Bev (bev) *also,* **bev.** *n.* a unit of energy equal to one billion electron volts. [From *B*(illion) *e*(lectron) *v*(olts).]

bev·a·tron (bev′ə tron′) *n.* a machine that accelerates protons to energies in the billions of electron volts.

bev·el (bev′əl) *n.* **1.** a slanting edge or surface, such as on a ruler, mirror, or a piece of plate glass. **2.** a tool consisting of an adjustable blade, used to measure the angle for shaping or cutting a slanting edge. —*v.t.,* **beveled, bev·el·ing;** *also, British,* **bev·elled, bev·el·ling.** to shape or cut a slanting edge on (something). —*adj.* slanting; oblique; sloping.

bevel gear, a gear fitting into another so that the shafts would intersect if extended.

bev·er·age (bev′ər ij) *n.* a liquid for drinking; drink. Milk, tea, coffee, and beer are beverages.

bev·y (bev′ē) *n. pl.,* **bev·ies.** **1.** a group, especially of girls or women. **2.** a flock of birds, especially of quail.

be·wail (bi wāl′) *v.t.* to feel or express deep sorrow for; mourn; lament: *The unfortunate man bewailed his fate.*

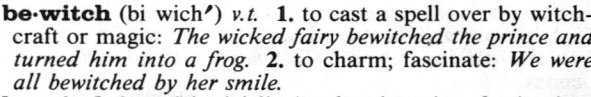

Bevel gears

be·ware (bi wer′) *v.i.* to be wary or careful: *Sailors should beware of the coming storm.* —*v.t.* to be wary or careful of: *Beware the dog!*

be·wil·der (bi wil′dər) *v.t.* to confuse or puzzle completely: *Her strange behavior bewildered me.* —**be·wil′der·ment,** *n.*

be·witch (bi wich′) *v.t.* **1.** to cast a spell over by witchcraft or magic: *The wicked fairy bewitched the prince and turned him into a frog.* **2.** to charm; fascinate: *We were all bewitched by her smile.*

be·witch·ing (bi wich′ing) *adj.* charming; fascinating: *She had a bewitching twinkle in her eye.* —**be·witch′-ing·ly,** *adv.*

bey (bā) *n.* a governor of a Turkish district or province.

be·yond (bē ond′) *prep.* **1.** on the other or far side of; farther on than: *The camp is beyond those hills.* **2.** later than: *The child was up well beyond his bedtime.* **3.** out of the reach or understanding of: *What the teacher said is beyond me.* **4.** more than: *These jewels are priced far beyond their worth.* —*adv.* farther on or away: *Beyond is the ocean.* —*n.* **the beyond** or **the great beyond.** life after death.

Bhu·tan (boo tän′) *n.* a country in south-central Asia, in the Himalayas. Capital, Thimbu. Area, 18,000 sq. mi. Pop. (1971 est.), 854,000.

bi- *prefix* **1.** having or involving two: *bicycle, bilateral.* **2.** twice; doubly: *biconvex.* **3.** coming or occurring every two: *bimonthly, biweekly.* [Latin *bi-* twice, two.]

Bi, the symbol for bismuth.

Bi·a·fra (bē äf′rə) *n.* the eastern part of Nigeria that seceded in 1967 from the main government. It was incorporated as part of Nigeria again in 1970. —**Bi·a′fran,** *adj., n.*

bi·an·nu·al (bī an′yōō əl) *adj.* happening twice a year; semiannual: *a biannual publication, a biannual trip.* —**bi·an′nu·al·ly,** *adv.*

   ▲ **Biannual** should not be confused with **biennial,** which means "occurring every two years."

bi·as (bī′əs) *n. pl.,* **bi·as·es.** **1.** a leaning too much toward one side or point of view; prejudice: *A good judge never shows bias. The newspaper article showed much bias against the candidate.* **2.** a slanting line cutting across the threads of a fabric: *The cloth for the dress was cut on the bias.* —*adj.* slanting across the threads of the fabric: diagonal. —*v.t.,* **bi·ased, bi·as·ing;** *also, British,* **bi·assed, bi·as·sing.** to cause to have a bias: *Tom's lie has biased me against him.*

bib (bib) *n.* **1.** a piece of cloth or plastic tied under the chin, especially of a baby, to protect the clothing from spilled food or drink. **2.** the upper front part of an apron or overalls.

Bi·ble (bī′bəl) *n.* **1.** the sacred writings of the Christian religion contained in the Old and New Testaments. **2.** the sacred writings of the Jewish religion contained in the Old Testament. **3.** a book or writings sacred to any religion. **4. bible.** any book used or accepted as an authority: *This book is a bible for baseball fans.*

bib·li·cal (bib′li kəl) *also,* **Bib·li·cal.** *adj.* of, relating to, or found in the Bible: *a biblical scholar, biblical names.* —**bib′li·cal·ly,** *adv.*

bib·li·og·ra·pher (bib′lē og′rə fər) *n.* a person who compiles bibliographies.

bib·li·og·ra·phy (bib′lē og′rə fē) *n. pl.,* **bib·li·og·ra·phies.** **1.** a list of books on a particular subject or person, or by a particular author. **2.** a study dealing with the description, comparison, and history of books and other

at; āpe; cär; end; mē; it; īce; hot; ōld; fôrk; wood; fŏŏl; oil; out; up; turn; sing; thin; **th**is; hw in white; zh in treasure. The symbol ə stands for the sound of **a** in about, **e** in taken, **i** in pencil, **o** in lemon, and **u** in circus.

writings. —**bib·li·o·graph·i·cal** (bib'lē ə graf'i kəl), *adj.* —**bib'li·o·graph'i·cal·ly**, *adv.*

bib·li·o·phile (bib'lē ə fīl') *n.* a person who loves books.

bi·cam·er·al (bī kam'ər əl) *adj.* having or consisting of two legislative chambers or houses: *The United States Congress is a bicameral legislature.*

bi·car·bo·nate (bī kär'bə nit) *n.* any salt containing the radical HCO₃, such as sodium bicarbonate.

bicarbonate of soda, another term for **sodium bicarbonate.**

bi·cen·ten·ni·al (bī'sen ten'ē əl) *adj.* happening once every 200 years. —*n.* a 200th anniversary or its celebration.

bi·ceps (bī'seps) *n. pl.,* **bi·ceps** or **bi·ceps·es.** the large muscle in the front of the upper arm.

bi·chlo·ride (bī klôr'īd) *n.* **1.** a compound that contains two atoms of chlorine; dichloride. **2.** see **bichloride of mercury.**

bichloride of mercury, a very poisonous white compound, used in photography.

bick·er (bik'ər) *v.i.* to quarrel noisily, especially about something unimportant: *The two brothers bickered over who would ride the bicycle.* —*n.* a quarrel.

Biceps

bi·con·cave (bī'kon kāv') *adj.* concave on both sides: *a biconcave lens.*

bi·con·vex (bī'kon veks') *adj.* convex on both sides: *a biconvex lens.*

bi·cus·pid (bī kus'pid) *n.* a tooth having two points; premolar. Human adults have eight bicuspids. —*adj.* having two points or cusps, as a crescent.

bi·cy·cle (bī'si kəl) *n.* a vehicle having two large wheels, one behind the other. A bicycle has a saddle seat for riding it, handlebars for steering it, and two foot pedals for making it go forward. —*v.i.,* **bi·cy·cled, bi·cy·cling.** to ride a bicycle. —**bi'cy·cler, bi'cy·clist,** *n.*

Bicycle

bid (bid) *v.,* (*v.t. defs. 1, 2, 5*) **bade** or **bid, bid·den** or **bid, bid·ding;** (*v.t. defs. 3, 4; v.i.*) **bid, bid·ding.** —*v.t.* **1.** to request or order, especially with authority; command: *The captain bid his men to advance.* **2.** to say as a greeting: *The children bade good-by to their friends.* **3.** to offer (an amount of money) as a price: *We bid fifty dollars for the lamp at the auction.* **4.** to state (the number of points or tricks) that one will try to make in return for declaring what is trump in a card game, such as bridge. **5.** to invite: *The host bade him to enter.* —*v.i.* to make an offer of an amount of money for something: *We didn't bid on the table at the auction.* —*n.* **1.** an offer of an amount of money for something. **2.** the amount offered. **3.** an attempt to win or get: *Governor Jones made a bid for the Presidency.* **4.a.** the number of tricks or points a player agrees to make in return for declaring what is trump in a card game, such as bridge. **b.** a player's turn to bid. **5.** an invitation. —**bid'der,** *n.*

bid·ding (bid'ing) *n.* **1.** an order or command: *John closed his book at the teacher's bidding.* **2.** invitation: *We came to the party at our friend's bidding.* **3.** the making of bids: *The bidding at the auction was slow.*

bide (bīd) *v.t.* **bid·ed** or **bode, bid·ed, bid·ing.** to wait.
to bide one's time. to wait patiently for the right moment or opportunity: *She is biding her time until spring to buy a winter coat on sale.*

bi·en·ni·al (bī en'ē əl) *adj.* **1.** happening once every two years: *a biennial election.* **2.** living for two years: *a biennial plant.* —*n.* **1.** a plant that lives for two years, usually producing flowers, fruit, and seeds in the second year. **2.** an event that happens once every two years. —**bi·en'ni·al·ly,** *adv.* ▲ See **biannual** for usage note.

bier (bēr) *n.* a stand on which a dead body or coffin is placed before burial.

bi·fo·cal (bī fō'kəl) *adj.* (of an eyeglass lens) having two parts, one for seeing close objects and one for seeing distant objects. —*n.* **1.** a lens ground with two parts. **2. bifocals.** a pair of eyeglasses having bifocal lenses.

big (big) *adj.,* **big·ger, big·gest. 1.** of great size, extent, amount, or degree; large: *New York is a big city. He raises wheat on a big farm.* **2.** of great importance: *a big banker, a big problem.* **3.** grown-up; mature: *He's a big boy now.* **4.** loud: *a big voice.* **5.** proud and boastful: *He is a big talker.* **6.** kind or generous: *Mrs. Brown has a big heart.* —*adv. Informal.* boastfully: *He talks big.* —**big'ness,** *n.*

big·a·mist (big'ə mist) *n.* a person who commits bigamy.

big·a·my (big'ə mē) *n.* the crime of marrying a person while married to someone else.

big-bang theory (big'bang') the theory that the universe began billions of years ago as the result of a huge cosmic explosion of a dense mass of material.

Big Dipper, a group of seven stars in the constellation Ursa Major, forming the outline of a dipper.

big game, large animals, such as elephants, lions, and tigers, hunted for sport.

big·heart·ed (big'här'tid) *adj.* having or showing kindness or generosity.

big·horn (big'hôrn') *n. pl.,* **big·horn** or **big·horns.** a wild sheep of the Rocky Mountains, having large, tightly curled horns. Also, **Rocky Mountain sheep.**

bight (bīt) *n.* **1.** a bend or curve, as in a river or coastline. **2.** a bay formed by such a bend in a coastline. **3.** a loop of a rope.

big·ot (big'ət) *n.* a person who is intolerant of any race, belief, or opinion differing from his or her own.

Bighorn

big·ot·ed (big'ə tid) *adj.* characteristic of a bigot; intolerant; prejudiced.

big·ot·ry (big'ə trē) *n. pl.,* **big·ot·ries.** a bigoted attitude or action.

big shot *Slang.* a person of importance.

big·wig (big'wig') *n. Informal.* a person of importance or influence. [*Big* + *wig;* from the large wigs formerly worn by men of importance.]

bike (bīk) *Informal. n.* a bicycle. —*v.i.,* **biked, bik·ing.** to ride a bicycle.

bi·ki·ni (bi kē'nē) *n.* a scanty two-piece bathing suit for women and girls. [From *Bikini,* an atoll in the Marshall Islands where the United States tested its first atomic weapons.]

bi·lat·er·al (bī lat'ər əl) *adj.* **1.** affecting two sides or parties: *a bilateral agreement.* **2.** arranged on two sides: *the bilateral symmetry of some leaves.* **3.** having two sides.

Bil·ba·o (bil bä'ō) *n.* a port city in northern Spain, near the Bay of Biscay. Pop. (1977 est.), 450,661.

B

bile (bīl) *n.* **1.** a bitter yellow or greenish liquid secreted by the liver to aid digestion, especially the digestion of fats. **2.** bad temper; anger.

bilge (bilj) *n.* **1.** the bottom part of the hull of a boat or ship. **2.** see **bilge water. 3.** the bulging part of a cask or barrel. **4.** *Informal.* nonsense; foolishness.

bilge water, stagnant water that collects in the bilge of a ship.

bi·lin·gual (bī ling′gwəl) *adj.* **1.** able to speak a foreign language as well or almost as well as one's native language. **2.** expressed or written in two languages: *a bilingual dictionary.* —**bi·lin′gual·ly,** *adv.*

bil·ious (bil′yəs) *adj.* **1.** bad-tempered; angry; cross: *The old man is a bilious person.* **2.** of or relating to bile. **3.** caused by or having some disorder of the liver. —**bil′ious·ly,** *adv.* —**bil′ious·ness,** *n.*

bilk (bilk) *v.t.* to cheat; swindle: *The dishonest salesman bilked Bob of $150.*

bill¹ (bil) *n.* **1.** a statement of money owed for things supplied or work done: *a grocery bill, a bill for repairs on a car.* **2.** a piece of paper money: *a five-dollar bill.* **3.** a printed advertisement or public notice; poster: *Do not post bills on the walls of this building.* **4.** a program of a performance or concert in a theater: *There is a good bill at the movie theater this weekend.* **5.** the draft of a proposed law: *Congress sent several bills to the President to be signed.* —*v.t.* **1.** to send (to someone) a statement of money owed: *The store billed us for the furniture we bought.* **2.** to announce or advertise by bills or posters: *The famous singer was billed as the main attraction.* [Medieval Latin *billa,* a form of *bulla* seal, document having a seal.]

   to fill the bill. to satisfy or meet the needs: *After ice-skating, a cup of hot chocolate really fills the bill.*

bill² (bil) *n.* **1.** the horny beak of a bird. **2.** an animal's beak resembling a bird's bill: *the bill of a turtle.* —*v.i.* (of birds) to join or touch bills. [Old English *bile* beak.]

   to bill and coo. to kiss and speak softly, as lovers do.

bill·board (bil′bôrd′) *n.* a large panel usually placed outdoors for posting advertisements or announcements.

bil·let¹ (bil′it) *n.* **1.** a lodging assigned to a soldier or serviceman. **2.** an order to provide lodging for a serviceman. —*v.t.* to lodge (a serviceman). [Old French *billette* a letter of safe-conduct, going back to Medieval Latin *billa* a document having a seal.]

bil·let² (bil′it) *n.* a small thick stick of wood, especially one used for fuel. [French *billette* a stick of wood.]

bil·let-doux (bil′ā doo′) *n. pl.,* **bil·lets-doux** (bil′ā-dooz′).** a love letter. [French *billet doux* literally, sweet letter.]

bill·fold (bil′fōld′) *n.* a folding case for paper money; wallet.

bil·liards (bil′yərdz) *n., pl.* **1.** a game played with three hard balls that are hit with a long stick called a cue. It is played on a cloth-covered rectangular table with cushions along the edges. **2.** any of several similar games such as pool. ▲ used with a singular verb in both definitions.

bil·lings·gate (bil′ingz-gāt′) *n.* language that is vulgar and insulting. [From *Billingsgate,* a fish market in London where much vulgar language was used.]

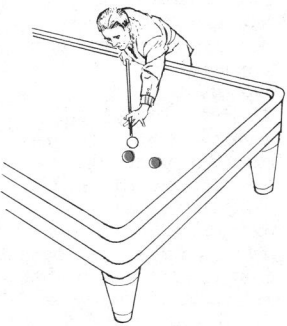
Billiards

bil·lion (bil′yən) *n.* **1.a.** in the United States and France, the cardinal number that is one thousand times one million. **b.** the symbol representing this number; 1,000,000,000. **2.a.** in Great Britain and Germany, the cardinal number that is one million times one million. **b.** the symbol representing this number; 1,000,000,000,000. —*adj.* numbering one billion.

bil·lion·aire (bil′yə ner′) *n.* a person who has a billion or more dollars, pounds, francs, or other kinds of currency.

bil·lionth (bil′yənth) *adj.* **1.** (the ordinal of billion) being last in a series of one billion. **2.** being one of a billion equal parts. —*n.* **1.** something that is last in a series of one billion. **2.** one of a billion equal parts.

bill of exchange, a written order to pay to a person a certain sum of money at a specified time.

bill of fare, a list of the foods served at a restaurant; menu.

bill of health, a certificate given to the captain of a ship indicating the conditions of health on board the ship or in the port at the time the ship departs.

   clean bill of health. *Informal.* a favorable report.

Bill of Rights 1. the first ten amendments to the Constitution of the United States, guaranteeing certain basic rights and liberties for all citizens, such as freedom of speech and freedom of religion. **2.** any declaration of the rights and liberties guaranteed to the citizens of a country.

bill of sale, a written statement transferring property from the person who sells it to the person who buys it.

bil·low (bil′ō) *n.* **1.** a great wave or swell of a body of water: *Ocean billows tossed the ship.* **2.** any great or surging mass: *Billows of smoke from the burning house choked the firemen.* —*v.i.* **1.** to rise or roll in billows; surge; swell. **2.** to swell out: *The sail billowed in the wind.* —*v.t.* to cause to swell out: *The wind billowed the girl's skirt.*

bil·low·y (bil′ō ē) *adj.,* **bil·low·i·er, bil·low·i·est.** full of or characterized by billows; swelling; surging: *a billowy sea.*

bil·ly (bil′ē) *n. pl.,* **bil·lies.** a policeman's stick or club; nightstick. Also, **billy club.**

billy goat *Informal.* a male goat.

bi·month·ly (bī munth′lē) *adj.* **1.** happening every two months. **2.** happening twice a month; semimonthly. —*n. pl.,* **bi·month·lies.** a bimonthly publication. —*adv.* **1.** every two months. **2.** twice a month; semimonthly.

▲ Although the adjective **bimonthly** has two different definitions, it is usually used to mean "happening every two months." If "happening twice a month" is meant, it is clearer to use the word **semimonthly,** which has only this meaning.

bin (bin) *n.* a receptacle or enclosed place for holding or storing something, such as grain or coal. —*v.t.,* **binned, bin·ning.** to store in a bin.

bi·na·ry (bī′nər ē) *adj.* **1.** consisting of, involving, or characterized by two things or parts. **2.** using or based on the binary system: *a binary numeral.* —*n. pl.,* **bi·na·ries.** see **binary star.**

binary star, a pair of stars revolving around a common center of gravity.

binary system, a number system with a base of two, in which any number may be expressed by 0 or 1 or by some combination of these.

---

at; āpe; cär; end; mē; it; īce; hot; ōld; fôrk; wood; fŏŏl; oil; out; up; turn; sing; thin; this; hw in white; zh in treasure. The symbol ə stands for the sound of **a** in about, **e** in taken, **i** in pencil, **o** in lemon, and **u** in circus.

bind (bīnd) *v.*, **bound, bind·ing.** —*v.t.* **1.** to tie, as with a rope; fasten together; secure: *to bind a package with twine, to bind wheat into bundles.* **2.** to fasten or wrap around; encircle: *A scarf bound her hair.* **3.** to bandage (often with *up*): *to bind up a wound.* **4.** to force or obligate; compel: *We are bound to obey the laws. The man was bound by the contract to work for the company for one full year.* **5.** to hamper or restrain; limit: *to be bound by tight clothing.* **6.** to cause to stick together: *Water binds particles of dirt to form mud.* **7.** to bring or hold together, as by ties of love, gratitude, or loyalty: *The team members were bound together by their desire for victory.* **8.** to strengthen or ornament by a border or edge: *She bound the hem of her dress with tape.* **9.** to fasten or enclose between covers: *to bind a book.* —*v.i.* **1.** to have the power to obligate or compel: *a rule that binds.* **2.** to stick together; cohere: *Water made the mixture bind.* —*n. Informal.* a difficult situation: *Receiving two invitations for the same night really put her in a bind.*

bind·er (bīn′dər) *n.* **1.** a person who binds, especially a bookbinder. **2.** anything that binds, such as string or glue. **3.** a removable cover that holds sheets of paper or other material together. **4.** a machine that reaps grain and ties it into bundles.

bind·er·y (bīn′dər ē) *n. pl.*, **bind·er·ies.** a place where books are bound.

bind·ing (bīn′ding) *n.* **1.** anything that binds. **2.** a cloth tape used to protect or finish raw edges, as of a garment, carpet, or blanket. **3.** a cover and backing holding together and enclosing the pages of a book. **4.** the act of binding. —*adj.* having the power to obligate or compel; obligatory: *He signed a binding agreement to pay back the loan in one year.*

bind·weed (bīnd′wēd′) *n.* a trailing or climbing plant with showy, trumpet-shaped flowers.

binge (binj) *n. Informal.* a period of unrestrained or extreme indulgence in some activity, such as eating, drinking, or spending money; spree.

bin·go (bing′gō) *n.* a game in which each player covers numbers on a card as they are called out. The winner is the first player to cover a row of numbers.

bin·na·cle (bin′ə kəl) *n.* a case or stand containing a ship's compass, usually placed near the helm.

bi·noc·u·lar (bə nok′yə lər) *adj.* **1.** for use by both eyes: *a binocular microscope.* **2.** using both eyes: *binocular vision.* —*n.* **binocu·lars.** an optical instrument for both eyes, used to magnify distant objects. Field glasses and opera glasses are binoculars.

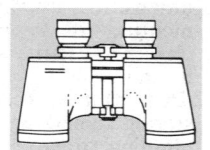
Binoculars

bi·no·mi·al (bī nō′mē əl) *adj.* consisting of two terms: *x – y* is a binomial expression. —*n.* **1.** a mathematical expression consisting of two terms joined by a plus or minus sign. The expressions *3x + 7y* and *8 + 2* are binomials. **2.** the scientific name for an animal or plant consisting of two terms. *Canis lupus,* the scientific name for the wolf, is a binomial.

bio- *combining form* of life or living things: *biology, biography.* [Greek *bios* life.]

bi·o·chem·i·cal (bī′o kem′ə kəl) *adj.* of or relating to biochemistry. —**bi′o·chem′i·cal·ly,** *adv.*

bi·o·chem·ist (bī′ō kem′ist) *n.* a student of or an expert in biochemistry.

bi·o·chem·is·try (bī′ō kem′is trē) *n.* the science dealing with the chemical structure and processes of living things.

bi·og·ra·pher (bī og′rə fər) *n.* a person who writes biographies.

bi·o·graph·i·cal (bī′ə graf′i kəl) *adj.* **1.** of or relating to a person's life: *a biographical novel.* **2.** of, relating to, or containing biography: *biographical writings.* Also, **bi·o·graph·ic** (bī′ə graf′ik). —**bi′o·graph′i·cal·ly,** *adv.*

bi·og·ra·phy (bī og′rə fē) *n. pl.*, **bi·og·ra·phies.** an account of a person's life.

bi·o·log·i·cal (bī′ə loj′i kəl) *adj.* of or relating to biology: *a biological experiment.* Also, **bi·o·log·ic** (bī′ə-loj′ik). —**bi′o·log′i·cal·ly,** *adv.*

biological warfare, warfare using bacteria, viruses, and other toxic biological products. Also, **germ warfare.**

bi·ol·o·gist (bī ol′ə jist) *n.* an expert in biology.

bi·ol·o·gy (bī ol′ə jē) *n.* the science of living organisms and their processes. Botany, zoology, and ecology are branches of biology.

bi·o·lu·mi·nes·cence (bī′ō lōō′mə nes′əns) *n.* a giving off of light by living organisms, such as fireflies.

bi·on·ic (bī on′ik) *adj.* having to do with a mechanical device that replaces or strengthens a part of the human body: *a bionic arm.*

bi·on·ics (bī on′iks) *n. pl.* the study of the parts of the bodies of human beings and other animals in order to make new mechanical or electronic devices or to improve old ones. The design of computers and artificial legs and arms is based on bionics. ▲ used with a singular verb.

bi·o·phys·i·cist (bī′ō fiz′ə sist) *n.* a student of or an expert in biophysics.

bi·o·phys·ics (bī′ō fiz′iks) *n., pl.* the science that applies the principles and methods of physics to the study of biological organisms and processes. ▲ used with a singular verb.

bi·op·sy (bī′op′sē) *n. pl.*, **bi·op·sies.** the surgical removal of a small amount of tissue from a living person or animal for microscopic examination.

bi·o·sphere (bī′ə sfēr′) *n.* the part of the earth and its atmosphere where life is found.

bi·o·tin (bī′ə tin) *n.* another name for **vitamin H.**

bi·par·ti·san (bī pär′tə zən) *adj.* composed of, representing, or supported by two parties, especially the Republican and Democratic parties: *a bipartisan bill.*

bi·par·tite (bī pär′tīt) *adj.* **1.** of or relating to two groups, nations, or the like: *a bipartite trade agreement.* **2.** consisting of two parts, especially two corresponding parts, as a leaf.

bi·ped (bī′ped′) *n.* an animal having two feet. Human beings and birds are bipeds. —*adj.* two-footed.

bi·plane (bī′plān′) *n.* an airplane with two sets of wings, one above the other.

birch (burch) *n. pl.*, **birch·es. 1.** any of a group of trees bearing saw-toothed leaves. The pale or white bark of this tree is easily peeled in thin papery strips and was used by American Indians to make canoes. **2.** the hard, close-grained wood of this tree. **3.** a branch or bundle of twigs from this tree, used as a whip.

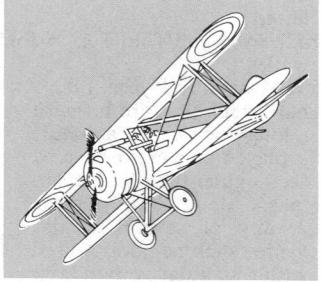
Biplane

bird (burd) *n.* **1.** any of a class of warm-blooded, egg-laying animals that have two legs, feathers, and wings. **2.** another word for **shuttlecock. 3.** *Informal.* a person: *He's an odd bird.* —**bird′like′,** *adj.*

bird·bath (burd′bath′) *n. pl.*, **bird·baths** (burd′bathz′, burd′baths′). a shallow basin filled with water for birds to bathe in and drink.

bird call **1.** the sound made by a bird; song of a bird. **2.** an instrument for imitating this sound.

bird dog, any of various dogs specially trained to hunt and retrieve game birds.

bird·house (burd′hous′) *n. pl.,* **bird·hous·es** (burd′hou′ziz). a small box in which birds may nest, often resembling a house.

bird·ie (bur′dē) *n.* **1.** *Informal.* a small bird. **2.** in golf, a score of one under par on a hole.

bird·lime (burd′līm′) *n.* a sticky substance that is smeared on twigs to catch small birds.

bird of paradise, a songbird of Australia, New Guinea, and neighboring islands. The male of the species is noted for its brilliant feathers.

bird of passage **1.** any bird that migrates. **2.** a person who does not stay in one place for long.

bird of prey, any of various birds that feed on animals and other birds, such as eagles, hawks, and owls.

bird·seed (burd′sēd′) *n.* a mixture of small seeds fed chiefly to caged birds.

bird's-eye (birdz′ī′) *adj.* **1.** seen from above: *From the airplane we had a bird's-eye view of the town.* **2.** having markings resembling birds' eyes: *The desk was made of bird's-eye maple.*

bird watcher, a person who observes and studies wild birds in their natural surroundings.

bi·ret·ta (bə ret′ə) *n.* a stiff, square cap worn by Roman Catholic clergymen. Its color is black for priests, purple for bishops, and red for cardinals.

Bir·ming·ham (*def. 1* bur′ming ham′; *def. 2* bur′ming əm) *n.* **1.** the largest city in Alabama, in the north-central part of the state. Pop. (1970), 300,910. **2.** a city in west-central England. Pop. (1971 est.), 1,013,420.

Biretta

birth (burth) *n.* **1.** the act or fact of being born. **2.** the act of bringing forth offspring. **3.** the beginning of anything; origin: *the birth of an idea, the birth of a nation.* **4.** descent; lineage; ancestry: *of German birth, of noble birth.*

  to give birth to. a. to bring forth (offspring): *The cat gave birth to six kittens.* **b.** to bring forth (anything); be the cause of: *The artist's work gave birth to a new style of painting.*

birth control, the control of the number of children a woman will have, especially by the preventing of conception.

birth·day (burth′dā′) *n.* **1.** the day of a person's birth. **2.** the anniversary of this day.

birth·mark (burth′märk′) *n.* a mark or blemish on the skin that is present at birth.

birth·place (burth′plās′) *n.* **1.** the place of a person's birth. **2.** any place of origin: *Greece is considered to be the birthplace of democracy.*

birth·rate (burth′rāt′) *also,* **birth rate.** *n.* the number of births occurring in a given population within a specified time. It is often expressed in terms of the number of live births per thousand of the population.

birth·right (burth′rīt′) *n.* a right, privilege, or possession that a person is entitled to by birth: *That farm is the eldest son's birthright when his father dies.*

birth·stone (burth′stōn′) *n.* a gem associated with a particular month of the year, supposed to bring good luck when it is worn by a person whose birthday falls in that month.

Bis·cay, Bay of (bis′kā) a broad inlet of the Atlantic Ocean, between western France and northern Spain.

bis·cuit (bis′kit) *n. pl.,* **bis·cuits** or **bis·cuit.** **1.** a small baked cake made of bread dough, usually raised with bak-

ing powder or soda. **2.** *British.* a cracker or thin cookie.

bi·sect (bī sekt′) *v.t.* **1.** to divide (a geometrical figure) into two equal parts: *to bisect a circle.* **2.** to cut in two. —**bi·sec·tion** (bī sek′shən), *n.* —**bi′sec′tor,** *n.*

bi·sex·u·al (bī sek′shoō əl) *adj.* **1.** having both male and female reproductive organs. **2.** of or relating to both sexes. —*n.* a person, animal, or plant that is bisexual. —**bi·sex′u·al·ly,** *adv.*

bish·op (bish′əp) *n.* **1.** a high-ranking clergyman who is the head of a church district or diocese. **2.** one of the pieces in the game of chess. It may be moved diagonally across any number of squares.

bish·op·ric (bish′ə prik) *n.* **1.** the office or rank of a bishop. **2.** a church district administered by a bishop; diocese.

Bis·marck (biz′märk) *n.* **1.** Ot·to von (ot′ō von). 1815–1898, German statesman. **2.** the capital of North Dakota, in the south-central part of the state. Pop. (1970), 34,703.

Bishop (def. 2)

Bismarck Archipelago, a large island group in the western Pacific Ocean, just east of New Guinea. It is administered by Australia. Land area, approx. 19,000 sq. mi. Pop. (1966), 225,100.

bis·muth (biz′məth) *n.* a brittle, grayish-white metallic element with a reddish tinge, used in alloys and in some drugs. Symbol: **Bi**

bi·son (bī′sən, bī′zən) *n. pl.,* **bi·son.** an animal of North America, resembling the ox and having a large head, short horns, humped shoulders, and a thick brown coat; buffalo.

bisque (bisk) *n.* a thick, creamy soup: *tomato bisque.*

bit[1] (bit) *n.* **1.** the metal piece of a bridle that goes into the horse's mouth. **2.a.** a boring or

Bison

drilling part that fits into a brace, drill, or similar tool. **b.** the cutting or end part of a tool. **3.** the part of a key that enters the lock and works the bolt and tumblers. [Old English *bite* a bite.]

bit[2] (bit) *n.* **1.** a small piece, part, or quantity: *I dropped the plate and it broke into bits.* **2.** a short while: *This will only take a bit. Wait a bit.* **3.** *Informal.* an amount equal to twelve and a half cents. ▲ used only in multiples of two, as *two bits, four bits.* —*adj.* small; insignificant: *He has only a bit part in the new play.* [Old English *bita* morsel, small piece bitten off.]

  a bit. somewhat: *He is a bit tired from mowing the lawn.* **bit by bit.** little by little; gradually.

bit[3] (bit) the past tense and a past participle of **bite.**

bitch (bich) *n.* the female of the dog, wolf, or other related animal.

at; āpe; cär; end; mē; it; īce; hot; ōld; fôrk; wood; fōōl; oil; out; up; turn; sing; thin; this; hw in white; zh in treasure. The symbol ə stands for the sound of a in about, e in taken, i in pencil, o in lemon, and u in circus.

bite (bīt) *v.,* **bit, bit·ten** or **bit, bit·ing.** —*v.t.* **1.** to cut, pierce, or seize with the teeth: *The girl bit the sandwich.* **2.** to remove with the teeth; cut or tear: *He bit off a piece of the candy bar.* **3.** to pierce the skin of with teeth, fangs, or similar parts: *I killed the mosquito before it could bite me.* **4.** to cause to smart or sting: *The icy wind bit our faces.* **5.** to take a firm hold on; grip: *The runners of the sled bit the snow.* —*v.i.* **1.** to cut, pierce, seize, or grip something: *The teeth of the saw bit into the wood.* **2.** to cause smarting or stinging. **3.** (of fish) to take the bait: *When the fish bites, pull back on the line.* —*n.* **1.** the act of biting. **2.** a wound made by biting or stinging: *a mosquito bite.* **3.** a piece bitten off; mouthful; morsel: *Do you want a bite of my apple?* **4.** *Informal.* a small meal; snack: *We stopped for a bite on the way home from school.* **5.** the effect or quality of biting; sting: *the bite of a cold wind.* **6.** the manner in which the upper and lower teeth meet. —**bi′ter,** *n.*

bit·ing (bī′ting) *adj.* **1.** sharp; stinging: *biting cold.* **2.** sarcastic; cutting: *The writer's biting wit often made people angry.* —**bit′ing·ly,** *adv.*

bit·ten (bit′ən) a past participle of **bite.**

bit·ter (bit′ər) *adj.* **1.** having a sharp, biting, unpleasant taste: *a bitter medicine.* **2.** unpleasant to the mind; hard to bear: *Carol refused to face the bitter truth that she had failed the test.* **3.** harsh or biting; sarcastic: *bitter humor.* **4.** causing or showing pain, misery, or discomfort: *the bitter cold, bitter tears.* **5.** having or showing intense anger, ill will, or hatred: *a bitter quarrel, bitter enemies.* **6.** full of resentment; unforgiving: *He was still bitter about not making the team.* —**bit′ter·ly,** *adv.* —**bit′ter·ness,** *n.*

bit·tern (bit′ərn) *n.* any of several marsh birds closely related to, but smaller than, the heron, and having a loud, booming cry.

bit·ter·root (bit′ər rōōt′, bit′ər root′) *n.* a low-growing plant having a circle of fleshy leaves at its base and a single white or rose-colored flower at the top, found in the northern Rocky Mountain region.

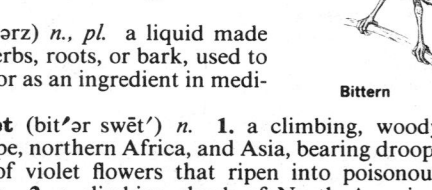

Bittern

bit·ters (bit′ərz) *n., pl.* a liquid made from bitter herbs, roots, or bark, used to flavor drinks or as an ingredient in medicine.

bit·ter·sweet (bit′ər swēt′) *n.* **1.** a climbing, woody plant of Europe, northern Africa, and Asia, bearing drooping clusters of violet flowers that ripen into poisonous scarlet berries. **2.** a climbing shrub of North America, bearing clusters of small, greenish flowers. —*adj.* **1.** both bitter and sweet: *bittersweet chocolate.* **2.** both pleasant and painful: *Bill had bittersweet memories of his first trip away from home and his family.*

bi·tu·men (bī tōō′mən, bī tyōō′mən) *n.* any of various dark brown or black substances that burn easily and are composed chiefly of hydrocarbons, such as asphalt, bituminous coal, or crude petroleum.

bi·tu·mi·nous (bī tōō′mə nəs, bī tyōō′mə nəs) *adj.* made of, containing, or like bitumen.

bituminous coal, a black coal that burns with a smoky flame and has a low carbon content. Also, **soft coal.**

bi·va·lent (bī vā′lənt) *adj.* having a valence of two.

bi·valve (bī′valv′) *n.* a mollusk whose shell consists of two parts, or valves, hinged together, such as the oyster or clam. —*adj.* having two shells hinged together.

biv·ou·ac (biv′ōō ak′) *n.* a temporary camp, especially one made by soldiers in the field, with or without shelter or tents. —*v.i.,* **biv·ou·acked, biv·ou·ack·ing.** to camp out in a bivouac.

bi·week·ly (bī wēk′lē) *adj.* **1.** happening every two weeks. **2.** happening twice a week; semiweekly. —*n. pl.,*

bi·week·lies. a biweekly publication. —*adv.* **1.** every two weeks. **2.** twice a week; semiweekly.

▲ Although the adjective **biweekly** has two different definitions, it is usually used to mean "happening every two weeks." If "happening twice a week" is meant, it is clearer to use the word **semiweekly,** which has only this meaning.

bi·year·ly (bī yēr′lē) *adj.* **1.** happening every two years. **2.** happening twice a year. —*adv.* **1.** every two years. **2.** twice a year; semiannually.

bi·zarre (bi zär′) *adj.* very odd or strange, as in manner or appearance; fantastic; grotesque.

Bk, the symbol for berkelium.

blab (blab) *v.,* **blabbed, blab·bing.** —*v.t.* to tell or reveal thoughtlessly: *to blab a secret.* —*v.i.* **1.** to chatter thoughtlessly. **2.** to tell or reveal a secret.

blab·ber (blab′ər) *v.i.* to chatter thoughtlessly or foolishly. —*n.* **1.** a person who blabs. **2.** thoughtless or foolish chatter.

blab·ber·mouth (blab′ər mouth′) *n. pl.,* **blab·ber·mouths** (blab′ər mouthz, blab′ər mouths). *Informal.* a person who talks thoughtlessly or foolishly.

black (blak) *adj.* **1.** having the darkest of all colors; having the color of coal; opposite of white: *a black car.* **2.** having no light; in darkness; dark: *the black depths of the ocean.* **3.** of, relating to, or belonging to a dark-skinned people, especially of African descent. **4.** gloomy; dismal: *When his business went bankrupt, the man's future looked black.* **5.** angry; sullen: *Fred gave a black look to the boy who pushed ahead of him in line.* **6.** dirty; soiled: *After the game his uniform was black.* **7.** morally evil; wicked: *a black deed.* —*n.* **1.** the darkest of all colors, reflecting no light; the opposite of white. Black is the color of coal. **2.** a black dye, paint, or the like. **3.** something black, as a black piece in a game of checkers. **4.** a member of a dark-skinned people, especially of African descent. **5.** dark clothes, especially those worn for mourning: *The widow was dressed in black.* —*v.t.* **1.** to make black; blacken: *Storm clouds blacked the sky.* **2.** to polish with blacking: *to black shoes.* —*v.i.* to become black. —**black′ly,** *adv.* —**black′ness,** *n.*

to **black out. a.** to lose consciousness temporarily.
b. to turn off or cover lights in, especially as a protection against air raids: *to black out a city.*

black-and-blue (blak′ən blōō′) *adj.* discolored as a result of ruptured blood vessels under the skin, as from a bruise.

black·ball (blak′bôl′) *v.t.* to vote against, especially to vote against letting (a person) become a member of some organization. —*n.* a vote against a person or thing. [From the ancient Greek practice of voting by using a small *black ball* to show disapproval.]

black bear, a North American bear having black or reddish-brown fur.

black·ber·ry (blak′ber′ē) *n. pl.,* **black·ber·ries. 1.** the sweet black fruit of any of several bramble bushes of the rose family. **2.** a thorny bush that bears this fruit.

black·bird (blak′burd′) *n.* **1.** any of various American birds that are all or mostly black or dark in color. **2.** a black or dark-brown thrush of Europe.

Blackberries

black·board (blak′bôrd′) *n.* a hard, smooth surface of slate or other material for writing or drawing on with chalk, originally black but now often green.

black body, a theoretical surface or body capable of absorbing all radiation falling on it and reflecting none.

black book, a book containing a blacklist.

black·damp (blak′damp′) *n.* a suffocating gaseous mixture consisting mostly of carbon dioxide, produced by explosions or fires in mines.

Black Death, an epidemic of bubonic plague that spread through Europe, Africa, and Asia in the fourteenth century. By 1352 it had wiped out one-third of the total population of Europe. [From the *black* spots on the body caused by the disease.]

black·en (blak′ən) *v.t.* **1.** to make black; darken: *Smoke blackened the walls of the building.* **2.** to speak evil of; defame: *False gossip blackened his good name.* —*v.i.* to become black or dark: *The sky blackened.*

black eye 1. a bruise on the skin around the eye, usually caused by a blow. **2.** *Informal.* a cause of disgrace; discredit.

black-eyed pea (blak′īd′) another word for **cowpea.**

black-eyed Su·san (sōō′zən) a flower having yellow petals surrounding a dark brown center, found in eastern Canada and the United States.

black·fish (blak′fish′) *n. pl.,* **black·fish** or **black·fish·es. 1.** any of various dark-colored saltwater fish, such as the sea bass. **2.** any of several small, dark toothed whales. **3.** a freshwater fish of the swamps and bogs of Alaska and Siberia, valued as a food fish.

Black-eyed Susan

black flag, see **Jolly Roger.**

Black·foot (blak′foot′) *n. pl.,* **Black·feet** or **Black·foot. 1.** a member of a tribe of plains Indians who lived east of the Rocky Mountains in Saskatchewan and Montana. **2.** the Algonquian language of the Blackfeet. [A translation of the Blackfoot word *Siksika,* possibly referring to their custom of blackening their moccasins.]

Black Forest, a wooded, mountain district in southwestern West Germany.

black·guard (blag′ärd) *n.* a low, dishonorable person; scoundrel. —**black′guard·ly** *adj.*

black·head (blak′hed′) *n.* a small, black piece of fatty matter in a pore in the skin.

Black Hills, a mountain range in southwestern South Dakota and northeastern Wyoming.

black·ing (blak′ing) *n.* a black polish, as for shoes.

black·jack (blak′jak′) *n.* **1.** a small club with a flexible handle, used as a weapon. **2.** a pirate's black flag. **3.** a card game in which the players play against the dealer, the winner being the person whose cards bear numbers adding up to twenty-one or to the closest number below that. If both the dealer and another player have twenty-one, the dealer wins. Also, **twenty-one.** —*v.t.* to strike with a blackjack.

black·list (blak′list) *n.* a list of persons or organizations boycotted, regarded as suspect, or punished in some way. —*v.t.* to place on a blacklist: *The actor was blacklisted because he was suspected of belonging to a subversive political group.*

black magic, magic used for evil purposes; witchcraft.

black·mail (blak′māl′) *n.* **1.** an attempt to get money or some special favor from a person by threatening to reveal information about him that would harm his reputation. **2.** the money obtained in this way. —*v.t.* to force or attempt to force (someone) to pay money or grant some special favor by threatening to reveal damaging information. —**black′mail′er,** *n.* [Compound of *black* and Scottish *mail* rent, payment; from the payment of cattle or grain made by farmers along the Scottish and English

borders to robbers and other outlaws in return for protection. *Black mail* was distinguished from *white mail,* which was paid in silver.]

black mark, a sign of something unfavorable or disgraceful on a person's record.

black market 1. the selling of goods illegally, especially in violation of price controls or rationing. **2.** a place where such selling is carried on.

Black Muslim, a member of an American Negro religious group that practices a form of the Muslim religion and advocates racial segregation.

black·out (blak′out′) *n.* **1.** a temporary loss of consciousness or sight. **2.** the temporary stopping or interruption of electric service in a certain area: *The power blackout was caused by a generator that failed.* **3.** the turning out or covering of lights as a protection against enemy air raids. **4.** a turning off of all lights on the stage of a theater, especially to mark a separation between scenes. **5.** a deliberate withholding of information: *a news blackout.*

black pepper, a hot, pungent spice made from the dried, ground berries of the pepper plant.

Black Power, the power of American blacks as a group to exert political, social, and economic pressure to achieve such goals as racial equality.

Black Sea, an inland sea between Europe and Asia, bordered by the Soviet Union, Turkey, Bulgaria, and Romania.

black sheep, a person who is regarded as a disgrace or discredit by the other members of the person's family or group.

black·smith (blak′smith′) *n.* a person who works with iron by heating it in a forge and then hammering it into shape on an anvil.

black·snake (blak′snāk′) *n.* a nonpoisonous snake of the eastern United States, having dull black scales.

black·thorn (blak′thôrn′) *n.* a thorny shrub of the rose family, found in Europe and Asia, bearing white flowers and deep blue fruit. Also, **sloe.**

black tie 1. a black bow tie, worn with a tuxedo. **2.** semiformal evening wear for men.

black·top (blak′top′) *n.* **1.** asphalt or similar material used to pave roads. **2.** a road paved with such a material. —*v.t.,* **black·topped, black·top·ping.** to pave with blacktop.

black widow, a glossy black spider commonly found in Central America and in southern and western parts of the United States. The female is poisonous, has a red hourglass-shaped marking on the underside of its abdomen, and is more than twice the size of the male. [From the female's practice of eating its mate.]

blad·der (blad′ər) *n.* **1.** a small, elastic sac in the body that stores urine received from the kidneys. **2.** something resembling a bladder, such as the inner bag of a football.

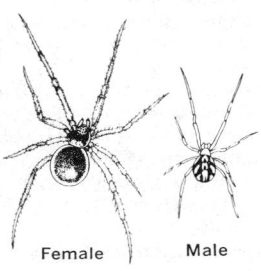
Female   Male
Black widow

at; āpe; cär; end; mē; it; īce; hot; ōld; fôrk; wood; fōōl; oil; out; up; turn; sing; thin; this; hw in white; zh in treasure. The symbol ə stands for the sound of **a** in about, **e** in taken, **i** in pencil, **o** in lemon, and **u** in circus.

blade (blād) *n.* **1.** the sharp-edged part of anything that cuts: *the blade of a knife, the blade of a sword.* **2.** a leaf, as of grass. **3.** the broad part of a leaf or petal. **4.** the broad, flat part of anything: *the blade of an oar, the blade of a propeller, the blades of a fan.* **5.** a sword. **6.** the sharp runner of an ice skate. **7.** a dashing young man. —**blade'like'**, *adj.*

Blake, William (blāk) 1757–1827, English poet, artist, and philosopher.

blame (blām) *v.t.,* **blamed, blam·ing. 1.** to find fault with: *I don't blame you for losing your temper.* **2.** to hold (someone or something) responsible: *Don't blame me for your mistakes.* —*n.* responsibility for something wrong or bad: *He took all the blame for the error upon himself.* —**blam'a·ble**, *adj.*

　to be to blame. to be at fault: *It was an accident, so no one is to blame.*

blame·less (blām'lis) *adj.* not deserving blame; innocent. —**blame'less·ly,** *adv.* —**blame'less·ness,** *n.*

blame·wor·thy (blām'wur'thē) *adj.* deserving blame: *No one who was involved in the affair is blameworthy.*

blanch (blanch) *v.i.* to become white; turn pale: *She blanched with fear when she saw the ghost.* —*v.t.* **1.** to remove color from; bleach. **2.** to make pale, as from fear or sickness. **3.** to remove the skin of by scalding: *to blanch almonds.*

bland (bland) *adj.* **1.** lacking excitement or interest; dull: *a bland book.* **2.** not irritating; soothing; mild: *a bland diet, a bland climate.* **3.** smoothly agreeable or pleasant: *a bland smile.* —**bland'ly,** *adv.* —**bland'ness,** *n.*

blan·dish (blan'dish) *v.t.* to coax with flattery.

blan·dish·ment (blan'dish mənt) *n.* a coaxing or flattering speech or action; coaxing; flattery.

blank (blangk) *adj.* **1.** not written or printed upon; unmarked: *a blank sheet of paper.* **2.** having spaces to be filled out: *a blank questionnaire.* **3.** lacking interest or thought; empty: *His mind is blank.* **4.** showing a lack of interest or thought; expressionless; vacant: *a blank stare.* —*n.* **1.** an empty space to be filled in, as in a printed form: *Fill in the blank with your name and address.* **2.** a form or document containing such spaces: *an application blank.* **3.** an empty space; void: *Her mind was a blank.* **4.** a cartridge containing powder, but no bullet. —*v.t.* to keep (an opponent) from scoring in a game: *Our baseball team was blanked for four games in a row.* —**blank'ly,** *adv.* —**blank'ness,** *n.*

blan·ket (blang'kit) *n.* **1.** a covering made of wool or other woven fabric, used to keep people or animals warm. **2.** anything that covers like a blanket: *a blanket of fog, a blanket of snow.* —*v.t.* to cover with a blanket.

blank verse **1.** unrhymed verse written in iambic pentameter. Much of Shakespeare's work is written in blank verse. **2.** any unrhymed verse.

blare (bler) *v.,* **blared, blar·ing.** —*v.i.* to make a loud, harsh sound: *The horns blared.* —*v.t.* to proclaim loudly and harshly: *The radio blared the news.* —*n.* a loud, harsh sound.

blar·ney (blär'nē) *n.* smooth, flattering talk. —*v.t.* to influence or try to influence with blarney; coax; wheedle. [From the *Blarney Stone.*]

Blarney Stone, a stone block in a wall of a castle in Ireland, said to give skill in flattery and coaxing to those who kiss it.

bla·sé (blä zā') *adj.* bored or wearied, as from too much of a pleasant experience.

blas·pheme (blas fēm') *v.,* **blas·phemed, blas·phem·ing.** —*v.t.* to speak of (God or anything sacred) with contempt or disrespect. —*v.i.* to speak with contempt and disrespect. —**blas·phem'er,** *n.*

blas·phe·mous (blas'fə məs) *adj.* characterized by or using blasphemy; irreverent: *a blasphemous statement.* —**blas'phe·mous·ly,** *adv.*

blas·phe·my (blas'fə mē) *n. pl.,* **blas·phe·mies.** an expression of contempt or disrespect for God or anything sacred.

blast (blast) *n.* **1.** a strong rush of wind or air; gust: *The chilling blasts swept over the lake.* **2.** a loud, explosive sound, as that made by a horn: *the blast of trumpets, the blast of a radio.* **3.** an explosion, as of dynamite: *The blast in the mine shaft caused a cave-in.* **4.** a current of compressed air directed into a blast furnace to aid combustion during smelting. —*v.t.* **1.** to blow up or shatter with an explosive. **2.** to cause to be damaged or ruined; wither: *The rain blasted our hopes for a successful picnic.* **3.** to cause to sound loudly. **4.** *Informal.* to criticize or scold severely. —*v.i.* to sound loudly or harshly: *The loudspeakers blasted.*

　at full blast. at top speed or operation: *Our neighbors complained because we had our radio on at full blast.*

　to blast off. (of a rocket or missile) to take off; begin flight.

blast furnace, a furnace used in smelting in which the heat is kept up by a blast of preheated air.

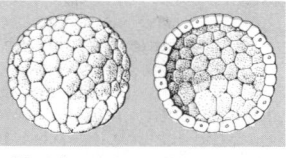

Blast furnace

blas·to·coele (blas'tə sēl') *also,* **blas·to·coel, blas·to·cele.** *n.* the cavity of a blastula.

blas·to·derm (blas'tə durm') *n.* a layer of cells forming the wall of the blastula.

blast-off (blast'ôf') *n.* the launching of a rocket or missile: *Today's blast-off will take place at 6:00 A.M.*

blas·tu·la (blas'chə lə) *n. pl.,* **blas·tu·lae** (blas'chə lē'). an early stage in the development of an animal embryo, usually consisting of a single layer of cells forming a hollow sphere.

bla·tant (blāt'ənt) *adj.* **1.** hard to overlook; very obvious: *blatant lies. His paper contains several blatant errors.* **2.** noisy in a coarse or vulgar way. —**bla'tan·cy,** *n.* —**bla'tant·ly,** *adv.*

Blastula exterior and cross section

blaze¹ (blāz) *n.* **1.** a bright flame or fire: *The blaze spread through the house before firemen could be called.* **2.** a bright, intense light or glow: *We shielded our eyes against the blaze of the sun.* **3.** a brilliant or striking display: *The parade was a blaze of color.* **4.** a strong, sudden outburst: *a blaze of fury.* —*v.i.,* **blazed, blaz·ing. 1.** to burn brightly: *Torches blazed through the night.* **2.** to shine brilliantly; be bright: *The city streets blazed with light.* **3.** to show strong feeling: *Sue's eyes blazed with anger.* [Old English *blæse* flame, torch.]

blaze² (blāz) *n.* **1.** a light-colored marking on the face of an animal. **2.** a mark made on a tree to show a trail or

B

boundary, as by chipping off a piece of bark. —*v.t.*, **blazed, blaz·ing. 1.** to mark (a tree) with blazes. **2.** to mark off (a trail) with blazes: *The hikers blazed a path through the forest.* **3.** to open up or take the lead in: *The invention of the microscope blazed the way for medical research.* [Probably from Middle Low German *bles* white spot.]

blaze³ (blāz) *v.t.*, **blazed, blaz·ing.** to make known; proclaim. [Old Norse *blāsa* to blow.]

blaz·er (blā′zər) *n.* a sports jacket, usually having a solid color or bright stripes.

bla·zon (blā′zən) *v.t.* **1.** to decorate with bright colors or displays; adorn. **2.** to make public; proclaim. —*n.* a coat of arms.

bldg. *pl.*, **bldgs.** building.

bleach (blēch) *v.t.* to make (something) white or colorless by exposing it to the sun or by the use of chemicals: *The sun bleached the sheets.* —*n. pl.*, **bleach·es. 1.** something used for bleaching, such as a chemical. **2.** the act or process of bleaching: *Those clothes need another bleach.*

bleach·er (blē′chər) *n.* **1.** a person or thing that bleaches. **2. bleachers.** a group of seats for spectators at sporting events, parades, and other activities. Bleachers in a stadium are usually low-priced seats that have no roof over them.

bleaching powder 1. a powder that bleaches. **2.** another name for **chloride of lime.**

bleak (blēk) *adj.* **1.** open and exposed to the wind; bare: *a bleak, barren desert.* **2.** cold; chilling: *a bleak December day.* **3.** not cheerful or hopeful; gloomy: *Our team's prospects for winning were bleak.* —**bleak′ly,** *adv.* —**bleak′ness,** *n.*

blear (blēr) *adj.* dimmed or blurred; bleary. —*v.t.* to dim or blur, as the eyes or vision.

blear·y (blēr′ē) *adj.*, **blear·i·er, blear·i·est.** dimmed or blurred: *He had bleary eyes.* —**blear′i·ness,** *n.*

blear·y-eyed (blēr′ē īd′) *adj.* having bleary eyes.

bleat (blēt) *n.* **1.** the cry of a sheep, goat, or calf. **2.** any sound like a bleat. —*v.i.* **1.** to utter the cry of a sheep, goat, or calf. **2.** to make a sound like a bleat. —*v.t.* to utter with a bleat or a sound like a bleat. —**bleat′er,** *n.*

bleed (blēd) *v.*, **bled** (bled), **bleed·ing.** —*v.i.* **1.** to lose or shed blood: *His cut finger bled.* **2.** to suffer wounds or die: *We honor those who bled on the battlefields.* **3.** to feel pity or sympathy: *My heart bled for the lost child.* **4.** to ooze sap or other fluid from an opening or cut. **5.** (of a dye or paint) to run. —*v.t.* **1.** to take blood from as a treatment for illness. **2.** to ooze (a fluid) from an opening or a cut: *The trees bled sap.* **3.** to drain or draw off a liquid or gas from: *to bleed a tire.*

bleed·er (blē′dər) *n.* a person who bleeds excessively, especially a hemophiliac.

blem·ish (blem′ish) *n. pl.*, **blem·ish·es.** something that spoils beauty or perfection: *skin blemishes. His character is without blemish.* —*v.t.* to spoil the beauty or perfection of; stain; mar: *One mistake was enough to blemish his good reputation.*

blench (blench) *v.i.* to shrink away; flinch.

blend (blend) *v.t.* **1.** to mix together thoroughly; combine so that the original ingredients cannot be separated: *We blended flour, milk, and eggs to make the pancake batter.* **2.** to make a mixture of different varieties of: *to blend tobacco.* —*v.i.* **1.** to mingle together; mix: *The voices of the choir blended well.* **2.** to pass or shade gradually into each other; merge: *Sea and sky seemed to blend on the horizon.* **3.** to fit together; harmonize: *The rug blends well with the other colors in the room.* —*n.* **1.** a thorough mixture: *a new blend of coffee.* **2.** a word formed by combining separate words or parts of separate words.

● In language, a **blend** is a word that is formed by combining separate words or parts of separate words. Blends are sometimes used to create new words that combine the meanings of the original words that are blended. Our word *brunch* is a combination of the words "breakfast" and "lunch" and as a meal is a combination of the two.

Blends are also formed when we need to describe something for which there had not previously been a word. Air pollution in cities is often called *smog,* which is a blend of the words "smoke" and "fog." After television was invented, the blend *telecast* was coined, combining the words "television" and "broadcast."

blend·er (blen′dər) *n.* **1.** an appliance for chopping and blending foods and drinks. **2.** a person or thing that blends.

bless (bles) *v.t.*, **blessed** (blest) or **blest, bless·ing. 1.** to declare holy: *The minister blessed the new chapel.* **2.** to ask God's favor or protection for: *The minister blessed the congregation.* **3.** to give something good or desirable to: *The entire family was blessed with good looks.* **4.** to bring happiness or pleasure to: *The kind old man blessed us with his presence.* **5.** to make the sign of the cross over.

bless·ed (bles′id, blest) *also,* **blest.** *adj.* **1.** made holy by a religious rite; sacred: *blessed water.* **2.** worthy of adoration or worship: *the blessed Trinity.* **3.** enjoying great happiness; fortunate. **4.** bringing happiness or pleasure: *It was a blessed relief to the mother to know that her lost child had finally been found.* —**bless′ed·ly,** *adv.* —**bless′ed·ness,** *n.*

Bless·ed Virgin (bles′id) the Virgin Mary.

bless·ing (bles′ing) *n.* **1.** a prayer asking for God's favor: *The priest pronounced a blessing at the end of the service.* **2.** a prayer of thanks, usually made before or after a meal. **3.** something that brings happiness or pleasure: *The boy enjoyed the blessings of a happy home.* **4.** approval; consent: *Her father gave his blessing to her marriage.* **5.** a wish for good fortune or success: *We send our blessings for the New Year.*

blest (blest) *v.* a past tense and past participle of **bless.**

blew (blōō) the past tense of **blow²** and **blow³.**

blight (blīt) *n.* **1.** any of several diseases that wither or kill plants. Mildew, rust, and smut are blights. **2.** the bacterium, fungus, or virus that causes such a disease. **3.** something that damages, ruins, or destroys: *These slums are a blight on our city.* —*v.t.* **1.** to cause to wither or decay: *Too much rain blighted the corn.* **2.** to damage, ruin, or destroy: *Lack of money blighted his hopes for a college education.*

blimp (blimp) *n. Informal.* a small airship whose body is not supported by a rigid framework.

blind (blīnd) *adj.* **1.** unable to see; sightless: *The blind man felt his way with a cane.* **2.** not easily seen; hidden from view: *a blind driveway.* **3.** done without the help of sight: *In his blind groping in the dark room, he knocked over a lamp.* **4.** done by using instruments only: *blind flying, a blind landing.* **5.** unable to notice or understand (often with *to*): *She was blind to her own faults.* **6.** lacking thought, control, or good judgment; reckless: *The cattle*

at; āpe; cär; end; mē; it; īce; hot; ōld; fôrk; wood; fōōl; oil; out; up; turn; sing; thin; this; hw in white; zh in treasure. The symbol ə stands for the sound of **a** in about, **e** in taken, **i** in pencil, **o** in lemon, and **u** in circus.

stampeded in blind terror after being frightened. **7.** not based on reason or intelligence: *The people's blind faith in their leaders led them to the brink of war.* **8.** closed at one end: *a blind alley.* —*n.* **1.** something that blocks sight or keeps out light, such as a window shade or shutter. **2.** a person, thing, or action used to conceal or mislead: *His government job was a blind for his activities as a spy.* **3.** a hiding place for hunters: *The hunter ducked into his blind as the birds flew overhead.* —*v.t.* **1.** to take away the power of sight from; make sightless: *The glare of the sun on the lake blinded him.* **2.** to take away the power to understand or judge well: *He was blinded by jealousy.* —*adv.* with little or no power of sight. —**blind′ly,** *adv.* —**blind′ness,** *n.*

blind date *Informal.* a date between a man and a woman who have never met before.

blind·er (blīn′dər) *n.* either of a pair of flaps attached to a horse's bridle to prevent him from seeing sideways. Also, **blinker.**

blind·fold (blīnd′fōld′) *v.t.* to cover the eyes of, especially with a cloth. —*n.* a cover for the eyes.

blind·man's buff (blīnd′manz′ buf′) a game in which a blindfolded player tries to catch and identify one of several other players.

blind spot **1.** a very small point on the retina of the eye that is not sensitive to light because the optic nerve enters there. **2.** an area or subject about which a person is very prejudiced or ignorant: *Her one blind spot is sports.* **3.** an area in which radio or television reception is poor. **4.** an area where sight is hindered or obscured: *a blind spot in a car's rear-view mirror.*

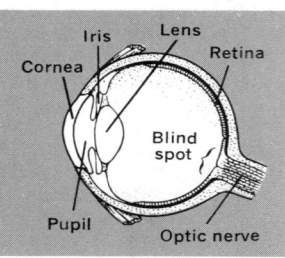

Blind spot in the human eye

(labels: Iris, Lens, Retina, Cornea, Blind spot, Pupil, Optic nerve)

blink (blingk) *v.i.* **1.** to wink rapidly, often not having meant to: *She blinked when the photographers' flash bulbs went off.* **2.** to flash on and off; glimmer; twinkle: *A star blinked in the sky.* —*v.t.* **1.** to wink (one's eyes). **2.** to cause to wink: *The policeman blinked his car lights as a signal.* —*n.* **1.** a rapid closing and opening of the eye. **2.** a sudden glimmer of light; twinkle.

on the blink. *Slang.* not working properly; out of order: *The radio is on the blink.*

to blink at. to deliberately overlook or ignore: *They blinked at any mistakes she made because it was her first day on the job.*

blink·er (bling′kər) *n.* **1.** a blinder. **2.** a light that blinks on and off, used to send messages or as a warning signal.

blintz (blints) *also,* **blintze** (blints, blint′sə). *n. pl.,* **blintz·es.** a thin pancake rolled around a filling, as of cheese or fruit, and then fried.

blip (blip) *n.* an image on a radar screen that indicates the presence of an object.

bliss (blis) *n.* great happiness or joy.

bliss·ful (blis′fəl) *adj.* full of, characterized by, or causing great happiness or joy: *a blissful marriage.* —**bliss′-ful·ly,** *adv.* —**bliss′ful·ness,** *n.*

blis·ter (blis′tər) *n.* **1.** a swelling of the skin that resembles a small bubble and is filled with watery matter. It is usually caused by rubbing or by a burn. **2.** any similar swelling, as on a plant, a painted surface, or molded plastic. —*v.t.* to raise blisters on: *Sunburn blistered his face.* —*v.i.* to have or develop blisters: *The paint blistered from the heat of the flames.* —**blis′ter·y,** *adj.*

blithe (blīth, blīth) *adj.* **1.** full of joy or gaiety; cheerful;

lighthearted: *the blithe laughter of children playing.* **2.** showing no concern, interest, or responsibility; thoughtless: *His blithe indifference to other people's feelings upset us.* —**blithe′ly,** *adv.* —**blithe′ness,** *n.*

blithe·some (blīth′səm, blīth′səm) *adj.* gay; cheerful; lighthearted. —**blithe′some·ly,** *adv.* —**blithe′some-ness,** *n.*

blitz (blits) *n. pl.,* **blitz·es.** **1.** see **blitzkrieg.** **2.** any sudden overwhelming attack: *a blitz of publicity for a new product.* —*v.t.* to attack with or overwhelm by a blitz.

blitz·krieg (blits′krēg′) *n.* warfare using sudden, violent, and overwhelming attacks intended to defeat the enemy quickly. [German *Blitzkrieg* literally, lightning war.]

bliz·zard (bliz′ərd) *n.* a severe, heavy snowstorm marked by a very strong wind and intense cold.

bloat (blōt) *v.t.* to cause to swell or expand: *Too much food bloated his stomach.* —*v.i.* to become swollen or expanded.

blob (blob) *n.* a drop or lump of a thick, soft, or sticky substance: *a blob of paint.*

bloc (blok) *n.* a group formed to promote a common interest or purpose: *the farm bloc in Congress.*

block (blok) *n.* **1.** a solid piece of wood, stone, or other material, often having one or more flat surfaces: *a block of ice, a child's building blocks. The butcher put the meat on his chopping block.* **2.a.** an area enclosed by four streets: *My brother jogs around the block every morning for exercise.* **b.** the length of a side of such an area: *Mother parked the car three blocks away from the store.* **3.** a group of buildings enclosed by streets: *an apartment block.* **4.** a number of things of the same kind, taken as a unit: *The club purchased a block of theater tickets so that everyone could sit together.* **5.** anything that hinders or stops movement or progress: *Beth's had a mental block about driving ever since she was in the car accident.* **6.** a mold or form upon which something is shaped or displayed: *a hat block.* **7.** a platform or stand where things are put up for sale at an auction. **8.** a pulley or system of pulleys mounted in a frame. —*v.t.* **1.** to hinder or stop movement or progress through (often with *up*): *After the storm, fallen trees blocked the road.* **2.** to stand in the way of; hinder: *The building next door blocks our view of the river.* **3.** to shape with a block: *You'll have to block the sweater after you finish knitting it.* **4.** *Sports.* to interfere with (an opponent's movement or his play). —*v.i. Sports.* to interfere with an opponent's movement.

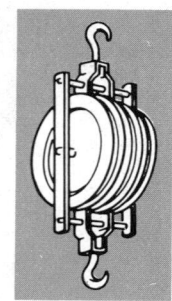

Block *(def. 8)*

to block out or **to block in.** to plan or outline roughly: *The author blocked out a new novel.*

block·ade (blo kād′) *n.* **1.** a shutting off of an area by troops or ships to prevent people or supplies from going into or out of it: *The enemy set up a blockade around the port.* **2.** the forces that carry on a blockade. **3.** something that shuts off or obstructs; obstacle. —*v.t.,* **block·ad·ed, block·ad·ing.** to subject to a blockade. —**block·ad′er,** *n.*
to run the blockade. to go through a blockade.

block·ade-run·ner (blo kād′run′ər) *n.* a person or ship that tries to go through a blockade.

block and tackle, an arrangement of pulley blocks and ropes, used for lifting or hauling.

block·bust·er (blok′bus′tər) *n. Informal.* **1.** a large aerial bomb. **2.** a person or thing that is remarkably impressive or successful: *The novel was a blockbuster and sold millions of copies.*

B

block·head (blok′hed′) *n.* a stupid or foolish person.

block·house (blok′hous′) *n. pl.*, **block·hous·es** (blok′-hou′ziz). **1.** a fortified building, originally made of timber or logs, having loopholes from which to fire weapons and an upper story built out over the lower one. **2.** a fortified building of concrete or other heavy material. **3.** a building made of strong, heavy material, serving as an observation and control center near the launching pad of a rocket or missile.

Blockhouse

bloke (blōk) *n. British. Slang.* a fellow; man.

blond (blond) *adj.* **1.** (of hair) having some shade of light yellow as its main color. **2.** *also,* **blonde.** (of a person, especially a woman) having such hair, often with light-colored skin and eyes. **3.** light-colored: *blond furniture, a blond complexion.* —*n. also,* **blonde.** a blond person. —**blond′ish**, *adj.* —**blond′ness;** *also,* **blonde′ness,** *n.*

blood (blud) *n.* **1.** the red fluid pumped by the heart through the arteries, veins, and capillaries, bringing oxygen and nourishment to all parts of the body and carrying away waste materials. **2.** the shedding of blood; murder: *The prince avenged the blood of his father.* **3.** descent from a common ancestor; kinship: *Susan is a cousin related by blood, not by marriage.* **4.** a related group or line of people; family: *Only a man of noble blood may marry the queen.* **5.** national or racial origin: *The scout was of Indian blood.* **6.** state of mind or temperament; disposition: *a man of hot blood.*

   in cold blood. without feeling or compassion: *to kill a man in cold blood.*

blood bank **1.** a place where whole blood or plasma is collected and stored for future use in giving people transfusions. **2.** the reserve of blood so stored.

blood bath, the merciless slaughter of many people; massacre.

blood count, a count of the number of red and white blood cells in a given sample of blood, used chiefly as a test to help diagnose or treat a disease.

blood·cur·dling (blud′kurd′ling) *adj.* causing great horror or fear; terrifying: *a bloodcurdling scream.*

blood group, one of the groups into which blood is classified according to the presence or absence of certain substances that either allow or prevent its mixing with other groups of blood. The four major blood groups are A, B, AB, and O. Also, **blood type.**

blood·hound (blud′hound′) *n.* a hunting dog having long, drooping ears, a wrinkled face, and a smooth coat, noted for its keen sense of smell. Bloodhounds are often used to track criminals or lost persons.

blood·less (blud′lis) *adj.* **1.** without bleeding or bloodshed: *a bloodless victory.* **2.** lacking blood; pale: *The frightened girl had bloodless lips.* **3.** lacking spirit or energy. **4.** lacking warmth; cold-hearted. —**blood′less·ly,** *adv.* —**blood′less·ness,** *n.*

blood·let·ting (blud′let′ing) *n.* **1.** the act of removing blood by opening a vein. **2.** bloodshed.

blood·line (blud′līn′) *n.* a line of direct descent, especially of an animal.

blood·mo·bile (blud′mə bēl′) *n.* a small truck equipped for the collection of blood from donors.

blood poisoning, a diseased condition of the blood caused by the presence of bacteria or poisonous material in it.

blood pressure, the force exerted by the blood against the inner walls of the arteries and other blood vessels. It is created by the pumping action of the heart and varies according to age, health, and other conditions.

blood·root (blud′rōōt′, blood′root′) *n.* a plant related to the poppy, having white or rose flowers and a root that yields a red sap.

blood·shed (blud′shed′) *n.* violence causing loss of blood or life: *We won the battle without much bloodshed.*

blood·shot (blud′shot′) *adj.* (of the eye) inflamed or marked with reddish streaks from the widening of the blood vessels.

blood·stain (blud′stān′) *n.* a spot or stain caused by blood. —**blood′stained′,** *adj.*

blood·stream (blud′strēm′) *n.* the blood as it flows through the body.

blood·suck·er (blud′suk′ər) *n.* an animal that sucks blood, especially a leech.

blood test, an analysis of a sample of a person's blood.

blood·thirst·y (blud′thurs′tē) *adj.* eager to shed blood; murderous; brutal: *a bloodthirsty pirate.* —**blood′thirst′-i·ly,** *adv.* —**blood′thirst′i·ness,** *n.*

blood type, another term for **blood group.**

blood vessel, any of the flexible tubes through which the blood flows, such as an artery, vein, or capillary.

blood·y (blud′ē) *adj.*, **blood·i·er, blood·i·est. 1.** stained or covered with blood: *a bloody knife.* **2.** losing blood; bleeding: *a bloody wound.* **3.** involving much bloodshed: *a bloody battle.* **4.** eager to shed blood; bloodthirsty. —*v.t.,* **blood·ied, blood·y·ing.** to stain or cover with blood; make bloody: *His nose was bloodied during the fight.* —**blood′i·ly,** *adv.* —**blood′i·ness,** *n.*

bloom (blōōm) *n.* **1.** the flower of a plant. **2.** the state or time of flowering: *The roses are in bloom.* **3.** the state or time of greatest health, beauty, or vigor: *She is in the bloom of youth.* **4.** a rosy glow of the cheeks or skin suggesting health and vigor. **5.** a powdery coating on certain fruits and leaves: *the bloom on a peach.* —*v.i.* **1.** to produce blossoms; flower: *Cherry trees bloom in the spring.* **2.** to be at or come to a state or time of greatest health, beauty, or vigor; flourish. **3.** to glow with health, beauty, or vigor. —**bloom′er,** *n.*

bloom·ers (blōō′mərz) *n., pl.* **1.** loose, baggy pants gathered at the knee, formerly worn by women or girls, chiefly for sports. **2.** women's underpants resembling these. [From Amelia J. *Bloomer*, 1818–1894, an American feminist who wore a costume consisting of a short skirt over loose pants gathered at the ankles.]

Bloomers

bloom·ing (blōō′ming) *adj.* **1.** in flower; blossoming. **2.** full of health, beauty, or vigor; flourishing: *She has a blooming complexion.* **3.** *Informal.* complete; utter: *He is a blooming fool.*

Bloom·ing·ton (blōō′ming tən) *n.* a city in southeastern Minnesota, a suburb of Minneapolis. Pop. (1970), 81,970.

blos·som (blos′əm) *n.* **1.** a flower, especially of a plant or tree that produces

at; āpe; cär; end; mē; it; īce; hot; ōld; fôrk; wood; fōōl; oil; out; up; turn; sing; thin; **th**is; hw in white; zh in treasure. The symbol ə stands for the sound of **a** in about, **e** in taken, **i** in pencil, **o** in lemon, and **u** in circus.

fruit: *an apple blossom.* **2.** the state or time of flowering; bloom: *a peach tree in blossom.* —*v.i.* **1.** to put forth blossoms; bloom: *All the trees in the garden are now blossoming.* **2.** to flourish; develop: *She was an awkward child who blossomed into a beautiful girl.*

blot (blot) *n.* **1.** a spot or stain, especially of ink. **2.** something that spoils or mars; blemish: *These billboards are a blot on the countryside.* —*v.,* **blot·ted, blot·ting.** —*v.t.* **1.** to spot or stain with or as if with ink. **2.** to dry or absorb with blotting paper: *I blotted every line I wrote so the ink wouldn't smear.* —*v.i.* **1.** to make blots: *The ink blotted.* **2.** to become stained or marked with a blot.

　to blot out. a. to cover up completely: *The clouds blotted out the moon.* **b.** to destroy completely: *The heavy snow blotted out all travel on the highways and roads. The shock of the accident blotted out her memory of what had happened.*

blotch (bloch) *n. pl.,* **blotch·es. 1.** a spot or stain, especially one that is large and irregular in shape: *The jelly left a blotch on the tablecloth.* **2.** a blemished or discolored patch on the skin: *The rash covered his arms with red blotches.* —*v.t.* to mark or cover with blotches. —**blotch'y,** *adj.*

blot·ter (blot'ər) *n.* **1.** a piece or pad of blotting paper. **2.** a book in which transactions or events are recorded in the order of their occurrence, such as a record of arrests and charges kept in a police station.

blotting paper, soft, absorbent paper used to soak up excess ink.

blouse (blous, blouz) *n.* **1.** a garment for women or girls that resembles a shirt and extends to the waist or below. **2.** a smock worn chiefly by certain European peasants and workmen. **3.** a jacket or tunic worn as part of the U.S. Army uniform.

Blouse *(def. 2)*

blow¹ (blō) *n.* **1.** a forceful, heavy stroke with the fist, a weapon, or some object: *A sudden blow to the jaw knocked the champion out.* **2.** a sudden, severe shock: *The bad news came as quite a blow to him.* **3.** a sudden, forceful attack, action, or effort: *The soldiers struck a blow at the enemy fort.* [Of uncertain origin.]

　at one blow. by a single action or effort.
　to come to blows. to begin fighting: *The angry boys came to blows.*

blow² (blō) *v.,* **blew, blown, blow·ing.** —*v.i.* **1.** (of wind or air) to be in motion; move with speed or force: *The wind blew against the sails.* **2.** to produce or send forth a current of air: *The fan was blowing. Blow on your hands to warm them.* **3.** to move or be carried by a current of air or wind: *His hat blew off as he ran to catch the bus.* **4.** to produce sound by a blast of air: *The whistle blows at noon.* **5.** to stop working properly; fail (often with *out*): *The tire blew out. The fuse blew.* **6.** (of a whale) to spout water and air: *Lookouts shouted "There she blows" whenever a whale came into sight.* —*v.t.* **1.** to drive by a current of air: *The wind blew the leaves across the yard.* **2.** to cause to sound by directing a blast of air: *to blow an automobile horn.* **3.** to form or shape by a current of air: *to blow bubbles.* **4.** to break, burst, or destroy, as by an explosion: *The dynamite blew the safe to bits.* **5.** to clear or empty by forcing air into or through: *to blow one's nose.* **6.** to melt (a fuse). **7.** *Slang.* to handle awkwardly or unsuccessfully: *You blew your chance to get that job when you were rude at the interview.* —*n.* **1.** the act of producing or directing a current of air. **2.** a sound resulting from producing or directing a blast of air. **3.** a strong wind; gale: *Yesterday's*

big blow knocked down the telephone wires. [Old English *blāwan* to send forth air.]

　to blow hot and cold. to change one's mind frequently: *That politician has blown hot and cold on the issue of income tax reform.*
　to blow in. *Informal.* to arrive; appear.
　to blow off steam. *Informal.* to release pent-up feelings noisily or violently.
　to blow out. to put out or be put out by a gust of air: *Make a wish and blow out the candles. The lantern blew out during the storm.*
　to blow over. a. to pass by or over; subside: *The storm finally blew over.* **b.** to be forgotten: *The scandal blew over quickly.*
　to blow the whistle on. to inform on; expose: *The thief blew the whistle on his accomplices.*
　to blow up. a. to explode: *The troops blew up the railroad tracks to cut the enemy's supply line.* **b.** to fill with air or gas: *to blow up a balloon.* **c.** *Informal.* to lose one's temper: *I really blew up at him when he told me to mind my own business.* **d.** to arise: *A storm blew up last night.* **e.** to enlarge (a photograph).

blow³ (blō) *v.i.,* **blew, blown, blow·ing.** *Archaic.* to blossom. ▲ Although the verb is archaic, the past participle **blown** is used, especially in the phrase *full-blown.* [Old English *blōwan* to blossom.]

blow·er (blō'ər) *n.* **1.** a machine for producing a current of air or for forcing air into a particular area: *They cooled the mine shaft with blowers.* **2.** a person or thing that blows: *a glass blower.*

blow·fly (blō'flī') *n. pl.,* **blow·flies.** any of various flies that deposit their larvae on the wounds, wastes, or flesh of animals.

blow·gun (blō'gun') *n.* a tube through which a person blows darts or other similar missiles. Also, **blowpipe, blow tube.**

blow·hole (blō'hōl') *n.* **1.** a breathing hole of certain whales, dolphins, and other similar animals, often located at the top of the head. **2.** an escape vent for gas or air, as in mines. **3.** a hole in the ice to which underwater animals, such as whales or seals, come to the surface in order to breathe.

blown (blōn) *v.* the past participle of **blow²** and **blow³.**

blow·out (blō'out') *n.* **1.** a sudden bursting of an automobile tire. **2.** the melting of an electric fuse caused by too much current.

blow·pipe (blō'pīp') *n.* **1.** a tube for blowing air or gas into a flame to increase its heat. **2.** another word for **blowgun.** **3.** another word for **blowtube** *(def. I).*

blow·torch (blō'tôrch') *n.* a device that produces and shoots out a very hot flame under pressure, used especially in melting metals and removing paint.

blow·tube (blō'tōōb', blō'tyōōb') *n.* **1.** a long metal tube used to shape molten glass. Also, **blowpipe.** **2.** another word for **blowgun.**

blow·up (blō'up') *n.* **1.** an explosion. **2.** *Informal.* an outburst of temper; quarrel. **3.** an enlargement, as of a snapshot.

Blowtorch

blowz·y (blou'zē) *adj.,* **blowz·i·er, blowz·i·est.** not clean, neat, or tidy; messy; slovenly.

blub·ber (blub'ər) *n.* **1.** a layer of fat in whales and certain other sea animals, used especially as a source of oil. **2.** a noisy weeping. —*v.i.* to weep and sob noisily. —**blub'ber·er,** *n.*

blub·ber·y (blub'ər ē) *adj.* of or like blubber; fat.

bludg·eon (bluj′ən) *n.* a short club, often heavier or thicker at one end. —*v.t.* to strike with a bludgeon.

blue (bloo) *n.* **1.** the color of the clear sky in the daytime; the color between green and violet in the spectrum. **2.** a blue dye or paint. **3.** *also,* **Blue.** a Union soldier in the Civil War. **4. the blue. a.** the sky. **b.** the sea. —*adj.,* **blu·er, blu·est. 1.** having the color blue: *blue eyes.* **2.** (of skin) of a bluish-purple color; discolored: *His face was blue from the cold.* **3.** unhappy and low in spirits; sad; melancholy: *Mike felt lonely and blue when most of his friends went away to camp.* See also **blues.** —*v.t.,* **blued, blu·ing** or **blue·ing. 1.** to treat with bluing. **2.** make blue. —**blue′ness,** *n.*

out of the blue. suddenly and unexpectedly.

blue·bell (bloo′bel′) *n.* any of various plants with blue flowers shaped like bells, such as the harebell of Scotland.

blue·ber·ry (bloo′ber′ē) *n. pl.,* **blue·ber·ries. 1.** a small, dark-blue, sweet berry with tiny seeds, grown on any of several shrubs. **2.** any of the shrubs bearing this berry.

blue·bird (bloo′burd′) *n.* any of several small songbirds of North America that are related to the thrush, having mainly blue feathers.

blue blood 1. aristocratic or royal descent. **2.** a person of such descent; aristocrat. [Translation of Spanish *sangre azul.* Spanish aristocrats had pale skin on which bluish veins were visible, while the common people had darker skin on which the veins were not as prominent.]

blue·bon·net (bloo′bon′it) *n.* any of several plants of North America having clusters of blue flowers shaped like bonnets.

blue·bot·tle (bloo′bot′əl) *n.* a large blowfly with a blue abdomen and hairy body.

blue·col·lar (bloo′kol′ər) *adj.* of or relating to workmen. [From the *blue* shirts worn by many workmen.]

blue·fish (bloo′fish′) *n. pl.,* **blue·fish** or **blue·fish·es.** a saltwater food and game fish having a bluish and silver body, found in coastal waters in various parts of the world.

blue flag, an iris with blue or purple flowers.

blue·grass (bloo′gras′) *n. pl.,* **bluegrass·es.** a popular name for any of various grasses with bluish-green

Bluebonnet

stems, widely raised as hay for pastures and as grass for lawns.

blue·ing (bloo′ing) another spelling of **bluing.**

blue·jack·et (bloo′jak′it) *n.* a sailor in the navy.

blue jay *also,* **blue·jay** (bloo′jā′). a jay of eastern North America, that has a crest and is mainly blue in color with black-and-white markings.

blue jeans, pants or overalls, usually made of blue denim.

blue law 1. one of the strict laws passed in colonial New England, forbidding recreation or business on Sunday. **2.** any law regulating Sunday activities.

Blue Nile, a river in northwestern Ethiopia and eastern Sudan, a tributary of the Nile.

Blue jay

blue·print (bloo′print′) *n.* **1.** a photographic print, usually showing white lines on a blue background, used especially for copying architectural plans and mechanical drawings. **2.** any detailed outline or plan of action: *The*

men who wrote the United States Constitution tried to set up a blueprint for democracy. —*v.t.* to make a blueprint of.

blue racer, a bluish-green blacksnake, found in the central and south-central United States.

blue ribbon, the highest honor or award in a contest or competition; first prize.

Blue Ridge Mountains, the eastern range of the Appalachian Mountains, extending from northeastern West Virginia to northern Georgia. Also, **Blue Ridge.**

blues (blooz) *n., pl.* **1. the blues.** *Informal.* low spirits; melancholy: *Jerry has had the blues since his best friend moved away.* **2.** *also,* **the blues.** music having a sad, melancholy quality and a jazz rhythm.

blu·et (bloo′it) *n.* a low-growing plant of North America, bearing light blue, white, or violet flowers with yellowish centers.

bluff¹ (bluf) *n.* a high, broad bank or cliff. —*adj.* **1.** rising with or having a flat, broad front: *bluff cliffs.* **2.** blunt or abrupt in a good-natured way; rough and hearty: *John's uncle greeted him with a bluff handshake.* [Possibly from Middle Dutch *blaf* broad, flat.] —**bluff′ly,** *adv.* —**bluff′ness,** *n.*

bluff² (bluf) *v.t.* **1.** to fool or deceive (someone) by putting on a false front of confidence or bravery: *George bluffed the other boys into thinking he was the strongest.* **2.** to gain or succeed with (something) by using deception or a false front: *The boy bluffed his way onto the team.* —*v.i.* to deceive by putting on a false front: *Susan is only bluffing when she says she can prove we're wrong.* —*n.* **1.** the act of bluffing. **2.** a person who bluffs. [Possibly from Dutch *bluffen* to boast.] —**bluff′er,** *n.*

to call someone's bluff. to challenge someone's statements or actions when it seems that he is bluffing: *I called his bluff and raced him to see if he were really a faster runner than I.*

blu·ing (bloo′ing) *also,* **blue·ing.** *n.* a blue liquid or powder used in laundering to keep white fabrics from turning yellow.

blu·ish (bloo′ish) *adj.* somewhat blue.

blun·der (blun′dər) *n.* a careless or stupid mistake: *Forgetting his mother's birthday was an awful blunder.* —*v.i.* **1.** to make a careless or stupid mistake: *The mayor blundered by raising taxes just before the election.* **2.** to move or act blindly or clumsily: *The lost campers blundered through the woods.* —**blun′der·er,** *n.*

blun·der·buss (blun′dər bus′) *n. pl.,* **blun·der·buss·es.** a short gun with a wide, flared muzzle for scattering shot at close range. It is no longer used.

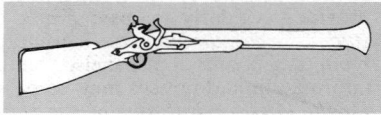

Blunderbuss

blunt (blunt) *adj.* **1.** having a dull edge or point; not sharp: *a blunt point on a pencil.* **2.** abrupt in speech or manner; outspoken; frank: *Being too blunt can hurt someone's feelings.* —*v.t.* to make less sharp or keen; dull: *He blunted his mother's scissors by using them to cut wire.* —*v.i.* to become blunt or dull. —**blunt′ly,** *adv.* —**blunt′ness,** *n.*

at; āpe; cär; end; mē; it; īce; hot; ōld; fôrk; wood; fool; oil; out; up; turn; sing; thin; this; hw in white; zh in treasure. The symbol ə stands for the sound of **a** in about, **e** in taken, **i** in pencil, **o** in lemon, and **u** in circus.

blur (blur) *v.*, **blurred, blur·ring.** —*v.t.* **1.** to make less clear or distinct in form or outline: *Fog blurred the skyline of the city.* **2.** to cause to smudge or smear: *Betty blurred the letter by folding it before the ink was dry.* **3.** to make dim: *Age had blurred the old man's eyesight.* —*v.i.* **1.** to become less clear or distinct in form or outline: *The road ahead blurred in the rain.* **2.** to smudge or smear: *The ink blurred where he had been resting his hand.* **3.** to dim: *The little girl's eyes blurred with tears.* —*n.* **1.** something indistinct or dim: *The houses along the road were just a blur as we sped by.* **2.** a smudge or smear; stain. —**blur′ry,** *adj.*

blurb (blurb) *n. Informal.* a brief advertisement or description: *The blurb on the book jacket tells all about the author.*

blurt (blurt) *v.t.* to say suddenly or without thinking: *to blurt out a secret.*

blush (blush) *v.i.* **1.** to become red in the face from shame, embarrassment, or modesty: *Mary blushed whenever the teacher called on her.* **2.** to be ashamed or embarrassed (often with *at* or *for*): *Bill blushed at his ridiculous mistake.* —*n. pl.*, **blush·es.** **1.** a reddening of the face from shame, embarrassment, or modesty. **2.** a rosy color: *the first blush of dawn.*

blus·ter (blus′tər) *v.i.* **1.** to blow with noise or stormy violence: *The storm blustered outside the house.* **2.** to talk in a noisy or threatening way. —*n.* **1.** a noisy, stormy blowing, as of the wind. **2.** noisy, threatening talk. —**blus′ter·er,** *n.* —**blus′ter·y,** *adj.*

blvd., boulevard.

bo·a (bō′ə) *n. pl.*, **bo·as.** **1.** any of various nonpoisonous snakes found in tropical and temperate regions, that kill their prey by squeezing it in their coils. **2.** a long scarf of fur or feathers.

boa constrictor, a large boa of Mexico and Central and South America, having light brown skin with dark brown marks on its back.

boar (bôr) *n. pl.*, **boars** or **boar.** **1.** a male pig or hog. **2.** see **wild boar.**

board (bôrd) *n.* **1.** a thin piece of sawed wood longer than it is wide. **2.** a flat piece of wood or other material used for some

Boa constrictor

particular purpose: *Get the board and we'll play a game of checkers.* **3.** a group of persons who direct or supervise an activity: *the board of directors of a bank.* **4.** meals provided regularly for pay: *Frank found good board for students near the campus.* ▲ usually used in the phrase *room and board.* **5.** a panel or similar surface on which information and notices may be posted: *Watch the board for the latest arrival time of her plane.* —*v.t.* **1.** to cover or close with boards: *They boarded up the windows of the summer cabin when they were ready to leave.* **2.** to provide with meals, or with lodging and meals, for pay. **3.** to get on (a ship, plane, or train): *We boarded the bus at the terminal.* —*v.i.* to get meals, or lodging and meals, for pay: *I boarded with friends of my parents last summer.*

on board. on or in a ship, plane, or train; aboard.

board·er (bôr′dər) *n.* a person who gets meals, or meals and lodging, for pay.

board foot *pl.*, **board feet.** a unit of measure for logs and lumber, equal to the volume of a board one foot square and one inch thick; 144 cubic inches.

board·ing (bôr′ding) *n.* wooden boards.

boarding house, a house at which meals, or lodging and meals, are furnished for pay.

boarding school, a school where the pupils live during the school year.

board·walk (bôrd′wôk′) *n.* a wide walk or promenade along a beach, usually made of boards.

boast (bōst) *v.i.* to speak with too much pride or with exaggeration about oneself or one's possessions; brag: *John is always boasting about being on the track team.* —*v.t.* **1.** to speak with too much pride or with exaggeration about (something); brag about: *Janet boasted that she would win the spelling contest.* **2.** to be proud of having: *The library boasts 500 new volumes.* —*n.* **1.** a bragging statement: *His boast that he is the best player on the team is not true.* **2.** something boasted of; cause for pride: *A new gymnasium is that school's boast.* —**boast′er,** *n.*

boast·ful (bōst′fəl) *adj.* characterized by or given to boasting; bragging. —**boast′ful·ly,** *adv.* —**boast′ful·ness,** *n.*

boat (bōt) *n.* **1.** a small vessel for use on water, moved by oars, sails, or a motor. **2.** a vessel of any size; ship: *His boat left the dock at noon.* **3.** an open dish shaped like a boat, as for gravy. —*v.i.* to travel in a boat. —*v.t.* to put or carry in a boat.

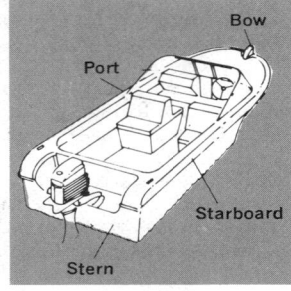

Boat

in the same boat. in the same situation or condition: *Neither of us has enough money to pay for the trip, so we're in the same boat.*

to miss the boat. to fail to make use of an opportunity: *You really missed the boat by not buying that coat while it was on sale.*

▲ In common usage, **boat** can refer to a vessel of any size. In nautical usage, **boat** means only a small vessel; **ship** applies to a larger vessel, such as an ocean liner.

boat·house (bōt′hous′) *n. pl.*, **boat·hous·es** (bōt′hou′-ziz). a building near the water's edge for sheltering or storing boats.

boat·ing (bō′ting) *n.* the act or practice of using a boat, especially for pleasure: *Eddie enjoys boating on the lake.*

boat·man (bōt′mən) *n. pl.*, **boat·men** (bōt′mən). a person who operates, works on, or deals with boats.

boat·swain (bō′sən, bōt′swān′) *also,* **bo's'n, bo·sun.** *n.* an officer on a ship who has charge of the rigging and anchors and directs the work of the crew.

bob[1] (bob) *v.*, **bobbed, bob·bing.** —*v.i.* **1.** to move up and down, or to and fro, with a short, jerky motion: *The cork bobbed in the water.* **2.** to try to snatch floating or dangling objects with the teeth: *to bob for apples.* —*v.t.* to move (something) up and down with a short, jerky motion: *The little boy bobbed his head in answer to his mother's question.* —*n.* a short, jerky motion. [Probably imitative of the sound suggested by this movement.]

bob[2] (bob) *n.* **1.** a short haircut for a woman or child. **2.** a small, hanging weight, as at the end of a pendulum or plumb line. **3.** a float or cork for a fishing line. —*v.*, **bobbed, bob·bing.** —*v.t.* to cut short, as hair or a tail. —*v.i.* to fish with a bob. [Middle English *bobbe* a bunch of hair; of uncertain origin.]

bob[3] (bob) *n. pl.*, **bob.** *British. Informal.* shilling. [Possibly from *Bob,* a nickname for Robert.]

bob·bin (bob′in) *n.* **1.** a spool around which thread or yarn is wound, used in weaving, machine sewing, or spinning. **2.** something resembling a bobbin in shape or use, such as a reel around which wire is coiled.

bob·by (bob′ē) *n. pl.*, **bob·bies.** *British. Informal.* a policeman. [From Sir *Robert* Peel, who reorganized the London police force in 1829.]

bobby pin, a flat hairpin with prongs that press close together to hold hair tightly.

bobby socks *Informal.* ribbed, often heavy, socks, usually folded just above the ankle.

bob·cat (bob′kat′) *n.* a North American lynx having a reddish-brown coat with dark spots. Also, **wildcat.**

bob·o·link (bob′ə lingk′) *n.* a songbird of North and South America, related to the blackbird. Also, **reedbird, ricebird.**

bob·sled (bob′sled′) *n.* **1.** a long racing sled with two sets of runners, a steering wheel, and a brake. **2.a.** a long sled made by attaching one short sled behind another. **b.** either of the short sleds so joined. —*v.i.,* **bob·sled·ded, bob·sled·ding.** to ride on a bobsled.

bob·tail (bob′tāl′) *n.* **1.** a tail that is cut short. **2.** an animal having such a tail. —*v.t.* to cut the tail of: *to bobtail a horse.* —*adj.* having a bobtail.

bob·white (bob′hwīt′, bob′wīt′) *n.* an American quail that has a reddish-brown body with markings of white, black, and buff.

Bobwhite

bock beer (bok) a strong, dark beer, usually brewed in the cold months and sold in the spring. Also, **bock.**

bode¹ (bōd) *v.t.,* **bod·ed, bod·ing.** to be an omen or sign of: *The dark sky boded a storm.*

to bode ill. to be a bad omen or sign: *The sickness of the team's best pitcher boded ill for its success in the play-off game.*

to bode well. to be a good omen or sign: *Jim's good work bodes well for his future in the business.*

bode² (bōd) a past tense of **bide.**

bod·ice (bod′is) *n.* **1.** the part of a woman's or girl's dress from the neckline to the waistline. **2.** a vest that laces up the front, worn over a woman's dress or blouse.

bod·i·less (bod′ē lis) *adj.* having no body.

bod·i·ly (bod′ə lē) *adj.* of or relating to the body: *The accident victim suffered almost no bodily harm.* —*adv.* **1.** in the flesh; in person. **2.** as a single body: *The audience rose bodily to applaud the singer.*

bod·kin (bod′kin) *n.* **1.** a small, pointed tool used for making holes in cloth. **2.** a long, ornamental hairpin. **3.** a large, blunt needle for pulling tape or other material through a hem. **4.** *Archaic.* a dagger.

bod·y (bod′ē) *n. pl.,* **bod·ies.** **1.** the whole physical structure and material of a human being, animal, or plant. **2.** the main portion of a human being or animal without the head and limbs; trunk. **3.** the main or central part of anything: *the body of an automobile, the body of a letter.* **4.** a dead person; corpse: *Detectives found the body in the bushes.* **5.** a group of persons or things considered as a whole: *a student body, a legislative body.* **6.** a distinct mass; portion of matter: *a body of water, a body of cold air.* **7.** substance; density; consistency: *This soup has very little body.*

bod·y·guard (bod′ē gärd′) *n.* a person or persons responsible for protecting someone from physical danger or attack.

Boer (bôr) *n.* a South African of Dutch descent. —*adj.* of or relating to the Boers.

Boer War, the war between Great Britain and the Boers, from 1899 to 1902, in which the Boers were defeated.

bog (bog) *n.* wet, spongy ground made up chiefly of decayed plant material; marsh; swamp. —*v.,* **bogged, bogging.** —*v.t.* to cause to become stuck in or as if in a bog: *Don't let all this work bog you down.* —*v.i.* to sink or stick in or as if in a bog: *They are always bogged down with money problems.* —**bog′gy,** *adj.*

bo·gey¹ (bō′gē) *n. pl.,* **bo·geys.** another spelling of **bogy¹.**

bo·gey² (bō′gē) *n. pl.,* **bo·geys.** in golf, one stroke over par for a hole. [Said to be from Colonel *Bogey,* an imaginary golf partner.]

bo·gey·man (boog′ē man′, boo′gē man′) *n. pl.,* **bo·gey·men** (boog′ē men′, boo′gē men′). a frightening imaginary figure, especially one described to children to threaten them.

bog·gle (bog′əl) *v.,* **bog·gled, bog·gling.** —*v.i.* **1.** to make a startled movement, as from fright or astonishment. **2.** to hesitate, as from doubt or confusion (with *at*): *Betty's father boggled at the idea of her staying out so late.* —*v.t.* to astound; startle: *That idea is so ridiculous it boggles the mind.*

bo·gie¹ (bō′gē) another spelling of **bogy.**

bo·gie² (bō′gē) *also,* **bo·gy.** *n.* **1.** a four-wheeled support under a railroad car. **2.** one of the wheels supporting the tread of a tractor or tank. [Of uncertain origin.]

Bo·go·tá (bō′gə tä′) *n.* the capital and largest city of Colombia, in the west-central part of the country. Pop. (1969 est.), 2,148,400.

bo·gus (bō′gəs) *adj.* not genuine; counterfeit; sham.

bo·gy (bō′gē) *also,* **bo·gey, bo·gie.** *n. pl.,* **bo·gies.** **1.** an evil spirit; goblin; specter. **2.** a frightening or dreaded person or thing.

Bo·he·mi·a (bō hē′mē ə) *n.* a historic region and ancient kingdom in western Czechoslovakia.

Bo·he·mi·an (bō hē′mē ən) *n.* **1.** a person who was born or is living in Bohemia. **2.** *also,* **bohemian.** a person who leads an unconventional life, especially an artist or writer. —*adj.* **1.** of or relating to Bohemia or its people. **2.** *also,* **bohemian.** characteristic of or relating to a bohemian: *to lead a bohemian life.*

Bohr, Niels (bôr; nēls) 1885–1962, Danish physicist.

boil¹ (boil) *v.i.* **1.** (of a liquid) to form bubbles that escape as vapor due to heating. **2.** to contain a boiling liquid: *The pot is boiling.* **3.** to reach the boiling point: *Turn off the flame as soon as the water boils.* **4.** to be stirred up or angry: *The bruised fighter boiled with rage.* **5.** to be in motion like boiling water; seethe: *The flood waters boiled over the river's banks.* —*v.t.* **1.** to bring to the boiling point: *Mary boiled water for tea.* **2.** to cook or prepare by boiling: *to boil potatoes.* —*n.* the act or state of boiling: *Bring the water to a boil.* [Old French *boillir* to form bubbles, be angry, from Latin *bullīre* to bubble.]

to boil down. a. to reduce or lessen by boiling. **b.** to shorten or be shortened: *to boil down a long report to a brief outline.*

to boil over. a. to overflow during boiling. **b.** to lose one's temper; show anger: *Bill boiled over at the insult.*

boil² (boil) *n.* a painful, pus-filled swelling beneath the skin, formed around a hard core. It is caused by bacterial infection. [Old English *bȳl* tumor.]

boil·er (boi′lər) *n.* **1.** a large container with a system of tubes in which water or other liquid is changed into steam for heating a building or running an engine. **2.** a container in which something is heated or boiled. **3.** a tank in which water is heated or hot water is stored.

at; āpe; cär; end; mē; it; īce; hot; ōld; fôrk; wood; fōōl; oil; out; up; turn; sing; thin; **this**; hw in white; zh in treasure. The symbol ə stands for the sound of **a** in about, **e** in taken, **i** in pencil, **o** in lemon, and **u** in circus.

boiling point **1.** the temperature at which a liquid begins to boil. The boiling point of water at sea level is 212 degrees Fahrenheit, or 100 degrees centigrade. **2.** *Informal.* the point at which a person loses his temper: *Eddie has a low boiling point.*

Boi·se (boi′sē) *n.* the capital of Idaho, in the southwestern part of the state. Pop. (1970), 74,990.

bois·ter·ous (bois′tər əs) *adj.* noisy and lively: *a boisterous party.* —**bois′ter·ous·ly,** *adv.* —**bois′ter·ous·ness,** *n.*

bo·la (bō′lə) *n.* a weapon used chiefly in South America, consisting of heavy balls tied to the ends of a cord. It is thrown to entangle and capture cattle or game.

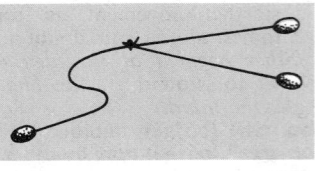

Bola

bold (bōld) *adj.* **1.** having courage; fearless: *a bold explorer.* **2.** showing or requiring spirit or courage; daring: *Rescuing the child from the burning house was a bold deed.* **3.** forward; rude; impudent: *The clerk's bold remarks to his employer almost cost him his job.* **4.** standing out prominently; distinct and striking: *Carol wore a dress with bold red stripes.* —**bold′ly,** *adv.* —**bold′ness,** *n.*

bold·face (bōld′fās′) *n.* a kind of printing type with heavy thick lines that make it stand out clearly. **This is printed in boldface.**

bole (bōl) *n.* the trunk of a tree.

bo·le·ro (bə ler′ō) *n. pl.,* **bo·le·ros. 1.** a lively dance in ¾ time that is usually accompanied by castanets. **2.** the music for this dance. **3.** a short, open jacket ending at or above the waistline.

Bol·eyn, Anne (bool′in, boo lin′) 1507?–1536, queen of England and second wife of Henry VIII.

Bo·lí·var, Si·món (bol′i vər, bō lē′vär; sē mōn′) 1783–1830, South American revolutionary leader and statesman, who fought for an end to Spanish rule.

Bo·liv·i·a (bə liv′ē ə) *n.* a landlocked country in central South America. Capitals, La Paz and Sucre. Area, 424,162 sq. mi. Pop. (1971 est.), 5,060,000. —**Bo·liv′i·an,** *adj., n.*

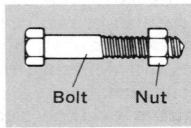

Bolero

boll (bōl) *n.* a rounded seed pod of a plant, as of cotton or flax.

boll weevil, a beetle with a long snout, whose larva lives in and causes damage to cotton bolls.

bo·lo (bō′lō) *n. pl.,* **bo·los.** a long, single-edged knife, used in the Philippines.

Bo·lo·gna (bə lōn′yə) *n.* a city in northern Italy. Pop. (1970 est.), 493,070.

bo·lo·gna (bə lō′nə, bə lō′nē) *also,* **ba·lo·ney, bo·lo·ney** (bə lō′nē). *n.* a smoked sausage made of beef, veal, and pork. [From *Bologna,* Italy.]

Bol·she·vik (bōl′shə vik) *also,* **bol·she·vik.** *n.* **1.** a member of the radical faction of the Socialist party in czarist Russia that in 1917, led by Lenin and Trotsky, gained control of the government. In 1918 the Bolsheviks formed the Communist Party of the Soviet Union. **2.** any extreme radical. —*adj.* **1.** relating to, or characteristic of the Bolsheviks or Bolshevism. **2.** extremely radical.

Bol·she·vism (bōl′shə viz′əm) *also,* **bol·she·vism.** *n.* **1.** the doctrines and policies of the Bolsheviks. **2.** extreme radicalism.

Bol·she·vist (bōl′shə vist) *also,* **bol·she·vist.** *n., adj.* another name for **Bolshevik.**

bol·ster (bōl′stər) *n.* **1.** a long, narrow pillow or cushion.

2. any cushion, pad, or pillow. —*v.t.* to support or strengthen: *The timbers bolstered the roof of the cabin. The good news bolstered Jack's spirits.*

bolt¹ (bōlt) *n.* **1.** a pin or rod used for holding things together, usually with a head at one end and threads for a nut to be attached on the other end. **2.** a sliding bar for fastening a door or gate. **3.** the part of a lock that is moved out or withdrawn by turning the key. **4.** a sudden spring or start: *The prisoner made a bolt for the door.* **5.** a stroke of lightning; thunderbolt. **6.** a roll of cloth or paper. **7.** a short, stout arrow, used with a crossbow. —*v.t.* **1.** to fasten or secure with a bolt: *Father bolted the door for the night.* **2.** to swallow (food) quickly or without chewing; gulp: *Frank bolted his dinner and ran out to play ball.* **3.** to break away from: *The mayor bolted his party and ran as an independent candidate.* —*v.i.* **1.** to spring or move suddenly: *He bolted up the stairs.* **2.** to break away from control; start and run off: *The horse bolted and threw its rider.* [Old English *bolt* arrow.]

bolt upright. stiffly straight and erect: *At the clap of thunder, I sat bolt upright in bed.*

bolt² (bōlt) *v.t.* to sift through a cloth or sieve: *to bolt flour.* [Old French *buleter* to sift; possibly of Germanic origin.]

bomb (bom) *n.* **1.** a container filled with an explosive, incendiary, or chemical substance, that is set off by dropping or throwing, by a fuse, or by a timing device: *The planes dropped bombs on the enemy's cities.* **2.** a container whose contents are stored under pressure for release as a fine spray or foam: *an insecticide bomb.* **3.** *Slang.* a total failure: *That play was a real bomb.* —*v.t.* to attack or destroy with a bomb or bombs: *Our planes bombed the village.*

bom·bard (bom bärd′) *v.t.* **1.** to attack with artillery or bombs: *The advancing army bombarded the fort.* **2.** to keep on attacking vigorously: *The reporters bombarded the movie star with questions.* **3.** *Physics.* to subject (atomic nuclei) to a stream of high-speed subatomic particles. —**bom·bard′ment,** *n.*

bom·bar·dier (bom′bər dēr′) *n.* the crew member of a bomber who works the bombsight and releases the bombs.

bom·bast (bom′bast) *n.* speech or writing that sounds important but has little meaning; pompous language: *The candidate's political bombast fooled many people.*

bom·bas·tic (bom bas′tik) *adj.* characterized by high-sounding or pompous speech or writing: *a bombastic speaker.* —**bom·bas′ti·cal·ly,** *adv.*

Bom·bay (bom bā′) *n.* the largest city and chief port of India, on the western coast of the country. Pop. (1971), 5,968,546.

bomb bay, the section in a bomber in which bombs are carried and from which they are dropped.

bomb·er (bom′ər) *n.* **1.** a military airplane used for dropping bombs. **2.** a person who drops or sets off bombs.

bomb·proof (bom′proof′) *adj.* safe from damage by bombs: *a bombproof shelter.*

bomb·shell (bom′shel′) *n.* **1.** a bomb. **2.** a person or thing that has a startling or overwhelming effect: *The discovery that the mayor had taken a bribe was a political bombshell.*

bomb shelter, a place, usually underground, where people may take refuge from an air raid.

bomb·sight (bom′sīt′) *n.* an instrument in a bomber used to sight the target and help the bombardier drop bombs accurately.

bo·na fide (bō′nə fīd′) **1.** in good faith; without fraud

B

or deception: *They made a bona fide offer for the used car.*
2. genuine; authentic: *He sold only bona fide Swiss watches.*

bo·nan·za (bə nan′zə) *n.* **1.** a rich mine or mass of ore.
2. any source of great wealth or profit.

Bo·na·parte, Napoleon (bō′nə pärt′) see **Napoleon I.**

bon·bon (bon′bon′) *n.* a piece of candy, especially one
with a chocolate coating and a smooth, creamy center.

bond (bond) *n.* **1.** something that binds, fastens, or holds
together: *The prisoner's bonds were made of rope.* **2.** a
binding or uniting force or influence; tie: *the bond of friendship.* **3.** a certificate issued by a government or corporation, promising to pay back a specified amount of money
with interest at a fixed future date: *The state issued bonds
to pay for the new highway.* **4.** *Law.* **a.** an obligation to
pay a specified sum of money if certain acts are or are not
performed. **b.** the amount of money so specified: *The accused man was released on $50,000 bond.* **5.** the storage
of imported goods in a warehouse until taxes upon them
are paid. **6.** an insurance policy covering an employer's
losses caused by the acts of an employee. **7.** *Chemistry.*
the force of attraction that holds together the atoms of a
molecule. The type of bond depends on the arrangement
of the electrons in the individual atoms. —*v.t.* **1.** to place
in or under bond. **2.** to furnish bond for: *to bond a prisoner.*
3. to bind together; unite. —*v.i.* to be held together.

bond·age (bon′dij) *n.* the condition of being under another's control against one's will; slavery.

bond·ed (bon′did) *adj.* guaranteed by a bond or bonds.

bond·hold·er (bond′hōl′dər) *n.* the owner of a bond
issued by a government or corporation.

bond·man (bond′mən) *n. pl.,* **bond·men** (bond′mən).
a slave or serf. —**bond′wo′man,** *n.*

bonds·man (bondz′mən) *n. pl.,* **bonds·men** (bondz′-
mən). **1.** a person who takes responsibility for another by
furnishing a bond. **2.** another word for **bondman.**

bone (bōn) *n.* **1.** one of the parts of the skeleton of an
animal with a backbone. **2.** the hard porous
substance of which such parts are composed. **3.** a substance resembling bone, such
as ivory or whalebone. **4.** **bones.** the body,
living or dead. —*v.t.,* **boned, bon·ing.** to
remove the bones from: *to bone a fish.*
—**bone′less,** *adj.* —**bone′like′,** *adj.*

  to feel in one's bones. to feel certain of
  something for no apparent reason.

  to have a bone to pick. to have something
  to argue or complain about.

  to make no bones about. to be direct or
  blunt about: *She made no bones about her dislike of
  homework.*

bone meal, crushed or ground animal bones, used as
fertilizer or feed.

bon·er (bō′nər) *n. Informal.* a foolish mistake: *Mailing
that letter without addressing it was a real boner.*

bon·fire (bon′fīr′) *n.* a large fire built in the open air.

bon·go drums (bong′gō) a pair of small drums, each
with a different pitch, played
with the hands while being
held between the knees. Also,
bon·gos (bong′gōz).

bo·ni·to (bə nē′tō) *n. pl.,* **bo·ni-
tos** or **bo·ni·to.** any of various
saltwater food fish closely
related to the tuna and mackerel.

bon jour (bōn zhoor′) *French.* good morning; good day.

Bonn (bon) *n.* the capital of West Germany, in the western part of the country. Pop. (1969 est.), 299,400.

Marrow cavity

**Bone
cross section**

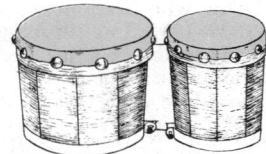
Bongo drums

bon·net (bon′it) *n.* **1.** a hat enclosing both the sides and
the back of the head and tied under the chin, worn especially by women and girls. **2.** a ceremonial headdress of
feathers worn by North American Indians. **3.** a cap worn
by men and boys in Scotland.

bon·ny (bon′ē) *also,* **bon·nie.** *adj.,* **bon·ni·er, bon·ni·est.**
Scottish. **1.** good-looking; handsome or pretty. **2.** fine;
pleasant. —**bon′ni·ly,** *adv.* —**bon′ni·ness,** *n.*

bo·nus (bō′nəs) *n. pl.,* **bo·nus·es.** something given in addition to what is usual or due; something extra: *Every
employee received a Christmas bonus.*

bon vo·yage (bon′ voi äzh′) pleasant trip; good-by.
[French *bon voyage* literally, good trip.]

bon·y (bō′nē) *adj.,* **bon·i·er, bon·i·est.** **1.** relating to or
like bone. **2.** having many bones: *a bony fish.* **3.** having
prominent bones; thin. —**bon′i·ness,** *n.*

boo (bōō) *n., interj.* a sound made to show dislike or
disapproval, or to frighten. —*v.,* **booed, boo·ing.** —*v.t.* to
show disapproval of by making this sound: *The crowd
booed the umpire.* —*v.i.* to make this sound.

boob (bōōb) *n. Slang.* a stupid or foolish person; dunce.

boo·by (bōō′bē) *n. pl.,* **boo·bies.** **1.** *Informal.* a stupid or
foolish person; dunce. **2.** any of several large tropical sea
birds having a long, straight bill and long, pointed wings.

booby prize, a prize, often a funny one, given to the
person who has done the worst in a competition or game.

booby trap **1.** a bomb set to explode when a harmless-
looking object attached to it is moved or touched by an
unsuspecting victim. **2.** any trick or device for causing
someone harm unexpectedly.

boog·ie-woog·ie (boog′ē woog′ē) *n.* a form of jazz
music.

boo·hoo (bōō′hōō′) *v.i.,* **boo·hooed, boo·hoo·ing.** to weep
noisily; blubber. —*n. pl.,* **boo·hoos.** a noisy sob; loud
weeping.

book (book) *n.* **1.** a written or printed work of some
length, especially on sheets bound together between two
covers. **2.** a set of blank or ruled sheets of paper bound
together: *an address book.* **3.** a section of a literary work:
a book of the Bible. **4.** a set of things bound together like
a book: *a book of matches, a book of stamps.* **5.** the words
or text of an opera or musical play. **6.** **books.** business
accounts or records. **7.** **the Book.** the Bible. —*v.t.*
1. to arrange for; engage; reserve: *He booked a table for
two at the restaurant. The theater manager booked the
singer for a week's engagement.* **2.** to enter charges against
(someone) in a police record.

  the book. the correct or accepted way of doing something: *Ken was an honest boy who did everything by the
  book.*

  to know like a book. to know completely and thoroughly: *Martha knew her old friend like a book.*

  to throw the book at. *Slang.* to punish severely: *The judge
  threw the book at the lawbreaker.*

book·bind·er (book′bīn′dər) *n.* a person whose business
is binding books.

book·case (book′kās′) *n.* a cabinet or set of shelves for
holding books.

book·end (book′end′) *n.* a support placed at the end of
a row of books to hold them upright.

at; āpe; cär; end; mē; it; īce; hot; ōld; fôrk;
wood; fōōl; oil; out; up; turn; sing; thin; this;
hw in white; zh in treasure. The symbol ə
stands for the sound of **a** in about, **e** in taken,
i in pencil, **o** in lemon, and **u** in circus.

book·ie (book′ē) *n. Informal.* see **bookmaker** (*def.* 1).

book·ish (book′ish) *adj.* **1.** fond of reading or study; studious. **2.** depending more on knowledge from books than on practical experience. **3.** too formal or scholarly in writing or speaking; stilted. —**book′ish·ly,** *adv.* —**book′ish·ness,** *n.*

book·keep·er (book′kē′pər) *n.* a person who keeps records of business accounts or transactions.

book·keep·ing (book′kē′ping) *n.* the work or system of keeping records of business accounts or transactions.

book·let (book′lit) *n.* a small, thin book, especially one with paper covers; pamphlet.

book·mak·er (book′mā′kər) *n.* **1.** a person who makes a business of taking bets, as on horse races and other sports events. Also, **bookie.** **2.** a person who prints or binds books.

book·mark (book′märk′) *n.* an object inserted between the pages of a book to mark the reader's place.

book·mo·bile (book′mə bēl′) *n.* a truck equipped to carry books and serve as a traveling library.

book·plate (book′plāt′) *n.* a printed label pasted in a book to show who owns it.

book·sell·er (book′sel′ər) *n.* a person whose business is selling books.

book·stall (book′stôl′) *n.* a stall or stand, often outdoors, where books are sold.

book·store (book′stôr′) *n.* a store where books are sold. Also, **book shop.**

book·worm (book′wurm′) *n.* **1.** any of various insect larvae that feed on the bindings or pages of books. **2.** a person who devotes a great deal of time or too much time to reading and studying.

boom[1] (boom) *n.* **1.** a deep, hollow, resonant sound: *the boom of crashing waves.* **2.** a period of rapid economic growth and prosperity: *That town is having a boom since the factory moved there.* **3.** a great or sudden increase, as in growth, importance, or popularity: *a boom in automobile sales.* —*v.i.* **1.** to make a deep, hollow resonant sound: *The cannon boomed in the distance.* **2.** to increase or grow suddenly and rapidly; flourish: *Business has been booming this year.* —*v.t.* **1.** to utter with a booming sound: *The loudspeaker boomed out his name.* **2.** to promote the growth, importance, or popularity of: *Supporters of the senator are booming him for governor.* —*adj.* caused by a boom: *boom prices.* [Imitative of the sound.]

boom[2] (boom) *n.* **1.** a long pole or beam used to extend the bottom of certain sails or to aid in handling cargo. **2.** the movable arm of a crane or derrick, from which the object to be moved is suspended. **3.** a long adjustable pole used to support a microphone. **4.** a chain, cable, or connection of timbers in a waterway, used to keep logs from floating away. [Dutch *boom* tree, pole.]

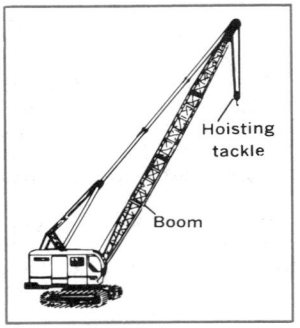

Hoisting tackle

Boom

Boom[2] *(def. 2)*

boom·er·ang (boo′mə rang′) *n.* **1.** a flat curved piece of wood that can be thrown so as to return to the thrower. It is used as a weapon by Australian natives and some Africans. **2.** something that returns to harm its originator: *Her unkind remark about Phil was a boomerang that cost her his friendship.* —*v.i.* to act as a boomerang: *The witness' false testimony boomeranged when the judge found out and sentenced him for perjury.*

boon[1] (boon) *n.* **1.** a great benefit; blessing: *His friend's help was a boon to him.* **2.** *Archaic.* favor; request. [Old Norse *bōn* petition.]

boon[2] (boon) *adj.* jolly; merry: *a boon companion.* [Old French *bon* good, from Latin *bonus* good.]

boon·docks (boon′doks′) *n., pl. Informal.* a remote or backwoods area. [Tagalog *bundok* mountain. American marines stationed in the Philippines used this word for the backwoods.]

Boone, Daniel (boon) 1734–1820, American frontiersman.

boor (boor) *n.* a crude, bad-mannered, or awkward person.

boor·ish (boor′ish) *adj.* crude, bad-mannered, or awkward: *David's boorish behavior offended everyone.* —**boor′ish·ly,** *adv.* —**boor′ish·ness,** *n.*

boost (boost) *n.* **1.** an upward shove or push: *Give me a boost over the wall.* **2.** something that supports, aids, or encourages: *The President's optimistic speech was intended to be a morale boost to the people.* **3.** an increase or rise: *a tax boost.* —*v.t.* **1.** to lift by pushing from below. **2.** to give support or aid to; promote or encourage: *The good news boosted my sagging spirits.* **3.** to raise; increase.

boost·er (boos′tər) *n.* **1.** an enthusiastic supporter: *The senator has many boosters for his reelection.* **2.** something that increases or reinforces power or effectiveness, such as an amplifier for a radio or television receiver. **3.** a first-stage engine of a rocket providing thrust for the launching and initial part of the flight.

booster shot, an additional inoculation of a vaccine or serum, given to prolong or reinforce immunity.

boot[1] (boot) *n.* **1.** a covering for the foot and part or most of the leg, usually made of leather or rubber. **2.** a blow with the foot or feet; kick: *Jim gave his little brother a playful boot in the seat of his pants.* **3.** something like a boot in shape or function. **4.** a thick patch put on the inner surface of an automobile tire. **5.** *British.* the trunk of an automobile. —*v.t.* **1.** to give a kick to: *to boot a football.* **2.** to put boots on. [Old French *bote* covering for the foot and leg; of uncertain origin.]

boot[2] (boot) *Archaic. v.t.* to be of use to. —*v.i.* to be useful. [Old English *bōt* advantage.]

to boot. in addition; besides: *Tom gave his younger brother a baseball glove and a bat to boot.*

boot·black (boot′blak′) *n.* a person whose work is polishing shoes and boots.

boot camp, a military camp for training new recruits.

boot·ee (boo′tē) *n.* an infant's soft shoe.

Bo·ö·tes (bō ō′tēz) *n.* a constellation in the northern sky containing the bright star Arcturus.

booth (booth) *n. pl.,* **booths** (boothz, booths). **1.** a small, enclosed space designed for a particular use: *a voting booth, a telephone booth, a ticket booth.* **2.** a small, partly enclosed space with a table and a set of seats, as in a restaurant. **3.** a stall for the display or sale of goods: *a refreshment booth at a church bazaar.*

Booth (booth) **1. John Wilkes** (wilks). 1838–1865, U.S. actor who assassinated Abraham Lincoln. **2. William.** 1829–1912, English founder of the Salvation Army.

boot·jack (boot′jak′) *n.* a device to hold a boot while the foot is pulled out.

boot·leg (boot′leg′) *v.,* **boot·legged, boot·leg·ging.** —*v.t.* to make, sell, or transport (liquor or other goods) illegally. —*v.i.* to bootleg liquor or other goods. —*adj.* made, sold, or transported illegally: *bootleg whiskey.* —*n.* a bootlegged article, especially liquor. [From the practice of smuggling products, especially liquor, in the legs of *boots.*] —**boot′leg·ger,** *n.*

boot·less (boot′lis) *adj.* unprofitable; useless.

boot·lick (boot′lik) *Informal. v.t., v.i.* to try to gain favor with (someone) by flattery or by acting in a servile manner.

boo·ty (boo′tē) *n. pl.,* **boo·ties. 1.** goods taken from an enemy in war. **2.** goods seized by violence and robbery; plunder: *a pirate's booty.* **3.** any rich prize or gain.

booze (booz) *Informal. n.* an alcoholic drink. —*v.i.,* **boozed, booz·ing.** to drink heavily. —**booz′er,** *n.*

bo·rax (bôr′aks) *n.* a compound of sodium, boron, and oxygen in the form of white or colorless crystals, used especially in soaps and cleansing powders.

Bor·deaux (bôr dō′) *n.* **1.** a port city in southwestern France. Pop. (1968), 266,662. **2.** any of several red or white wines produced in the region around Bordeaux.

bor·der (bôr′dər) *n.* **1.** a boundary line of a territory, country, or state: *A traveler must go through customs in order to cross the border.* **2.** a strip along an edge of anything, especially one that is ornamental: *a blue border on a dress.* **3.** an edge of anything, or the part near it; margin: *There was a path along the border of the river.* —*v.t.* **1.** to lie on or form the edge of; bound: *New York borders Pennsylvania.* **2.** to put a border or edging on.

  to border on or **to border upon. a.** to be next to or adjoining: *His land borders on mine.* **b.** to come close to: *His schemes for success border on madness.*

bor·der·land (bôr′dər land′) *n.* **1.** land lying near or at a border. **2.** an indefinite or vague region or area: *the borderland between fact and fiction.*

bor·der·line (bôr′dər līn′) *n.* a dividing line; boundary: *the borderline between Germany and France.* —*adj.* **1.** on or near a border or boundary: *a borderline river.* **2.** uncertain; indefinite: *a borderline case of flu.*

bore¹ (bôr) *v.,* **bored, bor·ing.** —*v.t.* **1.** to make (a hole or passage) by drilling or digging: *Workmen bored a tunnel through the mountain.* **2.** to make a hole in or through, as with a rotating tool: *to bore the ground for oil.* —*v.i.* **1.** to make a hole or passage: *The animal bored into the ground.* **2.** to be drilled by an instrument: *The wood bored easily.* —*n.* **1.** a hole made by boring. **2.** the long, hollow space inside a tube, pipe, or gun barrel. **3.** the diameter of a hole or the inside of a tube, pipe, or gun barrel. [Old English *borian* to make a hole.]

bore² (bôr) *v.t.,* **bored, bor·ing.** to make weary by being dull or monotonous: *Bill always bores me by telling the same jokes over and over again.* —*n.* a person or thing that bores: *That television program was a bore.* [Of uncertain origin.]

bore³ (bôr) the past tense of **bear¹.**

bore⁴ (bôr) *n.* a high wave or wall of tidal water that forms in a shallow bay or estuary and moves upstream with great force. [Possibly from Old Norse *bāra* wave.]

bore·dom (bôr′dəm) *n.* the state of being bored or uninterested: *His boredom with his job caused him to quit.*

bor·er (bôr′ər) *n.* **1.** a tool for boring holes. **2.** an insect or its wormlike larva that bores into wood, fruit, or other parts of plants.

bor·ic acid (bôr′ik) a compound of hydrogen, boron, and oxygen in the form of odorless white granules or colorless crystals, used as a mild antiseptic, especially for the eyes, and in manufacturing.

born (bôrn) *v.* a past participle of **bear¹.** —*adj.* **1.** brought into life or existence. **2.** by birth or nature; innate: *Larry's drawings showed that he was a born artist.*

borne (bôrn) a past participle of **bear¹.**

Bor·ne·o (bôr′nē ō′) *n.* a large island in the East Indies, southwest of the Philippines.

bo·ron (bôr′on) *n.* a nonmetallic element occurring in the form of yellowish-brown crystals or a dark brown powder, produced from borax and similar minerals. Symbol: **B**

bor·ough (bur′ō) *n.* **1.** in some states of the United States, an incorporated municipality smaller than a city. **2.** one of the five administrative divisions of New York City.

bor·row (bôr′ō, bor′ō) *v.t.* **1.** to take or get (something) with the understanding that it must be returned: *Bill borrowed a book from the library. I borrowed my brother's bicycle.* **2.** to take or adopt from another source and use as one's own: *The English word "debris" was borrowed from French.* **3.** in subtraction, to take (1) from a position in the minuend and add it as 10 to the position of the next lower denomination. To subtract 17 from 93, you borrow 1 from 90 and add it as 10 to the 3, so that the subtraction in the first column is 7 from 13. —**bor′row·er,** *n.*

borscht (bôrsht) *also,* **borsch** (bôrsh). *n.* a beet soup of Russian origin, eaten hot or cold.

bor·zoi (bôr′zoi) *n.* a dog having a narrow head, a long, curving tail, and a coat of long, silky hair. Borzois were originally raised in Russia for hunting wolves. Also, **Russian wolfhound.**

Borzoi

Bosch, Hie·ro·ny·mus (bosh; hē ron′ə məs) 1450?–1516, Flemish painter.

bosh (bosh) *n., interj. Informal.* foolish talk; nonsense.

bos·ky (bos′kē) *adj.,* **bosk·i·er, bosk·i·est. 1.** wooded. **2.** shaded by trees or shrubs: *a bosky lane.*

bo's'n (bō′sən) another spelling of **boatswain.**

bos·om (booz′əm, boo′zəm) *n.* **1.** the upper, front part of the human chest, especially of a woman. **2.** the upper, front part of a woman's garment. **3.** something thought of as giving protection, warmth, or privacy: *The child was happy in the bosom of her family.* **4.** the human breast thought of as the center of emotions and beliefs. —*adj.* close and dear: *a bosom friend.*

Bos·po·rus (bos′pər əs) *n.* a strait connecting the Black Sea and the Sea of Marmara.

boss¹ (bôs) *Informal. n. pl.,* **boss·es. 1.** a person who hires or supervises workers; employer or foreman. **2.** a politician who controls a political organization, as in a certain city. —*v.t.* to be the boss of; order: *He was a weak person who let everyone boss him around.* [Dutch *baas* master.]

boss² (bôs) *n. pl.,* **boss·es.** a raised ornamental knob or part on a flat surface, as on silver, ivory, or leather. —*v.t.* to ornament with bosses; emboss. [Old French *boce* bulge.]

boss·y (bô′sē) *adj.,* **boss·i·er, boss·i·est.** fond of bossing people around; domineering: *The little boy's older sister was very bossy.*

Bosses

Bosses on a Chinese bell

at; āpe; cär; end; mē; it; īce; hot; ōld; fôrk; wood; fool; oil; out; up; turn; sing; thin; this; hw in white; zh in treasure. The symbol ə stands for the sound of **a** in about, **e** in taken, **i** in pencil, **o** in lemon, and **u** in circus.

Bos·ton (bôs′tən) *n.* the capital of Massachusetts, in the eastern part of the state. Pop. (1970), 641,071. —**Bos·to·ni·an** (bôs tō′nē ən), *adj., n.*

Boston terrier, any of a breed of short-haired dogs having a smooth, black or brindled coat with white markings. Also, **Boston bull.**

bo·sun (bō′sən) another spelling of **boatswain.**

Bos·well, James (boz′wel′) 1740–1795, English biographer of Samuel Johnson, born in Scotland.

bo·tan·i·cal (bə tan′i kəl) *adj.* of or relating to plants or botany. Also, **bo·tan·ic** (bə tan′ik). —**bo·tan′i·cal·ly,** *adv.*

Boston terrier

botanical garden, grounds containing gardens and greenhouses, for the study and display of plants.

bot·a·nist (bot′ən ist) *n.* a student of or an expert in botany.

bot·a·ny (bot′ən ē) *n.* the science or study of plants. Botany deals with the origin, development, structure, function, and distribution of all forms of plant life.

botch (boch) *v.t.* to do or make in a poor or clumsy way; bungle: *Tom botched his history paper and had to do it over.* —*n. pl.,* **botch·es.** a poor piece of work.

both (bōth) *adj.* the two; the one and the other: *Both brothers made the basketball team. Both girls have blue eyes.* —*pron.* one and the other: *Why not invite both to the party?* —*conj.* alike; equally; as well: *Laura is both intelligent and beautiful.*

both·er (both′ər) *v.t.* **1.** to give trouble to; pester; annoy: *The mischievous boy kept bothering his sister.* **2.** to make uneasy or anxious: *Meeting new people bothers the shy girl.* —*v.i.* to take trouble; concern oneself: *Don't bother to see me to the door.* —*n.* a troublesome or annoying person or thing: *The child's constant questions were a bother to his older brother.*

both·er·some (both′ər səm) *adj.* causing trouble; annoying: *a bothersome noise, a bothersome delay, a bothersome swarm of insects.*

Bot·swa·na (bot swä′nə) *n.* a country in south-central Africa, formerly the British protectorate of Bechuanaland. Capital, Gaborone. Area, 238,605 sq. mi. Pop. (1980), 821,000.

Bot·ti·cel·li, San·dro (bot′i chel′ē; sän′drō) 1444?–1510, Italian painter.

bot·tle (bot′əl) *n.* **1.** a container for holding liquids, having a narrow neck or mouth that can be capped or stopped. Bottles are usually made of glass or plastic. **2.** the amount held by a bottle: *We drank a whole bottle of soda.* —*v.t.,* **bot·tled, bot·tling.** to put into a bottle or bottles. —**bot′·tler,** *n.*

to **bottle up.** to hold in or back; restrain: *Jean was a shy girl who bottled up all her feelings.*

bot·tle·neck (bot′əl nek′) *n.* **1.** a narrow opening or passageway. **2.** a situation or thing that hinders progress: *The traffic was slowed by a bottleneck on the highway where the road was being repaired.*

bot·tom (bot′əm) *n.* **1.** the lowest part of anything: *The automobile rolled to the bottom of the hill. His final average placed him at the bottom of the class.* **2.** the part on which something rests or stands: *the bottom of a plate.* **3.** the ground beneath a body of water, such as the ocean or a lake or river. **4.** *also,* **bottoms.** low land near a river. **5.** the seat of a chair. **6.** *Informal.* the buttocks. **7.** the fundamental or essential part of something; basis; foundation: *The detective tried to get to the bottom of the mystery.*

8. the part of a ship's hull below the surface of the water. —*adj.* at or on the bottom; lowest or last: *the bottom drawer of a dresser.*

bot·tom·less (bot′əm lis′) *adj.* **1.** having no bottom. **2.** seeming to have no bottom; very, very deep: *a bottomless well.*

bot·u·lism (boch′ə liz′əm) *n.* a food poisoning caused by certain bacteria that grow very rapidly in places where there is no air, such as in canned goods. Botulism can cause death.

bou·doir (bōōd′wär) *n.* a lady's bedroom, dressing room, or private sitting room. [French *boudoir* a lady's private room; literally, a place for sulking, from *bouder* to sulk.]

bouf·fant (bōō fänt′) *adj.* puffed out: *a bouffant skirt, a bouffant hairdo.*

bough (bou) *n.* a branch of a tree, especially a large or main branch.

bought (bôt) a past tense and past participle of **buy.**

bouil·la·baisse (bōōl′yə bäs′) *n.* a chowder made of fish and shellfish, vegetables, wine, and seasonings such as garlic and saffron.

bouil·lon (bool′yon) *n.* a clear, thin soup or broth, usually made from chicken or beef.

boul·der (bōl′dər) *n.* a large, rounded rock, especially one lying on the surface of the ground.

Boulder Dam, see Hoover Dam.

boul·e·vard (bool′ə värd′) *n.* a broad city street, often lined with trees.

bounce (bouns) *v.,* **bounced, bounc·ing.** —*v.i.* **1.** to spring back from a surface; rebound: *The rubber ball bounced off the sidewalk.* **2.** to move or walk in a springy or lively way: *The happy little girl bounced down the street.* **3.** *Informal.* (of a check) to be rejected for payment by a bank because the person who wrote it does not have enough money in his account to pay for it. —*v.t.* **1.** to cause (something) to spring back or rebound: *She bounced the ball.* **2.** *Slang.* to force (someone) to leave: *The noisy man was bounced from the restaurant.* —*n.* **1.** a springing back; rebound: *She hit the ball on the second bounce.* **2.** the ability to spring back or rebound: *This old basketball has lost its bounce.* **3.** liveliness; energy: *That young man has a lot of bounce.*

to **bounce back.** to recover, as from a blow or defeat: *After losing the first game, the team bounced back to win the second.*

bounc·er (boun′sər) *n.* **1.** something that bounces. **2.** *Slang.* a person employed to make disorderly persons leave a public place, such as a night club or bar.

bounc·ing (boun′sing) *adj.* big or strong; healthy; strapping: *a bouncing baby boy.*

bound¹ (bound) *v.* a past tense and past participle of **bind.** —*adj.* **1.** made fast; tied: *a bound prisoner.* **2.** certain; sure: *He is bound to fail the test if he doesn't study.* **3.** under obligation; obliged: *You are bound by your promise.* **4.** having a binding or cover: *a bound volume of poetry.* **5.** in language, designating a form that does not occur by itself as a separate word. The *-ly* in *gladly* and the *pre-* in *preschool* are bound forms. **6.** *Informal.* determined; resolved: *She is bound to have her way.* [Short for *bounden,* an earlier past participle of *bind.*]

bound up in or **bound up with. a.** closely connected with. **b.** deeply devoted to: *He is bound up in his work as a scientist.*

bound² (bound) *v.i.* **1.** to move by a series of leaps; spring; jump: *The children went bounding over the hill.* **2.** to spring back from a surface; rebound: *The ball bounded off the wall.* —*n.* **1.** a long or high leap: *With one great bound the deer cleared the stream.* **2.** a springing back; rebound: *the bound of a ball.* [Old French *bondir* to rebound.]

B

bound³ (bound) *n. also,* **bounds. 1.** a limiting line; boundary: *the bounds of a park.* **2.** an area near or within a boundary: *the vast bounds of a cattle ranch.* —*v.t.* **1.** to form the boundary of: *A river bounds his land on the north.* **2.** to name the boundaries of: *Can you bound your state?* —*v.i.* to have a boundary with another country or state. [Old French *bonde, bodne* boundary, limit.]
   out of bounds. a. beyond the boundary or limits, as of a playing field. **b.** not allowed; prohibited.

bound⁴ (bound) *adj.* going or intending to go; on the way: *The train is bound for California. He is homeward bound.* [Old Norse *būinn* ready.]

bound·a·ry (boun′dər ē, bound′rē) *n. pl.,* **bound·a·ries.** a line or thing that limits or marks a separation; border: *The boundary between Illinois and Iowa is the Mississippi River.*

bound·en (boun′dən) *adj.* that binds or obligates; binding.

bound·less (bound′lis) *adj.* having no bounds or limits; vast: *the boundless expanse of the universe. His energy seems boundless.* —**bound′less·ly,** *adv.* —**bound′less·ness,** *n.*

boun·te·ous (boun′tē əs) *adj.* **1.** plentiful; abundant: *a bounteous crop.* **2.** giving freely; generous: *He was a bounteous supporter of the hospital fund.* —**boun′te·ous·ly,** *adv.* —**boun′te·ous·ness,** *n.*

boun·ti·ful (boun′ti fəl) *adj.* **1.** plentiful; abundant: *a bountiful supply.* **2.** giving freely; generous: *A bountiful friend helped the poor old man.* —**boun′ti·ful·ly,** *adv.* —**boun′ti·ful·ness,** *n.*

boun·ty (boun′tē) *n. pl.,* **boun·ties. 1.** a reward or premium, especially one given by a government for the killing of certain animals or the raising of certain crops: *That state has a bounty on wolves.* **2.** generosity in giving: *Many poor people in the town were dependent on his bounty.* **3.** a gift generously given: *the bounties of Nature.*

bou·quet (bō kā′, boō kā′) *n.* **1.** a bunch of flowers, especially one arranged and fastened together. **2.** fragrance or aroma, especially of a wine.

bour·bon (bur′bən) *also,* **Bour·bon.** *n.* a whiskey distilled mainly from corn. [From *Bourbon* County, Kentucky, where it was first made.]

Bour·bon (boor′bən, boor bōn′) *n.* **1.** the royal family of France from 1589 to 1792 and from 1814 to 1848. **2.** any of the branches of this family in Spain, Naples, or Sicily.

bour·geois (boor zhwä′) *adj.* **1.** of or relating to the middle class. **2.** having the views and characteristics of the middle class: *a bourgeois custom.* **3.** having a narrow-minded and materialistic view of life: *a bourgeois greed for wealth and possessions.* —*n. pl.,* **bour·geois.** a member of the middle class.

bour·geoi·sie (boor′zhwä zē′) *n.* **1.** the social class between the working class and the very wealthy; middle class. **2.** in the political theory of Karl Marx, the capitalist class, as opposed to the proletariat.

bourn¹ (bôrn) *also,* **bourne.** *n.* a small stream; brook. [Old English *burna* stream.]

bourn² (bôrn, boorn) *also,* **bourne.** *n. Archaic.* **1.** a boundary; limit. **2.** goal; destination. [French *borne* boundary, limit, from Old French *bodne.*]

bout (bout) *n.* **1.** a trial of strength or skill; contest; match: *a boxing bout, a fencing bout.* **2.** a spell or period: *a bout of mumps, a bout of hot weather.*

bou·tique (boō tēk′) *n.* a small shop, especially one selling women's clothing.

bou·ton·niere (boō′tən yer′) *n.* a flower worn in the buttonhole of a lapel.

bo·vine (bō′vīn) *adj.* **1.** of or relating to an ox or cow.

2. like an ox or cow; dull, sluggish, or stupid. —*n.* an ox, cow, or other related animal.

bow¹ (bou) *v.i.* **1.** to bend the head or upper part of the body forward in respect, submission, or greeting: *The knight bowed to the king.* **2.** to give in; submit; yield: *The company bowed to the demands of the workers.* **3.** to bend, as under a weight: *The trees bowed in the wind.* —*v.t.* **1.** to cause to stoop or be bent: *Age had bowed his back.* **2.** to cause to bend forward in respect, submission, or greeting: *to bow one's head in prayer.* **3.** to show by bowing: *The host bowed a welcome to his guests.* —*n.* a forward bending of the head or upper part of the body in respect, submission, or greeting: *He made a graceful bow.* [Old English *būgan* to bend.]
   to bow and scrape. to be too polite or submissive.
   to bow out. to withdraw: *Harry had agreed to go on the picnic, but at the last minute he bowed out.*

bow² (bō) *n.* **1.** a weapon for shooting arrows, consisting of a strip of flexible wood that is bent and held by a taut string connecting the two ends. **2.** a knot with two or more loops extending from it: *a bow of ribbon.* **3.** a slender rod having horsehairs stretched tautly from one end to the other, used in playing the violin and related stringed instruments. **4.** something curved or bent, such as a rainbow. —*v.t.* **1.** to bend in the shape of a bow: *The hurricane bowed the trees.* **2.** to play by means of a bow: *to bow a cello.* —*v.i.* **1.** to curve in the shape of a bow: *His legs bow out.* **2.** to play a stringed instrument with a bow. [Old English *boga* this weapon, arch.] —**bow′like′,** *adj.*

Bows

bow³ (bou) *n.* **1.** the forward end of a boat, ship, or aircraft. **2.** the rower nearest the bow of a boat. [Of Germanic or Scandinavian origin.]

bowd·ler·ize (boud′lə rīz′) *v.t.,* **bowd·ler·ized, bowd·ler·iz·ing.** to edit (a book) by taking out words and passages considered to be obscene or otherwise objectionable. [From Thomas *Bowdler,* an English editor, who in 1818 published an edition of William Shakespeare's plays from which he had removed words and passages that he considered offensive.]

bow·el (bou′əl) *n.* **1.** a part of the intestines. **2.** *usually,* **bowels.** intestines; entrails. **3.** **bowels.** the inner or deepest part of something: *the bowels of the earth.*

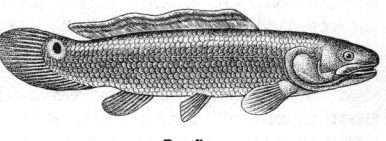

Bowfin

bow·er (bou′ər) *n.* a shelter of leafy branches; arbor.

bow·fin (bō′fin′) *n.* a large fish found in fresh waters of the eastern United States. It is the only surviving species of an ancient order of fish.

at; āpe; cär; end; mē; it; īce; hot; ōld; fôrk; wood; foōl; oil; out; up; turn; sing; thin; **this;** hw in white; zh in treasure. The symbol ə stands for the sound of **a** in about, **e** in taken, **i** in pencil, **o** in lemon, and **u** in circus.

bow·ie knife (bō′ē, boo′ē) a long, single-edged hunting knife. [From Colonel James *Bowie*, 1796–1836, U.S. frontiersman who used this kind of knife.]

bowl¹ (bōl) *n.* **1.** a deep, rounded dish used for holding food or liquid: *a salad bowl, a mixing bowl.* **2.** the amount such a container can hold; contents of a bowl: *a bowl of soup.* **3.** something shaped like a bowl; hollow, rounded thing or part: *the bowl of a spoon.* **4.** a stadium or other structure having the shape of a bowl. **5.** a football game played after the regular season between two specially selected teams. [Old English *bolla* a round container.]

Bowie knife

bowl² (bōl) *n.* **1.** a wooden ball that is weighted or shaped so that it will curve when rolled, used in the game of bowls. **2.** the act of rolling the ball in bowling or in bowls. —*v.i.* **1.** to take part in a game of bowling. **2.** to roll a ball in bowling. **3.** to move with a rapid and easy motion: *The truck bowled along on the open road.* —*v.t.* **1.** to roll (a ball or a bowl). **2.** to make (a certain score) in bowling: *She bowled 175 in the last game.* [French *boule* ball.]
  to bowl over. a. to knock over: *The swimmer was bowled over by the surging waves.* **b.** *Informal.* to confuse or overwhelm: *She was bowled over by the shocking news.*

bow·leg (bō′leg′) *n.* a leg that curves outward.

bow·leg·ged (bō′leg′id) *adj.* having legs that curve outward; having bowlegs: *The old cowboy was bowlegged from many years of horseback riding.*

bowl·er¹ (bō′lər) *n.* a person who bowls. [*Bowl²* + *-er¹*.]

bowl·er² (bō′lər) *n. British.* a derby hat. [From John *Bowler*, a nineteenth-century London hatmaker.]

bow·line (bō′lin) *n.* a knot used in making a loop that will not slip.

bowl·ing (bō′ling) *n.* **1.** a game in which ten wooden pins are set up at one end of a bowling alley and a player standing at the opposite end rolls a large, heavy ball at the pins in an attempt to knock them all down; tenpins. **2.** a similar game, such as duckpins and candlepins. **3.** see **bowls. 4.** the act of playing any of these games.

bowling alley 1. a long, narrow lane along which the ball is rolled in bowling. **2.** a building containing a number of these alleys.

bowling green, a smooth, level lawn for the game of bowls.

bowls (bōlz) *n.* a game played on a level lawn by rolling a weighted or slightly flattened wooden ball toward a smaller stationary ball. The object of the game is to roll the ball so that it stops as close as possible to the stationary ball. ▲ used with a singular verb. Also, **lawn bowling.**

bow·man (bō′mən) *n. pl.,* **bow·men** (bō′mən). a person who shoots with a bow and arrow; archer.

bow·sprit (bou′sprit′) *n.* a large pole or spar projecting forward from the bow of a sailing ship.

bow·string (bō′string′) *n.* a strong cord connecting the two ends of a bow.

bow tie (bō) a necktie tied in a bow.

box¹ (boks) *n. pl.,* **box·es. 1.** a container to hold or carry things, made of wood, cardboard, or some other stiff material, and usually having four sides, a bottom, and a lid or cover. **2.** the amount such a container can hold; contents of

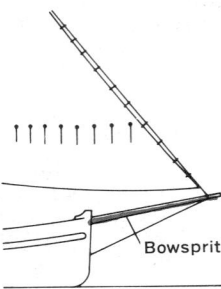

Bowsprit

a box: *He bought a box of crayons. The boys ate a box of crackers.* **3.** anything that resembles a box, such as a stall for a horse or a shelter for a sentry. **4.** an enclosed or separated area for one or more persons: *a jury box, a press box, a theater box.* **5.** any of certain designated areas on a baseball field, such as the marked-off space where the batter stands. —*v.t.* to place or pack in a box: *to box fruit.* [Old English *box* a container made of boxwood, from Latin *buxum* boxwood.] —**box′like′,** *adj.*
  to box in or **to box up.** to keep in; confine.

box² (boks) *n. pl.,* **box·es.** a blow struck with the open hand or the fist, especially on the ear or side of the head. —*v.t.* **1.** to strike with the hand or fist: *The bully boxed the little boy's ears.* **2.** to fight (someone) with the fists as a sport: *The champion boxed his opponent with great skill.* —*v.i.* to fight with the fists as a sport. [Possibly imitative of the sound made by this blow.]

box³ (boks) *n. pl.,* **box·es.** any of various evergreen trees or shrubs with small, oval, leathery leaves. Boxes are much used as hedges. [Old English *box* this tree.]

box·car (boks′kär′) *n.* a railroad freight car that can be completely enclosed, usually by a sliding door in the side.

box elder, a North American tree related to the maple, having low, spreading branches.

box·er (bok′sər) *n.* **1.** a person who boxes; prizefighter; pugilist. **2.** a short-haired dog having a smooth, tan or brindled coat, often with white markings, and a square, black muzzle.

box·ing (bok′sing) *n.* the act or sport of fighting with the fists in boxing gloves.

Boxer

boxing glove, a padded leather glove worn for boxing.

box office, a booth or window where admission tickets are sold, as in a theater, stadium, or the like.

box score, a summary of an athletic contest, as a baseball or basketball game, arranged in the form of a table listing each player and a statistical record of his performance.

box seat, a seat in a box at a theater, stadium, or the like.

box spring, a rectangular frame containing rows of coiled springs, used as a support for a mattress.

box·wood (boks′wood′) *n.* **1.** the hard, close-grained wood of the box tree or shrub. **2.** the tree or shrub itself.

boy (boi) *n.* **1.** a male child from birth to the time he is a young man. **2.** *Informal.* any man; fellow: *The boys at work gave a party for him.* **3.** a male servant.

boy·cott (boi′kot) *v.t.* **1.** to join with others in refusing to do business or have contact with (a person, group, or country): *The housewives boycotted the grocery store because its prices were too high.* **2.** to refuse to buy, sell, or use: *The American colonists sometimes boycotted British goods.* —*n.* a planned and organized refusal to have anything to do with a person, group, or nation: *Martin Luther King led a boycott of a city bus line to protest racial segregation.* [From Captain Charles *Boycott,* 1832–1897, an English land agent in Ireland. When he denied the Irish farmers' request to lower rents, they refused to have anything to do with him.]

boy·friend (boi′frend′) *n. Informal.* a male friend, especially a sweetheart.

boy·hood (boi′hood′) *n.* **1.** the time or state of being a boy: *Tom spent his boyhood in Virginia.* **2.** boys as a group.

boy·ish (boi′ish) *adj.* of, relating to, or fit for boys or boyhood: *boyish pranks, boyish enthusiasm.* —**boy′ish·ly,** *adv.* —**boy′ish·ness,** *n.*

Boyle, Robert (boil) 1627–1691, British scientist, born in Ireland.

boy scout, a member of the Boy Scouts.

Boy Scouts, a worldwide organization for boys whose intention is to promote physical fitness and outdoor skills, to develop qualities of leadership and good citizenship, and to encourage usefulness to others.

boy·sen·ber·ry (boi′zən ber′ē) n. pl., **boy·sen·ber·ries.** **1.** a large, soft, dark red or purple berry resembling a blackberry. **2.** the plant on which it grows. [From Rudolph *Boysen,* a twentieth-century American horticulturist who developed it.]

Br, the symbol for bromine.

bra (brä) n. see **brassiere.**

brace (brās) n. **1.** something that holds parts together or in place; thing that steadies or supports, such as a beam for strengthening a part of a building or a metal device for supporting a weak part of the body. **2.** pair; couple: *a brace of pheasants, a brace of pistols.* **3.** a tool resem-

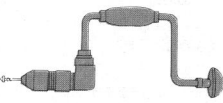

Brace *(def. 3)*

bling a handle, used for holding and turning a bit or drill. **4.** either of two curved lines,{ } , used in writing and printing to enclose words, letters, figures, staffs in music, or the members of a mathematical set. **5. braces.** metal wires used to straighten crooked teeth. **6. braces.** another word for **suspenders.** —v.t., **braced, brac·ing. 1.** to make strong, firm, or steady; support: *to brace a tree with wires.* **2.** to prepare to meet some form of shock: *Brace yourself for the bad news.* **3.** to give vigor and energy to; invigorate.

brace and bit, a tool for drilling or boring, consisting of a drill (the *bit*) fitted into a removable handle (the *brace*).

brace·let (brās′lit) n. an ornamental band or chain worn around the wrist, arm, or ankle.

brac·ing (brā′sing) adj. giving vigor and energy; refreshing; stimulating: *a bracing sea breeze.*

brack·en (brak′ən) n. another word for **brake³.**

brack·et (brak′it) n. **1.** a piece of wood, metal, or stone projecting from a wall, used as a support for a shelf or other object. **2.** a support joined or bent at an angle, especially at a right angle. **3.** a shelf supported by brackets. **4.** either of two symbols, [ ], used to enclose words, letters, or figures. **5.** a grouping or classification: *He is in a high income tax bracket.* —v.t. **1.** to supply or support with a bracket or brackets: *to bracket a shelf.* **2.** to enclose within brackets: *to bracket a word.* **3.** to group or classify together: *The employer bracketed job applicants according to past experience.*

brack·ish (brak′ish) adj. **1.** somewhat salty; briny: *brackish water, a brackish pond.* **2.** having an unpleasant taste; distasteful; nauseating. —**brack′ish·ness,** n.

bract (brakt) n. a leaf at or near the base of a flower or flower cluster. Some bracts are very colorful and showy and are frequently mistaken for flower petals.

brad (brad) n. a thin nail with a small head.

Brad·dock, Edward (brad′ək) 1695–1775, British general in the French and Indian War.

Brad·ford (brad′fərd) **1. William.** 1590?–1657, Pilgrim leader and a governor of the Plymouth Colony. **2.** a city in north-central England. Pop. (1968 est.), 294,400.

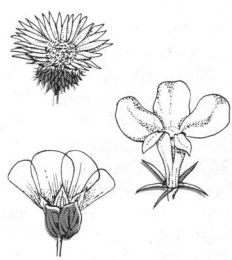

Bracts

brae (brā) n. *Scottish.* slope; hillside. [Old Norse *brā* eyelash (suggesting "the brow of a hill.")]

brag (brag) v.i., v.t., **bragged, brag·ging.** to praise oneself or one's possessions; boast: *He is always bragging about what a good athlete he is.* —n. a boast; boastful talk; bragging. —**brag′ger,** n.

brag·ga·do·ci·o (brag′ə dō′shē ō′) n. pl., **brag·ga·do·ci·os. 1.** empty boasting or bragging. **2.** a person who boasts; braggart.

brag·gart (brag′ərt) n. a person who brags a great deal; boaster. —adj. bragging; boastful.

Brah·ma (brä′mə) n. **1.** in the Hindu religion, the god who created the universe. **2.** any of a breed of cattle native to India, now raised widely in hot or tropical regions. It has a prominent hump over the shoulder and a deep fold of drooping skin under the throat.

Brah·man (brä′mən) n. pl., **Brah·mans.** a member of the highest, priestly caste of Hinduism. Also, **Brahmin.**

Brahma

Brah·man·ism (brä′mə niz′əm) n. the religious and social system of the Brahmans.

Brah·ma·pu·tra (brä′mə pōō′trə) n. a large river in southern Asia, flowing from southwestern Tibet to the Bay of Bengal.

Brah·min (brä′min) n. pl., **Brah·min. 1.** another spelling of **Brahman. 2.** a cultivated and intellectual member of the upper class.

Brahms, Jo·han·nes (brämz; yō hä′nəs) 1833–1897, German composer.

braid (brād) n. **1.** a ropelike strip or band in which three or more strands of hair, straw, leather, or the like are woven together. **2.** a band of fabric woven in this way, used for trimming or binding: *John's band uniform is trimmed with gold braid.* —v.t. **1.** to weave together three or more strands of (hair, straw, leather, or the like). **2.** to make (something) by such weaving: *He braided a belt out of thongs.* **3.** to trim or bind with braid. —**braid′er,** n.

braille (brāl) also, **Braille.** n. a system of writing and printing for the blind, in which the letters are represented by raised dots in patterns that may be recognized and read by touching them. [From Louis *Braille,* 1809–1852, a blind French teacher of the blind who developed the system.]

a	b	c	d	e	f	g	h	i	j	k	l	m

n	o	p	q	r	s	t	u	v	w	x	y	z

Braille alphabet

at; āpe; cär; end; mē; it; īce; hot; ōld; fôrk; wood; fōōl; oil; out; up; turn; sing; thin; this; hw in white; zh in treasure. The symbol ə stands for the sound of a in about, e in taken, i in pencil, o in lemon, and u in circus.

brain (brān) *n.* **1.** the main organ of the nervous system in man and other ani-
mals with backbones. It is enclosed in the skull and located at the upper end of the spinal cord. The brain is composed of a complex mass of nerves and supporting tissue and is divided into several different parts having different func-tions. The brain controls all the voluntary actions of the body and many of the involuntary actions, such as breathing, and in

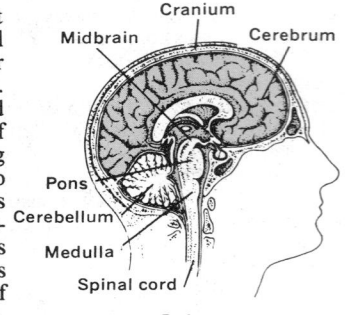

Brain

man it is the center of thought, memory, learning, and the emotions. **2.** *also,* **brains.** mind; intelligence: *That student has real brains.* **3.** *Informal.* a very intelligent person. —*v.t.* **1.** to kill by smashing the skull of. **2.** *Informal.* to hit on the head.
 to rack one's brains or **to cudgel one's brains.** to try hard to remember, understand, or solve something.
brain·child (brān′chīld′) *n. pl.,* **brain·chil·dren** (brān′-chil·drən). *Informal.* an invention, discovery, or original idea.
brain·less (brān′lis) *adj.* without intelligence; foolish; stupid. —**brain′less·ly,** *adv.* —**brain′less·ness,** *n.*
brain·storm (brān′stôrm′) *n. Informal.* a sudden inspi-ration or idea.
brain·wash (brān′wôsh′, brān′wosh′) *v.t.* **1.** to indoc-trinate (a person) so thoroughly that his beliefs, ideals, or way of acting are completely changed: *The captured soldier was brainwashed into accepting the political beliefs of the enemy.* **2.** to persuade (someone) by subtle or high-pres-sure methods: *The salesman brainwashed Paul into buying that car.*
brain·wash·ing (brān′wôsh′ing, brān′wosh′ing) *n.* the action or process by which a person is brainwashed.
brain·y (brā′nē) *adj.,* **brain·i·er, brain·i·est.** *Informal.* very intelligent; bright; clever. —**brain′i·ness,** *n.*
braise (brāz) *v.t.,* **braised, brais·ing.** to cook (meat or vegetables) by browning quickly on all sides in fat and then simmering in a covered pot or pan with a little liquid.
brake¹ (brāk) *n.* a device for slowing or stopping the motion of a wheel or vehicle, especially by means of fric-tion. —*v.,* **braked, brak·ing.** —*v.t.* to cause to slow up or stop by applying a brake: *to brake a bicycle, to brake an automobile.* —*v.i.* to apply a brake: *The driver braked suddenly when he saw the child in the middle of the road.* [Probably from Middle Dutch *braeke* a device for breaking or crushing something.]
brake² (brāk) *n.* an area overgrown with shrubs, bushes, or briers; thicket. [Middle Low German *brake* thicket.]
brake³ (brāk) *n.* a large, coarse fern. *Also,* **bracken.** [Probably short for *bracken;* possibly of Scandinavian ori-gin.]
brake band, a flexible band with a friction lining, ex-tending partially around a wheel or drum and exerting a braking force when tightened against the wheel or drum.
brake drum, a metal cylinder on the hub of a wheel, to which a brake band is applied in order to stop the wheel's motion.
brake·man (brāk′mən) *n. pl.,* **brake·men** (brāk′mən). a member of a train crew who assists the conductor and who formerly operated the brakes.
bram·ble (bram′bəl) *n.* any of a large group of shrubs and plants having thorny stems, such as the blackberry.

bram·bly (bram′ble) *adj.,* **bram·bli·er, bram·bli·est.** **1.** full of brambles. **2.** like a bramble; thorny.
bran (bran) *n.* the ground husks of wheat, rye, or other cereal grains, separated from the flour by sifting. Bran is used to feed livestock and in breakfast cereals and some other foods.
branch (branch) *n. pl.,* **branch·es. 1.** a woody part of a tree, shrub, or bush, growing out and away from the trunk or main stem, or from a main limb. **2.** anything that extends out or away from a main part: *a branch of a deer's antlers, a branch of a river, a branch of a railroad line.* **3.** any part or division of a main body: *a branch of the government, a branch of a family. Algebra is a branch of mathematics.* **4.** a part of an organization located apart from the main unit: *a neighborhood branch of a library, a suburban branch of a store.* —*v.i.* **1.** to put forth bran-ches; spread in branches. **2.** to separate or divide from a main route or body: *Turn left at the point where the path branches.*
 to branch off. to go off in different directions: *The trail branches off west of the stream.*
 to branch out. a. to give forth branches. **b.** to extend or enlarge one's activities, interests, or the like: *The movie company branched out and began making programs for television.*
brand (brand) *n.* **1.** the kind, quality, or make of a prod-uct: *a good brand of chocolate, a new brand of soap.* **2.** a manufacturer's mark identifying a product; trade-mark. **3.** a mark burned on the skin of cattle or other livestock with a hot iron to show who owns them. **4.** the iron used for this purpose. **5.** in former times, a mark burned on the skin of criminals. **6.** a mark of disgrace; stigma: *to bear the brand of a traitor.* **7.** a burning or partly burned piece of wood. —*v.t.* **1.** to mark with a brand: *to brand cattle.* **2.** to put a mark of disgrace on: *His actions in support of the enemy's cause branded him as a traitor.* —**brand′er,** *n.*
Bran·deis, Louis (bran′dīs) 1856–1941, associate jus-tice of the U.S. Supreme Court from 1916 to 1939.
Bran·den·burg (bran′dən burg′) *n.* a historic region of northeastern Germany, now divided between East Ger-many and Poland.
bran·dish (bran′dish) *v.t.* to wave, shake, or swing in a threatening way: *The guard brandished his club at the thief.*
brand-new (brand′nōō′, brand′nyōō′) *adj.* entirely new; newly made or acquired; unused: *a brand-new car, a brand-new house.*
Brandt, Wil·ly (brant; wil′ē) 1913—, German political leader, chancellor of West Germany since 1969.
bran·dy (bran′dē) *n. pl.,* **bran·dies.** an alcoholic beverage distilled from wine or fermented fruit juice. —*v.t.,* **bran-died, bran·dy·ing.** to treat, flavor, or preserve with brandy.
brant (brant) *n. pl.,* **brants** or **brant.** a small, dark wild goose that breeds in arctic regions.
Braque, Georges (bräk; zhôrzh) 1882–1963, French painter.
brash (brash) *adj.* **1.** not respect-ful; rudely bold; impudent: *a brash young man.* **2.** too hasty; rash; reckless: *a brash decision.* —**brash′ly,** *adv.* —**brash′ness,** *n.*
Bra·si·lia (brä sēl′yä) *n.* the capital of Brazil, in the east-cen-tral part of the country. Pop. (1970), 272,002.

Brant

brass (bras) *n. pl.,* **brass·es.**
1. a yellow alloy that is made by combining copper and

zinc. **2.** objects made of brass, such as utensils or ornaments. **3.** *also,* **brasses.** musical wind instruments made of brass or other metal, such as the trombone, trumpet, or tuba. **4.** *Informal.* extreme boldness or rudeness; impudence: *Bill had the brass to borrow his friend's bicycle without asking him.* **5.** *also,* **the brass.** *Informal.* persons of high rank or position, especially high-ranking military officers. —*adj.* made of brass: *a brass tray.*

bras·siere (brə zēr′) *n.* a woman's undergarment worn to support the breasts.

brass·y (bras′ē) *adj.,* **brass·i·er, brass·i·est. 1.** made of or resembling brass. **2.** harsh and loud in tone: *a brassy voice.* **3.** *Informal.* rude and bold; impudent. —**brass′-i·ly,** *adv.* —**brass′i·ness,** *n.*

brat (brat) *n.* a boy or girl who misbehaves or is ill-mannered; spoiled, rude child.

Bra·ti·sla·va (brä′tyi slä′vä) *n.* a city in southern Czechoslovakia, on the Danube River. Pop. (1970), 283,539.

bra·va·do (brə vä′dō) *n.* a showy display of boldness or confidence to hide a true feeling of fear or uncertainty: *The rookie player waited for his turn at bat with an air of bravado.*

brave (brāv) *adj.,* **brav·er, brav·est.** willing to face danger, pain, or difficulty; having or showing courage; without fear: *a brave explorer, brave deeds. The brave captain did not leave the burning ship until all the passengers were in lifeboats.* —*n.* a North American Indian warrior. —*v.t.,* **braved, brav·ing.** to face without fear; meet courageously; defy: *The boy braved the icy water to rescue his drowning friend.* —**brave′ly,** *adv.* —**brave′ness,** *n.*

brav·er·y (brā′vər ē) *n.* the quality of being brave; courage; fearlessness: *The troops showed great bravery in driving off the enemy.*

bra·vo (brä′vō) *interj.* well done; good; excellent. —*n. pl.,* **bra·vos.** a shout of "bravo."

bra·vu·ra (brə vyoor′ə) *n.* **1.** a musical piece or passage requiring great technical skill and power on the part of the performer. **2.** a display of daring; a show of boldness or spirit.

brawl (brôl) *n.* a noisy, rough fight or quarrel: *There was a brawl among the hockey players at the end of the game.* —*v.i.* to fight or quarrel noisily. —**brawl′er,** *n.*

brawn (brôn) *n.* **1.** muscular strength: *That player has more brawn than brains.* **2.** large, strong muscles.

brawn·y (brô′nē) *adj.,* **brawn·i·er, brawn·i·est.** strong; muscular: *a brawny football player.* —**brawn′i·ness,** *n.*

bray (brā) *n.* **1.** a loud, harsh cry made by a donkey or mule. **2.** any sound resembling such a cry: *the bray of trumpets.* —*v.i.* to make a loud, harsh cry or sound. —*v.t.* to make (a cry or sound) in loud, harsh tones: *The sergeant brayed out his orders.*

bra·zen (brā′zən) *adj.* **1.** made of or resembling brass. **2.** bold and impudent: *brazen behavior, a brazen lie.* **3.** loud; harsh. —**bra′zen·ly,** *adv.* —**bra′zen·ness,** *n.*

to brazen it out or **to brazen it through.** to face a situation boldly and without shame; behave defiantly: *The thief brazened it out and refused to confess despite all the evidence against him.*

bra·zier (brā′zhər) *n.* a metal container to hold burning charcoal or other coals, used for heating or lighting, or when furnished with a grill, for cooking food.

Bra·zil (brə zil′) *n.* the largest country in South America, in the northeastern part of the continent, on the Atlantic Ocean. Capital, Brasilia. Area, 3,286,487 sq. mi. Pop. (1971 est.), 95,700,000.

Bra·zil·ian (brə zil′yən) *n.* a person who was born or is living in Brazil. —*adj.* of or relating to Brazil or its people.

Brazil nut, a large, oily nut with a dark, hard shell and a triangular, cream-colored kernel. It is the seed of a large evergreen tree that is native to Brazil.

bra·zil·wood (brə zil′wood′) *n.* a deep red wood of any of several tropical trees native to Brazil. It yields red and purple dyes and is also used in making violin bows and furniture.

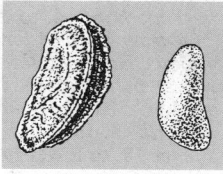

Brazil nut shell and nut

Braz·za·ville (braz′ə vil′) *n.* the capital of the Republic of the Congo, in the southeastern part of the country. Pop. (1970), 175,000.

breach (brēch) *n. pl.,* **breach·es. 1.** a break or gap made in something solid: *Water gushed forth through a breach in the dam.* **2.** a violation of or failure to live up to a law, promise, or obligation: *a breach of duty, to sue a person for breach of contract.* **3.** a breaking of friendly relations; quarrel: *There was a breach between the two brothers.* —*v.t.* to break through; make a gap in: *The attackers breached the enemy lines.*

breach of promise, a breaking of a promise, especially a promise to marry.

bread (bred) *n.* **1.** food made by mixing flour or meal with water or other liquid and then kneading and baking it. **2.** the means of living; livelihood: *He earns his bread by writing.* —*v.t.* to cover with bread crumbs before cooking: *to bread veal cutlets.*

to break bread. to eat, especially with someone else.

bread·bas·ket (bred′bas′kit) *n.* **1.** a basket for holding bread or rolls. **2.** a region that supplies much grain: *The Middle West is sometimes referred to as the breadbasket of the nation.* **3.** *Slang.* the stomach.

bread·fruit (bred′froot′) *n.* **1.** a round, starchy fruit of a tropical tree, native to southern Asia and Polynesia. When baked, it looks and tastes somewhat like bread. **2.** the tree bearing this fruit, having leathery, glossy green leaves and yellow flowers.

bread line, a line of needy people waiting to receive food distributed as charity or government relief.

bread·stuff (bred′stuf′) *n.* the grain, flour, or meal for making bread.

Breadfruit leaf and fruit

breadth (bredth) *n.* **1.** the measure of a thing from side to side; width: *The breadth of the rug is six feet.* **2.** something having a definite and regular width: *a breadth of silk.* **3.** spaciousness; largeness: *the breadth of the ocean.* **4.** freedom from narrowness in attitude or outlook: *The teacher showed great breadth of understanding in dealing with his students.*

bread·win·ner (bred′win′ər) *n.* a person who provides support for his or her family.

break (brāk) *v.,* **broke, bro·ken, break·ing.** —*v.t.* **1.** to make come apart by force; cause to separate into pieces: *He broke a glass. Jim broke his arm during football practice.* **2.** to open the surface of: *to break ground, to*

at; āpe; cär; end; mē; it; īce; hot; ōld; fôrk; wood; fōōl; oil; out; up; turn; sing; thin; **th**is; hw in white; zh in treasure. The symbol ə stands for the sound of **a** in about, **e** in taken, **i** in pencil, **o** in lemon, and **u** in circus.

break the skin. **3.** to put out of order by damaging; make useless: *The little boy broke the typewriter by hitting the keys too hard.* **4.** to destroy the order or completeness of: *The troops broke formation.* **5.** to fail to obey or keep; violate: *He broke the law by driving too fast. She broke her word.* **6.** to escape from: *The prisoner broke jail.* **7.** to weaken the force or effect of; lessen: *The pile of leaves broke his fall.* **8.** to cause to end; end: *Her scream broke the silence.* **9.** to lower in rank; demote: *The captain broke the soldier from sergeant to corporal.* **10.** to train to obey; tame: *The cowboy broke the wild horse.* **11.** to overwhelm with grief or sorrow; crush: *to break a person's heart.* **12.** to go beyond; surpass; excel: *Jim broke the school record in the mile run.* **13.** to make known; disclose: *She broke the news of her brother's car accident to the family.* **14.** to cause (someone) to stop a habit: *to break a child of sucking his thumb.* **15.** to divide (a bill or coin) into smaller units: *Can you break a five-dollar bill?* —*v.i.* **1.** to come apart by force; separate into pieces: *The mirror broke when she dropped it.* **2.** to become useless because of damage: *The clock broke.* **3.** to move away suddenly: *The runners broke from the starting line. The water broke through the dam.* **4.** to divide up or scatter: *The clouds broke and the sun shone again.* **5.** to take place, come into being, or become known: *The day is breaking. The story broke in the morning newspapers.* **6.** to change or fall off suddenly and abruptly: *His voice broke as he described his years of poverty.* **7.** to become overwhelmed with sorrow: *The little boy's heart broke when his dog died.* **8.** (of a pitched baseball) to curve near or over home plate. —*n.* **1.** the result of breaking; broken place; crack: *a break in a fence.* **2.** the act of breaking. **3.** a sudden rush or dash: *The prisoner made a break for freedom.* **4.** beginning; start: *the break of day.* **5.** a sudden change or interruption: *a break in the weather, a break in peaceful relations between countries.* **6.** a brief rest period; pause: *After an hour of marching the troops took a ten-minute break.* **7.** *Slang.* a stroke of luck; chance: *a lucky break, a bad break.*

to break away. a. to start before the starting signal is given. **b.** to escape suddenly; get away: *One of the prisoners broke away.*

to break down. a. to fail to work properly; stop working: *The car broke down and we had to walk.* **b.** to have a physical or mental collapse; become ill. **c.** to give way to emotion: *She broke down and cried when she learned of the tragedy.* **d.** to separate or divide into smaller or simpler parts; analyze: *to break down a chemical compound.*

to break in. a. to make ready for use or work: *to break in a new pair of shoes. The grocer broke in the new delivery boy.* **b.** to enter by force: *A thief broke in by the back door.* **c.** to interrupt: *He broke in with a question while the teacher was explaining the problem.*

to break into. a. to enter by force: *The robbers broke into the apartment while the family was away.* **b.** to interrupt: *The announcer broke into the regular program with a news bulletin.* **c.** to burst forth suddenly with: *The audience broke into laughter.*

to break off. a. to stop suddenly: *She broke off in the middle of her speech to turn a page of her notes.* **b.** to stop being friendly: *He has broken off with all his old friends since he moved away.*

to break out. a. to start suddenly and unexpectedly: *A fire broke out.* **b.** to become covered with a rash or pimples: *His back has broken out from poison ivy.* **c.** to make an escape: *to break out of jail.*

to break up. a. to separate or scatter: *The ice on the pond is breaking up.* **b.** to put an end to; stop: *The police broke up the fight.* **c.** to make or become upset: *The sad news*

broke her up. **d.** to end a relationship: *The two friends broke up.* **e.** *Informal.* to laugh or cause to laugh: *His jokes always break me up.*

to break with. to stop being friendly with: *Dick broke with John after their quarrel.*

break·a·ble (brā'kə bəl) *adj.* that can be broken: *a breakable glass.* —*n.* something that is easily broken.

break·age (brā'kij) *n.* **1.** the act of breaking. **2.** something broken. **3.** damage caused by breaking: *The store charged me for the breakage when I accidently dropped a dish.* **4.** the cost for such damage.

break·down (brāk'doun') *n.* **1.** a failure to work properly: *The breakdown of the car was caused by a broken axle.* **2.** a collapse of one's physical or mental health: *After the death of her father, she suffered a breakdown.* **3.** a separation of something into smaller or simpler parts; analysis: *The reporters were given a breakdown of the facts that the police had about the murder case.*

break·er (brā'kər) *n.* **1.** a large wave that foams as it breaks on the rocks or shore. **2.** a person or thing that breaks.

break·fast (brek'fəst) *n.* the first meal of the day, usually eaten in the morning. —*v.i.* to eat breakfast. [*Break* + *fast*²; because it is the meal that *breaks* the night's *fast.*]

break·neck (brāk'nek') *adj.* extremely dangerous: *The racer drove at a breakneck speed in order to win.*

break·through (brāk'throō') *n.* an important development, achievement, or discovery that helps to further progress in any field of knowledge or activity: *The invention of the microscope was a major breakthrough in science.*

break·up (brāk'up') *n.* **1.** a separation into smaller parts: *The warm weather caused the breakup of ice on the river.* **2.** a stopping or ending: *the breakup of a friendship.*

break·wa·ter (brāk'wô'tər) *n.* a wall or barrier that protects an area from the force of waves.

bream (brēm) *n. pl.,* **breams** or **bream.** **1.** any of various freshwater fish of Europe. **2.** a freshwater sunfish of the southeastern United States.

breast (brest) *n.* **1.** the front part of the human body between the neck and the abdomen; chest. **2.** the corresponding upper, front part of an animal's body. **3.** either of the two milk glands of women. **4.** something like the breast: *the breast of a hill.* **5.** the breast thought of as the center of emotions: *Pride filled his breast.* —*v.t.* to struggle against; oppose: *The lifeguard breasted the waves in an attempt to reach the drowning man.*

to make a clean breast of. to make complete confession of.

breast·bone (brest'bōn') *n.* the flat, narrow bone in the center of the breast to which the ribs are joined; sternum.

breast·plate (brest'plāt') *n.* a piece of armor worn to protect the chest.

breast stroke, a stroke made while swimming face down, in which both arms go out in front of the head, and then are swept in an arc to the sides and back.

breast·work (brest'wurk') *n.* a low, hastily built wall for defense.

breath (breth) *n.* **1.** air drawn into and forced out of the lungs in breathing. **2.** the act or process of breathing; respiration: *The swimmer held his breath as he swam underwater.* **3.** a single act or instance of breathing: *The sick old man's chest hurt with every breath he took.* **4.** the ability to breathe freely and easily: *After the race, the runner was out of breath.* **5.** air forced out from the lungs, especially in the form of vapor: *We blew on the window and saw our breath.* **6.** a slight current of air: *There is not a breath of air in this hot room.* **7.** a whisper or hint; suggestion: *the first breath of spring.*

below one's breath. in a whisper.

B

in the same breath or **in the next breath.** at almost the same time; immediately afterwards.

to catch one's breath. a. to stop or pause for breath; rest; relax. **b.** to gasp: *The boy caught his breath when the tightrope walker slipped and almost fell.*

to take one's breath away. to overwhelm or stun: *The view from the mountaintop took our breath away.*

under one's breath. in a very low voice; in a whisper: *He made an insulting remark under his breath as he left the room.*

breathe (breth) *v.,* **breathed, breath·ing.** —*v.i.* **1.** to draw air into the lungs and force it out: *The high altitude of the mountains often makes breathing difficult.* **2.** to be alive; live. **3.** to stop or pause for breath; rest; relax. **4.** to send out a fragrance or impression: *The field breathed of newly mowed hay. His manner breathed of self-confidence.* —*v.t.* **1.** to draw into and force out from the lungs, as air. **2.** to give out or instill: *Margaret's enthusiastic help breathed new life into John's campaign for class president.* **3.** to send out by breathing: *We breathed a sigh of relief when the lost child was found.* **4.** to whisper or say confidentially: *She promised not to breathe a word about his secret.* **5.** to allow to rest or recover breath: *The jockey breathed his horse after the race.*

to breathe one's last. to die.

breath·er (brē'thər) *n.* **1.** *Informal.* a short rest period: *Ted stopped studying and took a breather.* **2.** a person who breathes, especially in a particular way.

breathing space (brē'thing) a space or area in which a person can breathe or move about freely: *There was no breathing space in the crowded room.*

breath·less (breth'lis) *adj.* **1.** out of breath: *The mountain climbers were breathless when they reached the top.* **2.** in a state of fear or excitement; tense: *The children were breathless as they watched the lion-taming act.* —**breath'·less·ly,** *adv.* —**breath'less·ness,** *n.*

breath·tak·ing (breth'tā'king) *adj.* causing great excitement or pleasure; thrilling; overwhelming: *He gazed at the breathtaking beauty of the sunset reflected in the lake.*

Breck·in·ridge, John Cab·ell (brek'ən rij'; kab'əl) 1821–1875, the vice-president of the United States from 1857 to 1861. He later became a Confederate general.

bred (bred) the past tense and past participle of **breed.**

breech (brēch) *n. pl.,* **breech·es** (brē'chiz). **1.** the part of a gun or other firearm behind or at the rear of the barrel. **2.** the lower or back part of anything, such as a pulley. **3.** the lower, rear part of the body; buttocks.

breech·cloth (brēch'klôth') *n. pl.,* **breech·cloths** (brēch'-klôthz', brēch'klôths'). a piece of cloth worn to cover the loins; loincloth.

breech·clout (brēch'klout') *n.* another word for **breechcloth.**

breech·es (brich'iz) *n., pl.* **1.** trousers reaching to or just below the knees. **2.** *Informal.* any trousers.

breech·es buoy (brich'iz) a device consisting of a pair of short canvas pants attached to a life preserver, hung from a pulley that slides along a rope strung between two ships or between a ship and a shore point. It is used for rescuing people from sinking ships or for transferring them from one ship to another.

breech·load·er (brēch'lō'dər) *n.* a firearm that is loaded at the breech instead of at the muzzle.

breech·load·ing (brēch'lō'ding) *adj.* (of a firearm) loading at the breech instead of at the muzzle.

breed (brēd) *v.,* **bred, breed·ing.** —*v.t.* **1.** to raise (plants or animals), especially in order to develop new or improved kinds: *Mr. Jones breeds cattle.* **2.** to give rise to; cause; produce: *War and famine breed human misery.* **3.** to bring up or train; rear: *Jim was bred to be a good sport*

at all times. **4.** to mate: *They bred the stallion with the mare.* —*v.i.* **1.** to produce young: *Certain animals breed only in the winter.* **2.** to come into being; develop: *Disease breeds in poor living conditions.* —*n.* **1.** a particular strain or variety of a species of plant or animal. *Beagles are a breed of dog.* **2.** a kind or sort of anything; type: *The pioneers of the American West were a hardy breed of men.*

breed·er (brē'dər) *n.* **1.** a person who breeds plants or animals. **2.** a plant or animal that produces young, especially a plant or animal kept for this purpose.

breeder reactor, a nuclear reactor that produces at least as much fissionable material as it consumes. Also, **breeder pile.**

breed·ing (brē'ding) *n.* **1.** the bringing up or training of the young, especially as shown in a person's manners or behavior: *His breeding wouldn't allow him to do anything dishonest.* **2.** the act of producing young. **3.** the reproduction of plants or animals, usually to bring about improvements in the young.

Breed's Hill (brēdz) see **Bunker Hill.**

breeze (brēz) *n.* **1.** a light current of air; soft, gentle wind. **2.** *Informal.* something easy to do: *Sally thought the English test was a breeze.* —*v.i.,* **breezed, breez·ing.** *Informal.* to move in a relaxed or brisk manner: *Mary breezed into the room.*

to breeze through. to do or complete easily and quickly: *Sam breezed through his first job interview.*

breeze·way (brēz'wā') *n.* a roofed passageway, open at the sides, between two buildings or structures, as between a house and a garage.

breez·y (brē'zē) *adj.,* **breez·i·er, breez·i·est. 1.** having gentle winds: *breezy shores, a breezy day.* **2.** lively or carefree; cheerful: *a breezy manner of speaking.* —**breez'i·ly,** *adv.* —**breez'i·ness,** *n.*

Brem·en (brem'ən, brā'mən) *n.* a port city in northern West Germany. Pop. (1970), 582,300.

Bren·ner (bren'ər) *n.* a mountain pass in the Alps, on the border between Austria and Italy.

Bres·lau (bres'lou, brez'lou) *n.* see **Wroclaw.**

breth·ren (breth'rən) a plural of **brother.** ▲ used chiefly for people who belong to the same organization, especially a religious order or a fraternal society.

Bret·on (bret'ən) *n.* **1.** a person who was born or is living in Brittany. **2.** the Celtic language spoken by Bretons. —*adj.* of or relating to Brittany, its people, or their language.

breve (brēv) *n.* a mark (˘) placed over a vowel or syllable to show that it has a short sound.

bre·vi·ar·y (brē'vē er'ē) *n. pl.,* **bre·vi·ar·ies.** in the Roman Catholic and Orthodox churches, a book or books containing prayers, lessons, hymns, and special readings to be recited each day by priests and members of certain religious orders.

brev·i·ty (brev'ə tē) *n.* shortness, especially in speech or writing.

brew (broo) *v.t.* **1.** to make (beer, ale, or a similar beverage) by steeping, boiling, and fermenting malt and hops. **2.** to prepare (a nonalcoholic beverage, such as tea or coffee) by steeping, boiling, or mixing. **3.** to plan or bring about; plot: *to brew trouble* —*v.i.* **1.** to be brewed.

---

at; āpe; cär; end; mē; it; īce; hot; ōld; fôrk; wood; fōōl; oil; out; up; turn; sing; thin; this; hw in white; zh in treasure. The symbol ə stands for the sound of a in about, e in taken, i in pencil, o in lemon, and u in circus.

2. to form or develop: *There is a storm brewing in the west.* —*n.* **1.** a drink prepared by brewing. **2.** the amount that is brewed at one time.

brew·er (broo′ər) *n.* a person who brews, especially one whose business or trade is the brewing of beer or ale.

brew·er·y (broo′ər ē) *n. pl.,* **brew·er·ies.** a place where beer, ale, or other similar beverages are brewed.

brew·ing (broo′ing) *n.* **1.** the process by which beer, ale, or similar beverages are made. **2.** the amount brewed at one time.

Brezh·nev, Le·o·nid (brezh′nev; lā′ō nēd′) 1906—, Soviet Communist Party leader.

bri·ar¹ (brī′ər) *also,* **bri·er.** *n.* **1.** another word for **tree heath. 2.** the root of the tree heath, used for making tobacco pipes. **3.** a tobacco pipe made from this root. [French *bruyère* heath, heather; of Celtic origin.]

bri·ar² (brī′ər) another spelling of **brier¹.**

bri·ar·root (brī′ər root′, brī′ər root′) *also,* **bri·er·root.** *n.* another word for **briarwood.**

bri·ar·wood (brī′ər wood′) *also,* **bri·er·wood.** *n.* **1.** the wood of the root of the tree heath, used in making tobacco pipes. **2.** a tobacco pipe made from this wood.

bribe (brīb) *n.* **1.** money or gifts given or offered to a person in a position of trust or responsibility to persuade him to do something illegal or dishonest: *The speeder offered the policeman a bribe to let him go without a ticket.* **2.** anything that influences or persuades. —*v.t.,* **bribed, brib·ing. 1.** to give or offer a bribe to: *The murder suspect tried to bribe the witness to change his testimony.* **2.** to influence or persuade with a bribe.

brib·er·y (brī′bər ē) *n. pl.,* **bri·ber·ies.** the act or practice of giving, offering, or accepting a bribe.

bric-a-brac (brik′ə brak′) *n.* small decorative objects; knickknacks.

brick (brik) *n.* **1.** a molded, usually rectangular, block of clay baked by fire in a kiln or oven, or by the sun, used in building and paving. **2.** bricks as a material for building: *a fireplace made of brick.* **3.** something shaped like a brick: *a brick of gold.* —*v.t.* **1.** to enclose, cover or wall with bricks: *to brick up a doorway.* **2.** to build or pave with bricks. —*adj.* made of brick: *a brick house.*

brick·bat (brik′bat′) *n.* **1.** a piece of brick or other material, especially when thrown at someone. **2.** *Informal.* an insulting or critical remark.

brick·lay·er (brik′lā′ər) *n.* a person whose business or trade is building with bricks.

brick·lay·ing (brik′lā′ing) *n.* the act or business of building with bricks.

brick·work (brik′wurk′) *n.* work made of bricks.

brick·yard (brik′yärd′) *n.* a place where bricks are made or sold.

brid·al (brīd′əl) *adj.* of or relating to a bride or wedding: *a bridal bouquet, a bridal suite.*

bride (brīd) *n.* a woman newly married or about to be married.

bride·groom (brīd′groom′, brīd′groom′) *n.* a man newly married or about to be married.

brides·maid (brīdz′mād′) *n.* a woman who attends a bride at her wedding.

bridge¹ (brij) *n.* **1.** any structure built across a river, railroad track, highway, or other obstacle to allow passage for people or vehicles. **2.** the upper, bony ridge of the nose. **3.** the curved part of a pair of eyeglasses that joins the two lenses and rests on the bridge of the nose. **4.** one or more false teeth in a mounting fastened to the adjacent natural teeth. **5.** a raised structure on a deck of a ship, from which the ship is navigated and steered. **6.** in certain string instruments, such as violins and cellos, a thin piece of wood or other material over which the strings are stretched.

—*v.t.,* **bridged, bridg·ing. 1.** to build a bridge or bridges over: *to bridge a river.* **2.** to go across; span: *An overpass bridged the highway.* **3.** to serve as a way of overcoming: *Setting up a student exchange program may help to bridge the gap in understanding between the two countries.* [Old English *brycg* a structure over water.]

to burn one's bridges behind one or **to burn one's bridges.** to destroy all ways or chances for return.

bridge² (brij) *n.* a card game played by four players in teams of two. [Earlier *biritch* a card game, possibly from Russian *birich* announcer.]

bridge·head (brij′hed′) *n.* a military position established on enemy territory to which men and supplies may be sent so that further advance may be made.

Bridge·port (brij′pôrt′) *n.* a city in southwestern Connecticut. Pop. (1970), 156,542.

Bridge·town (brij′toun′) *n.* the capital and largest city of Barbados, on the southwestern coast of the island. Pop. (1970), 8,789.

bridge·work (brij′wurk′) *n.* a dental bridge or bridges.

bri·dle (brīd′əl) *n.* **1.** the part of a horse's harness that fits over the head, including the bit and reins, used to guide or control the animal. **2.** anything that restrains or controls. —*v.,* **bri·dled, bri·dling.** —*v.t.* **1.** to put a bridle on. **2.** to restrain or control; curb: *She could not bridle her anger at having been called a liar.* —*v.i.* to throw back the head and draw in the chin to show anger, indignation, or scorn: *Mrs. Smith bridled at the rude treatment she received from the saleslady.*

bridle path, a path for horseback riding.

brief (brēf) *adj.* **1.** short in time; ending quickly: *There was a brief interruption of the program for a news bulletin. His friend came for a brief visit.* **2.** using few words; concise: *The teacher asked Henry to give a brief summary of the story.* —*n.* **1.** a summary of the facts, points of law, and other material important to a case, prepared by a lawyer as the basis for arguing a case in court. **2. briefs.** short, close-fitting underpants. —*v.t.* to give important details to: *The scout leader briefed the boys before the camping trip.* —**brief′ly,** *adv.* —**brief′ness,** *n.*

in brief. in a few words; in short: *In brief, we had a wonderful time at the party.*

brief·case (brēf′kās′) *n.* a flat case with a handle, used especially for carrying papers and books.

bri·er¹ (brī′ər) *also,* **bri·ar.** *n.* **1.** any thorny shrub or plant, especially the wild rose. **2.** a thorny stem or a thorn on such a stem. [Old English *brær, brēr* this shrub.]

bri·er² (brī′ər) another spelling of **briar¹.**

bri·er·root (brī′ər root′, brī′ər root′) another spelling of **briarroot.**

bri·er·wood (brī′ər wood′) another spelling of **briarwood.**

brig (brig) *n.* **1.** a two-masted ship with square sails. **2.** a place on a ship for confining prisoners. **3.** a naval prison.

Brig. 1. Brigade. **2.** Brigadier.

bri·gade (bri gād′) *n.* **1.** a military unit made up of two or more battalions and forming part of a division. **2.** a group of people organized for a particular purpose or a specific function: *a fire brigade.*

Brig

brig·a·dier (brig′ə dēr′) *n.* see **brigadier general.**

brigadier general, a commissioned officer in the U.S. Army, Air Force, or Marines, ranking above a colonel and below a major general.

brig·and (brig′ənd) *n.* a robber or bandit, especially one who is a member of a band of roving outlaws.

brig·an·tine (brig′ən tēn′) *n.* a two-masted ship having a square-rigged foremast and a fore-and-aft-rigged mainmast.

bright (brīt) *adj.* **1.** giving or reflecting much light; filled with light; shining: *The sun was so bright it hurt your eyes when you looked out* (Ernest Hemingway). *The waxed floor had a bright finish.* **2.** of brilliant color; vivid: *a bright yellow dress.* **3.** having or showing much intelligence; quick-witted; clever: *a bright person, a bright reply.* **4.** favorable or hopeful: *a bright future.* **5.** lively; cheerful: *The children were bright and gay at the party.* —*adv.* in a bright manner; brightly: *The stars shone bright.* —**bright′ly,** *adv.* —**bright′ness,** *n.*

bright·en (brīt′ən) *v.t.* to make bright or brighter: *Painting the walls white brightened the room.* —*v.i.* to become bright or brighter: *The day brightened after the rain. Her face brightened with a smile.*

bril·liance (bril′yəns) *n.* the state or quality of being brilliant. Also, **bril·lian·cy** (bril′yən sē).

bril·liant (bril′yənt) *adj.* **1.** shining or sparkling with light or luster: *brilliant spotlights, brilliant stars.* **2.** splendid or outstanding; magnificent: *The hockey team played a brilliant game to win the championship.* **3.** having or showing much intelligence, ability, or talent: *He is a brilliant mathematician.* **4.** very rich in color; vivid: *Brilliant flags flew in the breeze.* —*n.* a gem, especially a diamond, cut with many facets to increase its sparkle. —**bril′liant·ly,** *adv.*

brim (brim) *n.* **1.** the upper edge or rim of a cup, bowl, or similar object: *My glass is filled to the brim.* **2.** a projecting edge or rim: *the brim of a hat.* —*v.i.,* **brimmed, brimming.** to be full to the brim; overflow: *Her eyes brimmed with tears.*

brim·ful (brim′fool′) *adj.* full to the brim; completely full: *a glass brimful of milk.*

brim·stone (brim′stōn′) *n.* another word for **sulfur.**

brin·dle (brind′əl) *adj.* brindled. —*n.* **1.** a brindled color. **2.** an animal having a brindled color.

brin·dled (brind′əld) *adj.* gray or brownish-yellow with irregular, dark streaks or spots: *a brindled cow.*

brine (brīn) *n.* **1.** water that is full of salt, used especially for pickling or preserving food. **2.** the sea or its water.

bring (bring) *v.t.,* **brought, bring·ing. 1.** to carry or cause (someone or something) to come with oneself: *Jerry brought Mike home from school with him. Bring all your books home.* **2.** to cause to come; attract; draw: *What brings you here? The news brought tears to her eyes.* **3.** to cause to reach a particular state or condition: *Bring the water to a boil. The firemen quickly brought the fire under control.* **4.** to cause to come about or happen; result in; produce: *The floods brought disaster to the town.* **5.** to cause (someone or oneself) to adopt a course of action or belief; persuade: *He couldn't bring himself to lie to his friend.* **6.** to sell for: *The car brought a high price.*

to bring about. to cause to happen; cause; accomplish: *Moving to a new town brought about many changes in his life.*

to bring around or **to bring round. a.** to cause (someone) to adopt a course of action or belief; convince; persuade. **b.** to bring back to consciousness; revive.

to bring forth. a. to produce (young or fruit). **b.** to make known; reveal: *The testimony of the new witness brought forth new evidence.*

to bring forward. to introduce; present: *The committee brought arguments forward in support of their plan to build a new gymnasium.*

to bring in. a. to produce, as profits: *The candy store brings in about $100 a day.* **b.** to give or submit (a verdict): *The jury brought in a verdict of "not guilty".*

to bring off. to accomplish successfully: *to bring off a business deal.*

to bring on. to lead to; cause: *The bad weather brought on my cold.*

to bring out. a. to make clear or evident; reveal: *That's not the point I want to bring out.* **b.** to introduce or present to the public: *to bring out a new movie.*

to bring to. to bring back to consciousness; revive.

to bring up. a. to take care of during childhood; rear or educate: *His grandmother brought him up after his parents died.* **b.** to introduce to notice or consideration: *May I bring up an important question?* **c.** to cause to pause or stop: *The rudeness of her reply brought him up short.*

▲ **Bring** and **take** both mean "to carry from one place to another." **Bring** usually describes carrying something *into* a place or *to* a person; **take** usually describes carrying something *away* from a place or *from* a person: *He took the books back to the library and brought me some new ones.*

brink (bringk) *n.* **1.** the edge or margin of a steep place, as of a cliff or the bank of a river. **2.** the point at which something is likely to happen or begin; verge: *The lost child was on the brink of tears.*

brin·y (brī′nē) *adj.,* **brin·i·er, brin·i·est.** of or like brine; salty.

bri·quette (bri ket′) also, **bri·quet.** *n.* a molded block of coal dust or other material, used for fuel.

Bris·bane (briz′bān) *n.* a port city in eastern Australia. Pop. (1969 est.), 693,100.

brisk (brisk) *adj.* **1.** quick and lively; energetic; vigorous: *The hikers walked at a brisk pace.* **2.** keen and bracing; invigorating: *a brisk autumn wind.* —**brisk′ly,** *adv.* —**brisk′ness,** *n.*

bris·ket (bris′kit) *n.* **1.** a cut of meat from the breast of an animal, especially a cow or steer. **2.** the breast of an animal.

bris·tle (bris′əl) *n.* **1.** a coarse, short, stiff hair, especially of a hog: *She had a brush made of hog bristles.* **2.** something resembling this: *My toothbrush has nylon bristles.* —*v.,* **bris·tled, bris·tling.** —*v.i.* **1.** to have the hairs on the back rise stiffly, as in fear, anger, excitement: *The cat bristled at the sight of the dog.* **2.** to show anger or irritation: *I bristled at his insults.* **3.** to rise stiffly: *The dog's hair bristled as we approached.* —*v.t.* **1.** to cause to rise stiffly: *The porcupine bristled his quills.* **2.** to furnish with bristles.

to bristle with. to be thick with or full of: *The shore bristled with boats. He bristled with excitement.*

bris·tly (bris′lē) *adj.,* **bris·tli·er, bris·tli·est. 1.** like bristles: *The tramp had bristly hairs on his chin.* **2.** easily angered or irritated: *Our neighbor is a bristly, old man.*

Bris·tol (bris′əl) *n.* a port city in southwestern England. Pop. (1971), 426,170.

Brit., Britain; British.

Brit·ain (brit′ən) *n.* see **Great Britain.**

Bri·tan·ni·a (bri tan′ē ə) *n.* **1.** Great Britain and Ireland. **2.** the British Empire. **3.** a female figure thought of as representing Great Britain or the British Empire.

at; āpe; cär; end; mē; it; īce; hot; ōld; fôrk; wood; fool; oil; out; up; turn; sing; thin; this; hw in white; zh in treasure. The symbol ə stands for the sound of **a** in about, **e** in taken, **i** in pencil, **o** in lemon, and **u** in circus.

britch·es (brich′iz) *n. Informal.* another spelling of **breeches.**

Brit·i·cism (brit′i siz′əm) *n.* a word, phrase, or idiom used only or mainly by the British. *Lorry* is a Briticism for *truck.*

Brit·ish (brit′ish) *adj.* of, relating to, or characteristic of Great Britain or its people. —*n.* **the British.** the people of Great Britain.

British Columbia, the westernmost province of Canada, on the Pacific Ocean. Area, 366,255 sq. mi. Pop. (1976), 2,466,608.

British Commonwealth of Nations, see **Commonwealth of Nations.**

British Empire, formerly, all the countries, colonies, dependencies, and protectorates that owed allegiance to the British Crown.

British English, the English language as spoken and written in Great Britain.

● The British writer George Bernard Shaw once said "England and America are two countries separated by the same language." He meant that, although they speak the same language, people from England and people from America sometimes have trouble understanding each other. Words in **British English** and American English sometimes differ in spelling, pronunciation, meaning, or usage. If you have ever read a newspaper from Great Britain, you may have noticed such words as *honour, centre,* or *traveller.* You were probably able to guess that these were the British spellings of *honor, center,* and *traveler.*

The pronunciation of British English differs from the pronunciation of American English in various ways. The most obvious difference is the British broad *a,* as in *brass, can't, bath* and *dance.* Other differences in British pronunciation appear in such words as *clerk* and *derby,* in which the *er* is said like the *ar* in *car,* and *schedule,* which begins with an *sh* sound rather than the *sk* sound that American speakers use.

Most words have the same meaning in Britain that they have in America. The greatest number of words that are not common to both British and American speakers are words that were created after the American Revolution, especially those words that describe industrial or scientific inventions or processes. In England, an elevator is called a *lift,* the hood of a car is called the *bonnet,* the trunk of a car is called the *boot,* and gasoline is called *petrol.*

The differences in grammar in British and American English are very slight. One very obvious difference is in the British use of a plural verb with a singular collective noun, as in *Manchester are confident of winning the soccer game.*

Despite all these differences, if you were to pick up an English newspaper there would probably be only a few words or phrases that you could not understand. In the last fifty or so years there has been increased communication between speakers of American English and British English. This greater communication, caused by the exchange of books, movies, popular music, and television shows, the stationing of American soldiers in Britain during wartime, and increased trade and travel between the two countries, has helped to make the differences between American and British English become smaller and smaller. As the differences are lessened, it becomes clear that we are joined to, rather than separated from, England by our speaking the same language.

Brit·ish·er (brit′i shər) *n.* a person who was born in or is a subject of Great Britain, especially of England.

British Guiana, see **Guyana.**

British Honduras, a former British possession on the northeastern coast of Central America, on the Caribbean, now Belize.

British Isles, a group of islands off the western coast of continental Europe, including Great Britain, Ireland, and many smaller islands.

British thermal unit, a unit for measuring the amount of heat needed to raise the temperature of one pound of water one degree Fahrenheit.

British West Indies, British islands in the West Indies, including the Bahamas, the Windward Islands, Leeward Islands, British Virgin Islands, and others.

Brit·on (brit′ən) *n.* **1.** a person who was born or who is living in Great Britain; Britisher. **2.** a member of an ancient Celtic people who lived in southern Britain at the time of the Roman invasion.

Brit·ta·ny (brit′ən ē) *n.* a historic region in northwestern France, between the English Channel and the Bay of Biscay.

brit·tle (brit′əl) *adj.* likely to break or snap; easily broken: *brittle twigs, brittle fingernails.*

bro., brother.

broach (brōch) *n. pl.,* **broach·es.** a pointed cutting tool driven or pulled through rough holes to enlarge or shape them. —*v.t.* **1.** to mention or suggest for the first time; introduce: *He broached the subject of going to camp for the summer to his parents.* **2.** to make a hole in so as to draw out a liquid; tap: *to broach a keg of wine.*

broad (brôd) *adj.* **1.** large from one side to the other; wide: *The broad highway had four traffic lanes.* **2.** large in size; spacious: *We drove across the broad plains for hours before seeing another car.* **3.** open-minded; tolerant: *a broad outlook on life.* **4.** having a wide range; not limited or narrow: *He has a broad knowledge of rocketry.* **5.** concerning the main parts or features; not detailed; general: *The witness could give only a broad description of the thief.* **5.** easy to understand; clear; obvious: *Sam gave us a broad hint that he knew about the surprise party.* **6.** clear and open: *A gang of men robbed the bank in broad daylight.* **7.** (of vowel sounds) formed with the mouth wide open and the back of the tongue in a low, flat position. The *a* in *father* is broad. —**broad′ly,** *adv.* —**broad′ness,** *n.*

broad·ax (brôd′aks′) *also,* **broad·axe.** *n. pl.,* **broad·ax·es.** **1.** an ax with a broad blade, used especially to cut logs. **2.** an ancient weapon with a wide blade.

broad·cast (brôd′kast′) *v.,* **broad·cast** or **broad·cast·ed,** **broad·cast·ing.** —*v.t.* **1.** to send out (information or entertainment) by radio or television. **2.** to make widely known or spread: *He broadcast the secret to the whole school.* **3.** to scatter over a large area: *to broadcast seed.* —*v.i.* to send out by radio or television: *That television channel does not broadcast early in the morning.* —*n.* **1.** something that is broadcast by radio or television, especially a program: *He will appear on tomorrow's news broadcast.* **2.** the act of broadcasting, especially by radio or television. —*adj.* **1.** relating to or sent by radio or television broadcast. **2.** scattered over a large area: *broadcast seed.* —*adv.* by scattering over a large area: *to sow broadcast.* —**broad′cast′er,** *n.*

broad·cloth (brôd′klôth′) *n.* **1.** a smooth, closely woven cotton or silk fabric, used especially in making shirts, pajamas, and dresses. **2.** a closely woven woolen fabric, used especially in suits and coats.

broad·en (brôd′ən) *v.t.* to make broad or broader: *The workmen broadened the road.* —*v.i.* to become broad or broader: *Mike's views of how other people live broadened after traveling in Europe for a year.*

broad jump **1.** a field event in which the contestant

jumps for distance from a running start or from a standing position. **2.** such a jump. Also, **long jump.**

broad·loom (brôd′lōōm′) *n.* a carpet woven on a wide loom, usually in widths ranging from six to eighteen feet.

broad·mind·ed (brôd′mīn′did) *adj.* tolerant of views, beliefs, and behavior that are unconventional or different from one's own; liberal; not bigoted: *My grandfather has a broad-minded attitude toward the opinions and actions of young people.* —**broad·′mind′ed·ly,** *adv.* —**broad·′mind′ed·ness,** *n.*

broad·side (brôd′sīd′) *n.* **1.** the whole side of a boat or ship above the water line. **2.** the firing of all the guns on one side of a ship at the same time. **3.** a written or spoken attack against someone or something: *The candidate for mayor delivered a broadside against his opponent.* —*adv.* with the side turned; on the side; sideward: *The wave caught the boat broadside, almost capsizing it.*

broad·sword (brôd′sôrd′) *n.* a sword with a broad, flat blade, made for cutting rather than thrusting.

Broad·way (brôd′wā′) *n.* a street running through New York City, noted for its brightly lighted entertainment and theater district and as the center of the American theater industry.

bro·cade (brō kād′) *n.* a heavy fabric woven with raised designs. —*v.t.,* **bro·cad·ed, bro·cad·ing.** to weave (fabric) with a raised design.

broc·co·li (brok′ə lē) *n.* **1.** the thick green stems and flower buds of a plant related to the cabbage, cooked and eaten as a vegetable. **2.** the plant itself.

bro·chure (brō shoor′) *n.* a small pamphlet; booklet.

Brock·ton (brok′tən) *n.* a city in southeastern Massachusetts. Pop. (1970), 89,040.

bro·gan (brō′gən) *n.* a heavy, sturdy shoe, especially one that reaches to the ankle.

brogue[1] (brōg) *n.* a thick or rough accent in the pronunciation of English, especially an Irish accent. [Possibly from Irish *barróg* hold, grip, in the sense of a hold on the tongue; possibly from *brogue*[2]; because the Irish and the Scottish people who spoke with this accent wore such shoes.]

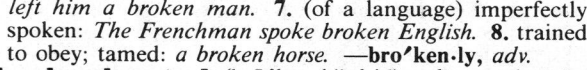

Broccoli

brogue[2] (brōg) *n.* **1.** a heavy, sturdy shoe of untanned hide, formerly worn in Ireland and Scotland. **2.** a shoe similar to an oxford, usually decorated with perforations. [Irish and Scottish Gaelic *brōg* shoe.]

broil (broil) *v.t.* **1.** to cook by fire or direct heat; grill: *to broil chicken on a charcoal grill.* **2.** to make very hot; scorch. —*v.i.* **1.** to be cooked by direct heat: *The meat broiled quickly.* **2.** to become very hot: *Our skin broiled under the hot sun at the beach.* —*n.* something broiled, especially meat.

broil·er (broi′lər) *n.* **1.** a pan, rack, or part of a stove used for broiling food. **2.** a chicken, usually young and tender, for broiling.

broke (brōk) *v.* the past tense of **break.** —*adj. Informal.* having little or no money.

bro·ken (brō′kən) *v.* the past participle of **break.** —*adj.* **1.** separated into pieces by force: *a broken window, a broken arm.* **2.** marked by interruptions; not complete: *a broken electrical circuit.* **3.** not smooth or even; rough: *We rode over miles of broken ground.* **4.** not kept or fulfilled: *a broken promise.* **5.** not working; damaged: *a broken television set.* **6.** overwhelmed by grief or sorrow; crushed, as in spirit or strength: *His many years in prison*

left him a broken man. **7.** (of a language) imperfectly spoken: *The Frenchman spoke broken English.* **8.** trained to obey; tamed: *a broken horse.* —**bro′ken·ly,** *adv.*

bro·ken-heart·ed (brō′kən här′tid) *adj.* crushed by grief or disappointment: *She was broken-hearted because she couldn't go to the party.* —**bro′ken-heart′ed·ly,** *adv.*

bro·ker (brō′kər) *n.* a person who arranges for the buying or selling of stocks, bonds, real estate, or other property, or handles business affairs for another person, receiving a fee for his services: *an insurance broker.*

bro·ker·age (brō′kər ij) *n.* the business of a broker.

bro·mide (brō′mīd) *n.* **1.** a compound of bromine and another element or radical. **2.** such a compound used to calm the nerves or to cause sleep. **3.** *Informal.* a commonplace or often-repeated saying; platitude.

bro·mine (brō′mēn) *n.* a reddish-brown nonmetallic liquid element of the halogen group having a disagreeable odor and irritating fumes and causing chemical burns on contact. It is used especially in gasoline, drugs, dyes, and photographic chemicals. Symbol: **Br**

bron·chi (brong′kī) the plural of **bronchus.**

bron·chi·a (brong′kē ə) *n., pl.* the larger tubes that are branches or subdivisions of the bronchi.

bron·chi·al (brong′kē əl) *adj.* of or relating to the bronchi, bronchia, or bronchioles.

bronchial tubes, the passages through which air flows to and from the lungs, consisting of the bronchi and their branching tubes.

bron·chi·ole (brong′kē ōl′) *n.* the smallest subdivision of a bronchus.

bron·chi·tis (brong kī′tis) *n.* an inflammation of the bronchial tubes.

bron·cho (brong′kō) *n. pl.,* **bron·chos.** another spelling of **bronco.**

bron·chus (brong′kəs) *n. pl.,* **bron·chi.** either of the two main divisions of the windpipe that allow the passage of air into the lungs.

bron·co (brong′kō) *also,* **bron·cho.** *n. pl.,* **bron·cos.** a small, untamed or partly tamed horse of the western United States.

Bron·të (bron′tē) the name of three English novelists who were sisters: **Anne,** 1820–1849, **Charlotte,** 1816–1855, and **Emily,** 1818–1848.

bron·to·sau·rus (bron′tə sôr′əs) *n. pl.* **bron·to·sau·rus·es.** a plant-eating dinosaur that lived during the Jurassic period. It was one of the largest land animals, growing to a length of eighty feet and weighing up to thirty-five tons. Also, **bron·to·saur** (bron′tə-sôr′). [Modern Latin *Brontosaurus,* from Greek *brontē* thunder + *sauros* lizard.]

Brontosaurus

Bronx, The (brongks) a borough of New York City, northeast of Manhattan. Area, 43.1 sq. mi. Pop. (1970), 1,472,216.

bronze (bronz) *n.* **1.** a strong, hard alloy of copper and tin. **2.** an alloy of copper and a metal other than tin, such as aluminum. **3.** a work of art made of bronze, as a bust or statue. **4.** a reddish-brown color like that of bronze. —*adj.* **1.** made of bronze: *a bronze door.* **2.** having the color bronze. —*v.,* **bronzed, bronz·ing.** —*v.t.* to give a bronze color or appearance to; brown: *The lifeguard's skin was bronzed by the sun.* —*v.i.* to become bronze in color; turn brown; tan.

Bronze Age, a stage in the development of civilization, from the end of the Stone Age to the Iron Age, characterized by the widespread use of bronze in making tools and weapons.

brooch (brōch, brōōch) *n.* an ornamental pin fastened by a clasp, usually worn at the neck or breast.

brood (brōōd) *n.* **1.** the young of a bird, hatched or cared for at the same time: *a brood of chicks.* **2.** all of the children in one family. —*v.i.* **1.** to sit on eggs in order to hatch them; incubate: *The hens are brooding.* **2.** to think in a worried or moody manner for a long time: *He brooded over his failure to pass the history test.* —*v.t.* to sit on (eggs) until they hatch; incubate.

brood·er (brōō'dər) *n.* **1.** a heated structure for keeping newly hatched chicks, usually for six to eight weeks. **2.** a hen that hatches eggs and cares for newly hatched chicks. **3.** a person who broods.

brook[1] (brook) *n.* a small stream. [Old English *brōc.*]

brook[2] (brook) *v.t.* to put up with; endure; tolerate: *That teacher brooks no nonsense from her students.* [Old English *brūcan* to use.]

brook·let (brook'lit) *n.* a small brook.

Brook·lyn (brook'lin) *n.* a borough of New York City, southeast of Manhattan. Area, 78.5 sq. mi. Pop. (1970), 2,601,852.

brook trout, a game fish of eastern North America, having speckles on its back. Also, **speckled trout.**

broom (brōōm, broom) *n.* **1.** a brush with a long handle, used for sweeping. **2.** a tree and shrub having long, slender branches and small leaves and bearing yellow, white, or purple flowers.

broom·corn (brōōm'kôrn', broom'kôrn') *n.* a grassy plant whose grain grows on long, strawlike stems that are used for making brooms.

broom·stick (brōōm'stik', broom'stik') *n.* the long handle of a broom.

bros., brothers.

broth (brôth) *n. pl.,* **broths** (brôths, brôthz). a thin soup made by boiling meat, fish, or vegetables in water.

broth·er (bruth'ər) *n. pl.,* **broth·ers** or *(defs. 3, 4)* **breth·ren. 1.** a boy or man having the same parents as another person of either sex. **2.** a fellow human being. **3.** a man who is a fellow member of a church, profession, or fraternal order. **4.** a man who is a member of a religious order, but who is not a priest.

broth·er·hood (bruth'ər hood') *n.* **1.** the state or quality of being a brother or brothers; brotherly relationship. **2.** all the men who are members of a church, profession, or fraternal order.

broth·er·in·law (bruth'ər in lô') *n. pl.,* **bro·thers·in·law. 1.** the brother of one's husband or wife. **2.** the husband of one's sister. **3.** the husband of the sister of one's wife or husband.

broth·er·ly (bruth'ər lē) *adj.* relating to, characteristic of, or befitting a brother; kind; affectionate: *There was a warm brotherly feeling between the two boys.* —**broth'er·li·ness,** *n.*

brougham (brōōm, brōō'əm) *n.* **1.** a closed, four-wheeled, horse-drawn carriage for two or four passengers having an uncovered, raised seat outside for the driver. **2.** an automobile having an enclosed passenger compartment, with the driver's seat outside. [From Lord *Brougham,* 1778–1868, a British statesman.]

Brougham

brought (brôt) the past tense and past participle of **bring.**

brow (brou) *n.* **1.** the part of the face above the eyes; forehead. **2.** *also,* **brows.** an arch of hair over the eye; eyebrow. **3.** the edge of a steep place: *the brow of a hill.*

brow·beat (brou'bēt') *v.t.,* **brow·beat, brow·beat·en, brow·beat·ing.** to frighten with stern looks or words; bully: *Henry browbeat us into telling him where we hid his book.*

brown (broun) *n.* a dark color like that of chocolate and coffee. —*adj.* **1.** having the color brown: *Betty has brown hair.* **2.** dark-complexioned; tanned. —*v.t.* to make brown: *to brown meat in an oven.* —*v.i.* to become brown: *The child browned in the sun.* —**brown'ish,** *adj.* —**brown'ness,** *n.*

Brown, John (broun) 1800–1859, U. S. abolitionist.

brown bear, any of various bears native to North America, Europe, and Asia, having fur that ranges from yellowish brown to very dark brown.

brown coal, another word for **lignite.**

brown·ie (brou'nē) *n.* **1.** an elf or goblin that does good deeds. **2.** a small, flat, sweet cake, usually chocolate, sometimes made with nuts or topped with frosting. **3. Brownie.** a girl between the ages of seven and nine who belongs to the junior division of the Girl Scouts.

Brown·ing (brou'ning) **1. Elizabeth Bar·rett** (bar'it). 1806–1861, English poet, wife of Robert Browning. **2. Robert.** 1812–1889, English poet.

brown rice, rice with the hulls removed, but with the layers of bran still intact.

brown·stone (broun'stōn') *n.* **1.** reddish-brown sandstone, used as a building material. **2.** a house having its outer walls made of brownstone.

brown sugar, partly refined sugar that still has traces of molasses, which gives it a dark or golden brown color.

browse (brouz) *v.,* **browsed, brows·ing.** —*v.i.* **1.** to glance through or look at something in a slow, casual manner: *She browsed through the magazine. We browsed through the antique shop.* **2.** to feed or nibble on grass, leaves, or twigs. —*v.t.* to cause to feed or nibble on grass, leaves, or twigs: *to browse cattle.* —*n.* grass, leaves, or twigs on which certain animals, such as cattle or deer, feed.

Bruce, Robert the (brōōs) 1274–1329, the king of Scotland from 1306 to 1329.

Brue·ghel, Pie·ter (broi'gəl; pē'tər) 1525?–1569, Flemish painter.

bru·in (brōō'in) *n.* a bear, especially a brown bear.

bruise (brōōz) *n.* **1.** an injury, as from a fall or blow, that discolors but does not break the surface of the skin. **2.** a discoloration on the outer surface of a fruit, vegetable, or plant caused by a similar injury. —*v.,* **bruised, bruis·ing.** —*v.t.* **1.** to cause a bruise on the surface of: *Sara bruised her arm on the edge of the table. The bananas were bruised in shipping.* **2.** to injure or hurt slightly: *The critics' bad comments bruised the actor's feelings.* —*v.i.* to become bruised: *Her skin bruises easily.*

bruit (bro͞ot) *v.t.* to spread a rumor or news of: *Reports of victory were bruited about.*

brunch (brunch) *n. pl.,* **brunch·es.** a meal combining breakfast and lunch, eaten late in the morning. —*v.i.* to eat brunch. [A blend of *br*(eakfast) and (l)*unch*.]

Bru·nei (bro͞o nī′) *n.* a British protectorate on the northern coast of Borneo. Area, 2226 sq. mi. Pop. (1971 est.), 140,000.

bru·nette (bro͞o net′) *also,* **bru·net.** *adj.* **1.** (of hair) having some shade of brown or brownish black as its main color. **2.** (of a person) having such hair, often with dark-colored skin and eyes. **3.** dark-colored: *a brunette complexion.* —*n.* a brunette person.

brunt (brunt) *n.* the worst or heaviest part: *Foot soldiers bore the brunt of the attack.*

brush¹ (brush) *n. pl.,* **brush·es. 1.** a tool having bristles, hairs, or wires set into a stiff back or attached to a handle, used especially for smoothing, scrubbing, painting, or cleaning: *a hair brush, a paint brush, a clothes brush.* **2.** the act of brushing: *Give the cat a good brush.* **3.** a light, touch in passing: *I felt a brush against my leg when the cat went by.* **4.** a brief encounter or fight: *He had a brush with the law over a parking ticket.* **5.** anything resembling a brush, such as the bushy tail of an animal. **6.** an electrical conductor that serves to make contact between fixed and moving parts of an electric motor or generator. —*v.t.* **1.** to use a brush on, as in smoothing, scrubbing, painting, or cleaning: *He brushed his hair.* **2.** to remove with or as with a brush: *Henry brushed the crumbs from his coat.* **3.** to touch (something) lightly in passing: *Leaves brushed my face as I walked through the woods.* —*v.i.* to touch lightly in passing: *She brushed against a chair as she rushed to answer the telephone.* [Old French *broisse* brushwood.]

to brush aside. to pay little or no attention to; disregard: *The coach brushed aside all criticism of the team.*

to brush off. to get rid of abruptly or ignore completely

to brush up. to go over again in order to refresh one's memory: *Mary brushed up on French verbs for the test.*

brush² (brush) *n.* **1.** a growth of shrubs, small trees, and bushes; thicket. **2.** cut or broken twigs or branches. **3.** thinly settled country; backwoods. [Old French *broche* brushwood.] —**brush′y,** *adj.*

brush·off (brush′ôf) *n. Informal.* an abrupt dismissal: *Jim asked a favor of his friend, but she gave him a brushoff.*

brush·wood (brush′wood′) *n.* **1.** cut or broken twigs or branches. **2.** a dense growth of shrubs, small trees, or bushes.

brusque (brusk) *adj.* blunt or rude in manner or speech: *a brusque person, a brusque reply.* —**brusque′ly,** *adv.* —**brusque′ness,** *n.*

Brus·sels (brus′əlz) *n.* the capital of Belgium, in the central part of the country. Pop. (1970 est.), 161,089.

Brussels sprouts 1. buds resembling small cabbages that grow on the stalk of a leafy plant, cooked and eaten as a vegetable. **2.** the plant bearing these buds.

bru·tal (bro͞ot′əl) *adj.* of or like a savage animal; cruel; inhuman: *The brutal man beat the dog.* —**bru′tal·ly,** *adv.*

bru·tal·i·ty (bro͞o tal′ə tē) *n. pl.,* **bru·tal·i·ties. 1.** brutal behavior; cruelty; inhumanity. **2.** a brutal act.

bru·tal·ize (bro͞ot′əl īz′) *v.,* **bru·tal·ized, bru·tal·iz·ing.** —*v.t.* to make brutal: *Harsh treatment brutalized the slave.* —*v.i.* to become brutal. —**bru′tal·i·za′tion,** *n.*

brute (bro͞ot) *n.* **1.** any animal.

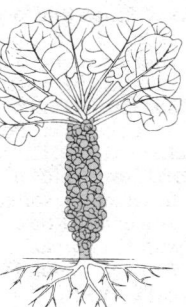

Brussels sprouts

2. a brutal person. —*adj.* **1.** like an animal; without reason: *the brute forces of nature.* **2.** brutal in character: *brute strength.*

brut·ish (bro͞o′tish) *adj.* of or like an animal that cannot reason; stupid and savage. —**brut′ish·ly,** *adv.* —**brut′ish·ness,** *n.*

Bru·tus, Mar·cus Jun·ius (bro͞o′təs; mär′kəs jo͞on′-yəs) 85?–42 B.C., Roman politician and soldier who helped to kill Julius Caesar.

Bry·an, William Jennings (brī′ən) 1860–1925, U.S. political leader who was the unsuccessful Democratic candidate for President three times.

Bry·ant, William Cullen (brī′ənt) 1794–1878, U.S. poet.

bry·o·phyte (brī′ə fīt′) *n.* any of a group of small plants including the mosses and liverworts.

b.s., bill of sale.

B.S. Bachelor of Science. Also, **B.Sc.**

btl., bottle.

btry., battery.

BTU, British thermal unit.

bu., bushel; bushels.

bub·ble (bub′əl) *n.* **1.** a thin film of liquid having the shape of a ball, filled with air or other gas: *The children blew soap bubbles with a pipe.* **2.** a small area in a solid or liquid that is round in shape and filled with air or another gas: *The glass is marred by bubbles. There are bubbles in carbonated soda.* —*v.i.,* **bub·bled, bub·bling. 1.** to rise in or form bubbles: *The boiling water bubbled rapidly.* **2.** to flow with or make a gurgling sound: *The creek bubbled along.* **3.** to show an emotion in a bright, happy manner: *She bubbled with joy when she saw the baby.* —**bub′bly,** *adj.*

to bubble over. to show excitement or enthusiasm.

bubble chamber, a device filled with a very hot liquid through which atomic particles leave trails of bubbles. By this means, the particles can be studied and identified.

bubble gum, chewing gum that can be blown into large bubbles.

bu·bon·ic plague (byo͞o bon′ik, bo͞o bon′ik) a very serious and dangerous disease marked by a high fever and swelling of the lymph glands. It is carried to humans by fleas from infected rats.

buc·ca·neer (buk′ə nēr′) *n.* **1.** a pirate. **2.** any of a group of pirates of the seventeenth and eighteenth centuries who attacked and robbed Spanish ships and settlements in America.

Bu·chan·an, James (byo͞o kan′ən) 1791–1868, the fifteenth president of the United States, from 1857 to 1861.

Bu·cha·rest (bo͞o′kə rest′, byo͞o′kə rest′) *n.* the capital and largest city of Romania, in the southern part of the country. Pop. (1970 est.), 1,475,050.

buck¹ (buk) *n.* **1.** the male of certain animals, especially the deer, antelope, rabbit, or goat. **2.** the act of jumping or kicking upward in order to throw off a rider or load. —*v.i.* to jump or kick upward with the back arched, in order to throw off a rider or load: *The donkey bucked.* —*v.t.* **1.** to throw by bucking. **2.** to make a charge at or against: *The football player bucked the line of the opposing team.* **3.** *Informal.* to oppose or resist stubbornly: *to buck*

at; āpe; cär; end; mē; it; īce; hot; ōld; fôrk; wood; fo͞ol; oil; out; up; turn; sing; thin; <u>th</u>is; hw in white; zh in treasure. The symbol ə stands for the sound of **a** in about, **e** in taken, **i** in pencil, **o** in lemon, and **u** in circus.

an unfair rule. [Old English *buc* a male deer and *bucca* a male goat.]

   to buck up. *Informal.* to cheer up: *Buck up; examinations are almost over.*

buck² (buk) *n. Slang.* a dollar. [Possibly because in poker silver dollars passed from one player to another to show whose turn it was to deal used to be called *bucks.*]

   to pass the buck. *Informal.* to shift the blame or responsibility to someone else.

buck·board (buk′-bôrd′) *n.* an open, four-wheeled carriage with the seat resting on a platform of long, flexible boards instead of on springs.

Buckboard

buck·et (buk′it) *n.* **1.** a round, hollow container with a flat bottom, used for carrying or holding water, sand, or other things; pail. **2.** anything like this, such as a scooplike device on a steam shovel. **3.** the amount that a bucket can hold; bucketful.

buck·et·ful (buk′it fool′) *n. pl.,* **buck·et·fuls.** the amount that a bucket can hold: *a bucketful of sand.*

bucket seat, a low, padded seat for one person, used especially in sports cars.

buck·eye (buk′ī′) *n.* **1.** a North American shrub or small tree related to the horse chestnut, bearing showy clusters of yellow, white, or red flowers. **2.** the shiny brown nutlike seed of this tree.

Buck·ing·ham Palace (buk′ing əm) the official London residence of British kings and queens.

buck·le (buk′əl) *n.* **1.** a clasp used to fasten together two loose ends, such as the ends of a belt or strap. **2.** something that resembles this, such as an ornament on a shoe. **3.** a bulge or bend: *a buckle in the surface of a road.* —*v.,* **buck·led, buck·ling.** **1.** to fasten with a buckle. **2.** to cause (something) to bulge or bend, especially from strain or heat. —*v.i.* **1.** to be fastened or joined by a buckle. **2.** to bulge or bend: *A beam supporting the building buckled.*

   to buckle down or **to buckle down to.** to begin working hard on: *He buckled down and finished all his homework.*

buck·ler (buk′lər) *n.* a small, round shield.

buck·ram (buk′rəm) *n.* a coarse cloth that has been stiffened with glue, used in bookbinding.

buck·saw (buk′sô) *n.* a saw set in a frame, used for sawing wood.

buck·shot (buk′shot′) *n.* large metal pellets for shotgun shells, used in hunting game.

buck·skin (buk′skin′) *n.* **1.** a strong, soft, yellowish-tan leather, made from the skins of deer or sheep. **2. buckskins.** clothing made of buckskin.

buck·tooth (buk′tooth′) *n. pl.,* **buck-teeth** (buk′tēth′). a projecting upper front tooth. —**buck′toothed′,** *adj.*

Bucksaw

buck·wheat (buk′hwēt′, buk′wēt′) *n.* **1.** the grain of any of a group of cereal plants. Buckwheat is used for animal feed or ground into flour. **2.** flour made from this grain. **3.** any of the plants that bear this grain, widely cultivated throughout the world.

buckwheat cake, a pancake made of buckwheat flour.

bu·col·ic (byoo kol′ik) *adj.* **1.** of or relating to shepherds; pastoral. **2.** relating to country life; rustic; rural. —*n.* a poem dealing with rural life.

bud (bud) *n.* **1.** a small swelling on a plant, that will later grow into a flower, stem, leaf, or branch. **2.** a flower that has not completely blossomed. **3.** a small swelling on certain plants or animals, such as the yeast, that later grows into a new plant or animal. **4.** the state or time of budding: *The cherry trees are in bud.* —*v.i.,* **bud·ded, bud·ding.** **1.** to put forth buds: *The apple trees have started to bud.* **2.** to begin to grow or develop.

   to nip in the bud. to stop (something) just as it is beginning: *The soldiers nipped the rebellion in the bud.*

Bu·da·pest (boo′də pest′) *n.* the capital and largest city of Hungary, in the north-central part of the country. Pop. (1970), 1,940,212.

Bud·dha (bood′ə, boo′də) 563?–483 B.C., the founder of Buddhism. Also, **Gautama.**

Bud·dhism (bood′iz′əm, boo′diz′əm) *n.* a religion originating in India that is based on the teachings of Buddha. It teaches that pain and evil are caused by desire and that to conquer desire is to attain a state of bliss, or nirvana.

Bud·dhist (bood′ist, boo′dist) *n.* a person who believes in Buddhism. —*adj.* of or relating to Buddha or Buddhism.

bud·dy (bud′ē) *n. pl.,* **bud·dies.** *Informal.* a close friend; pal.

budge (buj) *v.,* **budged, budg·ing.** —*v.i.* to move slightly or give way: *Harry wouldn't budge from the hammock.* —*v.t.* to cause to move slightly or give way: *We could not budge the heavy chest.*

budg·et (buj′it) *n.* a plan that shows the amount of money that will be received and the various purposes for which it will be spent in a given period of time: *Mother made a budget for household expenses. The cost of building highways and roads is a part of the budget of a state.* —*v.t.,* **budg·et·ed, budg·et·ing.** **1.** to plan for the spending of: *Father budgets his salary very carefully.* **2.** to plan for in a budget: *Jim was not able to budget a trip to Europe this year.* —**budg·et·ar·y** (buj′ə ter′ē), *adj.*

Bue·nos Ai·res (bwā′nəs ī′rās, bwā′nəs er′ēz) the capital, chief port, and largest city of Argentina, on the eastern coast of the country. Pop. (1970), 2,972,453.

buff¹ (buf) *n.* **1.** a soft, sturdy, yellowish-brown leather with a fuzzy surface, usually made from the hide of a buffalo or ox. **2.** a yellowish-brown color. **3.** a wheel or stick covered with leather, used for polishing. —*adj.* having the color buff; yellowish-brown. —*v.t.* to polish or clean, as with a wheel or stick covered with leather: *to buff shoes.* [French *buffle* buffalo, from Italian *bufalo* ox, going back to Greek *boubalos* antelope, wild ox.]

buff² (buf) *n.* a person who is an enthusiastic follower of something; fan; enthusiast: *a football buff, a movie buff.* [From *buff¹*; because nineteenth-century New York City volunteer firemen wore *buff* coats and were known as "fire buffs."]

buf·fa·lo (buf′ə lō′) *n. pl.,* **buf·fa·loes** or **buf·fa·los** or **buf·fa·lo.** **1.** the bison of North America. **2.** any of various wild or domesticated oxen of Europe, Asia, and Africa, such as the water buffalo.

Buf·fa·lo (buf′ə lō′) *n.* a port city in western New York, on Lake Erie. Pop. (1970), 462,768.

Buffalo Bill, see **Cody, William.**

buff·er¹ (buf′ər) *n.* a person or thing that comes between to lessen or soften the force or shock of something, such as a conflict or collision: *Mary listened to her brother's and sister's complaints against each other and acted as a buffer between them.* [Dialectal English *buff* to strike + -*er¹.*]

buff·er² (buf′ər) *n.* **1.** a person who polishes. **2.** a wheel, stick, or other object covered with a soft cloth or leather, used for polishing. [*Buff¹* + -*er¹.*]

B

buffer state, a small country lying between two larger countries that may be rivals or enemies, helping to reduce tensions or prevent conflicts between them.

buf·fet¹ (buf′it) *v.t.* **1.** to beat or strike with the hand or fist. **2.** to knock about: *The rough water buffeted the raft.* —*n.* **1.** a blow with the hand or fist. **2.** something that hits with the force of a blow; violent shock: *the buffet of a hurricane or a tornado.* [Old French *buffet,* a form of *buffe* blow.]

buf·fet² (bə fā′, boo fā′) *n.* **1.** a piece of furniture with a flat surface for serving food and with cabinets for storing dishes, silver, and table linen; sideboard. **2.** a meal laid out on a buffet or table so that guests may serve themselves. **3.** a counter where refreshments or light meals are served. [French *buffet;* of uncertain origin.]

buf·foon (bə foon′) *n.* a person who amuses others with pranks and jokes; clown.

bug (bug) *n.* **1.** any of a group of insects with or without wings, having beaklike sucking mouth parts, as a bedbug. **2.** any insect that crawls, such as an ant, spider, or cockroach. **3.** *Informal.* a germ that causes a disease: *a flu bug.* **4.** *Informal.* a defect or difficulty in a machine: *There is a bug in the television set.* **5.** *Slang.* a small hidden microphone used to overhear conversations. —*v.t.,* **bugged, bugging. 1.** *Slang.* to place a small hidden microphone in: *The spy bugged the enemy's conference room.* **2.** *Slang.* to annoy, bother, or worry (someone): *His constant complaining really bugs me.* —**bug′like′,** *adj.*

bug·a·boo (bug′ə boo′) *n. pl.,* **bug·a·boos.** a real or imaginary thing that a person fears.

bug·bear (bug′ber′) *n.* another word for **bugaboo.**

bug·gy (bug′ē) *n. pl.,* **bug·gies. 1.** a light, four-wheeled carriage with one large seat, and, sometimes, a top. **2.** a baby's carriage.

bu·gle (byoo′gəl) *n.* a brass wind instrument usually without keys or valves, used especially in the armed forces to give such calls as reveille or taps. —*v.i.,* **bu·gled, bu·gling.** to sound or play a bugle. —**bu′gler,** *n.*

build (bild) *v.,* **built, build·ing.** —*v.t.* **1.** to make (something) by putting materials or parts together; construct: *to build a house, to build a bridge. John built a bookcase.* **2.** to form over a length of time: *The druggist built a successful business.* —*v.i.* to construct a building: *He is planning to build on that vacant lot.* —*n.* the way in which someone or something is formed: *Hank has a sturdy build.*

   to build up. a. to increase or make stronger or better: *Jim built up his muscles by exercising. The dentist built up a good practice.* **b.** to fill with buildings or houses: *That area has been built up in recent years.*

build·er (bil′dər) *n.* **1.** a person who builds. **2.** a person whose work or business is constructing buildings or houses.

build·ing (bil′ding) *n.* **1.** something built. **2.** the act, process, or business of building.

build·up (bild′up′) *also,* **build-up.** *n.* **1.** an increasing, strengthening, or improving: *a buildup of weapons, a buildup of suspense in a detective story.* **2.** publicity or praise to make someone or something famous: *The young motion picture actor was given a big buildup in the newspapers.*

built (bilt) a past tense and past participle of **build:** *The boys built a raft.*

built-in (bilt′in′) *adj.* built as a permanent part of something; not removable: *The walls of his bedroom have built-in book shelves.*

Bu·jum·bu·ra (boo′zhoom boor′ä) *n.* the capital and chief port of Burundi, in the western part of the country. Pop. (1970 est.), 80,000.

bulb (bulb) *n.* **1.** a rounded, underground part of some plants, such as the onion or the lily, from which the plant grows. **2.** any rounded object or part resembling this: *an electric light bulb, a thermometer bulb.* —**bulb′like′,** *adj.*

bulb·ous (bul′bəs) *adj.* **1.** growing from bulbs: *Tulips are bulbous plants.* **2.** round or swollen: *The clown had a bulbous nose.*

Bul·gar·i·a (bul ger′ē ə, bool-ger′ē ə) *n.* a country in southeastern Europe, in the eastern part of the Balkan Peninsula. Capital, Sofia. Area, 42,823 sq. mi. Pop. (1971 est.), 8,540,000. —**Bul·gar′i·an,** *adj., n.*

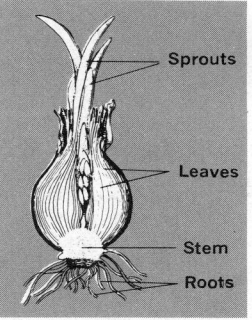

Cross section of a hyacinth bulb

bulge (bulj) *n.* a rounded part that swells out; swelling: *The ball made a bulge in Tom's coat pocket.* —*v.i.,* **bulged, bulg·ing.** to swell out: *The bag bulged with groceries.*

bulk (bulk) *n.* **1.** large size: *The fat man's bulk made it hard for him to move about.* **2.** the largest or main part: *The bulk of the land was cultivated. The millionaire left the bulk of his estate to charity.*

   in bulk. a. not packaged; loose: *to sell fruit in bulk.* **b.** in large quantities: *The bakery buys flour in bulk.*

bulk·head (bulk′hed′) *n.* **1.** one of the walls that divide a ship into compartments used to hold in check or prevent the spread of flood or fire. **2.** a wall or partition built to hold back earth, water, or gases.

bulk·y (bul′kē) *adj.,* **bulk·i·er, bulk·i·est. 1.** of great bulk; large. **2.** difficult to handle; clumsy: *The piano is too bulky to move.* —**bulk′i·ly,** *adv.* —**bulk′i·ness,** *n.*

bull¹ (bool) *n.* **1.** the mature male of any animal of the cattle family. **2.** the male of certain other large animals, such as the elephant, moose, whale, or seal. **3.** a person who believes that prices on the stock market are going to rise, especially one who buys stock with the hope of selling it back later at a higher price. [Old English *bula.*]

bull² (bool) *n.* a document containing an official pronouncement from the Pope. [Medieval Latin *bulla* seal, document.]

bull·dog (bool′dôg′) *n.* a heavily built dog having a large head, square jaws, short bowed legs, and a smooth coat. —*v.t.,* **bull·dogged, bull·dog·ging.** to wrestle (a steer) to the ground by taking hold of its horns and twisting its neck. —*adj.* characteristic of a bulldog: *bulldog courage.* [*Bull¹* + *dog;* possibly because this dog was once used to bait bulls.]

bull·doze (bool′dōz′) *v.t.,* **bull·dozed, bull·doz·ing. 1.** to move, clear, or level by using a bulldozer: *to bulldoze earth for a road.* **2.** to bully.

Bulldog

bull·doz·er (bool′dō′zər) *n.* a tractor with a powerful

---

at; āpe; cär; end; mē; it; īce; hot; ōld; fôrk;
wood; foōl; oil; out; up; turn; sing; thin; this;
hw in white; zh in treasure. The symbol ə
stands for the sound of **a** in about, **e** in taken,
i in pencil, **o** in lemon, and **u** in circus.

motor and a heavy metal blade mounted in front, used for moving earth and clearing land.

bul·let (bool′it) *n.* a small piece of rounded or pointed metal used for firing from a gun.

bul·le·tin (bool′it ən) *n.* **1.** a short account, statement, or report of news: *We heard a bulletin on the radio about the general's death.* **2.** a newspaper or magazine published regularly by a society, church, or other organization.

bulletin board, a board for posting notices, announcements, and pictures.

bul·let·proof (bool′it proof′) *adj.* able to keep a bullet from passing through: *a bulletproof vest, bulletproof glass.*

bull·fight (bool′fīt′) *n.* a sport in which a man fights a bull in an arena. Bullfights are popular in Spain, Portugal, and Latin America. —**bull′fight′er,** *n.* —**bull′fight′ing,** *n.*

bull·finch (bool′finch′) *n. pl.,* **bull·finch·es.** a songbird of Europe and Asia with a rose-colored breast, related to the cardinal.

bull·frog (bool′frôg′, bool′frog′) *n.* a large frog that makes a loud, bellowing croak. It is the largest frog in the United States.

bull·head (bool′hed′) *n.* any of a group of freshwater catfish of eastern North America, having a large flat head.

bull·head·ed (bool′hed′id) *adj.* foolishly stubborn. —**bull′head′ed·ness,** *n.*

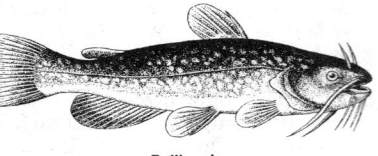
Bullhead

bull·ion (bool′yən) *n.* gold, silver, or other precious metal, especially in the form of bars.

bull·ish (bool′ish) *adj.* **1.** like a bull. **2.** expecting a rise in the price of stocks. —**bull′ish·ly,** *adv.* —**bull′ish·ness,** *n.*

bull·ock (bool′ək) *n.* an ox or steer.

Bull Run, a stream in northeastern Virginia, site of two Civil War battles, in 1861 and 1862, in which the Union forces were defeated.

bull's-eye (boolz′ī′) *n.* **1.** the central circle of a target. **2.** a shot that hits this circle. **3.** a round piece of thick glass set in a floor or ship's deck to let in light. **4.a.** a lens that curves outward. **b.** a lantern having such a lens.

bull terrier, a strong dog having broad pointed jaws, pointed ears, and a white or brindled coat.

bul·ly (bool′ē) *n. pl.,* **bul·lies.** a quarrelsome person who frightens, threatens, or hurts smaller or weaker people. —*v.t.,* **bul·lied, bul·ly·ing.** to frighten (someone) into doing something by threats. —*interj. Informal.* well done; good.

Bull terrier

bul·rush (bool′rush′) *n. pl.,* **bul·rush·es.** any of a group of coarse, relatively tall plants, having grasslike leaves. It grows in wet ground along shores, or in quiet, shallow water.

bul·wark (bool′wərk) *n.* **1.** a wall of earth, stone, or other material built for defense against an enemy. **2.** any means of defense or protection. **3.** a breakwater for protection against the force of waves. **4.** *also,* **bulwarks.** the part of a ship's side above the deck.

bum (bum) *n. Informal.* a person who is lazy or worthless; loafer; tramp. —*v.,* **bummed, bum·ming.** —*v.i.*

1. to live or be like a bum; loaf. **2.** to live off others. —*v.t.* to get (something) by begging: *to bum a cigarette, to bum a ride.* —*adj.,* **bum·mer, bum·mest.** worthless; bad: *bum luck, a bum leg.* —**bum′mer,** *n.*

bum·ble·bee (bum′bəl bē′) *n.* any of several species of thick-bodied, hairy bees closely related to honeybees. Bumblebees make a loud humming sound.

Bumblebee

bump (bump) *v.i.* **1.** to strike or knock suddenly; collide: *The two cars bumped into each other.* **2.** to move with a bump or series of bumps: *The wagon bumped down the dirt road.* —*v.t.* to hit suddenly; knock against: *He bumped his knee on the chair.* —*n.* **1.** a heavy blow or jolt; thump: *The bump on his head knocked him out.* **2.** a swelling or lump: *Mike had a bump on his forehead from the blow.* **3.** any uneven part that rises above the surrounding surface: *a bump in a road.*

bump·er (bum′pər) *n.* **1.** a heavy metal bar or strip attached to the front and rear ends of a car or truck to protect the body of the vehicle against damage or shock. **2.** a cup or glass filled to the brim, especially when drunk as a toast. —*adj.* very large or abundant: *a bumper crop of wheat.*

Bumper

bump·kin (bump′kin) *n.* a simple or awkward fellow from the country.

bump·tious (bump′shəs) *adj.* unpleasantly bold or conceited. —**bump′tious·ly,** *adv.* —**bump′tious·ness,** *n.*

bump·y (bum′pē) *adj.,* **bump·i·er, bump·i·est.** **1.** having bumps; full of bumps: *a bumpy piece of wood.* **2.** causing bumps or jolts: *a bumpy road.* —**bump′i·ly,** *adv.* —**bump′i·ness,** *n.*

bun (bun) *n.* **1.** a bread roll, variously shaped, sometimes sweetened or containing small pieces of fruit, such as raisins: *a breakfast bun.* **2.** a knot or roll of hair worn on the top or back of the head.

bunch (bunch) *n. pl.,* **bunch·es.** **1.** a number of things of the same kind growing, fastened, or grouped together; collection: *a bunch of bananas, a bunch of letters.* **2.** *Informal.* a group of people: *A bunch of us went to the movies.* —*v.i.* to place into or form a bunch or bunches; gather together: *The kittens bunched together to keep warm.* —*v.t.* to place or form into a bunch or bunches.

Bunche, Ralph (bunch) 1904–1971, U. S. statesman, educator, and United Nations official.

bun·dle (bund′əl) *n.* **1.** a number of things tied, wrapped, or bound together: *a bundle of old newspapers.* **2.** a package; parcel. —*v.,* **bun·dled, bun·dling.** —*v.t.* **1.** to wrap or bind together; make into a bundle: *Mary bundled some sheets for the laundry.* **2.** *Informal.* to send hastily: *Jane's mother bundled her off to school.* —*v.i.* to go hastily; hurry.

bung (bung) *n.* **1.** a stopper for closing the hole in a barrel or cask. **2.** another word for **bunghole.**

bun·ga·low (bung′gə lō′) *n.* a small house or cottage, usually of one story.

bung·hole (bung′hōl′) *n.* a hole in a barrel or cask through which it is filled or emptied.

bun·gle (bung′gəl) *v.,* **bun·gled, bun·gling.** —*v.i.* to work or act in a poor or clumsy way: *The repairman bungled, because the television set still doesn't work.* —*v.t.* to do or make (something) in a poor or clumsy way; botch: *He* bungled the model airplane. —*n.* a poor or clumsy performance, job, or piece of work. —**bun'gler,** *n.*

bun·ion (bun'yən) *n.* an inflamed and often painful swelling on the foot, at the base of the big toe.

bunk[1] (bungk) *n.* **1.** a narrow bed that is built into or against a wall. **2.** any narrow bed. —*v.i. Informal.* **1.** to sleep in a bunk. **2.** to sleep anywhere: *Hank bunked on the floor.* [Possibly from *bunker.*]

bunk[2] (bungk) *n. Informal.* empty, foolish talk; nonsense; humbug. [Shortened from *bunkum,* another spelling of *buncombe.* In 1820 the Congressman from *Buncombe* County, North Carolina, explained that a long-winded, pointless speech he had made was meant not for Congress but for Buncombe.]

bunk·er (bung'kər) *n.* **1.** a fortification built below ground and having walls usually of steel and concrete. **2.** an obstacle on a golf course, such as a sand trap or barrier of earth. **3.** a storage bin, such as for coal on a ship.

Bunk·er Hill (bung'kər) a hill in eastern Massachusetts, near Boston. The Battle of Bunker Hill, in 1775, the first major battle of the American Revolution, was actually fought on nearby Breed's Hill.

bunk·house (bungk'hous') *n. pl.,* **bunk·hous·es** (bungk'-hou'ziz). a building with sleeping quarters or bunks for workers or campers.

bun·ny (bun'ē) *n. pl.,* **bun·nies.** *Informal.* a rabbit.

Bun·sen burner (bun'sən) a gas burner with a very hot blue flame, used in laboratories. Openings at the base allow air to enter and mix with the gas. [From Robert W. *Bunsen,* 1811–1899, a German chemist who invented it.]

bunt (bunt) *v.t.* **1.** to tap (a pitched baseball) so that it goes only a short distance into the infield. **2.** to strike or push with the head or horns; butt. —*v.i.* **1.** to tap a pitched baseball. **2.** to strike or push with the head or horns. —*n.* **1.** the act of bunting. **2.** a ball hit by bunting. **3.** a push; butt. —**bunt'er,** *n.*

bunt·ing[1] (bun'ting) *n.* **1.** a blanket or wrapper for babies, made of wool, cotton, or other soft material. **2.** a light cloth used in making flags. **3.** banners or drapes printed with the colors or symbols of a country's flag. [Of uncertain origin.]

bunt·ing[2] (bun'ting) *n.* any of various songbirds related to and resembling the sparrow. [Of uncertain origin.]

Bun·yan (bun'yən) **1. John.** 1628–1686, English author. **2. Paul.** see **Paul Bunyan.**

bu·oy (boō'ē, boi) *n.* **1.** a floating object that is anchored and used to warn ships of sandbars, wrecks, or other hazards, or to show the way through a channel. **2.** see **life buoy.** —*v.t.* **1.** to prevent from sinking; keep afloat. **2.** to hold up or raise: *The victory buoyed up the morale of the team.*

buoy·an·cy (boi'ən sē) *n.* **1.** the power of something to float or rise in water: *Cork has great buoyancy.* **2.** the power of a liquid or gas to keep something afloat: *Salt water has more buoyancy than fresh water.* **3.** light-heartedness; cheerfulness: *Betty's buoyancy helped her brother stay in good spirits.*

buoy·ant (boi'ənt) *adj.* **1.** able to float or rise in water: *buoyant soap.* **2.** able to keep something afloat: *Salt water is buoyant* **3.** light-hearted; cheerful: *a buoyant personality.*

bur (bur) another spelling of **burr**[1].

Bur·bank, Luther (bur'bangk') 1849–1926, U. S. horticulturist who developed many new kinds of plants.

bur·ble (bur'bəl) *v.i.,* **bur·bled, bur·bling.** to make a bubbling sound; gurgle.

bur·den[1] (burd'ən) *n.* **1.** something that is carried; load: *The mule carried the burden easily.* **2.** something very difficult to bear: *The lazy young man was a burden to his parents.* —*v.t.* to put a heavy load on; load too heavily; oppress: *The poor man was burdened with debts.* [Old English *byrthen* load.]

bur·den[2] (burd'ən) *n.* **1.** the main topic, theme, or idea of something written or spoken: *the burden of an essay.* **2.** a refrain or chorus of a song or ballad. [Old French *bourdon* drone bee, from Late Latin *burdo;* imitative of the sound of the bee.]

burden of proof, the obligation of proving a statement or charge.

bur·den·some (burd'ən səm) *adj.* heavy or oppressive; hard to bear: *burdensome responsibilities, burdensome financial obligations.*

bur·dock (bur'dok) *n.* any of a small group of plants with coarse leaves and burrs.

bu·reau (byoor'ō) *n. pl.,* **bu·reaus** or **bu·reaux** (byoor'-ōz). **1.** a chest of drawers, especially for clothes, sometimes with a mirror. **2.** a department or agency of a government: *His father works for the bureau for Indian affairs.* **3.** an office or agency: *a credit bureau, a travel bureau.*

bu·reauc·ra·cy (byoo rok'rə sē) *n. pl.,* **bu·reauc·ra·cies.** **1.** government by bureaus and by the many officials who are appointed to direct or work in them. **2.** government officials as a group. **3.** too strict attention to rules and routine, often resulting in delay and inefficiency.

bu·reau·crat (byoor'ə krat') *n.* **1.** an official in a bureaucracy. **2.** an official in a government or business who pays too much attention to rules and routine.

bu·reau·crat·ic (byoor'ə krat'ik) *adj.* of or relating to a bureaucracy or a bureaucrat. —**bu'reau·crat'i·cal·ly,** *adv.*

burg (burg) *n. Informal.* a small town or city.

bur·geon (bur'jən) *v.i.* **1.** to put forth new leaves, buds, or shoots; sprout. **2.** to grow rapidly; flourish: *New factories and apartment buildings have burgeoned on what was once farmland.*

burg·er (burg'ər) *n. Informal.* a hamburger.

bur·gess (bur'jis) *n. pl.,* **bur·gess·es.** a member of the House of Burgesses, the popularly elected lower house of the legislature in colonial Virginia or Maryland.

burgh·er (bur'gər) *n.* a citizen of a town, especially a merchant city in feudal times.

bur·glar (bur'glər) *n.* a person who breaks into a building or home in order to steal something.

bur·glar·ize (bur'glə rīz') *v.t.,* **bur·glar·ized, bur·glar·iz·ing.** to break into (a building or home) in order to steal: *The thief burglarized Tom's home in the middle of the night.*

Lighted buoy   Spar buoy

Can buoy   Nun buoy
Buoys

Bunsen burner
Air
Gas

at; āpe; cär; end; mē; it; īce; hot; ōld; fôrk; wood; fōōl; oil; out; up; turn; sing; thin; this; hw in white; zh in treasure. The symbol ə stands for the sound of a in about, e in taken, i in pencil, o in lemon, and u in circus.

bur·glar·y (bur′glər ē) *n. pl.,* **bur·glar·ies.** the breaking into and entering of a building or home in order to steal.

bur·go·mas·ter (bur′gə mas′tər) *n.* the mayor of a town in the Netherlands, Flanders, Germany, or Austria.

Bur·goyne, John (bər goin′) 1722–1792, British general in the American Revolution.

Bur·gun·di·an (bər gun′dē ən) *adj.* of or relating to Burgundy or its people. —*n.* a person who was born or is living in Burgundy.

Bur·gun·dy (bur′gən dē) *n. pl.,* **Bur·gun·dies.** 1. a historic region in east-central France. 2. a red or white wine first produced in Burgundy.

bur·i·al (ber′ē əl) *n.* the act of putting a dead body in the earth, a tomb, or the sea. —*adj.* of or relating to burying: *a burial ceremony. We found some ancient relics in the Indian burial mound.*

bur·ied (ber′ēd) the past tense and past participle of **bury.**

Burke, Edmund (burk) 1729–1797, English statesman.

bur·lap (bur′lap) *n.* a coarse cloth made from jute or hemp, used for making sacks, curtains, and wall coverings.

bur·lesque (bər lesk′) *n.* 1. the comic treatment of a serious subject or the serious treatment of an unimportant or trivial subject: *The novel "Don Quixote" by Cervantes is a burlesque of medieval ideas of chivalry and romance.* 2. a stage show having vulgar entertainment. —*v.t.,* **bur·lesqued, bur·les·quing.** to make (something) appear comic or ridiculous, especially by imitating it.

bur·ly (bur′lē) *adj.,* **bur·li·er, bur·li·est.** big, strong, and sturdy: *a burly lumberjack.* —**bur′li·ness,** *n.*

Bur·ma (bur′mə) *n.* an Asian country between India and Thailand, south of China. Capital, Rangoon. Area, 261,790 sq. mi. Pop. (1977 est.), 31,512,000.

Bur·mese (bər mēz′) *n. pl.,* **Bur·mese.** 1. a person who was born or is living in Burma. 2. the language of Burma. —*adj.* of or relating to Burma, its people, their language, or their culture.

burn¹ (burn) *v.,* **burned** or **burnt, burn·ing.** —*v.t.* 1. to set on fire; consume by fire: *Joe burned the pile of leaves he had raked in the yard.* 2. to hurt, change, damage or destroy by fire, heat, or acid: *The child burned his hand on the hot stove.* 3. to make by fire, heat, or acid: *A cigarette spark burned a hole in the dress.* 4. to cause a sensation of heat in: *The chili burned Jim's mouth.* 5. to use for light or heat: *Our furnace burns oil.* 6. *Chemistry.* to cause to undergo combustion. —*v.i.* 1. to be on fire: *The candles burned very slowly.* 2. to be hurt, changed, or destroyed by fire, heat, or acid: *The steak burned on the outside.* 3. to give off light or heat: *The street lights burned all night.* 4. to feel or seem to be hot: *The child burned with a fever.* 5. to be filled with a strong emotion, such as love or anger. 6. *Chemistry.* to undergo combustion. —*n.* 1. an injury, change, or destruction caused by or as if by burning: *She got a burn on her arm from the hot stove. The burn on the rug is from a cigarette.* 2. the firing of one or more rocket engines of a spacecraft while in flight. [Partly from Old English *beornan* to be on fire; partly from Old English *bærnan* to set on fire.] —**burn′a·ble,** *adj.*

   to burn down. to destroy or be destroyed by fire: *to burn down a building.*

   to burn up. a. to destroy or be destroyed by fire. **b.** *Slang.* to make or become angry: *His habit of always being late burns me up.*

burn² (burn) *n. Scottish.* a stream. [Old English *burna.*]

burn·er (bur′nər) *n.* the part of a stove, furnace, or other device from which the flame comes.

bur·nish (bur′nish) *v.t.* to make smooth and shiny; polish: *Jim burnished the metal tray.* —*n.* a polish; gloss.

bur·noose (bər nōōs′, bur′nōōs′) *also,* **bur·nous.** *n.* a cloak with a hood, such as that worn by Arabs.

Burns, Robert (burnz) 1759–1796, Scottish poet.

burnt (burnt) a past tense and past participle of **burn¹.**

burp (burp) *Informal. n.* a belch. —*v.i.* to belch. —*v.t.* to cause (a baby) to belch.

burr¹ (bur) *also,* **bur.** *n.* 1. a prickly seed case covered with tiny barbs that cause it to stick to cloth or fur. 2. any plant bearing burrs, especially a weed. 3. a rough or sharp edge left on metal by a cutting or drilling tool. 4. any of several small cutting heads used on dentist's drills. [Possibly of Scandinavian origin.]

burr² (bur) *n.* 1. a rough, trilled pronunciation of *r,* as heard in Scotland and northern England. 2. a humming or whirring sound. —*v.t.* to pronounce (something) with a burr. —*v.i.* 1. to speak with a burr. 2. to make a humming or whirring sound. [Possibly imitative of the sound.]

Burnoose

Burr, Aaron (bur) 1756–1836, the vice-president of the United States from 1801 to 1805.

bur·ro (bur′ō) *n. pl.,* **bur·ros.** a small donkey.

bur·row (bur′ō) *n.* a hole dug in the ground by an animal, such as a rabbit or fox, for living or hiding in. —*v.i.* 1. to live or hide in a burrow. 2. to dig a burrow or burrows. 3. to hunt; search: *The woman burrowed into her purse for her keys.* —**bur′row·er,** *n.*

bur·sa (bur′sə) *n. pl.,* **bur·sae** (bur′sē) or **bur·sas.** a small sac in the body, especially one that is at a joint and filled with a lubricating fluid.

bur·sar (bur′sər, bur′sär) *n.* a treasurer, especially of a college.

bur·si·tis (bər sī′tis) *n.* a very painful condition resulting from inflammation of a bursa.

burst (burst) *v.,* **burst, burst·ing.** —*v.i.* 1. to fly apart or break open suddenly and violently, especially from pressure inside; explode: *The buds on the tree were ready to burst into bloom. The overstuffed grocery bag burst.* 2. to be full to the point of overflowing: *The closet was bursting with clothes.* 3. to come in or appear suddenly: *He burst into the room.* 4. to give in suddenly to an emotion: *Henry burst into tears.* —*v.t.* to cause to fly apart or break open suddenly and violently: *Marcia burst the balloon with a pin.* —*n.* 1. a bursting; outbreak: *a burst of gunfire, a burst of enthusiasm.* 2. a sudden effort or action; spurt: *a burst of speed.*

Bu·run·di (bə run′dē) *n.* a country in east-central Africa. Capital, Bujumbura. Area, 10,747 sq. mi. Pop. (1976 est.), 3,864,000.

bur·y (ber′ē) *v.t.,* **bur·ied, bur·y·ing.** 1. to put (a dead body) in the earth, a tomb, or the sea. 2. to cover up or hide: *The dog buried the bone. Mary buried her face in her hands and wept.* 3. to plunge by force: *The woodsman buried the ax in the tree trunk.* 4. to interest (oneself) in completely: *Roberta buried herself in the newspaper.* 5. to put out of one's mind; forget: *He buried his anger.*

bus (bus) *n. pl.,* **bus·es** or **bus·ses.** a motor vehicle with rows of seats for many passengers. —*v.,* **bused** or **bussed, bus·ing** or **bus·sing.** —*v.t.* to carry by bus: *to bus children to school.* —*v.i.* to travel by bus: *Chris bused to the city.*

bus·boy (bus′boi′) *also,* **bus boy.** *n.* a waiter's or waitress's assistant who sets and clears the table, fills glasses with water, and performs other duties.

B

bush (boosh) *n.* **1.** a woody plant smaller than a tree and having many stems that branch at or near the ground; shrub. **2.** a clump of shrubs or small trees; thicket. **3.** a wild, uncultivated or unsettled tract of land covered with shrubby growth: *The explorer crossed the Australian bush.* —*v.i.* to be or become thick or bushy; resemble a bush: *Her hair bushed out.*

   to beat around the bush. to speak or write around a subject without coming to the point: *Stop beating around the bush and tell the truth.*

Bush, George H. W. (boosh) 1924–, vice-president of the United States, since 1981.

bush·el (boosh′əl) *n.* **1.** a unit of measure equal to four pecks or thirty-two quarts, used for fruit, vegetables, grain, and other dry products. **2.** a container holding a bushel.

bush·ing (boosh′ing) *n.* a removable metal lining used in a machine part to lessen friction and wear.

Bush·man (boosh′mən) *n. pl.,* **Bush·men** (boosh′mən). a member of a group of wandering people living in the desert regions of southern Africa.

bush·mas·ter (boosh′mas′tər) *n.* a large poisonous snake found in Central and South America.

bush pilot, a pilot who flies a small plane to and from areas that are unsettled or only partly settled.

bush·whack (boosh′hwak) *v.t.* to attack from ambush. —**bush′whack′er,** *n.*

bush·y (boosh′ē) *adj.,* **bush·i·er, bush·i·est. 1.** like a bush; thick and spreading: *bushy eyebrows.* **2.** full of or overgrown with bushes: *bushy land.* —**bush′i·ness,** *n.*

bus·i·ly (biz′ə lē) *adv.* in a busy manner.

busi·ness (biz′nis) *n. pl.,* **busi·ness·es. 1.** work or activity that is a person's source of livelihood: *Mr. Brown's business is raising cattle.* **2.** a store, factory, or other commercial or industrial enterprise: *The druggist sold his business and retired.* **3.** the buying and selling of goods; trade: *Business was bad at the store.* **4.** something done or about to be done; matter; affair: *Moving to a new house can be a tiresome business.* **5.** private or personal concern or responsibility: *What business is it of yours how he wears his hair?* —*adj.* of or relating to business: *The usual business hours in this office are from nine to five.* —**busi′ness·like′,** *adj.*

   to mean business. *Informal.* to be in earnest: *When the coach says the team must practice every day, he means business.*

busi·ness·man (biz′nis man′) *n. pl.,* **busi·ness·men** (biz′nis men′). a man who owns, manages, or works in a business.

busi·ness·wom·an (biz′nis woom′ən) *n. pl.,* **busi·ness·wom·en** (biz′nis wim′ən). a woman who owns, manages, or works in a business.

bus·kin (bus′kin) *n.* **1.** a laced boot usually reaching to the middle of the calf. **2.** a thick-soled boot worn by actors in tragedies during Greek and Roman times.

Buskin

buss (bus) *Archaic. n. pl.,* **buss·es.** a kiss. —*v.t.* to kiss (someone).

bust¹ (bust) *n.* **1.** a piece of sculpture of a person's head, shoulders, and breast. **2.** the bosom of a woman. [French *buste,* from Italian *busto,* perhaps from Latin *būstum* tomb; possibly because tombs were often decorated with a bust of the deceased person.]

bust² (bust) *Slang. v.t.* **1.** to cause to come apart; burst or break. **2.** to hit; punch; sock. —*v.i.* to burst or break. —*n.* **1.** a complete failure; flop. **2.** a blow; hit. [A form of *burst.*]

bus·tard (bus′tərd) *n.* a game bird having long legs, a large, heavy body, and a long neck.

bus·tle¹ (bus′əl) *v.i.,* **bus·tled, bus·tling.** to move in a quick, excited, or noisy manner: *Mother bustled about, getting ready for the party.* —*n.* excited activity; stir: *She likes the noise and bustle of the city.* [Possibly a form of obsolete *buskle* to prepare.]

bus·tle² (bus′əl) *n.* a pad or frame formerly worn by women to add fullness to the back part of a skirt. [Of uncertain origin.]

Bustard

bus·y (biz′ē) *adj.,* **bus·i·er, bus·i·est. 1.** doing something; active: *Jean is busy making plans for the wedding.* **2.** full of activity: *Tomorrow is going to be a busy day.* **3.** in use: *When we phoned, the line was busy.* —*v.t.,* **bus·ied, bus·y·ing.** to make or keep busy; occupy (oneself): *He busied himself cleaning out the closets.*

bus·y·bod·y (biz′ē bod′ē) *n. pl.,* **bus·y·bod·ies.** a person who meddles into other people's affairs.

but (but) *conj.* **1.** on the other hand; in contrast: *He is tall, but she is short.* **2.** in spite of all; nevertheless: *It is early May, but it has begun snowing.* **3.** other than; except: *There was no direct route but through the center of town.* **4.** that: *There is no doubt but he will recover.* —*prep.* other than; except: *Everyone has signed but you.* —*adv.* only; merely; just: *I saw him but a few minutes ago.*

bu·ta·di·ene (byōō′tə dī′ēn) *n.* a colorless gas obtained from petroleum, used in making rocket fuels.

bu·tane (byōō′tān) *n.* a colorless gas that burns easily, used as a fuel and in making synthetic rubber.

butch·er (booch′ər) *n.* **1.** a person who kills animals and prepares their meat for market. **2.** a person who cuts up and sells meat. **3.** a person guilty of killing in a cruel or bloody manner. —*v.t.* **1.** to kill and prepare (animals) for market or for food. **2.** to kill in a cruel or bloody manner. **3.** to spoil by bad work; botch: *to butcher a job.*

butch·er·y (booch′ər ē) *n. pl.,* **butch·er·ies.** cruel or bloody killing; carnage.

but·ler (but′lər) *n.* a male servant, usually the head servant in a household.

butt¹ (but) *n.* **1.** the end of something, especially the thicker or larger end: *a rifle butt, the butt of a spear.* **2.** a leftover end, especially of a cigar or cigarette; stub. [Of uncertain origin.]

butt² (but) *n.* a person or thing that is the object of ridicule or jokes: *The fat boy was the butt of their teasing.* [Probably from Old French *but* goal; of uncertain origin.]

butt³ (but) *v.i.* to push or strike with the head or horns: *The goat butted at the gate.* —*v.t.* to strike or push (something) with the head or horns; ram. —*n.* a push or blow with the head or horns. [Anglo-Norman *buter* to push; of Germanic origin.]

   to butt in. *Informal.* to interrupt or meddle: *He always has to butt in whenever people are talking.*

butte (byōōt) *n.* a steep mountain or hill standing alone, usually having a flat top.

at; āpe; cär; end; mē; it; īce; hot; ōld; fôrk; wood; fōōl; oil; out; up; turn; sing; thin; this; hw in white; zh in treasure. The symbol ə stands for the sound of **a** in **a**bout, **e** in tak**e**n, **i** in penc**i**l, **o** in lem**o**n, and **u** in circ**u**s.

but·ter (but′ər) *n.* **1.** the yellowish fat obtained from cream or milk by churning, used especially as a spread or as a flavoring in cooking. **2.** any of various other foods used as spreads, such as peanut butter. —*v.t.* **1.** to spread with butter: *to butter bread.* **2.** *Informal.* to flatter: *We buttered him up so that he would lend us his football.*

but·ter·cup (but′ər kup′) *n.* **1.** a yellow flower having the shape of a cup. **2.** the plant bearing this flower.

but·ter·fat (but′ər fat′) *n.* the yellowish fat in milk, from which butter is made.

but·ter·fish (but′ər fish′) *n. pl.,* **but·ter·fish** or **but·ter·fish·es.** a saltwater fish having a silvery-blue body and a deeply forked tail, valued as a food fish.

but·ter·fly (but′ər flī′) *n. pl.,* **but·ter·flies.** **1.** any of various insects having a slender body and four large, usually bright-colored wings. **2.** a stroke in swimming. [Old English *butterflēge* this insect; possibly referring to the former belief that butterflies, and witches that took the form of butterflies, stole butter and milk.]

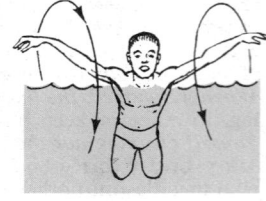

Butterfly stroke

but·ter·milk (but′ər milk′) *n.* the liquid that remains after cream or milk has been churned to make butter.

but·ter·nut (but′ər nut′) *n.* **1.** the oily nut of a tree of the walnut family. **2.** the tree bearing this nut.

but·ter·scotch (but′ər skoch′) *n.* a candy or flavoring made from brown sugar, butter, and corn syrup. —*adj.* made or flavored with butterscotch.

but·ter·y (but′ər ē) *adj.* **1.** having the look or taste of butter. **2.** spread with or containing butter.

but·tock (but′ək) *n.* **1.** either of the two fleshy hind parts of the body on which a person sits. **2.** **buttocks.** the rump.

but·ton (but′ən) *n.* **1.** a small disk or knob made of any of various materials, used to fasten or ornament clothing. **2.** anything resembling a button and worn on the clothing: *a campaign button.* **3.** a disk or knob that is turned or pushed to make something work: *Press the elevator button.* —*v.t.* to fasten with a button or buttons: *He buttoned his jacket.* —*v.i.* to be capable of being fastened with a button or buttons.

but·ton·hole (but′ən hōl′) *n.* a hole or slit through which a button passes. —*v.t.,* **but·ton·holed, but·ton·hol·ing. 1.** to make buttonholes in. **2.** to stop (a person) and make him listen to you as if by seizing the buttonhole of his coat.

but·ton·wood (but′ən wood′) *n.* the plane tree of North America; sycamore.

but·tress (but′ris) *n. pl.,* **but·tress·es.** a strong or heavy structure built against a wall to strengthen or support it. —*v.t.* to strengthen or support with a buttress.

bux·om (buk′səm) *adj.* (of women) plump and healthy. —**bux′om·ness,** *n.*

buy (bī) *v.,* **bought, buy·ing.** —*v.t.* **1.** to get (something) by giving money in return; purchase: *John bought a book for a dollar.* **2.** to serve as proper payment for; be a means of buying: *Money cannot buy health.* **3.** to bribe: *No one could buy our candidate with money or support.* —*v.i.* to make a purchase. —*n. Informal.* something bought at a lower price than usual; bargain: *That used car was a good buy.*

to buy off. to bribe: *The story was about the smugglers' failure to buy off the honest judge.*

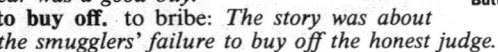

Buttress

to buy out. to buy all the shares, rights, or interests of: *He bought out his partner in the business.*

to buy up. to buy the entire supply of: *She bought up all the canned soup on sale.*

buy·er (bī′ər) *n.* **1.** a person who buys; purchaser. **2.** a person who buys merchandise for a business, especially for a store.

buzz (buz) *n. pl.,* **buzz·es. 1.** a continuous humming sound, such as that made by a bee. **2.** a low sound such as that made by many people talking: *The buzz of conversation in the theater stopped when the play began.* —*v.i.* **1.** to make a continuous humming sound: *A mosquito buzzed in my ear.* **2.** to talk or gossip excitedly, especially in low tones: *The entire village buzzed with the news.* —*v.t.* **1.** to signal with a buzzer: *He buzzed his secretary to come into his office.* **2.** to fly an airplane fast and low over: *The pilot buzzed the bridge.*

buz·zard (buz′ərd) *n.* **1.** any of various hawks having sharp, hooked beaks and long, sharp claws. **2.** any of various other birds, such as the turkey buzzard, vulture, or condor.

Buzzard

buzz·er (buz′ər) *n.* an electrical device used as a signal.

buzz saw, a power saw with a circular blade.

by (bī) *prep.* **1.** close to; near; beside: *A table is by the bed.* **2.** up to and beyond; past: *The bus sped by us.* **3.** through the means, action, or use of: *He came by train. The house was destroyed by fire. The book was written by Charles Dickens.* **4.** according to; in terms of: *We buy milk by the gallon. Jack plays every game by the rules.* **5.** by way of; through: *We came by the northern route.* **6.** during the course of: *Father likes to drive by day.* **7.** not later than: *Be here by eight o'clock.* **8.** after: *The children went into the room one by one.* **9.** in or to the extent or amount of: *Helen is older than her sister by five years.* **10.** combined in multiplication or measurement with: *Multiply 3 by 4. The rug measures nine feet by twelve feet.* —*adv.* **1.** close at hand; near: *His house is close by.* **2.** past: *Many years have gone by since we last met.* **3.** at or in another's house: *I'll stop by on my way to the store.*

by and by. at some future time; before long.

by and large. on the whole: *By and large, he did a good job.*

by the way or **by the by.** incidentally: *By the way, where is the book I lent you?*

by- *prefix* **1.** of less importance: *by-product.* **2.** near by: *bystander.* **3.** aside: *byway.* [From the adverb *by.*]

by-and-by (bī′ən bī′) *n.* a future time.

Bye·lo·rus·sia (byel′ō rush′ə) *n.* a republic of the Soviet Union, in the westernmost part of the country. Official name: **Byelorussian Soviet Socialist Republic.** Area, 80,150 sq. mi. Pop. (1970), 9,002,000. Also, **White Russia.** —**Bye′lo·rus′sian,** *adj., n.*

by·gone (bī′gôn′, bī′gon′) *adj.* gone by; past; former: *The old man thought of his bygone youth.* —*n.* **bygones.** something gone by or past.

to let bygones be bygones. to let past disagreements or hatreds be forgotten.

by·law (bī′lô′) *n.* a law or rule that is made by an organization, such as a corporation or club, to regulate its own affairs.

by·line (bī′līn′) *n.* a line at the beginning of an article in a newspaper or magazine with the writer's name.

by·pass (bī′pas′) *n. pl.,* **by·pass·es. 1.** a road that turns off the main road, especially one that goes around the center of a city. **2.** a pipe or channel for carrying a flow of a liquid or gas away from a main pipe or around an obstacle. —*v.t.* to go around or avoid by a bypass: *We bypassed the traffic jam on the highway by driving on a side road.*

by·path (bī′path′) *n. pl.,* **by·paths** (bī′pa__th__z′, bī′paths′). a side path.

by·play (bī′plā′) *n.* an action that takes place apart from or is not a direct part of the main action, especially in a stage production.

by-prod·uct (bī′prod′əkt) *n.* something useful that results from the manufacture of something else. Buttermilk is a by-product of the making of butter.

Byrd, Richard Evelyn (burd) 1888–1957, U. S. explorer.

by·road (bī′rōd′) *n.* a road that is out of the way or rarely used; side road.

By·ron, Lord (bī′rən) 1788–1824, English poet; born George Gordon.

by·stand·er (bī′stan′dər) *n.* a person who is present but does not take an active part: *Several bystanders watched the demonstration.*

by·way (bī′wā′) *n.* a road that is out of the way or rarely used; side road.

by·word (bī′wurd′) *n.* **1.** a common saying or proverb.

2. an object of contempt or scorn: *That shopkeeper became a byword for dishonesty.*

Byz·an·tine (biz′ən tēn′) *adj.* **1.** of or relating to Byzantium, the Byzantine Empire, or its art or culture. **2.** of or relating to a style of architecture developed in the Byzantine Empire, characterized by round arches, domes, and rich mosaic decorations. —*n.* a person who lived in Byzantium.

Byzantine Empire, the eastern part of the Roman Empire dating from A.D. 395, when the eastern and western parts were permanently divided, and lasting until 1453, when the capital, Constantinople, fell to the Ottoman Turks. Also, **Eastern Roman Empire.**

By·zan·ti·um (bi zan′shē əm, bi zan′tē əm) *n.* an ancient Greek city that became the capital of the Roman Empire in A.D. 330, and was later renamed Constantinople.

at; āpe; cär; end; mē; it; īce; hot; ōld; fôrk; wood; fo͞ol; oil; out; up; turn; sing; thin; __th__is; hw in white; zh in treasure. The symbol ə stands for the sound of **a** in about, **e** in taken, **i** in pencil, **o** in lemon, and **u** in circus.

1. Semitic	4. Etruscan
2. Early Hebrew	5. Latin Fourth Century B.C. Capitals
3. Greek Ninth Century B.C.	6. English

C is the third letter of the English alphabet. Although the letter **C,** as we use it now, was not developed until Roman times, it has its roots in the earliest alphabets. The earliest ancestor of **C** was *gimel* (**1**), the third letter of the ancient Semitic alphabet. The early Hebrew (**2**) form of *gimel* was borrowed by the Greeks, who called it *gamma* (**3**). Both *gimel* and *gamma* stood for the hard *g* sound, as the *g* in *game.* The Etruscans originally used a form of the Greek letter *kappa* to represent the *k* sound that **C,** as in the English word *cat,* sometimes has. This form of *kappa* was no longer used after about 400 B.C., and the Etruscans, who made no distinction between the hard *g* and *k,* began to use a form of *gamma* (**4**) to stand for both sounds. The Romans, whose alphabet came from the Etruscans, also used this letter for both the hard *g* and *k* sounds. In Latin the *k* sound was more common than the hard *g* sound. Because of this, the Roman letter **C** (**5**), which according to its early history should have been pronounced as a hard *g,* became more and more identified with the *k* sound. About 2200 years ago, the Romans began using **C** to represent only the *k* sound and devised a new letter, G, to stand for the hard *g* sound. Since that time, the capital letter **C** has been written almost exactly as we write it today (**6**).

c, C (sē) *n. pl.,* **c's, C's. 1.** the third letter of the English alphabet. **2.** something having the shape of this letter. **3.** the third item in a series or group. **4.** the Roman numeral for 100. **5.** *Music.* the first and last notes of the scale of C major.

C, the symbol for carbon.

c. 1. cent; cents. **2.** approximately; about. [Latin *circa.*] **3.** centimeter. **4.** cubic. **5.** century. **6.** copyright.

C. 1. Centigrade. **2.** Catholic. **3.** Conservative.

Ca, the symbol for calcium.

ca., approximately; about. [Latin *circa.*]

cab (kab) *n.* **1.** see **taxicab. 2.** any of various horse-drawn carriages for hire with a driver, such as a hansom. **3.** the enclosed or covered part of a truck, locomotive, steam shovel, or crane, where the controls and operator are housed.

ca·bal (kə bal') *n.* **1.** a small group of people secretly united to advance themselves or their aims by scheming. **2.** a secret scheme developed by such a group; plot. —*v.i.,* **ca·balled, ca·bal·ling.** to form or join in a cabal.

cab·al·le·ro (kab'əl yer'ō, kab'ə ler'ō) *n. pl.,* **cab·al·ler·ros. 1.** a Spanish gentleman, knight, or cavalier. **2.** a horseman. **3.** a lady's escort or admirer.

ca·ba·na (kə ban'ə) *n.* **1.** a small shelter at a swimming area, used as a bathhouse. **2.** a small cabin.

cab·a·ret (kab'ə rā') *n.* a restaurant or cafe providing food and drink, dancing, and entertainment; nightclub.

cab·bage (kab'ij) *n.* a plant having thick, green or reddish-purple leaves that are eaten as a vegetable.

cab·by (kab'ē) *also,* **cab·bie.** *n. pl.,* **cab·bies.** *Informal.* cabdriver.

cab·driv·er (kab'drī'vər) *n.* the driver of a taxicab.

cab·in (kab'in) *n.* **1.** a small, simply constructed house, usually having only one story. **2.** a room or compartment serving as living or working quarters on a ship. **3.** a compartment below the deck of a small boat, providing living quarters or shelter. **4.** an enclosed space for passengers, crew, or cargo in an aircraft.

cabin boy, a boy who waits on the officers and passengers of a ship.

cab·i·net (kab'ə nit) *n.* **1.** a piece of furniture fitted with shelves or drawers and often having doors, used for storing or displaying objects; cupboard: *a kitchen cabinet, a china cabinet.* **2.** *also,* **Cabinet.** the council that advises the chief executive or sovereign of a nation, usually made up of the heads of various departments of the government.

cab·i·net·mak·er (kab'ə nit mā'kər) *n.* a person who makes or repairs fine furniture and woodwork.

ca·ble (kā'bəl) *n.* **1.** a strong, thick rope, especially one made of wires twisted together. **2.** a bundle of wires enclosed in a protective covering, used to carry electric current. **3.** see **cablegram.** —*v.,* **ca·bled, ca·bling.** —*v.t.* **1.** to fasten with a cable. **2.** to furnish with a cable or cables. **3.** to transmit (a message) by underwater cable. **4.** to send a cablegram to: *Cable the hotel for reservations.* —*v.i.* to transmit a message by underwater cable.

cable car, a car drawn by an overhead cable or pulled along rails by an underground cable, used to carry passengers or cargo up and down steep grades.

ca·ble·gram (kā′bəl gram′) *n.* a message sent by underwater telegraph cable.

cable TV, a system for transmitting television programs by cable to the individual sets of subscribers who pay for such a service. Also, **cable television.**

ca·boose (kə boos′) *n.* a railroad car, usually at the rear of a freight train, used by the trainmen and workmen.

Cab·ot (kab′ət) **1. John.** 1450?–1498, Italian explorer of North America for England. **2. Sebastian.** 1476?–1557, his son; explorer of North America for England.

cab·ri·o·let (kab′rē ə lā′) *n.* a light, one-horse carriage, usually two-wheeled, with a folding top.

Cabriolet

ca·ca·o (kə kā′ō, kə kä′ō) *n. pl.,* **ca·ca·os. 1.** the seed of a tropical American evergreen tree, valued as the source of cocoa, chocolate, and cocoa butter. **2.** the tree that bears this seed.

cach·a·lot (kash′ə lot′) *n.* another word for **sperm whale.**

cache (kash) *n.* **1.** a hiding place, especially for provisions or treasure. **2.** something hidden or stored in such a place. —*v.t.,* **cached, cach·ing.** to hide or store in a cache.

cack·le (kak′əl) *v.i.,* **cack·led, cack·ling. 1.** to utter a shrill, broken cry, like the sound a hen makes after laying an egg. **2.** to laugh or talk with such a sound: *The old witch cackled.* —*n.* **1.** the act or sound of cackling. **2.** chatter.

ca·coph·o·ny (kə kof′ə nē) *n. pl.,* **ca·coph·o·nies.** a harsh or unpleasant sound; dissonance; discord.

cac·tus (kak′təs) *n. pl.,* **cac·tus·es** or **cac·ti** (kak′tī) any of a large group of plants found chiefly in desert regions of North and South America, usually having a central woody stem surrounded by thick, pulpy tissue, a leathery skin, and spines or scales instead of leaves. Many species bear beautiful flowers and fruit that can be eaten.

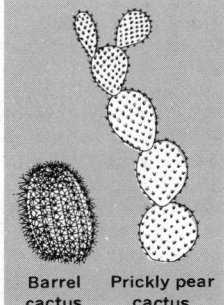

Barrel cactus Prickly pear cactus

Cactuses

cad (kad) *n.* a man who does not behave like a gentleman; ill-bred or ill-mannered man.

ca·dav·er (kə dav′ər) *n.* a dead body, especially a corpse prepared or used for dissection.

ca·dav·er·ous (kə dav′ər əs) *adj.* of, relating to, or like a corpse; pale; ghastly; gaunt.

cad·die (kad′ē) *also,* **cad·dy.** *n.* a person who assists a golfer, as by carrying his or her golf clubs. —*v.i.,* **cad·died, cad·dy·ing.** to act as a caddie.

cad·dis fly (kad′is) a small insect somewhat like a moth, whose larva lives in fresh water.

cad·dy¹ (kad′ē) *n. pl.,* **caddies.** a small box used to hold tea. [Malay *kātī* a weight of 1⅓ pounds.]

cad·dy² (kad′ē) *n. pl.,* **cad·dies,** *v.i.,* **cad·died, cad·dy·ing.** another spelling of **caddie.**

ca·dence (kād′əns) *n.* **1.** a rhythmic flow or pattern, as in poetry, speech, or natural sounds; rhythm: *the cadence of rushing water.* **2.** a measure or beat of any rhythmical movement, such as dancing or marching. **3.** the rising and falling of a sound, as of the voice at the end of a sentence. **4.** *Music.* a series of tones or chords that ends a phrase, passage, movement, or composition.

ca·den·za (kə den′zə) *n. Music.* an elaborate and technically difficult passage for a solo voice or instrument, usually near the end of a musical composition.

ca·det (kə det′) *n.* a student in a military academy in training for service as an officer.

Cá·diz (kə diz′, kā′diz) *n.* a port city in southwestern Spain. Pop. (1976), 148,200.

cad·mi·um (kad′mē əm) *n.* a soft, bluish-white metallic element resembling zinc. It is used especially to plate steel and other metals to give them a corrosion-resistant surface. Symbol: **Cd**

ca·du·ce·us (kə dōō′sē əs, kə dyōō′sē əs) *n. pl.,* **ca·du·ce·i** (kə dōō′sē ī′, kə dyōō′sē ī′). **1.** a winged staff with two snakes twined around it, carried by the god Mercury. **2.** a similar staff used as the emblem of the medical profession.

Caduceus

Cae·sar (sē′zər) *n.* **1. Ga·ius Jul·ius** (gā′əs jōōl′yəs). 100?–44 B.C., Roman statesman and general. The name *Caesar* was used as a title by the Roman emperors from Augustus to Hadrian and also by certain later rulers, such as the Holy Roman and Byzantine emperors. **2.** any emperor, tyrant, or dictator.

Cae·sar·e·an (si zer′ē ən) *also,* **Cae·sar·i·an.** *adj.* of or relating to Julius Caesar or the Caesars. —*n.* see **Cesarean section.**

Caesarean section, another spelling of **Cesarean section.**

cae·si·um (sē′zē əm) another spelling of **cesium.**

cae·su·ra (si zhoor′ə) *n. pl.,* **cae·su·ras, cae·su·rae** (si·zhoor′ē). a pause or break in a line of verse.

ca·fé (ka fā′) *n.* **1.** a coffee house or restaurant. **2.** a barroom, cabaret, or night club.

caf·e·te·ri·a (kaf′ə tēr′ē ə) *n.* a restaurant where customers buy food at a counter and serve themselves.

caf·feine (ka fēn′) *also,* **caf·fein.** *n.* an odorless, bitter, white substance found especially in coffee and tea. It is used as a stimulant.

cage (kāj) *n.* **1.** a boxlike structure or enclosure, usually having bars or made of wire mesh, used for confining birds or animals. **2.** anything like a cage, such as a cashier's window having bars. **3.** anything that confines or imprisons; prison. —*v.t.,* **caged, cag·ing.** to put or confine in a cage: *to cage a wild animal.*

cage·y (kā′jē) *also,* **cag·y.** *adj.,* **cag·i·er, cag·i·est.** *Informal.* wary of being tricked; shrewd; cautious. —**cag′i·ly,** *adv.* —**cag′i·ness,** *n.*

ca·hoots (kə hōōts′) *n.* **in cahoots.** *Slang.* in partnership, especially to plot secretly: *The king's most trusted friends were in cahoots with the men who tried to overthrow him.*

cai·man (kā′mən) *also,* **cay·man.** *n. pl.,* **cai·mans.** a large reptile of Central and South America, closely related to and resembling the alligator.

Caiman

Cain (kān) *n.* in the Old Testament, the oldest son of Adam and Eve. He murdered his brother Abel.

to raise Cain. *Slang.* to make a great disturbance.

at; āpe; cär; end; mē; it; īce; hot; ōld; fôrk; wood; fōōl; oil; out; up; turn; sing; thin; **th**is; hw in white; zh in treasure. The symbol ə stands for the sound of **a** in about, e in taken, i in pencil, o in lemon, and u in circus.

cairn (kern) *n.* a mound of stones piled up as a memorial or landmark.

Cai·ro (kī′rō) *n.* the capital of Egypt, in the northeastern part of the country. Pop. (1970 est.), 4,961,000.

cais·son (kā′sən, kā′son) *n.* **1.** a large, boxlike or cylindrical watertight structure in which men can carry on building or construction work under water. See **pneumatic caisson** for illustration. **2.** a watertight container that is attached to a sunken ship and filled with air. The buoyancy of the caisson helps to raise the ship to the surface. **3.** a two-wheeled ammunition wagon.

caisson disease, another name for **the bends.**

ca·jole (kə jōl′) *v.t.,* **ca·joled, ca·jol·ing.** to coax or persuade by flattery, soothing words, or false promises; wheedle: *The salesman tried to cajole the woman into buying a new vacuum cleaner.*

ca·jol·er·y (kə jō′lər ē) *n. pl.,* **ca·jol·er·ies.** persuasion by flattery, soothing words, or false promises.

Ca·jun (kā′jən) *n.* a descendant of the French who formerly lived in Acadia and settled in Louisiana in the eighteenth century.

cake (kāk) *n.* **1.** a baked mixture of various ingredients, such as flour, sugar, eggs, and flavoring, often covered with icing: *a chocolate cake.* **2.** a flat, thin portion of dough or batter that is baked or fried, as a pancake. **3.** any flat mass of food. **4.** a shaped, flattened, or compressed mass: *a cake of soap.* —*v.i.,* **caked, cak·ing.** to form into a hardened mass: *The wax caked where it had been applied too thickly.*

cake·walk (kāk′wôk′) *n.* **1.** formerly, a march or promenade in which a cake was awarded to the person who performed the most original and intricate steps. **2.** a dance developed from this promenade. **3.** the music for this dance. —*v.i.* to participate in a cakewalk.

Cal., California.

cal·a·bash (kal′ə bash′) *n.* **1.** another word for **gourd.** **2.** the dried fruit of a tropical American tree, used to make bowls, dippers, and water jugs. **3.** something made from this fruit, such as a bowl or tobacco pipe. **4.** the tree bearing this fruit.

cal·a·boose (kal′ə bōōs′) *n. Informal.* jail.

Cal·ais (kal′ā) *n.* a port city on the northern coast of France. It is the continental European city closest to England.

cal·a·mine (kal′ə mīn′) *n.* an odorless pink powder made from a mixture of zinc oxide and ferric oxide, used in skin lotions and ointments.

ca·lam·i·tous (kə lam′ə təs) *adj.* marked by or causing calamity; disastrous. —**ca·lam′i·tous·ly,** *adv.*

ca·lam·i·ty (kə lam′ə tē) *n. pl.,* **ca·lam·i·ties.** **1.** an event that causes great misfortune; disaster: *Fire, flood, and other calamities nearly destroyed the tiny village.* **2.** great suffering or distress; misery.

cal·car·e·ous (kal ker′ē əs) *adj.* consisting of or containing calcium, calcium carbonate, or lime; chalky.

cal·ci·fi·ca·tion (kal′sə fi kā′shən) *n.* **1.** the process of calcifying, especially the depositing of lime salts in body tissue. **2.** a calcified formation or structure.

cal·ci·fy (kal′sə fī′) *v.i.,* **cal·ci·fied, cal·ci·fy·ing.** to become hard or stony by the deposit of lime salts.

cal·ci·mine (kal′sə mīn′) *n.* a white or colored powder used especially to decorate plastered ceilings and walls. —*v.t.,* **cal·ci·mined, cal·ci·min·ing.** to cover with calcimine.

cal·cine (kal′sīn) *v.,* **cal·cined, cal·cin·ing.** —*v.t.* to cause (a substance) to lose moisture or impurities, or to be oxidized or reduced, by heating it to a high temperature. Limestone is calcined to make lime. —*v.i.* to become calcined. —**cal·ci·na′tion,** *n.*

cal·cite (kal′sīt) *n.* a very common mineral that is made up of calcium carbonate and is the chief component of limestone, chalk, and marble.

cal·ci·um (kal′sē əm) *n.* a soft, silvery-white metallic element that is essential for the growth of bones and teeth, as well as for plant growth. Symbol: **Ca**

calcium carbonate, a compound of calcium, carbon, and oxygen that occurs as a white powder or as colorless crystals in its pure state and, in nature, as chalk, limestone, marble, and several other mineral forms. It is used in medicines, baking powder, tooth powders, and cement.

cal·cu·la·ble (kal′kyə lə bəl) *adj.* that can be calculated.

cal·cu·late (kal′kyə lāt′) *v.,* **cal·cu·lat·ed, cal·cu·lat·ing.** —*v.t.* **1.** to determine by using mathematics; compute: *The scientists calculated the time required for a trip to the moon.* **2.** to figure out beforehand by reasoning; estimate: *The tennis player calculated his chances of winning the tournament.* **3.** *Informal.* to plan; intend: *The speech was calculated to win votes for the politician.* —*v.i.* **1.** to perform a mathematical process; compute. **2.** to rely or count (with *on* or *upon*): *The farmers were calculating on good weather.* [Late Latin *calculātus,* the past participle of *calculāre* to count, compute, from Latin *calculus* a small stone. In ancient times counting was often done with small stones.]

cal·cu·lat·ed (kal′kyə lā′tid) *adj.* done or attempted after estimating the probable results: *The general's attack on the enemy stronghold was a calculated risk.*

cal·cu·lat·ing (kal′kyə lā′ting) *adj.* **1.** given to careful or shrewd consideration of one's own interests; selfish; scheming. **2.** that calculates: *a calculating machine.*

cal·cu·la·tion (kal′kyə lā′shən) *n.* **1.** the act or process of calculating. **2.** the product or result of calculating. **3.** careful or shrewd planning.

cal·cu·la·tor (kal′kyə lā′tər) *n.* **1.** a person who calculates. **2.** a machine for performing mathematical operations mechanically.

cal·cu·lus (kal′kyə ləs) *n. pl.,* **cal·cu·li** (kal′kyə lī′) or **cal·cu·lus·es.** **1.** a method of calculation in advanced mathematics that uses a special system of algebraic symbols to solve problems. **2.** an abnormal hard mass of mineral matter formed in the body. Kidney stones are calculi.

Cal·cut·ta (kal kut′ə) *n.* a port city in northeastern India. Pop. (1971), 3,141,180.

cal·dron (kôl′drən) another spelling of **cauldron.**

cal·en·dar (kal′ən dər) *n.* **1.** a table showing the days, weeks, and months of a given year. **2.** a method of dividing time into fixed intervals, especially with reference to the beginning, length, and division of the year. **3.** a list, register, or schedule arranged in chronological order, such as a list of cases to be tried in court or of bills to be considered by a legislature.

calendar month, see **month** *(def. 1).*

calendar year, see **year** *(def. 1).*

cal·en·der (kal′ən dər) *n.* a machine consisting of a number of rollers through which cloth, paper, or other material is passed in order to produce a desired finish or a uniform thickness. —*v.t.* to press in a calender.

calf[1] (kaf) *n. pl.,* **calves.** **1.** a young cow or bull. **2.** the young of various other mammals, such as the elephant, whale, and seal. **3.** see **calfskin.** [Old English *cealf* a young cow or bull.]

calf[2] (kaf) *n. pl.,* **calves.** the fleshy part of the back of the leg between the knee and ankle. [Old Norse *kálfi.*]

calf·skin (kaf′skin′) *n.* **1.** the skin or hide of a calf. **2.** leather made from it.

Cal·ga·ry (kal′gər ē) *n.* a city in southwestern Canada, in the province of Alberta. Pop. (1971), 400,154.

Cal·houn, John Cald·well (kal hōōn′; käld′wel′) 1782–1850, U.S. political leader, the vice-president of the United States from 1825 to 1832.

Ca·li (kä′lē) *n.* a city in western Colombia. Pop. (1969 est.), 820,809.

cal·i·ber (kal′ə bər) *also,* **cal·i·bre.** *n.* **1.** the diameter of the inside of a hollow tube. **2.a.** the diameter of the bore of a gun. **b.** the diameter of a bullet or shell. **3.** a degree of merit, ability, or importance; quality: *The job requires a man of high caliber.*

cal·i·brate (kal′ə brāt′) *v.t.,* **cal·i·brat·ed, cal·i·brat·ing.** **1.** to determine, check, correct, or mark the scale of (a thermometer or similar measuring instrument). **2.** to determine the caliber of, as the interior of a thermometer tube. —**cal′i·bra′tion,** *n.*

cal·i·co (kal′ə kō′) *n. pl.,* **cal·i·coes** or **cal·i·cos.** a cotton fabric printed with small, usually brightly colored designs. —*adj.* **1.** made of calico. **2.** resembling calico; spotted: *a calico cat.*

ca·lif (kā′lif) another spelling of **caliph.**

Calif., California.

Cal·i·for·nia (kal′ə fôrn′yə, kal′ə fôr′nē ə) *n.* **1.** a state of the United States, on the Pacific coast. Capital, Sacramento. Area, 158,693 sq. mi. Pop. (1970), 19,953,134. Abbreviation, **Calif. 2. Gulf of.** a long inlet of the Pacific, just south of California, separating Lower California from the Mexican mainland. —**Cal′i·for′nian,** *adj., n.*

● **California** was originally the name of an imaginary island in a sixteenth-century Spanish story. When Spanish explorers landed on the southern tip of Lower California, they believed they were on an island, so they named it after the fabled island of Spanish literature. This name was carried north by other Spanish explorers and eventually included the whole territory that later became the state of California.

cal·i·for·ni·um (kal′ə fôr′nē əm) *n.* a radioactive element first produced in 1950. Symbol: **Cf**

cal·i·pers (kal′ə pərz) *also,* **cal·li·pers.** *n., pl.* a hinged instrument resembling a pair of tongs, used especially to measure the internal or external dimensions of a small object.

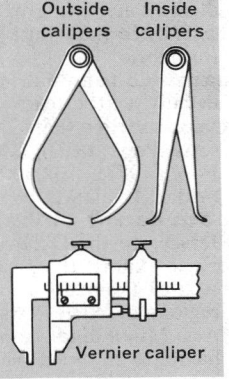

Outside calipers   Inside calipers

Vernier caliper

Calipers

ca·liph (kā′lif) *also,* **ca·lif.** *n.* formerly, the title given to the successors of Muhammad as the religious and secular heads of Islam.

ca·liph·ate (kā′lə fāt′) *n.* the office, reign, or government of a caliph or the land under his rule.

cal·is·then·ics (kal′is then′iks) *also,* **cal·lis·then·ics.** *n., pl.* **1.** light gymnastic exercises designed to develop strength and grace and to promote good health: *The athlete did calisthenics to keep in shape.* **2.** the science or practice of such exercises. ▲ used with a singular verb in definition 2. —**cal′is·then′ic,** *adj.*

calk¹ (kôk) another spelling of **caulk.**

calk² (kôk) *n.* **1.** one of the projecting pieces of a horseshoe that grips the ground and prevents the horse from slipping. **2.** a sharp, projecting piece of metal on the bottom of the heel or toe of a shoe or boot to prevent slipping. —*v.t.* to furnish with calks. [Short for earlier *calkin,* from Old French *calcain* heel.]

calk·er (kô′kər) another spelling of **caulker.**

call (kôl) *v.t.* **1.** to utter in a loud voice; proclaim; announce: *The teacher called my name.* **2.** to command, request, or cause to come; summon: *He was called to testify*

in the case. *We asked the doorman to call a cab for us.* **3.** to cause to assemble or begin officially: *to call a meeting, to call a strike.* **4.** to summon to a special duty, office, or activity: *My brother was called to serve in the army.* **5.** to arouse from sleep; waken: *Call me for breakfast at seven o'clock.* **6.** to make a telephone call to: *Call us from the airport when you arrive.* **7.** to give a name to; name: *She called the puppy "Daisy."* **8.** to describe or characterize in some way: *That's what I call a dirty trick.* **9.** to stop or suspend: *The game was called on account of darkness.* **10.** *Sports.* to rule on, as a pitch or a player's action: *The umpire called the pitch a strike.* —*v.i.* **1.** to speak loudly; cry; shout: *Did you hear someone call for help?* **2.** to make a short visit or stop: *We called at your house yesterday.* **3.** to make a telephone call: *Try to call before midnight.* —*n.* **1.** the act of calling; shout; cry. **2. a.** a characteristic sound or cry made by a bird or animal. **b.** a device that produces an imitation of such a sound in order to lure birds or animals. **3.** a summons; invitation: *The fiery speech was a call to revolution.* **4.** a signal or summons played on a drum or bugle: *Reveille is the first call of the day.* **5.** a need; occasion; cause: *There was no call for her to contribute so generously.* **6.** the act or instance of communicating by telephone: *Did I receive any calls while I was out?* **7.** *Sports.* a ruling by an official.

close call. a narrow escape: *The soldier has had many close calls with death.*

on call. a. available when summoned; ready: *The doctor is on call all night.* **b.** payable on demand.

to call back. a. to summon (a person) to return; bring back. **b.** to telephone again or in return.

to call for. a. to go and get; stop to obtain: *We called for the package at the post office.* **b.** to require or demand; need: *This problem calls for some careful thinking.*

to call forth. to bring into action; evoke.

to call in. a. to withdraw from circulation, as currency. **b.** to summon or invite, as for assistance or consultation: *The farmer called in a geologist to get his opinion of the land.*

to call off. a. to cancel: *to call off a trip, to call off an investigation.* **b.** to make go away: *Call off your dog.* **c.** to read aloud: *The judge called off the names of the winners.*

to call on or **to call upon. a.** to make a brief visit to. **b.** to appeal to: *The senator called on the voters to support her proposal.*

to call out. a. to utter or cry out in a loud voice. **b.** to summon into service; order into action: *to call out the Army Reserves.*

to call up. a. to telephone. **b.** to bring or summon into action or service: *Stan was called up for military duty.* **c.** to bring to mind: *The old letter called up pleasant memories.*

cal·la (kal′ə) *n.* any of several plants that bear tiny flowers on a spike inside a showy white or yellow spathe. Also, **calla lily.**

Cal·la·o (kä yä′ō) *n.* a city on the west coast of central Peru. Pop. (1972), 196,900.

call·er (kô′lər) *n.* **1.** a person who makes a short visit.

at; āpe; cär; end; mē; it; īce; hot; ōld; fôrk; wood; fōōl; oil; out; up; turn; sing; thin; **this**; hw in white; zh in treasure. The symbol ə stands for the sound of **a** in about, **e** in taken, **i** in pencil, **o** in lemon, and **u** in circus.

2. a person or thing that calls. **3.** a person who calls directions to dancers in a square dance.

cal·lig·ra·phy (kə lig′rə fē) *n.* **1.** beautiful or elegant handwriting. **2.** handwriting; penmanship.

call·ing (kô′ling) *n.* **1.** a vocation; profession. **2.** a strong impulse or urge to follow a certain course of action, especially of a religious nature: *The young man felt a calling to join the ministry.* **3.** the act of a person or thing that calls, especially crying or shouting aloud.

calling card, a small card with one's name on it, used for social or business purposes. Also, **visiting card.**

cal·li·o·pe (kə lī′ə pē′) *n.* **1.** a musical instrument consisting of a series of steam whistles, played by means of a keyboard. **2. Calliope.** *Greek Mythology.* the Muse of eloquence and epic poetry.

cal·li·pers (kal′ə pərz) another spelling of **calipers.**

cal·lis·then·ics (kal′is then′iks) another spelling of **calisthenics.**

call letters, the letters that identify a radio or television station.

cal·lous (kal′əs) *adj.* **1.** thickened and hardened, as a callus on the skin. **2.** hardened in mind or feelings; unfeeling; insensitive: *Carol was never callous about the troubles and cares of other people.* —*v.t., v.i.* to make or become callous. —**cal′lous·ly,** *adv.* —**cal′lous·ness,** *n.*

cal·low (kal′ō) *adj.* **1.** inexperienced; immature: *a callow young man who knew nothing of life.* **2.** (of birds) not having enough feathers for flight. —**cal′low·ness,** *n.*

cal·lus (kal′əs) *n. pl.,* **cal·lus·es.** a hardened and thickened area of the skin.

calm (käm) *adj.* **1.** without or nearly without wind or motion; not stormy: *a calm sea.* **2.** free from excitement, nervousness, or strong feeling; quiet; serene: *The police remained calm during the disturbance.* —*n.* **1.** the condition or period of being without motion or wind; stillness: *There was an eerie calm before the tornado hit the town.* **2.** freedom from excitement, nervousness, or strong feeling; tranquillity; serenity. —*v.t.* to make calm or quiet: *The mother calmed her child.* —*v.i.* to become calm or quiet (often with *down*): *The children calmed down soon after their fight.* —**calm′ly,** *adv.* —**calm′ness,** *n.*

cal·o·mel (kal′ə mel′) *n.* a compound of mercury and chlorine in the form of a white, tasteless powder. It is used as an insecticide, antiseptic, and laxative.

ca·lor·ic (kə lôr′ik) *adj.* relating to heat or calories.

cal·o·rie (kal′ər ē) *also,* **cal·o·ry.** *n. pl.,* **calories.** **1.** the quantity of heat required to raise the temperature of one gram of water one degree centigrade. Also, **small calorie.** **2.** the quantity of heat, equal to 1000 small calories, required to raise the temperature of one kilogram of water one degree centigrade. Also, **large calorie. 3.** a unit equal to the large calorie, used to measure the heat output of organisms or the energy-producing value of food. **4.** a quantity of food having such an energy-producing value.

cal·o·rif·ic (kal′ə rif′ik) *adj.* relating to or producing heat.

cal·o·rim·e·ter (kal′ə rim′ə tər) *n.* an apparatus for measuring the amount of heat given off or absorbed by a substance.

cal·u·met (kal′yə met′) *n.* another word for **peace pipe.**

ca·lum·ni·ate (kə lum′nē āt′) *v.t.,* **ca·lum·ni·at·ed, ca·lum·ni·at·ing.** to make false and harmful statements or accusations about; slander. —**ca·lum′ni·a′tion,** *n.* —**ca·lum′ni·a′tor,** *n.*

ca·lum·ni·ous (kə lum′nē əs) *adj.* containing or characterized by calumny; slanderous. —**ca·lum′ni·ous·ly,** *adv.*

cal·um·ny (kal′əm nē) *n. pl.,* **cal·um·nies.** a false and harmful statement or accusation intended to damage another person's reputation; slander.

Cal·va·ry (kal′vər ē) *n.* the hill near ancient Jerusalem where Jesus was crucified. Also, **Golgotha.**

calve (kav) *v.i.,* **calved, calv·ing.** to give birth to a calf.

calves (kavz) the plural of **calf.**

Cal·vin, John (kal′vin) 1509–1564, French theologian, the leader of the Protestant Reformation at Geneva.

Cal·vin·ism (kal′vi niz′əm) *n.* the religious teachings of John Calvin.

Cal·vin·ist (kal′vi nist) *n.* a person who believes in Calvinism.

ca·ly·ces (kal′ə sez, kā′lə sez) a plural of **calyx.**

ca·lyp·so (kə lip′sō) *n.* an improvised song, originally from the British West Indies, usually dealing with subjects that are humorous or of current interest.

ca·lyx (kā′liks, kal′iks) *n. pl.,* **ca·lyx·es** or **ca·ly·ces.** the outer circle of protective leaves, or sepals, that surround an unopened flower and usually fold back beneath the petals when the bud opens.

cam (kam) *n.* the projection on a revolving shaft that changes a circular motion into a back-and-forth motion.

ca·ma·ra·de·rie (kam′ə rad′ər ē, kä′mə rä′dər ē) *n.* friendliness and loyalty among comrades; fellowship; comradeship.

cam·bi·um (kam′bē əm) *n.* a layer of growth tissue between the bark and the wood of trees and woody plants. It gives rise to cells for new bark and new wood.

Cam

Cam·bo·di·a (kam bō′dē ə) *n.* a country in southeastern Asia, formerly part of French Indochina. Capital, Phnom Penh. It is officially known as the **Khmer Republic.** Area, 69,898 sq. mi. Pop. (1980 est.), 8,872,000. —**Cam·bo′di·an,** *adj., n.*

Cam·bri·an (kam′brē ən) *n.* the first geological period of the Paleozoic era. —*adj.* relating to this period.

cam·bric (kām′brik) *n.* a soft, lightweight linen or cotton fabric.

cambric tea, a drink made with water, milk, sugar, and usually a little tea.

Cam·bridge (kām′brij) *n.* **1.** a city in eastern Massachusetts. Pop. (1970), 100,361. **2.** a city in eastern England. Pop. (1978), 102,300. **3.** a famous university in Cambridge, England.

Cam·den (kam′dən) *n.* a city in southwestern New Jersey, on the Delaware River. Pop. (1970), 102,551.

came (kām) the past tense of **come.**

cam·el (kam′əl) *n.* a cud-chewing animal of the desert regions of Africa, Asia, Asia Minor, and Arabia, having a humped back, a sandy-white to deep-brown coat, and cloven hoofs. Camels are used for riding, as beasts of burden, and as a source of meat, milk, and leather. There are two species of camels: the dromedary, with one hump, and the Bactrian camel, with two humps.

Camel

ca·mel·lia (kə mēl′yə) *n.* **1.** a fragrant flower of any of a group of shrubs and trees, widely grown in warm, damp regions and having white, red, or pink petals. **2.** the woody plant bearing this flower.

Cam·e·lot (kam′ə lot′) *n.* the legendary site of King Arthur's court.

camel's hair, a soft fabric made of the hair of camels or of this hair in combination with wool. It usually has a distinctive tan color, and is used for coats, suits, and sweaters.

Cam·em·bert (kam′əm ber′) *n.* a rich, creamy, soft cheese. [From *Camembert,* a French village where it was first made.]

cam·e·o (kam′ē ō′) *n. pl.,* **cam·e·os.** a piece of jewelry made from a precious or semiprecious stone or a shell, having a carved, raised design on it. The stone often consists of different colored layers so that the darker layer can serve as a background for a figure, usually the head of a woman, that is carved in relief from the lighter part.

cam·er·a (kam′ər ə, kam′rə) *n. pl.,* **cam·er·as. 1.** a device for taking photographs, consisting of a light-proof box with a lens and shutter through which light is admitted and the image is focused on a film or plate that is sensitive to light. **2.** *Television.* a device that changes an image into electrical impulses for transmission.

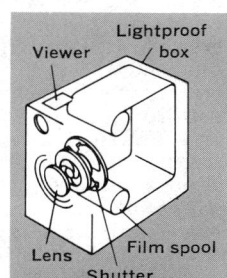

Camera

cam·er·a·man (kam′ər ə man′, kam′rə man′) *n. pl.,* **cam·er·a·men** (kam′ər ə men′, kam′rə men′). a person whose occupation is operating a motion picture or television camera.

Cam·er·oon (kam′ə rōōn′) *also,* **Cam·er·oun.** *n.* a country in west-central Africa made up of most of the territory of the former Cameroons. Capital, Yaoundé. Area, 183,569 sq. mi. Pop. (1971 est.), 5,900,000.

Cam·er·oons (kam′ə rōōnz′) *n.* two former United Nations trust territories, one under French administration, now Cameroon; the other under British administration, now divided between Cameroon and Nigeria.

cam·i·sole (kam′ə sōl′) *n.* a woman's undergarment that looks like the top of a slip, often trimmed with lace or ribbons.

cam·o·mile (kam′ə mīl′) *also,* **cham·o·mile.** *n.* any of several strong-smelling plants found in temperate regions, having flowers that resemble the daisy. The flowers of certain species are dried and used to make tea.

cam·ou·flage (kam′ə fläzh′) *n.* **1.** *Military.* the act or process of disguising or changing the appearance of troops, military equipment, or installations in order to conceal them from the enemy, especially by using paint, nets, or foliage to make them blend into the surroundings. **2.** any disguise, appearance, or behavior that serves to conceal or deceive, such as the protective coloring of an animal. —*v.t.,* **cam·ou·flaged, cam·ou·flag·ing.** to disguise or conceal by means of camouflage: *The soldiers camouflaged the tank by covering it with bushes and shrubs.*

camp (kamp) *n.* **1.** an outdoor site, often with tents, huts, or other structures, where people live or sleep temporarily, especially while traveling or marching: *The Indian scout made camp by the river. The army established a camp near the border.* **2.** a place, usually in the country, that provides supervised activities and is attended for a fixed period of time: *This summer Sam will be a counselor at a boys' camp.* **3.** a group of permanent structures in which a number of persons may be sheltered or confined: *a prisoner-of-war camp.* **4.** an area employed for or occupied by a camp. —*v.i.* to set up or live in a camp (often with *out*): *to camp out in the wilderness.*

   to break camp. to pack up camping equipment.

cam·paign (kam pān′) *n.* **1.** a series of related military operations carried on to accomplish a specific goal: *The general's campaign was designed to gain control of all of the enemy's territory.* **2.** an organized series of actions carried on for a particular purpose: *an election campaign, a fund-raising campaign.* —*v.i.* to carry on or serve in a campaign: *The candidate campaigned here last week. Volunteers campaigned for the mayor.* —**cam·paign′er,** *n.*

cam·pa·ni·le (kam′pə nē′lē) *n. pl.,* **cam·pa·ni·les** or **cam·pa·ni·li** (kam′pə nē′lē). a bell tower, especially one that stands separately from any other building.

camp·er (kam′pər) *n.* **1.** a person who stays at or lives in a camp. **2.** a vehicle or trailer built or designed for camping.

camp·fire (kamp′fīr′) *n.* **1.** an outdoor fire in a camp, used for warmth or cooking. **2.** a social gathering or meeting, as around a campfire.

Camp Fire Girls, a national organization for girls of ages seven through eighteen, that encourages participation in outdoor activities, sports, creative arts, and community service.

camp·ground (kamp′-ground′) *n.* a place for a camp or a camp meeting.

cam·phor (kam′fər) *n.* a white crystalline compound with a strong odor, used in mothballs, some medicines, and in the manufacture of plastics. Camphor is obtained from the wood of a kind of evergreen tree or made synthetically.

Campanile

camp meeting, a religious gathering, usually lasting several days, held outdoors or in a tent.

camp·site (kamp′sīt′) *n.* an area reserved for camping, usually having facilities for cooking and eating.

camp·stool (kamp′stōōl′) *n.* a light, portable, folding seat.

cam·pus (kam′pəs) *n. pl.,* **cam·pus·es.** the grounds, including buildings, of a school, college, or university. —*adj.* of or relating to a school, college, or university or to its students: *Dan was active in campus politics.* [Latin *campus* field; possibly because college grounds were originally located in open country.]

Ca·mus, Albert (ka mōō′) 1913–1960, French philosopher and writer.

can[1] (kan) *auxiliary verb.* Present tense: *sing.,* first person, **can;** second, **can** or (*archaic*) **canst;** third, **can;** *pl.,* **can.** Past tense: **could** or (*archaic*) **couldest** or **couldst. 1.** to be able to: *I can run faster than you. The car can hold five passengers.* **2.** to know how to: *Herb can speak French. Can you*

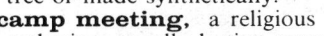

at; āpe; cär; end; mē; it; īce; hot; ōld; fôrk; wood; fōōl; oil; out; up; turn; sing; thin; this; hw in white; zh in treasure. The symbol ə stands for the sound of **a** in about, **e** in taken, **i** in pencil, **o** in lemon, and **u** in circus.

dance the waltz? **3.** to have the right to: *The general can give orders that must be obeyed.* **4.** *Informal.* to be permitted to; may: *Father says we can go to the movies.* [Old English *cunnan* to know, know how, be able.]

▲ In formal usage, **can** means to be able to do something, and **may** means to be allowed to do it. In informal usage, *can* is often used in place of *may.*

can² (kan) *n.* **1.** a metal container: *a garbage can.* **2.** a container, usually made of iron coated with tin, in which food or other products are sealed for preservation. **3.** the contents of a can: *He drank a can of root beer.* **4.** *Slang.* jail. —*v.t.,* **canned, can·ning.** **1.** to put or preserve in a can or jar: *to can peaches.* **2.** *Slang.* to fire from a job; discharge: *The boss canned him for being late too often.* [Old English *canne.*]

Can. **1.** Canada. **2.** Canadian.

Ca·naan (kā′nən) *n.* a region in Palestine between the Jordan River and the Mediterranean; the Promised Land.

Ca·naan·ite (kā′nə nīt′) *n.* a member of the Semitic people who lived in Canaan before its conquest by the Hebrews.

Can·a·da (kan′ə də) *n.* a country in northern North America, bordering the United States. Capital, Ottawa. Area, 3,851,809 sq. mi. Pop. (1980), 24,070,000. —**Ca·na·di·an** (kə nā′dē ən), *adj., n.*

Canada goose. a wild goose native to Arctic and temperate regions of North America, having a black head and neck, white patches on the face, and a brownish-gray body.

ca·nal (kə nal′) *n.* **1.** an inland waterway built to carry water for navigation, irrigation, drainage, or power. **2.** a tubelike passage in a plant or in the body of an animal. **3.** any of the long, faint, narrow markings on the planet Mars, as seen through a telescope.

Canal Zone. a strip of territory across the Isthmus of Panama, extending approximately five miles on each side of the Panama Canal. It was formerly administered by the United States. Also, **Panama Canal Zone.**

can·a·pé (kan′ə pē, kan′ə pā′) *n.* a cracker or thin piece of bread topped with cheese, meat, fish, or a seasoned spread and served hot or cold as an appetizer.

ca·nard (kə närd′) *n.* a false or exaggerated story, report, or rumor; hoax.

ca·nar·y (kə ner′ē) *n. pl.,* **ca·nar·ies.** **1.** a small yellow songbird, popular as a pet. **2.** see **canary yellow.**

Canary Islands. a Spanish island group in the North Atlantic, off the northwest coast of Africa. Also, **Canaries.** [Latin *Canāriae* (*insulae*) literally, (islands) of dogs. The ancient Romans found many dogs there.]

canary yellow. a light, bright yellow color.

ca·nas·ta (kə nas′tə) *n.* a form of rummy for two to six players, usually using two decks of fifty-two cards and four jokers.

Ca·nav·er·al, Cape (kə nav′ər əl) the site of the main U.S. launching and testing center for missiles and spacecraft, located on the Atlantic coast of Florida.

Can·ber·ra (kan′ber′ə) *n.* the capital of Australia, in the southeastern part of the country. Pop. (1976), 197,622.

can·can (kan′kan′) *n.* a dance that originated in Paris in the early nineteenth century, marked by high kicking.

can·cel (kan′səl) *v.,* **can·celed, can·cel·ing;** *also, British,* **can·celled, can·cel·ling.** —*v.t.* **1.** to do away with, withdraw, or stop; call off: *to cancel a dentist appointment.* **2.** to cross out or mark with a line or lines, especially to mark (a postage stamp) so that it cannot be used again. **3.** to make up for; balance; offset: *A vote in favor of something and a vote against it cancel each other.* **4.** *Mathematics.* to eliminate (a common factor) from the numerator and denominator of a fraction or from both sides of an equation. —*v.i.* to offset each other (with *out*).

can·cel·la·tion (kan′sə lā′shən) *n.* **1.** the act of canceling or the state of being canceled: *Rain caused the cancellation of the baseball game.* **2.** the marks used in canceling. **3.** something that is canceled.

can·cer (kan′sər) *n.* **1.** any of a group of frequently fatal diseases characterized by abnormal growth of cells that destroys healthy tissues and organs. **2.** any malignant tumor. **3.** any destructive or spreading evil. **4. Cancer. a.** see **Tropic of Cancer. b.** a constellation in the northern sky, thought to resemble a crab in shape. **c.** the fourth sign of the zodiac. —**can′cer·ous,** *adj.*

can·de·la (kan dē′lə) *n.* a unit for measuring the intensity of light.

can·de·la·bra (kand′əl ä′brə, kand′əl ā′brə) *n. pl.,* **can·de·la·bras.** see **candelabrum.**

can·de·la·brum (kand′əl ä′brəm, kand′əl ā′brəm) *n. pl.,* **can·de·la·bra** or **can·de·la·brums.** a large ornamental candlestick having several branches for holding candles.

can·did (kan′did) *adj.* **1.** honest and straightforward; frank; sincere: *a candid opinion.* **2.** not posed; informal: *a candid photograph.* —**can′did·ly,** *adv.* —**can′did·ness,** *n.*

Candelabrum

can·di·da·cy (kan′di də sē) *n. pl.,* **can·di·da·cies.** the state or fact of being a candidate.

can·di·date (kan′də dāt′) *n.* a person who seeks, or is put forward by others for, an office or honor: *The senator denied that he was a Presidential candidate.* [Latin *candidātus* a person dressed in white, candidate for office, from *candidus* white. In ancient Rome the color white was thought to represent honesty, and candidates for office wore white togas to show that they were honest.]

can·died (kan′dēd) *adj.* **1.** cooked in or coated with sugar: *candied yams.* **2.** wholly or partially crystallized into sugar.

can·dle (kand′əl) *n.* **1.** a mass of wax, tallow, or other solid fat formed around a wick, burned to give light or low heat. **2.** another word for **candela.** —*v.t.* **can·dled, can·dling.** to examine (eggs) for freshness and quality by holding them in front of a light.

to hold a candle to. to compare favorably with; be as good as: *As a musician, he can't hold a candle to his brother.*

can·dle·hold·er (kand′əl hōl′dər) *n.* another word for **candlestick.**

can·dle·light (kand′əl līt′) *n.* **1.** the light given by a candle or candles. **2.** twilight; dusk; nightfall.

Can·dle·mas (kand′əl məs) *n.* a church festival celebrating the purification of the Virgin Mary, during which candles for sacred use are blessed. It falls on February 2.

can·dle·pin (kand′əl pin′) *n.* **1.** a cylindrical wooden pin tapering slightly at the top and bottom, used in the game of candlepins. **2. candlepins.** a bowling game using ten of these pins, in which three balls are bowled in each frame and the pins that are knocked down are not removed until each frame is over. ▲ used with a singular verb.

can·dle·pow·er (kand′əl pou′ər) *n.* a measure of the intensity of a source of light, based on the light given off in a particular direction from that source. Candlepower is expressed in candelas.

can·dle·stick (kand′əl stik′) *n.* a holder with a cup or spike for a candle.

can·dle·wick (kand′əl wik′) *n.* the wick of a candle.

can·dor (kan′dər) *n.* frankness, as of speech; honesty; openness.

can·dy (kan′dē) *n. pl.,* **can·dies. 1.** a sweet food made chiefly of sugar or syrup combined with other ingredients, such as chocolate, milk, nuts, or fruit. **2.** a piece of this. —*v.,* **can·died, can·dy·ing.** —*v.t.* **1.** to preserve by cooking or coating with sugar. **2.** to cover with or as with sugar crystals. —*v.i.* to turn into or become covered with sugar.

can·dy·tuft (kan′dē tuft′) *n.* a plant of the mustard family, having narrow leaves and clusters of small white, purple, or pink flowers.

cane (kān) *n.* **1.** a stick or staff, usually made of wood, used as an aid in walking. **2.** the slender, woody, jointed stem of certain tall grasses, such as bamboo, reed, and rattan. **3.** any plant having such a stem. **4.** a material made of such stems, used in making furniture and wickerwork. **5.** see **sugarcane.** —*v.t.,* **caned, can·ing. 1.** to beat or flog with a cane. **2.** to make or repair with cane.

cane·brake (kān′brāk′) *n.* a thicket of cane.

cane sugar, sugar obtained from sugarcane.

ca·nine (kā′nīn) *adj.* **1.** of, resembling, or relating to a dog. **2.** of or relating to the dog family, which includes dogs, foxes, wolves, coyotes, and jackals. —*n.* **1.** a domestic dog. **2.** any member of the dog family. **3.** see **canine tooth.**

canine tooth, one of the four sharp-pointed teeth located between the incisors and the bicuspids in the upper and lower jaw. Also, **cuspid.**

can·is·ter (kan′is tər) *n.* a small box, can, or other container, usually made of metal, used especially for holding coffee, sugar, flour, or other dry foods.

can·ker (kang′kər) *n.* **1.** an open sore, especially on the mouth or lip. **2.** anything that corrupts or destroys.

can·ker·ous (kang′kər əs) *adj.* of or like a canker.

can·ker·worm (kang′kər wurm′) *n.* any of several caterpillars that are very destructive to shade and fruit trees.

can·na (kan′ə) *n.* **1.** a red or yellow flower of a tropical plant. **2.** the plant bearing this flower, having large, oblong leaves.

canned (kand) *adj.* **1.** preserved in a can or jar: *canned fruit.* **2.** *Informal.* on a record; recorded: *The television comedy was broadcast with canned laughter.*

can·ner (kan′ər) *n.* a person who cans food.

can·ner·y (kan′ər ē) *n. pl.,* **can·ner·ies.** a factory where foods are canned.

Cannes (kan, kanz) *n.* a resort in southeastern France, on the Mediterranean.

can·ni·bal (kan′ə bəl) *n.* **1.** a human being who eats human flesh. **2.** an animal that eats its own kind. —*adj.* **1.** of or relating to cannibals. **2.** given to cannibalism.

can·ni·bal·ism (kan′ə bə liz′əm) *n.* the act or practice of eating the flesh of one's own kind. —**can′ni·bal·is′tic,** *adj.*

can·ni·bal·ize (kan′ə bə līz′) *v.t.,* **can·ni·bal·ized, can·ni·bal·iz·ing.** to take parts from (something) to build, repair, or strengthen one or more other things: *The boys built their hot rod by cannibalizing abandoned cars.*

can·ning (kan′ing) *n.* the act, process, or business of preserving food by sealing it in airtight containers.

can·non (kan′ən) *n. pl.,* **can·nons** or **can·non.** a large gun or firearm that is mounted on a base.

can·non·ade (kan′ə nād′) *n.* **1.** a continuous firing of artillery. **2.** an attack with artillery. —*v.t.,* **can·non·ad·ed, can·non·ad·ing.** to attack with artillery.

can·non·ball (kan′ən bôl′) *n.* a heavy metal ball designed to be fired from a cannon.

can·non·eer (kan′ə nēr′) *n.* an artilleryman; gunner.

can·not (kan′ot, ka not′) can not.

can·ny (kan′ē) *adj.,* **can·ni·er, can·ni·est.** shrewd and cautious; wary. —**can′ni·ly,** *adv.* —**can′ni·ness,** *n.*

ca·noe (kə nōō′) *n.* a light, narrow boat, usually pointed at both ends, propelled by hand with a paddle. —*v.,* **ca·noed, ca·noe·ing.** —*v.i.* to paddle or go in a canoe. —*v.t.* to transport by canoe. —**ca·noe′ist,** *n.*

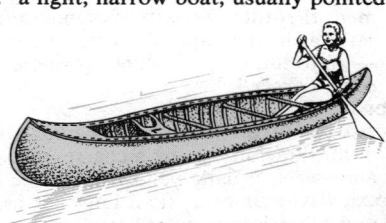

Canoe

can·on¹ (kan′ən) *n.* **1.** a law, rule, or decree of a church. **2.** a general rule, fundamental principle, or standard: *to be guided by the canons of good behavior.* **3.** a collection or list of the books of the Bible accepted by the church as genuine and divinely inspired. **4.** a list of saints officially recognized by the Roman Catholic Church and certain other churches. **5.** a musical composition in which a melody is begun and continued by different voices in succession. [Old English *canon* rule.]

can·on² (kan′ən) *n.* **1.** a clergyman serving in a cathedral. **2.** in the Middle Ages, a Roman Catholic clergyman living according to certain rules, or canons, of the church. [Old French *canonie* priest, from Church Latin *canōnicus* clergyman, a person belonging to the canon or rule.]

ca·ñon (can′yən) another spelling of **canyon.**

ca·non·i·cal (kə non′i kəl) *adj.* **1.** relating to, established by, or conforming to church law or rule. **2.** of or contained in the canon of the Bible.

canonical hours, the seven periods of the day fixed by church canon for prayer and devotion.

can·on·ize (kan′ə nīz′) *v.t.,* **can·on·ized, can·on·iz·ing.** to declare (a deceased person) a saint; place in the canon of saints: *Joan of Arc was canonized almost five hundred years after her death.* —**can′on·i·za′tion,** *n.*

canon law, in a Christian church, the body of law governing matters of faith and discipline.

Ca·no·pus (kə nō′pəs) *n.* the second brightest star in the sky.

can·o·py (kan′ə pē) *n. pl.,* **can·o·pies. 1.** a covering of cloth or other material, hung over a bed, throne, or entrance of a building, or supported on poles over a person or sacred object. **2.** an overhanging shelter or covering: *the canopy of the stars.* **3.** a transparent, sliding covering over an airplane cockpit. —*v.t.,* **can·o·pied, can·o·py·ing.** to cover with a canopy.

canst (kanst) *Archaic.* the present indicative, second person singular of **can.**

cant¹ (kant) *n.* **1.** talk that is insincere or trite, especially hypocritical religious or moral statements. **2.** words or language peculiar to a particular profession, class, or group: *The will was written in the legal cant of attorneys.* [Latin *cantus* song.]

Canopy

at; āpe; cär; end; mē; it; īce; hot; ōld; fôrk; wood; fōol; oil; out; up; turn; sing; thin; **this**; hw in white; zh in treasure. The symbol ə stands for the sound of a in about, e in taken, i in pencil, o in lemon, and u in circus.

cant² (kant) *n.* **1.** a slant or slope; tilt. **2.** a sudden movement that tilts or overturns something. —*v.t.* **1.** to put or set at an angle; slant; tilt. **2.** to give a sloping edge to; bevel. —*v.i.* to tilt, slant, or slope. [Middle Dutch *cant* a border, edge, corner.]

can't (kant) cannot.

can·ta·loupe (kan'tə lōp') *also,* **can·ta·loup.** *n.* a kind of muskmelon, having a coarse, pale green or yellow rind and sweet, usually yellowish-orange flesh.

can·tan·ker·ous (kan tang'kər əs) *adj.* ill-tempered and quarrelsome. —**can·tan'ker·ous·ly,** *adv.* —**can·tan'ker·ous·ness,** *n.*

can·ta·ta (kən tä'tə) *n.* a musical composition sung by a chorus. It is like an opera but is not acted.

can·teen (kan tēn') *n.* **1.** a small metal container for carrying water or other liquids. **2.** a place run by civilian volunteers where free food, beverages, and, usually, entertainment are provided for servicemen. **3.** another word for **post exchange. 4.** a place providing food and beverages, such as a snack bar at a factory.

can·ter (kan'tər) *n.* a slow, easy gallop. —*v.t., v.i.* to move or ride at a canter.

Can·ter·bur·y (kan'tər ber'ē) *n.* a city in southeastern England, the site of a famous cathedral. It is the seat of the spiritual leader of the Church of England.

Canterbury bell, a plant with tall stalks of bell-shaped flowers having white, pink, or blue-violet petals.

cant hook, a pole with a movable hooked arm at or near one end, used by loggers and linemen to grip and turn over logs or poles.

can·ti·cle (kan'ti kəl) *n.* a hymn whose words are usually taken directly from the Bible.

can·ti·le·ver (kant'əl ē'vər, kant'əl ev'ər) *n.* a projecting bracket, beam, or slab that is supported only at one end.

cantilever bridge, a bridge formed by two cantilevers whose projecting ends meet but do not support each other.

can·tle (kant'əl) *n.* the part of the seat of certain saddles that curves up at the back.

can·to (kan'tō) *n. pl.,* **can·tos.** one of the main divisions of a long poem.

can·ton (kan'tən, kan'ton) *n.* a small territorial district or political division of a country, especially one of the twenty-two states of the Swiss confederation.

Can·ton (*def. 1* kan'ton; *def. 2* kant'ən) *n.* **1.** a city in southeastern China. Pop. (1965 est.), 3,000,000. Also, **Guangzhou. 2.** a city in northeastern Ohio. Pop. (1970), 110,053.

Can·ton·ese (kan'tə nēz') *n. pl.,* **Can·ton·ese. 1.** a person who was born or is living in Canton, China. **2.** a Chinese dialect spoken in and around Canton, China. —*adj.* of or relating to Canton, China, its people, or their dialect.

can·ton·ment (kan tōn'mənt, kan ton'mənt) *n.* **1.** a military installation that includes quarters for servicemen and their families. **2.** temporary housing for troops.

can·tor (kan'tər) *n.* **1.** the chief singer of the liturgy in a synagogue. **2.** the singer who leads a choir or congregation.

Ca·nuck (kə nuk') *n. Slang.* **1.** Canadian. **2.** French Canadian. ▲ sometimes considered offensive.

can·vas (kan'vəs) *n. pl.,* **can·vas·es. 1.** a heavy cloth made of cotton, flax, or hemp, used to make items that must be strong and durable, such as tents, sails, boat and truck covers, and awnings. **2.** a piece of canvas on which a painting, especially an oil painting, is done. **3.** an oil painting done on canvas: *an artist's favorite canvas.*

Cant hook

can·vas·back (kan'vəs bak') *n.* a wild duck of North America. The male has black and brown feathers on most of its body and white feathers on its back.

can·vass (kan'vəs) *v.t.* **1.** to go through (a place) or among (people) trying to get votes, opinions, orders, or contributions: *The candidate's supporters canvassed the neighborhood.* **2.** to examine or discuss carefully or thoroughly: *to canvass a legal problem.* —*v.i.* to go about trying to get votes, opinions, orders, or contributions. —*n. pl.,* **can·vass·es. 1.** the act of canvassing. **2.** an examination; discussion. —**can'vass·er,** *n.*

can·yon (kan'yən) *also,* **cañon.** *n.* a deep valley with steep sides, usually with a stream running through it.

caou·tchouc (kou chook') *n.* natural rubber, especially in its crude form.

cap (kap) *n.* **1.** a soft, close-fitting head covering, usually without a brim or with a visor. **2.** a special head covering worn to show rank, membership, or occupation: *a nurse's cap.* **3.** something resembling a cap in shape, position, or use: *a bottle cap.* **4.** a paper wrapping or covering containing a small quantity of explosive, used in toy guns. **5.** see **percussion cap.** —*v.t.,* **capped, cap·ping. 1.** to put a cap on; cover: *to cap a bottle.* **2.** to form or serve as a cap, cover, or top for; lie on top of: *Clouds capped the mountains.* **3.** to follow with something equal to or better than; match; surpass: *He capped his friend's story with an even more exciting one.*

cap. **1.** *pl.,* **caps.** capital letter. **2.** capital.

ca·pa·bil·i·ty (kā'pə bil'ə tē) *n. pl.,* **ca·pa·bil·i·ties. 1.** the quality of being capable; ability; capacity: *Fred's capability as a leader is beyond question.* **2.** a quality or ability that may be used or developed; potentiality.

ca·pa·ble (kā'pə bəl) *adj.* having or showing ability; able; efficient; competent: *a capable doctor, a capable performance.* —**ca'pa·bly,** *adv.*

capable of a. having the capacity, ability, or quality needed for: *I think that our team is capable of winning the championship.* **b.** open or subject to: *The speaker made several statements that were capable of misunderstanding.*

ca·pa·cious (kə pā'shəs) *adj.* able to hold or contain much; roomy; spacious: *a capacious auditorium.* —**ca·pa'cious·ly,** *adv.* —**ca·pa'cious·ness,** *n.*

ca·pac·i·tance (kə pas'ə təns) *n.* the ratio of the amount of electric charge stored in a capacitor to the voltage across its terminals. Capacitance is measured in farads.

ca·pac·i·tor (kə pas'ə tər) *n.* a device for receiving and storing an electric charge, usually made of two metallic plates separated by a nonconductor. Also, **condenser.**

ca·pac·i·ty (kə pas'ə tē) *n. pl.,* **ca·pac·i·ties. 1.** the ability to receive or contain: *The auditorium has a very small seating capacity.* **2.** the maximum amount that can be held or contained in a space; content: *This car's gas tank has a capacity of twenty gallons.* **3.** the ability or power to do something: *Man has the capacity to do good or evil.* **4.** mental ability: *a scholar of great capacity.* **5.** a specific position, occupation, or function: *Mr. Smith is representing the company in the capacity of district manager.*

Rotors Stators
(movable)

Conductors

Capacitor

cap and bells, a cap trimmed with bells, worn by a court jester.

cap and gown, a flat cap and loose gown, worn by teachers and students at academic functions, especially at graduation ceremonies.

ca·par·i·son (kə par′ə sən) *n.* **1.** an ornamental covering for a horse. **2.** rich clothing. —*v.t.* **1.** to cover (a horse) with a caparison. **2.** to dress with rich clothing.

cape[1] (kāp) *n.* an outer garment without sleeves, which falls loosely over the shoulders and is worn in place of or attached to a jacket or coat. [French *cape* this garment, going back to Late Latin *cappa* hood, cloak.]

Caparison *(def. 1)*

cape[2] (kāp) *n.* a point of land extending out from the coastline into the sea or a lake. [French *cap*, going back to Latin *caput* head.]

Cape. Capes are entered in the dictionary under their proper names. For example, **Cape Horn** is listed in the H's.

ca·per[1] (kā′pər) *v.i.* to leap or jump about in a playful manner; prance. —*n.* **1.** a playful leap, skip, or jump. **2.** a prank; antic. **3.** *Slang.* an illegal act, such as a robbery or burglary. [Middle French *capriole* a leap, caper, from Italian *capriola* a leap like that of a goat, going back to Latin *caper* goat.]

ca·per[2] (kā′pər) *n.* **1.** the green flower bud of a Mediterranean shrub, pickled and used as a seasoning. **2.** the spiny shrub bearing this flower bud. [Latin *capparis* this shrub, from Greek *kapparis*.]

Cape Town *also,* **Cape·town.** a port city in the Republic of South Africa, on the southwestern coast of the country. Pop. (1971 est.), 721,350.

Cape Verde Islands, an island country in the North Atlantic Ocean, west of Cape Verde. Land area, 1,557 sq. mi. Pop. (1978 est.), 300,000.

cap·il·lar·i·ty (kap′ə lar′ə tē) *n.* another word for **capillary action.**

cap·il·lar·y (kap′ə ler′ē) *n. pl.,* **cap·il·lar·ies. 1.** any of the smallest blood vessels of the circulatory system, connecting the arteries and veins. **2.** a tube with a small, very narrow opening. —*adj.* **1.** of or like a hair; fine; slender. **2.** having a very small opening, as a tube. **3.** relating to or taking place in a capillary or capillaries.

capillary action, the rising or falling of a liquid where it touches a solid. When a lump of sugar is dipped into coffee, capillary action causes the coffee to rise in the lump. The tendency of liquids to rise in this way is called **capillary attraction;** the tendency to fall is called **capillary repulsion.** Also, **capillarity.**

cap·i·tal[1] (kap′it əl) *n.* **1.** a city or town in which the official seat of government of a country, state, or other political division is located: *Albany is the capital of New York State.* **2.** see **capital letter. 3.** the total amount of money or property owned or used by a corporation or individual. **4.** wealth in any form used or available for use in the production of more wealth. —*adj.* **1.** main, principal, or chief. **2.** being the official seat of government: *Madrid is Spain's capital city.* **3.** excellent; first-rate: *Jim is a capital fellow.* **4.** punishable by or involving the death penalty: *a capital offense.* **5.** of or relating to capital or wealth: *capital investments.* [Old French *capital* chief, going back to Latin *caput* head.]

to make capital of. to use to one's advantage.

▲ **Capital** is sometimes confused with **capitol. Capital** means the city in which a government is located: *Washington D.C. is the capital of the United States.* A **capitol** is the building in which a legislature meets: *The U.S. Congress meets in the Capitol.*

cap·i·tal[2] (kap′it əl) *n.* the top part of a column or pillar. [Late Latin *capitellum,* a form of Latin *caput* head.]

capital gain, the profit resulting from the sale of capital investments, such as stocks, bonds, or real estate.

cap·i·tal·ism (kap′it əl iz′əm) *n.* an economic system in which the means of production, such as land and factories, are privately owned and operated for profit, the wealth and goods passing freely between producers and consumers. Competition between producers determines the price of goods.

cap·i·tal·ist (kap′it əl ist) *n.* **1.** a person who has capital, especially capital that is available for, or being used in, some business activity. **2.** a supporter of capitalism. **3.** any wealthy or financially successful person. —**cap′i·tal·is′tic,** *adj.* —**cap′i·tal·is′ti·cal·ly,** *adv.*

cap·i·tal·i·za·tion (kap′it əl i zā′shən) *n.* **1.** the act or process of capitalizing. **2.** the total amount of capital used in a business.

cap·i·tal·ize (kap′it əl īz′) *v.,* **cap·i·tal·ized, cap·i·tal·iz·ing.** —*v.t.* **1.** to write or print with a capital letter or letters, or begin with a capital letter: *Always capitalize proper nouns.* **2.** to change into or use as capital. **3.** to provide capital for; finance. —*v.i.* to use to one's advantage; take advantage of: *The tennis player capitalized on his opponent's weak serve and won the match.*

capital letter, a large form of a letter of the alphabet, used especially as the first letter of a sentence or proper noun. A and B are capital letters.

● **Capital letters** as we use them today have been used for only a relatively short period of time. In early Greek and Latin writing, there were letters called capitals, but they were not used in combination with small letters. These early capital letters were used as a separate style of writing, such as we use script and printing separately today. It is believed that the modern use of capitals first developed in the Middle Ages, when the first letter of a paragraph was written in a large, ornate way. Later, people used two distinct styles of letters: capitals at the beginning of paragraphs and sentences, and small letters everywhere else. Eventually people began to use capital letters as we do today.

cap·i·tal·ly (kap′it əl ē) *adv.* in a capital manner; excellently; admirably.

capital punishment, the death penalty for a crime.

capital ship, a large warship, formerly a heavily armed sailing ship, now usually an aircraft carrier or battleship.

Cap·i·tol (kap′it əl) *n.* **1.** the building in which the U.S. Congress meets, in Washington, D.C. **2.** *also,* **capitol.** a building in which a state legislature meets. ▲ See **capital**[1] for usage note.

ca·pit·u·late (kə pich′ə lāt′) *v.i.,* **ca·pit·u·lat·ed, ca·pit·u·lat·ing.** to surrender or yield, especially on certain terms or conditions: *The rebels capitulated with the understanding that they would not be sent to prison.*

ca·pit·u·la·tion (kə pich′ə lā′shən) *n.* **1.** surrender, especially on certain terms or conditions. **2.** a statement of the main points of a subject; summary.

ca·pon (kā′pon) *n.* a young, castrated rooster.

Ca·pri (käp′rē, kə prē′) *n.* a small island off the southwestern coast of Italy, near Naples.

at; āpe; cär; end; mē; it; īce; hot; ōld; fôrk; wood; fōōl; oil; out; up; turn; sing; thin; this; hw in white; zh in treasure. The symbol ə stands for the sound of a in about, e in taken, i in pencil, o in lemon, and u in circus.

ca·price (kə prēs′) *n.* **1.** a sudden change of mind for no good or apparent reason; whim. **2.** a tendency to change one's mind in this way; capriciousness.

ca·pri·cious (kə prish′əs) *adj.* tending to change suddenly, unexpectedly, and for no apparent reason; guided by or as if by whim or fancy; unpredictable: *capricious weather.* —**ca·pri′cious·ly,** *adv.* —**ca·pri′cious·ness,** *n.*

Cap·ri·corn (kap′rə kôrn′) *n.* **1.** see Tropic of Capricorn. **2.** a constellation in the southern sky, thought to resemble a goat in shape. **3.** the tenth sign of the zodiac.

caps., capital letters.

cap·si·cum (kap′si kəm) *n.* any of a group of plants widely grown for their red or green pods containing sharptasting seeds. Peppers, pimientos, and chilies are kinds of capsicum.

cap·size (kap′sīz, kap sīz′) *v.,* **cap·sized, cap·siz·ing.** —*v.t.* to cause to overturn: *Rough waves capsized the boat.* —*v.i.* to overturn: *The boat capsized in the hurricane.*

cap·stan (kap′stən) *n.* a device with an upright spindle that is turned by hand or by motor to wind up a rope or cable, as in hoisting an anchor.

Capstan

cap·su·lar (kap′sə lər) *adj.* of, in, or resembling a capsule.

cap·sule (kap′səl) *n.* **1.** a small soluble case enclosing a dose of medicine. **2.** a detachable, sealed compartment of a spacecraft, designed to support life during flight and to be recovered after flight. **3.** a dry seedcase that opens when ripe. The seeds of the iris, azalea, and poppy develop in capsules. **4.** any membrane or membranous sac enclosing an organ or body part. —*adj.* in a brief form; concise: *The essay gave a capsule summary of the novel's plot.*

Capt., Captain.

cap·tain (kap′tən) *n.* **1.** a person who is in charge of or has authority over others; leader; chief: *Don is captain of the soccer team.* **2.** a person in command of a boat or ship. **3.** in the U. S. Navy and Coast Guard, an officer ranking below a commodore or a rear admiral and above a commander. **4.** in the U. S. Army, Air Force, and Marine Corps, an officer ranking below a major and above a first lieutenant. —*v.t.* to act as captain of; lead: *John will captain the basketball team this year.*

cap·tain·cy (kap′tən sē) *n. pl.,* **cap·tain·cies.** the rank or authority of a captain.

cap·tion (kap′shən) *n.* **1.** a title or written description for a picture. **2.** a title or heading, as at the beginning of a chapter, page, or article. —*v.t.* to furnish with a caption.

cap·tious (kap′shəs) *adj.* **1.** inclined to make much of unimportant faults or defects; difficult to please: *a captious critic.* **2.** designed to entrap or confuse: *a captious question.* —**cap′tious·ly,** *adv.* —**cap′tious·ness,** *n.*

cap·ti·vate (kap′tə vāt′) *v.t.,* **cap·ti·vat·ed, cap·ti·vat·ing.** to capture and hold the attention or affection of, as by beauty or excellence; charm; fascinate; enchant: *The audience was captivated by the actor's performance.* —**cap′ti·va′tion,** *n.*

cap·tive (kap′tiv) *n.* a person captured and held in confinement; prisoner: *The enemy captives were brought to the commanding officer for questioning.* —*adj.* **1.** taken or kept prisoner: *The captive soldiers were treated well.* **2.** kept under control; restrained; confined: *a captive balloon.*

cap·tiv·i·ty (kap tiv′ə tē) *n. pl.,* **cap·tiv·i·ties.** the state of being a captive: *Animals in a zoo live in captivity.*

cap·tor (kap′tər) *n.* a person who captures someone or something.

cap·ture (kap′chər) *v.t.,* **cap·tured, cap·tur·ing. 1.** to take or seize by force, surprise, or skill: *to capture an enemy gunboat, to capture a lion, to capture an opponent's chess piece.* **2.** to attract or catch: *The exciting novel captured my interest.* **3.** to represent in permanent form; reproduce: *The artist tried to capture his wife's beauty on canvas.* —*n.* **1.** the act of capturing. **2.** a person or thing that is captured.

cap·u·chin (kap′yə shin) *n.* **1.** any of various tree-dwelling monkeys having black or brown fur and a long tail that is used for grasping and climbing. Some have black hair on their head that resembles a monk's hood. **2. Capuchin.** a member of one of the branches of the Franciscan religious order of the Roman Catholic Church. A Capuchin monk usually is bearded and wears sandals and a brown habit with a long, pointed hood.

Capuchin

cap·y·ba·ra (kap′ə bär′ə) *n.* a South American rodent resembling a large guinea pig, and having a coarse coat of brownish, bristly hair. It grows to a length of three to four feet and is the largest living rodent.

car (kär) *n.* **1.** another word for **automobile. 2.** a vehicle designed to move on rails: *a railroad car.* **3.** any vehicle that moves on wheels. **4.** the part of an elevator that carries the passengers or cargo.

car·a·ba·o (kar′ə ba′ō) *n. pl.,* **car·a·ba·os.** a water buffalo of the Philippines.

car·a·bi·neer (kar′ə bə nēr′) *also,* **car·a·bi·nier.** *n.* formerly, a soldier in the cavalry armed with a carbine.

Ca·ra·cas (kə rä′kəs) *n.* the capital and largest city of Venezuela, in the northern part of the country. Pop. (1969 est.), 1,600,000.

car·a·cul (kar′ə kəl) *n.* the loosely curled fur of very young karakul lambs. Also, **karakul.**

ca·rafe (kə raf′) *n.* a glass bottle for water, wine, or other beverages; decanter.

car·a·mel (kar′ə məl, kär′məl) *n.* **1.** burnt sugar used for coloring and flavoring foods. **2.** a chewy candy made mainly from sugar, cream, and corn syrup, usually in the form of small squares.

car·a·pace (kar′ə pās′) *n.* the hard or bony covering on the back of some animals, such as turtles or lobsters.

car·at (kar′ət) *n.* **1.** a unit of weight equal to ⅕ of a gram, used chiefly in measuring the weight of gems. **2.** another spelling of **karat.**

car·a·van (kar′ə van′) *n.* **1.** a company of travelers, merchants, or pilgrims traveling together for safety and security, especially through deserts or dangerous regions. **2.** a number of vehicles traveling together: *The caravan of army trucks stopped to refuel.* **3.** *British.* a home on wheels; trailer.

car·a·van·sa·ry (kar′ə van′sər ē) *n. pl.,* **car·a·van·se·rai** (kar′ə van′sə rī′). **1.** in certain Oriental countries, an inn with a large central court, in which caravans can stay. **2.** any large inn or hotel.

car·a·vel (kar′ə vel′) *n.* any of several types of small, fast sailing ships developed in Portugal and Spain in the fifteenth century. Two of Christopher Columbus' ships were caravels.

car·a·way (kar′ə wā′) *n.* **1.** the fragrant, spicy seeds of a plant related to carrots and parsley, used as a spice. **2.** the plant bearing these seeds.

car·bide (kär′bīd) *n.* **1.** any of a large group of compounds that contain carbon and one other element, usually a metal. **2.** see **calcium carbide.**

car·bine (kär′bīn, kär′bēn) *n.* a lightweight automatic or semiautomatic rifle.

car·bo·hy·drate (kär′bō hī′drāt) *n.* a compound of carbon, hydrogen, and oxygen produced by green plants in the process of photosynthesis. Cellulose, sugars, and starches are carbohydrates.

car·bo·lat·ed (kär′bə lā′tid) *adj.* containing or treated with carbolic acid, or phenol.

car·bol·ic acid (kär bol′ik) *n.* another term for **phenol.**

car·bon (kär′bən) *n.* **1.** a common nonmetallic element occurring in crystalline forms, such as diamond and graphite, and in uncrystallized forms, such as charcoal. Carbon is present in all organic compounds and in many inorganic compounds. Symbol: **C 2.** a piece of carbon paper. **3.** see **carbon copy.**

carbon 12, the most common isotope of carbon, now used instead of oxygen as the standard for determining the atomic weight of chemical elements.

carbon 14, a radioactive isotope of carbon, used in archaeological dating.

car·bo·na·ceous (kär′bə nā′shəs) *adj.* of, relating to, or containing carbon.

car·bon·ate (kär′bə nāt′) *n.* a salt or ester of carbonic acid. —*v.t.,* **car·bon·at·ed, car·bon·at·ing.** to charge or treat (a substance) with carbon dioxide, especially to dissolve carbon dioxide in (a liquid) to make it effervescent.

car·bon·a·tion (kär′bə nā′shən) *n.* treatment or saturation with carbon dioxide, especially in manufacturing soda water.

carbon copy 1. a copy, as of a letter, made by using carbon paper. **2.** a close or exact replica; duplicate: *The boy is a carbon copy of his father.*

carbon dioxide, a colorless, odorless gas, made up of carbon and oxygen, that is present in the atmosphere. It is used commercially in soft drinks, fire extinguishers, and, in the form of dry ice, as a refrigerating agent. Carbon dioxide is exhaled by animals as a waste product and is absorbed by green plants as part of photosynthesis. Formula: CO_2

car·bon·ic (kär bon′ik) *adj.* of, containing, or obtained from carbon.

carbonic acid, a weak acid formed when carbon dioxide is dissolved in water.

Car·bon·if·er·ous (kär′bə nif′ər əs) *n.* the geological period of the Paleozoic era during which most of the coal-forming tropical forests flourished. —*adj.* **1.** of, relating to, or characteristic of this period. **2. carboniferous.** containing carbon or coal.

car·bon·ize (kär′bə nīz′) *v.t.,* **car·bon·ized, car·bon·iz·ing. 1.** to change (a substance) into carbon, as by burning. **2.** to cover, treat, or combine (something) with carbon. —**car′bon·i·za′tion,** *n.*

carbon monoxide, a colorless, odorless, very poisonous gas that is formed when carbon burns in an atmosphere not having enough oxygen for complete combustion. Carbon monoxide is found in the exhaust gases of automobiles.

carbon paper, a thin paper coated on one side with a preparation of carbon or another dark coloring substance. Carbon paper is placed between two sheets of paper to reproduce on the lower sheet any marks made by pressure, as of writing or typing, on the top sheet.

carbon tet·ra·chlo·ride (tet′rə klôr′īd) a colorless, poisonous, nonflammable liquid made from carbon and chlorine. It is used in refrigerants and propellants, in fire extinguishers, and as a cleaning fluid.

Car·bo·run·dum (kär′bə run′dəm) *n. Trademark.* an abrasive made of silicon carbide, used in grinding and polishing.

car·bun·cle (kär′bung′kəl) *n.* **1.** a hard, painful, pus-filled sore under the skin that resembles a boil, but is larger and more severe. Carbuncles are often accompanied by fever, headache, and loss of appetite. **2.** a smooth, deep-red garnet or other jewel.

car·bu·re·tor (kär′bə rā′tər) *also, British,* **car·bu·ret·tor.** *n.* a device in an internal-combustion engine that mixes a fine spray of gasoline with air to form a mixture that can be burned in the cylinders of the engine.

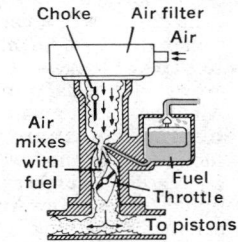

Carburetor

car·cass (kär′kəs) *n. pl.,* **car·cass·es. 1.** the dead body of an animal. **2.** *Informal.* the body of a human being. **3.** decaying or worthless remains, such as the ruined framework of a structure: *All that was left of the farm was the carcass of an old barn.*

car·cin·o·gen (kär sin′ə jən) *n.* any of various substances that are capable of causing or helping to cause cancer.

card¹ (kärd) *n.* **1.** a flat, usually rectangular piece of stiff paper or thin cardboard, used for any of various purposes, such as for identifying the owner of something: *Each person in our club had a membership card.* **2.** one of a set of such cards, marked with pictures, numbers, or symbols, used in playing various games; playing card. **3. cards. a.** a game played with such cards, such as poker or bridge. **b.** the playing of such a game: *David usually beats me at cards.* **4.** a piece of stiff paper or cardboard, usually decorated and bearing a message or greeting; greeting card: *a birthday card, a Christmas card.* **5.** see **post card** (def. 1). **6.** *Informal.* an amusing or witty person. [French *carte* a piece of stiff paper, playing card.]

in the cards. likely to happen.

to put one's cards on the table or **to lay one's cards on the table.** to be frank and open, as about one's intentions; be completely straightforward.

card² (kärd) *n.* a comb, brush, or similar device having metal or wire teeth, used to separate, comb, or straighten fibers, as of wool or cotton, before spinning. —*v.t.* to use a card on: *to card wool.* [French *carde* this device, going back to Latin *carduus* thistle. Thistles were originally used to make cards.] —**card′er,** *n.*

card·board (kärd′bôrd′) *n.* a thin pasteboard or other stiff material made of paper pulp. Cardboard is used to make such items as boxes and cards.

car·di·ac (kär′dē ak′) *adj.* of, relating to, or near the heart: *cardiac disease, a cardiac patient.*

Car·diff (kär′dif) *n.* the capital and chief city of Wales. Pop. (1971), 278,221.

car·di·gan (kär′di gən) *n.* a sweater that opens down the front and usually has no collar. [From the Earl of *Cardigan,* 1797–1868, a British army officer.]

---

at; āpe; cär; end; mē; it; īce; hot; ōld; fôrk; wood; fōōl; oil; out; up; turn; sing; thin; this; hw in white; zh in treasure. The symbol ə stands for the sound of **a** in **about**, **e** in **taken**, **i** in **pencil**, **o** in **lemon**, and **u** in **circus.**

car·di·nal (kärd′ən əl) *n.* **1.** in the Roman Catholic Church, one of a number of high officials ranking immediately below the Pope and appointed by him. When he dies, the cardinals meet to elect a new Pope. **2.** an American songbird related to the finch. The male cardinal has bright red feathers with a black patch around the bill. **3.** a deep, rich red color. —*adj.* **1.** of greatest importance; chief; principal. **2.** having the color cardinal; deep, rich red: *Cardinal autumn leaves covered the hillsides.*

Cardinal *(def. 2)*

cardinal flower **1.** the bright red flower of a plant that grows wild in damp regions of eastern and central North America. **2.** the plant bearing this flower.

cardinal number, a number that expresses how many, such as zero, one, two, three, and so forth.

▲ A **cardinal number** shows the number or total of something: *twelve boxes.* An **ordinal number** indicates the number that something is in a series: *the twelfth box.*

cardinal points, the four main directions of the compass; north, south, east, and west.

card·ing (kär′ding) *n.* the process of preparing textile fibers, such as wool, cotton, or flax, for spinning. During carding, the raw material is passed through rollers and brushes to clean, untangle, and straighten the fibers.

car·di·o·gram (kär′dē ə gram′) *n.* see **electrocardiogram.**

car·di·o·graph (kär′dē ə graf′) *n.* see **electrocardiograph.**

care (ker) *n.* **1.** a troubled state of mind, such as that arising from anxiety, doubt, or concern; worry; distress. **2.** the cause of such a state of mind: *She acts as though she doesn't have a care in the world.* **3.** close and serious attention: *The scientist used great care in handling the dangerous chemical.* **4.** keeping or charge; supervision; custody: *The sick child was under a doctor's care.* —*v.,* **cared, car·ing.** —*v.i.* **1.** to have or show interest; be anxious or concerned: *I care a great deal about the future of this country.* **2.** to have or feel a liking, fondness, or affection: *He doesn't care for spinach. The boy cares very much about his sister.* **3.** to want or wish; like: *Would you care to go the movies this evening?* **4.** to have an objection; mind. *Do you care if I borrow the book?* —*v.t.* to feel interest, concern, or distress about; pay attention to: *He doesn't care what people think of the way he dresses.* —**car′er,** *n.*

   in care of. at the address of: *The letter was sent to him in care of his former roommate.*

   to care for. to look after or provide for; take care of.

   to take care. to be careful: *Take care crossing the street.*

   to take care of. a. to look after or provide for; tend: *A nurse took care of Kathy while she was sick.* **b.** to attend to; deal with; finish: *Take care of the most important tasks first.*

ca·reen (kə rēn′) *v.i.* **1.** to sway from side to side while moving quickly; lurch: *The speeding car careened around the corner.* **2.** to lean to one side: *The ship careened as her sails caught the wind.* —*v.t.* to turn (a ship) over on its side in order to clean or repair the bottom.

ca·reer (kə rēr′) *n.* **1.** an occupation or profession: *Bob chose acting as his career. Joan hopes to have a career in medicine.* **2.** the course or progress of a person's life: *The newspaperman had met many interesting people in his career.* **3.** a swift or rushing movement or course; speed: *The horse galloped across the field in full career.* —*v.i.* to move or run with a swift, headlong motion: *The train careered down the tracks.*

care·free (ker′frē′) *adj.* free from care or worry; untroubled; lighthearted: *We spent a carefree day in the country.*

care·ful (ker′fəl) *adj.* **1.** showing caution and close attention; watchful; cautious: *Be careful not to trip on that last step. He was careful not to say anything about the surprise party.* **2.** done or made with great care or thoroughness; painstaking: *The scientist did careful research.* **3.** taking pains with or being attentive to one's work: *Careful writers try not to make spelling mistakes.* —**care′ful·ly,** *adv.* —**care′ful·ness,** *n.*

care·less (ker′lis) *adj.* **1.** not paying enough attention; not cautious or watchful; negligent: *The careless waiter spilled the soup.* **2.** caused by or done with a lack of care, attentiveness, or thoughtfulness: *Spelling that word wrong was a careless mistake.* **3.** free from care or worry; carefree: *The hobo led a simple and careless life.* —**care′less·ly,** *adv.* —**care′less·ness,** *n.*

ca·ress (kə res′) *v.t.* to touch or stroke gently and lovingly; pet: *The girl tenderly caressed her new puppy.* —*n.* **1.** a gentle, loving touch or stroke. **2.** a light, soothing touch: *the soft caress of a summer breeze.*

car·et (kar′it) *n.* a mark (∧) used in editing to indicate where something should be inserted, as in *The deer* ^ran^∧ *away.*

care·tak·er (ker′tā′kər) *n.* a person who takes care of a person, place, or thing, especially the custodian of a building or estate.

care·worn (ker′wôrn′) *adj.* showing the effects of worry or distress: *The old beggar's face was wrinkled and careworn.*

car·fare (kär′fer′) *n.* the amount a passenger must pay for a ride on a bus, subway, or the like.

car·go (kär′gō) *n. pl.,* **car·goes** or **car·gos.** the goods or merchandise carried by a ship, plane, or vehicle: *The freighter carried a cargo of rice.*

Car·ib (kar′ib) *n.* **1.** a member of one of several Indian tribes that live in the West Indies and northeastern South America. **2.** the family of South American Indian languages spoken chiefly in the West Indies and northeastern parts of South America.

Car·ib·be·an (kar′ə bē′ən, kə rib′ē ən) *n.* **1.** a sea bounded on the north and east by the West Indies, on the west by Central America, and on the south by South America. Also, **Caribbean Sea. 2. the Caribbean.** the region made up of this sea and those lands in and around it. —*adj.* **1.** of or relating to the Caribbean; **2.** of or relating to the Caribs, their languages, or their culture.

car·i·bou (kar′ə bōō′) *n. pl.,* **car·i·bous** or **car·i·bou.** any of a group of large deer that live in the northern regions of the world, having a coarse, heavy coat and large antlers. The caribou of Europe and Asia is usually called the reindeer.

car·i·ca·ture (kar′ə kə choor′) *n.* **1.** a picture or description that ridiculously exaggerates or distorts the characteristics, peculiarities, or striking features of a person or thing. **2.** the art or process of making such pictures or descriptions. —*v.t.,* **car·i·ca·tured, car·i·ca·tur·ing.** to make a caricature of.

car·i·ca·tur·ist (kar′ə ka choor′ist) *n.* a person who makes caricatures.

car·ies (ker′ēz) *n., pl.* decay of the teeth.

car·il·lon (kar′ə lon′) *n.* **1.** a set of bells usually played by means of a keyboard. **2.** a melody played on a carillon.

car·load (kär′lōd′) *n.* the amount that a car can hold or carry.

Car·lyle, Thomas (kär līl′) 1795–1881, Scottish essayist and historian.

Car·mel, Mount (kär mel′, kär′məl) a short, mountainous ridge in northwestern Israel.

C

Car·mel·ite (kär′mə līt′) *n.* a member of a religious order of friars and nuns founded in Palestine in the twelfth century. —*adj.* of or relating to the Carmelites or their order.

car·mine (kär′mən, kär′mīn) *n.* **1.** a deep red or purplish-red color; crimson. **2.** the crimson pigment obtained from the dye cochineal. —*adj.* having the color carmine; deep red or purplish-red.

car·nage (kär′nij) *n.* a great and bloody slaughter, as in battle: *The war caused terrible carnage.*

car·nal (kärn′əl) *adj.* **1.** relating to the passions and appetites of the body; sensual: *carnal pleasures.* **2.** not spiritual; worldly. —**car′nal·ly,** *adv.*

car·na·tion (kär nā′shən) *n.* **1.** the fragrant flower of a plant, grown commercially and as a garden flower. **2.** the plant bearing this flower, having grayish-green leaves that look like grass. **3.** a light red color. —*adj.* having the color carnation; light red.

Car·ne·gie, Andrew (kär nā′gē, kär′nə gē) 1835–1919, U.S. steel manufacturer and philanthropist, born in Scotland.

car·nel·ian (kär nēl′yən) *n.* a semiprecious stone that is red to reddish-orange in color.

Carnation

car·ni·val (kär′nə vəl) *n.* **1.** a public amusement show, usually one that travels, having rides, side-shows, games, and refreshments. **2.** any merrymaking or festival, such as an organized program of entertainment or sports. **3.** *also,* **Carnival.** the period of feasting and merrymaking that comes just before Lent. It varies from three days to a few weeks.

car·ni·vore (kär′nə vôr′) *n.* any of numerous animals having long, sharp teeth and sharp claws and generally feeding chiefly on flesh. Dogs, lions, bears, and weasels are carnivores.

car·niv·o·rous (kär niv′ər əs) *adj.* feeding chiefly on flesh; flesh-eating: *Wolves are carnivorous animals.* —**car·niv′o·rous·ly,** *adv.* —**car·niv′o·rous·ness,** *n.*

car·ol (kar′əl) *n.* a song of joy or praise, especially a Christmas song or hymn. —*v.,* **car·oled, car·ol·ing;** *also, British,* **car·olled, car·ol·ling.** —*v.i.* to sing joyously, especially to sing Christmas carols: *Our family carols every Christmas Eve.* —*v.t.* to sing (a song, carol, or the like) joyously. —**car′ol·er;** *also, British,* **car′ol·ler,** *n.*

Car·o·li·na (kar′ə lī′nə) *n.* **1.** a former British colony on the southern Atlantic coast of America, divided into North Carolina and South Carolina in 1729. **2.** North Carolina or South Carolina. **3. the Carolinas.** North Carolina and South Carolina.

Car·o·line Islands (kar′ə līn′) a group of islands in the western Pacific, north of New Guinea, administered by the United States.

car·om (kar′əm) *also,* **car·rom.** *n.* the act of striking and rebounding. —*v.i.* to strike and rebound: *The baseball caromed off the wall.*

ca·rous·al (kə rou′zəl) *n.* a noisy, jovial drinking party.

ca·rouse (kə rouz′) *v.i.,* **ca·roused, ca·rous·ing.** to drink freely and heavily; take part in a carousal. —*n.* a carousal. —**ca·rous′er,** *n.*

car·ou·sel (kar′ə sel′) *also,* **car·rou·sel.** *n.* see **merry-go-round** (*def. 1*).

carp¹ (kärp) *v.i.* to find fault or complain, especially unreasonably or repeatedly: *His boss carps at every small error.* [Old Norse *karpa* to brag.] —**carp′er,** *n.*

carp² (kärp) *n. pl.,* **carps** or **carp.** a freshwater fish used as food. [Old French *carpe,* from Late Latin *carpa.*]

car·pal (kär′pəl) *adj.* of, relating to, or near the wrist. —*n.* a bone of the wrist. See **hand** for illustration.

Car·pa·thi·an Mountains (kär pā′thē ən) the mountains in central and eastern Europe, extending from southwestern Czechoslovakia to central Romania. Also, **Car·pa·thi·ans** (kär pā′thē ənz).

car·pel (kär′pəl) *n.* the part of a flower that bears seeds; pistil.

car·pen·ter (kär′pən tər) *n.* a person who builds and repairs wooden structures and parts, as of houses.

car·pen·try (kär′pən trē) *n.* the business, trade, or work of a carpenter.

car·pet (kär′pit) *n.* **1.** a floor covering made of heavy, often woven fabric. **2.** the fabric used for such covering. **3.** any covering or surface resembling a carpet: *a carpet of snow.* —*v.t.* to cover or furnish with a carpet.
  on the carpet. before an authority for a scolding or reprimand: *The employee was called on the carpet by his supervisor for doing poor work.*

car·pet·bag (kär′pit bag′) *n.* a satchel or traveling bag, especially one made of carpeting.

car·pet·bag·ger (kär′pit bag′ər) *n.* a Northerner who went to the South immediately after the Civil War, especially one who tried to gain political or other advantages from the disorganized situation in the Southern states. [Because many of these people went South carrying clothes in *carpetbags.*]

car·pet·ing (kär′pi ting) *n.* **1.** the fabric used for carpets. **2.** a carpet or carpets: *wall-to-wall carpeting.*

car·port (kär′pôrt′) *n.* a shelter for an automobile, usually a roof projecting from the side of a building.

car·pus (kär′pəs) *n. pl.,* **car·pi** (kär′pī). the wrist, or the group of bones that make up the wrist.

car·riage (kar′ij) *n.* **1.** a wheeled vehicle for trans-

Carport

porting people, usually drawn by a horse or horses. **2.** a light, wheeled vehicle for a baby, designed to be pushed by a person on foot. **3.** a manner of carrying or holding the head and body: *The king has a stately carriage.* **4.** a movable part of a machine that supports or carries some other part: *the carriage of a typewriter.* **5.** a wheeled support for a gun or cannon. **6.** the act of carrying or transporting. **7.** the cost or price of transportation.

car·ri·er (kar′ē ər) *n.* **1.** a person or organization whose business it is to carry or transport something. Railroads, trucking companies, and shipping lines are carriers. **2.** a commercial or military vehicle used to carry or transport something: *a troop carrier.* **3.** a medium or device by which something is carried: *The blood serves as a carrier of oxygen to the cells.* **4.** any living thing that carries or transmits an infectious disease. A carrier may himself be immune to the germs he carries. **5.** see **carrier wave.** **6.** see **aircraft carrier.**

at; āpe; cär; end; mē; it; īce; hot; ōld; fôrk; wood; fōōl; oil; out; up; turn; sing; thin; this; hw in white; zh in treasure. The symbol ə stands for the sound of a in about, e in taken, i in pencil, o in lemon, and u in circus.

carrier pigeon, a homing pigeon used to carry messages.

carrier wave, an electromagnetic wave that can be modulated and carries signals to be transmitted, as through a radio system.

car·ri·on (kar′ē ən) *n.* dead and decaying flesh.

Car·roll, Lewis (kar′əl) 1832–1898, English author.

car·rom (kar′əm) another spelling of **carom.**

car·rot (kar′ət) *n.* **1.** the fleshy root of a plant related to parsley, eaten as a vegetable. **2.** the plant bearing this root.

car·rou·sel (kar′ə sel′) another spelling of **carousel.**

car·ry (kar′ē) *v.,* **car·ried, car·ry·ing.** —*v.t.* **1.** to bear or hold while moving, especially in order to transport or convey: *Evelyn carried the suitcase upstairs. The fireman carried the child out of the burning house.* **2.** to act or serve as a means of conveyance or transmission for: *This pipe carries oil. Air carries sound waves. Some insects carry diseases.* **3.** to have on one's person: *Robert always carries a pen.* **4.** to have as a characteristic, property, or consequence: *The old senator's opinion still carried great weight in Congress.* **5.** to bear the weight of; sustain: *I found it impossible to carry the heavy burden of responsibility* (King Edward VIII). **6.** to extend or continue: *You carried your teasing too far when you began to criticize his family.* **7.** to keep in stock for sale; deal in: *That store carries household supplies.* **8.** to pass or adopt (a motion or bill): *The motion was carried by a wide margin.* **9.** to be successful or victorious in; win or capture: *Franklin D. Roosevelt carried all but two states in the election of 1936.* **10.** to transfer and add, as a number or total from one column or page to another. **11.** to cause to go or come: *The hurricane carried the ship off course.* **12.** to sing (a melody or part) correctly: *Jerry can't carry a tune.* **13.** to hold (one's body or part of it) in a certain way: *The young princess carried herself regally.* —*v.i.* **1.** to go or travel for a distance: *The arrow carried for thirty yards. The actress' voice carried to the back of the theater.* **2.** to be approved by vote: *The proposed civil rights bill carried by a large majority.* **3.** to act as a bearer or carrier. —*n. pl.,* **car·ries. 1.** the range or distance covered or traveled by something, such as a gun or projectile. **2.** a portage between two bodies of water. **3.** the act of carrying: *The football player gained sixty yards in ten carries.*

  to carry away. to arouse strong feeling in: *The audience was so carried away by the musician's performance that they began to cheer.*

  to carry off. a. to win, as a prize or honor. **b.** to complete successfully; accomplish: *The thieves succeeded in carrying off their plan.* **c.** to cause the death of; kill.

  to carry on. a. to keep going; continue: *After the interruption we carried on with our work.* **b.** to engage in; conduct: *to carry on a debate.* **c.** *Informal.* to behave in a wild, foolish, or silly manner.

  to carry out. a. to obey; follow: *The soldier carried out his orders promptly.* **b.** to bring to completion; accomplish: *to carry out a plan.*

car·ry·all[1] (kar′ē ôl′) *n.* a lightweight, covered, one-horse carriage for several persons. [A form of *cariole.*]

car·ry·all[2] (kar′ē ôl′) *n.* a large bag, basket, or handbag. [*Carry* + *all.*]

car·ry·o·ver (kar′ē ō′vər) *n.* something retained or remaining: *Herb's interest in model trains is a carry-over from his childhood.*

car·sick (kär′sik′) *adj.* nauseated from riding in a car, train, or bus. —**car′sick′ness,** *n.*

Car·son, Kit (kär′sən; kit) 1809–1868, U.S. frontiersman and scout.

Carson City, the capital of Nevada, in the western part of the state. Pop. (1970), 15,468.

cart (kärt) *n.* **1.** a sturdy, two-wheeled vehicle for carrying heavy loads, usually drawn by horses or mules. **2.** a small, wheeled vehicle moved by hand; pushcart. **3.** a light, two-wheeled carriage. —*v.t.* to carry in a cart.

cart·age (kär′tij) *n.* **1.** the act of carting or transporting. **2.** the rate charged for this.

Car·ta·ge·na (kär′tə jē′nə) *n.* a port city in northwestern Colombia. Pop. (1973), 313,300.

carte blanche (kärt′ blänch′) *pl.,* **cartes blanches** (kärt′ blän′chiz). the complete authority or freedom to act as one wishes or thinks best. [French *carte blanche* literally, a blank card (to be filled in as one wishes).]

car·tel (kär tel′) *n.* an international group of companies or businesses formed to establish a monopoly by controlling prices and production.

Car·ter, Jimmy (kär′tər) 1924—, the thirty-ninth president of the United States, from 1977 to 1981. His full name is **James Earl Carter.**

Car·te·sian coordinate system (kär tē′zhən) *Mathematics.* a system of coordinates that locates a point in a plane by its distance from each of two perpendicular lines at right angles to each other.

Car·thage (kär′thij) *n.* an ancient city and state in North Africa, on the site of modern Tunisia. It was founded by the Phoenicians, and destroyed by the Romans in 146 B.C.

Car·tha·gin·i·an (kär′thə jin′ē ən) *adj.* of or relating to Carthage, its people, or its civilization. —*n.* a person who lived in Carthage.

Car·thu·sian (kär thōō′zhən) *n.* a member of a religious order of monks and nuns, founded in France in 1084.

Car·ti·er, Jacques (kär′tē ā′; zhäk) 1491–1557, the French navigator who discovered the St. Lawrence River.

car·ti·lage (kär′təl ij) *n.* **1.** the tough, flexible connective tissue in the skeleton of humans and other animals with backbones; gristle. **2.** a part or structure formed of cartilage.

car·ti·lag·i·nous (kärt′əl aj′ə nəs) *adj.* **1.** of or resembling cartilage. **2.** having a skeleton consisting mostly of cartilage.

car·tog·ra·pher (kär tog′rə fər) *n.* a person who makes maps or charts.

car·tog·ra·phy (kär tog′rə fē) *n.* the art or science of making maps or charts.

car·ton (kärt′ən) *n.* **1.** a container made of any of various materials, such as cardboard, wood, or plastic: *an egg carton, a milk carton.* **2.** the amount that a carton holds.

car·toon (kär tōōn′) *n.* **1.** a sketch or drawing, as in a magazine or newspaper, that shows an amusing situation, makes fun of some person or subject, or illustrates an opinion. **2.** see **animated cartoon. 3.** see **comic strip. 4.** the preliminary drawing of a design or picture, to be copied in a mosaic, tapestry, mural painting, or the like.

car·toon·ist (kär tōō′nist) *n.* a person who draws cartoons, especially one who draws cartoons as a profession.

car·tridge (kär′trij) *n.* **1.** a cylindrical case, usually made of metal or cardboard and containing a percussion cap, a propelling charge of gunpowder, and a bullet. **2.** a roll of camera film enclosed in a protective case that fits into a camera as a unit. **3.** a device that holds a phonograph needle and transforms its vibrations into an electric current as the needle follows the groove of a record. **4.** another word for **cassette** (*def. 2*). **5.** a small container designed for easy replacement as a unit: *an ink cartridge for a pen.*

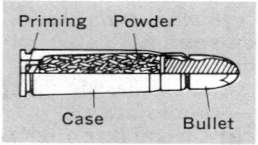

Cartridge

cart·wheel (kärt′hwēl′) *n.* **1.** the wheel of a cart. **2.** a sideways handspring in which the weight is put first on one hand and then on the other.

Cart·wright, Edmund (kärt′rīt′) 1743–1823, English inventor of the power-driven loom.

Ca·ru·so, En·ri·co (kə rōō′sō; en rē′kō) 1873–1921, Italian opera singer.

carve (kärv) *v.,* **carved, carv·ing.** —*v.t.* **1.** to cut (meat) into slices or pieces: *Mother carved the turkey.* **2.** to make or shape by or as if by cutting (often with *out*): *Grandfather carved a doll from a block of wood. The pioneers carved a new nation out of the wilderness.* **3.** to decorate by cutting figures or designs: *The old chest was carved with many strange designs.* —*v.i.* to cut meat into slices or pieces. —**carv′er,** *n.*

Car·ver, George Washington (kär′vər) 1864–1943, U. S. scientist and educator.

carv·ing (kär′ving) *n.* **1.** a carved work, such as a figure or design: *a wood carving of a dog.* **2.** the act or art of a person who carves.

carving knife, a knife used for carving, especially one used for carving meat.

car·y·at·id (kar′ē at′id) *n. pl.,* **car·y·at·ids** or **car·y·at·i·des** (kar′ē at′ə dēz) a statue of a draped female figure, serving as a column.

ca·sa·ba (kə sä′bə) *also,* **cas·sa·ba.** *n.* a melon having a creamy white pulp.

Cas·a·blan·ca (kas′ə blang′kə) *n.* the largest city and chief port of Morocco, in the northwestern part of the country. Pop. (1970 est.), 1,500,100.

cas·cade (kas kād′) *n.* **1.** a small waterfall or a series of small waterfalls. **2.** anything resembling this: *A cascade of ruffles came down the front of her blouse.* —*v.i.* **cas·cad·ed, cas·cad·ing.** to fall or flow in a cascade: *Water cascaded over the rocks. Martha's black hair cascaded over her shoulders.*

Cascade Range, a mountain range in the northwestern United States and southwestern Canada. Also, **Cas·cades** (kas kādz′).

cas·car·a (kas ker′ə) *n.* **1.** a North American tree having reddish-brown bark. **2.** a laxative made from dried strips of bark of this tree.

case[1] (kās) *n.* **1.** a specific example or occurrence; instance: *The fire was an obvious case of carelessness.* **2.** the actual state of affairs or circumstances: *If that's the case, there is nothing we can do.* **3.** an instance of a disease or injury: *The doctor treated many cases of the flu.* **4.** a person who has a disease or injury; patient. **5.** a statement or presentation, as of arguments or reasons: *The congressman presented his case for the proposed law.* **6.** a matter or problem, especially one under investigation: *The police were baffled by the case of the stolen painting.* **7.a.** an action or suit brought before a court of law for decision: *The judge found it difficult to rule on the case.* **b.** a statement of facts or circumstances presented for consideration in a court of law: *The attorney stated his case very simply.* **8.** *Grammar.* one of the various forms of a noun, pronoun, or adjective, used to show its relation to other words in a sentence by means of its ending or its position in the sentence. —*v.t.,* **cased, cas·ing.** *Informal.* to look over carefully, especially with criminal intent: *The thief cased the store before robbing it.* [Old French *cas* occurrence, event, from Latin *cāsus.*]

in any case. no matter what happens; anyhow; regardless.

in case. in the event that; if: *In case anything happens, call me immediately.*

in case of. in the event of: *In case of rain, we'll go to the movies instead of playing baseball.*

case[2] (kās) *n.* **1.** something designed to contain, enclose, or protect; box or other container: *The camera comes with a leather case.* **2.** the amount that a case can hold: *We ordered three cases of soda for the party.* **3.** *Printing.* a shallow tray divided into compartments, used for holding type. —*v.t.,* **cased, cas·ing.** to put in or cover with a case; encase. [Old French *casse* box, chest, from Latin *capsa.*]

case history, a collection of facts about a person or group, gathered together for the purpose of studying or dealing with some physical, mental, or social condition.

ca·sein (kā′sēn) *n.* the main protein present in milk, and the chief ingredient of cheese. Casein is also used in the manufacture of paints, plastics, fabrics, and adhesives.

case·ment (kās′mənt) *n.* **1.** the frame of a window that opens on hinges. **2.** a window having such a frame.

case·work (kās′wurk′) *n.* the work done by a caseworker.

case·work·er (kās′wur′kər) *n.* a social worker who is assigned to interview and give guidance and advice to an individual or family with social, psychological, or economic problems.

cash (kash) *n.* **1.** money in the form of coins or bills. **2.** money or its equivalent, such as a check, paid at the time of buying something: *Instead of charging the suit, I paid cash.* —*v.t.* to give or get cash for: *to cash a check.*

Casement

to cash in on. *Informal.* to use to one's advantage; take advantage of: *The explorer cashed in on his fame by writing a book.*

cash·ew (kash′ōō) *n.* **1.** a kidney-shaped nut that can be eaten. **2.** the tropical evergreen tree bearing this nut.

cash·ier[1] (ka shēr′) *n.* a person who is in charge of taking in and paying out money, as in a bank or business. [French *caissier,* from *casisse* money, box.]

cash·ier[2] (ka shēr′) *v.t.* to dismiss from service in disgrace: *The officer was cashiered for cowardice.* [Dutch *casseren,* from French *casser* to dismiss, break, from Latin *quassāre* to break in pieces, shatter.]

cashier's check, a check drawn by a bank on its own funds and signed by its cashier.

cash·mere (kazh′mēr, kash′mēr) *n.* **1.** a fine, soft, woolen fabric woven from the silky hair of a breed of goats of Kashmir. It is used to make coats, suits, and sweaters. **2.** a rare and expensive cloth made from this hair. [From *Kashmir,* a region in southern Asia.]

cash on delivery, immediate payment in cash upon delivery of merchandise.

cash register, a machine that automatically shows and records the amount of a sale, usually having a drawer for money.

cas·ing (kā′sing) *n.* **1.** something that covers, encloses, or protects, such as the outer covering of an automobile tire. **2.** a frame, especially of a door or window.

ca·si·no (kə sē′nō) *n. pl.,* **ca·si·nos. 1.** a building or room for public entertainment, especially for gambling. **2.** *also,* **cassino.** a card game for two, three, or four persons in

at; āpe; cär; end; mē; it; īce; hot; ōld; fôrk; wood; fōol; oil; out; up; turn; sing; thin; this; hw in white; zh in treasure. The symbol ə stands for the sound of a in about, e in taken, i in pencil, o in lemon, and u in circus.

which the player with the most points for cards taken is the winner.

cask (kask) *n.* **1.** a large wooden barrel, usually used to hold liquids. **2.** the amount contained in a cask.

cas·ket (kas′kit) *n.* **1.** a rectangular box of wood or metal, in which a dead body is placed for burial; coffin. **2.** a small box or chest, as for jewels.

Cas·pi·an Sea (kas′pē ən) an inland sea in the southern Soviet Union, bordering northern Iran. It is the largest inland body of water in the world.

casque (kask) *n.* a helmet.

cas·sa·ba (kə sä′bə) another spelling of **casaba.**

Cas·san·dra (kə san′drə) *n. Greek Legend.* a daughter of King Priam of Troy. Apollo, who was in love with her, gave her the gift of prophesy. When she refused to love him in return, he decreed that no one should believe her prophecies.

cas·sa·va (kə sä′və) *n.* **1.** a bushy shrub widely grown in tropical regions for its roots, which can be eaten. **2.** a nutritious starch obtained from these roots, from which tapioca and bread are made. Also, **manioc.**

cas·se·role (kas′ə rōl′) *n.* **1.** a deep baking dish, often of glass or earthenware, in which food can be cooked and served. **2.** any food prepared and served in a casserole. **3.** a small, deep dish with a handle, used in chemical laboratories for heating substances.

cas·sette (kə set′) *n.* **1.** another word for **cartridge** (*def. 2*). **2.** a small box designed to hold magnetic tape for easy insertion into a tape recorder or player.

cas·sia (kash′ə, kas′ē ə) *n.* **1.** the bark of an Asian tree, used as a substitute for cinnamon. **2.** the tree bearing this bark, having glossy, oblong leaves.

cas·si·no (kə sē′nō) another spelling of **casino** (*def. 2*).

Cas·si·o·pe·ia (kas′ē ə pē′ə) *n.* **1.** *Greek Legend.* the mother of Andromeda. **2.** a constellation in the northern sky, thought to resemble the seated figure of Cassiopeia.

cas·sock (kas′ək) *n.* an ankle-length garment worn by clergymen in the Roman Catholic and certain other churches. In the Roman Catholic Church the cassocks of priests are black, those of bishops violet, those of cardinals red, and that of the Pope white.

cas·so·war·y (kas′ə wer′ē) *n. pl.,* **cas·so·war·ies.** any of several birds of Australia and New Guinea that cannot fly. The cassowary is related to and resembles the ostrich, and has black feathers and a brilliantly colored head and neck.

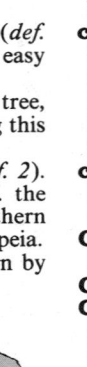

Cassock

cast (kast) *v.,* **cast, cast·ing.** —*v.t.* **1.** to throw through the air; hurl; fling: *The boy cast a handful of pebbles into the lake.* **2.** to cause to fall upon: *The statue cast a long shadow on the ground.* **3.** to direct or turn: *The teacher cast a glance in his direction.* **4.** to discard, dismiss, or ignore: *The daring pilot cast all caution aside.* **5.** to deposit or register: *to cast a vote.* **6.a.** to assign the parts of (a play, motion picture, or the like) to the actors: *to cast a new movie.* **b.** to select (an actor) for a particular part: *The director cast Bob in the play's leading role.* **7.a.** to shape (a substance) by pouring it into a mold to harden. **b.** to make (something) by this process: *to cast a statue.* **8.** to throw off; shed: *The snake cast its skin.* —*v.i.* **1.** to throw something, especially a fishing line. **2.** to take shape in a mold. —*n.* **1.** the act or manner of throwing. **2.** the distance a thing is thrown. **3.** something that is formed or shaped in a mold. **4.** the actors in a play, motion picture, or the like: *The cast of the new play is composed entirely of women.* **5.** a stiff, molded form, usually made of plaster of Paris, used to keep

a broken bone or badly sprained joint motionless while it heals. **6.** an impression formed by molding; mold: *The police made a cast of the footprints.* **7.** a tinge of color: *The sky had a bluish cast.* **8.** the form, appearance, or shape of something, such as physical features: *Steve's face had a stern cast.* **9.** a twist or turn to one side; squint: *The old man had a cast in one eye.*

to cast about for. to search for; look for: *We cast about for an explanation of the mystery.*

to cast off. to let loose; release: *The fishermen cast off the boat from its moorings.*

cas·ta·net (kas′tə net′) *n.* one of a pair of small, shell-shaped pieces, usually made of wood or ivory. Castanets are held in the hand and clicked together rhythmically, and are used especially as an accompaniment to certain Spanish music and dancing.

cast·a·way (kast′ə wā′) *n.* **1.** a person who is shipwrecked or set adrift at sea. **2.** an outcast. —*adj.* **1.** shipwrecked; cast adrift. **2.** thrown away; discarded.

caste (kast) *n.* **1.** one of the hereditary social classes into which Hindus are traditionally divided. **2.** any social system or set of principles that divides a society into classes on the basis of birth, wealth, rank, or religion. **3.** an exclusive social or professional group.

cas·tel·lat·ed (kas′təl ā′tid) *adj.* built with turrets and battlements like a castle.

cast·er (kas′tər) *n.* **1.** a person or thing that casts. **2.** *also, castor.* one of a set of wheels or rollers placed or fitted under a piece of furniture or other large, heavy object to make it easier to move. **3.** *also,* **castor. a.** a bottle for holding salt, mustard, vinegar, or the like; cruet. **b.** a stand for such bottles.

cas·ti·gate (kas′tə gāt′) *v.t.,* **cas·ti·gat·ed, cas·ti·gat·ing.** to criticize severely; rebuke; punish. —**cas′ti·ga′tion,** *n.* —**cas′ti·ga′tor,** *n.*

Cas·tile (kas tēl′) *n.* a region and former kingdom in north-central and central Spain.

Castile soap, a fine, hard soap made from olive oil.

Cas·til·ian (kas til′yən) *adj.* of or relating to Castile, its people, or their language. —*n.* **1.** the standard form of the Spanish language, based on the dialect of Castile. **2.** a person who was born or is living in Castile.

cast·ing (kas′ting) *n.* **1.** something that is shaped in a mold; cast. **2.** the act of a person or thing that casts: *The casting for the play has been completed.*

cast-i·ron (kast′ī′ərn) *adj.* **1.** made of cast iron. **2.** unyielding; inflexible: *cast-iron rules.* **3.** hardy; strong: *You have to have a cast-iron stomach to eat such spicy food.*

cast iron, a hard, brittle form of iron that contains a large amount of carbon and is shaped by casting.

cas·tle (kas′əl) *n.* **1.** a large fortified building or group of buildings serving as a stronghold or residence, as of a medieval prince or noble. **2.** any large, imposing house. **3.** *Chess.* another word for **rook².** —*v.t., v.i.,* **cas·tled, cas·tling.** *Chess.* to move (the king) two squares to the left or right and move the rook to the square passed over by the king.

Castle

castle in the air. something that is wished for but is not likely to happen; daydream: *The poor boy dreamed of owning a yacht and of other such castles in the air.*

cast·off (kast′ôf′) *adj.* discarded or abandoned; thrown away: *The charity collected castoff clothing to give to poor families.* —*n.* a person or thing that has been discarded or abandoned.

cas·tor[1] (kas′tər) another spelling of **caster** (*defs.* 2 and 3).

cas·tor[2] (kas′tər) *n.* an oily, strong-smelling substance produced by certain glands in beavers, used in making perfume. [Latin *castor* beaver.]

Cas·tor (kas′tər) *n. Greek and Roman Mythology.* one of the twin brothers usually regarded as sons of Leda and Zeus. Castor was traditionally thought to be mortal, and Pollux immortal.

castor bean, the oval bean of the castor-oil plant.

castor oil, a pale yellow or colorless oil obtained from castor beans, used as a strong laxative, a lubricant, and in the preparation of such products as paints and soaps.

cas·tor-oil plant (kas′tər oil′) a wide-leaved tropical plant whose beans yield castor oil.

cas·trate (kas′trāt) *v.t.,* **cas·trat·ed, cas·trat·ing.** to remove the sex glands of (a male); emasculate. —**cas·tra′tion,** *n.*

Cas·tro, Fi·del (käs′trō; fē del′) 1926—, Cuban revolutionary and political leader.

cas·u·al (kazh′ōō əl) *adj.* **1.** without serious intention or thought; offhand: *a casual remark.* **2.** happening by chance; unexpected; accidental: *a casual meeting.* **3.** designed for informal wear: *We wore casual clothes to the party.* **4.** unconcerned or indifferent; nonchalant: *He has a casual attitude toward his work.* **5.** temporary or irregular: *The farmer hired casual labor to help pick the crops.* —**cas′u·al·ly,** *adv.* —**cas′u·al·ness,** *n.*

cas·u·al·ty (kazh′ōō əl tē) *n. pl.,* **cas·u·al·ties. 1.** a serviceman who has been wounded, killed, or captured, or is missing in action. **2.** a person who is injured or killed in an accident. **3.** an accident, especially one involving a death.

cas·u·ist (kazh′ōō ist) *n.* a person who reasons cleverly but falsely.

cas·u·ist·ry (kazh′ōō is trē) *n. pl.,* **cas·u·ist·ries.** clever but false or misleading reasoning; sophistry.

cat (kat) *n.* **1.** a small, furry animal commonly kept as a pet or for catching mice and rats. **2.** any of a group of animals of the same family as the domestic cat, such as the lion, tiger, or leopard.

to let the cat out of the bag. to reveal a secret.

cat·a·clysm (kat′ə kliz′əm) *n.* **1.** a violent and sudden change in the ordinary processes of nature, such as a flood or earthquake. **2.** any violent change or sudden upheaval, such as a revolution or war.

cat·a·clys·mic (kat′ə kliz′mik) *adj.* of, relating to, or resembling a cataclysm.

cat·a·combs (kat′ə kōmz′) *n., pl.* an underground cemetery made up of rooms and passages with recesses in the walls for tombs.

Cat·a·lan (kat′əl an′) *n.* **1.** a person who was born or is living in Catalonia. **2.** a Romance language of Catalonia, Valencia, Andorra, the Balearic Islands, and some parts of southern France. —*adj.* of or relating to Catalonia, its people, or their language.

Cat·a·li·na (kat′əl ē′nə) *n.* another name for **Santa Catalina.** Also, **Catalina Island.**

cat·a·log (kat′əl ôg′, kat′əl og′) *also,* **cat·a·logue.** *n.* **1.** a list of books, names, subjects, or other items, usually in alphabetical order, that identifies and often describes each item. **2.** a publication containing such a list: *The store sent us a catalog of furniture.* —*v.t.* to make a catalog of; enter in a catalog: *to catalog the paintings in a museum.* —**cat′a log′er,** *n.*

cat·a·logue (kat′əl ôg′, kat′əl og′) *n., v.t.,* **cat·a·logued, cat·a·logu·ing.** another spelling of **catalog.** —**cat′a·logu′er,** *n.*

Cat·a·lo·ni·a (kat′əl ō′nē ə) *n.* a historic region in the northeastern corner of Spain.

ca·tal·pa (kə tal′pə) *n.* **1.** a tree found in North America and Asia, having large, heart-shaped leaves, white, pink, or yellow flowers, and pods that resemble beans. **2.** the coarse-grained, durable wood of this tree.

ca·tal·y·sis (kə tal′ə sis) *n. pl.,* **ca·tal·y·ses** (kə tal′ə sēz′). the speeding up of a chemical reaction by the presence of a substance that undergoes no permanent chemical change itself.

cat·a·lyst (kat′əl ist) *n.* **1.** a substance that causes the speeding up of a chemical reaction while remaining chemically unchanged itself. **2.** a person or thing that brings about or hastens a change: *The students' protests were a catalyst for reform in the school's policies.*

cat·a·lyt·ic (kat′əl it′ik) *adj.* relating to catalysis.

cat·a·ma·ran (kat′ə mə ran′) *n.* **1.** a sailboat or other boat having two hulls connected side by side by poles or by a platform that serves as a deck. **2.** a raft made of logs lashed together in the shape of a boat hull.

cat·a·mount (kat′ə mount′) *n.* any of several wild animals of the cat family, such as the cougar.

Ca·ta·nia (kə tän′yə) *n.* a port city on the eastern coast of Sicily. Pop. (1970 est.), 969,657.

cat·a·pult (kat′ə pult′) *n.* **1.** an ancient military weapon used to shoot or hurl stones, arrows, or other projectiles. **2.** a device for launching an airplane from the deck of a ship. **3.** *British.* another word for **slingshot.** —*v.t.* to hurl or shoot (something) from a catapult. —*v.i.* to move quickly or suddenly; leap; spring: *At the sound of the explosion Billy catapulted out of his chair.*

Catapult

cat·a·ract (kat′ə rakt′) *n.* **1.** a large, steep waterfall. **2.** the steep rapids in a river. **3.** a violent flood or downpour of water. **4.** a clouding of the lens of the eye, resulting in partial or total blindness.

ca·tarrh (kə tär′) *n.* an inflammation of a mucous membrane, especially that of the nose or throat, causing excessive production of mucus. —**ca·tarrh′al,** *adj.*

ca·tas·tro·phe (kə tas′trə fē′) *n.* a great and sudden disaster or misfortune: *The plane crash was a catastrophe.*

cat·a·stroph·ic (kat′əs trof′ik) *adj.* of, relating to, or resulting in a catastrophe; disastrous: *a catastrophic explosion, a catastrophic decision.* —**cat′a·stroph′i·cal·ly,** *adv.*

cat·bird (kat′burd′) *n.* a slate-gray songbird of North and Central America, related to the mockingbird and having a black cap and tail.

at; āpe; cär; end; mē; it; īce; hot; ōld; fôrk; wood; fōōl; oil; out; up; turn; sing; thin; this; hw in white; zh in treasure. The symbol ə stands for the sound of **a** in about, **e** in taken, **i** in pencil, **o** in lemon, and **u** in circus.

cat·boat (kat′bōt′) *n.* a sailboat with a single mast set well forward.

cat·call (kat′kôl′) *n.* a shrill cry or whistle expressing disapproval, scorn, or impatience: *The politician was showered with catcalls from the audience.* —*v.i.* to make catcalls: *The angry audience hissed and catcalled.*

catch (kach) *v.,* **caught, catch·ing.** —*v.t.* **1.** to capture or seize, as after a chase or search: *The police caught the thief. Tommy caught three fish.* **2.** to take or get hold of; grasp: *The woman caught my arm as I was leaving.* **3.** to stop or prevent the motion or passage of: *We used a pail to catch the water from the leaking roof.* **4.** to be in time for boarding; get aboard: *We will have to hurry to catch the train.* **5.** to cause to become stuck, entangled, or hooked: *The girl caught her sweater on a branch.* **6.** to hit; strike: *The bullet caught the fleeing criminal in the leg.* **7.** to come upon suddenly or unexpectedly; surprise or discover: *The boss caught the worker in the act of stealing.* **8.** to take or get suddenly or momentarily: *We caught a glimpse of the celebrity as he got into his car.* **9.** to become infected with: *to catch a cold.* **10.** to attract: *The brightly colored dress caught my eye.* —*v.i.* **1.** to become stuck, entangled, or hooked: *The fabric caught in the zipper.* **2.** to become fastened or take hold: *The bolt on the door didn't catch.* **3.** to become lighted; start to burn. **4.** to act as a catcher in baseball. —*n. pl.,* **catch·es. 1.** the act of catching: *The outfielder made a great catch.* **2.** a device that catches or fastens: *The repairman fixed the catch on the door.* **3.** something that is caught; amount caught: *a fisherman's catch.* **4.** a game in which an object, usually a ball, is thrown back and forth between players. **5.** a break in the voice, especially as a result of emotion. **6.** *Informal.* a hidden condition; trick or trap: *The offer seems too good; there must be a catch somewhere.*

to catch on. *Informal.* **a.** to understand: *Linda had to explain the answer to me three times before I caught on.* **b.** to become fashionable or popular: *That style of dressing caught on very quickly.*

to catch up. to come from behind so as to be even.

to catch up on. to get or become up to date: *Mother spent the evening trying to catch up on her reading.*

to catch up to. to come from behind so as to be even with or overtake: *Richard caught up to the leading runner near the end of the race.*

to catch up with. a. to come up to or overtake; catch up to. **b.** to get up to date; catch up on.

catch·all (kach′ôl′) *n.* **1.** anything that serves as a place to keep odds and ends: *The closet was a catchall.* **2.** a word or phrase used to cover various conditions or situations.

catch·er (kach′ər) *n.* **1.** a person or thing that catches. **2.** a baseball player who is positioned behind home plate to catch pitched balls.

catch·ing (kach′ing) *adj.* contagious; infectious: *Many diseases are catching.*

catch·up (kech′up, kach′əp) another spelling of **ketchup.**

catch·word (kach′wurd′) *n.* a word or phrase used repeatedly for effect, as by a political group; slogan.

catch·y (kach′ē) *adj.,* **catch·i·er, catch·i·est. 1.** catching the attention and easy to remember: *I keep humming that catchy tune.* **2.** tricky; deceptive: *a catchy question.*

cat·e·chism (kat′ə kiz′əm) *n.* **1.** a small book or manual in which the principles of a religion are set forth in the form of questions and answers. **2.** a similar book or manual about any subject. **3.** a series of questions used as an examination.

cat·e·chize (kat′ə kīz′) *v.t.,* **cat·e·chized, cat·e·chiz·ing. 1.** to instruct by questions and answers. **2.** to question closely.

cat·e·gor·i·cal (kat′ə gôr′i kəl) *adj.* without conditions or qualifications; absolute: *The accused man made a categorical denial of the charges against him.* —**cat′e·gor′i·cal·ly,** *adv.*

cat·e·go·ry (kat′ə gôr′ē) *n. pl.,* **cat·e·go·ries.** a group or division in a system of classification; class.

ca·ter (kā′tər) *v.i.* **1.** to provide food, supplies, and other services, such as entertainment: *This restaurant caters for large private parties.* **2.** to provide what is needed or desired: *That shop caters only to very wealthy people.* —*v.t.* to provide with food, supplies, and other services, such as entertainment: *to cater a wedding.*

cat·er-cor·ner (kat′ər kôr′nər) *also,* **cat·ty-cor·ner, kit·ty-cor·ner.** *adv.* in a diagonal position, usually in a corner.

cat·er-cor·nered (kat′ər kôr′nərd) *adv.* another word for **cater-corner.**

ca·ter·er (kā′tər ər) *n.* a person who caters, especially one who provides food and other services, as for a party.

cat·er·pil·lar (kat′ər pil′ər) *n.* a larva, especially of a butterfly or moth, that resembles a furry worm. [Old French *catepelose* literally, hairy cat.]

cat·er·waul (kat′ər wôl′) *v.i.* to howl or screech like a cat. —*n.* such a howl or screech.

cat·fish (kat′fish′) *n. pl.,* **cat·fish** or **cat·fish·es.** any of several usually scaleless fish having long feelers around the mouth that look like whiskers.

Caterpillar

cat·gut (kat′gut′) *n.* a tough string or cord that is made from the dried and twisted intestines of sheep and certain other animals. Catgut is used for surgical sutures and for stringing musical instruments and tennis rackets.

ca·thar·tic (kə thär′tik) *n.* a medicine that causes movement of the bowels; laxative. —*adj.* causing bowel movement; laxative.

Ca·thay (ka thā′) *n. Archaic.* another word for **China.**

ca·the·dral (kə thē′drəl) *n.* **1.** the official church of a bishop, containing his throne. **2.** any large or important church.

Cath·er·ine the Great (kath′ər in, kath′rin) 1729–1796, the empress of Russia from 1762 to 1796.

cath·ode (kath′ōd) *n.* **1.** an electrode through which electrons enter an electrical device or medium. When electricity is used to produce a chemical reaction, the negative electrode is the cathode, but when a chemical reaction is used to produce electricity, the positive electrode is the cathode. **2.** in electrolysis, an electrode that has an excess of electrons and is negatively charged. Positively charged ions are reduced at the cathode. **3.** an electrode from which electrons are given off.

cathode ray, a stream of electrons given off by the cathode in a vacuum tube.

cath·ode-ray tube (kath′ōd rā′) a vacuum tube in which a visible glowing pattern is produced on a luminescent screen by a cathode ray given off from an electron gun at the back of the tube. It is used in television sets, oscilloscopes, and radar sets.

Cath·o·lic (kath′ə lik) *adj.* **1.** of or relating to the Christian church under the authority of the Pope; Roman Catholic. **2.** of or relating to the ancient undivided Christian church, or those churches claiming unbroken descent from it, as the Roman, Orthodox, Eastern, and Anglican. **3. catholic.** of universal interest or use; broad: *Jill's taste in books is catholic.* —*n.* a member of a Catholic Church, especially the Roman Catholic Church.

Ca·thol·i·cism (kə thol′ə siz′əm) *n.* the beliefs, practices, and government of the Roman Catholic Church.

cat·i·on (kat′ī′ən) *n.* a positively charged ion of an electrolyte, attracted to the cathode in electrolysis.

cat·kin (kat′kin) *n.* a fuzzy spike of tiny flowers growing on certain trees, such as willows or birches. [Obsolete Dutch *katteken* literally, little cat; because the spike resembles a cat's tail.]

cat·nap (kat′nap′) *n.* a short nap. —*v.i.,* **cat·napped, cat·nap·ping.** to take a short nap.

cat·nip (kat′nip′) *n.* **1.** the dried leaves and stems of a plant of the mint family, used as a stuffing for cats' toys because cats are stimulated and attracted by its strong aroma. **2.** the strong-smelling plant that bears these leaves and stems.

Ca·to, Marcus Por·cius (kā′tō; pôr′shəs) 234–149 B.C., Roman statesman. Also, **Cato the Elder.**

cat-o'-nine-tails (kat′ə nīn′tālz′) *n. pl.,* **cat-o'-nine-tails.** a whip usually consisting of nine knotted cords fastened to a handle.

cat's cradle, a children's game in which a string is looped over the fingers of both hands in such a way as to form different patterns.

Cats·kill Mountains (kats′kil′) a mountain range in southeastern New York. It is part of the Appalachian mountain system. Also, **Cats·kills** (kats′kilz′).

cat's-paw (kats′pô′) *also,* **cats-paw.** *n.* **1.** a person used by another to do something difficult, dangerous, or unlawful; dupe. **2.** a light breeze that ruffles the surface of calm water.

cat·sup (kat′səp, kech′əp) another spelling of **ketchup.**

cat·tail (kat′tāl′) *n.* a tall marsh plant bearing long, narrow leaves and brown flowers clustered in spikes which turn velvety brown when mature.

cat·tle (kat′əl) *n.* animals of the ox family, such as cows, bulls, and steers, raised for meat and dairy products.

▲ Cattle is a plural noun that has no true singular form. If one animal is meant, the name of the particular kind of cattle is usually used, for example, *bull* or *cow.*

cat·tle·man (kat′əl mən) *n. pl.,* **cat·tle·men** (kat′əl-mən). a man who owns, raises, or deals in cattle.

cat·ty (kat′ē) *adj.,* **cat·ti·er, cat·ti·est. 1.** slyly malicious; spiteful: *a catty remark.* **2.** resembling a cat or cats. —**cat′ti·ly,** *adv.* —**cat′ti·ness,** *n.*

cat·ty-cor·ner (kat′ē kôr′nər) another spelling of **cater-corner.**

cat·walk (kat′wôk′) *n.* a narrow walking space or platform, as along a bridge.

Cau·ca·sia (kô kā′zhə) *n.* a region in the southern Soviet Union between the Black and Caspian seas. Also, **Caucasus.**

Cau·ca·sian (kô kā′zhən) *n.* **1.** a member of one of the major divisions of the human race, often referred to as the white race, with skin color ranging from pale pink to dark brown, and hair color from blond to dark brown. **2.** a person who was born or is living in Caucasia. —*adj.* **1.** of or relating to Caucasians. **2.** of or relating to Caucasia or its people.

Cau·ca·sus (kô′kə səs) *n.* **1.** a mountain range in the southern Soviet Union between the Black and Caspian Seas, usually thought of as part of the boundary between Europe and Asia. **2.** another name for **Caucasia.**

cau·cus (kô′kəs) *n. pl.,* **cau·cus·es.** a meeting of the members of a political party to choose party leaders, nominate candidates, and determine party policy. —*v.i.* to meet in or hold a caucus.

cau·dal (kôd′əl) *adj.* **1.** of, relating to, or near the tail: *the caudal fin of a fish.* **2.** like or resembling a tail.

caught (kôt) a past tense and past participle of **catch.**

caul·dron (kôl′drən) *also,* **cal·dron.** *n.* a large kettle or boiler.

cau·li·flow·er (kô′li flou′ər, kol′ē flou′ər) *n.* **1.** the white head of a plant related to the cabbage, eaten as a vegetable either raw or cooked. **2.** the low-growing plant bearing this head.

caulk (kôk) *also,* **calk.** *v.t.* to fill up (a seam, crack, or joint) with tar, oakum, or other substance so that it will not leak; make watertight or airtight.

caulk·er (kô′kər) *also,* **calk·er.** *n.* **1.** a person who caulks. **2.** a tool used for caulking.

caus·al (kô′zəl) *adj.* of, indicating, or acting as a cause: *There is often a causal relationship between poor study habits and poor grades.* —**caus′al·ly,** *adv.*

cau·sal·i·ty (kô zal′ə tē) *n. pl.,* **cau·sal·i·ties.** the principle that every effect requires a cause; the relationship between cause and effect.

cause (kôz) *n.* **1.** a person or thing that makes something happen or produces an effect: *The hurricane was the cause of great damage along the coast.* **2.** a basis or ground, as for action; reason; motive: *There is no cause for alarm.* **3.** something that is of concern or interest to an individual or group, and to which they give their support: *Helping the poor is a worthy cause.* —*v.t.,* **caused, caus·ing.** to make happen or result in; bring about: *The traffic jam caused him to be late for work. Careless driving causes many accidents.* —**cause′less,** *adj.*

cause·way (kôz′wā′) *n.* a raised road or path, as across a body of water.

caus·tic (kôs′tik) *adj.* **1.** capable of corroding or destroying animal tissue; corrosive: *a caustic chemical.* **2.** sarcastic; cutting; biting: *Paula's caustic remark hurt my feelings.* —*n.* a substance that destroys or corrodes animal tissue.

caus·ti·cal·ly (kôs′ti kə lē, kôs′tik lē) *adv.* in a caustic manner; sarcastically.

caustic soda, another term for **sodium hydroxide.**

cau·ter·ize (kô′tə rīz′) *v.t.,* **cau·ter·ized, cau·ter·iz·ing.** to sear with a hot iron or a caustic substance, especially in order to destroy dead tissue or prevent infection. —**cau′ter·i·za′tion,** *n.*

cau·tion (kô′shən) *n.* **1.** care with regard to danger or risk; prudence; wariness: *The scientist used extreme caution in working with the dangerous chemicals.* **2.** a warning. —*v.t.* to urge (someone) to be careful; warn: *Mother cautioned us not to play with matches.*

cau·tious (kô′shəs) *adj.* showing or characterized by caution; careful: *An inexperienced skier must be cautious when trying new slopes.* —**cau′tious·ly,** *adv.* —**cau′tious·ness,** *n.*

cav·al·cade (kav′əl kād′) *n.* **1.** a procession, especially of people on horseback or in vehicles. **2.** a large and impressive group or gathering: *A cavalcade of movie stars attended the award ceremony.*

cav·a·lier (kav′ə lēr′) *n.* **1.** a horseman, especially one who is armed; knight. **2.** a gallant or courteous gentleman, especially one serving as a lady's escort. **3. Cavalier.** a supporter of Charles I of England in his struggle with Parliament from 1641 to 1649. —*adj.* free and easy, sometimes in a haughty or disdainful manner: *a cavalier attitude.* —**cav′a·lier′ly,** *adv.*

---

at; āpe; cär; end; mē; it; īce; hot; ōld; fôrk; wood; fōōl; oil; out; up; turn; sing; thin; this; hw in white; zh in treasure. The symbol ə stands for the sound of **a** in about, **e** in taken, **i** in pencil, **o** in lemon, and **u** in circus.

cav·al·ry (kav′əl rē) *n. pl.,* **cav·al·ries. 1.** a military unit trained to fight on horseback. **2.** in some countries, a military unit made up of armored vehicles, such as tanks.

cav·al·ry·man (kav′əl rē mən) *n. pl.,* **cav·al·ry·men** (kav′əl rē mən). a member of the cavalry.

cave (kāv) *n.* a natural hollow chamber or hole beneath the earth's surface or in the side of a mountain. —*v.t.,* **caved, cav·ing.** to hollow out.
   to cave in. to fall or cause to fall in or down; collapse: *The walls of the old tunnel caved in.*

ca·ve·at emp·tor (kā′vē at′ emp′tôr) *Latin.* let the buyer beware.

cave dweller, another name for **cave man.**

cave-in (kāv′in′) *n.* **1.** a caving in or collapse, as of a mine or tunnel. **2.** the site of such a collapse.

cave man, a human being of the Stone Age who lived in caves.

cav·ern (kav′ərn) *n.* an underground cave, especially one of very great size.

cav·ern·ous (kav′ər nəs) *adj.* **1.** full of or containing caverns. **2.** like a cavern; hollow and deep.

cav·i·ar (kav′ē är′) *also,* **cav·i·are.** *n.* the eggs of sturgeon or certain other large fish, prepared and served as an appetizer.

cav·il (kav′əl) *v.i.,* **cav·iled, cav·il·ing;** *also, British,* **cav·illed, cav·il·ling.** to find fault unnecessarily; make petty objections; quibble. —*n.* trivial criticism.

cav·i·ty (kav′ə tē) *n. pl.,* **cav·i·ties. 1.** a hollow place; hole. **2.** a hollow space in a tooth caused by decay. **3.** a space within the body. The stomach; intestines, liver, and kidneys are located in the abdominal cavity.

ca·vort (kə vôrt′) *v.i. Informal.* to run and jump around playfully; frisk: *The puppies cavorted in the grass.*

ca·vy (kā′vē) *n. pl.,* **ca·vies.** any of several rodents of South America, having a rounded body, short legs, and small ears. The best-known kind of cavy is the guinea pig.

caw (kô) *n.* a harsh cry or call of a crow, raven, or similar bird. —*v.i.* to make this cry or call.

Cax·ton, William (kaks′tən) 1422?–1491, the first English printer.

cay (kā, kē) *n.* a low mound or island of sand and, often, coral fragments; key.

cay·enne (kī en′, kā en′) *n.* a hot spice made from the ground seeds and pods of any of several hot red peppers.

Cay·enne (kī en′, kā en′) *n.* the capital and largest city of French Guiana, on the northern coast. Pop. (1974), 30,461.

cay·man (kā′mən) another spelling of **caiman.**

Ca·yu·ga (kā yōō′gə, kī yōō′gə) *n. pl.,* **Ca·yu·ga** or **Ca·yu·gas.** a member of a tribe of Iroquois Indians formerly living in what is now New York State.

cay·use (kī yōōs′) *n.* an Indian pony of the western United States.

CB, radio communication on a designated frequency, intended for the use of the public for short-distance radio signaling by licensees. [Short for *C(itizens') B(and)* radio.]

Cb, the symbol for columbium.

cc., cubic centimeter; cubic centimeters.

C clef, a movable clef indicating that the line of the staff on which it is placed represents middle C.

Cd, the symbol for cadmium.

Ce, the symbol for cerium.

cease (sēs) *v.,* **ceased, ceas·ing.** —*v.i.* to come to an end; stop: *The rain had ceased by four o'clock.* —*v.t.* to put an end to; discontinue: *That factory will cease production.*

cease-fire (sēs′fīr′) *n.* a temporary halt of fighting by mutual agreement of opposing sides.

cease·less (sēs′lis) *adj.* never stopping; endless; continual. —**cease′less·ly,** *adv.* —**cease′less·ness,** *n.*

Ce·cil·ia, Saint (si sēl′yə) died A.D. 230?, Roman Christian martyr, the patron saint of music.

ce·cro·pi·a moth (si krō′pē ə) a large silkworm moth native to the eastern United States, having colorful markings.

ce·cum (sē′kəm) *n. pl.,* **ce·ca** (sē′kə). the pouch at the beginning of the large intestine, to which the appendix is attached.

ce·dar (sē′dər) *n.* **1.** any of several evergreen trees of the pine family, having rough, dark-gray bark and numerous branches that bear needle-shaped leaves. **2.** the durable fragrant wood of these trees, used for making chests and cabinets.

ce·dar·bird (sē′dər burd′) *n.* another name for **cedar waxwing.**

Cedar Rapids, a city in eastern Iowa. Pop. (1970), 110,642.

cedar waxwing, a crested bird native to North America, having brownish-gray feathers with yellow, black, and red markings. Also, **cedarbird.**

cede (sēd) *v.t.,* **ced·ed, ced·ing.** to give up possession of; surrender; yield: *Spain ceded the territory to France.*

ce·dil·la (si dil′ə) *n.* a mark (¸) placed under certain letters to indicate pronunciation. In English it is used especially under *c* to indicate the sound of *s,* as in *façade.*

ceil·ing (sē′ling) *n.* **1.** the interior, overhead covering or surface of a room. **2.** the maximum height at which an airplane can fly under standard air conditions. **3.** vertical visibility measured from sea level to the bottom of the lowest clouds. **4.** the highest or upper limit set on anything: *The government set a ceiling on prices.*
   to hit the ceiling. *Informal.* to lose one's temper; become very angry.

cel·an·dine (sel′ən dīn′) *n.* a plant of the poppy family that is sometimes grown as a garden plant because of its yellow flowers.

cel·e·brant (sel′ə brənt) *n.* **1.** a person who participates in a celebration. **2.** a priest who officiates at a Mass or other religious service.

cel·e·brate (sel′ə brāt′) *v.,* **cel·e·brat·ed, cel·e·brat·ing.** —*v.t.* **1.** to observe or commemorate (an event) with ceremonies or festivities: *We celebrated Ed's birthday by giving him a party.* **2.** to perform publicly with the proper ceremonies: *The priest celebrated Mass.* **3.** to honor or praise publicly; extol: *The soldier's courage was celebrated in all the newspapers.* —*v.i.* **1.** to observe or commemorate an event with ceremonies or festivities. **2.** *Informal.* to have a merry time.

cel·e·brat·ed (sel′ə brā′tid) *adj.* well-known; famous.

cel·e·bra·tion (sel′ə brā′shən) *n.* **1.** the act of celebrating. **2.** the ceremonies or festivities carried on to celebrate something: *All the members of the winning team were present at the victory celebration.*

ce·leb·ri·ty (sə leb′rə tē) *n. pl.,* **ce·leb·ri·ties.** a person who is well-known or much publicized: *The author's best-selling book made him a celebrity.*

ce·ler·i·ty (sə ler′ə tē) *n.* swiftness; speed: *Our request was answered with celerity.*

cel·er·y (sel′ər ē) *n.* **1.** the crisp, green or creamy-white leafstalks of a plant of the parsley family, eaten either raw or cooked. **2.** the plant bearing these leafstalks.

ce·les·ta (sə les′tə) *n.* a keyboard musical instrument resembling a small piano and having steel plates which are struck by hammers to produce bell-like tones.

ce·les·tial (sə les′chəl) *adj.* **1.** of or relating to the sky or heavens: *The planets are celestial bodies.* **2.** of heaven; heavenly; divine: *the celestial beauty of a Greek goddess.* —**ce·les′tial·ly,** *adv.*

celestial equator, the great circle formed by the intersection of the plane of the earth's equator and the celestial sphere.

ce·les·tial pole, either of the two intersections of the earth's axis with the celestial sphere.

ce·les·tial sphere, an imaginary sphere surrounding the earth and representing the entire sky. The stars, planets, and other heavenly bodies appear to be located on the surface of the celestial sphere.

cel·i·ba·cy (sel′ə bə sē) *n.* the state of being unmarried, especially in accordance with religious vows.

cel·i·bate (sel′ə bit) *n.* a person who remains unmarried, especially in accordance with religious vows. —*adj.* unmarried: *The church required that its priests be celibate.*

cell (sel) *n.* **1.** a small, usually plain, room, as in a prison, convent, or monastery. **2.** the basic unit of all living organisms, consisting of a mass of protoplasm with a nucleus near the center, and surrounded by a cell membrane or wall. **3.** a device that changes chemical, solar, or light energy into electrical energy. **4.** a small cavity or compartment, such as one of the six-sided compartments in a honeycomb.

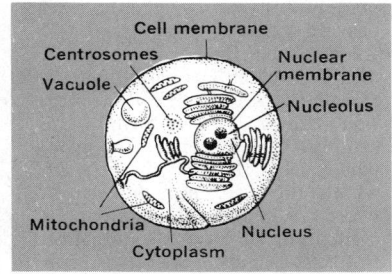

Cell membrane
Centrosomes
Nuclear membrane
Vacuole
Nucleolus
Mitochondria
Nucleus
Cytoplasm

Cell

cel·lar (sel′ər) *n.* **1.** a room or group of rooms, either wholly or partly underground, usually under a building and often used as a storage place. **2.** see **wine cellar.**

Cel·li·ni, Ben·ve·nu·to (chə lē′nē; ben′və nōō′tō) 1500–1571, Florentine author, sculptor, and goldsmith.

cel·list (chel′ist) *also,* **'cel·list.** *n.* a person who plays the cello. Also, **violoncellist.**

cell membrane, the very thin membrane that covers the entire surface of a cell.

cel·lo (chel′ō) *also,* **'cel·lo.** *n. pl.,* **cel·los.** an instrument of the violin family, between the viola and double bass in size and pitch. Also, **violoncello.**

cel·lo·phane (sel′ə fān′) *n.* a thin, flexible, usually transparent material made from cellulose, used especially as a wrapping material.

cel·lu·lar (sel′yə lər) *adj.* **1.** of, relating to, or resembling a cell or cells. **2.** consisting of cells.

Cel·lu·loid (sel′yə loid′) *n. Trademark.* a strong, transparent, flammable plastic made from nitrocellulose, alcohol, and camphor.

cel·lu·lose (sel′yə lōs′) *n.*

Cello

a compound of carbon, hydrogen, and oxygen in the form of a white solid that is insoluble in water. Cellulose is the major component of the walls of plant cells, and makes up the woody part of trees and plants. It is used especially to make paper, rayon, and other products.

cellulose acetate, a substance made by treating cellulose with acetic acid and other compounds, used to make synthetic acetate fibers.

cellulose nitrate, another term for **nitrocellulose.**

cell wall, in plants, the hard outer layer of cellulose that covers the cell membrane.

Cel·si·us scale (sel′sē əs) the official name of the **centigrade** scale. [From Anders *Celsius,* 1701–1744, a Swedish astronomer who established this scale.]

Celt (selt, kelt) *n.* **1.** a member of a Celtic-speaking people, including the Irish, Highland Scots, Welsh, Cornish, and Bretons. **2.** a member of an ancient people of central and western Europe, including the Gauls and Britons.

Celt·ic (sel′tik, kel′tik) *n.* a group of languages belonging to the Indo-European language family, including Irish, Scots Gaelic, Welsh, and Cornish. —*adj.* of or relating to the Celts, their languages, or their culture.

ce·ment (sə ment′) *n.* **1.** a material used in building, made by burning a mixture of limestone, clay or shale, silica, gypsum, and other substances to produce a powder that forms a slow-hardening paste when mixed with water. **2.** see **concrete** *(def. 3).* **3.** any soft substance, such as glue, that hardens to join things together. **4.** anything that joins together or unites; bond. —*v.t.* **1.** to fasten or join together with cement: *Rick cemented the wing to the model airplane.* **2.** to coat or cover with cement. **3.** to bind or unite: *This agreement cements their partnership.*

cem·e·ter·y (sem′ə ter′ē) *n. pl.,* **cem·e·ter·ies.** a place for burying the dead; graveyard.

Ce·no·zo·ic (sen′ə zō′ik) *n.* the most recent geological era, including the Tertiary and Quaternary periods; age of mammals. —*adj.* of, relating to, or characteristic of this era.

cen·ser (sen′sər) *n.* a container in which incense is burned.

cen·sor (sen′sər) *n.* **1.** a person employed by a government or organization to examine material, such as books, plays, or motion pictures, for the purpose of removing or suppressing anything that is considered improper, undesirable, or harmful. **2.** an official, usually employed by a government during wartime, who examines letters, literature, and other materials in order to remove any information that is confidential or dangerous to national security. **3.** in ancient Rome, one of the two officials who were in charge of taking the census and supervising public morals. —*v.t.* to examine and deal with as a censor: *Some governments censor books.*

▲ **Censor** should not be confused with **censure.** To **censor** is to remove or suppress material that is considered indecent or offensive: *Certain scenes of the movie were censored for its showing on television.* To **censure** is to express disapproval of or blame: *Congress censured the senator for revealing government secrets.*

cen·so·ri·ous (sen sôr′ē əs) *adj.* severely or harshly critical: *His censorious manner kept people away from him.* —**cen·so·ri·ous·ly,** *adv.* —**cen·so·ri·ous·ness,** *n.*

cen·sor·ship (sen′sər ship′) *n.* **1.** the act or system of censoring. **2.** the office or power held by a censor.

cen·sur·a·ble (sen′shər ə bəl) *adj.* worthy of censure.

cen·sure (sen′shər) *v.t.,* **cen·sured, cen·sur·ing.** to express disapproval of or find fault with; blame; condemn: *Journalists censured the athlete for his poor sportsmanship.* —*n.* an expression of disapproval or blame; condemnation, ▲ See **censor** for usage note. —**cen′sur·er,** *n.*

at; āpe; cär; end; mē; it; īce; hot; ōld; fôrk; wood; fōōl; oil; out; up; turn; sing; thin; this; hw in white; zh in treasure. The symbol ə stands for the sound of **a** in about, **e** in taken, **i** in pencil, **o** in lemon, and **u** in circus.

cen·sus (sen′səs) *n. pl.,* **cen·sus·es.** an official count of the people of a country or district, made in order to obtain certain statistics, such as age, sex, occupation, or economic status.

cent (sent) *n.* a coin of the United States equal to one-hundredth of a dollar.

cent. **1.** central. **2.** century. **3.** centigrade. **4.** centered.

cen·taur (sen′tôr) *n. Greek Mythology.* one of a race of creatures having the head, arms, and torso of a man, and the body and legs of a horse.

Centaur

cen·ta·vo (sen tä′vō) *n. pl.,* **cen·ta·vos.** one hundredth of various monetary units, as of the peso in certain Latin-American countries.

cen·te·nar·i·an (sen′tə ner′ē ən) *n.* a person who is one hundred years old or older.

cen·te·nar·y (sen′tə ner′ē, sen ten′ər ē) *n. pl.,* **cen·te·nar·ies.** **1.** another word for **centennial.** **2.** a period of one hundred years. —*adj.* of or relating to a period of one hundred years or to a hundredth anniversary; centennial.

cen·ten·ni·al (sen ten′ē əl) *n.* a hundredth anniversary or its celebration: *The town was settled in 1856 and had its centennial in 1956.* —*adj.* **1.** of or relating to a period of one hundred years. **2.** of or relating to a hundredth anniversary. —**cen·ten′ni·al·ly,** *adv.*

cen·ter (sen′tər) *also, British,* **cen·tre.** *n.* **1.** a point within a circle or sphere equally distant from all points of the circumference or surface. **2.** the middle point, part, or place of anything: *the center of a page, candies with chocolate centers, the center of a room.* **3.** a person or place around which interest, activity, or the like is concentrated: *The actor was the center of attention at the party. That city is a tourist center.* **4.** a point, line, or axis around which anything revolves, such as a wheel. **5.** *also,* **Center.** a group holding moderate political views. **6.** *Sports.* **a.** in football, the player who lines up in the middle of the offensive line and snaps the ball back to the quarterback. **b.** in basketball and hockey, the player whose position is in the center of the playing area. —*v.t.* **1.** to place or fix in or at the center: *We centered the picture on the wall.* **2.** to draw toward or gather around one point; concentrate: *She centered her attention on the main problem.* —*v.i.* to be centered or concentrated: *This story centers on the life of an astronaut.*

cen·ter·board (sen′tər bôrd′) *n.* a fin-shaped board or plate lowered through a slot in the bottom of a sailboat to prevent drifting.

center field *Baseball.* **1.** the middle section of the outfield behind second base. **2.** the position of the player stationed in this area.

center of gravity, the point in a body around which its mass is equally distributed.

cen·ter·piece (sen′tər pēs′) *n.* an ornamental object, such as a vase of flowers or a bowl of fruit, placed in the center of a table.

cen·tes·i·mal (sen tes′ə məl) *adj.* relating to or divided into hundredths. —**cen·tes′i·mal·ly,** *adv.*

centi- *combining form* **1.** hundred: *centipede.* **2.** a hundredth part of: *centigram, centimeter.*

cen·ti·grade (sen′tə grād′) *adj.* of, according to, or designating the temperature scale on which the freezing point is at zero degrees and the boiling point is at one hundred degrees under standard atmospheric pressure. A change of five degrees on the centigrade scale is equal to a change of nine degrees on the Fahrenheit scale.

cen·ti·gram (sen′tə gram′) *also, British,* **cen·ti·gramme.** *n.* a unit of metric weight equal to one-hundredth of a gram.

cen·time (sän′tēm) *n.* one-hundredth of any of various monetary units, such as the franc.

cen·ti·me·ter (sen′tə mē′tər) *also, British,* **cen·ti·me·tre.** *n.* a unit of metric measure equal to one-hundredth of a meter.

cen·ti·mo (sen′tə mō′) *n. pl.,* **cen·ti·mos.** one-hundredth of various monetary units.

cen·ti·pede (sen′tə pēd′) *n.* any of a group of small animals that resemble worms, having a flattened, long body made up of many segments, each bearing a pair of legs.

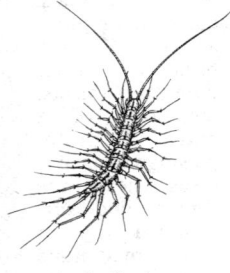

Centipede

cen·tral (sen′trəl) *adj.* **1.** in, at, or near the center or middle: *The railroad station has a central location in town.* **2.** of or forming the center. **3.** being the thing from which other things come or upon which they depend: *the central character of a book.* **4.** having a controlling or directing influence: *a central agency of the government.* —*n.* the main telephone exchange of an area, such as a town or city. —**cen′tral·ly,** *adv.*

Central African Republic, a country in central Africa. Capital, Bangui. Area, 240,535 sq. mi. Pop. (1971 est.), 1,640,000.

Central America, the region between the Pacific and the Caribbean, occupying the long isthmus of North America that links it with South America. Area, 205,087 sq. mi. —**Central American.**

Central Intelligence Agency, an executive agency that coordinates the intelligence activities of all the departments of the United States Government.

cen·tral·ize (sen′trə līz′) *v.,* **cen·tral·ized, cen·tral·iz·ing.** —*v.t.* **1.** to bring together at a center; make central. **2.** to bring or organize under one control or a central authority: *to centralize a country's government under a dictator.* —*v.i.* to come together at a center. —**cen′tral·i·za′tion,** *n.*

central nervous system, the part of the nervous system composed of the brain and the spinal cord.

Central Powers, the countries that fought against the Allies in World War I: Germany, Austria-Hungary, Bulgaria, and Turkey.

Central Standard Time, the standard time used in the central United States. It is six hours earlier than Greenwich Time.

cen·tre (sen′tər) *British. n., v.,* **cen·tred, cen·tring.** another spelling of **center.**

cen·trif·u·gal (sen trif′yə gəl, sen trif′ə gəl) *adj.* moving or directed away from a center. —**cen·trif′u·gal·ly,** *adv.*

centrifugal force, the force generated when a body is moving in a curved path, tending to move the body away from the center of the curve. If you whirl a ball on a string over your head, the outward pull you feel is centrifugal force.

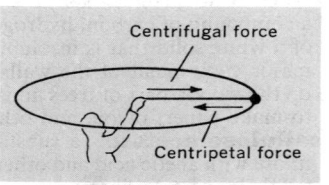

Centrifugal force

cen·tri·fuge (sen′trə fyōōj′) *n.* **1.** a device using centrifugal force to separate substances of different densities, as cream from milk, by spinning them at high speeds. **2.** a large machine that simulates the effects of gravity, usually consisting of a capsule or chair spun in a circle at the end of a long support. It is used in training astronauts to withstand the pull of gravity. —*v.t.*, **cen·tri·fuged, cen·tri·fug·ing.** to subject to the action of a centrifuge.

cen·tri·ole (sen′trē ōl′) *n.* a tiny cylindrical body in all animal cells and many plant cells, usually paired. Centrioles duplicate themselves just before mitosis and move to opposite ends of the cell during mitosis, where they form the poles of the spindle to which the chromosomes move.

cen·trip·e·tal (sen trip′ət əl) *adj.* moving or directed toward a center. —**cen·trip′e·tal·ly,** *adv.*

centripetal force, the force generated when a body is moving in a curved path, tending to move the body toward the center of the curve. If you whirl a ball on a string over your head, the inward pull exerted by your hand is centripetal force. If you remove the centripetal force by letting go of the string, the ball will fly off in a straight line rather than continue to spin. See **centrifugal force** for illustration.

cen·tro·some (sen′trə sōm′) *n.* an area in the cytoplasm of a cell that contains the centrioles.

cen·tu·ri·on (sen toor′ē ən, sen tyoor′ē ən) *n.* a commander of a century in the ancient Roman army.

cen·tu·ry (sen′chər ē) *n. pl.,* **cen·tu·ries. 1.** a period of one hundred years. From 1650 to 1750 is a century. **2.** a period of one hundred years reckoned forward or backward from some fixed date, especially from the birth of Christ: *the twentieth century A.D.* **3.** a unit of the ancient Roman army, originally consisting of one hundred men.

century plant, a desert plant found in Mexico and the southwestern United States, having thick, spiny-edged leaves and a flower stalk that grows to a height of twenty to forty feet. [It was formerly believed to bloom only once every *century.*]

ce·phal·ic (si fal′ik) *adj.* of or relating to the head.

ceph·a·lo·pod (sef′ə lə pod′) *n.* any of a group of sea animals including the octopus, squid, and cuttlefish, having a clearly defined head with large, well-developed eyes, a sharp beak, and muscular tentacles around the mouth that bear suckers.

ce·ram·ic (sə ram′ik) *adj.* of or relating to objects made of baked clay, such as pottery, earthenware, or porcelain. —*n.* an object made of baked clay.

ce·ram·ics (sə ram′iks) *n., pl.* the art or technique of making objects by shaping clay and then baking it at a high temperature. ▲ used with a singular verb.

cer·a·mist (ser′ə mist′, sə ram′ist) *n.* an expert in ceramics or an artist who makes ceramic objects.

Cer·ber·us (sur′bər əs) *n. Greek and Roman Mythology.* a three-headed dog guarding the entrance to Hades.

ce·re·al (sēr′ē əl) *n.* **1.** any grass, such as wheat, oats, rye, barley, or rice, that yields grains which are used for food. **2.** the grain of such a grass. **3.** a food made from this grain, especially a breakfast food such as oatmeal. —*adj.* of or relating to edible grain or to the grass that produces it.

Cerberus

cer·e·bel·lum (ser′ə bel′əm) *n. pl.,* **cer·e·bel·lums** or **cer·e·bel·la** (ser′ə bel′ə). the part of the brain that coordinates the activity of the muscles. It is located in the back of the skull.

cer·e·bral (ser′ə brəl, sə rē′brəl) *adj.* **1.** of or relating to the brain or to the cerebrum: *a cerebral hemorrhage.* **2.** relating to, involving, or appealing to the intellect rather than the emotions; intellectual.

cerebral palsy, lack of control over the muscles, resulting from damage to the brain before or during birth.

cer·e·bro·spi·nal (ser′ə brō spīn′əl) *adj.* of, relating to, or affecting the brain and spinal cord.

cer·e·brum (ser′ə brəm, sə rē′brəm) *n. pl.,* **cer·e·brums** or **cer·e·bra** (ser′ə brə, sə rē′brə). the largest part of the human brain, occupying the entire upper portion of the skull. The cerebrum controls voluntary movements and conscious mental activities.

cere·ment (sēr′mənt) *n.* a cloth used to wrap a dead body; shroud.

cer·e·mo·ni·al (ser′ə mō′nē əl) *adj.* **1.** relating to or showing ceremony; formal: *a ceremonial dinner.* **2.** used in connection with a ceremony: *ceremonial robes.* —*n.* a set of rites or formalities observed on or for some particular occasion; ritual. —**cer′e·mo′ni·al·ly,** *adv.*

cer·e·mo·ni·ous (ser′ə mō′nē əs) *adj.* **1.** very careful about ceremony; very polite: *a ceremonious person, a ceremonious bow.* **2.** marked by or done with ceremony: *a ceremonious occasion.* —**cer′e·mo′ni·ous·ly,** *adv.* —**cer′e·mo′ni·ous·ness,** *n.*

cer·e·mo·ny (ser′ə mō′nē) *n. pl.,* **cer·e·mo·nies. 1.** a formal act or set of acts done on a special or important occasion: *a wedding ceremony, a graduation ceremony, an inaugural ceremony.* **2.** very polite or formal conduct: *The guests got up and left without ceremony.*

to stand on ceremony. to behave with or insist on strict formality: *You needn't stand on ceremony with us.*

Ce·res (sēr′ēz) *n. Roman Mythology.* the goddess of grain and agriculture. In Greek mythology she was called Demeter.

ce·rise (sə rēs′) *n.* a bright red color resembling a ripe cherry. —*adj.* having the color cerise; bright red.

ce·ri·um (sēr′ē əm) *n.* a grayish metallic element that is used especially in refining processes and in alloys. It is the most abundant of the group of rare-earth elements. Symbol: **Ce**

cer·tain (surt′ən) *adj.* **1.** free from doubt; fully confident; positive; sure: *I am certain that I am correct.* **2.** beyond doubt or question; true: *It is now certain that he won the election.* **3.** bound to happen; inevitable: *Capture meant certain death to the spy.* **4.** agreed upon; settled; determined: *They plan to meet at a certain time.* **5.** that may be depended on; reliable; trustworthy: *a certain cure for a headache.* **6.** known, but not named or specified; particular: *Certain people didn't approve of your plan.* **7.** some, but not much: *There has been a certain amount of improvement in his health.*

for certain. without doubt; surely: *The police never knew for certain who had committed the crime.*

cer·tain·ly (surt′ən lē) *adv.* without a doubt; surely: *She certainly is pretty.*

at; āpe; cär; end; mē; it; īce; hot; ōld; fôrk; wood; fōol; oil; out; up; turn; sing; thin; **th**is; hw in white; zh in treasure. The symbol ə stands for the sound of **a** in about, **e** in taken, **i** in pencil, **o** in lemon, and **u** in circus.

cer·tain·ty (surt′ən tē) *n. pl.,* **cer·tain·ties. 1.** the quality, state, or fact of being certain: *There is no certainty that you will win the prize.* **2.** something certain; established fact: *It is a certainty that the earth revolves around the sun.*

cer·tif·i·cate (sər tif′ə kit) *n.* an official document declaring the truth of certain facts: *a birth certificate, a marriage certificate, a death certificate.*

cer·ti·fi·ca·tion (sur′tə fi kā′shən) *n.* **1.** the act of certifying or the state of being certified. **2.** a certified statement; certificate.

certified public accountant, an accountant who has received a certificate stating that he has met the requirements of the law of his state.

cer·ti·fy (sur′tə fī′) *v.t.,* **cer·ti·fied, cer·ti·fy·ing. 1.** to declare (something) to be true, accurate, or certain, especially by a signed statement or official document; testify to: *The document certified the date of her birth.* **2.** to guarantee the quality or value of: *to certify milk, to certify a check.*

cer·ti·tude (sur′tə tōōd′, sur′tə tyōōd′) *n.* a feeling of being certain.

ce·ru·le·an (sə rōō′lē ən) *n.* a sky-blue color; azure. —*adj.* having the color cerulean; sky-blue.

Cer·van·tes, Mi·guel de (sər vän′tēz; mē gel′ dā) 1547–1616, Spanish author.

cer·vi·cal (sur′vi kəl) *adj.* of or relating to a cervix.

cer·vix (sur′viks) *n. pl.,* **cer·vix·es** or **cer·vi·ces** (sur′və sēz). **1.** the neck. **2.** a neck-shaped part of the body, such as the outer end of the uterus.

Ce·sar·e·an (si zer′ē ən) *also,* **Ce·sar·i·an.** *n.* see **Cesarean section.**

Cesarean section *also,* **Caesarean section.** the delivery of a baby from its mother's uterus by a surgical incision made through the abdomen into the uterus. It is performed when normal delivery is impossible or dangerous. [From Julius *Caesar,* who supposedly was delivered in this way.]

ce·si·um (sē′zē əm) *also,* **cae·si·um.** *n.* a soft, silvery metallic element used especially in photoelectric cells. It is one of the rarest of metals. Symbol: **Cs**

ces·sa·tion (se sā′shən) *n.* a ceasing or halting; stop: *a cessation of fighting.*

ces·sion (sesh′ən) *n.* the act of ceding; giving up or surrendering to another: *a cession of territory, a cession of rights.*

cess·pool (ses′pōōl′) *n.* a pit, well, or other underground container for collecting sewage from the toilets and sinks of a house.

ce·ta·cean (si tā′shən) *adj.* of or relating to an order of mammals that resemble fish and live entirely in water, such as whales, dolphins, and porpoises. —*n.* any one of these mammals.

Cey·lon (si lon′) the former name of **Sri Lanka.** —**Cey·lo·nese** (sē′lə nēz′), *adj., n.*

Cé·zanne, Paul (sā zan′) 1839–1906, French painter.

Cf, the symbol for californium.

cf., compare. [Abbreviation of Latin *confer.*]

cg., centigram; centigrams. Also, **cg, cgm.**

ch. 1. chapter. **2.** church.

cha-cha (chä′chä′) *n.* **1.** a ballroom dance of Latin-American origin, similar to the mambo. **2.** the music for this dance.

Chad (chad) *n.* **1.** a country in north-central Africa, formerly a French colony. Capital, Ndjamena. Area, 495,800 sq. mi. Pop. (1975 est.), 4,030,000. **2. Lake.** a large lake in north-central Africa, at the southern edge of the Sahara Desert.

chafe (chāf) *v.,* **chafed, chaf·ing.** —*v.t.* **1.** to wear away or make sore by friction or rubbing: *The diaper chafed the baby's skin.* **2.** to make angry; irritate; annoy. **3.** to restore warmth to by rubbing: *We chafed her numb hands.* —*v.i.* **1.** to be worn away or made sore by friction or rubbing. **2.** to be irritated or annoyed: *He chafed under his sister's constant criticism.*

chaff[1] (chaf) *n.* **1.** the husks of wheat, oats, rye, and other grains, separated from the seed by threshing. **2.** finely cut hay or straw used as feed for livestock. **3.** any worthless matter; refuse. [Old English *ceaf.*]

chaff[2] (chaf) *v.t.* to tease or make fun of in a good-natured way: *The other golfers chaffed Ted when he swung and missed the ball.* —*n.* good-natured teasing. [Possibly a form of *chafe.*]

chaf·finch (chaf′inch) *n.* a European finch having a pleasant, short song, popular as a cage bird.

chafing dish, a pan or dish with a heating device underneath it, used for cooking or for keeping food warm at the table.

Cha·gall, Marc (shə gäl′) 1887—, Russian painter, living chiefly in France.

Chafing dish

cha·grin (shə grin′) *n.* a feeling of annoyance or distress because one has failed or been disappointed or embarrassed. —*v.t.* to annoy or distress by failure, disappointment, or embarrassment: *She was deeply chagrined by her failure.*

chain (chān) *n.* **1.** a series of connected links or rings, usually of metal, used chiefly to bind, hold, or pull something, or as an ornament: *The chain of a bicycle transmits power from the pedals to the wheels. She wore a chain of flowers around her neck.* **2.** a series of connected things: *a chain of mountains, the chain of events leading up to a war.* **3. chains.** anything that binds or restrains. **4.** a number of similar business establishments under the same ownership or management: *a chain of restaurants, a chain of movie theaters.* **5.** a measuring instrument consisting of 100 links of equal length, used by surveyors and engineers, and equal to either 66 feet (in surveying) or 100 feet (in engineering). —*v.t.* **1.** to fasten, secure, or connect with a chain: *He chained his bicycle to the post.* **2.** to restrain or confine; bind: *An unexpected amount of work chained him to his desk.*

chain gang, a group of convicts chained together, usually while at hard labor outdoors.

chain letter, a letter sent to a number of people, asking each to send a copy in turn to a specific number of other persons.

chain mail, flexible armor for the body, made of small metal rings or links joined together.

chain reaction 1. a series of atomic reactions that, once started, can sustain itself automatically. In a chain reaction, an atomic nucleus that has been split gives off neutrons, which strike other nuclei. This causes these nuclei to split and give off additional neutrons, which in turn collide with other nuclei, thus continuing the process. **2.** any series of events, each of which is caused by the preceding one and is the cause of the following one.

Chain mail

chair (cher) *n.* **1.** a piece of furniture designed to seat one person, usually having a back and legs and sometimes arms. **2.** an office or position of authority or dignity: *That professor holds the chair of French literature at the university.* **3.** a presiding officer; chairman: *The speaker rose to address the chair.* —*v.t.* to preside over; act as chairman of: *to chair a panel discussion.*

to take the chair. to take the position of chairman; preside at or open a meeting.

chair·man (cher′mən) *n. pl.,* **chair·men** (cher′mən). a person in charge of a meeting, committee, board, or organization. —**chair′wom′an,** *n.*

chair·man·ship (cher′mən ship′) *n.* the position, duties, or term of office of a chairman.

chair·per·son (cher′pur′sən) *n.* a chairman or chairwoman.

chaise (shāz) *n.* **1.** a light, usually two-wheeled carriage, often with a hood or folding top, usually seating one or two passengers. Also, **shay. 2.** see **chaise longue.**

chaise longue (shāz′lông′) a chair with a long, couch-like seat on which a person can sit with his legs outstretched. Also, **chaise lounge.** [French *chaise longue* lounging chair; literally, long chair.]

chal·ced·o·ny (kal sed′ən ē) *n. pl.,* **chal·ced·o·nies.** a variety of quartz having a waxy luster and occurring in various colors. Agate is a kind of chalcedony.

Chal·de·a (kal dē′ə) *n.* an ancient region in Babylonia, on the Tigris and Euphrates rivers, in what is now southern Iraq. —**Chal·de′an,** *adj., n.*

cha·let (sha lā′) *n.* **1.** a house having a wide, sloping roof with overhanging eaves, commonly found in Switzerland and other nearby regions. **2.** any house built in this style. **3.** any herdsman's hut or simple cottage in the Alps.

chal·ice (chal′is) *n.* **1.** a drinking cup or goblet. **2.** a cup or vessel containing the wine used in the Holy Communion service. **3.** a cup-shaped flower.

chalk (chôk) *n.* **1.** a soft, powdery, white or gray form of limestone that is made up mostly of tiny seashells. Chalk is used especially to make lime and cement and sometimes as a fertilizer. **2.** a piece of this substance or a similar material, usually in the form of a crayon and often colored, used for writing and drawing on a blackboard. —*v.t.* **1.** to mark, write, or draw with chalk: *He chalked his initials on the sidewalk.* **2.** to rub or treat with chalk. —**chalk′like′,** *adj.*
  to chalk up. a. to score or earn: *The player chalked up thirty points for his team.* **b.** to charge or credit: *You can chalk up his mistake to ignorance.*

chalk·board (chôk′bôrd′) *n.* another word for **blackboard.**

chalk·y (chô′kē) *adj.,* **chalk·i·er, chalk·i·est. 1.** resembling chalk: *a chalky taste.* **2.** of or containing chalk. —**chalk′i·ness,** *n.*

chal·lenge (chal′ənj) *v.t.,* **chal·lenged, chal·leng·ing. 1.** to invite or call to take part in a struggle or contest; dare to fight or compete: *The swordsman challenged his enemy to a duel. Fred challenged his friends to a race around the block.* **2.** to call into question; doubt or dispute: *to challenge a person's opinions.* **3.** to make demands on the talents or energy of; arouse the interest of: *This novel challenges the imagination. The science project challenged the entire class.* **4.** to stop and demand identification from: *The sentry challenged anyone who approached the gate.* **5.** *Law.* to object or take exception to: *to challenge a prospective juror.* —*n.* **1.** an invitation or call to take part in a fight or contest: *Our football team accepted their challenge.* **2.** a calling into question; doubting or disputing. **3.** something that demands the use of one's talents or energy: *He found chemistry to be a real challenge.* **4.** a demand for identification from a sentry. **5.** *Law.* a formal objection, especially to the qualifications of a juror. —**chal′leng·er,** *n.*

chal·lis (shal′ē) *also,* **chal·lie.** *n.* a soft, lightweight woolen, cotton, or rayon fabric, usually having a printed design, used especially for scarves and neckties.

cham·ber (chām′bər) *n.* **1.** a room, especially a bed-room. **2.** *also,* **chambers.** a room where a judge conducts business when not holding a court session, especially his or her private office. **3.** a hall where a legislature or other body meets. **4.** a legislative or judicial body or assembly: *The Senate is the upper chamber of Congress.* **5.** the reception room of a person of authority or rank, such as in a palace. **6.** a cavity or enclosed space in the body of an animal or plant: *the four chambers of the heart.* **7.** the rear portion of the barrel of a firearm, into which the cartridge or shell is inserted. —*v.t.* to provide with a chamber.

cham·ber·lain (chām′bər lin) *n.* **1.** a person in charge of the household of a king or nobleman; steward. **2.** a person who receives or keeps funds and revenues; treasurer.

cham·ber·maid (chām′bər mād′) *n.* a woman whose work is making beds and cleaning bedrooms, especially in a hotel, motel, or other place providing accommodation.

chamber music, music written for a small group of instruments and suitable for performance in a room or small hall.

chamber of commerce, an association organized to promote the business interests of a particular town, state, region, or country.

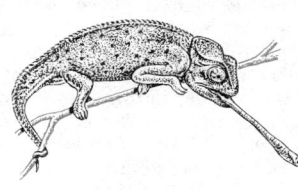

Chameleon

cham·bray (sham′brā) *n.* a cotton fabric woven with colored and white threads, used especially for dresses, shirts, and pajamas. [From *Cambrai,* a city in France.]

cha·me·leon (kə mēl′yən) *n.* **1.** a small lizard that can change the color of its skin to match that of its surroundings. **2.** a person who quickly changes his or her mood or opinions; changeable or fickle person.

cham·ois (sham′ē) *n. pl.,* **cham·ois** (sham′ēz). **1.** a small, goatlike antelope of the mountains of Europe and western Asia. It has a long, reddish-brown coat that turns dark brown in the winter. **2.** a soft, pliable leather, originally made from the skin of the chamois, now made from the skins of sheep, goats, and deer.

Chamois

cham·o·mile (kam′ə-mīl′) another spelling of **camomile.**

champ¹ (champ) *v.t.* **1.** to bite and chew vigorously and noisily; munch: *to champ popcorn.* **2.** to bite upon restlessly or impatiently: *The horse was champing its bit.* —*v.i.* to make biting or chewing movements with the jaws and teeth. [Probably in imitation of the sound made in chewing.]
  to champ at the bit. to show signs of restlessness or impatience: *The players were champing at the bit as they waited for the game to start.*

champ² (champ) *n. Informal.* champion.

---

at; āpe; cär; end; mē; it; īce; hot; ōld; fôrk; wood; fo̅o̅l; oil; out; up; turn; sing; thin; this; hw in white; zh in treasure. The symbol ə stands for the sound of **a** in about, **e** in taken, **i** in pencil, **o** in lemon, and **u** in circus.

C

cham·pagne (sham pān′) *n.* a sparkling, bubbling white or light pink wine. [From *Champagne*, a region in northeastern France.]

cham·paign (sham pān′) *n.* flat, open country; plain.

cham·pi·on (cham′pē ən) *n.* **1.** the winner of first place or first prize in a competition: *He is the heavyweight boxing champion. Our school is the league champion in basketball.* **2.** a person who fights for or defends a person or cause: *a champion of conservation, a champion of freedom of speech.* —*adj.* having won first place or first prize; superior to all others: *a champion wrestler, a champion chess player.* —*v.t.* to fight for or defend; support: *He champions the cause of civil rights.*

cham·pi·on·ship (cham′pē ən ship′) *n.* **1.** the position or honor of being a champion: *She won the tennis championship last year.* **2.** the act of championing; defense or support.

Cham·plain (sham plān′) *n.* **1. Samuel de.** 1567–1635, the French explorer who founded Quebec. **2. Lake.** a lake on the border between New York and Vermont, extending into southwestern Quebec.

chance (chans) *n.* **1.** the unknown cause of the way things take place; happening of events by accident; fate; luck; fortune: *I met her entirely by chance. He left matters to chance.* **2.** the likelihood of something happening; probability or possibility: *There's a chance he made a mistake. That team has little chance of winning the game.* **3.** an opportunity: *He saw the chance to escape. She has a chance to visit Europe.* **4.** a risk, gamble: *Don't take chances when you are swimming alone.* **5.** a ticket in a lottery, raffle, or similar contest. —*v.,* **chanced, chanc·ing.** —*v.i.* to happen by chance: *Our paths chanced to cross in the park.* —*v.t.* to take the chance of; risk: *The tourist chanced buying tickets at the last minute.* —*adj.* happening by chance; unplanned; accidental: *a chance meeting, a chance remark.*

to chance on or **to chance upon,** to find or meet unexpectedly or accidentally: *He chanced on the lost key while looking for a match. I chanced on an old friend today.*

chan·cel (chan′səl) *n.* the space around the altar of a church, used by the clergy and the choir. It is often set off by a railing, lattice, or screen.

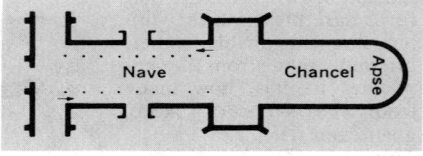

Chancel

chan·cel·ler·y (chan′- sə lər ē) *n. pl.,* **chan·cel·ler·ies. 1.** the position or office of a chancellor. **2.** the office of an embassy, legation, or consulate.

chan·cel·lor (chan′sə lər) *n.* **1.** the prime minister in certain European countries, such as West Germany and Austria. **2.** the president of certain American universities. **3.** the judge of a court of equity in some states of the United States. **4.** an official who serves as the chief secretary of a sovereign or embassy.

Chancellor of the Exchequer, the cabinet minister in the British government who is in charge of financial affairs.

chan·cel·lor·ship (chan′sə lər ship′) *n.* the position or term of office of a chancellor.

chan·cer·y (chan′sər ē) *n. pl.,* **chan·cer·ies. 1.** a court of law that deals with matters for which there are no fair remedies under the common law or the civil law. **2.** see **chancellery** (*defs. 2, 3*).

chanc·y (chan′sē) *adj.* **chanc·i·er, chanc·i·est.** *Informal.* subject to chance; uncertain; risky: *Prospecting for gold is a chancy job.*

chan·de·lier (shand′əl ēr′) *n.* a lighting fixture designed to be hung from a ceiling, usually having several lights arranged on projecting arms or branches.

chan·dler (chand′lər) *n.* **1.** a person who makes or sells candles. **2.** a dealer or merchant, especially one who deals in groceries or ship's supplies.

Chang (chäng) *n.* see **Yangtze.**

change (chānj) *v.,* **changed, chang·ing.** —*v.t.* **1.** to make different: *She changed the arrangement of the furniture. He has changed his attitude toward his work.* **2.** to replace (something) with another or others of the same or a similar kind: *to change one's shirt, to change one's job. The mechanic changed the oil in the car's engine.* **3.** to give and receive; exchange: *The two boys changed seats.* **4.** to give or receive the equivalent of (money) in smaller units: *Can you change a ten dollar bill for me?* —*v.i.* **1.** to become different: *The scenery changed as we drove farther south. He has changed since he became famous.* **2.** to put on other clothes: *The actors changed between scenes.* **3.** to transfer from one train, airplane, bus, or the like to another: *The passengers going from Washington to Albany had to change at New York.* —*n.* **1.** the act or fact of changing: *a change in plans, a change in the weather. The captain made a change in the ship's course.* **2.** something that may be substituted for another: *He brought along a change of clothing on the trip.* **3.** something different from the usual: *For a change he took his vacation in the winter.* **4.** coins as distinguished from paper money: *I've got lots of change in my pocket.* **5.** the money returned when the amount paid is more than the amount owed: *He gave the cashier a five dollar bill and got forty cents in change.* **6.** money equal in value to a coin or bill of a higher denomination: *He gave me ten dimes as change for a dollar bill.* —**chang′er,** *n.*

change·a·ble (chān′jə bəl) *adj.* **1.** likely to change; variable: *a changeable personality, a changeable mood.* **2.** that can be changed: *a changeable plan.* **3.** changing in color or appearance when looked at from different points of view: *changeable silk.* —**change′a·ble·ness,** *n.* —**change′a·bly,** *adv.*

change·ful (chānj′fəl) *adj.* full of changes; given to change; changeable; variable. —**change′ful·ly,** *adv.* —**change′ful·ness,** *n.*

change·less (chānj′lis) *adj.* that does not change; constant; enduring: *the changeless rhythm of the ocean tides.* —**change′less·ly,** *adv.* —**change′less·ness,** *n.*

change·ling (chānj′ling) *n.* **1.** a child secretly substituted for another. **2.** in folklore, a child left by fairies in place of a child they have stolen.

change·o·ver (chānj′ō′vər) *n.* a change, shift, or transfer, as from one activity, method, or way of managing, to another.

chan·nel (chan′əl) *n.* **1.** the deepest part of a river, harbor, or other waterway, often dredged and maintained as a passage for boats and ships. **2.** the bed of a stream, river, or other waterway. **3.** a body of water that connects two larger bodies of water; wide strait. **4.** a groove or furrow: *a channel for rain water.* **5.** the means by which something is directed or carried: *a channel of communication.* **6. channels.** a proper or official route or means, especially of communication: *The sergeant's request for new typewriters had to go through channels.* **7.** a band of frequencies assigned to a radio or television station for the transmission of electronic signals: *This old television set can only pick up one channel.* —*v.t.,* **chan·neled, chan·nel·ing;** *also, British,* **chan·nelled, chan·nel·ling. 1.** to cut out as a channel: *The stream channeled its way down the mountain.* **2.** to direct through a channel: *They channeled the stream onto the neighboring property.* **3.** to form a channel in.

Channel Islands, a group of British islands in the English Channel, off the northwestern coast of France.

chant (chant) *n.* **1.** a singing or shouting of words over and over, usually with a strong rhythm: *an Indian war chant. The crowd broke into a chant when the candidate appeared.* **2.** a simple melody in which a number of syllables or words are sung on one note. **3.** a religious text sung in this manner. —*v.t.* **1.** to sing or shout over and over: *She led the group in chanting their slogan.* **2.** to sing to a chant, as in a church service: *to chant a psalm.* **3.** to sing. —*v.i.* **1.** to recite or shout a chant: *The protesters chanted in the street below.* **2.** to sing a chant: *The choir chanted during the service.* —**chant′er,** *n.*

chan·teuse (shan toos′) *n. French.* a female singer, especially one who sings in a night club or cabaret.

chan·tey (shan′tē, chan′tē) *also,* **chan·ty, shan·tey, shan·ty.** *n. pl.,* **chan·teys.** a song sung by sailors in rhythm with their work.

chan·ti·cleer (chan′tə klēr′) *n.* a rooster. ▲ used chiefly as a proper name in fables and literature.

Chan·til·ly (shan til′ē) *n.* a delicate lace made of silk or other fibers, used chiefly for evening and bridal gowns. Also, **Chantilly lace.** [From *Chantilly,* a town in northern France where it was first made.]

chan·ty (shan′tē, chan′tē) *n. pl.,* **chan·ties.** another spelling of **chantey.**

Cha·nu·kah (hä′nə kə) another spelling of **Hanukkah.**

cha·os (kā′os) *n.* **1.** a state of complete confusion and disorder: *The village was in chaos after the earthquake struck.* **2. Chaos.** *Greek Mythology.* the confused and formless state that existed before the creation of the universe.

cha·ot·ic (kā ot′ik) *adj.* in complete confusion and disorder: *The candidate's headquarters was chaotic on the night of the election.* —**cha·ot′i·cal·ly,** *adv.*

chap[1] (chap) *v.,* **chapped, chap·ping.** —*v.t.* to split, crack, or make rough: *Her hands are chapped from washing all those dishes.* —*v.i.* to become split, cracked, or roughened: *My lips always chap in the winter.* [Middle English *chappen* to cut.]

chap[2] (chap) *n. Informal.* a man or boy; fellow. [Short for the earlier word *chapman* a peddler, from Old English *cēapman* a merchant.]

chap., chapter.

chap·ar·ral (shap′ə ral′) *n.* a dense thicket of low or shrubby trees or thorny shrubs, usually found in dry, sunny regions.

cha·peau (sha pō′) *n. pl.,* **cha·peaux** (sha pō′, sha pōz′) or **cha·peaus.** a hat. [French *chapeau.*]

chap·el (chap′əl) *n.* **1.** a place of worship that is smaller than a church. **2.** a room or space within a church, having its own altar and used for special or small services. **3.** a place of worship in a school, college, hospital, military post, or the like. **4.** religious services in a chapel, especially at a school or college: *Students were required to attend chapel twice each week.*

chap·er·on (shap′ə rōn′) *n.* **1.** an older or married person who attends and supervises a social gathering of young unmarried people. **2.** an older or married woman who accompanies a young unmarried woman in public. —*v.t.* to act as chaperon for: *Bill's mother and father chaperoned the dance.*

chap·er·one (shap′ə rōn′) *n., v.,* **chap·er·oned, chap·er·on·ing.** another spelling of **chaperon.**

chap·lain (chap′lin) *n.* a clergyman or clergywoman who performs religious functions for groups or organizations, such as a military unit, a prison, or a school.

chap·let (chap′lit) *n.* **1.** a wreath or garland worn on the head. **2.** a short rosary. **3.** any string of beads; necklace.

chaps (chaps, shaps) *n., pl.* strong leather leggings worn over trousers by cowboys to protect their legs while riding horseback. [Short for *chaparajos,* from Spanish *chaparral* chaparral; because they were worn as protection from the thorns of chaparral.]

chap·ter (chap′tər) *n.* **1.** a main division of a book or other writing. **2.** a main division or part of anything: *The Civil War was a tragic chapter in American history.* **3.** a local branch or division of an organization, such as a club, fraternity, or society.

Cha·pul·te·pec (chə pool′tə pek′) *n.* a rocky hill in Mexico City, captured by U.S. forces in 1847 in the last major battle of the Mexican War.

char (chär) *v.,* **charred, char·ring.** —*v.t.* **1.** to burn slightly or partially; scorch. **2.** to reduce to charcoal by burning: *to char wood.* —*v.i.* to become charred.

Chaps

char·ac·ter (kar′ik tər) *n.* **1.** all the qualities or features that are typical of or serve to distinguish a person, group, or thing; individual nature: *That author's stories have a gloomy character. The countryside has a different character as you travel west.* **2.** all the qualities of a person, good or bad, that make up his or her moral nature; moral quality: *He has a fine, honest character.* **3.** moral strength or excellence; integrity: *That judge is a woman of character.* **4.** a person represented in a novel, play, motion picture, or the like: *Hamlet is one of the most famous characters in literature.* **5.** any person; individual: *That man is the kindest looking character I've ever seen.* **6.** *Informal.* a person who is odd, eccentric, amusing, or very different. **7.** a position or function; capacity; status: *She signed the document in her character of president.* **8.** a mark or sign used as a symbol in writing or printing, such as a letter of the alphabet.

  in character. in keeping with a person's disposition or usual behavior.

  out of character. not in keeping with a person's disposition or usual behavior .

char·ac·ter·is·tic (kar′ik tə ris′tik) *n.* a quality or feature that is typical of or serves to distinguish a person, group, or thing from others: *Her kindness is her most outstanding characteristic. The ability to fly is a characteristic of bats.* —*adj.* relating to or indicating the character of a person or thing: *Lemons have a characteristic taste. Such a rude remark is not characteristic of her personality.* —**char′ac·ter·is′ti·cal·ly,** *adv.*

char·ac·ter·ize (kar′ik tə rīz′) *v.t.,* **char·ac·ter·ized, char·ac·ter·iz·ing.** **1.** to be a characteristic of; distinguish: *That disease is characterized by a high fever.* **2.** to describe the character or qualities of; portray: *The author characterizes his father as a highly amusing man.* —**char′ac·ter·i·za′tion,** *n.*

cha·rades (shə rādz′) *n., pl.* a game in which the players try to guess a word or phrase that another player acts out without speaking. To show the word *characterize,* a player might act out "care," "actor," and "eyes." ▲ used with a singular verb.

---

at; āpe; cär; end; mē; it; īce; hot; ōld; fôrk; wood; fool; oil; out; up; turn; sing; thin; this; hw in white; zh in treasure. The symbol ə stands for the sound of **a** in about, **e** in taken, **i** in pencil, **o** in lemon, and **u** in circus.

char·coal (chär′kōl′) *n.* a black, soft substance that is a form of carbon, made by partially burning wood or other plant or animal matter. It is used as a fuel, in filters, and as a pencil for drawing.

charge (chärj) *v.*, **charged, charg·ing.** —*v.t.* **1.** to fix or ask as a price: *The shop charged ten dollars to repair the radio.* **2.** to require payment from: *The neighbor charged Bill for the broken window.* **3.** to put off payment for (something) until a later time: *She charged the new dress at the shop.* **4.** to rush violently upon or toward in an attack: *The bull charged the farmer. The troops charged the fortress.* **5.** to bring an accusation against or put blame upon; accuse: *The police charged him with the theft.* **6.** to give a task, duty, or responsibility to: *The baby-sitter was charged with the care of the children while their parents were away.* **7.** to fill or load: *They charged the cannon with shot. Her reply was charged with emotion.* **8.** to supply with a quantity of electricity or electrical energy: *to charge a storage battery.* **9.** to command or order: *The judge charged the jury to disregard the witness' statement.* —*v.i.* **1.** to rush violently or go quickly: *He charged up the stairs after his little brother.* **2.** to fix or ask a price: *Does that store charge for delivery?* —*n.* **1.** the required payment; price asked or fixed: *The charge for admission was $1.50.* **2.** a purchase that is to be paid for at a later time. **3.** a violent or rushing attack: *The enemy's charge was turned back by the troops.* **4.** the signal or order for such an attack: *The bugler sounded the charge.* **5.** an accusation: *They were arrested on a charge of robbery.* **6.** care, custody, or management: *She had charge of her brother while their mother was out.* **7.** a person or thing under the care, custody, or management of another: *The orphan was made a charge of his uncle.* **8.** task, duty, or responsibility: *A child's education is the charge of his parents.* **9.** the quantity that something is fitted to receive and hold, such as the amount of gunpowder in a cartridge or shell. **10.** the amount of electrical energy possessed by an object. **11.** a command, order, or instruction: *a judge's charge to a jury.* —**charge′a·ble,** *adj.*

  in charge. in the position of authority or responsibility; in command.

  in charge of. in control of; responsible for: *He is in charge of the equipment for the hockey team.*

charge account, an arrangement by which a person may make purchases to be paid for at a later date: *She has a charge account at the department store.*

char·gé d' af·fairs (shär zhä′ də fer′) *pl.*, **char·gés d'af·fairs** (shär zhāz′də fer′). a diplomatic official who serves as a temporary substitute for an ambassador or minister. [French *chargé d'affaires* literally, (one) charged with affairs.]

charg·er (chär′jər) *n.* **1.** a horse trained for use in battle. **2.** a person or thing that charges. **3.** a device used to give an electrical charge to storage batteries.

char·i·ot (char′ē ət) *n.* a two-wheeled vehicle drawn by two, three, or four horses and driven from a standing position, used in ancient times in warfare, processions, and races.

char·i·ot·eer (char′ē ə·tēr′) *n.* the driver of a chariot.

cha·ris·ma (kə riz′mə) *n.* a rare personal quality that attracts the loyalty and devotion of a large following of people: *the charisma of a great political leader.*

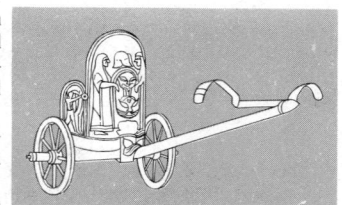

Chariot

char·is·mat·ic (kar′iz mat′ik) *adj.* having or showing charisma: *a charismatic leader.*

char·i·ta·ble (char′ə tə bəl) *adj.* **1.** of or for charity; giving help to the poor or needy: *The Red Cross is a charitable organization.* **2.** merciful, or forgiving in judging others; kindly; tolerant: *It was charitable of her to overlook his bad manners.* **3.** generous in giving help to the poor or needy. —**char′i·ta·ble·ness,** *n.* —**char′i·ta·bly,** *adv.*

char·i·ty (char′ə tē) *n. pl.*, **char·i·ties.** **1.** the giving of help to the poor or needy. **2.** money or other help given to the poor or needy: *The old woman refused to accept charity when her husband died.* **3.** a fund, institution, or organization for helping the poor or needy: *Give generously to your favorite charity.* **4.** mercy or forgiveness in judging others; kindness; tolerance: *With malice toward none; with charity for all* (Abraham Lincoln). **5.** love of one's fellow men; brotherly love: *And now abideth faith, hope, charity, these three; but the greatest of these is charity.* (I Corinthians 13:2).

char·la·tan (shär′lə tən) *n.* a person who pretends or claims to have knowledge or skill that he does not actually possess; quack; imposter.

Char·le·magne (shär′lə mān′) A.D. 742?–814, the king of the Franks from 768 to 814 and, as Charles I, the emperor of the Holy Roman Empire from 800 to 814. Also, **Charles the Great.**

Charles, Prince (chärlz) 1948—, the Prince of Wales, eldest son of Queen Elizabeth II, and heir to the throne of Great Britain.

Charles I, 1600–1649, the king of England, Scotland, and Ireland from 1625 until his execution in 1649; born Charles Stuart.

Charles II, 1630–1685, the king of England, Scotland, and Ireland from 1660 to 1685; son of Charles I.

Charles V, 1500–1558, the emperor of the Holy Roman Empire from 1519 to 1558 and, as Charles I, the king of Spain from 1516 to 1556.

Charles Mar·tel (mär tel′) A.D. 688?–741, ruler of the Franks and the grandfather of Charlemagne.

Charles the Great, another name for **Charlemagne.**

Charles·ton (chärl′stən) *n.* the capital of West Virginia, in the western part of the state. Pop. (1970), 71,505.

Charles·ton (chärl′stən) *n.* a lively dance in 4/4 time, popular especially in the 1920s. [From *Charleston,* a city in southeastern South Carolina.]

char·ley horse (chär′lē) stiffness or soreness of a muscle, especially in the leg. [Possibly from the use of *Charley* as a name for a lame horse.]

Char·lotte (shär′lət) *n.* a city in North Carolina, in the southern part of the state. Pop. (1970), 241,178.

Char·lotte A·ma·lie (shär′lət ä mä′lē) the capital, largest city, and chief port of the U.S. Virgin Islands, on the island of St. Thomas. Pop. (1970), 12,220.

Char·lotte·town (shär′lət toun′) *n.* the capital of Prince Edward Island, Canada. Pop. (1971), 18,631.

charm (chärm) *n.* **1.** the power to fascinate, attract, or delight greatly: *She is a woman of great charm. That ski resort holds much charm for winter vacationers.* **2.** any fascinating, attractive, or delightful quality or feature: *Her beautiful eyes were her greatest charm.* **3.** a small ornament or trinket, often worn on a chain bracelet. **4.** something worn to ward off evil or bring good luck; amulet: *He carries a rabbit's foot as a charm.* **5.** any action or formula that is supposed to have magic power. —*v.t.* **1.** to fascinate, attract, or delight greatly; captivate: *Her graciousness charmed everyone at the party.* **2.** to affect as if by magic; bewitch: *The playing of the flute charmed the cobra.* **3.** to endow with or protect by or as if by magic power: *to lead a charmed life.* —**charm′er,** *n.*

charm·ing (chär′ming) *adj.* full of charm; fascinating, attractive, or delightful: *a charming person, a charming little old house.* —**charm′ing·ly,** *adv.*

char·nel house (chärn′əl) a place in which the bones or bodies of the dead are placed.

Char·on (ker′ən, kar′ən) *n. Greek Mythology.* the boatman who ferried the souls of the dead across the river Styx to the entrance of Hades.

chart (chärt) *n.* **1.** a sheet showing information in the form of lists, diagrams, tables, graphs, or the like: *a weather chart, a population chart.* **2.** a map, especially one with information for sailors, such as the depth of water or the location of rocks, channels, harbors, and the like. —*v.t.* **1.** to make a map or chart of: *to chart a coastline.* **2.** to plan or map out: *to chart a course of action.*

char·ter (chär′tər) *n.* **1.** a formal written document issued by a government or a ruler to a person, a group of citizens, or to a corporation, granting the right to organize for carrying on some activity and imposing certain duties and obligations. **2.** a document setting forth the aims and principles of a body or organization, such as a group of nations. **3.** written permission from a society or organization to establish a new local chapter or branch. **4.** a leasing or renting of an aircraft, automobile, bus, or the like: *Those planes are available for charter.* —*v.t.* **1.** to lease or hire by charter: *Our school chartered three buses for the trip.* **2.** to grant a charter to; establish by charter: *The state chartered a bank.*

Char·tres (shär′trə) *n.* a city in north-central France, the site of a famous cathedral.

char·treuse (shär trōōz′, shär trōōs′) *n.* **1.** a pale yellowish-green color. **2.** a green, yellow, or white liqueur. —*adj.* having the color chartreuse; pale yellowish-green.

char·wom·an (chär′woom′ən) *n. pl.,* **char·wom·en** (chär′wim′ən). a woman hired to do cleaning and scrubbing in homes, offices, or public buildings.

char·y (cher′ē) *adj.,* **char·i·er, char·i·est. 1.** hesitant about danger or risks; careful; cautious; wary: *The fox was chary of hunters.* **2.** reluctant in granting or giving; not lavish; sparing. —**char′i·ly,** *adv.* —**char′i·ness,** *n.*

Cha·ryb·dis (kə rib′dis) *n. Greek Mythology.* a hideous monster having the form of a raging whirlpool, dwelling in the Strait of Messina opposite the cave of the monster Scylla. Sailors who were not devoured by Scylla were drowned by Charybdis.

chase (chās) *v.,* **chased, chas·ing.** —*v.t.* **1.** to go after and try to catch; pursue: *The cat chased the birds. The police chased the thief down the alley.* **2.** to cause to leave quickly or flee; drive: *He chased the children out of his yard.* —*v.i.* **1.** to follow in pursuit: *The boy chased after the ball that had rolled into the street.* **2.** *Informal.* to rush about; hurry: *She chased all over town looking for a new dress.* —*n.* **1.** the act of chasing; pursuit: *to join in a chase. They caught the puppy after a long chase.* **2. the chase.** the sport of hunting. **3.** something chased or hunted; quarry.

to give chase. to run or go after; chase; pursue.

chas·er (chā′sər) *n.* **1.** a person or thing that chases. **2.** *Informal.* a drink, as of water or beer, taken after a drink of hard liquor.

chasm (kaz′əm) *n.* **1.** a deep, yawning crack or gap in the earth's surface; gorge. **2.** a great difference of feelings, beliefs, opinions, or the like: *a chasm between two rival political parties.*

chas·sis (shas′ē, chas′ē) *n. pl.,* **chas·sis** (shas′ēz, chas′ēz). **1.** the part of a motor vehicle that supports the body, including the frame, wheels, engine, steering mechanism, and other mechanical parts. **2.** the frame that supports the body of an aircraft. **3.** the framework on which the parts of a radio or television set are mounted.

chaste (chāst) *adj.* **1.** pure in thought and action; moral, virtuous, or decent: *a chaste person.* **2.** simple in style; not ornate or extreme. —**chaste′ly,** *adv.* —**chaste′ness,** *n.*

chas·ten (chā′sən) *v.t.* **1.** to punish in order to correct or improve: *His father chastened him for spilling ink on the rug.* **2.** to restrain; subdue: *His speech chastened the crowd's desire for violence.* —**chas′ten·er,** *n.*

chas·tise (chas tīz′) *v.t.,* **chas·tised, chas·tis·ing.** to punish, reprimand, or discipline severely. —**chas·tise′ment,** *n.* —**chas·tis′er,** *n.*

chas·ti·ty (chas′tə tē) *n.* the state or quality of being chaste or pure.

chas·u·ble (chaz′yə bəl) *n.* a sleeveless outer garment worn by a priest officiating at Mass.

chat (chat) *v.i.,* **chat·ted, chat·ting.** to talk in a light, familiar, or informal manner: *The two friends chatted about the weather.* —*n.* **1.** informal, friendly talk. **2.** any of several songbirds having a chattering cry.

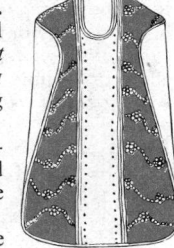

Chasuble

cha·teau (sha tō′) *n. pl.,* **cha·teaux** (sha tōz′). **1.** a French castle. **2.** a large and elaborate country house, especially one in France.

chat·e·laine (shat′əl ān′) *n.* **1.** the mistress or lady of a castle, chateau, or fashionable household. **2.** an ornamental chain or clasp, usually worn at a woman's waist, to which keys, a purse, or other articles may be attached.

Chat·ta·noo·ga (chat′ə nōō′gə) *n.* a city in southern Tennessee, on the Tennessee River. Pop. (1970), 119,082.

chat·tel (chat′əl) *n.* any article of personal property that can be moved, such as furniture, clothing, livestock, or an automobile.

chat·ter (chat′ər) *v.i.* **1.** to talk rapidly and foolishly, usually about matters of little importance; jabber: *She chattered on and on about her new dresses.* **2.** to click together quickly or uncontrollably: *My teeth chattered from the cold.* **3.** to make quick, short sounds: *The magpies chattered in the trees.* —*v.t.* to say rapidly or foolishly: *to chatter nonsense.* —*n.* **1.** rapid, foolish talk. **2.** the act or sound of chattering. —**chat′ter·er,** *n.*

chat·ter·box (chat′ər boks′) *n. pl.,* **chat·ter·box·es.** a person who talks too much.

chat·ty (chat′ē) *adj.,* **chat·ti·er, chat·ti·est. 1.** given to chatting; talkative. **2.** full of chat; light, familiar, and informal: *She received a chatty letter from her sister.* —**chat′ti·ly,** *adv.* —**chat′ti·ness,** *n.*

Chau·cer, Geof·frey (chô′sər; jef′rē) 1344?–1400, English poet.

chauf·feur (shō′fər, shō fur′) *n.* a person whose work is driving an automobile. —*v.t.* to act or work as a chauffeur for: *He chauffeured us to the airport.*

chau·tau·qua (shə tô′kwə) *also,* **Chau·tau·qua.** *n.* **1.** an educational movement begun in 1874 at Chautauqua, a city in New York State, that established summer programs of instruction in education, religion, and the arts. **2.** any of various similar programs.

chau·vin·ism (shō′və niz′əm) *n.* **1.** greatly exaggerated and boastful devotion to one's country or its military glory;

at; āpe; cär; end; mē; it; īce; hot; ōld; fôrk; wood; fōōl; oil; out; up; turn; sing; thin; this; hw in white; zh in treasure. The symbol ə stands for the sound of **a** in about, **e** in taken, **i** in pencil, **o** in lemon, and **u** in circus.

fanatical patriotism. **2.** greatly exaggerated pride in one's own group, race, or sex. [French *chauvinisme*, from Nicolas *Chauvin*, a French soldier noted for his blind patriotism and devotion to Napoleon I.]

chau·vin·ist (shō′və nist) *n.* **1.** a person who has a greatly exaggerated and boastful devotion to his country. **2.** a person who has a greatly exaggerated pride in his own group, race, or sex: *a male chauvinist.* —**chau′vin·ist′ic,** *adj.*

cheap (chēp) *adj.* **1.** low in price, especially as compared with its value: *Milk is cheap in that store. It was a good dinner and very cheap, too.* **2.** charging low prices: *a cheap dress shop.* **3.** of little value or worth; inferior in quality: *a cheap toy, a novel printed on cheap paper.* **4.** not willing to spend money; stingy: *He is too cheap to buy a new coat.* **5.** not worthy of respect; vulgar, common, or immoral: *All that gaudy make-up makes her look cheap.* **6.** costing little effort or trouble: *Talk is cheap.* —*adv.* at a low price: *He bought that used car cheap.* —**cheap′ly,** *adv.* —**cheap′ness,** *n.*

cheap·en (chē′pən) *v.t., v.i.* to make or become cheap.

cheap·skate (chēp′skāt′) *n. Informal.* a stingy person.

cheat (chēt) *v.t.* **1.** to treat in a dishonest manner; swindle or trick: *He won the last game by cheating his opponent. They cheated us out of our share of the money.* **2.** to escape from by cleverness or good luck: *to cheat death.* —*v.i.* to act in a dishonest manner: *He cheats at card games. They were accused of cheating on the test.* —*n.* **1.** a person who cheats. **2.** the act of cheating; fraud; deception. —**cheat′er,** *n.*

check (chek) *n.* **1.** a sudden stop: *Our lack of money put a check to our vacation plans.* **2.** a person or thing that stops, controls, or limits: *The leash was a check on the dog. His gloomy manner was a check on our enthusiasm.* **3.** a test or other means to see if something is as it should be; examination, inspection, or investigation: *The foreman made a check on the workers. A quick check of the facts showed that her story was true.* **4.** a mark (√) used to indicate that something has been approved, noted, or otherwise examined: *The teacher put a check next to the name of each pupil who was present.* **5.** a written order directing a bank to pay a stated amount of money from the account of the person who signs it: *She gave the store a check to pay for the new lamp.* **6.** a slip of paper listing an amount owed, especially in payment for a meal in a restaurant. **7.** a ticket, tag, or token that makes it possible for a person to reclaim something that has been left for temporary safekeeping: *He has the checks for our suitcases.* **8.** a pattern of squares like that of a checkerboard. **9.** one of these squares. **10.** *Chess.* the position of a king when it is under direct attack from one of the opposing pieces and is threatened with being captured on the next move. —*v.t.* **1.** to bring to a sudden stop: *The army checked the advance of the enemy troops.* **2.** to hold in control; restrain; curb: *to check one's temper. He checked his impulse to laugh at her mistake.* **3.** to compare for accuracy or agreement: *Check your answers with the ones in the back of the book.* **4.** to test (something) to see if it is as it should be; examine, inspect, or investigate: *He checked the references of all those applying for the job. The mechanic checked the engine to be sure it was running properly.* **5.** to mark with a check: *Please check the correct answer to each question.* **6.** to leave for temporary safekeeping, as in a checkroom: *to check one's coat, to check a package.* **7.** to mark with a pattern of small squares. **8.** *Chess.* to place (an opponent's king) in check. —*v.i.* **1.** to correspond accurately; agree: *My totals check with yours.* **2.** to make an examination, inspection, or investigation: *The doctor checked on the patient's condition.*

in check. under control or restraint: *Although she was annoyed, she kept her anger in check.*

to check in. to register as a guest at a hotel or motel.

to check out. a. to pay one's bill and depart from a hotel or motel. **b.** to prove to be true or correct: *The suspect's alibi checked out and he was set free.* **c.** to add up prices for payment, especially in a supermarket.

check·book (chek′book′) *n.* a book of blank checks issued by a bank.

check·er[1] (chek′ər) *n.* **1.** a person who checks. **2.** a cashier, especially in a supermarket. [*Check* + *er*[1].]

check·er[2] (chek′ər) *n.* **1.** one of the flat, circular, usually red or black pieces used in the game of checkers. **2.** a pattern of squares of alternating colors. **3.** one of these squares. —*v.t.* to mark with squares of alternating colors. [Old French *eschekier* chessboard, from *eschec* a check in chess.]

check·er·board (chek′ər bôrd′) *n.* a square board marked off into sixty-four alternately colored squares, used in playing checkers and chess.

check·ered (chek′ərd) *adj.* **1.** marked with squares of alternating colors: *a checkered scarf.* **2.** filled with changes of fortune: *The actor had had a checkered career.*

check·ers (chek′ərz) *n., pl.* a game for two people played on a checkerboard, each player having twelve pieces. The game is won when one of the players cannot make a move because all his pieces have been captured or blocked. ▲ used with a singular verb. Also, *British,* **draughts.**

checking account, a bank account against which checks may be drawn by the depositor.

check·mate (chek′māt′) *v.t.,* **check·mat·ed, check·mat·ing. 1.** *Chess.* to put (the opponent's king) in check from which no escape is possible, thus winning the game. **2.** to defeat or thwart completely. —*n.* **1.** *Chess.* a move that checkmates the opponent's king, or the position of a king when it has been checkmated. **2.** a complete defeat. [Old French *esche et mat,* going back to Persian *shāh-māt* literally, the king is dead.]

check·out (chek′out′) *n.* **1.** a checking out, as in a supermarket. **2.** a place for checking out.

check·point (chek′point′) *n.* a place where vehicles or travelers are stopped for inspection.

check·rein (chek′rān′) *n.* a short rein connecting a bit to a harness, used to keep a horse from lowering its head.

check·room (chek′rōōm′, chek′room′) *n.* a room in which personal property, such as hats, coats, or packages, may be left temporarily for safekeeping.

check·up (chek′up′) *n.* **1.** a complete physical examination. **2.** any thorough examination or inspection.

Ched·dar (ched′ər) *also,* **ched·dar.** *n.* any of several types of hard, smooth cheese, ranging in color from white to dark yellow and in taste from strong and sharp to mild. [From *Cheddar,* a village in England where this cheese was first made.]

cheek (chēk) *n.* **1.** either side of the face below the eye. **2.** something resembling this part of the face in shape or position. **3.** *Informal.* saucy or disrespectful boldness; insolence; impudence .

cheek·bone (chēk′bōn′) *n.* either of two bones at the upper part of the cheek, just below the eye.

cheek·y (chē′kē) *adj.,* **cheek·i·er, cheek·i·est.** *Informal.* saucy; insolent; impudent: *a cheeky young man.* —**cheek′i·ly,** *adv.* —**cheek′i·ness,** *n.*

cheep (chēp) *v.i.* to make a faint, shrill, chirping sound, as a young bird; peep. —*n.* such a sound.

cheer (chēr) *n.* **1.** a lively shout of approval, praise, encouragement, or joy: *A cheer arose from the crowd when the astronauts appeared.* **2.** a set of words or sounds used by spectators to encourage or show enthusiasm for a contestant or athletic team: *a school cheer.* **3.** gladness, joy, or gaiety: *There is a general feeling of cheer as the holiday season nears.* **4.** something that gives joy or gladness; comfort; encouragement: *The doctor spoke words of cheer to the sick child.* **5.** a state of mind or spirits; mood: *to be of good cheer.* —*v.t.* **1.** to salute or acclaim with cheers: *The crowd cheered the batter when he hit a home run.* **2.** to make hopeful or glad: *The mourners were cheered by the kind words. The good news cheered him up.* —*v.i.* **1.** to utter cheers: *We cheered as the runner neared the finish line.* **2.** to become hopeful or glad: *He cheered up at the thought of seeing her again.*

cheer·ful (chēr′fəl) *adj.* **1.** showing or feeling cheer; full of good spirits; happy; joyous: *a cheerful person, a cheerful smile.* **2.** bringing cheer: *a cheerful fire, a cheerful room.* **3.** ready to help; willing: *a cheerful worker.* —**cheer′·ful·ly,** *adv.* —**cheer′ful·ness,** *n.*

cheer·lead·er (chēr′lē′dər) *n.* a person who leads organized cheering, especially at a sports event.

cheer·less (chēr′lis) *adj.* without cheer; joyless; gloomy. —**cheer′less·ly,** *adv.* —**cheer′less·ness,** *n.*

cheer·y (chēr′ē) *adj.,* **cheer·i·er, cheer·i·est.** bringing or full of cheerfulness; gay: *She gave us a cheery greeting.* —**cheer′i·ly,** *adv.* —**cheer′i·ness,** *n.*

cheese (chēz) *n.* a food made from the curds of milk pressed into a solid mass or cake.

cheese·burg·er (chēz′bur′gər) *n.* a hamburger with cheese melted on top of the meat.

cheese·cake (chēz′kāk′) *n.* a rich, creamy cake made of cream cheese or cottage cheese, eggs, sugar, milk, and various flavorings.

cheese·cloth (chēz′klôth′) *n.* a thin, loosely woven cotton cloth, first used for wrapping cheese.

chees·y (chē′zē) *adj.,* **chees·i·er, chees·i·est.** **1.** of or like cheese. **2.** *Slang.* of inferior quality; poorly made; cheap.

chee·tah (chē′tə) *n.* an animal of the cat family that resembles a leopard and is found in Africa and southern Asia. It can run at speeds up to seventy miles per hour for short distances and is sometimes tamed and trained to hunt.

Cheetah

chef (shef) *n.* **1.** the head cook, as of a restaurant, hotel, or large household. **2.** any person who cooks.

chef-d'oeu·vre (shā dōō′vrə) *pl.,* **chefs-d'oeuvre** (shā-dōō′vrə) *n.* a masterpiece, especially one in art, literature, or music.

Che·khov, Anton (chek′ôf, chek′of; än tōn′) 1860–1904, Russian author.

che·la (kē′lə) *n. pl.,* **che·lae** (kē′lē). a claw of a lobster, crab, or scorpion.

chem. **1.** chemistry. **2.** chemical. **3.** chemist.

chem·i·cal (kem′i kəl) *adj.* of, relating to, or produced by chemistry. —*n.* a substance obtained by or used in a chemical process. —**chem′·i·cal·ly,** *adv.*

chemical engineering, the science or profession of applying chemical knowledge and principles to industrial processes.

chemical warfare, the use in war of chemicals or chemical products, such as poisonous gases, flame throwers, and incendiary bombs.

Lobster chela

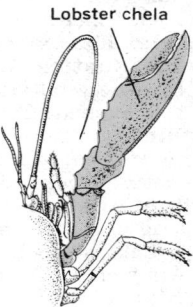
Chela

che·mise (shə mēz′) *n.* **1.** a loose, shirtlike undergarment worn by women. **2.** a loosely fitting dress that hangs straight from the shoulders.

chem·ist (kem′ist) *n.* **1.** a person who is a student of or expert in chemistry. **2.** *British.* another word for **druggist.**

chem·is·try (kem′is trē) *n. pl.,* **chem·is·tries.** **1.** the science that deals with the composition and properties of substances and the changes that take place when they react with other substances. **2.** chemical composition, property, or process: *the chemistry of carbon.*

chem·o·ther·a·py (kem′ō ther′ə pē) *n.* the use of chemical substances to treat diseases.

chem·ur·gy (kem′ər jē) *n.* the branch of chemistry that deals with the development of new industrial uses for plant and animal products.

che·nille (shə nēl′) *n.* **1.** a yarn, often made of cotton, silk, or worsted, with a velvety, fuzzy pile, used for embroidery, tassels, and fringes. **2.** a fabric woven from this yarn, used for such items as rugs and bedspreads.

Che·ops (kē′ops) the pharoah of ancient Egypt who built the largest of the pyramids as his tomb. He is believed to have ruled in about 2900 B.C. Also, **Khufu.**

cheque (chek) *n. British.* another spelling of **check** *(def. 5).*

cher·ish (cher′ish) *v.t.* **1.** to treat with affection; care for tenderly; hold dear: *The grandmother cherished her grandchild.* **2.** to hold or entertain in the mind; cling to: *She cherished the memory of her father.*

Cher·o·kee (cher′ə kē) *n. pl.,* **Cher·o·kees** or **Cher·o·kee.** **1.** a member of a tribe of North American Indians, formerly the largest tribe that lived in the southeastern United States, now living mostly in Oklahoma. **2.** the language of this tribe.

che·root (shə rōōt′) *n.* a cigar that is cut square at both ends.

cher·ry (cher′ē) *n. pl.,* **cher·ries.** **1.** a small, round or heart-shaped fruit of any of several trees or shrubs, grown in temperate regions of the world, having a smooth skin and a fleshy pulp enclosing a pit. **2.** the tree or shrub bearing this fruit, having clusters of white or pink flowers. **3.** the wood of this tree or shrub. **4.** a bright red color. —*adj.* having the color cherry; bright-red.

cher·ub (cher′əb) *n. pl.,* **(defs. 1, 2) cher·u·bim** (cher′-ə bim′) or **(def. 3) cher·ubs.** **1.** an angel of the second of the nine orders of angels. **2.** a representation of a cherub in art, usually as a chubby, winged child. **3.** a beautiful, innocent, or sweet child.

che·ru·bic (chə rōō′bik) *adj.* of or resembling a cherub.

cher·vil (chur′vəl) *n.* **1.** a plant related to parsley, whose leaves are used in salads and soups. **2.** a similar plant having a root that is eaten as a vegetable, either raw or cooked.

Ches·a·peake (ches′ə pēk′) *n.* a city in southeastern Virginia. Pop. (1970), 89,580.

Chesapeake Bay, a long arm of the Atlantic Ocean, extending into Virginia and Maryland.

chess (ches) *n.* a game for two played on a chessboard, each player having sixteen pieces. The players take turns moving their pieces, the object of the game being to checkmate the opponent's king.

at; āpe; cär; end; mē; it; īce; hot; ōld; fôrk; wood; fōol; oil; out; up; turn; sing; thin; **th**is; hw in white; zh in treasure. The symbol ə stands for the sound of a in about, e in taken, i in pencil, o in lemon, and u in circus.

chess·board (ches′bôrd′) *n.* a square board marked off into sixty-four alternately colored squares, used in playing chess or checkers.

chess·man (ches′man′) *n. pl.,* **chess·men** (ches′men′). any of the pieces used in playing chess.

chest (chest) *n.* **1.** the upper front part of the body in humans and other mammals, extending from the neck to the abdomen, enclosed by the ribs, breastbone, and spinal column, and containing the heart and lungs. **2.** a large, strong box with a lid, that is used for storing or shipping things: *a tool chest, a toy chest.* **3.** see **chest of drawers.**

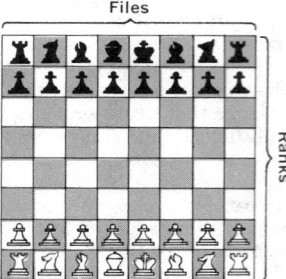

Files

Ranks

Chessboard

ches·ter·field (ches′tər fēld′) *n.* **1.** a single-breasted topcoat having concealed buttons and a velvet collar. **2.** a davenport or sofa, usually having upright, upholstered arms. [From the Earl of *Chesterfield.*]

chest·nut (ches′nut′) *n.* **1.** the smooth-shelled, sweet nut of a tree belonging to the beech family, having a reddish-brown color and growing inside a large, prickly burr. **2.** the tree producing this nut, having leathery, oblong leaves and fragrant flowers. **3.** the wood of this tree. **4.** a reddish-brown color. **5.** a reddish-brown horse. —*adj.* having the color chestnut; reddish-brown.

chest of drawers, a piece of furniture that consists of a frame containing a set of drawers, used for holding clothing, linens, or other articles.

chev·a·lier (shev′ə lēr′) *n.* **1.** a knight. **2.** a member of an order of merit.

Chev·i·ot (shev′ē ət, chev′ē ət) *n.* **1.** any of a small, hardy breed of sheep with thick, short wool. **2. cheviot. a.** a rough woolen fabric woven in raised diagonal lines, used for suits and coats, formerly made from the wool of Cheviots. **b.** a coarse cotton cloth resembling this. [From the *Cheviot* Hills, on the border between Scotland and England, where this breed of sheep originated.]

chev·ron (shev′rən) *n.* an emblem or insignia consisting of stripes meeting at an angle, worn on the sleeve of a military or police uniform to indicate rank, length of service, or some other distinction.

Chevrons

chew (chōō) *v.t.* **1.** to crush or grind with the teeth: *Chew your food thoroughly.* **2.** to make by chewing: *The puppy chewed a hole in the slipper.* —*v.i.* to crush or grind something with the teeth. —*n.* something that is chewed or is for chewing: *a chew of tobacco.*

chewing gum, a gummy preparation that is sweetened and flavored for chewing, usually made of chicle.

che·wink (chi wingk′) *n.* another word for **towhee.**

chew·y (chōō′ē) *adj.,* **chew·i·er, chew·i·est.** soft or sticky and needing much chewing, in order to be eaten: *chewy caramels.*

Chey·enne (shī en′, shī an′) *n. pl.,* **Chey·enne** or **Chey·ennes. 1.** a member of a tribe of North American Indians formerly living on the Great Plains, now living mainly in Montana and Oklahoma. **2.** the language of this tribe. **3.** the capital of Wyoming, in the southeastern part of the state. Pop. (1970), 40,914.

chg., charge.

Chiang Kai-shek (châng′ kī′shek′) 1886–1975, Chinese general and political leader.

chic (shēk) *adj.* attractive, tasteful, and fashionable in style; stylish; smart: *a chic dress.* —*n.* taste; elegance; style. [French *chic* stylish, smart.]

Chi·ca·go (shi kä′gō, shi kô′gō) *n.* a city in northeastern Illinois, on Lake Michigan. Pop. (1970), 3,366,957. —**Chi·ca′go·an,** *n.*

chi·can·er·y (shi kā′nər ē) *n. pl.,* **chi·can·er·ies.** the use of unfair or deceitful methods; trickery: *In spite of all the chicanery of his lawyer, he was found guilty.*

Chi·ca·no (chi kä′nō) *n., pl.* **Chi·ca·nos.** an American of Mexican birth or descent.

chick (chik) *n.* **1.** a young chicken. **2.** the young of certain other birds. **3.** a child. **4.** *Slang.* a young woman.

chick·a·dee (chik′ə dē′) *n.* a small North American bird, having gray or brown feathers with black, white, or brown markings and a black head.

Chick·a·mau·ga (chik′ə mô′gə) *n.* a creek flowing from northwestern Georgia into the Tennessee River, the site of a Confederate victory in the Civil War.

Chickadee

Chick·a·saw (chik′ə sô′) *n. pl.,* **Chick·a·saws** or **Chick·a·saw.** a member of a tribe of North American Indians formerly living in what is now Tennessee and northern Mississippi, now living in Oklahoma.

chick·en (chik′ən) *n.* **1.** a farm bird that is raised for its flesh and eggs; a hen or rooster. **2.** a young hen or rooster. **3.** the flesh of a chicken. **4.** any young bird. **5.** *Slang.* a cowardly person. —*adj. Slang.* cowardly.

chicken pox, a mild but highly contagious disease that is caused by a virus and usually occurs in children. It is characterized by a blotchy red rash that develops into blisters and, finally, scabs. Also, **varicella.**

chick·weed (chik′wēd′) *n.* a common weed found in temperate regions throughout the world, having a creeping root, small oval leaves, and tiny white flowers.

chic·le (chik′əl) *n.* a gum obtained from the milky juice of several evergreen trees of tropical America, used chiefly for making chewing gum.

chic·o·ry (chik′ər ē) *n. pl.,* **chic·o·ries. 1.** a plant that is related to lettuce, having blue flowers and lance-shaped leaves. **2.** the leaves of this plant, used as salad greens. **3.** the root of this plant, often roasted and ground to be mixed with coffee and used as a substitute for coffee.

chide (chīd) *v.t.,* **chid·ed** or **chid** (chid), **chid·ed** or **chid** or **chid·den** (chid′ən), **chid·ing.** to scold mildly.

chief (chēf) *n.* a person who is highest in rank or authority; head or leader of a group: *the chief of police, the chief of an Indian tribe.* —*adj.* **1.** highest in rank or authority: *the chief officer, the chief cook, the chief executive of a company.* **2.** most important; principal; main: *His chief reason for moving was the offer of a better job.*

in chief. of the highest rank or authority; at the head: *the editor in chief of a newspaper.*

Chief Executive, the President of the United States.

chief justice 1. the presiding or head judge of a court having several judges. **2. Chief Justice.** the head of the U.S. Supreme Court.

chief·ly (chēf′lē) *adv.* **1.** mainly; mostly: *The dish consisted chiefly of meat.* **2.** above all; especially: *Phil is chiefly interested in sports.*

chief of staff 1. in the armed forces, a senior officer or head of a staff; the principal assistant to a commander. **2. Chief of Staff.** the highest-ranking officer of the U.S. Army or Air Force.

chief·tain (chēf′tən) *n.* a chief or leader, especially of a tribe or clan: *a bandit chieftain.*

chief·tain·cy (chēf′tən sē) *n. pl.,* **chief·tain·cies.** the position or rank of a chieftain.

chif·fon (shi fon′) *n.* a sheer, lightweight fabric, usually of silk or rayon, used for such items as scarves and dresses. —*adj.* **1.** made of or resembling chiffon. **2.** made partially of beaten egg whites or gelatin, which give a light, airy consistency: *lemon chiffon pie.*

chif·fo·nier (shif′ə nēr′) *n.* a high bureau or chest of drawers, often having a mirror at the top.

chig·ger (chig′ər) *also,* **jig·ger.** *n.* **1.** the tiny, round, red larva of any of several kinds of mites. It pierces the skin and sucks out blood, leaving red spots and causing severe itching. **2.** see **chigoe** *(def. 1).*

chi·gnon (shēn′yon) *n.* a twist or knot of hair usually worn at the nape of the neck by women.

chig·oe (chig′ō) *n.* **1.** a small sand flea that sucks blood, found in tropical America and Africa. The female burrows under the skin, causing painful sores and itching. **2.** see **chigger** *(def. 1).*

Chi·hua·hua (chi wä′wə) *n.* **1.** a city in northern Mexico. Pop. (1970 est.), 257,000. **2. chihuahua.** a dog of a breed originally native to Mexico, having large, pointed ears and a smooth or wavy coat that is usually tan. It is the smallest breed of dog.

Chihuahua

chil·blain (chil′blān′) *n.* a painful, itchy swelling or reddening of the skin, especially the hands and feet, caused by exposure to cold.

child (chīld) *n. pl.,* **chil·dren. 1.** an offspring of a human being; son or daughter: *She is an only child. That couple has three children.* **2.** a boy or girl between birth and adolescence; young boy or girl: *That television program is intended for children.* **3.** a baby; infant. **4.** a descendant: *the children of Israel.* **5.** a person who is a product of a certain condition, place, or time: *a child of poverty.* —**child′less,** *adj.*

child·birth (chīld′burth′) *n.* the act of giving birth to a child or children.

child·hood (chīld′hood′) *n.* the period from birth to adolescence; time of being a child.

child·ish (chīl′dish) *adj.* **1.** of, like, or suitable for a child: *a childish dress.* **2.** immature; silly: *childish fears.* —**child′ish·ly,** *adv.* —**child′ish·ness,** *n.*

child·like (chīld′līk′) *adj.* relating to or suitable for a child; like a child; innocent; simple; trusting: *Katherine has a childlike affection for stray animals.*

chil·dren (chil′drən) the plural of **child.**

Children's Crusade, an unsuccessful crusade to recover the Holy Land from the Muslims, undertaken by thousands of French and German children in 1212.

child's play, anything that is easily done.

Chil·e (chil′ē) *n.* a country on the southwestern coast of South America. Capital, Santiago. Area, 292,258 sq. mi. Pop. (1971 est.), 8,990,000. —**Chil′e·an,** *adj., n.*

chil·i (chil′ē) *also,* **chil·e, chil·li.** *n. pl.,* **chil·ies. 1.** the dried pod of a kind of red pepper used to make a hot spice. **2.** the plant that this pod grows on, found in tropical America. **3.** see **chili con carne.**

chili con car·ne (kon kär′nē) *also,* **chile con car·ne.** a highly seasoned dish made of meat, red peppers, tomato sauce, and, usually, beans.

chili sauce, a highly spiced sauce used as a seasoning, made of red peppers, tomatoes, vinegar, sugar, and onions.

chill (chil) *n.* **1.** coldness, especially a mild but unpleasant coldness: *There was a chill in the air this morning.* **2.** a feeling of coldness in the body, usually accompanied by shivering: *He got a chill from sleeping without blankets.* **3.** a depressing or discouraging influence or effect; lack of warmth or friendliness: *The sick man's presence cast a chill over the party.* **4.** a feeling of fear or anxiety: *The horrible sight sent a chill through her.* —*v.t.* **1.** to make cold: *to chill wine.* **2.** to cause a sensation of cold in: *The night air chilled his bones.* **3.** to harden the surface of (a metal) by sudden cooling. —*v.i.* to become cold. —*adj.* chilly: *a chill wind.* —**chill′er,** *n.*

chill·y (chil′ē) *adj.,* **chill·i·er, chill·i·est. 1.** cold: *chilly night air.* **2.** affected by, sensitive to, or feeling cold: *She felt chilly without her sweater.* **3.** not friendly; lacking warmth: *a chilly welcome.* —**chill′i·ness,** *n.*

chime (chīm) *n.* **chimes. 1.** a set of large bells, tuned to a musical scale, that produce tones when swung or struck. **2. chimes.** a musical instrument made of a set of metal tubes that sound when struck with a mallet. **3.** a single bell, as in a clock. **4.** *also,* **chimes.** a sound or series of musical sounds made by a chime. —*v.,* **chimed, chim·ing.** —*v.t.* **1.** to produce a musical sound by striking; ring: *to chime bells.* **2.** to give or announce by ringing: *The clock chimed the hour.* —*v.i.* to ring.

to chime in. *Informal.* to join in or interrupt a conversation: *Susan chimed in with her opinions on what to do.*

Chi·me·ra (ki mēr′ə, kī mēr′ə) *also,* **Chi·mae·ra, Chi·me·ras. 1.** *Greek Mythology.* a fire-breathing monster with a lion's head, a goat's body, and a serpent's tail. **2. chimera. a.** any imaginary monster. **b.** a wild, ridiculous, or fantastic idea; silly fancy.

chi·mer·i·cal (ki mēr′i kəl) *adj.* **1.** not real; imaginary. **2.** filled with wild ideas; whimsical; fanciful.

chim·ney (chim′nē) *n. pl.,* **chim·neys. 1.** an upright structure used to carry smoke or vapor from a fireplace or furnace. **2.** the part of such a structure rising above a roof. **3.** a smokestack. **4.** a tube, usually of glass, surrounding the flame of a lamp.

chimney piece, see **mantel** *(def. 2).*

chimney sweep, a person whose work is cleaning out soot from chimneys.

chimney swift, a North American bird resembling a swallow and having narrow, crescent-shaped wings and dull feathers. It often builds its nest in unused chimneys.

chim·pan·zee (chim′pan zē′, chim pan′zē) *n.* a manlike ape native to western and central Africa, having brownish-black hair. It lives in trees and is smaller and more intelligent than a gorilla.

chin (chin) *n.* **1.** the part of the face below the mouth and above the neck. **2.** the middle, front part of the lower jaw. —*v.t.,* **chinned, chin·ning.** to lift (oneself) up to an overhead horizontal bar by pulling with the arms until the chin is level with or above the bar.

chi·na (chī′nə) *n.* **1.** a fine pottery composed chiefly of clay, feldspar, and flint, believed to have originated in

Chimpanzee

at; āpe; cär; end; mē; it; īce; hot; ōld; fôrk; wood; fōol; oil; out; up; turn; sing; thin; this; hw in white; zh in treasure. The symbol ə stands for the sound of a in about, e in taken, i in pencil, o in lemon, and u in circus.

China. China differs from porcelain in that it is baked twice. **2.** objects, especially dishes, that are made of this material. **3.** any pottery or dishes.

Chi·na (chī′nə) *n.* **1. People's Republic of.** a country in eastern Asia. It has the largest population of any country in the world. Capital, Peking. Area, 3,691,500 sq. mi. Pop. (1980), 939,000,000. Also, **Communist China. 2. Republic of.** a country made up of the island of Taiwan and nearby islands. The Chinese Nationalist government took refuge on Taiwan in 1949 when mainland China fell under Communist control. Capital, Taipei. Area, 13,885 sq. mi. Pop. (1975 est.), 16,000,000. Also, **Nationalist China, Taiwan.**

Chi·na·man (chī′nə mən) *n. pl.,* **Chi·na·men** (chī′nə-mən). see **Chinese** *(def. 1).* ▲ **Chinaman** is now generally considered to be offensive; **Chinese** is preferred.

Chi·nan (jē′nän′), another spelling of **Tsinan.**

China Sea, the part of the Pacific Ocean that borders on China.

Chi·na·town (chī′nə toun′) *n.* a Chinese section of any city outside China, as in San Francisco or New York.

chi·na·ware (chī′nə wer′) *n.* **1.** see **china** *(def. 2).* **2.** dishes of any kind.

chinch (chinch) *n. pl.,* **chinch·es. 1.** see **chinch bug. 2.** any bedbug.

chinch bug, a small black-and-white insect of North and Central America, that is very destructive to wheat, corn, and other cereal grasses, especially in dry weather.

chin·chil·la (chin chil′ə) *n.* **1.** a small, squirrellike rodent of the Andes, having large, dark eyes and broad ears rounded at the tip. **2.** the valuable, very fine, silver or bluish-gray fur of this animal, used to make women's coats and jackets, and to trim other apparel. **3.** a heavy fabric with a tufted finish, usually made partially or entirely of wool, that is used for such items as coats and women's suits.

Chinchilla

chine (chīn) *n.* **1.** the backbone; spine. **2.** a cut of meat including all or part of an animal's backbone.

Chi·nese (chī nēz′) *n. pl.,* **Chi·nese. 1.** a person who was born or is living in China. **2.** a person of Chinese descent. **3.** the language of China, consisting of many dialects. Mandarin, the dialect spoken in Peking, is the standard form of Chinese. —*adj.* of or relating to China, its people, their language, or their culture.

Chinese checkers, a game for two to six players, using marbles on a board shaped like a six-pointed star and containing holes in each triangle of the star. The object is to move the marbles filling one triangle to the opposite triangle.

Chinese Empire, China from the time of the first emperor, through the rule of various dynasties, until it became a republic in 1912.

Chinese lantern, a lantern of thin, usually decorated, paper that can be collapsed and folded flat.

Chinese puzzle 1. a puzzle that is complicated or hard to solve. **2.** anything that is complicated and hard to solve.

Chinese Wall, see **Great Wall of China.**

Ching·tao (ching′tou′) another spelling of **Tsingtao.**

chink¹ (chingk) *n.* a small, narrow opening; crack: *The chinks in the wall admitted light.* —*v.t.* to fill in the chinks of; plug: *to chink a wall with mud.* [Old English *cinu* crack.]

chink² (chingk) *n.* a short, sharp sound, as of metal or glass striking together. —*v.t.* to cause to make a short, sharp sound. —*v.i.* to make a short, sharp sound: *The ice cubes chinked in the glass.* [Imitative of this sound.]

Chi·nook (shi nook′) *n. pl.,* **Chi·nooks** or **Chi·nook. 1.** a member of a tribe of North American Indians who formerly lived near the mouth of the Columbia River in what is now the state of Washington. **2.** the language spoken by these people. **3. chinook. a.** a warm, moist, southwest wind that blows from the sea along the coasts of Washington and Oregon. **b.** a warm, dry wind that blows down from the Rocky Mountains to the neighboring plains of the western United States and Canada.

chintz (chints) *n.* a cotton fabric, usually having a glossy finish and printed with a colorful pattern, used for such items as curtains and slipcovers.

chintz·y (chint′sē) *adj.,* **chintz·i·er, chintz·i·est.** *Informal.* cheap; tawdry.

chin-up (chin′up′) *n.* the exercise of chinning.

chip (chip) *n.* **1.** a small, usually thin, piece that has been cut or broken off: *a chip of wood.* **2.** a place where such a piece has been cut or broken off: *a chip on the edge of a glass.* **3.** a small, usually thin, slice of food, such as a potato chip. **4.** a French-fried potato: *fish and chips.* **5.** a disk or counter used in place of money in certain games, such as poker. **6.** see **integrated circuit.** —*v.,* **chipped, chip·ping.** —*v.t.* **1.** to cut or break off a piece or pieces from: *to chip a bone, to chip a cup.* **2.** to shape or produce by cutting off small pieces. —*v.i.* to break off in small pieces: *The paint on the wall chipped.*

a chip off the old block. *Informal.* a person who is very much like one of his or her parents.

a chip on one's shoulder. *Informal.* an aggressive or hostile attitude or manner.

to chip in. *Informal.* to give one's share; contribute: *Everyone in the class chipped in to buy flowers for Mary when she was sick.*

chip·munk (chip′mungk′) *n.* a small North American rodent related to the squirrel, having brown or gray fur with stripes on the back and tail, large cheek pouches, and a slender, flattened tail.

chipped beef, beef that is sliced thinly and smoked or dried, sometimes served with a cream sauce.

chip·per (chip′ər) *adj. Informal.* lively or happy.

Chip·pe·wa (chip′ə wä′, chip′-ə wä′) *n. pl.,* **Chip·pe·wa** or **Chip·pe·was.** another name for **Ojibwa.**

Chipmunk

chipping sparrow, a sparrow of eastern and central North America that is reddish brown on the top of the head.

Chi·ron (kī′ron) *n. Greek Mythology.* a wise centaur, skilled in the arts, medicine, and prophecy. He was the teacher of many Greek heroes, including Jason, Achilles, and Hercules.

chi·rop·o·dist (kə rop′ə dist) *n.* another word for **podiatrist.**

chi·rop·o·dy (kə rop′ə dē) *n.* another word for **podiatry.**

chi·ro·prac·tic (kī′rə prak′tik) *n.* a system of treating disease by massaging and manipulating the joints by hand, especially those of the spinal column. —*adj.* of, relating to, or involving chiropractic: *a chiropractic school, chiropractic treatment.*

chi·ro·prac·tor (kī′rə prak′tər) *n.* a person who practices chiropractic.

chirp (churp) *n.* a short, sharp sound, such as that made by a bird. —*v.i.* to make such a sound.

chir·rup (chēr′əp, chur′əp) *n.* a sound of continuous chirping. —*v.i.* to chirp continuously.

chis·el (chiz'əl) *n.* a metal tool with a sharp edge at the end of a blade, used to cut or shape stone, wood, or metal. —*v.t.*, **chis·eled, chis·el·ing;** *also, British,* **chis·elled, chis·el·ling.** **1.** to cut or shape with a chisel. **2.** *Slang.* to cheat; swindle: *The dishonest cashier chiseled him out of ten dollars.* —**chis'el·er,** *also, British,* **chis'el·ler,** *n.*

Chis·holm Trail (chiz'əm) a cattle trail running from San Antonio, Texas, to Abilene, Kansas.

chit-chat (chit'chat') *n.* **1.** light, informal conversation. **2.** small talk; gossip. —*v.i.,* **chit-chat·ted, chit-chat·ting.** to talk informally: *The two friends chit-chatted about their plans for the coming summer vacation.*

chi·tin (kī'tin) *n.* a horny substance forming the hard outer covering in insects and certain other animals.

chit·ter·lings (chit'linz) *also,* **chit·lings, chit·lins.** *n., pl.* the small intestines of pigs, prepared as food.

chiv·al·rous (shiv'əl rəs) *adj.* **1.** having or showing the qualities characteristic of chivalry, such as gallantry, honor, and courtesy. **2.** of or relating to chivalry. —**chiv'al·rous·ly,** *adv.* —**chiv'al·rous·ness,** *n.*

chiv·al·ry (shiv'əl rē) *n.* **1.** the qualities of an ideal knight, such as gallantry, honor, courtesy, generosity, respect for women, protection of the weak, and skill in battle. **2.** the way of life of knights during the Middle Ages. **3.** a group of knights.

chive (chīv) *n.* **1.** the long, slender leaves of a plant related to the onion, used as a garnish or seasoning. **2.** the plant bearing these leaves.

chlo·ral (klôr'əl) *n.* **1.** a colorless, oily liquid having a strong odor, used especially in the manufacture of DDT. **2.** see **chloral hydrate.**

chloral hydrate, a white crystalline compound prepared from chlorine, ethyl alcohol, and water. It is used to produce sleep.

chlo·ride (klôr'īd) *n.* a compound of chlorine with another element or radical, especially a salt of hydrochloric acid.

chloride of lime, a white powder used for bleaching and disinfecting, prepared by treating slaked lime with chlorine. Also **bleaching powder.**

chlo·rin·ate (klôr'ə nāt') *v.t.,* **chlo·rin·at·ed, chlo·rin·at·ing.** to combine or treat with chlorine, especially in order to kill bacteria: *to chlorinate the water in a swimming pool.* —**chlo'rin·a'tion,** *n.*

chlo·rine (klôr'ēn) *n.* a nonmetallic element occurring naturally as a poisonous, greenish-yellow gas with an irritating, strong odor. Chlorine and its compounds are used in bleaching and disinfecting. Symbol: **Cl**

chlo·ro·form (klôr'ə fôrm') *n.* a compound of carbon, hydrogen, and chlorine in the form of a colorless non-burning liquid with a sweetish smell. Formerly used as an anesthetic, it is now used especially as a solvent to dissolve rubber, fats, and other substances. —*v.t.* to make unconscious or kill by means of chloroform.

Chlo·ro·my·ce·tin (klôr'ə mī sē'tin) *n. Trademark.* an antibiotic drug that is very effective in the treatment of certain diseases, especially typhoid fever.

chlo·ro·phyll (klôr'ə fil') *also,* **chlo·ro·phyl.** *n.* an organic compound of carbon, hydrogen, nitrogen, oxygen, and magnesium. It is the green coloring matter of plants and is needed by them for making food materials by changing carbon dioxide and water into sugar.

chlo·ro·plast (klôr'ə plast') *n.* any of the small bodies in a plant cell that contain chlorophyll.

chm., chairman. Also, **chmn.**

Chisel

chock (chok) *n.* a block or wedge put under or in front of something to keep it from moving, as in front of the wheels of an airplane on the ground. —*v.t.* to furnish or keep in position with a chock or chocks.

chock-a-block (chok'ə blok') *adj.* very crowded: *The museum's walls were chock-a-block with paintings.*

chock-full (chok'fool') *also,* **chuck-full.** *adj.* as full as can be; crammed: *The trunk was chock-full of old clothes.*

choc·o·late (chô'kə lit, chôk'ə lit) *n.* **1.** a food product made from ground and roasted cacao beans. **2.** a drink made by dissolving chocolate or cocoa in milk or water. **3.** a candy made of or coated with chocolate: *a box of chocolates.* **4.** a dark brown color. —*adj.* **1.** made of or flavored with chocolate: *a cake with chocolate icing.* **2.** having the color chocolate.

Choc·taw (chok'tô) *n. pl.,* **Choc·taws** or **Choc·taw.** **1.** a member of a tribe of North American Indians formerly living in parts of what are now Mississippi, Alabama, and Louisiana, now living in Oklahoma. **2.** the language of this tribe.

choice (chois) *n.* **1.** the act or instance of choosing: *It took her ten minutes to make a choice between the two dresses.* **2.** the power or opportunity to choose: *We were given a choice between the two movies.* **3.** a person or thing that is chosen: *The black horse is my choice to win the race.* **4.** a variety from which to choose: *a menu with a wide choice of dishes.* **5.** an alternative: *Our only choice was to go home.* —*adj.,* **choic·er, choic·est.** **1.** worthy of being chosen; select; excellent: *We searched through the forest until we found a choice spot for a picnic.* **2.** carefully selected: *The artist showed us a few choice samples of his work.* **3.** indicating a U.S. government grade of meat that is less tender than prime. —**choice'ly,** *adv.*

choir (kwīr) *n.* **1.** an organized group of singers, especially one used in a religious service. **2.** the part of a church set apart for the use of such singers.

choir·boy (kwīr'boi') *n.* a boy who sings in a choir.

choke (chōk) *v.,* **choked, chok·ing.** —*v.t.* **1.** to prevent or hinder the breathing of: *The dense smoke choked the people trapped in the burning building.* **2.** to stop up; block; clog: *Dirt choked the drain.* **3.** to fill completely: *The closet was choked with camping gear.* **4.** to stop the growth, progress, or action of: *to choke a fire with water.* **5.** to regulate the amount of air that enters (a gasoline engine) in order to enrich the fuel mixture. —*v.i.* to be prevented or hindered from breathing: *He almost choked on a bone.* —*n.* **1.** the act or sound of choking. **2.** a valve that regulates the amount of air that enters the carburetor of a gasoline engine.

to choke back. to hold back or repress; stifle: *Larry had to choke back his anger.*

to choke off. to put an end to; stop.

to choke up. a. to become speechless, as from sorrow or anger. **b.** *Informal.* to give a poor performance because of tension or nervousness: *The young actor choked up on opening night.*

choke·cher·ry (chōk'cher'ē) *n. pl.,* **choke·cher·ries.** **1.** the bitter cherrylike fruit of a tree or shrub of the rose family, used to make jams and jellies. **2.** the tree or shrub bearing this fruit.

at; āpe; cär; end; mē; it; īce; hot; ōld; fôrk; wood; fool; oil; out; up; turn; sing; thin; **this**; hw in white; zh in treasure. The symbol ə stands for the sound of **a** in about, **e** in taken, **i** in pencil, **o** in lemon, and **u** in circus.

chok·er (chō′kər) *n.* **1.** a person or thing that chokes. **2.** a necklace that fits tightly around the throat.

chol·er (kol′ər) *n.* irritability or anger.

chol·er·a (kol′ər ə) *n.* an infectious disease of the intestines, characterized by severe vomiting and diarrhea.

chol·er·ic (kol′ər ik) *adj.* easily irritated or angered.

cho·les·ter·ol (kə les′tə rôl′) *n.* a fatty material that is present in all body tissues, needed for the digestion of fats, the production of certain hormones, and the manufacture of vitamin D. It is believed that large amounts of this substance in the blood increase the possibility of hardening of the arteries.

Chong·qing (choong′ching′) another spelling of **Chungking.**

choose (chōōz) *v.,* **chose, cho·sen, choos·ing.** —*v.t.* **1.** to select from all that are available: *He chose the largest apples from the basket.* **2.** to prefer and decide (to do something): *We chose to leave the party early.* —*v.i.* **1.** to make a selection. **2.** to think fit. —**choos′er,** *n.*

choos·y (chōō′zē) also, **choos·ey.** *adj.,* **choos·i·er, choos·i·est.** *Informal.* very careful in making a choice; fussy; particular: *José is very choosy about the clothes he buys.*

chop¹ (chop) *v.,* **chopped, chop·ping.** —*v.t.* **1.** to cut by a quick blow or series of blows with a sharp instrument: *He chopped the tree down with an ax.* **2.** to make or form in this way: *The firefighter chopped a hole in the wall.* **3.** to cut into pieces: *to chop onions.* **4.** to make shorter in length or duration: *The reporter chopped the story by eliminating three paragraphs.* **5.** to hit (a ball) with a short, quick, downward stroke, as in tennis. —*v.i.* to make cutting strokes. —*n.* **1.** the act of chopping. **2.** a short, quick, downward cutting stroke or blow. **3.** a small cut of meat, as of lamb, pork, or veal, that usually includes a piece of the rib. [A form of *chap¹.*]

chop² (chop) *v.i.,* **chopped, chop·ping.** to change or shift suddenly. [A form of obsolete *chap* to exchange.]

chop³ (chop) also, **chops.** *n.* **1.** the jaw or cheek. **2.** the mouth. [Of uncertain origin.]

chop·house (chop′hous′) *n. pl.,* **chop·hous·es** (chop′hou′ziz). a restaurant that specializes in chops and steaks.

Cho·pin, Fré·dé·ric Fran·çois (shō′pan; fred′ər ik fran swä′) 1810–1849, Polish pianist and composer, living in France.

chop·per (chop′ər) *n.* **1.** a person or thing that chops. **2.** *Slang.* a helicopter.

chop·py¹ (chop′ē) *adj.,* **chop·pi·er, chop·pi·est.** **1.** rough with short, broken waves: *a choppy sea.* **2.** marked by short, jerky movements. [*Chop¹* + -*y¹.*] —**chop′pi·ness,** *n.*

chop·py² (chop′ē) *adj.,* **chop·pi·er, chop·pi·est.** changing or shifting suddenly: *a choppy wind.* [*Chop²* + -*y¹.*]

chop·sticks (chop′stiks′) *n., pl.* a pair of long, slender sticks, usually wood or ivory, that are held between the thumb and fingers and are used for eating. Chopsticks were first developed in China.

chop su·ey (chop′ sōō′ē) a dish of Chinese-American origin, consisting of vegetables such as mushrooms, onions, bean sprouts, and bamboo shoots, cooked with small pieces of meat, fish, or chicken, and usually served with rice. [Chinese *shap sui* odds and ends.]

cho·ral (*adj.,* kôr′əl; *n.,* kə ral′, kôr′əl) *adj.* **1.** of or relating to a choir or chorus. **2.** performed by or written for a choir or chorus: *choral music.* —*n.* another spelling of **chorale.**

cho·rale (kə ral′) also, **cho·ral.** *n.* **1.** a hymn having a plain melody and stately rhythm, usually sung in unison. **2.** a group of people singing such music; chorus.

chord¹ (kôrd) *n.* a combination of three or more musical tones or notes sounded at the same time to produce a harmony. [Earlier *cord,* short for *accord.*]

chord² (kôrd) *n.* **1.** a straight line segment joining any two points on a curve. **2.** a feeling or emotion: *Seeing someone in trouble strikes a sympathetic chord in me.* [Latin *chorda* catgut, a string of a musical instrument, from Greek *chordē.*]

Chord²
AB, CD are chords

chor·date (kôr′dāt) *n.* any animal of the group that includes all animals with backbones.

chore (chôr) *n.* **1.** a small or minor job: *The girl had several daily chores to do on her father's farm.* **2.** a hard or unpleasant task: *It's a real chore for him to have to mow the lawn.*

cho·re·a (kə rē′ə) *n.* another word for **Saint Vitus' dance.**

cho·re·o·graph (kôr′ē ə graf′) *v.t.* to create, arrange, or direct (dance movement), as for ballet.

cho·re·og·ra·pher (kôr′ē og′rə fər) *n.* a person who creates, arranges, or directs dance movements, as for ballet.

cho·re·og·ra·phy (kôr′ē og′rə fē) *n.* **1.** the art of creating, arranging, or directing dance movement. **2.** dancing or dance movement, as in a ballet.

chor·is·ter (kôr′is tər) *n.* **1.** a person who sings in a choir. **2.** a choirboy. **3.** a person who leads a choir.

cho·roid (kôr′oid) *n.* the membrane forming the middle coat of the eyeball and lying between the sclera and the retina. The choroid, in the front of the eye, forms the iris. Also, **choroid coat.** —*adj.* of or relating to the choroid.

chor·tle (chôrt′əl) *v.i.,* **chor·tled, chor·tling.** to laugh with a snorting chuckle. —*n.* such a laugh.

cho·rus (kôr′əs) *n. pl.,* **cho·rus·es. 1.** a large, organized group of people who sing together. **2.** a group of people who sing, dance, and often play minor parts, as in a musical comedy. **3.** a musical composition to be sung by a large group, usually written for four or more parts. **4.** a part of a song that is repeated after each stanza; refrain. **5.** a group of people who recite or speak at the same time: *the chorus in an ancient Greek drama.* **6.** the saying or uttering of something by a group of people all at the same time: *The joke produced a chorus of laughter.* —*v.t.,* **cho·rused, cho·rus·ing.** to sing or say at the same time.

chose (chōz) the past tense of **choose.**

cho·sen (chō′zən) *v.* the past participle of **choose.** —*adj.* selected by preference; select.

Chou En-lai (jō′ en lī′) 1898–1976, Chinese Communist political leader. Also, **Zhou Enlai.**

chow¹ (chou) *n. Slang.* food. [Short for *chow-chow,* a kind of spicy relish.]

chow² (chou) *n.* a dog of a breed originally developed in China, having a large head, a thick, usually brown or black coat, and a bluish-black tongue. Also, **chow chow.** [From a word in a Chinese dialect similar to Cantonese *kaú* dog.]

Chow

chow·der (chou′dər) *n.* a thick soup usually made of fish or shellfish, especially clams, with vegetables and sometimes milk.

chow mein (chou′ mān′) a dish of Chinese-American origin, made of shredded fish or meat and vegetables such as celery, onions, and bean sprouts. It is usually served with rice and fried noodles.

Christ (krīst) *n.* Jesus of Nazareth, the founder of the Christian religion.

Christ·church (krīst′church′) *n.* the largest city in New Zealand, on the eastern coast of South Island. Pop. (1976), 171,987.

chris·ten (kris′ən) *v.t.* **1.** to receive into a Christian church by baptism; baptize. **2.** to give a name to at baptism: *They christened their first child "Peter."* **3.** to give a name to: *to christen a ship.*

Chris·ten·dom (kris′ən dəm) *n.* **1.** the countries of the world in which Christianity is the main religion, considered as a group. **2.** Christians as a group.

chris·ten·ing (kris′ə ning) *n.* the act or ceremony of baptizing and naming a baby; baptism.

Chris·tian (kris′chən) *n.* a person who believes in and follows the teachings of Jesus; a member of the religion based on these teachings. —*adj.* **1.** of or relating to Jesus or His teachings. **2.** believing in Jesus and following His teachings; belonging to the religion based on these teachings: *Easter is celebrated by all the Christian people of the world.* **3.** of or relating to Christians or Christianity.

Chris·ti·an·i·ty (kris′chē an′ə tē) *n.* **1.** the religion based on the teachings of Jesus; the Christian religion. **2.** Christians as a group; Christendom.

Chris·tian·ize (kris′chə nīz′) *v.t.,* **Chris·tian·ized, Christian·iz·ing.** to make (someone) a Christian.

Christian name, the name given to a person at birth or baptism, as distinguished from the family name.

Christian Science, a religion founded by Mary Baker Eddy in 1866. It stresses healing by spiritual means.

Christian Scientist, a person who believes in Christian Science.

Christ·like (krīst′līk′) *adj.* having or showing the spirit of Jesus; like Jesus.

Christ·mas (kris′məs) *n.* the yearly celebration of the birth of Jesus. It falls on December 25. Also, **Christmas Day.**

Christmas Eve, the evening before Christmas.

Christ·mas·tide (kris′məs tīd′) *n.* the season of Christmas.

Christmas tree, an evergreen or artificial tree decorated with lights and ornaments at Christmas time.

Chris·to·pher, Saint (kris′tə fər) died A.D. 250?, Christian martyr, the patron saint of travelers.

chro·mat·ic (krō mat′ik) *adj.* **1.** of, relating to, or containing a color or colors. **2.** relating to the chromatic scale. —**chro·mat′i·cal·ly,** *adv.*

chromatic scale, a musical scale progressing entirely by half tones.

chro·ma·tin (krō′mə tin) *n.* the material in the cell nucleus that makes up the chromosomes during cell division.

chro·ma·tog·ra·phy (krō′mə tog′rə fē) *n.* the process for separating and analyzing the chemical compounds in a mixture by absorption.

chrome (krōm) *n.* **1.** another word for **chromium. 2.** something plated with chromium or an alloy of chromium.

chro·mic (krō′mik) *adj.* relating to or containing chromium.

chro·mi·um (krō′mē əm) *n.* a hard, brittle, silver-white metallic element that does not tarnish in air. It is used for plating other metals and in many alloys to provide strength and resistance to corrosion and heat. Symbol: **Cr**

chro·mo·some (krō′mə sōm′) *n.* a tiny structure in the nuclei of plant and animal cells, composed chiefly of proteins and DNA. Chromosomes carry the genes that determine sex, size, color, and many other characteristics.

chro·mo·sphere (krō′mə sfēr′) *n.* **1.** a gaseous layer several thousand miles thick that surrounds the sun and is visible as a red ring during a total solar eclipse. It is made up mostly of hydrogen, helium, and calcium. **2.** a similar gaseous layer around a star.

chron. **1.** chronological. **2.** chronology.

Chron., Chronicles.

chron·ic (kron′ik) *adj.* **1.** (of an illness) lasting a long time or coming back again and again: *chronic asthma.* **2.** done by habit; habitual; constant: *He is a chronic complainer.* —**chron′i·cal·ly,** *adv.*

chron·i·cle (kron′i kəl) *n.* a detailed record of events in the order in which they happened; history. —*v.t.* **chron·i·cled, chron·i·cling.** to record in a chronicle. —**chron′i·cler,** *n.*

Chron·i·cles (kron′i kəlz) *n., pl.* either of two books, I Chronicles and II Chronicles, of the Old Testament.

chron·o·log·i·cal (kron′ə loj′i kəl) *adj.* arranged according to the order in which events happened. —**chron′·o·log′i·cal·ly,** *adv.*

chro·nol·o·gy (krə nol′ə jē) *n.* *pl.,* **chro·nol·o·gies. 1.** the arrangement of events in the order in which they happened. **2.** a table or list arranged in this way. **3.** the science of arranging and recording the dates of events and the order in which they happened.

chro·nom·e·ter (krə nom′ə tər) *n.* a clock that is specially designed for keeping time very accurately, used for scientific purposes.

chrys·a·lid (kris′ə lid) *n.* *pl.,* **chry·sal·i·des** (kri sal′ə-dēs′). another word for **chrysalis.** —*adj.* of or relating to a chrysalis.

chrys·a·lis (kris′ə lis) *n.* *pl.,* **chrys·a·lis·es. 1.** an insect in the stage of metamorphosis during which it is enclosed in a cocoon and is undergoing changes in structure before emerging as a winged adult. **2.** a cocoon.

chry·san·the·mum (krə san′thə məm) *n.* **1.** the round, showy flower of any of a large group of plants growing in many different colors. **2.** the leafy plant bearing this flower, widely cultivated as a garden plant.

chub (chub) *n.* *pl.,* **chubs** or **chub.** any of several freshwater and saltwater fish, such as the minnow.

chub·by (chub′ē) *adj.,* **chub·bi·er, chub·bi·est.** round and plump. —**chub′bi·ness,** *n.*

chuck[1] (chuk) *n.* a gentle or playful pat or tap, especially under the chin. —*v.t.* **1.** to pat or tap gently or playfully, especially under the chin. **2.** *Informal.* to throw or toss. [Possibly from Old French *choquer* to knock, strike.]

chuck[2] (chuk) *n.* **1.** a device for holding a piece of work or a tool in a machine, such as a lathe or drill. **2.** a cut of beef including parts from the neck and the shoulder blade to the first three ribs. [A form of *chock.*]

chuck-full (chuk′fool′) *adj.* another word for **chock-full.**

chuck·le (chuk′əl) *v.i.,* **chuck·led, chuck·ling.** to laugh in a soft manner, especially to oneself: *John chuckled when he read the letter from his brother.* —*n.* a soft laugh.

chuck wagon, a wagon that carries cooking equipment and food, as for cowboys.

chuck·wal·la (chuk′wä′lə) *n.* a lizard related to the iguana, found in the southwestern United States and northwestern Mexico.

Chuck of a drill

chug (chug) *n.* a short, dull, explosive sound, such as that made by the exhaust of an engine. —*v.i.* **chugged, chug·ging.** to move with or make such sounds: *The old car chugged along down the highway.*

---

at; āpe; cär; end; mē; it; īce; hot; ōld; fôrk; wood; fōol; oil; out; up; turn; sing; thin; <u>th</u>is; hw in white; zh in treasure. The symbol ə stands for the sound of a in about, e in taken, i in pencil, o in lemon, and u in circus.

chum (chum) *n.* a close friend. —*v.i.,* **chummed, chum-ming.** to be close friends.

chum·my (chum′ē) *adj.,* **chum·mi·er, chum·mi·est.** *Informal.* very friendly; intimate.

chump (chump) *n. Slang.* a person who is easily fooled or taken advantage of.

Chung·king (choong′king′) *n.* a port city in west-central China, on the Yangtze River. Pop. (1961 est.), 2,165,000. Also, **Chong·qing.**

chunk (chungk) *n. Informal.* **1.** a thick piece or lump: *a chunk of wood, a chunk of ice.* **2.** an amount; quantity.

chunk·y (chung′kē) *adj.,* **chunk·i·er, chunk·i·est.** *Informal.* **1.** short and compact; stocky: *a chunky boy.* **2.** like a chunk; thick.

church (church) *n.* **1.** a building for public worship, especially one for Christian worship. **2.** Christian worship; religious services: *We go to church every Sunday.* **3.** Christians as a group. **4. Church.** a particular group of Christians having similar beliefs; denomination: *the Presbyterian Church, the Roman Catholic Church.* **5.** the profession of a clergyman or clergywoman.

church·go·er (church′gō′ər) *n.* a person who goes to church regularly.

Church·ill (chur′chil) **1. Sir Winston.** 1874–1965, British statesman and writer, the prime minister of Great Britain from 1940 to 1945 and from 1951 to 1955. **2. John.** see **Marlborough, Duke of.**

Church Latin, the form of Latin used by the Roman Catholic Church.

church·man (church′mən) *n. pl.,* **church·men** (church′-mən). **1.** a clergyman. **2.** a member of a church.

Church of Christ, Scientist, the official name of the Christian Science Church.

Church of England, the national church of England, headed by the British monarch. It was established by Henry VIII in the sixteenth century.

Church of Jesus Christ of Latter-day Saints, the official name of the Mormon Church.

church·war·den (church′wôrd′ən) *n.* in the Church of England and the Protestant Episcopal Church, an elected lay official whose duty is the management of church property, finances, and business affairs.

church·wom·an (church′woom′ən) *n. pl.,* **church-wom·en** (church′wim′ən). a woman who is a member of a church.

church·yard (church′yärd′) *n.* the ground around or adjoining a church, often used as a cemetery.

churl (churl) *n.* a surly, ill-bred person.

churl·ish (chur′lish) *adj.* surly; ill-bred; rude. —**churl′-ish·ly,** *adv.* —**churl′ish·ness,** *n.*

churn (churn) *n.* a vessel in which cream or milk is shaken or beaten to separate the fat in order to make butter. —*v.t.* **1.** to shake or beat (cream or milk) in a churn. **2.** to make (butter) in a churn. **3.** to stir or cause to move with violent motion: *The plow churned up the soil.* —*v.i.* **1.** to work or operate a churn. **2.** to move violently: *The water churned at the bottom of the waterfall.*

chute (shōot) *n.* **1.** an inclined or vertical trough or passage down or through which various things may be passed or carried: *a mail chute, a coal chute.* **2.** a waterfall or rapids in a river. **3.** a steep or curving slope, as for toboggans. **4.** *Informal.* see **para-chute.**

chut·ney (chut′nē) *n. pl.,* **chut·neys.** a sauce or relish made of fruits, herbs, spices, and vinegar.

chyme (kīm) *n.* the thick, pulpy mass, resulting from partly digested food that passes from the stomach into the small intestine.

CIA, Central Intelligence Agency.

ci·ca·da (si kā′də) *n. pl.,* **ci·ca·das** or **ci·ca·dae** (si kā′dē). a large insect with two pairs of transparent wings. The male makes a loud, shrill sound by means of two vibrating plates on its abdomen.

Cicada

Cic·e·ro, Marcus Tul·li·us (sis′ə rō′; tul′ē əs). 106–43 B.C., Roman orator, writer, and statesman.

Cid, The (sid) 1040?–1099, a Spanish soldier who fought against the Moors and became a national hero; born Rodrigo Diaz de Bivar.

-cide[1] *combining form* the act of killing: *homicide.* [Latin *-cīdium* a killing, from *caedere* to kill.]

-cide[2] *combining form* the killer of: *matricide.* [Latin *-cīda* killer, from *caedere* to kill.]

ci·der (sī′dər) *n.* the juice pressed from apples, used as a drink and in making certain products, such as vinegar.

ci·gar (si gär′) *n.* a roll of tobacco leaves prepared for smoking.

cig·a·rette (sig′ə ret′, sig′ə ret′) *also,* **cig·a·ret.** *n.* a small roll of finely shredded tobacco leaves, wrapped in thin paper, used for smoking.

cil·i·a (sil′ē ə) *n., pl. sing.,* **cilium. 1.** the eyelashes. **2.** the very small hairlike structures that line the two main branches of the windpipe and their smaller branching tubes. Cilia are constantly in motion and filter the air entering and leaving the lungs. **3.** similar hairlike structures on certain cells, such as paramecia, that move to and fro allowing the cell to move.

cil·i·ar·y (sil′ē er′ē) *adj.* **1.** relating to or like cilia; hairlike. **2.** of or relating to the ciliary body.

ciliary body, a portion of the membrane of the eye whose ligaments and muscles support and adjust the shape of the lens of the eyeball.

cil·i·um (sil′ē əm) the singular of **cilia.**

cinch (sinch) *n. pl.,* **cinch·es. 1.** a strap for fastening a saddle or pack on a horse. **2.** *Slang.* something sure or easy: *If you study hard, passing the test will be a cinch.* —*v.t.* **1.** to fasten a cinch around; bind firmly. **2.** *Slang.* to make sure of: *His hit cinched the victory for his team.*

cin·cho·na (sin kō′nə) *n.* **1.** any of a group of trees having smooth oblong leaves and pink or cream-colored flowers, found in South America, Asia, and Jamaica. **2.** the bark of this tree, which yields quinine and other similar drugs. Also *(def. 2),* **Peruvian bark.**

Cin·cin·nat·i (sin′sə nat′ē, sin′sə nat′ə) *n.* a city in southwestern Ohio, on the Ohio River. Pop. (1970), 452,524.

cinc·ture (singk′chər) *n.* a belt or girdle.

cin·der (sin′dər) *n.* **1.** a substance, especially coal, that is burning but is no longer flaming. **2.** a substance, such as wood or coal, that has burned but has not been reduced to ashes. **3. cinders.** the ashes from a fire. **4.** a speck, as of dirt or ash: *The wind was blowing and I got a cinder in my eye.*

cinder block, a building brick that is partially hollow, made from cinders and cement.

Cin·der·el·la (sin′də rel′ə) *n.* a girl in a fairy tale who was forced by her cruel stepmother and stepsisters to work very hard. With the help of her fairy godmother she later married a prince.

cin·e·ma (sin′ə mə) *n.* **1.** a motion-picture theater. **2.** motion pictures as a form of art. **3.** the business of making motion pictures. —**cin′e·mat′ic,** *adj.*

Churn

cin·e·ma·tog·ra·phy (sin′ə mə tog′rə fē) *n.* the art or process of photographing motion pictures.

cin·na·bar (sin′ə bär′) *n.* a red or brownish-red mineral that is the chief source of mercury.

cin·na·mon (sin′ə mən) *n.* **1.** a reddish-brown spice made from the dried inner bark of a tree grown in tropical regions. **2.** the inner bark itself, either ground or rolled into sheets. **3.** the tree yielding this bark. **4.** a light, reddish-brown color. —*adj.* having the color cinnamon; light reddish-brown.

CIO, Congress of Industrial Organizations.

ci·on (sī′ən) another spelling of **scion** (*def. 1*).

ci·pher (sī′fər) *also,* **cy·pher.** *n.* **1.** the number zero. **2.** the numeral representing this; 0. **3.** a person or thing that is of no value or importance. **4.** a system of secret writing that cannot be understood by those who do not have the key or pattern; code. —*v.t.* **1.** to write (a message) in cipher. —*v.i.* to do arithmetic.

cir·ca (sur′kə) *prep.* around; about. ▲ used especially to show an approximate date: *The poet Chaucer was born circa 1344.*

Cir·ce (sur′sē) *n. Greek Mythology.* a beautiful enchantress who lived on an island and who changed half of Odysseus's men into swine.

cir·cle (sur′kəl) *n.* **1.** a continuous, closed curved line, every point of which is equally distant from the center. **2.** a plane figure enclosed by such a line; the area within a circle. **3.** anything shaped like a circle, such as a halo, crown, or ring. **4.** a group of people sharing common interests: *He has a large circle of friends.* —*v.,* **cir·cled, cir·cling.** —*v.t.* **1.** to surround with a circle; encompass: *The enemy soldiers circled the camp.* **2.** to move around (someone or something) in a circle: *The airplane circled the landing field.* —*v.i.* to move around in a circle: *The outfielder circled under the high fly ball.*

cir·clet (sur′klit) *n.* **1.** a small circle. **2.** an ornamental ring or band worn about the head, neck, arm, or finger.

cir·cuit (sur′kit) *n.* **1.** the act of going around; a circular course; revolution: *The earth completes its circuit around the sun in a year.* **2.** a regular journey from one place to another, as by a judge or preacher. **3.** the district traveled through in such a journey, especially the district assigned to a judge for holding court. **4.** a system or part of a system of electronic parts through which an electric current flows; the path of an electric circuit. **5.** a group of theaters under one management, presenting movies or plays at the same time or in turn.

circuit breaker, a safety switch that automatically interrupts the flow of current through an electric circuit when the current becomes dangerously strong.

circuit court, a court that sits at intervals in various places within the territory over which it has jurisdiction.

cir·cu·i·tous (sər kyōō′ə təs) *adj.* not direct; roundabout: *We had to take a circuitous route downtown to avoid the traffic jam.* —**cir·cu′i·tous·ly,** *adv.* —**cir·cu′i·tous·ness,** *n.*

circuit rider, formerly, a minister who traveled over a circuit to preach.

cir·cu·lar (sur′kyə lər) *adj.* **1.** having the form of a circle; round: *a circular driveway, a necktie with a circular design.* **2.** moving in or forming a circle: *The skater moved in a circular path around the ice.* —*n.* printed material, such as a letter or advertisement, for general circulation: *The store distributed circulars advertising its spring sale.* —**cir′cu·lar·ly,** *adv.*

cir·cu·lar·i·ty (sur′kyə lar′ə tē) *n.* the state or quality of being circular.

cir·cu·lar·ize (sur′kyə lə rīz′) *v.t.,* **cir·cu·lar·ized, cir·cu·lar·iz·ing.** to send circulars to.

circular saw, a power saw having a thin, metal disk with a toothed edge mounted in a framework. The disk is rotated at a high speed.

Circular saw

cir·cu·late (sur′kyə lāt′) *v.,* **cir·cu·lat·ed, cir·cu·lat·ing.** —*v.i.* **1.** to move in a circular course back to the starting point: *Blood circulates in the body.* **2.** to move or pass from place to place or person to person; move freely: *Air circulates in a room.* —*v.t.* to cause to circulate: *The teacher circulated the picture around the room. The rumor was circulated through the office.*

circulating library, a library from which books may be borrowed or rented. Also, **lending library.**

cir·cu·la·tion (sur′kyə lā′shən) *n.* **1.** movement from place to place or person to person: *Gold coins are no longer in circulation in this country.* **2.** the movement of the blood to and from the heart through the blood vessels of the body. **3.** the number of copies of a newspaper or magazine that are distributed and sold: *The circulation of our city's newspaper is over 300,000.*

cir·cu·la·to·ry (sur′kyə lə tôr′ē) *adj.* of or relating to circulation, especially of the blood.

circulatory system, the network of tissues that carry blood and lymph throughout the body.

circum- *prefix* around; about: *circumnavigate.*

cir·cum·cise (sur′kəm sīz′) *v.t.,* **cir·cum·cised, cir·cum·cis·ing.** to remove the foreskin of.

cir·cum·ci·sion (sur′kəm sizh′ən) *n.* **1.** the act or rite of circumcising. **2. Circumcision.** a feast day commemorating the circumcision of the infant Jesus. It falls on January 1.

cir·cum·fer·ence (sər kum′fər əns) *n.* **1.** a line bounding any rounded plane figure, especially a circle. **2.** the measurement of this line; the distance around something: *the circumference of the earth.*

cir·cum·flex (sur′kəm fleks′) *n. pl.,* **cir·cum·flex·es.** a mark placed over a letter to show something about its pronunciation. In this dictionary, the mark ô over the letter *o* shows that it is pronounced as in the word *fork.* Also, **circumflex accent.** —*adj.* pronounced or marked with a circumflex.

cir·cum·lo·cu·tion (sur′kəm lō kyōō′shən) *n.* **1.** a roundabout or indirect way of speaking; use of too many words. **2.** an instance of this; roundabout expression: *"The bicycle that belongs to me" is a circumlocution for "my bicycle."*

cir·cum·nav·i·gate (sur′kəm nav′ə gāt′) *v.t.,* **cir·cum·nav·i·gat·ed, cir·cum·nav·i·gat·ing.** to sail completely around: *to circumnagivate the earth.* —**cir′cum·nav′i·ga′·tion,** *n.*

cir·cum·scribe (sur′kəm skrīb′) *v.t.,* **cir·cum·scribed, cir·cum·scrib·ing.** **1.** to draw a line around; form the boundaries of; encircle. **2.** to put restrictions on; limit: *The doctor circumscribed the amount of work Anita could do when she got out of the hospital.* **3.a.** to draw (a geometric figure) around another geometric figure so that the outer figure touches the inner at as many points as possible: *to*

---

at; āpe; cär; end; mē; it; īce; hot; ōld; fôrk; wood; fōōl; oil; out; up; turn; sing; thin; this; hw in white; zh in treasure. The symbol ə stands for the sound of a in about, e in taken, i in pencil, o in lemon, and u in circus.

circumscribe a circle around a pentagon. **b.** to enclose (a geometric figure) in this way.

cir·cum·spect (sur′kəm spekt′) *adj.* considering or examining carefully all sides of a problem before acting or making a decision; cautious. —**cir′cum·spect′ly,** *adv.*

cir·cum·spec·tion (sur′kəm spek′shən) *n.* circumspect action or behavior; caution; prudence.

cir·cum·stance (sur′kəm stans′) *n.* **1.** a condition, act, or event that is connected to and often affects another condition, act, or event: *Good weather and other circumstances made our picnic a success.* **2.** *also,* **circumstances.** the state of affairs surrounding and affecting a person or action: *Due to circumstances beyond our control, the football game was canceled.* **3.** a fact or event: *I don't know what circumstance made her leave so suddenly.* **4.** **circumstances.** financial condition: *Jim is determined to make a lot of money because of the poor circumstances of his youth.* **5.** a formal or splendid ceremony or display: *The crowning of the new queen was accompanied by great pomp and circumstance.* **6.** detail, especially full detail: *The scientist explained his discovery with great circumstance.*

under no circumstances. under no conditions; never.

under the circumstances. things being as they are: *Under the circumstances, we have no choice but to leave.*

cir·cum·stan·tial (sur′kəm stan′shəl) *adj.* **1.** relating to, affected by, or depending on circumstances: *The fact that he was seen leaving the victim's house the night of the murder is circumstantial.* **2.** not essential; incidental; secondary: *The author included many circumstantial details in his story.* **3.** full of details; particular: *a circumstantial account of the accident.* —**cir′cum·stan′tial·ly,** *adv.*

circumstantial evidence, evidence relating to the circumstances surrounding an event rather than to the event itself.

cir·cum·vent (sur′kəm vent′) *v.t.* **1.** to go around: *We took the long way home in order to circumvent the traffic accident.* **2.** to entrap or get the better of, as by trickery or cleverness: *Our soldiers circumvented the enemy by attacking at dawn.* —**cir′cum·ven′tion,** *n.*

cir·cus (sur′kəs) *n. pl.,* **cir·cus·es.** **1.** a traveling show, usually featuring acrobats, clowns, and both trained and wild animals. **2.** all the persons, animals, and equipment associated with such a show. **3.** a performance given by such a show. **4.** in ancient Rome, a long, open arena with rows of seats, used especially for horse and chariot races.

cir·rho·sis (si rō′sis) *n.* a disease of the liver marked by the growth of scar tissue and the destruction of normal liver cells. It causes the liver to gradually shrink and become hard.

cir·rus (sir′əs) *n. pl.,* **cir·ri** (sir′ī). a thin, white wispy cloud composed of ice crystals in small patches or bands, found at altitudes above 20,000 feet.

cis·tern (sis′tərn) *n.* a natural or man-made reservoir or tank for storing liquids, especially rain water.

cit·a·del (sit′əd əl) *n.* **1.** a fortress built so as to overlook or dominate a city. **2.** any refuge or fortified place.

ci·ta·tion (sī tā′shən) *n.* **1.** the act of citing or quoting. **2.** the passage or words quoted; quotation: *The author's lecture included a number of citations from his latest book.* **3.** a public commendation or award for bravery or outstanding achievement: *The fireman who saved the boy received a citation from the mayor.* **4.** a summons to appear before a court of law.

cite (sīt) *v.t.,* **cit·ed, cit·ing.** **1.** to quote (a passage or author), especially as an authority: *He cited an article in the encyclopedia in support of his statement.* **2.** to mention or refer to as support, proof, or confirmation: *The lawyer cited several previous decisions that had a bearing on the case being tried.* **3.** to give a public commendation or

award to for bravery or outstanding achievement. **4.** to summon to appear before a court of law.

cit·i·zen (sit′ə zən) *n.* **1.** a person who is born in a country or who chooses to become a member of a country by law, and who owes allegiance to and is granted rights and privileges by its government. **2.** a permanent resident, especially of a city or town: *the citizens of New York City.*

cit·i·zen·ry (sit′ə zən rē) *n. pl.,* **cit·i·zen·ries.** citizens as a group.

cit·i·zen·ship (sit′ə zən ship′) *n.* the status of being a citizen, including its rights, duties, and privileges.

cit·rate (sit′rāt) *n.* a salt or ester of citric acid.

cit·ric (sit′rik) *adj.* of or obtained from citrus fruits.

citric acid, a sour-tasting acid composed of carbon, hydrogen, and oxygen, found in almost all plants but especially in lemons, limes, and other citrus fruits. It is used especially as a flavoring and in medicines.

cit·ron (sit′rən) *n.* **1.** a large fruit resembling a lemon, valued mainly for its thick, yellow-green rind, which is used in desserts and in making liqueurs and perfumes. **2.** the shrub or tree bearing this fruit. **3.** the preserved or candied rind of this fruit, used especially in fruit cakes.

cit·ron·el·la (sit′rə nel′ə) *n.* **1.** a pale yellow oil obtained from the leaves of a plant of the grass family, having a lemon fragrance and used to make insect repellent and to scent soaps and cosmetics. **2.** the plant from which this oil is obtained.

cit·rus (sit′rəs) *n.* **1.** any of a group of shrubs and small trees valued for their fruit, grown in warm regions throughout the world. **2.** see **citrus fruit.** —*adj.* of or relating to such trees or their fruit.

citrus fruit, a fleshy, juicy fruit of any of a group of shrubs and small trees, such as the orange, lemon, lime, or grapefruit.

cit·y (sit′ē) *n. pl.,* **cit·ies.** **1.** an area where many people live and work, especially one that has its own local government; a large and important town. **2.** in the United States, any area of local government that is chartered by the state in which it is located. **3.** the people who live in a city. —*adj.* of or relating to a city.

city hall **1.** a building serving as the administrative headquarters of a city government. **2.** the governing body of a city: *City hall issued a statement on the problem of crime.*

city manager, an official appointed by a city council to manage the city's government.

cit·y-state (sit′ē stāt′) *n.* a self-governing political unit consisting of a city and sometimes the surrounding territory that it controls. Ancient Athens was a city-state.

Ci·u·dad Juá·rez (sē′oo däd′ wär′əz) a city at the northern border of Mexico, on the Rio Grande, opposite El Paso, Texas. Pop. (1976), 544,900. Also, **Juárez.**

Ci·u·dad Tru·jil·lo (sē′oo däd′ troo hē′yō) see **Santo Domingo.**

civ·et (siv′it) *n.* **1.** an animal related to the mongoose, native to the warmer regions of Africa, Europe, and Asia, having a narrow head, a pointed muzzle, and a slender body. Also, **civet cat.** **2.** the fur of this animal. **3.** a thick, yellowish substance secreted by the civet, having a strong musky odor. It is used in perfumes.

Civet

civ·ic (siv′ik) *adj.* **1.** of or relating to a city: *Keeping our city clean is a matter of civic pride.* **2.** of or relating to a citizen or citizenship: *It is a person's civic duty to vote.*

C

civ·ics (siv′iks) *n., pl.* the study of the function, services, and purpose of a government and of the duties, rights, and privileges of citizenship. ▲ used with a singular verb.

civ·il (siv′əl) *adj.* **1.** of or relating to a citizen or citizens. **2.** of or relating to the relations between a government and its citizens: *civil affairs.* **3.** taking place within the boundaries of a nation or among its citizens; domestic; internal: *civil strife.* **4.** not connected with the church or the military: *a civil wedding ceremony.* **5.** coolly polite; courteous. ▲ **Civil** and **polite** both mean having good manners. **Civil** merely indicates a lack of rudeness: *He gave me a civil answer even though he was angry.* **Polite** implies good manners and thoughtfulness: *The salesgirl was always polite to her customers.*

civil defense, organized plans for defense and protection to be carried out by civilians in case of enemy attack.

civil disobedience, a refusal to obey a law or laws as a means of protest against something regarded as being morally wrong.

civil engineer, a person whose profession is civil engineering.

civil engineering, the profession of designing and directing the construction of roads, bridges, and other public works.

ci·vil·ian (si vil′yən) *n.* **1.** a person who is not a member of the armed forces. **2.** a person who does not belong to a police force, fire-fighting unit, or similar organization. —*adj.* of or relating to civilians.

ci·vil·i·ty (si vil′ə tē) *n. pl.,* **ci·vil·i·ties. 1.** cool politeness. **2.** an act or expression of politeness or courtesy.

civ·i·li·za·tion (siv′ə li zā′shən) *n.* **1.** a stage of human society marked by a high level of social, cultural, political, and intellectual development. **2.** the countries and peoples that have reached such a stage of development. **3.** the way of life of a particular people, place, or time: *medieval civilization, ancient Greek civilization.* **4.** the act or process of civilizing or of becoming civilized.

civ·i·lize (siv′ə līz′) *v.t.,* **civ·i·lized, civ·i·liz·ing.** to bring out of a primitive or savage state or condition; educate in the arts, science, government, or the like.

civil law, the body of law of a state or country that controls and regulates the rights of citizens.

civil liberty, the freedom of a person to enjoy the individual rights guaranteed by the laws or constitution, such as freedom of speech, without undue interference by the government.

civ·il·ly (siv′ə lē) *adv.* in a coolly polite way.

civil marriage, a marriage performed by a government official instead of by a clergyman.

civil rights, the individual rights of a citizen, such as the right to vote, freedom of speech, and equal protection under the law.

civil servant, a person who is employed in the civil service.

civil service, the branch of governmental service that is not concerned with military, judicial, or legislative matters. Members of the civil service are hired on the basis of merit after proving their ability by passing certain examinations.

civil war 1. a war between two sections or groups within a country. **2. Civil War.** in the United States, the war between the North and the South from 1861 to 1865.

Cl, the symbol for chlorine.

cl. 1. class. **2.** clause. **3.** clearance. **4.** claim.

clab·ber (klab′ər) *n.* milk that has curdled in the process of souring. —*v.i.* to curdle while souring.

clack (klak) *v.i.* to make a short, sharp sound: *The typewriter clacked noisily.* —*v.t.* to cause to make a short, sharp sound. —*n.* a short, sharp sound.

clad (klad) a past tense and past participle of **clothe.**

claim (klām) *v.t.* **1.** to ask for or demand as one's own; assert one's right to: *The old man claimed the land. None of the passengers claimed the suitcase.* **2.** to declare as a fact or as true; maintain; contend: *Jim claimed he saw the accident.* **3.** to call for; require: *Work on his new book claimed the better part of the author's day.* —*n.* **1.** the right to something: *Her claim to the inheritance was questioned.* **2.** a declaration of something as a fact or as true; contention: *The police could not disprove his claims of innocence.* **3.** a demand for something due: *After the fire, the store's owner filed a claim with the insurance company.* **4.** something that is claimed, such as a piece of land.
   to lay claim to. to assert one's right to: *The old prospector laid claim to the abandoned mine.*

claim·ant (klā′mənt) *n.* a person who makes a claim.

clair·voy·ance (kler voi′əns) *n.* the supposed ability to see or know about objects or events that are not in sight or that cannot be seen.

clair·voy·ant (kler voi′ənt) *adj.* of, relating to, or having clairvoyance. —*n.* a person who is clairvoyant.

clam (klam) *n.* a soft-bodied animal without a backbone, having a hinged double shell. Clams are found in both salt and fresh water. Many clams are highly valued as food. —*v.i.,* **clammed, clam·ming.** to dig for clams.
   to clam up. *Slang.* to become or remain silent; stop talking.

clam·bake (klam′bāk′) *n.* an outdoor party at which clams and other kinds of seafood are served.

clam·ber (klam′bər) *v.i.* to climb by using both the hands and feet: *The explorers clambered up the steep mountainside.* —*n.* the act of clambering.

clam·my (klam′ē) *adj.,* **clam·mi·er, clam·mi·est.** cold and damp: *a clammy old basement.* —**clam′mi·ness,** *n.*

clam·or (klam′ər) *n.* **1.** a loud, noisy outcry or protest; uproar: *A clamor went up from the audience when they were told that the show was canceled.* **2.** any loud and continuous noise: *the clamor of trumpets.* —*v.i.* to make loud continuous cries or demands: *The crowd clamored for the box office to open.*

clam·or·ous (klam′ər əs) *adj.* **1.** loud and noisy: *a clamorous protest against the new school taxes.* **2.** making loud, noisy outcries or protests: *a clamorous audience.* —**clam′or·ous·ly,** *adv.* —**clam′or·ous·ness,** *n.*

clamp (klamp) *n.* a device that has two jaws that can be tightened to hold things firmly together. —*v.t.* to fasten with or place in a clamp or clamps.
   to clamp down on. *Informal.* to become more strict with.

clan (klan) *n.* **1.** a group of families in a community who claim descent from the same ancestor, as in the Scottish Highlands. **2.** a group of people closely united by a common interest; clique. **3.** *Informal.* a family: *The whole clan met at Christmas time.*

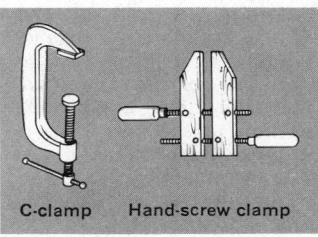

C-clamp   Hand-screw clamp

Clamps

at; āpe; cär; end; mē; it; īce; hot; ōld; fôrk; wood; fōōl; oil; out; up; turn; sing; thin; this; hw in white; zh in treasure. The symbol ə stands for the sound of **a** in about, **e** in taken, **i** in pencil, **o** in lemon, and **u** in circus.

clan·des·tine (klan des′tin) *adj.* secret, especially for an evil or illegal purpose: *The detectives uncovered a clandestine plot to blow up the chemical factory.* —**clan·des′·tine·ly,** *adv.*

clang (klang) *n.* a loud, harsh, ringing sound: *the clang of a fire alarm.* —*v.t.* to cause to make such a sound: *He clanged the school bell at noon.* —*v.i.* to make such a sound.

clan·gor (klang′gər, klang′ər) *n.* a continuous clanging: *The clangor of bells could be heard all over town.* —**clan′·gor·ous,** *adj.*

clank (klangk) *n.* a short, sharp, metallic sound: *the clank of chains.* —*v.t.* to cause to make such a sound. —*v.i.* to make such a sound: *The coins in Richard's pocket clanked as he walked.*

clan·nish (klan′ish) *adj.* **1.** relating to or characteristic of a clan. **2.** tending to stick closely together in a group; cliquish: *The people in this neighborhood are rather clannish.*

clans·man (klanz′mən) *n. pl.,* **clans·men** (klanz′mən). a member of a clan.

clap (klap) *n.* **1.** a short, sharp sound: *a clap of thunder, a clap of the hands.* **2.** a friendly slap: *a clap on the back.* —*v.,* **clapped, clap·ping.** —*v.t.* **1.** to strike (one's hands) together. **2.** to strike with a clap: *The child clapped the blocks together.* **3.** to strike in a friendly way with the palm of the hand. **4.** to put or place, especially with a sudden or forceful motion: *She clapped her hands to her face. The guard clapped the prisoner into a cell.* —*v.i.* **1.** to strike one's hands together, especially as an expression of approval or enjoyment; applaud: *The audience clapped at the end of the speech.* **2.** to make a short, sharp sound: *The shutters clapped in the strong wind.*

clap·board (klab′ərd, klap′bôrd′) *n.* a long, thin, narrow board, having one edge thicker than the other, used as siding on wooden buildings. —*v.t.* to cover with clapboards.

clap·per (klap′ər) *n.* **1.** the tongue of a bell. **2.** a person or thing that claps.

clap·trap (klap′trap′) *n.* nonsense; foolishness.

claque (klak) *n.* **1.** a person or organized group hired to applaud a performance, as in a theater. **2.** a group of people who fawn and flatter.

clar·et (klar′it) *n.* **1.** a dry red wine. **2.** a deep purplish-red color. —*adj.* having the color claret; deep purplish red.

clar·i·fy (klar′ə fī′) *v.,* **clar·i·fied, clar·i·fy·ing.** —*v.t.* **1.** to make more understandable; explain: *The candidate clarified his stand on the issue of prison reform.* **2.** to make pure and clear: *to clarify butter.* —*v.i.* **1.** to become more understandable. **2.** to become pure and clear. —**clar′i·fi·ca′tion,** *n.*

clar·i·net (klar′ə net′) *n.* a musical instrument of the woodwind family, having a single-reed mouthpiece and played by means of finger holes and keys. —**clar′i·net′ist,** *n.*

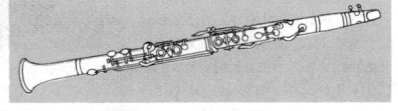
Clarinet

clar·i·on (klar′ē ən) *adj.* loud and clear: *the clarion sound of a bugle.* —*n.* a trumpet having a clear, shrill tone, popular in the seventeenth and eighteenth centuries.

clar·i·ty (klar′ə tē) *n.* the quality of being clear; clearness: *That writer is noted for his clarity of expression.*

Clark (klärk) **1. George Rogers.** 1752–1818, U.S. general and frontiersman. **2. William.** 1770–1838, brother of George; an explorer who led an expedition to the Pacific Northwest with Meriwether Lewis.

clash (klash) *n. pl.,* **clash·es. 1.** a loud, harsh, noise: *the clash of cymbals.* **2.** a strong disagreement or conflict: *There was a clash between the Republicans and the Democrats over the new bill.* —*v.i.* **1.** to come together with a clash: *The table fell over and the pots clashed to the floor.* **2.** to be in conflict: *The green rug and the purple chairs clash.* —*v.t.* to cause to strike together with a clash: *to clash cymbals.*

clasp (klasp) *n.* **1.** a fastening, such as a hook, used to hold two objects or parts together. **2.** a close or tight grasp or embrace. —*v.t.* **1.** to fasten together with a clasp. **2.** to hold or grasp closely or tightly: *She clasped the crying baby to her breast to comfort him. He clasped my hand when we were introduced.*

class (klas) *n. pl.,* **class·es. 1.** a number of persons or things that are grouped together because they are alike in some way: *a class of submarines.* **2.** a group of students taught or studying together: *The biology class took a field trip to the zoo.* **3.** a meeting of such a group: *Jane has a history class at nine o'clock.* **4.** a group of students in school or college who are ranked together or graduate in the same year: *She was a member of the class of 1972.* **5.** a rank or division of society having similar economic, educational, or social characteristics: *the working class, the upper class.* **6.** a level, grade, or quality: *Send this package by third class mail. We have reservations in the lowest class on the boat.* **7.** a group of related animals or plants forming a category that ranks below a phylum or division and above an order: *Man belongs to the class that includes mammals.* **8.** *Slang.* excellence or elegance, especially of style: *Her clothes have a lot of class.* —*v.t.* to place or group in a class; classify: *I would class him among the nicest people I have ever met.*

clas·sic (klas′ik) *adj.* **1.** serving or used as a standard, model, or guide: *That cathedral is a classic example of Gothic architecture.* **2.** simple, regular, and refined, as in style or lines: *This suit has a classic design.* **3.** typical or traditional: *the classic symptoms of a disease.* **4.** relating to ancient Greece or Rome; classical. —*n.* **1.** a work of art or literature considered to be of such high quality or excellence that it serves as a standard or model: *Many of the plays of Shakespeare are classics.* **2.** an author or artist who creates such a work. **3. the classics.** the literature of ancient Greece and Rome. **4.** any event that is considered typical or traditional: *The World Series is the classic of baseball.*

clas·si·cal (klas′i kəl) *adj.* **1.** relating to or characteristic of ancient Greece or Rome, and their art, literature, or culture: *a classical scholar.* **2.** *Music.* **a.** of or relating to usually serious music that conforms to certain established standards of form and style and is of long-lasting interest and value. Classical music differs from popular or folk music. **3.** considered to be standard and authoritative: *The course includes classical economic theories.* **4.** classic. —**clas′si·cal·ly,** *adv.*

clas·si·cism (klas′ə siz′əm) *n.* **1.** the principles of perfect order, harmony, and clarity found in the literature and art of ancient Greece and Rome, and present as ideals in all ages. **2.** adherence to these principles.

clas·si·cist (klas′ə sist) *n.* **1.** a person who follows the principles of classicism. **2.** a student of or an expert in the classics.

clas·si·fi·ca·tion (klas′ə fi kā′shən) *n.* **1.** the act of classifying. **2.** the result of classifying or being classified.

clas·si·fied (klas′ə fīd′) *adj.* **1.** arranged in groups or classes. **2.** secret, especially for reasons of national security: *The government has classified information on missile bases.* **3.** containing advertisements: *He looked in the classified section of the newspaper for a job.*

clas·si·fy (klas′ə fī′) *v.t.,* **clas·si·fied, clas·si·fy·ing.** **1.** to arrange or group in classes according to a system: *The librarian has a list of books that are classified according to subject matter.* **2.** to keep secret: *Governments classify many documents for reasons of national security.* —**clas′·si·fi′a·ble,** *adj.* —**clas′si·fi′er,** *n.*

class·mate (klas′māt′) *n.* a member of the same class in school or college: *My parents met when they were class-mates in high school.*

class·room (klas′room′, klas′room′) *n.* a room in which classes are held.

clat·ter (klat′ər) *n.* **1.** a loud rattling noise: *The clatter of dishes from the kitchen disturbed the customers in the restaurant.* **2.** noisy disorder; commotion: *the clatter of an angry mob in the streets.* **3.** noisy talk; chatter: *the clatter at a large party.* —*v.i.* **1.** to make a loud, rattling noise: *The pots and pans clattered as she put them away.* **2.** to move quickly with such a noise: *The wagon clattered over the wooden bridge.* **3.** to talk noisily; chatter. —*v.t.* to cause to clatter.

clause (klôz) *n.* **1.** a group of words containing a subject and predicate and forming part of a sentence. The two kinds of clauses are the independent clause and the dependent clause. **2.** a part of a formal or legal document, such as a contract or lease: *There is a clause in our lease that says that the landlord must paint our apartment every two years.*

claus·tro·pho·bi·a (klôs′trə fō′bē ə) *n.* an abnormal fear of being in any small, crowded, or enclosed place.

clav·i·chord (klav′ə kôrd′) *n.* a stringed musical instrument with a keyboard, whose tones are produced by the striking of brass wedges against metal strings. It was a forerunner of the piano.

clav·i·cle (klav′i kəl) *n.* either of the two long slender bones connecting the breast-bone and the shoulder blade; collarbone.

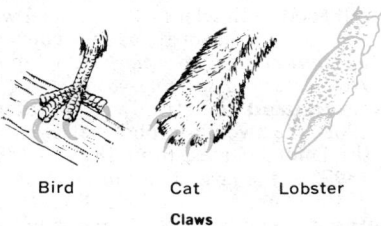
Clavichord

cla·vier (klə vēr′) *n.* **1.** any stringed musical instrument with a keyboard, such as the clavichord, harpsichord, or piano. **2.** the keyboard of a musical instrument, especially of a stringed instrument, such as a piano.

claw (klô) *n.* **1.a.** a sharp, usually curved nail on the foot of a bird or animal. **b.** a foot with such a nail or nails. **2.** one of the pincers of a shellfish, such as a lobster or crab. **3.** anything like a claw, such as the forked end of the head of a hammer. —*v.t.* to scratch or tear with claws: *The puppy was clawing the door.* —**claw′like′,** *adj.*

Bird   Cat   Lobster
Claws

clay (klā) *n.* a fine-grained earth that can be molded when wet, but hardens permanently when it is dried or baked. Clay is used in the making of pottery and bricks. —**clay′-like′,** *adj.*

Clay, Henry (klā) 1777–1852, U.S. statesman.

clay·ey (klā′ē) *adj.,* **clay·i·er, clay·i·est.** **1.** of, like, or containing clay. **2.** covered with clay.

clay pigeon, a clay disk tossed into the air as a target in trapshooting.

clean (klēn) *adj.* **1.** free from dirt or filth; unsoiled; unstained: *After playing football, he changed into clean clothes.* **2.** free from impure matter; pure: *clean water, clean air.* **3.** characterized by or having high moral standards; honorable: *He has always tried to live a clean life.* **4.** fair or within the rules: *a clean player, a clean basketball game.* **5.** smooth or even: *a clean cut. The sculpture has clean lines.* **6.** complete or thorough: *After getting out of prison, he tried to make a clean break with his past.* —*adv.* **1.** all the way; completely or thoroughly; entirely: *The arrow passed clean through the target.* **2.** in a clean manner. —*v.t.* **1.** to make free of dirt or impure matter: *to clean a car, to clean clothes by washing.* **2.** to remove or get rid of by cleaning: *to clean the dishes off a table.* **3.** to prepare (chicken, fish, or other food) for cooking. —*v.i.* to do or undergo cleaning. —**clean′ness,** *n.*

to clean out. a. to remove dirt, trash, or other matter from; make neat or clean. **b.** to make empty or use up: *We cleaned out our food supply this weekend.* **c.** *Informal.* to take away all the money of: *His last business deal cleaned him out.*

to clean up. a. to clear of dirt, trash, or other matter; make neat or clean. **b.** *Informal.* to make a lot of money: *John cleaned up in the card game.*

clean-cut (klēn′kut′) *adj.* **1.** clearly defined, as in outline or meaning; clear; definite: *The witness gave a clean-cut statement of the facts.* **2.** having a wholesome or pleasing appearance or personality: *He is a clean-cut young man.*

clean·er (klē′nər) *n.* **1.** a person whose work or business is cleaning, especially dry cleaning. **2.** something that cleans, as a machine or chemical substance.

clean·li·ness (klen′lē nis) *n.* **1.** the state of being clean. **2.** the habit of always being clean.

clean·ly¹ (klen′lē) *adj.,* **clean·li·er, clean·li·est.** habitually clean or kept clean: *a cleanly person.* [Old English *clænic* clean.]

clean·ly² (klēn′lē) *adv.* in a clean manner: *The bow of the motorboat cut the water cleanly.* [Old English *clænlīce* purely, entirely.]

cleanse (klenz) *v.t.,* **cleansed, cleans·ing.** **1.** to free from dirt, filth, or other matter: *to cleanse a wound.* **2.** to free from guilt or evil; make pure: *to cleanse one's soul.*

cleans·er (klen′zər) *n.* a substance that is used for cleaning, such as soap or detergent.

clear (klēr) *adj.* **1.** free from anything that darkens, dims, or clouds; bright: *a clear morning, a clear sky.* **2.** that can be easily seen through; not murky: *clear water, clear glass.* **3.** not having blemishes or flaws: *clear skin.* **4.** not blocked; open: *The road into town is now clear.* **5.** easily seen, heard, or understood; distinct: *a clear view, a clear voice. His directions were not very clear.* **6.** not to be doubted; obvious: *It was clear that he was lying.* **7.** free from confusion, uncertainty, or doubt: *clear thinking, a clear head.* **8.** not troubled or disturbed; free from guilt or blame: *a clear conscience.* **9.** with no further charges or expenses to be deducted; net: *We made a clear profit on the sale.* —*adv.* **1.** in a clear manner; plainly; distinctly: *She shouted for help loud and clear.* **2.** all the way; completely; entirely: *He climbed clear to the top of the tree.* —*v.t.* **1.** to free from anything that occupies, obstructs, or blocks: *Please clear*

at; āpe; cär; end; mē; it; īce; hot; ōld; fôrk; wood; fōōl; oil; out; up; turn; sing; thin; **this**; hw in white; zh in treasure. The symbol ə stands for the sound of **a** in about, e in taken, i in pencil, o in lemon, and u in circus.

the aisles. *The police cleared the street of traffic.* **2.** to remove (something) that occupies, obstructs, or blocks: *We cleared the snow from the driveway. Please clear the dishes off the table.* **3.** to pass by, over, or through without touching: *The plane barely cleared the trees.* **4.** to free from guilt, blame, or responsibility: *The new testimony cleared them of all wrongdoing.* **5.** to go through or pass, especially without difficulty: *The bill cleared the Senate.* **6.** to gain or receive as profit after all charges and expenses have been deducted: *She clears $10,000 a year after taxes.* —*v.i.* **1.** to become clear: *The sky cleared.* **2.** to pass away or disappear: *When the smoke cleared, we could see the people running out of the burning building.* —**clear′ly,** *adv.* —**clear′ness,** *n.*

  in the clear. *Informal.* free of guilt, blame, or responsibility.

  to clear out. *Informal.* to go away; leave: *We cleared out of the gym so the running team could practice.*

  to clear up. to make or become clear: *It rained all morning, but it cleared up in the afternoon. The detective cleared up the mystery of the missing jewels.*

clear·ance (klēr′əns) *n.* **1.** the act of clearing: *a ship's narrow clearance of a reef, the clearance of a school during a fire drill.* **2.** approval or authorization: *The scientist was given clearance to examine the secret plans.* **3.** the sale of merchandise at reduced prices. Also, **clearance sale.** **4.** permission to pass, as after having satisfied certain requirements: *The ship and its cargo received clearance to enter the port.* **5.** the space between two things, such as an overpass and the road underneath it: *This tunnel has a clearance of fifteen feet.*

clear-cut (klēr′kut′) *adj.* **1.** having a distinct outline: *a clear-cut profile.* **2.** completely evident or clear; obvious: *It was a clear-cut case of mistaken identity.*

clear-head·ed (klēr′hed′id) *adj.* not mentally confused; alert: *Although everyone around her panicked because of the fire, she remained clear-headed.*

clear·ing (klēr′ing) *n.* a piece of land, especially within a thickly wooded area, that is free of trees or brush.

cleat (klēt) *n.* **1.** a piece of rubber, leather, or metal attached to the sole of a shoe to prevent slipping. Shoes with cleats are used in football. **2.** a wedge-shaped piece of metal or wood with projections at both ends, used for controlling or fastening ropes, especially on the spar of a boat. **3.** a piece or strip of wood or iron fastened across a surface to give support or to prevent slipping, as on a ramp.

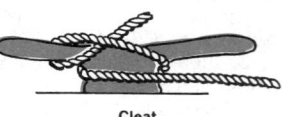

Cleat

cleav·age (klē′vij) *n.* **1.** the state or process of being cleft; split; division: *the cleavage of a log with an ax.* **2.** *Biology.* a series of cell divisions by which a fertilized egg splits into a number of smaller cells without increasing in overall size. This process changes the egg into an embryo. **3.** a tendency of certain crystals and rocks to split in a way that produces smooth plane surfaces.

cleave¹ (klēv) *v.,* **cleaved** or **cleft** or **clove, cleaved** or **cleft** or **clo·ven, cleav·ing.** —*v.t.* **1.** to split or part by force; divide: *Raoul cleaved the tree stump with a blow of the ax.* **2.** to pass through; pierce: *The ship's prow cleaved the waters.* **3.** to form by cutting: *The hikers cleaved a trail through the forest.* —*v.i.* **1.** to come apart; split: *The piece of wood cleaved in two.* **2.** to pass or go: *The ship cleaved through the waves.* [Old English *clēofan* to split.]

cleave² (klēv) *v.i.,* **cleaved, cleav·ing.** **1.** to stick fast; adhere: *Mud cleaved to his shoes.* **2.** to remain attached, devoted, or faithful: *He cleaves to his religious beliefs.* [Old English *cleofian* to stick, adhere.]

cleav·er (klē′vər) *n.* a short-handled tool with a broad blade, used for chopping meat, especially by butchers.

clef (klef) *n. Music.* a symbol placed on a staff to indicate the name and pitch of the notes on the various lines and spaces.

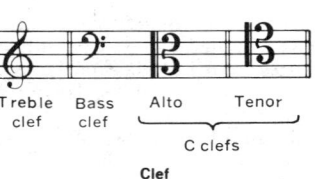

Clef

cleft (kleft) *v.* a past tense and past participle of **cleave¹.** —*n.* a space or opening made by splitting; crack: *a cleft in a rock.* —*adj.* partly or completely divided: *John has his grandfather's cleft chin.*

clem·a·tis (klem′ə tis) *n.* any of a group of climbing plants with showy white, red, blue, or purple flowers.

clem·en·cy (klem′ən sē) *n.* **1.** mercy in punishing or judging; leniency: *The judge showed clemency by giving a light sentence to the young thief.* **2.** mildness, as of weather or climate.

Cle·mens, Samuel Lang·horne (klem′ənz; lang′-hôrn′) see **Twain, Mark.**

clem·ent (klem′ənt) *adj.* **1.** forgiving, merciful, or understanding; lenient: *a clement judge.* **2.** mild; temperate: *clement weather.* —**clem′ent·ly,** *adv.*

clench (klench) *v.t.* **1.** to close or press together tightly: *to clench one's fists, to clench one's teeth.* **2.** to grasp or grip firmly; clutch: *She clenched her mother's hand as they entered the doctor's office.* **3.** another word for **clinch** (*v.t. defs.* 2,3). —*n. pl.,* **clench·es.** the act of clenching; firm grasp or grip.

Cle·o·pat·ra (klē′ə pat′rə) *n.* 69–30 B.C., the queen of Egypt from 51 to 49 B.C. and from 48 to 30 B.C.

cler·gy (klur′jē) *n. pl.,* **cler·gies.** persons ordained for religious service, such as ministers, priests, or rabbis.

cler·gy·man (klur′jē mən) *n. pl.,* **cler·gy·men** (klur′jē mən). a person ordained as a minister, priest, or rabbi; member of the clergy.

cler·gy·wom·an (klur′jē woom′ən) *n. pl.,* **cler·gy·wom·en** (klur′jē wim′ən). a woman member of the clergy.

cler·ic (kler′ik) *n.* a clergyman.

cler·i·cal (kler′i kəl) *adj.* **1.** of or relating to clerks or office workers or their work: *Typing is a clerical job.* **2.** of or characteristic of a member of the clergy or the clergy: *a clerical collar.* —**cler′i·cal·ly,** *adv.*

clerk (klurk) *n.* **1.** a person employed in an office to keep records, accounts, or files, and do other general office work, such as typing. **2.** a person employed in a store to sell goods; salesclerk. **3.** an official who keeps records and does routine business, as in a court of law or legislature: *a county clerk, a town clerk.* —*v.i.* to work or act as a clerk: *He clerks in a sporting goods store.*

Cleve·land (klēv′lənd) *n.* **1. (Stephen) Grover.** 1837–1908, the twenty-second and twenty-fourth president of the United States, from 1885 to 1889 and from 1893 to 1897. **2.** the largest city in Ohio, in the northeastern part of the state, on Lake Erie. Pop. (1970), 750,903.

clev·er (klev′ər) *adj.* **1.** mentally sharp and alert; quick-witted; shrewd: *a clever young man.* **2.** showing skill or mental sharpness; shrewd: *a clever scheme, a clever remark.* **3.** having or showing skill in doing something, especially with the hands: *He's very clever at making things out of wood.* —**clev′er·ly,** *adv.* —**clev′er·ness,** *n.*

clew (klōō) *n. British.* another spelling of **clue.**

cli·ché (klē shā′) *n.* an expression, phrase, or idea that has lost its originality or effect because it has been used too much. *As pretty as a picture* is a cliché.

click (klik) *n.* a light, sharp, often metallic sound: *We heard the click of his key in the lock.* —*v.t.* to cause to make a click or clicks: *The officer clicked his heels together*

C

and bowed to the ladies. —*v.i.* **1.** to move with a click; produce a click or clicks: *Her high heels clicked on the sidewalk.* **2.** *Informal.* to become understandable; make sense: *Everything suddenly clicked in the mystery story when I read the last chapter.* **3.** *Slang.* to be a success: *The new play clicked.*

cli·ent (klī'ənt) *n.* **1.** a person, group, or company that uses the professional services of another: *a lawyer's clients.* **2.** a customer of any business.

cli·en·tele (klī'ən tel') *n.* clients or customers as a group: *That restaurant caters to a wealthy clientele.*

cliff (klif) *n.* a high, steep face of rock or earth.

cliff dweller *also,* **Cliff Dweller.** a member of a tribe of prehistoric Indians who built their houses in ledges along the walls of cliffs. They were the ancestors of the Pueblo Indians of the southwestern United States.

cliff-hang·er (klif'hang'ər) *also,* **cliff·hang·er.** *n.* **1.** an exciting adventure serial whose parts or installments always end at a point full of suspense. **2.** any contest or situation having an outcome that is not known or settled until the very end: *The election was very close and turned into a real cliff-hanger.*

cliff swallow, a swallow that lives in colonies in mud nests under the eaves of buildings or against cliffs.

Clif·ton (klif'tən) *n.* a city in northeastern New Jersey. Pop. (1970), 82,437.

cli·mac·tic (klī mak'tik) *adj.* of, relating to, or forming a climax: *The third scene was a climactic one.*

cli·mate (klī'mit) *n.* **1.** the typical weather conditions of a particular place or region, usually considered in terms of average temperature, humidity, rainfall, and wind conditions. **2.** any place or region considered in terms of its typical weather conditions: *Florida has a mild climate.* **3.** the outlook, mood, or trend among a group of people; atmosphere: *The climate at school was one of excitement before the game.*

cli·mat·ic (klī mat'ik) *adj.* of or relating to climate. —**cli·mat'i·cal·ly,** *adv.*

cli·ma·tol·o·gy (klī'mə tol'ə jē) *n.* the branch of science dealing with the study of climate.

cli·max (klī'maks) *n. pl.,* **cli·max·es. 1.** the highest point, as of development, interest, or excitement: *The judge's appointment to the Supreme Court was the climax of his career.* **2.** the turning point or point of highest interest or excitement in the action or theme of a play, book, or similar work: *The climax in the film came when the detective discovered who the murderer was.* —*v.t.* to bring to a climax: *The evening was climaxed by the presentation of the awards.* —*v.i.* to reach a climax.

climb (klīm) *v.i.* **1.** to move upward or toward the top of something by using the hands or feet: *He climbed to the top of the tree.* **2.** to move or go by using the hands or feet: *to climb through a window, to climb into bed.* **3.** to go upward or move higher as if by climbing; rise: *The plane climbed to an altitude of 12,000 feet. Prices climbed last year.* **4.** to grow in an upward direction by twining around or clinging to another object for support: *The vines climbed up the side of the cottage.* —*v.t.* to move toward the top of (something) by using the hands or feet: *The workman climbed the ladder.* —*n.* **1.** the act or process of climbing: *Their climb up the hill took an hour.* **2.** the distance to be climbed: *It's only a short climb to the top from here.* **3.** a place or thing to be climbed: *That cliff is a dangerous climb.*

climb·er (klī'mər) *n.* **1.** a person or thing that climbs. **2.** any climbing plant, such as ivy.

clime (klīm) *n. Archaic.* country; region: . . . *that sweet golden clime where the traveler's journey is done* (William Blake).

clinch (klinch) *v.t.* **1.** to make final and definite; settle conclusively: *to clinch a business deal.* **2.** to fasten firmly, as a driven nail or bolt, by bending over or flattening the point that sticks out. **3.** to fasten (objects) together by using nails, bolts, or similar fastenings. Also *(defs. 2, 3),* **clench.** —*v.i.* to grasp or hold an opponent's arms or body, especially in boxing. —*n. pl.,* **clinch·es. 1.** the act of clinching: *The boxers went into a clinch.* **2.** a kind of knot in which the loose end is lashed back through a loop.

Clinch *(def. 2)*

clinch·er (klin'chər) *n.* **1.** a person or thing that clinches, especially a nail made for clinching. **2.** *Informal.* a final or deciding point, as one made in an argument: *Of all the reasons for not moving there, the high rent is the clincher.*

cling (kling) *v.i.,* **clung, cling·ing. 1.** to stick closely, as if glued: *The wet shirt clung to his back.* **2.** to hold tightly, as by grasping or embracing: *The shivering children clung to each other in fear.* **3.** to be or stay near, as if attached: *The car clung to the road as it rounded the curve.* **4.** to remain attached: *to cling to a routine, to cling to a belief.* —*n.* see **clingstone.**

cling·stone (kling'stōn') *n.* a fruit, especially a peach, in which the flesh or pulp is not easily separated from the pit or stone.

clin·ic (klin'ik) *n.* **1.** a place connected with a hospital or medical school, where patients come for treatment, often at a low cost or without charge. **2.** a place where specialists treat or study certain types of patients or certain diseases: *a maternity clinic, a cancer clinic.* **3.** a place offering advice or instruction in some field: *a reading clinic.* **4.** instruction given by doctors to medical students, in which a patient is examined and treated in the presence of the students.

clin·i·cal (klin'i kəl) *adj.* **1.** of or relating to a clinic. **2.** based on or dealing with the direct observation and treatment of patients rather than laboratory experimentation: *clinical psychology.* **3.** scientific and unemotional: *The novel contained a clinical description of the horrors of war.* —**clin'i·cal·ly,** *adv.*

clink (klingk) *v.t.* to cause to make a light, sharp, ringing sound: *They clinked their glasses together in a toast.* —*v.i.* to make a light, sharp ringing sound: *The coins clinked in his pocket as he walked.* —*n.* a light, sharp, ringing sound.

clink·er (kling'kər) *n.* **1.** a stony mass consisting of impurities that remain after coal is burned. **2.** *Slang.* a mistake; error.

Clin·ton, De Witt (klin'tən; di wit') 1769–1828, U.S. political leader who sponsored the building of the Erie Canal.

clip¹ (klip) *v.,* **clipped, clip·ping.** —*v.t.* **1.** to cut, with shears or scissors; remove or detach by cutting: *She clipped off the loose strands of thread when she finished sewing. He clipped the article out of the newspaper.* **2.** to make shorter by cutting; trim: *to clip one's nails, to clip a hedge.* **3.** to trim or cut the hair or fleece of: *to clip a poodle, to*

at; āpe; cär; end; mē; it; īce; hot; ōld; fôrk; wood; fo͞ol; oil; out; up; turn; sing; thin; *this;* hw in white; zh in treasure. The symbol ə stands for the sound of a in about, e in taken, i in pencil, o in lemon, and u in circus.

clip sheep. **4.** to make shorter: *The hero's last speech was clipped because the play was too long.* **5.** *Informal.* to hit with a quick, sharp blow: *to clip someone on the chin.* —*v.i.* to cut or trim. —*n.* **1.** the act of clipping. **2.** the amount of wool obtained from sheep at one shearing or during one season. **3.** *Informal.* a rate or pace: *The bus moved along at a rapid clip.* **4.** *Informal.* a quick, sharp blow or punch. [Old Norse *klippa* to cut off, cut short.]

clip² (klip) *n.* **1.** a device that grips or holds articles together: *a paper clip, a money clip.* **2.** a piece of jewelry that fastens with a clip or clasp: *a tie clip.* **3.** a holder for ammunition for certain firearms that fits into the magazine. —*v.t.,* **clipped, clip·ping.** to fasten with a clip: *He clipped the letters together.* [Old English *clyppan* to embrace, grip.]

clip·board (klip′bôrd′) *n.* a board with a spring clip at one end for holding paper or a pad, used as a portable writing surface.

clip·per (klip′ər) *n.* **1.** *also,* **clippers.** a tool or instrument for clipping, cutting, or shearing: *a barber's clippers.* **2.** a fast-sailing cargo ship developed in the United States in the nineteenth century, having a narrow beam and usually, three square-rigged masts. **3.** a person who clips.

Clipper

clip·ping (klip′ing) *n.* **1.** a piece that is cut off or out, especially an item cut from a newspaper or magazine. **2.** the act of cutting or trimming.

clique (klēk, klik) *n.* a small group of people friendly with each other, who stick together and are often unfriendly to outsiders.

cli·quish (klē′kish, klik′ish) *adj.* **1.** likely to form and stay within cliques: *The club members are all very cliquish.* **2.** having the characteristics of a clique: *a cliquish group.* —**cli′quish·ly,** *adv.* —**cli′quish·ness,** *n.*

clo·a·ca (klō ā′kə) *n. pl.,* **clo·a·cae** (klō ā′sē). a chamber found in birds, fish, reptiles, amphibians, and some other animals, into which the intestinal, urinary, and genital canals open.

cloak (klōk) *n.* **1.** a loose outer garment, with or without sleeves. **2.** something that covers or hides: *The robbery took place under the cloak of darkness.* —*v.t.* **1.** to cover with a cloak: *The actor cloaked himself in black.* **2.** to cover; hide; disguise: *The diplomats cloaked their meetings with the pretense of gathering socially.*

cloak·room (klōk′rōōm′, klōk′room′) *n.* a room in a restaurant, theater, or other place, where coats, hats, umbrellas, and the like may be left temporarily; coatroom.

clob·ber (klob′ər) *v.t. Slang.* **1.** to hit with great force. **2.** to defeat severely.

clock¹ (klok) *n.* a device for measuring and showing time, usually with hands that pass over a dial marked to show hours or minutes. A clock is not meant to be worn or carried about by a person as a watch is. —*v.t.* to find out or record the performance or speed of, as with a stopwatch; time: *to clock a race, to clock a runner.* [Middle Dutch *clocke* a clock, bell.]

clock² (klok) *n.* an ornamental design woven or embroidered on the side of a sock or stocking. [Probably from *clock¹*; because this design was originally shaped like a bell.]

clock·wise (klok′wīz′) *adv., adj.* in the direction in which the hands of a clock move.

clock·work (klok′wurk′) *n.* a mechanism made up of gears, wheels, and springs, such as that which runs a clock or other mechanical device.

like clockwork. with great regularity, precision, and smoothness: *We had rehearsed so long and so carefully that the first-night performance went like clockwork.*

clod (klod) *n.* **1.** a lump or mass, especially of earth or clay. **2.** a dull, awkward, or stupid person.

clod·hop·per (klod′hop′ər) *n.* **1.** *Informal.* a clumsy, awkward boor. **2. clodhoppers.** large, heavy shoes or boots.

clog (klog) *v.,* **clogged, clog·ging.** —*v.t.* **1.** to block or stop up: *Dirt clogged the pipes. Heavy traffic clogged the roads.* **2.** to hinder the progress or action of: *The snow clogged traffic.* —*v.i.* to become blocked or stopped up. —*n.* **1.** a shoe or sandal with a thick sole of wood or cork. **2.** anything that hinders or blocks progress or action.

clois·ter (klois′tər) *n.* **1.** a place of religious seclusion, such as a monastery. **2.** a covered walk along the wall or walls of a building, having a row of columns on one side. —*v.t.* to shut away in a quiet place.

clone (klōn) *n.* any of a group of genetically identical organisms reproduced asexually from a single ancestor. —*v.i., v.t.* to grow or cause to grow as a clone.

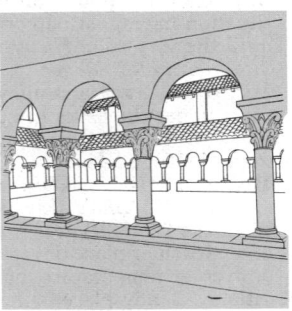
Cloister

close (*v., n. def. 1,* klōz; *adj., adv., n. def. 2,* klōs) *v.,* **closed, clos·ing.** —*v.t.* **1.** to move (something) so as to block or cover up an entrance, passage, or opening; shut: *to close a window, to close one's mouth.* **2.** to bring together the parts of so as to leave no opening or to form a whole: *to close a book. The troops closed ranks.* **3.** to fill or block; stop up: *Rocks from the landslide closed the mountain pass.* **4.** to keep or stop from operating: *The principal closed the school because of the blizzard.* **5.** to bring to an end; finish: *The speaker closed her lecture with a joke.* —*v.i.* **1.** to become shut: *The door closed with a bang.* **2.** to stop operation: *Banks close on legal holidays.* **3.** to come to an end; finish: *This story closes happily.* **4.** to come together, as parts of a whole: *The wound closed up after a week.* —*adj.,* **clos·er, clos·est. 1.** with little space or time between; near: *Our house is close to the school. This cloth has a close weave. Spring vacation is close.* **2.** not distant in relation, degree, or condition: *Michael's parents and mine are close relatives. The Spanish language is close to Italian.* **3.** attached or marked by strong affection or loyalty: *a close friend.* **4.** very much like another: *a close copy, a close resemblance.* **5.** careful and strict; exact; thorough: *Pay close attention to what I say. The police carried out a close investigation of the crime.* **6.** decided by a narrow margin: *a close race.* **7.** fitting tightly: *a close fit, close quarters.* **8.** lacking fresh or freely blowing air; stifling; stuffy: *It's very close in this room.* **9.** carefully guarded: *a close secret.* **10.** stingy: *She was never close with money.* —*adv.* in a close position or manner: *He held the child close in his arms. You're not parked close enough to the curb.* —*n.* **1.** end; finish: *We returned to our homes at the close of day.* **2.** an enclosed place, especially enclosed land beside a cathedral or other building. —**close·ly** (klōs′lē), *adv.* —**close·ness** (klōs′nis), *n.*

to close in or **to close in on.** to come near and surround: *Government frigates closed in on the pirate ship.*

C

to close out. to sell of (merchandise), usually at much lower prices: *The department store was closing out its summer clothes.*

close call (klōs) *Informal.* a narrow escape, as from danger or harm. Also, **close shave.**

closed circuit **1.** an electric circuit through which current can flow without interruption. **2.** a television system in which signals are sent out, usually by a cable, to a limited and selected number of receivers. Also (*def. 2*), **closed-circuit television.** —**closed´-cir´cuit,** *adj.*

closed shop, a factory or place of business in which only union members are hired and employed.

close-fist·ed (klōs´fis´tid) *adj.* stingy; miserly: *The close-fisted man wouldn't give a dime to charity.*

close-grained (klōs´grānd´) *adj.* having fine and closely arranged fibers, crystals, or particles: *close-grained wood.*

close-mouthed (klōs´mouthd´, klōs´moutht´) *adj.* not talking much; reserved; secretive: *He is very close-mouthed about his family.*

close·out (klōz´out´) also, **close-out.** *n.* a sale in which merchandise is sold at much lower prices: *The furniture store is having a closeout on rugs.*

close shave *Informal.* another term for **close call.**

clos·et (kloz´it) *n.* **1.** a small room or recess, usually with a door, for storing clothing. **2.** a cabinet, enclosed space, or small room for storing household utensils, food, or other articles: *a broom closet, a china closet.* **3.** a small, private room, especially one used for prayer or study. —*v.t.* to shut up in a room, as if for a conference or private talk: *The general was closeted with his officers, making plans for the attack.*

close-up (klōs´up´) *n.* **1.** a photograph, taken at close range or with a telescopic lens: *The toothpaste advertisement showed a close-up of two smiling people.* **2.** a close or detailed view or look: *a close-up of a problem.*

clo·sure (klō´zhər) *n.* **1.** the act of closing or the state of being closed. **2.** something that closes or shuts. **3.** another word for **cloture.**

clot (klot) *n.* a mass or lump formed by the thickening of a liquid: *a clot of blood.* —*v.,* **clot·ted, clot·ting.** —*v.i.* to form into clots: *The blood from the wound clotted.* —*v.t.* to cause to form into clots.

cloth (klôth) *n. pl.,* **cloths** (klôthz, klôths). **1.** material made by weaving, knitting, braiding, or pressing textile fibers; fabric: *a bolt of cloth.* **2.** a piece of such fabric, used for a particular purpose: *Put a cloth on the table before you set it.* **3. the cloth.** the clergy: *He is a man of the cloth.*

clothe (klōth) *v.t.,* **clothed** or **clad, cloth·ing.** **1.** to put clothes on; dress: *The baby was warmly clothed in a snowsuit.* **2.** to provide with clothes: *It takes a good deal of money to feed and clothe a large family.* **3.** to cover as if with clothing: *Snow clothed the field.* **4.** to have as a quality; endow: *The judge was clothed with dignity.*

clothes (klōz, klōthz) *n.,pl.* **1.** articles of clothing. **2.** see **bedclothes.**

clothes·horse (klōz´hôrs´, klōthz´hôrs´) *n.* **1.** a frame on which clothes are hung to dry or air. **2.** *Informal.* a person who takes great pleasure in owning and wearing many fashionable clothes.

clothes·line (klōz´līn´, klōthz´līn´) *n.* a rope or wire on which clothes and other laundry are hung to dry or air.

clothes moth, a small moth whose larva feeds on wool, fur, and other materials.

clothes·pin (klōz´pin´, klōthz´pin´) *n.* a clamp or forked piece of wood or plastic used to fasten clothes on a line.

clothes tree, an upright pole with hooks or pegs near the top on which to hang clothes.

cloth·ier (klōth´yər) *n.* a person who sells or makes cloth or clothing.

cloth·ing (klō´thing) *n.* **1.** articles worn to protect, cover, or adorn the body; clothes; garments. **2.** any covering.

clo·ture (klō´chər) *n.* a method of ending debate in a legislative body in order to bring a question to a vote. Also, **closure.**

cloud (kloud) *n.* **1.** a mass of water vapor or ice particles floating in the air high above the earth. **2.** any similar mass, as of smoke or steam: *The cowboys rode off in a cloud of dust.* **3.** a great number or mass of persons or things in motion: *A cloud of migrating birds filled the sky.* **4.** something that darkens, threatens, or troubles: *A cloud of gloom settled over the school when the team lost the championship.* —*v.t.* **1.** to cover with a cloud or clouds: *Mists clouded the sun. Smoke from the burning house clouded the street.* **2.** to darken or make dim or confused: *His judgment was clouded by the jealousy he felt.* **3.** to make gloomy or troubled: *Anger clouded his face.* **4.** to put under suspicion; sully: *The rumors clouded his reputation.* —*v.i.* to become cloudy: *The sky clouded up. Mother's face clouded with worry.* —**cloud´like´** *adj.*

cloud·burst (kloud´burst´) *n.* a sudden, heavy rainfall.

cloud chamber, a device used to make the paths of subatomic particles visible by means of a gas supersaturated with water vapor. The vapor condenses as the particles move through it, forming a cloudlike trail. Cloud chambers are used in the study of nuclear physics.

cloud·less (kloud´lis) *adj.* without clouds; clear; bright: *The sun shone brightly in the cloudless sky.* —**cloud´-less·ly,** *adv.* —**cloud´less·ness,** *n.*

cloud seeding, any of various methods for producing rain artificially by scattering particles, usually of dry ice or a chemical, into clouds.

cloud·y (klou´dē) *adj.,* **cloud·i·er, cloud·i·est.** **1.** covered with or hidden by clouds; overcast: *a cloudy sky.* **2.** having little sunshine: *a cloudy day.* **3.** not clear: *a cloudy pond, cloudy ideas.* —**cloud´i·ly,** *adv.* —**cloud´i·ness,** *n.*

clout (klout) *Informal. n.* a heavy blow, as with the hand: *During the scuffle, he received a clout on the side of the head.* —*v.t.* to hit, as with the hand.

clove¹ (klōv) *n.* **1.** the dried, unopened flower bud of a tropical evergreen tree, used as a spice. **2.** the tree bearing this bud, having oval, oblong leaves. [Old French *clou* (*de girofle*) literally, nail (of a clove tree); because this bud resembles a nail.]

clove² (klōv) *n.* one of the smaller sections of certain large plant bulbs: *a clove of garlic.* [Old English *clufu.*]

clove³ (klōv) a past tense of **cleave¹.**

clove hitch, a knot used to tie a rope around something, such as a spar or pole.

clo·ven (klō´vən) *v.* a past participle of **cleave¹.** —*adj.* split; divided: *the cloven hoof of a cow.*

clo·ver (klō´vər) *n.* any of a group of plants bearing leaves usually composed of three leaflets, and rounded heads or spikes of small red, white, yellow, or purple flowers, widely grown as food for cattle.

in clover. living in wealth and luxury: *After the success of his book the author was in clover.*

at; āpe; cär; end; mē; it; īce; hot; ōld; fôrk; wood; fōōl; oil; out; up; turn; sing; thin; this; hw in white; zh in treasure. The symbol ə stands for the sound of **a** in **a**bout, **e** in tak**e**n, **i** in penc**i**l, **o** in lem**o**n, and **u** in circ**u**s.

clo·ver·leaf (klō′vər lēf′) n. pl., **clo·ver·leaves** (klō′vər-lēvz). a highway intersection that consists of a series of curving ramps, usually shaped like a four-leaf clover, connecting highways crossing each other on different levels.

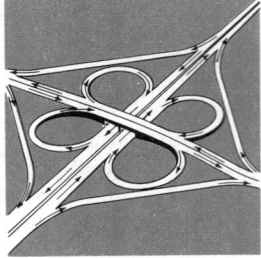

Cloverleaf

clown (kloun) n. **1.** a person in a circus, carnival, or similar show, who amuses the audience by playing tricks or jokes and is usually dressed in a ridiculous costume with funny make-up. **2.** any person who plays tricks or jokes: *He is the class clown.* —v.i. to act like a clown: *The boys stopped clowning when the teacher walked into the classroom.*

clown·ish (kloun′nish) adj. of or resembling a clown: *clownish behavior.* —**clown′ish·ly**, adv. —**clown′ish·ness**, n.

cloy (kloi) v.t. to make weary with too much of something pleasant: *All that cake will cloy your appetite.* —v.i. to weary from too much of something pleasant.

club (klub) n. **1.** a heavy stick, thicker at one end, used especially as a weapon. **2.** any of various sticks or bats used to hit a ball in certain games, such as golf. **3.** a group of people who meet together for pleasure or for some special purpose: *a social club, an athletic club.* **4.** a building or room where such a group meets. **5.a.** a playing card marked with one or more black figures shaped like this: (♣) **b. clubs.** the suit of such cards. —v., **clubbed, club·bing.** —v.t. to beat or strike with a club. —v.i. to unite for a common purpose.

club car, a railroad passenger car equipped with lounge chairs, card tables, and usually a bar or buffet.

club·foot (klub′foot′) n. pl., **club·feet. 1.** a condition in which the foot is deformed or twisted out of position, caused by abnormal development before birth. **2.** a deformed or twisted foot. —**club′foot′ed**, adj.

club·house (klub′hous′) n. pl., **club·hous·es** (klub′hou′ziz). a building used by a club.

club moss, a small evergreen plant that grows along the ground and bears small, upright branches covered with tiny, dark green leaves that look like pine needles.

club sandwich, a sandwich made with three slices of bread, usually toasted, and a filling of meat, lettuce, tomato, and a dressing.

club soda, another term for **soda water.**

cluck (kluk) n. **1.** a low sound made by a hen when sitting on eggs or calling her chicks. **2.** any similar sound. —v.i. **1.** to make the low sound of a hen. **2.** to make any similar sound. —v.t. to call or express by clucking.

clue (klōō) n. also, British. **clew.** a guide or key that aids in finding the solution to a problem or mystery: *The case stumped the police because they had few clues to follow.*

clump (klump) n. **1.** a small group of things of the same kind, gathered or lying close together: *The rabbit hopped out of a clump of bushes.* **2.** a thick mass or lump: *Clumps of earth clung to the roots of the plant.* **3.** a heavy, dull, thumping sound. —v.t. to gather or form into a clump. —v.i. to walk heavily and clumsily.

clum·sy (klum′zē) adj., **clum·si·er, clum·si·est. 1.** lacking grace or skill; awkward: *a clumsy dancer.* **2.** unskillfully or awkwardly shaped, done, or made: *clumsy boots, a clumsy remark.* —**clum′si·ly**, adv. —**clum′si·ness**, n.

clung (klung) the past tense and past participle of **cling.**

clus·ter (klus′tər) n. **1.** a group of things of the same kind growing or situated together: *Grapes grow in a cluster. The ring had a cluster of pearls.* **2.** any group of similar persons

or things: *There were clusters of people waiting for the parade to come.* —v.i. to group or form into a cluster or clusters: *The children clustered around the Christmas tree.*

clutch[1] (kluch) v.t. to grasp or hold tightly or firmly: *The little boy clutched the money in his hand on his way to the grocery store.* —v.i. to try to grasp or seize (with *at*): *He clutched at the railing as he started to fall.* —n. pl., **clutch·es. 1.** a strong hold; grip: *He felt a clutch on his arm.* **2.** a claw, paw, or hand that clutches: *The chicken could not escape from the clutches of the hawk.* **3. clutches.** control; power: *The messenger fell into the clutches of the enemy.* **4.** a device in a machine, such as an automobile, that connects or disconnects a motor to the drive shaft. **5.** the lever or pedal that operates such a device. **6.** *Informal.* a serious or crucial situation: *That player is at his best in the clutch.* [Old English *clyccan* to grasp or grip tightly.]

clutch[2] (kluch) n. pl., **clutch·es. 1.** the number of eggs laid at one time. **2.** a brood of chickens. [Earlier *cletch* a brood, from *cleck* to hatch.]

clut·ter (klut′ər) n. a confused or disorderly state or collection of things: *a clutter of papers on a street.* —v.t. to crowd or litter with a confused or disorderly collection of things: *The porch was cluttered with old newspapers.*

Clyde (klīd) n. a river in southwestern Scotland.

Cly·tem·nes·tra (klī′təm nes′trə) n. *Greek Legend.* the wife of Agamemnon, who killed him on his return from Troy and who was later killed by her son Orestes.

Cm, the symbol for curium.

cm, cm., centimeter; centimeters.

Co, the symbol for cobalt.

co- prefix **1.** with; together: *coexist.* **2.** fellow; joint: *copilot.* **3.** equally: *coextend.*

co., Co. 1. Company. **2.** County.

c.o. in care of. Also, **c/o.**

CO 1. Commanding Officer. **2.** conscientious objector.

coach (kōch) n. pl., **coach·es. 1.** a large, four-wheeled closed carriage drawn by horses, with seats inside for passengers and a raised seat outside for the driver. **2.** a railroad passenger car. **3.** a bus. **4.** a class of passenger accommodations offering the lowest rates for traveling, as on trains or airplanes. **5.** a teacher or trainer, as of an athlete or athletic team, singer, actor, or dancer: *a football coach.* —v.t. to act as a coach to; train or teach: *to coach a swimming team.* —v.i. to act as a coach.

Coach

coach·man (kōch′mən) n. pl., **coach·men** (kōch′mən). a person who drives a coach or carriage.

co·ad·ju·tor (kō aj′ə tər) n. **1.** an assistant; helper. **2.** a bishop appointed to assist another bishop.

co·ag·u·lant (kō ag′yə lənt) n. a substance that causes a liquid to coagulate.

co·ag·u·late (kō ag′yə lāt′) v., **co·ag·u·lat·ed, co·ag·u·lat·ing.** —v.t. to change (something) from a liquid into a thickened mass; clot. —v.i. to become changed from a liquid into a thickened mass. —**co·ag′u·la′tion**, n.

coal (kōl) n. **1.** a black or dark brown substance that burns easily and is widely used as a fuel. It is formed mostly of plant matter that has been buried deep in the earth for centuries and has undergone physical and chemical change because of great heat and pressure. **2.** a piece of this substance. **3.** any piece of fuel, such as wood or coal, that is glowing or burned. —v.t. to provide with coal: *to coal a ship.* —v.i. to take on a supply of coal.

coal·er (kō′lər) *n.* **1.** a ship or railroad that carries coal. **2.** a person who sells or supplies coal.

co·a·lesce (kō′ə les′) *v.i.,* **co·a·lesced, co·a·lesc·ing. 1.** to grow together so as to form one body; fuse: *The two parts of the broken bone coalesced.* **2.** to unite, as into one unit or organization; combine: *The factions coalesced to form a new political party.* —**co′a·les′cence,** *n.*

coal gas 1. a mixture of gases, made up chiefly of hydrogen and methane, produced by heating bituminous coal without air. It is used especially in open hearth furnaces and as a source of such compounds as ammonia and benzene. **2.** the gas given off by burning coal.

co·a·li·tion (kō ə lish′ən) *n.* an alliance of statesmen, political parties, or nations for some special purpose: *a liberal coalition.*

coal oil, another term for **kerosene.**

coal scuttle, a pail or other container, often with a wide, projecting lip, for carrying or holding coal.

coal tar, a black, sticky substance left after heating bituminous coal without air, used in many synthetic products, such as dyes, nylon, aspirin, and plastics.

coarse (kôrs) *adj.,* **coars·er, coars·est. 1.** lacking refinement or delicacy; crude; vulgar: *coarse behavior, coarse language.* **2.** lacking fineness of texture; thick or rough: *coarse cloth, coarse skin.* **3.** made of large parts or particles: *coarse sand.* **4.** of inferior or poor quality or worth. —**coarse′ly,** *adv.* —**coarse′ness,** *n.*

coars·en (kôr′sən) *v.t.* to make coarse: *Years of hard work had coarsened his hands.* —*v.i.* to become coarse.

coast (kōst) *n.* **1.** the land next to the sea: *Pirates roamed the coast, looking for victims to rob.* **2. the Coast.** a region of the United States bordering the Pacific Ocean. **3.** a slide down a hill or similar incline, as on a sled. —*v.i.* **1.** to ride or slide along an incline by the force of gravity: *to coast down a hill on a sled.* **2.** to continue to move after power has been shut off: *The car coasted after we turned off the engine.* **3.** to advance or move along without making any effort: *He tried to coast through high school.* **4.** to sail along or near a coast. —*v.t.* to sail along or near the coast of.

coast·al (kōst′əl) *adj.* of, at, near, or along a coast: *coastal waters.*

coast·er (kōs′tər) *n.* **1.** a small mat or tray placed under a glass or bottle to protect the surface beneath. **2.** a ship that engages in trade along a coast. **3.** a sled or toboggan.

Coast Guard 1. a military service responsible for preserving safety and order along the coasts and inland waterways of the United States. **2. coast guard.** any similar military service.

coast·line (kōst′līn′) *n.* the outline or contour of a coast.

coast·ward (kōst′wərd) *adj.* directed toward the coast: *a coastward course.* —*adv. also,* **coast·wards.** toward the coast: *to drift coastward.*

coast·wise (kōst′wīz′) *adj.* following or carried on along the coast: *coastwise trade.* —*adv.* by way of or along the coast.

coat (kōt) *n.* **1.** an outer garment with sleeves, usually designed to be worn outdoors over other clothing. **2.** a natural, external covering, such as the hair or fur of an animal: *A healthy dog usually has a glossy coat.* **3.** any layer that covers a surface: *a coat of paint.* —*v.t.* to cover with a layer: *The stove was coated with grease.*

co·a·ti (kō ä′tē) *n. pl.,* **co·a·tis.** an animal resembling a raccoon

Coati

and having a long body, yellowish-brown, gray, or red fur, a long, striped tail, and a flexible snout. It is found in Central and South America. Also, **co·a·ti·mun·di** (kō ä′tē mun′dē).

coat·ing (kō′ting) *n.* a layer covering a surface: *A thin coating of dust covered the furniture.*

coat of arms *pl.,* **coats of arms. 1.** a group of designs and figures arranged on a shield or other surface, serving as the emblem of some person, family, or institution. **2.** a shield, or a drawing of a shield, marked with such an emblem.

coat of mail *pl.,* **coats of mail.** a shirt or coat made of chainmail, formerly worn as armor.

coat·room (kōt′rōōm′, kōt′-room′) *n.* another word for **cloakroom.**

Coat of arms

co·au·thor (kō ô′thər) *n.* an author who writes with another author. —*v.t.* to write with another author: *The two writers coauthored a series of articles about colonial American history.*

coax (kōks) *v.t.* **1.** to persuade or try to persuade, as by flattery, pleasant manners, or soft, gentle speech: *He always coaxes people to do things his way.* **2.** to get by coaxing: *He coaxed extra money from his father.* —**coax′er,** *n.*

co·ax·i·al cable (kō ak′sē əl) a high-frequency telephone, telegraph, and television cable for sending out thousands of electronic signals at the same time, consisting of one or more thin metal tubes, each of which has a single wire running through it.

cob (kob) *n.* **1.** see **corncob** (*def. 1*). **2.** a thickset horse with short legs.

co·balt (kō′bôlt) *n.* a hard silver-white or pinkish metallic element, similar to nickel and iron, used especially in alloys and as a coloring agent for glass and ceramics. Symbol: **Co**

cobalt blue 1. a deep blue pigment made from cobalt. **2.** a deep blue color.

cobalt 60, a radioactive isotope of cobalt, used in medicine.

cob·ble[1] (kob′əl) *v.t.,* **cob·bled, cob·bling.** to mend or make (shoes or boots). [Probably from *cobbler.*]

cob·ble[2] (kob′əl) *n.* a cobblestone. —*v.t.,* **cob·bled, cob·bling.** to pave with cobblestones. [From dialectal *cob* lump; of uncertain origin.]

cob·bler (kob′lər) *n.* **1.** a person whose work is mending or making shoes. **2.** a fruit pie baked in a deep dish, having no bottom crust and a thick top crust.

cob·ble·stone (kob′əl stōn′) *n.* a naturally rounded stone, formerly used in paving streets.

co·bel·lig·er·ent (kō′bi lij′ər ənt) *n.* a nation that aids or cooperates with another in waging war, but is not bound by a formal alliance.

COBOL (kō′bôl′) *n.* a computer coding system designed for business use. [Short for *co*(mmon) *b*(usiness) *o*(riented) *l*(anguage).]

at; āpe; cär; end; mē; it; īce; hot; ōld; fôrk; wood; fōōl; oil; out; up; turn; sing; thin; **th**is; **hw** in white; **zh** in treasure. The symbol ə stands for the sound of **a** in about, **e** in taken, **i** in pencil, **o** in lemon, and **u** in circus.

co·bra (kō′brə) *n.* a large, poisonous snake found in Africa and Asia. When excited, it flattens its neck and raises its ribs so that its head takes on the appearance of a hood.

cob·web (kob′web′) *n.*
1. a web spun by a spider.
2. anything like a spider's web.

co·caine (kō kān′, kō′kān) *also,* **co·cain.** *n.* a habit-forming drug obtained from the leaves of a South American shrub, used especially as a local anesthetic.

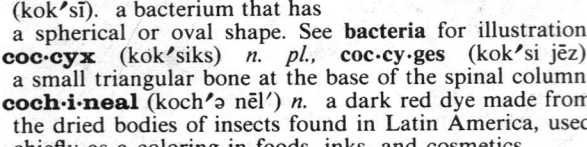
Cobra

coc·cus (kok′əs) *n. pl.,* **coc·ci** (kok′sī). a bacterium that has a spherical or oval shape. See **bacteria** for illustration.

coc·cyx (kok′siks) *n. pl.,* **coc·cy·ges** (kok′si jēz). a small triangular bone at the base of the spinal column.

coch·i·neal (koch′ə nēl′) *n.* a dark red dye made from the dried bodies of insects found in Latin America, used chiefly as a coloring in foods, inks, and cosmetics.

coch·le·a (kok′lē ə) *n. pl.,* **coch·le·ae** (kok′lē ē′). the tube of the inner ear, shaped somewhat like a snail shell, containing the sensory ends of the auditory nerve.

cock[1] (kok) *n.* **1.** a male chicken; rooster. **2.** the male of various other birds. **3.** the hammer of a firearm. **4.** the position into which the hammer of a firearm is brought when pulled back for firing. **5.** a device, as a faucet or valve, used to control the flow of a liquid or gas. —*v.t.* to pull back the hammer of (a firearm) to a firing position: *to cock a pistol.* [Old English *cocc* a male bird.]

cock[2] (kok) *v.t.* to turn up or upward or tilt to one side, especially in a jaunty, or lively way: *The dog cocked his ears when I whistled.* —*n.* an upward turn or tilt to one side: *the cock of a hat.* [From *cock*[1]; referring to the movement of a cock's head and chest when he crows.]

cock[3] (kok) *n.* a small, conical haystack. —*v.t.* to arrange in such stacks. [Possibly of Scandinavian origin.]

cock·ade (ko kād′) *n.* a knot of ribbon or similar ornament worn as a badge or sign of rank, especially on a hat.

cock·a·too (kok′ə tōō′) *n. pl.,* **cock·a·toos.** any of various crested parrots of Australia, the East Indies, and southwestern Asia, having white feathers.

cock·a·trice (kok′ə tris′) *n.* a legendary serpent, supposedly hatched from a cock's egg, whose glance was said to cause death.

cock·boat (kok′bōt′) *n.* a small rowboat, especially one on a ship.

cock·crow (kok′krō′) *n.* the time when roosters begin to crow; dawn.

cocked hat, a hat with the brim turned up so as to form two or more points.

Cocked hat

cock·er (kok′ər) *n.* a person who breeds fighting cocks.

cock·er·el (kok′ər əl) *n.* a young rooster less than one year old.

cocker spaniel, a spaniel having a short body, long, silky hair, and drooping ears, kept as a bird dog or house pet.

cock·eyed (kok′īd′) *adj.*
1. cross-eyed. **2.** *Slang.* tilted to one side; off-center: *Your cap is cockeyed.* **3.** *Slang.* absurd; foolish: *a cockeyed idea.*

cock·fight (kok′fīt′) *n.* a fight between gamecocks that are often fitted with spurs.

Cocker spaniel

cock·horse (kok′hôrs′) *n.* another word for **rocking horse.**

cock·le[1] (kok′əl) *n.* **1.** a shellfish related to the clam whose flesh is used for food. It is enclosed in two heart-shaped shells. **2.** see **cockleshell.** **3.** a wrinkle; pucker. —*v.t.,* **cock·led, cock·ling.** to wrinkle; pucker. [Old French *coquille* shell.]
to warm the cockles of one's heart. to make one very happy or pleased.

cock·le[2] (kok′əl) *n.* any of several weeds that grow in grain fields. [Old English *coccel.*]

cock·le·bur (kok′əl bur′) *n.* any of a group of weeds found widely in North America and Mexico and bearing spiny burs.

cock·le·shell (kok′əl shel′) *n.* **1.** the shell of a cockle. **2.** a small, light, shallow boat.

cock·ney (kok′nē) *also,* **Cock·ney.** *n. pl.,* **cock·neys.**
1. a person who was born or is living in the eastern district of London, England. **2.** the dialect spoken by cockneys. —*adj.* relating to cockneys or their dialect.

cock·pit (kok′pit′) *n.* **1.** the compartment in an airplane where the pilot and copilot sit. **2.** a pit or enclosed area for cockfights.

cock·roach (kok′rōch′) *n.* any of a group of brown or black insects, with oval, flattened bodies, bristly legs, and long antennae. Some species are common household pests.

cocks·comb (koks′kōm′) *n.* **1.** the comb or fleshy red crest on the head of a rooster. **2.** *also,* **coxcomb.** a jester's cap resembling this in shape. **3.** any of a group of plants having showy red, purple, or yellow flower spikes that resemble a rooster's comb.

cock·sure (kok′shoor′) *adj.* too confident or sure of oneself: *The conceited boy was cocksure that he would win.* —**cock′sure′ly,** *adv.* —**cock′sure′ness,** *n.*

cock·swain (kok′sən, kok′swān′) another spelling of **coxswain.**

cock·tail (kok′tāl′) *n.* **1.** an iced, alcoholic drink made by mixing liquor with flavorings, such as vermouth or fruit juices. **2.** any of various appetizers served at the beginning of a meal: *a shrimp cocktail.*

cock·y (kok′ē) *adj.,* **cock·i·er, cock·i·est.** *Informal.* too confident or sure of oneself; self-confident in a swaggering way: *That bully is a cocky boy.* —**cock′i·ly,** *adv.* —**cock′i·ness,** *n.*

co·co (kō′kō) *n. pl.,* **co·cos. 1.** see **coconut. 2.** see **coconut palm.**

co·coa (kō′kō) *n.* **1.** a brown powder made by drying, roasting, and grinding cacao seeds and removing the cocoa butter. It is used especially in making chocolate drinks. **2.** a chocolate drink made by mixing this powder with hot milk or water and sugar. **3.** a light, dull-brown color. —*adj.* having the color cocoa; light dull-brown.

cocoa butter, a yellowish-white fat obtained from cacao seeds, used in making chocolate, soap, and cosmetics.

co·co·nut (kō′kə nut′) *also,* **co·coa·nut.** *n.* **1.** the large, oval fruit of the coconut palm, having a smooth outer rind, a reddish-brown husk, and a hard inner shell lined with edible white meat and containing a milky fluid. **2.** the white meat of this fruit, often shredded for use in puddings, pies, and cakes. **3.** see **coconut palm.**

coconut oil, an oil obtained from the dried fruit of coconuts, used in making soap, shampoo, and many other products.

coconut palm, a tall palm tree with huge feathery leaves that bears coconuts.

co·coon (kə kōōn′) *n.* **1.** a protective case made of silk, leaves, or other materials that encloses the pupa of certain insects, such as the silkworm, while it is developing into an adult. **2.** any similar protective covering.

cod (kod) *n. pl.,* **cods** or **cod.** any of a group of food fish found in the colder northern waters of the Atlantic and Pacific Oceans. Also, **codfish.**

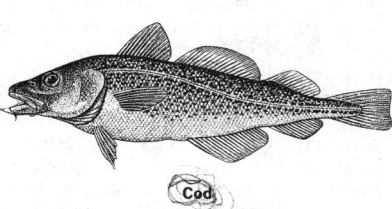

Cod

Cod, Cape (kod) a long, hook-shaped peninsula that is sixty-five miles long and is the easternmost part of Massachusetts.

c.o.d., C.O.D. collect on delivery.

co·da (kō′də) *n.* the passage at the end of a musical composition or movement that brings it to a formal close.

cod·dle (kod′əl) *v.t.,* **cod·dled, cod·dling.** **1.** to treat tenderly or too indulgently; pamper: *Even though she was an only child, her parents tried not to coddle her.* **2.** to cook gently in a liquid at or just below the boiling point; simmer: *to coddle eggs.*

code (kōd) *n.* **1.** a system of writing used to keep messages secret or brief, in which letters, words, numbers, or other symbols stand for the letters and words of the message: *During the war, all communications from headquarters were written in code.* **2.** a system of sending messages, in which sounds, light flashes, flags, or other signals stand for numbers, letters, or words: *In order to operate a telegraph, you must learn the code.* **3.** a collection of laws arranged in a systematic way: *the penal code.* **4.** any system or collection of principles and rules of conduct: *a moral code, a code of honor.* —*v.t.,* **cod·ed, cod·ing.** to put into the form of a code: *to code a message.*

co·deine (kō′dēn) *also,* **co·dein.** *n.* a habit-forming drug obtained from opium, used to relieve pain and coughing and to produce sleep.

cod·fish (kod′fish′) *n. pl.,* **cod·fish** or **cod·fish·es.** another word for **cod.**

codg·er (koj′ər) *n. Informal.* an odd or grumpy man, especially one who is old.

cod·i·cil (kod′ə sil) *n.* a part added to a will to add to, change, or explain something in it.

cod·i·fy (kod′ə fī′, kō′də fī′) *v.t.,* **cod·i·fied, cod·i·fy·ing.** to arrange in a systematic way; put into a code: *Napoleon Bonaparte codified the laws of France.* —**cod′i·fi·ca′tion,** *n.* —**cod′i·fi′er,** *n.*

cod·ling moth (kod′ling) a moth whose larvae destroy apples, pears, and other fruits.

cod-liv·er oil (kod′liv′ər) an oil obtained from the livers of cod and certain other fish, used as a source of vitamins A and D.

Co·dy, William Frederick (kō′dē) 1846–1917, U. S. scout and showman, known as **Buffalo Bill.**

co·ed (kō′ed′) *also,* **co-ed.** *Informal. n.* a female student, especially at a college. —*adj.* having both male and female students.

co·ed·u·ca·tion (kō′ej ə kā′shən) *n.* the education of both male and female students in the same school or college.

co·ed·u·ca·tion·al (kō′ej ə kā′shən əl) *adj.* educating male and female students together in the same school or college. —**co′ed·u·ca′tion·al·ly,** *adv.*

co·ef·fi·cient (kō′i fish′ənt) *n.* a number or algebraic expression put before and multiplying an algebraic expression. In $3x^2y$, 3 is the numerical coefficient of x^2y; in $3x^2(y + z)$, $3x^2$ is the coefficient of $(y + z)$.

coe·la·canth (sē′lə kanth′) *n.* a large, primitive fish having fleshy flippers shaped like paddles, found off the eastern coast of Africa. It is thought to be an important link in the evolution from sea to land animals.

coe·len·ter·ate (si len′tə rāt′) *n.* any of a group of animals having no backbone, including corals, jellyfish, and hydras, usually found in salt water. They have a body resembling a sac, with tentacles around a single mouth opening. —*adj.* belonging to or characteristic of this group.

co·erce (kō urs′) *v.t.,* **co·erced, co·erc·ing.** to force by violence or threats: *The pirates coerced their captives into serving them as slaves.* —**co·erc′er,** *n.*

co·er·cion (kō ur′shən) *n.* the use of force to compel or control: *The prisoner stated that the confession was obtained by coercion.*

co·er·cive (kō ur′siv) *adj.* tending or serving to coerce. —**co·er′cive·ly,** *adv.* —**co·er′cive·ness,** *n.*

co·e·val (kō ē′vəl) *adj.* of, belonging to, or living in the same age or time; contemporary.

co·ex·ist (kō′ig zist′) *v.i.* **1.** to exist in or at the same place or time as another: *Many species of animals coexisted in the jungle.* **2.** to live together peacefully, in spite of differences in policy or principle: *The two nations learned to coexist even though their systems of government were very different.* —**co′ex·ist′ence,** *n.* —**co′ex·ist′ent,** *adj.*

cof·fee (kô′fē) *n.* **1.** a dark brown beverage made from ground and roasted coffee beans and hot or boiling water. **2.** the coffee beans themselves, either whole or ground. **3.** any of a group of tropical evergreen shrubs and small trees that bear coffee beans. **4.** a rich, dark brown color. —*adj.* having the color coffee.

coffee bean, the seed of the coffee plant.

cof·fee·house (kô′fē hous′) *n. pl.,* **cof·fee·hous·es** (kô′fē hou′ziz). a place where coffee and other refreshments are served.

cof·fee·pot (kô′fē pot′) *n.* a container, usually with a cover, for making or serving coffee.

coffee shop, a restaurant, often having a counter, where coffee and food are served.

coffee table, a low table, usually placed in front of a sofa.

cof·fer (kô′fər) *n.* **1.** a box or chest, especially one used for holding money or other valuables. **2. coffers.** treasury; funds: *Years of war had emptied the coffers of the nation.*

cof·fer·dam (kô′fər dam′) *n.* a temporary watertight enclosure built in water and pumped dry so that foundations, bridge piers, or similar structures may be built.

cof·fin (kô′fin) *n.* a box or case into which a dead person is placed for burial.

cog (kog) *n.* **1.** one of a series of teeth on the rim of a wheel, that transmits or receives motion by locking into similar teeth on another wheel or on a track. **2.** see **cogwheel.**

co·gen·cy (kō′jən sē) *n.* the state or quality of being cogent.

co·gent (kō′jənt) *adj.* having the power to be convincing: *a cogent argument.* —**co′gent·ly,** *adv.*

cog·i·tate (koj′ə tāt′) *v.i.,* **cog·i·tat·ed, cog·i·tat·ing.** to think or consider carefully; meditate; ponder: *He cogitated a long time on the problem.* —**cog′i·ta′tion,** *n.*

co·gnac (kōn′yak) *n.* a brandy that is amber in color and has a mellow flavor. [From *Cognac,* a town in southwestern France, where it was originally made.]

at; āpe; cär; end; mē; it; īce; hot; ōld; fôrk; wood; fōōl; oil; out; up; turn; sing; thin; this; hw in white; zh in treasure. The symbol ə stands for the sound of **a** in about, **e** in taken, **i** in pencil, **o** in lemon, and **u** in circus.

cog·nate (kog′nāt) *adj.* **1.** related by having the same origin; coming from the same source: *cognate words, cognate languages.* **2.** related by having the same ancestor or parentage: *cognate families.* —*n.* a person or thing that is cognate: *The English word "father" and the Latin word "pater" are cognates.*

cog·ni·tion (kog nish′ən) *n.* the act or power of knowing or perceiving.

cog·ni·zance (kog′nə zəns) *n.* **1.** knowledge or perception: *That theory is beyond the cognizance of a child.* **2.** notice: *He took cognizance of those facts in making his decision.*

cog·ni·zant (kog′nə zənt) *adj.* having cognizance; aware: *After his injury, the man was barely cognizant of his surroundings.*

cog·no·men (kog nō′mən) *n.* **1.** a family name; surname. **2.** any name, especially a nickname.

cog·wheel (kog′hwēl′, kog′wēl′) *n.* a wheel with teeth on its rim, for transmitting or receiving motion.

co·here (kō hēr′) *v.i.,* **co·hered, co·her·ing.** **1.** to stick or hold together: *A mass of mud coheres.* **2.** to be logically connected or related.

co·her·ence (kō hēr′əns) *n.* **1.** logical connection: *There was no coherence to what the feverish old man tried to say.* **2.** the act of sticking or holding together. Also, **co·her·en·cy** (kō hēr′ən sē).

co·her·ent (kō hēr′ənt) *adj.* **1.** logically connected: *The terrified salesgirl could not give a coherent account of the robbery.* **2.** sticking or holding together. **3.** able to make sense or be understood; intelligible: *After the blow on his head, the man was barely coherent.* —**co·her′ent·ly,** *adv.*

co·he·sion (kō hē′zhən) *n.* **1.** the act or state of cohering: *There is cohesion between the bricks and the cement. The sentences in your essay lack cohesion.* **2.** the attraction between molecules of a substance, as a drop of water, that holds the substance together.

co·he·sive (kō hē′siv) *adj.* capable of, having, or causing cohesion. —**co·he′sive·ly,** *adv.* —**co·he′sive·ness,** *n.*

co·hort (kō′hôrt′) *n.* **1.** a companion, associate, or follower: *a thief and his cohorts.* **2.** any one of ten divisions that made up a legion in the ancient Roman army. **3.** any band, company, or group.

coif (koif) *n.* **1.** a cap that fits closely on the head. Some nuns wear coifs under their veils. Knights wore leather coifs under their helmets. **2.** see **coiffure.** —*v.t.* **1.** to cover with a coif. **2.** to dress or arrange (the hair).

coif·fure (kwä fyoor′) *n.* a way in which a woman's hair is worn or arranged: *The woman's elaborate coiffure was in keeping with her elegant gown.*

coil (koil) *n.* **1.** anything made up of a series of spirals or rings: *a coil of rope.* **2.** one of the spirals or rings of such a series. **3.** a pipe or a series of connected pipes arranged in rows, used to conduct heat or liquids, as in a radiator. **4.** any spiral wire for conducting electricity. —*v.i.* **1.** to form coils: *Ellen pinned her braids up so that they coiled around her head.* **2.** to move in a winding course: *The road coiled around the mountain.* —*v.t.* to wind in coils: *The sailor coiled the rope around the anchor.*

coin (koin) *n.* **1.** a piece of metal stamped with official government markings and of fixed weight and value, used as money. **2.** metal money. —*v.t.* **1.** to make (money) by stamping metal: *The government coins money at the mint.* **2.** to make (metal) into coins: *to coin copper into pennies.* **3.** to make up; invent: *to coin a new word.* —**coin′er,** *n.*

Cogwheels

coin·age (koi′nij) *n.* **1.** the act, process, or right of making coins. **2.** something that is coined; metal money. **3.** the act or process of making up or inventing: *"Skyjack" is a word of recent coinage.* **4.** something that is made up or invented.

● In language, **coinage** is the making up of a word. The word coinage is also used to describe the word that has been created. Coinage is used when we need a word to represent a new idea, object, or process for which there has not previously been a name. Such a coinage, or new word, can be created in various ways. Some coinages are created by combining foreign words, such as our word *telephone,* which was made by combining the Greek words for "far" and "sound." Existing English words can also be combined, such as in the word *railroad,* which is an eighteenth century coinage, and *motel,* which is a modern coinage made by blending "motor" and "hotel." Words are also coined from proper names, such as the electrical unit *watt,* which is a coinage from the name of the Scottish inventor James Watt. People also coin words in order to get a humorous or special effect in speaking or writing. Very often these words disappear from the language. Other such coinages, such as the words *discombobulate* and *hippie,* have become part of our language.

co·in·cide (kō′in sīd′) *v.t.,* **co·in·cid·ed, co·in·cid·ing.** **1.** to occur at the same time: *The football practice coincided with his appointment with the dentist.* **2.** to occupy the same area or place in space: *The two roads coincide after fifty miles.* **3.** to agree exactly; correspond: *Their views coincided.*

co·in·ci·dence (kō in′si dəns) *n.* **1.** a remarkable occurrence of events or circumstances at the same time and apparently by mere chance: *By coincidence I met my next-door neighbor in London last summer.* **2.** the fact or condition of coinciding: *The coincidence of two triangles.*

co·in·ci·dent (kō in′si dənt) *adj.* **1.** occurring at the same time: *Brad's birthday is coincident with his wedding anniversary.* **2.** occupying the same area or place in space: *coincident circles.* **3.** in exact agreement; corresponding: *She gave a description that was coincident with the facts.* —**co·in′ci·dent·ly,** *adv.*

co·in·ci·den·tal (kō in′si dent′əl) *adj.* characterized by, resulting from, or involving coincidence: *The police did not believe it was coincidental that the suspect was seen at the scene of the crime.* —**co·in′ci·den′tal·ly,** *adv.*

coke (kōk) *n.* a gray-black solid fuel that is obtained by heating bituminous coal in the absence of oxygen. It burns with much heat and little smoke or ash and is used especially in blast furnaces.

col-, a form of the prefix **com-** before *l,* as in *collateral.*

col. 1. column. **2.** color; colored. **3.** colony.

Col., Colonel.

col·an·der (kul′ən dər, kol′ən dər) *n.* a metal or plastic container with holes in the bottom and sides, used to rinse or drain liquid from food.

cold (kōld) *adj.* **1.** having a low temperature; lacking warmth or heat: *Canada has a cold climate. The ocean is cold today. My dinner is cold.* **2.** feeling a lack of warmth or heat; chilly: *The children were cold after playing outside.* **3.** not friendly or kind: *He is a cold person. She greeted us with a cold smile.* **4.** not fresh; stale or weak: *The bloodhounds could not follow the cold*

Colander

C

scent. **5.** *Informal.* unconscious: *Greg was knocked cold when he fell down the stairs.* —*n.* **1.** a lack of warmth or heat: *Many plants do not thrive in the cold.* **2.** the feeling caused by a lack of warmth or heat: *Cold always makes my teeth chatter.* **3.** a common illness marked by sneezing, coughing, and a running or stuffed nose. —*adv. Informal.* **1.** thoroughly; completely: *After studying for a week, I know this lesson cold.* **2.** without any knowledge or preparation ahead of time: *Charlie had to present his speech cold.* —**cold′ly,** *adv.* —**cold′ness,** *n.*

  cold feet. the lack or loss of courage: *He got cold feet at the last moment and ran away.*

  out cold. unconscious.

  out in the cold. ignored or neglected: *Joe felt himself out in the cold when his girlfriend started dating another boy.*

  to catch cold or **to take cold.** to become ill with a cold.

  to throw cold water on. to discourage: *He threw cold water on our vacation plans.*

cold-blood·ed (kōld′blud′id) *adj.* **1.** having blood that varies in temperature with the temperature of the surrounding air or water. Snakes and turtles are cold-blooded animals. **2.** lacking feeling or sympathy; cruel: *a cold-blooded criminal.* —**cold′-blood′ed·ly,** *adv.* —**cold′-blood′ed·ness,** *n.*

cold cream, a creamy substance used for cleansing and soothing the skin.

cold cuts, cooked meat that has been sliced and is served cold, such as roast beef, turkey, or ham.

cold front, the forward edge of a mass of cold air moving into an area of warmer air.

cold-heart·ed (kōld′här′tid) *adj.* without feeling or sympathy; unkind. —**cold′-heart′ed·ly,** *adv.* —**cold′-heart′ed·ness,** *n.*

cold shoulder *Informal.* a deliberate show of unfriendliness; snub; slight: *Doug's old girlfriend gave him the cold shoulder when she passed him on the street.*

cold sore, a blister in or near the mouth, often accompanying a cold or fever. Also, **fever sore, fever blister.**

cold storage, the storage of perishable objects in an artificially cooled chamber.

cold war 1. also, **Cold War.** the state of hostility and rivalry after World War II, between the United States and its allies on one side and the Soviet Union and its allies on the other, generally stopping short of military conflict. **2.** any state of intense political or economic rivalry between nations, stopping short of actual warfare.

cold wave, a period of sudden, unusually cold weather.

cole (kōl) *n.* any of various plants belonging to the same family as the cabbage, such as kale. Also, **cole·wort** (kōl′-wurt′).

Cole·ridge, Samuel Taylor (kōl′rij) 1772–1834, English poet and critic.

cole·slaw (kōl′slô′) *n.* a salad made of sliced, shredded, or grated raw cabbage, mixed with a dressing. Also, **slaw.**

col·ic (kol′ik) *n.* a sudden attack of severe pain in the stomach, especially in infants. —**col′ick·y,** *adj.*

col·i·se·um (kol′ə sē′əm) *n.* **1.** a large, usually oval building or stadium in which athletic contests and other entertainments are presented. Also, **colosseum. 2. Coliseum.** another spelling of **Colosseum.**

coll. 1. college. **2.** colleague. **3.** colloquial.

col·lab·o·rate (kə lab′ə rāt′) *v.i.,* **col·lab·o·rat·ed, col·lab·o·rat·ing. 1.** to work with another or others: *Marie Curie collaborated with her husband in doing scientific research.* **2.** to aid or cooperate with the enemy, especially with an enemy that is occupying one's country. —**col·lab′o·ra′tion,** *n.* —**col·lab′o·ra′tor,** *n.*

col·lage (kə läzh′) *n.* **1.** a work of art made by pasting paper, cloth, metal and other materials or objects together

on a surface. **2.** the art or technique of producing such works.

col·lapse (kə laps′) *v.,* **col·lapsed, col·laps·ing.** —*v.i.* **1.** to fall in; cave in: *The walls collapsed from the force of the explosion.* **2.** to fold together: *This cot collapses for easy storage.* **3.** to fail or break down completely or suddenly: *His plans collapsed. She collapsed from the heat. The messenger collapsed after finally reaching headquarters.* —*v.t.* to cause to collapse: *She collapsed the folding table and put it away.* —*n.* **1.** the act of falling in; a cave-in: *Hundreds of miners were injured in the collapse of the mining shaft.* **2.** any complete or sudden failure or breakdown: *The collapse of the talks with the union led to a strike.*

col·laps·i·ble (kə lap′sə bəl) *also,* **col·laps·a·ble.** *adj.* that can be folded together: *a collapsible dining table.*

col·lar (kol′ər) *n.* **1.** the part of a garment at the neckline, usually sewed on as a separate piece. **2.** a separate band of jewels, cloth, fur, or other material worn to decorate the neckline. **3.** a band of leather or metal placed around the neck of an animal, such as a dog. **4.** a cushioned band that fits over a horse's neck to bear the strain of the load he pulls.

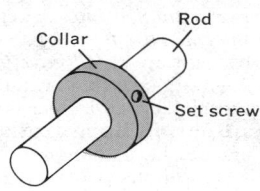

Collar *(def. 5)*

5. any of various devices that prevent or limit sideward motion, such as a ring on a rod or shaft. —*v.t.* **1.** to put a collar on: *to collar a dog.* **2.** *Informal.* to lay hold of; seize: *The police collared the thief a week after the robbery.*

col·lar·bone (kol′ər bōn′) *n.* either of two bones connecting the breastbone and the shoulder blade; clavicle.

col·late (kə lāt′, kol′āt) *v.t.,* **col·lat·ed, col·lat·ing. 1.** to arrange in proper order: *The secretary collated the pages of the report.* **2.** to compare critically and carefully.

col·lat·er·al (kə lat′ər əl) *n.* property given to a lender of money as security that the loan will be repaid. —*adj.* **1.** situated or placed side by side; parallel: *collateral railways.* **2.** connected with something, but secondary in importance: *His main interest is baseball, and his collateral interests include tennis and swimming.* **3.** guaranteed or backed by collateral: *a collateral loan.* **4.** descended from common ancestors, but in a different line: *Children of brothers are collateral relatives.* —**col·lat′er·al·ly,** *adv.*

col·la·tion (kə lā′shən) *n.* **1.** the act of collating. **2.** a light, informal, usually cold meal.

col·league (kol′ēg) *n.* a fellow member of a profession or other group; fellow worker or associate.

col·lect (kə lekt′) *v.t.* **1.** to gather (something) together; assemble: *My mother collected old clothes for the rummage sale.* **2.** to make a collection of as a hobby or for study: *Bob collects stamps.* **3.** to ask for and receive (payments or contributions): *The state collects tolls on this highway.* **4.** to call for and remove: *He collected the garbage at five o'clock.* **5.** to regain control of or summon up: *to collect one's thoughts.* —*v.i.* **1.** to gather together; assemble: *A large crowd collected to hear the speaker.* **2.** to pile up; accumulate: *Dust often collects under a bed.* **3.** to ask for and receive payments or contributions: *Mrs. Brown collects*

at; āpe; cär; end; mē; it; īce; hot; ōld; fôrk; wood; fo͞ol; oil; out; up; turn; sing; thin; this; hw in white; zh in treasure. The symbol ə stands for the sound of a in about, e in taken, i in pencil, o in lemon, and u in circus.

for charity. —*adj.* that is paid for at the time or place of delivery: *a collect telephone call.* —*adv.* so as to be paid for at the time or place of delivery: *to telephone someone collect.* —**col·lect′a·ble;** *also,* **col·lect′i·ble,** *adj.*

col·lect·ed (kə lek′tid) *adj.* in control of oneself; composed: *He always tries to remain calm and collected during a crisis.* —**col·lect′ed·ly,** *adv.*

col·lec·tion (kə lek′shən) *n.* **1.** the act or process of collecting: *The collection of trash is carried out by the sanitation department.* **2.** something gathered together, especially as a hobby or for study: *a coin collection.* **3.** a payment or contribution collected: *We took up a collection to buy a gift for the teacher.* **4.** something that has accumulated.

col·lec·tive (kə lek′tiv) *adj.* **1.** of, relating to, or done by a group of persons or things; common; united: *A collective effort on the part of all the players helped the team win the championship.* **2.** representing a whole or collection: *the collective needs of a community.* **3.** owned or managed by a group: *a collective farm.* —*n.* **1.** see **collective noun. 2.** an organization or undertaking marked by collectivism, especially a collective farm. —**col·lec′tive·ly,** *adv.*

collective bargaining, a negotiation between workers or their union representatives and employers about wages, hours, working conditions, or the like.

collective noun, a singular noun referring to a group of persons or things. It takes a singular verb if the group acts as a single unit: *The jury was unable to agree on a verdict.* It takes a plural verb if the group acts as individuals: *The jury were divided in their opinions.*

col·lec·tiv·ism (kə lek′ti viz′əm) *n.* an economic and political system in which the means of production and distribution are owned and controlled by the government or by the people as a group.

col·lec·tor (kə lek′tər) *n.* **1.** a person who collects objects of interest or value: *a rare book collector, a coin collector.* **2.** a person who is employed to collect money due: *a tax collector, a toll collector.* **3.** any thing that collects.

col·leen (kol′ēn, ko lēn′) *n.* a girl, especially an Irish girl.

col·lege (kol′ij) *n.* **1.** a school of higher education entered after high school, that grants degrees upon completion of courses of study. **2.** a major division in a university that offers a four-year course of study leading to a bachelor's degree. **3.** a school for training and instruction in a particular field: *a barber's college.* **4.** a group of persons having common duties and powers: *a college of surgeons.*

col·le·gian (kə lē′jən) *n.* a college student.

col·le·giate (kə lē′jit) *adj.* of or relating to college or college students: *collegiate clothing styles.*

col·lide (kə līd′) *v.i.,* **col·lid·ed, col·lid·ing. 1.** to come together with force; crash: *The car and the truck collided at the intersection.* **2.** to come into conflict; clash.

col·lie (kol′ē) *n.* a dog originally bred for tending sheep, having a long, narrow head, a slender body, and usually, a long-haired coat of white and tan or white, tan, and black.

col·lier (kol′yər) *n.* British. **1.** a coal miner. **2.** a ship for carrying coal.

col·lier·y (kol′yər ē) *n. pl.,* **col·lier·ies.** a coal mine with its buildings and equipment.

col·li·sion (kə lizh′ən) *n.* **1.** the act of coming together with force; act of colliding: *The bus driver broke his leg in the collision.* **2.** a conflict; clash.

Collie

col·loid (kol′oid) *n.* a substance evenly scattered through another substance in particles that are larger than ordinary molecules but that are too small to be visible to the naked eye. Both the particles and the medium in which they are scattered may be a gas, liquid, or solid. —**col·loi·dal** (kə loid′əl), *adj.* —**col·loi′dal·ly,** *adv.*

col·lo·qui·al (kə lō′kwē əl) *adj.* (of language) used in ordinary or familiar conversation, rather than formal speech or writing: *"Big wheel" is a colloquial term for "an important person."* —**col·lo′qui·al·ly,** *adv.* —**col·lo′qui·al·ness,** *n.*

col·lo·qui·al·ism (kə lō′kwē ə liz′əm) *n.* **1** a colloquial word or phrase: *"Hit the sack" is a colloquialism meaning "go to bed."* **2.** the use of colloquial words or phrases.

col·lo·quy (kol′ə kwē) *n. pl.,* **col·lo·quies.** a conversation, discussion, or conference, especially a formal one.

col·lu·sion (kə lōō′zhən) *n.* a secret agreement or cooperation between two or more people for an illegal or deceitful purpose.

Colo., Colorado.

Co·logne (kə lōn′) *n.* a city in the western part of West Germany, near Bonn. Pop. (1969 est.), 866,300.

co·logne (kə lōn′) *n.* a fragrant liquid made from alcohol and scented oils and used as perfume. [From *Cologne,* where it was first manufactured.]

Co·lom·bi·a (kə lum′bē ə) *n.* a country in northwestern South America, on the Pacific Ocean and the Caribbean Sea. Capital, Bogotá. Area, 439,513 sq. mi. Pop. (1971 est.), 21,770,000. —**Co·lom′bi·an,** *adj., n.*

Co·lom·bo (kə lum′bō) *n.* the capital and chief port of Ceylon, on the west coast of the island. Pop. (1968 est.), 558,500.

co·lon¹ (kō′lən) *n.* a mark of punctuation (:), used chiefly to introduce, set apart, or direct attention to something that follows, such as a list or series, a quotation, or an explanation. [Greek *kōlon* a limb or joint, later a clause of a sentence.]

co·lon² (kō′lən) *n. pl.,* **co·lons** or **co·la** (kō′lə). the lower part of the large intestine. [Latin *colon* large intestine, from Greek *kolon.*]

colo·nel (kurn′əl) *n.* a military officer usually ranking above a lieutenant colonel and below a brigadier general.

● It probably seems odd to you that the word **colonel** is spelled with an "l," but pronounced with an "r." The reason for this is that at one time there was another word in English, *coronel,* that had the same meaning as *colonel.* Somehow, the pronunciation of *coronel,* with an "r" sound, became attached to the spelling *colonel.*

---

co·lo·ni·al (kə lō′nē əl) *adj.* **1.** of or relating to a colony or colonies: *colonial government, a colonial empire.* **2.** *also,* **Colonial. a.** of or relating to the thirteen British colonies that became the United States of America. **b.** characteristic of this period in American history: *colonial architecture, colonial furniture.* —*n.* a person who was born in or is living in a colony. —**co·lo′ni·al·ly,** *adv.*

co·lo·ni·al·ism (kə lō′nē ə liz′əm) *n.* the policy of a nation seeking to acquire or keep control over other peoples or territories.

col·o·nist (kol′ə nist) *n.* **1.** a person who was born or is living in a colony. **2.** a person who helps to found or settle a colony.

col·o·nize (kol′ə nīz′) *v.,* **col·o·nized, col·o·niz·ing.** —*v.t.* **1.** to establish a colony or colonies in; send colonists to: *Spain colonized most of South America.* **2.** to travel to and settle in; occupy as a colony: *The Puritans colonized Plymouth.* —*v.i.* to establish a colony or colonies. —**col′·o·ni·za′tion,** *n.* —**col′o·niz′er,** *n.*

col·on·nade (kol′ə nād′) *n.* a series of columns, placed at regular intervals, usually supporting a roof or other structure.

col·o·ny (kol′ə nē) *n. pl.,* **col·o·nies. 1.** any territory that is under the control of another, usually distant, country. **2.** a body of settlers living in an area apart from, but under the control of, the country from which they came: *A colony of Puritans settled in Plymouth.* **3.** the area or land itself: *Plymouth was an English colony.* **4. the Colonies.** the thirteen British colonies that became the first states of the United States: New Hampshire, Massachusetts, Rhode Island, Connecticut, New York, New Jersey, Pennsylvania, Delaware, Maryland, Virginia, North Carolina, South Carolina, and Georgia. **5.** a group of people living or drawn together in an area because of common nationality, religion, or interests: *an American colony in Paris.* **6.** a group of animals or plants of the same kind, living or growing together in the same place: *a colony of bees.*

Colonnade

col·or (kul′ər) *also, British,* **col·our.** *n.* **1.** a quality of something resulting from the way it transmits or reflects light. Different colors, such as red, blue, or yellow, are caused when light of different wavelengths, reflected by an object, strikes the retina of the eye. **2.** one of the parts of the spectrum; a particular hue, tint, or shade: *Orange is her favorite color.* **3.** something used for coloring, such as a paint, dye, or pigment. **4.** the coloring of the skin, especially of the face; complexion: *Ellen regained her healthy color once she got well.* **5.** a skin pigmentation or complexion, especially when thought of as a racial feature: *That company hires workers without regard to race, creed, or color.* **6.** a vivid, lively, or interesting quality: *The professor's stories added color to his lecture. That baseball player has a lot of color.* **7. colors. a.** any color or pattern of colors, as of a badge or uniform: *My school's colors are red and black.* **b.** a flag or banner, especially the national flag: *The general saluted the colors as the parade passed by.* —*v.t.* **1.** to give or apply color to, as by painting, dyeing, or staining: *Paul colored the pictures with a yellow crayon.* **2.** to cause to appear different from reality: *The witness colored his testimony to protect his friend.* **3.** to change in character or nature; affect; influence: *Your judgment is being colored by your emotions.* —*v.i.* to become red in the face; blush; flush. —**col′or·er,** *n.*

to show one's true colors. to reveal one's true self or nature.

Col·o·rad·o (kol′ə rad′ō, kol′ə rä′dō) *n.* **1.** a state in the western United States. Capital, Denver. Area, 104,247 sq. mi. Pop. (1970), 2,207,259. Abbreviation, **Colo. 2.** a river flowing from northern Colorado into the Gulf of California. —**Col′o·rad′an,** *adj., n.*

• **Colorado** was named after the Colorado River, which originates in this state. The name of the river was first given to one of its tributaries by a Spanish exploration party and means "reddish river," referring to the reddish appearance of the water.

Colorado Springs, a city in central Colorado. The U.S. Air Force Academy is located there. Pop. (1970), 135,060.

col·o·ra·tion (kul′ə rā′shən) *n.* an arrangement of colors; coloring.

col·or·a·tu·ra (kul′ər ə toor′ə, kul′ər ə tyoor′ə) *n.* **1.** ornamental passages in vocal music, such as trills or runs. **2.** music characterized by such ornamentation. **3.** a high soprano voice having a wide range, trained for singing such music. **4.** a singer with such a voice. —*adj.* **1.** characterized by coloratura. **2.** able to sing coloratura: *a coloratura soprano.*

col·or·bear·er (kul′ər ber′ər) *n.* a person who carries the colors or flag, as in a ceremony or parade.

col·or-blind (kul′ər blīnd′) *adj.* affected by color blindness.

color blindness, a lack of ability to see colors. It is usually a difficulty in telling the difference between certain colors, such as red and green, but sometimes it is a total inability to distinguish any colors except black, white, and gray.

col·ored (kul′ərd) *adj.* **1.** having color, especially other than solid black or white: *This book has colored illustrations.* **2.** of a race other than the Caucasian or white race, especially of the Negro race. **3.** influenced, as by prejudice or emotion; distorted; slanted: *The defendant's brother gave a highly colored account of what had occurred.*

col·or·fast (kul′ər fast′) *adj.* (of fabrics) having color that will not fade or run.

col·or·ful (kul′ər fəl) *adj.* **1.** full of bright color: *a colorful tie.* **2.** vivid, lively, or interesting: *He told a colorful tale of his life as a cowboy.* —**col′or·ful·ly,** *adv.* —**col′or·ful·ness,** *n.*

col·or·ing (kul′ər ing) *n.* **1.** the way in which anything is colored: *the coloring of the autumn landscape, the coloring of spring flowers.* **2.** something used to give color: *food coloring.* **3.** the act or technique of applying color. **4.** a false appearance or show: *His lies have the coloring of truth.*

coloring book, a book of outline drawings for coloring with crayons or other materials.

col·or·less (kul′ər lis) *adj.* **1.** not vivid, lively, or interesting; dull: *a colorless personality.* **2.** without color: *a colorless liquid.* **3.** dull in color; pale: *His face was white and colorless.* —**col′or·less·ly,** *adv.* —**col′or·less·ness,** *n.*

co·los·sal (kə los′əl) *adj.* extremely large; gigantic; immense: *The pyramids of ancient Egypt are colossal structures.* —**col·los′sal·ly,** *adv.*

Col·os·se·um (kol′ə sē′əm) *n.* **1.** an oval-shaped amphitheater in Rome that was the site of games and fights between gladiators in ancient times. Part of it is still standing. Also, **Coliseum. 2. colosseum.** another spelling of **coliseum.**

Co·los·sians (kə lō′shəns) *n., pl.* a book of the New Testament, consisting of a letter written by Saint Paul to a Christian community in Asia Minor. ▲ used with a singular verb.

co·los·sus (kə los′əs) *n. pl.,* **co·los·si** (kə los′ī) or **co·los·sus·es. 1.** a gigantic statue. **2.** a person or thing of gigantic size or great power.

Colossus of Rhodes, a bronze statue of the sun god Helios that stood at the entrance to the harbor of Rhodes. It was built about 280 B.C. and was more than one hundred feet high.

col·our (kul′ər) *British.* another spelling of **color.**

---

at; āpe; cär; end; mē; it; īce; hot; ōld; fôrk; wood; fo͞ol; oil; out; up; turn; sing; thin; this; hw in white; zh in treasure. The symbol ə stands for the sound of **a** in about, **e** in taken, **i** in pencil, **o** in lemon, and **u** in circus.

colt (kōlt) *n.* **1.** a young horse, especially a male. **2.** the young of any similar animal, especially a male.

col·ter (kōl′tər) *also,* **coul·ter.** *n.* a sharp blade or disk attached to a plow to cut the earth in front of the plowshare.

Co·lum·bi·a (kə lum′bē ə) *n.* **1.** a river that flows into the Pacific Ocean, forming most of the border between Washington and Oregon. **2.** the capital of South Carolina, in the central part of the state. Pop. (1970), 113,542.

col·um·bine (kol′əm bīn′) *n.* **1.** a showy, drooping flower of any of a group of plants related to the buttercup. It grows in many colors and has five projecting petals that resemble tubes. **2.** the plant bearing this flower.

Columbine

Col·um·bine (kol′əm bīn′) *n.* a female character in pantomime and comedy, the sweetheart of Harlequin.

Co·lum·bus (kə lum′bəs) *n.* **1. Christopher.** 1451?–1506, the Italian explorer who discovered America and other lands for Spain in 1492. **2.** the capital of Ohio, in the central part of the state. Pop. (1970), 539,677. **3.** a city in western Georgia. Pop. (1970), 166,565.

Columbus Day, a legal holiday celebrated annually to commemorate the discovery of America by Christopher Columbus on October 12, 1492. This holiday is now celebrated on the second Monday in October.

col·umn (kol′əm) *n.* **1.** a written or printed group of items arranged one above the others: *a column of numbers.* **2.** a narrow, vertical section of printed or written words on a sheet or page, separated by lines or by blank spaces: *This page has two columns.* **3.** an article that appears regularly in a newspaper or magazine, usually written by one person and dealing with a particular subject: *a sports column, a fashion column.* **4.** a slender, upright structure serving as a support or ornament for part of a building, or standing alone as a monument. **5.** something resembling such a structure: *A column of smoke appeared above the hill.* **6.** a military formation in which the men, vehicles, or ships are arranged one behind the other in one or more rows.

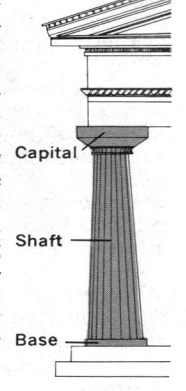

Capital

Shaft

Base

Column

co·lum·nar (kə lum′nər) *adj.* **1.** relating to or resembling a column. **2.** made of or with columns: *The archaeologist discovered ancient examples of columnar architecture.*

col·um·nist (kol′əm nist) *n.* a person who writes a column in a newspaper or magazine: *a political columnist.*

com- *prefix* in association with; together: *combine.*

com. 1. comedy. **2.** commerce. **3.** common; commonly.

Com. 1. Commissioner. **2.** Commission. **3.** Committee.

co·ma¹ (kō′mə) *n. pl.,* **co·mas.** a state of deep unconsciousness, caused by disease, injury, or poison. It may last for hours, days, or months, or in rare cases, for years. [Modern Latin *coma* deep unconsciousness, from Greek *kōma* deep sleep.]

co·ma² (kō′mə) *n. pl.,* **co·mae** (kō′mē). a mass of gases that resembles a cloud, found around the nucleus of a comet. [Latin *coma* hair.]

Co·man·che (kə man′chē) *n. pl.,* **Co·man·ches** or **Co·man·che. 1.** a member of a tribe of North American Indians formerly living in the southern part of the Great Plains, now living in Oklahoma. **2.** the language of this tribe.

comb (kōm) *n.* **1.** a piece of plastic, bone, metal, or other sturdy material, having teeth and used for smoothing, arranging, or fastening the hair. **2.** something resembling a comb in shape or use, such as a card for cleaning and separating fibers. **3.** a thick, usually reddish, fleshy growth on the head of roosters and other fowl. **4.** see **honeycomb. 5.** see **currycomb.** —*v.t.* **1.** to smooth or arrange (the hair) with a comb. **2.** to remove with a comb: *Linda combed the knots from her hair.* **3.** to search (something) thoroughly and with care; look everywhere in: *The police combed the woods looking for the lost child.*

Comb *(def. 3)*

com·bat (*n.,* kom′bat; *v.,* kəm bat′, kom′bat) *n.* **1.** fighting between enemy military forces: *The soldier was wounded in combat.* **2.** a fight, contest, or struggle: *The knight engaged in combat for his lady.* —*v.t.,* **com·bat·ed, com·bat·ing;** *also, British,* **com·bat·ted, com·bat·ting. 1.** to fight with; oppose in battle: *The troops combated the enemy.* **2.** to take measures or struggle against; oppose vigorously: *to combat inflation.* —**com·bat′er,** *n.*

com·bat·ant (kəm bat′ənt, kom′bət ənt) *n.* a person or group of persons fighting or ready to fight. —*adj.* ready or eager to fight.

com·bat·ive (kəm bat′iv) *adj.* ready or eager to fight. —**com·bat′ive·ly,** *adv.* —**com·bat′ive·ness,** *n.*

comb·er (kō′mər) *n.* **1.** a long, rolling wave that curls over or breaks at the crest. **2.** a person or thing that combs.

com·bi·na·tion (kom′bə nā′shən) *n.* **1.** something that is formed by combining; mixture; union: *The color pink is a combination of red and white.* **2.** a series of numbers or letters dialed in a certain sequence to open a combination lock: *Only the guard knows the combination to the safe.* **3.** the act of combining or the state of being combined. **4.** an alliance or association of persons or groups to further some common purpose. **5.** *Mathematics.* any of the possible arrangements of a certain number or of all the elements of a set. Some possible combinations of *x, y,* and *z* are *xyz, zxy,* and *yzx.*

combination lock, a lock opened by turning one or more dials to a series of numbers or letters in a certain sequence.

com·bine (*v.,* kəm bīn′; *n.,* kom′bīn) *v.,* **com·bined, com·bin·ing.** —*v.t.* **1.** to bring into close relationship; join together; unite: *The friends combined their efforts to get the work done faster.* **2.** to cause to mix together; mingle; blend: *She combined eggs, flour, and milk to make the batter.* **3.** to possess or show at the same time: *Julie combines kindness and a sense of humor in her personality.* —*v.i.* **1.** to join together; unite: *The thirteen colonies combined to form the United States. The two armies combined to defeat the enemy.* **2.** to unite to form a chemical compound: *One atom of carbon combines with two atoms of oxygen to form a molecule of carbon dioxide.* —*n.* **1.** an alliance of persons or groups for a common purpose. **2.** a farm machine that combines the functions of a harvester and a thresher by cutting, threshing, and cleaning grains and other field crops.

combining form, a word or a stem of a word, often of Greek or Latin origin, that is used only to form compound words and derivatives, such as *psycho-* in the word *psychoanalysis.*

com·bus·ti·ble (kəm bus′tə bəl) *adj.* that can catch fire and burn: *Paper and dry leaves are combustible.* —*n.* a substance that can catch fire and burn. —**com·bus′ti·bil′·i·ty,** *n.* —**com·bus′ti·bly,** *adv.*

com·bus·tion (kəm bus′chən) *n.* **1.** the act or process of burning. **2.a.** the rapid oxidation of a substance accompanied by the release of heat and sometimes light: *The combustion of gasoline in an engine.* **b.** the slow oxidation of a substance accompanied by little heat and no light: *the combustion of food in the body.*

Comdr., Commander.

come (kum) *v.i.,* **came, come, com·ing.** **1.** to move to or toward; draw near; approach: *Will you please come here? Jim is coming down the street now.* **2.** to reach a place; arrive: *The horse came to the first barrier and jumped over it.* **3.** to reach a particular state or condition: *The water came to a boil. The problem has already come to my attention.* **4.** to exist or occur at a particular place or position: *Five comes before six.* **5.** to reach; extend: *Her hair comes to her waist.* **6.** to be born; descend: *He comes from a well-known family.* **7.** to happen: *How did you come to meet her?* **8.** to exist or happen as a result: *No good will come of his lying.* **9.** to be offered, sold, or made: *This dress comes in several colors.* **10.** to prove or turn out to be: *The prediction came true.* **11.** to become: *The rope came untied.*
  to come about. to take place; happen; occur.
  to come across. to find or meet by chance: *I came across these old pictures while I was cleaning out the attic.*
  to come around. a. to become conscious again. **b.** to change one's opinion or position so as to agree with another's.
  to come by. to obtain; get: *How did he come by such wealth?*
  to come down. a. to be passed down through tradition: *The custom of Thanksgiving has come down to us from the Pilgrims.* **b.** to lose position or standing. **c.** to become ill with: *to come down with the flu.*
  to come forward. to offer or present oneself for work or duty: *A surprise witness came forward with new testimony.*
  to come in for. to receive or be subjected to; get: *He came in for a share of the blame.*
  to come into. to inherit: *Joel came into the property when his aunt died.*
  to come off. *Informal.* to take place; happen: *The party came off successfully.*
  to come out. a. to become known: *The truth has come out at last.* **b.** to declare oneself publicly: *The candidate came out for local control of public schools.* **c.** to be presented to the public: *That movie came out last year.* **d.** to turn out; end; result: *Everything will come out all right.* **e.** to make a formal social debut.
  to come through. a. to endure or finish successfully: *Only three out of ten men came through the training program.* **b.** *Informal.* to perform or do what is expected: *Fred always comes through when you need him.*
  to come to. a. to become conscious again. **b.** to be equal to; amount to: *The bill comes to five dollars.*
  to come up. to arise: *The question came up during our discussion.*
  to come upon. to find or meet with by chance.
  to come up with. *Informal.* to think of or produce.

come·back (kum′bak′) *n.* **1.** a return to a former favorable condition or position: *The ex-champion made a remarkable comeback and won the title.* **2.** a clever retort.

co·me·di·an (kə mē′dē ən) *n.* **1.** an entertainer who tells jokes or performs funny stunts or routines to make an audience laugh, as in a motion picture or television program. **2.** an actor who plays comic roles. **3.** *Informal.* a person who tries to make others laugh.

co·me·di·enne (kə mē′dē en′) *n.* a female comedian.

come·down (kum′doun′) *n.* a change for the worse in a person's position or status.

com·e·dy (kom′ə dē) *n. pl.,* **com·e·dies. 1.** a play, skit, or other dramatic presentation that is funny. **2.** a play that has a happy ending. **3.** the branch of drama composed of such plays. **4.** any humorous situation or action.

come·ly (kum′lē) *adj.,* **come·li·er, come·li·est.** pleasing in appearance; good-looking: *a comely young lady.* —**come′li·ness,** *n.*

com·er (kum′ər) *n.* **1.** a person who comes or arrives: *The boxing champion was willing to fight all comers.* **2.** *Informal.* a person or thing that shows great promise: *The sportswriters are saying that our team's new pitcher is a real comer.*

com·et (kom′it) *n.* a bright heavenly body made up of ice, frozen gases, and dust particles, and having a long, visible tail that points away from the sun. A comet travels around the sun in an elliptical orbit. [Old French *comete,* going back to Greek *komētes* having long hair; referring to the fact that the tail of a comet looks like long strands of hair.]

come·up·pance (kum′up′əns) *also,* **come·up·ance.** *n. Informal.* a punishment that one deserves.

com·fit (kum′fit, kom′fit) *n.* a piece of candy or candied fruit.

com·fort (kum′fərt) *n.* **1.** a state of ease or well-being with freedom from pain, distress, or want. **2.** relief from the distress caused by pain or sorrow: *Her cheerful letter brought comfort to her sick friend.* **3.** a person or thing that provides relief, ease, or well-being: *Jack was a comfort to his father after his mother's death.* **4.** the ability to give ease and well-being: *These soft pillows add to the comfort of the chair.* —*v.t.* to ease the grief or sorrow of; console: *We tried to comfort the crying child.*

com·fort·a·ble (kumf′tə bəl, kum′fər tə bəl) *adj.* **1.** giving ease or comfort: *a comfortable bed, a comfortable dress.* **2.** free from distress; at ease: *Susan never feels comfortable talking in front of a large group.* **3.** more than adequate: *a comfortable income. Our football team had a comfortable lead at half-time.* —**com′fort·a·ble·ness,** *n.* —**com′fort·a·bly,** *adv.*

com·fort·er (kum′fər tər) *n.* **1.** a person or thing that comforts. **2.** a quilted blanket or covering for a bed.

com·ic (kom′ik) *adj.* **1.** of or relating to comedy: *a comic actor.* **2.** causing laughter or mirth; amusing; funny: *a comic situation.* —*n.* **1.** a comedian. **2. comics.** comic strips. **3.** see **comic book.**

com·i·cal (kom′i kəl) *adj.* causing laughter or mirth; amusing; funny: *The children laughed at the clown's comical antics.* —**com′i·cal·ly,** *adv.*

comic book, a booklet of comic strips.

comic opera, a humorous opera or operetta, usually having a happy ending and some spoken dialogue.

comic strip, a series of cartoon drawings relating a story or incident, often printed regularly in a newspaper.

com·ing (kum′ing) *adj.* **1.** approaching; arriving: *Vacation starts this coming Monday.* **2.** *Informal.* on the way to being important or popular: *Space travel is the coming thing.* —*n.* approach; arrival: *the coming of spring, the coming of nightfall.*

com·ing-out (kum′ing out′) *n. Informal.* a formal social debut.

at; āpe; cär; end; mē; it; īce; hot; ōld; fôrk; wood; fōōl; oil; out; up; turn; sing; thin; **th**is; hw in white; zh in treasure. The symbol ə stands for the sound of **a** in about, **e** in taken, **i** in pencil, **o** in lemon, and **u** in circus.

C

com·i·ty (kom′ə tē) *n. pl.*, **com·i·ties.** mutual respect or courtesy; politeness: *comity between nations.*

com·ma (kom′ə) *n.* a punctuation mark (,) used to separate ideas or items in a series, and to set off certain grammatical constructions, such as main clauses.

com·mand (kə mand′) *v.t.* **1.** to give an order to; direct with authority: *The general commanded his troops to advance.* **2.** to have authority or power over; rule: *Great Britain once commanded the seas.* **3.** to deserve and get: *The teacher commanded our respect and admiration.* **4.** to control the position or location of: *The tower commanded the small town.* —*v.i.* to be in a position of authority or power; be in control: *He was born to command.* —*n.* **1.** the act of commanding: *At the sergeant's command, the troops halted.* **2.** something that is commanded; order: *My dog obeyed my command to sit.* **3.** the possession of authority; power to command: *He assumed complete command of the project.* **4.** control or mastery: *She has a good command of Italian.* **5.** the people, things, or area under a commander: *The general was relieved of his command.*

com·man·dant (kom′ən dant′) *n.* an officer in charge of a military installation or district.

com·man·deer (kom′ən dēr′) *v.t.* to seize (private property), especially for military use: *The army commandeered the hotel for use as a barracks.*

com·mand·er (kə man′dər) *n.* **1.** an officer in command of a military unit. **2.** in the U.S. Navy or Coast Guard, an officer ranking above a lieutenant commander and below a captain. **3.** a person who is officially in command; leader: *The sheriff was the commander of the search party.*

commander in chief, also, **Commander in Chief.** *pl.*, **commanders in chief.** the supreme commander of the armed forces of a country. In the United States, the President is the Commander in Chief.

com·mand·ing (kə man′ding) *adj.* **1.** demanding attention or respect: *The speaker had a commanding air about him.* **2.** in charge: *a commanding officer.*

com·mand·ment (kə mand′ment) *n.* **1.** also, **Commandment.** a law, especially one of the Ten Commandments. **2.** a command or order.

com·man·do (kə man′dō) *n. pl.*, **com·man·dos** or **com·man·does.** a soldier specially trained for scouting and quick raids.

com·mem·o·rate (kə mem′ə rāt′) *v.t.*, **com·mem·o·rat·ed, com·mem·o·rat·ing.** **1.** to serve as a memorial to: *The statue in the park commemorates the heroes of the Civil War.* **2.** to honor the memory of; celebrate: *Our class put on a pageant to commemorate Columbus Day.* —**com·mem′o·ra′tion**, *n.*

com·mem·o·ra·tive (kə mem′ə rā′tiv) *adj.* serving to commemorate: *David collects commemorative coins.*

com·mence (kə mens′) *v.*, **com·menced, com·menc·ing.** —*v.i.* to begin; start: *The program will commence at eight o'clock.* —*v.t.* to begin or start (something).

com·mence·ment (kə mens′mənt) *n.* **1.** a beginning; start. **2.** a ceremony in which a college or school gives degrees and diplomas to graduating students.

com·mend (kə mend′) *v.t.* **1.** to speak of with approval; praise: *The general commended the sergeant for his bravery.* **2.** to give over to someone's care; entrust: *Our neighbor commended her plants to us while she was away.* **3.** to recommend: *I commend this book to you.*

com·mend·a·ble (kə men′də bəl) *adj.* worthy of praise: *Alan's report was a commendable piece of work.*

com·men·da·tion (kom′ən dā′shən) *n.* **1.** the act of commending; praise. **2.** something that expresses approval or praise; citation: *The firemen received commendations for bravery.* —**com·men·da·to·ry** (kə men′də tôr′ē), *adj.*

com·men·sal (kə men′səl) *adj.* of or relating to commensalism. —*n.* a plant or animal living in commensalism.

com·men·sal·ism (kə men′sə liz′əm) *n.* a relationship between two organisms of different kinds in which one is benefited and the other is neither benefited nor harmed.

com·men·su·rate (kə men′sər it, kə men′shər it) *adj.* **1.** in proper proportion; equal to: *The reward for capturing the criminal was not commensurate with the risk involved.* **2.** having the same measure; of equal size: *The gambler's losses were commensurate with his winnings.* —**com·men′su·rate·ly**, *adv.*

com·ment (kom′ent) *n.* **1.** a brief statement or remark that explains, describes, or criticizes: *Our teacher's comments on the book made it sound interesting. Her sarcastic comments began to bother me.* **2.** gossip; discussion: *Mike's rude behavior was the subject of much comment.* —*v.i.* to make a comment or comments: *The coach took time to comment on last week's game.*

com·men·tar·y (kom′ən ter′ē) *n. pl.*, **com·men·tar·ies.** **1.** a series of notes or remarks that explain, describe, or criticize: *a commentary on Shakespeare's plays. We watched the news commentary on television.* **2.** anything that points out or serves as an example: *This sloppy report is a sad commentary on the student's lack of interest in the course.*

com·men·ta·tor (kom′ən tā′tər) *n.* a person who comments on something, especially one who comments on the news on radio or television.

com·merce (kom′ərs) *n.* the buying and selling of goods or services, especially on a large scale; business; trade.

com·mer·cial (kə mur′shəl) *adj.* **1.** of or relating to business or trade: *a commercial venture. He is taking accounting and other commercial subjects at school.* **2.** made for or concerned with financial profit: *commercial products. The book got bad reviews from the critics, but it was a commercial success.* **3.** supported by advertisers: *a commercial television station.* —*n.* an advertising message on radio or television: *The show was interrupted every few minutes by a commercial.* —**com·mer′cial·ly**, *adv.*

com·mer·cial·ism (kə mur′shə liz′əm) *n.* **1.** the placing of too much emphasis on financial profit. **2.** the methods and principles of commerce.

com·mer·cial·ize (kə mur′shə līz′) *v.t.*, **com·mer·cial·ized, com·mer·cial·iz·ing.** **1.** to make commercial or businesslike. **2.** to exploit for profit: *Some people feel that Christmas has been commercialized by the great emphasis on giving presents.* —**com·mer′cial·i·za′tion**, *n.*

com·min·gle (kə ming′gəl) *v.t., v.i.*, **com·min·gled, com·min·gling.** to mix together; mingle.

com·mis·er·ate (kə miz′ə rāt′) *v.*, **com·mis·er·at·ed, com·mis·er·at·ing.** —*v.i.* to feel or express sympathy: *We commiserated with Jean over the loss of her dog.* —*v.t.* to feel or express sympathy for; pity. —**com·mis′er·a′tion**, *n.*

com·mis·sar (kom′ə sär′) *n.* formerly, a head of a government department in the Soviet Union.

com·mis·sar·i·at (kom′ə ser′ē ət) *n.* formerly, a government department in the Soviet Union.

com·mis·sar·y (kom′ə ser′ē) *n. pl.*, **com·mis·sar·ies.** **1.** a store that sells food and supplies, as in a military camp. **2.** a place to eat, such as a cafeteria. **3.** a person who is acting for another; deputy; representative.

com·mis·sion (kə mish′ən) *n.* **1.** a group of persons appointed or elected to perform certain duties: *The President set up a commission to investigate the causes of crime.* **2.** a fee for services or work done, usually a percentage of the total price: *The salesman received a commission of fifty dollars on the sale.* **3.** the act of committing: *the commission of a crime.* **4.** a position of military rank and authority: *The officers received their commissions after completing training school.* **5.** the act of giving a person the authority to perform a task or duty. **6.** the task or duty for which authority is given. **7.** an assignment to create a work of art: *The artist received a commission to paint the king's portrait.* —*v.t.* **1.** to give military rank and authority to: *to commission an officer.* **2.** to give authority to; empower: *The company commissioned a private detective to investigate the theft.* **3.** to order a work of art: *The city commissioned a painting for the new library.* **4.** to put (a ship) into service.

in commission. in service or use; in working order.

out of commission. not in service or use; not in working order: *The bombing put three enemy ships out of commission.*

commissioned officer, in the United States, an officer of the armed forces who receives his commission from the President.

com·mis·sion·er (kə mish′ə nər) *n.* **1.** a member of a commission. **2.** an official in charge of a government department: *a parks commissioner, a highway commissioner.* **3.** an official who is the head of a professional sports league: *a baseball commissioner.*

com·mit (kə mit′) *v.t.*, **com·mit·ted, com·mit·ting. 1.** to do or perform (something wrong): *to commit a crime, to commit a mistake. The shortstop committed three errors in the game.* **2.** to put into the charge or keeping of another; entrust: *The doctor committed his patient to the hospital's care.* **3.** to put into official custody, as of a prison or mental institution: *The judge committed the convicted criminal for five years.* **4.** to devote or pledge; bind: *He committed himself fully to the plan.* —**com·mit′ta·ble,** *adj.*

to commit to memory. to learn by heart; memorize.

com·mit·ment (kə mit′mənt) *n.* **1.** the act of committing or the state of being committed. **2.** an obligation; pledge: *Our teacher's previous commitments will keep him from attending our school picnic.* Also, **com·mit·tal** (kə mit′əl).

com·mit·tee (kə mit′ē) *n.* a group of persons appointed or elected to perform certain duties: *The dance was planned by the club's social committee.*

com·mit·tee·man (kə mit′ē mən) *n. pl.,* **com·mit·tee·men** (kə mit′ē mən). a member of a committee. —**com·mit′tee·wom′an,** *n.*

com·mode (kə mōd′) *n.* **1.** a chest of drawers. **2.** a small piece of furniture containing a chamber pot or a washstand. **3.** see **toilet** *(def. 2).*

com·mo·di·ous (kə mō′dē əs) *adj.* having plenty of room; roomy; spacious: *a commodious apartment.* —**com·mo′di·ous·ly,** *adv.* —**com·mo′di·ous·ness,** *n.*

com·mod·i·ty (kə mod′ə tē) *n. pl.,* **com·mod·i·ties.** something that can be bought and sold; article of trade: *That country's chief exports are wheat, corn, and other agricultural commodities.*

com·mo·dore (kom′ə dôr′) *n.* **1.** in the U.S. Navy, an officer ranking above a captain and below a rear admiral. This rank has not been used since World War II. **2.** the president or head of a yacht club.

com·mon (kom′ən) *adj.* **1.** happening or appearing often; usual: *Tom made the common mistake of dialing a wrong number. Blond hair is common among people from northern Europe.* **2.** general; widespread: *Their quarrel is now a matter of common knowledge.* **3.** belonging equally to two or more; shared by all alike: *The club is made up of people with a common interest in music.* **4.** relating to the community as a whole; public: *the common good, to provide for the common defense.* **5.** not distinguished by special or outstanding characteristics; average; standard: *Replying to an invitation is a matter of common courtesy. Our mayor*

is interested in the problems of the common people. **6.** of coarse, poor quality; unrefined, or vulgar: *He has rather common manners.* —*n. also,* **commons.** a plot of land, such as a pasture or park, that is owned or used by the public. —**com′mon·ness,** *n.*

in common. in joint use or possession; shared equally: *The two friends had many interests in common.*

com·mon·al·ty (kom′ən əl tē) *n. pl.,* **com·mon·al·ties.** the common people, as opposed to royalty or the nobility.

common carrier, a railroad, steamship line, or other company that transports goods or people for a fee.

common cold, see **cold** *(n., def. 3).*

common denominator, a number that can be divided evenly by each of the denominators of a given group of fractions. The number 18 is a common denominator of $\frac{1}{3}$, $\frac{5}{6}$ and $\frac{2}{9}$, since $\frac{1}{3} = \frac{6}{18}$, $\frac{5}{6} = \frac{15}{18}$, and $\frac{2}{9} = \frac{4}{18}$.

common divisor, a number or algebraic expression that can divide two or more other numbers or algebraic expressions without leaving a remainder. The number 3 is a common divisor of 6, 9, 15, and 21. Also, **common factor.**

com·mon·er (kom′ə nər) *n.* a member of the common people, especially a person who is not of noble rank.

common fraction, a fraction whose numerator and denominator are whole numbers, such as $\frac{1}{4}$ or $\frac{3}{5}$.

common law, a system of law based on custom, usage, and court decisions rather than on laws that have been enacted.

common logarithm, a logarithm having a base of 10.

com·mon·ly (kom′ən lē) *adv.* **1.** usually; generally; ordinarily: *Alice commonly arrives at work on time.* **2.** in a common manner.

Common Market, an economic association formed in 1958 by France, West Germany, Italy, Belgium, the Netherlands, and Luxembourg to establish free trade among its members. Great Britain, Ireland, Norway, and Denmark became members in 1972.

common multiple, a number or algebraic expression that can be divided by two or more other numbers or algebraic expressions without leaving a remainder. The number 20 is a common multiple of 2, 4, 5, and 10.

common noun, a noun that names any one or all of the members of a class, rather than any one particular person, place, or thing. Common nouns can be used immediately after the word *the. Dog, dogs, street,* and *streets* are common nouns; *Elizabeth* and *Delaware* are not.

com·mon·place (kom′ən plās′) *adj.* not original, remarkable, or interesting; ordinary: *Snow is a commonplace occurrence in Maine, but not in Florida.* —*n.* **1.** an ordinary or obvious remark. **2.** anything ordinary or uninteresting; everyday thing. —**com′mon·place′ness,** *n.*

com·mons (kom′ənz) *n., pl.* **1.** a hall or building for dining, especially at a college or university. **2.** the food served in such a hall or building. **3. Commons.** see **House of Commons. 4.** the common people. ▲ used with a singular or plural verb. **5.** see **common.**

common sense, good sense and wisdom based on experience rather than special knowledge; sound practical judgment.

common stock, the stock of a corporation that has

at; āpe; cär; end; mē; it; īce; hot; ōld; fôrk; wood; fōōl; oil; out; up; turn; sing; thin; **th**is; hw in white; zh in treasure. The symbol ə stands for the sound of **a** in about, **e** in taken, **i** in pencil, **o** in lemon, and **u** in circus.

voting rights, but receives dividends only after the dividends due to preferred stock have been paid.

com·mon·weal (kom′ən wēl′) *n.* **1.** the general or public welfare; common good. **2.** *Archaic.* another word for **commonwealth.**

com·mon·wealth (kom′ən welth′) *n.* **1.** the people of a nation or state. **2.** a nation or state that is governed by the people; republic or democracy. **3.** any of certain states of the United States. Kentucky, Massachusetts, Pennsylvania, and Virginia use *commonwealth* rather than *state* as an official name. **4. the Commonwealth.** see **Commonwealth of Nations.**

Commonwealth of Nations, a worldwide association made up of Great Britain and the nations and territories that once were a part of the British Empire. Also, **the Commonwealth, British Commonwealth of Nations.**

com·mo·tion (kə mō′shən) *n.* a noisy disturbance or disorder; confusion: *There was commotion and rejoicing in the grandstand when the home team won.*

com·mu·nal (kə myōōn′əl) *adj.* **1.** of, relating to, or like a commune or community. **2.** belonging to the people of a community; public. —**com·mu′nal·ly,** *adv.*

com·mune[1] (kə myōōn′) *v.i.,* **com·muned, com·mun·ing.** to talk or be with closely: *to commune with nature.* [Old French *comuner* to share, make common.]

com·mune[2] (kom′yōōn) *n.* **1.** a community in which property is owned in common and work and living quarters are shared. **2.** the smallest unit of local government in certain European countries, such as France, Italy, and Belgium. **3. the Commune.** a revolutionary committee in Paris that governed France from 1792 to 1794. [French *commune* a unit of local government.]

com·mu·ni·ca·ble (kə myōō′ni kə bəl) *adj.* capable of being carried or passed along from one person to another: *Polio is a communicable disease.*

com·mu·ni·cant (kə myōō′ni kənt) *n.* **1.** a person who receives Holy Communion. **2.** a person who communicates.

com·mu·ni·cate (kə myōō′ni kāt′) *v.,* **com·mu·ni·cat·ed, com·mu·ni·cat·ing.** —*v.t.* **1.** to make known or understood; give knowledge or information of: *He communicated his ideas very well in the essay.* **2.** to carry or pass along: *to communicate a disease.* —*v.i.* **1.** to exchange or share feelings, thoughts, or information: *I've been communicating with her by mail.* **2.** to be connected or form a connecting passage: *This passageway communicates with the tunnel leading to the mine.* —**com·mu′ni·ca′tor,** *n.*

com·mu·ni·ca·tion (kə myōō′ni kā′shən) *n.* **1.** the transfer of information, such as facts, wishes, or emotions: *The Indians used smoke signals as a means of communication.* **2.** something communicated: *The reporter's communications were sent by telegram.* **3.** the act or process of communicating. **4. communications.** a system for communicating, especially one involving telephone, telegraph, radio, or television: *Communications in the flooded area are still not working.*

● **Communication** is the conveying of any kind of information from one person or place to another. This information can be facts, thoughts, orders, or anything else that can be known or felt. A crying baby, a smile, a handshake, a locked door, and a growling dog are all sources of communication for us. We receive some kind of information from each of them, even though the exact nature of the information may not be altogether clear. Facial expressions, gestures and physical actions such as a nod of the head, a wave of the hand, a shrug of the shoulders are all forms of body language, which allow for communication of a general nature.

Speech, first spoken, then both spoken and written, provides a means of conveying more precise information.

Language is probably the most important human achievement. Language, as opposed to the type of information that is transmitted by gestures, symbols, objects, or animals, can express our most complex thoughts and knowledge. In its written form, language has made it possible for us to store vast amounts of information that can be communicated to anyone who is able to read, or passed from one generation to another. It is the ability to communicate on a very high, complicated level, rather than the ability to use tools or manufacture things, that sets people apart from animals, plants, and machines.

---

communications satellite, a man-made satellite that relays radio or other signals between ground stations on earth.

com·mu·ni·ca·tive (kə myōō′ni kā′tiv) *adj.* ready to communicate or disclose information; talkative. —**com·mu′ni·ca′tive·ly,** *adv.* —**com·mu′ni·ca′tive·ness,** *n.*

com·mun·ion (kə myōōn′yən) *n.* **1.** a sharing of feelings or thoughts; fellowship: *There*

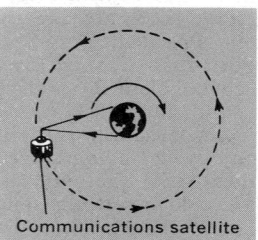
Communications satellite

was a close communion between the father and his son. **2.** a group of churches having common religious beliefs. **3. Communion. a.** see **Holy Communion. b.** the part of the Mass during which Holy Communion is received.

com·mu·ni·qué (kə myōō′ni kā′) *n.* an official communication or announcement: *A communiqué from the commanding general announced the surrender of the enemy.*

com·mu·nism (kom′yə niz′əm) *n.* **1.** a social and economic system based on the theories of Karl Marx and Friedrich Engels and later modified by Vladimir Lenin and others. Under this system, all property and goods are owned by the government or state and the products of labor are shared by all. **2.** also, **Communism. a.** a political movement working to promote this system. **b.** a system of government based on this, as in the Soviet Union. **3.** any social system in which goods and services are shared by all.

com·mu·nist (kom′yə nist) *also,* **Com·mu·nist.** *n.* **1.** a member of a Communist Party. **2.** a person who advocates or supports communism. —*adj.* relating to communism, communists, or a Communist Party. —**com′mu·nis′tic,** *adj.*

Communist China, see **China** *(def. 1).*

Communist Party, a political party that supports communism, as in the Soviet Union or the People's Republic of China.

com·mu·ni·ty (kə myōō′nə tē) *n. pl.,* **com·mu·ni·ties. 1.** a group of people living in the same area and under the same government; the people of a district or town: *Our community voted to build a new library.* **2.** the district or town itself. **3.** a number of people joined together by common interests: *the academic community, the business community.* **4.** society in general; the public: *We must consider the welfare of the community as a whole.* **5.** similarity; agreement. **6.** a group of animals and plants living together in the same area.

community center, a meeting place used by a community for recreational, social, and cultural activities.

community chest, a fund of voluntary contributions made by the people of a community for local charities and welfare activities.

community college, a junior college, especially one partially supported by the community it serves.

com·mu·ta·tion (kom′yə tā′shən) *n.* **1.** regular travel to and from work, especially over a long distance. **2.** a reduction or change, as of a prison sentence or penalty. **3.** a substitution, as of one type of payment for another.

commutation ticket, a discount ticket for a railroad or other form of transportation to be used for a specified number of rides or over a particular period of time.

com·mu·ta·tive (kom′yə tā′tiv) *adj.* *Mathematics.* relating to or designating a law stating that the sum or product of two or more quantities will be the same regardless of their order. For example: $2 + 5$ is the same as $5 + 2$, and $a \times b$ is the same as $b \times a$.

com·mu·ta·tor (kom′yə tā′tər) *n.* a device in an electric generator or motor that causes a change in direction of the current.

com·mute (kə myoot′) *v.,* **com·mut·ed, com·mut·ing.** —*v.i.* to travel regularly to and from work, especially over a long distance: *He commutes to the city from the suburbs.* —*v.t.* to reduce or change: *to commute a prison sentence.* —**com·mut′er,** *n.*

Com·o·ros (kä′mə rōz′) an island country off the southeastern coast of Africa. Land area, 838 sq. mi. Pop. (1978 est.), 330,000.

comp. 1. compound. **2.** compare. **3.** comparative.

com·pact¹ (*adj., v.,* kəm pakt′; *n.,* kom′pakt) *adj.* **1.** tightly packed together; dense: *Compact snow is good for making snowballs.* **2.** taking up a relatively small space or area: *A compact suitcase is convenient for traveling on an airplane.* **3.** said or written in few words; concise: *a compact article.* —*v.t.* to pack together closely and firmly; pack: *The gardener compacted the soil around the roots of the plants.* —*n.* **1.** a small case containing face powder and a mirror, designed to be carried in a purse. **2.** an automobile that is smaller than a standard model. [Latin *compactus* joined together.] —**com·pact′ly,** *adv.*

com·pact² (kom′pakt) *n.* an agreement or contract: *The Mayflower Compact was an agreement among the Pilgrims as to how their new colony would be governed.* [Latin *compactum* agreement.]

com·pan·ion (kəm pan′yən) *n.* **1.** a person who often goes along or associates with another; friend; comrade: *Steve and Tom were constant companions last summer.* **2.** any person who accompanies another. **3.** a person employed to stay with or assist another: *Jane was hired as a companion for the old woman.* **4.** something that matches something else; one of a pair: *I lost the companion to this glove at the theater.* [Old French *compaignon* friend, comrade, from Late Latin *compānio* literally, breadsharer.]

com·pan·ion·a·ble (kəm pan′yə nə bəl) *adj.* capable of being a good companion; easy to be with; sociable. —**com·pan′ion·a·bil′i·ty,** *n.* —**com·pan′ion·a·bly,** *adv.*

com·pan·ion·ship (kəm pan′yən ship′) *n.* the state of being companions; friendship; fellowship.

com·pan·ion·way (kəm pan′yən wā′) *n.* **1.** a stairway leading from the deck of a ship to the cabin or deck below. **2.** the space where such a stairway is located.

com·pa·ny (kum′pə nē) *n. pl.,* **com·pa·nies. 1.** a guest or guests: *We had company for dinner.* **2.** a business firm or establishment: *My father has been with the oil company for twelve years.* **3.** companionship; fellowship: *He was lonesome for the company of others.* **4.** a companion or companions: *Greg judges people by the company they keep.* **5.** a group of people gathered together: *The guide led the company of tourists through the museum.* **6.** a group of performers; troupe: *a theatrical company.* **7.** a military unit made up of two or more platoons, forming part of a battalion. **8.** a ship's crew, including the officers.

to keep company. a. to date; court: *My parents kept company for a long time before they were married.* **b.** to be with: *I kept her company while her parents were away.*

to part company. a. to separate and go in different directions. **b.** to end an association or friendship: *The partners finally parted company after a long dispute.*

compar., comparative.

com·pa·ra·ble (kom′pər ə bəl) *adj.* **1.** capable of being compared: *We bought gifts of comparable value for the twins. Human speech is not comparable to the sounds made by cats and dogs.* **2.** worthy of comparison: *Our school orchestra is not comparable to a professional one.* —**com′pa·ra·bly,** *adv.*

com·par·a·tive (kəm par′ə tiv) *adj.* **1.** that compares or involves comparison: *a comparative study of the structure of a frog and a worm.* **2.** judged by comparison; not absolute; relative: *He is a comparative stranger to me; I have met him only once.* **3.** *Grammar.* relating to or designating the comparative degree of an adjective or adverb. "Faster" is the comparative form of "fast." —*n. Grammar.* **1.** the degree of an adjective or adverb that indicates an increase in quantity, quality, or relation. **2.** a word or group of words expressing this degree. "Colder," "darker" and "higher" are comparatives. —**com·par′a·tive·ly,** *adv.*

● The **comparative** of an adjective or adverb in English is usually formed by adding *-er* to the root word, as in *deeper, richer,* and *greener.* Sometimes, the last letter of the word is doubled, as in *sadder.* For other words, the final letter is dropped or changed, as in *wider* and *funnier.* A few words have a comparative form that is completely different from the basic word, such as *better* for *good.*

The comparative of a word may also be shown by placing *more* in front of it. The comparative of *happy* may be either *happier* or *more happy.* For some long words, it is awkward to use the *-er* ending, and such words are compared by *more.* For example, *more courageous* sounds much more natural than "courageouser."

com·pare (kəm per′) *v.,* **com·pared, com·par·ing.** —*v.t.* **1.** to study in order to find likenesses and differences: *The police compared the fingerprints on the gun with those on the door.* **2.** to consider or speak of as similar or alike; liken: *The human brain has been compared to a giant computer.* **3.** *Grammar.* to form the positive, comparative, and superlative degrees of (an adjective or adverb). —*v.i.* to be worthy of being compared; be considered alike or similar: *His latest book does not compare with his first.*

▲ To **compare** is to show the likenesses and the differences between persons or things. To **contrast** is to show only the differences between persons or things.

com·par·i·son (kəm par′ə sən) *n.* **1.** the act of comparing or the state of being compared: *A comparison of the two teams seems to show that Saturday's game will be close.* **2.** a likeness; similarity: *There is no comparison between these two radios.* **3.** *Grammar.* a change in the form of an adjective or adverb to indicate the positive, comparative, or superlative degrees.

com·part·ment (kəm pärt′mənt) *n.* a division or sec-

C

at; āpe; cär; end; mē; it; īce; hot; ōld; fôrk; wood; fool; oil; out; up; turn; sing; thin; this; hw in white; zh in treasure. The symbol ə stands for the sound of **a** in about, **e** in taken, **i** in pencil, **o** in lemon, and **u** in circus.

tion of an enclosed space: *This wallet has a separate compartment for coins. There were ten compartments in each car of the train.*

com·part·men·tal·ize (kəm pärt′ment′əl īz′) *v.t.,* **com·part·men·tal·ized, com·part·men·tal·iz·ing.** to divide into separate compartments or categories.

com·pass (kum′pəs, kom′pəs) *n. pl.,* **com·pass·es.** 1. a device for showing directions, made up of a magnetized needle that is free to point to the north magnetic pole. 2. the outer limits or boundary of an enclosed area: *The children were told to stay within the compass of the school grounds.* 3. range within limits; scope: *That job is not within the compass of his abilities.* 4. also, **compasses.** a device for drawing circles and measuring distances, made up of two straight and equal legs connected at one end. 5. the range of tones of a voice or musical instrument. —*v.t.* 1. to make a circuit of; go around: *Magellan's voyage compassed the globe.* 2. to circle around; surround; encompass: *The mountains compassed the valley.* 3. to grasp mentally; understand: *He could not compass such a difficult idea.* 4. to accomplish or gain; achieve.

Compass (def. 4)

com·pas·sion (kəm pash′ən) *n.* sympathy for another's suffering or misfortune, combined with a desire to help.

com·pas·sion·ate (kəm pash′ə nit) *adj.* feeling or showing compassion; sympathetic. —**com·pas′sion·ate·ly,** *adv.*

com·pat·i·ble (kəm pat′ə bəl) *adj.* capable of existing well together; in harmony: *She and her roommate were not compatible.* —**com·pat′i·bil′i·ty,** *n.* —**com·pat′i·bly,** *adv.*

com·pa·tri·ot (kəm pā′trē ət) *n.* a person from one's own country; fellow countryman.

com·peer (kəm pēr′) *n.* 1. a person of equal rank; equal; peer. 2. a comrade; companion.

com·pel (kəm pel′) *v.t.,* **com·pelled, com·pel·ling.** 1. to drive or urge with force; oblige: *The rain compelled us to cancel our picnic.* 2. to obtain or bring about by force: *The sergeant compelled obedience to his orders.*

com·pen·di·ous (kəm pen′dē əs) *adj.* forming a summary; short but complete; concise: *a compendious handbook on camping.*

com·pen·di·um (kəm pen′dē əm) *n. pl.,* **com·pen·di·ums** or **com·pen·di·a** (kəm pen′dē ə). a brief summary covering a subject completely.

com·pen·sate (kom′pən sāt′) *v.,* **com·pen·sat·ed, com·pen·sat·ing.** —*v.t.* to make payment to (a person or persons) for work done, or for an injury or loss: *The company compensated her for the extra hours she worked. The insurance money could never fully compensate him for the loss of his house.* —*v.i.* to be a balance; make up: *The football player's speed compensated for his small size.* —**com′pen·sa′tive, com·pen·sa·to·ry** (kəm pen′sə tôr′ē), *adj.*

com·pen·sa·tion (kom′pən sā′shən) *n.* 1. the act of compensating. 2. something that makes payment for work done, or for an injury or loss: *He received compensation for the stolen car from his insurance company.* 3. salary or wages; pay.

com·pete (kəm pēt′) *v.i.,* **com·pet·ed, com·pet·ing.** to strive against another or others, as in a contest; vie: *The two girls competed with each other for the highest grade.*

com·pe·tence (kom′pət əns) *n.* 1. the state of being competent; ability; fitness: *He had to prove his competence as a pilot before he was licensed to fly alone.* 2. enough money to provide a comfortable living. Also, **com·pe·ten·cy** (kom′pət ən sē).

com·pe·tent (kom′pət ənt) *adj.* having or showing enough ability or knowledge; capable: *Only competent*

swimmers should use the deep end of the pool. Although the repairman was inexperienced, he did a competent job.* —**com′pe·tent·ly,** *adv.*

com·pe·ti·tion (kom′pə tish′ən) *n.* 1. the act of competing; rivalry: *The competition for scholarships was keen.* 2. something that tests or proves a person's skill or ability; contest: *Peggy entered the skating competition.*

com·pet·i·tive (kəm pet′ə tiv) *adj.* of, involving, or using competition: *a competitive sport, a highly competitive business.* —**com·pet′i·tive·ly,** *adv.* —**com·pet′i·tive·ness,** *n.*

com·pet·i·tor (kəm pet′ə tər) *n.* a person or thing that competes: *There were ten competitors in the race.*

com·pi·la·tion (kom′pə lā′shən) *n.* 1. the act of compiling. 2. something that has been compiled, such as a list or report.

com·pile (kəm pīl′) *v.t.,* **com·piled, com·pil·ing.** 1. to collect and put together in a list or report: *to compile statistics.* 2. to make or form by collecting material from various sources: *to compile an atlas of road maps.* —**com·pil′er,** *n.*

com·pla·cen·cy (kəm plā′sən sē) *n.* a feeling of self-satisfaction. Also, **com·pla·cence** (kəm plā′səns).

com·pla·cent (kəm plā′sənt) *adj.* pleased with oneself or one's position; self-satisfied: *The boxing champion was so complacent that he did not bother to train for his match with the challenger.* —**com·pla′cent·ly,** *adv.*

com·plain (kəm plān′) *v.i.* 1. to find fault; express dissatisfaction: *She complained that the exam was too hard.* 2. to talk about one's pains or ills. 3. to make an accusation or charge: *We complained to the police about our noisy neighbors.* —**com·plain′er,** *n.*

com·plain·ant (kəm plā′nənt) *n.* a person who files a formal complaint in a law suit.

com·plaint (kəm plānt′) *n.* 1. an expression of dissatisfaction: *We took our complaints to the store manager.* 2. a cause for complaining: *I have no complaint with the food in this restaurant.* 3. an illness; ailment: *She suffers from the common complaints of old age.* 4. a formal charge or accusation in a law suit.

com·plai·sance (kəm plā′zəns) *n.* a willingness to please others; agreeableness.

com·plai·sant (kəm plā′zənt) *adj.* willing to please others; obliging; agreeable. —**com·plai′sant·ly,** *adv.*

com·ple·ment (*n.,* kom′plə mənt; *v.,* kom′plə ment′) *n.* 1. something that makes complete: *The new table is just the right complement for the room.* 2. the required number or amount: *The football team now has its full complement of players.* 3. *Grammar.* a word or phrase that completes a sentence or predicate. In the sentence *The sky is blue, blue* is a complement. —*v.t.* to make complete: *The background music nicely complements the action in the movie.* ▲ *See* **compliment** for usage note.

com·ple·men·ta·ry (kom plə ment′trē) *adj.* making whole; completing: *The rubber boots were complementary to her rain outfit.*

complementary angle, either of two angles whose sum is 90 degrees.

complementary colors, two colors of the spectrum that produce white or gray light when combined. Red and green are complementary colors.

com·plete (kəm plēt′) *adj.* 1. having all its parts or elements; whole; entire: *a complete set of encyclopedias.* 2. ended; finished: *The report is now complete.* 3. total; thorough: *The show was a complete success.* —*v.t.,* **com·plet·ed, com·plet·ing.** 1. to make whole: *The delicious dinner completed a wonderful day.* 2. to bring to an end; finish: *Let's complete this book before we start another.* —**com·plete′ly,** *adv.* —**com·plete′ness,** *n.*

com·ple·tion (kəm plē′shən) *n.* the act of completing or the state of being completed.

com·plex (*adj.,* kəm pleks′, kom′pleks; *n.,* kom′pleks) *adj.* **1.** hard to understand or do: *a complex arithmetic problem.* **2.** made up of many related parts: *a complex piece of machinery.* —*n.* **1.** a whole made up of a combination of related parts: *The new housing complex will have a hotel as well as several apartment buildings.* **2.** a group of related ideas or feelings that a person may not know he has, which can influence his behavior to an abnormal degree. —**com·plex′ly,** *adv.*

complex fraction, a fraction having a common fraction, mixed number, or algebraic expression in the numerator, denominator, or in both. The fractions ½/2⅛ and ¾/1⅘ are complex fractions. Also, **compound fraction.**

com·plex·ion (kəm plek′shən) *n.* **1.** the color and general appearance of the skin, especially of the face. **2.** the general appearance or character of anything: *The addition of the two new players changed the complexion of the team.*

com·plex·i·ty (kəm plek′sə tē) *n. pl.,* **com·plex·i·ties. 1.** the state or quality of being complex: *The complexity of the mathematics problem baffled us all.* **2.** something complex.

complex sentence, a sentence that has one independent clause and one or more dependent clauses. For example: *After the girls played tennis for an hour, they decided to go for a swim.*

com·pli·ance (kəm plī′əns) *n.* **1.** the act of complying or giving in. **2.** readiness to give in to others. Also, **com·pli·an·cy** (kəm plī′ən sē).

in compliance with. in agreement with; according to: *She acted in compliance with our request.*

com·pli·ant (kəm plī′ənt) *adj.* complying or ready to comply; giving in; yielding. —**com·pli′ant·ly,** *adv.*

com·pli·cate (kom′plə kāt′) *v.t.,* **com·pli·cat·ed, com·pli·cat·ing.** to make hard to understand or do; make complex or difficult: *His little sister's clumsy help only complicated the boy's job.*

com·pli·cat·ed (kom′plə kā′tid) *adj.* hard to understand or do; complex: *The directions were too complicated to follow.*

com·pli·ca·tion (kom′plə kā′shən) *n.* **1.** the act of complicating. **2.** a complicated state or condition: *Train delays caused a complication of the plans for our departure.* **3.** something that complicates or causes difficulty: *Poor health and other complications kept him out of school for almost a month.*

com·plic·i·ty (kəm plis′ə tē) *n.* the state of being an accomplice, especially in wrongdoing: *He was proven guilty of complicity in the robbery.*

com·pli·ment (*n.,* kom′plə mənt; *v.,* kom′plə ment′) **1.** an expression of admiration or praise; flattering comment: *She receives many compliments on her cooking.* **2. compliments.** an expression of regard, greeting, or good wishes: *Extend my compliments to your mother.* —*v.t.* to pay a compliment to; praise; congratulate: *We complimented the bride on her beautiful dress.*

▲ **Compliment** and **complement** are often confused. To **compliment** is to admire or praise a person: *We complimented her on her new dress.* To **complement** is to complete something: *Her new pocketbook and shoes complemented her spring outfit.*

com·pli·men·ta·ry (kom′plə men′tər ē, kom′plə men′trē) *adj.* **1.** containing or expressing a compliment. **2.** without charge; free: *The coach gave us two complimentary tickets to the football game.*

com·ply (kəm plī′) *v.i.,* **com·plied, com·ply·ing.** to act in agreement, as with a request or rule: *I will comply with your wishes.*

com·po·nent (kəm pō′nənt) *n.* an essential part or ingredient: *We were given the components of a radio and we put them together ourselves.* —*adj.* being an essential part or ingredient: *the component parts of a machine.*

com·port (kəm pôrt′) *v.t.* to behave or conduct (oneself): *He comports himself well in the classroom.* —*v.i.* to suit or agree: *His joking attitude does not comport with his position as a judge.*

com·port·ment (kəm pôrt′mənt) *n.* behavior; conduct.

com·pose (kəm pōz′) *v.,* **com·posed, com·pos·ing.** —*v.t.* **1.** to be the elements or parts of; make up: *Twelve persons compose a jury. The fabric was composed of synthetic fibers.* **2.** to make or form from parts or elements; fashion: *He composed his paper from different sources.* **3.** to create (a musical work). **4.** to make quiet or calm: *She tried to compose herself after hearing the shocking news.* **5.** *Printing.* **a.** to set (type). **b.** to set the type for: *The printer composed the page of the book.* —*v.i.* to create a musical work.

com·posed (kəm pōzd′) *adj.* self-controlled, quiet, or calm. —**com·pos·ed·ly** (kəm pō′zid lē), *adv.*

com·pos·er (kəm pō′zər) *n.* a person who composes something, especially one who composes music.

com·pos·ite (kəm poz′it) *adj.* **1.** made up of various ous parts or elements: *a composite picture made up of parts of a few old snapshots.* **2.** belonging to a family of plants having flowers that are clustered together in dense flower heads. Chrysanthemums and daisies are composite flowers. —*n.* something that is composed of various parts or elements.

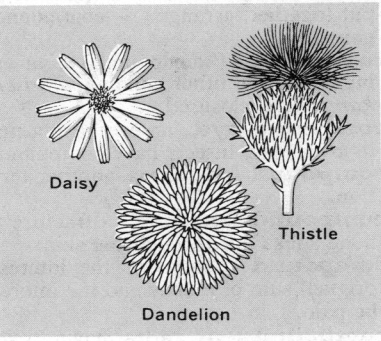

Daisy
Thistle
Dandelion

Composite flowers

composite number, a number that can be divided without a remainder by one or more numbers as well as by itself and 1. The numbers 4, 6, 8, 9, and 10 are composite numbers.

composite photograph, a photograph made by combining two or more photographs.

com·po·si·tion (kom′pə zish′ən) *n.* **1.** the act of forming parts into a whole; the act of composing, as a work of writing, art, or music: *The musician spent several years in the composition of his opera.* **2.** the parts that make up a whole: *The chemist analyzed the moon rock to determine its composition.* **3.** something composed, especially a work of writing, art, or music: *He wrote a composition about colonial America.* **4.** the way in which something is composed: *The prize-winning photograph has a balanced composition.* **5.** a mixture of substances: *The workmen used a composition containing gravel and asphalt to pave the road.* **6.** *Printing.* the setting of type.

at; āpe; cär; end; mē; it; īce; hot; ōld; fôrk; wood; fool; oil; out; up; turn; sing; thin; this; hw in white; zh in treasure. The symbol ə stands for the sound of a in about, e in taken, i in pencil, o in lemon, and u in circus.

com·pos·i·tor (kəm poz′ə tər) *n.* see **typesetter** (*def. 1*).

com·post (kom′pōst) *n.* a mixture of decayed plants and manure, used to fertilize soil.

com·po·sure (kəm pō′zhər) *n.* self-control; calmness: *Her composure during the fire had a calming influence on everyone around her.*

com·pote (kom′pōt) *n.* **1.** fruit that is stewed in syrup. **2.** a shallow bowl or dish having a stem, usually used for fruit or candy.

com·pound¹ (*adj.,* kom′pound′; *v.,* kəm pound′; *n.,* kom′pound′) *adj.* composed of two or more parts. —*v.t.* **1.** to mix (parts) to form something: *He compounded water, sand, and soil to form bricks.* **2.** to make (something) by combining various parts or ingredients: *The druggist compounded a medicine for the patient.* **3.** to add to: *She compounded her troubles at school by failing two subjects.* —*n.* **1.** a combination of two or more parts; mixture. **2.** a substance formed by the chemical combination of two or more elements: *A carbohydrate is a compound of carbon, hydrogen, and oxygen.* **3.** a word composed of two or more words that are written together or joined with a hyphen. The words *blueberry* and *fair-haired* are compounds. A combination of two words that has its own special meaning, such as *common sense,* may also be called a compound. [Middle French *compondre* to put together, arrange.] —**com·pound′a·ble,** *adj.* —**com·pound′er,** *n.*

com·pound² (kom′pound′) *n.* an enclosed area containing a house or other building: *a prison compound.* [Malay *kampong* enclosure.]

compound eye, an eye having many units, each with its own lens. Insects have compound eyes.

compound fraction, another term for **complex fraction.**

compound fracture, a fracture in which the broken bone sticks out through the skin.

compound interest, the interest paid on both the original sum of money and the interest already paid or to be paid.

compound leaf, a leaf having two or more leaflets on a common leafstalk.

compound sentence, a sentence that consists of two or more independent clauses, usually connected by a conjunction or conjunctions. For example: *John went to the store, and later he went to the movies.*

com·pre·hend (kom′pri hend′) *v.t.* **1.** to grasp with the mind; understand: *He was not able to comprehend the teacher's explanation of the mathematics problem.* **2.** to take in or contain; include: *The file comprehends every book in the library.*

com·pre·hen·si·ble (kom′pri hen′sə bəl) *adj.* that can be understood; understandable: *The injured man's words were not comprehensible.* —**com′pre·hen′si·bil′i·ty,** *n.* —**com′pre·hen′si·bly,** *adv.*

com·pre·hen·sion (kom′pri hen′shən) *n.* the act or power of grasping something with the mind; understanding: *Einstein's theory of relativity is beyond my comprehension.*

com·pre·hen·sive (kom′pri hen′siv) *adj.* **1.** covering a great deal; including much: *This book is a comprehensive study of the Civil War.* **2.** capable of understanding many things: *That teacher has a comprehensive mind.* —**com′pre·hen′sive·ly,** *adv.* —**com′pre·hen′sive·ness,** *n.*

com·press (*v.,* kəm pres′; *n.,* kom′pres′) *v.t.* to press or squeeze together; force into a smaller space: *The machine compressed cotton into bales.* —*n. pl.,* **com·press·es.** a pad or cloth used to apply pressure, heat, cold, or medicine to some part of the body. —**com·press′i·bil′i·ty,** *n.* —**com·press′i·ble,** *adj.*

compressed air, air that has been reduced in volume by compression. Its pressure when released is used to operate machinery, such as paint sprayers, pneumatic drills, and brakes.

com·pres·sion (kəm presh′ən) *n.* **1.** the act or process of compressing. **2.** the state of being compressed.

com·pres·sive (kəm pres′iv) *adj.* compressing or tending to compress.

com·pres·sor (kəm pres′ər) *n.* a person or thing that compresses, especially a machine that compresses gases: *an air compressor.*

com·prise (kəm prīz′) *v.t.,* **com·prised, com·pris·ing.** to consist of.

com·pro·mise (kom′prə mīz′) *n.* **1.** the settlement of an argument or disagreement by having each side agree to give up some part of its claims or demands. **2.** the result of such a settlement. —*v.,* **com·pro·mised, com·pro·mis·ing.** —*v.i.* to make a compromise: *The two brothers compromised and watched parts of both television programs.* —*v.t.* to expose to suspicion or danger: *She compromised her reputation.* —**com′pro·mis′er,** *n.*

comp·trol·ler (kən trō′lər) *n.* see **controller** (*def. 2*).

com·pul·sion (kəm pul′shən) *n.* **1.** the act of compelling or the state of being compelled. **2.** a strong impulse to do something: *Her compulsion to eat chocolates kept her from losing weight.*

com·pul·sive (kəm pul′siv) *adj.* of, relating to, or caused by compulsion: *He is a compulsive liar. That man is a compulsive gambler.* —**com·pul′sive·ly,** *adv.* —**com·pul′sive·ness,** *n.*

com·pul·so·ry (kəm pul′sər ē) *adj.* **1.** imposed as a requirement or duty; required: *In that company, retirement at age 65 is compulsory. Attendance at the lecture was compulsory for members of the class.* **2.** involving or using force.

com·punc·tion (kəm pungk′shən) *n.* an uneasiness caused by feelings of guilt; twinge of conscience: *He had no compunctions about borrowing his brother's bicycle without asking him.*

com·pu·ta·tion (kom′pyə tā′shən) *n.* **1.** the act, process, or method of computing. **2.** the result of computing.

com·pute (kəm pyōōt′) *v.t.,* **com·put·ed, com·put·ing.** to find out or calculate by using mathematics: *The builder computed the cost of the garage.*

com·put·er (kəm pyōō′tər) *n.* **1.** an electronic device that performs complex mathematical calculations rapidly, using information and instructions it receives and stores. **2.** any device or person that computes.

com·put·er·ize (kəm pyōō′tə rīz′) *v.t.,* **com·put·er·ized, com·put·er·iz·ing.** **1.** to control by or store in an electronic computer: *to computerize data.* **2.** to equip with electronic computers: *to computerize an office, to computerize a newspaper printing plant.*

com·rade (kom′rad) *n.* **1.** a close friend or companion. **2.** a person who works with or shares the same interests as another or others.

com·rade·ship (kom′rad ship′) *n.* fellowship; companionship.

con¹ (kon) *adv.* against: *We debated the problem pro and con.* —*n.* a reason, argument, or person against something: *The two friends discussed the pros and cons of buying the car.* [Short for Latin *contrā* against.]

con² (kon) *v.t.,* **conned, con·ning.** to study carefully; learn very well. [Old English *cunnian* to test, examine.]

con-, the form of the prefix **com-** before all consonants except *b, h, l, m, p, r,* and *w,* as in *concentrate, congenial.*

Con·a·kry (kon′ə krē) *n.* the capital and chief port of Guinea, in the western part of the country. Pop. (1967 est.), 197,267.

con·cave (*adj.*, kon kāv′, kon′kāv; *n.*, kon′kāv) *adj.* curving inward, as the inside of a bowl. —*n.* a concave surface. —**con·cave′ly**, *adv.* —**con·cave′ness**, *n.*

con·cav·i·ty (kon kav′ə tē) *n. pl.*, **con·cav·i·ties.** 1. the state of being concave. 2. a concave surface.

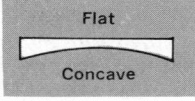
Flat
Concave

Concave lens

con·ceal (kən sēl′) *v.t.* 1. to put or keep out of sight; hide: *He concealed the car key under the dashboard.* 2. to keep secret: *She concealed her anger by smiling.* —**con·ceal′a·ble**, *adj.* —**con·ceal′er**, *n.*

con·ceal·ment (kən sēl′mənt) *n.* 1. the act of concealing or the state of being concealed. 2. a means or place for concealing.

con·cede (kən sēd′) *v.*, **con·ced·ed, con·ced·ing.** —*v.t.* 1. to admit as true: *Jack conceded defeat in the election for class president.* 2. to grant or yield: *His father conceded him the right to take the car on weekends.* —*v.i.* to make a concession; yield: *The candidate would not concede until all the votes were counted.*

con·ceit (kən sēt′) *n.* 1. a very high opinion of oneself or of one's achievements; vanity: *Fame and success went to her head and filled her with conceit.* 2. a witty or fanciful thought or expression.

con·ceit·ed (kən sē′tid) *adj.* having a very high opinion of oneself or of one's achievements; vain. —**con·ceit′ed·ly**, *adv.* —**con·ceit′ed·ness**, *n.*

con·ceiv·a·ble (kən sē′və bəl) *adj.* that can be thought of or imagined; imaginable. —**con·ceiv′a·bil′i·ty**, *n.* —**con·ceiv′a·bly**, *adv.*

con·ceive (kən sēv′) *v.*, **con·ceived, con·ceiv·ing.** —*v.t.* 1. to form or develop (something) in the mind; devise: *The engineers conceived a design for a new spacecraft.* 2. to picture (something) in the mind; think of or imagine: *We could not conceive his cheating on a test.* 3. to become pregnant with (a child). —*v.i.* 1. to form an idea; think: *The team could not conceive of losing the game.* 2. to become pregnant. —**con·ceiv′er**, *n.*

con·cen·trate (kon′sən trāt) *v.*, **con·cen·trat·ed, con·cen·trat·ing.** —*v.t.* 1. to bring or direct closely to one place, point, or goal; focus or fix on: *The team concentrated their efforts on winning the game.* 2. to make stronger or thicker: *She boiled down the sauce to concentrate its flavor.* —*v.i.* 1. to direct all of one's efforts or attention: *The student could not concentrate on his studies because the room was noisy.* 2. to come closely together in one place: *The soldiers concentrated outside the city for the attack.* —*n.* something that has been concentrated: *a concentrate of orange juice.* —**con′cen·tra′tor**, *n.*

con·cen·tra·tion (kon′sən trā′shən) *n.* 1. the act of concentrating or the state of being concentrated. 2. close attention: *A ringing telephone disturbed Jim's concentration on his studies.* 3. something concentrated: *There is a concentration of houses along the shore.* 4. the strength of something, such as a solution.

concentration camp, a camp that is fenced and guarded, used to confine prisoners of war or other persons by a government or military ruler.

con·cen·tric (kən sen′trik) *adj.* having a common center: *concentric circles.* Also, **con·cen·tri·cal** (kən sen′tri·kəl). —**con·cen′tri·cal·ly**, *adv.*

con·cept (kon′sept) *n.* a general idea, especially one based on a person's knowledge or experience: *He had no concept of honor.*

con·cep·tion (kən sep′shən) *n.* 1. the act of forming concepts. 2. a general idea; concept: *My conception of good manners is different from hers.* 3. the act of becoming pregnant.

con·cep·tu·al (kən sep′chōō əl) *adj.* of or relating to conceptions or concepts: *Thinking is conceptual.* —**con·cep′tu·al·ly**, *adv.*

con·cern (kən surn′) *v.t.* 1. to be of interest or importance to; have to do with: *What the President says and does concerns us all.* 2. to cause to worry; trouble: *Her illness concerns me very much.* —*n.* 1. something that is of interest or importance to: *What he reads is his concern, not yours.* 2. worried interest: *The neighbors showed much concern for the sick family.* 3. a business establishment; company: *Mr. Smith heads a large clothing concern.*

con·cerned (kən surnd′) *adj.* 1. interested; involved: *Tom is concerned with politics.* 2. having or showing worried interest: *He is concerned about his poor grades.*

con·cern·ing (kən sur′ning) *prep.* having to do with; relating to; regarding: *We watched a special program on television concerning deep-sea diving.*

con·cert (kon′sərt) *n.* a public performance of music: *a jazz concert.* —*adj.* of or relating to concerts: *a concert pianist, a concert hall.*

con·cert·ed (kən sur′tid) *adj.* planned or carried out by mutual agreement: *The team members made a concerted effort to improve their playing.*

con·cer·ti·na (kon′sər tē′nə) *n.* a musical instrument resembling an accordian.

con·cer·to (kən cher′tō) *n. pl.*, **con·cer·tos** or **con·cer·ti** (kən cher′tē). a musical composition for one or more solo instruments accompanied by an orchestra.

Concertina

con·ces·sion (kən sesh′ən) *n.* 1. the act of granting or conceding: *Father made a concession and allowed Jim to use the car on weekends.* 2. something granted or conceded: *The labor union demanded a number of concessions from the owner of the factory.* 3. a privilege or right granted by a government or other authority to operate a business at a certain place. 4. the business itself: *an ice-cream concession.*

con·ces·sion·aire (kən sesh′ə ner′) *n.* a person who has been granted a concession, as at an athletic stadium or fairground.

conch (kongk, konch) *n. pl.*, **conchs** (kongks) or **conch·es** (kon′chiz). 1. a saltwater animal having a large spiral shell. 2. the shell of this animal.

con·cil·i·ate (kən sil′ē āt′) *v.t.*, **con·cil·i·at·ed, con·cil·i·at·ing.** 1. to overcome the hostility or mistrust of; win over; placate: *The shopkeeper tried to conciliate the angry customer by giving her a refund.* 2. to make compatible; reconcile. —**con·cil′i·a′tion**, *n.* —**con·cil′i·a′tor**, *n.*

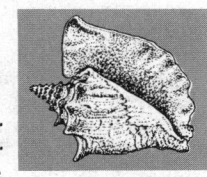
Conch

con·cil·i·a·to·ry (kən sil′ē ə tôr′ē) *adj.* meant to or tending to conciliate: *She has a conciliatory manner.*

con·cise (kən sīs′) *adj.* expressing much in few words; terse: *The instructions for using the machine were clear and concise.* —**con·cise′ly**, *adv.* —**con·cise′ness**, *n.*

at; āpe; cär; end; mē; it; īce; hot; ōld; fôrk; wood; fōōl; oil; out; up; turn; sing; thin; **th**is; **hw** in white; **zh** in treasure. The symbol ə stands for the sound of **a** in about, **e** in taken, **i** in pencil, **o** in lemon, and **u** in circus.

con·clave (kon′klāv) *n.* **1.** a private meeting. **2.** a meeting of the cardinals of the Roman Catholic Church to elect a pope.

con·clude (kən klōōd′) *v.,* **con·clud·ed, con·clud·ing.** —*v.t.* **1.** to bring to an end; finish: *The lecturer concluded his talk with a joke.* **2.** to arrange or settle finally: *The two countries concluded a treaty.* **3.** to come to an opinion about: *What do you conclude from these facts?* —*v.i.* **1.** to come to an end; close: *The church service concluded with the singing of a hymn.* **2.** to come to an opinion. —**con·clud′er,** *n.*

con·clu·sion (kən klōō′zhən) *n.* **1.** the final part of something; end: *The conclusion of the movie was very sad.* **2.** a final result or arrangement; settlement: *The conclusion of the sale of the house took place in the lawyer's office.* **3.** a final opinion reached by reasoning: *The judge's conclusion was that the evidence was true.*

con·clu·sive (kən klōō′siv) *adj.* that puts an end to argument or doubt; final: *The discovery of the arrowheads gave conclusive proof that Indians once lived in the area.* —**con·clu′sive·ly,** *adv.* —**con·clu′sive·ness,** *n.*

con·coct (kon kokt′) *v.t.* **1.** to prepare by mixing several ingredients: *She concocted a stew with beef, potatoes, and carrots.* **2.** to put together; devise: *The thieves concocted a plan to rob the bank.* —**con·coc′tion,** *n.*

con·com·i·tant (kon kom′ə tənt) *adj.* accompanying: *a concomitant event.* —*n.* something that happens with or accompanies something else. —**con·com′i·tant·ly,** *adv.*

con·cord (kon′kôrd, kong′kôrd) *n.* **1.** peace and harmony between persons, countries, or things; accord. **2.** a treaty establishing peace and harmony between countries.

Con·cord (kong′kərd) *n.* **1.** a town in eastern Massachusetts, site of one of the first battles of the American Revolution, on April 19, 1775. **2.** the capital of New Hampshire, in the southern part of the state. Pop. (1970), 30,022.

con·cord·ance (kon kôrd′əns) *n.* **1.** agreement; harmony. **2.** an alphabetical index of the important words of a book, such as the Bible, that gives the passages in which the words occur.

con·cord·ant (kon kôrd′ənt) *adj.* agreeing; harmonious: *His political views are concordant with mine.* —**con·cord′ant·ly,** *adv.*

con·cor·dat (kon kôr′dat) *n.* **1.** a formal agreement. **2.** a treaty between the Vatican and a country about church affairs.

con·course (kon′kôrs) *n.* **1.** a moving or coming together: *A concourse of atoms formed the universe.* **2.** a large gathering; crowd. **3.** a large, open place where crowds gather, as in a bus or train station.

con·crete (kon′krēt, kon krēt′) *adj.* **1.** of or relating to things or events that can be seen, felt, or experienced: *A chair is a concrete object.* **2.** of or relating to specific persons, things, or events: *The teacher asked for concrete facts about the fall of the Roman Empire.* **3.** made of a mixture of crushed stone, gravel, sand, or pebbles, and water, that becomes hard when it dries: *a concrete driveway.* —*n.* such a mixture, used for building or paving. —**con·crete′ly,** *adv.* —**con·crete′ness,** *n.*

con·cu·bine (kong′kyə bīn′) *n.* a woman who lives with a man without marrying him.

con·cur (kən kur′) *v.i.,* **con·curred, con·cur·ring. 1.** to have the same opinion; agree: *The two brothers concurred in their interest in sports.* **2.** to act or work together: *Hard work and intelligence concurred to make him a success.* **3.** to happen at the same time: *His birthday concurs with Thanksgiving Day this year.*

con·cur·rence (kən kur′əns) *n.* **1.** a sharing of the same opinion; agreement. **2.** an acting or working together. **3.** a happening at the same time.

con·cur·rent (kən kur′ənt) *adj.* **1.** existing or happening at the same time: *The early development of man was concurrent with the Ice Age.* **2.** acting together. **3.** in agreement: *concurrent ideas.* —**con·cur′rent·ly,** *adv.*

con·cus·sion (kən kush′ən) *n.* **1.** a violent shaking or jarring; shock: *The building shook from the concussion of the explosion.* **2.** an injury caused by a fall or blow, especially to the brain or spine.

con·demn (kən dem′) *v.t.* **1.** to disapprove of strongly: *They condemned his dishonesty.* **2.** to show or declare the guilt of; convict: *The thief was condemned by the jury.* **3.** to set the punishment of; sentence: *The judge condemned the criminal to ten years in jail.* **4.** to declare to be unfit for further use: *The slum building was condemned and torn down.* **5.** to take (private property) for public use: *to condemn land for a state highway.*

con·dem·na·tion (kon′dem nā′shən) *n.* **1.** the act of condemning or the state of being condemned. **2.** strong disapproval.

con·den·sa·tion (kon′den sā′shən) *n.* **1.** the act of condensing or the state of being condensed. **2.** something that results from condensing: *He read a condensation of the novel.* **3.** the changing of a gas to a liquid or solid form: *the condensation of steam into water.*

con·dense (kən dens′) *v.,* **con·densed, con·dens·ing.** —*v.t.* **1.** to make thicker or more compact; reduce the volume of: *to condense a sauce by boiling it.* **2.** to make shorter and more concise; abridge: *The writer condensed the novel to the length of a short story.* **3.** to change (a gas) into a liquid or solid form. —*v.i.* to become condensed. —**con·den′sa·ble,** *adj.*

condensed milk, sweetened cow's milk that has been thickened by boiling away part of the water.

con·dens·er (kən den′sər) *n.* **1.** a person or thing that condenses. **2.** a device that receives and stores an electric charge; capacitor. **3.** an apparatus for changing a gas into a liquid.

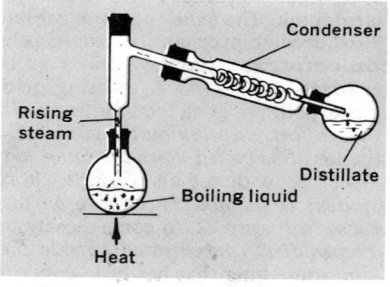

Condenser *(def. 3)*

con·de·scend (kon′di send′) *v.i.* **1.** to come down willingly to a humbler or lower level: *The great scientist condescended to give a talk to the school children.* **2.** to do something in a snobbish or superior way: *The haughty woman condescended to stand in line at the grocery store.*

con·de·scend·ing (kon′di sen′ding) *adj.* characterized by a snobbish or superior manner. —**con′de·scend′ing·ly,** *adv.*

con·de·scen·sion (kon′di sen′shən) *n.* **1.** a coming down to a humbler or lower level. **2.** a snobbish or superior attitude or manner.

con·di·ment (kon′də mənt) *n.* something used to make food more flavorful, such as a seasoning, spice, or sauce.

con·di·tion (kən dish′ən) *n.* **1.** the way that a person or thing is or exists: *The tramp's clothes were in shabby condition. The patient's condition was serious.* **2.** a state of physical fitness: *An athlete must keep in condition.* **3.** social position; rank: *a man of humble condition.* **4.** something needed before something else can take place or exist; something on which another thing depends: *Hard work is usu-*

ally a condition for getting good grades. **5.** something that limits or restricts: *Father set up several conditions for using the car.* **6.** *Informal.* a disease or ailment; illness: *His uncle has a heart condition.* **7. conditions.** circumstances that affect one's way of life or activities: *poor living conditions, working conditions.* —*v.t.* **1.** to put in a healthy or fit condition: *Regular exercise conditions the body.* **2.** to limit or restrict: *Laziness often conditions a person's success.* **3.** to accustom to: *Living in Alaska soon conditioned the boys to cold weather.* **4.** to cause to behave in a certain way: *The scientist conditioned the dog to bark when a bell rang.* —**con·di'tion·er,** *n.*

on condition that. provided that; if: *You may go on condition that you come home early.*

con·di·tion·al (kən dish'ən əl) *adj.* **1.** depending on a condition or conditions. **2.** *Grammar.* expressing a condition. In the sentence *If he goes, I will go too, If he goes* is a conditional clause. —**con·di'tion·al·ly,** *adv.*

con·di·tioned (kən dish'ənd) *adj.* **1.** having or subject to a condition or conditions. **2.** in good physical condition; fit. **3.** *Psychology.* caused by or relating to conditioning: *a conditioned response.*

con·dole (kən dōl') *v.i.,* **con·doled, con·dol·ing.** to express sympathy: *to condole with a widow.*

con·do·lence (kən dō'ləns) *n.* an expression of sympathy: *He sent his condolences to Mary's family when her father died.*

con·done (kən dōn') *v.t.,* **con·doned, con·don·ing.** to excuse or forgive; overlook: *I can't condone his bad behavior.*
▲ See **excuse** for usage note.

con·dor (kon'dər) *n.* a very large vulture having black-and-white feathers and a bare, dark gray head and neck. The condor is found in the mountains of South America and California.

con·duce (kən dōōs', kən dyōōs') *v.i.,* **con·duced, con·duc·ing.** to help bring about (with *to* or *toward*): *Getting enough sleep conduces to good health.*

con·du·cive (kən dōō'siv, kən dyōō'siv) *adj.* helping to bring about; leading (with *to*): *A brisk walk is conducive to a good appetite.* —**con·du'cive·ness,** *n.*

con·duct (*n.,* kon'dukt; *v.,* kən dukt') *n.* **1.** the way that a person behaves or acts: *The child's conduct was usually very good.* **2.** guidance or control; management: *His successful conduct of his business has made him rich.* —*v.t.* **1.** to take charge of; control; manage: *Mr. Brown conducted the affairs of his business very successfully.* **2.** to direct or lead, such as an orchestra, chorus, or other musical group: *Who will conduct the symphony orchestra next season?* **3.** to behave (oneself): *The spoiled child conducted himself badly in front of the guests.* **4.** to act as a guide: *My cousin conducted us safely to the station.* **5.** to transmit or carry: *Cast iron conducts heat evenly. The gutter conducts rain water from the roof.* —**con·duct'i·bil'i·ty,** *n.* —**con·duct'i·ble,** *adj.*

con·duc·tion (kən duk'shən) *n.* **1.** the flow of heat, electricity, or sound by the transmission of energy from one particle to another. **2.** a carrying or conveying: *the conduction of water by pipes.*

con·duc·tive (kən duk'tiv) *adj.* able to conduct heat, electricity, or sound.

con·duc·tiv·i·ty (kon'duk tiv'ə tē) *n.* the ability of a material or body to conduct heat, electricity, or sound: *The conductivity of rubber for electricity is poor.*

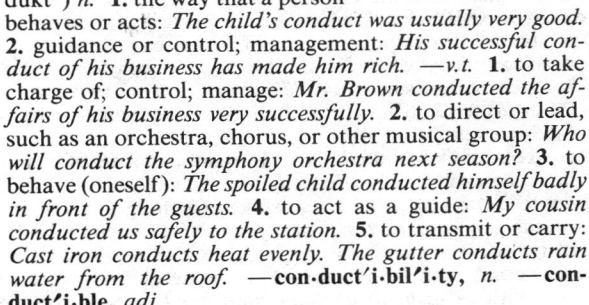

Condor

con·duc·tor (kən duk'tər) *n.* **1.** a person who conducts; director; guide; leader. **2.** the director of an orchestra, chorus, or other musical group. **3.** a person on a railroad train, streetcar, or bus, who collects the tickets or fares and announces stops. **4.** a material or body that conducts heat, electricity, or sound.

con·duit (kon'dit, kon'dōō it) *n.* **1.** a channel, pipe, or tube used to carry liquids. **2.** a tube or pipe that protects electric wires or cables.

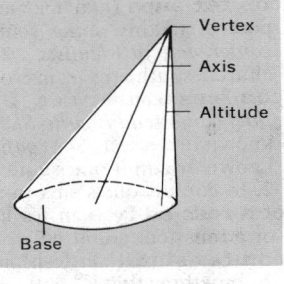

Cone

cone (kōn) *n.* **1.** a solid that narrows to a point from a circular base. **2.** an object shaped like a cone: *an ice-cream cone.* **3.** a fruit with scales that bear seeds, growing on a pine or other evergreen tree. **4.** a cell in the retina of the eye that is sensitive to color and bright light.

Con·es·to·ga wagon (kon'is tō'gə) a covered wagon with an arched canvas top and broad wheels, used by pioneers to cross the American prairies.

co·ney (kō'nē) *n. pl.,* **co·neys.** another spelling of **cony.**

con·fec·tion (kən fek'shən) *n.* any sweet food or mixture, such as a piece of candy, a preserve, or a pastry.

Conestoga wagon

con·fec·tion·er (kən fek'shə nər) *n.* a person who makes or sells confections, such as candy or pastry.

con·fec·tion·er·y (kən fek'shə ner'ē) *n. pl.,* **con·fec·tion·er·ies. 1.** a place where confections are made or sold. **2.** candies or sweets; confections.

con·fed·er·a·cy (kən fed'ər ə sē) *n. pl.,* **con·fed·er·a·cies. 1.** a union of countries, states, or persons joined together for a common purpose; league; alliance. **2. the Confederacy.** the Confederate States of America.

con·fed·er·ate (*n., adj.,* kən fed'ər it; *v.,* kən fed'ə rāt') *n.* **1.** a person or group joined with another for a common purpose; ally. **2. Confederate.** a person who supported the Confederate States of America. —*v.t., v.i.,* **con·fed·er·at·ed, con·fed·er·at·ing.** to unite in a confederacy. —*adj.* **1.** united in a confederacy. **2. Confederate.** relating to the Confederate States of America.

Confederate States of America, the union of the eleven southern states that seceded from the United States in 1860 and 1861. They were Alabama, Arkansas, Florida, Georgia, Louisiana, Mississippi, North Carolina, South Carolina, Tennessee, Texas, and Virginia.

con·fed·er·a·tion (kən fed'ə rā'shən) *n.* **1.** the act of confederating or the state of being confederated. **2.** an alliance of countries or states for a common purpose.

con·fer (kən fur') *v.,* **con·ferred, con·fer·ring.** —*v.i.* to meet and talk together; have a discussion: *The bankers*

at; āpe; cär; end; mē; it; īce; hot; ōld; fôrk; wood; fōōl; oil; out; up; turn; sing; thin; **th**is; hw in white; zh in treasure. The symbol ə stands for the sound of **a** in about, **e** in taken, **i** in pencil, **o** in lemon, and **u** in circus.

conferred before agreeing on the loan. —*v.t.* to give as a gift or honor: *The general conferred a medal on the soldier.*

con·fer·ence (kon'fər əns) *n.* **1.** a meeting for the purpose of talking about something of common interest: *a conference of dentists.* **2.** an association of schools, churches, athletic teams, or similar groups.

con·fess (kən fes') *v.t.* **1.** to make known or admit: *The thief confessed his guilt. She confessed her error.* **2.** to make known to a priest: *She confessed her sins.* —*v.i.* **1.** to make known or admit one's guilt: *The prisoner finally confessed.* **2.** to confess one's sins to a priest.

con·fess·ed·ly (kən fes'id lē) *adv.* by one's confession or admission; admittedly.

con·fes·sion (kən fesh'ən) *n.* **1.** the act of confessing. **2.** something that is confessed: *The court accepted the prisoner's confession.*

con·fes·sion·al (kən fesh'ən əl) *n.* a small enclosed area in a church where a priest hears confessions. —*adj.* of or relating to confession.

con·fes·sor (kən fes'ər) *n.* **1.** a priest who hears confessions. **2.** a person who confesses.

con·fet·ti (kən fet'ē) *n.* small bits of paper thrown about as a sign of celebration, as at a parade.

con·fi·dant (kon'fə dant') *n.* a person to whom one confides secrets or personal matters.

con·fide (kən fīd') *v.,* **con·fid·ed, con·fid·ing.** —*v.t.* **1.** to tell as a secret; trust with a personal matter: *She confided her fears to her friend.* **2.** to give into another's care; entrust: *The mother confided her baby into the nurse's care.* —*v.i.* **1.** to tell secrets or personal matters: *Mary always confided in her good friend.* **2.** to put trust or have faith: *They confide in your good judgment.* —**con·fid'er,** *n.*

con·fi·dence (kon'fə dəns) *n.* **1.** firm trust or faith; reliance: *He has confidence in his friend's honesty.* **2.** faith in oneself; self-assurance: *He is full of confidence.* **3.** something told in trust; secret: *She entrusted her friend with several confidences.*

in confidence. privately and as a secret: *She told her friend the news in confidence.*

con·fi·dent (kon'fə dənt) *adj.* **1.** firmly trusting; certain; sure: *Joe is confident that his team will win.* **2.** having faith in oneself; self-assured. —**con'fi·dent·ly,** *adv.*

con·fi·den·tial (kon'fə den'shəl) *adj.* **1.** told or kept in secrecy or privacy: *This letter is confidential.* **2.** suggesting confidence: *She has a confidential manner.* **3.** entrusted with secret or private matters: *The executive has a confidential secretary.* —**con'fi·den'tial·ly,** *adv.*

con·fid·ing (kən fī'ding) *adj.* tending to confide; trusting. —**con·fid'ing·ly,** *adv.*

con·fig·u·ra·tion (kən fig'yə rā'shən) *n.* form or shape resulting from the arrangement of parts.

con·fine (*v.,* kən fīn'; *n.,* kon'fīn) *v.t.,* **con·fined, con·fin·ing. 1.** to keep within limits; restrict: *She confined her letter to a single page.* **2.** to restrict to a particular place; keep or shut in: *The sheriff confined the prisoner in a cell. Her illness confined her to bed.* —*n.* usually, **confines.** a limit; boundary; border: *The dog was not permitted within the confines of the house.*

con·fine·ment (kən fīn'mənt) *n.* **1.** the act of confining or the state of being confined. **2.** the state of being confined because of childbirth.

con·firm (kən furm') *v.t.* **1.** to prove to be true or without mistakes; verify: *The senator confirmed the report that he would run for President.* **2.** to consent to officially; approve; ratify: *The senate confirmed his nomination as ambassador.* **3.** to make firm or firmer; strengthen: *The experiment confirmed the scientist's theory.* **4.** to admit to full membership in a church or synagogue.

con·fir·ma·tion (kon'fər mā'shən) *n.* **1.** the act of con-

firming. **2.** something that confirms; proof: *The newspaper waited for confirmation before printing the story.* **3.** the rite or ceremony for admitting someone to full membership in a church or synagogue.

con·firmed (kən furmd') *adj.* **1.** firmly established; proved. **2.** resulting from habit; habitual: *He is a confirmed bachelor.* —**con·firm·ed·ly** (kən fur'mid lē), *adv.*

con·fis·cate (kon'fis kāt') *v.t.,* **con·fis·cat·ed, con·fis·cat·ing.** to seize by authority: *Customs agents confiscated the smuggled goods.* —**con'fis·ca'tion,** *n.*

con·fla·gra·tion (kon'flə grā'shən) *n.* a very large fire that causes much damage.

con·flict (*n.,* kon'flikt; *v.,* kən flikt') *n.* **1.** a long fight; war: *A conflict broke out between the two countries.* **2.** a struggle between opposing views or ideas; disagreement: *The two reports of the fire in the newspapers are in conflict with one another.* —*v.i.* to be opposed; disagree: *The two accounts of the robbery conflict.*

con·flu·ence (kon'floo əns) *n.* **1.** a flowing together: *A confluence of streams forms the river.* **2.** a crowding or coming together of people or things.

con·flu·ent (kon'floo ənt) *adj.* flowing together: *confluent rivers.*

Confluence at Pittsburgh, Pa.

con·form (kən fôrm') *v.i.* **1.** to behave or think in agreement with a rule or standard: *The general told the soldiers to conform to local customs when stationed in a foreign country.* **2.** to be the same or similar; correspond: *The house conformed to the architect's plans.* —*v.t.* to bring into agreement; make the same: *Joe would not conform his taste in music to that of his friends.* —**con·form'er,** *n.*

con·form·a·ble (kən fôr'mə bəl) *adj.* **1.** corresponding; similar. **2.** obedient: *to be conformable to the rules.* —**con·form'a·bly,** *adv.*

con·form·ance (kən fôr'məns) *n.* another word for **conformity.**

con·for·ma·tion (kon'fôr mā'shən) *n.* **1.** the way in which the parts of something are arranged; shape or structure: *the conformation of a leaf.* **2.** the act of conforming or the state of being conformed.

con·form·ist (kən fôr'mist) *n.* a person who conforms to standard or popular beliefs or practices.

con·form·i·ty (kən fôr'mə tē) *n. pl.,* **con·form·i·ties. 1.** agreement or similarity: *The school insisted on conformity in dress.* **2.** behavior or thought in agreement with a rule or standard.

con·found (kon found') *v.t.* **1.** to put in a state of confusion; bewilder: *The difficult arithmetic problem confounded the student.* **2.** to mistake one thing for another; confuse: *to confound a dream for reality.* —**con·found'ed·ly,** *adv.*

con·front (kən frunt') *v.t.* **1.** to come or bring face to face with: *A difficult decision confronted him.* **2.** to face boldly or with defiance: *to confront the enemy.* —**con'fron·ta'tion,** *n.*

Con·fu·cian·ism (kən fyoo'shə niz'əm) *n.* a social and ethical system based on the teachings of Confucius and his followers, and emphasizing the maintenance of peace and justice and devotion to one's family and ancestors.

Con·fu·cius (kən fyoo'shəs) 551?–479? B.C., Chinese philosopher and the founder of Confucianism.

con·fuse (kən fyooz') *v.t.,* **con·fused, con·fus·ing.**

1. to fill with doubt or uncertainty; bewilder; perplex: *He was confused by the street signs and took the wrong turn.* **2.** to take (one person or thing) for another; mistake; mix up: *People are always confusing her with her cousin.* **3.** to throw into disorder: *to confuse the issues of an argument.* **4.** to embarrass. —**con·fus·ed·ly** (kən fyoō′zid lē), **con·fus′ing·ly,** *adv.*

con·fu·sion (kən fyoō′zhən) *n.* **1.** the state of being confused; bewilderment or disorder: *John's confusion prevented him from answering the question correctly. There was too much noise and confusion in the room to study.* **2.** a mistaking or mixing up of one person or thing for another. **3.** embarrassment: *Telling her she was pretty made her blush in confusion.*

con·fute (kən fyoōt′) *v.t.* to prove false or wrong; disprove: *Jim confuted Ted's argument. The two debaters confuted their opponents.* —**con·fut′a·ble,** *adj.* —**con·fut′er,** *n.*

Cong. **1.** Congressional. **2.** Congregational.

con·ga (kong′gə) *n.* **1.** a dance of Cuban origin in which dancers form a single line and follow each other across the dance floor. **2.** the fast music for this dance.

con·geal (kən jēl′) *v.i.* **1.** to change from a liquid to a solid by cooling or freezing: *Oil congeals in cold weather.* **2.** to thicken or coagulate. —*v.t.* to change (something) from a liquid to a solid. —**con·geal′a·ble,** *adj.* —**con·geal′er,** *n.* —**con·geal′ment,** *n.*

con·gen·ial (kən jēn′yəl) *adj.* **1.** having similar tastes and interests: *Martha and Joan are congenial friends.* **2.** to a person's liking; agreeable; pleasant: *He has a congenial job.* —**con·ge·ni·al·i·ty** (kən jē′nē al′ə tē), *n.* —**con·gen′ial·ly,** *adv.*

con·gen·i·tal (kən jen′ət əl) *adj.* existing before or from the time of birth: *He has a congenital heart defect.* —**con·gen′i·tal·ly,** *adv.*

con·ger (kong′gər) *n.* any of a group of large saltwater eels found in warm waters, valued as food. Also, **conger eel.**

con·gest (kən jest′) *v.t.* **1.** to fill so full as to overcrowd: *On weekends, automobiles congest all the highways near the city.* **2.** to fill with too great an amount of blood, mucus, or other matter. —*v.i.* to become congested.

con·ges·tion (kən jes′chən) *n.* **1.** an overcrowded condition: *There was much congestion of traffic on the highway.* **2.** too great an amount of blood, mucus, or other matter in an organ or part of the body: *He had a sore throat and congestion in his nasal passages.*

con·glom·er·ate (*v.,* kən glom′ə rāt′; *adj., n.,* kənglom′ər it) *v.,* **con·glomer·at·ed, con·glom·erat·ing.** —*v.t.* to collect together into a mass or heap. —*v.i.* to be collected together into a mass or heap. —*adj.* **1.** massed together. **2.** clustered into or forming a mass: *conglomerate rock.* —*n.* **1.** a mass formed of different parts. **2.** sedimentary rock formed of pebbles or gravel cemented together by some material, such as clay. **3.** a corporation formed of many different companies.

Conglomerate *(def. 2)*

con·glom·er·a·tion (kən glom′ə rā′shən) *n.* **1.** a mass formed of different parts. **2.** the act of conglomerating.

Con·go (kong′gō) *n.* **1.** a long river in central Africa, flowing into the Atlantic Ocean. Also, **Zaire. 2. Democratic Republic of the.** a former country in central Africa, formerly the Belgian Congo. See **Zaire. 3. Republic of the.** a country in west-central Africa, formerly a French

territory. Capital, Brazzaville. Area, 132,000 sq. mi. Pop. (1980), 1,537,000.

Con·go·lese (kong′gə lēz′) *n. pl.,* **Con·go·lese.** a person who was born or is living in either of the Congo countries. —*adj.* of or relating to either of the Congo countries, their people, or culture.

con·go snake (kong′gō) a salamander resembling an eel and having two pairs of small, weak legs. The congo snake is found in swampy regions of the southern United States. Also, **congo eel.**

Congo snake

con·grat·u·late (kən grach′ə lāt′) *v.t.,* **con·grat·u·lat·ed, con·grat·u·lat·ing.** to express one's happiness or pleasure at the success or good fortune of: *We congratulated the winner of the contest.*

con·grat·u·la·tion (kəngrach′ə lā′shən) *n.* **1.** the act of congratulating. **2. congratulations.** an expression of happiness or pleasure at another's success or good fortune.

con·grat·u·la·to·ry (kən grach′ə lə tôr′ē) *adj.* expressing congratulation: *a congratulatory telegram.*

con·gre·gate (kong′grə gāt′) *v.i.,* **con·gre·gat·ed, con·gre·gat·ing.** to come together in a crowd or mass; assemble: *The fans congregated around the movie star.*

con·gre·ga·tion (kong′grə gā′shən) *n.* **1.** the act of coming together in a crowd or mass. **2.** a gathering of people: *There was a small congregation at church Sunday.* **3.** a collection of things.

con·gre·ga·tion·al (kong′grə gā′shən əl) *adj.* **1.** of or relating to a congregation. **2. Congregational.** of or relating to a Protestant denomination holding that each church is independent and responsible only to Christ.

Con·gre·ga·tion·al·ist (kong′gre gā′shən əl ist) *n.* a member of a Congregational church.

con·gress (kong′gris) *n.* **1.** the lawmaking body of any of various countries, especially of a republic. **2. Congress.** a branch of the U.S. government that makes laws, made up of the Senate and the House of Representatives. **3.** a formal meeting of representatives to discuss a matter of common interest: *a medical congress.*

con·gres·sion·al (kən gresh′ən əl) *adj.* **1.** of or relating to a congress. **2. Congressional.** of or relating to Congress.

con·gress·man (kong′gris mən) *n. pl.,* **con·gress·men** (kong′gris mən). a member of Congress, especially of the House of Representatives. —**con′gress·wom′an,** *n.*

con·gru·ence (kong′groō əns) *n.* the state of being congruent; agreement. Also, **congruency.**

con·gru·ent (kong′groō ənt) *adj.* **1.** agreeing in every way; harmonious: *congruent beliefs.* **2.** *Geometry.* exactly alike in shape and size. Two triangles are congruent if the sides and angles of one are equal to the sides and angles of the other. —**con·gru′ent·ly,** *adv.*

con·gru·i·ty (kən groō′ə tē) *n.* the state of being congruous; agreement; harmony.

con·gru·ous (kong′groō əs) *adj.* harmoniously related; suitable; fitting. —**con′gru·ous·ness,** *n.*

---

at; āpe; cär; end; mē; it; īce; hot; ōld; fôrk; wood; foōl; oil; out; up; turn; sing; thin; this; hw in white; zh in treasure. The symbol ə stands for the sound of **a** in about, **e** in taken, **i** in pencil, **o** in lemon, and **u** in circus.

con·i·cal (kon′i kəl) *adj.* **1.** shaped like a cone. **2.** of or relating to a cone. Also, **con·ic** (kon′ik). —**con′i·cal·ly,** *adv.*

co·ni·fer (kon′ə fər, kō′nə fər) *n.* any of a large group of trees and shrubs that bear cones. Most conifers, such as the pines, spruces, and cedars, are evergreen and bear needle-shaped leaves.

co·nif·er·ous (kō nif′ər əs) *adj.* **1.** bearing cones. **2.** of or relating to the conifers.

conj. 1. conjunction. **2.** conjugation.

con·jec·tur·al (kən jek′chər əl) *adj.* based on or involving conjecture: *a conjectural solution to a problem.* —**con·jec′tur·al·ly,** *adv.*

con·jec·ture (kən jek′chər) *n.* **1.** the act of forming an opinion not based on proof. **2.** an opinion or conclusion so formed; guess: *Our conclusions about life on Mars are all conjecture.* —*v.,* **con·jec·tured, con·jec·tur·ing.** —*v.i.* to form an opinion not based on proof; guess: *The scientist conjectured about how the world began.* —*v.t.* to form an opinion about (something) without proof.

con·join (kən join′) *v.t.* to join together; unite. —*v.i.* to join together; unite: *The two countries conjoined to form an alliance.* —**con·join′er,** *n.*

con·joint (kən joint′) *adj.* joined together; united. —**con·joint′ly,** *adv.*

con·ju·gal (kon′jə gəl) *adj.* relating to marriage: *conjugal happiness.* —**con′ju·gal·ly,** *adv.*

con·ju·gate (*v.,* kon′jə gāt′; *adj.,* kon′jə git) *v.,* **con·ju·gat·ed, con·ju·gat·ing.** —*v.t.* to give the different forms of (a verb) in a certain order. The present tense of the verb "to be" is conjugated: *I am, you are, he is, we are, you are, they are.* —*v.i. Biology.* to join together in conjugation. —*adj.* joined together, especially in pairs; coupled.

con·ju·ga·tion (kon′jə gā′shən) *n.* **1.** the act of conjugating or the state of being conjugated. **2.** the different forms of a verb, indicating tense, person, number, and mood. **3.** *Biology.* the temporary joining together of two similar cells with an accompanying transfer of hereditary material.

con·junc·tion (kən jungk′shən) *n.* **1.** the act of joining together or the state of being joined together. **2.** a word used to connect words, phrases, clauses, or sentences. *And, but,* and *if* are conjunctions. **3.** *Astronomy.* the apparent meeting of two or more planets or other heavenly bodies at the same celestial longitude.

con·junc·ti·va (kon′jungk tī′və) *n. pl.,* **con·junc·ti·vas** or **con·junc·ti·vae** (kon′jungk tī′vē). the membrane that covers the front of the eyeball and lines the inner surface of the eyelids.

con·junc·tive (kən jungk′tiv) *adj.* joining together; connecting; uniting. —**con·junc′tive·ly,** *adv.*

con·junc·ti·vi·tis (kən jungk′tə vī′tis) *n.* an inflammation of the conjunctiva; pinkeye.

con·ju·ra·tion (kon′jə rā′shən, kun′jə rā′shən) *n.* **1.** a set form of words used in conjuring; incantation; spell. **2.** the practice or performance of magic. **3.** a summoning of supernatural beings by using a sacred name.

con·jure (kon′jər, kun′jər) *v.,* **con·jured, con·jur·ing.** —*v.t.* **1.** to summon or cause (something) to appear by using magic spells: *The sorcerer conjured spirits.* **2.** to bring about as if by magic: *Mother conjured up a delicious sauce for the ice cream.* —*v.i.* **1.** to summon demons or spirits by means of spells; practice sorcery. **2.** to perform magic tricks.

con·jur·er (kon′jər ər, kun′jər ər) *also,* **con·ju·ror.** *n.* **1.** a wizard; sorcerer. **2.** a person who does magic tricks; magician.

Conn., Connecticut.

con·nect (kə nekt′) *v.t.* **1.** to join or fasten together;

unite; link: *The workmen connected the boxcar to the freight train. A highway connects the two towns.* **2.** to think of as having a close relationship: *We often connect clowns with circuses.* —*v.i.* **1.** to be or become joined; meet: *This wire connects with the television antenna. The two rooms connect.* **2.** (of buses, trains, or airplanes) to be scheduled so that passengers can change from one route to another. —**con·nect′er;** *also,* **con·nec′tor,** *n.* —**con·nect′i·ble,** *adj.*

Con·nect·i·cut (kə net′i kit) *n.* a state in the northeastern United States. Capital, Hartford. Area, 5009 sq. mi. Pop. (1970), 3,032,217. Abbreviation, **Conn.**

● The name **Connecticut** comes from an Algonquian word meaning "beside the long tidal river" and indicated the area near what is now the Connecticut River. Settlers used the name for the river itself and later for nearby settlements, the colony, and eventually the state.

con·nec·tion (kə nek′shən) *n.* **1.** the act of connecting; linking up: *The connection of the pipes under the sink was difficult work.* **2.** the state of being connected; relationship or association: *The teacher's connection with the school lasted many years. The doctor studied the connection between living conditions in the slums and disease.* **3.** something that connects; connecting part; link: *The electrician looked for the faulty connection in the wiring.* **4.** a related person; distant relative: *She is a connection of his by marriage.* **5.** a person with whom one has a useful relationship: *He got the job through a business connection of his father's.* **6.** a scheduling of buses, trains, or airplanes that allows the passenger to change from one route to another: *He missed his airplane connection to Chicago.*

con·nec·tive (kə nek′tiv) *adj.* tending or serving to connect. —*n.* **1.** something that connects. **2.** a word used to connect words, phrases, and clauses. Conjunctions and relative pronouns are connectives.

connective tissue, tissue found throughout the body that serves to connect and support other tissues and organs.

con·ning tower (kon′ing) **1.** a structure on the deck of a submarine, used as an entrance and for observation. **2.** the armored pilot-house on the deck of a battleship.

Conning tower

con·niv·ance (kə nī′vəns) *n.* the act of conniving.

con·nive (kə nīv′) *v.i.,* **con·nived, con·niv·ing. 1.** to permit or encourage wrongdoing by overlooking or pretending not to know about it: *The boys connived at a classmate's cheating.* **2.** to cooperate secretly; conspire: *The bank clerk connived with the thief to rob the vault.* —**con·niv′er,** *n.*

con·nois·seur (kon′ə sur′) *n.* a person who is qualified to judge something, such as the fine arts, because of his good taste and expert knowledge.

con·no·ta·tion (kon′ə tā′shən) *n.* a meaning that a word or phrase suggests in addition to its literal meaning: *The word "politician" sometimes has an unfavorable connotation.*

con·note (kə nōt′) *v.t.,* **con·not·ed, con·not·ing.** to suggest a meaning in addition to the literal meaning: *The word "white" is the name of a color but it can also connote purity.* ▲ See **denote** for usage note. —**con′no·ta′tive,** *adj.*

con·nu·bi·al (kə no͞o′bē əl, kə nyo͞o′bē əl) *adj.* relating to or characteristic of marriage.

con·quer (kong′kər) *v.t.* **1.** to get possession of by force: *to conquer a country.* **2.** to overcome by force; defeat; vanquish: *to conquer an enemy.* **3.** to overcome by one's own effort: *She tried to conquer her shyness.* —*v.i.* to be victorious. —**con′quer·a·ble,** *adj.*

con·quer·or (kong′kər ər) *n.* a person who conquers.

con·quest (kon′kwest, kong′kwest) *n.* **1.** the act of conquering. **2.** something conquered: *Mexico was once a conquest of Spain.*

con·quis·ta·dor (kon kēs′tə dôr′, kon kwis′tə dôr′) *n. pl.,* **con·quis·ta·dors** or **con·quis·ta·do·res** (kon kēs′tə-dôr′ās, kon kēs′tə dôr′ēz). a Spanish conqueror in Mexico and Peru during the sixteenth century.

Con·rad, Joseph (kon′rad) 1857–1924, English novelist, born in Poland.

con·san·guin·i·ty (kon′sang gwin′ə tē) *n.* kinship by descent from the same ancestor; relationship by blood.

con·science (kon′shəns) *n.* a sense or understanding of what is right and what is wrong that prompts a person to do right.

con·sci·en·tious (kon′shē en′shəs) *adj.* **1.** guided by one's conscience: *That businessman is very conscientious in his dealings with people.* **2.** capable of or showing much thought and care; painstaking: *He is a conscientious student. She does conscientious work.* —**con′sci·en′tious·ly,** *adv.* —**con′sci·en′tious·ness,** *n.*

conscientious objector, a person whose religious beliefs or conscience will not allow him to fight in a war.

con·scious (kon′shəs) *adj.* **1.** knowing or realizing; aware: *He was conscious of a cat brushing against his leg.* **2.** awake and able to sense things: *Despite the blow on the head, the boy remained conscious.* **3.** felt by or known to oneself: *He was filled with a conscious but hidden anger at her remark.* **4.** done on purpose; deliberate: *She made a conscious effort to remain calm.* —**con′scious·ly,** *adv.*

con·scious·ness (kon′shəs nis) *n.* **1.** the state of being conscious; awareness: *He lost consciousness when he fell down the stairs.* **2.** all of a person's feelings and thoughts.

con·script (*v.,* kən skript′; *adj., n.,* kon′skript) *v.t.* to force (someone) by law to serve in the armed forces; draft. —*adj.* drafted. —*n.* a person who is forced by law to serve in the armed forces; draftee.

con·scrip·tion (kən skrip′shən) *n.* the forced enrollment of men in a country's armed forces by law; draft: *to raise an army by conscription.*

con·se·crate (kon′sə krāt′) *v.t.,* **con·se·crat·ed, con·se·crat·ing. 1.** to make or declare holy: *The priests consecrated the shrine.* **2.** to dedicate or devote to a particular purpose: *She consecrated her life to helping the poor.* —**con′se·cra′tion,** *n.* —**con′se·cra′tor,** *n.*

con·sec·u·tive (kən sek′yə tiv) *adj.* following one after another without a break: *1, 2, 3, and 4, are consecutive numbers. Our football team won thirty-three consecutive games.* —**con·sec′u·tive·ly,** *adv.* —**con·sec′u·tive·ness,** *n.*

con·sen·sus (kən sen′səs) *n.* a general agreement or opinion: *The consensus of the townspeople favored the new highway.* ▲ It is repetitious to say "consensus of opinion" because **consensus** means the general opinion.

con·sent (kən sent′) *v.i.* to give one's permission; agree to: *Her parents would not consent to her request to use the car.* —*n.* permission or agreement: *Jim had to get his father's consent to use the car.*

con·se·quence (kon′sə kwens′) *n.* **1.** something that results from an earlier action or happening; outcome: *He must suffer the consequences for his bad behavior.* **2.** importance: *Her opinion is of little consequence to me.*

con·se·quent (kon′sə kwent′) *adj.* following as a result or effect: *The heavy rainfall and consequent flood washed out the roads.*

con·se·quen·tial (kon′sə kwen′shəl) *adj.* **1.** following as a result or effect. **2.** of consequence; important: *That banker is a very consequential man in our town.* **3.** self-important. —**con′se·quen′tial·ly,** *adv.*

con·se·quent·ly (kon′sə kwent′lē) *adv.* as a result; therefore: *He didn't study, and consequently he failed the test.*

con·ser·va·tion (kon′sər vā′shən) *n.* a preserving or protecting from loss, harm, or waste, especially the preserving or protecting of natural resources, such as forests, rivers, and wildlife.

con·ser·va·tion·ist (kon′sər vā′shən ist) *n.* a person who supports the preserving or protecting of natural resources.

conservation of energy, a principle of physics stating that energy can neither be created nor destroyed, but can only be changed from one form to another.

conservation of mass, a principle of physics stating that mass can neither be created nor destroyed, and that the total mass of a system remains constant regardless of the interaction of its parts.

conservation of mass and energy, a principle of physics stating that the total amount of mass and energy in a system remains constant, although mass may be converted into energy and energy converted into mass within the system.

con·serv·a·tism (kən sur′və tiz′əm) *n.* a preference for things as they are or have been in the past; opposition to change.

con·serv·a·tive (kən sur′və tiv) *adj.* **1.** preferring things as they are or have been in the past; opposing change. **2.** *also,* **Conservative.** of or belonging to a political party that is opposed to major change and favors the preservation of existing institutions, traditions, and practices. **3.** cautious; moderate: *Mr. Brown is a conservative businessman.* **4.** showing traditional taste: *a conservative dresser, conservative clothes.* **5. Conservative.** relating to or designating the branch of Judaism that is midway between Orthodox and Reform. It follows ancient Hebrew law as expressed in the Torah, but also permits changes in traditional rituals and practices in the light of modern history. —*n.* **1.** a person who is conservative, especially in politics or religion. **2.** *also,* **Conservative.** a member of a conservative political party. —**con·serv′a·tive·ly,** *adv.* —**con·serv′a·tive·ness,** *n.*

con·serv·a·to·ry (kən sur′və tôr′ē) *n. pl.,* **con·serv·a·to·ries. 1.** a school of music or art. **2.** a small greenhouse for growing and displaying plants.

con·serve (*v.,* kən surv′; *n.,* kon′surv′) *v.t.,* **con·served, con·serv·ing. 1.** to preserve or protect from loss, harm, or waste; keep safe: *The athlete conserved his strength for the game.* **2.** to preserve with sugar: *Mother conserves fruit.* —*n. also,* **conserves.** preserves, especially a mixture of two or more fruits stewed in sugar, often with raisins and nuts.

con·sid·er (kən sid′ər) *v.t.* **1.** to think seriously or carefully about: *The coach asked Jim to consider playing on the basketball team.* **2.** to think to be; regard as; believe: *The*

at; āpe; cär; end; mē; it; īce; hot; ōld; fôrk; wood; fo͞ol; oil; out; up; turn; sing; thin; **th**is; hw in white; zh in treasure. The symbol ə stands for the sound of a in about, e in taken, i in pencil, o in lemon, and u in circus.

girls consider him very handsome. **3.** to take into account; keep in mind: *This car is in good shape, when you consider how old it is.* **4.** to think of; have regard for (others and their feelings): *He thinks only of himself and never considers anyone else.* —*v.i.* to think carefully: *Take time to consider before you make your decision.*

con·sid·er·a·ble (kən sid′ər ə bəl) *adj.* **1.** highly thought of; important: *John's father is a considerable man in the community.* **2.** great in amount or extent: *That pianist has considerable talent.* —**con·sid′er·a·bly,** *adv.*

con·sid·er·ate (kən sid′ər it) *adj.* having or showing regard for others and their feelings; thoughtful: *It was considerate of Tom to drive his aunt to the train station.* —**con·sid′er·ate·ly,** *adv.* —**con·sid′er·ate·ness,** *n.*

con·sid·er·a·tion (kən sid′ə rā′shən) *n.* **1.** the act of thinking seriously or carefully about something; careful thought: *After long consideration, Jim decided to take the trip.* **2.** something that should be considered; reason: *The used car's low price and good condition were two considerations for buying it.* **3.** regard for others and their feelings; thoughtfulness; respect: *Mary showed consideration for her grandmother by helping her up and down stairs.* **4.** something given in payment; fee: *The handyman refuses to do any extra work except for a consideration.*

in consideration of. a. because of; in view of. **b.** in return for: *Mr. Jones received a gold watch in consideration of his many years with the company.*

to take into consideration. to make allowances for; take into account: *In passing sentence, the judge took into consideration the fact that it was the man's first offense.*

under consideration. being considered: *Several people were under consideration for the job.*

con·sid·ered (kən sid′ərd) *adj.* carefully thought out: *a considered reply.*

con·sid·er·ing (kən sid′ər ing) *prep.* taking into account; in view of: *Considering that he didn't study, he did well on the test.*

con·sign (kən sīn′) *v.t.* **1.** to hand over formally; transfer or deliver: *Mr. Smith consigned his property to his son.* **2.** to send or deliver (merchandise): *The dealer consigned the toys to the storekeeper.* —**con·sign′a·ble,** *adj.*

con·sign·ment (kən sīn′mənt) *n.* **1.** the act of consigning or the state of being consigned. **2.** something sent or delivered: *A large consignment of Japanese radios arrived at the warehouse.*

con·sist (kən sist′) *v.i.* **1.** to be made up or composed: *Bricks consist mostly of clay.* **2.** to be contained or exist: *Good health consists partly in eating properly.*

con·sist·en·cy (kən sis′tən sē) *n. pl.,* **con·sist·en·cies. 1.** the degree of firmness, thickness, or stiffness: *That paint has a consistency like glue.* **2.** a keeping to a particular way of thinking or acting: *Since he was always changing his mind, his opinions showed little consistency over the years.* **3.** agreement or harmony: *There is a consistency between the old and new parts of the building.* Also, **con·sist·ence** (kən sis′təns).

con·sist·ent (kən sis′tənt) *adj.* **1.** keeping to a particular way of thinking or acting: *The boy remained consistent in his love of baseball.* **2.** in agreement or harmony: *The story he told the police was not consistent with the facts brought out in the trial.* —**con·sist′ent·ly,** *adv.*

con·sis·to·ry (kən sis′tər ē) *n. pl.,* **con·sis·to·ries.** a council or court of a church, especially a meeting of cardinals of the Roman Catholic Church for taking care of church business.

con·so·la·tion (kon sə lā′shən) *n.* **1.** the act of consoling. **2.** someone or something that consoles.

con·sole¹ (kən sōl′) *v.t.,* **con·soled, con·sol·ing.** to comfort or cheer (someone) in grief or sorrow; solace: *The*

mother tried to console the weeping child. [French *consoler* to comfort.] —**con·sol′a·ble,** *adj.* —**con·sol′er,** *n.*

con·sole² (kon′sōl) *n.* **1.** the cabinet of a radio, television set, or phonograph that rests on the floor. **2.** the desklike case of an organ, containing the keyboard, stops, and pedals. **3.** a table supported against a wall by brackets or by legs resembling brackets. [French *console.*]

con·sol·i·date (kən sol′ə dāt′) *v.t.* **con·sol·i·dat·ed, con·sol·i·dat·ing. 1.** to join together; unite; combine: *The two brothers consolidated their savings and bought a baseball bat.* **2.** to make secure or strong: *The army consolidated its position by building fortifications.*

con·sol·i·da·tion (kən sol′ə dā′shən) *n.* the act of consolidating or the state of being consolidated.

con·som·mé (kon′sə mā′) *n.* a clear soup made from the stock of meat, poultry, or vegetables.

con·so·nance (kon′sə nəns) *n.* **1.** harmony; agreement. **2.** a harmony of sounds, especially of tones in music.

con·so·nant (kon′sə nənt) *n.* **1.** a speech sound made by blocking the passage of air through the mouth with the lips, teeth, or tongue. **2.** any letter of the alphabet representing such a sound, such as *f, m,* or *p.* —*adj.* **1.** in agreement or harmony. **2.** consonantal. —**con′so·nant·ly,** *adv.*

con·so·nan·tal (kon′sə nant′əl) *adj.* relating to or having one or more consonants.

con·sort (*n.,* kon′sôrt; *v.,* kən sôrt′) *n.* **1.** a husband or wife; spouse. **2.** a ship that accompanies another. —*v.i.* to keep company; associate: *His parents don't want him to consort with people like that.*

con·spic·u·ous (kən spik′yōō əs) *adj.* **1.** easily seen: *The spilled ink left a conspicuous stain on the rug.* **2.** attracting attention; striking: *His bright red jacket was very conspicuous in the crowd. That boy is conspicuous for his good nature.* —**con·spic′u·ous·ly,** *adv.* —**con·spic′u·ous·ness,** *n.*

con·spir·a·cy (kən spir′ə sē) *n. pl.,* **con·spir·a·cies. 1.** the act of secretly planning together to perform some evil or illegal act. **2.** a plan that has been made; plot. **3.** a group making such a plan.

con·spir·a·tor (kən spir′ə tôr) *n.* a person who conspires; plotter.

con·spire (kən spīr′) *v.i.,* **con·spired, con·spir·ing. 1.** to plan a conspiracy; plot: *The rebels conspired to overthrow the government.* **2.** to work or act together: *All things conspired to make it a perfect day for the hike.* —**con·spir′er,** *n.*

con·sta·ble (kon′stə bəl, kun′stə bəl) *n.* **1.** a public officer in a town with somewhat less power than a sheriff. **2.** *British.* a policeman; patrolman.

con·stab·u·lar·y (kən stab′yə ler′ē) *n. pl.,* **con·stab·u·lar·ies. 1.** all the constables of a district. **2.** a police force organized on military lines, but not part of the regular army.

con·stan·cy (kon′stən sē) *n.* **1.** the condition of remaining unchanged: *The constancy of the good weather made her vacation a pleasant one.* **2.** unchanging devotion or loyalty; steadfastness; faithfulness: *She shows great constancy in her friendships.*

con·stant (kon′stənt) *adj.* **1.** not subject to change; remaining the same; unchanging: *The weather has been constant this week.* **2.** continuing without a break; happening over and over again; continual: *Her constant chatter annoyed us.* **3.** loyal; steadfast; faithful: *He is a constant friend.* —*n.* something that does not change: *The value of pi, or π, is a mathematical constant.* —**con′stant·ly,** *adv.*

Con·stan·tine the Great (kon′stən tīn′, kon′stən tēn′) A.D. 274?–337, the Roman emperor from A.D. 324–337, founder of Constantinople.

Con·stan·ti·no·ple (kon'stan tə nō'pəl) *n.* the capital of the Byzantine and Ottoman Empires, now known as Istanbul.

con·stel·la·tion (kon'stə lā'shən) *n.* **1.** a group of stars forming a pattern that suggests an object, animal, or mythological character: *Ursa Major is a constellation.* **2.** *Astrology.* a grouping of the planets and stars that are said to influence a person's character and fate. **3.** a brilliant or distinguished group of people.

con·ster·na·tion (kon'stər nā'shən) *n.* a feeling of alarm or amazement leading to confusion or fear: *We discovered to our consternation that the house was on fire.*

con·sti·pate (kon'stə pāt') *v.t.,* **con·sti·pat·ed, con·sti·pat·ing.** to cause constipation in.

con·sti·pa·tion (kon'stə pā'shən) *n.* a condition marked by difficult or irregular bowel movements.

con·stit·u·en·cy (kən stich'oo ən sē) *n. pl.,* **con·stit·u·en·cies. 1.** all the voters in a district who elect a legislator and are represented by him. **2.** the district represented.

con·stit·u·ent (kən stich'oo ənt) *adj.* **1.** needed as a part; serving to form a whole; component: *Hydrogen and oxygen are the constituent parts of water.* **2.** having the authority to appoint or elect a representative, or to create or amend a constitution: *a constituent assembly.* —*n.* **1.** a part that is needed to form a whole; component: *Wood pulp is an important constituent of paper.* **2.** a person who elects another as a representative; voter: *The congressman voted for the bill because his constituents were in favor of it.*

con·sti·tute (kon'stə toot', kon'stə tyoot') *v.t.,* **con·sti·tut·ed, con·sti·tut·ing. 1.** to make up; compose; form: *Four quarts constitute a gallon.* **2.** to appoint: *The club constituted a committee to plan the dance.* **3.** to set up; establish: *The city council constituted new traffic regulations.*

con·sti·tu·tion (kon'stə too'shən, kon'stə tyoo'shən) *n.* **1.** the way in which something is made up; physical make-up or composition: *The athlete has a strong constitution.* **2.** the fundamental principles by which a country, state, or other organized group is governed. **3. the Constitution.** the document containing the supreme law and plan of government of the United States. **4.** the act of constituting; establishment.

con·sti·tu·tion·al (kon'stə too'shən əl, kon'stə tyoo'shən əl) *adj.* **1.** of or relating to the constitution of a person or thing: *He has a constitutional weakness in his lungs.* **2.** of, coming from, in agreement with, or controlled by a constitution: *constitutional amendments, constitutional rights. The United States has a constitutional form of government.* —*n.* a walk taken for one's health. —**con'sti·tu'tion·al·ly,** *adv.*

con·sti·tu·tion·al·i·ty (kon'stə too'shə nal'ə tē, kon'stə tyoo'shə nal'ə tē) *n.* agreement with a constitution of a country, state, or other organized group: *The constitutionality of the new law was questioned.*

con·strain (kən strān') *v.t.* **1.** to make (someone) do something; force or obligate: *His conscience constrained him to do the right thing.* **2.** to hold back; restrain: *The prisoner was constrained by handcuffs. He tried to constrain his anger.* —**con·strain·ed·ly** (kən strā'nid lē), *adv.* —**con·strain'er,** *n.*

con·straint (kən strānt') *n.* **1.** a holding back of natural feelings; restraint: *The boy showed respectful constraint at church.* **2.** force or obligation: *The child behaved himself under constraint from his parents.*

con·strict (kən strikt') *v.t.* to make smaller or narrower by or as by pressing together; squeeze; compress: *to constrict a blood vessel.*

con·stric·tion (kən strik'shən) *n.* **1.** the act of constricting or the state of being constricted. **2.** something that constricts or is constricted. —**con·stric'tive,** *adj.*

con·stric·tor (kən strik'tər) *n.* **1.** any of various snakes, such as the python, boa, and anaconda, that kills by squeezing its prey in its coils. **2.** something that constricts, such as a muscle.

con·struct (kən strukt') *v.t.* to put together; build: *John and his father constructed a shed in the back yard.* —**con·struc'tor,** *n.*

con·struc·tion (kən struk'shən) *n.* **1.** the act of constructing: *The construction of the building was started a year ago.* **2.** the way in which something is constructed: *The old house is of good construction.* **3.** something constructed; structure. **4.** the way in which something is understood; interpretation; explanation: *He is always putting the wrong construction on their comments.* **5.** *Grammar.* the arrangement of words to form a sentence, clause, or phrase. —**con·struc'tion·al,** *adj.* —**con·struc'tion·al·ly,** *adv.*

con·struc·tive (kən struk'tiv) *adj.* **1.** serving to improve or help: *The teacher tries to give constructive criticism.* **2.** of or relating to construction; structural. —**con·struc'tive·ly,** *adv.* —**con·struc'tive·ness,** *n.*

con·strue (kən stroo') *v.t.,* **con·strued, con·stru·ing. 1.** to explain the meaning of; interpret: *Mary construed his words as a compliment.* **2.** to analyze (a sentence, clause, or phrase) in order to show how the words are used or arranged.

con·sul (kon'səl) *n.* **1.** an official appointed by his government to live in a foreign city in order to protect his country's citizens and commercial interests there. **2.** either of the two most important elected officials in the ancient Roman republic.

con·su·lar (kon'sə lar) *adj.* of or relating to a consul or consulate.

con·su·late (kon'sə lit) *n.* **1.** the official home or headquarters of a consul. **2.** the term of office of a consul.

con·sult (kən sult') *v.t.* **1.** to look to or seek for information or advice: *He consulted an encyclopedia to find the answer. When she felt ill, she consulted a doctor.* **2.** to have regard for; think of; consider: *He did not consult his wife when he made the decision.* —*v.i.* to meet in order to ask advice or share ideas or opinions: *The young doctor consulted with the specialist before treating his patient.*

con·sult·ant (kən sul'tənt) *n.* **1.** a person who gives professional advice. **2.** a person who seeks information or advice.

con·sul·ta·tion (kon'səl tā'shən) *n.* **1.** the act of consulting. **2.** a meeting to ask advice or share ideas or opinions: *The lawyers held a consultation to decide on the best defense for the accused man.*

con·sume (kən soom') *v.t.,* **con·sumed, con·sum·ing. 1.** to use up: *An automobile consumes gasoline.* **2.** to eat or drink up: *Jack consumed the whole cake.* **3.** to destroy, especially by fire: *Fire consumed the building.* **4.** to occupy all the attention of: *He was consumed with curiosity.* —**con·sum'a·ble,** *adj.*

con·sum·er (kən soo'mər) *n.* **1.** someone who buys and uses up things offered for sale, such as food, services, or clothing. **2.** a person or thing that consumes.

at; āpe; cär; end; mē; it; īce; hot; ōld; fôrk; wood; fool; oil; out; up; turn; sing; thin; **th**is; **hw** in white; **zh** in treasure. The symbol ə stands for the sound of **a** in about, **e** in taken, **i** in pencil, **o** in lemon, and **u** in circus.

con·sum·mate (*v.,* kon′sə māt′; *adj.,* kən sum′it, kon′-sə mit) *v.t.,* **con·sum·mat·ed, con·sum·mat·ing.** to complete or make perfect; finish or fulfill: *The architect consummated his life's work by designing the skyscraper.* —*adj.* reaching the highest degree; complete or perfect: *Michelangelo was an artist of consummate skill.* —**con·sum′mate·ly,** *adv.* —**con′su·ma′tion,** *n.*

con·sump·tion (kən sump′shən) *n.* **1.** the act of consuming or the state of being consumed. **2.** the amount consumed: *The consumption of gasoline is greater in some cars than in others.* **3.** a wasting disease, especially tuberculosis of the lungs.

con·sump·tive (kən sump′tiv) *adj.* **1.** of, relating to, or having consumption, especially tuberculosis of the lungs. **2.** tending to consume; destructive; wasteful. —*n.* a person having consumption. —**con·sump′tive·ly,** *adv.* —**con·sump′tive·ness,** *n.*

cont., continued. Also, **contd.**

con·tact (kon′takt) *n.* **1.** a touching or meeting: *The lamp is in contact with the table. The two cars stopped at the moment of contact.* **2.** the state of being in communication: *We lost contact with her until she finally wrote us a letter. The teacher comes in contact with many students.* **3.** a useful association: *a good business contact.* **4.** the point of connection between two conductors that permits an electrical current to flow, as in a switch. **5.** a device for opening or closing such a connection. —*v.t.* **1.** to bring into contact; touch. **2.** *Informal.* to communicate with: *Contact him tomorrow by telephone.*

contact lens, a thin plastic lens worn directly on the eye to help a person see better.

con·ta·gion (kən tā′jən) *n.* **1.** the spreading of disease by direct or indirect contact. **2.** a disease spread in this manner; contagious disease. **3.** the spreading of an idea or emotion: *A contagion of laughter spread through the crowd.*

con·ta·gious (kən tā′jəs) *adj.* **1.** spread by direct or indirect contact: *Everyone in the house caught the contagious disease.* **2.** readily spread: *Fear can be contagious.* —**con·ta′gious·ly,** *adv.* —**con·ta′gious·ness,** *n.*

con·tain (kən tān′) *v.t.* **1.** to have in it; hold inside itself: *The jar contains coffee.* **2.** to be made up of or include as a part: *A quart contains two pints. This salad dressing contains oil and vinegar.* **3.** to keep under control; hold back: *He tried to contain his anger at her insulting remarks.* —**con·tain′a·ble,** *adj.*

con·tain·er (kən tā′nər) *n.* a box, can, jar, or the like that contains or holds something; receptacle.

con·tain·ment (kən tān′mənt) *n.* the policy of preventing a hostile country from becoming too powerful politically or economically.

con·tam·i·nate (kən tam′ə nāt′) *v.t.,* **con·tam·i·nat·ed, con·tam·i·nat·ing.** to make unclean or impure by contact; pollute: *Garbage contaminated the water.* —**con·tam′i·na′tor,** *n.*

con·tam·i·na·tion (kən tam′ə nā′shən) *n.* **1.** the act of contaminating or the state of being contaminated; pollution: *Food should be kept covered to prevent contamination.* **2.** something that contaminates; impurity.

contd., continued.

con·temn (kən tem′) *v.t.* to treat with contempt; despise; scorn.

con·tem·plate (kon′təm plāt′) *v.,* **con·tem·plat·ed, con·tem·plat·ing.** —*v.t.* **1.** to give a great deal of attention to; look at or think about long and carefully: *The young man contemplated his future.* **2.** to have in mind; intend: *John is contemplating joining the Navy.* —*v.i.* to meditate; ponder: *The old man goes to the park everyday to sit and contemplate.*

con·tem·pla·tion (kon′təm plā′shən) *n.* **1.** the act of looking at or thinking about something long and carefully: *Helen spent a long time in contemplation of the painting.* **2.** meditation, especially religious meditation. **3.** expectation or intention: *She bought three dresses in contemplation of her trip.*

con·tem·pla·tive (kon′təm plā′tiv, kən tem′plə tiv) *adj.* of, relating to, or characterized by contemplation. —**con′tem·pla′tive·ly,** *adv.* —**con′tem·pla′tive·ness,** *n.*

con·tem·po·ra·ne·ous (kən tem′pə rā′nē əs) *adj.* belonging to or happening during the same period of time: *The Civil War and the Presidency of Abraham Lincoln were contemporaneous.* —**con·tem′po·ra′ne·ous·ly,** *adv.* —**con·tem′po·ra′ne·ous·ness,** *n.*

con·tem·po·rar·y (kən tem′pə rer′ē) *adj.* **1.** belonging to or living at the same time: *General de Gaulle and President Kennedy were contemporary figures.* **2.** belonging to the present time; current; modern: *contemporary art.* —*n. pl.,* **con·tem·po·rar·ies.** a person who belongs to or lives at the same time as another or others: *We are the contemporaries of the first men to walk on the moon.*

con·tempt (kən tempt′) *n.* **1.** a feeling that a person or thing is low, mean, or worthless; scorn; disdain: *They have contempt for the student who cheated on the test.* **2.** the state of being scorned or despised; disgrace: *He was held in contempt by everyone for his dishonesty.* **3.** disrespect for or disobedience of a law court or lawmaking body: *He was fined for contempt of court.*

con·tempt·i·ble (kən temp′tə bəl) *adj.* deserving of or held in contempt or scorn. —**con·tempt′i·ble·ness,** *n.* —**con·tempt′i·bly,** *adv.*

con·temp·tu·ous (kən temp′chōō əs) *adj.* showing contempt; scornful: *a contemptuous remark.* —**con·temp′tu·ous·ly,** *adv.* —**con·temp′tu·ous·ness,** *n.*

con·tend (kən tend′) *v.i.* to compete against another in or as in a contest: *The two athletes contended for first place in the race.* —*v.t.* to argue: *The defendant contended his innocence.* —**con·tend′er,** *n.*

to contend with. to deal or struggle with: *The Eskimos have to contend with harsh weather conditions.*

con·tent¹ (kon′tent) *n.* **1.** *usually,* **contents.** all that is contained inside: *The contents spilled out when the suitcase came open.* **2.** facts or topics discussed; subject matter: *What was the content of his letter? This book doesn't have a table of contents.* **3.** the ability to hold; capacity: *The content of the barrel is fifteen gallons.* [Latin *contentum* all that is contained.]

con·tent² (kən tent′) *adj.* wanting nothing else; free of desire for more; satisfied: *Jeff was content to eat only two meals a day.* —*v.t.* to make content; satisfy: *A word of praise will content him.* —*n.* contentment; satisfaction: *After eating, the baby went to sleep in complete content.* [Latin *contentus* satisfied.]

con·tent·ed (kən ten′tid) *adj.* enjoying contentment; satisfied. —**con·tent′ed·ly,** *adv.* —**con·tent′ed·ness,** *n.*

con·ten·tion (kən ten′shən) *n.* **1.** a disagreement or dispute; argument; quarrel. **2.** a point that a person supports or argues for: *It is Jack's contention that cheating on tests is immoral.*

con·ten·tious (kən ten′shəs) *adj.* fond of arguing; argumentative; quarrelsome: *The contentious bully was quick to pick a fight.* —**con·ten′tious·ly,** *adv.* —**con·ten′tious·ness,** *n.*

con·tent·ment (kən tent′mənt) *n.* the state of being happy and content; satisfaction.

con·test (*n.,* kon′test; *v.,* kən test′) *n.* **1.** something that tests or proves a person's skill or ability, such as a game or race; competition for a prize or honor: *Jim won the pie-eating contest. The senator entered the contest for gover-*

nor. **2.** a struggle or conflict: *a contest between nations.*
—*v.t.* **1.** to struggle in order to win (something); fight for:
The soldiers contested every bit of ground in the long battle.
2. to challenge or dispute: *The baseball player contested the
decision of the umpire.* —**con·test′a·ble,** *adj.*

con·test·ant (kən tes′tənt) *n.* a person who takes part
in a contest.

con·text (kon′tekst′) *n.* the words, phrases, or sentences
that surround a word, sentence, or passage and influence
or make clear its meaning: *It was difficult to understand
what the senator's statement meant because it was quoted
out of context. You can often understand the meaning of
an unfamiliar word from the context in which it is used.*

con·tex·tu·al (kən teks′chōō əl) *adj.* relating to or depending on the context. —**con·tex′tu·al·ly,** *adv.*

con·ti·gu·i·ty (kon′tə gyōō′ə tē) *n. pl.,* **con·ti·gu·i·ties.**
1. the state of being in actual contact. **2.** nearness.

con·tig·u·ous (kən tig′yōō əs) *adj.* **1.** in actual contact;
touching: *Our property is contiguous to the park along one
side.* **2.** close; near: *Carol's house is contiguous to her
friend's house, separated only by a low hedge.* —**con·tig′-
u·ous·ly,** *adv.* —**con·tig′u·ous·ness,** *n.*

con·ti·nence (kont′ən əns) *n.* self-restraint or moderation. Also, **con·ti·nen·cy** (kont′ən ən sē).

con·ti·nent[1] (kont′ən ənt) *n.* **1.** one of the seven great
land areas on the earth. The continents are Asia, Africa,
North America, South America, Antarctica, Europe, and
Australia. **2. the Continent.** the mainland of Europe.
[Latin *(terra) continēns* mainland, literally, (land) holding
together.]

con·ti·nent[2] (kont′ən ənt) *adj.* practicing self-restraint
or moderation. [Latin *continēns,* the present participle of
continēre to hold together, restrain.]

con·ti·nen·tal (kon′tə nent′əl) *adj.* **1.** *also,* **Continental.**
on or characteristic of the mainland of Europe; European:
She learned about continental cooking in Paris. **2. Continental.** of or relating to the American colonies during and
just after the American Revolution: *George Washington
commanded the Continental army.* **3.** of or resembling a
continent. —*n.* **1.** *also,* **Continental.** a person who lives
on the mainland of Europe; European. **2. Continental.**
a soldier in the American Army established by the Continental Congress.

Continental Congress, the assembly of delegates
from the American colonies that met from 1774 to 1781.

continental divide 1. an elevation of land that separates river systems flowing toward one side of a continent
from those flowing toward the other side. **2. Continental
Divide.** such an elevation in western North America
formed by the various peaks of the Rocky Mountains,
separating rivers flowing eastward from those flowing
westward. Also *(def. 2),* **Great Divide.**

con·tin·gen·cy (kən tin′jən sē) *n. pl.,* **con·tin·gen·cies.**
1. an event that can possibly take place; chance happening:
A mountain climber tries to prepare for every contingency.
2. the quality or state of being conditional or uncertain.

con·tin·gent (kən tin′jənt) *adj.* **1.** depending on an uncertain condition or event; conditional: *Tom's fall trip to
Europe is contingent upon his earning enough money this
summer.* **2.** likely to happen, but not certain; possible: *The
contingent result of Mary's interview is that she may get the
job.* **3.** happening by chance; accidental. —*n.* a group sent
by another, larger group as a share or quota: *a contingent
of soldiers.* —**con·tin′gent·ly,** *adv.*

con·tin·u·al (kən tin′yōō əl) *adj.* **1.** going on without a
break; continuous: *He could hear the continual rumble of
traffic from the streets below.* **2.** happening over and over
again; repeated: *The continual noise of a dog barking kept
him awake.* —**con·tin′u·al·ly,** *adv.*

con·tin·u·ance (kən tin′yōō əns) *n.* **1.** the act of continuing or the state of being continued. **2.** *Law.* a postponement of a pending court action to a future date.

con·tin·u·a·tion (kən tin′yōō ā′shən) *n.* **1.** a going on
or remaining without a break: *Many citizens were against
a continuation of the war.* **2.** a going on after a break;
resumption: *the continuation of school after the spring holiday.* **3.** something that continues anything already started;
added part: *This television program is a continuation of last
week's program.*

con·tin·ue (kən tin′yōō) *v.,* **con·tin·ued, con·tin·u·ing.**
—*v.i.* **1.** to keep on in a condition or action; go on; persist:
The snowfall continued for two days. **2.** to remain in a place
or position: *She chose to continue as principal at the school.*
3. to go on after a break; resume: *The meeting will continue
after lunch.* —*v.t.* **1.** to go on with; keep on with; persist
in: *He continued his work despite his illness.* **2.** to go on
with after a break; resume: *The professor will continue the
lecture tomorrow.* **3.** to cause to remain in a place or position; retain. **4.** *Law.* to postpone (a pending court action)
to a future date. —**con·tin′u·a·ble,** *adj.*

con·ti·nu·i·ty (kon′tə nōō′ə tē, kon′tə nyōō′ə tē) *n. pl.,*
con·ti·nu·i·ties. 1. the state or quality of being continuous. **2.** a logical connection, as of ideas; coherence: *The
story was hard to understand because it lacked continuity.*

con·tin·u·ous (kən tin′yōō əs) *adj.* going on without a
break; unbroken. —**con·tin′u·ous·ly,** *adv.* —**con·tin′u-
ous·ness,** *n.*

con·tort (kən tôrt′) *v.t.* to change the usual form or appearance of by twisting or bending out of shape; distort:
His face was contorted with pain.

con·tor·tion (kən tôr′shən) *n.* **1.** the act of contorting
or the state of being contorted. **2.** a twisted or bent shape:
The acrobat's body could take on some amazing contortions.

con·tor·tion·ist (kən tôr′shə nist) *n.* a person who con-
torts, especially a performer who twists and bends his body
into unusual positions.

con·tour (kon′toor) *n.* the shape of an object, figure, or
body, or the line representing this: *The contour of the earth
can be seen from an orbiting spacecraft.* —*adj.* **1.** following
the contours of hilly land when plowing or planting in
order to prevent soil erosion: *contour farming.* **2.** made to
fit the shape of something: *contour sheets for a bed.*

contour line, a line on a map connecting points of equal
elevation.

contour map, a map that shows the relative elevations
of a surface by means of contour
lines.

contra- *prefix* against; opposite:
contradiction.

con·tra·band (kon′trə band′) *n.*
1. goods forbidden by law from
being imported or exported;
smuggled goods: *The man was arrested for dealing in contraband.*
2. unlawful trade in such goods;
smuggling: *The government tried
to prevent contraband in drugs.*
—*adj.* forbidden by law from being imported or exported:
contraband goods.

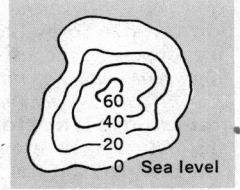

**Contour map
of a 60-foot hill**

at; āpe; cär; end; mē; it; īce; hot; ōld; fôrk;
wood; fōōl; oil; out; up; turn; sing; thin; **this;**
hw in white; zh in treasure. The symbol ə
stands for the sound of **a** in about, **e** in taken,
i in pencil, **o** in lemon, and **u** in circus.

C

con·tra·bass (kon′trə bās′) *n.* a musical instrument having a range below the bass; double bass.

con·tra·cep·tion (kon′trə sep′shən) *n.* the prevention of conception.

con·tra·cep·tive (kon′trə sep′tiv) *adj.* relating to or used for contraception: *a contraceptive device.* —*n.* a substance or device for preventing conception.

con·tract (*v.,* kən trakt′, *also* kon′trakt *for v.t. def. 3 and v.i. def. 2; n.,* kon′trakt) *v.t.* **1.** to draw together (the parts of a thing); make shorter or make smaller: *A frightened hedgehog contracts its body into a ball.* **2.** to get or acquire: *to contract pneumonia, to contract a debt.* **3.** to establish by agreement: *The two businesses contracted a merger.* **4.** to shorten (a word, syllable, or phrase) by omitting or combining sounds or letters. *Are not* can be contracted to *aren't.* —*v.i.* **1.** to draw together; become shorter or smaller: *The wet leather strap contracted as it dried.* **2.** to make or enter into an agreement: *The farmer contracted to lease his land.* —*n.* **1.** an agreement between two or more parties to do or not to do something, especially an agreement that is legally binding: *The strike finally ended when the labor union voted to accept the proposed contract.* **2.** a document containing the terms of such an agreement.

con·trac·tile (kən trakt′əl) *adj.* having the ability to contract or cause contraction: *a contractile muscle, the contractile force of cold.*

con·trac·tion (kən trak′shən) *n.* **1.** the act or process of contracting or the state of being contracted: *the contraction of a muscle, the contraction of a disease.* **2.** a shortened form of a word, syllable, or phrase. *Wouldn't* is a contraction of *would not.*

con·trac·tor (kon′trak′tər, kən trak′tər) *n.* a person who agrees to supply goods or do a job for a fixed price: *a building contractor.*

con·trac·tu·al (kən trak′chōō əl) *adj.* of, relating to, or having the force of a contract: *contractual agreements.*

con·tra·dict (kon′trə dikt′) *v.t.* **1.** to say the opposite of or deny (a statement); declare to be untrue: *The witness contradicted his earlier testimony.* **2.** to assert the opposite of or deny what is stated by (someone): *She contradicted her brother.* **3.** to be opposed to; disagree with: *Her words contradict her behavior.*

con·tra·dic·tion (kon′trə dik′shən) *n.* **1.** a statement that contradicts another: *That speech contains many contradictions.* **2.** the act of contradicting. **3.** opposition or disagreement; inconsistency: *There seems to be a contradiction between what he says and what he does.*

con·tra·dic·to·ry (kon′trə dik′tər ē) *adj.* **1.** contradicting; opposing; inconsistent: *The two witnesses gave contradictory accounts of the accident.* **2.** tending to contradict: *a contradictory person.*

con·tra·dis·tinc·tion (kon′trə dis tingk′shən) *n.* a distinction by contrast or opposition.

con·tral·to (kən tral′tō) *n. pl.,* **con·tral·tos. 1.** the lowest female voice; alto. **2.** a singer who has such a voice. **3.** a musical part for such a voice. —*adj.* **1.** able to sing contralto. **2.** for the contralto.

con·trap·tion (kən trap′shən) *n. Informal.* a mechanical device; gadget; contrivance.

con·trar·i·wise (kon′trer ē wīz′, kən trer′ē wīz′) *adv.* **1.** in the opposite direction or the opposite order. **2.** on the contrary.

con·trar·y (kon′trer ē, *also* kən trer′ē *for adj. def. 2*) *adj.* **1.** entirely different; opposite: *People from different parts of the world often have contrary ideas.* **2.** tending to oppose or contradict: *He is a contrary person who enjoys disagreeing with his friends.* **3.** unfavorable; adverse: *Contrary winds put the ship off its course.* —*n. pl.,* **con·trar·ies.** the

opposite: *I believe that the contrary of what he says is actually the truth.* —**con′trar·i·ly,** *adv.* —**con′trar·i·ness,** *n.* **on the contrary.** just the opposite: *On the contrary, we are not going to go to the party.*

con·trast (*v.,* kən trast′; *n.,* kon′trast) *v.t.* to compare in order to show differences: *The teacher contrasted two ancient civilizations in his lecture.* —*v.i.* to show differences when compared: *The white hat contrasted sharply with her black dress.* —*n.* **1.** the act of contrasting or the state of being contrasted: *The rich and poor sections of that city are in sharp contrast with each other.* **2.** a difference shown by contrasting: *the contrast between darkness and light.* **3.** a person or thing showing differences: *His new car is quite a contrast to the old one he used to own.* ▲ See **compare** for usage note.

con·trib·ute (kən trib′yōōt) *v.,* **con·trib·ut·ed, con·trib·ut·ing.** —*v.t.* **1.** to give along with others: *to contribute money to a hospital fund.* **2.** to write (an article, story, or the like) for a newspaper or magazine. —*v.i.* **1.** to give money, time, effort, or the like along with others: *to contribute to charity, to contribute to a discussion.* **2.** to write an article, story, or the like for a newspaper or magazine: *That professor often contributes to educational magazines.* **3.** to help bring about: *The young man's pleasing personality contributed to his success as a salesman.*

con·tri·bu·tion (kon′trə byōō′shən) *n.* **1.** the act of contributing: *A political campaign depends largely on the contribution of money or time by supporters.* **2.** something that is contributed: *He made a twenty-dollar contribution to charity.*

con·trib·u·tor (kən trib′yə tər) *n.* a person who contributes: *There were many contributors to the art museum's new building fund.*

con·trib·u·to·ry (kən trib′yə tôr′ē) *adj.* helping to bring about a result; contributing: *The king's cruelty was a contributing factor in his downfall.*

con·trite (kən trīt′, kon′trīt) *adj.* **1.** deeply sorry for one's faults or wrongdoings; remorseful; penitent: *He felt contrite about his rude behavior.* **2.** showing deep sorrow or regret: *a contrite apology.* —**con·trite′ly,** *adv.* —**con·trite′ness,** *n.*

con·tri·tion (kən trish′ən) *n.* deep sorrow or regret for one's faults or wrongdoings; penitence.

con·triv·ance (kən trī′vəns) *n.* **1.** something contrived, such as a plan, scheme, or mechanical device. **2.** the act of contriving.

con·trive (kən trīv′) *v.t.,* **con·trived, con·triv·ing. 1.** to plan in a clever or ingenious way; scheme; plot: *The gang contrived a bank robbery.* **2.** to bring about or manage, especially with difficulty: *They contrived to keep their plans secret.* **3.** to create or invent; design: *to contrive a new lock.* —**con·triv′er,** *n.*

con·trol (kən trōl′) *n.* **1.** the power to direct or regulate; authority: *The dictator had absolute control over the country.* **2.** a holding in check; restraint: *He had trouble keeping control of his temper.* **3.** a method or means of restraint; check: *The President proposed new controls over wages and prices.* **4.** *also,* **controls.** a device or system for operating, regulating, or guiding a machine, such as an airplane or spacecraft. **5.** a standard of comparison used to measure or check the results of a scientific experiment. —*v.t.,* **con·trolled, con·trol·ling. 1.** to have power to direct or regulate; have authority over: *The federal government controls interstate commerce.* **2.** to hold in check; curb; restrain: *to make an effort to control one's temper.* —**con·trol′la·ble,** *adj.*

con·trol·ler (kən trō′lər) *n.* **1.** a person who controls. **2.** *also,* **comptroller.** a person in charge of spending and finances, as in a bank or company.

control tower, a tower on an airfield from which aircraft and air traffic is directed, especially by radio.

con·tro·ver·sial (kon′trə·vur′shəl) *adj.* causing or characterized by controversy: *a controversial person, a controversial subject.* —**con′tro·ver·sial·ly,** *adv.*

con·tro·ver·sy (kon′trə·vur′sē) *n. pl.,* **con·tro·ver·sies.** a dispute, debate, or disagreement: *The new state tax caused widespread controversy.*

con·tro·vert (kon′trə·vurt′) *v.t.* to oppose or deny; contradict: *The facts controvert the testimony of the witness.* —**con′tro·vert′i·ble,** *adj.*

Control tower

con·tu·ma·cious (kon′tə·mā′shəs, kon′tyə·mā′shəs) *adj.* stubbornly and willfully disobedient; rebellious.

con·tu·ma·cy (kon′too·mə·sē, kon′tyoo·mə·sē) *n. pl.,* **con·tu·ma·cies.** a stubborn and willful disobedience of authority.

con·tu·me·ly (kon′too·mə·lē, kon′tyoo·mə·lē) *n. pl.,* **con·tu·me·lies.** **1.** rudeness in actions or speech; scornful insolence: *to treat a person with contumely.* **2.** an instance of such insolence; humiliating insult.

con·tu·sion (kən·too′zhən, kən·tyoo′zhən) *n.* an injury in which the skin is not broken; bruise.

co·nun·drum (kə·nun′drəm) *n.* **1.** a riddle whose answer involves a pun. For example: *What would an elephant bring on a trip? His trunk.* **2.** any puzzling or difficult problem.

con·va·lesce (kon′və·les′) *v.i.,* **con·va·lesced, con·va·lesc·ing.** to regain health and strength gradually after illness; recover: *He convalesced at home after his heart attack.*

con·va·les·cence (kon′və·les′əns) *n.* **1.** a gradual recovery of health and strength after illness. **2.** the period of this recovery.

con·va·les·cent (kon′və·les′ənt) *adj.* **1.** recovering from illness: *a convalescent patient.* **2.** for or relating to convalescence. —*n.* a person who is convalescing.

con·vec·tion (kən·vek′shən) *n.* **1.** the transfer of heat from one part of a gas or liquid to another by heated currents of the gas or liquid. Convection occurs because of differences in density. **2.** the act of conveying.

con·vene (kən·vēn′) *v.,* **con·vened, con·ven·ing.** —*v.i.* to come together, especially for a meeting; assemble: *The legislature convened.* —*v.t.* to cause to assemble: *The club president convened the members.*

con·ven·ience (kən·vēn′yəns) *n.* **1.** the quality of being convenient: *Mother appreciates the convenience of frozen foods.* **2.** ease; comfort: *An information service is provided for the convenience of visitors to the city.* **3.** something that gives ease or comfort: *A washing machine is one of many modern conveniences.*

at one's convenience. at a time or place, or under conditions, suited to one's needs or wishes.

con·ven·ient (kən·vēn′yənt) *adj.* **1.** suited to one's needs or purposes; giving ease or comfort: *It is convenient to have a dishwasher if you have a great many dishes to wash.* **2.** within easy reach; near: *My parents are looking for a home that is convenient to all transportation.* —**con·ven′ient·ly,** *adv.*

con·vent (kon′vent) *n.* **1.** a group of nuns living together under strict religious discipline. **2.** the building or buildings occupied by such a group, especially a nunnery.

con·ven·tion (kən·ven′shən) *n.* **1.** a formal meeting for a particular purpose: *a political convention.* **2.** the persons present at such a meeting. **3.** the generally accepted practices or standards of a society: *The young artist ignored convention in his way of life.* **4.** a generally accepted rule or custom: *Opening a door for a lady is a convention.* **5.** an agreement between countries or persons.

con·ven·tion·al (kən·ven′shən·əl) *adj.* **1.** following generally accepted practices or standards: *a conventional way of behaving.* **2.** following accepted custom or usage; customary: *conventional manners.* —**con·ven′tion·al·ly,** *adv.*

con·ven·tion·al·i·ty (kən·ven′shə·nal′ə·tē) *n. pl.,* **con·ven·tion·al·i·ties.** **1.** the quality or character of being conventional: *The conventionality of his opinions often becomes boring.* **2.** a conventional custom, practice, or rule.

con·verge (kən·vurj′) *v.,* **con·verged, con·verg·ing.** —*v.i.* to come together or tend to come together at a place or point: *Three major roads converge at the intersection.* —*v.t.* to cause to converge.

con·ver·gence (kən·vur′jəns) *n.* **1.** the act or process of converging. **2.** the point of converging.

con·ver·gent (kən·vur′jənt) *adj.* coming to a point; converging.

converging lens, a lens that is thicker in the middle than at the edges, causing light rays to converge and focus on a point. See **lens** for illustration.

con·ver·sant (kən·vur′sənt) *adj.* familiar or acquainted: *to be conversant with American history.*

con·ver·sa·tion (kon′vər·sā′shən) *n.* informal or friendly talk between people.

con·ver·sa·tion·al (kon′vər·sā′shən·əl) *adj.* **1.** of or characteristic of conversation: *a conversational tone.* **2.** fond of or good at conversation. —**con′ver·sa′tion·al·ly,** *adv.*

con·ver·sa·tion·al·ist (kon′vər·sā′shən·əl·ist) *n.* a person who is fond of or good at conversation.

con·verse¹ (kən·vurs′) *v.i.,* **con·versed, con·vers·ing.** to talk together in an informal and friendly way. [Old French *converser* to associate with, exchange words.]

con·verse² (*adj.,* kən·vurs′; *n.,* kon′vurs) *adj.* opposite in order, direction, or action; reversed; contrary. —*n.* **1.** something that is the opposite or contrary of something else: *Day is the converse of night.* **2.** a proposition in logic that is derived from another by interchanging the subject and predicate terms. The statement *Some doctors are women* is the converse of the statement *Some women are doctors.* [Latin *conversus,* the past participle of *convertere* to turn about.] —**con·verse′ly,** *adv.*

con·ver·sion (kən·vur′zhən) *n.* **1.** the act or process of converting; change in character, condition, or use: *the conversion of water into ice.* **2.** a change in a person's belief, opinion, or course of action: *a religious conversion.*

con·vert (*v.,* kən·vurt′; *n.,* kon′vurt) *v.t.* **1.** to change in character, condition, or use: *to convert matter into energy, to convert a couch into a bed.* **2.** to cause (someone) to change a belief, opinion, or course of action: *We will soon convert him to our way of thinking. Missionaries converted the tribe to Christianity.* **3.** to exchange for an equivalent: *He converted his Swiss francs into dollars.* —*v.i.* to change one's beliefs, course of action, or religion. —*n.* a person

at; āpe; cär; end; mē; it; īce; hot; ōld; fôrk; wood; fool; oil; out; up; turn; sing; thin; this; hw in white; zh in treasure. The symbol ə stands for the sound of **a** in about, **e** in taken, **i** in pencil, **o** in lemon, and **u** in circus.

who has been converted, as from one religious belief to another.

con·vert·er (kən vur′tər) *n.* **1.** a person or thing that converts. **2.** a machine for changing alternating electric current to direct current, or direct current to alternating current.

con·vert·i·ble (kən vur′tə bəl) *adj.* **1.** that can be converted: *A convertible bed also serves as a couch.* **2.** (of an automobile) having a roof that can be folded back. —*n.* an automobile having a roof that can be folded back. —**con·vert′i·bil′i·ty,** *n.* —**con·vert′i·bly,** *adv.*

con·vex (kon veks′, kon′veks) *adj.* curved outward, as the outside of a circle or sphere: *a convex lens.* —**con·vex′ly,** *adv.* —**con·vex′ness,** *n.*

con·vex·i·ty (kən vek′sə tē) *n. pl.,* **con·vex·i·ties. 1.** the quality or condition of being convex. **2.** a convex surface or thing.

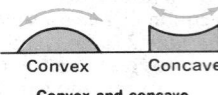

Convex   Concave

Convex and concave surfaces

con·vey (kən vā′) *v.t.* **1.** to take or carry from one place to another; transport: *The train conveyed the goods from the factory to the warehouse.* **2.** to serve as the medium for; transmit; conduct: *These pipes convey water from the reservoir to the city.* **3.** to express; communicate: *The author conveyed his feelings through his writing.* **4.** to transfer the ownership of, as property, from one person to another.

con·vey·ance (kən vā′əns) *n.* **1.** the act of conveying. **2.** something that transports or carries, especially a vehicle: *Buses and trains are public conveyances.* **3.** the transfer of the ownership of property from one person to another. **4.** the document by which such a transfer is made.

con·vey·or (kən vā′ər) *also,* **con·vey·er.** *n.* **1.** a person or thing that conveys. **2.** see **conveyor belt.**

conveyor belt *also,* **conveyer belt.** a mechanical device for transporting objects over relatively short distances, usually designed as a moving, continuous belt or a series of rollers.

con·vict (*v.,* kən vikt′; *n.,* kon′vikt) *v.t.* to find or prove (someone) guilty of a criminal charge: *The thief was convicted of robbery.* —*n.* a person serving a prison sentence.

con·vic·tion (kən vik′shən) *n.* **1.** the act of finding or proving (someone) guilty of a criminal charge. **2.** the state of being found or proved guilty. **3.** a firm belief or opinion: *He has the strong conviction that all men are equal.*

con·vince (kən vins′) *v.t.,* **con·vinced, con·vinc·ing.** to cause (someone) to believe or feel certain; persuade: *He convinced his brother to study hard for the test.*

con·vinc·ing (kən vin′sing) *adj.* having power to convince; persuasive: *The actor gave a convincing portrayal of Hamlet.* —**con·vinc′ing·ly,** *adv.*

con·viv·i·al (kən viv′ē əl) *adj.* **1.** fond of parties and good times with friends; sociable. **2.** festive: *The party had a convivial atmosphere.* —**con·viv·i·al·i·ty** (kən viv′ē al′ə tē), *n.* —**con·viv′i·al·ly,** *adv.*

con·vo·ca·tion (kon′və kā′shən) *n.* **1.** a group of persons called together; assembly: *There was a convocation of students before the graduation exercises.* **2.** a calling together of such a group; summons to assemble.

con·voke (kən vōk′) *v.t.,* **con·voked, con·vok·ing.** to call together; summon to meet or assemble: *to convoke a legislature.*

con·vo·lu·tion (kon′və lōō′shən) *n.* a coiling, twisting, or winding together: *the convolutions of a snake.*

con·voy (*n.,* kon′voi; *v.* kon′voi, kən voi′) *n.* **1.** a group of ships or vehicles traveling with a protective escort: *a convoy of troop carriers.* **2.** a group, as of warships, troops, or aircraft, that acts as a protective escort: *a convoy of destroyers escorted the aircraft carrier.* **3.** any group of persons or vehicles traveling together: *A convoy of oil*

trucks passed us on the highway. —*v.t.* to accompany or escort in order to provide protection.

con·vulse (kən vuls′) *v.t.,* **con·vulsed, con·vuls·ing. 1.** to shake or disturb violently: *His face was convulsed with anger. A revolution convulsed the nation.* **2.** to cause to shake with strong emotion or fits of laughter: *The clown's antics convulsed the children.* **3.** to throw into muscular convulsions.

con·vul·sion (kən vul′shən) *n.* **1.** a violent, involuntary contraction or series of contractions of the muscles; spasm. **2.** a fit of laughter. **3.** a violent shaking or disturbance; upheaval.

con·vul·sive (kən vul′siv) *adj.* **1.** of, like, or causing a convulsion or convulsions. **2.** having convulsions. —**con·vul′sive·ly,** *adv.*

co·ny (kō′nē) *also* **co·ney.** *n. pl.,* **co·nies. 1.** rabbit fur. **2.** a rabbit, especially the European rabbit.

coo (kōō) *n.* a soft, murmuring sound, such as that made by a pigeon or dove. —*v.i.,* **cooed, coo·ing. 1.** to make such a sound. **2.** to speak softly and lovingly.

cook (kook) *v.t.* to prepare (food) for eating by using heat, as by roasting, boiling, baking, or frying. —*v.i.* **1.** (of food) to be cooked; undergo cooking. **2.** to prepare food for eating; act as a cook: *She cooks well.* —*n.* a person who prepares food for eating.

Cook, James (kook) 1728–1779, English explorer.

cook·book (kook′book′) *n.* a book containing recipes and other information about food and its preparation.

cook·er (kook′ər) *n.* an apparatus or utensil for cooking food: *a steam cooker.*

cook·er·y (kook′ər ē) *n. pl.,* **cook·er·ies.** the art or practice of preparing and cooking food.

cook·ie (kook′ē) *also,* **cook·y.** *n.* a small, usually flat cake baked from sweetened dough.

cook·out (kook′out′) *n.* an outdoor gathering at which food is cooked and eaten.

cook·y (kook′ē) *n. pl.,* **cook·ies.** another spelling of **cookie.**

cool (kōōl) *adj.* **1.** lacking warmth but not very cold: *a cool breeze.* **2.** giving protection or relief from heat: *a cool summer dress.* **3.** not excited; calm; composed: *He remained cool in the face of danger.* **4.** lacking enthusiasm or warmth; not cordial: *The movie got a cool reception from the critics.* **5.** *Slang.* excellent; great. **6.** *Informal.* without exaggeration; actual: *a cool million dollars.* —*n.* **1.** something cool, as a time or place: *He took a walk in the cool of early morning.* **2.** *Slang.* calmness: *to keep one's cool.* —*v.t.* to make cool: *to cool soup by letting it stand.* —*v.i.* to become cool: *The air cooled over night. Her anger cooled as time passed.* —**cool′ly,** *adv.* —**cool′ness,** *n.*

cool·ant (kōō′lənt) *n.* a substance used to cool machinery, such as an automobile engine or a dentist's drill.

cool·er (kōō′lər) *n.* **1.** a container or apparatus for keeping or making something cool: *a cooler for soft drinks.* **2.** something that cools, such as an iced drink.

cool·head·ed (kōōl′hed′id) *adj.* not easily excited or disturbed; calm.

Cool·idge, Calvin (kōō′lij) 1872–1933, the thirtieth president of the United States, from 1923 to 1929.

coo·lie (kōō′lē) *n.* an unskilled Oriental laborer, especially one working for low wages.

coon (kōōn) *n.* see **raccoon.**

coop (kōōp, koop) *n.* a cage, pen, or enclosure for fowl or small animals: *a rabbit coop.* —*v.t.* to confine in a coop or any small space: *They cooped the dog up in the kitchen until the guests had gone.*

co-op (kō′op′) *n.* see **cooperative.**

coop·er (kōō′pər, koop′ər) *n.* a person who makes or repairs barrels, casks, and similar containers.

Coo·per, James Fen·i·more (kōō′per, koop′ər; fen′ə-môr′) 1789–1851, U.S. novelist.

co·op·er·ate (kō op′ə rāt′) *also,* **co-op·er·ate.** *v.i.,* **co·op·er·at·ed, co·op·er·at·ing.** to work or act with another or others for a common purpose; unite in action: *The three classes cooperated in planning a party.*

co·op·er·a·tion (kō op′ə rā′shən) *also,* **co-op·er·a·tion.** *n.* the act or process of cooperating; working with another or others for a common purpose.

co·op·er·a·tive (kō op′ər ə tiv, kō op′ə rā′tiv) *also,* **co-op·er·a·tive.** *adj.* **1.** willing to work together with another or others: *He is a very cooperative student.* **2.** of or characterized by cooperation: *The family made painting the house a cooperative effort.* **3.** of, relating to, or referring to a cooperative. —*n.* a business enterprise, such as a food store or apartment house, that is owned and operated by its members, who share its profits or benefits. —**co·op′er·a·tive·ly,** *adv.* —**co·op′er·a·tive·ness,** *n.*

co·or·di·nate (*v.,* kō ôr′də nāt′; *adj., n.,* kō ôr′də nit) *also,* **co-or·di·nate.** *v.,* **co·or·di·nat·ed, co·or·di·nat·ing.** —*v.t.* to cause to work well together; bring into proper working order; harmonize: *to coordinate the work of charitable agencies.* —*v.i.* to work well together; act in harmony. —*adj.* of equal rank or importance: *coordinate clauses.* —*n.* **1.** a person or thing that is equal in rank or importance to another. **2.** *Mathematics.* one of a set of numbers that give the position of a point in a line, in a plane, or in three-dimensional space. —**co·or′di·nate·ly,** *adv.* —**co·or′di·na′tor,** *n.*

co·or·di·na·tion (kō ôr′də nā′shən) *also,* **co-or·di·na·tion.** *n.* **1.** the act of coordinating or the state of being coordinated. **2.** a working well together, as of parts of the body: *Swimming requires good muscular coordination.*

Coot

coot (kōōt) *n.* **1.** a water bird having short wings and usually black or gray feathers. **2.** *Informal.* a foolish person, especially a foolish old man.

cop (kop) *n. Informal.* a policeman or policewoman.

cope¹ (kōp) *v.i.,* **coped, cop·ing.** to struggle or deal successfully: *She had trouble coping with the extra homework.* [Old French *colper* to strike, from *colp* a blow, going back to Latin *colaphus.*]

cope² (kōp) *n.* a long cape worn by bishops, priests, and other clergymen during processions and certain religious services. [Late Latin *cap(p)a* hood, cape.]

Co·pen·ha·gen (kō′pən hā′gən) *n.* the capital of Denmark, on the island of Zealand. Pop. (1970 est.), 627,800.

Co·per·ni·can (kə pur′ni kən) *adj.* of or relating to Copernicus or to his theory that the earth revolves around the sun and that the apparent movement of the stars is due to the earth's rotation on its axis.

Co·per·ni·cus, Nik·o·la·us (kə pur′ni-kəs; nik′ə lā′əs) 1473–1543, Polish astronomer.

cop·i·er (kop′ē ər) *n.* **1.** a person or thing that makes copies, especially a machine that makes copies of letters, documents, or other materials. **2.** a person who imitates.

co·pi·lot (kō′pī′lət) *n.* the assistant pilot in an aircraft, who assists and relieves the head pilot.

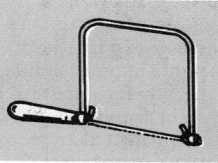

Coping saw

Cope²

cop·ing (kō′ping) *n.* a layer of brick or stone on the top of a wall, usually with a slope for shedding water.

coping saw, a narrow-bladed saw in a U-shaped frame, used for very fine work, such as cutting sharp angles or curves in wood.

co·pi·ous (kō′pē əs) *adj.* large in quantity; plentiful; abundant: *The lost child shed copious tears. We had a copious supply of food for the long hike.* —**co′pi·ous·ly,** *adv.* —**co′pi·ous·ness,** *n.*

Cop·land, Aaron (kōp′lənd) 1900—, U.S. composer.

cop·per (kop′ər) *n.* **1.** a reddish-brown metallic element that is easily shaped and is an excellent conductor of heat and electricity. Symbol: **Cu 2.** a reddish-brown color. **3.** a coin made of copper or bronze, as a penny. —*adj.* **1.** made of copper: *a copper pan.* **2.** having the color copper; reddish brown. —*v.t.* to cover or coat with copper. —**cop′per·y,** *adj.*

cop·per·as (kop′ər əs) *n.* a greenish crystalline compound of iron and sulfur, used in medicine, in photography, and in making inks and dyes.

cop·per·head (kop′ər hed′) *n.* **1.** a poisonous snake of the eastern United States, having a copper-colored head and a light brown body with dark brown markings. **2. Copperhead.** a Northerner who sympathized with the Confederacy during the Civil War.

cop·per·plate (kop′ər plāt′) *n.* **1.** a thin piece of copper etched or engraved with a picture, design, or writing. **2.** a print made from such a plate. **3.** a printing process using such plates.

cop·per·smith (kop′ər smith′) *n.* a person who works with copper, especially one who makes objects from copper.

cop·pice (kop′is) *n.* another word for **copse.**

cop·ra (kop′rə) *n.* the dried meat of the coconut. It is the source of coconut oil.

copse (kops) *n.* a thicket or grove of small trees or bushes. Also, **coppice.**

Copt (kopt) *n.* **1.** an Egyptian who is descended from the ancient Egyptians. **2.** a member of the Coptic Church.

cop·ter (kop′tər) *n. Informal.* see **helicopter.**

Cop·tic (kop′tik) *adj.* of or relating to the Copts, their language, or their culture. —*n.* a language descended from Egyptian, formerly spoken by the Copts. It is now used only in the services of the Coptic Church.

Coptic Church, the Christian church of Egypt and formerly of Ethiopia.

cop·u·late (kop′yə lāt′) *v.i.,* **cop·u·lat·ed, cop·u·lat·ing.** to have sexual intercourse. —**cop′u·la′tion,** *n.*

cop·y (kop′ē) *n. pl.,* **cop·ies. 1.** a reproduction of an original; duplicate; imitation: *a copy of a picture, a copy of a piece of furniture, a copy of a letter.* **2.** one of a number of books, magazines, newspapers, or the like: *He bought two copies of the book.* **3.** material to be set in type for printing in a newspaper, book, or the like. —*v.,* **cop·ied, cop·y·ing.** —*v.t.* **1.** to make a copy of (something): *to copy a letter, to copy a painting.* **2.** to make or do something

at; āpe; cär; end; mē; it; īce; hot; ōld; fôrk; wood; fōōl; oil; out; up; turn; sing; thin; this; hw in white; zh in treasure. The symbol ə stands for the sound of a in about, e in taken, i in pencil, o in lemon, and u in circus.

in imitation of: *Jean copied her older sister's style of dressing.* —*v.i.* to make a copy or copies.

cop·y·book (kop′ē book′) *n.* a book containing examples of handwriting for students to copy.

cop·y·ist (kop′ē ist) *n.* a person who makes copies, especially of documents or manuscripts.

cop·y·right (kop′ē rīt′) *n.* the sole right to produce, publish, or sell a literary, musical, or artistic work, granted by law for a certain number of years. —*v.t.* to get a copyright for: *to copyright a popular song.* —*adj.* relating to or protected by copyright.

cop·y·writer (kop′ē rī′tər) *n.* a person who writes copy, especially for advertisements.

co·quet·ry (kō′kə trē, kō ket′rē) *n. pl.,* **co·quet·ries.** the behavior or actions of a coquette; flirtation.

co·quette (kō ket′) *n.* a woman who flirts with men. —**co·quet′tish,** *adj.* —**co·quet′tish·ly,** *adv.* —**co·quet′tish·ness,** *n.*

co·qui·na (kō kē′nə) *n.* a soft, whitish limestone made up of fragments of seashells and corals, used for building.

cor·a·cle (kôr′ə kəl) *n.* a small, light boat made by stretching animal skins or other waterproof material over a frame.

cor·al (kôr′əl) *n.* **1.** a hard substance resembling limestone, usually found in tropical waters. It is secreted by certain tiny sea animals, called polyps. **2.** any of the polyps that secrete this substance. **3.** a mass or structure formed by the skeletons of these animals, such as a reef. **4.** a pinkish-red color. —*adj.* **1.** made of coral: *a coral reef.* **2.** having the color coral.

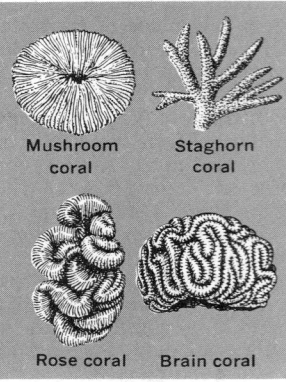

Mushroom coral

Staghorn coral

Rose coral

Brain coral

Types of coral

Coral Sea, a southwestern arm of the Pacific Ocean, off the coast of northeastern Australia. It was the site of an American victory over the Japanese in 1942, during World War II.

coral snake, a narrow-headed, poisonous American snake having red, black, and yellow bands.

cord (kôrd) *n.* **1.** a string or thin rope made of several strands twisted or woven together: *She tied the package with cord.* **2.** an insulated electric cable used to connect an appliance to an outlet or to make other electrical connections: *the cord of a lamp.* **3.** a structure in the body resembling a cord, such as the spinal cord. **4.** a rib or ridge on the surface of a fabric. **5.** a quantity of cut wood, equaling 128 cubic feet, usually arranged in a pile 4 feet wide, 4 feet high, and 8 feet long. —*v.t.* **1.** to bind or fasten with cord; furnish with a cord. **2.** to pile (wood) in cords. —**cord′like′,** *adj.*

Coral snake

cord·age (kôr′dij) *n.* **1.** cords or ropes, especially those in a ship's rigging. **2.** the quantity of cut wood measured in cords.

cord·ed (kôr′did) *adj.* **1.** fastened with cord. **2.** having ribs or ridges or twills; ribbed.

cor·dial (kôr′jəl) *adj.* warm and friendly; hearty. —*n.* a sweet alcoholic drink; liqueur. —**cor′dial·ly,** *adv.*

cor·di·al·i·ty (kôr′jē al′ə tē) *n. pl.,* **cor·di·al·i·ties.** warmth or friendliness; heartiness: *He welcomed us with great cordiality.*

cor·dil·le·ra (kôr dil′ər ə) *n.* a long series of mountain ranges, usually making up the main mountain chain of a large land area.

Cór·do·ba (kôr′də bə) *also,* **Cor·do·va** (kôr dō′və, kôr′də və). *n.* **1.** a city in southwestern Spain. Pop. (1970), 232,343. **2.** a city in north-central Argentina. Pop. (1970), 798,663.

cor·don (kôrd′ən) *n.* **1.** a line of men or barricades set up to guard or close off an area. **2.** a cord or ribbon worn diagonally across the chest as a badge of honor or rank. —*v.t.* to form or place a cordon around: *The police cordoned off an area for the parade.*

cor·do·van (kôr′də vən) *n.* **1.** a soft, fine-grained leather. **2.** a shoe made of this leather. [Spanish *cordobán* this leather, from *Córdoba,* Spain.]

cor·du·roy (kôr′də roi′) *n.* **1.** a fabric, usually made of cotton with a velvety, ribbed surface, used for clothing and upholstery. **2. corduroys.** slacks made of corduroy. —*adj.* made of corduroy.

corduroy road, a road constructed of logs laid crosswise, as over low, marshy ground.

cord·wood (kôrd′wood′) *n.* wood sold by the cord or cut for piling in cords.

core (kôr) *n.* **1.** the hard central part of certain fruits, such as apples and pears, that contains the seeds. **2.** the central, essential or innermost part of anything: *an argument built around a core of fact.* —*v.t.,* **cored, cor·ing.** to remove the core of: *to core an apple.* —**cor′er,** *n.*

CORE (kôr) Congress of Racial Equality.

Cor·fu (kôr′fyōō, kôr′fōō) *n.* a Greek island in the Ionian Sea, off the west coast of Greece.

Cor·inth (kôr′inth) *n.* a port city in southern Greece. Corinth was a major commercial and artistic center in ancient times.

Co·rin·thi·an (kə rin′thē ən) *adj.* **1.** of or relating to Corinth, its people, or their culture. **2.** of or relating to the most elaborate of the three orders of classical Greek architecture, characterized by columns having bell-shaped capitals decorated with acanthus leaves. —*n.* **1.** a person who was born or is living in Corinth. **2. Corinthians.** either of the two books of the New Testament written by the Apostle Paul to the Christians of Corinth.

Corinthian capital

cork (kôrk) *n.* **1.** the light, thick, porous outer bark of the cork oak, used especially as insulating material and for floats. **2.** something made of cork, especially a stopper for a bottle or other container. **3.** the tissue forming the outer bark of woody plants, acting as a protective covering. —*v.t.* to stop or provide with cork or a cork: *to cork a wine bottle.*

cork·er (kôr′kər) *n. Slang.* an outstanding or remarkable person or thing.

cork oak, an oak tree native to the Mediterranean region, from whose bark cork is obtained.

cork·screw (kôrk′skrōō′) *n.* a device for removing corks from bottles, usually having a pointed, metal spiral set in a handle. —*adj.* shaped like a corkscrew; spiral; winding: *a corkscrew mountain road.*

cork·y (kôr′kē) *adj.,* **cork·i·er, cork·i·est.** of, relating to, or like cork.

corm (kôrm) *n.* a thick, fleshy bulblike underground stem of certain plants, such as the crocus or gladiolus, producing leaves and buds at the tip and roots at the base.

cor·mo·rant (kôr′mər ənt) *n.* a large sea bird with dark feathers, having webbed feet, a hooked bill, and a pouch under the beak for holding fish.

corn[1] (kôrn) *n.* **1.** a grain that grows in rows on the large ears of a tall, coarse grass, used for food. **2.** the plant bearing this grain, having a jointed stalk and broad leaves. Also *(defs. 1, 2)*, **maize, Indian corn. 3.** an ear of this plant. **4.** *British.* any food grain or the plant it grows on. **5.** *Informal.* something considered old-fashioned, trite, or too sentimental. —*v.t.* to preserve or season (beef) in strong brine or with coarse, dry salt. [Old English *corn* grain.]

Cormorant

corn[2] (kôrn) *n.* a small hardening and thickening of the skin caused by friction or pressure, especially on a toe. [Old French *corn* horn, horny hardening of the skin.]

corn bread, bread made from cornmeal.

corn·cob (kôrn′kob′) *n.* **1.** the woody core of an ear of corn, on which the kernels grow in rows. **2.** a tobacco pipe with a bowl that is made from a hollowed, dried corncob.

corn·crib (kôrn′krib′) *n.* a bin or small building for storing cobs of corn, built with slats that are spaced for ventilation.

cor·ne·a (kôr′nē ə) *n.* the transparent outer covering or wall of the front of the eyeball, lying over the iris and the pupil.

corned (kôrnd) *adj.* (of beef) preserved or seasoned in strong brine or with coarse, dry salt.

cor·ner (kôr′nər) *n.* **1.** the point or place where two lines or surfaces meet; angle: *the sharp corners of a table, the corner of a room.* **2.** the place where two streets meet. **3.** a place that is hidden, secret, or private: *The little boy sulked in his own little corner of the house.* **4.** a region; part: *The politician campaigned in every corner of the state.* **5.** a place or position that is awkward or threatening, especially one from which escape is almost impossible: *The police had driven the robber into a corner.* **6.** the purchase or control of enough of a particular stock or commodity to raise the price: *to have a corner on grain.* —*adj.* **1.** at or near a corner: *the corner drugstore.* **2.** designed for or used in a corner: *a corner cabinet.* —*v.t.* **1.** to force or drive into an awkward or threatening place or position, especially one from which escape is almost impossible: *Police cornered the thieves in an abandoned warehouse.* **2.** to form or get a corner on (a stock or commodity): *to corner the wheat market.*

    to cut corners. to reduce time, effort, or expenses in doing something; economize: *The construction workers cut corners by using cheap materials to build the house.*

cor·ner·stone (kôr′nər stōn′) *n.* **1.** a stone that lies at the corner of a building. **2.** such a stone laid at a ceremony to mark the starting point in building. **3.** a fundamental principle or part; foundation; basis: *Freedom is the cornerstone of democracy.*

cor·net (kôr net′) *n.* a brass musical instrument that is very similar to the trumpet.

cor·net·tist (kôr net′ist) *also,* **cor·net·ist.** *n.* a person who plays a cornet.

corn·field (kôrn′fēld′) *n.* a field in which corn is grown.

corn·flow·er (kôrn′flou′ər) *n.* **1.** the blue, purple, pink, or white flower of a plant widely grown in North America. **2.** the plant bearing this flower.

corn·husk (kôrn′husk′) *n.* the coarse leaves or husk enclosing an ear of corn.

cor·nice (kôr′nis) *n.* **1.** a projecting ornamental molding along the top of a pillar, wall, or building. **2.** a molding along the walls of a room just below the ceiling.

Cor·nish (kôr′nish) *adj.* of or relating to Cornwall, its people, or their language. —*n.* a Celtic language that was formerly spoken in Cornwall. It became extinct in about 1800.

corn·meal (kôrn′mēl′) *also,* **corn meal.** *n.* meal made from coarsely ground corn.

corn pone, a simple corn bread that is baked or fried, usually made without milk or eggs.

corn·stalk (kôrn′stôk′) *n.* a stalk of corn.

corn·starch (kôrn′stärch′) *n.* a white, powdery starch made from corn, used in cooking as a thickening agent.

cor·nu·co·pi·a (kôr′nə kō′pē ə) *n.* **1.** a curved, twisted horn overflowing with fruit, grain, and vegetables. It is a symbol of abundance and prosperity. **2.** any container or ornament shaped like a horn or cone.

Corn·wall (kôrn′wôl′) *n.* a county in southwestern England. Pop. (1971 est.), 379,480.

Corn·wal·lis, Charles (kôrn wô′-lis, kôrn wol′is) 1738–1805, the British general in the American Revolution who surrendered to Washington at Yorktown, Virginia, in 1781.

Cornucopia

corn·y (kôr′nē) *adj.,* **corn·i·er, corn·i·est.** *Informal.* old-fashioned, trite, or too sentimental: *a corny joke. The audience was bored by the corny movie.*

co·rol·la (kə rol′ə) *n.* the petals of a flower.

cor·ol·lar·y (kôr′ə ler′ē) *n. pl.,* **cor·ol·lar·ies. 1.** a statement that follows naturally from a statement already proved and therefore requires no separate proof. **2.** anything that follows naturally; natural result.

co·ro·na (kə rō′nə) *n.* **1.** the ring of light seen around the sun, moon, or other heavenly body, caused by mist or clouds in the atmosphere. **2.** the outer atmosphere of the sun, seen as a ring of light during an eclipse.

Corolla

Cor·o·na·do, Fran·cis·co Vás·quez de (kôr′ə-nä′dō; fran sis′kō väs′kes dā) 1500?–1544, Spanish explorer of southwestern North America.

cor·o·nar·y (kôr′ə ner′ē) *adj.* of or relating to either of two arteries that branch from the aorta and supply blood to the muscular tissue of the heart. —*n. pl.,* **cor·o·nar·ies.** see **coronary thrombosis.**

coronary thrombosis, a blockage in either of the coronary arteries caused by formation of a blood clot.

cor·o·na·tion (kôr′ə nā′shən) *n.* the act or ceremony of crowning a king or queen.

cor·o·ner (kôr′ə nər) *n.* a local official whose chief duty is to investigate any death that is not clearly due to natural causes.

cor·o·net (kôr′ə net) *n.* **1.** a small crown worn by a noble

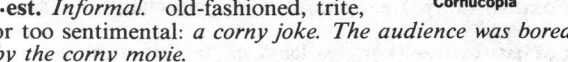

at; āpe; cär; end; mē; it; īce; hot; ōld; fôrk; wood; fool; oil; out; up; turn; sing; thin; this; hw in white; zh in treasure. The symbol ə stands for the sound of **a** in about, **e** in taken, **i** in pencil, **o** in lemon, and **u** in circus.

below the rank of king. **2.** a head ornament somewhat like a crown, especially one that is made with precious metals, jewels, or flowers.

Corp. 1. Corporation. **2.** Corporal.

cor·po·ral[1] (kôr′pər əl) *adj.* of or relating to the human body; physical: *corporal punishment.* [Old French *corporal.*] **—cor′po·ral·ly,** *adv.*

cor·po·ral[2] (kôr′pər əl, kôr′prəl) *n.* the lowest noncommissioned officer in the U.S. Army or Marine Corps, ranking below a sergeant. [Obsolete French *corporal,* going back to Latin *caput* head.]

cor·po·rate (kôr′pər it) *adj.* **1.** of, relating to, or forming a corporation: *a corporate business company.* **2.** of or relating to a united group; joint; collective: *The corporate action of a group of consumers brought about a lowering of food prices.* **—cor′po·rate·ly,** *adv.*

cor·po·ra·tion (kôr′pə rā′shən) *n.* an organization made up of a group of people who have been given the legal power to act as one person. A corporation is created by a government charter and has the right to buy and sell property and to enter into contracts.

cor·po·re·al (kôr pôr′ē əl) *adj.* **1.** of the body; not spiritual. **2.** having substance; material; tangible. **—cor·po′re·al·ly,** *adv.*

corps (kôr) *n. pl.,* **corps** (kôrz). **1.** a unit of a military service with a special function: *a medical corps.* **2.** a military unit consisting of a headquarters, two or more divisions, and additional support units, and forming part of a field army. **3.** a group of persons acting or working together: *a corps of workers, the diplomatic corps.*

corpse (kôrps) *n.* a dead body, especially of a human being.

cor·pu·lence (kôr′pyə ləns) *n.* fatness or stoutness of the body; obesity.

cor·pu·lent (kôr′pyə lənt) *adj.* fat or stout; obese.

Cor·pus Chris·ti (kôr′pəs kris′tē) a port city in southern Texas, on the Gulf of Mexico. Pop. (1970), 204,525.

cor·pus·cle (kôr′pus′əl) *n.* **1.** a particle in the blood or lymph, especially a red or white blood cell. **2.** any minute particle.

cor·ral (kə ral′) *n.* **1.** a fenced enclosure for cattle, horses, or other livestock. **2.** a circular area formed by wagons for defense against attack. **—v.t.,** **cor·ralled, cor·ral·ling. 1.** to drive into or enclose in a corral: *to corral a herd of horses.* **2.** to capture by surrounding or gathering together: *Police corralled the entire gang of thieves.* **3.** to form (wagons) into a corral.

cor·rect (kə rekt′) *adj.* **1.** agreeing with fact or truth; free from error; accurate: *This is the correct answer to the arithmetic problem.* **2.** according to the accepted or approved standard; proper: *A jacket and tie is the correct dress for the party.* **—v.t. 1.** to bring into agreement with fact or truth; make free from error: *He asked his sister to correct any spelling errors in his composition.* **2.** to note or mark the errors in: *The teacher corrected my spelling test.* **3.** to punish or scold in order to improve: *to correct a child for behaving badly.* **4.** to adjust to or make agree with a standard: *to correct poor eyesight with glasses.* **—cor·rect′ly,** *adv.* **—cor·rect′ness,** *n.*

cor·rec·tion (kə rek′shən) *n.* **1.** the act of correcting or the state of being corrected: *Correction of the trouble in the car's engine took several hours.* **2.** a change made to correct an error: *Keep a list of the corrections you make.* **3.** the act of punishing or scolding in order to improve.

cor·rec·tive (kə rek′tiv) *adj.* tending or meant to correct or improve: *corrective lenses, corrective criticism.* **—n.** something that corrects or tends to correct an error. **—cor·rec′tive·ly,** *adv.*

cor·re·late (kôr′ə lāt′, kor′ə lāt′) *v.,* **cor·re·lat·ed, cor-**

re·lat·ing. **—v.t.** to place in a meaningful relation; show a connection between: *The police tried to correlate the two accounts of the accident.* **—v.i.** to be meaningfully related: *These facts seem to correlate.*

cor·re·la·tion (kôr′ə lā′shən, kor′ə lā′shən) *n.* **1.** a meaningful relation; connection: *The speaker explained that there was a close correlation between poor sanitation and disease.* **2.** the act of correlating.

cor·rel·a·tive (kə rel′ə tiv) *adj.* **1.** having or involving a mutual relation: *He has correlative interests in nature and in conservation.* **2.** *Grammar.* complementing one another and commonly used together. In the sentence *I'll let you know either Tuesday or Wednesday,* either and or are correlative conjunctions. **—n. 1.** either of two correlative things. **2.** *Grammar.* a correlative word. **—cor·rel′a·tive·ly,** *adv.*

cor·re·spond (kôr′ə spond′) *v.i.* **1.** to be in agreement or harmony; match: *His taste in music does not correspond with hers.* **2.** to be similar or equivalent, as in character or function: *The gills of a fish correspond to the lungs of a man.* **3.** to communicate by exchanging letters: *The two friends corresponded for many years.*

cor·re·spon·dence (kôr′ə spon′dəns) *n.* **1.** agreement or similarity: *The detectives found a close correspondence between the stories of the two witnesses.* **2.** communication by exchange of letters. **3.** letters written or exchanged: *The congressman found that he did not have time to read all his correspondence.*

cor·re·spon·dent (kôr′ə spon′dənt) *n.* **1.** a person who communicates with another by letter. **2.** a person employed, as by a newspaper or magazine, to send news and commentary from a particular place or area: *He is the Moscow correspondent for a New York newspaper.* **—adj.** corresponding.

cor·re·spond·ing (kôr′ə spon′ding) *adj.* that corresponds; agreeing or similar: *The two neckties have a corresponding design.* **—cor·re·spond′ing·ly,** *adv.*

cor·ri·dor (kôr′ə dər) *n.* a long hallway or passageway in a building, often having rooms opening onto it: *a hotel corridor.*

cor·rob·o·rate (kə rob′ə rāt′) *v.t.,* **cor·rob·o·rat·ed, cor·rob·o·rat·ing.** to strengthen or support, as by giving additional proof; confirm: *The evidence given by several witnesses corroborated the defendant's story.* **—cor·rob·o·ra′tion,** *n.* **—cor·rob′o·ra′tive,** *adj.*

cor·rode (kə rōd′) *v.,* **cor·rod·ed, cor·rod·ing.** **—v.t.** to eat or wear away gradually, especially by chemical action: *This acid corrodes metal.* **—v.i.** to become corroded: *Some metals corrode easily.*

cor·ro·sion (kə rō′zhən) *n.* **1.** the act or process of corroding. **2.** the result of corroding.

cor·ro·sive (kə rō′siv) *adj.* tending to corrode; capable of producing corrosion: *a corrosive acid.* **—n.** a substance that corrodes. **—cor·ro′sive·ly,** *adv.* **—cor·ro′sive·ness,** *n.*

cor·ru·gate (kôr′ə gāt′) *v.,* **cor·ru·gat·ed, cor·ru·gat·ing.** **—v.t.** to shape into parallel ridges or folds; wrinkle. **—v.i.** to become corrugated.

corrugated paper, heavy paper or cardboard shaped into parallel ridges and used for packaging.

cor·ru·ga·tion (kôr′ə gā′shən) *n.* **1.** the act of corrugating or the state of being corrugated. **2.** one of a series of parallel ridges or folds; wrinkle.

cor·rupt (kə rupt′) *adj.* **1.** influenced by bribery; dishonest; crooked: *corrupt government officials.* **2.** wicked or immoral; depraved: *a corrupt life.* **3.** changed from the original or correct form or version, as by additions or errors: *a corrupt translation of a book.* **4.** rotten; decayed. **—v.t. 1.** to cause to act dishonestly, as by bribery: *That* *man cannot be corrupted.* **2.** to make morally wicked. **3.** to change from the original or correct form or version: *to corrupt the text of a manuscript.* **4.** to make rotten; decay. —*v.i.* to become corrupt. —**cor·rupt′er,** *n.* —**cor·rupt′ly,** *adv.* —**cor·rupt′ness,** *n.*

cor·rupt·i·ble (kə rup′tə bəl) *adj.* that can be corrupted. —**cor·rupt′i·bil′i·ty,** *n.* —**cor·rupt′i·bly,** *adv.*

cor·rup·tion (kə rup′shən) *n.* **1.** the act of corrupting or the state of being corrupted. **2.** dishonest behavior. **3.** wickedness; depravity. **4.** a corrupted form or version, as of a text or language. **5.** rot; decay.

cor·rup·tive (kə rup′tiv) *adj.* tending to corrupt; causing corruption: *The boy's dishonest friends had a corruptive influence on him.*

cor·sage (kôr säzh′) *n.* a flower or small bouquet of flowers worn by a woman, usually at the shoulder or waist.

cor·sair (kôr′ser′) *n.* **1.** a privateer or pirate, especially of the Barbary Coast. **2.** a privateering vessel or pirate ship.

cor·se·let (*def. 1* kôr′sə let′; *def. 2* kôrs′lit) *n.* **1.** a woman's undergarment similar to a corset. **2.** *also,* **cors·let.** a plate of armor for the upper part of the body.

cor·set (kôr′sit) *n.* a close-fitting undergarment worn chiefly by women to shape and support the waist and hips.

Cor·si·ca (kôr′si kə) *n.* a French island in the Mediterranean, southeast of France. —**Cor′si·can,** *adj., n.*

cor·tege (kôr tezh′) *also,* **cor·tège.** *n.* **1.** a ceremonial procession, especially a funeral procession. **2.** a group of followers or attendants; retinue.

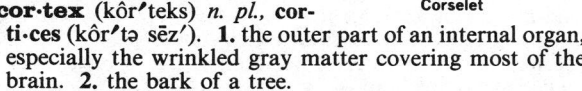

Corselet

cor·tex (kôr′teks) *n. pl.,* **cor·ti·ces** (kôr′tə sēz′). **1.** the outer part of an internal organ, especially the wrinkled gray matter covering most of the brain. **2.** the bark of a tree.

Cor·tez, Her·nan·do (kôr tez′; er nän′dō) *also,* **Cor·tés** (kôr tes′). 1485–1547, Spanish conqueror of Mexico.

cor·ti·cal (kôr′ti kəl) *adj.* of, relating to, or consisting of a cortex. —**cor′ti·cal·ly,** *adv.*

cor·ti·sone (kôr′tə zōn′) *n.* a hormone produced by the cortex of the adrenal gland or made synthetically, used to treat arthritis and various allergies.

co·run·dum (kə run′dəm) *n.* a mineral made up of aluminum oxide, second only to diamonds in hardness. The dark-colored variety is used for polishing and grinding; transparent varieties include such gems as sapphires and rubies.

cor·vette (kôr vet′) *also,* **cor·vet.** *n.* **1.** a fast armed ship, smaller than a destroyer, used especially to escort other ships. **2.** a former warship smaller than a frigate.

cor·ymb (kôr′imb, kôr′im, kor′imb) *n.* a type of flower arrangement in which each small stemmed flower grows individually at different levels on a main stem, but develops so that the flowers reach approximately the same height and form a flat-topped cluster, as in cherry blossoms.

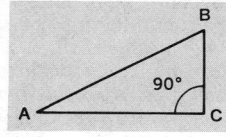

Cosecant of angle A = AB/BC

cos., cosine.

co·se·cant (kō sē′kənt, kō sē′kant) *n.* (of an acute angle in a right triangle) the ratio of the hypotenuse to the side opposite the angle.

co·sine (kō′sīn) *n.* (of an acute angle in a right triangle) the ratio of the angle's adjacent side to the hypotenuse.

cos·met·ic (koz met′ik) *n.* a preparation, such as lipstick, powder, or rouge, used to beautify the body, especially the face or hair. —*adj.* used to beautify the body.

cos·mic (koz′mik) *adj.* **1.** of or relating to the universe as a whole: *cosmic law.* **2.** of great extent; vast; endless: *The decision to drop the atomic bomb had cosmic implications.* **3.** of or from outer space. —**cos′mi·cal·ly,** *adv.*

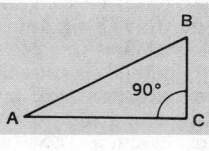

Cosine of angle A = AC/AB

cosmic rays, high-frequency rays of great penetrating force, consisting mainly of positively charged particles that come to the earth from outer space.

cos·mo·naut (koz′mə nôt′) *n.* an astronaut, especially one from the Soviet Union.

cos·mo·pol·i·tan (koz′mə pol′ə tən) *adj.* **1.** composed of or having characteristics or people from many different countries: *a cosmopolitan city.* **2.** not narrow in attitude, viewpoint, or interest; at home in all parts of the world: *a cosmopolitan person.* —*n.* a person who is cosmopolitan in attitude or viewpoint.

cos·mos (koz′məs) *n. pl.,* **cos·mos·es.** **1.** the universe considered as an ordered and harmonious system. **2.** any ordered and harmonious system.

Cos·sack (kos′ak) *n.* one of a people living mainly in the southeastern part of Russia, noted as horsemen and cavalrymen.

cost (kôst) *n.* **1.** an amount of money paid or charged for something; price; expense: *The cost of this used car is only $500.* **2.** a loss or sacrifice: *The war was won at a great cost of lives.* **3. costs.** the expenses of a lawsuit. —*v.t.,* **cost, cost·ing. 1.** to be obtained at the price of: *This book cost ten dollars.* **2.** to cause the loss or sacrifice of: *The accident almost cost him his life. The injury cost the team the services of its best player.*

at all costs or **at any cost.** regardless of the cost.

Cos·ta Ri·ca (kos′tə rē′kə) a country in Central America, between Nicaragua and Panama. Capital, San José. Area, 19,575 sq. mi. Pop. (1971 est.), 1,790,000. —**Costa Rican.**

cos·ter·mon·ger (kôs′tər mung′gər, kôs′tər mong′gər) *n. British.* a person who sells food, such as fruit, vegetables, or fish, in the street.

cost·ly (kôst′lē) *adj.,* **cost·li·er, cost·li·est.** costing much: *costly jewelry, a costly mistake.* —**cost′li·ness,** *n.*

cost of living, the average cost of goods and services in a typical family budget during a given period of time.

cos·tume (*n.,* kos′tōōm, kos′tyōōm; *v.,* kos tōōm′, kos tyōōm′) *n.* **1.** an outfit worn in order to portray someone else: *a Halloween costume, costumes for a play.* **2.** a style of dress, including accessories and hair style, belonging to a particular time, place, or people: *a peasant costume.* **3.** special clothing worn for a particular occasion or activity: *a riding costume.* —*v.t.,* **cos·tumed, cos·tum·ing.** to provide with a costume.

cos·tum·er (kos tōō′mər, kos tyōō′mər) *n.* a person who makes, sells, or rents costumes.

at; āpe; cär; end; mē; it; īce; hot; ōld; fôrk; wood; fōōl; oil; out; up; turn; sing; thin; this; hw in white; zh in treasure. The symbol ə stands for the sound of a in about, e in taken, i in pencil, o in lemon, and u in circus.

C

co·sy (kō′zē) *adj.*, **co·si·er, co·si·est,** *n. pl.,* **co·sies.** another spelling of **cozy.**

cot¹ (kot) *n.* a narrow bed, especially one made of canvas stretched on a folding frame. [Hindi *khat* bed, couch.]

cot² (kot) *n.* **1.** a small house; cottage. **2.** a small structure for shelter or protection, especially one for animals. [Old English *cot* cottage.]

co·tan·gent (kō tan′jənt, kō′tan′jənt) *n.* (of an acute angle in a right triangle) the ratio of the angle's adjacent side to the side opposite.

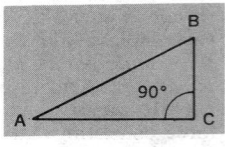
Cotangent of angle A = AC/BC

cote (kōt) *n.* a small shelter for animals or birds.

co·te·rie (kō′tər ē) *n.* a small group of people who share a particular interest and often meet socially.

co·til·lion (kə til′yən) *n.* **1.** an elaborate ballroom dance popular in the nineteenth century, usually led by one couple. **2.** the music for such a dance. **3.** a formal ball.

Co·to·pax·i (kō′tō päk′sē, kō′tō pä′hē) *n.* a volcano in the Andes in north-central Ecuador. It is one of the highest active volcanos in the world.

cot·tage (kot′ij) *n.* a small house, usually in the country or in a summer resort.

cottage cheese, an unripened, soft, white cheese made of strained and seasoned curds of sour skim milk.

cot·tag·er (kot′i jər) *n.* a person who lives or vacations in a cottage.

cot·ter (kot′ər) *also,* **cot·tar.** *n.* a Scottish tenant farmer.

cotter pin, a split pin whose ends are spread after it has been inserted in a hole or slot so that it will stay in place.

cot·ton (kot′ən) *n.* **1.** soft white, gray, or brown fibers that grow in a fluffy mass in large seed pods of certain plants, used in making textiles and other products. **2.** the woody, branching shrub bearing these fibers. **3.** thread made of cotton fibers. **4.** any fabric woven of cotton. —*adj.* having to do with or made of cotton.

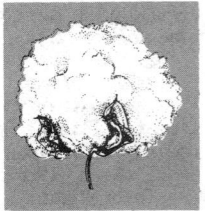
Cotton

cotton candy, a light, fluffy candy consisting of thin fibers of melted sugar spun or wound around a cone or stick.

cotton gin, a machine that separates the fibers of cotton from the seeds.

cot·ton·mouth (kot′ən mouth′) *n.* another word for **water moccasin.**

cot·ton·seed (kot′ən sēd′) *n. pl.,* **cot·ton·seeds** or **cot·ton·seed.** the seed of the cotton plant, from which cottonseed oil is extracted.

cottonseed oil, an oil extracted from cottonseed, used for cooking and in making soap and paints.

cot·ton·tail (kot′ən tāl′) *n.* an American rabbit that has brown or grayish fur and a short, fluffy white tail.

cot·ton·wood (kot′ən wood′) *n.* **1.** any of several North American trees related to the willow, having leathery, triangular leaves with toothed edges and tiny brown seeds covered with silky white hairs. **2.** the light, soft wood of this tree.

cot·ton·y (kot′ən ē) *adj.* like cotton; soft, downy, and white.

cot·y·le·don (kot′əl ēd′ən) *n.* the undeveloped leaf that forms part of a plant embryo. In many plants the cotyledon develops into the first leaf or one of the first pair of leaves to grow above the ground.

couch (kouch) *n. pl.,* **couch·es.** **1.** a piece of furniture, usually upholstered, for several people to sit on; sofa.

2. any place for sleeping or resting. —*v.t.* to put into words; express: *His argument was couched in careful phrases.*

cou·gar (kōō′gər) *n.* a tawny or grayish-brown wildcat of North, Central, and South America, having a small round head, long limbs, and a slender, muscular body. Also, **puma, mountain lion.**

cough (kôf) *v.i.* to force air from the lungs with a sudden sharp sound. —*v.t.* to expel by coughing: *to cough blood.* —*n.* **1.** the act or sound of coughing. **2.** an illness or condition that causes frequent coughing.

cough drop, a small medicated lozenge, usually flavored and sweetened, for relieving coughs.

could (kood) the past tense of **can¹.**

could·n't (kood′ənt) could not.

couldst (koodst) *Archaic.* the second person singular past tense of **can¹.**

cou·lee (kōō′lē) *n.* **1.** in the western United States, a deep gulch or ravine, often dry in summer, that has been formed by running water. **2.** a stream of lava.

cou·lomb (kōō′lom, kōō′lōm) *n.* a unit used as a measure of the quantity of electric charge. It is the amount of charge that in one second passes a given point in a wire carrying a current of one ampere.

coun·cil (koun′səl) *n.* **1.** a group of people called together to give advice, discuss a problem, or make a decision. **2.** a body of persons elected or appointed to govern or make laws in a city or town.

coun·cil·man (koun′səl mən) *n. pl.,* **coun·cil·men** (koun′səl mən). a member of a council, especially of the council of a city or town. —**coun′cil·wom′an,** *n.*

coun·ci·lor (koun′sə lər) *also, British,* **coun·cil·lor.** *n.* a member of a council; councilman or councilwoman.

coun·sel (koun′səl) *n.* **1.** an exchange of ideas, opinions, or advice; consultation; deliberation: *The leaders of the government met for counsel.* **2.** advice: *She failed to listen to the wise counsel of her friend.* **3.** a lawyer or group of lawyers giving legal advice: *the counsel for the defendant.* —*v.t.* **1.** to give advice to; advise: *He counseled his younger brother to study harder.* **2.** to recommend: *to counsel caution.*

   to take counsel. to seek or exchange ideas, opinions, or advice; consult: *to take counsel with friends.*

coun·se·lor (koun′sə lər) *also, British,* **coun·sel·lor.** *n.* **1.** a person who gives counsel or advice; adviser: *a guidance counselor in a high school.* **2.** a person who gives legal advice; lawyer. **3.** a person who supervises children at a summer camp.

count¹ (kount) *v.t.* **1.** to find out the total number of; add up: *She counted the eggs in the carton.* **2.** to list or say numbers in order up to (a certain number): *to count ten.* **3.** to take into account; include in counting: *There were forty people in the bus, counting the driver.* **4.** to believe to be; consider: *He counts Jack as his best friend.* —*v.i.* **1.** to list or say numbers in order: *to count up to five.* **2.** to be of value; have importance; matter: *Try to make every minute of your vacation count.* **3.** to be taken into account; be included in counting. —*n.* **1.** the act of counting; numbering: *The club chairman made a count of the members present.* **2.** a number obtained by counting; total. **3.** *Law.* each distinct charge in an accusation: *The robber pleaded innocent to the first two counts.* [Old French *co(u)nter* to reckon, tell.]

   to count in. to include: *If you're having a party, count me in.*

   to count off. to divide into equal groups by counting: *The coach told the gym students to count off by fours.*

   to count on or **to count upon.** to rely or depend on: *Can I count on you if I need help?*

to count out. a. to exclude; omit: *We'll have to count her out if we're going on a camping trip.* **b.** to declare (a fallen boxer) the loser when he cannot rise before a count of ten seconds is completed.

count² (kount) *n.* a European nobleman having a rank corresponding to that of a British earl. [Old French *conte*.]

count·down (kount′doun′) *n.* **1.** the act or process of counting backward from a given time to zero to indicate the time remaining before the launching of a spacecraft or missile. **2.** any act of counting in reverse numerical order.

coun·te·nance (koun′tə nəns) *n.* **1.** the face; features: *That actor has a handsome countenance.* **2.** an expression of the face; look: *The lost child had an unhappy countenance.* **3.** approval or support; encouragement: *His friends would not give countenance to his cheating.* —*v.t.,* **coun·te·nanced, coun·te·nanc·ing.** to give approval to; support; encourage: *His father does not countenance laziness.*

count·er¹ (koun′tər) *n.* **1.** a long table, as in a store, restaurant, or bank, where sales are made, business is conducted, or food or drinks are served. **2.** any long shelf or flat working area, as in a kitchen. **3.** a thing used in counting, especially a small disk used for keeping score in certain games. **4.** an imitation coin; token. [Anglo-Norman *counteour* counting table, counting house.]

count·er² (koun′tər) *n.* a person or thing that counts, especially a mechanical device for counting. [*Count¹* + *-er¹*.]

coun·ter³ (koun′tər) *adv.* in an opposite direction or way; opposite; contrary: *He acted counter to the rules.* —*adj.* opposite; contrary: *His plan is counter to mine.* —*v.t.* **1.** to go or act counter to; oppose: *They countered our proposal.* **2.** to deal a blow in boxing in return for (an opponent's blow). —*v.i.* **1.** to make an opposing move: *The debater countered with another argument.* **2.** to deal a blow in boxing in return for an opponent's blow: *The champion countered with a left to the head.* —*n.* **1.** something that is opposite or contrary. **2.** a boxing blow in return for an opponent's blow. **3.** a stiff piece on the inside of the heel of a shoe. [Old French *contre* against.]

counter- *combining form* **1.** in opposition to; against: *counteract.* **2.** in return: *counterattack.* **3.** corresponding: *counterpart.*

coun·ter·act (koun′tər akt′) *v.t.* to act against the effect or force of; neutralize; check: *The medicine could not counteract the effects of the disease.*

coun·ter·at·tack (koun′tər ə tak′) *n.* an attack made to counter another attack: *to launch a counterattack against an invading force.* —*v.i.* to make a counterattack. —*v.t.* to make a counterattack against.

coun·ter·bal·ance (*n.,* koun′tər bal′əns; *v.,* koun′tər-bal′əns) *n.* **1.** a weight used to balance another weight. **2.** any power or influence that balances or offsets an opposing power or influence: *Tom's easygoing nature is a counterbalance to Jim's quick temper.* —*v.t.,* **coun·ter·bal·anced, coun·ter·bal·anc·ing.** to act as a counterbalance to; offset.

coun·ter·check (koun′tər chek′) *n.* **1.** something that stops or opposes something else. **2.** a check made to confirm an earlier check; double check. —*v.t.* to confirm by a second check; double-check.

coun·ter·claim (koun′tər klām′) *n.* an opposing claim, especially an action by the defendant against the plaintiff in a lawsuit.

coun·ter·clock·wise (koun′tər klok′wīz′) *adv., adj.* in the direction opposite to the movement of a clock's hands.

coun·ter·es·pi·o·nage (koun′tər es′pē ə näzh′, koun′-tər es′pē ə nij) *n.* the use of espionage by a country to prevent and counteract espionage by another country.

coun·ter·feit (koun′tər fit′) *v.t.* **1.** to make a copy of in order to deceive or defraud: *It is a crime to counterfeit money.* **2.** to make a pretense of; pretend; feign: *to counterfeit sympathy.* —*v.i.* to make counterfeits. —*n.* a copy or imitation made in order to deceive or defraud; forgery. —*adj.* **1.** made in imitation of an original in order to deceive or defraud; not genuine: *a counterfeit hundred-dollar bill.* **2.** pretended; feigned: *counterfeit kindness.* —**coun′ter·feit·er,** *n.*

coun·ter·in·tel·li·gence (koun′tər in tel′ə jəns) *n.* actions carried on by a government to counteract espionage and sabotage activities of an enemy.

coun·ter·man (koun′tər man′) *n. pl.,* **coun·ter·men** (koun′tər men′). a man who waits on customers at a counter, especially in a cafeteria or restaurant.

coun·ter·mand (*v.,* koun′tər mand′; *n.,* koun′tər-mand′) *v.t.* to cancel or reverse (an order or command). —*n.* an order or command canceling or reversing an earlier order or command.

coun·ter·march (koun′tər märch′) *n. pl.,* **coun·ter·march·es.** a march back or in the opposite direction. —*v.i.* to perform a countermarch.

coun·ter·meas·ure (koun′tər mezh′ər) *n.* an action taken to counteract another action.

coun·ter·of·fen·sive (koun′tər ə fen′siv) *n.* an attack launched by a military force to turn back an enemy attack.

coun·ter·pane (koun′tər pān′) *n.* a quilt or cover for a bed; bedspread.

coun·ter·part (koun′tər pärt′) *n.* a person or thing corresponding to or closely resembling another: *The U.S. Congress is the counterpart of the British Parliament.*

coun·ter·point (koun′tər point′) *n.* **1.** the art or technique of composing music in which one or more melodies are played or sung at the same time in harmony with a main melody. **2.** one or more melodies added to a main melody in this way.

coun·ter·poise (koun′tər poiz′) *n.* **1.** a weight that balances another weight; counterbalance. **2.** any influence or power that balances or offsets an opposing influence or power. **3.** the state of being in balance. —*v.t.,* **coun·ter·poised, coun·ter·pois·ing.** to act as a counterpoise to; counterbalance.

coun·ter·rev·o·lu·tion (koun′tər rev′ə lōō′shən) *n.* a revolution opposed to an earlier revolution and seeking to reverse its effects: *The general led a counterrevolution against the rebels who had taken control of the government.*

coun·ter·rev·o·lu·tion·ar·y (koun′tər rev′ə lōō′shə-ner′ē) *adj.* relating to a counterrevolution. —*n. pl.,* **coun·ter·rev·o·lu·tion·ar·ies.** a person who takes part in or supports a counterrevolution.

coun·ter·sign (koun′tər sīn′) *n.* **1.** a secret sign or signal given in answer to another, especially a military password given in answer to the challenge of a guard or sentry. **2.** a signature added to a previously signed check or other document to confirm it or to show that it is authentic. —*v.t.* to sign (a document already signed by another) in order to confirm or authenticate it: *The treasurer of the company countersigned the checks.*

coun·ter·sink (koun′tər singk′) *v.t.,* **coun·ter·sunk, coun·ter·sink·ing. 1.** to enlarge the upper part of (a hole

at; āpe; cär; end; mē; it; īce; hot; ōld; fôrk; wood; fōōl; oil; out; up; turn; sing; thin; this; hw in white; zh in treasure. The symbol ə stands for the sound of **a** in about, **e** in taken, **i** in pencil, **o** in lemon, and **u** in circus.

or cavity) to make room for the head of a screw, bolt, rivet, or similar device. **2.** to set (a screw, bolt, or rivet) in a hole enlarged in this way. —*n.* **1.** a hole made in this way. **2.** a tool for making such a hole.

coun·ter·spy (koun′tər spī′) *n. pl.,* **coun·ter·spies.** a spy who is employed to detect and counteract the activities of enemy spies.

coun·ter·weight (koun′tər wāt′) *n.* a weight balancing another weight; counterbalance; counterpoise.

count·ess (koun′tis) *n. pl.,* **count·ess·es. 1.** the wife or widow of a count or, in Great Britian, of an earl. **2.** a woman holding in her own right a rank equal to that of a count or an earl.

counting house, a building, office, or room used for such purposes as bookkeeping, correspondence, or business transactions.

counting number, a number used in counting the numbers of a set; any whole number except 0. 1, 2, 3, 64, and 179 are counting numbers; ⅔ and ⁻5 are not.

count·less (kount′lis) *adj.* too many to be counted; innumerable: *There are countless stars in the sky.*

count noun, a noun that names something that can be counted. *Cat, chair,* and *sandwich* are count nouns. *Thunder* and *butter* are not, since we do not say "three thunders" or "two butters."

coun·tri·fied (kun′tri fīd′) *adj.* **1.** looking or acting like someone from the country. **2.** like the country or country life; rural; rustic.

coun·try (kun′trē) *n. pl.,* **coun·tries. 1.** an area of land; region, district, or territory: *farm country, mountain country.* **2.** an area of land that has definite boundaries and a common form of government; nation: *Brazil, Chile, and Argentina are countries in South America.* **3.** the land of a nation: *Much of the country of Egypt is desert.* **4.** the people of a nation: *The whole country feared the cruel dictator.* **5.** the land where a person was born or of which he is a citizen. **6.** the region outside of cities and towns; rural area: *On Sunday we went for a drive in the country.* —*adj.* of or relating to the country; rural: *country music, a country road, country property.*

country club, a private club, usually located in the country or a suburb, equipped with facilities for recreation, such as a golf course, a swimming pool, or tennis courts.

coun·try·folk (kun′trē fōk′) *n. pl.,* **coun·try·folk** or **coun·try·folks.** people who live in rural areas.

coun·try·man (kun′trē mən) *n. pl.,* **coun·try·men** (kun′trē mən). **1.** a person who was born or lives in one's own country; compatriot: *George Washington was said to have been "first in the hearts of his countrymen."* **2.** a person who lives in the country.

coun·try·seat (kun′trē sēt′) *n.* a mansion or estate in the country.

coun·try·side (kun′trē sīd′) *n.* **1.** a rural region or district; country. **2.** the people living in the country: *The whole countryside was at the county fair.*

coun·try·wom·an (kun′trē woom′ən) *n. pl.,* **coun·try·wom·en** (kun′trē wim′ən). **1.** a woman who was born or lives in one's own country. **2.** a woman who lives in the country.

coun·ty (koun′tē) *n. pl.,* **coun·ties. 1.** one of the sections into which a state of the United States is divided, having its own local government. **2.** one of the districts into which certain countries are divided, such as Great Britain and Ireland. **3.** the people of a county. [French *conté* a territory ruled by a count.]

county seat, a town or city that is the center of government for a county.

coup (kōō) *n. pl.,* **coups** (kōōz). **1.** a sudden, brilliant action; unexpected, clever maneuver; master stroke: *Get-*

ting the leader of the opposing party to support his plan was quite a coup for the President. **2.** see **coup d'etat.**

coup d'e·tat (kōō′dä tä′) *pl.,* **coups d'e·tat** (kōō′dä tä′). a sudden overthrow of a government. [French *coup d'état* literally, stroke of state.]

coupe (kōōp, kōō pā′) *also,* **cou·pé** (kōō pā′). *n.* **1.** a two-door automobile that is smaller than a sedan, seating two to six people. **2.** a short, four-wheeled, closed carriage with seats inside for two people and a seat outside for the driver.

Coupe *(def. 2)*

cou·ple (kup′əl) *n.* **1.** two things of the same kind joined together or thought of together; pair. **2.** a man and woman who are married, engaged, or are partners in a dance, game, or other activity. **3.** *Informal.* a small number; several; few: *We walked a couple of miles.* —*v.,* **cou·pled, cou·pling.** —*v.t.* to join or unite in a pair or pairs: *to couple two railroad cars.* —*v.i.* to join or unite in a pair or pairs.

cou·pler (kup′lər) *n.* **1.** a person or thing that couples. **2.** an interlocking device used to connect two railroad cars.

cou·plet (kup′lit) *n.* two successive lines of verse, usually rhyming and in the same meter, that form a unit. For example: *Earth, receive an honored guest;/William Yeats is laid to rest* (W. H. Auden).

cou·pling (kup′ling) *n.* **1.** the act of joining together. **2.** any of various devices for joining parts of machinery. **3.** see **coupler** *(def. 2).*

cou·pon (kōō′pon, kyōō′pon) *n.* **1.** a part of a ticket, certificate or printed advertisement that can be detached, giving the person holding it some right: *The record album will be sold at half price to anyone who presents this coupon.* **2.** a printed statement of the interest due on a bond, that can be detached and presented for payment at a specified time.

cour·age (kur′ij) *n.* a quality that makes it possible for a person to face danger or difficulties without fear; bravery; boldness: *She showed great courage in rescuing the drowning child. It took courage for the author to speak out against the dictator's policies.*

cou·ra·geous (kə rā′jəs) *adj.* having or showing courage; brave; fearless: *a courageous person, a courageous act.* —**cou·ra′geous·ly,** *adv.* —**cou·ra′geous·ness,** *n.*

cour·i·er (kur′ē ər, koor′ē ər) *n.* a messenger, especially one carrying an important or urgent message: *a diplomatic courier.*

course (kôrs) *n.* **1.** a moving from one point to the next; onward movement; progress; advance: *the course of history, in the course of human events. He grew four inches during the course of a year.* **2.** a line or path in which something moves; direction or route taken: *The ship sailed on a westward course.* **3.** a natural or regular order or development: *The disease has run its course.* **4.** a way of acting or proceeding: *Your wisest course would be to make no comment on what happened.* **5.** an area used for certain sports or games: *a race course.* **6.** a series or group of similar things: *a course of medical treatment.* **7.** a series of studies in a school, college, or university: *a secretarial course. Jim is taking a liberal arts course.* **8.** one of the subjects in such a series of studies: *a course in typing, a history course.* **9.** a part of a meal served at one time: *The main course was chicken.* —*v.i.,* **coursed, cours·ing.** to move swiftly; run; flow: *The tears coursed down her cheeks.*

of course. as is or was to be expected; naturally; certainly: *Of course I'll help you. Of course, there will have to be an inquiry into the matter.*

C

cours·er (kôr′sər) *n.* a swift or spirited horse. ▲ used in literature.

court (kôrt) *n.* **1.** an open space that is partly or entirely enclosed by walls or buildings; courtyard. **2.** a short street. **3.** a level space or area marked off for certain games: *a basketball court, a tennis court.* **4.** the residence of a king, queen, or other royal ruler; royal palace. **5.** the family, friends, and advisers of a king, queen, or other royal ruler. **6.** a royal ruler together with his officials and advisers, considered as a ruling power. **7.** a formal assembly held by a royal ruler: *The king held court at his summer palace.* **8.** a place where justice is carried out or trials are held; courtroom or courthouse. **9.** one or more persons appointed to hear legal cases and administer justice; judge or judges. **10.** an assembly of such persons to administer justice: *Court is held five days a week.* **11.** attention given to win favor, especially by a man to a woman. —*v.t.* **1.** to seek the love or affection of; woo. **2.** to pay flattering attention to (a person) to win his favor: *The movie producer courted the famous star.* **3.** to try to get or gain; seek: *to court flattery, to court a person's favor.* **4.** to act so as to invite: *to court danger, to court defeat.* —*v.i.* to carry on a courtship: *The young couple has courted for a year.*

cour·te·ous (kur′tē əs) *adj.* having or showing good manners; considerate of others; polite; gracious: *a courteous person, a courteous reply.* —**cour′te·ous·ly,** *adv.* —**cour′te·ous·ness,** *n.*

cour·te·san (kôr′tə zən, kur′tə zən) *n.* a prostitute, especially one who associates with men of wealth and high rank.

cour·te·sy (kur′tə sē) *n. pl.,* **cour·te·sies.** **1.** courteous behavior; politeness. **2.** a courteous act; favor.

court·house (kôrt′hous′) *n. pl.,* **court·hous·es** (kôrt′hou′ziz). **1.** a building in which courts of law are held. **2.** a building housing the main offices of a county government.

cour·ti·er (kôr′tē ər) *n.* **1.** a person who attends the court of a king, queen, or other royal ruler. **2.** a person who tries to win favor by flattery.

court·ly (kôrt′lē) *adj.,* **court·li·er, court·li·est.** suitable for a king's court; refined; elegant; polished: *a man with courtly manners.* —**court′li·ness,** *n.*

court-mar·tial (kôrt′mär′shəl) *n. pl.,* **courts-mar·tial.** **1.** a military court that tries members of the armed forces for offenses against military law. **2.** a trial by such a court. —*v.t.,* **court-mar·tialed, court-mar·tial·ing;** *also, British,* **court-mar·tialled, court-mar·tial·ling.** to try by court-martial: *The soldier was court-martialed for striking an officer.*

Court of St. James, the royal court of Great Britain.

court·room (kôrt′rōōm′, kôrt′room′) *n.* a room in which a court of law is held.

court·ship (kôrt′ship′) *n.* a courting; wooing: *The courtship of Robert Browning and Elizabeth Barrett has been described in books and movies.*

court tennis, a form of tennis played on an indoor court having high cement walls off which the ball may be hit.

court·yard (kôrt′yärd′) *n.* an open area surrounded by walls or buildings, in or next to a large building.

cou·sin (kuz′in) *n.* **1.** a son or daughter of one's uncle or aunt. **2.** any relative with whom one shares a common ancestor. ▲ First cousins have the same pair of grandparents; second cousins have great-grandparents in common.

cou·ture (kōō toor′) *n.* the designing, making, and selling of fashionable clothes for women.

co·va·lent bond (kō vā′lənt) a chemical bond formed when two neighboring atoms share a pair of electrons.

cove (kōv) *n.* **1.** a small, sheltered inlet or bay in a shoreline. **2.** a sheltered hollow, as in hills or a wood.

cov·en (kuv′ən) *n.* a gathering or assembly of witches.

cov·e·nant (kuv′ə nənt) *n.* an agreement between two or more persons or groups, especially a solemn and formal one: *A general association of nations must be formed under specific covenants* (Woodrow Wilson). —*v.i.* to enter into a covenant.

Cov·en·try (kuv′ən trē, kov′ən trē) *n.* **1.** a city in south-central England. During the English civil war Royalists were sent there to be imprisoned. Pop. (1971 est.), 333,000. **2.** a state of being completely ignored by one's associates; banishment or exclusion from society. ▲ used especially in the phrase *to send to Coventry.*

cov·er (kuv′ər) *v.t.* **1.** to put something over or upon: *She covered the table with a tablecloth. The workman covered the furniture before he painted the wall.* **2.** to be over the surface of; spread or extend over: *Snow covered the ground. The dog was covered with mud.* **3.** to hide from view or knowledge; conceal: *to cover a mistake with a lie. Darkness covered the thief's flight.* **4.** to protect against loss or harm: *This health insurance plan covers all the employees of the company.* **5.** to travel or pass over: *He covered the distance in fifteen minutes.* **6.** to deal with; treat; include: *This book covers the subject of the American Revolution.* **7.** to aim a firearm or other weapon at: *The policeman covered the thief with a pistol.* **8.** to get the details of; report: *This newspaper covers sports thoroughly.* **9.** *Sports.* **a.** to guard or defend against (an opposing player): *to cover a pass receiver in football.* **b.** to be responsible for defending (an area or position): *to cover a base in baseball.* —*n.* **1.** something that covers: *the covers on a bed, the cover of a box, the cover of a book.* **2.** protection or shelter: *The hikers took cover in a barn when the storm broke.* **3.** something that hides or disguises: *The thief escaped from the policemen under the cover of darkness.* **4.** a place setting for one person at a table, including silverware, dishes, and linens.

under cover. secret or secretly.

cov·er·age (kuv′ər ij) *n.* **1.** the extent or degree to which something is covered. **2.** all the risks covered by the terms of an insurance policy. **3.** the act or manner of gathering and reporting news: *The television networks provided full coverage of the election.*

cov·er·all (kuv′ər ôl′) *also,* **cov·er·alls.** *n.* a loose-fitting one-piece garment worn by workmen to protect their clothes.

cover crop, a crop planted in a field or orchard to protect the soil from erosion or to enrich the soil between plantings of other crops. Clover and rye are often planted as cover crops.

covered wagon, a large wagon with a canvas cover spread on hoops or other supports, used by pioneers traveling westward in the United States.

cov·er·ing (kuv′ər ing) *n.* anything that covers.

cov·er·let (kuv′ər lit) *n.* an outer covering for a bed.

cov·ert (kuv′ərt, kō′vərt) *adj.* kept out of sight; secret; concealed; hidden: *a covert glance. She made a covert attempt to communicate with the prisoner.* —*n.* **1.** a hiding place; shelter. **2.** a thicket that gives shelter to wild animals or game. —**cov′ert·ly,** *adv.* —**cov′ert·ness,** *n.*

cov·et (kuv′it) *v.t.* to have an eager desire for (something that belongs to another person): *He coveted his brother's new baseball glove.*

at; āpe; cär; end; mē; it; īce; hot; ōld; fôrk; wood; fōōl; oil; out; up; turn; sing; thin; this; hw in white; zh in treasure. The symbol ə stands for the sound of a in about, e in taken, i in pencil, o in lemon, and u in circus.

cov·et·ous (kuv′it əs) *adj.* eagerly desiring something belonging to another person: *He was covetous of his friend's new bicycle.* —**cov′et·ous·ly,** *adv.* —**cov′et·ous·ness,** *n.*

cov·ey (kuv′ē) *n. pl.,* **cov·eys. 1.** a small flock of partridges, quail, grouse, or similar birds. **2.** any small group: *a covey of students.*

cow[1] (kou) *n.* **1.** the full-grown female of domestic cattle, raised for its milk. **2.** the female of certain other large animals, such as the moose, elephant, or whale. [Old English *cū.*]

cow[2] (kou) *v.t.* to frighten with threats; make afraid; intimidate: *The bully cowed the smaller boys.* [Old Norse *kūga* to oppress.]

cow·ard (kou′ərd) *n.* a person who lacks courage; person who is very easily frightened, or who runs away from any form of danger or trouble.

cow·ard·ice (kou′ər dis) *n.* lack of courage; shameful fear of danger, difficulty, or pain.

cow·ard·ly (kou′ərd lē) *adj.* **1.** lacking courage; easily made afraid: *a cowardly person.* **2.** suitable for a coward; showing a lack of courage: *a cowardly act.* —**cow′ard·li·ness,** *n.*

cow·bell (kou′bel′) *n.* a small bell hung around a cow's neck to indicate where she is.

cow·bird (kou′burd′) *n.* a small blackbird of North and South America that is often found living near cattle. Cowbirds frequently lay their eggs in the nests of other birds.

cow·boy (kou′boi′) *n.* a man who herds and tends cattle on a ranch, usually riding on horseback to perform his work.

cow·catch·er (kou′kach′ər) *n.* a metal frame on the front of a locomotive or streetcar for clearing the tracks of obstructions.

cow·er (kou′ər) *v.i.* to crouch or cringe, as in fear or shame: *The dog cowered as the boy raised the stick to strike it.*

cow·girl (kou′gurl′) *n.* a woman whose work is like a cowboy's.

cow·hand (kou′hand′) *n.* another word for **cowboy.**

cow·herd (kou′hurd′) *n.* a person who herds or tends cattle.

cow·hide (kou′hīd′) *n.* **1.** the hide of a cow. **2.** leather made from it. **3.** a strong, flexible whip made of braided leather or rawhide.

cowl (koul) *n.* **1.** a hood attached to a monk's robe. **2.** a monk's robe with a hood. **3.** the top front part of an automobile body to which the windshield and dashboard are attached. **4.** see **cowling.**

cow·lick (kou′lik′) *n.* a tuft of hair that grows in a different direction from the rest of the hair and will not lie flat.

cowl·ing (kou′ling) *n.* a streamlined, metal covering for a section of an airplane, especially one designed to cover an engine.

co·work·er (kō′wur′kər) *n.* a person with whom one works; fellow worker.

cow·pea (kou′pē′) *n.* **1.** a bushy or trailing vine related to the bean, widely planted as a forage or cover crop. It bears long pods containing kidney-shaped seeds that are eaten as a vegetable. **2.** the seed of this plant. Also *(def. 2),* **black-eyed pea.**

cow·poke (kou′pōk′) *n. Informal.* a cowboy.

cow·pox (kou′poks′) *n.* a mild but very contagious disease of cows caused by the same kind of virus that causes smallpox in man. Smallpox vaccine is prepared from the cowpox virus.

cow·punch·er (kou′pun′chər) *n. Informal.* a cowboy.

cow·rie (kour′ē) *also,* **cow·ry.** *n. pl.,* **cow·ries. 1.** a small,

glossy, brightly colored shell of any of various sea snails commonly found in warm shallow waters of the Pacific and Indian Oceans. **2.** one of these snails.

cow·slip (kou′slip′) *n.* **1.** a wild plant related to the primrose, having fragrant yellow flowers. **2.** the flower of this plant. **3.** another word for **marsh marigold.**

cox·comb (koks′kōm′) *n.* **1.** a vain and pretentious person; conceited dandy. **2.** see **cockscomb** *(def. 2).*

cox·swain (kok′sən, kok′swān′) *also,* **cock·swain.** *n.* a person who steers a boat, especially the one who steers and gives directions to oarsmen in a racing shell.

coy (koi) *adj.* **1.** shy or modest; bashful. **2.** pretending to be shy or modest. —**coy′ly,** *adv.* —**coy′ness,** *n.*

coy·o·te (kī ō′tē, kī′ōt) *n. pl.,* **coy·o·tes** or **coy·o·te.** an animal of the prairies of central and western North America, resembling a wolf and known for its howling at night. Also, **prairie wolf.**

coy·pu (koi′pōō) *n. pl.,* **coy·pus** or **coy·pu.** a large South American rodent that lives near water, closely resembling the beaver. It is valued for its thick, light brown to black fur. Also, **nutria.**

Coyote

coz·en (kuz′ən) *v.t.* to cheat; deceive. —**coz′en·er,** *n.*

coz·en·age (kuz′ə nij) *n.* the act or practice of cozening: fraud.

co·zy (kō′zē) *also,* **co·sy.** *adj.,* **co·zi·er, co·zi·est.** warm and comfortable; snug: *The kitten found a cozy spot by the fire.* —*n. pl.,* **co·zies.** a padded cloth or knitted cover for keeping the contents of a teapot warm. —**co′zi·ly,** *adv.* —**co′zi·ness,** *n.*

cp., compare.

c.p., candle power.

C.P., Communist Party.

C.P.A., Certified Public Accountant.

cpd., compound.

Cpl., Corporal.

Cr, the symbol for chromium.

crab[1] (krab) *n.* **1.** any of a group of animals having a hard shell and no backbone and living in water, especially salt water. Crabs have a broad, flat body, four pairs of jointed legs, and a pair of pincer claws. Many kinds of crabs are highly valued as food. **2.** any of various similar animals, such as the horseshoe crab. **3.** a machine or apparatus for hoisting or hauling heavy weights. **4.** *Informal.* a cross, ill-tempered person. —*v.i.,* **crabbed, crab·bing. 1.** to fish for or catch crabs. **2.** *Informal.* to find fault; complain. [Old English *crabba.*] —**crab′ber,** *n.* —**crab′like′,** *adj.*

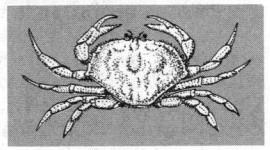
Crab

crab[2] (krab) *n.* see **crab apple.** [Of uncertain origin.]

crab apple 1. any of various small, hard, sour apples, used for making jelly. **2.** the tree bearing this apple.

crab·bed (krab′id) *adj.* **1.** cross or ill-tempered; crabby. **2.** (of handwriting) hard to read or make out; cramped. —**crab′bed·ly,** *adv.* —**crab′bed·ness,** *n.*

crab·by (krab′ē) *adj.,* **crab·bi·er, crab·bi·est.** ill-tempered; cross. —**crab′bi·ly,** *adv.* —**crab′bi·ness,** *n.*

crab grass, a coarse, hardy grass that spreads rapidly and is a common weed pest in lawns and gardens.

crack (krak) *n.* **1.** a break in something that does not cause its parts to separate completely: *a crack in a dish,* *a crack in the ice on a pond.* **2.** a sound like that made by something breaking; sudden, sharp noise: *the crack of a whip, the crack of a bat hitting a baseball.* **3.** *Informal.* a sharp, heavy blow: *He gave him a crack on the head.* **4.** a narrow opening: *There are cracks between the floor boards. Leave the window open just a crack.* **5.** *Informal.* an instant; moment: *He gets up at the crack of dawn.* **6.** *Informal.* a try; attempt: *Let me have a crack at opening that jar.* **7.** *Slang.* a witty or clever remark; joke; wisecrack: *He's always making cracks about her cooking.* —*v.i.* **1.** to break without completely separating into parts; become split: *The cup cracked when I dropped it on the floor.* **2.** to make a sudden, sharp noise, as in breaking: *The dry twig cracked under his foot.* **3.** to be harsh, shrill, or uneven; change suddenly in tone: *His voice cracked.* **4.** *Informal.* to break down; fail: *The soldier cracked under the pressure of being in combat.* —*v.t.* **1.** to cause to break without completely separating into parts: *The boiling water cracked the glass.* **2.** to cause to make a sudden, sharp sound: *He cracked the whip.* **3.** *Informal.* to hit or strike with a sharp blow: *I cracked my head against the low ceiling.* **4.** *Informal.* to break into; force open: *A thief cracked the safe.* **5.** to find the solution to; learn the meaning of: *During World War II the United States cracked the secret code used by the Japanese.* **6.** to subject (petroleum) to the process of cracking. —*adj. Informal.* excellent; first-rate: *The varsity team is made up of crack players.*

　cracked up to be. *Informal.* claimed or believed to be: *This new soap is not all it's cracked up to be.*

　to crack a joke. to make a witty or clever remark; tell a joke.

　to crack down. *Informal.* to take strict measures; become strict: *The candidate promised to crack down on spending if she won the election.*

　to crack up. *Informal.* **a.** to crash: *He cracked up the car.* **b.** to suffer a mental breakdown.

crack·down (krak′doun′) *n.* a sudden, strict enforcement of laws or rules: *a crackdown on illegal gambling.*

cracked (krakt) *adj.* **1.** having a crack or cracks; broken without a complete separation of parts: *a cracked dish.* **2.** broken into small pieces; crushed: *He put cracked ice in the drinks.* **3.** (of the voice) harsh, shrill, or uneven; changing in tone. **4.** *Informal.* crazy; insane.

crack·er (krak′ər) *n.* a thin, crisp biscuit.

crack·er·jack (krak′ər jak′) *Slang. n.* a person or thing of exceptional ability or quality. —*adj.* of exceptional ability or quality: *She is a crackerjack tennis player.*

crack·ing (krak′ing) *n.* the process of breaking down complex molecules of petroleum into simpler molecules by means of heat and pressure. Greater amounts of gasoline are obtained by cracking.

crack·le (krak′əl) *v.i.*, **crack·led, crack·ling.** to make a series of slight, sharp sounds: *The dry leaves crackled when we walked on them.* —*n.* **1.** one of a series of slight, sharp sounds: *the crackle of burning twigs.* **2.** a pattern of very small, irregular cracks in the surface of certain kinds of china or glassware.

crack·ling (krak′ling) *n.* **1.** a series of slight, sharp sounds. **2.** the crisp, browned skin of roasted pork. **3. cracklings.** the crisp part remaining after lard has been removed from hog's fat by frying.

crack·ly (krak′lē) *adj.* making a crackling sound: *crackly wrapping paper.*

crack·pot (krak′pot′) *Slang. n.* a very eccentric or crazy person. —*adj.* eccentric; crazy; foolish: *a crackpot scheme for making money.*

crack-up (krak′up′) *n.* **1.** a crash or collision, as of a car or airplane. **2.** *Informal.* a mental or physical breakdown.

Crac·ow (krak′ou) a former name for **Kraków.**

cra·dle (krād′əl) *n.* **1.** a small bed for a baby, usually on rockers. **2.** a place or region where something starts or begins to develop: *the cradle of civilization. Greece was the cradle of democracy.* **3.** a framework supporting something large, as a ship, while it is being constructed or repaired. **4.** the part of a telephone that is electrically connected to the wall outlet and holds the receiver. **5.** a box on rockers used to wash gold from earth. **6.** a frame with several long curved prongs, attached to a scythe for laying cut grain evenly. —*v.t.*, **cra·dled, cra·dling.** **1.** to put, rock, or hold in or as if in a cradle: *She cradled the child in her arms.* **2.** to support in or on a cradle, as a ship. **3.** to wash (earth containing gold) in a cradle. **4.** to cut (grain) using a cradle.

craft (kraft) *n.* **1.** special skill or ability: *The cabinetmaker worked with precision and craft.* **2.** skill in deceiving; deceit; guile; cunning. **3.** a trade or occupation requiring special skill or ability: *the craft of carpentry.* **4.** all the members of a trade collectively. **5.** a boat, ship, or aircraft: *a pirate craft.* **6.** boats, ships, or aircraft: *All small craft were warned to stay in the harbor until the storm passed.*

crafts·man (krafts′mən) *n. pl.*, **crafts·men** (krafts′mən). a person who has skill in a craft; a skilled worker; artisan. —**crafts′wom·an,** *n.*

crafts·man·ship (krafts′mən ship′) *n.* the skill or work of a craftsman or craftswoman.

craft union, a labor union that limits membership to workers in a single craft or occupation.

craft·y (kraf′tē) *adj.*, **craft·i·er, craft·i·est.** skillful in deceiving; sly; wily; cunning: *a crafty swindler, a crafty scheme to cheat people of their money.* —**craft′i·ly,** *adv.* —**craft′i·ness,** *n.*

crag (krag) *n.* a steep, rugged rock or cliff.

crag·gy (krag′ē) *adj.*, **crag·gi·er, crag·gi·est.** **1.** having many crags; steep and rugged: *Northern Scotland is a craggy area.* **2.** rough and uneven: *a face with craggy features.* —**crag′gi·ness,** *n.*

cram (kram) *v.*, **crammed, cram·ming.** —*v.t.* **1.** to fill (something) completely or with more than it normally or easily holds: *She crammed her closet with clothes.* **2.** to force or crowd (something) into a tight or crowded space: *We crammed more than a hundred books into the small bookcase.* —*v.i. Informal.* to study hastily and intensely for an examination or the like: *She is cramming for tomorrow's history test.*

cramp¹ (kramp) *n.* **1.** a sharp, painful tightening that occurs suddenly in a muscle or group of muscles: *The runner suffered a cramp in his leg and was forced to drop out of the race.* **2.** a temporary paralysis of certain muscles as a result of being used too much: *She got a cramp in her hand from writing too long.* **3. cramps.** sharp pains in the abdomen. —*v.t.* to cause to have a cramp or cramps. —*v.i.* to suffer a cramp. [Old French *crampe.*]

cramp² (kramp) *n.* **1.** a metal bar bent at the ends, used for holding together pieces of stone, timber, or the like. **2.** anything that confines or hinders. —*v.t.* **1.** to fasten or hold with a cramp. **2.** to confine or limit; restrict; hamper: *His vacation plans ʰwere cramped by a lack of money.* [Middle Dutch *crampe* hook.]

at; āpe; cär; end; mē; it; īce; hot; ōld; fôrk; wood; fŏŏl; oil; out; up; turn; sing; thin; **th**is; **hw** in white; **zh** in treasure. The symbol ə stands for the sound of **a** in about, **e** in taken, **i** in pencil, **o** in lemon, and **u** in circus.

cram·pon (kram′pən) *n.* **1.** an iron bar bent in the form of a hook, used in hinged pairs to lift heavy objects. **2. crampons.** spiked, iron plates attached to the soles of shoes or boots to help in climbing or walking on ice.

cran·ber·ry (kran′ber′ē) *n. pl.,* **cran·ber·ries. 1.** the sour, red berry of a low, creeping shrub, used for sauce, juice, and jelly. **2.** the shrub bearing this fruit, growing in bogs and swamps.

crane (krān) *n.* **1.** a large wading bird that lives in swamps and marshes, having very long, thin legs and a long neck and bill. **2.** a large machine for lifting and moving very heavy weights by means of cables attached to a long, movable arm. **3.** any of various devices in which a big movable arm is used to support something. —*v.,* **craned, cran·ing.** —*v.t.* to stretch out (the neck) in order to see better. —*v.i.* to stretch out the neck: *The people in the back row had to crane to see the stage.*

Crane, Stephen (krān) 1871–1900, U.S. novelist and short story writer.

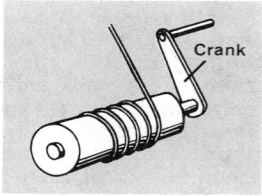
Crane

cra·ni·al (krā′nē əl) *adj.* of or relating to the skull: *The blow injured a cranial nerve.*

cra·ni·um (krā′nē əm) *n. pl.,* **cra·ni·ums** or **cra·ni·a** (krā′nē ə). **1.** the skull. **2.** the part of the skull that encloses the brain.

crank (krangk) *n.* **1.** a device that transmits motion from one part of a machine to another by turning. A crank has an arm or handle attached at right angles to the end of a shaft. **2.** *Informal.* a person with queer ideas; strange or eccentric person: *Police said that the odd telephone calls were the work of a crank.* **3.** *Informal.* a grouchy, ill-tempered person.

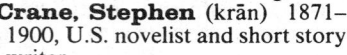
Crank

—*v.t.* to start or operate with a crank: *It was necessary to crank the engine of some old automobiles by hand.*

crank·case (krangk′kās′) *n.* a metal case enclosing the crankshaft of an engine, as in an automobile.

crank·shaft (krangk′shaft′) *n.* a shaft driven by or driving a crank. The crankshaft of an automobile engine serves to change the up-and-down motion of the pistons into the rotary motion of the shaft that drives the wheels.

crank·y (krang′kē) *adj.,* **crank·i·er, crank·i·est.** cross or ill-tempered; irritable; grouchy. —**crank′i·ly,** *adv.* —**crank′i·ness,** *n.*

cran·ny (kran′ē) *n. pl.,* **cran·nies.** a small, narrow opening; crack; crevice; chink.

crape (krāp) another spelling of **crepe.**

crap·pie (krap′ē) *n.* a North American freshwater fish related to the sunfish, used for food.

craps (kraps) *n.* a gambling game played with two dice.

crash¹ (krash) *n. pl.,* **crash·es. 1.** a sudden, loud noise, as of something shattering or breaking: *There was a crash when the ball went through the window.* **2.** a heavy fall or breaking with force: *the crash of a falling tree.* **3.** a violent, destructive collision or fall, as of a car or airplane: *There have been several crashes at that intersection.* **4.** a sudden ruin or collapse, as of a business: *He lost all his money in the stock market crash.* —*v.i.* **1.** to make a sudden, loud noise: *The thunder crashed overhead.* **2.** to fall or break with force and a loud noise: *The cups crashed to the floor.* **3.** to collide violently or destructively: *The car crashed into*

a tree. **4.** to land or fall so as to be damaged or destroyed: *The plane crashed during the storm.* **5.** to suffer sudden collapse or ruin: *His business crashed last year.* —*v.t.* **1.** to cause to break noisily and violently; smash; shatter: *He crashed the glass against the table.* **2.** to cause (an aircraft, automobile, or the like) to be in a crash: *The pilot crashed his plane into the enemy ship.* **3.** *Informal.* to enter (a dance, theater, stadium, or the like) without being invited or without having a ticket: *Some boys from out of town tried to crash the party.* —*adj.* carried out with all possible speed, effort, and resources: *The state started a crash program to build new housing.* [From a Middle English word imitating this sound.]

crash² (krash) *n.* a cotton or linen cloth made from uneven and irregular yarns, used for towels, tablecloths, curtains, and the like. [Short for Russian *krashenina* colored linen.]

crash-dive (krash′dīv′) *v.,* **crash-dived, crash-div·ing.** —*v.i.* to make a crash dive. —*v.t.* to cause to make a crash dive: *to crash-dive a submarine.*

crash dive, a sudden rapid dive made by a submarine, especially to avoid attack by an enemy aircraft or ship.

crash helmet, a padded helmet for protection against head injury, worn especially by motorcyclists, automobile racers, and pilots.

crash-land (krash′land′) *v.i., v.t.* to make or cause to make a crash landing: *The pilot had to crash-land his plane in a field because the landing gear failed to work.*

crash landing, the landing of an aircraft under emergency conditions that make a normal landing impossible, especially in a way that causes some damage to the aircraft.

crass (kras) *adj.* stupid, vulgar, or coarse: *crass behavior, a crass disregard for the feelings of others.* —**crass′ly,** *adv.* —**crass′ness,** *n.*

crate (krāt) *n.* a box, case or framework, usually of wooden slats, used for protecting things during shipping or storage: *an orange crate, a furniture crate.* —*v.t.,* **crat·ed, crat·ing.** to pack in a crate or crates: *The farmer crated the lettuce to be sent to the market.*

cra·ter (krā′tər) *n.* **1.** a bowl-shaped hollow area at the mouth of a volcano. **2.** any hole in the ground resembling this, such as one caused by the explosion of a bomb or by the impact of a meteorite. **3.** any of numerous circular depressions in the surface of the moon, usually surrounded by a high ridge and believed to be caused either by the impact of meteorites or by volcanic action.

Crater Lake, a lake in a crater on the site of a prehistoric volcano, in southwestern Oregon. It is the deepest lake in North America.

cra·vat (krə vat′) *n.* a necktie or a scarf worn as a necktie.

crave (krāv) *v.t.,* **craved, crav·ing. 1.** to long or yearn for; desire eagerly: *The artist craved recognition of his talents.* **2.** to need greatly; require: *The wound craved a doctor's attention.* **3.** to ask for earnestly; beg: *The knight craved a favor of his lord.*

cra·ven (krā′vən) *adj.* very cowardly. —*n.* a complete coward. —**cra′ven·ly,** *adv.* —**cra′ven·ness,** *n.*

crav·ing (krā′ving) *n.* an eager desire; longing; yearning: *The exhausted travelers had a craving for sleep.*

craw (krô) *n.* **1.** the crop of a bird or insect. **2.** the stomach of any animal.

craw·fish (krô′fish′) *n. pl.,* **craw·fish** or **craw·fish·es.** another word for **crayfish.**

crawl (krôl) *v.i.* **1.** to move slowly by dragging the body along the ground, as an earthworm does. **2.** to move slowly on hands and knees: *The baby crawled across the room.* **3.** to move slowly: *Traffic crawled through the city.* **4.** to swarm or be alive with crawling things: *The picnic* *table was crawling with ants.* **5.** to feel as if covered with crawling things: *The ghost story made my skin crawl.* —*n.* **1.** the act of crawling; slow crawling motion: *Traffic was slowed to a crawl during the snowstorm.* **2.** a rapid swimming stroke performed with the face down, in which the arms are lifted over the head one after the other and the feet kick continuously.

cray·fish (krā′fish′) *n. pl.,* **cray·fish** or **cray·fish·es.** any of various small shell-fish that closely resemble the lobster, found in fresh water in most parts of the world and frequently used as food. Also, **crawfish.**

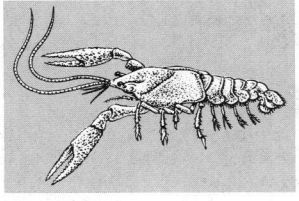

Crayfish

cray·on (krā′on, krā′ən) *n.* **1.** a colored stick or pencil of wax material, chalk, charcoal, or another substance, used for drawing and writing. **2.** a drawing made with a crayon or crayons. —*v.t.* to draw, color, or mark with a crayon or crayons: *She scolded the children because they crayoned the wall.*

craze (krāz) *n.* something that is very popular for a short time; fad: *Long skirts were a craze one year.* —*v.t.,* **crazed, craz·ing. 1.** to make insane: *The sudden tragedy almost crazed him.* **2.** to make very small cracks in the surface of (a piece of china or glassware): *to craze a vase.*

cra·zy (krā′zē) *adj.,* **cra·zi·er, cra·zi·est. 1.** not having a sound or normal mind; mentally ill; insane; mad: *The prisoner nearly became crazy from his years of confinement.* **2.** caused by or showing mental illness. **3.** *Informal.* not practical or sensible; foolish; silly: *That was a crazy idea.* **4.** very fond or enthusiastic: *That boy is crazy about cars.* —**cra·zi·ly,** *adv.* —**cra·zi·ness,** *n.*

crazy bone, another term for **funny bone.**

Crazy Horse, 1849?–1877, a Sioux chief who led the Indian forces at the battle of Little Bighorn.

crazy quilt a quilt made of pieces of cloth of different materials, shapes, colors, and patterns, that are sewed together without any regular pattern.

creak (krēk) *v.i.* to make a sharp, grating or squeaking sound: *The old rocking chair creaks.* —*n.* a sharp, grating or squeaking sound: *The rusty old gate swung open with a creak.*

creak·y (krē′kē) *adj.,* **creak·i·er, creak·i·est.** likely to creak; creaking: *an old staircase with creaky steps.* —**creak′i·ly,** *adv.* —**creak′i·ness,** *n.*

cream (krēm) *n.* **1.** the fatty, yellowish part of milk, that contains butterfat and rises to the top of milk that is not homogenized. **2.** a food made from or resembling this substance: *chocolate creams, cream of tomato soup.* **3.** a soft preparation used to cleanse or protect the skin: *hand cream, shaving cream.* **4.** the best or choicest part of anything: *the cream of the crop, the cream of society.* **5.** the color of cream; yellowish white. —*v.t.* **1.** to remove the cream from; skim: *to cream milk.* **2.** to cook with cream, milk, or a cream sauce: *to cream onions.* **3.** to blend into a soft, creamy mass: *to cream butter and sugar.* —*v.i.* to form cream or a creamy substance on the top. —*adj.* having the color of cream; yellowish-white: *The bride wore a dress of cream velvet.*

cream cheese, a soft, smooth, white cheese made from a mixture of milk and cream.

cream·er (krē′mər) *n.* a small pitcher used for serving cream.

cream·er·y (krē′mər ē) *n. pl.,* **cream·er·ies. 1.** a place where butter, cheese, and other dairy products are made. **2.** a place where milk, cream, and dairy products are sold.

cream of tar·tar (tär′tər) a white, powdery compound

containing potassium, hydrogen, carbon, and oxygen, used especially in baking powder, and also in medicine.

cream·puff (krēm′puf′) *n.* a very light pastry shell filled with custard or whipped cream.

cream sauce, a sauce made of cream or milk cooked with flour and butter.

cream·y (krē′mē) *adj.,* **cream·i·er, cream·i·est. 1.** containing cream; having much cream: *a rich, creamy dessert.* **2.** resembling cream, as in appearance or color: *She has smooth, creamy skin.* —**cream′i·ness,** *n.*

crease (krēs) *n.* **1.** a line or mark made by folding, wrinkling, or pressing cloth, paper, or the like; fold; ridge: *the crease in a pair of trousers.* **2.** any similar line or mark. —*v.,* **creased, creas·ing.** —*v.t.* **1.** to make a crease or creases on or in: *Years of exposure to the sun and wind had creased the old sailor's face.* **2.** to graze with a bullet. —*v.i.* to become creased: *Her clothes creased in the tightly-packed trunk.*

cre·ate (krē āt′) *v.t.,* **cre·at·ed, cre·at·ing. 1.** to bring into being; cause to exist: *In the beginning God created the heaven and the earth* (Genesis 1:1). **2.** to give rise to; bring about; cause: *His rude attitude created much ill will.* **3.** to produce by one's own thought or imagination: *Shakespeare created many famous characters.*

cre·a·tion (krē ā′shən) *n.* **1.** the act of creating: *The creation of the motion picture took many months.* **2.** anything that has been created, especially something that is produced by human intelligence or imagination: *Van Gogh's paintings are brilliant creations.* **3.** everything that has been created; the world and all things in it; universe. **4. the Creation.** God's act of creating the universe.

cre·a·tive (krē ā′tiv) *adj.* **1.** having the power to create: *A poet must have a creative imagination.* **2.** showing originality: *creative writing.* —**cre·a′tive·ly,** *adv.* —**cre·a′tive-ness,** *n.*

cre·a·tiv·i·ty (krē′ā tiv′ə tē) *n.* the quality of being creative; ability to create: *The artist possessed great creativity.*

cre·a·tor (krē ā′tər) *n.* **1.** a person or thing that creates: *Sir Arthur Conan Doyle was the creator of Sherlock Holmes.* **2. the Creator.** God.

crea·ture (krē′chər) *n.* **1.** any living being, especially an animal as distinct from man: *a sea creature, the creatures of the forest.* **2.** a human being: *She is a lazy creature.* **3.** a person who is completely dependent upon or under the influence of someone or something; tool: *Man is a creature of habit.*

crèche (kresh, krāsh) *n.* a model of the Nativity scene, often displayed at Christmas.

cre·dence (krēd′əns) *n.* belief: *He doesn't give credence to rumors.*

cre·den·tials (kri den′shəlz) *n., pl.* letters or documents that prove a person's identity or authority: *The ambassador presented his credentials to the king.*

cred·i·ble (kred′ə bəl) *adj.* that can be believed; believable; reliable: *Only one witness gave a credible account of the accident.* —**cred′i·bil′i·ty,** *n.* —**cred′i·bly,** *adv.*

cred·it (kred′it) *n.* **1.** belief in the truth of something; faith; trust: *His friends gave credit to his story.* **2.** a good reputation: *He is a man of great credit in our town.* **3.** praise for some action or quality: *She deserves great*

at; āpe; cär; end; mē; it; īce; hot; ōld; fôrk; wood; fo͞ol; oil; out; up; turn; sing; thin; this; hw in white; zh in treasure. The symbol ə stands for the sound of **a** in about, **e** in taken, **i** in pencil, **o** in lemon, and **u** in circus.

credit for working so hard to improve her marks. **4.** a person or thing that brings honor, approval, or praise: *That boy is a credit to his school.* **5. credits.** acknowledgments for work done or help given, as in a motion picture: *His name appeared in the credits as the producer of the film.* **6.** trust or confidence in a person's ability and intention to pay debts: *Several stores have extended credit to her.* **7.** a reputation in financial matters: *His credit was no longer good at the store, because he did not pay his bills.* **8.** Bookkeeping. **a.** an entry of an amount in an account as payment of an existing or future debt: *Carry that payment as a credit against next month's billing.* **b.** the right-hand side of an account where such entries are made. **9.** a balance in one's favor, as in a bank account. **10.** the time allowed for payment of a debt: *to have six months' credit.* **11.** an official entry on a student's record showing that he has satisfactorily completed a course of study: *He received credit for the history course.* **12.** a unit of such study: *He took three credits of math.* —*v.t.* **1.** to believe; trust: *Do you expect me to credit that silly story?* **2.** to give financial credit to: *He credited the checks to his account.* **3.** to attribute to: *History credits the Wright brothers with the first successful flight in a airplane.*
   on credit. with the understanding that one will pay at a future time.

cred·it·a·ble (kred′i tə bəl) *adj.* bringing honor or credit; praiseworthy: *He made a creditable effort to win the game for his team.* —**cred′it·a·ble·ness,** *n.* —**cred′it·a·bly,** *adv.*

credit card, a card entitling its holder to buy things or obtain services on credit.

cred·i·tor (kred′i tər) *n.* a person to whom a debt is owed.

cre·do (krē′dō, krā′dō) *n. pl.,* **cre·dos.** a statement of belief; creed.

cre·du·li·ty (kri dōō′li tē, kri dyōō′li tē) *n.* a readiness to believe, trust, or accept without proof; gullibility.

cred·u·lous (krej′ə ləs) *adj.* ready to believe, trust, or accept without proof; gullible. —**cred′u·lous·ly,** *adv.* —**cred′u·lous·ness,** *n.*

Cree (krē) *n. pl.,* **Crees** or **Cree. 1.** a member of a tribe of North American Indians, formerly living in eastern and central Canada, now living mainly in Manitoba. **2.** the language of this tribe.

creed (krēd) *n.* **1.** a formal statement or religious belief. **2.** any formal statement of belief, principles, or opinions: *a political creed.*

creek (krēk, krik) *n.* a small stream, usually larger than a brook and smaller than a river.

Creek (krēk) *n. pl.,* **Creeks** or **Creek. 1.** a member of a confederacy of North American Indian tribes, formerly living in Alabama, Georgia, and northern Florida, now living in Oklahoma. **2.** the language of these tribes.

creel (krēl) *n.* **1.** a fisherman's basket for holding fish. **2.** a wicker trap for catching fish, crabs, or lobsters.

creep (krēp) *v.i.,* **crept, creep·ing. 1.** to move with the body close to the ground, especially on hands and knees; crawl: *The baby crept across the room.* **2.** to move slowly, timidly, or stealthily: *Traffic crept along the highway. The burglar crept toward the open window.* **3.** to move or behave in a humble manner: *The embarassed boy crept from the room.* **4.** to feel as if things were crawling over the skin: *The howling of the wolves made my flesh creep.* **5.** (of a plant) to grow along a surface by sending out small tendrils or roots along the length of the stem: *Vines crept up the wall.* —*n.* **1.** the act of creeping; slow movement. **2. the creeps.** *Informal.* a feeling as if things were crawling over the skin, caused by fear or horror: *That horror movie gave me the creeps.*

creep·er (krē′pər) *n.* **1.** a person or thing that creeps. **2.** any plant that grows along a surface by sending out small tendrils or roots along the length of the steam, such as ivy. **3.** a small bird that creeps up and down tree trunks to find insects to feed on.

creep·y (krē′pē) *adj.,* **creep·i·er, creep·i·est. 1.** having or causing a feeling of things crawling over the skin, caused by fear or horror. **2.** moving slowly; creeping. —**creep′i·ly,** *adv.* —**creep′i·ness.** *n.*

cre·mate (krē′māt, kri māt′) *v.t.,* **cre·mat·ed, cre·mat·ing. 1.** to burn (a dead body) to ashes. **2.** to consume by fire; burn up. —**cre·ma′tion,** *n.*

cre·ma·to·ry (krē′mə tôr′ē, krem′ə tôr′ē) *n. pl.,* **cre·ma·to·ries.** a furnace or place for cremating.

Cre·ole (krē′ōl) *n.* **1.** a direct descendant of the first French and Spanish settlers of the Gulf Coast, especially Louisiana. **2.** a Spanish or French person born in the West Indies or Latin America. **3.** the dialect of French spoken by Creoles in Louisiana. **4.** a person who has both Negro and Creole ancestors. —*adj.* **1.** of or relating to Creoles. **2. creole.** (of food) prepared with sweet peppers, tomatoes, and onions and highly seasoned.

cre·o·sol (krē′ə sôl′) *n.* a colorless, oily, aromatic liquid used as an antiseptic.

cre·o·sote (krē′ə sōt′) *n.* **1.** a colorless or yellowish oily liquid obtained by distilling wood tar and used in medicines and antiseptics. **2.** a similar liquid obtained from coal tar and used as a wood perservative. —*v.t.,* **cre·o·sot·ed, cre·o·sot·ing.** to treat with creosote.

crepe (krāp) *n. also,* **crêpe, crape. 1.** any of various fabrics made of silk, cotton, rayon, and wool, and having a crinkled surface. **2.** a band of black crepe worn or hung as a sign of mourning.

crepe paper, a thin paper with a crinkled surface like crepe.

crepe rubber, rubber with a crinkled surface, used especially for the soles of shoes.

crept (krept) the past tense and past participle of **creep.**

cre·scen·do (kri shen′dō) *adj., adv.* with a gradual increase in loudness or force. —*n. pl.,* **cres·cen·dos. 1.** a gradual increase in loudness or force. **2.** *Music.* a crescendo passage.

cres·cent (kres′ənt) *n.* **1.** the shape of the visible part of the moon in its first or last quarter. **2.** anything crescent-shaped: *The row of houses was built in a crescent.* —*adj.* **1.** increasing; growing. **2.** shaped like the moon in its first or last quarter.

cress (kres) *n. pl.,* **cress·es. 1.** the pungent leaves of any of several plants, especially watercress, used as a garnish or in salads. **2.** any of these plants.

cres·set (kres′it) *n.* a metal container mounted on a pole or suspended from above, containing burning pitch-covered rope, oil, grease, wood, or other fuel to give light.

crest (krest) *n.* **1.** a comb, tuft, ridge, or other natural growth on the head, neck, or back of a bird or other animal. **2.** a plume or similar ornament on the top of a helmet. **3.** a decoration above a coat of arms. **4.** the highest point or stage of anything: *the crest of a hill, the crest of a wave. The politician reached the crest of his popularity just before the election.* —*v.i.* to reach the highest point or stage: *The flood crested late Sunday night.*

crest·ed (kres′tid) *adj.* having a crest.

crest·fall·en (krest′fô′lən) *adj.* dejected; discouraged; disheartened: *She was crestfallen because she wasn't invited to the party.*

Cre·ta·ceous (kri tā′shəs) *n.* the last geological period of the Mesozoic era, during which sandstone, limestone, and chalk deposits were formed. —*adj.* of, relating to, or characteristic of this period.

C

Cre·tan (krēt′ən) *adj.* of or relating to Crete or its people. —*n.* a person who was born or is living in Crete.

Crete (krēt) *n.* a Greek island in the eastern Mediterranean, southeast of Greece.

cre·tin (krēt′ən) *n.* a person having cretinism.

cre·tin·ism (krēt′ən iz′əm) *n.* a condition present at birth or developing in infancy, characterized by stunted physical and mental development. It is caused by a severe lack of thyroid secretion.

cre·tonne (krē′ton, kri ton′) *n.* a strong, medium-weight cotton fabric in bold print patterns, used for curtains, draperies, and slipcovers.

cre·vasse (kri vas′) *n.* a deep crack or crevice, especially in a glacier.

crev·ice (krev′is) *n.* a narrow crack into or through something: *The wind blew in through the crevices in the walls of the log cabin.*

crew[1] (krōō) *n.* **1.** all the persons who man a ship or aircraft. **2.** all of these persons except the officers. **3.** a group of people assigned to or working together on a job: *a road crew, a wrecking crew.* **4.** any group of people; crowd; company. **5.** the members of a rowing team. [Old French *creue* increase.]

crew[2] (krōō) a past tense of **crow**[1].

crew cut, a style of man's haircut in which the hair is closely cropped.

crew·el (krōō′əl) *n.* a loosely twisted, worsted yarn, used for embroidery.

crew·el·work (krōō′əl wurk′) *n.* embroidery done with wool yarn on linen or other fabric.

crib (krib) *n.* **1.** a baby's small bed with high sides, usually barred. **2.** a manger or rack used to hold food for cattle. **3.** a small building or bin used to store corn, grain, salt, or the like. **4.** a framework of wood or metal used to strengthen or support, as in a mine shaft. **5.** *Informal.* notes or other aids used dishonestly by students, especially during examinations. —*v.,* **cribbed, crib·bing.** —*v.t.* **1.** to close in a crib; confine. **2.** *Informal.* to use dishonestly (another's words or ideas). —*v.i. Informal.* to use notes or other aids dishonestly: *He cribbed on the history examination.*

crib·bage (krib′ij) *n.* a card game, usually for two, three, or four players. The score is kept on a small board into which pegs fit.

crick (krik) *n.* a painful stiffness or cramp of the muscles, especially of the neck or back.

crick·et[1] (krik′it) *n.* a hopping insect, related to the grasshopper, having strong hind legs and long slender antennae. The male of the species makes a chirping noise by rubbing the bases or edges of the forewings together. [Old French *criquet.*]

crick·et[2] (krik′it) *n.* **1.** a British game resembling baseball, played

Cricket

on a grass field with a ball, bats, and wickets by two teams of eleven players each. **2.** *Informal.* fair play; good sportsmanship. [Old French *criquet* a wicket or bat in a ball game.] —**crick′et·er,** *n.*

cried (krīd) the past tense and past participle of **cry.**

cri·er (krī′ər) *n.* **1.** a person who cries. **2.** an official who makes public announcements.

crime (krīm) *n.* **1.** an act that is forbidden by the law and for which a person can be punished. Murder, robbery, and blackmail are crimes. **2.** criminal activity: *There is much crime in the cities.*

Cri·me·a (krī mē′ə) *n.* a peninsula in the southern part of the Soviet Union, on the northern coast of the Black Sea. —**Cri·me′an,** *adj., n.*

crim·i·nal (krim′ən əl) *n.* a person guilty of or punished for a crime: *The criminal was sentenced to prison for robbery.* —*adj.* **1.** relating to crime or its punishment: *criminal law.* **2.** guilty of crime. **3.** of or like crime. —**crim′i·nal·ly,** *adv.*

crim·i·nol·o·gy (krim′ə nol′ə jē) *n.* the scientific study of crime and criminals.

crimp (krimp) *v.t.* to press into small, regular ridges, folds, or pleats: *to crimp paper.* —*n.* something that has been crimped; ridge; fold.

to put a crimp in. *Informal.* to prevent; hinder: *The rain put a crimp in their plans for a picnic.*

crimp·y (crim′pē) *adj.,* **crimp·i·er, crimp·i·est.** having small regular ridges, folds, or pleats.

crim·son (krim′zən) *n.* a deep red color. —*adj.* having the color crimson. —*v.i.* to become crimson.

cringe (krinj) *v.i.,* **cringed, cring·ing.** **1.** to shrink, flinch, or crouch, as in fear, pain, or horror: *She cringed when she saw the snake.* **2.** to behave in a humble manner; fawn. —**cring′er,** *n.*

crin·kle (kring′kəl) *v.,* **crin·kled, crin·kling.** —*v.i.* **1.** to form wrinkles or ripples; wrinkle: *Her nose crinkles when she laughs.* **2.** to make a rustling or crackling sound; crackle: *The fallen autumn leaves crinkled when we walked on them.* —*v.t.* **1.** to cause to form wrinkles or ripples; crumple: *He crinkled the paper when he sat on it.* **2.** to cause to rustle or crackle. —*n.* **1.** a wrinkle; ripple. **2.** a rustle; crackle. —**crin′kly,** *adj.*

cri·noid (krī′noid) *n.* any of a group of colorful, flower-shaped saltwater animals, having branched arms around a single mouth opening. Crinoids are usually found in deep tropical waters.

crin·o·line (krin′ə lin) *n.* **1.** a stiff petticoat worn to give fullness to a skirt or dress. **2.** a stiff fabric used as a lining for skirts, hats, or the like.

crip·ple (krip′əl) *n.* a person or animal that cannot move normally because of injury, defect, or the loss of a part of the body. —*v.t.,* **crip·pled, crip·pling.** **1.** to make a cripple of: *The injuries from the accident crippled him.* **2.** to disable; weaken: *The snowstorm crippled the airline service.* —**crip′pler,** *n.*

cri·sis (krī′sis) *n. pl.,* **cri·ses** (krī′sēz). **1.** an important and decisive turning point or event: *The young man's decision to go to college was a crisis in his career.* **2.** a condition or period of difficulty or danger: *The war caused a crisis in the nation's economic affairs.* **3.** a turning point in an acute disease, toward either recovery or death.

Crinoid

crisp (krisp) *adj.* **1.** easily crumbled or crushed; brittle: *crisp potato chips.* **2.** firm; fresh: *crisp lettuce.* **3.** keen and bracing; brisk; invigorating: *a cold, crisp autum day.* **4.** clear and short: *The general's orders were crisp and decided.* **5.** (of hair) curly, wavy, or wiry. —*v.t.* to make crisp. —**crisp′ly,** *adv.* —**crisp′ness,** *n.*

crisp·y (kris′pē) *adj.,* **crisp·i·er, crisp·i·est.** brittle; crisp. —**crisp′i·ness,** *n.*

---

at; āpe; cär; end; mē; it; īce; hot; ōld; fôrk; wood; fōōl; oil; out; up; turn; sing; thin; **th**is; hw in white; zh in treasure. The symbol ə stands for the sound of **a** in about, **e** in taken, **i** in pencil, **o** in lemon, and **u** in circus.

criss·cross (kris'krôs') *adj.* arranged in or marked with crossed lines; crossed; crossing. —*adv.* crosswise. —*n. pl.,* **criss·cross·es.** a mark or pattern made by crossing lines. —*v.t.* **1.** to mark with crossing lines. **2.** to cross repeatedly: *He crisscrossed the neighborhood looking for his dog.* —*v.i.* to form a crisscross: *The paths of the hikers crisscrossed in the snow.*

cri·te·ri·on (krī tēr'ē ən) *n. pl.,* **cri·te·ri·a** (krī tēr'ē ə) or **cri·te·ri·ons.** a rule or standard by which something or someone can be judged or measured: *Speed and strength are two criteria for judging the ability of a football player.*

crit·ic (krit'ik) *n.* **1.** a person who judges the merits or faults of books, plays, motion pictures, music, paintings, and the like, especially as a profession: *He read the newspapers to find out what the critics said about the new play.* **2.** a person who judges severely or unfavorably; faultfinder.

crit·i·cal (krit'i kəl) *adj.* **1.** inclined to find fault or judge severely or unfavorably: *He was critical of every plan that we suggested.* **2.** of or relating to critics or criticism: *a critical review of a new book.* **3.** of or relating to a crisis: *Winning the scholarship was a critical event in his life. The doctors announced that the patient's condition is now critical.* —**crit'i·cal·ly,** *adv.*

crit·i·cism (krit'ə siz'əm) *n.* **1.** the act of criticizing. **2.** disapproval; faultfinding. **3.** the art or profession of judging the merits or faults of something. **4.** a critical comment, article, or review: *The new play had favorable criticisms in the newspapers.*

crit·i·cize (krit'ə sīz') *v.,* **crit·i·cized, crit·i·ciz·ing.** —*v.i.* to judge harshly or unfavorably; find fault: *She is too quick to criticize.* —*v.t.* **1.** to find fault with: *They criticized her behavior.* **2.** to discuss, judge, or examine critically: *to criticize a poem, to criticize a motion picture.* —**crit'i·ciz'er,** *n.*

cri·tique (kri tēk') *n.* a critical comment, article, or review.

croak (krōk) *n.* a deep, hoarse sound like that made by a frog or raven. —*v.i.* **1.** to make a deep, hoarse sound. **2.** to speak in a deep, hoarse voice. —*v.t.* to say with a croak.

Cro·at (krō'at) *n.* **1.** a person who was born or is living in Croatia. **2.** the language of the Croats; Serbo-Croatian.

Cro·a·tia (krō ā'shə) *n.* a region in northwestern Yugoslavia. —**Cro·a'tian,** *adj., n.*

cro·chet (krō shā') *v.,* **cro·cheted** (krō shād'), **cro·chet·ing** (krō shā'ing). —*v.i.* to make interlocking loops or stitches using a single needle with a hook at one end. —*v.t.* to make by crocheting. —*n.* needlework done or made by crocheting.

crock (krok) *n.* an earthenware pot or jar.

crock·er·y (krok'ər ē) *n.* pots, dishes, and the like made of earthenware.

Crock·ett, David (krok'it) 1786–1836, U.S. frontiersman, known as **Davy Crockett.**

croc·o·dile (krok'ə dīl') *n.* a large, lizardlike reptile having a thick skin and a long, narrow snout. Crocodiles are found in both fresh water and salt water in swampy areas of tropical and semitropical Asia, Africa, and America, especially southern Florida. They have strong jaws with long rows of teeth. See **alligator** for illustration.

crocodile tears, pretended or insincere tears. [From an old saying that crocodiles moaned to attract victims and wept after they ate them.]

cro·cus (krō'kəs) *n. pl.,* **cro·cus·es** or **cro·ci** (krō'sī). **1.** a cup-shaped flower of any of a group of plants, grown as a garden flower of various colors. Most crocuses bloom in early spring. **2.** the plant bearing this flower, having a single flower stalk and grasslike leaves, growing directly from an underground bulblike stem.

Croe·sus (krē'səs) *n.* **1.** died 546? B.C., the king of Lydia from 560 to 546 B.C., famous for his great wealth. **2.** any very rich man.

croft (krôft) *n. British.* **1.** a small field for farming, especially one next to a house. **2.** a small rented farm.

croix de guerre (krwä də ger') a French military decoration awarded for distinguished service in war. [French *croix de guerre* literally, cross of war.]

Cro-Mag·non (krō mag'non) *n.* a member of a prehistoric group of men living in Europe and distinguished by a well-developed brain, tall, erect stature, and the use of stone and bone implements. Cro-Magnon man is one of the earliest examples of *Homo sapiens* yet found. —*adj.* of or belonging to this group. [From *Cro-Magnon,* a cave in southern France where remains of this form of man were found.]

Croix de guerre

Crom·well, Oliver (krom'wel) 1599–1658, English statesman and soldier, the ruler of England from 1653 to 1658.

crone (krōn) *n.* a withered old woman.

Cro·nus (krō'nəs) *n. Greek Mythology.* the youngest of the Titans, who overthrew his father, Uranus, to become ruler of the universe and was in turn overthrown by his son, Zeus. In Roman Mythology he was called Saturn.

cro·ny (krō'nē) *n. pl.,* **cro·nies.** a close friend; pal.

crook (krook) *n.* **1.** a bent, curved, or hooked thing or part: *the crook of the arm.* **2.** any bend, curve or turn: *The captain of the barge knew the crooks of the river by heart.* **3.** a shepherd's staff with a curve at one end. **4.** *Informal.* a person not to be trusted; thief; swindler. —*v.t.* to bend into a curved or hooked form: *She motioned to us to come into the house by crooking her finger.* —*v.i.* to be or become crooked; bend; curve.

crook·ed (krook'id) *adj.* **1.** not straight; bent; twisted: *a crooked path.* **2.** dishonest: *a crooked person, a crooked plan.* —**crook'ed·ly,** *adv.* —**crook'ed·ness,** *n.*

croon (kroon) *v.i.* **1.** to sing or hum in a soft, low tone: *The mother crooned a lullaby to her baby.* **2.** to sing in a soft and sentimental manner. —*v.t.* **1.** to sing or hum (a song or melody) in a soft, low tone. **2.** to sing (a popular song) in a soft and sentimental manner. —*n.* a soft, low singing or humming. —**croon'er,** *n.*

crop (krop) *n.* **1.** any plant product growing or gathered for use, such as wheat, corn, or cotton. **2.** the entire amount of any plant product gathered in one place or season: *The wheat crop was not large this year.* **3.** a group or collection of anything appearing or produced together: *a crop of new students, a crop of lies.* **4.** the act or result of cropping. **5.** a short haircut. **6.** a pouch in some birds' gullets in which food is prepared for digestion; craw. **7.** a short whip with a leather loop in place of a lash. —*v.t.,* **cropped, cropping. 1.** to bite off or cut the top end of: *Sheep crop grass very short. The gardener cropped the hedges.* **2.** to cut short; trim; clip: *The barber cropped the boy's hair.* **3.** to cause to bear a crop; raise crops on: *He cropped several acres with barley.*

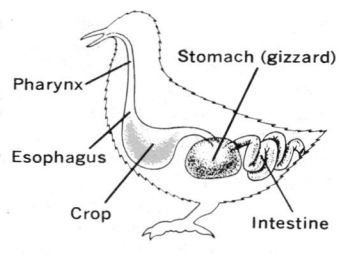

Crop *(def. 6)*

to crop up. to come up or appear unexpectedly: *Something cropped up and John had to cancel his plans.*

C

crop·dust·ing (krop′dus′ting) *n.* the spraying of pesticides on crops, as from an airplane.

crop·per (krop′ər) *n.* **1.** *Informal.* a heavy fall, as from a horse. **2.** *Informal.* a failure in an undertaking; collapse. **to come a cropper.** to fail miserably; collapse.

cro·quet (krō kā′) *n.* an outdoor game in which each player uses a mallet to drive a ball through small, bent wickets that are arranged in a particular order to form a course.

cro·quette (krō ket′) *n.* a small rounded or cone-shaped mass of chopped meat, fish, or vegetables, coated with beaten egg and bread crumbs and fried in deep oil.

cro·sier (krō′zhər) *n.* an ornamental staff carried as a symbol of office by or before bishops and archbishops during religious ceremonies.

cross (krôs) *n. pl.* **cross·es.** **1.** an upright stake with a horizontal bar across it. The ancient Romans used it as an instrument of torture and execution. **2. the Cross.** the cross on which Christ was crucified. **3.** a representation of the cross upon which Christ died, thought of as the symbol of Christianity. **4.** this representation mounted with the figure of Christ; crucifix. **5.** any object, figure, or mark formed by the crossing of two lines. **6.** any trouble, misfortune, or suffering. **7.** someone or something that combines the characteristics of two or more persons or things: *He is a cross between a businessman and a scholar.* **8.** an instance of a crossbreeding. **9.** the result of crossbreeding; hybrid: *A mule is a cross between a horse and a donkey.* —*v.t.* **1.** to move or pass from one to the other side of; go across: *The ship crossed the ocean in seven days.* **2.** to place or lay one thing or part over another: *to cross one's legs.* **3.** to pass (each other) so as to intersect: *That street crosses the railroad tracks.* **4.** to draw a line or lines through or across: *Cross all your "t's" neatly.* **5.** to cancel by drawing a line or lines across: *Cross his name off the list. She crossed out her mistake.* **6.** to extend across; span: *The bridge crosses the river.* **7.** to pass while going in different directions: *Your letter must have crossed mine in the mail.* **8.** to interfere with; oppose: *Cross him and he will be angry.* **9.** to make the sign of the cross upon or over: *The girl crossed herself as she entered the church.* **10.** to crossbreed (animals or plants). —*v.i.* **1.** to move, pass, or extend across: *The trail crosses through the woods.* **2.** to pass so as to intersect; lie or be crosswise: *The friends met where the two roads crossed.* —*adj.* **1.** bad-tempered; peevish: *a cross word, a cross look. His little brother was cross because he did not get his way.* **2.** lying or passing across or crosswise: *cross ventilation, cross streets.* —**cross′ly,** *adv.* —**cross′ness,** *n.*

cross·bar (krôs′bär′) *n.* **1.** a bar fixed across a structure: *the crossbar on a bicycle.* **2.** a line going across: *the crossbar on the letter "H."*

cross·beam (krôs′bēm′) *n.* any large beam that crosses another or crosses from wall to wall.

cross·bill (krôs′bil′) *n.* a songbird resembling the finch, having a sharply curved bill with overlapping tips.

cross·bones (krôs′bōnz′) *n.,pl.* see **skull and crossbones.**

Crosier

Latin   Papal

Maltese   Celtic

Crosses

cross·bow (krôs′bō′) *n.* a weapon widely used in the Middle Ages, consisting of a bow mounted crosswise at the front of a grooved stock along which arrows, stones, or other missiles are released.

Crossbow

cross·breed (krôs′brēd′) *v.t.,* **cross·bred** (krôs′bred′), **cross·breed·ing.** to breed (plants or animals) with those of different kinds in order to produce hybrids. —*n.* an individual or type that is produced by crossbreeding; a hybrid plant or animal.

cross·coun·try (krôs′kun′trē) *adj.* **1.** across open country or fields instead of following roads: *He won the cross-country ski race.* **2.** from one end of a country to the other: *a cross-country flight.* —*adv.* in a cross-country course: *to travel cross-country.*

cross·cut (krôs′kut′) *adj.* made or used for cutting crosswise: *a crosscut blade.* —*n.* a course or path across. —*v.t.,* **cross·cut, cross·cut·ting.** to cut across.

crosscut saw, a saw having beveled teeth shaped like knives, used for cutting wood across the grain.

cross·ex·am·ine (krôs′ig zam′in) *v.t.,* **cross·ex·am·ined, cross·ex·am·in·ing.** **1.** to question (a witness who has already testified for the opposing side) to check the reliability of his testimony or character. **2.** to question closely to check the reliability of previous answers: *The reporters cross-examined the senator about his plans to run for a second term.* —**cross′-ex·am′i·na′tion,** *n.* —**cross′-ex·am′in·er,** *n.*

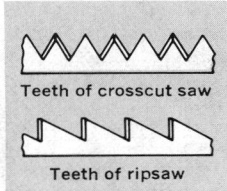

Teeth of crosscut saw

Teeth of ripsaw

Crosscut saw

cross·eyed (krôs′īd′) *adj.* having one or both eyes turned inward toward the nose.

cross·fer·ti·li·za·tion (krôs′furt′əl i zā′shən) *n.* another word for **cross-pollination.**

cross·grained (krôs′grānd′) *adj.* **1.** having the grain running crosswise or irregularly: *cross-grained wood.* **2.** stubborn; contrary.

cross·hatch (krôs′hach′) *v.t.* to mark or shade with parallel lines that cross each other.

cross·ing (krô′sing) *n.* **1.** the act of going across: *The ship made an Atlantic crossing.* **2.** a place or point of intersection, as of roads. **3.** a place where something, as a street or river, may be crossed. **4.** the act of crossbreeding.

cross·leg·ged (krôs′leg′id, krôs′legd′) *adv.* with the ankles crossed and the knees out: *The children sat cross-legged on the floor.*

cross·patch (krôs′pach′) *n. Informal.* a bad-tempered person; grouch.

cross·piece (krôs′pēs′) *n.* a piece of any material placed or lying across something else.

cross·pol·li·na·tion (krôs′pol′ə nā′shən) *n.* the fertilization of a flower or plant by pollen carried from another by wind, water, insects, or birds.

cross·pur·pose (krôs′pur′pəs) *n.* an opposing or conflicting purpose.
  at cross-purposes. opposing or hindering each other's efforts through misunderstanding.

cross·ques·tion (krôs′kwes′chən) *v.t.* to question closely or repeatedly; cross-examine.

cross-ref·er·ence (krôs′ref′ər əns) *n.* a reference from one part of a book or index to another part, pointing out where additional information can be found. The phrase "see **skull and crossbones**" under the entry **crossbones** is a cross reference.

cross·road (krôs′rōd′) *n.* **1.** a road crossing another or a road leading from one main road to another. **2.** **crossroads.** **a.** a place where roads cross. **b.** a point where an important decision must be made. ▲ used with either a singular or plural verb in definition 2.

cross section **1.** a plane section produced by cutting across an object, especially at right angles to its length. **2.** a piece cut in this manner. **3.** a sampling of people or things considered representative or typical of the whole: *A cross section of public opinion in the state showed that the senator would be reelected.*

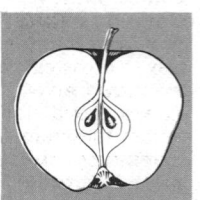

Cross section
of an apple

cross-stitch (krôs′stitch′) *n. pl.,* **cross-stitch·es.** **1.** a stitch made by crossing over another, forming an X. **2.** needlework made with this stitch. —*v.t.* to sew with a cross-stitch.

cross·trees (krôs′trēz′) *n.,pl.* two horizontal bars attached near the top of the mast on a sailing ship to spread the rigging and support the top.

cross·walk (krôs′wôk′) *n.* a lane marked off for use by pedestrians in crossing a street.

cross·way (krôs′wā′) *n.* another word for **crossroad.**

cross·wise (krôs′wīz′) *also,* **cross·ways.** *adv.* **1.** so as to cross; across: *The bridge was built crosswise over the stream.* **2.** in the form of a cross: *The logs were laid crosswise in the fireplace.*

cross·word puzzle (krôs′wurd′) a puzzle in which words or phrases are filled in on a pattern of numbered squares in answer to a list of clues having corresponding numbers. The words usually intersect each other in such a way that they read both across and down.

crotch (kroch) *n. pl.,* **crotch·es.** **1.** the place where the body divides into the two legs. **2.** the place where limbs or branches divide: *the crotch of a tree.*

crotch·et (kroch′it) *n.* **1.** an odd notion; whim. **2.** a small hook or hooked instrument.

crotch·et·y (kroch′ə tē) *adj.* full of odd notions or whims: *a crotchety old man.* —**crotch′et·i·ness,** *n.*

crouch (krouch) *v.i.* **1.** to stoop or bend low, especially with the knees bent, as an animal does when about to spring or when trying to hide: *The tiger crouched in the bushes waiting for its prey.* **2.** to cringe or cower: *The frightened puppy crouched at the feet of his master.* —*n. pl.,* **crouch·es.** **1.** the act or manner of crouching. **2.** a crouching position.

croup[1] (krōōp) *n.* an inflammation of the throat and windpipe, especially in children, characterized by a high-pitched, barking cough and difficult breathing. It is caused by infection or allergy. [Imitative of the barking sound of the cough.] —**croup′y,** *adj.*

croup[2] (krōōp) *n.* the rump of a horse or other animal. [Old French *croupe.*]

crou·ton (krōō′ton, krōō ton′) *n.* a small cube of toasted or fried bread, often served in soup or salads.

crow[1] (krō) *v.i.,* **crowed** or *(def. 1)* **crew, crowed, crow·ing.** **1.** to utter the shrill cry of a rooster. **2.** to utter a delighted, happy cry. **3.** to boast in triumph; exult: *He crowed when he won the contest.* —*n.* **1.** the cry of a rooster. **2.** a delighted, happy cry. [Old English *crāwan.*]

crow[2] (krō) *n.* **1.** a bird having glossy black feathers and a harsh, croaking cry or caw. **2.** any of various similar birds, such as the raven, magpie, or jay. [Old English *crāwe.*]
  as the crow flies. in a straight line: *That town is only twenty miles away as the crow flies, but it's a forty-mile trip over the winding mountain roads.*

Crow² *(def. 1)*

  to eat crow. *Informal.* to be forced to humble oneself: *He ate crow by admitting his mistake.*

Crow (krō) *n. pl.,* **Crows** or **Crow.** **1.** a member of a tribe of North American Indians formerly living along the Missouri River in the Great Plains. **2.** the language of the Crow, a member of the Siouan language family.

crow·bar (krō′bär′) *n.* a bar of iron or steel with a wedge-shaped end that is sometimes slightly bent and forked, used as a lever or pry.

crowd (kroud) *n.* **1.** a large number of people gathered together; throng: *We tried to make our way through the crowd at the scene of the accident.* **2.** *Informal.* a particular group of people; set; clique: *My cousin and her crowd are too young for me.* **3.** people in general; the masses. —*v.t.* **1.** to push or shove: *Please don't crowd me.* **2.** to fill too full: *He crowded the shelves with books. Swimmers crowded the beaches.* **3.** to press or force (into a close space); cram: *He crowded everything into the suitcase and then could not close it.* —*v.i.* **1.** to gather closely or in large numbers: *We crowded around the table to get our food.* **2.** to press forward; advance by pushing: *The passengers crowded into the bus.*

crown (kroun) *n.* **1.** a covering for the head worn by a king or queen, often of jewels and precious metal. **2.** a wreath, band, or other circular ornament for the head: *She wore a crown of flowers.* **3.** the power or authority of a monarch. **4.** *also,* **the Crown.** a sovereign ruler; monarch. **5.** the highest part of anything; top: *They climbed to the crown of a hill.* **6.** the head. **7.** the upper part of a hat or other head covering. **8.** an honor; reward: *He won the middleweight boxing crown.* **9.** the part of a tooth visible above the gum. **10.** an artificial substitute for this part, usually made of gold, porcelain, or plastic. **11.** a former British silver coin, worth five shillings. —*v.t.* **1.** to make a monarch of; enthrone: *They crowned the new king shortly after his father's death.* **2.** to be the top part of: *Whipped cream crowned the dessert.* **3.** to add the finishing touch to; complete: *Fame crowned his career.* **4.** to recognize officially as: *He was crowned heavyweight champion.* **5.** to put an artificial crown on (a tooth).

crown colony, a colony that is under the authority of the British Crown and is administered by the British government.

crown prince, the male heir to a throne.

crown princess **1.** the wife of a crown prince. **2.** a woman or girl who is the heir to a throne.

crow's-feet (krōz′fēt′) *n., pl.* wrinkles near the outer corners of the eyes.

crow's-nest (krōz′nest′) *n.* a small enclosed platform or other structure near the top of a ship's mast, used for a lookout.

cru·cial (krōō′shəl) *adj.* very important; critical; decisive: *a crucial battle, a crucial game. The candidate's strong opposition to the rise in crime proved to be a crucial issue in the election.* —**cru′cial·ly,** *adv.*

cru·ci·ble (krōō′sə bəl) *n.* **1.** a container that can resist very great heat, used for melting chemicals, metals, and ores. **2.** a severe test or trial.

cru·ci·fix (krōō′sə fiks′) *n. pl.,* **cru·ci·fix·es. 1.** a cross with the crucified figure of Christ upon it. **2.** a cross considered as a Christian symbol.

cru·ci·fix·ion (krōō′sə fik′shən) *n.* **1.** the act of crucifying or the state of being crucified. **2. Crucifixion. a.** the execution of Christ on the Cross. **b.** a picture, statue, or other representation of this.

cru·ci·fy (krōō′sə fī′) *v.t.,* **cru·ci·fied, cru·ci·fy·ing. 1.** to put to death by nailing or binding the hands and feet to a cross. **2.** to treat cruelly; persecute; torment. —**cru′·ci·fi′er,** *n.*

crude (krōōd) *adj.,* **crud·er, crud·est. 1.** in a natural or raw state; unrefined: *crude oil, crude rubber.* **2.** done or made without skill; rough: *The boys built a crude shack in the woods.* **3.** lacking tact, taste, or refinement; rude: *crude behavior, a crude joke.* —**crude′ly,** *adv.* —**crude′ness,** *n.*

cru·di·ty (krōō′də tē) *n. pl.,* **cru·di·ties. 1.** the quality or state of being crude. **2.** something crude, such as a remark or act.

cru·el (krōō′əl) *adj.* **1.** willing or ready to cause suffering or pain to others: *The cruel man beat his horse.* **2.** causing suffering or pain: *The cold was cruel this winter.* —**cru′el·ly,** *adv.* —**cru′el·ness,** *n.*

cru·el·ty (krōō′əl tē) *n. pl.,* **cru·el·ties. 1.** the quality or state of being cruel: *His cruelty toward animals was unforgivable.* **2.** a cruel act or acts.

cru·et (krōō′it) *n.* a small glass bottle for holding vinegar, oil, or other dressings.

cruise (krōōz) *v.,* **cruised, cruis·ing.** —*v.i.* **1.** to sail from place to place without any special destination, as for pleasure or business: *The yacht cruised about the Greek islands.* **2.** to move or ride from place to place: *The police car cruised through the area.* **3.** to move at the speed of maximum efficiency, as an aircraft or automobile. —*v.t.* to cruise over or around in: *The pleasure boat cruised the Mediterranean.* —*n.* a sea voyage, especially one taken for pleasure.

Cruet

cruis·er (krōō′zər) *n.* **1.** a warship that is less heavily armed than a battleship and designed for speed. **2.** a motorboat having a cabin equipped for living on board, used for short cruises. **3.** a police squad car. **4.** a person or thing that cruises.

cruising speed, the speed at which an aircraft, powered boat, or automobile operates with maximum efficiency.

crul·ler (krul′ər) *n.* a small cake made of sweetened dough cut into strips that are twisted together and fried in deep fat.

crumb (krum) *n.* **1.** a tiny piece, as of bread, cake, or similar food. **2.** a small bit of something; scrap: *He would give us only crumbs of information about his trip.* **3.** the soft inner part of bread. —*v.t.* **1.** to break into crumbs. **2.** to prepare for cooking by covering or dressing with crumbs.

crum·ble (krum′bəl) *v.,* **crum·bled, crum·bling.** —*v.t.* to break into small pieces: *She crumbled the bread and fed it to the pigeons.* —*v.i.* **1.** to fall into small pieces: *The yellowed pages of the old letter crumbled when I touched them.* **2.** to fall apart or be destroyed: *Our hopes for winning the game crumbled when our best player was injured.*

crum·bly (krum′blē) *adj.,* **crum·bli·er, crum·bli·est.** apt to crumble; easily crumbled: *crumbly bread.* —**crum′·bli·ness,** *n.*

crum·pet (krum′pit) *n.* a soft, unsweetened batter cake that is baked on a griddle, then usually toasted and buttered.

crum·ple (krum′pəl) *v.,* **crum·pled, crum·pling.** —*v.t.* to press or crush (something) into wrinkles or folds: *to crumple paper.* —*v.i.* **1.** to become wrinkled or creased: *The fender crumpled when the car hit the wall.* **2.** to give way; collapse: *The wounded soldier crumpled to the ground.* —*n.* a wrinkle or fold.

crunch (krunch) *v.t.* **1.** to chew or bite with a crushing or crackling sound: *to crunch carrots.* **2.** to crush or grind noisily: *The car wheels crunched the gravel.* —*v.i.* **1.** to chew noisily: *He crunched on some celery.* **2.** to give out a crunching or crackling sound: *The dry leaves crunched under our feet.* **3.** to move with a crunching or crackling sound. —*n. pl.,* **crunch·es.** the act or sound of crunching.

crunch·y (krun′chē) *adj.,* **crunch·i·er, crunch·i·est.** making a crackling sound: *crunchy potato chips.*

crup·per (krup′ər) *n.* **1.** a leather strap attached to the back of a saddle and passing over the horse's back and around its tail to prevent the saddle from sliding forward. **2.** the rump of a horse; croup.

cru·sade (krōō sād′) *n.* **1.** also, **Crusade.** any of the military expeditions undertaken by European Christians between 1096 and 1270 to recover the Holy Land from the Muslims. **2.** any vigorous campaign for the advancement of a cause, especially for reform or improvement: *The new mayor promised a crusade against crime in the city.* —*v.i.,* **cru·sad·ed, cru·sad·ing.** to take part in a crusade. —**cru·sad′er,** *n.*

cruse (krōōz) *n. Archaic.* an earthenware jug, pot, or bottle.

crush (krush) *v.t.* **1.** to press or squeeze forcefully so as to break, put out of shape, or damage: *The shock of the impact crushed the racing car.* **2.** to break into small pieces by pressing, grinding, or pounding: *a machine that crushes rock.* **3.** to put down; subdue: *The dictator crushed the rebel uprising by military force. His spirits were crushed when he failed the examination.* **4.** to crowd or press: *He was crushed against the door of the bus by the mob of passengers.* —*v.i.* to become wrinkled or be put out of shape by pressure: *Her clothes crushed because she packed them too tightly in the suitcase.* —*n. pl.,* **crush·es. 1.** the act of crushing or the state of being crushed. **2.** a closely packed crowd of people: *I was caught in the crush at the parade.* **3.** *Informal.* a sudden and, sometimes, foolish love or liking for a person: *She had a crush on the new boy at school.* —**crush′er,** *n.*

Cru·soe, Robinson (krōō′sō) see **Robinson Crusoe.**

crust (krust) *n.* **1.** the outside, often hard or crisp, part of bread. **2.** a piece of this. **3.** any dry, hard piece of bread. **4.** the outer coating or layer of certain foods: *This fried chicken has a thick crust on it.* **5.** any hard or brittle outer coating: *The lake was covered with a thin crust of ice.* **6.** the hard outer layer of the earth. —*v.t.* **1.** to cover with a crust: *Ice crusted the highway.* **2.** to form into a crust: *to crust pie dough.* —*v.i.* to become covered with a crust.

crus·ta·cean (krus tā′shən) *n.* any of a group of animals having hard shells and jointed bodies, that usually live in water and breathe through gills. Lobsters, crabs, shrimp,

---

at; āpe; cär; end; mē; it; īce; hot; ōld; fôrk; wood; fōōl; oil; out; up; turn; sing; thin; **this**; hw in white; zh in treasure. The symbol ə stands for the sound of **a** in about, **e** in taken, **i** in pencil, **o** in lemon, and **u** in circus.

and barnacles are crustaceans. —*adj.* of or relating to crustaceans.

crust·y (krus′tē) *adj.,* **crust·i·er, crust·i·est. 1.** having or resembling a crust: *crusty rolls.* **2.** bad-tempered and harsh in manner or speech: *The crusty old man made a nasty reply.* —**crust′i·ly,** *adv.* —**crust′i·ness,** *n.*

crutch (kruch) *n. pl.,* **crutch·es. 1.** a staff or support used to help a lame person in walking, especially one having a grip for the hand and either a crosspiece that fits under the armpit or a curved piece that fits around the forearm. **2.** anything that gives support: *His parents' financial help was a welcome crutch when he lost his job.*

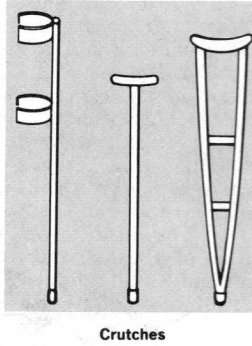
Crutches

crux (kruks) *n. pl.,* **crux·es. 1.** the most important, fundamental, or decisive point: *the crux of an argument.* **2.** a difficult or perplexing problem.

cry (krī) *v.,* **cried, cry·ing.** —*v.i.* **1.** to shed tears; weep: *The baby cried whenever he was hungry.* **2.** to call loudly; shout: *The drowning man cried for help.* **3.** (of an animal) to make its characteristic call: *The seagulls cried as they glided above the beach.* —*v.t.* **1.** to call loudly; shout: *He cried, "Fire!"* **2.** to announce or advertise publicly as being for sale: *The sidewalk vendor cried his wares.* —*n. pl.,* **cries. 1.** a loud call or shout: *The child gave a cry of joy when she saw the presents under the Christmas tree.* **2.** a fit of weeping: *She had a good cry over the sad movie.* **3.** a call for help: *The lifeguard heard the drowning man's cry and rescued him.* **4.** a public outcry; clamor: *a cry for justice.* **5.** a rallying call or slogan. **6.** the characteristic call of an animal or bird: *the cry of a coyote, the cry of a seagull.*

a far cry. a long distance: *The amount of money that we collected is a far cry from the amount we need.*

in full cry. in full pursuit, as a pack of hounds.

to cry for. to be in great need of; demand: *The problem of overcrowded slums cries for attention.*

cry·ba·by (krī′bā′bē) *n. pl.,* **cry·ba·bies.** a person, especially a child, who cries or complains often.

cry·ing (krī′ing) *adj.* demanding immediate attention or remedy: *There is a crying need for more doctors in that country.*

cry·o·gen·ics (krī′ə jen′iks) *n., pl.* the branch of physics dealing with the structure and properties of materials at very low temperatures. ▲ used with a singular verb.

crypt (kript) *n.* an underground chamber or vault, especially one beneath the main floor of a church, used chiefly as a burial place.

cryp·tic (krip′tik) *adj.* having a puzzling or hidden meaning: *a cryptic remark.* —**cryp′ti·cal·ly,** *adv.*

cryp·to·gram (krip′tə gram′) *n.* a message written in a secret code or cipher.

cryp·to·graph (krip′tə graf′) *n.* **1.** another word for **cryptogram. 2.** a system of secret writing; cipher.

cryp·tog·ra·pher (krip tog′rə fər) *n.* a person who specializes in cryptography.

cryp·tog·ra·phy (krip tog′rə fē) *n.* the science of writing and reading cryptograms.

crys·tal (kris′təl) *n.* **1.** a clear, colorless variety of quartz; rock crystal. **2.** a solid body bounded by flat surfaces, whose atoms, molecules, or ions are arranged in an orderly and repeated pattern: *crystals of salt.* **3.** very transparent and brilliant glass. **4.** drinking glasses, bowls, vases, or

other objects made of this glass. **5.** the transparent covering over the face of a watch. —*adj.* **1.** made of crystal: *a crystal goblet.* **2.** resembling crystal; clear; transparent: *crystal waters.*

crystal ball, a ball of transparent glass, crystal, or similar material, believed to reveal future events when looked into.

crys·tal·line (kris′təl in) *adj.* **1.** made of crystal or crystals. **2.** having the structure of a crystal. **3.** resembling crystal; clear: *a crystalline lake.*

crys·tal·lize (kris′təl īz′) *v.,* **crys·tal·lized, crys·tal·liz·ing.** —*v.t.* **1.** to cause to form crystals or become crystalline: *The student crystallized salt as part of his chemistry experiment.* **2.** to give a definite or fixed form to: *He crystallized his ideas before he began writing the story.* —*v.i.* **1.** to form into crystals; become crystalline. **2.** to assume a definite or fixed form: *Her suspicions about his dishonesty crystallized when she found the missing watch in his room.* —**crys′tal·li·za′tion,** *n.*

crys·tal·log·ra·phy (kris′təl og′rə fē) *n.* the branch of science that deals with the form, structure, and physical and chemical properties of crystals.

Cs, the symbol for cesium.

CS 1. Civil Service. **2.** Christian Science.

CST, Central Standard Time.

ct., cent.

Ct., Connecticut.

cts., cents.

Cu, the symbol for copper. [Late Latin *cuprum.*]

cu., cubic.

cub (kub) *n.* **1.** the young of certain animals, such as bears, foxes, wolves, lions, and tigers. **2.** a beginner or apprentice, especially in the newspaper business. **3.** see **cub scout.**

Cu·ba (kyōō′bə) *n.* an island country in the Caribbean, the largest and westernmost island of the West Indies. Capital, Havana. Area, 44,218 sq. mi. Pop. (1971 est.), 8,600,000. —**Cu′ban,** *adj., n.*

cub·by·hole (kub′ē hōl′) *n.* a small, enclosed space.

cube (kyōōb) *n.* **1.** a solid figure with six equal, square sides. **2.** something resembling this figure in shape: *a cube of sugar, an ice cube.* **3.** the product of a number or quantity that is multiplied by itself twice; the third power of a number. The cube of 2 is 8, that is, $2^3 = 2 \times 2 \times 2 = 8$. —*v.t.,* **cubed, cub·ing. 1.** to cut or form into cubes: *to cube potatoes.* **2.** to raise (a number or quantity) to the third power.

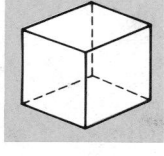
Cube

cube root, a number or quantity that produces a given number or quantity when multiplied by itself twice. The cube root of 8 is 2.

cu·bic (kyōō′bik) *adj.* **1.** of or having length, breadth, and thickness. **2.** relating to or involving the cube of a number; of the third power: *a cubic equation.* **3.** shaped like a cube; cubical.

cu·bi·cal (kyōō′bi kəl) *adj.* shaped like a cube.

cu·bi·cle (kyōō′bi kəl) *n.* a small room, compartment, or partitioned area.

cubic measure, a unit or system of units for measuring volume.

cub·ism (kyōō′biz′əm) *n.* a movement in art, especially painting, begun in the early twentieth century, characterized by the use of basic geometric forms to represent objects.

cu·bit (kyōō′bit) *n.* an ancient unit of measure based on the length of the forearm from the elbow to the fingertips. Its value usually ranged between 18 and 22 inches.

cu·boi·dal (kyōō boid′əl) *adj.* shaped like a cube.

cub scout, a member of the Cub Scouts.

Cub Scouts, the junior division of the Boy Scouts, for boys from eight to ten years of age.

cuck·oo (kook′koo, kook′oo) *n. pl.,* **cuck·oos. 1.** any of a group of slender, long-tailed birds having a two-note call, found in tropical and temperate regions throughout the world. The European cuckoo lays its eggs in the nests of other birds. **2.** the call of the cuckoo, or an imitation of it. —*adj. Informal.* crazy; silly: *That was really a cuckoo idea.*

Cuckoo

cuckoo clock, a clock with a toy cuckoo that pops out, usually on the hour, and announces the time by making a sound similar to a cuckoo's call.

cu. cm., cubic centimeter; cubic centimeters.

cu·cum·ber (kyoo′kum·bər) *n.* **1.** a fleshy, green vegetable, usually eaten in salads or pickled. **2.** the vine bearing this vegetable.

cud (kud) *n.* the partially digested, barely chewed food that cattle and certain other animals bring up from the first stomach back into the mouth for a thorough second chewing.

cud·dle (kud′əl) *v.,* **cud·dled, cud·dling.** —*v.i.* to lie close and snug; nestle; snuggle: *The two kittens cuddled together in the basket.* —*v.t.* to hold (someone or something) closely in one's arms, especially to make warm and snug: *The little girl cuddled the doll.* —*n.* a warm or fond embrace.

cudg·el (kuj′əl) *n.* a short, thick stick used as a weapon; club. —*v.t.,* **cudg·eled, cudg·el·ing;** *also, British,* **cudg·elled, cudg·el·ling.** to beat with a cudgel.

  to cudgel one's brains. to think hard: *The boy cudgeled his brains trying to remember the answer to the question.*

cue¹ (kyoo) *n.* **1.** a signal, before or during a stage performance, for an actor to speak or begin some action: *The slamming of a door was the actor's cue to go onstage.* **2.** any similar signal to begin or do something: *The candidate's appearance in the hall was the band's cue to begin to play.* **3.** a guiding suggestion or hint as to what to do or how to behave: *Take a cue from me and leave the room when I do.* —*v.t.,* **cued, cu·ing.** to give a cue to: *She stood backstage and cued the actors.* [Possibly from the letter *q* as an abbreviation of Latin *quando* when; formerly used in the scripts of plays to let actors know when to go on stage.]

cue² (kyoo) *n.* **1.** a long, tapering stick used to hit the ball in billiards and pool. **2.** see **queue** *(def. 2).* [Old French *coe, cue* tail.]

cue ball, in billiards and pool, the ball intended to be hit by the cue and then in turn to strike and move one or more of the other balls.

cuff¹ (kuf) *n.* **1.** a band, fold, or similar piece at the bottom of a sleeve, usually at the wrist. **2.** a turned-up fold on the bottom of a trouser leg. **3.** see **handcuff.** [Middle English *cuffe* glove.]

  off the cuff. *Informal.* with little or no preparation: *Since he did not expect to be called on, he had to give an answer off the cuff.*

  on the cuff. *Informal.* on credit: *to pay for something on the cuff.*

cuff² (kuf) *v.t.* to strike with the hand. —*n.* a blow, especially with the hand. [Possibly from Middle English *cuffe* glove. The original meaning was probably "to strike with a glove."]

cuff link, one of a pair of linked fastenings for the cuffs of a shirt.

cu. ft., cubic foot; cubic feet.

cu. in., cubic inch; cubic inches.

cui·rass (kwi ras′) *n. pl.,* **cui·rass·es.** a piece of armor consisting of a breastplate and a back plate.

cui·sine (kwi zēn′) *n.* **1.** the manner or style of cooking or preparing food: *the cuisine of Spain.* **2.** the food prepared, especially at a restaurant: *The cuisine at the hotel is excellent.*

cuisse (kwis) *n.* the part of a suit of plate armor used to protect the thigh.

cul-de-sac (kul′də sak′) *n. pl.,* **culs-de-sac** or **cul-de-sacs.** a street or passage closed at one end; blind alley; dead end.

Cuirass

cu·li·nar·y (kyoo′lə ner′ē) *adj.* of, relating to, or used in cooking or the kitchen: *Jane went to cooking school to improve her culinary skills.*

cull (kul) *v.t.* **1.** to pick out from a group; select: *He culled the newest books from the library shelves.* **2.** to look over carefully and make a selection; pick over: *Mother culled the basket of peaches.* —*n.* something selected, especially to be put aside as inferior.

culm (kulm) *n.* the jointed, usually hollow, stem of certain grasses.

cul·mi·nate (kul′mə nāt′) *v.,* **cul·mi·nat·ed, cul·mi·nat·ing.** —*v.i.* to reach the highest or final point; come to a climax: *The border clashes between the two countries culminated in a full-scale war.* —*v.t.* to bring to a close or to the highest point; complete; climax: *The committee chairman culminated his speech with a plea for money.*

cul·mi·na·tion (kul′mə nā′shən) *n.* the point at which something culminates; highest point; climax.

cu·lotte (koo′lot, kyoo′lot) *also,* **cu·lottes.** *n.* women's wide trousers that may be short or long, designed to look like a skirt.

cul·pa·ble (kul′pə bəl) *adj.* deserving blame: *Littering is a culpable act.* —**cul′pa·bil′i·ty,** *n.* —**cul′pa·bly,** *adv.*

cul·prit (kul′prit) *n.* **1.** a person guilty of some offense or crime: *The police caught the culprit in the bank robbery.* **2.** a person who has been charged with a crime, as in a court of law.

cult (kult) *n.* **1.** a particular form or system of religious worship: *Ancient civilizations had many cults of the sun.* **2.** the enthusiastic devotion of a group to a particular person, thing, or idea: *A cult grew up around the movie star.* **3.** the followers or members of a cult.

cul·ti·vate (kul′tə vāt′) *v.t.,* **cul·ti·vat·ed, cul·ti·vat·ing. 1.** to prepare and use (land) for raising crops; till. **2.** to plant and improve the growth of by labor and care: *to cultivate roses, to cultivate corn.* **3.** to loosen the soil around (growing plants) in order to uproot the weeds and reduce water loss. **4.** to improve or develop by education or training: *to cultivate good eating habits, to cultivate one's mind.* **5.** to seek the friendship of: *The ambitious young man cultivated people who could help him.*

cul·ti·vat·ed (kul′tə vā′tid) *adj.* **1.** (of soil) prepared and used for growing crops. **2.** produced or improved by cultivation; not wild: *cultivated flowers.* **3.** improved by education or training. **4.** cultured; refined.

---

at; āpe; cär; end; mē; it; īce; hot; ōld; fôrk; wood; fool; oil; out; up; turn; sing; thin; this; hw in white; zh in treasure. The symbol ə stands for the sound of **a** in about, e in taken, i in pencil, o in lemon, and u in circus.

cul·ti·va·tion (kul′tə vā′shən) *n.* **1.** the act of cultivating soil or plants. **2.** the improvement or development of something by education or training: *the cultivation of one's manners.* **3.** culture; refinement.

cul·ti·va·tor (kul′tə vā′tər) *n.* **1.** a person who cultivates. **2.** a tool or machine for uprooting weeds and loosening the ground around growing plants.

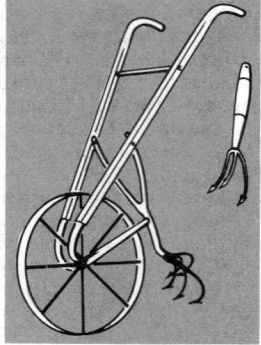
Cultivators

cul·tur·al (kul′chər əl) *adj.* of, relating to, or tending to develop culture: *cultural activities.* —**cul′tur·al·ly,** *adv.*

cul·ture (kul′chər) *n.* **1.** the way of life of a group of people at a particular time, including their customs, beliefs, and arts: *the culture of the ancient Greeks.* **2.** a knowledge of intellectual and artistic accomplishments and of what is considered to be fine in taste and manners: *He is a man of culture.* **3.** the improvement or development of the mind or body, as by education or training: *physical culture.* **4.** the cultivation of the soil. **5.** the care and raising of plants or animals, especially with an interest in improving them: *the culture of silkworms.* **6.** the result of this: *a silkworm culture.* **7.** the growth of living cells or organisms, as viruses or bacteria, in a special preparation for scientific study.

cul·tured (kul′chərd) *adj.* **1.** having or showing culture; educated; refined: *a cultured man, cultured speech.* **2.** produced or raised by cultivation: *a cultured pearl.*

cul·vert (kul′vərt) *n.* a drain for water under roads, sidewalks, and railroads.

cum·ber (kum′bər) *v.t.* to hinder; encumber.

Cum·ber·land Gap (kum′bər land) a natural pass through the Cumberland Mountains near the point where Tennessee, Virginia, and Kentucky meet.

Culvert

Cumberland Mountains, the rugged plateau in the Appalachian Mountains that extends from southwestern West Virginia to northwestern Alabama.

cum·ber·some (kum′bər səm) *adj.* not easily managed or carried; clumsy; unwieldy: *a cumbersome package.* —**cum′ber·some·ly,** *adv.* —**cum′ber·some·ness,** *n.*

cum·brous (kum′brəs) *adj.* unwieldy; cumbersome. —**cum′brous·ly,** *adv.* —**cum′brous·ness,** *n.*

cum lau·de (koom lou′dē, kum lô′də) with honors or praise: *He graduated from college cum laude.* [Modern Latin *cum laude.*]

cum·mer·bund (kum′ər bund′) *n.* a broad sash worn around the waist, especially with a tuxedo.

cum·quat (kum′kwot) another spelling of **kumquat.**

cu·mu·la·tive (kyōō′myə lə tiv) *adj.* increasing in size, strength, or value by constant additions: *The cumulative evidence against the suspect finally led to his arrest.* —**cu′mu·la·tive·ly,** *adv.* —**cu′mu·la·tive·ness,** *n.*

cu·mu·lus (kyōō′myə ləs) *n. pl.,* **cu·mu·li** (kyōō′myə lī′). a dense cloud made up of rounded mounds billowing upward from a flat base. In the sunlight they appear brilliant white.

Cummerbund

cu·ne·i·form (kyōō nē′ə fôrm′) *n.* a system of writing distinguished by wedge-shaped characters, used in ancient times by the Sumerians, Babylonians, Assyrians, and Persians. —*adj.* wedge-shaped.

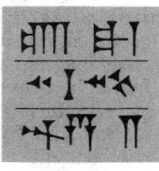
Cuneiform

cun·ning (kun′ing) *adj.* **1.** clever or skilled in deceiving; tricky; sly: *a cunning thief.* **2.** *Informal.* cute or appealing; charming: *a cunning baby.* —*n.* **1.** cleverness or skill in deception; craftiness; slyness: *His plan showed a good deal of cunning.* **2.** skill in workmanship; expertness. —**cun′ning·ly,** *adv.* —**cun′ning·ness,** *n.*

cup (kup) *n.* **1.** a small, open container, usually bowl-shaped and having a handle, used chiefly for drinking. **2.** the amount contained in a cup; cupful: *I'd like a cup of soup.* **3.** a unit of measure equal to eight fluid ounces or half a pint. **4.** an ornamental cup or cup-shaped vase given as a prize, especially in sports. **5.** anything resembling a cup in shape. **6. a.** a metal container in a hole on a golf course. **b.** the hole itself. —*v.t.,* **cupped, cup·ping. 1.** to shape like a cup: *to cup one's hands.* **2.** to place in or as if in a cup: *He cupped his chin in his hand.*

cup·bear·er (kup′ber′ər) *n.* formerly, a person who filled and served cups of wine.

cup·board (kub′ərd) *n.* **1.** a closet or cabinet with shelves, especially for dishes or food. **2.** any small closet or cabinet.

cup·cake (kup′kāk′) *n.* a small cake baked in a cup-shaped container.

cup·ful (kup′fool′) *n. pl.,* **cup·fuls.** the amount that a cup holds.

Cu·pid (kyōō′pid) *n.* **1.** *Roman Mythology.* the god of love and son of Venus, usually pictured as a winged boy with a bow and arrows. In Greek mythology he was called Eros. **2.** *also,* **cupid.** any picture or other representation of a naked winged boy, especially with a bow and arrows, considered as a symbol of love.

cu·pid·i·ty (kyōō pid′ə tē) *n.* an eager desire for possession, especially of wealth; greed.

cu·po·la (kyōō′pə lə) *n.* **1.** a rounded or dome-shaped structure rising above a roof. **2.** a rounded roof or ceiling; dome.

cur (kur) *n.* **1.** a worthless or bad-tempered dog; mongrel. **2.** a nasty, worthless person.

cur·a·ble (kyoor′ə bəl) *adj.* that can be cured: *a curable disease.* —**cur′a·bil′i·ty,** *n.*

Cu·ra·çao (koor′ə sou′, kyoor′ə sō′) *n.* an island off the coast of Venezuela.

cu·rate (kyoor′it) *n.* a clergyman who assists the pastor, rector, or vicar of a parish.

Cupola

cur·a·tive (kyoor′ə tiv) *adj.* **1.** having the tendency or power to cure or remedy: *curative treatment.* **2.** of, relating to, or used in the cure of disease: *curative medicine.* —*n.* something that cures; remedy.

cu·ra·tor (kyoor rā′tər) *n.* a person in charge of all or part of the collection or exhibit at a museum, art gallery, or zoo.

curb (kurb) *n.* **1.** a border of concrete, stone, or other material along the edge of a street or sidewalk; outer edge of a sidewalk. **2.** something that restrains or controls; check: *The club's treasurer recommended a curb on spending.* **3.** a chain or strap fastened to a horse's bit and passing under its lower jaw, used to hold back or control the horse when the reins are pulled. —*v.t.* to hold back or control; check: *to curb one's anger, to curb inflation.*

curb·ing (kur′bing) *n.* the material forming or used for making a curb along a street or sidewalk.

curb·stone (kurb′stōn′) *n.* a stone or row of stones along the edge of a street or sidewalk.

curd (kurd) *also,* **curds.** *n.* the thick, clotted portion of milk that separates from the watery part when the milk sours, used in making cheese.

cur·dle (kurd′əl) *v.,* **cur·dled, cur·dling.** —*v.i.* to form into curd: *The milk curdled.* —*v.t.* to cause to form into curd: *You'll curdle the sauce if you get it too hot.*

to make (one's) blood curdle. to fill (someone) with horror or fear; terrify.

cure (kyoor) *n.* **1.** a return to a healthy or sound condition; recovery: *The patient's cure was hastened by plenty of rest.* **2.** something, such as a medicine or method of treatment, that restores health; remedy: *There is no known cure for that disease.* **3.** anything that corrects an unwanted or harmful condition or situation: *Seeing your old friends may be the cure for your loneliness.* —*v.,* **cured, cur·ing.** —*v.t.* **1.** to restore to a healthy or sound condition; make well: *The doctor cured the patient.* **2.** to get rid of: *This medicine might cure your sore throat.* **3.** to preserve or prepare for use, as by drying, smoking, or chemically treating: *to cure fish, to cure tobacco.* —*v.i.* to be or become preserved or processed by curing: *The meat was hung up in the smokehouse to cure.*

cu·ré (kyoo rā′) *n. French.* a parish priest.

cure-all (kyoor′ôl′) *n.* something that is thought to cure all diseases or evils.

cur·few (kur′fyoo) *n.* **1.** an order or rule requiring certain persons to be indoors or at home before a fixed time, especially at night. **2.** the hour at which such an order or rule becomes effective. **3.** the sounding of a bell at evening time as a signal. In medieval European towns, a curfew was a signal to the people to put out lights and fires and go to bed.

cu·rie (kyoor′ē, kyoo rē′) *n.* a unit of measurement of radioactivity. [From Marie *Curie.*]

Cu·rie (kyoor′ē, kyoo rē′) **1. Marie.** 1867–1934, Polish chemist and physicist who lived and worked in France. With her husband, she discovered radium in 1898. **2. Pierre** (pyer). 1859–1906, her husband; French physicist and chemist.

cu·ri·o (kyoor′ē ō′) *n. pl.,* **cu·ri·os.** an object valued as a curiosity: *She collects old china figurines and other such curios.*

cu·ri·os·i·ty (kyoor′ē os′ə tē) *n. pl.,* **cu·ri·os·i·ties. 1.** the desire for knowledge, especially of something new, strange, or unknown. **2.** an object that arouses interest because it is strange, rare, or unusual.

cu·ri·ous (kyoor′ē əs) *adj.* **1.** eager to know or learn: *Most young children have very curious natures.* **2.** strange, rare, or unusual: *There were curious markings on the wall of the cave.* —**cu′ri·ous·ly,** *adv.* —**cu′ri·ous·ness,** *n.*

cu·ri·um (kyoor′ē əm) *n.* a radioactive element produced artificially. Symbol: **Cm** [From Pierre and Marie *Curie.*]

curl (kurl) *v.t.* **1.** to twist or form into coils or ringlets: *to curl one's hair.* **2.** to bend or form into a curved or spiral shape: *She curled the ribbon around her finger.* —*v.i.* **1.** to take the form of coils or ringlets: *My hair curls when it gets wet.* **2.** to move in a curved or spiral shape: *The smoke curled up from his pipe.* —*n.* **1.** a coiled or curved lock of hair; ringlet. **2.** something having a curved or spiral shape: *We decorated the cake with chocolate curls.*

to curl up. to sit or lie down in a comfortable position, as with the back curved and the legs drawn up.

curl·er (kur′lər) *n.* a device on which hair is wound to make it curl.

cur·lew (kur′loo) *n.* a wading bird of arctic and temperate regions, having long legs, a long, slender, curved bill, and usually, brown feathers.

Curlew

curl·i·cue (kur′li kyoo′) *n.* a fancy curve, twist, or flourish, as in handwriting.

curl·ing (kur′ling) *n.* a game played on ice, in which large, rounded stones are slid toward a circular target, the object being to come as close as possible to the target.

curl·y (kur′lē) *adj.,* **curl·i·er, curl·i·est. 1.** curling or tending to curl: *curly hair.* **2.** having curls: *a curly head.* —**curl′i·ness,** *n.*

cur·rant (kur′ənt) *n.* **1.** a small, sour berry of any of several shrubs, used especially for making jelly, syrup, and wine. **2.** the shrub on which this berry grows. **3.** a small, seedless raisin used especially in cakes, pies, and buns.

cur·ren·cy (kur′ən sē) *n. pl.,* **cur·ren·cies. 1.** the money that is used in a country. **2.** general use or acceptance: *That custom has little currency in this country.* **3.** a passing from person to person; circulation: *That piece of gossip gained wide currency.*

cur·rent (kur′ənt) *adj.* **1.** of or belonging to the present time; in progress: *We plan to move during the current year. My current address is on the envelope.* **2.** commonly used or accepted; prevalent: *The current belief is that there is probably no life on the planet Venus.* **3.** passing from person to person; in wide circulation. —*n.* **1.** a portion of a body of water or of air continuously flowing in approximately the same path: *The ocean's current swept the bottle out to sea. A cold current of air came into the room when he opened the door.* **2.** the flow of electricity in an electric circuit or through any conducting body or medium. **3.** a general course, movement, or tendency; trend: *the current of political thought in a country.*

cur·rent·ly (kur′ənt lē) *adv.* at the present time: *He is currently away on a trip.*

cur·ric·u·lar (kə rik′yə lər) *adj.* of or relating to a curriculum.

cur·ric·u·lum (kə rik′yə ləm) *n. pl.,* **cur·ric·u·lums** or **cur·ric·u·la** (kə rik′yə lə). all the courses of study offered at a school, college, or university.

cur·ry¹ (kur′ē) *v.t.,* **cur·ried, cur·ry·ing.** to rub down and clean (a horse or other animal) with a brush or currycomb. [Old French *correier* to prepare, arrange.]

to curry favor. to try to win favor, as by flattery: *The courtier tried to curry favor with the king by praising his mastery of hunting and horsemanship.*

cur·ry² (kur′ē) *n. pl.,* **cur·ries. 1.** a very spicy powder made from various dried, ground spices. Also, **curry powder. 2.** a spicy sauce made from this. **3.** food seasoned with this powder or sauce. —*v.t.,* **cur·ried, cur·ry·ing.** to flavor or prepare (food) with curry. [Tamil *kari* sauce.]

cur·ry·comb (kur′ē kōm′) *n.* a brush with rows of teeth rather than bristles, usually of metal or rubber, for currying a horse or similar animal. —*v.t.* to rub down or groom with a currycomb.

at; āpe; cär; end; mē; it; īce; hot; ōld; fôrk; wood; fool; oil; out; up; turn; sing; thin; **this**; **hw** in white; **zh** in treasure. The symbol ə stands for the sound of **a** in about, **e** in taken, **i** in pencil, **o** in lemon, and **u** in circus.

curse (kurs) *n.* **1.** a wish that evil or harm may come to someone or something. **2.** the evil or harm that has been wished for. **3.** a word or words used in swearing; profane language. **4.** something that brings or causes evil or harm. —*v.,* **cursed** or **curst, curs·ing.** —*v.t.* **1.** to call down evil or harm upon; damn. **2.** to use profane language against; swear at. **3.** to cause evil, harm, or suffering to: *He was cursed with constant ill health.* —*v.i.* to utter a curse or curses; swear.

curs·ed (kur′sid, kurst) *also,* **curst.** *v.* a past tense and past participle of **curse.** —*adj.* **1.** deserving a curse; evil; hateful. **2.** under a curse; damned.

cur·sive (kur′siv) *adj.* written or printed with the letters joined together: *cursive handwriting.* —**cur′sive·ly,** *adv.*

cur·so·ry (kur′sər ē) *adj.* not thorough; rapid; hasty: *He gave the letter a cursory reading.* —**cur′so·ri·ly,** *adv.*

curst (kurst) a past tense and past participle of **curse.**

curt (kurt) *adj.* rudely brief or abrupt: *A curt nod was the only greeting he gave me.* —**curt′ly,** *adv.* —**curt′ness,** *n.*

cur·tail (kər tāl′) *v.t.* to cut short or cut down; lessen; reduce: *to curtail expenses.* —**cur·tail′ment,** *n.*

cur·tain (kur′tin) *n.* **1.** a piece or pieces of cloth or other material hung at a window or door as a decoration or screen. **2.** the hanging screen or drapery used to conceal the major part of the stage of a theater from the view of the audience. **3.** the lowering or closing of the curtain in a theater to indicate the end of a performance, act, or scene. **4.** anything that screens or covers like a curtain: *A curtain of fog hid the tops of the buildings.* —*v.t.* to provide, shut off, or cover with a curtain.

curt·sey (kurt′sē) *n. pl.,* **curt·seys.** another spelling of **curtsy.**

curt·sy (kurt′sē) *n. pl.,* **curt·sies.** a gesture of respect or greeting by women and girls, made by bending the knees and lowering the body slightly. —*v.i.,* **curt·sied, curt·sy·ing.** to make a curtsy.

cur·va·ture (kur′və chər) *n.* **1.** the quality or condition of being curved: *The curvature of the earth could be seen in the satellite photograph.* **2.** something curved. **3.** an abnormal curving, as of the spine.

curve (kurv) *n.* **1.** a continuously bent line having no straight parts or angles, such as an arc of a circle. **2.** something having the shape of a curve: *a curve in a road.* **3.** a baseball or softball pitched so that it swerves from a straight path as it passes the batter. **4.** *Mathematics.* any set of points that satisfy a certain mathematical condition. —*v.,* **curved, curv·ing.** —*v.i.* **1.** to have or take the form of a curve: *The driveway curves as it nears the house.* **2.** to move in a curve: *The ball curved to the left.* —*v.t.* to cause to curve.

cush·ion (koosh′ən) *n.* **1.** a pillow or soft pad, used to sit, rest, or lie on. **2.** something like a cushion in shape or use: *We sat on a cushion of leaves.* **3.** anything that absorbs shock or protects against harm: *His savings account will be a nice cushion until he finds another job.* —*v.t.* **1.** to absorb or lessen the shock or effect of: *The pile of leaves cushioned my fall.* **2.** to place or seat on a cushion; support: *Mother cushioned the baby's head on her arm.* **3.** to provide with a cushion or cushions. —**cush′ion·like′,** *adj.*

cusp (kusp) *n.* **1.** a point or pointed end: *A crescent moon has two cusps.* **2.** a point or pointed end on the grinding surface or crown of a tooth.

cus·pid (kus′pid) *n.* another word for **canine tooth.**

cus·pi·dor (kus′pə dôr′) *n.* another word for **spittoon.**

cuss (kus) *Informal. v.t.* to swear at: *The angry man cussed the driver of the car that bumped into him.* —*v.i.* to swear; curse. —*n. pl.,* **cuss·es. 1.** an odd person or animal. **2.** a curse.

cus·tard (kus′tərd) *n.* a sweet dessert made from eggs, sugar, milk, and flavoring, either baked or boiled.

Cus·ter, George Arm·strong (kus′tər; ärm′strông′) 1839–1876, U.S. general who was killed in the battle of Little Bighorn, along with his entire command of troops.

cus·to·di·an (kəs tō′dē ən) *n.* **1.** a person who has care or custody of a person or thing; guardian; keeper. **2.** a person responsible for the care of a building; janitor.

cus·to·dy (kus′tə dē) *n. pl.,* **cus·to·dies. 1.** keeping; care; guardianship: *She was in her grandmother's custody after her parents died.* **2.** the state of being in the charge of the police; imprisonment: *The police took the suspect into custody immediately after the robbery.*

cus·tom (kus′təm) *n.* **1.** an accepted social habit or pattern of behavior of a group. Customs are learned and passed from one generation to another. Trimming trees and giving presents at Christmas is a custom in this country. **2.** the usual way of acting or doing things; habit: *It is her custom to clean house every Saturday.* **3.** the regular business given to a store or other business establishment: *We give our custom to the grocer on the corner.* **4. customs. a.** taxes or duties imposed by a government on goods imported from foreign countries. **b.** the government agency that inspects imported goods and collects the taxes or duties on them. —*adj.* **1.** making things to order: *a custom tailor.* **2.** made-to-order; custom-made.

cus·tom·ar·y (kus′tə mer′ē) *adj.* according to or based on custom; usual; habitual: *It is customary in our family to have Thanksgiving dinner at our grandmother's house.* —**cus′tom·ar′i·ly,** *adv.*

cus·tom·er (kus′tə mər) *n.* **1.** a person who shops or buys, especially a person who deals regularly at a particular store. **2.** *Informal.* anyone with whom a person has to deal: *That boy is a tough customer.*

cus·tom·house (kus′təm hous′) *n. pl.,* **cus·tom·hous·es** (kus′təm hou′ziz). a government office or building where customs on imported goods are collected and where ships or their cargoes are cleared.

cus·tom-made (kus′təm mād′) *adj.* made especially for a particular person; made-to-order: *a custom-made suit.*

cut (kut) *v.,* **cut, cut·ting.** —*v.t.* **1.** to separate or divide into parts with a sharp-edged instrument: *to cut a rope, to cut a pie into slices.* **2.** to pierce, slit, or wound with a sharp instrument or edge; make an opening in: *I cut my foot on the jagged rock.* **3.** to remove or take away with a sharp-edged instrument: *He cut the dead branches from the tree.* **4.** to make shorter by removing a part or parts: *to cut hair, to cut grass, to cut a speech.* **5.** to make or shape by cutting: *to cut a pattern for a dress, to cut a hole in a fence.* **6.** to make smaller or less; reduce: *We have to cut expenses this year. The store cut its prices during the sale.* **7.** to leave out or remove: *The director cut out her part from the play.* **8.** to put an end to or stop: *He cut the motor and removed the key. The troops cut off the enemy's retreat.* **9.** to go across or through: *A road cuts the field.* **10.** to hurt the feelings of: *Her rudeness cut me deeply.* **11.** to have (a tooth or teeth) grow through the gum. **12.** *Informal.* to be absent from, especially without permission: *to cut classes.* **13.** *Informal.* to pretend not to recognize or know; snub: *She cut him in the street without a word.* —*v.i.* **1.** to act or do the work of a sharp-edged instrument: *This saw cuts well.* **2.** to be cut: *Silk cuts easily.* **3.** to go or move by the shortest or most direct route: *He cut through the park on the way home.* **4.** to cross or pass: *The road cuts through the swamp.* **5.** to change direction suddenly or sharply; swerve: *The driver of the car cut to the right to avoid hitting the dog.* **6.** to go through or pierce like a sharp-edged instrument: *The cold wind cut through her* *thin coat.* —*n.* **1.** an opening or wound made with a sharp instrument or edge: *He got a cut on his hand from the broken glass.* **2.** a slice, stroke, or blow with a sharp-edged instrument: *He severed the rope with one clean cut of his knife.* **3.** a piece or part, cut or cut off: *a good cut of beef.* **4.** a reduction, as in price; decrease: *a cut in salary, a cut in prices.* **5.** the way or shape in which a thing is cut; style: *The cut of that dress makes her look slimmer.* **6.** a remark or action that hurts the feelings. **7.** a passage or channel made by cutting, digging, or blasting. **8.** a stroke or swing at a ball, as in baseball. **9.a.** an engraved block or plate from which a picture is printed. **b.** a picture made from such a block or plate. **10.** *Informal.* a share or part, as of profits: *The salesman got a seven percent cut on all sales.* —*adj.* that has been cut: *a cut foot, cut flowers.*

cut and dried. a. arranged or settled beforehand. **b.** not interesting; dull; boring: *a cut and dried speech.*

cut out. suited or fit by nature: *He's not cut out for that kind of work.*

to cut back. to reduce, as prices.

to cut down. a. to cause to fall by cutting: *to cut down a tree.* **b.** to reduce in size or amount.

to cut in. a. to break or move into suddenly or out of turn: *He cut in at the head of the line.* **b.** to interrupt, as a conversation. **c.** to interrupt a dancing couple in order to take the place of one partner.

to cut up. *Informal.* to behave in a mischievous boisterous way.

cut·a·way (kut′ə wā′) *n.* a man's formal coat for daytime wear, cut so as to slope back from the waistline in front to the tails in back.

cut·back (kut′bak′) *n.* a reduction: *a cutback in government spending.*

cute (kyoot) *adj.,* **cut·er, cut·est.** *Informal.* **1.** charmingly pretty or attractive; adorable: appealing: *a cute baby.* **2.** clever; shrewd: *a very cute trick.* —**cute′ly,** *adv.* —**cute′ness,** *n.*

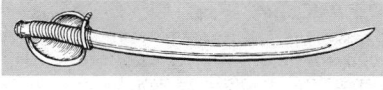

cu·ti·cle (kyoo′ti kəl) *n.* **1.** the tough skin surrounding the base and sides of a fingernail or toenail. **2.** the outer layer of skin; epidermis.

cut·lass (kut′ləs) *n. pl.,* **cut·lass·es.** a short sword with a wide, flat, slightly curved blade.

cut·ler·y (kut′- lər ē) *n.* **1.** cutting instruments, such as knives and scissors. **2.** knives, forks, and other utensils used in eating or serving food.

Cutlass

cut·let (kut′lit) *n.* **1.** a thin slice of meat, usually of veal, that is cut from the leg or ribs and is broiled or fried. **2.** a flat cake made of chopped meat, fish, or other food: *veal cutlets.*

cut·off (kut′ôf′) *n.* **1.** a stopping or cutting off of something, especially the flow of steam or other fluid into the cylinder of an engine. **2.** the point at which this is done. **3.** a device for cutting off the flow of something, as steam or other fluid. **4.** a shorter road or route cutting across or through something; short cut. —*adj.* at or during which something ends or expires: *The cutoff date for contest entries is May 6.*

cut·out (kut′out′) *n.* **1.** something cut out or designed to be cut out: *The book has paper cutouts of fairy tale figures.* **2.** a device for letting the exhaust gases from an automobile engine pass directly into the air rather than through the muffler.

cut·rate (kut′rāt′) *adj.* sold or selling at reduced or cheap prices: *a cut-rate drugstore.*

cut·ter (kut′ər) *n.* **1.** a person who cuts, especially a person whose job is cutting: *a diamond cutter, a dress cutter.* **2.** a device or machine for cutting. **3.** a single-masted sailboat. **4.** a small, fast ship used by the Coast Guard. **5.** a small, light sleigh, usually made to be drawn by one horse.

cut·throat (kut′thrōt′) *n.* a murderer or murderous thug. —*adj.* ruthless; merciless: *cutthroat thieves, cutthroat business methods.*

cut·ting (kut′ing) *adj.* **1.** able to cut; sharp: *the cutting edge of a knife.* **2.** that hurts the feelings; sarcastic: *a cutting remark.* —*n.* **1.** the act of a person or thing that cuts. **2.** a small shoot or other part cut from a plant and used to grow a new plant. **3.** a newspaper or magazine clipping.

cut·tle·bone (kut′əl bōn′) *n.* the hard inner shell or plate of cuttlefish, used for making polishing powder. It is often placed in bird cages to provide the birds with minerals.

cut·tle·fish (kut′əl fish′) *n. pl.,* **cut·tle·fish** or **cut·tle·fish·es.** a saltwater animal found in warm, shallow waters of the Atlantic and Indian Oceans. It has arms with suckers and a hard inner shell. When in danger, it may release an inky fluid.

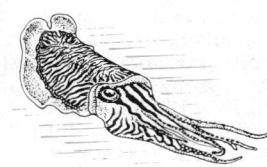

Cuttlefish

cut·up (kut′up′) *n. Informal.* a person who clowns, plays tricks, or behaves in a mischievous or boisterous way, especially to attract attention.

cut·worm (kut′wurm′) *n.* the larva or caterpillar of any of several moths. The cutworm feeds at night on the leaves and stems of cultivated crops and garden plants.

cwt., hundredweight.

-cy *suffix* (used to form nouns) **1.** the quality, state, condition, or fact of being: *bankruptcy.* **2.** the office, position, or rank of: *captaincy.*

cy·a·nide (sī′ə nīd′, sī′ə nid) *n.* any of several very poisonous compounds, used especially as pesticides and in the extraction of metal from ore.

cy·ber·net·ics (sī′bər net′iks) *n., pl.* the science dealing with communication and control processes in man and other animals and in electronic machines, especially computers. ▲ used with a singular verb.

cyc·la·men (sī′klə mən, sik′lə mən) *n.* **1.** the showy flower of any of a group of plants, having pink, purple, rose, or white petals. **2.** the plant bearing this flower, having heart-shaped leaves.

cy·cle (sī′kəl) *n.* **1.** a complete course or series of events or phenomena that occur over and over again in a definite order: *the cycle of the four seasons.* **2.** a period of time during which such a course or series occurs and completes itself. **3.** a bicycle, tricycle, or motorcycle. **4.** a group of stories, poems, or plays about a particular figure, event, or theme: *The Arthurian cycle deals with the adventures of King Arthur and his knights.* **5.** *Physics.* a complete round or series of changes in a quantity that varies periodically, as alternating current. —*v.i.,* **cy·cled, cy·cling.** to ride a cycle, especially a bicycle.

at; āpe; cär; end; mē; it; īce; hot; ōld; fôrk; wood; fool; oil; out; up; turn; sing; thin; this; hw in white; zh in treasure. The symbol ə stands for the sound of **a** in about, e in taken, i in pencil, o in lemon, and u in circus.

cy·clic (sī′klik) *adj.* **1.** moving or coming in cycles: *the cyclic changing of the seasons.* **2.** of or relating to a cycle. **3.** of, relating to, or characterized by an arrangement of atoms in a ring or closed chain. Also, **cy·cli·cal** (sī′kli·kəl). —**cy′cli·cal·ly,** *adv.*

cy·clist (sī′klist) *n.* a person who rides a bicycle, tricycle, or motorcycle.

cy·clone (sī′klōn) *n.* **1.** a disturbance in the atmosphere in which winds rotate around a moving center of low air pressure. Cyclone winds circle clockwise in the Northern Hemisphere and counterclockwise in the Southern Hemisphere. **2.** any violent windstorm, such as a hurricane or tornado.

cy·clon·ic (sī klon′ik) *adj.* **1.** of or relating to a cyclone: *cyclonic winds.* **2.** like a cyclone; destructive.

cy·clo·pe·di·a (sī′klə pē′dē ə) *also,* **cy·clo·pae·di·a.** *n.* another word for **encyclopedia.**

cy·clo·pe·dic (sī′klə pē′dik) *also,* **cy·clo·pae·dic.** *adj.* another word for **encyclopedic.**

Cy·clops (sī′klops) *n. pl.,* **Cy·clo·pes** (sī klō′pēz). *Greek Mythology.* one of a race of giants having only one eye, located in the center of the forehead.

cy·clo·tron (sī′klə tron′) *n.* a device that accelerates charged atomic particles to very high speeds.

cyg·net (sig′nit) *n.* a young swan.

cyl., cylinder.

cyl·in·der (sil′ən dər) *n.* **1.** a solid geometric figure bounded by two equal, parallel circles and a curved surface that is formed by a straight line moving parallel to itself with its ends always on the circumferences of the circles. **2.** something resembling a cylinder in shape, such as a can. **3.** the rotating part of a revolver that contains chambers for cartridges. **4.** a chamber in which the piston of an engine or pump moves up and down.

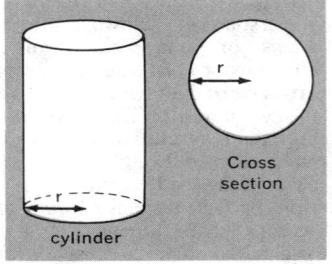

Cylinder

cy·lin·dri·cal (sə lin′dri kəl) *adj.* having the form of a cylinder; shaped like a cylinder: *a cylindrical can.* —**cy·lin′dri·cal·ly,** *adv.*

cym·bal (sim′bəl) *n.* a musical instrument consisting of a circular, slightly concave metal plate that produces a ringing sound when clashed against another cymbal or struck, as with a drumstick.

cyn·ic (sin′ik) *n.* a person who tends to doubt the sincerity, goodness, or unselfishness of human motives and actions. —*adj.* cynical.

cyn·i·cal (sin′i kəl) *adj.* having or showing disbelief in or doubt about the sincerity, goodness, or unselfishness of human motives and actions: *a cynical young man, a cynical attitude, a cynical smile.* —**cyn′i·cal·ly,** *adv.*

cyn·i·cism (sin′ə siz′əm) *n.* **1.** a cynical disposition, character, or quality. **2.** a cynical remark, act, or opinion.

cy·no·sure (sī′nə shoor′) *n.* a person or thing that attracts attention; center or object of attraction, interest, or admiration: *The beautiful movie star was the cynosure of all those present.*

cy·pher (sī′fər) another spelling of **cipher.**

cy·press (sī′prəs) *n.* **1.** any of a group of evergreen trees or shrubs found in southern Europe, Asia, and North America, having closely overlapping, scalelike leaves and woody cones. **2.** a cone-bearing tree found especially in swampy lands in the southern United States. It has conical root projections when it grows in water. **3.** the wood of these trees.

Cypress *(def. 2)*

Cyp·ri·an (sip′rē ən) *n.* another word for **Cypriot.**

Cyp·ri·ot (sip′rē ət) *also,* **Cyp·ri·ote.** *n.* **1.** a person who was born or is living in Cyprus. **2.** the ancient or modern Greek dialect of Cyprus. —*adj.* of or relating to Cyprus, its people, their language, or their culture.

Cy·prus (sī′prəs) *n.* an island country in the eastern Mediterranean Sea, south of Turkey. Capital, Nicosia. Area, 3572 sq. mi. Pop. (1970 est.), 633,000.

Cy·rus the Great (sī′rəs) died 529 B.C., the king of Persia from 558? to 529 B.C. and the founder of the Persian empire.

cyst (sist) *n.* **1.** an abnormal sac in the body, usually containing a liquid substance. **2.** a protective outer covering formed around an organism, such as a protozoan, during reproduction or in an inactive stage.

cyst·ic (sis′tik) *adj.* **1.** of, relating to, or resembling a cyst. **2.** having or containing a cyst or cysts. **3.** of or relating to the gall bladder or to the urinary bladder.

cystic fibrosis, an inherited disease, usually appearing during childhood, that affects the ducts of certain glands. It is often characterized by inadequate functioning of the pancreas and lungs.

cy·tol·o·gist (sī tol′ə jist) *n.* a student of or an expert in cytology.

cy·tol·o·gy (sī tol′ə jē) *n.* the branch of biology that deals with the study of cells, including their formation, structure, and function.

cy·to·plasm (sī′tə plaz′əm) *n.* all the protoplasm of a cell, outside the nucleus.

C.Z., Canal Zone.

czar (zär) *also,* **tsar, tzar.** *n.* **1.** any of the emperors of Russia before the Revolution of 1917. **2.** a person having great or absolute power or authority: *He is a czar of the motion picture industry.*

cza·ri·na (zä rē′nə) *also,* **tsa·ri·na, tza·ri·na.** *n.* the wife of a Russian czar; an empress of Russia.

Czech (chek) *n.* **1.** a member of branch of the Slavic people, including the Bohemians and Moravians. **2.** see **Czechoslovak. 3.** the language of Czechoslovakia. —*adj.* of or relating to Czechoslovakia, its people, or their language.

Czech·o·slo·vak (chek′ə slō′vak, chek′ə slō′väk) *n.* a person who was born or is living in Czechoslovakia. —*adj.* of or relating to Czechoslovakia, its people, or their language. Also, **Czechoslovakian.**

Czech·o·slo·va·ki·a (chek′ə slə vä′kē ə) *n.* a country in central Europe. Capital, Prague. Area, 49,370 sq. mi. Pop. (1971 est.), 14,500,000. —**Czech′o·slo·va′ki·an,** *adj., n.*

D

1. Semitic △ ◁ △ ▷|

2. Phoenician ◁ ◁

3. Early Hebrew △ △

4. Greek Eighth Century B.C. ◁ △

5. Greek Classical Capitals △

6. Etruscan ◁ ▷

7. Latin Fourth Century B.C. Capitals ▷

8. English ▷

D is the fourth letter of the English alphabet. The ancient Semitic letter *daleth* (1), meaning "door," is the earliest letter that corresponds to our modern letter **D**. *Daleth* probably came from an Egyptian hieroglyphic that was the symbol for "door." The early alphabets, including Phoenician (2) and early Hebrew (3), that developed from the ancient Semitic, all used some form of triangle as the basic shape of this letter. The Greeks borrowed *daleth*, making only slight changes in its shape, and called it *delta* (4). In later centuries, *delta* was written in the form of an equilateral triangle (5). We use *delta* in English to mean something triangular, especially the triangular deposits of silt that builds up at the mouth of a river. The Etruscans (6) changed the shape of delta by rounding two of the triangle's sides. This form was used, with only slight changes, in the Latin alphabet (7). By about the fourth century B.C., the Romans were writing this letter almost exactly as we write the capital letter **D** today (8).

d, D (dē) *n. pl.,* **d's, D's. 1.** the fourth letter of the English alphabet. **2.** the fourth item in a series or group. **3.** the Roman numeral for 500. **4.** *Music.* the first and last notes of the scale of D major.

D 1. the symbol for deuterium. **2.** *Physics.* density.

d. 1. died. **2.** penny; pence: *6d.* [Latin *denarius*.] **3.** dead. **4.** dime. **5.** dollar. **6.** day; days. **7.** date. **8.** diameter. **9.** degree.

D. 1. Democrat. **2.** December. **3.** Dutch. **4.** department. **5.** Doctor.

D.A., district attorney.

dab (dab) *v.,* **dabbed, dab·bing.** —*v.t.* **1.** to pat or stroke gently with something soft or moist: *The nurse dabbed his wound with cotton.* **2.** to apply with a light, quick touch: *The artist dabbed green paint on the canvas.* —*v.i.* to pat or stroke gently, as with something soft or moist: *The girl dabbed at the stain on her dress with a wet cloth.* —*n.* **1.** a small, moist mass of something: *a dab of clay, a dab of paint.* **2.** a little bit: *a dab of mashed potatoes.* **3.** a light, quick pat: *She gave her nose a dab with a powder puff.*

dab·ble (dab′əl) *v.,* **dab·bled, dab·bling.** —*v.i.* **1.** to do something occasionally or in a casual manner: *to dabble in politics, to dabble at painting.* **2.** to splash or play gently, as in water. —*v.t.* to splash or dip (something) gently, as in water. —**dab′bler,** *n.*

Dac·ca (dak′ə) *n.* the capital and largest city of Bangladesh. Pop. (1970 est.), 600,000.

dace (dās) *n. pl.,* **dac·es** or **dace.** any of various minnows commonly found in small streams of North America and Europe.

da·cha (dä′shə) *n.* a Russian country house.

Dach·au (dä′kou) *n.* a city in southern Germany, near Munich, the site of a Nazi concentration camp.

dachs·hund (däks′hoont′, däks′hoond′) *n.* a small dog having a long body, very short legs, drooping ears, and a red, tan, or black-and-tan coat. [German *Dachshund,* from *Dachs* badger + *Hund* dog; because this dog was once used for hunting badgers.]

Dachshund

Da·cron (dā′kron, dak′- ron) *n. Trademark.* **1.** a strong synthetic textile fiber that does not wrinkle or stretch, used especially for clothing. **2.** a yarn or fabric made of this fiber.

dac·tyl (dakt′əl) *n.* **1.** in modern English verse, a metrical foot consisting of one accented syllable followed by two unaccented syllables. The line *Think of her mournfully, gently and humanly* (Thomas Hood) contains four dactyls. **2.** a line of verse made up of such feet.

dad (dad) *n. Informal.* father.

dad·dy (dad′ē) *n. pl.,* **dad·dies.** *Informal.* father.

dad·dy-long·legs (dad′ē lông′legz′) *n. pl.,* **dad·dy-long- legs.** an animal related to the spider and having long, slender legs. The daddy-longlegs does not spin a web.

Daed·a·lus (ded′əl əs) *n. Greek Legend.* a skillful craftsman and inventor who designed the Labyrinth in Crete and was later imprisoned in it with his son Icarus. Daedalus then invented artificial wings, made out of feathers and wax, with which he and his son escaped.

Daddy-longlegs

daf·fo·dil (daf′ə dil′) *n.* **1.** the flower of any of several plants, having yellow or white petals that surround the base of a trumpet-shaped center. **2.** the plant bearing this flower, having tall, stiff, slender leaves and growing from a bulb.

daff·y (daf′ē) *adj.,* **daff·i·er, daff·i·est.** *Informal.* **1.** silly; foolish. **2.** crazy; insane.

daft (daft) *adj. British.* **1.** crazy; insane. **2.** silly; foolish. —**daft′ly,** *adv.* —**daft′ness,** *n.*

da Ga·ma, Vas·co (də gä′mə; väs′kō) 1469?–1524, Portuguese navigator.

dag·ger (dag′ər) *n.* **1.** a small weapon having a pointed blade, used for stabbing. **2.** a mark (†) used in printing to indicate a reference to a footnote or other note.

da·guerre·o·type (də ger′ə tīp′) *n.* **1.** an early method of taking photographs by using silver-coated copper plates that were sensitive to light. **2.** a picture made in this way. [French *daguerréotype,* from Louis *Daguerre,* 1789–1851, the French inventor of this method.]

dahl·ia (dal′yə, däl′yə) *n.* **1.** a showy flower growing in various bright colors. **2.** the leafy plant bearing this flower. [Modern Latin *Dahlia,* from Anders *Dahl,* an eighteenth-century Swedish botanist.]

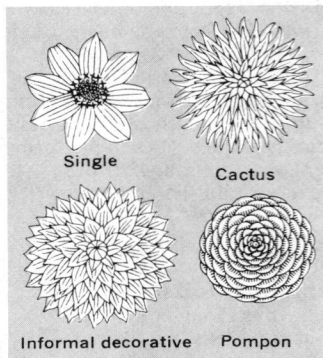

Single Cactus

Informal decorative Pompon

Dahlias

Da·ho·mey (də hō′mē) *n.* a country in western Africa. Capital, Porto-Novo. Area, 44,713 sq. mi. It is now called **Benin.** —**Da·ho′man,** *adj., n.*

dai·ly (dā′lē) *adj.* appearing, done, or happening every day or every weekday: *a daily newspaper, a daily routine, daily pay.* —*n. pl.,* **dai·lies.** a newspaper published every day or every weekday. —*adv.* day after day; every day: *That newspaper column is published daily.*

dain·ty (dān′tē) *adj.,* **dain·ti·er, dain·ti·est. 1.** delicately beautiful or graceful: *a dainty porcelain vase.* **2.** having delicate tastes or fussy habits; refined: *She is a dainty eater.* **3.** pleasing to the taste; delicious: *dainty cakes.* —*n. pl.,* **dain·ties.** a delicious bit of food; delicacy. —**dain′ti·ly,** *adv.* —**dain′ti·ness,** *n.*

Dai·ren (dī′ren′) *n.* a city in southern Manchuria, part of the municipality of Lüda. Pop. (1965 est.), 600,000.

dair·y (der′ē) *n. pl.,* **dair·ies. 1.** a room or building where milk and milk products are made and stored. **2.** a store or company that sells milk and milk products. **3.** see **dairy farm.**

dairy cattle, cows bred and raised especially for milk production.

dairy farm, a farm where dairy cattle are raised and milk and milk products are produced.

dair·y·maid (der′ē mād′) *n.* a girl or woman who works in a dairy; milkmaid.

da·is (dā′is, dās) *n. pl.,* **da·is·es** (dā′ə sēz). a slightly raised platform, as for a throne, speaker's desk, or seats for guests of honor.

dai·sy (dā′zē) *n. pl.,* **dai·sies. 1.** a flower having pink or white petals surrounding a yellow center. **2.** the plant bearing this flower.

Da·kar (dä kär′) *n.* the capital and largest city of Senegal. Pop. (1970 est.), 581,000.

Da·ko·ta (də kō′tə) *n.* **1.** a former territory of the United States, made up of what is now North Dakota and South Dakota. **2. the Dakotas.** North Dakota and South Dakota. **3.** a member of a Siouan tribe of North American Indians formerly living on the Great Plains. Also, **Sioux. 4.** the language of this tribe. —**Da·ko′tan,** *adj., n.*

Da·lai La·ma (dä lī′ lä′mə) the spiritual and political leader of the Buddhists of Tibet.

dale (dāl) *n.* a small valley.

Dal·las (dal′əs) *n.* a city in northeastern Texas. Pop. (1970), 844,401.

dal·li·ance (dal′ē əns) *n.* **1.** the act of wasting time; delaying. **2.** a flirtation or trifling.

dal·ly (dal′ē) *v.,* **dal·lied, dal·ly·ing.** —*v.i.* **1.** to waste time; linger; delay: *If she dallies any longer, we will miss the bus.* **2.** to flirt or play; trifle: *to dally with danger.* —*v.t.* to waste (time): *He dallied away the entire morning.*

Dal·ma·tia (dal mā′shə) *n.* a region in western Yugoslavia, on the coast of the Adriatic Sea.

Dalmatian

Dal·ma·tian (dal mā′shən) *n.* **1.** a large dog of a breed believed to have been developed in Dalmatia, having a short-haired white coat speckled with small black or brown spots. **2.** a person who was born or is living in Dalmatia. —*adj.* of or relating to Dalmatia or its people.

dam¹ (dam) *n.* **1.** a structure made of concrete, earth, or other material, built across a stream or river to hold back flowing water. **2.** the body of water held back by a dam. —*v.t.,* **dammed, dam·ming. 1.** to hold back by a dam; furnish with a dam: *to dam a river.* **2.** to hold or keep back; restrain: *The boy tried to dam up his anger.* [Of Germanic origin.]

dam² (dam) *n.* the female parent of a four-footed animal, such as a horse or cow. [A form of *dame.*]

Dam¹

dam·age (dam′ij) *n.* **1.** harm or injury that causes loss: *The tornado caused great damage to the farms in the area.* **2. damages.** *Law.* the money claimed or allowed as payment to make up for injury or loss. —*v.t.,* **dam·aged, dam·ag·ing.** to cause damage to; harm or injure: *to damage a car, to damage a person's reputation.*

Da·mas·cus (də mas′kəs) *n.* the capital and largest city of Syria, one of the oldest cities in the world. Pop. (1970), 836,179.

Damascus steel, a tough steel whose surface is decorated with a wavy pattern, originally made at Damascus. Damascus steel was used for sword blades during the Middle Ages.

dam·ask (dam′əsk) *n.* **1.** a reversible cloth made of various fibers woven with elaborate patterns or designs, used especially for tablecloths and napkins. **2.** another word for **Damascus steel. 3.** a deep pink or rose color. —*adj.* **1.** made of or resembling damask. **2.** having the color damask.

dame (dām) *n.* **1.** *British.* **a.** a woman having an honorary rank corresponding to that of a knight. **b.** the wife or widow of a knight or baronet. **2.** formerly, a woman of rank, position, or authority; lady. **3.** an elderly woman. **4.** *Slang.* any woman or girl.

damn (dam) *v.t.* **1.** to declare (something) to be bad, worthless, or a failure: *The critics damned the play.* **2.** to curse or swear at. **3.** to condemn to eternal punishment in hell. —*n.* the saying of "damn" as an expression of anger, annoyance, or disappointment. —*adv. Informal.* very. —*interj.* an expression of anger, annoyance, or disappointment.

dam·na·ble (dam′nə bəl) *adj.* deserving to be damned; outrageous; detestable. —**dam′na·bly,** *adv.*

dam·na·tion (dam nā′shən) *n.* **1.** the act of damning or the state of being damned. **2.** condemnation to eternal punishment in hell. —*interj.* damn.

damned (damd) *adj.* **1.** condemned as bad, worthless, or a failure. **2.** condemned to eternal punishment in hell. —*adv. Informal.* very.

Dam·o·cles (dam′ə klēz′) *n. Greek Legend.* a courtier of the king of Syracuse, who praised the happiness of kings. The king showed Damocles the dangers of wealth and power by inviting him to a magnificent feast which Damocles enjoyed until he saw a sword suspended above his head by a single hair.

Da·mon (dā′mən) *n. Roman Legend.* a Greek youth who pledged his life for his friend Pythias, who had been condemned to death.

damp (damp) *adj.* slightly wet; moist: *a damp cloth, a damp cellar, damp weather.* —*n.* **1.** moisture; humidity: *The damp made the walls peel.* **2.** something that checks, discourages, or saddens; damper. **3.** a harmful gas found especially in mines. —*v.t.* **1.** to make damp; dampen. **2.** to lessen in force or strength; check: *to damp a fire, to damp one's spirits.* —**damp′ly,** *adv.* —**damp′ness,** *n.*

damp·en (dam′pən) *v.t.* **1.** to make damp; moisten. **2.** to lessen the force or strength of; check; depress: *The bad weather dampened our enthusiam over the picnic.* —*v.i.* to become damp. —**damp′en·er,** *n.*

damp·er (dam′pər) *n.* **1.** a person or thing that checks, discourages, or saddens: *Lack of money put a damper on our vacation plans.* **2.** a movable plate used to control the draft in a fireplace, stove, or furnace. **3.** a device for deadening vibration, especially of piano strings.

dam·sel (dam′zəl) *n.* a young girl; maiden.

damsel fly, a brightly colored insect that closely resembles the dragonfly, having a slender body and four wings folded over its back when at rest.

dam·son (dam′zən) *n.* **1.** a small, round, dark purple fruit of a plum tree, having a tart flavor and used mainly in preserves. **2.** the tree bearing this fruit.

Damsel fly

Dan (dan) *n.* in the Bible: **a.** a tribe of Israel that settled in northern Palestine. **b.** the northernmost city of Palestine. It is now a village in northeastern Israel.

Da·na, Richard Henry (dā′nə) 1815–1882, U.S. author.

dance (dans) *v.,* **danced, danc·ing.** —*v.i.* **1.** to move the body or feet rhythmically, usually in time to music. **2.** to move about in a lively or excited way; leap about: *The presents made the little girl dance with joy.* **3.** to move or bob up and down: *The sunlight danced on the water's surface.* —*v.t.* **1.** to perform or take part in (a dance): *to dance the polka.* **2.** to cause to dance: *The bride's father*

danced her around the room. —*n.* **1.** a definite series of rhythmical steps or movements, usually done to music: *The waltz is a well-known dance.* **2.** the act or instance of dancing. **3.** *also,* **the dance.** the art of dancing: *to study the dance.* **4.** a social gathering for dancing: *There will be a dance Friday night at the high school.* **5.** one round of dancing: *He was her partner for the last dance.* **6.** a piece of music written for dancing.

danc·er (dan′sər) *n.* a person who dances, especially a person whose profession is dancing.

dan·de·li·on (dand′əl ī′ən) *n.* **1.** a yellow flower of any of a group of plants. **2.** the plant bearing this flower, having a cluster of long, jagged leaves around the base of a hollow stalk. The leaves may be eaten in salads or cooked as a vegetable. [French *dent de lion* literally, tooth of the lion; from the toothlike shape of its leaves.]

dan·der (dan′dər) *n. Informal.* temper; anger.
to get one's dander up. to make or become angry.

dan·dle (dand′əl) *v.t.,* **dan·dled, dan·dling. 1.** to move (someone) up and down on one's knees or in one's arms: *She dandled the baby on her knee.* **2.** to fondle; pamper; pet. —**dan′dler,** *n.*

dan·druff (dan′drəf) *n.* small, white or grayish scales of dead skin shed from the scalp.

dan·dy (dan′dē) *n. pl.,* **dan·dies. 1.** a man who is too fussy or concerned about the elegance of his clothes and appearance; fop. **2.** *Informal.* something very good. —*adj.,* **dan·di·er, dan·di·est.** *Informal.* very good; excellent.

Dane (dān) *n.* a person who was born or is living in Denmark.

dan·ger (dān′jər) *n.* **1.** the chance or risk of harm, injury, evil, or loss; peril: *The children knew the danger in skating on the thin ice.* **2.** an instance or cause of harm, risk, or peril: *Narrow, winding roads are a danger to drivers.*

dan·ger·ous (dān′jər əs) *adj.* **1.** full of danger; risky; hazardous: *Driving too fast is dangerous.* **2.** likely to cause harm: *A tiger can be a dangerous animal.* —**dan′ger·ous·ly,** *adv.* —**dan′ger·ous·ness,** *n.*

dan·gle (dang′gəl) *v.,* **dan·gled, dan·gling.** —*v.i.* **1.** to hang or swing loosely: *Tinsel dangled from the Christmas tree.* **2.** to follow longingly or closely: *Many men dangled after the beautiful girl.* —*v.t.* to make (something) hang or swing loosely: *He dangled his feet over the side of the pool.* —**dan′gler,** *n.*

dangling participle, a participle that does not clearly relate to the word it is supposed to modify. In the sentence *After working all morning cleaning the yard, lunch was brought out to us, working* is a dangling participle because it does not modify the word *lunch.*

Dan·iel (dan′yəl) *n.* **1.** in the Bible, a Hebrew prophet who was held captive in Babylon and whose faith in God saved him from death in the lions' den. **2.** a book of the Old Testament containing the story of Daniel and his prophecies.

Dan·ish (dā′nish) *adj.* of or relating to Denmark, its people, or their language. —*n.* the language of Denmark.

dank (dangk) *adj.* disagreeably damp; moist and cold: *a dank basement.* —**dank′ly,** *adv.* —**dank′ness,** *n.*

Dan·te (dan′tē, dän′tā) 1265–1321, Italian poet.

at; āpe; cär; end; mē; it; īce; hot; ōld; fôrk; wood; fōōl; oil; out; up; turn; sing; thin; this; hw in white; zh in treasure. The symbol ə stands for the sound of a in about, e in taken, i in pencil, o in lemon, and u in circus.

Dan·ube (dan'yoōb) *n.* a river in Europe, flowing eastward from southern West Germany to the Black Sea.

Dan·zig (dan'sig) *n.* see **Gdansk**.

Daph·ne (daf'nē) *n.* *Greek Mythology.* a nymph who escaped from her pursuer, Apollo, by being changed into a laurel tree.

dap·per (dap'ər) *adj.* fashionable and attractive in dress or appearance; neat; trim.

dap·ple (dap'əl) *adj.* having spots; spotted: *a dapple horse.* Also, **dap·pled** (dap'əld). —*n.* **1.** a spot or dot, as on an animal's skin or coat. **2.** an animal having a spotted coat. —*v.,* **dap·pled, dap·pling.** —*v.t.* to mark with spots: *Sunlight dappled the lawn.* —*v.i.* to become marked with spots.

Dar·da·nelles (därd'ən elz') *n.* the narrow strait between European Turkey and Asian Turkey, connecting the Aegean Sea with the Sea of Marmara. In ancient times it was known as the Hellespont.

dare (der) *v.,* **dared** or (*archaic*) **durst, dar·ing.** —*v.t.* **1.** to challenge (someone) to do something, especially as proof of courage or ability: *Bill dared Dick to dive off the high board.* **2.** to be bold enough to try; have courage for: *to dare to climb a mountain.* **3.** to meet boldly and defiantly: *He dared the elements by sailing through the storm.* —*v.i.* to have enough boldness or courage to do or try something: *No one dared to skate on the thin ice.* —*n.* a challenge: *She took my dare and rode the horse bareback.* —**dar'er,** *n.*

I dare say. I suppose or believe; I have no doubt.

dare·dev·il (der'dev'əl) *n.* a reckless, daring person. —*adj.* reckless; rash: *The acrobats performed daredevil stunts.*

Dar es Sa·laam (där' es sə läm') the capital and largest city of Tanzania. Pop. (1970 est.), 344,900.

dar·ing (der'ing) *n.* adventurous courage; boldness. —*adj.* courageous and adventurous; fearless: *The soldier received a medal for his daring attempt to save his friend's life.* —**dar'ing·ly,** *adv.*

Da·ri·us I (də rī'əs) 549?–485? B.C., the king of Persia from 521 to 485. Also, **Darius the Great.**

dark (därk) *adj.* **1.** having little or no light: *a dark night, a dark room.* **2.** not light-colored: *a dark complexion, dark hair, a dark blue.* **3.** gloomy; cheerless; dismal: *She always looks on the dark side of things.* **4.** hidden from view or knowledge; secret; mysterious: *The rebels kept their plot dark.* **5.** evil; wicked; heinous: *dark deeds.* —*n.* **1.** a partial or total absence of light: *The child was afraid of the dark.* **2.** night; nightfall: *The thieves crept away after dark.* **3.** a dark color or shade: *There are many lights and darks in that painting.* —**dark'ly,** *adv.* —**dark'ness,** *n.*

in the dark. **a.** hidden or secret: *The senator kept his political plans in the dark.* **b.** in a state of ignorance; uninformed: *We were in the dark about his schemes.*

Dark Ages also, **dark ages.** the period in European history from about A.D. 476 to about A.D. 1000, between the fall of the Western Roman Empire and the rise of the Middle Ages. It was thought of as a time when learning and culture were neglected and civilization did not advance.

dark·en (där'kən) *v.t.* to make or become dark or darker: *Storm clouds darkened the sky.* —**dark'en·er,** *n.*

dark horse **1.** an unexpected winner in a horse race, about whom little is known and whose chances of winning had been considered small. **2.** a person who unexpectedly receives a nomination for political office.

dark·ish (där'kish) *adj.* somewhat dark.

dark·ling (därk'ling) *adv.* in the dark. —*adj.* dark; dim; obscure: *We are here as on a darkling plain* (Matthew Arnold). ▲ used in literature.

dark·room (därk'rōom', därk'room') *n.* a room in which photographs are developed, arranged so that all outside light is kept out.

dar·ling (där'ling) *n.* **1.** a person who is very dear or much loved. **2.** a favorite: *That actress was once the darling of movie audiences.* —*adj.* **1.** dearly loved; cherished. **2.** *Informal.* charmingly attractive; cute: *What a darling dress!*

darn¹ (därn) *v.t.* to mend by weaving stitches across the hole: *to darn the toe of a sock.* —*n.* a place mended by darning. [Of uncertain origin.]

darn² (därn) *Informal.* another word for **damn.**

darning needle **1.** a long needle with a large eye, used for darning. **2.** another term for **dragonfly.**

dart (därt) *n.* **1.** a long, slender, pointed object resembling an arrow, used in playing certain games. **2. darts.** a game in which these objects are thrown at a target. **3.** a slender, pointed weapon to be thrown by hand or shot from a blowgun. **4.** a sudden, swift movement. **5.** a tapered tuck sewn in a garment to give it a better fit. —*v.i.* to spring or move suddenly and swiftly: *The rabbit darted from the bushes.* —*v.t.* **1.** to throw or move suddenly and rapidly: *The lizard darted its tongue at the insect.* **2.** to send suddenly: *She darted an angry look at her friend.*

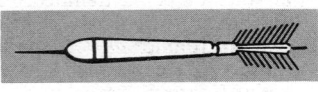

Dart

Dar·win, Charles (där'win) 1809–1882, English naturalist and pioneer in the study of evolution.

dash (dash) *v.i.* **1.** to move with speed; rush: *The dog dashed after the rabbit.* **2.** to strike or hit with violence; smash: *Waves dashed against the ship.* —*v.t.* **1.** to strike violently against: *The waves dashed the shore.* **2.** to shatter or break with force or violence; smash: *The storm dashed the ship against the rocks.* **3.** to splash; spatter: *The boys dashed each other with water.* **4.** to ruin or destroy: *The bad news dashed her hopes.* —*n. pl.,* **dash·es. 1.** a sudden rush or movement: *The hikers made a dash for cover when the rain started.* **2.** a small amount added or mixed in: *Add another dash of salt to the stew.* **3.** a short race that is run or swum at top speed: *the 50-yard dash.* **4.** spirited energy and style: *That young actor has dash.* **5.** a short horizontal line (—) used in writing or printing, as for showing a pause or break in a sentence or indicating that something has been left out. **6.** *Telegraphy.* a long signal used with a shorter one to represent numbers or letters, as in Morse code. **7.** see **dashboard.**

to dash off. a. to hurry away; leave quickly. **b.** to make, write, or complete quickly or hastily: *He dashed off a letter to his friend.*

dash·board (dash'bôrd') *n.* a panel equipped with instruments and gauges, located in front of the driver in an automobile or similar vehicle.

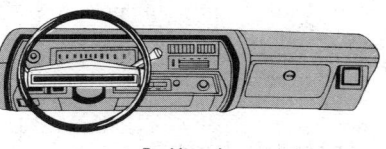

Dashboard

dash·ing (dash'ing) *adj.* **1.** courageous and spirited: *the dashing young hero of a movie.* **2.** showy; stylish: *dashing costumes.* —**dash'ing·ly,** *adv.*

das·tard (das'tərd) *n.* a mean, base coward. —*adj.* see **dastardly.**

das·tard·ly (das'tərd lē) *adj.* mean and cowardly; sneaking. —**das'tard·li·ness,** *n.*

da·ta (dā'tə, dat'ə) *n.,pl. sing.,* **da·tum.** information from which conclusions can be drawn; facts and figures.

▲ used with either a singular or plural verb: *The data indicate that our theory is wrong. The data for our science project has been collected.*

data processing, the rapid organization and analysis of large amounts of information by computers or other machines.

date¹ (dāt) *n.* **1.** a day of the month or year: *Today's date is January 21.* **2.** a specific point or period of time when something happened or is to happen: *The date of her birth is April 3, 1945. The date for the party is June 12.* **3.** an inscription stating when something was written or made: *The cornerstone of the building bears the date 1954.* **4.** *Informal.* an appointment or social engagement for a specified time or place: *The friends made a date for next Tuesday.* **5.** *Informal.* a person of the opposite sex with whom such an appointment or engagement is made: *John picked up his date for the party at seven o'clock* —*v.*, **dat·ed, dat·ing.** —*v.t.* **1.** to furnish or mark with a date: *The secretary dated the letter.* **2.** to determine or fix the time of; give a date to: *Archaeologists dated the statue after much study.* **3.** *Informal.* to go on a date with (someone): *She is dating my brother.* —*v.i.* **1.** to belong to, or come from, a particular time or era: *This custom dates from the seventeenth century.* **2.** to have appointments or engagements with members of the opposite sex. [Old French *date* a specific point of time, going back to Latin *data;* from the expression used to date a letter in ancient Rome: *(epistola) data Romae* (letter) given or written in Rome.]

out of date. no longer in fashion or use; unfashionable: *The old woman's dress was out of date.*

to date. up to and including the present time.

up to date. a. according to the latest style or thought; modern. **b.** including the newest facts or information: *Samuel kept his diary up to date by writing in it each night.*

date² (dāt) *n.* **1.** the oval fruit of the date palm, having thick, sweet flesh that can be eaten. **2.** see **date palm.** [Old French *date* this fruit.]

dat·ed (dā'tid) *adj.* **1.** marked with a date: *a dated letter.* **2.** old-fashioned: *The clothes in that old movie are dated.*

date·less (dāt'lis) *adj.* **1.** without a date; bearing no date: *The letter was dateless.* **2.** having no limit or end: *the dateless beauty of an ancient Greek statue.*

date·line (dāt'līn') *n.* a line in a piece of printed material, such as an article or newspaper, that gives its date and place of origin.

date line, see **International Date Line.**

date palm, a tall, tropical tree related to the palm, having a straight, shaggy trunk topped with divided leaves and bearing thick clusters of fruit.

da·tive (dā'tiv) *n.* **1.** the grammatical case in Latin, Russian, and certain other languages that indicates the indirect object of a verb. **2.** a word in this case. —*adj.* of or belonging to the dative.

da·tum (dā'təm, dat'əm) *n. pl.,* **da·ta.** a known or assumed fact from which a conclusion can be made.

daub (dôb) *v.t.* **1.** to coat, cover, or smear with a soft substance, such as grease or clay: *to daub the cracks in a wall with plaster.* **2.** to spread (a soft adhesive substance) on or over a surface: *to daub paint on a canvas.* **3.** to paint (something) crudely or poorly. —*v.i.* to paint coarsely or poorly. —*n.* **1.** a smear or smudge; spot: *The boys had daubs of dirt on their legs.* **2.** a substance used for daubing, such as plaster or clay. **3.** a crudely painted picture.

daugh·ter (dô'tər) *n.* **1.** a female child, considered in relation to one or both of her parents. **2.** any female descendant. **3.** a female considered in relation to something, as a child is related to a parent: *She is a daughter of Scotland.*

daugh·ter-in-law (dô'tər in lô') *n. pl.,* **daugh·ters-in-law.** the wife of one's son.

daugh·ter·ly (dô'tər lē) *adj.* of, relating to, or proper for a daughter: *daughterly affection.*

daunt (dônt) *v.t.* to frighten or dishearten: *The explorer was not daunted by the dangers of the voyage.*

daunt·less (dônt'lis) *adj.* having no fear; courageous; daring. —**daunt'less·ly,** *adv.* —**daunt'less·ness,** *n.*

dau·phin (dô'fin) *n.* the oldest son of a king of France, used as a title from 1349 to 1830.

dav·en·port (dav'ən pôrt') *n.* **1.** a large upholstered sofa, especially one that converts into a bed. **2.** a writing desk or table, often with drawers.

Dav·en·port (dav'ən pôrt') *n.* a city in eastern Iowa. Pop. (1970), 98,469.

Da·vid (dā'vid) 1040?–970? B.C., the second king of Judah and Israel, from about 1010 to about 970 B.C. He was the successor to Saul and the father of Solomon.

da Vinci, Leonardo, see **Leonardo da Vinci.**

Da·vis, Jefferson (dā'vis) 1808–1889, the president of the Confederate States of America.

dav·it (dav'it, dā'vit) *n.* **1.** one of a pair of movable or curved arms that can project over the stern or side of a boat or ship, used especially for raising or lowering a small boat. **2.** a similar device used for raising or lowering the anchor of a ship.

Da·vy Jones (dā'vē jōnz') the spirit of the sea; the sailor's devil.

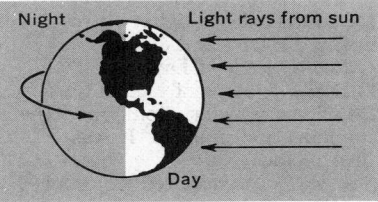

Davits

Davy Jones's locker, the bottom of the ocean, especially as the grave of those who drown at sea.

daw (dô) *n.* see **jackdaw.**

daw·dle (dôd'əl) *v.,* **daw·dled, daw·dling.** —*v.i.* to waste time; linger: *The child dawdled over his breakfast.* —*v.t.* to waste (time); idle: *to dawdle the afternoon away.* —**daw'dler,** *n.*

dawn (dôn) *n.* **1.** the first appearance of light in the morning; daybreak. **2.** the beginning or first appearance: *the dawn of a new era, the dawn of civilization.* —*v.i.* **1.** to begin to grow light in the morning; to become day. **2.** to begin to be clear, understood, or perceived: *It suddenly dawned on him that he was being tricked.* **3.** to begin to appear, develop, or open: *The space age dawned in the twentieth century.*

day (dā) *n.* **1.** the period of light between the rising and setting of the sun: *In the Northern Hemisphere, June 21 is the longest day of the year.* **2.** the light of day; daylight. **3.** the length of time required for the earth to complete one rotation on its axis, approximately 24 hours. **4.** the length of time

Day and night

at; āpe; cär; end; mē; it; īce; hot; ōld; fôrk; wood; fŏŏl; oil; out; up; turn; sing; thin; this; hw in white; zh in treasure. The symbol ə stands for the sound of **a** in about, **e** in taken, **i** in pencil, **o** in lemon, and **u** in circus.

required by any heavenly body to complete one rotation on its axis. **5.** the part of a day passed in a particular way or place: *a school day.* **6.** the hours of a day devoted to work. **7.** *also,* **Day.** a specific period of 24 hours set aside for a particular purpose: *Tomorrow is her wedding day. November 7 is Election Day this year.* **8.** a period of existence, success, or influence: *Knighthood has had its day.* **9.** *also,* **days.** a particular time or period; era: *Television had not been invented in the days when my grandfather was a boy.*

day·break (dā′brāk′) *n.* the time each morning when daylight first appears; dawn.

day care center, another term for **day nursery.**

day·dream (dā′drēm′) *n.* a fanciful, dreamy imagining: *She had a daydream of being a movie star.* —*v.i.* to have daydreams. —**day′dream′er,** *n.*

day·light (dā′līt′) *n.* **1.** the light of day: *During the morning the room was filled with daylight.* **2.** the daytime. **3.** the dawn; daybreak: *The farmer was up doing his chores before daylight.* **4.** public view: *The reporter brought the matter out into the daylight.* **5. daylights.** *Informal.* wits; sense: *That horror movie scared the daylights out of me.*

day·light-sav·ing time (dā′līt′sā′ving) a system of time in which clocks are set one or more hours ahead of standard time. It is used especially during summer months to provide more hours of daylight at the end of the working day.

day nursery, a nursery for the care of small children during the day, especially those of mothers who work. Also, **day care center.**

Day of Atonement, another term for **Yom Kippur.**

day school 1. a school that holds classes only during the day. **2.** a private school whose students live at home.

day·time (dā′tīm′) *n.* the period of time between the rising and setting of the sun.

Day·ton (dāt′ən) *n.* a city in southwestern Ohio. Pop. (1970), 243,601.

daze (dāz) *v.t.,* **dazed, daz·ing.** to stun or confuse, as by a blow; bewilder: *His opponent's punch dazed the boxer.* —*n.* a dazed state or condition: *The accident left him in a daze.*

daz·zle (daz′əl) *v.t.,* **daz·zled, daz·zling. 1.** to dim the vision of or make almost blind with too much light: *The bright morning sun dazzled him.* **2.** to overpower or impress, as by brilliance, splendor, or the like: *The quarterback's outstanding play dazzled the fans.* —*n.* the act of dazzling or the state of being dazzled. —**daz′zler,** *n.* —**daz′zling·ly,** *adv.*

DC, D.C., d.c., direct current.

D.C., District of Columbia.

D.D., Doctor of Divinity.

D.D.S., Doctor of Dental Surgery.

DDT, a powdery compound that is very poisonous to humans and animals. It was formerly much used as an insecticide.

de- *prefix* **1.** removed from; away; off: *defrost, dethrone.* **2.** down: *devalue, degrade.* **3.** to do the opposite of, reverse, or undo: *decode, decompose.* **4.** thoroughly; completely: *despoil.*

dea·con (dē′kən) *n.* **1.** in certain Christian churches, a clergyman or layman who assists the priest or minister. **2.** a clergyman ranking next below a priest.

dea·con·ess (dē′kə nis) *n. pl.,* **dea·con·ess·es.** a woman who is a church assistant.

dead (ded) *adj.* **1.** no longer living; having died; lifeless: *A dead plant cannot bloom.* **2.** like death; still: *a dead sleep.* **3.** not having life; inanimate: *Minerals are dead matter.* **4.** lacking power, force, usefulness, or interest: *a dead law,*

a dead tennis ball. **5.** no longer active, working, or in use: *a dead volcano, a dead language. The telephone is dead.* **6.** complete; absolute: *a dead silence.* **7.** without error; sure; certain: *a dead shot.* **8.** exact; direct: *He hit the target at dead center.* **9.** *Informal.* very tired; exhausted. —*adv.* **1.** completely; absolutely; entirely: *The hikers were dead tired. You are dead right.* **2.** directly; straight: *The exit from the highway is dead ahead.* —*n.* **1.** dead persons as a group: *We here highly resolve that these dead shall not have died in vain* (Abraham Lincoln). **2.** the time of greatest intensity, as of coldness, darkness, or quiet: *the dead of night, the dead of winter.* —**dead′ness,** *n.*

dead·beat (ded′bēt′) *n. Slang.* **1.** a person who avoids paying his bills. **2.** an idle person; loafer.

dead·en (ded′ən) *v.t.* **1.** to make less active, forceful, or intense; weaken: *to deaden sound, to deaden pain.* **2.** to make less sensitive; numb; dull: *The dentist used a drug to deaden the nerve of the tooth.*

dead-end (ded′end′) *adj.* being a dead end: *a dead-end street.*

dead end 1. a street, alley, or passage closed at one end. **2.** a situation or point from which no progress can be made: *The negotiations had reached a dead end.*

dead heat, a race in which two or more competitors tie.

dead letter 1. a letter that is unclaimed or cannot be delivered, especially because of a wrong address. **2.** something that is not as important as it once was.

dead·line (ded′līn′) *n.* a set time by which something must be completed; time limit: *The deadline for the first edition of the newspaper was five o'clock in the morning.*

dead·lock (ded′lok′) *n.* a standstill that results when two opposing sides are of equal strength and are unable to reach an agreement. —*v.t., v.i.* to bring or come to a deadlock.

dead·ly (ded′lē) *adj., dead·li·er, dead·li·est.* **1.** causing or tending to cause death; fatal: *a deadly blow, a deadly poison.* **2.** aiming or intending to kill or destroy; mortal: *deadly enemies.* **3.** extremely effective or dangerous: *The soldier took deadly aim.* **4.** like death: *His skin has a deadly pallor.* **5.** very great; extreme: *a deadly silence.* —*adv.* **1.** in a manner resembling death: *His face was deadly pale.* **2.** *Informal.* very; extremely: *deadly serious.* —**dead′li·ness,** *n.*

deadly nightshade, see **belladonna** *(def. 1).*

dead·pan (ded′pan′) *adj. Informal.* showing or expressing no emotion: *a deadpan comedian, a deadpan remark.*

dead pan *Informal.* a face that shows no emotion.

dead reckoning, the calculation of the position of a boat, ship, or aircraft, by using the records of its speed and last known position and the compass readings of the course steered.

Dead Sea, a salt lake between Israel and Jordan.

Dead Sea Scrolls, ancient manuscripts, dating from 100 B.C. to A.D. 100, found in caves near the western shore of the Dead Sea. The Dead Sea Scrolls contain parts of almost all the books of the Old Testament.

dead weight 1. a heavy, oppressive weight, as of a lifeless body or thing. **2.** a heavy or oppressive burden: *The man struggled under the dead weight of debt.* **3.** the weight of a ship, truck, or other means of transportation when not loaded.

dead·wood (ded′wood′) *n.* **1.** the dead portion of a woody plant. **2.** a person or thing that has little or no use or value.

deaf (def) *adj.* **1.** wholly or partly unable to hear. **2.** unwilling to hear or listen; heedless: *He was deaf to their pleas for help.* —**deaf′ly,** *adv.* —**deaf′ness,** *n.*

deaf·en (def′ən) *v.t.* **1.** to make deaf. **2.** to stun or overwhelm with noise: *The noise in the factory deafened us.*

deaf-mute (def′myo͞ot′) *n.* a person who cannot hear or speak.

deal (dēl) *v.,* **dealt, deal·ing.** —*v.i.* **1.** to be engaged or concerned; have to do: *This book deals with dogs.* **2.** to act or behave: *The police dealt roughly with the rioters.* **3.** to take action; consider: *I will deal with the problem right away.* **4.** to do business; trade: *That store deals in antiques.* **5.** to give out cards to the players of a card game: *It's your turn to deal.* —*v.t.* **1.** to give out (cards) to the players of a card game: *He dealt seven cards to each player.* **2.** to give to a person as a share; distribute: *She dealt out cookies to the children.* **3.** to give or deliver: *The fighter dealt his opponent a heavy blow.* —*n.* **1.** *Informal.* a transaction or arrangement, especially in business: *My uncle made a deal to sell his house.* **2.** a bargain: *He got a good deal on that used car.* **3.** *Informal.* a treatment: *to get a fair deal.* **4.** the act of giving out cards to the players of a card game.
  a great deal or **a good deal. a.** a large amount or quantity: *She spent a good deal of time writing that letter.* **b.** to a great extent or degree; very much: *She travels a great deal.*

deal·er (dē′lər) *n.* **1.** a person who buys or sells something: *an antique dealer.* **2.** a person who gives out the cards in a card game.

deal·ing (dē′ling) *n.* **1.** a way of acting. **2. dealings.** relations, transactions, or communications with others, especially in business: *The storekeeper was always honest in his dealings.*

dealt (delt) the past tense and past participle of **deal**[1].

dean (dēn) *n.* **1.** a person at a college or university who is in charge of the discipline, activities, studies, and guidance of the students: *the academic dean, the dean of women.* **2.** the head of a faculty or division of a school, college, or university: *the dean of a law school.* **3.** the chief official of a cathedral. **4.** a person who has been a member the longest, as of an association or group: *He is the dean of American sports writers.*

dear (dēr) *adj.* **1.** greatly loved; beloved: *a dear friend.* **2.** highly esteemed. ▲ used as a form of address in letters: *Dear Sir.* **3.** high-priced; costly; expensive: *Mother would buy that dress if it weren't so dear.* —*n.* a beloved person; darling. —*adv.* **1.** affectionately; fondly: *She held him very dear.* **2.** at a high price. —*interj.* an exclamation of emotion, as surprise or distress. —**dear′ly,** *adv.* —**dear′ness,** *n.*

Dear·born (dēr′bərn, dēr′bôrn) *n.* a city in southeastern Michigan, near Detroit. Pop. (1970), 104,199.

dearth (durth) *n.* a scant supply; scarcity; lack: *a dearth of food, a dearth of information.*

dear·y (dēr′ē) *also,* **dear·ie.** *n. pl.,* **dear·ies.** *Informal.* dear one; darling.

death (deth) *n.* **1.** the permanent stop of all vital functions in a plant or animal; the end of life; dying. **2.** the state or condition of being dead. **3.** the ending or destruction of anything; extinction: *the death of the Holy Roman Empire, the death of silent movies.* **4.** the cause of dying: *Financial worries will be the death of him.*
  at death's door. close to death; dying.
  to put to death. to kill or execute.
  to death. to the extreme; excessively: *The sudden clap of thunder scared her to death.*

death·bed (deth′bed′) *n.* **1.** the bed on which a person dies. **2.** the last hours of life.

death·blow (deth′blō′) *n.* **1.** a blow that causes death. **2.** something that causes the end or destruction of something: *The eruption of the volcano was the deathblow to the small village.*

death·less (deth′lis) *adj.* never dying; immortal; eternal:
the deathless writings of Shakespeare. —**death′less·ness,** *n.*

death·like (deth′līk′) *adj.* characteristic of or like death.

death·ly (deth′lē) *adj.* **1.** characteristic of or like death: *a deathly pallor.* **2.** causing death; deadly: *a deathly blow.* —*adv.* **1.** in a deathlike manner. **2.** extremely; very: *The girl was deathly afraid of snakes.*

death rate, the proportion of the number of deaths to the total number of people in a given area, usually stated in terms of the number of deaths per thousand people per year.

death's-head (deths′hed′) *n.* the human skull, or a figure representing it, used to symbolize death.

Death Valley, a deep desert basin in southeastern California. Death Valley is the hottest and driest place in the United States and contains the lowest point in the Western Hemisphere.

de·ba·cle (di bä′kəl, di bak′əl) *n.* a sudden and complete downfall or collapse; rout; ruin: *The last battle was a great debacle and the army was forced to surrender.*

de·bar (di bär′) *v.t.,* **de·barred, de·bar·ring.** to shut out; exclude; prohibit; bar: *A person who is not a citizen is debarred from voting.* —**de·bar′ment,** *n.*

de·bark (di bärk′) *v.i.* to land; disembark: *The passengers debarked in New York.* —*v.t.* to unload from a ship or airplane: *to debark cargo.* —**de·bar·ka·tion** (dē bär kā′-shən), *n.*

de·base (di bās′) *v.t.,* **de·based, de·bas·ing.** to lower in quality, value, or character: *to debase coinage, to debase oneself by lying.* —**de·base′ment,** *n.*

de·bat·a·ble (di bā′tə bəl) *adj.* open to discussion or dispute; that can be debated: *The merits of his plan are debatable.*

de·bate (di bāt′) *n.* **1.** a discussion or argument; dispute: *There was much debate about the new tax law.* **2.** a formal discussion of the arguments for and against a question or issue, especially a public contest in which two people or teams argue opposite sides of a given topic. —*v.,* **de·bat·ed, de·bat·ing.** —*v.t.* **1.** to argue about or discuss, as at a public meeting: *The two candidates debated the issue of controlling crime in big cities.* **2.** to think about; consider: *They debated whether or not they would go to the movies.* —*v.i.* **1.** to discuss or argue a matter. **2.** to consider: *to debate about buying a new car.* —**de·bat′er,** *n.*

de·bauch (di bôch′) *v.t.* to lead away from morality; corrupt; deprave. —*v.i.* to indulge in too much eating, drinking, or revelry; dissipate. —*n.* **1.** another word for **debauchery.** **2.** an instance of debauching: *The party turned into a drunken debauch.* —**de·bauch′er,** *n.*

de·bauch·er·y (di bô′chər ē) *n. pl.,* **de·bauch·er·ies.** too much indulgence in eating, drinking, or revelry.

de·bil·i·tate (di bil′ə tāt′) *v.t.,* **de·bil·i·tat·ed, de·bil·i·tat·ing.** to lessen the strength or vitality of; weaken: *The disease debilitated him.* —**de·bil′i·ta′tion,** *n.*

de·bil·i·ty (di bil′ə tē) *n. pl.,* **de·bil·i·ties.** lack of strength or vigor; feebleness.

deb·it (deb′it) *n.* **1.** the entry of a debt in an account. **2.** an item entered in an account as a debt. **3.** the left-hand side or column of an account where such entries are recorded. —*v.t.* **1.** to enter (a debt) in an account. **2.** to charge with a debt: *to debit an account with $300.*

---

at; āpe; cär; end; mē; it; īce; hot; ōld; fôrk; wood; fo͞ol; oil; out; up; turn; sing; thin; **th**is; hw in white; zh in treasure. The symbol ə stands for the sound of **a** in about, **e** in taken, **i** in pencil, **o** in lemon, and **u** in circus.

D

deb·o·nair (deb′ə ner′) *also,* **de·bo·naire.** *adj.* gaily courteous, charming, and pleasant: *a debonair young man.* —**deb′o·nair′ly,** *adv.* —**deb′o·nair′ness,** *n.*

de·brief (dē′brēf′) *v.t.* to question or instruct a person, as a pilot or astronaut, at the end of a mission or term of service.

de·bris (də brē′, dā′brē) *also,* **dé·bris.** *n.* scattered remains, as of something broken or destroyed; rubbish: *The earthquake left the streets filled with debris.*

debt (det) *n.* **1.** something that is owed to another: *a debt of $1000.* **2.** the obligation to pay or give something to another. **3.** the condition of owing or being obligated: *to be in debt, to get out of debt.*

debt·or (det′ər) *n.* a person who owes something to another.

de·bunk (di bungk′) *v.t. Informal.* to expose or ridicule as false, pretentious, or exaggerated: *to debunk the claims made in an advertisement.*

De·bus·sy, Claude (deb′yoo sē′; klôd) 1862–1918, French composer.

de·but (dā byoo′) *also,* **dé·but.** *n.* **1.** a first public appearance, as of a performer on stage. **2.** a formal introduction of a young lady into society. **3.** a beginning, as of a career or course of action.

deb·u·tante (deb′yoo tänt′) *also,* **dé·bu·tante.** *n.* a young lady who is making her formal entrance into society.

Dec., December.

deca- *combining form* ten: *decagon.*

dec·ade (dek′ād) *n.* a period of ten years.

dec·a·dence (dek′əd əns) *n.* **1.** the process of decay; decline; deterioration: *the gradual decadence of an empire.* **2.** a period or condition of decline, as in morals, art, or literature.

dec·a·dent (dek′əd ənt) *adj.* characterized by or undergoing deterioration, as in morals, art, or literature: *a decadent society.* —*n.* a person who is decadent. —**dec′a·dent·ly,** *adv.*

dec·a·gon (dek′ə gon′) *n.* a plane figure having ten sides and ten angles.

dec·a·he·dron (dek′ə hē′drən) *n. pl.,* **dec·a·he·drons** or **dec·a·he·dra** (dek′ə hē′drə). a solid figure having ten plane surfaces.

de·cal (dē′kal, di kal′) *n.* a design or picture on specially treated paper, that can be transferred to glass, wood, or other surfaces.

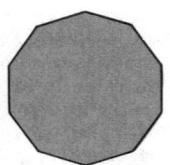
Regular decagon

dec·al·co·ma·ni·a (di kal′kə mā′nē ə) *n.* **1.** the art or process of transferring designs or pictures from specially treated paper to glass, wood, and other surfaces. **2.** another word for **decal.**

dec·a·li·ter (dek′ə lē′tər) *also,* **dec·a·li·tre.** *n.* a metric measure of volume, equal to ten liters.

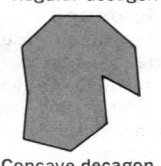
Concave decagon

Decagons

Dec·a·logue (dek′ə lôg′, dek′ə log′) *also,* **Dec·a·log.** *n.* in the Bible, the Ten Commandments.

de·camp (di kamp′) *v.i.* **1.** to leave a camp; break camp. **2.** to depart quickly or secretly; run away: *The robbers decamped under the cover of night.* —**de·camp′ment,** *n.*

de·cant (di kant′) *v.t.* **1.** to pour off (a liquid) gently without disturbing the sediment: *to decant wine.* **2.** to pour from one container to another.

de·cant·er (di kan′tər) *n.* a decorative glass bottle with a stopper, usually used for wine or liquor.

de·cap·i·tate (di kap′ə tāt′) *v.t.,* **de·cap·i·tat·ed, de·cap·i·tat·ing.** to cut off the head of; behead. —**de·cap′i·ta′tion,** *n.*

de·cath·lon (di kath′lon) *n.* an athletic contest consisting of ten different track and field events. The contestant scoring the highest total points for all events is the winner.

De·ca·tur (də kā′tər) *n.* a city in central Illinois. Pop. (1970), 90,397.

de·cay (di kā′) *n.* **1.** a rotting; decomposition, as of vegetable or animal matter: *tooth decay.* **2.** a gradual decline, as in strength or quality: *a decay in health, the decay of an empire.* **3.** *Physics.* the changing of an atomic nucleus of a radioactive element into another isotope of the same element or into a nucleus of a different element. —*v.i.* **1.** to rot; decompose: *The potatoes had decayed in the storage bin.* **2.** to decline gradually, as in quality or strength. **3.** *Physics.* to undergo decay.

de·cease (di sēs′) *n.* the act of dying; death. —*v.i.,* **deceased, de·ceas·ing.** to die.

de·ceased (di sēst′) *adj.* dead. —*n.* **the deceased.** dead person or persons: *Friends and relatives of the deceased went to the funeral.*

de·ce·dent (di sēd′ənt) *n. Law.* a dead person: *The decedent left his property to his son.*

de·ceit (di sēt′) *n.* **1.** the act or practice of deceiving; deception; lying: *He believed that deceit was the only way to be successful in his business.* **2.** something that is meant to deceive; trick. **3.** the quality of being deceitful; deceitfulness: *She was full of deceit.*

de·ceit·ful (di sēt′fəl) *adj.* **1.** given to deceiving; lying: *a deceitful person.* **2.** meant to deceive; false: *a deceitful answer.* —**de·ceit′ful·ly,** *adv.* —**de·ceit′ful·ness,** *n.*

de·ceive (di sēv′) *v.,* **de·ceived, de·ceiv·ing.** —*v.t.* to make (someone) believe something that is false; mislead: *The thief deceived the man by pretending to be his friend.* —*v.i.* to use deceit; lie. —**de·ceiv′er,** *n.*

de·cel·er·ate (dē sel′ə rāt′) *v.,* **de·cel·er·at·ed, de·cel·er·at·ing.** —*v.t.* to decrease the speed of: *The driver decelerated the car when he turned off the main highway.* —*v.i.* to decrease speed; slow down. —**de·cel′er·a′tion,** *n.* —**de·cel′er·a′tor,** *n.*

De·cem·ber (di sem′bər) *n.* the twelfth and last month of the year, having thirty-one days. [Latin *December* the tenth month in the early Roman calendar, from *decem* ten.]

de·cen·cy (dē′sən sē) *n. pl.,* **de·cen·cies. 1.** proper behavior, as in speech, actions, or dress: *He had the decency to admit his error.* **2. decencies.** the things that are needed for a respectable or comfortable manner of living.

de·cent (dē′sənt) *adj.* **1.** according to the standards of society, as in morality or social conduct; respectable: *a decent family.* **2.** according to the standards of good taste; proper: *It is not decent to pry into other people's business.* **3.** kind; generous: *It was very decent of her to help him.* **4.** fairly good; passable; satisfactory: *She makes a decent salary. He gets decent grades.* —**de′cent·ly,** *adv.* —**de′cent·ness,** *n.*

de·cen·tral·ize (dē sen′trə līz′) *v.t.,* **de·cen·tral·ized, de·cen·tral·iz·ing.** to redistribute most of the centralized power, authority, or production of (a government, industry, or other body) by giving it to smaller groups or units: *to decentralize a school system.* —**de·cen′tral·i·za′tion,** *n.*

de·cep·tion (di sep′shən) *n.* **1.** the act of deceiving or the state of being deceived. **2.** something that deceives or is meant to deceive; trick.

de·cep·tive (di sep′tiv) *adj.* characterized by deception; meant to deceive: *She hid her anger with a deceptive smile.* —**de·cep′tive·ly,** *adv.* —**de·cep′tive·ness,** *n.*

deci- *combining form* one tenth of: *deciliter, decimeter.*

dec·i·bel (des′ə bel′) *n.* a unit for measuring the loudness of sounds.

de·cide (di sīd′) *v.,* **de·cid·ed, de·cid·ing.** —*v.i.* **1.** to make up one's mind; resolve: *They decided to go home by bus.* **2.** to make a judgment; come to a conclusion: *The judge decided in favor of the defendant.* —*v.t.* **1.** to determine or settle, as a dispute or question: *The umpire decided the question in our team's favor.* **2.** to determine the result of: *The last touchdown decided the game.* **3.** to cause (someone) to come to a decision: *What decided her against buying that coat?*

de·cid·ed (di sī′did) *adj.* **1.** definite; unquestionable: *The taller basketball player had a decided edge over the others.* **2.** determined; sure: *to speak in a decided tone of voice.* —**de·cid′ed·ly,** *adv.* —**de·cid′ed·ness,** *n.*

de·cid·u·ous (di sij′ōō əs) *adj.* **1.** (of a tree, shrub, or other plant) shedding its leaves each year: *A maple is a deciduous tree.* **2.** falling off or shed at a particular season or stage of growth: *deciduous leaves, deciduous antlers.*

dec·i·gram (des′ə gram′) *n.* a metric unit of weight, equal to one tenth of a gram.

dec·i·li·ter (des′ə lē′tər) *also,* **dec·i·li·tre.** *n.* a metric measure of volume, equal to one tenth of a liter.

dec·i·mal (des′ə məl) *adj.* relating to or based on the number 10; proceeding by tens. —*n.* see **decimal fraction.**

decimal fraction, a fraction whose denominator is equal to ten or a multiple of ten. The fractions 5/10 and 75/100 expressed as decimal fractions are .5 and .75.

decimal point, a period placed before a decimal fraction, which indicates, by the number of figures following it, the size of the denominator.

decimal system, a system of computation having the number 10 as its base.

dec·i·mate (des′ə māt′) *v.t.,* **dec·i·mat·ed, dec·i·mat·ing.** to destroy or kill a large number or proportion of: *The fire decimated the trees in the forest.* [Latin *decimātus,* the past participle of *decimāre* to select every tenth man for punishment. In ancient Rome an army revolt was punished by taking every tenth soldier and executing him.] —**dec′i·ma′tion,** *n.*

dec·i·me·ter (des′ə mē′tər) *also,* **dec·i·me·tre.** *n.* a metric measure of length, equal to one tenth of a meter.

de·ci·pher (di sī′fər) *v.t.* **1.** to make out the meaning of (something illegible or difficult to understand): *to decipher messy handwriting, to decipher a riddle.* **2.** to interpret or translate (something written in code) by using a key; decode: *The expert deciphered the enemy's message.* —**de·ci′pher·a·ble,** *adj.*

de·ci·sion (di sizh′ən) *n.* **1.** the act of making up one's mind: *Jim hesitated because of the difficulty of the decision.* **2.** the act of reaching a conclusion or making a judgment about something, as a controversy or question: *The decision will be left to the jury.* **3.** a judgment or conclusion reached or given: *The umpire's decision was final.* **4.** the quality of being decided; firmness; determination: *He is a man of decision who rarely changes his mind.*

de·ci·sive (di sī′siv) *adj.* **1.** settling something finally and completely; conclusive: *a decisive victory.* **2.** characterized by decision; resolute: *Tom disagreed in a decisive tone of voice.* —**de·ci′sive·ly,** *adv.* —**de·ci′sive·ness,** *n.*

deck (dek) *n.* **1.** a platform or other flat surface serving as a floor or level in a boat or ship. **2.** any similar platform or flat surface. **3.** a set of playing cards. —*v.t.* **1.** to dress or adorn; ornament: *The woman decked herself in furs.* **2.** to provide with a deck. **3.** *Slang.* to knock down: *The fighter decked his opponent.*

on deck. *Informal.* **a.** on hand and ready for use or action. **b.** ready and waiting for one's turn: *The next batter was on deck.*

deck hand, a sailor who performs manual tasks.

de·claim (di klām′) *v.i.* **1.** to speak or recite publicly; give an oration. **2.** to speak in a loud, showy way: *The speaker declaimed against capital punishment.* —*v.t.* to say or recite (something) in a loud, showy way: *The actor declaimed his lines.* —**de·claim′er,** *n.*

dec·la·ma·tion (dek′lə mā′shən) *n.* **1.** the act of declaiming. **2.** the art of speaking or reciting publicly; public speaking. **3.** a formal, prepared public speech or recitation.

de·clam·a·to·ry (di klam′ə tôr′ē) *adj.* **1.** of or relating to declamation. **2.** loud and showy: *a declamatory speech against injustice.*

dec·la·ra·tion (dek′lə rā′shən) *n.* **1.** the act of declaring. **2.** something that is declared; announcement. **3.** a formal statement: *Congress issued a declaration of war.* **4.** a statement of goods that may be taxed.

Declaration of Independence, the document declaring the thirteen American colonies independent of Great Britain, written mainly by Thomas Jefferson and adopted on July 4, 1776, by the Second Continental Congress.

de·clar·a·tive (di klar′ə tiv) *adj.* making a statement or affirmation: *"I like ice cream" is a declarative sentence.*

de·clare (di kler′) *v.,* **de·clared, de·clar·ing.** —*v.t.* **1.** to make known publicly or formally; announce; proclaim: *The legislature declared a new state holiday.* **2.** to state positively or strongly; assert: *He declared that he was right.* **3.** to make a full statement or account of (goods that may be taxed). —*v.i.* to announce, as an opinion or choice: *The newspaper declared for the Republican candidate.*

de·clen·sion (di klen′shən) *n.* **1.** the changing of the forms or endings of nouns, pronouns, and adjectives to show case, gender, and number. **2.** a group of words whose inflections are the same.

dec·li·na·tion (dek′lə nā′shən) *n.* **1.** a leaning, bending, or sloping downward; inclination. **2.** an angular difference between the direction in which a magnetic compass points and the direction of the true North Pole. **3.** a polite refusal.

de·cline (di klīn′) *v.,* **de·clined, de·clin·ing.** —*v.t.* **1.** to refuse (something) politely: *to decline an invitation.* **2.** to give the inflected forms of (a noun, pronoun, or adjective). —*v.i.* **1.** to refuse politely. **2.** to fall into an inferior or poor condition; weaken: *His health was declining.* **3.** to fall or become less: *Prices on the stock market declined.* **4.** to bend or slope downward. —*n.* **1.** a decrease, as in influence, strength, value, or amount: *The census showed a decline in the town's population.* **2.** a downward bend or slope. **3.** a period during which something is drawing to a close or weakening.

de·cliv·i·ty (di kliv′ə tē) *n. pl.,* **de·cliv·i·ties.** a downward slope.

de·code (dē kōd′) *v.t.,* **de·cod·ed, de·cod·ing.** to interpret or translate from code into ordinary language by using a key: *to decode a secret message.*

de·com·pose (dē′kəm pōz′) *v.,* **de·com·posed, de·com·pos·ing.** —*v.i.* **1.** to decay; rot: *The old tree stump was decomposing.* **2.** to separate into basic parts or elements. —*v.t.* **1.** to cause to decay or rot. **2.** to separate (something) into its basic parts or elements: *to decompose a chemical compound.* —**de·com·po·si·tion** (dē′kom pə zish′ən), *n.*

at; āpe; cär; end; mē; it; īce; hot; ōld; fôrk; wood; fōōl; oil; out; up; turn; sing; thin; this; hw in white; zh in treasure. The symbol ə stands for the sound of **a** in about, **e** in taken, **i** in pencil, **o** in lemon, and **u** in circus.

de·com·press (dē′kəm pres′) *v.t.* to cause to undergo decompression.

de·com·pres·sion (dē′kəm presh′ən) *n.* the reduction or removal of pressure, especially of high atmospheric pressure on the human body. Deep-sea divers must undergo gradual decompression as they return to the surface.

de·con·tam·i·nate (dē′kən tam′ə nāt′) *v.t.,* **de·con·tam·i·nat·ed, de·con·tam·i·nat·ing.** to make (a contaminated area or object) safe by removing harmful materials, such as poison gas, bacteria, or radioactive wastes: *We had to decontaminate the water before we drank it.* —**de′con·tam′i·na′tion,** *n.*

de·con·trol (dē′kən trōl′) *v.t.,* **de·con·trolled, de·con·trol·ling.** to remove controls from, especially government controls: *to decontrol rents.* —*n.* the removal of controls.

dé·cor (dā kôr′) *also,* **de·cor.** *n.* **1.** a decorative plan and style, as of a room. **2.** scenery, as in a theatrical or television presentation.

dec·o·rate (dek′ə rāt′) *v.t.,* **dec·o·rat·ed, dec·o·rat·ing. 1.** to make more beautiful; ornament; adorn: *The children decorated the Christmas tree.* **2.** to plan and execute the style and design of (a room or rooms), as by selecting and arranging furniture, choosing fabrics, paint, wallpaper, or adding ornamentation. **3.** to honor, as with a medal: *The army decorated the soldier for bravery.*

dec·o·ra·tion (dek′ə rā′shən) *n.* **1.** the act or process of decorating. **2.** something used to decorate; ornament; adornment. **3.** a mark of honor, as a medal or ribbon.

Decoration Day, another term for **Memorial Day.**

dec·o·ra·tive (dek′ər ə tiv) *adj.* serving to decorate; ornamental: *The room was filled with small, decorative objects.* —**dec′o·ra·tive·ly,** *adv.* —**dec′o·ra·tive·ness,** *n.*

dec·o·ra·tor (dek′ə rā′tər) *n.* a person who decorates, especially an interior decorator.

dec·o·rous (dek′ər əs) *adj.* characterized by decorum; in good taste; proper; suitable. —**dec′o·rous·ly,** *adv.* —**dec′o·rous·ness,** *n.*

de·co·rum (di kôr′əm) *n.* good taste, as in behavior or speech; propriety.

de·coy (*n.,* dē′koi, di koi′; *v.,* di koi′) *n.* **1.** an artificial bird used to lure birds into a trap or within gunshot range. **2.** a person or thing that lures, as into danger: *She was used as a decoy to trap the murderer.* **3.** a trick; deception. —*v.t.* **1.** to lure (birds or other animals) into a trap or within gunshot range. **2.** to lure into danger by a decoy.

de·crease (*v.,* di krēs′; *n.,* dē′krēs′, di krēs′) *v.,* **de·creased, de·creas·ing.** —*v.i.* to become less; diminish; abate: *The number of traffic accidents decreased last year.* —*v.t.* to cause to become less; reduce: *to decrease the speed of an automobile, to decrease prices.* —*n.* **1.** the act or process of decreasing; lessening: *A decrease in sales lowered the store's profits.* **2.** the amount by which something decreases or is decreased: *From noon to midnight there was a decrease of ten degrees in temperature.*

de·cree (di krē′) *n.* **1.** *Law.* a decision or order issued by a court: *a divorce decree.* **2.** any official decision or order; edict: *The king sent out a decree raising taxes.* —*v.t.,* **de·creed, de·cree·ing.** to order, decide, or appoint by decree: *The President decreed a national holiday.*

dec·re·ment (dek′rə mənt) *n. Mathematics.* the amount by which the value of a variable quantity decreases.

de·crep·it (di krep′it) *adj.* broken down or feeble because of old age or overuse: *a decrepit old house.* —**de·crep′it·ly,** *adv.*

de·crep·i·tude (di krep′ə tōōd′, di krep′ə tyōōd′) *n.* the condition of being decrepit.

de·cre·scen·do (dē′krə shen′dō) *n. pl.,* **de·cre·scen·dos.** *Music.* **1.** a gradual decrease in loudness or force. **2.** a passage in which this occurs. —*adj.* with a gradual decrease in loudness or force. —*adv.* gradually decreasing in loudness or force.

de·cry (di krī′) *v.t.,* **de·cried, de·cry·ing. 1.** to express strong disapproval of; speak out against; condemn: *The teacher decried cheating on exams.* **2.** to try to lower the value of; belittle: *to decry a college education.*

ded·i·cate (ded′ə kāt′) *v.t.,* **ded·i·cat·ed, ded·i·cat·ing. 1.** to set apart for or devote to a special purpose or use: *Part of the building was dedicated to chemical research. The temple was dedicated to Athena.* **2.** to give or devote: *The doctor dedicated himself to finding a cure for cancer.* **3.** to inscribe (a book or other artistic composition) to a friend or patron in order to show respect, gratitude, or affection: *The author dedicated his book to his wife.*

ded·i·ca·tion (ded′ə kā′shən) *n.* **1.** the act of dedicating or the state of being dedicated. **2.** an inscription in a book or other artistic work, dedicating it to a friend or patron.

ded·i·ca·to·ry (ded′ə kə tôr′ē) *adj.* of or serving as a dedication.

de·duce (di dōōs′, di dyōōs′) *v.t.,* **de·duced, de·duc·ing.** to reach or draw (a conclusion) from something known or assumed; infer: *She deduced from George's frown that he was unhappy.* —**de·duc′i·ble,** *adj.*

de·duct (di dukt′) *v.t.* to take away or subtract from a total: *The company deducted income taxes from his salary.* —**de·duct′i·ble,** *adj.*

de·duc·tion (di duk′shən) *n.* **1.** the act of deducting; subtraction. **2.** something that is deducted: *a tax deduction.* **3.** the act or method of reaching a conclusion by reasoning from a general principle to particular cases or facts. **4.** something that is deduced; conclusion; inference.

de·duc·tive (di duk′tiv) *adj.* of, using, or based on deduction. —**de·duc′tive·ly,** *adv.*

deed (dēd) *n.* **1.** something done; act; action: *Helping the old woman across the street was a good deed.* **2.** a legal document showing or proving ownership of real estate. —*v.t.* to transfer (real estate) by deed: *They deeded their house to their children.*

deem (dēm) *v.t.* to think; believe; judge: *He deemed it wise to accept the new job.*

deep (dēp) *adj.* **1.** going or reaching far downward from the surface or top: *a deep well, deep water, a deep hole, a deep cut.* **2.** great in degree; intense; extreme: *a deep sleep.* **3.** going or reaching far inward or backward from the front or outer edge: *a deep closet, deep woods.* **4.** difficult to understand; obscure: *That book is too deep for me.* **5.** completely occupied; absorbed; engrossed: *He didn't hear the doorbell ring because he was deep in thought.* **6.** strongly felt; profound: *deep sorrow.* **7.** dark and rich in color: *a deep brown.* **8.** low in pitch: *a deep voice, the deep tones of an organ.* **9.** having a specified dimension downward, inward, or backward: *a pool twelve feet deep.* —*adv.* **1.** in, at, to, or with a great depth; deeply: *The explorers went deep into the jungle.* **2.** far on in time; late: *The meeting continued deep into the night.* —*n.* **1.** the part or time of greatest intensity, as of coldness, darkness, or quiet: *the deep of winter, the deep of night.* **2. the deep.** the sea. —**deep′ly,** *adv.* —**deep′ness,** *n.*

deep·en (dē′pən) *v.t., v.i.* to make or become deep or deeper: *The workmen deepened the hole by digging.*

deep-root·ed (dēp′rōō′tid, dēp′root′id) *adj.* firmly fixed; deep-seated: *a deep-rooted friendship.*

deep-sea (dēp′sē′) *adj.* of, in, or relating to the deeper parts of the ocean: *deep-sea fishing, a deep-sea diver.*

deep-seat·ed (dēp′sē′tid) *adj.* firmly fixed; deeply rooted: *a deep-seated fear of snakes.*

deep-set (dēp′set′) *adj.* placed or fixed deeply: *deep-set eyes.*

deer (dēr) *n. pl.,* **deer.** any of various swift, cud-chewing animals, as the moose, the elk, and the reindeer. All male deer and some female deer have antlers that are shed each year. [Old English *dēor* animal, beast, deer.]

deer mouse, a mouse of North and Central America, having tan or brown fur with white markings on the underside.

deer·skin (dēr′skin′) *n.* **1.** the hide of a deer. **2.** the leather made from this hide.

Deer

def. 1. definition. **2.** defense.

de·face (di fās′) *v.t.,* **de·faced, de·fac·ing.** to spoil or mar the surface or appearance of: *to deface a monument with chalk marks.* —**de·face′ment,** *n.*

de fac·to (dē fak′tō) existing in reality, with or without legal right; actual: *de facto racial segregation. During the king's illness, the queen was the de facto ruler of the country.* [Latin *dē factō* from the fact.]

def·a·ma·tion (def′ə mā′shən) *n.* the act of defaming; slander or libel.

de·fam·a·to·ry (di fam′ə tôr ē) *adj.* damaging to the reputation; slanderous or libelous.

de·fame (di fām′) *v.t.,* **de·famed, de·fam·ing.** to attack or ruin the good name or reputation of; slander or libel. —**de·fam′er,** *n.*

de·fault (di fôlt′) *n.* a failure to do something required, especially failure to take part in or complete a scheduled game or contest: *If he doesn't arrive for the chess match, he will lose by default.* —*v.i.* to fail or neglect to do something required: *He defaulted in his payment of the debt.* —**de·fault′er,** *n.*

de·feat (di fēt′) *v.t.* **1.** to overcome in a contest or conflict of any kind; win a victory over: *to defeat an opponent in tennis, to defeat the enemy in battle.* **2.** to prevent the success of; frustrate; thwart: *to defeat a purpose, to defeat a person's hopes.* —*n.* the act of overcoming or the state of being overcome in a contest or conflict.

de·feat·ism (di fē′tiz′əm) *n.* the state of mind or behavior characteristic of a defeatist.

de·feat·ist (di fē′tist) *n.* a person who expects defeat or who accepts it too readily or soon. —*adj.* characteristic of a defeatist: *a defeatist attitude.*

def·e·cate (def′ə kāt′) *v.i.,* **def·e·cat·ed, def·e·cat·ing.** to excrete waste from the bowels. —**def′e·ca′tion,** *n.*

de·fect (*n.,* dē′fekt, di fekt′; *v.,* di fekt′) *n.* **1.** an imperfection, flaw, or weakness; fault; blemish: *The only defect in the glass bowl is that small chip.* **2.** the lack of something necessary for completeness or perfection; deficiency: *a speech defect.* —*v.i.* to desert a group, country, or cause, especially for another that is opposed to it: *The spy defected to the enemy.* —**de·fec′tor,** *n.*

de·fec·tion (di fek′shən) *n.* the act of deserting a group, country, or cause, especially for another that is opposed to it.

de·fec·tive (di fek′tiv) *adj.* **1.** having a defect or defects; imperfect; incomplete: *Defective wiring can be the cause of fires.* **2.** having less than normal mental or physical ability. —*n.* a person who has less than normal mental or physical ability. —**de·fec′tive·ly,** *adv.* —**de·fec′tive·ness,** *n.*

de·fence (di fens′) *British.* another spelling of **defense.**

de·fend (di fend′) *v.t.* **1.** to guard against attack, injury, or danger; protect: *The troops defended the city.* **2.** to support, justify, or argue for by word or deed: *to defend one's rights.* **3.** *Law.* to plead the case or cause of (an accused person): *The lawyer defended the prisoner in court.* —**de·fend′er,** *n.*

de·fend·ant (di fen′dənt) *n.* a person against whom a civil or criminal action is brought in a court of law.

de·fense (di fens′) *also, British,* **de·fence.** *n.* **1.** the act of guarding against attack, injury, or danger; protection: *All the citizens were armed for the defense of the city against enemy invasion.* **2.** a person or thing that protects; means of protection: *The dike was the town's only defense against floods.* **3.** support or justification by word or deed: *The governor spoke in defense of his new proposal.* **4.** an argument, speech, or writing that supports or justifies: *The scientist's defense of his theory lacked definite proof.* **5.** the defending team, players, or side in a game. **6.a.** the arguments presented by a defendant or his lawyer. **b.** a defendant and his lawyer or lawyers.

de·fense·less (di fens′lis) *adj.* having no defense; helpless; unprotected: *The mother cat guarded her defenseless kitten.* —**de·fense′less·ly,** *adv.* —**de·fense′less·ness,** *n.*

de·fen·si·ble (di fen′sə bəl) *adj.* **1.** that can be defended; justifiable: *a defensible action.* **2.** that can be defended against attack, injury, or danger: *a defensible coastline.* —**de·fen′si·bil′i·ty,** *n.* —**de·fen′si·bly,** *adv.*

de·fen·sive (di fen′siv) *adj.* **1.** serving to defend; protective: *defensive armor.* **2.** having or using defenses: *a defensive attitude, a defensive person.* —*n.* a position or attitude of defense. —**de·fen′sive·ly,** *adv.* —**de·fen′sive·ness,** *n.*
  on the defensive. assuming a protective attitude: *She was always on the defensive when criticized.*

de·fer¹ (di fur′) *v.t.,* **de·ferred, de·fer·ring.** to put off to a future time; postpone: *The court will defer judgment until all the facts are known.* [Old French *differer* to postpone.] —**de·fer′ra·ble,** *adj.*

de·fer² (di fur′) *v.i.,* **de·ferred, de·fer·ring.** to yield in judgment or opinion; give in respectfully: *He deferred to his friend's wishes.* [French *déférer* to yield.]

def·er·ence (def′ər əns) *n.* a courteous respect or regard: *to have deference for one's elders.*
  in deference to. out of respect for: *Flags were lowered in deference to the dead leader.*

def·er·en·tial (def′ə ren′shəl) *adj.* characterized by or showing deference; respectful: *a deferential attitude.* —**def′er·en′tial·ly,** *adv.*

de·fer·ment (di fur′mənt) *n.* the act of putting off or delaying; postponement: *a deferment from military service.* Also, **de·fer·ral** (di fur′əl).

de·fi·ance (di fī′əns) *n.* bold or open resistance to authority, an opponent, or an opposing force; contempt of opposition or authority: *The boys showed their defiance by deliberately breaking the rules.*

de·fi·ant (di fī′ənt) *adj.* characterized by or showing defiance; boldly or openly resisting: *a defiant act.* —**de·fi′ant·ly,** *adv.*

de·fi·cien·cy (di fish′ən sē) *n. pl.,* **de·fi·cien·cies.** **1.** the condition of being deficient; lack of something necessary: *a mental deficiency, a vitamin deficiency.* **2.** the amount by which something is lacking; deficit: *a deficiency of ten dollars.*

at; āpe; cär; end; mē; it; īce; hot; ōld; fôrk; wood; fōōl; oil; out; up; turn; sing; thin; this; hw in white; zh in treasure. The symbol ə stands for the sound of a in about, e in taken, i in pencil, o in lemon, and u in circus.

deficiency disease, a disease, as scurvy or rickets, caused by the lack of some necessary vitamin or other element in the diet.

de·fi·cient (di fish'ənt) *adj.* **1.** not adequate in quantity or supply; insufficient: *a diet deficient in vitamins.* **2.** lacking something necessary; incomplete; imperfect: *When John went to college he found that he was deficient in science.* —**de·fi'cient·ly,** *adv.*

def·i·cit (def'ə sit) *n.* the amount by which something, especially a sum of money, falls short of what is due, required, or expected; shortage: *There was a ten dollar deficit in our food budget, because we budgeted fifty dollars and owed the grocer sixty dollars.*

de·fi·er (di fī'ər) *n.* a person who defies.

de·file¹ (di fīl') *v.t.,* **de·filed, de·fil·ing. 1.** to spoil the purity of; taint: *to defile a sacred temple.* **2.** to make filthy, dirty, or impure; pollute: *to defile a stream with garbage.* [Middle English *defoulen* to trample on, crush.] —**de·file'ment,** *n.*

de·file² (di fīl') *v.i.,* **de·filed, de·fil·ing.** to march in a narrow column or single line. —*n.* a narrow passage in a mountain region, especially one that permits travel only in a narrow column or single line. [French *défiler* to march in this manner.]

de·fine (di fīn') *v.t.,* **de·fined, de·fin·ing. 1.** to state the meaning or meanings of (a word or phrase): *Can you define the word "love"?* **2.** to describe, fix, or set forth exactly or authoritatively: *The Constitution of the United States defines the powers of the President.* **3.** to determine or fix the limits or extent of: *The river defined the boundary between the two countries.* **4.** to make clear or distinct in outline or form: *The bright sky boldly defined the mountain.* —**de·fin'a·ble,** *adj.* —**de·fin'er,** *n.*

def·i·nite (def'ə nit) *adj.* **1.** clearly defined; precise; exact: *He has definite ideas on the subject of education.* **2.** positive; certain; sure: *It is definite that Mrs. Robinson will be the new principal.* **3.** having fixed limits: *a definite boundary.* —**def'i·nite·ly,** *adv.* —**def'i·nite·ness,** *n.*

definite article, the article *the.*

def·i·ni·tion (def'ə nish'ən) *n.* **1.** a statement of the meaning of a word or phrase. **2.** a statement of the true nature or characteristics of a thing. **3.** sharpness of outline; distinctness; clearness: *This photograph lacks definition.*

⬤ In dictionary making, an ideal **definition** would include everything that a word means and nothing that it doesn't mean. That is, a definition of the word *dog* should be general enough to cover anything that is a dog, and also specific enough to leave out everything that is not a dog. If you were to try to define "dog" using this method, you would have very little trouble deciding what a dog *isn't* and leaving everything it isn't out of your definition. But if you try to say everything that a dog *is,* you will probably have given more facts than a reader really needs or wants to know, and you may have included things that are true of some dogs but not all dogs.

Most early dictionaries dealt with this problem by saying very little in their definitions. One book defined a dog as a "well-known creature" and another defined it as a "well-known domestic quadruped." These definitions could also be used to describe a cow, a horse, and a cat. In a good modern dictionary, a definition of the word "dog" would include those facts that would help the reader understand what a dog, as opposed to any other animal, is and would leave out those facts that, although they are correct, are not necessary.

The most difficult type of word to define is an abstract word. Abstract words, such as "beauty," "sorrow," and "kindness," do not describe something that exists, but rather what we think or feel about a thing that exists. Because of this, there are no "facts," such as those about a dog, that we can use in defining abstract words. Therefore such words are defined in general, rather than specific, terms. Showing how an abstract word is used in a sentence is one of the ways in which a dictionary can best help you to understand what the word means.

de·fin·i·tive (di fin'ə tiv) *adj.* **1.** most nearly correct and complete: *the definitive biography of Charles Dickens.* **2.** conclusive; final; decisive: *a definitive answer.* —**de·fin'i·tive·ly,** *adv.* —**de·fin'i·tive·ness,** *n.*

de·flate (di flāt') *v.,* **de·flat·ed, de·flat·ing.** —*v.t.* **1.** to let out the air or gas of: *to deflate a tire, to deflate a balloon.* **2.** to reduce in importance: *to deflate a boastful person's ego.* **3.** to reduce the amount, size, or level of: *to deflate prices.* —*v.i.* to collapse or become smaller, as through loss of air or gas.

de·fla·tion (di flā'shən) *n.* **1.** the act of deflating or the state of being deflated. **2.** a decline in the general level of prices, resulting from a reduction in money supply or spending.

de·flect (di flekt') *v.t.* to cause to turn aside or change direction; bend from a straight course: *The boxer's raised arm deflected his opponent's blow.* —*v.i.* to turn aside or change direction.

de·flec·tion (di flek'shən) *n.* **1.** the act of deflecting or the state of being deflected; deviation. **2.** the amount of such turning or deviation. **3.** the amount that an indicator on a measuring instrument moves or deviates from the zero reading on its scale.

De·foe, Daniel (də fō') 1660?–1731, English author.

de·fo·li·ate (dē fō'lē āt') *v.t.,* **de·fo·li·at·ed, de·fo·li·at·ing. 1.** to strip of leaves: *to defoliate plants.* **2.** to destroy (a forest, jungle, or other area of vegetation). —**de·fo'li·a'tion,** *n.*

de·for·est (dē fôr'ist, dē for'ist) *v.t.* to clear or strip of forests or trees. —**de·for'est·a'tion,** *n.*

De For·est, Lee (də fôr'əst, də for'əst) 1873–1961, U.S. inventor.

de·form (di fôrm') *v.t.* **1.** to spoil the form or shape of: *Shoes that were too tight deformed the baby's feet.* **2.** to make ugly; mar the beauty of; disfigure.

de·for·ma·tion (dē'fôr mā'shən) *n.* **1.** the act of deforming or the state of being deformed. **2.** a result or condition of being deformed; deformity.

de·formed (di fôrmd') *adj.* improperly formed; especially distorted: *He was born with a deformed leg.*

de·form·i·ty (di fôr'mə tē) *n. pl.,* **de·form·i·ties. 1.** an improperly formed or distorted part of the body. **2.** the condition of being deformed.

de·fraud (di frôd') *v.t.* to take something away from (a person) by fraud; cheat; swindle: *He defrauded the old lady of her savings.*

de·fray (di frā') *v.t.* to pay (costs or expenses): *The college raised its tuition to help defray additional expenses.*

de·frost (di frôst') *v.t.* **1.** to make free of frost or ice: *to defrost a refrigerator.* **2.** to thaw: *to defrost frozen meat.* —*v.i.* **1.** to become free of frost or ice: *The refrigerator will defrost overnight.* **2.** to become thawed.

de·frost·er (di frôs'tər) *n.* a device that removes or prevents the formation of ice or frost, as on an automobile windshield.

deft (deft) *adj.* skillful and nimble; adroit: *the deft fingers of a pianist. Her deft handling of the difficult situation prevented a crisis.* —**deft'ly,** *adv.* —**deft'ness,** *n.*

de·funct (di fungkt') *adj.* no longer existing or active; dead; extinct: *a defunct business.*

de·fy (di fī') *v.t.,* **de·fied, de·fy·ing. 1.** to resist (opposition or authority) boldly or openly; face with contempt: *to defy the law.* **2.** to resist completely or successfully; withstand: *That problem defies solution.* **3.** to challenge; dare: *He defied his opponent to equal his swimming record.* [Old French *defier* to challenge; earlier, to renounce faith in God.]

deg., degree; degrees.

De·gas, Ed·gar (dā gä′; ed gär′) 1834–1917, French painter.

de Gaulle, Charles (də gōl′, də gôl′; shärl) 1890–1970, French general and political leader, the president of France from 1959 to 1969.

de·gen·er·a·cy (di jen′ər ə sē) *n.* **1.** the state of being degenerate, especially in moral character. **2.** the process of degenerating; deterioration.

de·gen·er·ate (*v.,* di jen′ə rāt′; *adj., n.,* di jen′ər it) *v.t.,* **de·gen·er·at·ed, de·gen·er·at·ing.** to become worse or inferior in condition, character, or quality; deteriorate: *His health gradually degenerated as he grew old.* —*adj.* having become worse or inferior in condition, character, or quality; deteriorated; degraded: *a degenerate society.* —*n.* a person who is morally degraded. —**de·gen′er·ate·ly** (di jen′ər it lē), *adv.* —**de·gen′er·a′tion,** *n.*

de·gen·er·a·tive (di jen′ə rā′tiv) *adj.* relating to, characterized by, or causing degeneration: *a degenerative disease.*

deg·ra·da·tion (deg′rə dā′shən) *n.* **1.** the act of degrading or the state of being degraded. **2.** a degraded condition.

● In language, **degradation** means the changing of the meaning of a word from something good or neutral to something bad. Degradation, which is also called *degeneration,* is one of the basic ways in which our language is constantly changing. Although a word itself is neither bad nor good, the meaning of a word can be whatever people choose it to be. For example, *silly,* which originally had the meaning "deserving pity or sympathy," now has come to mean "foolish." The word *counterfeit* once had a neutral meaning, "to copy"; but it is now used to refer to dishonest copying that is done to deceive, especially illegal copying of money. The meaning of various words has changed as people took a different view of the person or thing to which the words applied. The word *boor* originally meant "farmer." Later this word was used humorously to refer to any person from the country rather than the city. By the process of degradation, *boor* has now come to mean "a crude, bad-mannered, or awkward person."

---

de·grade (di grād′) *v.t.,* **de·grad·ed, de·grad·ing.** **1.** to lower in character, quality, or estimation; debase: *Lying degrades a man.* **2.** to lower in rank or position, especially as a punishment.

de·gree (di grē′) *n.* **1.** one of a series of stages or steps in a process or course: *The child learned to walk by degrees.* **2.** intensity, amount, or extent: *a high degree of intelligence, a burn of the first degree.* **3.** social rank or position: *a man of low degree.* **4.** a rank or title given by a school, college, or university to a student for completion of a course of study or to a person as an honor: *a master's degree in history.* **5.** a unit of measurement for temperature, varying according to the scale used. ▲ The symbol for degrees (○) is often used with figures: *70° Fahrenheit.* **6.** *Mathematics.* a unit of measurement for angles or arcs, equal to 1/360 of the circumference of a circle. **7.** *Algebra.* **a.** the rank of a monomial term as determined by the sum of the exponents of the variables. The terms x^4 and xy^3 are both of the fourth degree. **b.** the rank of

Degree
(def. 6)

a polynomial as determined by the sum of the exponents of the term of the highest degree. The equation $xy^4 + yz$ is of the fifth degree. **8.** *Grammar.* one of the three forms of comparison of adjectives or adverbs. For the adjective *good, good* is the positive degree, *better* is the comparative degree, and *best* is the superlative degree. **9.** *Law.* the relative seriousness of a particular crime: *murder in the first degree.*

de·gree-day (di grē′dā′) *n.* a unit representing the amount of difference between the average temperature for a given day and a standard, usually 65 degrees Fahrenheit, used for estimating fuel and power requirements.

de·hu·mid·i·fy (dē′hyōō mid′ə fī′) *v.t.,* **de·hu·mid·i·fied, de·hu·mid·i·fy·ing.** to remove moisture from (air or other gases). —**de′hu·mid′i·fi·ca′tion,** *n.* —**de′hu·mid′i·fi′er,** *n.*

de·hy·drate (dē hī′drāt) *v.,* **de·hy·drat·ed, de·hy·drat·ing.** —*v.t.* to remove water or moisture from: *to dehydrate milk.* —*v.i.* to lose water or moisture; become dry. —**de′hy·dra′tion,** *n.*

de·ice (dē īs′) *v.t.,* **de·iced, de·ic·ing.** to remove ice from or prevent ice from forming on: *to deice a windshield.*

de·ic·er (dē ī′sər) *n.* a device or substance that prevents or removes formations of ice, as on an airplane wing.

de·i·fi·ca·tion (dē′ə fi kā′shən) *n.* the act of deifying or the state of being deified.

de·i·fy (dē′ə fī′) *v.t.,* **de·i·fied, de·i·fy·ing.** **1.** to make a god of: *The ancient Egyptians deified the sun.* **2.** to worship as a god; regard as an object of worship: *to deify an emperor, to deify wealth.*

deign (dān) *v.i.* to think worthy of oneself; condescend: *He would not deign to consider such an offer.* —*v.t.* to see fit to grant or give: *He deigned no reply.*

de·ism (dē′iz′əm) *n.* the belief that the universe and its natural laws were created by God, but that the natural laws govern its operation, not the will of God.

de·ist (dē′ist) *n.* a person who believes in deism.

de·i·ty (dē′ə tē) *n. pl.,* **de·i·ties. 1.** a god or goddess; divine being. **2.** divine nature or condition; divinity. **3. the Deity.** God.

de·ject (di jekt′) *v.t.* to make low in spirits; dishearten; depress: *The defeat dejected the team.*

de·ject·ed (di jek′tid) *adj.* characterized by or showing low spirits; disheartened; depressed: *a dejected person, a dejected look.* —**de·ject′ed·ly,** *adv.* —**de·ject′ed·ness,** *n.*

de·jec·tion (di jek′shən) *n.* lowness of spirits; depression; sadness.

de ju·re (dē joor′ē) by right; according to law: *a de jure ruler.* [Latin *dē jūre.*]

Del., Delaware.

Del·a·ware (del′ə wer′) *n.* **1.** a state in the eastern United States. Capital, Dover. Area, 2057 sq. mi. Pop. (1970), 548,104. Abbreviation, **Del. 2.** a river in the eastern United States, flowing from southeastern New York State between Pennsylvania and New Jersey into Delaware Bay. —**Del′a·war′e·an,** *adj., n.*

● The name **Delaware** comes from the name of one of the governors of the colony of Virginia, Thomas West, Lord De la Warr. An English navigator named a cape near

at; āpe; cär; end; mē; it; īce; hot; ōld; fôrk; wood; fōōl; oil; out; up; turn; sing; thin; **this;** hw in white; zh in treasure. The symbol ə stands for the sound of **a** in about, **e** in taken, **i** in pencil, **o** in lemon, and **u** in circus.

present-day Delaware after the governor, and later English settlers transferred the name to the bay, the river, and, after the English had defeated the Dutch, to the colony itself.

Delaware Bay, an inlet of the Atlantic Ocean between Delaware and New Jersey.

de·lay (di lā′) v.t. **1.** to put off to a future time; postpone: *The officials delayed the start of the baseball game because of the rain.* **2.** to make late; hinder the progress of; detain: *Heavy traffic delayed us.* —v.i. to put off or slow down action; linger: *Jane will miss the bus if she delays any longer.* —n. **1.** the act of delaying or the state of being delayed: *The train's delay was caused by a derailment.* **2.** the amount of time something is delayed: *There will be a brief delay before the show begins.*

de·lec·ta·ble (di lek′tə bəl) adj. highly pleasing or delightful, especially to the taste; delicious: *a delectable chocolate cake.*

del·e·gate (n., del′ə gāt′, del′ə git; v., del′ə gāt′) n. a person given authority to represent or act for another or others; representative; deputy: *Every chapter sent delegates to the club's national convention.* —v.t., **del·e·gat·ed, del·e·gat·ing. 1.** to give (power, authority, or responsibility) to another or others. **2.** to appoint or send as a delegate: *The club delegated Bill to head its fund-raising drive.*

del·e·ga·tion (del′ə gā′shən) n. **1.** a group of delegates: *A delegation of war veterans marched in the parade.* **2.** the act of delegating or the state of being delegated.

de·lete (di lēt′) v.t., **de·let·ed, de·let·ing.** to cross out or take out (something written or printed); omit; cancel: *Jane deleted Sam's name from the list of volunteers.*

del·e·te·ri·ous (del′i tēr′ē əs) adj. causing harm; injurious; hurtful: *a deleterious drug.* —**del′e·te′ri·ous·ly,** adv. —**del′e·te′ri·ous·ness,** n.

de·le·tion (di lē′shən) n. **1.** the act of deleting or the state of being deleted. **2.** something that has been deleted.

delft (delft) n. glazed earthenware decorated in patterns inspired by Chinese porcelains. [From *Delft,* a city in the Netherlands where it was first made.]

Del·hi (del′ē) n. a city in northern India, near New Delhi. Pop. (1971), 3,694,451. Also, **Old Delhi.**

Delft plate

de·lib·er·ate (adj., di lib′ər it; v., di lib′ə rāt′) adj. **1.** carefully thought out or planned; intentional; studied: *He made a deliberate attempt to ignore their rude comments.* **2.** careful and slow in deciding; not hasty or rash: *The businessman was deliberate in his dealings with others.* **3.** unhurried in action or movement; slow: *The old man walked with deliberate steps.* —v., **de·lib·er·at·ed, de·lib·er·at·ing.** —v.i. to think or consider carefully: *She deliberated whether or not she should go to the party.* —v.t. to think over or discuss carefully; debate: *The Senate has been deliberating the question for three days.* —**de·lib′er·ate·ly,** adv. —**de·lib′er·ate·ness,** n.

de·lib·er·a·tion (di lib′ə rā′shən) n. **1.** careful thought or consideration: *She decided to go only after much deliberation.* **2.** a discussion and consideration by a group of people of the reasons for and against something: *He reported on the deliberations of the jury.* **3.** slowness and care in decision or action: *He spoke with deliberation.*

de·lib·er·a·tive (di lib′ə rā′tiv) adj. relating to deliberation: *The state legislature is a deliberative assembly.*

del·i·ca·cy (del′i kə sē) n. pl., **del·i·ca·cies. 1.** fineness of structure, quality, texture, or form; daintiness; frailty:

the delicacy of lace. **2.** a rare or choice food: *Caviar is a delicacy.* **3.** physical weakness: *His delicacy kept him from participating in sports.* **4.** requiring tact, skill, or care in treatment or handling: *the delicacy of a situation, a matter of great delicacy.* **5.** fineness of taste, skill, or feeling. **6.** sensitivity to what is becoming, proper, or modest.

del·i·cate (del′i kit) adj. **1.** fine or dainty in structure, quality, texture, or form: *a delicate piece of lace, a face with delicate features.* **2.** pleasing to the senses in a soft, mild, or subtle way: *a delicate perfume, a delicate color, a delicate flavor.* **3.** easily damaged; fragile: *a delicate flower, a delicate crystal wine glass.* **4.** very susceptible to disease or injury: *a delicate child.* **5.** requiring tact, skill, or care in treatment or handling; difficult: *a delicate topic of conversation, a delicate brain operation.* **6.** finely skilled or sensitive: *a delicate touch, a delicate measuring instrument.* —**del′i·cate·ly,** adv. —**del′i·cate·ness,** n.

del·i·ca·tes·sen (del′i kə tes′ən) n. **1.** a store that sells prepared foods, such as cooked meats, salads, and cheeses. **2.** the foods sold in such a store.

de·li·cious (di lish′əs) adj. highly pleasing or delightful, especially to the taste or smell: *delicious fruit, a delicious meal.* —**de·li′cious·ly,** adv. —**de·li′cious·ness,** n.

de·light (di līt′) n. **1.** a high degree of pleasure; joy: *She could not conceal her delight at seeing him again.* **2.** something that gives great pleasure: *The dancer's performance was a delight to watch.* —v.t. to give great pleasure or joy to; please highly: *The puppet show delighted the children.* —v.i. to have or take great pleasure: *He delighted in helping others.*

de·light·ed (di lī′tid) adj. highly pleased; gratified: *Mary said she would be delighted to come to the party.* —**de·light′ed·ly,** adv.

de·light·ful (di līt′fəl) adj. highly pleasing; giving delight: *a delightful story, a delightful person.* —**de·light′ful·ly,** adv. —**de·light′ful·ness,** n.

de·lin·e·ate (di lin′ē āt′) v.t., **de·lin·e·at·ed, de·lin·e·at·ing. 1.** to draw or show the outline of; sketch: *The map delineated the boundaries between the two countries.* **2.** to describe in words; portray: *The author of the novel delineated the characters clearly.*

de·lin·e·a·tion (di lin′ē ā′shən) n. **1.** the act or process of delineating. **2.** something that delineates, such as a drawing or description.

de·lin·quen·cy (de ling′kwən sē) n. pl., **de·lin·quen·cies. 1.** a failure or neglect of duty or obligation. **2.** a fault; offense; misdeed. **3.** see **juvenile delinquency.**

de·lin·quent (di ling′kwənt) adj. **1.** failing in or neglectful of a duty or obligation: *He was always delinquent in paying his bills.* **2.** guilty of a fault, offense, or misdeed. **3.** due and unpaid: *delinquent taxes.* —n. a person who is delinquent. —**de·lin′quent·ly,** adv.

de·lir·i·ous (di lēr′ē əs) adj. **1.** temporarily out of one's mind; raving: *The fever made him delirious.* **2.** wildly excited: *He was delirious with happiness when he won the award.* —**de·lir′i·ous·ly,** adv. —**de·lir′i·ous·ness,** n.

de·lir·i·um (di lēr′ē əm) n. **1.** a temporary disturbance of the mind, occurring during high fevers or intoxication. Delirium is characterized by confusion, restlessness, excitement, and hallucinations. **2.** wild excitement or emotion.

de·liv·er (di liv′ər) v.t. **1.** to carry or take to a particular place or person: *to deliver mail, to deliver groceries.* **2.** to give forth in words or sound; utter; pronounce: *to deliver a speech.* **3.** to strike: *to deliver a blow.* **4.** to throw; pitch: *The pitcher delivered a curve ball.* **5.** to surrender or hand over: *The man he thought of as a friend delivered him to the authorities.* **6.** to help in the birth of: *The doctor delivered the twins.* **7.** to set free; rescue; save: *to deliver* *slaves from bondage.* —*v.i.* to make deliveries: *Does that supermarket deliver?* —**de·liv′er·er,** *n.*

de·liv·er·ance (di liv′ər əns) *n.* **1.** the act of setting free; rescue. **2.** a judgment or opinion expressed formally or publicly.

de·liv·er·y (di liv′ər ē) *n. pl.,* **de·liv·er·ies. 1.** the act of carrying or taking something to a particular place or person: *That laundry makes deliveries to its customers.* **2.** something carried or brought: *The eggs were missing from the grocery delivery.* **3.** a manner of speaking or singing: *The singer's delivery was too weak.* **4.** the act or manner of sending forth, discharging, or striking: *The pitcher had an awkward delivery.* **5.** the act of giving birth. **6.** the act of giving up; handing over; surrender. **7.** the act of setting free or saving; rescue.

dell (del) *n.* a small, usually wooded, glen or valley.

Del·phi (del′fī) *n.* an ancient city in central Greece, the site of the Delphic oracle.

Del·phic (del′fik) *adj.* **1.** relating to Delphi, the oracle of Apollo at Delphi, or Apollo himself. **2.** *also,* **delphic.** having more than one meaning; ambiguous.

Delphic oracle, the oracle or prophetess of Apollo at Delphi, famed for giving advice or prophecies having more than one meaning.

del·phin·i·um (del fin′ē əm) *n.* a plant having dense spikes of flowers, usually blue or purple. Also, **larkspur.**

del·ta (del′tə) **1.** the fourth letter of the Greek alphabet (Δ, δ), corresponding to English *D, d.* **2.** something having the triangular shape of this letter. **3.** an area of land that is formed by deposits of silt, sand, and pebbles at the mouth of a river and is usually triangular in shape.

del·ta·wing (del′tə wing′) *adj.* (of an airplane) having triangular-shaped wings.

de·lude (di lōōd′) *v.t.,* **de·lud·ed, de·lud·ing.** to mislead the mind or judgment of; deceive: *The dishonest politician attempted to delude the voters by promising impossible reforms.*

del·uge (del′yōōj) *n.* **1.** a great flood. **2.** a heavy rain; downpour: *They were drenched by the deluge before they could reach shelter.* **3.** anything that overwhelms or rushes like a flood: *That resort has a deluge of tourists during the holiday season.* **4. the Deluge.** in the Old Testament, the great flood in the time of Noah. —*v.t.,* **del·uged, del·ug·ing. 1.** to flood with water: *The heavy rain deluged the valley.* **2.** to overwhelm by any great rush: *The magazine was deluged with angry letters from its readers.*

de·lu·sion (di lōō′zhən) *n.* **1.** a false idea or belief: *He had the delusion that wealth always leads to happiness.* **2.** the act of deluding or the state of being deluded.

de·lu·sive (di lōō′siv) *adj.* tending to mislead the mind or judgment. —**de·lu′sive·ly,** *adv.* —**de·lu′sive·ness,** *n.*

de·luxe (di luks′) *adj.* exceptionally fine in quality or elegance: *The couple had a deluxe room at the hotel.*

delve (delv) *v.i.,* **delved, delv·ing. 1.** to make a careful investigation or search for information: *The detectives delved into the facts of the crime.* **2.** *Archaic.* to dig.

Dem., Democrat; Democratic.

de·mag·net·ize (dē mag′nə tīz′) *v.t.,* **de·mag·net·ized, de·mag·net·iz·ing.** to remove the magnetism from. —**de·mag′net·i·za′tion,** *n.*

dem·a·gog·ic (dem′ə goj′ik) *adj.* of, relating to, or characteristic of a demagogue.

dem·a·gogue (dem′ə gog′) *also,* **dem·a·gog.** a public leader or agitator who appeals to the emotions and prejudices of the people in order to gain or keep power.

dem·a·gogu·er·y (dem′ə gog′ər ē) *n.* the actions, practices, or principles of a demagogue.

de·mand (di mand′) *v.t.* **1.** to ask for urgently: *The angry customer demanded a refund.* **2.** to ask for with authority; claim as a right: *The judge demanded silence in the courtroom.* **3.** to require as necessary or useful; call for; need: *This job demands careful attention.* —*n.* **1.** the act of demanding: *His demand for a raise in salary was turned down.* **2.** something demanded: *His job makes many demands on his time.* **3.** the desire for a product together with the ability to buy it: *The demand for the new novel was greater than the supply of copies the publisher had in stock.* —**de·mand′er,** *n.*

in demand. sought after; wanted: *The singer's new recording was much in demand.*

de·mar·ca·tion (dē′mär kā′shən) *n.* **1.** the marking or fixing of limits or boundaries: *the demarcation of public parks in a state.* **2.** separation; distinction: *the demarcation between youth and old age.*

de·mean¹ (di mēn′) *v.t.* to lower the dignity or status of; degrade; debase: *The old man would not demean himself by asking for charity.* [*De-* + *mean².*]

de·mean² (di mēn′) *v.t.* to behave or conduct (oneself): *The boy demeaned himself well at his new school.* [Old French *demener* to conduct.]

de·mean·or (di mē′nər) *n.* the way a person behaves or conducts himself; manner: *He has a calm demeanor.*

de·ment·ed (di men′tid) *adj.* having a severe mental illness; insane. —**de·ment′ed·ly,** *adv.*

de·mer·it (dē mer′it) *n.* **1.** a mark against a person for bad work or behavior: *The teacher gave him a demerit for being late for school.* **2.** something that deserves blame; fault.

de·mesne (di mān′, di mēn′) *n.* **1.** the manor house and land belonging to a feudal lord. **2.** domain; realm.

De·me·ter (di mē′tər) *n. Greek Mythology.* the goddess of agriculture and the fertility and fruits of the earth. In Roman mythology she was called Ceres.

dem·i·god (dem′ē god′) *n.* **1.** an inferior or lesser god. **2.** the child of a god or goddess and a mortal.

dem·i·john (dem′ē jon′) *n.* a narrow-necked bottle of glass or earthenware, usually enclosed in wicker and holding from one to ten gallons.

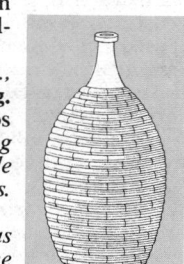

de·mil·i·tar·ize (dē mil′ə tə rīz′) *v.t.,* **de·mil·i·tar·ized, de·mil·i·tar·iz·ing.** to remove military installations or troops from (an area or zone): *The two warring nations agreed to demilitarize a four-mile strip of land between their countries.* —**de·mil′i·ta·ri·za′tion,** *n.*

de·mise (di mīz′) *n.* **1.** death: *She was eighty years old at her demise.* **2.** end: *the demise of slavery.*

dem·i·tasse (dem′ē tas′) *n.* **1.** a small cup of black, usually strong, coffee. **2.** a small cup in which such coffee is commonly served.

Demijohn

de·mo·bi·lize (dē mō′bə līz′) *v.t.,* **de·mo·bi·lized, de·mo·bi·liz·ing. 1.** to disband or dismiss from military service: *The government demobilized the troops when the war*

at; āpe; cär; end; mē; it; īce; hot; ōld; fôrk; wood; fōōl; oil; out; up; turn; sing; thin; this; hw in white; zh in treasure. The symbol ə stands for the sound of a in about, e in taken, i in pencil, o in lemon, and u in circus.

ended. **2.** to change from a state of readiness for war; put on a peacetime basis: *The country demobilized its industries after the war.* —**de·mo′bi·li·za′tion,** *n.*

de·moc·ra·cy (di mok′rə sē) *n. pl.,* **de·moc·ra·cies.** **1.** a government that is run by the people, who rule either directly, or indirectly. **2.** a nation or state having such a government. **3.** the belief that all people are equal socially and politically. [Middle French *democratie;* going back to Greek *dēmos* people + *-kratiā* rule.]

▲ **Democracy** and **republic** do not always mean the same thing. In a **democracy** the people may rule directly, as in ancient Athens, or they may have indirect control through elected representatives, as in the United States. In a **republic** power is always held by elected representatives, rather than by the people themselves.

dem·o·crat (dem′ə krat′) *n.* **1.** a person who believes in or supports democracy as a principle of government. **2.** a person who believes that all people are equal socially and politically. **3. Democrat.** a member of the Democratic Party.

dem·o·crat·ic (dem′ə krat′ik) *adj.* **1.** of, relating to, or supporting democracy. **2.** believing all people are equal socially and politically. **3. Democratic.** of, relating to, or characteristic of the Democratic Party. —**dem′o·crat′i·cal·ly,** *adv.*

Democratic Party, one of the two major political parties in the United States.

de·moc·ra·tize (di mok′rə tīz′) *v.t., v.i.,* **de·moc·ra·tized, de·moc·ra·tiz·ing.** to make or become democratic.

de·mol·ish (di mol′ish) *v.t.* **1.** to tear down or apart; destroy the structure of: *The wreckers demolished the old apartment building.* **2.** to destroy or ruin completely: *New evidence demolished the defense lawyer's case.* —**de·mol′ish·ment,** *n.*

dem·o·li·tion (dem′ə lish′ən) *n.* the act of demolishing or the state of being demolished.

de·mon (dē′mən) *n.* **1.** an evil spirit; devil. **2.** a very wicked or cruel person. **3.** a person who shows great skill or energy in some activity: *Bobby is a demon on ice skates. John is a demon for work.*

de·mo·ni·ac (di mō′nē ak′) *adj.* **1.** of or like a demon or evil spirit; devilish. **2.** caused by a demon or evil spirit. Also, **de·mo·ni·a·cal** (dē′mə nī′ə kəl). —*n.* a person supposedly possessed by a demon. —**de·mo·ni·a·cal·ly** (dē′mə nī′ik lē), *adv.*

de·mon·stra·ble (di mon′strə bəl) *adj.* that can be proved, shown, or made clear: *a demonstrable theory.* —**de·mon′stra·bil′i·ty,** *n.* —**de·mon′stra·bly,** *adv.*

dem·on·strate (dem′ən strāt′) *v.,* **dem·on·strat·ed, dem·on·strat·ing.** —*v.t.* **1.** to prove or make clear: *The recent election demonstrated the voters' support of the mayor's policies.* **2.** to describe, explain, or show by use of experiments or examples: *The teacher demonstrated the principle of static electricity.* **3.** to make a show of; express openly: *She demonstrated her love for the kitten by cuddling it.* **4.** to show the uses or merits of (a product): *The salesman demonstrated the record player in the department store.* —*v.i.* to hold or take part in a public meeting or parade to show feelings toward a particular issue or person: *A group of citizens demonstrated against pollution.*

dem·on·stra·tion (dem′ən strā′shən) *n.* **1.** something that proves clearly: *His rescue of the child from the burning house was a demonstration of his bravery.* **2.** an explaining or showing by the use of experiments or examples: *The science teacher gave a demonstration of the law of gravity.* **3.** an open show or expression of feeling or emotion: *The prisoner reacted to the judge's sentence with a demonstration of anger.* **4.** a public meeting or parade to show feeling toward a particular issue or person: *The workers held a*

demonstration to demand a raise in wages. **5.** the act of showing the uses or merits of a product: *a demonstration of a sewing machine.*

de·mon·stra·tive (di mon′strə tiv) *adj.* **1.** showing one's feelings or emotions openly, especially affectionate ones: *The demonstrative child hugged and kissed her parents.* **2.** showing or explaining clearly: *a demonstrative experiment of the properties of magnetism.* **3.** *Grammar.* pointing out a particular person or thing. In the sentence *This is my book and that is yours, this* and *that* are demonstrative pronouns. —**de·mon′stra·tive·ly,** *adv.* —**de·mon′stra·tive·ness,** *n.*

dem·on·stra·tor (dem′ən strā′tər) *n.* **1.** a person who demonstrates, especially a person who takes part in a demonstration of public feeling. **2.** something used for demonstration, such as a sample product used in demonstrations to customers.

de·mor·al·ize (di môr′ə līz′, di mor′ə līz′) *v.t.,* **de·mor·al·ized, de·mor·al·iz·ing.** **1.** to lower or destroy the morale of; deprive of courage, confidence, or hope; dishearten: *A series of defeats demoralized the team.* **2.** to lower the morals of; corrupt. —**de·mor′al·iz·a′tion,** *n.*

De·mos·the·nes (də mos′thə nēz′) 384?–322 B.C., Greek orator and statesman.

de·mote (di mōt′) *v.t.,* **de·mot·ed, de·mot·ing.** to reduce to a lower grade or rank: *to demote a soldier from corporal to private.* —**de·mo·tion** (di mō′shən) *n.*

de·mur (di mur′) *v.i.,* **de·murred, de·mur·ring.** to make an objection; show disapproval: *The boy demurred at being told to do extra homework.* —*n.* the act of demurring; an objection raised.

de·mure (di myoor′) *adj.,* **de·mur·er, de·mur·est.** **1.** quiet and modest; shy; reserved: *a demure young girl.* **2.** pretending to be shy or modest; coy. —**de·mure′ly,** *adv.* —**de·mure′ness,** *n.*

den (den) *n.* **1.** a place where a wild animal lives; lair: *a bear's den.* **2.** a hideout or secret place, especially one in which criminals have their headquarters. **3.** a private room, usually small and cozy, for relaxation or study. **4.** a group of about eight cub scouts.

de·na·ture (dē nā′chər) *v.t.,* **de·na·tured, de·na·tur·ing.** **1.** to make (a substance) unfit for drinking or eating without destroying its other useful properties: *to denature alcohol.* **2.** to change the nature of. —**de·na′tur·a′tion,** *n.*

den·drite (den′drīt) *n.* a small branched fiber in a nerve cell that conducts impulses to the cell body.

de·ni·al (di nī′əl) *n.* **1.** the act of saying something is untrue; contradiction: *The judge listened to the defendant's denial of the charges against him.* **2.** the act of refusing something asked for or desired: *His denial of their request for a contribution was disappointing.* **3.** a refusal to acknowledge a connection with or responsibility for. **4.** a refusal to accept or believe in something: *He wrote a denial of his former belief in communism.*

Dendrites

Cell body

Nucleus

Nucleolus

Dendrite

den·i·grate (den′ə grāt′) *v.t.,* **den·i·grat·ed, den·i·grat·ing.** to blacken the reputation of; slander. —**den′i·gra′tion,** *n.*

den·im (den′im) *n.* **1.** a heavy, twilled cotton fabric used for such items as work clothes and sportswear. **2. denims.** overalls or trousers made of this fabric. [Short for French (serge) de Nîm(es) (serge) of Nîmes, a French city where the fabric was first made.]

den·i·zen (den'ə zən) n. a person or animal that lives in a place; inhabitant; dweller: *Wolves are denizens of the forest.*

Den·mark (den'märk) n. a country in northern Europe, between the North and Baltic seas. Capital, Copenhagen. Area, 16,619 sq. mi. Pop. (1971 est.), 4,970,000.

de·nom·i·nate (di nom'ə nāt') v.t., **de·nom·i·nat·ed, de·nom·i·nat·ing.** to give a name to; name; designate.

de·nom·i·nate number (di nom'ə nit) a number that specifies a quantity by limiting a unit of measurement. In the expression *5 pounds, 5* is a denominate number.

de·nom·i·na·tion (di nom'ə nā'shən) n. **1.** a religious group or sect: *He is of the Lutheran denomination.* **2.** one kind of unit in a system of numbers, measures, or values: *A dime and a nickel are coins of different denominations.* **3.** a name for a group or class of things; designation.

de·nom·i·na·tion·al (di nom'ə nā'shən əl) adj. relating to or controlled by a religious denomination or sect: *a denominational school.* —**de·nom'i·na'tion·al·ly,** adv.

de·nom·i·na·tor (di nom'ə nā'tər) n. a number below or to the right of the line in a fraction, indicating the number of equal parts into which the whole is divided; divisor. In the fraction ½, 2 is the denominator.

de·no·ta·tion (dē'nō tā'shən) n. **1.** the exact and literal meaning of a word or phrase, as distinct from what it suggests. **2.** the act of denoting or the state of being denoted.

de·note (di nōt') v.t., **de·not·ed, de·not·ing. 1.** to be a sign of; indicate: *A rapidly falling barometer denotes an approaching storm.* **2.** to be a name for; mean: *The word "dentist" denotes a doctor whose work is the care of teeth.* **3.** to be a mark or symbol for: *The sign* ° *denotes degrees.* ▲ **Denote** and **connote** both refer to the meaning of a word. To **denote** is to give the literal meaning of a word. To **connote** is to refer to what a word suggests in addition to its literal meaning. The word "lion" *denotes* a large animal of the cat family, but it *connotes* strength and courage.

de·noue·ment (dā'noo män') n. the final outcome or solution of the plot in a play or story, or of a complex or difficult situation.

de·nounce (di nouns') v.t., **de·nounced, de·nounc·ing. 1.** to attack or speak against publicly or openly: *The senator denounced the rise in food prices.* **2.** to inform against; accuse: *He denounced the forger to the police.* **3.** to announce formally the end of (a treaty, armistice, or other agreement). —**de·nounce'ment,** n. —**de·nounc'er,** n.

dense (dens) adj., **dens·er, dens·est. 1.** having parts closely packed together; thick; compact: *a dense forest, a dense crowd.* **2.** *Informal.* stupid or dull. —**dense'ly,** adv. —**dense'ness,** n.

den·si·ty (den'sə tē) n. pl., **den·si·ties. 1.** the quality or condition of being closely packed together; thickness; compactness: *The density of the jungle made traveling difficult.* **2.** *Physics.* the ratio of the mass of a substance to its volume: *Iron has a greater density than wood.* **3.** quantity per unit of area, volume, length, or time: *The density of population in that region of the country is very high.* **4.** *Informal.* stupidity.

dent (dent) n. **1.** a hollow or depression in a surface made by a blow or pressure: *a dent in an automobile fender.* **2.** headway; progress: *He worked all night, but barely made a dent in the work.* —v.t. to make a hollow or depression in. —v.i. to become dented: *This metal dents easily.*

den·tal (dent'əl) adj. **1.** of, for, or relating to the teeth. **2.** of, relating to, or used in dentistry: *dental equipment.*

den·ti·frice (den'tə fris) n. a paste, powder, or liquid used for cleaning the teeth.

den·tin (den'tin) *also,* **den·tine** (den'tēn, den tēn'). n. the hard, bony material forming the major part of a tooth, covered by the enamel.

den·tist (den'tist) n. a doctor who specializes in the health, care, and treatment of the teeth and gums.

den·tist·ry (den'tis trē) n. **1.** the branch of medical science dealing with the health, care, and treatment of the teeth and gums. **2.** the work done by a dentist.

den·ture (den'chər) n. a false tooth or set of false teeth.

de·nude (di nōōd', di nyōōd') v.t., **de·nud·ed, de·nud·ing.** to strip of all covering; make bare: *The heavy bombing denuded the land of all plant growth.*

de·nun·ci·a·tion (di nun'sē ā'shən) n. **1.** a public expression of disapproval; open condemnation. **2.** the act of informing against; accusation.

Den·ver (den'vər) n. the capital and largest city of Colorado, in the north-central part of the state. Pop. (1970), 514,678.

de·ny (di nī') v.t., **de·nied, de·ny·ing. 1.** to declare (something) to be untrue; contradict: *She denied that she had spent her whole allowance.* **2.** to refuse to believe or accept as being true or valid; reject: *to deny a superstition.* **3.** to refuse to give or grant: *His boss denied his request for a raise.* **4.** to refuse to acknowledge; disavow: *to deny one's family.*

to deny oneself. to do without things that one wants: *She denied herself desserts in order to lose weight.*

de·o·dor·ant (dē ō'dər ənt) n. a substance that destroys or covers up unpleasant odors. —adj. that can destroy or cover up unpleasant odors: *a deodorant soap.*

de·o·dor·ize (dē ō'də rīz') v.t., **de·o·dor·ized, de·o·dor·iz·ing.** to destroy or cover up the unpleasant odor of. —**de·o'dor·i·za'tion,** n. —**de·o'dor·iz'er,** n.

de·ox·i·dize (dē ok'sə dīz') v.t., **de·ox·i·dized, de·ox·i·diz·ing.** to remove oxygen from, especially chemically combined oxygen. —**de·ox'i·di·za'tion,** n. —**de·ox'i·diz'er,** n.

de·ox·y·ri·bo·nu·cle·ic acid (dē ok'sē rī'bō nōō-klē'ik, dē ok'sē rī'bō nyōō klē'ik) see **DNA.**

de·part (di pärt') v.i. **1.** to go away; leave: *The plane departs at nine o'clock. She departed in a hurry.* **2.** to differ or change: *He departed from his usual habit of arriving at school early and was an hour late.*

de·part·ed (di pär'tid) adj. past; gone: *departed fame.* —n. a person or persons who have died.

de·part·ment (di pärt'mənt) n. **1.** a separate part or division of an organization or government: *the police department of a city, the sales department of a company, the English department of a school.* **2.** an administrative district of France.

de·part·men·tal (dē'pärt ment'əl) adj. of or relating to a department: *a departmental meeting.*

department store, a large retail store selling a variety of merchandise arranged in separate departments.

de·par·ture (di pär'chər) n. **1.** the act of departing or leaving: *The departure of the plane was on time.* **2.** a change, as from a standard or usual course of action; deviation: *a departure from habit.* **3.** the act of setting out, as on a course of action: *This law marks a new departure in civil rights legislation.* **4.** *Archaic.* death.

---

at; āpe; cär; end; mē; it; īce; hot; ōld; fôrk; wood; fōōl; oil; out; up; turn; sing; thin; **th**is; **hw** in white; **zh** in treasure. The symbol ə stands for the sound of **a** in about, **e** in taken, **i** in pencil, **o** in lemon, and **u** in circus.

de·pend (di pend´) v.i. **1.** to place confidence; rely: *She could always depend on Jim to help.* **2.** to rely for what is needed or wanted: *While he was a student he depended on his parents for support.* **3.** to be influenced or determined: *Whether he takes the job depends on what the salary is.*

de·pen·da·ble (di pen´də bəl) adj. that can be depended on; reliable: *He is a dependable worker.* —**de·pen·da·bil·i·ty,** n. —**de·pen·da·bly,** adv.

de·pen·dence (di pen´dəns) n. **1.** the state of relying on another for what is needed or wanted: *the dependence of a baby on his mother.* **2.** the state of being influenced or determined by something else: *the dependence of crops on rain.* **3.** trust; reliance.

de·pen·den·cy (di pen´dən sē) n. pl., **de·pen·den·cies.** **1.** a country or territory that is governed by another country but is not part of the governing country: *Puerto Rico is a dependency of the United States.* **2.** another word for **dependence.**

de·pen·dent (di pen´dənt) adj. **1.** relying on another for what is needed or wanted: *He was dependent on his uncle for his college tuition.* **2.** influenced or determined by something: *Our plans for the picnic are dependent on the weather.* —n. a person who depends on another for support or help. —**de·pen´dent·ly,** adv.

dependent clause, a clause that functions as a noun, adjective, or adverb within a sentence and cannot stand alone. In the sentence *After the girls had played tennis for an hour, they decided to go for a swim,* the clause *After the girls had played tennis for an hour* is a dependent clause. Also, **subordinate clause.**

de·pict (di pikt´) v.t. **1.** to represent by drawing or painting; picture; portray: *The artist depicted the ocean.* **2.** to represent in words; describe: *The poet depicted the sound of the waves.* —**de·pic´tion,** n.

de·pil·a·to·ry (di pil´ə tôr´ē) n. pl., **de·pil·a·to·ries.** a substance for removing hair. —adj. that can remove hair: *a depilatory cream.*

de·plane (dē plān´) v.i., **de·planed, de·plan·ing.** to get out of an airplane after landing.

de·plete (di plēt´) v.t., **de·plet·ed, de·plet·ing.** to reduce in amount; use up: *The campers depleted their food supply after three days. At the end of the long hike his strength was depleted.* —**de·ple´tion,** n.

de·plor·a·ble (di plôr´ə bəl) adj. **1.** that should be deplored: *His behavior in the classroom was deplorable.* **2.** wretched; miserable: *There were deplorable living conditions in the slums of the city.* —**de·plor´a·bly,** adv.

de·plore (di plôr´) v.t., **de·plored, de·plor·ing.** **1.** to disapprove of strongly: *The minister deplored the use of violence to bring about changes in society.* **2.** to be very sorry about; regret deeply; lament: *He deplored the death of his friend.*

de·ploy (di ploi´) v.t. **1.** to spread out (troops or ships) in a long line of battle. **2.** to spread out according to a plan: *The newspaper deployed reporters all over the country to cover the election.* —**de·ploy´ment,** n.

de·pop·u·late (dē pop´yə lāt´) v.t., **de·pop·u·lat·ed, de·pop·u·lat·ing.** to reduce the population of, as by death: *Heavy bombing depopulated the city.* —**de·pop´u·la´·tion,** n.

de·port (di pôrt´) v.t. **1.** to force to leave a country; expel: *The authorities deported the criminal as an undesirable alien.* **2.** to behave or conduct (oneself) in a specified way: *Mary always deports herself like a lady.*

de·por·ta·tion (dē´pôr tā´shən) n. expulsion from a country.

de·port·ment (di pôrt´mənt) n. the way in which a person acts or behaves; conduct; bearing: *the deportment of a soldier.*

de·pose (di pōz´) v.t., **de·posed, de·pos·ing.** **1.** to remove from a throne or other high office: *The rebels deposed the king.* **2.** Law. to declare under oath, especially in a written statement.

de·pos·it (di poz´it) v.t. **1.** to put (money or valuables) in a bank or other place for safekeeping: *He deposited five dollars in his savings account.* **2.** to set or lay down; place: *She deposited the groceries on the table.* **3.** to leave as a layer: *The river deposited silt at its mouth.* —n. **1.** something put in a place for safekeeping, especially money in a bank. **2.** something given as part payment or security: *He made a deposit of $150 on a new car.* **3.** something that has settled: *a deposit of dust on the window sill.* **4.** a natural layer, as of a mineral: *a large deposit of iron ore.*

dep·o·si·tion (dep´ə zish´ən) n. **1.** removal from a throne or other high office. **2.** a sworn, written statement given by a witness out of court, intended to be used as testimony in court. **3.** the act or process of laying down: *The delta at the mouth of the river was formed by the deposition of silt.* **4.** something deposited; deposit.

de·pos·i·tor (di poz´ə tər) n. a person who makes a deposit, especially a person who deposits money in a bank.

de·pos·i·to·ry (di poz´ə tôr´ē) n. pl., **de·pos·i·to·ries.** a place where something is deposited for safekeeping.

de·pot (def. 1 dē´pō; defs. 2, 3 dep´ō) n. **1.** a railroad station or bus terminal. **2.** a place where military supplies and equipment are stored. **3.** a storage place; storehouse; warehouse.

de·prave (di prāv´) v.t., **de·praved, de·prav·ing.** to make morally bad; corrupt.

de·praved (di prāvd´) adj. morally bad; corrupt; perverted: *a depraved man.*

de·prav·i·ty (di prav´ə tē) n. pl., **de·prav·i·ties.** **1.** the state of being depraved; corruption. **2.** a depraved act or practice.

dep·re·cate (dep´rə kāt´) v.t., **dep·re·cat·ed, dep·re·cat·ing.** to express disapproval of; disparage; belittle: *The critic deprecated the author's latest novel.* —**dep´re·ca´·tion,** n.

dep·re·ca·to·ry (dep´rə kə tôr´ē) adj. expressing disapproval: *deprecatory remarks.*

de·pre·ci·ate (di prē´shē āt´) v., **de·pre·ci·at·ed, de·pre·ci·at·ing.** —v.t. **1.** to lower the price or value of. **2.** to represent as of little value; belittle: *He depreciated our efforts to help.* —v.i. to fall in price or value: *The value of the dollar sometimes depreciates.* —**de·pre´ci·a´tor,** n.

de·pre·ci·a·tion (di prē´shē ā´shən) n. a decrease in value as a result of wear, age, or use: *the depreciation of a car over the years.*

dep·re·da·tion (dep´rə dā´shən) n. the act of plundering or destroying; ravaging.

de·press (di pres´) v.t. **1.** to lower in spirits; make gloomy; sadden: *The death of his dog depressed the boy.* **2.** to lessen in force, vigor, or activity; weaken: *The medicine depressed the patient's pulse rate.* **3.** to press or push down: *to depress the accelerator in an automobile.*

de·pres·sant (di pres´ənt) n. **1.** a drug or other substance that reduces or slows down nervous, muscular, or other body activities. Anesthetics, sedatives, and narcotics are depressants. **2.** anything that depresses.

de·pressed (di prest´) adj. **1.** low in spirits; sad: *He was very depressed when he failed the exam.* **2.** decreased in activity, force, value, or price. **3.** having a high rate of unemployment and a low standard of living: *a depressed area of a country.* **4.** pressed down: *a depressed key on a typewriter.*

de·pres·sion (di presh´ən) n. **1.** a sunken place or surface; hollow: *The car bumped over the depression in the road.* **2.** lowness of spirits; sadness; dejection: *His failure* caused a fit of depression. **3.** a period marked by a severe reduction in business activity, a rise in unemployment, and falling wages and prices. **4.** the act of pressing down.

dep·ri·va·tion (dep′rə vā′shən) n. the act of depriving or the state of being deprived.

de·prive (di prīv′) v.t., **de·prived, de·priv·ing. 1.** to take away from: *The proposed highway will deprive the children of their playground.* **2.** to keep from having or enjoying: *to deprive a citizen of his or her right to vote.*

dept., department.

depth (depth) n. **1.** the distance downward, inward, or from front to back: *The depth of the pool was twelve feet at the deep end. The depth of the building lot was 250 feet.* **2.** the quality of being deep; deepness: *The mother's depth of understanding helped her son with his problems.* **3.** deepness of feeling or thought: *That movie is amusing, but it has no depth.* **4.** also, **depths. a.** the deepest, lowest, or furthest part: *The treasure lay buried in the depths of the ocean.* **b.** the most intense or extreme state or stage: *the depths of sorrow.*

depth charge, an explosive charge designed to go off under water at a certain depth, used especially against submarines. Also, **depth bomb.**

dep·u·ta·tion (dep′yə tā′shən) n. **1.** a person or persons authorized to represent another or others; delegation: *A deputation from the striking miners demanded higher wages.* **2.** the act of deputing or the state of being deputed.

de·pute (di pyo͞ot′) v.t., **de·put·ed, de·put·ing. 1.** to appoint as one's substitute, delegate, or agent. **2.** to transfer, as work or authority, to another.

dep·u·tize (dep′yə tīz′) v.t., **dep·u·tized, dep·u·tiz·ing.** to appoint as deputy.

dep·u·ty (dep′yə tē) n. pl., **dep·u·ties.** a person appointed or authorized to act for or take the place of another or others: *The sheriff appointed deputies to help him capture the criminal.*

de·rail (dē rāl′) v.t. to cause to run off the rails: *to derail a train.* —v.i. to run off the rails. —**de·rail′ment,** n.

de·range (di rānj′) v.t., **de·ranged, de·rang·ing. 1.** to disturb the order or arrangement of. **2.** to make insane.

de·range·ment (di rānj′mənt) n. **1.** mental illness; insanity. **2.** disturbance of order or arrangement; disorder.

der·by (dur′bē) n. pl., **der·bies. 1.** a hard, round man's hat with a narrow rolled brim. **2. Derby. a.** a race for three-year-old horses, held annually near London, England. **b.** any similar horse race: *the Kentucky Derby.* **3.** any large race or contest.

der·e·lict (der′ə likt′) n. **1.** a homeless, wandering person; vagrant; tramp. **2.** property abandoned by the owner or guardian, especially a ship abandoned at sea. —adj. **1.** neglectful of one's duty; negligent: *The sentry was derelict in failing to notice the approach of the enemy.* **2.** abandoned by the owner: *a derelict ship.*

Derby

der·e·lic·tion (der′ə lik′shən) n. **1.** neglect of one's duty: *The guard's dereliction allowed the prisoners to escape.* **2.** the act of abandoning or the state of being abandoned; desertion.

de·ride (di rīd′) v.t., **de·rid·ed, de·rid·ing.** to treat with contempt or scorn; laugh at; ridicule: *Some people deride traditional customs as being old-fashioned.*

de·ri·sion (di rizh′ən) n. scornful contempt; mockery; ridicule.

de·ri·sive (di rī′siv) adj. showing or characterized by derision; mocking; ridiculing: *derisive laughter.* —**de·ri′sive·ly,** adv. —**de·ri′sive·ness,** n.

der·i·va·tion (der′ə vā′shən) n. **1.** the act of deriving or the state of being derived. **2.** a source or origin: *This legend is of Irish derivation.* **3.** something derived; derivative: *This custom is a derivation from an earlier English one.* **4.** the process of tracing the origin and development of a word. **5.** a statement of this; etymology. **6.** the formation of a new word from an existing word, root, or stem, especially by the addition of a prefix or suffix, such as *kindness* from *kind.*

In language, **derivation** usually refers to the forming of a word by adding a prefix or a suffix to an existing word. Because of derivation, there is almost no limit to the number of words that can exist in our language. Not all the derivations that are possible are in use in our language or recorded in a dictionary, but these derivations could exist and would be easily understood by someone reading or hearing them. If you take *friend* as a root word, you can make the common words *friendly, friendliness, friendless, friendship, befriend, unfriendly,* and *unfriendliness* and the uncommon or nonexistent words *ex-friend, nonfriend, antifriend, semifriend,* and *friendhood.*

de·riv·a·tive (di riv′ə tiv) adj. not original; derived: *a derivative theory.* —n. **1.** something derived. **2.** a word formed from another by derivation.

de·rive (di rīv′) v., **de·rived, de·riv·ing.** —v.t. **1.** to obtain from a source or origin: *to derive pleasure from reading.* **2.** to trace the origin of (something) from or to its source: *to derive a word.* —v.i. to come from a source; originate: *The word "democracy" derives from Greek.*

der·ma (dur′mə) n. another word for **dermis.**

der·mal (dur′məl) adj. of or relating to the skin.

der·ma·tol·o·gist (dur′mə tol′ə jist) n. a doctor who specializes in dermatology.

der·ma·tol·o·gy (dur′mə tol′ə jē) n. the branch of medical science dealing with the skin and its diseases.

der·mis (dur′mis) n. the layer of skin beneath the epidermis. Also, **derma.**

der·o·gate (der′ə gāt′) v.t., **der·o·gat·ed, der·o·gat·ing.** to lessen the importance or merit of; belittle: *The writer derogated the works of other authors.* —**der′o·ga′tion,** n.

de·rog·a·to·ry (di rog′ə tôr′ē) adj. lessening in importance or estimation; disparaging; belittling: *Derogatory comments usually make people angry.*

der·rick (der′ik) n. **1.** a machine for lifting and moving heavy objects, consisting of a vertical support to which a slanted boom with hoisting tackle is attached. **2.** the framework over an oil well or other drill hole that supports the drilling machinery. [From *Derrick,* a seventeenth-century hangman in London; the modern derrick is shaped like a gallows.]

der·ring-do (der′ing do͞o′) n. courageous behavior or deeds; daring: *The pirate tale was full of derring-do.*

Derrick (labeled: Guy, Hoisting tackle, Vertical support, Boom)

at; āpe; cär; end; mē; it; īce; hot; ōld; fôrk; wood; fo͞ol; oil; out; up; turn; sing; thin; this; hw in white; zh in treasure. The symbol ə stands for the sound of **a** in about, **e** in taken, **i** in pencil, **o** in lemon, and **u** in circus.

der·rin·ger (der′in jər) *n.* a pistol having a short barrel and a large caliber. [From Henry *Deringer*, a nineteenth-century American gunsmith, who invented it.]

Der·ry (der′ē) *n.* see **Londonderry.**

der·vish (dur′vish) *n. pl.*, **der·vish·es.** a member of any of various Muslim religious orders known for certain violent forms of worship, such as howling and whirling.

de·sal·i·nate (dē sal′ə nāt′) *v.t.*, **de·sal·i·nat·ed, de·sal·i·nat·ing.** to remove salt from: *to desalinate sea water.*

des·cant (*n.*, des′kant; *v.*, des kant′) *n. Music.* a melody that is sung or played above another melody, usually by several soprano voices or instruments. —*v.i.* to speak at length.

Des·cartes, Re·né (dā kärt′; rə nā′) 1596–1650, French philosopher and mathematician.

de·scend (di send′) *v.i.* 1. to move or pass from a higher place to a lower one; come or go downward: *They rode up the hill on horseback, but descended on foot.* 2. to slope or extend downward: *The hikers walked along a mountain path that descended to a lake.* 3. to be handed down by inheritance: *The property descended from the father to his son.* 4. to come down from an earlier source or ancestor: *His family descends from the first French colonists.* 5. to come in force or in overwhelming numbers: *The vultures descended on their prey.* 6. to lower oneself; stoop: *He was so hungry that he descended to robbery in order to get food.* —*v.t.* to come or go downward on or along: *to descend a mountain trail.*

de·scen·dant (di sen′dənt) *n.* a person who is descended from a particular ancestor or group of ancestors: *Queen Elizabeth is a descendant of Queen Victoria.* —*adj.* coming or going downward.

de·scent (di sent′) *n.* 1. movement from a higher place to a lower one: *the descent of an elevator.* 2. downward slope or inclination: *a hill with a steep descent.* 3. ancestry or birth: *Our family is of English descent.* 4. a sudden attack.

de·scribe (di skrīb′) *v.t.*, **de·scribed, de·scrib·ing.** 1. to give a picture of in words; tell or write about: *The boy's essay described his adventures at camp during the previous summer. Can you describe the man you saw at the window?* 2. to draw or trace the outline of: *to describe a circle with a compass.*

de·scrip·tion (di skrip′shən) *n.* 1. the act of giving a picture of in words: *The bank teller's description of the robber was very complete and accurate.* 2. a statement or account that describes. 3. kind; sort; variety: *There were dogs of every description in the show.* 4. the act of tracing in outline.

de·scrip·tive (di skrip′tiv) *adj.* giving a picture in words: *The tourists were given descriptive pamphlets about places to visit in England.* —**de·scrip′tive·ly,** *adv.* —**de·scrip′tive·ness,** *n.*

● In dictionary making, the term **descriptive** refers to a method of recording and defining words and explaining their usage according to the way people actually write and speak. Another approach to writing a dictionary is the **prescriptive** method. The statements in a dictionary following the prescriptive method are based on how the author or authors think words should be used. All early dictionaries tried to be prescriptive by telling the reader exactly what the author thought about the words he defined. Samuel Johnson stated in a dictionary he published in 1755 that *budge, coax,* and *touchy* were "low" words and that *chaperon* was "an affected word." Although Johnson began his work with the idea of following the prescriptive method, he came to realize that it was impossible to say with authority exactly what was right and wrong in language.

Modern writers of dictionaries understand that our language is constantly growing and changing, and that a dictionary must reflect these changes. They feel that the real purpose of a dictionary is to make communication easier by helping us to understand what our language really is, not what someone might want it to be.

de·scry (di skrī′) *v.t.*, **de·scried, de·scry·ing.** to catch sight of; make out from afar: *The sailor descried land in the distance.*

des·e·crate (des′ə krāt′) *v.t.*, **des·e·crat·ed, des·e·crat·ing.** to destroy the sacredness of; treat with irreverence; profane: *to desecrate a tomb.* —**des′e·crat·er,** *n.* —**des′e·cra′tion,** *n.*

de·seg·re·gate (dē seg′rə gāt′) *v.t.*, **de·seg·re·gat·ed, de·seg·re·gat·ing.** to do away with racial segregation in: *to desegregate a city's public school system.* —**de·seg′re·ga′tion,** *n.*

des·ert¹ (dez′ərt) *n.* 1. a hot, dry, sandy region with little or no plant or animal life. 2. any area of land with little or no plant or animal life. —*adj.* 1. relating to or living in a desert: *desert cactuses.* 2. not lived in or on; uninhabited; desolate: *a desert island.* [Old French *desert;* going back to Latin *dēserere* to abandon, forsake.]

de·sert² (di zurt′) *v.t.* to go away from (someone or something), especially one that should not be left; abandon; forsake: *The man deserted his wife and children. The soldier deserted his regiment. His friend deserted him when he needed help.* —*v.i.* to go away from one's duty, post, or cause: *The soldier deserted.* [French *déserter;* going back to Latin *dēserere* to abandon, forsake.] —**de·sert′er,** *n.*

de·sert³ (di zurt′) *n. also*, **de·serts.** a deserved reward or punishment: *When he was put in prison he got his just deserts for robbing the bank.* [Old French *deserte;* going back to Latin *dēservire* to serve well.]

de·ser·tion (di zur′shən) *n.* the act of deserting or the state of being deserted: *desertion from the army.*

de·serve (di zurv′) *v.t.*, **de·served, de·serv·ing.** to have a right to; be worthy of; merit: *The child's rude behavior deserves punishment. The boy deserves praise for getting such good marks at school.*

de·serv·ed·ly (di zur′vid lē) *adv.* according to merit; justly; rightfully: *He was deservedly praised for his great achievements.*

de·serv·ing (di zur′ving) *adj.* 1. worthy: *This plan is deserving of your attention.* 2. worthy of help, especially financial help: *The scholarship will be given to a deserving student.*

des·ic·cate (des′i kāt′) *v.t.*, **des·ic·cat·ed, des·ic·cat·ing.** to dry up completely: *The brook was desiccated by the long drought.*

de·sign (di zīn′) *n.* 1. a plan, sketch, or outline made to serve as a guide or pattern: *an architect's design for a house.* 2. an arrangement or combination of parts, details, or colors; pattern: *a blue and green design in a carpet, a floral design.* 3. the art of making designs: *a school of design.* 4. a plan, scheme, or project to be carried out: *His design for success was hard work.* 5. *also*, **designs.** a secret or evil plot or scheme: *The greedy man had designs on her fortune.* —*v.t.* 1. to make a first plan, sketch, or outline of; make a pattern for: *to design a spacecraft, to design an automobile.* 2. to plan and make with artistic skill; arrange the parts, details, or colors of: *to design a dress.* 3. to form in the mind; plan; conceive: *to design a plot for a novel.* 4. to have as an aim or purpose; intend: *He wrote a book designed for younger readers.*

des·ig·nate (dez′ig nāt′) *v.t.*, **des·ig·nat·ed, des·ig·nat·ing.** **1.** to point out or indicate by a distinctive mark, sign, or name; specify; signify: *The boundaries of the state are designated on the map.* **2.** to call by a particular name or title: *The head of the government of the United States is designated "President."* **3.** to select for a particular purpose, duty, or office; appoint: *My mother was designated chairman of the school board.*

designated hitter, a baseball player who bats in place of the pitcher, usually a powerful hitter.

des·ig·na·tion (dez′ig nā′shən) *n.* **1.** the act of pointing out or indicating something: *the designation of a place to meet.* **2.** a distinguishing name, title, or mark: *the designation of "Your Majesty."* **3.** selection for a particular purpose, duty, or office; appointment: *The president of the company is responsible for the designation of department heads.*

de·sign·ed·ly (di zī′nid lē) *adv.* on purpose.

de·sign·er (di zī′nər) *n.* a person who designs, especially a person who creates patterns for manufacture or construction: *a dress designer, an automobile designer.*

de·sign·ing (di zī′ning) *adj.* **1.** having low motives; scheming: *a crafty, designing person.* **2.** showing planning or forethought. —*n.* the practice or art of making designs or patterns.

de·sir·a·ble (di zīr′ə bəl) *adj.* worth having or wishing for; pleasing: *That busy corner is a desirable location for a drugstore.* —**de·sir′a·bil′i·ty,** *n.* —**de·sir′a·bly,** *adv.*

de·sire (di zīr′) *v.t.,* **de·sired, de·sir·ing. 1.** to have a strong wish for; long for; crave: *to desire success.* **2.** to express a wish for; request: *He desired information about vacationing in the mountains.* —*n.* **1.** a longing; wish: *a desire for wealth.* **2.** an expressed wish; request. **3.** something desired: *His main desire was to have his own car.*

de·sir·ous (di zīr′əs) *adj.* having desire; desiring: *The young actor was desirous of fame.*

de·sist (di zist′, di sist′) *v.i.* to cease some action; stop: *The two armies desisted from fighting and signed a truce.*

desk (desk) *n.* **1.** a piece of furniture having a flat or sloping surface and usually drawers or compartments, used especially for reading or writing. **2.** a booth or counter at which certain duties or services are performed, such as the place in a hotel where guests register. **3.** a division or department of an organization or office: *the city desk of a newspaper.*

Des Moines (də moin′) the capital and largest city of Iowa, in the south-central part of the state. Pop. (1970), 200,587.

des·o·late (*adj.,* des′ə lit; *v.,* des′ə lāt′) *adj.* **1.** lacking inhabitants; deserted: *a desolate ghost town, a desolate beach.* **2.** left alone; without companionship; lonely: *We felt desolate after our cousins moved away.* **3.** laid waste; devastated: *The forest was left desolate by the fire.* **4.** miserable; cheerless; dreary: *Living conditions for the early settlers in the North were desolate.* —*v.t.,* **des·o·lat·ed, des·o·lat·ing. 1.** to lay waste; devastate: *The tornado desolated the area.* **2.** to make miserable, wretched, or forlorn: *The news of his friend's illness desolated him.*

des·o·la·tion (des′ə lā′shən) *n.* **1.** the act of making desolate; devastation. **2.** loneliness; sadness: *Her desolation grew as days passed and the lost dog was not found.* **3.** a ruined or deserted condition: *He found the old house in complete desolation.* **4.** a desolate place or region.

De So·to, Her·nan·do (də sō′tō; er nän′dō) 1500?–1542, the Spanish explorer who discovered the Mississippi River.

de·spair (di sper′) *n.* **1.** a complete loss of hope: *Hope replaced despair when she got a job.* **2.** a person or thing that causes loss of hope: *The naughty child was the despair of his mother.* —*v.i.* to lose hope; be without hope: *After three days, she despaired of ever finding the lost puppy.*

des·patch (dis pach′) another spelling of **dispatch.**

des·patch·er (dis pach′ər) another spelling of **dispatcher.**

des·per·a·do (des′pə rä′dō) *n. pl.,* **des·per·a·does** or **des·per·a·dos.** a bold, desperate, or reckless criminal.

des·per·ate (des′pər it) *adj.* **1.** reckless because of hopelessness; ready or willing to take any risk; rash: *We made a desperate race to get out of the path of the storm.* **2.** done without regard to what happens afterward; irresponsible: *a desperate act.* **3.** having little or no hope of improvement or recovery; extremely bad; hopeless: *a desperate illness.* **4.** deep; extreme: *desperate concern.* —**des′per·ate·ly,** *adv.* —**des′per·ate·ness,** *n.*

des·per·a·tion (des′pə rā′shən) *n.* recklessness arising from loss of hope: *A rock crumbled and, in desperation, the mountaineer grasped a tree root from the ledge above.*

des·pi·ca·ble (des′pi kə bəl, di spik′ə bəl) *adj.* to be scorned; hateful; contemptible: *Cruelty to animals is despicable.* —**des′pi·ca·ble·ness,** *n.* —**des′pi·ca·bly,** *adv.*

de·spise (di spīz′) *v.t.,* **de·spised, de·spis·ing.** to look down on as hateful; scorn: *She always tells the truth and despises dishonesty in any form.*

de·spite (di spīt′) *prep.* in spite of; notwithstanding: *He went to work despite his sickness.*

de·spoil (di spoil′) *v.t.* to take away all the possessions of by force; rob; pillage; plunder: *The soldiers despoiled the enemy town.* —**de·spoil′er,** *n.*

de·spond (di spond′) *v.i.* to lose heart or hope; be depressed: *Although he failed the test, he did not despond.*

de·spon·den·cy (di spon′dən sē) *n. pl.,* **de·spon·den·cies.** loss of heart or hope; depression; dejection. Also, **de·spon·dence** (di spon′dəns).

de·spon·dent (di spon′dənt) *adj.* having lost heart or hope; depressed; dejected: *She was despondent when her brother became ill.* —**de·spon′dent·ly,** *adv.*

des·pot (des′pət) *n.* **1.** a ruler who governs with unlimited authority; absolute ruler; autocrat. **2.** any person who rules with unlimited authority; tyrant; oppressor.

des·pot·ic (dis pot′ik) *adj.* of or like a despot or despotism; tyrannical. —**des·pot′i·cal·ly,** *adv.*

des·pot·ism (des′pə tiz′əm) *n.* **1.** the rule of a despot. **2.** a government or state ruled by a despot.

des·sert (di zurt′) *n.* a course served at the end of a meal, usually a sweet food, such as cake, pie, fruit, or ice cream.

des·ti·na·tion (des′tə nā′shən) *n.* a place to which a person is going or a thing is sent: *The airplane's destination is Paris.*

des·tine (des′tin) *v.t.,* **des·tined, des·tin·ing. 1.** to set apart for a particular purpose or use; intend: *That land is destined for the new hospital.* **2.** to fix beforehand; predetermine: *He is destined for greatness in the field of medical research.*

des·ti·ny (des′tə nē) *n. pl.,* **des·ti·nies. 1.** what happens to a person or thing; lot; fortune: *It was his destiny to become a great leader.* **2.** what is fated to happen; course of events determined beforehand: *He felt that it was his destiny to work hard all his life.*

at; āpe; cär; end; mē; it; īce; hot; ōld; fôrk; wood; fōōl; oil; out; up; turn; sing; thin; this; hw in white; zh in treasure. The symbol ə stands for the sound of **a** in about, **e** in taken, **i** in pencil, **o** in lemon, and **u** in circus.

D

des·ti·tute (des′tə tōōt′, des′tə tyōōt′) *adj.* **1.** lacking the things necessary for life; in great need: *The villagers were left destitute by the flood.* **2.** entirely lacking; wanting: *The barren plain was destitute of trees.*

des·ti·tu·tion (des′tə tōō′shən, des′tə tyōō′shən) *n.* **1.** extreme poverty; great need. **2.** a being without; lack.

de·stroy (di stroi′) *v.t.* **1.** to break into pieces; ruin completely; wreck: *The earthquake destroyed the city. Locusts destroyed the crops.* **2.** to put an end to; do away with: *His failure at the football tryouts destroyed his hopes of being a member of the team.* **3.** to kill: *Our veterinarian destroys animals that are hopelessly ill, using a painless injection.*

de·stroy·er (di stroi′ər) *n.* **1.** a person or thing that destroys. **2.** a small, fast warship, armed with guns, depth charges, torpedoes, and sometimes guided missiles.

de·struct (di strukt′) *n.* the intentional destruction of a rocket or other missile that fails to function properly after it has been launched. —*adj.* designed to destroy such a rocket or missile: *a destruct mechanism.* —*v.i.* to be destroyed automatically. —*v.t.* to destroy.

de·struc·ti·ble (di struk′tə bəl) *adj.* that can be destroyed. —**de·struc′ti·bil′i·ty,** *n.*

de·struc·tion (di struk′shən) *n.* **1.** the act of destroying: *The police charged him with the destruction of other people's property.* **2.** the fact or state of being destroyed; ruin: *The total destruction of the city was a result of the earthquake.* **3.** something that destroys.

de·struc·tive (di struk′tiv) *adj.* **1.** causing destruction: *Boll weevils are destructive to cotton bolls.* **2.** tending to tear down or discredit: *destructive criticism.* —**de·struc′tive·ly,** *adv.* —**de·struc′tive·ness,** *n.*

des·ul·to·ry (des′əl tôr′ē) *adj.* shifting or jumping from one thing to another; without plan or method; irregular; disconnected: *They had a desultory conversation about many things.* —**des′ul·to′ri·ly,** *adv.* —**des′ul·to′ri·ness,** *n.*

de·tach (di tach′) *v.t.* **1.** to unfasten and separate; disconnect: *The engineer detached three cars from the train. The salesclerk detached the price tag from the gift.* **2.** to send away on a special mission: *The commanding officer detached a patrol to search the area for enemy soldiers.*

de·tach·a·ble (di tach′ə bəl) *adj.* that can be detached: *a shirt with a detachable collar.* —**de·tach′a·bil′i·ty,** *n.* —**de·tach′a·bly,** *adv.*

de·tached (di tacht′) *adj.* **1.** not connected; unattached: *The detached house was surrounded by a large yard.* **2.** not interested; indifferent; aloof; unconcerned: *He had a detached attitude toward the problem.* **3.** lacking prejudice; impartial: *The reporter was a detached observer at the trial.*

de·tach·ment (di tach′mənt) *n.* **1.** the act of detaching or the state of being detached; separation. **2.** a group of soldiers or ships assigned to special duty: *A detachment of ten men remained behind to guard the prisoners.* **3.** a standing apart; indifference; aloofness. **4.** the lack of prejudice or bias; impartiality: *The judge was able to consider the case with detachment.*

de·tail (di tāl′, dē′tāl) *n.* **1.** a small or secondary part of a whole; item; particular: *Modern scholars know few details of the life of Shakespeare.* **2.** treatment of matters item by item; attention to particulars: *The detail in the portrait was painted with great care.* **3.** a small group of men assigned to some special duty: *A detail of policemen patrolled the troubled area.* —*v.t.* **1.** to tell or describe item by item: *He detailed his camping experiences to the class.* **2.** to assign to or send on special duty: *Troops were detailed to guard the frontier.*

in detail. part by part; minutely: *He described the day's events in detail.*

de·tailed (di tāld′, dē′tāld) *adj.* **1.** having many details: *The witness gave a detailed description of the accident.* **2.** showing careful attention to detail: *The detective made a detailed examination of the room.*

de·tain (di tān′) *v.t.* **1.** to keep from going; hold back; delay: *A flat tire detained him on his way home.* **2.** to keep in custody; confine: *The police detained the robbery suspect.* —**de·tain′ment,** *n.*

de·tect (di tekt′) *v.t.* to find out; discover: *to detect smoke, to detect a secret plot.* —**de·tect′a·ble;** *also,* **de·tect′i·ble,** *adj.*

de·tec·tion (di tek′shən) *n.* the act of finding out or the state of being found out; discovery.

de·tec·tive (di tek′tiv) *n.* a police officer or other person who makes investigations to get evidence and information, especially in order to solve crimes and arrest criminals. —*adj.* **1.** relating to detectives and their work: *a detective story.* **2.** used for the purpose of detection: *She used detective methods to solve the crime.*

de·tec·tor (di tek′tər) *n.* **1.** a person or thing that detects. **2.** a device, as in a radio receiver, that helps convert radio waves into sound waves. **3.** any device that indicates the presence of radioactivity, an electric current, or the like.

de·ten·tion (di ten′shən) *n.* **1.** the act of detaining or holding back. **2.** the state of being detained; delay. **3.** a keeping in custody; confinement: *He had a long detention in the city jail before his trial.*

de·ter (di tur′) *v.t.,* **de·terred, de·ter·ring.** to discourage from acting or going ahead, especially by arousing fear or doubt: *The huge waves deterred him from going swimming.* —**de·ter′ment,** *n.*

de·ter·gent (di tur′jənt) *n.* any cleaning agent, especially one that is man-made and resembles soap in its cleansing action but not in its chemical composition.

de·te·ri·o·rate (di tēr′ē ə rāt′) *v.,* **de·te·ri·o·rat·ed, de·te·ri·o·rat·ing.** —*v.i.* to lessen in character, quality, condition, or value; become worse: *Steve's car deteriorated with age.* —*v.t.* to make worse: *The damp climate deteriorated the shingles of the house.* —**de·te′ri·o·ra′tion,** *n.*

de·ter·mi·na·ble (di tur′mi nə bəl) *adj.* that can be determined.

de·ter·mi·nant (di tur′mi nənt) *n.* something that determines: *The low cost of the house was the determinant that made him decide to buy it.* —*adj.* determining.

de·ter·mi·nate (di tur′mi nit) *adj.* having defined limits; fixed; definite: *a determinate quantity in mathematics.* —**de·ter′mi·nate·ly,** *adv.* —**de·ter′mi·nate·ness,** *n.*

de·ter·mi·na·tion (di tur′mi nā′shən) *n.* **1.** a fixed and firm purpose: *His determination to succeed was not affected by the obstacles he met.* **2.** the act of reaching a decision; deciding or settling beforehand: *The campers' determination of what to take on their hike took some time.* **3.** the act of finding out something by observation, calculation, or investigation: *the determination of the amount of uranium in an ore.*

de·ter·mine (di tur′min) *v.t.,* **de·ter·mined, de·ter·min·ing. 1.** to decide or settle definitely or beforehand: *The members of the committee determined the date for the next meeting.* **2.** to find out by observation, calculation, or investigation: *The botanist determined the species of the plant.* **3.** to decide firmly; resolve: *He determined to be a success as an author.* **4.** to be the cause or deciding factor of: *The number of votes each candidate receives will determine the result of the election.*

de·ter·mined (di tur′mind) *adj.* having or showing determination or fixed purpose; resolute: *The basketball team made a determined effort to win.* —**de·ter′mined·ly,** *adv.* —**de·ter′mined·ness,** *n.*

de·ter·min·er (di tur'mi nər) *n.* **1.** a person or thing that determines. **2.** *Grammar.* a word belonging to a class of noun modifiers that includes articles, demonstratives, possessive adjectives, and other words. Determiners always precede the noun they modify, occupying either the first position in a noun phrase or the second position after another determiner. *Our* in the phrase *our house* and *the* in the phrase *the blue car* are determiners.

de·ter·rence (di tur'əns) *n.* the act of deterring.

de·ter·rent (di tur'ənt) *adj.* discouraging; deterring; restraining: *Citronella has a deterrent effect on mosquitos.* —*n.* a person or thing that deters: *The harsh climate of the North was a deterrent to possible settlers.*

de·test (di test') *v.t.* to dislike very much; hate; loathe: *Many Puritans detested finery as a show of vanity.*

de·test·a·ble (di tes'tə bəl) *adj.* deserving to be detested; hateful; abominable: *Skyjacking is a detestable crime.* —**de·test'a·ble·ness,** *n.* —**de·test'a·bly,** *adv.*

de·tes·ta·tion (dē'tes tā'shən) *n.* **1.** a very great hatred or dislike. **2.** a person or thing that is detested.

de·throne (dē thrōn') *v.t.,* **de·throned, de·thron·ing.** **1.** to remove from a throne; depose: *The police uncovered a plot to dethrone the king.* **2.** to remove from any high position: *The young boxer dethroned the champion by winning the bout.* —**de·throne'ment,** *n.*

det·o·nate (det'ən āt') *v.,* **det·o·nat·ed, det·o·nat·ing.** —*v.t.* to cause to explode suddenly and with a loud noise: *to detonate dynamite.* —*v.i.* to explode suddenly and with a loud noise: *The dynamite detonated.* —**det'o·na'tion,** *n.*

det·o·na·tor (det'ən ā'tər) *n.* a device or small explosive used to detonate a large quantity of explosive material.

de·tour (dē'toor) *n.* **1.** a road used temporarily when the main road cannot be traveled. **2.** a roundabout or indirect way. —*v.i.* to make a detour: *The driver detoured around the construction on the highway.* —*v.t.* to cause to make a detour: *The police detoured the traffic because of the accident ahead.*

de·tract (di trakt') *v.i.* to lessen in value, quality, importance, or reputation: *The worn old rug detracted from the appearance of the otherwise beautifully decorated room.* —**de·trac'tion,** *n.* —**de·trac'tor,** *n.*

det·ri·ment (det'rə mənt) *n.* **1.** damage, injury, or harm: *He is able to pursue several hobbies without detriment to his studies.* **2.** something that causes damage, injury, or harm: *His lack of political experience is a detriment to his candidacy for mayor.*

det·ri·men·tal (det'rə ment'əl) *adj.* causing damage; injurious; harmful: *Poor eating habits can be detrimental to health.* —**det'ri·men'tal·ly,** *adv.*

de·tri·tus (di trī'təs) *n.* fragments of rock, as gravel or sand, torn away from a larger mass by such forces as erosion or glacial ice.

De·troit (di troit') *n.* a city in Michigan, in the southeastern part of the state. Pop. (1970), 1,511,482.

deuce¹ (dōōs, dyōōs) *n.* **1.** a playing card having two symbols of the suit it represents. **2.** the face of a die having two spots. **3.** a throw of the dice that totals two. **4.** *Tennis.* a tie score of forty points or more each in a game, or five games or more in a set. [Old French *deus.*]

deuce² (dōōs, dyōōs) *interj. Informal.* bad luck; the devil. ▲ used as a mild oath or exclamation: *What the deuce was that?* [Probably from *deuce¹,* the lowest throw in dice.]

Deut., Deuteronomy.

deu·te·ri·um (dōō tēr'ē əm, dyōō tēr'ē əm) *n.* an isotope of hydrogen having one neutron and one proton in the nucleus and about twice the atomic weight of ordinary hydrogen. Symbol: **D** Also, **heavy hydrogen.**

Deu·ter·on·o·my (dōō'tə ron'ə mē, dyōō'tə ron'ə mē) *n.* the fifth book of the Old Testament.

deut·sche mark (doi'chə) the unit of money of West Germany.

Deutsch·land (doich'länt') *n.* the German name of Germany.

De Va·le·ra, Ea·mon (dev'ə ler'ə; ā'mən) 1882–1975, Irish political leader, born in the United States.

de·val·u·ate (dē val'yōō āt') *v.t.,* **de·val·u·at·ed, de·val·u·at·ing.** **1.** to lower the legal value of (a currency): *to devaluate the dollar.* **2.** to lessen the value of. —**de·val'u·a'tion,** *n.*

de·val·ue (dē val'yōō) *v.t.,* **de·val·ued, de·val·u·ing.** another word for **devaluate.**

dev·as·tate (dev'əs tāt') *v.t.,* **dev·as·tat·ed, dev·as·tat·ing.** **1.** to lay waste; make desolate; destroy; ravage: *Locusts devastated the crops.* **2.** to overwhelm, as with surprise: *She devastated him with the news of her marriage.* —**dev'as·tat'ing·ly,** *adv.* —**dev'as·ta'tor,** *n.*

dev·as·ta·tion (dev'əs tā'shən) *n.* the act of devastating or the state of being devastated; destruction.

de·vel·op (di vel'əp) *v.t.* **1.** to bring into being or activity: *He developed an interest in sports at an early age.* **2.** to change (someone or something) gradually: *The demand for speed and comfort has developed the automobile greatly over the past forty years.* **3.** to cause to grow or expand: *He developed his muscles by exercise. Only by hard work can he develop his skills as a painter.* **4.** to put to use: *develop the natural resources of a country.* **5.** to build houses or other buildings on (land). **6.** to work out in detail: *The rest of the book developed the ideas of the first chapter.* **7.** to make known; reveal; disclose. **8.** to treat (an exposed photographic film, plate, or print) with a chemical developer to make the picture visible. —*v.i.* **1.** to come into being or activity: *A rash developed on his skin after he ate the fruit.* **2.** to change gradually: *The small river port developed into one of the country's largest cities.* **3.** to grow: *He developed into a strong leader.* **4.** to become known: *Several new facts developed after the case had already been decided.*

de·vel·op·er (di vel'ə pər) *n.* **1.** a person or thing that develops. **2.** *Photography.* the chemical solution that makes visible the picture on a film, plate, or print.

de·vel·op·ment (di vel'əp mənt) *n.* **1.** the act or process of developing: *The development of this spacecraft took many years.* **2.** the state of having been developed: *He exercised to improve his muscular development.* **3.** an event or happening: *The radio station reported the newest political developments.* **4.** a group of houses or other buildings, often of similar design and usually built by one builder.

de·vi·ate (dē'vē āt') *v.i.,* **de·vi·at·ed, de·vi·at·ing.** to turn aside from a course of action, line of thought, or the like: *He deviated from the truth when he told that story.*

de·vi·a·tion (dē'vē ā'shən) *n.* **1.** the act of deviating: *Getting up at five o'clock is a deviation from his usual routine.* **2.** the amount of deviating.

de·vice (di vīs') *n.* **1.** something made or invented for a particular purpose; mechanism: *a device to open a can.* **2.** a plan or scheme; trick. **3.** an ornamental figure or design, especially on a coat of arms.

to leave (someone) to his own devices. to permit (someone) to do as he wishes.

at; āpe; cär; end; mē; it; īce; hot; ōld; fôrk; wood; fōōl; oil; out; up; turn; sing; thin; **th**is; **hw** in white; **zh** in treasure. The symbol ə stands for the sound of **a** in about, **e** in taken, **i** in pencil, **o** in lemon, and **u** in circus.

dev·il (dev′əl) *n.* **1.** *also,* **Devil, the Devil.** a supernatural being thought to be the supreme ruler of hell, the chief spirit of evil, the opponent of God, and the spiritual enemy of man, often represented as a creature having horns, a tail, and cloven feet; Lucifer; Satan. **2.** any evil spirit; demon. **3.** a wicked, cruel, or ill-natured person. **4.** a person of great cleverness, energy, impudence, or recklessness. **5.** a wretched or pitiful person: *The poor devil hasn't any decent clothing to wear.* **6.** an apprentice or errand boy in a printing shop. Also, **printer's devil.** —*v.t.,* **dev·iled, dev·il·ing;** *also, British,* **dev·illed, dev·il·ling. 1.** to tease; torment: *She deviled her mother to let her go to the party.* **2.** to prepare (food) by using hot seasonings, especially with mustard or pepper: *to devil eggs.*

dev·il·fish (dev′əl fish′) *n. pl.,* **dev·il·fish** or **dev·il·fish·es. 1.** another word for **manta. 2.** a large octopus.

dev·il·ish (dev′ə lish) *adj.* **1.** relating to or like the Devil or a devil; evil; cruel. **2.** full of mischief; mischievous. —**dev′il·ish·ly,** *adv.* —**dev′il·ish·ness,** *n.*

dev·il-may-care (dev′əl mā ker′) *adj.* carefree or reckless: *He has a devil-may-care attitude toward his work.*

dev·il·ment (dev′əl mənt) *n.* devilish activity; mischief.

dev·il·ry (dev′əl rē) *n. pl.,* **dev·il·ries.** another word for **deviltry.**

Devil's Island, an island off the coast of French Guiana, formerly a French penal colony.

dev·il·try (dev′əl trē′) *n. pl.,* **dev·il·tries. 1.** evilness; wickedness. **2.** mischievous behavior.

de·vi·ous (dē′vē əs) *adj.* **1.** turning aside from the direct way; roundabout; wandering: *They took a devious route home in order to avoid the heavy traffic on the highway.* **2.** not straightforward, frank, or direct: *He gave a devious explanation for being late.* —**de′vi·ous·ly,** *adv.* —**de′vi·ous·ness,** *n.*

de·vise (di vīz′) *v.t.,* **de·vised, de·vis·ing. 1.** to think out; invent; plan: *to devise a secret code.* **2.** to give or leave (property) by a will. —**de·vis′er,** *n.*

de·void (di void′) *adj.* entirely without; lacking (with *of*): *The expedition was disorganized and devoid of leadership.*

de·volve (di volv′) *v.,* **de·volved, de·volv·ing.** —*v.t.* to transfer (work or responsibility) to another: *The chairman devolved his authority to the vice-chairman.* —*v.i.* to pass on to another; be transferred: *When he retired, the business devolved on his son.*

Dev·on (dev′ən) *n.* a county in southwestern England.

De·vo·ni·an (də vō′nē ən) *n.* the fourth period of the Paleozoic era, characterized by an abundance of primitive fish and the appearance of amphibians. —*adj.* of, relating to, or characteristic of this period.

de·vote (di vōt′) *v.t.,* **de·vot·ed, de·vot·ing. 1.** to give or apply, as oneself or one's time, effort, or attention, to some person or purpose: *She devoted all her energies to her family. He devoted himself to study.* **2.** to set apart for a particular use or purpose: *They devoted one room in the house to a playroom.*

de·vot·ed (di vō′tid) *adj.* **1.** loyal; faithful: *a devoted friend.* **2.** dedicated to some purpose. —**de·vot′ed·ly,** *adv.* —**de·vot′ed·ness,** *n.*

dev·o·tee (dev′ə tē′) *n.* a person devoted to anything; enthusiast: *a devotee of baseball.*

de·vo·tion (di vō′shən) *n.* **1.** a strong attachment or affection; loyalty; faithfulness: *parents' devotion to their children.* **2.** the act of devoting or the state of being devoted. **3.** religious piety; devoutness. **4. devotions.** religious worship; prayers.

de·vo·tion·al (di vō′shən əl) *adj.* relating to religious devotion; used in worship. —**de·vo′tion·al·ly,** *adv.*

de·vour (di vour′) *v.t.* **1.** to eat up with great greed or vigor: *The hungry lion devoured its prey. The boy devoured his dinner.* **2.** to waste or destroy: *Fire devoured the house.* **3.** to take in greedily or eagerly with the ears, eyes, or the mind: *to devour a book.* **4.** to absorb or engross completely: *to be devoured by grief.* —**de·vour′ing·ly,** *adv.*

de·vout (di vout′) *adj.* **1.** devoted to worship and prayer; religious; pious: *a devout order of monks.* **2.** showing devotion or piety: *devout prayer.* **3.** earnest; sincere: *devout wishes for success.* —**de·vout′ly,** *adv.* —**de·vout′ness,** *n.*

dew (dōō, dyōō) *n.* **1.** moisture from the air that condenses in small drops on cool surfaces at night. **2.** any light moisture in small drops, such as tears or perspiration. **3.** anything fresh, pure, or refreshing like dew: *the dew of youth.* —*v.t.* to moisten with or as if with dew.

dew·ber·ry (dōō′ber′ē, dyōō′ber′ē) *n. pl.,* **dew·ber·ries. 1.** the sweet, black berry of any of several trailing or climbing shrubs of the rose family, similar to the blackberry. **2.** the shrub bearing this berry.

dew·claw (dōō′klô′, dyōō′klô′) *n.* **1.** the small inner toe on the foot of certain dogs. **2.** the false hoof above the true hoof in deer, cattle, hogs, and other animals.

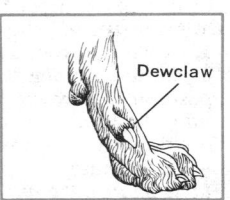

Dewclaw on a dog's leg

dew·drop (dōō′drop′, dyōō′drop′) *n.* a drop of dew.

Dew·ey decimal system (dōō′ē, dyōō′ē) the system used in libraries for classifying books and other publications according to subject matter. It uses the numbers 000 to 999 to designate major categories and decimal numbers to indicate special subdivisions of these fields. [From Melvil *Dewey,* 1851–1931, a U.S. librarian who devised it.]

dew·lap (dōō′lap′, dyōō′lap′) *n.* the loose fold of skin under the throat of cattle and certain other animals.

DEW line (dōō, dyōō) a chain of radar stations across North America above the Arctic Circle, maintained to provide advance warning of the approach of hostile aircraft or missiles. [Abbreviation of *D*(istant) *E*(arly) *W*(arning).]

dew point, the temperature at which dew forms or vapor condenses into liquid.

dew·y (dōō′ē, dyōō′ē) *adj.,* **dew·i·er, dew·i·est. 1.** moist with dew: *dewy grass.* **2.** resembling or suggesting dew. —**dew′i·ly,** *adv.* —**dew′i·ness,** *n.*

dex·ter (deks′tər) *adj.* of or on the right-hand side.

dex·ter·i·ty (deks ter′ə tē) *n.* skill in using the hands, body, or mind: *The gymnast's performance showed great dexterity. The diplomat handled the matter with dexterity.*

dex·ter·ous (deks′tər əs) *adj.* having or showing skill in using the hands, body, or mind: *Magicians and acrobats are dexterous.* Also, **dextrous.** [Latin *dexter* on the right-hand side.] —**dex′ter·ous·ly,** *adv.* —**dex′ter·ous·ness,** *n.*

dex·trin (deks′trin) *also,* **dex·trine** (deks′trēn, deks′trin). *n.* a gummy substance obtained from the partial chemical breakdown of starch, used especially as an adhesive.

dex·trose (deks′trōs) *n.* a colorless, crystalline sugar found in many plants and in blood. Also, **grape sugar.**

dex·trous (deks′trəs) *n.* another word for **dexterous.**

DH, designated hitter.

di- *prefix* twofold; twice; double: *dicotyledon.*

di·a·be·tes (dī′ə bē′tis, dī′ə bē′tēz) *n.* a disease characterized by a deficiency of insulin and a resulting excess of sugar in the blood.

di·a·bet·ic (dī'ə bet'ik) *adj.* of, relating to, or having diabetes. —*n.* a person having diabetes.

di·a·bol·i·cal (dī'ə bol'i kəl) *adj.* **1.** befitting the devil; very cruel or wicked; fiendish: *The detectives uncovered a diabolical plot to blow up the airplane.* **2.** relating to the devil or devils. Also, **di·a·bol·ic** (dī'ə bol'ik). —**di·a·bol'i·cal·ly**, *adv.* —**di·a·bol'i·cal·ness**, *n.*

di·a·crit·ic (dī'ə krit'ik) *n.* see **diacritical mark**. —*adj.* another word for **diacritical**.

di·a·crit·i·cal (dī'ə krit'i kəl) *adj.* serving to distinguish, as the sounds of letters.

diacritical mark, a mark or sign (such as ¨, ^, ¯, ´, or `) placed over, under, or across a letter to indicate pronunciation or as part of the spelling.

di·a·dem (dī'ə dem') *n.* **1.** a crown. **2.** a cloth headband, often set with jewels and precious metals, formerly worn as a crown by Oriental rulers.

di·ag·nose (dī'əg nōs') *v.,* **di·ag·nosed, di·ag·nos·ing.** —*v.t.* to make a diagnosis of: *The doctor diagnosed the patient's illness as pneumonia.* —*v.i.* to make a diagnosis.

di·ag·no·sis (dī'əg nō'sis) *n. pl.,* **di·ag·no·ses** (dī'əg nō'sēz). **1.** the act or process of finding out the nature of a disease or other harmful condition by careful examination and study of symptoms: *The doctor's diagnosis revealed that Jane had the measles.* **2.** an investigation and study of facts to find out the basic characteristics of something: *He made a complete diagnosis of the housing problem.* **3.** the conclusion reached by careful examination of symptoms or study of facts: *His diagnosis was that the city urgently needed more housing.*

di·ag·nos·tic (dī'əg nos'tik) *adj.* relating to, helpful in, or used in diagnosis: *diagnostic procedures, diagnostic equipment.*

di·ag·nos·ti·cian (dī'əg nos tish'ən) *n.* a person who makes diagnoses, especially one who specializes in medical diagnoses.

di·ag·o·nal (dī ag'ən əl) *adj.* **1.** *Geometry.* **a.** connecting two nonadjacent angles of a figure. **b.** connecting two nonadjacent edges of a solid figure. **2.** having a slanting direction: *The fabric has a diagonal weave.* —*n.* **1.** a diagonal straight line or plane. **2.** anything slanting. —**di·ag'o·nal·ly**, *adv.*

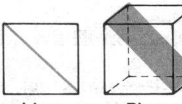

Line   Plane

Diagonals

di·a·gram (dī'ə gram') *n.* a figure, plan, sketch, or set of lines giving the outline or general scheme of something to show how it is put together or how it works, or to show the course or results of an action: *a diagram of the floors of a building, a diagram of a machine part, a diagram of troop movements during a battle.* —*v.t.,* **di·a·gramed, di·a·gram·ing;** *also, British,* **di·a·grammed, di·a·gram·ming.** to show by a diagram; make a diagram of: *to diagram a sentence.*

di·a·gram·mat·ic (dī'ə grə mat'ik) *adj.* **1.** in the form of a diagram: *a diagrammatic sketch of an engine.* **2.** in outline; sketchy. Also, **di·a·gram·mat·i·cal** (dī'ə grə mat'i kəl). —**di·a·gram·mat'i·cal·ly**, *adv.*

di·al (dī'əl, dīl) *n.* **1.** the surface on which the amount or degree of something is shown by a pointer moving over numbers, letters, or other marks. The faces of clocks, compasses, and meters are dials. **2.** the movable disk or other device on a radio or television for tuning in to a station or channel. **3.** the disk on the front of certain telephones, that is rotated to signal the numbers and letters of the telephone being called. **4.** see **sundial.** —*v.t.,* **di·aled, di·al·ing;** *also, British,* **di·alled, di·al·ling 1.** to tune in (a radio or television station or program): *Dial the channel that the movie is being shown on.* **2.** to call by means of a telephone dial: *to dial a wrong number.* **3.** to select or

operate by means of a dial: *to dial the combination of a safe.* —*v.i.* to operate or use a dial, as in telephoning: *If you get a bad connection, hang up and dial again.*

di·a·lect (dī'ə lekt') *n.* a form of a language that is spoken in a particular area or by a particular group, and differs from other forms of the same language in some of its grammar, pronunciation, vocabulary, or idioms.

● The term **dialect** refers to a special way that a language, any language, is spoken by a group of people. Some mistakenly believe that the term designates an inferior variety of a language. Actually, everyone speaks a dialect, and, to a student of language, no one dialect is "better" than or superior to any other.

For the most part, dialects are regional, used by most people in a given area. Speech often enables a listener to identify the region of the country from which the speaker comes. In the United States, for example, people who live in the South, the New England states, and the Middle West use different dialects. New Englanders often do not pronounce the *r* in *park* or *car,* and a Midwesterner's pronunciation of *wash* may sound like *worsh* to someone from another part of the country.

Within a regional dialect, further pronunciation and usage patterns may depend on the individual speaker's occupation, social class, and degree of education.

It is sometimes hard to tell whether two ways of speaking are different languages, or different dialects of the same language. Scholars often use this general rule: if two people who have different ways of speaking can understand each other, then each is speaking a dialect of the same language (such as the Scottish and Irish dialects of English). If they cannot understand each other, then they are speaking entirely different languages (such as Spanish and French).

di·a·lec·tal (dī'ə lekt'əl) *adj.* relating to or characteristic of a dialect.

di·a·logue (dī'ə lôg', dī'ə log') *also,* **di·a·log.** *n.* **1.** the parts that are conversation in a play, novel, or similar work: *a comedy with witty dialogue.* **2.** a conversation between two or more persons: *The two friends who had not seen each other for a long time carried on a lengthy dialogue.* **3.** a literary work written in the form of a conversation between two or more persons: *Plato wrote many dialogues.* **4.** an exchange of ideas: *There was a dialogue between different groups in the community before the election.*

dial tone, the steady humming sound in a telephone, indicating to the user that a call may be dialed.

diam., diameter.

di·am·e·ter (dī am'ə tər) *n.* **1.** a straight line passing through the center of a circle or sphere, from one side to the other. **2.** the length of such a line; the width or thickness of something: *the diameter of the earth.*

di·a·met·ri·cal (dī'ə met'ri kəl) *adj.* **1.** of or along a diameter: *The surveyor took a diametrical measurement of the tree.* **2.** directly opposite; completely contrary: *The two candidates have diametrical views on that issue.* Also, **di·a·met·ric** (dī'ə met'rik).

Center

Diameter

Diameter

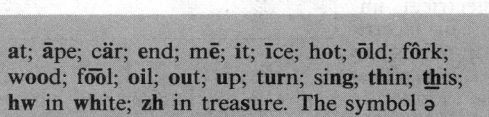

at; āpe; cär; end; mē; it; īce; hot; ōld; fôrk; wood; fо̄о̄l; oil; out; up; turn; sing; thin; **this**; hw in white; zh in treasure. The symbol ə stands for the sound of **a** in about, **e** in taken, **i** in pencil, **o** in lemon, and **u** in circus.

di·a·met·ri·cal·ly (dī′ə met′rik əl ē, dī′ə met′rik lē) *adv.* **1.** along a diameter; straight through: *The apple was cut diametrically.* **2.** directly; completely: *While the two politicians were diametrically opposed on most issues, occasionally they could agree.*

dia·mond (dī′mənd, dī′ə mənd) *n.* **1.** a mineral that is usually colorless, consisting of pure carbon in a crystalline form. It is the hardest natural substance known. Diamonds are used as precious gems when cut and polished and in industry for cutting and grinding. **2.** a piece cut from this mineral, especially when cut and polished for use as a gem. **3.** *Geometry.* a plane figure with four equal sides, forming two acute and two obtuse angles. **4.a.** a playing card marked with one or more red figures (♦) in the shape of a diamond. **b. diamonds.** the suit of such cards. **5.** *Baseball.* **a.** the infield. **b.** the entire field. —*adj.* **1.** resembling, made of, or set with a diamond or diamonds: *a diamond necklace.* **2.** of or being the sixtieth or seventy-fifth anniversary of an event: *a diamond wedding anniversary.*

dia·mond·back (dī′mənd bak′, dī′ə mənd bak′) *n.* **1.** a large, poisonous rattlesnake having diamond-shaped markings on its back, found in the southeastern United States. **2.** *also,* **diamond-back terrapin.** a turtle with diamond-shaped markings on its shell, found in Atlantic coastal waters.

Diamondback

Di·an·a (dī an′ə) *n. Roman Mythology.* the goddess of the moon, the woods, and of hunting. In Greek mythology she was called Artemis.

di·a·pa·son (dī′ə pā′zən) *n.* **1.** either of two principal stops in a pipe organ that extend through the entire range of the organ. **2.** the entire range of a voice or instrument. **3.** a fixed standard of musical pitch. **4.** another word for **tuning fork. 5.** an outpouring of harmonious sound.

dia·per (dī′pər, dī′ə pər) *n.* **1.** a baby's undergarment consisting of a soft, absorbent, thickly folded cloth or other material, drawn up between the legs and fastened at the waist. **2.** a pattern made up of small, constantly repeated, geometric figures. **3.** white cotton or linen cloth woven with such a pattern. —*v.t.* to put a diaper on (a baby).

di·aph·a·nous (dī af′ə nəs) *adj.* sheer enough to be seen through or to let light through: *diaphanous cloth.*

di·a·phragm (dī′ə fram′) *n.* **1.** a membrane of muscle and connective tissue between the chest cavity and abdominal cavity, used in inhaling and exhaling. **2.** any member or partition that serves to separate. **3.** a disk used in converting sound to electrical impulses or electrical impulses to sound, as in a telephone or microphone. **4.** a mechanism that can be adjusted to control the amount of light entering the lens of a camera, microscope, or similar equipment.

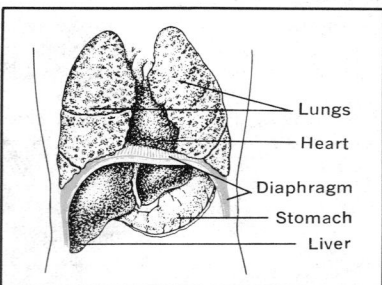

Lungs

Heart

Diaphragm

Stomach

Liver

Diaphragm

di·a·rist (dī′ər ist) *n.* a person who keeps a diary.

di·ar·rhe·a (dī′ə rē′ə) *also,* **di·ar·rhoe·a.** *n.* a condition marked by frequent and loose bowel movements and, often, stomach pains, low fever, and nausea.

di·a·ry (dī′ər ē) *n. pl.,* **di·a·ries. 1.** a daily record of events, especially of the writer's personal experiences and observations. **2.** a book in which such a record is kept.

Di·as, Bar·tho·lo·me·u (dē′əs; bär′too loo mā′oo) 1450–1500, the Portuguese navigator who was the first to sail around the southern tip of Africa.

di·as·to·le (dī as′tə lē′) *n.* the period of expansion or relaxation of the heart during which the heart chambers are filled with blood. These periods alternate rhythmically with systoles, or periods of contraction.

di·a·stol·ic (dī′ə stol′ik) *adj.* relating to, involving, or taken during the diastole: *diastolic blood pressure.*

di·a·tom (dī′ə tom′) *n.* any of a large group of microscopic, one-celled algae that live in fresh and salt water and have cell walls made up mostly of silica.

di·a·ton·ic (dī′ə ton′ik) *adj. Music.* of or relating to the standard major or minor scale that has eight tones.

di·a·tribe (dī′ə trīb′) *n.* a bitter, violent, often lengthy criticism: *The candidate's speech was a diatribe against his opponent.*

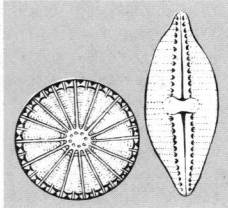
Diatoms

Di·az, Bartholomew (dē′əs) see **Dias, Bartholomeu.**

dib·ble (dib′əl) *n.* a pointed hand tool used to make holes in the ground for planting seeds or young plants.

dice (dīs) *n., pl. sing.,* **die. 1.** small cubes of wood, plastic, or other material, marked on each side with from one to six spots, used in games of chance, usually in a pair. **2.** a gambling game played with dice. —*v.t.,* **diced, dic·ing.** to cut into small cubes: *to dice potatoes.*

dick·ens (dik′inz) *interj.* the devil; deuce. ▲ used as a mild oath or exclamation: *Where the dickens is my coat?*

Dick·ens, Charles (dik′inz) 1812–1870, English novelist.

Dick·en·si·an (di ken′zē ən) *adj.* of, relating to, or similar to Charles Dickens or his writings.

dick·er (dik′ər) *v.i.* to trade by bargaining or haggling in a petty way: *The old lady and the grocer spent a long time dickering over the price of a head of lettuce.* —*n.* **1.** petty bargaining. **2.** a petty bargain.

dick·ey (dik′ē) *also,* **dick·y.** *n. pl.,* **dick·eys. 1.** an article of clothing, usually having a collar and covering part of the chest, designed to fill in the neckline and be worn under a shirt, jacket, sweater, or other garment. **2.** a false shirt front. **3.** any small bird.

Dick·in·son, Emily (dik′in sən) 1830–1886, U.S. poet.

Dick test (dik) a test to find out whether a person can contract scarlet fever, made by injecting scarlet fever toxin into the skin. [From George and Gladys *Dick,* the U.S. doctors who devised it in 1923.]

dick·y (dik′ē) *n. pl.,* **dick·ies.** another spelling of **dickey.**

di·cot·y·le·don (dī kot′əl ēd′ən) *n.* a plant that has two cotyledons, or seed leaves, in the embryo. Dicotyledons make up one of the two classes of flowering plants. Also, **di·cot** (dī′kot). —**di·cot′y·le·don·ous,** *adj.*

dic·ta (dik′tə) a plural of **dictum.**

Dic·ta·phone (dik′tə fōn′) *n. Trademark.* an instrument to record and reproduce speech, used especially for the recording or dictating of business letters that are to be typed at a later time.

dic·tate (*v.,* dik′tāt, dik tāt′; *n.,* dik′tāt) *v.,* **dic·tat·ed, dic·tat·ing.** —*v.t.* **1.** to say or read (something) aloud to be written down or recorded by another: *He dictated the letter* *to his secretary.* **2.** to order or make necessary, with or as if with authority: *The victorious nation dictated the conditions of peace.* —*v.i.* **1.** to say or read aloud something to be written down or recorded by another: *The teacher dictated in French to the class.* **2.** to give orders or exercise authority. —*n.* a principle, rule, or command that must be followed: *Everyone is subject to the dictates of the law.*

dic·ta·tion (dik tā′shən) *n.* **1.** the act of dictating something to be written down or recorded by another: *The students listened carefully to the teacher's dictation.* **2.** material that is dictated or recorded: *Part of the French exam was a dictation.* **3.** the act of giving orders with authority.

dic·ta·tor (dik′tā′tər) *n.* **1.** a ruler who has absolute power and authority, especially one who is cruel, unjust, or tyrannical. **2.** a person who has great authority in some field or about some subject: *a dictator of fashion.* **3.** a person who dictates something to be written down or recorded.

dic·ta·to·ri·al (dik′tə tôr′ē əl) *adj.* **1.** relating to or characteristic of a dictator: *dictatorial powers.* **2.** tending to give orders or be tyrannical; overbearing: *a dictatorial football coach.* —**dic′ta·to′ri·al·ly,** *adv.*

dic·ta·tor·ship (dik′tā′tər ship′) *n.* **1.** the period of time during which a dictator rules; office of a dictator: *During the general's dictatorship, freedom of the press was abolished.* **2.** a state or government ruled by a dictator: *That country was a dictatorship until civil war broke out.* **3.** a form of government in which absolute power is held by a dictator.

dic·tion (dik′shən) *n.* **1.** the way in which ideas are expressed in words; choice and arrangement of words in speaking or writing: *The diction of poetry is often different from ordinary conversation.* **2.** a manner of saying or pronouncing words: *An actor must have clear diction.*

dic·tion·ar·y (dik′shə ner′ē) *n. pl.,* **dic·tion·ar·ies. 1.** a book containing words of a language arranged in alphabetical order, together with information about them, such as what they mean, how they are pronounced, how they are used, and where they came from. **2.** a book containing words of one language arranged in alphabetical order, and giving their meanings in another language: *an Italian-English dictionary.* **3.** a book containing and defining words used in a special area of interest or knowledge, usually arranged in alphabetical order: *a sports dictionary, a dictionary of cooking terms.*

● In relation to the long history of written language, the **dictionary** is a new invention. The earliest ancestors of modern dictionaries were probably glossaries made by Romans who were reading the works of Greek authors. These ancient glossaries, like most early dictionaries, contained only foreign or difficult words and did not attempt to record all the words of a language. These glossaries also differed from a modern dictionary in that they usually gave only synonyms, rather than definitions, for the words that were listed.

Before the invention of printing, it was almost impossible to produce a book of the length of a dictionary. One of the first large-scale English glossaries was a book finished in 1440 that translated 10,000 English words into Latin. The first real English dictionary was published in 1552 and contained not only the Latin equivalents of English words but the English definitions as well.

In 1755, the first great dictionary of the English language was published. This book, written by Samuel Johnson, is called *A Dictionary of the English Language.* The first great American dictionary was *An American Dictionary of the English Language,* written by Noah Webster and published in 1828. His purpose in writing the dictionary was to show and record the differences that had grown up between American English and British English.

Because our language is always changing and people's needs for a dictionary vary greatly, new dictionaries are constantly being written. Among the specialized dictionaries published are technical dictionaries that record and define the language of a particular science or profession, slang dictionaries, and student dictionaries. In a student dictionary, certain technical and archaic words that a standard dictionary might include are eliminated, many more illustrations are used to aid the reader in understanding definitions, and extra information on usage is given in order to help the student use language in the clearest, most effective way.

dic·tum (dik′təm) *n. pl.,* **dic·tums** or **dic·ta. 1.** a formal authoritative statement or opinion: *The dictums of the king were regarded as law.* **2.** a popular saying: *He always followed the dictum "A penny saved is a penny earned."*

did (did) the past tense of **do¹.**

di·dac·tic (dī dak′tik) *adj.* **1.** intended to instruct or to guide moral behavior: *This story is a didactic one and its moral is that "Crime does not pay."* **2.** often tending to moralize or to instruct or lecture others: *The man's didactic manner often offended people.* —**di·dac′ti·cal·ly,** *adv.*

did·n't (did′ənt) did not.

Di·do (dī′dō) *n. Greek and Roman Legend.* a queen of Carthage, who fell in love with Aeneas and killed herself when he left her.

didst (didst) *Archaic.* the second person singular, past tense of **do¹.**

die¹ (dī) *v.i.,* **died, dy·ing. 1.** to stop living; become dead: *Millions of soldiers died in World War II.* **2.** to pass out of existence; come to an end (often with *out*): *The pony express died with the coming of the telegraph. Knighthood died out centuries ago.* **3.** to lose force or strength; stop being active: *The wind suddenly died as the sailboat neared shore.* **4.** to stop functioning or operating: *The engine died just before the car reached the finish line.* **5.** to end, pass, or fade gradually (often with *away, out,* or *down*): *The music died away in the distance.* **6.** *Informal.* to suffer terribly: *I was dying of boredom when I had to stay in with the flu.* **7.** *Informal.* to want very much; desire strongly: *She is dying to see him again.* [Old Norse *deyja.*]

to die off. to die one by one until all are gone: *All the mice died off during the experiment.*

die² (dī) *n. pl., (def. 1)* **dice** or *(def. 2)* **dies. 1.** one of a pair of dice. **2.** any of various machines or devices used to shape, stamp, or cut out an object, especially a metal block or plate used to stamp designs on coins. [Old French *de.*]

the die is cast. the decision is made and cannot be avoided or changed.

die-hard (dī′härd′) *also,* **die·hard.** *adj.* resisting stubbornly to the very end; refusing to change or give in: *a die-hard bigot.* —*n.* a person who refuses to give in or change his views.

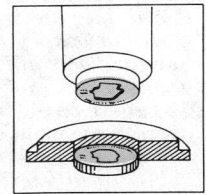

Die²
Die for stamping one side of a coin

at; āpe; cär; end; mē; it; īce; hot; ōld; fôrk; wood; fōōl; oil; out; up; turn; sing; thin; <u>th</u>is; hw in white; zh in treasure. The symbol ə stands for the sound of **a** in about, **e** in taken, **i** in pencil, **o** in lemon, and **u** in circus.

Dien·bien·phu (dyen′byen′foo′) *n.* a town in northwestern North Vietnam. The capture of Dienbienphu from the French by the Vietminh in 1954 marked the end of French military power in Indochina.

di·er·e·sis (dī er′ə sis) *n. pl.,* **di·er·e·ses** (dī er′ə sēz′). two dots (¨) placed over a vowel to show that it is pronounced in a separate syllable, as in naïve.

die·sel (dē′zəl) *also,* **Die·sel.** *n.* **1.** see **diesel engine. 2.** a vehicle powered by a diesel engine. —*adj.* of or for a diesel engine: *diesel fuel.*

diesel engine *also,* **Diesel engine.** an internal-combustion engine in which heat produced by the compression of air in the engine's cylinder ignites the fuel oil. Also, **diesel motor.** [From Rudolf *Diesel,* 1858–1913, a German engineer who invented it.]

Di·es I·rae (dē′ās ēr′ā) a medieval Latin hymn that describes Judgment Day, usually sung at masses for the dead. [Latin *diēs īrae* literally, the day of wrath, the first two words of this hymn.]

di·et[1] (dī′ət) *n.* **1.** food and drink usually eaten by a person or animal: *Her diet includes meat, vegetables, and fruit. A lion's diet consists of meat.* **2.** a regulated selection of food and drink chosen for reasons of health or weight control: *People with high blood pressure are sometimes put on salt-free diets. My uncle lost twenty pounds the first month of his diet.* —*v.i.* to eat according to a particular diet, especially in order to lose weight: *She dieted for several weeks and lost twelve pounds.* [Old French *diete,* going back to Greek *diaita* way of living.] —**di′et·er,** *n.*

di·et[2] (dī′ət) *n.* **1.** a formal assembly or meeting for discussion: *A diet of church officials met to consider changes in the service.* **2.** a lawmaking body or council, such as the national legislature of Japan. [Medieval Latin *dīeta* a public assembly, day for meeting, from Latin *diēs* day.]

di·e·tar·y (dī′ə ter′ē) *adj.* relating to diet: *Certain dietary rules must be observed for good health.*

di·e·tet·ic (dī′ə tet′ik) *adj.* **1.** relating to diet or to regulation of the use of food. **2.** prepared for use in special diets, especially diets followed to produce a loss in weight: *Dietetic sweets are made without sugar.* —**di′e·tet′i·cal·ly,** *adv.*

di·e·tet·ics (dī′ə tet′iks) *n., pl.* the branch of science dealing with diet and nutrition, with meal planning, and with the preparation and serving of food. ▲ used with a singular verb.

di·e·ti·tian (dī′ə tish′ən) *also,* **di·e·ti·cian.** *n.* a person trained in dietetics, usually employed by a hospital, school, or similar place.

dif·fer (dif′ər) *v.i.* **1.** to be not the same; be unlike: *Although they are brothers, Michael and Christopher differ greatly in looks.* **2.** to have a difference of opinion; disagree: *The candidate differs with the other members of his party on that issue.*

dif·fer·ence (dif′ər əns, dif′rəns) *n.* **1.** the state or quality of being unlike or different: *Was there a difference between her answers and his?* **2.** an instance of this: *He noticed a difference in her attitude after he apologized.* **3.** a distinguishing characteristic: *The only difference between the two cars is the price.* **4.** the amount by which one quantity is greater or less than another; remainder left after subtracting one quantity from another: *The difference between 16 and 12 is 4.* **5.** a disagreement in opinion: *They managed to settle their differences without a fight.* **6.** an instance of disagreement; dispute: *A difference arose between the neighbors over the exact boundary line between their property.*

  to make a difference. to affect or change a situation; matter: *Getting enough sleep makes a difference in how one feels and looks.*

dif·fer·ent (dif′ər ənt, dif′rənt) *adj.* **1.** not alike or similar: *She and her husband have very different taste in furniture.* **2.** not the same; separate; distinct: *It rained two different times this afternoon.* **3.** not like most others; not ordinary; unusual: *Her approach to raising children is quite different.* —**dif′fer·ent·ly,** *adv.*

▲ The word *from* is usually used after **different**: *His handwriting is very different from mine.* "Different *than*" is also used, although it is not as common, especially in writing. In Great Britain, the phrase "different *to*" is often used.

dif·fer·en·tial (dif′ə ren′shəl) *adj.* relating to, involving, or based on a difference or differences: *differential rates on freight charges.* —*n.* **1.** a differential amount, factor, wage, or rate. **2.** *also,* **differential gear.** a system of gears that enables the opposite driving wheels of a motor vehicle to turn at different speeds when the vehicle rounds a curve. —**dif′fer·en′tial·ly,** *adv.*

dif·fer·en·ti·ate (dif′ər en′shē āt′) *v.,* **dif·fer·en·ti·at·ed, dif·fer·en·ti·at·ing.** —*v.t.* **1.** to form or make up the difference in; serve to distinguish between: *Different coloring helps differentiate the male from the female in some species of birds.* **2.** to see or tell the differences in (something); distinguish between: *Not many people could differentiate this counterfeit bill from real money.* —*v.i.* **1.** to become different or specialized. **2.** to see or tell a difference: *Only their parents can always differentiate between the twins.* —**dif′fer·en′ti·a′tion,** *n.*

dif·fi·cult (dif′ə kult′) *adj.* **1.** hard to do or perform; demanding effort; not easy: *Crossing the river during the rain was a difficult task.* **2.** hard to solve or understand: *a difficult problem, a difficult poem.* **3.** hard to deal with, get along with, or please: *She was the most difficult customer the salesman had to wait on that day.*

dif·fi·cul·ty (dif′ə kul′tē) *n. pl.,* **dif·fi·cul·ties. 1.** the fact or condition of being difficult: *the difficulty of learning to drive a car. Walking on your hands is a trick of great difficulty.* **2.** something that is difficult to do, understand, or deal with; obstacle: *The hikers encountered many difficulties during the trip.* **3.** considerable effort; struggle: *She speaks French with difficulty. Heather had difficulty fitting everything into her suitcase.* **4.** embarrassing or troublesome state of affairs, especially a financial dilemma. **5.** a disagreement; conflict; trouble: *There was always some difficulty between John and his sister.*

dif·fi·dence (dif′ə dəns) *n.* a lack of confidence in oneself; shyness.

dif·fi·dent (dif′ə dənt) *adj.* lacking confidence in oneself; shy. —**dif′fi·dent·ly,** *adv.*

dif·fract (di frakt′) *v.t.* **1.** to break in pieces; break up. **2.** to cause to undergo diffraction.

dif·frac·tion (di frak′shən) *n.* **1.** the bending of the path of a ray of light as it passes close to the edge of an object or through a narrow slit. The light wave bent in this way will spread out to form a series of light and dark bands or the colored bands of the spectrum. **2.** the similar bending of other kinds of waves, such as sound, electricity, or X rays.

dif·fuse (*adj.,* di fyoos′; *v.,* di fyooz′) *adj.* **1.** widely spread out; scattered: *diffuse light.* **2.** using many words; wordy: *a diffuse writer.* —*v.,* **dif·fused, dif·fus·ing.** —*v.t.* **1.** to scatter in all directions; spread widely: *The colors of the sunset were diffused across the sky. He so diffused his talents that he never became a success in anything.* **2.** to cause (gases or liquids) to mix together by diffusion. —*v.i.* **1.** to be or become scattered; spread out: *The warmth from the fire diffused throughout the room.* **2.** to mix together by diffusion: *Every gas diffuses at a certain rate.* —**dif·fuse·ly** (di fyoos′lē) *adv.* —**dif·fuse·ness** (di fyoos′nis), *n.*

dif·fu·sion (di fyōo′zhən) *n.* **1.** the act of diffusing or the state of being diffused; dispersion: *The diffusion of knowledge was greatly aided by the coming of radio and television.* **2.** wordiness in speech or writing. **3.** a gradual mixing together of the molecules of gases or of liquids. Diffusion is due to the movement of the molecules from an area where there are many of them to an area where there are few.

dig (dig) *v.,* **dug, dig·ging.** —*v.t.* **1.** to break up or turn over and remove (earth), as with a shovel, the hands, or claws. **2.** to make or form by digging; hollow out: *to dig a hole, to dig a tunnel.* **3.** to obtain or remove by digging: *to dig potatoes.* **4.** to discover or obtain by search or investigation: *It took the reporter weeks to dig up the information he needed for the article.* **5.** to poke; prod: *He dug the horse with his spurs.* **6.** to thrust or plunge: *The bronco dug his hooves into the ground and bucked.* **7.** *Slang.* **a.** to understand. **b.** to like or appreciate. —*v.i.* **1.** to break up or turn over and remove the earth, as with a shovel, the hands, or claws: *The dog was digging in the yard for bones.* **2.** to make a way by or as if by digging: *The workers dug through the mountain to complete the highway.* —*n.* **1.** a thrust or poke: *a dig in the ribs.* **2.** *Informal.* a sarcastic remark; cutting statement: *Nick made a dig about his sister's new hair style.* **3.** the site of an archaeological excavation.
  to dig in. a. to dig trenches or holes for military defense. **b.** to begin to eat.

di·gest (*v.,* di jest′, dī jest′; *n.,* dī′jest) *v.t.* **1.** to break down (food materials) by the process of digestion. **2.** to think over or understand fully so as to absorb in the mind: *It took her a while to digest the surprising news of her daughter's engagement.* —*v.i.* to go through digestion: *Protein digests slowly.* —*n.* a collection or summary of literary, historical, legal, or scientific material.

di·gest·i·ble (di jes′tə bəl, dī jes′tə bəl) *adj.* capable of being digested; easily digested. —**di·gest′i·bil′i·ty,** *n.*

di·ges·tion (di jes′chən, dī jes′chən) *n.* **1.** the process by which food materials are broken down into simple compounds so as to be used or absorbed by the body. **2.** the ability to digest food: *The patient's digestion is good.*

di·ges·tive (di jes′tiv, dī jes′tiv) *adj.* relating to, for, or aiding digestion: *the digestive system.*

dig·ger (dig′ər) *n.* **1.** a person who digs. **2.** a tool or machine for digging.

dig·gings (dig′ingz) *n.,pl.* **1.** a place where digging is done, such as a mine. **2.** materials dug out. **3.** *Informal.* living quarters.

dig·it (dij′it) *n.* **1.** a finger or toe. **2.** any of the ten Arabic numerals 0 through 9. Sometimes 0 is excluded.

dig·i·tal (dij′it əl) *adj.* **1.** relating to or resembling a digit or digits. **2.** having digits. —*n.* a key on a keyboard instrument played with the finger.

digital computer, a computer that operates with numbers, particularly the digits 0 and 1, or with alphabetical symbols of language, used especially to solve problems that require exact answers.

dig·i·tal·is (dij′i tal′is) *n.* **1.** a drug used for stimulating the heart, prepared from the dried leaves of the foxglove. **2.** the plant from which this drug is made; foxglove.

dig·ni·fied (dig′nə fīd′) *adj.* marked by or showing dignity of manner or style; noble; stately.

dig·ni·fy (dig′nə fī′) *v.t.,* **dig·ni·fied, dig·ni·fy·ing. 1.** to give dignity to; make noble; honor: *The governor dignified the ceremony by his presence.* **2.** to give undeserved distinction or attention to: *Don't dignify the rumor by admitting to having heard it.*

dig·ni·tar·y (dig′nə ter′ē) *n. pl.,* **dig·ni·tar·ies.** a person who has a high position or office, as in government or the church: *Several foreign dignitaries were entertained by the President.*

dig·ni·ty (dig′nə tē) *n. pl.,* **dig·ni·ties. 1.** nobility of character or manner; stateliness, serenity, or self-respect: *Throughout great hardship and poverty their mother kept her dignity.* **2.** the state or quality of being worthy, honorable, or noble: *The real dignity of a man lies in what he is, not in what he owns.* **3.** degree of excellence or importance: *The judge swore to uphold the dignity of the court.* **4.** a high office, rank, or title.

di·graph (dī′graf′) *n.* two letters used to represent one sound, such as *oa* in *boat* or *sh* in *ship.*

di·gress (di gres′, dī gres′) *v.i.* to depart or wander from the main subject in speaking or writing: *The professor digressed during his lecture to tell stories of his childhood.*

di·gres·sion (di gresh′ən, dī gresh′ən) *n.* **1.** the act of digressing: *The speaker's frequent digressions soon bored the audience.* **2.** something that digresses: *The next chapter is a long digression about the author's view of politics.*

di·gres·sive (di gres′iv, dī gres′iv) *adj.* tending to digress; marked by digression. —**di·gres′sive·ly,** *adv.* —**di·gres′sive·ness,** *n.*

dike (dīk) *n.* a high bank, wall, or other structure built to prevent flooding by holding back the waters of a sea or river. —*v.t.,* **diked, dik·ing.** to provide, protect, or surround with a dike or dikes.

Dike

di·lap·i·dat·ed (di lap′ə dā′tid) *adj.* fallen into ruin or decay; broken down: *a dilapidated old tool shed.*

di·lap·i·da·tion (di lap′ə dā′shən) *n.* a condition of ruin or decay: *They found several of the slum houses in complete dilapidation.*

di·late (dī lāt′) *v.,* **di·lat·ed, di·lat·ing.** —*v.t.* to make larger or wider; cause to expand: *Taking a deep breath will dilate your chest.* —*v.i.* **1.** to become larger or wider; expand: *The kitten's eyes dilated with fear when she was startled.* **2.** to speak or write at length: *The returning explorer dilated upon his adventures for over an hour.* —**di·la′tion,** *n.*

dil·a·to·ry (dil′ə tôr′ē) *adj.* **1.** tending to delay or be negligent: *He is often dilatory in paying his bills.* **2.** tending to cause delay, gain time, or postpone action: *The senator used dilatory tactics to prevent passage of the bill.* —**dil′a·to′ri·ly,** *adv.* —**dil′a·to′ri·ness,** *n.*

di·lem·ma (di lem′ə) *n.* a situation requiring a choice between two or more things that are equally unpleasant or unsatisfactory; difficult choice: *Her dilemma was in deciding whether to take the bad-tasting cough medicine or to let her terrible coughing continue.*

dil·et·tante (dil′ə tänt′) *n. pl.,* **dil·et·tantes** or **dil·et·tan·ti** (dil′ə tän′tē). a person who pursues an art or science in a superficial way or merely for amusement.

dil·i·gence (dil′ə jəns) *n.* serious, constant attention and effort: *He is a worker who checks every detail with diligence.*

dil·i·gent (dil′ə jənt) *adj.* **1.** careful and hard-working in whatever is done: *a diligent student.* **2.** showing or carried out with painstaking care and effort: *a diligent search.* —**dil′i·gent·ly,** *adv.*

dill (dil) *n.* **1.** the dried seedlike fruit and fresh or dried leaves of a plant related to parsley, used chiefly as a spice to flavor pickles and other foods. **2.** the plant bearing this fruit.

dill pickle, a pickled cucumber flavored with dill.

dil·ly-dal·ly (dil′ē dal′ē) *v.i.,* **dil·ly-dal·lied, dil·ly-dal·ly·ing.** to waste time: *He dilly-dallied all day and never finished his work.*

di·lute (di loot′, dī loot′) *v.t.,* **di·lut·ed, di·lut·ing. 1.** to thin or weaken by adding a liquid: *to dilute fruit juice with water, to dilute paint with turpentine.* **2.** to weaken or reduce the strength or purity of by adding something else: *The addition of six new teams to the professional hockey league diluted the quality of play.* —*adj.* diluted; weak: *a dilute acid.*

di·lu·tion (di loo′shən, dī loo′shən) *n.* **1.** the act of diluting or the state of being diluted. **2.** something that is or has been diluted.

dim (dim) *adj.,* **dim·mer, dim·mest. 1.** having or giving little light; not bright: *a dim light bulb, a dim corner of a basement.* **2.** not clear to the senses; indistinct; faint: *He saw the dim outline of a figure in the distance.* **3.** not clear to the mind; vague; confused: *She had only a dim recollection of the accident.* **4.** not seeing, hearing, or understanding clearly: *Her eyes were dim with tears.* **5.** not favorable; discouraging: *Mother takes a dim view of our idea.* —*v.,* **dimmed, dim·ming.** —*v.t.* to make dim: *He dimmed the car's headlights.* —*v.i.* to grow or become dim. —**dim′ly,** *adv.* —**dim′ness,** *n.*

dime (dīm) *n.* a coin of the United States equal to ten cents or one-tenth of a dollar.

di·men·sion (di men′shən) *n.* **1.** any extent that can be measured, such as length, breadth, thickness, or height: *The room's dimensions are twenty feet by twelve feet by ten feet.* **2.** size, scope, or importance: *The dimensions of this problem have not yet been fully realized by the public.*

di·men·sion·al (di men′shən əl) *adj.* relating to or having a dimension or dimensions.

dime store, another term for **five-and-ten.**

di·min·ish (di min′ish) *v.t.* to make smaller or less, as in size, amount, importance, or degree: *The decision to raise taxes diminished the governor's popularity.* —*v.i.* to become smaller or less: *The campers' food supply gradually diminished as the days wore on.*

di·min·u·en·do (di min′yoo en′dō) *Music. adj.* with gradually decreasing loudness or force. —*adv.* with gradually decreasing loudness or force. —*n. pl.,* **di·min·u·en·dos. 1.** a gradual decrease in loudness or force. **2.** a passage played with a gradual decrease in loudness or force.

dim·i·nu·tion (dim′ə noo′shən, dim′ə nyoo′shən) *n.* the act of diminishing or the state of being diminished; reduction; decrease.

di·min·u·tive (di min′yə tiv) *adj.* **1.** small in size; tiny: *the diminutive hands of a baby.* **2.** *Grammar.* expressing smallness, familiarity, or affection. For example, -*let* in *droplet* and -*y* in *Bobby* are diminutive suffixes. —*n.* **1.** a small kind or variety of something. **2.** a word formed from another either by change in structure or by the addition of a suffix, expressing smallness, familiarity, or affection. *Piglet* is a diminutive of *pig.* The nickname *Joe* is a diminutive of *Joseph.*

dim·i·ty (dim′ə tē) *n. pl.,* **dim·i·ties.** a sheer, crisp, cotton fabric, usually woven with heavy, raised threads forming a striped or checkered arrangement, used for such items as blouses, dresses, or curtains.

dim·mer (dim′ər) *n.* a device that dims an electric light, especially a stage light or automobile headlight.

dim·ple (dim′pəl) *n.* a small, slight hollow in the surface of the human body, especially as formed in the chin, or in the cheek in the act of smiling. —*v.,* **dim·pled, dim·pling.** —*v.t.* to mark with dimples: *A smile dimpled her cheeks.* —*v.i.* to form dimples: *Her face dimpled when she smiled.*

din (din) *n.* a rattle or clatter that goes on for some time; loud, continuous noise: *the din of machines in a factory, the din of a New Year's Eve party.* —*v.,* **dinned, din·ning.** —*v.t.* to say over and over in a persistent way: *He is always dinning his complaints into her ear.* —*v.i.* to make a din.

di·nar (di när′) *n.* **1.** a unit of money in various countries, such as Yugoslavia, Iraq, Iran, Algeria, and Tunisia. **2.** an ancient gold coin used in Arab countries.

dine (dīn) *v.,* **dined, din·ing.** —*v.i.* **1.** to eat dinner: *The family always dines at six o'clock. Mother and Dad dined out to celebrate their anniversary.* **2.** to eat (with *on* or *upon*): *to dine on roast beef.* —*v.t.* to provide with dinner; give a dinner for: *to dine an important guest.*

din·er (dī′nər) *n.* **1.** a person who dines. **2.** another word for **dining car. 3.** a restaurant designed to resemble a dining car.

di·nette (dī net′) *n.* an alcove or small room used for dining.

ding (ding) *n.* **1.** a sound made by a bell. **2.** any similar sound. —*v.i.* to make a ringing sound. —*v.t.* to cause (something) to make a ringing sound.

ding-dong (ding′dông′, ding′dong′) *n.* **1.** the sound of a bell when it is struck repeatedly. **2.** any similar sound.

din·gey (ding′gē) *n. pl.,* **din·geys.** another spelling of **dinghy.**

din·ghy (ding′gē) *also,* **din·gey, din·gy.** *n. pl.,* **din·ghies.** a small open boat, propelled either by oars or by an outboard motor or fitted with a small mast for sailing. Dinghies are often used as tenders for larger boats.

din·gle (ding′gəl) *n.* a small, wooded valley; dell.

din·go (ding′gō) *n. pl.,* **din·goes.** a wild dog of Australia resembling a wolf, having pointed ears, reddish-brown fur, and a long, bushy tail with a white tip.

Dingo

din·gy¹ (din′jē) *adj.,* **din·gi·er, din·gi·est.** having a dirty, dull, or dreary appearance; not bright and fresh: *The sheets looked dingy even after she washed them. The old man lived in a dingy one-room apartment.* [Of uncertain origin.] —**din′gi·ly,** *adv.* —**din′gi·ness,** *n.*

din·gy² (ding′gē) *n. pl.,* **din·gies.** another spelling of **dinghy.**

dining car, a railroad car in which meals are served to passengers. Also, **diner.**

dining room, a room in which meals are served and eaten, as in a home or hotel.

dink·y (ding′kē) *adj.,* **dink·i·er, dink·i·est.** *Informal.* of little value, size, or importance; small or insignificant.

din·ner (din′ər) *n.* **1.** the principal meal of the day: *He ate dinner at his grandmother's house every Sunday.* **2.** a formal meal in honor of some person or occasion; banquet: *There was a dinner after the wedding ceremony.*

din·ner·ware (din′ər wer′) *n.* the dishes, glasses, and utensils used to eat a meal.

din·o·saur (dī′nə sôr′) *n.* a member of a large group of extinct reptiles that lived millions of years ago. Dinosaurs were of all sizes and some were the largest land animals that ever lived, growing to eighty-seven feet in length and weighing up to fifty tons.

dint (dint) *n.* **1.** force; power. ▲ now used chiefly in the phrase *by dint of: by dint of argument, by dint of effort.* **2.** another word for **dent.** —*v.t.* to make a dent in.

di·oc·e·san (dī os′ə sən) *adj.* of or relating to a diocese. —*n.* the bishop of a diocese.

di·o·cese (dī′ə sis, dī′ə sēs′) *n.* the church district under a bishop's authority.

di·ode (dī′ōd) *n.* a vacuum tube or semiconductor with two terminals, used especially to convert alternating current into direct current.

Di·og·e·nes (dī oj′ə nēz′) 412?–323 B.C., Greek philosopher.

Di·o·ny·sus (dī′ə nī′səs) *also,* **Di·o·ny·sos.** *n. Greek Mythology.* the god of fertility and wine. In Roman mythology he was called Bacchus.

di·o·ram·a (dī′ə ram′ə) *n.* **1.** a picture viewed from a distance through a small opening, in which various realistic effects are produced by means of lighting and other devices. **2.** an exhibit consisting of sculptured figures, stuffed animals, or other lifelike models, placed in a realistic setting against a curved, painted background.

di·ox·ide (dī ok′sīd) *n.* an oxide containing two atoms of oxygen in each molecule.

dip (dip) *v.,* **dipped** or **dipt, dip·ping.** —*v.t.* **1.** to put or let down into something, especially a liquid, for a moment: *She dipped the brush into the paint. He dipped his hand into the bowl to pick the winning ticket.* **2.** to obtain or lift up and out by scooping: *to dip water from a boat.* **3.** to lower and raise again quickly: *to dip a flag in a salute.* **4.** to immerse (sheep or other animals) in a disinfectant solution. **5.** to dye by immersing in a liquid. **6.** to make (a candle) by plunging a wick into melted tallow or wax over and over again. —*v.i.* **1.** to plunge into and then emerge from water or other liquid, especially quickly. **2.** to sink or go down: *The sun dipped below the horizon. Prices on the stock market dipped at the end of the week.* **3.** to slope downward: *The land dips as it meets the sea.* **4.** to reach into, especially in order to take something out: *She dipped into her purse to get her keys.* —*n.* **1.** the act of dipping, expecially a brief immersion in water: *She took a dip in the ocean.* **2.** a liquid preparation into which something is dipped, as for dyeing or disinfecting. **3.** a sudden drop or decline. **4.** a downward slope: *a dip in a road.* **5.** a creamy mixture of foods intended to be scooped up on crackers or similiar food. **6.** the quantity of something taken out or up by dipping: *a dip of ice cream.*

diph·the·ri·a (dif thēr′ē ə, dip thēr′ē ə) *n.* a serious contagious disease characterized by fever and by the formation of material that may block the throat and interfere with breathing.

diph·thong (dif′thông′, dif′thong′) *n.* a blend of two vowel sounds in one syllable that is pronounced as one speech sound. The *ou* in *mouse* and the *oy* in *boy* are diphthongs.

di·plo·ma (di plō′mə) *n.* a certificate given by a school or college to a graduating student, showing that a program of study has been completed or that a degree has been granted.

di·plo·ma·cy (di plō′mə sē) *n.* **1.** the art or practice of managing political relations between nations and carrying on negotiations between governments. **2.** skill or tact in dealing with other people or with situations, especially so as to avoid anything that would be awkward or unpleasant: *He showed diplomacy in not pointing out her mistake in front of other people.*

dip·lo·mat (dip′lə mat′) *n.* **1.** a person who is employed or skilled in managing relations between nations, especially an official representing his or her government to a foreign country or international assembly. **2.** any person skilled in dealing with others; tactful person. Also, **diplomatist.**

dip·lo·mat·ic (dip′lə mat′ik) *adj.* **1.** of, relating to, or connected with relations between nations: *diplomatic affairs.* **2.** having or showing skill or tact in dealing with other people. —**dip′lo·mat′i·cal·ly,** *adv.*

diplomatic immunity, the freedom from taxes, duties, and legal proceedings that is granted to diplomats stationed in a foreign country.

dip·lo·ma·tist (di plō′mə tist) *n.* another word for **diplomat.**

dip·per (dip′ər) *n.* **1.** a person or thing that dips. **2.** a cup-shaped container having a long, straight handle, used for scooping up liquids; ladle. **3. Dipper.** the Big Dipper or the Little Dipper.

Dipper

dipt (dipt) a past tense and a past participle of **dip.**

dip·ter·ous (dip′tər əs) *adj.* of or belonging to an order of insects that have only one pair of wings, including the gnat, mosquito, and housefly.

dip·tych (dip′tik) *n.* a double painting or carving consisting of two panels hinged together, especially one depicting a religious subject.

Diptych

dire (dīr) *adj.,* **dir·er, dir·est. 1.** causing great fear or suffering; dreadful; horrible: *a dire calamity, dire poverty.* **2.** extremely urgent; desperate: *The wounded soldier was in dire need of medical attention.* —**dire′ly,** *adv.* —**dire′ness,** *n.*

di·rect (di rekt′, dī rekt′) *v.t.* **1.** to manage or control the course or affairs of: *to direct traffic, to direct the affairs of a country.* **2.** to give instructions to; order; command: *The general directed the troops to attack.* **3.** to tell or show (someone) the way: *Can you direct me to the nearest police station?* **4.** to cause to move in a particular direction; turn; aim: *She directed her gaze to where he was pointing.* **5.** to intend (words) to be heard by someone; address: *The teacher directed his remarks to the entire class.* **6.** to lead, guide, or supervise the production or performance of: *to direct a film.* —*adj.* **1.** going in a straight line or by the shortest course: *a direct route.* **2.** with nothing or no one between; immediate: *direct contact.* **3.** straightforward; plain; honest: *a direct question.* **4.** in an unbroken line of descent: *a direct ancestor.* **5.** exact; absolute; complete: *the direct opposite.* **6.** in the exact words of the speaker or author: *a direct quotation.* **7.** of or by the action of the people or electorate without the work of representatives: *the direct election of senators.* —*adv.* directly: *This flight goes direct to New York.* —**di·rect′ness,** *n.*

at; āpe; cär; end; mē; it; īce; hot; ōld; fôrk; wood; fōōl; oil; out; up; turn; sing; thin; this; hw in white; zh in treasure. The symbol ə stands for the sound of **a** in about, **e** in taken, **i** in pencil, **o** in lemon, and **u** in circus.

direct current, an electric current in which the flow of electrons is in one direction only.

di·rec·tion (di rek′shən, dī rek′shən) *n.* **1.** management or control; guidance: *The recruits are under the direction of a sergeant.* **2.** a line or course along which something moves, faces, or lies: *The direction of the airplane changed from north to northeast. He was walking in the direction of the park.* **3.** *also,* **directions.** an order or instruction about how to proceed or act: *Follow the doctor's directions. The directions on the package say to put the vegetables in boiling water.* **4.** a tendency or line of development: *That senator has made efforts in the direction of reform.* **5.** the supervision and organization of the parts and presentation of a play, film, or other performance.

di·rec·tion·al (di rek′shən əl, dī rek′shən əl) *adj.* **1.** of, relating to, or showing direction: *the directional signals of an automobile.* **2.** *Electronics.* able to send or receive signals from one direction only: *a directional antenna.*

direction finder, a radio receiving device that determines the direction of incoming radio signals, usually by means of a rotating antenna in the form of a loop or rectangle.

di·rec·tive (di rek′tiv, dī rek′tiv) *n.* an order, regulation, or instruction, especially one issued by a higher authority: *On the day of the invasion, all officers received directives from headquarters.*

di·rect·ly (di rekt′lē, dī rekt′lē) *adv.* **1.** in a direct line or manner; straight: *The car headed directly toward them.* **2.** without anything or anyone between: *The new clerk was directly responsible for the confusion.* **3.** without delay; at once: *He returned directly.* **4.** exactly; absolutely: *His political views are directly opposed to hers.*

direct object, a word or words indicating the person or thing that receives the action expressed by a verb. In the sentence *George hit Joe,* the direct object is *Joe.*

di·rec·tor (di rek′tər, dī rek′tər) *n.* **1.** a person or thing that manages or controls: *a camp director, a funeral director.* **2.** a person who supervises and guides the performers and technicians in the production of a film, play, television program, or other show or performance. **3.** one of a group of board members chosen to control or govern the affairs of a company or institution.

di·rec·tor·ate (di rek′tər it, dī rek′tər it) *n.* **1.** the office or position of director. **2.** a group of directors.

di·rec·to·ri·al (di rek′tôr′ē əl, dī′rek′tôr′ē əl) *adj.* **1.** of or relating to a director or directorate: *directorial duties.* **2.** that directs; directive: *a directorial memo.*

di·rec·to·ry (di rek′tər ē, dī rek′tər ē) *n.* an alphabetical or classified list, as of the names, addresses, or occupations of a group of people: *a telephone directory.*

direct primary, an election in which registered members of a political party vote directly for the candidates of their party, rather than for delegates who will nominate such candidates at a convention.

direct proportion, the mathematical relationship of two variables when one equals the other multiplied by a constant. For example, if $a = bc,$ and c is a constant, then a and b are in direct proportion.

di·rec·trix (di rek′triks, dī rek′triks) *n. pl.,* **di·rec·trix·es.** *Geometry.* a fixed line that guides the motion of another line as it generates a surface or guides the motion of a point as it generates a curve.

direct tax, a tax levied directly on the persons who must pay it, such as an income tax.

dire·ful (dīr′fəl) *adj.* dire; dreadful; terrible. —**dire′ful·ly,** *adv.* —**dire′ful·ness,** *n.*

dirge (durj) *n.* a song, hymn, or tune of grief or mourning, especially one performed at a funeral.

dir·i·gi·ble (dir′ə jə bəl, də rij′ə bəl) *n.* a rigid, cigar-shaped airship that is driven by motors and can be steered.

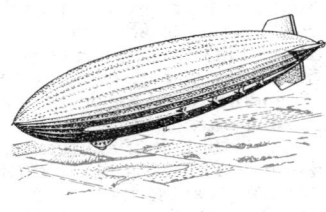
Dirigible

dirk (durk) *n.* another word for **dagger.**

dirn·dl (durnd′əl) *n.* **1.** a woman's dress with a fitted bodice and a full skirt gathered at the waist. **2.** a full skirt gathered at the waist.

dirt (durt) *n.* **1.** mud, dust, or other material that soils or makes something unclean: *Mother told Tommy to wash the dirt off his hands before he came to the dinner table.* **2.** earth or soil, especially when loose: *The gardener filled all the flowerpots with dirt.* **3.** something despised or worthless: *His old friends treated him like dirt after he was convicted of the crime.* **4.** indecent writing, pictures, or speech. **5.** *Informal.* gossip, especially of a nasty or shocking nature.

dirt·y (dur′tē) *adj.,* **dirt·i·er, dirt·i·est. 1.** soiled with dirt; not clean; filthy: *a dirty towel.* **2.** tending to soil or make unclean: *Digging the hole was a hard and dirty job.* **3.** low or nasty; despicable: *a dirty trick.* **4.** not decent; vulgar; obscene: *a dirty joke.* **5.** not sportsmanlike; unfair: *a dirty fighter.* **6.** *Informal.* full of spite; resentful; insulting: *He gave them a dirty look when they laughed at his mistake.* **7.** (of weather) stormy; unsettled. —*v.t., v.i.,* **dirt·ied, dirt·y·ing.** to make or become dirty: *White shoes dirty easily.* —**dirt′i·ness,** *n.*

dis- *prefix* **1.** opposite or lack of; not: *disobedience.* **2.** undoing of; reverse of: *disconnect.* **3.** deprivation of; removal from: *dispossession.*

dis·a·bil·i·ty (dis′ə bil′ə tē) *n. pl.,* **dis·a·bil·i·ties. 1.** the loss or lack of ability; disabled condition: *The insurance policy covers disability arising from injury.* **2.** something that disables; handicap: *Not having a high school diploma can be a disability when looking for a job.*

dis·a·ble (dis ā′bəl) *v.t.,* **dis·a·bled, dis·a·bling.** to take ability or power away from; make unable to move, work, or act as usual: *A broken leg disabled him for months.* —**dis·a′ble·ment,** *n.*

dis·a·bled (dis ā′bəld) *adj.* having a disability; crippled: *These funds will finance a training program for disabled veterans.*

dis·ad·van·tage (dis′əd van′tij) *n.* **1.** something that interferes with or prevents success; drawback; handicap: *Being short is a disadvantage to a basketball player.* **2.** a loss; injury; harm: *It will be to her disadvantage if she turns down such a generous offer.*

dis·ad·van·taged (dis′əd van′tijd) *adj.* lacking a decent standard of living: *Many disadvantaged families live in slums.*

dis·ad·van·ta·geous (dis ad′vən tā′jəs) *adj.* causing disadvantage; unfavorable. —**dis·ad′van·ta′geous·ly,** *adv.* —**dis·ad′van·ta′geous·ness,** *n.*

dis·af·fect (dis′ə fekt′) *v.t.* to destroy the affection or loyalty of; make unfriendly: *The brutal tactics of the new government disaffected many who had supported it.* —**dis′af·fec′tion,** *n.*

dis·a·gree (dis′ə grē′) *v.i.,* **dis·a·greed, dis·a·gree·ing. 1.** to differ in opinion: *The teacher disagreed with John's statement.* **2.** to quarrel; argue: *They disagreed violently, and she ran out crying.* **3.** to fail to agree or harmonize: *The various newspaper accounts of the robbery disagreed.* **4.** to cause physical discomfort or ill effects (with *with*): *Hot weather disagrees with her. Spicy foods disagree with my stomach.*

dis·a·gree·a·ble (dis′ə grē′ə bəl) *adj.* **1.** not to one's taste or liking; unpleasant: *a disagreeable odor, a disagreeable task.* **2.** having a bad temper; nasty; quarrelsome: *She's always disagreeable in the morning.* —**dis′a·gree′a·ble·ness,** *n.* —**dis′a·gree′a·bly,** *adv.*

dis·a·gree·ment (dis′ə grē′mənt) *n.* **1.** a difference of opinion. **2.** a quarrel; argument. **3.** a failure to agree; difference: *The disagreement between the suspects' stories aroused the suspicion of the police.*

dis·al·low (dis′ə lou′) *v.i.* **1.** to deny the truth or validity of: *to disallow a claim.* **2.** to refuse to allow; prohibit: *to disallow gambling.*

dis·ap·pear (dis′ə pēr′) *v.i.* **1.** to pass from sight; vanish: *The sun disappeared below the horizon.* **2.** to cease to exist or be known: *The dinosaur disappeared centuries ago.*

dis·ap·pear·ance (dis′ə pēr′əns) *n.* the act or fact of disappearing.

dis·ap·point (dis′ə point′) *v.t.* **1.** to fail to fulfill the hope, desire, or expectation of: *His poor showing in the race disappointed his coach.* **2.** to prevent the realization or fulfillment of (something); thwart; frustrate: *to disappoint a person's hopes.*

dis·ap·point·ment (dis′ə point′mənt) *n.* **1.** the state or feeling of being disappointed: *She couldn't hide her disappointment when Paul did not come to the party.* **2.** a person or thing that disappoints: *He was a disappointment to his family.* **3.** the act or fact of disappointing.

dis·ap·pro·ba·tion (dis ap′rə bā′shən) *n.* disapproval.

dis·ap·prov·al (dis′ə prōō′vəl) *n.* **1.** the act of disapproving. **2.** an unfavorable opinion or feeling; dislike: *He showed his disapproval by frowning.*

dis·ap·prove (dis′ə prōōv′) *v.,* **dis·ap·proved, dis·ap·prov·ing.** —*v.t.* **1.** to have or express an unfavorable opinion of (something); condemn: *Mother disapproves his rude behavior.* **2.** to refuse to approve; reject: *The boss disapproved her request for a vacation.* —*v.i.* to have or express an unfavorable opinion: *Jan disapproves of practical jokes that hurt people's feelings.* —**dis′ap·prov′ing·ly,** *adv.*

dis·arm (dis ärm′) *v.t.* **1.** to take a weapon or weapons from: *The sheriff disarmed the prisoners.* **2.** to do away with the anger, hostility, or suspicion of: *The stranger's charming manner disarmed the frightened woman.* **3.** to make harmless by removing the means to injure or attack: *to disarm a bomb.* —*v.i.* **1.** to lay down arms: *The rebels agreed to disarm.* **2.** to reduce, limit, or do away with military weapons or forces.

dis·ar·ma·ment (dis är′mə mənt) *n.* the act of disarming, especially the reduction, limitation, or elimination of military weapons or forces.

dis·arm·ing (dis är′ming) *adj.* tending to do away with anger, hostility, or suspicion: *a disarming smile.* —**dis·arm′ing·ly,** *adv.*

dis·ar·range (dis′ə rānj′) *v.t.,* **dis·ar·ranged, dis·ar·rang·ing.** to disturb the order or arrangement of; create disorder in: *She disarranged everything in the closet looking for her missing shoe.* —**dis′ar·range′ment,** *n.*

dis·ar·ray (dis′ə rā′) *n.* **1.** a condition of disorder or confusion; lack of orderly arrangement: *The burglars left the apartment in complete disarray.* **2.** a condition of disorder or incompleteness of dress: *When the fire broke out in the dormitory, the students ran from their rooms in disarray.* —*v.t.* to throw into disorder or confusion.

dis·as·sem·ble (dis′ə sem′bəl) *v.t.,* **dis·as·sem·bled, dis·as·sem·bling.** to take apart: *to disassemble an engine.*

dis·as·so·ci·ate (dis′ə sō′shē āt′, dis′ə sō′sē āt′) *v.t.,* **dis·as·so·ci·at·ed, dis·as·so·ci·at·ing.** to cut off association or connection with; separate from: *The candidate disassociated himself from his party's stand on that issue.* —**dis′as·so′ci·a′tion,** *n.*

dis·as·ter (di zas′tər) *n.* any event causing much suffering, distress, or loss; sudden or great misfortune. [French *désastre,* going back to Latin *dis-* against + *astrum* star; referring to the belief that the stars control human fate, and when they are against a person, great misfortune occurs.]

dis·as·trous (di zas′trəs) *adj.* causing or accompanied by disaster: *a disastrous flood, a disastrous mistake.* —**dis·as′trous·ly,** *adv.*

dis·a·vow (dis′ə vou′) *v.t.* to deny knowledge or responsibility for: *The government disavowed the spy when his capture was announced.*

dis·a·vow·al (dis′ə vou′əl) *n.* the act of disavowing.

dis·band (dis band′) *v.t.* to break up the organization of: *to disband a regiment.* —*v.i.* to stop functioning as an organized body; break up: *The club disbanded after only three meetings.* —**dis·band′ment,** *n.*

dis·bar (dis bär′) *v.t.,* **dis·barred, dis·bar·ring.** to expel (a lawyer) officially from the legal profession. —**dis·bar′ment,** *n.*

dis·be·lief (dis′bi lēf′) *n.* lack of belief; refusal to believe: *Nancy's face showed disbelief when she was told the news.*

dis·be·lieve (dis′bi lēv′) *v.,* **dis·be·lieved, dis·be·liev·ing.** —*v.t.* to fail to believe in (someone or something): *The police disbelieved the suspect's alibi.* —*v.i.* to fail to believe in someone or something: *to disbelieve in the existence of ghosts.* —**dis′be·liev′er,** *n.*

dis·bur·den (dis burd′ən) *v.t.* **1.** to rid of a burden or load: *to disburden a ship, to disburden an animal.* **2.** to relieve of something burdensome or oppressive: *to disburden one's conscience by telling the truth.*

dis·burse (dis burs′) *v.t.,* **dis·bursed, dis·burs·ing.** to pay out (funds). —**dis·burs′er,** *n.*

dis·burse·ment (dis burs′mənt) *n.* **1.** the act of disbursing or paying out. **2.** the money paid out.

disc (disk) *n.* **1.** a phonograph record. **2.** another spelling of **disk.**

dis·card (*v.,* dis kärd′; *n.,* dis′kärd′) *v.t.* **1.** to reject or give up as useless, worthless, or unwanted; cast aside: *The scientists discarded the old theory when the new one proved correct. He discarded his overcoat as soon as he entered the heated room.* **2.** *Card Games.* **a.** to throw away or put aside (an unwanted card or cards). **b.** to play (a card other than a trump or the suit led). —*n.* **1.** the act of discarding or the state of being discarded. **2.** a person or thing that is discarded. **3.** a card or cards discarded.

dis·cern (di surn′, di zurn′) *v.t.* **1.** to recognize as different and distinct; to separate or distinguish mentally: *to discern good from evil.* **2.** to make out or recognize: *She could barely discern the figure of a man in the fog.* —*v.i.* to see a difference; distinguish: *to discern between truth and falsehood.* —**dis·cern′er,** *n.*

dis·cern·i·ble (di sur′nə bəl, di zur′nə bəl) *adj.* that can be discerned. —**dis·cern′i·bly,** *adv.*

dis·cern·ing (di sur′ning, di zur′ning) *adj.* having or showing keen perception, judgment, or understanding: *a discerning judge of character, discerning taste in art.* —**dis·cern′ing·ly,** *adv.*

dis·cern·ment (di surn′mənt, di zurn′mənt) *n.* **1.** the

at; āpe; cär; end; mē; it; īce; hot; ōld; fôrk; wood; fōōl; oil; out; up; turn; sing; thin; this; hw in white; zh in treasure. The symbol ə stands for the sound of a in about, e in taken, i in pencil, o in lemon, and u in circus.

act of discerning. **2.** keenness of perception, judgment, or understanding; insight.

dis·charge (*v.,* dis chärj′; *n.,* dis′chärj′) *v.,* **dis·charged, dis·charg·ing.** —*v.t.* **1.** to release from service, office, or employment; dismiss: *to discharge a worker, to discharge a soldier from the army.* **2.** to release from care or custody; set at liberty: *to discharge a prisoner, to discharge a patient from the hospital.* **3.** to let go or clear out; remove or unload: *The boat discharged its passengers at the pier.* **4.** to fulfill the requirements of; carry out: *to discharge an errand, to discharge a duty.* **5.** to fire; shoot: *to discharge a bow, to discharge a gun.* **6.** to send forth: *The river discharged its water into the bay.* **7.** to relieve of responsibility, duty, or obligation: *to discharge a jury.* **8.** to pay off; settle: *to discharge a debt.* **9.** to rid of an electric charge; withdraw electricity from: *to discharge a battery.* —*v.i.* **1.** to send forth contents: *The smaller pipes discharged into the main one.* **2.** to go off, as a firearm; fire. **3.** to lose an electrical charge. —*n.* **1.** a dismissal from service, office, or employment. **2.** release from care or custody: *the discharge of a prisoner.* **3.** something that dismisses or releases, such as a certificate discharging a person from military service. **4.** the act of firing or going off, as a weapon. **5.** the act of carrying out; performance: *to be faithful in the discharge of one's duties.* **6.** the act of flowing or letting out: *the discharge of pus from a wound.* **7.** something that is discharged or sent forth: *a watery discharge from an open sore.* **8.** the act of paying off or settling: *the discharge of a debt.* **9.** the act of removing contents or a burden; unloading: *the discharge of cargo.* **10.** the transference of electricity between two charged bodies.

dis·ci·ple (di sī′pəl) *n.* **1.** a follower of a particular teacher or doctrine: *Plato was a disciple of Socrates.* **2.** any of the early followers of Jesus, especially one of the Apostles.

dis·ci·pli·nar·i·an (dis′ə pli ner′ē ən) *n.* a person who enforces or is in favor of strict discipline: *The captain was a stern disciplinarian who was feared by all his men.*

dis·ci·pli·nar·y (dis′ə pli ner′ē) *adj.* of, relating to, or used in discipline: *disciplinary measures.*

dis·ci·pline (dis′ə plin) *n.* **1.** training that molds, corrects, or perfects something, such as the mind or moral character. **2.** orderly, obedient, or restrained conduct; self-control: *The students showed excellent discipline during the fire drill.* **3.** punishment given to train or correct: *The child's rude behavior demanded severe discipline.* **4.** a branch of instruction or knowledge; field of study: *Mathematics and physics are related disciplines.* **5.** a set or system of rules for conduct: *Cadets at the academy must observe strict discipline.* —*v.t.,* **dis·ci·plined, dis·ci·plin·ing. 1.** to train to be obedient; keep in order or under control: *to discipline troops.* **2.** to develop or train, as by instruction or exercise: *to discipline one's mind.* **3.** to punish.

disc jockey also, **disk jockey.** an announcer or master of ceremonies on a radio program of recorded music.

dis·claim (dis klām′) *v.t.* **1.** to deny any claim to, responsibility for, or connection with; refuse to accept as one's own: *The driver disclaimed any responsibility for the accident.* **2.** to give up a legal right or claim to: *He disclaimed a share in his uncle's estate.* —**dis·claim′er,** *n.*

dis·close (dis klōz′) *v.t.,* **dis·closed, dis·clos·ing. 1.** to make known; reveal: *to disclose a secret, to disclose one's intentions.* **2.** to expose to view; lay bare; uncover: *The excavation disclosed the ruins of an ancient city.*

dis·clo·sure (dis klō′zhər) *n.* **1.** the act of disclosing: *The disclosure of such information is against company rules.* **2.** something that is disclosed: *The news of the President's illness was a startling disclosure.*

dis·col·or (dis kul′ər) *v.t.* to change or spoil the color of; stain: *Heat and smoke had discolored the kitchen wallpaper.* —*v.i.* to become changed or spoiled in color: *This fabric will discolor if washed in hot water.*

dis·col·or·a·tion (dis kul′ə rā′shən) *n.* **1.** the act of discoloring or the state of being discolored. **2.** a discolored spot or mark; stain.

dis·com·bob·u·late (dis′kəm bob′yə lāt′) *v.t.,* **dis·com·bob·u·lat·ed, dis·com·bob·u·lat·ing.** *Informal.* to confuse; upset.

dis·com·fit (dis kum′fit) *v.t.* **1.** to throw into confusion; embarrass: *He was quite discomfited by the reporter's rude question.* **2.** to defeat the plans or expectations of; frustrate: *The arrival of the police discomfited the holdup men.* **3.** to defeat or overthrow in battle; rout.

dis·com·fi·ture (dis kum′fi chər) *n.* the act of discomfiting or the state of being discomfited.

dis·com·fort (dis kum′fərt) *n.* **1.** lack of comfort; uneasiness: *The question caused him much discomfort because he did not know the answer.* **2.** something that causes discomfort: *Sleeping on the couch for one night shouldn't be a discomfort for him.* —*v.t.* to make uncomfortable or uneasy.

dis·com·mode (dis′kə mōd′) *v.t.,* **dis·com·mod·ed, dis·com·mod·ing.** to cause inconvenience to; disturb; trouble.

dis·com·pose (dis′kəm pōz′) *v.t.,* **dis·com·posed, dis·com·pos·ing.** to disturb the calm or composure of; make nervous or uneasy: *The jeers of the crowd did not discompose the speaker.*

dis·com·po·sure (dis′kəm pō′zhər) *n.* the state of being discomposed: *The more they laughed at his mistake, the more his discomposure increased.*

dis·con·cert (dis′kən surt′) *v.t.* **1.** to disturb the self-possession or composure of; embarrass; confuse: *Their rude laughter disconcerted him.* **2.** to throw into disorder; upset or frustrate. —**dis′con·cert′ing·ly,** *adv.*

dis·con·nect (dis′kə nekt′) *v.t.* to break the connection of or between: *The repairman disconnected the television set before fixing it. The workmen disconnected the locomotive from the train.* —**dis′con·nec′tion,** *n.*

dis·con·nect·ed (dis′kə nek′tid) *adj.* **1.** lacking order, connection, or logic: *a disconnected speech, disconnected thoughts.* **2.** not connected: *a disconnected telephone.* —**dis′con·nect′ed·ly,** *adv.* —**dis′con·nect′ed·ness,** *n.*

dis·con·so·late (dis kon′sə lit) *adj.* so sad as to be without cheer, hope, or comfort: *The little boy was disconsolate after his dog's death.* —**dis·con′so·late·ly,** *adv.* —**dis·con′so·late·ness,** *n.*

dis·con·tent (dis′kən tent′) *n.* lack of contentment; dissatisfaction; restlessness: *Overcrowded conditions in the jails caused much discontent among the prisoners.* Also, **discontentment.** —*v.t.* to make discontented. —*adj.* discontented: *He was discontent with the way the manager ran the team.*

dis·con·tent·ed (dis′kən ten′tid) *adj.* uneasy in mind; not contented; dissatisfied; restless. —**dis′con·tent′ed·ly,** *adv.* —**dis′con·tent′ed·ness,** *n.*

dis·con·tent·ment (dis′kən tent′mənt) *n.* another word for **discontent.**

dis·con·tin·u·a·tion (dis′kən tin′yōo ā′shən) *n.* the act of discontinuing or the state of being discontinued. Also, **dis·con·tin·u·ance** (dis′kən tin′yōo əns).

dis·con·tin·ue (dis′kən tin′yōo) *v.,* **dis·con·tin·ued, dis·con·tin·u·ing.** —*v.t.* to put an end or halt to; stop: *He discontinued his subscription to the magazine.* —*v.i.* to come to an end: *Publication of the newspaper discontinued.*

dis·con·ti·nu·i·ty (dis′kon tə nōō′ə tē, dis′kon tə nyōō′ə tē) *n. pl.,* **dis·con·ti·nu·i·ties. 1.** a lack of continuity. **2.** a gap or break.

dis·con·tin·u·ous (dis′kən tin′yo͞o əs) *adj.* not continuous; interrupted; broken. —**dis′con·tin′u·ous·ly,** *adv.*

dis·cord (dis′kôrd) *n.* **1.** a lack of agreement or harmony; disagreement; conflict: *There was constant discord among the members of the committee.* **2.** harsh, clashing, or unpleasant sounds. **3.** *Music.* lack of harmony in notes sounded at the same time; dissonance.

dis·cord·ant (dis kôrd′ənt) *adj.* **1.** not in agreement or harmony; disagreeing; conflicting: *discordant opinions.* **2.** harsh, clashing, or unpleasant in sound: *discordant noises.* —**dis·cor′dance,** *n.* —**dis·cord′ant·ly,** *adv.*

dis·co·thèque (dis′kō tek′) *n.* a nightclub or other place for dancing, especially to recorded music.

dis·count (*n.,* dis′kount′; *v.,* dis′kount′, dis kount′) *n.* a deduction of a specified amount or percentage, as from a price or other amount: *to sell a radio at a 25% discount.* —*v.t.* **1.** to offer for sale at a reduced rate: *That store discounts all its merchandise.* **2.** to take off or deduct (a specified amount or percentage) from the total amount charged or owed: *The dealer discounted 15% from the price of the car.* **3.** to view as exaggerated or not entirely true: *Discount most of his stories about his athletic ability.*

dis·coun·te·nance (dis kount′ən əns) *v.t.,* **dis·coun·te·nanced, dis·coun·te·nanc·ing. 1.** to look upon with disfavor or disapproval; discourage: *The school discountenanced the students' plans for raising money.* **2.** to make ashamed or embarrassed: *The discovery of her error discountenanced her.*

dis·cour·age (dis kur′ij) *v.t.,* **dis·cour·aged, dis·cour·ag·ing. 1.** to lessen the courage, hope, or confidence of; dishearten: *Failing his first test did not discourage him.* **2.** to try to prevent by expressing disapproval of; frown upon: *The principal discouraged unexcused absences.* **3.** to prevent, interfere with, or hinder: *Bad weather discouraged them from going on a picnic. Strict laws were passed in an attempt to discourage crime.*

dis·cour·age·ment (dis kur′ij mənt) *n.* **1.** the act of discouraging. **2.** the state or feeling of being discouraged: *The team was filled with discouragement by the defeat.* **3.** something that discourages: *His failure to pass the examination was a discouragement to him.*

dis·course (*n.,* dis′kôrs; *v.,* dis kôrs′) *n.* **1.** a formal speech or writing, as a lecture or sermon: *The guest speaker gave a discourse on prehistoric man.* **2.** conversation; talk. —*v.i.,* **dis·coursed, dis·cours·ing.** to speak or write formally and at length on a subject: *The police chief discoursed on the need for more public cooperation in fighting crime.*

dis·cour·te·ous (dis kur′tē əs) *adj.* not courteous; rude; impolite: *a discourteous reply.* —**dis·cour′te·ous·ly,** *adv.* —**dis·cour′te·ous·ness,** *n.*

dis·cour·te·sy (dis kur′tə sē) *n. pl.,* **dis·cour·te·sies. 1.** lack of courtesy; rudeness; impoliteness: *Her mother disapproved of discourtesy in any form.* **2.** a discourteous act: *It would be a discourtesy to leave the party without thanking the hostess.*

dis·cov·er (dis kuv′ər) *v.t.* **1.** to come upon or see (something) for the first time: *DeSoto discovered the Mississippi River.* **2.** to learn of; come to know of: *He discovered his mistake too late.* —**dis·cov′er·er,** *n.*

dis·cov·er·y (dis kuv′ər ē) *n. pl.,* **dis·cov·er·ies. 1.** the act of discovering: *His discovery of the error was too late.* **2.** something discovered: *Finding the dollar in his pocket was a pleasant discovery.*

dis·cred·it (dis kred′it) *v.t.* **1.** to cause to be doubted or disbelieved; destroy belief, confidence, or trust in: *New facts discredited the old theory.* **2.** to damage the credit or reputation of; disgrace: *The unsportsmanlike conduct of the football team discredited the entire school.* **3.** to refuse to

believe or give credit to: *Susan discredited all rumors.* —*n.* **1.** lack or loss of credit or reputation: *Her conduct brought discredit on her whole family.* **2.** lack or loss of belief, confidence, or trust; doubt: *His habit of lying brought everything he said into discredit.* **3.** something that discredits: *His dishonest activities were a discredit to his business partners.*

dis·cred·it·a·ble (dis kred′i tə bəl) *adj.* bringing discredit; disgraceful: *Lying is a discreditable act.* —**dis·cred′it·a·bly,** *adv.*

dis·creet (dis krēt′) *adj.* having or showing tact and careful judgment in speech and action; prudent: *Nick was discreet enough not to reveal the secret.* —**dis·creet′ly,** *adv.* —**dis·creet′ness,** *n.*

▲ **Discreet** and **discrete** are pronounced alike, but they have different meanings. **Discreet** means prudent or careful: *The diplomat had to be discreet when he discussed his country's foreign policy.* **Discrete** means separate or distinct: *An apple and an orange are discrete objects.*

dis·crep·an·cy (dis krep′ən sē) *n. pl.,* **dis·crep·an·cies.** lack of agreement or consistency; difference; contradiction: *There was a wide discrepancy in the testimony of the two witnesses.*

dis·crete (dis krēt′) *adj.* detached from others; separate; distinct: *The word "heart" has several discrete meanings.* ▲ See **discreet** for usage note. —**dis·crete′ly,** *adv.* —**dis·crete′ness,** *n.*

dis·cre·tion (dis kresh′ən) *n.* **1.** the quality of being discreet; good judgment; caution; prudence: *He showed much discretion in not revealing who told him the story.* **2.** the freedom or power to act according to one's own judgment: *The students left the choice of how much to spend on the teacher's gift up to Ann's discretion.*

dis·cre·tion·ar·y (dis kresh′ə ner′ē) *adj.* left to or determined by one's own judgment or discretion: *The delegate to the conference was given discretionary powers.*

dis·crim·i·nate (dis krim′ə nāt′) *v.i.,* **dis·crim·i·nat·ed, dis·crim·i·nat·ing. 1.** to act or treat differently on the basis of unfair feelings; show prejudice: *It is against the law to discriminate against people because of their race or religion.* **2.** to notice a difference; make a distinction: *to discriminate between good and bad poetry.*

dis·crim·i·nat·ing (dis krim′ə nā′ting) *adj.* **1.** noticing and making distinctions with accuracy; keen: *a discriminating judge of character.* **2.** noticing or paying attention to small details; particular: *to be discriminating in one's choice of clothes.* **3.** making or forming a difference: *The color of their eyes is a discriminating feature between the twins.* **4.** showing prejudice. —**dis·crim′i·nat′ing·ly,** *adv.*

dis·crim·i·na·tion (dis krim′ə nā′shən) *n.* **1.** the act of discriminating. **2.** unfair difference in treatment; prejudice: *The applicants were judged without discrimination as to race, color, or creed.* **3.** the ability to make distinctions with accuracy; keen judgment: *She showed taste and discrimination in furnishing her home.*

dis·crim·i·na·to·ry (dis krim′ə nə tôr′ē) *adj.* showing or marked by prejudice, especially racial prejudice: *Discriminatory practices in hiring people for jobs are against the law.* —**dis·crim′i·na·to′ri·ly,** *adv.*

at; āpe; cär; end; mē; it; īce; hot; ōld; fôrk; wood; fo͞ol; oil; out; up; turn; sing; thin; this; hw in white; zh in treasure. The symbol ə stands for the sound of **a** in about, e in taken, i in pencil, o in lemon, and u in circus.

dis·cur·sive (dis kur′siv) *adj.* wandering from one subject to another: *The professor's discursive lecture soon bored or confused most of the students.*

dis·cus (dis′kəs) *n.* a heavy circular plate, usually of wood with a smooth metal rim around its edges. It is used in athletic contests to see who can throw it the farthest distance.

dis·cuss (dis kus′) *v.t.* to exchange or present ideas or opinions about; consider in conversation or writing: *The council discussed plans for a new city hall. This article discusses the American Revolution.*

dis·cus·sion (dis kush′ən) *n.* **1.** the act of discussing: *The student's question at the end of the speech started a discussion.* **2.** an instance of discussing: *The book's discussion of the Middle Ages was thirty pages long.*

dis·dain (dis dān′) *n.* a feeling of contempt and dislike for something or someone thought of as unworthy or beneath one; scorn: *He treated the younger boys with disdain.* —*v.t.* to consider unworthy or beneath oneself; look down on; scorn: *Despite his poverty the old man disdained all help.*

dis·dain·ful (dis dān′fəl) *adj.* feeling or showing disdain; scornful. —**dis·dain′ful·ly**, *adv.*

dis·ease (di zēz′) *n.* **1.** a disturbance in the function of an organ or an organism resulting from a specific cause or causes, such as infection, and characterized by particular symptoms: *Chicken pox is a childhood disease. Rust is a disease of plants.* **2.** any harmful condition: *Poverty is a disease of society.* —**dis·eased′**, *adj.*

dis·em·bark (dis′em bärk′) *v.i.* to get off a ship or airplane: *The tourists from Europe disembarked at New York.* —*v.t.* to put or let off a ship or airplane: *to disembark passengers at a port.* —**dis·em·bar·ka·tion** (dis em′bär kā′shən), *n.*

dis·em·bod·ied (dis′em bod′ēd) *adj.* separated from the body: *disembodied spirits.*

dis·em·bow·el (dis′em bou′əl) *v.t.* to take out the bowels or entrails of. —**dis′em·bow′el·ment**, *n.*

dis·en·chant (dis′en chant′) *v.t.* to free from enchantment or pleasant illusion: *She had pictured the author as young and handsome, but she was disenchanted when she met him.* —**dis′en·chant′ment**, *n.*

dis·en·cum·ber (dis′en kum′bər) *v.t.* to relieve or free from something that burdens or troubles: *The tired old woman disencumbered herself of her packages and sat down to rest.*

dis·en·fran·chise (dis′en fran′chīz) *v.t.*, **dis·en·fran·chised, dis·en·fran·chis·ing.** to take away a right or privilege from, especially the right to vote. Also, **disfranchise.** —**dis′en·fran′chise·ment**, *n.*

dis·en·gage (dis′en gāj′) *v.*, **dis·en·gaged, dis·en·gag·ing.** —*v.t.* **1.** to release or loosen from something that holds, connects, or entangles: *She disengaged her hand from his.* **2.** to free, as from an engagement, promise, or obligation: *He disengaged himself from the business deal as soon as he realized it was a fraud.* —*v.i.* to release, detach, or free oneself: *The two wrestlers disengaged.* —**dis′en·gage′ment**, *n.*

dis·en·tan·gle (dis′en tang′gəl) *v.*, **dis·en·tan·gled, dis·en·tan·gling.** —*v.t.* to free from tangles or confusion: *The boy disentangled the kite string. The detective tried to disentangle the witness' story.* —*v.i.* to become free from tangles or confusion. —**dis′en·tan′gle·ment**, *n.*

dis·es·teem (dis′is tēm′) *v.t.* to have a low opinion of. —*n.* lack of esteem; disfavor: *That theory is held in disesteem by most scientists.*

dis·fa·vor (dis fā′vər) *n.* **1.** displeasure or lack of favor; dislike; disapproval: *The students looked with disfavor on the plan to shorten the spring vacation.* **2.** the state of being

regarded unfavorably: *The boy fell into disfavor with his team because of his lack of sportsmanship.* **3.** an unkind, unfair, or damaging act: *He did his friend a disfavor by not sticking up for him.* —*v.t.* to dislike; disapprove.

dis·fig·ure (dis fig′yər) *v.t.*, **dis·fig·ured, dis·fig·ur·ing.** to spoil or destroy the beauty or appearance of: *Scars from the accident disfigured his face. Billboards disfigured the landscape along the highway.* —**dis·fig′ure·ment**, *n.*

dis·fran·chise (dis fran′chīz) *v.t.*, **dis·fran·chised, dis·fran·chis·ing.** another word for **disenfranchise.** —**dis·fran′chise·ment**, *n.*

dis·gorge (dis gôrj′) *v.t.*, **dis·gorged, dis·gorg·ing.** **1.** to throw up (something swallowed); vomit. **2.** to throw or pour (something) forth, especially with force: *The volcano disgorged lava and smoke. The crowded bus disgorged its passengers at the station.*

dis·grace (dis grās′) *n.* **1.** loss of honor, respect, or favor; shame: *His arrest brought disgrace upon the entire family.* **2.** the state of being dishonored or out of favor: *The president of the company resigned in disgrace when the fraud was discovered.* **3.** a person or thing that brings about shame, dishonor, or reproach: *These slum conditions are a disgrace to the city.* —*v.t.*, **dis·graced, dis·grac·ing.** **1.** to bring shame, dishonor, or reproach to or upon: *to disgrace one's family.* **2.** to dismiss from favor or grace; treat with disfavor: *The king disgraced his disloyal adviser in front of the entire court.*

dis·grace·ful (dis grās′fəl) *adj.* characterized by, deserving, or causing disgrace; shameful: *disgraceful behavior.* —**dis·grace′ful·ly**, *adv.* —**dis·grace′ful·ness**, *n.*

dis·grun·tle (dis grunt′əl) *v.t.*, **dis·grun·tled, dis·grun·tling.** to put in a bad humor; make dissatisfied, displeased, or cross: *He was disgruntled because he had to wash the floor.* —**dis·grun′tle·ment**, *n.*

dis·guise (dis gīz′) *v.t.*, **dis·guised, dis·guis·ing.** **1.** to change the appearance or dress to hide the identity of: *The children disguised themselves as ghosts on Halloween.* **2.** to hide; conceal: *Mother disguised the taste of the cough medicine by mixing it with orange juice. She disguised her sadness with a happy smile.* —*n.* **1.** something that disguises: *A mustache was part of the thief's disguise.* **2.** the act of disguising: *The spy was a master of disguise.* **3.** the state of being disguised: *a blessing in disguise.*

dis·gust (dis gust′) *n.* a sickening feeling of strong dislike or distaste: *It filled her with disgust when she heard the rumors.* —*v.t.* to cause strong distaste or loathing in; sicken: *His selfishness disgusts everyone who has to work with him.*

dis·gust·ed (dis gus′tid) *adj.* filled with or showing disgust: *a disgusted look, a disgusted person.* —**dis·gust′ed·ly**, *adv.*

dis·gust·ing (dis gus′ting) *adj.* causing disgust; offensive. —**dis·gust′ing·ly**, *adv.*

dish (dish) *n. pl.*, **dish·es.** **1.** a plate, shallow bowl, or other container used for holding or serving food. **2.** a single serving of food on or in a dish; dishful: *to have a dish of ice cream for dessert.* **3.** food prepared in a particular way: *Spaghetti is his favorite dish.* **4.** a radio, radar, or television antenna with a reflector shaped like a bowl. —*v.t.* to put or serve in a dish (usually with *up* or *out*): *The cook dished up dinner as soon as everyone sat down.*

dish·cloth (dish′klôth′) *n.* a cloth for washing dishes. Also, **dishrag.**

dis·heart·en (dis härt′ən) *v.t.* to cause to lose hope or courage; discourage; depress: *Losing the game disheartened the team.* —**dis·heart′en·ing·ly**, *adv.*

di·shev·eled (di shev′əld) *also,* **di·shev·elled.** *adj.* not neat or in order; rumpled; tousled; untidy: *disheveled hair, a disheveled appearance.*

dish·ful (dish′fool′) *n. pl.,* **dish·fuls.** the amount that a dish holds.

dis·hon·est (dis on′ist) *adj.* **1.** given to lying, stealing, or cheating; not honest: *He is a dishonest man.* **2.** characterized by or showing a lack of honesty: *The salesman used dishonest methods to sell his product.* —**dis·hon′est·ly,** *adv.*

dis·hon·es·ty (dis on′is tē) *n. pl.,* **dis·hon·es·ties. 1.** lack of honesty. **2.** a dishonest act or statement.

dis·hon·or (dis on′ər) *n.* **1.** lack or loss of honor or reputation; shame; disgrace: *to prefer death to dishonor.* **2.** a person or thing that causes shame or disgrace: *It is no dishonor to admit you are wrong if you make a mistake.* —*v.t.* to bring shame or disgrace to: *The traitor dishonored his regiment.*

dis·hon·or·a·ble (dis on′ər ə bəl) *adj.* **1.** characterized by or causing dishonor; shameful; disgraceful: *dishonorable conduct.* **2.** lacking honor; without honor: *a dishonorable man, a dishonorable discharge from the army.* —**dis·hon′or·a·ble·ness,** *n.* —**dis·hon′or·a·bly,** *adv.*

dish·rag (dish′rag′) *n.* another word for **dishcloth.**

dish·tow·el (dish′tou′əl) *n.* a towel for drying dishes.

dish·wash·er (dish′wô′shər, dish′wosh′ər) *n.* **1.** a machine for washing dishes and cooking utensils. **2.** a person who washes dishes and cooking utensils, especially in a restaurant.

dis·il·lu·sion (dis′i loo′zhən) *v.t.* to free from an illusion or false idea, especially a false idea about the truth or goodness of someone or something: *The scandals in the mayor's administration disillusioned many of his admirers.* —*n.* freedom from illusion; disillusionment.

dis·il·lu·sion·ment (dis′i loo′zhən mənt) *n.* the act of disillusioning or the state of being disillusioned.

dis·in·cli·na·tion (dis in′klə nā′shən) *n.* a slight distaste or unwillingness: *The lazy boy had a disinclination to do hard work.*

dis·in·cline (dis′in klīn′) *v.t.,* **dis·in·clined, dis·in·clin·ing.** to make unwilling: *He was disinclined to accept the job because of the low salary.*

dis·in·fect (dis′in fekt′) *v.t.* to destroy disease-causing microorganisms in: *to disinfect a hospital room.* —**dis′in·fec′tion,** *n.*

dis·in·fect·ant (dis′in fek′tənt) *n.* a substance used to destroy disease-causing microorganisms. —*adj.* serving to disinfect: *a disinfectant soap.*

dis·in·her·it (dis′in her′it) *v.t.* to deprive (an heir) of an inheritance or of the right to inherit: *His father threatened to disinherit him if he married at such a young age.* —**dis′in·her′it·ance,** *n.*

dis·in·te·grate (dis in′tə grāt′) *v.,* **dis·in·te·grat·ed, dis·in·te·grat·ing.** —*v.i.* **1.** to break up into particles, fragments, or parts: *This type of rock disintegrates under pressure.* **2.** to fall apart or be destroyed by breaking into parts: *The empire disintegrated under his rule.* **3.** *Physics.* to undergo a nuclear change as a result of radioactive decay. —*v.t.* to cause to disintegrate: *The floodwaters disintegrated the foundations of the house.* —**dis·in′te·gra′tion,** *n.*

dis·in·ter (dis′in tur′) *v.t.,* **dis·in·terred, dis·in·ter·ring. 1.** to remove from a grave or tomb; dig up: *to disinter a body.* **2.** to bring to light; reveal: *The reporter disinterred unknown facts about the author's early life.* —**dis′in·ter′ment,** *n.*

dis·in·ter·est·ed (dis in′tris tid, dis in′tər is tid, dis in′tə res′tid) *adj.* not having a personal interest in a matter; not influenced by selfish motives; impartial: *A judge should take a disinterested view of the cases that come before him.* ▲ See **uninterested** for usage note. —**dis·in′ter·est·ed·ly,** *adv.* —**dis·in′ter·est·ed·ness,** *n.*

dis·joint (dis joint′) *v.t.* **1.** to take apart or separate at the joints: *to disjoint a turkey.* **2.** to put out of joint; dislocate: *He fell and disjointed his shoulder during football practice.* **3.** to disturb or destroy the order, connection, or unity of: *Racial or religious conflict disjoints a society.* —*adj. Mathematics.* (of sets) having no members in common. The sets [A, B, C], [1, 2, 3], and [½, ¼, ⅛] are disjoint.

dis·joint·ed (dis join′tid) *adj.* **1.** lacking order, connection, or unity; disconnected; incoherent: *The dazed man could give only a disjointed description of the accident.* **2.** taken apart or separated at the joints: *a disjointed chicken.* —**dis·joint′ed·ly,** *adv.* —**dis·joint′ed·ness,** *n.*

disk (disk) *also,* **disc.** *n.* **1.** a flat, thin, circular object, such as a coin, plate, or phonograph record. **2.** something that resembles a disk in appearance, such as the round, flat shape that a heavenly body seems to have when viewed from the earth: *the disk of the sun.* **3.** a flat, circular part of a plant or animal, such as the center of a daisy and certain other flowers, or the rings of elastic tissue between the bones of the spinal column. —**disk′like′,** *adj.*

Disk of a sunflower

disk harrow, a farm tool that is used to break up and cultivate the soil, consisting of a series of sharp disks that are set on a rotating shaft.

disk jockey, another spelling of **disc jockey.**

dis·like (dis līk′) *n.* a feeling of not liking or being opposed to something; attitude of disapproval or displeasure; distaste: *She has a strong dislike for cold weather.* —*v.t.,* **dis·liked, dis·lik·ing.** to have a feeling against; consider disagreeable; not like: *She dislikes doing housework.*

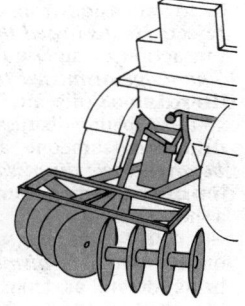
Disk harrow

dis·lo·cate (dis′lō kāt′) *v.t.,* **dis·lo·cat·ed, dis·lo·cat·ing. 1.** to upset the order of; throw into confusion; disrupt: *The nation's economy was dislocated by war.* **2.** to put out of proper place or order; displace: *to dislocate a book on a library shelf.* **3.** to put (a bone) out of joint: *The man dislocated his hip when he slipped and fell on the ice.* —**dis′lo·ca′tion,** *n.*

dis·lodge (dis loj′) *v.t.,* **dis·lodged, dis·lodg·ing.** to move or force out of a place or position: *The avalanche dislodged large rocks from the cliff. The hounds managed to dislodge the fox from its hiding place.*

dis·loy·al (dis loi′əl) *adj.* not loyal; unfaithful: *It was disloyal of them to hope that their own team would lose the game.* —**dis·loy′al·ly,** *adv.*

dis·loy·al·ty (dis loi′əl tē) *n. pl.,* **dis·loy·al·ties. 1.** lack of loyalty; unfaithfulness: *He was greatly saddened by the disloyalty of his friends during his time of need.* **2.** a disloyal act.

dis·mal (diz′məl) *adj.* **1.** causing gloom or depression;

at; āpe; cär; end; mē; it; īce; hot; ōld; fôrk; wood; fool; oil; out; up; turn; sing; thin; this; hw in white; zh in treasure. The symbol ə stands for the sound of **a** in about, **e** in taken, **i** in pencil, **o** in lemon, and **u** in circus.

277

dreary; miserable: *It was a damp and dismal winter day. The forest was a dismal sight after the fire.* **2.** feeling gloom; depressed: *She was dismal because she had failed the test.* **3.** very bad; dreadful; terrible: *The project was a dismal failure.* [Anglo-Norman *dis mal* evil days; originally referring to certain days being marked as unlucky on calendars of the Middle Ages.] —**dis′mal·ly,** *adv.* —**dis′mal·ness,** *n.*

dis·man·tle (dis mant′əl) *v.t.,* **dis·man·tled, dis·man·tling. 1.** to pull down or take apart; disassemble: *to dismantle a machine.* **2.** to strip of covering, furniture, or equipment: *to dismantle a ship.* —**dis·man′tle·ment,** *n.*

dis·may (dis mā′) *v.t.* **1.** to fill with fear or alarm; take away the courage of; make afraid: *The sight of the enemy forces dismayed the soldier.* **2.** to trouble or discourage greatly; depress; dishearten: *The audience's lack of interest dismayed the speaker.* —*n.* a feeling of alarm or uneasiness; frightened amazement: *He was filled with dismay when he heard the bad news.*

dis·mem·ber (dis mem′bər) *v.t.* **1.** to cut or tear off the limbs of; tear limb from limb: *The lion dismembered the dead antelope.* **2.** to divide into parts or sections: *The conquering nations dismembered the defeated country.* —**dis·mem′ber·ment,** *n.*

dis·miss (dis mis′) *v.t.* **1.** to send away or allow to leave: *The teacher dismissed the class.* **2.** to discharge, as from a position or job; fire: *to dismiss an employee for stealing.* **3.** to put aside from attention or serious consideration; reject: *He dismissed the story as a mere rumor.* **4.** to send (an action or suit) out of court without further hearing: *The judge dismissed the case because of lack of evidence.*

dis·miss·al (dis mis′əl) *n.* **1.** the act of dismissing or the state of being dismissed. **2.** a written or spoken order dismissing someone, as from a job: *Those employees will be given their dismissal at the end of the week.*

dis·mount (dis mount′) *v.i.* to get off or down, as from a horse; alight: *The rider dismounted from his bicycle.* —*v.t.* **1.** to remove (something) from its setting, support, or mounting: *to dismount a cannon.* **2.** to knock off or bring down, as from a horse; unseat: *The knight dismounted his enemy.* **3.** to take apart; disassemble; dismantle: *to dismount a machine.*

Dis·ney, Walt(er) (diz′nē) 1901–1966, U.S. motion-picture producer.

dis·o·be·di·ence (dis′ə bē′dē əns) *n.* a refusal or failure to obey an order or rule: *The child was punished for disobedience.*

dis·o·be·di·ent (dis′ə bē′dē ənt) *adj.* refusing or failing to obey; not obedient: *The disobedient boy ignored the teacher's request to be quiet.* —**dis′o·be′di·ent·ly,** *adv.*

dis·o·bey (dis′ə bā′) *v.t.* to refuse or fail to obey (someone or something): *The soldier disobeyed the lieutenant's orders.* —*v.i.* to refuse to obey: *That child always disobeys.*

dis·o·blige (dis′ə blīj′) *v.t.,* **dis·o·bliged, dis·o·blig·ing.** to act contrary to the wishes of; refuse to oblige: *I don't like to disoblige you, but I won't be able to attend your party.*

dis·or·der (dis ôr′dər) *n.* **1.** lack of order or regular arrangement; confusion: *The room was in disorder after the police searched it for the missing jewels.* **2.** a breach of peace or public order, such as a riot; public disturbance: *The police tried to quiet the disorders in the streets.* **3.** a physical or mental sickness; ailment: *a disorder of the stomach, a nervous disorder.* —*v.t.* **1.** to disturb the order or regular arrangement of; throw into confusion: *Noisy demonstrations disordered the political convention.* **2.** to make physically or mentally sick.

dis·or·der·ly (dis ôr′dər lē) *adj.* **1.** lacking order or regular arrangement; messy; untidy: *The papers lay in a disorderly pile.* **2.** causing a public disturbance; uncon-

trolled; unruly: *a disorderly crowd.* **3.** guilty of disorderly conduct: *He was arrested for being drunk and disorderly.* —**dis·or′der·li·ness,** *n.*

disorderly conduct, any behavior that is considered to be a minor violation of public peace, order, or decency.

dis·or·gan·ize (dis ôr′gə nīz′) *v.t.,* **dis·or·gan·ized, dis·or·gan·iz·ing.** to upset or destroy the organization, arrangement, or order of; throw into confusion and disorder: *Heavy shelling by the enemy disorganized the army's retreat.* —**dis·or′gan·i·za′tion,** *n.*

dis·or·gan·ized (dis ôr′gə nīzd′) *adj.* lacking organization, arrangement, or order: *a disorganized project, a novel with a badly disorganized plot.*

dis·or·i·ent (dis ôr′ē ent′) *v.t.* to disturb the sense of direction or position of; cause to lose one's bearings; mix up; confuse: *He was disoriented after wandering through the narrow, winding streets of the old city.* —**dis·o′ri·en·ta′tion,** *n.*

dis·own (dis ōn′) *v.t.* to refuse to recognize as one's own; deny responsibility for or connection with; reject: *The man disowned his son and left his fortune to his nephew.*

dis·par·age (dis par′ij) *v.t.,* **dis·par·aged, dis·par·ag·ing. 1.** to speak critically or slightingly of; belittle: *The candidate for mayor disparaged his opponent's record in office.* **2.** to bring discredit upon; lower in reputation. —**dis·par′age·ment,** *n.*

dis·par·ag·ing (dis par′ij ing) *adj.* that disparages; belittling; slighting: *He made disparaging remarks about her singing ability.* —**dis·par′ag·ing·ly,** *adv.*

dis·par·ate (dis par′it, dis′pər it) *adj.* different in kind; unlike; dissimilar: *The two political parties have disparate points of view on that issue.* —**dis·par′ate·ly,** *adv.*

dis·par·i·ty (dis par′ə tē) *n. pl.,* **dis·par·i·ties.** lack of agreement or similarity; inequality or difference: *There is a great disparity between the report and what happened.*

dis·pas·sion·ate (dis pash′ə nit) *adj.* free from prejudice or strong feeling; unbiased; impartial: *an honest, dispassionate judge.* —**dis·pas′sion·ate·ly,** *adv.* —**dis·pas′sion·ate·ness,** *n.*

dis·patch (dis pach′) *also,* **des·patch.** *v.t.* **1.** to send off quickly to a certain place or for a certain purpose: *to dispatch a telegram, to dispatch an official messenger.* **2.** to finish or dispose of quickly or promptly: *to dispatch a business deal.* **3.** to put to death; kill. —*n., pl.* **dis·patch·es. 1.** the act of dispatching: *the dispatch of a messenger.* **2.** prompt or quick action; quickness; speed: *The urgency of the situation called for great dispatch.* **3.** a written message sent off quickly or promptly, especially an official government or military communication. **4.** a news story or report, as by a special reporter or from a news service: *The newspaper received a dispatch from its correspondent in London.*

dis·patch·er (dis pach′ər) *also,* **des·patch·er.** *n.* **1.** a person who dispatches. **2.** a person who schedules and directs the arrivals and departures of trains, buses, taxicabs, and other means of transportation.

dis·pel (dis pel′) *v.t.,* **dis·pelled, dis·pel·ling.** to drive away or cause to disappear; scatter; disperse: *The wind dispelled the smoke. His reassuring words dispelled her doubts.*

dis·pen·sa·ble (dis pen′sə bəl) *adj.* that can be done without; not essential; unimportant: *Because his suitcase was too heavy, he removed all the dispensable items.* —**dis·pen′sa·bil′i·ty,** *n.*

dis·pen·sa·ry (dis pen′sər ē) *n. pl.,* **dis·pen·sa·ries. 1.** a room in which medicines and medical supplies are given out or dispensed: *a hospital dispensary.* **2.** a place where medicines and medical treatment are given without charge or for a small fee.

dis·pen·sa·tion (dis′pən sā′shən) *n.* **1.** the act of dispensing; giving out; distribution: *The dispensation of supplies in the disaster area was delayed.* **2.** something that is dispensed or distributed: *His widow received a financial dispensation from the government.* **3.** a system of administration; management; rule: *the dispensation of justice.* **4.** official permission to disregard a law, especially a church law: *a papal dispensation.*

dis·pense (dis pens′) *v.t.,* **dis·pensed, dis·pens·ing. 1.** to give or deal out in portions; distribute: *Various charities dispense clothing to the needy. This machine dispenses gum.* **2.** to prepare and give out (medicine), especially by prescription. **3.** to carry out or apply; administer: *to dispense justice.*

to dispense with. a. to get along without: *He can dispense with a coat now that the weather is warm.* **b.** to do away with; make unnecessary: *The committee dispensed with formalities and started the discussion right away.*

dis·pens·er (dis pen′sər) *n.* **1.** a person or thing that dispenses. **2.** a container or mechanical device that dispenses something in convenient units or portions: *a chewing gum dispenser.*

dis·per·sal (dis pur′səl) *n.* the act of dispersing or the state of being dispersed; breaking up; scattering.

dis·perse (dis purs′) *v.,* **dis·persed, dis·pers·ing.** —*v.t.* **1.** to break up and send off in different directions; scatter: *The police dispersed the crowd.* **2.** to drive away or cause to vanish; dispel: *The winds dispersed the smoke.* **3.** *Physics.* to separate (radiation) into its component parts according to frequency or wavelength. A beam of white light can be dispersed into the spectrum by being passed through a prism. —*v.i.* to break up and go in different directions; scatter; dissipate: *The congregation dispersed when the service ended.*

dis·per·sion (dis pur′zhən) *n.* **1.** the act of dispersing or the state of being dispersed. **2.** *Physics.* the separation of radiation into its component parts according to frequency or wavelength.

dis·pir·it (dis pir′it) *v.t.* to depress or lower the spirits of; discourage: *The failure of his experiments greatly dispirited the scientist.*

dis·pir·it·ed (dis pir′ə tid) *adj.* depressed; dejected; discouraged: *The dispirited candidate conceded that his opponent had won the election.* —**dis·pir′it·ed·ly,** *adv.* —**dis·pir′it·ed·ness,** *n.*

dis·place (dis plās′) *v.t.,* **dis·placed, dis·plac·ing. 1.** to take the place of; replace: *Television has displaced motion pictures as America's most popular form of entertainment.* **2.** to move or shift from the usual or proper place or position. **3.** to remove from a position or office: *to displace an officer of the government.* **4.** *Physics.* to take or occupy the space of (a certain weight or volume of fluid): *A floating object displaces an amount of water equal to its own weight.*

displaced person, a homeless person driven or taken from his own country or region, usually as a result of war.

dis·place·ment (dis plās′mənt) *n.* **1.** the act of displacing or the state of being displaced. **2.** the distance that something has moved from its original place or position. **3.** *Physics.* the weight or volume of fluid displaced by a body floating or immersed in it. The weight of the fluid displaced by a floating body equals the weight of the body itself.

dis·play (dis plā′) *v.t.* **1.** to expose to view; cause to be seen; exhibit; show: *to display a poster, to display a flag.* **2.** to make obvious; reveal: *to display fear, to display one's ignorance.* **3.** to make a show of; show off; flaunt: *The woman proudly displayed her furs.* —*n.* **1.** the act of displaying: *a display of anger.* **2.** an exhibition or show: *The*

museum had a display of early American furniture. **3.** something that is displayed or exhibited: *The display of flowers at the show was beautifully arranged.* **4.** a showing off: *The man's neighbors were offended by his display of wealth.*

dis·please (dis plēz′) *v.,* **dis·pleased, dis·pleas·ing.** —*v.t.* to fail to please; cause annoyance to; offend; irritate: *His rude conduct displeased his family.* —*v.i.* to cause displeasure or annoyance.

dis·pleas·ure (dis plezh′ər) *n.* the state or feeling of being displeased; annoyance; disapproval: *Her frown showed her displeasure with his behavior.*

dis·port (dis pôrt′) *v.t.* to amuse or divert (oneself): *The puppies disported themselves in the yard.* —*v.i.* to play; frolic.

dis·pos·a·ble (dis pō′zə bəl) *adj.* **1.** made to be thrown away after being used: *disposable paper napkins, disposable diapers.* **2.** free to be used; at hand; available: *disposable income.*

dis·pos·al (dis pō′zəl) *n.* **1.** the act of getting rid of something; throwing away: *the disposal of garbage.* **2.** the act of dealing with or settling something: *the disposal of certain business matters.* **3.** a transferring of something to another, as by gift or sale: *the disposal of money in a will, the disposal of merchandise.*

at one's disposal. available for use as one pleases: *His father's car will be at his disposal this week.*

dis·pose (dis pōz′) *v.,* **dis·posed, dis·pos·ing.** —*v.t.* **1.** to make inclined or willing: *His prejudice disposed him to decide the contest in their favor.* **2.** to make susceptible or subject: *His frailness disposed him to frequent illness.* **3.** to place in a particular order or position; arrange: *The farmer disposed the plants in rows.* —*v.i.* to determine or control the course of events; ordain: *Man proposes, God disposes* (Thomas à Kempis).

to dispose of. a. to get rid of; throw away: *to dispose of garbage.* **b.** to attend to or finish with; settle: *He quickly disposed of his work.* **c.** to part with, as by gift or sale; transfer to another: *The widow disposed of her husband's property.* **d.** to consume (food or drink).

dis·posed (dis pōzd′) *adj.* having a tendency; willing or inclined: *That lazy boy is not disposed to work hard.*

dis·po·si·tion (dis′pə zish′ən) *n.* **1.** a person's general or usual way of acting, thinking, or feeling; temperament; nature: *an irritable disposition, a pleasant disposition.* **2.** a tendency or inclination: *He has a disposition to accept the ideas of others too readily.* **3.** a placing or being placed in a particular order; arrangement: *the orderly disposition of trees in an orchard.* **4.** management or settlement: *the disposition of business affairs.* **5.** a transferring of something to another, as by gift or sale: *the disposition of property after a death.*

dis·pos·sess (dis′pə zes′) *v.t.* to put out of possession of something, especially by legal action: *The landlord dispossessed the tenants for not paying their rent.* —**dis′pos·ses′sion,** *n.*

dis·proof (dis proof′) *n.* **1.** the act of disproving; refutation: *There has been no disproof of his evidence as yet.* **2.** something that disproves.

dis·pro·por·tion (dis′prə pôr′shən) *n.* lack of proper

at; āpe; cär; end; mē; it; īce; hot; ōld; fôrk; wood; fōol; oil; out; up; turn; sing; thin; this; hw in white; zh in treasure. The symbol ə stands for the sound of a in about, e in taken, i in pencil, o in lemon, and u in circus.

proportion or symmetry; disparity: *There is a disproportion between the price of that house and its actual value.*

dis·pro·por·tion·ate (dis′prə pôr′shə nit) *adj.* out of proportion in size, amount, or degree; lacking proportion: *The two arms of the statue are disproportionate to the body. Her salary is disproportionate to the amount of work she does.* —**dis′pro·por′tion·ate·ly,** *adv.* —**dis′pro·por′tion·ate·ness,** *n.*

dis·prove (dis proov′) *v.t.,* **dis·proved, dis·prov·ing.** to prove to be false or incorrect; refute: *The photograph disproved the witness's claim that he had never met the defendant.*

dis·put·a·ble (dis pyoo′tə bəl, dis′pyə tə bəl) *adj.* that can be disputed or called into question; debatable: *Whether or not he is really guilty is disputable.*

dis·pu·tant (dis pyoo′tənt) *n.* a person who takes part in a dispute, debate, or argument.

dis·pu·ta·tion (dis′pyoo tā′shən) *n.* 1. the act of disputing. 2. a debate or argument.

dis·pute (dis pyoot′) *v.,* **dis·put·ed, dis·put·ing.** —*v.t.* 1. to debate or quarrel about; discuss; argue: *The issue was disputed at the council meeting.* 2. to deny or question the validity, accuracy, or existence of; express doubt or opposition to: *to dispute someone's authority, to dispute a statement.* 3. to fight or compete for the possession of; strive or contend for: *The two countries disputed the territory located at their common border.* —*v.i.* to take part in argument, discussion, or debate: *The politicians disputed with each other on various issues.* —*n.* 1. a difference of opinion; argument or debate: *A judge had to settle the dispute over the ownership of the house.* 2. a quarrel: *a bitter dispute between two neighbors.*

dis·qual·i·fi·ca·tion (dis kwol′ə fi kā′shən) *n.* 1. the act of disqualifying or the state of being disqualified. 2. something that disqualifies: *Deafness is a disqualification from military service.*

dis·qual·i·fy (dis kwol′ə fī′) *v.t.,* **dis·qual·i·fied, dis·qual·i·fy·ing.** 1. to make or declare unfit, unqualified, or unsuitable: *Poor eyesight disqualified him from military service. Her age disqualifies her from voting.* 2. to bar from competition or from winning a prize or contest: *The officials disqualified him from the race for knocking down another runner.*

dis·qui·et (dis kwī′it) *v.t.* to make uneasy, anxious, or restless; disturb; alarm: *The bad news disquieted him.* —*n.* lack of calm or peacefulness; uneasiness; unrest: *There was a feeling of disquiet among the ship's passengers as the storm approached.*

dis·qui·e·tude (dis kwī′i tood′, dis kwī′i tyood′) *n.* a state of uneasiness or unrest; anxiety; disquiet.

dis·qui·si·tion (dis kwə zish′ən) *n.* a formal discussion or essay; dissertation.

Dis·rae·li, Benjamin (diz rā′lē) 1804–1881, English statesman.

dis·re·gard (dis′ri gärd′) *v.t.* to pay no attention to; treat without regard or respect; ignore: *She disregarded the gossip and rumors. He disregarded everyone else's feelings in the matter.* —*n.* lack of attention or regard; neglect: *His actions show a disregard for the school's regulations.*

dis·re·pair (dis′ri per′) *n.* the state of being in need of repairs; poor, run-down condition: *The old house had fallen into disrepair.*

dis·rep·u·ta·ble (dis rep′yə tə bəl) *adj.* 1. not having a good reputation; not reputable, respectable, or decent: *a disreputable company, a disreputable businessman.* 2. not respectable in appearance; shabby: *a disreputable old jacket.* —**dis·rep′u·ta·ble·ness,** *n.* —**dis·rep′u·ta·bly,** *adv.*

dis·re·pute (dis′ri pyoot′) *n.* lack or loss of reputation

or regard; ill repute; discredit; disfavor: *That scientific theory is now in disrepute.*

dis·re·spect (dis′ri spekt′) *n.* lack of respect, reverence, or courtesy: *The boy's rude and selfish actions showed his disrespect for the rights of others.*

dis·re·spect·ful (dis′ri spekt′fəl) *adj.* having or showing disrespect; rude; impolite: *It was disrespectful of him to make such critical remarks about his parents.* —**dis′re·spect′ful·ly,** *adv.* —**dis′re·spect′ful·ness,** *n.*

dis·robe (dis rōb′) *v.,* **dis·robed, dis·rob·ing.** —*v.t.* to undress (someone): *The mother disrobed her baby.* —*v.i.* to undress.

dis·rupt (dis rupt′) *v.t.* to throw into disorder or confusion; break up or apart; upset: *His behavior disrupted the class.* —**dis·rupt′er,** *n.*

dis·rup·tion (dis rup′shən) *n.* 1. the act of disrupting or the state of being disrupted. 2. a break; interruption.

dis·rup·tive (dis rup′tiv) *adj.* causing disruption: *a disruptive influence.* —**dis·rup′tive·ly,** *adv.* —**dis·rup′tive·ness,** *n.*

dis·sat·is·fac·tion (dis′sat is fak′shən) *n.* a condition or feeling of being dissatisfied; discontent: *The people expressed their dissatisfaction with the policies of the government by participating in nationwide demonstrations.*

dis·sat·is·fac·to·ry (dis′sat is fak′tər ē) *adj.* another word for **unsatisfactory.**

dis·sat·is·fied (dis sat′is fīd′) *adj.* 1. not satisfied; displeased: *The dissatisfied workers struck for higher wages.* 2. showing discontent or displeasure: *a dissatisfied look.*

dis·sat·is·fy (dis sat′is fī′) *v.t.,* **dis·sat·is·fied, dis·sat·is·fy·ing.** to fail to satisfy; cause discontent to; disappoint; displease: *The actor's poor performance dissatisfied the film's director.*

dis·sect (di sekt′, dī sekt′) *v.t.* 1. to cut apart or divide into parts for the purpose of study or scientific examination: *The biology student dissected a frog.* 2. to examine carefully and critically; analyze in great detail: *The teacher dissected the poem and explained it to the class.*

dis·sec·tion (di sek′shən, dī sek′shən) *n.* 1. the act of dissecting: *the dissection of an earthworm to study its parts.* 2. something that has been dissected, as an animal being studied. 3. a detailed analysis or criticism.

dis·sem·ble (di sem′bəl) *v.,* **dis·sem·bled, dis·sem·bling.** —*v.t.* 1. to disguise or conceal the true nature of (one's character, feelings, or intentions): *He dissembled his excitement by acting bored.* 2. to put on a false appearance of; pretend; feign: *The corrupt man dissembled honesty.* —*v.i.* to disguise or conceal one's true character, feelings, or intentions by false pretense. —**dis·sem′bler,** *n.*

dis·sem·i·nate (di sem′ə nāt′) *v.t.,* **dis·sem·i·nat·ed, dis·sem·i·nat·ing.** to scatter widely; spread abroad; diffuse: *to disseminate information, to disseminate news.* —**dis·sem′i·na′tion,** *n.*

dis·sen·sion (di sen′shən) *n.* a strong difference of opinion or feeling; disagreement; conflict: *There was dissension among the king's advisors.*

dis·sent (di sent′) *v.i.* 1. to differ in opinion or feeling; withhold approval; disagree: *Many people dissented from the policy of the government.* 2. to refuse to conform to the rules, doctrines, or beliefs of an established church. —*n.* 1. strong difference of opinion or feeling; disagreement: *A dictatorship does not permit dissent in political matters.* 2. refusal to conform to the rules, doctrines, or beliefs of an established church.

dis·sent·er (di sen′tər) *n.* 1. a person who dissents. 2. *also,* **Dissenter.** a person who refuses to conform to the rules, doctrines, or beliefs of an established church, especially the Church of England.

dis·ser·ta·tion (dis′ər tā′shən) *n.* a long, formal essay or discussion on a particular subject, especially one written to obtain the degree of doctor from a university.

dis·serv·ice (dis sur′vis) *n.* harm; injury: *The politician did his party a great disservice by his dishonest actions.*

dis·sev·er (di sev′ər) *v.t.* to cut or divide into parts; sever; separate.

dis·si·dence (dis′ə dəns) *n.* dissent; disagreement.

dis·si·dent (dis′ə dənt) *adj.* not agreeing; dissenting: *dissident views on an issue.* —*n.* a person who disagrees; dissenter.

dis·sim·i·lar (di sim′ə lər) *adj.* not similar or alike; different: *A deer and a bear are dissimilar animals. He and his sister have dissimilar interests.* —**dis·sim′i·lar·ly,** *adv.*

dis·sim·i·lar·i·ty (di sim′ə lar′ə tē) *n. pl.,* **dis·sim·i·lar·i·ties.** lack of similarity; difference: *There is great dissimilarity between the clothes of today and those worn in colonial times.*

dis·sim·u·late (di sim′yə lāt′) *v.t., v.i.,* **dis·sim·u·lat·ed, dis·sim·u·lat·ing.** to disguise or conceal (feelings or intentions) by pretense; dissemble. —**dis·sim′u·la′tion,** *n.*

dis·si·pate (dis′ə pāt′) *v.,* **dis·si·pat·ed, dis·si·pat·ing.** —*v.t.* **1.** to disperse or drive away; scatter; dispel: *The winds dissipated the haze.* **2.** to spend wastefully or foolishly; squander: *In three years he dissipated the family fortune.* —*v.i.* **1.** to become dispersed or scattered; be dispelled: *By noon the mist had dissipated.* **2.** to indulge in foolish or extravagant pleasures, especially so as to harm oneself.

dis·si·pat·ed (dis′ə pā′tid) *adj.* given to indulging in harmful or foolish pleasures; intemperate.

dis·si·pa·tion (dis′ə pā′shən) *n.* **1.** the act of scattering or dispersing. **2.** indulgence in harmful or foolish pleasures.

dis·so·ci·ate (di sō′shē āt′, di sō′sē āt′) *v.t.,* **dis·so·ci·at·ed, dis·so·ci·at·ing.** to break the association or connection of; separate: *He dissociated himself from the club.*

dis·so·ci·a·tion (di sō′shē ā′shən, di sō′sē ā′shən) *n.* the act of dissociating or the state of being dissociated.

dis·sol·u·ble (di sol′yə bəl) *adj.* that can be dissolved.

dis·so·lute (dis′ə lōōt′) *adj.* evil in conduct; immoral; corrupt: *a dissolute young man, a dissolute life.* —**dis′so·lute′ly,** *adv.* —**dis′so·lute′ness,** *n.*

dis·so·lu·tion (dis′ə lōō′shən) *n.* **1.** a breaking up; ending: *the dissolution of a business.* **2.** the act or process of changing from a solid or liquid to a gas. **3.** separation into parts; disintegration.

dis·solve (di zolv′) *v.,* **dis·solved, dis·solv·ing.** —*v.t.* **1.** to cause (a substance) to change from a solid or gas into a liquid; cause to pass into solution with a liquid: *He dissolved the sugar in water.* **2.** to separate into parts; disintegrate. **3.** to put an end to; terminate: *to dissolve a partnership.* —*v.i.* **1.** to pass into solution; become liquid: *Salt dissolves in water.* **2.** to dwindle or disappear gradually; fade away: *His prospects for winning the election were dissolving rapidly.* **3.** to break up; disperse: *The fog dissolved.* **4.** in motion pictures and television, to change scenes by having one image gradually fade out of view as the next image gradually appears. —**dis·solv′a·ble,** *adj.*

dis·so·nance (dis′ə nəns) *n.* **1.** a harsh or unpleasant sound or combination of sounds; discord. **2.** lack of harmony or agreement; disagreement.

dis·so·nant (dis′ə nənt) *adj.* **1.** harsh or unpleasant in sound; not harmonious. **2.** lacking harmony or agreement; at variance; disagreeing: *dissonant views on a subject.* —**dis′so·nant·ly,** *adv.*

dis·suade (di swād′) *v.t.,* **dis·suad·ed, dis·suad·ing.** to keep (someone) from doing something by persuasion or advice: *He dissuaded her from resigning her job.*

dis·sua·sion (di swā′zhən) *n.* the act of dissuading.

dis·sua·sive (di swā′siv) *adj.* tending or meant to dissuade. —**dis·sua′sive·ly,** *adv.* —**dis·sua′sive·ness,** *n.*

dist. **1.** distance. **2.** district.

dis·taff (dis′taf) *n.* a stick on which wool, flax, cotton, or other fibers are held for use in spinning, either by hand or with a spinning wheel.

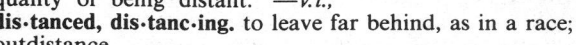
Distaff

Spindle

distaff side, the mother's side of a family.

dis·tance (dis′təns) *n.* **1.** the amount of space between two things, objects, or points: *The distance from Jane's house to the school is two blocks. Astronomers can measure the distance of the moon from the earth.* **2.** a far-off point or place; distant region or position: *The driver saw another car in the distance.* **3.** the fact or quality of being distant. —*v.t.;* **dis·tanced, dis·tanc·ing.** to leave far behind, as in a race; outdistance.

to keep one's distance. to remain aloof or reserved: *The new boy kept his distance from his classmates.*

dis·tant (dis′tənt) *adj.* **1.** far off or away in space; not near: *Pluto is a distant planet. His ranch is distant from the nearest town.* **2.** away: *The highway is eight miles distant from the house.* **3.** far away in time: *King Solomon lived in the distant past.* **4.** to or from a distance: *a distant rumble of thunder.* **5.** far apart or remote in relationship, connection, or degree: *Franklin D. Roosevelt and his wife Eleanor were distant cousins.* **6.** not friendly or familiar; cool in manner; aloof; reserved: *She's been very distant toward him since their argument.* —**dis′tant·ly,** *adv.*

dis·taste (dis tāst′) *n.* lack of taste or liking for something; dislike: *She has a distaste for spinach. Guy has a distaste for hard work.*

dis·taste·ful (dis tāst′fəl) *adj.* causing dislike; unpleasant; disagreeable; offensive. —**dis·taste′ful·ly,** *adv.* —**dis·taste′ful·ness,** *n.*

dis·tem·per (dis tem′pər) *n.* a highly contagious disease of dogs and certain other animals, caused by a virus. Distemper often causes death, especially among puppies.

dis·tend (dis tend′) *v.t.* to enlarge by pressure from within; stretch out; swell; expand: *Water pressure had distended the weak spot in the hose.* —*v.i.* to become distended; swell: *His stomach distended during the course of his illness.*

dis·til (dis til′) *v.,* **dis·tilled, dis·til·ling.** *British.* another spelling of **distill.**

dis·till (dis til′) *also, British,* **dis·til.** *v.t.* **1.** to heat (a liquid or other substance) until evaporation takes place and then condense the vapor given off: *to distill water in order to purify it.* **2.** to produce by distilling: *to distill whiskey, to distill alcohol from grain.* **3.** to obtain as if by distilling; extract the essence of: *to distill wisdom from experience, to distill a moral from a story.* —*v.i.* **1.** to undergo distillation. **2.** to fall in drops; trickle.

dis·til·late (dist′əl it, dist′əl āt′) *n.* a product obtained by distillation.

---

at; āpe; cär; end; mē; it; īce; hot; ōld; fôrk; wood; fōōl; oil; out; up; turn; sing; thin; this; hw in white; zh in treasure. The symbol ə stands for the sound of **a** in about, **e** in taken, **i** in pencil, **o** in lemon, and **u** in circus.

D

dis·til·la·tion (dist′əl ā′shən) *n.* **1.** the act or process of separating the parts of a liquid or other substance that boil at a lower temperature from those that boil at a higher temperature, by heating until evaporation takes place and then condensing the vapor given off. **2.** something that is distilled; distillate. **3.** the state of being distilled.

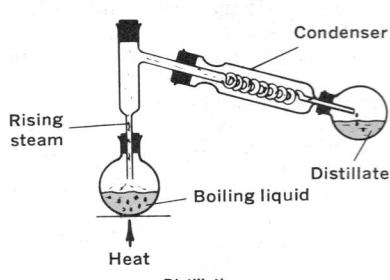

Rising steam · Condenser · Distillate · Boiling liquid · Heat

Distillation

dis·till·er (dis til′ər) *n.* **1.** a person or thing that distills. **2.** a person or company that makes distilled liquors, such as rye, bourbon, or vodka.

dis·till·er·y (dis til′ər ē) *n. pl.,* **dis·till·er·ies.** a place where distilling is performed, especially an industrial plant where distilled liquors are made.

dis·tinct (dis tingkt′) *adj.* **1.** not the same; not identical; separate: *The twins had distinct personalities.* **2.** different in quality or kind: *The Spanish language is distinct from Portuguese.* **3.** clearly seen, heard, or understood; clear; plain: *The sound of the drums was distinct even from a distance.* **4.** unquestionable; definite; unmistakable: *There has been a distinct improvement in his work.* —**dis·tinct′ly,** *adv.* —**dis·tinct′ness,** *n.*

dis·tinc·tion (dis tingk′shən) *n.* **1.** the act of making or noting a difference: *to make a distinction between truth and fiction.* **2.** the condition or quality of being distinct; difference: *The distinction between a dog and a cat is clear.* **3.** a distinguishing mark or characteristic: *That boy has the distinction of being the fastest runner in the school.* **4.** a quality that makes a person worthy of special recognition or honor; excellence; superiority: *The soldier was decorated for his many acts of distinction.* **5.** a mark or symbol of special recognition or honor.

dis·tinc·tive (dis tingk′tiv) *adj.* serving to distinguish or having a distinguishing quality; characteristic: *the distinctive scent of roses.* —**dis·tinc′tive·ly,** *adv.* —**dis·tinc′tive·ness,** *n.*

dis·tin·guish (dis ting′gwish) *v.t.* **1.** to recognize or indicate as different: *to distinguish gold from brass, to distinguish a counterfeit bill from a genuine one.* **2.** to be a distinctive characteristic or quality of; characterize: *Brilliant red plumage distinguishes the male cardinal from the female.* **3.** to see or hear clearly; discern; perceive: *They could see three men walking toward them but could not distinguish their faces in the fog.* **4.** to make famous or worthy of special notice: *The senator has distinguished himself as an advocate of civil rights.* —*v.i.* to recognize or know a difference: *to distinguish between a poisonous snake and a harmless one.* —**dis·tin′guish·a·ble,** *adj.*

dis·tin·guished (dis ting′gwisht) *adj.* **1.** famous for significant achievement or excellent qualities; eminent; celebrated: *Winston Churchill was a distinguished statesman.* **2.** having the look of a famous or important person; dignified: *That fur coat makes her look quite distinguished.*

dis·tort (dis tôrt′) *v.t.* **1.** to twist or bend out of shape; change the natural or usual form of: *The curved mirror distorted Bobby's image.* **2.** to change so as to give a false impression; misrepresent: *The editor distorted the author's meaning when he rewrote the sentence.*

dis·tor·tion (dis tôr′shən) *n.* **1.** the act of distorting. **2.** the state of being distorted. **3.** something that is distorted: *That account of the trial is filled with distortions.*

dis·tract (dis trakt′) *v.t.* **1.** to turn away the mind or attention of; divert: *Noise distracted the boy from his homework.* **2.** to confuse or perplex; unsettle; disturb: *A continual series of questions from customers distracted the new salesgirl.* **3.** to disturb or agitate the mind of: *Worry about her missing son distracted the mother.*

dis·trac·tion (dis trak′shən) *n.* **1.** the act of turning away the mind or attention. **2.** something that draws away the mind or attention: *The parade outside was a distraction to the students in the classroom.* **3.** great confusion or agitation of the mind: *Her brother's constant teasing nearly drove the girl to distraction.* **4.** something that relieves or relaxes the mind; amusement; diversion: *Building model airplanes is a pleasant distraction for him.*

dis·traught (dis trôt′) *adj.* **1.** mentally confused or bewildered; very upset; distracted: *The passengers were distraught with fear as the storm approached.* **2.** crazed; mad.

dis·tress (dis tres′) *n.* **1.** great suffering of body or mind; pain or sorrow; misery: *The famine brought distress to the people.* **2.** something that causes pain or suffering: *Her mother's illness was a great distress to her.* **3.** a condition or situation of danger, trouble, or great need. —*v.t.* to cause pain, suffering, or sorrow to: *The bad news from home distressed him.* —**dis·tress′ing·ly,** *adv.*

dis·tress·ful (dis tres′fəl) *adj.* causing or bringing distress; painful. —**dis·tress′ful·ly,** *adv.*

dis·trib·ute (dis trib′yoot) *v.t.,* **dis·trib·ut·ed, dis·trib·ut·ing.** **1.** to divide and give out in shares; deal out: *The teacher distributed books to the students.* **2.** to scatter or spread out over an area or surface: *The farmer distributed seed over the plowed land.* **3.** to divide or arrange into groups or categories; classify: *The scientist distributed the plants he had found according to their species.*

dis·tri·bu·tion (dis′trə byoo′shən) *n.* **1.** the act of distributing: *the distribution of clothes and food to flood victims.* **2.** the way in which something is distributed: *an uneven distribution of work.* **3.** something that is distributed. **4.** the process or system by which goods are sent from those who produce them to those who use them.

dis·trib·u·tive (dis′trib′yə tiv) *adj.* **1.** of or relating to distribution. **2.** *Grammar.* referring to each member of a group considered individually. *Each* and *every* are distributive words. **3.** *Mathematics.* relating to a law or principle stating that the product of multiplication is the same when the operation is performed on a whole set as when it is performed on the individual members of the set. For example: $4 \times (2 + 5) = 4 \times 2 + 4 \times 5$ and a $\times$ (b + c) = (a $\times$ b) + (a $\times$ c). —*n. Grammar.* a distributive word or expression. —**dis·trib′u·tive·ly,** *adv.*

dis·trib·u·tor (dis trib′yə tər) *n.* **1.** a person or thing that distributes. **2.** a person or company that sells goods to retailers or consumers. **3.** a device that distributes electric current to the spark plugs of a gasoline engine so that they fire in proper sequence.

Distributor · Rotor · Electrical source · Spark plugs

Distributor

dis·trict (dis′trikt) *n.* **1.** a division of a country, state, city, or other area, marked off for a special purpose: *a school district, an election district.* **2.** any region or locality having a particular characteristic: *the theater district of a city.* —*v.t.* to divide or organize into districts. [Late Latin *districtus* a territory ruled by a lord.]

district attorney, a lawyer who acts as an attorney for the government in a certain district, such as a county. A district attorney prosecutes persons accused of crime.

District of Columbia, a federal district in the eastern United States between Maryland and Virginia, consisting of the city of Washington. Area, 69 sq. mi. Pop. (1970), 756,510. Abbreviation, **D.C.**

dis·trust (dis trust′) *v.t.* to have no trust or confidence in; be suspicious of; doubt: *John distrusts many television commercials.* —*n.* lack of trust or confidence; suspicion; doubt.

dis·trust·ful (dis trust′fəl) *adj.* having or showing distrust; suspicious; doubtful: *She has a distrustful nature.* —**dis·trust′ful·ly,** *adv.* —**dis·trust′ful·ness,** *n.*

dis·turb (dis turb′) *v.t.* **1.** to make uneasy or anxious: *The news of the accident disturbed him.* **2.** to break in upon; interrupt; bother: *Don't disturb her while she's working.* **3.** to interfere with the peace or quiet of: *The noisy trucks disturbed the neighborhood.* **4.** to upset the order or arrangement of: *The child disturbed the toys on the shelf.* —**dis·turb′er,** *n.*

dis·turb·ance (dis tur′bəns) *n.* **1.** the act of disturbing or the state of being disturbed. **2.** something that disturbs: *Their noisy laughter was a disturbance to the others in the room.* **3.** noise and confusion; uproar: *The policeman went to see what the disturbance was about.*

di·sul·fide (dī sul′fīd) *n.* a compound in which two atoms of sulfur are combined with another atom or radical.

dis·un·ion (dis yōōn′yən) *n.* **1.** a breaking into parts; separation. **2.** lack of agreement or unity; disagreement.

dis·u·nite (dis′yōō nīt′) *v.,* **dis·u·nit·ed, dis·u·nit·ing.** —*v.t.* **1.** to break into parts; separate. **2.** to cause to disagree. —*v.i.* to come apart; become separate.

dis·u·ni·ty (dis yōō′nə tē) *n.* lack of unity; disunion.

dis·use (dis yōōs′) *n.* lack of use: *The books have collected dust from disuse.*

ditch (dich) *n. pl.,* **ditch·es.** a long, narrow hole dug in the ground; trench. —*v.t.* **1.** to land (a disabled airplane) on water. **2.** to throw into a ditch. **3.** to dig a ditch in or around. **4.** *Slang.* to get rid of; get away from: *The bank robbers ditched the stolen car.* —*v.i.* to land a disabled airplane on water.

dith·er (dith′ər) *n.* the condition of being stirred up, excited, and confused: *The news of her winning the contest threw her into a dither.*

dit·to (dit′ō) *n. pl.,* **dit·tos. 1.** the same as appeared or was mentioned before, represented by ditto marks. **2.** see **ditto mark. 3.** a copy; duplicate.

ditto mark, one of a pair of small marks (″) placed under something written or printed to show that it is to be repeated.

dit·ty (dit′ē) *n. pl.,* **dit·ties.** a short, light song.

di·ur·nal (dī urn′əl) *adj.* **1.** occurring every day; daily: *the diurnal ebb and flow of the tides.* **2.** of, occurring, or active during the daytime: *An animal that hunts during the day is diurnal.* **3.** (of a flower) opening during the day and closing at night. —**di·ur′nal·ly,** *adv.*

di·va (dē′və) *n. pl.,* **di·vas.** a famous female opera singer; prima donna.

di·van (di van′, dī′van) *n.* a long, low couch or sofa, usually having no back or arms.

dive (dīv) *v.,* **dived** or **dove, dived, div·ing.** —*v.i.* **1.** to plunge headfirst, as into water: *He dived into the pool.* **2.** to plunge downward rapidly at a steep angle: *The submarine dived. The bomber dove toward its target.* **3.** to go, dash, or drop suddenly and quickly: *The frightened children dived under the covers when they heard the thunder.* **4.** to enter deeply into something: *Walter dove into his studies.* —*v.t.* to send (an airplane) into a dive. —*n.* **1.** a headfirst or downward plunge, as into water. **2.** a steep, rapid plunge. **3.** *Informal.* a cheap, low nightclub, tavern, or bar.

dive bomber, a fighter plane that dives down steeply toward the target as the bombs are released.

div·er (dī′vər) *n.* **1.** a person or thing that dives. **2.** a person who works or explores underwater. **3.** any of various diving birds, such as the loon.

di·verge (di vurj′, dī vurj′) *v.,* **di·verged, di·verg·ing.** —*v.i.* **1.** to move in different directions from a common point or from each other; draw apart; branch out: *The two roads ran side by side for several miles, and then diverged.* **2.** to differ, as in opinion: *The two friends' tastes in music diverge.* **3.** to turn aside or deviate, as from a rule or standard. —*v.t.* to cause to diverge.

di·ver·gence (di vur′jəns, dī vur′jəns) *n.* **1.** the act of moving out in different directions from a common point. **2.** a difference, as of opinion. **3.** a turning aside or deviation, as from a rule or standard.

di·ver·gen·cy (di vur′jən sē, dī vur′jən sē) *n. pl.,* **di·ver·gen·cies.** another word for **divergence.**

di·ver·gent (di vur′jənt, dī vur′jənt) *adj.* **1.** moving in different directions; diverging: *divergent paths.* **2.** differing, as in opinion. **3.** turning aside or deviating, as from a rule or standard. —**di·ver′gent·ly,** *adv.*

diverging lens, a lens that is thinner in the middle than at the edges. These lenses form virtual images rather than real images.

di·vers (dī′vərz) *adj.* various; several: *There are divers ways of doing the job.*

di·verse (di vurs′) *adj.* **1.** different; unlike: *diverse opinions. The students in the class come from diverse backgrounds.* **2.** of different kinds; varied; diversified: *Martin has a diverse collection of shells. Helen has diverse interests.* —**di·verse′ly,** *adv.* —**di·verse′ness,** *n.*

Diverging lens

di·ver·si·fi·ca·tion (di vur′sə fi kā′shən) *n.* the act of diversifying or the state of being diversified.

di·ver·si·fy (di vur′sə fī′) *v.,* **di·ver·si·fied, di·ver·si·fy·ing.** —*v.t.* to make diverse; give variety to; vary: *The hotel diversified its menu with Japanese, French, and Greek food.* —*v.i.* to deal in different products: *The company diversified, and began manufacturing toys as well as radios.*

di·ver·sion (di vur′zhən) *n.* **1.** the act of diverting or the state of being diverted. **2.** something that distracts the attention: *The thieves' accomplice created a diversion so that they could escape from the bank.* **3.** amusement; entertainment; pastime: *Ted's favorite diversion is playing golf.*

di·ver·si·ty (di vur′sə tē) *n. pl.,* **di·ver·si·ties. 1.** the condition of being diverse: *the diversity of a group of people.* **2.** variety: *a diversity of opinion.*

di·vert (di vurt′) *v.t.* **1.** to change the direction or course of; turn aside: *The policeman diverted traffic from the scene of the accident.* **2.** to distract the attention of. **3.** to amuse; entertain: *The children were diverted by the clown's antics.*

di·vest (di vest′) *v.t.* **1.** to deprive (someone or oneself) as of a right. **2.** to strip, as of clothing or ornament.

di·vide (di vīd′) *v.,* **di·vid·ed, di·vid·ing.** —*v.t.* **1.** to separate into parts or pieces; split up: *The child divided the orange into four parts.* **2.** to separate into parts or pieces

at; āpe; cär; end; mē; it; īce; hot; ōld; fôrk; wood; fōōl; oil; out; up; turn; sing; thin; this; hw in white; zh in treasure. The symbol ə stands for the sound of a in about, e in taken, i in pencil, o in lemon, and u in circus.

and give out; distribute; share: *Jane divided the candy among her friends.* **3.** to cause to be separated into parts: *The fence divides his land from theirs.* **4.** to separate or arrange into groups: *The teacher divided the children in the class according to their reading level.* **5.** to separate into opposing sides or opinions; disunite: *The argument divided the friends.* **6.** *Mathematics.* to show how many times (one number) contains another number. For example, when you divide 8 by 2, you get 4 (8 ÷ 2 = 4), showing that 8 contains the number 2 four times. —*v.i.* **1.** to become separated into parts. **2.** to become separated into opposing sides: *The Senate divided on that issue.* —*n.* a ridge or other raised area of land separating two regions drained by different rivers and their tributaries; watershed.

div·i·dend (div′ə dend′) *n.* **1.** the number or quantity that is to be divided by another number or quantity. When you divide 15 by 3, the dividend is 15. **2.** the money earned by a corporation for a particular period of time, divided among the stockholders as their share of the profits of the business. **3.** a share of such money given to a stockholder.

di·vid·er (di vī′dər) *n.* **1.** a person or thing that divides. **2. dividers.** an instrument for measuring and marking distances.

div·i·na·tion (div′ə nā′shən) *n.* **1.** the art or practice of foretelling the future or the unknown by interpreting signs or omens or by magic. **2.** the act of divining. **3.** something that is divined; prophecy.

di·vine (di vīn′) *adj.* **1.** of or relating to God or a god: *divine will.* **2.** given by or coming from God or a god: *divine forgiveness.* **3.** directed toward or devoted to God or a god; sacred; religious: *divine worship.* **4.** having the nature or characteristics of God or a god; heavenly: *divine beauty.* **5.** excellent or extremely talented: *a divine poet.* **6.** *Informal.* extremely delightful. —*v.t.,* **di·vined, di·vin·ing. 1.** to foretell (the future or the unknown) by interpreting signs or omens or by magic. **2.** to guess: *Ann divined that her friend had planned the surprise party for her.* —*n.* a clergyman; priest. —**di·vine′ly,** *adv.* —**di·vine′-ness,** *n.* —**di·vin′er,** *n.*

diving bell, a large, hollow, watertight container open at the bottom and filled with air, used for work underwater.

diving board, a springy board fastened at one end and jutting out over water, especially over a swimming pool. Diving boards are used by swimmers to jump from.

diving suit, a waterproof suit with a helmet, used for working under water. Air is supplied through tubes from the surface or from portable tanks worn by the diver.

divining rod, a forked branch or stick held by the ends and thought to be able to show where underground water or minerals can be found by bending downward at such a point.

Diving bell

di·vin·i·ty (di vin′ə tē) *n. pl.,* **di·vin·i·ties. 1.** the state or quality of being God or a god: *the divinity of Christ.* **2.** a divine being; deity; god. **3.** the study of God and religion; theology: *Michael is a student of divinity at the university.* **4. the Divinity.** God.

di·vis·i·ble (di viz′ə bəl) *adj.* **1.** capable of being divided: *a divisible quantity.* **2.** capable of being divided without a remainder: *The number 8 is divisible by 2 and 4.* —**di·vis′i·bil′i·ty,** *n.*

di·vi·sion (di vizh′ən) *n.* **1.** the act of dividing or the state of being divided. **2.** one of the parts into which something is divided: *Poetry and grammar are two divisions of this English course.* **3.** something that divides: *The fence formed a division between the two yards.* **4.** lack of agreement: *The divisions among the club members caused the club to disband.* **5.** in modern armies, a unit that is part of a corps and is composed of different regiments. **6.** *Mathematics.* the process of dividing two numbers to show how many times one number contains the other number.

di·vi·sion·al (di vizh′ən əl) *adj.* of or relating to a division.

di·vi·sive (di vī′siv) *adj.* causing or tending to cause disagreement or discord: *divisive policies.* —**di·vi′sive·ly,** *adv.* —**di·vi′sive·ness,** *n.*

di·vi·sor (di vī′zər) *n.* **1.** the number or quantity by which another number or quantity is to be divided. When you divide 15 by 3, the divisor is 3. **2.** a number that divides another without leaving a remainder.

di·vorce (di vôrs′) *n.* **1.** the legal ending of a marriage. **2.** any complete separation. —*v.t.,* **di·vorced, di·vorc·ing. 1.** to free oneself from (one's spouse) by divorce: *He divorced his wife.* **2.** to legally dissolve the marriage of: *The judge divorced the couple.* **3.** to separate; sever: *He divorced himself from the quarrel.*

di·vor·cé (di vôr′sā′) *n.* a divorced man.

di·vor·cée (di vôr′sē′, di vôr′sā′) *n.* a divorced woman.

div·ot (div′ət) *n.* a piece of sod torn up by a golf club in making a stroke.

di·vulge (di vulj′) *v.t.,* **di·vulged, di·vulg·ing.** to make known; disclose: *Carol divulged the secret to her friend.*

Dix·ie (dik′sē) *n.* the South, especially the part of the South that was in the Confederacy.

Dix·ie·land (dik′sē land′) *n.* a style of jazz developed in New Orleans.

diz·zy (diz′ē) *adj.,* **diz·zi·er, diz·zi·est. 1.** having the feeling of whirling and falling; giddy: *The children twirled until they were dizzy.* **2.** causing or tending to cause giddiness: *a dizzy height.* **3.** having a feeling of confusion or bewilderment. —*v.t.* to make dizzy. —**diz′zi·ly,** *adv.* —**diz′zi·ness,** *n.*

Dja·kar·ta (jə kär′tə) *also,* **Ja·kar·ta.** *n.* the capital and largest city of Indonesia. Pop. (1971 est.), 5,899,000.

DNA, nucleic acid found in the chromosomes of all living cells, consisting of a ladder-shaped strand made up of alternating units of sugar and phosphate connected by a nitrogen base. It carries hereditary information from parent to child, and determines the exact structure of all the protein produced by the cells. [Abbreviation of *d*(eoxyribo) *n*(ucleic) *a*(cid).]

Dne·pro·pe·trovsk (dnye′prō pe trôfsk′) *n.* a city in the southwestern Soviet Union, in the Ukraine. Pop. (1970 est.), 862,000.

Dnie·per (nē′pər, dnye′per) *n.* a river flowing through the western part of the Soviet Union into the Black Sea.

Dnies·ter (nēs′tər, dnyes′ter) *n.* a river flowing through the southwestern part of the Soviet Union into the Black Sea.

do¹ (dσσ) *v.,* **did** or (*archaic*) **didst, done, do·ing.** Present tense: *sing.,* first person **do;** second, **do** or (*archaic*) **do·est** or **dost;** third, **does** or (*archaic*) **do·eth** or **doth;** *pl.,* **do.** —*v.t.* **1.** to carry out or perform: *He always does his duty. The nurses did everything they could to make the patient comfortable.* **2.** to produce or create; make: *The artist did a sketch. She did her report on the causes of the American Revolution.* **3.** to bring to an end; complete; finish: *She interrupted him before his speech was done.* **4.** to deal with or take care of; attend to: *to do one's hair.* **5.** to work out; solve: *The students couldn't do the algebra problem.*

6. to bring about or be the cause of: *It'll do Father good to take a vacation.* **7.** to give or grant: *John did his friend a good turn.* **8.** to work at, especially as a job: *What is Harry planning to do when he graduates from college?* **9.** to satisfy the needs of; serve; suffice: *The extra money from home will do him for a while.* **10.** to travel at a speed of: *The car did seventy-five miles an hour.* —*v.i.* **1.** to behave or act in a certain way: *The rude child never did as he was told.* **2.** to fare or manage; get along: *The patient is doing well.* **3.** to serve the purpose; be satisfactory: *That light jacket won't do for skiing.* —*auxiliary verb.* **1.** used without specific meaning: **a.** to ask a question: *Does she need a new coat?* **b.** to form an expression with not: *He does not want any. She did not find the book.* **2.** used to give emphasis: *Do be quiet! They do enjoy his company.* **3.** used in place of a verb already used, to avoid repetition: *Jane speaks French as well as Tom does.* [Old English *dōn.*]

to do away with. a. to kill. **b.** to put an end to: *to do away with slavery.*

to do in. *Informal.* **a.** to kill. **b.** to tire out: *All that walking really did her in.*

to do up. a. to tie or wrap up: *The salesgirl did up the package.* **b.** to put in order; arrange: *Jean did up her hair.*

to make do. to get along or manage: *They can make do without the extra money.*

do² (dō) *n. Music.* **1.** the first and last note of the major scale. **2.** the note C. [Italian *do,* said to be a reversal and changed form of *ut,* the original first note of the scale. The names of the notes of the scale are from syllables in a Latin hymn: *Ut* queant laxis *re*sonare *fi*bris, *Mi*ra gestorum *fa*muli tuorum, *Sol*ve polluti *la*bii reatum, *Sancte* Johannes.]

Do²
Notes of the scale

do., ditto.

dob·bin (dob'in) *n.* a horse, especially a gentle, plodding one.

Do·ber·man pin·scher (dō'bər mən pin'shər) a dog belonging to a breed originally developed in Germany, having a long head, slender legs, and usually a sleek, black or brown coat. [From Ludwig *Dobermann,* a nineteenth-century German dog breeder.]

Doberman pinscher

doc·ile (dos'əl) *adj.* easily managed, trained, or taught: *a docile pet, a docile child.* —**doc'ile·ly,** *adv.*

do·cil·i·ty (do sil'ə tē) *n.* the state or quality of being docile.

dock¹ (dok) *n.* **1.** a structure built along the shore or out from the shore, used as a landing place where boats and ships can be tied up and passengers and cargo loaded and unloaded; wharf; pier. **2.** an area of water between two piers where boats and ships can be moored; slip. **3.** see **dry dock.** —*v.t.* **1.** to bring (a boat or ship) to a dock. **2.** to bring together (two or more orbiting objects, such as spacecraft) in space. —*v.i.* **1.** to come into a dock: *The ship docked last night.* **2.** (of orbiting objects) to come together in space. [Middle Dutch *docke* pier.]

dock² (dok) *n.* **1.** the solid, fleshy part of an animal's tail. **2.** the stump of a tail left after clipping or cropping. —*v.t.* **1.** to cut the end off or shorten: *to dock a horse's tail.* **2.** to deduct from: *The company docked his wages for missing a day of work.* [Possibly from Old English -*docca,* a word root used in such words as *fingerdocca* finger muscle.]

dock³ (dok) *n.* the place in a criminal court where the defendant stands or sits during a trial. [Flemish *dok* cage.]

dock⁴ (dok) *n.* any of a group of plants related to buckwheat, usually having large, wavy-edged leaves. [Old English *docce.*]

dock·age (dok'ij) *n.* **1.** the amount charged for using a dock. **2.** the facilities for docking a boat or ship.

dock·et (dok'it) *n.* **1.** a list of cases that are to be tried by a court of law. **2.** a list of legal judgments given in a particular court. **3.** any list or calendar of things to be done; agenda. **4.** a label or tag attached to something, such as a package or document, and listing its contents. —*v.t.* **1.** to enter in a docket. **2.** to put a label or tag on (something, such as a package or document).

dock·yard (dok'yärd') *n.* a place containing docks, workshops, and warehouses where boats and ships can be built, equipped, and repaired.

doc·tor (dok'tər) *n.* **1.** a person who is licensed to practice any of various branches of medicine, such as pediatrics or psychiatry; physician or surgeon. **2.** a person who is licensed to practice any of various related sciences, such as dentistry, osteopathy, or veterinary medicine. **3.** a person who holds the highest graduate degree given by a university. —*v.t.* **1.** to treat with medicine; try to cure: *Pam doctored her brother when he had the flu.* **2.** to tamper with: *The clerk doctored the records by changing the dates.*

doc·tor·al (dok'tər əl) *adj.* of, relating to, or studying for a doctorate: *a doctoral thesis, a doctoral student.*

doc·tor·ate (dok'tər it) *n.* **1.** the highest graduate degree given by a university. **2.** such a degree awarded as an honor.

doc·tri·nal (dok'trin əl) *adj.* of, relating to, or based on doctrine: *a doctrinal controversy.*

doc·trine (dok'trin) *n.* **1.** a belief or set of beliefs held by a particular group, such as a church or political party: *the doctrines of Catholicism.* **2.** something that is taught; teachings: *political doctrine.*

doc·u·ment (*n.,* dok'yə mənt; *v.,* dok'yə ment') *n.* something written or printed that gives information, support, or proof about a particular object or matter. Deeds, maps, and official records are documents. —*v.t.* to support or prove with facts, evidence, or examples: *The research scientist documented his findings.*

doc·u·men·ta·ry (dok'yə men'tər ē) *adj.* **1.** relating to, supported by, or consisting of documents: *Does he have documentary evidence for his statement?* **2.** dealing with or giving facts: *The children watched a documentary program about wolves on television.* —*n. pl.,* **doc·u·men·ta·ries.** a documentary motion picture, television program, or radio program.

doc·u·men·ta·tion (dok'yə mən tā'shən) *n.* **1.** the preparation of documents. **2.** documentary proof: *There was no documentation for his statement.*

dod·der (dod'ər) *v.i.* **1.** to move feebly and shakily; totter: *The old man doddered down the street.* **2.** to tremble or shake, as from age.

at; āpe; cär; end; mē; it; īce; hot; ōld; fôrk; wood; fōōl; oil; out; up; turn; sing; thin; this; hw in white; zh in treasure. The symbol ə stands for the sound of a in about, e in taken, i in pencil, o in lemon, and u in circus.

dodge (doj) v., **dodged, dodg·ing.** —v.t. **1.** to keep away from or avoid by moving aside quickly or suddenly: *to dodge a blow.* **2.** to get out of or evade by trickery or cunning: *The senator dodged the reporter's question about his campaign finances.* —v.i. to move quickly or suddenly: *The fleeing thief dodged in and out of the crowd.* —n. **1.** the act of dodging. **2.** a trick used to cheat or deceive. **3.** a clever scheme.

dodg·er (doj′ər) n. **1.** a person who dodges, especially one who uses trickery or cunning: *a tax dodger.* **2.** a type of bread or cake made of cornmeal and baked or fried. **3.** a small handbill.

Dodg·son, Charles L. (doj′sən) see **Carroll, Lewis.**

do·do (dō′dō) n. pl., **do·dos** or **do·does.** an extinct, flightless bird, having a large head, a heavy hooked bill, and a short tail of curly feathers. [Portuguese *doudo* stupid, silly; from its awkward appearance.]

doe (dō) n. the female of the deer, antelope, and certain other animals.

do·er (dōō′ər) n. a person who does something, especially a person of action: *a doer of brave deeds.*

does (duz) the present indicative, third person singular, of **do¹.**

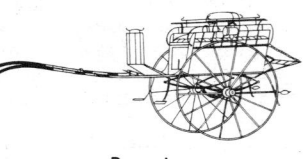
Dodo

doe·skin (dō′skin′) n. **1.** the skin of a female deer. **2.** leather made from this. **3.** a fabric made of wool, cotton, or rayon, having a napped surface, used for coats, suits, and sportswear.

does·n't (duz′ənt) does not.

do·est (dōō′ist) *Archaic.* the present indicative, second person singular, of **do¹.**

do·eth (dōō′ith) *Archaic.* the present indicative, third person singular, of **do¹.**

doff (dof) v.t. to take off, especially to lift (the hat) as a polite gesture.

dog (dôg) n. **1.** a four-footed, meat-eating animal of which there are more than 200 distinct breeds that vary greatly in appearance. Dogs are usually kept as pets or guardians. **2.** any of a group of animals related to the dog, such as the wolf or fox. **3.** the male of any of these animals. **4.** any of various mechanical devices used to fasten, hold, or grip. **5.** *Informal.* person: *He's a sly dog.* —v.t., **dogged, dog·ging.** to follow closely or pursue; hound. —**dog′·like,** adj.

dog·bane (dôg′bān′) n. any of a group of plants having clusters of small, white or pink bell-shaped flowers.

dog·cart (dôg′kärt′) n. **1.** a light, open, one-horse carriage, usually two-wheeled, having two seats set back to back. **2.** a small cart drawn by one or more dogs.

dog·catch·er (dôg′-kach′ər) n. a person employed to pick up stray or unlicensed dogs.

Dogcart

dog days, the hot, sultry days of July and August. [Because the ancient Romans believed that the star Sirius, called the *Dog Star,* caused excessive heat during these months.]

doge (dōj) n. the chief magistrate in the former republics of Genoa and Venice.

dog-ear (dôg′ēr′) n. the turned-down corner of a page of a book or magazine. —v.t. to turn down the corner of (a page). —**dog′-eared′,** adj.

dog·fight (dôg′fīt′) n. **1.** a fight between dogs, or a fight resembling this; rough, violent dispute or brawl. **2.** combat between fighter planes.

dog·fish (dôg′fish′) n. pl., **dog·fish** or **dog·fish·es.** a small shark having a long, slender, grayish-green body, a pointed snout, and a large forked tail.

Dogfish

dog·ged (dô′gid) adj. not yielding; stubborn; persevering: *dogged courage.* —**dog′ged·ly,** adv. —**dog′ged·ness,** n.

dog·ger·el (dô′gər əl) n. poetry having little or no artistic worth. —adj. resembling or composed of such poetry.

dog·gy (dô′gē) also, **dog·gie.** n. pl., **dog·gies.** a dog, especially a little dog.

dog·house (dôg′hous′) n. pl., **dog·hous·es** (dôg′hou′ziz). a small house for a dog.
   in the doghouse. *Informal.* in disfavor.

do·gie (dō′gē) n. in the western United States, a stray calf on the range.

dog·ma (dôg′mə) n. pl., **dog·mas** or **dog·ma·ta** (dôg′mə tə). **1.** a doctrine accepted as true and as having the authority of a church. **2.** any doctrine accepted as true and having authority: *a political dogma.*

dog·mat·ic (dôg mat′ik) adj. **1.** stating opinions or beliefs in a positive and haughty manner: *The dogmatic lecturer would not let anyone question his statements.* **2.** of or relating to dogma; doctrinal. Also, **dog·mat·i·cal** (dôg mat′i kəl). —**dog·mat′i·cal·ly,** adv.

dog·ma·tism (dôg′mə tiz′əm) n. a positive and haughty statement of opinions or beliefs.

dog·ma·tist (dôg′mə tist) n. a person who expresses dogmas or who is dogmatic.

do-good·er (dōō′good′ər) n. *Informal.* a person who is idealistic and eager to change things for the better.

dog-pad·dle (dôg′pad′əl) v.i., **dog-pad·dled, dog-pad·dling.** to use the dog paddle in swimming.

dog paddle, a stroke in swimming with the body in an almost upright position, the hands paddling at the surface, and the legs kicking.

Dog Star, another name for **Sirius.**

dog·trot (dôg′trot′) n. a gentle, easy trot.

dog·wood (dôg′wood′) n. **1.** a tree bearing greenish-yellow flowers surrounded by pink or white petallike leaves. **2.** the hard, heavy wood of this tree.

Do·ha (dō′hə) n. the capital of the sheikdom of Qatar. Pop. (1971 est.), 95,000.

doi·ly (doi′lē) n. pl., **doi·lies.** a small piece of

Dogwood flowers and fruit

linen, lace, paper or other material, placed under something, such as a vase or lamp, as a decoration or to protect a table surface.

do·ings (dōō′ingz) n. **1.** activities, deeds, or events: *social doings.* **2.** behavior; conduct.

dol·drums (dôl′drəmz, dol′drəmz) n., pl. **1.** dull or depressed mood; low spirits. **2.** certain regions of the ocean near the equator that are calm, with light winds and frequent tropical showers.

dole (dōl) n. **1.** something given out in charity, such as money, food, or clothing. **2.** anything given in little amounts; small portion. —v.t., **doled, dol·ing. 1.** to give out in charity. **2.** to give in little amounts: *She doled out the cookies to the children one by one.*

dole·ful (dōl′fəl) *adj.* full of or expressing grief or sorrow; sad: *a doleful cry, a doleful look.* —**dole′ful·ly,** *adv.* —**dole′ful·ness,** *n.*

doll (dol) *n.* **1.** a child's toy made to look like a human being, especially a baby or child. **2.** a pretty or delightful child. —*v.t. Informal.* to dress smartly (with *up*): *Jane dolled herself up for the party.*

dol·lar (dol′ər) *n.* **1.** the standard unit of money in the United States, equal to one hundred cents. **2.** the standard unit of money in certain other countries, such as Canada, New Zealand, and Australia. **3.** a piece of paper currency or silver or gold coin equal to one dollar.

doll·y (dol′ē) *n. pl.,* **doll·ies. 1.** a child's word for a doll. **2.** any of several kinds of low frames or platforms with wheels, used for moving heavy loads.

dol·men (dōl′mən, dol′mən) *n.* a prehistoric structure consisting of a large stone slab resting on two or more stones placed upright.

Dolmen

do·lo·mite (dō′lə mīt′, dol′ə mīt′) *n.* **1.** a mineral whose crystals are usually pink or white in color. **2.** a rock resembling limestone and consisting mainly of dolomite.

do·lor (dō′lər) *n.* sorrow; grief.

do·lor·ous (dō′lər əs, dol′ər əs) *adj.* causing or expressing sorrow or grief: *a dolorous cry.* —**do′lor·ous·ly,** *adv.* —**do′lor·ous·ness,** *n.*

dol·phin (dol′fin) *n.* **1.** any of a group of highly intelligent animals related to the whale, found in all seas and in some freshwater rivers. Dolphins have scaleless black, brown, or gray skin, two flippers, and usually a beaklike snout. **2.** a saltwater fish found in warm waters, used as food. Dolphins are remarkable for their changes of color when taken from the water.

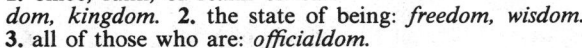
Dolphin

dolt (dōlt) *n.* a dull, stupid person. —**dolt′ish,** *adj.* —**dolt′ish·ly,** *adv.* —**dolt′ish·ness,** *n.*

-dom *suffix* (used to form nouns) **1.** office, rank, or realm of: *earldom, kingdom.* **2.** the state of being: *freedom, wisdom.* **3.** all of those who are: *officialdom.*

do·main (dō mān′) *n.* **1.** the land controlled or governed by a ruler or government; realm. **2.** a field of knowledge or interest: *the domain of science.* **3.** the land owned by one person or family; estate.

dome (dōm) *n.* **1.** a round roof resembling a hemisphere, built on a circular or many-sided base. **2.** something like this in shape: *the dome of a mountain.* —*v.t.,* **domed, dom·ing.** to cover with a dome.

do·mes·tic (də mes′tik) *adj.* **1.** of or relating to the home, household, or family: *domestic life, domestic problems.* **2.** devoted to or fond of things having to do with the home and family: *a domestic person.* **3.** living with or near man and cared for by him; domesticated; tame: *The*

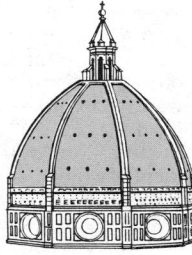
Dome

cat is a domestic animal. **4.** of or made in one's own country: *domestic wine.* —*n.* a household servant. —**do·mes′ti·cal·ly,** *adv.*

do·mes·ti·cate (də mes′tə kāt′) *v.t.,* **do·mes·ti·cat·ed, do·mes·ti·cat·ing. 1.** to adapt, tame, or develop for man's use. **2.** to make fond of or used to a home, household affairs, and family life. —**do·mes′ti·ca′tion,** *n.*

do·mes·tic·i·ty (dō′mes tis′ə tē) *n. pl.,* **do·mes·tic·i·ties. 1.** home and family life. **2.** devotion to one's home and family. **3. domesticities.** household affairs.

domestic science, another term for **home economics.**

dom·i·cile (dom′ə sīl′) *n.* **1.** a place where one lives; home; dwelling. **2.** an official or legal residence. —*v.t.,* **dom·i·ciled, dom·i·cil·ing.** to establish in a domicile.

dom·i·nance (dom′ə nəns) *n.* the state or fact of being dominant.

dom·i·nant (dom′ə nənt) *adj.* **1.** having the main influence, authority, or control; most important: *Great Britain was the dominant country in the world for many years.* **2.** most prominent or striking: *Blue is the dominant color in this room.* **3.** *Music.* of, based upon, or relating to the fifth tone of a scale. **4.** relating to or indicating one of a pair of hereditary characteristics appearing in an organism, that hides or dominates the other when both are present. —*n.* **1.** *Music.* the fifth tone of a scale. G is the dominant in the key of C. **2.** a dominant hereditary characteristic. —**dom′i·nant·ly,** *adv.*

dom·i·nate (dom′ə nāt′) *v.,* **dom·i·nat·ed, dom·i·nat·ing.** —*v.t.* **1.** to have the main influence, authority, or control over: *Because of his forceful personality he dominates people around him.* **2.** to have a commanding or towering position over; tower over: *Skyscrapers dominate New York's skyline.* —*v.i.* **1.** to have the main influence, authority, or control: *France dominated in Europe during the time of Napoleon.* **2.** to have a commanding or towering position. —**dom′i·na′tor,** *n.*

dom·i·na·tion (dom′ə nā′shən) *n.* **1.** the act of dominating or the state of being dominated. **2.** influence, authority, or control; rule; sway: *The weak country was under the stronger country's domination.*

dom·i·neer (dom′ə nēr′) *v.i.* to control or rule others in an arrogant or harsh way; be overbearing or like a tyrant: *The bully domineered over the other children.* —*v.t.* to control or rule (others) in an arrogant or harsh way; tyrannize: *Peasants in Europe were once domineered by dukes, princes, and kings.*

dom·i·neer·ing (dom′ə nēr′ing) *adj.* tending to domineer; overbearing; tyrannical. —**dom′i·neer′ing·ly,** *adv.*

Dom·i·nic, Saint (dom′ə nik) 1170–1221, the founder of the Roman Catholic order of Dominicans.

Do·min·i·can (də min′i kən) *adj.* **1.** of or relating to Saint Dominic or to the religious order founded by him. **2.** of, relating to, or characteristic of the Dominican Republic. —*n.* **1.** a member of the Roman Catholic order founded by Saint Dominic in 1215. **2.** a person who was born or is living in the Dominican Republic.

Dominican Republic, a country in the Caribbean, on the eastern part of the island of Hispaniola. Capital, Santo Domingo. Area, 18,816 sq. mi. Pop. (1971 est.), 4,190,000.

dom·i·nie (dom′ə nē) *n. Scottish.* a schoolmaster.

at; āpe; cär; end; mē; it; īce; hot; ōld; fôrk; wood; fōōl; oil; out; up; turn; sing; thin; this; hw in white; zh in treasure. The symbol ə stands for the sound of **a** in about, **e** in taken, **i** in pencil, **o** in lemon, and **u** in circus.

do·min·ion (də min′yən) *n.* **1.** the power or right to rule; supreme authority: *The dying king gave his son dominion over all the land.* **2.** a territory or country controlled or governed by a particular ruler or government. **3.** *also,* **Dominion.** any of a group of self-governing states belonging to the British Commonwealth, such as Canada or Australia.

dom·i·no (dom′ə nō′) *n. pl.,* **dom·i·noes. 1.** a small black tile divided into halves, each half being either blank or having from one to six white dots, used in playing certain games. **2. dominoes.** a game played with these tiles.

Dom·ré·my (dôn rə mē′) *n.* a village in northeastern France, the birthplace of Joan of Arc.

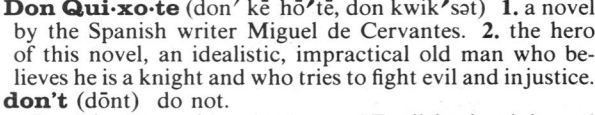

Dominoes

don¹ (don) *n.* **1. Don.** Sir. ▲ Spanish form of respectful or polite address for a man, usually used before the first name only: *Don Jose.* **2.** a Spanish nobleman or gentleman. **3.** a head or tutor of a college at Oxford or Cambridge University. [Spanish *don,* from Latin *dominus* master, lord.]

don² (don) *v.t.,* **donned, don·ning.** to put on: *He donned his coat.* [A contraction of the phrase *do on.*]

Don (don) *n.* a river flowing through the central Soviet Union into the Sea of Azov.

do·ña (dōn′yə) *n.* **1. Doña.** Lady; Madam. ▲ Spanish form of respectful or polite address for a married woman, usually used before the first name only: *Doña Maria.* **2.** a Spanish noblewoman or lady. [Spanish *doña,* from Latin *domina* mistress, lady.]

do·nate (dō′nāt) *v.t.,* **do·nat·ed, do·nat·ing.** to give to; contribute: *She donated the painting to a museum.*

Don·a·tel·lo (don′ə tel′ō) 1386?–1466, Florentine sculptor.

do·na·tion (dō nā′shən) *n.* **1.** the act of giving; contributing: *Many students took part in the yearly donation of clothing to the poor.* **2.** a gift; contribution: *She gave a large donation to charity.*

done (dun) *v.* the past participle of **do.** —*adj.* **1.** completed; finished: *The work is done.* **2.** cooked: *The potatoes are done.*

don·jon (dun′jən, don′jən) *n.* the strong, inner tower of a castle; keep.

Don Juan (don wän′, don hwän′) a legendary Spanish nobleman, famous for his many love affairs.

don·key (dong′kē, dung′kē) *n. pl.,* **don·keys. 1.** a domestic animal that resembles a small horse but has longer ears and a shorter mane; ass. The donkey is often used as a beast of burden. **2.** a stupid or stubborn person.

don·na (don′ə, dō′nə) *n.* **1. Donna.** lady; madam. ▲ Italian form of respectful or polite address for a married woman, usually used before the first name only. **2.** an Italian noblewoman or lady. [Italian *donna,* from Latin *domina* mistress, lady.]

Donne, John (dun) 1573?–1631, English poet.

don·ny·brook (don′ē brook′) *n.* a rough, noisy brawl; free-for-all. [From *Donnybrook,* a fair formerly held in Ireland, at which such brawls were common.]

Donkey

do·nor (dō′nər) *n.* a person who donates: *a blood donor.*

Don Qui·xo·te (don′ kē hō′tē, don kwik′sət) **1.** a novel by the Spanish writer Miguel de Cervantes. **2.** the hero of this novel, an idealistic, impractical old man who believes he is a knight and who tries to fight evil and injustice.

don't (dōnt) do not.

▲ **Don't** is not considered to be good English when it is used in place of **doesn't.**

doo·dle (doōd′əl) *v.,* **doo·dled, doo·dling.** —*v.i.* to draw or scribble idly or aimlessly: *He doodled all over the paper while talking on the telephone.* —*v.t.* to draw or scribble (something) in an idle or aimless manner: *She doodled a face in the margin of her paper.* —*n.* a design or drawing made by doodling. —**doo′dler,** *n.*

doo·dle·bug (doōd′əl bug′) *n.* the larva of the ant lion.

doom (doōm) *n.* **1.** something that cannot be escaped, especially something bringing pain, ruin, or death. **2.** a harsh sentence or judgment: *The judge pronounced the man's doom.* —*v.t.* **1.** to pronounce a harsh judgment against; condemn. **2.** to destine, especially to a bad or tragic end: *He was doomed to fail.*

Dooms·day (doōmz′dā′) *also,* **dooms·day.** *n.* **1.** another name for **Judgment Day. 2.** any day of final judgment.

door (dôr) *n.* **1.** a structure, usually made of wood, glass, or metal, that serves to open or close an entrance or opening in something, such as a building or automobile. **2.** doorway: *She's standing in the door.* **3.** a room or building: *Her room is four doors away. The Smiths live two doors down the street.* **4.** any means of entrance or exit: *Many people think of college as the door to business success.* —**door′like′,** *adj.*

door·bell (dôr′bel′) *n.* a bell or buzzer that makes a sound when a button or handle on or near a door is pressed or pulled by someone wanting to come in.

door·jamb (dôr′jam′) *n.* the vertical piece forming the side of a doorway.

door·knob (dôr′nob′) *n.* the handle on a door, used to open it.

door·man (dôr′mən) *n. pl.,* **door·men** (dôr′mən). a man at the door of a building, such as a hotel, department store, or apartment house, who helps people entering and leaving.

door·mat (dôr′mat′) *n.* a mat placed before a doorway, used by people coming in for wiping their shoes.

door·nail (dôr′nāl′) *n.* a nail having a large head, used to strengthen or decorate doors.

dead as a doornail. dead beyond a doubt.

door·plate (dôr′plāt′) *n.* a plate, usually of metal, placed on or near a door of an apartment, office, or house, and bearing the occupant's name and apartment or street number.

door·sill (dôr′sil′) *n.* the sill of a door.

door·step (dôr′step′) *n.* a step or steps leading from an outside door to the ground or sidewalk.

door·way (dôr′wā′) *n.* **1.** an opening in a wall that is closed by a door. **2.** any means of entrance.

door·yard (dôr′yärd′) *n.* the yard around a house, especially near the door.

dope (dōp) *n.* **1.** *Informal.* a stupid, dull-witted person. **2.** *Informal.* a drug or narcotic. **3.** *Slang.* secret information. **4.** a clear mixture used to fasten a covering to an object, as tissue to a model airplane, and to strengthen or waterproof it. —*v.t.,* **doped, dop·ing.** *Slang.* to give dope to; drug.

do·pey (dō′pē) *adj.,* **do·pi·er, do·pi·est.** *Informal.* mentally slow; stupid.

Dop·pler effect (dop′lər) *Physics.* the change in the frequency of a sound, light, or other wave as the distance between the source of the wave and the observer changes. The frequency becomes lower as the distance between the source and the observer becomes greater, and higher as the distance between the source and the observer becomes less. [From Christian J. *Doppler,* 1803–1853, an Austrian physicist who described this change.]

Dor·ic (dôr′ik, dor′ik) *adj.* of or relating to the first and simplest of the three orders of classical Greek architecture, characterized by columns having no base and very plain capitals. —*n.* one of the three principal dialects of ancient Greece.

Doric capital

dorm (dôrm) *n. Informal.* see **dormitory.**

dor·man·cy (dôr′mən sē) *n.* the state of being dormant:*Plants do not grow during dormancy.*

dor·mant (dôr′mənt) *adj.* **1.** temporarily quiet or inactive: *a dormant volcano.* **2.** in a sleeping or inactive condition.

dor·mer (dôr′mər) *n.* **1.** a window that projects from a sloping roof. Also, **dormer window. 2.** a roofed projection containing such a window.

dor·mi·to·ry (dôr′mə tôr′ē) *n. pl.,* **dor·mi·to·ries. 1.** a building having many bedrooms, as for students at a college to live and sleep in. **2.** a room containing a number of beds, as in a school.

dor·mouse (dôr′mous′) *n. pl.,* **dor·mice** (dôr′mīs′). a rodent found in Europe, Africa, and Asia, resembling a squirrel and usually having brown or gray fur. Dormice hibernate for up to six months of the year.

Dormouse

dor·sal (dôr′səl) *adj.* of, on, or near the back: *a dorsal fin.*

Dort·mund (dôrt′moont′) *n.* a city in northwestern West Germany. Pop. (1969 est.), 648,900.

do·ry (dôr′ē) *n. pl.,* **do·ries.** a deep, flat-bottomed rowboat having high sides sloping upward and outward, used by fishermen.

dos·age (dō′sij) *n.* **1.** the amount of a medicine or other medical treatment in a single dose. **2.** the giving of such a dose.

dose (dōs) *n.* **1.** the amount of a medicine or other medical treatment prescribed to be given or taken at one time. **2.** an amount, especially of something painful or unpleasant: *The bully was given a dose of his own medicine when the older boy beat him up.* —*v.t.,* **dosed, dos·ing.** to give (medicine) to: *to dose a person with antibiotics.*

dos·si·er (dô′sē ā′) *n.* a collection of detailed documents or papers relating to some subject or person.

dost (dust) *Archaic.* the present indicative, second person singular, of **do¹.**

Dos·to·yev·sky, Feo·dor (dos′tə yef′skē; fyô′dôr) 1821–1881, Russian novelist and short-story writer.

dot (dot) *n.* **1.** a small, usually round, mark; speck or very small spot: *He made a dot on the paper with the tip of his pencil.* **2.** *Telegraphy.* the shorter of the two signals used to represent numbers or letters, as in Morse code. —*v.t.,* **dot·ted, dot·ting. 1.** to mark with a dot or dots: *The artist dotted the canvas with yellow and blue.* **2.** to be scattered over or about: *Houses dotted the hillside.*

on the dot. at exactly the specified time: *The train left the station at seven o'clock on the dot.*

dot·age (dō′tij) *n.* the state of being feeble-minded, especially because of old age; senility.

dot·ard (dō′tərd) *n.* a person whose mind is feeble, especially from old age.

dote (dōt) *v.i.,* **dot·ed, dot·ing. 1.** to lavish extreme or excessive affection: *The grandparents doted on the child.* **2.** to be feeble-minded, especially because of old age.

doth (duth) *Archaic.* the present indicative, third person singular, of **do¹.**

Dou·ay Bible (doo̅′ā) an English translation from Latin of the Roman Catholic Vulgate Bible of St. Jerome. Also, **Douay Version.** [From *Douai,* a city in France where this translation was first published.]

dou·ble (dub′əl) *adj.* **1.** twice as great, as many, or as much, as in size, amount, or strength: *She paid double fare for a first-class ticket.* **2.** having or forming two like or identical parts; paired: *People formed a double line in front of the theater. The room has double doors that open out onto the garden.* **3.** having or combining two parts, intentions, uses, or the like: *This statement has a double meaning. The secret agent led a double life.* **4.** *Botany.* having more than one set of petals. —*adv.* in pairs or twos; doubly: *to see double.* —*n.* **1.** something that is twice as much: *Ten is the double of five.* **2.** a person or thing that closely resembles or looks exactly like another: *Louis is the double of his father.* **3.** *Baseball.* a hit that enables a batter to reach second base safely. **4. doubles.** a game, as of tennis, having two players on each side. —*v.,* **dou·bled, dou·bling.** —*v.t.* **1.** to make twice as great, as much, or as many, as in size or amount: *Increased efficiency doubled the company's profits in five years.* **2.** to fold or bend, as to make two layers: *to double a sheet of paper, to double a blanket.* **3.** to be or contain twice the number or amount of. **4.** to clench (the fist): *to double one's fist in rage.* **5.** (of a ship) to sail or go around: *to double a cape.* —*v.i.* **1.** to become twice as great, as much, or as many: *The price of this product has doubled over the last three years.* **2.** to serve two purposes or functions: *This sofa doubles as a bed.* **3.** to turn, especially sharply or suddenly, and trace the same or similar course: *The fleeing criminal doubled back across the field in hopes of escaping his pursuers.* **4.** to fold or bend: *to double up with pain, to double over with laughter.* **5.** to be a substitute: *to double for the star in a play.* **6.** *Baseball.* to hit a double: *Henry doubled to left field.*

on the double. *Informal.* quickly: *Deliver this message and get back here on the double.*

to double up. *Informal.* to share living quarters with another: *If there's only one room left, Brad and Walter will double up.*

double bar *Music.* see **bar** (def. 9c).

double bass (bās) the largest and deepest-toned instrument of the violin family, usually having four strings, and played in an upright position. Also, **bass viol, contrabass.**

double bassoon, a large bassoon, the largest and deepest-toned instrument of the oboe family, pitched an octave lower than the ordinary bassoon.

double bed, a bed large enough for two adults, having a standard width of fifty-four inches.

double boiler, a cooking utensil consisting of a pair of pots, one fitting into the other. The upper pot contains the food that is cooked gently by the heat from boiling water in the lower pot.

dou·ble-breast·ed (dub′əl bres′tid) *adj.* (of garments such as coats or jackets) overlapping enough to make two thicknesses across the breast and having two rows of buttons.

at; āpe; cär; end; mē; it; īce; hot; ōld; fôrk; wood; fōol; oil; out; up; turn; sing; thin; **th**is; hw in white; zh in treasure. The symbol ə stands for the sound of **a** in about, **e** in taken, **i** in pencil, **o** in lemon, and **u** in circus.

dou·ble-check (dub′əl chek′) *v.t.*, *v.i.* to check again, especially for accuracy: *The student double-checked her addition before handing in her paper.*

double chin, a fat fold of flesh under the chin.

dou·ble-cross (dub′əl krôs′) *v.t. Informal.* to deceive or betray (someone) by failing to act as one has promised; be treacherous to. —**dou′ble-cross′er,** *n.*

double cross *Informal.* an act of betrayal; treachery.

dou·ble-deal·er (dub′əl dē′lər) *n.* a person who acts in a deceitful, dishonest, or treacherous way.

dou·ble-deal·ing (dub′əl dē′ling) *n.* deceitful, dishonest, or treacherous behavior or action. —*adj.* given to or characterized by such behavior or action.

double eagle, a former gold coin of the United States, worth twenty dollars.

dou·ble en·ten·dre (dōō′bəl än tän′drə) a word or expression having two meanings, one of which is usually indecent or improper. [Obsolete French *double entendre* double meaning.]

dou·ble-head·er (dub′əl hed′ər) *n.* two games played on the same day in close succession, as in baseball.

double jeopardy, the condition of being tried again for the same offense for which one has already been tried and judged.

dou·ble-joint·ed (dub′əl join′tid) *adj.* having extremely flexible joints that permit movement of the body into unusual angles or positions.

double negative, the use in the same statement of two negative words or phrases, especially to express one negative idea.

▲ At one time, the use of a **double negative** was common in English. Famous writers often used double, and even triple negatives, such as *Thou hast spoken no word this while, nor understood none neither* (Shakespeare, *Love's Labour's Lost*). Today, however, a double negative is not generally considered to be good English, and is used only in special contexts, such as *I am not unaware of his problems.*

dou·ble-park (dub′əl pärk′) *v.t.*, *v.i.* to park (a motor vehicle) next to one that is already parked parallel to the curb.

double play, a baseball play in which two base runners are put out.

double pneumonia, pneumonia affecting both lungs.

dou·ble-quick (dub′əl kwik′) *adj.* very quick; hurried; rapid. —*n.* see **double time** *(def. 1).*

double standard, a standard that is applied more strictly to one group than to another, especially a code of moral behavior whereby women are permitted less freedom than men.

double star, two stars that appear to be one unless viewed through a telescope.

dou·blet (dub′lit) *n.* **1.** a close-fitting waist-length jacket, with or without sleeves, worn especially by men in Western Europe from about 1400 to 1650. **2.** one of two or more words derived from the same original source, but in different ways. The words *custom* and *costume* are doublets.

double take, a delayed reaction, as to a joke or surprising situation.

double talk, deliberately deceptive or meaningless talk, often mixing actual words with meaningless syllables.

dou·ble-time (dub′əl tīm′) *v.*, **dou·ble-timed,** **dou·ble-tim·ing.** —*v.i.* to move in double time. —*v.t.* to cause to move in double time.

double time 1. *Military.* a rapid marching rate of 180

Doublet

three-foot steps per minute. **2.** a rate of pay that is twice one's normal pay rate.

dou·bloon (dub lōōn′) *n.* a former Spanish gold coin.

dou·bly (dub′lē) *adv.* in a twofold manner or degree; twice as: *He rechecked his calculations to make doubly sure there was no error.*

doubt (dout) *v.t.* to be unconvinced, uncertain, or distrustful about; hesitate to believe or accept; question: *He doubted the truth of her story.* —*v.i.* to be unconvinced or undecided in opinion or belief; be unconvinced, uncertain, or distrustful. —*n.* **1.** a feeling of disbelief, uncertainty, or distrust: *He had doubts about her sincerity.* **2.** the state or condition of being unconvinced, uncertain, or distrustful: *The outcome of the election was in doubt.* —**doubt′er,** *n.*

no doubt. a. without question; certainly. **b.** most likely; probably.

without doubt. without question; certainly: *That was without doubt the best book I've ever read.*

doubt·ful (dout′fəl) *adj.* **1.** having, showing, or experiencing doubt: *She had a doubtful look on her face. His friends were doubtful about his chances of success.* **2.** subject to or causing doubt; not clear or sure; uncertain: *The outcome of the war was doubtful. It's doubtful whether they'll go to the party.* **3.** of questionable character: *a doubtful reputation.* —**doubt′ful·ly,** *adv.* —**doubt′ful·ness,** *n.*

doubting Thomas, a person who is habitually doubtful and refuses to believe anything without proof; skeptic. [From St. *Thomas,* because he doubted the resurrection of Christ.]

doubt·less (dout′lis) *adv.* **1.** unquestionably; certainly. **2.** probably. Also, **doubt·less·ly** (dout′lis lē). —*adj.* free from doubt or uncertainty.

douche (dōōsh) *n.* **1.** a jet of water or other liquid directed into or onto a body part, organ, or cavity for cleansing or medicinal purposes. **2.** a device, as a spray or syringe, for administering a douche.

dough (dō) *n.* **1.** a soft, thick mass worked or kneaded from a mixture of flour or meal, liquid, and other ingredients, used in baking. **2.** any soft, thick, pasty mass. **3.** *Slang.* money.

dough·nut (dō′nut′) *n.* a small, usually ring-shaped, cake made of dough, usually leavened and sweetened, cooked by frying in deep fat.

dough·ty (dou′tē) *adj.*, **dough·ti·er,** **dough·ti·est.** steadfast and courageous; valiant. —**dough′ti·ly,** *adv.* —**dough′ti·ness,** *n.*

dough·y (dō′ē) *adj.*, **dough·i·er,** **dough·i·est.** of or like dough, as in appearance; pasty: *The sick man's face had a doughy complexion.*

Doug·las, Stephen A. (dug′ləs) 1813–1861, U.S. political leader who was Abraham Lincoln's major opponent in the presidential election of 1860.

Douglas fir 1. an evergreen timber tree of the pine family, found in western North America, having reddish-brown ridged bark and bearing oval cones. It may grow to a height of 200 feet. **2.** the hard, strong wood of this tree, used chiefly in building construction.

Doug·lass, Frederick (dug′ləs) 1817–1895, U.S. writer, orator, and abolitionist.

dour (door, dour) *adj.* **1.** sullenly gloomy; grim; forbidding: *a dour look.* **2.** unyielding; stern. —**dour′ly,** *adv.* —**dour′ness,** *n.*

douse (dous) *v.t.*, **doused, dous·ing. 1.** to plunge into water or other liquid: *He doused the burning rag in a bucket of water.* **2.** to throw water or other liquid over; drench: *The children doused each other with the hose.* **3.** *Informal.* to put out; extinguish: *Douse the lights.*

dove¹ (duv) *n.* **1.** any of various small or medium-sized birds related to the pigeon, including the mourning dove and turtledove. A dove is often used as a symbol of peace. **2.** a person who favors or supports resolving international conflicts by peaceful means, as through negotiation. [Possibly from Old Norse *dūfa*.]

dove² (dōv) a past tense of **dive.**

dove·cote (duv′kōt′) *also,* **dove·cot** (duv′kot′). *n.* a small house or shelter for doves or pigeons, usually having compartments and placed on a pole or other structure.

Do·ver (dō′vər) *n.* **1.** the capital of Delaware, in the east-central part of the state. Pop. (1970), 17,488. **2.** a port town in southeastern England, noted for its white cliffs. **3. Strait of.** a strait separating southeastern England from northern France, and connecting the English Channel with the North Sea.

dove·tail (duv′tāl′) *n.* **1.** a wedge-shaped projection designed to interlock with a mortise or corresponding opening, as in a piece of wood, to form a strong joint. **2.** a joint formed by the interlocking of such pieces. —*v.t.* to fit together or join, as two boards, by means of dovetails. —*v.i.* to fit together precisely, compactly, or harmoniously: *Their travel plans dovetailed and they decided to tour Europe together.*

dow·a·ger (dou′ə jər) *n.* **1.** a widow who holds property or a title from her deceased husband. **2.** a dignified, elderly lady.

dow·dy (dou′dē) *adj.,* **dow·di·er, dow·di·est.** not stylish or smart in appearance or dress; unfashionable or shabby: *a dowdy woman. The poor old lady wore a dowdy dress.* —*n. pl.,* **dow·dies.** a dowdy woman. —**dow′di·ly,** *adv.* —**dow′di·ness,** *n.*

dow·el (dou′əl) *n.* a peg or pin designed to fit into corresponding holes in two adjacent pieces to hold them together. —*v.t.,* **dow·eled, dow·el·ing;** *also, British,* **dow·elled, dow·el·ling.** to fasten or furnish with dowels.

dow·er (dou′ər) *n.* **1.** the part of a deceased man's property that is given by law to his widow. **2.** another word for **dowry.** —*v.t.* to provide with a dower.

down¹ (doun) *adv.* **1.** from a higher to a lower place, level, or position; in a descending direction; toward the ground: *He stepped down from the ladder. We looked down upon the valley.* **2.** to or on the ground, floor, or bottom: *The boxer knocked his opponent down.* **3.** to, toward, or in a lower place, position, direction, or condition: *She pulled the shades down. They drove down from New York to Florida. He cut his expenses down. The train slowed down.* **4.** to or in a calmer or less active or intense state: *The crowd quieted down.* **5.** with seriousness; earnestly: *to get down to work.* **6.** from an earlier time or individual: *The dress was handed down to her sister.* **7.** at the time of purchase; in cash: *He paid thirty dollars down and the rest in installments.* **8.** in writing; on paper: *She took down their names.* —*adj.* **1.** going or directed downward; descending: *a down staircase.* **2.** in a lower place, level, or position: *The shades are down.* **3.** sick; ill; ailing: *He's down with a cold.* **4.** depressed; dejected: *Bob felt down about losing the game.* —*prep.* in a descending direction along, through, or into: *to walk down a lane, to glance down a page.* —*v.t.* **1.** to bring, throw, knock, or put down; cause to fall: *The fighter downed his opponent. The guns downed four planes.* **2.** *Informal.* to swallow, especially quickly: *He downed his milk and ran out.* **3.** *Informal.* to defeat,

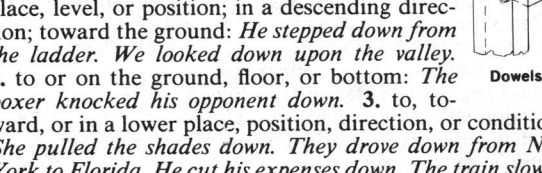

Dovetails

Dowels

as in a game. —*n.* **1.** a downward movement; descent. **2.** unfavorable change or reversal, as of fortune: *Life has its ups and downs.* **3.** *Football.* any of four successive plays during which a team must advance the ball at least ten yards in order to keep possession of it. [Old English *dūne,* short for *of-dūne* literally, from the hill.]

down and out. in a state of misery or wretchedness because of a complete lack of money or friends.

down on. *Informal.* angry at, annoyed with, or hostile to: *Cheryl was down on him for playing that joke on her.*

down with. do away with; eliminate: *Down with tyranny!*

down² (doun) *n.* **1.** fine, soft feathers, as on young birds or under the outside feathers of certain adult birds. **2.** any fine, soft hair or fuzz. [Old Norse *dūnn.*]

down³ (doun) *also,* **downs.** *n.* open, rolling, grassy land, especially in southern and southeastern England. [Old English *dūn.*]

down·beat (doun′bēt′) *n. Music.* **1.** a downward gesture made by a conductor to indicate the first accented beat in a measure. **2.** the first beat or the first accented beat in a measure.

down·cast (doun′kast′) *adj.* **1.** low or dejected in spirit; sad; depressed. **2.** directed downward: *She sat quietly with downcast eyes.*

Dow·ney (dou′nē) *n.* a city in southern California. Pop. (1970), 88,445.

down·fall (doun′fôl′) *n.* **1.** a descent to a lower position or standing; fall, as from power or prosperity; ruin: *The downfall of the government was caused by the corruption of its officials.* **2.** a person or thing causing this. **3.** a fall of rain or snow, especially when sudden or heavy.

down·grade (doun′grād′) *n.* a downward or descending slope, as of a hill or road. —*v.t.,* **down·grad·ed, down·grad·ing.** **1.** to lower in rank, position, or salary; demote. **2.** to lessen the importance or worth of; belittle: *to downgrade a person's achievements.*

on the downgrade. becoming worse; declining: *His reputation as an author is on the downgrade.*

down·heart·ed (doun′här′tid) *adj.* depressed or discouraged in spirit; sad; dejected. —**down′heart′ed·ly,** *adv.* —**down′heart′ed·ness,** *n.*

down·hill (doun′hil′) *adv.* **1.** in a descending or downward direction; toward the bottom of a hill: *The wagon rolled downhill.* **2.** into or toward a lower or worse level or condition: *His physical condition has been going downhill rapidly.* —*adj.* sloping or going downward on or as if on a hill: *a downhill road, a downhill race.*

Down·ing Street (dou′ning) **1.** a street in London that is the site of several official residences and offices of the British government. The home and residence of the prime minister is at 10 Downing Street. **2.** the British government or cabinet.

down·pour (doun′pôr′) *n.* a heavy fall of rain.

down·right (doun′rīt′) *adj.* **1.** thorough; absolute; utter: *This article is downright nonsense. He's a downright liar.* **2.** frankly direct; straightforward: *a downright reply.* —*adv.* thoroughly; utterly.

down·stairs (doun′sterz′) *adv.* **1.** down the stairs. **2.** on or to a lower floor or level. —*adj.* situated on a lower or main floor: *a downstairs room, a downstairs neighbor.*

at; āpe; cär; end; mē; it; īce; hot; ōld; fôrk; wood; fōōl; oil; out; up; turn; sing; thin; this; hw in white; zh in treasure. The symbol ə stands for the sound of **a** in about, **e** in taken, **i** in pencil, **o** in lemon, and **u** in circus.

291

down·stream (doun′strēm′) *adv., adj.* in the direction of the current or flow of a stream: *The canoe drifted slowly downstream.*

down-to-earth (doun′tŏŏ urth′) *adj.* realistic, practical: *a mature, down-to-earth young woman.*

down·town (doun′toun′) *adv.* to, toward, or in the business center or geographically lower part of a town or city: *Her father works downtown.* —*adj.* of or relating to the business center or geographically lower part of a town or city: *a downtown office, a downtown branch of a bank.*

down·trod·den (doun′trod′ən) *adj.* abused or oppressed, as by those in power: *the downtrodden serfs of the feudal period.*

down under *Informal.* a nickname for **Australia** or **New Zealand.**

down·ward (doun′wərd) *also,* **down·wards.** *adv.* **1.** from a higher to a lower place, level, or condition. **2.** from an earlier time or individual: *This custom has been passed downward through many generations.* —*adj.* moving from a higher to a lower place, level, or condition.

down·wind (doun′wind′) *adj.* in the direction in which the wind is blowing.

down·y (dou′nē) *adj.,* **down·i·er, down·i·est. 1.** of or covered with down. **2.** like down; soft; fluffy. —**down′i·ness,** *n.*

dow·ry (dour′ē) *n. pl.,* **dow·ries.** the money or property that a woman brings to her husband at the time of her marriage.

dox·ol·o·gy (dok sol′ə jē) *n. pl.,* **dox·ol·o·gies.** a hymn praising God.

Doyle, Sir Arthur Co·nan (doil; kô′nən) 1859–1930, English writer.

doz., dozen; dozens.

doze (dōz) *v.i.,* **dozed, doz·ing. 1.** to sleep lightly or for a short while; be half asleep; nap: *She's dozing on the couch.* **2.** to fall into a light, brief sleep: *He dozed off while reading.* —*n.* a light or brief sleep.

doz·en (duz′ən) *n. pl.,* **doz·ens** or **doz·en.** a group of twelve.

doz·enth (duz′ənth) *adj.* another word for **twelfth.**

DP, displaced person.

dpt., department.

Dr. 1. Doctor. **2.** Drive.

drab (drab) *n.* **1.** a dull, yellowish-brown or gray color. **2.** a thick, strong woolen or cotton cloth of this color, often woven with a twill. —*adj.,* **drab·ber, drab·best. 1.** lacking brightness; dull or cheerless: *He lived a very drab life.* **2.** having the color drab. —**drab′ly,** *adv.* —**drab′ness,** *n.*

drach·ma (drak′mə) *n. pl.,* **drach·mas** or **drach·mae** (drak′mē). **1.** the basic unit of money in Greece. **2.** a silver coin of ancient Greece. **3.** a unit of weight of ancient Greece. **4.** any of several modern weights, especially a dram.

draft (draft) *also,* **draught.** *n.* **1.** a current of air in an enclosed space or area: *She felt a draft on her back from the open window.* **2.** a device for regulating the flow of air, as in a stove. **3.** the first or rough version of something written: *a draft of a proposed law, a draft of an essay.* **4.** a sketch, plan, or design of something to be made, such as a building. **5.** the act or process of selecting an individual or individuals for some special purpose: *The senator accepted his party's draft and outlined his campaign plans.* **6.** the act or process of selecting persons for compulsory military service: *Men over a certain age are not eligible for the draft.* **7.** a written order directing the payment of a specified amount of money, as from one person or bank to another. **8.** the act of drawing or pulling something, such as a loaded wagon. **9.** the act of drinking. **10.** the amount taken in one drink. **11.** the act of drawing in a fishnet. **12.** the amount of fish taken in a net at one time. **13.** *Nautical.* the depth of water required for a ship to float. —*v.t.* **1.** to prepare a first or rough sketch or version of; make an outline or plan of: *to draft a speech.* **2.** to select for some special purpose, especially for compulsory military service: *David was drafted into the army after he graduated from college.* —*adj.* **1.** used for pulling loads: *a draft animal.* **2.** drawn or ready to be drawn from a tap; not bottled: *draft beer.*

draft·ee (draf tē′) *n.* a person who is drafted for military service.

drafts·man (drafts′mən) *also,* **draughts·man** *n. pl.,* **drafts·men** (drafts′mən). a person who draws or designs plans for machinery, buildings, and other structures and facilities.

drafts·man·ship (drafts′mən ship′) *n.* the work or skill of a draftsman.

draft·y (draf′tē) *also,* **draught·y** *adj.,* **draft·i·er, draft·i·est.** exposed to or admitting drafts of air: *a drafty hallway.* —**draft′i·ly,** *adv.* —**draft′i·ness,** *n.*

drag (drag) *v.,* **dragged, drag·ging.** —*v.t.* **1.** to pull or draw heavily, slowly, or with great effort; haul: *He dragged the heavy suitcase along the ground.* **2.** to search the bottom of, as with a net or hook; dredge: *to drag a lake for a sunken boat.* **3.** to continue for a painfully long period of time: *to drag out a story.* —*v.i.* **1.** to be pulled or drawn along: *The prisoner's chains dragged behind him.* **2.** to move heavily, slowly, or with great effort: *His feet dragged as he walked along wearily.* **3.** to pass or move slowly or painfully: *The lonely old man's days dragged on, one by one.* —*n.* **1.** a person or thing that hinders or slows down: *His lack of ambition proved to be a drag on his career.* **2.** something that is used in searching the bottom of a body of water, such as a net, hook, or dredge. **3.** something that is pulled or hauled along a surface. **4.** *Slang.* a person or thing that is dull or boring.

drag·gle (drag′əl) *v.,* **drag·gled, drag·gling.** —*v.t.* to make wet or dirty, as by dragging through mud. —*v.i.* to become wet or dirty, as by being dragged through mud.

drag·net (drag′net′) *n.* **1.** a net, usually bag-shaped, to be towed over the bottom of a body of water for catching fish or the like. **2.** a system or operation for locating, gathering in, or catching something or someone, such as a wanted criminal.

drag·on (drag′ən) *n.* an imaginary monster somewhat like a huge lizard, usually having claws and wings, and often represented as breathing fire and smoke.

drag·on·fly (drag′ən flī′) *n. pl.,* **drag·on·flies.** any of a large group of slender-bodied insects found near fresh water and feeding on mosquitoes and other insects. Dragonflies have broad heads, compound eyes, and two pairs of thin, veined wings. Also, **darning needle.**

Dragonfly

dra·goon (drə gōōn′) *n.* **1.** a heavily armed cavalryman. **2.** formerly, a mounted infantryman armed with a musket. —*v.t.* to force or pressure into doing something: *His colleagues dragooned the senator into voting for the tax bill.*

drag race *Slang.* a race on a short, straight course between automobiles beginning from a dead stop, the winner being the car that accelerates the fastest.

drain (drān) *v.t.* **1.** to draw water or other liquid from; empty or dry by drawing off liquid: *to drain a pool, to drain a bathtub.* **2.** to draw off (a liquid) gradually or completely: *to drain water from a pool.* **3.** to use up; exhaust: *All feeling had been drained out of him in the fight* (Ernest Hemingway). *The long hike drained his strength.* **4.** to drink all the liquid from; empty by drinking: *He drained his glass.* —*v.i.* **1.** to become dry or empty by the flowing off or away of liquid: *The dishes drained on the counter.* **2.** to flow off or away gradually: *The water drained out of the hole in the pail.* **3.** to release or discharge waters: *The river drains into the sea.* —*n.* **1.** a channel, pipe, or similar device for drawing off water or other liquid: *The bathtub drain is clogged.* **2.** a thing that uses up or exhausts: *The project was a drain on the institute's funds.*

drain·age (drā′nij) *n.* **1.** the act or process of draining. **2.** a system of natural or artificial drains. **3.** something that is drained off.

drain·pipe (drān′pīp′) *n.* a pipe for draining water or other liquid.

drake (drāk) *n.* a male duck.

Drake, Sir Francis (drāk) 1540?–1596, English admiral and explorer, the commander of the first English voyage around the world.

dram (dram) *n.* **1.** an apothecaries' weight equal to sixty grains, or one-eighth of an ounce. **2.** an avoirdupois weight equal to 27.343 grams. **3.** see **fluid dram**. **4.** a small drink, especially of alcoholic liquor.

dra·ma (drä′mə, dram′ə) *n.* **1.** a literary work telling a story and written to be performed; play. **2.** the branch of literature made up of such works. **3.** the art or profession of writing, acting in, or producing plays. **4.** a situation or series of events having dramatic qualities: *The history of space exploration is an exciting drama.* **5.** a dramatic state, quality, or effect: *The witness' revealing testimony was filled with drama.*

dra·mat·ic (drə mat′ik) *adj.* **1.** of, relating to, or characteristic of drama or plays. **2.** like a drama, as in emotional impact; exciting; striking: *a dramatic appeal for mercy, the dramatic events leading to the revolution.* —**dra·mat′i·cal·ly**, *adv.*

dra·mat·ics (drə mat′iks) *n.* **1.** the art or activity of producing or performing plays. ▲ used with a singular verb. **2.** exaggerated or theatrical behavior. ▲ used with a plural verb: *Her dramatics are beginning to annoy her friends.*

dram·a·tist (dram′ə tist) *n.* a person who writes dramas; playwright.

dram·a·ti·za·tion (dram′ə ti zā′shən) *n.* **1.** the act of dramatizing. **2.** something that is dramatized; dramatized version or representation: *a dramatization of the life of Christ.*

dram·a·tize (dram′ə tīz′) *v.t.*, **dram·a·tized, dram·a·tiz·ing.** **1.** to put into the form of a play; adapt for dramatic performance: *to dramatize a novel.* **2.** to express in an exaggerated or theatrical way; cause to seem exciting or spectacular: *She dramatizes all her problems.*

drank (drangk) a past tense of **drink**.

drape (drāp) *v.*, **draped, drap·ing.** —*v.t.* **1.** to cover or decorate with cloth hanging in loose folds: *to drape an altar.* **2.** to place or arrange, as cloth or clothing, in loose, graceful folds. **3.** to arrange, spread, or let fall casually or carelessly: *He draped his feet over the chair.* —*v.i.* to hang or fall in loose folds. —*n.* **1.** *usually,* **drapes.** drapery: *He pulled the drapes back.* **2.** the way in which cloth hangs.

drap·er (drā′pər) *n.* a dealer in cloth or dry goods.

dra·per·y (drā′pər ē) *n. pl.,* **dra·per·ies. 1.** cloth hung or arranged in loose, graceful folds, especially when used as a window curtain. **2.** the draping or arranging of cloth.

dras·tic (dras′tik) *adj.* having a forceful or severe effect; rigorous; extreme: *The President resorted to drastic measures to curb inflation.* —**dras′ti·cal·ly**, *adv.*

draught (draft) another spelling of **draft**.

draughts (drafts, dräfts) *n. British.* the game of checkers. ▲ used with a singular verb.

draughts·man (drafts′mən) *n. pl.,* **draughts·men** (drafts′-mən). another spelling of **draftsman**.

draught·y (draf′tē) *adj.,* **draught·i·er, draught·i·est.** another spelling of **drafty**.

draw (drô) *v.*, **drew, drawn, draw·ing.** —*v.t.* **1.** to cause to move in a particular direction or to a particular position by pulling: *She drew the blankets over her head.* **2.** to cause to follow behind by the use of force or effort; drag; haul: *Two oxen drew the wagon.* **3.** to remove or bring out, as by pulling from a holder; take out: *The policeman drew his revolver. He drew the cork from the bottle.* **4.** to create a picture or likeness of with pen, pencil, or the like: *The artist drew a cat.* **5.** to describe or represent in words: *The speaker drew a grim picture of conditions in the slums.* **6.** to cause (a liquid) to flow forth: *to draw water for a bath.* **7.** to stretch, extend, or pull tight: *He drew the bowstring and fired the arrow.* **8.** to cause to come; bring; attract: *This band always draws a large audience. She drew his attention to the mistake.* **9.** to bring forth or result in; evoke: *His actions drew criticism from his superiors.* **10.** to close; shut: *Please draw the drapes.* **11.** to write out or draft formally or in proper form: *to draw a contract, to draw up a will.* **12.** to take in, as by inhaling or sucking: *She drew a deep breath.* **13.** to take out (funds); withdraw: *to draw thirty dollars from a bank account.* **14.** (of a ship) to require (a certain depth of water) in order to float. —*v.i.* **1.** to create a picture or likeness: *This artist draws beautifully.* **2.** to approach; come; move: *The train drew near the station. He drew back in terror.* **3.** to wrinkle or pucker; become contracted: *Her eyebrows drew together in a frown.* **4.** to cause or allow a current of air to pass: *The chimney is not drawing well.* **5.** to tie, as in a game. —*n.* **1.** the act of drawing. **2.** something that is drawn. **3.** a game or contest in which there is no winner; tie. **4.** a gully or ravine into or through which water drains.

to draw away. to move ahead, as in a race.

to draw out. a. to extend or lengthen; prolong: *He draws out his stories until they become boring.* **b.** to cause or persuade to talk freely: *to draw out a shy person.*

to draw up. a. to come or bring to a stop: *The car drew up in front of the bank.* **b.** to arrange: *The general drew up the troops in battle order.*

draw·back (drô′bak′) *n.* an unpleasant or objectionable feature or characteristic; shortcoming; disadvantage: *The main drawback of that house is that it is so small.*

draw·bridge (drô′brij′) *n.* a bridge that can be wholly or partly raised, lowered, or drawn aside so as to permit or prevent passage.

drawer (*def. 1* drôr; *def. 2* drô ər) *n.* **1.** a sliding box, usually with a handle, that fits into a piece of furniture, such as a bureau, and is drawn out to be opened and pushed in to be closed. **2.** a person who draws.

drawers (drôrz) *n.,pl.* another word for **underpants**.

draw·ing (drô′ing) *n.* **1.** the act of a person or thing that draws. **2.** a picture, sketch,

Drawbridge

or design, usually made by the use of pencil, pen, crayon, or similar material: *an ink drawing of a bird.* **3.** the art or technique of making such a picture, sketch, or design: *John's drawing has improved.* **4.** the selection of the winning chance or chances in a lottery or raffle: *The drawing will be held next Saturday.*

drawing board, a board on which paper or other material is placed or mounted for making drawings.

drawing room, a room for receiving or entertaining guests, such as a parlor or formal reception room.

drawl (drôl) *v.i.* to speak slowly, especially with a drawing out of the vowel sounds. —*v.t.* to pronounce in a drawling manner. —*n.* the act or manner of speech of a person who drawls: *Many people from Texas speak with a drawl.*

drawn (drôn) the past participle of **draw.**

drawn butter, melted butter, often thickened and seasoned, used as a sauce for food.

draw·string (drô′string′) *n.* a string, cord, or tape run through a hem, casing, or eyelets, as at the mouth of a bag, which, when pulled, draws together or closes an opening.

dray (drā) *n.* a low, strong cart with detachable sides, used for carrying heavy loads. —*v.t.* to carry or transport by dray.

dray·man (drā′mən) *n. pl.,* **dray·men** (drā′mən). a person whose work is driving a dray.

dread (dred) *v.t.* **1.** to look forward to with fear or anxiety; fear greatly: *He dreads going to the doctor.* **2.** to look forward to with misgiving or distaste: *He dreaded telling her the bad news.* —*n.* a fear or uneasiness, as over something that will or may happen. —*adj.* causing fear, terror, or awe: *a dread disease.*

dread·ful (dred′fəl) *adj.* **1.** causing fear or awe; terrible: *a dreadful monster.* **2.** *Informal.* very bad; awful: *a dreadful headache, a dreadful movie.* —**dread′ful·ly,** *adv.* —**dread′ful·ness,** *n.*

dread·nought (dred′nôt′) *also,* **dread·naught.** *n.* a battleship with heavy armor and high-powered guns.

dream (drēm) *n.* **1.** a series of thoughts, images, and sensations seen or experienced during sleep: *She had a frightening dream last night.* **2.** a fanciful thought entertained while awake, especially a wild or vain fancy; daydream. **3.** a strong or earnest hope or desire; cherished goal: *Her one great dream was to become a movie star.* **4.** something having great beauty or charm. —*v.,* **dreamed** or **dreamt, dream·ing.** —*v.i.* **1.** to have a dream or dreams: *She dreamt about him last night.* **2.** to have daydreams or fantasies: *He dreams of going to Europe.* **3.** to think of as at all possible: *He wouldn't dream of going to her party.* —*v.t.* **1.** to see or imagine in a dream: *He dreamt he was a millionaire.* **2.** to believe possible; suppose; imagine: *They never dreamed the movie would be so long.* —*adj. Informal.* exactly as wished for; ideal: *That's her dream house.*

   to dream up. *Informal.* to create or devise in one's imagination; concoct: *to dream up an excuse for being late.*

dream·er (drē′mər) *n.* **1.** a person who dreams. **2.** a person who seems to live in a world of dreams or fantasy.

dream·land (drēm′land′) *n.* **1.** the place where a person is said to be while sleeping; realm of dreams. **2.** a delightful or ideal place existing only in the imagination.

dreamt (dremt) a past tense and past participle of **dream.**

dream·y (drē′mē) *adj.,* **dream·i·er, dream·i·est. 1.** like a dream; vague; indistinct: *a dreamy recollection.* **2.** given to dreaming or daydreaming: *a dreamy frame of mind.* **3.** soothing; pleasing; soft: *dreamy music.* **4.** of, relating to, or full of dreams. —**dream′i·ly,** *adv.* —**dream′i·ness,** *n.*

drear (drēr) *adj. Archaic.* another word for **dreary.**

drear·y (drēr′ē) *adj.,* **drear·i·er, drear·i·est. 1.** causing or characterized by sadness or gloom; dismal; depressing: *a dreary room, the dreary prospects of a lonely life.* **2.** dull or uninteresting; monotonous: *She thinks that Monday is the dreariest day of the week.* —**drear′i·ly,** *adv.* —**drear′i·ness,** *n.*

dredge¹ (drej) *n.* **1.** a machine equipped for scooping up or removing mud, sand, and other substances from the bottom of a body of water. **2.** an apparatus equipped with a net for gathering shellfish and other objects from the bottom of a harbor, bay, or other body of water. —*v.,* **dredged, dredg·ing.** —*v.t.* **1.** to clear out, deepen, or enlarge with a dredge: *to dredge a harbor.* **2.** to gather or remove with or as if with a dredge (often with *up*): *to dredge mud, to dredge up facts.* —*v.i.* to use a dredge. [Possibly going back to Old English *dragan* to pull, drag.]

Dredge¹

dredge² (drej) *v.t.,* **dredged, dredg·ing.** to sprinkle or coat with a powdered substance, especially sugar or flour: *Jane dredged the chicken with flour before frying.* [From obsolete *dredge* sweetmeat.]

dredg·er¹ (drej′ər) *n.* **1.** a person or thing that dredges. **2.** a boat used in dredging. [*Dredge¹* + *-er¹*.]

dredg·er² (drej′ər) *n.* a container with holes in its lid, used for sprinkling powdered substances, as sugar or flour, on food. [*Dredge²* + *-er¹*.]

dregs (dregz) *n., pl.* **1.** small pieces of matter that settle at the bottom of a liquid, especially a beverage: *the dregs of coffee.* **2.** the most worthless or undesirable part: *the dregs of society.*

Drei·ser, Theodore (drī′sər, drī′zər) 1871–1945, U.S. novelist.

drench (drench) *v.t.* to wet (someone or something) thoroughly; soak: *The sudden rainfall drenched her on the way home from work.*

Dres·den (drez′dən) *n.* **1.** a city in southern East Germany. Pop. (1971), 500,051. **2.** a fine porcelain decorated with elaborate, brightly colored designs, made near Dresden.

dress (dres) *v.,* **dressed** or **drest, dress·ing.** —*v.t.* **1.** to put clothes on; clothe: *The little girl dressed her dolls.* **2.** to decorate; adorn; trim: *to dress a store window.* **3.** to clean or prepare for use or sale: *to dress a chicken.* **4.** to treat (a wound or sore): *to dress a burn.* **5.** to comb and arrange (hair). **6.** to groom or curry (an animal). **7.** to arrange in a straight line, as a line of soldiers. —*v.i.* **1.** to put on clothes: *He dresses very slowly in the morning.* **2.** to select and wear clothes: *She dresses well.* **3.** to put on or wear formal clothes. —*n. pl.,* **dress·es. 1.** a garment for a woman or girl, cut to appear as one piece and usually extending from the neck to above or below the knees. **2.** clothing; apparel; attire: *soldiers in battle dress.* **3.** a style or choice of clothing; manner of wearing clothes: *Ed is very conservative in his dress.* —*adj.* **1.** of or for a dress: *dress material, a dress pattern.* **2.** relating to or suitable for a formal or ceremonial occasion: *a dress suit, a dress uniform.*

   to dress down. *Informal.* to scold severely.

   to dress up. to put on clothing more elaborate or fancy than that usually worn.

dress·er¹ (dres′ər) *n.* **1.** a person who dresses something: *a window dresser.* **2.** a person who assists another in dressing, as for the stage. **3.** a person who dresses in a particular way: *a fancy dresser.* [*Dress* + *-er¹*.]

dress·er² (dres′ər) *n.* **1.** a chest of drawers, often with a mirror; bureau. **2.** a sideboard or set of shelves for holding dishes and kitchen utensils. [Old French *dresseur*.]

dress·ing (dres′ing) *n.* **1.** the act of a person or thing that dresses. **2.** a sauce, especially for salads. **3.** a medication or bandage applied to a wound or sore. **4.** a mixture of bread or cracker crumbs and other ingredients, usually seasoned, used to stuff poultry, fish, or roasts; stuffing.

dress·ing-down (dres′ing doun′) *n. Informal.* a severe scolding: *Ann got a dressing-down from her mother for coming in late.*

dressing gown, a robe, especially a long, loose one, usually worn before or while dressing or for lounging.

dressing room, a room for dressing, as in a theater.

dressing table, a table, often with drawers, having a mirror for use while grooming and dressing oneself.

dress·mak·er (dres′mā′kər) *n.* a person whose work is making and altering dresses or other articles of clothing for women.

dress·mak·ing (dres′mā′king) *n.* the work or skill of a dressmaker.

dress rehearsal, a full rehearsal in costume of a theatrical presentation or similar performance, especially the final rehearsal.

dress·y (dres′ē) *adj.,* **dress·i·er, dress·i·est. 1.** suitable for formal occasions; elegant; elaborate: *That outfit is much too dressy to wear to a picnic.* **2.** stylish; fashionable: *a dressy social affair.* **—dress′i·ness,** *n.*

drest (drest) a past tense and past participle of **dress.**

drew (drōō) the past tense of **draw.**

Drey·fus, Alfred (drā′fəs, drī′fəs) 1859–1935, French army officer convicted of treason and imprisoned in 1895, acquitted in 1906.

drib·ble (drib′əl) *v.,* **drib·bled, drib·bling. —v.i. 1.** to fall or flow in drops or small quantities; trickle: *Rain dribbled through the cracks in the roof.* **2.** to let saliva run from the mouth; drivel; drool. **3.** to come little by little or in small amounts: *Contributions dribbled in day by day.* **4.** to move a ball by a succession of bounces or kicks, as in basketball or soccer. —*v.t.* **1.** to let fall or flow in drops or small quantities: *The faucet is dribbling cold water.* **2.** to move (a ball) by a succession of bounces or kicks, as in basketball or soccer. —*n.* **1.** a small quantity of a liquid falling in drops or flowing in a thin stream. **2.** the act of dribbling a ball. **—drib′bler,** *n.*

drib·let (drib′lit) *also,* **drib·blet.** *n.* a small amount or part; bit.

dried (drīd) the past tense and past participle of **dry.**

dri·er (drī′ər) *adj.* the comparative of **dry.** —*n.* **1.** a person or thing that dries. **2.** another spelling of **dryer.**

dri·est (drī′ist) *adj.* the superlative of **dry.**

drift (drift) *v.i.* **1.** to be moved, driven, or carried along by currents of water or air: *The boat drifted downstream. Columns of smoke drifted toward the sky.* **2.** to move or seem to move aimlessly and without any particular goal or purpose: *The tramp drifted from town to town. Some people drift through life.* **3.** to gather or accumulate in heaps by the force of wind or water: *The snow drifted against the garage.* —*v.t.* to cause to drift: *The wind drifted the snow.* —*n.* **1.** an act or instance of being driven along by currents of water or air. **2.** the direction of movement or drifting, especially a current of water. **3.** something driven along or heaped up by air or water currents. **4.** a general course of movement; tendency; trend: *The drift of the discussion changed from history to politics.* **5.** a meaning or intent: *They did not quite understand the drift of his remark.* **6.** material, such as sand, gravel, or rocks, that has been moved from one place and deposited in another by a glacier or by the melted water from a glacier.

7. the movement off course of a ship, aircraft, or missile, due especially to water or air currents.

drift·er (drif′tər) *n.* a person or thing that drifts, especially a person who moves aimlessly from one job or place to another.

drift·wood (drift′wood′) *n.* wood drifting on or washed ashore by water.

drill¹ (dril) *n.* **1.** a tool with cutting edges or a pointed end, used for boring holes in wood, plaster, concrete, or other hard substances. **2.** the machine operating such a tool. **3.** strict training or instruction by repeated exercises and practice: *military drill. The class got a lot of drill in alegbra.* —*v.t.* **1.** to pierce or bore a hole in (something) with a drill. **2.** to make (a hole) by boring: *He drilled three holes in the wall for the brackets of the shelf.* **3.** to train or instruct by repeated exercises and practice: *to drill soldiers in marching. The teacher drilled the class in math all morning.* —*v.i.* **1.** to bore or make a hole with a drill: *to drill for oil.* **2.** to go through or perform drills: *The band drills for two hours every day after school.* [Middle Dutch *drillen* to bore.] **—drill′er,** *n.*

Drill¹
Electric hand drill

drill² (dril) *n.* **1.** a machine that plants seeds by making a hole or furrow, dropping in the seed and sometimes fertilizer or other soil preparation, and then covering it with soil. **2.** a small furrow in which seeds are planted. —*v.t.* to sow (seed) in rows. [Of uncertain origin.]

drill press, a machine tool consisting of one or more drills mounted on a column and having an adjustable horizontal table on which the material that is to be drilled is placed.

dri·ly (drī′lē) another spelling of **dryly.**

drink (dringk) *v.,* **drank, drunk, drink·ing. —v.t. 1.** to take into the mouth and swallow: *He drinks milk with his meals.* **2.** to take in or soak up; absorb: *The sponge drank up the water. The plants drank in the rain.* **3.** to swallow the contents of: *He quickly drank a cup of coffee and ran out.* **4.** to take in through the senses or the mind: *He drank in the beauty of the woodland scene.* **5.** to give or join in (a toast): *The guests drank a toast to the bride and groom.* —*v.i.* **1.** to take liquid into the mouth and swallow it. **2.** to drink alcoholic liquor. **3.** to make or join in a toast: *They drank to his success.* —*n.* **1.** a liquid for drinking; beverage: *Lemonade is a favorite cold drink.* **2.** a portion of liquid swallowed: *He stopped for a drink of water.* **3.** a portion of alcoholic liquor. **4.** alcoholic liquor. **—drink′er,** *n.*

drink·a·ble (dring′kə bəl) *adj.* suitable or safe for drinking: *That stream is polluted, so its water is no longer drinkable.*

drip (drip) *v.,* **dripped, drip·ping. —v.i. 1.** to fall in drops: *The rain came through the roof and dripped from the ceiling.* **2.** to have moisture or liquid falling in drops: *The leaky bucket dripped all over the floor.* —*v.t.* to let (something) fall in drops: *She accidentally dripped paint from the brush.* —*n.* **1.** a falling of liquid in drops. **2.** a liquid

at; āpe; cär; end; mē; it; īce; hot; ōld; fôrk; wood; fōōl; oil; out; up; turn; sing; thin; this; hw in white; zh in treasure. The symbol ə stands for the sound of **a** in about, **e** in taken, **i** in pencil, **o** in lemon, and **u** in circus.

falling in drops. **3.** the sound made by a liquid falling in drops: *He could hear the drip of rain outdoors.*

drip-dry (drip′drī′) *adj.* of or referring to a fabric or garment that dries quickly when hung dripping wet and requires little or no ironing: *a drip-dry shirt.*

drip-pings (drip′ingz) *n.,pl.* the melted fat and juices that drip from meat, fowl, or fish while cooking.

drive (drīv) *v.,* **drove, driv-en, driv-ing.** —*v.t.* **1.** to cause to move by physical force: *The waves drove the ship onto the rocks. They drove their attackers off.* **2.** to force into some act or condition: *He complained that the noise was driving him crazy.* **3.** to put in motion and direct the movement of; steer: *to drive a car.* **4.** to carry in a car or other vehicle: *He drove the children to the party.* **5.** to cause to penetrate by force: *to drive a nail into wood.* **6.** to force to work hard; overwork: *He's been driving himself lately and needs a vacation badly.* **7.** to carry on or bring about with force or vigor: *She certainly drives a hard bargain.* **8.** to cause to go rapidly, as by hitting or throwing with force: *He drove the baseball over the fence.* **9.** *Golf.* to strike (the ball) forcefully, especially from a tee. **10.** to set or keep in motion or operation; supply the power for: *Electricity drives this machine.* **11.** to form or produce by making an opening: *to drive a tunnel through a mountain.* —*v.i.* **1.** to operate and steer a car or other vehicle: *He drives too fast.* **2.** to go or be carried in a car or other vehicle: *They drove through the park.* **3.** to rush, dash, or move forcefully or violently: *The hurricane winds drove against the house.* —*n.* **1.** a trip in a car or other vehicle: *They took a drive in the country.* **2.** a driveway or a public road on which to drive: *The winding drive to the house was covered with gravel.* **3.** the act of driving, especially a gathering together and moving forward: *a cattle drive.* **4.** an organized group effort for some specific purpose; campaign: *a drive to collect clothing for flood victims.* **5.** forceful energy; vigor: *His drive and enthusiasm helped make the project a success.* **6.** a strong, motivating force that moves an animal or person to action: *the hunger drive.* **7.** the act or instance of driving a ball or other object; forceful blow or stroke: *The batter hit a drive to left field.* **8.** the way in which power is transmitted to the wheels in a motor vehicle: *rear-wheel drive.*

    to drive at, to mean or intend to say; suggest: *What was he driving at when he made that remark?*

drive-in (drīv′in′) *n.* **1.** an outdoor motion picture theater where patrons remain in their parked cars while viewing a movie projected on a large screen. **2.** any place of business, such as a bank or restaurant, designed to serve customers while they remain in their cars. —*adj.* designed to give service to customers while they remain in their cars: *a drive-in bank.*

driv-el (driv′əl) *v.i.,* **driv-eled, driv-el-ing;** *also, British,* **driv-elled, driv-el-ling. 1.** to let saliva run from the mouth; dribble; slobber. **2.** to talk in a childish or foolish way; talk nonsense. —*n.* **1.** childish, foolish, or ridiculous talk; nonsense. **2.** saliva flowing from the mouth.

driv-en (driv′ən) the past participle of **drive.**

driv-er (drī′vər) *n.* **1.** a person or thing that drives, especially a person who drives a car or other vehicle. **2.** a golf club with a wooden head used to drive balls long distances from the tee. **3.** any machine part that transmits motion or power.

drive shaft, a shaft that transmits power from a source to wheels or to other parts to be driven.

drive-way (drīv′wā′) *n.* a private road leading to a house, garage, or other building from a road or street.

driz-zle (driz′əl) *v.i.,* **driz-zled, driz-zling.** to rain steadily in fine, misty drops. —*n.* a fine, misty rain. —**driz′zly,** *adj.*

droll (drōl) *adj.* amusingly odd or quaint: *a droll fellow.* —**droll′ly,** *adv.* —**droll′ness,** *n.*

droll-er-y (drō′lər ē) *n. pl.,* **droll-er-ies. 1.** the quality of being droll; quaint humor. **2.** something droll, as a story. **3.** the behavior or antics of a droll person; jesting.

drom-e-dar-y (drom′ə der′ē) *n. pl.,* **drom-e-dar-ies.** a single-humped camel native to Arabia and North Africa.

Dromedary

drone¹ (drōn) *n.* **1.** a male bee, especially a honeybee, that develops from an unfertilized egg and does no work. The drone mates once with the queen bee and then dies. **2.** a person who lives on the work of others; idler; loafer. [Old English *drān.*]

drone² (drōn) *v.,* **droned, dron-ing. 1.** to make a continuous, low, humming sound: *The planes droned overhead.* **2.** to talk in a dull, monotonous tone: *The speaker droned on and on.* —*v.t.* to say (something) in a dull, monotonous tone. —*n.* a dull, continuous buzzing or humming sound: *The drone of the mosquitoes kept him awake.* [Possibly from *drone¹,* in imitation of the sound made by a bee.]

drool (drool) *v.i.* **1.** to let saliva run from the mouth; drivel: *The baby drooled all over his bib.* **2.** to water at the mouth, as in anticipation of food: *He drooled at the thought of a steak dinner.* **3.** *Informal.* to show great delight or enthusiasm: *He drooled over his brother's new motorcycle.*

droop (droop) *v.i.* **1.** to hang or sink down: *The dead flowers drooped over the side of the vase.* **2.** to become weak; lose energy or vigor: *His spirits drooped at the thought of losing the game.* **3.** to become discouraged or depressed. —*v.t.* to let hang or sink down: *The sleepy child drooped his head.* —*n.* the act or fact of drooping; drooping position.

droop-y (droo′pē) *adj.,* **droop-i-er, droop-i-est. 1.** that droops or tends to droop. **2.** gloomy; discouraged: *a droopy face.* —**droop′i-ly,** *adv.* —**droop′i-ness,** *n.*

drop (drop) *v.,* **dropped** or **dropt, drop-ping.** —*v.i.* **1.** to fall in small amounts, as a liquid: *Beads of perspiration dropped from his forehead as he worked.* **2.** to fall or go down, especially rapidly or suddenly: *The wet dish dropped from his hand. The runner dropped to his knees after the race.* **3.** to fall or decline in amount or degree; become less: *Business in the summer resort dropped during the winter.* **4.** to fall or move to a position that is lower, inferior, or further back: *He dropped behind the other runners.* **5.** to cease to be of concern; come to an end: *He suggested that they let the matter drop.* **6.** to pay a casual or unexpected visit: *John is going to drop by this evening.* **7.** to fall or pass into a particular state, condition, or activity: *After two hours of tossing and turning, he finally dropped off to sleep.* —*v.t.* **1.** to let fall by letting go of: *He dropped his keys on the floor.* **2.** to cause to move or go down; lower: *When she realized she was being stared at, the shy girl dropped her eyes.* **3.** to let fall in small amounts: *The leaky pail dropped water all over the floor.* **4.** to stop pursuing or dealing with: *to drop a course in school, to drop a subject of discussion.* **5.** to write and send: *John dropped his parents a postcard when he arrived at camp.* **6.** to say or refer to in a casual or incidental way: *to drop a hint.* **7.** to let out or leave: *The bus dropped the children in front of the school.* **8.** (of animals) to give birth to. **9.** to cause to fall, as by striking or shooting: *The hunter dropped the deer with one shot.* **10.** to leave out; omit: *to drop a stitch in knitting.*

11. to break off an association or connection with: *The company dropped ten employees.* 12. *Slang.* to lose: *He dropped $100 at the racetrack.* —*n.* 1. a small quantity of liquid that is shaped like a tiny ball or pear: *a drop of water, a drop of blood.* 2. any very small amount of liquid: *There was only a drop of soda left in the bottle.* 3. a very small amount: *He didn't have a drop of strength left after the long hike.* 4. something resembling a drop of liquid in shape or size, such as a piece of candy. 5. an act or instance of dropping; descent; fall. 6. a sudden decline or decrease: *a drop in prices, a drop in temperature.* 7. **drops.** a liquid medicine to be administered in drops: *eye drops.* 8. the distance between a higher and a lower level; distance or depth to which anything drops: *There was a forty-foot drop from the third floor to the street.* 9. a slit or other opening, as in a mail box, into which something is inserted or dropped.

to drop out. to withdraw; quit: *The boy dropped out of school.*

drop·let (drop′lit) *n.* a tiny drop.

drop·out (drop′out′) *also,* **drop-out.** *n.* 1. a student who withdraws from school, especially high school, before graduating. 2. a person who drops out or withdraws: *a dropout from society.*

drop·per (drop′ər) *n.* 1. a glass tube with a rubber bulb at one end and a small opening at the other end, used for measuring, transferring, or applying liquids in drops. 2. a person or thing that drops.

drop·sy (drop′sē) *n.* an abnormal accumulation of a watery fluid in body tissues or cavities; edema.

dropt (dropt) a past tense and past participle of **drop.**

dro·soph·i·la (drō sof′ə lə) *n. pl.,* **dro·soph·i·lae** (drō-sof′ə lē′). another word for **fruit fly.**

dross (drôs) *n.* 1. the waste or impure matter that rises to the surface of molten metals. 2. any worthless matter; refuse; waste.

drought (drout) *also,* **drouth** (drouth). *n.* a long period of dry weather; prolonged lack of rainfall.

drove[1] (drōv) the past tense of **drive.**

drove[2] (drōv) *n.* 1. a group of animals moving or driven along together: *a drove of cattle, a drove of sheep.* 2. a group of human beings moving or acting together; crowd: *On a hot, muggy day people head for the beaches in droves.* [Old English *dráf* herd.]

dro·ver (drō′vər) *n.* 1. a person who takes a drove of cattle, sheep, or other animals to market. 2. a sheep or cattle dealer.

drown (droun) *v.i.* to die by suffocation in water or other liquid. —*v.t.* 1. to kill by suffocation in water or other liquid. 2. to cover with a flood; drench: *The dam broke and its waters drowned the entire valley. He drowned his pancakes in syrup.* 3. to lessen or smother the sound of by greater loudness; muffle: *The roar of the train drowned out his words.* 4. to get rid of: *He tried to drown his sorrow by working day and night.*

drowse (drouz) *v.i.,* **drowsed, drows·ing.** to be half asleep; doze: *He was drowsing during class.* —*n.* the state of being half asleep.

drow·sy (drou′zē) *adj.,* **drow·si·er, drow·si·est.** 1. sleepy or inclined to sleep; half asleep: *Everyone felt drowsy after the large dinner.* 2. characterized by quiet peacefulness: *a drowsy little village.* 3. causing sleepiness: *drowsy summer days.* —**drow′si·ly,** *adv.* —**drow′si·ness,** *n.*

drub (drub) *v.t.,* **drubbed, drub·bing.** 1. to beat severely, as with a stick; thrash. 2. to defeat decisively; rout.

drudge (druj) *n.* a person who works hard at wearying, boring, or menial tasks. —*v.i.,* **drudged, drudg·ing.** to work hard at wearying, boring, or menial tasks.

drudg·er·y (druj′ər ē) *n. pl.,* **drudg·er·ies.** wearying, boring, or menial labor: *Her whole life seemed to be spent in drudgery.*

drug (drug) *n.* 1. any chemical agent that affects living cells, especially one used to treat disease in man and animals. 2. a substance to which a person may become addicted; narcotic. —*v.t.,* **drugged, drug·ging.** 1. to give drugs to, especially narcotic drugs: *to drug a patient before an operation.* 2. to add a drug or drugs to (food or drink), especially a narcotic or poisonous drug. 3. to affect or overcome as if with a drug.

drug addict, a person who is addicted to a narcotic drug, such as heroin.

drug·gist (drug′ist) *n.* 1. a person licensed to fill prescriptions; pharmacist. 2. a person who owns or operates a drugstore.

drug·store (drug′stôr′) *n.* a store where medicines, drugs, medical supplies, and various other items are sold; pharmacy.

dru·id (drōō′id) *also,* **Dru·id.** *n.* a member of an order of priests among the ancient Celts of Gaul and the British Isles.

drum (drum) *n.* 1. a percussion instrument usually consisting of a hollow cylinder or frame with a membrane stretched tightly over one or both ends, played by beating on the membrane with sticks or the hands. 2. a sound produced when a drum is beaten. 3. any similar sound: *The drum of her fingers on the table made him nervous.* 4. something resembling a drum in shape. 5. a cylindrical metal container, as for oil. 6. a metal cylinder around which something, as cable, is wound. 7. see **eardrum.** —*v.,* **drummed, drum·ming.** —*v.i.* 1. to beat or play a drum. 2. to beat or tap rhythmically or repeatedly: *He drummed on the desk with his fingers.* 3. to sound like a drum; pound; resound: *The noise drummed in her ears.* —*v.t.* to perform or play on or as if on a drum.

to drum into. to drive or force into by repetition: *The teacher drummed the mathematical formulas into their heads.*

to drum out of. to expel or dismiss from in disgrace: *to be drummed out of the army.*

to drum up. to obtain or create by much effort: *The Senator tried to drum up support for reelection.*

drum·beat (drum′bēt′) *n.* the sound of a stroke on a drum.

drum·lin (drum′lin) *n.* an oval mound formed from glacial deposits.

drum major, a person who leads or directs a marching band.

drum majorette, a girl who twirls a baton while marching with a band in a parade.

drum·mer (drum′ər) *n.* 1. a person who plays a drum. 2. *Informal.* a traveling salesman.

drum·stick (drum′stik′) *n.* 1. a stick for beating a drum. 2. the lower part of the leg of a fowl, especially when cooked.

drunk (drungk) *v.* the past participle of **drink.** —*adj.* 1. without normal control of one's faculties because of too much drinking of alcoholic liquor; intoxicated. 2. powerfully affected; overwhelmed: *drunk with success, drunk with joy.* —*n. Informal.* 1. a person who is drunk, espe-

at; āpe; cär; end; mē; it; īce; hot; ōld; fôrk; wood; fōōl; oil; out; up; turn; sing; thin; this; hw in white; zh in treasure. The symbol ə stands for the sound of a in about, e in taken, i in pencil, o in lemon, and u in circus.

cially one who habitually drinks too much alcoholic liquor. **2.** a drinking spree; binge.

drunk·ard (drung′kərd) *n.* a person who habitually drinks too much alcoholic liquor; person who is often drunk.

drunk·en (drung′kən) *adj.* **1.** drunk; intoxicated. **2.** caused by being drunk: *a drunken rage, a drunken stupor.* —**drunk′en·ly,** *adv.* —**drunk′en·ness,** *n.*

drunk·o·me·ter (drung kom′ə tər) *n.* a device that chemically analyzes a person's breath to determine the alcoholic content of his blood.

dry (drī) *adj.,* **dri·er, dri·est. 1.** not wet or damp; free from moisture: *After a few hours in the sun, the bathing suits were dry.* **2.** empty of water or other liquid: *The well has been dry for a month.* **3.** not under or in water: *They stepped from the boat onto dry land.* **4.** having or characterized by little or no rainfall: *It was the driest summer in years.* **5.** free from tears: *dry eyes.* **6.** thirsty: *He was dry after the long hike.* **7.** without butter or other spreads: *dry toast.* **8.** not giving milk: *a dry cow.* **9.** witty in an ironic, matter-of-fact way: *a dry sense of humor.* **10.** not interesting; dull; boring: *a dry book.* **11.** not liquid; solid: *dry cereal.* **12.** not sweet or fruity: *dry wine.* **13.** *Informal.* prohibiting the manufacture, sale, or use of alcoholic beverages: *a dry state.* —*v.,* **dried, dry·ing.** —*v.t.* to make dry; remove moisture from: *She dried the dishes. The sun dried up the puddles.* —*v.i.* to become dry; lose moisture: *Her wet hair dried in the sun. The creek dried up last summer.* —**dry′ness,** *n.*

dry·ad (drī′əd) *also,* **Dry·ad.** *n. Greek Mythology.* a nymph living in trees; wood nymph.

dry cell, an electric cell in which the electrolyte is in a form that does not spill, such as a paste or jelly.

dry-clean (drī′klēn′) *v.t.* to clean (clothes or other cloth articles) with chemical solvents instead of water.

dry cleaner 1. a person or business that does dry cleaning. **2.** a substance used in dry cleaning.

dry cleaning, the act or process of cleaning clothes or other cloth articles with chemical solvents instead of water.

Dry·den, John (drīd′ən) 1631–1700, English poet.

dry dock, any of various watertight structures in which a ship can be docked to allow for such work as repairs, inspection, or cleaning.

dry·er (drī′ər) *also,* **dri·er.** *n.* **1.** a device or appliance for drying: *a hair dryer, a clothes dryer.* **2.** a substance added to paints, varnishes, and other materials to make them dry more quickly.

dry goods, fabrics and related items, as thread, ribbon, or lace.

dry ice, an extremely cold solid, made by compressing

Ship in dry dock

and then cooling carbon dioxide. Dry ice is widely used as a refrigerant because it changes from a solid back to a gas without becoming liquid. Trademark: **Dry Ice.**

dry·ly (drī′lē) *also,* **dri·ly.** *adv.* in a dry manner.

dry measure, a system of units for measuring the volume of dry commodities, as grain, vegetables, or fruit.

dry rot, decay of seasoned timber resulting in its crumbling to a dry powder, caused by any of various fungi.

dry run, a practice session; trial; rehearsal.

dry-shod (drī′shod′) *adj.* having or keeping one's shoes or feet dry; without getting the feet wet.

DST, Daylight Saving Time.

du·al (dōō′əl, dyōō′əl) *adj.* **1.** composed or consisting of two; twofold; double: *dual controls.* **2.** referring or relating to two.

dub[1] (dub) *v.t.,* **dubbed, dub·bing. 1.** to confer knighthood upon by tapping on the shoulder with a sword; make a knight. **2.** to give a title or nickname to; name: *His friends dubbed him "Freckles."* **3.** to speak of or refer to as: *He was dubbed a fool.* [Old English *dubbian.*]

dub[2] (dub) *v.t.,* **dubbed, dub·bing. 1.** to provide (a film or other recording) with a new sound track, especially one in which the dialogue is in another language: *The French movie was dubbed with English.* **2.** to insert or substitute (music, dialogue, or other sounds) in the sound track of a film or other recording. [Short for *double.*]

du·bi·ous (dōō′bē əs, dyōō′bē əs) *adj.* **1.** feeling or showing doubt or uncertainty; hesitant; skeptical: *His friends were dubious about his chances of winning.* **2.** of questionable character; suspect: *a man of dubious reputation.* **3.** causing doubt; not clear: *a dubious reply.* —**du′bi·ous·ly,** *adv.* —**du′bi·ous·ness,** *n.*

Dub·lin (dub′lin) *n.* the capital and largest city of the Republic of Ireland, in the eastern part of the country. Pop. (1971), 566,034.

du·cal (dōō′kəl, dyōō′kəl) *adj.* of or relating to a duke or duchy.

duc·at (duk′ət) *n.* any of several gold or silver coins formerly used in certain European countries.

duch·ess (duch′is) *n. pl.,* **duch·ess·es. 1.** the wife or widow of a duke. **2.** a woman holding in her own right a rank equal to a duke's, especially the female sovereign of a duchy.

duch·y (duch′ē) *n. pl.,* **duch·ies.** the territory under the rule of a duke or duchess; dukedom.

duck[1] (duk) *n.* **1.** any of various wild or domestic waterbirds having a relatively short neck and legs, webbed feet, and usually a broad, flat bill. **2.** a female duck. **3.** the flesh of a duck used as food. [Old English *dūce.*]

duck[2] (duk) *v.t.* **1.** to plunge or thrust under water quickly or suddenly: *The boys ducked the swimming instructor in the lake.* **2.** to lower or bend (the head or body) suddenly and quickly: *The batter ducked his head to avoid being hit by the ball.* **3.** to avoid or evade: *to duck a punch, to duck a question.* —*v.i.* **1.** to lower the head or body quickly or suddenly, as to avoid being hit: *Everyone ducked when they heard the gun shots.* **2.** to move quickly; dart: *The thief ducked around the corner when he saw the policeman coming.* —*n.* the act of ducking. [From an Old English word whose original meaning is not recorded.]

Duck[1]

duck[3] (duk) *n.* **1.** a very strong cotton fabric similar to, but lighter in weight than, canvas, used for making small sails, tents, and clothes. **2. ducks.** trousers made of this fabric. [Dutch *doek* linen cloth, canvas.]

duck[4] (duk) *n.* a military truck that can travel on land and water, used especially during World War II. [From its code name, *DUKW.*]

duck·bill (duk′bil′) *n.* another word for **platypus.** Also, **duck-billed platypus.**

duck-billed (duk′bild′) *adj.* having a bill like a duck's.

ducking stool, a device for punishment formerly used in England and colonial America, consisting of a long plank with a chair at the end in which offenders were tied to be plunged into water.

duck·ling (duk′ling) *n.* a young duck.

duck·pin (duk′pin′) *n.* **1. duckpins.** a bowling game played with pins smaller than those used in tenpins, and a smaller ball. ▲ used with a singular verb. **2.** a pin used in this game.

duck·weed (duk′wēd′) *n.* any of various very small, stemless green plants that float on still water, often forming a coating on the surface.

duct (dukt) *n.* **1.** a tube, pipe, or channel that carries something, such as a liquid or gas. **2.** a tube or channel for carrying a body fluid, especially a fluid secreted by a gland. **3.** a pipe or channel for electric wires or cables. —**duct′less,** *adj.*

duc·tile (dukt′əl) *adj.* **1.** that can be hammered out thin or drawn out into wire without breaking; malleable: *ductile metals.* **2.** easily molded or shaped; pliable: *Modeling clay is ductile.* **3.** easily controlled or influenced; tractable: *a ductile person.* —**duc·til·i·ty** (duk til′ə tē), *n.*

ductless gland, any of various glands without ducts that secrete hormones directly into the blood or lymph; endocrine gland.

dud (dud) *n.* **1.** a bomb or shell that fails to explode. **2. duds.** *Informal.* another word for **clothing. 3.** *Slang.* a person or thing that is a failure.

dude (dood, dyood) *n.* **1.** a man who is too concerned with his clothes. **2.** *Informal.* a city-bred person, especially an easterner visiting the western United States.

dude ranch, a ranch operated as a resort for tourists.

dudg·eon (duj′ən) *n.* a feeling of anger, resentment, or offense. ▲ used chiefly in the phrase *in high dudgeon: After the argument, she stalked out of the room in high dudgeon.*

due (doo, dyoo) *adj.* **1.** owed or owing as a debt; owed and expected to be paid; payable: *The rent will be due on the first of the month. The final payment on the loan is due.* **2.** owed or owing, as by right or custom; appropriate; proper: *The lawyer addressed the judge with all due respect.* **3.** as much as is necessary; adequate; sufficient: *The children were cautioned to use due care when crossing the street.* **4.** required or expected to arrive, be present, or be ready: *The train is due at 5:30.* —*n.* **1.** something that is due or owed. **2. dues.** a fee or charge, especially one paid to a group or organization for the rights of membership. —*adv.* straight; directly; exactly: *The ship sailed due north.*
  due to. a. caused by: *The delay was due to heavy traffic.* **b.** because of: *The project was abandoned due to lack of support.*

du·el (doo′əl, dyoo′əl) *n.* **1.** a formal fight between two people with swords or pistols. Duels are arranged to settle an argument or decide a point of honor and are fought in the presence of two witnesses called seconds. **2.** any contest or struggle between two opponents: *a duel of wits.* —*v.,* **du·eled, du·el·ing;** *also, British,* **du·elled, du·el·ling.** —*v.i.* to fight a duel. —*v.t.* to fight a duel with (someone). —**du′el·er;** *also, British,* **du′el·ler,** *n.*

du·el·ist (doo′ə list, dyoo′ə list) *also, British,* **du·el·list.** *n.* a person who fights a duel.

du·en·na (doo en′ə, dyoo en′ə) *n.* **1.** an elderly woman who serves as the chaperon or escort of a young unmarried girl in a Spanish or Portuguese family. **2.** any chaperon.

due process of law, the carrying out of the law according to established legal principles and in such a way that the rights of the individual are protected. Also, **due process.**

du·et (doo et′, dyoo et′) *n.* **1.** a musical composition for two voices or instruments. **2.** two musical performers.

duf·fel (duf′əl) *n.* **1.** a coarse woolen cloth with a thick nap. **2.** equipment or supplies, especially for camping.

duffel bag, a large bag, usually of canvas, used for carrying clothes, equipment, or other belongings.

dug (dug) the past tense and past participle of **dig.**

du·gong (doo′gong′) *n.* a plant-eating sea mammal having a blunt snout, a short, flat tail, and a pair of front flippers.

dug·out (dug′out′) *n.* **1.** a rough shelter or dwelling formed by digging a hole in the ground or in a hillside or other slope, often covered by sod, logs, or other material. **2.** a long, three-sided, roofed structure in which baseball players sit when not at bat or in the field. **3.** a canoe or boat made by hollowing out a large log.

Dugong

Duis·burg (doos′boork′) *n.* a city in northwestern West Germany. Pop. (1969 est.), 457,900.

duke (dook, dyook) *n.* **1.** a British nobleman of the highest rank. **2.** a nobleman of certain other European countries having a similar rank. **3.** a prince who rules an independent duchy.

duke·dom (dook′dəm, dyook′dəm) *n.* **1.** the territory ruled by a duke; duchy. **2.** the title or rank of a duke.

dul·cet (dul′sit) *adj.* soothing or agreeable, especially to the ear; sweet; pleasant: *the dulcet tones of a voice.*

dul·ci·mer (dul′sə mər) *n.* a musical instrument having metal strings and played by striking the strings with two leather-covered hammers.

dull (dul) *adj.* **1.** not sharp or pointed; blunt: *a dull blade, a pencil with a dull point.* **2.** not interesting; boring; tedious: *a dull speech, a dull subject.* **3.** lacking in intelligence or mental quickness; slow to learn or understand: *a dull student.* **4.** not keenly felt; not intense: *a dull ache.* **5.** not bright, clear, or vivid: *a dull red, a dull finish on a floor.* **6.** not distinct or ringing in sound; muffled: *a dull thud.* —*v.t.* to make dull: *to dull a blade.* —*v.i.* to become dull: *The razor dulled when he used it to cut wood.* —**dull′ness,** *n.* —**dul′ly,** *adv.*

Dulcimer

dull·ard (dul′ərd) *n.* a person who is stupid or slow-witted; dolt.

Du·luth (də looth′) *n.* a city in northeastern Minnesota. Pop. (1970), 100,578.

du·ly (doo′lē, dyoo′le) *adv.* **1.** in a fitting or proper manner; suitably; rightfully: *The sheriff's deputies were duly sworn in.* **2.** to the extent or degree that is due; adequately; sufficiently: *These proposals should be duly considered.* **3.** when due; at the proper time: *The bill was duly paid.*

Du·mas (doo mä′) **1. A·le·xan·dre** (ä lek sän′drə). 1802–1870, French novelist and playwright. **2. Alexandre.** 1824–1895, his son; French playwright.

dumb (dum) *adj.* **1.** lacking the power of speech; mute: *a person who is deaf and dumb.* **2.** temporarily speechless: *Ed was struck dumb when he heard the story.* **3.** not speaking; silent; taciturn: *The prisoner remained dumb, refusing to answer questions.* **4.** *Informal.* stupid. —**dumb′ly,** *adv.* —**dumb′ness,** *n.*

at; āpe; cär; end; mē; it; īce; hot; ōld; fôrk; wood; fool; oil; out; up; turn; sing; thin; this; hw in white; zh in treasure. The symbol ə stands for the sound of **a** in about, **e** in taken, **i** in pencil, **o** in lemon, and **u** in circus.

dumb·bell (dum′bel′) *n.* **1.** a bar with heavy, usually metal, balls or discs at either end, used for exercising. **2.** *Slang.* a stupid person.

dumb·found (dum′found′) another spelling of **dumfound.**

dumb show, gestures without speech; pantomime.

dumb·wait·er (dum′wā′tər) *n.* **1.** a small elevator used to carry dishes, food, rubbish, or other articles from one floor to another. **2.** a movable serving table or stand.

dum·dum (dum′dum′) *n.* a bullet with a soft nose made so that it will expand on impact, causing a large wound. Also, **dumdum bullet.** [From *Dum Dum,* a town near Calcutta, India, where it was formerly manufactured.]

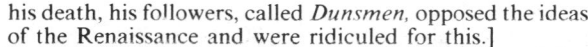
Dumbbell

dum·found (dum′found′) *also,* **dumb·found.** *v.t.* to strike dumb, as with amazement; astonish: *He was dumfounded when he found out that he had passed the test.*

dum·my (dum′ē) *n. pl.,* **dum·mies. 1.** the figure of the human body used to represent or serve as a real person: *department store dummies, a ventriloquist's dummy.* **2.** something made to resemble the real thing: *The actor's gun was a dummy.* **3.** a person seeming to act independently or for his own interests but really controlled by another. **4.** a player, as in bridge, whose cards are laid face up on the table and played by his partner. **5.** a sample, as of a book or magazine, usually consisting of blank pages, arranged to show the size and appearance of the final version. **6.** *Informal.* a stupid person; dolt. —*adj.* **1.** imitation; sham: *a dummy rifle.* **2.** seeming to act independently but really serving or controlled by another: *a dummy president of a corporation.*

dump (dump) *v.t.* **1.** to throw down or let fall in a heap or mass; fling down or drop heavily or suddenly: *The truck dumped the gravel in the driveway. She dumped her books on the bed.* **2.** to unload or empty the contents of (a container), as by overturning: *He dumped out his briefcase on the table.* **3.** *Informal.* to get rid of or throw away by dumping: *He went to dump the garbage.* —*n.* **1.** a place where rubbish or garbage is deposited. **2.** a pile or heap of rubbish or other discarded materials. **3.** a place for temporary storage of military supplies: *an ammunition dump.* **4.** *Slang.* a messy, shabby, or unattractive place: *The hotel was a real dump.*

dump·ling (dump′ling) *n.* **1.** a ball of dough that is boiled or steamed and usually served with meat. **2.** a dessert made by enclosing fruit in a piece of dough and baking or steaming it.

dumps (dumps) *n.,pl.* a gloomy or depressed state of mind; low spirits: *After they lost the big game, the whole team was down in the dumps.*

dump truck, a truck having a rear portion that can be tilted so that its load slides down through an open tailgate.

dump·y (dum′pē) *adj.,* **dump·i·er, dump·i·est.** short and stout; squat. —**dump′i·ness,** *n.*

dun¹ (dun) *v.t.,* **dunned, dun·ning.** to make repeated demands upon (someone) for payment of a debt: *The department store kept dunning him for his past due bills.* —*n.* **1.** the repeated demand for payment of a debt. **2.** a person who duns. [Of uncertain origin.]

dun² (dun) *n.* a dull grayish-brown color. —*adj.* having the color dun. [Old English *dunn* dark.]

dunce (duns) *n.* a person who is slow at learning; dull-witted or ignorant person. [From John *Duns* Scotus, 1266?–1308, Scottish theologian and philosopher. After

his death, his followers, called *Dunsmen,* opposed the ideas of the Renaissance and were ridiculed for this.]

dune (dōōn, dyōōn) *n.* a mound, hill, or ridge of sand that is heaped up by the wind.

dung (dung) *n.* solid waste matter that is eliminated by animals; manure.

dun·ga·ree (dung′gə rē′) *n.* **1.** a denim fabric used for such items as work clothes, sportswear, and sails. **2. dungarees.** trousers or work clothes made of this fabric. [Hindi *dūngrī,* from the name of a village that is now part of Bombay, India.]

dun·geon (dun′jən) *n.* a dark cell or prison, especially one underground: *the dungeon of a castle.*

dung·hill (dung′hil′) *n.* a heap of dung.

dunk (dungk) *v.t.* **1.** to dip (something to eat) into a liquid: *to dunk doughnuts into coffee.* **2.** to push or plunge (someone) underwater briefly; duck: *John dunked Susan in the pool.*

Dun·kirk (dun′kurk′) *n.* a seaport in northern France, scene of the evacuation of Allied troops in 1940.

du·o (dōō′ō, dyōō′ō) *n. pl.,* **du·os. 1.** another word for **duet. 2.** a pair; couple.

du·o·dec·i·mal (dōō′ə des′ə məl, dyōō′ə des′ə məl) *adj.* relating to or based on twelfths or the number twelve; proceeding by twelves: *duodecimal multiplication.* —*n.* a number in a duodecimal system.

duodecimal system, a system of numbers in which the base is twelve, rather than ten, as in the decimal system.

du·o·de·nal (dōō′ə dēn′əl, dyōō′ə dēn′əl) *adj.* of or relating to the duodenum: *a duodenal ulcer.*

du·o·de·num (dōō′ə dē′nəm, dyōō′ə dē′nəm) *n. pl.,* **du·o·de·na** (dōō′ə dē′nə, dyōō′ə dē′nə). the first section of the small intestine, extending from the final portion of the stomach.

dupe (dōōp, dyōōp) *n.* a person who is easily tricked or deceived, or who unknowingly is used by another: *He was a dupe of the racketeers.* —*v.t.,* **duped, dup·ing.** to make a dupe of; trick or deceive: *He was duped into helping the thieves escape after the robbery.*

du·ple (dōō′pəl, dyōō′pəl) *adj.* **1.** double; twofold. **2.** *Music.* having two, or a multiple of two, beats to the measure: *duple time, duple meter.*

du·plex (dōō′pleks, dyōō′pleks) *adj.* having two parts; double; twofold. —*n.* a duplex house or apartment.

duplex apartment, an apartment having rooms on two floors.

duplex house, a house having two separate single-family units.

du·pli·cate (*adj., n.,* dōō′pli kit, dyōō′pli kit; *v.,* dōō′pli kāt′, dyōō′pli kāt′) *adj.* **1.** exactly like something else; being an exact copy of an original: *a duplicate list, a duplicate key.* **2.** having or consisting of two corresponding or identical parts; double; twofold. —*n.* **1.** a copy exactly like an original; exact copy: *The secretary kept a duplicate of the business letter.* **2.** something corresponding in every way to something else; counterpart; double: *Jane's jacket is a duplicate of Susan's.* —*v.t.,* **du·pli·cat·ed, du·pli·cat·ing. 1.** to make an exact copy of; reproduce: *to duplicate a letter.* **2.** to do again; repeat: *The tennis champion tried to duplicate his past victory.*

in duplicate, in two identical copies: *The secretary typed the letter in duplicate.*

du·pli·ca·tion (dōō′pli kā′shən, dyōō′pli kā′shən) *n.* **1.** the act of duplicating or the state of being duplicated. **2.** a copy or counterpart; duplicate.

du·pli·ca·tor (dōō′pli kā′tər, dyōō′pli kā′tər) *n.* a machine for making copies, especially of pages of written or typed material.

du·plic·i·ty (dōō plis′ə tē, dyōō plis′ə tē) *n. pl.,* **du·plic·i·ties.** an acting in a way that is opposite to one's true feelings or beliefs in order to deceive: *The duplicity of the police informer was discovered by the gang.*

du·ra·bil·i·ty (door′ə bil′ə tē, dyoor′ə bil′ə tē) *n.* the quality of being durable; ability to resist wear, decay, or change.

du·ra·ble (door′ə bəl, dyoor′ə bəl) *adj.* **1.** able to resist wear or decay: *a durable floor covering, durable shoes.* **2.** able to resist change or stress; stable; enduring: *a durable friendship.* —**du′ra·ble·ness,** *n.* —**du′ra·bly,** *adv.*

du·rance (door′əns, dyoor′əns) *n.* forced confinement or imprisonment. ▲ used chiefly in the phrase *in durance vile.*

du·ra·tion (doo rā′shən, dyoo rā′shən) *n.* the length of time during which anything continues or exists: *He fought in Europe for the duration of the war. The peace between the two countries was of short duration.*

Dur·ban (dur′bən) *n.* a port city in eastern South Africa. Pop. (1971 est.), 725,577.

Dür·er, Al·brecht (door′ər, dyoor′ər; äl′brekt) 1471–1528, German artist and engraver.

du·ress (doo res′, dyoo res′) *n.* **1.** the use of force to make someone do something: *The prisoner signed the confession under duress.* **2.** unlawful confinement or imprisonment.

Dur·ham (dur′əm) *n.* a city in north-central North Carolina. Pop. (1970), 95,438.

dur·ing (door′ing, dyoor′ing) *prep.* **1.** throughout the time or duration of: *He lives in the country during the summer.* **2.** at some point in the course of: *He arrived at the theater during the second act.*

durst (durst) *Archaic.* a past tense of **dare.**

du·rum (door′əm, dyoor′əm) *n.* a type of wheat having hard, amber-colored kernels used in producing a high-quality flour from which macaroni, spaghetti, and similar products are made. Also, **durum wheat.**

dusk (dusk) *n.* **1.** the time of day just before nightfall; twilight. **2.** shade or gloom; darkness: *in the dusk of the forest.* —*adj.* dark or gloomy.

dusk·y (dus′kē) *adj.,* **dusk·i·er, dusk·i·est. 1.** dark in color: *The dress was a dusky brown.* **2.** without light; shadowy; dim: *a dusky day, a dusky room.* —**dusk′i·ly,** *adv.* —**dusk′i·ness,** *n.*

Düs·sel·dorf (doos′əl dôrf′) *n.* a city in northwestern West Germany. Pop. (1970), 663,600.

dust (dust) *n.* **1.** fine, dry particles of earth or other matter: *The passing car raised a cloud of dust.* **2.** ground, especially as the burial place of the dead; earth. **3.** what remains of something, as a dead body, after decay or destruction. —*v.t.* **1.** to remove dust from, as by brushing or wiping: *to dust a table.* **2.** to cover or sprinkle: *to dust a cake with powdered sugar, to dust crops with insecticide.* —*v.i.* to remove dust, especially from furniture: *She dusted every day.*

to bite the dust. to be killed, especially in battle.

to throw dust in (someone's) eyes. to deceive or mislead (someone).

dust bowl *also,* **Dust Bowl.** an area of dry, dusty land having irregular rainfall and frequent dust storms, especially such an area that developed in the western plains of the United States in the 1930s.

dust·er (dus′tər) *n.* **1.** a person or thing that dusts. **2.** a cloth, brush, or other device for removing dust from objects. **3.** a loose-fitting, knee-length housecoat. **4.** a long, lightweight coat formerly worn in open automobiles to protect clothing from dust.

dust jacket, a removable, usually illustrated paper cover for a book.

dust·pan (dust′pan′) *n.* a broad, short-handled pan resembling a shovel, used for collecting dust swept from a floor.

dust storm, a strong wind that carries clouds of dust across dry plains or desert regions.

dust·y (dus′tē) *adj.,* **dust·i·er, dust·i·est. 1.** full of or covered with dust: *a dusty old trunk.* **2.** like dust; powdery: *a dusty snow.* **3.** having the color of dust; grayish: *a dusty pink.* —**dust′i·ness,** *n.*

Dutch (duch) *adj.* of or relating to the Netherlands, its people, or their language. —*n.* **1. the Dutch.** the people of the Netherlands. **2.** the language of the Netherlands.

in Dutch. *Informal.* in trouble or disfavor: *He's in Dutch with his parents for coming home late.*

to go Dutch. *Informal.* to have each person pay for himself, as on a date.

Dutch Guiana, see **Surinam.**

Dutch·man (duch′mən) *n. pl.,* **Dutch·men** (duch′mən). a person who was born or is living in the Netherlands.

Dutch oven 1. a heavy metal or ceramic pot with a tight-fitting cover, used chiefly for cooking meats and stews. **2.** a metal box having one side that opens, placed before a fire for cooking by reflected heat.

Dutch treat *Informal.* a meal, entertainment, or outing at which each person pays his own expenses.

du·te·ous (dōō′tē əs, dyōō′tē əs) *adj.* dutiful; obedient. —**du′te·ous·ly,** *adv.* —**du′te·ous·ness,** *n.*

du·ti·a·ble (dōō′tē ə bəl, dyōō′tē ə bəl) *adj.* subject to the payment of customs duty or taxes: *a shipment of dutiable imports.*

du·ti·ful (dōō′ti fəl, dyōō′ti fəl) *adj.* **1.** doing one's duty or duties; obedient; respectful: *a dutiful child, a dutiful subject of the king.* **2.** showing or resulting from a sense of duty: *The store manager displayed a dutiful interest in the customers' complaints.* —**du′ti·ful·ly,** *adv.* —**du′ti·ful·ness,** *n.*

du·ty (dōō′tē, dyōō′tē) *n. pl.,* **du·ties. 1.** something that a person is bound to do; obligation: *It is the duty of parents to care for their children properly.* **2.** a sense of what is right: *He was motivated by duty, and not by any hope of reward when he returned the wallet he found.* **3.** an act or action that is required by or is a part of a person's work or position: *One of the duties of a secretary is typing letters.* **4.** the tax on goods that are brought into or taken out of a country.

Dvo·řák, An·ton (dvôr′zhäk; än′tōn) 1841–1904, Czech composer.

dwarf (dwôrf) *n. pl.,* **dwarfs** or **dwarves** (dwôrvz). **1.** a fully grown person, animal, or plant of less than normal size for its kind. **2.** in folklore, a little man, often represented as ugly and deformed, having unusual or magical powers or skills. —*v.t.* **1.** to cause to seem small, as by contrast or comparison: *Most professional basketball players dwarf other men.* **2.** to keep from growing to the normal size; stunt: *to dwarf a tree.* —*adj.* of unusually small size; diminutive: *dwarf trees.*

dwarf·ish (dwôr′fish) *adj.* like a dwarf; unusually small. —**dwarf′ish·ly,** *adv.* —**dwarf′ish·ness,** *n.*

dwell (dwel) *v.i.,* **dwelt** or **dwelled, dwell·ing. 1.** to make one's home; live; reside: *to dwell in the suburbs, to dwell*

---

at; āpe; cär; end; mē; it; īce; hot; ōld; fôrk; wood; fŏol; oil; out; up; turn; sing; thin; <u>th</u>is; hw in white; zh in treasure. The symbol ə stands for the sound of **a** in about, **e** in taken, **i** in pencil, **o** in lemon, and **u** in circus.

in a cottage by the sea. **2.** to exist or be present: *The memory of those childhood years dwells in our hearts.* —**dwell′er,** *n.*

   to dwell on or **to dwell upon.** to think, write, or speak about for a long time: *The speaker dwelt at length upon his final point. He dwells too much on painful memories.*

dwell·ing (dwel′ing) *n.* a place where a person lives; house; abode.

dwelt (dwelt) a past tense and past participle of **dwell.**

dwin·dle (dwind′əl) *v.i.,* **dwin·dled, dwin·dling.** to become gradually smaller or less; shrink; diminish: *After the parade was over, the crowd began to dwindle. Hopes for their safety dwindled.*

Dy, the symbol for dysprosium.

dye (dī) *n.* **1.** a coloring matter used to give a particular color to cloth, hair, food, or other materials. Dye is either obtained from natural substances in plants, animals, and minerals, or produced artificially from coal-tar substances. **2.** a color or hue, especially as produced by dyeing. —*v.,* **dyed, dye·ing.** —*v.t.* to give a particular color to, especially by soaking in a liquid dye: *Sarah dyed the curtains green.* —*v.i.* to take on color in dyeing. —**dy′er,** *n.*

dyed-in-the-wool (dīd′in thə wool′) *adj.* thoroughgoing; absolute; complete: *a dyed-in-the-wool political conservative.*

dye·ing (dī′ing) *n.* the act, process, or trade of coloring cloth, hair, or other materials with dye.

dye·stuff (dī′stuf′) *n.* a substance used as a dye or as a source of dye.

dy·ing (dī′ing) *v.* the present participle of **die¹.** —*adj.* **1.** approaching death; about to die: *the confession of a dying man.* **2.** of or associated with death or dying; at death: *dying words.* **3.** coming to an end; fading: *a dying flame.*

dyke (dīk) *n., v.,* **dyked, dyk·ing.** another spelling of **dike.**

dy·nam·ic (dī nam′ik) *adj.* **1.** characterized by or full of energy and vigor; forceful: *a dynamic personality, a dynamic person.* **2.** characterized by change or activity: *a dynamic new government.* **3.** of or relating to energy or force in motion. **4.** of or relating to dynamics. —**dy·nam′i·cal·ly,** *adv.*

dy·nam·ics (dī nam′iks) *n.,pl.* **1.** the branch of physics dealing with bodies in motion. ▲ used with a singular verb. **2.** the motivating or governing forces operating in any field

or activity: *the dynamics of human behavior.* ▲ used with a plural verb.

dy·na·mite (dī′nə mīt′) *n.* an explosive consisting of an absorbent material saturated with nitroglycerin, usually packed in cylindrical sticks. —*v.t.,* **dy·na·mit·ed, dy·na·mit·ing.** to blow up or destroy with dynamite. —**dy′na·mit′er,** *n.*

dy·na·mo (dī′nə mō′) *n. pl.,* **dy·na·mos.** **1.** an electric generator or motor, especially one that produces a direct current. **2.** *Informal.* an energetic, forceful person.

dy·nas·tic (dī nas′tik) *adj.* of or relating to a dynasty.

dy·nas·ty (dī′nəs tē) *n. pl.,* **dy·nas·ties.** **1.** a line of rulers who belong to the same family. **2.** the period of time during which a dynasty rules.

dyne (dīn) *n. Physics.* a unit of force equal to the amount of force that must be applied to a mass of one gram to produce an acceleration of one centimeter per second for each second that the force is applied.

dys·en·ter·y (dis′ən ter′ē) *n.* any of several diseases of the intestines, characterized by severe diarrhea, often with mucus and bloody discharges, pain, and cramps. Dysentery is caused by various organisms, such as bacteria, parasites, or viruses.

dys·pep·si·a (dis pep′sē ə, dis pep′shə) *n.* poor digestion; indigestion.

dys·pep·tic (dis pep′tik) *adj.* **1.** of, relating to, or suffering from dyspepsia. **2.** gloomy or irritable. —*n.* a person who has dyspepsia.

dys·pro·si·um (dis prō′sē əm) *n.* a rare-earth element that is more magnetic than any other known substance. Symbol: **Dy** [Modern Latin *dysprosium,* from Greek *dysprositos* hard to get at; because it was discovered only after great difficulty.]

dz., dozen; dozens.

at; āpe; cär; end; mē; it; īce; hot; ōld; fôrk; wood; fōōl; oil; out; up; turn; sing; thin; this; hw in white; zh in treasure. The symbol ə stands for the sound of a in about, e in taken, i in pencil, o in lemon, and u in circus.

1. Egyptian Hieroglyphics	5. Greek Ninth Century B.C.
2. Semitic	6. Etruscan
3. Phoenician	7. Latin Fourth Century B.C. Capitals
4. Early Hebrew	8. English

E is the fifth letter of the English alphabet. The earliest ancestor of our modern capital letter **E** was an Egyptian hieroglyphic (1) that depicted a human figure with its arms outstretched. In the ancient Semitic alphabet, this symbol was simplified and adapted for the letter *he* (2), which represented an **h** sound. In both design and pronunciation, *he* was similar to the letter *cheth,* the ancient Semitic letter from which our modern **H** developed. *He* was used, with only slight changes in its shape, in the Phoenician (3) and early Hebrew (4) alphabets. When the early Greeks borrowed *he,* they called it *epsilon* (5), at first using it to stand for both the consonant sound *h* and the vowel sound *e.* Because the Greeks had another letter, *eta,* that represented the *h* sound, *epsilon* eventually was used to stand for only the vowel sound *e.* This later form of *epsilon* was adopted by the Etruscans (6), who, by reversing it, gave it its modern shape. Both the design and pronunciation of this letter were used in the Latin alphabet (7). By about 2300 years ago, the Latin **E** was being written almost exactly as we write the capital letter **E** today (8).

e, E (ē) *n. pl.,* **e's, E's. 1.** the fifth letter of the English alphabet. **2.** the fifth item in a series or group. **3.** *Music.* the third note of the scale of C major.

E *Physics.* energy.

E. 1. East. **2.** Eastern. **3.** English.

ea., each.

each (ēch) *adj.* being one of two or more things or persons considered separately or singly: *Each house on the street has a small yard. Each player on the team has his own uniform.* —*pron.* every individual person or thing, as of a group or number. ▲ used with a singular verb and a singular pronoun: *Each of his friends is going to camp for the summer.* —*adv.* for each; apiece: *These cookies are a nickel each.*

   each other. the one the other; one another: *They have known each other for twenty years.*

ea·ger (ē'gər) *adj.* **1.** filled with desire; wanting very much: *She was eager to start her vacation.* **2.** characterized by or showing much interest or enthusiasm: *He had an eager look on his face. The two boys are eager hockey fans.* **ea'·ger·ly,** *adv.* —**ea'ger·ness,** *n.*

ea·gle (ē'gəl) *n.* **1.** any of a group of birds of prey related to the hawk, having very sharp eyesight, a sharply hooked bill, and strong claws. **2.** a representation of an eagle, often used as a symbol or emblem. **3.** a former gold coin of the United States. It was worth ten dollars.

Eagle

ea·gle-eyed (ē'gəl īd') *adj.* able to see clearly; sharp-sighted.

ea·glet (ē'glit) *n.* a young eagle.

ear¹ (ēr) *n.* **1.** the organ of the body by which people and animals hear. In mammals, the ear has three parts: the external ear, the middle ear, and the inner ear. **2.** in man and other mammals, the outer, visible part of this organ of hearing: *The dog pricked up his ears at the noise.* **3.** the sense of hearing: *Tom has a keen ear. Her voice is pleasing to the ear.* **4.** the ability to hear and understand the differences in sounds, especially musical sounds: *That girl has no ear for music.* **5.** attention: *to have someone's ear.* **6.** something resembling the outer part of the ear in shape or position, such as the handle of a pitcher. [Old English *ēare.*]

   to be all ears. to listen eagerly: *He was all ears when he heard his father mention a camping trip.*

   to play by ear. to play (a musical instrument) without following written music.

ear² (ēr) *n.* the part of a cereal plant, such as corn or wheat, on which the grains or seeds grow. [Old English *ēar.*]

ear·ache (ēr'āk') *n.* a pain in the middle or inner ear.

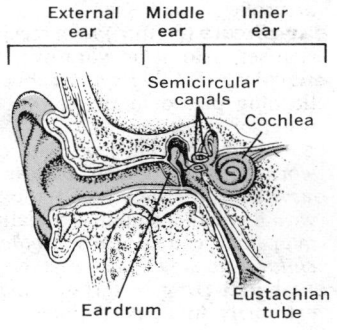

External ear   Middle ear   Inner ear

Semicircular canals

Cochlea

Eardrum

Eustachian tube

Human ear

303

ear·drum (ēr′drum′) *n.* a thin membrane that separates the external ear from the middle ear and vibrates when sound waves strike it; tympanic membrane.

earl (url) *n.* a British nobleman ranking below a marquis and above a viscount.

earl·dom (url′dəm) *n.* the rank, title, or lands of an earl.

ear lobe, the lower, fleshy part of the outer ear.

ear·ly (ur′lē) *adj.,* **ear·li·er, ear·li·est. 1.** happening in or near the beginning; belonging to the first part: *The house was built in the early part of the twentieth century.* **2.** happening or doing something before the customary or expected time: *The farmer is an early riser.* —*adv.* **1.** in or near the beginning: *It's still too early to know who will win the World Series.* **2.** before the customary or expected time: *He arrived at work early.* —**ear′li·ness,** *n.*

early bird *Informal.* a person who does something earlier than others, especially a person who gets up early.

ear·mark (ēr′märk′) *n.* **1.** a mark of identification, usually a cut, made on the ear of an animal. **2.** a distinguishing mark or feature; characteristic; sign: *This book has all the earmarks of a great novel.* —*v.t.* **1.** to make an earmark on. **2.** to set aside for a specific purpose: *Dad earmarked that money for our summer vacation.*

ear·muffs (ēr′mufs′) *n., pl.* a pair of coverings worn to protect the ears against the cold.

earn (urn) *v.t.* **1.** to receive (something as payment) in return for work done: *Jim earns twenty-five dollars a week mowing lawns.* **2.** to get what is deserved; be worthy of: *She really earned her high grades.* **3.** to produce as income; yield: *His savings account earns five percent interest a year.* —**earn′er,** *n.*

ear·nest¹ (ur′nist) *adj.* **1.** sincere or serious in purpose or feeling: *Helen is an earnest student.* **2.** showing or characterized by sincere feeling: *John offered her an earnest apology for his rude remark.* [Old English *earnoste.*] —**ear′nest·ly,** *adv.* —**ear′nest·ness,** *n.*

ear·nest² (ur′nist) *n.* something given as an indication or pledge of something to come, such as a deposit of money. [A changed form of earlier *erles,* going back to Hebrew *'ērābōn* a pledge of something, security.]

earn·ings (ur′ningz) *n., pl.* money earned, such as wages or profit.

ear·phone (ēr′fōn′) *n.* a receiver, as for a radio or television set, held at or worn over the ear.

ear·plug (ēr′plug′) *n.* a rubber or plastic plug placed in the ear to keep out water or noise.

ear·ring (ēr′ring′) *n.* an ornament worn on or hung from the ear lobe.

ear·shot (ēr′shot′) *n.* the distance within which a sound, especially the human voice, can be heard: *Mother told the children to stay within earshot.*

ear·split·ting (ēr′split′ing) *adj.* extremely loud; deafening: *an earsplitting crash.*

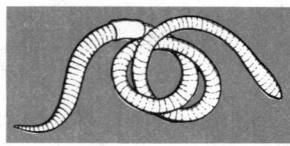

Earphone

earth (urth) *n.* **1.** *also,* **Earth.** the planet on which man lives, the fifth largest planet of the solar system and third in order of distance from the sun. **2.** the ground; dry land: *After the long sea voyage, the sailors were glad to feel the earth under their feet again.* **3.** soil; dirt: *The gardener loosened the earth around the plants.* **4.** the people who live on the planet earth: *The Lord reigneth; let the earth rejoice* (Psalms 97:1).

down to earth. simple, practical, and straightforward.

earth·en (ur′thən) *adj.* **1.** made of earth. **2.** made of baked clay: *The earthen jug has a reddish-brown color.*

earth·en·ware (ur′thən wer′) *n.* pottery made of clay baked at a low temperature.

earth·ling (urth′ling) *n.* an inhabitant of the earth; human being.

earth·ly (urth′lē) *adj.,* **earth·li·er, earth·li·est. 1.** of or relating to the earth rather than to heaven; worldly: *He lost all his earthly possessions in the fire.* **2.** possible: *These worn-out shoes are of no earthly use.* —**earth′li·ness,** *n.*

earth·quake (urth′kwāk′) *n.* a movement of a part of the earth's surface, caused by the sudden shifting of rock along a fault, or by volcanic or other disturbances.

earth·ward (urth′wərd) *adj.* moving toward the earth: *an earthward motion.* —*adv. also,* **earthwards.** toward the earth: *The plane plunged earthward.*

earth·work (urth′wurk′) *n.* a fortification made of earth.

earth·worm (urth′wurm′) *n.* a worm that has a long, segmented body and lives in the soil. Also, **angleworm.**

earth·y (ur′thē) *adj.,* **earth·i·er, earth·i·est. 1.** of, containing, or like soil: *an earthy smell, an earthy color.* **2.** natural and hearty; simple: *The farmer and his wife are earthy people.* **3.** unrefined; coarse: *earthy language.* —**earth′i·ness,** *n.*

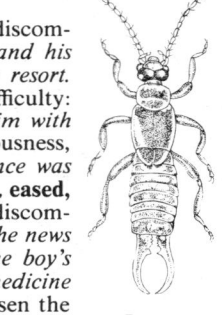

Earthworm

ear·wig (ēr′wig′) *n.* an insect having a hard, slender body and a pair of pincers at the end of its abdomen.

ease (ēz) *n.* **1.** freedom from pain, discomfort, toil, or worry; comfort: *Jim and his parents lived a life of ease at the resort.* **2.** freedom from great effort or difficulty: *While at camp, Mike learned to swim with ease.* **3.** freedom from stiffness, nervousness, or embarrassment: *His self-confidence was shown by the ease of his manner.* —*v.,* **eased, eas·ing.** —*v.t.* **1.** to free from pain, discomfort, or worry; comfort or relieve: *The news of his parents' safe arrival eased the boy's mind.* **2.** to make less; lighten: *The medicine eased the ache in his back.* **3.** to lessen the pressure or strain of (something); loosen: *to ease a tight waistband, to ease a rope.* **4.** to move or place (something) slowly and carefully: *He eased the car onto the ramp of the ferry boat.* —*v.i.* to move slowly and carefully.

at ease. a. free from stiffness or nervousness: *The host's friendly manner helped his guests feel at ease.* **b.** *Military.* in a relaxed standing position with the feet apart and the hands behind the back. ▲ often used as a command.

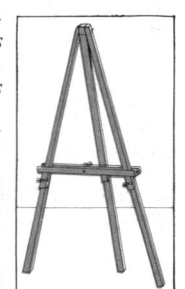

Earwig

ea·sel (ē′zəl) *n.* an upright frame or tripod, used especially to hold an artist's canvas.

eas·i·ly (ē′zə lē) *adv.* **1.** without difficulty, discomfort, or great effort: *He is well trained and can do the work easily.* **2.** without a doubt; certainly: *Jim is easily the best player on the team.*

eas·i·ness (ē′zē nis) *n.* the quality or state of being easy.

east (ēst) *n.* **1.** the direction a person faces when he watches the sun rise. East is one of the four main points of the compass, located directly opposite west. **2.** *also,* **East.** any region or place lying in this direction. **3. the East. a.** a region in the United States along the Atlantic coast, especially the area east of the Allegheny Mountains and north of Maryland. **b.** Asia and

Easel

the islands close to it; the Orient. —*adj.* **1.** toward or in the east. **2.** from the east: *an east wind.* —*adv.* toward the east: *to drive east.*

East Berlin, the capital of East Germany, in northeastern Germany. Pop. (1971) 1,084,866.

east·bound (ēst′bound′) *adj.* going east: *an eastbound freight train.*

East·er (ēs′tər) *n.* **1.** a Christian holy day celebrating the resurrection of Christ. Easter comes on the Sunday after the first full moon on or following March 21st. **2.** the Sunday on which this holy day is celebrated. Also *(def. 2),* **Easter Sunday.**

Easter Island, an island in the eastern South Pacific, belonging to Chile. It is noted for the enormous ancient stone statues found there.

east·er·ly (ēs′tər lē) *adj., adv.* **1.** toward the east: *an easterly direction.* **2.** from the east: *an easterly wind.*

east·ern (ēs′tərn) *adj.* **1.** toward or in the east: *the eastern part of the state.* **2.** *also,* **Eastern.** of, relating to, or characteristic of the east or East. **3.** coming from the east: *an eastern breeze.* **4. Eastern.** Oriental: *Eastern philosophy.*

Eastern Church 1. another term for **Orthodox Church. 2.** any of various Christian churches, such as the Coptic Church in Africa, deriving from the church of the Byzantine Empire.

east·ern·er (ēs′tər nər) *n.* **1.** a person who was born or is living in the east. **2.** *usually,* **Easterner.** a person who was born or is living in the eastern part of the United States.

Eastern Hemisphere, the eastern half of the earth that includes Europe, Asia, Africa, and Australia.

east·ern·most (ēs′tərn mōst′) *adj.* farthest east.

Eastern Orthodox Church, another term for **Orthodox Church.**

Eastern Roman Empire, another term for **Byzantine Empire.**

Eastern Standard Time, the local time used in the eastern United States. It is five hours earlier than Greenwich time.

East Germany, a country in north-central Europe. Capital, East Berlin. Area, 41,815 sq. mi. Pop. (1971) 17,040,926. Official name: **German Democratic Republic.**

East Indies, a group of islands in the Pacific Ocean between Australia and southeastern Asia; Malay Archipelago. Also, **East India.**

East Pakistan, see **Bangladesh.**

east·ward (ēst′wərd) *adv. also,* **east·wards.** toward the east: *to travel eastward.* —*adj.* toward or in the east. —*n.* an eastward direction, point, or place.

eas·y (ē′zē) *adj.,* **eas·i·er, eas·i·est. 1.** needing little effort; not hard to do: *an easy job.* **2.** free from discomfort, trouble, or worry: *an easy life.* **3.** not demanding, harsh, or strict; lenient: *She is an easy teacher.* **4.** comfortable or restful: *This car has an easy ride.* **5.** not stiff, formal, or awkward: *He has an easy manner.* **6.** not hurried: *The boys hiked along at an easy pace.* —*adv. Informal.* easily.

to take it easy. *Informal.* **a.** to keep from too much effort or activity; relax. **b.** to stay calm.

easy chair, a comfortable chair, especially a padded armchair.

eas·y·go·ing (ē′zē gō′ing) *adj.* tending to be calm and unhurried; good-natured; relaxed.

eat (ēt) *v.,* **ate, eat·en, eat·ing.** —*v.t.* **1.** to take in through the mouth and swallow, especially to chew and swallow: *Tom ate three slices of cake.* **2.** to destroy or wear away gradually: *Rust has eaten away the surface of the metal lawn furniture.* **3.** to use up or waste: *Gambling quickly ate up his savings.* **4.** to make as if by eating: *The acid ate holes in the material. The termites ate their way through*

the log. —*v.i.* **1.** to take or eat food; have a meal: *Her family eats at six o'clock.* **2.** to destroy or wear away gradually, as by gnawing or corroding: *The acid ate into the copper plate.* **3.** to chew or bore: *The termites ate through the floor.* —**eat′er,** *n.*

eat·a·ble (ē′tə bəl) *adj.* fit to be eaten; edible. —*n. also,* **eatables.** something fit to be eaten; food.

eaves (ēvz) *n., pl.* the overhanging edge or edges of a sloping roof.

eaves·drop (ēvz′drop′) *v.i.,* **eaves·dropped, eaves·drop·ping.** to listen to the private conversation of others without their knowing it. —**eaves′·drop′per,** *n.*

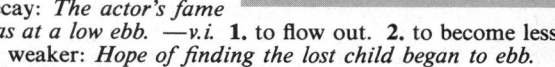

Eaves

ebb (eb) *n.* **1.** the flowing out of the tide from shore. **2.** a point or condition of decline or decay: *The actor's fame was at a low ebb.* —*v.i.* **1.** to flow out. **2.** to become less or weaker: *Hope of finding the lost child began to ebb.*

ebb tide, the tide that flows out from shore.

eb·on (eb′ən) *n., adj. Archaic.* another word for **ebony.**

eb·on·ite (eb′ə nīt′) *n.* a hard, black rubber treated with sulfur, used for plumbing, electrical equipment, and bowling balls.

eb·on·y (eb′ə nē) *n. pl.,* **eb·on·ies. 1.** a hard, black wood, used especially for piano keys, knife handles, and cabinets. **2.** the tree yielding this wood, found in Africa, Ceylon, and the East Indies. —*adj.* **1.** made of ebony. **2.** like ebony, especially in color.

e·bul·lient (i bul′yənt) *adj.* overflowing or bubbling over with excitement or enthusiasm: *The winner of the contest was ebullient.* —**e·bul′lience, e·bul′lien·cy,** *n.* —**e·bul′lient·ly,** *adv.*

ec·cen·tric (ek sen′trik) *adj.* **1.** not conforming to normal or usual practices or behavior; peculiar; odd: *The eccentric man always carried his parrot on his shoulder wherever he went.* **2.** *Mathematics.* not having the same center: *eccentric circles.* **3.** having its axis set off center: *an eccentric wheel.* —*n.* **1.** a person who is eccentric. **2.** a wheel set off center on a revolving shaft, used to change circular motion into an up-and-down or back-and-forth motion. —**ec·cen′tri·cal·ly,** *adv.*

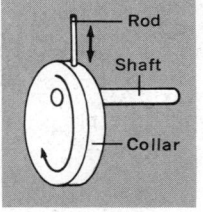

Eccentric *(def. 2)*

ec·cen·tric·i·ty (ek′sen tris′ə tē) *n. pl.,* **ec·cen·tric·i·ties. 1.** the state or quality of being eccentric. **2.** an act or trait that is unusual or odd; peculiarity. **3.** the amount or degree by which something is eccentric.

Ec·cle·si·as·tes (i klē′zē as′tēz) *n.* a book of the Old Testament, thought to have been written by King Solomon.

ec·cle·si·as·tic (i klē′zē as′tik) *n.* a clergyman. —*adj.* another word for **ecclesiastical.**

ec·cle·si·as·ti·cal (i klē′zē as′ti kəl) *adj.* of or relating

at; āpe; cär; end; mē; it; īce; hot; ōld; fôrk; wood; fōōl; oil; out; up; turn; sing; thin; this; hw in white; zh in treasure. The symbol ə stands for the sound of **a** in about, **e** in taken, **i** in pencil, **o** in lemon, and **u** in circus.

to the church or the clergy: *ecclesiastical books, ecclesiastical garments.* —**ec·cle′si·as′ti·cal·ly,** *adv.*

ech·e·lon (esh′ə lon′) *n.* **1.** a formation of soldiers, ships, or airplanes in a steplike arrangement. **2.** a particular level of command, authority, or responsibility: *the high echelon of a military organization, the lower echelons of a bureaucracy.* [French *échelon* a rung of a ladder.]

e·chid·na (i kid′nə) *n. pl.,* **e·chid·nas** or **e·chid·nae** (i kid′nē). any of a group of egg-laying anteaters native to Australia, Tasmania, and New Guinea, having thick, grayish-brown fur, yellow spines, and a long snout.

Echidna

e·chi·no·derm (i kī′nə durm′) *n.* any of a group of saltwater animals, such as the starfish and sea urchin, having a spiny skin and a body made up of equal parts that radiate from a central point.

Ech·o (ek′ō) *n. Greek Mythology.* a mountain nymph who was deprived by the goddess Hera of her power of speech, except to repeat the final words of others.

ech·o (ek′ō) *n. pl.,* **ech·oes. 1.** the repetition of a sound made by sending back sound waves from a surface that blocks them. **2.** any repetition or close imitation of something, such as the ideas or opinions of another. —*v.t.* **1.** to send back the sound of: *The cavern walls echoed his cries.* **2.** to repeat or closely imitate: *The students echoed the thoughts of their teacher.* —*v.i.* **1.** to send back an echo: *The corridor of the school echoed with voices and footsteps.* **2.** to be repeated by an echo: *His laughter echoed through the house.* [From *Echo.*]

é·clair (ā kler′) *n.* an oblong pastry shell filled with whipped cream or custard, and usually topped with chocolate icing.

é·clat (ā klä′) *n.* **1.** a brilliant or striking effect or success: *The guitarist performed with great éclat.* **2.** great applause or praise; acclaim: *The new play was received with éclat.*

ec·lec·tic (ek lek′tik) *adj.* taking what seems best from different sources: *an eclectic painter, an eclectic musical program.* —*n.* a person who uses an eclectic method or approach. —**ec·lec′ti·cal·ly,** *adv.*

ec·lec·ti·cism (ek lek′tə siz′əm) *n.* an eclectic method, system, or philosophy.

e·clipse (i klips′) *n.* a partial or total darkening or hiding of a planet, moon, or sun. In a solar eclipse the moon passes between the sun and the earth, partly or totally blocking the sun's rays and darkening certain areas of the earth, and causing the sun to be partially or totally hidden from those areas of the earth. In a lunar eclipse the earth moves between the sun and the moon, blocking the sun's rays and partially or totally darkening the moon. —*v.t.* **e·clipsed, e·clips·ing. 1.** to cause an eclipse of: *The moon eclipsed the sun.* **2.** to overshadow or dim; outshine; surpass: *His achievements eclipsed those of his brother.*

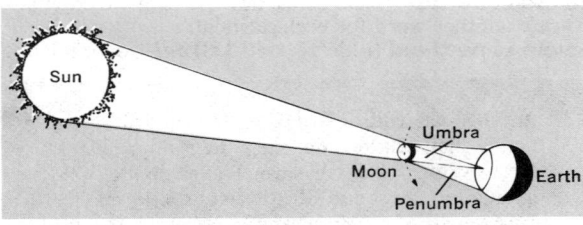
Solar eclipse

e·clip·tic (i klip′tik) *n.* the path that the sun appears to follow in a year around the celestial sphere. —*adj. also,* **e·clip·ti·cal** (i klip′ti kəl). of or relating to eclipses or to the ecliptic. —**e·clip′ti·cal·ly,** *adv.*

e·co·cide (ē′kə sīd′, ek′ə sīd′) *n.* the destruction of the earth's environment by pollution.

ec·o·log·i·cal (ek′ə loj′i kəl, ē′kə loj′i kəl) *adj.* of or relating to ecology. Also, **ec′o·log·ic.** —**ec′o·log′i·cal·ly,** *adv.*

e·col·o·gist (ē kol′ə jist) *n.* a student of or an expert in ecology.

e·col·o·gy (ē kol′ə jē) *n.* a branch of biology that deals with the relationships of living things to their surroundings and to each other.

ec·o·nom·ic (ek′ə nom′ik, ē′kə nom′ik) *adj.* **1.** of or relating to the science of economics: *economic theory.* **2.** of or relating to money matters or concerns; financial: *They sold the house because of economic considerations.*

ec·o·nom·i·cal (ek′ə nom′i kəl, ē′kə nom′i kəl) *adj.* careful or cautious in the use of money, goods, or other resources; frugal; thrifty: *Jim is very economical and always saves his money.* —**ec′o·nom′i·cal·ly,** *adv.*

ec·o·nom·ics (ek′ə nom′iks, ē′kə nom′iks) *n.,pl.* the science that deals with the production, distribution, and use of goods, money, natural resources, and services. ▲ used with a singular verb.

e·con·o·mist (i kon′ə mist) *n.* a student of or an expert in economics.

e·con·o·mize (i kon′ə mīz′) *v.,* **e·con·o·mized, e·con·o·miz·ing.** —*v.i.* to be careful or cautious in the use of money, goods, or other resources; be frugal and thrifty: *He economized and managed to save money toward a trip to Europe.* —*v.t.* to use carefully and wisely:

e·con·o·my (i kon′ə mē) *n. pl.,* **e·con·o·mies. 1.** a system, method, or result of managing the production, distribution, and use of money, goods, natural resources, and services: *That nation's economy is growing rapidly.* **2.** the careful or cautious use of money, goods, or other resources; thrift. [Latin *oeconomia* the management of a household.]

ec·ru (ek′rōō) *n.* a pale yellowish-brown color. —*adj.* having the color ecru.

ec·sta·sy (ek′stə sē) *n. pl.,* **ec·sta·sies.** a feeling or state of overwhelming joy or delight; rapture: *The children were in ecstasy at the thought of going to the circus.*

ec·stat·ic (ek stat′ik) *adj.* **1.** overwhelmed with joy or delight; enraptured: *Mary was ecstatic when she was told that she had won the contest.* **2.** of, resulting from, or causing ecstasy: *She had an ecstatic expression on her face.* —**ec·stat′i·cal·ly,** *adv.*

ec·to·derm (ek′tə durm′) *n.* the outermost of the three cell layers of an embryo in an early stage of its development. The ectoderm develops into the outer layer of skin, the nervous system, and the sense organs.

Ec·ua·dor (ek′wə dôr′) *n.* a country on the northwestern coast of South America. Capital, Quito. Area, 109,483 sq. mi. Pop. (1974), 6,500,845. —**Ec′ua·do′ri·an,** *adj., n.*

ec·u·men·i·cal (ek′yə men′i kəl) *adj.* **1.** including the entire world; worldwide; universal. **2.** of or relating to all Christian churches: *an ecumenical church.* **3.** promoting worldwide Christian unity: *an ecumenical movement.*

ec·ze·ma (ek′si mə, eg zē′mə) *n.* a skin disorder characterized by redness, itching, and scaly patches. It is often caused by an allergy. [Greek *ekzema,* from *ekzein* to boil over.]

-ed[1] *suffix* (used to form the past tense of regular verbs): *He walked to work last week.* [Old English *-de, -ede, -ode, -ade.*]

-ed² *suffix* **1.** (used to form the past participle of regular verbs): *He has walked to work every day this month.* **2.** (used to form adjectives from nouns): **a.** characterized by or having: *a blue-eyed baby.* **b.** having the characteristics of; like: *a prejudiced man, a dogged pursuit.* [Old English *-ed, -od, -ad.*]

ed. **1.** edition. **2.** editor. **3.** edited.

E·dam cheese (ē′dəm, ē′dam) a mild, yellow cheese, usually round and covered with red wax. [From *Edam*, a Dutch village where it was first made.]

ed·dy (ed′ē) *n. pl.*, **ed·dies.** a current of air or water moving against the main current, especially with a circular or whirling motion; small whirlwind or whirlpool. —*v.i.*, **ed·died, ed·dy·ing.** to move with a circular or whirling motion; whirl: *Smoke eddied from the chimney.*

Ed·dy, Mary Baker (ed′ē) 1821–1910, the founder of the Christian Science Church.

e·del·weiss (ād′əl vīs′) *n.* **1.** a flower having tiny yellow petals surrounded by white leaves. **2.** a small plant bearing this flower, found on high mountains in Europe and Asia.

e·de·ma (i dē′mə) *n. pl.*, **e·de·ma·ta** (i dē′mə tə). another word for **dropsy.**

E·den (ēd′ən) *n.* **1.** see **Garden of Eden.** **2.** a place of extreme delight or happiness; paradise.

edge (ej) *n.* **1.** a line or place where an object or area begins or ends; extreme or outermost border: *John sat on the edge of his chair. We walked down to the edge of the lake.* **2.** a thin,

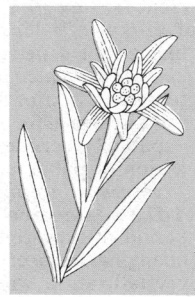

Edelweiss

cutting side of a blade, as of a knife or tool: *He cut himself on the knife's sharp edge.* **3.** strength or intensity: *Eating the crackers took the edge off his appetite.* **4.** *Informal.* a better position; advantage: *Our candidate has a slight edge on his opponent.* —*v.*, **edged, edg·ing.** —*v.t.* **1.** to furnish with a border; form a border on: *The seamstress edged the fabric with fringe.* **2.** to move slowly or gradually: *The workman edged the large crate across the floor.* —*v.i.* to move slowly or gradually: *He edged toward the door.*

on edge. very impatient, tense, or nervous: *The players were on edge as they waited for the game to begin.*

edge·wise (ej′wīz′) *adv.* **1.** with the edge forward. **2.** on or toward the edge. Also, **edge·ways** (ej′wāz′).

edg·ing (ej′ing) *n.* something that forms an edge or is joined to an edge; trimming.

edg·y (ej′ē) *adj.*, **edg·i·er, edg·i·est.** very impatient, tense, or nervous; on edge. —**edg′i·ness,** *n.*

ed·i·ble (ed′ə bəl) *adj.* that can be eaten; fit to eat: *These mushrooms are edible.* —*n. also,* **edibles.** something fit to eat; food. —**ed′i·ble·ness,** *n.*

e·dict (ē′dikt) *n.* an official command or order from a ruler or other person having authority.

ed·i·fi·ca·tion (ed′ə fi kā′shən) *n.* moral instruction or improvement: *The young man reads the classics for his own edification.*

ed·i·fice (ed′ə fis) *n.* a building, especially a large and impressive one.

ed·i·fy (ed′ə fī′) *v.t.*, **ed·i·fied, ed·i·fy·ing.** to instruct or improve, especially morally or spiritually: *That story edifies all who read it.*

Ed·in·burgh (ed′ən bur′ō) *n.* the capital of Scotland, in the east-central part of the country. Pop. (1971), 453,422.

Ed·i·son, Thomas Al·va (ed′i sən; al′və) 1847–1931, U. S. inventor.

ed·it (ed′it) *v.t.* **1.** to correct, improve, and otherwise prepare for publication: *She edited the manuscript of the textbook.* **2.** to review, cut, and arrange for presentation: *The student edited his film before showing it to the class.* **3.** to be in charge of preparing for publication: *Henry's father edits the town newspaper.*

e·di·tion (i dish′ən) *n.* **1.** the form in which a book is published: *That dictionary is now published in a two-volume edition.* **2.** the total number of copies of a publication printed from the same plates or type: *The first edition of the book sold quickly.* **3.** a single copy of such a publication: *Jim bought the morning edition of the newspaper.*

ed·i·tor (ed′ə tər) *n.* a person who edits.

ed·i·to·ri·al (ed′ə tôr′ē əl) *n.* an article in a newspaper or magazine, or a statement on television or radio, expressing the opinion or viewpoint of the editor, publisher, or owner on a particular topic. —*adj.* of or relating to an editor or an editorial: *editorial freedom, editorial responsibility.* —**ed′i·to′ri·al·ly,** *adv.*

ed·i·tor·ship (ed′ə tər ship′) *n.* the position, functions, or authority of an editor.

Ed·mon·ton (ed′mən tən) *n.* the capital and largest city of the province of Alberta, Canada. Pop. (1971), 434,116.

ed·u·ca·ble (ej′ə kə bəl) *adj.* able to be educated.

ed·u·cate (ej′ə kāt′) *v.t.*, **ed·u·cat·ed, ed·u·cat·ing.** **1.** to give knowledge or skill to; teach or train. **2.** to provide schooling for; send to school: *The cost of educating children is very high.*

ed·u·ca·tion (ej′ə kā′shən) *n.* **1.** the act or process of educating: *A person's education at college usually takes four years.* **2.** the knowledge or skill that a person gains by being educated: *a man of little education.* **3.** study of the problems and methods of teaching and learning: *His sister majored in education at college.*

ed·u·ca·tion·al (ej′ə kā′shən əl) *adj.* **1.** of or relating to education: *an educational institution, a person's educational background.* **2.** giving knowledge or skill; instructive: *an educational television program.* —**ed′u·ca′tion·al·ly,** *adv.*

ed·u·ca·tive (ej′ə kā′tiv) *adj.* **1.** that educates or tends to educate; educational. **2.** of or relating to education: *the educative process.*

ed·u·ca·tor (ej′ə kā′tər) *n.* **1.** a person whose profession is to educate others. **2.** a person who is an expert or authority in the field of education.

e·duce (i dōōs′, i dyōōs′) *v.t.*, **e·duced, e·duc·ing.** to bring out; draw forth: *The supervisor was able to educe good work from the men under him. He educed her real feelings from her expression rather than from her words.* —**e·duc′i·ble,** *adj.*

Ed·ward VII (ed′wərd) 1841–1910, the king of England from 1901 to 1910, son of Queen Victoria.

Edward VIII, 1894–1972, the King of England in 1936, who abdicated and received the title Duke of Windsor.

Ed·ward·i·an (ed wär′dē ən, ed wôr′dē ən) *adj.* relating to or characteristic of the reign of Edward VII: *Edwardian architecture, Edwardian fashions.*

-ee *suffix* (used to form nouns from verbs) **1.** a person to whom something is done or given: *payee.* **2.** a person who performs some action or is in some condition: *standee.*

at; āpe; cär; end; mē; it; īce; hot; ōld; fôrk; wood; fōōl; oil; out; up; turn; sing; thin; this; hw in white; zh in treasure. The symbol ə stands for the sound of a in about, e in taken, i in pencil, o in lemon, and u in circus.

E

307

eel (ēl) *n. pl.*, **eels** or **eel.** any of a group of fish having a long body with a smooth skin not covered by scales.

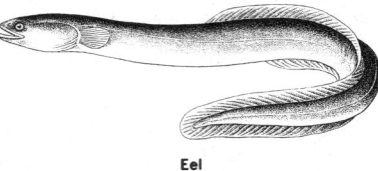

Eel

eel·grass (ēl′gras′) *n.* a grass that grows in shallow water and has branching stems with long, ribbonlike leaves, used by birds as a major source of food.

e'en (ēn) *adv. Archaic.* another word for **even.**

e'er (er) *adv. Archaic.* another word for **ever.**

-eer *suffix* **1.** (used to form nouns) **a.** a person who makes: *pamphleteer, profiteer.* **b.** a person who has to do with: *auctioneer, engineer.* **2.** (used to form verbs) to have to do with: *electioneer.*

ee·rie (ēr′ē) also, **ee·ry.** *adj.*, **ee·ri·er, ee·ri·est. 1.** strange and frightening; weird; uncanny: *The Halloween decorations gave an eerie look to the room.* **2.** nervously uneasy; fearful: *After seeing the horror movie, Phil had an eerie feeling.* —**ee′ri·ly,** *adv.* —**ee′ri·ness,** *n.*

ef-, the form of the prefix **ex-** before *f*, as in *efficient.*

ef·face (i fās′) *v.t.*, **ef·faced, ef·fac·ing.** to destroy by or as if by rubbing out; erase: *The name on the old sign has been effaced by the wind and rain. He tried to efface the bad memory.* —**ef·face′ment,** *n.* —**ef·fac′er,** *n.*

ef·fect (i fekt′) *n.* **1.** something brought about by a cause or agent; result: *His blindness was one of the effects of the accident.* **2.** the power or ability to influence or bring about a result: *The bad news had no effect on her.* **3.** the state or fact of being in force: *The club members wanted to put their plan into effect.* **4.** an impression made on the mind or senses: *This painter achieves dramatic effects by his use of color.* **5.** something used to make such an impression: *Tom is in charge of lighting effects for the play.* **6. effects.** property; possessions: *He quickly packed his personal effects and left the hotel.* ▲ See **affect** for usage note. —*v.t.* to bring about; produce as a result; cause: *Congress effected a program to provide health care for elderly people.*

for effect. in order to make an impression; for show.

in effect. in actual fact; in reality: *Mark is, in effect, the only good player on the team.*

to take effect. to begin to do or accomplish something; start to have results: *The pill should take effect in an hour.*

ef·fec·tive (i fek′tiv) *adj.* **1.** bringing about or able to bring about a desired effect: *Her argument was very effective because everyone now agrees with her.* **2.** in force or operation: *The new sales tax will not be effective until later this summer.* **3.** making a striking impression; impressive: *John is an effective speaker.* —**ef·fec′tive·ly,** *adv.* —**ef·fec′tive·ness,** *n.*

ef·fec·tu·al (i fek′chŏo əl) *adj.* bringing about or able to bring about a desired effect. —**ef·fec′tu·al·ly,** *adv.*

ef·fec·tu·ate (i fek′chŏo āt′) *v.t.*, **ef·fec·tu·at·ed, ef·fec·tu·at·ing.** to bring about or cause; accomplish.

ef·fem·i·na·cy (i fem′ə nə sē) *n.* the state or quality of being effeminate.

ef·fem·i·nate (i fem′ə nit) *adj.* (of a man or boy) having the appearance, behavior, or traits suitable to or usual in a woman; womanish; unmanly. —**ef·fem′i·nate·ly,** *adv.* —**ef·fem′i·nate·ness,** *n.*

ef·fer·ent (ef′ər ənt) *adj.* carrying away from a central organ or point: *efferent nerve fibers.*

ef·fer·vesce (ef′ər ves′) *v.i.*, **ef·fer·vesced, ef·fer·vesc·ing. 1.** to give off bubbles of gas, as carbonated water does. **2.** to be gay, bright, and full of life. —**ef·fer·ves·cence** (ef′ər ves′əns), *n.*

ef·fer·ves·cent (ef′ər ves′ənt) *adj.* **1.** giving off bubbles of gas; bubbling. **2.** gay, bright, and lively: *Sally was very effervescent at the party.*

ef·fete (e fēt′) *adj.* without strength or vigor; worn out; exhausted: *an effete and decadent civilization.* —**ef·fete′·ness,** *n.*

ef·fi·ca·cious (ef′i kā′shəs) *adj.* bringing about or able to bring about a desired effect; effective. —**ef′fi·ca′cious·ly,** *adv.*

ef·fi·ca·cy (ef′i kə sē) *n. pl.*, **ef·fi·ca·cies.** the power to bring about a desired effect; effectiveness.

ef·fi·cien·cy (i fish′ən sē) *n. pl.*, **ef·fi·cien·cies. 1.** the quality of being efficient. **2.** the ratio of the useful work done by a machine to the energy that is supplied to it.

ef·fi·cient (i fish′ənt) *adj.* bringing about or able to bring about a desired effect with as little effort or waste as possible; effective or competent: *This machine is very efficient. Tom is a capable and efficient worker.* —**ef·fi′·cient·ly,** *adv.*

ef·fi·gy (ef′i jē) *n. pl.*, **ef·fi·gies. 1.** a representation or likeness of a person, especially a sculptured image: *The citizens dedicated a bronze effigy of the general.* **2.** a crude representation of a disliked or hated person.

to burn in effigy or **to hang in effigy.** to burn or hang publicly a crude representation of someone as an expression of public contempt: *The angry citizens burned the governor in effigy.*

ef·flo·res·cence (ef′lə res′əns) *n.* **1.** the act, state, or period of flowering. **2.** *Chemistry.* the act or process of changing from crystals to a powder by loss of water of crystallization when exposed to air. **3.** any eruption or rash on the skin.

ef·fort (ef′ərt) *n.* **1.** the use of the strength of the body or the power of the mind to do something: *Climbing the stairs took much effort for the old man.* **2.** an attempt, especially a strong attempt: *Ruth made an effort to get to school on time.* **3.** the product or result of hard work: *This painting is the artist's first effort.*

ef·fort·less (ef′ərt lis) *adj.* showing or needing little or no effort; easy: *an effortless task.* —**ef′fort·less·ly,** *adv.* —**ef′fort·less·ness,** *n.*

ef·fron·ter·y (i frun′tər ē) *n.* shameless boldness or rudeness; insolence: *She had the effrontery to ask him a favor after she had insulted him.*

ef·ful·gence (i ful′jəns) *n.* great brightness; radiance or splendor.

ef·ful·gent (i ful′jənt) *adj.* bright; radiant.

ef·fu·sion (i fyŏo′zhən) *n.* **1.** the act of pouring out: *The doctor stopped the effusion of blood from the cut.* **2.** something that pours out. **3.** an unrestrained pouring forth of ideas, feelings, or words.

ef·fu·sive (i fyŏo′siv) *adj.* showing more feeling than is called for or desired; gushing: *Her effusive expression of thanks seemed insincere.* —**ef·fu′sive·ly,** *adv.* —**ef·fu′·sive·ness,** *n.*

eft (eft) *n.* a young newt that lives on land until it matures.

e.g., for example. [Abbreviation of Latin *exemplī grātiā.*]

egg¹ (eg) *n.* **1.** an oval or round reproductive body produced in the female sex organs of most animals, from which a young animal hatches: *The butterfly laid its eggs on the leaf.* **2.** a hard-shelled oval body produced by a bird, especially a hen, used as food: *Jerry went to the store to get a dozen eggs.* **3.** the contents of this: *She beat the egg and added milk.* **4.** the reproductive cell produced in the female sex organs of most animals; ovum. Also, **egg cell. 5.** *Slang.* a person; fellow: *Jack is a good egg.* [Old Norse *egg.*]

egg² (eg) *v.t.* to encourage to do some action; urge; incite: *His friends egged him on to play the trick.* [Old Norse *eggja.*]

egg·beat·er (eg′bē′tər) *n.* a kitchen utensil with rotary blades, used for beating eggs, whipping cream, and mixing cooking ingredients.

egg·nog (eg′nog′) *n.* a drink made of raw eggs mixed with milk or cream, sugar, and spices, and often containing an alcoholic beverage such as rum.

egg·plant (eg′plant′) *n.* **1.** the oval-shaped fruit of a bushy plant, usually blackish-purple in color, cooked and eaten as a vegetable. **2.** the plant bearing this fruit.

egg·shell (eg′shel′) *n.* **1.** the hard, thin shell of a bird's egg. **2.** a pale yellow, tan, or ivory color. —*adj.* **1.** having the color eggshell; pale yellow, tan, or ivory. **2.** thin and fragile: *an eggshell porcelain cup.*

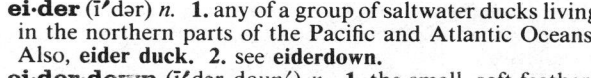

Eggplant

e·gis (ē′jis) another spelling of **aegis.**

eg·lan·tine (eg′lən tīn′) *n.* another word for **sweetbrier.**

e·go (ē′gō) *n. pl.,* **e·gos. 1.** a person's awareness of his or her needs and desires, and of everything else that makes him or her different and separate from others; a person's own distinct self. **2.** *Informal.* self-centeredness or conceit.

e·go·ism (ē′gō iz′əm) *n.* **1.** too much concern with one's own welfare and interests; selfishness or self-centeredness. **2.** conceit; egotism.

e·go·ist (ē′gō ist) *n.* **1.** a selfish or self-centered person. **2.** a conceited person; egotist.

e·go·is·tic (ē′gō is′tik) *adj.* relating to or characterized by egoism. Also, **egoistical.** —**e′go·is′ti·cal·ly,** *adv.*

e·go·tism (ē′gə tiz′əm) *n.* **1.** a very high opinion of oneself; conceit. **2.** a great tendency to talk or write about oneself, especially in a bragging or boastful manner. **3.** selfishness; egoism.

e·go·tist (ē′gə tist) *n.* **1.** a conceited, boastful person. **2.** a selfish or self-centered person; egoist.

e·go·tis·tic (ē′gə tis′tik) *adj.* relating to or characterized by egotism. Also, **egotistical.** —**e′go·tis′ti·cal·ly,** *adv.*

e·gre·gious (i grē′jəs) *adj.* openly or outrageously bad; flagrant: *He made an egregious error by lying to the judge in court.* —**e·gre′gious·ly,** *adv.* —**e·gre′gious·ness,** *n.*

e·gress (ē′gres) *n.* **1.** the act of going out. **2.** a place or means of going out; way out; exit.

e·gret (ē′grit) *n.* **1.** a large, white bird having tufts of long, lacy feathers. **2.** a feather of this bird.

E·gypt (ē′jipt) *n.* a country in northeastern Africa. Ancient Egypt was the center of one of the world's earliest and greatest civilizations. From 1958 to 1971 it was known as the **United Arab Republic.** Capital, Cairo. Area, approx. 386,000 sq. mi. Pop. (1971 est.), 34,130,000.

E·gyp·tian (i jip′shən) *n.* **1.** a person who was born or is living in Egypt. **2.** a person who lived in ancient Egypt. **3.** the language of the ancient Egyptians. —*adj.* of or relating to Egypt, its people, or their culture.

Egyptian cotton, a fine, silky cotton with long fibers, grown chiefly in Egypt.

eh (ā) *interj.* used to express surprise, doubt, or failure to hear what was said: *Eh, speak up please; I can't hear you.*

Egret

ei·der (ī′dər) *n.* **1.** any of a group of saltwater ducks living in the northern parts of the Pacific and Atlantic Oceans. Also, **eider duck. 2.** see **eiderdown.**

ei·der·down (ī′dər doun′) *n.* **1.** the small, soft feathers from the breast of the female eider, used to stuff pillows and quilts. **2.** a quilt filled with eiderdown.

eight (āt) *n.* **1.** the cardinal number that is one more than seven. **2.** a symbol representing this number, such as 8 or VIII. **3.** something having this many units or things, such as a playing card. —*adj.* numbering one more than seven.

eight·een (ā′tēn′) *n.* **1.** the cardinal number that is eight more than ten. **2.** a symbol representing this number, such as 18 or XVIII. **3.** something having this many units or things. —*adj.* numbering eight more than ten.

eight·eenth (ā′tēnth′) *adj.* **1.** (the ordinal of eighteen) next after the seventeenth. **2.** being one of eighteen equal parts. —*n.* **1.** something that is next after the seventeenth. **2.** one of eighteen equal parts; 1/18.

eight·fold (āt′fōld′) *adj.* **1.** eight times as great or numerous. **2.** having or consisting of eight parts. —*adv.* so as to be eight times greater or more numerous.

eighth (ātth) *adj.* **1.** (the ordinal of eight) next after the seventh. **2.** being one of eight equal parts. —*n.* **1.** something that is next after the seventh. **2.** one of eight equal parts; 1/8. **3.** *Music.* see **octave** *(defs. 1a, b, c).* —*adv.* in the eighth place.

eighth note *Music.* a note that is sounded for one-eighth as long as a whole note.

eight·i·eth (ā′tē ith) *adj.* **1.** (the ordinal of eighty) next after the seventy-ninth. **2.** being one of eighty equal parts. —*n.* **1.** something that is next after the seventy-ninth. **2.** one of eighty equal parts; 1/80.

eight·y (ā′tē) *n. pl.,* **eight·ies. 1.** the cardinal number that is eight times ten. **2.** a symbol representing this number, such as 80 or LXXX. —*adj.* numbering eight times ten.

Ein·stein, Albert (īn′stīn) 1879–1955, the physicist who developed the theory of relativity, born in Germany and later living in the United States.

ein·stein·i·um (īn stī′nē əm) *n.* a radioactive element produced artificially. Symbol: **Es** [From Albert *Einstein.*]

Eir·e (er′ə) *n.* see **Ireland, Republic of.**

Ei·sen·how·er, Dwight D. (ī′zən hou′ər; dwīt) 1890–1969, U. S. military and political leader, the thirty-fourth president of the United States, from 1953 to 1961.

ei·ther (ē′thər, ī′thər) *adj.* **1.** one or the other: *She didn't want either gift.* **2.** one and the other; each: *There were no houses on either side of the road.* —*pron.* one or the other: *Either is fine with me.* —*conj.* one or the other. ▲ used with *or* before the first of two or more possibilities: *Either be quiet or leave. He may telephone either now, tonight, or tomorrow.* —*adv.* any more so; also. ▲ used for emphasis after a negative: *He can't do this kind of work, and she can't either.*

e·jac·u·late (i jak′yə lāt′) *v.t.,* **e·jac·u·lat·ed, e·jac·u·lat·ing.** to utter suddenly and briefly; blurt out; exclaim. —**e·jac′u·la′tion,** *n.*

e·ject (i jekt′) *v.t.* to give off, force out, or throw out: *The rifle ejects empty cartridges automatically. The manager ejected the noisy customer from the store.* —**e·jec′tor,** *n.*

at; āpe; cär; end; mē; it; īce; hot; ōld; fôrk; wood; fōol; oil; out; up; turn; sing; thin; **this;** hw in white; zh in treasure. The symbol ə stands for the sound of **a** in about, **e** in taken, **i** in pencil, **o** in lemon, and **u** in circus.

e·jec·tion (i jek′shən) *n.* **1.** the act of ejecting or the state of being ejected. **2.** something ejected, such as lava from a volcano.

eke (ēk) *v.t.,* **eked, ek·ing. to eke out. 1.** to barely manage to make (a living): *He was able to eke out a living by selling used clothing.* **2.** to add to in order to make barely enough: *The old woman eked out her income by renting rooms to students.*

e·lab·o·rate (*adj.,* i lab′ər it; *v.,* i lab′ə rāt′) *adj.* **1.** worked out with great care and in great detail: *The scientist developed an elaborate theory concerning the origin of life.* **2.** highly detailed or ornamented; ornate: *She prefers fancy and elaborate furniture.* —*v.,* **e·lab·o·rat·ed, e·lab·o·rat·ing.** —*v.i.* to give greater detail or fuller treatment to something spoken or written; work out further: *The speaker was asked to elaborate on his last comment.* —*v.t.* to work out carefully and in greater detail: *The artist elaborated his sketch for the painting.* —**e·lab·o·rate·ly** (i lab′ər it lē), *adv.* —**e·lab′o·rate·ness,** *n.*

e·lab·o·ra·tion (i lab′ə rā′shən) *n.* **1.** the act of elaborating or the state of being elaborated. **2.** something added, as a detail: *The design is good, but it has too many elaborations.*

e·land (ē′lənd) *n.* a large antelope found in southern Africa, having humped shoulders and long, twisted horns.

e·lapse (i laps′) *v.i.,* **e·lapsed, e·laps·ing.** (of time) to slip by; pass: *Three years elapsed before he returned.*

e·las·tic (i las′tik) *adj.* **1.** capable of returning to its original size or shape after being stretched, twisted, or squeezed: *A rubber band is elastic.* **2.** capable of changing to fit new conditions; flexible; accommodating: *His schedule is very elastic, and he can change his plans at a moment's notice.* —*n.* **1.** a fabric made stretchable by having rubber threads or strands running through it. **2.** a rubber band. —**e·las′ti·cal·ly,** *adv.*

Eland

e·las·tic·i·ty (i las tis′ə tē, ē′las tis′ə tē) *n.* the state or quality of being elastic.

e·late (i lāt′) *v.t.,* **e·lat·ed, e·lat·ing.** to put in high spirits; make joyful or proud: *The good news elated us.*

e·lat·ed (i lā′tid) *adj.* in high spirits; filled with joy or pride. —**e·lat′ed·ly,** *adv.*

e·la·tion (i lā′shən) *n.* a feeling of joy or pride: *We were filled with elation at his good fortune.*

El·ba (el′bə) *n.* an Italian island between Italy and Corsica, the site of Napoleon Bonaparte's exile in 1814 and 1815.

El·be (el′bə) *n.* a river flowing from Czechoslovakia through Germany into the North Sea.

el·bow (el′bō) *n.* **1.** the joint between the lower arm and the upper arm. **2.** something having a bend like the elbow, such as a curved pipe. —*v.t.* **1.** to push with or as if with the elbows; shove aside: *The rude man elbowed her in order to pass.* **2.** to make or force (one's way) by pushing with or as if with the elbows. —*v.i.* to go forward by pushing with or as if with the elbows: *He elbowed through the crowd.*

elbow grease *Informal.* much energy or effort; hard work.

el·bow·room (el′bō rōōm′, el′bō room′) *n.* enough room, especially to move or work in.

El·brus, Mount (el′brōōs) the highest peak of Europe, in the southwestern Soviet Union. It is part of the Caucasus Mountains.

eld·er[1] (el′dər) *adj.* born earlier; older: *an elder sister.* —*n.* **1.** a person who is older. **2.** an older, influential member, as of a family or community: *The tribe's elders met to decide on important matters.* **3.** an officer in any of various churches. [Old English *eldra.*]

eld·er[2] (el′dər) *n.* any of a group of shrubs and small trees bearing red or purplish-black berries that can be eaten. Also, **elderberry.** [Old English *ellærn.*]

el·der·ber·ry (el′dər ber′ē) *n. pl.,* **el·der·ber·ries. 1.** the berry of the elder, used especially for making wines, jellies, and pies. **2.** see **elder**[2].

el·der·ly (el′dər lē) *adj.* past middle age; rather old.

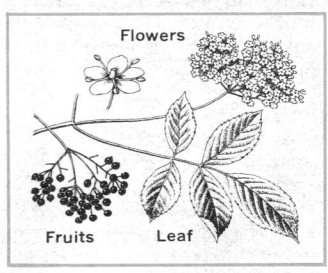

Flowers

Fruits   Leaf

Elder[2]

elder statesman, a retired statesman who advises government leaders.

eld·est (el′dist) *adj.* born first; oldest: *She is the eldest of three children.*

El Do·ra·do (el də rä′dō) *also,* **El·do·ra·do.** *n.* **1.** a legendary place in South America, sought by sixteenth-century Spanish explorers because they believed that it was full of gold and jewels. **2.** any place of fabulous wealth.

e·lect (i lekt′) *v.t.* **1.** to choose by voting: *The townspeople elected a new mayor.* **2.** to select or decide; choose: *Jack elected biology as his major subject in college.* —*adj.* elected to an office but not yet formally installed. ▲ used in combination after a noun: *senator-elect.* —*n.* **the elect. 1.** people who belong to a special group. **2.** people chosen by God for salvation.

e·lec·tion (i lek′shən) *n.* **1.** the act of electing or the state of being elected. **2.** the process of choosing a person or persons, especially for an office, by voting: *Did your father vote in the election last year?*

e·lec·tion·eer (i lek′shə nēr′) *v.i.* to work or campaign for the election of a candidate or political party.

e·lec·tive (i lek′tiv) *adj.* **1.** chosen or filled by vote: *an elective office.* **2.** open to choice; not required: *an elective course in school.* **3.** having the power or right to choose by vote: *an elective body.* —*n.* a subject or course that is not required and may be chosen by a student in high school or college: *Marsha chose the art course as an elective.*

e·lec·tor (i lek′tər) *n.* **1.** a person who has the right to vote in an election. **2.** a member of the U. S. electoral college. Before an election, a slate of electors is selected by each political party in each state and pledged to the party's candidate. Voters on election day cast their ballots for one of the presidential candidates, and thus for one of the slates of electors pledged to that candidate.

e·lec·tor·al (i lek′tər əl) *adj.* of or relating to an election or electors: *the electoral vote.*

electoral college, a group of representatives, called electors, chosen by vote in an election, who formally elect the President and Vice-President of the United States.

e·lec·tor·ate (i lek′tər it) *n.* all the persons who have the right to vote in an election.

e·lec·tric (i lek′trik) *adj.* **1.** of or relating to electricity. **2.** carrying or operated by electricity: *an electric iron, electric wires.* **3.** caused by electricity: *an electric shock.*

4. producing electricity: *an electric generator.* **5.** exciting; thrilling: *an electric sensation.*

e·lec·tri·cal (i lek′tri kəl) *adj.* **1.** another word for **electric** (*defs. 1–4*). **2.** dealing with electricity: *electrical engineering.* —**e·lec′tri·cal·ly,** *adv.*

electric eel, a long freshwater fish that resembles an eel and is able to give off strong electric shocks to protect itself and to catch its prey.

electric eye, a photoelectric cell used to open a door, to ring a bell, or to do similar tasks.

e·lec·tri·cian (i lek trish′ən) *n.* a person who designs, installs, or repairs electric wiring or equipment.

e·lec·tric·i·ty (i lek tris′ə tē) *n.* **1.** energy carried especially by electrons and protons and capable of driving motors and of producing light and heat. **2.** an electric current.

e·lec·tri·fi·ca·tion (i lek′trə fi kā′shən) *n.* the act of electrifying or the state of being electrified.

e·lec·tri·fy (i lek′trə fī′) *v.t.,* **e·lec·tri·fied, e·lec·tri·fy·ing. 1.** to charge with electricity: *The farmer electrified the fence around the cow pasture.* **2.** to equip for the use of electricity. **3.** to excite; thrill; startle: *The acrobat's daring feat electrified the crowd.*

electro- *combining form* of, relating to, or by means of electricity: *electromagnet, electrocute.*

e·lec·tro·car·di·o·gram (i lek′trō kär′dē ə gram′) *n.* a record of the heart's actions as it beats, made on a graph by an electrocardiograph.

e·lec·tro·car·di·o·graph (i lek′trō kär′dē ə graf′) *n.* an instrument that receives and records electrical impulses sent out by the heart as it beats.

e·lec·tro·cute (i lek′trə kyōōt′) *v.t.,* **e·lec·tro·cut·ed, e·lec·tro·cut·ing.** to execute or kill by electricity. —**e·lec′-tro·cu′tion,** *n.*

e·lec·trode (i lek′trōd) *n.* part of an electric circuit through which electrons enter or leave a gas or liquid solution.

e·lec·trol·y·sis (i lek trol′ə sis) *n.* **1.** the breaking down of a liquified or dissolved substance into its component parts by passage of an electric current through the substance. **2.** the permanent removal of unwanted body hair by destroying the root cells with an electrified needle.

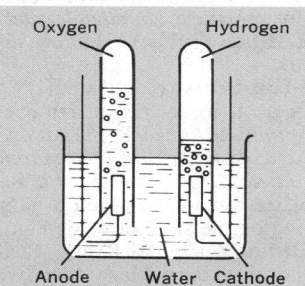

Electrolysis of water

e·lec·tro·lyte (i lek′-trə līt′) *n.* **1.** any nonmetallic substance that will conduct an electric current, especially a liquid solution. **2.** a chemical compound that, when liquified or in solution, will separate into ions and conduct an electric current.

e·lec·tro·lyze (i lek′trə līz′) *v.t.,* **e·lec·tro·lyzed, e·lec·tro·lyz·ing.** to break down by electrolysis.

e·lec·tro·mag·net (i lek′trō mag′nit) *n.* a piece of iron with insulated wire wound around it, that becomes a magnet when an electric current is passed through the wire.

e·lec·tro·mag·net·ic (i lek′trō mag net′ik) *adj.* **1.** of or produced by an electromagnet. **2.** of or relating to electromagnetism.

electromagnetic wave, a wave of energy that is made up of electric and magnetic fields and that can travel through empty space at around 186,000 miles per second. Radio waves, light rays, and X rays are electromagnetic waves.

e·lec·tro·mag·net·ism (i lek′trō mag′nə tiz′əm) *n.* **1.** magnetism produced by a current of electricity. **2.** a branch of physics that studies the relation between magnetism and electricity.

e·lec·tro·mo·tive (i lek′trə mō′tiv) *adj.* **1.** producing a flow of electricity. **2.** of or relating to electromotive force.

electromotive force 1. a force that causes an electric current to flow in a circuit. **2.** the amount of energy derived from an electric source.

e·lec·tron (i lek′tron) *n.* a subatomic particle that carries the smallest negative electric charge.

electron gun, a device that sends out and focuses a beam of electrons. An electron gun at one end of a television picture tube sends out a beam of electrons to the picture screen.

e·lec·tron·ic (i lek tron′ik) *adj.* of or relating to electrons or electronics. —**e·lec′tron′i·cal·ly,** *adv.*

e·lec·tron·ics (i lek tron′iks) *n., pl.* a branch of physics dealing with the motion of electrons and other charged particles in a vacuum and in gases. The study of electronics has led to the development of the radio, television, and many other inventions.

electron microscope, a device that makes extremely small things visible by means of a beam of electrons rather than a beam of light. It has much higher power than an ordinary microscope.

electron tube, a sealed container of glass or metal in which electrons move through a vacuum or gas. An electron tube produces, amplifies, or regulates electrical signals.

electron volt, the amount of energy gained by an electron when it is accelerated through a potential difference of one volt.

e·lec·tro·plate (i lek′trə plāt′) *v.t.,* **e·lec·tro·plat·ed, e·lec·tro·plat·ing.** to apply a metal coating to the surface of (an object) by means of electrolysis.

e·lec·tro·scope (i lek′trə skōp′) *n.* an instrument used to discover and measure electric charges.

e·lec·tro·ther·a·py (i lek′trō ther′ə pē) *n.* the use of electricity in the treatment of various mental or physical disorders.

e·lec·tro·type (i lek′trə tīp′) *n.* **1.** a metal plate used in printing, made by the electroplating process that duplicates the original plate. **2.** a print made from such a plate. *v.t.,* **e·lec·tro·typed, e·lec·tro·typ·ing.** to make such a plate or plates of.

el·e·gance (el′ə gəns) *n.* the state or quality of being elegant.

el·e·gant (el′ə gənt) *adj.* **1.** showing richness and good taste; luxurious: *The woman wore an elegant mink coat.* **2.** showing grace, dignity, and refinement in manners, taste, or style; polished: *Those people are very elegant.* —**el′e·gant·ly,** *adv.*

el·e·gi·ac (el′ə jī′ak, i lē′jē ak) *adj.* of, relating to, or suitable for an elegy.

el·e·gize (el′ə jīz′) *v.,* **el·e·gized, el·e·giz·ing.** —*v.t.* to mourn in an elegy. —*v.i.* to write an elegy.

el·e·gy (el′ə jē) *n. pl.,* **el·e·gies.** a mournful or sad poem or musical work, especially one written to mourn someone who has died.

at; āpe; cär; end; mē; it; īce; hot; ōld; fôrk; wood; fōōl; oil; out; up; turn; sing; thin; **this**; hw in white; zh in treasure. The symbol ə stands for the sound of **a** in about, **e** in taken, **i** in pencil, **o** in lemon, and **u** in circus.

el·e·ment (el′ə mənt) *n.* **1.** a substance, such as iron, carbon, oxygen, or hydrogen, that cannot be changed into a simpler substance by ordinary chemical means. Elements consist entirely of atoms having the same atomic number. **2.** a basic part from which something is made or formed: *Jerry learned the elements of arithmetic.* **3.** the natural or most comfortable environment: *The ocean is the whale's element.* **4.** *Mathematics.* a member of a set. **5. the elements.** the forces of the atmosphere, such as rain, wind, or snow.

el·e·men·tal (el′ə ment′əl) *adj.* **1.** of or relating to a force of nature: *The elemental power of the hurricane caused much destruction.* **2.** like a force of nature; natural, primitive, or unrestrained: *elemental feelings.* **3.** being a basic part of anything: *an elemental substance.*

el·e·men·ta·ry (el′ə men′tər ē, el′ə men′trē) *adj.* of, relating to, or dealing with the simple basic parts or beginnings of something: *Carl's knowledge of science is very elementary. Tom is studying elementary French.*

elementary particle, see **subatomic particle.**

elementary school, a school that includes the first six or eight grades, and sometimes kindergarten. Also **grade school, grammar school.**

el·e·phant (el′ə fənt) *n. pl.,* **el·e·phants** or **el·e·phant.** the largest and most powerful land animal, native to the tropical regions of Africa and Asia, having a massive head and body, thick skin, a long, muscular trunk, and a pair of ivory tusks.

African elephant   Indian elephant

el·e·phan·tine (el′ə fan′tin, el′ə fan′tīn) *adj.* **1.** like an elephant in size, strength, or movement. **2.** of or relating to an elephant.

el·e·vate (el′ə vāt′) *v.t.,* **el·e·vat·ed, el·e·vat·ing. 1.** to lift up; raise: *The mechanic elevated the car so that he could repair the brakes.* **2.** to raise or improve the mental or moral level of: *The minister's inspiring sermon elevated the congregation.* **3.** to raise in rank or position: *Tom was elevated from clerk to manager.*

el·e·va·tion (el′ə vā′shən) *n.* **1.** the act of elevating or the state of being elevated. **2.** something elevated, such as a raised place or surface. **3.** height above the earth's surface or above sea level.

● In language, **elevation** means the changing of the meaning of a word from something bad or neutral to something good. Elevation, which is also called *amelioration,* is one of the basic ways in which our language is constantly changing. Although a word itself is neither bad nor good, the meaning of a word can be whatever people choose it to be. The meaning of words such as *knight,* which originally meant "boy" or "servant," and *squire,* which originally meant "shield-bearer," was changed by elevation after the institution of chivalry in the Middle Ages. This change was due to the higher status that a knight or squire had in the eyes of society. In modern England, a knight is a man who has been honored by being given a title and a squire is a country gentleman or landowner. The names of certain religious groups have also undergone elevation. Both the names *Methodist* and *Quaker* were originally used contemptuously. As these groups have become accepted by society, the names for them have taken on a neutral quality.

el·e·va·tor (el′ə vā′tər) *n.* **1.** a car, platform, or cage and the machinery for raising or lowering it, used for carrying people and things from one level to another, especially from one floor to another in a building. **2.** a building used for handling and storing grain or other crops. **3.** one of two movable flat pieces attached to the tail of an airplane. When the elevators are lowered, the tail of the plane rises and the nose drops.

el·ev·en (i lev′ən) *n.* **1.** the cardinal number that is one more than ten. **2.** a symbol representing this number, such as 11 or XI. **3.** something having this many units or things, such as a football or soccer team. —*adj.* numbering one more than ten.

el·ev·enth (i lev′ənth) *adj.* **1.** (the ordinal of eleven) next after the tenth. **2.** being one of eleven equal parts. —*n.* **1.** something that is next after the tenth. **2.** one of eleven equal parts; 1/11.

eleventh hour, the last possible moment, just before it is too late: *The strike was prevented at the eleventh hour.*

elf (elf) *n. pl.,* **elves.** a small, often mischievous fairy or sprite having magical powers.

elf·in (el′fin) *adj.* of or like an elf; impish; mischievous: *an elfin grin.*

elf·ish (el′fish) *adj.* of or like an elf; elfin. —**elf′ish·ly,** *adv.* —**elf′ish·ness,** *n.*

El Gre·co (el grek′ō) 1541?–1614, Spanish painter; born in Crete.

e·lic·it (i lis′it) *v.t.* to bring out or draw forth: *The teacher finally elicited the right answer from the student.*

▲ **Elicit** and **illicit** are pronounced alike, but they have different meanings. **Elicit** is a verb that means to bring out: *Her greeting elicited no reply from the stranger.* **Illicit** is an adjective that means illegal: *A smuggler brings goods into a country by illicit means.*

el·i·gi·bil·i·ty (el′i jə bil′ə tē) *n.* the state or quality of being eligible.

el·i·gi·ble (el′i jə bəl) *adj.* **1.** qualified or meeting the requirements for something: *A person under 35 is not eligible to run for the Senate.* **2.** desirable or suitable, especially for marriage: *an eligible bachelor.* —**el′i·gi·bly,** *adv.*

E·li·jah (i lī′jə) Hebrew prophet of the ninth century B.C.

e·lim·i·nate (i lim′ə nāt′) *v.t.,* **e·lim·i·nat·ed, e·lim·i·nat·ing. 1.** to get rid of; remove: *The President promised to eliminate hunger in the nation.* **2.** to leave out of consideration; disregard: *In their search for a new home, they eliminated all houses without a backyard.*

e·lim·i·na·tion (i lim′ə nā′shən) *n.* the act of eliminating or the state of being eliminated.

El·i·ot (el′ē ət, el′yət) **1. George.** 1819–1880, English novelist; born Mary Ann Evans. **2. T(homas) S(tearns).** 1888–1965, English poet and critic; born in the United States.

E·li·sha (i lī′shə) Hebrew prophet of the ninth century B.C. He was the successor of Elijah.

e·li·sion (i lizh′ən) *n.* the leaving out or slurring over of a vowel or a syllable in pronunciation, such as the leaving out of the *ha* sound of *has* in *She's already gone home.*

e·lite (i lēt′, ā lēt′) *also,* **é·lite.** *n.* **1.** the best or finest members, as of a society or social group. **2.** a size of type for typewriters.

e·lit·ist (i lēt′ist, ā lēt′ist) *n.* **1.** a person who is a member of an elite. **2.** a person who regards himself or herself as a member of an elite.

e·lix·ir (i lik′sər) *n.* **1.** a substance that alchemists in former times believed could extend life forever and change base metals, such as iron and lead, into gold. **2.** a sweetened alcoholic solution containing medicine. **3.** a universal remedy; cure-all.

E·liz·a·beth (i liz′ə bəth) *n.* a city in northeastern New Jersey. Pop. (1970), 112,654.

Elizabeth I, 1533–1603, the queen of England from 1558 to 1603; daughter of Henry VIII and Anne Boleyn.

Elizabeth II, 1926—, the queen of Great Britain, since 1952.

E·liz·a·be·than (i liz′ə bē′thən, i liz′ə beth′ən) *adj.* of or relating to Queen Elizabeth I or the time in which she lived. —*n.* an English person of this time, especially a writer.

elk (elk) *n. pl.,* **elk** or **elks**. **1.** a large deer of the mountain regions of western North America, having a coat that is mainly fawn colored. The male has antlers measuring more than 5 feet across. Also, **wapiti. 2.** any of several other deer of northern Europe and Asia.

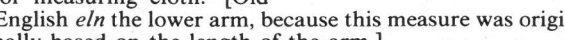

Elk

ell¹ (el) *n.* **1.** the letter L. **2.** something shaped like an L, such as an addition to the main part of a building.

ell² (el) *n.* an old measure of length ranging from 27 to 45 inches, used especially for measuring cloth. [Old English *eln* the lower arm, because this measure was originally based on the length of the arm.]

el·lipse (i lips′) *n.* a closed curve resembling an oval, but having both ends alike. It consists of a set of points whose distances from two fixed points add up to a fixed sum.

el·lip·sis (i lip′sis) *n. pl.,* **el·lip·ses** (i lip′sēz). **1.** the leaving out of a word or words strictly required by grammatical rules to complete the construction of a sentence, but not necessary for the understanding of its meaning. For example, *He arrived sooner than expected* instead of *He arrived sooner than he had been expected to arrive,* is an ellipsis. **2.** a mark such as (. . ., * * *, or —) used to show that something has been left out in writing or printing.

el·lip·ti·cal (i lip′ti kəl) *adj.* **1.** of or shaped like an ellipse. **2.** of or relating to ellipsis; with a word or words left out. Also, **el·lip·tic** (i lip′tik). —**el·lip′ti·cal·ly,** *adv.*

El·lis Island (el′is) an island in New York Bay, formerly a reception center for immigrants.

elm (elm) *n.* **1.** a tall, hardy tree, often grown for ornament or shade. **2.** the hard, heavy wood of this tree.

el·o·cu·tion (el′ə-kyōō′shən) *n.* **1.** the art of public speaking or reading. **2.** a manner of speaking or reading in public.

Elm leaves and flowers

e·lon·gate (i lông′gāt) *v.,* **e·lon·gat·ed, e·lon·gat·ing.** —*v.t.* to make longer; stretch; lengthen. —*v.i.* to become longer or stretched out. —*adj.* long and thin; lengthened. —**e′lon·ga′tion,** *n.*

e·lope (i lōp′) *v.i.,* **e·loped, e·lop·ing.** to run away secretly to get married. —**e·lope′ment,** *n.*

el·o·quence (el′ə kwəns) *n.* **1.** language that is expressive and effective: *The speech was full of eloquence and wit.* **2.** the ability to use language effectively: *Winston Churchill's eloquence was well-known.* **3.** the quality of being expressive and effective: *The eloquence of his plea aroused the jury's sympathy.*

el·o·quent (el′ə kwənt) *adj.* having or showing elo-

quence: *an eloquent orator, an eloquent plea.* —**el′o·quent·ly,** *adv.*

El Pas·o (el pas′ō) a city in western Texas, on the Rio Grande River. Pop. (1970), 322,261.

El Sal·va·dor (el sal′və dôr′) a country in western Central America. Capital, San Salvador. Area, 8260 sq. mi. Pop. (1971), 3,541,010. Also, **Salvador.**

else (els) *adj.* **1.** other; different: *I mistook him for someone else.* **2.** additional; more; further: *If anyone else comes, we won't have enough chairs.* —*adv.* **1.** in another time, place, or manner; instead: *Where else did you go?* **2.** under other circumstances; if not; otherwise: *Dress warmly, or else you'll catch cold.*

else·where (els′hwer′, els′wer′) *adv.* in, at, or to another place; somewhere else: *You'll have to look elsewhere for that information.*

e·lu·ci·date (i lōō′sə dāt′) *v.t.,* **e·lu·ci·dat·ed, e·lu·ci·dat·ing.** to make clear; explain: *The debater elucidated his point by giving several examples.* —**e·lu′ci·da′tion,** *n.*

e·lude (i lōōd′) *v.t.,* **e·lud·ed, e·lud·ing. 1.** to avoid or escape, as by cleverness or trickery; evade: *The bandit eluded the police.* **2.** to be beyond the memory or understanding of: *The answer to the riddle eluded him.*

e·lu·sion (i lōō′zhən) *n.* the act of eluding; evasion.

e·lu·sive (i lōō′siv) *adj.* **1.** hard to explain or understand: *an elusive idea.* **2.** hard to catch or follow: *an elusive criminal.* Also, **e·lu·so·ry** (i lōō′sər ē). —**e·lu′sive·ly,** *adv.* —**e·lu′sive·ness,** *n.*

el·ver (el′vər) *n.* a young eel.

elves (elvz) the plural of **elf.**

E·ly·sian (i lizh′ən, i liz′ē ən) *adj.* **1.** of or relating to Elysium. **2.** blissful; happy.

E·ly·sium (i lizh′əm, i liz′ē əm) *n.* **1.** *Greek Mythology.* a happy land where heroes and virtuous people lived after death. Also, **Elysian Fields. 2.** any place of perfect happiness; paradise.

'em (əm) *pron. Informal.* another word for **them.**

em-, the form of the prefix **en-** used before *b, p,* and sometimes *m,* as in *embroider, empower.*

e·ma·ci·ate (i mā′shē āt′) *v.t.,* **e·ma·ci·at·ed, e·ma·ci·at·ing.** to cause to become abnormally thin; cause to lose much weight or flesh: *The long illness emaciated him.* —**e·ma′ci·a′tion,** *n.*

em·a·nate (em′ə nāt′) *v.i.,* **em·a·nat·ed, em·a·nat·ing.** to come forth; arise; originate: *The smoke emanated from the chimney.* —**em′a·na′tion,** *n.*

e·man·ci·pate (i man′sə pāt′) *v.t.,* **e·man·ci·pat·ed, e·man·ci·pat·ing.** to free from control or restraint; liberate: *to emancipate a slave.* [Latin *ēmancipātus,* going back to *ex* away + *manus* hand + *capere* to take. In ancient Rome, a father would take his son by the hand and then let go to show that the son was released from his father's control.] —**e·man′ci·pa′tion,** *n.* —**e·man′ci·pa′tor,** *n.*

Emancipation Proclamation, a proclamation by President Abraham Lincoln on January 1, 1863, that freed all slaves in the territory still at war with the Union.

e·mas·cu·late (*v.,* i mas′kyə lāt′; *adj.,* i mas′kyə lit, i mas′kyə lāt′) *v.t.,* **e·mas·cu·lat·ed, e·mas·cu·lat·ing. 1.** to remove the sex glands of (a male); castrate. **2.** to deprive of strength, force, or vigor; weaken. —*adj.* de-

at; āpe; cär; end; mē; it; īce; hot; ōld; fôrk; wood; fōōl; oil; out; up; turn; sing; thin; this; hw in white; zh in treasure. The symbol ə stands for the sound of **a** in about, **e** in taken, **i** in pencil, **o** in lemon, and **u** in circus.

prived of strength, force, or vigor. —e·mas′cu·la′tion, n.

em·balm (em bäm′) v.t. to treat (a dead body) with certain chemicals to temporarily keep it from decaying. —em·balm′er, n.

em·bank (em bangk′) v.t. to protect or enclose with an embankment, dike, or similar structure.

em·bank·ment (em bangk′mənt) n. 1. a bank of earth, stones, or other materials, used to support a roadbed or to hold back water. 2. the act of embanking.

em·bar·go (em bär′gō) n. pl., em·bar·goes. 1. an order by a government preventing merchant ships from entering or leaving its ports. 2. a restriction put on trade by law, especially upon the import, export, or sale of certain goods: *an embargo on the sale of arms*

Embankment

to warring countries. 3. any restriction or prohibition. —v.t., em·bar·goed, em·bar·go·ing. to put an embargo on.

em·bark (em bärk′) v.i. 1. to go aboard a ship for a trip: *The passengers embarked at San Francisco.* 2. to begin or set out, as on an adventure: *The explorers embarked upon a dangerous expedition.* —v.t. to put or take on board a ship. —em′bar·ka′tion, n.

em·bar·rass (em bar′əs) v.t. 1. to cause to feel uncomfortable or ashamed: *Her foolish mistake embarrassed her.* 2. to make difficult; hinder; impede.

em·bar·rass·ing (em bar′ə sing) adj. that embarrasses: *an embarrassing situation.* —em·bar′rass·ing·ly, adv.

em·bar·rass·ment (em bar′əs mənt) n. 1. the act of embarrassing or the state of being embarrassed. 2. something that embarrasses.

em·bas·sy (em′bə sē) n. pl., em·bas·sies. 1. the official home and office of an ambassador in a foreign country. 2. an ambassador and his staff: *The embassy gave a party for the visiting statesmen.* 3. the position or duties of an ambassador.

em·bat·tled (em bat′əld) adj. 1. armed and ready for battle: *The embattled troops awaited the outbreak of war.* 2. fortified against battle: *an embattled fortress.*

em·bed (em bed′) also, im·bed. v.t., em·bed·ded, em·bed·ding. 1. to set or enclose in surrounding matter: *The workmen embedded the pole in cement. The arrow was embedded in the tree.* 2. to place or plant firmly, as in the mind: *The idea was embedded in her memory.*

em·bel·lish (em bel′ish) v.t. 1. to make beautiful by adding ornament; decorate; adorn: *The jeweler embellished the case with pearls and rubies.* 2. to make (a story) more interesting by adding interesting or fanciful details. —em·bel′lish·ment, n.

em·ber (em′bər) n. 1. a piece of wood or coal glowing in the ashes of a fire. 2. embers. the glowing remains of a fire.

em·bez·zle (em bez′əl) v.t., em·bez·zled, em·bez·zling. to steal (money entrusted to one's care): *The bank official embezzled thousands of dollars.* —em·bez′zle·ment, n. —em·bez′zler, n.

em·bit·ter (em bit′ər) v.t. to make bitter or resentful: *Mr. Wallace's repeated business failures embittered him.*

em·bla·zon (em blā′zən) v.t. 1. to adorn or decorate, as with bright colors or the symbols of heraldry: *to emblazon a shield with a coat of arms.* 2. to praise; celebrate: *Achilles' deeds were emblazoned by the poet Homer.*

em·blem (em′bləm) n. an object or figure that identifies

or represents something: *The soldier wore the emblem of his regiment. The crown is an emblem of monarchy.*

em·blem·at·ic (em′blə mat′ik) adj. of, relating to, or being an emblem; symbolic: *A gold medal is emblematic of first place in the Olympic games.* Also, **emblematical.**

em·bod·i·ment (em bod′ē mənt) n. 1. the act of embodying or the state of being embodied. 2. a person or thing that embodies something: *Satan is the embodiment of evil.*

em·bod·y (em bod′ē) v.t., em·bod·ied, em·bod·y·ing. 1. to give concrete or visible form to: *The statue embodies the sculptor's idea of beauty.* 2. to collect into or make part of an organized whole; incorporate: *The report embodied the experiments of ten scientists.*

em·bold·en (em bōld′ən) v.t. to make bold or bolder; encourage.

em·bo·lism (em′bə liz′əm) n. the blockage of a blood vessel by material carried in the blood, such as a blood clot or a mass of fat.

em·bo·lus (em′bə ləs) n. pl., em·bo·li (em′bə lī′). a blood clot, mass of fat, or other material that causes a blockage of a blood vessel.

em·bos·om (em booz′əm) v.t. 1. to take to one's heart; embrace. 2. to surround and protect; shelter.

em·boss (em bôs′) v.t. 1. to decorate or cover (a surface) with a design that is raised: *Her stationery was embossed with her initials.* 2. to raise (a design) on a surface: *The printer embossed her return address on the envelope.*

em·bow·er (em bou′ər) v.t. to shelter in a bower.

em·brace (em brās′) v., em·braced, em·brac·ing. —v.t. 1. to take or hold in the arms as a sign of love or affection; hug: *Susan embraced her mother before she left.* 2. to take up as one's own; adopt: *Andrew embraced medicine as his career.* 3. to take willingly: *to embrace an opportunity.* 4. to include; contain: *Botany embraces the study of all plant life.* —v.i. to hug one another: *The children embraced before they parted.* —n. the act of holding in the arms; hug: *The child welcomed his mother's embrace.*

em·bra·sure (em brā′zhər) n. an opening in a wall through which a gun may be fired. The sides usually spread outward to permit the gun to be swung from side to side.

em·broi·der (em broi′dər) v.t. 1. to decorate with a design in needlework: *Jane embroidered napkins for Christmas presents.* 2. to make (a design) in needlework: *The store embroidered her initials on the new towels.* 3. to make (a story) more interesting by adding details. —v.i. to do embroidery.

em·broi·der·y (em broi′dər ē) n. pl., em·broi·der·ies. 1. the act or art of decorating with raised designs done in needlework. 2. an embroidered design or work: *The embroidery on her dress is beautiful.*

em·broil (em broil′) v.t. 1. to involve in conflict or difficulty: *He tried to embroil his friend in his quarrel.* 2. to throw into confusion or disorder: *The bus strike embroiled the whole city.*

em·bry·o (em′brē ō′) n. pl., em·bry·os. 1. an organism in the early stages of its development, after fertilization and before hatching or birth. The human embryo is called a fetus after the first eight weeks of development. 2. an undeveloped plant within a seed. 3. the beginning stage or form of anything: *It was still an embryo of an idea.* —adj. another word for **embryonic.**

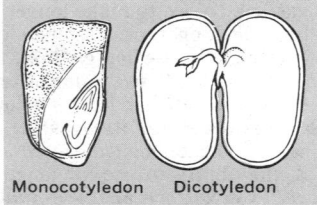

Monocotyledon Dicotyledon

Embryos of seeds

em·bry·ol·o·gist (em′brē ol′ə jist) *n.* a person who specializes in embryology.

em·bry·ol·o·gy (em′brē ol′ə jē) *n.* the branch of biology dealing with the formation and development of embryos.

em·bry·on·ic (em′brē on′ik) *adj.* of, relating to, or like an embryo: *embryonic development, the embryonic stages of a program.*

em·cee (em′sē′) *Informal. n.* a master of ceremonies. —*v.t., v.i.* to act as master of ceremonies.

e·mend (i mend′) *v.t.* to remove errors from or make changes in; correct: *The editors emended the text before it was published.*

e·men·da·tion (ē′mən dā′shən) *n.* 1. the act of emending. 2. an alteration or correction.

em·er·ald (em′ər əld) *n.* 1. a bright green precious stone. 2. a bright green color. —*adj.* having the color emerald; bright green.

Emerald Isle, another name for **Ireland.**

e·merge (i murj′) *v.i.,* **e·merged, e·merg·ing.** 1. to come into view: *Ten people emerged from the elevator.* 2. to come into being or notice: *New facts emerged from the investigation.* 3. to rise or come out, as from a difficult situation: *He emerged from the accident unharmed.*

e·mer·gence (i mur′jəns) *n.* the act or process of emerging: *This season saw the emergence of a new football star.*

e·mer·gen·cy (i mur′jən sē) *n. pl.,* **e·mer·gen·cies.** a situation or happening that requires immediate action: *The police acted quickly in the traffic emergency.* —*adj.* for use in an emergency: *an emergency exit, emergency funds.*

e·mer·gent (i mur′jənt) *adj.* coming into view or being: *the emergent nations of the world.*

e·mer·i·tus (i mer′i təs) *adj.* retired from service, usually because of age, while keeping rank and title: *professor emeritus.* —*n. pl.,* **e·mer·i·ti** (i mer′i tī′). a person who is emeritus.

Em·er·son, Ralph Waldo (em′ər sən) 1803–1882, U.S. essayist, poet, and philosopher.

em·er·y (em′ər ē) *n.* a hard black or brown mixture of minerals, used chiefly in powdered form for grinding and polishing.

emery board, a piece of cardboard coated with powdered emery, used in filing the fingernails.

e·met·ic (i met′ik) *n.* a medicine that causes vomiting. —*adj.* causing vomiting: *an emetic drug.*

em·i·grant (em′ə grənt) *n.* a person who leaves one place or country to live in another: *His ancestors were emigrants from Scotland.* —*adj.* leaving one place or country to live in another.

▲ **Emigrant** and **immigrant** are sometimes confused. An **emigrant** is a person who leaves his country to live in another country. An **immigrant** is a person who enters a new country to live there.

em·i·grate (em′ə grāt′) *v.i.,* **em·i·grat·ed, em·i·grat·ing.** to leave one place or country to live in another: *Albert Einstein emigrated from Germany to the United States.*

em·i·gra·tion (em′ə grā′shən) *n.* 1. the act or process of emigrating: *The population of Ireland has decreased because of emigration.* 2. emigrants as a group: *Small emigrations left this country periodically over the years.*

em·i·gré (em′i grā′) *also,* **é·mi·gré.** *n.* a person who leaves one country or place to live in another, usually for political reasons. [French *émigré.*]

em·i·nence (em′ə nəns) *n.* 1. high rank or standing; position above all others: *The scientist achieved eminence in his field.* 2. a high place on the earth's surface: *The architect built the house on an eminence to take advantage*

of the view. 3. **Eminence.** a title or form of address used in speaking or referring to a cardinal of the Roman Catholic Church. ▲ usually preceded by *His* or *Your.*

em·i·nent (em′ə nənt) *adj.* above all others, as in rank, power, or achievement; distinguished: *an eminent writer, an eminent accomplishment.* —**em′i·nent·ly,** *adv.*

eminent domain, the power or right of a government to take privately owned land for public use after paying the owner.

e·mir (ə mēr′) *n.* 1. a chief, prince, or military leader in certain Arab or Muslim countries. 2. a descendant of Muhammad. 3. formerly, any of certain high Turkish officials.

em·is·sar·y (em′ə ser′ē) *n. pl.,* **em·is·sar·ies.** an agent, as of a government, sent on a mission: *The nation's emissaries to the international conference were met at the airport by the press.*

e·mis·sion (i mish′ən) *n.* 1. the act or process of emitting. 2. something that is emitted: *light, heat, and other emissions from the sun.*

e·mis·sive (i mis′iv) *adj.* that emits; emitting.

e·mit (i mit′) *v.t.,* **e·mit·ted, e·mit·ting.** 1. to send forth or give off; discharge: *Boiling water emits steam. Fireflies emit light but not heat.* 2. to utter: *He was in severe pain, but he did not emit a sound.*

Em·man·u·el (i man′yōō əl) another spelling of **Immanuel.**

e·mol·lient (i mol′yənt) *adj.* soothing and softening, especially to the skin. —*n.* something that softens and soothes: *Lanolin is an emollient for the skin.*

e·mote (i mōt′) *v.i.,* **e·mot·ed, e·mot·ing.** to show emotion, especially in an exaggerated or affected way.

e·mo·tion (i mō′shən) *n.* 1. a strong feeling: *Richard read the poem with emotion.* 2. any feeling, as love, hate, happiness, or sorrow: *The actress was able to show many emotions convincingly.*

e·mo·tion·al (i mō′shən əl) *adj.* 1. of, relating to, or showing emotion: *an emotional quarrel, an emotional outburst.* 2. easily influenced by emotion: *an emotional person.* 3. appealing to or arousing emotion: *The lawyer made an emotional plea to the jury.* —**e·mo′tion·al·ly,** *adv.*

e·mo·tion·al·ism (i mō′shən əl iz′əm) *n.* 1. a tendency to show or be affected by emotion too easily. 2. an appeal to the emotions: *The speech was full of emotionalism.*

e·mo·tive (i mō′tiv) *adj.* 1. showing, causing, or appealing to emotion. 2. of or relating to emotion.

em·pan·el (em pan′əl) another spelling of **impanel.**

em·pa·thize (em′pə thīz′) *v.i.,* **em·pa·thized, em·pa·thiz·ing.** to experience empathy: *The newspaper reporter was able to empathize with the farm workers.*

em·pa·thy (em′pə thē) *n.* a sharing of another's feelings or state of mind without actually going through the same experiences.

em·per·or (em′pər ər) *n.* the male ruler of an empire.

em·pha·sis (em′fə sis) *n. pl.,* **em·pha·ses** (em′fə sēz′). 1. special importance given to something: *Too little emphasis was placed on the safety regulations.* 2. something that is given special importance: *Faith was the emphasis of the sermon.* 3. vocal stress given to a particular syllable, word, or phrase.

E

at; āpe; cär; end; mē; it; īce; hot; ōld; fôrk; wood; fōōl; oil; out; up; turn; sing; thin; **this**; hw in white; zh in treasure. The symbol ə stands for the sound of a in about, e in taken, i in pencil, o in lemon, and u in circus.

em·pha·size (em′fə sīz′) *v.t.*, **em·pha·sized, em·pha·siz- ing.** to give emphasis to; stress: *His speech emphasized the need for conservation of wildlife.*

em·phat·ic (em fat′ik) *adj.* **1.** spoken or done with em- phasis: *The senator issued an emphatic denial of the news- paper story.* **2.** forceful; insistent: *He remained emphatic on that point.* **3.** striking; definite: *The mayor suffered an emphatic defeat in the last election.* **—em·phat′i·cal·ly,** *adv.*

em·phy·se·ma (em′fə sē′mə) *n.* a disease that hinders breathing, characterized by enlargement of the air sacs in the lungs.

em·pire (em′pīr) *n.* **1.** a group of countries or territories ruled or controlled by the government of one country. **2.** a country or group of countries or territories ruled by an emperor or empress. **3.** absolute power or authority. **4.** a large territory or business controlled by one person or a group of people: *The millionaire had built up a vast real estate empire.*

em·pir·ic (em pir′ik) *n.* a person whose knowledge is based entirely on practical experience, experiments, or what can actually be seen. *—adj.* another word for **empiri- cal.**

em·pir·i·cal (em pir′i kəl) *adj.* based on practical ex- perience, experiments, or what can actually be seen: *The results of the experiments were empirical proof of the scien- tist's theories.* **—em·pir′i·cal·ly,** *adv.*

em·pir·i·cism (em pir′ə siz′əm) *n.* **1.** a method or prac- tice based on practical experience, experiments, or what can actually be seen. **2.** a theory in philosophy that all knowledge is based on experience gained through the senses.

em·pir·i·cist (em pir′ə sist) *n.* a person who practices or supports empiricism.

em·place·ment (em plās′mənt) *n.* a place or position prepared for heavy guns.

em·ploy (em ploi′) *v.t.* **1.** to give work to (someone) for pay; hire: *The store employed extra workers at Christmas.* **2.** to make use of: *The gardener employed a shovel, a hoe, and a spade in his work.* **3.** to take up or fill; occupy: *His hobby employs much of his time.* *—n.* the state or condi- tion of being employed: *The agent was in the employ of a foreign country.* **—em·ploy′a·ble,** *adj.*

em·ploy·ee (em ploi′ē, em′ploi ē′) *also,* **em·ploy·e.** *n.* a person who works for a person or business for pay.

em·ploy·er (em ploi′ər) *n.* a person or business that employs a person or a group of people for pay.

em·ploy·ment (em ploi′mənt) *n.* **1.** the act of employ- ing or the state of being employed. **2.** work that a person does; job: *It was hard for him to find employment this summer.*

em·po·ri·um (em pôr′ē əm) *n. pl.,* **em·po·ri·ums** or **em- po·ri·a** (em pôr′ē ə). **1.** a large store selling many differ- ent kinds of things. **2.** a principal center of trade or com- merce.

em·pow·er (em pou′ər) *v.t.* **1.** to give power or authority to; authorize: *The ambassador was empowered to sign the treaty.* **2.** to make possible; enable; permit: *Scientific ad- vances have empowered man to explore space.*

em·press (em′pris) *n. pl.,* **em·press·es.** **1.** the wife or widow of an emperor. **2.** a woman who rules an empire.

emp·ty (emp′tē) *adj.,* **emp·ti·er, emp·ti·est.** **1.** having nothing in it; lacking what is usually inside: *an empty glass, an empty room.* **2.** lacking force or meaning; hollow: *an empty promise, an empty threat.* *—v.,* **emp·tied, emp·ty- ing.** *—v.t.* **1.** to take out the contents of; make empty: *to empty a wastebasket.* **2.** to take out (the contents of some- thing): *Empty the water out of the bathtub.* *—v.i.* **1.** to become empty: *The theater emptied when the movie ended.*

2. to pour or flow out; discharge: *That river empties into the sea.* *—n. pl.,* **emp·ties.** *Informal.* something that is empty, such as a container or bottle. **—emp′ti·ly,** *adv.* **—emp′ti·ness,** *n.*

emp·ty-hand·ed (emp′tē han′did) *adj.* **1.** with nothing in the hands. **2.** with nothing gotten or gained: *The union representatives came away from the negotiations empty- handed.*

empty set *Mathematics.* a set that has no members. The set of even numbers between 8 and 10 is an empty set.

em·pyr·e·al (em pir′ē əl, em′pə rē′əl) *adj.* of or relat- ing to the empyrean; celestial.

em·py·re·an (em′pə rē′ən) *n.* **1.** the highest heaven in ancient and medieval astronomy. **2.** the visible heavens; sky. *—adj.* another word for **empyreal.**

e·mu (ē′myōō) *n.* a bird of Australia, related to the os- trich. The emu cannot fly, but it can run as fast as forty miles per hour.

Emu

em·u·late (em′yə lāt′) *v.t.,* **em·u·lat·ed, em·u·lat- ing.** to try to equal or go beyond: *The younger play- ers emulated the team's star player.* **—em′u·la′tor,** *n.*

em·u·la·tion (em′yə lā′- shən) *n.* the effort or desire to equal or go beyond some- one.

em·u·lous (em′yə ləs) *adj.* eager to equal or go beyond; competitive. **—em′u·lous·ly,** *adv.* **—em′u·lous·ness,** *n.*

e·mul·si·fy (i mul′sə fī′) *v.t.,* **e·mul·si·fied, e·mul·si·fy- ing.** to make into an emulsion. **—e·mul′si·fi·ca′tion,** *n.* **—e·mul′si·fi′er,** *n.*

e·mul·sion (i mul′shən) *n.* **1.** a mixture made up of very small droplets of one liquid suspended, rather than dis- solved, in another liquid. **2.** a coating on photographic film, plates, or paper that is sensitive to light.

en- *prefix* **1.** (used to form verbs from nouns) **a.** to put in, into, or on: *encase, enthrone.* **b.** to cover or surround with: *encircle, enshroud.* **2.** (used to form verbs from ad- jectives and nouns) to cause to be or be like; make: *enable, enslave.*

-en[1] *suffix* **1.** (used to form verbs from adjectives) to cause to be or become: *sharpen, madden, harden.* **2.** (used to form verbs from nouns) to cause or come to have: *heighten, strengthen, lengthen.* [Old English *-nian.*]

-en[2] *suffix* (used to form adjectives from nouns) made of or resembling: *silken, wooden, golden.* [Old English *-en* made of.]

-en[3] *suffix* used in the past participles of certain verbs: *risen, written.* [Old English *-en.*]

-en[4] *suffix* used in the plural of some nouns: *children, brethren, oxen.* [Old English *-an.*]

en·a·ble (i nā′bəl) *v.t.,* **en·a·bled, en·a·bling.** to give enough power, ability, or opportunity to; make able: *Extra study enabled him to pass the test.*

en·act (i nakt′) *v.t.* **1.** to make into law: *Congress enacted a bill on education this year.* **2.** to act out on stage; per- form: *Sandra enacted the part of the queen in this year's class play.*

en·act·ment (i nakt′mənt) *n.* **1.** a making into law: *the enactment of a bill in Congress.* **2.** something that is enacted.

e·nam·el (i nam′əl) *n.* **1.** a hard, glossy substance used to decorate or protect a surface, such as metal or pottery, to which it is fused. **2.** paint that dries to form a hard, glossy coating. **3.** the hard, glossy substance that is the

outer covering of a tooth. —*v. t.*, **e·nam·eled, e·nam·el·ing;**
also, British, **e·nam·elled, e·nam·el·ling.** to cover with
enamel or any hard, glossy coating.

e·nam·el·ware (i nam′əl wer′) *n.* objects coated with
enamel, such as kitchenware or dinnerware.

en·am·ored (en am′ərd) *adj.* taken by love; charmed;
captivated: *The enamored knight would perform any feat
to protect his lady.*

> **to be enamored of.** to be in love with: *He was enamored
> of the actress.*

en·camp (en kamp′) *v. i.* to settle in a camp; make camp:
The scouts encamped in the valley. —*v. t.* to place in a
camp: *The soldiers were encamped near the river.*

en·camp·ment (en kamp′mənt) *n.* **1.** a place occupied
by a camp; camp. **2.** the act of encamping or the state of
being encamped.

en·case (en kās′) *also,* **in·case.** *v. t.,* **en·cased, en·cas·ing.**
to enclose in or as if in a case: *The jewels were encased in
a glass box. His broken leg was encased in a plaster cast.*

-ence *suffix* (used to form nouns from adjectives ending
in *-ent*) the action, quality, state, or condition of being:
violence, existence, independence, absence.

en·ceph·a·li·tis (en sef′ə lī′tis) *n.* an inflammation of
the brain.

en·ceph·a·lon (en sef′ə lon′) *n.* the brain.

en·chain (en chān′) *v. t.* to bind with or as if with chains.

en·chant (en chant′) *v. t.* **1.** to cast a spell on; bewitch:
The witch had enchanted the handsome prince. **2.** to charm
or delight greatly: *Everyone was enchanted by the child's
performance in the play.* —**en·chant′er,** *n.*

en·chant·ing (en chan′ting) *adj.* very charming or
delightful: *The children's ballet was enchanting.* —**en·
chant′ing·ly,** *adv.*

en·chant·ment (en chant′mənt) *n.* **1.** the act of enchanting or the state of being enchanted. **2.** something that
enchants.

en·chan·tress (en chan′tris) *n. pl.,* **en·chan·tress·es.**
1. a woman who casts spells; witch; sorceress. **2.** any
charming or fascinating woman.

en·chase (en chās′) *v. t.,* **en·chased, en·chas·ing.** **1.** to
decorate (a surface), as with engraved work. **2.** to engrave
or carve (a design) on a surface: *The jeweler enchased the
family crest on the silver box.*

en·chi·la·da (en′chi lä′də) *n.* a Mexican dish made of
a tortilla filled with meat or cheese, served with a spicy
tomato or chili sauce. [Spanish *enchilada.*]

en·cir·cle (en sur′kəl) *v. t.,* **en·cir·cled, en·cir·cling.**
1. to form a circle around; surround: *The soldiers encircled
the enemy camp.* **2.** to move in a circle around: *Many
satellites encircle the earth today.* —**en·cir′cle·ment,** *n.*

en·clave (en′klāv) *n.* **1.** a territory surrounded by the
territory of another country: *Vatican City is an enclave.*
2. a district inhabited by a minority group: *a Chinese enclave in an American city.*

en·close (en klōz′) *also,* **in·close.** *v. t.,* **en·closed, en·clos·
ing.** **1.** to close in on all sides; surround: *The field was
enclosed by trees.* **2.** to include with a letter or parcel: *She
enclosed a picture of the children with her letter.* **3.** to
contain: *The letter enclosed a check.*

en·clo·sure (en klō′zhər) *also,* **in·clo·sure.** *n.* **1.** the act
of enclosing or the state of being enclosed. **2.** something
that is enclosed. **3.** something that encloses, such as a fence
or wall.

en·code (en kōd′) *v. t.,* **en·cod·ed, en·cod·ing.** to put into
code: *The general encoded his message before sending it.*
—**en·cod′er,** *n.*

en·co·mi·um (en kō′mē əm) *n. pl.,* **en·co·mi·ums** or **en·
co·mi·a** (en kō′mē ə). high praise expressed in a formal
way; eulogy.

en·com·pass (en kum′pəs, en kom′pəs) *v. t.* **1.** to form
a circle around; encircle; surround: *A moat encompassed
the castle.* **2.** to contain or include: *The autobiography
encompasses every aspect of the writer's life.*

en·core (äng′kôr, än′kôr) *interj.* again. ▲ used as a call
to a performer or performers to perform again. —*n.*
1. a call made by an audience to a performer or performers
to perform again. **2.** something that is performed in response to such a call: *The pianist played three encores.*
—*v. t.,* **en·cored, en·cor·ing.** to call for an encore from.

en·coun·ter (en koun′tər) *v. t.* **1.** to meet unexpectedly;
come upon: *Tom encountered his old piano teacher at the
concert.* **2.** to meet in conflict; confront in battle: *The
soldiers encountered the enemy and defeated them.*
3. to be faced with; experience: *The club chairman encountered little resistance to his plan.* —*n.* **1.** an unexpected
or casual meeting: *Susan's encounter with the movie star
left her breathless.* **2.** a meeting of enemies in conflict;
skirmish: *Repeated encounters with the enemy had tired the
troops.*

en·cour·age (en kur′ij) *v. t.,* **en·cour·aged, en·cour·ag·
ing.** **1.** to inspire with courage, hope, or confidence;
hearten: *The good news encouraged her.* **2.** to give support
to; help; promote: *The bank lowered its interest rate on
loans to encourage borrowing.*

en·cour·age·ment (en kur′ij mənt) *n.* **1.** the act of
encouraging or the state of being encouraged. **2.** something that encourages: *His father's faith in him was an
encouragement to him.*

en·cour·ag·ing (en kur′i jing) *adj.* giving courage,
hope, or confidence: *encouraging news, an encouraging
smile.* —**en·cour′ag·ing·ly,** *adv.*

en·croach (en krōch′) *v. i.* **1.** to intrude on the property
or rights of another; trespass: *He felt that his neighbors
encroached on his privacy.* **2.** to go beyond usual or natural
limits: *Every spring the river encroached farther on the land.*
—**en·croach′ment,** *n.*

en·crust (en krust′) *also,* **in·crust.** *v. t.* **1.** to cover with
a crust or hard coating: *Dried mud encrusted his shoes.*
2. to cover or decorate, as with jewels: *The sword handle
was encrusted with diamonds and gold.*

en·crus·ta·tion (en′krus tā′shən) *also,* **in·crus·ta·tion.**
n. **1.** the act of encrusting or the state of being encrusted.
2. something that encrusts: *An encrustation of gold, pearls,
and jewels covered the jewelry box.*

en·cum·ber (en kum′bər) *also,* **in·cum·ber.** *v. t.* **1.** to
hinder the motion or action of, as with a burden: *The bulky
packages encumbered her.* **2.** to weigh down or burden,
as with cares or duties: *Financial worries encumbered him.*
3. to block or obstruct, as with obstacles: *Discarded furniture encumbered the hallway.*

en·cum·brance (en kum′brəns) *also,* **in·cum·brance.** *n.*
something that hinders; burden.

-ency *suffix* (used to form nouns from adjectives ending
in *-ent*) the act, fact, quality, or state of being: *dependency,
fluency.*

en·cyc·li·cal (en sik′li kəl) *n.* a letter written by a pope
to his bishops about important matters relating to the
church.

en·cy·clo·pe·di·a (en sī′klə pē′dē ə) *also,* **en·cy·clo·pae-**

---

at; āpe; cär; end; mē; it; īce; hot; ōld; fôrk;
wood; fōōl; oil; out; up; turn; sing; thin; this;
hw in white; zh in treasure. The symbol ə
stands for the sound of a in about, e in taken,
i in pencil, o in lemon, and u in circus.

di·a. *n.* a reference work in one or more volumes, containing information on all branches of knowledge or on a special subject, usually in articles arranged alphabetically.

en·cy·clo·pe·dic (en sī′klə pē′dik) *also,* **en·cy·clo·pae·dic.** *adj.* covering a broad range of subjects or information: *His knowledge of history is encyclopedic.*

end (end) *n.* **1.** the point or part at which something that has length starts or stops: *They each held an end of the rope.* **2.** the part that concludes; final part: *Jane liked the end of the book better than the beginning.* **3.** the point at which something is over or no longer exists: *The end of the war is in sight.* **4.** the outermost limit; boundary: *Tom lived at the end of town.* **5.** the result of an action; purpose; goal: *The end does not always justify the means.* **6.** death or destruction: *The pilot came to a sudden and violent end when the plane crashed.* **7.** *also,* **ends.** a part left over; remnant; fragment: *The store had put its carpet ends on sale.* **8.** *Football.* either of the two players or positions on the left or right end of the line. —*v.t.* **1.** to bring to an end; conclude; finish: *The club chairman ended the meeting.* **2.** to be or form the end of: *The clown act ended each circus performance.* —*v.i.* **1.** to come to an end: *The play ended at ten o'clock.* **2.** to reach a final state or condition: *He will probably end as the winner of the race.*

at loose ends. in an unsettled or confused state.

on end. a. in an upright position. **b.** without stopping; in succession: *The committee worked for days on end.*

to end up. to be in a final position or state; become: *He will end up wealthy someday.*

en·dan·ger (en dān′jər) *v.t.* to put in danger; imperil: *He endangered his own life to save the drowning child.*

en·dear (en dēr′) *v.t.* to make dear or beloved: *The puppy endeared itself to the children.* —**en·dear′ing·ly,** *adv.*

en·dear·ment (en dēr′mənt) *n.* **1.** the act of endearing or the state of being endeared. **2.** an action or word that expresses love or affection: *The child whispered endearments to her doll.*

en·deav·or (en dev′ər) *also, British,* **en·deav·our.** *v.i.* to make an effort; strive; try: *The senator endeavored to gain support for his bill.* —*n.* a serious attempt to do or accomplish something; effort.

en·dem·ic (en dem′ik) *adj.* occurring in or restricted to a particular place or group of people: *Malaria is an endemic disease.* —*n.* an endemic disease.

end·ing (en′ding) *n.* a final part; conclusion: *The story has a sad ending.*

en·dive (en′dīv) *n.* **1.** creamy white or curly green leaves of a plant related to chicory, usually eaten raw in salads. **2.** the plant bearing these leaves.

end·less (end′lis) *adj.* **1.** having no limit or end; boundless: *endless space.* **2.** never stopping; constant; incessant: *endless repetition, endless interruptions.* **3.** having the ends joined so as to form a circle or loop; continuous: *an endless chain.* —**end′less·ly,** *adv.* —**end′less·ness,** *n.*

end·most (end′mōst′) *adj.* at or nearest to the end; farthest: *We sat in the endmost seats in the row.*

en·do·car·di·um (en′dō kär′dē əm) *n. pl.,* **en·do·car·di·a** (en′dō kär′dē ə). a thin membrane lining the heart.

en·do·crine (en′də krin, en′də krīn′) *adj.* **1.** producing secretions that pass directly into the bloodstream or lymph. **2.** of or relating to an endocrine gland or its secretion. —*n.* **1.** see **endocrine gland. 2.** a secretion of an endocrine gland; hormone.

endocrine gland, any of various glands

Endive leaves and root

without ducts, such as the thyroid and pituitary, that secrete hormones directly into the bloodstream or lymph; ductless gland.

en·do·cri·nol·o·gy (en′də kri nol′ə jē, en′də krī nol′ə jē) *n.* a branch of medicine dealing with the endocrine glands and their secretions.

en·do·derm (en′də durm′) *n.* the innermost of the three cell layers of an embryo in an early stage of its development. The endoderm develops into the lining of the stomach, intestines, and lungs, and into certain internal organs, such as the liver and pancreas.

en·do·plasm (en′də plaz′əm) *n.* a grainy inner portion of the cytoplasm of a cell, containing the nucleus.

en·dorse (en dôrs′) *also,* **in·dorse.** *v.t.,* **en·dorsed, en·dors·ing. 1.** to sign one's name on the back of (a check, note, or similar document): *She had to endorse the check before the bank would cash it.* **2.** to give support to; approve: *The senator enthusiastically endorsed the President's statement.* —**en·dors′er,** *n.*

en·dorse·ment (en dôrs′mənt) *also,* **in·dorse·ment.** *n.* **1.** the act of endorsing. **2.** writing, as a signature or comments, on the back of a check, note, or similar document. **3.** approval; support.

en·do·skel·e·ton (en′dō skel′ə tən) *n.* the inner skeleton which supports the body of certain animals. Fish, dogs, humans, and other animals with backbones all have endoskeletons.

en·do·sperm (en′də spurm′) *n.* food material in a plant seed that surrounds and gives nourishment to the embryo.

en·dow (en dou′) *v.t.* **1.** to give money or property to as a source of income: *Several wealthy families endowed the new library.* **2.** to provide with an ability, talent, or quality: *The dancer was endowed with natural grace.*

en·dow·ment (en dou′mənt) *n.* **1.** money or property given to provide a source of income, as for a church or college: *That college has a large endowment.* **2.** talent, ability, or quality: *He has a keen mind, a sharp wit, and other natural endowments.* **3.** the act of endowing.

en·dur·a·ble (en door′ə bəl, en dyoor′ə bəl) *adj.* that can be endured; bearable: *The pain was constant, but endurable.* —**en·dur′a·bly,** *adv.*

en·dur·ance (en door′əns, en dyoor′əns) *n.* **1.** the power of bearing up under hardships or difficulties, such as pain, stress, or fatigue: *A long-distance runner must have a great amount of endurance.* **2.** the power of lasting; continued existence: *the endurance of a custom through the ages.*

en·dure (en door′, en dyoor′) *v.,* **en·dured, en·dur·ing.** —*v.t.* **1.** to undergo without yielding; stand; bear: *She endured the hike through the forest without complaint.* **2.** to put up with; tolerate: *She can't endure his rudeness.* —*v.i.* **1.** to continue to be; last: *Though they were apart, their friendship endured.* **2.** to suffer without yielding; hold out: *The family endured throughout all its financial troubles.*

end·ways (end′wāz′) *adv.* **1.** with the end forward. **2.** on end; upright. **3.** lengthwise. **4.** end to end. Also, **end·wise** (end′wīz′).

end zone, the area at either end of a football field between the goal line and the final boundary of the field. It is ten yards long.

en·e·ma (en′ə mə) *n.* **1.** a forcing of liquid into the rectum, usually to help cleanse the bowels. **2.** the liquid used for this.

en·e·my (en′ə mē) *n. pl.,* **en·e·mies. 1.** a person who has hatred for, or wishes to cause harm to, another: *The dictator's harsh policies made him many enemies.* **2.** a hostile nation or military force: *The enemy attacked at dawn.* **3.** a person belonging to such a nation or force. **4.** something dangerous or harmful: *Disease is an enemy of mankind.* —*adj.* of or relating to a hostile nation or military force: *enemy troops, an enemy camp.*

en·er·get·ic (en′ər jet′ik) *adj.* having, using, or showing energy; vigorous; forceful: *an energetic worker.* —**en′er·get′i·cal·ly,** *adv.*

en·er·gize (en′ər jīz′) *v.t.,* **en·er·gized, en·er·giz·ing.** to give energy or power to. —**en′er·giz′er,** *n.*

en·er·gy (en′ər jē) *n. pl.,* **en·er·gies. 1.** the ability or tendency to act with energy: *The child had more energy than his parents.* **2.** *also,* **energies.** power used in action or work: *It took a lot of energy to move the furniture. He put all his energies into helping her.* **3.** *Physics.* the capacity for doing work. Energy takes various different forms, such as radiant energy, electrical energy, chemical energy, and mechanical energy.

en·er·vate (en′ər vāt′) *v.t.,* **en·er·vat·ed, en·er·vat·ing.** to lessen the strength or vitality of; weaken: *Frequent attacks of malaria enervated him.* —**en′er·va′tion,** *n.*

en·fee·ble (en fē′bəl) *v.t.,* **en·fee·bled, en·fee·bling.** to make feeble; weaken: *The long illness enfeebled the old man.* —**en·fee′ble·ment,** *n.*

en·fold (en fōld′) *also,* **in·fold.** *v.t.* **1.** to wrap in folds; envelop: *The saleswoman enfolded the fragile cups in tissue paper.* **2.** to embrace; clasp: *The child enfolded the puppy in his arms.*

en·force (en fôrs′) *v.t.,* **en·forced, en·forc·ing. 1.** to make certain that (a law or rule) is observed; force obedience to: *The police in that town enforce the laws strictly.* **2.** to obtain by force: *Monitors in the halls enforce silence.* **3.** to give force to; strengthen: *The lawyer enforced his case with new evidence.* —**en·force′a·ble,** *adj.*

en·force·ment (en fôrs′mənt) *n.* the act or process of enforcing: *The club president believed in strict enforcement of the rules.*

en·fran·chise (en fran′chīz) *v.t.,* **en·fran·chised, en·fran·chis·ing. 1.** to give the right to vote to: *Women were not enfranchised in the United States until the twentieth century.* **2.** to set free; liberate: *to enfranchise slaves.* —**en·fran′chise·ment,** *n.*

eng. 1. engine. **2.** engineer; engineering.

Eng. 1. England. **2.** English.

en·gage (en gāj′) *v.,* **en·gaged, en·gag·ing.** —*v.t.* **1.** to hire (a person) or secure (services): *The company engaged two new employees. The builder engaged the professional skills of an electrician.* **2.** to obtain the use of; reserve: *to engage a hotel room.* **3.** to attract and hold (one's attention or interest); involve: *The story engaged the children's interest.* **4.** to keep busy; occupy: *Housework engages much of her time.* **5.** to bind or pledge (oneself): *He engaged himself to fulfill certain duties when he accepted the job.* **6.** to pledge to marry; betroth: *Harry and Anne were engaged in January and married in June.* **7.** to meet in combat; encounter and fight: *The soldiers engaged the enemy forces at dawn.* **8.** *Mechanics.* to interlock with; mesh. —*v.i.* **1.** to occupy or involve oneself; take part: *He engaged in a serious study of the problem.* **2.** to pledge oneself; promise: *He engaged to pay the costs of the project.* **3.** to enter into combat. **4.** *Mechanics.* to interlock; mesh: *The gears engaged.*

en·gage·ment (en gāj′mənt) *n.* **1.** the act of engaging or the state of being engaged. **2.** a promise to marry; betrothal. **3.** a meeting or a promise to meet with someone at a certain time; appointment: *Tim has an engagement for dinner this evening.* **4.** employment or period of employment: *The singer signed a contract for a two-week engagement at the nightclub.* **5.** a meeting of enemy forces; battle. **6.** a pledge or agreement: *The bankrupt company had failed to fulfill all its engagements.*

en·gag·ing (en gā′jing) *adj.* pleasingly attractive; winning; charming: *Joan has an engaging smile.* —**en·gag′ing·ly,** *adv.*

En·gels, Frie·drich (eng′əlz; frē′drik) 1820–1895, German socialist writer, an associate of Karl Marx.

en·gen·der (en jen′dər) *v.t.* to bring into being; cause; produce: *His hostile attitude engendered much ill will among his fellow workers.*

en·gine (en′jin) *n.* **1.** a machine that converts energy into mechanical work. **2.** a railroad locomotive. **3.** any mechanical device: *Cannons are engines of war.*

en·gi·neer (en′ji nēr′) *n.* **1.** a person who is skilled in one of the branches of engineering: *an electrical engineer, an aeronautical engineer.* **2.** a person who drives or manages an engine, especially a railroad locomotive. **3.** any skillful manager; shrewd leader: *The general was the chief engineer of the victory.* —*v.t.* **1.** to plan, construct, or manage as an engineer: *to engineer the building of a bridge.* **2.** to manage or lead skillfully or shrewdly: *The politician engineered a successful campaign.*

en·gi·neer·ing (en′ji nēr′ing) *n.* the science or profession of putting matter and energy to use for man.

Eng·land (ing′glənd) *n.* the largest political division of the United Kingdom, in the southern part of the island of Great Britain. Capital, London. Area, 50,873 sq. mi. Pop. (1971), 45,870,062.

Eng·lish (ing′glish) *n.* **1.** a language spoken in the United Kingdom, the United States, Canada, Australia, New Zealand, and in various other parts of the world. **2. the English.** the people of England. **3.** *also,* **english.** a spin given to a ball by striking it off-center or by throwing or bowling it with a twist of the wrist. —*adj.* **1.** of or relating to England or its people. **2.** of, relating to, or expressed in the English language. See **Old English** for further information.

English Channel, a channel between England and France, connecting the North Sea with the Atlantic Ocean.

English horn, a woodwind instrument similar to the oboe, but having a lower pitch.

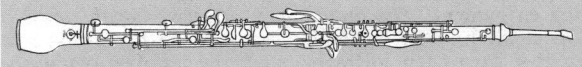

English horn

Eng·lish·man (ing′glish mən) *n. pl.,* **Eng·lish·men** (ing′glish mən). a person who was born or is living in England. —**Eng′lish·wom′an,** *n.*

english muffin, a round, flat, unsweetened muffin, usually eaten toasted.

en·graft (en graft′) *also,* **in·graft.** *v.t.* **1.** to graft (a shoot from one tree or plant) into or onto another. **2.** to set firmly; implant.

en·grave (en grāv′) *v.t.,* **en·graved, en·grav·ing. 1.** to cut or carve letters, figures, or the like into: *to engrave a tombstone.* **2.** to cut or carve (letters, figures, or the like) into an object or surface: *The boy engraved his initials on the tree.* **3.** to cut (letters, figures, or the like) into a metal plate or other material for printing. **4.** to print (something) from a metal plate or other material cut in this way: *to engrave*

at; āpe; cär; end; mē; it; īce; hot; ōld; fôrk;
wood; fo͞ol; oil; out; up; turn; sing; thin; this;
hw in white; zh in treasure. The symbol ə
stands for the sound of a in about, e in taken,
i in pencil, o in lemon, and u in circus.

an invitation. **5.** to impress deeply; fix permanently: *His dying words were engraved in her mind.* —**en·grav′er,** *n.*

en·grav·ing (en grā′ving) *n.* **1.** the art or process of creating a design, inscription, or picture by cutting letters or lines into a metal plate, stone, wood, or other material. **2.** the design, inscription, or picture engraved in this way. **3.** an engraved printing plate. **4.** a printed impression made from such a plate.

en·gross (en grōs′) *v.t.* **1.** to occupy all the attention of; absorb: *The scientist was engrossed in his work. The audience was completely engrossed by the actor's performance.* **2.** to write or copy out (a document or the like) in large letters or in a formal manner.

en·gulf (en gulf′) *v.t.* to swallow up or completely surround; overwhelm: *The avalanche engulfed the small cabin. Civil war engulfed the country.*

en·hance (en hans′) *v.t.,* **en·hanced, en·hanc·ing.** to make greater, as in quality or value; heighten: *The reviews of the poet's most recent book enhanced his reputation.* —**en·hance′ment,** *n.*

e·nig·ma (i nig′mə) *n.* a person or thing that is puzzling or hard to understand; riddle; mystery: *The origin of the universe remains an enigma. He was a total enigma to all but his closest friends.*

en·ig·mat·ic (en′ig mat′ik) *adj.* of or like an enigma; mysterious; puzzling: *The woman in the painting has an enigmatic smile.* Also, **enigmatical.**

En·i·we·tok (en′ə wē′tok) *n.* a large atoll in the Marshall Islands, used by the U.S. as a testing ground for nuclear weapons.

en·join (en join′) *v.t.* **1.** to order, direct, or urge: *She enjoined the children to be careful in crossing the street.* **2.** to order (a person or group) to do or to keep from doing some act, as by a court order: *The court enjoined the union from striking for a period of thirty days.*

en·joy (en joi′) *v.t.* **1.** to experience joy, pleasure, or satisfaction in: *The class enjoyed the party.* **2.** to have the use or benefit of: *to enjoy good health.*

  to enjoy oneself. to have a good time.

en·joy·a·ble (en joi′ə bəl) *adj.* giving or capable of giving enjoyment: *The family spent a very enjoyable day in the country.* —**en·joy′a·ble·ness,** *n.* —**en·joy′a·bly,** *adv.*

en·joy·ment (en joi′mənt) *n.* **1.** the act of enjoying: *the enjoyment of prosperity.* **2.** something that gives joy, pleasure, or satisfaction: *His work is enjoyment for him.* **3.** joy, pleasure, or satisfaction.

en·kin·dle (en kind′əl) *v.t.,* **en·kin·dled, en·kin·dling.** another word for **kindle.**

en·lace (en lās′) *v.t.,* **en·laced, en·lac·ing. 1.** to bind with or as if with laces; encircle; enfold. **2.** to intertwine; entangle.

en·large (en lärj′) *v.,* **en·larged, en·larg·ing.** —*v.t.* to increase the size or amount of; make larger: *The school has decided to enlarge its library. She had the photographs of the graduation enlarged.* —*v.i.* to become larger: *Bus service increased as the town enlarged.*

  to enlarge on or **to enlarge upon.** to write or say something in more detail: *The coach enlarged upon his earlier comments about yesterday's game*

en·large·ment (en lärj′mənt) *n.* **1.** the act of enlarging or the state of being enlarged. **2.** a thing that enlarges by being added; addition. **3.** an enlarged form of something else, such as a photograph that is larger than the original.

en·larg·er (en lär′jər) *n.* a device for making photographic prints larger than the original negatives.

en·light·en (en līt′ən) *v.t.* to give knowledge or wisdom to; free from prejudice, ignorance, or superstition.

en·light·en·ment (en līt′ən mənt) *n.* the act of enlightening or the state of being enlightened.

en·list (en list′) *v.i.* **1.** to join the armed forces voluntarily: *My sister enlisted in the army and is serving on a post in Europe.* **2.** to join in some cause: *The entire class enlisted in the community fund drive.* —*v.t.* **1.** to enroll (someone) for military service; induct. **2.** to get; obtain: *He enlisted the aid of his friends when he moved.*

en·list·ed (en lis′tid) of or relating to the part of a military or naval force below commissioned or warrant officers.

enlisted man, any man in the armed forces who is not a commissioned officer, warrant officer, or cadet.

en·list·ment (en list′mənt) *n.* **1.** the act of enlisting or the state of being enlisted. **2.** a period of time for which a person enlists.

en·liv·en (en lī′vən) *v.t.* to make lively or cheerful; animate: *His witty comments enlivened the discussion.*

en masse (än mas′, en mas′) in a group; all together: *The club's officers resigned en masse.* [French *en masse.*]

en·mesh (en mesh′) *v.t.* to catch or entangle, as in a net: *A struggle for power enmeshed the leader when the king died.*

en·mi·ty (en′mə tē) *n. pl.,* **en·mi·ties.** a bitter feeling, as between enemies; ill will; hatred: *The enmity between the two countries is giving way to harmony.*

en·no·ble (i nō′bəl) *v.t.,* **en·no·bled, en·no·bling. 1.** to raise in nature, quality, or reputation: *The soldier's brave deeds ennobled him in the eyes of his comrades.* **2.** to give a title of nobility to. —**en·no′ble·ment,** *n.*

en·nui (än wē′) *n.* a feeling of listlessness and unhappiness resulting from a lack of interesting things to think about or do; boredom. [French *ennui.*]

e·nor·mi·ty (e nôr′mə tē) *n. pl.,* **e·nor·mi·ties. 1.** extreme wickedness: *The enormity of his crime shocked the townspeople.* **2.** something extremely wicked or outrageous; atrocity. **3.** great size; hugeness.

e·nor·mous (i nôr′məs) *adj.* much greater than the usual size, amount, or degree; extremely large: *Some dinosaurs were enormous. The war caused an enormous amount of suffering.* —**e·nor′mous·ly,** *adv.* —**e·nor′mous·ness,** *n.*

e·nough (i nuf′) *adj.* as much or as many as needed or desired: *There is not enough room for her in the car. There were enough players for a baseball game.* —*n.* a quantity or amount that satisfies a need or desire: *There is enough here to feed the whole family.* —*adv.* **1.** in an amount or degree that satisfies a need or desire: *The steak is not cooked enough. Is he feeling well enough to travel?* **2.** quite; very: *The path up the mountain is certainly steep enough.* —*interj.* that's enough; stop.

en·quire (in kwīr′) another spelling of **inquire.**

en·quir·y (in kwīr′ē, in′kwər ē) *n. pl.,* **en·quir·ies.** another spelling of **inquiry.**

en·rage (en rāj′) *v.t.,* **en·raged, en·rag·ing.** to put into a rage; make very angry: *Reckless drivers enrage him.*

en·rapt (en rapt′) *adj.* charmed; enraptured.

en·rap·ture (en rap′chər) *v.t.,* **en·rap·tured, en·rap·tur·ing.** to bring into a state of rapture; delight greatly: *The circus enraptured adults as well as children.*

en·rich (en rich′) *v.t.* **1.** to make rich or richer: *Money from the school fair enriched the scholarship fund. The guide's comments enriched their appreciation of the old castle.* **2.** to improve, as by adding desirable elements or ingredients. —**en·rich′ment,** *n.*

en·roll (en rōl′) *also,* **en·rol.** *v.,* **en·rolled, en·roll·ing.** —*v.t.* **1.** to make a member: *The teacher enrolled seven new students in the class.* **2.** to put or record (a name) on a list. —*v.i.* **1.** to become a member; join: *Her older sister will enroll at the university in the fall.* **2.** to have or put one's name on a list.

en·roll·ment (en rōl′mənt) *also,* **en·rol·ment.** *n.*

1. the act of enrolling or the state of being enrolled. **2.** the number of persons enrolled: *Enrollment in that college declined this year.*

en route (än rōōt′) on the way: *They will stop for lunch en route to the museum.* [French *en route.*]

en·sconce (en skons′) *v.t.,* **en·sconced, en·sconc·ing. 1.** to settle comfortably and securely: *Father ensconced himself in the chair by the fireplace.* **2.** to hide or shelter: *The children ensconced themselves in the tree house during the rainstorm.*

en·sem·ble (än säm′bəl) *n.* **1.** all the parts of something considered as a whole; total effect: *The furniture made a charming ensemble.* **2.** a set of matching clothes; costume: *Her ensemble consisted of a dress, shoes, a hat, and a coat.* **3.** a small group of musicians performing together: *The string ensemble gave three concerts during the week.* **4.** a group of musicians or other performers in a production; supporting cast: *The whole ensemble joined the star for a curtain call.*

en·shrine (en shrīn′) *v.t.,* **en·shrined, en·shrin·ing. 1.** to enclose in or as if in a shrine. **2.** to hold sacred; cherish: *His words were enshrined in her memory.* **—en·shrine′ment,** *n.*

en·shroud (en shroud′) *v.t.* to hide from view; conceal: *Darkness enshrouded the house.*

en·sign (*defs. 1, 3* en′sīn, en′sən; *def. 2* en′sən) *n.* **1.** a flag or banner, especially a national or a naval flag. **2.** in the U.S. Navy or Coast Guard, the lowest-ranking commissioned officer, ranking below a lieutenant junior grade. **3.** an emblem of rank or office.

en·si·lage (en′sə lij) *n.* another word for **silage.**

en·slave (en slāv′) *v.t.,* **en·slaved, en·slav·ing.** to make a slave of; reduce to slavery: *The harsh conquerors tried to enslave the entire population. Financial worries enslaved the struggling businessman.* **—en·slave′ment,** *n.*

en·snare (en sner′) *also,* **in·snare.** *v.t.,* **en·snared, en·snar·ing.** to catch in a snare; trap.

en·sue (en sōō′) *v.i.,* **en·sued, en·su·ing. 1.** to come or happen afterward; follow: *The first chapters were better than those that ensued.* **2.** to happen as a result: *The two rival gangs met, and a brief fight ensued.*

en·sure (en shoor′) *also,* **in·sure.** *v.t.,* **en·sured, en·sur·ing. 1.** to make sure or certain; guarantee: *Careful planning helped to ensure the success of the project.* **2.** to make safe or secure; protect: *Vaccinations ensure people against diseases.*

-ent *suffix* **1.** (used to form adjectives) being or acting in a particular state or manner: *independent, persistent.* **2.** (used to form nouns) a person or thing that performs a particular action: *president, superintendent.*

en·tab·la·ture (en tab′lə chər) *n.* a horizontal structure used in Greek and Roman architecture, supported on columns and composed of the architrave, frieze, and cornice.

en·tail (en tāl′) *v.t.* to impose or require; involve: *His work entails much traveling.* **—en·tail′ment,** *n.*

en·tan·gle (en tang′gəl) *v.t.,* **en·tan·gled, en·tan·gling. 1.** to catch in a tangle or net; ensnare: *The swimmer's legs were entangled in seaweed.* **2.** to involve, as in difficulties: *An innocent bystander became entangled in the argument.* **3.** to cause to become knotted

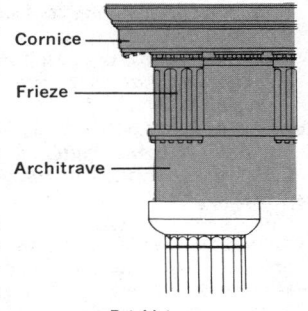

Cornice

Frieze

Architrave

Entablature

or tangled; snarl: *The kitten entangled the yarn.* **4.** to confuse or complicate: *His reasoning was hopelessly entangled.*

en·tan·gle·ment (en tang′gəl mənt) *n.* **1.** the act of entangling or the state of being entangled. **2.** something that entangles.

en·tente (än tänt′) *n.* **1.** an understanding or agreement between countries. An entente is less binding than a formal alliance. **2.** countries having such an understanding or agreement.

en·ter (en′tər) *v.t.* **1.** to go or come into: *The bride and her father entered the church. A sudden thought entered his mind.* **2.** to pass through a surface; penetrate; pierce: *The bullet entered his left shoulder.* **3.** to become a member or participant in; join: *Lynn will enter the university in the fall.* **4.** to cause to be admitted or accepted; enroll: *He entered his dog in the competition.* **5.** to set down in writing; make a record of; register: *She entered her name in the guest book at the reception.* **6.** to take the first steps in; begin; start: *The cadets entered a new phase of their training.* **—v.i. 1.** to go or come in: *The actor entered when he heard his cue.* **2.** to pierce; penetrate: *The bullet entered above the shoulder.*

to enter into. a. to begin to take part in; engage in: *He entered into politics as a young man.* **b.** to form a part of: *Many factors entered into his decision not to go.*

to enter on or **to enter upon.** to set out on; begin; start: *The travelers entered upon the voyage eagerly.*

en·ter·i·tis (en′tə rī′tis) *n.* an inflammation of the lining of the intestines.

en·ter·prise (en′tər prīz′) *n.* **1.** a project or undertaking, especially one that is difficult or important: *His father is involved with the oil company's overseas enterprises.* **2.** readiness to take part in such undertakings; energy; initiative: *The assignment called for a man of enterprise and tact.*

en·ter·pris·ing (en′tər prī′zing) *adj.* showing energy and initiative; venturesome: *An enterprising salesman will be able to sell this product easily.*

en·ter·tain (en′tər tān′) *v.t.* **1.** to hold the attention of pleasantly; divert, interest, or amuse: *The clown entertained the children.* **2.** to have or receive as a guest; give hospitality to: *Every summer they entertain the neighbors at an outdoor party.* **3.** to bear in mind; maintain: *He entertains some strange notions.* **—v.i.** to have or receive guests: *That family entertains often.*

en·ter·tain·er (en′tər tā′nər) *n.* a person who entertains, especially a professional performer.

en·ter·tain·ing (en′tər tā′ning) *adj.* that entertains; engaging; amusing: *The play was long, but entertaining.* **—en′ter·tain′ing·ly,** *adv.*

en·ter·tain·ment (en′tər tān′mənt) *n.* **1.** the act of entertaining. **2.** something that entertains, especially a performance: *The school's marching band provided the entertainment.* **3.** the receiving of guests; hospitality.

en·thrall (en thrôl′) *also,* **en·thral.** *v.t.,* **en·thralled, en·thrall·ing. 1.** to hold spellbound; captivate; charm: *Everyone in the audience was enthralled by the skill and beauty of the young actress.* **2.** to make a slave of; enslave. **—en·thrall′ment,** *n.*

at; āpe; cär; end; mē; it; īce; hot; ōld; fôrk; wood; fōōl; oil; out; up; turn; sing; thin; this; hw in white; zh in treasure. The symbol ə stands for the sound of **a** in about, **e** in taken, **i** in pencil, **o** in lemon, and **u** in circus.

en·throne (en thrōn′) *v.t.,* **en·throned, en·thron·ing.**
1. to place on a throne in a ceremony: *to enthrone a king.*
2. to place in a position of authority or reverence: *The old man was enthroned as the head of the family.* —**en·throne′· ment,** *n.*

en·thuse (en thōōz′) *v.,* **en·thused, en·thus·ing.** *Informal.*
—*v.i.* to show enthusiasm. —*v.t.* to make enthusiastic.

en·thu·si·asm (en thōō′zē az′əm) *n.* eager or fervent interest; zeal: *He showed great enthusiasm for the plan.*

en·thu·si·ast (en thōō′zē ast′) *n.* a person who is filled with enthusiasm; zealous supporter or follower: *Her uncle is a great golf enthusiast.*

en·thu·si·as·tic (en thōō′zē as′tik) *adj.* full of enthusiasm; zealous: *A crowd of enthusiastic admirers surrounded the singer.* —**en·thu′si·as′ti·cal·ly,** *adv.*

en·tice (en tīs′) *v.t.,* **en·ticed, en·tic·ing.** to attract by offering pleasure or reward; tempt: *The promise of a good deal of money enticed him into taking part in the crooked scheme.* —**en·tice′ment,** *n.*

en·tire (en tīr′) *adj.* **1.** having all the parts or elements; total; complete; whole: *The entire team was present at the awards ceremony. He donated the entire sum to charity.*
2. not broken; in one piece; intact: *Only one house remained entire after the flood.*

en·tire·ly (en tīr′lē) *adv.* without exception; completely: *He was entirely without blame in the accident.*

en·tire·ty (en tīr′tē) *n. pl.,* **en·tire·ties. 1.** the state of being whole or complete: *The opera was too long to be performed in its entirety.* **2.** something that is entire; whole: *He spent the entirety of his day cleaning the yard.*

en·ti·tle (en tīt′əl) *v.t.,* **en·ti·tled, en·ti·tling. 1.** to give the title of; call: *The author has not yet entitled his new book.* **2.** to give a claim or right to; qualify: *His high score entitled him to a prize. What entitles her to criticize him?*

en·ti·ty (en′tə tē) *n. pl.,* **en·ti·ties.** something with real existence; an actual thing: *The house and the property were sold as separate entities.*

en·tomb (en tōōm′) *also,* **in·tomb.** *v.t.* **1.** to place in a tomb; bury. **2.** to serve as a tomb for: *The snow from the avalanche entombed the mountain climbers.* —**en·tomb′· ment,** *n.*

en·to·mo·log·i·cal (en′tə mə loj′i kəl) *adj.* of or relating to entomology. Also, **en·to·mo·log·ic** (en′tə mə· loj′ik).

en·to·mol·o·gist (en′tə mol′ə jist) *n.* a student of or an expert in entomology.

en·to·mol·o·gy (en′tə mol′ə jē) *n.* a branch of zoology dealing with insects.

en·tou·rage (än′too räzh′) *n.* a group of attendants, followers, or companions, especially one accompanying a person of high rank: *The queen never traveled without her entourage.*

en·trails (en′trālz, en′trəlz) *n., pl.* the inner parts of a man or animal, especially the intestines.

en·train (en trān′) *v.i.* to go aboard a train: *The soldiers entrained at dawn.* —*v.t.* to put aboard a train.

en·trance¹ (en′trəns) *n.* **1.** the act of entering: *Everyone rose at the judge's entrance. The campaign marked his entrance into politics.* **2.** a place or means for entering: *One entrance to the building was kept open at night.* **3.** the right or power of entering; admittance: *High school students were given free entrance to the basketball game.* [Old French *entrance.*]

en·trance² (en trans′) *v.t.,* **en·tranced, en·tranc·ing.**
1. to put into a trance. **2.** to fill with delight or wonder; charm: *The actress entranced the audience.* [*En*¹- + *trance.*]

en·trant (en′trənt) *n.* **1.** a person who enters a contest; contestant: *All the entrants were judged by a panel of experts.* **2.** a person who enters anything.

en·trap (en trap′) *v.t.,* **en·trapped, en·trap·ping. 1.** to catch in a trap. **2.** to bring into difficulty or danger by trickery: *The detectives entrapped the suspect into admitting his guilt.*

en·treat (en trēt′) *v.t.* to ask earnestly; beg; beseech: *The prisoner entreated the king for mercy.*

en·treat·y (en trē′tē) *n. pl.,* **en·treat·ies.** an earnest request; plea.

en·tree (än′trā) *also,* **en·trée.** *n.* **1.** a main dish or course at a meal. **2.** the freedom or right to enter; access; admission: *The reporters finally gained entree into the senator's office.*

en·trench (en trench′) *also,* **in·trench.** *v.t.* **1.** to place in a trench; surround with trenches: *The troops entrenched themselves well beyond the range of enemy fire.* **2.** to establish firmly or securely: *The idea became entrenched in his mind.*

en·trench·ment (en trench′mənt) *also,* **in·trench·ment.**
n. **1.** the act of entrenching. **2.** a trench or a series of trenches, usually with a bank of earth built along the side facing the enemy.

en·tre·pre·neur (än′trə prə nur′) *n.* a person who organizes and controls a business or other financial enterprise.

en·trust (en trust′) *also,* **in·trust.** *v.t.* **1.** to put something in the trust of; charge with a responsibility: *Mary entrusted her friend with the care of her pet for the weekend.*
2. to give over the care of; assign responsibility for: *The chemist entrusted the completion of the work to his assistant.*

en·try (en′trē) *n. pl.,* **en·tries. 1.** the act or instance of entering: *His unexpected entry into the race surprised the spectators.* **2.** a place for entering; entrance: *Barricades blocked the entry to the building.* **3.** a written item included in a book, diary, list, or other record: *an entry in a ship's log.* **4.** something that is entered in a contest or race: *All entries must be submitted before May 1.* **5.** a word or phrase that is defined or otherwise explained in a dictionary, usually printed in heavy, dark type.

en·twine (en twīn′) *v.t.,* **en·twined, en·twin·ing.** to twine together; twist or twine around: *The children entwined their arms around each other. Flowers were entwined in her hair.*

e·nu·mer·ate (i nōō′mə rāt′, i nyōō′mə rāt′) *v.t.,* **e·nu·mer·at·ed, e·nu·mer·at·ing. 1.** to name one by one; list: *He enumerated the reasons for his decision.* **2.** to find the number of; count. —**e·nu′mer·a′tor,** *n.*

e·nu·mer·a·tion (i nōō′mə rā′shən, i nyōō′mə rā′· shən) *n.* **1.** the act of enumerating. **2.** a list or catalogue.

e·nun·ci·ate (i nun′sē āt′) *v.,* **e·nun·ci·at·ed, e·nun·ci·at·ing.** —*v.t.* **1.** to pronounce (words or speech sounds), especially in a particular manner; articulate: *It is often difficult to understand someone who does not enunciate his words clearly.* **2.** to state definitely; announce. —*v.i.* to pronounce words or speech sounds, especially in a particular manner: *That actor enunciates beautifully.* —**e·nun′ci· a′tor,** *n.*

e·nun·ci·a·tion (i nun′sē ā′shən) *n.* **1.** a way of pronouncing: *His enunciation is poor.* **2.** a statement; declaration: *an enunciation of rules.*

en·vel·op (en vel′əp) *v.t.* to wrap up or cover completely: *Clouds enveloped the mountain peak.*

en·ve·lope (en′və lōp′, än′və lōp′) *n.* **1.** a flat wrapper or container made of paper, used especially for mailing letters. **2.** something that envelops; covering; wrapper.
3. the outer covering of a balloon or airship.

en·vel·op·ment (en vel′əp mənt) *n.* **1.** the act of enveloping or the state of being enveloped. **2.** something that envelops; covering; wrapping.

en·ven·om (en ven′əm) *v.t.* **1.** to fill with venom; make poisonous. **2.** to fill with hate or vindictiveness; embitter: *Mistreatment of animals envenoms most people.*

en·vi·a·ble (en′vē ə bəl) *adj.* worthy of envy; desirable: *Jim has an enviable record in school.*

en·vi·ous (en′vē əs) *adj.* having, feeling, or showing envy: *Martha is envious of her sister's popularity.* —**en′vi·ous·ly,** *adv.* —**en′vi·ous·ness,** *n.*

en·vi·ron·ment (en vī′rən mənt) *n.* **1.** all of the objects, influences, and conditions that surround and affect the development of an animal or plant: *In order to survive, an animal must be able to adapt to changes in its environment. A farm child and a city child grow up in different environments.* **2.** surroundings: *That school has a nice environment.*

en·vi·ron·men·tal (en vī′rən ment′əl) *adj.* of or relating to environment —**en·vi′ron·men′tal·ly,** *adv.*

en·vi·ron·men·tal·ist (en vī′rən ment′əl ist) *n.* a person who is concerned about the quality of the environment, especially about the effects of pollution of the earth's air, land, and water and the depletion of the earth's natural resources.

en·vi·rons (en vī′rənz) *n., pl.* the surrounding districts of a town or city; outskirts.

en·vis·age (en viz′ij) *v.t.,* **en·vis·aged, en·vis·ag·ing.** to form a mental picture of: *Helen tried to envisage how her room would look after she repainted it.*

en·vi·sion (en vizh′ən) *v.t.* to form an idea of; imagine: *Can you envision what life will be like in a hundred years?*

en·voy (en′voi, än′voi) *n.* **1.** a representative sent by one country to another, ranking next below an ambassador. **2.** anyone sent as messenger or representative of another.

en·vy (en′vē) *n. pl.,* **en·vies. 1.** a feeling of resentment, jealousy, or desire brought on by another person's abilities, possessions, or good fortune. **2.** the object of this feeling: *Sam's new bicycle made him the envy of his friends.* —*v.t.,* **en·vied, en·vy·ing. 1.** to feel envy toward (someone); regard with envy. **2.** to feel envy because of: *His friends envy his good grades.* —**en′vi·er,** *n.*

en·wrap (en rap′) *v.t.,* **en·wrapped, en·wrap·ping.** to enfold; envelop.

en·zyme (en′zīm) *n.* a chemical substance produced in the living cells of all plants and animals. Some enzymes control activities within the cells that provide energy and materials for rebuilding and repair. Others control such activities outside the cell as digestion and blood clotting.

E·o·cene (ē′ə sēn′) *n.* the second geological epoch of the Tertiary period of the Cenozoic era, when such animals as the horse, the elephant, and the camel first appeared. —*adj.* of, relating to, or characteristic of this epoch.

e·o·hip·pus (ē′ō hip′əs) *n.* the small, early ancestor of the horse, found as a fossil in Eocene deposits in North America and Europe.

e·on (ē′ən, ē′on) *also,* **ae·on.** *n.* **1.** a very long, indefinite period of time. **2.** the largest division of geological time, including at least two eras.

ep·au·let (ep′ə let′) *also,* **ep·au·lette.** *n.* an ornament worn on the shoulder of a uniform, such as a military uniform.

e·phed·rine (i fed′rin) *n.* a drug used especially to treat low blood pressure and to relieve hay fever and asthma.

e·phem·er·a (i fem′ər ə) *n. pl.,* **e·phem·er·as** or **e·phem·er·ae** (i fem′ər ē). an ephemeral person or thing.

e·phem·er·al (i fem′ər əl) *adj.* **1.** lasting for a very short time; short-lived; fleeting: *the ephemeral beauty of a rainbow after a rainstorm.* **2.** *Biology.* lasting for a day.

Epaulets

E·phe·sian (i fē′zhən) *adj.* of, relating to, or characteristic of Ephesus. —*n.* **1.** a person who lived in Ephesus. **2. Ephesians.** a book of the New Testament, written as an epistle by the Apostle Paul to the Christians in Ephesus.

Eph·e·sus (ef′i səs) *n.* an ancient city on the west coast of Asia Minor.

ep·ic (ep′ik) *n.* a long, narrative poem that tells of the adventures and achievements of heroes in legend or history. *The Odyssey* by the Greek poet Homer is an epic. —*adj. also,* **ep·i·cal** (ep′i kəl). **1.** of, relating to, or like an epic: *an epic poem.* **2.** suitable for an epic; heroic: *the epic events of westward expansion in the United States.* —**ep′i·cal·ly,** *adv.*

ep·i·cot·yl (ep′ə kot′əl) *n.* the part of the stem of a plant embryo or seedling above the cotyledons.

ep·i·cure (ep′i kyoor′) *n.* a person who has developed a refined taste for good food and drink.

ep·i·cu·re·an (ep′i kyoo rē′ən) *adj.* **1.** having refined tastes or habits, especially in eating and drinking. **2.** fit or suitable for an epicure: *an epicurean meal.* —*n.* another word for **epicure.**

ep·i·dem·ic (ep′ə dem′ik) *n.* **1.** the rapid spread or sudden, widespread appearance of a disease among many people at the same time: *an epidemic of measles.* **2.** the rapid spread or sudden, widespread appearance of anything: *an epidemic of burglaries.* —*adj.* spreading among and affecting many people at the same time; widespread: *an epidemic disease.*

ep·i·der·mis (ep′ə dur′mis) *n.* **1.** a protective outer layer of the skin of animals with backbones. The epidermis does not contain blood vessels or nerves. **2.** a protective outer layer of cells of seed plants and ferns.

ep·i·glot·tis (ep′ə glot′is) *n.* a thin, triangular flap of cartilage that blocks the entrance to the windpipe during swallowing, preventing foreign matter from entering the lungs.

ep·i·gram (ep′ə gram′) *n.* **1.** a brief, pointed statement expressing a thought in a witty manner. For example: *There is only one thing in the world worse than being talked about, and that is not being talked about* (Oscar Wilde). **2.** a short poem with a witty, clever ending.

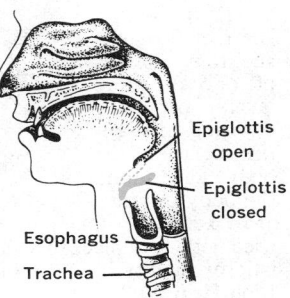
Epiglottis open
Epiglottis closed
Esophagus
Trachea

ep·i·gram·mat·ic (ep′i grə mat′ik) *adj.* **1.** of, relating to, or using epigrams. **2.** like or suitable to an epigram; witty, pointed, and brief.

ep·i·lep·sy (ep′ə lep′sē) *n.* a disorder of the brain, characterized by seizures that may take the form of convulsions or loss of consciousness.

ep·i·lep·tic (ep′ə lep′tik) *adj.* of, relating to, or having epilepsy: *an epileptic seizure.* —*n.* a person who has epilepsy.

ep·i·logue (ep′ə lôg′, ep′ə log′) *also,* **ep·i·log.** *n.* **1.** a passage or section added to the end of a story, poem, or other written work as an explanation, summary, or conclu-

at; āpe; cär; end; mē; it; īce; hot; ōld; fôrk; wood; fo͞ol; oil; out; up; turn; sing; thin; **this;** **hw** in white; **zh** in treasure. The symbol ə stands for the sound of **a** in about, **e** in taken, **i** in pencil, **o** in lemon, and **u** in circus.

sion. **2.** a speech or short poem addressed to the audience by one of the actors at the end of a play.

ep·i·neph·rine (ep'ə nef'rēn) *n.*   another word for **adrenalin.**

E·piph·a·ny (i pif'ə nē) *n.*   a Christian holy day celebrating the appearance of Christ on earth. It falls on January 6. In the Western Church, it celebrates the visit of the Three Wise Men to the infant Jesus. In the Eastern Church, it celebrates the baptism of Jesus.

ep·i·phyte (ep'ə fīt') *n.*   any of various plants that grow on other plants for support, but usually do not harm the plant on which they live. Also, **air plant.**

Epis. **1.** Episcopal. **2.** Episcopalian. **3.** Epistle.

e·pis·co·pal (i pis'kə pəl) *adj.* **1.** of or relating to bishops. **2.** governed by bishops. **3.** **Episcopal.** of or relating to the Church of England or the Protestant Episcopal Church.

E·pis·co·pa·lian (i pis'kə pāl'yən) *n.*   a member of an Episcopal church, such as the Protestant Episcopal Church. —*adj.* another word for **Episcopal.**

ep·i·sode (ep'ə sōd') *n.* **1.** an incident or event that stands out in a series of events. **2.** an incident or event that is separate from the main plot or subject of a novel or other written work. **3.** an installment of a play, story, or the like that is presented in serial form, as on television.

e·pis·tle (i pis'əl) *n.* **1.** a long, formal letter. **2.** **Epistle.** any one of the letters written by an Apostle and contained in the New Testament. **3.** a selection from one of these, read as part of a Christian service.

ep·i·taph (ep'ə taf') *n.*   a brief statement, usually inscribed on a tombstone or other monument in memory of a dead person.

ep·i·the·li·um (ep'ə thē'lē əm) *n. pl.,* **ep·i·the·li·ums** or **ep·i·the·li·a** (ep'ə thē'lē ə). a thin sheet of body tissue that consists of one or more layers of cells, covering the entire surface of the body and lining the body cavities.

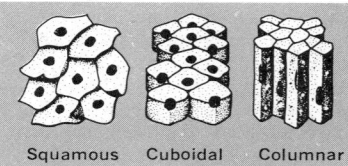

Squamous   Cuboidal   Columnar

Epithelium cells

ep·i·thet (ep'ə thet') *n.*   a descriptive word or phrase used with or in place of a name to indicate some characteristic or quality, as "the Lion-Hearted" in "Richard the Lion-Hearted."

e·pit·o·me (i pit'ə mē) *n.* **1.** a person or thing that has or represents all the qualities or characteristics of something: *He is the epitome of a gentleman in his manner and dress.* **2.** a short account or summary of a speech, book, or other written work; abridgment.

e·pit·o·mize (i pit'ə mīz') *v.t.,* **e·pit·o·mized, e·pit·o·miz·ing. 1.** to be the epitome of: *The king epitomized the wise ruler.* **2.** to make a short account or summary of (a written work).

e plu·ri·bus u·num (ē' ploor'ə bəs yōō'nəm) *Latin.* out of many, one. It is the motto on the official seal of the United States.

ep·och (ep'ək) *n.* **1.** a period of time marked by some particular characteristic, development, or course of events. **2.** a division of geological time smaller than a period.

Ep·som salts (ep'səm) *also,* **Epsom salt.** a bitter compound consisting of colorless crystals, used especially as a laxative and in baths for sore muscles or minor infections. [From *Epsom,* a town in England where the compound was first obtained from the water of a mineral spring.]

eq. 1. equal. **2.** equivalent. **3.** equation. **4.** equator.

eq·ua·ble (ek'wə bəl) *adj.* **1.** not easily disturbed or upset; tranquil: *an equable state of mind.* **2.** not changing; unvarying; steady: *an equable temperature.* —**eq'ua·bly,** *adv.*

e·qual (ē'kwəl) *adj.* **1.** the same, as in amount, number, rank, or size: *Four quarts are equal to one gallon.* **2.** having the same rights, privileges, and responsibilities: *All people are equal under the law.* **3.** evenly matched or balanced; even: *Their chances to win are equal.* **4.** *Mathematics.* (of sets) having exactly the same members. The sets [12, 23, 59, 74] and [59, 12, 74, 23] are equal. —*n.* a person or thing that is equal: *Joan is his equal as a tennis player.* —*v.t.,* **e·qualed, e·qual·ing;** *also, British,* **e·qualled, e·qual·ling. 1.** to be equal to: *Two plus two equals four.* **2.** to make or do something equal to: *No one has equaled his service to the community. She never again equaled her record in sports or school work.* —**e'qual·ly,** *adv.*

equal to. having the strength or ability necessary for: *He was not equal to the job.*

e·qual·i·ty (i kwol'ə tē) *n.*   the state or quality of being equal, especially having the same rights, privileges, and responsibilities.

e·qual·ize (ē'kwə līz') *v.t.,* **e·qual·ized, e·qual·iz·ing.** to make equal: *to equalize water pressure.* —**e'qual·i·za'tion,** *n.* —**e'qual·li'zer,** *n.*

equal sign, a mathematical symbol (=) used to show that two quantities or expressions are equal, as in $1 + 6 = 7$.

e·qua·nim·i·ty (ē'kwə nim'ə tē, ek'wə nim'ə tē) *n.* evenness of mind or temper; calmness: *The candidate accepted the news of his defeat with equanimity.*

e·quate (i kwāt') *v.t.,* **e·quat·ed, e·quat·ing. 1.** to consider, treat, or represent as equal: *He equates good manners with politeness to others.* **2.** to consider or represent as related: *Some people equate wealth and happiness.* **3.** *Mathematics.* to state the equality of; put in the form of an equation.

e·qua·tion (i kwā'zhən) *n.* **1.** *Mathematics.* a statement of equality between two quantities or expressions, especially one using an equal sign. $9 + 6 = 15$ and $3x - y = 0$ are equations. **2.** *Chemistry.* an expression representing a chemical reaction indicated by the symbol (=) or (→), as in $FeS + 2HCl = FeCl_2 + H_2S$.

e·qua·tor (i kwā'tər) *n.*   an imaginary line encircling the earth halfway between the North and South Poles. The equator is the line from which degrees of latitude are measured.

e·qua·to·ri·al (ē'kwə tôr'ē əl, ek'wə tôr'ē əl) *adj.* **1.** of, at, or near the equator: *an equatorial country.* **2.** characteristic of the equator: *equatorial heat.*

Equatorial Guinea, a country in west-central Africa, on the Gulf of Guinea, formerly a Spanish colony. Capital, Malabo. Area, 10,831 sq. mi. Pop. (1980), 363,000.

eq·uer·ry (ek'wər ē) *n. pl.,* **eq·uer·ries. 1.** formerly, an officer of a royal or noble household in charge of the horses. **2.** a personal attendant to any of the members of the British royal family.

e·ques·tri·an (i kwes'trē ən) *adj.* **1.** of or relating to horsemen or horsewomen, horsemanship, or horseback riding. **2.** mounted on horseback: *an equestrian performer in a circus.* **3.** showing a person mounted on horseback: *an equestrian statue.* —*n.* a rider, especially a performer on horseback in a circus or other show.

e·ques·tri·enne (i kwes'trē en') *n.*   a woman who is an equestrian.

equi- *combining form* **1.** equal: *equilibrium.* **2.** equally: *equidistant.*

e·qui·dis·tant (ēk'wə dis'tənt) *adj.* equally distant: *The two houses are equidistant from the road.*

e·qui·lat·er·al (ēk′wə lat′ər əl) *adj.* having all sides equal in length: *an equilateral triangle.*

e·qui·lib·ri·um (ē′kwə lib′rē əm) *n.* **1.** a state of balance, especially between forces acting on or within a body or system: *A scale having equal weights on each side is in equilibrium.* **2.** mental and emotional balance: *He maintains his equilibrium no matter what problems arise.*

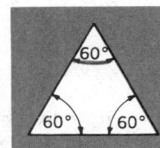
Equilateral triangle

e·quine (ēk′wīn) *adj.* of, relating to, or like a horse.

e·qui·noc·tial (ēk′wə nok′shəl) *adj.* **1.** of or relating to an equinox. **2.** happening at or near the time of an equinox: *an equinoctial storm.*

e·qui·nox (ē′kwə noks′) *n. pl.,* **e·qui·nox·es.** either of the two times of the year when day and night are of equal length all over the earth. During these two times the sun is directly above the equator. In the Northern Hemisphere, the vernal equinox takes place about March 21, and marks the beginning of spring. The autumnal equinox takes place about September 23, and marks the beginning of autumn.

e·quip (i kwip′) *v.t.,* **e·quipped, e·quip·ping.** to provide or outfit with whatever is necessary for a particular purpose or use: *He equipped his boat for a long cruise.*

eq·ui·page (ek′wə pij) *n.* **1.** equipment, as for an army or camp; gear. **2.** a carriage, especially when fully outfitted with horses, driver, and attendants.

e·quip·ment (i kwip′mənt) *n.* **1.** anything that is necessary or provided for a particular purpose or use; supplies; gear: *camping equipment, sports equipment.* **2.** the act of equipping or the state of being equipped.

e·qui·poise (ek′wə poiz′, ek′wə poiz′) *n.* **1.** a state of balance or equilibrium. **2.** a weight or force that balances another; counterbalance.

eq·ui·ta·ble (ek′wə tə bəl) *adj.* fair or just: *an equitable law.* —**eq′ui·ta·bly,** *adv.*

eq·ui·ty (ek′wə tē) *n. pl.,* **eq·ui·ties. 1.** the quality of being fair and just: *the equity of a law.* **2.** something that is fair and just.

e·quiv·a·lence (i kwiv′ə ləns) *n.* the state or condition of being equivalent.

e·quiv·a·lent (i kwiv′ə lənt) *adj.* **1.** equal, as in value, force, effect, or meaning; corresponding: *A quarter is equivalent to five nickels. Shaking one's head is equivalent to saying no.* **2.** *Mathematics.* (of sets) having the same number of members. The sets [1,2,3,4] and [2,4,6,8] are equivalent. —*n.* something that is equivalent: *Ten dimes are the equivalent of one dollar.*

e·quiv·o·cal (i kwiv′ə kəl) *adj.* **1.** capable of being understood in more than one way; having more than one possible meaning; ambiguous: *an equivocal answer.* **2.** undecided or uncertain; doubtful: *The evidence gathered by the detective was of equivocal value.* **3.** of a suspicious nature; questionable: *equivocal behavior.* —**e·quiv′o·cal·ly,** *adv.*

e·quiv·o·cate (i kwiv′ə kāt′) *v.i.,* **e·quiv·o·cat·ed, e·quiv·o·cat·ing.** to express oneself in language having more than one possible meaning, especially in order to mislead others or to avoid committing oneself: *The senator has equivocated on that issue for many years.* —**e·quiv′o·ca′tor,** *n.*

e·quiv·o·ca·tion (i kwiv′ə kā′shən) *n.* **1.** the act of equivocating. **2.** an equivocal statement.

Er, the symbol for erbium.

-er¹ *suffix* **1.** (used to form nouns from verbs) a person or thing that carries out the action of the verb: *driver, grater.* **2.** (used to form nouns) **a.** a person who was born or is living in: *northerner, New Yorker.* **b.** a person who

makes or is concerned with: *hatter, biographer.* **c.** a person or thing that is or is characterized by: *foreigner.* [Old English *-ere.*]

-er² *suffix* used to form the comparative degree of adjectives and adverbs: *colder, sooner.* [Old English *-ra.*]

e·ra (êr′ə, er′ə) *n.* **1.** a period of time marked by certain events, conditions, ideas, persons, or things: *The reign of Queen Victoria is called the Victorian era.* **2.** a period of time measured from or beginning with a particular event: *the Christian era.* **3.** one of the major divisions of geological time, including several epochs.

e·rad·i·cate (i rad′ə kāt′) *v.t.,* **e·rad·i·cat·ed, e·rad·i·cat·ing.** to remove or destroy completely; eliminate; abolish: *to eradicate weeds, to eradicate a disease.* —**e·rad′i·ca′tion,** *n.* —**e·rad′i·ca′tor,** *n.*

e·rase (i rās′) *v.,* **e·rased, e·ras·ing.** —*v.t.* **1.** to rub, scrape, or scratch out; wipe off: *He erased the notes he had written in the margin.* **2.** to remove marks, writing, or recorded information from: *Will you erase the blackboard?* **3.** to remove or destroy completely as if by rubbing or blotting out: *Time had not erased his memories of the war.* —*v.i.* **1.** to be capable of being erased: *Make light pencil lines so that they will erase easily.* **2.** to remove marks, writing, or recorded information: *The tape recorder erases if it is operated in reverse.* —**e·ras′a·ble,** *adj.*

e·ras·er (i rā′sər) *n.* a device for erasing, especially a piece of rubber for removing marks, such as those made with a pencil or pen.

E·ras·mus (i raz′məs) 1466?–1536, Dutch scholar and theologian.

e·ra·sure (i rā′shər) *n.* **1.** the act of erasing. **2.** something that has been erased, such as a word or letter. **3.** the place or mark left where something has been erased.

er·bi·um (ur′bē əm) *n.* a metallic element of the group of rare-earth elements. Symbol: Er [Modern Latin *erbium,* from *Ytterby,* a town in Sweden where it was first found.]

ere (êr) *Archaic. prep.* before in time. —*conj.* **1.** before. **2.** rather than.

e·rect (i rekt′) *adj.* in a vertical or upright position; raised: *The dog was trained to stand with his ears and tail erect.* —*v.t.* **1.** to build; construct: *The construction company is erecting an apartment house on that lot.* **2.** to raise or put in a vertical or upright position: *It takes only a few minutes to erect this tent.* —**e·rect′ly,** *adv.* —**e·rect′ness,** *n.*

e·rec·tion (i rek′shən) *n.* **1.** the act of erecting or the state of being erected. **2.** something that is erected, such as a building or other structure.

erg (urg) *n. Physics.* a unit of work equal to the work done by a force of one dyne acting through a distance of one centimeter.

er·go (ur′gō) *adv., conj. Latin.* therefore.

Er·ic·son, Leif (er′ik sən; lēf) the Norse explorer believed to have landed in North America about 1000; son of Eric the Red.

Er·ic the Red (er′ik) born 950?, the Norse explorer who discovered Greenland about 982.

E·rie (êr′ē) *n.* **1. Lake.** the southernmost of the Great Lakes, on the U.S.-Canadian border. **2.** a city in northwestern Pennsylvania, on Lake Erie. Pop. (1970), 129,231.

---

at; āpe; cär; end; mē; it; īce; hot; ōld; fôrk; wood; fōōl; oil; out; up; turn; sing; thin; this; hw in white; zh in treasure. The symbol ə stands for the sound of **a** in about, **e** in taken, **i** in pencil, **o** in lemon, and **u** in circus.

Erie Canal, a waterway across New York, connecting the Hudson River with Lake Erie. It is now part of the New York State Barge Canal.

Er·in (er′in) *n.* another name for **Ireland.**

er·mine (ur′min) *n. pl.,* **er·mines** or **er·mine. 1.** a weasel having a brown coat that usually changes to white in winter. **2.** the white winter fur of this animal, used especially for women's coats and for trimming on royal or judges' robes in some European countries.

Ermine

e·rode (i rōd′) *v.,* **e·rod·ed, e·rod·ing.** —*v.t.* **1.** to wear or wash away gradually, as by rubbing or friction: *The heavy rains eroded the topsoil on the hills.* **2.** to eat into or away; corrode: *Salt water collected in the bottom of the boat and eroded the metal parts.* **3.** to form (a channel or the like) by a gradual eating or wearing away: *The glacier had eroded a valley in the side of the mountain.* —*v.i.* to become eroded; undergo erosion.

E·ros (ēr′os, er′os) *n. Greek Mythology.* the god of love and son of Aphrodite. In Roman mythology he was called Cupid.

e·ro·sion (i rō′zhən) *n.* a gradual wearing, washing, or eating away, especially of the soil and rock of the earth's surface by glaciers, running water, waves, or wind: *Sand dunes help prevent the erosion of the shore by the ocean waves.*

e·ro·sive (i rō′siv) *adj.* causing erosion; eroding.

err (ur, er) *v.i.* **1.** to do something wrong; make a mistake; be in error: *He erred in making his decision before he knew all the facts.* **2.** to do something that is morally wrong; commit a sin.

er·rand (er′ənd) *n.* **1.** a short trip to do something, usually for someone else: *She was kept busy all morning, running errands for her mother.* **2.** what a person is sent to do; the purpose or object of such a trip.

er·rant (er′ənt) *adj.* **1.** traveling or roaming in search of adventure; wandering; roving: *the errant knights of the Middle Ages.* **2.** straying from the proper place or correct behavior; erring: *an errant child, errant conduct.*

er·rat·ic (ə rat′ik) *adj.* **1.** acting or moving in an irregular or confused way: *the erratic path of a tornado.* **2.** straying from the accepted or usual standard; eccentric: *erratic behavior.* —**er·rat′i·cal·ly,** *adv.*

er·ro·ne·ous (ə rō′nē əs) *adj.* marked by or containing error; mistaken; incorrect: *an erroneous conclusion.* —**er·ro′ne·ous·ly,** *adv.* —**er·ro′ne·ous·ness,** *n.*

er·ror (er′ər) *n.* **1.** something incorrectly done, believed, or stated; mistake: *There is an error in his subtraction. There were five spelling errors on her test paper.* **2.** the state or condition of being mistaken or incorrect: *They are in error if they think that she is coming to the party.* **3.** the amount by which something is wrong: *How large was the error in his calculations?* **4.** *Baseball.* a misplay by a fielder that allows a base runner to reach a base safely or a batter to remain at bat when, if the play had been made properly, the runner or batter would have been put out.

erst·while (urst′hwīl′, urst′wīl′) *adj.* former: *an erstwhile friend.* —*adv. Archaic.* formerly.

er·u·dite (er′oo dīt′, er′yoo dīt′) *adj.* having or showing much knowledge or learning; scholarly; learned: *an erudite speaker.* —**er′u·dite′ly,** *adv.* —**er′u·dite′ness,** *n.*

er·u·di·tion (er′oo dish′ən, er′yoo dish′ən) *n.* much knowledge or learning; scholarship.

e·rupt (i rupt′) *v.i.* **1.** to throw forth something suddenly and violently: *The geyser erupts every few hours.* **2.** to burst or be thrown forth: *Enough lava had erupted from the volcano to bury the entire village.* **3.** to break out suddenly and violently: *A fight erupted during the game between the opposing teams.* **4.** to break out, as in a rash: *Many youngsters erupt with acne.* —*v.t.* to throw forth (something, such as steam, water, or lava) suddenly and violently.

e·rup·tion (i rup′shən) *n.* **1.** the act of erupting: *The last eruption of that volcano was in 1900.* **2.** a slight inflammation of the skin; rash.

e·rup·tive (i rup′tiv) *adj.* **1.** bursting forth; tending to erupt: *an eruptive geyser.* **2.** causing or characterized by a rash, such as certain diseases. **3.** of or relating to volcanic eruptions; formed by a volcano.

-ery *suffix* (used to form nouns) **1.** a place of business or place where something is made, stored, or sold: *bakery, brewery.* **2.** a place or home for: *nunnery.* **3.** the art, practice, or profession of: *thievery, cookery, archery.* **4.** the state or condition of: *slavery.* **5.** the characteristics, practices, or principles of: *knavery, trickery.* **6.** a collection or group of: *greenery, crockery.*

Es, the symbol for einsteinium.

E·sau (ē′sô) *n.* in the Old Testament, the son of Isaac and Rebecca who sold his birthright to his younger twin brother, Jacob, for a dish of food.

es·ca·late (es′kə lāt′) *v.,* **es·ca·lat·ed, es·ca·lat·ing.** —*v.t.* to increase or enlarge by stages: *to escalate a war.* —*v.i.* to be increased or enlarged by stages: *The quarrel between the two boys escalated into a fight.* —**es′ca·la′tion,** *n.*

es·ca·la·tor (es′kə lā′tər) *n.* a moving stairway made up of a series of steps attached to a continuous chain, used for carrying passengers from one floor or level to another.

es·cal·lop (es kol′əp) *n.* another word for **scallop.**

es·ca·pade (es′kə pād′) *n.* action or behavior that is wild, reckless, or full of adventure.

es·cape (es kāp′) *v.,* **es·caped, es·cap·ing.** —*v.i.* **1.** to get away or free; gain or regain liberty: *The bird escaped from the cage.* **2.** to avoid or remain free, as from capture, punishment, harm, or danger: *They chased the bank robber, but he escaped in the crowd.* **3.** to leak or flow out from a container or enclosure: *Gas escaped from the pipe.* —*v.t.* **1.** to get away or free from; elude: *The actress escaped her fans outside the theater by going out the back door.* **2.** to avoid or remain free from: *The driver of the car narrowly escaped death.* **3.** to fail to be noticed or remembered by; slip by or away from: *Her name escapes me at the moment.* —*n.* **1.** the act of escaping: *Their escape was by way of the sea.* **2.** the fact or state of having escaped. **3.** a way of escaping: *A rope ladder served as an escape from the burning house.* **4.** a way of temporarily avoiding or forgetting problems, worries, or the like: *Reading detective stories is his escape.*

es·cape·ment (es kāp′mənt) *n.* **1.** a device in a clock or watch made up of a small toothed wheel and a catch. The back-and-forth movement of the catch allows one tooth of the wheel to escape at each swing, thus controlling the regular movement of a system of gears that moves the hands. **2.** a mechanism that regulates the movement of a typewriter carriage during use.

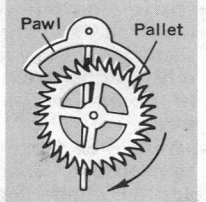

Escapement

escape velocity, the minimum speed that something, such as a rocket, must reach to escape the gravitational pull of the earth or another body: *Escape velocity from earth is about seven miles per second.*

es·cap·ism (es kā′piz′əm) *n.* the tendency to escape the dull routine and responsibilities of daily life by daydreaming or by reading, watching television, or the like.

es·ca·role (es′kə rōl′) *n.* a plant bearing curly green leaves, used especially in salads.

es·carp·ment (es kärp′mənt) *n.* 1. a steep slope or cliff. 2. a fortification consisting of a man-made steep slope.

es·chew (es chōō′) *v.t.* to keep away from; avoid; shun: *to eschew wickedness.*

es·cort (*n.,* es′kôrt; *v.,* es kôrt′) *n.* 1. a person or persons who accompany another or others as a courtesy, honor, or protection: *The visiting king had an escort of armed guards.* 2. a man or boy who accompanies a woman or girl to a party, dance, or the like. 3. one or more ships or airplanes accompanying or protecting another. —*v.t.* to accompany as a courtesy, honor, or protection; act as an escort to: *John escorted Ann to the party. The police escorted the senator to his car after the rally.*

es·crow (es′krō, es krō′) *Law. n.* a deed or bond, or money or other property, held by a third person until certain conditions are fulfilled.

in escrow. held by a third person until certain conditions are fulfilled: *They placed the money for rent in escrow until the landlord repaired the hot water heater.*

es·cutch·eon (es kuch′ən) *n.* a shield or shield-shaped surface carrying a coat of arms.

-ese *suffix* 1. (used to form nouns) a. a person who was born or is living in: *Burmese.* b. the language of: *Japanese.* 2. (used to form adjectives) of, relating to, or coming from: *Chinese.*

Es·ki·mo (es′kə mō′) *n. pl.,* **Es·ki·mos** or **Es·ki·mo.** 1. a member of a Mongoloid race of people living in Alaska, northern Canada, Greenland, and northeastern Siberia. 2. the language spoken by these people. —*adj.* of or relating to the Eskimos, their language, or their culture. Also, **Inuit.**

Escutcheon

Eskimo dog. a dog of a breed native to Greenland and northern Canada, having a thick, shaggy coat, broad chest, and curved bushy tail, used by the Eskimos to draw heavy sleds. The name is often also applied to other dogs used by the Eskimos, such as the Alaskan malamute, Siberian husky, and Samoyed.

e·soph·a·gus (i sof′ə gəs) *n. pl.,* **e·soph·a·gi** (i sof′ə jī′). a passageway or tube through which food passes from the mouth to the stomach; gullet.

es·o·ter·ic (es′ə ter′ik) *adj.* 1. understood by or intended for a small and select group of people; of or for a chosen few: *esoteric rites, an esoteric doctrine.* 2. hard to understand: *an esoteric discussion on the meaning of life.* 3. kept secret; private; confidential. —**es′o·ter′i·cal·ly,** *adv.*

Esophagus

esp., especially.

ESP, extrasensory perception.

es·pe·cial (es pesh′əl) *adj.* special; particular: *What he thinks is of especial importance to her.*

es·pe·cial·ly (es pesh′ə lē) *adv.* particularly; principally; exceptionally: *The sea is rough here, especially in the winter. She called especially to speak to her brother.*

Es·pe·ran·to (es′pə rän′tō, es′pə ran′tō) *n.* an artificial language based on the major European languages, having a simplified system of grammar.

es·pi·o·nage (es′pē ə näzh′, es′pē ə nij) *n.* the practice of spying, especially the use of spies by one country to discover the military or political secrets of other countries.

es·pla·nade (es′plə näd′, es′plə näd′) *n.* an open, level space, especially along a shore, used as a public walkway or roadway; promenade.

es·pous·al (es pou′zəl) *n.* 1. the act of espousing; adoption; advocacy: *the espousal of a political doctrine.* 2. also, **espousals.** a ceremony of engagement or marriage.

es·pouse (es pouz′) *v.t.,* **es·poused, es·pous·ing.** 1. to take up or adopt; advocate or embrace: *to espouse a religious belief.* 2. to marry; wed. 3. to promise or give in marriage.

es·prit (es prē′) *n.* a lively wit; spirit; vivacity.

es·prit de corps (es prē′ de kôr′) a feeling of pride, loyalty, and devotion found in a group and among its members. [French *esprit de corps* spirit of a body.]

es·py (es pī′) *v.t.,* **es·pied, es·py·ing.** to catch sight of (something hidden or at a distance); see: *She espied the children in the bushes.*

Esq., Esquire.

es·quire (es kwīr′, es′kwīr) *n.* 1. a young attendant to a medieval knight; squire. 2. a man belonging to the English gentry, ranking next below a knight. 3. **Esquire.** Mr. or Dr. ▲ a form of respectful or polite address used in writing. It is placed after a man's last name and a comma, and it is usually abbreviated as *Esq.: Thomas Williams, Esq.*

-ess *suffix* used to form feminine nouns: *lioness.*

es·say (*n.,* es′ā, *def. 2 also* e sā′; *v.,* e sā′) *n.* 1. a short written composition on a particular subject. 2. an effort or attempt to do something; endeavor. —*v.t.* to try; attempt.

es·say·ist (es′ā ist) *n.* a writer of essays.

Es·sen (es′ən) *n.* a city in northwestern West Germany. Pop. (1976 est.), 670,200.

es·sence (es′əns) *n.* 1. something that makes a thing what it is; necessary and basic part: *The essence of poetry is invention* (Samuel Johnson). 2. a substance containing, in concentrated form, the basic parts of the thing from which it is taken; extract: *essence of peppermint.* 3. a perfume.

es·sen·tial (i sen′shəl) *adj.* 1. very important or necessary: *It is essential that we arrive early for the surprise party.* 2. forming or being the basis of something; fundamental: *Having a good sense of balance is essential to riding a bike.* —*n.* a necessary or basic part: *He outlined the essentials of his plan.* —**es·sen′tial·ly,** *adv.*

essential oil, any of various oils that give a plant its characteristic flavor or fragrance. Essential oils are extracted from plant tissues and used to make perfumes and flavorings.

-est¹ *suffix* 1. (used to form the superlative degree of adjectives) most: *coldest.* 2. (used to form the superlative degree of adverbs) most: *soonest.* [Old English *-est, -ost.*]

-est² *suffix* used to form the archaic second person singular of verbs: *doest.* [Old English *-est, -ast.*]

est. 1. established. 2. estate. 3. estimated.

EST, Eastern Standard Time.

es·tab·lish (es tab′lish) *v.t.* 1. to set up permanently; found: *to establish a colony in a new land, to establish a university.* 2. to settle (oneself) securely or permanently, as in a business: *The lawyer established himself in his new*

at; āpe; cär; end; mē; it; īce; hot; ōld; fôrk; wood; fōōl; oil; out; up; turn; sing; thin; this; hw in white; zh in treasure. The symbol ə stands for the sound of a in about, e in taken, i in pencil, o in lemon, and u in circus.

E

327

offices. **3.** to introduce and win permanent acceptance for; gain recognition of: *to establish a law, to establish one's reputation.* **4.** to show or prove to be true: *to establish a motive, to establish a fact.*

established church, a church recognized as the official church of a particular nation.

es·tab·lish·ment (es tab′lish mənt) *n.* **1.** the act of establishing or the state of being established. **2.** something established, such as a household, business, or institution: *Stores and restaurants are private establishments; the police and fire departments are public establishments.* **3. the Establishment.** a group of people or institutions that have the most influence or control in a nation or society.

es·tate (es tāt′) *n.* **1.** a piece of land with a large house; landed property: *He spends his summers at his country estate.* **2.** all the property or possessions of a person, especially at his death. **3.** a condition or stage in life: *When I am grown to man's estate, I shall be very proud and great* (Robert Louis Stevenson).

es·teem (es tēm′) *v.t.* **1.** to consider good or important; have high regard or respect for; value highly: *to esteem someone's opinion.* **2.** to judge to be; consider; regard: *He esteemed himself lucky.* —*n.* **1.** high regard or respect: *His acts of charity won him much esteem in the community.* **2.** judgment; consideration: *In Pauline's esteem, the movie was bad.*

es·ter (es′tər) *n.* an organic compound formed by the reaction of an alcohol with an acid, occurring naturally as animal or vegetable fat, oil, or wax.

Es·ther (es′tər) *n.* **1.** in the Old Testament, the Jewish queen of the king of Persia. She saved her people from being slaughtered. **2.** the book of the Old Testament that tells her story.

es·thete (es′thēt) another spelling of **aesthete.**

es·thet·ic (es thet′ik) another spelling of **aesthetic.**

es·thet·ics (es thet′iks) another spelling of **aesthetics.**

es·ti·ma·ble (es′tə mə bəl) *adj.* worthy of or deserving high regard or respect: *The senator has an estimable reputation for honesty.* —**es′ti·ma·bly,** *adv.*

es·ti·mate (*n.,* es′tə mit; *v.,* es′tə māt′) *n.* **1.** a judgment or opinion, as of the value, quality, extent, size, or cost of something: *an estimate of the height of a mountain, an estimate of the age of an antique.* **2.** a written statement of this: *The mechanic gave Dad an estimate on repairing the car.* —*v.t.,* **es·ti·mat·ed, es·ti·mat·ing.** to form a judgment or opinion of: *He estimated that the trip would take three hours.*

es·ti·ma·tion (es′tə mā′shən) *n.* **1.** a judgment or opinion: *The plan was a good one in their estimation.* **2.** the act of estimating. **3.** a favorable opinion; regard or respect; esteem: *He is held in the highest estimation by everyone.*

Es·to·ni·a (es tō′nē ə) *n.* a republic of the Soviet Union, in the northwestern part of the country, on the Baltic Sea. Official name: **Estonian Soviet Socialist Republic.** Area 17,400 sq. mi. Pop. (1970), 1,356,000.

Es·to·ni·an (es tō′nē ən) *adj.* of or relating to Estonia or its people. —*n.* **1.** a person who was born or is living in Estonia. **2.** the language of Estonia.

es·trange (es trānj′) *v.t.,* **es·tranged, es·trang·ing. 1.** to turn (someone) from kind or friendly feelings to unkind or unfriendly feelings; alienate: *He estranged his friends by arguing with them constantly.* **2.** to keep apart: *He estranged himself from the group.* —**es·trange′-ment,** *n.*

es·tu·ar·y (es′chōō er′ē) *n. pl.,* **es·tu·ar·ies. 1.** the mouth or lower course of a river where the current meets the sea and is affected by the tides. **2.** an arm or inlet of the sea.

-et *suffix* (used to form nouns) small: *islet.*

etc., et cetera: *At the zoo we saw many kinds of animals: lions, tigers, monkeys, bears, etc.*

et cet·er·a (et set′ər ə) and so forth; and the rest; and others. [Latin *et cetera* and other things.]

etch (ech) *v.t.* **1.** to engrave (a picture or design) on a surface by means of acid. **2.** to sketch or outline on (a metal plate) by this method. —*v.i.* to engage in the art of etching.

etch·ing (ech′ing) *n.* **1.** the art or process of engraving a picture or design on a surface, as of metal, by means of acid. The surface of the plate is covered with wax, and the design is scratched into the wax with a needle, thus exposing parts of the metal plate. The plate is then dipped into an acid solution, which eats away the exposed parts. **2.** an etched figure, design, or plate. **3.** an impression or print made by covering an etched plate with ink and running it through a printing press, thus transferring the design to a piece of paper.

e·ter·nal (i turn′əl) *adj.* **1.** without beginning or end; lasting forever. **2.** forever the same; never changing: *the eternal laws of nature.* **3.** seeming to last or continue forever; perpetual: *She complained about the eternal noise of the construction next door.* —*n.* **the Eternal.** God. —**e·ter′nal·ly,** *adv.*

e·ter·ni·ty (i tur′nə tē) *n. pl.,* **e·ter·ni·ties. 1.** time without beginning or end; infinite time. **2.** all future time, especially the time after death. **3.** a seemingly endless length of time: *He waited an eternity for her.*

-eth *suffix* used to form the archaic third person singular of verbs: *doeth.*

e·ther (ē′thər) *n.* a colorless, flammable liquid with a strong, sweetish odor, used especially as an anesthetic and as a solvent.

e·the·re·al (i thēr′ē əl) *adj.* **1.** very light and delicate; airy: *ethereal music.* **2.** of or relating to heaven or the heavens; heavenly. —**e·the′re·al·ly,** *adv.*

eth·i·cal (eth′i kəl) *adj.* **1.** of or relating to ethics or standards of right and wrong. **2.** according to accepted standards of conduct, especially the standards or code of a profession: *It is not ethical for a lawyer to reveal information a client has told him in confidence.* —**eth′i·cal·ly,** *adv.*

eth·ics (eth′iks) *n., pl.* **1.** a branch of philosophy that deals with human conduct, the meaning of moral codes, and the standards for judging right and wrong. ▲ used with a singular verb. **2.** standards of conduct, as of a profession: *the ethics of the legal profession.* ▲ used with a plural verb.

E·thi·o·pi·a (ē′thē ō′pē ə) *n.* a country in eastern Africa, formerly known as **Abyssinia.** Capital, Addis Ababa. Area, 457,268 sq. mi. Pop. (1971 est.), 25,250,000. —**E′thi·o′pi·an,** *adj., n.*

eth·nic (eth′nik) *adj.* of or relating to a group of people having certain characteristics in common, such as language, culture, history, race, or national origin.

eth·no·log·i·cal (eth′nə loj′i kəl) *adj.* of or relating to ethnology. —**eth′no·log′i·cal·ly,** *adv.*

eth·nol·o·gy (eth nol′ə jē) *n.* the study of the various racial and ethnic groups of mankind, and of their origin, characteristics, customs, cultures, and distribution.

eth·yl (eth′əl) *n.* a chemical radical present in many compounds, such as ether and ethyl alcohol.

ethyl alcohol, see **alcohol** *(def. 1).*

et·i·quette (et′i kit, et′i ket′) *n.* **1.** forms of proper or polite behavior in society; good manners. **2.** rules for proper or formal conduct in a specific area, such as a profession or official ceremony: *the etiquette of diplomacy.*

Et·na, Mount (et′nə) a high, active volcano in northeastern Sicily.

E·ton College (ēt′ən) a famous preparatory school for boys, located at Eton, a town near London, England.

E·tru·ri·a (i troor′ē ə) *n.* an ancient country in west-central Italy.

E·trus·can (i trus′kən) *adj.* of, like, or relating to Etruria. —*n.* **1.** a person who lived in Etruria. **2.** the language of Etruria.

-ette *suffix* (used to form nouns) **1.** small: *kitchenette.* **2.** female: *usherette.* **3.** a substitute for or imitation of: *Leatherette.*

é·tude (ā′tood, ā′tyood) *n.* a musical composition for a solo instrument, intended mainly for practice. [French *étude* study, exercise.]

et·y·mo·log·i·cal (et′ə mə loj′i kəl) *adj.* of or relating to etymology. —**et′y·mo·log′i·cal·ly,** *adv.*

et·y·mol·o·gist (et′ə mol′ə jist) *n.* a student of or an expert in etymology.

et·y·mol·o·gy (et′ə mol′ə jē) *n. pl.,* **et·y·mol·o·gies. 1.** the history of a word, tracing it from its origin to its present form, including the changes in spelling and meaning that have taken place. **2.** the study of the history of words.

● An **etymology** traces the history of a word from its earliest roots to its modern form in our language. People originally felt that the purpose of tracing the history of a word was to learn its "true" meaning and "proper" usage. The belief that the correct meaning of a word is its original meaning was rejected in the nineteenth century. At that time, etymologies were studied by scholars who were interested in discovering the origin of words, not in establishing how the words should be used. Modern scholars go even further in their study of etymologies. They study a word not only in terms of its own history, but in terms of the history, culture, and language of the people who have created and used the word.

It is often relatively easy to trace the etymology of the older words in our language. Many of these words came from simple words in the earlier forms of English or from the French language which the Normans brought with them when they invaded England in the eleventh century.

Although you would not guess it to be so, the etymologies of these older words are often more easily discovered than the etymologies of modern words. With increased travel and modern forms of mass communication such as radio and television, words come into, and sometimes leave, our language at a faster rate than at any other time in history. For example, the etymology of the word *hip* that refers to a part of the body is known, even though this is one of the oldest words in our language. But the origin of the slang word *hip* that means "well-informed" or "aware" is not known, even though this is a very modern word and is the source of the even newer term *hippie.*

Although some words have interesting etymologies, such as *boycott, tantalize,* and *candidate,* most words can be traced back to simple origins that are of interest mainly to professional language scholars. Because of this, we have omitted many etymologies from this book that would not be of special interest and have included those etymologies that provide an interesting or surprising story about the history of a word.

eu- *prefix* good, well, or pleasing: *eulogy.*

Eu, the symbol for europium.

Eu·boe·a (yoo bē′ə) *n.* the largest Greek island in the Aegean Sea, just off the eastern coast of the Greek peninsula.

eu·ca·lyp·tus (yoo′kə lip′təs) *n. pl.,* **eu·ca·lyp·tus·es** or **eu·ca·lyp·ti** (yoo′kə lip′tī). any of a large group of evergreen trees or shrubs widely grown in warm climates for its hard, durable wood, resins, and oils.

Eu·cha·rist (yoo′kə rist) *n.* another term for **Holy Communion.**

Eu·cha·ris·tic (yoo′kə ris′tik) *adj.* of or relating to the Eucharist.

Eu·clid (yoo′klid) 323?–285 B.C., Greek mathematician.

Eu·gene (yoo jēn′) *n.* a city in western Oregon. Pop. (1970), 76,346.

eu·gen·ic (yoo jen′ik) *adj.* **1.** relating to the improvement of the human race according to the principles of eugenics. **2.** of or relating to eugenics. —**eu·gen′i·cal·ly,** *adv.*

eu·gen·ics (yoo jen′iks) *n., pl.* the science that deals with improving the human race by controlling heredity, as by a careful selection of parents. ▲ used with a singular verb.

eu·gle·na (yoo glē′nə) *n.* a microscopic, green, one-celled organism that lives in water.

eu·lo·gist (yoo′lə jist) *n.* a person who eulogizes.

eu·lo·gis·tic (yoo′lə jis′tik) *adj.* of or relating to eulogy; praising.

eu·lo·gize (yoo′lə jīz′) *v.t.,* **eu·lo·gized, eu·lo·giz·ing.** to praise highly in speech or writing; deliver a eulogy about.

eu·lo·gy (yoo′lə jē) *n. pl.,* **eu·lo·gies.** a speech or writing in praise of a person or thing: *The President delivered a eulogy for the dead general.*

eu·nuch (yoo′nək) *n.* **1.** a castrated man. **2.** a castrated man in the service of an Oriental ruler as a court official or harem guard.

eu·phe·mism (yoo′fə miz′əm) *n.* **1.** the use of a mild word or expression in place of a blunt or harsh one. **2.** a word or expression used in this way. For example, in the sentence *He put the dog to sleep, put to sleep* is a euphemism for *killed.*

● A **euphemism** is a mild, vague, or polite word or phrase that is used in place of one that is more precise, blunt, and realistic. Every society judges some action, thing, or concept to be too disagreeable, offensive, or shocking to be referred to directly. When something is thought of in this way, so are the words that refer to it. Euphemisms are created to replace these unacceptable or forbidden words. One of the characteristics of a euphemism, however, is that it often tends to lose its euphemistic quality and take on the significance and connotation of the stronger term and then become, itself, considered unacceptable. For example, it was once acceptable to refer to a country that was not as economically, educationally, and politically advanced as our own as *primitive* or *backward.* These words were rejected as sounding too arrogant and disdainful and were replaced by the milder term *underdeveloped.* This word was also in turn rejected, and the more positive term *emerging* is now being used in its place. Obviously, the condition being described had not changed. What had changed was the way that people felt about the words that described the condition.

In the nineteenth century, many words that referred to the body and to sex were considered taboo. For example, the word *leg* was replaced by the euphemism *limb.* This prudishness was sometimes carried to ridiculous lengths.

at; āpe; cär; end; mē; it; īce; hot; ōld; fôrk; wood; fool; oil; out; up; turn; sing; thin; **this;** hw in white; zh in treasure. The symbol ə stands for the sound of **a** in about, **e** in taken, **i** in pencil, **o** in lemon, and **u** in circus.

An English novelist visiting America in 1837 wrote with surprise of having heard the legs of a piano being called its limbs. Words that describe certain specifically male or female animals, such as *boar, buck, ram, stallion,* and *sow,* temporarily disappeared almost completely from our language. For example, such euphemisms as *cow-creature* and *seed-ox* often replaced the word *bull.*

The most difficult and frightening things for most people to talk about are aging and death, and a great many of our modern euphemisms refer to them. We say that people *depart, pass on, pass away,* or *are no longer with us* because these words sound less harsh and final than the word *die.* A person who is over sixty-five years old is no longer *aged* or *old,* but a *senior citizen.* Poverty is another subject that, particularly in a land of great wealth, we try to treat euphemistically. So we often refer to the poor as being *underprivileged, economically deprived,* or *members of a low-income group,* rather than simply as being *poor.* A *slum* is called a *depressed area* or even *the inner city.*

Euphemisms are often used by politicians in order to soften harsh truths. A serious economic decline is referred to as a *recession,* because the word *depression* reminds people too much of the desperate economic problems of the Depression of the 1930s. You will often hear *atomic weapons* referred to euphemistically as *nuclear deterrents,* because it is more acceptable to consider the devastating power of these weapons being used defensively rather than offensively.

The purpose of language is to communicate, but the use of euphemisms is often, at best, an attempt not to communicate and, at worst, can be an attempt to deceive.

---

eu·phe·mis·tic (yŏŏ′fə mis′tik) *adj.* of or using euphemisms; serving as a euphemism. —**eu′phe·mis′ti·cal·ly,** *adv.*

eu·pho·ni·ous (yŏŏ fō′nē əs) *adj.* pleasant and agreeable in sound; pleasant to hear: *A nightingale has a more euphonious call than a crow.* —**eu·pho′ni·ous·ly,** *adv.*

eu·pho·ny (yŏŏ′fə nē) *n. pl.,* **eu·pho·nies.** the quality of having a pleasant sound.

eu·pho·ri·a (yŏŏ fôr′ē ə) *n.* a feeling of well-being and happiness.

Eu·phra·tes (yŏŏ frā′tēz) *n.* a river in southwestern Asia, flowing from east-central Turkey through Syria and Iraq into the Persian Gulf. The Euphrates joins the Tigris River in southeastern Iraq.

Eur. 1. Europe. 2. European.

Eur·a·sia (yoo rā′zhə) *n.* Europe and Asia, considered as a single continent.

Eur·a·sian (yoo rā′zhən) *adj.* 1. of or relating to Eurasia. 2. of mixed European and Asian descent. —*n.* a person who is of mixed European and Asian descent.

eu·re·ka (yoo rē′kə) *interj.* used as an exclamation of triumph upon the sudden discovery of something or the solving of a problem. [Greek *heurēka* I have found (it); said to have been exclaimed by Archimedes when he discovered a test for the purity of gold.]

Eu·rip·i·des (yoo rip′ə dēz′) 485?–406 B.C., Greek dramatist.

Eu·rope (yoor′əp) *n.* the continent between Asia and the Atlantic Ocean. Area, 4,063,000 sq. mi. Pop. (1971 est.), 466,000,000.

Eu·ro·pe·an (yoor′ə pē′ən) *adj.* of or relating to Europe or its people. —*n.* 1. a person who was born or is living in Europe. 2. a person of European descent.

eu·ro·pi·um (yoo rō′pē əm) *n.* a metallic element of the rare-earth group, used especially in nuclear reactors and in tubes for color television. Symbol: **Eu**

Eu·sta·chi·an tube (yŏŏ stā′kē ən, yŏŏ stā′shən) a canal or passage extending from the pharynx to the middle ear. The Eustachian tube equalizes the air pressure on the inside of the eardrum with the atmospheric pressure on the outside. [From Bartolommeo *Eustachio,* a sixteenth-century Italian anatomist who discovered it.]

eu·tha·na·sia (yŏŏ′thə nā′zhə) *n.* the painless killing of a person suffering from a painful and incurable disease.

EVA, extravehicular activity.

e·vac·u·ate (i vak′yŏŏ āt′) *v.t.,* **e·vac·u·at·ed, e·vac·u·at·ing.** 1. to leave or make empty; vacate: *The troops evacuated their position. Police evacuated the theater.* 2. to cause to leave; remove: *Firemen evacuated the tenants from the burning building.* 3. to discharge waste matter from: *to evacuate the bladder.* 4. to discharge (waste matter): *to evacuate urine from the bladder.*

e·vac·u·a·tion (i vak′yŏŏ ā′shən) *n.* 1. the act of evacuating or the state of being evacuated. 2. the discharge of waste matter from the body, especially from the bladder or bowels.

e·vac·u·ee (i vak′yŏŏ ē′) *n.* a person removed from an area of danger or disaster: *The evacuees from the flooded area were housed in the school.*

e·vade (i vād′) *v.t.,* **e·vad·ed, e·vad·ing.** 1. to avoid, as by trickery or cunning; elude: *The fox evaded the hounds and hunters.* 2. to escape or avoid the responsibility of: *to evade taxes.* 3. to avoid answering: *to evade a question.*

e·val·u·ate (i val′yŏŏ āt′) *v.t.,* **e·val·u·at·ed, e·val·u·at·ing.** 1. to establish the value or amount of; appraise: *to evaluate a stamp collection.* 2. to determine the meaning or importance of; assess: *The diplomat was asked to evaluate the peace talks.*

e·val·u·a·tion (i val′yŏŏ ā′shən) *n.* 1. the act or process of evaluating. 2. the result of evaluating; appraisal or judgment.

ev·a·nes·cence (ev′ə nes′əns) *n.* a gradual passing, or fading away: *the evanescence of a rainbow.*

ev·a·nes·cent (ev′ə nes′ənt) *adj.* tending to pass or fade away gradually; fleeting.

e·van·gel·i·cal (ē′van jel′i kəl) *adj.* 1. of, in, or according to the four Gospels or the New Testament. 2. teaching that faith in Christ is the only way to achieve salvation, and that the Bible is the sole religious authority: *an evangelical church.* —**e′van·gel′i·cal·ly,** *adv.*

e·van·gel·ism (i van′jə liz′əm) *n.* enthusiastic preaching or spreading of the Gospel, as by traveling preachers or at revival meetings; work of evangelists.

e·van·gel·ist (i van′jə list) *n.* 1. a preacher of the Gospel, especially one who travels from place to place and holds religious meetings. 2. **Evangelist.** one of the four authors of the Gospels: Matthew, Mark, Luke, or John.

e·van·gel·is·tic (i van′jə lis′tik) *adj.* 1. of or relating to the Evangelists. 2. of or relating to evangelists or evangelism.

Ev·ans, Mary Ann (ev′ənz) see **Eliot, George.**

Ev·ans·ton (ev′ən stən) *n.* a city in northeastern Illinois, a suburb of Chicago. Pop. (1970), 79,808.

Ev·ans·ville (ev′ənz vil′) *n.* a city in southwestern Indiana. Pop. (1970), 138,764.

e·vap·o·rate (i vap′ə rāt′) *v.,* **e·vap·o·rat·ed, e·vap·o·rat·ing.** —*v.i.* 1. to be changed from a liquid or solid into a vapor: *Water evaporates when boiled.* 2. to fade away or disappear; vanish: *His anger evaporated when Susan explained why she was late.* —*v.t.* 1. to cause (a liquid or solid) to change into a vapor: *The sun soon evaporated the morning dew.* 2. to remove moisture from, as by heating: *to evaporate milk.*

evaporated milk, unsweetened canned milk, made by removing some of the water from whole milk.

e·vap·o·ra·tion (i vap′ə rā′shən) *n.* **1.** a change from a liquid or solid state into a vapor; vaporization. **2.** the removal of moisture or liquid.

e·vap·o·ra·tor (i vap′ə rā′tər) *n.* an apparatus for removing moisture or liquid.

e·va·sion (i vā′zhən) *n.* **1.** the act of evading a duty, question, or the like: *He was charged with income tax evasion.* **2.** the means of evading something: *Changing the subject in response to a question is an evasion.*

e·va·sive (i vā′siv) *adj.* that evades or tends to evade; characterized by evasion: *evasive answers, an evasive person.* —**e·va′sive·ly,** *adv.* —**e·va′sive·ness,** *n.*

eve (ēv) *n.* **1.** the evening or day just before a holiday or other important day. **2.** the period just before: *the eve of an election, the eve of an invasion.* **3.** evening.

Eve (ēv) *n.* in the Bible, the first woman, Adam's wife.

e·ven[1] (ē′vən) *adj.* **1.** without slope or hills; completely flat; level: *an even piece of ground, even countryside.* **2.** at the same level; of uniform height: *The two mountain peaks looked even in the distance.* **3.** the same throughout; equally distributed: *an even coat of paint.* **4.** free from variations or sudden changes; regular; constant: *an even rhythm, an even heartbeat.* **5.** not easily excited; calm: *an even disposition.* **6.** the same or equal, as in amount, size, or quantity: *The score in the game was even.* **7.** that can be divided exactly by two: *Four is an even number.* —*adv.* **1.** at the very same moment; while; just: *He called even as you came in the door.* **2.** as a matter of fact; actually; indeed: *She was happy, even joyous.* **3.** though it may seem unlikely: *He was always generous, even to strangers.* **4.** in comparison; still; yet: *Her idea is even better than his.* —*v.t.* to make even: *The workmen evened the road surface. The last touchdown evened the score of the game.* [Old English *efen* level.] —**e′ven·ly,** *adv.* —**e′ven·ness,** *n.*

to get even with. to get revenge upon: *He promised to get even with them for trying to cheat him.*

e·ven[2] (ē′vən) *n.* evening. ▲ used in literature. [Old English *æēfen.*]

eve·ning (ēv′ning) *n.* **1.** the late afternoon and early nighttime; period from twilight to bedtime. **2.** the last part or closing period, as of a life. —*adj.* of, relating to, or occurring in the evening: *evening classes, the evening meal.*

evening star, the first planet, most often Venus or rarely Mercury, to appear after sunset in the western sky.

e·ven·song (ē′vən sông′) *n.* **1.** in the Anglican Church, a prayer service said or sung at evening. **2.** in the Roman Catholic Church, vespers.

e·vent (i vent′) *n.* **1.** anything that happens, especially a happening of some importance. **2.** any of the contests in a program or series of sports: *The mile run was the main event in the track meet.* **3.** the outcome of anything; result; conclusion.

in any event. in any case; at any rate; whatever happens.

in the event of. if something should occur; in case of: *In the event of rain, the game will be played tomorrow.*

e·ven-tem·pered (ē′vən tem′pərd) *adj.* not easily disturbed, excited, or angered; calm.

e·vent·ful (i vent′fəl) *adj.* **1.** marked by important or interesting happenings: *an eventful year.* **2.** having important results; momentous: *an eventful meeting.*

e·ven·tide (ē′vən tīd′) *n.* evening. ▲ used in literature.

e·ven·tu·al (i ven′chōō əl) *adj.* **1.** happening at some time in the future; bound to occur: *The eventual consequence of the friction between the two groups will be civil war.* **2.** resulting from events that go before; final; ultimate: *The eventual outcome of the project will depend on how much money is raised.*

e·ven·tu·al·i·ty (i ven′chōō al′ə tē) *n. pl.,* **e·ven·tu·al·i·ties.** a possible event or condition; possibility.

e·ven·tu·al·ly (i ven′chōō ə lē) *adv.* in the end; ultimately; finally.

ev·er (ev′ər) *adv.* **1.** at any time: *Did she ever go to Ireland?* **2.** at all times; always: *He is ever willing to help his friends.* **3.** throughout all time: *They lived happily ever after.* **4.** in any possible way: *How can we ever repay you?*

ever so. *Informal.* very; exceedingly; extremely: *The salesman was ever so helpful.*

Ev·er·est, Mount (ev′ər ist) the highest mountain in the world, located in the Himalayas on the border between Nepal and Tibet.

ev·er·glade (ev′ər glād′) *n.* **1.** a large region of low, marshy land partly covered with tall grass. **2. Everglades.** a large region of marshy lands and swamps in southern Florida.

ev·er·green (ev′ər grēn′) *adj.* (of shrubs, trees, or other plants) having green leaves or needles throughout the year. —*n.* an evergreen shrub, tree, or other plant.

ev·er·last·ing (ev′ər las′ting) *adj.* **1.** existing, continuing, or lasting forever; eternal: *The mighty God, the everlasting Father* (Isaiah 9:6). **2.** lasting for a long time: *everlasting joy.* —*n.* **1.** past and future; eternity: *From everlasting to everlasting thou art God* (Psalms: 90). **2. the Everlasting.** God.

ev·er·more (ev′ər môr′) *adv.* for and at all times; forever; eternally.

ev·er·y (ev′rē) *adj.* **1.** each of the individual members or units that make up a group or whole; each without excepting any: *Every student in the class was present today.* **2.** all possible; the utmost: *I have every confidence in his ability.* **3.** at a regular interval of: *The pills should be taken every four hours.*

every bit. in every way; entirely; quite: *She's every bit as good a cook as her mother.*

every now and then or **every now and again.** from time to time; occasionally: *He comes to visit us every now and then.*

every other. each alternate; each second: *That program is broadcast every other week.*

every so often. from time to time; occasionally.

eve·ry·bod·y (ev′rē bod′ē, ev′rē bud′ē) *pron.* every person. ▲ **Everybody** and **everyone** are both singular. In formal usage, they are used with a singular pronoun: *Everyone should do his share of the work.* In informal usage, they are sometimes used with a plural pronoun: *Everybody raised their hands to answer the question.*

eve·ry·day (ev′rē dā′) *adj.* **1.** of or relating to every day; daily: *the everyday business of one's life.* **2.** suitable for ordinary days: *everyday clothes.* **3.** not unusual; commonplace; ordinary: *an everyday occurrence.*

eve·ry·one (ev′rē wun′) *pron.* every person; everybody: *Everyone agreed that it was a good movie.* ▲ See **everybody** for usage note.

eve·ry·thing (ev′rē thing′) *pron.* **1.** all things; all: *She showed her mother everything she had bought.* **2.** what is important, highly valued, or very much wanted: *Her happiness means everything to him.*

eve·ry·where (ev′rē hwer′, ev′rē wer′) *adv.* in every place; in all places: *They traveled everywhere in England.*

e·vict (i vikt′) *v.t.* to throw out or remove (a tenant) from

at; āpe; cär; end; mē; it; īce; hot; ōld; fôrk; wood; fōōl; oil; out; up; turn; sing; thin; **th**is; hw in white; zh in treasure. The symbol ə stands for the sound of **a** in about, **e** in taken, **i** in pencil, **o** in lemon, and **u** in circus.

E

a building or other property; dispossess: *The tenant was evicted for not paying his rent.* —e·vic′tion, *n.*

ev·i·dence (ev′ə dəns) *n.* **1.** something that serves to prove or disprove a belief or conclusion; proof: *He produced much research as evidence for his theory.* **2.** an indication or sign: *Her silence was evidence of her unhappiness.* —*v.t.* **ev·i·denced, ev·i·denc·ing.** to give proof of; show clearly; demonstrate: *Lines of people waiting to buy tickets evidenced the play's success.*

ev·i·dent (ev′ə dənt) *adj.* easily seen or understood; clear; apparent: *It was evident that he didn't like the play.*

ev·i·dent·ly (ev′ə dənt lē) *adv.* clearly; apparently; obviously: *It is cloudy and windy outside, so evidently a storm is approaching.*

e·vil (ē′vəl) *adj.* **1.** morally bad; wicked; sinful: *an evil person, evil thoughts.* **2.** causing trouble or injury; harmful: *an evil custom, evil laws.* **3.** characterized by or threatening misfortune or suffering; disastrous; unlucky: *an evil omen, evil times.* —*n.* **1.** the state or condition of being morally bad; wickedness; sin: *The dictator's rule was full of evil. The sermon was about good and evil.* **2.** something that causes trouble or injury; something harmful: *War is a great evil.* —e′vil·ly, *adv.* —e′vil·ness, *n.*

e·vince (i vins′) *v.t.,* **e·vinced, e·vinc·ing.** to make evident; show clearly: *He evinced his anger by banging his fist on the table.*

e·vis·cer·ate (i vis′ə rāt′) *v.t.,* **e·vis·cer·at·ed, e·vis·cer·at·ing.** to remove the internal organs, especially the intestines, from; disembowel. —e·vis′cer·a′tion, *n.*

ev·o·ca·tion (ē′vō kā′shən, ev′ə kā′shən) *n.* the act of evoking.

e·voke (i vōk′) *v.t.,* **e·voked, e·vok·ing.** to call forth or bring out; elicit: *The reporter's question evoked an angry response. The song evoked happy memories.*

ev·o·lu·tion (ev′ə lōō′shən) *n.* **1.** a gradual process of development, growth, or change through a series of stages: *the evolution of music, the evolution of a society.* **2.** *Biology.* the theory that all living plants and animals arose from earlier and simpler forms of life, and that they gradually developed into widely different and more complicated forms through natural processes of change over millions of generations. **3.** *Mathematics.* the process of extracting the root of a number.

ev·o·lu·tion·ar·y (ev′ə lōō′shə ner′ē) *adj.* **1.** of, relating to, or resulting from gradual development or growth. **2.** of, relating to, or agreeing with the theory of evolution.

ev·o·lu·tion·ist (ev′ə lōō′shə nist) *n.* a person who believes in or supports the theory of evolution.

e·volve (i volv′) *v.,* **e·volved, e·volv·ing.** —*v.t.* to develop gradually; work out: *to evolve a new scientific theory.* —*v.i.* **1.** to undergo gradual development or growth. **2.** *Biology.* to undergo evolution.

ewe (yōō) *n.* a female sheep.

ew·er (yōō′ər) *n.* a wide-mouthed pitcher, used especially for holding or pouring water.

ex- *prefix* **1.** out of or from: *exhale, exit, export.* **2.** thoroughly; completely: *exasperate.* **3.** former; previous. ▲ followed by a hyphen and another word to form a compound: *ex-president, ex-employee.*

ex. **1.** example. **2.** examined.

Ex., Exodus.

ex·act (eg zakt′) *adj.* **1.** very accurate; precise; correct: *The clock gives the exact time. She gave the salesman a check for the exact amount.* **2.** being the same in every way: *an exact copy.* **3.** characterized by or showing accuracy: *an exact thinker.* —*v.t.* to demand and get by force or authority:

Ewer

to exact payment of a debt, to exact obedience to a command. —ex·act′ness, *n.*

ex·act·ing (eg zak′ting) *adj.* **1.** very demanding; strict; severe: *an exacting teacher.* **2.** requiring great skill, accuracy, care, or attention: *an exacting task.*

ex·ac·tion (eg zak′shən) *n.* **1.** the act of exacting. **2.** something that is exacted, such as taxes, duties, or tribute.

ex·act·i·tude (eg zak′tə tōōd′, eg zak′tə tyōōd′) *n.* the quality of being exact; accuracy; precision.

ex·act·ly (eg zakt′lē) *adv.* **1.** in an exact manner; accurately; precisely: *He followed my instructions exactly.* **2.** entirely or quite: *The accident happened exactly as the witness described it.*

ex·ag·ger·ate (eg zaj′ə rāt′) *v.,* **ex·ag·ger·at·ed, ex·ag·ger·at·ing.** —*v.t.* to make (something) seem more, larger, or greater than it is; overstate: *to exaggerate the seriousness of a problem, to exaggerate a person's faults.* —*v.i.* to make something seem more, larger, or greater than it is; overstate: *Fishermen often exaggerate when describing the fish they have caught.*

ex·ag·ger·a·tion (eg zaj′ə rā′shən) *n.* **1.** the act of exaggerating or the state of being exaggerated. **2.** an instance of exaggerating; overstatement: *Her statement of how much the dress cost was an exaggeration.*

ex·alt (eg zôlt′) *v.t.* **1.** to praise; glorify; extol: *He exalted honesty above all other virtues.* **2.** to raise, as in rank, position, character, or esteem.

ex·al·ta·tion (eg′zôl tā′shən, ek′sôl tā′shən) *n.* **1.** the act of exalting or the state of being exalted. **2.** a feeling of great joy, delight, or pride; elation.

ex·am (eg zam′) *n. Informal.* see **examination.**

ex·am·i·na·tion (eg zam′ə nā′shən) *n.* **1.** the act or process of examining: *The examination lasted one hour.* **2.** a test, especially of knowledge, skill, or qualifications: *She has an examination in chemistry.* **3.** a checking and testing of the body or a part of the body, as by a dentist or physician. **4.** a questioning of a witness in a court of law.

ex·am·ine (eg zam′in) *v.t.,* **ex·am·ined, ex·am·in·ing.** **1.** to look at closely and carefully; investigate; inspect: *She examined the merchandise before buying it.* **2.** to test, especially in order to check or learn the knowledge or skill of: *to examine applicants for a job.* **3.** to subject (a person or body part) to medical checking and testing. **4.** to question (a witness) in a court of law. —ex·am′in·er, *n.*

ex·am·ple (eg zam′pəl) *n.* **1.** one particular thing belonging to a group of things, that serves to show what the others are like; sample; illustration: *The art teacher hung several examples of the painter's work on the wall.* **2.** a person or thing that is worthy of imitation; model: *His politeness is a good example for others to follow.* **3.** a problem or exercise used to illustrate a rule, method, or process, as in arithmetic. **4.** something used to serve as a warning to others: *The judge made an example of the criminal by giving him a harsh sentence.*

for example. by way of illustration; for instance.

to set an example. to serve as a model for others.

ex·as·per·ate (eg zas′pə rāt′) *v.t.,* **ex·as·per·at·ed, ex·as·per·at·ing.** to irritate greatly; provoke to anger; infuriate: *Constant interruption of his work exasperated him.*

ex·as·per·a·tion (eg zas′pə rā′shən) *n.* the act of exasperating or the state of being exasperated.

ex·ca·vate (eks′kə vāt′) *v.t.,* **ex·ca·vat·ed, ex·ca·vat·ing.** **1.** to remove by digging: *The workman excavated the dirt at the housing site with a steam shovel.* **2.** to uncover by digging; unearth: *The archaeologists excavated the ruins of an ancient city.* **3.** to make by hollowing out; dig: *The miners excavated a tunnel in the side of the mountain.*

4. to make a hole in; hollow out: *They excavated the mountainside for a tunnel.*

ex·ca·va·tion (eks′kə vā′shən) *n.* **1.** the act or process of excavating. **2.** a hole made by excavating: *A new building will go up on the site of the excavation.* **3.** something uncovered by excavating, such as ruins.

ex·ca·va·tor (eks′kə vā′tər) *n.* a person or thing that excavates, especially a machine used for digging, such as a steam shovel.

Excavator

ex·ceed (ek sēd′) *v.t.* **1.** to go beyond the limit of: *The driver exceeded the speed limit. The contributions exceeded $10,000.* **2.** to be greater than or superior to; surpass; excel: *His knowledge of history exceeds mine.*

ex·ceed·ing (ek sē′ding) *Archaic. adj.* unusually great; surpassing. —*adv.* another word for **exceedingly.**

ex·ceed·ing·ly (ek sē′ding lē) *adv.* unusually; extremely.

ex·cel (ek sel′) *v.,* **ex·celled, ex·cel·ling.** —*v.t.* to be better or greater than, as in ability or quality; surpass; outdo: *He excelled everyone in his class in sports.* —*v.i.* to be better or greater than others; surpass others: *She excels in music and art.*

ex·cel·lence (ek′sə ləns) *n.* the fact or state of excelling; superiority, as in ability or quality: *His excellence as a skier was known to all his friends.*

ex·cel·len·cy (ek′sə lən sē) *n. pl.,* **ex·cel·len·cies. 1.** another word for **excellence. 2. Excellency.** a title of honor or form of address used in speaking or referring to governors, ambassadors, or other high officials. ▲ often preceded by *His* or *Your.*

ex·cel·lent (ek′sə lənt) *adj.* remarkably good; superior; exceptional. —**ex′cel·lent·ly,** *adv.*

ex·cel·si·or (ek sel′sē ər) *n.* fine shavings, as of wood or paper, used as a packing material or stuffing.

ex·cept (ek sept′) *prep.* with the exception of; excluding; but: *All the boys went home except Jack.* —*conj.* only; but: *He would go with us, except that he has to work.* —*v.t.* to leave out; exclude or omit: *Certain students were excepted from the final examination because their marks during the year were so high.*

ex·cept·ing (ek sep′ting) *prep.* with the exception of; except: *The store is open every day excepting Sundays and holidays.*

ex·cep·tion (ek sep′shən) *n.* **1.** the act of excepting or the state of being excepted. **2.** a person or thing that is left out or is different from others.

to take exception. to object; protest: *He took exception to the insulting remark.*

ex·cep·tion·a·ble (ek sep′shə nə bəl) *adj.* tending to cause objection; objectionable: *an insulting, exceptionable comment.* —**ex·cep′tion·a·bly,** *adv.*

ex·cep·tion·al (ek sep′shən əl) *adj.* out of the ordinary; unusual; extraordinary: *The pianist has exceptional talent. She is an exceptional student.* —**ex·cep′tion·al·ly,** *adv.*

ex·cerpt (*n.,* ek′surpt; *v.,* ek surpt′) *n.* a passage or scene selected from a larger work: *He read excerpts from his book. They saw excerpts from the new film.* —*v.t.* to take out a passage or scene from; extract; quote: *to excerpt a novel.*

ex·cess (ek′ses, ek ses′) *n. pl.,* **ex·cess·es. 1.** an amount greater than what is usual, needed, or desired; more than enough: *An excess of water in the river caused a flood.* **2.** an amount or degree by which one thing is greater than another: *He spent an excess of ten dollars over his budget.* **3.** a doing of any action to a harmful degree: *to avoid excess in eating candy.* —*adj.* being greater than what is usual, needed, or desired; extra: *We had excess baggage on the airplane and had to pay an extra amount of money for it.*

in excess of. to a greater amount or degree than: *His bank balance was in excess of $500.*

to excess. too much: *to eat to excess.*

ex·ces·sive (ek ses′iv) *adj.* beyond what is necessary, usual, or proper; immoderate: *He spends an excessive amount of money on clothes.* —**ex·ces′sive·ly,** *adv.* —**ex·ces′sive·ness,** *n.*

ex·change (eks chānj′) *v.t.,* **ex·changed, ex·chang·ing. 1.** to give for something else: *He exchanged American dollars for British pounds before his trip to London.* **2.** to give up for something in return: *By going to prison, he exchanged a life of ease for one of hard labor.* **3.** to return (a purchase) for something else: *She exchanged the blouse for a smaller one.* —*n.* **1.** the act of giving or receiving: *an exchange of prisoners of war.* **2.** the act of giving one thing in return for another: *the exchange of a purchase.* **3.** something that is given or received in return for something else: *a poor exchange.* **4.** a place where things, such as commodities or securities, are bought, sold, or traded: *a jewelry exchange.* **5.** a central office where telephone lines are connected for a town or part of a large city.

ex·change·a·ble (eks chān′jə bəl) *adj.* that can be exchanged: *Merchandise bought on sale is not exchangeable.* —**ex·change′a·bil′i·ty,** *n.*

ex·cheq·uer (eks chek′ər) *n.* **1.** a royal or national treasury. **2.** any treasury, as of an organization. **3. Exchequer.** the department of the British government that manages the national finances, including the collection and spending of the public revenue.

ex·cise[1] (ek′sīz) *n.* an indirect tax on the manufacture, sale, or use of certain things, such as liquor, tobacco, or gasoline. Also, **excise tax.** [Probably from Middle Dutch *excijs.*]

ex·cise[2] (ek sīz′) *v.t.,* **ex·cised, ex·cis·ing.** to remove by cutting: *to excise a tumor, to excise a paragraph from an essay.* [Latin *excīsus,* the past participle of *excīdere* to cut out.] —**ex·ci·sion** (ek sizh′ən), *n.*

ex·cit·a·ble (ek sī′tə bəl) *adj.* easily excited: *She is a very excitable child.* —**ex·cit′a·bil′i·ty, ex·cit′a·ble·ness,** *n.* —**ex·cit′a·bly,** *adv.*

ex·cite (ek sīt′) *v.t.,* **ex·cit·ed, ex·cit·ing. 1.** to stir up the mind or feelings of: *The idea of a picnic excited the children. His inflammatory speech excited the crowd.* **2.** to call forth: *to excite fear, to excite curiosity.* **3.** to increase the activity of (an organ or organism); stimulate.

ex·cit·ed (ek sī′tid) *adj.* stirred up; aroused; agitated. —**ex·cit′ed·ly,** *adv.*

ex·cite·ment (ek sīt′mənt) *n.* **1.** the act of exciting or the state of being excited. **2.** something that excites.

ex·cit·ing (ek sī′ting) *adj.* causing excitement; stirring; thrilling: *He told exciting stories about his trip to Africa.*

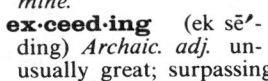

at; āpe; cär; end; mē; it; īce; hot; ōld; fôrk; wood; fo͞ol; oil; out; up; turn; sing; thin; ᴛʜis; hw in white; zh in treasure. The symbol ə stands for the sound of **a** in about, **e** in taken, **i** in pencil, **o** in lemon, and **u** in circus.

ex·claim (eks klām') *v.t.* to speak or cry out suddenly, as in anger or surprise: *"You took my baseball bat without asking me!" exclaimed Phil to his brother.*

ex·cla·ma·tion (eks'klə mā'shən) *n.* **1.** the act of exclaiming. **2.** something exclaimed.

exclamation point, a punctuation mark (!) used after a word, phrase, or sentence to indicate an exclamation, as of anger or surprise. Also, **exclamation mark.**

ex·clam·a·to·ry (eks klam'ə tôr'ē) *adj.* using, containing, or expressing exclamation.

ex·clude (eks klōōd') *v.t.,* **ex·clud·ed, ex·clud·ing. 1.** to keep from entering; shut out: *All those under sixteen years of age were excluded from seeing the movie.* **2.** to leave out; omit: *The publisher excluded certain passages from the original book in the new edition.*

ex·clu·sion (eks klōō'zhən) *n.* the act of excluding or the state of being excluded.

ex·clu·sive (eks klōō'siv) *adj.* **1.** belonging to a single individual or group; not divided or shared: *Mr. Brown has exclusive ownership of the hotel.* **2.** open to or admitting only a certain select group: *He belongs to an exclusive club.* **3.** complete; entire: *The matter will be given our exclusive attention.* —**ex·clu'sive·ly,** *adv.* —**ex·clu'sive·ness,** *n.*

  exclusive of, leaving out; excluding: *The price is fifty dollars, exclusive of the sales tax.*

ex·com·mu·ni·cate (eks'kə myōō'nə kāt') *v.t.,* **ex·com·mu·ni·cat·ed, ex·com·mu·ni·cat·ing.** to expel (a person) from membership in a church. —**ex'com·mu'ni·ca'tion,** *n.*

ex·co·ri·ate (eks kôr'ē āt') *v.t.,* **ex·co·ri·at·ed, ex·co·ri·at·ing. 1.** to strip off or scrape the skin of. **2.** to scold harshly. —**ex·co'ri·a'tion,** *n.*

ex·cre·ment (eks'krə mənt) *n.* waste matter discharged from the body, especially from the bowels.

ex·cres·cence (eks kres'əns) *n.* any abnormal growth or addition, such as a wart or mole.

ex·crete (eks krēt') *v.t.,* **ex·cret·ed, ex·cret·ing.** to discharge (waste matter) from the body.

ex·cre·tion (eks krē'shən) *n.* **1.** the act of excreting. **2.** matter excreted, such as sweat or urine.

ex·cre·to·ry (eks'krə tôr'ē) *adj.* of, relating to, or for excretion: *an excretory organ.*

ex·cru·ci·at·ing (eks krōō'shē ā'ting) *adj.* causing extreme pain or suffering; agonizing; torturous. —**ex·cru'ci·at'ing·ly,** *adv.*

ex·cul·pate (eks'kul pāt') *v.t.,* **ex·cul·pat·ed, ex·cul·pat·ing.** to declare free from blame or a charge of guilt; exonerate. —**ex'cul·pa'tion,** *n.*

ex·cur·sion (eks kur'shən) *n.* **1.** a short trip made for a special purpose or for pleasure: *The class made an excursion to the museum to see the new American Indian exhibits. The family made an excursion into the country for a picnic.* **2.** a round trip on a train, ship, or other public conveyance at a reduced rate: *They took the weekend train excursion to the seashore.*

ex·cus·a·ble (eks kyōō'zə bəl) *adj.* that can be forgiven; pardonable: *an excusable error.* —**ex·cus'a·bly,** *adv.*

ex·cuse (*v.,* eks kyōōz'; *n.,* eks kyōōs') *v.t.,* **ex·cused, ex·cus·ing. 1.** to give pardon or forgiveness to: *Please excuse us for bothering you.* **2.** to release from duty, obligation, or attendance: *The judge excused the jury. He was excused from football practice because of a bruised knee.* **3.** to accept as understandable; disregard; overlook: *Knowing how upset she was, we excused her rudeness.* **4.** to serve as a reason or explanation for; justify. —*n.* **1.** a reason given in explanation; justification: *Oversleeping is not a good excuse for being late.* **2.** the act of excusing. **3.** *Informal.* example; sample: *That's a poor excuse for a sailboat.*

  to excuse oneself. a. to make an apology for oneself. **b.** to ask to be released, as from attendance or duty.

▲ **Excuse, forgive, condone** mean to overlook a fault or mistake, without wanting to blame or punish. **Excuse** often means to overlook a fault or mistake of little importance: *The boss excused her lateness after she explained that her car had broken down.* **Forgive** usually refers to pardoning a person for a serious fault or mistake, without any feeling of resentment toward that person: *He forgave his enemies.* **Condone** suggests overlooking a serious wrong, and thus silently accepting it: *The mother could not condone her son's stealing.*

ex·e·cra·ble (ek'sə krə bəl) *adj.* **1.** that deserves disgust or hatred; abominable; detestable: *Lynching is an execrable practice.* **2.** of poor quality; very bad: *an execrable movie.* —**ex'e·cra·ble·ness,** *n.* —**ex'e·cra·bly,** *adv.*

ex·e·crate (ek'sə krāt') *v.t.,* **ex·e·crat·ed, ex·e·crat·ing. 1.** to condemn severely; curse. **2.** to have disgust or hatred for; abominate; detest.

ex·e·cra·tion (ek'sə krā'shən) *n.* **1.** the act of execrating. **2.** a curse. **3.** a person or thing that is execrated.

ex·e·cute (ek'sə kyōōt') *v.t.,* **ex·e·cut·ed, ex·e·cut·ing. 1.** to carry out; fulfill: *to execute an order.* **2.** to put into effect; administer; enforce: *to execute a law.* **3.** to put to death, especially according to a legal sentence: *to execute a convicted murderer.* **4.** to produce, especially according to a plan or design: *A well-known artist executed that painting.* **5.** to carry out or make valid by doing whatever is legally required: *The lawyer executed the will.*

ex·e·cu·tion (ek'sə kyōō'shən) *n.* **1.** the act of carrying out or putting into effect: *the execution of a plan.* **2.** the act of putting a person to death, especially by a legal sentence. **3.** a production or performance, as of a work of art or piece of music. **4.** a carrying out or making valid by doing whatever is legally required: *the execution of a will.*

ex·e·cu·tion·er (ek'sə kyōō'shə nər) *n.* a person who executes someone.

ex·ec·u·tive (eg zek'yə tiv) *adj.* **1.** of, relating to, or suitable for the management of affairs in business or industry: *He held an executive position as vice-president of the company.* **2.** concerned with the administration of government or the enforcement of laws. —*n.* **1.** a person who directs or manages affairs, as of a corporation: *A meeting of the company's executives was called.* **2.** the branch of government responsible for administering laws and for managing the affairs of a nation. **3.** a person or persons that make up this branch of government.

ex·ec·u·tor (eg zek'yə tər; *def. 2 also* ek'sə kyōō'tər) *n.* **1.** a person named in a will to carry out its terms. **2.** a person who carries out something or puts something into effect.

ex·em·pla·ry (eg zem'plər ē) *adj.* **1.** serving as a model or example; worthy of imitation: *exemplary behavior.* **2.** serving as a warning: *exemplary punishment.*

ex·em·pli·fi·ca·tion (eg zem'plə fi kā'shən) *n.* **1.** the act of exemplifying. **2.** something that exemplifies; model or example.

ex·em·pli·fy (eg zem'plə fī') *v.t.,* **ex·em·pli·fied, ex·em·pli·fy·ing.** to serve as a model or example of; show by example.

ex·empt (eg zempt') *v.t.* to free from a duty or requirement; excuse: *He was exempted from the final examination because of his good grades.* —*adj.* freed from a duty or requirement; excused: *Church property is exempt from real estate taxes.*

ex·emp·tion (eg zemp'shən) *n.* **1.** the act of exempting or the state of being exempted. **2.** a deduction from taxable income allowed for oneself and for each of one's dependents.

ex·er·cise (ek'sər sīz') *n.* **1.** physical activity that trains or improves the body: *Walking is good exercise.* **2.** an activity or lesson designed or done to improve the mind: *The book has arithmetic exercises at the end of each chapter.* **3.** active use or performance: *the exercise of patience, the exercise of power.* **4.** *also,* **exercises.** a ceremony, program, or proceedings: *The graduation exercises included speeches and the presentation of awards.* —*v.,* **ex·er·cised, ex·er·cis·ing.** —*v.t.* **1.** to train or improve by means of exercise: *to exercise one's body.* **2.** to make active use of; employ: *A person should exercise his rights as a citizen by voting.* **3.** to perform or fulfill: *to exercise the duties of governor.* —*v.i.* to perform exercises: *He exercises in the gymnasium three times a week.*

ex·ert (eg zurt′) *v.t.* to make active use of: *He exerted his influence in obtaining free tickets to the concert.*

  to exert oneself. to make a great effort; try hard: *He exerted himself to make his guests feel welcome.*

ex·er·tion (eg zur′shən) *n.* **1.** great effort: *Climbing a mountain involves much physical exertion.* **2.** the act or process of putting forth or into action: *Solving the problem demanded the exertion of much thought.*

ex·ha·la·tion (eks′hə lā′shən) *n.* **1.** the act or process of exhaling. **2.** something that is exhaled, such as air or an odor.

ex·hale (eks hāl′) *v.,* **ex·haled, ex·hal·ing.** —*v.t.* **1.** to breathe out (air) from the lungs. **2.** to give off (vapor or an odor): *to exhale cigarette smoke.* —*v.i.* to breathe out air from the lungs: *We inhale and exhale in breathing.*

ex·haust (eg zôst′) *v.t.* **1.** to make very weak or tired: *The long, hot hike exhausted the children.* **2.** to use up completely: *The campers exhausted their supply of water. The child's bad behavior exhausted his mother's patience.* **3.** to study, develop, or treat thoroughly: *The writer exhausted that subject in his book.* **4.** to draw out: *to exhaust a gas from a container.* —*n.* **1.** the escape or discharge of used steam or gases from an engine. **2.** waste products, such as steam or gases, that escape or are discharged. **3.** a pipe or other means of passage, by which such waste products escape or are discharged. —**ex·haust′ed·ly,** *adv.* —**ex·haust′i·bil′i·ty,** *n.* —**ex·haust′i·ble,** *adj.*

ex·haus·tion (eg zôs′chən) *n.* **1.** the act of exhausting or the state of being exhausted. **2.** a lack of strength or energy; extreme fatigue.

ex·haus·tive (eg zôs′tiv) *adj.* overlooking or omitting nothing; thorough: *an exhaustive survey.* —**ex·haus′-tive·ly,** *adv.* —**ex·haus′tive·ness,** *n.*

ex·haust·less (eg zôst′lis) *adj.* that cannot be exhausted: *an exhaustless supply.* —**ex·haust′less·ly,** *adv.* —**ex·haust′less·ness,** *n.*

ex·hib·it (eg zib′it) *v.t.* **1.** to put on public display; show publicly: *The gallery exhibited the artist's paintings.* **2.** to make known; show; reveal: *He exhibited great talent in playing the piano.* —*n.* **1.** a public display: *We went to see the exhibit of sculpture.* **2.** a thing or things displayed publicly: *His science exhibit won first prize.* **3.** a document or thing used as evidence: *The bank robber's gun was marked as an exhibit and shown to the jury.* —**ex·hib′-it·er,** *n.*

ex·hi·bi·tion (ek′sə bish′ən) *n.* **1.** the act of exhibiting: *an exhibition of bravery.* **2.** a public display: *a skiing exhibition, an automobile exhibition.*

ex·hi·bi·tion·ism (ek′sə bish′ə niz′əm) *n.* the act of attracting attention to oneself by behaving in an intentionally conspicuous manner.

ex·hi·bi·tion·ist (ek′sə bish′ə nist) *n.* a person who intentionally attracts attention to himself; show-off.

ex·hib·i·tor (eg zib′i tər) *n.* a person or thing that exhibits or presents an exhibition.

ex·hil·a·rate (eg zil′ə rāt′) *v.t.,* **ex·hil·a·rat·ed, ex·hil·a·rat·ing.** to make cheerful, lively, or excited; stimulate:

Their trip to the amusement park exhilarated them all. —**ex·hil′a·rat′ing·ly,** *adv.*

ex·hil·a·ra·tion (eg zil′ə rā′shən) *n.* **1.** an exhilarated feeling or condition. **2.** the act of exhilarating.

ex·hort (eg zôrt′) *v.t.* to try to persuade by appeal, argument, or warning; urge strongly: *He exhorted the crew of the ship to mutiny.*

ex·hor·ta·tion (eg′zôr tā′shən, ek′sôr tā′shən) *n.* **1.** the act of exhorting. **2.** something that exhorts or is intended to exhort, such as a sermon.

ex·hor·ta·tive (eg zôr′tə tiv) *adj.* serving or intended to exhort.

ex·hu·ma·tion (eks′hyōō mā′shən) *n.* the act of exhuming: *The medical examiner ordered the exhumation of the man's body because new evidence suggested that he had been murdered.*

ex·hume (eks hyōōm′) *v.t.,* **ex·humed, ex·hum·ing.** **1.** to remove (something buried, especially a corpse) from the earth; dig up. **2.** to bring to light; disclose; reveal: *The detective exhumed hidden facts about the crime.*

ex·i·gen·cy (ek′sə jən sē) *n. pl.,* **ex·i·gen·cies.** **1.** a situation requiring prompt action, assistance, or attention; emergency: *She met the exigency by calling an ambulance for the injured man.* **2.** *also,* **exigencies.** urgent needs: *the exigencies of survival.*

ex·i·gent (ek′sə jənt) *adj.* requiring prompt action, assistance, or attention; urgent; pressing: *exigent needs.*

ex·ile (eg′zīl, ek′sīl) *v.t.,* **ex·iled, ex·il·ing.** to send away (a person) from his country or home by law or decree: *The government exiled him because of his political activities.* —*n.* **1.** the state of being exiled: *Exile was the fate of many aristocrats after the French Revolution.* **2.** a person who is expelled from his country or home.

ex·ist (eg zist′) *v.i.* **1.** to be real; have reality: *He does not believe that ghosts exist.* **2.** to continue to have being or life: *The prisoners could not exist on bread and water.* **3.** to be present or found; occur: *Outside of zoos, koalas exist only in Australia.*

ex·ist·ence (eg zis′təns) *n.* **1.** the state or fact of existing. **2.** a condition or way of existing; living; life: *The early colonists in America had a hard struggle for existence.* **3.** all that exists.

ex·ist·ent (eg zis′tənt) *adj.* **1.** now existing; present. **2.** having existence; living: *Dinosaurs are no longer existent.*

ex·it (eg′zit, ek′sit) *n.* **1.** the way out: *We left the theater by the rear exit.* **2.** the act of leaving; departure. **3.** the departure of a performer from the stage: *The actor made his exit amid much applause.* —*v.i.* to leave; go out; depart: *They exited by the back door.*

Exod., Exodus.

ex·o·dus (ek′sə dəs) *n.* **1.** a departure, especially of a great many people: *an exodus from the cities to the suburbs.* **2. the Exodus.** the departure of the Israelites from Egypt under the leadership of Moses. **3. Exodus.** the second book of the Old Testament, containing an account of this departure.

ex of·fi·ci·o (eks′ ə fish′ē ō′) by virtue of or because of one's office or position: *A governor of a state is ex officio in command of the state's militia and police force.*

ex·on·er·ate (eg zon′ə rāt′) *v.t.,* **ex·on·er·at·ed, ex·on·**

---

at; āpe; cär; end; mē; it; īce; hot; ōld; fôrk;
wood; fōōl; oil; out; up; turn; sing; thin; this;
hw in white; zh in treasure. The symbol ə
stands for the sound of a in about, e in taken,
i in pencil, o in lemon, and u in circus.

er·at·ing. to free from blame or guilt; prove or declare innocent: *The new evidence fully exonerated the accused man.* —**ex·on′er·a′tion,** *n.*

ex·or·bi·tance (eg zôr′bə təns) *n.* a going beyond proper, reasonable, or usual limits: *She was angered by the exorbitance of the food prices at that supermarket.*

ex·or·bi·tant (eg zôr′bə tənt) *adj.* going beyond proper, reasonable, or usual limits; excessive: *exorbitant prices, exorbitant demands.* —**ex·or′bi·tant·ly,** *adv.*

ex·or·cise (ek′sôr sīz′) *also,* **ex·or·cize.** *v.t.,* **ex·or·cised, ex·or·cis·ing. 1.** to drive out (an evil spirit), as by prayer or magic. **2.** to free (a person or place) from an evil spirit. —**ex′or·cis′er,** *n.*

ex·or·cism (ek′sôr siz′əm) *n.* **1.** the act or fact of exorcising. **2.** prayers or incantations used in exorcising.

ex·or·cist (ek′sôr sist) *n.* a person who exorcises.

ex·or·cize (ek′sôr sīz′) *v.t.,* **ex·or·cized, ex·or·ciz·ing.** another spelling of **exorcise.**

ex·o·skel·e·ton (ek′sō skel′ə tən) *n.* an external skeleton, such as that of insects or lobsters.

ex·o·sphere (ek′sō sfēr′) *n.* the outermost layer of the earth's atmosphere, beginning at an altitude of about 400 miles and gradually merging with outer space.

ex·o·spher·ic (ek′sō sfer′ik) *adj.* of or relating to the exosphere.

ex·ot·ic (eg zot′ik) *adj.* **1.** of or belonging to another part of the world; not native; foreign: *exotic flowers, exotic birds.* **2.** strangely beautiful or fascinating; strikingly unusual: *an exotic painting.* —**ex·ot′i·cal·ly,** *adv.*

ex·pand (eks pand′) *v.t.* **1.** to make larger, as in size; enlarge: *Heat expands metal.* **2.** to stretch or spread (something) out; unfold: *The bird expanded its wings and flew away.* **3.** to develop or express (something) in fuller form or greater detail: *to expand an idea.* **4.** to develop a number or algebraic expression to its completed or fullest form according to given rules. The algebraic expression $(a + b)^3$, when expanded, is $a^3 + 3a^2b + 3ab^2 + b^3$. —*v.i.* **1.** to grow larger in size, extent, or scope: *Metal expands when heated. The baseball league expanded by adding four new teams.* **2.** to stretch or spread out; unfold. —**ex·pand′a·ble,** *adj.*

to expand on. to discuss in greater detail: *The teacher expanded on the causes of the American Revolution.*

ex·panse (eks pans′) *n.* a wide, unbroken stretch or area: *a vast expanse of desert.*

ex·pan·si·ble (eks pan′sə bəl) *adj.* capable of being expanded. —**ex·pan′si·bil′i·ty,** *n.*

ex·pan·sion (eks pan′shən) *n.* **1.** the act of expanding or the state of being expanded. **2.** the amount or degree of enlargement or increase: *An eagle has a wing expansion of up to six feet.* **3.** something expanded: *This television play is an expansion of a short story.* **4.** a number or algebraic expression in its expanded form. The expansion of $(x + y)^2$ is $x^2 + 2xy + y^2$; the expansion of *125* is $(1 \times 10 \times 10) + (2 \times 10) + (5 \times 1)$.

ex·pan·sive (eks pan′siv) *adj.* **1.** that can expand. **2.** extending widely; broad; extensive. **3.** generous and outgoing; demonstrative; open: *He was an expansive host who made his guests feel welcome.* —**ex·pan′sive·ly,** *adv.* —**ex·pan′sive·ness,** *n.*

ex·pa·ti·ate (eks pā′shē āt′) *v.i.,* **ex·pa·ti·at·ed, ex·pa·ti·at·ing.** to write or speak at length or in detail: *The explorer expatiated for hours on his adventures.*

ex·pa·tri·ate (*v.,* eks pā′trē āt′; *n.,* eks pā′trē it, eks-pā′trē āt′) *v.t.,* **ex·pa·tri·at·ed, ex·pa·tri·at·ing. 1.** to force (a person) out of his native country. **2.** to voluntarily withdraw (oneself) from one's native country: *Many American writers expatriated themselves to Europe after World War I.* —*n.* a person who is expatriated.

ex·pect (eks pekt′) *v.t.* **1.** to look forward to: *They had expected a larger group at the party.* **2.** to look for as just, necessary, or right: *The teacher expected an explanation for the student's lateness.* **3.** *Informal.* to think; suppose: *I expect he isn't coming.*

ex·pect·an·cy (eks pek′tən sē) *n. pl.,* **ex·pect·an·cies. 1.** the state of expecting. **2.** something that is expected.

ex·pect·ant (eks pek′tənt) *adj.* **1.** having or showing expectation: *an expectant look.* **2.** waiting in expectation: *He was expectant of a promotion.* —**ex·pect′ant·ly,** *adv.*

ex·pec·ta·tion (eks′pek tā′shən) *n.* **1.** the act of expecting. **2.** the state of expecting; expectancy. **3.** *also,* **expectations.** a reason or ground for expecting; hope, as of future good or success: *He had expectations of getting a good job after graduating from college.*

ex·pec·to·rate (eks pek′tə rāt′) *v.t., v.i.,* **ex·pec·to·rat·ed, ex·pec·to·rat·ing.** to cough up and spit out something from the throat or lungs. —**ex·pec′to·ra′tion,** *n.*

ex·pe·di·en·cy (eks pē′dē ən sē) *n. pl.,* **ex·pe·di·en·cies. 1.** the state or quality of being expedient. **2.** a concern for personal gain or advantage rather than for what is right or just: *In making his campaign promises, the politician was influenced more by the expediency of winning the election than by the needs of the people.* **3.** something that is expedient. Also, **ex·pe·di·ence** (eks pē′dē əns).

ex·pe·di·ent (eks pē′dē ənt) *adj.* **1.** based on personal gain or advantage rather than on what is right or just. **2.** suitable or useful for a given situation or purpose; appropriate. —*n.* something used to bring about a desired result. —**ex·pe′di·ent·ly,** *adv.*

ex·pe·dite (eks′pə dīt′) *v.t.,* **ex·pe·dit·ed, ex·pe·dit·ing. 1.** to speed up the process or progress of: *to expedite a shipment.* **2.** to do quickly and efficiently: *to expedite a task.* —**ex′pi·dit′er,** *n.*

ex·pe·di·tion (eks′pə dish′ən) *n.* **1.** a journey made for a specific purpose: *The explorers made an expedition to the North Pole.* **2.** the people, ships, or equipment, involved in such a journey. **3.** prompt and efficient action; promptness; dispatch: *to perform one's work with expedition.*

ex·pe·di·tion·ar·y (eks′pə dish′ə ner′ē) *adj.* of, relating to, or making up an expedition: *an expeditionary force.*

ex·pe·di·tious (eks′pə dish′əs) *adj.* quick and efficient: *He used the most expeditious means possible to finish the job on time.* —**ex′pe·di′tious·ly,** *adv.* —**ex′pe·di′tious·ness,** *n.*

ex·pel (eks pel′) *v.t.,* **ex·pelled, ex·pel·ling. 1.** to force to leave: *to expel a student from school.* **2.** to drive out or discharge by force; force out: *to expel one's breath.*

ex·pend (eks pend′) *v.t.* **1.** to pay out; spend: *A great deal of money was expended for the new hospital.* **2.** to use up; consume: *to expend one's energy.*

ex·pend·a·ble (eks pen′də bəl) *adj.* **1.** that can be expended. **2.** that may be sacrificed, often in order to gain a larger advantage: *The general regarded some of the troops as expendable, and sent them out to hold off the enemy while the rest of the army retreated.*

ex·pend·i·ture (eks pen′di chər) *n.* **1.** the act of expending. **2.** something that is expended, such as money, time, or effort.

ex·pense (eks pens′) *n.* **1.** the spending of money; expenditure: *Remodeling the house involved great expense.* **2.** the cause of spending money: *The rent on his apartment was his biggest monthly expense.* **3.** money spent in order to buy or do something; cost: *We cannot afford the expense of a new car.* **4.** loss, injury, or sacrifice: *The war was won at great expense to both countries.* **5.** **expenses.** money spent in doing something, especially an assigned job or task: *The salesman was given traveling expenses by his company.*

ex·pen·sive (eks pen′siv) *adj.* high in price; very costly: *an expensive fur coat, an expensive car.* —**ex·pen′sive·ly**, *adv.* —**ex·pen′sive·ness**, *n.*

ex·pe·ri·ence (eks pēr′ē əns) *n.* **1.** something that a person has seen, done, or taken part in: *He told us of his experiences in the war.* **2.** knowledge, skill, or wisdom gained through seeing, doing, or taking part in something, often over a period of time: *The job requires three years' experience as an accountant. She doesn't have any experience in dealing with children.* —*v.t.,* **ex·pe·ri·enced, ex·pe·ri·enc·ing.** to have happen to one; undergo: *He experienced real fear when the plane developed engine trouble.*

ex·pe·ri·enced (eks pēr′ē ənst) *adj.* made skillful, knowledgeable, or wise through experience: *an experienced politician, an experienced carpenter.*

ex·per·i·ment (*n.,* eks per′ə mənt; *v.,* eks per′ə ment′) *n.* a test or trial to discover or illustrate something: *Benjamin Franklin's experiments showed that lightning is an electrical discharge.* —*v.i.* to make an experiment or experiments: *Gregor Mendel developed his theories of heredity by experimenting with garden peas.* —**ex·per′i·ment·er**, *n.*

ex·per·i·men·tal (eks per′ə ment′əl) *adj.* **1.** relating to, derived from, or based on experiments: *experimental evidence in chemistry.* **2.** used for experimentation: *an experimental drug.* **3.** of or like an experiment; tentative: *He took an experimental dip in the cold stream.* —**ex·per′i·men′tal·ly**, *adv.*

ex·per·i·men·ta·tion (eks per′ə mən tā′shən) *n.* the act or process of experimenting.

ex·pert (eks′purt, *adj., also* eks purt′) *n.* a person having special skill or knowledge in something; specialist; authority: *an expert in mathematics, an expert on foreign affairs.* —*adj.* **1.** highly skilled or knowledgeable: *He is an expert skier. That soldier is an expert marksman.* **2.** characteristic of or from an expert; authoritative: *expert advice.* —**ex·pert′ly**, *adv.* —**ex·pert′ness**, *n.*

ex·per·tise (eks′pər tēz′) *n.* special skill or knowledge.

ex·pi·ate (eks′pē āt′) *v.t.,* **ex·pi·at·ed, ex·pi·at·ing.** to make amends for; atone for: *He tried to expiate his failure by doing the job over again.*

ex·pi·a·tion (eks′pē ā′shən) *n.* **1.** the act of expiating. **2.** something that expiates; means of atonement.

ex·pi·ra·tion (eks′pə rā′shən) *n.* **1.** closing or ending; termination: *The expiration of the union contract is at the end of the month.* **2.** the act of breathing out air; exhalation.

ex·pire (eks pīr′) *v.i.,* **ex·pired, ex·pir·ing. 1.** to come to an end; terminate: *The lease on our apartment expires on May 1. Her magazine subscription expires with the March issue.* **2.** to force out air from the lungs; exhale. **3.** to die.

ex·plain (eks plān′) *v.t.* **1.** to make clear or understandable: *The pilot explained that the plane's departure would be delayed by the storm.* **2.** to tell the meaning of; interpret: *to explain the plot of a novel.* **3.** to give the reason or reasons for; account for: *Can you explain her strange behavior?*

ex·pla·na·tion (eks′plə nā′shən) *n.* **1.** the act or process of explaining: *a teacher's explanation of an arithmetic problem.* **2.** something that makes a thing clear or understandable.

ex·plan·a·to·ry (eks plan′ə tôr′ē) *adj.* that explains or makes clear: *The explanatory notes at the end of each chapter are very helpful.*

ex·ple·tive (eks′plə tiv) *n.* an exclamation or oath. *"Darn!"* is an expletive.

ex·plic·a·ble (eks plik′ə bəl, eks′plə kə bəl) *adj.* that can be explained: *His rudeness is not explicable.*

ex·pli·cate (eks′plə kāt′) *v.t.,* **ex·pli·cat·ed, ex·pli·cat·ing.** to explain clearly and in detail.

ex·pli·ca·tion (eks′plə kā′shən) *n.* **1.** the act or process of explicating. **2.** an explanation, as of a passage in a text; interpretation. **3.** a detailed account or description.

ex·plic·it (eks plis′it) *adj.* clearly stated or expressed: *He gave explicit instructions not to be disturbed.* —**ex·plic′it·ly**, *adv.* —**ex·plic′it·ness**, *n.*

ex·plode (eks plōd′) *v.,* **ex·plod·ed, ex·plod·ing.** —*v.i.* **1.** to burst suddenly and violently with a loud noise; blow up: *The sealed bottle exploded in the fire. The firecracker exploded on the sidewalk.* **2.** to expand suddenly and violently, giving off light, heat, and noise: *The nitroglycerin exploded on impact.* **3.** to break forth violently or noisily: *He exploded with rage.* **4.** to increase rapidly: *That country's population has exploded in the last few years.* —*v.t.* **1.** to cause (something) to burst suddenly and violently with a loud noise. **2.** to cause to expand suddenly and violently, giving off light, heat, and noise. **3.** to prove wrong: *The theory that the earth was flat was exploded long ago.*

ex·ploit (*n.,* eks′ploit; *v.,* eks ploit′) *n.* a heroic deed or act; bold feat: *That general's exploits in the war are well-known.* —*v.t.* **1.** to use unjustly or unfairly for selfish profit or advantage: *That factory owner exploits his workers by underpaying them.* **2.** to make practical use of; use or develop profitably: *to exploit the natural resources of a region* —**ex·ploit′a·ble**, *adj.* —**ex·ploit′er**, *n.*

ex·ploi·ta·tion (eks′ploi tā′shən) *n.* **1.** use or development: *the exploitation of water as a source of power.* **2.** unjust or unfair use for selfish reasons: *the exploitation of migrant workers.*

ex·plo·ra·tion (eks′plə rā′shən) *n.* the act or instance of exploring, especially for the purpose of discovering or investigating unknown or unfamiliar regions.

ex·plor·a·to·ry (eks plôr′ə tôr′ē) *adj.* of, relating to, or for exploration: *an exploratory voyage.*

ex·plore (eks plôr′) *v.t.,* **ex·plored, ex·plor·ing. 1.** to travel over or in (unknown or unfamiliar regions) in order to discover or investigate: *to explore the surface of the moon.* **2.** to examine or look through or into closely; scrutinize: *The historian explored the causes of the Civil War.*

ex·plor·er (eks plôr′ər) *n.* a person who explores.

ex·plo·sion (eks plō′zhən) *n.* **1.** the act of bursting or expanding suddenly and violently: *an atomic explosion.* **2.** a loud noise caused by exploding: *The explosion of the dynamite was deafening.* **3.** a sudden, violent outburst of emotion: *an explosion of rage.* **4.** a large, rapid increase: *a population explosion.*

ex·plo·sive (eks plō′siv) *adj.* **1.** of, relating to, or like an explosion. **2.** tending or liable to explode or cause an explosion: *A bomb is an explosive device. He has an explosive temper.* —*n.* a substance that can explode: *Dynamite is an explosive.* —**ex·plo′sive·ly**, *adv.* —**ex·plo′sive·ness**, *n.*

ex·po·nent (eks pō′nənt) *n.* **1.** a person who explains or interprets something: *He was an early exponent of abstract painting.* **2.** a person or thing that represents something, such as an idea, principle, or cause: *Patrick Henry was an exponent of liberty.* **3.** a numeral or symbol placed at the upper right side of another numeral or symbol to indicate

at; āpe; cär; end; mē; it; īce; hot; ōld; fôrk; wood; fōol; oil; out; up; turn; sing; thin; this; hw in white; zh in treasure. The symbol ə stands for the sound of a in about, e in taken, i in pencil, o in lemon, and u in circus.

the power to which the latter is to be raised or how many times it is to be taken as a factor. In 4^3 the exponent is 3, indicating $4 \times 4 \times 4;$ in A^2 the exponent is 2, indicating $A \times A;$ in 5^x the exponent is x, indicating 5 multiplied by itself x times.

ex·port (*v.,* eks pôrt′, eks′pôrt′; *n.,* eks′pôrt′) *v.t.* to carry or send goods or products to other countries for sale or trade: *Colombia exports coffee to the United States.* —*n.* **1.** something that is exported: *Wool is an important Australian export.* **2.** the act or process of exporting. —**ex·port′er,** *n.*

ex·por·ta·tion (eks′pôr tā′shən) *n.* **1.** the act of exporting: *the exportation of wheat.* **2.** something that is exported.

ex·pose (eks pōz′) *v.t.,* **ex·posed, ex·pos·ing. 1.** to place or leave open to the action or influence of: *She has never been exposed to the mumps.* **2.** to leave (oneself) open to: *He exposed himself to the taunts of the crowd.* **3.** to make known; disclose; reveal: *to expose a conspiracy, to expose a crime.* **4.** to allow light to reach (a photographic film or plate). —**ex·pos′er,** *n.*

ex·po·sé (eks′pō zā′) *n.* **1.** a public disclosure of something secret or shameful, such as a scandal or crime. **2.** a book or article making such a disclosure.

ex·po·si·tion (eks′pə zish′ən) *n.* **1.** a large public show or display, as of industrial products. **2.** the act or process of setting forth or explaining facts or ideas. **3.** a detailed statement or explanation of facts or ideas, especially in writing. **4.** the first section in certain musical forms in which the theme of the movement or composition is introduced.

ex·pos·i·tor (eks poz′ə tər) *n.* a person who explains something.

ex·pos·i·to·ry (eks poz′ə tôr′ē) *adj.* relating to, like, or containing an explanation; explanatory.

ex·pos·tu·late (eks pos′chə lāt′) *v.i.,* **ex·pos·tu·lat·ed, ex·pos·tu·lat·ing.** to present reasons against something one opposes. —**ex·pos′tu·la′tion,** *n.* —**ex·pos·tu·la·to·ry** (eks pos′chə lə tôr′ē) *adj.*

ex·po·sure (eks pō′zhər) *n.* **1.** the act of exposing or the state of being exposed. **2.** a lack of protection from the elements resulting in harm, especially serious harm: *One of the stranded mountain climbers died of exposure to the extreme cold.* **3.** a position in relation to a point of the compass: *a room with a southern exposure.* **4.** the act or process of exposing a photographic film or plate to light. **5.** the length of time needed for this. **6.** a section of film that is exposed to light.

exposure meter, another term for **light meter.**

ex·pound (eks pound′) *v.t.* **1.** to set forth in detail: *to expound a theory.* **2.** to make clear the meaning of; explain; interpret. —**ex·pound′er,** *n.*

ex·press (eks pres′) *v.t.* **1.** to put into words: *She expressed her opinions.* **2.** to show or reveal outwardly; indicate: *He expressed his happiness by smiling.* **3.** to make known; communicate: *The artist's work expresses his love of nature.* **4.** to represent, as by a figure, symbol, or formula; indicate: *The sign ÷ expresses division.* **5.** to send (something) by a system of rapid transportation or delivery: *to express a package.* **6.** to press out; squeeze out: *to express the juice from grapes in order to make wine.* —*adj.* **1.** particular or sole; special: *He came here for the express purpose of seeing her.* **2.** clear and unmistakable: *to give express orders.* **3.** of or relating to a system of rapid transportation or delivery: *an express bus, an express company.* —*adv.* by a system of rapid transportation or delivery: *to send a package express.* —*n. pl.,* **ex·press·es. 1.** a system for the rapid and direct transportation or delivery of goods or money. **2.** a company engaged in such

transportation or delivery. **3.** a train, bus, or elevator that is quick and direct and makes few or no stops. —**ex·press′i·ble,** *adj.*

to express oneself. to put one's thoughts or opinions into words: *He expressed himself eloquently.*

ex·pres·sion (eks presh′ən) *n.* **1.** the act of expressing or putting something into words, such as thoughts, opinions, or ideas. **2.** an outward show; indication: *Crying is an expression of grief.* **3.** a particular look that expresses a thought or feeling: *His face wore an expression of disapproval.* **4.** a particular tone of voice that expresses a thought or feeling. **5.** a particular word or phrase: *"Look before you leap"* is a familiar expression. **6.** a symbol or combination of symbols used to indicate a mathematical quantity or operation.

ex·pres·sion·less (eks presh′ən lis) *adj.* showing little or no thought or feeling: *an expressionless face.*

ex·pres·sive (eks pres′iv) *adj.* **1.** that expresses; expressing: *He spoke in a manner expressive of his anger.* **2.** full of expression: *an expressive tone of voice, an expressive look.* **3.** of, relating to, or concerned with expression. —**ex·pres′sive·ly,** *adv.* —**ex·pres′sive·ness,** *n.*

ex·press·ly (eks pres′lē) *adv.* **1.** particularly or solely; specially: *He went to the party expressly to see her.* **2.** in clear terms; plainly: *The children were expressly warned against feeding the bears.*

ex·press·man (eks pres′mən) *n. pl.,* **ex·press·men** (eks pres′mən). a person who works for an express company.

ex·press·way (eks pres′wā′) *n.* a wide, usually divided highway built for rapid and direct traveling.

ex·pro·pri·ate (eks prō′prē āt′) *v.t.,* **ex·pro·pri·at·ed, ex·pro·pri·at·ing.** to take (private property) from a person or business by official authority, especially for public use. —**ex·pro′pri·a′tion,** *n.*

ex·pul·sion (eks pul′shən) *n.* the act of expelling or the state of being expelled.

ex·punge (eks punj′) *v.t.,* **ex·punged, ex·pung·ing.** to delete or erase: *to expunge passages from a manuscript.* —**ex·pung′er,** *n.*

ex·pur·gate (eks′pər gāt′) *v.t.,* **ex·pur·gat·ed, ex·pur·gat·ing.** to remove objectionable passages or words from: *to expurgate a book.* —**ex′pur·ga′tion,** *n.*

ex·qui·site (eks′kwi zit, eks kwiz′it) *adj.* **1.** of great beauty, charm, or perfection: *an exquisite face.* **2.** of great excellence or high quality: *a vase of exquisite workmanship, exquisite taste in clothes.* **3.** intensely sharp; keen: *exquisite delight.* —**ex′qui·site·ly,** *adv.* —**ex′qui·site·ness,** *n.*

ex·tant (eks′tənt, eks tant′) *adj.* not lost, destroyed, or extinct; still existing: *The only extant copy of the book is in a private collection.*

ex·tem·po·ra·ne·ous (eks tem′pə rā′nē əs) *adj.* spoken, made, or done with little or no preparation; impromptu: *The winner of the scholarship made a few extemporaneous remarks.* —**ex·tem′po·ra′ne·ous·ly,** *adv.* —**ex·tem′po·ra′ne·ous·ness,** *n.*

ex·tem·po·re (eks tem′pər ē) *adv.* with little or no preparation; offhand; extemporaneously: *The politician spoke extempore.* —*adj.* spoken, made, or done with little or no preparation; extemporaneous; impromptu.

ex·tem·po·rize (eks tem′pə rīz′) *v.t.,* **ex·tem·po·rized, ex·tem·po·riz·ing.** to speak, make, or do (something) with little or no preparation; improvise: *The mayor extemporized a welcoming speech.* —**ex·tem′po·ri·za′tion,** *n.*

ex·tend (eks tend′) *v.t.* **1.** to make longer; lengthen: *The builders extended the road for three more miles. We extended our visit.* **2.** to stretch out: *The bird extended its wings. The dancer extended her leg.* **3.** to offer or give: *We extended our sympathy to the family. The store extended credit to them.* **4.** to increase, as in size or scope: *The*

ancient Romans extended their empire into Asia and Africa.
—*v.i.* to continue in distance or time; stretch out: *The driveway extends from the house to the main road.*

ex·ten·sion (eks ten′shən) *n.* **1.** the act of extending or the state of being extended. **2.** something that extends. **3.** an additional telephone connected to the same line as the main one.

ex·ten·sive (eks ten′siv) *adj.* **1.** covering or extending over a large area; great in extent; vast: *an extensive ranch.* **2.** broad, as in scope, effect, or range: *The senator has extensive influence in his state. The scholar has done extensive research in American history.* **3.** large in amount, degree, or number: *He has an extensive fortune.* —**ex·ten′sive·ly,** *adv.* —**ex·ten′sive·ness,** *n.*

ex·ten·sor (eks ten′sôr) *n.* any muscle that straightens or stretches out a part of the body, especially an arm or leg.

ex·tent (eks tent′) *n.* the space, amount, degree, or limit to which something extends or is extended: *What is the extent of his duties? She agrees with us to a certain extent.*

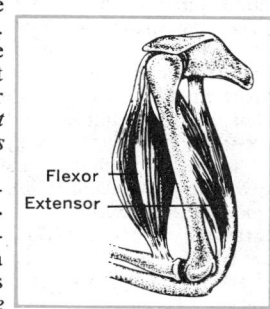

Flexor
Extensor

Extensor in the arm

ex·ten·u·ate (eks ten′yōō·āt′) *v.t.,* **ex·ten·u·at·ed, ex·ten·u·at·ing.** to lessen the seriousness of (something, such as a fault or offense), by serving as an excuse or explanation: *The boy's youth does not extenuate his crime.* —**ex·ten′u·a′tion,** *n.*

ex·te·ri·or (eks tēr′ē ər) *n.* **1.** the outer surface or part; outside: *The exterior of the building is made of marble.* **2.** an outward look or manner: *He has a calm exterior.* —*adj.* **1.** of, relating to, or on the outside; outer; external: *The exterior paint of the house was white.* **2.** coming or acting from the outside: *exterior help, exterior causes.*

ex·ter·mi·nate (eks tur′mə nāt′) *v.t.,* **ex·ter·mi·nat·ed, ex·ter·mi·nat·ing.** to wipe out; destroy: *to exterminate household pests.* —**ex·ter′mi·na′tion,** *n.*

ex·ter·mi·na·tor (eks tur′mə nā′tər) *n.* a person or thing that exterminates, especially a person whose business is exterminating cockroaches, termites, rats, and the like.

ex·ter·nal (eks turn′əl) *adj.* **1.** of, relating to, or on the outside; outer: *He put an external coat of paint on the house.* **2.** from without: *an external force, external causes.* **3.** relating to outward appearance: *an external calm, an external beauty.* **4.** on or to be used on the outside of the body: *Rubbing alcohol is for external use only.* —*n., pl.* **externals.** outward form, appearance, feature, or circumstance: *He puts too much emphasis on externals in judging people.* —**ex·ter′nal·ly,** *adv.*

external ear, the outer, visible part of the ear and the passage leading to the eardrum; outer ear.

ex·tinct (eks tingkt′) *adj.* **1.** no longer in existence: *The dodo is extinct.* **2.** no longer active; inactive; extinguished: *an extinct volcano.*

ex·tinc·tion (eks tingk′shən) *n.* **1.** the state or condition of being or becoming extinct: *Efforts have been made to prevent the extinction of the buffalo.* **2.** the act of extinguishing or the state of being extinguished.

ex·tin·guish (eks ting′gwish) *v.t.* **1.** to put out: *to extinguish a fire, to extinguish all the lights in a house.* **2.** to put an end to; destroy: *Rain did not extinguish the high spirits of the picnickers.* —**ex·tin′guish·a·ble,** *adj.*

ex·tin·guish·er (eks ting′gwi shər) *n.* **1.** a person or thing that extinguishes. **2.** see **fire extinguisher.**

ex·tir·pate (eks′tər pāt′) *v.t.,* **ex·tir·pat·ed, ex·tir·pat·ing. 1.** to remove or destroy completely: *The government*

tried to extirpate bad living conditions in the slums by providing new housing. **2.** to tear up by the roots; uproot.

ex·tol (eks tōl′) *also,* **ex·toll.** *v.t.,* **ex·tolled, ex·tol·ling.** to praise highly; laud: *The teacher extolled Shakespeare's ability as a poet.*

ex·tort (eks tôrt′) *v.t.* to obtain (something) by threats or force: *to extort money by blackmail, to extort a confession.* —**ex·tort′er,** *n.*

ex·tor·tion (eks tôr′shən) *n.* **1.** an obtaining of money or another valuable thing by threat or force. **2.** something that is extorted.

ex·tor·tion·ate (eks tôr′shə nit) *adj.* very excessive; exorbitant: *We can't afford such extortionate prices.*

ex·tor·tion·ist (eks tôr′shə nist) *n.* a person who is guilty of or practices extortion. Also, **ex·tor·tion·er** (eks·tôr′shə nər).

ex·tra (eks′trə) *adj.* more than what is usual, expected, or needed; additional: *to work extra hours, to receive extra pay.* —*n.* **1.** something in addition to what is usual, expected, or needed. **2.** a special edition of a newspaper that carries an account of an unusually important news event: *The paper published an extra to announce the outbreak of war.* **3.** a person hired to play a minor, usually nonspeaking, part in a motion picture or other production. —*adv.* unusually: *an extra large size, extra dry wine.*

extra- *prefix* outside; beyond; besides: *extraordinary, extracurricular.*

ex·tract (*v.,* eks trakt′; *n.,* eks′trakt) *v.t.* **1.** to draw or pull out by effort or force: *The dentist extracted her tooth.* **2.** to obtain (a substance) by pressing, cooking, distilling, or some other means: *to extract salt from sea water, to extract wine from grapes.* **3.** to obtain by force, threats, or similar oppression; extort: *I liked the scene in which the villain extracted the hero's promise to leave town.* **4.** to derive (something) from a particular source: *He extracted great pleasure from winning the award.* **5.** to take out or select: *to extract a passage from a book.* —*n.* something that is extracted: *an extract from a book, vanilla extract.*

ex·trac·tion (eks trak′shən) *n.* **1.** the act of extracting or the state of being extracted. **2.** ancestry or birth; descent; lineage: *He is of Swedish extraction.*

ex·trac·tor (eks trak′tər) *n.* a person or thing that extracts.

ex·tra·cur·ric·u·lar (eks′trə kə rik′yə lər) *adj.* not part of the regular course of study: *Working on the school paper and playing on the football team are extracurricular activities.*

ex·tra·dite (eks′trə dīt′) *v.t.,* **ex·tra·dit·ed, ex·tra·dit·ing. 1.** to surrender or turn over (a person accused of a crime) to the authorities of another nation or state where the crime was committed. **2.** to obtain the extradition of (a person accused of a crime) from another nation or state.

ex·tra·di·tion (eks′trə dish′ən) *n.* the act of extraditing.

ex·tra·mu·ral (eks′trə myoor′əl) *adj.* involving participants from more than one school or organization.

ex·tra·ne·ous (eks trā′nē əs) *adj.* **1.** that has little or nothing to do with the subject; not pertinent; irrelevant: *That statement is extraneous to this discussion.* **2.** coming from the outside; not belonging; foreign: *He has some extraneous matter in his eye.*

E

at; āpe; cär; end; mē; it; īce; hot; ōld; fôrk; wood; fōōl; oil; out; up; turn; sing; thin; this; hw in white; zh in treasure. The symbol ə stands for the sound of **a** in about, e in taken, i in pencil, o in lemon, and u in circus.

ex·traor·di·nar·y (eks trôr′də ner′ē, eks′trə ôr′də-ner′ē) *adj.* beyond or above the usual or ordinary; very unusual or remarkable; exceptional: *His extraordinary height made him stand out among the rest of the basketball players. She is a woman of extraordinary intelligence.* —**ex·traor′di·nar′i·ly,** *adv.*

ex·tra·sen·sor·y perception (eks′trə sen′sər ē) the ability to perceive external objects, thoughts, or events without the aid of the senses.

ex·tra·ter·ri·to·ri·al (eks′trə ter′ə tôr′ē əl) *adj.* outside the legal jurisdiction of the country in which it is located.

ex·trav·a·gance (eks trav′ə gəns) *n.* **1.** lavish or wasteful spending of money: *She lived very simply and avoided any extravagance.* **2.** going beyond reasonable limits, as in speech or behavior: *The extravagance of his praise made her doubt his sincerity.* **3.** an instance of excess or wastefulness: *Buying all that jewelry was an extravagance.*

ex·trav·a·gant (eks trav′ə gənt) *adj.* **1.** lavish or wasteful in the spending of money: *The extravagant man only bought the most expensive clothes.* **2.** beyond reasonable limits; unrestrained: *extravagant demands.* —**ex·trav′a·gant·ly,** *adv.*

ex·trav·a·gan·za (eks trav′ə gan′zə) *n.* a lavish, elaborate show or production, as in a theater; spectacle.

ex·tra·ve·hic·u·lar activity (eks′trə vē hik′yə lər) any of various maneuvers or experiments performed by an astronaut outside a vehicle in outer space.

ex·treme (eks trēm′) *adj.,* **ex·trem·er, ex·trem·est.** **1.** of the greatest or highest degree; very great or severe: *The wounded man was in extreme pain. The mountain climbers were in extreme danger because of a possible avalanche.* **2.** going beyond what is usual, reasonable, or average: *The mayor took extreme measures to halt crime in the streets.* **3.** farthest: *His house was at the extreme end of the block.* —*n.* **1.** the greatest or highest degree: *Starvation is the extreme of hunger.* **2.** the farthest point: *The light house was at one extreme of the island.* **3. extremes.** complete opposites. **4.** *Mathematics.* the first or last term of a proportion. In the proportion *a:b-c:d, a* and *d* are the extremes. —**ex·treme′ly,** *adv.* —**ex·treme′ness,** *n.*

to go to extremes. to use extreme measures; do something drastic.

extremely high frequency, a radio frequency between 30,000 and 300,000 megacycles.

ex·trem·ist (eks trē′mist) *n.* a person who supports extreme measures or holds extreme views, especially in politics. —*adj.* of or relating to extremists.

ex·trem·i·ty (eks trem′ə tē) *n. pl.,* **ex·trem·i·ties.** **1.** the farthest or last part or point; very end: *The Cape of Good Hope is near the southern extremity of Africa.* **2. extremities.** the hands and feet. **3.** greatest or highest degree: *the extremity of grief.* **4.** an extreme action or measure: *The people of the town were forced to the extremity of fleeing their homes when the flood waters rose.* **5.** a condition of extreme danger or distress.

ex·tri·ca·ble (eks′tri kə bəl) *adj.* that can be extricated.

ex·tri·cate (eks′trə kāt′) *v.t.,* **ex·tri·cat·ed, ex·tri·cat·ing.** to set free or remove, as from entanglement or difficulty: *He extricated the rabbit from the trap. He extricated himself from debt by taking a second job.* —**ex′tri·ca′tion,** *n.*

ex·trin·sic (eks trin′sik) *adj.* **1.** not essential to the nature of a thing; extraneous: *That statement is extrinsic to the discussion.* **2.** coming or acting from without; external: *an extrinsic force.* —**ex·trin′si·cal·ly,** *adv.*

ex·tro·vert (eks′trə vurt′) *n.* an outgoing person who is more interested in other people and what goes on around him than in his own thoughts or feelings.

▲ An **extrovert** is the opposite of an **introvert.** An introvert is a person concerned mainly with himself rather than with other people and events.

ex·tro·vert·ed (eks′trə vur′tid) *adj.* tending to be more interested in other people and what goes on around one than in one's own thoughts or feelings.

ex·trude (eks trōōd′) *v.,* **ex·trud·ed, ex·trud·ing.** —*v.t.* **1.** to force or push out, as by squeezing: *The volcano extruded lava.* **2.** to shape (plastic or metal) by forcing through a die or mold. —*v.i.* to stick out.

ex·tru·sion (eks trōō′zhən) *n.* the act or process of extruding.

ex·u·ber·ance (eg zōō′bər əns) *n.* the state or quality of being exuberant.

ex·u·ber·ant (eg zōō′bər ənt) *adj.* **1.** overflowing with high spirits, enthusiasm, or vigor; elated: *He was exuberant when he heard the news that he had won the award.* **2.** abundant or lavish: *exuberant praise.* **3.** luxuriant in growth: *exuberant tropical foliage.* —**ex·u′ber·ant·ly,** *adv.*

ex·u·da·tion (eks′yoo dā′shən) *n.* **1.** the act of exuding. **2.** something that is exuded, such as sweat.

ex·ude (eg zōōd′, ek syōōd′) *v.,* **ex·ud·ed, ex·ud·ing.** —*v.t.* **1.** to discharge (a substance) gradually: *The hard work made him exude sweat.* **2.** to give forth: *to exude warmth, to exude charm.* —*v.i.* to come out gradually; ooze out: *Sap exuded from the pine tree.*

ex·ult (eg zult′) *v.i.* to rejoice greatly; be joyful: *The basketball players exulted in their victory.* —**ex·ult′ing·ly,** *adv.*

ex·ult·ant (eg zult′ənt) *adj.* triumphantly joyful; jubilant; elated. —**ex·ult′ant·ly,** *adv.*

ex·ul·ta·tion (eg′zul tā′shən, ek′sul tā′shən) *n.* triumphant joy; jubilation; elation: *There was great exultation when the home team won.*

eye (ī) *n.* **1.** the organ of the body by which people and animals see. **2.** the colored part of this organ; iris: *She has blue eyes.* **3.** the area surrounding the eye, including the eyelids: *a swollen eye.* **4.** a look; glance; gaze: *He cast an envious eye at his friend's new bicycle.* **5.** a careful or close watch: *Please keep an eye on the road when you drive.* **6.** the ability to judge with the eye: *to have an eye for beauty.* **7.** *also,* **eyes.** a point of view; opinion; judgment: *In the eyes of his fellow citizens, he was an honest man.* **8.** something resembling the eye in shape, position, or use, such as the bud of a potato or the hole at the end of a needle through which the thread passes. **9.** the small, cloudless center of a hurricane, having very light winds and low pressure. —*v.t.,* **eyed, ey·ing** or **eye·ing.** to watch carefully or closely: *The detective eyed the suspect's every movement.*

an eye for an eye. punishment or revenge similar or equal to the injury or damage suffered.

in the public eye. often noticed by the public; widely known.

to catch (someone's) eye. to attract (someone's) attention: *He tried to catch her eye by waving.*

to see eye to eye. to agree completely: *They didn't see eye to eye on the strategy for the game.*

to set eyes on or **to lay eyes on.** to catch sight of; see: *She hadn't set eyes on her old school friend in years.*

with an eye to. with a view to; with the purpose of: *He is saving his allowance with an eye to buying a new movie camera.*

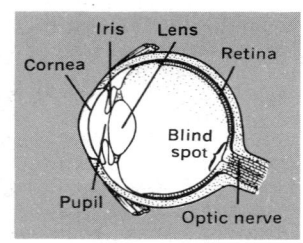

Human eye

eye·ball (ī′bôl′) *n.* the ball-shaped portion of the eye, enclosed by the eyelids and the eye socket.

eye·brow (ī′brou′) *n.* **1.** the bony ridge over the eye. **2.** the fringe of hair growing on this.

eye·cup (ī′kup′) *n.* a small cup with a rim shaped to fit closely over the eye, used in washing the eyes or applying medicine to them.

eye·drop·per (ī′drop′ər) *n.* a dropper for applying medicine to the eye.

eye·glass (ī′glas′) *n. pl.,* **eye·glass·es. 1.** a lens to improve a person's eyesight. **2. eyeglasses.** a pair of glass lenses mounted in frames, used to improve a person's eyesight. **3.** an eyepiece.

eye·lash (ī′lash′) *n. pl.,* **eye·lash·es. 1.** one of the stiff hairs growing on the edge of the eyelid. **2.** *also,* **eyelashes.** a fringe of these hairs.

eye·less (ī′lis) *adj.* without eyes or blind.

eye·let (ī′lit) *n.* **1.** a small hole in a material, such as leather or cloth, for a cord or lace to go through: *Shoelaces are passed through eyelets.* **2.** a metal or plastic ring lining such a hole to strengthen it. **3.** a small hole edged with stitches, used to make a pattern or edging in embroidery. **4.** any of various fabrics, especially cotton, decorated with this pattern.

eye·lid (ī′lid′) *n.* a movable, protective fold of skin that can close over the eyeball.

eye opener *Informal.* something surprising or revealing: *Our team's victory over the league champion was an eye opener to many people.*

eye·piece (ī′pēs′) *n.* the lens or combination of lenses nearest to the eye of the user in an optical instrument, especially a telescope or microscope.

eye shadow, a tinted cosmetic cream, powder, or liquid applied to the eyelids.

eye·sight (ī′sīt′) *n.* **1.** the power or ability to see; sight; vision: *A hawk has very keen eyesight.* **2.** the distance that the eye can see: *The ocean was within eyesight of the house.*

eye socket, the bony cavity in which the eyeball is located; orbit.

eye·sore (ī′sôr′) *n.* something ugly or unpleasant to look at: *That old shack is an eyesore.*

eye·spot (ī′spot′) *n.* a simple organ of sight in many lower animals, such as flatworms.

eye·stalk (ī′stôk′) *n.* a jointed, movable stalk with a compound eye on its tip, as in lobsters, crayfish, and shrimp.

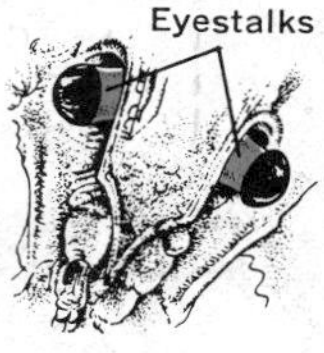

Eyestalks

eye·strain (ī′strān′) *n.* a tired condition of the eyes.

eye·tooth (ī′tōōth′) *n. pl.,* **eye·teeth** (ī′tēth′). either one of the two canine teeth in the upper jaw between the incisors and the bicuspids.

Head of a crayfish

eye·wit·ness (ī′wit′nis) *n. pl.,* **eye·wit·ness·es.** a person who has actually seen something happen and therefore can testify about it: *She was an eyewitness to the bank robbery.*

ey·rie (er′ē, ēr′ē) *also,* **ey·ry.** *n. pl.,* **ey·ries.** another spelling of **aerie.**

E·ze·ki·el (i zē′kē əl) *n.* **1.** Hebrew prophet of the sixth century B.C. **2.** a book of the Old Testament containing his writings and prophecies.

Ez·ra (ez′rə) *n.* **1.** Hebrew scribe and prophet of the fifth century B.C., who led a revival of Judaism among the Jews returning to Jerusalem from the Exile. **2.** a book of the Old Testament that is believed to have been written by him.

E

at; āpe; cär; end; mē; it; īce; hot; ōld; fôrk; wood; fōōl; oil; out; up; turn; sing; thin; this; hw in white; zh in treasure. The symbol ə stands for the sound of a in about, e in taken, i in pencil, o in lemon, and u in circus.

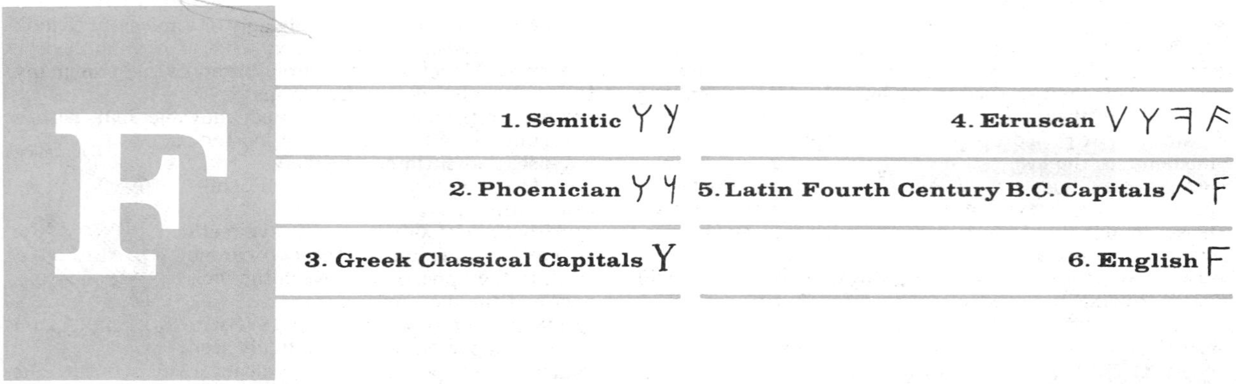
F
1. Semitic
2. Phoenician
3. Greek Classical Capitals
4. Etruscan
5. Latin Fourth Century B.C. Capitals
6. English

F is the sixth letter of the English alphabet. Although the *f* sound, as the *f* in *fish*, was not represented in early alphabets, the shape of the letter **F**, like the letters **U, V, W,** and **Y** developed from the ancient Semitic letter *waw* (1), that depicted a hook and stood for the *w* sound as the *w* in *water.* When the Phoenicians (2) borrowed *waw,* they used it to represent both the consonant sound *w* and the vowel sound *u,* as the *u* in *rude.* The Greeks adopted *waw* and called it *upsilon* (3), writing it as the capital letter **Y** is written today. *Upsilon* was used to represent only the vowel sound *u,* the *w* sound being represented by a letter called *digamma,* which looked something like a modern capital letter **F.** The Etruscans (4) borrowed modified forms of *upsilon* and *digamma,* and used them both to stand for the *f* sound. This was probably the first time in the history of the alphabet that the *f* sound appeared. The Etruscan form of *digamma* was adopted to represent the *f* sound in the Latin alphabet (5). By about 2300 years ago, the Roman letter **F** was written almost exactly as we write it today (6).

f, F (ef) *n. pl.,* **f's, F's. 1.** the sixth letter of the English alphabet. **2.** the sixth item in a series or group. **3.** *Music.* the fourth note of the scale of C major.

F, the symbol for fluorine.

f. 1. female. **2.** feminine. **3.** forte. **4.** franc.

F. 1. Fahrenheit. **2.** French. **3.** Friday. **4.** February.

fa (fä) *n. Music.* **1.** the fourth note of the major scale. **2.** the note F.

fa·ble (fā′bəl) *n.* **1.** a short story meant to teach a moral or lesson, especially one using animals as characters. **2.** legend; myth. **3.** a story or statement that is not true; falsehood.

fa·bled (fā′bəld) *adj.* **1.** told about or described in fables; mythical; legendary: *a fabled hero.* **2.** not real; fictitious; made up.

fab·ric (fab′rik) *n.* **1.** a material that is woven, knitted, or produced in a similar way, made from natural or synthetic fibers; cloth. Tweed, flannel, jersey, and felt are fabrics. **2.** a system of connected or related parts; framework; structure: *the fabric of society.*

fab·ri·cate (fab′rə kāt′) *v.t.,* **fab·ri·cat·ed, fab·ri·cat·ing. 1.** to make up; invent: *She fabricated an excuse to explain her lateness for class.* **2.** to make, manufacture, or build by putting parts together: *to fabricate a spacecraft.* **—fab′ri·ca′tion,** *n.*

fab·u·list (fab′yə list) *n.* a person who makes up or writes fables.

fab·u·lous (fab′yə ləs) *adj.* **1.** amazing; incredible: *She spent fabulous sums of money on her clothes.* **2.** *Informal.* exceptionally good; wonderful: *We had a fabulous time at the party.* **3.** of or like a fable; imaginary; legendary: *She read about a winged dragon and other fabulous monsters.* **—fab′u·lous·ly,** *adv.* **—fab′u·lous·ness,** *n.*

fa·cade (fə säd′) *also,* **fa·çade.** *n.* **1.** the front of a building. **2.** a false front or outward appearance; illusion; pretense: *The poor man kept up a facade of prosperity.*

face (fās) *n.* **1.** the front of the head. The eyes, nose, and mouth are parts of the face. **2.** a look or expression; countenance: *The boy's face was happy when he saw his new bicycle.* **3.** a queer or twisted look or expression; grimace: *to make faces in the mirror.* **4.** *Informal.* boldness; impudence: *She had the face to insult him in front of everybody at the party.* **5.** dignity; self-respect: *to lose face, to save face.* **6.** the front, main, or outward surface of something: *the face of a cliff, on the face of a clock.* **7.** *Geometry.* one of the surfaces or sides of a solid: *a cube has six faces.* **8.** *Printing.* **a.** the surface of a piece of type, on which the letter or character to be printed is cut. **b.** the style or design of this surface. **—***v.,* **faced, fac·ing. —***v.t.* **1.** to have or turn the face toward; front on: *Please face the camera. The house faces the park.* **2.** to cause to turn in a particular direction: *Face the plant toward the light.* **3.** to meet openly; confront: *to face a problem, to face an enemy.* **4.** to realize and admit; accept: *to face the facts.* **5.** to cover or line (a surface): *to face the collar of a coat with fur, to face the walls of a room with wood paneling.* **—***v.i.* to be turned or placed with the face in a particular direction: *The house faced west. He faced left.*

face to face. facing each other.

in the face of. a. in the presence of: *He ran in the face of danger.* **b.** in spite of: *The prisoner said he was innocent in the face of evidence that proved him guilty.*

to face up to. a. to meet or oppose boldly: *to face up to danger.* **b.** to admit and accept: *to face up to a mistake.*

to one's face. directly and boldly in one's presence: *Would you ever say that to his face?*

face card, a jack, queen, or king in a deck of playing cards.

face lifting 1. plastic surgery to tighten sagging or wrinkled skin of the face. **2.** a repairing, alteration, or renovation: *The old city hall was getting a face lifting.*

fac·et (fas′it) *n.* **1.** any of the small, polished plane surfaces of a cut gem. **2.** any of various sides or aspects: *the many facets of a problem, the many facets of a person's personality.* **3.** any of the segments of the external surface of the compound eye of insects and certain animals.

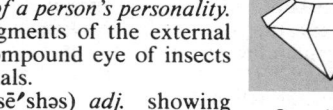

Gem with nine facets showing

fa·ce·tious (fə sē′shəs) *adj.* showing light humor; not meant to be serious; frivolously amusing: *a facetious young man, a facetious comment.* —**fa·ce′tious·ly,** *adv.* —**face′tious·ness,** *n.*

face value 1. the value appearing on currency, stamps, bonds, banknotes, and the like. **2.** apparent value: *We accepted his promises at face value.*

fa·cial (fā′shəl) *adj.* of, for, or relating to the face. —*n.* a massage or other treatment to beautify the face. —**fa′cial·ly,** *adv.*

fac·ile (fas′əl) *adj.* **1.** acting or working with skill and ease: *a facile writer, a facile mind.* **2.** requiring little effort; easily done: *a facile task, a facile victory.* **3.** having a mild disposition; easygoing: *She had a facile nature.* —**fac′ile·ly,** *adv.* —**fac′ile·ness,** *n.*

fa·cil·i·tate (fə sil′ə tāt′) *v.t.,* **fa·cil·i·tat·ed, fa·cil·i·tat·ing.** to make easier; aid in the operation of; assist: *Zip codes are used to facilitate mail service.*

fa·cil·i·ty (fə sil′ə tē) *n. pl.,* **fa·cil·i·ties. 1.** the ease of doing; freedom from difficulty: *This new car can be driven with great facility.* **2.** skill or ability; aptitude: *That carpenter has great facility.* **3.** *often,* **facilities.** something, as a building or piece of equipment, that provides a convenience or serves a particular purpose: *a cabin with cooking facilities, playground facilities.*

fac·ing (fā′sing) *n.* **1.a.** a piece of fabric sewn inside or outside along an edge of a garment to strengthen or trim it. **b.** the fabric used for this. **2.** a covering in front for ornamentation, protection, or other purposes: *a house with marble facing.* **3. facings.** the cuffs, collar, and trimmings of certain military coats.

fac·sim·i·le (fak sim′ə lē) *n.* an exact copy or reproduction: *The history book contained a facsimile of the Declaration of Independence.*

fact (fakt) *n.* **1.** something known to be true or real; something that has actually happened: *He supported his argument with facts. The police investigated the facts of the crime.* **2.** the quality or state of being actual; reality; truth: *to distinguish fact from fiction.* **3.** a thing done, especially a criminal or evil act: *His shame came after the fact.*
  as a matter of fact. actually; really: *As a matter of fact, the job was much easier than they thought it would be.*
  in fact. actually; really.

fac·tion (fak′shən) *n.* **1.** a group of people within an organization, as a political party, government, or church, that acts against other such groups to promote its own ends. **2.** strife or disagreement within an organization.

fac·tion·al (fak′shən əl) *adj.* of or characteristic of a faction.

fac·tious (fak′shəs) *adj.* **1.** tending to cause disagreement: *a factious political leader.* **2.** of, relating to, or characterized by faction: *factious disputes.* —**fac′tious·ly,** *adv.* —**fac′tious·ness,** *n.*

fac·ti·tious (fak tish′əs) *adj.* not natural or real; artificial: *a factitious show of friendship.* —**fac·ti′tious·ly,** *adv.* —**fac·ti′tious·ness,** *n.*

fac·tor (fak′tər) *n.* **1.** one of several elements that brings about a result or is part of the formation of a thing or circumstance: *Sunny weather and good food were factors of the success of the picnic.* **2.** any of the numbers or algebraic expressions which, when multiplied together, form a product. The factors of $14xy$ are 2, 7, x, and y. —*v.t.* to separate (a mathematical product) into its factors.

fac·to·ri·al (fak tôr′ē əl) *n.* the product of an integer and all lower positive integers. The factorial of 3, written as $3!$, is $3 \times 2 \times 1 = 6.$

fac·to·ry (fak′tər ē) *n. pl.,* **fac·to·ries.** a building or group of buildings where goods are manufactured.

fac·to·tum (fak tō′təm) *n.* a person employed to do all kinds of work.

fac·tu·al (fak′chōō əl) *adj.* **1.** of or relating to facts. **2.** consisting of or based on facts: *The witness gave a factual account of the accident.* —**fac′tu·al·ly,** *adv.*

fac·ul·ty (fak′əl tē) *n. pl.,* **fac·ul·ties. 1.** one of the natural powers of the mind or body: *the faculty of speech, to be in full possession of one's faculties.* **2.** a special skill or aptitude; talent: *The elderly woman had a faculty for putting young people at their ease.* **3.** the teaching staff of a school, college, or university. **4.** a department of learning at a college or university: *A new professor has been appointed to the faculty of law.*

fad (fad) *n.* a popular practice, interest, or fashion followed enthusiastically for a short time.

fade (fād) *v.,* **fad·ed, fad·ing.** —*v.i.* **1.** to lose color, brightness, or distinctness: *Some fabrics fade in the wash.* **2.** to lose freshness, vigor, or strength; wither: *The roses faded after three days.* **3.** to disappear gradually; die down: *The sound of the footsteps faded away.* —*v.t.* to cause to fade: *Sunlight faded my curtains.*
  to fade in. in motion pictures, radio, and television, to become gradually clearer or louder, as an image or sound.
  to fade out. in motion pictures, radio, and television, to become gradually less clear or loud.

fade-in (fād′in′) *n.* in motion pictures, radio, and television, the gradual appearance of an image or sound.

fade-out (fād′out′) *n.* in motion pictures, radio, and television, the gradual disappearance of an image or sound: *The movie ended with a fade-out of the hero winning the race.*

faer·ie (fer′ē) *n. Archaic.* another spelling of **fairy.**

fag (fag) *v.t.,* **fagged, fag·ging.** to tire by hard work; exhaust: *After the race, the runner was completely fagged out.* —*n. British. Informal.* a boy who does menial work for an older boy, as in certain English public schools.

fag end 1. a frayed or unfinished end, as of a piece of cloth or rope. **2.** the last and worst part of anything; remnant: *the fag end of a tiring day.*

fag·ot (fag′ət) *also,* **fag·got.** *n.* a bundle of sticks, twigs, or branches, used especially for fuel.

Fahr·en·heit (far′ən hīt′) *adj.* of, according to, or designating the temperature scale on which the freezing point of water is at 32 degrees and the boiling point is at 212 degrees under standard atmospheric pressure. [From Gabriel D. *Fahrenheit,* 1686–1736, a German physicist who devised this scale.]

at; āpe; cär; end; mē; it; īce; hot; ōld; fôrk; wood; fōōl; oil; out; up; turn; sing; thin; this; hw in white; zh in treasure. The symbol ə stands for the sound of **a** in about, **e** in taken, **i** in pencil, **o** in lemon, and **u** in circus.

F

fail (fāl) *v.i.* **1.** to be unsuccessful in doing or achieving something attempted, desired, or expected: *The plan failed when it was tested.* **2.** to be unsuccessful in passing an examination or subject. **3.** to become weaker, as in health or strength: *The old man's eyesight failed.* **4.** to stop working; die out: *The plane crashed because the engines failed.* **5.** to be insufficient; fall short; run out: *The water supply failed.* **6.** to go bankrupt. —*v.t.* **1.** to neglect or not do: *He failed to get to school on time.* **2.** to prove to be of no use or help to; disappoint: *His friends failed him when he needed them.* **3.** to abandon; desert: *His courage failed him.* **4.** to receive a grade of failure in (an examination or subject). **5.** to give a grade of failure to (a student).
without fail. definitely; certainly: *We will be there without fail.*

fail·ing (fā′ling) *n.* a shortcoming; fault: *His chief failing is rudeness.* —*prep.* in the absence of; without: *Failing a reply, the magazine canceled his subscription.*

faille (fīl) *n.* a ribbed fabric, usually made with silk or rayon yarn, used for clothing.

fail·ure (fāl′yər) *n.* **1.** being unable to achieve something attempted, desired, or expected: *The author was discouraged by his failure to write a successful novel.* **2.** a person or thing that is unsuccessful: *The play was a failure and closed after two performances.* **3.** omission or neglect (of something required): *a failure to pay one's bills.* **4.** a failing to pass an examination or subject. **5.** a grade or mark indicating this. **6.** a ceasing to work; dying out: *a power failure.* **7.** a falling short; insufficiency: *a crop failure.* **8.** bankruptcy.

fain (fān) *Archaic. adv.* with pleasure; gladly. —*adj.* glad; willing.

faint (fānt) *adj.* **1.** dim; indistinct: *a faint light, a faint cry.* **2.** without enthusiasm or strength; feeble: *faint praise, a faint attempt to be friendly.* **3.** weak and dizzy; likely to faint: *The workman was faint with hunger by noon.* —*n.* a brief loss of consciousness caused by a temporary decrease in the amount of blood that flows to the brain. —*v.i.* to lose consciousness briefly. —**faint′ly,** *adv.* —**faint′ness,** *n.*

faint-heart·ed (fānt′här′tid) *adj.* lacking courage; timid. —**faint′-heart′ed·ly,** *adv.* —**faint′-heart′ed·ness,** *n.*

fair[1] (fer) *adj.* **1.** free from prejudice; just; impartial: *The judge made a fair decision.* **2.** according to accepted rules or standards: *a fair play in a game.* **3.** moderately good or acceptable; average: *He has a fair chance of winning.* **4.** light in coloring: *a fair complexion.* **5.** not cloudy; clear; bright; sunny: *The forecast says we will have fair weather for the weekend.* **6.** pleasing in appearance; attractive; beautiful. **7.** legitimately open to attack or pursuit: *Deer are fair game in the hunting season.* —*adv.* in a fair manner; according to the rules: *A good sportsman always plays fair.* [Old English *fæger* beautiful.] —**fair′ness,** *n.*
to bid fair. to seem likely or favorable: *He bids fair to win the election.*

fair[2] (fer) *n.* **1.** an exhibition, as of livestock and farming products or of cultural and industrial displays of different nations. Fairs often have shows, competitions, and other entertainment. **2.** the exhibition and sale of articles for some charitable cause; bazaar: *a church fair.* **3.** a gathering of people to exhibit and sell goods: *a book fair.* [Old French *feire.*]

fair ball, a batted baseball that is not a foul.

Fair·banks (fer′bangks′) *n.* a city in east-central Alaska.

fair·ground (fer′ground′) *n. often,* **fairgrounds.** an outdoor place where fairs are held.

fair-haired (fer′herd′) *adj.* having light-colored hair.

fair·ish (fer′ish) *adj.* moderately good, well, or large.

fair·ly (fer′lē) *adv.* **1.** in a fair manner; justly; impartially; honestly: *The fans did not think that the umpire had called the ball fairly.* **2.** somewhat; moderately: *The boy had saved a fairly large amount of money.* **3.** actually; completely: *The audience fairly roared its approval.*

fair-mind·ed (fer′mīn′did) *adj.* not prejudiced or biased; impartial; just: *a fair-minded judge.* —**fair′-mind′-ed·ness,** *n.*

fair trade, trade under an agreement that forbids a seller to sell certain products for less than a minimum price set by the manufacturer or distributor.

fair·way (fer′wā′) *n.* the mowed area on a golf course between the tee and putting green.

fair·y (fer′ē) *n. pl.,* **fair·ies.** a tiny imaginary creature supposed to possess magic powers. —*adj.* **1.** of or relating to fairies. **2.** like or having the magic powers of a fairy: *a fairy godmother.*

fair·y·land (fer′ē land′) *n.* **1.** the imaginary land of the fairies. **2.** any enchanting, beautiful place.

fairy tale 1. a story, usually for children, about fairies. **2.** an unbelievable or highly imaginative story or lie.

fait ac·com·pli (fā tä kôm plē′) something done that no longer can be changed or reversed [French *fait accompli* accomplished fact.]

faith (fāth) *n.* **1.** a belief not based on proof: *His friends accepted his excuse on faith.* **2.** reliance or trust: *to have faith in one's doctor.* **3.** a belief in God or the doctrines of a religion. **4.** a system of religious belief: *the Protestant faith.*
▲ *Faith* and **belief** both mean the acceptance of something as true or real. *Faith* is based on emotion; *belief* is based on thought and reason.

faith·ful (fāth′fəl) *adj.* **1.** steadfast in loyalty and devotion; trustworthy: *a faithful friend.* **2.** accurate; true; exact: *a faithful copy of a document.* —*n.* **the faithful. a.** the followers or supporters of a religion. **b.** the loyal followers or supporters of any cause or group. —**faith′-ful·ly,** *adv.* —**faith′ful·ness,** *n.*

faith·less (fāth′lis) *adj.* **1.** not trustworthy or loyal: *a faithless friend.* **2.** without faith or belief, especially religious belief. —**faith′less·ly,** *adv.* —**faith′less·ness,** *n.*

fake (fāk) *n.* a person or thing that is not genuine; fraud; sham: *It's not a genuine antique; it's a fake.* —*v.t.,* **faked, fak·ing. 1.** to pretend; feign: *He faked illness in order to stay home from school.* **2.** to make (something) seem genuine in order to deceive; counterfeit: *The accounts were faked to show a profit that didn't exist.* —*adj.* not genuine; false: *a fake fireplace, a fake moustache.* —**fak′er,** *n.*

fak·er·y (fā′kə rē) *n. pl.,* **fak·er·ies. 1.** the act of faking. **2.** something that is faked: *The expert said the painting was a fakery.*

fa·kir (fə kēr′, fā′kər) *n.* a member of a Muslim sect who takes vows of poverty and supports himself by begging.

fal·chion (fôl′chən) *n.* a sword with a broad, curved blade, used in the Middle Ages.

fal·con (fôl′kən, fal′kən, fô′kən) *n.* **1.** any of various swift-flying birds of prey that resemble hawks, having a short, hooked bill. **2.** a hawk that has been trained to hunt birds and small game.

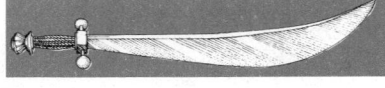

Falchion

fal·con·er (fôl′kə nər, fal′kə nər, fô′kə nər) *n.* **1.** a person who hunts with falcons. **2.** a breeder or trainer of falcons.

fal·con·ry (fôl′kən rē, fal′kən rē, fô′kən rē) *n.* **1.** the sport of hunting with falcons; hawking. **2.** the art of training falcons to hunt birds and small game.

fal·de·ral (fal′də ral′) *also,* **fal·de·rol** (fal′də rol′). *n.* another spelling of **folderol.**

fall (fôl) *v.i.,* **fell, fall·en, fall·ing. 1.** to come down from a higher place by the force of gravity; drop: *The book fell off the shelf. Snow fell during the night.* **2.** to come down suddenly or involuntarily from a standing position: *to fall on one's knees before a king, to faint and fall.* **3.** to become lower or less, as in quantity, quality, or strength: *His voice fell to a whisper. Production at the factory fell sharply.* **4.** to strike or land: *The arrow fell wide of the target.* **5.** to take place; happen; occur: *Christmas falls on December 25th.* **6.** to come as if by dropping from a higher place: *Night fell upon the town.* **7.** to pass into a particular condition; become: *to fall ill, to fall in love.* **8.** to be defeated, captured, or overthrown: *The city fell after the long siege.* **9.** to be wounded or killed, as in battle. **10.** to give in to temptation; sin: *Adam fell when he ate the apple.* **11.** to be classified or divided: *His book report falls into three parts.* **12.** to show sadness or disappointment: *Her face fell.* **13.** to hang down: *The dress fell in soft folds. Her hair fell around her shoulders.* **14.** to pass by inheritance or right: *The estate falls to the eldest son.* **15.** to be said: *Angry words fell from his lips.* —*n.* **1.** the act of coming down from a higher place by the force of gravity: *the fall of a meteor.* **2.** the amount of anything that comes down: *a six-inch fall of rain.* **3.** the distance through which anything falls: *It's a short fall from the branch of the tree to the ground.* **4.** a sudden or involuntary drop from a standing position: *The skater took a fall on the ice.* **5.** capture, destruction, or defeat; overthrow: *the fall of the Roman Empire.* **6.** a decline in reputation, rank, or dignity: *a fall from favor.* **7.** the act of yielding to temptation; sin. **8.** a decrease, as in value, quality, or quantity: *a fall in prices.* **9.** another word for **autumn. 10. falls.** waterfall; cascade. ▲ usually used with a singular verb. **11.** a woman's hairpiece, usually worn to add length or fullness. **12.** in wrestling, the act of throwing and holding one's opponent on his back with both shoulders touching the mat for a specified number of seconds. **13. the Fall.** the sin of disobedience to God by Adam and Eve in eating the forbidden fruit. —*adj.* of, relating to, or suitable for the autumn: *fall clothing.*

   to fall back. to retreat; withdraw: *The enemy's forces fell back.*

   to fall back on. a. to rely on for help. **b.** to retreat or go back to.

   to fall behind. to fail to keep up: *to fall behind in one's work.*

   to fall for. *Informal.* to be deceived or tricked by: *He fell for the swindler's plan.*

   to fall in. a. to take a place in line. **b.** to cave in.

   to fall in with. a. to meet and join company with: *He fell in with some amusing people on the airplane trip.* **b.** to agree with; be favorable to: *The new ruling falls in with popular demand for lower prices.*

   to fall off. to become less; diminish; drop: *The demand for the product fell off.*

   to fall on or **to fall upon. a.** to attack vigorously; assault. **b.** to come upon; discover; find: *He fell upon an interesting book in the library.*

   to fall out. a. to have a quarrel; argue: *Dan and Bill fell out over whose turn it was to wash the dog.* **b.** to leave a place in line.

   to fall short. to fail to meet a certain standard, goal, or requirement (with *of*).

   to fall through. to come to nothing; fail: *Their plans fell through.*

   to fall to. a. to set about; begin: *He fell to work.* **b.** to begin to attack. **c.** to start eating.

   to fall under. a. to be classified as; be included in: *That book falls under the heading of fiction.* **b.** to be or come under the influence of: *to fall under a spell.*

fal·la·cious (fə lā′shəs) *adj.* **1.** based on or containing a fallacy; not logical. **2.** deceptive; misleading: *fallacious hopes.* —**fal·la′cious·ly,** *adv.* —**fal·la′cious·ness,** *n.*

fal·la·cy (fal′ə sē) *n. pl.,* **fal·la·cies. 1.** a false or mistaken belief; misconception: *Columbus disproved the ancient fallacy that the world was flat.* **2.** false reasoning; unsound argument.

fall·en (fô′lən) *v.* the past participle of **fall.** —*adj.* **1.** having come down from a higher place; dropped: *fallen snow.* **2.** degraded or disgraced: *a fallen idol.* **3.** captured, overthrown, or defeated: *a fallen village.* **4.** having died, especially in battle: *a fallen hero.*

fal·li·ble (fal′ə bəl) *adj.* liable to be deceived or mistaken: *There is no one in the world who isn't fallible.* —**fal·li·bil′i·ty,** *n.* —**fal′li·bly,** *adv.*

falling star, another term for **meteor.**

fall line, the boundary between two plateaus or other land masses, often marked by waterfalls and rapids.

fall·out (fôl′out′) *n.* the radioactive dust particles that are caused by nuclear explosions and fall to the earth from the atmosphere.

fal·low (fal′ō) *adj.* (of land) tilled and left without being planted for one or more growing seasons. —*n.* fallow land.

fallow deer, a small European deer that usually has a yellowish coat with white spots.

Fall River, a city in southeastern Massachusetts. Pop. (1970), 96,898.

false (fôls) *adj.,* **fals·er, fals·est. 1.** not true; incorrect: *a false statement, a false accusation.* **2.** not genuine or natural; artificial: *false modesty.* **3.** misleading; deceptive: *a false impression.* **4.** disloyal; unfaithful: *a false friend.* **5.** untruthful; dishonest: *a false witness.* —**false′ly,** *adv.* —**false′ness,** *n.*

Fallow deer

false·hood (fôls′hood′) *n.* **1.** a false statement; lie: *to tell falsehoods about one's past.* **2.** the quality of being false; absence of truth: *to distinguish between falsehood and truthfulness.* **3.** something that is false, as a theory or idea.

false teeth, a complete or partial set of artificial teeth used in place of real teeth.

fal·set·to (fôl set′ō) *n. pl.,* **fal·set·tos. 1.** an unnaturally high-pitched voice used by a male singer, especially a tenor. **2.** a singer who has such a voice. —*adj.* of or for such a voice.

fal·si·fy (fôl′sə fī′) *v.,* **fal·si·fied, fal·si·fy·ing.** —*v.t.* **1.** to change in order to deceive; make false: *to falsify the date of one's birth, to falsify an accident report.* **2.** to give a false account of; misrepresent: *This book falsifies the events of the Civil War.* —*v.i.* to tell falsehoods; lie. —**fal′si·fi·ca′tion,** *n.* —**fal′si·fi′er,** *n.*

at; āpe; cär; end; mē; it; īce; hot; ōld; fôrk; wood; fōōl; oil; out; up; turn; sing; thin; this; hw in white; zh in treasure. The symbol ə stands for the sound of a in about, e in taken, i in pencil, o in lemon, and u in circus.

F

fal·si·ty (fôl′sə tē) *n. pl.,* **fal·si·ties. 1.** the state or quality of being false; untruthfulness. **2.** something that is false; falsehood.

Fal·staff, Sir John (fôl′staf) the fat, boastful, swaggering old knight, given to drinking, jesting, and good-natured lying, in Shakespeare's *Henry IV* and *The Merry Wives of Windsor.*

Fal·staff·i·an (fôl staf′ē ən) *adj.* of or characteristic of Falstaff or his band of ragged soldiers and comrades.

fal·ter (fôl′tər) *v.i.* **1.** to act with hesitation or uncertainty; waver: *The baby faltered for a moment before trying to take a step.* **2.** to speak with hesitation; stammer: *He faltered every time he spoke of the accident.* —**fal′ter·er,** *n.* —**fal′ter·ing·ly,** *adv.*

fame (fām) *n.* a widespread reputation, especially for great achievement: *The athlete's fame had spread around the world.*

famed (fāmd) *adj.* well-known; famous.

fa·mil·iar (fə mil′yər) *adj.* **1.** commonly seen, heard, or experienced; well-known: *I can't remember the name of the song, although it is a familiar tune. Smog is a familiar sight in some cities.* **2.** well-acquainted: *He is familiar with the book.* **3.** close; intimate: *to be on familiar terms with one's neighbors.* **4.** informal; friendly: *an easy and familiar manner.* **5.** too friendly or intimate; presumptuous; forward. —*n.* **1.** a close friend or associate. **2.** *Folklore.* a spirit or demon supposed to wait on a person, as a witch. —**fa·mil′iar·ly,** *adv.*

fa·mil·i·ar·i·ty (fə mil′ē ar′ə tē) *n. pl.,* **fa·mil·i·ar·i·ties. 1.** a close acquaintance with something: *to have familiarity with a subject.* **2.** friendliness or intimacy: *to be on terms of familiarity.* **3.** friendliness that is too bold; forwardness. **4.** an action suitable only for a person of close acquaintance: *to resent the familiarities of a stranger.*

fa·mil·iar·ize (fə mil′yə rīz′) *v.t.,* **fa·mil·iar·ized, fa·mil·iar·iz·ing. 1.** to make (oneself or someone else) accustomed or well-acquainted: *He familiarized himself with the duties of his new job.* **2.** to make (something) well known: *Advertising familiarized the new soft drink.* —**fa·mil′iar·i·za′tion,** *n.*

fam·i·ly (fam′ə lē, fam′lē) *n. pl.,* **fam·i·lies. 1.** parents and their children: *Twenty families live on our street.* **2.** the children of the same parents: *My parents raised a large family.* **3.** a group of people connected by blood or marriage; relatives. **4.** a group of people descended from a common ancestor; house, line, or clan. **5.** a group of things related by common or similar characteristics: *a family of musical instruments.* **6.** *Biology.* a group of related animals or plants, ranking below an order and above a genus. Zebras, asses, and horses belong to the horse family. **7.** a group of related languages descended from a common language. The English language belongs to the Indo-European family. —*adj.* of, relating to, or suitable for a family: *a family gathering at Thanksgiving.*

family name, a last name; surname.

family tree, a chart or diagram showing the ancestry, relationships, and descent of all the members of a family.

fam·ine (fam′in) *n.* **1.** a very great and widespread lack or scarcity of food: *Many children died of starvation during the famine.* **2.** a great scarcity of anything; dearth: *a fuel famine.*

fam·ished (fam′isht) *adj.* very hungry; starving: *They were famished after their long hike.*

fa·mous (fā′məs) *adj.* having great fame; very well-known; renowned: *a famous author, a famous play.*

fa·mous·ly (fā′məs lē) *adv.* very well; splendidly: *We got along famously.*

fan[1] (fan) *n.* **1.** a device shaped like part of a circle, that is waved by hand to make a small current of air. Fans are often collapsible and are made of various materials, such as paper, ivory, or feathers. **2.** anything resembling an open fan, such as the tail of a peacock. **3.** a mechanical device having several blades which are attached to a central hub and rotated by a motor. Fans are used for producing a current of air to cool, heat, or ventilate. —*v.,* **fanned, fan·ning.** —*v.t.* **1.** to move (air) with or as with a fan: *The bird's wings fanned the air.* **2.** to direct a current of air upon or toward with a fan: *to fan the flames of a fire.* **3.** to blow gently or refreshingly upon: *The cool breeze fanned his hot face.* **4.** to stir up; excite; stimulate: *The touchdown fanned the crowd's enthusiasm.* **5.** to spread out like a fan: *The magician fanned the deck of cards.* **6.** *Baseball.* to cause (a batter) to strike out. —*v.i.* **1.** to spread out like a fan. **2.** *Baseball.* to strike out. [Old English *fann* a device for separating grain from chaff.] —**fan′like′,** *adj.*

fan[2] (fan) *n. Informal.* an enthusiastic devotee or admirer, as of a sport or performer: *Bob is a real baseball fan.* [Short for *fanatic.*]

fa·nat·ic (fə nat′ik) *n.* a person whose devotion to a cause or belief is unreasonably strong or enthusiastic: *a religious fanatic, to be a fanatic about correct grammar.* —*adj.* another word for **fanatical.**

fa·nat·i·cal (fə nat′i kəl) *adj.* unreasonably enthusiastic or devoted. —**fa·nat′i·cal·ly,** *adv.*

fa·nat·i·cism (fə nat′ə siz′əm) *n.* unreasonable enthusiasm or zeal.

fan·cied (fan′sēd) *adj.* imagined; imaginary: *To the little boy the dark room was filled with fancied dangers.*

fan·ci·er (fan′sē ər) *n.* a person who has a special liking for or interest in something: *a cat fancier.*

fan·ci·ful (fan′si fəl) *adj.* **1.** suggested by fancy; imaginary; unreal: *She told the children a fanciful story about knights slaying dragons.* **2.** showing imagination: *a fanciful costume.* **3.** influenced by fancy; imaginative; whimsical: *He has a fanciful mind.* —**fan′ci·ful·ly,** *adv.* —**fan′ci·ful·ness,** *n.*

fan·cy (fan′sē) *n. pl.,* **fan·cies. 1.** the imagination, especially of a whimsical kind: *The unicorn is a creature of fancy.* **2.** something that is imagined by the fancy. **3.** an idea or opinion based on few or no facts; notion; supposition: *a mere fancy.* **4.** a preference or inclination; fondness; liking: *Andrew has a fancy for cowboy movies. The two boys took a fancy to each other.* —*adj.,* **fan·ci·er, fan·ci·est. 1.** made to please the fancy; highly decorated; ornamental; elaborate: *a shirt with fancy embroidery.* **2.** of highest quality; superior; choice: *fancy fruits and vegetables.* **3.** *Informal.* very high; extravagant: *That store charges fancy prices.* **4.** showing or requiring great skill or grace; intricate: *fancy diving.* —*v.t.,* **fan·cied, fan·cy·ing. 1.** to picture in the mind; imagine: *He fancies himself a great writer.* **2.** to have a fondness for; like: *Which of these dresses do you fancy the most?* —**fan′ci·ly,** *adv.* —**fan′ci·ness,** *n.*

fan·cy·work (fan′sē wurk′) *n.* ornamental needlework, as embroidery or tatting.

fan·fare (fan′fer′) *n.* **1.** a short tune sounded by bugles, trumpets, or other brass instruments, used especially for military and ceremonial occasions. **2.** a great noise, excitement, fuss, or activity, as in celebration of something: *The team's victory was greeted with much fanfare.*

Fangs

fang (fang) *n.* **1.** a long, pointed tooth with which an animal slashes or holds its prey. **2.** one of the two sharp, slender teeth with which a poisonous snake injects venom. **3.** any pointed, tapered projection.

fan·light (fan′līt′) *n.* a semicircular window over a door or larger window.

fan·tail (fan′tāl′) *n.*
1. a tail, end, or part resembling an open fan.
2. a domestic pigeon having a fan-shaped tail.

fan·tas·tic (fan tas′-tik) *adj.* 1. very unusual or strange; odd; grotesque: *Driftwood sometimes takes on fantastic shapes.* 2. existing in the mind only; imaginary: *the fantastic fears of children.* 3. *Informal.* particularly good; splendid: *The climbers had a fantastic view of the town from the mountain top.* 4. extraordinary; remarkable; amazing: *to eat a fantastic amount of food.* Also, **fan·tas·ti·cal** (fan tas′ti kəl). —**fan·tas′ti·cal·ly,** *adv.*

Fanlight

fan·ta·sy (fan′tə sē) *also,* **phan·ta·sy.** *n. pl.,* **fan·ta·sies.**
1. imagination or fancy. 2. an unreal or grotesque fancy: *fantasies brought on by a high fever.* 3. a fanciful or imaginative creation or invention: *He wrote a fantasy about life on Mars.*

far (fär) *adv.,* **far·ther** or **fur·ther,** **far·thest** or **fur·thest.** 1. at or to a great distance in space: *to travel far from home.* 2. at or to a distant time, degree, or extent: *He worked far into the night. The job is far from finished.* 3. to or at a certain distance, time, or degree: *Billy's practical jokes always go too far.* 4. to a great degree; very much: *It would be far better if you stayed until the rain stopped.* —*adj.,* **far·ther** or **fur·ther, far·thest** or **fur·thest.** 1. distant in time or space: *the far future, the far north.* 2. more distant; farther: *the far side of the moon.* 3. going or reaching over a long distance or time: *a far journey.*

Fantail (def. 2)

as far as. to the distance, degree, or extent that: *Read as far as you can in ten minutes.*
by far. very much: *That is by far the best choice.*
far and away. without a doubt; very much: *Tom is far and away the best player on the team.*
in so far as. to the degree or extent that: *In so far as I know, he arrives next week.*
so far. a. up to now: *I've saved five dollars so far.* **b.** up to a certain point or extent: *You can go just so far in being frank.*
so far as. to the degree or extent that.

far·ad (far′əd) *n.* a unit of electrical capacitance. An object that stores one coulomb of charge when raised to a potential of one volt has a capacitance of one farad.

far·a·day (far′ə dā) *n.* in electrolysis, the quantity of electricity necessary to deposit or dissolve an amount of a substance equivalent to one gram. One faraday is equal to about 96,500 coulombs. [From Michael *Faraday*, 1791–1867, English physicist.]

far·a·way (fär′ə wā′) *adj.* 1. at a great distance; remote: *The old sailor had traveled to faraway places.* 2. dreamy; pensive: *She had a faraway look in her eyes.*

farce (färs) *n.* 1. a humorous play in which the situation and characters are greatly exaggerated. 2. an absurd pretense; mockery: *The meeting turned out to be a farce.*

far·ci·cal (fär′si kəl) *adj.* of, relating to, or characteristic of a farce; absurd; ludicrous. —**far·ci·cal·i·ty** (fär′si kal′-ə tē), *n.* —**far′ci·cal·ly,** *adv.*

far cry, a great distance; long way: *His statement was a far cry from the truth.*

fare (fer) *n.* 1. the cost of a ride on a bus, train, airplane, or other conveyance. 2. a passenger who pays a fare: *How many fares can that bus carry?* 3. food and drink: *The restaurant served English fare.* —*v.i.,* **fared, far·ing.** 1. to get along; do: *He is faring well at school.* 2. to turn out; result; happen: *It fared badly with us on our camping trip.*

Far East, the countries of eastern Asia, including Japan, Korea, and China.

fare·well (fer′wel′) *interj.* good-by and good luck. —*n.* 1. parting word; good-by: *The guests said their farewells and left.* 2. the act of parting; departure; leave-taking. —*adj.* of or relating to a farewell; last: *a farewell dinner, a farewell speech.*

far-fetched (fär′fetcht′) *adj.* not natural or reasonable; forced; strained: *The prisoner's alibi was so far-fetched that the police did not believe it.*

far-flung (fär′flung′) *adj.* covering a great distance or area; widespread: *a far-flung empire.*

fa·ri·na (fə rē′nə) *n.* a flour or meal made from cereal grains, nuts, or starchy roots, used as a breakfast cereal or in puddings.

farm (färm) *n.* 1. an area of land used to raise crops, livestock, or poultry. 2. a tract of water used for the cultivation of fish or other forms of marine life: *an oyster farm.* —*v.t.* to cultivate (land). —*v.i.* to grow crops or raise livestock or poultry: *The people in this valley farm for a living.*

farm·er (fär′mər) *n.* a person who lives on and runs a farm.

farm·hand (färm′hand′) *n.* a person who works on a farm, especially a hired laborer.

farm·house (färm′hous′) *n. pl.,* **farm·hous·es** (färm′-hou′ziz). a house on a farm, especially one in which the owner or manager lives.

farm·ing (fär′ming) *n.* the business of raising crops, livestock, or poultry; agriculture.

farm·stead (färm′sted′) *n.* a farm and its buildings.

farm team, a minor-league team owned by or associated with a major-league club.

farm·yard (färm′yärd′) *n.* a yard enclosed by or surrounding farm buildings.

far-off (fär′ôf′) *adj.* distant; remote: *to visit far-off lands.*

far-out (fär′out′) *adj. Slang.* unconventional; extreme: *He has far-out taste in clothing.*

far-reach·ing (fär′rē′ching) *adj.* having wide influence, effect, or range: *The government's new plan included far-reaching reforms.*

far·ri·er (far′ē ər) *n. British.* a blacksmith who shoes horses.

far·row (far′ō) *n.* a litter of pigs. —*v.i.* to give birth to a litter of pigs.

far·see·ing (fär′sē′ing) *adj.* 1. able to see distant objects. 2. having or showing foresight and careful planning; far-sighted: *a farseeing businessman, a farseeing program to improve public education.*

far·sight·ed (fär′sī′tid) *adj.* 1. able to see distant objects more clearly than those nearby. 2. having or showing foresight and careful planning; prudent: *a farsighted leader.* —**far′sight′ed·ly,** *adv.* —**far′sight′ed·ness,** *n.*

at; āpe; cär; end; mē; it; īce; hot; ōld; fôrk; wood; fōōl; oil; out; up; turn; sing; thin; this; hw in white; zh in treasure. The symbol ə stands for the sound of a in about, e in taken, i in pencil, o in lemon, and u in circus.

F

far·ther (fär′thər) a comparative of **far.** —*adv.*
1. at or to a more distant point in space: *The raft drifted farther and farther from the dock.* **2.** to a greater degree or extent; more completely. —*adj.* **1.** more distant: *They live at the farther side of the town.* **2.** more; additional; further.

▲ **Farther** or **further** can be used interchangeably. **Farther** is somewhat more common when distance is referred to: *Carol jumped two feet farther than Ann.* **Further** is used more often than *farther* in the sense of "additional": *The district attorney called for a further investigation into the charges of corruption.*

far·ther·most (fär′thər mōst′) *adj.* most distant or remote; farthest.

far·thest (fär′thist) a superlative of **far.** —*adv.* **1.** at or to the most distant point in space: *Jane sat farthest from the teacher.* **2.** to the greatest degree or extent; most completely. —*adj.* most distant: *the farthest hill.*

far·thing (fär′thing) *n.* a former British coin, equal to one-fourth of a penny.

far·thin·gale (fär′thing gāl) *n.* a framework for holding out a woman's skirt, worn in the sixteenth and seventeenth centuries.

fas·ci·nate (fas′ə nāt′) *v.t.,* **fas·ci·nat·ed, fas·ci·nat·ing.**
1. to attract and hold the close interest of by some special quality or charm; captivate: *The magician's tricks fascinated the children in the audience.* **2.** to hold motionless or paralyze by terror or awe: *The snake fascinated its prey.* —**fas′ci·na′tor,** *n.*

fas·ci·nat·ing (fas′ə nā′ting) *adj.* very interesting or captivating: *a fascinating man, a fascinating story.* —**fas′ci·nat′ing·ly,** *adv.*

fas·ci·na·tion (fas′ə nā′shən) *n.* **1.** the act of fascinating or the state of being fascinated. **2.** very strong attraction; charm; enchantment.

fas·cism (fash′iz əm) *n.* **1. Fascism.** a political movement that controlled Italy from 1922 to 1943 under the dictatorship of Benito Mussolini. Fascism established strict economic controls and attempted to organize most phases of Italian life. **2.** any similar movement, such as Naziism, that advocates a nationalist dictatorship, private ownership of property but state control of the economy, and suppression of opposing political movements. **3.** the doctrines or methods of any such movement.

fas·cist (fash′ist) *n.* **1. Fascist.** a member of the ruling political party in Italy under the dictatorship of Benito Mussolini. **2.** a member of any similar political party. **3.** a person who believes in and supports fascism. —*adj.* also, **Fascist.** of, relating to, or supporting fascism or fascists.

fash·ion (fash′ən) *n.* **1.** clothing; apparel: *The department store was showing spring fashions.* **2.** the current custom or style, as in dress, speech, or behavior: *the latest fashion in men's clothing, a slang word that is no longer in fashion.* **3.** manner; way: *to act in a carefree fashion.* —*v.t.* to give form to; shape; mold: *The cobbler fashioned a boot out of leather.*
   after a fashion or **in a fashion.** to some extent, but not completely or too well: *The boy washed the car after a fashion.*

fash·ion·a·ble (fash′ə nə bəl) *adj.* **1.** following current styles or practices; in fashion; stylish: *a fashionable hairdo, a fashionable coat.* **2.** of, relating to, or used by people who set or follow styles: *a fashionable restaurant.* —**fash′ion·a·bly,** *adv.*

fast¹ (fast) *adj.* **1.** acting, moving, or done with speed; quick; rapid: *a fast train, a fast thinker, a fast game.* **2.** (of a clock or watch) ahead of the correct time. **3.** wild and dissipated: *to lead a fast life, a fast group of*

people. **4.** firmly attached; secure; tight: *a fast knot, to have a fast grip on a rope.* **5.** loyal; faithful; steadfast: *fast friends.* **6.** (of colors) not easily faded. —*adv.* **1.** in a firm manner; securely; tightly: *The tent was held fast by stakes driven into the ground. This stamp will not stick fast.* **2.** soundly; deeply: *to be fast asleep.* **3.** with speed; quickly; rapidly: *The horse ran fast.* **4.** in a wild, dissipated manner. [Old English *fæst* firm, fixed, quick.]

fast² (fast) *v.i.* to eat little or no food or only certain kinds of food, especially as a religious observance. —*n.* **1.** the act of fasting. **2.** a day or period of fasting. [Old English *fæstan.*]

fas·ten (fas′ən) *v.t.* **1.** to attach firmly; connect; join: *to fasten a pin to a dress. The team fastened the blame for their defeat on poor pitching.* **2.** to make fast; close tightly; secure: *to fasten a door, to fasten a seat belt, to fasten a dress with a zipper.* **3.** to direct steadily or fix: *Joan fastened her attention on her book.* —*v.i.* **1.** to become attached or firmly joined: *This snap won't fasten.* **2.** to take a firm hold; concentrate: *to fasten on a plan.* —**fas′ten·er,** *n.*

fas·ten·ing (fas′ə ning) *n.* **1.** something that fastens, as a hook, bolt, or button. **2.** the act of making fast.

fast-food (fast′fōōd′) *adj.* serving foods that can be cooked quickly, such as hamburgers, frankfurters, and fried chicken: *a fast-food restaurant.*

fas·tid·i·ous (fas tid′ē əs) *adj.* difficult to please or satisfy, particularly in matters of taste: *a person who is fastidious about clothing, a fastidious eater.* —**fas·tid′i·ous·ly,** *adv.* —**fas·tid′i·ous·ness,** *n.*

fast·ness (fast′nis) *n. pl.,* **fast·ness·es.** **1.** the quality or state of being securely fixed. **2.** swiftness; rapidity: *We prefer sureness to fastness.* **3.** stronghold: *The fort was an impenetrable fastness.*

fat (fat) *n.* **1.** any of a group of oily or greasy substances that are white or yellow in color, found especially in deposits in certain tissues of animals and some plants, for which they serve as reserve sources of energy. Fats are compounds of carbon, hydrogen, and oxygen. **2.** animal tissue consisting mainly of such a substance. **3.** a fat or oil used in cooking: *to fry potatoes in deep fat.* **4.** too much weight; obesity. —*adj.,* **fat·ter, fat·test. 1.** having much flesh or fat; obese or plump: *a fat man, a fat turkey.* **2.** containing much fat, oil, or grease; fatty: *fat hamburger, fat gravy.* **3.** containing much; full; abundant: *a fat wallet.* **4.** profitable. —*v.t.,* **fat·ted, fat·ting.** to fatten. —**fat′ness,** *n.*

fa·tal (fāt′əl) *adj.* **1.** causing death: *a fatal injury, a fatal accident.* **2.** causing destruction or harm; disastrous: *a fatal mistake.* **3.** very important or decisive; fateful: *Finally, the fatal day of the championship match arrived.*

fa·tal·ism (fāt′əl iz′əm) *n.* **1.** the belief that all events are determined beforehand by fate and cannot be changed by people. **2.** the acceptance of this belief.

fa·tal·ist (fāt′əl ist) *n.* a person who believes in fatalism.

fa·tal·is·tic (fāt′əl is′tik) *adj.* relating to or believing in fatalism. —**fa′tal·is′ti·cal·ly,** *adv.*

fa·tal·i·ty (fā tal′ə tē) *n. pl.,* **fa·tal·i·ties. 1.** a death resulting from a disaster; fatal accident: *Highway fatalities were high over the holiday weekend.* **2.** the ability to cause death; deadly influence or effect: *the fatality of a disease.*

fa·tal·ly (fāt′əl ē) *adv.* so as to cause death or disaster; mortally: *to be fatally ill.*

fat·back (fat′bak′) *n.* a fatty strip of meat from the back of a hog, usually salted and dried.

fate (fāt) *n.* **1.** the power that is believed to determine events before they happen and over which humans have no control. **2.** something that is believed to be caused by fate; unavoidable lot or fortune; destiny: *It was his fate to die young.* **3.** the final state; outcome: *The defendant awaited the fate of an appeal to a higher court.*

fat·ed (fā′tid) *adj.* **1.** determined in advance by fate; destined: *Our team was fated to win.* **2.** destined to disaster; doomed.

fate·ful (fāt′fəl) *adj.* **1.** of great importance; decisive; momentous: *a fateful battle, a fateful decision.* **2.** showing or telling what will happen; prophetic: *fateful words.* **3.** causing death or disaster; deadly. —**fate′ful·ly,** *adv.* —**fate′ful·ness,** *n.*

Fates (fāts) *n.,pl. Greek and Roman Mythology.* the three goddesses who controlled human life and destiny.

fa·ther (fä′thər) *n.* **1.** a male parent. **2.** a man who acts or is thought of as a male parent; guardian or provider. **3.** a man who originates, invents, or founds something: *Gutenberg was the father of printing. George Washington has been called "the father of his country."* **4.** a man who is an important leader: *the town fathers.* **5.** *also,* **Father.** a title of respect used to address a priest or another clergyman. **6. Father.** God. **7.** a male ancestor; forefather. —*v.t.* **1.** to be the father of: *Mr. Johnson fathered two sons and a daughter.* **2.** to act as a father toward: *to father an orphan.* **3.** to originate, invent, or found: *The revolutionists fathered a new form of government.*

fa·ther·hood (fä′thər hood′) *n.* the state of being a father.

fa·ther·in·law (fä′thər in lô′) *n. pl.,* **fa·thers·in·law.** the father of one's husband or wife.

fa·ther·land (fä′thər land′) *n.* the country in which a person or his ancestors were born.

fa·ther·less (fä′thər lis) *adj.* **1.** having no living father. **2.** having no known father.

fa·ther·ly (fä′thər lē) *adj.* **1.** of, relating to, or characteristic of a father: *fatherly advice.* **2.** like a father: *a fatherly uncle.* —**fa′ther·li·ness,** *n.*

Father's Day, a day set aside in honor of fathers, celebrated each year on the third Sunday in June.

fath·om (fath′əm) *n. pl.,* **fath·oms** or **fath·om.** a unit of measure equal to six feet, used especially in nautical measurements, as for the depth of water. —*v.t.* **1.** to measure the depth of (water); sound. **2.** to understand fully: *Jim could not fathom the meaning of the poem.* —**fath′om·a·ble,** *adj.*

fath·om·less (fath′əm lis) *adj.* **1.** too deep to be measured. **2.** difficult or impossible to be understood; incomprehensible.

fa·tigue (fə tēg′) *n.* **1.** a loss of strength that is caused by hard work or mental effort; weariness; exhaustion. **2.** the cause of such weariness; toil; exertion. **3.** manual labor done by military personnel. Also, **fatigue duty.** **4. fatigues.** a two-piece work uniform worn by military personnel. —*v.t.,* **fa·tigued, fa·ti·guing.** to cause weariness in; tire out: *The hard work fatigued him.*

fat·ten (fat′ən) *v.t.* to make fat or plump; fill out: *to fatten turkeys for market.* —*v.i.* to grow or become fat.

fat·ty (fat′ē) *adj.,* **fat·ti·er, fat·ti·est.** **1.** made of or containing fat, especially in large amounts. **2.** like fat; greasy; oily. —**fat′ti·ness,** *n.*

fatty acid, any of several organic compounds that make up a large part of animal and plant fat.

fa·tu·i·ty (fə tōō′ə tē, fə tyōō′ə tē) *n. pl.,* **fa·tu·i·ties.** **1.** smug stupidity or foolishness. **2.** something that is fatuous, as an action or statement.

fat·u·ous (fach′ōō əs) *adj.* smugly stupid or foolish; inane: *He answered the question with a fatuous remark.* —**fat′u·ous·ly,** *adv.* —**fat′u·ous·ness,** *n.*

fau·cet (fô′sit) *n.* a device that controls the flow of water or another liquid from a pipe or container by means of a valve.

Faulk·ner, William (fôk′nər) 1897–1962, U.S. novelist and short story writer.

fault (fôlt) *n.* **1.** something that spoils character, appearance, or structure; flaw: *The roof collapsed because of a fault in the beams. His bad temper is his main fault.* **2.** the responsibility for a mistake or wrongdoing: *The accident was no one's fault.* **3.** mistake; error: *He corrected the faults in his arithmetic.* **4.** *Geology.* a break in a rock mass. The mass on one side of the break is displaced with respect to the mass on the other side. **5.** a failure to serve the ball into the correct area of the court in tennis, squash, and similar games. —*v.t.* **1.** to find fault with; blame. **2.** *Geology.* to cause or produce a fault in. —*v.i. Geology.* to develop a fault.

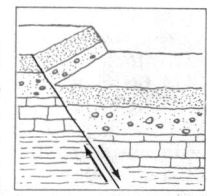

Fault *(def. 4)*

at fault. deserving blame; wrong: *The boys are not at fault in this case.*

to a fault. excessively; extremely: *He is generous to a fault.*

to find fault. to look for and point out a fault; complain: *You are always finding fault.*

to find fault with. to criticize: *John's aunt seems to find fault with everything.*

fault·find·er (fôlt′fīn′dər) *n.* a person who looks for and points out faults; person who criticizes too much.

fault·find·ing (fôlt′fīn′ding) *n.* the act or habit of criticizing or pointing out faults. —*adj.* tending to point out faults; critical.

fault·less (fôlt′lis) *adj.* without a fault; perfect. —**fault′less·ly,** *adv.* —**fault′less·ness,** *n.*

fault·y (fôl′tē) *adj.,* **fault·i·er, fault·i·est.** having faults or defects: *a faulty motor.* —**fault′i·ly,** *adv.* —**fault′i·ness,** *n.*

faun (fôn) *n. Roman Mythology.* a minor god of the woods and fields, having the body of a man and the ears, horns, legs, and tail of a goat. In Greek mythology it was called a satyr.

fau·na (fô′nə) *n. pl.,* **fau·nas** or **fau·nae** (fô′nē). the animals characteristic of a particular region, time, or environment: *the fauna of the African plains.*

Faust (foust) *n. German Legend.* a magician and philosopher who sold his soul to the devil in return for knowledge and power.

faux pas (fō′ pä′) *pl.,* **faux pas** (fō′ päz′, fō′ pä′). an embarrassing mistake, especially a social one: *Forgetting my host's name was a silly faux pas.* [French *faux pas* false step.]

fa·vor (fā′vər) *n.* **1.** an act of kindness or good will: *He did her the favor of lending her his book.* **2.** friendly regard; approval; liking: *The teacher looked on his students with favor.* **3.** special consideration or kindness; partiality: *The judge never showed favor to his friends.* **4.** the condition of being liked, highly regarded, or approved: *That politician is in favor with the people.* **5.** something given, as a souvenir at a party; gift. **6.** the state of being ahead of one's opponent in a contest: *The score is 12 to 6, in our favor.* —*v.t.* **1.** to show favor to; oblige: *Please favor us with a reply.* **2.** to approve of; like: *to favor long hair.* **3.** to show special consideration for; be partial to: *to favor one son over*

at; āpe; cär; end; mē; it; īce; hot; ōld; fôrk; wood; fool; oil; out; up; turn; sing; thin; this; hw in white; zh in treasure. The symbol ə stands for the sound of a in about, e in taken, i in pencil, o in lemon, and u in circus.

F

another, a law that favors rural areas. **4.** to prove advantageous to; make easy; assist: *Crowded conditions favor the spread of disease.* **5.** to treat with gentleness; spare: *to favor a sprained ankle.* **6.** to look like; resemble: *The baby favors his father.*

　in favor of. a. in support of; supporting: *The students were in favor of longer vacations.* **b.** to the advantage of: *The jury decided in favor of the defendant.*

　in one's favor. to one's advantage or interest.

fa·vor·a·ble (fā′vər ə bəl) *adj.* **1.** approving; complimentary: *That movie received a favorable review.* **2.** in one's favor; advantageous: *They had favorable weather conditions for sailing. The speaker made a favorable impression on the audience.* **3.** granting something desired or requested: *I hope that my application for a job will receive a favorable reply.* —**fa′vor·a·ble·ness,** *n.* —**fa′vor·a·bly,** *adv.*

fa·vor·ite (fā′vər it) *adj.* looked upon with special liking or favor; liked best: *a favorite baseball team. Spring is her favorite time of the year.* —*n.* **1.** a person or thing that is liked best: *Mystery stories are my favorites. Of all my teachers, she is my favorite.* **2.** in a contest, the competitor that is most likely to win: *That horse is a favorite in the next race.*

fa·vor·it·ism (fā′vər i tiz′əm) *n.* the unfair favoring of one or more persons over others; partiality.

fawn[1] (fôn) *n.* **1.** a deer less than one year old. **2.** a light yellowish-brown color. —*adj.* having the color fawn. [Old French *faon* a young animal.]

fawn[2] (fôn) *v.i.* **1.** to seek favor by acting in a slavish manner: *People fawned on the wealthy man.* **2.** (of dogs) to show affection, as by wagging the tail. [Middle English *faunen.*]

fay (fā) *n.* a fairy or elf.

faze (fāz) *v.t.,* **fazed, faz·ing.** *Informal.* to upset; disconcert: *Being called on to answer a question never fazes him.*

FBI, Federal Bureau of Investigation.

F clef *Music.* another term for **bass clef.**

Fe, the symbol for iron. [Abbreviation of Latin *ferrum.*]

fe·al·ty (fē′əl tē) *n. pl.,* **fe·al·ties.** the loyalty and duty owed by a vassal or feudal tenant to his lord.

fear (fēr) *n.* **1.** a strong feeling caused by the awareness or threat of danger, pain, or evil; dread: *They trembled with fear at the sight of the gunman.* **2.** the state of feeling fear: *to live in fear.* **3.** a feeling of concern or anxiety: *The boy had a fear that his sick dog would not get well.* **4.** a cause for fear or alarm; danger: *There was no fear of his failing the exam.* —*v.t.* **1.** to be afraid of; dread: *Many children fear the dark.* **2.** to feel concerned or anxious about: *He feared that we would be late for the show.* —*v.i.* **1.** to feel fear; be afraid. **2.** to be concerned or anxious: *to fear for one's safety.*

fear·ful (fēr′fəl) *adj.* **1.** feeling fear; afraid: *The child was fearful of the barking dog.* **2.** causing fear; dreadful; frightening: *The blizzard was fearful.* **3.** showing fear: *a fearful look.* **4.** *Informal.* very bad; offensive: *He has fearful table manners.* —**fear′ful·ly,** *adv.* —**fear′ful·ness,** *n.*

fear·less (fēr′lis) *adj.* showing or feeling no fear; brave. —**fear′less·ly,** *adv.* —**fear′less·ness,** *n.*

fear·some (fēr′səm) *adj.* **1.** causing fear; frightening. **2.** feeling fear; frightened. —**fear′some·ly,** *adv.* —**fear′some·ness,** *n.*

fea·si·ble (fē′zə bəl) *adj.* **1.** capable of being done or carried out; practicable: *a feasible design for a bridge.*

2. capable of being used successfully; suitable: *a feasible site for a dam.* **3.** likely; probable: *Tom had a feasible explanation for being absent.* —**fea′si·bil′i·ty,** *n.* —**fea′si·bly,** *adv.*

feast (fēst) *n.* **1.** an elaborate and rich meal, especially one prepared for many guests on a special occasion: *a wedding feast.* **2.** a religious celebration or festival: *the feast of the Annunciation.* **3.** something that gives great pleasure; treat: *The snow-capped mountains were a feast for the climbers' eyes.* —*v.t.* **1.** to give great pleasure to: *to feast one's eyes on an apple orchard in bloom.* **2.** to provide a feast for; entertain richly. —*v.i.* to have or partake of a feast; eat richly: *to feast on turkey.*

feat (fēt) *n.* an act or deed, especially one showing great skill, strength, or courage: *Climbing that mountain was quite a feat.*

feath·er (feth′ər) *n.* **1.** one of the light outgrowths that cover a bird's skin. A feather consists of a horny hollow shaft with soft, flexible barbs on either side. **2.** something like a feather in appearance or lightness, as a fringe of hair on the leg of a dog. —*v.t.* **1.** to provide with feathers: *to feather a dart.* **2.** to turn (the blade of an oar) parallel to the water's surface after a stroke. **3.** to bring (an airplane propeller blade) parallel to the line of flight in order to decrease wind resistance. —**feath′er·like′,** *adv.*

　feather in one's cap. an act to be proud of: *Winning the game was a feather in the team's cap.*

feather bed, a soft, warm quilt or mattress filled with feathers.

feath·er·bed·ding (feth′ər bed′ing) *n.* the requiring of an employer to hire or continue to employ more people than are needed to do a job, especially as practiced by some labor unions to preserve jobs.

feath·er·weight (feth′ər wāt′) *n.* **1.** a boxer competing in the second from the lowest weight class. **2.** a wrestler or weight lifter in a similar class. **3.** a person or thing that is very small or unimportant.

feath·er·y (feth′ər ē) *adj.* **1.** covered with or having feathers. **2.** like a feather; light and soft.

fea·ture (fē′chər) *n.* **1.** an important or distinctive part or characteristic of something: *Great speed is a feature of this sports car.* **2.** a part of the face, as the eyes, nose, mouth, or chin. **3.** a full-length motion picture, especially one shown as a main attraction. **4.** anything presented as a main or special attraction: *The feature of the circus will be the trapeze act.* **5.** a story, article, or column of special interest, appearing in a newspaper or magazine. —*v.,* **featured, fea·tur·ing.** —*v.t.* to give an important place to: *The concert features a guitarist and a singer.* —*v.i.* to play an important part: *Local school issues featured prominently in the campaign.*

Feb., February.

Feb·ru·ar·y (feb′rōō er′ē, feb′yōō er′ē) *n. pl.,* **Feb·ru·ar·ies.** the second month of the year, having twenty-eight days in regular years and twenty-nine days in leap years. [Latin *Februārius* the month of purification, from *februa* the Roman festival of purification, which was held on February 15.]

fe·ces (fē′sēz) *n., pl.* the waste matter discharged from the bowels; excrement.

feck·less (fek′lis) *adj.* **1.** weak; feeble. **2.** irresponsible; careless: *a feckless young man.*

fe·cund (fē′kənd, fek′ənd) *adj.* fertile; fruitful; productive: *fecund earth, a fecund mind.*

Fawn

Feather

fe·cun·di·ty (fi kun′də tē) *n.* the quality of being fecund; fertility; fruitfulness; productiveness.

fed (fed) the past tense and past participle of **feed.**

fed up. *Informal.* disgusted, annoyed, or bored: *After waiting for him for an hour, we got fed up and left.*

fed·er·al (fed′ər əl) *adj.* **1.** of, relating to, or formed by an agreement between states or other groups establishing a central government to control matters of common concern, with each of the states or groups keeping control over its own affairs. **2.** of or relating to a central government formed in this way. **3.** *also,* **Federal.** of or relating to the central government of the United States, as distinguished from the governments of the individual states. **4. Federal.** of, relating to, or supporting the Union during the Civil War. —*n.* **Federal.** a person who supported the Union during the Civil War, especially a Union soldier.

Federal Bureau of Investigation, an agency of the United States Department of Justice that investigates violations of federal law and subversive activities against the United States.

fed·er·al·ism (fed′ər ə liz′əm) *n.* **1.** the principle or system of federal government. **2.** the belief in or support of such a system of government. **3. Federalism.** the principles of the Federalist Party.

fed·er·al·ist (fed′ər ə list) *n.* **1.** a person who believes in or supports a federal system of government. **2. Federalist.** a member or supporter of the Federalist Party.

Federalist Party, a political party in the United States from 1788 to 1816, that supported the adoption of the Constitution and advocated a strong central government. Its principal leader was Alexander Hamilton.

fed·er·al·ize (fed′ər ə līz′) *v.t.,* **fed·er·al·ized, fed·er·al·iz·ing. 1.** to unite in a federal union. **2.** to place under the control of a federal government.

Federal Republic of Germany, see **West Germany.**

fed·er·ate (*v.,* fed′ə rāt′; *adj.,* fed′ər it) *v.,* **fed·er·at·ed, fed·er·at·ing.** —*v.t.* to unite in a federal union. —*v.i.* to form a federal union: *The states federated to form one nation.* —*adj.* united in a federation.

fed·er·a·tion (fed′ə rā′shən) *n.* **1.** the act of forming a federal union by agreement between states, nations, or other groups. **2.** a union formed in this way, especially as a form of government: *a federation of nations to promote peace, a federation of labor unions.*

fe·do·ra (fi dôr′ə) *n.* a soft felt hat for men with a curved brim and a lengthwise crease in the top.

fee (fē) *n.* **1.** a charge or payment for a service or privilege: *a license fee, a registration fee.* **2.** an estate in land held from a feudal lord; fief. **3.** see **fee simple.**

fee·ble (fē′bəl) *adj.,* **fee·bler, fee·blest. 1.** lacking physical strength; weak: *The feeble old woman used a cane.* **2.** lacking force, strength, or effectiveness: *a feeble cry, a feeble try.* —**fee′ble·ness,** *n.* —**fee′bly,** *adv.*

fee·ble·mind·ed (fē′bəl mīn′did) *adj.* having less than normal intelligence; not intelligent; stupid. —**fee′-ble·mind′ed·ly,** *adv.* —**fee′ble·mind′ed·ness,** *n.*

feed (fēd) *v.,* **fed, feed·ing.** —*v.t.* **1.** to give food or nourishment to: *to feed a baby.* **2.** to provide as food or nourishment: *to feed grain to cattle.* **3.** to provide with something that is used for growth: *Melting snow from the mountains feeds the rivers each spring.* **4.** to supply (material to be used or consumed): *to feed data into a computer, to feed fuel into an engine.* —*v.i.* (of animals) to eat: *Cows are feeding in that pasture. Vultures feed on dead animals.* —*n.* **1.** food for animals; fodder. **2.** *Informal.* a meal; food.

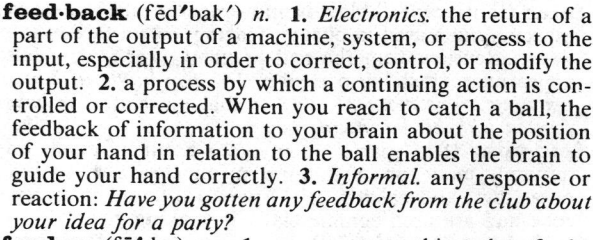
Fedora

feed·back (fēd′bak′) *n.* **1.** *Electronics.* the return of a part of the output of a machine, system, or process to the input, especially in order to correct, control, or modify the output. **2.** a process by which a continuing action is controlled or corrected. When you reach to catch a ball, the feedback of information to your brain about the position of your hand in relation to the ball enables the brain to guide your hand correctly. **3.** *Informal.* any response or reaction: *Have you gotten any feedback from the club about your idea for a party?*

feed·er (fē′dər) *n.* **1.** a person or thing that feeds. **2.** anything that supplies or leads into a main line, such as a tributary of a river, a branch of a railroad, or a side road leading into a highway.

feel (fēl) *v.,* **felt, feel·ing.** —*v.t.* **1.** to sense or examine by touching or handling; touch: *to feel the difference between satin and velvet. The doctor felt the patient's pulse.* **2.** to be aware of by touch: *to feel the cold, to feel the rain on one's face.* **3.** to be affected by: *She felt pity for the victims of the famine.* **4.** to hold as an opinion; believe: *Many students felt that the rule was unfair.* **5.** to try to find (one's way) by touching; grope: *The blind boy felt his way up the stairs.* —*v.i.* **1.** to be aware of being: *to feel happy, to feel hot.* **2.** to produce the sensation or feeling of being; seem: *The water feels warm. Today feels like spring.* **3.** to search or explore by touch; grope: *He felt in his pocket for his wallet. The doctor felt for broken bones.* **4.** to have sympathy or compassion: *She felt deeply for the crippled child.* —*n.* a quality that is sensed or learned by touching: *the cold feel of snow.*

to feel like. to have an interest in or desire for: *Do you feel like playing baseball today?*

to feel out. to try to discover in a cautious way: *to feel out one's boss for a raise in pay, to feel out used car prices.*

to feel up to. to feel able to or ready for: *The swimmer had a cold and did not feel up to racing.*

feel·er (fē′lər) *n.* **1.** an organ of touch in an animal's body, especially the antenna of an insect. **2.** an act, remark, or plan used to feel out a person or group: *After years of battle, a peace feeler was sent to the enemy.*

feel·ing (fē′ling) *n.* **1.** the ability to feel by touching; sense of touch: *He rubbed his numb foot to bring back the feeling.* **2.** a sensation: *a feeling of dampness, a feeling of hunger.* **3.** an emotion, as joy, fear, or anger. **4.** an awareness; impression: *The child had a feeling of security when his mother was near.* **5. feelings.** the sensitive part of one's character or nature: *The criticism hurt his feelings.* **6.** tender emotion, especially sympathy or pity: *a man of deep feeling, to have great feeling for the disabled.* **7.** opinion; belief; sentiment: *It is my feeling that you are right about what happened.* —**feel′ing·ly,** *adv.*

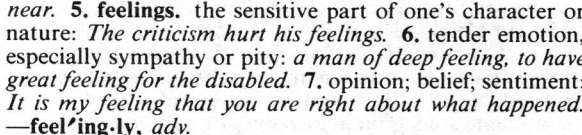
Feelers

fee simple, an estate in land, over which the owner has complete rights.

feet (fēt) the plural of **foot.**

feign (fān) *v.t.* to put on a false appearance of; pretend: *to feign sickness, to feign friendliness.* —*v.i.* to make believe; pretend.

at; āpe; cär; end; mē; it; īce; hot; ōld; fôrk; wood; fōōl; oil; out; up; turn; sing; thin; this; hw in white; zh in treasure. The symbol ə stands for the sound of **a** in about, e in taken, i in pencil, o in lemon, and u in circus.

F

feint (fānt) *n.* **1.** a blow or movement meant to deceive, especially one used in boxing, fencing, or warfare to take away attention from the real point of attack. **2.** a false appearance or show; pretense: *The boy made a feint of listening to his mother.* —*v.i.* to make a feint: *The boxer feinted with his left hand.*

feld·spar (feld′spär′) *n.* any of a group of crystalline minerals made up of aluminum silicates with sodium, potassium, and calcium. Feldspars are found in igneous rock and are used commercially in making glass.

fe·lic·i·tate (fi lis′ə tāt′) *v.t.*, **fe·lic·i·tat·ed, fe·lic·i·tat·ing.** to wish happiness to; congratulate.

fe·lic·i·ta·tion (fi lis′ə tā′shən) *n.* an expression of pleasure over another's happiness or good fortune; congratulation.

fe·lic·i·tous (fi lis′ə təs) *adj.* **1.** suitable to the occasion; appropriate; apt: *a felicitous reply, a felicitous choice of words.* **2.** showing skill at appropriate expression: *The congressman was a felicitous speaker.* —**fe·lic′i·tous·ly,** *adv.* —**fe·lic′i·tous·ness,** *n.*

fe·lic·i·ty (fi lis′ə tē) *n. pl.,* **fe·lic·i·ties.** **1.** great happiness; bliss. **2.** a source of happiness; blessing. **3.** skill at appropriate expression: *to write with felicity.* **4.** a suitable or appropriate expression.

fe·line (fē′līn) *adj.* **1.** of or relating to cats or the cat family. **2.** like a cat: *The dancer moved with feline grace.* —*n.* an animal belonging to the cat family, such as a lion, tiger, or leopard.

fell[1] (fel) the past tense of **fall.**

fell[2] (fel) *v.t.* **1.** to strike and knock down; cause to fall: *He felled his opponent with one blow. The hunter felled the deer.* **2.** to cut down (a tree or trees). **3.** in sewing, to finish (a seam) by joining the edges, turning them under, and stitching them to the fabric. [Old English *fellan.*]

fell[3] (fel) *adj.* **1.** cruel; savage; dreadful: *a fell pirate.* **2.** destructive; deadly: *a fell disease.* [Old French *fel.*]

fell[4] (fel) *n.* the skin or hide of an animal; pelt. [Old English *fel* or *fell.*]

fel·lah (fel′ə) *n. pl.,* **fel·la·hin** (fel′ə hēn′). a peasant or laborer in Arabic-speaking countries.

fel·loe (fel′ō) *n.* another word for **felly.**

fel·low (fel′ō) *n.* **1.** a man or boy: *What a clever fellow he is.* **2.** a person in general; individual; anyone: *He won't give a fellow a chance.* **3.** companion; comrade; associate: *He was happy with his fellows.* **4.** a member of a learned society. **5.** a graduate student who holds a fellowship at a university or college. **6.** one of a pair, as of shoes or gloves; mate; match. —*adj.* belonging to the same class, group, or condition: *fellow workers, fellow Americans.*

fel·low·ship (fel′ō ship′) *n.* **1.** companionship; friendliness: *the warm fellowship between brothers.* **2.** a group of people joined by common interests, beliefs, or goals; brotherhood; society. **3.** a position or sum of money given to a graduate student in a university or college to allow him to continue his studies.

fel·ly (fel′ē) *n. pl.,* **fel·lies.** the rim or a section of the rim of a wheel, into which the outer ends of the spokes fit. Also, **felloe.**

fel·on (fel′ən) *n.* a person who has committed a felony; criminal.

fe·lo·ni·ous (fə lō′nē əs) *adj.* of, relating to, or classified as a felony: *a felonious assault.* —**fe·lo′ni·ous·ly,** *adv.* —**fe·lo′ni·ous·ness,** *n.*

fel·o·ny (fel′ə nē) *n. pl.,* **fel·o·nies.** any of various crimes, as murder, rape, or burglary, designated by law to be more serious than a misdemeanor.

felt[1] (felt) the past tense and past participle of **feel.**

felt[2] (felt) *n.* a fabric, usually composed of wool, hair, or fur, made by pressing together layers of fibers, rather than by weaving or knitting them. —*adj.* made of felt: *a felt hat.* [Old English *felt.*]

fem., female; feminine.

fe·male (fē′māl) *adj.* **1.** of or relating to the sex that bears young or produces eggs. **2.** of or characteristic of the female sex; feminine. **3.** of or relating to a plant that bears flowers that have only pistils. **4.** (of an object or device) having a hollowed part into which a corresponding part fits, as an electric socket. —*n.* a female person, animal, or plant.

fem·i·nine (fem′ə nin) *adj.* **1.** of, characteristic of, or relating to a woman: *feminine taste, feminine interests.* **2.** having qualities or characteristics regarded as womanly, such as gentleness and delicateness. **3.** (of a man) effeminate; womanish. **4.** of or relating to the female sex. **5.** *Grammar.* of the gender that includes words applying to females or things classified as female.

fem·i·nin·i·ty (fem′ə nin′ə tē) *n.* **1.** the quality or state of being feminine. **2.** effeminacy; womanishness.

fem·i·nism (fem′ə niz′əm) *n.* **1.** the principle that women are entitled to the same social, economic, and political rights as men. **2.** a movement to obtain such rights for women.

fem·i·nist (fem′ə nist) *n.* a person who believes in or supports feminism. —**fem′i·nis′tic,** *adj.*

fe·mur (fē′mər) *n. pl.,* **fe·murs** or **fem·o·ra** (fem′ər ə). the long bone of the upper leg, extending from the pelvis to the knee; thighbone.

fen (fen) *n.* a marshy lowland; swamp; bog.

fence (fens) *n.* **1.** a structure, often made of wire or wood, used to bound, surround, or protect an area: *a fence around a yard, a fence around a pasture, a fence around a construction site.* **2.** a person who receives and sells stolen goods. —*v.,* **fenced, fenc·ing.** —*v.t.* to surround or separate with a fence or other enclosure: *to fence a garden, to fence in cattle, to fence off an area of a park for a ball field.* —*v.i.* to practice the sport of fencing.

on the fence. undecided about something: *to be on the fence about an issue.*

fenc·er (fen′sər) *n.* a person who fights with a foil or sword.

fenc·ing (fen′sing) *n.* **1.** the art or sport of fighting with a foil or sword. **2.** the material used in making fences. **3.** a fence or fences.

Fencing

fend (fend) *v.i.* to resist; defend.

to fend for oneself. to provide for or take care of oneself.

to fend off. to ward off; defend against: *The boxer fended off his opponent's blow.*

fend·er (fen′dər) *n.* **1.** a metal guard projecting over the wheel of an automobile, bicycle, or other vehicle to protect against splashed water or mud. **2.** a metal frame or screen placed in front of a fireplace to protect against escaping coals or sparks. **3.** a metal frame projecting from the front of a locomotive or streetcar, used to push obstacles from the tracks.

fen·nel (fen′əl) *n.* **1.** the fragrant seeds of a plant which taste like licorice and are used as a flavoring in certain foods and liqueurs. **2.** the plant itself, bearing bright green feathery leaves and clusters of yellow flowers.

fer-de-lance (fer′də lans′) *n.* a very poisonous, tropical American snake related to the rattlesnake.

Fer·di·nand V (furd′ən and′) 1452–1516, the king of Spain from 1474 to 1516. He and his queen, Isabella I, sponsored the voyages of Columbus.

fer·ment (v., fər ment′; n., fur′ment) v.i. **1.** to undergo chemical fermentation. **2.** to be excited or agitated; seethe. —v.t. **1.** to cause chemical fermentation in. **2.** to excite or agitate; stir up: *to ferment a revolution.* —n. **1.** a substance or agent causing chemical fermentation, as the enzymes secreted by yeast or certain bacteria. **2.** a state of excitement, agitation, or unrest: *the political ferment of an election year.*

fer·men·ta·tion (fur′men tā′shən) n. **1.** a chemical reaction or series of chemical reactions in carbohydrates caused by enzymes, resulting in the formation of bubbles of gas. Fermentation causes milk to turn sour and the juice of grapes to turn into wine. **2.** the process of undergoing this reaction. **3.** excitement; agitation; unrest.

Fer·mi, En·ri·co (fur′mē; en rē′kō) 1901–1954, American physicist, born in Italy. He directed the building of the first nuclear reactor.

fer·mi·um (fur′mē əm) n. a radioactive element produced artificially. Symbol: **Fm** [Modern Latin *fermium,* from Enrico *Fermi.*]

fern (furn) n. any of a large group of plants that lack flowers, have large, feathery leaves, and reproduce by spores instead of seeds.

Fern

fe·ro·cious (fə rō′shəs) adj. **1.** savage; fierce: *ferocious beasts, ferocious warriors.* **2.** Informal. very intense: *a ferocious headache.* —**fe·ro′cious·ly,** adv. —**fe·ro′cious·ness,** n.

fe·roc·i·ty (fə ros′ə tē) n. pl., **fe·roc·i·ties.** the state or quality of being ferocious; fierceness: *the ferocity of a wild animal.*

fer·ret (fer′it) n. an animal resembling a weasel, usually having yellowish-white fur and pink eyes. It is sometimes trained to hunt rats, mice, and rabbits. —v.t. **1.** to hunt (game) with ferrets: *to ferret rabbits.* **2.** to bring to light; search; hunt: *to ferret out the facts.* —v.i. **1.** to hunt with ferrets: *to ferret for rabbits.* **2.** to search: *He ferreted through old bookshops to find rare books.*

fer·ric (fer′ik) adj. of or containing iron.

Ferret

Fer·ris wheel (fer′is) a large, upright, revolving wheel with seats hung within its rim, used as an amusement ride. [From George W. G. *Ferris,* 1859–1896, an American engineer who invented it.]

fer·rous (fer′əs) adj. of or containing iron.

fer·rule (fer′əl, fer′ool) also, **fer·ule.** n. a metal ring or cap put around the end of a cane, tool handle, stem of a pipe, or umbrella, to give added strength or protect against splitting.

fer·ry (fer′ē) n. pl., **fer·ries. 1.** a boat or other craft used to carry people, vehicles, and goods across a river or other narrow body of water. **2.** a docking place for a ferry. —v., **fer·ried, fer·ry·ing.** —v.t. **1.** to carry across a narrow body of water by a boat or other craft: *They ferried the storm victims to the mainland.* **2.** to cross (a body of water) in a ferryboat: *to ferry the Mississippi.* **3.** to deliver (an airplane) by flying it to a particular destination. —v.i. to cross a body of water in a ferryboat.

fer·ry·boat (fer′ē bōt′) n. a boat used as a ferry.

fer·ry·man (fer′ē mən) n. pl., **fer·ry·men** (fer′ē mən). a person who owns, operates, or works on a ferry.

fer·tile (furt′əl) adj. **1.** producing or able to produce crops or vegetation abundantly: *fertile soil.* **2.** able to produce young, eggs, seeds, pollen, or the like: *a fertile animal.* **3.** able to develop into a new individual: *a fertile egg.* **4.** mentally productive; inventive: *The writer had a fertile imagination.*

Fertile Crescent, a crescent-shaped region of fertile land extending from the eastern coast of the Mediterranean to the northern coast of the Persian Gulf, site of several early civilizations.

fer·til·i·ty (fər til′ə tē) n. the state or quality of being fertile; productiveness.

fer·ti·li·za·tion (furt′əl i zā′shən) n. **1.** the act of fertilizing or the state of being fertilized. **2.** *Biology.* the uniting of a sperm cell with an egg cell to form a cell that will develop into a new individual.

fer·ti·lize (furt′əl īz′) v.t., **fer·ti·lized, fer·ti·liz·ing. 1.** to make fertile or productive. **2.** to put fertilizer on: *to fertilize a field.* **3.** *Biology.* to make (an egg cell) capable of reproducing a new individual.

fer·ti·liz·er (furt′əl ī′zər) n. a substance, such as manure or certain chemicals, added to the soil to make it more productive.

fer·ule[1] (fer′əl, fer′ool) n. a flat stick, as a ruler, used to punish school children by striking them, especially on the hand. —v.t., **fer·uled, fer·ul·ing.** to punish with a ferule. [Late Latin *ferula.*]

fer·ule[2] (fer′əl, fer′ool) another spelling of **ferrule.**

fer·ven·cy (fur′vən sē) n. great warmth or intensity of feeling; ardor.

fer·vent (fur′vənt) adj. having or showing great warmth or intensity of feeling; ardent: *fervent prayers. The lawyer made a fervent appeal for justice.* —**fer′vent·ly,** adv.

fer·vid (fur′vid) adj. very intense in feeling; impassioned; fervent: *fervid devotion to a cause.* —**fer′vid·ly,** adv. —**fer′vid·ness,** n.

fer·vor (fur′vər) n. great warmth or intensity of feeling; ardor: *patriotic fervor.*

fes·tal (fest′əl) adj. of or suitable for a feast or holiday; joyous; festive.

fes·ter (fes′tər) v.i. **1.** to form pus, as a wound. **2.** to become increasingly strong, as a feeling of resentment or anger: *Jealousy of her sister's beauty festered in the girl's mind.* —n. a small sore that forms pus.

fes·ti·val (fes′tə vəl) n. **1.** a feast, holiday, or celebration, especially one that takes place every year: *a harvest festival, a religious festival.* **2.** a period or program of activities or cultural events: *a Shakespeare festival, a film festival.*

fes·tive (fes′tiv) adj. relating to or suitable for a festival; festal; gay: *A birthday is always a festive occasion at our house.* —**fes′tive·ly,** adv.

fes·tiv·i·ty (fes tiv′ə tē) n. pl., **fes·tiv·i·ties. 1.** the rejoicing and gaiety typical of a celebration or other joyous occasion. **2. festivities.** festive activities; merrymaking: *wedding festivities.*

fes·toon (fes toon′) n. **1.** an ornamental string or chain, as of flowers, leaves, or ribbons, hanging in a curve between two points. **2.** a carved, molded, or painted orna-

at; āpe; cär; end; mē; it; īce; hot; ōld; fôrk; wood; fŏŏl; oil; out; up; turn; sing; thin; this; hw in white; zh in treasure. The symbol ə stands for the sound of **a** in about, **e** in taken, **i** in pencil, **o** in lemon, and **u** in circus.

F

ment resembling this. —*v.t.* **1.** to decorate with festoons: *The walls were festooned with crepe paper and balloons for the dance.* **2.** to arrange in festoons.

fe·tal (fēt′əl) *adj.* of, relating to, or characteristic of a fetus.

fetch (fech) *v.t.* **1.** to go after and bring back; come and take back; get: *to fetch a chair from another room.* **2.** to cause to come; succeed in bringing; draw forth: *to fetch an answer.* **3.** to be sold for: *The car should fetch at least $2000.* —*v.i.* to go after or get something and bring it back: *to teach a dog to fetch.*

fetch·ing (fech′ing) *adj. Informal.* attractive; charming. —**fetch′ing·ly,** *adv.*

fete (fāt) *also,* **fête.** *n.* a festival or large celebration. —*v.t.,* **fet·ed, fet·ing.** to entertain or honor with a fete.

fet·id (fet′id, fē′tid) *adj.* having a bad smell; stinking: *a fetid swamp.* —**fet′id·ly,** *adv.* —**fet′id·ness,** *n.*

fet·ish (fet′ish, fē′tish) *n. pl.,* **fet·ish·es. 1.** an object believed to have magical or supernatural powers. **2.** anything to which unreasonable devotion, concern, or reverence is given: *He made a fetish of keeping his hair combed.*

fet·ish·ism (fet′i shiz′əm, fē′ti shiz′əm) *n.* **1.** a belief in or devotion to fetishes. **2.** an unreasonable concern with or devotion to something.

fet·lock (fet′lok′) *n.* **1.** a tuft of hair on the back part of the leg of a horse or similar animal, just above the hoof. **2.** the part of the leg where this tuft grows.

fet·ter (fet′ər) *n.* **1.** a chain or shackle placed on the feet to restrain movement. **2.** anything that confines or restrains: *The students rebelled against the fetters of the school's strict rules.* —*v.t.* **1.** to bind with fetters; shackle: *The jailers fettered the prisoner to prevent his escape.* **2.** to bind; confine; restrain: *to feel fettered by regulations.*

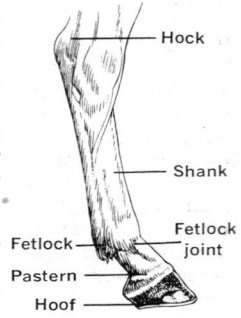

Fetlock
Parts of a horse's leg

Hock

Shank

Fetlock joint

Pastern

Hoof

fet·tle (fet′əl) *n.* a condition or state of the body or mind: *After a month's vacation in the mountains, he is in fine fettle.*

fe·tus (fē′təs) *also,* **foe·tus.** *n. pl.,* **fe·tus·es.** an animal embryo in its later stages of development in the womb or egg, especially a human embryo after the eighth week of pregnancy until birth.

feud[1] (fyood) *n.* **1.** a bitter quarrel between families, tribes, or clans, usually lasting for many years and marked by violent and deadly clashes. **2.** bitter and lasting hatred or conflict between individuals or groups: *a feud between two candidates for political office.* —*v.i.* to carry on a feud. [Old French *fede* or *feide.*]

feud[2] (fyood) *n.* another word for **fief.** [Medieval Latin *feudum.*]

feu·dal (fyood′əl) *adj.* **1.** relating to or characteristic of feudalism: *feudal law.* **2.** of or relating to a fief: *feudal rights.*

feu·dal·ism (fyood′əl iz′əm) *n.* a political, economic, and social system in western Europe during the Middle Ages. It was based upon the relation between a lord who provided land and protection and a vassal who in return pledged military and certain other services to the lord.

feu·dal·is·tic (fyood′əl is′tik) *adj.* of or relating to feudalism.

feudal system, another term for **feudalism.**

feu·da·to·ry (fyood′ə tôr′ē) *adj.* owing feudal allegiance to a lord: *a feudatory noble.* —*n. pl.,* **feu·da·to·ries.** a person holding land by feudal law; vassal.

fe·ver (fē′vər) *n.* **1.** a body temperature higher than normal. **2.** any of various diseases marked by higher than normal body temperature, such as yellow fever. **3.** a state of great excitement, anxiety, or restlessness: *The children were in a fever of anticipation on Christmas Eve.*

fever blister, another term for **cold sore.**

fe·vered (fē′vərd) *adj.* having or affected by fever.

fe·ver·ish (fē′vər ish) *adj.* **1.** having a fever, especially a slight degree of fever: *a feverish patient.* **2.** showing, characteristic of, or caused by fever: *feverish symptoms, feverish dreams.* **3.** causing fever. **4.** excited or restless, as if from fever: *There was feverish activity in the barracks as the men prepared for the general's visit.* —**fe′ver·ish·ly,** *adv.* —**fe′ver·ish·ness,** *n.*

fever sore, another term for **cold sore.**

few (fyōō) *adj.* not many: *Few people attended the meeting.* —*n.* **1.** not many persons or things; a small number: *Many were invited to the party, but few actually came. He sold only a few of the papers.* **2. the few.** the minority: *Tom is among the few in the class who do not like sports.* ▲ See **less** for usage note.

quite a few. *Informal.* a large number; good many: *Quite a few of my friends have stopped smoking.*

fez (fez) *n. pl.,* **fez·zes.** a brimless felt cap, usually red, having a flat crown and ornamented with a tassel, worn especially by men in the Middle East.

ff., and the following (pages, lines, sections, or the like).

fi·an·cé (fē′än sā′) *n.* a man to whom a woman is engaged to be married.

fi·an·cée (fē′än sā′) *n.* a woman to whom a man is engaged to be married.

fi·as·co (fē as′kō) *n. pl.,* **fi·as·cos** or **fi·as·coes.** a complete or humiliating failure: *The ski trip turned into a fiasco when it began to rain.*

Fez

fi·at (fī′ət, fī′at) *n.* an official order or decree.

fib (fib) *n.* a lie about something unimportant; trivial lie. —*v.i.,* **fibbed, fib·bing.** to tell a fib. —**fib′ber,** *n.*

fi·ber (fī′bər) *also, British,* **fi·bre.** *n.* **1.** any fine threadlike part of a substance: *cotton fibers, a nerve fiber.* **2.** a substance composed of such parts: *The rope was made of hemp fiber.* **3.** the composition or structure of such a substance; texture: *cloth of coarse fiber.* **4.** essential character, nature, or strength: *moral fiber, a man of weak fiber.*

fi·ber·board (fī′bər bôrd′) *n.* a material made of fibers, especially of wood, compressed into sheets and used for panels, partitions, or the like.

fi·ber·glass (fī′bər glas′) *n.* a durable, nonflammable material made of fine threads of glass, used for insulation, textiles, boat bodies, and many other purposes. Trademark: **Fiberglas.**

fi·bre (fī′bər) *British.* another spelling of **fiber.**

fi·brin (fī′brin) *n.* a fibrous, insoluble substance formed during the clotting of blood.

fi·brin·o·gen (fī brin′ə jen′) *n.* a soluble protein in the blood plasma from which fibrin is formed.

fi·broid (fī′broid) *adj.* made up of or resembling fibers or fibrous tissue: *a fibroid tumor.*

fi·brous (fī′brəs) *adj.* made up of, having, or resembling fibers.

fib·u·la (fib′yə lə) *n. pl.,* **fib·u·lae** (fib′yə lē) or **fib·u·las.** the outer and more slender of the two bones of the human lower leg, extending from the knee to the ankle.

-fic *suffix* (used to form adjectives) making; causing: *terrific.*

-fication *suffix* (used to form nouns) the act of making: *purification.*

fick·le (fik′əl) *adj.* that cannot be relied upon or pre-

dicted; changeable; capricious: *a fickle friend, fickle fate.*
—**fick′le·ness,** *n.*

fic·tion (fik′shən) *n.* **1.** prose works, such as novels and short stories, that tell about imaginary characters and events. **2.** something made up or imagined, as a story, explanation, or statement: *A newspaper reporter must be able to distinguish fact from fiction.*

fic·tion·al (fik′shən əl) *adj.* relating to or like fiction. —**fic′tion·al·ly,** *adv.*

fic·tion·al·ize (fik′shən əl īz′) *v.t.,* **fic·tion·al·ized, fic·tion·al·iz·ing.** to make into fiction; give a fictional account of: *to fictionalize a period of history in a novel.* —**fic′tion·al·i·za′tion,** *n.*

fic·ti·tious (fik tish′əs) *adj.* not real or true; made-up: *a fictitious character, a fictitious excuse.* —**fic·ti′tious·ly,** *adv.* —**fic·ti′tious·ness,** *n.*

fid·dle (fid′əl) *n. Informal.* a violin or other instrument of the violin family. —*v.,* **fid·dled, fid·dling.** —*v.i.* **1.** *Informal.* to play a fiddle. **2.** to make aimless or nervous movements, as with the fingers or hands; fidget: *She fiddled nervously with her pencil.* —*v.t.* **1.** *Informal.* to play (a tune) on a fiddle. **2.** to waste in an idle or trifling way: *to fiddle away one's time.* —**fid′dler,** *n.*

fiddler crab, any of a group of burrowing crabs, the male of which has one claw much larger than the other. [Possibly because it seems to hold its large claw like a *fiddle.*]

fid·dle·sticks (fid′əl stiks′) *interj.* nonsense.

fi·del·i·ty (fi del′ə tē, fī del′ə tē) *n. pl.,* **fi·del·i·ties. 1.** faithfulness to duties, obligations, or vows; steadfast loyalty. **2.** accuracy, as in writing or copying something; correctness: *The novel*

Fiddler crab

was written with strict fidelity to historical facts. **3.** the degree of accuracy with which electronic devices, such as radios or record players, reproduce original sound.

fidg·et (fij′it) *v.i.* to make restless movements; be nervous or uneasy: *The audience fidgeted in their seats.* —*n.* **1.** a person who fidgets. **2. the fidgets.** a state of restlessness or uneasiness, often characterized by nervous movements: *I had the fidgets all morning waiting for my interview.*

fidg·et·y (fij′ə tē) *adj.* restless; uneasy.

fie (fī) *interj.* for shame: *Fie on you!*

fief (fēf) *n.* the land held by a vassal in return for military and certain other services given to the feudal lord owning it. Also, **fee.**

field (fēld) *n.* **1.** a piece of land having few or no trees. **2.** a piece of cleared land, usually bounded, used or suitable for cultivation or pasture: *a wheat field.* **3.** a region or area containing and yielding some natural resource: *an oil field.* **4.** a broad, level expanse: *a field of snow.* **5.** a place of battle. **6.** a battle: *The field was won after four hours of fighting.* **7.** an area or region of active military operations: *Early in the spring, the army took to the field.* **8.** *Sports.* **a.** an enclosed piece of ground, or one with defined boundaries, on which games are played or events are held: *a baseball field, a football field.* **b.** a portion or division of such an area, usually surrounded by or next to a track, where such contests as the pole vault, broad jump, discus throw, and shot put are held. **c.** all those who take part in a particular event or contest: *The winning runner finished five yards ahead of the field.* **9.** the surface on which something is shown: *The artist painted his white figures against a field of black.* **10.** a range or area of interest; sphere of activity: *He was one of the pioneers in the field*

of medicine. **11.** *Physics.* the area or space within which a particular effect or property, as electricity, magnetism, or gravity, may be measured at every point. **12.** the space or range within which objects are visible through the lens of a telescope, microscope, or other optical instrument. —*v.t.* **1.** to catch, stop, or pick up (a ball in play), especially in baseball. **2.** to put or send (a team or player) into a position in the field. —*v.i.* to act as a fielder, especially in baseball. —*adj.* of, relating to, or growing in: *field flowers.*

field day 1. a day set aside for athletic contests, games, and races. **2.** a day or time of unusual opportunity, as for fun: *The children had a field day when their parents went away for the weekend.*

field·er (fēl′dər) *n.* **1.** *Baseball.* any of the players in the field attempting to put out the team at bat. **2.** any player with such defensive duties in softball, cricket, or similar ball games.

field glasses, small binoculars, used especially outdoors. Also, **field glass.**

field goal 1. *Football.* a play in which the ball is kicked over the crossbar and between the posts of the opponent's goal. It scores three points. **2.** *Basketball.* a goal made while the ball is in play. It scores two points.

field hockey, a game played on a field by two teams of eleven players each. Wooden sticks with curved ends are used to hit the ball along the ground, the object being to drive the ball into the opponent's goal.

field hospital, a temporary military hospital close to a combat area.

field house, a building near an athletic field, having dressing rooms, showers, and the like for the athletes, and room for storing sports equipment.

Field·ing, Henry (fēl′ding) 1707–1754, English novelist.

field magnet, a magnet used to produce and maintain a magnetic field, especially in an electric motor or generator.

field marshal, an officer of highest rank in the army of Great Britain and in the armies of certain other nations.

field mouse, any of various mice living in fields and meadows.

field trip, a trip away from the classroom for firsthand observation and study, as to a museum, factory, or farm.

fiend (fēnd) *n.* **1.** an evil spirit; devil; demon. **2. the Fiend,** the Devil; Satan. **3.** a very wicked or cruel person. **4.** *Informal.* a person who is devoted to a particular field, interest, or activity: *a chess fiend.* **5.** *Informal.* a person who is addicted to a practice or habit, especially one that is harmful: *a dope fiend.*

fiend·ish (fēn′dish) *adj.* very wicked or cruel; devilish. —**fiend′ish·ly,** *adv.* —**fiend′ish·ness,** *n.*

fierce (fērs) *adj.,* **fierc·er, fierc·est. 1.** cruel or violent in nature or behavior; savage; ferocious: *a fierce grizzly bear.* **2.** violent or intense in force or activity; raging: *a fierce storm, fierce fighting.* —**fierce′ly,** *adv.* —**fierce′ness,** *n.*

fier·y (fīr′ē) *adj.,* **fier·i·er, fier·i·est. 1.** containing or made up of fire; aflame; flaming: *a fiery furnace.* **2.** hot as fire; burning: *the fiery sun.* **3.** like fire; flashing; glowing:

at; āpe; cär; end; mē; it; īce; hot; ōld; fôrk; wood; fōōl; oil; out; up; turn; sing; thin; **th**is; hw in white; zh in treasure. The symbol ə stands for the sound of **a** in about, **e** in taken, **i** in pencil, **o** in lemon, and **u** in circus.

a fiery red, a fiery sunset, fiery eyes. **4.** full of feeling; ardent; passionate: *a fiery speech.* **5.** excitable; irritable: *a fiery temper.* —**fier′i·ly,** *adv.* —**fier′i·ness,** *n.*

fi·es·ta (fē es′tə) *n.* **1.** a religious festival, especially a saint's day as celebrated in Spain or Latin America. **2.** any festive celebration; holiday.

fife (fīf) *n.* a shrill-toned musical instrument of the flute family, often used with drums in marching bands. —*v.,* **fifed, fif·ing.** —*v.t.* to play (a tune) on a fife. —*v.i.* to play a fife. —**fif′er,** *n.*

fif·teen (fif′tēn′) *n.* **1.** the cardinal number that is five more than ten. **2.** the symbol representing this number, as 15 or XV. **3.** something having this many units or things. —*adj.* numbering five more than ten.

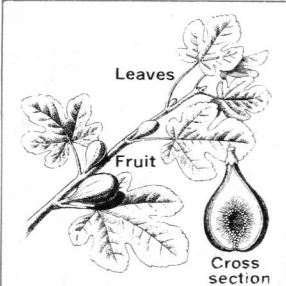

Fife

fif·teenth (fif′tēnth′) *adj.* **1.** (the ordinal of fifteen) next after the fourteenth. **2.** being one of fifteen equal parts. —*n.* **1.** something that is next after the fourteenth. **2.** one of fifteen equal parts; 1/15.

fifth (fifth) *adj.* **1.** (the ordinal of five) next after the fourth. **2.** being one of five equal parts. —*n.* **1.** something that is next after the fourth. **2.** one of five equal parts; 1/5. **3.** one-fifth of a gallon, used as a measure of liquor. **4.** *Music.* **a.** a note that is a total of three whole steps and one half step above a given note. G is the fifth of C. **b.** an interval of three whole steps and one half step. **c.** a combination of two notes that are separated by this interval. —*adv.* in the fifth place.

fifth column, a group of persons within a country who secretly aid its enemies. [From a statement by a general during the Spanish Civil War that he had four columns marching on Madrid and a *fifth column* of sympathizers and agents within Madrid.]

fifth columnist, a person who is a member of a fifth column.

fif·ti·eth (fif′tē ith) *adj.* **1.** (the ordinal of fifty) next after the forty-ninth. **2.** being one of fifty equal parts. —*n.* **1.** something that is next after the forty-ninth. **2.** one of fifty equal parts; 1/50.

fif·ty (fif′tē) *n. pl.,* **fif·ties. 1.** the cardinal number that is five times ten. **2.** the symbol representing this number, as 50 or L. —*adj.* numbering five times ten.

fif·ty-fif·ty (fif′tē fif′tē) *Informal. adj.* **1.** sharing equally; equal: *a fifty-fifty division of the profits.* **2.** as likely to turn out one way as another; even: *Our team has a fifty-fifty chance of winning the game.* —*adv.* equally: *to share expenses fifty-fifty.*

fig (fig) *n.* **1.** a small, sweet fruit having many tiny seeds. **2.** the shrub or small tree bearing this fruit, grown mainly in the Mediterranean region and California. **3.** the smallest amount; least bit: *I don't care a fig for your idea.*

fig., figure.

fight (fīt) *n.* **1.** a physical struggle between two opposing individuals or groups; battle; conflict: *There was a fight between the two gangs.* **2.** a contest between two boxers; boxing match. **3.** dispute; quarrel; argument: *The two sisters had a fight over who should wash*

Leaves

Fruit

Cross section

Fig

the dishes. **4.** any struggle, especially one to gain some objective or goal: *a fight for control of a government.* **5.** the power or will to carry on a struggle: *The dazed boxer had no fight left in him.* —*v.,* **fought, fight·ing.** —*v.t.* **1.** to take part in a physical struggle or combat with: *The British fought the Americans in 1776.* **2.** to oppose in a boxing match: *The champion fought three opponents last year.* **3.** to struggle against: *Firemen fought the blaze for hours.* **4.** to carry on or wage (a battle, contest, or struggle): *The battle was fought on an open plain.* **5.** to gain or make (one's way) by struggle: *The celebrity fought his way through the crowd of fans.* —*v.i.* **1.** to take part in a physical struggle or combat: *The two armies fought for days.* **2.** to struggle, as to reach a goal: *to fight for equal rights, to fight for one's life.*

to fight off. a. to drive away or defend against by fighting: *The defenders of the town fought off the invading army.* **b.** to struggle to get rid of or avoid: *to fight off a cold.*

fight·er (fī′tər) *n.* **1.** a person who fights. **2.** a professional boxer. **3.** a fast, maneuverable airplane designed for use against enemy airplanes or ground forces, usually with a crew of one or two men.

fig·ment (fig′mənt) *n.* something imagined or made up; fiction: *The boy's story of seeing a dragon was a figment of his imagination.*

fig·u·ra·tive (fig′yər ə tiv) *adj.* **1.** using, based on, or characteristic of a figure of speech; not literal; metaphorical. *To throw caution to the wind* is a figurative expression. **2.** containing or using many figures of speech; flowery: *figurative poetry.* **3.** representing by a symbol or by a figure or likeness: *a figurative ceremony.* —**fig′ur·a·tive·ly,** *adv.* —**fig′ur·a·tive·ness,** *n.*

fig·ure (fig′yər) *n.* **1.** a symbol representing a number, such as 0, 1, 2, 3, 4, 5. **2. figures.** the use of such symbols in calculating; arithmetic: *She is good at figures.* **3.** an amount or value as expressed in figures; price; sum: *The figure asked for the house was too high.* **4.** a visible form or appearance of anything; shape; outline: *He saw the figure of a child silhouetted in the window.* **5.** a human body or form: *a slender figure, a fine figure of a man.* **6.** a person as he appears or looks to others: *His strange clothes made him seem a comical figure.* **7.** a person, especially one of importance; character: *a figure of evil, a figure of strength. The mayor is a public figure.* **8.** a picture, likeness, or representation, as of a human form: *The figure of a man's head appears on this coin.* **9.** a diagram; illustration; drawing: *This figure shows an automobile engine.* **10.** a design; pattern: *The cloth had bold figures woven into it.* **11.** *Geometry.* a bounded surface or space; series of lines, solids, or surfaces having a definite shape: *The circle is a plane figure. The sphere is a solid figure.* **12.** a set or series of movements, as in dancing or skating. **13.** see **figure of speech.** —*v.,* **fig·ured, fig·ur·ing.** —*v.t.* **1.** to solve or find out by using numbers; calculate; compute: *to figure the cost of a trip, to figure the solution to an arithmetic problem.* **2.** to ornament or cover with a design or pattern: *The wallpaper was figured with roses.* **3.** *Informal.* to think or believe: *They figured he was the best man for the job.* —*v.i.* to appear or be prominent: *Several well-known politicians figured in the news yesterday.*

to figure on. *Informal.* **a.** to depend on; plan on: *They figured on him to do his part of the job. They figured on getting a loan so they could buy the car.* **b.** to take into consideration: *We had not figured on the possibility of rain.*

to figure out. to arrive at the explanation of; understand: *He figured out who the murderer was before the end of the book.*

argument: *The two sisters had a fight over who should wash*

fig·ure·head (fig′yər hed′) *n.* **1.** a person having a position of authority but no real power or responsibility: *The emperor of Japan is a figurehead.* **2.** a carved, ornamental figure, usually of wood, on the bow of a ship.

figure of speech, a form of expression in which words are used out of their literal sense to produce a vivid, forceful, or poetic effect. Similes and metaphors are figures of speech.

● In language, a **figure of speech** is a word or phrase that is used to give a special effect in writing or speaking. The meaning of the words in a figure of speech is usually not the literal meaning. Figures of speech are very often used in poetry and other creative writing in order to express feelings and experiences in a fresh, vivid, or artistic way. You probably use figures of speech in your everyday speaking and writing without realizing it. We often use **simile,** which is a very common type of figure of speech: *He is as strong as ten men. She eats like a bird.* **Metaphor** is also a frequently used figure of speech: *Their holiday in Europe was heaven.* Another kind of figure of speech is called **hyperbole:** *It took her a year and a day to answer the telephone.*

Figures of speech are tools for using language creatively, but when they are used excessively or carelessly they become trite or confusing. A figure of speech that has been overused is called a **cliche.** Because the purpose of a figure of speech is to make writing and speaking more fresh and expressive, cliches should be avoided whenever possible. Examples of cliches are: *white as snow, fit as a fiddle, to swim like a fish,* and *the long arm of the law.* When figures of speech are used carelessly the result can be silly or illogical: *The politician threw in the sponge when the storm of protest broke.*

fig·ur·ine (fig′yə rēn′) *n.* a small carved or molded figure; statuette.

Fi·ji (fē′jē) *n.* an island country in the southwestern Pacific Ocean. Land area, 7036 sq. mi. Pop. (1978 est.), 612,000.

fil·a·ment (fil′ə mənt) *n.* **1.** a very fine thread or a part like a thread; fiber: *a filament of a spider's web.* **2.** a fine wire in an electric bulb, that gives off light when an electric current passes through it. **3.** the wire in a vacuum tube that sends out electrons when heated by the passage of an electric current and that often acts as a cathode.

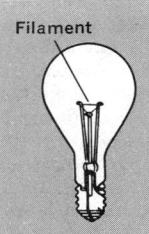

Filament

fil·bert (fil′bərt) *n.* **1.** a thick-shelled nut. Also, **hazelnut. 2.** the shrub bearing this nut.

filch (filch) *v.t.* to steal, especially something of little value; pilfer: *The boy filched some candy from the box. Ann filched some cake once her mother left.* —**filch′er,** *n.*

file¹ (fīl) *n.* **1.** any device, as a folder, drawer, or cabinet, in which papers, cards, records, or documents are arranged in order for easy reference. **2.** a set of such items arranged in order. **3.** a line of persons, animals, or things placed one behind another: *a file of soldiers.* —*v.,* **filed, fil·ing.** —*v.t.* **1.** to keep (papers or similar items) arranged in order. **2.** to place in a file: *The clerk filed the letter in its proper alphabetical place.* **3.** to hand in legally or officially; enter on a record: *to file a report, to file one's income tax return.* —*v.i.* **1.** to march or move in a file: *The soldiers filed out of the barracks.* **2.** to make an application: *He filed for a hunting permit.* [In some meanings from Old French *file* row; in other meanings from Old French *fil* thread.] —**fil′er,** *n.*

file² (fīl) *n.* a steel tool having one or more closely ridged surfaces, used to cut, smooth, or grind down hard substances. —*v.t.,* **filed, fil·ing.** to cut, smooth, or grind down with a file. [Old English *fēol, fīl.*] —**fil′er,** *n.*

fi·let (fi lā′, fil′ā) *n.* **1.** net or lace with a square mesh. **2.** see **fillet** *(def. 3).*

fi·let mi·gnon (fi lā′ min yon′) a small, thick steak from the tip of the tenderloin, noted for its tenderness. [French *fillet mignon* literally, dainty fillet.]

File²

fil·i·al (fil′ē əl) *adj.* relating or suitable to a son or daughter: *filial love.* —**fil′i·al·ly,** *adv.*

fil·i·bus·ter (fil′ə bus′tər) *n.* a method of delaying or stopping action on a legislative issue by the use of lengthy speeches, prolonged debate, or other delaying tactics. —*v.i., v.t.* to hinder or block legislative action by use of a filibuster, as by prolonged speeches. —**fil′i·bus′ter·er,** *n.*

fil·i·gree (fil′ə grē′) *n.* **1.** delicate ornamental work of intertwined gold or silver wire. **2.** anything ornamental, delicate, or fanciful, such as a pattern or design: *The sun shining through the leaves made a green and gold filigree.* —*adj.* like, made of, or ornamented with filigree: *filigree earrings.* —*v.t.,* **fil·i·greed, fil·i·gree·ing.** to adorn with filigree.

fil·ings (fī′lingz) *n.,pl.* particles removed by a file.

Fil·i·pi·no (fil′ə pē′nō) *n. pl.,* **Fil·i·pi·nos.** a person who was born or is living in the Philippine Islands. —*adj.* another word for **Philippine.**

fill (fil) *v.t.* **1.** to supply with as much as can be held or contained; make full, as a container or space: *to fill a bucket with water.* **2.** to take up or occupy the whole capacity or space of: *Flowers filled the garden. The crowd filled the auditorium.* **3.** to spread over or throughout: *Smoke filled the room. Angry shouts filled the air.* **4.** to fulfill; satisfy; meet: *to fill the requirements of a job.* **5.** to supply or make up whatever is required or asked for: *to fill a grocery order, to fill a prescription.* **6.** to stop up or close by putting something in; plug: *to fill a hole in a wall with plaster.* **7.** to put a filling in (a tooth). **8.** to hold or occupy, as a position or office: *to fill the office of treasurer.* **9.** to put or place a person into: *to fill a vacancy on the Supreme Court.* —*v.i.* to become full: *The room filled with smoke.* —*n.* **1.** a quantity that is enough to fill or satisfy a desire or need: *Eat your fill.* **2.** something used to fill: *Stone and gravel were used as fill for the hole.*

to fill in. a. to fill completely with something: *The men filled in the hole with sand.* **b.** to complete by inserting something: *to fill in a questionnaire.* **c.** to insert to make something complete: *Don't forget to fill in your name on the application form.* **d.** to act as a substitute: *Tom filled in for the chairman during the meeting.*

to fill out. a. to complete by inserting something: *to fill out an order form.* **b.** to become larger, fuller, or more rounded: *The thin child gradually filled out as he grew older.*

to fill up. to make or become completely full: *The man*

at; āpe; cär; end; mē; it; īce; hot; ōld; fôrk; wood; fōōl; oil; out; up; turn; sing; thin; **th**is; hw in white; zh in treasure. The symbol ə stands for the sound of **a** in about, **e** in taken, **i** in pencil, **o** in lemon, and **u** in circus.

F

filled up the gas tank of the car. The bathtub filled up with water in a few minutes.

to have one's fill. to have enough or too much: *The weary soldier had had his fill of war.*

fill·er (fil′ər) *n.* **1.** a person or thing that fills. **2.** a material used to fill something. **3.** an item, especially a brief paragraph, used to fill space in a newspaper or magazine. **4.** paper for a looseleaf notebook.

fil·let (fil′it; *n., def. 3, v., def. 2* fi lā′) *n.* **1.** a narrow band or ribbon for binding or adorning the hair. **2.** a narrow band or strip of any material. **3.** *also,* **fi·let.** a lean, boneless piece or slice of fish or meat. —*v.t.* **1.** to bind or adorn with a fillet. **2.** to cut (fish or meat) into fillets.

fill·ing (fil′ing) *n.* **1.** a thing used to fill something: *pie filling.* **2.** a substance used to fill a cavity in a tooth. **3.** the act of filling.

filling station, another term for **gas station.**

fil·lip (fil′ip) *n.* **1.** the snap of a finger that has been pressed down by the thumb and suddenly released. **2.** something that arouses, excites, or enlivens; stimulus: *That good news was a fillip to my spirits.* —*v.t.* **1.** to tap or strike with a fillip. **2.** to move by a fillip.

Fill·more, Mil·lard (fil′môr; mil′ərd) 1800–1874, the thirteenth president of the United States, from 1850 to 1853.

fil·ly (fil′ē) *n. pl.,* **fil·lies.** a female colt.

film (film) *n.* **1.** a thin layer, sheet, or covering: *The windows were covered with a film of dirt.* **2.** a thin, flexible roll or strip of material coated with a substance sensitive to light, used in making photographs. **3.** such a roll or strip containing pictures to be projected on a screen. **4.** a motion picture: *We saw a good western film.* **5.** a thin veil or haze that blurs: *a film of tears.* —*v.t.* **1.** to cover with a thin layer or haze. **2.** to photograph with a motion-picture camera: *He filmed the football game.* **3.** to make a motion picture of: *to film a popular novel.* —*v.i.* **1.** to become covered or blurred by a thin layer or haze: *The windows of the car filmed with dust from the road.* **2.** to be suitable for filming: *Some plays do not film well.*

film·strip (film′strip′) *n.* a length of film containing still pictures for projection on a screen, often used as a teaching aid.

film·y (fil′mē) *adj.,* **film·i·er, film·i·est. 1.** composed of or resembling a thin layer; gauzy: *The curtains were made of a filmy material.* **2.** covered with a thin layer of something; hazy: *a filmy mirror.* —**film′i·ness,** *n.*

fil·ter (fil′tər) *n.* **1.** a device for straining solids or impurities from a liquid or gas. **2.** a porous material used in such a device, such as sand, charcoal, or paper. **3.** a device that allows waves of certain frequencies to pass and stops the passage of others. —*v.t.* **1.** to pass (a liquid or gas) through a filter; strain: *The water was filtered through charcoal.* **2.** to act as a filter for. **3.** to separate or remove by a filter: *The solid particles were filtered from the solution.* —*v.i.* to pass slowly: *Sunlight filtered through the leaves.*

fil·ter·a·ble (fil′tər ə bəl) *also,* **fil·tra·ble** (fil′trə bəl). *adj.* **1.** capable of being filtered. **2.** capable of passing through a filter that stops bacteria: *a filterable virus.*

filth (filth) *n.* **1.** disgusting dirt or refuse: *Industrial filth pollutes the air and water.* **2.** a dirty or foul condition: *Poor people are sometimes forced to live in filth.* **3.** something offensive or indecent; obscenity. **4.** obscene language.

filth·y (fil′thē) *adj.,* **filth·i·er, filth·i·est. 1.** covered with or containing filth; dirty; foul: *filthy streets.* **2.** offensive; obscene. **3.** highly unpleasant or objectionable; contemptible: *That was a filthy lie.* —**filth′i·ly,** *adv.* —**filth′i·ness,** *n.*

fil·trate (fil′trāt) *n.* liquid that has been passed through a filter. —*v.t.,* **fil·trat·ed, fil·trat·ing.** to pass through a filter. —**fil·tra′tion,** *n.*

fin (fin) *n.* **1.** one of the movable winglike parts extending from the body of a fish. A fish uses its fins to propel, guide, and balance itself in the water. **2.** a similar structure of other water animals, such as whales and some porpoises. **3.** something resembling a fin in shape or use. **4.** a vertical surface attached to an aircraft or rocket to provide stability in flight.

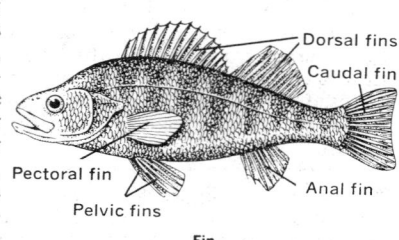

Dorsal fins
Caudal fin
Pectoral fin
Anal fin
Pelvic fins
Fin

fi·na·gle (fi nā′gəl) *v.,* **fi·na·gled, fi·na·gling.** *Informal.* —*v.t.* **1.** to get or manage (something) by trickery or deceit; wangle: *He finagled a free ticket to the game.* **2.** to cheat or trick (someone): *The swindler finagled them out of their money.* —*v.i.* to use trickery or deceit; cheat.

fi·nal (fīn′əl) *adj.* **1.** coming at the end; last: *the final chapter of a novel, the final days of his life, the final score of a game.* **2.** allowing no further action, discussion, or change; deciding completely; conclusive: *The decision of the judges is final.* —*n. also,* **finals. 1.** the last examination of a school or college course: *He is studying for the history finals.* **2.** the last and decisive game, match, or event in a series of athletic contests: *Our team reached the finals of the basketball tournament.*

fi·na·le (fi nä′lē) *n.* **1.** the last part or conclusion. **2.** the concluding part of a piece of music or a play.

fi·nal·ist (fīn′əl ist) *n.* a person who takes part in the final match or event of a series of games or contests.

fi·nal·i·ty (fī nal′ə tē) *n. pl.,* **fi·nal·i·ties. 1.** the state or quality of being final, settled, or complete; conclusiveness: *She stated her position with finality.* **2.** something final.

fi·nal·ize (fīn′əl īz′) *v.t.,* **fi·nal·ized, fi·nal·iz·ing.** to put into final or finished form; bring to completion: *We must finalize our plans.* —**fi′nal·i·za′tion,** *n.*

fi·nal·ly (fīn′əl ē) *adv.* **1.** at the end; at last; in conclusion: *We finally reached our destination. Finally, she thanked us all and left.* **2.** decisively; conclusively: *We must deal with this problem effectively and finally.*

fi·nance (fi nans′, fī′nans) *n.* **1.** the management of money affairs of individuals, businesses, or governments. **2. finances.** the money affairs or resources of a government, organization, or individual; funds; revenue; income. —*v.t.,* **fi·nanced, fi·nanc·ing.** to provide money for: *His parents financed his college education.*

fi·nan·cial (fi nan′shəl fī nan′shəl) *adj.* relating to money matters or finance: *a financial crisis, the financial section of a newspaper.* —**fi·nan′cial·ly,** *adv.*

fin·an·cier (fin′ən sēr′, fī′nan sēr′) *n.* **1.** a person skilled in financial matters, such as a banker. **2.** a person active in financial operations on a large scale.

finch (finch) *n.* any of a large group of songbirds that have a cone-shaped bill and stout body, as the sparrow, bunting, and canary.

find (fīnd) *v.t.,* **found, find·ing. 1.** to come upon accidentally; meet with by chance; happen on: *He found a wallet on the sidewalk. She found many friends at the new school.* **2.** to get or learn by calculation; obtain (the solution to a problem): *to find the sum of several numbers.* **3.** to discover or learn: *to find a place to live, to find a cure for a disease. I found I couldn't study well*

Finch

without a good night's sleep. **4.** to recover (something lost): *She found her missing necklace under the couch.* **5.** to get by arrangement or management: *I haven't found time to read that book.* **6.** to arrive at; reach: *The arrow found its target.* **7.** to determine and declare: *The jury found the defendant guilty.* **8.** to feel or think to be; consider; regard: *Many people find the climate here too humid.* —*n.* something that is found, especially something of value: *The ancient sculpture was a priceless find.*

  to find oneself. to discover one's abilities or talents and the best way to use them: *After changing jobs many times, he finally found himself.*

  to find out. to learn; discover: *He found out that prices were much higher in the city.*

find·er (fīn′dər) *n.* **1.** a person or thing that finds. **2.** a small, extra lens or other device built in or attached to a camera for sighting the object or area to be photographed. Also, **viewfinder. 3.** a small telescope attached to a larger one to help sight the objects to be viewed.

find·ing (fīn′ding) *n.* **1.** the act of a person or thing that finds; discovery. **2.** something found. **3.** *also,* **findings.** the result or conclusions of an investigation or inquiry: *The pollution researchers will publish their findings next week.*

fine¹ (fīn) *adj.,* **fin·er, fin·est. 1.** of high grade or quality; very good; excellent: *a fine speech, a fine musician, fine foods.* **2.** very satisfactory; enjoyable: *We had a fine time at the party.* **3.** refined; elegant; polished: *fine manners, a fine gentleman.* **4.** delicate, as in structure, texture, or workmanship: *fine facial features, fine linen, fine embroidery.* **5.** subtle: *to make a fine distinction in an argument.* **6.** very thin; slender: *a fine thread.* **7.** very small: *fine sand. That book has fine print.* **8.** sharp; keen: *the fine edge of a razor.* **9.** free from clouds or rain; clear; bright: *fine weather.* **10.** free from impurities or foreign matter; pure: *fine gold.* —*adv. Informal.* very well: *He is doing fine in school.* [Old French *fin* perfect, exact.] —**fine′ly,** *adv.* —**fine′ness,** *n.*

fine² (fīn) *n.* a sum of money to be paid as punishment for an offense: *There is a fine of fifty dollars for littering.* —*v.t.,* **fined, fin·ing.** to punish by a fine: *to fine a motorist for speeding.* [Old French *fin* end, settlement.]

fine arts, those arts concerned mainly with the creation of beauty, including painting, drawing, and sculpture, and sometimes architecture, literature, music, drama, and the dance.

fin·er·y (fī′nər ē) *n. pl.,* **fin·er·ies.** fine or showy clothes or ornaments.

fi·nesse (fi nes′) *n.* **1.** refinement or skill in doing something: *The violinist played the difficult piece with remarkable finesse.* **2.** the smooth or skillful handling of a difficult or awkward situation: *The labor mediator showed great finesse in settling the dispute.*

fin·ger (fing′gər) *n.* **1.** one of the five separate parts at the end of the hand, especially the four other than the thumb; digit. **2.** the part of a glove which is made to cover one of these. **3.** anything like a finger in shape or use: *fingers of sunlight.* —*v.t.* **1.** to touch, feel, or handle with the fingers; toy with: *She fingered the silk gently.* **2.** *Music.* to play with the fingers: *to finger a guitar, to finger a chord.*

  to put one's finger on. to indicate or point out precisely or correctly: *He put his finger on the cause of the problem.*

fin·ger·board (fing′gər bôrd′) *n.* a strip of wood on the neck of a violin, guitar, or similar instrument, against which the strings are pressed by the fingers.

finger bowl, a small bowl containing water for rinsing the fingers during or after a meal.

fin·ger·ing (fing′gər ing) *n.* **1.** the act of touching or handling with the fingers. **2.** *Music.* **a.** the action or

method of using the fingers in playing a musical instrument: *a difficult fingering on the guitar.* **b.** numerals or other notations on a piece of music indicating which fingers are to be used in playing its notes.

fin·ger·nail (fing′gər nāl′) *n.* a horny substance that forms a hard layer on the upper surface of the end of a finger.

finger painting 1. a method of painting by spreading paint on dampened paper with the fingers or palms. **2.** a painting made in this way.

fin·ger·print (fing′gər print′) *n.* an impression of the markings on the inner surface of the tip of a finger, especially such an impression made with ink and used for purposes of identification. —*v.t.* to take the fingerprints of.

fin·i·cal (fin′i kəl) *adj.* another word for **finicky.** —**fin′i·cal·ly,** *adv.*

fin·ick·y (fin′i kē) *adj.* too particular; fussy: *She is a finicky eater.*

fi·nis (fin′is, fī′nis) *n.* end; conclusion. [Latin *finis.*]

fin·ish (fin′ish) *v.t.* **1.** to bring to an end; come to the end of; complete; end: *to finish speaking, to finish a meal, to finish a job.* **2.** to use up or consume completely: *to finish up a jar of jam.* **3.** to treat the surface of in a certain way: *He used clear varnish to finish the cabinet.* —*v.i.* to reach or come to an end: *She finished before the time was up.* —*n. pl.,* **fin·ish·es. 1.** the last stage of anything; conclusion; end: *the finish of a race, a fight to the finish.* **2.** the surface or texture of something: *The table has a shiny finish.* **3.** a material used to coat or finish a surface, such as varnish. —**fin′ish·er,** *n.*

  to finish off. a. to complete; end: *She finished off the thread with a knot.* **b.** to defeat, destroy, or kill: *The boxer finished off his opponent with a blow to the jaw.*

  to finish up. to complete; end: *Finish up what you are working on as soon as possible.*

fin·ished (fin′isht) *adj.* **1.** ended; completed: *It took the company several years of research and testing to develop the finished product.* **2.** polished; perfected: *a finished work of art.* **3.** highly skilled or accomplished: *a finished dancer.*

fi·nite (fī′nīt) *adj.* **1.** having a beginning and an end; having limits or bounds: *The lifetime of a human being is finite.* **2.** *Mathematics.* **a.** that can be completed by counting: *a finite number, a finite set.* **b.** not infinite or infinitesimal: *a finite width.* **3.** *Grammar.* of a verb, limited by person, number, tense, or mood. In the sentence *He attends school, attends* is a finite verb. —**fi′nite·ly,** *adv.*

Fin·land (fin′lənd) *n.* **1.** a country in northeastern Europe, on the Baltic Sea. Capital, Helsinki. Area, 130,119 sq. mi. Pop. (1971 est.), 4,680,000. **2. Gulf of.** an arm of the Baltic Sea between Finland and Estonia.

Finn (fin) *n.* a person who was born or is living in Finland.

fin·nan had·die (fin′ən had′ē) smoked haddock.

Finn·ish (fin′ish) *n.* the language spoken principally in Finland. —*adj.* of or relating to Finland, its people, or their language.

fin·ny (fin′ē) *adj.* **1.** having fins. **2.** like a fin. **3.** relating to or abounding in fish: *finny waters.*

fiord (fyôrd) *also,* **fjord.** *n.* a deep, narrow inlet of the sea

---

at; āpe; cär; end; mē; it; īce; hot; ōld; fôrk;
wood; fōōl; oil; out; up; turn; sing; thin; this;
hw in white; zh in treasure. The symbol ə
stands for the sound of a in about, e in taken,
i in pencil, o in lemon, and u in circus.

F

between high, steep banks or cliffs, especially one along the coast of Norway.

fir (fur) *n.* **1.** any of a group of evergreen trees of the same family as the pine, bearing cones. **2.** the wood of such a tree.

fire (fīr) *n.* **1.** the flame, heat, and light given off in burning. **2.** something burning, as wood, coal, or other fuel: *He added another log to the fire.* **3.** destructive burning: *The carelessly thrown match started a forest fire.* **4.** an intense emotion, feeling, or spirit; fervor; passion: *the fire of enthusiasm, eyes full of fire.* **5.** the discharge of firearms; shooting: *the crackle of rifle fire.* —*v.,* **fired, fir·ing.** —*v.t.* **1.** to supply with fuel; tend the fire of: *to fire a furnace.* **2.** to set on fire: *to fire a heap of dead leaves.* **3.** to treat by the use of heat; bake: *to fire pottery.* **4.** to shoot: *to fire a shotgun.* **5.** to arouse the feelings or passions of; inflame; excite: *to fire one's anger. Stories about pirates fired the boy's imagination.* **6.** *Informal.* to direct or throw suddenly or with force: *He fired the ball to home plate. The lawyer fired questions at the witness.* **7.** *Informal.* to dismiss from a job; discharge: *The firm fired seven employees.* —*v.i.* to discharge firearms; shoot: *The enemy fired on the town.*

on fire. a. burning; ignited. **b.** full of intense emotion, feeling, or spirit; passionate.

to catch fire. to begin to burn.

to fire up. to start a fire, as in an engine, furnace, or boiler.

under fire. a. exposed to the enemy's shooting or attack. **b.** exposed to criticism or blame: *She remained calm under fire.*

fire alarm **1.** a signal calling attention to a fire. **2.** a device for giving such a signal.

fire·arm (fīr′ärm′) *n.* a weapon from which a shot is discharged by an explosive charge, especially one that can be carried and fired by one man, as a rifle, pistol, or shotgun.

fire·ball (fīr′bôl′) *n.* **1.** something resembling a ball of fire, as the sun. **2.** a brilliant meteor; shooting star. **3.** a luminous cloud of hot gases produced by a nuclear explosion.

fire·boat (fīr′bōt′) *n.* a boat equipped with apparatus for fighting fires.

fire·brand (fīr′brand′) *n.* **1.** a piece of burning wood. **2.** a person who stirs up feelings of unrest or anger; agitator.

fire·bug (fīr′bug′) *n. Informal.* a person who purposely sets destructive fires; pyromaniac.

fire·crack·er (fīr′krak·ər) *n.* a paper cylinder containing an explosive and an attached fuse, exploded as a noisemaker.

fire·damp (fīr′damp′) *n.* a gas formed in coal mines that is dangerously explosive when mixed with certain proportions of air.

fire·dog (fīr′dôg′) *n.* another word for **andiron.**

fire drill, a practice drill, especially in school or aboard ship, involving the procedures to be followed in case of fire.

fire engine, a truck designed to carry equipment with which to fight fire, especially one that has a pumping apparatus to spray water or chemicals on a fire.

fire escape, a metal stairway attached to the outside of a building for use as a means of escape in case of fire.

fire extinguisher, an apparatus containing chemicals that can be sprayed on a fire to put it out.

fire·fight·er (fīr′fī′tər) *n.* a person employed to put out and prevent fires. Also, **fireman** (def. 1).

Fir twig with cone

fire·fly (fīr′flī′) *n. pl.,* **fire·flies.** any of a number of small beetles that give off flashes of phosphorescent light as a mating signal. Also, **lightning bug.**

fire·house (fīr′hous′) *n. pl.,* **fire·hous·es** (fīr′hou′ziz). a building housing firemen and equipment for putting out fires. Also, **fire station.**

fire hydrant, see **hydrant.**

fire·light (fīr′līt′) *n.* the light from a fire, especially an open fire.

fire·man (fīr′mən) *n. pl.,* **fire·men** (fīr′mən). **1.** a person employed to put out and prevent fires. Also, **firefighter. 2.** a person who tends the fire in a furnace or steam engine, especially on a locomotive; stoker. **3.** an enlisted man in the navy who tends engineering machinery.

fire·place (fīr′plās′) *n.* **1.** an opening in a room at the base of a chimney, in which fires are built. **2.** a structure outdoors in which a fire is built.

fire·plug (fīr′plug′) *n.* a hydrant for supplying water in case of fire.

fire·proof (fīr′proof′) *adj.* resistant to fire; that will not burn: *a fireproof building.* —*v.t.* to make fireproof.

fire screen, a metal screen placed in front of a fireplace to prevent sparks from entering the room.

fire·side (fīr′sīd′) *n.* **1.** the space around a fireplace; hearth. **2.** home or home life. —*adj.* of, in, or near the hearth or home.

fire station, another term for **firehouse.**

fire tower, a tower, usually overlooking a forest, where a lookout is posted to watch for and report fires.

fire·trap (fīr′trap′) *n.* a building that is likely to catch on fire easily or lacks adequate means of escape in case of fire.

fire·wood (fīr′wood′) *n.* wood used for fuel.

fire·works (fīr′wurks′) *n.,pl.* **1.** devices that are designed to be burned or exploded to produce a brilliant display of light or loud noises, as during an outdoor celebration. **2.** a show or display in which such devices are set off.

firing pin, the part of a firearm that strikes the primer to explode the charge.

firm[1] (furm) *adj.* **1.** not yielding to pressure; solid: *firm ground.* **2.** not easily moved; securely fixed: *a firm foundation.* **3.** fixed or settled; not changing: *It is my firm belief that all people are equal. The price of wheat is firm this year.* **4.** steadfast and constant; unwavering: *a firm friendship.* **5.** steady or determined: *a firm voice, a firm hand.* —*adv.* firmly: *The workmen stood firm in their demands.* —*v.t.* to make firm: *Exercise will firm up your muscles.* —*v.i.* to become firm. [Old French *ferme* strong.] —**firm′ly,** *adv.* —**firm′ness,** *n.*

firm[2] (furm) *n.* a company or partnership of two or more persons for carrying on a business; business establishment: *a law firm.* [Italian *firma.*]

fir·ma·ment (fur′mə mənt) *n.* the heavens; sky.

first (furst) *adj.* **1.** (the ordinal of one) before all others in an order or series: *Our team finished in first place.* **2.** before all others in time; earliest: *George Washington was the first President of the United States.* **3.** before all others in importance or excellence; superior; highest; best: *He was first among writers of his time.* **4.** *Music.* (of a performer or instrument) playing or singing the part of highest pitch or principal melodic importance: *first violin, first tenor.* —*adv.* **1.** before all other persons or things, as in order or importance: *She was ranked first in the skiing competition.* **2.** before any other action, time, or event: *Apologize to him first.* **3.** for the first time: *I first heard the news yesterday.* **4.** rather; sooner: *He would starve first.* —*n.*

1. a person or thing that is first, as in importance, order, time, or place: *This invention is the first of its kind.* **2.** the first day of a month: *Our rent is due on the first.* **3.** beginning: *He was a troublemaker from the first.* **4.** the lowest forward gear, as of an automobile.

first-aid (furst′ād′) *adj.* of or for first aid: *a first-aid kit.*

first aid, emergency treatment given to an ill or injured person before full medical care can be obtained.

first-born (furst′bôrn′) *adj.* born first; eldest. —*n.* the first-born child.

first-class (furst′klas′) *adj.* **1.** of the highest rank or best quality: *The actress gave a first-class performance.* **2.** of or relating to a class of mail consisting primarily of letters, parcels, and other written or sealed matter. **3.** of or relating to the best-equipped or most luxurious accommodations on a ship, airplane, or train. —*adv.* by first-class mail or travel accommodations: *to send a package first-class, to travel first-class.*

first class **1.** first-class travel accommodations. **2.** first-class mail.

first-hand (furst′hand′) *adj.* direct from the original source: *He has first-hand knowledge of the event.* —*adv.* from the original source: *to learn of something first-hand.*

first lady **1.** the wife of the President of the United States or of a state governor. **2.** a leading or outstanding woman in a particular field or profession: *the first lady of the theater.*

first lieutenant, an officer in the U.S. Army, Air Force, or Marine Corps, ranking above a second lieutenant and below a captain.

first-ly (furst′lē) *adv.* in the first place; first.

first person, a verb, pronoun, or inflected form that indicates the speaker. *I* and *we* are pronouns of the first person.

first-rate (furst′rāt′) *adj.* **1.** of the highest class, quality, or importance: *a first-rate military power.* **2.** *Informal.* excellent; very good: *a first-rate tennis player.* —*adv. Informal.* excellently.

firth (furth) *n.* a long, narrow arm of the sea.

fis-cal (fis′kəl) *adj.* **1.** relating to the treasury, finances, or revenues of a government: *fiscal policy.* **2.** relating to money matters; financial. —**fis′cal·ly,** *adv.*

fiscal year, any twelve-month period used as a basis for settling financial accounts in a business or government.

fish (fish) *n. pl.,* **fish** or **fish·es.** **1.** a cold-blooded water animal having a backbone, gills for breathing, fins, and, usually, a scaly outer covering for protection. **2.** the flesh of fish used as food. —*v.i.* **1.** to catch or try to catch fish: *to fish for trout.* **2.** to get or try to get something by cunning or indirect means: *She fished for an invitation to the party.* **3.** to search: *He fished around in his pocket for a nickel.* —*v.t.* **1.** to catch or try to catch fish in: *to fish a stream.* **2.** to catch or try to catch (fish). **3.** to find and bring out: *She fished her keys out of her purse.*

fish-er (fish′ər) *n.* **1.** a person who fishes; fisherman. **2.** any animal that catches fish for food. **3.** a meat-eating North American animal related to the marten, having a long body, short legs, and a pointed face. **4.** the dark-brown fur of this animal.

fish-er-man (fish′ər mən) *n. pl.,* **fish·er·men** (fish′ər mən). a person who fishes as an occupation or for sport.

fish-er-y (fish′ər ē) *n. pl.,* **fish·er·ies.** **1.** the occupation or business of catching fish. **2.** a place for catching fish. **3.** fish hatchery.

Fisher *(def. 3)*

fish hatchery, a place where fish are bred under controlled conditions.

fish hawk, another term for **osprey.**

fish-hook (fish′hook′) *n.* a hook, usually barbed, for catching fish.

fish-ing (fish′ing) *n.* **1.** the occupation or sport of catching fish. **2.** a place to catch fish.

fishing rod, a long pole, usually made of wood, metal, or fiberglass, with a line, hook, and usually a reel attached to it, used to catch fish.

fishing tackle, the equipment used by a fisherman, such as rods, lines, hooks, and nets.

fish-mon-ger (fish′mung′gər) *n.* a person who deals in fish.

fish-pond (fish′pond′) *n.* a pond containing fish, especially a pond stocked with fish for sport or food.

fish-wife (fish′wīf′) *n. pl.,* **fish·wives** (fish′wīvz′). **1.** a woman who sells fish. **2.** a coarse, abusive woman.

fish-y (fish′ē) *adj.,* **fish·i·er, fish·i·est.** **1.** like a fish, as in odor or taste. **2.** consisting of fish. **3.** full of fish. **4.** *Informal.* unlikely or suspicious: *The boy gave the teacher a fishy excuse for being late.* **5.** without expression; dull: *a fishy stare.* —**fish′i·ness,** *n.*

fis-sion (fish′ən) *n.* **1.** the act of splitting or breaking apart. **2.** *Physics.* the splitting of an atomic nucleus into two parts, occurring when the nucleus is bombarded by and absorbs a neutron. Fission is accompanied by the release of large amounts of energy. **3.** *Biology.* a method of reproduction in which the parent cell divides to form two or more new individuals. Many single-celled plants and animals reproduce by means of fission.

fis-sion-a-ble (fish′ən ə bəl) *adj.* capable of undergoing nuclear fission. Uranium and plutonium are fissionable materials.

fis-sure (fish′ər) *n.* a long, narrow opening; crack: *a fissure in a rock.*

fist (fist) *n.* a hand tightly closed with fingers doubled into the palm.

fist-ful (fist′fool′) *n. pl.,* **fist·fuls.** another word for **handful.**

fist-i-cuffs (fis′ti kufs′) *n.,pl.* **1.** a fight with the fists. **2.** the art of boxing.

fis-tu-la (fis′chə lə) *n. pl.,* **fis·tu·las** or **fis·tu·lae** (fis′chə lē). a passage that connects body cavities or organs that are normally not connected. A fistula can be present from birth or be the result of the improper healing of a wound or abscess.

fit¹ (fit) *adj.,* **fit·ter, fit·test.** **1.** adapted to or qualified for an end, object, or purpose; suited: *This water is not fit to drink.* **2.** right or proper: *Such behavior is not fit for a public official.* **3.** having the necessary qualifications; competent: *He is fit for the job.* **4.** ready: *The fruit will be fit to eat in three days.* **5.** in good physical or mental condition; healthy: *A person must exercise to keep fit.* —*v.,* **fit·ted, fit·ting.** —*v.t.* **1.** to be suitable or proper for; be adapted to: *Let the punishment fit the crime.* **2.** to be of the proper or correct size or shape for: *The coat fits her well.* **3.** to make fit or suitable; alter; adjust: *to fit a speech to the occasion.* **4.** to supply with what is necessary or suitable; equip: *The campers were fitted out with all the*

at; āpe; cär; end; mē; it; īce; hot; ōld; fôrk; wood; fōol; oil; out; up; turn; sing; thin; this; hw in white; zh in treasure. The symbol ə stands for the sound of a in about, e in taken, i in pencil, o in lemon, and u in circus.

F

supplies needed for their trip. **5.** to adjust, join, or insert: *to fit the pieces of a jigsaw puzzle together.* —*v.i.* **1.** to be suitable or proper. **2.** to be of the proper size or shape: *The shirt fits perfectly.* **3.** to be in harmony: *The abstract painting did not fit in with the other pictures in the room.* —*n.* **1.** the way in which something fits: *The jacket had a loose fit.* **2.** a thing that fits or is fitted: *The dress is a perfect fit.* [Middle English *fitten* to set (troops) in an order.] —**fit′ly,** *adv.* —**fit′ness,** *n.*

fit² (fit) *n.* **1.** a sudden, acute attack of illness: *an epileptic fit.* **2.** a sudden seizure or attack: *a coughing fit.* **3.** a sudden outburst of emotion or feeling: *a fit of anger, a fit of laughter.* [Old English *fitt* conflict.]

by fits and starts or **in fits and starts.** in an irregular way: *to work by fits and starts.*

fitch (fich) *n.* **1.** the European polecat. **2.** its fur, used to make coats and jackets.

fit·ful (fit′fəl) *adj.* not regular; restless: *fitful sleep.* —**fit′ful·ly,** *adv.* —**fit′ful·ness,** *n.*

fit·ter (fit′ər) *n.* **1.** a person who fits or alters garments. **2.** a person who supplies, installs, and fixes parts, machinery, or fittings: *a pipe fitter.*

fit·ting (fit′ing) *adj.* suitable; proper; appropriate: *fitting praise, a fitting end to a story.* —*n.* **1.** the act of a person who fits. **2.** the trying on of an article of clothing so that it can be marked for alterations. **3.** an accessory part or attachment used to adjust something: *a pipe fitting.* —**fit′ting·ly,** *adv.* —**fit′ting·ness,** *n.*

Fitz·ger·ald, F(rancis) Scott (Key) (fits jer′əld) 1896–1940, U.S. novelist and short story writer.

five (fīv) *n.* **1.** the cardinal number that is one more than four. **2.** a symbol representing this number, such as 5 or V. **3.** something having this many units or things, as a playing card. —*adj.* numbering one more than four.

five-and-ten (fīv′ən ten′) *n.* a store offering a wide variety of inexpensive merchandise. Also, **dime store, five-and-dime.** [Because such stores originally sold articles costing *five* or *ten* cents.]

five·fold (fīv′fōld′) *adj.* **1.** five times as great or numerous. **2.** having or consisting of five parts. —*adv.* so as to be five times greater or more numerous.

Five Nations, see Iroquois.

fix (fiks) *v.t.* **1.** to make firm, stable, or secure; fasten tightly: *The campers fixed the stakes for the tent in the ground.* **2.** to settle or arrange definitely; establish; set: *to fix a price, to fix a date for the wedding.* **3.** to direct or hold steadily: *He fixed his gaze on her.* **4.** to place or put: *Police fixed responsibility for the accident on the driver.* **5.** to mend; repair: *to fix a broken chair.* **6.** to treat so as to make permanent or lasting: *to fix colors in a fabric.* **7.** *Photography.* to treat (a photograph) with a chemical solution so that it will not fade. **8.** *Informal.* to put in order; get ready; arrange: *She fixed up the room for her guest.* **9.** *Informal.* to influence the result of (a contest) to one's advantage, as by a bribe: *to fix a race, to fix a boxing match.* **10.** to prepare (food or a meal): *to fix dinner.* **11.** *Informal.* to get revenge upon; get even with; punish: *I'll fix him for what he did.* —*n. pl.,* **fix·es.** **1.** *Informal.* a position from which it is difficult to escape; difficulty; predicament: *She got herself into quite a fix by accepting two dates for the same dance.* **2.** *Slang.* a dosage of a narcotic. **3.** the position of a ship or aircraft, as determined by observations or from radio signals. —**fix′a·ble,** *adj.* —**fix′er,** *n.*

to fix on or **to fix upon.** to decide on; choose; select: *to fix on a date.*

to fix up. *Informal.* **a.** to mend; repair. **b.** to provide what is needed for: *We fixed him up with a place to spend the night.*

fix·a·tion (fik sā′shən) *n.* **1.** the act of fixing or the state of being fixed. **2.** a treatment to make a dye or color permanent, as in photographic film. **3.** a strong and persistent attachment to a person or thing.

fix·a·tive (fik′sə tiv) *n.* something that fixes or makes permanent, especially a substance sprayed on a charcoal or crayon drawing to preserve it. —*adj.* fixing or making permanent.

fixed (fikst) *adj.* **1.** made firm in position; securely placed or fastened; not movable: *the fixed seats in a motion picture theater.* **2.** steadily directed; not moving: *a fixed stare.* **3.** not changing; settled: *a fixed rate of interest.* **4.** definite; resolute: *a fixed purpose.* **5.** *Informal.* prearranged dishonestly as to result or decision: *a fixed race* —**fix·ed·ly** (fik′sid lē), *adv.* —**fix′ed·ness,** *n.*

fixed star, a star that appears to remain in the same position in relation to other stars, because of its great distance from the earth.

fix·ture (fiks′chər) *n.* **1.** anything fixed or securely fastened into place, especially a permanently attached part or accessory of a house: *bathroom fixtures, a light fixture.* **2.** a person or thing permanently associated with a particular place or job: *That old professor is a fixture at the college.*

fizz (fiz) *v.i.* to make a hissing or sputtering sound. —*n.* **1.** a hissing sound. **2.** an effervescent or bubbling beverage, as champagne or soda water.

fiz·zle (fiz′əl) *v.i.,* **fiz·zled, fiz·zling. 1.** to make a hissing or sputtering sound: *The wet wood fizzled in the fireplace.* **2.** *Informal.* to fail or end feebly, especially after a good start: *All our plans fizzled out.* —*n.* **1.** a hissing or sputtering sound. **2.** *Informal.* a person or thing that does not succeed; failure.

fiz·zy (fiz′ē) *adj.,* **fizz·i·er, fizz·i·est.** fizzing; bubbling.

fjord (fyôrd) another spelling of **fiord.**

Fl, the symbol for fluorine.

Fla., Florida.

flab·ber·gast (flab′ər gast′) *v.t. Informal.* to overwhelm with surprise or amazement; astonish: *The news that he had won the contest flabbergasted him.*

flab·by (flab′ē) *adj.,* **flab·bi·er, flab·bi·est.** lacking firmness or force; soft: *flabby muscles, a flabby mind.* —**flab′bi·ly,** *adv.* —**flab′bi·ness,** *n.*

flac·cid (flak′sid) *adj.* lacking firmness; limp; weak: *flaccid muscles.* —**flac·cid′i·ty,** *n.*

fla·con (flak′ən, fla kōn′) *n.* a small bottle or flask that is closed with a stopper: *a flacon of perfume.*

flag¹ (flag) *n.* a piece of cloth having various colors and designs on it that is used as a symbol of a country or organization, or as a signal. —*v.t.,* **flagged, flag·ging. 1.** to put a flag or flags on; decorate with flags. **2.** to stop or signal: *to flag a taxicab.* [Possibly from *flag³.*]

flag² (flag) *n.* **1.** any of various irises having sword-shaped leaves and blue, yellow, purple, or white flowers. **2.** a flower of any of these plants. [Middle English *flagge* rush, reed.]

flag³ (flag) *v.i.,* **flagged, flag·ging.** to grow weak or tired; lose vigor: *His interest flagged.* [Possibly from Old Norse *flakka* to flutter.]

flag⁴ (flag) *n.* see **flagstone.** —*v.t.,* **flagged, flag·ging.** to pave with flagstones. [Old Norse *flaga* a slab of stone.]

Flag Day, the anniversary of the day in 1777 when the Stars and Stripes was made the official flag of the United States. It falls on June 14.

flag·el·late (flaj′ə lāt′) *adj.* **1.** having a flagellum or flagella. **2.** shaped like a flagellum. —*v.t.,* **flag·el·lat·ed, flag·el·lat·ing.** to whip; scourge. —**flag′el·la′tion,** *n.*

fla·gel·lum (flə jel′əm) *n. pl.,* **fla·gel·la** (flə jel′lə) or **fla-**

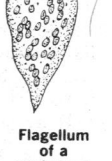

Flagellum of a protozoan

gel·lums. **1.** a long whiplike tail or part that enables certain cells, bacteria, and protozoa to move. **2.** a whip.

flag·eo·let (flaj′ə let′) *n.* a wind instrument like a flute, having six finger holes, four on the top and two below.

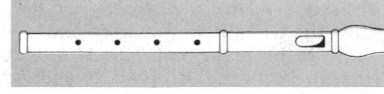

Flageolet

flag·man (flag′-mən) *n. pl.,* **flag-men** (flag′mən). a person who signals with a flag or lantern, especially at a railroad crossing.

flag officer, a naval officer above the rank of captain, entitled to display a flag showing his rank.

flag·on (flag′ən) *n.* **1.** a large container for liquids, having a handle, a spout, and usually a cover. **2.** the contents of a flagon: *to drink a flagon of ale.*

flag·pole (flag′pōl′) *n.* a pole on which a flag is raised and flown. Also, **flagstaff.**

fla·grant (flā′grənt) *adj.* openly bad or wrong; scandalous: *flagrant violations of the law, a flagrant display of cowardice.* —**fla′gran·cy,** *n.* —**fla′grant·ly,** *adv.*

flag·ship (flag′ship′) *n.* a ship carrying the commanding officer of a fleet and flying his flag.

flag·staff (flag′staf′) *n.* another word for **flagpole.**

flag·stone (flag′stōn′) *n.* a large, flat stone, used for paving.

flail (flāl) *n.* a device used for threshing grain by hand. It is made of a wooden staff at the end of which a wide, short stick is hung so as to swing freely. —*v.t.* **1.** to strike with a flail; thresh. **2.** to wave or swing, especially violently or quickly: *The woman flailed her arms at the bees swarming around her.*

flair (fler) *n.* **1.** an ability to choose what is good; discernment: *The room had been decorated with flair.* **2.** a natural talent: *George has a flair for acting.*

flak (flak) *n.* **1.** antiaircraft fire. **2.** fragments from exploding shells fired at enemy aircraft. **3.** *Slang.* criticism or abuse: *The senator's proposal met with much flak from the newspapers.*

flake (flāk) *n.* a small, thin, flat piece: *a flake of snow, flakes of paint peeling off a wall.* —*v.,* **flaked, flak·ing.** —*v.t.* to chip or peel off in flakes: *to flake paint from a wall.* —*v.i.* to peel off in flakes: *The plaster cracked and flaked.*

flak·y (flā′kē) *adj.,* **flak·i·er, flak·i·est. 1.** consisting of flakes: *Mica is a flaky mineral.* **2.** separating easily into flakes: *The pie crust was flaky and light.* —**flak′i·ly,** *adv.* —**flak′i·ness,** *n.*

flam·boy·ance (flam boi′əns) *n.* the quality of being flamboyant.

flam·boy·ant (flam boi′ənt) *adj.* **1.** overly decorated; showy; florid: *a flamboyant writing style, flamboyant fashions.* **2.** brilliant; colorful: *a flamboyant sunset.* **3.** having wavy or flamelike lines or curves, as some Gothic architecture. —**flam·boy′ant·ly,** *adv.*

flame (flām) *n.* **1.** one of the tongues of light given off by a fire: *The flames from the burning house shot out in every direction.* **2.** ignited gas or vapor that gives off light and heat: *Lower the flame under the frying pan.* **3.** the condition or state of burning: *The house burst into flame.* **4.** something like a flame: *The sun was a flame on the horizon.* **5.** strong emotional feeling; passion; ardor: *the flame of love.* —*v.i.,* **flamed, flam·ing. 1.** to burn with flames; burst into flame; blaze: *The fire flamed intensely.* **2.** to light up or glow as if with flames: *His face flamed with embarrassment.* **3.** to break out with violence or passion: *She flamed with rage at his insulting remark.* —**flame′like′,** *adj.*

fla·men·co (flə meng′kō) *n.* a Spanish gypsy style of dancing, characterized by stamping of the feet, clapping of the hands, and the use of castanets.

flame thrower, a weapon or instrument that throws a stream of burning fuel.

flam·ing (flā′ming) *adj.* **1.** in flames; blazing; fiery. **2.** brilliant: *flaming colors.* **3.** ardent; passionate: *a flaming speech.* —**flam′ing·ly,** *adv.*

fla·min·go (flə ming′gō) *n. pl.,* **fla·min·gos** or **fla·min-goes.** any of various wading birds of tropical and subtropical regions, having a long thin neck and legs, webbed feet, and feathers that range from pinkish white to deep crimson.

flam·ma·ble (flam′ə bəl) *adj.* able to be set on fire easily; combustible. —*n.* something that is flammable. —**flam′ma·bil′i·ty,** *n.*

Flan·ders (flan′dərz) *n.* a historic region of northwestern Europe, in western Belgium, northern France, and the southwestern Netherlands.

Flamingo

flange (flanj) *n.* a projecting rim or collar on an object, designed to keep it in place, to attach it to another object, or to strengthen it. The wheels of a railroad car have flanges to keep them on the tracks.

flank (flangk) *n.* **1.** the part between the ribs and the hip on either side of a human being or animal. **2.** a cut of meat, especially beef, from this part of an animal. **3.** the right or left side of a military unit, formation, position, or fortification. **4.** the side of anything: *the flank of a building.* —*v.t.* **1.** to be located at the side of: *Two statues flanked the entrance of the library.* **2.** to attack or move around the flank of: *to flank an enemy fleet.*

flank·er (flang′kər) *n.* **1.** a person or thing that flanks. **2.** *Football.* an offensive back who lines up in a flanking position.

flan·nel (flan′əl) *n.* **1.** a soft cotton fabric, having a nap on one or both sides, used for such items as nightgowns, infants' wear, and shirts. Also, **flannelette. 2.** a soft woolen fabric having a slight nap. **3. flannels.** clothes made of flannel.

flan·nel·ette (flan′əl et′) *n.* see **flannel** *(def. 1).*

flap (flap) *v.,* **flapped, flap·ping.** —*v.t.* to move up and down, especially with a muffled, slapping sound: *The birds flapped their wings.* —*v.i.* **1.** to move the wings or arms up and down, especially with a muffled, slapping sound. **2.** to sway or wave loosely, especially with noise: *The curtains flapped in the breeze.* —*n.* **1.** a flapping motion. **2.** the muffled slapping sound made when something flaps. **3.** the part of an envelope folded down in closing or sealing it. **4.** a piece of material attached at one edge only so that it may move, especially one covering the opening of a pocket. **5.** a hinged section on the back edge of an airplane wing that is used to increase lift during a take-off or a landing.

flap·jack (flap′jak′) *n.* another word for **pancake.**

at; āpe; cär; end; mē; it; īce; hot; ōld; fôrk; wood; fōōl; oil; out; up; turn; sing; thin; this; hw in white; zh in treasure. The symbol ə stands for the sound of **a** in about, **e** in taken, **i** in pencil, **o** in lemon, and **u** in circus.

F

flap·per (flap′ər) *n.* **1.** a person or thing that flaps. **2.** *Informal.* a young woman of the 1920s who was unconventional in dress and behavior.

flare (fler) *v.i.,* **flared, flar·ing. 1.** to burn with a sudden, very bright light, especially for only a short time: *The match flared in the darkness and then went out.* **2.** to break out in sudden or violent emotion: *Her temper flared at his remark.* **3.** to open or spread outward: *This skirt flares from the waist.* —*n.* **1.** a sudden, bright light, usually lasting only a short time. **2.** a fire or blaze of light used to signal or provide light. **3.** a sudden outburst, as of emotion or activity: *a flare of temper.* **4.** a widening or spreading outward: *the flare of a skirt.*

   to flare up. to become suddenly angry or excited.

flare-up (fler′up′) *n.* **1.** a sudden outburst of flame or light. **2.** *Informal.* a sudden or violent activity or emotion: *a flare-up of violence.*

flash (flash) *n. pl.,* **flash·es. 1.** a sudden, brief burst, as of light or flame: *a flash of lightning.* **2.** a very brief period of time; instant; moment: *He was there in a flash.* **3.** a sudden outburst or brief display: *a flash of merriment, a flash of inspiration.* **4.** a brief bulletin or report of very recent or urgent news. —*v.i.* **1.** to burst forth in sudden, brief light or fire: *Lightning flashed in the sky.* **2.** to reflect or burst forth with light; shine; gleam: *Her eyes flashed with anger.* **3.** to burst suddenly into view or perception: *An idea flashed into his mind.* **4.** to come or move suddenly or quickly: *The car flashed by.* —*v.t.* **1.** to cause to flash: *He flashed the light in her eyes.* **2.** to communicate by flashes, as by telegraph or radio: *The news was flashed all over the country.* —*adj.* happening or done very quickly; lasting for a short time: *A flash fire destroyed the house.* —**flash′er,** *n.*

   flash in the pan. a person or something that at first seems promising or successful, but in the end is a failure.

flash·back (flash′bak′) *n.* **1.** a break in the normal time sequence of a motion picture, radio script, novel, or play, during which a scene describing earlier events is introduced. **2.** a scene or episode that is introduced in this way.

flash bulb, an electric bulb that gives off a single very bright flash, used for taking photographs.

flash·card (flash′kärd′) *n.* any of a set of cards having words, numbers, or other information on them, used in classroom drills or in private study.

flash flood, a sudden, violent flood caused by heavy rainfall.

flash gun, a device used to hold and set off a flash bulb.

flash·light (flash′līt′) *n.* a portable electric light powered by batteries.

flash·y (flash′ē) *adj.,* **flash·i·er, flash·i·est. 1.** brilliant for a short time; sparkling; flashing. **2.** showy; gaudy: *a flashy car, flashy clothes.* —**flash′i·ly,** *adv.* —**flash′i·ness,** *n.*

flask (flask) *n.* **1.** a small, flattened bottle, as for holding liquor, made to be carried in the pocket. **2.** a rounded glass container with a long neck, used in laboratory work.

flat¹ (flat) *adj.,* **flat·ter, flat·test. 1.** smooth or even; level: *a flat field. It is easy to bicycle on a flat road.* **2.** lying or stretched at full length; spread out: *He was lying flat on his back.* **3.** having little depth or thickness; shallow: *a flat sheet of metal.* **4.** plain; positive; absolute: *a flat denial, a flat refusal.* **5.** fixed; unchangeable: *a flat rate.* **6.** lacking in interest or vigor; lifeless; dull: *a flat performance.* **7.** not shiny or glossy: *flat paint.* **8.** containing little or no air; deflated: *a flat tire.* **9.** *Music.* **a.** below the true, regular, or intended pitch. **b.** one half note lower than natural pitch. **c.** having a flat in the signature. —*n.* **1.** a flat part or surface: *the flat of a sword, the flat of the hand.* **2.** a tract of low-lying, level land. **3. flats.** women's shoes having low heels. **4.** *Informal.* a tire from which air is

escaping or has escaped. **5.** *Music.* **a.** a tone or note lowered one half note below its natural pitch. **b.** a symbol (♭) that indicates such a tone or note. —*adv.* **1.** in a flat manner; flatly: *The cat lay flat on the ground.* **2.** exactly; precisely: *He ran a mile in four minutes flat.* **3.** *Music.* below the true pitch: *She sang flat.* —*v.,* **flat·ted, flat·ting.** —*v.t.* **1.** to make flat. **2.** *Music.* to sing or play flat. —*v.i.* to become flat. [Old Norse *flatr* level.] —**flat′ly,** *adv.* —**flat′ness,** *n.*

flat² (flat) *n.* an apartment or suite of rooms on one floor of a building. [Middle English *flet* floor.]

flat·boat (flat′bōt′) *n.* a large boat with a flat bottom and square ends, used for carrying freight on rivers or canals.

flat·car (flat′kär′) *n.* a railroad car consisting of a platform without a roof or sides, used for carrying freight.

flat·fish (flat′fish′) *n. pl.,* **flat·fish** or **flat·fish·es.** any of a group of fish that have flattened bodies. In the adult both eyes are on the upper side of the body. Halibut, flounder, and sole are flatfish.

flat·foot (flat′foot′) *n. pl.,* **flat·feet. 1.** a condition in which the arch of the foot is abnormally low and most or all of the sole touches the ground. **2.** a foot with an abnormally low arch. **3.** *Slang.* a policeman, especially a patrolman.

flat·foot·ed (flat′foot′id) *adj.* **1.** having flat feet. **2.** *Informal.* off one's guard; not ready; unprepared: *to be caught flat-footed.* —**flat′-foot′ed·ly,** *adv.* —**flat′-foot′ed·ness,** *n.*

flat·i·ron (flat′ī′ərn) *n.* a heavy iron for pressing clothes, especially one that must be heated in an oven or fireplace before it can be used.

flat·ten (flat′ən) *v.t.* **1.** to make flat or flatter. **2.** to knock down: *The boxer flattened his opponent.* —*v.i.* **1.** to become flat or flatter. **2.** to fall or lie flat. —**flat′ten·er,** *n.*

flat·ter (flat′ər) *v.t.* **1.** to praise too much or insincerely. **2.** to try to please or gain the favor of by praising too much or insincerely. **3.** to cause to be pleased; compliment: *She was flattered by the invitation.* **4.** to show favorably, especially to show as more attractive than is actually the case: *The photograph flatters him.* —**flat′ter·er,** *n.* —**flat′ter·ing·ly,** *adv.*

flat·ter·y (flat′ər ē) *n. pl.,* **flat·ter·ies. 1.** the act of flattering. **2.** a flattering remark or speech.

flat·tish (flat′ish) *adj.* somewhat flat.

flat·top (flat′top′) *n. Informal.* an aircraft carrier.

flat·ware (flat′wer′) *n.* **1.** table utensils, such as knives, forks, and spoons. **2.** dishes that are more or less flat, such as plates, platters, or saucers.

flat·worm (flat′wurm′) *n.* any of a large group of soft, flat-bodied worms, including the tapeworm.

flaunt (flônt) *v.i.* **1.** to show off in order to impress others; make a gaudy display. **2.** to wave or flutter freely: *Banners were flaunting at the stadium entrance.* —*v.t.* to show or display boldly or boastfully: *He is always flaunting his wealth.* —*n.* the act of flaunting. —**flaunt′ing·ly,** *adv.*

▲ **Flaunt** and **flout** are spelled and pronounced in a similar way, but they have different meanings. **Flaunt** means to show off in a boastful way in order to impress others: *He flaunted his wealth by buying an expensive new car every year.* **Flout** means to defy or treat with contempt: *He flouted the law by refusing to pay his taxes.*

flau·tist (flô′tist) *n.* another word for **flutist.**

fla·vor (flā′vər) *also, British,* **fla·vour.** *n.* **1.** a particular or characteristic taste: *Adding pepper to the stew will give it a spicy flavor.* **2.** flavoring; seasoning: *That ice-cream is made with chocolate, vanilla and other flavors.* **3.** characteristic, distinctive, or main quality; aura: *That story has a quaint flavor.* —*v.t.* to give flavor to: *to flavor apple pie with cinnamon.* —**fla′vor·ful,** *adj.*

fla·vor·ing (flā′vər ing) *n.* something added to food or drink to give or heighten flavor: *She added lemon flavoring to the cookies.*

flaw (flô) *n.* something that takes away from or spoils completeness, soundness, or perfection: *His quick temper is a flaw in his character. The glass had a flaw in it.* —*v.t.* to make defective.

flaw·less (flô′lis) *adj.* having no flaw; perfect: *a flawless emerald, a flawless complexion, a flawless performance.* —**flaw′less·ly**, *adv.* —**flaw′less·ness**, *n.*

flax (flaks) *n.* **1.** a fiber that is obtained from the stem of a plant and prepared to be spun into thread. Flax is used to make linen and such products as rope and rugs. **2.** the plant itself.

flax·en (flak′sən) *adj.* **1.** made of flax: *flaxen thread.* **2.** having a pale yellow color like that of flax fiber: *flaxen hair.*

flax·seed (flaks′sēd′) *n.* the seed of flax, used to make linseed oil; linseed.

flay (flā) *v.t.* **1.** to strip off the skin or outer covering of, as by lashing. **2.** to criticize or scold severely or harshly.

flea (flē) any of a large group of wingless insects that feed on the blood of warm-blooded animals. They have strong legs for leaping and sharp mouth parts for piercing the skin and sucking blood. Fleas may transmit certain diseases, such as bubonic plague.

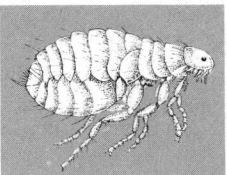

Flea

fleck (flek) *n.* **1.** a small patch or streak of light or color; spot: *flecks of sunlight, black marble with flecks of white in it.* **2.** a small particle; flake; speck: *flecks of dust.* —*v.t.* to mark with flecks; spot: *to fleck a wall with paint.*

fled (fled) the past tense and past participle of **flee.**

fledge (flej) *v.*, **fledged, fledg·ing. 1.** to provide (an arrow) with feathers. **2.** to rear (a young bird) until it is able to fly. —*v.i.* (of a young bird) to grow the feathers needed for flight.

fledg·ling (flej′ling) also, **fledge·ling.** *n.* **1.** a young bird just fledged. **2.** a young or inexperienced person.

flee (flē) *v.*, **fled, flee·ing.** —*v.i.* **1.** to run away, as from danger or pursuit; take flight: *The robbers fled down the alley.* **2.** to move or pass away swiftly: *Color fled from her cheeks.* —*v.t.* to run away or try to escape from: *The family fled the burning house.* —**fle′er**, *n.*

fleece (flēs) *n.* **1.** a coat of wool covering a sheep or similar animal. **2.** the quantity of wool sheared from a sheep or similar animal at any one time. **3.** something resembling fleece: *a fleece of snow.* **4.** a fabric with a thick nap or pile resembling the wool of a sheep, used for lining clothes. —*v.t.*, **fleeced, fleec·ing. 1.** to shear the fleece from. **2.** to deprive of money or property by deception; cheat; swindle. —**fleec′er**, *n.*

fleec·y (flē′sē) *adj.*, **fleec·i·er, fleec·i·est. 1.** made of or covered with fleece. **2.** like fleece: *fleecy clouds.* —**fleec′i·ness**, *n.*

fleet¹ (flēt) *n.* **1.** a group of warships under one command. **2.** a group of boats or vehicles working together or under one management: *a fleet of taxis.* [Old English *flēot* a ship or group of ships.]

fleet² (flēt) *adj.* swift; fast: *The deer is a fleet animal.* —*v.i.* to move or pass swiftly. [Possibly from Old Norse *fljotr* swift.] —**fleet′ly**, *adv.* —**fleet′ness**, *n.*

fleet admiral, an officer in the U.S. Navy of the highest rank.

fleet·ing (flē′ting) *adj.* passing quickly; very brief: *a fleeting glimpse, a fleeting moment.* —**fleet′ing·ly**, *adv.* —**fleet′ing·ness**, *n.*

Flem·ing (flem′ing) *n.* **1.** a Belgian whose native language is Flemish. **2.** one of the people of the region of Flanders.

Flem·ing, Sir Alexander (flem′ing) 1881–1955, Scottish bacteriologist, the discoverer of penicillin.

Flem·ish (flem′ish) *n.* **1. the Flemish.** the people of Flanders. **2.** a Germanic language resembling Dutch and spoken chiefly in northern Belgium and northwestern France. —*adj.* of or relating to Flanders, its people, or their language.

flesh (flesh) *n.* **1.** the soft part of the body of a human being or animal that covers the bones, consisting mainly of muscle and fat. **2.** the parts of an animal used as food; meat. **3.** the soft, pulpy part of fruits or vegetables used as food: *the flesh of a peach.* **4.** the body of man, as distinguished from his soul or spirit: *The spirit indeed is willing, but the flesh is weak* (Matthew XXV:41). **5.** a light yellowish pink color.

flesh and blood. family or other close relatives.

in the flesh. present before one's eyes; in person: *He's taller in the flesh than he looks in pictures.*

flesh·ly (flesh′lē) *adj.*, **flesh·li·er, flesh·li·est. 1.** sensual; carnal: *fleshly desires.* **2.** of or relating to the flesh or body; bodily; physical. —**flesh′li·ness**, *n.*

flesh·y (flesh′ē) *adj.*, **flesh·i·er, flesh·i·est. 1.** having much flesh; plump; fat. **2.** of or like flesh. **3.** firm and pulpy: *a fleshy fruit, fleshy leaves.* —**flesh′i·ness**, *n.*

fleur-de-lis (flur′də lē′) *n. pl.*, **fleurs-de-lis** (flur′də lēz′). **1.** a heraldic design representing an iris, used as an emblem by the former royal family of France. **2.** see **iris** *(defs. 2, 3).*

Fleurs-de-lis

flew (flōō) the past tense of **fly²**: *The bird flew to its nest in the tree.*

flex (fleks) *v.t.* **1.** to bend: *to flex one's arm. The archers flexed their bows.* **2.** to tighten or contract: *to flex a muscle.*

flex·i·ble (flek′sə bəl) *adj.* **1.** able to bend without breaking; not stiff or rigid: *Rubber is flexible.* **2.** able to adjust easily to change; adaptable: *a flexible schedule, flexible rules.* —**flex′i·bil′i·ty, flex′i·ble·ness**, *n.* —**flex′i·bly**, *adv.*

flex·ion (flek′shən) *n.* the act of bending a limb or muscle.

flex·or (flek′sər) *n.* any muscle that bends a limb or other part of the body.

flick (flik) *n.* **1.** a light, quick, snapping movement or stroke: *a flick of the wrist, a flick with a whip.* **2.** a sound made by such a movement or stroke. —*v.t.* **1.** to hit or remove (something) with a light, quick, snapping movement or stroke: *to flick crumbs from one's lap, to flick a horse's rump with a whip.* **2.** to make a quick, snapping movement with: *to flick a towel at someone.*

flick·er¹ (flik′ər) *v.i.* **1.** to shine or burn with an unsteady or wavering light: *The match flickered in the breeze.* **2.** to move back and forth with a quick, fluttering movement; quiver; tremble: *Shadows flickered on the wall.*

at; āpe; cär; end; mē; it; īce; hot; ōld; fôrk; wood; fōōl; oil; out; up; turn; sing; thin; this; hw in white; zh in treasure. The symbol ə stands for the sound of **a** in **about, e** in **taken, i** in **pencil, o** in **lemon,** and **u** in **circus.**

F

—*n.* **1.** an unsteady or wavering light. **2.** a slight indication; brief appearance: *a flicker of hope, a flicker of interest.* **3.** a quick fluttering or quivering movement: *the flicker of an eyelid.* [Old English *flicorian.*]

flick·er² (flik′ər) *n.* a North American woodpecker having yellow markings on its wings and tail. [Possibly imitative of its cry.]

flied (flīd) a past tense and past participle of **fly²** (*v.i. def. 7*).

fli·er (flī′ər) *also,* **fly·er.** *n.* **1.** a person or thing that flies: *That sea gull is a graceful flier.* **2.** an aviator. **3.** a thing that moves swiftly, such as an express train. **4.** a small handbill or leaflet, especially one used in advertising.

flies (flīz) *n.* the plural of **fly¹** and **fly².** —*v.* the third person singular, present tense of **fly².**

flight¹ (flīt) *n.* **1.** the act, manner, or power of flying: *We watched the graceful flight of the butterfly.* **2.** the distance or course traveled by something flying, as an airplane or bird. **3.** a group of things flying or passing through the air together: *a flight of swallows.* **4.** a trip made by or in an aircraft: *He took the ten o'clock flight to Washington.* **5.** a passing above or beyond the ordinary: *a flight of fancy.* **6.** a series of stairs or steps between floors or landings. [Old English *flyht.*]

flight² (flīt) *n.* the act of fleeing. [Middle English *fliht.*]
to put to flight. to cause to flee; rout: *to put enemy troops to flight.*

flight attendant, a person who serves passengers on an airplane.

flight·less (flīt′lis) *adj.* (of birds) not able to fly: *The ostrich is flightless.*

flight·y (flī′tē) *adj.,* **flight·i·er, flight·i·est.** given to sudden whims or impulses; frivolous; giddy.

flim·sy (flim′zē) *adj.,* **flim·si·er, flim·si·est.** **1.** lacking strength or substance; thin; frail: *The blouse was made of a flimsy material.* **2.** not convincing or adequate; weak: *a flimsy excuse, a flimsy argument.* —**flim′si·ly,** *adv.*

flinch (flinch) *v.i.* to draw back or away, as from something painful, dangerous, or unpleasant; shrink; wince: *She always flinches at loud noises.*

fling (fling) *v.,* **flung, fling·ing.** —*v.t.* **1.** to throw with force or violence; hurl: *He flung up his hands in disgust.* **2.** to send or put suddenly or violently; thrust: *to fling a letter onto one's desk.* —*v.i.* to move suddenly or violently; rush headlong. —*n.* **1.** the act of flinging. **2.** a period of freely indulging oneself, as in pleasures: *to have a fling before settling down.* **3.** a lively or spirited dance, especially the Highland fling.
to have a fling at or **to take a fling at.** to have a try at; make an attempt at.

flint (flint) *n.* **1.** a hard variety of quartz, usually dull gray in color, that produces sparks when struck against steel. **2.** a piece of this used for kindling a fire.

Flint (flint) *n.* a city in southeastern Michigan. Pop. (1970), 193,317.

flint·lock (flint′lok′) *n.* **1.** a gunlock in which a flint is struck against steel to produce sparks and ignite gunpowder. **2.** an old-fashioned firearm with such a gunlock.

flint·y (flin′tē) *adj.,* **flint·i·er, flint·i·est.** **1.** consisting of or containing flint. **2.** hard; unyielding; cruel: *a flinty heart, a flinty look.* —**flint′i·ly,** *adj.* —**flint′i·ness,** *n.*

flip (flip) *v.,* **flipped, flip·ping.** **1.** to toss with a quick, jerking movement so as to cause to turn over in the air: *to flip a coin.* **2.** to turn over, especially with a quick, jerking movement: *Ed flipped the pages of the book.*

3. to move with a quick, jerking movement: *to flip a switch.* —*v.i.* to move or turn with a jerk: *The fish flipped onto its back. She flipped through the magazine.* —*n.* a quick turning or jerking movement. —*adj.,* **flip·per, flip·pest.** *Informal.* impertinent; saucy; flippant: *a flip remark.*

flip·pant (flip′ənt) *adj.* lacking proper respect or seriousness: *a flippant answer, a flippant attitude.* —**flip′pant·ly,** *adv.*

flip·per (flip′ər) *n.* **1.** a broad, flat limb, as of a seal, dolphin, penguin, or turtle, that is adapted for swimming. **2.** one of a pair of broad, paddle-shaped rubber shoes, worn as an aid to swimming or skin diving.

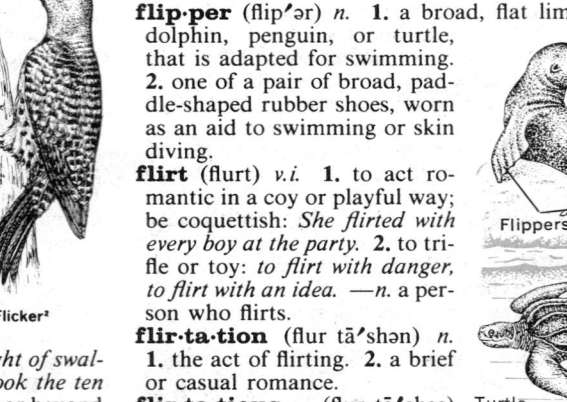

Sea lion

Flippers

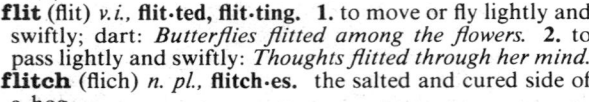

Turtle

Flippers

Flipper

flirt (flurt) *v.i.* **1.** to act romantic in a coy or playful way; be coquettish: *She flirted with every boy at the party.* **2.** to trifle or toy: *to flirt with danger, to flirt with an idea.* —*n.* a person who flirts.

flir·ta·tion (flur tā′shən) *n.* **1.** the act of flirting. **2.** a brief or casual romance.

flir·ta·tious (flur tā′shəs) *adj.* **1.** inclined to flirt or be coquettish: *a flirtatious girl.* **2.** characteristic of a flirt: *flirtatious behavior.* —**flir·ta′tious·ly,** *adv.* —**flir·ta′tious·ness,** *n.*

flit (flit) *v.i.,* **flit·ted, flit·ting.** **1.** to move or fly lightly and swiftly; dart: *Butterflies flitted among the flowers.* **2.** to pass lightly and swiftly: *Thoughts flitted through her mind.*

flitch (flich) *n. pl.,* **flitch·es.** the salted and cured side of a hog.

float (flōt) *v.i.* **1.** to rest on or at the surface of a liquid: *Sailboats floated on the lake. He was floating on his back in the pool. The cork floated.* **2.** to drift or be carried along in the air: *The clouds floated across the sky. Leaves floated down from the trees.* **3.** to hover or move as if carried along in this manner: *The rumors were floating all about town.* —*v.t.* **1.** to cause to float: *to float lumber down a river.* **2.** to offer for sale, as stocks or bonds; put on the market: *to float an issue of stock.* —*n.* **1.** a thing that floats or helps something else to float, such as a raft. **2.** an exhibit carried on a vehicle or wheeled platform in parades or pageants. **3.** a hollow metal ball or other device that floats on the surface of a body of liquid and regulates the level, supply, or outflow of the liquid, as in a carburetor or boiler. —**float′er,** *n.*

floating rib, a rib attached to the backbone but not to the breastbone. In human beings the bottom two pairs of ribs are floating ribs.

flock (flok) *n.* **1.** a group of animals of one kind gathered or herded together: *a flock of crows, a shepherd and his flock.* **2.** a large number or group: *a flock of reporters.* **3.** the members of a church; congregation: *a pastor and his flock.* —*v.i.* to move or gather in crowds: *People flocked to the beaches during the hot weather.*

floe (flō) *n.* a mass or sheet of floating ice. Also, **ice floe.**

flog (flog) *v.t.,* **flogged, flog·ging.** to beat or whip severely, especially as punishment.

flood (flud) *n.* **1.** a great flow or overflowing of water, especially over normally dry land. **2.** a great outpouring of anything: *a flood of tears, a flood of words.* **3.** *also,* **the Flood.** in the Old Testament, the great flood that occurred in the time of Noah. —*v.t.* **1.** to cover or cause to be covered with a flood; inundate: *The valley was flooded*

Flicker²

when the dam broke. **2.** to fill or overwhelm, as with a flood: *The box office was flooded with requests for tickets.* —*v.i.* to rise in a flood; overflow.

flood·gate (flud′gāt′) *n.* a gate in a waterway designed to control the flow of water.

flood·light (flud′līt′) *n.* **1.** a lamp that provides a broad beam of bright light. **2.** a broad beam of light projected by such a lamp. —*v.t.,* **flood·light·ed** or **flood·lit, flood·light·ing.** to light with a floodlight.

flood plain, a plain along a river, made by deposits of earth from floodwaters.

flood tide, the tide that is flowing in toward the shore.

flood·wa·ter (flud′wô′tər, flud′wot′ər) *n.* the water flooding normally dry land.

floor (flôr) *n.* **1.** the lower surface of a room on which one stands or walks. **2.** any surface like a floor in position or use; bottom surface: *the ocean floor, the forest floor.* **3.** a story of a building: *Anita's office is on the second floor of the building.* **4.** a part of a room or building, as in a legislative house, where members sit, speak, and carry on business: *The bill was debated at length on the floor of the Senate.* **5.** the right or privilege to speak to an assembly: *The chairman gave him the floor.* —*v.t.* **1.** to cover or furnish with a floor: *to floor a porch.* **2.** to knock down: *The boxer floored his opponent.* **3.** *Informal.* to bewilder or surprise completely; dumbfound: *He was floored by the news that he had won the contest.*

floor·ing (flôr′ing) *n.* **1.** material for making floors. **2.** a floor or floors: *The kitchen had a tile flooring.*

floor·walk·er (flôr′wô′kər) *n.* a person employed in a store to supervise sales and services.

flop (flop) *v.i.,* **flopped, flop·ping. 1.** to drop or fall loosely, clumsily, or heavily: *to flop into a chair, to flop into bed.* **2.** to move, swing, or flap about loosely or clumsily: *The spaniel's ears flopped about its face.* **3.** *Informal.* to be completely unsuccessful; fail: *The play flopped.* —*n.* **1.** the act of flopping: *He took a flop on the ice.* **2.** *Informal.* a failure.

flop·py (flop′ē) *adj.,* **flop·pi·er, flop·pi·est.** *Informal.* that flops or tends to flop: *She wore a large straw hat with a floppy brim.* —**flop′pi·ly,** *adv.* —**flop′pi·ness,** *n.*

flo·ra (flôr′ə) *n. pl.,* **flo·ras** or **flo·rae** (flôr′ē). the plants or plant life characteristic of a particular region or period. [From *Flora,* the Roman goddess of flowers.]

flo·ral (flôr′əl) *adj.* of, relating to, or like flowers: *a floral arrangement, a perfume with a floral fragrance.*

Flor·ence (flôr′əns, flor′əns) *n.* a city in central Italy. It was one of the world's greatest centers of Renaissance art. Pop. (1970 est.), 460,944.

Flor·en·tine (flôr′ən tēn′, flor′ən tēn′) *n.* a person who was born or is living in Florence. —*adj.* of or relating to Florence, its people, or their culture.

flo·ret (flôr′it) *n.* **1.** a small flower. **2.** *Botany.* one of the small flowers that make up the head of a composite plant, such as the dandelion.

flor·id (flôr′id, flor′id) *adj.* **1.** flushed with redness; ruddy: *a florid complexion.* **2.** too elaborate; ornate; flowery: *The author has a very florid style of writing.* —**flor′id·ly,** *adv.* —**flor′id·ness,** *n.*

Flor·i·da (flôr′ə də, flor′ə də) *n.* a state mostly on the southeastern peninsula of the United States. Capital, Tallahassee. Area, 58,560 sq. mi. Pop. (1970), 6,789,443. Abbreviation, **Fla.**

● **Florida** is a Spanish word meaning "flowery." The name was given to this region by the Spanish explorer Ponce de Leon, who landed there during *Pasqua florida*— the Spanish festival of flowers, which takes place at Easter.

flor·in (flôr′in, flor′in) *n.* any of various European coins, such as a former British coin worth two shillings.

flo·rist (flôr′ist, flor′ist) *n.* a person who sells flowers and ornamental plants.

floss (flôs′, flos′) *n.* **1.** short silk fibers. **2.** a soft, loosely twisted silk thread made from such fibers, used for embroidery. **3.** the soft, silky fibers of fluff found in cotton, corn, milkweed, and other plants.

floss·y (flô′sē) *adj.,* **floss·i·er, floss·i·est.** of, relating to, or like floss.

flo·til·la (flō til′ə) *n.* **1.** a fleet of small vessels: *a flotilla of sailboats.* **2.** a small fleet. **3.** in the U.S. Navy, a group of small ships, as destroyers, usually consisting of two or more squadrons.

flot·sam (flot′səm) *n.* the wreckage of a ship or its cargo, found floating on the sea.

flounce[1] (flouns) *v.t.,* **flounced, flounc·ing.** to go or move with an abrupt or impatient motion of the body: *She flounced out of the room in anger.* —*n.* an abrupt or impatient motion of the body: *She sat down with a flounce.* [Probably of Scandinavian origin.]

flounce[2] (flouns) *n.* a wide strip of cloth, gathered along one edge and attached as a trimming, as on the hem of a skirt. —*v.t.,* **flounced, flounc·ing.** to trim or furnish with a flounce or flounces. [Earlier *frounce* a wrinkle, fold, pleat.]

floun·der[1] (floun′dər) *v.i.* **1.** to move or struggle with stumbling or plunging motions: *The hikers floundered about in the mud.* **2.** to struggle in an embarrassed, awkward, or confused way: *The shy boy floundered through his speech.* [Possibly a blend of *founder*[1] + *blunder.*]

floun·der[2] (floun′dər) *n. pl.,* **floun·ders** or **floun·der.** a flatfish used for food. [Old French *flondre.*]

flour (flour) *n.* a fine, powdery meal made by grinding and sifting grain, especially wheat. Flour is used to make baked goods. —*v.t.* to cover or sprinkle with flour.

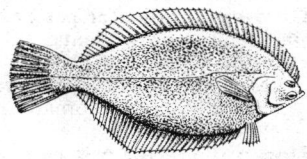

Flounder

flour·ish (flur′ish) *v.i.* **1.** to grow or develop strongly or prosperously; thrive: *Crops flourish in rich soil. His business is flourishing.* **2.** to reach or be at the highest point of development or achievement: *The Aztec civilization flourished hundreds of years ago.* —*v.t.* to wave about with bold or sweeping gestures; brandish: *to flourish a flag.* —*n. pl.,* **flour·ish·es 1.** a fancy or showy action or display. **2.** a decorative stroke in writing. **3.** a passage or series of notes added to a musical work.

flout (flout) *v.t.* to treat with contempt; show no respect for; scoff at; defy: *to flout the law, to flout tradition.* —**flout′er,** *n.* ▲ See **flaunt** for usage note.

flow (flō) *v.i.* **1.** to move or pass along steadily in a stream: *The river flows northward. The electricity flowed through the wire.* **2.** to move along smoothly or continuously: *Conversation at the party flowed freely. Crowds flowed toward the stadium.* **3.** to be full or plentiful; overflow: *Her heart was flowing with happiness.* **4.** to hang, fall, or ripple

at; āpe; cär; end; mē; it; īce; hot; ōld; fôrk;
wood; fōōl; oil; out; up; turn; sing; thin; this;
hw in white; zh in treasure. The symbol ə
stands for the sound of **a** in about, **e** in taken,
i in pencil, **o** in lemon, and **u** in circus.

F

loosely: *Her hair flowed to her waist.* **5.** to rise, as the tide: *The waters ebb and flow.* —*n.* **1.** the act or way of flowing: *to stop the flow of blood from a cut.* **2.** any continuous movement; outpouring; stream: *a heavy flow of traffic.* **3.** something that flows.

flow·er (flou′ər) *n.* **1.** the part of certain plants that is composed of the reproductive organs and their surrounding, usually brightly colored petals; blossom; bloom. **2.** a plant grown for the beauty of its blossoms: *Roses and tulips are my favorite flowers.* **3.** the condition or time of blossoming: *an apple orchard in flower.* **4.** the finest or choicest part or example: *the flower of a country's youth.* **5.** the finest or most active period: *in the flower of manhood, the days when knighthood was in flower.* —*v.i.* **1.** to produce flowers; bloom: *Cherry trees flower in the early spring.* **2.** to be at or reach fullest development or growth: *The poet's writing ability flowered early.* —**flow′er·like′,** *adj.*

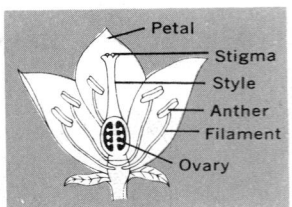

Petal
Stigma
Style
Anther
Filament
Ovary

Parts of a flower

flow·ered (flou′ərd) *adj.* having flowers or decorated with a design of flowers: *a flowered hillside, a flowered blouse.*

flow·er·et (flou′ər it) *n.* a small flower.

flowering plant, any of a large group of plants including trees and shrubs whose seeds are enclosed in an ovary. Flowering plants make up the largest division of the plant kingdom, including more than half of all known plants. Also, **angiosperm.**

flow·er·pot (flou′ər pot′) *n.* a pot, usually made of clay, in which to grow plants.

flow·er·y (flou′ər ē) *adj.,* **flow·er·i·er, flow·er·i·est.** **1.** covered with or like flowers. **2.** using or containing fancy, elegant, or ornate language: *a flowery letter.* —**flow′er·i·ness,** *n.*

flown (flōn) the past participle of **fly².**

fl. oz., fluid ounce; fluid ounces.

flu (flōō) *n.* see **influenza.**

fluc·tu·ate (fluk′chōō āt′) *v.i.,* **fluc·tu·at·ed, fluc·tu·at·ing.** to rise and fall; change; waver: *The patient's temperature fluctuated. Prices on the stock market fluctuate daily.* —**fluc′tu·a′tion,** *n.*

flue (flōō) *n.* a passage through which smoke, hot air, or waste gases pass, as in a chimney.

flu·en·cy (flōō′ən sē) *n.* ease or smoothness in speaking or writing.

flu·ent (flōō′ənt) *adj.* **1.** spoken or written smoothly and easily: *fluent poetry.* **2.** capable of speaking or writing smoothly and effortlessly: *He is fluent in Spanish.* —**flu′ent·ly,** *adv.*

fluff (fluf) *n.* **1.** a soft, light, downy material. **2.** a soft, downy mass: *A fluff of brown hair surrounded her face.* **3.** *Informal.* an error or blunder, especially one made by a performer in speaking his lines. —*v.t.* **1.** to shake, pat, or puff out into a soft mass: *to fluff up a pillow. The bird fluffed its feathers.* **2.** *Informal.* to make an error or blunder in: *The actor fluffed his lines.*

fluff·y (fluf′ē) *adj.,* **fluff·i·er, fluff·i·est.** consisting of, covered with, or resembling fluff: *a fluffy sweater.* —**fluff′i·ly,** *adv.* —**fluff′i·ness,** *n.*

flu·id (flōō′id) *n.* **1.** a substance, as a liquid or gas, that is capable of flowing, has no definite shape, and adapts itself to the shape of any container that confines it. **2.** any liquid: *The doctor told her to stay in bed and drink plenty of fluids.* —*adj.* **1.** capable of flowing; not solid; liquid or gaseous. **2.** of, relating to, or consisting of fluids: *a fluid diet.* **3.** changing readily; not fixed, firm, or stable: *The plans for the dance are still fluid.* —**flu′id·ly,** *adv.* —**flu′id·ness,** *n.*

fluid dram, a liquid measure of capacity equal to ⅛ of a fluid ounce.

flu·id·i·ty (flōō id′ə tē) *n.* the condition or quality of being fluid.

fluid ounce, a liquid measure of capacity equal to 1/16 of a pint.

fluke¹ (flōōk) *n.* **1.** either of the two flat, triangular pieces on an anchor that catch in the ground underwater. **2.** a barb or barbed head, as of an arrow, harpoon, or spear. **3.** either of the two horizontal fins of a whale's tail. [Possibly from *fluke³.*]

fluke² (flōōk) *n.* an unexpected or accidental stroke or turn, especially of good luck; chance happening: *We met by a fluke.* [Of uncertain origin.]

fluke³ (flōōk) *n.* **1.** any of various flatfish, especially a flounder. **2.** any of a group of parasitic flatworms that live in many kinds of animals; trematode. [Old English *flōc* this fish.]

flume (flōōm) *n.* **1.** a deep, narrow passage or ravine through which a stream runs. **2.** an artificial chute or trough that carries water, as for moving logs or furnishing water power.

flung (flung) the past tense and past participle of **fling.**

flunk (flungk) *Informal. v.t.* **1.** to fail to pass; fail: *to flunk a test, to flunk a course.* **2.** to give a failing grade or mark to: *His teacher flunked him.* —*v.i.* to fail, as in an examination.

to flunk out. to be dismissed, as from a school, because of failing grades.

flunk·ey (flung′kē) *n. pl.,* **flunk·eys.** another spelling of **flunky.**

flunk·y (flung′kē) *n. pl.,* **flunk·ies. 1.** a person who fawns on or does menial tasks for another. **2.** formerly, a footman or other male servant.

flu·o·resce (floo res′) *v.i.,* **flu·o·resced, flu·o·resc·ing.** to produce or show fluorescence.

flu·o·res·cence (floo res′əns) *n.* **1.** a giving off of light from a substance that is absorbing radiant energy, such as X rays or ultraviolet rays. Fluorescence continues only as long as the substance is exposed to the source of energy. **2.** a light given off in this way.

flu·o·res·cent (floo res′ənt) *adj.* producing, resulting from, or showing fluorescence.

fluorescent lamp, an electric lamp that produces ultraviolet light and converts it into visible light.

flu·o·ri·date (floor′ə dāt′) *v.t.,* **flu·o·ri·dat·ed, flu·o·ri·dat·ing.** to add a fluoride to (drinking water), especially in order to reduce tooth decay. —**flu′o·ri·da′tion,** *n.*

flu·o·ride (floor′īd) *n.* a compound consisting of fluorine and another element or radical.

flu·o·rine (floor′ēn) *n.* a greenish-yellow, poisonous, very corrosive gas that is the most reactive nonmetallic element. Symbol: F

flu·o·ro·scope (floor′ə skōp′) *n.* an instrument used to examine internal structures or parts, as of the body. It consists of an X-ray machine and a fluorescent screen that shows patterns of light and shadow cast by the different amounts of X rays allowed to pass through the internal structures or parts. —*v.t.,* **flu·o·ro·scoped, flu·o·ro·scop·ing.** to examine with a fluoroscope.

flur·ry (flur′ē) *n. pl.,* **flur·ries. 1.** a sudden commotion; stir: *a flurry of activity, a flurry of excitement.* **2.** a light, scattered snowfall, usually accompanied by gusts of wind. **3.** a brief, sudden gust: *a flurry of wind.* —*v.t.,* **flur·ried, flur·ry·ing.** to excite, confuse, or agitate.

flush¹ (flush) *v.i.* **1.** to turn red; blush; glow: *His face flushed with embarrassment. He flushed when he answered the question incorrectly.* **2.** to flow or rush suddenly: *Water flushed through the pipes.* —*v.t.* **1.** to cause to redden: *Fever flushed the child's face.* **2.** to clean, empty, or wash with a sudden, rapid rush or flow, as of water: *to flush out a drain, to flush a toilet.* **3.** to make proud or excited: *He was flushed with success.* —*n. pl.,* **flush·es. 1.** a reddish color or glow. **2.** a rush or surge of pride, excitement, or other emotion. **3.** a flowing vigor or freshness: *the first flush of spring.* **4.** a rapid, sudden rush or flow, as of water. [Possibly a blend of *flash* and *blush.*]

flush² (flush) *adj.* **1.** having direct contact; touching: *The table was flush against the wall.* **2.** even or level, as with a surface: *The house is flush with the road.* **3.** well supplied, especially with money. —*adv.* **1.** in immediate or direct contact: *He set the bureau flush against the wall.* **2.** in an even or level manner: *They placed the second picture flush with the first.* **3.** directly; squarely: *to hit someone flush on the chin.* [Probably from *flush¹.*]

flush³ (flush) *v.t.* to drive from cover or from a hiding place: *We flushed a covey of quail under a high clay bank* (Ernest Hemingway). [Of uncertain origin.]

flush⁴ (flush) *n.* in poker, a hand in which all of the cards are of the same suit. [French *flux* a flowing.]

flus·ter (flus'tər) *v.t.* to cause to be embarrassed or nervous; agitate and confuse: *The laughter of the audience flustered the speaker.* —*n.* a state of agitated or nervous confusion.

flute (flōōt) *n.* **1.** a musical instrument of the woodwind family, consisting of a hollow tube with keys along its length and played by blowing through a mouth hole near one end. **2.** a shallow, rounded groove on the shaft of a column. **3.** any similar groove, especially a decorative one. —*v.,* **flut·ed, flut·ing.** —*v.i.* **1.** to play on a flute. **2.** to make a sound like that of a flute: —*v.t.* **1.** to utter with a sound like that of a flute. **2.** to make flutes in: *to flute the edges of a pie crust.*

Flute

flut·ing (flōō'ting) *n.* **1.** a decoration with flutes or grooves. **2.** a groove or a series of grooves.

flut·ist (flōō'tist) *also,* **flau·tist.** *n.* a person who plays the flute.

flut·ter (flut'ər) *v.i.* **1.** to wave or flap quickly and lightly: *The flag fluttered in the breeze.* **2.** to fly, hover, or flap the wings lightly, gracefully, and quickly: *Butterflies fluttered among the flowers.* **3.** to fall or move with light, irregular motion: *Leaves fluttered to the ground.* **4.** to move about lightly, quickly, or in a nervous, excited way: *She fluttered about the room.* **5.** to beat quickly and irregularly, as the heart. —*v.t.* to cause to flutter: *She fluttered her eyelashes at him.* —*n.* **1.** a quick, light movement: *the flutter of a bird's wings.* **2.** a condition of nervous confusion or excitement: *The children were in a flutter as they waited to open their Christmas presents.* —**flut'ter·er,** *n.*

flux (fluks) *n. pl.,* **flux·es. 1.** constant change or movement: *His plans for the future were in a state of flux.* **2.** a flowing or flow. **3.** a substance, such as lime, that makes metals melt more easily, used chiefly in metal refining. **4.** a substance, such as rosin, used in soldering to help the fusion of metals by preventing oxidation. **5.** *Physics.* **a.** the rate of flow of fluids, particles, or energy, such as light or other radiant energy, through a given area. **b.** see **magnetic flux. 6.** an abnormal, excessive discharge of liquid matter from the body.

fly¹ (flī) *n. pl.,* **flies. 1.** any of a large group of insects, including houseflies, mosquitoes, and gnats, that have sucking mouth parts and one pair of transparent wings. **2.** any of various other flying insects. **3.** a fishhook that is decorated with feathers or other material, so that it looks like an insect. [Old English *flȳge, flēoge* a winged insect.]

fly² (flī) *v., (v.i. defs. 1–6, v.t.)* **flew, flown, fly·ing** or *(v.i. def. 7)* **flied, fly·ing.** —*v.i.* **1.** to move through the air by using wings, as a bird does. **2.** to operate, move, or travel in an aircraft or spacecraft: *The pilot flew to Chicago. They flew to Los Angeles last night.* **3.** to pass, move, or be propelled through the air by the wind or other force: *The ocean spray flew into our faces.* **4.** to wave or flutter in the air: *A flag flew from the ship's mast.* **5.** to move or pass swiftly; speed: *She flew up the stairs when she heard the child crying.* **6.** to change rapidly and suddenly from one state, condition, or position to another: *to fly into a rage. The door flew open.* **7.** *Baseball.* to hit a fly ball: *The batter flied to left field.* —*v.t.* **1.** to cause to move through the air: *The boy went to the park to fly his kite.* **2.** to operate (an aircraft or spacecraft): *He flew a bomber during the war.* **3.** to travel or pass over, as in an aircraft: *They flew the Atlantic Ocean in five hours.* **4.** to carry or transport by air: *They flew supplies to the flooded town.* —*n. pl.,* **flies. 1.** a flap of material covering a zipper or row of buttons on a piece of clothing, especially on the front of a pair of trousers. **2.** *Baseball.* see **fly ball. 3.** a piece of canvas put up in front of or over a tent to provide extra protection. [Old English *flēogan.*]
    on the fly. while still in flight; before touching the ground: *He caught the ball on the fly.*
    to let fly. to throw or shoot: *to let fly a stone.*

fly ball *Baseball.* a ball hit high into the air.

fly·catch·er (flī'kach'ər) *n.* any of various birds that feed on insects that they catch while flying.

fly·er (flī'ər) another spelling of **flier.**

flying boat, a seaplane having a body shaped like the hull of a boat.

flying buttress, an arched support between a pier or other structure and the wall of a building, used to help the wall bear the weight of the roof.

flying fish, any of a group of saltwater fish that are found in warm waters and have one or two pairs of winglike fins that enable them to leap into the air and glide for some distance.

flying jib, a small, triangular sail set out in front of the jib.

flying saucer, any of various unidentified flying objects that are said to be shaped like a saucer and thought by some people to be from outer space.

flying squirrel, any of various squirrels having membranes between the front and hind legs that resemble wings and which enable them to make long, gliding leaps through the air.

fly·leaf (flī'lēf') *n. pl.,* **fly·leaves** (flī'lēvz').

Flying buttress

at; āpe; cär; end; mē; it; īce; hot; ōld; fôrk;
wood; fōōl; oil; out; up; turn; sing; thin; **this;**
hw in white; zh in treasure. The symbol ə
stands for the sound of **a** in about, **e** in taken,
i in pencil, **o** in lemon, and **u** in circus.

a blank sheet of paper at the beginning or end of a book.

fly·pa·per (flī′pā′pər) *n.* paper covered with a sticky or poisonous substance, used to catch or kill flies.

fly·speck (flī′spek′) *n.* **1.** a tiny spot of dirt left by a fly. **2.** any very small spot.

fly swatter, a device for killing flies or other insects, usually a square piece of mesh attached to a long handle.

fly·trap (flī′trap′) *n.* any of various plants that trap insects, such as the Venus's-flytrap.

fly·way (flī′wā′) *n.* a particular air route along which birds regularly migrate.

fly·weight (flī′wāt′) *n.* an athlete competing in the lightest weight class in boxing and wrestling.

fly·wheel (flī′hwēl′, flī′wēl′) *n.* a heavy wheel that regulates the speed of an engine.

Fm, the symbol for fermium.

FM 1. a method of radio broadcasting by which a signal is transmitted over radio carrier waves by altering the frequency of the waves. **2.** a broadcasting system using this method. **3.** of, relating to, or using an FM broadcasting system: *an FM radio, an FM station.* [Abbreviation of *f*(requency) *m*(odulation).]

f number, in photography, a number obtained by dividing the focal length of a lens by its diameter. The f number expresses the size to which the lens opening in a camera is adjusted and indicates the amount of light let in by the lens at that setting. The lower the f number, the wider the lens opening.

foal (fōl) *n.* a young horse, donkey, zebra, or other member of the horse family, especially one less than one year of age. —*v.i.* to give birth to a foal: *The mare foaled in the spring.*

foam (fōm) *n.* a frothy mass of bubbles, as that formed on the surface of a liquid: *the foam formed by breaking waves, the foam left in a glass of beer.* —*v.i.* **1.** to form or produce foam: *The water foamed and bubbled when the soap flakes were added.* **2.** to flow or gush in a foam.

foam rubber, a spongy rubber used for mattresses, upholstery, and insulation.

foam·y (fō′mē) *adj.,* **foam·i·er, foam·i·est.** covered with, consisting of, or like foam: *foamy waves.* —**foam′i·ness,** *n.*

fob¹ (fob) *n.* **1.** a short chain or ribbon attached to a watch, often worn hanging from a watch pocket. **2.** an ornament worn at the end of such a chain or ribbon. **3.** a small pocket for holding a watch, as in the front of a vest or just below the waist in trousers. [Probably of Germanic origin.]

fob² (fob) *v.t.,* **fobbed, fob·bing.** to trick; cheat. [Middle English *fobben* to trick, deceive, cheat.]

to fob off. a. to get rid of (something worthless) by trickery or deception: *to fob off counterfeit money.* **b.** to put (someone) off by trickery or deception.

F.O.B., free on board.

fo·cal (fō′kəl) *adj.* of, at, or relating to a focus. —**fo′cal·ly,** *adv.*

focal length, the distance from the center of a lens or mirror to the focus. Also, **focal distance.**

fo·cus (fō′kəs) *n. pl.,* **fo·cus·es,** or **fo·ci** (fō′sī). **1.** the point at which converging rays, especially light rays, meet after being refracted by a lens or reflected by a mirror. **2.** the point from which diverging rays, especially light rays, appear to originate, after having undergone such refraction or reflection. **3.** another word

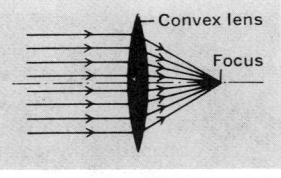

Focus

for **focal length. 4.** an adjustment, as of a lens or the eye, necessary to produce a clear image: *These binoculars are not in focus.* **5.** the condition of being clear or understandable: *His explanation brought the meaning of the events into focus for us.* **6.** a central point or center, as of activity, interest, or importance: *The speaker was the focus of attention.* **7.** *Geometry.* a fixed point or one of two fixed points used in determining an ellipse, parabola, or hyperbola. **8.** the center or point of origin of an earthquake. —*v.,* **focused, fo·cus·ing;** *also, British,* **fo·cussed, fo·cus·sing.** —*v.t.* **1.** to bring to a focus or into focus: *The photographer focused the camera.* **2.** to fix; concentrate: *The audience focused its attention on the speaker.* —*v.i.* to become focused. [Latin *focus* hearth; because the hearth was the center of the Roman home.]

fod·der (fod′ər) *n.* food for livestock, made by cutting and drying various grasses, such as alfalfa, or the stalks and leaves of corn.

foe (fō) *n.* enemy; adversary: *You shall judge a man by his foes as well as by his friends* (Joseph Conrad).

foe·tus (fē′təs) *n. pl.,* **foe·tus·es.** another spelling of **fetus.**

fog (fog) *n.* **1.** a cloud of very small water droplets in the air, at or close to the earth's surface. **2.** any hazy condition: *a fog of dust, a fog of smoke.* **3.** a condition of confusion or bewilderment; daze: *He was really in a fog after the long exam.* —*v.,* **fogged, fog·ging.** —*v.t.* **1.** to cover or obscure with fog: *The tops of the skyscrapers were fogged.* **2.** to confuse; bewilder: *The heat fogged his brain.* —*v.i.* to become covered or obscured with fog.

fog·gy (fog′ē) *adj.,* **fog·gi·er, fog·gi·est. 1.** full of or obscured by fog: *a foggy day.* **2.** confused or unclear; vague: *foggy thinking.* —**fog′gi·ly,** *adv.* —**fog′gi·ness,** *n.*

fog·horn (fog′hôrn′) *n.* a horn or similar device that is used for sounding warning signals during a fog, as to boats.

fo·gy (fō′gē) *also,* **fo·gey.** *n. pl.,* **fo·gies.** a person who has old-fashioned ideas, habits, or ways.

foi·ble (foi′bəl) *n.* a minor weakness of character; shortcoming: *Always being late is one of her foibles.*

foil¹ (foil) *v.t.* to interfere with or stop from being successful: *The police foiled the robbery attempt.* [Old French *fouler* to trample on, hurt.]

foil² (foil) *n.* **1.** metal hammered or rolled into a very thin, flexible sheet: *aluminum foil.* **2.** a person or thing that sets off another by comparison or contrast: *Her black dress was the perfect foil for her blonde hair.* [Old French *foil* a leaf of metal.]

foil³ (foil) *n.* a long, flexible fencing sword that tapers from the hilt to the point. The point of a foil is blunted or padded to prevent injury. [Of uncertain origin.]

foist (foist) *v.t.* to pass off or offer (something false or worthless) as genuine or valuable: *The salesman tried to foist a broken radio on us.*

fold¹ (fōld) *v.t.* **1.** to bend or double over on itself: *Fold the paper in half. Fold the chairs up and lean them against the wall.* **2.** to bring together close to the body: *She folded her hands in her lap. The bird folded its wings.* **3.** to put the arms around; embrace; clasp: *The mother folded the crying child in her arms.* **4.** *Cooking.* to add or blend (an ingredient) into a mixture by repeatedly turning one part over another gently: *Next fold the egg whites in.* —*v.i.* **1.** to be or become folded: *Paper folds more easily than cardboard.* **2.** *Informal.* to end or close, especially as a result of financial failure: *His business folded. The play folded up within a month.* —*n.* **1.** a part that is folded; pleat: *Her dress hung in graceful folds.* **2.** a mark or crease made by folding: *Cut the paper along the fold.* [Old English *fealdan.*]

fold² (fōld) *n.* **1.** a pen or other enclosure for livestock, especially for sheep. **2.** a group, such as the congregation of a church or a political party, under the guidance of a leader or having common beliefs, aims, or values. [Old English *falod.*]

-fold *suffix* **1.** (a specified number of) times as much or as great: *a tenfold increase.* **2.** having (a specified number of) parts: *a twofold problem.*

fold·er (fōl′dər) *n.* **1.** a holder or container for loose papers, usually a folded sheet of light cardboard. **2.** a sheet of printed material, as a circular, timetable, or map, folded into a number of pages: *The travel folder showed pictures of London.* **3.** a person or thing that folds.

fol·de·rol (fol′də rol′) *also,* **fal·de·ral.** *n.* foolish talk; nonsense.

fo·li·age (fō′lē ij) *n.* the growth of leaves on a tree or other plant.

fo·li·a·tion (fō′lē ā′shən) *n.* the act or process of putting forth leaves.

fol·ic acid (fō′lik) a vitamin of the vitamin B complex, used in treating certain forms of anemia.

fo·li·o (fō′lē ō′) *n. pl.,* **fo·li·os. 1.** a sheet of paper folded once to form two leaves, or four pages, of a book. **2.** a book usually more than eleven inches in height, made up of sheets folded in this way. **3.** a page number of a book. —*adj.* of or having the size or form of a folio.

folk (fōk) *n. pl.,* **folk** or **folks. 1.** *also,* **folks.** people: *city folk, old folks.* **2. folks.** *Informal.* one's family or relatives, especially one's parents: *During the vacation he is going home to see his folks.* **3.** a nation or race; people. —*adj.* of or coming from the common people: *a folk custom, folk art.*

folk dance 1. a dance originating among the common people of a region or country and handed down from generation to generation. **2.** the music for such a dance.

folk etymology 1. a change in the form of a word because of an incorrect assumption about its origin. **2.** a popular but incorrect belief about the origin of a word.

● In language, a **folk etymology** is a commonly accepted wrong idea about the origin or meaning of a word. In certain cases, however, a folk etymology can become so generally accepted that changes take place in the spelling or meaning of a word as a result. For example, the article of furniture called a *chaise longue* takes its name from the French words meaning "long chair." But because this chair is used for lounging, many people now call it a *chaise lounge.* People tend to change unfamiliar words to connect them with words that are more familiar to them, and the word *lounge* is well known, while *longue* is not.

The cut of beef that we call *sirloin* is another example of folk etymology. Many people believe that its name comes from an English king knighting the loin of beef, because a knight is given the title *sir.* In fact, *sirloin* came from a French word *surlonge,* meaning "over or above the loin."

An area in which folk etymologies are quite common is *acronyms,* which are words made by combining the first letter or letters of a series of words. Acronyms are a relatively new feature of our language and are rarely formed to make common words. Despite this, many people believe that some of the old and common words of our language developed this way. For example, the informal word *cop,* meaning a policeman, is often thought of as being an acronym formed from Constable of Police, the words that used to be written on a policeman's hat. Actually, *cop* is a much older word, going all the way back to the Latin word *capere,* meaning "to take."

folk·lore (fōk′lôr′) *n.* the tales, beliefs, customs, or other traditions of a people, handed down from generation to generation.

folk music, the traditional music of the common people of a region or country.

folk singer, a singer who performs folk songs.

folk song 1. a traditional song, usually originating among the common people and handed down from generation to generation. Folk songs often have a simple tune and appear in different versions. **2.** a modern song written in imitation of a traditional folk song.

folk·sy (fōk′sē) *adj.,* **folk·si·er, folk·si·est.** *Informal.* friendly and simple. —**folk′si·ly,** *adv.* —**folk′si·ness,** *n.*

folk tale, a story that is part of the folklore of a people and often appears in different versions.

folk·way (fōk′wā′) *n.* a tradition or custom of a people or group.

fol·li·cle (fol′i kəl) *n.* **1.** a small cavity, sac, or gland in the body. Hair grows from follicles. **2.** a dry fruit that splits open along one seam when it is ripe and releases its seeds.

fol·low (fol′ō) *v.t.* **1.** to go or come after: *The dog followed the boy obediently. Spring follows winter.* **2.** to go along: *Follow the river to the fork.* **3.** to act according to; obey: *to follow orders. Follow the directions on the package.* **4.** to watch or observe closely: *The police followed the suspect's movements from across the street. We followed his career as a singer closely.* **5.** to understand: *I don't follow your reasoning.* **6.** to use as a guide or model; imitate: *Follow his example.* **7.** to make a living from: *to follow the legal profession.* **8.** to result from: *Disaster followed the flood.* **9.** to try to overtake or capture; pursue: *The detective followed the suspect for three days.* —*v.i.* to go, come, or happen after some person or thing: *He entered the house and his friend followed.*

  to follow through. a. to continue with to an end; complete: *to follow through an assignment.* **b.** to continue the motion of a stroke after hitting the ball, as in tennis or golf.

  to follow up. a. to pursue to an end: *The reporter followed up on the story.* **b.** to add to the effect of by doing something more: *The enemy followed up the battle with a surprise attack.*

fol·low·er (fol′ō ər) *n.* **1.** a person or thing that follows. **2.** a person who follows the beliefs or ideas of another, as a supporter, disciple, or admirer: *That civil rights leader is a follower of Martin Luther King.*

fol·low·ing (fol′ō ing) *adj.* coming after or next in order or time: *the following morning.* —*n.* **1.** a body of followers: *That author has a large following.* **2. the following.** those about to be mentioned: *The following are the boys who will be in the play.*

fol·ly (fol′ē) *n. pl.,* **fol·lies. 1.** a lack of good sense or understanding; foolishness. **2.** something foolish.

fo·ment (fō ment′) *v.t.* to stir up; incite: *to foment rebellion, to foment trouble.* —**fo·ment′er,** *n.*

fond (fond) *adj.* **1.** liking or loving: *to be fond of animals, a fond smile.* **2.** too loving or indulgent; doting: *a fond aunt.* **3.** deeply felt; cherished: *a fond wish.* —**fond′ly,** *adv.* —**fond′ness,** *n.*

at; āpe; cär; end; mē; it; īce; hot; ōld; fôrk; wood; fōōl; oil; out; up; turn; sing; thin; this; hw in white; zh in treasure. The symbol ə stands for the sound of **a** in about, **e** in taken, **i** in pencil, **o** in lemon, and **u** in circus.

fon·dant (fon′dənt) *n.* a smooth, creamy mixture made of sugar, used as a filling or icing or eaten as candy.

fon·dle (fond′əl) *v.t.,* **fon·dled, fon·dling.** to stroke or touch lovingly or tenderly; caress: *The boy fondled his dog's ears.* —**fon′dler,** *n.*

font[1] (font) *n.* **1.** a basin or other receptacle, often made of stone, used to hold the water for baptism. **2.** a basin or other receptacle for holy water. **3.** a fountain; source: *The old man was a font of wisdom.* [Old English *font.*]

font[2] (font) *n. Printing.* a complete assortment of type of one size and style. [French *fonte* a casting (of metals).]

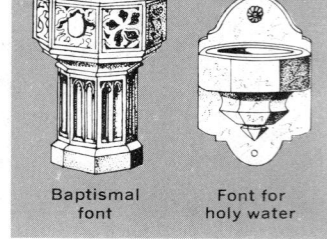

Baptismal font   Font for holy water

Fonts[1]

Foo·chow (fōō′chou′) *n.* a port city in southeastern China, opposite Taiwan. Pop. (1958 est.), 623,000. Also, **Fuzhou.**

food (fōōd) *n.* **1.** something that is eaten or taken in by a plant or animal to sustain life, provide energy, and aid in growth and repair of tissues; nourishment. **2.** nourishment that is eaten rather than drunk: *There was food and drink at the party.* **3.** something that stimulates or aids an activity: *The interesting book was food for thought.*

food chain, a sequence of the plants and animals of a community, in which each plant or animal in the sequence feeds upon the one below it. An example of a food chain is plant—plant louse—ladybug—spider—small bird—hawk—and so on. Each dash in the food chain means "is eaten by."

food poisoning, a sickness caused by eating foods that have been contaminated by harmful bacteria.

food·stuff (fōōd′stuf′) *n.* a substance used as food.

fool (fōōl) *n.* **1.** a person who lacks judgment or good sense; unwise or silly person. **2.** a clown formerly kept by a king or nobleman to entertain the household; jester. —*v.t.* to deceive; trick: *His Santa Claus disguise did not fool the children.* —*v.i.* **1.** to act like a fool; be silly: *Stop fooling and get to work.* **2.** to act or speak in a jesting or playful manner; tease; joke: *Don't be angry; I was only fooling.* —*adj. Informal.* foolish; silly: *a fool notion.*

to fool around. *Informal.* to spend time idly or aimlessly: *The team was just fooling around on the court and not really practicing.*

to fool with. to play or meddle aimlessly or thoughtlessly with: *Do not fool with that gun.*

fool·er·y (fōōl′ər ē) *n. pl.,* **fool·er·ies.** foolish behavior.

fool·har·dy (fōōl′här′dē) *adj.,* **fool·har·di·er, fool·har·di·est.** bold or daring in a foolish way; rash; reckless: *a foolhardy young man, a foolhardy thing to do.* —**fool′·har′di·ly,** *adv.* —**fool′har′di·ness,** *n.*

fool·ish (fōō′lish) *adj.* **1.** showing a lack of understanding or good sense; unwise; silly: *Buying that old car was foolish.* **2.** ridiculous; absurd: *You look foolish in that dress.* —**fool′ish·ly,** *adv.* —**fool′ish·ness,** *n.*

fool·proof (fōōl′prōōf′) *adj.* so simple or safe as to make error, misuse, or failure impossible: *a foolproof plan.*

fools·cap (fōōlz′kap′) *n.* **1.** writing paper varying in size from about 12 by 15 inches to 13½ by 17 inches. **2.** another spelling of **fool's cap.**

fool's cap, a jester's cap or hood, usually having several drooping peaks from which bells are hung.

fool's gold, any of various minerals that look like gold, such as pyrite.

foot (foot) *n. pl.,* **feet. 1.** the end part of the leg, on which man and certain other animals stand or walk. **2.** any similar part or organ in other animals and plants. **3.** something like a foot in shape, position, or use. **4.** the lowest or supporting part: *the foot of a mountain, the foot of a ladder.* **5.** the part far from or opposite the head: *the foot of a bed.* **6.** a part that covers the foot: *the foot of a stocking.* **7.** a measure of length equal to twelve inches. **8.** a basic unit of rhythm in poetry, consisting of a group of accented and unaccented syllables. The line *The time/you won/your town/the race* has four feet. —*v.t. Informal.* to pay, as a bill: *We footed the cost of the party.*

on foot. walking or running: *Rather than drive, I came on foot.*

to put one's foot down. to make up one's mind and act firmly: *She put her foot down and refused to go.*

under foot. in the way: *The kittens were always under foot.*

foot·ball (foot′bôl′) *n.* **1.** a game played between two teams of eleven players each on a field one hundred yards long with goals at each end. Points are made by getting the ball across the opponent's goal line. **2.** the oval ball used in this game, usually having an inflatable rubber bladder inside a leather covering. **3.** any of several similar games, such as soccer. **4.** a ball used in any of these games.

foot·bridge (foot′brij′) *n.* a bridge for pedestrians only.

foot·can·dle (foot′kand′əl) *also,* **foot·can·dle.** *n.* a unit for measuring illumination, equal to the amount of light produced by one candle on a surface at a distance of one foot.

foot·ed (foot′id) *adj.* **1.** having a foot or feet: *a footed goblet.* **2.** having a specified kind or number of feet. ▲ used in combination in definition 2: *flat-footed, a four-footed animal.*

foot·fall (foot′fôl′) *n.* a footstep or its sound.

foot·hill (foot′hil′) *n.* a low hill at the foot of a mountain or mountain range.

foot·hold (foot′hōld′) *n.* **1.** a place where one may stand or walk securely; hold or support for the feet: *The climber used cracks in the cliff as footholds.* **2.** a firm or secure position from which it is possible to go forward: *Once the disease gained a foothold, it spread rapidly.*

foot·ing (foot′ing) *n.* **1.** the secure or firm placing of the feet: *to lose one's footing.* **2.** a hold or support for the feet: *The icy ledge provided no footing.* **3.** a secure position or condition: *to put a business on a sound footing.*

foot·less (foot′lis) *adj.* **1.** lacking a foot or feet. **2.** having no basis; insubstantial: *footless daydreams.*

foot·lights (foot′līts′) *n., pl.* lights in one or more rows along the front of a stage.

foot·loose (foot′lōōs′) *adj.* free to travel about or live as one pleases; free from responsibilities.

foot·man (foot′mən) *n. pl.,* **foot·men** (foot′mən). a male servant in uniform who assists a butler with various jobs.

foot·note (foot′nōt′) *n.* a note, comment, or explanation, usually at the bottom of a page and indicated in the text by a number or symbol referring to it.

foot·path (foot′path′) *n. pl.,* **foot·paths** (foot′pathz′). a path for pedestrians.

foot·pound (foot′pound′) *n.* a unit of work or energy, equal to the amount of energy required to raise one pound a distance of one foot.

foot·print (foot′print′) *n.* a mark or impression made by a foot: *footprints in the sand. The little boy made dirty footprints all over the kitchen floor.*

foot·rest (foot′rest′) *n.* something, as a small stool or platform, on which the feet may be rested.

foot soldier, a soldier trained or equipped to fight on foot; infantryman.

foot·sore (foot′sôr′) *adj.* having sore or tired feet, as from much walking.

foot·step (foot′step′) *n.* **1.** a step or tread of the foot: *a baby's first awkward footsteps.* **2.** the sound made by this: *I heard his footsteps in the hall.* **3.** the distance covered in a step.

   to follow in someone's footsteps. to imitate or follow the same course as someone: *Dan followed in his father's footsteps and became a teacher.*

foot·stool (foot′stool′) *n.* a low stool on which to place the feet when sitting.

foot·wear (foot′wer′) *n.* coverings to be worn on the feet, such as shoes or slippers.

foot·work (foot′wurk′) *n.* the use of the feet, as in boxing or dancing.

fop (fop) *n.* a man or boy who is too vain about his appearance and has affected manners; dandy.

fop·per·y (fop′ər ē) *n. pl.,* **fop·per·ies.** the behavior, clothing, or manner of a fop.

fop·pish (fop′ish) *adj.* like a fop. —**fop′pish·ly,** *adv.* —**fop′pish·ness,** *n.*

for (fôr; *unstressed* fər) *prep.* **1.** as long as: *The maid worked for an hour.* **2.** as far as: *The boys hiked for five miles.* **3.** used with or made for: *That closet is for canned goods.* **4.** as a result of; because of: *He was praised for his good work.* **5.** in support or defense of: *He is willing to fight for what he believes in.* **6.** to or in the amount of: *He received a check for fifty dollars.* **7.** at the cost or price of: *Ted bought the book for five dollars.* **8.** in order to become or do: *The senator is running for President.* **9.** in order to go toward or reach: *Helen has already left for school.* **10.** sent to; given to; belonging to: *This letter is for Mary.* **11.** in place of; instead of: *He used a cardboard carton for a table.* **12.** on behalf of: *The lawyer spoke for his client.* **13.** considering the usual nature or characteristics of: *It is quite cool for August.* **14.** with the purpose of: *His parents are saving for his college education.* **15.** serving as: *We had eggs for breakfast.* —*conj.* seeing that; because: *We should go, for it is late.*

for·age (fôr′ij, for′ij) *n.* **1.** hay, grain, and other food for cows, horses, and similar animals. **2.** a search for food or supplies. —*v.,* **for·aged, for·ag·ing.** —*v.i.* **1.** to hunt or search for food or supplies: *The birds foraged in the snow.* **2.** to make a search. —*v.t.* **1.** to get by hunting or searching: *to forage a meal.* **2.** to get food or supplies from: *The troops foraged the countryside.* —**for′ag·er,** *n.*

for·ay (fôr′ā, for′ā) *n.* an attack or raid, especially for plunder. —*v.i.* to raid; plunder: *The soldiers forayed in the enemy's lands.*

for·bad (fər bad′) a past tense of **forbid.**

for·bade (fər bad′, fər bād′) a past tense of **forbid.**

for·bear¹ (fôr ber′) *v.,* **for·bore, for·borne, for·bear·ing.** —*v.i.* **1.** to keep oneself from doing something; hold back; refrain: *He forbore from arguing with his younger brother.* **2.** to control oneself or be patient: *When your friends are exasperating, try to forbear, if you can.* —*v.t.* to keep oneself from (doing something); refrain from: *Tom could not forbear smiling at his embarrassed friend.* [Old English *forberan* to hold back.]

for·bear² (fôr′ber) another spelling of **forebear.**

for·bear·ance (fôr ber′əns) *n.* **1.** the act of forbearing. **2.** self-control or patience: *Jim showed great forbearance during his long illness.*

for·bid (fər bid′) *v.t.,* **for·bade** or **for·bad, for·bid·den** or *(archaic)* **for·bid, for·bid·ding.** to order not to do something; refuse to allow; prohibit: *I forbid you to go out. The school forbids eating in the classrooms.*

for·bid·ding (fər bid′ing) *adj.* looking unfriendly or dangerous; frightening; grim: *The old house was dark and forbidding.* —**for·bid′ding·ly,** *adv.*

for·bore (fôr bôr′) the past tense of **forbear¹.**

for·borne (fôr bôrn′) the past participle of **forbear¹.**

force (fôrs) *n.* **1.** power, strength, or energy: *The batter struck the ball with great force. The force of the explosion broke windows in nearby buildings.* **2.** the use of such power, strength, or energy; violence: *The sheriff dragged the outlaw off by force.* **3.** the power to convince, influence, or control: *The force of her argument won us over.* **4.** a group of people organized or available for some purpose or activity: *a police force, a military force, a work force.* **5.** *Physics.* something that causes a body to move or to change or stop its motion: *the force of gravity.* —*v.t.,* **forced, forc·ing.** **1.** to make (someone) do something: *Your question forced me to solve the problem. The Board of Directors forced the president to leave.* **2.** to get by force: *My friend's arguments forced a change in my ideas.* **3.** to bring forth by an effort: *The sick man forced a smile.* **4.** to cause to open or give way by using force; break open: *Jim forced the lock on his suitcase because he had lost the key.* **5.** to make by force: *The man tried to force his way through the crowd.* **6.** *Baseball.* to cause (a base runner) to be put out by hitting the ball so that he is forced to run toward the next base. —**forc′er,** *n.*

   in force. in operation or effect: *The rule against smoking is still in force at school.*

forced (fôrst) *adj.* **1.** done because of the use of force: *The road was built long ago by forced labor.* **2.** affected; strained: *a forced smile.* **3.** done because of an emergency: *The plane made a forced landing.*

force·ful (fôrs′fəl) *adj.* full of or having much force; powerful; vigorous; effective: *a forceful personality.* —**force′ful·ly,** *adv.* —**force′ful·ness,** *n.*

for·ceps (fôr′seps) *n. pl.,* **for·ceps.** pincers used for holding or pulling, especially by dentists or surgeons.

for·ci·ble (fôr′sə bəl) *adj.* **1.** done by force; resulting from force: *The burglar made a forcible entry into the apartment.* **2.** having force; powerful; effective: *a forcible argument.* —**for′ci·bly,** *adv.*

ford (fôrd) *n.* a shallow place where a river, stream, or other body of water may be crossed. —*v.t.* to cross (a body of water) at a shallow place. —**ford′able,** *adj.*

Ford (fôrd) **1. Gerald R.** 1913—, the thirty-eighth president of the United States, from 1974–1977. **2. Henry.** 1863–1947, U.S. automobile manufacturer.

fore¹ (fôr) *adj.* at or toward the front; forward: *the fore part of a ship.* —*n.* the bow of a boat or ship. —*adv.* at or toward the bow of a boat or ship. [Old English *fore* for, before.]

   to the fore. into view or a prominent position: *Mona came to the fore as the best athlete in school.*

fore² (fôr) *interj.* a warning cry made on a golf course to persons ahead just before the ball is hit. [Probably short for *before.*]

fore- *prefix* **1.** in front: *foremast, forelock.* **2.** coming beforehand: *forenamed, foretell.*

fore-and-aft (fôr′ən aft′) *adj.* from bow to stern of a ship: *a fore-and-aft sail.*

F

373

fore and aft **1.** from bow to stern of a ship. **2.** in, at, or toward both the bow and the stern of a ship.

fore·arm[1] (fôr′ärm′) *n.* the part of the arm between the elbow and wrist. [*Fore-* + *arm*[1].]

fore·arm[2] (fôr ärm′) *v.t.* to prepare beforehand for something, especially for trouble. [*Fore-* + *arm*[2].]

fore·bear (fôr′ber) *also,* **for·bear** *n.* an ancestor; forefather.

fore·bode (fôr bōd′) *v.t.,* **fore·bod·ed, for·bod·ing. 1.** to be a warning of: *The primitive people believed that certain omens forboded disaster.* **2.** to have a feeling of (something evil or bad to come). —**fore·bod′er,** *n.*

fore·bod·ing (fôr bō′ding) *n.* a feeling that something evil or bad is going to happen.

fore·cast (fôr′kast′) *v.t.,* **fore·cast** or **fore·cast·ed, fore·cast·ing.** to tell what may or will happen; make known ahead of time; predict: *to forecast the weather.* —*n.* a prediction: *a weather forecast.* —**fore′cast′er,** *n.*

fore·cas·tle (fōk′səl, fôr′kas′əl) *n.* **1.** the part of the upper deck of a ship that is in front of the foremast. **2.** sailors' quarters located in the forward section of a ship.

fore·close (fôr klōz′) *v.,* **fore·closed, fore·clos·ing.** —*v.t.* **1.** to take away the right to pay off (a mortgage). **2.** to prevent; stop: *The speaker foreclosed all discussion by refusing to answer questions.* —*v.i.* to foreclose a mortgage: *The bank foreclosed, and the farmer lost his property.*

fore·clo·sure (fôr klō′zhər) *n.* a legal proceeding that takes away a person's right to pay off a mortgage and to keep possession of his mortgaged property, because he has failed to meet the conditions of the mortgage.

fore·deck (fôr′dek′) *n.* the forward part of a ship's main deck.

fore·doom (fôr dōōm′) *v.t.* to doom ahead of time.

fore·fa·ther (fôr′fä′thər) *n.* an ancestor.

fore·fin·ger (fôr′fing′gər) *n.* the finger next to the thumb; index finger.

fore·foot (fôr′foot′) *n. pl.,* **fore·feet.** one of the front feet of an insect or a four-legged animal.

fore·front (fôr′frunt′) *n.* a place in the front; first or most important position: *the forefront of a battle, the forefront of a reform movement.*

fore·gath·er (fôr gath′ər) another spelling of **forgather.**

fore·go (fôr gō′) *v.t.,* **fore·went, fore·gone, fore·go·ing.** another spelling of **forgo.**

fore·go·ing (fôr gō′ing) *adj.* going before; preceding: *the foregoing example.*

fore·gone (fôr′gôn′, fôr′gon′) *adj.* **1.** that has gone before or gone by; previous; past: *in a foregone era.* **2.** that is settled or known ahead of time; certain; inevitable: *a foregone conclusion.*

fore·ground (fôr′ground′) *n.* **1.** the part of a picture or view nearest to a person's eye. **2.** the most important position; forefront.

fore·hand (fôr′hand′) *adj.* made with the arm held outward from the body and the palm of the hand toward the front: *a forehand stroke in tennis.* Also, **fore·hand·ed** (fôr′han′did). —*n.* a forehand stroke, as in tennis.

fore·head (fôr′id, fôr′hed′) *n.* the part of the face above the eyes.

for·eign (fôr′ən, for′ən) *adj.* **1.** of or from another country; not native: *a foreign accent.* **2.** outside a person's own country: *Have you ever visited foreign lands?* **3.** with or related to other countries: *foreign policy, foreign trade.* **4.** not belonging or characteristic: *Selfishness is foreign to her nature.* —**for′eign·ness,** *n.*

● One of the most important characteristics of the English language is its ability continually to absorb **foreign words.** This borrowing from foreign languages began with Old English, the earliest form of our language, which was brought to England by Germanic tribes of Angles, Saxons, and Jutes when they invaded from northwestern Europe in the middle of the fifth century. About one fifth of our modern English vocabulary is derived from Old English. When Roman missionaries brought Christianity to England in the sixth century, they introduced some Latin words. Invasions by the Vikings, which occurred between the ninth and eleventh centuries, brought Scandinavian elements into the language.

The single most important event in the history of the development of our language was the Norman invasion of England in 1066. The Normans brought to England the benefit of two languages. They brought French, their native language, and Latin, the language of the continental Christian Church. English borrowed from both languages. A revived interest in classical learning in the fifteenth and sixteenth centuries brought Greek words and additional Latin words into the English vocabulary. It is estimated that half of the words in English have their roots in Latin.

In the following centuries, words continued to be borrowed as international trade brought the English into contact with many other languages. The spreading of the British Empire, the growth of American commerce, and the immigration of large numbers of people to America caused many foreign words to be borrowed and absorbed from languages which had rarely or never before contributed to the English language. Among these new words, most of which came into English in the nineteenth century, are *tycoon,* from Japanese; *khaki,* from Hindi; *boomerang,* from the native Australian language; *sarong,* from Malay; *taboo,* from Polynesian; *quinine,* from the South American Indian language Quechua; and *safari,* from Arabic through Swahili.

for·eign·er (fôr′ə nər, for′ə nər) *n.* a person born in another country; citizen of another country.

fore·know (fôr nō′) *v.t.,* **fore·knew** (fôr nōō′, fôr-nyōō′), **fore·known, fore·know·ing.** to know (something) ahead of time.

fore·knowl·edge (fôr′nol′ij, fôr nol′ij) *n.* knowledge of something before it happens or exists.

fore·leg (fôr′leg′) *n.* one of the front legs of an insect or a four-legged animal.

fore·limb (fôr′lim′) *n.* a front limb of an animal.

fore·lock (fôr′lok′) *n.* a lock or tuft of hair growing above the forehead.

fore·man (fôr′mən) *n. pl.,* **fore·men** (fôr′mən). **1.** a worker who supervises a group of workers, as in a factory or plant. **2.** a person who is chairman and spokesman of a jury.

fore·mast (fôr′mast′, fôr′məst) *n.* the mast nearest the bow of a ship.

fore·most (fôr′mōst′) *adj.* first in position, rank, or importance: *Charles Dickens was the foremost novelist of his time.* —*adv.* before anything else.

fore·noon (fôr′nōōn′) *n.* the period of time between sunrise and noon; morning.

fo·ren·sic (fə ren′sik) *adj.* of, relating to, or used in courts of law or public discussion and debate: *forensic arguments.* —**fo·ren′si·cal·ly,** *adv.*

fore·or·dain (fôr′ôr dān′) *v.t.* to fix or decide ahead of time; predestine. —**fore′or·dain′ment,** *n.*

fore·part (fôr′pärt′) *n.* the first, front, or early part.

fore·paw (fôr′pô′) *n.* a front paw.

fore·quar·ter (fôr′kwôr′tər) *n.* **1.** the front section of a side of beef or other meat, including the leg and shoulder. **2.** **forequarters.** the forelegs, shoulders, and nearby parts of an animal.

fore·run·ner (fôr′run′ər) *n.* **1.** a person or thing that comes before another; predecessor; ancestor: *The bicycle was the forerunner of the motorcycle.* **2.** a sign of something to come: *A brisk wind is often the forerunner of rain.* **3.** a person who is sent to announce the approach of something or someone; herald.

fore·sail (fôr′sāl′, fôr′səl) *n.* **1.** the lowest sail on the foremast of a square-rigged ship. **2.** the principal sail on the foremast of a schooner.

fore·see (fôr sē′) *v.t.,* **fore·saw** (fôr sô′), **fore·seen, fore·see·ing.** to know or see ahead of time: *We foresaw the difficulty of climbing the mountain but made the climb anyway.* —**fore·see′a·ble,** *adj.* —**fore·se′er,** *n.*

fore·shad·ow (fôr shad′ō) *v.t.* to suggest or indicate beforehand.

fore·short·en (fôr shôrt′ən) *v.t.* to shorten (lines or objects) in a drawing or painting to create an impression of depth and distance to the eye.

fore·sight (fôr′sīt′) *n.* **1.** care or thought for the future: *The boys showed foresight in bringing enough food and water for the long hike.* **2.** the ability to know or see ahead of time what is likely to happen.

fore·sight·ed (fôr′sī′tid, fôr sī′tid) *adj.* having or showing foresight. —**fore′sight′ed·ly,** *adv.* —**fore′sight′ed·ness,** *n.*

fore·skin (fôr′skin′) *n.* the fold of skin that covers the end of the penis. It is removed in circumcision.

for·est (fôr′ist, for′ist) *n.* a heavy growth of trees and other plants, usually covering a large area of land. —*v.t.* to plant or cover with trees; make into a forest.

fore·stall (fôr stôl′) *v.t.* to hinder or prevent by taking action in advance: *Careful planning forestalled failure.* —**fore·stall′er,** *n.*

for·est·er (fôr′is tər, for′is tər) *n.* a person whose work is managing, developing, and protecting forests.

forest ranger, an officer in charge of the protection of a forest, especially a public forest.

for·est·ry (fôr′is trē, for′is trē) *n.* the science that deals with the management, development, and protection of forests.

fore·taste (fôr′tāst′) *n.* a brief taste or sample of something to come: *The cold October day gave them a foretaste of winter.*

fore·tell (fôr tel′) *v.t.,* **fore·told, fore·tell·ing.** to tell of ahead of time; give a prophecy of: *The prophet foretold the king's death.*

fore·thought (fôr′thôt′) *n.* care or thought for the future; planning in advance; foresight.

fore·top (fôr′top′, fôr′təp) *n.* a platform at the top of a foremast.

for·ev·er (fô rev′ər, fə rev′ər) *adv.* **1.** throughout all time; without ever coming to an end; eternally. **2.** without letting up; always; constantly: *She is forever complaining.*

for·ev·er·more (fô rev′ər môr′, fə rev′ər môr′) *adv.* for always; forever.

fore·warn (fôr wôrn′) *v.t.* to warn ahead of time.

fore·went (fôr went′) the past tense of **forego.**

fore·wom·an (fôr′woom′ən) *n. pl.,* **fore·wom·en** (fôr′wim′ən). **1.** a woman who supervises a group of workers, as in a factory. **2.** a woman chairman or spokesman of a jury.

fore·word (fôr′wurd′, fôr′wərd) *n.* a short statement found at the opening of a book; preface.

for·feit (fôr′fit) *v.t.* to lose as a penalty for some fault, mistake, or misdeed: *The team forfeited the game because it did not show up to play.* —*n.* something lost as a penalty for some fault, mistake, or misdeed.

for·fei·ture (fôr′fi chər) *n.* **1.** the act of forfeiting. **2.** something that is forfeited.

for·gath·er (fôr gath′ər) *also,* **fore·gath·er.** *v.i.* to meet or gather together; assemble.

for·gave (fər gāv′) the past tense of **forgive.**

forge¹ (fôrj) *n.* **1.** a furnace or hearth in which metal is heated and softened so that it can be hammered into shape. **2.** a workshop in which metals are heated in such a furnace or hearth and then hammered into shape; smithy. —*v.,* **forged, forg·ing.** —*v.t.* **1.** to heat (metal) in a forge and then hammer into shape. **2.** to make or form; fashion: *to forge an agreement.* **3.** to make or copy (something) with the intention of deceiving or cheating someone; counterfeit; falsify: *to forge a document, to forge a signature.* —*v.i.* **1.** to commit forgery. **2.** to work at a forge. [Old French *forge.*] —**forg′er,** *n.*

forge² (fôrj) *v.i.,* **forged, forg·ing.** to move forward slowly but steadily: *The ferry forged through the choppy water of the bay. We forged ahead on the difficult project.* [Of uncertain origin.]

for·ger·y (fôr′jər ē) *n. pl.,* **for·ger·ies. 1.** the crime of making or copying something, such as a document or signature, with the intention of deceiving or cheating someone. **2.** something that is forged: *The signature on the document was a forgery.*

for·get (fər get′) *v.t.,* **for·got, for·got·ten** or **for·got, for·get·ting. 1.** to be unable to remember; fail to recall: *He forgot her telephone number.* **2.** to fail to think of or do, especially through carelessness or thoughtlessness; neglect; overlook: *He forgot his keys.* —**for·get′ta·ble,** *adj.* —**for·get′ter,** *n.*

for·get·ful (fər get′fəl) *adj.* **1.** likely to forget; having a poor memory: *He is very forgetful and is always losing his glasses.* **2.** failing to think of or do something; neglectful; careless. —**for·get′ful·ly,** *adv.* —**for·get′ful·ness,** *n.*

for·get-me-not (fər get′mē not′) *n.* **1.** a small blue or white flower resembling a trumpet in shape and growing in clusters. **2.** the small plant that bears these flowers, widely cultivated in gardens.

for·give (fər giv′) *v.,* **for·gave, for·giv·en, for·giv·ing.** —*v.t.* **1.** to cease to blame or feel resentment toward (someone): *His father forgave him for breaking the window.* **2.** to pardon; excuse. *He forgave the insult.* —*v.i.* to grant pardon. —**for·giv′a·ble,** *adj.* —**for·giv′er** *n.* ▲ See **excuse** for usage note.

Forget-me-not

for·give·ness (fər giv′nis) *n.* **1.** the act of forgiving or the state of being forgiven. **2.** a willingness to forgive.

for·giv·ing (fər giv′ing) *adj.* having or showing ness: *She has a forgiving nature.* —fo... —**for·giv′ing·ness,** *n.*

for·go (fôr gō′) *also,* **fore·go.** ... **for·go·ing.** to keep oneself fro... *intend to forgo lunch today.* —...

for·got (fər got′) the past ... **forget.**

at; āpe; cär; end; ...
wood; fōol; oil; ou...
hw in white; zh i...
stands for the so...
i in pencil, o in l...

for·got·ten (fər got′ən) a past participle of **forget.**

fork (fôrk) *n.* **1.** a utensil having a handle at one end and two or more prongs at the other, used especially for lifting or handling food. **2.** something resembling a fork in shape, such as a tool used for digging or lifting. **3.** a branching or dividing into branches: *a fork of a road, a fork of a river, a fork of a tree where the branches begin.* **4.** one of the branches into which a thing divides. —*v.t.* to lift, spear, or pitch with a fork: *We forked the hay into the wagon.* —*v.i.* to divide into branches: *The road forks further ahead.* —**fork′like′,** *adj.*

  to fork over, to fork out, or **to fork up.** *Informal.* to hand over: *When the policeman caught him, the thief forked over the stolen jewelry.*

forked (fôrkt) *adj.* shaped like a fork; divided into forks: *The snake had a forked tongue.*

for·lorn (fôr lôrn′) *adj.* **1.** unhappy or wretched, as from being lost and lonely: *The little boy with the ragged clothes looks so forlorn.* **2.** abandoned; forsaken; deserted. —**for·lorn′ly,** *adv.* —**for·lorn′ness,** *n.*

form (fôrm) *n.* **1.** the outline of something; shape: *He could see the faint form of a skyscraper through the fog.* **2.** a body or figure: *The football player had a powerful form.* **3.** the outward appearance of something: *In that myth, the god Zeus took the form of a bull.* **4.** the particular condition something is in: *a medicine in liquid form.* **5.** kind; type; variety: *The tree is a form of plant.* **6.** a way of doing something: *Dick worked to improve his form in diving.* **7.** fitness of mind or body; condition: *The athlete is in top form.* **8.** a document having blank spaces for filling in required information: *The student applying for the summer job filled out a form.* **9.** a way of behaving or conducting oneself: *It was bad form to act so rudely.* **10.** a traditional practice or ritual: *a form followed in a church service.* **11.** a grade or class in a secondary school. **12.** *Grammar.* any of the ways in which a word may appear, usually as a result of a change in the spelling or pronunciation. *Men* is the plural form of *man; went* is a form of the verb *go.* —*v.t.* **1.** to give form to; make or produce; fashion: *The artist formed a figure out of clay.* **2.** to make up: *Students formed the majority of the crowd.* **3.** to think of; conceive: *to form a plan.* **4.** to develop: *to form a habit.* **5.** *Grammar.* to make, as by changing spelling or pronunciation: *to form the past tense of a verb by adding "-ed."* —*v.i.* **1.** to take shape: *The water formed into icicles.* **2.** to come into being; be produced: *Mold formed on the stale bread.*

for·mal (fôr′məl) *adj.* **1.** very stiff, proper, or polite in behavior: *formal manners.* **2.** requiring strict form or ceremony, or elaborate dress: *a formal banquet.* **3.** suitable for a formal event: *a formal dress.* **4.** done or made with authority; official: *The businessman drew up a formal con-* [t]r[act.] —*n.* something that is formal, such as a dance or [gown.] —**for′mal·ly,** *adv.*

  [a] language that, although it is correct [in cer]tain situations, is not the language [of conversat]ion. If you have ever seen a legal [document,] a university, a wedding invita[tion, or an] address by a President of the [United States, you no]ticed that many of the words [are very for]mal. These words are used [because the formal]ness of the event requires [them.]

  [Very often the] formal words or phrases [should be avoided b]ecause they will sound [stiff or stuffy. A] wedding invitation may [read: We request] the pleasure of your [company. To ask] two friends to come to [a party, this word]ing would be much too

formal and should be replaced by a simpler phrase. As in the case of most problems of usage in our language, there are no real "rights" and "wrongs" in using formal as opposed to ordinary language, but only a question of what is appropriate or inappropriate.

form·al·de·hyde (fôr mal′də hīd′) *n.* a colorless, poisonous gas, used especially in solution to preserve and disinfect.

for·mal·ism (fôr′mə liz′əm) *n.* the strict observance of or attention to conventional or traditional forms.

for·mal·i·ty (fôr mal′ə tē) *n. pl.,* **for·mal·i·ties.** **1.** the state or quality of being formal. **2.** a proper or very polite way of behaving: *The hostess treated all of us with great formality.* **3.** a correct or official procedure: *All the legal formalities were followed in carrying out the will.* **4.** something that is a matter of form only: *He was certain of getting an A in math, and the final test was a mere formality.*

for·mal·ize (fôr′mə līz′) *v.t.,* **for·mal·ized, for·mal·iz·ing.** **1.** to make formal. **2.** to give a definite or official form to: *to formalize an agreement.* —**for′mal·i·za′tion,** *n.* —**for′mal·iz′er,** *n.*

for·mat (fôr′mat) *n.* **1.** the way a book, magazine, or other publication is formed, including arrangement of parts, size, and kind of type used. **2.** the way in which something is organized or planned.

for·ma·tion (fôr mā′shən) *n.* **1.** the act or process of forming: *the formation of ice from water.* **2.** something formed: *a rock formation.* **3.** the way in which something is formed: *The troops lined up in parade formation.*

form·a·tive (fôr′mə tiv) *adj.* **1.** giving or capable of giving form: *a formative influence.* **2.** of or relating to growth or development: *the formative years of childhood.*

for·mer (fôr′mər) *adj.* **1.** the first of two mentioned. ▲ used with **latter,** which refers to the second of two mentioned: *Jack and Bill are both on the football team; the former* (Jack) *is a guard and the latter* (Bill) *is a tackle.* **2.** belonging to or happening in the past; previous; earlier: *our former governor, in former times.*

for·mer·ly (fôr′mər lē) *adv.* in time past; once; previously: *Trains were formerly pulled by steam locomotives.*

For·mi·ca (fôr mī′kə) *n. Trademark.* a plastic covering made in thin layers, used especially to cover counters and other surfaces in kitchens and bathrooms.

for·mi·da·ble (fôr′mi də bəl) *adj.* **1.** causing fear, dread, or awe: *a formidable opponent.* **2.** difficult to deal with or do: *Painting the house was a formidable job.* —**for′mi·da·bil′i·ty,** *n.* —**for′mi·da·bly,** *adv.*

form·less (fôrm′lis) *adj.* without a definite or regular shape; shapeless. —**form′less·ly,** *adv.* —**form′less·ness,** *n.*

For·mo·sa (fôr mō′sə) *n.* another name for **Taiwan.**

for·mu·la (fôr′myə lə) *n. pl.,* **for·mu·las** or **for·mu·lae** (fôr′myə lē). **1.** a set method for doing something; fixed rule: *There is no formula for making friends.* **2.** a set order or form of words, used in conventional expressions: *"Yours truly"* is a formula for closing a letter. **3.** an expression using symbols and numbers for a chemical compound: *The formula for carbon dioxide is* CO_2. **4.** an expression of a relationship, fact, or rule in mathematical symbols: *The formula for the circumference of a circle is* $c = \pi d$.

for·mu·late (fôr′myə lāt′) *v.t.,* **for·mu·lat·ed, for·mu·lat·ing.** **1.** to develop or state in a clear, exact, or systematic way: *The general formulated a plan of attack.* **2.** to express in a formula. —**for′mu·la′tion,** *n.* —**for′mu·la′tor,** *n.*

for·sake (fôr sāk′) *v.t.,* **for·sook** (fôr sook′), **for·sak·en, for·sak·ing.** **1.** to give up completely: *He forsook his old beliefs.* **2.** to leave or desert: *His friends have forsaken him.* —**for·sak′er,** *n.*

F

for·sooth (fôr sōōth′) *adv. Archaic.* in truth; indeed.

for·swear (fôr swer′) *v.,* **for·swore** (fôr swôr′), **for·sworn, for·swear·ing.** —*v.t.* to swear to give up: *The young man forswore smoking.* —*v.i.* to swear falsely.

for·syth·i·a (fôr sith′ē ə) *n.* any of a group of shrubs having bell-shaped yellow flowers that grow in clusters along the stems. [From William *Forsyth,* 1737–1804, an English botanist who introduced it from China.]

fort (fôrt) *n.* a fortified building or area that can be defended against an enemy; fortification.

For·ta·le·za (fôrt′əl ä′zə) *n.* a city on the northeastern coast of Brazil. Pop. (1975 est.), 1,109,837.

Fort-de-France (fôr də fräns′) *n.* the capital and largest city of Martinique. Pop. (1974), 98,807.

forte[1] (fôrt) *n.* something a person does especially well; strong point: *Mathematics is his forte.* [French *fort.*]

for·te[2] (fôr′tā) *Music. adj.* loud and forceful. —*adv.* loudly and forcefully. [Italian *forte.*]

Forsythia

forth (fôrth) *adv.* **1.** forward in time or place; onward: *from this day forth. She came forth to receive her degree.* **2.** out into view: *The tree put forth leaves.*

forth·com·ing (fôrth′kum′ing) *adj.* **1.** about to happen or appear: *My brother is old enough to vote in the forthcoming election.* **2.** ready when needed or expected: *Relief will be forthcoming for those left homeless by the flood.*

forth·right (fôrth′rīt′) *adj.* going straight to the point; straightforward; frank. —**forth′right′ly,** *adv.* —**forth′right′ness,** *n.*

forth·with (fôrth′with′, fôrth′with′) *adv.* without delay; at once; immediately: *The doctor came forthwith.*

for·ti·eth (fôr′tē ith) *adj.* **1.** (the ordinal of forty) next after the thirty-ninth. **2.** being one of forty equal parts. —*n.* **1.** something that is next after the thirty-ninth. **2.** one of forty equal parts; 1/40.

for·ti·fi·ca·tion (fôr′tə fi kā′shən) *n.* **1.** the act of fortifying. **2.** something that fortifies, such as a wall or ditch. **3.** a fortified place or building.

for·ti·fy (fôr′tə fī′) *v.t.,* **for·ti·fied, for·ti·fy·ing.** **1.** to protect with a wall, ditch, or other fortification. **2.** to strengthen the structure of; make strong or stronger: *The men fortified the dam against the flood.*

for·tis·si·mo (fôr tis′i mō′) *Music. adj.* very loud. —*adv.* very loudly.

for·ti·tude (fôr′tə tōōd′, fôr′tə tyōōd′) *n.* courage or strength in the face of pain, danger, or misfortune.

Fort-La·my (fôr lä mē′) *n.* see **Ndjamena.**

Fort Lau·der·dale (fôrt lô′dər dāl′) a city in southeastern Florida. Pop. (1970), 139,590.

fort·night (fôrt′nīt′) *n.* two weeks.

fort·night·ly (fôrt′nīt′lē) *adv.* once every two weeks. —*adj.* happening or appearing every two weeks. —*n. pl.,* **fort·night·lies.** something published every two weeks, such as a magazine.

for·tress (fôr′tris) *n. pl.,* **for·tress·es.** **1.** a fortified place; stronghold; fort. **2.** a person or thing that protects or gives security: *God is our fortress* (Shakespeare, *Henry VI*).

for·tu·i·tous (fôr tōō′ə təs, fôr tyōō′ə təs) *adj.* **1.** happening by chance; accidental: *A fortuitous meeting on a bus was the start of their friendship.* **2.** fortunate; lucky: *a fortuitous happening.* —**for·tu′i·tous·ly,** *adv.* —**for·tu′i·tous·ness,** *n.*

for·tu·nate (fôr′chə nit) *adj.* **1.** having good fortune; lucky: *He is very fortunate to have won the scholarship.* **2.** bringing good fortune; favorable: *You arrived at a fortunate time.* —**for′tu·nate·ly,** *adv.*

for·tune (fôr′chən) *n.* **1.** something that happens or is going to happen to a person, whether good or bad; fate: *The gypsy told his fortune by looking into a crystal ball.* **2.** luck, especially when good: *It was his good fortune to meet her when he did.* **3.** great wealth; riches: *Mr. Smith has a fortune in stocks and bonds.*

for·tune-tell·er (fôr′chən tel′ər) *n.* a person who claims to be able to tell another person's fortune.

Fort Wayne (wān) a city in northeastern Indiana. Pop. (1970), 177,671.

Fort Worth (wurth) a city in northeastern Texas. Pop. (1970), 393,467.

for·ty (fôr′tē) *n. pl.,* **for·ties.** **1.** the cardinal number that is four times ten. **2.** a symbol representing this number, such as 40 or XL. —*adj.* numbering four times ten.

for·ty-nin·er (fôr′tē nī′nər) *n.* a person who went to California seeking gold in the gold rush of 1849.

fo·rum (fôr′əm) *n.* **1.** the public square or marketplace of an ancient Roman city, where important activities took place. **2.** an assembly or meeting for the discussion of issues or questions of public interest: *An open forum was held at the school to discuss the new rules.* **3.** a court of law.

for·ward (fôr′wərd) *adv.* **1.** *also,* **forwards.** toward what is ahead or in front; onward: *The athlete stepped forward to accept the trophy.* **2.** toward the future: *We are looking forward to the trip.* **3.** into view; forth: *John brought forward an opinion.* —*adj.* **1.** in, at, near, or toward the front: *He stayed in one of the forward cabins of the ship.* **2.** moving or directed toward a point in front: *The football player made a forward pass.* **3.** advanced or progressive: *He has forward ideas.* **4.** bold or rude: *She is a very forward young lady.* —*v.t.* **1.** to send onward or ahead, especially to a new address: *His parents forwarded his mail to his camp address.* **2.** to help along; promote; advance: *They were interested in forwarding the cause of peace.* —*n.* a player whose position is at or near the front line in certain games, such as basketball or hockey.

for·ward·ly (fôr′wərd lē) *adv.* boldly or rudely.

for·ward·ness (fôr′wərd nis) *n.* **1.** boldness or rudeness. **2.** the condition of being advanced or progressive.

for·went (fôr went′) the past tense of **forgo.**

fos·sil (fos′əl) *n.* **1.** the remains or traces of an animal or plant that lived long ago: *The boys found fossils of prehistoric sea animals in some rocks.* **2.** *Informal.* a person or thing that is old-fashioned, outmoded, or belonging to the past. —*adj.* of, relating to, or forming a fossil.

fos·sil·ize (fos′ə līz′) *v.,* **fos·sil·ized, fos·sil·iz·ing.** —*v.t.* to change into a fossil. —*v.i.* to become a fossil: *The bones of the dinosaur fossilized.* —**fos′sil·i·za′tion,** *n.*

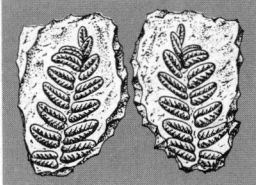

Fossil

fos·ter (fôs′tər) *v.t.* **1.** to help the growth or development of: *The teacher fostered the student's interest in science.*

---

at; āpe; cär; end; mē; it; īce; hot; ōld; fôrk;
wood; fōōl; oil; out; up; turn; sing; thin; this;
hw in white; zh in treasure. The symbol ə
stands for the sound of **a** in about, **e** in taken,
i in pencil, **o** in lemon, and **u** in circus.

2. to bring up; rear: *to foster a child.* —*adj.* brought up in or belonging to a family without being adopted or related by blood: *He was a foster child.*

Fos·ter, Stephen Col·lins (fôs′tər; kol′inz) 1826–1884, U.S. composer of popular songs.

foster parent, a man or woman who brings up a child not his or her own.

fought (fôt) the past tense and past participle of **fight.**

foul (foul) *adj.* **1.** very unpleasant or disgusting: *a foul odor.* **2.** containing dirt or filth: *foul air, foul water.* **3.** cloudy, rainy, or stormy: *foul weather.* **4.** very bad; evil; vile: *a foul deed.* **5.** breaking the rules; unfair: *a foul blow in boxing.* **6.** *Baseball.* outside the foul line: *The ball was foul.* —*n.* **1.** a breaking of rules: *The athlete committed a foul.* **2.** see **foul ball.** —*v.t.* **1.** to make dirty; soil: *They fouled the water by throwing in garbage.* **2.** to tangle: *The boy fouled the fishing line.* **3.** *Sports.* to commit a foul against: *The boxer fouled his opponent by hitting him below the belt.* **4.** *Baseball.* to hit (a ball) into foul territory. —*v.i.* **1.** to be or become dirty. **2.** to become tangled: *The rope fouled on the anchor.* **3.** *Sports.* to break a rule of a game. **4.** *Baseball.* to hit a foul ball. —*adv.* afoul: *He ran foul of the law.* —**foul′ly,** *adv.* —**foul′ness,** *n.*

fou·lard (foo lärd′) *n.* a soft, lightweight fabric made of silk, rayon, cotton, or other, similar fibers, used especially for neckties, scarves, and dresses.

foul ball *Baseball.* a batted ball that goes outside the foul lines.

foul line 1. *Baseball.* either of the lines that extend from home plate through first or third base to the limits of the playing field. **2.** *Basketball.* another term for **free throw line.**

foul play, dishonest or treacherous action, especially when violent.

found[1] (found) the past tense and past participle of **find.**

found[2] (found) *v.t.* **1.** to bring into being; start or set up: *The students founded a science club.* **2.** to set firmly; base; ground: *My argument is founded on fact.* [Old French *fonder.*]

found[3] (found) *v.t.* **1.** to melt and pour (metal) into a mold. **2.** to form or make by pouring molten metal into a mold; cast. [Old French *fondre.*]

foun·da·tion (foun dā′shən) *n.* **1.** the act of founding or the state of being founded; establishment. **2.** something serving as a base or support; basis: *the foundations of a building, the foundations of society.* **3.** an organization that has been endowed especially to support worthwhile causes, such as scientific, artistic, or scholarly work. **4.** the fund endowed for such an organization; endowment.

foun·der[1] (foun′dər) *v.i.* **1.** to fill with water and sink: *The boat foundered in the storm.* **2.** to fall down: *Several buildings foundered in the earthquake.* **3.** to fail completely: *The business foundered.* **4.** to stumble and become lame or disabled: *The horse foundered on the rocky path.* —*v.t.* to cause to founder. [Old French *fondrer.*]

found·er[2] (foun′dər) *n.* a person who founds, starts, or sets up something: *His grandfather was the founder of the business.* [*Found*[2] + *-er*[1].]

found·er[3] (foun′dər) *n.* a person who melts and casts metal. [*Found*[3] + *-er*[1].]

found·ling (found′ling) *n.* a deserted infant whose parents are not known.

found·ry (foun′drē) *n. pl.,* **found·ries. 1.** a place where metal is melted and cast. **2.** the act or process of founding metal.

fount (fount) *n.* **1.** source: *That book is a fount of knowledge.* **2.** fountain; spring.

foun·tain (foun′tən) *n.* **1.** a stream of water made to rise or shoot up in order to provide water for drinking or to serve as a decoration. **2.** a structure designed for such a stream: *A large marble fountain was built in the park.* **3.** a spring of water coming out of the earth. **4.** the source of anything: *That boy is a fountain of facts about baseball.* **5.** see **soda fountain.**

foun·tain·head (fount′ən hed′) *n.* **1.** a spring from which a stream flows; source of a stream. **2.** the primary source or origin of anything.

fountain pen, a pen having a reservoir that holds and feeds ink to the writing point.

four (fôr) *n.* **1.** the cardinal number that is one more than three. **2.** a symbol representing this number, such as 4 or IV. **3.** something having this many units or things, such as a playing card. —*adj.* numbering one more than three.
　on all fours. a. on all four feet: *The cat landed on all fours.* **b.** on hands and knees: *We were on all fours looking for the lost contact lens.*

four·fold (fôr′fōld′) *adj.* **1.** four times as great or numerous. **2.** having or consisting of four parts. —*adv.* so as to be four times greater or more numerous.

Four-H clubs (fôr′āch′) *also,* **4-H clubs.** an organization for youth, sponsored by the U.S. Department of Agriculture, to teach skills in agriculture and home economics. [From its purpose of improving the *h*ead, *h*earts, *h*ands, and *h*ealth of its members.]

four-leaf clover (fôr′lēf′) a clover with four leaflets, considered to bring good luck to a person who finds it.

four-post·er (fôr′pōs′tər) *n.* a bedstead with four tall corner posts to support a canopy or curtains.

four·score (fôr′skôr′) *adj., n.* four times twenty; eighty.

four·some (fôr′səm) *n.* **1.** a group of four persons. **2.** something played or done by four persons, such as a round of golf.

four·square (fôr′skwer′) *adj.* **1.** square. **2.** frank; forthright. **3.** firm; forthright. —*adv.* squarely; firmly.

four·teen (fôr′tēn′) *n.* **1.** the cardinal number that is four more than ten. **2.** a symbol representing this number, such as 14 or XIV. **3.** something having this many units or things. —*adj.* numbering four more than ten.

four·teenth (fôr′tēnth′) *adj.* **1.** (the ordinal of fourteen) next after the thirteenth. **2.** being one of fourteen equal parts. —*n.* **1.** something that is next after the thirteenth. **2.** one of fourteen equal parts; 1/14.

fourth (fôrth) *adj.* **1.** (the ordinal of four) next after the third. **2.** being one of four equal parts. —*n.* **1.** something that is next after the third. **2.** one of four equal parts; 1/4. **3.** *Music.* **a.** a note that is a total of two whole steps and one half step above a given note. F is the fourth of C. **b.** an interval of two whole steps and one half step. **c.** a combination of two notes that are separated by this interval. **4.** the fourth forward gear, as of an automobile. —*adv.* in the fourth place.

fourth estate, the press; journalists or journalism.

Fourth of July, another term for **Independence Day.**

fowl (foul) *n. pl.,* **fowl** or **fowls. 1.** a hen or rooster; chicken. **2.** any of various related birds, such as a turkey, pheasant, or duck. **3.** the flesh of a fowl used as food. **4.** any bird.

fox (foks) *n. pl.,* **fox·es. 1.** any of a group of wild animals belonging to the dog family, having a pointed nose, large erect ears, a bushy tail, and a thick coat. **2.** the fur of a fox. **3.** a sly, crafty person. —*v.t. Informal.* to trick or

Fox

deceive; outwit: *The escaped prisoner foxed his pursuers by hiding until they had passed by.* —**fox′like′**, *adj.*

Fox, George (foks) 1624–1691, English religious leader, founder of the Society of Friends, or Quakers.

fox·glove (foks′gluv′) *n.* a plant bearing white, yellow, or purple thimble-shaped flowers on long spikes. The dried leaves of the foxglove are used in making the drug digitalis.

fox·hole (foks′hōl′) *n.* a hole dug in the ground by soldiers to give themselves shelter from enemy fire.

fox·hound (foks′hound′) *n.* a large hound with a keen sense of smell, usually having a tan, black, and white coat, trained especially to hunt foxes.

fox·tail (foks′tāl′) *n.* **1.** the tail of a fox. **2.** any of various grasses bearing flower spikes that resemble the tail of foxes.

fox terrier, a dog having a long head, short tail, and a smooth or wiry white coat with tan or black and tan markings. Fox terriers were once used to drive foxes from their burrows.

fox·trot (foks′trot′) *v.i.*, **fox·trot·ted, fox·trot·ting.** to dance the fox trot.

fox trot **1.** a dance that combines slow steps and short, quick steps. **2.** the music for this dance.

fox·y (fok′sē) *adj.*, **fox·i·er, fox·i·est.** like a fox; sly; crafty. —**fox′i·ly**, *adv.* —**fox′i·ness**, *n.*

foy·er (foi′ər) *n.* **1.** the lobby of a theater, hotel, or other public building. **2.** the entrance hall in a house or apartment.

Fr, the symbol for francium.

fr. **1.** fragment. **2.** franc. **3.** from.

Fr. **1.** Father. **2.** France. **3.** French. **4.** Friday.

fra·cas (frā′kəs) *n. pl.*, **fra·cas·es.** a loud quarrel or fight; brawl.

Smooth-haired fox terrier

frac·tion (frak′shən) *n.* **1.** a part of a whole; small part: *Only a fraction of the people attending the game left before it was over.* **2.** *Mathematics.* a quantity expressing the division of one number by a second number, written as two numerals separated by a line, such as $\frac{2}{3}$, $\frac{3}{4}$, or $\frac{11}{16}$.

frac·tion·al (frak′shən əl) *adj.* **1.** of, relating to, or forming a fraction or fractions: *Four inches is a fractional part of a foot.* **2.** small or unimportant: *He has made only a fractional improvement in his work.*

frac·tious (frak′shəs) *adj.* **1.** difficult to control; unruly. **2.** bad-tempered or quarrelsome; cranky. —**frac′tious·ly**, *adv.* —**frac′tious·ness**, *n.*

frac·ture (frak′chər) *v.*, **frac·tured, frac·tur·ing.** —*v.t.* to crack, split, or break (something): *He fractured his ankle playing ice hockey.* —*v.i.* to crack, split, or break: *His arm fractured in the accident.* —*n.* **1.** the act of breaking or the state of being broken. **2.** a crack, split, or break, as in a bone.

frag·ile (fraj′əl) *adj.* tending to break easily: *That porcelain cup is very fragile.* —**frag′ile·ly**, *adv.* —**fra·gil·i·ty** (frə jil′ə tē) *n.*

frag·ment (*n.*, frag′mənt; *v.*, frag′ment) *n.* **1.** a part broken off; small piece: *The archaeologists found fragments of pottery.* **2.** a part of something left incomplete or unfinished: *a fragment of a novel, fragments of conversation.* —*v.t.* to break (something) into fragments: *He fragmented the glass pitcher when he dropped it.* —*v.i.* to break into fragments.

frag·men·tar·y (frag′mən ter′ē) *adj.* made up of fragments; broken; incomplete: *the fragmentary remains of a deserted house. The police had only a fragmentary report of the crime.*

frag·men·ta·tion (frag′mən tā′shən) *n.* the act or process of breaking into fragments.

fra·grance (frā′grəns) *n.* a sweet or pleasing smell: *The flowers have a pleasant fragrance.*

fra·grant (frā′grənt) *adj.* having a sweet or pleasing smell: *a fragrant garden.* —**fra′grant·ly**, *adv.*

frail (frāl) *adj.* **1.** lacking in strength; weak: *The child was too frail to take part in active sports.* **2.** easily broken or torn; delicate; fragile: *frail, old lace.* —**frail′ness**, *n.*

frail·ty (frāl′tē) *n. pl.*, **frail·ties.** **1.** the state or quality of being frail; weakness. **2.** a fault resulting from moral weakness: *One of his frailties is gambling.*

frame (frām) *n.* **1.** a structure that holds or borders something: *a window frame, a picture frame, frames for eyeglasses.* **2.** a structure that gives shape or supports something; framework: *the metal frame of a bed, the wooden frame of a house.* **3.** the way in which one's body is formed; build: *She has a thin frame.* **4.** one of the pictures on a roll of motion-picture film. **5.** one of the ten divisions of a game of bowling. —*v.t.*, **framed, fram·ing.** **1.** to set in a border: *The artist framed his painting.* **2.** to form, draw up, or make: *The lawyer framed his questions clearly.* **3.** *Slang.* to cause (an innocent person) to appear guilty by using false evidence. —**fram′er**, *n.*

frame house, a house constructed on a wooden framework, usually covered with boards or shingles.

frame of mind, the state of a person's mind or feeling; mood: *Losing his job put him in a low frame of mind.*

frame-up (frām′up′) *n. Slang.* a scheme to make an innocent person appear guilty through the use of false evidence.

frame·work (frām′wurk′) *n.* **1.** a structure that gives shape or support to something: *the framework of a building.* **2.** arrangement of parts: *the framework of a novel.*

franc (frangk) *n.* a monetary unit and coin of France, Belgium, Switzerland, Luxembourg, and several African countries.

France (frans) *n.* a country in western Europe. Capital, Paris. Area, 210,039 sq. mi. Pop. (1971 est.), 51,260,000.

fran·chise (fran′chīz) *n.* **1.** the right to vote; suffrage: *The United States government has given the franchise to persons who are eighteen years old.* **2.** the right to have or do something, given to an individual or group, especially by a government or business firm: *a franchise to operate a bus service, a franchise to sell a certain product.* **3.** the geographical area for which such a privilege is given.

Fran·cis·can (fran sis′kən) *adj.* **1.** of or relating to Saint Francis of Assisi or to the religious order that he founded. **2.** belonging to this order: *a Franciscan monk.* —*n.* a member of this order.

Francis Ferdinand, 1863–1914, the archduke of Austria whose assassination led to World War I.

Francis of As·si·si, Saint (ə sē′zē) 1181?–1226, an Italian friar, founder of the Franciscan order.

fran·ci·um (fran′sē əm) *n.* a rare, radioactive metallic element. Symbol: Fr

F

at; āpe; cär; end; mē; it; īce; hot; ōld; fôrk; wood; fo͞ol; oil; out; up; turn; sing; thin; this; hw in white; zh in treasure. The symbol ə stands for the sound of **a** in about, **e** in taken, **i** in pencil, **o** in lemon, and **u** in circus.

Fran·co, Fran·cis·co (frang′kō; fran sis′kō) 1892–1975, Spanish general, the ruler of Spain from 1939–1975.

frank¹ (frangk) *adj.* honest and open in expressing one's thoughts and feelings; outspoken; candid: *Let me be frank with you and tell you what I really think.* —*v.t.* **1.** to mark (a letter, package, or other mail) for delivery without charge. **2.** to send (mail) without charge. —*n.* **1.** the right or privilege to send mail without charge. **2.** a mark indicating this right or privilege. —**frank′ly,** *adv.* —**frank′ness,** *n.*

frank² (frangk) *n. Informal.* see **frankfurter.**

Frank (frangk) *n.* a member of a Germanic people who conquered Gaul in the late fifth century A.D., and who gave their name to present-day France.

Frank·en·stein (frang′kən stīn′) *n.* **1.** a young scientist in Mary Shelley's novel *Frankenstein,* who creates a monster that eventually destroys him. **2.** the monster created by him. **3.** anything that threatens or destroys its creator.

Frank·fort (frangk′fərt) *n.* the capital of Kentucky, in the north-central part of the state. Pop. (1970), 21,356.

Frank·furt (frangk′fərt) *n.* a city in central West Germany. Pop. (1977 est.), 632,565. Also, **Frank·furt am Main** (frängk′foort äm mīn′).

frank·furt·er (frangk′fər tər) *n.* **1.** a reddish sausage made of beef or beef and pork mixed and shaped like a cylinder. **2.** such a sausage served hot in a long, soft roll, often with mustard, relish, or sauerkraut. Also, **hot dog.** [German *Frankfurter* of or from Frankfurt.]

frank·in·cense (frang′kin sens′) *n.* a resin from certain Asian and African trees, burned as an incense.

Frank·ish (frang′kish) *adj.* of or relating to the Franks. —*n.* the language of the Franks.

Frank·lin, Benjamin (frangk′lin) 1706–1790, U.S. statesman, scientist, author, and inventor.

fran·tic (fran′tik) *adj.* wildly excited by worry, grief, fear, or anger; frenzied: *The mother was frantic when her child became lost.* —**fran′ti·cal·ly;** also, **fran′tic·ly,** *adv.* —**fran′tic·ness,** *n.*

frap·pé (*adj., n., def. 1* fra pā′; *n., def. 2* frap) *adj.* iced; chilled. —*n.* **1.** a beverage that is partly frozen or served over shaved ice. **2. frappe.** a beverage made with ice cream, such as a milkshake.

fra·ter·nal (frə turn′əl) *adj.* **1.** of or relating to a brother or brothers; brotherly. **2.** of or relating to an association of men who join together for fellowship or because of common interests. —**fra·ter′nal·ly,** *adv.*

fraternal twins, twins of the same or opposite sex that develop from two separate fertilized egg cells and therefore do not necessarily look alike. Fraternal twins are different from identical twins, which develop from the same fertilized egg cell and therefore look alike.

fra·ter·ni·ty (frə tur′nə tē) *n. pl.,* **fra·ter·ni·ties. 1.** a social organization of men or boys, often having student chapters in colleges. **2.** the state or quality of being brotherly; brotherhood. **3.** a group of people sharing the same interests or profession: *the medical fraternity.*

frat·er·nize (frat′ər nīz′) *v.i.,* **frat·er·nized, frat·er·nizing.** to associate closely with someone in a friendly or brotherly way: *The players were told they could not fraternize with the other team before the game.* —**frat′er·ni·za′tion,** *n.*

frat·ri·cide¹ (frat′rə sīd′) *n.* the act of killing one's brother or sister. [Latin *frātricīdium,* from *frāter* brother + *-cīdium* a killing.]

frat·ri·cide² (frat′rə sīd′) *n.* a person who kills his brother or sister. [Latin *frātricīda,* from *frāter* brother + *-cīda* a killer.]

Frau (frou) *n. pl.,* **Fraus** or *(German)* **Frau·en** (frou′ən) a married woman; wife. ▲ German form of respectful or polite address for a married woman.

fraud (frôd) *n.* **1.** deceit or trickery, especially the tricking of another person in order to cheat him of his rights or property. **2.** a person or thing that deceives; imposter or sham.

fraud·u·lent (frô′jə lənt) *adj.* **1.** given to or using fraud; deceitful; dishonest: *He is a fraudulent businessman and cheats his customers.* **2.** characterized by or done by fraud: *a fraudulent business deal.* —**fraud′u·lence, fraud′u·len·cy,** *n.* —**fraud′u·lent·ly,** *adv.*

fraught (frôt) *adj.* filled: *The spy's mission was fraught with danger.*

Fräu·lein (froi′līn) *n. pl.,* **Fräu·leins** or *(German)* **Fräu·lein.** an unmarried woman; young lady. ▲ German form of respectful or polite address for an unmarried woman.

fray¹ (frā) *n.* a noisy quarrel or fight: *The boy jumped into the fray and got a bloody nose.* [A form of *affray.*]

fray² (frā) *v.t.* **1.** to cause (something, such as cloth or rope) to separate into loose threads, especially along the edges; ravel: *Hard wear had frayed the cuffs of his coat.* **2.** to strain or irritate: *Her nerves are frayed from all the excitement.* —*v.i.* to become frayed; ravel. [French *frayer* to rub against.]

freak (frēk) *n.* **1.** a person, animal, or plant that has not developed normally; monstrosity. **2.** anything odd or unusual. —*adj.* not normal; odd or unusual; bizarre: *a freak accident.*

freak·ish (frē′kish) *adj.* **1.** of or relating to a freak; abnormal. **2.** odd or unusual: *a freakish turn of events.* —**freak′ish·ly,** *adv.* —**freak′ish·ness,** *n.*

freck·le (frek′əl) *n.* a small brownish spot on the skin, often caused by exposure to the sun. —*v.,* **freck·led, freckling.** —*v.t.* to mark (something) with freckles. —*v.i.* to become marked with freckles.

Fred·er·ick the Great (fred′ər ik) 1712–1786, the king of Prussia from 1740 to 1786.

free (frē) *adj.,* **fre·er, fre·est. 1.** having one's liberty; not under the control or domination of another; not a slave. **2.** having a government that allows such liberty: *a free country.* **3.** not held back, restrained, or confined: *The movements of the dancer were free and graceful. He is free to come and go as he pleases.* **4.** relieved of something that causes worry, pain, or effort: *free from care.* **5.** without cost or payment: *We received free tickets to the show.* **6.** not busy; available: *free time.* **7.** not following regular rules, patterns, or words: *a free translation.* **8.** not subject to custom duties or other taxes: *free trade.* **9.** *Chemistry.* not part of a compound; not combined: *free oxygen.* —*adv.* **1.** without cost or payment: *Children were admitted free to the theater.* **2.** in a free manner; easily: *The colts ran free across the meadow.* —*v.t.,* **freed, free·ing. 1.** to make free; set loose: *The child freed the trapped animal.* **2.** to save from or relieve of something: *The prize money helped free him from his debts.* —**free′ly,** *adv.* —**free′ness,** *n.*

free·board (frē′bôrd′) *n.* the part of the side of a ship that is out of the water.

free·boot·er (frē′boo′tər) *n.* a person who plunders; pirate.

free·born (frē′bôrn′) *adj.* not born in slavery; born free.

freed·man (frēd′mən) *n. pl.,* **freed·men** (frēd′mən). a person who is freed from slavery. —**freed′wom′an,** *n.*

free·dom (frē′dəm) *n.* **1.** the condition of being free: *The American colonists struggled for their freedom.* **2.** a setting free, as from slavery or prison. **3.** ease of movement or action. **4.** openness or frankness in manner or speech. **5.** full use: *His guests were given the freedom of his home.*

free enterprise, an economic system in which people

are able to own and operate businesses with little control by the government. Also, **private enterprise.**

free fall **1.** the fall of a body through air when the only checking force on it is gravity. **2.** the part of a parachute jump before the parachute is opened.

free-for-all (frē′fər ôl′) *n.* a noisy fight or quarrel.

free·hand (frē′hand′) *adj.* drawn or sketched by hand without measuring or using a drawing instrument, such as a ruler. —*adv.* by hand without measuring or using a drawing instrument.

free·hand·ed (frē′han′did) *adj.* openhanded; generous.

free·hold (frē′hōld′) *n.* **1.** a piece of land held for life with the right to give it to one's heirs. **2.** the holding of land in this way. —**free′hold′er,** *n.*

free-lance (frē′lans′) *adj.* of, relating to, or working as a free lance. —*v.i.,* **free-lanced, free-lanc·ing.** to work as a free lance. —**free′-lanc′er,** *n.*

free lance, a trained person, especially a writer or artist, who does not work for one employer, but sells his or her work to anyone who will buy it. [In the Middle Ages, a *free lance* was a knight who would fight for anyone who paid his price.]

free·man (frē′mən) *n. pl.,* **free·men** (frē′mən). **1.** a person who is free from bondage or slavery; a free man or woman. **2.** a person who is a citizen.

Free·ma·son (frē′mā′sən) *n.* a member of a secret organization that teaches brotherly love and mutual aid. Also, **Mason.**

Free·ma·son·ry (frē′mā′sən rē) *n.* **1.** the beliefs and practices of the Freemasons. **2.** Freemasons as a group. Also, **Masonry.**

free on board, delivered onto a ship, train, or the like by the seller without charge to the buyer.

Free-Soil Party (frē′soil′) a U.S. political party formed in 1848 that was against bringing slavery into the western territories and admitting new slave states into the Union.

free·spo·ken (frē′spō′kən) *adj.* given to speaking frankly; outspoken.

Free State, a U.S. state in which slavery was not allowed during the period before the Civil War.

free·stone (frē′stōn′) *adj.* having a pit that comes out easily from the flesh of the fruit: *a freestone peach.* —*n.* **1.** any fine-grained stone, such as limestone or sandstone, that can be cut easily in any direction without splitting. **2.** a freestone fruit, such as a plum.

free·style (frē′stīl′) *adj.* in swimming, using or allowing any stroke the swimmer chooses. —*n.* a free-style swimming race or event.

free·think·er (frē′thing′kər) *n.* a person whose opinions are based on his or her own thinking or judgment instead of on tradition or the opinions of others.

Free·town (frē′toun′) *n.* the capital of Sierra Leone, on the western coast of the country. Pop. (1970 est.), 178,600.

free verse, poetry that does not have a regular meter or rhyme scheme.

free·way (frē′wā′) *n.* a highway with more than two lanes and no toll charges, usually divided for fast and direct driving.

free·will (frē′wil′) *adj.* given or done freely; voluntary: *a freewill offering.*

free will **1.** the power of choosing freely what one is going to do without being directed or influenced by others; free choice: *He did it of his own free will.* **2.** the doctrine that people have free choice and are responsible for what they do.

freeze (frēz) *v.,* **froze, fro·zen, freez·ing.** —*v.i.* **1.** to change into a solid state or form by cold. When water freezes, it becomes ice. **2.** to become covered or blocked with ice: *The lake froze over last night. The water pipes froze.* **3.** to be or become very cold: *He almost froze waiting for the bus in the snowstorm.* **4.** to become fixed because of cold: *The windshield wiper froze to the window.* **5.** to be unable to move because of fear or shock: *He froze in his tracks when he saw the escaped bear.* **6.** to be damaged, destroyed, or killed by frost or extreme cold: *The orange crop froze this winter.* **7.** to become unfriendly, formal, or aloof: *The child froze up around strangers.* —*v.t.* **1.** to cause to change to a solid state or form by cold; cause to become ice: *to freeze water.* **2.** to cover or block (something) with ice: *The cold weather froze the lake.* **3.** to preserve (food) by quickly lowering its temperature: *to freeze a steak.* **4.** to cause to become fixed to something by the cold. **5.** to damage, destroy, or kill by frost or extreme cold. **6.** to fix or set at a particular amount or level: *The government froze food prices.* —*n.* **1.** the act of freezing or the state of being frozen. **2.** a period of extremely cold weather.

freeze-dry (frēz′drī′) *v.t.,* **freeze-dried, freeze-dry·ing.** to dry while frozen under high vacuum for preservation: *to freeze-dry coffee.*

freez·er (frē′zər) *n.* **1.** a refrigerator or section in a refrigerator that freezes food rapidly and keeps it from spoiling for long periods of time. **2.** a machine for freezing ice cream.

freezing point, the temperature at which a liquid freezes. The freezing point of water at sea level is 32 degrees Fahrenheit or zero degrees centigrade.

freight (frāt) *n.* **1.** the transportation of goods by means of land, air, or water. **2.** the goods transported by such means; cargo. **3.** the charge for the transportation of goods by such means. **4.** see **freight train.** —*v.t.* **1.** to load with goods for transportation. **2.** to send by freight.

freight car, a railroad car for carrying freight.

freight·er (frā′tər) *n.* **1.** a ship used mainly for transporting cargo. **2.** a person who receives and transports freight.

freight train, a railroad train composed of freight cars.

Fré·mont, John Charles (frē′mont) 1813–1890, U.S. explorer, soldier, and politician.

French (french) *n.* **1.** the French. the people of France. **2.** the language of France. It is also spoken in parts of Belgium, Switzerland, and Canada. —*adj.* of or relating to France, its people, their language, or culture.

● The most important single event in the shaping of the English language was the introduction of **French** to England by the Norman invaders in 1066. Since the Normans brought Church Latin along with their native French, they contributed the richness of two languages to English. As conquerors the Normans soon established French as the language of the court, the military, the law, and the upper classes. English continued to be spoken by the native population. England had, in effect, two languages, each representing a different segment of society. By looking at specific groups of French and English words, we can determine the relative social status suggested by various words. The word for an animal that had to be raised or hunted, such as *calf, ox, pig,* and *deer,* usually came from

at; āpe; cär; end; mē; it; īce; hot; ōld; fôrk; wood; fōōl; oil; out; up; turn; sing; thin; this; hw in white; zh in treasure. The symbol ə stands for the sound of a in about, e in taken, i in pencil, o in lemon, and u in circus.

English. When these animals were served as food, they were called *veal, beef, pork,* and *venison,* which were all originally French words. Although the English words *king* and *queen* remained in the language, most other words that indicated noble rank, such as *prince, duke, baron,* and *countess,* came from the Normans.

For about two hundred years after the Norman Conquest it seemed likely that French would completely take the place of English. But by 1362, the year in which the opening of Parliament was first conducted in English, English had once again become the national language. This was a very different English from the language spoken before the Conquest. The language had been greatly changed and enriched by the addition of French.

This blending of two languages is the main reason that English is so rich in synonyms. Usually, in a pair of synonyms in which one was derived from Old English and the other from Norman French, the simpler, more concrete word will be from the Old English, while the more difficult or abstract word will be of French origin. Examples of such pairs of words are *room* and *chamber, hide* and *conceal, feed* and *nourish,* and *begin* and *commence.*

French and Indian War, a war in North America in which the French and their Indian allies fought against the English, from 1754 to 1763.

French cuff, the cuff of a sleeve that is folded back and fastened with a cuff link.

French doors, a pair of doors with glass panes. The doors are hinged at opposite sides of a doorway and open in the middle.

French dressing, a salad dressing made of oil, vinegar, and spices.

French fried, fried in deep fat until brown and crisp: *French fried onion rings.*

French fries, potatoes cut into thin strips and fried in deep fat until brown and crisp.

French doors

French Guiana, a French overseas territory on the northeastern coast of South America. Area, 35,135 sq. mi. Pop. (1980 est.), 71,000.

French Guinea, see **Guinea** (*def. 1*).

French horn, a brass musical instrument that has a long, coiled tube ending in a flared bell, and makes a rich, mellow tone.

French Indochina, a former French dependency in Southeast Asia, comprising the present countries of Vietnam, Laos, and Cambodia.

French·man (french′mən) *n. pl.,* **French·men** (french′mən). a man who was born or is living in France.

French horn

French Revolution, a revolution in France from 1789 to 1799 that overthrew the monarchy and aristocracy and resulted in the establishment of a republic.

French toast, bread dipped in a mixture of egg and milk and then fried.

French windows, a pair of doorlike windows hinged at opposite sides and opening in the middle.

French·wom·an (french′woom′ən) *n. pl.,* **French·wom·en** (french′wim′ən). a woman who was born or is living in France.

fre·net·ic (fri net′ik) *adj.* frenzied; frantic: *frenetic activity.* —**fre·net′i·cal·ly,** *adv.*

fren·zied (fren′zēd) *adj.* marked by frenzy; frantic.

fren·zy (fren′zē) *n. pl.,* **fren·zies.** a state of great emotion or wild excitement: *The mother went into a frenzy of grief at the news of her child's kidnapping.*

fre·quen·cy (frē′kwən sē) *n. pl.,* **fre·quen·cies.** **1.** the state of happening or taking place again and again. **2.** the number of times something happens or takes place during a period of time; rate of occurrence: *The frequency of the heartbeat in a grown person is between sixty and ninety beats a minute.* **3.** *Mathematics.* the ratio of the number of times an event occurs to the total number of possible occurrences. **4.** the number of cycles per second of an alternating current, electromagnetic radiation, or sound.

● In language, **frequency** refers to the number of times that a letter or word appears. The frequency of a letter or word is determined by examining how many times it occurs in books, magazines, and other writing, or how often it is used in conversation. In a recent study of reading matter, particularly that used in schools, the ten words that appeared most often were *the, of, and, a, to, in, is, you, that,* and *it.* These words are among the first that we learn in beginning to read, and they are basic building blocks of our language.

The letter of the alphabet with the highest frequency in our language is the letter *e.* The most frequent *initial letter* is *s.* This means that more words in our language begin with *s* than with any other letter. The second most common initial letter is *c.* More than 20% of the words in this book begin with either *c* or *s.* The least commonly used initial letters are *q, x, y,* and *z.* Less than 2% of the words in this book begin with *q, x, y,* or *z.*

frequency modulation, see **FM.**

fre·quent (*adj.,* frē′kwənt; *v.,* fri kwent′, frē′kwənt) *adj.* **1.** taking place again and again; happening often: *There are frequent thunder storms here.* **2.** appearing often; regular; habitual: *He is a frequent visitor at our house.* —*v.t.* to go to often; be at or in regularly: *He frequented the theater when he was in New York.* —**fre·quent′er,** *n.* —**fre′·quent·ly,** *adv.*

fres·co (fres′kō) *n. pl.,* **fres·coes** or **fres·cos.** **1.** the art or method of painting on a surface of wet plaster. **2.** a picture or design painted using this method. —*v.t.,* **fres·coed, fres·co·ing.** to paint by using this method.

fresh (fresh) *adj.* **1.** newly done, made, gathered, or obtained: *a fresh coat of paint, fresh vegetables, a fresh wound.* **2.** not known, seen, or used before; new: *a fresh day, fresh news, a fresh start.* **3.** clean: *fresh air, a fresh shirt.* **4.** different; additional; another: *a fresh start.* **5.** not faded; vivid: *His words remained fresh in my mind.* **6.** looking healthy or youthful: *a fresh complexion.* **7.** cool and pleasant; refreshing: *a fresh breeze.* **8.** (of water) not salty. **9.** not tired; rested: *He felt fresh after sleeping for an hour.* **10.** *Informal.* showing rudeness or boldness; impudent: *The little girl was very fresh to her parents.* —**fresh′ly,** *adv.* —**fresh′ness,** *n.*

fresh·en (fresh′ən) *v.t.* to make fresh: *The rain freshened the air.* —*v.i.* **1.** to become fresh. **2.** to make oneself fresh, as by washing or changing clothes: *We freshened up before going to the party.*

fresh·et (fresh′it) *n.* **1.** the sudden rise or overflow of a stream, caused by heavy rains or melted snow. **2.** a stream of fresh water flowing into the sea.

fresh·man (fresh′mən) *n. pl.,* **fresh·men** (fresh′mən). a student in his or her first year of high school or college.

fresh·wa·ter (fresh'wô'tər) *adj.* of, relating to, or living in fresh water: *a freshwater fish.*

Fres·no (frez'nō) *n.* a city in central California. Pop. (1970), 165,972.

fret¹ (fret) *v.,* **fret·ted, fret·ting.** —*v.i.* to be upset, unhappy, or worried: *Don't fret about what happened.* —*v.t.* **1.** to make upset, unhappy, or worried. **2.** to wear away: *The acid fretted the metal.* —*n.* **1.** the condition of being upset or worried. **2.** the act of wearing away. [Old English *fretan* to eat up.]

fret² (fret) *n.* a decorative pattern, usually having short, straight lines within a band or border. —*v.t.,* **fret·ted, fret·ting.** to decorate with a fret. [Old French *frete.*]

fret³ (fret) *n.* one of a series of bars or ridges of wood, metal, or other material across the neck of such instruments as the guitar or banjo, used to help the player place the fingers correctly. [Of uncertain origin.]

fret·ful (fret'fəl) *adj.* tending to fret; irritable. —**fret'ful·ly,** *adv.* —**fret'ful·ness,** *n.*

fret·work (fret'wurk') *n.* decorative openwork made of frets.

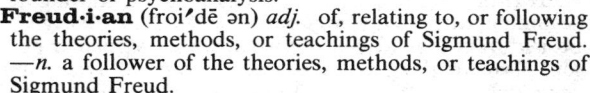

Frets²

Freud, Sig·mund (froid; sig'mənd) 1856–1939, Austrian physician, the founder of psychoanalysis.

Freud·i·an (froi'dē ən) *adj.* of, relating to, or following the theories, methods, or teachings of Sigmund Freud. —*n.* a follower of the theories, methods, or teachings of Sigmund Freud.

Fri., Friday.

fri·a·ble (frī'ə bəl) *adj.* easily crumbled or crushed into powder: *friable rock.* —**fri'a·bil'i·ty, fri'a·ble·ness,** *n.*

fri·ar (frī'ər) *n.* a man who is a member of any of the monastic orders of the Roman Catholic Church, such as the Franciscans or Dominicans.

fri·ar·y (frī'ər ē) *n. pl.,* **fri·ar·ies. 1.** a building or group of buildings where friars live. **2.** a brotherhood of friars.

fric·as·see (frik'ə sē') *n.* a dish made up of meat, especially chicken, that is stewed, and served in a sauce made with its own gravy. —*v.t.,* **fric·as·seed, fric·as·see·ing.** to make (meat) into a fricassee.

fric·tion (frik'shən) *n.* **1.** the rubbing of one object against another: *the friction of a rope on one's hand.* **2.** *Physics.* a force that resists movement between two surfaces that are touching one another: *The friction between the parts of a machine can be reduced by oiling.* **3.** anger or ill will caused by conflict or disagreement: *There was much friction between the two rival teams.*

fric·tion·al (frik'shən əl) *adj.* of, relating to, or brought about by friction. —**fric'tion·al·ly,** *adv.*

friction tape, a moisture-proof adhesive tape, used especially to protect and insulate exposed electric wires.

Fri·day (frī'dē, frī'dā) *n.* the sixth day of the week. [Old English *Frīgedæg* literally, the day of Frig, a Norse goddess.]

fried (frīd) the past tense and past participle of **fry¹.**

friend (frend) *n.* **1.** a person who is known well and regarded with affection by another; person one knows well and likes. **2.** a person who supports: *Her name was on the list of friends of the museum.* **3. Friend.** a member of the Society of Friends. Also, **Quaker.**

　to make friends with. to become a friend of.

friend·less (frend'lis) *adj.* having no friends. —**friend'less·ness,** *n.*

friend·ly (frend'lē) *adj.,* **friend·li·er, friend·li·est. 1.** of, relating to, or characteristic of a friend: *friendly*

advice, a friendly letter. **2.** showing friendship, kindness, or warmth of feeling: *a friendly person, a friendly gesture.* **3.** not hostile: *friendly relations between nations.* **4.** helpful or favorable: *a friendly breeze.* —**friend'li·ness,** *n.*

friend·ship (frend'ship') *n.* **1.** the state or fact of being friends. **2.** a mutual liking or attachment between friends.

frieze (frēz) *n.* **1.** a horizontal band, often decorated with sculpture or other ornamentation, between the cornice and architrave of a building. **2.** any decorative horizontal band, as around the top of a wall or building.

Frigate

frig·ate (frig'it) *n.* **1.** formerly, a three-masted, square-rigged sailing warship. **2.** a warship used for escort and patrol duties.

frigate bird, any of various tropical sea birds having long, pointed wings, dark feathers, and a thin, hooked bill.

fright (frīt) *n.* **1.** sudden, violent alarm or terror: *The people in the burning building were seized with fright.* **2.** *Informal.* a person or thing that is ugly, shocking, or ridiculous in appearance: *He looked a fright after three months of camping in the mountains.*

Frigate bird

fright·en (frīt'ən) *v.t.* **1.** to make suddenly alarmed or afraid; terrify or scare: *The explosion frightened them.* **2.** to drive or force by terrifying or scaring: *The dog frightened away the squirrels.* —*v.i.* to become suddenly alarmed or afraid: *That timid girl frightens easily.* —**fright'en·ing·ly,** *adv.*

fright·ful (frīt'fəl) *adj.* **1.** causing fright; terrifying: *a frightful enemy.* **2.** disgusting, shocking, or revolting: *The living conditions in the slums were frightful.* **3.** *Informal.* very unpleasant or disagreeable: *a frightful headache. The children were making a frightful racket.* **4.** *Informal.* extreme; great: *He was in a frightful rush to catch the train.* —**fright'ful·ly,** *adv.* —**fright'ful·ness,** *n.*

frig·id (frij'id) *adj.* **1.** very cold: *a frigid winter.* **2.** lacking warmth of feeling or enthusiasm; unfriendly or indifferent: *a frigid welcome.* —**fri·gid'i·ty, frig'id·ness,** *n.* —**frig'id·ly,** *adv.*

Frigid Zone, either of two extremely cold regions, one lying within the Arctic Circle and the other within the Antarctic Circle.

fri·jol (frē'hōl) *also,* **fri·jo·le** (frē hō'lē). *n. pl.,* **fri·joles** (frē'hōlz, frē hō'lēz). any of various beans used for food, especially in the southwestern United States, Mexico, and other Central and South American countries.

frill (fril) *n.* **1.** an ornamental trimming consisting of a strip of material, such as lace, gathered and attached along

at; āpe; cär; end; mē; it; īce; hot; ōld; fôrk; wood; fōōl; oil; out; up; turn; sing; thin; this; hw in white; zh in treasure. The symbol ə stands for the sound of a in about, e in taken, i in pencil, o in lemon, and u in circus.

F

one edge and left free along the other; ruffle. **2.** *also,* **frills.** anything showy or unnecessary: *a plain meal with no frills.* —**frill′y,** *adj.*

fringe (frinj) *n.* **1.** a border or trimming consisting of hanging threads, cords, tassels, or the like. **2.** anything like such a border or trimming: *A fringe of bushes lined the driveway.* **3.** an outer edge; border; margin: *The factory is on the fringe of the city.* —*v.t.,* **fringed, fring·ing. 1.** to provide with a fringe. **2.** to serve as a fringe for: *Flowers fringed the path to the house.*

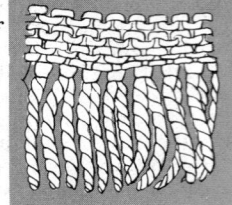

Fringe

fringe benefit, any benefit received by an employee in addition to wages or salary, such as pensions, health insurance, or paid vacations.

frip·per·y (frip′ər ē) *n. pl.,* **frip·per·ies. 1.** cheap, showy clothes or ornaments. **2.** showiness or pretense.

Fris·bee (friz′bē) *n. Trademark.* a plastic disk that is thrown back and forth through the air between players.

frisk (frisk) *v.i.* to leap, skip, or move about playfully; gambol; frolic: *The kittens frisked in the yard.* —*v.t. Informal.* to search (someone), especially for concealed weapons, by running the hand quickly over the pockets and clothing.

frisk·y (fris′kē) *adj.,* **frisk·i·er, frisk·i·est.** playful; lively. —**frisk′i·ly,** *adv.* —**frisk′i·ness,** *n.*

frit·ter¹ (frit′ər) *v.t.* to waste little by little: *to fritter away money. He frittered away his time doing nothing.* [Possibly a form of the older word *fitter* to break into pieces.] —**frit′ter·er,** *n.*

frit·ter² (frit′ər) *n.* a small cake made of fried batter, often containing fruit, vegetables, meat, or fish: *an apple fritter, a corn fritter.* [Old French *friture* something fried.]

fri·vol·i·ty (fri vol′ə tē) *n. pl.,* **fri·vol·i·ties. 1.** the quality or condition of being frivolous. **2.** a frivolous act or thing.

friv·o·lous (friv′ə ləs) *adj.* **1.** lacking seriousness or sense; silly. **2.** of little importance; trivial: *The scientist was too busy with her research to pay attention to frivolous matters.* —**friv′o·lous·ly,** *adv.* —**friv′o·lous·ness,** *n.*

frizz (friz) *also,* **friz.** *v.,* **frizzed, friz·zing.** —*v.t.* to form into small, tight curls: *to frizz one's hair.* —*v.i.* to become frizzed: *Her hair frizzes when it gets wet.* —*n. pl.,* **frizz·es.** something frizzed, especially hair.

friz·zle¹ (friz′əl) *v.,* **friz·zled, friz·zling.** —*v.t.* to form into small, tight curls; frizz. —*v.i.* to become frizzled. —*n.* something frizzed, especially hair. [*Frizz + -le.*]

friz·zle² (friz′əl) *v.,* **friz·zled, friz·zling.** —*v.t.* to fry (food) until crisp: *to frizzle bacon.* —*v.i.* to fry or cook with a sizzling noise. [Possibly a blend of *fry¹* and *sizzle.*]

friz·zly (friz′lē) *adj.,* **friz·zli·er, friz·zli·est.** another word for **frizzy.**

friz·zy (friz′ē) *adj.,* **friz·zi·er, friz·zi·est.** having small, tight curls. —**friz′zi·ly,** *adv.* —**friz′zi·ness,** *n.*

fro (frō) *adv.* **to and fro.** in different directions; back and forth: *The children ran to and fro across the playground.*

frock (frok) *n.* **1.** a woman's or girl's dress. **2.** a long, loose robe, especially one worn by monks and friars.

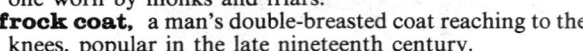

Frock coat

frock coat, a man's double-breasted coat reaching to the knees, popular in the late nineteenth century.

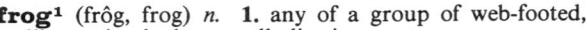

frog¹ (frôg, frog) *n.* **1.** any of a group of web-footed, tailless animals that usually live in or near water and have strong hind legs adapted for leaping. **2.** a triangular horny pad on the sole of a horse's foot. **3.** a device that permits the wheels of a railroad car to pass over the junction at intersecting tracks without difficulty. **4.** *Informal.* a slight irritation of the throat causing hoarseness. [Old English *frogga.*]

Frog²

frog² (frôg, frog) *n.* an ornamental fastening for clothing, usually made of braid that forms a loop on one side and a button on the other. [Of uncertain origin.]

frog·man (frôg′man′, frog′man′) *n. pl.,* **frog·men** (frôg′men′, frog′men′). a swimmer who is specially equipped and trained for underwater work, especially for military purposes.

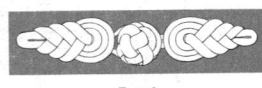

Frog¹

frol·ic (frol′ik) *v.i.,* **frol·icked, frol·ick·ing.** to move about or play with spirit or gaiety; make merry: *The children were frolicking in the yard.* —*n.* **1.** gay or spirited activity; romp. **2.** merriment; gaiety.

frol·ic·some (frol′ik səm) *adj.* gay and spirited; merry.

from (from, frum; *unstressed* frəm) *prep.* **1.** starting at; beginning with: *We flew from New York to Chicago. I worked from nine o'clock to five.* **2.** with a particular person, place, or thing as the source or origin: *a letter from John, light from the sun.* **3.** out of: *He took the money from his pocket.* **4.** out of the control, keeping, or possession of: *The rabbit escaped from the trap.* **5.** out of the whole of: *to subtract two from five.* **6.** at a distance of; out of contact with: *She lives about ten miles from my house.* **7.** by reason of; because of: *He acted from a sense of duty. She shivered from cold.*

frond (frond) *n.* **1.** the leaf of a fern or palm. **2.** a leaflike part of certain other plants, such as seaweed.

front (frunt) *n.* **1.** the part that faces forward: *the front of the body. The jacket had a zipper in the front.* **2.** the first or foremost part: *The introduction is in the front of the book.* **3.** a place or position ahead of or before: *She sat in front of me.* **4.** a person's attitude or manner when facing anything: *a bold front.* **5.** a large movement uniting various groups for the achievement of a common goal: *the labor front.* **6.** land facing or lying along a street, river, or the like; frontage: *We rented a cabin on the lake front.* **7.** the line or area of fighting between two enemy forces. **8.** *Informal.* an apparently respectable person or thing used to hide unlawful dealings or activities: *The real estate business was a front for the gang's gambling activities.* **9.** the boundary between two air masses of different origin and temperatures: *a warm front, a cold front.* —*adj.* at, on, or near the front: *the front door of a house, the front page of a newspaper.* —*v.t.* **1.** to face toward: *The cottage fronts the lake.* **2.** to provide with a front: *They fronted the building with red brick.* **3.** to meet face to face; defy; oppose: *to front an enemy.* —*v.i.* to have the front toward; face: *The house fronts on the street.*

front·age (frun′tij) *n.* **1.** the front of a building or lot. **2.** the length of this. **3.** land between a building and a street. **4.** land facing or lying along a street, river, or the like: *The house was built on ocean frontage.*

fron·tal (frunt′əl) *adj.* **1.** of, on, in, or at the front: *The enemy made a frontal attack.* **2.** of or relating to the forehead. —*n.* the bone of the front of the skull, forming the forehead. —**front′al·ly,** *adv.*

fron·tier (frun tēr′) *n.* **1.** the settled region of a country lying along the border of unsettled or undeveloped territory. **2.** that part of a country lying along the border of another country; border: *the frontier between Canada and the United States.* **3.** *also,* **frontiers.** any new or unexplored area: *the frontiers of medicine.* —*adj.* of, at, or on the frontier: *a frontier town.*

fron·tiers·man (frun tērz′mən) *n. pl.,* **fron·tiers·men** (frun tērz′mən). a person who lives on the frontier.

fron·tis·piece (frun′tis pēs′) *n.* an illustration facing the title page of a book or division of a book.

front·let (frunt′lit) *n.* **1.** a band or ornament worn on the forehead, especially a decorative headband of the Middle Ages. **2.** the forehead of an animal or bird.

frost (frôst) *n.* **1.** a deposit of minute ice crystals formed by the freezing of dew or water vapor on the surface of an exposed object or on the ground. **2.** a freezing condition of the atmosphere; severe cold: *Frost damaged the orange crop.* **3.** the act of freezing. —*v.t.* **1.** to cover with frost. **2.** to damage or destroy by frost. **3.** to cover with something like frost: *to frost glass.* **4.** to cover with frosting: *to frost a cake.*

Frost, Robert (frôst) 1874–1963, U.S. poet.

frost·bite (frôst′bīt′) *n.* a frozen or partly frozen condition of some part of the body as a result of too much exposure to extreme cold. —*v.t.,* **frost·bit** (frost′bit′), **frost·bit·ten, frost·bit·ing.** to damage or destroy by freezing: *The explorer's fingers and toes were frostbitten by the cold.*

frost·ed (frôs′tid) *adj.* **1.** covered with frost: *frosted window panes.* **2.** covered with frosting; iced: *a frosted cake.* **3.** having a dull surface like frost: *frosted glass.*

frost·ing (frôs′ting) *n.* **1.** a mixture of sugar, a liquid, butter, flavoring, and sometimes egg whites, used to cover baked goods; icing. **2.** a dull finish like frost on glass or metal.

frost·y (frôs′tē) *adj.,* **frost·i·er, frost·i·est. 1.** producing frost; freezing: *frosty weather.* **2.** covered with frost: *frosty windows.* **3.** cold in manner or feeling: *a frosty welcome.* —**frost′i·ly,** *adv.* —**frost′i·ness,** *n.*

froth (frôth) *n.* **1.** a mass of bubbles formed in or on a liquid; foam: *the froth on a glass of soda. There was froth at the mouth of the tired horse.* **2.** something light, trivial, or worthless, as ideas or conversation. —*v.i.* to give out or form froth; foam: *The rabid dog frothed at the mouth.* —*v.t.* to cause to foam.

froth·y (frô′thē) *adj.,* **froth·i·er, froth·i·est. 1.** covered with or full of froth; foamy. **2.** light, trivial, or worthless: *a frothy speech, a frothy newspaper column.* —**froth′i·ly,** *adv.* —**froth′i·ness,** *n.*

fro·ward (frō′wərd) *adj.* not easily managed; stubborn or disobedient: *a froward child.* —**fro′ward·ly,** *adv.* —**fro′ward·ness,** *n.*

frown (froun) *n.* **1.** a wrinkling of the brow, as in anger, thought, or disapproval. **2.** any expression of anger or disapproval. —*v.i.* **1.** to wrinkle the brow, as in anger, thought, or disapproval: *The teacher frowned at the rude boy.* **2.** to look with anger or disapproval: *His parents frowned on his staying out late.* —*v.t.* to show by wrinkling the brow: *to frown one's annoyance.*

frowz·y (frou′zē) *adj.,* **frowz·i·er, frowz·i·est. 1.** having a dirty or messy look; unkempt: *frowzy hair.* **2.** having an unpleasant smell; musty. —**frowz′i·ly,** *adv.* —**frowz′i·ness,** *n.*

froze (frōz) the past tense of **freeze.**

fro·zen (frō′zən) *v.* the past participle of **freeze.** —*adj.* **1.** changed into ice; made hard by cold. **2.** covered or clogged with ice: *a frozen lake, frozen water pipes.* **3.** unable to move: *frozen with fear.* **4.** (of food) preserved by freezing quickly: *a frozen turkey.* **5.** damaged or destroyed by frost or extreme cold: *frozen crops.* **6.** very cold; frigid: *a frozen climate.* **7.** fixed or set at a particular amount or level: *frozen wages.* **8.** cold and unfeeling: *a frozen stare.*

fruc·tose (fruk′tōs) *n.* a simple sugar occurring naturally in fruits and honey. Also, **fruit sugar.**

fru·gal (frōō′gəl) *adj.* **1.** not wasteful; economical; saving: *a frugal woman.* **2.** of little cost or amount; meager; spare: *a frugal meal.* —**fru′gal·ly,** *adv.*

fru·gal·i·ty (frōō gal′ə tē) *n.* the quality or condition of being frugal.

fruit (frōōt) *n. pl.,* **fruit** or **fruits. 1.** any plant product that can be eaten, such as an orange, apple, or pear. **2.** the part of a plant that contains the seeds. Nuts, grains, and pea pods are fruits. **3.** any useful plant product: *the fruits of the fields.* **4.** the result of an action: *His success was the fruit of hard work.* —*v.i.* to have or bear fruit.

fruit·age (frōō′tij) *n.* **1.** the state or process of producing fruit. **2.** a crop of fruit. **3.** the result of any action.

fruit cake, a rich cake containing preserved or dried fruit, nuts, and spices, and sometimes wine or brandy.

fruit fly, a small fly whose larvae feed chiefly on decaying fruit. Also, **drosophila.**

fruit·ful (frōōt′fəl) *adj.* **1.** producing good results; profitable: *a fruitful discussion.* **2.** bearing much fruit or many offspring: *a fruitful tree.* —**fruit′ful·ly,** *adv.* —**fruit′ful·ness,** *n.*

fru·i·tion (frōō ish′ən) *n.* **1.** the accomplishment of one's efforts; fulfillment: *After many years the inventor brought his ideas to fruition.* **2.** the bearing of fruit.

fruit·less (frōōt′lis) *adj.* **1.** having no effect or result; useless: *a fruitless effort.* **2.** bearing no fruit or offspring; barren: *a fruitless tree.* —**fruit′less·ly,** *adv.* —**fruit′less·ness,** *n.*

fruit sugar, another term for **fructose.**

fruit·y (frōō′tē) *adj.,* **fruit·i·er, fruit·i·est.** of, relating to, or like fruit, as in taste or smell. —**fruit′i·ness,** *n.*

frump (frump) *n.* a dowdy, often ill-tempered woman.

frus·trate (frus′trāt) *v.t.,* **frus·trat·ed, frus·trat·ing. 1.** to keep from doing or achieving something; disappoint or thwart: *He was frustrated by his inability to find a job.* **2.** to prevent (something) from being fulfilled; defeat: *The rainy weather frustrated our plans for a hike.*

frus·tra·tion (frus trā′shən) *n.* **1.** the act of frustrating or the state of being frustrated. **2.** something that frustrates.

fry[1] (frī) *v.,* **fried, fry·ing.** —*v.t.* to cook (something) in hot fat, usually over direct heat: *to fry potatoes.* —*v.i.* to cook in hot fat, usually over direct heat: *The potatoes fried quickly.* —*n. pl.,* **fries.** a social gathering, usually outdoors, at which food is fried and eaten: *a fish fry.* [Old French *frire.*]

fry[2] (frī) *n. pl.,* **fry.** a newly hatched fish. [Probably from Anglo-Norman *frie* fish eggs.]

fry·er (frī′ər) *n.* **1.** a young chicken suitable for frying. **2.** a deep pan for frying food. **3.** a person or thing that fries.

frying pan, a shallow pan, used for frying food.

ft. 1. feet; foot. **2.** fort. **3.** fortification.

---

at; āpe; cär; end; mē; it; īce; hot; ōld; fôrk; wood; fōōl; oil; out; up; turn; sing; thin; <u>th</u>is; hw in white; zh in treasure. The symbol ə stands for the sound of **a** in about, **e** in taken, **i** in pencil, **o** in lemon, and **u** in circus.

F

fuch·sia (fyōō′shə) *n.* **1.** any of a large group of tropical American shrubs or small trees, bearing pink, red, or purple clusters of funnel-shaped drooping flowers. **2.** a bright purplish-pink color. —*adj.* having the color fuchsia. [Modern Latin *Fuchsia,* from Leonhard *Fuchs,* 1501–1566, a German botanist.]

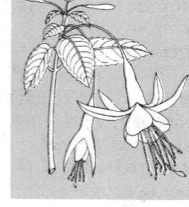

Fuchsia

fud·dle (fud′əl) *v.t.,* **fud·dled, fud·dling.** to muddle or confuse, as with liquor; befuddle.

fudge (fuj) *n.* **1.** a soft candy made of sugar, milk, butter, flavoring, and sometimes nuts **2.** empty talk; nonsense; foolishness.

Fueh·rer (fyoor′ər) another spelling of **Führer.**

fu·el (fyōō′əl) *n.* **1.** a substance burned as a source of heat and power, such as coal, wood, or oil. **2.** something that keeps alive or increases an emotion: *Her rude words added fuel to his anger.* —*v.,* **fu·eled, fu·el·ing;** also, British, **fu·elled, fu·el·ling.** —*v.t.* to supply with fuel: *to fuel an airplane.* —*v.i.* to take in fuel.

fuel cell, a device that produces electricity by a direct chemical reaction between a fuel and an oxidizer.

fu·gi·tive (fyōō′jə tiv) *n.* a person who flees or has fled, as from danger or pursuit: *a fugitive from the law.* —*adj.* **1.** fleeing or having fled. **2.** not lasting; fleeting: *fugitive thoughts.*

fugue (fyōōg) *n.* a musical composition based on one or more short themes or subjects that are repeated by different voices or instruments and developed according to the rules of counterpoint.

Füh·rer (fyoor′ər) *also,* **Fueh·rer.** *n. German.* **1.** a leader. **2. der Führer.** the title of Adolf Hitler as head of Nazi Germany.

Fu·ji (fōō′jē) *n.* the highest mountain in Japan, in the south-central part of the island of Honshu. Also, **Fu·ji·ya·ma** (fōō′jē yä′mə).

-ful *suffix* **1.** full of or characterized by: *graceful, peaceful.* **2.** tending or able to: *forgetful, helpful.* **3.** having the qualities of: *manful.* **4.** the number or amount that fills or will fill: *spoonful, glassful.*

ful·crum (fool′krəm) *n. pl.,* **ful·crums** or **ful·cra** (fool′-krə). the support or point of support upon which a lever rests, or about which it turns when in use.

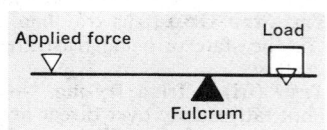

Fulcrum

ful·fill (fool fil′) *also,* **ful·fil.** *v.t.,* **ful·filled, ful·fill·ing. 1.** to carry out or bring to completion; cause to happen: *to fulfill a dream, to fulfill a promise.* **2.** to meet or satisfy: *She could not fulfill the necessary requirements for the job.* **3.** to bring to an end (a period of time or a task); finish: *to fulfill a homework assignment.* **4.** to do or perform (a duty or request).

ful·fill·ment (fool fil′mənt) *also,* **ful·fil·ment.** *n.* **1.** the act or process of being fulfilled. **2.** something that fulfills.

full (fool) *adj.* **1.** containing as much or as many as possible; with no empty space: *a full glass of water.* **2.** having or containing a large number, quantity, or amount: *a house full of people. His report was full of spelling errors.* **3.** complete, as in extent, quantity, or number; entire: *a full dozen, a full day, a full set of dishes.* **4.** having reached the greatest possible size, degree, or amount: *full strength, full speed.* **5.** filled with enough food or drink: *I am full.* **6.** having a rounded outline; well filled out; plump: *full*

hips, *a full face.* **7.** strong, clear, and rich: *full tones, a full voice.* **8.** having loose, wide folds or much cloth: *a full skirt.* —*adv.* **1.** straight; directly: *He looked her full in the face.* **2.** to the greatest possible degree or extent; completely; entirely: *He filled the bag full.* **3.** very; exceedingly: *You know full well that I am right.* —**full′ness,** *n.*

in full. a. to or for the entire amount: *He paid the bill in full.* **b.** without shortening or cutting: *They reprinted the document in full.*

to the full. completely; entirely: *His grandfather enjoyed life to the full.*

full·back (fool′bak′) *n. Football.* a player on the offensive team who usually lines up farthest behind the front line.

full-blood·ed (fool′blud′id) *adj.* **1.** of unmixed race, breed, or ancestry. **2.** full of energy or vigor; hearty.

full-blown (fool′blōn′) *adj.* **1.** (of flowers) in full bloom: *a full-blown rose.* **2.** fully developed or perfected.

full dress, formal attire, as worn for ceremonial occasions.

Ful·ler·ton (fool′ər tən) *n.* a city in southern California. Pop. (1970), 85,826.

full-fledged (fool′flejd′) *adj.* **1.** having full rank or status: *a full-fledged citizen.* **2.** fully developed or mature: *a full-fledged bird.*

full-grown (fool′grōn′) *adj.* having reached full size or maturity; fully grown: *a full-grown horse.*

full-length (fool′lengkth′) *adj.* **1.** showing or covering the whole length of an object or figure: *a full-length mirror, a full-length dress.* **2.** not shortened or cut: *a full-length novel.*

full moon 1. the moon when the whole of its face is illuminated, as seen from the earth. **2.** the time of month when this occurs.

full-rigged (fool′rigd′) *adj.* (of a ship) having complete rigging for three or more masts and a full set of sails.

full-scale (fool′skāl′) *adj.* **1.** of the same size as the original; of actual size: *a full-scale drawing.* **2.** not limited; complete: *a full-scale war.*

ful·ly (fool′ē) *adv.* **1.** to the fullest extent or degree; completely; entirely: *to be fully aware of the facts.* **2.** at least; not less than: *He was fully two hours late.*

ful·mi·nate (fool′mə nāt′) *v.,* **ful·mi·nat·ed, ful·mi·nat·ing.** —*v.i.* **1.** to make loud and violent threats, protests, or denunciations: *The speaker fulminated against the increase in crime.* **2.** to explode with sudden violence. —*v.t.* **1.** to threaten, protest, or denounce violently. **2.** to cause (something) to explode with sudden violence. —*n.* any of several explosive substances used as detonators. —**ful′mi·na′tion,** *n.*

ful·some (fool′səm) *adj.* so much as to be offensive to good taste: *fulsome praise.* —**ful′some·ly,** *adv.* —**ful′some·ness,** *n.*

Ful·ton, Robert (foolt′ən) 1765–1815, U.S. inventor who developed the first successful steamboat.

fum·ble (fum′bəl) *v.,* **fum·bled, fum·bling.** —*v.i.* **1.** to search or grope about clumsily: *He fumbled for his wallet.* **2.** to make an awkward or clumsy attempt: *He fumbled at opening the lock.* **3.** to handle or finger something clumsily or aimlessly: *She fumbled nervously with her necklace.* **4.** in sports, to catch and then lose hold of a ball. —*v.t.* **1.** to handle or deal with awkwardly: *She fumbled her chances.* **2.** in sports, to catch and then lose hold of (a ball). —*n.* **1.** the act of fumbling. **2.** a ball that is fumbled. —**fum′bler,** *n.*

fume (fyōōm) *n.* **1.** *also,* **fumes.** a smoke, gas, or vapor, especially when irritating or offensive: *the fumes of a car's exhaust.* **2.** a strongly penetrating odor: *fumes from the city dump.* —*v.,* **fumed, fum·ing.** —*v.i.* **1.** to give off fumes. **2.** to be filled with anger or irritation: *The man fumed as he waited in the heavy traffic jam.* —*v.t.* to expose to or treat with fumes.

fu·mi·gate (fyōō′mə gāt′) *v.t.,* **fu·mi·gat·ed, fu·mi·gat·ing.** to expose to fumes, especially so as to disinfect: *She fumigated the room to kill the mosquitoes.* —**fu′mi·ga′tion,** *n.* —**fu′mi·ga′tor,** *n.*

fun (fun) *n.* **1.** amusement or enjoyment; diversion; recreation: *The children had fun riding their sleds.* **2.** playfulness or gaiety: *He is full of fun.*

for fun or **in fun.** not seriously; in jest; playfully.

to make fun of or **to poke fun at.** to laugh at; ridicule.

func·tion (fungk′shən) *n.* **1.** the proper or natural action or use of anything; purpose: *The function of the kidneys is to excrete wastes from the body.* **2.** a special duty or action required of a person: *What is his function on the committee?* **3.** a formal social gathering or official ceremony. **4.** *Mathematics.* **a.** a quantity whose value depends on the value of another quantity. **b.** the relationship between two sets in which at least one element of the second set is paired with one element of the first set. —*v.i.* **1.** to work; act: *The motor functions best when it is kept well oiled.* **2.** to perform the role of something else; serve: *The box functioned as a table.*

func·tion·al (fungk′shən əl) *adj.* **1.** of or relating to a function or functions: *That machine has functional problems. He has a functional disorder of the stomach.* **2.** having a function: *a functional kitchen.* **3.** *Mathematics.* relating to or designating a function. —**func′tion·al·ly,** *adv.*

func·tion·ar·y (fungk′shə ner′ē) *n. pl.,* **func·tion·ar·ies.** a public official: *The mayor and other functionaries welcomed the astronauts.*

function word, a word used to express grammatical relationship in a sentence or phrase, such as a conjunction, preposition, or auxiliary verb.

● You can divide all the words of our language into two basic types: **function words,** or **functors,** and **contentive words.** Function words, which never change their form, are unusual in that their primary importance lies not in their vocabulary meaning but in their use or function in a phrase or sentence. The primary importance of contentive words, on the other hand, does lie in their vocabulary meaning, or content. Function words, such as *the, of, some,* or *for* give us information about contentive words. Contentive words include nouns, such as *dogs, chairs,* or *friends,* verbs, such as *run, sleep,* or *swim,* and adjectives, such as *strong, happy,* or *cold.*

You might find it difficult to define function words like *the, of,* or *some,* but you can easily observe how they affect the meaning of the contentive words with which they are used. For example, the phrases *the dogs, of dogs,* and *some dogs* all have quite different meanings.

The number of function words in English is relatively small, and there has been almost no change in this group of words for hundreds of years. Contentives, on the other hand, are an enormously large group of words, and new ones are constantly being added to the language. Nevertheless, function words are the most commonly used words in English. As a matter of fact, they are the building blocks of our language. Consider this phrase: *girl cut finger.* This phrase could mean, among other things, *a girl cut a finger; some girl cut some finger; the girl cut some finger.* Each of these sentences means something different because the function words in each connect the contentive words in quite different ways.

To understand the difference between function words and contentives, think of the language people use in sending telegrams. Since each word used in a telegram costs money, people usually leave out any word that is not necessary to convey the vocabulary meaning of what they want to say. For example, a person might send a telegram saying "Missed plane Chicago. New arrival time La Guardia seven P.M. Friday. Please meet airport lounge." Although this telegram contains no grammatically correct sentences, you can easily understand its meaning. But in order to convert it to a series of normal English sentences, we would have to add many function words: "*I* missed *my* plane *in* Chicago. *My* new arrival time *at* La Guardia *is* seven P.M. Friday. Please meet *me at the* airport lounge."

func·tor (fungk′tər) *n.* another term for **function word.**

fund (fund) *n.* **1.** a sum of money set aside for a specific purpose: *a fund for a political campaign.* **2.** a stock or supply: *This book has a fund of information on American Indians.* **3. funds.** money that is readily available: *What funds does he have to finance that business?* —*v.t.* **1.** to provide money for a longer period of payment of (a debt). **2.** to provide a fund or money for: *to fund an organization.*

fun·da·men·tal (fun′də ment′əl) *adj.* relating to or serving as a foundation; basic; essential: *Learning the rules is a fundamental part of a game.* —*n.* **1.** anything that forms or serves as the basis of a system, principle, rule, or law: *the fundamentals of arithmetic.* **2.** *Physics.* the component of a wave that has the lowest frequency. —**fun′da·men′tal·ly,** *adv.*

Fun·dy, Bay of (fun′dē) an inlet of the Atlantic Ocean in eastern Canada, noted for its very high tides.

fu·ner·al (fyōō′nər əl) *n.* **1.** the burial or cremation of the body of a dead person, together with religious services or other accompanying ceremonies. **2.** the procession accompanying the body of a dead person to the place of burial or cremation. —*adj.* of or suitable for a funeral: *a funeral service.*

fu·ne·re·al (fyōō nēr′ē əl) *adj.* **1.** of, relating to, or suitable for a funeral. **2.** sad; gloomy; dismal: *a funereal atmosphere.* —**fu·ne′re·al·ly,** *adv.*

fun·gi (fun′jī) a plural of **fungus.**

fun·gi·cide (fun′jə sīd′) *n.* any substance used in destroying fungi.

fun·gous (fung′gəs) *adj.* **1.** of, relating to, or caused by a fungus: *a fungous disease.* **2.** springing up or spreading suddenly.

fun·gus (fung′gəs) *n. pl.,* **fun·gi** or **fun·gus·es. 1.** any of a large group of plants that lack flowers, leaves, or chlorophyll and live on other plants or animal matter. Mildews, mushrooms, and molds are fungi. **2.** a diseased, spongy growth on the body.

fu·nic·u·lar (fyōō nik′yə lər) *n.* a railway system in which two cars attached to both ends of a cable along a steep slope move alternately up and down the slope by counterbalancing and pulling each other.

fun·nel (fun′əl) *n.* **1.** a utensil

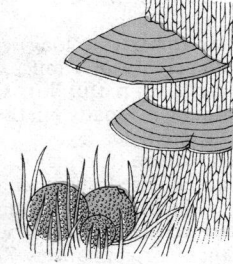

Fungi

at; āpe; cär; end; mē; it; īce; hot; ōld; fôrk; wood; fōōl; oil; out; up; turn; sing; thin; this; hw in white; zh in treasure. The symbol ə stands for the sound of a in about, e in taken, i in pencil, o in lemon, and u in circus.

with a tube at one end and a wide, cone-shaped mouth at the other, used for pouring a substance into a container with a small opening. **2.** a round chimney or smokestack, as on a steamship or locomotive. —*v.,* **fun·neled, fun·nel·ing;** *also, British,* **fun·nelled, fun·nel·ling.** —*v.t.* to cause (something) to pass through a funnel: *to funnel water into a jar.* —*v.i.* to pass through a funnel: *The water funneled down the drainpipe.*

fun·nies (fun′ēz) *n., pl.* **1.** comic strips. **2.** the section of a newspaper containing them.

fun·ny (fun′ē) *adj.,* **fun·ni·er, fun·ni·est. 1.** causing laughter or amusement; comical: *a funny joke.* **2.** *Informal.* strange or suspicious; odd: *She gave me a funny look when I came into the room.* —**fun′ni·ly,** *adv.* —**fun′ni·ness,** *n.*

funny bone, a part of the elbow where a nerve passes very close to the skin. When it is struck, a sharp, tingling sensation is felt in the arm and hand. Also, **crazy bone.**

fur (fur) *n.* **1.** the soft, thick, hairy coat of certain animals. **2.** a piece of animal skin with such a coat, prepared for use in clothing, rugs, and other items. **3.** an article of clothing, as a coat, made of such skin. **4.** a coating of fuzzy foul matter, as on the tongue of a sick person. —*v.,* **furred, fur·ring.** —*v.t.* **1.** to cover, trim, or line with fur. **2.** to coat with a fuzzy deposit of foul matter. —*v.i.* to become coated with a fuzzy deposit of foul matter. —**fur′like′,** *adj.*

fur·be·low (fur′bə lō′) *n.* **1.** a frill, ruffle, or similar trimming, especially on women's clothing. **2.** *also,* **furbe·lows.** any showy or useless trimming. —*v.t.* to furnish or trim with furbelows.

fur·bish (fur′bish) *v.t.* **1.** to make bright by rubbing; polish; burnish: *We furbished the old silver mug.* **2.** to restore to a fresh or usable condition; renovate: *to furbish an old chair.* —**fur′bish·er,** *n.* —**fur′bish·ment,** *n.*

Fu·ries (fyoor′ēz) *n. Greek and Roman Mythology.* three hideous female spirits who punished wrongdoers.

fu·ri·ous (fyoor′ē əs) *adj.* **1.** extremely angry; full of rage: *He was furious at her insulting remarks.* **2.** extremely violent or intense: *Summer is frequently a time of furious thunderstorms.* **3.** unrestrained, as in activity, speed, or energy: *The car raced down the highway at a furious speed.* —**fu′ri·ous·ly,** *adv.* —**fu′ri·ous·ness,** *n.*

furl (furl) *v.t.* to roll up and fasten, as to a staff or mast: *to furl a sail.* —*v.i.* to become furled. —*n.* **1.** the act of furling or the state of being furled. **2.** a rolled-up section, as of a flag.

fur·long (fur′lông) *n.* a measure of distance equal to one-eighth of a mile, or 220 yards.

fur·lough (fur′lō) *n.* an official leave of absence from duty, especially in the armed services. —*v.t.* to give a furlough to.

fur·nace (fur′nis) *n.* a structure or apparatus containing an enclosed chamber in which intense heat is produced, as for heating buildings or melting metals.

fur·nish (fur′nish) *v.t.* **1.** to equip with furniture, fixtures, or appliances: *The family finally finished furnishing their new home.* **2.** to supply with whatever is necessary or wanted; provide: *The book furnished us with facts about the Civil War.* —**fur′nish·er,** *n.*

fur·nish·ings (fur′ni shingz) *n., pl.* **1.** furniture, fixtures, or appliances, as for a house or office. **2.** articles of clothing and accessories: *men's furnishings.*

fur·ni·ture (fur′ni chər) *n.* movable articles, such as tables, chairs, or beds, used to make a room suitable for use.

fu·ror (fyoor′ôr) *n.* **1.** a great outburst of enthusiasm or

Funnel

excitement; commotion: *There was a great furor at the bank when the theft was discovered.* **2.** frenzy or rage.

fur·ri·er (fur′ē ər) *n.* a person who deals in or works with furs.

fur·row (fur′ō) *n.* **1.** a long, narrow groove or channel made in the ground by a plow. **2.** any long, narrow groove or channel, as a rut: *There were furrows in the dusty road made by cars.* —*v.t.* **1.** to make a furrow or furrows in, as with a plow. **2.** to make deep wrinkles in: *Age had furrowed the old woman's face.*

fur·ry (fur′ē) *adj.,* **fur·ri·er, fur·ri·est. 1.** made of or like fur: *a furry rug.* **2.** covered with fur. —**fur′ri·ness,** *n.*

fur·ther (fur′thər) *adj.* a comparative of **far. 1.** additional; more: *without further delay, further discussion.* **2.** more distant in time, space, or degree; farther. —*adv.* a comparative of **far. 1.** at or to a more distant point in time or space; farther. **2.** to a greater degree or extent; more: *to inquire further into a problem.* **3.** in addition; moreover. —*v.t.* to help forward; promote or support: *to further the cause of peace.* ▲ See **farther** for usage note.

fur·ther·ance (fur′thər əns) *n.* the act of furthering; advancement; promotion.

fur·ther·more (fur′thər môr′) *adv.* in addition; moreover; besides.

fur·ther·most (fur′thər mōst′) *adj.* most distant; furthest.

fur·thest (fur′thist) *adv.* a superlative of **far. 1.** at or to the most distant point in time or space: *He threw the ball furthest of all the players.* **2.** to the greatest degree or extent; most. —*adj.* a superlative of **far.** most distant in time, space, or degree.

fur·tive (fur′tiv) *adj.* **1.** done by stealth; secret: *a furtive glance.* **2.** shifty; sly: *furtive eyes.* —**fur′tive·ly,** *adv.* —**fur′tive·ness,** *n.*

fu·ry (fyoor′ē) *n. pl.,* **fu·ries. 1.** violent, uncontrollable anger. **2.** a fit of such anger: *He was in a fury at the insult.* **3.** violence; fierceness: *the fury of a storm.* **4.** a person having a violent or uncontrollable temper. **5. Fury.** one of the Furies.

furze (furz) *n.* any of a group of spiny shrubs found in Europe, Asia, and parts of North America, bearing yellow flowers. Also, **gorse.**

fuse[1] (fyooz) *also,* **fuze.** *n.* **1.** a strip of metal inserted in an electric circuit. It melts and breaks the circuit if the current becomes too strong. **2.** a length of cord or tubing filled or soaked with material that will burn, used to set off an explosive charge: *the fuse on a stick of dynamite.* [Italian *fuso* a rod used to hold thread.]

fuse[2] (fyooz) *v.,* **fused, fus·ing.** —*v.t.* **1.** to melt (something), especially by heating. **2.** to blend or unite by melting together: *to fuse metals.* —*v.i.* **1.** to melt, especially by heating. **2.** to be or become united by melting together: *The two committees fused into one to raise money for the new school.* [Latin *fūsus.*]

fu·see (fyoo zē′) *n.* **1.** a match with a large head that will burn in a wind. **2.** a red or green flare used as a railroad signal.

fu·se·lage (fyoo′sə läzh′, fyoo′sə lij) *n.* the main body of an airplane carrying the passengers, cargo, and crew.

fu·si·ble (fyoo′zə bəl) *adj.* capable of being fused or melted: *a fusible metal.* —**fu′si·bil′i·ty,** *n.*

fu·sil·ier (fyoo′zə lēr′) *also,* **fu·sil·eer. 1.** a soldier of any of several regiments of the British army. **2.** formerly, a soldier armed with a light flintlock musket.

fu·sil·lade (fyoo′sə lād′) *n.* **1.** the discharge or firing of firearms at the same time or continuously. **2.** anything like this: *a fusillade of rain, a fusillade of criticism.*

fu·sion (fyoo′zhən) *n.* **1.** the act or process of fusing; melting together: *the fusion of metals.* **2.** the state of being fused: *metals in fusion.* **3.** the union or blending together of different things, as of political parties. **4.** something formed by fusing; fused mass. **5.** *Physics.* the combining of two light nuclei to form a heavier nucleus. Fusion occurs when the light nuclei are heated to extremely high temperatures, releasing huge amounts of energy, as in the explosion of a hydrogen bomb.

fusion bomb, another term for **hydrogen bomb.**

fuss (fus) *n. pl.,* **fuss·es. 1.** unnecessary stir or bother over small or unimportant things: *There was a great fuss in the school when the holiday was canceled.* **2.** a slight quarrel or dispute; spat: *The children had a fuss about who would be the leader.* **3.** a protest or complaint: *The passengers will make a fuss if the train is late again.* —*v.i.* **1.** to make an unnecessary stir: *She fussed over dinner for her guests.* **2.** to have a slight quarrel or dispute. —**fuss′er,** *n.*

fuss·y (fus′ē) *adj.,* **fuss·i·er, fuss·i·est. 1.** hard to please; finicky: *She is very fussy about food.* **2.** requiring much attention to details: *He had a fussy job to finish.* **3.** elaborately made or trimmed: *a fussy dress.* —**fuss′i·ly,** *adv.* —**fuss′i·ness,** *n.*

fust·y (fus′tē) *adj.,* **fust·i·er, fust·i·est. 1.** having a stale smell; musty; moldy: *a fusty old trunk.* **2.** old-fashioned in appearance or behavior; not up-to-date. —**fust′i·ly,** *adv.* —**fust′i·ness,** *n.*

fu·tile (fyōot′əl) *adj.* useless or hopeless; ineffective; vain: *The workers and the owners of the factory made futile efforts at reaching an agreement that would settle the strike.* —**fu′tile·ly,** *adv.*

fu·til·i·ty (fyōo til′ə tē) *n. pl.,* **fu·til·i·ties. 1.** the quality of being futile. **2.** something that is futile.

fu·ture (fyōo′chər) *adj.* **1.** that is to be or happen in time to come: *He hoped his future work would be better.* **2.** *Grammar.* indicating a state or action in time to come. —*n.* **1.** time that is to come: *In the future, please call if you are going to be late.* **2.** something that will be or

happen in time to come: *No one can predict the future with certainty.* **3.** the opportunity of success or prosperity in time to come: *He has a good future in business.* **4.** *Grammar.* the future tense or a verb in this tense.

future perfect 1. a verb tense expressing an action or state of being that is completed before a specified time in the future. It is formed in English with "will have" or "shall have." In the sentence *He will have finished the job by tomorrow, will have finished* is in the future perfect tense. **2.** a verb form in this tense.

future tense 1. a verb tense expressing an action or state happening or existing in time to come. In the sentence *John will come tomorrow, will come* is in the future tense. **2.** a verb form in this tense.

fu·tu·ri·ty (fyōo toor′ə tē, fyōo tyoor′ə tē) *n. pl.,* **fu·tu·ri·ties. 1.** the future. **2.** the state or quality of being future. **3.** a future event.

fuze (fyōoz) another spelling of **fuse**[1].

Fu·zhou (fōo′jō′) another spelling of **Foochow.**

fuzz (fuz) *n.* fine, loose particles, hair, or fibers: *peach fuzz.*

fuzz·y (fuz′ē) *adj.,* **fuzz·i·er, fuzz·i·est. 1.** having or covered with fuzz. **2.** resembling fuzz. **3.** not clear; indistinct; blurred: *fuzzy thinking.* —**fuzz′i·ly,** *adv.* —**fuzz′i·ness,** *n.*

-fy *suffix* (used to form verbs) **1.** to cause to be or become; make: *simplify, pacify.* **2.** to become: *solidify.* **3.** to make similar to: *countrify.*

at; āpe; cär; end; mē; it; īce; hot; ōld; fôrk; wood; fōol; oil; out; up; turn; sing; thin; this; hw in white; zh in treasure. The symbol ə stands for the sound of a in about, e in taken, i in pencil, o in lemon, and u in circus.

F

1. Semitic 7⌐	**4. Latin Fourth Century B.C. Capitals** ⟨ C
2. Greek Ninth Century B.C. ⌐7	**5. Classical Latin** G
3. Etruscan 7 ⟨ ⟨	**6. English** G

G is the seventh letter of the English alphabet. Although the modern letter **G** was developed from the Latin letter **C**, it has its roots in the earliest alphabets. The oldest form of **G** was *gimel* (1), the third letter of the ancient Semitic alphabet. *Gimel* was passed down, with only slight changes, through various alphabets and adopted by the Greeks, who called it *gamma* (2). Both *gimel* and *gamma* represented a hard *g* sound, as the *g* in *game*. The Etruscans (3) borrowed *gamma* and, because they made no distinction between a hard *g* and a *k*, used it to represent both sounds. When the Romans adopted the Etruscan alphabet, they also used a form of *gamma*, which had begun to look very much like a modern capital letter **C**, to stand for both the hard *g* and *k* sounds. In Latin the *k* sound was more common than the hard *g* sound. As a result of this, the Latin letter **C** (4), which according to its early history should have been pronounced as a hard *g*, became more and more identified with the *k* sound. About 2200 years ago, the Romans began to use **C** to represent only the *k* sound and devised a new letter (5) to represent the hard *g* sound. This letter, which was made by adding a short line to the letter **C**, was written almost exactly as we write the capital letter **G** today (6).

g, G (jē) *n. pl.*, **g's, G's. 1.** the seventh letter of the English alphabet. **2.** *Music.* the fifth note of the scale of C major. **3.** the unit of measurement of the force acting on bodies undergoing acceleration. It is equal to the acceleration of gravity, approximately 32.2 feet per second per second at sea level.

g. 1. gram; grams. **2.** gauge.

G. 1. specific gravity. **2.** Gulf.

Ga, the symbol for gallium.

Ga., Georgia.

G.A., General Assembly.

gab (gab) *v.i.*, **gabbed, gab·bing.** *Informal.* to talk idly or too much; chatter: *I gabbed on the telephone with my best friend for over an hour.* —*n.* idle or excessive talk; chatter. —**gab′ber,** *n.*

gab·ar·dine (gab′ər dēn′) *n.* **1.** strong, closely woven fabric, having slanting ribs on its surface. It is used for such items as sportswear, coats, and suits. **2.** another spelling of **gaberdine** (*def. 1*).

gab·ble (gab′əl) *v.,* **gab·bled, gab·bling.** —*v.i.* to talk rapidly or foolishly without making sense; jabber. —*v.t.* to say (something) rapidly or foolishly without making sense: *The student quickly gabbled his excuses for arriving late in class.* —*n.* rapid, foolish, or meaningless talk. —**gab′bler,** *n.*

gab·by (gab′ē) *adj.,* **gab·bi·er, gab·bi·est.** *Informal.* very talkative.

gab·er·dine (gab′ər dēn′) *n.* **1.** a loose cloak or smock worn by men in the Middle Ages. **2.** another spelling of **gabardine** (*def. 1*).

Ga·be·ro·nes (gä′bə rō′nəs) *n.* see **Gaborone.**

ga·ble (gā′bəl) *n.* **1.** the section of an outside wall surface, usually triangular, between the sides of a sloped roof. **2.** any architectural feature having the form of a gable, as over a door or window.

ga·bled (gā′bəld) *adj.* having or built with a gable or gables.

gable roof, a ridged roof that forms a gable either at one or both ends.

Gables

Ga·bon (gä bōn′) *n.* a country on the west coast of central Africa. Capital, Libreville. Area, 103,347 sq. mi. Pop. (1980), 551,000. —**Gab′o·nese′,** *adj., n.*

Ga·bo·rone (gä′bə rōn′) *n.* the capital of Botswana. Pop. (1971), 18,799.

Ga·bri·el (gā′brē əl) *n.* in the Bible, the archangel chosen by God as His divine messenger.

gad (gad) *v.i.*, **gad·ded, gad·ding.** to move about restlessly or aimlessly, as in search of fun or excitement; roam.

gad·a·bout (gad′ə bout′) *n. Informal.* a person who moves about restlessly or aimlessly, especially in search of fun or excitement.

gad·fly (gad′flī′) *n. pl.*, **gad·flies. 1.** a large blood-sucking fly that bites animals, especially horses and cattle. **2.** a person who constantly annoys, irritates, or stirs up others.

gad·get (gaj′it) *n. Informal.* a small mechanical device.

gad·o·lin·i·um (gad′əl in′ē əm) *n.* a metallic element, one of the rare-earth elements. Symbol: **Gd** [Modern Latin *gadolinium*, from Johann *Gadolin*, 1760–1852, a Finnish chemist.]

Gae·a (jē′ə) *also,* **Gai·a.** *n.* *Greek Mythology.* the earth goddess who was the mother and wife of Uranus and mother of the Cyclopes and Titans.

Gael (gāl) *n.* **1.** see **Highlander** *(def. 2a).* **2.** one of the Celtic people of Scotland, Ireland, or the Isle of Man.

Gael·ic (gā′lik) *adj.* of or relating to the Gaels or their languages. —*n.* any of the languages of the Gaels.

gaff (gaf) *n.* **1.** a large, sharp hook at the end of a pole, used to help pull large fish out of the water. **2.** a pole having such a hook. **3.** a spar for extending the upper edge of a fore-and-aft sail. —*v.t.* to hook or land (a fish) with a gaff.

gaf·fer (gaf′ər) *n.* an old man.

gag (gag) *n.* **1.** something stuffed into or put over the mouth to prevent a person from talking or crying out. **2.** anything used to restrain or suppress freedom of speech. **3.** *Slang.* an amusing act or remark; joke. —*v.,* **gagged, gag·ging.** —*v.t.* **1.** to prevent from speaking or crying out by means of a gag: *The kidnapers gagged and bound the child.* **2.** to restrain or suppress freedom of speech; silence: *The government gagged the revolutionary newspaper.* —*v.i.* to heave with nausea; choke; retch: *John gagged when he took the medicine.*

Ga·ga·rin, Yu·ri (gä gär′in; yŏŏ′rē) 1934–1968, Russian cosmonaut, the first man to fly in outer space.

gage¹ (gāj) *n.* something given as security that an obligation or promise will be fulfilled; pledge. [Old French *gage* or *guage* pledge.]

gage² (gāj) another spelling of **gauge.**

Gage, Thomas (gāj) 1721–1787, British general in the American Revolution.

Gai·a (jē′ə) another spelling of **Gaea.**

gai·e·ty (gā′ə tē) *also,* **gay·e·ty.** *n. pl.,* **gai·e·ties.** **1.** the state or quality of being gay; cheerfulness. **2.** merry-making; festivity: *We look forward to taking part in the gaieties of the holiday season.* **3.** brightness or showiness, as of appearance or dress.

gai·ly (gā′lē) *also,* **gay·ly.** *adv.* in a gay manner.

gain (gān) *v.t.* **1.** to get by effort; obtain; secure: *to gain the advantage in an argument, to gain time by stalling.* **2.** to get or develop as an increase, addition, advantage, or profit: *to gain weight, to gain strength.* **3.** to get in competition or combat; win: *They gained the battle but lost many men.* **4.** to get to; arrive at; reach: *The ship gained the port before the storm struck.* —*v.i.* **1.** to improve, progress, or advance: *to gain in health.* **2.** to advance nearer, as to an opponent in a race; come closer: *The black horse is gaining on the brown one.* —*n.* **1.** something that is gained: *a ten-pound gain in weight. The halfback made a gain of ten yards on that last play.* **2. gains.** something acquired as profits, earnings, or winnings. **3.** the act of gaining; acquisition.

gain·er (gā′nər) *n.* **1.** a person or thing that gains. **2.** a dive in which the diver faces the water and then does a full backward somersault, entering the water feet first. **3.** a dive in which the diver does a half backward somersault and enters the water head first.

gain·ful (gān′fəl) *adj.* bringing or producing gain; profitable. —**gain′ful·ly,** *adv.*

gain·say (gān′sā′) *v.t.,* **gain·said** (gān′sād′, gān′sed′), **gain·say·ing.** to deny or contradict: *Do not gainsay the facts.*

Gains·bor·ough, Thomas (gānz′bur′ō) 1727–1788, English painter.

gainst (genst) *also,* **'gainst.** *prep. Archaic.* against.

gait (gāt) *n.* **1.** a particular manner of moving on foot:

The young boy walked with a slow and easy gait. **2.** any of the particular ways in which a horse steps or runs.

gai·ter (gā′tər) *n.* **1.** a covering made of cloth or leather for the ankle, and sometimes the lower leg, worn over the top of a shoe. **2.** a shoe with elastic inserts on the sides. **3.** an overshoe with a cloth top.

gal., gallon; gallons.

ga·la (gā′lə, gal′ə) *adj.* of, relating to, or suitable for a festive occasion; festive: *Her birthday was marked with a gala celebration.* —*n.* a festive occasion or celebration.

ga·lac·tic (gə lak′tik) *adj.* of or relating to a galaxy or galaxies, especially the Milky Way.

Gal·a·had, Sir (gal′ə had′) in the legends of King Arthur, the purest and most virtuous knight of the Round Table. According to one story, he was the only knight to find the Holy Grail.

Ga·lá·pa·gos Islands (gə lä′pə gōs′) an island group in the eastern Pacific, west of and belonging to Ecuador.

Gal·a·te·a (gal′ə tē′ə) *n. Greek Legend.* the statue of a maiden carved by Pygmalion, who then fell in love with it. Aphrodite brought the statue to life in answer to Pygmalion's prayers.

Ga·la·tians (gə lā′shənz) *n.* a book of the New Testament, an epistle written by the Apostle Paul.

gal·ax·y (gal′ək sē) *n. pl.,* **gal·ax·ies.** **1.** any of the vast groupings of stars, dust, and gases scattered throughout the universe. **2.** *also,* **Galaxy.** the Milky Way. **3.** a brilliant or splendid group: *The opening of the show was attended by a galaxy of celebrities.*

gale (gāl) *n.* **1.** a very strong wind, especially one having a velocity of from thirty-two to sixty-three miles per hour. **2.** a noisy outburst, as of laughter.

ga·le·na (gə lē′nə) *n.* a gray metallic ore. It is the principal source of lead and an important source of silver.

Ga·li·cia (gə lish′ə) *n.* **1.** a historic region in east-central Europe, now divided between Poland and the Ukraine. **2.** a region and ancient kingdom in northwestern Spain. —**Ga·li′cian,** *adj., n.*

Gal·i·le·an (gal′ə lē′ən) *adj.* of or relating to Galilee or its people. —*n.* a person who was born or is living in Galilee. **2. the Galilean.** another name for **Jesus.**

Gal·i·lee (gal′ə lē′) *n.* **1.** a small region in northernmost Palestine. Jesus spent much of his life in Galilee. **2. Sea of.** a small, freshwater lake in northeastern Israel. Also *(def. 2),* **Lake Tiberias.**

Gal·i·le·o (gal′ə lē′ō) 1564–1642, Italian astronomer, physicist, and mathematician; full name, Galileo Galilei.

gall¹ (gôl) *n.* **1.** see **bile** *(def. 1).* **2.** something bitter or unpleasant: *the gall of disappointment.* **3.** bitterness of feeling; hatred. **4.** *Informal.* impudence; nerve: *He had the gall to talk back to his grandfather.* [Old English *galla, gealla* bile.]

gall² (gôl) *v.t.* **1.** to make sore by rubbing or chafing. **2.** to annoy or irritate: *It galled her to hear her friend insulted.* —*v.i.* to become sore or chafed. —*n.* a sore spot on the skin caused by rubbing or chafing. [Old English *gealla.*]

gall³ (gôl) *n.* an abnormal growth or swelling on a plant, usually caused by insects, fungi, or other plant parasites. [Old French *galle.*]

---

at; āpe; cär; end; mē; it; īce; hot; ōld; fôrk; wood; fōōl; oil; out; up; turn; sing; thin; this; hw in white; zh in treasure. The symbol ə stands for the sound of **a** in about, **e** in taken, **i** in pencil, **o** in lemon, and **u** in circus.

G

gal·lant (*adj., def. 1* gal′ənt; *adj., def. 2, n.,* gə lant′, gal′ənt) *adj.* **1.** brave or noble in spirit or conduct; heroic: *a gallant soldier.* **2.** polite and attentive to women; courtly. —*n.* **1.** a chivalrous, brave, or noble man. **2.** a fashionable or dashing young man. **3.** a man who is particularly polite and attentive to women. —**gal′lant·ly,** *adv.*

gal·lant·ry (gal′ən trē) *n. pl.,* **gal·lant·ries. 1.** bravery or nobleness of spirit or conduct; heroism: *The soldier received a medal for gallantry in combat.* **2.** courtly politeness and attentiveness to women. **3.** courtly or polite action or speech: *The men exchanged a few gallantries with the women.*

gall bladder, a small, muscular sac that is attached to the liver and in which bile is stored.

gal·le·on (gal′ē ən) *n.* a large sailing ship, usually having four masts with square sails, a square stern, and three or four decks. It was used from the fifteenth to the seventeenth centuries.

Galleon

gal·ler·y (gal′ər ē) *n. pl.,* **gal·ler·ies. 1.** a narrow platform or passage, usually roofed and open on one side; balcony. **2.** a room or building where works of art are shown or sold. **3.** a platform or floor projecting from the rear inside wall or side of a building, especially the highest of a series of such floors in a theater, usually containing the cheapest seats. **4.** the part of the audience occupying the highest gallery of a theater. **5.** a group of spectators, as at a sports event: *The gallery applauded when the golfer made a difficult putt.* **6.** a long, narrow corridor or passage, often open or having windows on one side. **7.** a room or building used for a particular activity, such as target shooting.

gal·ley (gal′ē) *n. pl.,* **gal·leys. 1.** a long, low ship of ancient and medieval times, propelled chiefly by a row of oars on either side or sometimes by several rows, one above the other. **2.** the kitchen of a ship or airplane. **3.** *Printing.* **a.** see **galley proof. b.** a long, shallow metal tray for holding type that has been set.

Galley

galley proof *Printing.* a proof printed from type set in a galley, used especially for making corrections in the printed matter before it is made up into pages.

Gal·lic (gal′ik) *adj.* **1.** of or relating to Gaul or its people. **2.** of or relating to France or its people; French.

gall·ing (gô′ling) *adj.* extremely annoying; irritating; exasperating: *a galling defeat.*

Gal·lip·o·li (gə lip′ə lē) *n.* a peninsula in northwestern Turkey, forming the northern shore of the Dardanelles.

gal·li·um (gal′ē əm) *n.* a rare, bluish-white, metallic element, found in aluminum ore and zinc ore. It has a very low melting point. Symbol: **Ga**

gal·li·vant (gal′ə vant′) *v.i.* to wander about or travel in search of fun or excitement; gad.

gall·nut (gôl′nut′) *n.* a nut-shaped growth or swelling, especially on oak trees.

gal·lon (gal′ən) *n.* a liquid measure of capacity. In the United States it is equal to four quarts, 231 cubic inches, or 128 fluid ounces.

gal·lop (gal′əp) *n.* **1.** the fastest gait of a horse or other four-footed animal, in which all four feet are off the ground at the same time during each leaping stride. **2.** a ride or run at a gallop. —*v.i.* **1.** to ride or move at a gallop: *The zebra galloped away from the lion.* **2.** to go or act very fast; hurry; race. —*v.t.* to cause to gallop: *She galloped the horse around the corral.* —**gal′lop·er,** *n.*

gal·lows (gal′ōz) *n. pl.,* **gal·lows·es** or **gal·lows. 1.** a framework from which criminals are hanged, usually consisting of upright beams supporting a crossbar. **2.** punishment or death by hanging: *to be sentenced to the gallows.*

gall·stone (gôl′stōn′) *n.* a small, hard mass that sometimes forms in the gall bladder or its ducts. When a gallstone becomes lodged in a duct, it produces severe pain.

ga·lore (gə lôr′) *adv.* in large or plentiful amounts: *There was entertainment galore at the circus.*

ga·losh·es (gə losh′iz) *n.,pl.* rubber overshoes reaching above the ankles, usually worn in wet or snowy weather.

gals., gallons.

gal·van·ic (gal van′ik) *adj.* of or relating to direct electric current, especially when produced by chemical action.

gal·va·nism (gal′və niz′əm) *n.* **1.** direct current electricity, especially when produced by chemical action. **2.** the use of such electricity in medicine. [French *galvanisme,* from Luigi *Galvani,* 1737–1798, an Italian physician and physicist who discovered it.]

gal·va·nize (gal′və nīz′) *v.t.,* **gal·va·nized, gal·va·niz·ing. 1.** to stimulate by the application of electric current. **2.** to rouse suddenly; startle; excite: *The unexpected news galvanized him into action.* **3.** to cover (metal, especially iron or steel) with a protective coating of zinc to prevent rusting. —**gal′va·ni·za′tion,** *n.*

gal·va·nom·e·ter (gal′və nom′ə tər) *n.* an instrument for detecting and measuring electric current and determining the direction of its flow.

Gam·bi·a (gam′bē ə) *n.* a country on the western coast of Africa, formerly a British colony. Capital, Banjul. Area, 4,361 sq. mi. Pop. (1980), 603,000.

gam·bit (gam′bit) *n.* **1.** in chess, an opening move in which a pawn or other piece is risked or sacrificed to gain some advantage. **2.** any opening move or maneuver designed to gain an advantage.

gam·ble (gam′bəl) *v.,* **gam·bled, gam·bling.** —*v.i.* **1.** to play games of chance, especially for money. **2.** to take a risk: *The coach gambled when he used an inexperienced pitcher in the championship game.* —*v.t.* **1.** to bet or wager (something of value): *I gambled a dollar at the church bingo game.* **2.** to lose or squander by gambling: *He gambled away his fortune.* —*n.* any risk or uncertain undertaking. —**gam′bler,** *n.*

gam·bol (gam′bəl) *v.i.,* **gam·boled, gam·bol·ing;** *also, British,* **gam·bolled, gam·bol·ling.** to run, skip, or leap about in play; frolic: *The children loved to gambol in the woods.* —*n.* running, skipping, or leaping about in play; frolic.

gam·brel roof (gam′brəl) a ridged roof having two slopes on each side, the lower slope being steeper than the upper.

game¹ (gām) *n.* **1.** a form of playing; pastime; amusement: *Hide-and-seek is a children's game.* **2.** a contest or other competitive play in which the players must follow specific rules: *the game of baseball, the game of poker.* **3.** a single match between two opposing players or teams: *Our school won the football game.* **4.** one of several parts in a fixed series or number of contests: *The tennis player won the first game of the set.* **5.** the score at any given point in a competition: *In the third inning the game was tied.*

6. the materials or equipment used in playing certain games: *The man bought several toys and games for his children.* **7.** a plan, scheme, or trick: *Some people's game is pretending to be what they aren't.* **8.** wild animals, birds, or fish, hunted or caught for sport or for food: *He hunted zebra, antelope, and other game in Africa.* **9.** the flesh of such animals used for food. **10.** *Informal.* a profession, activity, or undertaking: *The senator has been in the political game for twenty years.* —*adj.,* **gam·er, gam·est. 1.** having a fighting spirit; courageous; plucky: *He was a game fighter.* **2.** *Informal.* having enough spirit or will; ready: *Are you game for a swim in the cold water?* —*v.i.,* **gamed, gam·ing.** to play games of chance, especially for money; gamble. [Old English *gamen* fun, amusement.]

game² (gām) *adj. Informal.* lame or injured: *a game leg.* [Of uncertain origin.] —**game′ly,** *adv.* —**game′ness,** *n.*

game·cock (gām′kok′) *n.* a rooster bred and trained for fighting.

game·keep·er (gām′kē′pər) *n.* a person employed to breed, protect, and care for game in a government preserve or on private lands.

game·ster (gām′stər) *n.* a person who gambles; gambler.

gam·ete (gam′ēt, gə mēt′) *n. Biology.* either of two mature reproductive cells, the sperm or the ovum, capable of uniting to form a new plant or animal.

ga·me·to·phyte (gə mē′tə fīt′) *n. Botany.* the stage in the life cycle of plants during which sex cells, or gametes, are produced.

game warden, a public official who enforces the hunting and fishing laws in a given district.

gam·in (gam′in) *n.* a neglected or homeless child left to roam about the streets; urchin.

gam·ing (gā′ming) *n.* the act or practice of playing games of chance, especially for money; gambling.

gam·ma (gam′ə) *n.* the third letter of the Greek alphabet (Γ, γ) corresponding to the English letter G, g.

gamma glob·u·lin (glob′yə lin) any of a group of proteins in blood plasma. Most gamma globulins are antibodies that protect the body against a recurrence of certain diseases, such as measles or polio. Gamma globulin is sometimes given as an injection to immunize a person who has been exposed to a disease.

gamma ray, electromagnetic radiation similar to X rays but of shorter wavelength and greater penetrating power, given off by the nuclei of radioactive atoms.

gam·ut (gam′ət) *n.* **1.** the entire range, scope, or extent of anything: *The actress ran the gamut of emotions in the play.* **2.** the entire series of recognized notes or tones in modern music.

gam·y (gā′mē) *adj.,* **gam·i·er, gam·i·est. 1.** having the taste or smell of game, especially game that has been kept uncooked until slightly spoiled. **2.** brave; plucky; courageous. —**gam′i·ly,** *adv.* —**gam′i·ness,** *n.*

gan·der (gan′dər) *n.* an adult male goose.

Gan·dhi (gän′dē, gan′dē) **1. In·di·ra** (in dēr′ə). 1917—, the prime minister of India from 1966 to 1977 and since 1980. **2. Mo·han·das K.** (mō′han däs′). 1869–1948, Indian political, social, and religious leader; called Mahatma Gandhi.

gang (gang) *n.* **1.** a group of people who work together for illegal or criminal purposes: *The bank was held up by a gang of robbers.* **2.** a group of laborers working together under one foreman; crew. **3.** *Informal.* a group of people who are friends: *Our gang went to the party after the football game.* **4.** a group of youths from one neighborhood who band together, especially to fight other such groups. —*v.i. Informal.* to form a group or gang.

   to gang up on. *Slang.* to attack or oppose together or as a group: *We ganged up on the intruder.*

Gan·ges (gan′jēz) *n.* a river in northern India and Bangladesh, flowing from the Himalayas to the Bay of Bengal. It is considered sacred by the Hindus.

gan·gling (gang′gling) *adj.* awkwardly tall and skinny.

gan·gli·on (gang′glē ən) *n. pl.,* **gan·gli·a** (gang′glē ə) or **gan·gli·ons.** a group of nerve cell bodies outside the brain or spinal cord.

gang·plank (gang′plangk′) *n.* a movable bridge between a ship and a wharf, used for boarding or leaving the ship.

gan·grene (gang′-grēn′) *n.* the death and decay of body tissue caused when the blood supply is cut off or as a result of certain bacterial infections. —*v.,* **gan·grened, gan·gren·ing.** —*v.t.* to cause gangrene in. —*v.i.* to become affected with gangrene. —**gan′gre·nous,** *adj.*

Gangplank

gang·ster (gang′stər) *n. Informal.* a member of a gang of criminals.

gang·way (*n.,* gang′wā′; *interj.,* gang′wā′) *n.* **1.** a passageway. **2.** a passageway on either side of the upper deck of a ship. **3.** an opening in the side of a ship for boarding passengers or loading freight. **4.** a gangplank. —*interj.* get out of the way; make room.

gan·net (gan′it) *n.* any of various web-footed sea birds of coastal islands and waters of most temperate regions. Gannets have long, pointed bills and mainly white feathers, and are able to fly long distances.

gant·let¹ (gônt′lit) another spelling of **gauntlet¹.**

gant·let² (gônt′lit) another spelling of **gauntlet².**

gan·try (gan′trē) *n. pl.,* **gan·tries. 1.** a framework consisting of a horizontal bridge set on upright supports that may be stationary or mounted on wheels. Gantries are used especially to support movable cranes and railroad signals. **2.** see **gantry scaffold.**

gantry crane, a crane mounted on a gantry.

gantry scaffold, a movable scaffold, used to assemble and service a space rocket on its launching pad.

Gan·y·mede (gan′ə mēd′) *n. Greek Mythology.* a beautiful youth who was the favorite of Zeus and cupbearer to the Olympian gods.

gaol (jāl) *n. British.* another spelling of **jail.** —**gaol′er,** *n.*

gap (gap) *n.* **1.** a break, crack, or opening, as in a wall. **2.** a deep ravine or pass through a mountain ridge. **3.** an unfilled part or space; break in continuity: *There were gaps of a week or more in her diary.* **4.** a wide difference or divergence, as of opinion, character, or ideas: *There is a large gap between what he says and what he actually does.* —*v.t., v.i.,* **gapped, gap·ping.** to make or form a gap.

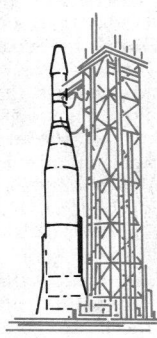
Gantry scaffold

at; āpe; cär; end; mē; it; īce; hot; ōld; fôrk; wood; fōōl; oil; out; up; turn; sing; thin; this; hw in white; zh in treasure. The symbol ə stands for the sound of a in about, e in taken, i in pencil, o in lemon, and u in circus.

gape (gāp) *v.i.*, **gaped, gap·ing 1.** to stare with the mouth open, as in wonder or surprise: *The children gaped at the beautiful Christmas tree.* **2.** to open the mouth wide, as when yawning. **3.** to open or be opened wide, as a gap or hole. —*n.* the act of gaping. [Old Norse *gapa* to open the mouth.] —**gap′er,** *n.*

ga·rage (gə räzh′, gə räj′; *British* gar′ij) *n.* a private or commercial building where motor vehicles are kept, repaired, or serviced. —*v.t.,* **ga·raged, ga·rag·ing.** to put or keep in a garage.

garb (gärb) *n.* clothing or attire, especially a particular or distinctive form of dress: *military garb.* —*v.t.* to clothe; dress: *The actress was garbed in a flowing gown of black and white lace.*

gar·bage (gär′bij) *n.* **1.** waste material, especially animal or vegetable matter that has been thrown away as food scraps from a kitchen. **2.** anything worthless or offensive: *The book she's reading is garbage.*

garbage disposal, a machine that is attached to a sink and disposes of garbage by grinding it up to be carried away with the waste water.

gar·ble (gär′bəl) *v.t.,* **gar·bled, gar·bling. 1.** to make unfair or misleading selections from (facts or a text) in order to give a false impression or to distort: *The witness garbled his account of the accident.* **2.** to confuse or mix up unintentionally: *to garble a telephone message.* —*n.* the act of garbling. —**gar′bler,** *n.*

Gar·cí·a Lor·ca, Fer·nan·do (gär sē′ə lôr′kə; fer-nän′dō) 1899–1936, Spanish poet and dramatist.

gar·çon (gär sōn′) *n. pl.,* **gar·çons** (gär sōn′). *French.* **1.** a waiter. **2.** a young man; boy.

gar·den (gärd′ən) *n.* **1.** a plot of ground where flowers, vegetables, herbs, or other plants are grown. **2.** *also,* **gardens.** a park or other piece of ground used by the public for recreation or amusement: *The class went to the botanical gardens.* —*adj.* relating to or grown in a garden: *Petunias and lilies of the valley are common garden flowers.* —*v.i.* to work in a garden: *Dad gardens on weekends.* —*v.t.* to cultivate as a garden: *He gardened the lot behind his house.*

garden apartment 1. a ground-floor apartment rented with an adjoining garden. **2.** an apartment building, usually having landscaped grounds and only a few stories of apartments.

gar·den·er (gärd′nər) *n.* a person who cultivates or tends a garden as a job or hobby.

Garden Grove, a city in southern California, near Los Angeles. Pop. (1970), 122,524.

gar·de·nia (gär dēn′yə) *n.* **1.** a fragrant yellow or white flower having waxy, dish-shaped petals. **2.** the evergreen shrub or tree bearing this flower. [Modern Latin *Gardenia,* from Alexander *Garden,* 1730–1791, U.S. botanist.]

Garden of Eden, in the Bible, the original home of Adam and Eve.

Gar·field, James A. (gär′fēld′) 1831–1881, the twentieth president of the United States, from March 4 to September 19, 1881.

gar·gan·tu·an (gär gan′chōō ən) *adj.* of enormous size; gigantic; huge: *a gargantuan redwood tree.* [From *Gargantua,* the giant in François Rabelais' satire *Gargantua and Pantagruel* + *-an.*]

gar·gle (gär′gəl) *v.,* **gar·gled, gar·gling.** —*v.i.* to wash or rinse the throat or mouth with a liquid kept in motion by an exhalation of the breath. —*v.t.* **1.** to use (a liquid)

Gardenia
(cape jasmine)

for gargling: *to gargle salt water.* **2.** to wash or rinse (the throat or mouth) by gargling. —*n.* a liquid used for gargling.

gar·goyle (gär′goil) *n.* a waterspout, usually in the form of a grotesque human or animal figure, projecting from the gutter of a building to carry off rainwater.

Gargoyle

Gar·i·bal·di, Giu·sep·pe (gar′ə-bôl′dē; jōō zep′ē) 1807–1882, Italian patriot and general.

gar·ish (ger′ish, gar′ish) *adj.* too bright or ornate; flashy; gaudy. —**gar′ish·ly,** *adv.* —**gar′ish·ness,** *n.*

gar·land (gär′lənd) *n.* a wreath of flowers, leaves, vines, or similar materials, usually worn about the head for decoration, especially as a token of honor. —*v.t.* to decorate with a garland or garlands.

Gar·land (gär′lənd) *n.* a city in northeastern Texas, a suburb of Dallas. Pop. (1970), 81,437.

gar·lic (gär′lik) *n.* **1.** the strong tasting bulb of a plant that is widely cultivated in most parts of the world, used to season food. The bulb is composed of separate sections called cloves. **2.** the plant bearing this bulb, having long, flat, ridged leaves and bearing clusters of small pink or purple flowers.

gar·ment (gär′mənt) *n.* an article of clothing.

gar·ner (gär′nər) *v.t.* to gather and store in or as if in a granary; accumulate; reap: *The farmers garnered grain during the harvest. The businessman garnered large profits from the sale.* —*n.* **1.** a place for storing grain; granary. **2.** a store of anything: *a great garner of knowledge.*

gar·net (gär′nit) *n.* **1.** any of a group of hard minerals found in various colors. The deep-red variety is most commonly used as a gem. **2.** a deep red color. —*adj.* having the color garnet; deep red.

gar·nish (gär′nish) *v.t.* **1.** to decorate or trim: *The queen's robes were garnished with gems and fur.* **2.** to decorate (food) with something that improves its appearance or flavor: *The cook garnished the fish with lemon slices.* —*n. pl.,* **gar·nish·es. 1.** something placed on or around food to improve its appearance or flavor: *to serve steak with a garnish of parsley.* **2.** a decoration or trimming.

gar·nish·ee (gär′ni shē′) *v.t.,* **gar·nish·eed, gar·nish·ee·ing.** to hold or seize (a person's money or property) by legal authority in payment of a debt.

gar·ret (gar′it) *n.* the uppermost floor or room of a house directly below the roof; attic.

Gar·rick, David (gar′ik) 1717–1779, English actor.

gar·ri·son (gar′ə sən) *n.* **1.** a military post. **2.** the soldiers stationed in a town or post. —*v.t.* **1.** to station soldiers in (a town or post): *to garrison a village to protect it from the enemy.* **2.** to station (soldiers) in a garrison.

Gar·ri·son, William Lloyd (gar′ə sən) 1805–1879, U.S. editor and abolitionist.

gar·ru·li·ty (gə rōō′lə tē) *n.* the quality of being garrulous; talkativeness.

gar·ru·lous (gar′ə ləs) *adj.* given to too much talking, especially about unimportant matters; talkative. —**gar′ru·lous·ly,** *adv.* —**gar′ru·lous·ness,** *n.*

gar·ter (gär′tər) *n.* **1.** a band or strap, usually elastic, worn to hold up a stocking or sock. **2. Garter. a.** see **Order of the Garter. b.** the badge of this order. —*v.t.* to fasten or support with a garter.

garter snake, any of a group of harmless, brownish or greenish snakes found in North and Central America, usually having yellow stripes along the body.

Gar·y (ger′ē, gar′ē) *n.* a city in northwestern Indiana. Pop. (1970), 175,415.

gas (gas) *n. pl.,* **gas·es. 1.** the form of matter that is neither solid nor liquid, characterized by the ability of its atoms or molecules to move about easily and independently. It has no definite shape or volume and expands to fill its container. **2.** any gas or gaseous mixture other than air. **3.** any gas or gaseous mixture that will burn, used for heating or lighting, such as natural gas. **4.** any gas or gaseous mixture used as an anesthetic, such as laughing gas. **5.** a chemical substance, such as mustard gas or tear gas, that is intentionally released in the air to irritate, stun, or kill. **6.** see **gasoline.** —*v.t.,* **gassed, gas·sing. 1.** to irritate, stun, or kill with gas, as in chemical warfare. **2.** to supply with gas or gasoline: *Dad gassed the car up before the long drive.*

gas chamber, a sealed room in which people are executed by poisonous gas.

gas·e·ous (gas′ē əs, gash′əs) *adj.* relating to or in the form of gas: *a gaseous state, a gaseous substance.*

gash (gash) *n. pl.,* **gash·es.** a long, deep cut or wound: *The doctor closed the gash with ten stitches.* —*v.t.* to make a gash in: *The swimmer gashed his foot on a rock.*

gas·ket (gas′kit) *n.* a ring, disk, or other piece of packing used to seal a joint or closure, as in a pipe or piston.

gas·light (gas′līt′) *n.* **1.** the light produced by the burning of gas. **2.** something that burns gas, such as a lamp.

gas mask, a mask having a filter, worn over the mouth, nose, and eyes to protect the wearer from breathing in harmful substances.

gas·o·hol (gas′ə hôl′) *n.* a fuel used in motor vehicles, made from gasoline and alcohol.

gas·o·line (gas′ə lēn′, gas′ə lēn′) *also,* **gas·o·lene.** *n.* a fuel for internal-combustion engines in automobiles, etc. It is obtained from petroleum or natural gas.

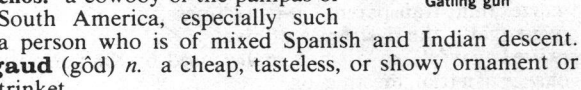
Gas mask

gasp (gasp) *v.i.* to draw in the breath suddenly, sharply, or with difficulty, as in fear, surprise, or exhaustion. —*v.t.* to utter while gasping: *The excited child gasped the news to us.* —*n.* the act or instance of gasping.

gas station, an establishment that sells gasoline, oil, and other things necessary to keep motor vehicles operating, often having repair facilities as well. Also, **filling station, service station.**

gas·sy (gas′ē) *adj.,* **gas·si·er, gas·si·est.** full of, containing, or like gas: *a gassy mixture.*

gas·tric (gas′trik) *adj.* of, relating to, or near the stomach.

gastric juice, a digestive fluid secreted by glands in the stomach lining, containing hydrochloric acid and certain enzymes, such as pepsin and rennin.

gas·tro·nom·ic (gas′trə nom′ik) *adj.* of or relating to gastronomy. Also, **gas·tro·nom·i·cal** (gas′trə nom′i kəl).

gas·tron·o·my (gas tron′ə mē) *n.* the art or science of good eating.

gas·tro·pod (gas′trə pod′) *n.* any of a group of animals, including the snail, slug, and whelk, that move by means of a muscular foot on the undersurface of the body. Most gastropods have a single-chambered, usually spiral, shell. —*adj.* of or relating to gastropods.

gat (gat) *Archaic.* a past tense of **get.**

gate (gāt) *n.* **1.** a movable barrier, usually swinging on hinges, used to close off a passage, as in a wall or fence. **2.** an opening in a wall or fence for entering or leaving, especially such an opening equipped with a gate. **3.** a device used to control the flow of a fluid, especially water, as through a pipe, dam, or lock. **4.** the number of people who pay to see a sports event, play, or other contest or performance. **5.** the total amount of money received from these people: *The race drew in a gate of $2,000.*

gate crasher, a person who gains admittance to a party or other private gathering without being invited, or to a performance or game without having a ticket.

gate·house (gāt′hous′) *n. pl.,* **gate·hous·es** (gāt′hou′ziz). a house or other structure built next to or over a gate, used especially as the gatekeeper's quarters.

gate·keep·er (gāt′kē′pər) *n.* a person in charge of a gate.

gate·post (gāt′pōst′) *n.* either of two posts on each side of a gate. The gate is hinged or fastened to one side and closes against the other.

Gates, Ho·ra·tio (gāts; hə rā′shō) 1728–1806, U.S. general during the American Revolution.

gate·way (gāt′wā′) *n.* **1.** an opening in a wall or fence that may be closed with a gate, used for entering or leaving. **2.** the means of entering someplace or achieving something: *the gateway to the West, the gateway to happiness.*

gath·er (gath′ər) *v.t.* **1.** to bring together in one place or group: *The general gathered his army and marched forward.* **2.** to get or collect from various places or sources; accumulate: *The bird gathered twigs for its nest.* **3.** to pick and harvest (fruit or crops): *The farmer gathered the corn in August.* **4.** to increase little by little; gain gradually: *The ball gathered speed as it rolled down the hill.* **5.** to learn or realize by observation or reasoning; conclude: *We gathered from the evidence that he was guilty.* **6.** to take and hold; enfold: *She gathered the child in her arms.* **7.** to draw (cloth) into pleats, folds, or puckers along a line of stitching: *She gathered the skirt at the waist.* —*v.i.* **1.** to come together or assemble: *Students gathered in the auditorium.* **2.** to increase or collect gradually: *Sweat gathered on his brow.* —*n.* a pleat, fold, or pucker made by gathering. —**gath′er·er,** *n.*

gath·er·ing (gath′ər ing) *n.* **1.** the act of a person or thing that gathers. **2.** a meeting, assembly, or crowd: *A large gathering of reporters waited outside the courtroom.*

Gat·ling gun (gat′ling) the earliest machine gun, consisting of from six to ten barrels mounted in a circle on a frame. The entire assembly was rotated by a hand crank. [From Richard J. *Gatling,* 1818–1903, its American inventor.]

gauche (gōsh) *adj.* lacking social grace; awkward or tactless. [French *gauche* left, left-handed.]

gau·cho (gou′chō) *n. pl.,* **gau·chos.** a cowboy of the pampas of South America, especially such a person who is of mixed Spanish and Indian descent.

Gatling gun

gaud (gôd) *n.* a cheap, tasteless, or showy ornament or trinket.

gaud·y (gô′dē) *adj.,* **gaud·i·er, gaud·i·est.** tastelessly bright or ornate; showy or cheap: *The yellow and pink shawl with gold tassels was gaudy.* —**gaud′i·ly,** *adv.* —**gaud′i·ness,** *n.*

gauge (gāj) *also,* **gage.** *n.* **1.** a standard measure or scale

at; āpe; cär; end; mē; it; īce; hot; ōld; fôrk; wood; fōōl; oil; out; up; turn; sing; thin; this; hw in white; zh in treasure. The symbol ə stands for the sound of **a** in about, **e** in taken, **i** in pencil, **o** in lemon, and **u** in circus.

G

of measurements. **2.** an instrument or device used for measuring or indicating measurements: *a gasoline gauge.* **3.** a means of estimating or judging; standard: *The students' performance on this test is a gauge of their reading ability.* **4.** the distance between two rails on a railroad. The standard U.S. gauge is 56.5 inches. **5.** the diameter of the bore of a gun, especially a shotgun. —*v.t.,* **gauged, gaug·ing. 1.** to determine accurately the dimensions, amount, force, or capacity of, especially with a gauge; measure: *to gauge the depth of a well, to gauge the speed of the wind.* **2.** to estimate or judge; appraise: *The jeweler gauged the worth of the gem.* —**gauge′a·ble,** *adj.* —**gaug′er,** *n.*

Gau·guin, Paul (gō gan′) 1848–1903, French painter.

Gaul (gôl) *n.* **1.** an ancient region in western Europe, consisting of present-day France, Belgium, northern Italy, and parts of Germany, Switzerland, and the Netherlands. **2.** one of the Celtic people who lived in this region. **3.** a Frenchman.

gaunt (gônt) *adj.* **1.** extremely thin and hollow-eyed, as from hunger or illness; haggard. **2.** bare and gloomy; grim; bleak: *a gaunt stretch of desert.* —**gaunt′ly,** *adv.* —**gaunt′ness,** *n.*

gaunt·let[1] (gônt′lit) *also,* **gant·let.** *n.* **1.** a heavy glove, usually made of leather covered with armor plate or mail, used in medieval times to protect the hand. **2.** a glove having a long, flaring cuff extending above the wrist. [Old French *gantelet.*]

　to take up the gauntlet. to accept a challenge.

　to throw down the gauntlet. to challenge, as to combat.

gaunt·let[2] (gônt′lit) *also,* **gant·let.** *n.* a form of punishment in which the offender is made to run between two rows of men who strike him with clubs, whips, or other weapons as he passes. [From earlier *gantlope,* from Swedish *gatlopp.*]

　to run the gauntlet. a. to undergo the punishment of the gauntlet. **b.** to be subjected to a series of difficulties or severe opposition or criticism.

Gau·ta·ma (gô′tə mə, gou′tə mə) another name for **Buddha.**

gauze (gôz) *n.* a very thin, light-weight cloth woven from any of various fibers, used for such items as bandages, surgical dressings, and curtains.

gauz·y (gô′zē) *adj.,* **gauz·i·er, gauz·i·est.** resembling gauze; thin; transparent. —**gauz′i·ness,** *n.*

gave (gāv) the past tense of **give.**

gav·el (gav′əl) *n.* a small mallet used by the person in charge of a trial, meeting, or other gathering to call for attention or order.

ga·votte (gə vot′) *n.* **1.** a dance of French origin, resembling the minuet, but much faster and livelier. **2.** the music for this dance.

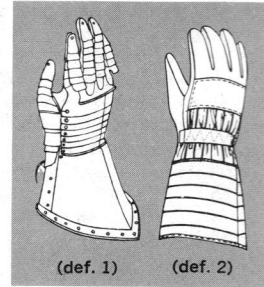
Gauntlets
(def. 1)　**(def. 2)**

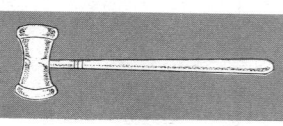
Gavel

Ga·wain (gä′win, gə wān′) *n.* in the legends of King Arthur, a knight of the Round Table and the nephew of King Arthur.

gawk (gôk) *v.i. Informal.* to stare stupidly; gape.

gawk·y (gô′kē) *adj.,* **gawk·i·er, gawk·i·est.** awkward; clumsy. —**gawk′i·ly,** *adv.* —**gawk′i·ness,** *n.*

gay (gā) *adj.,* **gay·er, gay·est. 1.** full of joy and fun; merry; happy. **2.** brightly colored or showy: *a gay design.* —**gay′ness,** *n.*

gay·e·ty (gā′ə tē) another spelling of **gaiety.**

gay·ly (gā′lē) another spelling of **gaily.**

Ga·za (gä′zə, gaz′ə) *n.* a historic city in the Gaza Strip.

Gaza Strip, the territory on the southeastern coast of the Mediterranean Sea, between Egypt and Israel, formerly part of Palestine.

gaze (gāz) *v.i.,* **gazed, gaz·ing.** to look long and steadily, as in admiration or wonder. —*n.* a long, steady look.

ga·zelle (gə zel′) *n. pl.,* **ga·zelles** or **ga·zelle.** any of various graceful antelopes found in hot, dry regions of northern Africa and southern Asia. The gazelle has a fawn-colored coat with black and white markings, curving horns, and large, shining eyes. It can run as fast as sixty miles per hour.

ga·zette (gə zet′) *n.* **1.** a newspaper or similar periodical. **2.** an official publication, as of a government or institution. —*v.t.,* **ga·zet·ted, ga·zet·ting.** to publish, list, or announce in a gazette.

gaz·et·teer (gaz′ə tēr′) *n.* a book or list of geographical names.

Gazelle

G.B., Great Britain.

G clef, the clef placed on the second line of the staff, showing that this line corresponds to the note G above middle C; treble clef.

Gd, the symbol for gadolinium.

Gdansk (gə dänsk′) *n.* a port city in northern Poland, formerly known as **Danzig.** Pop. (1970), 364,200.

Ge, the symbol for germanium.

gear (gēr) *n.* **1.** a wheel having a toothed edge designed to mesh with or fit into the teeth of another similar wheel. **2.** a mechanical arrangement or assembly of such wheels, used for transmitting or changing motion, as in an automobile: *low gear.* **3.** a mechanism or part of a mechanism within a machine, performing a specific function: *steering gear.* **4.** any equipment used for a specific purpose: *fishing gear, camping gear.* —*v.t.* **1.** to furnish or equip with gears. **2.** to adapt, change, or regulate (something) in order to make it conform to or suit something else: *The candidate geared his campaign to capture the middle-class vote.* —*v.i.* to come into or be in gear; mesh: *The teeth of the wheels gear into each other.*

　in gear. connected or engaged, as one gear with another or with a motor.

　out of gear. not connected or engaged, as one gear with another or with a motor.

gear·ing (gēr′ing) *n.* a system of gears for transmitting motion or power.

gear·shift (gēr′shift′) *n.* a device for connecting or disconnecting any of several sets of gears in a transmission system, as in an automobile.

gear·wheel (gēr′hwēl′, gēr′wēl′) *n.* a wheel having a toothed edge; cogwheel.

geck·o (gek′ō) *n. pl.,* **geck·os** or **geck·oes.** a harmless tropical lizard having pads on the bottom of the toes covered with thousands of very tiny hooks that enable it to walk on walls and ceilings.

gee[1] (jē) *interj.* to the right. ▲ used to direct horses, mules, and certain other animals. —*v.i., v.t.,* **geed, gee·ing.** to turn or cause to turn to the right.

gee[2] (jē) *interj.* used to express enthusiasm or surprise.

geese (gēs) a plural of **goose.**

Gei·ger counter (gī′gər) an electronic device that is used to detect and measure the intensity of ionizing radiation. This radiation may be in the form of X rays, gamma rays, or cosmic rays. [From Hans *Geiger*, 1882–1945, a German physicist who was one of its inventors.]

gei·sha (gā′shə, gē′shə) *n. pl.*, **gei·shas** or **gei·sha**. a Japanese girl who has been trained to sing, dance, and provide entertainment in a teahouse.

gel·a·tin (jel′ət ən) *also*, **gel·a·tine.** *n.* **1.** a colorless, tasteless protein substance obtained from skin, bones, and other animal tissues. Gelatin dissolves in hot water and forms a jellylike mass when it cools. It is used in jellies, desserts, and other foods, and in the manufacture of drugs and photographic film. **2.** a preparation or product made with or resembling gelatin.

gel·a·tine (jel′ət ən, jel′ə tēn′) another spelling of **gelatin**.

ge·lat·i·nous (jə lat′ən əs) *adj.* **1.** of or like gelatin. **2.** containing gelatin.

geld (geld) *v.t.*, **geld·ed** or **gelt, geld·ing.** to castrate (a horse or similar animal).

geld·ing (gel′ding) *n.* a gelded animal, especially a gelded horse.

gelt (gelt) a past tense and past participle of **geld**.

gem (jem) *n.* **1.** a cut and polished precious stone; jewel. **2.** a person or thing that is considered perfect, extremely beautiful, or precious: *This novel is a gem.* —*v.t.*, **gemmed, gem·ming.** to set or adorn with or as if with gems: *Tiny white blossoms gemmed the branches of the cherry trees in the orchard.*

Gem·i·ni (jem′ə nī′) *n.,pl.* **1.** a constellation in the northern sky, thought to resemble the twin brothers, Castor and Pollux. **2.** the third sign of the zodiac. ▲ used with a singular verb in both definitions.

gems·bok (gemz′bok′) *n. pl.*, **gems·bok** or **gems·boks.** a southern African antelope having very long, straight horns, a long, tufted tail, and a sandy-gray coat with dark markings on the side and brown and white markings on the face.

gem·stone (jem′stōn′) *n.* a mineral or petrified material that can be used in jewelry.

gen. 1. gender. **2.** general. **3.** genitive. **4.** genus.

Gen., General.

Gemsbok

gen·darme (zhän′därm) *n. pl.*, **gen·darmes** (zhän′-därmz). **1.** an armed policeman in France and French-speaking parts of certain other European countries. **2.** *Informal.* any policeman.

gen·der (jen′dər) *n. Grammar.* **1.** the classification of words that distinguishes chiefly between masculine, feminine, and neuter. **2.** any one of such classes.

gene (jēn) *n.* one of the units located on a chromosome that determine the characteristics which an organism inherits from its parent or parents.

ge·ne·a·log·i·cal (jē′nē ə loj′i kəl) *adj.* of or relating to genealogy: *a genealogical trait.* —**ge′ne·a·log′i·cal·ly,** *adv.*

ge·ne·al·o·gist (jē′nē ol′ə jist, jē′nē al′ə jist) *n.* a person who traces or studies genealogies.

ge·ne·al·o·gy (jē′nē ol′ə jē, jē′nē al′ə jē) *n. pl.*, **ge·ne·al·o·gies. 1.** the study of the descent of persons or families from an ancestor or ancestors. **2.** an account or chart of such a descent for a particular person or family: *Her gene-*

alogy went back to the American Revolution. **3.** a direct descent from an ancestor or ancestors; pedigree; lineage.

gen·er·a (jen′ər ə) a plural of **genus**.

gen·er·al (jen′ər əl) *adj.* **1.** concerned with or affecting all or the whole: *a general election, to work for the general welfare of the people.* **2.** common or occurring among many or most; widespread; prevalent: *a word in general use.* **3.** not limited to a particular group, use, or area: *a general rule.* **4.** not concerned with details or specifics: *a general idea, to speak in a general way.* —*n.* **1.** the commander of a large army; military officer of the highest rank: *Napoleon and Julius Caesar are two of history's greatest generals.* **2.** in the U.S. Army and Air Force, an officer ranking below general of the army or general of the air force and above lieutenant general. **3.** in the U.S. Marine Corps, an officer of the highest rank. **4.** any officer ranking above a colonel.

in general. for the most part; commonly.

General Assembly, the main body of the United Nations, in which every member nation has one vote.

general delivery 1. the department of the post office that handles mail picked up at a post office window by the person to whom it is addressed. **2.** the mail sent through this department.

gen·er·al·is·si·mo (jen′ər ə lis′ə mō′) *n. pl.*, **gen·er·al·is·si·mos.** the commander in chief of all the military forces of a country, or of several armies in the field.

gen·er·al·i·ty (jen′ə ral′ə tē) *n. pl.*, **gen·er·al·i·ties. 1.** a statement, phrase, or idea that is not concerned with details or specifics, especially one that is too broad or vague to be meaningful: *to speak in generalities.* **2.** the greater part or number; main body; majority. **3.** the quality or condition of being general.

gen·er·al·i·za·tion (jen′ər ə li zā′shən) *n.* **1.** the act of generalizing. **2.** a general statement, idea, or rule: *To say that all firefighters are brave is a generalization.*

● In language, **generalization** means the changing of the definition of a word from a narrow, specific meaning to a broader, more general one. Generalization is one of the ways in which our language is constantly changing and growing. For example, the word *arrive,* originally came from the Latin words *ad,* meaning "to," and *ripa,* meaning "shore," and meant to land on the shore at the end of a voyage. Over the years, people began to use *arrive* to refer to the ending of any journey or action. Because of this process of generalization, we now have several meanings of this word: *Jack arrived at school after a long walk. The time for action has arrived. The argument ended when the two sides arrived at an agreement.*

gen·er·al·ize (jen′ər ə līz′) *v.*, **gen·er·al·ized, gen·er·al·iz·ing.** —*v.i.* **1.** to treat a subject without going into details or specifics; speak in or use generalities. **2.** to form a general rule or principle from particular facts or instances. —*v.t.* to give a more general form to; state in general terms.

gen·er·al·ly (jen′ər ə lē) *adv.* **1.** in most cases; as a rule; usually: *I generally walk to school.* **2.** for the most part; commonly: *That theory is generally accepted by scientists.*

---

at; āpe; cär; end; mē; it; īce; hot; ōld; fôrk; wood; fŏŏl; oil; out; up; turn; sing; thin; this; hw in white; zh in treasure. The symbol ə stands for the sound of **a** in about, **e** in taken, **i** in pencil, **o** in lemon, and **u** in circus.

G

3. without regard to specific details: *Generally speaking, the book was good.*

general of the air force, in the U.S. Air Force, an officer of the highest rank.

general of the army, in the U.S. Army, an officer of the highest rank.

general practitioner, a doctor who does not limit his or her practice to a specific branch of medicine.

gen·er·al·ship (jen′ər əl ship′) *n.* **1.** the military skill of a general. **2.** skill in management of any sort; leadership. **3.** the rank of general.

general store, a store that carries a large variety of items but is not divided into departments.

gen·er·ate (jen′ə rāt′) *v.t.,* **gen·er·at·ed, gen·er·at·ing.** to produce or cause to be; bring into existence: *to generate electricity. The advertising campaign generated much interest in the new film.*

gen·er·a·tion (jen′ə rā′shən) *n.* **1.** a group of individuals born at about the same time: *the younger generation.* **2.** one step or degree in the line of natural descent, as of people, animals, or plants. Grandfather, father, and son make up three generations. **3.** the period of time, usually about thirty years, between the birth of one generation and the next. **4.** the act or process of causing to be or bringing into existence; production.

gen·er·a·tive (jen′ə rā′tiv) *adj.* **1.** of or relating to production of offspring. **2.** having the ability or power to produce or bring into existence.

gen·er·a·tor (jen′ə rā′tər) *n.* **1.** a device that changes mechanical energy into electrical energy. **2.** an apparatus for the production of gas or steam. **3.** a person or thing that generates.

ge·ner·ic (jə ner′ik) *adj.* **1.** of, relating to, or applied to a whole kind, class, or group; general: *"Fruit" is a generic term.* **2.** of, relating to, or characteristic of a genus of plants or animals. **3.** not under trademark registration: *generic drugs, generic canned goods.* —**ge·ner′i·cal·ly,** *adv.*

gen·er·os·i·ty (jen′ə ros′ə tē) *n. pl.,* **gen·er·os·i·ties.** **1.** willingness to give or share freely; quality of being unselfish. **2.** the quality of being noble-minded and free from meanness; graciousness. **3.** a generous act.

gen·er·ous (jen′ər əs) *adj.* **1.** having or showing a willingness to give or share freely; unselfish: *a generous gift, a generous person.* **2.** noble-minded and gracious; free from meanness: *a generous nature.* **3.** large or plentiful; abundant: *a generous helping of food.* —**gen′er·ous·ly,** *adv.*

gen·e·sis (jen′ə sis) *n. pl.,* **gen·e·ses** (jen′ə sēz′). the coming into being of anything; beginning; origin.

Gen·e·sis (jen′ə sis) *n.* the first book of the Old Testament, giving an account of the origin of the world, of man, and of the Hebrew people.

ge·net·ic (jə net′ik) *adj.* **1.** of or relating to genetics. **2.** of, relating to, or produced by a gene or genes: *a genetic trait.* **3.** of or relating to the origin and development of anything. —**ge·net′i·cal·ly,** *adv.*

genetic code, the arrangement of the sections of a DNA molecule that determines the characteristics of an organism.

ge·net·i·cist (jə net′ə sist) *n.* a student of or an expert in genetics.

ge·net·ics (jə net′iks) *n.,pl.* the branch of biology that deals with the principles of heredity and the inherited similarities and differences found in organisms. ▲ used with a singular verb.

Ge·ne·va (jə nē′və) *n.* **1.** a city in southwestern Switzerland. Pop. (1977 est.), 152,600. **2. Lake.** a narrow lake between southwestern Switzerland and eastern France.

Geneva Convention, an international agreement regulating the wartime treatment of sick and wounded soldiers and prisoners of war. It was first adopted in 1864 at Geneva, Switzerland.

Gen·ghis Khan (jeng′gis kän′) 1162–1227, Mongol conqueror of central Asia.

gen·ial (jēn′yəl) *adj.* **1.** pleasant and cheerful; friendly; cordial: *a genial host.* **2.** favorable to life or growth; pleasantly warm and comfortable: *a genial climate.* —**gen′ial·ly,** *adv.*

ge·ni·al·i·ty (jē′nē al′ə tē) *n.* the quality or condition of being genial.

ge·nie (jē′nē) *also,* **jin·ni.** *n.* in Arab folklore and literature, a spirit having magic powers, capable of assuming human or animal form.

ge·ni·i (jē′nē ī′) the plural of **genius** *(def. 7).*

gen·i·tal (jen′ət əl) *adj.* of or relating to the sex organs or to reproduction.

gen·i·ta·li·a (jen′ə tā′lē ə) *n.,pl.* another word for **genitals.**

gen·i·tals (jen′ət əlz) *n.,pl.* the reproductive organs, especially the external sex organs.

gen·i·tive (jen′ə tiv) *n.* **1.** the grammatical case in Latin, Greek, and certain other languages that indicates possession, source, or origin, or the object of certain prepositions. It corresponds to the possessive case in English. **2.** a word or construction in this case. —*adj.* of, relating to, or indicating this case.

gen·ius (jēn′yəs) *n. pl., (defs. 1–6)* **gen·ius·es** or *(def. 7)* **ge·ni·i.** **1.** extraordinary mental power, especially as shown by creativity or inventiveness in science or the arts: *Leonardo da Vinci was a man of genius.* **2.** a person who has such power: *Beethoven was a genius.* **3.** a person having a very high intelligence quotient. **4.** a great natural ability or talent for a particular thing: *She has a genius for drawing.* **5.** a person who has such an ability or talent: *He is a genius at diplomatic negotiations.* **6.** a person who has a powerful influence over another: *an evil genius.* **7.** a guardian spirit, as of a person or place.

Gen·o·a (jen′ō ə) *n.* a port city in northwestern Italy. Pop. (1976 est.), 800,500.

gen·o·cide (jen′ə sīd′) *n.* the extermination or destruction of an entire national, cultural, or racial group.

Gen·o·ese (jen′ō ēz′) *n. pl.,* **Gen·o·ese.** a person who was born or is living in Genoa. —*adj.* of or relating to Genoa or its people.

gen·re (zhän′rə) *n.* **1.** a particular class or style, especially a class or style of work in literature or art: *O. Henry was a master of the genre of the short story.* **2.** a style of painting showing or dealing with scenes and events from everyday life. —*adj.* being or relating to a genre: *a genre painting, a genre film.*

gen·teel (jen tēl′) *adj.* **1.** polite in manner or behavior; well-bred or refined: *a genteel person.* **2.** of, relating to, or suitable for those who are well-bred or refined: *genteel manners.* **3.** artificially or excessively refined or polite. —**gen·teel′ness,** *n.*

gen·tian (jen′shən) *n.* a plant found in temperate and mountainous regions, bearing leaves without stalks and blue flowers.

gen·tile (jen′tīl) *also,* **Gen·tile.** *n.* a person who is not a Jew, especially a Christian as distinguished from a Jew. —*adj.* of or relating to a gentile or gentiles; not Jewish.

gen·til·i·ty (jen til′ə tē) *n. pl.,* **gen·til·i·ties.** **1.** the refinement or good manners characteristic of a person who is well-bred. **2.** the position or condition of belonging to the upper classes; social superiority.

gen·tle (jent′əl) *adj.,* **gen·tler, gen·tlest.** **1.** mild and kindly in manner, nature, or tone: *She was gentle when she spoke to the young child.* **2.** not severe, rough, or loud; soft;

moderate: *We could hear the gentle tapping of the rain on the roof.* **3.** easily handled; tame: *a gentle horse.* **4.** not extreme or abrupt; gradual: *a gentle slope.* **5.** of good family or birth; wellborn. **6.** characteristic of or like one of good family; polite or refined. —**gen′tle·ness,** *n.* —**gen′tly,** *adv.*

gen·tle·folk (jent′əl fōk′) *n.,pl.* people of good family and breeding.

gen·tle·man (jent′əl mən) *n. pl.,* **gen·tle·men** (jent′əl-mən). **1.** a man who is honorable, courteous, and considerate. **2.** a man of good family and high social standing. **3.** any man: *There is a gentleman at the door.* **4. gentlemen.** a form of respectful or polite address, used especially in speaking or writing to a group of men.

gen·tle·man·ly (jent′əl mən lē) *adj.* having the character, behavior, or appearance of a gentleman; courteous; well-bred. —**gen′tle·man·li·ness,** *n.*

gentleman's agreement, an unwritten agreement guaranteed only by the honor of the people or groups involved. It is not legally binding. Also, **gentlemen's agreement.**

gen·tle·wom·an (jent′əl woom′ən) *n. pl.,* **gen·tle·wom·en** (jent′əl wim′ən). **1.** a woman of good family and high social standing. **2.** a well-mannered, refined woman; lady. **3.** formerly, a woman attending a lady of rank.

gen·try (jen′trē) *n.* **1.** people of good family or high social standing. **2.** the social class ranking below the nobility. **3.** the people of any particular area, class, or group.

gen·u·flect (jen′yoo flekt′) *v.i.* to bend the knee, as in worship or respect.

gen·u·flec·tion (jen′yoo flek′shən) *n.* the act of bending the knee, as in worship or respect.

gen·u·ine (jen′yoo in) *adj.* **1.** actually being what it is claimed to be; real; true: *genuine pearls, a genuine antique.* **2.** free from pretense or dishonesty; sincere: *a genuine expression of sympathy, a genuine effort to help.* —**gen′u·ine·ly,** *adv.* —**gen′u·ine·ness,** *n.*

ge·nus (jē′nəs) *n. pl.,* **gen·er·a** or **gen·us·es.** **1.** the category of animal and plant classification ranking next below a family and next above a species. **2.** any group of related things; kind; sort; class.

geo- *combining form* relating to the earth: *geophysics.*

ge·o·cen·tric (jē′ō sen′trik) *adj.* **1.** as measured or viewed from the earth's center. **2.** based on the idea that the earth is the center of the universe: *a geocentric system of astronomy.*

ge·o·chem·is·try (jē′ō kem′is trē) *n.* the branch of chemistry dealing with the chemical composition of the earth's crust and the chemical changes that take place there.

ge·o·des·ic (jē′ə des′ik, jē′ə dē′sik) *n.* the shortest line segment that joins two points lying on a surface, especially a curved surface. —*adj.* **1.** of or relating to geodesy. **2.** of or relating to geodesic lines.

geodesic dome, a light, strong, dome-shaped structure, usually made of a framework of triangular shapes and covered with plastic sheeting.

ge·od·e·sy (jē od′ə sē) *n.* the science concerned with determining the shape and measurements of the earth and with the mapping of large areas of its surface.

geog., geography; geographical; geographer.

ge·og·ra·pher (jē og′rə fər) *n.* a student of or an expert in geography.

ge·o·graph·i·cal (jē′ə graf′i kəl) *adj.* of or relating to geography. Also, **ge·o·graph·ic** (jē′ə graf′ik). —**ge′o·graph′i·cal·ly,** *adv.*

geographical mile, a measure of length equal to ¹⁄₆₀ of a degree of the earth's equator, or approximately 6080 feet.

ge·og·ra·phy (jē og′rə fē) *n. pl.,* **ge·og·ra·phies. 1.** the study of the characteristics of and differences between particular places on the surface of the earth, and of all the physical and cultural factors affecting these characteristics. Geography includes the study of the earth's natural surface, its climate, the distribution of plant, animal, and human life, and man's use of and relationship to his environment. **2.** the surface or natural features of a particular place or region: *the geography of Siberia, the geography of Nebraska.*

geol., geology; geological; geologist.

ge·o·log·i·cal (jē′ə loj′i kəl) *adj.* of or relating to geology. Also, **ge·o·log·ic** (jē′ə log′ik). —**ge′o·log′i·cal·ly,** *adv.*

ge·ol·o·gist (jē ol′ə jist) *n.* a student of or an expert in geology.

ge·ol·o·gy (jē ol′ə jē) *n. pl.,* **ge·ol·o·gies. 1.** the science that deals with the earth's structure, composition, and history, including the changes that have taken place on the earth's surface and the processes, such as erosion, by which such changes have occurred. **2.** the structure and composition of the earth in a particular area.

geom., geometry; geometric; geometrician.

ge·o·met·ric (jē′ə met′rik) *adj.* **1.** of or relating to geometry. **2.** made up of or decorated with straight lines, angles, circles, triangles, or similar forms: *a geometric design.* Also, **ge·o·met·ri·cal** (jē′ə met′ri kəl). —**ge′o·met′-ri·cal·ly,** *adv.*

ge·om·e·tri·cian (jē om′ə trish′ən) *n.* a student of or an expert in geometry.

geometric progression *Mathematics.* a series in which each number is multiplied by a given factor in order to obtain the next number. 1½, 3, 6, 12, 24 is a geometric progression in which the given factor is 2.

ge·om·e·try (jē om′ə trē) *n. pl.,* **ge·om·e·tries. 1.** the branch of mathematics that deals with the properties, measurements, and relations of points, lines, angles, plane figures, and solids. **2.** shape or design: *the geometry of a building.*

ge·o·mor·phol·o·gy (jē′ō môr fol′ə jē) *n.* the science that deals with the physical features of the surface of the earth and the geological processes by which they are produced.

ge·o·phys·i·cal (jē′ō fiz′i kəl) *adj.* of or relating to geophysics.

ge·o·phys·i·cist (jē′ō fiz′ə sist) *n.* a student of or an expert in geophysics.

ge·o·phys·ics (jē′ō fiz′iks) *n., pl.* the branch of earth science that deals with the physical nature, motions, atmosphere, and oceans of the earth. ▲ used with a singular verb.

George (jôrj) *n.* **1. David Lloyd.** see **Lloyd George. 2. Saint.** died A.D. 303?, Christian martyr; the patron saint of England. **3. Lake.** a lake in eastern New York.

George I, 1660–1727, the king of England from 1714 to 1727. He was the first king from the house of Hanover.

George II, 1683–1760, the king of England from 1727 to 1760.

George III, 1738–1820, the king of England from 1760 to 1820.

G

at; āpe; cär; end; mē; it; īce; hot; ōld; fôrk; wood; fōōl; oil; out; up; turn; sing; thin; this; hw in white; zh in treasure. The symbol ə stands for the sound of a in about, e in taken, i in pencil, o in lemon, and u in circus.

George IV, 1762–1830, the king of England from 1820 to 1830.

George V, 1865–1936, the king of England from 1910 to 1936.

George VI, 1895–1952, the king of England from 1936 to 1952.

George·town (jôrj′toun′) *n.* the capital of Guyana, on the northern coast of the country. Pop. (1970), 66,070.

George Town *also,* **George·town.** see **Penang.**

Geor·gia (jôr′jə) *n.* **1.** a state in the southeastern United States. Capital, Atlanta. Area, 58,876 sq. mi. Pop. (1970), 4,589,575. Abbreviation, **Ga. 2.** a republic of the Soviet Union, in the southwestern part of the country, bordering Turkey and the Black Sea. Official name: **Georgian Soviet Socialist Republic.** Area, approx. 26,900 sq. mi. Pop. (1970), 4,686,000.

● **Georgia** was named after King George II of England, who gave its trustees the right to start a colony in the southern part of what is now the state of Georgia.

Geor·gian (jôr′jən) *adj.* **1.** of or relating to the reigns of the first four kings of England named George, who ruled from 1714 to 1830. **2.** of or relating to the state of Georgia. **3.** of or relating to the republic of Georgia or its people. —*n.* a person who was born or is living in the state or republic of Georgia.

ge·ot·ro·pism (jē ot′rə piz′əm) *n.* the movement or growth of plants and certain other organisms in response to the force of gravity.

Ger., German; Germany.

ge·ra·ni·um (jə rā′nē əm) *n.* **1.** any of a group of plants, widely grown for their showy clusters of red, pink, or white flowers. **2.** any of various related plants, having lobed leaves and small, usually white or purple, flowers. **3.** the flower of any of these plants.

Geranium

ger·bil (jur′bil) *n.* a rodent that lives in burrows, native to desert regions of southern Africa and Asia. It has a slender, tufted tail and a short, soft coat that is usually gray, brown, or reddish. Gerbils are sometimes kept as pets.

ger·fal·con (jər fal′kən, jər fôl′kən) another spelling of **gyrfalcon.**

ger·i·at·rics (jer′ē at′riks) *n., pl.* the branch of medicine that deals with the diseases of old age and the care and treatment of old people. ▲ used with a singular verb.

germ (jurm) *n.* **1.** any tiny living organism, especially one that causes disease. Germs can only be seen with the aid of a microscope. **2.** the earliest form or stage in the development of an organism. **3.** the earliest form or stage of anything: *the germ of a plan.*

Ger·man (jur′mən) *n.* **1.** a person who was born or is living in Germany. **2.** the Germanic language spoken mainly in Germany, Austria, and parts of Switzerland. —*adj.* of or relating to Germany, its people, their language, or their culture.

German Democratic Republic, see **East Germany.**

ger·mane (jər mān′) *adj.* directly or closely related; pertinent; relevant: *His comments are in no way germane to the subject under discussion.*

Ger·man·ic (jər man′ik) *n.* the branch of related languages that includes English, German, Dutch, Flemish, Norwegian, Swedish, Danish, and Icelandic. Also, **Teutonic.** —*adj.* **1.** of or relating to this family of languages. **2.** another word for **German. 3.** another word for **Teutonic.**

● The English language is classified as a **Germanic** language because in its earliest forms it is closely related to German, Dutch, and Flemish. The earliest known forms of our language were the Germanic dialects of the Angles, Saxons, and Jutes, which were tribes of people living in northwestern Europe. In the fifth century, members of these tribes invaded England, bringing with them their language. This language, which is known as Old English or Anglo-Saxon, became the native language of England, replacing Latin, which had been brought by Roman colonists, and Celtic, which had been the native tongue. About a fifth of modern English words can be traced back to Old English. The modern English vocabulary contains many words that are very similar to the corresponding modern German words. These English words, which are usually simple and very common, include *man, house, sleep, by, under, when, I,* and *good.*

ger·ma·ni·um (jər mā′nē əm) *n.* a grayish-white metallic element, widely used in the manufacture of transistors. Symbol: **Ge**

German measles, a contagious disease usually producing a pink blotchy rash; rubella. It is most common in young people and is especially serious for women early in pregnancy.

German shepherd, a dog of a breed developed in Germany, having a thick coat of black, brown, or gray fur. It is often trained for use as a watchdog, guard dog, or Seeing Eye dog. Also, **police dog, Alsatian.**

German silver, another term for **nickel silver.**

German shepherd

Ger·ma·ny (jur′mə nē) *n.* a country in north-central Europe, divided into West Germany and East Germany since 1949. Also, *German,* **Deutschland.**

germ cell, a male or female reproductive cell; sperm or egg.

ger·mi·cid·al (jur′mə sī′dəl) *adj.* that kills germs: *a germicidal substance.*

ger·mi·cide (jur′mə sīd′) *n.* a chemical substance that kills germs, especially germs that cause disease.

ger·mi·nate (jur′mə nāt′) *v.,* **ger·mi·nat·ed, ger·mi·nating.** —*v.i.* to start to grow or develop, as from a seed; sprout. —*v.t.* to cause to grow or develop: *Warmth and moisture germinate seeds.* —**ger′mi·na′tion,** *n.*

germ plasm, a substance in germ cells that contains the material of heredity.

germ warfare, another term for **biological warfare.**

Ge·ron·i·mo (jə ron′ə mō′) 1829?–1909, Apache Indian chief.

ger·ry·man·der (jer′ē man′dər, ger′ē man′dər) *n.* **1.** the arrangement of voting districts in a state or other political unit to give one political party an unfair advantage. **2.** a district arranged in this way. —*v.t.* to arrange (the voting districts of a state or other political unit) in order to give one political party an unfair advantage. [Coined in 1812 from the name Elbridge *Gerry,* 1744–1814, governor of Massachusetts when the legislature rearranged voting districts to give his party an unfair advantage + (sala)*mander;* because the shape of one of the new districts suggested a salamander.]

Gersh·win, George (gursh′win) 1898–1937, U.S. composer.

ger·und (jer′ənd) *n.* a verb form that ends with -*ing* and is used as a noun. In the sentence *Swimming is good exercise,* the word *swimming* is a gerund.

Ge·sta·po (gə stä′pō) *n.* the secret police force of Nazi Germany.

ges·ta·tion (jes tā′shən) *n.* **1.** the period from conception to birth, during which the unborn young are carried in the uterus; pregnancy. **2.** the developing or conceiving of something, such as a project, plan, or idea.

ges·tic·u·late (jes tik′yə lāt′) *v.i.,* **ges·tic·u·lat·ed, ges·tic·u·lat·ing.** to make or use gestures to express a thought or feeling or to emphasize something, as in speaking.

ges·tic·u·la·tion (jes tik′yə lā′shən) *n.* **1.** an emphatic or expressive gesture. **2.** the act of gesticulating.

ges·ture (jes′chər) *n.* **1.** a movement of the head, body, or limbs, used to express a thought or feeling, or to emphasize what is said: *He used hand gestures to indicate the size of the fish he had caught.* **2.** something said or done for effect or as a symbol: *to shake hands as a gesture of friendship.* —*v.i.,* **ges·tured, ges·tur·ing.** to make or use gestures: *The police officer gestured to us to stop.*

Ge·sund·heit (gə zoont′hīt′) *interj. German.* used to wish good health to someone who has just sneezed.

get (get) *v.,* **got, got** or **got·ten, get·ting.** —*v.t.* **1.** to obtain possession of; receive or acquire: *to get a new coat, to get an idea.* **2.** to achieve; earn; gain: *The team got three touchdowns.* **3.** to go for and return with; fetch: *Please get me a glass of water.* **4.** to cause to be done or become: *to get a haircut, to get into trouble.* **5.** to become ill with; suffer from; catch: *to get the mumps.* **6.** to make ready; prepare: *to get lunch.* **7.** to possess; have: *I've got a new dress.* **8.** to be obliged: *You've got to clean up your room.* **9.** *Informal.* to understand; comprehend: *I get the idea.* —*v.i.* **1.** to come to or reach: *to get to shore safely, to get to work on time.* **2.** to move, come, or go: *to get into an elevator, to get down from a ladder.* **3.** to be or become: *to get lost, to get ready to leave.*

to get along. a. to be on good terms: *Iris does not get along with her sister.* **b.** to manage: *to get along on little money.*

to get around. a. to move or go from place to place. **b.** to be circulated; become known: *The rumor got around quickly.* **c.** to avoid; evade.

to get at. a. to arrive at; reach. **b.** to attempt to express; mean: *I don't see what you're getting at.*

to get away. a. to leave; depart. **b.** to escape.

to get away with. *Informal.* to do (something) without being noticed, caught, or punished: *to get away with a mistake.*

to get back. a. to return: *to get back from a trip.* **b.** to recover: *to get back one's strength.*

to get back at. *Slang.* to take revenge on.

to get in. a. to go in; enter. **b.** to come in; arrive: *The train got in at noon.* **c.** to put in; insert: *He talks so much that I can never get in a word.*

to get off. a. to move down from or out of. **b.** to start; depart. **c.** to be released or escape: *The students got off with a severe lecture on the sin of being late.*

to get on. a. to move up on or into: *to get on a horse.* **b.** to get along.

to get out. a. to go away; depart. **b.** to get away; escape. **c.** to become known: *No one knew how the secret got out.* **d.** to publish; issue: *to get out a daily newspaper.*

to get out of. to escape: *to get out of an embarrassing situation.*

to get over. to recover from: *to get over a cold.*

to get together. a. to come together, especially informally. **b.** to come to an agreement.

to get up. a. to rise from bed or sleep. **b.** to sit or stand up.

get·a·way (get′ə wā′) *n. Informal.* **1.** the act of escaping: *The couple made a fast getaway after the wedding.* **2.** the start of a race.

Geth·sem·a·ne (geth sem′ə nē) *n.* in the New Testament, a garden east of Jerusalem, the scene of Jesus' agony, betrayal, and arrest.

get-to·geth·er (get′tə geth′ər) *n. Informal.* an informal meeting, gathering, or party.

Get·tys·burg (get′iz burg′) *n.* a town in southern Pennsylvania, the site of a decisive Union victory during the Civil War, in 1863.

get-up (get′up′) *n. Informal.* **1.** a dress or costume, especially an unusual one; outfit. **2.** the style or way in which something is made or arranged; arrangement.

get-up-and-go (get′up′ən gō′) *n. Informal.* drive; vigor; energy.

gew·gaw (gyōo′gô′) *n.* a gaudy, worthless plaything or ornament; showy trifle; bauble. —*adj.* showy but without value; gaudy.

gey·ser (gī′zər) *n.* a natural hot spring from which steam and hot water shoot into the air after being heated below the surface by surrounding masses of hot rock.

Gha·na (gä′nə) *n.* a country in western Africa, consisting of the former British territories of the Gold Coast and Togoland. Capital, Accra. Area, 92,100 sq. mi. Pop. (1980), 11, 680,000.

ghast·ly (gast′lē) *adj.,* **ghast·li·er, ghast·li·est. 1.** horrible; dreadful: *the ghastly sights of war.* **2.** deathly pale; like a ghost: *The frightened man's face bore a ghastly look.*

Geyser

3. *Informal.* extremely bad or unpleasant: *a ghastly mistake.* —*adv.* in a ghastly manner; dreadfully. —**ghast′li·ness,** *n.*

gher·kin (gur′kin) *n.* a small, prickly, many-seeded cucumber used for making pickles.

ghet·to (get′ō) *n. pl.,* **ghet·tos** or **ghet·toes. 1.** the section of a European city where Jews were required to live. **2.** the section of a city, especially a slum area, in which members of a minority group live because of social discrimination or economic pressure.

ghost (gōst) *n.* **1.** the spirit of a dead person, thought of as making its presence known to the living in a visible form or in some other way; specter. **2.** a shadowy outline or likeness: *a ghost of a smile.* **3.** slightest bit: *He doesn't have a ghost of a chance of winning the election.*

to give up the ghost. to die.

ghost·ly (gōst′lē) *adj.,* **ghost·li·er, ghost·li·est.** relating to or like a ghost: *The scarecrow took on a ghostly shape in the dim light.* —**ghost′li·ness,** *n.*

ghost town, a town that has been deserted, especially a mining town in the western United States abandoned after the nearby mines closed.

ghost-writ·er (gōst′rī′tər) *n.* a person who writes a

at; āpe; cär; end; mē; it; īce; hot; ōld; fôrk; wood; fōol; oil; out; up; turn; sing; thin; this; hw in white; zh in treasure. The symbol ə stands for the sound of **a** in about, **e** in taken, **i** in pencil, **o** in lemon, and **u** in circus.

G

speech, article, book, or other work for another person who gets credit for the work.

ghoul (gōōl) *n.* **1.** *Oriental Legend.* a horrible demon believed to rob graves and feed on human corpses. **2.** anyone who robs graves. **3.** a person who enjoys revolting acts or horrible things. —**ghoul'ish,** *adj.* —**ghoul'-ish·ly,** *adv.* —**ghoul'ish·ness,** *n.*

GI (jē'ī') *n. pl.,* **GI's, GIs.** *Informal.* an enlisted man in the U.S. military service, especially the Army. —*adj.* **1.** of, relating to, or characteristic of GI's: *a GI haircut.* **2.** issued by the U.S. government for use by the armed forces: *GI boots.* [Originally used as an abbreviation for *galvanized iron* by U.S. Army clerks in entering items made of this metal. It was later used as an abbreviation for *government issue* or *general issue.*]

gi·ant (jī'ənt) *n.* **1.** in folklore and legend, a huge and powerful creature having human form. **2.** a person or thing that is extraordinary in strength, importance, size, or ability: *Isaac Newton was an intellectual giant. That company is a giant in the field of electronics.* —*adj.* extremely large or great; huge: *a giant telescope.* —**gi'ant·ess,** *n.*

giant panda, see **panda** *(def. 1).*

giant star, any of a group of very bright, large stars.

gib·ber (jib'ər) *v.i.* to speak rapidly and senselessly; jabber. —*n.* gibberish.

gib·ber·ish (jib'ər ish) *n.* **1.** rapid senseless chatter. **2.** meaningless speech or writing; nonsense.

gib·bet (jib'it) *n.* **1.** a gallows. **2.** an upright post with a projecting part from which the bodies of executed criminals were hung. —*v.t.,* **gib·bet·ed, gib·bet·ing. 1.** to hang (a corpse) on a gibbet. **2.** to put (a person) to death by hanging.

gib·bon (gib'ən) *n.* any of various small, tree-dwelling apes of southeastern Asia and the East Indies, having long slender limbs and no tail.

gib·bous (gib'əs) *adj.* of or relating to that phase of the moon or a planet in which it appears more than half full but less than full.

gibe (jīb) *also,* **jibe.** *n.* a mocking remark; jeer; taunt. —*v.,* **gibed, gib·ing.** —*v.i.* to utter gibes; jeer. —*v.t.* to utter gibes at.

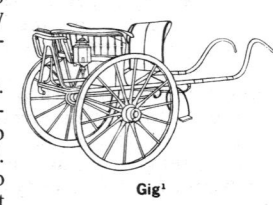
Gibbon

gib·let (jib'lit) *n. usually,* **gib-lets.** any of the internal parts of a fowl that can be eaten, such as the heart, liver, or gizzard.

Gi·bral·tar (ji brôl'tər) *n.* **1.** a British colony and seaport near the southern tip of Spain, the site of a large, heavily fortified naval base. **2. Rock of.** a great rock formation where this colony is located. **3. Strait of.** a body of water connecting the Mediterranean Sea with the Atlantic Ocean, separating northern Africa from the southern tip of Spain.

gid·dy (gid'ē) *adj.,* **gid·di·er, gid·di·est. 1.** having a spinning sensation in one's head; dizzy. **2.** causing or tending to cause dizziness. **3.** lacking seriousness; frivolous; flighty. —**gid'di·ly,** *adv.* —**gid'di·ness,** *n.*

Gide, An·dré (zhēd; än drā') 1869–1951, French novelist, essayist, dramatist, and critic.

gift (gift) *n.* **1.** something given; present; donation: *a wedding gift.* **2.** natural ability; talent: *a gift for writing.* **3.** the act or power of giving.

gift·ed (gif'tid) *adj.* having natural ability; talented: *a gifted artist.*

gig¹ (gig) *n.* **1.** a light, open, two-wheeled carriage drawn by a single horse. **2.** a long, light, ship's boat propelled by oars, sails, or a motor. [Possibly of Scandinavian origin.]

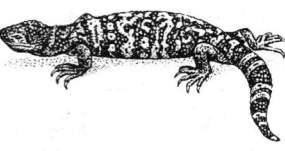
Gig¹

gig² (gig) *n.* **1.** a fishing spear. **2.** a device made of hooks fastened back to back, used to catch fish by their bodies. —*v.i.,* **gigged, gig·ging.** to catch (fish) with a gig. [Short for *fishgig* fishing spear.]

gi·gan·tic (jī gan'tik) *adj.* like or resembling a giant, especially in size; huge; enormous: *A gigantic wave washed over the boat.*

gig·gle (gig'əl) *v.i.,* **gig·gled, gig·gling.** to laugh in a silly, high-pitched, or nervous way. —*n.* silly, high-pitched, or nervous laughter. —**gig'gler,** *n.*

Gi·la monster (hē'lə) a large, poisonous lizard found in desert regions of northern Mexico and the southwestern United States. It has a black or brown scaly body with orange or yellow blotches. [From the *Gila* River in Arizona, where this lizard is found.]

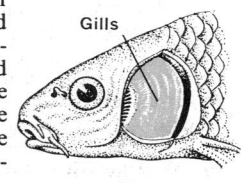
Gila monster

Gil·bert, Sir William Schwenck (gil'bərt; shwenk) 1836–1911, English poet and librettist who collaborated with the composer Sir Arthur Sullivan on comic operas.

gild¹ (gild) *v.t.,* **gild·ed** or **gilt, gild·ing. 1.** to coat with a thin layer of gold. **2.** to adorn, especially with a golden light or color; brighten attractively. **3.** to make (something) seem better than it is. [Old English *gyldan.*]

gild² (gild) another spelling of **guild.**

Gil·e·ad (gil'ē əd) *n.* a mountainous region in ancient Palestine, east of the Jordan River.

gill¹ (gil) *n.* **1.** the organ of breathing for fish and most other water animals, consisting of a thin layer of tissue well supplied with blood. It is capable of absorbing oxygen from the water and releasing carbon dioxide from the blood. **2.** one of the thin, bladelike structures on the underside of the cap of a mushroom. [Of Scandinavian origin.]

Gills

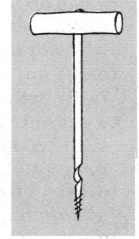
Gill¹

gill² (jil) *n.* a liquid measure that is equal to one fourth of a pint. [Old French *gille.*]

gilt (gilt) *v.* a past tense and past participle of **gild¹.** —*adj.* covered with gold or having a golden color; gilded. —*n.* gold or similar material used in gilding.

gim·crack (jim'krak') *n.* a gaudy, useless object; trifle.

gim·let (gim'lit) *n.* a small tool with a screw point and a cross handle, used for boring holes.

gim·mick (gim'ik) *n. Slang.* **1.** a clever feature or idea, especially one that is used to attract attention. **2.** a small device or gadget.

Gimlet

gin¹ (jin) *n.* a strong alcoholic liquor that is distilled from grains and flavored with juniper berries. [Short for earlier *geneva,* from obsolete Dutch *genever* juniper.]

gin² (jin) *n.* a machine for separating cotton from its seed. —*v.t.,* **ginned, gin·ning.** to separate (cotton) from its seeds with a gin. [Shortened from Old French *engin* a machine, engine, from Latin *ingenium* skill.] —**gin'ner,** *n.*

gin³ (jin) *n.* see **gin rummy.**

gin·ger (jin′jər) *n.* **1.** any of a group of plants grown in tropical and subtropical regions for their roots, which can be eaten. **2.** a spice that is ground from these roots, used in cooking and in medicine. **3.** the root itself, often candied or preserved in syrup. **4.** *Informal.* liveliness; high spirits; pep.

ginger ale, a carbonated soft drink that is flavored with ginger.

ginger beer, a carbonated soft drink made with yeast and flavored with ginger.

gin·ger·bread (jin′jər bred′) *n.* **1.** a dark, sweet cake or cookie flavored with ginger and molasses. **2.** gaudy and tasteless ornamentation, as on furniture or buildings. —*adj.* cheap and showy; gaudy.

gin·ger·ly (jin′jər lē) *adv.* with extreme caution; carefully; timidly: *to walk gingerly on thin ice.* —*adj.* extremely cautious or wary: *gingerly steps.*

gin·ger·snap (jin′jər snap′) *n.* a thin, crisp cookie flavored with ginger and molasses.

ging·ham (ging′əm) *n.* a strong, medium-weight, dyed cotton fabric, usually woven in checks, stripes, or plaids.

gink·go (ging′kō) *n. pl.,* **gink·goes.** *also,* **ging·ko.** a large tree with fan-shaped leaves, native to China. Ginkgoes are often planted as ornamental or shade trees.

gin rummy, a variation of the card game rummy, in which two players form matched sets of cards until one of the players has matched all his cards or has ten points or fewer of unmatched cards.

gin·seng (jin′seng) *n.* **1.** either of two low plants grown in North America and Asia, having a thick branched root and bearing toothed leaves and small, pale green flowers. **2.** the root of this plant, used in medicine by the Chinese.

Giot·to (jot′ō) 1266?–1337, Italian painter.

Gip·sy (jip′sē) another spelling of Gypsy.

gipsy moth, another spelling of **gypsy moth.**

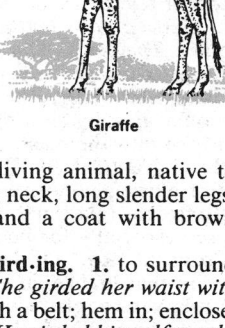
Giraffe

gi·raffe (jə raf′) *n.* the tallest living animal, native to Africa. The giraffe has a very long neck, long slender legs, two or four small bony horns, and a coat with brown patches outlined with white.

gird (gurd) *v.t.,* **girt** or **gird·ed, gird·ing. 1.** to surround or encircle with a belt or girdle: *She girded her waist with a gold chain.* **2.** to encircle as if with a belt; hem in; enclose. **3.** to prepare (oneself) for action: *He girded himself to take the examination.*

gird·er (gur′dər) *n.* a large horizontal beam usually made of steel, used as a support, as for a floor or the framework of a bridge or building.

gir·dle (gurd′əl) *n.* **1.** a flexible undergarment worn especially by women to support or shape the waist, abdomen, or hips; corset. **2.** a belt or band worn around the waist. **3.** anything that encircles in the manner of a belt. —*v.t.* **gir·dled, gir·dling. 1.** to encircle with a belt or girdle. **2.** to encircle as if with a belt; surround: *Trees girdled the lake.*

girl (gurl) *n.* **1.** a female child

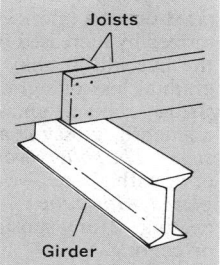
Joists

Girder

Girder

from birth to the time she is a young woman. **2.** a young woman. **3.** a female servant. **4.** *Informal.* a sweetheart. **5.** *Informal.* any woman.

girl·friend (gurl′frend′) *n. Informal.* a female friend, especially a sweetheart.

girl·hood (gurl′hood′) *n.* **1.** the time or state of being a girl. **2.** girls as a group.

girl·ish (gur′lish) *adj.* of, relating to, or fit for girls or girlhood. —**girl′ish·ly,** *adv.* —**girl′ish·ness,** *n.*

girl scout, a member of the Girl Scouts.

Girl Scouts, a worldwide organization for young girls, founded to develop character and physical fitness and encourage helpfulness to others.

girt (gurt) a past tense and past participle of **gird.**

girth (gurth) *n.* **1.** the distance around something; circumference: *the girth of a column, the girth of a person's waist.* **2.** a strap or band that is passed under the belly of a horse or other animal to keep a saddle or pack in place. —*v.t.* **1.** to fasten or fit with a girth. **2.** to surround; encircle; gird.

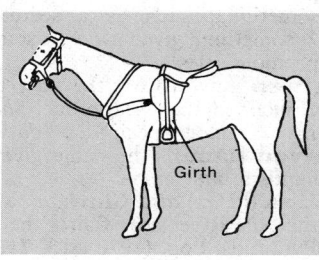
Girth

Girth

gist (jist) *n.* a main idea; central point: *the gist of a speech.*

give (giv) *v.,* **gave, giv·en, giv·ing.** —*v.t.* **1.** to hand over to another as a present: *Linda gave Dennis a sweater for his birthday.* **2.** to transfer ownership of (something) in exchange for something else, especially to sell for payment: *The dealer gave the car to Mr. Smith for $2000.* **3.** to hand over or deliver: *The secretary gave the letter to her boss. Please give this money to my brother.* **4.** to confer as an honor: *to give first prize to the winner of a contest.* **5.** to grant: *to give permission.* **6.** to communicate to another; transmit; send: *Please give my regards to your mother.* **7.** to assign or allot: *The teacher gave the job of handing out the papers to John.* **8.** to administer: *to give medicine to a baby.* **9.** to provide; supply: *to give food to the hungry, to give evidence in court.* **10.** to issue forth in words, sound, or motion: *to give a shout, to give the signal to start.* **11.** to arrange and carry out: *to give a party.* **12.** to sacrifice; surrender: *to give one's life in war.* —*v.i.* **1.** to make a donation; contribute: *to give to charity.* **2.** to move or bend under pressure; yield: *The dam gave under the heavy rainfall, and the town was flooded.* —*n.* the quality of being elastic; flexibility: *This fabric has a lot of give.* —**giv′er,** *n.*

to give away. a. to give as a gift; donate: *The aging millionaire gave away all his money.* **b.** to present (the bride) to the bridegroom in a marriage ceremony: *Her father gave her away.* **c.** to reveal; expose: *The boy gave away his hiding place when he sneezed.*

to give back. to return: *She gave back the money she borrowed.*

to give in. to stop opposing; yield: *The father gave in and let his son drive the car.*

at; āpe; cär; end; mē; it; īce; hot; ōld; fôrk; wood; fo͞ol; oil; out; up; turn; sing; thin; this; hw in white; zh in treasure. The symbol ə stands for the sound of **a** in about, **e** in taken, **i** in pencil, **o** in lemon, and **u** in circus.

G

to give off. to put forth; emit: *The flowers gave off a sweet fragrance.*

to give out. a. to distribute or issue: *to give out free samples.* **b.** to make public; announce: *to give out information.* **c.** to become exhausted, broken down, or used up: *The swimmer gave out after ten laps.*

to give up. a. to yield; surrender. **b.** to stop; cease: *to give up smoking.* **c.** to acknowledge that one has failed and stop trying. **d.** to abandon as hopeless or useless: *to give up the search for a lost dog.* **e.** to devote completely: *to give up one's life to medical research.*

to give way. to yield under pressure; break down.

give-and-take (giv′ən tāk′) *n.* **1.** a mutual yielding or concession; compromise. **2.** a good-natured exchange of talk; banter.

give·a·way (giv′ə wā′) *n. Informal.* **1.** the revealing of something, such as a secret, accidentally; exposure. **2.** something given away or sold at a very low price, as to promote sales.

giv·en (giv′ən) *v.* the past participle of **give.** —*adj.* **1.** inclined; disposed; prone: *She is given to spreading gossip.* **2.** stated; specified: *to do something at a given time.*

given name, the name given to a person at birth or baptism; first name.

Gi·za (gē′zə) *also,* **Gi·zeh.** *n.* a city in northern Egypt, on the Nile River near Cairo, the site of the Sphinx and the Pyramids. Pop. (1970 est.), 712,000.

giz·zard (giz′ərd) *n.* the muscular second part of the stomach of a bird, in which partially digested food from the first part of the stomach is finely ground.

gla·cial (glā′shəl) *adj.* **1.** of, relating to, or produced by ice or glaciers. **2.** of or relating to a period of time when glaciers covered large areas of the earth, especially the Pleistocene epoch. **3.** cold; icy: *glacial rivers, a glacial manner.* —**gla′cial·ly,** *adv.*

glacial epoch, see **ice age** *(def. 1).*

gla·cier (glā′shər) *n.* a large mass of ice moving slowly over some land surface or down a valley. A glacier is formed over a long period of time from the accumulation of snow in areas where the amount of snow that falls is greater than the amount that melts.

glad (glad) *adj.,* **glad·der, glad·dest. 1.** feeling or expressing joy, pleasure, or satisfaction; happy: *I am very glad to meet you. We were glad to hear of his success.* **2.** causing joy or pleasure; pleasing: *glad tidings.* **3.** very willing: *Tom will be glad to go with us.* —**glad′ly,** *adv.* —**glad′ness,** *n.*

glad·den (glad′ən) *v.t.* to make glad.

glade (glād) *n.* an open space in a wood or forest.

glad·i·a·tor (glad′ē ā′tər) *n.* a slave, captive, or paid professional who took part in public combat in the arenas of ancient Rome.

glad·i·o·lus (glad′ē ō′ləs) *n. pl.,* **glad·i·o·li** (glad′ē ō′lī) or **glad·i·o·lus·es. 1.** a funnel-shaped, showy flower that grows in long clusters. **2.** the leafy plant bearing this flower, having stiff, sword-shaped leaves. Also, **glad·i·o·la** (glad′ē ō′lə). [Latin *gladiolus* a little sword.]

glad·some (glad′səm) *adj.* causing joy or pleasure.

glam·or·ize (glam′ə rīz′) *v.t.,* **glam·or·ized, glam·or·iz·ing.** to make glamorous: *He criticized the movie because he felt that it glamorized crime.*

glam·or·ous (glam′ər əs) *adj.* full of glamour; fascinatingly attractive; alluring: *a glamorous film star.* —**glam′or·ous·ly,** *adv.* —**glam′or·ous·ness,** *n.*

glam·our (glam′ər) *also,* **glam·or.** *n.* alluring excite-

Gladiolus

ment or charm; fascinating attraction: *the glamour of the movie industry.*

glance (glans) *n.* a brief or hurried look: *She gave me an angry glance when I made that remark.* —*v.i.,* **glanced, glanc·ing. 1.** to take a brief or hurried look: *The girls glanced in the store windows as they walked by.* **2.** to strike a surface and move off at a slant: *The bullet glanced off the rock.*

gland (gland) *n.* an organ, tissue, or cell that produces and discharges one or more substances that are used by or discharged from the body. Important glands include the thyroid and pituitary glands and the liver, kidneys, and pancreas.

glan·du·lar (glan′jə lər) *adj.* **1.** of, relating to, or affecting a gland: *a glandular disease.* **2.** consisting of or containing a gland or glands: *glandular tissue.*

glare (gler) *n.* **1.** a strong, usually unpleasant light, as from sunlight reflected on a shiny surface. **2.** a piercing, hostile look or stare. —*v.,* **glared, glar·ing.** —*v.i.* **1.** to shine with a strong, harsh light. **2.** to look or stare piercingly and with hostility: *The angry fighter glared at his opponent.* —*v.t.* to express with a glare: *The accused man glared his defiance at the jury.*

glar·ing (gler′ing) *adj.* **1.** giving off or reflecting a harsh light; unpleasantly bright. **2.** extremely conspicuous; flagrant: *a glaring mistake.* **3.** staring piercingly and with hostility. —**glar′ing·ly,** *adv.*

glar·y (gler′ē) *adj.,* **glar·i·er, glar·i·est.** dazzling; glaring.

Glas·gow (glas′gō, glas′kō) *n.* the largest city in Scotland, a port in the southern part of the country. Pop. (1971), 896,958.

glass (glas) *n. pl.,* **glass·es. 1.** a hard, brittle, usually transparent material made by melting a mixture of sand, soda, and lime. **2.** an open container, especially of glass and usually without a handle, used chiefly for drinking. **3.** a glassful: *He drank half a glass of water.* **4.** something partly or entirely made of glass, such as a window, a mirror, or telescope. **5. glasses.** see **eyeglasses.** —*adj.* made of glass: *a glass bottle.* —*v.t.* to enclose or protect with glass: *They glassed in the open porch.*

glass blower, a person whose work is glass blowing.

glass blowing, the art or process of shaping a mass of molten glass by blowing a controlled stream of air through a tube into the mass.

glass·ful (glas′fool′) *n. pl.,* **glass·fuls.** the amount that a drinking glass can hold.

glass·ine (gla sēn′) *n.* a thin, glazed translucent paper, used especially for book jackets and envelope windows.

glass snake, a legless lizard resembling a snake, having a tail that breaks off easily into small pieces.

glass·ware (glas′wer′) *n.* objects of glass made by hand or produced by machine, especially drinking glasses.

glass·y (glas′ē) *adj.,* **glass·i·er, glass·i·est. 1.** resembling glass; smooth and shiny: *the glassy surface of a lake on a windless day.* **2.** fixed, expressionless, or lifeless: *a glassy stare, glassy eyes.* —**glass′i·ly,** *adv.* —**glass′i·ness,** *n.*

glau·co·ma (glô kō′mə) *n.* a serious eye disease characterized by increased pressure in, and gradual hardening of, the eyeball. It may lead to damage of the retina and gradual loss of sight.

glaze (glāz) *v.,* **glazed, glaz·ing.** —*v.t.* **1.** to cover with a smooth, glossy coating: *She glazed the doughnuts with sugar. The pottery was glazed to make it shiny.* **2.** to furnish or fit with glass. —*v.i.* to become glassy or glazed: *His eyes glazed with pain.* —*n.* **1.** a smooth, glossy covering or coating. **2.** any substance used to produce such a covering or coating.

gla·zier (glā′zhər) *n.* a person who installs panes of glass, as in windows and doors.

gleam (glēm) *n.* **1.** a flash or beam of bright light: *We could see the gleam of a flashlight in the distance.* **2.** reflected brightness, as from a polished surface: *the gleam of a new car.* **3.** a faint or brief appearance or sign: *a gleam of hope.* —*v.i.* to shine or reflect light: *The knight's armor gleamed in the sunlight.*

glean (glēn) *v.t.* **1.** to collect slowly and with great effort: *to glean information.* **2.** to gather (grain) left on a field after reaping. —**glean′er,** *n.*

glean·ings (glē′ningz) *n.,pl.* things obtained by gleaning.

glee (glē) *n.* **1.** joy or delight; merriment: *The little boy laughed with glee when he opened his present.* **2.** a song for three or more male voices, without accompaniment, popular in the eighteenth century.

glee club, a group organized for singing choral music.

glee·ful (glē′fəl) *adj.* full of glee; merry; joyous. —**glee′ful·ly,** *adv.* —**glee′ful·ness,** *n.*

glen (glen) *n.* a small, narrow, usually secluded valley.

Glen·dale (glen′dāl′) *n.* a city in southwestern California, adjoining Los Angeles. Pop. (1970), 132,752.

glen·gar·ry (glen gar′ē) *n. pl.,* **glen·gar·ries.** a Scottish cap made of wool, having straight sides and a crease lengthwise across the top.

Glenn, John (glen) 1921—, U.S. astronaut, the first American to orbit the earth.

glib (glib) *adj.,* **glib·ber, glib·best.** speaking or spoken with little thought or sincerity: *The car salesman was a glib talker. She always has a glib excuse for being late.* —**glib′ly,** *adv.* —**glib′ness,** *n.*

glide (glīd) *v.i.,* **glid·ed, glid·ing. 1.** to move smoothly, continuously, and effortlessly: *The figure skater glided over the ice.* **2.** to pass gradually and unnoticed: *The time glided by.* **3.** to maintain flight or descend slowly without the use of power. —*n.* **1.** the act of moving smoothly and effortlessly. **2.** the act of gliding.

glid·er (glī′dər) *n.* **1.** an aircraft made of light materials and designed to fly without the aid of an engine, relying on rising air currents to remain aloft. **2.** a person or thing that glides. **3.** a piece of furniture resembling a couch, usually used outdoors. It is suspended from a frame so that it can swing backward and forward.

glim·mer (glim′ər) *n.* **1.** a dim, unsteady light. **2.** a faint hint or sign; inkling: *a glimmer of hope.* —*v.i.* to shine with dim, unsteady light; flicker.

glimpse (glimps) *n.* a brief view; passing glance: *He caught a glimpse of the driver's face as the car sped by.* —*v.,* **glimpsed, glimps·ing.** —*v.t.* to catch a brief view of; see for a moment: *We glimpsed the actress as she entered the studio.* —*v.i.* to look quickly; glance: *to glimpse at a road sign.*

glint (glint) *n.* a bright, quick flash; gleam; sparkle. —*v.i.* to shine; gleam.

glis·san·do (gli sän′dō) *n. pl.,* **glis·san·di** (gli sän′dē). *Music.* **1.** a gliding effect performed in various ways, as by rapidly running one finger over the white keys of a piano or sliding one finger along the string of a stringed instrument. **2.** a passage performed with such an effect. —*adj.* of or performed with a gliding effect.

Glider

glis·ten (glis′ən) *v.i.* to shine or sparkle with reflected light: *The snow glistened in the sun. Tears glistened on the man's cheeks.* —*n.* a gleam; sparkle.

glit·ter (glit′ər) *v.i.* **1.** to shine with a bright light; sparkle: *The jewels glittered.* **2.** to be attractive or showy. —*n.* **1.** sparkling brightness or light: *the glitter of jewelry.* **2.** showiness; splendor: *the glitter of New York City's theater district.* **3.** small bits of sparkling material, used for ornamentation. —**glit′ter·y,** *adj.*

gloam·ing (glō′ming) *n.* twilight; dusk.

gloat (glōt) *v.i.* to think about with satisfaction or wicked delight: *He gloated over his victory in the boxing match.* —**gloat′er,** *n.* —**gloat′ing·ly,** *adv.*

glob (glob) *n.* a rounded mass, lump, or drop: *a glob of paint.*

glob·al (glō′bəl) *adj.* **1.** of or relating to the entire world; worldwide: *global warfare.* **2.** shaped like a globe; spherical. —**glob′al·ly,** *adv.*

globe (glōb) *n.* **1.** the earth; world. **2.** a sphere on which a map of the earth or of the heavens is drawn. **3.** a solid spherical body; sphere. **4.** anything resembling a sphere in shape, such as a glass covering for a light bulb.

glo·bose (glō′bōs) *adj.* having the form of a globe.

glob·u·lar (glob′yə lər) *adj.* **1.** having the shape of a globe; spherical. **2.** made up of globules.

glob·ule (glob′yool) *n.* a small ball or drop: *a globule of oil.*

glock·en·spiel (glok′ən spēl′) *n.* a musical instrument consisting of a series of metal bars mounted in a frame, played by being struck with two small hammers.

gloom (gloom) *n.* **1.** a depressing or dismal atmosphere: *the frightening gloom of a cemetery late at night.* **2.** sadness or dejection; low spirits: *The defeated candidate's gloom was reflected in his voice.* **3.** complete or partial darkness; dimness: *The car's headlights pierced the gloom.* —*v.i.* **1.** to be or look sad, depressed, or displeased. **2.** to be or become dark or dismal.

gloom·y (gloo′mē) *adj.,* **gloom·i·er, gloom·i·est. 1.** sad or depressing; dismal; dreary: *There was a gloomy atmosphere in the losing team's locker room.* **2.** low in spirits; melancholy; depressed; dejected: *He was gloomy after he lost the race.* **3.** dark; dim: *a gloomy hallway.* —**gloom′i·ly,** *adv.* —**gloom′i·ness,** *n.*

Glockenspiel

Glo·ri·a (glôr′ē ə) *n.* **1.** any of several hymns of praise to God that begin with the Latin word *Gloria.* **2.** a musical setting for any of these.

glo·ri·fi·ca·tion (glôr′ə fi kā′shən) *n.* the act of glorifying or the state of being glorified.

glo·ri·fy (glôr′ə fī′) *v.t.,* **glo·ri·fied, glo·ri·fy·ing. 1.** to exalt with praise; honor or worship: *The Romans glorified Julius Caesar.* **2.** to bring honor or distinction to; give glory to: *The achievements of the three brothers glorified their family name.* **3.** to cause to appear more glorious or splendid than it actually is: *The writer glorified the life of a soldier in his war novel.* —**glo′ri·fi′er,** *n.*

Glengarry

at; āpe; cär; end; mē; it; īce; hot; ōld; fôrk; wood; fōōl; oil; out; up; turn; sing; thin; this; hw in white; zh in treasure. The symbol ə stands for the sound of a in about, e in taken, i in pencil, o in lemon, and u in circus.

G

glo·ri·ous (glôr'ē əs) *adj.* **1.** magnificent; splendid: *a glorious day, a glorious sunset.* **2.** having or deserving glory; famous: *a glorious work of art.* **3.** bringing glory: *a glorious deed.* **4.** *Informal.* extremely enjoyable or delightful: *We had a glorious time at the birthday party.* —**glo'ri·ous·ly,** *adv.*

glo·ry (glôr'ē) *n. pl.,* **glo·ries. 1.** great praise, honor, or distinction; fame; renown: *The scientist's assistant actually made the discovery, but the scientist received all the glory.* **2.** a person or thing that brings praise, honor, distinction, or renown; source of pride: *The glory of the tropical island was its climate.* **3.** great beauty or splendor; magnificence: *The sun shone in all its glory.* **4.** the state or condition of greatest magnificence or prosperity: *That country was in its glory during the years just before the war.* **5.** the highest degree of self-satisfaction or pleasure: *The actor was in his glory in front of the television cameras.* **6.** praise and honor offered in worship or adoration: *Give glory to God.* **7.** the splendor and bliss of heaven. —*v.i.,* **glo·ried, glo·ry·ing.** to rejoice proudly or triumphantly; exult: *He gloried in his victory.*

gloss¹ (glôs) *n. pl.,* **gloss·es. 1.** the surface shine of something; luster: *the gloss of a waxed floor.* **2.** a deceptive appearance: *After his gloss of politeness wore off, she found he was actually rather rude.* —*v.t.* **1.** to put a shine or luster on. **2.** to minimize or attempt to hide: *to gloss over a mistake.* [Possibly of Scandinavian origin.]

gloss² (glôs) *n. pl.,* **gloss·es. 1.** an explanation or interpretation, as of a text; commentary. **2.** a glossary. **3.** a translation of a foreign word or phrase, as in an etymology in a dictionary. —*v.t.* to explain or comment on, as a word or text. [Latin *glossa* an explanation.]

glos·sa·ry (glos'ər ē) *n. pl.,* **glos·sa·ries.** an alphabetized list of explanations or definitions, especially of specialized, foreign, or obscure words.

gloss·y (glô'sē) *adj.,* **gloss·i·er, gloss·i·est.** having a shiny surface; lustrous. —*n. pl.,* **gloss·ies.** a photograph printed on smooth, glossy paper. —**gloss'i·ly,** *adv.* —**gloss'i·ness,** *n.*

glot·tis (glot'is) *n. pl.,* **glot·tis·es** or **glot·ti·des** (glot'ə-dēz). a narrow opening in the larynx between the vocal cords.

glove (gluv) *n.* **1.** a covering for the hand usually made of fabric or leather with separate sections for each finger. **2.** any of several coverings for the hand used in various sports, such as baseball, hockey, or golf. **3.** see **boxing glove.** —*v.t.,* **gloved, glov·ing. 1.** to cover or provide with a glove or gloves. **2.** to catch in a glove: *The shortstop gloved the ball and threw it to first base.*

glove compartment, a small storage space in the dashboard of an automobile.

glow (glō) *n.* **1.** the light or shine from a heated substance. **2.** a similar light or shine without heat: *the glow given off by a firefly.* **3.** brightness or warmth of color: *Her face had the glow of good health.* **4.** a warm, ardent feeling or appearance: *a glow of pleasure.* —*v.i.* **1.** to shine from intense heat: *The candle glowed brightly.* **2.** to shine without heat: *The face of my watch glows in the dark.* **3.** to show a bright or warm color: *Her cheeks glowed with health and happiness.* **4.** to show or be filled with enthusiasm or emotion: *The man's eyes glowed with pride when he heard of his daughter's accomplishments.*

glow·er (glou'ər) *v.i.* to look at angrily or threateningly; scowl: *The motorist glowered at the driver who had cut in front of him.* —*n.* an angry or threatening stare. —**glow'-er·ing·ly,** *adv.*

glow·worm (glō'wurm') *n.* any of various insects or larvae that give off light, such as the larva of the firefly.

glu·cose (gloo'kōs) *n.* **1.** a simple sugar occurring in plants and in the blood of man and animals. It is an important source of energy for the body. **2.** a thick, yellowish syrup made from starch, used in foods, in intravenous feedings, in the curing of tobacco, and in the tanning industry.

glue (gloo) *n.* **1.** a substance used to join or stick things together, made by boiling animal hooves, bones, and skins. **2.** any sticky substance used for the same purpose. —*v.t.,* **glued, glu·ing. 1.** to attach or fasten with glue: *She glued the broken pieces of pottery together.* **2.** to attach or fasten firmly: *He glued his eyes to the road while driving in the heavy rain.*

glu·ey (gloo'ē) *adj.,* **glu·i·er, glu·i·est. 1.** like or resembling glue; sticky. **2.** full of or smeared with glue: *a gluey surface.*

glum (glum) *adj.,* **glum·mer, glum·mest.** gloomy; sullen. —**glum'ly,** *adv.* —**glum'ness,** *n.*

glut (glut) *v.t.,* **glut·ted, glut·ting. 1.** to satisfy completely or to excess: *Henry glutted himself at dinner.* **2.** to supply (a market) with goods to excess; oversupply. —*n.* a supply that is greater than needed.

glu·ten (gloot'ən) *n.* a tough, sticky protein substance obtained from wheat, rye, and other grains, used to make bread dough rise.

glu·ti·nous (gloot'ən əs) *adj.* like glue; sticky.

glut·ton (glut'ən) *n.* **1.** a person who eats too much or takes pleasure in eating excessively. **2.** a person who has great fondness or capacity for something: *a glutton for work, a glutton for punishment.*

glut·ton·ous (glut'ən əs) *adj.* given to overeating; greedy. —**glut'ton·ous·ly,** *adv.* —**glut'ton·ous·ness,** *n.*

glut·ton·y (glut'ən ē) *n. pl.,* **glut·ton·ies.** excess in eating; greediness.

glyc·er·in (glis'ər in) *also,* **glyc·er·ine.** *n.* a colorless, syrupy, sweet liquid obtained from fats or produced synthetically, used especially in making nitroglycerin, medicines, soaps, and certain plastics.

glyc·er·ol (glis'ə rôl') *n.* another word for **glycerin.**

gly·co·gen (glī'kə jən) *n.* a white substance that is one of the forms in which sugar is stored in the body of animals. When needed for use by the body, it is changed into glucose.

gm., gram; grams.

G-man (jē'man') *n. pl.,* **G-men** (jē'men'). *Informal.* an agent of the Federal Bureau of Investigation. [Short for *g*(overnment) *man.*]

gnarl (närl) *n.* a knot or lump, as on a tree.

gnarled (närld) *adj.* **1.** having many rough, twisted knots, as a tree trunk or branches. **2.** (of the hands) rough or rugged in appearance.

gnash (nash) *v.t.* to strike, grate, or grind (the teeth) together, as in anger or pain.

gnat (nat) *n.* any of various small, winged insects that have sharp, piercing mouth parts. Some gnats suck blood, while others feed on plants.

gnaw (nô) *v.,* **gnawed, gnawed** or **gnawn, gnaw·ing.** —*v.t.* **1.** to bite (something) repeatedly with the teeth: *The dog gnawed the bone.* **2.** to make by gnawing: *The puppy gnawed a hole through the box.* **3.** to cause constant discomfort, pain, or trouble to. —*v.i.* **1.** to bite repeatedly: *The lion gnawed on the bars of his cage.* **2.** to torment or trouble: *The man's secret crime gnawed at his conscience.*

gneiss (nīs) *n.* a rock composed of layers of light-colored feldspar and quartz, alternating with darker layers of other minerals.

gnome (nōm) *n.* in folklore, a dwarf who lives in the earth and guards treasures of precious metals and stones.

GNP, gross national product.

gnu (nōō, nyōō) *n. pl.*, **gnus** or **gnu.** any of several swift antelopes of Africa having a head like that of an ox, short horns that curve sharply upward, and a long tail. Also, **wildebeest.**

Gnu

go (gō) *v.*, **went, gone, going.** —*v.i.* **1.** to move or pass along; travel: *The car is going too fast.* **2.** to move away; depart; leave: *I have to go now.* **3.** to advance or move toward someone or something, or in a particular direction: *In the fall the war was always there but we did not go to it any more* (Ernest Hemingway). **4.** to be in action; operate: *The machines are kept going day and night.* **5.** to be given or awarded: *The money went to his children when he died.* **6.** to be or continue in a particular state or condition: *His goodness will not go unrewarded.* **7.** to pass or enter into a particular state or condition; become: *to go insane, to go into hiding.* **8.** to be spent, used, or applied: *Most of the money went for food.* **9.** to proceed or be guided: *We have to go by the rules.* **10.** to extend, reach, or lead: *The road goes east from here.* **11.** to be suitable; harmonize; match: *These shoes go with that dress.* **12.** to pass; elapse: *When you are busy, time goes quickly.* **13.** to be sold: *The sofa went for fifty dollars at the auction.* **14.** to proceed or end in a specified manner: *Things went well at the meeting today.* **15.** to fail, break down, or give way: *His eyesight started to go as he grew older.* **16.** to be expressed or phrased: *Do you remember how that song goes?* **17.** to have a usual or proper place; belong: *These sheets go in the linen closet.* **18.** to be able to be contained; fit: *Will all these books go into that box?* **19.** to be capable of being divided: *Eight goes into forty five times.* —*v.t.* to move, travel, or proceed along: *Are you going my way?* —*n. pl.*, **goes.** *Informal.* **1.** spirit; energy; vigor: *She is always full of go.* **2.** a try; attempt: *I'll have a go at fixing the radio.* **3.** a success: *He was determined to make a go of the business.*

no go. *Informal.* not to be done; useless; hopeless.

on the go. *Informal.* constantly active or in motion: *Mother was on the go all day long.*

to go. remaining; left: *There are only six days to go before the holidays.*

to go about. a. to be occupied with or busy at: *to go about one's business.* **b.** to change direction.

to go along. to agree or cooperate: *We go along with your idea.*

to go around. to be enough: *Is there enough food to go around?*

to go back on. *Informal.* to fail to keep or be loyal to: *The girl went back on her word.*

to go by. to pass unnoticed or be disregarded: *We'll let the error go by this time.*

to go down. to be recorded or remembered: *The scientist's discovery will go down in history.*

to go for. *Informal.* **a.** to try to get or obtain. **b.** to favor or support. **c.** to be strongly attracted by or interested in.

to go in for. *Informal.* to like or engage in: *to go in for sports.*

to go into. a. to examine or discuss: *We can't go into that problem now.* **b.** to enter or take up, as a profession or study: *She went into medicine.*

to go off. a. to explode or be discharged: *The gun went off accidentally.* **b.** to ring: *My alarm went off at 6 A.M.* **c.** *Informal.* to take place; happen; occur.

to go on. a. to continue or proceed: *The meeting went on until midnight.* **b.** to take place; happen; occur: *What's going on here?* **c.** to approach; near: *It's going on two years since we last saw her.*

to go out. a. to be extinguished: *The fire went out.* **b.** to take part in social affairs or date: *Linda goes out with several boys.* **c.** to be a candidate; try: *Bob went out for the soccer team.*

to go over. a. to examine carefully: *The accountant went over the company's books.* **b.** to read, rehearse, or review: *He went over his notes before the exam.*

to go through. a. to undergo; experience: *She went through one hardship after another.* **b.** to search or examine thoroughly: *The thief went through all the drawers.* **c.** to be accepted or approved: *Her application went through and she was hired.* **d.** to spend or wear out completely.

to go through with. to carry out to the end; complete.

to go together. to harmonize; match: *The blouse and the skirt go together.*

to go to pieces. to become extremely upset.

to go under. to fail: *His business went under.*

to go with. to date one person for a long period of time.

to let go. a. to release or set free. **b.** to allow to pass by without taking action or notice.

to let oneself go. a. to give way to one's feelings or desires. **b.** to fail to take care of oneself properly.

goad (gōd) *n.* **1.** a sharp-pointed stick used for driving cattle or oxen. **2.** anything that drives or urges. —*v.t.* to drive or urge with a goad.

go·a·head (gō'ə hed') *n. Informal.* a signal, order, or permission to proceed: *The captain gave the go-ahead to his soldiers.*

goal (gōl) *n.* **1.** an end to which effort is directed; aim: *Steve's goal in life was to become a successful writer.* **2.** an area or object into or through which players in certain games try to get a ball or puck in order to score. **3.** the act of getting a ball or puck into or through such an area or object. **4.** the point or points made by such an act.

goal·ie (gō'lē) *n.* another word for **goaltender.**

goal·keep·er (gōl'kē'pər) *n.* another word for **goaltender.**

goal line, either of two lines marking the goals in a game.

goal post, a structure consisting of a pair of posts and a crossbar, used as the goal in football and certain other games.

goal·tend·er (gōl'ten'dər) *n.* the player who defends the goal in certain games, such as ice hockey, lacrosse, and soccer. Also, **goalie, goalkeeper.**

Goat

goat (gōt) *n. pl.*, **goats** or **goat.** **1.** any of various cud-chewing animals related to the sheep, having hollow horns and frequently a tuft of hair under the chin. **2.** *Informal.* **a.** a person who is made to take the blame or punishment for others; scapegoat. **b.** a person who is the butt of a joke. —**goat'like'**, *adj.*

---

at; āpe; cär; end; mē; it; īce; hot; ōld; fôrk; wood; fōōl; oil; out; up; turn; sing; thin; **this**; **hw** in white; **zh** in treasure. The symbol ə stands for the sound of **a** in about, **e** in taken, **i** in pencil, **o** in lemon, and **u** in circus.

G

goat·ee (gō tē′) *n.* a small pointed beard on a man's chin.

goat·herd (gōt′hurd′) *n.* a person who tends goats.

goat·skin (gōt′skin′) *n.* **1.** the skin of a goat. **2.** the leather made from this skin. **3.** a container made from this leather, used especially for wine.

gob¹ (gob) *n. Informal.* **1.** a mass or lump. **2. gobs.** a large quantity; a lot: *She always puts gobs of butter on her toast.* [Old French *gobe.*]

gob² (gob) *n. Informal.* a sailor in the U.S. Navy. [Of uncertain origin.]

gob·ble¹ (gob′əl) *v.t.,* **gob·bled, gob·bling. 1.** to eat (food) rapidly and greedily. **2.** *Informal.* to seize eagerly or greedily. [*Gob¹* + *-le.*]

gob·ble² (gob′əl) *v.i.,* **gob·bled, gob·bling.** to make the throaty sound characteristic of a male turkey. —*n.* such a sound. [Imitative of this sound.]

gob·ble·dy·gook (gob′əl dē gook′) *n. Informal.* speech or writing that is wordy, complicated, and hard to understand.

gob·bler (gob′lər) *n.* a male turkey.

go·be·tween (gō′bi twēn′) *n.* a person who goes back and forth between persons or groups to make arrangements, conduct business, or settle disputes.

Go·bi (gō′bē) *n.* a large desert in east-central Asia.

gob·let (gob′lit) *n.* a drinking glass with a base and stem.

gob·lin (gob′lin) *n.* an ugly, mischievous sprite or elf, especially one that is evil or wicked.

go·cart (gō′kärt′) *n.* **1.** a small wagon for young children to ride in or pull. **2.** a small, light framework mounted on rollers, used to support a baby learning to walk. **3.** a light carriage. **4.** a handcart.

God (god) *n.* **1.** The Supreme Being in monotheistic religions considered as the eternal, all-powerful creator and ruler of the universe. **2. god. a.** any of various beings, as in Greek and Roman mythology, believed to have special powers over the lives and affairs of man. **b.** a male god. **c.** an image of a god that is an object of worship; idol. **d.** a person or thing that is made an object of worship, devotion, or admiration.

god·child (god′chīld′) *n. pl.,* **god·chil·dren** (god′chil′drən). a person for whom another person acts as sponsor at baptism.

god·daugh·ter (god′dô′tər) *n.* a female godchild.

god·dess (god′is) *n. pl.,* **god·dess·es. 1.** a female god. **2.** an extremely beautiful woman.

god·fa·ther (god′fä′thər) *n.* a man who sponsors a child at baptism.

God·head (god′hed′) *n.* **1.** God. **2.** *also,* **godhead.** divine nature; divinity.

god·less (god′lis) *adj.* **1.** not believing in God or a god. **2.** wicked. —**god′less·ness,** *n.*

god·like (god′līk′) *adj.* suitable to or like God or a god.

god·ly (god′lē) *adj.,* **god·li·er, god·li·est.** faithful to God and obeying God's laws; pious. —**god′li·ness,** *n.*

god·moth·er (god′muth′ər) *n.* a woman who sponsors a child at baptism.

god·par·ent (god′per′ənt) *n.* a godfather or godmother.

God's acre, a cemetery, especially in a churchyard.

god·send (god′send′) *n.* something that is needed or desired and arrives or happens unexpectedly, as if sent by God: *The inheritance was a godsend to the poor girl.*

god·son (god′sun′) *n.* a male godchild.

God·speed (god′spēd′) *n.* success; good luck.

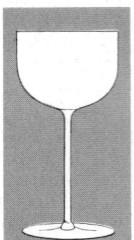

Man with a goatee

Goblet

Goe·thals, George W. (gō′thəlz) 1858–1928, U.S. army engineer in charge of constructing the Panama Canal.

Goe·the, Jo·hann Wolf·gang von (goo′tə; yō′hän vôlf′gäng′) 1749–1832, German poet, playwright, and novelist.

go·get·ter (gō′get′ər) *n. Informal.* a person who is full of energy and ambition.

gog·gle (gog′əl) *n.* **goggles.** large, close-fitting eyeglasses used to protect the eyes, as from wind, dust, or sparks. Skiers, motorcyclists, and welders often wear goggles. —*v.i.,* **gog·gled, gog·gling.** to roll one's eyes or stare with bulging eyes. —*adj.* (of eyes) rolling, bulging, or staring.

gog·gle-eyed (gog′əl īd′) *adj.* having rolling, bulging, or staring eyes.

Gogh, Vincent Van, see Van Gogh, Vincent.

Go·gol, Ni·ko·lai (gō′gol; ni kə lī′) 1809–1852, Russian author.

go·ing (gō′ing) *n.* **1.** the act of moving away or departing: *Her going was unexpected.* **2.** the condition of a surface or the environment, as for walking, driving, or flying: *The going was muddy because of heavy rain.* —*adj.* **1.** in action or movement; functioning: *My watch is in going condition.* **2.** operating successfully: *The shop is a going business.* **3.** current; prevailing: *What is the going price for that type of car?* **4.** *Informal.* in existence; around: *I think that is the funniest joke going.*

goings on, actions, behavior, or incidents, especially when disapproved of: *Police investigated the strange goings on at the old house.*

goi·ter (goi′tər) *also,* **goi·tre.** *n.* an enlargement of the thyroid gland causing a swelling in the neck. It is often caused by improper functioning of the thyroid or a deficiency of iodine in the diet.

gold (gōld) *n.* **1.** a heavy, soft, yellow metallic element, used especially as a standard for currency and in the making of jewelry and coins. Symbol: **Au 2.** coins made of this metal. **3.** wealth; riches. **4.** a bright yellow color. **5.** anything resembling or compared to gold, as in worth or beauty: *a heart of gold.* —*adj.* **1.** relating to, containing, or made of gold: *a gold bracelet, a gold tooth.* **2.** having the color gold; bright yellow.

gold·brick (gōld′brik′) *v.i. Slang.* to get out of or avoid work or duty, as by pretending to be ill. —*n.* a person, especially in the armed forces, who gets out of or avoids work or duty. —**gold′brick′er,** *n.*

Gold Coast, a former British possession in western Africa, now part of Ghana.

gold·en (gōld′ən) *adj.* **1.** made of or containing gold: *a golden locket.* **2.** having the color or luster of gold: *the golden sun.* **3.** excellent or very valuable: *a golden opportunity.* **4.** very happy and prosperous; flourishing: *the golden age of a country's history.* **5.** of or marking the fiftieth year or event in a series: *Ann's grandparents recently celebrated their golden wedding anniversary.*

golden eagle, an eagle of the Northern Hemisphere, having dark-brown feathers with golden tints on the head and back of the neck.

Golden Fleece *Greek Legend.* the sheepskin from a golden ram, kept in a grove guarded by a dragon. It was stolen by Jason and the Argonauts.

golden mean, a course or way that avoids extremes; moderation.

gold·en·rod (gōld′ən rod′) *n.* a plant having clusters of small yellow flowers on tall, branching stalks.

golden rule, the rule of conduct that one should treat others as one wishes to be treated.

gold-filled (gōld′fild′) *adj.* made of or containing metal covered with a layer of gold.

gold·finch (gōld′finch′) *n. pl.,* **gold·finch·es. 1.** a European songbird having yellow markings on its wings. **2.** an American finch, the male of which is bright yellow with black markings.

Goldfinch

gold·fish (gōld′fish′) *n. pl.,* **goldfish** or **gold·fish·es.** a freshwater fish native to southeastern Asia, ranging in color from gold to black. Many varieties are raised in home aquariums and outdoor ponds.

gold leaf, gold beaten into extremely thin sheets, used in gilding.

gold rush, a sudden rush of people to an area where gold has been discovered, as to California in 1849.

gold·smith (gōld′smith′) *n.* a person who makes or deals in objects of gold, such as jewelry.

Gold·smith, Oliver (gōld′smith′) 1730–1774, English poet, novelist, and playwright.

golf (golf) *n.* a game played on a golf course with a small, hard ball and a set of golf clubs. The object of the game is to hit the ball into a series of holes with as few strokes as possible. —*v.i.* to play the game of golf. —**golf′er,** *n.*

golf club, any of various clubs with long thin shafts and wooden or iron heads, used to hit the ball in golf.

golf course, an area of land for playing golf, usually having eighteen holes. Also, **golf links.**

Gol·go·tha (gol′gə thə) *n.* another name for **Calvary.**

Go·li·ath (gə lī′əth) *n.* in the Old Testament, the Philistine giant whom David killed with a stone shot from a sling.

Go·mor·rah (gə môr′ə) *n.* see **Sodom.**

Gom·pers, Samuel (gom′pərz) 1850–1924, U.S. labor leader.

go·nad (gō′nad) *n.* a male or female sex organ in which reproductive cells develop and in which sex hormones are produced. The ovaries are the female gonads, and the testes are the male gonads.

gon·do·la (gon′də lə) *n.* **1.** a long, narrow, flat-bottomed boat with high peaks at the ends, propelled at the stern by one man with an oar or pole. It is used to carry passengers on the canals of Venice. **2.** see **gondola car. 3.** a car suspended under a dirigible or balloon.

Gondola with gondolier

gondola car, a railroad freight car with low sides and no top.

gon·do·lier (gon′də lēr′) *n.* a man who rows or poles a gondola.

gone (gôn, gon) *v.* the past participle of **go.** —*adj.* **1.** moved away; left; departed: *He is gone for the summer.* **2.** used up or spent: *The cake is all gone.* **3.** dead. **4.** beyond hope or recovery; lost; ruined. **5.** characterized by weakness or faintness: *a gone feeling.*

gon·er (gô′nər, gon′ər) *n. Informal.* a person or thing that is dying, ruined, lost, or beyond help or recovery.

gong (gông, gong) *n.* **1.** an Oriental musical instrument consisting of a metal disk that makes a loud, resonant tone when struck. **2.** a saucer-shaped bell sounded by a mechanical hammer.

gon·or·rhe·a (gon′ə rē′ə) *also,* **gon·or·rhoe·a.** *n.* a contagious venereal disease that causes inflammation of the genital and urinary organs. It can usually be cured with penicillin, but if left untreated, leads to serious complications.

goo (gŏo) *n. Informal.* any sticky substance, such as glue.

goo·ber (gŏo′bər) *n. Informal.* a peanut.

good (good) *adj.,* **bet·ter, best. 1.** above average in quality; not bad or poor: *good food, a good movie.* **2.** agreeable; pleasant: *good news.* **3.** kind or helpful; considerate: *The queen was good to her subjects.* **4.** skillful; talented: *She is a good dancer.* **5.** honorable: *John has a good reputation among his colleagues.* **6.** safe or correct; reliable: *a good investment, good advice.* **7.** genuine or valid: *He had a good excuse for his lateness.* **8.** beneficial; advantageous: *The new trade agreement was good for the country's economy.* **9.** representative; typical: *That is a good example of Greek architecture.* **10.** not impaired; sound: *good eyesight, good health.* **11.** fairly great, as in amount or extent; considerable: *There were a good number of people at the party.* **12.** well-behaved; obedient: *She was always good as a child.* **13.** thorough: *Her parents gave her a good scolding.* **14.** not spoiled; fresh: *Is the meat still good?* —*n.* **1.** benefit; advantage: *I am telling you this for your own good.* **2.** moral goodness; virtue. —*adv. Informal.* well.

as good as. almost; practically: *The game is as good as over.*

for good. finally; permanently: *Joan said she was leaving for good.*

good and. *Informal.* completely or extremely; thoroughly: *His comments made me good and angry.*

good for. a. able to last or remain valid or functioning for: *The offer is good for another month.* **b.** able or willing to pay or give.

no good. worthless or useless.

to make good. a. to keep or fulfill: *He made good his promise to pay the money back.* **b.** to make up for; repay or replace: *The driver of the car agreed to make good the damage he had done.* **c.** to be successful.

to the good. as a profit or advantage.

Good Book, the Bible.

good·by (good′bī′) *also,* **good·by, good-bye.** *interj.* farewell. —*n. pl.,* **good-bys.** farewell: *After the necessary good-bys, we left the house.* [A shortening of *God be with you.*]

good day, an expression of greeting or farewell used in the daytime.

good evening, an expression of greeting or farewell used in the evening.

good-for-noth·ing (good′fər nuth′ing) *adj.* useless or worthless. —*n.* a person who is idle, worthless, or useless.

Good Friday, the Friday before Easter, commemorating the crucifixion of Jesus.

good-heart·ed (good′här′tid) *adj.* kind or generous. —**good′-heart′ed·ly,** *adv.* —**good′-heart′ed·ness,** *n.*

Good Hope, Cape of a cape at the southernmost tip of Africa, on the Atlantic.

good-hu·mored (good′hyŏo′mərd) *adj.* having or showing a cheerful, pleasant, or friendly mood or feeling. —**good′-hu′mored·ly,** *adv.*

good-look·ing (good′look′ing) *adj.* pleasing or attractive in appearance; beautiful or handsome.

good·ly (good′lē) *adj.,* **good·li·er, good·li·est.** fairly large, as in amount or degree: *Their trip cost them a goodly sum of money.* —**good′li·ness,** *n.*

G

at; āpe; cär; end; mē; it; īce; hot; ōld; fôrk; wood; fōol; oil; out; up; turn; sing; thin; this; hw in white; zh in treasure. The symbol ə stands for the sound of **a** in about, **e** in taken, **i** in pencil, **o** in lemon, and **u** in circus.

good·man (good′mən) *n. pl.,* **good·men** (good′mən). *Archaic.* **1.** the master or male head of a household. **2.** a title of respect for a man below the rank of gentleman; mister.

good morning, an expression of greeting or farewell used in the morning.

good-na·tured (good′nā′chərd) *adj.* having or showing a pleasant or kindly disposition; agreeable. —**good′-na′-tured·ly,** *adv.* —**good′-na′tured·ness,** *n.*

good·ness (good′nis) *n.* **1.** the state or quality of being good. **2.** kindness or generosity: *He helped us out of the goodness of his heart.* —*interj.* used to express surprise.

goods (goodz) *n.,pl.* **1.** things that are sold; merchandise; wares. **2.** personal property; belongings: *They lost all their worldly goods in the fire.* **3.** fabric; cloth.

Good Samaritan **1.** in the New Testament, a traveler who aided a fellow traveler who had been beaten and robbed. **2.** any person who is compassionate and helpful toward others.

good·wife (good′wīf′) *n. pl.,* **good·wives** (good′wīvz′). *Archaic.* **1.** the mistress of a household. **2.** a woman below the rank of lady.

good will *also,* **good·will** (good′wil′). **1.** kindness or friendliness: *a feeling of good will toward others.* **2.** cheerful consent; willingness: *He accepted the task with good will.* **3.** the advantage that a business has as a result of the good relations it has established with the public.

good·y (good′ē) *n. pl.,* **good·ies.** *Informal.* something very tasty and sweet, such as candy or cookies. —*interj.* used to express delight or pleasure.

goo·ey (gōō′ē) *adj.,* **goo·i·er, goo·i·est.** *Informal.* sticky.

goof (gōōf) *Informal. n.* **1.** a stupid or clumsy mistake; blunder. **2.** a stupid, silly, or blundering person. —*v.i.* to make a stupid or clumsy mistake; blunder. —*v.t.* to make a mess of: *He really goofed up that assignment.*
   to goof off. to avoid work or duty or do nothing: *The secretary spent most of the day goofing off.*

goof·y (gōō′fē) *adj.,* **goof·i·er, goof·i·est.** *Slang.* stupid, silly, or ridiculous. —**goof′i·ness,** *n.*

goon (gōōn) *n. Slang.* **1.** a hoodlum or thug. **2.** a stupid, rough, or clumsy person.

goose (gōōs) *n. pl.,* **geese.** **1.** any of various wild or tame web-footed water birds found throughout most of the world, resembling, but larger than, a duck and usually having a longer neck. **2.** a female goose. A male goose is called a gander. **3.** the flesh of a goose, used as food. **4.** *Informal.* a foolish, silly person.
   to cook one's goose. *Informal.* to ruin one's chances.

Goose

goose·ber·ry (gōōs′ber′ē) *n. pl.,* **goose·ber·ries.** **1.** a tart berry of any of a group of thorny shrubs widely grown in many parts of Europe and North America. **2.** the shrub bearing this berry.

goose flesh, a temporary, rough condition of the skin caused by the contraction of tiny muscles near the surface, usually resulting from cold or fear. Also, **goose bumps, goose pimples.**

goose·neck (gōōs′nek′) *n.* something long and curved like a goose's neck, such as a flexible support for a desk lamp.

goose-step (gōōs′step′) *v.i.,* **goose-stepped, goose-stepping.** to march in a goose step.

goose step, a marching step in which the legs are held straight and kicked high with the knees unbent.

G.O.P., Grand Old Party; the Republican Party.

go·pher (gō′fər) *n.* **1.** any of various burrowing rodents found throughout North and Central America, having large cheek pouches. **2.** a ground squirrel.

Gopher

Gor·di·an knot (gôr′dē ən) *Greek Legend.* an intricate knot that could be untied only by the person who should rule Asia. Alexander the Great, instead of trying to untie the knot, cut through it with his sword.
   to cut the Gordian knot. to find and use quick or bold means to solve a problem or difficulty.

gore[1] (gôr) *n.* blood that has been shed, especially when thick or clotted. [Old English *gor* dirt.]

gore[2] (gôr) *v.t.,* **gored, gor·ing.** (of an animal) to pierce with a horn or tusk: *The bull gored the matador.* [Possibly from Old English *gār* spear.]

gore[3] (gôr) *n.* a triangular piece of fabric, used to add fullness, especially in making umbrellas, sails, or certain skirts. —*v.t.,* **gored, gor·ing.** to make or furnish with a gore or gores: *The seamstress gored the skirt.* [Old English *gāra* a triangular piece of land.]

gorge (gôrj) *n.* **1.** a deep, narrow opening or passage between steep and rocky sides of walls or mountains. **2.** a mass which stops up or clogs a passage: *an ice gorge.* **3.** *Archaic.* the throat; gullet. —*v.,* **gorged, gorg·ing.** —*v.t.* **1.** to stuff with food: *He gorged himself at dinner.* **2.** to swallow or eat greedily: *He gorged his food.* —*v.i.* to stuff oneself with food. —**gorg′er,** *n.*
   to make one's gorge rise. to cause to feel anger or disgust.

gor·geous (gôr′jəs) *adj.* **1.** richly or brilliantly colored: *gorgeous autumn leaves.* **2.** *Informal.* beautiful, attractive, or delightful: *a gorgeous woman.* —**gor′geous·ly,** *adv.* —**gor′geous·ness,** *n.*

gor·get (gôr′jit) *n.* a piece of armor used to protect the throat.

Gor·gon (gôr′gən) *n. Greek Legend.* any one of three sisters who had snakes for hair and whose faces were so horrible that anyone who looked at them was turned to stone.

go·ril·la (gə ril′ə) *n.* an ape of Africa, having a large, heavy body, short legs, long arms, and a gray or black coat. It is the largest and most powerful anthropoid ape. [Greek *gorilla* a wild, hairy person; because some early explorers in Africa thought that gorillas were primitive people instead of animals.]

gor·mand·ize (gôr′mən dīz′) *v.i.,* **gor·mand·ized, gor·mand·iz·ing.** to eat like a glutton; gorge. —**gor′mand·iz′er,** *n.*

gorse (gôrs) *n.* another word for **furze.**

Gorilla

gor·y (gôr′ē) *adj.,* **gor·i·er, gor·i·est.** **1.** covered with gore; bloody. **2.** characterized by bloodshed: *a gory clash of two armies.* **3.** like gore; disgusting; horrible: *He spared us the gory details of the accident.* —**gor′i·ly,** *adv.* —**gor′i·ness,** *n.*

gosh (gosh) *interj.* used to express pleasure or surprise.

gos·hawk (gos′hôk′) *n.* a powerful, short-winged hawk of northern North America, Europe, and Asia, formerly used in falconry.

Go·shen (gō′shən) *n.* **1.** in the Old Testament, a fertile region in northern Egypt where the Israelites lived before the Exodus. **2.** any land of plenty and peace.

gos·ling (goz′ling) *n.* a young goose.

gos·pel (gos′pəl) *n.* **1.** the teachings of Jesus and the

Apostles. **2. Gospel. a.** any one of the first four books of the New Testament, believed to have been written by Matthew, Mark, Luke, and John. **b.** a part of one of these books read in a religious service. **3.** something accepted as absolutely true or serving as a guide for action: *The rebels preached the gospel of revolution.* —*adj.* of, relating to, or according to the gospel: *a gospel singer.*

gos·sa·mer (gos′ə mər) *n.* **1.** a fine filmy cobweb, seen especially in autumn floating in the air or suspended from bushes or grass. **2.** any light or filmy substance. **3.** a light, delicate, gauzelike fabric. —*adj.* of or like gossamer; light, filmy, or delicate.

gos·sip (gos′ip) *n.* **1.** idle talk or rumors, often unfriendly, about the personal affairs of other people. **2.** a person who is fond of repeating gossip. —*v.,* **gos·siped, gos·sip·ing.** —*v.i.* to repeat gossip: *to gossip about one's friends.* —*v.t.* to repeat as gossip: *The old woman gossiped the story all over town.* —**gos′sip·er,** *n.*

gos·sip·y (gos′ə pē) *adj.* **1.** fond of gossip: *a gossipy person.* **2.** full of gossip: *a gossipy newspaper column.*

got (got) the past tense and a past participle of **get.**

Gö·te·borg (yoo′tə bôr′yə) *n.* a port city in southwestern Sweden. Pop. (1970), 451,806. Also, **Goth·en·burg** (goth′ən burg′).

Goth (goth) *n.* a member of a Germanic people that invaded the Roman Empire in the third, fourth, and fifth centuries A.D.

Goth·ic (goth′ik) *adj.* **1.** of or relating to a style of architecture developed in Europe between the twelfth and sixteenth centuries, characterized by pointed arches, rib vaulting, and flying buttresses. **2.** of or relating to the Goths, their language, or culture. **3.**

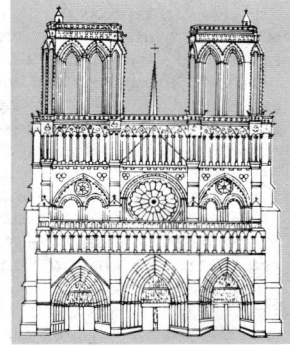

Gothic cathedral

also, **gothic.** of, relating to, or characteristic of a literary style emphasizing the grotesque, horrible, violent, and mysterious. —*n.* the language of the Goths.

got·ten (got′ən) a past participle of **get.**

gouge (gouj) *n.* **1.** a tool like a chisel but having a curved, hollow blade, used for cutting rounded grooves or holes in wood. **2.** a groove or hole made by gouging. **3.** *Slang.* the act of cheating or defrauding. —*v.t.,* **gouged, goug·ing. 1.** to cut or scoop out with or as with a gouge. **2.** to dig, tear, or poke (with *out*): *to gouge out an eye.* **3.** *Slang.* to cheat or defraud.

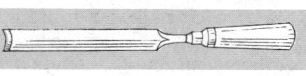

Gouge

gou·lash (gōō′läsh) *n. pl.,* **gou·lash·es.** a stew made of beef or veal and vegetables, usually seasoned with paprika.

gourd (gôrd) *n.* **1.** the hard-shelled fruit of any of a group of trailing or climbing vines. **2.** the vine bearing this fruit. **3.** the dried shell of a gourd, used as a dipper, cup, or bowl.

gour·mand (goor′mənd, goor mand′) *n.* a person who loves fine food and drink.

gour·met (goor mā′, goor′-mā) *n.* a person who is expert in choosing and judging fine food and drink.

gout (gout) *n.* **1.** a disease

Gourds

characterized by painful swelling of the joints, especially the big toe. **2.** a drop or clot: *a gout of blood.*

gout·y (gou′tē) *adj.,* **gout·i·er, gout·i·est. 1.** of, relating to, or like gout. **2.** caused by or causing gout. —**gout′i·ly,** *adv.* —**gout′i·ness,** *n.*

gov., Gov. 1. governor. **2.** government.

gov·ern (guv′ərn) *v.t.* **1.** to rule, control, or direct by right of authority: *The President and the Congress govern the nation.* **2.** to direct or influence; guide: *Concern for his own welfare governed his actions.* **3.** to hold in check; restrain; curb: *Govern your temper.* —**gov′ern·a·ble,** *adj.*

gov·ern·ess (guv′ər nis) *n. pl.,* **gov·ern·ess·es.** a woman employed to teach and train children in their home.

gov·ern·ment (guv′ərn mənt, guv′ər mənt) *n.* **1.** an organization or body that rules, controls, or directs a city, state, nation, or other political unit. **2.** a system or form of ruling by which a given political unit is governed: *parliamentary government, democratic government.* **3.** control or authority over the affairs of a state, city, or other political unit; rule. **4.** a body of elected officials holding power. —**gov′ern·men′tal,** *adj.* —**gov′ern·men′tal·ly,** *adv.*

gov·er·nor (guv′ər nər) *n.* **1.** an official elected as the chief executive of a state or commonwealth of the United States. **2.** an official appointed to govern a province, colony, or territory. **3.** a person who manages or directs a social organization or financial institution: *the board of governors of a club, a governor of a bank.* **4.** an automatic device for regulating the speed of an engine by controlling the rate at which fuel or steam is supplied to the engine.

gov·er·nor·ship (guv′ər nər ship′) *n.* the duties, position, or term of office of a governor.

govt., Govt., government.

gown (goun) *n.* **1.** a woman's dress, especially a formal dress. **2.** a long, loose outer garment worn to show the wearer's office, profession, or status; robe. **3.** a nightgown or dressing gown.

Go·ya, Fran·cis·co (gô′yə; fran sis′kō) 1746–1828, Spanish painter and etcher.

gr. 1. grade. **2.** grain. **3.** gram; grams. **4.** gross.

Gr. 1. Greek. **2.** Greece. **3.** Grecian.

grab (grab) *v.,* **grabbed, grab·bing.** —*v.t.* to grasp or snatch suddenly: *Tom grabbed the candy bar away from his brother.* —*v.i.* to make a grasping or snatching motion: *The drowning man grabbed desperately for the life preserver.* —*n.* the act of grabbing: *The baseball player made a grab at the ball.* —**grab′ber,** *n.*

grab bag, a bag filled with wrapped articles, from which a person takes one without knowing what it is.

grace (grās) *n.* **1.** harmony or beauty of form, movement, or manner: *The ballerina danced with grace.* **2.** a short prayer or blessing before or after a meal. **3.** good manners; consideration: *He had the grace to apologize for leaving the party early.* **4.** the favor and love of God. **5.** an attractive or charming quality or feature: *Speaking French and playing the piano are social graces.* **6.** see **grace period. 7. Grace.** worship; eminence. ▲ used to address or speak of royalty, nobility, or clergy: *Your Grace.* **8. Graces.** *Greek Mythology.* three young and beautiful sister goddesses who brought loveliness, happiness, and charm to men, gods, and nature. —*v.t.,* **graced, grac·ing. 1.** to add

at; āpe; cär; end; mē; it; īce; hot; ōld; fôrk; wood; fōōl; oil; out; up; turn; sing; thin; **this**; hw in white; zh in treasure. The symbol ə stands for the sound of **a** in about, **e** in taken, **i** in pencil, **o** in lemon, and **u** in circus.

G

grace or beauty to; adorn: *The lovely park graced the city.*
2. to favor or honor (something): *The wife of the President graced the luncheon with her presence.*

   in the bad graces of. disliked or disapproved by; in disfavor with.

   in the good graces of. liked or approved by; in favor with.

grace·ful (grās′fəl) *adj.* having beauty or harmony of form, movement, or manner: *a graceful dancer.* —**grace′·ful·ly,** *adv.* —**grace′ful·ness,** *n.*

grace·less (grās′lis) *adj.* **1.** without beauty or harmony of form, movement, or manner. **2.** without a sense of what is right or proper. —**grace′less·ly,** *adv.* —**grace′less·ness,** *n.*

grace note *Music.* a note added to ornament the melody or harmony.

grace period, an allowance of extra time: *That company allows a three week grace period to pay a bill after it is due.*

gra·cious (grā′shəs) *adj.* **1.** having or showing kindness and courtesy: *The man was a gracious host who made his guests feel welcome.* **2.** prosperous, leisurely, and comfortable: *gracious living.* **3.** merciful; kindly. —**gra′cious·ly,** *adv.* —**gra′cious·ness,** *n.*

grack·le (grak′əl) *n.* any of several North American blackbirds having a long, wedge-shaped tail and shiny black feathers.

gra·da·tion (grā dā′shən) *n.*
1. a gradual change by a series of steps, stages, or degrees: *The volume control of a radio can be used to produce gradations of sound from loud to soft.* **2.** a step, stage, or degree in such a series: *a gradation of the color green.*

Grackle

grade (grād) *n.* **1.** any one of the divisions of study in an elementary or high school, usually one year's work: *Bob is eight years old and is in the third grade.* **2.** a number or letter showing how well a student has done in work at school: *Mary got a grade of eighty on her geography paper.* **3.** a degree or step in quality, value, rank, or order: *a grade of beef. The soldier reached the grade of sergeant.* **4.** the slope of a road or railroad track: *a steep grade on a mountain road.* —*v.,* **grad·ed, grad·ing.** —*v.t.* **1.** to arrange or sort in grades; classify: *The farmer graded the eggs by size and color.* **2.** to give a grade to: *The teacher was grading term papers.* **3.** to make (ground) more level; lessen the slope of: *The bulldozer graded the new road.* —*v.i.* to pass through a series of stages or degrees; change gradually: *The colors graded from dark red to bright pink.*

grade crossing, a place where a railroad track crosses a road or another railroad track at the same level.

grad·er (grā′dər) *n.* **1.** a person or thing that grades. **2.** a pupil in a certain grade in school: *a twelfth grader.*

grade school, another term for **elementary school.**

gra·di·ent (grā′dē ənt) *n.* **1.** the amount or degree of slope, as of a road or railroad track. **2.** a sloping surface. **3.** *Physics.* the rate at which a variable quantity, such as temperature or pressure, changes.

grad·u·al (graj′ōō əl) *adj.* **1.** moving, changing, or happening slowly or by degrees: *The change in the weather was so gradual that we hardly noticed it until the storm was about to break.* **2.** not steep or abrupt: *There is a gradual rise in the road around the bend.* —**grad′u·al·ly,** *adv.* —**grad′u·al·ness,** *n.*

grad·u·ate (*v.,* graj′ōō āt′; *n., adj.,* graj′ōō it) *v.,* **grad·u·at·ed, grad·u·at·ing.** —*v.i.* to receive a diploma or degree after the completion of a course of study: *He graduated from high school last year.* —*v.t.* **1.** to give an academic

diploma or degree to (someone) for the completion of a course of study. **2.** to mark with or divide into degrees, units, or similar divisions. —*n.* a person who has been given a diploma or degree for completion of a course of study. —*adj.* **1.** that has graduated: *a graduate student.* **2.** relating to or for graduates: *graduate courses.*

grad·u·a·tion (graj′ōō ā′shən) *n.* **1.** the act of graduating or the state of being graduated. **2.** the ceremony of giving diplomas or degrees, as at a school or university. **3.** a mark or series of marks showing degrees or quantity, used for measuring: *graduations on a thermometer.*

graf·fi·ti (grə fē′tē) *n., pl., sing.,* **graf·fi·to** (grə fē′tō). words or drawings on walls, fences, sidewalks, etc.

graft¹ (graft) *v.t.* **1.** to put a shoot, bud, or branch from one plant, especially a tree, into a cut or slit in another so that the two pieces will grow together and eventually form one plant. **2.** to transplant (skin or bone) from one part of the body to another or from one person to another: *The doctors grafted new skin on his burned arm.* —*n.* **1.** a shoot, bud, or branch that has been grafted. **2.** a piece of skin or bone surgically transplanted from one part of the body to another, or from one person to another. **3.** the act or process of grafting. [Earlier *graff,* from Old French *grafe.*] —**graft′er,** *n.*

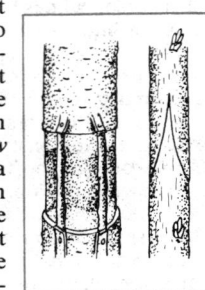

Graft¹

graft² (graft) *n.* **1.** the gaining of money or advantages by dishonest means, especially through one's political influence or position. **2.** something gained by such means. —*v.i.* to gain money or advantages by dishonest means. [Of uncertain origin.] —**graft′er,** *n.*

gra·ham (grā′əm) *adj.* made from or consisting of unsifted whole-wheat flour: *graham crackers.*

Grail (grāl) *n.* see **Holy Grail.**

grain (grān) *n.* **1.** the seed of various cereal grasses, such as rye, wheat, oats, or corn. **2.** the plants bearing such seeds. **3.** a tiny, hard particle: *a grain of sand, a grain of sugar.* **4.** the markings or patterns in wood, stone, cloth or other materials caused by the arrangement of fibers or layers. **5.** a very small unit of weight, equal to 64.8 milligrams. **6.** the smallest possible amount; tiny bit: *There isn't a grain of truth in what he said.*

grain alcohol, see **alcohol** *(def. 1).*

grain elevator, a building for the storage of grain.

grain·y (grā′nē) *adj.,* **grain·i·er, grain·i·est. 1.** of or like grains; granular. **2.** having a grain: *grainy wood.* —**grain′·i·ness,** *n.*

gram (gram) *also, British,* **gramme.** *n.* a unit of mass or weight in the metric system, equal to ¹⁄₂₈ of an ounce.

-gram¹ *combining form* something written or drawn: *telegram, diagram.* [Greek *gramma.*]

-gram² *combining form* of a gram; grams: *centigram, kilogram.* [From *gram.*]

gram atom, the quantity of a chemical element having a weight in grams numerically equal to the atomic weight of the element. One gram atom of aluminum, which has an atomic weight of 27, weighs 27 grams.

gram·mar (gram′ər) *n.* **1.** a system of rules describing how the users of a language form sentences to communicate with each other. **2.** the study of how a language is used in order to produce such a system of rules. **3.** a book containing rules or principles of grammar. **4.** grammar as part of a course of study in school: *He was never very interested in grammar.* **5.** the use of words according to accepted or standard principles; usage: *Many people think that "ain't" is bad grammar.*

● **Grammar** is the system of arranging words so that the meaning of what is said is clearly communicated. This system is based on a series of rules, most of which come naturally to us as we use our language and hear it used. The words in the sentence "Give me Tom's red pencil" can be arranged 120 different ways. Yet we instinctively know in what order the words should go. Young children learn to speak long before they have any idea of the rules of grammar. They hear language and quickly learn how to make themselves understood. In early times, English grammar existed in only this way; there was little if any interest in setting down rules.

The first real interest in the systematic study of English grammar began in the fifteenth and sixteenth centuries, during which there was a great revival of interest in the Greek and Latin languages. The study of Latin grammar, in particular, deeply influenced later attitudes and theories about English grammar, even though Latin grammar was unrelated to English grammar. Beginning in the late seventeenth century, there was great interest among English scholars in "purifying" the language. Following the example set in Italy and France, which had established academies that were responsible for setting strict standards of grammar and usage, English scholars began presenting new rules and refinements of grammar.

For example, the rule that *shall* is used for the first person and *will* for the second and third person in a simple future statement, but that *will* is used for the first person and *shall* for the second and third person when a statement expresses determination, was set down by an English grammarian in 1653. An eighteenth century rule condemned the use of a double negative, stating that two negatives would counteract each other rather than add further negative emphasis. The fact that many great writers, including Shakespeare, had used the double negative did not change the feeling that its use was incorrect.

Beginning in the nineteenth century, linguists rejected such ideas and studied grammar by tracing the historical development of English in its own terms, rather than in relationship to Latin or to fixed rules. They began to see English grammar in terms of English usage; they realized that what is actually said, rather than what artificial rules require to be said, is the true basis for grammar.

Modern grammar focuses mainly on communication. For this reason, there has been a trend toward eliminating those rules that make using language difficult and complicated, and emphasizing those rules or concepts that make communication through language simple, natural, and effective.

---

gram·mar·i·an (grə mer′ē ən) *n.* a student of or an expert in grammar.

grammar school 1. another term for **elementary school.** 2. a secondary school, especially in England, in which college preparatory subjects are emphasized.

gram·mat·i·cal (grə mat′i kəl) *adj.* 1. of or relating to grammar. 2. following the rules of grammar: *The sentence "I bought a shirt white" is not grammatical.* —**gram·mat′i·cal·ly,** *adv.* —**gram·mat′i·cal·ness,** *n.*

gramme (gram) another spelling of **gram.**

gram·o·phone (gram′ə fōn′) *n.* a phonograph. Trademark: Gramophone.

gram·pus (gram′pəs) *n. pl.,* **gram·pus·es.** a large dolphin found in all seas except those in polar regions.

Gra·na·da (grə nä′də) *n.* a historic city in southern Spain, formerly the capital of a Moorish kingdom.

gra·na·ry (grā′nər ē, gran′ər ē) *n. pl.,* **gra·na·ries.** a storehouse for grain.

Gran Cha·co (grän′ chä′kō) a vast lowland region in south-central South America.

grand (grand) *adj.* 1. large and impressive: *a grand palace.* 2. noble or dignified: *The judge was a grand old man.* 3. including everything; complete: *The grand total of his winnings was three thousand dollars.* 4. most important; main; principal: *The dance was held in the grand ballroom.* 5. *Informal.* very good or excellent: *We had a grand time at the party.* —*n.* 1. see **grand piano.** 2. *Slang.* a thousand dollars. —**grand′ly,** *adv.* —**grand′ness,** *n.*

grand·aunt (grand′ant′, grand′änt′) *n.* the aunt of one's father or mother. Also, **great-aunt.**

Grand Bank *also,* **Grand Banks.** a shoal off the eastern coast of Newfoundland, in the North Atlantic Ocean. It is a major fishing area.

Grand Canyon, a large canyon on the upper course of the Colorado River, in northwestern Arizona, regarded as one of the most spectacular natural wonders of the world.

grand·child (grand′chīld′) *n. pl.,* **grand·chil·dren** (grand′chil′drən). the child of one's son or daughter.

Grand Cou·lee (kōō′lē) a large dam on the Columbia River, in east-central Washington.

grand·daugh·ter (gran′dô′tər) *n.* the daughter of one's son or daughter.

grand duchess 1. the wife or widow of a grand duke. 2. a woman ruling a grand duchy. 3. in czarist Russia, a princess of the royal family.

grand duchy, a territory under the rule of a grand duke or grand duchess.

grand duke 1. the ruler of a grand duchy. 2. in czarist Russia, a prince of the royal family.

gran·dee (gran dē′) *n.* 1. a Spanish or Portuguese nobleman of the highest rank. 2. any person of high rank or great importance.

gran·deur (gran′jər) *n.* the state or quality of being majestic or imposing; magnificence; splendor.

grand·fa·ther (grand′fä′thər) *n.* 1. the father of one's father or mother. 2. a forefather; ancestor.

grandfather clock *also,* **grandfather's clock.** a clock having a pendulum and enclosed in a tall, usually wooden, cabinet that stands on the floor.

grand·fa·ther·ly (grand′fä′thər lē) *adj.* like or characteristic of a grandfather; kindly; benevolent.

gran·dil·o·quence (gran dil′ə kwəns) *n.* the quality of being grandiloquent.

gran·dil·o·quent (gran dil′ə kwənt) *adj.* using or characterized by a pompous or pretentious style in speech or writing. —**gran·dil′o·quent·ly,** *adv.*

gran·di·ose (gran′dē ōs′) *adj.* 1. imposing or impressive; magnificent. 2. trying to seem grand; pompous or pretentious: *He wrote in a grandiose style.* —**gran′di·ose·ly,** *adv.*

grand jury, a jury chosen to hear accusations in criminal cases and bring indictments if there is enough evidence for a trial in a court of law.

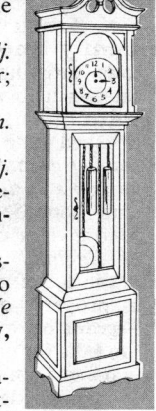

Grandfather clock

grand·ma (grand′mä′, gram′ə) *n. Informal.* grandmother.

grand·moth·er (grand′muth′ər) *n.* **1.** the mother of one's father or mother. **2.** a female ancestor.

grand·moth·er·ly (grand′muth′ər lē) *adj.* like or characteristic of a grandmother; kindly; benevolent.

grand·neph·ew (grand′nef′yōō) *n.* the son of one's nephew or niece. Also, **great-nephew.**

grand·niece (grand′nēs′) *n.* the daughter of one's nephew or niece. Also, **great-niece.**

Grand Old Party, the Republican Party of the United States.

grand opera, an opera in which the entire text is sung.

grand·pa (grand′pä′, gram′pə) *n. Informal.* grandfather.

grand·par·ent (grand′per′ənt) *n.* a grandfather or grandmother.

grand piano, a piano having horizontally arranged strings in a harp-shaped case.

Grand Rapids, a city in western Michigan. Pop. (1970), 197,649.

grand·sire (grand′sīr′) *n. Archaic.* **1.** a grandfather. **2.** an old man.

grand slam **1.** *Bridge.* the winning of all thirteen tricks in a round of play. **2.** *Baseball.* a home run hit with the bases loaded.

grand·son (grand′sun′) *n.* the son of one's son or daughter.

grand·stand (grand′stand′) *n.* **1.** a seating area for spectators, as at an outdoor sports event or parade. **2.** the spectators seated in such an area.

grand·un·cle (grand′ung′kəl) *n.* the uncle of one's father or mother. Also, **great-uncle.**

grange (grānj) *n.* **1.** *British.* a farm and the buildings on it. **2. Grange.** a fraternal organization, founded in 1867, to promote the interests and welfare of farm families and rural communities in the United States.

gran·ite (gran′it) *n.* a hard, durable igneous rock that is composed of feldspar and quartz with specks of darker minerals, often used for buildings and monuments.

gran·ny (gran′ē) *also,* **gran·nie.** *n. pl.,* **gran·nies.** *Informal.* **1.** a grandmother. **2.** an old woman.

granny knot, a knot like a square knot but with the ends crossing the wrong way, causing it to jam easily.

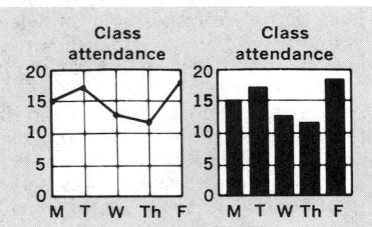

Granny knot

grant (grant) *v.t.* **1.** to give (what is asked for); allow; confer: *The teacher granted him permission to go home early.* **2.** to admit to be true; concede: *I'll grant that your argument is correct.* **3.** to give or confer, especially by a formal act: *The king of England granted a charter to the colonists.* —*n.* **1.** the act of granting. **2.** something that is granted, such as property or a right or privilege. —**grant′a·ble,** *adj.* —**grant′er,** *n.*

to take for granted. a. to assume to be true. **b.** to accept, possess, or regard without thought, consideration, or acknowledgment: *She took her friend's help for granted and wasn't really grateful for it.*

Grant, Ulysses S(impson) (grant) 1822–1885, U.S. general and the eighteenth president of the United States, from 1869 to 1877.

grant·ee (gran′tē) *n.* a person to whom a grant is made.

grant·or (gran′tər, gran tôr′) *n.* a person who makes a grant.

gran·u·lar (gran′yə lər) *adj.* **1.** consisting of, containing, or like grains or granules: *Sugar is granular.* **2.** having a granulated surface.

gran·u·late (gran′yə lāt′) *v.t.,* **gran·u·lat·ed, gran·u·lat·ing.** **1.** to form into grains or granules. **2.** to roughen the surface of. —**gran′u·la′tion,** *n.*

gran·ule (gran′yōōl) *n.* a very small particle; grain.

grape (grāp) *n.* **1.** a smooth, thin-skinned fruit of any of a group of climbing woody vines. Grapes grow in large clusters and are usually green or purple in color. They are used to make wine and eaten dried as raisins or raw as a fruit. **2.** the vine bearing this fruit, grown in warm and temperate regions throughout the world.

grape·fruit (grāp′frōōt′) *n.* **1.** a large, round, citrus fruit of an evergreen tree. It has a thick skin that ranges in color from pale yellow to reddish brown and a tart, pink or white, juicy pulp. **2.** the tree that bears this fruit.

grape·shot (grāp′shot′) *n.* a cluster of small iron balls used as a charge for cannon.

grape sugar, another term for **dextrose.**

grape·vine (grāp′vīn′) *n.* **1.** a vine bearing grapes. **2.** *Informal.* a secret or informal way of spreading news or information: *The thief learned that the police were after him through the underworld grapevine.*

graph (graf) *n.* **1.** a diagram showing the changes of and the relationship between two or more things by a series of dots, bars, or lines. **2.** *Mathematics.* a representation of a function or equation plotted on coordinate axes. —*v.t.* to show or represent by a graph.

Line graph   Bar graph

-graph *combining form* **1.** a machine or other apparatus that writes or records: *telegraph, seismograph.* **2.** something that is written or recorded: *autograph.*

graph·ic (graf′ik) *adj.* **1.** vividly described; lifelike: *The book gave such a graphic description of the battle that I felt as if I had actually been there.* **2.** of, relating to, or represented by a graph. **3.** of or relating to the graphic arts. **4.** of or relating to writing: *Letters of the alphabet are graphic symbols.* —**graph′i·cal·ly,** *adv.*

graphic arts, painting, photography and other arts in which forms are represented visually, especially those arts in which impressions are made from blocks, plates, and the like, such as etching or lithography.

graph·ite (graf′īt) *n.* a soft, black crystalline form of carbon, commonly used as a lubricant when mixed with oil and as lead for pencils when mixed with clay.

graph paper, paper ruled in small squares on which graphs, charts, and diagrams can be drawn.

-graphy *combining form* **1.** a process or form of writing, describing, or recording: *photography, biography.* **2.** a descriptive science: *oceanography.*

grap·nel (grap′nəl) **1.** another word for **grappling iron.** **2.** a small anchor with three to six hooks.

grap·ple (grap′əl) *v.,* **grap·pled, grap·pling.** —*v.t.* to seize or hold with a grappling iron. —*v.i.* to struggle; wrestle: *The fighter grappled with his opponent. He grappled with the problem of how to start his term paper.* —*n.* **1.** the act of grappling. **2.** see **grappling iron.**

grappling iron, any of various devices having one or more hooks or clamps, used especially for seizing or holding something.

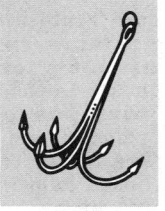

Grapnel

grasp (grasp) *v.t.* **1.** to take hold of firmly with the hand: *The batter grasped the baseball bat.* **2.** to understand; comprehend: *Geometry is sometimes hard for students to grasp.* —*n.* **1.** the act or instance of grasping. **2.** the power or ability to grasp: *Happiness was within his grasp.* **3.** understanding: *He has a good grasp of algebra.* **4.** firm control; possession: *The patriots freed the country from the grasp of the enemy.*

grasp·ing (gras'ping) *adj.* **1.** greedy. **2.** that grasps. —**grasp'ing·ly,** *adv.* —**grasp'ing·ness,** *n.*

grass (gras) *n. pl.,* **grass·es.** **1.** any of a large group of plants having jointed, usually hollow, stems, narrow leaves called blades, and often bearing spikes of small flowers. Wheat, rye, oats, corn, sugarcane, rice, and bamboo are grasses. **2.** any of a number of such plants covering lawns, pastures, or fields. **3.** the land on which grass grows, such as a lawn or pasture. —**grass'like',** *n.*

grass·hop·per (gras'hop'ər) *n.* any of a group of chirping, winged insects having long, powerful hind legs used for jumping.

grass·land (gras'land') *n.* land on which grass grows, used for pasture.

Grasshopper

grass·roots (gras'rōōts') *adj.* of, relating to, or coming from the common people, especially in rural areas: *He had grass-roots support for his candidacy for the governorship.*

grass·y (gras'ē) *adj.,* **grass·i·er, grass·i·est.** **1.** covered with or having much grass. **2.** consisting of or containing grass. **3.** like grass, especially in color. —**grass'i·ness,** *n.*

grate¹ (grāt) *n.* **1.** a framework of crossed bars set in or over an opening, as in a window, door, or drain; grating. **2.** a framework or basket of iron bars to hold burning fuel, as in a fireplace or furnace. **3.** a fireplace. —*v.t.,* **grat·ed, grat·ing.** to fit or furnish with a grate or grating. [Medieval Latin *grata.*]

grate² (grāt) *v.,* **grat·ed, grat·ing.** —*v.t.* **1.** to make into small pieces or shreds by rubbing against a rough surface: *to grate cheese, to grate carrots.* **2.** to rub together so as to produce a harsh, scraping sound; grind: *to grate one's teeth.* —*v.i.* **1.** to make a harsh, scraping sound by rubbing: *The old iron gate grated on its rusty hinges.* **2.** to have an annoying or irritating effect: *Her selfish attitude grates on my nerves.* [Old French *grater* to scratch, scrape.]

grate·ful (grāt'fəl) *adj.* **1.** thankful and appreciative because of kindness or favors received: *The old man was grateful for his friend's hospitality.* **2.** pleasing; welcome: *a grateful shower of rain.* —**grate'ful·ly,** *adv.* —**grate'ful·ness,** *n.*

grat·er (grā'tər) *n.* **1.** a kitchen utensil having a rough surface of sharp, raised edges used to grate vegetables, cheese, spices, and other foods. **2.** a person or thing that grates.

grat·i·fi·ca·tion (grat'ə fi kā'shən) *n.* **1.** the act of gratifying or the state of being gratified. **2.** something that causes pleasure or satisfaction.

grat·i·fy (grat'ə fī') *v.t.,* **grat·i·fied, grat·i·fy·ing.** **1.** to give pleasure or satisfaction to; please: *I was gratified by the news that my grandfather had recovered from his illness.* **2.** to satisfy, indulge, or humor, as a feeling, need, or desire: *She gratified her grandchild's every whim.* —**grat'i·fi·er,** *n.*

grat·i·fy·ing (grat'ə fī'ing) *adj.* that gratifies; pleasing or satisfying. —**grat'i·fy'ing·ly,** *adv.*

grat·ing¹ (grā'ting) *n.* a framework of parallel or crossed bars set in or over an opening, such as a window or sewer, and serving as a cover, guard, or screen. [*Grate¹* + *-ing¹.*]

grat·ing² (grā'ting) *adj.* **1.** making a harsh or irritating sound: *a grating door hinge.* **2.** annoying; irritating: *She had a grating habit of snapping her gum when she chewed it.* [*Grate²* + *-ing².*]

grat·is (grat'is, grā'tis) *adv.* without charge, cost, or payment; free: *I got two tickets to the ball game gratis.* —*adj.* given or provided without charge, cost, or payment.

grat·i·tude (grat'ə tōōd', grat'ə tyōōd') *n.* the quality or condition of being grateful, as for a kindness or favor.

gra·tu·i·tous (grə tōō'ə təs, grə tyōō'ə təs) *adj.* **1.** given without payment or return; free. **2.** without good reason or cause; unjustifiable: *a gratuitous insult.* —**gra·tu'i·tous·ly,** *adv.* —**gra·tu'i·tous·ness,** *n.*

gra·tu·i·ty (grə tōō'ə tē, grə tyōō'ə tē) *n. pl.,* **gra·tu·i·ties.** a gift, especially of money, given in return for services; tip.

grave¹ (grāv) *n.* **1.** a hole dug in the earth for the burial of a body. **2. the grave.** death. [Old English *græf.*]

grave² (grāv; *def. 4 also* gräv) *adj.,* **grav·er, grav·est.** **1.** of great importance; weighty: *The President had to make grave decisions when war broke out.* **2.** of a threatening nature; dangerous; critical: *a grave illness.* **3.** earnest and dignified; sober; sedate: *a grave, humorless man.* **4.** marked or pronounced with a grave accent. [Latin *gravis.*] —**grave'ly,** *adv.* —**grave'ness,** *n.*

grave³ (grāv) *v.t.,* **graved, graved** or **grav·en, grav·ing.** to form or shape by carving; sculpt; engrave. [Old English *grafan.*]

grave accent (grāv, gräv) a mark (`) placed over a vowel to show correct pronunciation, as in French *père,* or to show the difference between two words spelled the same way, as in French *a* and *à,* or to show in English that a final syllable is pronounced.

grav·el (grav'əl) *n.* pebbles and small pieces of rock, often mixed with sand, used especially for roads and walks. —*v.t.,* **grav·eled, grav·el·ing;** *also, British,* **grav·elled, grav·el·ling.** to cover or lay with gravel: *to gravel a driveway.*

grav·el·ly (grav'ə lē) *adj.* **1.** of or like gravel. **2.** (of the voice) harsh; grating.

grav·en (grā'vən) a past participle of **grave³.**

grave·stone (grāv'stōn') *n.* a stone marking a grave.

grave·yard (grāv'yärd') *n.* a cemetery.

grav·i·tate (grav'ə tāt') *v.i.,* **grav·i·tat·ed, grav·i·tat·ing.** **1.** to move or tend to move by the force of gravity. **2.** to move or be attracted by a strong influence: *The two new students in the class gravitated toward each other.* **3.** to sink or fall: *The sediment in the wine bottle gravitated to the bottom.*

grav·i·ta·tion (grav'ə tā'shən) *n.* **1.** the force of attraction that exists between any two objects in the universe. Gravitation keeps the stars on their courses and the planets in their orbits. It also keeps people and objects on the surface of the earth. **2.** the act or process of gravitating. **3.** a movement toward or attraction to someone or something as the result of a strong influence. —**grav'i·ta'tion·al,** *adj.* —**grav'i·ta'tion·al·ly,** *adv.*

grav·i·ty (grav'ə tē) *n. pl.,* **grav·i·ties.** **1.** the force that pulls things toward the center of the earth. It is gravity that causes objects to fall when they are dropped and pulls them back to earth when they are thrown upward. The pull

at; āpe; cär; end; mē; it; īce; hot; ōld; fôrk; wood; fōōl; oil; out; up; turn; sing; thin; this; hw in white; zh in treasure. The symbol ə stands for the sound of **a** in about, **e** in taken, **i** in pencil, **o** in lemon, and **u** in circus.

G

of gravity on a body is called the weight of the body.
2. another word for **gravitation. 3.** weight; heaviness: *an object's center of gravity.* **4.** serious nature: *The teacher didn't seem aware of the gravity of student unrest at the school.* **5.** seriousness; solemnness.

gra·vy (grā′vē) *n. pl.,* **gra·vies. 1.** the juice that comes out from meat during and after cooking. **2.** a thickened sauce made by mixing this juice with other ingredients, such as flour and seasonings.

gray (grā) *also,* **grey.** *n.* a color made by mixing black and white. —*adj.* **1.** having the color gray. **2.** dark, gloomy, or dismal: *a gray day.* **3.** having gray hair. —*v.t., v.i.* to make or become gray: *The old man's hair was graying.* —**gray′ly,** *adv.* —**gray′ness,** *n.*

Gray, Thomas (grā) 1716–1771, English poet.

gray·beard (grā′bērd′) *n.* an old man.

gray·ish (grā′ish) *adj.* somewhat gray: *At dawn the sky was grayish.*

gray·lag (grā′lag′) *n.* a wild, gray, European goose.

gray·ling (grā′ling) *n.* a silver-blue or purple fish related to the trout, found in cold, running streams, and valued as both a food and a game fish.

gray matter 1. a grayish tissue in the brain and spinal cord containing some cell fibers and nerve cells. **2.** *Informal.* intelligence; brains.

graze¹ (grāz) *v.,* **grazed, graz·ing.** —*v.i.* to feed on growing grass: *Cattle and sheep grazed in the meadow.* —*v.t.* **1.** to put (livestock) to feed on growing grass: *They grazed the herd in the north pasture.* **2.** to feed on (growing grass). [Old English *grasian.*]

graze² (grāz) *v.,* **grazed, graz·ing.** —*v.t.* **1.** to scrape the skin from slightly: *The bullet grazed the young soldier's arm.* **2.** to touch or rub against lightly in passing. —*v.i.* to move so as to touch, rub, or scrape something lightly. —*n.* **1.** the act or instance of grazing. **2.** a scratch, scrape, or slight wound caused by grazing. [Possibly from *graze¹,* in the sense of a bullet coming close to or touching grass.]

graz·ing (grā′zing) *n.* pasture land; pasturage.

grease (*n.,* grēs; *v.,* grēs, grēz) *n.* **1.** soft animal fat, especially when it has been melted: *lamb grease, bacon grease.* **2.** a thick, oily substance, used especially as a lubricant. —*v.t.,* **greased, greas·ing.** to smear or lubricate with grease: *to grease the wheels of an automobile.* —**greas′er,** *n.*

grease paint, a thick make-up having a heavy oil or wax base, used by actors and actresses.

greas·y (grē′sē, grē′zē) *adj.,* **greas·i·er, greas·i·est. 1.** smeared or soiled with grease: *The mechanic's overalls were greasy after he repaired the car.* **2.** containing much grease or fat. **3.** like grease. —**greas′i·ly,** *adv.* —**greas′i·ness,** *n.*

great (grāt) *adj.* **1.** very large, as in size or number: *A great crowd gathered to welcome the astronauts to the city.* **2.** unusual in ability or achievement: *Shakespeare was a great writer.* **3.** important; remarkable: *The scientist's discovery of the new drug was a great event.* **4.** more than usual; extreme: *There is often great poverty in the slums of a city.* **5.** *Informal.* very good; excellent: *We had a great vacation in the mountains.* —**great′ness,** *n.*

great-aunt (grāt′ant′, grāt′änt′) *n.* another word for **grandaunt.**

Great Barrier Reef, the largest barrier reef in the world, along the northeastern coast of Australia.

Great Bear, another term for **Ursa major.**

Great Britain 1. an island off the western coast of Europe, comprising England, Scotland, and Wales. It is the largest of the British Isles. Area, 94,214 sq. mi. Pop. (1971), 55,521,534. Also, **Britain. 2.** see **United Kingdom.**

great circle, any circle on a sphere formed by a plane intersecting the surface of the sphere and passing through the center of the sphere.

great·coat (grāt′kōt′) *n.* a heavy overcoat.

Great Dane, a dog of a breed noted for its size and strength, having a square muzzle and a smooth, short-haired coat.

Great Divide, another term for **Continental Divide.**

Great Dane

great·er (grā′tər) *adj.* **1.** the comparative of **great. 2.** of or relating to a city and its suburbs: *the greater metropolitan area.*

Greater Antilles, an island group of the West Indies, including Cuba, Jamaica, Hispaniola, and Puerto Rico.

Greater London, an administrative unit of England comprising the City of London and the thirty-two London boroughs. Area, 616 sq. mi. Pop. (1971), 7,379,014.

great-grand·child (grāt′gran′chīld′) *n. pl.,* **great-grand·chil·dren** (grāt′grand′chil′drən). the child of one's grandchild.

great-grand·daugh·ter (grāt′gran′dô′tər) *n.* the daughter of one's grandchild.

great-grand·fa·ther (grāt′grand′fä′th̲ər) *n.* the father of one's grandmother or grandfather.

great-grand·moth·er (grāt′grand′muth̲′ər) *n.* the mother of one's grandmother or grandfather.

great-grand·par·ent (grāt′grand′per′ənt) *n.* the mother or father of one's grandmother or grandfather.

great-grand·son (grāt′grand′sun′) *n.* the son of one's grandchild.

great-heart·ed (grāt′här′tid) *adj.* **1.** having a generous and forgiving nature; noble. **2.** brave.

great horned owl, a dark-brown horned owl found throughout North and South America.

Great Lakes, a group of five large freshwater lakes along the border between the United States and Canada, including Lakes Superior, Michigan, Huron, Erie, and Ontario.

great·ly (grāt′lē) *adv.* **1.** in or to a great degree; very much: *I was greatly impressed by her performance.* **2.** in a great manner.

great-neph·ew (grāt′nef′yōō) *n.* another word for **grandnephew.**

great-niece (grāt′nēs′) *n.* another word for **grandniece.**

Great Plains, a vast plateau region in western North America, extending for about 2,500 miles from Alberta, Canada, to Texas, consisting mostly of flat or rolling, usually treeless, plains.

Great Salt Lake, a lake in northwestern Utah, the largest salt lake in North America and one of the saltiest bodies of water in the world.

Great Smoky Mountains, a mountain range in the southeastern United States, between Tennessee and North Carolina, part of the Appalachian Mountains. Also, **Smoky Mountains, Great Smokies.**

Great Spirit, the chief god of the religion of certain North American Indian tribes.

great-un·cle (grāt′ung′kəl) *n.* another word for **granduncle.**

Great Wall of China, a wall extending about 1500 miles along the boundary between north and northwest China and Mongolia. It was originally built in the third century B.C. as a defense against Huns and other invaders from Mongolia. Also, **Great Wall, Chinese Wall.**

greave (grēv) *n.* armor for the leg below the knee.

grebe (grēb) *n.* any of various water birds related to the loon and having soft, shiny feathers.

Gre·cian (grē′shən) *adj., n.* another word for **Greek.**

Gre·co–Ro·man (grē′kō rō′mən) *adj.* of or characteristic of ancient Greece and Rome: *Greco-Roman art.*

Greece (grēs) *n.* a country at the southern end of the Balkan Penin-

Grebe

sula. Ancient Greece was a great intellectual and artistic center and had a major influence on Western culture. Capital, Athens. Area, 50,944 sq. mi. Pop. (1971), 8,745,084.

greed (grēd) *n.* a very great, usually selfish, desire to have or get something: *The dictator's greed for power was soon revealed to the people of the nation.*

greed·y (grē′dē) *adj.,* **greed·i·er, greed·i·est. 1.** eager to have or get something; wanting more than one's share: *to be greedy for money.* **2.** wanting to eat or drink too much or too quickly; gluttonous. —**greed′i·ly,** *adv.* —**greed′i·ness,** *n.*

Greek (grēk) *adj.* of or relating to Greece, its people, their language, or culture. —*n.* **1.** a person who was born or is living in Greece. **2.** a person who lived in ancient Greece. **3.** the language of Greece.

● **Greek** is one of several languages that have played a large part in the shaping of our modern English vocabulary. While not contributing as much to our common vocabularly as Old English, French, and Latin, the Greek language is the source of about half of the vocabulary of the modern sciences. Although there were Greek words that had come into English through languages that had borrowed and absorbed some of the Greek vocabulary, the earliest large-scale adoption of Greek into English came in the fifteenth century. At that time, there was a great revival of interest in classical culture in particular, and in the liberal arts, science, and religion, in general. Among the Greek words that came into our language are *epic, drama, tragedy, comedy, history, biography,* and *music* in the liberal arts; *physics, energy, atom,* and *diagnosis* in science; and *theology* and *dogma* in religion.

Greek cross, a cross having four arms of equal length.

Greek Orthodox Church 1. see **Orthodox Church. 2.** the established church of Greece, a self-governing member of the Orthodox Church.

Gree·ley, Horace (grē′lē) 1811–1872, U.S. journalist, author, and politician.

Greek cross

green (grēn) *n.* **1.** the color of growing grass and of leaves in spring and summer. It is between yellow and blue in the spectrum. **2.** a grassy, usually level, piece of land used for a particular purpose: *a village green.* **3.** *Golf.* the area around a cup, having very thick, closely cut grass. Also, **putting green. 4. greens. a.** the green leaves or stems of certain plants, such as turnips, lettuce, spinach, or dandelions, used for food: *salad greens.* **b.** freshly cut leaves or branches used for decoration: *The mantelpiece was decorated with greens for the holiday.* —*adj.* **1.** having the color green: *a green coat.* **2.** covered with growing plants, grass, or green leaves: *green pastures.* **3.** not fully grown or mature; not ripe: *green tomatoes.* **4.** consisting of edible green leaves or other plant parts: *a*

green salad. **5.** having little or no training or experience; immature: *a green recruit in the marines.* **6.** having a pale, sickly color, as from illness or fear: *The children's faces were green when they came off the roller coaster.* **7.** not dried, cured, or otherwise ready for use: *green lumber.* —**green′ness,** *n.*

green·back (grēn′bak′) *n.* a paper currency with the back printed in green.

Greenback Party, a U.S. political party organized in 1874 and active through the 1880s, that favored the use of paper currency that could not be converted into gold and silver.

Green Bay, a port city in east-central Wisconsin. Pop. (1970), 87,809.

green bean, another term for **string bean.**

Greene, Nathanael (grēn) 1742–1786, U.S. general in the American Revolution.

green·er·y (grē′nər ē) *n. pl.,* **green·er·ies.** green plants or leaves.

green-eyed (grēn′īd′) *adj.* **1.** having green eyes. **2.** jealous: *The boy was green-eyed because his older brother got a new bicycle.*

green·gage (grēn′gāj′) *n.* a sweet plum having a greenish-yellow skin and pulp. [From Sir William *Gage,* a botanist who brought this fruit to England from France in about 1725.]

green·gro·cer (grēn′grō′sər) *n. British.* a person who sells fresh vegetables and fruit.

green·horn (grēn′hôrn′) *n. Informal.* **1.** an inexperienced person; person without training. **2.** a person who is easily fooled. [Originally referring to a young animal with horns that were not fully grown.]

green·house (grēn′hous′) *n. pl.,* **green·hous·es** (grēn′hou′ziz). a building having the roof and sides of glass or transparent plastic that traps the heat of the sun, and in which plants can be cultivated all year; hothouse.

green·ing (grē′ning) *n.* any of several apples having a greenish-yellow skin when ripe and a tart flavor, used especially for cooking.

green·ish (grē′nish) *adj.* somewhat green.

Green·land (grēn′lənd) *n.* a Danish island northeast of the mainland of North America, lying mostly within the Arctic Circle. It is the largest island in the world. Area, 840,000 sq. mi. Pop. (1980 est.), 52,000.

green light 1. a green traffic light that gives permission to go ahead. **2.** *Informal.* the permission to go ahead with a particular project or activity: *Mother gave us the green light to go on the camping trip.*

Green Mountains, a mountain range extending along the length of central Vermont, a part of the Appalachian Mountains.

green onion, see **scallion.**

green pepper, an unripe sweet pepper.

Greens·bor·o (grēnz′bur′ō) *n.* a city in north-central North Carolina. Pop. (1970), 144,076.

green soap, a soft soap used especially in treating skin disorders.

green·sward (grēn′swôrd′) *n.* green grass or grassy ground.

green thumb, a special talent for making plants grow.

---

at; āpe; cär; end; mē; it; īce; hot; ōld; fôrk;
wood; fōōl; oil; out; up; turn; sing; thin; this;
hw in white; zh in treasure. The symbol ə
stands for the sound of **a** in about, **e** in taken,
i in pencil, **o** in lemon, and **u** in circus.

Green·wich (gren′ich) *n.* a borough of Greater London, England, the former site of an astronomical observatory. The prime meridian passes through Greenwich. Pop. (1970 est.), 226,130.

Greenwich Time, the time at the prime meridian in Greenwich, England, used as the standard time by which the time zones of the world are established.

Greenwich Village, a section of lower Manhattan, New York City, noted as an artists' and writers' quarter.

green·wood (grēn′wood′) *n.* a forest when the leaves are green, as in the summer.

greet (grēt) *v.t.* **1.** to speak to or welcome in a friendly or polite way: *The hostess greeted her guests at the door.* **2.** to meet or receive: *The famous pianist was greeted with applause.* **3.** to present itself to; appear to: *The morning sun greeted us as we came out on the deck of the boat.* —**greet′er,** *n.*

greet·ing (grē′ting) *n.* **1.** the act or words of a person who greets another or others. **2. greetings.** friendly wishes or message, especially from someone absent: *My friend sent greetings on my birthday.* —*interj.* **greetings.** hello.

greeting card, see **card**[1] *(def. 4).*

gre·gar·i·ous (gri ger′ē əs) *adj.* **1.** enjoying and happy to be with others; sociable; outgoing: *The man was very gregarious and enjoyed giving parties.* **2.** living in flocks, herds, or groups: *Sheep are gregarious.* —**gre·gar′i·ous·ly,** *adv.* —**gre·gar′i·ous·ness,** *n.*

Gre·go·ri·an (gri gôr′ē ən) *adj.* of, relating to, or introduced by one of several popes named Gregory, especially Pope Gregory I or Pope Gregory XIII.

Gregorian calendar, a calendar now in use in most countries of the world. Introduced as a reform of the Julian calendar by Pope Gregory XIII in 1582, it provides for an ordinary year of 365 days and a leap year of 366.

Gregorian chant, the music used in the liturgy of the Roman Catholic and certain other churches, introduced by Pope Gregory I.

Greg·o·ry I, Saint (greg′ər ē) A.D. 540?–604, the pope from 590 to 604. Also, **Gregory the Great.**

grem·lin (grem′lin) *n.* a small, mischievous spirit blamed for sudden or unaccountable troubles, especially in airplane engines.

Gre·na·da (gri nä′ də) *n.* an island country in the West Indies, one of the Windward Islands. Land area, 133 sq. mi. Pop. (1978 est.), 100,000.

gre·nade (gri nād′) *n.* a small bomb that can be thrown by hand or fired by a rifle.

gren·a·dier (gren′ə dēr′) *n.* **1.** a member of the first regiment of infantry in the British Army attached to the royal household. **2.** formerly, a soldier who threw hand grenades.

grew (grōō) the past tense of **grow.**

grey (grā) another spelling of **gray.**

grey·hound (grā′hound′) *n.* a slender, swift dog, having a smooth blue-gray, black, white, brown, or red short-haired coat, raised especially for racing or hunting.

Greyhound

grid (grid) *n.* **1.** an arrangement of parallel or intersecting bars or wires with openings between them; grating: *The hot air came through grids in the floor.* **2.** a pattern of intersecting parallel lines used to divide a map or chart into small squares. **3.** a metal plate that forms an electrode in a storage battery. **4.** an electrode in a vacuum tube, used to control the flow of electrons.

grid·dle (grid′əl) *n.* a heavy, flat metal pan used especially for cooking pancakes. —*v.t.,* **grid·dled, grid·dling.** to cook on a griddle.

grid·dle·cake (grid′əl kāk′) *n.* a pancake.

grid·i·ron (grid′ī′ərn) *n.* **1.** a football field. **2.** see **grill** *(def. 1).*

grief (grēf) *n.* **1.** very great sadness or deep sorrow: *a mother's grief at the death of a child.* **2.** the cause of such sadness or sorrow: *The loss of her dog was the greatest grief the child had known.*

to come to grief. to meet with disaster; fail: *The expedition came to grief when two mountain climbers were hurt.*

grief-strick·en (grēf′strik′ən) *adj.* overcome by grief; deeply anguished: *We were grief-stricken by the news of his untimely death.*

Grieg, Ed·vard (grēg; ed′värd) 1843–1907, Norwegian composer.

griev·ance (grē′vəns) *n.* a real or imagined wrong that causes anger, resentment, or distress: *The striking construction workers wrote down a list of their grievances about working conditions.*

grieve (grēv) *v.,* **grieved, griev·ing.** —*v.t.* to feel grief; mourn: *The parents grieved over the death of their son.* —*v.t.* to cause to feel grief; sadden deeply.

griev·ous (grē′vəs) *adj.* **1.** causing grief, deep sorrow, or great pain: *Her son's death was a grievous loss.* **2.** of a very serious nature; grave; outrageous: *Murder is a grievous crime.* **3.** showing or full of grief; sorrowful; mournful: *a grievous cry of pain.* —**griev′ous·ly,** *adv.* —**griev′ous·ness,** *n.*

grif·fin (grif′ən) *also,* **grif·fon.** *n.* a mythical creature with the head and wings of an eagle and the body and legs of a lion.

Griffin

Grif·fith, D(avid) W(ark) (grif′ith; wôrk) 1875–1948, U.S. motion picture director and producer.

grill (gril) *n.* **1.** a cooking utensil having a framework of parallel metal bars or wires on which food is placed to be broiled over an open fire. Also, **gridiron. 2.** food, especially meat, that has been broiled on a grill. **3.** a restaurant that specializes in grilled foods. —*v.t.* **1.** to broil on a grill: *The campers grilled hamburgers for supper.* **2.** to question closely and relentlessly: *The police grilled the suspected bank robber for eight hours.*

grille (gril) *n.* a grating, of ornamental metalwork, used to cover or enclose a space as a screen or gate.

grill·work (gril′wurk′) *n.* a grille or a pattern of grilles: *the grillwork of an automobile.*

Grille

grilse (grils) *n. pl.,* **grilse.** a young salmon on its first return from the sea to fresh water.

grim (grim) *adj.,* **grim·mer, grim·mest. 1.** having a stern or forbidding quality or look: *The old house was grim and dirty. Her face had a cold, grim expression.* **2.** not yielding; resolute: *The team played with grim determination to win the game.* **3.** without mercy; fierce: *a grim battle.* **4.** horrifying; ghastly: *The soldier told grim stories about his experiences in the war.* —**grim′ly,** *adv.* —**grim′ness,** *n.*

gri·mace (grim′əs, gri mās′) *n.* a twisting of the face showing pain, disgust, or displeasure: *The girl made a grimace when she tasted the bitter medicine.*

grime (grīm) *n.* dirt covering or rubbed into a surface: *The windows were black with grime.* —*v.t.,* **grimed, griming.** to cover with grime; soil: *The walls were grimed from the smoke and grease in the air.*

Grimm, Ja·kob (grim; yä′kop) 1785–1863 and his brother **Wil·helm** (vil′helm) 1786–1859, German language scholars and collectors of fairy tales.

grim·y (grī′mē) *adj.,* **grim·i·er, grim·i·est.** full of or covered with grime; filthy: *Windows often become grimy in the city.* —**grim′i·ness,** *n.*

grin (grin) *v.i.,* **grinned, grin·ning.** **1.** to smile broadly: *The boy grinned when his father said they were going fishing.* **2.** to draw back the lips and show the teeth, as in scorn or anger: *The cat spat and grinned angrily when the fireman tried to get her down from the roof.* —*n.* a broad smile.

grind (grīnd) *v.t.,* **ground, grind·ing.** **1.** to crush or chop into small pieces or powder: *to grind corn into meal.* **2.** to make or produce by crushing: *to grind pepper from peppercorns.* **3.** to wear down, smooth, or sharpen by rubbing against something rough: *to grind the lens for a telescope.* **4.** to rub together, press down, or move in a harsh or noisy way: *He ground his teeth in anger.* **5.** to work by turning a crank: *to grind a coffee mill.* —*n.* **1.** the size of the pieces of a material that has been crushed: *There are several different grinds of coffee.* **2.** the act of grinding. **3.** hard, long work or study: *the grind of working a 12-hour day.* **4.** *Informal.* a person who is thought to spend too much time and effort at his studies or work.

grind·er (grīn′dər) *n.* **1.** a person or thing that grinds: *a coffee grinder.* **2.** any one of the back teeth; molar.

grind·stone (grīnd′stōn′) *n.* a stone disk that can be turned on an axle to sharpen tools, as knives or axes, or to polish or smooth things.

to keep one's nose to the grindstone. to work steadily or very hard at one's job.

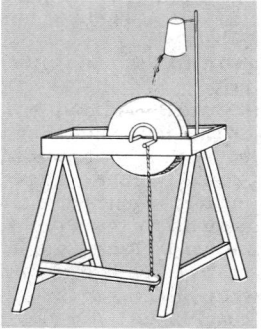
Grindstone

grip (grip) *n.* **1.** a firm hold; tight grasp: *I kept a good grip on the dog's collar when he tried to jump at the stranger.* **2.** the ability to hold firmly. **3.** a way of holding or taking hold of something, such as a golf club or tennis racket, or other piece of sports equipment. **4.** a special manner of shaking or clasping hands, especially one used by members of a secret or fraternal organization. **5.** firm control; power: *The people were in the grip of the dictator.* **6.** a mental grasp; knowledge: *He is just beginning to get a grip on algebra.* **7.** the part of certain pieces of sports equipment by which they are intended to be held. **8.** a small suitcase. —*v.t.,* **gripped, grip·ping.** **1.** to take hold of firmly and tightly: *He gripped the rifle between his knees.* **2.** to attract and keep the interest of: *The movie about racing cars really gripped him.* —**grip′per,** *n.*

to come to grips with. to face and deal with in a firm, decisive manner: *to come to grips with a difficult problem.*

gripe (grīp) *v.,* **griped, grip·ing.** *Informal.* —*v.i.* to complain; grumble: *The boy griped about all the extra homework he had to do.* —*v.t.* to irritate; annoy: *The umpire's decision griped the team. Informal.* —*n.* a complaint: *Lawrence had many gripes about his new job.*

grippe (grip) *n.* a disease resembling influenza.

gris·ly (griz′lē) *adj.,* **gris·li·er, gris·li·est.** causing horror, revulsion, or fear; gruesome: *a grisly sight.* —**gris′li·ness,** *n.*

grist (grist) *n.* grain that is to be ground.

gris·tle (gris′əl) *n.* a tough tissue found in meat; cartilage.

gris·tly (gris′lē) *adj.,* **gris·tli·er, gris·tli·est.** consisting of, containing, or like gristle.

grist mill, a mill for grinding grain.

grit (grit) *n.* **1.** very small, hard particles of sand or stone. **2.** strength of mind and spirit; courage. **3.** a coarse sandstone. —*v.t.,* **grit·ted, grit·ting.** to grind or tightly clamp together (the teeth).

grits (grits) *n., pl.* **1.** coarsely ground hominy, used as a cereal and in bread and puddings. Also, **hominy grits.** **2.** coarsely ground, hulled grain.

grit·ty (grit′ē) *adj.,* **grit·ti·er, grit·ti·est.** **1.** of, containing, or like grit. **2.** covered or soiled with grit. **3.** having or showing strength of mind and spirit; courageous. —**grit′ti·ness,** *n.*

griz·zled (griz′əld) *adj.* **1.** gray or mixed with gray: *The old man had a grizzled beard.* **2.** gray-haired.

griz·zly (griz′lē) *n. pl.,* **griz·zlies.** a grizzly bear. —*adj.,* **griz·zli·er, griz·zli·est.** grayish; grizzled.

grizzly bear, a long-clawed bear of western North America, having a large head and body and usually brown or gray fur.

Grizzly bear

groan (grōn) *n.* a deep, sad sound, as of grief, pain, or disapproval; moan. —*v.i.* **1.** to make such a sound: *The football player groaned when he tried to move his injured leg.* **2.** to make a sound like this: *The roof creaked and groaned under the weight of the snow.* **3.** to be overburdened or strained: *The shelves groaned with books.* —*v.t.* to express or say with a groan: *The fans groaned their disappointment when their team lost.* —**groan′er,** *n.*

groat (grōt) *n.* an English silver coin, used from the thirteenth through the seventeenth centuries.

gro·cer (grō′sər) *n.* a person who owns or manages a grocery.

gro·cer·y (grō′sər ē) *n. pl.,* **gro·cer·ies.** **1.** a store that sells food and household supplies. **2. groceries.** goods, especially food, sold by such a store.

grog (grog) *n.* **1.** a drink made by mixing rum or whiskey with water. **2.** any alcoholic beverage. [From "Old *Grog,*" the nickname of an eighteenth-century British admiral who gave an order that the rum given to sailors should be mixed with water.]

grog·gy (grog′ē) *adj.,* **grog·gi·er, grog·gi·est.** not fully alert or awake; in a dazed or unsteady condition: *John is groggy this morning because he went to bed so late last night.* —**grog′gi·ly,** *adv.* —**grog′gi·ness,** *n.*

groin (groin) *n.* **1.** a hollow on either side of the front of the body where the thigh joins the abdomen. **2.** a curved

at; āpe; cär; end; mē; it; īce; hot; ōld; fôrk; wood; fōol; oil; out; up; turn; sing; thin; this; hw in white; zh in treasure. The symbol ə stands for the sound of a in about, e in taken, i in pencil, o in lemon, and u in circus.

G

edge formed by the intersection of two vaults on a ceiling. —*v.t.* to build with groins.

grom·met (grom′it) *n.* **1.** a ring, as of metal or plastic, that reinforces a hole in material. **2.** a ring of rope or metal to hold oars in place or to fasten the edges of sails to spars.

Gro·my·ko, An·drei An·dre·ie·vich (grō mē′kō; än drā′ än drā′yə vich) 1909—, Soviet diplomat and statesman.

groom (grōōm, groom) *n.* **1.** see **bridegroom. 2.** a person who washes, curries, and otherwise takes care of horses. —*v.t.* **1.** to wash, curry, and otherwise take care of (horses). **2.** to make neat, tidy, and attractive in appearance: *She groomed her hair and fingernails carefully before the party.* **3.** to train or prepare (someone) for some purpose, such as political office: *The young congressman was being groomed for the Senate.*

grooms·man (grōōmz′mən, groomz′mən) *n. pl.,* **grooms·men** (grōōmz′mən, groomz′mən). a man who attends the bridegroom at a wedding.

groove (grōōv) *n.* **1.** a long, narrow channel or depression in a surface: *The car wheels made grooves on the dirt road. A phonograph record has grooves.* **2.** a narrow, limited way of doing things; routine; rut: *He has been too thoroughly trained to progress along a certain groove ever to question it* (Eugene O'Neill). —*v.t.,* **grooved, groov·ing.** to make a groove or grooves in.

grope (grōp) *v.,* **groped, grop·ing.** —*v.i.* **1.** to feel about with the hands: *He groped for the door handle in the dark hall.* **2.** to search blindly and uncertainly: *He groped for a solution to his problem.* —*v.t.* to find (one's way) by groping. —**grop′ing·ly,** *adv.*

Gro·pi·us, Walter (grō′pē əs) 1883–1969, German architect.

gros·beak (grōs′bēk′) *n.* a bird of the finch family, having a large cone-shaped bill.

gros·grain (grō′grān′) *n.* a closely woven, ribbed fabric, often of silk or rayon, used chiefly for ribbons.

Grosbeak

gross (grōs) *adj.* **1.** with nothing taken away; total; entire: *From gross monthly earnings of $1000, his net income was $650.* **2.** very obvious; glaring; flagrant: *a gross mistake, a gross injustice.* **3.** not refined; coarse; vulgar: *gross behavior, a gross joke.* **4.** thick or heavy: *gross tropical vegetation.* —*n. pl.,* **gross·es** *(def. 1);* **gross** *(def. 2).* **1.** the total amount, as of income, before deductions: *The company's gross for the year was five million dollars.* **2.** twelve dozen. —*v.t.* to earn a total of before deductions: *That motion picture grossed more than ten million dollars.* —**gross′ly,** *adv.* —**gross′ness,** *n.*

gross national product, the total value of all the goods and services produced by a country during a certain period of time.

gro·tesque (grō tesk′) *adj.* **1.** distorted, deformed, unnatural, or ugly in shape or appearance: *The movie showed all kinds of grotesque monsters.* **2.** amusingly absurd; ludicrous: *She wore her hat at a grotesque angle over one ear.* —**gro·tesque′ly,** *adv.* —**gro·tesque′ness,** *n.*

grot·to (grot′ō) *n. pl.,* **grot·toes** or **grot·tos. 1.** a cave. **2.** a structure made to resemble a cave, as for a shrine.

grouch (grouch) *n. pl.,* **grouch·es. 1.** a person who is very irritable, sulky, or ill-tempered: *That old man is a grouch.* **2.** a sulky or grumbling mood. —*v.i.* to grumble or sulk: *The boy grouched because his mother made him dry the dishes.*

grouch·y (grou′chē) *adj.,* **grouch·i·er, grouch·i·est.** in a bad mood; irritable; sulky. —**grouch′i·ly,** *adv.* —**grouch′i·ness,** *n.*

ground¹ (ground) *n.* **1.** the solid surface of the earth; soil; land: *The ground was covered with snow.* **2. grounds.** the land surrounding a house, institution, or other building: *The school grounds were beautifully planted with trees and flowers.* **3.** *also,* **grounds.** an area or piece of land put aside for a particular use: *a parade ground, picnic grounds.* **4.** *also,* **grounds.** a reason; basis; foundation: *grounds for suspicion.* **5.** an underlying surface or background: *The wallpaper is printed with a red floral design on a green ground.* **6. grounds.** the particles or bits that settle at the bottom of a liquid or are left over in the container that held it; dregs: *Throw out the coffee grounds.* **7.** a connection between an electric conductor and the earth. —*v.t.* **1.** to place or set on the ground; cause to touch the ground. **2.** to provide a firm foundation or basis for; base: *Their fears were grounded on superstition.* **3.** to instruct in the first or basic principles or elements of a subject: *He grounded himself thoroughly in mathematics.* **4.** to forbid (a person or aircraft) to fly; keep on the ground: *The plane was grounded for three hours because of bad weather.* **5.** to connect (an electric wire or other conductor) with the earth. **6.** to cause (a boat or ship) to run aground: *The captain grounded his ship on the shoal.* —*v.i.* **1.** to fall to or strike the ground. **2.** (of a boat or ship) to run aground. **3.** *Baseball.* to hit a ground ball: *He grounded to the shortstop.* [Old English *grund.*]

to break ground. to begin building something.

to gain ground. to make progress: *The railroad gained ground in its effort to end the engineers' strike.*

to give ground. to withdraw from attack; retreat; yield: *The army had to give ground after the enemy's attack.*

to ground out. in baseball, to hit a ground ball that puts one out at first base.

to hold one's ground. to maintain one's position; not retreat, yield, or withdraw.

to lose ground. to move farther away from a goal; go backwards.

ground² (ground) the past tense and past participle of grind.

ground ball *Baseball.* a batted ball that strikes the ground in the infield and then rolls or moves along in low bounces. Also, **grounder.**

ground crew, the personnel responsible for the servicing and maintenance of aircraft.

ground·er (groun′dər) *n.* another word for **ground ball.**

ground floor, the floor in a building that is level or nearly level with the ground.

ground·hog (ground′hog′) *n.* another word for **woodchuck.**

Groundhog Day, the day when the groundhog, according to popular belief, comes out of hibernation. The tradition is that if he sees his shadow, he returns underground for six more weeks of winter. It falls on February 2.

ground·less (ground′lis) *adj.* having no real cause or reason: *The child had a groundless fear of the dark.* —**ground′less·ly,** *adv.* —**ground′less·ness,** *n.*

ground·nut (ground′nut′) *n.* **1.** any of several plants of the pea family having underground parts used for food, especially the peanut. **2.** the underground parts of such a plant.

ground pine, any of several club mosses.

ground speed, the speed of an aircraft relative to the ground over which it is traveling.

ground squirrel 1. any of various rodents that live in burrows in the ground, usually having gray or light brown fur, often with striped or spotted markings. Also, **gopher. 2.** a chipmunk or prairie dog.

ground swell, broad, deep waves or a rolling sea, caused by a distant storm or earthquake.

ground water, water that has flowed or seeped beneath the surface of the earth and saturated the soil and other porous material below. It is the source of water for wells and underground springs.

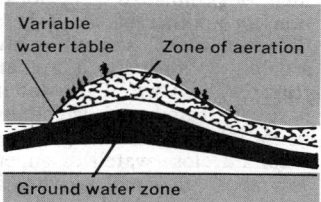

Variable water table   Zone of aeration

Ground water zone

Ground water

ground·work (ground'wurk') *n.* the first work or material on which something is built or based; foundation: *The student completed the groundwork for his term paper in the library.*

group (grōop) *n.* **1.** a number of persons or things found together or thought of as forming a unit: *A group of employees drew up a petition protesting working conditions.* **2.** a number of persons or things classed together because of similarities: *The Italians and the Irish are two of the ethnic groups that emigrated to this country in large numbers.* **3.** a military unit consisting of two or more battalions or squadrons. **4.** a number of chemical elements having similar characteristics and arranged in a column on the periodic table. **5.** an arrangement of atoms attached to different molecules, giving similar characteristics to a family of compounds. —*v.t.* to arrange or place in a group: *The counselor grouped the younger children together.* —*v.i.* to form or belong to a group: *The skiers grouped around the fire. The tourists grouped at the airport.*

group·er (grōo'pər) *n. pl.,* **group·ers** or **group·er.** any of a number of saltwater fish having huge mouths and sharp teeth. Many are food fish and some may weigh as much as 1000 pounds.

Grouper

group·ing (grōo'ping) *n.* **1.** the act of placing in a group. **2.** a set of things arranged in a group: *There was an attractive grouping of paintings on one wall.*

group therapy, a form of psychological therapy in which a group of patients, usually with the help of a therapist, try to understand and deal with their emotional problems by openly discussing them.

grouse (grous) *n. pl.,* **grouse** or **grous·es.** any of a group of game birds, including the ruffed grouse and prairie chicken, having brown, black, or gray feathers, often with white markings, and feathered legs.

grove (grōv) *n.* **1.** a small group of trees without underbrush: *The frightened rabbit scampered off into the grove.* **2.** a group of fruit trees, especially citrus trees: *an orange grove.*

grov·el (gruv'əl, grov'əl) *v.i.,* **grov·eled, grov·el·ing;** *also,* British, **grov·elled, grov·el·ling.** **1.** to act in a cringing or humble way, as through fear or the desire to please or flatter: *The old man's nephew always groveled in his presence in hopes of getting an inheritance.* **2.** to lie or crawl face downward, as in fear or humility: *The subjects groveled before their king.* —**grov'el·er;** *also,* British, **grov'el·ler,** *n.*

grow (grō) *v.,* **grew, grown, grow·ing.** —*v.i.* **1.** to mature or become larger by a natural process of development: *Jack grew two inches this year.* **2.** to expand or increase, as in size, amount, or degree: *His savings account began to grow rapidly.* **3.** to be produced and develop; thrive; flourish:

Orchids grow wild in the jungles of South America. **4.** to come into existence; arise: *Bitter feelings grew from the argument.* **5.** to come to be by degrees; become: *My uncle grew rich as his business expanded.* —*v.t.* **1.** to cause to grow; raise; cultivate: *That farmer grows tomatoes.* **2.** to allow to grow: *He grew a mustache.* **3.** to cover with a growth: *The lawn was grown with weeds.*

to grow out of. a. to outgrow: *The child has grown out of all his baby clothes.* **b.** to develop or arise from: *Arguments often grow out of misunderstandings.*

to grow up. to become an adult: *He wants to be a fireman when he grows up.*

grow·er (grō'ər) *n.* **1.** a person who grows something: *His father is the largest wheat grower in the state.* **2.** a plant that grows in a certain way: *a rapid grower.*

growl (groul) *v.i.* **1.** to make a deep, harsh, rumbling sound in the throat, in anger or as a threat: *The bear growled as we approached his cage.* **2.** to speak or make an angry sound or sounds like this. —*v.t.* to express or say with a deep, harsh, rumbling sound. —*n.* **1.** a deep, harsh, rumbling sound made by an angry animal. **2.** any sound resembling this.

grown (grōn) *v.* the past participle of **grow.** —*adj.* having reached full growth or maturity; adult: *My older sister is a grown woman.*

grown-up (*adj.,* grōn'up'; *n.,* grōn'up') *adj.* **1.** adult; mature: *She seems more grown-up this year.* **2.** characteristic of or suitable for adults: *grown-up behavior.* —*n.* an adult: *The grown-ups watched as the children swam in the pool.*

growth (grōth) *n.* **1.** the process of growing; development: *We studied human growth in biology class. The puppy has reached its full growth.* **2.** increase, as in size, importance, or power: *the growth of a company. That politician has experienced a rapid growth in popularity.* **3.** something that grows or has grown: *They cleared a growth of weeds from the garden.* **4.** a mass of new tissue that results from an abnormal increase in cells and serves no useful function for the body; tumor.

grub (grub) *n.* **1.** a soft larva, especially of a beetle, that resembles a worm. **2.** *Informal.* food. —*v.,* **grubbed, grubbing.** —*v.i.* **1.** to dig in the ground; root: *Pigs grub for food with their hooves and snouts.* **2.** to work very hard, especially doing menial or dreary work. —*v.t.* to dig up by the roots: *to grub out the mushrooms in a lawn.* —**grub'ber,** *n.*

grub·by (grub'ē) *adj.,* **grub·bi·er, grub·bi·est.** dirty; grimy; filthy. —**grub'bi·ness,** *n.*

grub·stake (grub'stāk') *n.* money or supplies advanced to a prospector in return for a share of his profits. —*v.t.,* **grub·staked, grub·stak·ing.** to supply with a grubstake.

grudge (gruj) *n.* a strong feeling of ill will, anger, or resentment. —*v.t.,* **grudged, grudg·ing.** to give or allow unwillingly; begrudge. —**grudg'ing·ly,** *adv.*

gru·el (grōo'əl) *n.* a thin porridge made by boiling meal, especially oatmeal, in water or milk.

gru·el·ing (grōo'ə ling) *also,* **gru·el·ling.** *adj.* very difficult or punishing; exhausting: *The marathon is a grueling race.*

G

at; āpe; cär; end; mē; it; īce; hot; ōld; fôrk; wood; fōol; oil; out; up; turn; sing; thin; this; hw in white; zh in treasure. The symbol ə stands for the sound of **a** in about, **e** in taken, **i** in pencil, **o** in lemon, and **u** in circus.

grue·some (grōō′səm) *adj.* causing horror, disgust, or fear; frightful; repulsive. —**grue′some·ly**, *adv.* —**grue′-some·ness**, *n.*

gruff (gruf) *adj.* **1.** (of the voice) deep and rough. **2.** abrupt or stern; bluff: *Underneath his gruff manner he's really very kind.* —**gruff′ly**, *adv.* —**gruff′ness**, *n.*

grum·ble (grum′bəl) *v.*, **grum·bled, grum·bling.** —*v.i.* to mutter in discontent; complain in a grouchy manner. —*v.t.* to express or say by grumbling. —*n.* **1.** a mutter of discontent or complaint. **2.** a rumble. —**grum′bler**, *n.*

grump (grump) *n.* an ill-tempered, complaining person.

grump·y (grum′pē) *adj.*, **grump·i·er, grump·i·est.** in an irritable or gloomy mood; ill-tempered: *He is grumpy when he first gets up in the morning.* —**grump′i·ly**, *adv.* —**grump′i·ness**, *n.*

grunt (grunt) *n.* **1.** a short, deep, hoarse sound, such as that made by a hog. **2.** any of a group of tropical saltwater fish that make a similar sound by rubbing their teeth together. —*v.i.* **1.** to make the short, deep, hoarse sound of a hog. **2.** to make a similar sound: *The tired boys grunted as they pushed the stalled car along.* —*v.t.* to say or express with a grunt: *He grunted hello as we came into the room.*

Gt. Br. *also,* **Gt. Brit.** Great Britain.

Gua·da·la·ja·ra (gwäd′əl ə här′ə) *n.* a city in southwestern Mexico. Pop. (1970), 1,194,646.

Gua·dal·ca·nal (güäd′əl kə nal′) *n.* an island in the southwestern Pacific Ocean, one of the Solomon Islands. It was the scene of fighting between American and Japanese forces in World War II.

Gua·de·loupe (gwäd′əl ōōp′) *n.* **1.** a French overseas department consisting of a group of islands in the Leeward Islands. **2.** the largest island in this group.

Guam (gwäm) *n.* an island in the western Pacific, east of the Philippines. It is administered by the United States.

gua·na·co (gwä nä′kō) *n. pl.,* **gua·na·cos.** a long-legged animal of South America, having a long, slender neck and large, pointed ears.

Guang·zhou (gwäng′jō′) another spelling of **Canton.**

gua·nine (gwä′nēn) *n.* a purine base that is an essential constituent of DNA and RNA.

gua·no (gwä′nō) *n. pl.,* **gua·nos. 1.** the waste matter of sea birds, widely used as fertilizer, found in large deposits on islands off the coast of Peru. **2.** any similar fertilizer.

Guanaco

Guan·tá·na·mo Bay (gwän tä′nə mō′) an inlet of the Caribbean Sea in southeastern Cuba, the site of a U.S. naval base.

guar·an·tee (gar′ən tē′) *n.* **1.** an assurance or pledge given by a seller to a buyer that his product is what it is claimed to be or that it will be repaired or replaced if anything goes wrong with it within a certain period of time; warranty. **2.** anything that assures a certain outcome or condition: *Beauty is no guarantee of happiness.* **3.** a person who receives a guaranty. **4.** see **guaranty** *(defs. 1,2).* —*v.t.,* **guar·an·teed, guar·an·tee·ing. 1.** to give assurance of the quality of; give a guarantee for. **2.** to agree to be responsible for the debts or obligations of another; make a guaranty. **3.** to make sure or certain: *Having that band appear will guarantee the success of the dance.* **4.** to state or affirm (something); promise: *I guarantee the work will be finished on time.*

guar·an·tor (gar′ən tôr′) *n.* a person who makes or gives a guarantee.

guar·an·ty (gar′ən tē′) *n. pl.,* **guar·an·ties. 1.** an agreement or promise to be responsible for the debts or obligations of another person if he should fail to take care of them himself. **2.** something given or taken as security for a debt or obligation. **3.** a guarantee; warranty.

guard (gärd) *v.t.* **1.** to watch over or tend carefully to keep safe from harm; defend; protect: *The dog guarded the house. Secret Service agents guard the President.* **2.** to maintain close watch or supervision over, as to prevent escape or to control activity: *The policeman guarded the prisoners. Two soldiers guarded the gate of the fort.* **3.** in certain sports, to attempt to prevent (an opponent) from scoring. **4.** to provide a cover, shield, or other protective device for: *Using this lotion will guard your skin against the sun.* —*v.i.* to take precautions or care: *to guard against illness, to guard against repeating a mistake.* —*n.* **1.** a person or group that guards: *a prison guard, a museum guard.* **2.** a cover, attachment, or other device that protects against loss, injury, or damage. **3.** careful or restraining watch or supervision: *A sentry kept guard at the door.* **4.** something that guards or protects; defense; safeguard: *Brushing your teeth after each meal is a good guard against tooth decay.* **5.** *Football.* one of two players positioned at the right and the left of the center. **6.** *Basketball.* one of two players whose usual position is toward the rear of the court.

on one's guard. prepared or watchful; alert.

off one's guard. not alert; unprepared: *The troops were caught off guard by the enemy.*

to stand guard. a. to serve as a sentry. **b.** to keep a protective watch.

guard cell *Botany.* one of a pair of bean-shaped cells found next to a pore on the outer surface of a leaf. Their reactions to heat and light control the movement of gases into and out of the leaf through the pores.

guard·ed (gär′did) *adj.* **1.** cautious; prudent: *The lawyer gave a guarded reply to any questions the reporters asked about his client.* **2.** closely watched, defended, or restrained. —**guard′ed·ly**, *adv.*

guard·house (gärd′hous′) *n. pl.,* **guard·hous·es** (gärd′-hou′ziz). **1.** a building used as a temporary jail for military prisoners. **2.** a building used to house people on military guard duty.

guard·i·an (gär′dē ən) *n.* **1.** a person or thing that guards or watches over; protector: *The judge felt it was his duty to act as a guardian of justice.* **2.** a person who is entrusted by law to take care of the person, property, or rights of someone who cannot take care of them himself: *After the young girl's parents died, her uncle became her guardian.* —*adj.* protecting: *a guardian angel.* —**guard′-i·an·ship′**, *n.*

guard·rail (gärd′rāl′) *n.* a railing for support or protection, as on a staircase or a highway.

guard·room (gärd′rōōm′, gärd′room′) *n.* a room used by people on military guard duty.

guards·man (gärdz′mən) *n. pl.,* **guards·men** (gärdz′-mən). **1.** a man who serves as a guard. **2.** a soldier in the National Guard. **3.** a soldier in a guards regiment of the British army.

Gua·te·ma·la (gwä′tə mä′lə) *n.* **1.** the northernmost country of Central America. Capital, Guatemala City. Area, 42,042 sq. mi. Pop. (1980), 7,260,000. **2.** Guatemala City. —**Gua′te·ma′lan**, *adj., n.*

Guatemala City, the capital and principal city of Guatemala, in the southern part of the country. It is the largest city in Central America. Pop. (1973), 700,504.

gua·va (gwä′və) *n.* **1.** a round or pear-shaped fruit, having a sweet, firm flesh, that is used for making jellies and other sweets. **2.** the tree or shrub bearing this fruit, grown in tropical America, having large oval leaves and white flowers.

Guay·a·quil (gwī'ə kēl') *n.* the largest city and chief port of Ecuador, in the western part of the country. Pop. (1970 est.), 794,300.

gu·ber·na·to·ri·al (gōō'bər nə tôr'ē əl) *adj.* of or relating to a governor or the office of governor: *a gubernatorial election.*

gudg·eon (guj'ən) *n.* **1.** a freshwater fish of Europe, easily caught and often used for bait. **2.** any of various similar fish, as the minnow.

Guern·sey (gurn'zē) *n. pl.*, **Guern·seys. 1.** a British island in the English Channel. **2.** any of a breed of dairy cattle originally developed in the Channel Islands, typically having a reddish or tan coat with white markings.

guer·ril·la (gə ril'ə) *also,* **gue·ril·la.** *n.* a member of a band of fighters, usually not part of a regular army, who combat the enemy with such acts as sabotage, ambushes, and sudden raids. —*adj.* of, relating to, or involving guerrillas: *guerrilla warfare.*

guess (ges) *v.t.* **1.** to form an opinion or estimate of (something) without complete or certain knowledge or evidence: *Without a clock he could only guess what time it was.* **2.** to judge (something) correctly by doing this: *She managed to guess the answer to the teacher's question.* **3.** to think; believe; suppose: *I guess he forgot about the meeting.* —*v.i.* to make a guess: *We guessed at her age.* —*n. pl.,* **guess·es.** an opinion, estimate, or conclusion formed by guessing: *My guess is that Peterson will win the election.* —**guess'er,** *n.*

guess·work (ges'wurk') *n.* the process or result of guessing: *He arrived at the answer by guesswork.*

guest (gest) *n.* **1.** a person who is received and entertained by another, as for a party, meal, or visit. **2.** a person who pays for lodgings, food, and other services, as at a hotel, boarding house, or restaurant.

guf·faw (gu fô') *n.* a loud, hearty burst of laughter. —*v.i.* to laugh loudly and heartily: *He guffawed when I fell into the swimming pool.*

Gui·a·na (gē ä'nə, gē an'ə) *n.* a region in northeastern South America, on the Atlantic Ocean, including Guyana, French Guiana, Surinam, and parts of Venezuela and Brazil.

guid·ance (gīd'əns) *n.* **1.** the act or process of guiding; leadership; direction: *She wrote a term paper under her teacher's guidance.* **2.** something that guides. **3.** counseling and advice dealing with educational and career plans and personal problems, especially that given to pupils by school services. **4.** a device or other means by which a missile can be guided while in flight.

guide (gīd) *n.* **1.** a person who shows the way or directs, especially someone employed to lead or conduct tours, hunting trips, or other outings. **2.** a person or thing that directs conduct or a course of action: *Let your conscience be your guide.* **3.** see **guidebook. 4.** a book explaining or outlining the basic elements of some subject: *a guide to medieval literature.* **5.** a part of a machine serving to steady or direct motion. —*v.t.,* **guid·ed, guid·ing. 1.** to show the way to; lead; conduct: *The scout guided the hunters through the forest.* **2.** to direct the course or motion of: *The driver guided the truck around the curves in the road.* **3.** to lead or direct the actions, affairs, or motives of; regulate: *He always lets his common sense guide him.*

guide·book (gīd'book') *n.* a book of directions and information for travelers and tourists.

guided missile, a missile that is guided during its flight by electronic signals or other means.

guide·post (gīd'pōst') *n.* a post at a roadside or intersection bearing a sign giving directions for travelers.

guide word, one of the two or more words appearing at the top of a page or set of pages in a dictionary or other reference book, used to show what the first and last entries on a page are. The guide words on this page are **Guayaquil** and **guinea fowl.**

guild (gild) *also,* **gild.** *n.* **1.** in the Middle Ages, a group of merchants or artisans in one trade or craft, organized to maintain standards of work and to protect the interests of members. **2.** any organization of persons with similar interests or aims: *an actors' guild.*

guil·der (gil'dər) *n.* **1.** the basic unit of money in the Netherlands. **2.** any of several coins formerly used in the Netherlands, Germany, and Austria. Also, **gulden.**

guild·hall (gild'hôl') *n.* a hall in which a guild meets.

guile (gīl) *n.* cunning; deceit; slyness.

guile·ful (gīl'fəl) *adj.* full of guile; cunning; deceitful.

guile·less (gīl'lis) *adj.* without guile; sincere; honest.

guil·lo·tine (*n.,* gil'ə tēn'; *v.,* gil'ə tēn') *n.* a machine consisting of a heavy blade that falls between two grooved posts, used for beheading people. It was widely used to execute people in France during the French Revolution. —*v.t.,* **guil·lo·tined, guil·lo·tin·ing.** to behead by the guillotine. [French *guillotine,* from Joseph I. *Guillotin,* 1738–1814, a French doctor who urged its use as a swift and relatively painless method of execution.]

Guillotine

guilt (gilt) *n.* **1.** the state or fact of having done wrong, especially of having committed a crime: *The new evidence definitely proved the man's guilt.* **2.** a feeling of regret, shame, or of being to blame for having done wrong: *He felt overwhelmed by guilt after he ignored the old man's request.* —**guilt'less,** *adj.*

guilt·y (gil'tē) *adj.,* **guilt·i·er, guilt·i·est. 1.** having done wrong; deserving of blame or punishment: *We are all guilty of losing our temper sometimes.* **2.** convicted of a crime: *The jury found him guilty of arson.* **3.** feeling or showing guilt or a sense of guilt: *a guilty conscience, a guilty look.* —**guilt'i·ly,** *adv.*

guin·ea (gin'ē) *n.* **1.** a former English gold coin last minted in 1813, fixed in value at twenty-one shillings. **2.** in England, a sum of money equal to twenty-one shillings.

Guin·ea (gin'ē) *n.* **1.** a country in western Africa, on the Atlantic Ocean, formerly known as **French Guinea.** Capital, Conakry. Area, 94,925 sq. mi. Pop. (1978 est.), 5,900,000. **2. Gulf of.** a very large bay of the Atlantic Ocean, on the west coast of Africa.

Guinea fowl

Guinea Bis·sau (bi sou') a country in western Africa. Area, 13,944 sq. mi. Pop. (1978 est.), 550,000.

guinea fowl, a fowl similar to the pheasant and native to Africa, having dark-gray feathers speckled with white. They are widely domesticated and raised for food.

at; āpe; cär; end; mē; it; īce; hot; ōld; fôrk; wood; fōōl; oil; out; up; turn; sing; thin; this; hw in white; zh in treasure. The symbol ə stands for the sound of **a** in about, **e** in taken, **i** in pencil, **o** in lemon, and **u** in circus.

G

guinea hen **1.** a female guinea fowl. **2.** a guinea fowl.
guinea pig **1.** a small, plump animal having a large head, small rounded ears, and a long or short coat that may be solid or spotted or streaked with different colors. It is widely used in experiments for biological and medical research and is often kept as a pet. **2.** any person or thing used in experimentation: *I'm always my sister's guinea pig when she cooks a new dish.*

Guinea pig

Guin·e·vere (gwin′ə vēr′) *n.* the beautiful wife of King Arthur. She was loved by Lancelot, a knight of the Round Table.
guise (gīz) *n.* **1.** an outward appearance; semblance: *The mayor presented an old approach to the problem of unemployment in a new guise.* **2.** an assumed or false appearance; pretense: *Under the guise of friendship, he betrayed all the people who had trusted him.* **3.** *Archaic.* a style or manner of dress.
gui·tar (gi tär′) *n.* a musical instrument having a long neck, six or more strings, and a body shaped somewhat like a violin. It is played by plucking or strumming the strings with the fingers or a plectrum.

Guitar

gulch (gulch) *n. pl.,* **gulch·es.** a deep, narrow ravine with steep sides, especially one marking the course of a stream or torrent.
gul·den (gool′dən) *n. pl.,* **gulden** or **gul·dens.** another word for **guilder.**
gulf (gulf) *n.* **1.** a body of water forming an indentation in the shoreline of an ocean or sea, usually larger and deeper than a bay. **2.** a deep hollow in the earth; chasm. **3.** any wide separation: *There is a great gulf between the rich and the poor in that country.*
Gulf States, the five Southern states bordering the Gulf of Mexico: Florida, Alabama, Mississippi, Louisiana, and Texas.
Gulf Stream, a warm ocean current flowing from the Gulf of Mexico across the North Atlantic Ocean, along the eastern coast of North America to the northern coast of Europe. It is the world's largest warm ocean current system.
gull¹ (gul) *n.* any of several long-winged birds found on most seacoasts and near large bodies of water, having webbed feet, a thick, slightly hooked beak, and usually gray and white feathers with black wing tips. Also, **sea gull.** [Of Celtic origin.]
gull² (gul) *v.t.* to trick; cheat; dupe: *Swindlers gulled him into giving them money.* —*n.* a person who is easily tricked or cheated; dupe. [Of uncertain origin.]
gul·let (gul′it) *n.* **1.** the tube or passage through which food passes from the mouth to the stomach; esophagus. **2.** the throat.

Gull¹

gul·li·ble (gul′ə bəl) *adj.* believing or trusting in almost anything; easily tricked, cheated, or duped: *You would have to be very gullible to believe such a silly story.* —**gul′·li·bil′i·ty,** *n.* —**gul′li·bly,** *adv.*
gul·ly (gul′ē) *n. pl.,* **gul·lies.** a ditch or channel cut in the earth by running water; small ravine: *After the rain storm there were deep gullies along the sides of the road.*

gulp (gulp) *v.t.* to swallow hastily, greedily, or in large amounts: *Eddie gulped his sandwich and ran out to catch the bus.* —*v.i.* to draw in or swallow air, as in surprise or fear. —*n.* **1.** the act of gulping: *to drink a glass of milk in two gulps.* **2.** the amount swallowed at one time; mouthful.
gum¹ (gum) *n.* **1.** a thick sticky juice produced by various plants and trees, that dissolves or softens in cold water and hardens when exposed to air or heat. **2.** any similar plant or tree substance, such as resin. **3.** a preparation made from such substances, used in manufacturing textiles, adhesives, dyes, and paints. **4.** see **chewing gum. 5.** a glue or other substance used to make paper stick to something else: *There is no gum on the back of this stamp.* **6.** see **gum tree.** —*v.,* **gummed, gum·ming.** —*v.t.* to coat, clog, stiffen, or glue with gum or a gummy substance: *The machine gummed the back of the stamps.* —*v.i.* to become coated, clogged, stiffened, or glued with gum or a gummy substance. [Old French *gomme.*]
gum² (gum) *also,* **gums.** *n.* the tough fleshy tissue surrounding the teeth. [Old English *gōma* the roof of the mouth.]
gum arabic, a gum obtained from any of several trees, used chiefly in the manufacture of candies, adhesives, inks, textiles, and medicines. Also, **acacia.**
gum·bo (gum′bō) *n. pl.,* **gum·bos. 1.** the okra plant and its pods. **2.** a soup thickened with okra pods and usually containing other vegetables and meat or fish. **3.** a fine soil that becomes very sticky when wet.
gum·drop (gum′drop′) *n.* a small, jellylike piece of candy made of gum arabic or gelatin that is sweetened and usually coated with sugar.
gum·my (gum′ē) *adj.,* **gum·mi·er, gum·mi·est. 1.** of, containing, or resembling gum; sticky. **2.** covered or clogged with gum or something sticky. —**gum′mi·ness,** *n.*
gump·tion (gump′shən) *n. Informal.* determined courage and energy; initiative; nerve: *It took a lot of gumption to stand up to that bully.*
gum resin, a mixture of gum and resin, usually obtained by cutting the outer covering of certain plants.
gum tree, any tree that produces gum, such as certain eucalyptus trees.
gun (gun) *n.* **1.** any of various weapons, such as a pistol, rifle, or cannon, made up of a metal tube through which a bullet or other projectile is shot by the force of an explosive. **2.** any device resembling a gun in shape or use: *a dart gun, a spray gun.* **3.** the firing of a gun as a signal or salute. —*v.,* **gunned, gun·ning.** —*v.t.* **1.** *Informal.* to shoot (a person or animal) with a gun (often with *down*). **2.** *Informal.* to open the throttle of so as to increase the speed: *The driver gunned the engine.* —*v.i.* to shoot or hunt with a gun.
　to stick to one's guns. to be firm in spite of opposition; refuse to retreat or yield.
gun·boat (gun′bōt′) *n.* a small, armed ship used for patrolling rivers and coastal waters.
gun·cot·ton (gun′kot′ən) *n.* an explosive made by treating cotton with a mixture of concentrated nitric and sulfuric acids.
gun·fire (gun′fīr′) *n.* the shooting of a gun or guns.
gung ho (gung′ hō′) *Slang.* very enthusiastic; eager.
gun·lock (gun′lok′) *n.* the part of the mechanism in certain guns by which the charge is exploded.
gun·man (gun′mən) *n. pl.,* **gun·men** (gun′mən). a man armed with a gun, especially a criminal: *Three gunmen robbed the bank.*
gun metal **1.** any of various metallic alloys with a grayish color, used for making such items as chains, buckles, and other trinkets. **2.** a kind of bronze formerly used for

making guns. **3.** a dark-gray color with a bluish tinge. —**gun′-met′al,** *adj.*

gun·nel (gun′əl) another spelling of **gunwale.**

gun·ner (gun′ər) *n.* **1.** a soldier or other member of the armed forces who operates or helps to operate guns or artillery. **2.** a naval warrant officer in charge of guns or artillery. **3.** a person who hunts with a gun.

gun·ner·y (gun′ər ē) *n.* the use and firing of guns.

gun·ny (gun′ē) *n. pl.,* **gun·nies.** a strong, coarse fabric made of jute or hemp, used especially for making sacks or bags.

gun·ny·sack (gun′ē sak′) *n.* a sack or bag made of gunny or other coarse material.

gun·point (gun′point′) *n.* the end of a gun barrel.
  at gunpoint. under threat of being shot: *He was held up at gunpoint.*

gun·pow·der (gun′pou′dər) *n.* an explosive made up of charcoal, sulfur, and potassium nitrate, used especially in bullets, artillery shells, fireworks, and blasting.

gun·shot (gun′shot′) *n.* **1.** a bullet or other shot fired from a gun. **2.** the distance within which a gun will shoot accurately; range of a gun. **3.** the firing of a gun: *We could hear gunshots in the distance.*

gun·smith (gun′smith′) *n.* a person who makes or repairs firearms.

gun·stock (gun′stok′) *n.* a wooden support or handle to which the barrel of a gun is attached.

gun·wale (gun′əl) *also,* **gun·nel.** *n.* the upper edge of the side of a ship or boat.

gup·py (gup′ē) *n. pl.,* **gup·pies.** a small, slender fish native to tropical fresh waters of Trinidad and northern South America, the male of which is brightly colored. It is widely raised in home aquariums. [From R. J. L. *Guppy,* a British clergyman in Trinidad, who gave specimens of the fish to the British Museum.]

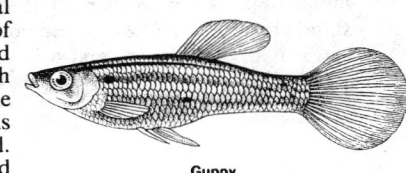

Guppy

gur·gle (gur′gəl) *v.,* **gur·gled, gur·gling.** —*v.i.* **1.** to flow or rush in an irregular current and with a bubbling sound: *The stream gurgled around the rocks.* **2.** to make a similar sound: *The baby cooed and gurgled with delight.* —*v.t.* to utter with a gurgling sound: *The baby gurgled her satisfaction.* —*n.* the act or sound of gurgling.

gu·ru (gōō′rōō, goo rōō′) *n.* **1.** a holy man and religious and spiritual teacher, especially in the Hindu religion. **2.** *Informal.* a respected leader or teacher.

gush (gush) *v.i.* **1.** to flow or rush out suddenly and abundantly: *Water gushed from the broken pipe.* **2.** *Informal.* to speak or write with too much feeling or enthusiasm in a foolish way: *The young poet's work gushed with sentimentality.* —*v.t.* to give forth in a sudden and abundant flow: *The cut gushed blood.* —*n. pl.,* **gush·es.** a sudden rush or outflow: *a gush of water.*

gush·er (gush′ər) *n.* an oil well that gives forth oil abundantly without being pumped.

gush·y (gush′ē) *adj.,* **gush·i·er, gush·i·est.** showing too much feeling or enthusiasm in a foolish way: *a gushy greeting, a gushy person.* —**gush′i·ness,** *n.*

gus·set (gus′it) *n.* **1.** a triangular piece of material inserted into a garment or other article to strengthen or expand some part of it. **2.** a triangular metal brace or bracket that is used to strengthen a corner or angle of a structure.

gust (gust) *n.* **1.** a sudden, strong rush of wind or air.

2. any sudden burst or outflow, as of rain or fire. **3.** an outburst of emotion, as anger or enthusiasm.

gus·ta·to·ry (gus′tə tôr′ē) *adj.* of or relating to the sense of taste.

gus·to (gus′tō) *n.* great enthusiasm or enjoyment: *The boys ate with gusto after returning from their hike.*

gust·y (gus′tē) *adj.,* **gust·i·er, gust·i·est.** characterized by or coming in gusts; windy; blustery: *the gusty weather of March.* —**gust′i·ly,** *adv.* —**gust′i·ness,** *n.*

gut (gut) *n.* **1.** the digestive tract or any part of it, especially the stomach or intestine. **2. guts. a.** *Slang.* courage; pluck: *She had the guts to admit she was wrong. It took guts to play when he was injured.* **b.** entrails; bowels. **3.** see **catgut.** —*v.t.,* **gut·ted, gut·ting. 1.** to remove the entrails of. **2.** to destroy the inside of: *Fire gutted the house.*

Gu·ten·berg, Jo·hann (gōōt′ən bûrg′; yō′hän) 1400?–1468?, German printer, thought to be the inventor of printing from movable type.

gut·ta-per·cha (gut′ə pur′chə) *n.* a pliable, pale-gray material obtained from the milky juice of several evergreen trees found in Malaya and the East Indies. It is used especially in electrical insulation, in dentistry, and as water-proofing.

gut·ter (gut′ər) *n.* **1.** a narrow channel, ditch, or low area along the side of a street or road to carry off surface water. **2.** a trough fixed under or along the eaves of a roof to carry off rain water. **3.** any channel or groove, as at the side of a bowling alley. —*v.t.* to form gutters in or furnish with gutters. —*v.i.* **1.** to flow in streams. **2.** (of a candle) to melt rapidly so that the wax or tallow runs down the sides in channels.

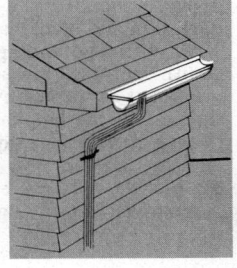

Gutter

gut·tur·al (gut′ər əl) *adj.* **1.** of or relating to the throat. **2.** having a harsh, rasping quality, as a sound produced in the throat: *a fierce, guttural growl.* **3.** pronounced with the back of the tongue raised toward the soft palate. The *g* in *go* is a guttural sound. —*n.* a guttural sound. —**gut′tur·al·ly,** *adv.*

guy¹ (gī) *n.* a rope, chain, wire, or rod used to steady or secure something. —*v.t.,* **guyed, guy·ing.** to steady or secure with a guy. [Old French *guie* guide.]

guy² (gī) *Informal. n.* a man; fellow. —*v.t.,* **guyed, guy·ing.** to make fun of; tease. [From *Guy* Fawkes, 1570–1606, the leader of a plot to blow up the British Parliament in 1605; the original meaning of this word was an effigy of Guy Fawkes displayed and burned on November 5, the anniversary of the plot.]

Guy·an·a (gī an′ə) *n.* a country on the northeastern coast of South America, formerly known as **British Guiana.** Capital, Georgetown. Area, 83,000 sq. mi. Pop. (1980), 884,000.

guz·zle (guz′əl) *v.t., v.i.,* **guz·zled, guz·zling.** to drink (something) greedily or excessively. —**guz′zler,** *n.*

gym (jim) *n.* **1.** see **gymnasium. 2.** a course in physical education in a school or college.

G

at; āpe; cär; end; mē; it; īce; hot; ōld; fôrk; wood; fōōl; oil; out; up; turn; sing; thin; <u>th</u>is; hw in white; zh in treasure. The symbol ə stands for the sound of **a** in about, **e** in taken, **i** in pencil, **o** in lemon, and **u** in circus.

gym·na·si·um (jim nā′zē əm) *n. pl.,* **gym·na·si·ums** or **gym·na·si·a** (jim nā′zē ə). a room or building having equipment for physical exercise or training and for indoor sports.

gym·nast (jim′nast) *n.* a person skilled in gymnastics.

gym·nas·tic (jim nas′tik) *adj.* of or relating to gymnastics.

gym·nas·tics (jim nas′tiks) *n., pl.* **1.** physical exercises designed to develop strength, agility, coordination, and balance. **2.** the art, practice, or sport of such exercises. ▲ used with a singular verb in definition 2.

gym·no·sperm (jim′nə spurm′) *n.* any of a large group of plants whose seeds are not enclosed in ovaries and are generally borne in cones. Gymnosperms include pines, spruces, and junipers.

gy·ne·col·o·gist (gī′nə kol′ə jist, jin′ə kol′ə jist) *n.* a doctor who specializes in gynecology.

gy·ne·col·o·gy (gī′nə kol′ə jē, jin′ə kol′ə jē) *n.* the branch of medicine dealing with the functions and disorders of the female reproductive system.

gyp (jip) *Slang. v.t.,* **gypped, gyp·ping.** to cheat or swindle. —*n.* **1.** a fraud; swindle. **2.** a cheat; swindler.

gyp·sum (jip′səm) *n.* a common mineral used especially in cements, in plaster of Paris, and as a fertilizer.

Gyp·sy (jip′sē) *also,* **Gip·sy.** *n. pl.,* **Gyp·sies. 1.** *also* **gypsy.** a member of a wandering Caucasian people having dark skin and black hair, who left northwestern India over 1000 years ago and appeared in Europe around the fourteenth century. Now scattered throughout the world, they are noted as musicians, fortune tellers, horse traders, and tinkers. **2.** the language spoken by Gypsies; Romany.

gypsy moth *also,* **gipsy moth.** a moth native to Europe and Japan, and now found in the northeastern United States, whose larvae eat the leaves of trees.

gy·rate (jī′rāt) *v.i.,* **gy·rat·ed, gy·rat·ing.** to move in a circle or spiral, especially around an axis or fixed point; whirl; rotate: *The dancing couple gyrated around the room.*

gy·ra·tion (jī rā′shən) *n.* the act of gyrating; circular or spiral motion.

gyr·fal·con (jur′fal′kən, jur′fôl′kən) *also,* **ger·fal·con.** *n.* a powerful falcon living mainly in the Arctic. It is the largest of the falcons.

gy·ro (jī′rō) *n. pl.,* **gy·ros. 1.** see **gyrocompass. 2.** see **gyroscope.**

gy·ro·com·pass (jī′rō kum′pəs, jī′rō kom′pəs) *n. pl.,* **gy·ro·com·pass·es.** a compass that uses a spinning gyroscope to indicate true north rather than magnetic north.

gy·ro·scope (jī′rə skōp′) *n.* a wheel mounted so that the axis on which it spins can point in any direction. When the wheel is spinning, the axis sets itself in a fixed direction and resists changes from that direction. Gyroscopes are used in ships and airplanes as stabilizers, compasses, and automatic pilots.

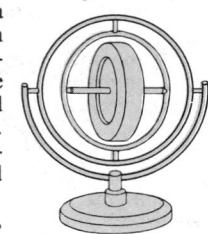

Gyroscope

gyve (jīv) *n.* a fetter or shackle, especially for the leg. —*v.t.,* **gyved, gyv·ing.** to bind with or as if with fetters; shackle: *I will gyve thee in thine own courtship* (Shakespeare, *Othello*).

at; āpe; cär; end; mē; it; īce; hot; ōld; fôrk; wood; fōōl; oil; out; up; turn; sing; thin; this; hw in white; zh in treasure. The symbol ə stands for the sound of **a** in about, **e** in taken, **i** in pencil, **o** in lemon, and **u** in circus.

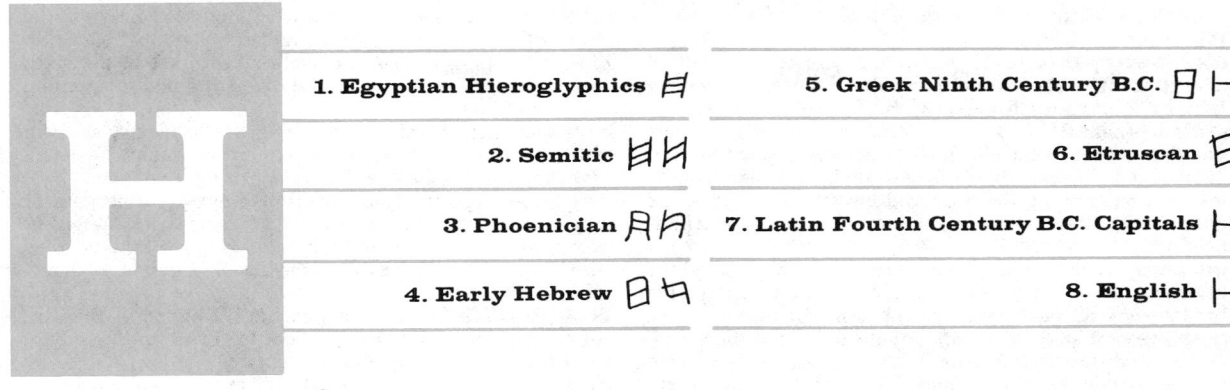

1. Egyptian Hieroglyphics	5. Greek Ninth Century B.C.
2. Semitic	6. Etruscan
3. Phoenician	7. Latin Fourth Century B.C. Capitals
4. Early Hebrew	8. English

H is the eighth letter of the English alphabet. The earliest form of the letter **H** was probably an Egyptian hieroglyphic (1) meaning "fence." This symbol was simplified in the ancient Semitic (2), Phoenician (3), and early Hebrew (4) alphabets, in which it became the letter *cheth,* or *het. Cheth,* which also may have meant "fence," represented an *h* sound made at the back of the throat. When the ancient Greeks borrowed *cheth,* they called it *eta* (5). The early form of *eta* looked very much like a square modern capital letter **B.** Later, the Greeks gave it the modern form of two tall lines connected by a short bar. The Etruscans (6) borrowed the earlier form of *eta,* writing it much as it had been written in the early Hebrew alphabet. Although most of the Latin letters came from the Etruscan alphabet, the Latin letter **H** (7) came directly from the later form of the Greek *eta.* By about 2300 years ago this letter was being written almost exactly the way we write the capital letter **H** today (8).

h, H (āch) *n. pl.,* **h's, H's.** the eighth letter of the English alphabet.

H, the symbol for hydrogen.

H. 1. hour; hours. **2.** height. **3.** hundred.

ha (hä) *interj.* **1.** *also,* **hah.** used to express a sudden feeling, as of surprise, joy, triumph, or scorn. **2.** used to express laughter.

ha·be·as cor·pus (hā′bē əs kôr′pəs) a writ or order to bring a prisoner before a court or judge to determine if he is being held lawfully. [Latin *habeās corpus* you may have the person.]

hab·er·dash·er (hab′ər dash′ər) *n.* a person who sells clothing, especially for men.

hab·er·dash·er·y (hab′ər dash′ər ē) *n. pl.,* **hab·er·dash·er·ies. 1.** the goods sold by a haberdasher. **2.** a haberdasher's shop.

hab·er·geon (hab′ər jən) *n.* **1.** a sleeveless jacket or short coat of mail or scale armor. **2.** another word for **hauberk.**

ha·bil·i·ment (hə bil′ə mənt) *n.* clothing; dress.

hab·it (hab′it) *n.* **1.** an action done so often or for so long a time that one does not think about it and usually cannot stop or control it: *Biting one's nails is a bad habit.* **2.** a customary or usual way of acting: *It is her father's habit to read the paper before dinner. The book's third chapter deals with the eating habits of animals.* **3.** an addiction: *The program helps those with a drug habit.* **4.** a characteristic type of dress: *a nun's habit, a riding habit.* —*v.t.* to dress or clothe (oneself): *The king's messengers habited themselves in blue and gold.*

hab·it·a·ble (hab′ə tə bəl) *adj.* suitable for living in; able to be lived in or on: *The planet Jupiter is not habitable by man.*

hab·i·tant (hab′ə tənt) *n.* an inhabitant; dweller.

hab·i·tat (hab′ə tat′) *n.* **1.** the area or region in which an animal or plant naturally lives or grows: *The desert is the habitat of the cactus.* **2.** a place where a person or thing is most frequently found.

hab·i·ta·tion (hab′ə tā′shən) *n.* **1.** the place where one lives; living quarters. **2.** the act of inhabiting; occupancy: *These slums are not fit for human habitation.*

ha·bit·u·al (hə bich′ōō əl) *adj.* **1.** done by or resulting from habit: *his habitual optimism.* **2.** being or acting in a certain way by habit: *a habitual smoker, a habitual latecomer.* **3.** commonly occurring or used; usual; regular: *a habitual diet.* —**ha·bit′u·al·ly,** *adv.*

ha·bit·u·ate (hə bich′ōō āt′) *v.t.,* **ha·bit·u·at·ed, ha·bit·u·at·ing.** to make used to something; accustom: *Living near a busy highway habituated them to noise.*

ha·bit·u·é (hə bich′ōō ā′) *n.* a person who goes regularly or frequently to a particular place.

ha·ci·en·da (hä′sē en′də) *n.* **1.** a landed estate, country house, ranch, or plantation. **2.** in the southwestern United States and Spanish America, a low, sprawling ranch house with wide porches.

hack¹ (hak) *v.t.* to cut or chop unevenly or crudely with heavy blows, as with a hatchet or cleaver: *Jeff hacked the dead limbs off the tree.* —*v.i.* **1.** to make uneven or crude cuts or chops; deal cutting blows: *The gardener hacked at the branches to trim them off the tree.* **2.** to give short, harsh, repeated coughs. —*n.* **1.** an uneven or crude cut or chop made with a heavy blow. **2.** a short, harsh, repeated cough. [Old English *-haccian* to cut or chop.] —**hack′er,** *n.*

hack² (hak) *n.* **1.** a person who hires himself out to do dull or routine work solely for money. **2.** a carriage for hire; hackney. **3.** an old, worn-out horse. **4.** *Informal.* a taxicab. **5.** a horse kept for hire or for general work.

427

—*v.i. Informal.* to drive a taxicab. —*adj.* **1.** working or done solely for money: *a hack writer, a hack job.* **2.** typical of such a hack or his work; dull or routine: *hack writing.* [Short for *hackney.*]

hack·ber·ry (hak′ber′ē) *n. pl.,* **hack·ber·ries. 1.** any of a large group of shrubs and trees related to the elm, having gray bark and tiny flowers. **2.** the fruit of this tree.

hack·le (hak′əl) *n.* **1.** any of the long, slender feathers on the neck of certain birds, especially the rooster. **2.** an artificial fishing fly made with such feathers. **3. hackles.** the hairs along the neck and back of a dog or other animal that stand up when the animal is angry or frightened.

hack·ney (hak′nē) *n. pl.,* **hack·neys. 1.** a horse used for ordinary or everyday riding or driving. **2.** a carriage for hire. —*adj.* let out, employed, or done for hire.

hack·neyed (hak′nēd) *adj.* made dull or ordinary by being used too often; trite: *"As busy as a bee" is a hackneyed phrase.* [From *hackney* a horse used for everyday riding, because such a horse was often worn out from being overused.]

hack·saw (hak′sô′) *n.* a saw having a narrow, fine-toothed blade held firm in a frame, used especially for cutting metal.

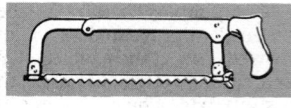
Hacksaw

had (had; *unstressed* həd, əd) the past tense and past participle of **have.** ▲ often used to show what is preferred or necessary. *Had rather* means "would prefer to": *I had rather leave now. Had better* means "ought to": *You had better study if you want to pass the test.*

had·dock (had′ək) *n. pl.,* **had·dock** or **had·docks.** a food fish of the northern Atlantic related to the cod, having five fins and a black line running along each side of the body from the gills to the tail.

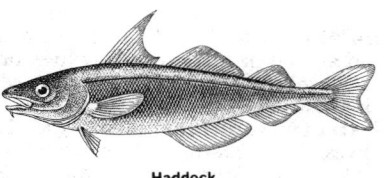
Haddock

Ha·des (hā′dēz) *n.* **1.** *Greek Mythology.* a place where the spirits of the dead dwell; underworld. **2.** the god who ruled the underworld; Pluto. **3. hades.** hell.

had·n't (had′ənt) had not.

Ha·dri·an (hā′drē ən) A.D. 76–138, Roman emperor from 117 to 138.

hadst (hadst) *Archaic.* the second person singular past tense of **have.**

haf·ni·um (haf′nē əm) *n.* a gray metallic element used to control the consumption of nuclear fuel in atomic submarines and nuclear power plants. Symbol: **Hf**

haft (haft) *n.* the handle of a knife, sword, or other tool or weapon.

hag (hag) *n.* **1.** an ugly, often evil or vicious old woman. **2.** a witch. **3.** see **hagfish.**

hag·fish (hag′fish′) *n. pl.,* **hag·fish** or **hag·fish·es.** any of a group of saltwater fish that resemble eels, having a round, sucking mouth surrounded by tentacles. Some hagfish attach themselves by mouth to other fish, bore into their bodies, and feed on their organs, often leaving only skin and bones.

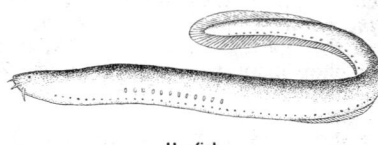
Hagfish

Hag·ga·dah (hə gä′də) *also,* **Hag·ga·da.** *n. pl.,* **Hag·ga·doth** (hə gä′dōt). a book of services for the celebration of the Jewish festival of Passover, including prayers, the story of the Exodus, legends, and songs.

Hag·ga·i (hag′ē ī′) *n.* **1.** Hebrew prophet of the sixth century B.C. **2.** the book of the Old Testament containing his prophecies.

hag·gard (hag′ərd) *adj.* having a worn look, as from fatigue, anxiety, hunger, or suffering; gaunt. —**hag′gard·ly,** *adv.* —**hag′gard·ness,** *n.*

hag·gle (hag′əl) *v.i.,* **hag·gled, hag·gling.** to bargain or argue in a petty way: *She always haggles with the grocer about his prices. The children haggled over who was going to ride the bicycle first.* —*n.* the act of haggling. —**hag′gler,** *n.*

Hague, The (hāg) a city in the Netherlands, the seat of the national government. Pop. (1979 est.), 458,242.

hah (hä) another spelling of **ha.**

ha-ha (hä′hä′) *interj.* used to express amusement or scorn.

Hai·fa (hī′fə) *n.* a port city in northwestern Israel, on the Mediterranean Sea. Pop. (1977 est.), 227,800.

hai·ku (hī′kōō) *n. pl.,* **hai·ku.** a form of Japanese poetry containing seventeen syllables, usually on a subject from nature.

hail¹ (hāl) *v.t.* **1.** to greet by calling or shouting: *He hailed his friend across the street.* **2.** to attract the attention of through motions or calls: *He hailed a taxi.* **3.** to acknowledge with a greeting; salute: *Many people hailed the astronauts.* —*n.* **1.** a greeting. **2.** a motion or call intended to attract attention. —*interj.* used as an expression of acclaim, welcome, or salutation: *Hail to the victor!* [Middle English *hailen.*] —**hail′er,** *n.*

  to hail from. to come from: *He hails from Detroit.*

hail² (hāl) *n.* **1.** small, usually round, pieces of ice that fall in a shower, especially during thunderstorms. **2.** a heavy shower of anything: *The robbers escaped in a hail of bullets.* —*v.i.* to pour down hail: *It hailed for an hour.* —*v.t.* to pour down or shower heavily: *The bully hailed blows upon him.* [Old English *hægl, hagol.*]

Hai·le Se·las·sie (hī′lē sə las′ē) 1892–1975, the emperor of Ethiopia from 1930 to 1936, and from 1941 to 1974.

Hail Mary, another term for **Ave Maria.**

hail·stone (hāl′stōn′) *n.* a pellet of hail.

hail·storm (hāl′stôrm′) *n.* a storm in which hail falls.

Hai·phong (hī′fong′) *n.* a port city in northeastern Vietnam. Pop. (1969), 500,000.

hair (her) *n.* **1.** a fine, threadlike growth on the skin of man and other mammals. **2.** a mass of such growths, as on the head of humans or the bodies of animals. **3.** a fine, threadlike growth on the outer layer of plants. **4.** an extremely small amount or distance; least degree: *The arrow missed the bull's-eye by a hair.* —*adj.* **1.** of or containing hair: *a hair mattress.* **2.** for the hair: *a hair dryer.* —**hair′less,** *adj.* —**hair′like′,** *adj.*

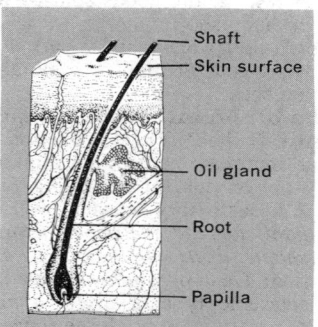
Root of a hair

  to let one's hair down. to relax completely: *He could really let his hair down with his friends.*

  to split hairs. to make very fine or petty distinctions.

hair·breadth (her′bredth′) another spelling of **hair's-breadth.**

hair·brush (her′brush′) *n., pl.* **hair·brush·es.** a brush used for grooming the hair.

hair·cloth (her′klôth′) *n.* a stiff, coarse cloth made of horsehair or camel's hair, used chiefly for upholstering furniture and for stiffening clothing.

hair·cut (her′kut′) *n.* the act of cutting hair, or the style in which it is cut.

hair·do (her′dōō′) *n. pl.,* **hair·dos.** the style in which the hair, especially of a woman, is arranged.

hair·dress·er (her′dres′ər) *n.* a person whose job is to style, cut, and arrange hair, especially women's hair.

hair·line (her′līn′) *n.* 1. the line where hair growth ends on the head, especially around the forehead. 2. a very thin or fine line, as in printing.

hair·piece (her′pēs′) *n.* a quantity of real or artificial hair made into a removable wig, toupee, or fall and worn to cover baldness or as part of a hair style.

hair·pin (her′pin′) *n.* a small, U-shaped pin, usually made of wire, shell, or plastic, used by a woman to keep her hair or hairpiece in place. —*adj.* shaped like a hairpin; U-shaped: *There is a hairpin curve in the road at the top of the mountain.*

hair·rais·ing (her′rā′zing) *adj. Informal.* causing great fear; terrifying.

hair's-breadth (herz′bredth′) *also,* **hairs·breadth, hair·breadth.** *n.* an extremely small space or margin: *to lose by a hair's-breadth.* —*adj.* very narrow or close.

hair·spring (her′spring′) *n.* a fine, coiled spring in a watch or clock that regulates the movement of the balance wheel.

hair trigger, a trigger that can set off a firearm with very slight pressure.

hair·y (her′ē) *adj.,* **hair·i·er, hair·i·est.** 1. covered with hair; having much hair. 2. of or resembling hair. —**hair′·i·ness,** *n.*

Hai·ti (hā′tē) *n.* 1. a country in the Caribbean Sea, on the western part of the island of Hispaniola. Capital, Port-au-Prince. Area, 10,714 sq. mi. Pop. (1980), 5,820,000. 2. see **Hispaniola.**

Hai·tian (hā′shən, hā′tē ən) *n.* 1. a person who was born or is living in Haiti. 2. a dialect of French spoken in Haiti. —*adj.* of or relating to Haiti, its people, or their dialect.

hake (hāk) *n. pl.,* **hake** or **hakes.** a valuable food fish related to the cod, found in cold and temperate seas.

hal·berd (hal′-bərd) *also,* **hal·bert** (hal′bərt) *n.* a weapon in the form of a long spear with a hook-shaped blade at the top, used especially in fifteenth- and sixteenth-century Europe.

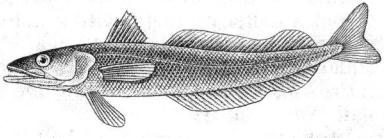
Hake

hal·cy·on (hal′sē ən) *adj.* peaceful and happy: *The old man yearned for the halcyon days of his youth.* —*n.* a mythical bird identified with the kingfisher, that supposedly had the power of calming the winds and sea so that it could build its nest in the water.

hale[1] (hāl) *adj.,* **hal·er, hal·est.** in good physical condition; healthy; robust. ▲ used chiefly in the phrase *hale and hearty.* [Old English *hāl* healthy.]

hale[2] (hāl) *v.t.,* **haled, hal·ing.** 1. to force (someone) to go: *He haled the thief into court.* 2. to drag or pull, especially by force. [Old French *haler.*]

Hale, Na·than (hāl; nā′thən) 1755–1776, U.S. patriot, hanged as a spy by the British.

half (haf) *n. pl.,* **halves.** 1. either of two equal parts into which anything is or may be divided: *A pint is half of a quart. She will be away for a year and a half.* 2. *Sports.* **a.** either of two time periods into which certain games are divided. **b.** an intermission between these two periods, such as in football or basketball. **c.** one of the two divisions of an inning in baseball. **d.** see **halfback.** —*adj.* 1. being one of two equal parts; forming a half: *a half gallon of ice cream.* 2. lacking in some part; incomplete; partial: *a half truth.* —*adv.* not completely; partially: *The theater was half empty.*

in half. into two equal parts.

half·back (haf′bak′) *adj.* an offensive football player whose position is behind the line of scrimmage.

half-baked (haf′bākt′) *adj.* 1. not completely cooked or baked. 2. *Informal.* showing a lack of planning, intelligence, or common sense: *Peter presented only a half-baked plan to the committee.*

half-breed (haf′brēd′) *n.* a person whose parents are of different races, especially the child of one Caucasian and one American Indian parent. ▲ considered offensive.

half brother, a brother related through one parent only.

half-caste (haf′kast′) *n.* a person whose parents are of different races, especially the child of one European and one Asian parent. ▲ considered offensive.

half dollar, a coin of the United States, equal to fifty cents.

half-heart·ed (haf′här′tid) *adj.* lacking interest or enthusiasm: *a half-hearted attempt.* —**half′-heart′ed·ly,** *adv.* —**half′-heart′ed·ness,** *n.*

half hitch, a knot made by passing the end of a rope around itself, then through the loop thus formed, and finally drawing the end tight.

half-hour (haf′our′) *n.* 1. a half of an hour; thirty minutes. 2. a point thirty minutes past a given hour: *The bus runs on the half-hour.* —*adj.* of, lasting for, or occurring at the half-hour: *a half-hour ride.*

half-life (haf′līf′) *n.* the time it takes for any given amount of a radioactive isotope to decay to half that amount. Different radioactive materials decay at different rates.

half-mast (haf′mast′) *n.* the position of a flag about halfway down from the top of a mast, staff, or pole, used especially as a sign of mourning or as a distress signal. Also, **half-staff.**

half·moon (haf′mōōn′) *n.* 1. the moon when only half of its disk appears bright. 2. anything in the shape of a half moon.

half note, a musical note that is sounded for one half as long a time as a whole note.

half·pen·ny (hā′pə nē, hāp′nē) *n. pl.,* **half·pence** (hā′pəns) or **half·pen·nies.** a coin of Great Britain equal to half a penny.

half sister, a sister related through one parent only.

half-staff (haf′staf′) *n.* another word for **half-mast.**

half step *Music.* the difference in pitch between any two keys next to each other on a keyboard instrument. Also, **half tone, semitone.**

half-tone (haf′tōn′) *n.* in art or photography, any tone between a high light and a deep shadow.

H

at; āpe; cär; end; mē; it; īce; hot; ōld; fôrk; wood; fōol; oil; out; up; turn; sing; thin; this; hw in white; zh in treasure. The symbol ə stands for the sound of a in about, e in taken, i in pencil, o in lemon, and u in circus.

half tone, another term for **half step.**

half-track (haf′trak′) *also,* **half·track.** *n.* an armored military vehicle having wheels in front and tracks like those on a tractor in the rear.

half·way (haf′wā′) *adv.* **1.** at or to the midway point; half the distance: *to climb halfway up a mountain.* **2.** not completely; partially: *The movie is halfway over.* —*adj.* **1.** midway between two points: *As the racers reached the halfway mark, Jack was out in front.* **2.** incomplete; partial: *Halfway measures will not solve the problem.*

half-wit (haf′wit′) *n.* **1.** a feeble-minded person. **2.** a foolish or stupid person. —**half′wit·ted,** *adj.*

hal·i·but (hal′ə bət) *n. pl.,* **hal·i·but** or **hal·i·buts.** a large flatfish found in northern waters of the Atlantic and Pacific Oceans and highly valued as a source of food and vitamin oil. Halibuts often weigh up to several hundred pounds.

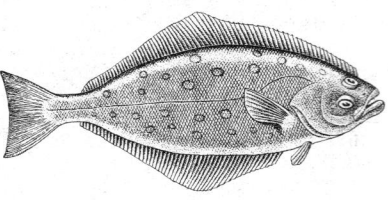

Halibut

Hal·i·car·nas·sus (hal′ə kär nas′əs) *n.* an ancient city in southwestern Asia Minor, site of the famous mausoleum that was one of the Seven Wonders of the World.

Hal·i·fax (hal′ə faks′) *n.* a port city in southeastern Canada and the capital of Nova Scotia. Pop. (1971), 121,086.

hal·ite (hal′īt, hā′līt) *n.* another word for **rock salt.**

hal·i·to·sis (hal′ə tō′sis) *n.* a condition in which the breath has a bad odor.

hall (hôl) *n.* **1.** a passageway onto which rooms open in a house or building; corridor. **2.** a passageway or room at the entrance to a building; vestibule or lobby. **3.** a room or building in which public meetings, entertainment, or lectures are held: *a concert hall.* **4.** a room or building in a school, college, or university set aside for a particular purpose: *a dining hall.*

Hal·le (hä′lə) *n.* a city in west-central East Germany. Pop. (1977 est.), 231,480.

hal·le·lu·jah (hal′ə loo′yə) *also,* **hal·le·lu·iah, al·le·lu·ia.** *interj.* praise ye the Lord. ▲ used to express praise or joy, as in prayers and hymns. —*n.* a hymn or other musical composition based on the word *hallelujah.*

Hal·ley′s comet (hal′ēz) a comet that can be seen from the earth every seventy-six years. It was last seen in 1910. [From Edmund *Halley,* 1656–1742, an English astronomer who studied this comet and predicted when it could be seen from the earth.]

hall·mark (hôl′märk′) *n.* **1.** an official symbol stamped on gold and silver items to guarantee their high quality or purity. **2.** any mark that indicates high quality, purity, or genuineness. **3.** a distinguishing quality or characteristic: *Suspense is a hallmark of a good mystery.* —*v.t.* to stamp with a hallmark. [From the *mark* showing quality or purity that was stamped on gold or silver articles in the Goldsmiths' *Hall,* the center of the guild of goldsmiths, in London.]

hal·loa (hə lō′) another spelling of **halloo.**

hall of fame, a room or building containing tablets, busts, or other items honoring famous or outstanding people: *the baseball hall of fame.*

hal·loo (hə loo′) *also,* **hal·loa.** *interj.* used to attract attention or to urge on hounds in fox hunting. —*n. pl.,* **hal·loos.** a call or cry of *halloo.* —*v.i.,* **hal·looed, hal·loo·ing.** **1.** to call or shout, especially to attract attention. **2.** to urge on hounds with cries of *halloo.*

hal·low (hal′ō) *v.t.* to make sacred or holy; sanctify: *The church officials hallowed the ground for burial.*

hal·lowed (hal′ōd) *adj.* **1.** made holy; sanctified. **2.** regarded as sacred or holy. —**hal′lowed·ness,** *n.*

Hal·low·een (hal′ə wēn′, hal′ō ēn′) *also,* **Hal·low·e'en.** *n.* the eve of All Saints' Day, now celebrated especially by children in costumes and masks. It falls on October 31.

Hal·low·mas (hal′ō məs) *n.* another word for **All Saints' Day.**

hal·lu·ci·nate (hə loo′sə nāt′) *v.i.,* **hal·lu·ci·nat·ed, hal·lu·ci·nat·ing.** to have hallucinations.

hal·lu·ci·na·tion (hə loo′sə nā′shən) *n.* **1.** the experience of seeing or hearing something that is not really there. **2.** something seen or heard in such an experience: *The voices he heard were actually hallucinations.*

hal·lu·ci·na·to·ry (hə loo′sə nə tôr′ē) *adj.* of, relating to, or causing hallucinations; hallucinogenic.

hal·lu·cin·o·gen (hə loo′si nə jen′) *n.* any of several drugs that cause hallucinations, such as LSD.

hal·lu·cin·o·gen·ic (hə loo′si nə jen′ik) *adj.* of, relating to, or causing hallucinations; *a hallucinogenic drug.*

hall·way (hôl′wā′) *n.* **1.** a passageway in a house or building; corridor. **2.** an entrance hall; foyer.

ha·lo (hā′lō) *n. pl.,* **ha·los** or **ha·loes.** **1.** in art, a ring or disk of light surrounding the head of a saint, angel, or other sacred figure. **2.** a circle of light that appears to surround the sun, moon, or another heavenly body, caused by the reflection and refraction of light by ice crystals in the earth's upper atmosphere.

hal·o·gen (hal′ə jən) *n.* any of the five very active elements that combine readily with metals to form salts. They are fluorine, chlorine, iodine, bromine, and astatine.

halt[1] (hôlt) *n.* a temporary stop in movement or activity: *Production at the factory came to a halt because of the strike.* —*v.t.* to cause to stop: *The captain halted his horse.* —*v.i.* to come to a stop: *The parade halted in front of the mayor's reviewing stand.* [German *Halt.*]

halt[2] (hôlt) *v.i.* **1.** to hesitate or be in doubt; waver; falter: *Her voice halted as she tried to hold back her tears.* **2.** *Archaic.* to be lame; limp. —*adj. Archaic.* unable to walk without limping; lame. [Old English *haltian, healtian* to be lame.] —**halt′ing,** *adj.* —**halt′ing·ly,** *adv.*

hal·ter (hôl′tər) *n.* **1.** a rope or strap used for leading or tying an animal, usually designed to fit around the animal's nose and over or behind its ears. **2.** a garment resembling a blouse, worn by women and girls, that usually fastens behind the neck, leaving the arms and back bare. —*v.t.* to put a halter on or tie with a halter: *to halter a horse.*

halve (hav) *v.t.,* **halved, halv·ing.** **1.** to divide into two equal parts: *to halve an apple.* **2.** to share equally: *Bill halved his food with me during the hike.* **3.** to lessen by half: *Susan halved the recipe.*

halves (havz) the plural of **half.**

hal·yard (hal′yərd) *n. Nautical.* a rope or tackle used for hoisting or lowering something, such as a sail, yard, or flag.

ham (ham) *n.* **1.** the meat from the hind leg or shoulder of a hog, usually cured and smoked. **2.** the hind leg of an animal, especially a hog. **3. hams.** the back part of the thighs and buttocks. **4.** *Informal.* an actor who performs in a showy or exaggerated way. **5.** *Informal.* an amateur radio operator. —*v.i.,* **hammed, ham·ming.** *Informal.* (of an actor) to act in a showy or exaggerated way.

Ham (ham) *n.* in the Old Testament, the second son of Noah, thought to be the ancestor of the African races.

Ham·burg (ham′burg′) *n.* a port city in northern West Germany, on the Elbe River. Pop. (1977 est.), 1,680,300.

ham·burg·er (ham′bur′gər) *n.* **1.** ground beef: *The recipe calls for half a pound of hamburger.* **2.** a round patty of such meat, broiled or fried and often served as a sandwich on a bun or roll. Also, **ham·burg** (ham′burg′). [Short for *Hamburger steak,* from *Hamburg,* Germany.]

Ham·il·ton (ham′əl tən) *n.* **1. Alexander.** 1757–1804, U.S. statesman and first Secretary of the Treasury. **2.** a port city in southeastern Ontario, Canada, at the western end of Lake Ontario. Pop. (1971), 307,473. **3.** the capital of Bermuda. Pop. (1970), 2127.

ham·let (ham′lit) *n.* a cluster of houses in the country; small village.

Ham·let (ham′lit) *n.* the central character in William Shakespeare's play *Hamlet,* a prince of Denmark who avenges his father's murder.

Ham·mar·skjöld, Dag (ham′ər shöld′; däg) 1905–1961, Swedish statesman, Secretary General of the United Nations from 1953 to 1961.

ham·mer (ham′ər) *n.* **1.** a tool with a solid head of metal or other material set crosswise on a handle, usually used for driving nails and beating or shaping metal. **2.** anything resembling such a tool in shape or function, such as the lever that strikes a bell in a clock or a small gavel used by an auctioneer. **3.** the part of a gun that strikes the firing pin, causing the gun to go off. **4.** the largest and outermost of the three small bones in the middle ear, shaped like a hammer; malleus. **5.** a metal ball attached to a wire, thrown for distance in athletic contests. —*v.t.* **1.** to strike again and again with or as if with a hammer; drive; pound: *to hammer nails into a board, to hammer a wall with one's fist.* **2.** to pound into shape or form with a hammer: *to hammer a bowl out of metal.* **3.** to force by repetition: *They could not hammer any sense into him.* —*v.i.* to strike blows again and again with or as if with a hammer: *The angry man hammered at the door with his fists.* —**ham′mer·er,** *n.*

ham·mer·head (ham′ər hed′) *n.* a shark whose head extends on each side in a broad, flat lobe, resembling a double-headed hammer.

Hammerhead

hammer lock, a wrestling hold in which an opponent's arm is twisted and held up tightly in a right-angle position behind his back.

ham·mock (ham′ək) *n.* a swinging bed made from a long piece of canvas, leather, or netting hung between two supports, such as trees or poles.

Ham·mond (ham′ənd) *n.* a city in northwestern Indiana. Pop. (1970), 107,790.

Ham·mu·ra·bi (hä′moo rä′bē) Babylonian king of the eighteenth century B.C., noted for the code of laws he issued to his people.

ham·per[1] (ham′pər) *v.t.* to interfere with the action or progress of: *Stalled cars hampered efforts to remove the snow.* [Of uncertain origin.]

ham·per[2] (ham′pər) *n.* a large basket or other container, usually with a cover: *a picnic hamper, a hamper for soiled clothes.* [Earlier *hanaper,* from Old French *hanapier* a case that holds cups.]

Hamp·ton (hamp′tən) *n.* a city in southeastern Virginia. Pop. (1970), 120,779.

Hampton Roads, a channel of the Chesapeake Bay in southeastern Virginia, site of the battle in 1862 between the iron-clad warships the *Monitor* and the *Merrimac.*

ham·ster (ham′stər) *n.* a rodent that resembles a mouse, having a stout body, stumpy tail, and large cheek pouches.

ham·string (ham′string′) *n.* **1.** in man, the tendon at the back of the knee. **2.** in animals with four legs, the great tendon at the back of the hock. —*v.t.,* **ham·strung** (ham′strung′), **ham·string·ing. 1.** to cripple (a person or animal) by cutting the hamstring. **2.** to destroy the efficiency or power of; make ineffective: *The project was hamstrung by a lack of funds.*

Han·cock, John (han′kok′) 1737–1793, U.S. patriot and statesman, the first signer of the Declaration of Independence.

hand (hand) *n.* **1.** the end part of the arm from the wrist down, consisting of the palms, fingers, and thumb. **2.** anything resembling a hand in shape or function, such as the pointers on a clock. **3.** *also,* **hands.** personal possession or control: *He took the law into his own hands.* **4.** a direction in relation to one of the hands; side: *She was at his left hand.* **5.** a workman who does manual labor; laborer: *the hands on a farm.* **6.** a member of a group or crew: *All hands were ordered on deck.* **7.** a way of doing something: *Russell has a deft hand at juggling.* **8.** an active part or influence in something; share; role: *Each club member had a hand in the final decision.* **9.** help; assistance: *He gave me a hand in moving the piano.* **10.** a round of applause; clapping: *The audience gave the singer a big hand.* **11.a.** a single round of a card game: *We have time to play another hand.* **b.** the cards held by a player during a round. **c.** the players in a card game: *We need one more hand to play.* **12.** handwriting style; penmanship. **13.** a promise or pledge of marriage: *He asked her father for her hand.* **14.** a unit of measure equal to four inches, used in expressing the height of a horse: *The mare stands sixteen hands high.* —*v.t.* **1.** to give or pass with the hand: *He handed the book to the librarian.* **2.** to lead or help with the hand. —*adj.* **1.** of, relating to, or for the hand or hands: *hand lotion.* **2.** done or operated by hand: *a hand tool.* **3.** suited to be held in the hand: *a hand mirror.*

at hand. a. nearby or ready for use. **b.** near in time; close.

at the hand of or **at the hands of.** by the action of: *The captured troops suffered at the hands of the enemy.*

by hand. with the hands, rather than with machinery: *to wash clothes by hand.*

from hand to hand. from one person to another.

from hand to mouth. without considering or providing for the future.

hand and foot. a. with both hands and feet tied or confined. **b.** totally: *to wait on someone hand and foot.*

hand in hand. a. holding each other's hand: *to walk hand in hand.* **b.** in close association; together: *Good study habits and good grades usually go hand in hand.*

hand over fist. rapidly and in great quantity: *to make money hand over fist.*

hands down. with great ease; without effort: *to win hands down.*

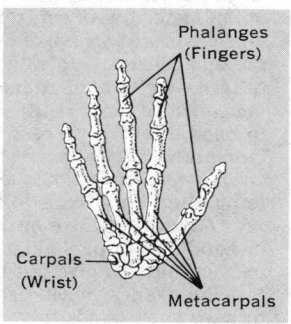

Phalanges (Fingers)

Carpals (Wrist)

Metacarpals

Bones of the hand

at; āpe; cär; end; mē; it; īce; hot; ōld; fôrk; wood; fōōl; oil; out; up; turn; sing; thin; **th**is; hw in white; zh in treasure. The symbol ə stands for the sound of **a** in about, **e** in taken, **i** in pencil, **o** in lemon, and **u** in circus.

in hand. a. in one's possession. **b.** under one's control: *The police had the mob well in hand.*

off one's hands. out of one's control or responsibility: *The salesman offered to take the car off our hands.*

on hand. a. readily available for use: *to have cash on hand.* **b.** present: *A large crowd was on hand for the speech.*

on one hand or **on the one hand.** from one side or viewpoint.

on one's hands. in one's possession or control.

on the other hand. from another side or viewpoint.

out of hand. out of control: *Things got out of hand at the rally and a fight broke out.*

the upper hand. superior position; advantage.

to force one's hand. to make someone act before he had intended to act.

to hand down. a. to pass along, as from one generation to another. **b.** to make and announce (a decision): *The Supreme Court handed down a decision on the new law.*

to hand in. to give, as to someone in authority; deliver: *He handed in his resignation.*

to hand on. to pass along; hand down.

to hand out. to give out to people; distribute.

to hand over. to yield or give up to another.

to have one's hands full. to be busy with as much as or more than one can do: *The mother has her hands full with five small children.*

to lay one's hand on. a. to get possession of; seize. **b.** to injure or harm; attack.

to tie one's hands. to hinder one's efforts; prevent one from acting.

to try one's hand at. to make an attempt at (doing something): *She tried her hand at acting.*

to turn one's hand to. to begin to work at: *He turned his hand to writing novels when he was past forty.*

to wash one's hands of. to refuse to associate with or be responsible for any longer.

hand·bag (hand′bag′) *n.* **1.** a bag or case used by women for carrying small articles, such as cosmetics and a wallet; pocketbook. **2.** a small suitcase.

hand·ball (hand′bôl′) *n.* **1.** a game in which the players take turns hitting a small rubber ball against a wall with the hand. **2.** the ball used in this game.

hand·bar·row (hand′bar′ō) *n.* a flat, rectangular frame having handles at each end, used for lifting and carrying loads.

hand·bill (hand′bil′) *n.* a printed announcement or advertisement, intended to be given out to people by hand.

hand·book (hand′book′) *n.* a book containing basic information or instructions on a particular subject.

hand·cart (hand′kärt′) *n.* a small cart moved by hand.

hand·cuff (hand′kuf′) *n.* either of a pair of metal rings joined by a short chain and locked around the wrist of a person to be restrained, such as a prisoner. —*v.t.* to put handcuffs on: *The policemen handcuffed the thief and led him away.*

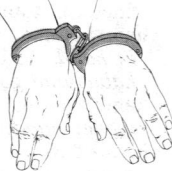
Handcuffs

hand·ed (han′did) *adj.* **1.** characterized by or done with (a specified) hand. ▲ used in combination: *a left-handed pitch.* **2.** characterized by or done with (a specified number of) hands or people. ▲ used in combination: *We played a game of two-handed bridge.*

Han·del, George Frederick (hand′əl) 1685–1759, British composer, born in Germany.

hand·ful (hand′fool′) *n. pl.*, **hand·fuls. 1.** the amount the hand can hold at one time: *He grabbed a handful of peanuts.* **2.** a small number or quantity: *Only a handful of people showed up for the lecture.*

hand grenade, a small explosive device designed to be thrown by hand, set off by a fuse.

hand·gun (hand′gun′) *n.* a firearm that can be held and fired with one hand; pistol; revolver.

hand·i·cap (han′dē kap′) *n.* **1.** a race, contest, or game in which some contestants are given certain advantages or disadvantages so that all have an equal chance of winning. **2.** an advantage or disadvantage given in such a race, contest, or game. **3.** anything that places a person at a disadvantage and hampers his achievement: *Being short can be a handicap in playing basketball.* —*v.t.,* **hand·i·capped, hand·i·cap·ping. 1.** to place at a disadvantage; hamper: *His poor eyesight handicaps him in his work.* **2.** (in a contest) to give one or more handicaps to: *to handicap an opponent.* —**hand′i·cap′per,** *n.*

hand·i·capped (han′dē kapt′) *adj.* having a handicap; disabled: *a handicapped person.* —*n.* handicapped persons considered as a group.

hand·i·craft (han′dē kraft′) *n.* **1.** a trade, occupation, or art in which great skill with the hands is required, such as weaving or pottery. **2.** skill in working with the hands. **3.** an object made or work done by a skilled hand.

hand·i·work (han′dē wurk′) *n.* **1.** work done by hand: *My grandmother did embroidered handiwork for years.* **2.** the product of one's work or action: *Her hurt feelings are the handiwork of his thoughtless remarks.*

hand·ker·chief (hang′kər chif′) *n.* **1.** a soft piece of cloth, usually square, used especially to wipe the nose or brow or worn as an ornament. **2.** a larger piece of cloth worn around the head or neck; kerchief.

han·dle (hand′əl) *n.* the part of an object that is made to be grasped by the hand: *to carry a suitcase by the handle.* —*v.,* **han·dled, han·dling.** —*v.t.* **1.** to touch or hold with the hand or hands: *Please do not handle the glassware.* **2.** to work at with the hands: *to handle clay.* **3.** to manage, control, or train: *She knows how to handle dogs.* **4.** to act on or toward; deal or cope with: *to handle a problem.* —*v.i.* to act in a certain way or respond to being handled: *This car handles nicely.* —**han′dler,** *n.*

to fly off the handle. to become very angry suddenly.

han·dle·bar mustache (hand′əl bär′) a thick mustache extending in a prominent curve to either side.

han·dle·bars (hand′əl bärz′) *also,* **han·dle·bar.** *n.* a curved steering bar connected with the front wheel of a bicycle, motorcycle, or similar vehicle, having right and left ends extending toward the rider, often with a grip for the rider to hold.

Handlebar mustache

hand·made (hand′mād′) *adj.* made by hand rather than by machine: *a handmade sweater.*

hand·maid (hand′mād′) *n.* a female servant or personal attendant. Also, **hand·maid·en** (hand′mād′ən).

hand·me·down (hand′mē doun′) *n.* something, especially a piece of clothing, previously owned or used by one person and then given to another person for additional use.

hand organ, a portable musical instrument combining features of an organ and a music box, played by means of a hand crank. Also, **barrel organ.**

hand·out (hand′out′) *n.* **1.** food, clothing, or money given out to a beggar. **2.** a prepared news story or statement released to the press for free publicity. **3.** anything handed out without charge, such as a pamphlet or leaflet.

hand·rail (hand′rāl′) *n.* a railing that may be grasped by the hand, used especially as a guard on stairs or at the edge of a balcony.

hand·saw (hand′sô′) *n.* a saw used with one hand.

hand·shake (hand′shāk′) *n.* the act of clasping and shaking a person's hand as a sign of greeting, friendliness, or agreement: *The two businessmen ended their discussion with a handshake.*

hand·some (han′səm) *adj.,* **hand·som·er, hand·som·est.**
1. having a pleasing, often masculine or dignified appearance; good-looking: *a handsome man, a handsome desk.*
2. considerable in size or quantity; fairly large: *The lawyer was paid a handsome fee for his services.* **3.** characterized by generosity; gracious. **—hand′some·ly,** *adv.* **—hand′-some·ness,** *n.*

hand·spike (hand′spīk′) *n.* a bar used as a lever.

hand·spring (hand′spring′) *n.* a kind of somersault in which a person springs onto both hands and then returns to a standing position.

hand·stand (hand′stand′) *n.* the act of balancing the body in an upright position on the hands.

hand-to-hand (hand′tə hand′) *adj.* in direct contact; at close quarters: *hand-to-hand combat.*

hand-to-mouth (hand′tə mouth′) *adj.* without considering or providing for the future, especially because of a lack of money: *a hand-to-mouth existence.*

hand·work (hand′wurk′) *n.* work done by hand; handiwork.

hand·writ·ing (hand′rī′ting) *n.* **1.** writing done by hand; writing that is not typewritten or printed. **2.** the style or manner of writing; penmanship: *The boy's handwriting was hard to read.*

hand·writ·ten (hand′rit′ən) *adj.* written by hand: *handwritten invitations.*

hand·y (han′dē) *adj.,* **hand·i·er, hand·i·est. 1.** within reach; at hand; nearby: *He always keeps pen and paper handy.* **2.** able to use the hands skillfully: *Mike is very handy with tools.* **3.** convenient or easy to use or handle: *a handy carrying case.* **—hand′i·ly,** *adv.* **—hand′i·ness,** *n.*
to come in handy. to be helpful: *His ability to speak French will come in handy when he travels to Europe this summer.*

Han·dy, W(illiam) C(hristopher) (han′dē) 1873–1958, U.S. blues musician and composer.

hand·y·man (han′dē man′) *n. pl.,* **hand·y·men** (han′dē-men′).** a person who is skilled in doing or working at various small jobs.

hang (hang) *v.,* **hung** or *(v.t. def. 3; v.i. def. 3)* **hanged, hanging. —v.t. 1.** to fasten or attach (an object) from above only, without any support from below: *to hang wet towels on a clothesline.* **2.** to attach (an object) with a hinge, so as to swing or move freely: *to hang a garden gate.* **3.** to suspend (a person) by the neck, as from a gallows, until he is dead. **4.** to bend forward or downward; droop: *He hung his head in shame.* **5.** to furnish, cover, or decorate with anything that is suspended or attached: *to hang a room with tapestries.* **6.** to attach or suspend for decoration or display: *to hang wallpaper, to hang pictures on a wall.* **—v.i. 1.** to be attached to or suspended from something above; dangle: *A wire hung from the ceiling.* **2.** to be fastened so as to swing or move freely. **3.** to die by hanging. **4.** to cling, especially for support; hold fast: *The fisherman hung onto the capsized boat.* **5.** to depend: *The defendant's fate hung on the jury's decision.* **6.** to bend forward or downward; droop: *The tree hangs over the pond.* **7.** to float or be suspended: *Polluted air hung over the city.* **—n. 1.** the way in which something hangs or falls: *the hang of a dress.* **2.** a particular way of doing something; knack: *to get the hang of riding a bicycle.* **3.** a general meaning: *to get the hang of a conversation.*
to hang back. to be reluctant to move forward; hesitate: *The shy girl hung back in the doorway.*

to hang out. a. to lean out of: *The dog hung out the car window.* **b.** *Slang.* to spend much time: *They usually hang out at Bob's house.*

to hang together. a. to keep together; be united: *Those who were opposed to the proposal hung together.* **b.** to be related in a logical or understandable way.

to hang up. a. to suspend from a hanger or peg: *Hang up the coats in the bedroom.* **b.** to end a telephone conversation by replacing the receiver in its cradle. **c.** to hinder the progress of; delay.

han·gar (hang′ər) *n.* a building for sheltering and servicing aircraft.

Hang·chow (hang′chou′) *n.* a port city in eastern China. Pop. (1958 est.), 794,000. Also, **Hang·zhou.**

hang·dog (hang′dôg′) *adj.* having an ashamed, defeated, or cringing manner or appearance.

hang·er (hang′ər) *n.* **1.** a frame or device on which something is hung, especially one that fits under the shoulders of a coat or other garment. **2.** a loop or ring for hanging something, as at the back of the neck of a coat. **3.** a person who hangs something: *a wallpaper hanger.*

hang·er-on (hang′ər ôn′, hang′er on′) *n. pl.,* **hang·ers-on.** someone who clings to a person or group, especially for personal gain.

hang glider 1. a diamond-shaped sail beneath which a person hangs face down in a harness, used for hang gliding. **2.** a person who engages in hang gliding.

hang gliding, the sport of gliding and soaring in the air with a hang glider, launched from a hill or cliff.

hang·ing (hang′ing) *n.* **1.** an execution in which a person is hanged, as from a gallows. **2.** *also,* **hangings.** a drape or other fabric that hangs as a decoration, as from a wall or window. **—adj. 1.** attached to something above: *a hanging lamp.* **2.** leaning over; overhanging: *a hanging balcony.* **3.** placed on a steep slope: *hanging gardens.*

hang·man (hang′mən) *n. pl.,* **hang·men** (hang′mən). a person who hangs criminals condemned to death.

hang·nail (hang′nāl′) *n.* a piece of skin partially torn away and hanging loose at the side or base of a fingernail.

hang·out (hang′out′) *n. Informal.* a place where a person or group spends much time.

hang·o·ver (hang′ō′vər) *n.* **1.** a feeling of being sick that follows drunkenness, marked by nausea or a headache. **2.** something remaining from a past time or condition.

hang-up (hang′up′) *n. Informal.* **1.** an emotional problem or confusion that seemingly cannot be cleared up or removed. **2.** anything that hampers or delays progress.

Hang·zhou (häng′jō′) another spelling of **Hangchow.**

hank (hangk) *n.* **1.** a loop or coil, as of hair. **2.** a length of yarn, thread, or similar material, especially one of yarn containing a specific number of yards. A hank of cotton or silk yarn contains 840 yards; a hank of worsted yarn contains 560 yards.

han·ker (hang′kər) *v.i.* to desire strongly; yearn or crave.

han·ker·ing (hang′kər ing) *n.* a strong desire; yearning.

Han·ni·bal (han′ə bəl) 247?–183? B.C., the general who led Carthage against Rome and invaded Italy by crossing the Alps.

Ha·noi (ha noi′) *n.* the capital of Vietnam, in the northeastern part of the country. Pop. (1969 est.), 1,200,000.

H

at; āpe; cär; end; mē; it; īce; hot; ōld; fôrk; wood; fōōl; oil; out; up; turn; sing; thin; **th**is; hw in white; zh in treasure. The symbol ə stands for the sound of **a** in about, **e** in taken, **i** in pencil, **o** in lemon, and **u** in circus.

Han·o·ver (han′ō′vər) *n.* **1.** a historic region and former province of Prussia, in the northern part of present-day West Germany. **2.** a city in northern West Germany. Pop. (1970), 523,900. **3.** the royal family that reigned in Great Britain from 1714 to 1901, beginning with George I and ending with Queen Victoria.

Han·o·ve·ri·an (han′ō ver′ē ən) *n.* **1.** a person who was born or is living in Hanover. **2.** a member or supporter of the English royal family of Hanover. —*adj.* **1.** of, like, or relating to Hanover. **2.** of or relating to the English royal family of Hanover: *George I was a Hanoverian king.*

han·som (han′səm) *n.* a low, two-wheeled, covered carriage for two passengers, drawn by one horse and having the driver's seat raised behind the cab. [From Joseph A. *Hansom,* a nineteenth-century English architect who designed it.]

Hansom

Ha·nuk·kah (hä′nə kə) *also,* **Cha·nu·kah.** *n.* a Jewish holiday commemorating the restoration of the Temple of Jerusalem after the victory of the Maccabees over the king of ancient Syria. It is celebrated by lighting candles on eight successive nights. [Hebrew *hanukkāh* dedication.]

hap (hap) *Archaic. n.* chance; luck. —*v.i.,* **happed, happing.** to occur by chance; happen.

hap·haz·ard (hap′haz′ərd) *adj.* characterized by a lack of order, direction, or planning: *Phil threw his clothes into the closet in a haphazard manner.* —**hap′haz′ard·ly,** *adv.* —**hap′haz′ard·ness,** *n.*

hap·less (hap′lis) *adj.* unlucky; unfortunate. —**hap′less·ly,** *adv.* —**hap′less·ness,** *n.*

hap·ly (hap′lē) *adv. Archaic.* by chance; perhaps.

hap·pen (hap′ən) *v.i.* **1.** to take place; occur: *The accident happened last week.* **2.** to take place without plan or reason; occur by chance: *His birthday just happens to be the same day as mine.* **3.** to come or go by chance: *A policeman happened along just after the accident.*

   to happen on or **to happen upon.** to meet or find accidentally: *The scientist happened on his discovery.*

   to happen to. a. to be done to; befall: *Something must have happened to the phone, because I can't get a dial tone.* **b.** to become of: *What ever happened to her?*

hap·pen·ing (hap′ə ning) *n.* something that happens; event; occurrence.

hap·pi·ly (hap′ə lē) *adv.* **1.** with pleasure, joy, or contentment: *They lived happily on their little farm.* **2.** luckily; fortunately: *Happily, no one was hurt in the fire.*

hap·pi·ness (hap′ē nis) *n.* **1.** the quality or state of being joyous, glad, or contented. **2.** good fortune; luck.

hap·py (hap′ē) *adj.,* **hap·pi·er, hap·pi·est. 1.** having, showing, or bringing pleasure, joy, or contentment: *a happy man, a happy home.* **2.** lucky; fortunate: *a happy discovery.* **3.** well-suited; apt: *a happy choice of words.*

hap·py-go-luck·y (hap′ē gō luk′ē) *adj.* free from care or worry; carefree; light-hearted.

Haps·burg (haps′bûrg′) *n.* a ruling family in Europe from 1273 to 1918, which governed Austria from 1282 to 1918, the Holy Roman Empire from 1438 to 1806, Spain from 1516 to 1700, and Hungary from 1526 to 1918.

har·a·kir·i (har′ə kēr′ē) *also,* **har·a·kar·i** (har′ə kar′ē), **har·i·kar·i** *n.* suicide by cutting open the abdomen with a knife. It is a form of ritual suicide in Japan.

ha·rangue (hə rang′) *n.* a long, noisy, often pompous speech, delivered with anger or strong feeling. —*v.,* **ha·rangued, ha·rangu·ing.** —*v.t.* to address with a harangue:

The camp counselor harangued the boys about their practical jokes. —*v.i.* to deliver a harangue. —**ha·rangu′er,** *n.*

har·ass (har′əs, hə ras′) *v.t.* **1.** to bother or annoy repeatedly; torment: *The workers on the picket line complained that they had been harassed by the crowd.* **2.** to trouble (an enemy) by repeated raids or attacks. —**har′ass·ment,** *n.*

Har·bin (här′bin) *n.* a city in northeastern China. Pop. (1971 est.), 1,600,000.

har·bin·ger (här′bin jər) *n.* a person or thing that goes before to announce or indicate what is coming: *A robin is a harbinger of spring.* —*v.t.* to act as a harbinger of.

har·bor (här′bər) *n.* **1.** a protected place on the coastline of a sea, lake, or river, used as a shelter for ships and boats. **2.** any place of shelter. —*v.t.* **1.** to give shelter or protection to; conceal: *to harbor a criminal.* **2.** to keep or foster in the mind: *to harbor a grudge.* —*v.i.* to take shelter in a harbor.

har·bor·age (här′bər ij) *n.* **1.** a shelter for ships and boats. **2.** any shelter.

hard (härd) *adj.* **1.** not easily pierced, dented, or crushed; solid and firm to the touch: *the hard surface of a concrete floor.* **2.** requiring or involving much physical or mental effort to do, make, or deal with: *a hard task, a hard decision, a hard man to get along with.* **3.** not easy to understand, master, or explain: *a hard problem.* **4.** causing sorrow, pain, or discomfort; severe; harsh: *a hard life.* **5.** without sympathy or sensitivity; stern; strict: *a hard heart.* **6.** showing or carried on with great energy or vigor: *a hard day's work.* **7.** having great force or strength: *a hard blow.* **8.** containing much alcohol: *hard liquor.* **9.** (of water) containing minerals that interfere with the sudsing and cleansing action of soap. **10.** (of currency) easily converted into gold or other currencies. **11.** *Phonetics.* (of *c* and *g*) pronounced with the sound of *k* in *cat* and *g* in *good.* —*adv.* **1.** with effort or energy; strenuously; persistently: *to work hard.* **2.** with force or strength: *It rained hard yesterday.* **3.** with difficulty: *The runner breathed hard after the race.* **4.** with a deep emotional reaction: *She took the tragic news hard.* —**hard′ness,** *n.*

   hard and fast. that cannot be changed or put aside; fixed; strict: *a hard and fast rule.*

   hard of hearing. partially deaf.

   hard up. *Informal.* in need of (something): *He was hard up for a job.*

   to be hard put to. to have much difficulty or trouble: *He was hard put to find an excuse for his lateness.*

hard-bit·ten (härd′bit′ən) *adj.* not easily moved by the emotions; tough: *He is an experienced and hard-bitten newspaper reporter.*

hard-boiled (härd′boild′) *adj.* **1.** (of eggs) boiled until the yolk and white are solid. **2.** *Informal.* not sympathetic or sensitive; tough: *a hard-boiled detective.*

hard coal, another term for **anthracite.**

hard·en (härd′ən) *v.i.* **1.** to become solid and firm to the touch: *The clay hardened in the sun.* **2.** to become strong, tough, or rigid: *The recruits hardened during basic training.* **3.** to become less sympathetic or sensitive. —*v.t.* **1.** to make solid and firm to the touch. **2.** to make less sympathetic or sensitive: *Years of loneliness have hardened him.* **3.** to make strong, tough, or rigid.

hard-head·ed (härd′hed′id) *adj.* **1.** not easily tricked or moved by the emotions; practical; shrewd: *a hard-headed businessman.* **2.** stubborn; willful: *He was hard-headed and would not admit a mistake.* —**hard′-head′ed·ly,** *adv.* —**hard′-head′ed·ness,** *n.*

hard-heart·ed (härd′här′tid) *adj.* without sympathy or sensitivity; lacking pity; cruel; unfeeling. —**hard′-heart′ed·ly,** *adv.* —**hard′-heart′ed·ness,** *n.*

har·di·hood (här′dē hood′) *n.* boldness, daring, and firmness of character: *The hardihood of the settlers was put to the test during their first winter.*

har·di·ness (här′dē nis) *n.* **1.** physical endurance; strength. **2.** boldness; daring.

Har·ding, Warren Ga·ma·liel (här′ding; gə mäl′-yəl) 1865–1923, the twenty-ninth president of the United States, from 1921 to 1923.

hard landing, the landing of a spacecraft on the moon or another body in outer space at so high a speed that the vehicle or its equipment is damaged.

hard·ly (härd′lē) *adv.* **1.** only just; barely: *We could hardly see in the dim light.* **2.** not quite; not likely.

hard palate, the bony part of the palate at the front of the roof of the mouth, separating the mouth from the nasal cavity.

hard·pan (härd′pan′) *n.* **1.** a layer of hard earth underneath soft soil through which roots cannot penetrate. **2.** hard, unbroken ground. **3.** a firm foundation.

hard sauce, an uncooked, creamy mixture of butter, sugar, and flavoring, used as a topping for dishes.

hard·ship (härd′ship′) *n.* the cause or condition of difficulty, pain, or suffering, such as poverty or illness: *The lack of rain caused great hardship to the farmers.*

hard·tack (härd′tak′) *n.* a hard, dry biscuit, traditionally eaten by sailors. Also, **sea biscuit, ship biscuit.**

hard·top (härd′top′) *n.* an automobile having the general design of a convertible, but with a rigid top that does not fold back.

hard·ware (härd′wer′) *n.* **1.** metal articles or parts, such as tools, nails and screws, or cutlery. **2.** weapons, especially heavy equipment. **3.** the physical equipment of a computer as distinguished from its programs, data, or the like.

hard·wood (härd′wood′) *n.* **1.** any of a large group of trees having broad leaves that are shed every year, such as the oak, beech, or maple. **2.** the wood of such a tree, usually denser, heavier, and harder than softwood, used to make such items as furniture, flooring, and athletic equipment. **3.** any hard, compact, heavy wood.

har·dy (här′dē) *adj.,* **har·di·er, har·di·est. 1.** able to endure hardship or harsh physical conditions; strong; robust. **2.** (of plants) able to endure the cold of winter without protection.

Har·dy, Thomas (här′dē) 1840–1928, English novelist and poet.

hare (her) *n. pl.,* **hares** or **hare.** an animal similar to but usually larger than a rabbit, having very long ears, powerful hind legs and feet, and a short tail.

hare·bell (her′bel′) *n.* a plant having a slender stem with bright blue flowers shaped like bells.

hare·brained (her′brānd′) *adj.* showing a lack of common sense and careful thought; foolish; reckless: *a harebrained scheme.*

hare·lip (her′lip′) *n.* a birth defect in which the upper lip is split, often impairing speech. —**hare′-lipped′,** *adj.*

Hare

har·em (her′əm) *n.* **1.** the part of a Muslim house where the women live. **2.** the women of a Muslim household. [Arabic *haram, harīm* forbidden; because men are forbidden to enter.]

har·i·kar·i (har′ē kar′ē) another spelling of **hara-kiri.**

hark (härk) *v.i.* to listen. ▲ used chiefly as a command.
to hark back. to go back, as to a previous time in one's memory: *The custom harks back to the last century.*

hark·en (här′kən) also, **heark·en.** *v.i.* to pay close attention; listen carefully: *to harken to a plea.*

Har·lem (här′ləm) *n.* a district of New York City, in Manhattan, including one of the largest Negro and Spanish-American communities in the United States.

har·le·quin (här′lə kwin, här′lə kin) *n.* **1. Harlequin.** a stock character in pantomime and comedy, traditionally appearing in a costume of many bright colors, and wearing a mask. **2.** a clown; buffoon. —*adj.* having a brightly colored pattern; parti-colored.

har·lot (här′lət) *n.* a prostitute or other woman of loose or immoral behavior.

har·lot·ry (här′lə trē) *n.* the state or quality of being a harlot; behavior of a harlot.

harm (härm) *n.* **1.** the cause of damage, pain, or loss; injury; hurt: *The guards were there to make sure that no harm would come to the royal family.* **2.** a moral injury or offense; evil; wrong: *The bad man saw no harm in lying to his friends.* —*v.t.* to do damage to; hurt: *The gunmen said that they wouldn't harm the hostages.*

harm·ful (härm′fəl) *adj.* causing or capable of causing harm; injurious or damaging: *Smoking may be harmful to your health.* —**harm′ful·ly,** *adv.* —**harm′ful·ness,** *n.*

harm·less (härm′lis) *adj.* not capable of causing harm; not injurious or damaging: *a harmless prank.* —**harm′-less·ly,** *adv.* —**harm′less·ness,** *n.*

har·mon·ic (här mon′ik) *adj.* **1.** of, relating to, or characterized by musical harmony. **2.** of or relating to a higher tone or tones produced with the main tone or tones when a musical note is played. —*n. Music.* see **overtone.**

har·mon·i·ca (här mon′i kə) *n.* a musical wind instrument consisting of a small slotted case that contains a series of metal reeds. It is played by inhaling and exhaling through the slots. Also, **mouth organ.**

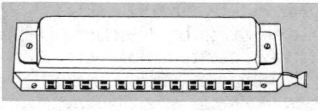
Harmonica

har·mo·ni·ous (här mō′nē əs) *adj.* **1.** characterized by agreement in feelings, thoughts, or actions; in accord; friendly: *There has always been a harmonious relationship between the people in our neighborhood.* **2.** having elements that combine agreeably or pleasingly: *There is a harmonious mixture of colors in the painting.* **3.** agreeable or pleasing to the ear; sweet-sounding. —**har·mo′ni·ous·ly,** *adv.*

har·mo·ni·um (här mō′nē əm) *n.* another word for **reed organ.**

har·mo·nize (här′mə nīz′) *v.,* **har·mo·nized, har·mo·niz·ing.** —*v.i.* **1.** to arrange, sing, or play in harmony: *The voices of the quartet harmonized in song.* **2.** to be in agreement; combine agreeably or pleasingly: *The color scheme in the living room harmonizes with the one in the dining room.* —*v.t.* **1.** to bring into agreement; make harmonious. **2.** to add notes, usually of lower pitch (to a melody), so as to form chords; add harmony to. —**har′mo·ni′-zer,** *n.*

har·mo·ny (här′mə nē) *n. pl.,* **har·mo·nies. 1.** a combination of musical notes sounded together so as to form chords. **2.** the science or study of this. **3.** any sweet or

H

pleasant sound. **4.** an agreement of feeling, thoughts, or actions; good relations: *to live in harmony.* **5.** an agreeable or pleasing combination of elements: *a harmony of colors.*

har·ness (här′nis) *n. pl.,* **har·ness·es.** **1.** the gear of a draft animal, including a combination of straps and bands by which the animal is attached to the load it is pulling, and the headgear by which the animal is controlled and guided. **2.** any combination of straps and bands resembling this: *a dog's harness.* **3.** *Archaic.* the armor for a knight, soldier, or horse. —*v.t.* **1.** to put a harness on. **2.** to control and make use of: *to harness water power to generate electricity.*

harp (härp) *n.* a musical instrument consisting of a series of strings set in an upright, triangular frame with a curved top, played by plucking the strings with the fingers. —*v.i.* to play on a harp.

> **to harp on.** to refer to over and over again; talk about too much: *He is always harping on how much tax he has to pay to the federal government.*

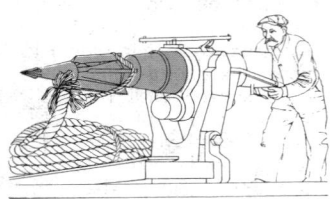
Harp

Har·pers Ferry (här′pərz) a town in northeastern West Virginia, the site of John Brown's raid on a government arsenal in 1859.

harp·ist (här′pist) *n.* a person who plays the harp.

har·poon (här poon′) *n.* a barbed weapon resembling a spear with a rope attached, used to kill or capture whales and other sea animals. It is thrown by hand or shot from a gun. —*v.t.* to strike, catch, or kill with a harpoon: *The men harpooned the whale after a long chase.* —**har·poon′er,** *n.*

Harpoon

harp·si·chord (härp′sə kôrd′) *n.* a stringed musical instrument with a keyboard, that was widely used in the sixteenth through eighteenth centuries. It resembles a grand piano, but has wire strings plucked by leather or quill points, and produces a tone like that of a guitar.

Har·py (här′pē) *n. pl.,* **Har·pies.** **1.** *Greek Mythology.* one of several foul-smelling, ugly monsters having an old woman's head and the body, wings, and claws of a bird. **2. harpy.** a disagreeable, shrewish woman.

har·que·bus (här′kwə bəs) *also,* **ar·que·bus.** *n. pl.,* **har·que·bus·es.** an early portable firearm, used in the fifteenth and sixteenth centuries, later replaced by the musket.

har·ri·dan (har′id ən) *n.* a mean, old woman.

har·ri·er¹ (har′ē ər) *n.* **1.** a hunting dog of a breed developed in England, originally raised for hunting hares. **2.** a runner in a cross-country race. [*Hare* + -*ier.*]

har·ri·er² (har′ē ər) *n.* **1.** a person or thing that harries. **2.** any of various hawks that prey on rodents, frogs, and other small animals. [*Harry* + -*er¹*.]

Har·ris·burg (har′is burg′) *n.* the capital of Pennsylvania, in the southeastern part of the state. Pop. (1970), 68,061.

Har·ri·son (har′i sən) **1. Benjamin.** 1833–1901, the twenty-third president of the United States, from 1889 to 1893. **2. William Henry.** 1773–1841, the ninth president of the United States, from March 4 to April 4, 1841; grandfather of Benjamin Harrison.

har·row (har′ō) *n.* a heavy frame with upright disks or teeth, drawn by a horse or tractor to break up and level plowed land. —*v.t.* **1.** to draw a harrow over (land).

2. to cause (someone) much pain, fright, or distress. —**har′row·er,** *n.*

har·ry (har′ē) *v.t.* **har·ried, har·ry·ing.** **1.** to trouble constantly; torment; vex: *The defense attorney harried the witness with many difficult questions.* **2.** to rob or pillage, as in a raid or attack.

harsh (härsh) *adj.* **1.** rough or unpleasant to any of the physical senses: *The sergeant snarled his orders in a loud, harsh voice. The towel felt harsh against my sunburned skin.* **2.** very cruel; severe: *The prisoners received harsh treatment at the hands of their captors.* —**harsh′ly,** *adv.* —**harsh′ness,** *n.*

hart (härt) *n. pl.,* **harts** or **hart.** a stag, especially a male red deer after its fifth year.

Harte, (Francis) Bret (härt; bret) 1839–1902, U.S. short story writer.

har·te·beest (här′tə bēst′) *n. pl.,* **har·te·beests** or **har·te·beest.** a reddish-brown African antelope having a long, narrow head and ringed, U-shaped horns that bend backward at the tips.

Hartebeest

Hart·ford (härt′fərd) *n.* the capital and largest city in Connecticut, in the central part of the state. Pop. (1970), 158, 017.

har·um-scar·um (har′əm skar′əm) *adj.* reckless or rash: *His brother is a harum-scarum boy.* —*adv.* in a reckless or rash manner: *The boys raced harum-scarum down the block.*

Har·vard (här′vərd) *n.* a private university in Cambridge, Massachusetts, the oldest college in the United States.

har·vest (här′vist) *n.* **1.** the act of gathering a crop when it is ripe: *The men soon finished the harvest of the wheat.* **2.** the crop that is gathered; season's yield of a crop: *the farmer had a large wheat harvest.* **3.** the time of year when ripened crops are gathered. **4.** the result of any action, effort, or labor: *a harvest of good will.* —*v.t.* **1.** to gather, as a crop: *to harvest corn.* **2.** to gather the crop from: *to harvest the wheat fields.* **3.** to get as a result of: *to harvest the benefits of a long, productive life.* —*v.i.* to gather a crop.

har·vest·er (här′vis tər) *n.* **1.** any of various machines for harvesting field crops, especially a reaper. **2.** a person who harvests.

harvest moon, the full moon occurring nearest the autumnal equinox.

Har·vey, William (här′vē) 1578–1657, English physiologist who discovered that blood circulates through the body.

has (haz) the third person singular present indicative of **have.**

has-been (haz′bin′) *n. Informal.* a person or thing that is no longer popular, powerful, or effective: *The star of that old movie is now a has-been.*

hash (hash) *n. pl.,* **hash·es.** **1.** a mixture of cooked meat, potatoes, and often onions or other vegetables, usually chopped fine and fried. **2.** a mess; jumble; muddle: *The new typist made such a hash of the letter that it had to be redone.* —*v.t.* **1.** to chop into small pieces. **2.** to discuss; review: *The friends hashed over the plans for their trip.*

hash·ish (hash′ēsh) *also,* **hash·eesh.** *n.* the dried flowering top parts of a hemp plant, smoked or chewed as a narcotic.

has·n't (haz′ənt) has not.

hasp (hasp) *n.* any of several clasps or fastenings, especially a hinged metal clasp that fits over a staple and is fastened by a pin or padlock, used to keep a door, window, or box closed.

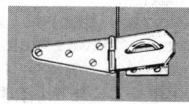

Hasp

has·sle (has′əl) *Informal.* *n.* 1. a heated argument; squabble. 2. a bother; irritation; struggle: *Getting home during the heavy rainstorm was quite a hassle.* —*v.,* **has·sled, has·sling.** —*v.i.* to squabble; fight. —*v.t.* to bother or irritate.

has·sock (has′ək) *n.* 1. a low, cushioned stool or other piece of furniture used to rest the feet on, or to sit or kneel on. 2. a tuft of coarse grass.

hast (hast) *Archaic.* the second person singular present indicative of **have.** ▲ used with *thou.*

haste (hāst) *n.* quickness or speed in moving or acting; hurry: *She departed in great haste in order to make the train.*

　to make haste. to move quickly; hurry.

has·ten (hā′sən) *v.t.* to cause to move or act quickly; speed up: *Treating his subjects with great cruelty hastened the dictator's downfall.* —*v.i.* to move or act quickly; hurry.

Has·tings (hās′tingz) *n.* a city in southeastern England, on the English Channel, the site of William the Conqueror's victory over the Saxons in 1066.

hast·y (hās′tē) *adj.,* **hast·i·er, hast·i·est.** 1. swift in motion or action; hurried; quick: *a hasty meal.* 2. characterized by careless hurry; rash: *He made some hasty remarks that he later regretted.* —**hast′i·ly,** *adv.* —**hast′i·ness,** *n.*

hasty pudding, a mush made of flour, cornmeal, or oatmeal boiled with water or milk.

hat (hat) *n.* a covering for the head, usually having a brim and crown. —*v.t.,* **hat·ted, hat·ting.** to furnish or cover with a hat.

　to pass the hat. to take up a collection; ask for contributions.

　to take off one's hat to. to praise or congratulate.

　to talk through one's hat. to speak ignorantly; talk nonsense.

　to toss one's hat into the ring. to enter into a contest, especially as a candidate for office.

　under one's hat. as a secret; in confidence: *He kept the news of her engagement under his hat.*

hat·band (hat′band′) *n.* a cloth band around the crown of a hat, just above the brim.

hat·box (hat′boks′) *n. pl.,* **hat·box·es.** a box or piece of luggage for holding a hat.

hatch¹ (hach) *v.t.* 1. to cause young to be brought forth from (an egg): *to hatch eggs in an incubator.* 2. to bring forth (young) from the egg: *The hen hatched the chicks yesterday.* 3. to devise or bring forth, as a plan or plot. —*v.i.* 1. to come forth from the egg: *The chicks hatched by pecking through their shells.* 2. (of eggs) to produce young: *All the eggs hatched today.* —*n. pl.,* **hatch·es.** 1. the act of hatching. 2. a brood of young that have been hatched. [Middle English *hacchen.*]

hatch² (hach) *n. pl.,* **hatch·es.** 1. an opening in the deck of a ship leading to lower decks or to the hold. Also, **hatchway.** 2. a cover or trap door for such an opening. 3. the lower half of a door or gate with two movable parts. [Old English *hæc* a gate, wicket.]

hatch·er·y (hach′ər ē) *n. pl.,* **hatch·er·ies.** a place where eggs are hatched, especially fish or poultry eggs.

hatch·et (hach′it) *n.* 1. a small ax with a short handle, designed to be used with one hand. 2. a tomahawk.

　to bury the hatchet. to stop fighting; make peace.

hatch·way (hach′wā′) *n.* see **hatch²** *(def. 1).*

hate (hāt) *v.,* **hat·ed, hat·ing.** —*v.t.* 1. to have very strong feelings against; have an intense dislike for: *He hates cruel people.* 2. to think of as unpleasant or distasteful; dislike: *She hates to sew.* —*v.i.* to feel intense dislike. —*n.* 1. an intense dislike or bitterness: *The men's hate for prison life grew as time went on.* 2. a person or thing that is hated. —**hat′er,** *n.*

hate·ful (hāt′fəl) *adj.* 1. deserving or causing hatred; detestable: *a hateful practice.* 2. feeling or showing hate; full of hate: *a hateful remark, a hateful stare.* —**hate′ful·ly,** *adv.* —**hate′ful·ness,** *n.*

hath (hath) *Archaic.* the third person singular present indicative of **have.**

hat·pin (hat′pin′) *n.* a long, sometimes ornamental pin for fastening a woman's hat to her hair.

hat·rack (hat′rak′) *n.* a rack or pole with hooks, used to hold hats or other garments.

ha·tred (hā′trid) *n.* a strong feeling against someone or something; great dislike or bitterness.

hat·ter (hat′ər) *n.* a person who makes, sells, or repairs hats.

Hat·ter·as, Cape (hat′ər əs) a cape on an island off the eastern coast of North Carolina.

hau·berk (hô′burk′) *n.* a long coat of chain mail or scale armor worn in medieval Europe. Also, **habergeon.**

haugh·ty (hô′tē) *adj.,* **haugh·ti·er, haugh·ti·est.** having or showing much pride in oneself: *a haughty queen.* —**haugh′ti·ly,** *adv.* —**haugh′ti·ness,** *n.*

haul (hôl) *v.t.* 1. to pull or draw with force; drag; tug: *We hauled the cart up the hill.* 2. to transport, as in a truck or car: *Railroads haul freight across the country.* —*v.i.* to pull; tug. —*n.* 1. the act of hauling: *It was an easy haul by truck from the farm to the town.* 2. something that is gotten or taken, as by catching or winning: *The fisherman came home with a big haul of fish.* 3. the distance over which a load is hauled: *From here to the warehouse is a long haul.* —**haul′er,** *n.*

haunch (hônch) *n. pl.,* **haunch·es.** 1. a part of the body including the hip, buttock, and upper thigh in man and four-footed animals. 2. the leg and loin of an animal, such as a deer or sheep, used for food.

haunt (hônt) *v.t.* 1. (of ghosts or spirits) to visit or inhabit: *A ghost haunts that house.* 2. to come often to the mind of so as to trouble or bother: *Memories of the shipwreck haunted the old sailor.* 3. to visit often; frequent: *She used to haunt the antique shops in town.* —*n.* 1. a place often visited; hangout: *The barn was our haunt during rainy summer days.* 2. *Informal.* a ghost.

haunt·ed (hôn′tid) *adj.* visited or inhabited by ghosts: *a haunted house.*

haunt·ing (hôn′ting) *adj.* appearing or coming to the mind often; hard to forget: *a haunting melody.* —**haunt′ing·ly,** *adv.*

haut·boy (hō′boi′) *n.* another word for **oboe.**

hau·teur (hō tur′) *n.* a haughty or arrogant manner; arrogance: *With much hauteur, she told him to mind his own business.*

Ha·van·a (hə van′ə) *n.* the capital and chief port of Cuba, on the northwestern coast of the island. Pop. (1970), 1,755,400.

at; āpe; cär; end; mē; it; īce; hot; ōld; fôrk; wood; fool; oil; out; up; turn; sing; thin; this; hw in white; zh in treasure. The symbol ə stands for the sound of **a** in about, **e** in taken, **i** in pencil, **o** in lemon, and **u** in circus.

H

have (hav) *v.t.*, **had, hav·ing.** Present tense: *sing.*, first person, **have**; second, **have** or *(archaic)* **hast**; third, **has** or *(archaic)* **hath**; *pl.*, **have. 1.** to own or be in possession of: *They have a house in the country. The girl has a scarf around her neck.* **2.** to contain or be characterized by: *The year has twelve months.* **3.** to hold or keep in the mind: *Do you have any doubts? He has much patience.* **4.** to engage in; carry on or out: *The family had a discussion about vacation plans.* **5.** to experience; undergo: *We had a good time at the party. Liza had the mumps when she was ten years old.* **6.** to give birth to: *His older sister had a little boy yesterday.* **7.** to be obligated: *I have to go to the grocery store.* **8.** to receive, take, or obtain: *She had a telephone call from him last night.* **9.** used as an auxiliary verb with past participles to form the perfect tenses, expressing completed action: *We have done the work. We had done the work. We shall have done the work.*

> **to have done.** to get through; stop: *Let's pay all the bills now and have done with them.*
>
> **to have it in for.** *Informal.* to have or hold a grudge against.
>
> **to have it out.** to settle a matter once and for all, as by discussion.
>
> **to have to do with.** to be connected or associated with; relate to.

ha·ven (hā′vən) *n.* **1.** a sheltered harbor; port. **2.** a place of safety or shelter; refuge.

have-not (hav′not′) *n.* a person or country that has little or no property, wealth, or resources.

have·n't (hav′ənt) have not: *We haven't been introduced.*

hav·er·sack (hav′ər sak′) *n.* a bag worn over the shoulders or suspended at one's side by a strap, used to carry food and other supplies, as by a soldier or hiker.

hav·oc (hav′ək) *n.* great destruction; devastation; ruin: *The floodwaters caused much havoc throughout the countryside.*

Ha·vre (hä′vrə) *n.* another name for **Le Havre.**

haw[1] (hô) *n.* **1.** the fruit of a hawthorn. **2.** another word for **hawthorn.** [Old English *haga.*]

haw[2] (hô) *v.i.* to hesitate in speaking; grope for words. ▲ usually used in the phrase *to hem and haw.* —*n.* a stammering sound made by a speaker when hesitating between words. [Imitative of this sound.]

Haversack

haw[3] (hô) *interj.* to the left. ▲ used to direct horses, mules, and certain other animals. —*v.t.* to cause to turn to the left. —*v.i.* to turn to the left. [Of uncertain origin.]

Ha·wai·i (hə wī′ē) *n.* **1.** a state of the United States, made up of the Hawaiian Islands. It is the only island state and the only state not on the North American continent. Capital, Honolulu. Land area, 6424 sq. mi. Pop. (1970), 768,561. **2.** the largest of the Hawaiian Islands. Area, 4021 sq. mi. Pop. (1970), 63,468.

● **Hawaii** comes from the Hawaiian name for one of the eight main islands of the state. It is thought to be a form of the Polynesians' name for the mythical homeland of their ancestors.

Ha·wai·ian (hə wī′ən) *n.* **1.** a person who was born or is living in Hawaii. **2.** a Polynesian language spoken chiefly in Hawaii. —*adj.* of or relating to Hawaii, its people, their language, or their culture.

Hawaiian Islands, an island chain in the north Pacific Ocean.

hawk[1] (hôk) *n.* **1.** a bird of prey having a sharp, hooked beak, strong talons, and short, rounded wings. **2.** any of various other birds of prey, such as the eagle, buzzard, or kite. **3.** a person who favors or supports the use of military force to resolve international conflicts. —*v.i.* to hunt game with trained hawks. [Old English *hafoc.*] —**hawk′ish,** *adj.*

Hawk

hawk[2] (hôk) *v.t.* to offer (goods) for sale by calling out in public: *The peddler hawked his goods in the marketplace.* [From *hawker*[2].]

hawk[3] (hôk) *v.i.* to clear the throat noisily by coughing. —*v.t.* to bring up (phlegm) by coughing. —*n.* a noisy effort to clear the throat. [Imitative of this sound.]

hawk·er[1] (hô′kər) *n.* a person who uses trained hawks in hunting; falconer. [Old English *hafocere.*]

hawk·er[2] (hô′kər) *n.* a person who offers goods for sale by calling out in public. [Low German *höker.*]

hawse (hôz) *n.* the part of a ship's bow having holes through which hawsers or cables may go.

haw·ser (hô′zər) *n.* a heavy rope or cable used especially for mooring and towing ships.

haw·thorn (hô′thôrn′) *n.* any of a large group of thorny shrubs or trees related to the rose, bearing small red, yellow, or black berries.

Haw·thorne, Nathaniel (hô′-thôrn′) 1804–1864, U.S. novelist and short story writer.

Hawser

Hawse

hay (hā) *n.* any of various plants, such as grass, alfalfa, or clover, cut and dried for use as feed for livestock. —*v.i.* to mow, dry, and store hay. —*v.t.* to feed with hay.

> **to hit the hay.** *Slang.* to go to bed: *We didn't hit the hay until after midnight.*
>
> **to make hay while the sun shines.** to take full advantage of an opportunity.

hay·cock (hā′kok′) *n.* a small, cone-shaped pile of hay.

Hay·dn, Franz Joseph (hīd′ən; fränts) 1732–1809, Austrian composer.

Hayes, Rutherford B. (hāz) 1822–1893, the nineteenth president of the United States, from 1877 to 1881.

hay fever, an allergy caused by breathing the pollen in the air, characterized by a stopping up of the nostrils, itching of the eyes, and sneezing.

hay·fork (hā′fôrk′) *n.* **1.** a pitchfork. **2.** a mechanical device for moving or loading hay.

hay·loft (hā′lôft′) *n.* a loft or upper section in a stable or barn, used for storing hay.

hay·mow (hā′mou′) *n.* **1.** another word for **hayloft. 2.** a pile of hay stored in a barn.

hay·rack (hā′rak′) *n.* **1.** a rack or frame for holding hay on which livestock may feed. **2.** a framework mounted on a wagon, used for holding hay or other bulky material.

hay·rick (hā′rik′) *n.* another word for **haystack.**

hay·ride (hā′rīd′) *n.* a pleasure ride in a wagon partly filled with hay, taken by a group as an outing.

hay·seed (hā′sēd′) *n.* **1.** the seed of any of various grasses. **2.** clinging bits of straw, chaff, and seed that fall from hay when it is moved. **3.** *Slang.* a person from the country; bumpkin; hick.

hay·stack (hā′stak′) *n.* a pile of hay stacked outdoors. Also, **hayrick.**

Hay·ward (hā′wərd) *n.* a city in western California, a suburb of Oakland. Pop. (1970), 93,058.

hay·wire (hā′wīr′) *n.* wire used for baling hay. —*adj. Informal.* **1.** out of order; broken down. **2.** crazy or upset.

haz·ard (haz′ərd) *n.* **1.** a chance of danger, harm, or loss; risk; peril: *the hazards of mountain climbing.* **2.** a source of danger or harm: *Icy roads are a hazard to motorists.* **3.** any obstruction on a golf course, such as sand or water. —*v.t.* **1.** to dare to put forth; to venture: *I'll hazard a guess as to how old he is.* **2.** to expose to danger, harm, or loss; risk: *to hazard one's life.*

haz·ard·ous (haz′ər dəs) *adj.* involving danger, harm, or loss; risky: *a hazardous journey.* —**haz′ard·ous·ly,** *adv.* —**haz′ard·ous·ness,** *n.*

haze[1] (hāz) *n.* **1.** mist, smoke, dust, or the like in the air: *An early morning haze hid the city's skyline.* **2.** vagueness of mind; mental confusion. [From *hazy.*]

haze[2] (hāz) *v.t.,* **hazed, haz·ing.** to humiliate and play pranks on, especially as part of initiation in a college or a college fraternity. [Of uncertain origin.]

ha·zel (hā′zəl) *n.* **1.** any of a group of shrubs or trees of the United States and Europe, bearing nuts that can be eaten, and having oval, tooth-edged leaves and clusters of small flowers. **2.** a light-brown color, like that of the hazelnut. —*adj.* **1.** of or relating to the hazel. **2.** having the color hazel; light brown: *Vera has beautiful hazel eyes.*

ha·zel·nut (hā′zəl nut′) *n.* the light brown, round or oval, edible nut of a hazel. Also, **filbert.**

ha·zy (hā′zē) *adj.,* **ha·zi·er, ha·zi·est.** **1.** full of or blurred by haze: *a hazy day, a hazy view.* **2.** not clear; vague; confused: *His knowledge of physics is hazy.* —**ha′zi·ly,** *adv.* —**ha′zi·ness,** *n.*

Hazelnut

H-bomb (āch′bom′) *n.* another word for **hydrogen bomb.**

he (hē) *pron.* **1.** a male person or animal that has been mentioned or spoken about before: *Russell promised that he would be on time.* **2.** a person; anyone: *He that hath ears to hear, let him hear* (Matthew 11:15). —*n. pl.,* **hes.** a male person or animal: *Is the kitten you found a he or a she?*

He, the symbol for helium.

head (hed) *n. pl.,* **heads** or *(def. 9)* **head.** **1.** in humans and other animals having a backbone, the upper part of the body that contains the brain and the eyes, ears, nose, and mouth. **2.** a similar part of any other animal or organism. **3.** the top or uppermost part of anything: *Jane paused at the head of the stairs.* **4.** the foremost part of anything; front: *the head of a line.* **5.** the leading or commanding part, position, or rank: *Father sat at the head of the table. The young army officer was put at the head of the division.* **6.** any part resembling a head in position or shape: *the head of a pin, the head of a hammer.* **7.** a person above others in rank; chief; leader: *The old man was the head of the tribe.* **8.** mental ability; aptitude: *Jack has a good head for figures.* **9.** a single person or animal, especially when considered as one of a number: *The cowboys rounded up fifty head of cattle after the stampede.* **10. heads.** the side of a coin bearing the main design; usually stamped with an image of a person's head. **11.** foam or froth on the surface of certain liquids, especially beer. **12.** a firm cluster of leaves, as of cabbage or lettuce, growing from a main stem. **13.** the tip or point, as of a boil or pimple. **14.** pressure, as of a fluid: *a head of steam.* **15.** a tightly stretched membrane covering the end or ends of a drum, tambourine, or similar instrument. **16.** a title or topic; heading: *The report is divided under five main heads.* **17.** *Nautical.* **a.** the forward part of a ship; bow. **b.** the upper corner or top of a sail. **c.** a toilet. —*adj.* **1.** chief; principal; commanding: *the head lifeguard.* **2.** situated at the top or front. **3.** coming from in front: *head winds.* —*v.t.* **1.** to be or go at the top or front of: *The bishop headed the church procession. Her name heads the list.* **2.** to be the chief or leader of; be in charge of; direct. **3.** to turn or direct the course of: *The captain headed the ship northward.* **4.** to fit or furnish with a head or heading. —*v.i.* to move in a certain direction or toward a specified point: *The ship headed for the open sea.*

head and shoulders above. greatly superior to: *The pitcher was head and shoulders above the other players.*

head over heels. a. in a somersault: *He tumbled head over heels down the stairs.* **b.** completely; thoroughly: *He was head over heels in love with her.*

one's head off. *Informal.* too much; excessively: *She talked her head off at the party.*

on one's head. as one's responsibility.

out of one's head or **off one's head.** *Informal.* crazy; insane.

over one's head. beyond one's power or ability to understand, handle, or manage: *Mathematics has always been way over my head.*

to go over someone's head. to bypass (someone) and go to a higher authority: *She went over the teacher's head and complained to the principal.*

to go to one's head. a. to make one dizzy or intoxicated: *The wine went to his head.* **b.** to make one conceited: *All those compliments will go to her head.*

to head off. to get in front of and turn back or aside: *The sheriff's men tried to head off the robbers.*

to keep one's head above water. to manage to avoid disaster, loss, or failure.

to make head or tail of. to understand: *He wasn't able to make head or tail of what she said.*

to turn one's head. to make one conceited: *All the attention she got at the dance turned her head.*

head·ache (hed′āk′) *n.* **1.** a pain in the head. **2.** *Informal.* a source or cause of annoyance, trouble, or worry: *The flat tire was an added headache on the long drive.*

head·band (hed′band′) *n.* a narrow band, usually of cloth, worn around the head to hold the hair in place or as an ornament.

head·board (hed′bôrd′) *n.* a board at the head of a bed.

head·dress (hed′dres′) *n. pl.,* **head·dress·es.** a covering or decoration for the head.

head·ed (hed′id) *adj.* **1.** having a head or heading. **2.** grown or formed into a head, such as cabbage. **3.** having a specified kind of head. ▲ used in combination: *red-headed.* **4.** having a specified number of heads. ▲ used in combination: *a two-headed monster.*

head·er (hed′ər) *n.* **1.** a person or thing that removes heads, especially a machine that removes the heads from grain. **2.** a person or thing that puts on or makes heads, as for rivets or nails.

to take a header. to fall or plunge headfirst.

at; āpe; cär; end; mē; it; īce; hot; ōld; fôrk; wood; fōōl; oil; out; up; turn; sing; thin; this; hw in white; zh in treasure. The symbol ə stands for the sound of **a** in about, **e** in taken, **i** in pencil, **o** in lemon, and **u** in circus.

H

head·first (hed'furst') *adv.* **1.** with the head going in front: *He dove headfirst into the lake.* Also, **head·fore·most** (hed'fôr'mōst'). **2.** hastily and without thinking; rashly: *He always jumps headfirst into difficult situations.*

head·gear (hed'gēr') *n.* a covering for the head, especially one worn for protection: *Football players wear special headgear.*

head·ing (hed'ing) *n.* **1.** a title or subtitle that describes or sets apart a section of a written work. **2.** a part serving as or forming the top or front of anything. **3.** a direction or course, as of a ship or aircraft, as indicated on a compass.

head·land (hed'lənd) *n.* a point of land jutting out into the water; cape.

head·less (hed'lis) *adj.* **1.** having no head; beheaded. **2.** having no leader or chief.

head·light (hed'līt') *n.* a bright light on the front of an automobile, motorcycle, or other vehicle.

head·line (hed'līn') *n.* one or more lines printed in large or heavy type at the top of an article, as in a newspaper, that tells what the article is about. —*v.t.,* **head·lined, head·lin·ing. 1.** to provide with a headline. **2.** to be the main attraction of (a theatrical presentation): *A magic act headlined the show.*

head·lock (hed'lok') *n.* a wrestling hold in which the arm or arms encircle the opponent's head.

head·long (hed'lông') *adv.* **1.** with the head foremost; headfirst. **2.** without giving much thought; rashly; recklessly: *He rushed headlong into a new business deal.* —*adj.* **1.** made or moving with the head foremost: *He took a headlong dive into the lake.* **2.** rash; reckless.

head·man (hed'man') *n. pl.,* **head·men** (hed'men'). a chief; leader.

head·mas·ter (hed'mas'tər) *n.* a man who is the principal or head of a school, especially a private elementary or secondary school. —**head'mis'tress,** *n.*

head-on (hed'ôn', hed'on') *adj., adv.* with the head or front end foremost: *to narrowly escape a head-on collision, to collide head-on.*

head·phone (hed'fōn') *n.* a radio or telephone receiver held against or worn over the ear by means of a band that fits over the head.

head·piece (hed'pēs') *n.* **1.** a covering for the head, such as a hat, cap, or helmet. **2.** a pair of headphones.

head·quar·ters (hed'kwôr'tərz) *n.,pl.* **1.** the center of operations from which a commanding officer, chief, or other leader issues orders. **2.** any center of operations, as of a business; main office: *The firm's headquarters is in New York.* **3.** the entire staff of a center of operations. ▲ used with a singular or plural verb.

head·rest (hed'rest') *n.* a support for the head.

heads·man (hedz'mən) *n. pl.,* **heads·men** (hedz'mən). a person who beheads condemned criminals; public executioner.

head·stand (hed'stand') *n.* the balancing of the body on the head in an upside-down vertical position, usually with the help of the hands.

head start 1. the advantage of starting a race ahead of others. **2.** a similar advantage in any competition.

head·stone (hed'stōn') *n.* **1.** a stone set at the head of a grave; tombstone. **2.** the principal stone in a structure, such as a cornerstone or keystone.

head·strong (hed'strông') *adj.* **1.** determined to have one's own way or do as one pleases; willful. **2.** characterized by or resulting from stubbornness; rash: *His headstrong decisions always get him into trouble.*

head·wait·er (hed'wā'tər) *n.* a man who is in charge of the waiters in a restaurant and sometimes is responsible for taking reservations and seating customers.

head·wa·ters (hed'wô'tərz) *n., pl.* small streams at the source of a river that join to form the main channel.

head·way (hed'wā') *n.* **1.** forward motion or progress: *The ship made little headway in the storm.* **2.** clear space overhead, as under a bridge.

head wind (wind) a wind blowing from the direction in which something, such as a ship, is moving.

head·y (hed'ē) *adj.,* **head·i·er, head·i·est. 1.** tending to make one dizzy or giddy; intoxicating: *a heady wine.* **2.** headstrong; willful. —**head'i·ness,** *n.*

heal (hēl) *v.i.* to become whole or sound; get well: *The wound healed without leaving a scar. Her arm healed quickly.* —*v.t.* **1.** to return to health or soundness; make well; cure: *The doctor healed the sick child.* **2.** to remedy, repair, or remove: *Nothing could heal the rift between the two friends.* —**heal'er,** *n.*

health (helth) *n.* **1.** soundness of body and mind; freedom from defect or disease. **2.** the condition of body or mind: *The doctor said the boy was in very good health.* **3.** a toast drunk in a person's honor, expressing a wish for his well-being.

health·ful (helth'fəl) *adj.* **1.** promoting or good for the health; wholesome: *a healthful diet.* **2.** having good health; healthy. —**health'ful·ly,** *adv.* —**health'ful·ness,** *n.*

health·y (hel'thē) *adj.,* **health·i·er, health·i·est. 1.** having good health; well: *a healthy young woman.* **2.** characteristic of or showing good health or sound condition: *a healthy appearance, a healthy outlook on life.* **3.** promoting or good for the health; healthful. **4.** *Informal.* considerable or great: *She kept a healthy distance from the growling dog.* —**health'i·ly,** *adv.* —**health'i·ness,** *n.*

heap (hēp) *n.* **1.** a collection of things piled together; mass: *a heap of clothes on the floor.* **2.** also, **heaps.** *Informal.* a large number or quantity; a lot: *He has heaps of money.* —*v.t.* **1.** to make into a heap; pile: *Mother heaped the dirty clothes on the bed.* **2.** to fill (something) full or more than full: *She heaped the dish with mashed potatoes.* **3.** to give or cast in large amounts: *He heaped insults on everyone at the meeting.*

hear (hēr) *v.,* **heard** (hurd), **hear·ing.** —*v.t.* **1.** to receive or be able to receive (sound) by means of the ear: *I heard someone call my name. Did you hear a noise?* **2.** to pay attention to; listen to: *He heard both sides of the argument before he made a decision.* **3.** to be informed of; become aware of: *She heard the news from her neighbor.* **4.** to give a formal, official, or legal hearing to: *The judge heard the testimony of the witness.* —*v.i.* **1.** to receive or be able to receive sound by means of the ear: *She can't hear well, so you will have to speak loudly.* **2.** to receive information or be told: *I haven't heard from her yet.* —**hear'er,** *n.*

to hear of. to allow, consider, or agree to: *She would not hear of our leaving so early.*

to hear out. to listen to until the end: *He promised to hear me out before he decided.*

hear·ing (hēr'ing) *n.* **1.** the faculty or sense by which sound is perceived; ability to hear: *She has very good hearing.* **2.** the act or process of perceiving sound. **3.** the opportunity to be heard; audience: *We were granted a hearing to present our version of what happened.* **4.** a formal, official, or legal investigation or trial. **5.** the distance within which sound may be heard; earshot.

hearing aid, a small electronic device that makes sounds louder, worn to improve poor hearing.

heark·en (här'kən) another spelling of **harken.**

hear·say (hēr'sā') *n.* information that has been received by word of mouth instead of by personal knowledge; gossip; rumor.

hearse (hurs) *n.* a vehicle for carrying a dead person from one place to another before or after a funeral service.

heart (härt) *n.* **1.** in man and other animals having a backbone, the hollow, muscular organ that pumps the blood through the body by beating regularly. **2.** a similar part in any other animal or organism. **3.** the region of the body containing the heart; bosom. **4.** the heart considered as the center of a person's innermost feelings, thoughts, or emotions: *He spoke from his heart when he thanked them for their help.* **5.** love and affection: *The little puppy won our hearts.* **6.** disposition; nature: *She has a kind heart.* **7.** mental state; mood: *He told us of the accident with a heavy heart.* **8.** firmness of will; spirit; courage: *The team lost heart after their defeat.* **9.** the center or innermost part of anything: *The tranquil waterway seemed to lead into the heart of an immense darkness* (Joseph Conrad). **10.** the main, vital, or most important part: *Let's get to the heart of the matter.* **11.** anything shaped like the heart: *The children cut out paper hearts.* **12.a.** a playing card marked with one or more red figures (♥) in the shape of a heart. **b. hearts.** the suit of such playing cards. **13. hearts.** a card game in which the players try to win either none or all of the cards of this suit.

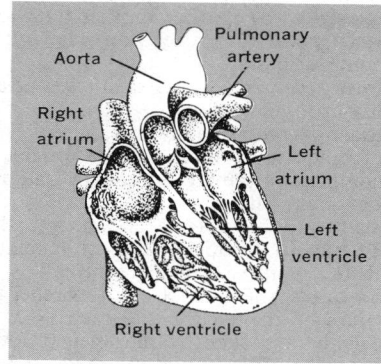

Human heart

   after one's own heart. corresponding or conforming perfectly to one's own ideas, tastes, or desires.
   at heart. in one's innermost thoughts or feelings: *He is a good man at heart.*
   by heart. by or from memory: *to know a poem by heart.*
   to break one's heart. to cause one to feel great sorrow, disappointment, or grief.
   to set one's heart on. to desire strongly; long for.
   to take to heart. a. to consider seriously or carefully. **b.** to be deeply affected or worried by.
   with all one's heart. a. with great sincerity or earnestness. **b.** very willingly; gladly.
heart·ache (härt′āk′) *n.* great sorrow or grief.
heart·beat (härt′bēt′) *n.* a beat of the heart, consisting of one complete contraction and relaxation.
heart·break (härt′brāk′) *n.* overwhelming sorrow or grief.
heart·break·ing (härt′brā′king) *adj.* causing overwhelming sorrow or grief: *heartbreaking news.*
heart·bro·ken (härt′brō′kən) *adj.* overwhelmed with sorrow or grief. —**heart′bro′ken·ly,** *adv.*
heart·burn (härt′burn′) *n.* a burning sensation under the breastbone, usually caused by too much acid in the stomach.
heart·ed (här′tid) *adj.* having or marked by a (specified kind of) disposition. ▲ used in combination: *heavy-hearted, good-hearted.*
heart·en (härt′ən) *v.t.* to give heart to; encourage; cheer.
heart·felt (härt′felt′) *adj.* deeply and earnestly felt; sincere; genuine: *heartfelt thanks.*
hearth (härth) *n.* **1.** the floor of a fireplace, often extending out into the room. **2.** home; fireside. **3.** the lowest part of a blast furnace in which molten metal and slag collect.
hearth·stone (härth′stōn′) *n.* **1.** the stone forming a hearth. **2.** the family circle; home; fireside.

heart·i·ly (härt′əl ē) *adv.* **1.** with genuine sincerity or friendliness; earnestly: *He welcomed his guests heartily.* **2.** with enthusiasm or vigor; eagerly; vigorously: *to laugh heartily.* **3.** with a good appetite: *After the day's labors, the farmer ate heartily.* **4.** completely; thoroughly; exceedingly: *We heartily support their plan.*
heart·less (härt′lis) *adj.* without kindness, sympathy, or pity; unfeeling; cruel: *a heartless remark, a heartless ruler.* —**heart′less·ly,** *adv.* —**heart′less·ness,** *n.*
heart-rend·ing (härt′ren′ding) *adj.* causing much sorrow or anguish: *a heart-rending story.*
hearts·ease (härts′ēz′) also, **heart's-ease.** *n.* peace of mind; tranquility.
heart·sick (härt′sik′) *adj.* deeply depressed or unhappy.
heart·strings (härt′stringz′) *n., pl.* strongest or deepest feelings or affections: *The sad story touched their heartstrings.*
heart-to-heart (härt′tə härt′) *adj.* frank; sincere: *The father had a heart-to-heart talk with his daughter.*
heart·wood (härt′wood′) *n.* the hard, central portion of the wood of a tree.
heart·y (här′tē) *adj.,* **heart·i·er, heart·i·est. 1.** full of affection, warmth, or kindness; cordial; friendly: *a hearty welcome.* **2.** very enthusiastic; vigorous; unrestrained: *a hearty laugh.* **3.** of sound health; strong and well. **4.** satisfying to the appetite; full; nourishing: *a hearty meal.* **5.** needing or using much food: *a hearty appetite.* —*n. pl.,* **heart·ies.** a bold, good fellow or comrade. —**heart′i·ness,** *n.*

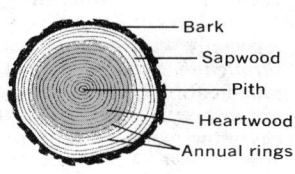

Heartwood

heat (hēt) *n.* **1.** the state or quality of being hot. **2.** degree of hotness; temperature. **3.** great warmth; high temperature: *The heat in the room is unbearable.* **4.** a heating mechanism that provides warmth for a house or other building: *We turned on the heat as soon as we got home.* **5.** the most intense or violent stage; point of greatest excitement or activity: *in the heat of battle.* **6.** *Physics.* a form of energy represented by the random motion of molecules, atoms, or smaller particles of a body. It is transferred from body to body by contact or by radiation. **7.** a single trial or effort in a contest, as a race, used to determine which contestants will compete in the finals. —*v.t., v.i.* to make or become hot or warm: *to heat milk. The milk heated quickly.*
heat·ed (hē′tid) *adj.* very angry or excited: *a heated argument.* —**heat′ed·ly,** *adv.*
heat·er (hē′tər) *n.* an apparatus, such as a stove, furnace, or radiator, that produces or gives heat or warmth.
heath (hēth) *n.* **1.** a flat, open wasteland overgrown with heather or low bushes; moor. **2.** any plant or shrub growing on such land, especially heather. **3.** any of a large group of shrubs grown in southern Africa and the Mediterranean region, bearing needle-shaped leaves and tiny white, pink, or red flowers.
hea·then (hē′thən) *n. pl.,* **hea·thens** or **hea·then. 1.** a person who does not believe in the God of the Christians, Jews, or Muslims. **2.** an uncivilized or uncultured

H

at; āpe; cär; end; mē; it; īce; hot; ōld; fôrk;
wood; fōōl; oil; out; up; turn; sing; thin; this;
hw in white; zh in treasure. The symbol ə
stands for the sound of a in about, e in taken,
i in pencil, o in lemon, and u in circus.

person. —*adj.* **1.** of or relating to heathens; pagan: *heathen gods.* **2.** uncivilized or uncultured. [Old English *hǣthen* originally, a dweller on a heath, from *hǣth* an open wasteland; probably because people who lived in remote areas were the last to be converted to Christianity.]

hea·then·dom (hē′thən dəm) *n.* **1.** heathen practices or beliefs; paganism. **2.** heathen countries or people.

hea·then·ish (hē′thə nish) *adj.* **1.** of or relating to heathens. **2.** characteristic of heathens; uncivilized.

heath·er (heth′ər) *n.* **1.** a low, evergreen shrub bearing small purple or pink bell-shaped flowers in dense clusters. It grows wild and is found especially in Scotland. **2.** the flower of this shrub.

heat shield, the covering on a spacecraft designed to protect it against the intense heat caused by friction during reentry into the earth's atmosphere.

heat wave, a period of extremely hot weather.

Heather

heave (hēv) *v.,* **heaved, heav·ing.** —*v.t.* **1.** to lift or raise with force or effort: *The men heaved bales of hay onto the truck.* **2.** to throw, especially with great effort: *He heaved a rock through the window.* **3.** to utter or give out with much effort: *He heaved a sigh of relief when he heard that she was safe.* —*v.i.* **1.** to rise and fall continuously in a rhythmic manner. **2.** to rise and swell; bulge. **3.** to retch; vomit. —*n.* **1.** the act or effort of heaving. **2. heaves.** a chronic, respiratory disease of horses. ▲ used with a singular verb.

  to heave in sight or **to heave into sight.** to come into view over the horizon, as a ship.
  to heave to. to bring a ship to a standstill.

heav·en (hev′ən) *n.* **1.** in the Christian religion, the dwelling place of God, the angels, and those who are saved. **2. Heaven.** the Supreme Being; God. **3.** *also,* **heavens.** the space above and around the earth; sky. **4.** any place or condition of happiness or beauty.

heav·en·ly (hev′ən lē) *adj.* **1.** of, belonging to, or in heaven; divine; holy: *Angels are heavenly beings.* **2.** of, relating to, or in the sky: *The sun and moon are heavenly bodies.* **3.** fit for or characteristic of heaven; happy, pleasing, or beautiful: *This is a heavenly spot for a picnic.* —**heav′en·li·ness,** *n.*

heav·en·ward (hev′ən wərd) *adv. also,* **heav·en·wards.** toward heaven. —*adj.* directed toward heaven.

Heav·i·side layer (hev′ē sīd′) the second layer of the atmosphere, existing at fifty-five to seventy-five miles above the earth. Certain radio waves can be transmitted by repeated bouncing between the earth and this layer. [From Oliver *Heaviside,* 1850–1925, English physicist.]

heav·y (hev′ē) *adj.,* **heav·i·er, heav·i·est. 1.** hard to lift or move; of great weight: *The furniture was very heavy.* **2.** having more than the usual weight: *heavy paper, heavy cloth, a heavy blanket.* **3.** of an unusually large amount, size, volume, or quantity: *a heavy snow, heavy traffic, a heavy eater.* **4.** difficult to do, accomplish, or deal with: *a heavy responsibility.* **5.** showing or feeling grief; sorrowful; sad: *a heavy heart.* **6.** considerable or pronounced: *The German girl spoke English with a heavy accent.* **7.** acting or moving slowly, clumsily, or with difficulty: *to walk with a heavy gait.* **8.** overcast; gloomy: *heavy skies.* **9.** loud and deep; resounding: *a heavy bass voice.* **10.** hard to travel over or through: *heavy underbrush.* —*adv.* in a heavy manner; heavily: *His troubles weigh heavy upon him.* —**heav′i·ly,** *adv.* —**heav′i·ness,** *n.*

  to hang heavy. to pass slowly, as time.

heav·y-du·ty (hev′ē dōō′tē, hev′ē dyōō′tē) *adj.* designed, made, or constructed for sturdiness and long wear.

heav·y-heart·ed (hev′ē här′tid) *adj.* full of or showing sadness; depressed. —**heav′y-heart′ed·ness,** *n.*

heavy hydrogen, another term for **deuterium.**

heav·y·set (hev′ē set′) *adj.* having a solid, sturdy, and compact build.

heavy water, water composed of deuterium and ordinary oxygen.

heav·y·weight (hev′ē wāt′) *n.* **1.** a person or animal of much more than average weight. **2.** an athlete who competes in the highest weight class in boxing, wrestling, or weight lifting.

He·be (hē′bē) *n. Greek Mythology.* the goddess of youth.

He·bra·ic (hi brā′ik) *adj.* of or relating to the Hebrews, their language, or their culture.

He·brew (hē′brōō) *n.* **1.** a member of one of the Jewish tribes of ancient times; Israelite. **2.** a Semitic language originally spoken by the ancient Jews. It is the official language of Israel and the religious language of Judaism. —*adj.* another word for **Hebraic.**

He·brews (hē′brōōz) *n.* a book of the New Testament, thought to have been written by Saint Paul.

Heb·ri·des (heb′rə dēz′) *n.* a group of islands off the northwestern coast of Scotland.

Hec·a·te (hek′ə tē) *n. Greek Mythology.* the goddess who had power over the moon, the earth, and the realm of the dead. She was also associated with witchcraft and magic.

hec·a·tomb (hek′ə tōm′) *n.* **1.** in ancient Greece and Rome, a public sacrifice of a hundred oxen or other animals at one time. **2.** any great slaughter or sacrifice.

heck·le (hek′əl) *v.t.,* **heck·led, heck·ling.** to harass (a speaker) with questions, taunts, and noises. —**heck′ler,** *n.*

hec·tic (hek′tik) *adj.* **1.** characterized by great excitement, agitation, haste, and activity: *a hectic day.* **2.** flushed and feverish, as from illness.

hec·tor (hek′tər) *v.t.* to threaten or bully. —*n.* a brawling, swaggering fellow; bully.

Hec·tor (hek′tər) *n. Greek Legend.* the eldest son of King Priam of Troy, killed by Achilles.

he'd (hēd) **1.** he had. **2.** he would.

hedge (hej) *n.* **1.** a row of shrubs or small trees planted close together, forming a fence or barrier. **2.** any barrier or boundary. **3.** the act or means of protecting oneself against loss or risk: *He saved his money as a hedge against unexpected expenses.* —*v.,* **hedged, hedg·ing.** —*v.t.* **1.** to surround, enclose, or separate with a hedge. **2.** to protect oneself from losing money on (a bet or investment) by making another bet or investment that would make up for any possible loss on the first. **3.** to surround with a barrier to prevent or obstruct free movement. —*v.i.* to avoid giving a direct answer or committing oneself: *The politician hedged when questioned about his stand on the proposed tax increase.*

hedge·hog (hej′hog′) *n.* an insect-eating animal having a pointed snout and a thick mass of sharp, hard spines on its back and sides. When frightened or attacked, it rolls up into a tight ball with only its spines exposed.

hedge·row (hej′rō′) *n.* a row of shrubs or small trees planted close together, used as boundary markers, screens, or decorations; hedge.

Hedgehog

heed (hēd) *v.t.* to pay careful attention to; mind: *Heed my advice.* —*v.i.* to pay careful attention; listen. —*n.* careful attention; notice: *The children paid no heed to her.*

heed·ful (hēd′fəl) *adj.* giving or taking heed; attentive; mindful. —**heed′ful·ly,** *adv.* —**heed′ful·ness,** *n.*

heed·less (hēd′lis) *adj.* not paying careful attention; unmindful. —**heed′less·ly,** *adv.* —**heed′less·ness,** *n.*

hee·haw (hē′hô′) *n.* **1.** the braying sound made by a donkey. **2.** a loud, rude laugh. —*v.i.* **1.** to make the braying sound of a donkey. **2.** to laugh in a loud, rude manner.

heel[1] (hēl) *n.* **1.** the rounded, projecting rear part of the human foot, below the ankle. **2.** the fleshy, rounded part of the palm of the hand, near the wrist. **3.** that part of a stocking, shoe, or other piece of footwear that covers the heel. **4.** the thick part of a shoe or boot that is under or raises the heel: *Certain shoe styles have low heels.* **5.** anything resembling the heel of the human foot in shape, use, or position. **6.** *Informal.* a low or hateful person. —*v.t.* **1.** to furnish with a heel or heels: *to heel a shoe.* **2.** to follow on the heels of. —*v.i.* to follow closely: *The dog was taught to heel.* [Old English *hēla.*]

  down at the heel or **down at the heels.** poor or shabby.
  on the heels of. close behind or immediately after.
  to take to one's heels. to run away; flee.

heel[2] (hēl) *v.i.* to lean to one side: *The ship heeled in the rough seas.* —*v.t.* to cause to lean to one side. —*n.* the act of heeling; list. [Old English *hieldan* to lean.]

heft (heft) *Informal. v.t.* **1.** to lift up; heave: *The movers hefted the sofa onto the truck.* **2.** to test the weight of by lifting: *to heft a grapefruit.* —*n.* **1.** weight; heaviness. **2.** the greater part; bulk.

heft·y (hef′tē) *adj.,* **heft·i·er, heft·i·est.** *Informal.* **1.** big and strong; muscular. **2.** heavy; weighty.

heif·er (hef′ər) *n.* a young cow that has not given birth to a calf.

heigh-ho (hī′hō′) *interj. Archaic.* used to express surprise, happiness, sadness, or weariness.

height (hīt) *n.* **1.** the distance or measurement from bottom to top: *The height of the statue is eleven feet.* **2.** the state or condition of being relatively tall or high: *Height is an advantage in playing basketball.* **3.** the distance above a given level, such as the sea or horizon. **4.** *also,* **heights.** a high point or place: *The little girl was afraid of heights.* **5.** greatest degree; culmination: *the height of fashion.* **6.** the highest point or part of something; summit: *He died at the height of his career.*

height·en (hīt′ən) *v.t.* **1.** to make high or higher; increase the height of. **2.** to increase (something) in amount, degree, or intensity: *The disappearance of the witness heightened the suspense of the murder trial.* —*v.i.* **1.** to become high or higher. **2.** to increase, as in amount, degree, or intensity.

hei·nous (hā′nəs) *adj.* extremely wicked; hateful; atrocious: *The dictator was guilty of committing heinous crimes.* —**hei′nous·ly,** *adv.* —**hei′nous·ness,** *n.*

heir (er) *n.* a person who inherits or is entitled to inherit money, property, or the like after the death of the owner.

heir apparent *pl.,* **heirs apparent.** a person who will become heir to a throne, title, or inheritance if he outlives the former owner or ancestor.

heir·ess (er′is) *n. pl.,* **heir·ess·es.** a woman who inherits or is entitled to inherit money, property, or the like, especially one who has inherited or will inherit great wealth.

heir·loom (er′lōōm′) *n.* a personal possession handed down in a family from generation to generation.

heir presumptive *pl.,* **heirs presumptive.** a person who will become heir to a throne, title, or inheritance if an heir more closely related to the ancestor is not born: *The king's nephew is the heir presumptive.*

He·jaz (hē jaz′) *n.* a former independent kingdom in the northwestern part of the Arabian peninsula, on the Red Sea, now part of Saudi Arabia.

held (held) the past tense and past participle of **hold**[1].

Hel·e·na (hel′ə nə) *n.* the capital of Montana, in the west-central part of the state. Pop. (1970), 22,730.

Helen of Troy *Greek Legend.* the very beautiful queen of King Menelaus of Sparta. When she was carried off by Paris, the Greeks, in revenge, waged war against Troy.

hel·i·cal (hel′i kəl) *adj.* of, relating to, or having the form of a helix. —**hel′i·cal·ly,** *adv.*

hel·i·ces (hel′ə sēz′) a plural of **helix.**

hel·i·con (hel′ə kon′) *n.* a very large tuba that is carried over the shoulder, used especially in marching bands.

hel·i·cop·ter (hel′ə kop′tər) *n.* an aircraft supported in the air by one or more motor-driven rotors that rotate horizontally above the craft.

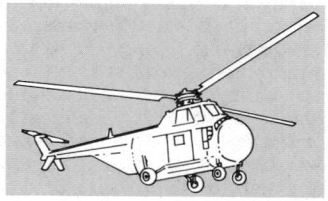
Helicopter

he·li·o·cen·tric (hē′lē ō sen′trik) *adj.* having or regarding the sun as the center of the planetary system or universe.

he·li·o·graph (hē′lē ə graf′) *n.* an instrument for signaling by means of mirrors that reflect light from the sun. The signal may be interrupted by a shutter to form a code. —*v.t.* to signal by means of a heliograph.

He·li·os (hē′lē os′) *n. Greek Mythology.* the god of the sun. In Roman mythology he was called Sol.

he·li·o·trope (hē′lē ə trōp′) *n.* **1.** any of a group of plants and shrubs growing wild in warm regions of the world, bearing clusters of fragrant, tube-shaped white or purple flowers. **2.** a reddish-purple color. —*adj.* having the color heliotrope; reddish purple.

he·li·ot·ro·pism (hē′lē ot′rə piz′əm) *n.* a response of plants and certain other organisms that causes them to move or turn toward the sunlight.

hel·i·port (hel′ə pôrt′) *n.* a place, as on the top of a building, for helicopters to take off and land.

he·li·um (hē′lē əm) *n.* an inert, nonmetallic, extremely light gaseous element with no color or odor, used especially to inflate balloons, blimps, and dirigibles, and to dilute oxygen and other gases. Symbol: **He**

he·lix (hē′liks) *n. pl.,* **hel·i·ces** or **he·lix·es.** **1.** anything having a spiral shape, such as the thread of a screw. **2.** a curve lying along the surface of a cylinder or cone at a fixed angle.

hell (hel) *n.* **1.** in the Christian religion, the dwelling place of Satan and the fallen angels, where the wicked will be punished after death. **2.** in various religions, the dwelling place of the dead; Hades. **3.** any place or condition of great evil, torment, or misery: *The prison was a hell on earth.*

he'll (hēl) **1.** he will. **2.** he shall.

Hel·las (hel′əs) *n.* another name for **Greece.**

hell·bend·er (hel′ben′dər) *n.* a large salamander that lives in the rivers and streams of the eastern and southern United States.

hel·le·bore (hel′ə bôr′) *n.* **1.** any of a group of thick-rooted plants often grown for their large attractive flowers that grow at the ends of long stalks. **2.** a tall, poisonous plant related to the lily.

Hel·lene (hel′ēn) *n.* a Greek.

at; āpe; cär; end; mē; it; īce; hot; ōld; fôrk;
wood; fōōl; oil; out; up; turn; sing; thin; this;
hw in white; zh in treasure. The symbol ə
stands for the sound of **a** in about, **e** in taken,
i in pencil, **o** in lemon, and **u** in circus.

H

Hel·len·ic (he len′ik) *adj.* of or relating to Greece, especially ancient Greece before the time of Alexander the Great. —*n.* a branch of the Indo-European language family, to which Greek and its dialects, both ancient and modern, belong.

Hel·le·nis·tic (hel′ə nis′tik) *adj.* of or relating to the period in Greek history after the death of Alexander the Great in 323 B.C. until the first century B.C.

Hel·les·pont (hel′is pont′) *n.* see **Dardanelles.**

hell·ish (hel′ish) *adj.* like, relating to, or fit for hell; horrible; fiendish: *a hellish crime.* —**hell′ish·ly,** *adv.* —**hell′ish·ness,** *n.*

hel·lo (he lō′) *interj.* used to express greeting, attract attention, or show surprise. —*n. pl.,* **hel·los.** the saying of *hello: They gave us a loud hello when we arrived.* —*v.t., v.i.,* **hel·loed, hel·lo·ing.** to say, call, or shout hello.

helm[1] (helm) *n.* **1.** the tiller, wheel, or entire steering apparatus of a ship. **2.** a place or position of control or authority; head: *John will take over the helm of the business when his father retires.* [Old English *helma* a handle.]

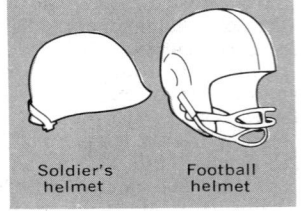

Helm[1]

helm[2] (helm) *n. Archaic.* another word for **helmet.** [Old English *helm.*]

hel·met (hel′mit) *n.* any of various protective coverings for the head, such as those worn by soldiers or by players in various sports, such as football or hockey.

helms·man (helmz′mən) *n. pl.,* **helms·men** (helmz′-mən). a person who steers a ship; steersman.

hel·ot (hel′ət) *n.* **1.** *also,* **Helot.** one of a class of serfs in ancient Sparta, who had no rights or privileges of their own. **2.** any serf.

Soldier's helmet   Football helmet

help (help) *v.t.* **1.** to provide with support or aid, as in doing a task; be of service to: *He helped his brother paint the room. She helped the old woman up the stairs.* **2.** to assist (someone or something) in accomplishing a goal or achieving a desired result: *The coach's advice helped the team to win.* **3.** to make better or cure: *Nothing really helped his cold.* **4.** to prevent or put an end to: *I can't help his rudeness.* **5.** to keep from; avoid: *I couldn't help smiling when I heard the story.* —*v.i.* to provide support or aid, as in doing a task; be of service. —*n.* **1.** the act of providing support, aid, or service: *Do you need help?* **2.** a source of support, aid, or service: *He was a great help to me when I was in trouble.* **3.** a person or group of persons hired to work for another or others: *How much does he pay his help at the store?* **4.** the means of improving, remedying, or preventing: *There is no help for his condition.*

  cannot help but. *Informal.* cannot but: *I cannot help but admire your courage.*
  to help oneself to. to take, especially without permission: *The thief helped himself to all the jewels.*
  to help out. to provide support, aid, or service: *He helped out when she got behind in her work.*

help·er (hel′pər) *n.* a person or thing that provides support, aid, or service, as in doing a task.

help·ful (help′fəl) *adj.* giving or providing support, aid, or service; useful. —**help′ful·ly,** *adv.* —**help′ful·ness,** *n.*

help·ing (hel′ping) *n.* an individual portion of food.

helping verb, another term for **auxiliary verb.**

help·less (help′lis) *adj.* **1.** unable to take care of oneself; dependent: *He was made helpless by the accident.* **2.** without power or strength: *The doctor felt helpless when he could not save the dying man.* **3.** without a source or means of relief, protection, or support. **4.** showing confusion or bewilderment: *With a helpless look, he shrugged and walked away.* —**help′less·ly,** *adv.* —**help′less·ness,** *n.*

help·mate (help′māt′) *n.* a companion and helper, especially a wife or husband. Also, **help·meet** (help′mēt′).

Hel·sin·ki (hel′sing′kē) *n.* the capital, largest city, and chief port of Finland, on the southern coast of the country. Pop. (1971 est.), 528,800.

hel·ter-skel·ter (hel′tər skel′tər) *adj.* hurried, confused, and disorderly. —*adv.* in a helter-skelter manner: *She threw her books and papers helter-skelter on the table.*

helve (helv) *n.* a handle, as of an ax, hatchet, or hammer.

hem[1] (hem) *n.* **1.** that part of a garment or piece of cloth made by turning the unfinished edge back and fastening it down, usually by sewing. **2.** the edge formed by this: *The hem is uneven.* —*v.t.,* **hemmed, hem·ming.** to turn back the unfinished edge of (a garment or piece of cloth) and fasten it down, usually by sewing: *to hem a dress.* [Old English *hem* or *hemm,* which probably originally meant an enclosed piece of land.]

  to hem in or **to hem about** or **to hem around.** to enclose in; encircle; surround: *The valley was hemmed in by steep cliffs.*

hem[2] (hem) *n., interj.* a sound resembling the clearing of the throat, made to attract attention or to show hesitation, doubt, or embarrassment. —*v.i.,* **hemmed, hem·ming.** to make this sound. [Imitative of this sound.]

  to hem and haw. to hesitate in speaking, especially in order to avoid making a definite or clear statement.

hem·a·tite (hem′ə tīt′) *n.* a hard mineral that ranges in color from reddish brown to black, and is the principal ore of iron.

hemi- *prefix* half: *hemisphere.*

Hem·ing·way, Ernest (hem′ing wā′) 1899–1961, U.S. novelist and short story writer.

hem·i·sphere (hem′is fēr′) *n.* **1.** one-half of the earth, as divided by the equator or the Greenwich meridian. The equator divides the earth into the Northern and Southern Hemispheres; the Greenwich meridian divides the earth into the Eastern and Western Hemispheres. **2.** one-half of a sphere.

hem·i·spher·ic (hem′is fer′ik) *adj.* of, relating to, or shaped like a hemisphere. Also, **hem·is·pher·i·cal** (hem′is-fer′i kəl).

hem·line (hem′līn′) *n.* the bottom edge of a skirt or dress.

hem·lock (hem′lok′) *n.* **1.** a tall evergreen tree related to the pine, having reddish bark and flat, blunt needles. **2.** the soft, coarse-grained wood of this tree. **3.** a poisonous plant related to parsley, having speckled, hollow stems with many branches and finely divided leaves, and bearing clusters of white flowers. **4.** the poison prepared from this plant.

he·mo·glo·bin (hē′mə glō′bin, hem′ə glō′bin) *n.* the iron-bearing protein matter in the red blood cells, carrying oxygen from the lungs to the tissues and carbon dioxide from the tissues to the lungs.

he·mo·phil·i·a (hē′mə fil′ē ə) *n.* a hereditary disease that prevents the blood from clotting normally, so that a small injury may result in excessive bleeding.

he·mo·phil·i·ac (hē′mə fil′ē ak′) *n.* a person who has hemophilia.

hem·or·rhage (hem′ər ij) *n.* a discharge of blood, especially one that is severe. —*v.i.,* **hem·or·rhaged, hem·or·rhag·ing.** to lose a large amount of blood.

hem·or·rhoids (hem′ə roidz′) *n., pl.* enlarged veins on or within the lower part of the rectum; piles.

hemp (hemp) *n.* **1.** a strong, tough fiber obtained from the stem of a tall plant, used chiefly to make rope and twine. **2.** the plant from which this fiber is obtained, having a hollow, thin stem and large leaves. **3.** any of various drugs obtained from this plant, such as hashish.

hemp·en (hem′pən) *adj.* made of or resembling hemp.

hem·stitch (hem′stich′) *v.t.* to stitch across an area of cloth from which cross threads have been removed, gathering several of the remaining threads at a time into small bundles. —*n. pl.,* **hem·stitch·es. 1.** ornamental needlework that has been hemstitched, often used to decorate borders and hems. Also, **hem·stitch·ing** (hem′stich′ing). **2.** a single stitch made by hemstitching.

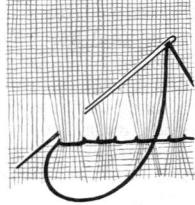

Hemstitch

hen (hen) *n.* **1.** the mature female of the domestic fowl. **2.** the female of various other birds.

hence (hens) *adv.* **1.** as a consequence or result; therefore: *He studied for several years in France, and hence learned to speak French fluently.* **2.** from this time: *We plan to meet three weeks hence.* **3.** away from this place; from here.

hence·forth (hens′fôrth′) *adv.* from this time on; from now on. Also, **hence·for·ward** (hens′fôr′wərd).

hench·man (hench′mən) *n. pl.,* **hench·men** (hench′mən). **1.** a willing partner in crime: *The duke was the evil king's henchman.* **2.** a trusted follower.

hen·e·quen (hen′ə kin) *n.* **1.** a strong fiber obtained from a Mexican plant, used for making twine or rope. **2.** the plant that yields this fiber.

hen·house (hen′hous′) *n. pl.,* **hen·hous·es** (hen′hou′ziz). a house, coop, or shelter for poultry.

hen·na (hen′ə) *n.* **1.** a reddish-brown dye obtained from the dried leaves of a shrub of Asia and Africa, used to color hair. **2.** the tall, slender shrub from whose leaves this dye is obtained. **3.** a reddish-brown or copper color. —*v.t.* **hen·naed, hen·na·ing.** to color or tint with henna. —*adj.* having the color henna; reddish brown.

hen·peck (hen′pek′) *v.t.* to dominate (one's husband) by constant nagging.

hen·ry (hen′rē) *n. pl.,* **hen·ries** or **hen·rys.** *Physics.* a unit of inductance in an electric circuit. One henry is the amount of inductance that produces a force of one volt when the current changes at the rate of one ampere per second. [From Joseph *Henry,* 1797–1878, an American physicist.]

Hen·ry (hen′rē) **1. O.** 1862–1910, U.S. short story writer; born William Sidney Porter. **2. Patrick.** 1736–1799, American patriot, statesman, and orator.

Henry II 1. 1133–1189, the king of England from 1154 to 1189. **2.** 1519–1559, the king of France from 1547 to 1559.

Henry IV 1. 1367–1413, the king of England from 1399 to 1413. **2.** 1553–1610, the king of France from 1589 to 1610. Also, **Henry of Navarre.**

Henry V, 1387–1422, the king of England from 1413 to 1422.

Henry VII, 1457–1509, the king of England from 1485 to 1509.

Henry VIII, 1491–1547, the king of England from 1509 to 1547; founder of the Church of England.

Henry of Na·varre (nə vär′) another name for **Henry IV** of France.

he·pat·i·ca (hi pat′i kə) *n.* a low-growing plant, bearing three-lobed leaves and small purple, pink, or white flowers.

hep·a·ti·tis (hep′ə tī′tis) *n.* an inflammation of the liver, that is usually caused by a virus. Hepatitis produces such symptoms as fever, weakness, and often jaundice.

hep·ta·gon (hep′tə gon′) *n.* a plane figure with seven sides and seven angles.

her (hur) *pron.* the form of **she** used as the object of a verb or preposition: *I gave the book to her. We called her and offered her a ride.* —*adj.* of or belonging to her: *her blouse, her piano, her accomplishments.*

He·ra (hēr′ə) *n. Greek Mythology.* the goddess of marriage and the protector of married women, who was the sister and wife of Zeus. In Roman mythology she was called Juno.

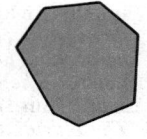

Irregular heptagon

Her·a·cles (her′ə klēz′) *also,* **Her·a·kles.** *n.* another name for **Hercules.**

her·ald (her′əld) *v.t.* to proclaim, be a sign of, or announce; usher in: *Trumpets heralded the hero's arrival.* —*n.* **1.** formerly, an officer who carried messages between princes or rulers. **2.** a person who proclaims or announces; messenger. **3.** a person or thing that announces or is a sign of someone or something to come: *The robin is the herald of spring.*

he·ral·dic (he ral′dik) *adj.* of or relating to heraldry or heralds.

her·ald·ry (her′əl drē) *n. pl.,* **her·ald·ries. 1.** the science or art of describing and designing coats of arms or of tracing family descent. **2.** a coat of arms.

herb (urb, hurb) *n.* **1.** any plant whose leaves, stems, seeds, or roots are used in cooking for their flavor, or are used in making medicines. **2.** any flowering plant that does not form a woody stem, but instead dies at the end of each growing season.

her·ba·ceous (hur bā′shəs) *adj.* of, relating to, or having the characteristics of an herb or herbs.

herb·age (ur′bij, hur′bij) *n.* **1.** herbs or grass, especially when used for grazing. **2.** the green leaves and stems of herbaceous plants.

herb·al (hur′bəl, ur′bəl) *adj.* of, relating to, made of, or containing herbs: *a herbal tea.*

her·bar·i·um (hur ber′ē əm) *n. pl.,* **her·bar·i·ums** or **her·bar·i·a** (hur ber′ē ə). **1.** a collection of dried plant specimens. **2.** a place in which such a collection is kept.

her·bi·cide (hur′bə sīd′) *n.* a chemical compound used to kill plants.

her·bi·vore (hur′bə vôr′) *n.* any animal that feeds chiefly on plants, such as a cow or a kangaroo.

her·biv·o·rous (hur biv′ər əs) *adj.* feeding chiefly on plants: *A cow is a herbivorous animal.*

Her·cu·la·ne·um (hur′kyə lā′nē əm) *n.* an ancient city in southwestern Italy, buried when Mount Vesuvius erupted in A.D. 79.

her·cu·le·an (hur′kyə lē′ən, hər kyŏŏ′lē ən) *adj.* **1.** requiring great strength or effort: *Moving the boulder was a herculean task.* **2.** *also,* **Herculean.** like Hercules, especially in strength or courage. **3. Herculean.** of or relating to Hercules.

Her·cu·les (hur′kyə lēz′) *n. Greek and Roman Legend.* a mortal son of Zeus, a hero celebrated for his exceptional strength and courage. Also, **Heracles, Herakles.**

at; āpe; cär; end; mē; it; īce; hot; ōld; fôrk; wood; fōōl; oil; out; up; turn; sing; thin; this; hw in white; zh in treasure. The symbol ə stands for the sound of a in about, e in taken, i in pencil, o in lemon, and u in circus.

H

herd¹ (hurd) *n.* **1.** a group of animals, especially large animals, such as cattle, sheep, reindeer, or elephants, feeding, traveling, or being kept together. **2.** a large number of people; crowd: *A herd of autograph seekers waited outside the theater for the star.* —*v.t.* **1.** to group (persons or animals) in a herd: *The cowboys herded the cattle and drove them to market.* **2.** to lead or drive in a herd: *The guide herded the tourists into the bus.* —*v.i.* to group or join in a herd: *The cows herded together.* [Old English *heord.*]

herd² (hurd) *n.* see **herdsman.** —*v.t.* to take care of; tend: *The old man herds goats in the mountains.* [Old English *hierde.*]

herds·man (hurdz′mən) *n. pl.,* **herds·men** (hurdz′mən). a man who owns, tends, or drives a herd. Also, **herd·er** (hur′dər).

here (hēr) *adv.* **1.** at or in this place: *We come here every year.* **2.** to or toward this place: *Bring the book here.* **3.** at this point, as in time or place: *I suggest we stop here and read the rest tomorrow.* **4.** now to be presented; as follows: *Here is my answer to your question.* **5.** in the present life. —*n.* **1.** this place: *How can I get to her house from here?* **2.** this life: *the here and now.* —*interj.* used as an exclamation, as in answering a roll call, calling an animal, or attracting attention.

  here and there. in various places: *The balloons were hung here and there for the party.*

  neither here nor there. not related to the matter being discussed; not relevant or important.

here·a·bout (hēr′ə bout′) *also,* **here·a·bouts.** *adv.* about or near this place; in this vicinity.

here·af·ter (hēr′af′tər) *adv.* **1.** from now on; after this: *When you see her hereafter, be kind to her.* **2.** after the present life. —*n.* **the hereafter.** the life after the present life; future life.

here·by (hēr′bī′) *adv.* by means of this: *I hereby resign.*

he·red·i·tar·y (hə red′ə ter′ē) *adj.* **1.** passed on or capable of being passed on genetically from an animal or plant to its offspring: *a hereditary disease.* **2.** taken or coming from persons or groups of earlier times; inherited: *a hereditary custom, a hereditary right.* **3.** passed or capable of being passed from an ancestor to an heir according to rules of descent: *a hereditary title.*

he·red·i·ty (hə red′ə tē) *n. pl.,* **he·red·i·ties. 1.** the process by which characteristics are passed on genetically from an animal or plant to its offspring. **2.** all the characteristics passed on in this way.

Here·ford (hur′fərd) *n.* any of a breed of beef cattle having a thick, curly red coat, a white face, and white body markings.

here·in (hēr′in′) *adv.* in this place, matter, or circumstance; in this: *Herein lies his mistake.*

here·of (hēr′uv′) *adv.* of or concerning this.

here·on (hēr′ôn′, hēr′on′) *adv.* on this or immediately after this; hereupon.

her·e·sy (her′ə sē) *n. pl.,* **her·e·sies. 1.** a religious belief or doctrine that is contrary to accepted church doctrine. **2.** the holding of such a belief or doctrine.

her·e·tic (her′ə tik) *n.* a person who holds a religious belief or doctrine that is contrary to accepted church doctrine.

he·ret·i·cal (hə ret′i kəl) *adj.* of, relating to, or characterized by heresy: *heretical beliefs, a heretical movement within a church.* —**he·ret′i·cal·ly,** *adv.*

here·to (hēr′tōō′) *adv.* to this matter, subject, point, or place.

here·to·fore (hēr′tə fôr′) *adv.* before now; until this time.

here·un·to (hēr′un tōō′) *adv.* to this matter, subject, point, or place; hereto.

here·up·on (hēr′ə pon′) *adv.* upon this or immediately following this.

here·with (hēr with′, hēr with′) *adv.* **1.** along or together with this. **2.** by means of this; hereby.

her·it·a·ble (her′ə tə bəl) *adj.* that can be inherited. —**her′it·a·bil′i·ty,** *n.*

her·it·age (her′ə tij) *n.* **1.** something that is handed down from previous generations or from the past; tradition: *The right to vote is part of the American heritage.* **2.** all the property that has been or may be inherited by someone, including possessions or land.

her·maph·ro·dite (hur maf′rə dīt′) *n.* an animal or plant that has both male and female reproductive organs. Many species of worms are hermaphrodites.

Her·mes (hur′mēz) *n. Greek Mythology.* the god of science and invention, who was the swift messenger of the gods, usually pictured with winged sandals and helmet. In Roman mythology he was called Mercury.

her·met·ic (hur met′ik) *adj.* not allowing air or gas to get in or out; airtight: *a hermetic seal.* Also, **her·met·i·cal** (hur met′i kəl).

her·met·i·cal·ly (hur met′ik lē) *adv.* so as to be airtight: *a hermetically sealed container.*

her·mit (hur′mit) *n.* a person who lives alone, away from other people, often for religious reasons.

her·mit·age (hur′mi tij) *n.* **1.** a place where a hermit lives. **2.** any dwelling place that is solitary or secluded.

hermit crab, any of a group of soft-bodied, mostly ocean-dwelling crabs that occupy the empty shells of snails and similar animals for protection.

hermit thrush, a North American thrush having a brown body, white-and-brown spotted breast, and reddish tail, noted for its melodious song.

Snail shell

Hermit crab

her·ni·a (hur′nē ə) *n. pl.,* **her·ni·as** or **her·ni·ae** (hur′nē ē′). a condition in which a part of an organ bulges out through the wall of its body cavity; rupture.

he·ro (hēr′ō) *n. pl.,* **he·roes. 1.** a person who is looked up to and admired for bravery and other noble qualities. **2.** a man or boy who performs a difficult or courageous act. **3.** the chief male character in a story, play, or poem. **4.** a sandwich made of a small loaf of bread filled with meat, cheese, and vegetables.

Her·od (her′əd) **1.** another name for **Herod the Great. 2.** another name for **Herod Antipas.**

Herod An·ti·pas (an′tə pas′) 20 B.C.?–A.D. 39, the ruler of Judea from 4 B.C. to A.D. 39, son of Herod the Great.

He·rod·o·tus (hə rod′ə təs) 484?–425? B.C., Greek historian, known as the father of history.

Herod the Great, 73?–4 B.C., the king of Palestine from 37 to 4 B.C. Also, **Herod.**

he·ro·ic (hi rō′ik) *adj.* **1.** of, like, or suitable to a hero; courageous: *The firefighter made a heroic attempt to save the child's life.* **2.** relating to or describing the deeds of heroes and heroines from myth and legend: *a heroic poem.* Also, **he·ro·i·cal** (hi rō′i kəl). —*n.* **heroics.** words or actions that are overly dramatic, noble, or grand and are made for effect. —**he·ro′i·cal·ly,** *adv.*

her·o·in (her′ō in) *n.* a white, crystalline drug made from morphine. It is habit-forming and, if too much is taken, may be fatal.

her·o·ine (her′ō in) *n.* **1.** a woman admired and looked up to for her bravery or noble qualities. **2.** a woman or girl who performs a difficult or courageous act. **3.** the chief female character in a story, play, or poem.

her·o·ism (her′ō iz′əm) *n.* **1.** the qualities of a hero or heroine; bravery; fortitude. **2.** brave conduct that saves or protects someone.

her·on (her′ən) *n.* any of various wading birds having a long slender neck, long pointed bill, and long thin legs.

Heron

he·ron·ry (her′ən rē) *n. pl.,* **he·ron·ries.** a place where herons congregate during the breeding season.

her·pe·tol·o·gy, (hur′pə tol′ə jē) *n.* a branch of zoology that deals with reptiles and amphibians. **—her′pe·tol′o·gist,** *n.*

Herr (her) *n. pl.,* **Her·ren** (her′ən). mister; sir. ▲ German form of respectful or polite address for a man.

Her·rick, Robert (her′ik) 1591–1674, English poet.

her·ring (her′ing) *n. pl.,* **her·ring** or **her·rings.** a bony, saltwater fish highly valued as food.

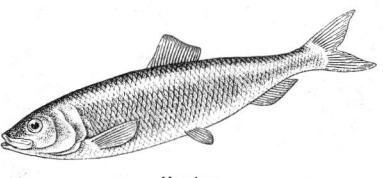

Herring

her·ring·bone (her′ing bōn′) *n.* a pattern of short lines slanting back from either side of a longer line, forming a design resembling the spine of a herring. *—adj.* having or making this pattern: *a herringbone suit.*

hers (hurz) *pron.* the one or ones that belong or relate to her: *My room was neat; hers was messy. —adj.* of or belonging to her.

her·self (hur self′) *pron.* **1.** the form of **she** or **her** used to give emphasis to the word it goes with: *She herself was opposed to the idea.* **2.** the form of **she** or **her** used to show that the subject and direct object of a verb are the same: *She blamed herself for the accident.* **3.** her usual or normal self: *She has not been herself lately.*

hertz (hurts) *n. pl.,* **hertz.** in the metric system, a unit for measuring the frequency of vibrations and waves, equal to one cycle per second.

Hertz·i·an wave (hurt′sē ən) an electromagnetic wave, such as a radio wave, produced by the speeding up or vibration of an electric charge. [From Heinrich *Hertz,* 1857–1894, a German physicist who discovered this wave.]

he's (hēz) **1.** he is. **2.** he has.

hes·i·tan·cy (hez′ət ən sē) *n. pl.,* **hes·i·tan·cies.** the quality or condition of being hesitant. Also, **hes·i·tance** (hez′ət əns).

hes·i·tant (hez′ət ənt) *adj.* lacking certainty or willingness; doubtful; reluctant. **—hes′i·tant·ly,** *adv.*

hes·i·tate (hez′ə tāt′) *v.i.,* **hes·i·tat·ed, hes·i·tat·ing.** **1.** to wait or stop a moment; pause briefly: *The salesman hesitated and then rang the doorbell again.* **2.** to be unwilling: *I hesitate to ask her because I know she will refuse.* **3.** to fail to take action or to delay an action because of fear, uncertainty, or doubt. **—hes′i·tat′ing·ly,** *adv.*

hes·i·ta·tion (hez′ə tā′shən) *n.* **1.** a delay due to fear, uncertainty, or doubt: *The actress accepted the part without hesitation.* **2.** the act or instance of stopping; pause: *In this dance there is a hesitation after each step.*

Hes·per·i·des (hes per′ə dēz′) *n., pl.* Greek Mythology. the daughters of Atlas who guarded the golden apples given to Hera when she married Zeus.

Hes·per·us (hes′pər əs) *n.* the evening star.

Hesse (hes, hes′ə) *n.* a political subdivision of West Germany in the central part of the country.

Hes·sian (hesh′ən) *n.* **1.** a person who was born or is living in Hesse. **2.** a soldier from Hesse who was hired to fight for the British during the American Revolution. **3.** any hired soldier. *—adj.* of or relating to Hesse or its people.

hetero- *combining form* not the same: *heterodox.*

het·er·o·dox (het′ər ə doks′) *adj.* **1.** not the same as accepted beliefs or doctrines; unorthodox. **2.** holding opinions that are not the same as accepted beliefs or doctrines.

het·er·o·dox·y (het′ər ə dok′sē) *n. pl.,* **het·er·o·dox·ies.** **1.** the state or quality of being heterodox. **2.** a heterodox belief or doctrine.

het·er·o·ge·ne·ous (het′ər ə jē′nē əs) *adj.* **1.** made up of unlike or unrelated parts or elements; not homogeneous: *a heterogeneous nation.* **2.** differing in kind or nature; dissimilar: *a heterogeneous group of people.* **—het′er·o·ge′ne·ous·ly,** *adv.* **—het′er·o·ge′ne·ous·ness,** *n.*

het·er·o·sex·u·al (het′ər ə sek′shōō əl) *adj.* of, relating to, or characterized by heterosexuality. *—n.* a heterosexual person.

het·er·o·sex·u·al·i·ty (het′ər ə sek′shōō al′ə tē) *n.* sexual desire for members of the opposite sex.

hew (hyōō) *v.,* **hewed, hewed** or **hewn** (hyōōn), **hew·ing.** *—v.t.* **1.** to make or shape with cutting blows, as from an ax: *The farmer hewed fence posts from logs.* **2.** to strike or cut, as with an ax or sword; chop; hack: *He hewed off the dead branches of the tree. —v.i.* to conform or adhere: *The young man hewed to accepted standards of behavior.* **—hew′er,** *n.*

hex (heks) *v.t.* to put an evil spell on; bewitch. *—n. pl.,* **hex·es.** **1.** an evil spell. **2.** a witch.

hex·a·gon (hek′sə gon′) *n.* a plane figure having six sides and six angles.

hex·ag·o·nal (hek sag′ən əl) *adj.* of, relating to, or having the shape of a hexagon.

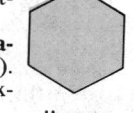

Hexagon

hex·a·he·dron (hek′sə hē′drən) *n. pl.,* **hex·a·he·drons** or **hex·a·he·dra** (hek′sə hē′drə). a solid figure having six faces. A regular hexahedron is a cube.

hex·am·e·ter (hek sam′ə tər) *n.* a line of verse consisting of six metrical feet. For example: *Ghosts′ of the / fear′ some O′ / Fla′ hertys / ride′ through the / val′-leys of Gal′ way.*

hey (hā) *interj.* used to attract attention or to express a sudden feeling, as of surprise, pleasure, or annoyance.

hey·day (hā′dā′) *n.* a period of greatest strength, popularity, or prosperity: *In her heyday she was a famous actress.*

Hf, the symbol for hafnium.

hf. 1. half. **2.** high frequency.

Hg, the symbol for mercury. [Modern Latin *hydrargyrum,* going back to Greek *hydor* water + *argyros* silver.]

H.H. 1. His (or Her) Highness. **2.** His Holiness.

hi (hī) *interj. Informal.* hello.

H.I., Hawaiian Islands.

hi·a·tus (hī ā′təs) *n. pl.,* **hi·a·tus·es** or **hi·a·tus.** a break, gap, or empty space, as in time: *After a brief hiatus, the argument flared up again.*

Hi·a·wath·a (hī′ə woth′ə) *n.* an Indian brave who is the hero of a poem by Henry Wadsworth Longfellow.

at; āpe; cär; end; mē; it; īce; hot; ōld; fôrk;
wood; fōōl; oil; out; up; turn; sing; thin; this;
hw in white; zh in treasure. The symbol ə
stands for the sound of **a** in about, e in taken,
i in pencil, o in lemon, and u in circus.

H

hi·ba·chi (hi bä′chē, hē bä′chē) *n.* a utensil for cooking, consisting of a grill covering a deep container in which charcoal is burned. [Japanese *hibachi,* from *hi* fire + *bachi* bowl.]

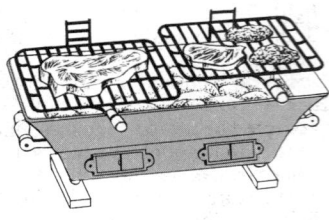

Hibachi

hi·ber·nate (hī′bər-nāt′) *v.i.,* **hi·ber·nat·ed, hi·ber·nat·ing.** to spend the winter in a dormant or inactive state, as do many animals, such as bears, squirrels, snakes, most amphibians, a few fish and birds, and certain insects. —**hi′ber·na′tion,** *n.*

hi·bis·cus (hī bis′kəs) *n. pl.,* **hi·bis·cus·es.** any of a large group of plants, shrubs, or trees bearing large, bell-shaped flowers of various colors.

hic·cup (hik′up) *also,* **hic·cough** (hik′up). *n.* **1.** a spasm of involuntary inhaling of the breath that is stopped suddenly by a closing of the vocal cords. **2.** the sharp sound caused by this spasm. **3. hiccups.** the condition of being affected by such spasms: *to have the hiccups.* —*v.i.,* **hic·cupped, hic·cup·ping.** to inhale with a spasm, with a sharp sound like a catch in the voice.

hick (hik) *Informal. n.* a person who is awkward or naive, especially one from a rural area. —*adj.* of or characteristic of a hick.

Hick·ok, Wild Bill (hik′ok) 1837–1876, U.S. frontier marshal; born James Butler Hickok.

hick·o·ry (hik′ər ē) *n. pl.,* **hick·o·ries. 1.** any of a group of tall trees found in North America, having gray bark and hard nuts. **2.** the hard, strong wood of this tree, used especially for tool handles. **3.** the round or oblong nut of this tree, which can be eaten.

hid·den (hid′ən) *v.* a past participle of **hide**[1]. —*adj.* not easily seen, found, or known; concealed or secret.

hide[1] (hīd) *v.,* **hid** (hid), **hid·den** or **hid, hid·ing.** —*v.t.* **1.** to put or keep out of sight: *Maria's parents hid the presents for her birthday.* **2.** to keep from the knowledge of others; keep secret: *Sometimes it is difficult to hide your feelings.* **3.** to prevent from being seen; cover up: *The heavy snowfall hid the animals' tracks.* —*v.i.* to keep oneself out of sight; conceal oneself: *The rabbit hid in the high grass.* [Old English *hȳdan.*]

hide[2] (hīd) *n.* **1.** the skin of an animal, either raw or tanned. **2.** *Informal.* the human skin. —*v.i.,* **hid·ed, hid·ing.** *Informal.* to give a severe beating to; thrash. [Old English *hȳd* skin.]

> **neither hide nor hair.** absolutely nothing: *They could find neither hide nor hair of him.*

hide-and-seek (hīd′ən sēk′) *n.* a children's game in which one of the players has to find all of the others who have hidden themselves.

hide·a·way (hīd′ə wā′) *n.* a secret or secluded place where one may hide or be alone.

hide·bound (hīd′bound′) *adj.* stubbornly narrow-minded.

hid·e·ous (hid′ē əs) *adj.* very ugly; horrible; detestable: *a hideous creature, hideous crimes.* —**hid′e·ous·ly,** *adv.* —**hid′e·ous·ness,** *n.*

hide·out (hīd′out′) *n.* a place where one can hide, especially where a criminal can hide from the police.

hid·ing[1] (hī′ding) *n.* **1.** a state or place of concealment. **2.** the act of concealing. [From **hide**[1].]

hid·ing[2] (hī′ding) *n. Informal.* a severe beating or thrashing. [From **hide**[2].]

hie (hī) *v.,* **hied, hie·ing** or **hy·ing.** *Archaic.* —*v.t.* to hurry; hasten: *to hie oneself home.* —*v.i.* to go quickly; hurry.

hi·er·ar·chi·cal (hī′ə rär′ki kəl) *adj.* of, relating to, or consisting of a hierarchy.

hi·er·ar·chy (hī′ə rär′kē) *n. pl.,* **hi·er·ar·chies. 1.** an organization of persons or things by rank: *the governmental hierarchy.* **2.** a body of clergy organized in this manner. **3.** church government by such a body of clergy.

hi·er·o·glyph (hī′ər ə glif′) *n.* see **hieroglyphic.**

hi·er·o·glyph·ic (hī′ər ə glif′ik) *n.* **1.** a picture or symbol representing an object, word, syllable, or sound, used in writing by certain ancient peoples, especially the Egyptians. **2.** a system of writing that uses hieroglyphics. **3.** any writing that is difficult to read. —*adj.* **1.** of, relating to, or resembling hieroglyphics. **2.** written in hieroglyphics. —**hi′er·o·glyph′i·cal·ly,** *adv.*

Hieroglyphics

hi-fi (hī′fī′) *n.* **1.** see **high fidelity. 2.** equipment for reproducing sound with high fidelity. —*adj.* of or relating to high fidelity.

hig·gle·dy-pig·gle·dy (hig′əl dē pig′əl dē) *adv.* in jumbled confusion or disorder. —*adj.* jumbled; confused.

high (hī) *adj.* **1.** reaching upward a great distance; tall: *The walls around the fort were high and strong. The mountain was too high to climb in a day.* **2.** being or elevated some distance above the ground or other surface: *The bridge is high above the water.* **3.** having a specified height: *The building is forty stories high.* **4.** reaching to or made from a great height: *a high dive, a high jump.* **5.** great or above average, as in force, amount, or degree: *high winds, high speed, high hopes.* **6.** above or more important than others, as in rank or position: *a high church official.* **7.** of a noble or lofty nature: *high ideals.* **8.** very good or favorable: *She has a high opinion of you.* **9.** very happy; joyful: *She was in high spirits after the party.* **10.** raised above the middle range in pitch; shrill: *The soprano sang a high note.* —*adv.* at or to a high position, point, or degree: *He climbed high up the mountain.* —*n.* **1.** a high position, point, or degree: *The temperature reached a new high.* **2.** an arrangement of gears that produces the greatest speed, as in an automobile engine.

> **high and dry. a.** completely up out of water: *The ship was stranded high and dry on the rocks.* **b.** without aid or assistance; alone; abandoned: *He left them high and dry.*
> **high and low.** in every place; everywhere: *We looked high and low for the missing book.*

high·born (hī′bôrn′) *adj.* of noble birth.

high·boy (hī′boi′) *n.* a tall chest of drawers supported on legs.

high·brow (hī′brou′) *Informal. n.* a person who has or seems to have cultivated tastes or interests. —*adj.* of, relating to, or suitable for a highbrow: *highbrow music.*

high·chair (hī′cher′) *n.* a chair for feeding an infant or young child, having high legs and a tray placed across the arms.

high·er-up (hī′ər up′) *n. Informal.* a person having a high rank or position.

high·fa·lu·tin (hī′fə lōōt′ən) *adj. Informal.* pompous or overly refined, as in speech or manner.

high fidelity, the reproduction of sound, as on a phonograph, so that the original sound is almost exactly duplicated. —**high′-fi·del′i·ty,** *adj.*

high-flown (hī′flōn′) *adj.* lofty or extravagant, as in ambitions, ideas, or language.

high frequency, a radio frequency between 3 and 30 megacycles. —**high′-fre′quen·cy,** *adj.*

High German, the literary and official form of the German language.

high-grade (hī′grād′) *adj.* of the highest quality.

high-hand·ed (hī′han′did) *adj.* acting or done in a haughty way without consideration for others; arrogant and ruthless: *The businessman used high-handed methods.* —**high′-hand′ed·ly,** *adv.* —**high′-hand′ed·ness,** *n.*

high-hat (hī′hat′) *Informal.* *v.t.,* **high-hat·ted, high-hat·ting.** to treat snobbishly; snub. —*adj.* snobbish.

high jinks (jingks) lively, good-natured pranks or fun.

high jump 1. a field event in which the contestant jumps over a crossbar set between two uprights. **2.** such a jump.

high·land (hī′lənd) *n.* **1.** *also,* **highlands.** a hilly or mountainous region of a country. **2.** a portion of land, such as a hill or plateau, rising above the land around it. **3. Highlands.** a rugged, mountainous region of northern and central Scotland. —*adj.* **1.** of, relating to, or characteristic of such a region or portion of land. **2. Highland.** of or relating to the Highlands of Scotland.

high·land·er (hī′lən dər) *n.* **1.** a person living in a highland. **2. Highlander. a.** a member of the Gaelic people who live in the Highlands of Scotland. **b.** a soldier of a regiment recruited from the Highlands of Scotland.

Highland fling, a lively Scottish folk dance that originated in the Highlands.

high·light (hī′līt′) *n.* **1.** a point or area in a painting or picture that is represented as brightly lighted. **2.** the most important, interesting, or memorable part of something: *The lighting of the Christmas tree was the highlight of Christmas eve.* —*v.t.,* **high·light·ed, high·light·ing. 1.** to give a highlight or highlights to. **2.** to give emphasis or importance to.

high·ly (hī′lē) *adv.* **1.** in or to a high degree; very much: *He is a highly ambitious person.* **2.** with much approval or praise; very favorably: *The teacher thinks highly of his work.* **3.** at a high price: *The actor is highly paid.*

high-mind·ed (hī′mīn′did) *adj.* having or characterized by noble ideals or feelings. —**high′-mind′ed·ness,** *n.*

high·ness (hī′nis) *n.* **1.** the state or quality of being high; loftiness. **2. Highness.** a form of address used in speaking to or of a member of a royal family, preceded by *His, Her,* or *Your.*

high-pitched (hī′picht′) *adj.* **1.** having a high pitch; shrill. **2.** (of a roof) having a steep slope.

high-pres·sure (hī′presh′ər) *adj.* **1.** having, using, or able to withstand pressure higher than normal. **2.** having high atmospheric pressure. **3.** *Informal.* using aggressive methods of persuasion: *a high-pressure sales approach.* —*v.t.,* **high-pres·sured, high-pres·sur·ing.** to use aggressive methods of persuasion on: *The salesman tried to high-pressure Dad into buying the car.*

high-rise (hī′rīz′) *n.* a building with many stories. —*adj.* having many stories: *a high-rise apartment house.*

high·road (hī′rōd′) *n.* a main road; highway.

high school, a school attended after elementary school, usually comprising grades nine through twelve or ten through twelve, or sometimes seven through twelve.

high seas, those portions of the seas and oceans that are not within the territorial boundaries of any country.

high-sound·ing (hī′soun′ding) *adj.* having an important or pretentious sound: *a high-sounding name.*

high-spir·it·ed (hī′spir′i tid) *adj.* having a proud, courageous, or fiery spirit.

high-strung (hī′strung′) *adj.* very tense or nervous; excitable.

high-ten·sion (hī′ten′shən) *adj.* having or using a high voltage: *a high-tension wire.*

high tide 1. the tide at its highest level. **2.** the time when this level is reached.

high time, later than the proper time but not too late: *It is high time that he start thinking about his future.*

high treason, treason against one's own government or monarch.

high·way (hī′wā′) *n.* a public road, especially one that is extensive and a major route of travel.

high·way·man (hī′wā′mən) *n. pl.,* **high·way·men** (hī′wā′mən). a robber who holds up travelers on a public road.

hi·jack (hī′jak′) *v.t.* **1.** to seize or take (a vehicle in transit) by force: *Two men hijacked the airplane.* **2.** to steal (cargo) from a vehicle in transit: *The thieves hijacked a truckload of tires.* —**hi′jack′er,** *n.*

hike (hīk) *v.,* **hiked, hik·ing.** —*v.i.* to walk a long distance, especially for pleasure or exercise. —*v.t.* **1.** to raise or pull up, especially with a sharp movement: *He was continually hiking up his trousers.* **2.** to increase sharply: *The bus company hiked its fare to forty cents.* —*n.* **1.** a long walk or march. **2.** an increase: *a hike in rent.* —**hik′er,** *n.*

hi·la (hī′lə) the plural of **hilum.**

hi·lar·i·ous (hi ler′ē əs) *adj.* **1.** extremely funny; very amusing: *hilarious stories.* **2.** noisily gay or cheerful: *a hilarious party.* —**hi·lar′i·ous·ly,** *adv.* —**hi·lar′i·ous·ness,** *n.*

hi·lar·i·ty (hi ler′ə tē) *n.* **1.** great merriment or laughter; boisterous gaiety. **2.** an extremely humorous quality or aspect; funniness.

hill (hil) *n.* **1.** a part of the earth's surface that is usually rounded and raised above the surrounding land, but is not as high as a mountain. **2.** a small heap or mound: *a hill made by ants.* **3.** a small mound or pile of earth in which seed is planted: *a hill of beans.*

hill·bil·ly (hil′bil′ē) *n. pl.,* **hill·bil·lies.** *Informal.* a person who lives in or comes from the backwoods or mountain country, especially from such an area in the southern United States.

hill·ock (hil′ək) *n.* a small hill or mound.

hill·side (hil′sīd′) *n.* the side or slope of a hill.

hill·top (hil′top′) *n.* the top of a hill.

hill·y (hil′ē) *adj.,* **hill·i·er, hill·i·est. 1.** having many hills: *hilly country, a hilly road.* **2.** like a hill; steep. —**hill′i·ness,** *n.*

hilt (hilt) *n.* the handle of a sword, dagger, or similar weapon.

to the hilt. thoroughly; completely: *He is involved in the scandal to the hilt.*

hi·lum (hī′ləm) *n. pl.,* **hi·la.** a mark or scar formed on a seed at the point where it was attached to the cone or flower.

him (him; *unstressed* im) *pron.* the form of **he** used as the object of a verb or preposition: *We saw him last night at the theater. I lent the book to him.*

Him·a·la·yas (him′ə lā′əz) *n.* the highest mountain system in the world, extending across Asia from the northeastern border of Afghanistan through northern India and Tibet to the northwestern border of Burma. Also, **Himalaya Mountains.** —**Him′a·la′yan,** *adj.*

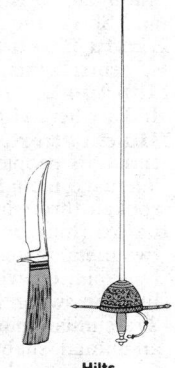

Hilts

at; āpe; cär; end; mē; it; īce; hot; ōld; fôrk; wood; fo͞ol; oil; out; up; turn; sing; thin; this; hw in white; zh in treasure. The symbol ə stands for the sound of **a** in about, **e** in taken, **i** in pencil, **o** in lemon, and **u** in circus.

H

him·self (him self′) *pron.* **1.** the form of **he** or **him** used to give emphasis to the word it goes with: *The President himself was unable to solve the problem.* **2.** the form of **he** or **him** used to show that the subject and direct object of a verb of a sentence are the same: *He has the habit of talking to himself.* **3.** his usual or normal self: *The great DiMaggio is himself again* (Ernest Hemingway).

hind¹ (hīnd) *adj.,* **hind·er, hind·most** or **hind·er·most.** at the back; rear: *The dog hurt one of its hind legs.* [Probably from *hinder².*]

hind² (hīnd) *n. pl.,* **hinds** or **hind.** a doe, especially a female red deer in and after its third year. [Old English *hind.*]

hin·der¹ (hin′dər) *v.t.* to delay or make difficult the movement or progress of; hold back: *The storm hindered the search for the missing child. Her stubbornness hinders her in friendships with other people.* [Old English *hindrian.*]

hin·der² (hīn′dər) *adj.* at the back or rear. [Old English *hinder.*]

hind·er·most (hīn′dər mōst′) *adj.* another word for **hindmost.**

Hin·di (hin′dē) *n.* a language of the Indo-European family of languages, spoken in northern India. It is the official language of India.

hind·most (hīnd′mōst′) *adj.* farthest back; nearest the rear. Also, **hindermost.**

hind·quar·ter (hīnd′kwôr′tər) *n.* **1.** the back half of a side of beef, lamb, veal, or other meat, including the leg and loin. **2. hindquarters.** the rear part of an animal.

hin·drance (hin′drəns) *n.* **1.** a person or thing that hinders; obstacle: *His lack of education will be a hindrance to him in the future.* **2.** the act of hindering.

hind·sight (hīnd′sīt′) *n.* the understanding of an event after it is over, especially of what should have been done.

Hin·du (hin′dōō) *n.* **1.** a person who believes in the teachings, beliefs, or practices of Hinduism. **2.** a person who was born or is living in India, especially northern India. —*adj.* of, relating to, or characteristic of Hindus or Hinduism.

Hin·du·ism (hin′dōō iz′əm) *n.* the chief religious, philosophical, and social system of India. The goal of Hinduism is salvation through communion with the Supreme Being, or Brahman, who appears in the form of the three major gods: Brahma, the creator; Vishnu, the sustainer; and Shiva, the destroyer.

Hindu Kush Mountains (koosh) a mountain system of central Asia, largely in northeastern Afghanistan.

Hin·du·stan (hin′dōō stan′) *n.* **1.** an area of northern India where Hindi is spoken. **2.** the Indian subcontinent.

Hin·du·sta·ni (hin′dōō stan′ē) *adj.* of or relating to India, its people, their languages, or their culture. —*n.* a language including elements of Hindi and Urdu, that is spoken throughout most parts of India.

hinge (hinj) *n.* **1.** a movable joint, usually consisting of two metal plates attached to one another by a pin, on which a door, gate, or the like can swing, turn, or otherwise move. **2.** a similar joint in the body of man or an animal, such as the elbow or knee, or that between the halves of a clam shell. —*v.,* **hinged, hing·ing.** —*v.t.* to furnish with or attach by a hinge or hinges. —*v.i.* to depend: *The fate of the prisoner hinges upon the jury's decision.*

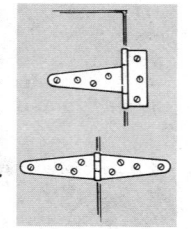

Hinges

hint (hint) *n.* a slight sign, indication, or suggestion: *There was a hint of spring in the morning air.* —*v.t.* to give a slight sign, indication, or suggestion of: *She hinted to me that she knew about the party.* —*v.i.* to make a hint. —**hint′er,** *n.*

hin·ter·land (hin′tər land′) *n.* **1.** a region or district lying inland from the coast. **2.** a region that is far from cities and towns; back country.

hip¹ (hip) *n.* **1.** the projecting part of each side of the human body, where the top of the thighbone joins the side of the pelvis. **2.** the corresponding part of the body of animals. **3.** the joint between the thighbone and the pelvic bone. [Old English *hype* this part of the human body.]

hip² (hip) *n.* the ripe fruit of a rosebush. [Old English *hēope* this fruit.]

hip³ (hip) *adj.,* **hip·per, hip·pest.** *Slang.* familiar with or informed about what is happening or what is new: *He is hip to the latest dance steps.* [Of uncertain origin.]

hip·bone (hip′bōn′) *n.* either of two large, irregularly shaped bones forming the two sides of the pelvic cavity; ilium.

hip·pie (hip′ē) *n.* any of a number of young people who, especially in the 1960s, turned away from many of the traditional values and practices of conventional society, and developed their own style of behavior and dress.

Hip·poc·ra·tes (hi pok′rə tēz) 460?–370? B.C., Greek physician known as the father of medicine.

Hip·po·crat·ic oath (hip′ə krat′ik) a vow taken by most beginning physicians that sets forth an ethical code for medical practice.

hip·po·drome (hip′ə drōm′) *n.* **1.** in ancient Greece and Rome, an outdoor arena for horse races and chariot races. **2.** an arena or similar structure for circuses, horse shows, or other spectacles.

hip·po·pot·a·mus (hip′ə pot′ə məs) *n. pl.,* **hip·po·pot·a·mus·es** or **hip·po·pot·a·mi** (hip′ə pot′ə mī′). a very large plant-eating animal, native to central and southern Africa, living in and near rivers and lakes, and having a massive, thick-skinned, hairless body, short legs, and the largest mouth of any land animal. [Latin *hippopotamus,* going back to Greek *hippos* horse + *potamos* river.]

Hippopotamus

hire (hīr) *v.t.,* **hired, hir·ing. 1.** to pay for the services of (a person): *The school hired two new science teachers.* **2.** to pay for the use of (a thing): *They hired a car for the trip.* **3.** to give the use of (a thing) or the services of (a person) in return for payment: *He hired out his boat for the summer.* —*n.* **1.** payment for the use of an object, services rendered, or labor performed. **2.** the act of hiring.
   for hire. available for use or work in return for payment.

hire·ling (hīr′ling) *n.* a person who works only for the sake of money, especially a person who can be hired to do something unpleasant or dishonest. —*adj.* of or like a hireling; mercenary.

Hir·o·hi·to (hēr′ō hē′tō) 1901—, the emperor of Japan since 1926.

Hir·o·shi·ma (hēr′ō shē′mə) *n.* a port city in southwestern Japan, on the island of Honshu. In 1945 it was devastated by an atomic bomb. Pop. (1970), 541,998.

hir·sute (hur′sōōt) *adj.* having much hair; hairy. —**hir′sute·ness,** *n.*

his (hiz) *pron.* the one or ones that belong or relate to him: *We went to the movies with my sisters and his.* —*adj.* of or belonging to him: *His dog is his constant companion.*

His·pa·ni·a (his pā′nē ə) *n.* another name for **Spain.**

His·pan·ic (his pan′ik) *adj.* of or relating to Spain or to Spanish America: *a person of Hispanic descent.*

His·pan·io·la (his′pən yō′lə) *n.* an island in the Greater Antilles, in the Caribbean Sea, divided into the Dominican Republic and Haiti.

hiss (his) *v.i.* **1.** to make a sound like a prolonged *s: The startled snake hissed.* **2.** to make such a sound to show disapproval or dislike: *The angry crowd hissed when the man spoke.* —*v.t.* **1.** to show disapproval by hissing: *The fans hissed the umpire.* **2.** to say or express by hissing. —*n. pl.,* **hiss·es.** a sound like a prolonged *s.*

hist. **1.** history. **2.** historian. **3.** historical.

his·ta·mine (his′tə mēn′) *n.* a chemical compound found in certain plant and animal cells, which, when released, has certain effects on the body, such as lowering the blood pressure. Histamine is also released by the body in allergic reactions and causes tissues to swell.

his·tol·o·gy (his tol′ə jē) *n.* the study of plant and animal tissues through a microscope.

his·to·ri·an (his tôr′ē ən) *n.* **1.** a person who writes history. **2.** a student of or an expert in history.

his·tor·ic (his tôr′ik) *adj.* **1.** famous or important in history: *a historic old fort.* **2.** another word for **historical.**

his·tor·i·cal (his tôr′i kəl) *adj.* **1.** of or relating to history: *historical events.* **2.** based on the facts or events of history: *a historical novel.* —**his·tor′i·cal·ly,** *adv.*

his·to·ry (his′tər ē) *n. pl.,* **his·to·ries.** **1.** the story or record of what has happened in the past, especially of a country, people, or person: *a history of the United States, a history of the American Indians.* **2.** all past events in general: *human history.* **3.** the branch of knowledge or study dealing with past events: *a class in history.* **4.** the recorded or known past of something: *That old house has an interesting history.*

his·tri·on·ic (his′trē on′ik) *adj.* **1.** overly emotional or theatrical in behavior or speech. **2.** of or relating to actors or acting.

his·tri·on·ics (his′trē on′iks) *n.,pl.* **1.** overly emotional or theatrical behavior or speech. ▲ used with a plural verb. **2.** a dramatic representation; acting; dramatics. ▲ used with a singular verb.

hit (hit) *v.,* **hit, hit·ting.** —*v.t.* **1.** to give a blow to; strike: *Jim hit the ball over the fence. Bill hit his brother.* **2.** to come against or strike (someone or something) with force: *The car hit the tree. The bullet hit the target.* **3.** to cause (something) to come against or strike someone or something with force: *He hit his fist against the wall.* **4.** to come to; reach: *The car hit ninety miles per hour.* **5.** to have a painful or bad effect on: *The lack of jobs hit the town hard that winter.* **6.** to become suddenly plain or clear to: *The truth hit me at the last moment.* **7.** *Baseball.* to make (a base hit): *He hit a home run in the third inning.* —*v.i.* **1.** to give a blow. **2.** to come against someone or something with force; collide: *The cars hit with a loud crash.* **3.** to arrive or appear: *The tornado hit without warning.* **4.** to discover or arrive at: *We hit upon the solution to the problem.* —*n.* **1.** a blow or strike: *The bomber made a direct hit on the town.* **2.** a person or thing that is successful: *His guitar playing made him a hit at the party. That popular song was a hit.* **3.** see **base hit.** —**hit′ter,** *n.*

to hit it off. to like or get along well with one another.

hit-and-run (hit′ən run′) *adj.* of or relating to an accident in which a driver hits someone or something and then drives away from the scene of the accident.

hitch (hich) *v.t.* **1.** to attach, as with a hook, rope, or strap; fasten; tie: *The farmer hitched the horse to the wagon.* **2.** to raise with a quick jerky movement: *He hitched up his suspenders.*

Clove   Timber   Rolling

Types of hitch knots

3. *Informal.* to get by hitchhiking: *He hitched a ride to the* station. —*v.i.* **1.** to become fastened or caught: *The fisherman's line hitched onto a branch of a tree.* **2.** *Informal.* to hitchhike. —*n. pl.,* **hitch·es.** **1.** something used to connect two things together; fastening; catch: *The hitch between the car and the trailer broke.* **2.** an unexpected delay or obstacle: *The class play went without a hitch.* **3.** a quick, jerky movement: *The boy gave his trousers a hitch.* **4.** any of various knots used for temporary fastenings. **5.** *Informal.* time spent in military service: *a three-year hitch in the navy.*

hitch·hike (hich′hīk′) *v.i.,* **hitch·hiked, hitch·hik·ing.** *Informal.* to travel by getting free rides from passing cars or trucks. —**hitch′hik′er,** *n.*

hitching post, a railing or pole to which animals, especially horses, may be tied.

hith·er (hith′ər) *adv.* to or toward this place: *Come hither.* —*adj.* on or toward this side; nearer.

hith·er·to (hith′ər tōō′) *adv.* up to this time; until now: *A hitherto unknown actress became the star of the new movie.*

hith·er·ward (hith′ər wərd) *adv.* to or toward this place; hither.

Hit·ler, Ad·olf (hit′lər; ad′olf) 1889–1945, German dictator born in Austria, the ruler of Nazi Germany from 1933 to 1945.

Hit·tite (hit′īt) *n.* **1.** a member of a people whose civilization dominated Asia Minor and part of Syria between 2000 and 1200 B.C. **2.** an ancient language of the Hittites, belonging to the Indo-European family of languages. —*adj.* of or relating to the Hittites, their language, or their culture.

hive (hīv) *n.* **1.** a box or house for bees, especially honeybees, to build a nest in. **2.** a colony of bees living in a hive. **3.** a place swarming with busy people: *The airport was a hive of activity.* —*v.t.,* **hived, hiv·ing.** to put (bees) into a hive.

 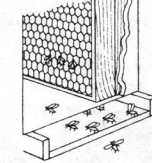

Natural hive   Man-made hive

hives (hīvz) *n.,pl.* an itching skin rash, usually caused by an allergy. ▲ used with a singular or plural verb.

H.M.S., His (or Her) Majesty's Ship.

ho (hō) *interj.* **1.** used to express pleasure, laughter, surprise, or doubt. **2.** used to attract attention or call attention to: *Land ho!*

Ho, the symbol for holmium.

hoar (hôr) *adj.* another word for **hoary.** —*n.* another word for **hoarfrost.**

hoard (hôrd) *v.t.* to save and store or hide away: *He hoarded his allowance until he had enough money to buy a camera.* —*n.* a thing or things saved and stored or hidden away, especially for future use: *She had a hoard of canned goods in the cupboard.* —**hoard′er,** *n.*

hoar·frost (hôr′frôst′) *n.* frost, especially when it forms a white coating on a surface.

hoar·hound (hôr′hound′) another spelling of **horehound.**

---

at; āpe; cär; end; mē; it; īce; hot; ōld; fôrk; wood; fōōl; oil; out; up; turn; sing; thin; this; hw in white; zh in treasure. The symbol ə stands for the sound of **a** in about, **e** in taken, **i** in pencil, **o** in lemon, and **u** in circus.

H

hoarse (hôrs) *adj.,* **hoars·er, hoars·est. 1.** sounding deep and harsh or grating: *After his cold, he had a hoarse voice.* **2.** having a harsh or grating voice. —**hoarse′ly,** *adv.* —**hoarse′ness,** *n.*

hoar·y (hôr′ē) *adj.,* **hoar·i·er, hoar·i·est. 1.** white or gray: *the hoary beard of an old man, leaves hoary with frost.* **2.** old; ancient. —**hoar′i·ness,** *n.*

hoax (hōks) *n. pl.,* **hoax·es.** a trick or deception, meant as a practical joke or to fool others: *The report that a serpent had been sighted in the lake was a hoax.* —*v.t.* to trick or deceive by a hoax. —**hoax′er,** *n.*

hob¹ (hob) *n.* a shelf or ledge at the back or side of the inside of a fireplace, used for keeping food warm. [Of uncertain origin.]

hob² (hob) *n.* hobgoblin; elf. [From *Hob,* an earlier nickname for *Robin* or *Robert.*]

    to play hob with or **to raise hob with.** *Informal.* to make trouble for; do mischief to: *His slowness in getting ready played hob with our plan to leave early.*

Hobbes, Thomas (hobz) 1588–1679, English philosopher.

hob·ble (hob′əl) *v.,* **hob·bled, hob·bling.** —*v.i.* to move or walk awkwardly with a limp: *He had to hobble around in his cast for a month.* —*v.t.* **1.** to tie the front legs or hind legs of (a horse or other animal) together to prevent it from moving far. **2.** to hinder or hamper: *Lack of time hobbled him in his work.* —*n.* **1.** a rope or strap used to hobble an animal. **2.** an awkward walk or movement; limp.

hob·ble·de·hoy (hob′əl dē hoi′) *n.* a young boy, especially one who is awkward or gawky.

hob·by (hob′ē) *n. pl.,* **hob·bies.** an activity or interest that is pursued for pleasure in one's spare time: *The doctor's hobby was collecting stamps.*

hob·by·horse (hob′ē hôrs′) *n.* **1.** a toy consisting of a horse's head that is attached to a pole that a child can straddle and pretend to ride. **2.** another word for **rocking horse.**

hob·gob·lin (hob′gob′lin) *n.* **1.** a mischievous goblin or elf. **2.** an imaginary thing that causes fear; bogy.

hob·nail (hob′nāl′) *n.* a nail with a large head, used to protect the soles of heavy boots or shoes.

hob·nob (hob′nob′) *v.i.,* **hob·nobbed, hob·nob·bing.** to be on close or familiar terms; be friendly: *Her family hobnobs with the most important people in the city.*

ho·bo (hō′bō) *n. pl.,* **ho·bos** or **ho·boes.** a person who wanders from place to place and usually begs or does odd jobs for a living; tramp.

Ho Chi Minh (hō′ chē′ min′) 1890?–1969, the president of North Vietnam from 1954 to 1969.

Ho Chi Minh City, see **Saigon.**

hock¹ (hok) *n.* the joint in the hind leg of a horse or cow or similar animal, that is above the fetlock joint and corresponds to the ankle in man. [Old English *hōh* heel.]

hock² (hok) *v.t. Informal.* to pawn. [Dutch *hok* a pen for animals, prison.]

    in hock. *Informal.* **a.** in the possession of a pawnbroker. **b.** in debt.

hock·ey (hok′ē) *n.* **1.** a game played on ice by two teams of six players wearing skates. The players hit a rubber disk, called a puck, with hockey sticks, the object being to get the puck into the opponent's goal. Also, **ice hockey. 2.** see **field hockey.**

hockey stick, a long stick with a flat curved blade, used to hit the puck in ice hockey.

ho·cus-po·cus (hō′kəs pō′kəs) *n.* **1.** meaningless words used in performing magic tricks. **2.** any bit of trickery or nonsense.

hod (hod) *n.* **1.** a long-handled tool that consists of a V-shaped container that is closed at one end, used for carrying bricks, mortar, and similar materials on the shoulder. **2.** a coal scuttle.

hodge·podge (hoj′poj′) *n.* a confused mixture; mess; jumble: *The attic was filled with a hodgepodge of old clothes, furniture, toys, trunks, books, and magazines.*

hoe (hō) *n.* a tool with a wide, thin blade set at an angle to a long handle, used especially for weeding and loosening soil. —*v.,* **hoed, hoe·ing.** —*v.t.* to dig or cultivate with a hoe: *The farmer's wife hoed her vegetable garden.* —*v.i.* to use a hoe. —**ho′er,** *n.*

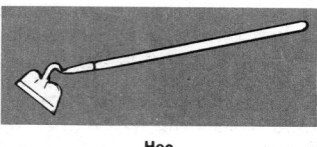

Hoe

hoe·cake (hō′kāk′) *n.* a coarse bread made of cornmeal.

hog (hog) *n.* **1.** a full-grown pig, raised for its meat. **2.** *Informal.* a greedy or filthy person. —*v.t.,* **hogged, hogging.** *Informal.* to take more than one's share of: *His brother hogged the cookies. The truck hogged the road.*

ho·gan (hō′gän) *n.* a dwelling used by the Navaho Indians, usually made of timber and branches and covered with earth.

Ho·garth, William (hō′gärth) 1697–1764, English painter and engraver.

hog·gish (hog′ish) *adj.* greedy or filthy. —**hog′gish·ly,** *adv.* —**hog′gish·ness,** *n.*

Hogan

hog·nose snake (hog′nōz′) any of several thick-nosed, harmless North American snakes.

hogs·head (hogz′hed′) *n.* **1.** a large cask or barrel, especially one that can contain from 63 to 140 gallons. **2.** a liquid measure, especially one equal to 63 gallons.

hog·wash (hog′wosh′, hog′wôsh′) *n.* **1.** worthless or nonsensical talk or writing. **2.** refuse fed to hogs; swill.

Hoh·en·zol·lern (hō′ən zol′ərn) *n.* the German royal family founded by Frederick I, that included the kings of Prussia from 1701 to 1918 and the emperors of Germany from 1871 to 1918.

hoist (hoist) *v.t.* to lift or pull up, especially by means of ropes and pulleys or a crane: *The sailors hoisted the cargo on board.* —*n.* **1.** an apparatus used for hoisting, such as a block and tackle. **2.** the act of hoisting.

Hok·kai·do (ho kī′dō) *n.* the northernmost and second largest island of Japan.

Hol·bein (hōl′bīn) **1. Hans (the Elder)** (häns). 1460?–1524, German painter. **2. Hans (the Younger).** 1497–1543, his son; German painter and engraver.

hold¹ (hōld) *v.,* **held, hold·ing.** —*v.t.* **1.** to take and keep in the hands or arms; clasp; grip: *He held the packages while I unlocked the door.* **2.** to support or bear: *Will that chair hold his weight?* **3.** to keep in a certain position; maintain: *The photographer asked her to hold the pose for a few minutes longer.* **4.** to have control or influence over: *The play held the audience's attention.* **5.** to keep under control; check: *The dam held back the flooding river.* **6.** to be able to contain: *A sponge holds water. This bus can hold fifty people.* **7.** to keep or have in the mind: *to hold an opinion, to hold a grudge.* **8.** to keep by force against an enemy; defend: *The troops held the fort.* **9.** to carry on or engage in: *to hold a conversation, to hold a meeting.* **10.** to believe to be; think; consider: *They hold him responsible for the accident.* —*v.i.* **1.** to remain fast: *The anchor held even in the rough seas.* **2.** to keep one's clasp or grip: *She held tightly to the railing as she came down the steps.* **3.** to stay faithful or attached; adhere: *to hold to a promise.*

He held to his beliefs. **4.** to remain or continue in a state, position, or condition. —*n.* **1.** the act of holding; grasp; grip: *The climber's tight hold on the rope saved him from a fall.* **2.** a controlling force; strong influence: *The dictator kept a tight hold on his people.* **3.** something that can be grasped, as for support: *The boy found enough holds to climb the side of the cliff.* **4.** *Music.* a sign or symbol indicating a pause. [Old English *healdan* or *haldan* to keep, retain, support, defend.]

  to hold down. a. to keep under control: *The policemen held down the crowd.* **b.** to have and work at: *to hold down a job.*

  to hold forth. a. to talk at great length: *to hold forth on a subject.* **b.** to offer; propose.

  to hold in. a. to keep in check; curb; restrain. **b.** to control or hide (one's feelings).

  to hold off. to keep away or at a distance.

  to hold on. *Informal.* **a.** to keep one's hold or grasp on something. **b.** to continue; last. **c.** to stop; wait: *Hold on!*

  to hold one's own. to keep one's condition, advantage, or position; stand one's ground.

  to hold out. a. to last; continue: *The food supply held out for a week.* **b.** to continue to resist: *The troops in the fort held out for two weeks.*

  to hold over. a. to keep for future action or consideration; postpone: *The proposal was held over for the next meeting.* **b.** to stay or keep beyond the regular time: *The movie was held over for another week because it was so popular.*

  to hold up. a. *Informal.* to rob. **b.** to bring or point attention to: *She held him up as an example of a good student to the class.* **c.** to stop or delay.

  to hold with. to approve of: *He did not hold with their plan.*

hold² (hōld) *n.* an area or space where cargo is stowed in a ship or airplane. A ship's hold is below the main deck. [Middle Dutch *hol.*]

hold·er (hōl′dər) *n.* **1.** a person who holds something, especially an owner of property or a title. **2.** something to hold something else with: *She used a holder to take the hot pan from the oven.*

hold·ing (hōl′ding) *n.* **1.** *also,* **holdings.** property owned, especially land, or stocks or bonds. **2.** *Sports.* the act of illegally hindering the movement of an opposing player with the hands or arms, as in football or basketball.

hold·up (hōld′up′) *n.* **1.** a robbery by someone who is armed. **2.** a stoppage or delay: *There was a holdup of traffic on the road to the bridge.*

hole (hōl) *n.* **1.** a hollow place or cavity in something solid; pit: *The workmen filled in a hole in the street.* **2.** an opening in or through something: *He had holes in the elbows of his sweater.* **3.** a small, dingy, filthy place. **4.** a flaw; defect; fault: *There were many holes in the prisoner's alibi.* **5.** *Informal.* an awkward or embarrassing position: *He tried to help his friend out of a hole by lending him money.* **6.** *Golf.* **a.** a small cup sunk into a green, into which the ball is hit. **b.** one of the divisions of a golf course. —*v.t.,* **holed, hol·ing. 1.** to make a hole or holes in: *The ground was holed along the road for telephone posts.* **2.** to hit or drive (a golf ball) into a hole.

  to hole up. a. to hibernate: *The bear holed up for the winter.* **b.** to hide oneself: *The fugitive holed up in an abandoned house.*

hol·i·day (hol′ə dā′) *n.* **1.** a day on which most people do not work, especially a day that is fixed by custom or law to celebrate a special event: *The Fourth of July and Thanksgiving Day are American holidays.* **2.** *also,* **holidays.** a period of rest or freedom from work; vacation: *He*

is home for the Christmas holidays. **3.** a holy day. —*adj.* relating or suited to a holiday: *holiday shopping.*

ho·li·ness (hō′lē nis) *n.* **1.** the state or quality of being holy. **2. Holiness.** the title for the pope. ▲ used with **Your** when speaking to the pope and with **His** when speaking of him.

Hol·land (hol′ənd) *n.* another name for **the Netherlands.**

Hol·land·er (hol′ən dər) *n.* see **Dutchman.**

hol·ler (hol′ər) *Informal. v.t.* to shout loudly. —*v.i.* to cry out loudly. —*n.* a loud shout.

hol·low (hol′ō) *adj.* **1.** having a hole or space inside; not solid: *A water pipe is hollow. The squirrel lived in an old, hollow tree trunk.* **2.** having a shape like a cup or bowl; scooped out: *The car bounced over a hollow place in the road.* **3.** deeply set; sunken: *hollow cheeks.* **4.** deep and muffled: *Their footsteps made a hollow sound as they walked through the cave.* **5.** without sincerity or truth; false: *The defeated team's praise of the winning team's victory was hollow.* —*n.* **1.** a hollow or empty space; hole: *She tripped over the hollow in the path.* **2.** a valley: *The farm was set in a hollow surrounded by rolling hills.* —*v.t.* **1.** to form by making hollow: *The workmen hollowed out a tunnel in the hill.* **2.** to make hollow: *The tree trunk was hollowed out by age.* —**hol′low·ly,** *adv.* —**hol′low·ness,** *n.*

hol·ly (hol′ē) *n. pl.,* **hol·lies. 1.** any of a group of trees or woody shrubs with glossy, spiny-toothed leaves and bright red berries. **2.** the leaves and berries that grow on this tree, widely used as Christmas decorations.

hol·ly·hock (hol′ē hok′) *n.* **1.** a stalk of large showy flowers of various colors, growing on a tall plant that has wrinkled leaves and a strong, hairy stem. **2.** the plant bearing these flowers.

Hol·ly·wood (hol′ē wood′) *n.* **1.** a section of Los Angeles, known as the center of the U.S. motion-picture and television industries. **2.** a city in southeastern Florida, on the Atlantic Ocean. Pop. (1970), 106,873.

holm (hōm) *n.* see **holm oak.**

Holmes (hōmz) **1. Oliver Wen·dell** (wend′əl). 1809–1894, U.S. author and physician. **2. Oliver Wendell, Jr.** 1841–1935, his son; an associate justice of the U.S. Supreme Court from 1902 to 1932. **3.** see **Sherlock Holmes.**

Hollyhock

hol·mi·um (hōl′mē əm) *n.* a lustrous metallic element, one of the rare-earth elements. Symbol: **Ho**

holm oak, an evergreen oak grown in warm regions of the world, and having broad, leathery leaves.

hol·o·caust (hol′ə kôst′) *n.* **1.** a great or complete destruction, especially by fire. **2.** a sacrifice that is entirely consumed by fire.

Hol·o·cene (hol′ə sēn′) *n.* the Recent geological epoch. —*adj.* of, relating to, or characteristic of this epoch.

hol·o·gram (hol′ə gram′) *n.* a type of photograph made by exposing film to certain kinds of light, such as laser beams. When properly lit, the hologram produces a three-dimensional picture.

---

at; āpe; cär; end; mē; it; īce; hot; ōld; fôrk; wood; fōōl; oil; out; up; turn; sing; thin; **th**is; **hw** in white; zh in treasure. The symbol ə stands for the sound of **a** in about, **e** in taken, **i** in pencil, **o** in lemon, and **u** in circus.

hol·o·graph (hol′ə graf′) *adj.* written entirely in the handwriting of the person who signed it: *a holograph document.* —*n.* any document written in this way.

Hol·stein (hōl′stīn′, hōl′stēn′) *n.* any of a breed of black-and-white dairy cattle. It is the largest dairy breed.

hol·ster (hōl′stər) *n.* a leather case for a firearm, especially one attached to a belt at the waist or shoulder for a pistol.

ho·ly (hō′lē) *adj.,* **ho·li·er, ho·li·est. 1.** belonging to, dedicated to, or coming from God; sacred: *a holy altar.* **2.** free from sin; pious; saintly: *A church is a holy place to many people.* **3.** worthy of or inspiring reverence.

Holy City, a city considered sacred by the followers of a particular religion.

Holy Communion 1. a church service in which bread and wine are consecrated and distributed to members of the congregation in commemoration of the Last Supper. **2.** the bread and wine used in this service.

holy day, a day set apart for religious observance.

Holy Father, a title and form of address used in speaking or referring to the pope.

Holy Ghost, the third person of the Trinity.

Holy Grail *Medieval Legend.* the sacred cup or dish used by Christ at the Last Supper, and by one of His followers to catch drops of the blood of Christ at the Crucifixion. King Arthur's Knights of the Round Table searched for the Holy Grail.

Holy Land, another name for **Palestine.**

holy of holies, the innermost chamber of the Temple in ancient Jerusalem. It housed the Ark of the Covenant and could be entered only by the high priest on the Day of Atonement.

Holy Roman Empire, an empire in western and central Europe that was founded by Charlemagne in 800 and that lapsed into anarchy late in the ninth century. It was revived by Otto I of Germany in 962 and lasted until 1806.

Holy Scripture, see Bible *(def. 1).*

Holy See, the office, authority, or jurisdiction of the pope.

Holy Spirit, another term for **Holy Ghost.**

ho·ly·stone (hō′lē stōn′) *n.* a flat piece of soft sandstone, used for scouring the wooden decks of ships. —*v.t.,* **ho·ly·stoned, ho·ly·ston·ing.** to scrub with a holystone.

holy water, water blessed by a priest, used in religious services.

Holy Week, the week before Easter, beginning with Palm Sunday.

Holy Writ, see Bible *(def. 1).*

hom·age (hom′ij, om′ij) *n.* **1.** honor, respect, or reverence: *The university paid homage to the professor by establishing a scholarship in his name.* **2.** the formal acknowledgment of allegiance and obligation by a feudal vassal to his lord.

hom·bre (ōm′brā, ōm′brē) *n. Informal.* man; fellow.

home (hōm) *n.* **1.** the place in which a person lives; residence: *His home is in that apartment house.* **2.** the home thought of as a family unit; family; household: *a happy home, a broken home.* **3.** a country, region, town, or locality where one was born or raised or where one lives: *New York has been his home for five years now.* **4.** a place or region where something is commonly found: *Australia is the home of the koala bear and the kangaroo.* **5.** an institution or establishment for the shelter and care of certain people: *a home for orphans, a home for the aged.* **6.** a goal or place of safety in certain sports and games. **7.** see **home**

plate. —*adv.* **1.** at, to, or toward home: *He wrote home every week.* **2.** to the place or mark aimed at: *The bullet struck home.* **3.** to the very heart or center: *Her criticism hit home.* —*v.,* **homed, hom·ing.** —*v.i.* **1.** to go or return home. **2.** to have a home. —*v.t.* to cause to go toward a particular point or target: *to home an airplane by radar.* —**home′like′,** *adj.*

at home. a. at one's ease; comfortable: *She always felt at home in her friend's house.* **b.** ready to receive visitors.

home base, another term for **home plate.**

home economics, the science, art, and study of managing a household, including such subjects as cooking, budgeting household money, and child care.

home·land (hōm′land′) *n.* a country where a person was born or has his home.

home·less (hōm′lis) *adj.* having no home.

home·ly (hōm′lē) *adj.,* **home·li·er, home·li·est. 1.** having plain features; not good-looking; unattractive. **2.** of a familiar or everyday nature; simple: *homely manners, homely food.* —**home′li·ness,** *n.*

home·made (hōm′mād′) *adj.* **1.** made at home: *homemade cookies.* **2.** crudely or simply done.

home·mak·er (hōm′mā′kər) *n.* a person who manages a household, especially a housewife.

home plate *Baseball.* a slab beside which a baseball player stands to hit a pitched ball, and which he must touch after rounding the bases in order to score a run.

hom·er (hō′mər) *n. Informal.* another term for **home run.**

Ho·mer (hō′mər) **1.** Greek poet who lived in about the eighth century B.C., believed to be the author of the *Iliad* and the *Odyssey.* **2. Wins·low** (winz′lō). 1836–1910, U.S. painter.

Ho·mer·ic (hō mer′ik) *adj.* of, relating to, or characteristic of Homer, his poetry, or the period of Greek history about which he wrote.

home·room (hōm′rōōm′, hōm′room′) *n.* **1.** a classroom to which the students of a class report to have their attendance checked and to hear school announcements. **2.** the time during which such a class meets.

home rule, a system under which one political unit within a larger one, as a city within a state, is granted power to manage its own affairs.

home run 1. a hit made by a baseball player that allows him to round the bases and score a run. **2.** a score made in such a way.

home·sick (hōm′sik′) *adj.* sad or ill because one is away from one's home or family; longing for home. —**home′-sick′ness,** *n.*

home·spun (hōm′spun′) *adj.* **1.** spun or made at home. **2.** simple and plain in character: *homespun jokes.* —*n.* **1.** a fabric woven of yarn spun at home or by hand. **2.** any of various coarse fabrics woven to resemble this.

home·stead (hōm′sted′) *n.* **1.** a house with its buildings and the land they are on. **2.** a parcel of 160 acres of public land granted by the United States government to a settler for farming. —*v.t.* to settle on and claim (land). —*v.i.* to settle and claim a homestead. —**home′stead′er,** *n.*

home stretch 1. the straight part of a track between the last turn and the finish line. **2.** the last part of any trip or effort.

home·ward (hōm′wərd) *adv.* also, **homewards.** toward home: *The hikers turned homeward.* —*adj.* directed toward home: *a homeward trip.*

home·work (hōm′wurk′) *n.* **1.** a school lesson to be studied or prepared outside the classroom, usually at home. **2.** any work done at home.

home·y (hō′mē) *adj.,* **hom·i·er, hom·i·est.** *Informal.* informal and friendly; cozy; comfortable.

hom·i·cid·al (hom'ə sīd'əl) *adj.* **1.** of or relating to homicide. **2.** tending to homicide; murderous: *a homicidal maniac, a homicidal rage.*

hom·i·cide¹ (hom'ə sīd') *n.* the killing of one human being by another. [Old French *homicide,* going back to Latin *homō* man + *-cīdium* a killing.]

hom·i·cide² (hom'ə sīd') *n.* a person who kills another. [Old French *homicide,* going back to Latin *homō* man + *-cīda* killer.]

hom·i·ly (hom'ə lē) *n. pl.,* **hom·i·lies. 1.** a sermon, especially one based on some portion of the Bible. **2.** a solemn and usually long talk, especially about morals.

homing pigeon, a pigeon trained to fly home, often used to carry messages. Also, **carrier pigeon.**

hom·i·ny (hom'ə nē) *n.* kernels of white corn that have been dried and hulled, prepared for eating by being mixed with water and boiled.

hominy grits, see grits *(def. 1).*

homo- *combining form* same: *homograph, homogenize.*

ho·mo·ge·ne·i·ty (hō'mə jə nē'ə tē) *n.* the state or quality of being homogeneous.

ho·mo·ge·ne·ous (hō'mə jē'nē əs) *adj.* **1.** of the same kind; similar or identical: *two homogeneous parts.* **2.** having a similar character or similar parts throughout: *a homogeneous mixture.* —**ho'mo·ge'ne·ous·ly,** *adv.* —**ho'mo·ge'ne·ous·ness,** *n.*

ho·mog·e·nize (hə moj'ə nīz') *v.t.,* **ho·mog·e·nized, ho·mog·e·niz·ing.** to make homogeneous.

homogenized milk, milk in which the fat particles are distributed evenly throughout and do not separate and rise to the top as cream.

hom·o·graph (hom'ə graf') *n.* a word with the same spelling as another, but with a different origin, meaning, and, sometimes, pronunciation. *Bear* meaning "to hold up or carry" and *bear* meaning "a large, heavy animal" are homographs; as are *bow* meaning "to bend forward at the waist" and *bow* meaning "a weapon for shooting arrows."

ho·mol·o·gous (hə mol'ə gəs) *adj.* corresponding, as in position, proportion, function, or structure. The human arm, the wing of a bird, and the foreleg of a horse are homologous.

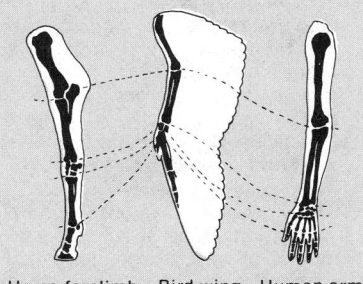

Horse forelimb　Bird wing　Human arm

Homologous structures

hom·o·nym (hom'ə nim') *n.* a word with the same pronunciation as another, but with a different meaning and, often, a different spelling. *Lean* meaning "to bend" and *lean* meaning "thin" are homonyms, as are *boar* and *bore.*

hom·o·phone (hom'ə fōn') *n.* **1.** a letter or group of letters having the same sound as another. The letters *ks* and *x* are homophones. **2.** a word with the same pronunciation as another, but with a different meaning and spelling. *Know* and *no* are homophones. **3.** any word with the same pronunciation as another; homonym.

ho·mop·ter·ous (hə mop'tər əs) *adj.* of or belonging to a group of insects including aphids and cicadas, characterized by sucking mouth parts and membranous wings.

Ho·mo sa·pi·ens (hō'mō sā'pē ənz) the human being viewed as the only living species of the genus *Homo.* [Modern Latin *Homo sapiens* wise man.]

ho·mo·sex·u·al (hō'mə sek'shōō əl) *adj.* of, relating to, or showing homosexuality. —*n.* a homosexual person.

ho·mo·sex·u·al·i·ty (hō'mə sek'shōō al'ə tē) *n.* sexual attraction toward members of one's own sex.

Hon. 1. Honorable. **2.** Honorary.

Hon·du·ras (hon door'əs, hon dyoor'əs) *n.* a country in northern Central America with coastlines on the Caribbean Sea and the Pacific Ocean. Capital, Tegucigalpa. Area, 43,277 sq. mi. Pop. (1980), 3,693,000.

hone (hōn) *n.* a whetstone with a fine grain, used to sharpen the cutting edges of tools, as razors or scissors. —*v.t.,* **honed, hon·ing.** to sharpen on or as on a hone.

hon·est (on'ist) *adj.* **1.** truthful, fair, or trustworthy, as in character or actions: *an honest person, an honest effort.* **2.** earned or gotten fairly and without deceit: *to make an honest living.* **3.** sincere; frank; open: *The young boy had an honest face.* —**hon'est·ly,** *adv.* —**hon'est·ness,** *n.*

hon·es·ty (on'is tē) *n.* **1.** the state or quality of being honest: *The honesty of his answer is not in question.* **2.** truthfulness; sincerity; fairness: *He could not, in all honesty, agree to their terms.*

hon·ey (hun'ē) *n. pl.,* **hon·eys. 1.** a thick, sweet liquid, made by bees from the nectar they collect from flowers, used for food and as a sweetening agent. **2.** a sweet quality; sweetness. **3.** sweet one; darling; dear. —*adj.* of, like, or containing honey; sweet. —*v.t.,* **hon·eyed** or **hon·ied, hon·ey·ing. 1.** to sweeten with honey. **2.** to talk to in a sweet or flattering manner.

hon·ey·bee (hun'ē bē') *n.* any bee that makes and stores honey.

hon·ey·comb (hun'ē kōm') *n.* **1.** a wax structure formed by bees, consisting of six-sided cells arranged back to back, used for storing honey, pollen, eggs, and larvae. **2.** anything resembling this in appearance or structure.

Honeybee

—*adj.* like a honeycomb: *Termites chew wood in a honeycomb pattern.* —*v.t.* to make full of holes or cavities like a honeycomb: *Secret passages honeycombed the castle.*

hon·ey·dew (hun'ē dōō', hun'ē dyōō') *n.* **1.** see **honeydew melon. 2.** a sweet substance secreted on leaves and stems by aphids and certain other plant-sucking insects. **3.** a sweet substance that oozes from the leaves of certain plants in hot weather.

honeydew melon, a muskmelon having a smooth, creamy-yellow rind and sweet, light green flesh.

hon·ey·moon (hun'ē mōōn') *n.* a vacation taken by a newly married couple, usually immediately after the wedding. —*v.i.* to go or be on a honeymoon. —**hon'ey·moon'er,** *n.*

hon·ey·suck·le (hun'ē suk'əl) *n.* any of a group of erect or climbing shrubs bearing fragrant, bell-shaped, white, yellow, or pink flowers.

Hong Kong (hong' kong') **1.** a British crown colony off the southeastern coast of China. Area, 398 sq. mi. Pop. (1976), 4,402,990. **2.** another name for **Victoria,** the capital of this colony.

Ho·ni·ar·a (hō'nē är'ə) *n.* the capital of the Solomon Islands. Pop. (1970), 11,191.

at; āpe; cär; end; mē; it; īce; hot; ōld; fôrk; wood; fōōl; oil; out; up; turn; sing; thin; <u>th</u>is; hw in white; zh in treasure. The symbol ə stands for the sound of **a** in about, **e** in taken, **i** in pencil, **o** in lemon, and **u** in circus.

H

hon·ied (hun′ēd) a past tense and past participle of **honey.**

honk (hongk) *n.* **1.** the cry of a goose. **2.** any similar sound, especially that made by the horn of an automobile. —*v.i.* to utter or make such a sound. —*v.t.* to cause (something) to make such a sound: *Stop honking the horn!* —**honk′er,** *n.*

Hon·o·lu·lu (hon′ə loō′loō) *n.* the capital, major city, and chief port of Hawaii, on the southern coast of Oahu. Pop. (1970), 324,871.

hon·or (on′ər) *also, British,* **hon·our.** *n.* **1.** a sense of what is right or moral; integrity: *A man of honor would not behave in such a cowardly way.* **2.** a good name or reputation; position of being respected; credit: *The businessman's honor was at stake.* **3.** a source or cause of respect, esteem, or pride: *It was a great honor to receive the award.* **4.** glory; renown; fame: *The fewer men, the greater share of honor* (Shakespeare, *Henry V*). **5. Honor.** a title of respect used in speaking or referring to certain officials, such as a judge or mayor, preceded by *His* or *Your.* **6. honors.** something done or given as a sign of respect, esteem, or distinction: *The hero was buried with full military honors.* **7. honors.** special recognition given to a student by a school or college for outstanding academic achievement: *He was graduated with highest honors.* —*v.t.* **1.** to regard with great respect or esteem: *Honor thy father and thy mother* (Exodus 20:12). **2.** to give honor to; favor; dignify. **3.** to accept as valid for payment or credit: *The store would not honor my credit card.*

hon·or·a·ble (on′ər ə bəl) *adj.* **1.** characterized by or having a sense of what is right or moral: *an honorable man.* **2.** bringing honor or distinction; creditable: *an honorable achievement.* **3.** worthy of honor and respect: *an honorable profession.* **4.** having high rank or position; noble; illustrious: *He is descended from an honorable family.* **5.** done with honor or respect: *The soldier received an honorable discharge at the end of the war.* **6. Honorable.** a title of respect used in speaking of certain government officials, such as members of Congress and cabinet officers, or certain members of the nobility. —**hon′or·a·ble·ness,** *n.* —**hon′or·a·bly,** *adv.*

hon·o·rar·i·um (on′ə rer′ē əm) *n. pl.,* **hon·o·rar·i·ums** or **hon·o·rar·i·a** (on′ə rer′ē ə). a fee for services given, especially by a professional person: *The visiting lecturer received an honorarium of $300.*

hon·or·ar·y (on′ə rer′ē) *adj.* **1.** given as an honor: *an honorary degree from a university.* **2.** holding a title or position as an honor without the usual duties or a salary: *an honorary chairman of a fund drive.*

hon·our (on′ər) *British.* another spelling of **honor.**

Hon·shu (hon′shoō) *n.* the largest island of Japan.

hood¹ (hood) *n.* **1.** a covering for the head and back of the neck, often attached to the neckline of a coat, jacket, or other garment. **2.** anything resembling a hood in shape or use, such as the loose skin on the neck of a cobra. **3.** a movable metal covering over the engine of an automobile. **4.** a fold of cloth worn over the back of an academic gown. —*v.t.* to cover or furnish with a hood. [Old English *hōd* covering for the head and back of the neck.] —**hood′like′,** *adj.*

hood² (hood) *n. Slang.* hoodlum.

Hood, Mount, a mountain in the Cascade Range, in northwestern Oregon.

Hood¹ *(def. 4)*

-hood *suffix* **1.** the state, quality, or condition of being: *childhood, motherhood.* **2.** the entire group, class, or body of: *priesthood, brotherhood.*

hood·ed (hood′id) *adj.* **1.** having, wearing, or covered with a hood. **2.** shaped like a hood.

hood·lum (hood′ləm) *n. Informal.* **1.** a young ruffian or rowdy. **2.** a gangster; thug.

hood·wink (hood′wingk′) *v.t.* **1.** to trick or deceive. **2.** *Archaic.* to blindfold.

hoof (hoof, hoof) *n. pl.,* **hooves** or **hoofs.** **1.** a hard, horny covering on the feet of certain animals, as horses, cattle, pigs, or deer. **2.** the whole foot of such an animal.
  on the hoof. (of livestock) not butchered; alive.

hoof·beat (hoof′bēt′, hoof′bēt′) *n.* the sound made by a hoofed animal when it walks, trots, or runs.

hoofed (hooft, hooft) *adj.* having hooves.

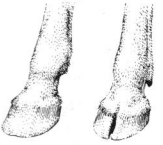

Single-toe hoof   Cloven hoof

hook (hook) *n.* **1.** a sharply bent piece of metal, wood, or other firm material, having one or more free ends used for catching, hanging, fastening, or holding something: *a coat hook.* **2.** a curved piece of wire with a barb at one end, used for catching fish; fishhook. **3.** something like a hook in shape or use. **4.** a sharp bend or angle in the length or course of something, as in a river. **5.** a projecting point or spit of land. **6.** *Golf.* a stroke in which the ball curves to the left if the golfer is right-handed, and to the right if he is left-handed. **7.** *Boxing.* a short, swinging blow made with the arm bent. **8.** *Baseball.* a pitch that curves. —*v.t.* **1.** to attach, fasten, or hang with a hook or hooks: *The sailor hooked the line to the side of the boat.* **2.** to catch or take hold of with a hook: *The fisherman hooked three trout in the stream.* **3.** to make into the shape of a hook; bend; crook: *The boy hooked his leg over the arm of the chair.* **4.** to make, as a rug or mat, by pulling yarn or strips of cloth through a piece of fabric by means of a hook. **5.** *Golf.* to hit (a ball) so that it hooks. —*v.i.* **1.** to have the form of a hook; curve. **2.** to be attached, fastened, or hung with a hook or hooks: *The skirt hooks on the side.* —**hook′like′,** *adj.*
  by hook or by crook. by any means, fair or foul; in any way possible: *The dishonest politician was determined to win the election by hook or by crook.*
  on one's own hook. *Informal.* by oneself; independently: *She got the job on her own hook without any help from her parents.*
  to hook up. to assemble (a mechanical or electrical device) and connect it to a source of power: *The electrician hooked up the doorbell.*

hook·ah (hook′ə) *n.* a tobacco pipe of Oriental origin, having a long tube attached to a container of water through which the smoke is drawn and cooled.

hook and eye, a clothing fastener consisting of a metallic or plastic hook and a loop or bar to which the hook may be attached.

hooked (hookt) *adj.* **1.** curved or bent like a hook. **2.** having a hook or hooks.

hooked rug, a rug made by looping yarn or strips of cloth through a piece of fabric, as canvas or burlap.

hook·up (hook′up′) *n.* **1.** the arrangement and connection of electric or electronic parts or circuits, such as a network of television stations. **2.** any arrangement, relationship, or connection of separate or related parts.

Hookah

hook·worm (hook′wurm′) *n.* **1.** any of several small, threadlike, parasitic worms that live in the intestines of man and other animals. It bites into blood vessels and feeds on the blood. **2.** a disease that is caused by hookworms. It is characterized by anemia and weakness.

hook·y (hook′ē) *n. Informal.* **to play hooky.** to stay out of school without permission or a good excuse.

hoop (hoop, hoop) *n.* **1.** a circular band or ring, as of wood or metal, for holding together the staves of a barrel. **2.** a child's toy consisting of a large circular band of wood, metal, or plastic which can be rolled along the ground or spun around the body. **3.** a flexible, circular band of whalebone or metal, formerly used to make a woman's skirt stand out from her body. —*v.t.* to bind or fasten with a hoop or hoops.

hoop skirt, a woman's skirt worn over a framework of flexible hoops connected by tapes to make the skirt stand out.

hoo·ray (hoo rā′) another spelling of **hurrah.**

hoot (hoot) *n.* **1.** the cry of an owl. **2.** a cry or shout, especially one expressing scorn or disapproval: *His appearance on stage was greeted with hoots from the audience.* **3.** *Informal.* a very small or insignificant amount; the least bit: *His advice isn't worth a hoot.* —*v.i.* **1.** to utter the cry of an owl. **2.** to cry or shout out, as in scorn or disapproval: *The fans hooted at the outfielder's error.* —*v.t.* **1.** to drive away by hooting: *The audience hooted the actor off the stage.* **2.** to show scorn or disapproval of by hooting: *The crowd hooted the congressman's speech.*

Hoo·ver, Herbert Clark (hoo′vər) 1874–1964, the thirty-first president of the United States, from 1929 to 1933.

Hoover Dam, a large dam on the Colorado River between Nevada and Arizona, formerly known as **Boulder Dam.**

hooves (hoovz, hoovz) a plural of **hoof.**

hop¹ (hop) *v.,* **hopped, hop·ping.** —*v.i.* **1.** to make a short leap or series of leaps on one foot. **2.** to move in short leaps on both or all feet at once: *The frog hopped along the edge of the pond.* **3.** to rise or get up quickly. —*v.t.* **1.** to jump over: *The rabbit hopped the fence.* **2.** *Informal.* to board and ride in (a vehicle), especially without paying: *The hobo hopped a freight train that took him to Houston.* —*n.* **1.** the act of hopping. **2.** *Informal.* a trip, especially in an airplane. **3.** *Informal.* a dance or dancing party. **4.** *Informal.* a bounce or rebound: *The ball took a bad hop and the shortstop could not catch it.* [Old English *hoppian* to leap, dance.]

hop² (hop) *n.* **1. hops.** the cone-shaped, greenish-yellow fruits of any of a group of plants related to the mulberry, containing bitter-tasting oils and used in the brewing of beer and other malt beverages. **2.** a long-stemmed, climbing plant bearing this fruit. —*v.t.,* **hopped, hop·ping.** to flavor or treat with hops. [Middle Dutch *hoppe.*]

hope (hōp) *v.,* **hoped, hop·ing.** —*v.t.* **1.** to desire with expectation of fulfillment: *Susan hoped her book would be published.* **2.** to wish, believe, or trust: *I hope you will enjoy your vacation.* —*v.i.* to have expectation or desire: *The politician hoped for the support of all the people in his state.* —*n.* **1.** a desire accompanied by expectation of fulfillment: *He has hopes of going to college.* **2.** something that is hoped for: *The senator staked his career on the hope of winning reelection.* **3.** a person or thing on which hopes are placed or centered.

hope·ful (hōp′fəl) *adj.* **1.** full of or showing hope. **2.** inspiring hope; promising fulfillment: *a hopeful sign.* —*n.* a person who is considered likely to succeed or who desires success: *Many young hopefuls tried out for the play.* —**hope′ful·ly,** *adv.* —**hope′ful·ness,** *n.*

hope·less (hōp′lis) *adj.* **1.** having or feeling no hope: *After he lost his job he felt hopeless.* **2.** inspiring no hope: *The patient's condition is hopeless.* —**hope′less·ly,** *adv.* —**hope′less·ness,** *n.*

Ho·pi (hō′pē) *n. pl.,* **Ho·pis** or **Ho·pi. 1.** a member of a tribe of Pueblo Indians living in northeastern Arizona and New Mexico. **2.** the language spoken by the Hopis.

hop·per (hop′ər) *n.* **1.** a person or thing that hops, such as a grasshopper. **2.** a container with a narrow opening at the bottom, used to hold grain, coal, or other material, and to empty it into another container or part.

hop·scotch (hop′skoch′) *n.* a children's game played on a course usually consisting of a pattern of numbered squares drawn on the pavement or ground. The players hop into the squares in sequence and try to pick up a stone or other object that has been tossed into one of the squares.

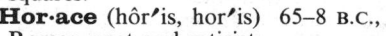

Hopper

Hor·ace (hôr′is, hor′is) 65–8 B.C., Roman poet and satirist.

horde (hôrd) *n.* **1.** a large group; swarm; multitude: *A horde of people poured out of the stadium when the football game ended.* **2.** a group of wandering people; nomadic tribe or clan: *a horde of Mongols.*

hore·hound (hôr′hound′) *also,* **hoar·hound.** *n.* **1.** a bitter, aromatic plant related to the mint, having whitish, woolly leaves and stems and bearing clusters of small flowers. **2.** a candy or cough medicine flavored with an extract obtained from the leaves of this plant.

ho·ri·zon (hə rī′zən) *n.* **1.** the line where the sky and the earth or sea seem to meet: *Two ships were barely visible on the horizon.* **2.** the limit or range of knowledge, interest, or experience: *Meeting new people widened the young man's horizon.*

hor·i·zon·tal (hôr′ə zont′əl, hor′ə zont′əl) *adj.* **1.** parallel to the horizon; level. **2.** of, relating to, or near the horizon. —*n.* something horizontal, such as a line, plane, or direction. —**hor′i·zon′tal·ly,** *adv.*

hor·mone (hôr′mōn) *n.* any of numerous chemical substances formed in and by the endocrine glands, which enter the bloodstream directly and affect the activity of other organs. Hormones regulate body growth, control sexual activity and development, and maintain the body's chemical balance.

horn (hôrn) *n.* **1.** a hard, permanent growth on the head of various hoofed animals, including cattle, sheep, antelope, and rhinoceroses. **2.** one of the antlers of a deer. **3.** a hornlike projection on the head of various other animals, such as the tuft of feathers on a horned owl. **4.** the substance or material of which horn is composed. **5.** a container formed from or shaped like a horn. **6.** *Music.* **a.** any of various brass instruments usually consisting of a coiled metal tube that gradually widens into a flaring bell, especially the French horn. **b.** *Informal.* any brass instrument, especially a trumpet. **c.** any wind instrument resembling or originally made from the horn of an animal.

at; āpe; cär; end; mē; it; īce; hot; ōld; fôrk; wood; fool; oil; out; up; turn; sing; thin; **th**is; hw in white; zh in treasure. The symbol ə stands for the sound of **a** in about, **e** in taken, **i** in pencil, **o** in lemon, and **u** in circus.

H

7. a device used to sound a warning signal: *The bus driver honked his horn at the children in the street.* **8.** something shaped like a horn, such as a cape or peninsula. **9.** either of the pointed ends of a crescent, as of the moon. —**horn′less**, *adj.* —**horn′like′**, *adj.*

   to horn in. *Slang.* to enter without being invited; butt in; intrude: *to horn in on a conversation.*

Horn, Cape, a cape on an island of Tierra del Fuego, forming the southernmost tip of South America.

horn·bill (hôrn′bil′) *n.* any of various birds living in forests of Africa, Asia, and the East Indies, usually having a large, colorful bill with a horny growth on top. Hornbills range from two to five feet in length.

horn·blende (hôrn′blend′) *n.* a mineral, usually dark green or black, found in granite and various igneous and metamorphic rocks.

horn·book (hôrn′book′) *n.* a primer consisting of a page with the alphabet and a prayer or numerals on it, covered with a sheet of transparent horn and fastened in a frame with a handle. It was formerly used, mainly in England in the fifteenth through eighteenth centuries, in teaching children to read.

horned (hôrnd) *adj.* having a horn, horns, or hornlike growths: *a horned moon, a horned snail.*

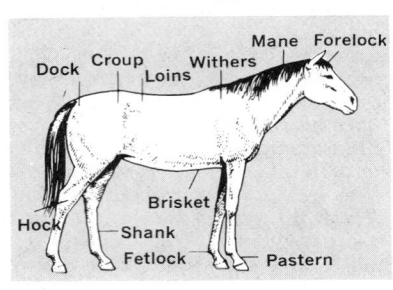

Hornbill

horned owl, any of various owls having hornlike tufts of feathers on the top of the head. It is one of the largest owls and is noted for its fierceness and strength.

horned toad, an insect-eating lizard common in dry areas of the western United States, having spiny horns on the head and fringed scales along the sides of the body.

hor·net (hôr′nit) *n.* any of various large wasps that live in colonies and are often reddish-brown or black with dull markings.

Horned toad

Female hornets have stingers and can give a painful sting.

horn of plenty, another term for **cornucopia.**

horn·pipe (hôrn′pīp′) *n.* **1.** a lively British folk dance, usually done by one person, formerly popular among sailors. **2.** the music for such a dance.

horn·y (hôr′nē) *adj.,* **horn·i·er, horn·i·est. 1.** made of horn or of something like it. **2.** having a horn, horns, or hornlike growths. **3.** hard like horn; calloused.

hor·o·scope (hôr′ə skōp′, hor′ə skōp′) *n.* **1.** a prediction about one's personal future, often containing advice, especially for a particular day. It is based on an interpretation of the positions of the planets at a given time. **2.** the relative positions of the planets at any particular moment, especially at the time of a person's birth. **3.** a diagram of the twelve signs of the zodiac with relation to the positions of the planets, used to predict the future.

hor·ren·dous (hô ren′dəs, ho ren′dəs) *adj.* horrible; dreadful; frightful. —**hor·ren′dous·ly,** *adv.*

hor·ri·ble (hôr′ə bəl, hor′ə bəl) *adj.* **1.** causing or tending to cause horror; terrible; dreadful: *The scene of the accident was horrible.* **2.** *Informal.* extremely unpleasant, disagreeable, shocking, or ugly: *She has a horrible temper.* —**hor′ri·ble·ness,** *n.* —**hor′ri·bly,** *adv.*

hor·rid (hôr′id, hor′id) *adj.* **1.** causing horror; dreadful. **2.** *Informal.* extremely unpleasant, disagreeable, or shocking. —**hor′rid·ly,** *adv.* —**hor′rid·ness,** *n.*

hor·ri·fy (hôr′ə fī′, hor′ə fī′) *v.t.,* **hor·ri·fied, hor·ri·fy·ing. 1.** to cause to feel horror: *The news of the war horrified the country.* **2.** *Informal.* to shock greatly and unpleasantly.

hor·ror (hôr′ər, hor′ər) *n.* **1.** a feeling of great fear and dread; terror. **2.** a great dislike; loathing: *She has a horror of snakes.* **3.** the quality of causing horror: *the horror of war.* **4.** a person or thing that causes horror. **5.** *Informal.* something that is very disagreeable, shocking, or ugly: *That blue dress is a horror.*

hors d'oeuvre (ôr durv′) *pl.,* **hors d'oeuvres** (ôr durvz′). a hot or cold appetizer, such as olives, celery, or cheese, that is served before the main courses of a meal. [French *hors d'oeuvre* a side dish, something out of the ordinary course, literally, outside the work.]

horse (hôrs) *n. pl.,* **hors·es. 1.** a four-legged, hoofed animal having a long, flowing mane and tail. Horses are used for pulling and carrying loads and for riding. **2.** a full-grown male horse. **3.** a gymnastic apparatus consisting of a leather-covered block mounted on four legs, used for vaulting and other exercises. **4.** a frame or structure, usually having four legs, used for holding or supporting something. **5.** mounted troops; cavalry. —*v.t.,* **horsed, hors·ing.** to furnish with a horse or horses.

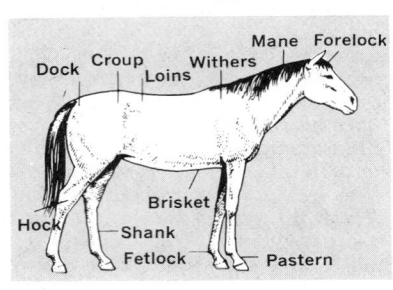

Horse

horse·back (hors′bak′) *n.* the back of a horse. —*adv.* on a horse: *to ride horseback.*

horse chestnut 1. a large tree widely grown in Europe and the United States, bearing clusters of white flowers. **2.** the nut of this tree, containing two large, shiny, brown seeds.

horse·flesh (hôrs′flesh′) *n.* **1.** horses as a group: *That trainer is a good judge of horseflesh.* **2.** the flesh of a horse.

horse·fly (hôrs′flī′) *n. pl.,* **horse·flies.** a large fly having a stout, hairy, usually black or brown body. The female attacks various animals, including man, and gives a painful bite.

horse·hair (hôrs′her′) *n.* **1.** the hair of a horse, especially from the mane or tail. **2.** a stiff fabric made with this hair, usually in combination with other fibers, used especially for upholstery. —*adj.* made of, covered, or stuffed with horsehair.

horse·hide (hôrs′hīd′) *n.* **1.** the hide of a horse. **2.** the leather made from this hide.

horse latitudes, two regions of high atmospheric pressure and mainly calm, dry weather, extending over the oceans at about 30 degress north and south of the equator.

horse·laugh (hôrs′laf′) *n.* a loud, coarse or boisterous laugh.

horse·man (hôrs′mən) *n. pl.,* **horse·men** (hôrs′mən). **1.** a man who rides on horseback. **2.** a man skilled in riding or handling horses.

horse·man·ship (hôrs′mən ship′) *n.* the art of riding or handling horses.

horse·play (hôrs′plā′) *n.* rough, boisterous play or fun.

horse·pow·er (hôrs′pou′ər) *n.* a unit for measuring power, or rate of work, as of an engine. One horsepower is equal to 550 foot-pounds per second or 746 watts.

horse·rad·ish (hôrs′rad′ish) *n.* **1.** the sharp-tasting white root of a plant, used as a relish. **2.** the plant bearing this root, widely grown in southeastern Europe and North America.

horse sense *Informal.* plain, practical common sense.

horse·shoe (hôrs′shoo′) *n.* **1.** a U-shaped piece of metal curved to fit the shape of a horse's hoof, attached by means of nails driven into the hard, horny, outer shell of the hoof. **2.** something shaped like a horseshoe. **3. horseshoes.** a game for two or more players in which the object is to pitch a U-shaped piece so that it encircles a stake, normally placed 40 feet away from the pitcher, or lands closest to the stake. ▲ used with a singular verb. —*v.t.,* **horse·shoed, horse·shoe·ing.** to provide with horseshoes.

horseshoe crab, a saltwater animal having a hard horseshoe-shaped shell and a stiff spine.

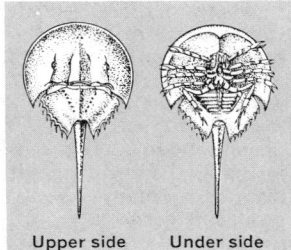

Upper side   Under side

Horseshoe crab

horse·whip (hôrs′hwip′, hôrs′wip′) *n.* a whip used for driving or controlling horses. —*v.t.,* **horse·whipped, horse·whip·ping.** to beat with or as if with a horsewhip.

horse·wom·an (hôrs′woom′ən) *n. pl.,* **horse·wom·en** (hôrs′wim′ən). **1.** a woman who rides on horseback. **2.** a woman who is skilled in the art of riding or handling horses.

hors·y (hôr′sē) *adj.,* **hors·i·er, hors·i·est.** *also,* **hors·ey. 1.** relating to or suggestive of a horse or horses: *a horsy smell.* **2.** interested in or fond of horses or sports involving horses. —**hors′i·ly,** *adv.* —**hors′i·ness,** *n.*

hor·ta·to·ry (hôr′tə tôr′ē) *adj.* serving to urge or encourage.

hor·ti·cul·tur·al (hôr′tə kul′chər əl) *adj.* of or relating to horticulture.

hor·ti·cul·ture (hôr′tə kul′chər) *n.* **1.** the art or science of growing flowers, fruits, vegetables, and ornamental plants. **2.** the growing of a garden.

hor·ti·cul·tur·ist (hôr′tə kul′chər ist) *n.* a student of or an expert in horticulture.

ho·san·na (hō zan′ə) *interj.* praise to God. —*n.* a cry of *hosanna.*

hose (hōz) *n. pl.,* **hose** or *(def. 1)* **hos·es. 1.** a flexible tube of rubber, canvas, or other material, used for carrying water or other liquids to a desired point. **2.** stockings or socks. **3.** close-fitting trousers resembling tights, formerly worn by men. —*v.t.,* **hosed, hos·ing.** to spray, wash, or water with a hose.

Ho·se·a (hō zē′ə) *n.* **1.** a Hebrew prophet of the eighth century B.C. **2.** a book of the Old Testament believed to have been written by him.

ho·sier·y (hō′zhər ē) *n.* stockings and socks.

hos·pice (hos′pis) *n.* a place of lodging for travelers or pilgrims, especially one kept by monks.

hos·pi·ta·ble (hos′pi tə bəl, hos pit′ə bəl) *adj.* **1.** characterized by or giving a friendly and generous welcome to guests or strangers: *The hotel staff was very hospitable.* **2.** receptive or open in mind or outlook: *The committee members were hospitable to my plan.* —**hos′pi·ta·bly,** *adv.*

hos·pi·tal (hos′pit əl) *n.* a place giving medical, surgical, or psychiatric treatment for the sick or injured.

hos·pi·tal·i·ty (hos′pə tal′ə tē) *n. pl.,* **hos·pi·tal·i·ties.** the act, practice, or quality of being hospitable.

hos·pi·tal·i·za·tion (hos′pit əl i zā′shən) *n.* **1.** the act of hospitalizing or the state of being hospitalized. **2.** the period of time during which a person is hospitalized. **3.** a form of insurance providing part or total payment of a patient's hospital expenses.

hos·pi·tal·ize (hos′pit əl īz′) *v.t.,* **hos·pi·tal·ized, hos·pi·tal·iz·ing.** to put in a hospital as a patient: *The skier was hospitalized with a broken leg.*

host¹ (hōst) *n.* **1.** a man who receives or entertains others, usually as guests in his own home. **2.** the keeper of an inn or hotel. **3.** a living plant or animal in or upon which a parasite lives and gets nourishment. —*v.t.* to be or serve as host for: *to host a birthday party for a friend.* [Old French *hoste.*]

host² (hōst) *n.* a large number; multitude: *On a clear night you can see a host of stars in the sky.* [Old French *host* army.]

host³ (hōst) *also,* **Host.** *n.* a wafer of unleavened bread used for Holy Communion in the Roman Catholic Church and certain other churches. [Old French *oiste* or *hoiste.*]

hos·tage (hos′tij) *n.* a person held or given as security that certain promises or conditions will be fulfilled: *The general was held as a hostage by the enemy until the peace treaty was signed.*

hos·tel (host′əl) *n.* a lodging place, especially a supervised lodging place for young people on hiking or bicycling trips.

host·ess (hōs′tis) *n. pl.,* **host·ess·es. 1.** a woman who receives or entertains others, usually as guests in her own home. **2.** a woman employed, as by a restaurant or nightclub, to greet and assist customers. **3.** a stewardess. **4.** a woman who keeps an inn or hotel.

hos·tile (host′əl) *adj.* **1.** feeling or showing hatred or dislike: *The speaker was shouted down by the hostile crowd.* **2.** of or belonging to an enemy: *The battalion encountered hostile forces in the valley.* —**hos′tile·ly,** *adv.*

hos·til·i·ty (hos til′ə tē) *n. pl.,* **hos·til·i·ties. 1.** the state of being hostile; antagonism. **2.** a hostile act. **3. hostilities.** acts of war; warfare; war: *The hostilities ended when the truce was signed.*

hos·tler (hos′lər, os′lər) *also,* **os·tler.** *n.* a person who takes care of horses at an inn or stable.

hot (hot) *adj.,* **hot·ter, hot·test. 1.** having a high temperature; having much warmth or heat: *It was surprisingly hot for an autumn day.* **2.** feeling warmth or heat: *He was hot after playing basketball for an hour.* **3.** having a burning or spicy taste; pungent; sharp: *Some Mexican food is very hot.* **4.** having or carrying an electrical current or charge, especially one of high voltage: *a hot wire.* **5.** characterized by or showing anger; angry: *The candidates exchanged hot words over the controversial issue.* **6.** very active; violent; raging: *a hot battle.* **7.** following very closely; close behind: *The police were hot on the heels of the robber.* **8.** in hunting, strong or fresh: *The trail of the fox was hot.* **9.** *Informal.* in demand; popular: *Skis are a hot item during the winter.* **10.** *Slang.* recently stolen or illegally gotten: *The thief tried to sell the hot jewelry.* —*adv.* in a hot manner; violently. —**hot′ly,** *adv.* —**hot′ness,** *n.*

hot air *Slang.* empty or boastful talk or writing.

hot·bed (hot′bed′) *n.* **1.** a bed of earth protected by a frame of glass, used for growing plants. The soil is heated by decaying manure or by electricity, steam, or hot water pipes. **2.** a place where anything grows or develops rapidly, especially something bad: *The investigation of the police department exposed a hotbed of crime in the city.*

at; āpe; cär; end; mē; it; īce; hot; ōld; fôrk; wood; fool; oil; out; up; turn; sing; thin; this; hw in white; zh in treasure. The symbol ə stands for the sound of a in about, e in taken, i in pencil, o in lemon, and u in circus.

H

hot·blood·ed (hot′blud′id) *adj.* very excitable; passionate; impulsive; rash.

hot cake, a pancake; griddlecake.

  to go like hot cakes or **to sell like hot cakes.** *Informal.* to be sold quickly and in great quantity.

hot cross bun, a sweet bun containing small bits of dried fruit, such as raisins, marked with a cross made of icing and traditionally eaten during Lent.

hot dog *Informal.* another term for **frankfurter.**

ho·tel (hō tel′) *n.* a place that rents rooms to travelers and usually provides a restaurant and other services.

hot·foot (hot′foot′) *v.i.* to go very quickly; hurry. —*adv.* in great haste.

hot·head (hot′hed′) *n.* a hot-headed person.

hot·head·ed (hot′hed′id) *adj.* **1.** easily angered. **2.** reckless; rash: *a hot-headed decision.* —**hot′·head′·ed·ly,** *adv.* —**hot′·head′ed·ness,** *n.*

hot·house (hot′hous′) *n. pl.,* **hot·hous·es** (hot′hou′ziz). a heated building, made mainly of glass, where plants are grown; greenhouse. —*adj.* grown in a hothouse: *hothouse flowers.*

hot plate, a small electrical device usually consisting of one or two burners, used for cooking or heating food.

hot rod *Slang.* an automobile, especially an older car rebuilt for high speeds.

Hot·ten·tot (hot′ən tot′) *n.* **1.** a member of a southern African people. **2.** the language of the Hottentots. —*adj.* of or relating to the Hottentots or their language.

hot water *Informal.* a state of difficulty; trouble.

hound (hound) *n.* **1.** any of various dogs that were originally bred and trained to hunt, such as the beagle and bloodhound. **2.** any dog. —*v.t.* **1.** to chase or pursue without stopping: *The police hounded the thief.* **2.** *Informal.* to urge persistently; nag; pester: *Mother hounded me about cleaning my room.*

hour (our) *n.* **1.** a unit of time equal to 1/24 of a day; sixty minutes. **2.** one of the twelve points on a clock or watch indicating such a unit of time. **3.** a definite time of day as indicated by a clock or watch: *At what hour should we leave?* **4.** a particular time for some activity: *the dinner hour.* **5.** an indefinite period of time: *He helped us in our hour of need.* **6. hours.** a fixed time devoted to one's work or other regular activity: *The doctor has office hours four days a week.* **7.** the amount of distance that can be traveled in an hour: *We were an hour away from home.* **8.** in colleges and universities, a unit of academic credit, one of which is usually given for each class hour per week.

hour·glass (our′glas′) *n. pl.,* **hour·glass·es.** a device for measuring time, consisting of a glass container with a narrow passage in the middle, through which a quantity of sand or mercury runs from the upper to lower part in exactly one hour.

hour hand, the short hand on a clock or watch indicating the hour.

hour·ly (our′lē) *adj.* **1.** done, occurring, or counted every hour: *There are hourly airplane departures for Chicago.* **2.** done in the course of or computed on the basis of an hour: *hourly wages.* —*adv.* every hour: *The nurse looked in on the patient hourly.*

house (*n.,* hous; *v.,* houz) *n. pl.,* **hous·es** (hou′ziz). **1.** a building in which people

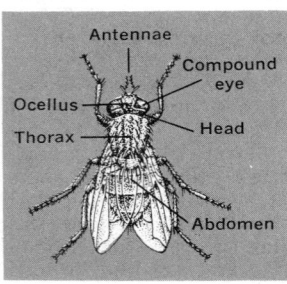

Hourglass

live. **2.** people, especially a family, living in a house; household. **3.** a building used for a particular purpose: *a movie house.* **4.** an audience, as in a theater. **5.** also, **House.** a legislative or deliberative body: *Both houses of Congress passed the bill.* **6.** also, **House.** a royal or noble

family: *Queen Elizabeth II of England is a member of the House of Windsor.* —*v.t.,* **housed, hous·ing. 1.** to provide with a house; shelter; lodge: *The soldiers were housed in the old mansion.* **2.** to store or keep in a house or building: *The art collection was housed in the museum.*

  on the house. at the expense of the owner; free: *Our dinner in the restaurant was on the house.*

  to clean house. a. to clean a house or put it in order. **b.** to do away with a person or thing that is undesirable.

  to keep house. to manage and take care of a house.

house·boat (hous′bōt′) *n.* a boat or barge that is fitted out as a place to live.

house·break·ing (hous′brā′king) *n.* the act of breaking into and entering a house with intent to steal or commit some other crime. —**house′break′er,** *n.*

house·bro·ken (hous′brō′kən) *adj.* (of a household pet) trained to live indoors.

house·coat (hous′kōt′) *n.* a robe or similar garment worn at home.

house·fly (hous′flī′) *n. pl.,* **house·flies.** a fly that lives in and around houses, feeding on food and garbage. It may carry many disease-producing germs.

house·hold (hous′hōld′) *n.* all the people who live in a house. —*adj.* **1.** of or relating to a household; domestic: *household chores.* **2.** familiar; common: *The actor's name became a household word.*

house·hold·er (hous′hōl′dər) *n.* **1.** a person who owns or lives in a house. **2.** the head of a family.

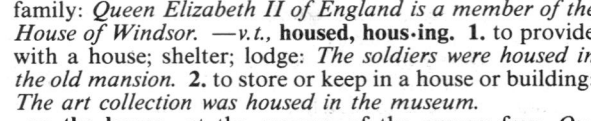

Housefly

house·keep·er (hous′kē′pər) *n.* a woman who manages the affairs of a household, especially a woman who is hired to do it.

house·keep·ing (hous′kē′ping) *n.* the maintenance of a household and the managing of its affairs.

house·maid (hous′mād′) *n.* a woman hired to do housework.

house·moth·er (hous′muth′ər) *n.* a woman who supervises a group of young people living together, as in a dormitory.

House of Commons, the lower, elective house of either the British or Canadian Parliament. Also, **Commons.**

house of correction, a place for the confinement and rehabilitation of persons convicted of minor offenses.

House of Lords, the upper house of the British Parliament, composed of the nobility and high-ranking clergymen.

House of Representatives, the lower, elective house of the U.S. Congress and of many state legislatures, in which representation is based on population.

house·plant (hous′plant′) *n.* any plant grown indoors.

house sparrow, a sparrow found throughout warm and temperate regions of the world, having dull gray-and-brown feathers with black-and-white markings. Also, **English sparrow.**

house·top (hous′top′) *n.* the roof or top of a house.

house·warm·ing (hous′wôr′ming) *n.* a party given when people move into a house.

house·wife (hous′wīf′) *n. pl.,* **house·wives** (hous′wīvz′). a woman, especially a married woman, who manages a home and its affairs.

house·work (hous′wurk′) *n.* work done in housekeeping, such as washing, ironing, cleaning, and cooking.

hous·ing¹ (hou′zing) *n.* **1.** houses as a group: *The city built new housing for poor families.* **2.** the act of sheltering or of providing houses. **3.** any shelter or covering. **4.** a frame, plate, or casing which supports, secures, or contains a machine or part of a machine. [*House* + *-ing.*]

hous·ing² (hou′zing) *n.* an ornamental covering for a horse. [Middle English *house.*]

Hous·man, A(lfred) E(dward) (hous′mən) 1859–1936, English poet and scholar.

Hous·ton (hyōos′tən) *n.* **1.** Samuel. 1793–1863, U.S. soldier and statesman, twice president of Texas before it became a state. **2.** a city in southeastern Texas. Pop. (1970), 1,232,802.

hove (hōv) a past tense and past participle of **heave.**

hov·el (huv′əl, hov′əl) *n.* **1.** a small, very poor house or shack; hut. **2.** an open shed, as for sheltering cattle or tools.

hov·er (huv′ər, hov′ər) *v.i.* **1.** to remain suspended in the air over or around a particular spot: *The bird hovered over its nest.* **2.** to linger or remain nearby: *to hover over a sick child.* **3.** to continue in an indeterminate state; waver: *to hover between tears and laughter.*

hov·er·craft (huv′ər kraft′) *n.* a vehicle that can travel over land or water on a thin cushion of high-pressure air created beneath the craft by means of fans or rotors. Trademark: **Hovercraft.**

how (hou) *adv.* **1.** in what manner or way; by what means: *How do you plan to get home?* **2.** to what degree, amount, or extent: *How hot is it today? How did you like the movie?* **3.** in what state or condition: *How are you today?* **4.** for what reason or purpose; why: *How did he happen to be there?* **5.** with what meaning; to what effect: *How did she mean her last statement?*

  how about. what do you think of; would you like: *How about coming to the party with us?*

  how come. *Informal.* how does it happen that: *How come he wasn't in school yesterday?*

how·be·it (hou bē′it) *adv. Archaic.* however it may be; nevertheless.

how·dah (hou′də) *n.* a seat, usually with a railing and canopy, used for riding on the back of an elephant or camel.

how·dy (hou′dē) *n. pl.,* **how·dies.** *Informal.* hello.

Howe, Elias (hou) 1819–1867, U.S. inventor of the sewing machine.

how·ev·er (hou ev′ər) *conj.* nevertheless; yet; notwithstanding: *Jack and Bob both passed the test; however, Dick failed.* —*adv.* **1.** in whatever way; by whatever means: *You may do the job however you like.* **2.** to whatever degree or extent: *However far our dog wanders, he always comes home.*

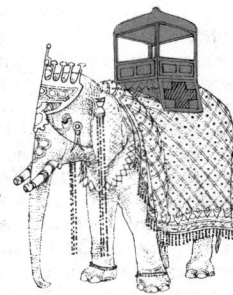

Howdah

how·itz·er (hou′it sər) *n.* a cannon of medium length, used to fire shells at high angles of elevation.

howl (houl) *v.i.* **1.** to make a loud, wailing cry as that of a dog or wolf: *The dog howled at night. The wind howled.* **2.** to utter such a cry: *He howled when he stubbed his toe. The joke made us howl with laughter.* —*v.t.* **1.** to utter or express with howling. **2.** to force or drive by howling: *The audience howled the actor off the stage.* —*n.* **1.** a loud, wailing cry, as of a dog or wolf. **2.** any howling sound.

How·rah (hou′rä) *n.* a city in northeastern India, near Calcutta. Pop. (1971), 740,622.

how·so·ev·er (hou′sō ev′ər) *adv.* **1.** in whatever way; by whatever means. **2.** to whatever degree or extent.

hoy·den (hoid′ən) *n.* a boisterous, ill-mannered, or saucy girl or woman. —**hoy′den·ish,** *adj.*

hp, Hp, horsepower.

HQ, hq, headquarters.

hr., hour.

H.R., House of Representatives.

H.R.H., His (or Her) Royal Highness.

H.S., High School.

ht., height.

Huang He (hwäng′hu′) another spelling of **Hwang Ho.**

hub (hub) *n.* **1.** the central part of a wheel into which the axle is inserted. **2.** a central point of interest, importance, or activity.

hub·bub (hub′ub) *n.* a loud, confused noise, as of many voices or sounds; uproar.

hub·cap (hub′kap′) *n.* a removable metal disk covering the hub of a wheel.

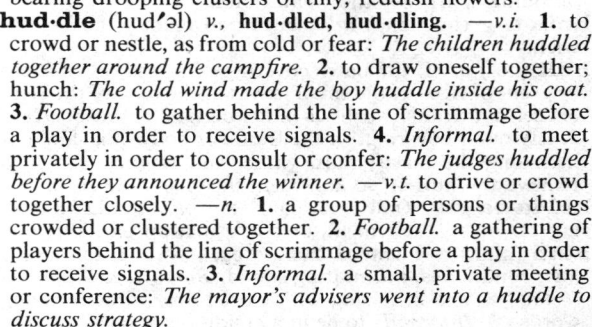

Hub

huck·le·ber·ry (huk′əl ber′ē) *n. pl.,* **huck·le·ber·ries. 1.** a small, shiny, blue or black berry resembling the blueberry but smaller and darker in color. **2.** the low shrub bearing this fruit, growing wild in North and South America and bearing drooping clusters of tiny, reddish flowers.

hud·dle (hud′əl) *v.,* **hud·dled, hud·dling.** —*v.i.* **1.** to crowd or nestle, as from cold or fear: *The children huddled together around the campfire.* **2.** to draw oneself together; hunch: *The cold wind made the boy huddle inside his coat.* **3.** *Football.* to gather behind the line of scrimmage before a play in order to receive signals. **4.** *Informal.* to meet privately in order to consult or confer: *The judges huddled before they announced the winner.* —*v.t.* to drive or crowd together closely. —*n.* **1.** a group of persons or things crowded or clustered together. **2.** *Football.* a gathering of players behind the line of scrimmage before a play in order to receive signals. **3.** *Informal.* a small, private meeting or conference: *The mayor's advisers went into a huddle to discuss strategy.*

Hud·son (hud′sən) *n.* **1.** Henry. died 1611, English navigator and explorer of North America. **2.** a river in eastern New York, flowing southward into New York Bay.

Hudson Bay, a large inland sea in northeastern Canada, connected with the Atlantic Ocean by the Hudson Strait.

Hudson Strait, the strait connecting Hudson Bay with the Atlantic Ocean.

hue¹ (hyōo) *n.* one part of the spectrum; a color or shade. [Old English *hīw* or *hīew* appearance, color.]

hue² (hyōo) *n.* **hue and cry.** a public stir or outcry, as of alarm or opposition: *The newspaper raised a great hue and cry when the scandal was disclosed.* [Old French *hu* a cry.]

huff (huf) *n.* a sudden, temporary feeling of anger or indignation: *Cindy walked off in a huff when Dan insulted her.* —*v.i.* to puff; blow: *She huffed and puffed and blew out the birthday candles.* —*v.t.* to make angry; offend: *The writer was huffed by the critic's unfavorable comment.*

huff·y (huf′ē) *adj.,* **huff·i·er, huff·i·est. 1.** easily offended; touchy. **2.** offended; sulking. —**huff′i·ly,** *adv.* —**huff′i·ness,** *n.*

hug (hug) *v.t.,* **hugged, hug·ging. 1.** to clasp the arms

at; āpe; cär; end; mē; it; īce; hot; ōld; fôrk; wood; fōol; oil; out; up; turn; sing; thin; **th**is; hw in white; zh in treasure. The symbol ə stands for the sound of **a** in about, **e** in taken, **i** in pencil, **o** in lemon, and **u** in circus.

around and hold close, especially in affection; embrace closely. **2.** to grasp and squeeze tightly with the arms, as a bear does. **3.** to keep close to: *The bicycle rider hugged the curb.* —*n.* a strong clasp with the arms, especially as a sign of affection; embrace.

huge (hyōōj) *adj.,* **hug·er, hug·est.** of great size, extent, or degree; extremely large. —**huge′ly,** *adv.* —**huge′- ness,** *n.*

Hughes, Lang·ston (hyōōz; lang′stən) 1902–1967, U.S. poet.

Hu·go, Victor (hyōō′gō) 1802–1885, French poet, novelist, and dramatist.

Hu·gue·not (hyōō′gə not′) *n.* a French Protestant of the sixteenth or seventeenth century.

huh (hu) *interj.* used to express surprise, contempt, or doubt.

hu·la (hōō′lə) *n.* a traditional Hawaiian dance in which movements of the dancers' arms and hands are used to relate a story. Also, **hu·la-hu·la** (hōō′lə hōō′lə).

hulk (hulk) *n.* **1.** a large, clumsy person or thing. **2.** the body of an old, wrecked or dismantled ship. **3.** the shell of something that has been abandoned, wrecked, or gutted: *Only the hulk of the building remained after the explosion.* **4.** a ship used for a prison, storehouse, or similar purpose other than sailing.

hulk·ing (hul′king) *adj.* huge and clumsy; bulky; unwieldy.

hull (hul) *n.* **1.** the outer covering of a seed, as of a nut or grain of rice. **2.** the small leaves at the base of the stem of certain fruits, such as strawberries or raspberries. **3.** any outer covering. **4.** the frame or body of a ship, not including the masts, sails, yards, and rigging. —*v.t.* to remove the hull of: *to hull raspberries.* —**hull′er,** *n.*

hul·la·ba·loo (hul′ə bə lōō′) *n. pl.,* **hul·la·ba·loos.** a great noise, excitement, or confusion; uproar.

hum (hum) *v.,* **hummed, hum·ming.** —*v.i.* **1.** to make a low, continuous, murmuring sound: *Bumblebees hummed in the garden.* **2.** to sing with closed lips, without saying words. **3.** *Informal.* to be in a condition of busy activity: *Things were really humming at the newspaper offices on election night.* —*v.t.* to sing (something) with closed lips, without saying words: *to hum a tune.* —*n.* **1.** a low, continuous, murmuring sound: *The hum of machinery could be heard throughout the factory.* **2.** a singing with closed lips, without saying words.

hu·man (hyōō′mən) *adj.* **1.** of or relating to human beings or humanity: *the human body, human life, a human trait.* **2.** having or showing the qualities characteristic of human beings: *human nature, human kindness, human weaknesses.* **3.** consisting of human beings: *The police formed a human wall around the building.* —*n.* see **human being.** —**hu′man·ness,** *n.*

human being, a member of the human race; person; man or woman.

hu·mane (hyōō mān′) *adj.* having or showing sympathy and compassion; kind; merciful: *The doctor fought for humane treatment of the mentally retarded.* —**hu·mane′ly,** *adv.* —**hu·mane′ness,** *n.*

hu·man·ism (hyōō′mə niz′əm) *n.* any system of thought or action concerned with human interests, needs, values, and ideals.

hu·man·ist (hyōō′mə nist) *n.* **1.** a follower or student of any philosophy concerned primarily with human interests, needs, values, and ideals. **2.** a student of the humanities, especially a classical scholar.

hu·man·i·tar·i·an (hyōō man′ə ter′ē ən) *adj.* concerned with or promoting the general welfare of humanity. —*n.* a person who devotes himself or herself to the welfare of humanity.

hu·man·i·tar·i·an·ism (hyōō man′ə ter′ē ə niz′əm) *n.* humane or humanitarian principles or action.

hu·man·i·ty (hyōō man′ə tē) *n. pl.,* **hu·man·i·ties.** **1.** human beings as a group; the human race; mankind. **2.** the quality or condition of being human; human character or nature. **3.** the quality of being humane; kindness; benevolence. **4. the humanities.** a branch of learning concerned with human culture, including languages, literature, philosophy, and art.

hu·man·ize (hyōō′mə nīz′) *v.t.,* **hu·man·ized, hu·man·iz·ing.** **1.** to give or attribute a human character to; make human. **2.** to cause to be kind, merciful, or benevolent; make humane. —**hu′man·i·za′tion,** *n.*

hu·man·kind (hyōō′mən kīnd′) *n.* the human race; humanity; mankind.

hu·man·ly (hyōō′mən lē) *adv.* **1.** within human ability or power; by human means: *It isn't humanly possible to run that far in two minutes.* **2.** in accordance with human nature; in a human manner: *to act humanly.*

hum·ble (hum′bəl) *adj.,* **hum·bler, hum·blest. 1.** having or showing a low estimate or opinion of one's importance or worth; not proud. **2.** low in position, station, or condition; not pretentious: *a humble house.* **3.** courteous or respectful: *The letter was signed "Your humble servant."* —*v.t.,* **hum·bled, hum·bling. 1.** to make humble in spirit; humiliate. **2.** to make lower in position, station, or condition. —**hum′ble·ness,** *n.* —**hum′bly,** *adv.*

hum·bug (hum′bug′) *n.* **1.** foolish or empty talk; nonsense. **2.** something intended to deceive or trick; hoax; sham. **3.** a person who tries to deceive or trick others; imposter; fraud. —*v.t.,* **hum·bugged, hum·bug·ging.** to deceive or trick; cheat.

hum·drum (hum′drum′) *adj.* lacking variety or excitement; monotonous; dull: *humdrum routine, a humdrum life.* —*n.* a person or thing that is monotonous or dull.

Hume, David (hyōōm) 1711–1776, Scottish philosopher and historian.

hu·mer·us (hyōō′mər əs) *n. pl.,* **hu·mer·i** (hyōō′mə rī′). the long bone in the upper arm or forelimb, extending from the shoulder to the elbow.

hu·mid (hyōō′mid) *adj.* containing or characterized by the presence of much water vapor; moist; damp: *a hot and humid summer day.*

hu·mid·i·fy (hyōō mid′ə fī′) *v.t.,* **hu·mid·i·fied, hu·mid·i·fy·ing.** to make more humid or moist, as the air in a room. —**hu·mid′i·fi′er,** *n.*

hu·mid·i·ty (hyōō mid′ə tē) *n.* **1.** moistness or dampness, especially of the atmosphere. **2.** *Meteorology.* the ratio, expressed as a percentage, of the amount of water vapor present in the air to the maximum amount the air could hold at the same temperature; relative humidity.

hu·mi·dor (hyōō′mə dôr′) *n.* a container or storage room for cigars or other tobacco products, containing a device that keeps the air and tobacco moist.

hu·mil·i·ate (hyōō mil′ē āt′) *v.t.,* **hu·mil·i·at·ed, hu·mil·i·at·ing.** to lower the pride or dignity of; cause to seem foolish or worthless: *His inability to succeed humiliated him.*

hu·mil·i·a·tion (hyōō mil′ē ā′shən) *n.* **1.** a feeling of shame or extreme embarrassment. **2.** the act of humiliating or the state of being humiliated.

hu·mil·i·ty (hyōō mil′ə tē) *n.* the quality of being humble; lack of pride or arrogance.

Humerus
Radius
Ulna

hum·ming·bird (hum'ing burd') *n.* a small, brightly colored American bird having a slender, pointed bill, and narrow wings that beat very rapidly when it flies. It is capable of flying sideways and backwards. [From the *humming* sound made by its rapidly moving wings.]

Hummingbird

hum·mock (hum'ək) *n.* **1.** a low mound of earth or rock; knoll. **2.** a bump or ridge on an ice field. —**hum'mock·y**, *adj.*

hu·mor (hyōo'mər) *also, British,* **hu·mour.** *n.* **1.** the quality of something that makes it amusing or funny. **2.** the ability to appreciate or express what is amusing or funny: *George has a good sense of humor.* **3.** a speech, writing, or action that is amusing or funny. **4.** a temporary state of mind; mood: *The thought of a vacation put Ruth in a good humor.* —*v.t.* to give in to the moods, wishes, or whims of (someone); indulge: *We humored the old man and listened to his story again.* [Old French *umor, humor* the fluid that determined a person's health and temperament. In former times, the body was thought to be made up of four liquids, the mixture of which determined a person's health and disposition.]

hu·mor·ist (hyōo'mər ist) *n.* **1.** a professional writer or performer of humorous material. **2.** a person with a good sense of humor.

hu·mor·less (hyōo'mər lis) *adj.* without a sense of humor or humorous qualities. —**hu'mor·less·ness,** *n.*

hu·mor·ous (hyōo'mər əs) *adj.* characterized by or full of humor; funny; comical: *a humorous writer, a humorous situation.* —**hu'mor·ous·ly,** *adv.* —**hu'mor·ous·ness,** *n.*

hump (hump) *n.* **1.** a rounded lump, as on the back of a camel. **2.** a hillock; mound. —*v.t.* to bend or arch so as to form a hump.

hump·back (hump'back') *n.* a hunchback. —**hump'-backed',** *adj.*

hu·mus (hyōo'məs) *n.* a dark substance in the soil, consisting of decayed animal or vegetable matter and containing nitrogen and other plant nutrients.

Hun (hun) *n.* **1.** a member of a wandering Asian people who invaded Europe in the fourth and fifth centuries A.D., and helped to destroy the Roman Empire. **2.** a barbarous, willfully destructive person.

hunch (hunch) *v.t.* to draw up, raise, or bend: *The cold air made him hunch his shoulders.* —*v.i.* to assume a bent, stooped, or crouched posture. —*n. pl.,* **hunch·es. 1.** *Informal.* a guess or feeling. **2.** a rounded lump; hump.

hunch·back (hunch'bak') *n.* **1.** a person who has a hump on his back caused by a curving of the spine. **2.** a back having such a hump. —**hunch'backed',** *adj.*

hun·dred (hun'drid) *n. pl.,* **hun·dreds** or **hun·dred. 1.** the cardinal number that is ten times ten. **2.** a symbol representing this number, such as 100 or C. —*adj.* numbering ten times ten.

hun·dredth (hun'dridth) *adj.* **1.** (the ordinal of hundred) next after the ninety-ninth. **2.** being one of a hundred equal parts. —*n.* **1.** something that is next after the ninety-ninth. **2.** one of a hundred equal parts; 1/100.

hun·dred·weight (hun'drid wāt') *n. pl.,* **hun·dred·weights** or **hun·dred·weight.** a unit of weight equal to 100 pounds avoirdupois in the United States or 112 pounds in England.

hung (hung) a past tense and past participle of **hang.**

Hun·gar·i·an (hung ger'ē ən) *n.* **1.** a person who was born or is living in Hungary. **2.** the language of the Hungarians. Also *(def. 2),* **Magyar.** —*adj.* of or relating to Hungary, its people, their language, or their culture.

Hun·ga·ry (hung'gər ē) *n.* a country in east-central Europe. Capital, Budapest. Area, 35,919 sq. mi. Pop. (1971 est.), 10,360,000.

hun·ger (hung'gər) *n.* **1.** discomfort, pain, or weakness caused by lack of food: *to die of hunger.* **2.** a desire or craving for food: *The candy bar satisfied Ruth's hunger for chocolate.* **3.** any strong desire or craving: *a hunger for praise.* —*v.i.* **1.** to have or feel a need or desire for food. **2.** to have a strong desire or craving: *That child hungers for affection.*

hung jury, a jury so divided in opinion that it is unlikely it could ever agree on a verdict and is therefore dismissed by the judge.

hun·gry (hung'grē) *adj.,* **hun·gri·er, hun·gri·est. 1.** desiring or needing food. **2.** caused by or suggestive of a lack of or desire for food: *Cassius has a lean and hungry look* (Shakespeare, *Julius Caesar*). **3.** having a strong desire or craving; eager; longing: *hungry for companionship.* —**hun'gri·ly,** *adv.* —**hun'gri·ness,** *n.*

hunk (hungk) *n. Informal.* a large lump or piece; chunk: *The keeper fed the lion a hunk of meat.*

hunt (hunt) *v.t.* **1.** to chase (game) for the purpose of killing or catching: *to hunt deer, to hunt lions.* **2.** to try to get or find; search for: *to hunt for a book in the library.* **3.** to search (a place) carefully and thoroughly: *to hunt the prairie for buffalo, to hunt the woods for an escaped prisoner.* —*v.i.* **1.** to chase game for the purpose of killing or catching. **2.** to look for; seek: *to hunt for buried treasure.* **3.** to search thoroughly or carefully: *Susan hunted through her purse for some change.* —*n.* **1.** the act or instance of hunting game. **2.** a group of persons hunting game together. **3.** the act or instance of looking for something; search.

hunt·er (hun'tər) *n.* **1.** a person who hunts game. **2.** a person who searches for something. **3.** a horse or dog used in hunting.

hunt·ing (hun'ting) *n.* the act or sport of chasing game for the purpose of killing or catching.

Hunt·ing·ton Beach (hun'ting tən) a city in southern California, on the Pacific Ocean. Pop. (1970), 115,960.

hunt·ress (hun'tris) *n. pl.,* **hunt·ress·es.** a female hunter.

hunts·man (hunts'mən) *n. pl.,* **hunts·men** (hunts'mən). **1.** a person who hunts game; hunter. **2.** a person who manages a hunt, especially a fox hunt.

Hunts·ville (hunts'vil') *n.* a city in northern Alabama. Pop. (1970), 137,802.

hur·dle (hurd'əl) *n.* **1.** an obstacle over which a runner must leap in certain track events. **2.** **hurdles.** a race in which the contestants must leap over hurdles while running. **3.** an obstacle, difficulty, or problem: *Getting a college education was the biggest hurdle before him.* **4.** a movable frame made of sticks or narrow boards, used as a temporary fence or pen. —*v.t.,* **hur·dled, hur·dling. 1.** to jump over (a hurdle or similar obstacle)

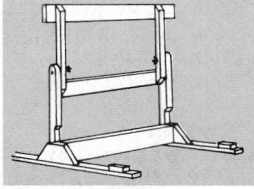

Hurdle

at; āpe; cär; end; mē; it; īce; hot; ōld; fôrk; wood; fōol; oil; out; up; turn; sing; thin; this; hw in white; zh in treasure. The symbol ə stands for the sound of **a** in about, **e** in taken, **i** in pencil, **o** in lemon, and **u** in circus.

in a race. **2.** to overcome or surmount (an obstacle or difficulty). —**hur′dler,** *n.*

hur·dy-gur·dy (hur′dē gur′dē) *n. pl.,* **hur·dy-gur·dies.** any of various mechanical musical instruments played by turning a handle or crank.

hurl (hurl) *v.t.* **1.** to throw with violence or force; fling: *He hurled a rock through the window.* **2.** to utter or emit with vehemence: *The senator's opponent hurled insults at him.* —*n.* the action of throwing forcefully or violently. —**hurl′er,** *n.*

hurl·y-burl·y (hur′lē bur′lē) *n. pl.,* **hurl·y-burl·ies.** noisy disorder; tumult; turmoil.

Hu·ron (hyoor′ən) *n.* **1. Lake.** the second largest of the Great Lakes, on the U.S.-Canadian border. **2.** a member of a tribe of North American Indians, formerly living east of Lake Huron, now living in Oklahoma. **3.** the language of this tribe.

hur·rah (hə rä′) *also,* **hoo·ray, hur·ray** (hə rā′). *interj.* used to express joy, triumph, praise, or encouragement. —*n.* a shout of joy, triumph, praise, or encouragement. —*v.i.* to shout hurrah; cheer: *The spectators hurrahed when our team won the game.*

hur·ri·cane (hur′ə kān′) *n.* **1.** a storm with violent winds of more than seventy-five miles per hour that spin around a calm center and are accompanied by heavy rain, high tides, and flooding in coastal regions. **2.** something resembling a hurricane in force or speed; violent outburst: *a hurricane of emotion.*

hur·ried (hur′ēd) *adj.* done, made, or carried on quickly or too quickly: *a hurried glance, a hurried letter full of spelling mistakes.* —**hur′ried·ly,** *adv.* —**hur′ried·ness,** *n.*

hur·ry (hur′ē) *v.,* **hur·ried, hur·ry·ing.** —*v.i.* to move or act with speed; go faster than is easy or natural: *Because we were late we had to hurry. If we don't hurry, we'll miss the train.* —*v.t.* **1.** to cause or urge to act, move, or go with greater speed: *Mother hurried the children along so they wouldn't miss the bus.* **2.** to cause or urge to act, move, or go too quickly; rush: *The judge would not be hurried into making a decision.* —*n.* **1.** the act of hurrying. **2.** the state or condition of wanting or needing to act, move, or go with greater speed: *He had to leave because he was in a hurry.*

hurt (hurt) *v.,* **hurt, hurt·ing.** —*v.t.* **1.** to cause physical pain or injury to: *He slipped and hurt his back.* **2.** to do harm to; damage: *The scandal hurt the mayor's chance for reelection.* **3.** to cause mental pain or suffering to; injure the feelings of: *The insult hurt her deeply.* —*v.i.* **1.** to be painful: *His knee hurts.* **2.** to cause or inflict pain or injury: *The doctor said that the injection wouldn't hurt much.* —*n.* any pain or suffering: *The medication will ease the hurt in your arm.*

hurt·ful (hurt′fəl) *adj.* causing hurt; painful; injurious: *He unintentionally made a hurtful remark.* —**hurt′ful·ly,** *adv.* —**hurt′ful·ness,** *n.*

hur·tle (hurt′əl) *v.i.,* **hur·tled, hur·tling.** **1.** to strike, especially violently or noisily: *The car went out of control and hurtled against the fence.* **2.** to move rapidly, especially with much force or noise: *The arrow hurtled through the air.*

hus·band (huz′bənd) *n.* the man in a married couple; married man. —*v.t.* to manage carefully; use or spend economically: *to husband one's time and energy.*

hus·band·ry (huz′bən drē) *n.* **1.** the cultivation of the soil and the breeding and raising of livestock; agriculture; farming. **2.** careful management; thrift.

hush (hush) *n. pl.,* **hush·es.** a silence or stillness, especially after noise or commotion has ceased: *A hush fell over the audience.* —*v.t.* **1.** to quiet, silence, or calm: *The teacher hushed the noisy children.* **2.** to keep knowledge or discussion of (something) from spreading: *The principal hushed the information about our teacher's leaving until the end of school.* —*interj.* be quiet; be calm.

husk (husk) *n.* **1.** the dry outer covering of certain seeds or fruits, such as an ear of corn. **2.** the outer shell or covering of something, especially when it is useless or worthless. —*v.t.* to remove the husk of: *to husk corn.* —**husk′er,** *n.*

husk·y¹ (hus′kē) *adj.,* **husk·i·er, husk·i·est.** **1.** big and strong: *a husky fellow.* **2.** hoarse and deep in tone: *a husky voice.* —*n. pl.,* **husk·ies.** *Informal.* a big, strong person. [*Husk* + *-y¹*.] —**husk′i·ly,** *adv.* —**husk′i·ness,** *n.*

husk·y² (hus′kē) *also,* **Husk·y.** *n. pl.,* **husk·ies.** see **Siberian husky.**

Huss, John (hus) 1369?–1415, Bohemian religious reformer.

hus·sar (hə zär′) *n.* a member of a light cavalry regiment in any of several European armies.

hus·sy (huz′ē, hus′ē) *n. pl.,* **hus·sies.** **1.** a woman of improper behavior or low character. **2.** a saucy, mischievous girl.

hus·tle (hus′əl) *v.,* **hus·tled, hus·tling.** —*v.i.* **1.** to move or work quickly or energetically: *She had to hustle to finish the job on time.* **2.** *Slang.* to make money by clever or dishonest means. —*v.t.* to hasten along by force; move hurriedly: *The nurse hustled patients in and out of the office.* —*n.* *Informal.* energy and enthusiasm; drive: *A good athlete has to have lots of hustle.*

hus·tler (hus′lər) *n.* *Informal.* **1.** a person who works hard or energetically. **2.** a person who earns a living by scheming, begging, or cheating.

hut (hut) *n.* a small, roughly or simply built house or shelter.

hutch (huch) *n. pl.,* **hutch·es.** **1.** a covered pen or box for keeping rabbits or other small animals. **2.** a cupboard with open shelves. **3.** a chest or bin that is used for storing things, such as china or linen.

Hux·ley (huks′lē) **1. Al·dous** (ôl′dəs). 1894–1963, English author. **2. Thomas Henry.** 1825–1895, English biologist; grandfather of Aldous.

huz·za (hə zä′) another word for **hurrah.**

Hwang Ho (hwäng′ hō′) a large river in China flowing from the Tibetan highlands into the Yellow Sea. Also, **Huang He, Yellow River.**

hwy., highway.

hy·a·cinth (hī′ə sinth′) *n.* **1.** a fragrant flower of any of a group of plants related to the lily. It is shaped like a funnel and grows in long clusters. **2.** the plant bearing this flower.

hy·brid (hī′brid) *n.* **1.** the offspring of two animals or plants of different varieties, lines, or breeds, that combines the differing qualities of the parents. **2.** anything derived from different sources or made up of unlike elements. —*adj.* of, relating to, or of the nature of a hybrid: *a hybrid flower.*

hy·brid·ism (hī′bri diz′əm) *n.* **1.** the condition, quality, or fact of being hybrid. **2.** the production of hybrids.

hy·brid·ize (hī′bri dīz′) *v.t.,* **hy·brid·ized, hy·brid·iz·ing.** to cause to produce hybrids. —**hy′brid·i·za′tion,** *n.*

Hyacinth

Hy·der·a·bad (hī′dər ə bad′) *n.* **1.** a city in south-central India. Pop. (1971), 1,798,910. **2.** a city in southeastern Pakistan. Pop. (1972), 600,796.

hy·dra (hī′drə) *n. pl.*, **hy·dras** or **hy·drae** (hī′drē).
1. Hydra. *Classical Mythology.* a deadly monster that resembled a snake and had nine heads and the power to grow two more whenever one was cut off. **2.** a small freshwater animal having a tube-shaped body with a single mouth opening. The mouth is surrounded by thin tentacles bearing clusters of stinging cells that carry poison. If a hydra is cut into pieces, each piece will develop into a complete, new animal.

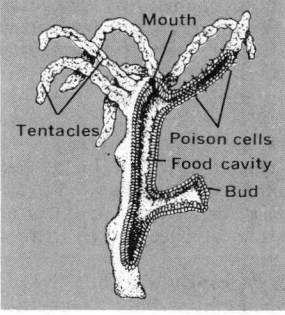

Hydra *(def. 2)*

hy·dran·gea (hī drān′jə) *n.* **1.** a large, showy flower that grows in clusters of usually white, blue, or pink blossoms. **2.** the shrub or vine bearing this flower.

hy·drant (hī′drənt) *n.* a street fixture for drawing water directly from a water main, consisting of an upright pipe with spouts to which hoses may be attached. Also, **fire hydrant.**

hy·drate (hī′drāt) *n.* any crystalline substance formed by the union of a chemical compound with molecules of water in a definite ratio. —*v.t.*, **hy·drat·ed, hy·drat·ing.** to combine (a chemical compound) with water to form a hydrate. —**hy·dra′tion,** *n.*

hy·drau·lic (hī drô′lik) *adj.* **1.** operated by water or some other fluid: *hydraulic brakes.* **2.** of or relating to the forces exerted by fluids in motion and at rest, or to the science of hydraulics. **3.** hardening under water: *hydraulic cement.* —**hy·drau′li·cal·ly,** *adv.*

hydraulic ram, a pump that uses the energy of moving water to pump part of the water to a higher level.

hy·drau·lics (hī drô′liks) *n., pl.* the branch of science that deals with fluids in motion and at rest, and their use to perform work. ▲ usually used with a singular verb.

hy·dra·zine (hī′drə zēn′) *n.* a colorless, poisonous liquid that has an odor like ammonia. It is a compound of nitrogen and hydrogen and is used especially as a rocket fuel.

hy·dride (hī′drīd) *also,* **hy·drid** (hī′drid). *n.* a compound of hydrogen with an element or radical.

hydro- *combining form* **1.** of or relating to water: *hydrodynamics, hydroplane.* **2.** *Chemistry.* combined with or made up of hydrogen: *hydrocarbon.*

hy·dro·car·bon (hī′drə kär′bən) *n.* any of a large group of organic compounds composed solely of the chemical elements hydrogen and carbon.

hy·dro·chlo·ric acid (hī′drə klôr′ik) a poisonous, highly corrosive solution of hydrogen chloride in water. Its fumes cause severe irritation of the eyes and nose.

hy·dro·cy·an·ic acid (hī′drō sī an′ik) a weak, colorless, poisonous acid having an odor like bitter almonds. It is a solution of a compound of hydrogen, carbon, and nitrogen in water and is used to make plastics and pesticides. Also, **prussic acid.**

hy·dro·dy·nam·ic (hī′drō dī nam′ik) *adj.* of or relating to the forces exerted by fluids in motion or to the science of hydrodynamics. —**hy′dro·dy·nam′i·cal·ly,** *adv.*

hy·dro·dy·nam·ics (hī′drō dī nam′iks) *n.,pl.* the branch of science that deals with the forces exerted by fluids in motion. ▲ usually used with a singular verb.

hy·dro·e·lec·tric (hī′drō i lek′trik) *adj.* of or relating to electricity generated by water power.

hy·dro·foil (hī′drə foil′) *n.* **1.** a blade or wing-shaped structure under a motor-powered boat. The hydrofoil raises the hull of the boat out of the water when the boat reaches a certain speed, eliminating the resistance of the water against the hull and increasing the speed of the boat. **2.** a boat fitted with hydrofoils.

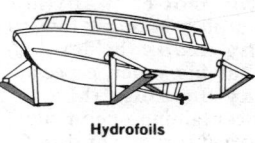

Hydrofoils

hy·dro·gen (hī′drə jən) *n.* a nonmetallic element that is a highly flammable gas at normal temperatures. It is colorless, tasteless, and odorless, and is the lightest chemical element. Symbol: H —**hy·drog·e·nous** (hī droj′ə nəs), *adj.*

hy·dro·gen·ate (hī′drə jə nāt′, hī droj′ə nāt′) *v.t.,* **hy·dro·gen·at·ed, hy·dro·gen·at·ing.** to combine or treat with hydrogen: *Oils are hydrogenated to produce margarine.* —**hy′dro·gen·a′tion,** *n.*

hydrogen bomb, a bomb whose enormous destructive power is caused by the fusion of hydrogen atoms to form helium atoms. Its destructive force is similar to, but much greater than that of an atomic bomb. Also, **H-bomb, fusion bomb.**

hydrogen peroxide, a colorless, unstable liquid that is an active oxidizing agent, diluted for use as a bleach and antiseptic. It is highly explosive in concentrated form.

hy·drog·ra·phy (hī drog′rə fē) *n.* the scientific measurement, charting, and description of oceans, lakes, rivers, and other surface waters, especially to determine their use for navigation. —**hy·dro·graph·ic** (hī′drə graf′ik), *adj.*

hy·drol·y·sis (hī drol′ə sis) *n. pl.,* **hy·drol·y·ses** (hī·drol′ə sēz′). a chemical reaction in which one of the reactants is water. Starch undergoes hydrolysis to form glucose.

hy·drom·e·ter (hī drom′ə tər) *n.* an instrument for measuring the specific gravity of liquids.

hy·dro·pho·bi·a (hī′drə fō′bē ə) *n.* **1.** see **rabies.** **2.** an excessive, abnormal fear of water.

hy·dro·plane (hī′drə plān′) *n.* **1.** a motorboat whose hull is designed to skim over the surface of the water rather than push through it. Hydroplanes are used especially in racing. **2.** another word for **seaplane.**

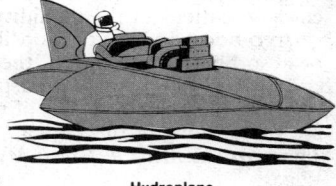

Hydroplane

hy·dro·pon·ics (hī′drə pon′iks) *n.,pl.* the science or practice of cultivating plants in a chemical solution rather than in soil. ▲ used with a singular verb.

hy·dro·sphere (hī′drə sfēr′) *n.* **1.** all the water on the surface of the earth. **2.** all the moisture in the atmosphere surrounding the earth.

hy·dro·stat·ic (hī′drə stat′ik) *adj.* of or relating to the science of hydrostatics.

hy·dro·stat·ics (hī′drə stat′iks) *n., pl.* the branch of physics dealing with the forces exerted by fluids at rest. ▲ used with a singular verb.

at; āpe; cär; end; mē; it; īce; hot; ōld; fôrk; wood; fōol; oil; out; up; turn; sing; thin; this; hw in white; zh in treasure. The symbol ə stands for the sound of **a** in about, **e** in taken, **i** in pencil, **o** in lemon, and **u** in circus.

H

465

hy·dro·ther·a·py (hī′drō ther′ə pē) *n.* the scientific treatment of disease by means of water.

hy·drot·ro·pism (hī drot′rə piz′əm) *n.* the tendency of a plant to grow toward moisture.

hy·drous (hī′drəs) *adj.* (of a chemical compound) containing water, especially in chemical combination.

hy·drox·ide (hī drok′sīd) *n.* any chemical compound containing one or more hydroxyl radicals.

hy·drox·yl (hī drok′sil) *n.* a chemical ion or group consisting of one atom of oxygen and one of hydrogen.

hy·dro·zo·an (hī′drə zō′ən) *n.* any of various saltwater and freshwater animals, including hydra and coral, generally existing in two unlike forms, that of a jellyfish and that of an unattached polyp. —*adj.* of or relating to hydrozoans.

hy·e·na (hī ē′nə) *n.* a wolflike animal native to Africa and Asia, having a large head, strong jaws, and front legs that are longer than the back ones. A hyena feeds chiefly on decaying carcasses by day and hunts live prey at night.

Hyena

hy·giene (hī′jēn) *n.* **1.** practices or conditions that aid good health. **2.** the science that deals with the maintenance of good health and the prevention of infection and disease.

hy·gi·en·ic (hī′jē en′ik) *adj.* **1.** free from anything dangerous to good health; sanitary. **2.** of or relating to health or hygiene. —**hy′gi·en′i·cal·ly,** *adv.*

hy·gien·ist (hī jē′nist) *n.* a person who is trained or expert in the principles of hygiene.

hy·grom·e·ter (hī grom′ə tər) *n.* an instrument for determining the humidity of the atmosphere.

hy·gro·met·ric (hī′grə met′rik) *adj.* of or relating to hygrometry or a hygrometer.

hy·grom·e·try (hī grom′ə trē) *n.* the study of the moisture of the atmosphere.

hy·gro·scope (hī′grə skōp) *n.* an instrument that records variations in the humidity of the atmosphere.

hy·gro·scop·ic (hī′grə skop′ik) *adj.* readily attracting or absorbing moisture from the atmosphere.

hy·ing (hī′ing) a present participle of **hie.**

hy·men (hī′mən) *n.* a fold of membrane partially covering the opening of the vagina.

Hy·men (hī′mən) *n. Greek Mythology.* the god of marriage.

hymn (him) *n.* **1.** a song of praise to God or a god. **2.** any song or ode of praise or joy.

hym·nal (him′nəl) *n.* a book or collection of hymns for use in a religious service. Also, **hymn·book** (him′book′).

hyper- *prefix* excessive or excessively: *hypercritical, hypertension.*

hy·per·a·cid·i·ty (hī′pər ə sid′ə tē) *n.* excessive acidity, especially of gastric juice.

hy·per·bo·la (hī pur′bə lə) *n.* an open curve with two branches consisting of a set of points in a plane whose distances from two fixed points, or foci, differ by a constant value.

hy·per·bo·le (hī pur′bə lē) *n.* a figure of speech consisting of an extreme exaggeration not meant to be taken literally. For example: *I shopped in a million stores today.*

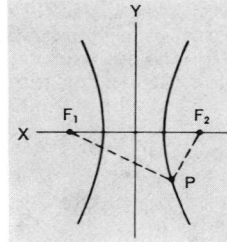

Hyperbola
P = any point on
hyperbola; F₁F₂ = foci;
PF₁ − PF₂ = a constant.

● In language, **hyperbole** is used to give special emphasis to a statement by exaggerating it. Hyperbole is often used in common speaking and writing. The difference between hyperbole and simple exaggeration is that the exaggeration used in hyperbole is so great that no one would take it literally or believe it to be true. For example, if you say "I'm so hungry I could eat a horse," people will understand that you are just using a colorful expression to convey the idea that you are very hungry. If you simply exaggerate and say "I'm so hungry I could eat four sandwiches," then it is not clear whether what you are saying is to be accepted as truth or exaggeration.

hy·per·bol·ic (hī′pər bol′ik) *adj.* **1.** of, relating to, or using hyperbole; exaggerated or exaggerating. **2.** of, relating to, or having the form of a hyperbola.

hy·per·crit·i·cal (hī′pər krit′i kəl) *adj.* too critical. —**hy′per·crit′i·cal·ly,** *adv.*

hy·per·sen·si·tive (hī′pər sen′sə tiv) *adj.* overly or abnormally sensitive: *hypersensitive skin, to be hypersensitive to criticism.* —**hy′per·sen′si·tive·ness,** *n.* —**hy′per·sen′si·tiv′i·ty,** *n.*

hy·per·son·ic (hī′pər son′ik) *adj.* of or relating to the speed of an object that is moving at a speed of at least five times the speed of sound.

hy·per·ten·sion (hī′pər ten′shən) *n. Medicine.* a condition characterized by high blood pressure.

hy·per·tro·phy (hī pur′trə fē) *n. pl.,* **hy·per·tro·phies.** abnormal or excessive growth, especially of a body part or organ.

hy·phen (hī′fən) *n.* a punctuation mark (-) used to connect two or more elements or words to form a compound word, or to join the syllables of a word that have been separated, as at the end of a line.

hy·phen·ate (hī′fə nāt′) *v.t.,* **hy·phen·at·ed, hy·phen·at·ing.** to separate, connect, or write with a hyphen: *to hyphenate a word.* —**hy′phen·a′tion,** *n.*

hyp·no·sis (hip nō′sis) *n. pl.,* **hyp·no·ses** (hip nō′sēz). **1.** an artificially produced state resembling deep sleep, characterized by extreme responsiveness to suggestion and loss of will power. It is sometimes used to produce anesthesia. **2.** another word for **hypnotism** *(def. 1).*

hyp·not·ic (hip not′ik) *adj.* **1.** of or relating to hypnosis or hypnotism: *a hypnotic trance.* **2.** tending to produce sleep or a trance that is like sleep: *The speaker had a droning, hypnotic voice. The long, straight highway had a hypnotic effect on drivers.* —*n.* **1.** something, as a drug, that produces sleep. **2.** a person who is or can be easily hypnotized. —**hyp·not′i·cal·ly,** *adv.*

hyp·no·tism (hip′nə tiz′əm) *n.* **1.** the science, practice, or act of inducing hypnosis. **2.** another word for **hypnosis** *(def. 1).*

hyp·no·tist (hip′nə tist) *n.* a person who induces hypnosis.

hyp·no·tize (hip′nə tīz′) *v.t.,* **hyp·no·tized, hyp·no·tiz·ing.** **1.** to put (someone) in a hypnotic trance; induce hypnosis in: *The doctor hypnotized his patient.* **2.** to fascinate; enthrall: *He was hypnotized by her beauty.* —**hyp′no·tiz′er,** *n.*

hy·po (hī′pō) *n. pl.,* **hy·pos.** *Informal.* a hypodermic syringe or injection.

hy·po·chon·dri·a (hī′pə kon′drē ə) *n.* a neurotic disorder that is characterized by excessive worry over one's health, imagined diseases and symptoms, and extreme depression.

hy·po·chon·dri·ac (hī′pə kon′drē ak′) *n.* a person who suffers from hypochondria. —*adj.* of, relating to, or suffering from hypochondria.

hy·po·cot·yl (hī′pə kot′əl) *n.* a part of the stem below the cotyledons in the embryo or seedling stage of a plant.

hy·poc·ri·sy (hi pok′rə sē) *n. pl.,* **hy·poc·ri·sies.** the act or practice of presenting one's character, feelings, or beliefs as being other than they really are, especially by pretending to be good or pious.

hyp·o·crite (hip′ə krit′) *n.* a person who is given to or practices hypocrisy. —**hyp′o·crit′i·cal,** *adj.* —**hyp′o·crit′i·cal·ly,** *adv.*

hy·po·der·mic (hī′pə dur′mik) *adj.* **1.** lying beneath the skin. **2.** made to be injected under the skin. —*n.* **1.** see **hypodermic syringe. 2.** an injection given with a needle or syringe.

hypodermic syringe, a syringe with a hollow needle that is inserted underneath the skin in order to inject or remove fluids. Also, **hypodermic needle.**

hy·po·sul·fite (hī′pə sul′fīt) *n.* another word for **sodium thiosulfate.**

hy·pot·e·nuse (hī pot′ən ōōs′, hī pot′ən yōōs′) *n.* the side of a right triangle opposite the right angle.

hy·po·thal·a·mus (hī′pə thal′ə·məs) *n. pl.,* **hy·po·thal·a·mi** (hī pə·thal′ə mī′). the part of the brain that controls various body functions, such as the heartbeat and body temperature.

hy·poth·e·sis (hī poth′ə sis) *n. pl.,* **hy·poth·e·ses** (hī poth′ə sēz′). an unproved, temporary explanation or supposition that is based on known facts and can be used as a basis for further experimentation or investigation; theory.

hy·poth·e·size (hī poth′ə sīz′) *v.i.,* **hy·poth·e·sized, hy·poth·e·siz·ing.** to make a hypothesis.

hy·po·thet·i·cal (hī′pə thet′i kəl) *adj.* of the nature of, involving, or based on a hypothesis or theory; theoreti-

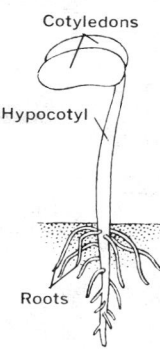

Cotyledons

Hypocotyl

Roots

Hypocotyl

Hypotenuse

90°

cal: *a hypothetical example.* Also, **hy·po·thet·ic** (hī′pə·thet′ik). —**hy′po·thet′i·cal·ly,** *adv.*

hy·rax (hī′raks) *n. pl.,* **hy·rax·es** or **hy·ra·ces** (hī′rə·sēz′). any of various animals of Africa and the Middle East that closely resemble rabbits and have claws that are like hooves, sharp canine teeth, and a coarse black, brownish-gray, or tan coat.

hys·sop (his′əp) *n.* **1.** a stiff plant related to the mint, having leaves with a pungent odor that were formerly used for flavoring food and for medicinal purposes. **2.** in the Old Testament, a plant whose twigs were used for sprinkling water in purification ceremonies.

hys·te·ri·a (his ter′ē ə) *n.* **1.** excessive, uncontrollable terror, panic, or other strong emotion; frenzy: *The riot was caused by an outbreak of mob hysteria.* **2.** an emotional disorder characterized by excitability and disturbances in normal functions, such as loss of sight or the ability to walk, for which no medical cause can be found. [Modern Latin *hysteria,* going back to Greek *hysterā* womb; originally applied to the emotional behavior of women who were thought to be suffering from disturbances of the womb.]

hys·ter·ic (his ter′ik) *n.* a person who suffers from hysteria. —*adj.* another word for **hysterical.**

hys·ter·i·cal (his ter′i kəl) *adj.* **1.** resembling or caused by hysteria; uncontrollably emotional; frenzied: *a hysterical outburst, a fit of hysterical sobbing.* **2.** of, characteristic of, or occurring as a symptom of hysteria: *hysterical blindness.* **3.** suffering from or prone to hysteria. **4.** *Informal.* extremely funny. —**hys·ter′i·cal·ly,** *adv.*

hys·ter·ics (his ter′iks) *n.,pl.* a fit of uncontrollable emotion, especially of laughing and crying at the same time. ▲ usually used with a singular verb.

at; āpe; cär; end; mē; it; īce; hot; ōld; fôrk; wood; fōōl; oil; out; up; turn; sing; thin; this; hw in white; zh in treasure. The symbol ə stands for the sound of **a** in about, **e** in taken, **i** in pencil, **o** in lemon, and **u** in circus.

H

1. Egyptian Hieroglyphics \\ 𝓎	5. Greek Classical Capitals Ⅰ
2. Semitic 𝟐	6. Etruscan (
3. Phoenician Ⅰ	7. Latin Fourth Century B.C. Capitals |
4. Greek Ninth Century B.C. |	8. English Ⅰ

I is the ninth letter of the English alphabet. The earliest form of the letter **I** was an Egyptian hieroglyphic (1) that probably represented a hand. In the ancient Semitic alphabet this symbol was altered and called *yod* (2), meaning "hand." The Phoenicians (3) borrowed *yod* and simplified it by making it a tall vertical line with a short horizontal stroke at the top and bottom. The early Greeks adopted *yod* and called it *iota.* At first, *iota* was written as a single vertical line (4). By about the fifth century B.C., the Greeks had added a short horizontal stroke at the top and bottom of the letter (5), writing it much as the Phoenicians had. The Etruscans (6) and the Romans (7) adopted the earlier form of *iota.* Our modern capital letter **I** (8) is almost always written like the classical Greek *iota,* having a short horizontal stroke at the top and bottom of the vertical line.

The dot that we write over the small letter **i** was not used until about 1000 years ago. In the style of writing used at the time, the small letters **m** and **n** were made up of strokes that each looked like a small letter **i.** Because of this, a word containing a combination of these letters, such as the Latin "minimus," was very hard to read. The addition of a dot over the small letter **i** helped the eye to distinguish the letters and made reading less difficult.

i, I (ī) *n. pl.,* **i's, I's. 1.** the ninth letter of the English alphabet. **2.** something having the shape of this letter. **3.** the Roman numeral for 1.

I (ī) *pron.* the person who is speaking or writing: *I called her yesterday. I am very grateful for all you have done for me.*

I, the symbol for iodine.

i., intransitive.

I. 1. Island; Islands. **2.** Isle; Isles.

Ia., Iowa.

-ial, the form of the suffix **-al**[1] after stressed syllables, as in *celestial.*

i·amb (ī′amb) *n.* **1.** in poetry, a metrical foot in verse consisting of an unaccented or short syllable followed by an accented or long syllable. The line *That fought/with us/upon/Saint Cris/pin's day* (Shakespeare, *Henry V*) contains five iambs. **2.** a line of verse that is made up of such feet.

i·am·bic (ī am′bik) *adj.* of, relating to, or containing iambs. —*n.* **1.** an iamb. **2.** *usually,* **iambics.** poetry written in iambs.

-ian, a form of the suffix **-an,** as in *Australian.*

ib., ibid.

I·ba·dan (ē bä′dän) *n.* the largest city of Nigeria, in the southwestern part of the country. Pop. (1971 est.), 627,379.

I·be·ri·a (ī bēr′ē ə) *n.* a large peninsula of southwestern Europe, between the Atlantic Ocean and the Mediterranean Sea, made up of Spain and Portugal. Also, **Iberian Peninsula.** —**I·be′ri·an,** *adj., n.*

i·bex (ī′beks) *n. pl.,* **i·bex·es** or **i·bex.** a wild goat that lives in the mountains of Europe, Asia, and northern Africa, having ridged, curving horns which in the male may grow to as much as five feet in length.

ibid., in the work previously mentioned or cited. [From Latin *ibidem* in the same place.]

-ibility, a form of the suffix **-ability,** as in *sensibility, flexibility.*

i·bis (ī′bis) *n. pl.,* **i·bis·es** or **i·bis.** a long-legged wading bird related to the stork and heron and having a long, downward curving bill.

-ible, a form of the suffix **-able,** as in *convertible.*

Ib·sen, Hen·rik (ib′sən; hen′rik) 1828–1906, Norwegian dramatist.

-ic *suffix* **1.** (used to form adjectives from nouns) **a.** of or relating to: *dramatic, Celtic.* **b.** having the qualities of; being or like: *athletic, angelic.* **c.** made of or containing: *alcoholic, iambic.* **d.** produced or caused by: *volcanic.* ▲ Many words ending in *-ic* have more than one of the above meanings. **2.** *Chemistry.* having a higher valence than a related compound or ion whose name ends in *-ous: ferric.*

-ical *suffix* **1.** (used to form adjectives from nouns) of, relating to, characterized by, or caused by: *economical,*

Ibex

468

philosophical. **2.** (used to form adjectives from nouns ending in -*ic*) of, relating to, or characterized by: *musical.*

Ic·a·rus (ik′ər əs) *n. Greek Mythology.* a youth who escaped from Crete on wings made by his father, Daedalus. The wax holding the wings melted when he flew too near to the sun, and he fell into the sea.

ICBM, a ballistic missile with a range of over 3000 miles. [Abbreviation of *i*(nter) *c*(ontinental) *b*(allistic) *m*(issile).]

ice (īs) *n.* **1.** the solid state of water, normally produced at or below 32 degrees Fahrenheit. **2.** the frozen surface of a body of water, such as a lake: *The fisherman cut a hole in the ice.* **3.** something that looks or feels like ice. **4.** a frozen dessert made of sweetened water and fruit flavoring or fruit juice. —*v.,* **iced, ic·ing.** —*v.i.* to become covered with ice: *The lake iced over.* —*v.t.* **1.** to cause ice to form on; cover with ice. **2.** to chill or keep cold, especially with ice: *to ice lemonade.* **3.** to cover or decorate with icing; frost. **4.** to change into ice.

on thin ice. in a dangerous or risky situation.

ice age 1. any period of time when glaciers covered much of the surface of the earth. **2. Ice Age.** another term for **Pleistocene.**

ice·berg (īs′burg′) *n.* a large mass of floating ice that has broken off from a glacier or polar icecap.

ice·boat (īs′bōt′) *n.* **1.** a light, often triangular, frame equipped with runners and sails for sailing on ice. **2.** another word for **ice-breaker.**

ice·bound (īs′bound′) *adj.* **1.** obstructed by ice: *an icebound coast.* **2.** held fast or surrounded by ice: *an icebound ship.*

ice·box (īs′boks′) *n. pl.,* **ice-box·es. 1.** a box or chest cooled by blocks of ice, used for storing food and drinks. **2.** a refrigerator.

Iceberg

ice·break·er (īs′brā′kər) *n.* a ship with a strong prow, used in harbors, rivers, and other waterways to break or open a channel through ice. Also, **iceboat.**

ice·cap (īs′kap′) *n.* a cone-shaped or dome-shaped glacier covering a land area and moving out from the center in all directions.

ice cream, a frozen dessert made chiefly of milk products, sweeteners, and flavoring.

ice field, a large mass of floating ice, found especially in polar regions.

ice floe, see **floe.**

ice hockey, see **hockey** *(def. 1).*

ice·house (īs′hous′) *n. pl.,* **ice·hous·es** (īs′hou′ziz). a building for storing ice.

Ice·land (īs′lənd) *n.* an island country in the North Atlantic, between Greenland and Norway, formerly a possession of Denmark. Capital, Reykjavik. Area, 39,800 sq. mi. Pop. (1971 est.), 210,000. —**Ice·land·er** (īs′lan′dər), *n.*

Ice·lan·dic (īs lan′dik) *adj.* of or relating to Iceland, its people, their language, or their culture. —*n.* the Germanic language spoken in Iceland.

ice·man (īs′man′) *n. pl.,* **ice·men** (īce′men′). a person whose job or business is selling or delivering ice.

ice pack 1. a bag or folded cloth filled with ice and applied to parts of the body to relieve pain or lessen swelling. **2.** another term for **pack ice.**

ice pick, a pointed tool used to break or chip ice.

ice sheet, a thick layer of ice covering a large area of land for a long period of time.

ice-skate (īs′skāt′) *v.i.,* **ice-skat·ed, ice-skat·ing.** to skate on ice.

ice skate 1. a runner, usually of metal, mounted in a frame that has straps and clamps for attaching to the sole of a shoe, used for skating on ice. **2.** a shoe, usually covering the ankle, with such a runner permanently attached to it.

ice skater, a person who ice-skates.

ich·neu·mon (ik nōō′mən) *n.* **1.** a mongoose native to Africa, having a gray body and brownish-black feet. It was considered sacred by the ancient Egyptians. **2.** see **ichneumon fly.**

ichneumon fly, any of a large group of insects resembling wasps, found throughout the world. Its larvae destroy many destructive crop pests.

ich·thy·ol·o·gist (ik′thē ol′ə jist) *n.* a student of or an expert in ichthyology.

ich·thy·ol·o·gy (ik′thē ol′ə jē) *n.* the branch of zoology that deals with fish.

ich·thy·o·saur (ik′thē ə sôr′) *n.* any of an extinct group of marine reptiles that resembled fish. The ichthyosaur had a large head with a long, thin snout and four paddlelike flippers.

ich·thy·o·sau·rus (ik′thē ə sôr′əs) *n. pl.,* **ich·thy·o·sau·ri** (ik′thē ə sôr′ī) or **ich·thy·o·sau·rus·es.** another word for **ichthyosaur.**

Ichthyosaur

i·ci·cle (ī′si kəl) *n.* a pointed, hanging piece of ice formed by water that freezes as it drips.

i·ci·ly (ī′sə lē) *adv.* in an icy manner: *She stared icily at the rude stranger.*

i·ci·ness (ī′sē nis) *n.* the state or quality of being icy.

ic·ing (ī′sing) *n.* a mixture of sugar, butter, flavoring, a liquid, and sometimes egg whites, used to cover or decorate cakes or other baked goods; frosting.

i·con (ī′kon) *also,* **i·kon.** *n.* a painted picture or other representation of a holy person, such as Christ, the Virgin Mary, or a saint. Icons are considered sacred by Christians in the Eastern Church.

i·con·o·clast (ī kon′ə klast′) *n.* **1.** a person who attacks traditional or cherished ideas, beliefs, or institutions as being false or harmful. **2.** a person who destroys icons and is against their religious use.

i·con·o·clas·tic (ī kon′ə klas′tik) *adj.* of or relating to iconoclasts.

-ics *suffix* (used to form nouns) **1.** an art, science, or field of study: *physics, mathematics.* **2.** methods, systems, practices, or activities: *gymnastics.*

i·cy (ī′sē) *adj.,* **i·ci·er, i·ci·est. 1.** made of, containing, or covered with ice: *an icy sidewalk.* **2.** very cold: *icy winds, icy hands.* **3.** without warmth of feeling; cold and unfriendly: *an icy welcome.*

I'd (īd) **1.** I had. **2.** I would. **3.** I should.

ID, identification.

Ida., Idaho.

I·da·ho (ī′də hō′) *n.* a state in the western United States. Capital, Boise. Area, 83,557 sq. mi. Pop. (1970), 712,567. Abbreviation, **Ida.** —**I′da·ho′an,** *adj., n.*

at; āpe; cär; end; mē; it; īce; hot; ōld; fôrk; wood; fōōl; oil; out; up; turn; sing; thin; this; hw in white; zh in treasure. The symbol ə stands for the sound of a in about, e in taken, i in pencil, o in lemon, and u in circus.

I

• **Idaho** probably comes from an Apache name for the Comanche Indians. It first appeared in present-day Colorado, but the Senate chose it as the name for the new state of Idaho.

i·de·a (ī dē′ə) *n.* **1.** something formed by or in the mind; thought: *The author had an idea for a new novel.* **2.** a belief or opinion: *The old man had strong ideas about religion.* **3.** a plan of action or intention: *She had the idea of becoming an artist.* **4.** the aim or purpose of something: *The idea of the game of golf is to hit the ball into the hole.*

i·de·al (ī dē′əl) *n.* **1.** an idea or standard of perfection or excellence: *The Declaration of Independence contains many of the ideals of our forefathers.* **2.** a person or thing regarded as being perfect or excellent and worthy of imitation or admiration: *The famous football player was the ideal of many young boys.* **3.** the best or most satisfactory situation; aim or goal. —*adj.* **1.** being exactly what one would wish or hope for; most desirable or suitable: *The breeze makes it an ideal day for sailing.* **2.** existing only in the mind.

i·de·al·ism (ī dē′ə liz′əm) *n.* **1.** an action or belief that is in keeping with one's own ideas or standards of perfection or excellence. **2.** a theory in philosophy that reality is essentially mental or spiritual rather than physical. Idealists believe either that nothing is real except what exists in a person's mind, or that reality exists in ideal forms that are outside of a person's mind.

i·de·al·ist (ī dē′ə list) *n.* **1.** a person who thinks or acts according to his ideals. **2.** a person who thinks that things are better than they are. **3.** a person who believes in or follows idealism in philosophy. —**i′de·al·is′tic,** *adj.* —**i′de·al·is′ti·cal·ly,** *adv.*

i·de·al·ize (ī dē′ə līz′) *v.t.,* **i·de·al·ized, i·de·al·iz·ing.** to think of or represent as perfect: *The old man idealized his early days on his father's farm.* —**i′de·al·i·za′tion,** *n.*

i·de·al·ly (ī dē′ə lē) *adv.* **1.** in the best possible manner; perfectly or very well: *His new school suits him ideally.* **2.** under the best or most desirable conditions; in theory: *Ideally, each child should receive three shots of the vaccine.*

i·den·ti·cal (ī den′ti kəl) *adj.* **1.** one and the same; the very same: *She wore the identical dress at both parties.* **2.** exactly alike: *identical uniforms, identical answers.* —**i·den′ti·cal·ly,** *adv.*

identical twins, twins of the same or opposite sex that develop from a single fertilized egg cell and therefore look alike.

i·den·ti·fi·ca·tion (ī den′tə fi kā′shən) *n.* **1.** the act of identifying or the state of being identified. **2.** something used to prove or to establish one's identity: *John carried his passport as identification.*

i·den·ti·fy (ī den′tə fī′) *v.,* **i·den·ti·fied, i·den·ti·fy·ing.** —*v.t.* **1.** to prove that (someone or something) is a particular person or thing: *The witness identified the suspect by the scar on his face. How many species of birds can you identify?* **2.** to regard or treat as identical; assume to be one and the same: *The Roman goddess Venus is identified with the Greek goddess Aphrodite.* **3.** to connect closely; associate: *He identifies money with success.* —*v.i.* to become as one with another or others: *She always identifies with the heroine of the book she is reading.* —**i·den′ti·fi′a·ble,** *adj.*

i·den·ti·ty (ī den′tə tē) *n. pl.,* **i·den·ti·ties. 1.** a person's sense of being different from other persons; individuality. **2.** the fact or condition of being a certain person or thing; being who or what one or it is: *His driver's license established his identity.* **3.** the state or condition of being identical: *the identity of two accounts of an accident.*

4. *Mathematics.* a statement of equality that is true for all values of a variable. The equation $3x + 2x = 5x$ is true for all values of x and is therefore an identity.

identity element, an element in a set that, when added to or multiplied by another element, yields that element. For addition, 0 is the identity element, since $7 + 0 = 7$. For multiplication, 1 is the identity element, since $7 \times 1 = 7$.

id·e·o·gram (id′ē ə gram′) *n.* another word for **ideograph.**

id·e·o·graph (id′ē ə graf′) *n.* a written symbol that stands for an object or idea rather than for a word, used in certain languages, such as Chinese.

id·e·o·log·i·cal (ī′dē ə loj′i kəl, id′ē ə loj′i kəl) *adj.* of or based on ideologies or an ideology.

id·e·ol·o·gy (ī′dē ol′ə jē, id′ē ol′ə jē) *n. pl.,* **id·e·ol·o·gies.** all the beliefs, attitudes, ideas, and doctrines that are held by the members of a group, such as a political party.

ides (īdz) *n., pl.* in the ancient Roman calendar, the fifteenth day of March, May, July, or October, and the thirteenth day of the other months.

id·i·o·cy (id′ē ə sē) *n.* **1.** severe mental retardation. **2.** great silliness or stupidity.

id·i·om (id′ē əm) *n.* **1.** an expression whose meaning cannot be understood from the meanings of the individual words composing it. **2.** the language or dialect of a particular people or a specific region: *the idiom of the American Southwest.* **3.** the characteristic way in which words are used in a particular language.

• Because **idioms** are part of our everyday speaking and writing, we rarely think about the fact that they don't make sense according to the meanings of their individual words. It is only because we learn to speak our own language instinctively that the idioms in English don't seem strange to us. Try to imagine what a foreigner learning English would think if, for the first time, he heard someone say "I don't believe you; you're just pulling my leg." Most of us have used the phrase "you're pulling my leg" without thinking about how foolish it would sound to someone who knows only the literal meaning of the individual words. Idioms are defined in this dictionary because you would be unable to understand their meaning by separately looking up each of the words that are in them.

All languages have their own special idioms. For example, the Spanish phrase equivalent to our English phrase "You're welcome" is *"De nada."* The literal meaning of the words in this phrase is "of nothing." The Spanish idiom *"Que tal?",* which is equivalent to English "How are you?" literally means "What such?"

id·i·o·mat·ic (id′ē ə mat′ik) *adj.* **1.** having the nature of or containing an idiom or idioms: *an idiomatic expression.* **2.** characterized by the use of idioms: *He is an idiomatic writer.* **3.** following the characteristic pattern of a particular language: *idiomatic English.* —**id′i·o·mat′i·cal·ly,** *adv.*

id·i·o·syn·cra·sy (id′ē ə sing′krə sē) *n. pl.,* **id·i·o·syn·cra·sies.** an unusual or distinguishing characteristic of an individual, such as a habit or mannerism; peculiarity.

id·i·ot (id′ē ət) *n.* **1.** a person who is mentally retarded and cannot develop beyond a mental age of four years. **2.** a very silly or stupid person; fool. [Old French *idiote* an ignorant person, going back to Greek *idiōtēs* a person not holding public office; because the ancient Greeks considered people not holding public office to be ignorant or ill-informed.]

id·i·ot·ic (id′ē ot′ik) *adj.* very silly or stupid; foolish: *Her idiotic behavior embarrassed us.* —**id′i·ot′i·cal·ly,** *adv.*

i·dle (īd′əl) *adj.*, **i·dler, i·dlest.** **1.** not working, in use, or busy: *an idle machine.* **2.** not willing to work; lazy. **3.** having little worth, usefulness, or importance: *an idle pastime, idle chatter.* —*v.*, **i·dled, i·dling.** —*v.i.* **1.** to spend time doing nothing; be inactive: *He idled around the house all morning.* **2.** (of machines) to run slowly, out of gear, or without transmitting power: *The car motor idled.* —*v.t.* to spend (time) doing nothing; waste: *He idled away his entire vacation.* —**i′dle·ness,** *n.* —**i′dly,** *adv.*

i·dler (īd′lər) *n.* a person who is lazy; loafer.

i·dol (īd′əl) *n.* **1.** an image or representation of a god, used as an object of worship. **2.** a person who is greatly loved or admired: *The athlete was the idol of many fans.*

i·dol·a·ter (ī dol′ə tər) *n.* a person who worships an idol or idols. —**i·dol′a·tress,** *n.*

i·dol·a·trous (ī dol′ə trəs) *adj.* **1.** of, relating to, or characteristic of idolatry. **2.** given to worshiping an idol or idols: *an idolatrous tribe.* **3.** admiring and loving very much. —**i·dol′a·trous·ly,** *adv.*

i·dol·a·try (ī dol′ə trē) *n. pl.*, **i·dol·a·tries.** **1.** the worship of idols. **2.** very great admiration or love.

i·dol·ize (īd′əl īz′) *v.t.*, **i·dol·ized, i·dol·iz·ing.** **1.** to have very great admiration or love for: *The teenagers idolized the singer.* **2.** to worship as an idol. —**i′dol·i·za′tion,** *n.*

i·dyll (īd′əl) *also,* **i·dyl.** *n.* **1.** a short poem or work of prose that describes peaceful, simple events or scenes of country life. **2.** an event or scene suitable for such a work.

i·dyl·lic (ī dil′ik) *adj.* **1.** of, relating to, or having the nature of an idyll. **2.** peaceful, simple, and charming: *His home was in an idyllic setting of woods and fields.*

i.e., that is. [An abbreviation of Latin *id est.*]

-ier *suffix* (used to form nouns) a person who has to do with: *cashier, financier.*

if (if) *conj.* **1.** in case that; supposing that: *If I hurt your feelings, I'm sorry. If he is sick, he won't be able to come.* **2.** granting that: *Even if it rains, the game will still be played.* **3.** on condition that: *I will sing, if you will accompany me.* **4.** whether: *I don't know if he will be there.* **5.** even though; although: *It was a nice, if humid, day.* **6.** used to express a wish, surprise, or annoyance: *If we had only known.*

ig·loo (ig′lōō) *n. pl.*, **ig·loos.** a dome-shaped hut used by Eskimos, usually built of blocks of hardened snow.

Ig·na·tius of Loyola, Saint (ig nā′shəs) 1491–1556, the founder of the Society of Jesus.

ig·ne·ous (ig′nē əs) *adj.* **1.** relating to or characteristic of fire. **2.** produced by great heat or volcanic action: *an igneous rock.*

Igloo

ig·nite (ig nīt′) *v.*, **ig·nit·ed, ig·nit·ing.** —*v.t.* to burn or set on fire; kindle: *We ignited the pile of dead leaves with a match.* —*v.i.* to begin to burn; catch on fire: *Oily rags will ignite easily.*

ig·ni·tion (ig nish′ən) *n.* **1.** the act of igniting or the state of being ignited. **2.** a device or system for igniting the fuel and air mixture within the cylinders of an internal-combustion engine.

ig·no·ble (ig nō′bəl) *adj.* **1.** without honor or worth; mean; base: *Cheating is an ignoble act.* **2.** of low birth or position. —**ig·no′ble·ness,** *n.* —**ig·no′bly,** *adv.*

ig·no·min·i·ous (ig′nə min′ē əs) *adj.* **1.** marked by or involving dishonor or disgrace; shameful: *ignominious punishment, an ignominious defeat.* **2.** deserving shame or contempt: *ignominious behavior.* —**ig′no·min′i·ous·ly,** *adv.* —**ig′no·min′i·ous·ness,** *n.*

ig·no·min·y (ig′nə min′ē) *n. pl.*, **ig·no·min·ies.** **1.** disgrace or dishonor. **2.** something that causes or deserves disgrace or dishonor.

ig·no·ra·mus (ig′nə rā′məs, ig′nə ram′əs) *n. pl.*, **ig·no·ra·mus·es.** an ignorant person. [From *Ignoramus*, an ignorant character in a play by George Ruggle, written in 1615.]

ig·no·rance (ig′nər əns) *n.* the state or quality of being ignorant.

ig·no·rant (ig′nər ənt) *adj.* **1.** lacking in knowledge or education. **2.** not informed or aware: *She was ignorant of the fact that we were not going to the game.* **3.** showing lack of knowledge or education: *an ignorant statement.* —**ig′no·rant·ly,** *adv.*

ig·nore (ig nôr′) *v.t.*, **ig·nored, ig·nor·ing.** to refuse to take notice of or recognize; pay no attention to: *He ignored my question.*

i·gua·na (i gwä′nə) *n.* a large, greenish-brown lizard, found in tropical America. The iguana usually lives in trees and has a large fold of skin hanging from its throat and a ridge of scales down the center of the back.

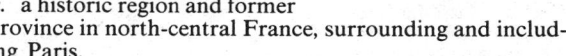

Iguana

i·kon (ī′kon) another spelling of **icon.**

il-, the form of the prefix **in-**[1] before *l*, as in *illegitimate.*

Ile-de-France (ēl′də fräns′) *n.* a historic region and former province in north-central France, surrounding and including Paris.

il·e·um (il′ē əm) *n. pl.*, **il·e·a** (il′ē ə). the last section of the small intestine.

Il·i·ad (il′ē əd) *n.* an ancient Greek epic poem describing some of the events of the Trojan War. It is believed to have been written by Homer.

il·i·um (il′ē əm) *n. pl.*, **il·i·a** (il′ē ə). the broad upper portion of the hipbone.

Il·i·um (il′ē əm) *n.* see **Troy** *(def. 1).*

ilk (ilk) *n.* kind; sort; class: *He does not associate with liars and others of that ilk.*

ill (il) *adj.*, **worse, worst.** **1.** not healthy or well; sick: *He is absent because he is ill.* **2.** not satisfactory; poor: *ill health, ill fortune.* **3.** hostile, cruel, or unfriendly: *ill feeling.* **4.** causing harm, destruction, or evil: *The war had many ill consequences.* —*adv.* **1.** in a harmful or unkind manner; badly: *Do not speak ill of him.* **2.** scarcely; hardly: *We can ill afford the time wasted.* —*n.* **1.** *usually,* **ills.** trouble, evil, or misfortune: *the ills of mankind.* **2.** a sickness or ailment: *Arthritis is a common ill.*

ill at ease. nervous and uncomfortable: *The shy girl felt ill at ease with strangers.*

I'll (īl) **1.** I will. **2.** I shall.

ill. **1.** illustrated. **2.** illustration.

Ill., Illinois.

ill-ad·vised (il′əd vīzd′) *adj.* acting or done without sound advice or enough thought or consideration; unwise.

ill-bred (il′bred′) *adj.* badly brought up or trained; unmannerly; rude.

at; āpe; cär; end; mē; it; īce; hot; ōld; fôrk; wood; fŏŏl; oil; out; up; turn; sing; thin; this; hw in white; zh in treasure. The symbol ə stands for the sound of **a** in about, **e** in taken, **i** in pencil, **o** in lemon, and **u** in circus.

I

il·le·gal (i lē′gəl) *adj.* **1.** not legal; unlawful. **2.** against the official rules, as in sports. —**il·le′gal·ly,** *adv.*

il·le·gal·i·ty (il′ē gal′ə tē) *n. pl.,* **il·le·gal·i·ties.** **1.** the state or quality of being illegal; unlawfulness. **2.** an illegal act.

il·leg·i·ble (i lej′ə bəl) *adj.* difficult or impossible to read; not legible: *The tiny handwriting on the envelope was illegible.* —**il·leg′i·bil′i·ty,** *n.* —**il·leg′i·bly,** *adv.*

il·le·git·i·ma·cy (il′i jit′ə mə sē) *n. pl.,* **il·le·git·i·ma·cies.** the state or quality of being illegitimate.

il·le·git·i·mate (il′i jit′ə mit) *adj.* **1.** not authorized; not lawful: *an illegitimate ruler.* **2.** born to a woman who is not married: *an illegitimate child.* —**il′le·git′i·mate·ly,** *adv.*

ill-fat·ed (il′fā′tid) *adj.* **1.** having a bad fate or end; doomed from the start: *The ill-fated play closed after the second performance.* **2.** characterized by or causing misfortune; unlucky: *an ill-fated day.*

ill-fa·vored (il′fā′vərd) *adj.* unpleasant in appearance; ugly: *an ill-favored woman.*

ill-got·ten (il′got′ən) *adj.* gotten by evil or dishonest means: *ill-gotten money.*

ill-hu·mored (il′hyōo′mərd) *adj.* having or showing a bad temper or humor; irritable; cross.

il·lib·er·al (i lib′ər əl) *adj.* **1.** narrow-minded; bigoted; intolerant. **2.** not generous in giving; stingy.

il·lic·it (i lis′it) *adj.* forbidden by law; not allowed. —**il·lic′it·ly,** *adv.* —**il·lic′it·ness,** *n.* ▲ See **elicit** for usage note.

il·lim·it·a·ble (i lim′i tə bəl) *adj.* not capable of being limited or bounded; limitless: *an illimitable amount.* —**il·lim′it·a·bly,** *adv.*

Il·li·nois (il′ə noi′, il′ə noiz′) *n.* **1.** a state in the north-central United States. Capital, Springfield. Area, 56,400 sq. mi. Pop. (1970), 11,113,976. Abbreviation, **Ill. 2.** a river flowing from northeastern Illinois into the Mississippi River. —**Il′li·nois′an,** *adj., n.*

● The name **Illinois** is the French form of an Algonquian word meaning "men" or "tribe of superior men." This word was the name of an Indian tribe that once lived in what is now Illinois.

il·lit·er·a·cy (i lit′ər ə sē) *n. pl.,* **il·lit·er·a·cies. 1.** a lack of the ability to read or write. **2.** a lack of education or knowledge.

il·lit·er·ate (i lit′ər it) *adj.* **1.** unable to read or write. **2.** lacking or showing a lack of education or knowledge: *an illiterate book.* —*n.* a person who is illiterate. —**il·lit′er·ate·ly,** *adv.*

ill-man·nered (il′man′ərd) *adj.* having bad manners; rude.

ill-na·tured (il′nā′chərd) *adj.* having or showing a disagreeable or cross disposition. —**ill′-na′tured·ly,** *adv.*

ill·ness (il′nis) *n. pl.,* **ill·ness·es. 1.** a condition or period of being ill: *During her illness, she stayed home from school.* **2.** a sickness; disease.

il·log·i·cal (i loj′i kəl) *adj.* showing a lack of good sense or reasoning. —**il·log′i·cal·ly,** *adv.*

ill-starred (il′stärd′) *adj.* ill-fated or unlucky.

ill-suit·ed (il′sōo′tid) *adj.* not fitting; inappropriate: *His silly behavior was ill-suited to the seriousness of the occasion.*

ill-tem·pered (il′tem′pərd) *adj.* irritable; cross.

ill-timed (il′tīmd′) *adj.* coming at the wrong or a bad time.

ill-treat (il′trēt′) *v.t.* to treat badly or cruelly; abuse. —**ill′-treat′ment,** *n.*

il·lu·mi·nate (i lōo′mə nāt′) *v.t.,* **il·lu·mi·nat·ed, il·lu·mi·nat·ing. 1.** to give light to; light up: *The sun illuminates the sky.* **2.** to decorate with lights: *to illuminate a fountain at night.* **3.** to make clear; explain: *The teacher's descriptions illuminate history more than any book.* **4.** to decorate (a scroll, manuscript, or page) with ornamental designs and pictures in gold, silver, and brilliant colors, as in medieval times.

il·lu·mi·na·tion (i lōo′mə nā′shən) *n.* **1.** the act of illuminating or the state of being illuminated. **2.** an amount or supply of light: *This lamp gives poor illumination.* **3.** decoration with lights. **4.** the decoration of a scroll, manuscript, or page of a book with ornamental designs and figures in gold, silver, and brilliant colors, as in medieval times.

il·lu·mine (i lōo′min) *v.t.,* **il·lu·mined, il·lu·min·ing.** to light up; illuminate.

illus. 1. illustrated. **2.** illustrator.

ill-use (*v.,* il′yōoz′; *n.,* il′yōos′) *v.t.,* **ill-used, ill-us·ing.** to treat badly, cruelly, or unfairly; abuse. —*n.* bad, cruel, or unfair treatment.

il·lu·sion (i lōo′zhən) *n.* **1.** a false or misleading idea or belief; misconception: *She had many illusions about what life in a foreign country would be like.* **2.** an impression of the nature or appearance of something that is contrary to fact or reality: *The color red gives the illusion of heat.*

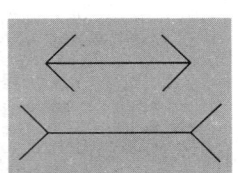

il·lu·sive (i lōo′siv) *adj.* false or misleading; illusory. —**il·lu′sive·ly,** *adv.* —**il·lu′sive·ness,** *n.*

il·lu·so·ry (i lōo′sər ē) *adj.* caused by or causing an illusion; false or misleading.

Illusion (def. 2)
Optical illusion in which the two horizontal lines are equal in length although they appear unequal

illust. 1. illustration. **2.** illustrated.

il·lus·trate (il′əs trāt′, i lus′trāt′) *v.t.,* **il·lus·trat·ed, il·lus·trat·ing. 1.** to make clear or explain, as by the use of examples or comparisons: *The teacher illustrated how the human eye works by comparing it to a camera.* **2.** to provide with pictures, drawings, or diagrams that explain or decorate: *to illustrate a book.* **3.** to be or serve as an example, explanation, or instance of: *These paintings illustrate the artist's early work.*

il·lus·tra·tion (il′əs trā′shən) *n.* **1.** something used to make clear or explain, such as an example or comparison. **2.** a picture, diagram, or drawing used to explain or decorate written or printed matter. **3.** the act or art of illustrating.

il·lus·tra·tive (i lus′trə tiv, il′əs trā′tiv) *adj.* used or serving to illustrate: *This book contains much illustrative material.* —**il·lus′tra·tive·ly,** *adv.*

il·lus·tra·tor (il′əs trā′tər) *n.* **1.** an artist who makes illustrations, as for books or magazines. **2.** a person or thing that illustrates.

il·lus·tri·ous (i lus′trē əs) *adj.* **1.** distinguished or famous: *an illustrious statesman.* **2.** marked by or giving greatness, distinction, or glory: *illustrious acts.* —**il·lus′tri·ous·ly,** *adv.* —**il·lus′tri·ous·ness,** *n.*

ill will, unfriendly feeling.

I'm (īm) I am.

im-¹, the form of the prefix **in-¹** before *b, m, p,* as in *immoral.*

im-², the form of the prefix **in-²** before *b, m, p,* as in *imbibe.*

im·age (im′ij) *n.* **1.** a picture, statue, or other likeness of a person, animal, or thing: *The ancient coin had an image of the emperor on one side.* **2.** a picture or idea held in the mind of a person or thing that is not actually present: *I had formed an image of her before we met.* **3.** a person or thing that closely resembles another: *He is the image* of his father. **4.** a typical example; picture: *He is the image of good health.* **5.** a description or figure of speech, especially a metaphor or simile. **6.** an impression created by a person, group, or organization on the basis of its attitudes, policies, and practices: *The politician wanted to change his public image.* **7.** a picture of an object produced when light rays from the object are focused on a surface, as by a lens or mirror. —*v.t.,* **im·aged, im·ag·ing.** to make or form an image of.

im·age·ry (im′ij rē) *n. pl.,* **im·age·ries. 1.** images formed in the mind, as by memory or imagination. **2.** the use of descriptions or figures of speech in writing or speech.

i·mag·i·na·ble (i maj′i nə bəl) *adj.* that can be imagined: *He used every argument imaginable to convince them to stay longer.* —**i·mag′i·na·bly,** *adv.*

i·mag·i·nar·y (i maj′ə ner′ē) *adj.* **1.** existing only in the imagination; unreal. **2.** of or relating to imaginary numbers.

imaginary number, a number whose square is negative.

i·mag·i·na·tion (i maj′ə nā′shən) *n.* **1.** the power or process of forming images in the mind of things that are not actually present: *She relived last summer's vacation in her imagination.* **2.** the mental power or ability to create new images or ideas of things never experienced or to use and combine past images and ideas to form new ones: *It took great imagination to write that poem.*

i·mag·i·na·tive (i maj′ə nə tiv) *adj.* **1.** having or showing creative ability or a good imagination: *an imaginative child.* **2.** produced or characterized by creativity or imagination: *an imaginative story.* —**i·mag′i·na·tive·ly,** *adv.* —**i·mag′i·na·tive·ness,** *n.*

i·mag·ine (i maj′in) *v.,* **i·mag·ined, i·mag·in·ing.** —*v.t.* **1.** to picture (someone or something) in the mind; form a mental picture of: *She cannot imagine life on another planet.* **2.** to suppose; guess: *I don't imagine they will come if it rains.* —*v.i.* to picture in the mind; think: *The book was different from what I had imagined.*

i·ma·go (i mā′gō) *n. pl.,* **i·ma·gos** or **i·mag·i·nes** (i maj′-ə nēz). an insect in the adult stage.

im·bal·ance (im bal′əns) *n.* a lack of balance.

im·be·cile (im′bə sil) *n.* **1.** a person who is mentally retarded and cannot develop beyond a mental age of eight years. **2.** a stupid or foolish person. —*adj.* another word for **imbecilic.**

im·be·cil·ic (im′bə sil′ik) *adj.* stupid or foolish: *imbecilic behavior.*

im·be·cil·i·ty (im′bə sil′ə tē) *n. pl.,* **im·be·cil·i·ties. 1.** the condition of being an imbecile. **2.** stupidity or foolishness.

im·bed (im bed′) *v.t.,* **im·bed·ded, im·bed·ding.** another spelling of **embed.**

im·bibe (im bīb′) *v.,* **im·bibed, im·bib·ing.** —*v.t.* **1.** to take into the mouth and swallow (liquid); drink. **2.** to take in as if by drinking; absorb: *The dry soil imbibed the water.* **3.** to take into the mind and keep: *to imbibe knowledge.* —*v.i.* to drink something, especially liquor.

im·bro·glio (im brōl′yō) *n. pl.,* **im·bro·glios. 1.** a complicated argument or disagreement: *The two neighbors got into an imbroglio over the boundaries of their property.* **2.** a confused or complicated situation.

im·bue (im byoo′) *v.t.,* **im·bued, im·bu·ing. 1.** to fill or inspire, as with emotions, ideals, or opinions: *The young lawyer was imbued with the spirit of justice.* **2.** to fill completely, as with color; saturate.

im·i·tate (im′ə tāt′) *v.t.,* **im·i·tat·ed, im·i·tat·ing. 1.** to follow or try to follow the example of: *The child imitated her older sister.* **2.** to copy the behavior or mannerisms of; mimic: *He imitated the famous singer.* **3.** to

make a copy or duplicate of: *The forger imitated her handwriting.* **4.** to have the appearance of; look like; resemble: *The floors were painted to imitate marble.*

im·i·ta·tion (im′ə tā′shən) *n.* **1.** the act of imitating: *an imitation of a bird's call.* **2.** a copy, especially one that is of poor quality: *That is not a genuine antique clock, but only an imitation.* —*adj.* made to look like something genuine or superior; not real: *imitation mink.*

im·i·ta·tive (im′ə tā′tiv) *adj.* **1.** imitating or tending to imitate: *Children are very imitative of their elders.* **2.** characterized by or showing imitation: *The word "chirp" is imitative of the sound made by a bird.* **3.** not real: *imitative jewelry.* —**im′i·ta′tive·ly,** *adv.* —**im′i·ta′tive·ness,** *n.*

im·i·ta·tor (im′ə tā′tər) *n.* a person who imitates.

im·mac·u·late (i mak′yə lit) *adj.* **1.** free from dust, grime, or clutter; very clean or neat: *Her house is always immaculate.* **2.** free from fault or blemish; flawless: *He is an immaculate dresser.* **3.** free from sin; pure. —**im·mac′u·late·ly,** *adv.* —**im·mac′u·late·ness,** *n.*

Immaculate Conception, the Roman Catholic doctrine that the Virgin Mary was conceived free from original sin.

Im·man·u·el (i man′yoo əl) *also,* **Em·man·u·el.** *n.* another name for the **Messiah.**

im·ma·te·ri·al (im′ə tēr′ē əl) *adj.* **1.** of little or no importance or value; unimportant: *It is immaterial to me whether she comes or not.* **2.** not consisting of matter; not material; spiritual. —**im′ma·te′ri·al·ly,** *adv.* —**im′ma·te′ri·al·ness,** *n.*

im·ma·ture (im′ə choor′, im′ə toor′, im′ə tyoor′) *adj.* **1.** not having reached full growth or development; not mature: *an immature plant.* **2.** foolish or childish: *immature behavior.* —**im′ma·ture′ly,** *adv.*

im·ma·tu·ri·ty (im′ə choor′ə tē, im′ə toor′ə tē, im′ə tyoor′ə tē) *n.* the state or quality of being immature.

im·meas·ur·a·ble (i mezh′ər ə bəl) *adj.* that cannot be measured. —**im·meas′ur·a·bly,** *adv.*

im·me·di·a·cy (i mē′dē ə sē) *n.* the state or quality of being immediate.

im·me·di·ate (i mē′dē it) *adj.* **1.** done or happening without delay; instant: *We received an immediate answer to our question.* **2.** of or relating to the present time: *I have no immediate plans.* **3.** close in time or space; near: *We do not plan on moving in the immediate future.* **4.** nearest in relationship: *They only invited the immediate family to the wedding.* **5.** with nothing coming between; direct: *The evidence of the witness had no immediate bearing on the case.* —**im·me′di·ate·ly,** *adv.* —**im·me′di·ate·ness,** *n.*

im·me·mo·ri·al (im′ə môr′ē əl) *adj.* going back beyond memory or record; ancient. —**im′me·mo′ri·al·ly,** *adv.*

im·mense (i mens′) *adj.* of great size, extent, or degree; very large; huge: *an immense building. The book was an immense success.* —**im·mense′ly,** *adv.* —**im·mense′ness,** *n.*

im·men·si·ty (i men′sə tē) *n.* the state or quality of being immense; hugeness; vastness: *the immensity of the ocean.*

im·merse (i murs′) *v.t.,* **im·mersed, im·mers·ing. 1.** to plunge or dip into water or other liquid so as to cover

at; āpe; cär; end; mē; it; īce; hot; ōld; fôrk; wood; foōl; oil; out; up; turn; sing; thin; **this;** hw in white; zh in treasure. The symbol ə stands for the sound of **a** in about, **e** in taken, **i** in pencil, **o** in lemon, and **u** in circus.

completely. **2.** to baptize by immersion. **3.** to involve deeply; absorb: *She was immersed in her book.*

im·mer·sion (i mur′zhən) *n.* **1.** the act of immersing or the state of being immersed. **2.** a method of baptism in which all or part of the body is placed under water.

im·mi·grant (im′ə grənt) *n.* a person who immigrates. ▲ See **emigrant** for usage note.

im·mi·grate (im′ə grāt′) *v.i.,* **im·mi·grat·ed, im·mi·grat·ing.** to enter a country or region in which one was not born in order to make a permanent home there. —**im′mi·gra′tion,** *n.*

im·mi·nent (im′ə nənt) *adj.* about to happen; impending: *The darkening sky showed that a thunderstorm was imminent.* —**im′mi·nence,** *n.* —**im′mi·nent·ly,** *adv.*

im·mo·bile (i mō′bil) *adj.* **1.** not able to move or be moved; fixed. **2.** not moving; motionless. —**im′mo·bil′i·ty,** *n.*

im·mo·bi·lize (i mō′bə līz′) *v.t.,* **im·mo·bi·lized, im·mo·bi·liz·ing.** to make immobile; fix in place. —**im·mo′bi·li·za′tion,** *n.*

im·mod·er·ate (i mod′ər it) *adj.* going beyond usual or proper limits; not moderate: *immoderate demands.* —**im·mod′er·ate·ly,** *adv.*

im·mod·est (i mod′ist) *adj.* **1.** lacking or showing a lack of modesty. **2.** tending to take too much praise or credit; boastful. —**im·mod′est·ly,** *adv.*

im·mod·es·ty (i mod′is tē) *n.* the state or quality of being immodest.

im·mo·late (im′ə lāt′) *v.t.,* **im·mo·lat·ed, im·mo·lat·ing.** to offer in sacrifice, especially to kill as a sacrifice. —**im′mo·la′tion,** *n.*

im·mor·al (i môr′əl, i mor′əl) *adj.* characterized by or showing wickedness or indecency; not moral: *immoral actions, an immoral person.* —**im·mor′al·ly,** *adv.*

im·mo·ral·i·ty (im′ə ral′ə tē) *n. pl.,* **im·mo·ral·i·ties.** **1.** immoral character or quality. **2.** an immoral act.

im·mor·tal (i môrt′əl) *adj.* **1.** never dying; living forever: *The ancient Greeks believed that the gods were immortal.* **2.** remembered or famous through future time: *the immortal works of Shakespeare.* —*n.* **1.** an immortal being. **2.** a person remembered or famous through future time. —**im·mor′tal·ly,** *adv.*

im·mor·tal·i·ty (im′ôr tal′ə tē) *n.* **1.** the supposed power of living on after death. **2.** the fact of being remembered or famous through future time; everlasting fame.

im·mor·tal·ize (i môrt′əl īz′) *v.t.,* **im·mor·tal·ized, im·mor·tal·iz·ing.** to make remembered or famous through future time: *The poet immortalized his love for her in many poems.*

im·mov·a·ble (i mōō′və bəl) *adj.* **1.** not able to move or be moved; stationary. **2.** not easily changed or shaken; steadfast; unyielding: *Grandfather was immovable in his opinions.* —*n.* **immovables.** property that cannot be moved from place to place, such as land. —**im·mov′a·bil′i·ty,** *n.* —**im·mov′a·bly,** *adv.*

im·mune (i myōōn′) *adj.* **1.** protected from a disease or infection, as by inoculation: *immune to measles.* **2.** not affected by something, especially something disagreeable or harmful: *immune to threats.*

im·mu·ni·ty (i myōō′nə tē) *n. pl.,* **im·mu·ni·ties.** **1.** resistance to a disease or infection, especially as a result of vaccination or inoculation: *immunity to smallpox.* **2.** freedom or protection from anything disagreeable or harmful: *immunity from attack.* **3.** a special exemption, as from laws or taxes: *Foreign diplomats are often granted immunity from some of the laws of a country.*

im·mu·nize (im′yə nīz′) *v.t.,* **im·mu·nized, im·mu·niz·ing.** to make immune, especially to a disease. —**im′mu·ni·za′tion,** *n.*

im·mu·nol·o·gy (im′yə nol′ə jē) *n.* the branch of medicine dealing with immunity to disease.

im·mure (i myoor′) *v.t.,* **im·mured, im·mur·ing.** to enclose within walls, as in a prison. —**im·mure′ment,** *n.*

im·mu·ta·ble (i myōō′tə bəl) *adj.* that cannot be changed; unchanging: *It is an immutable law of nature that a stone dropped from the hand will fall to the ground.* —**im·mu′ta·bil′i·ty, im·mu′ta·ble·ness,** *n.* —**im·mu′ta·bly,** *adv.*

imp (imp) *n.* **1.** a young or small demon; mischievous spirit. **2.** a mischievous child.

imp. **1.** imperative. **2.** imperfect. **3.** imported; importer.

im·pact (im′pakt) *n.* **1.** the force or action of one object striking against another: *The glass shattered upon impact with the floor.* **2.** a strong effect or influence: *Her pleas for forgiveness had little impact on him.*

im·pact·ed (im pak′tid) *adj.* **1.** (of a tooth) pressed between the jawbone and another tooth so that it cannot grow out. **2.** closely packed together or wedged in.

im·pair (im per′) *v.t.* to lessen the quality, strength, or value of; damage; weaken: *The accident impaired his vision.* —**im·pair′ment,** *n.*

im·pal·a (im pal′ə) *n.* a small, slender African antelope having a reddish or golden-brown coat. The impala is known for its ability to leap great distances.

Impala

im·pale (im pāl′) *v.t.,* **im·paled, im·pal·ing.** **1.** to fix on a stake or other pointed object by piercing: *The boy mounted the dead insects in his collection by impaling them on pins.* **2.** to torture or put to death by fixing on a stake. —**im·pale′ment,** *n.*

im·pal·pa·ble (im pal′pə bəl) *adj.* **1.** that cannot be felt by the sense of touch: *impalpable shadows.* **2.** not easily understood or grasped by the mind; incomprehensible: *impalpable distinctions.* —**im·pal′pa·bil′i·ty,** *n.* —**im·pal′pa·bly,** *adv.*

im·pan·el (im pan′əl) *also,* **em·pan·el.** *v.t.,* **im·pan·eled, im·pan·el·ing;** *also, British,* **im·pan·elled, im·pan·el·ling.** **1.** to place (someone) on a panel or list, as for jury duty. **2.** to select (a jury) from such a list. —**im·pan′el·ment,** *n.*

im·part (im pärt′) *v.t.* **1.** to make known; tell; disclose: *to impart information.* **2.** to give; bestow: *The judge's presence imparted a sense of dignity to the committee.*

im·par·tial (im pär′shəl) *adj.* not favoring one more than another; without prejudice; unbiased: *The judges of a contest should be impartial.* —**im·par′tial·ly,** *adv.*

im·par·ti·al·i·ty (im pär′shē al′ə tē) *n.* freedom from bias; fairness.

im·pass·a·ble (im pas′ə bəl) *adj.* that cannot be passed or traveled over, across, or through: *The road was impassable after the snowstorm.* —**im·pass′a·bil′i·ty,** *n.* —**im·pass′a·bly,** *adv.*

im·passe (im′pas′) *n.* a position or situation from which it is impossible to advance or go on; deadlock: *The workmen and the company officials reached an impasse in their negotiations.*

im·pas·sioned (im pash′ənd) *adj.* filled with passion or strong feeling; fiery; ardent: *The speaker made an impassioned plea for justice.*

im·pas·sive (im pas′iv) *adj.* not feeling or showing emotion; unmoved: *The accused murderer remained impassive throughout the trial.* —**im·pas′sive·ly,** *adv.* —**im·pas′sive·ness,** *n.*

im·pa·tience (im pā′shəns) *n.* **1.** irritation or annoy-

ance because of delay or opposition; lack of patience.
2. restless eagerness, as for change or activity.

im·pa·tient (im pā′shənt) *adj.* **1.** irritated or annoyed by delay or opposition: *She was very impatient because he was late.* **2.** showing lack of patience: *an impatient answer.* **3.** restlessly eager: *The children were impatient for the weekend to come.* —**im·pa′tient·ly,** *adv.*

im·peach (im pēch′) *v.t.* **1.** to bring formal charges against (a public official) for crime or misconduct in office. **2.** to question, challenge, or cast doubt on: *The defense attorney impeached the honesty of the witness.* —**im·peach′ment,** *n.*

im·pec·ca·ble (im pek′ə bəl) *adj.* free from error or defect; without fault; flawless: *impeccable manners, impeccable judgment.* —**im·pec′ca·bil′i·ty,** *n.* —**im·pec′ca·bly,** *adv.*

im·pe·cu·ni·ous (im′pi kyōō′nē əs) *adj.* having no money; poor; penniless. —**im′pe·cu′ni·ous·ly,** *adv.*

im·pede (im pēd′) *v.t.,* **im·ped·ed, im·ped·ing.** to obstruct, hinder, or delay: *The rough seas impeded the ship's progress.* [Latin *impedīre* literally, to chain the feet of; originally referring to the chaining of slaves' feet to hinder their movements.]

im·ped·i·ment (im ped′ə mənt) *n.* **1.** something that impedes; obstruction; obstacle. **2.** a physical defect: *a speech impediment.*

im·pel (im pel′) *v.t.,* **im·pelled, im·pel·ling. 1.** to drive or urge to some action: *War impelled them to leave the country.* **2.** to propel or cause to move forward: *The boat was impelled by a strong wind.*

im·pend (im pend′) *v.i.* to be about to happen; threaten: *All ships have been warned that a storm impends.*

im·pend·ing (im pen′ding) *adj.* about to happen; threatening: *an impending crisis.*

im·pen·e·tra·ble (im pen′ə trə bəl) *adj.* **1.** that cannot be pierced, entered, or passed through: *an impenetrable forest.* **2.** that cannot be easily understood: *an impenetrable mystery.* —**im·pen′e·tra·bil′i·ty,** *n.* —**im·pen′e·tra·bly,** *adv.*

im·pen·i·tent (im pen′ə tənt) *adj.* not penitent or sorry for having done wrong. —**im·pen′i·tent·ly,** *adv.*

imper., imperative.

im·per·a·tive (im per′ə tiv) *adj.* **1.** not to be avoided; absolutely necessary; urgent: *It is imperative that we leave at once.* **2.** of the nature of or expressing a command; commanding; authoritative: *an imperative tone of voice.* **3.** *Grammar.* of, relating to, or indicating the mood of a verb used to express commands, requests, or pleas. In the sentence *Go to your room, go* is in the imperative mood. —*n.* **1.** something that is imperative, as a command or obligation. **2.** *Grammar.* **a.** the imperative mood. **b.** a verb or verb form in this mood. —**im·per′a·tive·ly,** *adv.* —**im·per′a·tive·ness,** *n.*

im·per·cep·ti·ble (im′pər sep′tə bəl) *adj.* too slight or gradual to be easily seen or noticed: *an imperceptible change.* —**im′per·cep′ti·bil′i·ty,** *n.* —**im′per·cep′ti·bly,** *adv.*

imperf., imperfect.

im·per·fect (im pur′fikt) *adj.* **1.** having a fault or flaw; not perfect; faulty: *an imperfect diamond.* **2.** not fully developed, formed, or done; incomplete: *He has an imperfect understanding of the problem.* **3.** in certain languages, relating to or indicating the tense of a verb that expresses continuous or incomplete action in the past. —*n.* the imperfect tense. —**im·per′fect·ly,** *adv.* —**im·per′fect·ness,** *n.*

im·per·fec·tion (im′pər fek′shən) *n.* **1.** the state or quality of being imperfect. **2.** a fault; flaw: *There was an imperfection in the cloth.*

im·pe·ri·al (im pēr′ē əl) *adj.* **1.** of or relating to an em-

pire or to the rule of an emperor or empress. **2.** of or relating to a country's military, political, or economic power or control over other countries or colonies. **3.** of great size or superior quality. —*n.* a small, pointed beard growing below the lower lip. —**im·pe′ri·al·ly,** *adv.*

im·pe·ri·al·ism (im pēr′ē ə liz′əm) *n.* **1.** the policy of extending a country's power or control over other countries or colonies by military, political, or economic means. **2.** an imperial system of government; rule of an emperor.

im·pe·ri·al·ist (im pēr′ē ə list) *n.* a person who favors or supports imperialism. —*adj.* of or relating to imperialism: *imperialist policies.* —**im·pe′ri·al·is′tic,** *adj.* —**im·pe′ri·al·is′ti·cal·ly,** *adv.*

im·per·il (im per′əl) *v.t.,* **im·per·iled, im·per·il·ing;** *also,* **British, im·per·illed, im·per·il·ling.** to put in danger; expose to peril: *The driver's foolish actions imperiled the lives of the passengers.*

im·pe·ri·ous (im pēr′ē əs) *adj.* **1.** haughty or arrogant; domineering; overbearing: *That elderly lady has an imperious way of speaking.* **2.** imperative; urgent: *an imperious need.* —**im·pe′ri·ous·ly,** *adv.* —**im·pe′ri·ous·ness,** *n.*

im·per·ish·a·ble (im per′i shə bəl) *adj.* not subject to destruction or decay; not perishable; enduring: *imperishable foods.* —**im·per′ish·a·bil′i·ty,** *n.* —**im·per′ish·a·bly,** *adv.*

im·per·ma·nent (im pur′mə nənt) *adj.* subject to change; not permanent; temporary: *an impermanent situation.* —**im·per′ma·nence,** *n.* —**im·per′ma·nent·ly,** *adv.*

im·per·me·a·ble (im pur′mē ə bəl) *adj.* that cannot be penetrated; impenetrable.

im·per·son·al (im pur′sən əl) *adj.* **1.** not concerned with or referring to a particular person or persons; not personal: *impersonal criticism.* **2.** not existing as a person. **3.** *Grammar.* **a.** (of a verb) denoting an action by an unspecified subject, used in the third person singular. In the sentence *It snowed today, snowed* is an impersonal verb. **b.** (of a pronoun) referring to an indefinite subject. —**im·per′son·al·ly,** *adv.*

im·per·son·ate (im pur′sə nāt′) *v.t.,* **im·per·son·at·ed, im·per·son·at·ing. 1.** to take on or copy the appearance, behavior, or mannerisms of: *He was arrested for impersonating a police officer.* **2.** to act the part or character of, as in a play. —**im·per′son·a′tion,** *n.* —**im·per′son·a′tor,** *n.*

im·per·ti·nence (im purt′ən əns) *n.* **1.** boldness and rudeness; insolence. **2.** an impertinent act or remark. **3.** lack of relevance or appropriateness.

im·per·ti·nent (im purt′ən ənt) *adj.* **1.** offensively bold and rude; insolent: *an impertinent young girl.* **2.** not relevant or appropriate. —**im·per′ti·nent·ly,** *adv.*

im·per·turb·a·ble (im′pər tur′bə bəl) *adj.* not easily excited or disturbed; calm. —**im′per·turb′a·bil′i·ty,** *n.* —**im′per·turb′a·bly,** *adv.*

im·per·vi·ous (im pur′vē əs) *adj.* **1.** not easily affected, influenced, or disturbed: *He is impervious to criticism.* **2.** not allowing passage; impenetrable: *This material is impervious to water.* —**im·per′vi·ous·ly,** *adv.* —**im·per′vi·ous·ness,** *n.*

im·pe·ti·go (im′pə tī′gō) *n.* a contagious skin disease characterized by blisters that break open and release pus.

---

at; āpe; cär; end; mē; it; īce; hot; ōld; fôrk;
wood; fōōl; oil; out; up; turn; sing; thin; this;
hw in white; zh in treasure. The symbol ə
stands for the sound of **a** in about, **e** in taken,
i in pencil, **o** in lemon, and **u** in circus.

I

im·pet·u·os·i·ty (im pech′o͞o os′ə tē) *n. pl.,* **im·pet·u·os·i·ties.** **1.** the state or quality of being impetuous. **2.** an impetuous act.

im·pet·u·ous (im pech′yo͞o əs) *adj.* **1.** rushing headlong into things; impulsive and energetic: *an impetuous person.* **2.** made or done impulsively and suddenly; rash: *an impetuous choice.* **3.** moving with great force or violence; rapid; furious: *the impetuous winds of a gale.* —**im·pet′u·ous·ly,** *adv.* —**im·pet′u·ous·ness,** *n.*

im·pe·tus (im′pə təs) *n. pl.,* **im·pe·tus·es.** **1.** the momentum of a moving body. **2.** the force that puts a body in motion. **3.** energy, strength, or other moving force; stimulus: *The rise in crime in the state gave impetus to demands for stricter law enforcement.*

im·pi·e·ty (im pī′ə tē) *n. pl.,* **im·pi·e·ties.** **1.** a lack of reverence or respect. **2.** an impious act.

im·pinge (im pinj′) *v.i.,* **im·pinged, im·ping·ing.** **1.** to interfere with; encroach; infringe: *That proposed law impinges on freedom of speech.* **2.** to strike or hit: *The light from the movie projector impinged on the screen.* —**im·pinge′ment,** *n.*

im·pi·ous (im′pē əs) *adj.* lacking reverence or respect. —**im′pi·ous·ly,** *adv.* —**im′pi·ous·ness,** *n.*

imp·ish (im′pish) *adj.* of or like an imp; mischievous: *an impish grin.* —**imp′ish·ly,** *adv.* —**imp′ish·ness,** *n.*

im·plac·a·ble (im plak′ə bəl, im plā′kə bəl) *adj.* that cannot be calmed or pacified: *implacable anger.* —**im·plac′a·bil′i·ty,** *n.* —**im·pla′ca·bly,** *adv.*

im·plant (*v.,* im plant′; *n.,* im′plant′) *v.t.* **1.** to fix firmly and deeply; instill: *He has implanted fear of strangers in all his children.* **2.** to plant or root firmly: *The old tree stump was implanted in the ground.* **3.** to insert (living tissue or a device) in the body by surgery, as in grafting. —*n.* living tissue or a device inserted in the body by surgery. —**im′plan·ta′tion,** *n.*

im·plau·si·ble (im plô′zə bəl) *adj.* not believable; unlikely: *an implausible explanation.* —**im·plau′si·bil′i·ty,** *n.* —**im·plau′si·bly,** *adv.*

im·ple·ment (*n.,* im′plə mənt; *v.,* im′plə ment′) *n.* something used in performing a task or other work; tool; instrument: *kitchen implements, gardening implements.* —*v.t.* to put into effect; carry out: *to implement a law. The new mayor implemented many reform measures.* —**im′·ple·men·ta′tion,** *n.*

im·pli·cate (im′plə kāt′) *v.t.,* **im·pli·cat·ed, im·pli·cat·ing.** to claim or show to be involved, as in a crime: *The robbery suspect implicated his friends by testifying that they helped him.*

im·pli·ca·tion (im′plə kā′shən) *n.* **1.** something that is implied; indirect suggestion. **2.** the act of implicating or the state of being implicated, as in a crime. **3.** the act of implying or the state of being implied.

im·plic·it (im plis′it) *adj.* **1.** suggested or understood, though not directly expressed: *Her disapproval was implicit in the frown on her face.* **2.** without reservation or doubt; unquestioning; absolute: *He had implicit faith in the loyalty of his friend.* —**im·plic′it·ly,** *adv.* —**im·plic′it·ness,** *n.*

im·plore (im plôr′) *v.t.,* **im·plored, im·plor·ing.** **1.** to plead with; ask earnestly; beg: *They implored the whole school to contribute to the fund.* **2.** to beg or pray for earnestly: *to implore forgiveness.*

im·ply (im plī′) *v.t.,* **im·plied, im·ply·ing.** **1.** to suggest or express indirectly: *Are you implying that I caused the trouble?* **2.** to involve as a necessary part, condition, or consequence: *"John has left" implies "John has been here."* ▲ See **infer** for usage note.

im·po·lite (im′pə līt′) *adj.* not having or showing good manners; not courteous; rude. —**im′po·lite′ly,** *adv.* —**im′po·lite′ness,** *n.*

im·pol·i·tic (im pol′ə tik) *adj.* not conforming to good judgment or policy; not politic; unwise.

im·pon·der·a·ble (im pon′dər ə bəl) *adj.* that cannot be weighed or evaluated with certainty. —*n.* an imponderable thing or factor: *There are too many imponderables for us to make a decision.* —**im·pon′der·a·ble·ness,** *n.* —**im·pon′der·a·bly,** *adv.*

im·port (*v.,* im pôrt′; *n.,* im′pôrt′) *v.t.* **1.** to bring in (goods) from a foreign country for sale or use: *to import tea from India.* **2.** to have as a meaning: *What do his words import?* —*n.* **1.** something that is imported for sale or use. **2.** the act of importing goods; importation. **3.** meaning; significance: *What was the import of his remark?* **4.** consequence; importance: *That is a matter of great import.*

im·por·tance (im pôrt′əns) *n.* the state or quality of being important.

im·por·tant (im pôrt′ənt) *adj.* **1.** having special value, consequence, or meaning: *Her friendship is very important to him.* **2.** having special authority, social position, or influence: *He is an important member of the city council.* **3.** acting important; giving the impression of being important: *He had an important air about him.* —**im·por′·tant·ly,** *adv.*

im·por·ta·tion (im′pôr tā′shən) *n.* **1.** the act of importing. **2.** something that is imported.

im·port·er (im pôr′tər) *n.* a person or company in the business of importing goods.

im·por·tu·nate (im por′chə nit) *adj.* annoyingly or stubbornly persistent; insistent: *an importunate salesman.* —**im·por′tu·nate·ly,** *adv.* —**im·por′tu·nate·ness,** *n.*

im·por·tune (im′pôr to͞on′, im′pôr tyo͞on′) *v.t.,* **im·por·tuned, im·por·tun·ing.** to trouble with constant requests or demands.

im·por·tu·ni·ty (im′pôr to͞o′nə tē, im′pôr tyo͞o′nə tē) *n. pl.,* **im·por·tu·ni·ties.** the act of importuning or the state of being importunate.

im·pose (im pōz′) *v.,* **im·posed, im·pos·ing.** —*v.t.* **1.** to establish or apply by legal means as an obligation: *to impose taxes, to impose a penalty.* **2.** to inflict or force: *to impose one's will on others.* **3.** to thrust (oneself) upon others: *He was always imposing himself on his friends.* —*v.i.* to thrust oneself upon others; intrude. —**im·pos′er,** *n.*

im·pos·ing (im pō′zing) *adj.* causing awe or admiration because of great size or dignity; impressive: *an imposing building.* —**im·pos′ing·ly,** *adv.*

im·po·si·tion (im′pə zish′ən) *n.* **1.** the act of imposing. **2.** something that is imposed.

im·pos·si·bil·i·ty (im pos′ə bil′ə tē) *n. pl.,* **im·pos·si·bil·i·ties.** **1.** the state or quality of being impossible. **2.** something that is impossible.

im·pos·si·ble (im pos′ə bəl) *adj.* **1.** not capable of being or happening; not possible: *It is impossible for a man to live forever.* **2.** not capable of being realized or done: *That is an impossible scheme.* **3.** not capable of being endured; very objectionable: *He is an impossible person to work with. This is an impossible situation.* **4.** not acceptable as truth: *an impossible explanation.* —**im·pos′si·bly,** *adv.*

im·post (im′pōst′) *n.* a tax or duty, especially on imported goods.

im·pos·tor (im pos′tər) *n.* a person who deceives by taking on the name or character of someone else: *It was soon discovered that he was not the duke but an impostor.*

im·pos·ture (im pos′chər) *n.* a deception, especially by taking on the name or character of someone else.

im·po·tent (im′pə tənt) *adj.* **1.** lacking force or effectiveness; helpless: *Without the air force's help the troops were impotent against enemy attack.* **2.** physically weak. —**im′po·tence,** *n.* —**im′po·tent·ly,** *adv.*

im·pound (im pound′) *v.t.* **1.** to shut up in a pound: *to impound a stray dog.* **2.** to seize and put in the custody of a court of law: *The court ordered that all the businessman's papers and records be impounded until after the investigation.* **3.** to collect (water), as in a reservoir. —**im·pound′er**, *n.* —**im·pound′ment**, *n.*

im·pov·er·ish (im pov′ər ish) *v.t.* **1.** to make very poor: *Loss of crops by drought impoverished the farmers.* **2.** to take away the strength, richness, or resources of: *Poor farming methods impoverished the land.* —**im·pov′er·ish·ment**, *n.*

im·prac·ti·ca·ble (im prak′ti kə bəl) *adj.* **1.** not capable of being accomplished, carried out, or put into practice: *an impracticable plan.* **2.** not capable of being used; unserviceable: *an impracticable machine.* —**im·prac′ti·ca·bil′i·ty**, *n.* —**im·prac′ti·ca·bly**, *adv.*

im·prac·ti·cal (im prak′ti kəl) *adj.* lacking good sense or usefulness; not practical.

im·prac·ti·cal·i·ty (im prak′ti kal′ə tē) *n. pl.,* **im·prac·ti·cal·i·ties.** **1.** the state or quality of being impractical. **2.** something impractical.

im·pre·ca·tion (im′pri kā′shən) *n.* **1.** the act of calling down a curse or other evil on someone. **2.** a curse.

im·pre·cise (im′pri sīs′) *adj.* not precise; inexact; vague. —**im′pre·cise′ly**, *adv.*

im·preg·na·ble (im preg′nə bəl) *adj.* **1.** not capable of being taken by force; able to resist attack: *an impregnable fortress.* **2.** not capable of being moved, shaken, or overcome; firm: *an impregnable argument.* —**im·preg′na·bil′i·ty**, *n.* —**im·preg′na·bly**, *adv.*

im·preg·nate (im preg′nāt) *v.t.,* **im·preg·nat·ed, im·preg·nat·ing.** **1.** to make pregnant; cause to conceive. **2.** to make fertile; fertilize. **3.** to cause to be saturated with; permeate: *to impregnate wood with furniture polish.* —**im′preg·na′tion**, *n.*

im·pre·sa·ri·o (im′prə sär′ē ō′) *n. pl.,* **im·pre·sa·ri·os.** a person who organizes or manages live entertainment events, especially ballets, operas, or concerts.

im·press¹ (*v.,* im pres′; *n.,* im′pres′) *v.t.* **1.** to influence or produce a strong effect on the mind or feelings of: *The speaker's honesty impressed us.* **2.** to fix firmly in the mind: *He impressed on his son the importance of being truthful.* **3.** to form or make a mark or design on (something) by pressing or stamping: *to impress wax with a seal.* **4.** to form or make by pressing or stamping: *to impress figures on coins.* —*n. pl.,* **im·press·es.** **1.** the act of forming or making a mark or design on something by pressing or stamping. **2.** a mark or design made in this way. [Latin *impressus,* the past participle of *imprimere* to press on or into.]

im·press² (im pres′) *v.t.* **1.** to force by illegal means to enter military service, especially the navy. **2.** to take (property) by force for public use. [*Im-²* + *press².*] —**im·press′ment**, *n.*

im·pres·sion (im presh′ən) *n.* **1.** an effect or influence produced on the mind, senses, or feelings: *The experience of flying for the first time left a lasting impression on me.* **2.** a feeling or judgment about someone or something: *My first impression of him proved to be correct.* **3.** a notion or belief: *I was under the impression that they were brothers.* **4.** a mark or design produced by pressing or stamping: *We made impressions of our hands in the wet concrete.* **5.** an impersonation; imitation: *The young child gave his impression of a monkey.* **6.** the act or process of impressing.

im·pres·sion·a·ble (im presh′ə nə bəl) *adj.* easily impressed or influenced: *an impressionable young man.*

im·pres·sion·ism (im presh′ə niz′əm) *n.* **1.** a method or school of painting developed in the late nineteenth century by French painters, such as Claude Monet and Pierre Auguste Renoir. It is characterized by a careful study of nature and the direct observation of the effects of light and color on a subject at a given moment. **2.** a method and style of musical composition of the late nineteenth and early twentieth centuries in which rich harmonies are used to create mood and atmosphere.

im·pres·sion·ist (im presh′ə nist) *n.* a person who practices impressionism, especially in painting.

im·pres·sion·is·tic (im presh′ə nis′tik) *adj.* of, relating to, or characteristic of impressionism.

im·pres·sive (im pres′iv) *adj.* producing or tending to produce a strong impression on the mind; exciting attention, emotion, or admiration: *an impressive feat of strength. She wore an impressive display of jewels.* —**im·pres′sive·ly**, *adv.* —**im·pres′sive·ness**, *n.*

im·print (*n.,* im′print′; *v.,* im print′) *n.* **1.** a mark or depression produced by pressing or stamping. **2.** an effect or mark: *Years of poverty left an imprint on his personality.* **3.** a publisher's or printer's name, the place and date of publication, and sometimes a trademark, printed on the title page of a book. —*v.t.* **1.** to make or produce (a mark or design) by pressing or stamping. **2.** to produce a mark or design on by pressing or stamping; print. **3.** to fix firmly in the mind or memory.

im·pris·on (im priz′ən) *v.t.* **1.** to put or keep in prison. **2.** to confine or restrain in any way. —**im·pris′on·ment**, *n.*

im·prob·a·bil·i·ty (im prob′ə bil′ə tē) *n. pl.,* **im·prob·a·bil·i·ties.** **1.** the quality of being improbable; unlikelihood. **2.** something improbable.

im·prob·a·ble (im prob′ə bəl) *adj.* not probable; unlikely: *an improbable story.* —**im·prob′a·bly**, *adv.*

im·promp·tu (im promp′tōō, im promp′tyōō) *adj.* made or done on the spur of the moment; without preparation or previous thought; offhand: *The chairman made some impromptu remarks.* —*n.* anything made or done on the spur of the moment. —*adv.* without preparation or previous thought: *to speak impromptu.* [French *impromptu* unprepared.]

im·prop·er (im prop′ər) *adj.* **1.** not according to fact, truth, or established usage; not correct. **2.** not according to accepted standards of decency or good taste: *improper behavior.* —**im·prop′er·ly**, *adv.*

improper fraction, a fraction whose numerator is greater than, or equal to, its denominator, such as $8/5$ or $6/6$.

improper subset, any subset that is not a proper subset.

im·pro·pri·e·ty (im′prə prī′ə tē) *n. pl.,* **im·pro·pri·e·ties.** **1.** the quality of being improper. **2.** an improper act or behavior.

im·prove (im prōōv′) *v.,* **im·proved, im·prov·ing.** —*v.t.* to make better: *I am taking lessons to improve my singing.* —*v.i.* to become better: *That player has improved greatly since last season.* —**im·prov′a·ble**, *adj.*
  to improve on or **to improve upon,** to do or make something better or more perfect than: *They improved on the original plan.*

im·prove·ment (im prōōv′mənt) *n.* **1.** the act of improving or the state of being improved. **2.** a change or

at; āpe; cär; end; mē; it; īce; hot; ōld; fôrk; wood; fōōl; oil; out; up; turn; sing; thin; this; hw in white; zh in treasure. The symbol ə stands for the sound of **a** in about, **e** in taken, **i** in pencil, **o** in lemon, and **u** in circus.

I

addition that improves something, as in quality or value: *The new curtains are an improvement to the room.* **3.** a person or thing that is better or more perfect than another: *The team's new manager is an improvement over the past one.*

im·prov·i·dent (im prov'ə dənt) *adj.* not cautious in providing for future needs; lacking foresight: *He was improvident in spending his salary.* —**im·prov'i·dence,** *n.* —**im·prov'i·dent·ly,** *adv.*

im·prov·i·sa·tion (im prov'ə zā'shən) *n.* **1.** the act or art of improvising. **2.** something that is improvised.

im·pro·vise (im'prə vīz') *v.t.,* **im·pro·vised, im·pro·vis·ing. 1.** to make up and perform on the spur of the moment: *The children in the class improvised a skit for the visiting parents.* **2.** to make or construct from whatever materials are on hand: *to improvise a bookcase out of wooden crates.* —**im'pro·vis'er,** *n.*

im·pru·dent (im prood'ənt) *adj.* lacking prudence; unwise; rash. —**im·pru'dence,** *n.* —**im·pru'dent·ly,** *adv.*

im·pu·dence (im'pyə dəns) *n.* **1.** the quality of being impudent; rudeness; insolence. **2.** impudent speech or behavior.

im·pu·dent (im'pyə dənt) *adj.* rudely bold or forward; insolent: *an impudent child.* —**im'pu·dent·ly,** *adv.*

im·pugn (im pyōon') *v.t.* to suggest there is something bad about; call into question; doubt: *They impugned his reasons for giving the gift.*

im·pulse (im'puls) *n.* **1.** a force or feeling that makes a person act without planning or thinking: *A sudden, generous impulse led him to give his new baseball mitt to his brother.* **2.** a sudden force that causes motion; thrust; push: *The impulse of falling water turns the water wheel.* **3.** the motion caused by the sudden application of force. **4.** a brief surge or pulsation of power or energy: *an electrical impulse.* **5.** a signal produced and carried by nerve cells to or from the central nervous system, serving to control activity in the body.

im·pul·sion (im pul'shən) *n.* **1.** the act of impelling. **2.** a driving motion. **3.** an impulse to act.

im·pul·sive (im pul'siv) *adj.* **1.** tending to act on impulse: *an impulsive person.* **2.** resulting from impulse: *He later regretted his impulsive decision.* **3.** having the power of producing motion; thrusting. —**im·pul'sive·ly,** *adv.* —**im·pul'sive·ness,** *n.*

im·pu·ni·ty (im pyōo'nə tē) *n.* freedom from punishment, penalty, injury, or loss: *You cannot continually cheat with impunity.*

im·pure (im pyoor') *adj.* **1.** dirty; unclean: *impure water.* **2.** containing another substance that is foreign or inferior: *an impure blend of tobacco.* **3.** bad; corrupt: *impure thoughts, impure actions.*

im·pu·ri·ty (im pyoor'ə tē) *n. pl.,* **im·pu·ri·ties. 1.** the state or quality of being impure. **2.** a substance that makes something impure: *There are many impurities in the air we breathe.*

im·pu·ta·tion (im'pyə tā'shən) *n.* **1.** the act or instance of imputing. **2.** something that is imputed: *an imputation of guilt.*

im·pute (im pyōot') *v.t.,* **im·put·ed, im·put·ing.** to charge or lay the blame for: *They imputed the team's defeat to lack of practice.*

in (in) *prep.* **1.** within; inside: *The suitcase is in the closet. The bird is in the cage.* **2.** through or into: *Go in the door on your left.* **3.** while, during, or after: *The weather here is cold in the winter. He will call back in twenty minutes.* **4.** covered by or wearing: *My sister is the girl in the pink dress.* **5.** out of: *One in every four children examined had bad teeth.* **6.** affected by or having: *He is in bad health.* **7.** with the purpose or result of; for: *The suspected murderer said that he had acted in self-defense.* **8.** with respect to; as regards: *The two students differ in ability.* —*adv.* **1.** to or toward a point or place inside: *to come in out of the cold.* **2.** at a specific place, especially one's home or office: *She stayed in because she had a cold. Is the doctor in?* —*adj.* **1.** having power or control: *the in political party.* **2.** relating to or understood only by a particular group: *an in joke.* **3.** leading or going in: *the in door.* **4.** *Informal.* in style; fashionable or popular: *Hats are in this year.* —*n.* **1.** *usually,* **ins.** the people in office or in power. **2.** a means of influencing or approaching: *He has an in with the boss.*

ins and outs. all the details: *He knows the ins and outs of his father's business.*

in that. because; since.

to be in for. to be due or certain to have or receive: *We are in for some bad weather.*

to have it in for. to hold a grudge against.

In, the symbol for indium.

in-[1] *prefix* without; not: *inactivity, inaccurate.* [Latin *in-* not.]

in-[2] *prefix* in; into: *indent, intrust.* [Latin *in* in, into, within, on, toward.]

in-[3] *prefix* in; within; into: *insight, indoors.* [Old English *in* within.]

in., inch; inches.

in·a·bil·i·ty (in'ə bil'ə tē) *n.* lack of power, means, or ability: *an inability to walk.*

in·ac·ces·si·ble (in'ək ses'ə bəl) *adj.* difficult or impossible to reach or approach; not accessible. —**in'ac·ces'si·bil'i·ty,** *n.* —**in'ac·ces'si·bly,** *adv.*

in·ac·cu·ra·cy (in ak'yər ə sē) *n. pl.,* **in·ac·cu·ra·cies. 1.** the quality or condition of being inaccurate. **2.** an error; mistake.

in·ac·cu·rate (in ak'yər it) *adj.* not accurate; wrong. —**in·ac'cu·rate·ly,** *adv.*

in·ac·tion (in ak'shən) *n.* lack of action; idleness; inertness.

in·ac·tive (in ak'tiv) *adj.* not active; idle; inert: *an inactive volcano. Bats are inactive throughout most of the daytime.* —**in·ac'tive·ly,** *adv.*

in·ac·tiv·i·ty (in'ak tiv'ə tē) *n.* lack of activity; idleness.

in·ad·e·qua·cy (in ad'ə kwə sē) *n. pl.,* **in·ad·e·qua·cies. 1.** the state or quality of being inadequate. **2.** something that is inadequate.

in·ad·e·quate (in ad'ə kwit) *adj.* less than required; not adequate: *an inadequate water supply. He gave an inadequate excuse for being late.* —**in·ad'e·quate·ly,** *adv.*

in·ad·mis·si·ble (in'əd mis'ə bəl) *adj.* not to be admitted, considered, or allowed; not admissible: *The judge ruled that the testimony of the witness was inadmissible as evidence.* —**in'ad·mis'si·bil'i·ty,** *n.*

in·ad·ver·tence (in'əd vurt'əns) *n.* **1.** the quality of being inadvertent. **2.** a result of being inadvertent; mistake.

in·ad·ver·tent (in'əd vurt'ənt) *adj.* not intended; accidental: *an inadvertent discovery.* —**in'ad·ver'tent·ly,** *adv.*

in·ad·vis·a·ble (in'əd vī'zə bəl) *adj.* not advisable; unwise. —**in'ad·vis·a·bil'i·ty,** *n.* —**in'ad·vis'a·bly,** *adv.*

in·al·ien·a·ble (in āl'yə nə bəl) *adj.* that cannot be given up, taken away, or transferred: *The pursuit of happiness is an inalienable right of every citizen.* —**in·al'ien·a·bil'i·ty,** *n.* —**in·al'ien·a·bly,** *adv.*

in·ane (i nān') *adj.* lacking intelligence; empty of meaning; silly and senseless: *His speech was full of inane remarks.* —**in·ane'ly,** *adv.*

in·an·i·mate (in an'ə mit) *adj.* **1.** not moving, growing, or feeling; not having the functions of life; not alive: *Rocks are inanimate objects.* **2.** lacking spirit; dull. —**in·an'i·mate·ly,** *adv.* —**in·an'i·mate·ness,** *n.*

in·an·i·ty (i nan′ə tē) *n. pl.,* **in·an·i·ties.** **1.** the state or quality of being inane. **2.** something inane, as a remark or act.

in·ap·pli·ca·ble (in ap′li kə bəl, in ə plik′ə bəl) *adj.* not relevant or suitable; not applicable: *The rule is inapplicable in this case.* —**in·ap′pli·ca·bil′i·ty,** *n.*

in·ap·pre·cia·ble (in′ə prē′shə bəl) *adj.* too small to be given attention; slight; unimportant. —**in′ap·pre·cia·bly,** *adv.*

in·ap·pro·pri·ate (in′ə prō′prē it) *adj.* not appropriate; unsuitable: *It was inappropriate to laugh at such a serious moment.* —**in′ap·pro′pri·ate·ly,** *adv.* —**in′ap·pro′pri·ate·ness,** *n.*

in·apt (in apt′) *adj.* not suitable; inappropriate: *an inapt remark.* —**in·apt′ly,** *adv.* —**in·apt′ness,** *n.*

in·ap·ti·tude (in ap′tə tood′, in ap′tə tyood′) *n.* lack of aptitude or skill.

in·ar·tic·u·late (in′är tik′yə lit) *adj.* **1.** not clearly expressed or pronounced: *The boy's speech was inarticulate because his mouth was full of food.* **2.** not able to express oneself in a clear or meaningful way. **3.** not fully expressed; not made definite and clear: *inarticulate anger.* **4.** not capable of speech or expression; mute. **5.** *Biology.* not jointed. —**in′ar·tic′u·late·ly,** *adv.* —**in′ar·tic′u·late·ness,** *n.*

in·ar·tis·tic (in′är tis′tik) *adj.* not artistic; lacking taste. —**in′ar·tis′ti·cal·ly,** *adv.*

in·as·much as (in′əz much′) in view of the fact that; since: *Inasmuch as she is here, she might as well stay for dinner.*

in·at·ten·tion (in′ə ten′shən) *n.* lack of attention.

in·at·ten·tive (in′ə ten′tiv) *adj.* not attentive; neglectful: *He is inattentive to details.* —**in′at·ten′tive·ly,** *adv.* —**in′at·ten′tive·ness,** *n.*

in·au·di·ble (in ô′də bəl) *adj.* that cannot be heard. —**in·au′di·bly,** *adv.*

in·au·gu·ral (in ô′gyər əl) *adj.* of, relating to, or for an inauguration: *an inaugural ball.* —*n.* a speech or address made by a person being inaugurated, especially one made by a President of the United States.

in·au·gu·rate (in ô′gyə rāt′) *v.t.,* **in·au·gu·rat·ed, in·au·gu·rat·ing.** **1.** to install in office with a formal ceremony: *to inaugurate a governor.* **2.** to begin formally: *to inaugurate a new policy.* **3.** to open for public use with a formal ceremony: *to inaugurate a new highway.* —**in·au′gu·ra′tion,** *n.*

in·aus·pi·cious (in′ôs pish′əs) *adj.* not favorable for success; unlucky: *an inauspicious beginning.* —**in′aus·pi′cious·ly,** *adv.*

in·board (in′bôrd′) *adj.* inside the hull of a ship: *an inboard engine.* —*adv.* inside the hull or within the sides of a ship: *to stow cargo inboard.*

in·born (in′bôrn′) *adj.* born in a person; natural.

in·bound (in′bound′) *adj.* inward bound: *an inbound train.*

in·bred (in′bred′) *adj.* **1.** resulting from inbreeding. **2.** inborn; natural: *The child had an inbred curiosity.*

in·breed (in′brēd′) *v.t.,* **in·bred, in·breed·ing.** to breed (closely related animals): *to inbreed a strain of cows.*

in·breed·ing (in′brē′ding) *n.* the breeding of closely related animals, resulting in certain traits becoming more dominant.

inc., incorporated.

In·ca (ing′kə) *n.* **1.** a member of a highly civilized Indian people who ruled a large empire in Peru and other parts of South America. The Incas were conquered by the Spanish in the sixteenth century. **2.** a ruler or a member of the ruling family of this people. —**In′can,** *adj., n.*

in·cal·cu·la·ble (in kal′kyə lə bəl) *adj.* **1.** too much or too many to be calculated: *There are an incalculable number of stars in the sky.* **2.** impossible to calculate beforehand; not predictable. —**in·cal′cu·la·bly,** *adv.*

in·can·des·cent (in′kən des′ənt) *adj.* **1.** glowing with heat. **2.** brightly shining; brilliant; sparkling. —**in′can·des′cence,** *n.*

incandescent lamp, a light bulb in which light is produced by passing an electric current through a thin high-resistance wire or filament, causing it to glow.

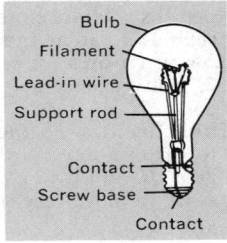

Incandescent lamp

in·can·ta·tion (in′kan tā′shən) *n.* **1.** a formula of words spoken or chanted in casting a spell or performing other magic. **2.** the use of such a formula.

in·ca·pa·ble (in kā′pə bəl) *adj.* not capable: *an incapable employee. A baby is incapable of walking.* —**in·ca′pa·bil′i·ty,** *n.*

in·ca·pac·i·tate (in′kə pas′ə tāt′) *v.t.,* **in·ca·pac·i·tat·ed, in·ca·pac·i·tat·ing.** to take away or limit the power or ability of: *A broken ankle incapacitated him.*

in·ca·pac·i·ty (in′kə pas′ə tē) *n. pl.,* **in·ca·pac·i·ties.** lack of power or ability.

in·car·cer·ate (in kär′sə rāt′) *v.t.,* **in·car·cer·at·ed, in·car·cer·at·ing.** to put in prison. —**in·car′cer·a′tion,** *n.*

in·car·nate (*adj.* in kär′nit, in kär′nāt; *v.,* in kär′nāt) *adj.* in human form; personified: *He thought of himself as wisdom incarnate.* —*v.t.,* **in·car·nat·ed, in·car·nat·ing.** **1.** to embody in human form; personify. **2.** to be a real or true example of; typify.

in·car·na·tion (in′kär nā′shən) *n.* **1.** the taking on of human form by a supernatural being. **2.** a person or thing that is a real or true example of some quality or ideal: *The old woman was the incarnation of loneliness.* **3. the Incarnation.** the taking on of human flesh and nature by the Son of God in the person of Jesus Christ.

in·case (in kās′) *v.t.,* **in·cased, in·cas·ing.** another spelling of **encase.**

in·cau·tious (in kô′shəs) *adj.* not cautious; heedless. —**in·cau′tious·ly,** *adv.* —**in·cau′tious·ness,** *n.*

in·cen·di·ar·y (in sen′dē er′ē) *adj.* **1.** causing or designed to cause a fire: *incendiary grenades.* **2.** tending to excite, inflame, or anger; inflammatory: *an incendiary speech.* **3.** of or relating to arson. —*n. pl.,* **in·cen·di·ar·ies.** **1.** an arsonist. **2.** a bomb, shell, grenade, or other device designed to cause a fire.

in·cense¹ (in′sens′) *n.* **1.** any of several substances that produce a fragrant aroma when burned. **2.** the aroma or smoke produced by the burning of such a substance. **3.** any pleasant aroma: *the incense of a meadow.* [Late Latin *incēnsum* literally, something burnt.]

in·cense² (in sens′) *v.t.,* **in·censed, in·cens·ing.** to make very angry; enrage: *It incensed her when she realized that he was lying.* [Latin *incēnsus,* the past participle of *incendere* to burn, enrage.]

in·cen·tive (in sen′tiv) *n.* something that urges to action; stimulus: *The possibility of a raise was offered as an incentive to do extra work.*

I

at; āpe; cär; end; mē; it; īce; hot; ōld; fôrk; wood; fo͞ol; oil; out; up; turn; sing; thin; this; hw in white; zh in treasure. The symbol ə stands for the sound of **a** in about, **e** in taken, **i** in pencil, **o** in lemon, and **u** in circus.

in·cep·tion (in sep′shən) *n.* the point of beginning or being begun; commencement: *That television program was popular from its inception.*

in·ces·sant (in ses′ənt) *adj.* continuing without interruption; continuous; unceasing: *The campers were bothered by the incessant buzz of mosquitoes.* —**in·ces′sant·ly,** *adv.*

in·cest (in′sest′) *n.* a sexual relationship between two persons who are closely related and cannot legally marry, such as a parent and child or a brother and sister.

in·ces·tu·ous (in ses′chōō əs) *adj.* **1.** involving incest. **2.** guilty of incest. —**in·ces′tu·ous·ly,** *adv.* —**in·ces′tu·ous·ness,** *n.*

inch (inch) *n. pl.,* **inch·es. 1.** a measure of length, equal to $1/12$ of a foot. **2.** the smallest distance, amount, or degree: *He wouldn't budge an inch from his seat to help us.* —*v.i.* to move very slowly: *The snake inched through the grass.*

every inch. in every way; totally: *He is every inch a sailor.*

inch by inch. little by little.

within an inch of. very close to: *The driver came within an inch of having an accident.*

In·chon (in′chon′) *n.* a port city in northwestern South Korea, on the Yellow Sea. During the Korean War it was the site of an important landing by United Nations troops. Pop. (1971 est.), 610,000.

inch·worm (inch′wurm′) *n.* a caterpillar that moves by drawing the rear of the body up toward the front, forming a loop, and then stretching the front end forward. Also, **measuring worm.**

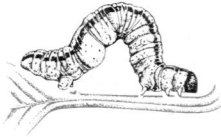

Inchworm

in·ci·dence (in′sə dəns) *n.* **1.** the rate, frequency, or range in which something happens: *Our town has a low incidence of crime.* **2.** the act or fact of happening; occurrence. **3.** the falling of a ray of light or a projectile on a surface.

in·ci·dent (in′sə dənt) *n.* **1.** an event or act; happening: *a funny incident.* **2.** a minor disturbance or conflict: *The protest march proceeded through town without incident.* —*adj.* naturally connected with; belonging to as a part.

in·ci·den·tal (in′sə dent′əl) *adj.* **1.** belonging to as a part, especially as a minor part: *There are many problems incidental to traveling in space.* **2.** happening without being expected, or without being connected with anything else: *The incidental expenses of our visit to New York were more than we had thought.* —*n. often,* **incidentals.** something that is incidental or unimportant: *Just bring the necessary supplies; we can buy the incidentals on the way.*

in·ci·den·tal·ly (in′sə dent′lē) *adv.* **1.** in an incidental manner. **2.** by the way: *Incidentally, have you heard about his new job?*

in·cin·er·ate (in sin′ə rāt′) *v.t.,* **in·cin·er·at·ed, in·cin·er·at·ing.** to burn (something) to ashes. —**in·cin′er·a′tion,** *n.*

in·cin·er·a·tor (in sin′ə rā′tər) *n.* a piece of equipment, such as a furnace, used to dispose of garbage or other waste material by burning it to ashes.

in·cip·i·ent (in sip′ē ənt) *adj.* just beginning to appear: *the incipient stage of a disease.* —**in·cip′i·ence,** *n.*

in·cise (in sīz′) *v.t.,* **in·cised, in·cis·ing. 1.** to cut into. **2.** to carve; engrave.

in·ci·sion (in sizh′ən) *n.* **1.** the act of incising. **2.** a cut, especially as made by a scalpel in surgery.

in·ci·sive (in sī′siv) *adj.* penetrating; sharp: *an incisive mind, an incisive comment.* —**in·ci′sive·ly,** *adv.* —**in·ci′sive·ness,** *n.*

in·ci·sor (in sī′zər) *n.* any of the front teeth of the upper or lower jaw having sharp flattened edges, used for cutting food.

Incisors

in·cite (in sīt′) *v.t.,* **in·cit·ed, in·cit·ing. 1.** to move or urge; rouse: *The sounding of the alarm incited us to action.* **2.** to cause by urging or arousing: *to incite a riot.* —**in·cit′er,** *n.*

in·cite·ment (in sīt′mənt) *n.* **1.** the act of inciting. **2.** something that incites.

in·ci·vil·i·ty (in′sə vil′ə tē) *n. pl.,* **in·ci·vil·i·ties. 1.** lack of politeness and courtesy. **2.** an impolite act.

incl. 1. inclosure. **2.** including. **3.** inclusive.

in·clem·ent (in klem′ənt) *adj.* **1.** cold or stormy: *The inclement weather kept us in the house all weekend.* **2.** not having or showing mercy; harsh: *an inclement ruler.* —**in·clem′en·cy,** *n.* —**in·clem′ent·ly,** *adv.*

in·cli·na·tion (in′klə nā′shən) *n.* **1.** a natural tendency; bent: *He has an inclination to thinness.* **2.** a preference or liking: *He has an inclination for all sports.* **3.** the act of bending or slanting. **4.** a slope; slant.

in·cline (*v.,* in klīn′; *n.,* in′klīn′, in klīn′) *v.,* **in·clined, in·clin·ing.** —*v.i.* **1.** to be or go at an angle; slope; slant: *The road inclines upward.* **2.** to bend or lean: *The old man inclined forward on his cane.* **3.** to have a preference or liking for something: *He inclines toward becoming a mechanic.* —*v.t.* **1.** to cause to bend, lean, slope, or slant. **2.** to give (someone) a preference or liking for something: *Her interests inclined her toward dress design.* —*n.* a surface that is at an angle: *The wagon rolled down the incline.*

in·clined (in klīnd′) *adj.* **1.** having an inclination or tendency. **2.** sloping or leaning.

inclined plane, any plane surface, such as a ramp, set at an angle of less than ninety degrees with a horizontal surface. An inclined plane is a simple machine that allows an object to be raised by less force than is needed to raise it vertically.

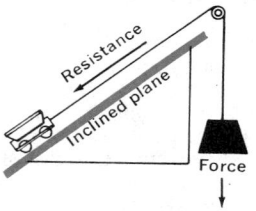

Inclined plane

in·close (in klōz′) *v.t.,* **in·closed, in·clos·ing.** another spelling of **enclose.**

in·clo·sure (in klō′zhər) another spelling of **enclosure.**

in·clude (in klōōd′) *v.t.,* **in·clud·ed, in·clud·ing. 1.** to have as part of the whole; contain: *The book includes an index.* **2.** to put in a group or total: *He included the whole class in the list.*

in·clu·sion (in klōō′zhən) *n.* **1.** the act of including or the state of being included. **2.** something that is included.

in·clu·sive (in klōō′siv) *adj.* **1.** including the specified limits and everything in between: *We will be gone five days, Monday to Friday inclusive.* **2.** including everything; comprehensive: *an inclusive list of schools in an area.* —**in·clu′sive·ly,** *adv.* —**in·clu′sive·ness,** *n.*

in·cog·ni·to (in′kog nē′tō, in kog′ni tō′) *adv.* having one's identity hidden so as to be unknown; in disguise. —*adj.* being in disguise. [Italian *incognito* unknown, from Latin *incognitus.*]

in·co·her·ent (in′kō hēr′ənt) *adj.* **1.** characterized by confused speech or thought; not understandable: *The patient was incoherent when he was brought to the hospital.* **2.** not sticking together; disconnected. —**in′co·her′ence,** *n.* —**in′co·her′ent·ly,** *adv.*

in·com·bus·ti·ble (in′kəm bus′tə bəl) *adj.* that cannot burn. —*n.* an incombustible substance. —**in′com·bus′ti·bil′i·ty,** *n.*

in·come (in′kum′) *n.* **1.** payment in money for services or labor, or from property or investments. **2.** the amount of such payment: *a low income.*

income tax, a tax on yearly income.

in·com·ing (in′kum′ing) *adj.* coming in: *the incoming tide, incoming telephone calls.*

in·com·men·su·rate (in′kə men′shər it) *adj.* **1.** not in proportion; not of equal size: *His wages are incommensurate to his needs.* **2.** not measurable. —**in′com·men′su·rate·ly,** *adv.*

in·com·mode (in′kə mōd′) *v.t.,* **in·com·mod·ed, in·com·mod·ing.** to bother or annoy; inconvenience.

in·com·mu·ni·ca·ble (in′kə myōō′ni kə bəl) *adj.* that cannot be told or communicated.

in·com·mu·ni·ca·do (in′kə myōō′nə kä′dō) *adv.* without the right or means of communicating with others: *The prisoner was held incommunicado.*

in·com·pa·ra·ble (in kom′pər ə bəl) *adj.* **1.** having no equal; matchless: *The great soprano has an incomparable voice.* **2.** that cannot be compared. —**in·com′pa·ra·bly,** *adv.*

in·com·pat·i·ble (in′kəm pat′ə bəl) *adj.* not able to exist or work together in harmony. —**in′com·pat′i·bil′i·ty,** *n.* —**in′com·pat′i·bly,** *adv.*

in·com·pe·tent (in kom′pət ənt) *adj.* not having or showing enough ability; not capable: *an incompetent typist, an incompetent repair job.* —*n.* **1.** a person who lacks ability. **2.** a person who is not legally able to act for himself, because of insanity, severe illness, or old age. —**in·com′pe·tence,** *n.* —**in·com′pe·tent·ly,** *adv.*

in·com·plete (in′kəm plēt′) *adj.* not complete. —**in′com·plete′ly,** *adv.* —**in′com·plete′ness,** *n.*

in·com·pre·hen·si·ble (in′kom pri hen′sə bəl) *adj.* that cannot be understood: *This page of Chinese writing is incomprehensible to me.* —**in′com·pre·hen′si·bil′i·ty,** *n.* —**in′com·pre·hen′si·bly,** *adv.*

in·com·pre·hen·sion (in′kom prə hen′shən) *n.* the fact of not understanding.

in·con·ceiv·a·ble (in′kən sē′və bəl) *adj.* that is hard or impossible to imagine or think of: *Space travel to other galaxies is at present inconceivable.* —**in′con·ceiv′a·bil′i·ty,** *n.* —**in′con·ceiv′a·bly,** *adv.*

in·con·clu·sive (in′kən klōō′siv) *adj.* that does not end argument or doubt; not conclusive. —**in′con·clu′sive·ly,** *adv.* —**in′con·clu′sive·ness,** *n.*

in·con·gru·i·ty (in′kən grōō′ə tē) *n. pl.,* **in·con·gru·i·ties.** **1.** the quality or condition of being incongruous. **2.** something that is incongruous.

in·con·gru·ous (in kong′grōō əs) *adj.* not harmoniously related or joined; not suitable: *High-heeled shoes and blue jeans look incongruous together.* —**in·con′gru·ous·ly,** *adv.*

in·con·se·quence (in kon′sə kwens′) *n.* the condition or quality of being inconsequential.

in·con·se·quen·tial (in kon′sə kwen′chəl) *adj.* **1.** not leading to anything important; trivial. **2.** not following from anything; unrelated. —**in′con·se·quen′tial·ly,** *adv.*

in·con·sid·er·a·ble (in′kən sid′ər ə bəl) *adj.* small or not worth considering. —**in′con·sid′er·a·bly,** *adv.*

in·con·sid·er·ate (in′kən sid′ər it) *adj.* having or showing little thought for others: *It was very inconsiderate of her to hang up in the middle of our telephone conversation.* —**in′con·sid′er·ate·ly,** *adv.* —**in′con·sid′er·ate·ness,** *n.*

in·con·sist·en·cy (in′kən sis′tən sē) *n. pl.,* **in·con·sist·en·cies.** **1.** the quality or condition of being inconsistent. **2.** something that is inconsistent.

in·con·sist·ent (in′kən sis′tənt) *adj.* **1.** not in agreement; contradictory: *That country's practice of praising*

peace while waging war is inconsistent. **2.** not keeping to the same thoughts or course of action. —**in′con·sist′ent·ly,** *adv.*

in·con·sol·a·ble (in kən sō′lə bəl) *adj.* that cannot be consoled; grief-stricken: *The mother was inconsolable when her child died.* —**in·con·sol′a·bly,** *adv.*

in·con·spic·u·ous (in′kən spik′yōō əs) *adj.* likely to escape notice; not easily seen. —**in′con·spic′u·ous·ly,** *adv.* —**in′con·spic′u·ous·ness,** *n.*

in·con·stan·cy (in kon′stən sē) *n.* the state or quality of being inconstant.

in·con·stant (in kon′stənt) *adj.* **1.** not faithful or steadfast; fickle. **2.** likely to change; changeable. —**in·con′stant·ly,** *adv.*

in·con·test·a·ble (in′kən tes′tə bəl) *adj.* that cannot be disputed or questioned: *incontestable evidence.* —**in′con·test′a·bly,** *adv.*

in·con·ti·nence (in kont′ən əns) *n.* the condition of being incontinent.

in·con·ti·nent (in kont′ən ənt) *adj.* lacking self-control.

in·con·tro·vert·i·ble (in kon′trə vur′tə bəl) *adj.* that cannot be argued against or debated; certain: *incontrovertible proof.* —**in′con·tro·vert′i·bly,** *adv.*

in·con·ven·ience (in′kən vēn′yəns) *n.* **1.** the state or quality of being inconvenient. **2.** an inconvenient situation or thing: *Not having a telephone is an inconvenience.* —*v.t.,* **in·con·ven·ienced, in·con·ven·ienc·ing.** to cause (someone) to have difficulty or trouble: *We hope the delay will not inconvenience you.*

in·con·ven·ient (in′kən vēn′yənt) *adj.* not favorable or suitable for one's needs or purposes; not convenient; troublesome. —**in′con·ven′ient·ly,** *adv.*

in·cor·po·rate (in kôr′pə rāt′) *v.,* **in·cor·po·rat·ed, in·cor·po·rat·ing.** —*v.t.* **1.** to include (something) as a part: *The proposed law incorporates many changes.* **2.** to form into a corporation: *to incorporate a business.* —*v.i.* to become or form a corporation. —**in·cor′po·ra′tion,** *n.*

in·cor·po·rat·ed (in kôr′pə rā′tid) *adj.* formed into a corporation.

in·cor·po·re·al (in′kôr pôr′ē əl) *adj.* having no material body; spiritual. —**in′cor·po′re·al·ly,** *adv.*

in·cor·rect (in′kə rekt′) *adj.* **1.** not agreeing with fact or truth; not accurate: *an incorrect answer.* **2.** not conforming to an approved standard; not proper. —**in′cor·rect′ly,** *adv.* —**in′cor·rect′ness,** *n.*

in·cor·ri·gi·ble (in kôr′ə jə bəl, in kor′ə jə bəl) *adj.* that cannot be made better or reformed; bad beyond or almost beyond all hope of correction: *an incorrigible criminal.* —*n.* a person who is incorrigible. —**in·cor′ri·gi·bil′i·ty,** *n.* —**in·cor′ri·gi·bly,** *adv.*

in·cor·rupt·i·ble (in′kə rup′tə bəl) *adj.* **1.** that cannot be corrupted; morally strong: *an incorruptible public official.* **2.** that does not decay or become rotten: *an incorruptible substance.* —**in′cor·rupt′i·bil′i·ty,** *n.* —**in′cor·rupt′i·bly,** *adv.*

in·crease (*v.,* in krēs′; *n.,* in′krēs) *v.,* **in·creased, in·creas·ing.** —*v.t.* to make greater, as in number or size: *The library has increased its collection of books.* —*v.i.* to become greater, as in number or size: *The school's enroll-*

at; āpe; cär; end; mē; it; īce; hot; ōld; fôrk; wood; fōōl; oil; out; up; turn; sing; thin; this; hw in white; zh in treasure. The symbol ə stands for the sound of **a** in about, **e** in taken, **i** in pencil, **o** in lemon, and **u** in circus.

I

ment has increased. —*n.* **1.** the act or process of increasing; becoming greater. **2.** the amount by which something is increased: *He got a salary increase of ten dollars per week.* **on the increase.** increasing.

in·creas·ing·ly (in krē′sing lē) *adv.* to a greater and greater extent; more and more.

in·cred·i·ble (in kred′ə bəl) *adj.* hard or impossible to believe: *an incredible story, an incredible feat.* —**in·cred′i·bil′i·ty,** *n.* —**in·cred′i·bly,** *adv.*

in·cre·du·li·ty (in′krə dōō′lə tē, in′krə dyōō′lə tē) *n.* refusal to believe; doubt.

in·cred·u·lous (in krej′ə ləs) *adj.* **1.** not able to believe something; skeptical; unbelieving: *When the discovery was first announced, many people were incredulous.* **2.** showing disbelief: *an incredulous gasp.* —**in·cred′u·lous·ly,** *adv.*

in·cre·ment (ing′krə mənt) *n.* **1.** something that is added to something; increase. **2.** an amount that is added.

in·crim·i·nate (in krim′ə nāt′) *v.t.,* **in·crim·i·nat·ed, in·crim·i·nat·ing. 1.** to charge with a crime or fault. **2.** to suggest or show the guilt of: *The fact that he ran away seemed to incriminate the boy.* —**in·crim′i·na′tion,** *n.* —**in·crim′i·na·to·ry,** *adj.*

in·crust (in krust′) another spelling of **encrust.**

in·crus·ta·tion (in′krus tā′shən) another spelling of **encrustation.**

in·cu·bate (ing′kyə bāt′) *v.t.,* **in·cu·bat·ed, in·cu·bat·ing. 1.** to sit on and keep (eggs) warm for hatching: *A hen incubates her eggs.* **2.** to form or develop gradually: *He incubated the idea in his mind before writing it down.*

in·cu·ba·tion (ing′kyə bā′shən) *n.* **1.** the process of incubating or the state of being incubated. **2.** the stage of a disease from the time of infection to the first appearance of symptoms.

in·cu·ba·tor (ing′kyə bā′tər) *n.* **1.** a boxlike apparatus of glass or clear plastic that provides a steady, warm temperature for babies who are sick or born too soon. **2.** a heated container used to hatch eggs or grow bacteria.

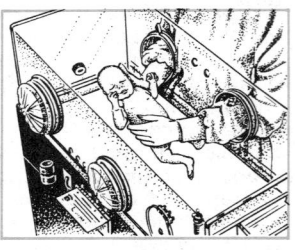
Incubator

in·cu·bus (ing′kyə bəs) *n. pl.,* **in·cu·bi** (ing′kyə bī′) or **in·cu·bus·es. 1.** a demon supposed to do evil to sleeping people. **2.** any oppressive burden. **3.** a nightmare.

in·cu·des (ing kyōō′dēz) the plural of **incus.**

in·cul·cate (in kul′kāt) *v.t.,* **in·cul·cat·ed, in·cul·cat·ing.** to fix firmly in the mind or memory by example or by repeated teaching: *The parents inculcated a love of music in their children.* —**in·cul′ca′tion,** *n.*

in·cum·ben·cy (in kum′bən sē) *n. pl.,* **in·cum·ben·cies. 1.** the act of holding an office and performing its duties. **2.** the term of office of an incumbent.

in·cum·bent (in kum′bənt) *adj.* **1.** imposed as a duty or obligation: *It was incumbent upon the witness to tell the truth.* **2.** holding an office: *an incumbent president.* **3.** lying, leaning, or resting upon something. —*n.* a person who holds an office.

in·cum·ber (in kum′bər) another spelling of **encumber.**

in·cum·brance (in kum′brəns) another spelling of **encumbrance.**

in·cur (in kur′) *v.t.,* **in·curred, in·cur·ring.** to bring (something) on oneself by one's own actions: *The king incurred the wrath of the people.*

in·cur·a·ble (in kyoor′ə bəl) *adj.* that cannot be cured or healed: *an incurable disease.* —*n.* a person who has a

disease that cannot be cured or healed. —**in·cur′a·bil′i·ty,** *n.* —**in·cur′a·bly,** *adv.*

in·cur·sion (in kur′zhən) *n.* a sudden attack or raid: *an incursion of wild animals, an incursion of soldiers.*

in·cus (ing′kəs) *n. pl.,* **in·cu·des.** one of the three small bones of the middle ear; anvil.

Ind. 1. Indiana. **2.** India. **3.** Indian.

in·debt·ed (in det′id) *adj.* **1.** owing gratitude; in the debt of: *I am indebted to her for all she has done.* **2.** owing money; in debt.

in·debt·ed·ness (in det′id nis) *n. pl.,* **in·debt·ed·ness·es. 1.** the state of being indebted. **2.** an amount owed.

in·de·cen·cy (in dē′sən sē) *n. pl.,* **in·de·cen·cies. 1.** the quality or condition of being indecent. **2.** something that is indecent.

in·de·cent (in dē′sənt) *adj.* **1.** not modest or moral; obscene: *indecent language.* **2.** not conforming to the standards of good taste; improper. —**in·de′cent·ly,** *adv.*

in·de·ci·sion (in′di sizh′ən) *n.* the inability to decide or to make up one's mind.

in·de·ci·sive (in′di sī′siv) *adj.* **1.** not able to decide; hesitating: *an indecisive leader.* **2.** not leading to a decision: *an indecisive contest.* —**in′de·ci′sive·ly,** *adv.* —**in′de·ci′sive·ness,** *n.*

in·dec·o·rous (in dek′ər əs) *adj.* not conforming to the standards of good taste; improper. —**in·dec′o·rous·ly,** *adv.* —**in·dec′o·rous·ness,** *n.*

in·deed (in dēd′) *adv.* really; truly: *He is indeed grateful to her.* —*interj.* used to express surprise, disbelief, or contempt: *The king marry a commoner? Indeed!*

indef., indefinite.

in·de·fat·i·ga·ble (in′di fat′ə gə bəl) *adj.* that does not become tired: *an indefatigable worker.* —**in′de·fat′i·ga·bil′i·ty,** *n.* —**in′de·fat′i·ga·bly,** *adv.*

in·de·fen·si·ble (in′di fen′sə bəl) *adj.* **1.** that cannot be defended against attack: *The troops' position on the battlefield became indefensible.* **2.** that cannot be proved, justified, or excused: *Their acts are indefensible.* —**in′de·fen′si·bly,** *adv.*

in·de·fin·a·ble (in′di fī′nə bəl) *adj.* that cannot be defined. —**in′de·fin′a·bly,** *adv.*

in·def·i·nite (in def′ə nit) *adj.* **1.** not clearly defined; not exact: *His plans for the summer are still indefinite.* **2.** having no limits; unmeasured: *a line of indefinite length.* **3.** *Grammar.* not specifying or determining the person, thing, place, time, or manner; not exact or precise. *Some, any,* and *other* are indefinite pronouns. —**in·def′i·nite·ly,** *adv.* —**in·def′i·nite·ness,** *n.*

indefinite article, the article *a* or *an.*

in·del·i·ble (in del′ə bəl) *adj.* **1.** that cannot be removed or taken away: *indelible ink, indelible memories.* **2.** that makes indelible writing or marks: *an indelible pen.* —**in·del′i·bil′i·ty,** *n.* —**in·del′i·bly,** *adv.*

in·del·i·ca·cy (in del′ə kə sē) *n. pl.,* **in·del·i·ca·cies. 1.** the quality of being indelicate. **2.** something that is indelicate.

in·del·i·cate (in del′ə kit) *adj.* **1.** not tactful or considerate; coarse; crude: *indelicate behavior.* **2.** not proper or modest; offensive: *indelicate language.* —**in·del′i·cate·ly,** *adv.* —**in·del′i·cate·ness,** *n.*

in·dem·ni·fy (in dem′nə fī′) *v.t.,* **in·dem·ni·fied, in·dem·ni·fy·ing. 1.** to compensate for damage, loss, expense, or injury: *The airline indemnified the passenger for the loss of his suitcase.* **2.** to protect against future damage, loss, or expense; insure. —**in·dem′ni·fi·ca′tion,** *n.*

in·dem·ni·ty (in dem′nə tē) *n. pl.,* **in·dem·ni·ties. 1.** a compensation given for damage, loss, expense, or injury. **2.** protection against future damage, loss, or expense; insurance.

in·dent¹ (*v.*, in dent′; *n.*, in′dent′, in dent′) *v.t.* **1.** to start (a line of writing, typing, or printing) farther in than the other lines, as at the beginning of a paragraph. **2.** to cut or make toothlike notches on. —*n.* an indentation. [Old French *endenter*.]

in·dent² (in dent′) *v.t.* to make a dent in. [*In-²* + *dent*.]

in·den·ta·tion (in′den tā′shən) *n.* **1.** the act of indenting or the state of being indented. **2.** a part that is set or pushed back from the rest; dent or recess.

in·den·tion (in den′shən) *n.* **1.** the starting of a line of writing, typing, or printing farther in than the other lines: *to begin each new paragraph with an indention.* **2.** the empty or blank space left by this. **3.** a dent or recess.

in·den·ture (in den′chər) *n.* a contract that binds a person, such as an apprentice, to work for another person for a stated period of time. —*v.t.*, **in·den·tured, in·den·tur·ing.** to bind (a person) by such a contract: *an indentured servant.*

in·de·pend·ence (in′di pen′dəns) *n.* the state or quality of being independent: *The American colonies fought to win independence from England.*

In·de·pend·ence (in′di pen′dəns) *n.* a city in western Missouri, near Kansas City. Pop. (1970), 111,662.

Independence Day, a holiday observed on July 4, commemorating the adoption of the Declaration of Independence on July 4, 1776. Also, **Fourth of July.**

in·de·pend·ent (in′di pen′dənt) *adj.* **1.** not easily influenced or controlled by another or others: *an independent mind, an independent person.* **2.** not subject to the political control or rule of another or others: *an independent country.* **3.** not connected with another; separate: *independent research, an independent grocery store.* **4.** not connected with or supporting any political party: *an independent voter.* **5.** having or providing enough to live on without working: *an independent income.* —*n.* a person or thing that is independent. —**in′de·pend′ent·ly,** *adv.*

independent clause, a clause in a sentence that can stand alone as a complete sentence. In the sentence *After the girls had played tennis for an hour, they decided to go for a swim,* the clause *they decided to go for a swim* is an independent clause. Also, **main clause.**

in·de·scrib·a·ble (in′di skrī′bə bəl) *adj.* that cannot be described in words; beyond description: *a sunset of indescribable beauty.* —**in′de·scrib′a·bly,** *adv.*

in·de·struc·ti·ble (in′di struk′tə bəl) *adj.* that cannot be destroyed. —**in′de·struc′ti·bil′i·ty,** *n.* —**in′de·struc′ti·bly,** *adv.*

in·de·ter·mi·na·ble (in′di tur′mi nə bəl) *adj.* that cannot be defined, decided, or determined: *a man of indeterminable age.* —**in′de·ter′mi·na·bly,** *adv.*

in·de·ter·mi·nate (in′di tur′mi nit) *adj.* without defined limits; indefinite or vague: *We will be away for an indeterminate length of time.* —**in′de·ter′mi·nate·ly,** *adv.* —**in′de·ter′mi·nate·ness,** *n.*

in·dex (in′deks) *n. pl.,* **in·dex·es** or **in·di·ces. 1.** an alphabetical list in a published work, such as a book or magazine, that gives the page where a reference to a particular subject or name can be found. **2.** something that shows or indicates: *His work is an index of his ability.* **3.** a pointer or indicator, as the needle on the dial of a compass. —*v.t.* **1.** to make an index for: *to index a book.* **2.** to enter in an index: *to index a word.* —**in′dex·er,** *n.*

index finger, the finger next to the thumb; forefinger.

In·di·a (in′dē ə) *n.* **1.** a country in southern Asia. Capital, New Delhi. Area, 1,226,860 sq. mi. Pop. (1971), 547,367,926. **2.** a large peninsula in southern Asia, bounded by the Arabian Sea, Indian Ocean, and Bay of Bengal. It contains India, Pakistan, Bangladesh, and several smaller countries.

India ink, ink made from a black pigment, used for both writing and drawing.

In·di·an (in′dē ən) *n.* **1.** a member of one of the tribes of original inhabitants of North and South America. Also, **American Indian. 2.** any one of the languages of these peoples. **3.** a person who was born or is living in India. —*adj.* **1.** of or relating to American Indians. **2.** of or relating to India or its people. [When Columbus discovered America, he mistakenly thought he had reached India, and so he called the native people he met *Indians.*]

● Many of the words we use today came into English from the languages of the American **Indians.** When the European explorers and settlers came to America, they used Indian words for two basic reasons. First, because they found many new things that they had not seen before, and they needed names for these things. That is how we got words like *tobacco, raccoon, canoe, tomato,* and *maize.* Second, because they had no names for the rivers, lakes, and other places that they found. That is how more than half of our fifty states came to have names that trace back to Indian words.

There are a great many different American Indian languages. Within the past fifty years, scholars have made a careful study of these languages. From their study, they have learned many important things about how people use language. In fact, studies of non-Indo-European languages like those of the Indians have contributed greatly to advances in the science of language.

In·di·an·a (in′dē an′ə) *n.* a state in the north-central United States. Capital, Indianapolis. Area, 36,291 sq. mi. Pop. (1970), 5,193,669. Abbreviation, **Ind.** —**In′di·an′i·an,** *adj., n.*

● **Indiana** comes from either a Modern Latin or a Spanish adjective meaning "Indian." When the name was first used, the region was still Indian territory.

In·di·an·ap·o·lis (in′dē ə nap′ə lis) *n.* the capital and largest city of Indiana, in the central part of the state. Pop. (1970), 744,624.

Indian club, a bottle-shaped club used in arm exercises.

Indian corn, see **corn¹** *(defs. 1, 2).*

Indian Ocean, an ocean south of Asia, between Africa and Australia.

Indian clubs

Indian pipe, a waxy, white leafless plant with one bell-shaped flower, growing wild.

Indian summer, a period of warm, mild weather occurring in autumn, usually after the first frost.

India paper, a thin, strong paper, used chiefly for Bibles.

India rubber also, **india rubber.** see **rubber** *(def. 1).*

in·di·cate (in′di kāt′) *v.t.,* **in·di·cat·ed, in·di·cat·ing. 1.** to be a sign of; show: *A high fever indicates the*

I

at; āpe; cär; end; mē; it; īce; hot; ōld; fôrk; wood; fo͞ol; oil; out; up; turn; sing; thin; **th**is; hw in white; zh in treasure. The symbol ə stands for the sound of **a** in about, **e** in taken, **i** in pencil, **o** in lemon, and **u** in circus.

presence of a disease. **2.** to direct attention to; point out: *The guide indicated the best trail for us to take.* **3.** to state or express briefly: *He indicated that he might go to camp this summer.*

in·di·ca·tion (in′di kā′shən) *n.* **1.** the act of indicating. **2.** something that indicates; sign: *There are many indications that she will do well in high school.*

in·dic·a·tive (in dik′ə tiv) *adj.* **1.** that points out, suggests, or expresses: *We gave him a gift indicative of our high regard for him.* **2.** *Grammar.* of or relating to the mood of a verb that expresses a fact or asks a question of fact. In the sentences *The water is hot* and *Did she buy the dress?, is* and *buy* are in the indicative mood. *—n. Grammar.* **1.** the indicative mood. **2.** a verb in this mood. *—in·dic′a·tive·ly, adv.*

in·di·ca·tor (in′di kā′tər) *n.* **1.** a person or thing that indicates. **2.** any of various instruments that measure or record something, such as a dial in an airplane that indicates the plane's speed. **3.** a pointer on the dial of such an instrument. **4.** a substance, such as litmus, that indicates a chemical condition or change, especially by changing color.

in·di·ces (in′də sēz′) a plural of **index**.

in·dict (in dīt′) *v.t.* **1.** to accuse of an offense; criticize harshly. **2.** (of a grand jury) to accuse formally of a crime. *—in·dict′er;* also, **in·dict′or,** *n.*

in·dict·ment (in dīt′mənt) *n.* **1.** a formal, written accusation by a grand jury. **2.** any accusation or criticism.

In·dies (in′dēz) *n.* **1.** see **East Indies**. **2.** see **West Indies**.

in·dif·fer·ence (in dif′ər əns, in dif′rəns) *n.* **1.** lack of feeling, concern, or care: *He showed complete indifference to the old woman's poverty.* **2.** lack of importance: *What he thinks is a matter of indifference to her.*

in·dif·fer·ent (in dif′ər ənt, in dif′rənt) *adj.* **1.** having or showing a lack of feeling, concern, or care: *He is indifferent to other people's troubles.* **2.** not particularly good; routine; average: *The actor gave an indifferent performance.* *—in·dif′fer·ent·ly, adv.*

in·di·gence (in′di jəns) *n.* extreme need; poverty.

in·dig·e·nous (in dij′ə nəs) *adj.* originating, growing, or living naturally in a particular place; not brought in from outside; native: *Coyotes are indigenous to North America.* *—in·dig′e·nous·ly, adv.*

in·di·gent (in′di jənt) *adj.* not having enough to live on; poor; needy.

in·di·gest·i·ble (in′di jes′tə bəl) *adj.* impossible or difficult to digest. *—in′di·gest′i·bil′i·ty, n.*

in·di·ges·tion (in′di jes′chən) *n.* difficulty or discomfort in digesting food.

in·dig·nant (in dig′nənt) *adj.* filled with indignation: *He was indignant at his son for telling a lie.* *—in·dig′nant·ly, adv.*

in·dig·na·tion (in′dig nā′shən) *n.* anger aroused by something unfair, cruel, or evil: *The students felt indignation at the boy who cheated on the test.*

in·dig·ni·ty (in dig′nə tē) *n. pl.,* **in·dig·ni·ties.** an act or remark that humiliates, insults, or injures: *The little boy suffered the indignity of being called names by the bully.*

in·di·go (in′di gō′) *n. pl.,* **in·di·gos** or **in·di·goes. 1.** a very dark blue dye obtained from various plants or made by man. **2.** any of the plants from which this dye is obtained. **3.** a deep violet-blue color. *—adj.* having the color indigo; violet-blue.

in·di·rect (in′də rekt′) *adj.* **1.** not in a straight line; roundabout: *an indirect route.* **2.** having or depending on something that comes between; not immediate: *an indirect result.* **3.** not straightforward and open; devious: *She gave an indirect answer.* *—in′di·rect′ly, adv.* *—in′di·rect′ness, n.*

indirect object, a person or thing indirectly affected by an action. In the sentence *I gave him a book, him* is the indirect object.

indirect tax, a tax on goods that is paid indirectly by the consumer because it is included in the price of the goods. The excise tax is an indirect tax.

in·dis·creet (in′dis krēt′) *adj.* lacking tact or careful judgment; not discreet: *She is very indiscreet in discussing her personal affairs.* *—in′dis·creet′ly, adv.* *—in′dis·creet′ness, n.*

in·dis·cre·tion (in′dis kresh′ən) *n.* **1.** the quality of being indiscreet. **2.** something that is indiscreet: *to commit an indiscretion.*

in·dis·crim·i·nate (in′dis krim′ə nit) *adj.* **1.** not noticing differences or making wise choices: *He is an indiscriminate television fan who will watch any program.* **2.** random or confused. *—in′dis·crim′i·nate·ly, adv.*

in·dis·pen·sa·ble (in′dis pen′sə bəl) *adj.* that cannot be done without; necessary or essential: *Good soil, water, and sunshine are indispensable to a successful garden.* *—in′dis·pen′sa·bil′i·ty, n.* *—in′dis·pen′sa·bly, adv.*

in·dis·posed (in′dis pōzd′) *adj.* **1.** slightly ill. **2.** unwilling; disinclined: *She was indisposed to help us.*

in·dis·po·si·tion (in dis′pə zish′ən) *n.* **1.** a slight illness: *Her indisposition kept her from going out last night.* **2.** the condition of being unwilling; unwillingness.

in·dis·put·a·ble (in′dis pyōō′tə bəl) *adj.* that cannot be disputed; unquestionable: *These facts are indisputable.* *—in′dis·put′a·bil′i·ty, n.* *—in′dis·put′a·bly, adv.*

in·dis·sol·u·ble (in′di sol′yə bəl) *adj.* that cannot be dissolved or destroyed: *Our friendship is indissoluble.*

in·dis·tinct (in′dis tingkt′) *adj.* not clear or sharp; not distinct. *—in′dis·tinct′ly, adv.* *—in′dis·tinct′ness, n.*

in·dis·tin·guish·a·ble (in′dis ting′gwish shə bəl) *adj.* **1.** that cannot be told apart: *The two houses are indistinguishable from one another.* **2.** that cannot be seen or recognized: *an indistinguishable difference.*

in·di·um (in′dē əm) *n.* a soft, silvery, rare metallic element, used in alloys for jewelry, bearings, and dentures. Symbol: **In**

in·di·vid·u·al (in′də vij′ōō əl) *adj.* **1.** single and distinct; separate: *Each individual house has its own yard.* **2.** for or by one only: *This play is an individual effort.* **3.** characteristic of one only: *He has an individual style of dressing.* *—n.* **1.** a person: *He is a strange individual.* **2.** a single person or thing. *—in′di·vid′u·al·ly, adv.*

in·di·vid·u·al·ism (in′də vij′ōō ə liz′əm) *n.* **1.** the theory and practice that emphasizes the worth, freedom, and well-being of the individual and his right to think and live as he sees fit without the control or direction of others, especially of a government. **2.** action or thought by each person for his or her own ends without regard for others.

in·di·vid·u·al·ist (in′də vij′ōō ə list) *n.* **1.** a person who thinks and acts in an independent manner. **2.** a person who practices or supports individualism.

in·di·vid·u·al·is·tic (in′də vij′ōō ə lis′tik) *adj.* relating to individualism or to individualists.

in·di·vid·u·al·i·ty (in′də vij′ōō al′ə tē) *n. pl.,* **in·di·vid·u·al·i·ties. 1.** a quality that makes one person or thing different from others; individual character: *Her paintings show much individuality.* **2.** the condition of being an individual.

in·di·vis·i·ble (in′də viz′ə bəl) *adj.* **1.** that cannot be divided. **2.** that cannot be divided without a remainder: *5 is indivisible by 2.* *—in′di·vis′i·bil′i·ty, n.* *—in′di·vis′i·bly, adv.*

In·do·chi·na (in′dō chī′nə) *n.* **1.** a peninsula in southeast Asia between the Bay of Bengal and the South China Sea, consisting of the Malay Peninsula and the countries of Vietnam, Burma, Laos, Cambodia, and Thailand. **2.** see **French Indochina.** —**In·do·chi·nese** (in′dō chī nēz′) *adj., n.*

in·doc·tri·nate (in dok′tri nāt′) *v.t.,* **in·doc·tri·nat·ed, in·doc·tri·nat·ing.** to teach (someone) a theory, belief, or principle. —**in·doc′tri·na′tion,** *n.*

In·do-Eu·ro·pe·an (in′dō yoor′ə pē′ən) *n.* a family of languages that includes most languages spoken in Europe and the Americas and many of those spoken in Asia. English, Russian, Italian, Persian, and Hindi are Indo-European languages. —*adj.* of or relating to this family of languages.

● The **Indo-European** language family includes most of the languages spoken from northern India to western Europe. Indo-European languages are also spoken in North America, South America, Australia, Africa, and parts of Asia. Approximately one-half of the world's population speaks an Indo-European language. These languages include English, German, French, Spanish, Italian, Russian, Greek, Celtic, Persian, and Hindustani.

If you have ever seen or heard any of these languages, you will probably find it hard to believe that they are related to English or to each other. But as early as the sixteenth century, language scholars had begun to notice that these languages had certain basic words in common. Among the words that were similarly pronounced or spelled in various Indo-European languages were the terms for family members and for the numerals one through ten. For example, the English word *brother* is similar to the German *bruder,* Irish *bhrathair,* Latin *frater,* Greek *phrater,* Russian *brat,* Sanskrit *bhrata,* and Persian *biradar.* The English word *seven* is similar to the German *sieben,* Irish *seacht,* French *sept,* Latin *septem,* Greek *hepta,* and Slavic *sedm'.* Very basic words like these are usually not borrowed by one language from another; they exist in the earliest roots of a language. Therefore, scholars reasoned that all Indo-European languages came from a single prehistoric language. The different Indo-European languages that exist today are believed to have been the result of successive migrations of groups of people who spoke the original Indo-European language. As they lost contact with each other these groups developed different forms of their language. Over the centuries, these forms changed so greatly that they became separate languages.

This theory, which is generally accepted, does not answer the question as to where this original Indo-European language was spoken. Although no one has been able to establish precisely the original Indo-European homeland, scholars have done detective work that has produced some general ideas. The oldest recorded form of an Indo-European language dates from about 2000 B.C. From this and from other early sources it has been found that the ancient Indo-European language had many words relating to cold, northern regions, such as *snow, bear, wolf, salmon, birch,* and *beech.* Such words as *grape, olive, lion,* and *camel,* relating to warmer regions, appear to be later additions. The beech tree did not grow in Asia and salmon existed mainly in the Baltic Sea. The early appearance of such words as *sheep, cow,* and *horse* suggests that the original Indo-European language developed in an area of grassy plains. From all this evidence, some scholars have suggested that the original Indo-European homeland was in eastern Europe on the plains and uplands between the Baltic and Black Seas. Because there are no surviving ancient records in writing to prove this theory, the roots of the Indo-European language family will probably never be definitely known.

in·do·lent (ind′əl ənt) *adj.* having or showing a dislike of work or effort; lazy; idle. —**in′do·lence,** *n.* —**in′do·lent·ly,** *adv.*

in·dom·i·ta·ble (in dom′ə tə bəl) *adj.* that cannot be conquered: *an indomitable will.* —**in·dom′i·ta·bly,** *adv.*

In·do·ne·sia (in′də nē′zhə) *n.* a country in southeastern Asia composed of islands in the Malay Archipelago. Capital, Djakarta. Area, 735,268 sq. mi. Pop. (1980), 153, 000,000.

In·do·ne·sian (in′də nē′zhən) *adj.* of or relating to Indonesia or its people. —*n.* a person who was born or is living in Indonesia.

in·door (in′dôr′) *adj.* used or done within a house or building: *an indoor swimming pool. Bowling is an indoor sport.*

in·doors (in′dôrz′) *adv.* in or into a house or building: *We moved the party indoors when it started to rain.*

in·dorse (in dôrs′) *v.t.,* **in·dorsed, in·dors·ing.** another spelling of **endorse.**

in·dorse·ment (in dôrs′mənt) another spelling of **endorsement.**

in·du·bi·ta·ble (in dōō′bə tə bəl, in dyōō′bə tə bəl) *adj.* not to be doubted; certain. —**in·du′bi·ta·bly,** *adv.*

in·duce (in dōōs′, in dyōōs′) *v.t.,* **in·duced, in·duc·ing. 1.** to persuade to do something; influence: *They could not induce him to stay.* **2.** to bring about; bring on; produce; cause: *The nurse gave Ned a drug to induce sleep.* **3.** to produce (electric current) by induction. **4.** to reason by induction.

in·duce·ment (in dōōs′mənt, in dyōōs′mənt) *n.* **1.** something attractive that leads someone to do something: *The extra money was an inducement for him to work harder.* **2.** the act of inducing or the state of being induced.

in·duct (in dukt′) *v.t.* **1.** to take into the armed forces: *to be inducted into the army.* **2.** to bring into a group; admit: *The club inducted four new members.* **3.** to install formally in an office: *to induct a new mayor.*

in·duc·tance (in duk′təns) *n.* the ability of an electric circuit to produce an electromotive force when the current in the circuit or in a neighboring circuit is changing.

in·duc·tee (in duk′tē′) *n.* a person who is being inducted, especially into the armed forces.

in·duc·tion (in duk′shən) *n.* **1.** the process by which a person is taken into the armed forces. **2.** the process or ceremony of being brought into a group or installed in an office: *We attended the induction of the new club president.* **3.** the act of inducing: *the induction of a hypnotized state.* **4.** *Electricity.* **a.** the process by which a body having electric or magnetic properties produces electric or magnetic properties in another body without touching it. **b.** the act or process of magnetizing an object by placing it in a magnetic field. **c.** the act or process of producing an electric current in a conductor by moving it through a magnetic field, or by moving the magnetic field itself. **5.** the act or method of reasoning from particular cases or facts to a general principle or conclusion.

induction coil, an electrical device that converts low-voltage direct current into high-voltage pulses.

in·duc·tive (in duk′tiv) *adj.* **1.** of or using induction: *We attempted to reach a conclusion by inductive reasoning.*

at; āpe; cär; end; mē; it; īce; hot; ōld; fôrk; wood; fōōl; oil; out; up; turn; sing; thin; this; hw in white; zh in treasure. The symbol ə stands for the sound of **a** in about, **e** in taken, **i** in pencil, **o** in lemon, and **u** in circus.

I

2. relating to, producing, or produced by electrical or magnetic induction. —**in·duc'tive·ly,** adv.

in·dulge (in dulj') v., **in·dulged, in·dulg·ing.** —v.t. **1.** to give way to; yield to: He often indulges his craving for ice cream. **2.** to yield to the whims or wishes of; give in to: The grandparents indulge the child. —v.i. to allow oneself to have, do, or enjoy something: The students often indulge in card playing during study periods.

in·dul·gence (in dul'jəns) n. **1.** the act of indulging. **2.** something that is indulged in: Record albums are his main indulgence. **3.** something given by a person who is indulgent; favor. **4.** in the Roman Catholic Church, pardon from punishment for the sin that remains after the guilt has been forgiven.

in·dul·gent (in dul'jənt) adj. characterized by indulgence: an indulgent parent. —**in·dul'gent·ly,** adv.

In·dus (in'dəs) n. a river flowing from Tibet through Kashmir and Pakistan into the Arabian Sea.

in·dus·tri·al (in dus'trē əl) adj. **1.** relating to, connected with, or produced by industry: industrial workers, industrial wastes. **2.** having highly developed industry: an industrial society. **3.** made for the use of industry: industrial buildings, industrial equipment. —**in·dus'tri·al·ly,** adv.

in·dus·tri·al·ist (in dus'trē ə list) n. a person who owns, manages, or has to do with industry.

in·dus·tri·al·ize (in dus'trē ə līz') v.t., **in·dus·tri·al·ized, in·dus·tri·al·iz·ing.** to set up or develop industry in: to industrialize an area, to industrialize a country's economy. —**in·dus'tri·al·i·za'tion,** n.

Industrial Revolution, the changes in the way of living and the economy of people in Europe and the United States, beginning in the eighteenth century in England. It resulted from the development of factories with machines for manufacturing products, and the use of power from steam, oil, or electricity in place of human and animal power.

in·dus·tri·ous (in dus'trē əs) adj. hard-working; diligent: a nation of industrious people. —**in·dus'tri·ous·ly,** adv. —**in·dus'tri·ous·ness,** n.

in·dus·try (in'dəs trē) n. pl., **in·dus·tries. 1.** manufacturing plants and other businesses considered as a whole: The townspeople are interested in attracting industry to their area. **2.** a particular branch of business, trade, or manufacturing: the tourist industry, the aircraft industry. **3.** hard work; steady effort; diligence: He shows much industry in performing his job.

-ine suffix (used to form adjectives from nouns) of, like, or relating to: Alpine.

in·e·bri·ate (v., i nē'brē āt'; n., i nē'brē it) v.t., **in·e·bri·at·ed, in·e·bri·at·ing.** to make drunk. —n. a person who is drunk. —**in·e·bri·a'tion,** n.

in·ed·i·ble (in ed'ə bəl) adj. not fit as food; unsuitable for eating: The burned meat was inedible.

in·ef·fa·ble (in ef'ə bəl) adj. that cannot be fully described in words: The view from the mountain at dawn is one of ineffable beauty. —**in·ef·fa·bil'i·ty,** n. —**in·ef'fa·bly,** adv.

in·ef·fec·tive (in'i fek'tiv) adj. **1.** not able to bring about a desired effect; not effective: The method he suggested for curing hiccups was ineffective. **2.** not able or competent: He is an ineffective person. —**in'ef·fec'tive·ly,** adv. —**in'ef·fec'tive·ness,** n.

in·ef·fec·tu·al (in'i fek'choo əl) adj. that cannot or does not produce a desired effect: ineffectual action, ineffectual advice. —**in'ef·fec'tu·al·ly,** adv.

in·ef·fi·cien·cy (in'i fish'ən sē) n. the state, quality, or fact of being inefficient.

in·ef·fi·cient (in'i fish'ənt) adj. involving, causing, or resulting in too much effort or waste; not efficient. —**in'ef·fi'cient·ly,** adv.

in·e·las·tic (in'i las'tik) adj. not elastic. —**in'e·las·tic'i·ty,** n.

in·el·e·gant (in el'ə gənt) adj. not elegant. —**in·el'e·gance,** n. —**in·el'e·gant·ly,** adv.

in·el·i·gi·ble (in el'i jə bəl) adj. not qualified to be chosen: He is ineligible for the team because of his poor grades. —n. a person who is ineligible. —**in·el'i·gi·bil'i·ty,** n. —**in·el'i·gi·bly,** adv.

in·ept (i nept') adj. **1.** awkward or clumsy: He is inept at changing a tire. **2.** out of place; not suitable: That is an inept remark. —**in·ept'ly,** adv. —**in·ept'ness,** n.

in·ep·ti·tude (i nep'tə tood', i nep'tə tyood') n. **1.** the quality of being inept. **2.** an inept act or remark.

in·e·qual·i·ty (in'i kwol'ə tē) n. pl., **in·e·qual·i·ties. 1.** the fact or condition of not being equal. **2.** a mathematical statement showing that two numbers are not equal or that one number is greater or less than another number.

in·eq·ui·ta·ble (in ek'wə tə bəl) adj. not fair and just; not equitable. —**in·eq'ui·ta·bly,** adv.

in·eq·ui·ty (in ek'wə tē) n. pl., **in·eq·ui·ties. 1.** injustice; unfairness. **2.** something that is unfair and unjust.

in·e·rad·i·ca·ble (in'i rad'i kə bəl) adj. that cannot be eradicated or gotten rid of. —**in'e·rad'i·ca·bly,** adv.

in·ert (i nurt') adj. **1.** without power to move or act; not moving. **2.** not reacting or combining readily with other substances; chemically inactive: Helium is an inert gas. **3.** not active; sluggish; slow.

in·er·tia (i nur'shə) n. **1.** the tendency not to move or change: His inertia kept him from beginning his work. **2.** Physics. the property of all matter that causes it to remain in a state of rest if at rest, or, if moving, to continue moving in a straight line at a constant speed, unless acted upon by an outside force.

in·es·cap·a·ble (in'is kā'pə bəl) adj. that cannot be escaped or avoided; certain: inescapable defeat. —**in'es·cap'a·bly,** adv.

in·es·ti·ma·ble (in es'tə mə bəl) adj. that cannot be estimated, measured, or valued; very great: His friendship is of inestimable worth to me. —**in·es'ti·ma·bly,** adv.

in·ev·i·ta·ble (i nev'ə tə bəl) adj. that cannot be avoided; obvious or certain: an inevitable result. —**in·ev'i·ta·bil'i·ty,** n. —**in·ev'i·ta·bly,** adv.

in·ex·act (in'ig zakt') adj. not exact; not completely correct. —**in'ex·act'ly,** adv. —**in'ex·act'ness,** n.

in·ex·cus·a·ble (in'iks kyōo'zə bəl) adj. that cannot be excused or justified: Cruelty to animals is completely inexcusable. —**in'ex·cus'a·bly,** adv.

in·ex·haust·i·ble (in'ig zôs'tə bəl) adj. **1.** that cannot be used up easily: He seemed to have an inexhaustible supply of paper in his desk. **2.** that does not become easily worn out or tired out; tireless: He is an inexhaustible swimmer. —**in'ex·haust'i·bil'i·ty,** n. —**in'ex·haust'i·bly,** adv.

in·ex·o·ra·ble (i nek'sər ə bəl) adj. that does not change, stop, or yield, no matter what anyone says or does; unyielding: Fate is inexorable. —**in·ex'o·ra·bil'i·ty,** n. —**in·ex'o·ra·bly,** adv.

in·ex·pe·di·ent (in'iks pē'dē ənt) adj. not suitable or useful for a given purpose; not expedient. —**in'ex·pe'di·en·cy,** n. —**in'ex·pe'di·ent·ly,** adv.

in·ex·pen·sive (in'iks pen'siv) adj. not costing much; cheap: an inexpensive dress. —**in'ex·pen'sive·ly,** adv. —**in'ex·pen'sive·ness,** n.

in·ex·pe·ri·ence (in'iks pēr'ē əns) n. lack of experience, or of the knowledge or skill that comes with experience.

in·ex·pe·ri·enced (in'iks pēr'ē ənst) adj. lacking experience, knowledge, or skill: *an inexperienced swimmer.*

in·ex·pert (in eks′purt) *adj.* not expert; unskilled. —**in·ex′pert·ly,** *adv.* —**in·ex′pert·ness,** *n.*

in·ex·plic·a·ble (in′iks plik′ə bəl, in eks′pli kə bəl) *adj.* that cannot be explained: *His odd behavior is inexplicable.* —**in′ex·plic′a·bil′i·ty,** *n.* —**in′ex·plic′a·bly,** *adv.*

in·ex·press·i·ble (in′iks pres′ə bəl) *adj.* that cannot be put into words: *inexpressible feelings.* —**in′ex·press′i·bil′i·ty,** *n.* —**in′ex·press′i·bly,** *adv.*

in·ex·pres·sive (in′iks pres′iv) *adj.* having or showing little feeling or meaning; not expressive.

in·ex·tin·guish·a·ble (in′iks ting′gwi shə bəl) *adj.* that cannot be put out or destroyed: *an inextinguishable flame.* —**in′ex·tin′guish·a·bly,** *adv.*

in·ex·tri·ca·ble (in eks′tri kə bəl) *adj.* **1.** that cannot be cleared up or untangled: *an inextricable knot, inextricable confusion.* **2.** that cannot be escaped from: *His lying got him in an inextricable situation.* —**in·ex′tri·ca·bly,** *adv.*

in·fal·li·ble (in fal′ə bəl) *adj.* **1.** not able to make a mistake: *No one is infallible.* **2.** reliable; unfailing; sure: *an infallible solution.* —**in·fal′li·bil′i·ty,** *n.* —**in·fal′li·bly,** *adv.*

in·fa·mous (in′fə məs) *adj.* **1.** widely known for wrongdoing; having a wicked reputation: *an infamous criminal.* **2.** having or deserving condemnation; very bad: *infamous crimes.* —**in′fa·mous·ly,** *adv.*

in·fa·my (in′fə mē) *n. pl.,* **in·fa·mies. 1.** the condition of being widely known for wrongdoing. **2.** the quality of being extremely bad: *The great infamy of these crimes will live long in history.* **3.** an infamous act: *the infamies of war.*

in·fan·cy (in′fən sē) *n. pl.,* **in·fan·cies. 1.** the condition or period of being an infant. **2.** the earliest period of development of anything: *Twenty years ago the electronic computer was still in its infancy.*

in·fant (in′fənt) *n.* **1.** a child during the earliest period of life; baby. **2.** *Law.* a person who has not reached the age of legal responsibility; minor. —*adj.* **1.** of, relating to, or for an infant: *infant care, infant toys.* **2.** in the earliest period of development: *an infant industry.* [Latin *īnfāns* baby; literally, a person not yet able to speak.]

in·fan·ti·cide[1] (in fan′tə sīd′) *n.* the killing of an infant. [Late Latin *īnfanticīdium,* from Latin *īnfāns* an infant + *-cīdium* a killing.]

in·fan·ti·cide[2] (in fan′tə sīd′) *n.* a person who kills an infant. [Late Latin *īnfanticīda,* from Latin *īnfāns* an infant + *-cīda* a killer.]

in·fan·tile (in′fən tīl′) *adj.* **1.** too much like an infant; childish: *His behavior is infantile when he can't get his way.* **2.** of, relating to, or belonging to infancy.

infantile paralysis, another term for **poliomyelitis.**

in·fan·try (in′fən trē) *n. pl.,* **in·fan·tries. 1.** soldiers trained and equipped to fight on foot. **2.** the branch of an army made up of such soldiers.

in·fan·try·man (in′fən trē mən) *n. pl.,* **in·fan·try·men** (in′fən trē mən). a man who is in the infantry.

in·fat·u·ate (in fach′ōō āt′) *v.t.,* **in·fat·u·at·ed, in·fat·u·at·ing.** to cause to have a foolish or childish attraction or passion: *She was infatuated with the captain of the football team.* —**in·fat′u·a′tion,** *n.*

in·fect (in fekt′) *v.t.* **1.** to cause disease in or contaminate by introducing germs: *The filthy bandage infected the wound.* **2.** to affect or influence: *His happiness infected those around him.*

in·fec·tion (in fek′shən) *n.* **1.** the entering of part of the body by certain germs that cause disease. **2.** a disease or other harmful condition resulting from this. **3.** the state of being infected.

in·fec·tious (in fek′shəs) *adj.* **1.** (of a disease) that can

be spread by infection. **2.** that can affect or influence others: *infectious laughter.* —**in·fec′tious·ly,** *adv.* —**in·fec′tious·ness,** *n.*

infectious mononucleosis, a contagious, but usually not serious, blood disease in which there are too many of a certain kind of white blood cell in the blood. It is characterized by fever, loss of appetite, and tiredness, and is thought to be caused by a virus.

in·fe·lic·i·tous (in′fə lis′ə təs) *adj.* **1.** not appropriate or suitable; unfitting: *an infelicitous comment.* **2.** unfortunate; unhappy: *an infelicitous happening.*

in·fe·lic·i·ty (in′fə lis′ə tē) *n. pl.,* **in·fe·lic·i·ties. 1.** the state or quality of being infelicitous. **2.** something that is infelicitous.

in·fer (in fur′) *v.t.,* **in·ferred, in·fer·ring.** to come to (an opinion) by reasoning from facts or observations: *From his grades I inferred that he was a good student.* ▲ **Infer** and **imply** have different meanings. To **infer** is to draw a conclusion from something that is known or hinted at: *They inferred from his frown that he was upset.* To **imply** is to suggest something without stating it directly: *His frown implied that he was upset.*

in·fer·ence (in′fər əns) *n.* **1.** something that is inferred; conclusion. **2.** the act or process of inferring.

in·fe·ri·or (in fēr′ē ər) *adj.* **1.** of poor quality; below average: *The food at that restaurant is inferior.* **2.** low or lower in quality, value, rank, or importance: *She always felt inferior to her older sister.* —*n.* a person who is inferior to others, as in rank or importance.

in·fe·ri·or·i·ty (in fēr′ē ôr′ə tē, in fēr′ē or′ə tē) *n.* the quality or condition of being inferior.

inferiority complex, a general feeling that one is of little worth or importance. At times a person with an inferiority complex tries to cover up such a feeling with arrogant, aggressive behavior.

in·fer·nal (in furn′əl) *adj.* **1.** of, relating to, or characteristic of hell. **2.** like or appropriate to hell; hellish: *infernal cruelty.* **3.** *Informal.* hateful: *an infernal nuisance.* —**in·fer′nal·ly,** *adv.*

in·fer·no (in fur′nō) *n. pl.,* **in·fer·nos. 1.** hell. **2.** any place resembling hell: *The furnace room was an inferno.*

in·fer·tile (in furt′əl) *adj.* not fertile; barren. —**in′fer·til′i·ty,** *n.*

in·fest (in fest′) *v.t.* to grow, spread, or exist in large numbers so as to cause trouble or harm: *Weeds infested the garden.* —**in′fes·ta′tion,** *n.*

in·fi·del (in′fəd əl) *n.* **1.** a person who does not believe in any religion. **2.** among Muslims, a person who does not accept Islam. **3.** among Christians, a person who does not accept Christianity. —*adj.* **1.** having no religious beliefs. **2.** not accepting a particular faith, such as Christianity or Islam.

in·fi·del·i·ty (in′fi del′ə tē) *n. pl.,* **in·fi·del·i·ties. 1.** lack of religious faith. **2.** unfaithfulness in marriage; adultery.

in·field (in′fēld′) *n. Baseball.* **1.** the area bounded by the paths connecting the bases. **2.** the first, second, and third basemen and the shortstop.

in·field·er (in′fēl′dər) *n. Baseball.* a player who plays a position in the infield.

I

at; āpe; cär; end; mē; it; īce; hot; ōld; fôrk; wood; fōōl; oil; out; up; turn; sing; thin; this; hw in white; zh in treasure. The symbol ə stands for the sound of **a** in about, **e** in taken, **i** in pencil, **o** in lemon, and **u** in circus.

in·fil·trate (in fil′trāt, in′fil trāt′) *v.*, **in·fil·trat·ed**, **in·fil·trat·ing.** —*v.t.* **1.** to move gradually and secretly into or through: *to infiltrate enemy lines. Members of the secret police infiltrated the revolutionary organization.* **2.** to filter into or through; permeate. —*v.i.* to pass into or through a substance by filtering. —**in′fil·tra′tion,** *n.*

infin., infinitive.

in·fi·nite (in′fə nit) *adj.* **1.** having no limits or end; boundless: *Outer space seems to be infinite.* **2.** very great; immense; vast: *She takes infinite pains with her work.* **3.** *Mathematics.* of or designating a quantity larger than any assigned number. —*n.* **1.** something that is infinite. **2.** *Mathematics.* an infinite quantity. **3. the Infinite.** God. —**in′fi·nite·ly,** *adv.* —**in′fi·nite·ness,** *n.*

in·fi·ni·tes·i·mal (in′fi nə tes′ə məl) *adj.* so small as to be hard or impossible to measure: *an infinitesimal speck of dust.* —**in′fi·ni·tes′i·mal·ly,** *adv.*

in·fin·i·tive (in fin′ə tiv) *n.* a simple verb form that does not indicate person or number and is often preceded by *to.* In the sentences *He likes to run* and *We must leave, to run* and *leave* are infinitives.

in·fin·i·tude (in fin′ə tōod′, in fin′ə tyōod′) *n.* **1.** the quality of being infinite. **2.** an infinite quantity.

in·fin·i·ty (in fin′ə tē) *n. pl.,* **in·fin·i·ties. 1.** the state or quality of being infinite. **2.** something that is infinite, such as space or time. **3.** a very great amount or number: *an infinity of details.* **4.** *Mathematics.* a quantity of unlimited magnitude, larger than any assigned number, represented by the symbol ∞.

in·firm (in furm′) *adj.* **1.** physically weak, as from old age: *an infirm old man.* **2.** lacking firmness of will, purpose, or character. —**in·firm′ly,** *adv.* —**in·firm′ness,** *n.*

in·fir·ma·ry (in fur′mər ē) *n. pl.,* **in·fir·ma·ries.** a place for the care or treatment of the sick or injured. Schools and factories have infirmaries.

in·fir·mi·ty (in fur′mə tē) *n. pl.,* **in·fir·mi·ties. 1.** the state or quality of being infirm; physical weakness; feebleness. **2.** a physical defect or ailment.

in·flame (in flām′) *v.t.,* **in·flamed, in·flam·ing. 1.** to excite to great emotion; stir up: *The speaker inflamed his listeners with his speech.* **2.** to make hot, red, swollen, or painful: *The infection inflamed his finger.*

in·flam·ma·ble (in flam′ə bəl) *adj.* **1.** that can be set on fire easily: *an inflammable fluid.* **2.** easily excited or aroused: *an inflammable temper.* —*n.* something that can be set on fire easily. —**in·flam′ma·bil′i·ty,** *n.*

in·flam·ma·tion (in′flə mā′shən) *n.* **1.** a condition of a part of the body caused by a reaction to injury, infection, or irritation, and characterized by heat, redness, swelling, and pain. **2.** the act of inflaming or the state of being inflamed.

in·flam·ma·to·ry (in flam′ə tôr′ē) *adj.* **1.** tending to excite strong emotion or violent action: *an inflammatory speech.* **2.** relating to or characterized by inflammation.

in·flat·a·ble (in flā′tə bəl) *adj.* that can be inflated: *an inflatable rubber raft.*

in·flate (in flāt′) *v.,* **in·flat·ed, in·flat·ing.** —*v.t.* **1.** to cause to swell by filling with air or gas: *to inflate a balloon.* **2.** to cause to puff up, especially with pride: *His sudden fame inflated his ego.* **3.** to increase beyond usual levels: *to inflate prices.* —*v.i.* to become inflated. —**in·flat′er; also, in·fla′tor,** *n.*

in·fla·tion (in flā′shən) *n.* **1.** the act of inflating or the state of being inflated. **2.** a rise in the usual price level for goods and services, usually caused by an increase in money supply without a corresponding increase in the supply of goods and services.

in·fla·tion·ar·y (in flā′shə ner′ē) *adj.* of, relating to, or causing inflation.

in·flect (in flekt′) *v.t.* **1.** to change or vary the tone or pitch of (the voice). **2.** to vary the form of (a word) to show tense, number, case, and the like. **3.** to turn from a direct line or course; bend: *to inflect rays of light.*

in·flec·tion (in flek′shən) *also, British,* **in·flex·ion.** *n.* **1.** a change or variation in the tone or pitch of the voice: *A person usually raises the inflection of his voice to ask a question.* **2.** *Language.* a process by which the form of a word is changed to show tense, number, case, and the like. **3.** the act of inflecting or the state of being inflected. **4.** a bend or angle.

● In language, **inflection** is the changing of the form of a word in order to show that there is a change in the use or meaning of the word in a sentence. In English, nouns, pronouns, verbs, adjectives and adverbs are inflected. The inflections of a noun are called its *declension.* The forms of a noun tell you whether the noun is singular or plural and whether or not it is possessive, such as *girl, girls, girl's,* and *girls'.* Pronouns are inflected to indicate the possessive form, the subjective form, and the objective form, such as *our, we,* and *us.*

The inflected forms of a verb are called its *conjugation.* The verb *dance* is conjugated *dance, dances* (for the third person singular), *danced,* and *dancing.* The inflected forms of an English adjective or adverb show comparison and are called the *comparative* and the *superlative* forms. The adjective *tall* has the comparative form *taller* and the superlative form *tallest.* Adverbs are inflected less often than adjectives. We usually use the words *more* or *most* before an adverb in order to produce the same effect that inflection has, as in *quickly, more quickly,* and *most quickly.* Some adverbs, such as *fast,* whose inflected forms are *faster* and *fastest,* are inflected in the same way that most adjectives are.

in·flec·tion·al (in flek′shən əl) *also, British,* **in·flex·ion·al.** *adj.* of or showing grammatical inflection.

in·flex·i·ble (in flek′sə bəl) *adj.* **1.** that cannot be bent; stiff; rigid: *an inflexible metal rod.* **2.** unyielding in mind or purpose; adamant: *Chris is an inflexible person who never admits he is wrong.* **3.** that cannot be changed or altered. —**in·flex·i·bil′i·ty,** *n.* —**in·flex′i·bly,** *adv.*

in·flict (in flikt′) *v.t.* **1.** to cause: *to inflict pain, to inflict a wound.* **2.** to impose (something unwelcome) on someone: *to inflict a burden, to inflict punishment.*

in·flic·tion (in flik′shən) *n.* **1.** the act of inflicting. **2.** something that is inflicted, such as punishment.

in·flo·res·cence (in′flô res′əns) *n.* a cluster of flowers on a stem or stems, or the arrangement of flowers in such a cluster.

in·flow (in′flō′) *n.* **1.** the act of flowing in. **2.** something that flows in.

in·flu·ence (in′flōo əns) *n.* **1.** the power or ability of a person or thing to produce an effect on others: *Ted's brother has great influence over him.* **2.** an effect produced in this way: *That teacher had a great influence on his career.* **3.** a person or thing that has the power to affect others: *His friends were a bad influence on him.* —*v.t.,* **in·flu·enced, in·flu·enc·ing. 1.** to change or affect the thought

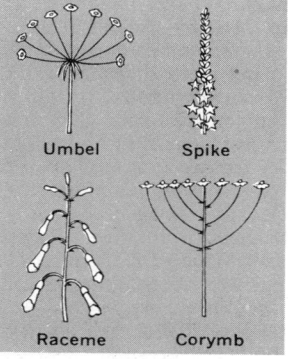

Umbel   Spike

Raceme   Corymb

Inflorescence

or behavior of; persuade; sway: *He influenced his friend to stop smoking.* **2.** to have or produce an effect on; modify: *Her opinions influence my thinking.*

in·flu·en·tial (in′flōō en′shəl) *adj.* having or using influence: *Mr. Brown is a very influential person in that community.*

in·flu·en·za (in′flōō en′zə) *n.* a highly contagious disease, characterized by fever, headache, coughing, exhaustion, and inflammation of the mucous membranes. Also, **flu.** [Italian *influenza,* a fluid that supposedly flowed from the stars and affected people; because the disease was once thought to be caused by this fluid.]

in·flux (in′fluks′) *n.* a continual flowing in: *the influx of goods into a country.*

in·fold (in fōld′) another spelling of **enfold.**

in·form (in fôrm′) *v.t.* to give information to; tell: *Please inform me when the train arrives.* —*v.i.* to reveal something secret or damaging: *The thief informed on the other members of the gang.*

in·for·mal (in fôr′məl) *adj.* **1.** not marked by, needing, or following fixed rules or ceremonies; not formal; relaxed: *informal behavior, an informal wedding.* **2.** suitable for everyday or ordinary use or occasions: *informal clothes, an informal conversation.* **3.** suitable for everyday speaking or writing. —**in·for′mal·ly,** *adv.*

● **Informal** language is language that, although it is correct, is not appropriate for all situations. If you were making a speech, writing a book report, or being introduced to an important person, you probably would not use quite the same words that you would use in your everyday conversations with your friends or family. This is not because these words are wrong, but because the situation is formal. Most people use different words in different situations without even being aware of it. For example, try to imagine the times when you would say *hi,* rather than *how do you do; thanks a lot,* rather than *I thank you very much;* or *it was loads of fun,* rather than *I had a very enjoyable time.* Although each of these examples is correct English, you can see that they would be used in different ways. Most of us use informal language as our normal way of speaking and writing. As in the case of most other problems of usage in our language, there are no real "rights" and "wrongs" in using informal or formal language, but only a question of what kind of language is most appropriate to the situation.

---

in·for·mal·i·ty (in′fôr mal′ə tē) *n. pl.,* **in·for·mal·i·ties. 1.** the state or quality of being informal. **2.** an informal act.

in·form·ant (in fôr′mənt) *n.* a person who gives information.

in·for·ma·tion (in′fər mā′shən) *n.* **1.** knowledge or facts about something: *He asked for information about the train schedule. She got her information on that subject from an encyclopedia.* **2.** the act of informing or the state of being informed. **3.** a person or service that answers questions and gives facts: *Henry called information for the telephone number.*

in·form·a·tive (in fôr′mə tiv) *adj.* giving information; instructive: *an informative book.*

in·form·er (in fôr′mər) *n.* **1.** a person who informs on others, often for money: *He was an informer for the secret police.* **2.** any person who informs; informant.

in·frac·tion (in frak′shən) *n.* the act of breaking a law or rule; violation: *He committed an infraction of the law when he threw litter in the street.*

in·fra·red (in′frə red′) *adj.* of or relating to electromagnetic radiation whose wavelengths are longer than those

of visible light but shorter than those of radio waves. When a body absorbs infrared radiation, the body becomes heated.

in·fre·quent (in frē′kwənt) *adj.* not happening or appearing often; not frequent; rare: *He makes infrequent visits to his old home town.* —**in·fre′quen·cy,** *n.* —**in·fre′quent·ly,** *adv.*

in·fringe (in frinj′) *v.,* **in·fringed, in·fring·ing.** —*v.i.* to go or thrust in without a right; encroach; trespass: *That law infringes on the rights of the people.* —*v.t.* to break or violate: *to infringe a law.* —**in·fringe′ment,** *n.* —**in·fring′er,** *n.*

in·fu·ri·ate (in fyoor′ē āt′) *v.t.,* **in·fu·ri·at·ed, in·fu·ri·at·ing.** to make furious; enrage: *The bully's taunts infuriated him.* —**in·fu′ri·a′tion,** *n.*

in·fuse (in fyooz′) *v.t.,* **in·fused, in·fus·ing. 1.** to put in gradually; instill: *The officer infused courage into his troops.* **2.** to inspire; imbue: *The boys' mother infused them with a sense of responsibility.* **3.** to steep or soak in a liquid: *She infused the tea leaves in the hot water.*

in·fu·sion (in fyoo′zhən) *n.* **1.** the act or process of infusing. **2.** a substance that is obtained by infusion: *a strong infusion of tea.*

-ing[1] *suffix* **1.** (used to form nouns from verbs) **a.** the act, art, process, or instance of performing the action of the root verb: *her sewing, their meeting, our skating.* **b.** the result of such action: *to make a drawing, to give a reading.* **2.** material used for a particular purpose: *lining, roofing, scaffolding.* **3.** something that does the action of the root verb: *bedding, covering.* [Old English *-ing, -ung.*]

-ing[2] *suffix* **1.** used to form the present participle of verbs: *He is walking. We were talking.* **2.** used to form adjectives from the present participle of verbs: *a charming woman, a leading citizen.* [Middle English *-ing, -inge,* a form of *-ind, -end,* from Old English *-ende.*]

in·gen·ious (in jēn′yəs) *adj.* **1.** made with or showing cleverness, originality, or imagination: *an ingenious plan, an ingenious mechanical toy.* **2.** having creative ability; imaginative; inventive: *an ingenious designer, an ingenious mystery writer.* —**in·gen′ious·ly,** *adv.* —**in·gen′ious·ness,** *n.*

in·gé·nue (än′jə nōō′) *also,* **in·ge·nue.** *n. pl.,* **in·gé·nues. 1.** an innocent or naive girl or young woman. **2.** the role of such a person in a play. **3.** an actress who plays such a role. [French *ingénue.*]

in·ge·nu·i·ty (in′jə nōō′ə tē) *n.* the quality of being ingenious; cleverness or originality: *The boy showed great ingenuity in building the radio from old parts.*

in·gen·u·ous (in jen′yōō əs) *adj.* **1.** honest and frank; straightforward; candid: *He was ingenuous with us, and told us exactly what happened.* **2.** innocent and simple; naive: *The child has an ingenuous manner.* —**in·gen′u·ous·ly,** *adv.* —**in·gen′u·ous·ness,** *n.*

in·gest (in jest′) *v.t.* to take or put (food) into the body for digestion. —**in·ges′tion,** *n.*

in·gle·nook (ing′gəl nook′) *n.* a corner beside a chimney or fireplace.

in·glo·ri·ous (in glôr′ē əs) *adj.* bringing no glory or honor; shameful; disgraceful: *an inglorious past.* —**in·glo′ri·ous·ly,** *adv.* —**in·glo′ri·ous·ness,** *n.*

---

at; āpe; cär; end; mē; it; īce; hot; ōld; fôrk; wood; fōōl; oil; out; up; turn; sing; thin; this; hw in white; zh in treasure. The symbol ə stands for the sound of **a** in about, **e** in taken, **i** in pencil, **o** in lemon, and **u** in circus.

in·got (ing′gət) *n.* a mass of metal cast into a shape, such as a bar or block.

in·graft (in graft′) another spelling of **engraft**.

in·grain (in grān′) *v.t.* to set or place deeply and lastingly; fix firmly.

in·grained (in grānd′) *adj.* deeply and lastingly fixed: *ingrained prejudice, an ingrained habit.*

in·grate (in′grāt′) *n.* an ungrateful person.

in·gra·ti·ate (in grā′shē āt′) *v.t.,* **in·gra·ti·at·ed, in·gra·ti·at·ing.** to bring (oneself) into another's favor: *The boy tried to ingratiate himself with the football star by running errands for him.* —**in·gra′ti·at′ing·ly,** *adv.*

in·grat·i·tude (in grat′ə tōōd′, in grat′ə tyōōd′) *n.* lack of gratitude or appreciation.

in·gre·di·ent (in grē′dē ənt) *n.* **1.** any one of the parts of a mixture: *Flour, eggs, and sugar are the ingredients of this cake.* **2.** a part of anything: *Working at a job that one enjoys is an ingredient of a happy life.*

in·gress (in′gres) *n. pl.,* **in·gress·es. 1.** the act of going in; entrance. **2.** a place of entrance. **3.** the right to go in: *Everyone in town has ingress to the park.*

in·grown (in′grōn′) *adj.* grown into the flesh, as a hair or toenail.

in·hab·it (in hab′it) *v.t.* to live in or on: *Many birds inhabit the forest.*

in·hab·it·a·ble (in hab′i tə bəl) *adj.* that can be lived in or on: *an inhabitable planet.*

in·hab·it·ant (in hab′ət ənt) *n.* a person or animal that lives permanently in a place; resident.

in·hal·ant (in hā′lənt) *n.* a medicine to be inhaled. —*adj.* used for inhaling.

in·ha·la·tion (in′hə lā′shən) *n.* the act of inhaling.

in·ha·la·tor (in′hə lā′tər) *n.* a device used for inhaling medicine.

in·hale (in hāl′) *v.,* **in·haled, in·hal·ing.** —*v.t.* to draw into the lungs: *He inhaled the fresh, clean mountain air.* —*v.i.* to draw something, such as air or tobacco smoke, into the lungs.

in·hal·er (in hā′lər) *n.* **1.** another word for **inhalator**. **2.** a device used to filter air that is breathed. **3.** a person who inhales something.

in·har·mo·ni·ous (in′här mō′nē əs) *adj.* not in harmony or agreement: *inharmonious sounds, an inharmonious family.* —**in′har·mo·ni·ous·ly,** *adv.* —**in′har·mo·ni·ous·ness,** *n.*

in·her·ent (in hēr′ənt, in her′ənt) *adj.* forming a permanent or basic part of a person or thing: *Her inherent good judgment kept her from making many mistakes.* —**in·her′ent·ly,** *adv.*

in·her·it (in her′it) *v.t.* **1.** to receive from a former owner at his or her death: *She inherited the jewelry from her aunt.* **2.** to receive from one's parent or parents: *The little boy inherited his mother's good temper.* **3.** to receive or come into possession of in any way: *He inherited the old furniture when he bought the house.*

in·her·it·ance (in her′it əns) *n.* **1.** something that is or may be inherited; legacy: *He received a large inheritance from his aunt.* **2.** the act or fact of inheriting.

inheritance tax, a tax that is imposed on inherited property.

in·her·i·tor (in her′i tər) *n.* a person who inherits something; heir.

in·hib·it (in hib′it) *v.t.* to hold back; check; restrain: *Shyness inhibited him when he was with strangers.*

in·hi·bi·tion (in′hi bish′ən) *n.* **1.** a restraint or check on some activity or on one's natural impulses: *The young man's inhibitions kept him from speaking up.* **2.** the act of inhibiting or the state of being inhibited.

in·hos·pi·ta·ble (in hos′pi tə bəl, in′hos pit′ə bəl) *adj.*

1. not offering hospitality to guests or visitors; not hospitable; unfriendly. **2.** not providing food, shelter, or other accommodation: *The arid land was very inhospitable to the settlers.* —**in·hos′pi·ta·bly,** *adv.*

in·hu·man (in hyōō′mən) *adj.* **1.** lacking kindness, pity, or compassion; cruel; brutal: *inhuman treatment, an inhuman punishment.* **2.** not like or characteristic of a human being. —**in·hu′man·ly,** *adv.*

in·hu·mane (in′hyōō mān′) *adj.* not feeling or showing kindness, pity, or compassion for other human beings or animals; not humane. —**in′hu·mane′ly,** *adv.*

in·hu·man·i·ty (in′hyōō man′ə tē) *n. pl.,* **in·hu·man·i·ties. 1.** the quality or condition of being inhuman or inhumane; lack of kindness, pity, or compassion. **2.** an instance of this.

in·im·i·cal (in im′i kəl) *adj.* **1.** unfriendly; hostile: *She was inimical to my suggestion.* **2.** causing harm; injurious: *Lack of sleep is inimical to good health.* —**in·im′i·cal·ly,** *adv.*

in·im·i·ta·ble (in im′ə tə bəl) *adj.* that cannot be imitated; matchless: *the inimitable beauty of a sunset.* —**in·im′i·ta·bil′i·ty,** *n.* —**in·im′i·ta·bly,** *adv.*

in·iq·ui·tous (in ik′wə təs) *adj.* unjust or wicked: *an iniquitous act.* —**in·iq′ui·tous·ly,** *adv.* —**in·iq′ui·tous·ness,** *n.*

in·iq·ui·ty (in ik′wə tē) *n. pl.,* **in·iq·ui·ties. 1.** a great injustice or wickedness: *the iniquity of a dictatorship.* **2.** a wicked or unjust act or deed.

i·ni·tial (i nish′əl) *adj.* of, relating to, or occurring at the beginning; first: *"R" is the initial letter of the word "rug."* —*n.* the first letter of a word or a name. —*v.t.,* **i·ni·tialed, i·ni·tial·ing;** *also, British,* **i·ni·tialled, i·ni·tial·ling.** to mark or sign with one's initial or initials: *He initialed the report after reading it.*

i·ni·tial·ly (i nish′ə lē) *adv.* at the beginning.

i·ni·ti·ate (*v.,* i nish′ē āt′; *n.,* i nish′ē it) *v.t.,* **i·ni·ti·at·ed, i·ni·ti·at·ing. 1.** to introduce or begin: *The librarian initiated a policy of lending books for a month.* **2.** to admit (a person) into an organization or group, especially with formal ceremonies: *He was initiated into the club.* **3.** to introduce or instruct in some subject or practice: *The scoutmaster initiated the boys in knot tying.* —*n.* a person who has been initiated into an organization or group. —**i·ni′ti·a·tor,** *n.*

i·ni·ti·a·tion (i nish′ē ā′shən) *n.* **1.** the act of initiating or the state of being initiated. **2.** the ceremonies by which one is admitted to an organization or group.

i·ni·tia·tive (i nish′ə tiv) *n.* **1.** the first step in doing or beginning something; lead: *She took the initiative by introducing herself first.* **2.** the ability to take a first step in beginning or doing something: *He did not have much initiative.* **3.** the right of citizens to introduce or enact a new law. **4.** the procedure by which this is done.

in·ject (in jekt′) *v.t.* **1.** to force (fluid) through the skin into a muscle, vein, or the like: *to inject serum into the bloodstream.* **2.** to throw in; introduce: *That lecturer often tries to inject humor into his talks.* —**in·jec′tor,** *n.*

in·jec·tion (in jek′shən) *n.* **1.** the act or process of injecting. **2.** the fluid that is injected.

in·ju·di·cious (in′jōō dish′əs) *adj.* showing lack of judgment; not judicious: *an injudicious decision.* —**in′ju·di′cious·ly,** *adv.* —**in′ju·di′cious·ness,** *n.*

in·junc·tion (in jungk′shən) *n.* **1.** a court order requiring or forbidding some act: *The mayor asked for an injunction against the strike.* **2.** a command; order.

in·jure (in′jər) *v.t.,* **in·jured, in·jur·ing. 1.** to do or cause damage to; harm: *He injured himself by falling off his bicycle.* **2.** to do wrong to: *She injured his reputation by spreading rumors about him.*

in·ju·ri·ous (in joor′ē əs) *adj.* causing harm or damage: *Pollution in the rivers is injurious to fish.* —**in·ju′ri·ous·ly,** *adv.* —**in·ju′ri·ous·ness,** *n.*

in·ju·ry (in′jər ē) *n. pl.,* **in·ju·ries.** damage or harm done to a person or thing: *The accident caused a slight injury to his leg.*

in·jus·tice (in jus′tis) *n.* **1.** the lack of justice; unfairness: *He protested the injustice of the court's ruling.* **2.** an unjust act: *He did his friend an injustice by calling him a liar.*

ink (ingk) *n.* **1.** a colored fluid or paste used for writing, drawing, or printing. **2.** a dark pigment ejected by cuttlefish, squids, and other sea animals for protection when frightened. —*v.t.* to mark, cover, or color with ink.

ink·horn (ingk′hôrn′) *n.* a small container made of horn or similar material, formerly used to hold ink.

ink·ling (ingk′ling) *n.* **1.** a vague idea or notion: *She had no inkling of what we were talking about.* **2.** a slight suggestion; hint: *They gave us no inkling of their plans.*

ink·stand (ingk′stand′) *n.* **1.** a stand or rack for holding containers of ink and pens. **2.** another word for **inkwell.**

ink·well (ingk′wel′) *n.* a container for ink, especially on a desk.

ink·y (ing′kē) *adj.,* **ink·i·er, ink·i·est. 1.** dark or black in color. **2.** marked, covered, or stained with ink. —**ink′i·ness,** *n.*

Inkwell

in·laid (in′lād′) *v.* the past participle of **inlay.** —*adj.* **1.** set into a surface as a decoration: *The box had inlaid ivory on the lid.* **2.** decorated with a material, such as gold or ivory, set into the surface: *The table had an inlaid top.*

in·land (in′lənd) *adj.* of, relating to, or located in the interior of a country or region; away from the coast or border: *an inland city, an inland waterway.* —*adv.* in or toward the interior of a country or region: *He drove inland from the coast for many miles.* —*n.* the interior part of a country or region.

in-law (in′lô′) *n. Informal.* a relative by marriage.

in·lay (*v.,* in lā′; *n.,* in′lā) *v.t.,* **in·laid, in·lay·ing. 1.** to set into the surface of something so as to form a decorative design: *The craftsman inlaid gold into the picture frame.* **2.** to decorate with a material set into the surface: *to inlay a cabinet with ivory.* —*n.* **1.** an inlaid design or material: *The jewel box is decorated with gold inlay.* **2.** a filling of gold, porcelain, or the like for a tooth.

in·let (in′let′) *n.* a narrow body of water between islands or leading inland from a larger body of water.

in·mate (in′māt′) *n.* a person confined in a prison, asylum, or similar place.

in me·mo·ri·am (in′mə môr′ē əm) as a memorial to; in memory of. [Latin *in memoriam.*]

in·most (in′mōst′) *adj.* farthest in; innermost.

inn (in) *n.* **1.** a small hotel, especially in the country. **2.** a restaurant or tavern.

in·nate (i nāt′, in′āt′) *adj.* **1.** that one has at birth; natural; inborn: *Her innate intelligence helped her make wise decisions.* **2.** being or forming a basic characteristic: *the innate humor of a situation.* —**in·nate′ly,** *adv.* —**in·nate′ness,** *n.*

in·ner (in′ər) *adj.* **1.** located farther in: *His desk was in the inner office.* **2.** of or relating to the mind or soul: *one's inner life.* **3.** more private or intimate; personal: *one's inner feelings.*

inner ear, the innermost part of the ear, behind the middle ear, containing the cochlea, the semicircular canals, and the vestibule.

in·ner·most (in′ər mōst′) *adj.* **1.** farthest from the outside; most inward: *the innermost part of a building.* **2.** most private or intimate; deepest: *one's innermost feelings.*

inner tube, a rubber tube used inside a tire to hold air.

in·ning (in′ing) *n.* a division of a baseball game in which both teams bat, the visiting team first, until three men on each team are put out.

inn·keep·er (in′kē′pər) *n.* a person who owns or manages an inn.

in·no·cence (in′ə səns) *n.* the state or quality of being innocent.

in·no·cent (in′ə sənt) *adj.* **1.** free from guilt or wrongdoing: *A defendant in a criminal case is innocent until proven guilty.* **2.** free from or knowing nothing of sin or evil; pure. **3.** not arising from or involving any bad motive; harmless: *an innocent prank, an innocent remark.* —*n.* a person, especially a child, who is free from or knows nothing of sin or evil. —**in′no·cent·ly,** *adv.*

in·noc·u·ous (i nok′yōō əs) *adj.* harmless; innocent. —**in·noc′u·ous·ly,** *adv.*

in·no·vate (in′ə vāt′) *v.,* **in·no·vat·ed, in·no·vat·ing.** —*v.t.* to introduce (something new): *to innovate a method of doing a job.* —*v.i.* to introduce something new; make changes in something. —**in′no·va′tor,** *n.*

in·no·va·tion (in′ə vā′shən) *n.* **1.** something newly introduced; change: *Anesthesia was a great innovation in medicine.* **2.** the act of innovating.

in·nu·en·do (in′yōō en′dō) *n. pl.,* **in·nu·en·does.** a hint or suggestion, especially one that is meant to cause harm or damage to a person's reputation: *Her comments were filled with innuendoes about his early life.*

in·nu·mer·a·ble (i nōō′mər ə bəl, i nyōō′mər ə bəl) *adj.* too many to be counted: *There are innumerable stars in the sky.* —**in·nu′mer·a·ble·ness,** *n.* —**in·nu′mer·a·bly,** *adv.*

in·oc·u·late (in ok′yə lāt′) *v.t.,* **in·oc·u·lat·ed, in·oc·u·lat·ing. 1.** to infect (a person or animal) with an organism that causes a disease, in order to produce that disease in a mild form so that immunity to the disease will result. **2.** to use (the organism that causes a disease) to prevent or cure that disease.

in·oc·u·la·tion (in ok′yə lā′shən) *n.* **1.** the act of inoculating. **2.** an injection given in order to produce immunity to a disease.

in·of·fen·sive (in′ə fen′siv) *adj.* not offensive; harmless: *an inoffensive person, inoffensive remarks.* —**in′of·fen′sive·ly,** *adv.* —**in′of·fen′sive·ness,** *n.*

in·op·er·a·tive (in op′ər ə tiv, in op′ə rā′tiv) *adj.* not working or producing an effect; not operative: *inoperative equipment, inoperative laws.*

in·op·por·tune (in op′ər tōōn′, in op′ər tyōōn′) *adj.* coming or happening at a bad time; untimely or inconvenient: *He chose an inopportune moment to visit us, just as we were leaving.* —**in·op′por·tune′ly,** *adv.* —**in·op′por·tune′ness,** *n.*

in·or·di·nate (in ôr′də nit) *adj.* beyond what is necessary or proper; too great; excessive: *inordinate demands.* —**in·or′di·nate·ly,** *adv.*

in·or·gan·ic (in′ôr gan′ik) *adj.* **1.** not related to, including, or made by animals or plants; not living: *Minerals are*

I

at; āpe; cär; end; mē; it; īce; hot; ōld; fôrk; wood; fōōl; oil; out; up; turn; sing; thin; this; hw in white; zh in treasure. The symbol ə stands for the sound of **a** in about, **e** in taken, **i** in pencil, **o** in lemon, and **u** in circus.

inorganic substances. **2.** of or relating to matter that is not organic: *Inorganic compounds include water and salt. Inorganic chemistry is the study of elements and compounds that do not contain carbon.* —**in′or·gan′i·cal·ly,** *adv.*

in·put (in′poot′) *n.* **1.** anything put or taken in. **2.** the power or energy that is put into something, such as a machine. **3.** the information fed into a computer.

in·quest (in′kwest) *n.* an inquiry made by a jury or other body appointed by law, especially one made to find out the cause of a sudden or violent death.

in·quire (in kwīr′) *also,* **en·quire.** *v.,* **in·quired, in·quir·ing.** —*v.i.* **1.** to seek knowledge or information by asking a question or questions: *We inquired about his health.* **2.** to make an investigation, search, or examination: *The police inquired into the suspect's background.* —*v.t.* to seek knowledge or information about by asking a question or questions: *We stopped at a gas station to inquire the way.* —**in·quir′er,** *n.* —**in·quir′ing·ly,** *adv.*

in·quir·y (in kwīr′ē, in′kwər ē) *also,* **en·quir·y.** *n. pl.,* **in·quir·ies.** **1.** the act of inquiring. **2.** an investigation, search, or examination: *scientific inquiry, an inquiry made by the police.* **3.** a question.

in·qui·si·tion (in′kwə zish′ən) *n.* **1.** strict or thorough inquiry or questioning. **2. the Inquisition.** the Roman Catholic court established in the thirteenth century to discover and punish heretics.

in·quis·i·tive (in kwiz′ə tiv) *adj.* **1.** eager for knowledge; curious: *He is an inquisitive child, always asking questions.* **2.** too curious; nosy; prying: *She is inquisitive about other people's business.* —**in·quis′i·tive·ly,** *adv.* —**in·quis′i·tive·ness,** *n.*

in·quis·i·tor (in kwiz′ə tər) *n.* **1.** a person who makes or conducts an inquisition or inquiry. **2. Inquisitor.** an official of the Inquisition.

in·road (in′rōd′) *n.* **1.** a sudden attack or raid. **2.** *also,* **inroads.** an advance that causes loss or injury to something or someone: *Paying the bills made inroads on her savings.*

in·rush (in′rush′) *n.* a sudden rushing or pouring in, as of water.

ins., inches.

in·sane (in sān′) *adj.* **1.** not having a sound or healthy mind; mentally ill; crazy. **2.** of or for insane people: *an insane asylum.* **3.** very foolish; senseless: *What an insane thing to do!* —**in·sane′ly,** *adv.*

in·san·i·tar·y (in san′ə ter′ē) *adj.* bad for health; not sanitary; unclean.

in·san·i·ty (in san′ə tē) *n. pl.,* **in·san·i·ties.** **1.** the state of being insane; mental illness. **2.** extreme folly; senselessness: *It was insanity to drive in that blizzard.*

in·sa·tia·ble (in sā′shə bəl) *adj.* that cannot be satisfied: *an insatiable thirst.* —**in·sa′tia·bly,** *adv.*

in·scribe (in skrīb′) *v.t.,* **in·scribed, in·scrib·ing.** **1.** to write, carve, engrave, or mark (words or characters) on something: *The stonecutter inscribed the date on the tombstone.* **2.** to write, carve, engrave, or mark words or characters on: *The jeweler inscribed the locket with the girl's initials.* **3.** to write a message or note on (something, such as a book) in giving it to someone. **4.** to draw (a geometric figure) within another figure so that the inner intersects the outer in as many points as possible: *to inscribe a circle within a square.* —**in·scrib′er,** *n.*

in·scrip·tion (in skrip′shən) *n.* **1.** something inscribed: *an inscription on a ring.* **2.** a message or note written on something, such as a book, in giving it to someone. **3.** the act of inscribing.

in·scru·ta·ble (in skrōō′tə bəl) *adj.* that cannot be easily understood; mysterious: *His inscrutable behavior left us all baffled.* —**in·scru′ta·bil′i·ty,** *n.* —**in·scru′ta·bly,** *adv.*

in·sect (in′sekt) *n.* **1.** any of a group of small animals without a backbone, having a body divided into three parts. Insects have three pairs of legs and, in the adult, usually two pairs of wings. Flies, ants, grasshoppers, and beetles are insects. **2.** any of various similar animals, such as ticks or spiders.

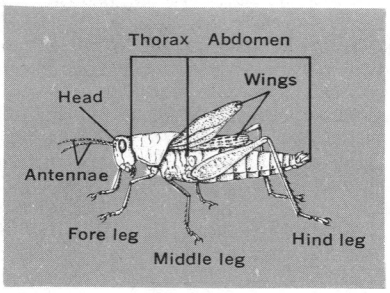

Thorax Abdomen

Wings

Head

Antennae

Fore leg   Middle leg   Hind leg

Parts of an insect

in·sec·ti·cide (in sek′tə sīd′) *n.* a chemical for killing insects and similar pests.

in·sec·ti·vore (in sek′tə vôr′) *n.* **1.** an animal, such as the hedgehog, mole, or shrew, that feeds chiefly on insects. **2.** a plant that feeds chiefly on insects.

in·sec·tiv·o·rous (in′sek tiv′ər əs) *adj.* feeding chiefly on insects.

in·se·cure (in′si kyoor′) *adj.* **1.** liable to give way or fail; unstable or unsafe: *The knot was very insecure.* **2.** not assured; uncertain: *His position on the team was very insecure.* **3.** lacking in self-confidence: *an insecure person.* —**in′se·cure′ly,** *adv.*

in·se·cu·ri·ty (in′si kyoor′ə tē) *n. pl.,* **in·se·cu·ri·ties.** **1.** the state or quality of being insecure. **2.** a lack of self-confidence; self-doubt: *His insecurity made it difficult for him to travel alone.*

in·sen·sate (in sen′sāt) *adj.* **1.** without life or sensation; inanimate: *insensate rocks.* **2.** lacking feeling or sensitivity: *He is insensate to beautiful music.* **3.** lacking sense or reason; stupid; foolish. —**in·sen′sate·ly,** *adv.*

in·sen·si·ble (in sen′sə bəl) *adj.* **1.** not able to feel or perceive: *insensible to pain, insensible to the suffering of others.* **2.** not aware: *They were insensible of the risks involved.* **3.** unconscious: *He was insensible for several minutes after being struck on the head.* **4.** too slight or gradual to be easily perceived; imperceptible: *insensible changes in temperature.* —**in·sen′si·bil′i·ty,** *n.* —**in·sen′si·bly,** *adv.*

in·sen·si·tive (in sen′sə tiv) *adj.* **1.** not capable of feeling or perceiving: *insensitive to beauty, insensitive to pain.* **2.** lacking feeling, sensitivity, or perception: *He is a cruel and insensitive person.* —**in·sen′si·tive·ly,** *adv.* —**in·sen′si·tive·ness, in·sen′si·tiv′i·ty,** *n.*

in·sep·a·ra·ble (in sep′ər ə bəl) *adj.* that cannot be separated: *The boy and his dog were inseparable.* —**in·sep′a·ra·bil′i·ty,** *n.* —**in·sep′a·ra·bly,** *adv.*

in·sert (*v.,* in surt′; *n.,* in′surt) *v.t.* to put, set, or place in: *to insert a bookmark into a book, to insert a cork into a bottle.* —*n.* something inserted or to be inserted, such as an extra section in a newspaper or magazine.

in·ser·tion (in sur′shən) *n.* **1.** the act of inserting. **2.** something inserted. **3.** a band of lace or embroidery to be sewed at each edge between parts of other material.

in·set (*v.,* in set′; *n.,* in′set′) *v.t.,* **in·set, in·set·ting.** to set, put, or place in; insert. —*n.* **1.** something inset or to be inset; insertion. **2.** a small map, diagram, or other illustration inserted within the borders of a larger one.

in·shore (in′shôr′) *adj.* **1.** near the shore. **2.** moving toward the shore. —*adv.* toward the shore.

in·side (in sīd′, in′sīd′) *n.* **1.** the inner side, surface, or part; interior: *the inside of a car.* **2. insides.** *Informal.* the internal organs of the body. —*adj.* **1.** situated on or in the inside: *an inside seat on a train.* **2.** known to only a few; confidential: *The reporter got the inside story on the* *crime.* —*adv.* **1.** on, in, or toward the inside; within: *She opened the door and stepped inside.* **2.** indoors: *The children played inside all day.* —*prep.* in or into the inside of; within: *I looked inside the closet.*

  inside of. a. inside. **b.** within the space or limits of: *He ran the race inside of an hour.*

  inside out. a. so that the inside is facing out: *She turned her jacket inside out.* **b.** thoroughly; totally: *He knew his work inside out.*

in·sid·er (in sī′dər) *n.* **1.** a person who is a member of a certain group, society, or organization. **2.** a person who has or can obtain information that is known to only a few.

in·sid·i·ous (in sid′ē əs) *adj.* **1.** slyly treacherous or deceitful: *an insidious plot to overthrow a government.* **2.** working in a hidden but harmful manner: *an insidious disease.* —**in·sid′i·ous·ly,** *adv.* —**in·sid′i·ous·ness,** *n.*

in·sight (in′sīt′) *n.* **1.** the ability to see into and understand the true character or hidden nature of things: *She had great insight into his problems.* **2.** an instance of such understanding.

in·sig·ni·a (in sig′nē ə) *n. pl.,* **in·sig·ni·a** or **in·sig·ni·as.** an emblem, badge, medal, or other distinguishing mark of office, honor, or position: *The officer wore an insignia on his collar.*

in·sig·nif·i·cance (in′sig nif′i kəns) *n.* the state or quality of being insignificant.

in·sig·nif·i·cant (in′sig nif′i kənt) *adj.* **1.** having little or no meaning or importance; not significant: *My problems seem insignificant compared to the difficulties she faces.* **2.** small in size or amount: *an insignificant sum of money.* —**in′sig·nif′i·cant·ly,** *adv.*

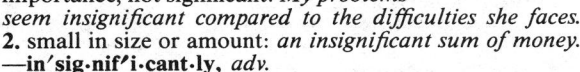

Insignia

in·sin·cere (in′sin sēr′) *adj.* not sincere, as in expressing one's feelings; dishonest or hypocritical. —**in′sin·cere′ly,** *adv.*

in·sin·cer·i·ty (in′sin ser′ə tē) *n. pl.,* **in·sin·cer·i·ties.** **1.** the quality of being insincere. **2.** an instance of being insincere.

in·sin·u·ate (in sin′yōō āt′) *v.t.,* **in·sin·u·at·ed, in·sin·u·at·ing. 1.** to suggest indirectly; imply; hint: *The prosecutor insinuated that the witness was lying.* **2.** to get in or introduce by an indirect or subtle way: *The new employee insinuated himself into the boss's favor.* —**in·sin′u·a′tion,** *n.*

in·sip·id (in sip′id) *adj.* **1.** lacking qualities that arouse interest or excite; dull; colorless: *an insipid person, an insipid novel.* **2.** without much taste or flavor; bland: *insipid food.* —**in·sip′id·ness,** *n.* —**in·sip′id·ly,** *adv.*

in·sist (in sist′) *v.t.* **1.** to demand (something) firmly and strongly: *The doctor insisted that the patient get plenty of rest.* **2.** to declare or maintain persistently and positively: *He insisted that he was the best man for the job.* —*v.i.* **1.** to demand firmly and strongly: *She insisted on our coming to the party.* **2.** to continue in a course of action: *If he insists on shouting, I shall leave.*

in·sis·tence (in sis′təns) *n.* **1.** the act or instance of insisting: *Her insistence on using correct grammar often made me nervous.* **2.** the quality of being insistent.

in·sis·tent (in sis′tənt) *adj.* **1.** firm or persistent, as in some demand: *Although she was having a good time, her friend was insistent on going home.* **2.** demanding attention or notice: *The insistent ringing of the doorbell woke us.* —**in·sis′tent·ly,** *adv.*

in·snare (in sner′) *v.t.,* **in·snared, in·snar·ing.** another spelling of **ensnare.**

in·so·far as (in′sō fär′) to such an extent as: *Insofar as we know, he is coming to the party.*

in·sole (in′sōl′) *n.* **1.** the inner sole of a shoe or boot. **2.** a layer of material laid on the sole inside a shoe or boot for warmth, waterproofing, or for a better fit.

in·so·lence (in′sə ləns) *n.* **1.** offensive rudeness or boldness. **2.** insolent speech or behavior.

in·so·lent (in′sə lənt) *adj.* offensively rude or bold: *The child made an insolent reply.* —**in′so·lent·ly,** *adv.*

in·sol·u·ble (in sol′yə bəl) *adj.* **1.** that cannot be dissolved: *an insoluble chemical.* **2.** that cannot be solved or explained: *an insoluble crime.* —**in·sol′u·bil′i·ty,** *n.* —**in·sol′u·bly,** *adv.*

in·sol·vent (in sol′vənt) *adj.* not able to pay one's debts. —**in·sol′ven·cy,** *n.*

in·som·ni·a (in som′nē ə) *n.* the inability to sleep.

in·so·much (in′sō much′) *adv.* to such an extent or degree.

  insomuch as. inasmuch as; since.

in·spect (in spekt′) *v.t.* **1.** to look at closely and carefully, especially for errors, faults, or flaws: *The mechanic inspected the automobile for possible defects.* **2.** to examine formally or officially: *The general inspected the troops.*

in·spec·tion (in spek′shən) *n.* **1.** the act of inspecting, especially for errors, faults, or flaws. **2.** a formal or official examination.

in·spec·tor (in spek′tər) *n.* **1.** a person, especially an appointed official, who inspects. **2.** a police officer ranking next below a superintendent.

in·spi·ra·tion (in′spə rā′shən) *n.* **1.** the stimulation of the mind, feelings, or imagination: *The beauty of nature gave inspiration to the painter.* **2.** a person or thing that inspires: *The writer's wife was the inspiration for all his heroines.* **3.** something inspired, such as an idea or action. **4.** the act of breathing in; inhalation.

in·spi·ra·tion·al (in′spə rā′shən əl) *adj.* **1.** giving or tending to give inspiration; inspiring. **2.** resulting from inspiration; inspired.

in·spire (in spīr′) *v.,* **in·spired, in·spir·ing.** —*v.t.* **1.** to have a rousing effect or influence on; stimulate; stir: *The minister's words inspired his congregation.* **2.** to be the force or influence that results in (something specified): *The author's wife inspired his first novel.* **3.** to produce or arouse, as a thought or feeling: *Grandfather inspired love and respect.* **4.** to cause to have a specified thought or feeling: *His success inspired him with hope for the future.* —*v.i.* to inhale. —**in·spir′er,** *n.*

in·sta·bil·i·ty (in′stə bil′ə tē) *n.* lack of stability.

in·stall (in stôl′) *v.t.* **1.** to put in position for service or use: *The serviceman installed the air conditioner.* **2.** to place (a person) in an office, rank, or position with ceremony: *We installed the new club president today.* **3.** to establish in a place or position; settle: *The policeman installed himself at the front door.*

in·stal·la·tion (in′stə lā′shən) *n.* **1.** the act of installing or the state of being installed. **2.** a mechanical system or apparatus placed in position for use. **3.** a military base, including personnel, buildings, and equipment.

in·stall·ment¹ (in stôl′mənt) *also,* **in·stal·ment.** *n.* **1.** one of the portions of a sum of money owed to be paid at regular intervals: *Father paid for our car in thirty installments.* **2.** any of several parts issued or presented at regu-

---

at; āpe; cär; end; mē; it; īce; hot; ōld; fôrk; wood; fōol; oil; out; up; turn; sing; thin; this; hw in white; zh in treasure. The symbol ə stands for the sound of **a** in about, **e** in taken, **i** in pencil, **o** in lemon, and **u** in circus.

I

lar intervals: *The novel appeared in the magazine in weekly installments.* [*In-²* + obsolete *stall* to arrange a payment.]

in·stall·ment² (in stôl′mənt) *also,* **in·stal·ment.** *n.* the act of installing or the state of being installed; installation. [*Install* + *-ment.*]

installment plan, a system of paying for goods or services in specified amounts at regular intervals.

in·stance (in′stəns) *n.* an example or case: *His action was an instance of great courage.*

 for instance. by way of illustration; for example: *He enjoys team sports, for instance, baseball, hockey, and basketball.*

in·stant (in′stənt) *n.* **1.** a very short period of time; moment: *We saw him for just an instant.* **2.** a particular moment or point in time: *I want to leave this instant.* —*adj.* **1.** without delay: *The computer gave us an instant reply.* **2.** pressing; urgent: *an instant need.* **3.** (of food products) prepared beforehand and packaged, often in powdered form, and requiring only the addition of a liquid, as water or milk, for final preparation: *instant oatmeal, instant coffee.*

in·stan·ta·ne·ous (in′stən tā′nē əs) *adj.* happening, done, or coming in an instant or without delay: *His reaction was instantaneous.* —**in′stan·ta′ne·ous·ly,** *adv.*

in·stant·ly (in′stənt lē) *adv.* without delay; at once.

in·stead (in sted′) *adv.* in place of the person or thing mentioned; as a substitute or alternative: *The recipe called for butter, but we used margarine instead.*

 instead of. rather than; in place of: *We went for a walk instead of going straight home.*

in·step (in′step′) *n.* **1.** the arched upper surface of the human foot between the toes and the ankle. **2.** the part of a shoe, stocking, or other footwear that covers the instep.

in·sti·gate (in′stə gāt′) *v.t.,* **in·sti·gat·ed, in·sti·gat·ing. 1.** to cause by stirring up or urging; incite: *to instigate a riot.* **2.** to urge on to some action: *to instigate someone to commit a crime.* —**in′sti·ga′tion,** *n.* —**in′sti·ga′tor,** *n.*

in·still (in stil′) *also,* **in·stil.** *v.t.,* **in·stilled, in·stil·ling. 1.** to put in or introduce gradually or little by little: *The English teacher instilled a love of literature into his students.* **2.** to pour in by drops.

in·stinct (in′stingkt) *n.* **1.** a natural tendency to act in a certain way: *Birds build nests by instinct.* **2.** a natural aptitude; talent: *The boy had a definite instinct for painting.*

in·stinc·tive (in stingk′tiv) *adj.* **1.** arising from or done by instinct: *instinctive behavior.* **2.** of or relating to instinct. —**in·stinc′tive·ly,** *adv.*

in·sti·tute (in′stə tōōt′, in′stə tyōōt′) *v.t.,* **in·sti·tut·ed, in·sti·tut·ing.** to set up or put into operation; establish; start: *to institute a new set of rules.* —*n.* **1.** an organization, school, or society set up to promote and carry on work in a particular field: *a music institute, a cancer research institute.* **2.** the building or buildings housing such an organization.

in·sti·tu·tion (in′stə tōō′shən, in′stə tyōō′shən) *n.* **1.** an organization, society, or similar establishment devoted to a particular purpose, especially one of a social, educational, or religious nature. **2.** the building or buildings housing such an establishment. **3.** the act of instituting; establishment. **4.** an established practice, custom, law, or system: *Slavery was an institution in the South before the Civil War.* —**in′sti·tu′tion·al,** *adj.*

in·sti·tu·tion·al·ize (in′stə tōō′shən əl īz′, in′stə tyōō′shən əl īz′) *v.t.* **1.** to make into an institution. **2.** to place in an institution, especially one for the care and treatment of an illness.

in·struct (in strukt′) *v.t.* **1.** to provide with knowledge, information, or skill; teach: *My father instructed me in the* correct use of woodworking tools. **2.** to give directions or orders to: *He instructed us to lock the door.*

in·struc·tion (in struk′shən) *n.* **1.** the act of teaching. **2. instructions.** explanations, directions, or orders: *If you follow my instructions, you won't get lost.* **3.** knowledge or information given; lesson. —**in·struc′tion·al,** *adj.*

in·struc·tive (in struk′tiv) *adj.* giving or providing knowledge or information; serving to instruct: *The lecture was interesting as well as instructive.* —**in·struc′tive·ly,** *adv.*

in·struc·tor (in struk′tər) *n.* **1.** a person who instructs; teacher. **2.** a teacher in a college or university who is of lower rank than a professor. —**in·struc′tress,** *n.*

in·stru·ment (in′strə mənt) *n.* **1.** a tool, especially one designed or used for precise or careful work: *A scalpel is a surgical instrument.* **2.** a device for producing musical sounds: *She plays the guitar, the flute, and several other instruments.* **3.** a device for measuring, controlling, or a similar purpose: *navigational instruments.* **4.** the means by which something is done or brought about: *The king's evil brother was the instrument of his downfall.* **5.** a formal or legal document, such as a contract, deed, or will.

in·stru·men·tal (in′strə ment′əl) *adj.* **1.** serving as a means; helpful: *A small band of revolutionaries was instrumental in overthrowing the dictatorship.* **2.** relating to, composed for, or performed on musical instruments: *He composed both vocal and instrumental music.* —*n.* a composition for one or more musical instruments. —**in′stru·men′tal·ly,** *adv.*

in·stru·men·tal·ist (in′strə ment′əl ist) *n.* a person who plays a musical instrument.

in·stru·men·tal·i·ty (in′strə men tal′ə tē) *n.* **1.** the state or quality of being instrumental. **2.** something that serves or is used for some purpose; means.

in·stru·men·ta·tion (in′strə men tā′shən) *n.* **1.** an arrangement or composition of music for instruments, especially for an orchestra. **2.** the use of scientific, surgical, or other instruments.

in·sub·or·di·nate (in′sə bôrd′ən it) *adj.* not yielding to or obeying authority; disobedient. —**in′sub·or′di·nate·ly,** *adv.*

in·sub·or·di·na·tion (in′sə bôrd′ən ā′shən) *n.* the refusal to yield to or obey authority; disobedience: *The soldier who ignored the captain's orders was charged with insubordination.*

in·sub·stan·tial (in′səb stan′shəl) *adj.* **1.** not real; imaginary: *insubstantial hopes.* **2.** not strong, solid, or firm; flimsy: *insubstantial evidence.* —**in′sub·stan′tial·ly,** *adv.*

in·suf·fer·a·ble (in suf′ər ə bəl) *adj.* not to be endured; not tolerable; unbearable: *As a public speaker, he was an insufferable bore.* —**in·suf′fer·a·bly,** *adv.*

in·suf·fi·cien·cy (in′sə fish′ən sē) *n. pl.,* **in·suf·fi·cien·cies.** a lack or deficiency, as in amount or quality.

in·suf·fi·cient (in′sə fish′ənt) *adj.* not enough; inadequate: *Profits were insufficient to keep the business going.* —**in′suf·fi′cient·ly,** *adv.*

in·su·lar (in′sə lər) *adj.* **1.** of, relating to, or characteristic of an island or its people. **2.** living or situated on an island. **3.** composing or forming an island. **4.** standing alone; isolated. **5.** narrow-minded; prejudiced: *an insular way of thinking.*

in·su·lar·i·ty (in′sə lar′ə tē) *n.* **1.** the condition of being an island. **2.** narrow-mindedness; prejudice.

in·su·late (in′sə lāt′) *v.t.,* **in·su·lat·ed, in·su·lat·ing. 1.** to cover or surround with a material that does not conduct electricity, heat, or sound, such as rubber: *to insulate an electric wire.* **2.** to install a layer of material, such as rubber, between the exterior and interior walls of (a building, refrigerator, or other structure) to reduce or prevent the passage of heat. **3.** to protect or isolate: *Parents often try to insulate their children from the harshness of life.*

in·su·la·tion (in′sə lā′shən) *n.* **1.** the material used in insulating. **2.** the act of insulating or the condition of being insulated.

in·su·la·tor (in′sə lā′tər) *n.* something that insulates, especially a material or device that prevents the passage of electric current.

in·su·lin (in′sə lin) *n.* **1.** a hormone that is secreted by the pancreas and regulates the body's use and storage of sugar and other carbohydrates. **2.** a preparation containing this hormone, used in treating diabetes. It is obtained from the pancreas of cattle, sheep, or pigs or is produced artificially. Trademark: **Insulin.**

in·sult (*v.,* in sult′; *n.,* in′sult) *v.t.* to speak to or treat in a rude, disrespectful, or scornful way; hurt the feelings or pride of: *He insulted his friend when he accused him of stealing.* —*n.* an insulting remark or act. —**in·sult′ing·ly,** *adv.*

in·su·per·a·ble (in soo′pər ə bəl) *adj.* that cannot be overcome or surmounted: *insuperable obstacles.* —**in·su′per·a·bly,** *adv.*

in·sur·a·ble (in shoor′ə bəl) *adj.* capable of being or fit to be insured.

in·sur·ance (in shoor′əns) *n.* **1.** protection against risk or loss by means of a contract between two parties whereby the insurer guarantees to pay a sum of money to the insured in case of death, accident, fire, theft, or the like in return for the regular payment of small amounts by the insured. **2.** a contract guaranteeing such protection. **3.** the amount for which someone or something is insured. **4.** the amount paid for insurance; premium. **5.** the business of insuring persons or property. **6.** any protection against risk, harm, or loss.

in·sure (in shoor′) *v.t.,* **in·sured, in·sur·ing. 1.** to protect against risk or loss by means of insurance; cover with insurance: *to insure a car, to insure a diamond ring.* **2.** another spelling of **ensure.**

in·sured (in shoord′) *n.* a person who is protected or covered by insurance.

in·sur·er (in shoor′ər) *n.* a person or company that insures.

in·sur·gence (in sur′jəns) *n.* the act of rebelling against established authority; revolt.

in·sur·gent (in sur′jənt) *n.* **1.** a person who rebels against established authority. **2.** a member of a political party who rebels against the policies and decisions of the party. —*adj.* rising in revolt against authority; rebellious.

in·sur·mount·a·ble (in′sər moun′tə bəl) *adj.* that cannot be overcome: *insurmountable difficulties.* —**in′sur·mount′a·bly,** *adv.*

in·sur·rec·tion (in′sə rek′shən) *n.* a rebellion against established authority, especially against a government; revolt. —**in′sur·rec′tion·ist,** *n.*

in·tact (in takt′) *adj.* untouched or whole; not damaged or injured: *The tornado left few buildings intact.*

in·take (in′tāk′) *n.* **1.** the act of taking in. **2.** the amount taken in: *The doctors restricted his intake of liquids.* **3.** a place in a channel, pipe, or other narrow opening where fluid is taken in.

in·tan·gi·ble (in tan′jə bəl) *adj.* **1.** not easily defined or grasped by the mind; vague: *The soul is an intangible concept.* **2.** not capable of being perceived by the sense of touch: *Love and other emotions are intangible.* —*n.* something intangible. —**in·tan′gi·bil′i·ty,** *n.* —**in·tan′gi·bly,** *adv.*

in·te·ger (in′tə jər) *n.* any positive or negative whole number, or zero.

in·te·gral (in′tə grəl) *adj.* **1.** necessary to the completeness of a whole; essential: *A carburetor is an integral part of an automobile engine.* **2.** having no part or element missing; entire. **3.** relating to or being an integer.

in·te·grate (in′tə grāt′) *v.,* **in·te·grat·ed, in·te·grat·ing.** —*v.t.* **1.** to make available to all racial groups; desegregate: *to integrate a school, to integrate a neighborhood.* **2.** to bring (parts) together into a whole. **3.** to make whole by adding or bringing together all necessary parts. —*v.i.* to become available to all racial groups.

integrated circuit, an electronic circuit formed on a minute slice of silicon called a chip, containing many thousands of transistors and other devices. Integrated circuits are used in computers.

in·te·gra·tion (in′tə grā′shən) *n.* **1.** the elimination of racial segregation, as in schools or housing. **2.** the act of integrating parts into a whole.

in·te·gra·tion·ist (in′tə grā′shə nist) *n.* a person who believes in or favors racial integration.

in·teg·ri·ty (in teg′rə tē) *n.* **1.** moral uprightness; honesty; sincerity: *The witness's false testimony put his integrity in question.* **2.** the state of being complete.

in·teg·u·ment (in teg′yə mənt) *n.* the natural covering of an animal or plant, such as a skin, husk, shell, or rind.

in·tel·lect (int′əl ekt′) *n.* **1.** the power of the mind to know, understand, and reason. **2.** intelligence or mental ability, especially when highly developed. **3.** a person of great intelligence.

in·tel·lec·tu·al (int′əl ek′chōō əl) *adj.* **1.** of or relating to the intellect: *a woman of great intellectual ability.* **2.** appealing to, involving, or using the intellect: *Reading great literature is an intellectual pursuit.* **3.** possessing or showing intellect: *an intellectual young man.* —*n.* an intellectual person. —**in′tel·lec′tu·al·ly,** *adv.*

in·tel·li·gence (in tel′ə jəns) *n.* **1.** the ability to learn, understand, and reason. **2.** secret information, especially about an enemy. **3.** the agency engaged in collecting such information.

intelligence quotient, a number used to estimate a person's intelligence level. It is obtained by dividing a person's mental age, as shown by tests, by his real age, and multiplying by 100.

intelligence test, a test used to measure a person's mental development in relation to that of others.

in·tel·li·gent (in tel′ə jənt) *adj.* having or showing intelligence; bright: *That was a very intelligent question to ask.* —**in·tel′li·gent·ly,** *adv.*

in·tel·li·gent·si·a (in tel′ə jent′sē ə) *n., pl.* a group of persons having or regarded as having superior intelligence.

in·tel·li·gi·ble (in tel′ə jə bəl) *adj.* capable of being understood; comprehensible: *His statement was not intelligible.* —**in·tel′li·gi·bil′i·ty,** *n.* —**in·tel′li·gi·bly,** *adv.*

in·tem·per·ance (in tem′pər əns) *n.* a lack of moderation or restraint, as in the use of alcoholic beverages.

in·tem·per·ate (in tem′pər it, in tem′prit) *adj.* **1.** lacking moderation, restraint, or self-control, as in the use of alcoholic beverages; excessive. **2.** harsh; extreme: *intemperate weather.* —**in·tem′per·ate·ly,** *adv.*

in·tend (in tend′) *v.t.* **1.** to have in mind as a purpose; plan: *He intends to leave for the camp next week.* **2.** to

at; āpe; cär; end; mē; it; īce; hot; ōld; fôrk; wood; fōōl; oil; out; up; turn; sing; thin; this; hw in white; zh in treasure. The symbol ə stands for the sound of **a** in about, **e** in taken, **i** in pencil, **o** in lemon, and **u** in circus.

I

make or mean for a particular purpose, use, or person: *The movie is intended for adults only.*

in·tend·ed (in ten′did) *adj.* **1.** meant or planned; intentional: *an intended insult.* **2.** that is to be; prospective: *We met his intended wife.* —*n.* an intended husband or wife.

in·tense (in tens′) *adj.* **1.** of a very high degree; very great or strong: *intense heat, an intense desire.* **2.** having or showing strong or earnest feeling: *an intense person, an intense look.* —**in·tense′ly,** *adv.*

in·ten·si·fi·er (in ten′sə fī′ər) *n. Grammar.* an intensive.

in·ten·si·fy (in ten′sə fī′) *v.,* **in·ten·si·fied, in·ten·si·fy·ing.** —*v.t.* to make intense or more intense; increase greatly: *The police intensified their search for the missing boy.* —*v.i.* to become intense or more intense; grow in strength, amount, or degree: *The heat intensified as the fire began to spread.* —**in·ten·si·fi·ca′tion,** *n.*

in·ten·si·ty (in ten′sə tē) *n. pl.,* **in·ten·si·ties. 1.** the state or quality of being intense: *The light shone with great intensity.* **2.** strength, amount, or degree, as of force or feeling: *The pain increased in intensity. The intensity of her anger frightened me.* **3.** the amount of strength of a form of energy, such as heat, light, or sound, per unit of area, volume, or mass.

in·ten·sive (in ten′siv) *adj.* **1.** thorough or concentrated: *The hospital patient needed intensive care.* **2.** *Grammar.* giving force or emphasis. In the sentence *I myself did it, myself* is an intensive pronoun. —*n. Grammar.* an intensive element, word, or phrase. The word *very* is an intensive in the sentence *That very man committed the crime.* —**in·ten′sive·ly,** *adv.*

in·tent[1] (in tent′) *n.* **1.** an intention; aim: *Her intent has always been to go to college.* **2.** meaning; significance: *What was the intent of his remark?* [Old French *entent* aim.]
   to all intents and purposes or **for all intents and purposes.** in almost every way; practically.

in·tent[2] (in tent′) *adj.* **1.** having the mind firmly fixed on something: *Is he intent on leaving? She was intent on her book.* **2.** firmly directed or fixed: *an intent look.* [Latin *intentus,* the past participle of *intendere* to stretch out.] —**in·tent′ly,** *adv.*

in·ten·tion (in ten′shən) *n.* something that is intended; purpose; plan: *I have no intention of going to her party. The king had good intentions, but he was a weak ruler.*

in·ten·tion·al (in ten′shən əl) *adj.* carefully thought out or planned; done on purpose: *My leaving his name off this list was intentional.* —**in·ten′tion·al·ly,** *adv.*

in·ter (in tur′) *v.t.,* **in·terred, in·ter·ring.** to put (a dead body) into a grave or tomb; bury.

inter- *prefix* **1.** one with the other; together: *interact.* **2.** between or among: *intercollegiate, interchange.*

in·ter·act (in′tə rakt′) *v.i.* to act on or influence each other. —**in′ter·ac′tion,** *n.*

in·ter·breed (in′tər brēd′) *v.t.,* **in·ter·bred** (in′tər bred′), **in·ter·breed·ing.** to breed (animals or plants) with those of different varieties or lines; crossbreed.

in·ter·cede (in′tər sēd′) *v.i.,* **in·ter·ced·ed, in·ter·ced·ing. 1.** to plead on behalf of another or others: *The teacher interceded with the principal for the boy who was in trouble.* **2.** to come between opposing parties in an effort to end or settle a dispute.

in·ter·cept (in′tər sept′) *v.t.* **1.** to seize or stop on the way: *to intercept a forward pass, to intercept a note.* **2.** to stop the course or progress of; check: *to intercept the flight of a missile.* **3.** *Mathematics.* to mark off, as between two points or lines. —**in′ter·cep′tion,** *n.*

in·ter·cep·tor (in′tər sep′tər) *n.* **1.** a person or thing that intercepts. **2.** a fast-climbing airplane designed to intercept attacking enemy aircraft.

in·ter·ces·sion (in′tər sesh′ən) *n.* **1.** the act of interceding. **2.** a prayer or plea that is made on behalf of another or others.

in·ter·ces·sor (in′tər ses′ər) *n.* a person who intercedes.

in·ter·change (*v.,* in′tər chānj′; *n.,* in′tər chānj′) *v.,* **in·ter·changed, in·ter·chang·ing.** —*v.t.* **1.** to put each of (two things) in the place or position of the other: *She interchanged the two chairs.* **2.** to give and receive mutually; exchange: *They interchanged gifts at Christmas.* —*v.i.* to change places one with the other. —*n.* **1.** the act or instance of interchanging: *an interchange of ideas.* **2.** a place where a vehicle may enter or leave a major highway without interfering with the flow of traffic on the highway.

in·ter·change·a·ble (in′tər chān′jə bəl) *adj.* capable of being put or used in place of each other: *interchangeable machine parts.* —**in′ter·change′a·bly,** *adv.*

in·ter·col·le·giate (in′tər kə lē′jit) *adj.* carried on or occurring between colleges or universities: *intercollegiate baseball.*

in·ter·com (in′tər kom′) *n.* a radio or telephone system that provides communication within or between given areas, as between rooms or different parts of a building.

in·ter·com·mu·ni·cate (in′tər kə myōō′nə kāt′) *v.i.,* **in·ter·com·mu·ni·cat·ed, in·ter·com·mu·ni·cat·ing.** to communicate with each other or one another. —**in′ter·com·mu′ni·ca′tion,** *n.*

in·ter·con·nect (in′tər kə nekt′) *v.t.* to connect one with the other: *to interconnect wires.* —*v.i.* to be connected one with the other. —**in′ter·con·nec′tion,** *n.*

in·ter·con·ti·nen·tal (in′tər kon′tə nent′əl) *adj.* **1.** traveling or capable of traveling from one continent to another: *an intercontinental missile.* **2.** of, relating to, or involving more than one continent: *intercontinental trade.*

in·ter·course (in′tər kôrs′) *n.* **1.** communication, relations, or dealings between individuals or groups; interchange, as of thoughts, ideas, or feelings: *cultural intercourse between nations.* **2.** sexual relations.

in·ter·de·nom·i·na·tion·al (in′tər di nom′ə nā′shən əl) *adj.* between, among, or involving different religious denominations: *an interdenominational religious service.*

in·ter·de·pen·dent (in′tər di pen′dənt) *adj.* dependent on each other or one another; mutually dependent. —**in′ter·de·pen′dence,** *n.* —**in′ter·de·pend′ent·ly,** *adv.*

in·ter·dict (*v.,* in′tər dikt′; *n.,* in′tər dikt′) *v.t.* **1.** to prohibit; forbid. **2.** in the Roman Catholic Church, to exclude from certain rites and sacraments. —*n.* **1.** an official prohibition. **2.** in the Roman Catholic Church, a punishment in which a person, district, or country is excluded from certain rites and sacraments. —**in′ter·dic′tion,** *n.*

in·ter·est (in′trist, in′tər ist) *n.* **1.** a feeling of concern, involvement, or curiosity: *He has a great interest in sports.* **2.** the cause or source of such feeling: *His career is his main interest at the moment.* **3.** the power to arouse such feeling: *That book about sports cars had little interest for her.* **4.** *also,* **interests.** advantage; benefit; welfare: *She only cares about her own interests.* **5.** money paid for the use or borrowing of money: *to pay interest on a loan.* **6.** a legal right, claim, or share: *He has a controlling interest in the business.* **7.** something in which a person has such a right, claim, or share. **8.** *usually,* **interests.** a group having a common concern, especially in a business or industry: *the mining interests.* —*v.t.* **1.** to arouse or hold the curiosity or attention of: *History interests him greatly.* **2.** to cause (a person) to take an interest in something: *Mother tried to interest me in cooking.*

in·ter·est·ed (in′tris tid, in′tə res′tid) *adj.* **1.** having or showing interest: *an interested listener.* **2.** having an interest or share. —**in′ter·est·ed·ly,** *adv.*

in·ter·est·ing (in′tris ting, in′tə res′ting) *adj.* arousing or holding interest or attention: *an interesting face, an interesting magazine.* —**in′ter·est·ing·ly,** *adv.*

in·ter·fere (in′tər fēr′) *v.i.,* **in·ter·fered, in·ter·fer·ing.** **1.** to concern oneself with or intrude in the affairs of others without having been asked; meddle: *I wish she would stop interfering in my private life.* **2.** to interrupt, hinder, or disturb: *His guitar playing interferes with my studying.*

in·ter·fer·ence (in′tər fēr′əns) *n.* **1.** the act of interfering. **2.** in radio and television, the disruption of a signal by other signals. **3.** *Football.* **a.** the blocking of opposing players in order to make way for the ball carrier. **b.** the player or players who provide such blocking. **4.** *Sports.* the illegal hindering of an opposing player, as in football or hockey.

in·ter·fuse (in′tər fyōoz′) *v.t.,* **in·ter·fused, in·ter·fus·ing.** **1.** to mix together thoroughly; blend. **2.** to spread through; permeate. **3.** to cause to pass into or spread throughout. —**in′ter·fu′sion,** *n.*

in·ter·im (in′tər im) *n.* the time between; meantime. —*adj.* for or happening during an interim; temporary: *an interim settlement of a dispute.*

in·te·ri·or (in tēr′ē ər) *n.* **1.** the inner side, surface, or part: *The interior of the cave was dark.* **2.** the part of a region or country that is away from the coast or border: *The interior of that country is mostly jungle.* **3.** the internal or domestic affairs of a country: *the Department of the Interior of the United States.* —*adj.* **1.** of, relating to, or on the inside. **2.** away from the coast or border; inland.

interior decoration, the art or business of planning, designing, and furnishing interiors, as of homes or offices, to provide beauty, comfort, and convenience.

interior decorator, a person whose business is interior decoration.

interj., interjection.

in·ter·ject (in′tər jekt′) *v.t.* to put or throw in; insert abruptly: *to interject a comment in a discussion.*

in·ter·jec·tion (in′tər jek′shən) *n.* **1.** a word or phrase belonging to that part of speech that expresses emotion and is capable of standing alone. *Oh!* and *alas!* are interjections. **2.** the act of interjecting. **3.** something interjected, as a remark or question.

in·ter·lace (in′tər lās′) *v.,* **in·ter·laced, in·ter·lac·ing.** —*v.t.* to join by or as if by weaving together; intertwine: *to interlace garlands of flowers.* —*v.i.* to intertwine.

in·ter·lard (in′tər lärd′) *v.t.* to give variety to by mixing in or inserting something different: *to interlard a speech with Biblical quotations.*

in·ter·lock (in′tər lok′) *v.i.* to lock or fit together closely: *The parts of this machine interlock.* —*v.t.* to cause to lock or fit together closely: *The bulls interlocked horns.*

in·ter·lop·er (in′tər lō′pər) *n.* a person who interferes in the affairs of others; meddler; intruder.

in·ter·lude (in′tər lōod′) *n.* **1.** anything that fills time between two events: *a brief interlude of rest in a busy day.* **2.** a short piece of music played between parts of a church service, acts of a play, or sections of a long musical composition.

in·ter·mar·riage (in′tər mar′ij) *n.* a marriage between persons of different religious faiths, races, or ethnic backgrounds.

in·ter·mar·ry (in′tər mar′ē) *v.i.,* **in·ter·mar·ried, in·ter·mar·ry·ing.** **1.** to marry outside one's religious, racial, or ethnic group. **2.** to become connected by marriage, as two families, tribes, or races. **3.** to marry within one's own family.

in·ter·me·di·ar·y (in′tər mē′dē er′ē) *n. pl.,* **in·ter·me·di·ar·ies.** a person who comes between two or more opposing parties in order to bring about an agreement or com-

promise; mediator. —*adj.* **1.** acting as a mediator: *an intermediary agent.* **2.** being or coming between; intermediate: *an intermediary step in a process.*

in·ter·me·di·ate (in′tər mē′dē it) *adj.* being or coming in the middle or between: *a skier of intermediate skill.* —*n.* something that is intermediate.

in·ter·ment (in tur′mənt) *n.* the act of interring; burial.

in·ter·mez·zo (in′tər met′sō, in′tər med′zō) *n. pl.,* **in·ter·mez·zos** or **in·ter·mez·zi** (in′tər met′sē, in′tər med′zē). **1.** a short musical composition played between the acts of a play or opera. **2.** *Music.* **a.** a short, slow movement between the main parts of a long composition, as a symphony. **b.** a short, independent instrumental composition.

in·ter·mi·na·ble (in tur′mi nə bəl) *adj.* endless or seeming to be endless: *The politician's boring speech was interminable.* —**in·ter′mi·na·bly,** *adv.*

in·ter·min·gle (in′tər ming′gəl) *v.t., v.i.,* **in·ter·min·gled, in·ter·min·gling.** to mix or mingle together.

in·ter·mis·sion (in′tər mish′ən) *n.* **1.** the interval or time between events or periods of activity: *There was a short intermission after the first act of the play.* **2.** an interruption; pause: *The rain continued for hours with no intermission.*

in·ter·mit·tent (in′tər mit′ənt) *adj.* alternately stopping and starting again; coming at intervals: *intermittent rain.* —**in′ter·mit′tent·ly,** *adv.*

in·tern[1] (in turn′) *v.t.* to confine or restrict to a particular place, especially during a war. [French *interner.*]

in·tern[2] (in′turn′) *n. also,* **in·terne.** a recently graduated doctor serving in a hospital or clinic under the supervision of experienced doctors. —*v.i.* to be an intern. [French *interne.*]

in·ter·nal (in turn′əl) *adj.* **1.** of, relating to, or being on the inside; interior: *the stomach and other internal organs.* **2.** of or relating to the domestic matters or concerns of a country: *internal affairs.* **3.** to be taken internally: *internal medication.* —**in·ter′nal·ly,** *adv.*

in·ter·nal-com·bus·tion engine (in turn′əl kəm bus′chən) an engine in which fuel is burned within the engine itself, usually in cylinders.

in·ter·na·tion·al (in′tər nash′ən əl) *adj.* **1.** of, relating to, or concerning two or more countries: *an international trade agreement.* **2.** of or relating to relations between countries. —**in′ter·na′tion·al·ly,** *adv.*

International Date Line *also,* **international date line.** an imaginary line running approximately along the 180th meridian, marking the time boundary between one day and the next. Also, **date line.**

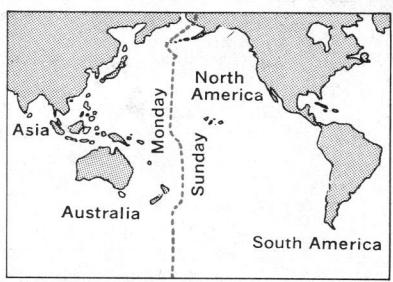

International Date Line

in·ter·na·tion·al·ism (in′tər nash′ən əl iz′əm) *n.* the doctrine of mutual

I

cooperation among countries and peoples for the benefit of all mankind. —**in·ter·na·tion·al·ist,** *n.*

in·ter·na·tion·al·ize (in′tər nash′ən əl īz′) *v.t.,* **in·ter·na·tion·al·ized, in·ter·na·tion·al·iz·ing.** to bring under international control; make international.

in·terne (in′turn′) another spelling of **intern²** *(n.).*

in·ter·ne·cine (in′tər nes′ēn, in′tər nē′sīn) *adj.* **1.** harmful to both sides. **2.** characterized by much bloodshed.

in·tern·ee (in′tur nē′) *n.* a person who is or has been interned, especially during a war.

in·tern·ment (in turn′mənt) *n.* the act of interning or the state of being interned, especially during a war.

in·tern·ship (in′turn ship′) *n.* the period during which a person serves as an intern in a hospital or clinic.

in·ter·plan·e·tar·y (in′tər plan′ə ter′ē) *adj.* between the planets: *interplanetary travel.*

in·ter·play (in′tər plā′) *n.* action or influence on each other; interaction: *The story's suspense arises from the interplay of the two main characters.*

in·ter·po·late (in tur′pə lāt′) *v.t.,* **in·ter·po·lat·ed, in·ter·po·lat·ing. 1.** to alter (a text) by putting in new material. **2.** to put (new or false material) into a text: *The actor interpolated several lines of his own into the play.* **3.** *Mathematics.* to find the value of (a function, as a logarithm) between two known values. —**in·ter·po·la′tion,** *n.*

in·ter·pose (in′tər pōz′) *v.,* **in·ter·posed, in·ter·pos·ing.** —*v.t.* **1.** to introduce into a conversation or speech: *to interpose an unnecessary remark.* **2.** to place between; insert. **3.** to put forth or assert in order to interfere or intervene: *to interpose an objection.* —*v.i.* to come between; intervene. —**in′ter·po·si′tion,** *n.*

in·ter·pret (in tur′prit) *v.t.* **1.** to make clear or understandable; reveal the meaning of: *to interpret a dream.* **2.** to translate: *He interpreted the foreign visitor's remarks for us.* **3.** to understand or regard: *The policeman interpreted the offer as a bribe.* **4.** to perform so as to bring out the meaning: *The pianist interpreted the concerto with great feeling.* —*v.i.* to act as an interpreter.

in·ter·pre·ta·tion (in tur′prə tā′shən) *n.* **1.** the act of interpreting. **2.** the meaning that results from interpreting: *The student gave an imaginative interpretation of the poem.* **3.** a performance that brings out the meaning of something, as of a musical composition or dramatic role.

in·ter·pre·ta·tive (in tur′prə tā′tiv) *adj.* serving to interpret; explanatory. Also, **interpretive.**

in·ter·pret·er (in tur′prə tər) *n.* **1.** a person who interprets. **2.** a person who gives oral translations from one language to another.

in·ter·pre·tive (in tur′prə tiv) *adj.* another word for **interpretative.**

in·ter·ra·cial (in′tər rā′shəl) *adj.* **1.** between or involving members of different races: *an interracial marriage.* **2.** of or for members of different races: *interracial sports facilities.*

in·ter·reg·num (in′tər reg′nəm) *n. pl.,* **in·ter·reg·nums** or **in·ter·reg·na** (in′tər reg′nə). **1.** the time between the end of a ruler's reign and the beginning of the reign of his successor. **2.** any period of time without the usual ruling power or authority.

in·ter·re·late (in′tər ri lāt′) *v.t., v.i.,* **in·ter·re·lat·ed, in·ter·re·lat·ing.** to bring or come into mutual or close relation. —**in′ter·re·la′tion, in′ter·re·la′tion·ship′,** *n.*

in·ter·re·lat·ed (in′tər ri lā′tid) *adj.* closely or mutually related to each other: *interrelated laws.*

in·ter·ro·gate (in ter′ə gāt′) *v.,* **in·ter·ro·gat·ed, in·ter·ro·gat·ing.** —*v.t.* to examine by questioning formally and methodically: *The policeman interrogated the prisoner for hours.* —*v.i.* to ask questions. —**in·ter·ro·ga′tion,** *n.*

interrogation point, question mark. Also, **interrogation mark.**

in·ter·rog·a·tive (in′tə rog′ə tiv) *adj.* **1.** relating to or having the form of a question: *an interrogative sentence.* **2.** expressing or introducing a question. In the sentence *Who is it?* the word "who" is an interrogative pronoun. —*n.* a word or construction used in asking a question. —**in′ter·rog′a·tive·ly,** *adv.*

in·ter·rog·a·to·ry (in′tə rog′ə tôr′ē) *adj.* expressing or asking a question; questioning.

in·ter·rupt (in′tə rupt′) *v.t.* **1.** to break in upon or stop (someone) in the course of an action or speech: *Please do not interrupt me when I am talking.* **2.** to stop or break off (activity or speech): *She interrupted her work to answer the phone.* **3.** to interfere with or make a break in: *The tall trees interrupted our view of the valley.* —*v.i.* to break in upon or stop an action or speech: *That child always interrupts when someone is speaking.*

in·ter·rup·tion (in′tə rup′shən) *n.* **1.** the act of interrupting or the state of being interrupted. **2.** something that interrupts: *His question was an unnecessary interruption.*

in·ter·scho·las·tic (in′tər skə las′tik) *adj.* between or among schools: *interscholastic sports.*

in·ter·sect (in′tər sekt′) *v.t.* to divide by passing through or cutting across: *The river intersected the valley.* —*v.i.* to meet and cross each other: *Parallel lines never intersect.*

in·ter·sec·tion (in′tər sek′shən, in′tər sek′shən) *n.* **1.** the place of intersecting, especially where two or more roads or streets meet and cross. **2.** the act of intersecting or the state of being intersected. **3.** *Mathematics.* **a.** the points contained in common by two geometrical figures. **b.** the set of all the elements that are found in two or more given sets.

Intersection

in·ter·sperse (in′tər spurs′) *v.t.,* **in·ter·spersed, in·ter·spers·ing. 1.** to scatter or insert (something) here and there among other things: *The author interspersed poems among the short stories in his book.* **2.** to vary by scattering or inserting something here and there: *He interspersed his remarks with literary quotations.* —**in·ter·sper·sion** (in′tər spur′shən), *n.*

in·ter·state (in′tər stāt′) *adj.* between or among two or more states of the United States: *interstate highways.*

in·ter·stel·lar (in′tər stel′ər) *adj.* between or among the stars: *interstellar space.*

in·ter·stice (in tur′stis) *n. pl.,* **in·ter·sti·ces** (in tur′stə siz, in tur′stə sēz′). a narrow space or opening between things or parts; crevice.

in·ter·twine (in′tər twīn′) *v.t., v.i.,* **in·ter·twined, in·ter·twin·ing.** to twine or twist together.

in·ter·val (in′tər vəl) *n.* **1.** time or space between: *An interval of a year passed before we were able to return.* **2.** *Music.* a difference in pitch between any two notes.

at intervals. a. with spaces between; here and there: *Signs were placed at intervals along the road.* **b.** from time to time; now and then.

in·ter·vene (in′tər vēn′) *v.i.*, **in·ter·vened, in·ter·ven·ing.**
1. to come between certain events or points in time: *Many years intervened before they met again.* **2.** to come between opposing parties; intercede: *The young man intervened in her behalf.* **3.** to come in or between so as to affect, change, or prevent: *The man had made many plans, but his sudden illness intervened.* **4.** to interfere in the affairs of another country. —**in·ter·ven·tion** (in′tər ven′shən), *n.*

in·ter·view (in′tər vyoo′) *n.* **1.** a meeting between a writer or reporter and a person from whom information is wanted. **2.** a broadcast or published report resulting from such a meeting. **3.** a meeting for a specific purpose, as to discuss employment: *a job interview.* —*v.t.* to have an interview with: *to interview a famous actress.* —**in′ter·view′er,** *n.*

in·ter·weave (in′tər wēv′) *v.t., v.i.*, **in·ter·wove** (in′tər wōv′) or **in·ter·weaved, in·ter·wo·ven** (in′tər wō′vən) or **in·ter·wove** or **in·ter·weaved, in·ter·weav·ing.** to weave, mix, or blend together.

in·tes·tate (in tes′tāt) *adj.* without making a will: *to die intestate.*

in·tes·ti·nal (in tes′tən əl) *adj.* of, relating to, or affecting the intestines. —**in·tes′ti·nal·ly,** *adv.*

in·tes·tine (in tes′tin) *n. usually,* **intestines.** that part of the alimentary canal extending from the stomach to the anus. The intestines are divided into the large intestine and the small intestine.

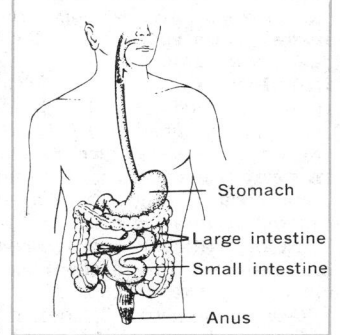

Stomach

Large intestine

Small intestine

Anus

in·ti·ma·cy (in′tə mə-sē) *n. pl.,* **in·ti·ma·cies.** **1.** the state of being intimate; closeness. **2.** an instance of this.

in·ti·mate¹ (in′tə mit) *adj.* **1.** closely or personally associated; well-acquainted: *The two men have been intimate friends for years.* **2.** of or resulting from great familiarity or closeness: *He has an intimate knowledge of the business.* **3.** personal or private: *She kept a diary of her most intimate thoughts.* —*n.* a very close friend or associate. [Influenced by *intimate²*, a form of earlier *intime,* from French *intime* inward, close.] —**in′ti·mate·ly,** *adv.*

in·ti·mate² (in′tə māt′) *v.t.*, **in·ti·mat·ed, in·ti·mat·ing.** to make known indirectly; hint; imply: *The mayor intimated that he might not seek reelection.* [Late Latin *intimātus.*] —**in′ti·ma′tion,** *n.*

in·tim·i·date (in tim′ə dāt′) *v.t.*, **in·tim·i·dat·ed, in·tim·i·dat·ing.** **1.** to make fearful or timid: *The child was intimidated by the fury of the storm.* **2.** to influence or frighten by threats or violence: *The thieves intimidated the shopkeeper by threatening to beat him.* —**in·tim′i·da′tion,** *n.* —**in·tim′i·da′tor,** *n.*

in·to (in′too, in′tə) *prep.* **1.** to or toward the inside of: *He bit into the apple. She came into the kitchen.* **2.** against so as to meet head on: *He bumped into the door.* **3.** to the state or form of: *The water turned into ice. The dish broke into pieces.* **4.** dividing: *8 into 16 is 2.*

in·tol·er·a·ble (in tol′ər ə bəl) *adj.* not to be endured; unbearable: *The living conditions in the city's slums were intolerable.* —**in·tol′er·a·bly,** *adv.*

in·tol·er·ance (in tol′ər əns) *n.* **1.** an unwillingness to allow or accept differences of opinion or practice: *religious intolerance.* **2.** the inability to resist or endure the effects of something: *an intolerance to penicillin.*

in·tol·er·ant (in tol′ər ənt) *adj.* **1.** unwilling to allow or accept differences of opinion or practice; not tolerant: *He was very intolerant of people who disagreed with his religious beliefs.* **2.** unable to resist or endure the effects: *She was intolerant of extreme heat.* —**in·tol′er·ant·ly,** *adv.*

in·to·na·tion (in′tō nā′shən) *n.* **1.** the act of intoning. **2.** the manner in which the voice rises and falls in pitch in speaking. **3.** *Music.* the production of tones that are accurate in pitch.

in·tone (in tōn′) *v.t., v.i.,* **in·toned, in·ton·ing.** to recite in a singing voice or monotone; chant.

in·tox·i·cant (in tok′sə kənt) *n.* any substance that intoxicates, especially alcoholic liquor.

in·tox·i·cate (in tok′sə kāt′) *v.t.*, **in·tox·i·cat·ed, in·tox·i·cat·ing.** **1.** to make drunk. **2.** to excite greatly: *The very sounds and smells of the country intoxicated him.* —**in·tox′i·ca′tion,** *n.*

intra- *prefix* inside of; within: *intrastate, intravenous.*

in·trac·ta·ble (in trak′tə bəl) *adj.* **1.** not easily managed; not tractable; stubborn: *an intractable child.* **2.** not easily treated, handled, used, or worked: *an intractable problem, an intractable subject.* —**in·trac′ta·bil′i·ty,** *n.* —**in·trac′ta·bly,** *adv.*

in·tra·mu·ral (in′trə myoor′əl) *adj.* consisting of or limited to participants from the same school or organization: *intramural basketball.*

in·tran·si·gent (in tran′sə jənt) *adj.* refusing to give in or compromise. —*n.* a person who is uncompromising. —**in·tran′si·gence,** *n.* —**in·tran′si·gent·ly,** *adv.*

in·tran·si·tive (in tran′sə tiv) *adj. Grammar.* of or relating to an action that does not require a direct object. The verb *die* is intransitive. —**in·tran′si·tive·ly,** *adv.*

in·tra·state (in′trə stāt′) *adj.* existing or happening within a state, especially of the United States.

in·tra·ve·nous (in′trə vē′nəs) *adj.* within or into a vein: *The doctor administered the medicine by an intravenous injection.* —**in′tra·ve′nous·ly,** *adv.*

in·trench (in trench′) another spelling of **entrench.**

in·trench·ment (in trench′mənt) another spelling of **entrenchment.**

in·trep·id (in trep′id) *adj.* having or showing great bravery; courageous; fearless: *The intrepid explorers moved deeper into the jungle.* —**in·trep′id·ly,** *adv.* —**in·trep′id·ness,** *n.*

in·tri·ca·cy (in′tri kə sē) *n. pl.,* **in·tri·ca·cies.** **1.** the state or quality of being intricate: *The design was drawn with great intricacy.* **2.** something intricate: *the intricacies of a legal document.*

in·tri·cate (in′tri kit) *adj.* **1.** very involved or complicated: *an intricate machine.* **2.** difficult to understand: *an intricate problem.* —**in′tri·cate·ly,** *adv.*

in·trigue (*n.,* in′trēg, in trēg′; *v.,* in trēg′) *n.* **1.** the use of underhanded and devious means: *There was much plotting and intrigue before the outbreak of war.* **2.** a secret scheme or plot: *a political intrigue.* **3.** a secret love affair. —*v.,* **in·trigued, in·trigu·ing.** —*v.t.* to arouse the curiosity or interest of; fascinate: *The story of the sailor's adventures intrigued the boys.* —*v.i.* to carry on an underhanded and devious scheme or plot: *The palace guards intrigued against the king.*

at; āpe; cär; end; mē; it; īce; hot; ōld; fôrk; wood; fōōl; oil; out; up; turn; sing; thin; **this;** hw in white; zh in treasure. The symbol ə stands for the sound of **a** in about, **e** in taken, **i** in pencil, **o** in lemon, and **u** in circus.

in·trin·sic (in trin′zik, trin′sik) *adj.* belonging or basic to something by its very nature: *the intrinsic beauty of a rose.* —**in·trin′si·cal·ly,** *adv.*

intro- *prefix* into; inward; within: *introvert.*

in·tro·duce (in′trə doos′, in′trə dyoos′) *v.t.,* **in·tro·duced, in·tro·duc·ing.** **1.** to make acquainted formally: *Our host introduced us to the other guests.* **2.** to bring into use, knowledge, or notice: *He introduced a new method of manufacturing the product.* **3.** to give first knowledge or experience to: *She introduced him to the ballet.* **4.** to bring forward for consideration; propose: *He introduced a motion to adjourn the meeting.* **5.** to bring or put in; insert: *The botanist introduced a new species of plant to the region.* **6.** to start; open; begin: *She introduced her lecture with a short poem.* —**in′tro·duc′er,** *n.*

in·tro·duc·tion (in′trə duk′shən) *n.* **1.** the act of introducing or the state of being introduced. **2.** something that serves to introduce, such as the preface of a book. **3.** something introduced.

in·tro·duc·to·ry (in′trə duk′tər ē) *adj.* serving to introduce; preliminary: *The senator began his speech with a few introductory remarks.*

in·tro·spec·tion (in′trə spek′shən) *n.* the examination of one's own thoughts or feelings.

in·tro·spec·tive (in′trə spek′tiv) *adj.* of, characterized by, or given to introspection. —**in′tro·spec′tive·ly,** *adv.*

in·tro·vert (in′trə vurt′) *n.* a person who is chiefly concerned with his or her own thoughts and feelings rather than with other people and what goes on around him or her. ▲ See **extrovert** for usage note.

in·tro·vert·ed (in′trə vurt′əd) *adj.* tending to be more concerned with one's own thoughts and feelings rather than with other people and what goes on around one.

in·trude (in trood′) *v.,* **in·trud·ed, in·trud·ing.** —*v.i.* to come in as a disturbing or unwelcome addition; enter without being asked or wanted: *The inconsiderate young man intruded upon their privacy.* —*v.t.* to thrust or force in or upon: *to intrude one's opinion into someone else's conversation.* —**in·trud′er,** *n.*

in·tru·sion (in troo′zhən) *n.* **1.** the act of intruding or the state of being intruded upon. **2.** an instance of intruding.

in·tru·sive (in troo′siv) *adj.* intruding or tending to intrude: *intrusive questions.* —**in·tru′sive·ly,** *adv.*

in·trust (in trust′) another spelling of **entrust.**

in·tu·i·tion (in′too ish′ən, in′tyoo ish′ən) *n.* **1.** a direct or immediate perception or understanding of truth without reasoning: *She knew by intuition that her friend was upset.* **2.** the knowledge or insight resulting from such perception.

in·tu·i·tive (in too′ə tiv, in tyoo′ə tiv) *adj.* **1.** of or relating to intuition: *intuitive ability.* **2.** coming from or characterized by intuition: *intuitive knowledge.* **3.** having intuition: *an intuitive person.* —**in·tu′i·tive·ly,** *adv.*

I·nu·it (in′oo it′, in′yoo it′) Another word for **Eskimo.**

in·un·date (in′ən dāt′) *v.t.,* **in·un·dat·ed, in·un·dat·ing.** **1.** to cover with a flood: *The river overflowed its banks and inundated the valley.* **2.** to overwhelm: *The newspaper was inundated with responses to its ad.* —**in′un·da′tion,** *n.*

in·ure (in yoor′) *v.t.,* **in·ured, in·ur·ing.** to make tough or hardy by experience; accustom: *The arctic climate inured him to extreme cold.*

in·vade (in vād′) *v.,* **in·vad·ed, in·vad·ing.** —*v.t.* **1.** to enter and attack with an armed force, as for conquest: *Germany invaded France in 1940.* **2.** to enter and overrun as if to take possession: *Rabbits invaded the garden during the night.* **3.** to interfere with; infringe upon; violate: *to invade the privacy of others.* **4.** to penetrate and spread with harmful effects; infect: *Disease germs had invaded his body.* —*v.i.* to make an invasion. —**in·vad′er,** *n.*

in·va·lid[1] (in′və lid) *n.* a person who is disabled by disease or injury. —*adj.* **1.** disabled by disease or injury. **2.** of, relating to, or for invalids. —*v.t.* to make an invalid of; disable. [French *invalide* sick, disabled.]

in·val·id[2] (in val′id) *adj.* without force, basis, or authority; not valid: *an invalid contract, an invalid excuse.* [Latin *invalidus* not strong, weak.]

in·val·i·date (in val′ə dāt′) *v.t.,* **in·val·i·dat·ed, in·val·i·dat·ing.** to make invalid: *This contract invalidates our previous agreement.* —**in·val′i·da′tion,** *n.*

in·va·lid·i·ty (in′və lid′ə tē) *n.* lack of validity.

in·val·u·a·ble (in val′yoo ə bəl, in val′yə bəl) *adj.* of greater value or worth than can be measured; priceless. —**in·val′u·a·bly,** *adv.*

in·var·i·a·ble (in ver′ē ə bəl, in var′ē ə bəl) *adj.* unchanging or unchangeable; not variable; constant; uniform: *the invariable heat of the tropics.* —**in·var′i·a·bil′i·ty,** *n.* —**in·var′i·a·bly,** *adv.*

in·va·sion (in vā′zhən) *n.* **1.** the entrance of an armed force, as into a country, in order to conquer or pillage. **2.** the act of invading or the state of being invaded. **3.** an intrusion or violation; infringement: *an invasion of one's rights.*

in·vec·tive (in vek′tiv) *n.* a violent accusation or verbal attack; harsh, abusive language: *The candidate for mayor directed his invective against the present mayor.*

in·veigh (in vā′) *v.i.* to utter a violent attack: *to inveigh against dictatorship.*

in·vei·gle (in vā′gəl, in vē′gəl) *v.t.,* **in·vei·gled, in·vei·gling.** to persuade or lure by deceit, coaxing, or flattery: *The man inveigled his friend into lending him a large sum of money.* —**in·vei′gler,** *n.*

in·vent (in vent′) *v.t.* **1.** to make or devise for the first time; create or originate: *to invent a new kind of automobile engine, to invent a new word.* **2.** to make up (something false or fictitious): *to invent rumors.*

in·ven·tion (in ven′chən) *n.* **1.** the act or process of inventing: *The invention of the computer has had a great effect on industry.* **2.** something that is invented: *The phonograph was one of Edison's most important inventions.* **3.** a fictitious account; false statement: *His story is nothing but invention.* **4.** the ability to invent; inventiveness.

in·ven·tive (in ven′tiv) *adj.* **1.** skillful and resourceful; able to invent: *an inventive person.* **2.** of, relating to, or characterized by invention: *inventive ability.* —**in·ven′tive·ly,** *adv.* —**in·ven′tive·ness,** *n.*

in·ven·tor (in ven′tər) *n.* a person who invents, especially one who makes or devises a new device or process: *Alexander Graham Bell was the inventor of the telephone.*

in·ven·to·ry (in′vən tôr′ē) *n. pl.,* **in·ven·to·ries.** **1.** a detailed list of articles in stock at a given time: *The inventory revealed that the store had too much merchandise on hand.* **2.** any detailed list of articles: *an inventory of books in a library.* **3.** the articles so listed. **4.** the act or process of making up such a list: *The store was closed for inventory.* —*v.t.,* **in·ven·to·ried, in·ven·to·ry·ing.** to make a detailed list of.

in·verse (in vurs′, in′vurs′) *adj.* opposite or reversed, as in order, position, direction, or effect. —*n.* **1.** the direct opposite; reverse. **2.** *Mathematics.* an element in a set which, when added to or multiplied by a given element, yields the identity element for addition or multiplication respectively. The **additive inverse** of 3 is −3; the **multiplicative inverse** of 3 is 1/3. Also *(def. 2),* **inverse element.** —**in·verse′ly,** *adv.*

in·ver·sion (in vur′zhən) *n.* **1.** the act of inverting or the state of being inverted. **2.** something that is inverted.

in·vert (in vurt′) *v.t.* **1.** to turn upside down: *The lens inverted the image.* **2.** to reverse the order, position, or relation of: *If you invert the letters of the word "star" you have "rats."* —**in·vert′i·ble,** *adj.*

in·ver·te·brate (in vur′tə brit, in vur′tə brāt′) *adj.* of or relating to an animal having no backbone. —*n.* an invertebrate animal.

in·vest (in vest′) *v.t.* **1.** to put (money) to use for the purpose of obtaining profit or income: *to invest one's savings in stocks.* **2.** to give or devote (time, effort, or the like), especially for personal benefit or advantage: *He invested much time and effort in the project.* **3.** to give power, authority, or privilege to: *Public officials are invested with certain powers.* **4.** to formally put in an office, rank, or position: *to invest a new school principal.* **5.** to give a certain quality to: *Her manner of speaking invested every word with great dignity.* —*v.i.* to make an investment: *to invest in a new business.* —**in·ves′tor,** *n.*

in·ves·ti·gate (in ves′tə gāt′) *v.,* **in·ves·ti·gat·ed, in·ves·ti·gat·ing.** —*v.t.* to look into carefully in order to uncover facts or gain information; make a thorough examination of: *to investigate a murder.* —*v.i.* to make an investigation.

in·ves·ti·ga·tion (in ves′tə gā′shən) *n.* the act or process of investigating; careful, thorough examination or search: *Police continued their investigation of the crime.*

in·ves·ti·ga·tor (in ves′tə gā′tər) *n.* a person who investigates, such as a detective.

in·ves·ti·ture (in ves′tə chər) *n.* the act or ceremony of formally putting a person in an office, rank, or position.

in·vest·ment (in vest′mənt) *n.* **1.** the act of investing, especially the use of money to obtain profit or income. **2.** the amount of money that is invested. **3.** something in which money is invested: *That stock is a good investment.*

in·vet·er·ate (in vet′ər it) *adj.* **1.** confirmed in a habit or practice; habitual: *an inveterate gambler.* **2.** firmly established by tradition or custom; deep-rooted: *inveterate prejudices.* —**in·vet′er·ate·ly,** *adv.*

in·vid·i·ous (in vid′ē əs) *adj.* **1.** arousing or liable to arouse ill will or hatred; odious: *an invidious task, an invidious remark.* **2.** unfairly or offensively biased: *She made an invidious comparison between her work and mine.* —**in·vid′i·ous·ly,** *adv.*

in·vig·o·rate (in vig′ə rāt′) *v.t.,* **in·vig·o·rat·ed, in·vig·o·rat·ing.** to fill with strength and energy; give vigor to: *The mountain air invigorated and refreshed him.* —**in·vig′o·rat′ing·ly,** *adv.* —**in·vig′o·ra′tion,** *n.*

in·vin·ci·ble (in vin′sə bəl) *adj.* not capable of being conquered or overcome; unconquerable: *an invincible army.* —**in·vin′ci·bil′i·ty,** *n.* —**in·vin′ci·bly,** *adv.*

in·vi·o·la·ble (in vī′ə bəl) *adj.* **1.** that must not be violated: *an inviolable oath.* **2.** that cannot be harmed or destroyed. —**in·vi′o·la·bil′i·ty,** *n.* —**in·vi′o·la·bly,** *adv.*

in·vi·o·late (in vī′ə lit, in vī′ə lāt′) *adj.* not broken; not violated: *Their friendship remained strong and inviolate through the years.*

in·vis·i·ble (in viz′ə bəl) *adj.* not capable of being seen; not visible: *The children believed that an invisible ghost haunted the old house.* —**in·vis′i·bil′i·ty,** *n.* —**in·vis′i·bly,** *adv.*

in·vi·ta·tion (in′və tā′shən) *n.* **1.** the act of inviting. **2.** the written or spoken form by which a person is invited: *to receive an invitation to a wedding.*

in·vite (in vīt′) *v.t.,* **in·vit·ed, in·vit·ing. 1.** to make a courteous or formal request for the presence or participation of: *He invited his friends to a party.* **2.** to ask for; request: *The editor invited comments from the readers of the magazine.* **3.** to tend to bring on; encourage or foster: *Her rude behavior can only invite trouble.* **4.** to attract; tempt: *The peacefulness of the lake invited them to pause in their hike and rest for a while.* —**in·vit′er,** *n.*

in·vit·ing (in vī′ting) *adj.* tempting; attractive: *The lake's clear water looked inviting on such a hot day.* —**in·vit′ing·ly,** *adv.*

in·vo·ca·tion (in′və kā′shən) *n.* **1.** the act of invoking, especially the calling upon in prayer for aid or protection; supplication. **2.** a prayer used in invoking, especially one spoken at the beginning of a public ceremony or formal religious service. **3.** an incantation used to summon a devil or spirit.

in·voice (in′vois′) *n.* an itemized list of goods sent to a buyer, indicating the quantities shipped, prices, and shipping charges. —*v.t.,* **in·voiced, in·voic·ing.** to make an invoice of: *to invoice a shipment of goods.*

in·voke (in vōk′) *v.t.,* **in·voked, in·vok·ing. 1.** to call upon in prayer for aid or protection: *to invoke God.* **2.** to call or beg for earnestly: *to invoke God's mercy.* **3.** to call forth by charms or incantation; conjure: *to invoke the spirits of the dead.* **4.** to call into use for support: *to invoke a law.*

in·vol·un·tar·y (in vol′ən ter′ē) *adj.* **1.** not done willingly or by choice; not voluntary: *an involuntary confession.* **2.** occurring without conscious control: *Breathing is an involuntary action.* —**in·vol′un·tar′i·ly,** *adv.*

in·volve (in volv′) *v.t.,* **in·volved, in·volv·ing. 1.** to include as a necessary part, condition, or result: *Winning the race involves both skill and speed.* **2.** to draw or bring into an unfortunate or difficult situation: *The young man's remark involved him in the quarrel.* **3.** to occupy completely; absorb: *He was involved in reading the book all evening.* **4.** to make complex; complicate: *a long, involved arithmetic problem.* —**in·volve′ment,** *n.*

in·vul·ner·a·ble (in vul′nər ə bəl) *adj.* not capable of being harmed or injured; safe against attack: *an invulnerable mountain fortress.* —**in·vul′ner·a·bil′i·ty,** *n.* —**in·vul′ner·a·bly,** *adv.*

in·ward (in′wərd) *adv. also,* **in·wards. 1.** toward the inside, interior, or center: *The front door opens inward.* **2.** into or toward the mind or self: *When she is unhappy, her thoughts usually turn inward.* —*adj.* **1.** toward the inside: *an inward push.* **2.** located within; inner; internal: *an inward pain.* **3.** in the mind or thought: *inward fears.*

in·ward·ly (in′wərd lē) *adv.* **1.** in, on, or toward the inside; within. **2.** in the mind or thought: *Although he seemed very calm, he was inwardly terrified.*

i·o·dide (ī′ə dīd′) *n.* a chemical compound of iodine with another element or radical.

i·o·dine (ī′ə dīn′, ī′ə dēn′) *n.* **1.** a nonmetallic element consisting of shiny, grayish crystals that vaporize in air, giving off a violet-colored vapor. Iodine is used in medicine and photography. Symbol: **I 2.** an antiseptic consisting of iodine dissolved in an alcohol solution.

i·o·dize (ī′ə dīz′) *v.t.,* **i·o·dized, i·o·diz·ing.** to treat with iodine or an iodide: *iodized salt.*

i·on (ī′ən) *n.* an atom or group of atoms that has an electrical charge resulting from a loss or gain of one or more electrons. Positive ions are formed by a loss of electrons; negative ions are formed by a gain of electrons.

-ion *suffix* (used to form nouns from verbs) **1.** the act of: *discussion, completion.* **2.** the state of being: *depression, damnation.* **3.** the result of: *pollution, fusion.*

at; āpe; cär; end; mē; it; īce; hot; ōld; fôrk; wood; fo͞ol; oil; out; up; turn; sing; thin; **th**is; hw in white; zh in treasure. The symbol ə stands for the sound of **a** in about, **e** in taken, **i** in pencil, **o** in lemon, and **u** in circus.

I·o·ni·a (ī ō′nē ə) *n.* an ancient region on the western coast of Asia Minor, colonized by the ancient Greeks. —**I·o′ni·an,** *adj., n.*

i·on·ic (ī on′ik) *adj.* of or relating to ions.

I·on·ic (ī on′ik) *adj.* **1.** of or relating to one of the three orders of classical Greek architecture, characterized by columns having scrolls on the capitals. **2.** of or relating to Ionia, its people, their language, or their culture.

i·on·ize (ī′ə nīz′) *v.,* **i·on·ized, i·on·iz·ing.** —*v.t.* to produce ions in. —*v.i.* to be changed into ions. —**i′on·i·za′tion,** *n.*

i·on·o·sphere (ī on′ə sfēr′) *n.* a region of ionized gases in the earth's atmosphere, occurring approximately 40 to 300 miles above the earth's surface. The ionosphere reflects certain radio waves, making it possible to transmit radio communications over long distances on earth.

i·o·ta (ī ō′tə) *n.* **1.** the ninth letter of the Greek alphabet (Ι, ι), corresponding to the English letter I, i. **2.** a very small amount; bit: *He hasn't an iota of proof to support what he said.*

IOU (ī′ō′yōō′) *n.* an informal written promise to pay a debt. [From the phrase "I owe you."]

I·o·wa (ī′ə wə) *n.* a state in the north-central United States. Capital, Des Moines. Area, 56,290 sq. mi. Pop. (1970), 2,825,041. Abbreviation, Ia. —**I′o·wan,** *adj., n.*

● **Iowa** comes from a shortened French version of the Dakota Indian word meaning "sleepy ones." It was the Dakota's scornful name for another Indian tribe that lived in what is now Iowa. The name went through a common process of being given first to a principal river of the region, then to the territory as a whole, and finally to the state.

IQ, see **intelligence quotient.**

Ir, the symbol for iridium.

ir-¹, a form of the prefix **in-¹** before *r,* as in *irregular.*

ir-², a form of the prefix **in-²** before *r,* as in *irruption.*

I·ran (i ran′, ē rän′) *n.* a country in southwestern Asia, formerly known as Persia. Capital, Tehran. Area, 636,300 sq. mi. Pop. (1980), 38,100,000.

I·ra·ni·an (i rā′nē ən) *n.* **1.** a person who was born or is living in Iran. **2.** the language of Iran. —*adj.* of or relating to Iran, its people, their language, or their culture.

I·raq (i rak′, i räk′) *n.* a country in southwestern Asia. Capital, Baghdad. Area, 167,925 sq. mi. Pop. (1980), 13,080,000. —**I·ra·qi** (i rak′ē, i rä′kē), *adj., n.*

i·ras·ci·ble (i ras′ə bəl) *adj.* easily irritated or made angry; irritable. —**i·ras′ci·bil′i·ty,** *n.* —**i·ras′ci·bly,** *adv.*

i·rate (ī rāt′) *adj.* angry; enraged: *A group of irate citizens demanded to see the mayor.* —**i·rate′ly,** *adv.*

IRBM, a ballistic missile with a range of between 300 and 1500 miles. [Abbreviation of *i*(ntermediate) *r*(ange) *b*(allistic) *m*(issile).]

ire (īr) *n.* anger; wrath.

ire·ful (īr′fəl) *adj.* full of ire; angry; wrathful: *an ireful glance.* —**ire′ful·ly,** *adv.*

Ire·land (īr′lənd) *n.* **1.** one of the British Isles, consisting of the Republic of Ireland and Northern Ireland. Area, 32,596 sq. mi. **2. Republic of.** a country in northwestern Europe occupying most of the island of Ireland, formerly known as Eire. Capital, Dublin. Area, 27,137 sq. mi. Pop. (1980), 3,037,000.

ir·i·des·cent (ir′ə des′ənt) *adj.* displaying shimmering and changing colors, like those reflected by soap bubbles. —**ir′i·des′cence,** *n.* —**ir′i·des′cent·ly,** *adv.*

i·rid·i·um (i rid′ē əm) *n.* an extremely hard, brittle, silver-white metallic element of the platinum family. It is used especially in alloys of platinum and for electrical contacts and chemical apparatus. Symbol: **Ir**

i·ris (ī′ris) *n. pl.,* **i·ris·es. 1.** the circular, colored membrane between the cornea and the lens that controls the amount of light entering the eye. **2.** a showy flower having three erect petals and three drooping petals. **3.** the plant bearing this flower, grown as a house and garden plant, usually having long, sword-shaped leaves. **4.** a rainbow. [From *Iris,* the Greek goddess of the rainbow.]

I·rish (ī′rish) *n.* **1. the Irish.** the people of Ireland or their close descendants. **2.** see **Irish Gaelic. 3.** the dialect of English spoken by the Irish.

Irish Gaelic, Gaelic as spoken in Ireland.

Iris

I·rish·man (ī′rish mən) *n. pl.,* **I·rish·men** (ī′rish mən). a person who was born or is living in Ireland. —**I′rish·wom′an,** *n.*

Irish potato, the common white potato.

Irish Sea, an arm of the Atlantic Ocean between Ireland and England.

Irish setter, a dog of a breed that originated in Ireland, having a coat of silky, reddish hair.

Irish terrier, a short-haired dog having a reddish, wiry coat.

Irish wolfhound, a very large, tall dog having a rough, wiry, usually gray, coat.

irk (urk) *v.t.* to annoy; vex; bother: *It irks me to hear her talk about herself all the time.*

Irish setter

irk·some (urk′səm) *adj.* annoying; tiresome: *an irksome job.* —**irk′some·ly,** *adv.* —**irk′some·ness,** *n.*

i·ron (ī′ərn) *n.* **1.** a gray-white metallic element that is very ductile, highly magnetic, and a good conductor of heat and electricity. Iron is the most important metal, and its alloys, such as steel, are the most widely used. Symbol: Fe **2.** anything that is hard, strong, or unyielding: *muscles of iron.* **3.** something made from iron or an alloy of iron. **4.** an appliance having a flat surface that is heated and used to press or smooth clothing and fabrics. **5.** a golf club with a metal head. **6. irons.** fetters or shackles: *The prisoner was in irons.* —*adj.* **1.** of or relating to iron: *The lion's cage had iron bars.* **2.** strong or unyielding: *an iron will.* —*v.t.* to smooth or press with a heated iron: *to iron a shirt.* —*v.i.* to iron fabric, especially clothing.

to iron out. to smooth out; settle: *We talked things over and ironed out our differences.*

Iron Age, the stage in the development of civilization following the Bronze Age, characterized by the widespread use of iron in tools and weapons.

i·ron·clad (ī′ərn klad′) *adj.* **1.** covered or protected with iron or steel plates. **2.** difficult to change or break: *an ironclad regulation.* —*n.* a nineteenth-century warship covered wholly or partially with iron plates for protection.

iron curtain, an imaginary barrier of censorship and secrecy, regarded as separating the Soviet Union and other European Communist countries from the non-Communist world. [Popularized by Winston Churchill in a speech in Fulton, Missouri, in 1946.]

i·ron·ic (ī ron′ik) *adj.* **1.** of, relating to, or characterized by irony: *an ironic situation, an ironic remark.* **2.** given to the use of irony: *an ironic writer.* Also, **i·ron·i·cal** (ī ron′i kəl). —**i·ron′i·cal·ly,** *adv.*

ironing board, a padded board, usually on a folding frame, on which fabrics or clothing may be ironed.

iron lung, an apparatus used to maintain breathing when normal respiration is impaired, as when a person's chest muscles are paralyzed. An iron lung consists of a cylindrical tank that encloses the body, except the head, and air pumps that increase and decrease the air pressure in the tank.

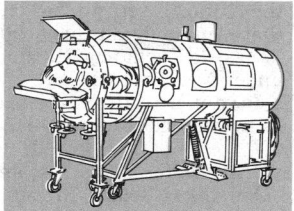
Iron lung

i·ron·ware (ī′ərn wer′) *n.* articles that are made of iron, such as pots.

i·ron·wood (ī′ərn wood′) *n.* **1.** any of a number of trees having hard, close-grained wood. **2.** the hard, durable wood of any of these trees, used especially for making tool handles and similar equipment.

i·ron·work (ī′ərn wurk′) *n.* things made of iron.

i·ron·work·er (ī′ərn wur′kər) *n.* **1.** a person whose work is smelting iron or manufacturing iron objects. **2.** a person who builds or repairs steel frameworks, as of bridges.

i·ron·works (ī′ərn wurks′) *n., pl.* a place where iron is smelted or where iron objects are manufactured.

i·ro·ny (ī′rə nē) *n. pl.,* **i·ro·nies. 1.** a form of expression in which the intended meaning is the opposite of that expressed in words, as when a person says "Oh, wonderful!" upon hearing bad news. **2.** an event or outcome of events opposite to what was, or might naturally have been, expected. **3.** the fact that such an unexpected event or outcome has occurred: *The fireman whose home had burned down was unable to appreciate the irony of his situation.*

Ir·o·quois (ir′ə kwoi′) *n. pl.,* **Ir·o·quois. 1.** a member of a confederation of North American Indian tribes formerly living in what is now the state of New York. Originally called the Five Nations (the Seneca, Cayuga, Onondaga, Oneida, and Mohawk), the Iroquois became the Six Nations in 1722 when the Tuscaroras joined the confederation. **2.** a member of a tribe belonging to this confederation. **3.** any of the languages spoken by these Indians. —*adj.* of or relating to the Iroquois or their languages.

ir·ra·di·ate (i rā′dē āt′) *v.t.,* **ir·ra·di·at·ed, ir·ra·di·at·ing. 1.** to shed light upon; brighten; illuminate: *Brilliant flashes of lightning irradiated the night sky.* **2.** to expose (something) to or treat with radiation. **3.** to send out in or as if in rays; radiate. —**ir·ra′di·a′tion,** *n.*

ir·ra·tion·al (i rash′ən əl) *adj.* **1.** lacking reason; not rational: *The survivors of the crash wandered about in a confused and irrational state.* **2.** contrary to reason; illogical; absurd: *The man's remarks were totally irrational.* —**ir·ra′tion·al·ly,** *adv.*

ir·ra·tion·al·i·ty (i rash′ə nal′ə tē) *n.* the condition or quality of being irrational.

irrational number, a number that cannot be expressed as a quotient of integers or as an integer. $\sqrt{2}$ and π are irrational numbers.

Ir·ra·wad·dy (ir′ə wod′ē) *n.* a river in eastern Asia, flowing through Burma into the Bay of Bengal.

ir·re·claim·a·ble (ir′i klā′mə bəl) *adj.* that cannot be reclaimed: *irreclaimable land.* —**ir′re·claim′a·bly,** *adv.*

ir·rec·on·cil·a·ble (i rek′ən sī′lə bəl) *adj.* **1.** that cannot be restored to friendly relations: *irreconcilable enemies.* **2.** that cannot be brought into agreement: *irreconcilable differences.* —**ir·rec′on·cil′a·bly,** *adv.*

ir·re·cov·er·a·ble (ir′i kuv′ər ə bəl) *adj.* that cannot be recovered or remedied: *an irrecoverable loss, irrecoverable damage.* —**ir′re·cov′er·a·bly,** *adv.*

ir·re·deem·a·ble (ir′i dē′mə bəl) *adj.* **1.** that cannot be bought back or paid off: *an irredeemable mortgage.* **2.** that cannot be converted into coin, such as certain kinds of paper money. **3.** that cannot be changed or remedied; hopeless: *an irredeemable criminal, an atmosphere of irredeemable gloom.* —**ir′re·deem′a·bly,** *adv.*

ir·re·duc·i·ble (ir′i dōō′sə bəl, ir′i dyōō′sə bəl) *adj.* that cannot be reduced or simplified; not reducible. —**ir′re·duc′i·bly,** *adv.*

ir·ref·u·ta·ble (i ref′yə tə bəl, ir′i fyōō′tə bəl) *adj.* that cannot be refuted or disproved; indisputable: *irrefutable evidence.* —**ir·ref′u·ta·bly,** *adv.*

ir·reg·u·lar (i reg′yə lər) *adj.* **1.** not conforming to standards, custom, or usual practice; unusual: *irregular behavior.* **2.** not evenly or uniformly shaped, arranged, or spaced; uneven: *the irregular surface of the moon.* **3.** *Grammar.* not according to the usual or most common pattern of inflection. The verb *be* is irregular. —**ir·reg′u·lar·ly,** *adv.*

ir·reg·u·lar·i·ty (i reg′yə lar′ə tē) *n. pl.,* **ir·reg·u·lar·i·ties. 1.** the state or quality of being irregular. **2.** something that is irregular.

ir·rel·e·vance (i rel′ə vəns) *n.* **1.** the quality or fact of being irrelevant. **2.** something that is irrelevant. Also, **ir·rel·e·van·cy** (i rel′ə vən sē).

ir·rel·e·vant (i rel′ə vənt) *adj.* not bearing upon or connected with the matter at hand; not pertinent; inappropriate: *Many of his remarks were irrelevant to the conversation.* —**ir·rel′e·vant·ly,** *adv.*

ir·re·li·gious (ir′i lij′əs) *adj.* **1.** indifferent to or lacking religion; not religious. **2.** showing disrespect to religious principles; profane. —**ir′re·li′gious·ly,** *adv.*

ir·re·me·di·a·ble (ir′i mē′dē ə bəl) *adj.* that cannot be remedied or cured. —**ir′re·me′di·a·bly,** *adv.*

ir·rep·a·ra·ble (i rep′ər ə bəl) *adj.* that cannot be repaired, restored, or made right: *The hurricane did irreparable damage to the house.* —**ir·rep′a·ra·bly,** *adv.*

ir·re·place·a·ble (ir′i plā′sə bəl) *adj.* that cannot be replaced: *irreplaceable works of art.*

ir·re·press·i·ble (ir′i pres′ə bəl) *adj.* that cannot be repressed or restrained: *She was a cheerful girl with irrepressible high spirits.* —**ir′re·press′i·bly,** *adv.*

ir·re·proach·a·ble (ir′i prō′chə bəl) *adj.* free from blame or criticism; above reproach; faultless: *irreproachable conduct.* —**ir′re·proach′a·bly,** *adv.*

ir·re·sist·i·ble (ir′i zis′tə bəl) *adj.* that cannot be resisted or opposed: *The chocolate cake was an irresistible temptation to the dieting woman.* —**ir′re·sis′ti·bil′i·ty,** *n.* —**ir′re·sist′i·bly,** *adv.*

ir·res·o·lute (i rez′ə lōōt′) *adj.* lacking decisiveness or certainty; hesitating: *The weak, irresolute king was never sure what to do.* —**ir·res′o·lute′ly,** *adv.* —**ir·res′o·lute′ness, ir·res′o·lu′tion,** *n.*

ir·re·spec·tive (ir′i spek′tiv) *adv.* regardless: *Anyone can apply for this job, irrespective of age or sex.*

ir·re·spon·si·ble (ir′i spon′sə bəl) *adj.* **1.** not trustworthy or dependable; unreliable: *a careless and irresponsi-*

at; āpe; cär; end; mē; it; īce; hot; ōld; fôrk; wood; fōol; oil; out; up; turn; sing; thin; this; hw in white; zh in treasure. The symbol ə stands for the sound of **a** in about, **e** in taken, **i** in pencil, **o** in lemon, and **u** in circus.

I

ble worker. **2.** not carefully considered: *an irresponsible decision, irresponsible behavior.* —**ir·re·spon·si·bil·i·ty,** *n.* —**ir·re·spon′si·bly,** *adv.*

ir·re·triev·a·ble (ir′i trē′və bəl) *adj.* that cannot be retrieved or recovered. —**ir′re·triev′a·bly,** *adv.*

ir·rev·er·ence (i rev′ər əns) *n.* **1.** lack of reverence or respect. **2.** an irreverent act or statement.

ir·rev·er·ent (i rev′ər ənt) *adj.* not feeling or showing reverence or respect; disrespectful: *an irreverent attitude toward religion.* —**ir·rev′er·ent·ly,** *adv.*

ir·re·vers·i·ble (ir′i vur′sə bəl) *adj.* that cannot be reversed, changed, or undone; irrevocable: *an irreversible decision.* —**ir′re·vers′i·bly,** *adv.*

ir·rev·o·ca·ble (i rev′ə kə bəl) *adj.* that cannot be revoked or recalled; unalterable: *The general's order was irrevocable.* —**ir·rev′o·ca·bly,** *adv.*

ir·ri·gate (ir′ə gāt′) *v.t.,* **ir·ri·gat·ed, ir·ri·gat·ing.** **1.** to supply (land) with water by means of channels, streams, or pipes: *to irrigate a desert so that crops can be grown.* **2.** to cleanse (a wound or body cavity) with a constant flow of some liquid. —**ir′ri·ga′tion,** *n.*

ir·ri·ta·bil·i·ty (ir′ə tə bil′ə tē) *n. pl.,* **ir·ri·ta·bil·i·ties.** **1.** the state or quality of being irritable: *The child's irritability was caused by his weariness.* **2.** *Biology.* the ability to respond to a stimulus.

ir·ri·ta·ble (ir′ə tə bəl) *adj.* **1.** easily excited to impatience or anger: *Michael is irritable when he is very tired.* **2.** very sensitive: *She has irritable skin.* **3.** *Biology.* able to respond to stimuli. —**ir′ri·ta·ble·ness,** *n.* —**ir′ri·ta·bly,** *adv.*

ir·ri·tant (ir′ə tənt) *n.* something that causes irritation. —*adj.* causing irritation.

ir·ri·tate (ir′ə tāt′) *v.t.,* **ir·ri·tat·ed, ir·ri·tat·ing. 1.** to make impatient or angry; vex: *The constant arguing of his friends irritated the young man.* **2.** to make sore or inflamed: *Smoke irritates the eyes.* —**ir′ri·tat′ing·ly,** *adv.* —**ir′ri·ta′tor,** *n.*

ir·ri·ta·tion (ir′ə tā′shən) *n.* **1.** the act or process of irritating or the state of being irritated; vexation. **2.** an inflamed or painful condition: *a skin irritation.*

Ir·ving (ur′ving) *n.* **1. Washington.** 1783–1859, U.S. author. **2.** a city in northeastern Texas, near Dallas. Pop. (1970), 97,260.

is (iz) the third person singular, present indicative, of **be.**

is., island.

I·saac (ī′zək) *n.* in the Old Testament, the son of Abraham and Sarah and the father of Jacob and Esau.

Is·a·bel·la I (iz′ə bel′ə) 1451–1504, Spanish queen of Castile. See **Ferdinand V.**

I·sai·ah (ī zā′ə) *n.* **1.** Hebrew prophet of the eighth century B.C. **2.** a book of the Old Testament believed to have been written by him.

Is·car·i·ot (is kar′ē ət) see **Judas** *(def. 1).*

is·chi·um (is′kē əm) *n. pl.,* **is·chi·a** (is′kē ə). the lowest portion of the hipbone.

Is·fa·han (is′fə hän′) *n.* a city in west-central Iran, the capital of Persia during the seventeenth and eighteenth centuries. Pop. (1966), 424,045.

-ish *suffix* (used to form adjectives) **1.** of, belonging to, or relating to: *Jewish.* **2.** of the nature or character of; like: *childish, foolish.* **3.** tending or inclined to: *bookish.* **4.** somewhat: *bluish, youngish.*

Ish·ma·el (ish′mē əl) *n.* **1.** in the Old Testament, the son of Abraham, who was cast out into the wilderness. **2.** any outcast.

i·sin·glass (ī′zin glas′) *n.* **1.** a white, odorless, very pure form of gelatin obtained from the air bladders of fish, especially sturgeon, used to make glue and clarify liquors. **2.** mica in thin sheets.

I·sis (ī′sis) *n.* the Egyptian goddess of fertility. She was the wife and sister of Osiris.

Is·lam (is′lam, is läm′) *n.* **1.** the religion based on the teachings and writings of Muhammad as they appear in the Koran, asserting that there is only one god, Allah, and that Muhammad is his prophet. **2.** the whole of the Muslim world, including Muslim civilization, and the countries under Muslim rule.

Is·lam·a·bad (is läm′ä bäd′) *n.* the capital of Pakistan, in the northern part of the country. Pop. (1970 est.), 60,000.

Is·lam·ic (is lam′ik, is läm′ik) *adj.* of, relating to, or belonging to Islam; Muslim.

is·land (ī′lənd) *n.* **1.** a body of land entirely surrounded by water and smaller than a continent. **2.** anything resembling an island: *an island of floating ice.*

is·land·er (ī′lən dər) *n.* a person who was born or is living on an island.

isle (īl) *n.* an island, especially a small island.

Isle of Man, see **Man, Isle of.**

is·let (ī′lit) *n.* a little island.

islet of Lang·er·hans (lang′ər häns′) any of the small masses of endocrine cells in the pancreas that secrete insulin. Also, **island of Langerhans.**

ism (iz′əm) *n.* a doctrine, theory, or system.

-ism *suffix* (used to form nouns) **1.** an action or practice: *criticism, baptism.* **2.** a state or condition: *parallelism, pessimism.* **3.** characteristic conduct or behavior: *patriotism, barbarism, heroism.* **4.** a distinguishing feature, aspect, or manner, as of language: *colloquialism.* **5.** a doctrine, system, or principle: *socialism, paganism.*

is·n't (iz′ənt) is not.

i·so·bar (ī′sə bär′) *n.* a line on a weather map connecting points having the same barometric pressure.

i·so·late (ī′sə lāt′) *v.t.,* **i·so·lat·ed, i·so·lat·ing.** to place or set apart; separate from others: *Persons with contagious diseases were isolated from the other hospital patients.*

i·so·la·tion (ī′sə lā′shən) *n.* the act of isolating or the state of being isolated.

i·so·la·tion·ism (ī′sə lā′shə niz′əm) *n.* the policy of avoiding political, economic, or military involvements with foreign countries.

i·so·la·tion·ist (ī′sə lā′shə nist) *n.* a person who supports, or is in favor of isolationism.

i·so·mer (ī′sə mər) *n.* any of two or more chemical compounds having the same molecular formula and thus the same composition, but differing in properties because their atoms are arranged differently.

i·so·met·ric (ī′sə met′rik) *adj.* of or relating to the contraction of a muscle in which there is increased tension rather than change in length: *isometric exercises.*

i·sos·ce·les (ī sos′ə lēz′) *adj.* of a triangle, having two sides whose lengths are equal.

i·so·therm (ī′sə thurm′) *n.* a line on a weather map connecting points having the same average temperature.

i·so·tope (ī′sə tōp′) *n.* any of two or more kinds of atoms of the same element having the same atomic number but different mass numbers.

Is·ra·el (iz′rē əl) *n.* **1.** a country in southwestern Asia, at the eastern end of the Mediterranean Sea. Capital, Jerusalem. Area, 7993 sq. mi. Pop. (1971 est.), 3,010,000. **2.** in the Old Testament, the patriarch Jacob. **3.** the people descended from Jacob; the Hebrew people. **4.a.** an ancient kingdom of Hebrew people, ruled by David and Solomon in the eleventh and tenth centuries B.C. **b.** the northern portion of this, established as a separate kingdom after Solomon's death.

Is·rae·li (iz rā′lē) *n. pl.,* **Is·rae·lis.** a person who was born or is living in modern Israel. —*adj.* of or relating to modern Israel, its people, their language, or their culture.

Is·ra·el·ite (iz'rē ə līt') *n.* a descendant of the patriarch Jacob; Hebrew. —*adj.* of or relating to the Hebrews.

is·su·ance (ish'ōō əns) *n.* the act of issuing.

is·sue (ish'ōō) *n.* **1.** the act of sending or giving out: *an issue of licenses, an issue of supplies.* **2.** the act of going, passing, or flowing out: *an issue of blood from a wound.* **3.** something that is sent or given out, such as a certain quantity of magazines, newspapers, stamps, or books, printed and distributed at one time. **4.** an individual copy of a magazine. **5.** a subject under discussion or consideration: *The raising of taxes was the issue under debate.* **6.** offspring: *The money was willed to Mr. Brown and his issue.* **7.** the outcome of an action or course of events; result; consequence. —*v.,* **is·sued, is·su·ing.** —*v.t.* **1.** to send or give out: *to issue coins, to issue a statement.* **2.** to send forth; discharge; emit. **3.** to publish: *to issue a magazine.* —*v.i.* to go or come out; flow out; pour forth. —**is'su·er,** *n.*

-ist *suffix* (used to form nouns) **1.** a person who does or makes: *tourist, novelist.* **2.** a person who practices or has as a profession: *machinist, violinist.* **3.** a person who supports or is in favor of: *idealist, socialist.*

Is·tan·bul (is'tan bōōl') *n.* the largest city of Turkey, located on both sides of the Bosporus. It was formerly called Constantinople and, in ancient times, Byzantium. Pop. (1970), 2,247,600.

isth·mus (is'məs) *n. pl.,* **isth·mus·es.** a narrow strip of land bordered by water and connecting two larger bodies of land.

it (it) *pron. sing.,* nominative, **it;** possessive, **its;** objective, **it;** *pl.,* nominative, **they;** possessive, **their, theirs;** objective, **them. 1.** a thing or animal previously mentioned: *He threw me the ball and I caught it.* **2.** the subject of an impersonal verb: *It snowed last night.* **3.** the grammatical subject of a verb introducing a phrase or dependent clause that is the actual subject: *It is obvious that he is lying.* —*n.* in certain children's games, the person who has to do something special. In playing tag, the person who is *it* has to chase the other players.

ital., italic; italics.

I·tal·ian (i tal'yən) *n.* **1.** a person who was born or is living in Italy. **2.** the language spoken in Italy and in parts of Switzerland. —*adj.* of, relating to, or characteristic of Italy, its people, their language, or their culture.

i·tal·ic (i tal'ik) *adj.* of or relating to a style of type whose letters slant to the right: *This sentence is printed in italic type.* —*n. also,* **italics.** italic type.

i·tal·i·cize (i tal'ə sīz') *v.t.,* **i·tal·i·cized, i·tal·i·ciz·ing.** to print in italic type.

It·a·ly (it'əl ē) *n.* a country in southern Europe, on the Mediterranean Sea. Capital, Rome. Area, 116,303 sq. mi. Pop. (1971 est.), 54,080,000.

itch (ich) *n. pl.,* **itch·es. 1.** a tickling or stinging feeling in the skin that is relieved by scratching or rubbing. **2.** a restless, uneasy desire for something: *He had an itch to travel across the country.* —*v.i.* **1.** to have or cause a tickling or stinging sensation in the skin: *The rash on my hand itches.* **2.** to have a restless, uneasy desire: *He is itching for a fight.*

itch·y (ich'ē) *adj.,* **itch·i·er, itch·i·est.** characterized by, having, or causing an itch. —**itch'i·ness,** *n.*

-ite *suffix* (used to form nouns) **1.** a person who was born or is living in: *Israelite.* **2.** a supporter or follower of: *laborite.* **3.** a mineral or rock: *calcite, bauxite.*

i·tem (ī'təm) *n.* **1.** a unit or article included in a group, series, or list: *There are many valuable items in his stamp collection.* **2.** a bit of information, or a brief newspaper article or paragraph containing such information: *There*

was an item in the newspaper about the senator's speech.

i·tem·ize (ī'tə mīz') *v.t.,* **i·tem·ized, i·tem·iz·ing.** to give each item of; list by items: *She itemized her expenses before making up a budget for the month.*

it·er·ate (it'ə rāt') *v.t.,* **it·er·at·ed, it·er·at·ing.** to say or do again; repeat. —**it'er·a'tion,** *n.*

i·tin·er·ant (ī tin'ər ənt) *adj.* traveling from place to place, especially for business or duty: *an itinerant preacher.* —*n.* a person who travels from place to place, especially for business or duty. —**i·tin'er·ant·ly,** *adv.*

i·tin·er·ar·y (ī tin'ə rer'ē) *n. pl.,* **i·tin·er·ar·ies. 1.** a planned course or route of travel, as for a journey: *Rome and Paris were included in her itinerary.* **2.** an account or record of travel. **3.** a guidebook for travelers.

-itis *suffix* (used to form nouns) inflammation of: *tonsillitis, bronchitis.*

it'll (it'əl) **1.** it will. **2.** it shall.

its (its) *adj.* of or belonging to it: *The cat licked its paw.*

it's (its) **1.** it is: *It's cold today.* **2.** it has: *It's been nice to see you.*

it·self (it self') *pron.* **1.** the form of **it** used to give emphasis to the word it goes with: *The yard is overgrown with weeds, but the house itself is in good condition.* **2.** the form of **it** used to show that the subject and direct object of a verb in a sentence are the same: *The cat can wash itself.*

-ity *suffix* (used to form nouns) the state, condition, or quality of being: *formality, inferiority.*

I·van III (ī'vən) 1440–1505, the ruler of Russia from 1462 to 1505. Also, **Ivan the Great.**

Ivan IV, 1530–1584, the czar of Russia from 1547 to 1584. Also, **Ivan the Terrible.**

I've (īv) I have: *I've no money.*

-ive *suffix* (used to form adjectives) **1.** given to: *active, assertive, instructive.* **2.** of, relating to, or of the nature of: *massive, instinctive.*

i·vo·ry (ī'vər ē) *n. pl.,* **i·vo·ries. 1.** a smooth, hard, white substance that forms the tusks of elephants, walruses, and certain other animals. **2.** something made of this substance: *The museum has a fine collection of medieval ivories.* **3.** a creamy white color. **4. ivories.** *Slang.* the keys of a piano. —*adj.* **1.** of or resembling ivory. **2.** having the color ivory.

Ivory Coast, a country in western Africa, on the Gulf of Guinea. Capital, Abidjan. Area, 124,504 sq. mi. Pop. (1969 est.), 4,200,000.

i·vy (ī'vē) *n. pl.,* **i·vies. 1.** any of several climbing or creeping vines with shiny leaves, widely grown as decorative coverings for walls. **2.** any of various other climbing plants, such as poison ivy.

ivy

-ize *suffix* (used to form verbs) **1.** to act upon; make: *civilize, legalize.* **2.** to treat like: *idolize.* **3.** to treat or affect with: *oxidize.* **4.** to form into; become: *crystallize.* **5.** to be concerned with or engaged in: *economize.*

Iz·mir (iz'mēr, iz mēr') *n.* a port city in western Turkey, on the Aegean Sea, formerly known as Smyrna. Pop. (1970 est.), 520,700.

---

at; āpe; cär; end; mē; it; īce; hot; ōld; fôrk; wood; fōōl; oil; out; up; turn; sing; thin; this; hw in white; zh in treasure. The symbol ə stands for the sound of **a** in about, **e** in taken, **i** in pencil, **o** in lemon, and **u** in circus.

I

1. Egyptian Hieroglyphics \\ ⫻	5. Greek Classical Capitals Ɪ
2. Semitic ⁊	6. Etruscan ( ))
3. Phoenician Ɪ	7. Latin Fourth Century B.C. Capitals │
4. Greek Ninth Century B.C. │	8. English J

J is the tenth letter of the English alphabet. It is one of only three letters that we use today that did not come from Latin or from an earlier alphabet. Because the letter **J** developed as a variation of the letter **I,** they can be said to share the same early history. The earliest ancestor of **I** and **J** was an Egyptian hieroglyphic (1) that probably represented a hand. In the ancient Semitic alphabet, this symbol was altered and called *yod* (2), meaning "hand." The Phoenicians (3) simplified *yod* by making it a tall vertical line with a short horizontal stroke at the top and bottom. The Greek form of *yod* was called *iota*. At first, *iota* was written as a single vertical line (4). By about the fifth century B.C., the Greeks had added a short horizontal stroke at the top and bottom of the letter (5), writing it much as the Phoenicians had. The earlier form of *iota* was adopted in the Etruscan (6) and the Latin (7) alphabets. In the Latin alphabet, from which our alphabet developed, the letter **I,** like our modern letter **Y,** stood for both a vowel sound and a consonant sound. In the Middle Ages, it became customary to lengthen the small letter **i** below the line when it appeared as the first letter of a word. Two distinct forms of the letter **I** were soon recognized, the new form being written almost exactly as the letter **J** is written today (8). By about 400 years ago, the letter **I** was used to represent only the vowel sound, and the letter **J,** which was placed after I in the alphabet, was used only for the consonant sound. The close relationship between I and J can best be seen when they are written in lower case, as **i** and **j,** because they are the only letters of the alphabet that are written with a dot.

j, J (jā) *n. pl.,* **j's, J's. 1.** the tenth letter of the English alphabet. **2.** something having the shape of this letter.

jab (jab) *v.,* **jabbed, jab·bing.** —*v.t.* **1.** to poke or thrust at sharply, as with something pointed: *I accidentally jabbed her with a pin.* **2.** to punch or strike at (something) with short, quick blows: *to jab a punching bag.* —*v.i.* **1.** to poke or thrust sharply. **2.** to punch or strike with short, quick blows. —*n.* a sharp, quick thrust or blow.

jab·ber (jab′ər) *v.i.* to talk rapidly, indistinctly, or foolishly; chatter. —*n.* rapid, indistinct, or foolish talk; gibberish. —**jab′ber·er,** *n.*

ja·bot (zha′bō) *n.* a ruffle or similar decoration of lace or other material, usually worn down the front of a dress or shirt.

jack (jak) *n.* **1.** any of various devices, usually portable, that are used for raising heavy objects a short distance. **2.** a playing card on which there is a picture of a young man. Also, **knave. 3.a. jacks.** a game in which the object is to pick up a number of small, six-pointed metal pieces or similar objects while bouncing and catching a small rubber ball with the same hand. Also, **jackstones.** ▲ used with a singular verb. **b.** one of the playing pieces used in this game. Also, **jackstone. 4.** a male donkey; jackass. **5.** a small flag flown by a ship, usually to show what

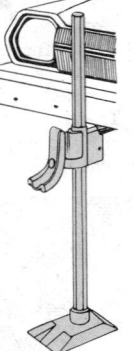

Jack

country it is from. **6.** an electrical device into which a plug may be inserted to make a connection. —*v.t.* **1.** to raise or move with a jack: *to jack up an automobile.* **2.** *Informal.* to increase: *The club jacked up its monthly dues to five dollars.*

jack·al (jak′əl) *n.* any of various animals of Africa, Asia, and southeastern Europe, that have a pointed face, a bushy tail, and usually gray, buff, or reddish-black fur. Jackals often feed on the remains of another animal's prey.

jack·a·napes (jak′ə nāps′) *n.* a bold, rude, or conceited fellow.

jack·ass (jak′as′) *n. pl.,* **jack·ass·es. 1.** a male donkey. **2.** a stupid or foolish person; blockhead.

Jackal

jack·boot (jak′boot′) *also,* **jack boot.** *n.* a sturdy boot reaching above the knee, originally designed to be worn by cavalrymen.

jack·daw (jak′dô′) *n.* a crow of Europe, Asia, and northern Africa, having glossy black feathers with a gray band around the throat and a gray underside. Also, **daw.**

jack·et (jak′it) *n.* **1.** a short coat that usually does not extend below the hips. **2.** an outer covering or casing, such as a removable paper cover for a book or a cardboard cover for a phonograph record. —*v.t.* to cover with a jacket; put a jacket on.

Jack Frost, frost or freezing cold weather thought of as a person.

jack·ham·mer (jak′ham′ər) *n.* a machine that is powered by compressed air, used to drill rock, pavement, or similar hard materials.

jack-in-the-box (jak′in′<u>th</u>ə boks′) *n. pl.,* **jack-in-the-box·es.** a toy consisting of a box containing a doll, often in the form of a clown, that springs up when the lid of the box is opened.

jack-in-the-pul·pit (jak′in <u>th</u>ə pul′pit) *n. pl.,* **jack-in-the-pul·pits.** a tall plant of eastern North America, bearing tiny flowers that are enclosed within a leaf that is shaped like a hood.

jack·knife (jak′nīf′) *n. pl.,* **jack·knives** (jak′nīvz). **1.** a large pocketknife. **2.** a dive in which the diver bends at the waist and, keeping his legs straight, touches his feet with his hands before straightening out and entering the water. —*v.t., v.i.,* **jack·knifed, jack·knif·ing.** to double up or bend like a jackknife.

jack-of-all-trades (jak′əv ôl′trādz′) *n. pl.,* **jacks-of-all-trades.** a person who can do many different kinds of work.

jack-o’-lan·tern (jak′ə lan′tərn) *n. pl.,* **jack-o’-lan·terns.** a pumpkin that has been hollowed out and carved so as to resemble a human face, used as a decoration or lantern at Halloween.

jack·pot (jak′pot′) *n.* the top prize in a game or contest: *That quiz show has a $100,000 jackpot.*
  to hit the jackpot. a. to win a jackpot. **b.** to have great success or unexpected good fortune.

jack rabbit, any of several North American hares having very long ears and long, powerful hind legs.

jack·screw (jak′skrōō′) *n.* a jack for raising objects, operated by means of a screw.

Jack·son (jak′sən) *n.* **1. Andrew.** 1767–1845, the seventh president of the United States, from 1829 to 1837. **2. Stone·wall** (stōn′wôl′). 1824–1863, Confederate general in the Civil War; born Thomas Jonathan Jackson. **3.** the capital and largest city of Mississippi, in the central part of the state. Pop. (1970), 153,968.

Jack·son·ville (jak′sən vil′) *n.* the largest city in Florida, a port on the northeastern coast of the state. Pop. (1970), 528,865.

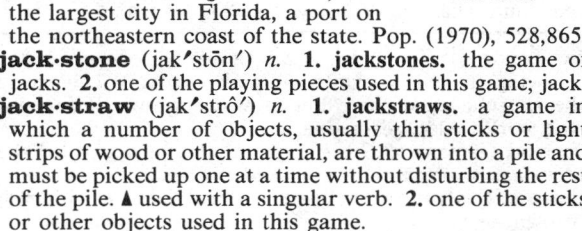
Jack rabbit

jack·stone (jak′stōn′) *n.* **1. jackstones.** the game of jacks. **2.** one of the playing pieces used in this game; jack.

jack·straw (jak′strô′) *n.* **1. jackstraws.** a game in which a number of objects, usually thin sticks or light strips of wood or other material, are thrown into a pile and must be picked up one at a time without disturbing the rest of the pile. ▲ used with a singular verb. **2.** one of the sticks or other objects used in this game.

Ja·cob (jā′kəb) *n.* in the Old Testament, a Hebrew patriarch who was the son of Isaac and twin brother of Esau. Jacob's twelve sons founded the twelve tribes of Israel.

jade¹ (jād) *n.* **1.** either of the two very hard minerals that are most commonly deep green to greenish-white in color and are used for jewelry and carved ornaments. **2.** a deep green to greenish-white color. —*adj.* having the color jade. [French *jade.*]

jade² (jād) *n.* **1.** an old, worthless, or ill-tempered horse. **2.** a disreputable or worthless woman. —*v.,* **jad·ed, jad·**

ing. —*v.t.* to make dull, tired, or worn-out: *The large amount of candy he ate that day jaded his appetite for sweets.* —*v.i.* to become dull, tired, or worn-out. [Of uncertain origin.]

jad·ed (jā′did) *adj.* **1.** tired or worn-out: *a jaded animal.* **2.** dulled, as from overindulgence; sated: *After watching television for a long time, his interest became jaded.* —**jad′ed·ly,** *adv.* —**jad′ed·ness,** *n.*

Jaf·fa (jaf′ə) *n.* a port on the Mediterranean coast of Israel, combined with Tel Aviv in 1950 as one city.

jag (jag) *n.* a sharp, projecting point. —*v.t.,* **jagged, jagging. 1.** to cut notches in. **2.** to make uneven or ragged by cutting or tearing.

jag·ged (jag′id) *adj.* having sharp, projecting points or uneven edges: *a piece of jagged rock, a jagged rip in cloth.* —**jag′ged·ly,** *adv.* —**jag′ged·ness,** *n.*

jag·uar (jag′wär) *n.* a large animal of the cat family, native to the southwestern United States, Mexico, and Central and South America, having a coat of short, tawny or golden fur with black spots.

Jaguar

jai a·lai (hī′ lī′, hī′ə lī′) a game similar to handball, in which the ball is hurled and caught with a long, curved basket strapped to the wrist. It is popular especially in Spain and Latin America. [Spanish *jai alai,* from Basque *jai* festival + *alai* merry.]

jail (jāl) *also, British,* **gaol.** *n.* a building in which people who have been accused or convicted of breaking the law are confined. —*v.t.* to put or keep in jail; imprison.

jail·er (jā′lər) *also,* **jail·or;** *British,* **gaol·er.** *n.* the keeper of a jail.

Jai·pur (jī′poor) *n.* a city in northwestern India. Pop. (1971), 613,144.

Ja·kar·ta (jə kär′tə) another spelling of **Djakarta.**

ja·lop·y (jə lop′ē) *n. pl.,* **ja·lop·ies.** *Informal.* an old or broken-down automobile.

jal·ou·sie (jal′ə sē) *n.* a series of horizontal overlapping slats, often made of glass, that can be adjusted to regulate the passage of air and light.

jam¹ (jam) *v.,* **jammed, jam·ming.** —*v.t.* **1.** to squeeze, force, or press into or through a tight or close space: *Ed jammed all his clothes into one small suitcase.* **2.** to fill or block up completely: *Shoppers jammed the stores at Christmas time.* **3.** to push, place, or thrust violently: *Jim jammed on the brakes to stop the car.* **4.** to cause to become stuck or wedged so as to be unworkable: *Rust and dirt had jammed the lock on the gate.* **5.** to bruise or crush: *The girl jammed her hand when she closed the drawer on it.* **6.** to interfere with (electronic signals), as by operating radio equipment at the same frequency. —*v.i.* **1.** to become stuck or wedged: *The key jammed in the lock.* **2.** to become unworkable through the sticking or wedging of some part: *The soldier's rifle jammed.* **3.** to force one's way into a confined space: *Thousands of people jam into the subways during rush hour.* —*n.* **1.** a mass of people or things so tightly crowded together that it is difficult or

at; āpe; cär; end; mē; it; īce; hot; ōld; fôrk;
wood; fōōl; oil; out; up; turn; sing; thin; <u>th</u>is;
hw in white; zh in treasure. The symbol ə
stands for the sound of **a** in about, **e** in taken,
i in pencil, **o** in lemon, and **u** in circus.

J

impossible to move. **2.** the act of jamming or the state of being jammed. **3.** *Informal.* a difficult or troublesome situation; fix: *He was in a real jam for having told a lie.* [Possibly imitative of the sound made by a jamming movement.]

jam² (jam) *n.* a food made by boiling fruit with sugar until it is thick, used as a spread on bread and other foods. [Probably from *jam¹*; referring to the fact that jam is made by pressing fruit into a tight space.]

Ja·mai·ca (jə māʹkə) *n.* an island country of the Greater Antilles, in the Caribbean, south of Cuba. Capital, Kingston. Area, 4232 sq. mi. Pop. (1971 est.), 1,900,000. —**Ja·maiʹcan,** *adj., n.*

jamb (jam) *also,* **jambe.** *n.* a post or surface forming the side of a doorway, window, or other opening.

jam·bo·ree (jamʹbə rēʹ) *n.* **1.** a noisy or festive gathering or celebration. **2.** a large national or international assembly of Boy Scouts.

James (jāmz) *n.* **1.** in the New Testament, one of Christ's Apostles. Also, **James the Greater. 2.** in the New Testament, one of Christ's Apostles. Also, **James the Less. 3.** an Epistle of the New Testament. **4. Henry.** 1843–1916, U.S. novelist and short story writer. **5. William.** 1842–1910, U.S. philosopher and psychologist; brother of Henry James.

James I, 1566–1625, the king of England from 1603 to 1625, and, as James VI, the king of Scotland from 1567 to 1625.

James II, 1633–1701, the king of England, Scotland, and Ireland from 1685 to 1688.

James·town (jāmzʹtounʹ) *n.* a village in southeastern Virginia, the first permanent English settlement in America, founded in 1607.

Jam·mu and Kashmir (jumʹōō) see **Kashmir.**

jam session, a gathering of jazz musicians in which they improvise freely.

Jan., January.

jan·gle (jangʹgəl) *v.,* **jan·gled, jan·gling.** —*v.i.* to make a harsh or unpleasant sound: *I woke up when the telephone jangled.* —*v.t.* **1.** to cause to make a harsh or unpleasant sound. **2.** to have an upsetting or irritating effect on: *The constant noise jangled his nerves.* —*n.* a harsh or unpleasant sound.

jan·i·tor (janʹə tər) *n.* a person employed to clean and service a building or establishment, such as an apartment house, school, or office.

Jan·u·ar·y (janʹyōō erʹē) *n. pl.,* **Jan·u·ar·ies.** the first month of the year, having thirty-one days. [Latin *Jānuārius (mēnsis)* the (month) of the god Janus; because Janus had two faces, he was thought of as looking back on the old year and ahead to the new.]

Ja·nus (jāʹnəs) *n. Roman Mythology.* the god of gates and doors, usually represented as having two faces looking in opposite directions.

Jap. 1. Japan. **2.** Japanese.

ja·pan (jə panʹ) *n.* **1.** any of various durable, glossy, black lacquers or varnishes, originally from Japan. **2.** a work varnished and decorated with this. —*adj.* relating to or varnished with japan. —*v.t.,* **ja·panned, japan·ning.** to varnish or lacquer with japan.

Ja·pan (jə panʹ) *n.* **1.** an island country in the North Pacific, off the eastern coast of Asia. Capital, Tokyo. Land area, 142,727 sq. mi. Pop. (1971 est.), 104,660,000. Also, **Nippon. 2. Sea of.** the arm of the Pacific separating Japan from the Asian mainland.

Jap·a·nese (japʹə nēzʹ) *n. pl.,* **Jap·a·nese. 1.** a person who was born or is living in Japan. **2.** the language of Japan. —*adj.* of or relating to Japan, its people, their language, or their culture.

Japanese beetle, a small, destructive beetle introduced into the United States from Japan. It has red wings and a green and brown oval body, and feeds on various plants.

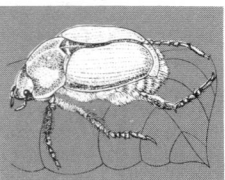

Japanese beetle

jar¹ (jär) *n.* **1.** a cylindrical container that usually has a wide mouth, and is made of glass or earthenware. **2.** the amount contained in a jar; contents of a jar: *The boy ate a whole jar of jam.* [French *jarre.*]

jar² (jär) *v.,* **jarred, jar·ring.** —*v.t.* **1.** to cause to move suddenly by impact or shock; shake; vibrate: *The explosion jarred the building.* **2.** to have a harsh, disturbing, or unpleasant effect on: *The sudden clatter jarred her nerves.* —*v.i.* **1.** to have an irritating or upsetting effect: *His loud laugh jars on my nerves.* **2.** to clash; conflict: *This verse . . . jars with the words which precede and follow* (Matthew Arnold). **3.** to make a harsh or discordant sound. —*n.* **1.** a shake or sudden movement; shock; jolt. **2.** a sudden disturbing effect on the mind or senses. **3.** a harsh or discordant sound or combination of sounds. [Probably imitative of a jarring sound.]

jar·gon (järʹgən) *n.* **1.** the technical or specialized language of a particular profession, sect, or other group. **2.** confused, unclear, or meaningless speech or writing; gibberish. **3.** a mixture of two or more languages or dialects, especially a mixture that helps people who speak different languages to talk with each other.

● **Jargon** is the special vocabulary used by a group of people who are in the same profession or share some other special interest. The use of jargon comes from the need to have words that describe all the things that one deals with. If you were a doctor, you would need to know and use many more words relating to medicine than other people would, because you would be dealing with medicine in a much more complicated way. The same is true for lawyers, chefs, carpenters, musicians, and anyone else who is involved in a particular field.

The word jargon is often used in a negative sense, because people feel that jargon is difficult to understand. Jargon or any other type of specialized language should be used only when it effectively conveys information that simpler language could not. When two doctors discuss a medical problem it is perfectly natural that they will use jargon. But if one of these doctors were to use jargon in speaking to a patient, the patient would probably not understand what the doctor was saying.

---

jas·mine (jazʹmin) *n.* **1.** a fragrant bell-shaped flower growing in yellow, white, or pink clusters. **2.** a shrub bearing clusters of these flowers, widely grown throughout the world. Also, **jessamine.**

Ja·son (jāʹsən) *n. Greek Legend.* the hero who led the Argonauts in search of the Golden Fleece.

jas·per (jasʹpər) *n.* an opaque quartz that is usually red, brown, or yellow.

jaun·dice (jônʹdis) *n.* **1.** a yellow discoloration of the skin, the whites of the eyes, and the mucous membranes, caused by an excess of bile pigment in the blood. **2.** a state of mind or feeling that affects the point of view or distorts the judgment. —*v.t.,* **jaun·diced, jaun·dic·ing.** to affect the point of view or distort the judgment of; prejudice: *Bitterness toward women jaundiced his view of marriage.*

jaun·diced (jônʹdist) *adj.* **1.** affected with jaundice. **2.** affected by envy, jealousy, bitterness, or similar feeling; prejudiced.

jaunt (jônt) *n.* a short trip, especially one taken for pleasure. —*v.i.* to take such a trip.

jaun·ty (jôn′tē) *adj.,* **jaun·ti·er, jaun·ti·est. 1.** lively, carefree, or self-confident in air or manner; sprightly: *He whistled a jaunty tune as he walked home.* **2.** smart; stylish: *He wore a jaunty cap and jacket.* —**jaun′ti·ly,** *adv.* —**jaun′ti·ness,** *n.*

Ja·va (jä′və, jav′ə) *n.* **1.** a large island of Indonesia, in the Malay Archipelago. Area, approx. 50,000 sq. mi. Pop. (1975 est.), 79,929,325. **2.** the coffee grown on Java and other nearby islands. **3.** *also,* **java.** *Informal.* any coffee.

Java man, an extinct primitive man that resembled an ape but was able to walk erect. His fossil remains, dating from the early Ice Age, were found in central Java. Also, **Pithecanthropus.**

Jav·a·nese (jav′ə nēz′) *n. pl.,* **Jav·a·nese. 1.** a person who was born or is living in Java. **2.** the language spoken in Java. —*adj.* of or relating to Java, its people, their language, or their culture.

jave·lin (jav′lin) *n.* **1.** a light spear, used chiefly as a weapon. **2.** a lightweight metal shaft that resembles a spear. It is thrown for distance in athletic contests. **3.** the contest in which it is thrown.

Javelin

jaw (jô) *n.* **1.** either of the two bony structures forming the framework of the mouth and holding the teeth, especially the lower of these structures. **2.** *also,* **jaws.** the part of the face covering these structures; the mouth and its related parts. **3.** either of a pair of parts, as of a tool, than can be closed to grasp or hold something: *the jaws of a vise.* —*v.i. Slang.* to talk; chatter. —**jaw′like′,** *adj.*

jaw·bone (jô′bōn′) *n.* one of the bones of the jaw, especially the mandible.

jaw·break·er (jô′brā′kər) *n.* **1.** very hard candy or chewing gum. **2.** *Informal.* a word that is difficult to pronounce.

jay (jā) *n.* any of various noisy birds related to crows and magpies. Most jays have a crest and brightly colored feathers.

Jay, John (jā) 1745–1829, the first chief justice of the U.S. Supreme Court, from 1789 to 1795.

jay·walk (jā′wôk′) *v.i.* to cross a street without paying attention to traffic laws or signals. —**jay′walk′er,** *n.*

jazz (jaz) *n.* **1.** music of a style that was originated by American blacks late in the nineteenth century. Jazz is characterized by improvisation, strong rhythm, and syncopation. **2.** *Slang.* exaggerated, insincere, or idle talk; nonsense. —*v.t.* to play or arrange (music) as jazz.

    to jazz up. to make more lively or exciting: *He jazzed up his bedroom with brightly colored posters.*

jeal·ous (jel′əs) *adj.* **1.** fearful or suspicious of losing to someone else what one wishes to gain or keep, especially the love or affection of another person: *Don't be jealous of your best friend's accomplishments.* **2.** envious or resentful of a person or of a person's achievements or advantages: *The girl was jealous of her friend's success.* **3.** careful in guarding or keeping something: *The people were jealous of their hard-won freedoms.* —**jeal′ous·ly,** *adv.* —**jeal′ous·ness,** *n.*

jeal·ous·y (jel′ə sē) *n. pl.,* **jeal·ous·ies.** the state or quality of being jealous; jealous feeling or attitude.

jean (jēn) *n.* **1.** a strong cotton fabric, used chiefly for sportswear and work clothes. **2. jeans.** trousers or overalls made of this fabric or denim; dungarees.

Jeanne d'Arc (zhän′därk′) another spelling of **Joan of Arc.**

jeep (jēp) *n.* a small, powerful motor vehicle used chiefly by the armed forces.

jeer (jēr) *v.i.* to speak or shout in a scornful or mocking manner; scoff: *The other boys jeered at the boastful boy.* —*v.t.* to treat or speak to (someone) with scorn or mockery; taunt: *The fans jeered the player when he dropped the ball.* —*n.* a scornful or mocking remark; taunt.

Jef·fer·son, Thomas (jef′ər sən) 1743–1826, the third president of the United States, from 1801 to 1809.

Jefferson City, the capital of Missouri, in the central part of the state. Pop. (1970), 32,407.

Jef·fer·so·ni·an (jef′ər sō′nē ən) *adj.* of or relating to Thomas Jefferson or his political principles.

Je·ho·vah (ji hō′və) *n.* in the Old Testament, God.

Jehovah's Witnesses, a Christian religious sect, founded in the United States in the late nineteenth century.

je·june (ji jōōn′) *adj.* lacking interest, significance, or value; dull or empty: *a jejune speech.*

je·ju·num (ji jōō′nəm) *n. pl.,* **je·ju·na** (ji jōō′nə). the middle section of the small intestine, extending from the duodenum to the ileum.

jell (jel) *v.i.* **1.** to change from a liquid to a solid resembling jelly. **2.** *Informal.* to assume definite form; become clear: *His ideas began to jell.*

jel·ly (jel′ē) *n. pl.,* **jel·lies. 1.** any food preparation consisting mainly of gelatin or pectin and having a smooth, firm, elastic consistency, especially such a preparation made of boiled fruit juice and sugar: *The boy put grape jelly on the toast.* **2.** anything having the consistency of or resembling jelly. —*v.t.,* **jel·lied, jel·ly·ing. 1.** to make into jelly. **2.** to spread or prepare with jelly. —**jel′ly·like′,** *adj.*

jel·ly·bean (jel′ē bēn′) *n.* a small egg-shaped candy having a hard outer coating and a jellylike center.

jel·ly·fish (jel′ē fish′) *n. pl.,* **jel·ly·fish** or **jel·ly·fish·es.** any of a group of animals that are found chiefly in salt water and are shaped like an umbrella. A jellyfish has a soft, jellylike body with long, thin tentacles that have stinging cells.

Jen·ner, Edward (jen′ər) 1749–1823, English physician who discovered vaccination as a means of producing immunity to smallpox.

jen·net (jen′it) *n.* a small Spanish horse.

Jellyfish

jen·ny (jen′ē) *n. pl.,* **jen·nies. 1.** see **spinning jenny. 2.** the female of certain animals, especially a donkey.

jeop·ard·ize (jep′ər dīz′) *v.t.,* **jeop·ard·ized, jeop·ard·iz·ing.** to expose to loss or injury; endanger; imperil: *The scandal jeopardized his reputation.*

jeop·ard·y (jep′ər dē) *n.* the danger of loss, injury, or death; peril: *The fireman put his own life in jeopardy to save the child.*

---

at; āpe; cär; end; mē; it; īce; hot; ōld; fôrk; wood; fōōl; oil; out; up; turn; sing; thin; **this**; hw in white; zh in treasure. The symbol ə stands for the sound of **a** in about, **e** in taken, **i** in pencil, **o** in lemon, and **u** in circus.

J

jer·bo·a (jər bō′ə) *n.* a small animal related to the mouse, native to desert regions of Asia and Africa. Jerboas have very long hind legs, a long tail with a tuft on the end, and a silky buff-colored coat.

Jerboa

Jer·e·mi·ah (jer′ə mī′ə) *n.* **1.** Hebrew prophet of the seventh and sixth centuries B.C. **2.** a book of prophecies in the Old Testament, thought to have been written by Jeremiah.

Jer·i·cho (jer′ə kō′) *n.* an ancient Palestinian city near the northern tip of the Dead Sea. According to the Old Testament, it was captured by Joshua, whose soldiers toppled the walls of the city by sounding their trumpets.

jerk¹ (jurk) *n.* **1.** a sudden, sharp pull, twist, or push. **2.** a sudden contraction of a muscle, caused by reflex action. **3.** *Informal.* a stupid or foolish person. —*v.t.* to move or throw (something) with a sudden, sharp motion; give a sudden, sharp pull, twist, or push to: *The child jerked his hand away from the hot stove.* —*v.i.* to move with a sudden, sharp motion or series of such motions: *The car jerked forward when I stepped on the gas.* [Probably imitative of the sound made by a jerking movement.]

jerk² (jurk) *v.t.* to cure (meat) by cutting it into strips and drying it, usually in the sun. [Spanish *charquear.*]

jer·kin (jur′kin) *n.* a short, tight jacket or waistcoat, usually sleeveless and often made of leather. It was worn chiefly in the sixteenth and seventeenth centuries.

jerk·y¹ (jur′kē) *adj.,* jerk·i·er, jerk·i·est. **1.** characterized by abrupt movements; moving with sudden starts and stops: *a jerky subway ride.* **2.** *Informal.* stupid or foolish. [*Jerk¹* + *-y¹.*] —**jerk′i·ly,** *adv.* —**jerk′i·ness,** *n.*

jerk·y² (jur′kē) *n.* meat, especially beef, that has been cured and dried. [From *jerk².*]

Je·rome, Saint (jə rōm′) A.D. 342?–420, monk and author of the Vulgate Bible.

jer·ry-built (jer′ē bilt′) *adj.* built or put together carelessly, hastily, or with poor materials: *a jerry-built cottage.*

Jerkin

Jer·sey (jur′zē) *n. pl.,* **Jer·seys. 1.** a British island in the English Channel, off the coast of France, the largest of the Channel Islands. **2.** one of a breed of usually light-brown dairy cattle originally developed on this island.

jer·sey (jur′zē) *n. pl.,* **jer·seys. 1.** a machine-knitted fabric made of wool, cotton, silk, or synthetic fibers, used for clothing. **2.** a knitted sweater, usually a pullover, made of this or a similar fabric. [From the island of *Jersey,* where this fabric was first made.]

Jersey City, a port city in northeastern New Jersey, opposite New York City. Pop. (1970), 260,545.

Je·ru·sa·lem (jə rōō′sə ləm) *n.* a historic city in central Palestine, now the capital of Israel. It is a holy city for Jews, Christians, and Muslims. Pop. (1975 est.), 355,500.

jes·sa·mine (jes′ə min) another spelling of **jasmine.**

jest (jest) *n.* **1.** something said or done to cause laughter; prank; joke. **2.** a playful mood or manner; playfulness; fun. **3.** an object of laughter or mockery. —*v.i.* to speak or act in a playful manner.

jest·er (jes′tər) *n.* a person who jests, especially a clown formerly kept in royal courts and noble households.

Jes·u·it (jezh′ōō it, jes′ōō it) *n.* a member of the Society of Jesus, a Roman Catholic religious order for men.

Je·sus (jē′zəs) 4 B.C.?–A.D. 29?, the founder of the Christian religion.

Jesus Christ, another name for **Jesus.**

jet¹ (jet) *n.* **1.** a stream of liquid, gas, or vapor, forcefully or suddenly shot forth from a nozzle, spout, or narrow opening. **2.** something shot forth in such a stream. **3.** the nozzle or spout from which such a stream comes: *the gas jets of a stove.* **4.** see **jet plane. 5.** see **jet engine.** —*v.,* jet·ted, jet·ting. —*v.i.* **1.** to be shot forth in a stream. **2.** to travel by jet plane. —*v.t.* **1.** to shoot (something) forth in a stream. **2.** to transport by jet plane. [Old French *jeter* to throw.]

jet² (jet) *n.* **1.** a dense, black coal that can be highly polished, formerly used to make jewelry. **2.** any of several other materials, such as black quartz or glass, imitating this, used to make jewelry. **3.** a deep-black color. —*adj.* **1.** made of or resembling jet. **2.** jet-black. [Old French *jaiet* black coal.]

jet-black (jet′blak′) *adj.* black as jet; deep black.

jet engine 1. an engine that produces power by burning a mixture of fuel and oxygen that is ejected out of the rear as hot exhaust gases. **2.** any engine that produces power by ejecting a stream of fuel.

[Diagram labels: Air intake, Combustion chamber, Fuel intake, Hot gases, Compressor, Fuel intake, Nozzle, Turbine]

Gas turbine jet engine

jet plane, an airplane driven by jet propulsion.

jet-pro·pelled (jet′prə peld′) *adj.* driven by jet propulsion: *a jet-propelled rocket.*

jet propulsion 1. propulsion by means of a jet of fluid, such as hot gas. When the jet of fluid is ejected in one direction, it causes the body or vehicle from which it was ejected to move in the opposite direction. **2.** propulsion by means of one or more jet engines.

jet·sam (jet′səm) *n.* **1.** cargo or equipment thrown overboard in order to lighten a ship in distress. **2.** such discarded cargo or equipment found washed ashore. **3.** discarded, worthless, or miscellaneous things.

jet stream 1. a high-speed air current, usually found between seven and nine miles above the earth's surface. It moves generally west to east at speeds reaching over 200 miles per hour. **2.** a high-speed stream of gas or other fluid ejected from a jet engine.

jet·ti·son (jet′ə sən) *v.t.* **1.** to throw (cargo or equipment) overboard or off, especially in order to lighten a ship or aircraft in distress. **2.** to get rid of or discard (something unwanted, useless, or burdensome).

jet·ty (jet′ē) *n. pl.,* **jet·ties. 1.** a structure of timber, concrete, steel, or a combination of these materials, built out into a body of water in order to affect the current or protect a harbor or coast. **2.** a wharf; pier.

Jew (jōō) *n.* **1.** a member of a people descended from the group of Semitic tribes who lived in and around ancient Palestine, and among whom the beliefs and laws of Judaism were developed and followed; Hebrew. Jews now live in Israel and many other countries. **2.** a person whose religion is Judaism. —**Jew′ess,** *n.*

jew·el (jōō′əl) *n.* **1.** a precious stone; gem. **2.** any article of personal adornment, such as a ring, bracelet, or brooch, usually made of cut and polished gems in a setting of precious metal. **3.** a person or thing of great value or excellence. **4.** a gem or substitute for a gem used as a bearing in a watch.

jew·el·er (jōō′ə lər) *also, British,* **jew·el·ler.** *n.* a person who makes, repairs, or deals in jewelry.

jew·el·ry (jōō′əl rē) *also, British,* **jew·el·ler·y** *n.* precious stones or other articles, as of gold, silver, or glass, for personal ornamentation; jewels as a group.

Jew·ish (jōō′ish) *adj.* of, relating to, or characteristic of the Jews or their culture.

Jew·ry (jōō′rē) *n. pl.,* **Jew·ries.** Jews as a group; the Jewish people.

jew's-harp (jōōz′härp′) *also,* **jews'-harp.** *n.* a small musical instrument that consists of a lyre-shaped metal frame and a flexible metal strip. It is held between the teeth when played, and produces a twanging tone when the free end of the metal strip is plucked with the finger.

Jez·e·bel (jez′ə bel′) *n.* **1.** in the Old Testament, the wicked wife of Ahab, king of Israel. **2.** *also,* **jezebel.** a shameless or wicked woman.

jib (jib) *n.* a triangular sail set on a stay in front of the mast or foremast, usually smaller than the mainsail.

jibe¹ (jīb) *v.i.,* **jibed, jib·ing.** to shift a fore-and-aft sail or its boom from one side of a boat or ship to the other when sailing before the wind. [Dutch *gijpen.*]

jibe² (jīb) *n., v.,* **jibed, jib·ing.** another spelling of **gibe.**

jibe³ (jīb) *v.i.,* **jibed, jib·ing.** *Informal.* to be in harmony or accord; agree: *The witnesses' stories don't jibe.* [Of uncertain origin.]

Jib

Jib

jif·fy (jif′ē) *n. pl.,* **jif·fies.** *Informal.* a very short time; moment; instant.

jig (jig) *n.* **1.** a fast, lively dance, usually in triple time. **2.** the music for this dance. **3.** a device used for guiding a tool, such as a drill, or for holding in place material to be worked on with such a tool. —*v.i.,* **jigged, jig·ging. 1.** to dance or play a jig. **2.** to move with a rapid jerking or bobbing motion.

jig·ger (jig′ər) *n.* **1.** small glass or cup used to measure liquor, holding about an ounce and a half. **2.** the amount contained in a jigger.

jig·gle (jig′əl) *v.,* **jig·gled, jig·gling.** —*v.t.* to move (something) up and down or to and fro with quick, slight jerking motions. —*v.i.* to move up and down or to and fro with quick, slight jerking motions. —*n.* a jiggling motion.

jig·saw (jig′sô′) *n.* a saw with a narrow blade set in a frame, used to cut curved or irregular lines.

jigsaw puzzle, a puzzle made up of a set of irregularly shaped cardboard or wooden pieces that can be fitted together to form a picture.

jilt (jilt) *v.t.* to cast off or desert (a lover or sweetheart). —*n.* a person who jilts a lover or sweetheart. —**jilt′er,** *n.*

Jim Crow *also,* **jim crow.** *Informal.* segregation of or discrimination against blacks. [From *Jim Crow,* a name in a nineteenth-century Afro-American song.]

jim·my (jim′ē) *n. pl.,* **jim·mies.** a short crowbar used especially by burglars. —*v.t.,* **jim·mied, jim·my·ing.** to force or pry open with a jimmy.

jim·son·weed (jim′sən wēd′) *n.* a poisonous plant related to the nightshade, found in the tropics and many parts of North America. It has large oval leaves and white or purple trumpet-shaped flowers.

Ji·nan (jē′ nän′) another spelling of **Tsinan.**

jin·gle (jing′gəl) *v.,* **jin·gled, jin·gling.** —*v.i.* to make a light, metallic tinkling or ringing sound: *The coins jingled in his pocket.* —*v.t.* to cause to make a tinkling or ringing sound: *to jingle keys.* —*n.* **1.** a light, metallic tinkling or

ringing sound: *the jingle of a cowboy's spurs.* **2.** a catchy or repeated series of words or sounds, especially a short, catchy song or verse: *He often hums the musical jingles used in advertising.*

jin·go (jing′gō) *n. pl.,* **jin·goes.** a person who supports or favors an aggressive, warlike foreign policy.

jin·ni (jin nē′, jin′ē) *n. pl.,* **jinn** (jin). another spelling of **genie.**

jin·rick·sha (jin rik′shô) *also,* **jin·rik·i·sha.** *n.* another word for **ricksha.**

jinx (jingks) *Informal. n. pl.,* **jinx·es. 1.** a person or thing that brings or is believed to bring bad luck. **2.** a spell of bad luck; hex: *to put a jinx on someone.* —*v.t.* to bring or try to bring bad luck to; hex.

jit·ney (jit′nē) *n. pl.,* **jit·neys.** *Informal.* a car or bus that carries passengers for a small fare, usually over a short regular route.

jit·ter (jit′ər) *Informal. v.i.* to be nervous or uneasy; fidget. —*n.* **jitters.** a fit of nervousness; extreme anxiety. —**jit′ter·y,** *adj.*

jit·ter·bug (jit′ər bug′) *Informal. n.* **1.** a lively, fast dance, popular especially during the 1930s and 1940s. **2.** a person who does this dance. —*v.i.,* **jit·ter·bugged, jit·ter·bug·ging.** to dance the jitterbug.

jiu·jit·su (jōō jit′sōō) *n.* another spelling of **jujitsu.**

jive (jīv) *Slang. n.* **1.** jazz music, especially of the late 1930s and 1940s. **2.** the special terms or way of speaking used by jazz musicians and fans. **3.** deceptive, glib, or meaningless talk.

Joan of Arc (jōn′ əv ärk′) 1412–1431, French national heroine and military leader. She was condemned as a witch and heretic and burned at the stake. In 1920 she was made a saint. Also, **Jeanne d'Arc.**

job (job) *n.* **1.** a position of work; employment: *She took a job in a store for the summer.* **2.** something that has to be done; task, duty, or responsibility: *It's his job to feed the dog.* **3.** a specific activity or piece of work: *The repair job will cost $300.*

Job (jōb) *n.* **1.** in the Old Testament, a righteous man who patiently accepted the trials that God inflicted upon him to test his faith. **2.** the book of the Old Testament that tells his story.

job·ber (job′ər) *n.* a person who buys goods, as from a manufacturer, and sells them to retailers.

job·less (job′lis) *adj.* without a job; unemployed.

jock·ey (jok′ē) *n. pl.,* **jock·eys.** a person who rides horses in races, especially as a profession. —*v.,* **jock·eyed, jock·ey·ing.** —*v.i.* **1.** to maneuver, especially in order to gain an advantage: *The runner jockeyed for position.* **2.** to ride a horse in a race. —*v.t.* **1.** to maneuver (someone or something): *to jockey a car into a parking space.* **2.** to ride (a horse) in a race.

jo·cose (jō kōs′) *adj.* given to or characterized by joking and jesting; merry; playful. —**jo·cose′ly,** *adv.* —**jo·cose′ness,** *n.*

jo·cos·i·ty (jō kos′ə tē) *n. pl.,* **jo·cos·i·ties. 1.** the state or quality of being jocose. **2.** a jocose act or remark; joke or jest.

joc·u·lar (jok′yə lər) *adj.* **1.** given to or characterized by joking and jesting; merry; playful. **2.** of the nature of or

J

at; āpe; cär; end; mē; it; īce; hot; ōld; fôrk; wood; fōōl; oil; out; up; turn; sing; thin; this; hw in white; zh in treasure. The symbol ə stands for the sound of a in about, e in taken, i in pencil, o in lemon, and u in circus.

meant as a joke; humorous: *a jocular remark.* —**joc′u·lar·ly,** *adv.*

joc·u·lar·i·ty (jok′yə lar′ə tē) *n. pl.,* **joc·u·lar·i·ties.**
1. the state or quality of being jocular; merriment.
2. a jocular act or remark; joke or jest.

joc·und (jok′ənd) *adj.* cheerful; merry; carefree.

jo·cun·di·ty (jō kun′də tē) *n. pl.,* **jo·cun·di·ties.**
1. the state or quality of being jocund; cheerfulness.
2. a jocund act or remark.

Jodh·pur (jōd′poor′) *n.* a city in northwestern India.
Pop. (1971), 317,612.

jodh·purs (jod′pərz) *n., pl.* trousers that are loose above
the knee and close-fitting from knee to an-
kle, used for horseback riding. [From *Jodh-
pur,* where they were first popular.]

Jo·el (jō′əl) *n.* **1.** Hebrew prophet of the
Old Testament. **2.** a book of the Old Testament thought to have been written by him.

jog (jog) *v.,* **jogged, jog·ging.** —*v.i.*
to run or move at a slow, steady pace or trot:
The runners jogged lazily around the track.
—*v.t.* **1.** to cause to move by shaking or
jerking; jolt. **2.** to give a slight shake or
push to; nudge. **3.** to stir or stimulate: *to jog
the memory.* —*n.* **1.** a shake, push, or
nudge. **2.** a slow, steady, jolting pace or
motion. —**jog′ger,** *n.*

jog·gle (jog′əl) *v.t., v.i.,* **jog·gled, jog·gling.**
to shake slightly. —*n.* the act of joggling.

Jo·han·nes·burg (jō han′is burg′) *n.* a
city in the Republic of South Africa, in the northeastern
part of the country. Pop. (1971 est.), 1,274,418.

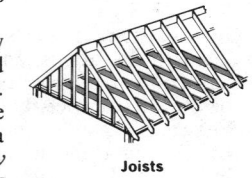

Jodhpurs

John (jon) *n.* **1.** in the New Testament, one of Christ's
Apostles. **2.** the fourth book of the New Testament,
thought to have been written by him. **3.** see **John the
Baptist. 4.** 1167?–1216, the king of England from 1199 to
1216 who signed the Magna Carta in 1215.

John XXIII, 1881–1963, the pope from 1958 to 1963.

John Bull, personification of England or the English.

John Doe 1. an unknown or fictitious person. ▲ used
especially in legal documents to designate a fictitious person or a person whose real name is not known. **2.** the
average man.

John Han·cock (han′kok) *Informal.* a person's signature or autograph. [From the large signature of *John Han-
cock* on the Declaration of Independence.]

John·ny Ap·ple·seed (jon′ē ap′əl sēd′) 1774–1845,
U.S. frontiersman, noted for sowing apple seeds throughout the Ohio River valley; born John Chapman.

john·ny·cake (jon′ē kāk′) *n.* a flat, crisp bread made
of cornmeal, water or milk, flour, and, sometimes, eggs.

John Paul I, 1912–1978, the pope from August to September, 1978.

John Paul II, 1920—, the pope since 1978.

John·son (jon′sən) **1. Andrew.** 1808–1875, the seven-
teenth president of the United States, from 1865 to 1869.
He was impeached and acquitted in 1868. **2. Lyn·don B.**
(lin′dən). 1908–1973, the thirty-sixth president of the
United States, from 1963 to 1969. **3. Samuel.** 1709–1784,
English poet, essayist, critic, and lexicographer.

● **Samuel Johnson** was the greatest and most famous English lexicographer, or dictionary-maker. Modern dictionaries are produced by large staffs of people, sometimes
up to 100, but the two-volume, 2300-page work *A Dictionary of the English Language* was written entirely by Dr.
Johnson himself. It was published in 1755 after eight years
of work, and it was the standard English dictionary for
more than a century.

Today Dr. Johnson's dictionary is best remembered for
its humorous or eccentric definitions. For example: "*oats:*
a grain, which in England is generally given to horses, but
in Scotland supports the people;" "*excise:* a hateful tax
. . . adjudged by wretches hired by those to whom excise
is paid" and "*lexicographer:* a harmless drudge." When a
woman asked the reason why he had defined a certain
word incorrectly, Johnson replied "Ignorance, Madam,
sheer ignorance."

Actually, Dr. Johnson was a brilliant student of language and a superb definer. Many of the methods he introduced to dictionary-making are still used today.

John the Baptist, in the New Testament, the prophet
who foretold the coming of Jesus and baptized Him.

join (join) *v.t.* **1.** to bring, put, or fasten together so as to
become one: *I joined the ends of the rope in a knot. We
joined hands and formed a circle.* **2.** to come into contact
or union with: *This road joins the main highway just ahead.*
3. to become a member or part of: *to join the army.*
4. to come or enter into the company of: *He joined us at
our table when he'd finished eating.* —*v.i.* **1.** to take part
with others; participate: *We joined in the celebration.*
2. to become united or associated: *All members of the
community joined to fight the epidemic.* **3.** to come into
or be in contact or union: *At what point do the rivers join?*
—*n.* a place or line of joining; seam; joint; junction.

join·er (joi′nər) *n.* **1.** *Informal.* a person who joins many
clubs, committees, or other organized activities. **2.** a
craftsman or carpenter who makes woodwork and furniture. **3.** any person or thing that joins.

join·er·y (joi′nər ē) *n.* **1.** the skill of a joiner. **2.** woodwork, furniture, or other articles made by a joiner.

joint (joint) *n.* **1.** the place or part where two or more
bones meet or join, usually able to move freely. **2.** any
place or part at or by which two or more things are joined
or fitted together. **3.** a part or section between such places
or structures. **4.** one of the portions into which meat is
cut by a butcher, especially one containing the bone.
5. *Botany.* the point on a stem from which a leaf or branch
grows. **6.** *Slang.* a cheap or disreputable bar, restaurant,
or other gathering place. —*adj.* **1.** belonging to or used
by two or more; held or shared in common: *a joint bank
account.* **2.** performed or produced by two or more working or acting together: *joint efforts, a joint attack.* **3.** sharing or acting with another or others: *joint owners.* **4.** of
or involving both houses or branches of a legislature: *a
joint session of Congress.* —*v.t.* **1.** to connect with a joint
or joints. **2.** to divide or cut at the joints, as meat.

Joint Chiefs of Staff, the principal military advisors
to the President of the United States. The group consists
of a chairman, the chiefs of staff of the Army and of the
Air Force, the head of the Navy, and, usually, the com-
mandant of the Marine Corps.

joint·ed (join′tid) *adj.* having a joint or joints.

joint·ly (joint′lē) *adv.* in conjunction; together: *The island is administered jointly by the two countries.*

joist (joist) *n.* one of a series of parallel beams to which
the boards of a floor or the laths
of a ceiling are fastened.

joke (jōk) *n.* **1.** a story, usually
ending with a funny line, intended
to cause laughter or amusement.
2. anything said or done to cause
laughter or amusement, such as a
funny remark or a prank: *My
brother hid the keys to the house as
a joke.* **3.** a person or thing causing amusement or ridicule.
—*v.i.,* **joked, jok·ing.** to tell or make jokes.

Joists

jok·er (jō′kər) *n.* **1.** a person who jokes or is given to joking. **2.** either of two extra playing cards provided with a standard deck, often having a picture of a jester on it. Jokers are used in certain card games as a wild card or as trump.

Jo·li·et (jō′lē et′) *n.* a city in northeastern Illinois. Pop. (1970), 80,378.

Jol·li·et, Louis (jō′lē et′) *also,* **Jo·li·et.** 1645–1700, French-Canadian explorer of the Mississippi River.

jol·li·ty (jol′ə tē) *n.* the state or quality of being jolly.

jol·ly (jol′ē) *adj.,* **jol·li·er, jol·li·est. 1.** full of fun, good humor, and high spirits: *a jolly old man.* **2.** characterized by or causing mirth, gaiety, or good cheer: *a jolly song, jolly laughter.* —*v.t.,* **jol·lied, jol·ly·ing.** *Informal.* to amuse, humor, or flatter so as to put or keep in a good mood. —**jol′li·ness,** *n.*

Jol·ly Rog·er (jol′ē roj′ər) a black flag with a white skull and crossbones on it, flown especially by pirates.

jolt (jōlt) *v.t.* to cause to move with a rough, jerky motion; jar or shake up with a sudden bump or blow: *The impact of the collision jolted us out of our seats.* —*v.i.* to move with sudden bumpy jerks: *The carriage jolted along the dirt road.* —*n.* **1.** a rough, jerky motion: *The wagon stopped with a jolt.* **2.** an abrupt surprise or shock: *The news gave me quite a jolt.*

Jo·nah (jō′nə) *n.* **1.** in the Old Testament, the Hebrew prophet who, because he had disobeyed God, was thrown overboard during a storm and swallowed by a large fish. Three days later he was cast up on land unharmed. **2.** the book of the Old Testament containing his story and prophecies.

Jones, John Paul (jōnz) 1747–1792, Scottish-born U.S. naval hero in the American Revolution; born John Paul.

jon·quil (jong′kwil) *n.* **1.** a yellow flower of a plant resembling the daffodil, having six petal-like segments surrounding a shallow, cup-shaped structure. **2.** the slender plant bearing this flower.

Jon·son, Ben (jon′sən) 1573?–1637, English dramatist and poet.

Jor·dan (jôrd′ən) *n.* **1.** a country in southwestern Asia, east of and bordering Israel. It was formerly known as Transjordan. Capital, Amman. Area, 37,738 sq. mi. Pop. (1971 est.), 2,400,000. **2.** a river in southwestern Asia flowing between Israel and Jordan into the Dead Sea. —**Jor·da·ni·an** (jôr dā′nē ən), *adj., n.*

Jo·seph (jō′zəf, jō′səf) *n.* **1.** in the Old Testament, a son of Jacob who was sold into slavery by his jealous brothers and who later became a high official in Egypt. **2.** in the New Testament, the husband of the Virgin Mary.

Jo·se·phine (jō′zə fēn′, jō′sə fēn′) 1763–1814, first wife of Napoleon Bonaparte and empress of France from 1804 to 1809.

josh (josh) *Informal. v.t.* to make fun of in a nice way; tease playfully. —*v.i.* to indulge in playful teasing.

Josh·u·a (josh′ōō ə) *n.* **1.** in the Old Testament, the successor of Moses who led the Israelites into Canaan. **2.** the book of the Old Testament containing the history of the Israelites from the death of Moses to the settlement in Canaan.

jos·tle (jos′əl) *also,* **jus·tle.** *v.t.,* **jos·tled, jos·tling.** to bump, push, or shove roughly, as with the elbows: *He jostled his way across the crowded room.* —*n.* a bump, push, or shove; a jostling. —**jos′tler,** *n.*

Jonquil

jot (jot) *n.* the least or smallest bit: *Her bragging didn't impress me a jot.* —*v.t.,* **jot·ted, jot·ting.** to make a brief and hasty note of: *The witness jotted down the license number of the car that left the scene of the accident.*

joule (jōōl, joul) *n. Physics.* a unit of work or energy in the meter-kilogram-second system of units, equal to the work done by a force of one newton acting through a distance of one meter. One joule is equivalent to 10^7 ergs. [From James P. *Joule,* 1818–1889, an English physicist.]

jounce (jouns) *v.t., v.i.,* **jounced, jounc·ing.** to move or shake up and down roughly: *The old wagon jounced along the road.* —*n.* a sudden, rough bump; bounce; jolt.

jour·nal (jurn′əl) *n.* **1.** a record or account, especially one written every day, of events, experiences, or thoughts; diary. **2.** an official record, usually one written every day, of proceedings or transactions, such as the register of a legislative body. **3.** a magazine or periodical, especially one dealing with matters of current interest in a particular area: *The medical journal published a report on the doctor's discovery.* **4.** a newspaper, especially one published every day. **5.** the part of a shaft or axle turning within a bearing.

jour·nal·ism (jurn′əl iz′əm) *n.* the collecting, presenting, or interpreting of facts and opinions about current events and topics of public interest, especially the writing or publishing of such facts and opinions in newspapers or magazines.

jour·nal·ist (jurn′əl ist) *n.* a person whose occupation is journalism, especially a person who edits or writes for a newspaper or magazine.

jour·nal·is·tic (jurn′əl is′tik) *adj.* of, relating to, or characteristic of journalism or journalists.

jour·ney (jur′nē) *n. pl.,* **jour·neys. 1.** a trip, especially one over a long distance or taking a long time: *a journey across the United States.* **2.** the distance that is traveled, or that can be traveled, in a specified time: *That village is four days' journey from here.* —*v.i.,* **jour·neyed, jour·ney·ing.** to make a trip; travel: *to journey through Europe.*

jour·ney·man (jur′nē mən) *n. pl.,* **jour·ney·men** (jur′nē-mən). **1.** a person who has completed his apprenticeship in a trade, craft, or skill, and works for another. **2.** an experienced and skilled workman.

joust (joust) *also,* **just.** *n.* a formal combat, often part of a tournament, between two knights on horseback or other persons armed with lances and other weapons. —*v.i.* to take part in a joust. —**joust′er,** *n.*

Jove (jōv) *n.* see **Jupiter** *(def. 1).*

jo·vi·al (jō′vē əl) *adj.* characterized by hearty good humor; merry; jolly. —**jo′vi·al·ly,** *adv.*

jo·vi·al·i·ty (jō′vē al′ə tē) *n.* the state or quality of being jovial; jollity; merriment.

Jo·vi·an (jō′vē ən) *adj.* of, relating to, or like Jove.

jowl¹ (joul) *n.* **1.** flabby, sagging flesh hanging from or under the lower jaw. **2.** any similar fleshy part, such as the dewlap of a moose or the wattle of a fowl. [Old English *ceole* throat.]

jowl² (joul) *n.* **1.** the jawbone or jaw, especially the lower jaw. **2.** the cheek. [Old English *ceafl* jaw.]

joy (joi) *n.* **1.** a strong feeling of happiness or delight. **2.** someone or something that is the source or cause of such feeling: *The kind, good-natured girl is a joy to her family.*

J

at; āpe; cär; end; mē; it; īce; hot; ōld; fôrk; wood; fōōl; oil; out; up; turn; sing; thin; **th**is; hw in white; zh in treasure. The symbol ə stands for the sound of **a** in about, **e** in taken, **i** in pencil, **o** in lemon, and **u** in circus.

Joyce, James (jois) 1882–1941, Irish novelist, poet, and short story writer.

joy·ful (joi'fəl) *adj.* feeling, showing, or causing joy: *joyful children, a joyful look in one's eyes, a joyful sight.* —**joy'ful·ly,** *adv.* —**joy'ful·ness,** *n.*

joy·less (joi'lis) *adj.* feeling, showing, or causing no joy: *a joyless smile, a joyless life.* —**joy'less·ly,** *adv.* —**joy'less·ness,** *n.*

joy·ous (joi'əs) *adj.* feeling, showing, or causing joy; marked by rejoicing: *Her marriage was a joyous occasion.* —**joy'ous·ly,** *adv.* —**joy'ous·ness,** *n.*

jr., junior.

Juá·rez (wär'ez) *n.* **1. Be·ni·to Pa·blo** (be nē'tō pä'blō). 1806–1872, Mexican statesman, president of Mexico from 1858 to 1865 and from 1867 to 1872. **2.** see **Ciudad Juárez.**

ju·bi·lant (jōō'bə lənt) *adj.* joyfully happy or triumphant; exultant: *After the game the victors were jubilant.* —**ju'bi·lant·ly,** *adv.*

ju·bi·la·tion (jōō'bə lā'shən) *n.* **1.** a feeling of joyful happiness or triumph. **2.** the act of rejoicing.

ju·bi·lee (jōō'bə lē') *n.* **1.** a special anniversary, especially a twenty-fifth or fiftieth anniversary. **2.** a year, season, or occasion of joyful celebration and rejoicing.

Ju·dae·a (jōō dē'ə) *n.* another spelling of **Judea.** —**Ju·dae'an,** *adj., n.*

Ju·dah (jōō'də) *n.* **1.** in the Old Testament, the fourth son of Jacob and founder of one of the twelve tribes of Israel. **2.** the tribe descended from him, the most powerful of the twelve tribes of Israel. **3.** a Hebrew kingdom in Palestine, consisting of the tribes of Judah and Benjamin.

Ju·da·ic (jōō dā'ik) *adj.* of or relating to Jews or Judaism.

Ju·da·ism (jōō'dē iz'əm) *n.* the religion of the Jews, based chiefly on a belief in one God and the teachings of the Old Testament and the Talmud.

Ju·das (jōō'dəs) *n.* **1.** in the New Testament, the Apostle who betrayed Jesus for thirty pieces of silver. Also, **Judas Iscariot. 2.** *also,* **judas.** any betrayer or traitor.

Jude (jōōd) *n.* **1.** one of the twelve Apostles of Jesus. **2.** a book of the New Testament thought to have been written by him.

Ju·de·a (jōō dē'ə) *also,* **Ju·dae·a.** *n.* the southern part of ancient Palestine, especially when it was under Roman rule. —**Ju·de'an,** *adj., n.*

Ju·de·o-Chris·tian (jōō dā'ō kris'chən) *adj.* Jewish and Christian.

judge (juj) *v.,* **judged, judg·ing.** —*v.t.* **1.** to hear and decide in a court of law and with legal authority the merits or guilt of: *to judge a case, to judge an accused person.* **2.** to settle or decide: *to judge a beauty contest.* **3.** to form an opinion or evaluation of: *Judge him by what he does, not by his appearance.* **4.** to criticize; condemn; censure: *He is too quick to judge other people.* **5.** to think; suppose; consider: *I judge him to be loyal.* —*v.i.* **1.** to form an opinion or evaluation: *I will listen to both sides of the story and judge for myself.* **2.** to act or decide as a judge: *He'll have to judge between four contestants.* —*n.* **1.** an appointed or elected official who has authority to hear and decide cases in a court of law. **2.** a person appointed to decide the winner or victor in any contest, competition, or dispute: *The judges at the dog show awarded first prize to a beagle.* **3.** a person who is qualified to give an opinion about a particular subject: *He is a good judge of horses.* —**judg'er,** *n.*

Judg·es (juj'iz) *n.* the book of the Old Testament containing the history of the Israelites from the death of Joshua to the birth of Samuel.

judge·ship (juj'ship') *n.* the position, function, or term of office of a judge.

judg·ment (juj'mənt) *also,* **judge·ment.** *n.* **1.** the ability to judge wisely: *She shows good judgment.* **2.** the act of judging. **3.** an opinion or conclusion reached through judging: *I will form my own judgment of what's going on.* **4.** *Law.* a decree, verdict, order, or sentence handed down by a court of law.

Judgment Day *also,* **judgment day.** in certain religions, the day of God's final judgment of mankind, which is to occur on the day the world ends. Also, **Last Judgment, Doomsday.**

ju·di·cial (jōō dish'əl) *adj.* **1.** of or relating to courts of law and the administration of justice: *the judicial branch of the government.* **2.** of, relating to, or appropriate to a judge: *judicial robes, judicial authority.* **3.** decreed or enforced by a judge or a court: *a judicial decision.* —**ju·di'cial·ly,** *adv.*

ju·di·ci·ar·y (jōō dish'ē er'ē) *n. pl.,* **ju·di·ci·ar·ies. 1.** the branch of government that has judicial power and that interprets and applies the law. **2.** the system of courts of a country. **3.** the judges of these courts as a group. —*adj.* of or relating to judges, courts of law, or the administration of justice.

ju·di·cious (jōō dish'əs) *adj.* having or showing good judgment; wise; sensible: *a judicious commander of troops, a judicious plan.* —**ju·di'cious·ly,** *adv.* —**ju·di'cious·ness,** *n.*

ju·do (jōō'dō) *n.* **1.** a method of unarmed combat and self-defense related to jujitsu and karate. It originated in the Orient and developed from jujitsu. **2.** the sport of fighting by this method.

jug (jug) *n.* **1.** a rounded container of earthenware, glass, or other material, having a handle and a narrow neck that usually has a stopper or cap, used chiefly for holding liquids. **2.** a pitcher or similar container for liquids. **3.** the contents of a jug. —*v.t.,* **jugged, jug·ging.** to put or cook in a jug.

jug·ger·naut (jug'ər nôt') *n.* **1.** any overpowering force or object that advances relentlessly and destroys whatever is in its path. **2.** a custom, belief, or the like to which people blindly devote or sacrifice themselves.

jug·gle (jug'əl) *v.,* **jug·gled, jug·gling.** —*v.t.* **1.** to keep (two or more balls or other objects) in continuous motion from the hands into the air by skillfully tossing and catching in rapid succession: *He can juggle four oranges at once.* **2.** to change or manipulate in order to deceive or defraud: *The embezzler juggled the company's financial records.* —*v.i.* **1.** to perform or entertain as a juggler. **2.** to practice trickery with the intent of deceiving or defrauding. —*n.* **1.** the act of juggling. **2.** deception or fraud.

jug·gler (jug'lər) *n.* **1.** a person whose work or occupation is juggling: *a circus juggler.* **2.** a person who practices deception or fraud.

Ju·go·slav (yōō'gō släv') *adj.* another spelling of **Yugoslav.**

Ju·go·sla·vi·a (yōō'gō slä'vē ə) *n.* another spelling of **Yugoslavia.** —**Ju'go·sla'vi·an,** *adj., n.*

jug·u·lar (jug'yə lər) *adj.* **1.** of or relating to the neck or throat. **2.** of or relating to the jugular vein. —*n.* see **jugular vein.**

jugular vein, either of the two large blood vessels on either side of the neck that return blood from the head and neck to the heart.

juice (jōōs) *n.* **1.** the fluid contained in a plant or in plant tissues, especially the fluid that is pressed or squeezed from a fruit or vegetable for use as a drink. **2.** the fluid contained in animal flesh or tissues: *Mother let the roast cook in its own juice.* **3.** the fluid secreted in animal tissue: *gastric juices, intestinal juices.* **4.** *Slang.* electric current. —*v.t.,* **juiced, juic·ing.** to press or squeeze the juice from.

juic·y (jōō′sē) *adj.,* **juic·i·er, juic·i·est.** having much juice: *a juicy orange.* —**juic′i·ly,** *adv.* —**juic′i·ness,** *n.*

ju·jit·su (jōō jit′sōō) *also,* **jiu·jit·su, ju·jut·su.** *n.* a method of unarmed self-defense or combat that originated in Japan, related to judo and karate. It uses the strength and weight of an opponent to his disadvantage.

juke·box (jōōk′boks′) *n. pl.,* **juke·box·es.** an automatic phonograph enclosed in a cabinet and usually operated by inserting coins and pushing one or more buttons to select a record.

Jul·ian calendar (jōōl′yən) the calendar established by Julius Caesar, providing for 365 days in a year with every fourth year having 366 days. The number of days in each month and the order of months in the year correspond to the present-day Gregorian calendar.

ju·li·enne (jōō′lē en′) *adj.* cut into thin strips: *julienne carrots.* —*n.* a clear soup containing vegetables cut in such a manner.

Ju·liet (jōōl′yət, jōō′lē et′) *n.* the heroine of Shakespeare's tragedy *Romeo and Juliet.*

Jul·ius Cae·sar (jōōl′yəs sē′zər) see **Caesar.**

Ju·ly (joo lī′) *n. pl.,* **Ju·lies.** the seventh month of the year, having thirty-one days. [Old French *Jule,* from Latin *Jūlius,* from *Jūlius* Caesar, who was born in this month.]

jum·ble (jum′bəl) *v.t.,* **jum·bled, jum·bling.** to mix or throw into confusion and disorder: *All the toys were jumbled together in the box.* —*n.* **1.** a confused or disordered mixture, collection, or mass. **2.** a state of confusion or disorder.

jum·bo (jum′bō) *Informal. adj.* extremely large: *a jumbo bar of candy.* —*n. pl.,* **jum·bos.** a person, animal, or thing that is unusually large.

jump (jump) *v.i.* **1.** to spring into the air: *Billy jumped up to catch a ball.* **2.** to move or go suddenly or abruptly: *They jumped to their feet when they heard the alarm go off.* **3.** to move suddenly as in surprise or fright: *Natalie always jumps when the phone rings.* **4.** to increase or rise suddenly: *His temperature jumped sharply.* **5.** to come or pass abruptly, as by leaving out the necessary steps: *She jumped to a hasty conclusion before learning the facts.* **6.** to accept or grab hastily and eagerly: *to jump at a chance, to jump at an offer.* —*v.t.* **1.** to cause to jump: *Keith jumped his pony across the brook.* **2.** to spring or pass over or by (something): *He jumped the fence.* **3.** *Informal.* to attack by surprise; pounce upon: *The thief jumped him as he opened the door.* **4.** *Informal.* to board hastily or by jumping. —*n.* **1.** the act of jumping; spring; leap. **2.** a place or thing to be jumped over or across: *There were five jumps in the race.* **3.** the distance or space covered by a jump: *a jump of eight feet.* **4.** a sudden start or jerk, as in surprise or fright. **5.** a sudden increase or rise: *a jump in prices.* **6.** any of a number of sports contests in jumping. **7.** a leap by parachute from an airplane.

  to get the jump on or **to have the jump on.** to get or have a head start or advantage over.

  to jump the gun. to start too quickly or too soon: *Take time to read the instructions before you jump the gun.*

jump ball, a basketball tossed by the referee between two opposing players who must jump up and tap the ball to put it into play.

jump·er[1] (jum′pər) *n.* **1.** a person or thing that jumps. **2.** a cable, wire, or other conductor used, usually temporarily, to complete or bypass a circuit. [*Jump* + *-er*[1].]

jump·er[2] (jum′pər) *n.* **1.** a one-piece, sleeveless dress, usually worn over a blouse or sweater. **2.** a loose shirt, smock, or jacket worn over other clothes to protect them, as by sailors or workmen. **3.** **jumpers.** a loose, one-piece garment worn by young children; rompers. [Probably from dialectal *jump* a type of short coat.]

jumping bean, a seed of any of several plants native to Mexico. It contains a small moth larva whose movements cause the seed to jump. Also, **Mexican jumping bean.**

jumping jack, a toy figure of a man or animal having jointed limbs that can be made to move by pulling attached strings or a lever.

jump shot, a basketball shot in which a player jumps into the air and shoots the ball toward the basket at the highest point of his jump.

jump·suit (jump′sōōt′) *n.* **1.** a one-piece garment, combining shirt and trousers, designed to be worn as coveralls by paratroopers. **2.** any garment resembling this.

jump·y (jum′pē) *adj.,* **jump·i·er, jump·i·est.** **1.** nervous; jittery. **2.** moving by jumps or sudden sharp movements. —**jump′i·ness,** *n.*

jun·co (jung′kō) *n. pl.,* **jun·cos** or **jun·coes.** any of various North American finches, usually having gray and white feathers. Also, **snow bunting.**

junc·tion (jungk′shən) *n.* **1.** a place or station where railroad lines meet or cross. **2.** any place or point where two or more things join or meet. **3.** the act of joining or the state of being joined.

June (jōōn) *n.* the sixth month of the year, having thirty days. [Old French *juin,* from Latin *Jūnius (mēnsis)* the month of the goddess Juno.]

Ju·neau (jōō′nō) *n.* the capital of Alaska, in the southeastern part of the state. Pop. (1970), 13,556.

June bug, any of several brown beetles that emerge as adults in late spring or early summer, and are destructive to shrubs and trees. Their larvae feed on the roots of many crops. Also, **June beetle.**

Jung, Carl Gus·tav (yoong; goos′täf) 1875–1961, Swiss psychiatrist.

jun·gle (jung′gəl) *n.* **1.** a dense and tangled mass of tropical vegetation, usually consisting of vines, ferns, low bushes, and young trees. **2.** land overgrown with such a mass, usually inhabited by wild animals. **3.** any wild, confused, or tangled growth or mass: *a jungle of skyscrapers.* **4.** a scene of ruthless competition or of a fierce struggle for survival: *a career in the jungle of big business.*

jun·ior (jōōn′yər) *adj.* **1.** the younger of two. ▲ used after the name of a son whose father has the same name: *James Jones, Junior.* **2.** of lower position, rank, or standing, or of more recent appointment or election: *a junior member of a law firm, the junior senator from New York.* **3.** relating to, enrolled in, or designating the third year of a four-year high school or college program: *the junior class.* —*n.* **1.** a person who is younger than another: *She's my junior by three years.* **2.** a person who is of lower position, rank, or standing or of more recent appointment. **3.** a student in the third year of a four-year high school or college.

junior college, a school having a two-year course equivalent to the first two years of a four-year college.

junior high school, a school that usually includes grades seven and eight, and sometimes six or nine; any school between elementary school and senior high school.

June bug

J

at; āpe; cär; end; mē; it; īce; hot; ōld; fôrk; wood; fōōl; oil; out; up; turn; sing; thin; this; hw in white; zh in treasure. The symbol ə stands for the sound of **a** in **about,** **e** in **taken,** **i** in **pencil,** **o** in **lemon,** and **u** in **circus.**

ju·ni·per (jōō′nə pər) *n.* any of a group of ornamental evergreen shrubs or trees related to the cypress. Junipers bear purple fruits that look like berries, some of which yield an oil used to flavor gin.

junk¹ (jungk) *n.* **1.** old or discarded material, such as metal, wood, or rags. **2.** *Informal.* anything worthless or useless; rubbish; trash. **3.** *Slang.* a narcotic drug, especially heroin. —*v.t. Informal.* to throw away or discard as junk; scrap: *to junk an old car.* [Middle English *jonke* a piece of worn or poor rope or cable.]

junk² (jungk) *n.* a large flat-bottomed sailing vessel developed in China, having a square prow and lugsails. [Portuguese *junco* from Javanese *jong* a large boat.]

Junk²

jun·ket (jung′kit) *n.* **1.** a trip or excursion, such as one made by a government official or businessman, paid for by public funds and supposedly for the purpose of making an inspection or for other official business. **2.** a trip or tour, especially one made for pleasure. **3.** a food similar to custard, made of flavored and sweetened milk curdled by rennet. —*v.i.* to go on a junket.

junk·ie (jung′kē) also, **junk·y.** *n. pl.,* **junk·ies.** *Slang.* a narcotics addict, especially one who is addicted to heroin.

junk·man (jungk′man′) *n. pl.,* **junk·men** (jungk′men′). a person who buys or sells scrap material, such as metal, glass, paper, and rags.

junk·yard (jungk′yärd′) *n.* a place where junk is collected, stored, or resold.

Ju·no (jōō′nō) *n. Roman Mythology.* the goddess who was the wife and sister of Jupiter and queen of the gods. She was also the protectress of women and marriage. In Greek mythology she was called Hera.

jun·ta (hoon′tə, jun′tə) *n.* **1.** a group that rules a country after the overthrow of a government. **2.** a legislative or administrative council or committee, especially in Latin America.

jun·to (jun′tō) *n. pl.,* **jun·tos.** a small, usually secret group that gathers for some common purpose, especially for political intrigue.

Ju·pi·ter (jōō′pə tər) *n.* **1.** *Roman Mythology.* the god who was the ruler of gods and men, and was associated with rain and thunder. In Greek mythology he was called Zeus. Also, **Jove. 2.** the largest planet of the solar system and fifth in order of distance from the sun. It has twelve known moons.

Ju·ras·sic (joo ras′ik) *n.* the middle geological period of the Mesozoic era, during which the first known birds and flowering plants appeared. —*adj.* of, relating to, or characteristic of this period.

ju·ris·dic·tion (joor′is dik′shən) *n.* **1.** the limits within which judicial or other authority may be exercised; range or extent of authority. **2.** the territory over which authority is exercised. **3.** the legal right to exercise authority, especially the authority to interpret or apply the law.

ju·ris·pru·dence (joor′is prood′əns) *n.* **1.** the science or philosophy of law. **2.** a body or system of laws. **3.** a branch or department of law: *medical jurisprudence.*

ju·rist (joor′ist) *n.* a person who is expert or skilled in the law, such as a lawyer or judge.

ju·ror (joor′ər) *n.* a member of a jury.

ju·ry (joor′ē) *n. pl.,* **ju·ries. 1.** a group of persons selected according to law to hear evidence on a matter submitted to them in a court of law and to make a decision according to the law and the evidence. **2.** a committee chosen to select the winners and award the prizes in a contest, exhibition, or other competition.

ju·ry·man (joor′ē mən) *n. pl.,* **ju·ry·men** (joor′ē mən). a male juror. —**ju′ry·wom′an,** *n.*

just¹ (just) *adj.* **1.** that is fair, right, and moral: *a stern but just ruler, a legal system providing for just treatment of suspects.* **2.** rightly due or given; deserved; merited: *a just reward.* **3.** having a sound, reasonable, or adequate basis; well-founded: *just indignation.* **4.** legally valid; lawful; legitimate: *a just claim to the throne.* —*adv.* **1.** exactly; precisely: *It's just as I thought.* **2.** a very little while ago; very recently: *I just saw him.* **3.** by very little; by a narrow margin: *He arrived just in time.* **4.** only; merely: *It is just a cold.* **5.** *Informal.* simply; completely; positively: *That movie was just awful.* [From French *juste* fair.] —**just′ly,** *adv.* —**just′ness,** *n.*

just² (just) another spelling of **joust.**

jus·tice (jus′tis) *n.* **1.** the state or quality of being just; fairness. **2.** the maintenance or administration of law: *a court of justice.* **3.** a judge of the Supreme Court of the United States.

to do justice to. a. to treat or deal with (someone or something) in a just manner. **b.** to represent or show (someone or something) truly or well: *That picture doesn't do you justice.*

justice of the peace, a local public official who has the power to try minor cases, hold inquests and hearings, perform civil marriages, and carry out certain other duties.

jus·ti·fi·a·ble (jus′tə fī′ə bəl) *adj.* that can be justified.

jus·ti·fi·ca·tion (jus′tə fi kā′shən) *n.* **1.** the act of justifying or the state of being justified. **2.** something that justifies: *His rudeness was justification for our anger.*

jus·ti·fy (jus′tə fī′) *v.t.,* **jus·ti·fied, jus·ti·fy·ing. 1.** to show to be just or reasonable; vindicate: *His great success justified our faith in him.* **2.** to declare or prove blameless; absolve. **3.** *Printing.* to adjust (lines of type) to the proper length by spacing.

Jus·tin·i·an I (jus tin′ē ən) A.D. 483–565, the emperor of the Byzantine Empire from 527 to 565. During his reign, an important code of Roman law was compiled.

jus·tle (jus′əl) another spelling of **jostle.**

jut (jut) *v.i.,* **jut·ted, jut·ting.** to stick out; project; protrude: *A piece of rock jutted from the face of the cliff.*

jute (jōōt) *n.* **1.** a strong flexible fiber, chiefly used to make burlap and twine. **2.** either of the two plants yielding this fiber, grown chiefly in India and Pakistan.

Jute (jōōt) *n.* a member of a Germanic tribe, some of whom, along with the Angles and Saxons, invaded and settled in Britain during the fifth century.

Jut·land (jut′lənd) *n.* a peninsula in northern Europe, comprising the mainland of Denmark and the adjoining part of West Germany.

ju·ve·nile (jōō′vən əl, jōō′və nīl′) *adj.* **1.** of or suitable for children or young people: *a juvenile book, juvenile fashions.* **2.** childish; immature: *temper tantrums and other juvenile behavior.* **3.** young; youthful. —*n.* **1.** a young person; youth. **2.** an actor who plays youthful parts.

juvenile court, the court of law that handles cases involving children or adolescents under a certain age, usually eighteen.

juvenile delinquency, unlawful behavior by children or adolescents, usually under eighteen years of age.

juvenile delinquent, a child or adolescent, usually under eighteen years of age, who is guilty of unlawful behavior but is too young to be held criminally responsible.

jux·ta·pose (juks′tə pōz′) *v.t.,* **jux·ta·posed, jux·ta·pos·ing.** to place (two or more things) side by side or close together, especially for contrast or comparison. —**jux′ta·po·si′tion,** *n.*

1. Egyptian Hieroglyphics ⌣ᴼ	**5. Greek Ninth Century B.C.** ⅄
2. Semitic Ⴤ ↓	**6. Greek Classical Capitals** K
3. Phoenician ⅄ ⅄	**7. Latin Fourth Century B.C. Capitals** K
4. Early Hebrew ⅄ ⅄	**8. English** K

K is the eleventh letter of the English alphabet. The earliest form of **K** was an Egyptian hieroglyphic (1) that resembled a bowl or a cupped hand. The ancient Semitic form of this symbol was the letter *kaph* (2), meaning "hand" or "fist." When the Phoenicians (3) and early Hebrews (4) borrowed *kaph,* they made only slight changes in its shape. The ancient Greeks adopted *kaph* and called it *kappa* (5). In ancient times, the Greeks wrote from right to left or in alternating rows of right to left and left to right. Later, when they began to write from left to right, the shape of certain letters, including *kappa,* was reversed (6). This new form of *kappa* was borrowed by the Romans (7) who, by about 2300 years ago, were writing it almost exactly as we write the capital letter **K** today (8).

k, K (kā) *n. pl.,* **k's, K's.** the eleventh letter of the English alphabet.

K, the symbol for potassium. [Modern Latin *kalium.*]

Kaa·ba (kä′bə) *n.* a sacred Muslim shrine at Mecca. It is a small cubical structure containing a black stone said to have been given to Abraham by the archangel Gabriel.

Ka·bu·ki (kə bōō′kē) *n.* a form of Japanese drama, originating in the late sixteenth century, characterized by elaborate costumes and stylized acting, singing, and dancing.

Ka·bul (kä′bool) *n.* the capital and largest city of Afghanistan, in the east-central part of the country. Pop. (1971 est.), 318,094.

kai·ak (kī′ak) another spelling of **kayak.**

Kai·ser (kī′zər) *n.* **1.** any of the emperors of Germany from 1871 to 1918. **2.** any of the emperors of Austria from 1804 to 1918. **3.** any of the emperors of the Holy Roman Empire from 962 to 1806.

Kal·a·ma·zoo (kal′ə mə zōō′) *n.* a city in southwestern Michigan. Pop. (1970), 85,555.

kale (kāl) *n.* **1.** the broad, curly, bluish-green leaves of a plant of the cabbage family, eaten cooked or raw as a vegetable. **2.** the plant itself.

ka·lei·do·scope (kə lī′də skōp′) *n.* **1.** a tube-shaped toy containing loose bits of colored glass or other small objects which are reflected by a set of mirrors as a series of continually changing patterns when the tube is held to the eye and turned. **2.** anything having continually changing patterns or phases. —**ka·lei·do·scop·ic** (kə lī′də skop′ik), *adj.* —**ka·lei′do·scop′i·cal·ly,** *adv.*

Ka·li·nin·grad (kə lē′nin grad′) *n.* a port city in the westernmost part of the Soviet Union. It was once the capital of the former German province of East Prussia. Pop. (1970 est.), 297,000.

ka·mi·ka·ze (kä′mə kä′zē) *n.* one of a group of Japanese pilots in World War II whose mission was to dive their planes onto a ship or other target in a suicidal attempt

to destroy it. [Japanese *kamikaze* literally, divine wind.]

Kam·pa·la (käm pä′lə) *n.* the capital of Uganda, in the southern part of the country. Pop. (1969), 331,889.

Kan., Kansas.

kan·ga·roo (kang′gə rōō′) *n. pl.,* **kan·ga·roos** or **kan·ga·roo.** an Australian animal having small forelimbs, powerful hind legs adapted for leaping, and a long, muscular tail. For about six months after birth, the baby kangaroo is carried in the mother's pouch.

kangaroo rat, any of various jumping rodents of Mexico and western North America.

Kan·pur (kän′poor′) *n.* a city in north-central India. Pop. (1971), 1,151,975.

Kangaroo

Kans., Kansas.

Kan·sas (kan′zəs) *n.* a state in the west-central United States. Capital, Topeka. Area, 82,264 sq. mi. Pop. (1970), 2,249,071. Abbreviations, **Kans., Kan.** —**Kan′san,** *adj., n.*

● **Kansas** was named from the principal river in the state. The river's name came from the French version of the Siouan name for an Indian tribe that once lived in what is now northeastern Kansas.

Kansas City **1.** a city in western Missouri. Pop. (1970), 507,087. **2.** a city in eastern Kansas adjoining it. Pop. (1970), 168,213.

Kant, Im·ma·nu·el (kant, känt; i mä′nyōō el′) 1724–1804, German philosopher.

ka·o·lin (kā′ə lin) *n.* a fine white clay used to make porcelain.

517

ka·pok (kā′pok) *n.* a light, fluffy fiber obtained from the seedpods of a tropical tree. It is used as a stuffing for life preservers, pillows, and mattresses, and as an insulating material.

Ka·ra·chi (kə rä′chē) *n.* the largest city of Pakistan, a port on the Arabian Sea. Pop. (1975 est.), 2,800,000.

kar·a·kul (kar′ə kəl) *n.* **1.** a sheep of a breed originally native to central Asia, having a narrow body and a broad tail. The young karakul has a coat of curled, gray or glossy black fur. **2.** another spelling of **caracul.** [From *Kara Kul,* a lake in Turkestan, where it was first raised.]

kar·at (kar′ət) *also,* **car·at.** *n.* a unit of measure used to express the degree of purity of gold. Twenty-four karats is pure gold. Fourteen-karat gold is 14 parts gold and 10 parts alloy.

ka·ra·te (kə rä′tē) *n.* a Japanese system of unarmed self-defense in which the hands, elbows, knees, and feet are used to strike an opponent at vulnerable points of the body. [Japanese *karate* literally, empty hand; because weapons are not used in this system of defense.]

Kash·mir (kash′mēr, kash mēr′) *n.* an area in southern Asia, north of India, disputed by India and Pakistan. Also, **Jammu and Kashmir.**

Kashmir goat, a goat native to India, Tibet, and other regions in Asia, raised especially for its soft undercoat, which is used to make cashmere wool.

Ka·tan·ga (kə täng′gə) *n.* a region in southeast Zaire, now known as **Shaba.**

Kat·man·du (kät′män dōō′) *n.* the capital of Nepal, in the central part of the country. Pop. (1971), 153,405.

ka·ty·did (kā′tē did′) *n.* a large green grasshopper having long, threadlike antennae. The male makes a shrill, rasping noise by rubbing its wings together.

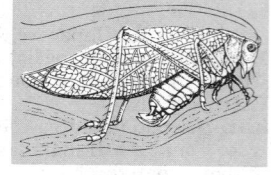

Katydid

Kau·ai (kou′ī) *n.* the northernmost island of Hawaii.

kay·ak (kī′ak) *also,* **kai·ak.** *n.* **1.** an Eskimo canoe made of animal skins stretched over a light framework of wood or whalebone, having a small opening in the center for a paddler. **2.** a light canoe resembling this.

ke·a (kē′ə) *n.* a large, green parrot of New Zealand, having a sharp, hooked bill.

Keats, John (kēts) 1795–1821, English poet.

keel (kēl) *n.* **1.** the main timber or steel piece extending lengthwise along the center of the bottom of a ship or boat and supporting the entire frame. **2.** the part in an aircraft resembling a ship's keel.

  on an even keel. steady; balanced: *His calmness helped keep everyone on an even keel during the fire.*

  to keel over. a. to turn bottom up; capsize. **b.** to fall over suddenly; topple; collapse: *to keel over in a faint.*

Keel

keel·haul (kēl′hôl′) *v.t.* **1.** to drag (a person) under the keel of a ship from one side or end to the other as a punishment. **2.** to rebuke or punish severely.

keen¹ (kēn) *adj.* **1.** having a sharp cutting edge or point; able to cut or pierce easily: *a keen knife.* **2.** having or showing great mental sharpness; quick: *a keen mind.* **3.** very sensitive or acute: *That hound has a keen sense of smell.* **4.** very strong; intense: *He has a keen interest in sports.* **5.** piercing or cutting: *A keen wind blew in from the ocean.* **6.** full of enthusiasm; eager: *Kate is keen about*

traveling. [Old English *cēne* wise, brave.] —**keen′ly,** *adv.* —**keen′ness,** *n.*

keen² (kēn) *Irish. n.* a wailing lament for the dead. —*v.i.* to wail loudly for the dead. [Irish *caoine.*]

keep (kēp) *v.,* **kept, keep·ing.** —*v.t.* **1.** to continue to have and hold: *The little girl kept the kitten that followed her home.* **2.** to cause to continue in a certain condition, place, or relation: *The mother kept her sick child in bed. The refrigerator kept the meat fresh.* **3.** to store, put, or hold: *The child kept his toys in the closet.* **4.** to make regular entries in: *to keep a diary.* **5.** to hold back: *The cold weather may keep the plants from budding.* **6.** to be faithful to; fulfill: *The boy kept his promise and mowed the lawn for his father.* **7.** to look after the affairs of; manage: *to keep house.* **8.** to take care of; watch over: *The shepherd kept the flock of sheep.* —*v.i.* **1.** to stay or continue in a certain condition, place, or relation: *The teacher told the class to keep quiet.* **2.** to hold back; refrain: *Ruth couldn't keep from crying at the sad movie.* **3.** to stay in good condition; last without spoiling: *Will this meat keep until tomorrow?* —*n.* **1.** something needed for a person to live, as food and shelter: *The boy earned his keep by working.* **2.** the strongest part of a castle or fortress.

  to keep to oneself. to stay away from the company of others.

  to keep up. a. to go at the same speed or rate: *The small boy could not keep up with his older brother.* **b.** to continue: *The noise of the machinery kept up all through the night.*

  to keep up with. a. to go at the same speed or rate as. **b.** to continue to be informed about: *He always keeps up with current events.*

keep·er (kē′pər) *n.* a person who protects, takes care of, or is responsible for someone or something: *a keeper at a zoo, the keeper of an inn.* ▲ often used in combination: *a shopkeeper, a gamekeeper.*

keep·ing (kē′ping) *n.* care, charge, or possession: *The jewels were placed in my keeping.*

  in keeping with. in harmony with; appropriate: *Greg's silly behavior was not in keeping with the solemn occasion.*

keep·sake (kēp′sāk′) *n.* something given or kept to remind one of the giver; memento.

keg (keg) *n.* **1.** a small barrel, usually holding five to ten gallons. **2.** a unit of weight for nails that is equal to 100 pounds.

Kel·ler, Helen (kel′ər) 1880–1968, U.S. writer and lecturer who was deaf and blind from infancy.

kelp (kelp) *n.* **1.** any of a large group of brown seaweeds growing along the coasts of the Atlantic and Pacific Oceans. **2.** the ashes of such seaweed, formerly a major source of potassium and iodine, now used mainly as a fertilizer.

Kel·vin scale (kel′vin) a temperature scale in which one degree is equal in size to a centigrade degree and zero degrees represents absolute zero ($-273.15°$ centigrade). [From Lord *Kelvin,* 1824–1907, a British scientist who introduced this scale.]

ken (ken) *n.* range of sight, knowledge, or understanding: *I'm afraid that the subject of calculus is beyond my ken.* —*v.i.,* **kenned, ken·ning.** *Scottish.* to know or understand.

Ken·ne·dy, John Fitzgerald (ken′ə dē) 1917–1963, the thirty-fifth president of the United States, from 1961 to 1963.

ken·nel (ken′əl) *n.* **1.** a shelter for a dog or dogs. **2.** *also,* **kennels.** a place where dogs are bred, trained, or boarded. —*v.t.* to put or keep in a kennel.

Kent (kent) *n.* **1.** a county in southeastern England. **2.** an ancient kingdom in southeastern England.

Ken·tuck·y (kən tuk′ē) *n.* a state in the east-central United States. Capital, Frankfort. Area, 40,395 sq. mi. Pop. (1970), 3,219,311. Abbreviation, **Ky.** —**Ken·tuck′-i·an,** *adj., n.*

● **Kentucky** comes from an Iroquois word that probably meant "meadowland" or "level land." This name was used also for the river running through this land. The name was later given to a county organized by the state of Virginia in 1776, and was kept when this county became the state of Kentucky.

Ken·ya (ken′yə, kēn′yə) *n.* a country in eastern Africa, formerly a British colony and protectorate. Capital, Nairobi. Area, 224,960 sq. mi. Pop. (1971 est.), 11,690,000. —**Ken′yan,** *adj., n.*

Kep·ler, Jo·hann (kep′lər; yō′hän) 1571–1630, German astronomer.

kept (kept) the past tense and past participle of **keep.**

ker·a·tin (ker′ə tin) *n.* a tough, fibrous protein present in the skin tissue of all vertebrates. It forms the main part of horns, hoofs, hair, nails, and feathers.

ker·chief (kur′chif) *n.* 1. a piece of cloth, usually square, worn over the head or around the neck. 2. see **handkerchief** (*def. 1*).

ker·nel (kurn′əl) *n.* 1. the grain or seed of various plants, such as wheat or corn. 2. the softer, inner part of a seed or fruit. 3. the central, most valuable, or most important part.

ker·o·sene (ker′ə sēn′) *also,* **ker·o·sine.** *n.* a colorless, highly volatile liquid distilled from petroleum, widely used as a fuel and cleaning solvent. It consists of a mixture of hydrocarbons.

ketch (kech) *n. pl.,* **ketch·es.** a fore-and-aft-rigged sailing ship with two masts, similar to a yawl, but having the mizzenmast farther forward.

ketch·up (kech′əp) *also,* **catch·up, cat·sup.** *n.* a thick, seasoned sauce which is made of tomatoes, onions, salt, sugar, and spices and is used with many types of food.

ket·tle (ket′əl) *n.* 1. any metal container used for boiling liquids or for cooking in liquid; pot. 2. a teakettle.

ket·tle·drum (ket′əl drum′) *n.* a drum consisting of a hollow brass or copper hemisphere with a parchment top that can be tuned to a definite pitch.

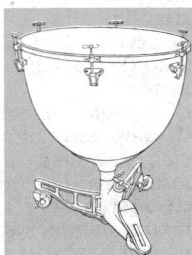

Kettledrum

key[1] (kē) *n. pl.,* **keys.** 1. an instrument that opens or closes a lock by moving a bolt or tumblers. 2. anything like this instrument in use or shape: *a roller skate key, a key that winds a clock, a key to open a can of sardines.* 3. something that solves or explains: *The detectives finally found the key to the crime. A key to the pronunciations in this dictionary appears at the bottom of the page.* 4. something that leads to or is a way of getting something: *Hard work can sometimes be the key to success in business.* 5. a place or position that gives control of entry or possession: *Gibraltar is the key to the Mediterranean Sea.* 6. a person or thing that is thought of as the main or controlling force: *The quarterback was the key to the team.* 7. a part pressed down in working a machine or instrument: *a piano key, a telegraph key, a typewriter key.* 8. *Music.* a scale or system of notes in which all the notes bear a definite relationship to, and are based on and named for, a given note which is the keynote: *a symphony in the key of F sharp.* 9. a tone or pitch of the voice: *to speak in a high key.* —*adj.* of great or chief importance; major;

basic: *The manufacture of automobiles is a key industry of this country.* —*v.t.,* **keyed, key·ing.** 1. *Music.* to regulate the pitch or tone of: *to key an instrument to B flat.* 2. to regulate or adjust (something) to suit a particular activity or occasion. [Old English *cǣg.*]

to key up. to make nervous, tense, or excited: *He was keyed up from thinking about the final exam.*

key[2] (kē) *n. pl.,* **keys.** a low, coastal island or reef, as along the southern tip of Florida. [Spanish *cayo.*]

Key, Francis Scott (kē) 1799–1843, the author of *The Star-Spangled Banner.*

key·board (kē′bôrd′) *n.* an arrangement or set of keys, as in a piano, typewriter, or key punch.

key·hole (kē′hōl′) *n.* a hole through which a key is inserted into a lock.

key·note (kē′nōt′) *n.* 1. *Music.* the note on which a scale or system of tones is based; tonic. 2. the main or dominant idea, principle, theme, or mood: *Economic expansion was the keynote of the nation's foreign policy.* —*v.t.,* **key·not·ed, key·not·ing.** to give or set the keynote of.

keynote speech, a speech, as at the convention of a political party, in which important issues and the basic policy to be followed are presented. Also, **keynote address.**

key punch, a machine operated from a keyboard and used to record information in data processing by means of holes punched in cards.

key signature *Music.* the sharps or flats placed after the clef at the beginning of each staff, or at any point where there is a change of key, indicating the key of the music which follows.

key·stone (kē′stōn′) *n.* 1. the central, topmost stone of an arch, that locks the remaining stones of the arch together. It is usually the last stone to be set in place. 2. the main or basic element or part upon which related parts depend: *Singapore was the keystone of the power of the British Empire in the Far East.*

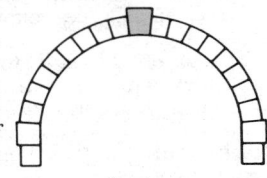

Keystone

Key West, an island off the coast of southwestern Florida, in the Gulf of Mexico.

kg., kilogram; kilograms.

khak·i (kak′ē, kä′kē) *n. pl.,* **khak·is.** 1. a dull, yellowish-brown or tan color. 2. a sturdy, twilled cotton cloth of this color. 3. **khakis.** a garment made of this fabric, especially a military uniform.

khan (kän) *n.* 1. any of the medieval emperors of China who also ruled the Tartar, Turkish, and Mongol tribes. 2. a ruler or official of high rank in Iran, Afghanistan, and central Asia.

Khar·kov (kär′kof) *n.* a city in the southwestern Soviet Union, in the Ukraine. Pop. (1970 est.), 1,248,000.

Khar·toum (kär tōm′) *n.* the capital of Sudan, in the north-central part of the country, on the Nile. Pop. (1970 est.), 261,840.

khe·dive (kə dēv′) *n.* the title of the Turkish viceroys of Egypt from 1867 to 1914.

Khmer Republic (kə mer′) the official name of **Cambodia.**

K

at; āpe; cär; end; mē; it; īce; hot; ōld; fôrk; wood; fōōl; oil; out; up; turn; sing; thin; **th**is; hw in white; zh in treasure. The symbol ə stands for the sound of **a** in about, **e** in taken, **i** in pencil, **o** in lemon, and **u** in circus.

Khrush·chev, Ni·ki·ta (kroosh′chef′; ni kē′tə) 1894–1971, the premier of the Soviet Union from 1958 to 1964.

Khu·fu (kōo′fōo) *n.* another name for **Cheops.**

Khy·ber Pass (kī′bər) a mountain pass between Pakistan and Afghanistan.

kib·butz (ki boots′) *n. pl.,* **kib·but·zim** (ki boot′sēm). a collective farm or settlement in modern Israel.

kib·itz (kib′its) *v.i. Informal.* to act as a kibitzer.

kib·itz·er (kib′it sər) *n. Informal.* **1.** a person who looks on at a card game and gives unwanted advice to the players. **2.** anyone who gives unwanted advice or meddles in the affairs of others.

kick (kik) *v.t.* **1.** to strike with the foot or feet: *to kick a pebble on the beach.* **2.** to drive or move by striking with the foot or feet: *to kick a tin can into a sewer.* **3.** *Sports.* to score (a goal or point) by kicking the ball over the goal posts or into the goal, as in football or soccer. **4.** (of firearms) to spring back when fired; recoil. —*v.i.* **1.** to strike out with the foot or feet: *The swimmer increased his speed by kicking faster.* **2.** *Sports.* to put the ball in play or attempt to score or gain ground by kicking the ball, as in football or soccer. **3.** (of firearms) to recoil when fired. **4.** *Informal.* to complain; rebel: *Mike kicked at having to dry the dishes.* —*n.* **1.** the act or power of kicking the foot or feet: *Pete shut the door with a kick.* **2.** the sudden springing back of a gun when fired. **3.** *Sports.* **a.** the act or instance of kicking a ball. **b.** a kicked ball: *to block a kick.* **c.** the distance a ball travels when kicked: *a fifty-yard kick.* **4.** *Slang.* a complaint; objection. **5.** *Slang.* a pleasing or exciting feeling; thrill. —**kick′er,** *n.*

to kick back. *Slang.* to pay back (a portion of money received as a fee, commission, salary, or the like) as a kickback.

to kick off. *Football.* to make a kickoff.

to kick out. *Informal.* to expel or eject forcefully or suddenly: *He was kicked out of school for cheating on a test.*

kick·back (kik′bak′) *n.* an illegal or secret payment made by a seller of goods or services to the person who sent a buyer or client to him.

kick·off (kik′ôf′) *n.* **1.** a kick that puts the ball in play in football. **2.** *Informal.* the beginning; commencement: *The dance marked the kickoff of the charity's fund drive.*

kid (kid) *n.* **1.** a young goat. **2.** see **kidskin. 3.** *Informal.* a young person; child; youngster. —*adj. Informal.* (of a brother or sister) younger: *The boy took his kid brother to the circus.* —*v., kid·ded, kid·ding. Informal.* —*v.t.* **1.** to make fun of; tease: *They kidded Jim about his freckles.* **2.** to deceive (someone) as a joke; fool: *Sam tried to kid us into believing his story.* —*v.i.* to engage in good-humored fooling or teasing; joke. —**kid′der,** *n.*

kid·nap (kid′nap′) *v.t.,* **kid·naped** or **kid·napped, kid·nap·ing** or **kid·nap·ping.** to seize or hold (a person) against his will, especially for the purpose of getting a ransom. —**kid′nap′er;** *also,* **kid′nap′per,** *n.*

kid·ney (kid′nē) *n. pl.,* **kid·neys. 1.** either of a pair of organs located at the back of the abdominal cavity. They filter wastes out of the bloodstream, forming urine which is collected in the bladder. **2.** the kidney of certain animals, used as food. **3.** kind or disposition: *a man of my kidney* (Shakespeare, *The Merry Wives of Windsor).*

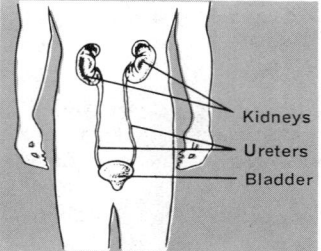

kidney bean 1. the kidney-shaped seed of any of various varieties of a plant of the pea family, cooked and eaten as a vegetable. **2.** the plant bearing this seed.

kid·skin (kid′skin′) *n.* a leather made from the skin of young goats, used for such items as gloves and shoes.

Kiel (kēl) *n.* a city in northern West Germany. Pop. (1970), 271,700.

Ki·ev (kē′ef) *n.* a port city on the Dnieper River, in the southwestern Soviet Union, the capital and largest city of the Ukraine. Pop. (1971 est.), 1,693,000.

Ki·ga·li (ki gä′lē) *n.* the capital of Rwanda, in the central part of the country. Pop. (1970 est.), 60,000.

Kil·i·man·ja·ro, Mount (kil′ə mən jär′ō) the highest mountain in Africa, in northeastern Tanzania.

kill¹ (kil) *v.t.* **1.** to take away the life of; cause the death of: *Automobile accidents kill thousands of Americans every year.* **2.** to put an end to; destroy: *Failing the examination killed his chances of winning the scholarship.* **3.** to cancel or stop the publication of: *The editor killed the story in the late edition.* **4.** to pass (time) aimlessly or unproductively: *Ed killed an hour by wandering through the town.* **5.** *Informal.* to affect with severe pain, discomfort, or fatigue: *My back is killing me.* —*v.i.* to cause death; be fatal: *An overdose of this drug can kill.* —*n.* **1.** the act or instance of killing, especially in hunting: *The hunters moved in for the kill.* **2.** the animal or animals killed: *The tiger dragged its kill into the jungle.* [Middle English *cullen, killen.*]

kill² (kil) *n.* a channel, creek, or stream. [Dutch *kil.*]

kill·deer (kil′dēr′) *n. pl.,* **kill·deers** or **kill·deer.** a North American wading bird, having brownish feathers with two black bands across the breast.

kill·er (kil′ər) *n.* a person, animal, or thing that kills.

killer whale, a black-and-white whale that preys on fish, penguins, seals, sea lions, and even other whales.

Killdeer

kill·ing (kil′ing) *n.* **1.** the act of killing. **2.** *Informal.* a sudden great profit or success: *Her father made a killing in the stock market.*

kill·joy (kil′joi′) *n.* a person who spoils or lessens the enjoyment or fun of others.

kiln (kil, kiln) *n.* a furnace or oven for burning, baking, or drying, used in making bricks, pottery, or charcoal.

ki·lo (kē′lō, kil′ō) *n. pl.,* **ki·los. 1.** a kilogram. **2.** a kilometer.

kilo- *prefix* one thousand: *kilocycle, kiloliter.*

kil·o·cy·cle (kil′ə sī′kəl) *n.* **1.** a unit equal to 1000 cycles. **2.** a unit equal to 1000 cycles per second, used in measuring the frequency of electromagnetic waves.

kil·o·gram (kil′ə gram′) *n.* a unit of mass and weight in the metric system equal to 1000 grams, or 2.2046 pounds avoirdupois.

kil·o·gram-me·ter (kil′ə gram′mē′tər) *n.* a unit of work or energy, equal to about 7.2 foot-pounds. A kilogram-meter is the amount of energy required to raise a mass of one kilogram to a height of one meter.

kil·o·li·ter (kil′ə lē′tər) *n.* a unit of capacity in the metric system equal to 1000 liters, or one cubic meter; 264.17 U.S. gallons or 1.308 cubic yards.

ki·lom·e·ter (ki lom′ə tər, kil′ə mē′tər) *n.* a unit of length in the metric system equal to 1000 meters, or 3280.8 feet.

kil·o·ton (kil′ə tun′) *n.* **1.** a unit of weight equal to 1000 tons. **2.** a unit of explosive force equivalent to that produced by the detonation of 1000 tons of TNT.

kil·o·watt (kil′ə wot′) *n.* a unit of electrical power equal to 1000 watts.

kil·o·watt-hour (kil′ə wot′our′) *n.* a unit of electrical energy equal to the energy consumed by a machine working at a constant rate of one kilowatt for one hour.

kilt (kilt) *n.* a pleated skirt usually made of tartan and reaching to the knees, especially one worn by men in the Scottish Highlands.

kil·ter (kil′tər) *n.* **out of kilter.** out of order; not in good condition: *The toaster is out of kilter.*

ki·mo·no (ki mō′nə) *n. pl.,* **ki·mo·nos. 1.** a loose robe or gown tied with a sash, worn by Japanese men and women. **2.** a loose dressing gown similar to this.

kin (kin) *n.* **1.** a person's whole family; relatives; kindred; kinsfolk. **2.** a kinsman; relative. —*adj.* related: *She is not kin to me.*
  next of kin. a person or persons most closely related to one: *The police immediately notified the injured man's next of kin.*

-kin *suffix* little; small: *lambkin.*

kind¹ (kīnd) *adj.* **1.** gentle, considerate, and friendly in nature or behavior; good-hearted: *The boy was always kind to animals. It was kind of you to help her.* **2.** from or showing good-heartedness: *kind words, a kind act.* [Old English *cynde, gecynde* natural, native.]

kind² (kīnd) *n.* a class, sort, or grouping; variety; type: *The whale is a kind of mammal. That store has many different kinds of sports equipment.* [Old English *cynd, gecynd* type, nature.]
  in kind. a. in goods or produce, rather than in money. **b.** with something of the same sort: *She insulted him, and he repaid her in kind.*
  kind of. *Informal.* somewhat; rather: *I'm feeling kind of hungry.*

kin·der·gar·ten (kin′dər gärt′ən) *n.* a class or division of school for children from four to six years old, coming before the first grade of elementary school. [German *Kindergarten* literally, a children's garden.]

kind-heart·ed (kīnd′här′tid) *adj.* having or showing kindness or sympathy: *a kind-hearted person, kind-hearted actions.* —**kind′-heart′ed·ly,** *adv.* —**kind′-heart′ed·ness,** *n.*

kin·dle (kind′əl) *v.,* **kin·dled, kin·dling.** —*v.t.* **1.** to set on fire; light: *The campers kindled the logs of the campfire.* **2.** to arouse, stir up, or excite: *The boy's rude behavior kindled his father's anger.* **3.** to make bright or glowing; light up: *The setting sun kindled the evening sky.* —*v.i.* **1.** to catch fire; begin to burn: *A dry forest is likely to kindle with the smallest spark.* **2.** to become aroused or stirred up. **3.** to become bright or glowing. Also, **enkindle.** —**kin′dler,** *n.*

kin·dling (kind′ling) *n.* material for starting a fire, especially small pieces of dry wood or twigs.

kind·ly (kīnd′lē) *adj.,* **kind·li·er, kind·li·est. 1.** having or showing kindness; kind; benevolent: *The old man had a kindly face.* **2.** pleasant; agreeable: *a kindly breeze on a hot day.* —*adv.* **1.** in a kind or gentle manner: *The policeman spoke kindly to the lost child.* **2.** favorably; agreeably. **3.** as a favor; please: *Kindly mail this letter for me.* **4.** enthusiastically; cordially: *We thank you kindly for your help.* —**kind′li·ness,** *n.*
  to take kindly to. to like or accept: *John does not take kindly to criticism.*

kind·ness (kīnd′nis) *n. pl.,* **kind·ness·es. 1.** the quality or state of being kind: *I have always depended on the kindness of strangers* (Tennessee Williams). **2.** a kind act; favor:

The guests thanked their hostess for her many kindnesses.

kin·dred (kin′drid) *n.* a person's whole family; relatives. —*adj.* **1.** like; similar: *a kindred spirit, kindred pursuits.* **2.** related by history or derivation; having common ancestors: *Spanish, French, and Italian are kindred languages.*

kine (kīn) *n., pl. Archaic.* cows; cattle.

kin·e·mat·ics (kin′ə mat′iks) *n.* the branch of mechanics dealing with the motion of moving bodies, without reference to the mass or force that is involved in the motion.

kin·e·scope (kin′ə skōp′) *n.* **1.** a motion-picture record of a television program. **2.** the picture tube of a television set. —*v.t.,* **kin·e·scoped, kin·e·scop·ing.** to make a kinescope of.

ki·net·ic (ki net′ik) *adj.* **1.** of or relating to motion. **2.** produced or caused by motion.

kinetic energy, the energy that a body has because of its motion.

ki·net·ics (ki net′iks) *n.* the branch of physics that deals with the effects of forces in causing or changing the motion of bodies.

kin·folk (kin′fōk′) *also,* **kin·folks.** another spelling of **kinsfolk.**

king (king) *n.* **1.** a male ruler who holds limited or absolute power over a nation or state for life, usually by hereditary rights. **2.** a person or thing that is supreme or is the best of its class: *The lion is often thought of as the king of the jungle. That man owns so many oil wells that he is known as an oil king.* **3.** a playing card bearing a picture of a king. **4.** a principal piece in the game of chess, capable of moving one square in any direction. The object of chess is to checkmate the opponent's king. **5.** a piece in the game of checkers that has moved across the board to the opponent's side and can now move both forward and backward. —**king′like′,** *adj.*

King *(def. 4)*

King. Kings are entered in the dictionary under their proper name. For example, **King John** is listed under **John.**

King, Martin Luther, Jr. (king) 1928–1968, U.S. clergyman and civil rights leader.

King Arthur, see **Arthur** *(def. 1).*

king·bird (king′burd′) *n.* any of various birds found throughout North and South America, related to the flycatcher.

king·bolt (king′bōlt′) *n.* a vertical bolt connecting the body of a wagon or other vehicle with the front axle of its body. Also, **kingpin.**

king crab, a large crab having a small triangular body and very long legs. It is found in the northern Pacific Ocean.

king·dom (king′dəm) *n.* **1.** a nation or state ruled by a king or queen. **2.** a realm, region, or sphere in which some condition or quality is supreme or prevails: *a cattle kingdom.* **3.** one of the three primary divisions of nature: *the animal kingdom, the vegetable kingdom, and the mineral kingdom.*

king·fish (king′fish′) *n. pl.,* **king·fish** or **king·fish·es.** any of several saltwater food and game fish found along

K

at; āpe; cär; end; mē; it; īce; hot; ōld; fôrk; wood; fōōl; oil; out; up; turn; sing; thin; this; hw in white; zh in treasure. The symbol ə stands for the sound of a in about, e in taken, i in pencil, o in lemon, and u in circus.

Kilt

the Atlantic coast of the United States, having a dark-gray body.

king·fish·er (king'fish'ər) *n.* any of various brightly colored birds having a large, usually crested head and a long, pointed bill. It eats fish, insects, reptiles, and sometimes small animals or birds.

King James Version, an English translation of the Bible, authorized by King James I and first published in 1611.

king·ly (king'lē) *adj.,* **king·li·er, king·li·est.** characteristic of, like, or suitable for a king; royal; regal: *The old man had a kingly way of walking.* —*adv.* in a kingly manner; regally; royally. —**king'li·ness,** *n.*

king·pin (king'pin') *n.* **1.** the pin that is positioned in the center and in front of the other pins in bowling. **2.** another word for **kingbolt. 3.** *Informal.* the chief person in a group or sphere: *That man is a kingpin of organized crime.*

Kings (kingz) *n.* **1.** in the Protestant Bible, either of two books (I Kings or II Kings) of the Old Testament, containing the history of the Jewish monarchy from the reign of Solomon to the fall of Jerusalem in 586 B.C. **2.** in the Douay Bible, one of four books of the Old Testament, equivalent to I and II Samuel and I and II Kings of the Protestant Bible.

king salmon, a large salmon found throughout the northern Pacific Ocean, important as a food fish.

King's English, standard, correct, or accepted usage of English in Great Britain.

● **King's English,** or **Queen's English** as it is often called when a queen rules, is the form of English that is considered to be correct in Great Britain. The term refers to the way educated British people use the language, and not necessarily to the way a king or queen actually speaks. Not all the rulers of Britain have spoken King's English themselves. King George I, who was German, could not speak English at all. Rather, this form of English got its name because of the idea that it had the official approval of the king or queen.

King's English is called a *prestige dialect,* which means that people consider it to be superior to other dialects, which are the different ways in which a language is spoken. In Great Britain, as in any other country, the way in which the most prominent, most successful, and best-educated people speak is thought to be the correct way. This does not mean that this way of speaking is really correct while others are wrong; it simply means that social custom has established this as the standard form of the language.

---

king·ship (king'ship') *n.* **1.** the position, office, or dignity of a king. **2.** government by a king; monarchy.

king-size (king'sīz') *adj.* larger or longer than is ordinary: *a king-size cigarette.*

king snake, a nonpoisonous snake found from southern Canada to northern South America. It feeds on other snakes and on rodents, lizards, frogs, and other small animals.

Kings·ton (king'stən) *n.* the capital, largest city, and chief port of Jamaica, on the southeastern coast of the island. Pop. (1976 est.), 635,100.

kink (kingk) *n.* **1.** a tight curl or sharp twist, as in a hair, wire, or rope. **2.** a painful muscle spasm or cramp; crick: *He got a kink in his back after lifting the heavy weight.* **3.** *Informal.* an imperfection or flaw, as in the plan or operation of something: *The engineer got the kinks out of the design of the car.* **4.** *Informal.* a mental quirk or whim. —*v.t.* to cause to form a kink or kinks. —*v.i.* to form a kink or kinks.

kin·ka·jou (king'kə joo') *n.* a small, slender, yellowish-brown animal of Mexico and Central and South America that is related to the raccoon, having a long tail and soft woolly fur.

Kinkajou

kink·y (king'kē) *adj.,* **kink·i·er, kink·i·est.** full of kinks; tightly curled or twisted: *kinky hair.* —**kink'i·ness,** *n.*

kins·folk (kinz'fōk') *also,* **kin·folk, kin·folks.** *n., pl.* a person's relatives; family.

Kin·sha·sa (kin shä'sə) *n.* the capital and largest city of Zaire, a port in the western part of the country. It was formerly known as Léopoldville. Pop. (1975 est.), 2,202,000.

kin·ship (kin'ship') *n.* **1.** a family relationship. **2.** any relationship or close connection.

kins·man (kinz'mən) *n. pl.,* **kins·men** (kinz'mən). a male relative.

kins·wom·an (kinz'woom'ən) *n. pl.,* **kins·wom·en** (kinz'wim'ən). a female relative.

ki·osk (kē'osk, kē osk') *n.* a small structure with one or more open sides, used especially as a newsstand, bandstand, telephone booth, or subway entrance.

Kip·ling, Rud·yard (kip'-ling; rud'yərd) 1865–1936, English poet, short story writer, and novelist.

kip·per (kip'ər) *v.t.* to cure (fish) by splitting, cleaning, and salting, and then drying, smoking, or preserving. —*n.* **1.** any of various kinds of fish,

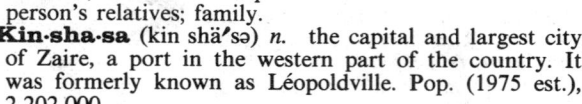

Kiosk

especially herring, salmon, or sea trout, that have been kippered. **2.** a male salmon or sea trout during or shortly after spawning.

Kir·ghiz or **Kir·giz** (kir gēz') *n.* a republic in the south-central Soviet Union. Also, **Kirghiz Soviet Socialist Republic.** Pop. (1976 est.), 3,368,000.

kirk (kurk) *n. Scottish.* a church.

kis·met (kiz'met') *n.* fate; destiny.

kiss (kis) *v.t.* **1.** to touch with the lips as a sign of greeting, affection, desire, or respect: *The mother kissed her child.* **2.** to touch lightly or softly: *When the sweet wind did gently kiss the trees* (Shakespeare, *Merchant of Venice*). —*v.i.* to touch with the lips. —*n. pl.,* **kiss·es. 1.** a touching with the lips as a sign of greeting, affection, desire, or respect. **2.** a light or gentle touch. **3.** a small candy, as of chocolate.

kit (kit) *n.* **1.** a set of tools, instruments, or equipment for a specific purpose: *a repair kit, a first-aid kit.* **2.** a collection of personal articles packed for traveling. **3.** a container for storing or carrying a kit: *The television repairman kept spare tubes in his kit.* **4.** a set of parts or materials to be assembled: *a model rocket kit.*

Kit·a·kyu·shu (kē'tä kyoo'shoo) *n.* a city at the northwestern tip of Kyushu, Japan. Pop. (1978 est.), 1,067,612.

kitch·en (kich'ən) *n.* **1.** a room or place specially equipped or set apart for the preparation and cooking of food. **2.** the facilities, equipment, or staff of a kitchen.

kitch·en·ette (kich'ə net') *n.* a small kitchen.

kitchen police *Military.* **1.** the duty of helping the cook by performing kitchen chores. **2.** the enlisted personnel assigned to such duty.

kitch·en·ware (kich'ən wer') *n.* kitchen utensils, such as pots and pans.

kite (kīt) *n.* **1.** a lightweight frame, usually of wood covered with paper, plastic, or cloth, flown in the air at the end of a long string for sport or recreation. **2.** any of various hawks having a hooked bill, a forked tail, and long, narrow wings.

kith (kith) *n.* **kith and kin.** a person's friends, acquaintances, and relatives.

kit·ten (kit′ən) *n.* a young cat.

kit·ty¹ (kit′ē) *n. pl.*, **kit·ties.** a kitten or cat.

kit·ty² (kit′ē) *n. pl.*, **kit·ties.** money contributed by a group of people for some special purpose: *The boys put money into the kitty to pay for the party.* [*Kit* + -*y²*.]

kit·ty-cor·ner (kit′ē kôr′nər) *n.* another word for **catty-corner.**

Kitty Hawk, a village in northeastern North Carolina where the first successful airplane flight was made in 1903 by Wilber and Orville Wright.

Kiu·shu (kyōō′shōō) another spelling of **Kyushu.**

ki·wi (kē′wē) *n. pl.*, **ki·wis.** a bird of New Zealand that cannot fly, having a rounded body, a very long, slender bill, and brownish-gray, furlike feathers.

KKK, Ku Klux Klan.

klep·to·ma·ni·a (klep′tə mā′-nē ə) *n.* a very strong impulse or tendency to steal, especially when a person has no need for the thing stolen.

klep·to·ma·ni·ac (klep′tə mā′-nē ak′) *n.* a person who has kleptomania.

klieg light (klēg) a bright arc lamp used especially in filming motion pictures.

Klon·dike (klon′dīk) *n.* a gold-mining region in the west-central Yukon, Canada.

km., kilometer; kilometers.

knack (nak) *n.* a special skill, ability, or method for doing something easily: *My uncle has a knack for repairing things.*

knap·sack (nap′sak′) *n.* a bag, usually of canvas or leather, for carrying clothes, equipment, or other supplies, strapped over the shoulders and carried on the back.

knave (nāv) *n.* **1.** a deceitful or dishonest, disloyal man; scoundrel. **2.** in card games, a jack. **3.** *Archaic.* **a.** a male servant. **b.** a man of humble birth.

knav·er·y (nā′vər ē) *n. pl.*, **knav·er·ies.** behavior characteristic of a knave; deceitfulness; trickery.

knav·ish (nā′vish) *adj.* of, relating to, or characteristic of a knave; deceitful; dishonest. —**knav′ish·ly,** *adv.* —**knav′ish·ness,** *n.*

knead (nēd) *v.t.* **1.** to mix or work (a substance, such as dough or clay) into a uniform mass, especially by pressing and squeezing with the hands. **2.** to press and squeeze with the hands; massage: *The team's trainer kneaded the pitcher's sore arm.* **3.** to make or shape by kneading: *to knead a statue of clay.* —**knead′er,** *n.*

knee (nē) *n.* **1.** the joint of the human leg between the thigh and the lower leg. **2.** the region around this joint. **3.** any joint similar or corresponding to the human knee, such as the joint in the foreleg of hoofed mammals. **4.** the part of a garment covering the knee. —*v.t.,* **kneed, knee·ing.** to strike or touch with the knee.

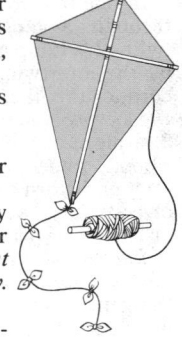
Kite

Kiwi

Knapsack

knee·cap (nē′kap′) *n.* a flat, triangular, movable bone at the front of the knee, protecting the joint from injury. Also, **kneepan, patella.**

knee-deep (nē′dēp′) *adj.* **1.** so deep as to reach the knees: *The river is only knee-deep at this point.* **2.** sunk to the knees: *The hikers trudged almost knee-deep in mud.* **3.** deeply involved or concerned: *He is knee-deep in the scandal.*

knee-high (nē′hī′) *adj.* so high or tall as to reach the knees: *The meadow was covered with knee-high grass.*

kneel (nēl) *v.i.,* **knelt** or **kneeled, kneel·ing.** to go down on a bent knee or knees: *to kneel down to scrub the floor, to kneel before an altar.* —**kneel′er,** *n.*

knee·pad (nē′pad′) *n.* a protective covering for the knee worn in certain sports, such as football or ice hockey.

knee·pan (nē′pan′) *n.* another word for **kneecap.**

knell (nel) *n.* **1.** the tolling of a bell, rung slowly and solemnly, as after a death or at a funeral. **2.** a warning of death or failure. **3.** any mournful sound. —*v.i.* (of a bell) to ring slowly and solemnly, as after a death or at a funeral; toll.

knelt (nelt) a past tense and past participle of **kneel.**

knew (nōō, nyōō) the past tense of **know.**

Knick·er·bock·er (nik′ər bok′ər) *n.* **1.** a descendant of the early Dutch settlers of New York. **2.** a New Yorker. [From Diedrich *Knickerbocker,* the name under which Washington Irving wrote the book *History of New York* (1809).]

knick·ers (nik′ərz) *n., pl.* loose-fitting trousers ending just below the knee. Also, **knick·er·bock·ers** (nik′ər-bok′ərz).

knick·knack (nik′nak′) *also,* **nick·nack.** *n.* a small decorative object.

knife (nīf) *n. pl.,* **knives. 1.** a tool for cutting, consisting of a sharp-edged blade attached to a handle. **2.** the cutting blade of a tool or machine. —*v.,* **knifed, knif·ing.** —*v.t.* **1.** to cut or stab with a knife. **2.** *Informal.* to slander, betray, or harm (someone) in an underhanded way. —*v.i.* to move or cut a way through something as if with a knife: *The boat knifed through the water.* —**knife′like′,** *adj.*

knight (nīt) *n.* **1.** in the Middle Ages, a mounted soldier who gave military service to a king or lord in return for the right to hold land, especially such a soldier who first served an apprenticeship as a page and squire. **2.** a man raised to honorary rank by a king or queen in recognition of personal merit or for services rendered to the crown or country. In Great Britain a knight is entitled to use *Sir* before his name. **3.** a piece in the game of chess shaped like a horse's head. —*v.t.* to raise to the rank of knight: *The king knighted the soldier for his courage.*

Knight *(def. 3)*

knight-er·rant (nīt′er′ənt) *n. pl.,* **knights-er·rant.** a medieval knight who traveled in search of adventure to show his military skill, bravery, and chivalry.

knight·hood (nīt′hood′) *n.* **1.** the rank or occupation of a knight. **2.** the behavior or qualities befitting a knight; chivalry. **3.** knights as a group.

at; āpe; cär; end; mē; it; īce; hot; ōld; fôrk;
wood; fōōl; oil; out; up; turn; sing; thin; this;
hw in white; zh in treasure. The symbol ə
stands for the sound of **a** in about, **e** in taken,
i in pencil, **o** in lemon, and **u** in circus.

K

knight·ly (nīt′lē) *adj.* of, relating to, or characteristic of a knight: *knightly deeds.* —**knight′li·ness,** *n.*

knit (nit) *v.,* **knit·ted** or **knit, knit·ting.** —*v.t.* **1.** to make (a fabric or garment) by interlocking loops of yarn or thread, either by hand or by the use of knitting needles, or by machine. **2.** to join or fasten closely and securely: *Love knitted the family together.* **3.** to draw (the brows) together in wrinkles; furrow. —*v.i.* **1.** to make a cloth or garment by interlocking loops of yarn or thread. **2.** to come together closely: *The broken bone in his leg knitted well.* —*n.* a fabric or garment made by knitting. —**knit′ter,** *n.*

knit·ting (nit′ing) *n.* a knitted cloth or garment.

knitting needle, a long, slender rod, either straight or curved, having a blunt point at one or both ends, used in knitting.

knit·wear (nit′wer′) *n.* clothing made of knitted cloth.

knives (nīvz) the plural of **knife.**

knob (nob) *n.* **1.** a rounded lump or part that sticks out: *He had a knob on his head where the ball hit him.* **2.** a rounded handle or dial, as for opening a door or drawer or for operating a radio or television. **3.** a rounded hill or mountain. —**knob′like′,** *adj.*

knob·by (nob′ē) *adj.,* **knob·bi·er, knob·bi·est. 1.** covered with knobs or lumps. **2.** shaped like a knob: *knobby knees.*

knock (nok) *v.t.* **1.** to strike with a sharp, hard blow; hit: *The falling branch knocked him on the head.* **2.** to drive or force by hitting: *The batter knocked the ball out of the park.* **3.** to drive or bring (something) violently against something else; cause to collide: *Dan knocked his leg against the table.* **4.** to hit or push so as to cause to fall: *to knock over a chair.* **5.** to make by striking: *to knock a hole in a wall.* **6.** *Informal.* to find fault with: *All the critics knocked the play.* —*v.i.* **1.** to strike a noisy blow or series of blows: *I knocked on the door but no one answered.* **2.** to come into collision; bump: *His nervousness made his knees knock.* **3.** to make a pounding, clanking, or rattling sound: *The engine of the old car knocked.* —*n.* **1.** the act of knocking; a sharp, hard blow: *Bill got a knock on the head in the football game.* **2.** the sound made by a blow: *There was a knock on the door.* **3.** a pounding, clanking, or rattling sound, especially one in an automobile engine caused by faulty combustion. **4.** *Informal.* a misfortune; setback.

to knock about. *Informal.* to wander from place to place.

to knock off. *Informal.* **a.** to stop or discontinue: *to knock off work for lunch.* **b.** to deduct (an amount or sum): *to knock off ten dollars from the price of an item.* **c.** to kill.

to knock out. a. to make unconscious: *A blow on the head knocked him out.* **b.** *Informal.* to tire or exhaust completely: *The long hike really knocked me out.* **c.** *Informal.* to destroy: *The storm knocked out electricity in the town.*

knock·a·bout (nok′ə bout′) *n.* a small, one-masted sailboat, rigged with a mainsail and a jib. —*adj.* **1.** suitable for rough use or wear: *an old knockabout jacket.* **2.** rough; noisy; boisterous: *knockabout comedy.*

knock·er (nok′ər) *n.* **1.** a person or thing that knocks. **2.** a hinged knob, ring, or other device, usually made of metal, fastened to a door for use in knocking.

knock-kneed (nok′nēd′) *adj.* having the legs curved inward so that the knees rub together in walking.

knock·out (nok′out′) *n.* **1.** the defeat of an opponent in boxing by a blow that knocks him down so that he cannot rise to his feet before the referee counts to ten. **2.** a blow that causes unconsciousness. —*adj.* causing a knockout: *a knockout punch.*

knoll (nōl) *n.* a small, rounded hill or mound.

knot (not) *n.* **1.** a fastening made by intertwining rope, string, or the like, especially with one free end being passed through a loop and drawn tight. **2.** a lump or tangle made by the intertwining of thread, cord, or the like: *Ethel combed the knots out of her hair.* **3.** a piece of material, such as ribbon, folded or tied into a knot and worn as an ornament or accessory. **4.** a small group or cluster of persons or things: *A knot of people waited on the platform for the train.* **5.** something intricate, involved, or difficult to solve: *It is too hard a*

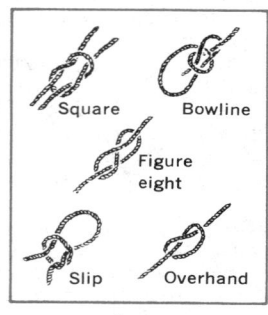

Knots

knot for me (Shakespeare, *Twelfth Night*). **6.** a hard, cross-grained lump of wood formed in a tree trunk at the point where a branch grows out from the tree. **7.** a cross section of such a lump, that shows as a roundish, cross-grained section in a board. **8.** a lump or swelling, as in a muscle or gland. **9. a.** a unit of speed of one nautical mile per hour, approximately equal to 6080 feet per hour, or 1.15 statue miles. **b.** one nautical mile. —*v.,* **knot·ted, knot·ting.** —*v.t.* **1.** to tie in a knot; form a knot or knots in: *Carol knotted the string around the package.* **2.** to fasten with or by a knot. —*v.i.* to become tangled or snarled.

knot·hole (not′hōl′) *n.* a hole in a board or other piece of cut wood where a knot has fallen out or been removed.

knot·ty (not′ē) *adj.,* **knot·ti·er, knot·ti·est. 1.** having, covered with, or full of knots or bumps, as wood: *knotty pine.* **2.** hard to understand, solve, or explain; puzzling: *a knotty problem.* —**knot′ti·ness,** *n.*

know (nō) *v.t.,* **knew, known, know·ing. 1.** to understand clearly; be certain of the facts or truth of: *Do you know the solution to this problem? Jim knew that he was a good baseball player.* **2.** to be aware of: *He knows exactly what he is doing.* **3.** to be acquainted or familiar with: *I know him well, but I don't know his sister.* **4.** to have skill in or experience with: *She knows how to type very well.* **5.** to have learned by memorizing; have in the mind: *The actress knew her part perfectly.* **6.** to be able to tell the difference between; distinguish: *That critic knows good music from bad.* **7.** to meet with or experience: *The old man had known much sorrow and poverty during his life.* —**know′a·ble,** *adj.* —**know′er,** *n.*

in the know. *Informal.* having special or secret information.

know-how (nō′hou′) *n. Informal.* the knowledge of how to do something; practical skill.

know·ing (nō′ing) *adj.* **1.** suggesting secret or private knowledge about something: *a knowing smile.* **2.** showing discernment or cunning; shrewd: *She is a knowing judge of human nature.* **3.** having knowledge; well-informed: *He is very knowing about horses.* —**know′ing·ly,** *adv.*

knowl·edge (nol′ij) *n.* **1.** what is known from understanding, experience, study, or awareness: *Her knowledge of physics is limited.* **2.** the fact of knowing: *The knowledge that the car might skid on the icy road made Bill drive more slowly.*

to one's knowledge or **to the best of one's knowledge.** so far as one is aware: *I have never been to this town before to the best of my knowledge.*

knowl·edge·a·ble (nol′i jə bəl) *adj.* having knowledge; well-informed: *Joe is very knowledgeable about politics.* —**knowl′edge·a·bil′i·ty, knowl′edge·a·ble·ness,** *n.* —**knowl′edge·a·bly,** *adv.*

known (nōn) the past participle of **know.**

Knox, John (noks) 1505?–1572, Scottish religious reformer, the founder of Presbyterianism.

Knox·ville (noks'vil') *n.* a city in eastern Tennessee, on the Tennessee River. Pop. (1970), 174,587.

knuck·le (nuk'əl) *n.* **1.** a joint of a finger, especially one connecting a finger to the hand. **2.** a cut of meat, especially of ham or veal, consisting of the knuckle joint and the flesh immediately above and below it. —*v.t.,* **knuck·led, knuck·ling.** to press, rub, or hit with the knuckles.

to knuckle under. to give in; submit; yield: *The general would not knuckle under to the enemy's terms for peace.*

KO (kā'ō') *n. Slang.* a knockout in boxing.

ko·a·la (kō ä'lə) *n.* an animal of Australia, having a chubby, tailless body covered with grayish-blue fur, large, bushy ears, and a black nose. Koalas live mainly in trees, and the female carries her young in a pouch.

Koala

Ko·be (kō'bē) *n.* a port city in Japan, on the southern coast of Honshu. Pop. (1971 est.), 1,266,000.

Koch, Robert (kok) 1843–1910, German bacteriologist and physician.

Ko·di·ak (kō'dē ak') *n.* a U.S. island off the coast of southwestern Alaska.

kohl·ra·bi (kōl rä'bē) *n. pl.,* **kohl·ra·bies.** a plant of the cabbage family, having a white or purple, thick, round stem that looks like a turnip and is eaten as a vegetable.

ko·la (kō'lə) *n.* **1.** a tropical evergreen tree having leathery oval leaves and bearing nuts and clusters of small bell-shaped yellow flowers. **2.** its nuts, used chiefly to flavor soft drinks.

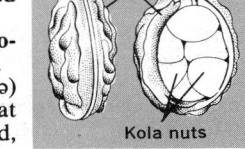
Pod
Kola nuts

koo·doo (kō'dōō) *n. pl.,* **koo·doos.** another spelling of **kudu.**

kook·a·bur·ra (kook'ə bur'ə) *n.* a kingfisher of Australia that has a cry that sounds like loud, harsh laughter.

ko·peck (kō'pek) *also,* **ko·pek.** *n.* a copper or bronze coin of the Soviet Union, equal to ¹/₁₀₀ of a ruble.

Ko·ran (kô ran', kô rän') *n.* the sacred book of the Muslims, containing the religious and moral code of Islam. Muslims believe it contains the word of Allah, revealed by the archangel Gabriel to the prophet Muhammad.

Ko·re·a (kô rē'ə) *n.* a country in eastern Asia, divided into North Korea and South Korea in 1948. Area, 85,030 sq. mi.

Ko·re·an (kô rē'ən) *n.* **1.** a person who was born or is living in Korea. **2.** the language of Korea. —*adj.* of or relating to Korea, its people, or their language.

Korean War, the war between North Korea, aided by Communist China, and South Korea, aided by the United States and other United Nations members, which lasted from June 1950 until July 1953.

Kos·ci·us·ko, Thad·de·us (kos'ē us'kō; thad'ē əs) 1746–1817, Polish patriot who served in the American army during the American Revolution.

ko·sher (kō'shər) *adj.* **1.** according to Jewish ceremonial law, especially those laws relating to food and its preparation: *kosher meat.* **2.** serving or preparing food according to Jewish ceremonial law: *a kosher restaurant.* —*v.t.* to prepare (food) according to Jewish ceremonial law.

Ko·sy·gin, A·lek·sei (kō sē'gin; ä lek sā') 1904–, the premier of the Soviet Union since 1964.

kow·tow (kou'tou) *v.i.* **1.** to kneel and touch the forehead to the ground to show deep respect, submission, or worship. **2.** to show slavish respect: *The young man*

refused to kowtow to his boss. —*n.* the act of kowtowing.

KP, kitchen police.

Kr, the symbol for krypton.

kraal (kräl) *n.* **1.** a village of South African natives, usually surrounded by a fence or stockade. **2.** a pen for livestock, as cattle or sheep, in South Africa.

Krak·ow (krak'ou) *n.* a city in southern Poland. Pop. (1971 est.), 577,000.

Krem·lin (krem'lin) *n.* **1.** the former residence of the czars in Moscow. It now houses the major offices of the Soviet government. **2.** the Soviet government.

Krish·na (krish'nə) *n.* a Hindu god worshiped as an incarnation of Vishnu.

Kriss Krin·gle (kris' kring'gəl) another name for **Santa Claus.**

kryp·ton (krip'ton) *n.* a colorless, inert gaseous element used especially to fill some electric light bulbs. Symbol: **Kr**

Kua·la Lum·pur (kwä'lə loom poor') the capital of Malaysia, on the Malay Peninsula. Pop. (1970), 451,728.

Ku·blai Khan (kōō'blī kän') 1215?–1294, ruler of the Mongol empire from 1260 to 1294.

ku·dos (kōō'dōs, kyōō'dōs) *n.* praise; renown.

ku·du (kōō'dōō) *also,* **koo·doo.** *n.* an African antelope having long, spirally twisted horns.

Kui·by·shev (kwē'bə shef') *n.* a city in the European Soviet Union, on the Volga River, formerly known as Samara. Pop. (1971), 1,069,000.

Ku Klux Klan (kōō' kluks' klan', kyōō' kluks' klan') an organization founded in the southern United States after the Civil War to reestablish the political and social dominance that white Southerners lost under Reconstruction.

Greater kudu

kum·quat (kum'kwot) *also,* **cum·quat.** *n.* **1.** a small, oval orange or yellow fruit of any of a group of evergreen shrubs or trees, having a sweet rind and a sour pulp. **2.** a shrub or tree bearing this fruit.

Kun·ming (koon'ming') *n.* a city in southwestern China. Pop. (1958 est.), 900,000.

Ku·wait (kə wāt') *n.* **1.** a country in the northeastern part of the Arabian peninsula, formerly a British protectorate. Capital, Kuwait. Area, 8000 sq. mi. Pop. (1971 est.), 830,000. **2.** the capital and chief city of this country. Pop. (1970), 80,008.

kw., kilowatt; kilowatts.

Ky., Kentucky.

ky·mo·graph (kī'mə graf') *n.* an instrument used for measuring and recording variations in fluid pressure, as in blood pressure or the pulse.

Kyo·to (kyō'tō) *n.* a city in the west-central part of Honshu, Japan, former capital of the country. Pop. (1971 est.), 1,431,000.

Kyu·shu (kyōō'shōō) *n.* the southernmost island of Japan.

K

at; āpe; cär; end; mē; it; īce; hot; ōld; fôrk; wood; fŏŏl; oil; out; up; turn; sing; thin; this; hw in white; zh in treasure. The symbol ə stands for the sound of a in about, e in taken, i in pencil, o in lemon, and u in circus.

1. **Egyptian Hieroglyphics**	5. **Greek Classical Capitals**
2. **Semitic**	6. **Etruscan**
3. **Early Hebrew**	7. **Latin Fourth Century B.C. Capitals**
4. **Greek Ninth Century B.C.**	8. **English**

L is the twelfth letter of the English alphabet. The earliest form of L was an Egyptian hieroglyphic (1) representing a lion. This symbol was greatly simplified in the ancient Semitic alphabet (2), being given the shape it has kept throughout most of the history of the alphabet. In the early Hebrew alphabet (3), this letter was called *lamedh,* meaning "staff" or "rod." The ancient Greeks borrowed *lamedh* and, by reversing it and turning it upside-down, formed a new letter that they called *lambda* (4). By about the 5th century B.C., *lambda* was being written as an upside-down letter **V** (5). This design was not adopted by the Etruscans who wrote their letter L (6) very much as *lamedh* had been written. The Romans (7), who adopted the Etruscan alphabet, also based their letter L on *lamedh,* rather than *lambda.* By about 2300 years ago, the Romans were writing this letter almost exactly the way we write the capital letter L today (8).

l, L (el) *n. pl.,* **l's, L's. 1.** the twelfth letter of the English alphabet. **2.** something having the shape of this letter. **3.** the Roman numeral for 50.

l. 1. left. **2.** length. **3.** liter.

L., Latin.

la (lä) *n. Music.* **1.** the sixth note of the major scale. **2.** the note A.

La, the symbol for lanthanum.

La., Louisiana.

L.A., Los Angeles.

lab (lab) *n. Informal.* laboratory.

la·bel (lā′bəl) *n.* **1.** a piece of cloth or paper that is fastened to something, such as a garment, package, or can, giving its name, manufacturer, contents, or other information. **2.** a short word or phrase used to describe, characterize, or classify a person, thing, or idea. —*v.t.,* **la·beled, la·bel·ing;** *also, British,* **la·belled, la·bel·ling. 1.** to put a label on. **2.** to describe or characterize by means of a label: *to label a chemical poisonous, to label a person a thief.* —**la′bel·er;** *also, British,* **la′bel·ler,** *n.*

la·bi·al (lā′bē əl) *adj.* **1.** of, relating to, or characteristic of the lips. **2.** *Phonetics.* made primarily by the lips in speaking. The sounds of the letters *m, p,* and *b* are labial sounds. —*n. Phonetics.* a vowel or consonant sound made by the lips.

la·bor (lā′bər) *also, British,* **la·bour.** *n.* **1.** physical or mental effort; work; toil. **2.** a specific task: *Hercules was given twelve labors to do.* **3.** persons who do manual work for a living, as a group. **4.** labor unions as a group. **5.** the effort of childbirth. —*v.i.* **1.** to do work; perform labor: *He labors in the coal mine.* **2.** to move slowly and with difficulty: *The old man labored up the steep hill.* —*v.t.* to spend too much time on, or to work out in too

Label

much detail: *The speaker labored the point of his speech.*

lab·o·ra·to·ry (lab′rə tôr′ē) *n. pl.,* **lab·o·ra·to·ries.** a room, building, or workshop for teaching science or for making scientific experiments or tests.

Labor Day, a legal holiday in honor of working people, observed in the United States on the first Monday in September.

la·bored (lā′bərd) *adj.* done with effort; not easy; forced: *labored breathing, a labored style of writing.*

la·bor·er (lā′bər ər) *n.* a worker, especially one who does manual work for a living.

la·bo·ri·ous (lə bôr′ē əs) *adj.* needing much work: *Checking all the names was a slow, laborious job.* —**la·bo′ri·ous·ly,** *adv.* —**la·bo′ri·ous·ness,** *n.*

la·bor-sav·ing (lā′bər sā′ving) *adj.* that saves people work: *The dishwasher is a labor-saving appliance.*

labor union, an association of workers formed to protect and advance their interests, as by bargaining with employers for better wages and working conditions.

la·bour (lā′bər) *British.* another spelling of **labor.**

Lab·ra·dor (lab′rə dôr′) *n.* **1.** a region in eastern Canada, on the Atlantic Ocean, part of the province of Newfoundland and Labrador. **2.** a peninsula in eastern Canada, between the Atlantic Ocean and Hudson Bay.

la·bur·num (lə bur′nəm) *n.* any of a group of shrubs or small trees related to the pea, bearing hanging clusters of yellow flowers.

lab·y·rinth (lab′ə rinth′) *n.* **1.** a place with winding and connected passages or pathways in which it is easy to lose one's way; maze. **2. Labyrinth.** *Greek Mythology.* an underground maze in Crete designed by Daedalus to contain the Minotaur.

lab·y·rin·thine (lab′ə rin′thin) *adj.* of or like a labyrinth; intricate; complicated. Also, **lab·y·rin·thi·an** (lab′ə-rin′thē ən).

lac (lak) *n.* a reddish-brown substance resembling resin that is left on trees by an Asian insect, used to make shellac and varnish.

lace (lās) *n.* **1.** a string, cord, or strip of leather passed or threaded through holes or eyelets to pull or hold together the edges or parts of something, such as a shoe. **2.** an ornamental, patterned fabric made by weaving together fine thread. —*v.*, **laced, lac·ing.** —*v.t.* **1.** to pull together or tighten with a lace or laces. **2.** to ornament or trim with lace. **3.** to fold together; interlace. —*v.i.* to fasten by means of a lace or laces.

Lac·e·dae·mon (las'ə dē'mən) *n.* another name for **Sparta.** —**Lac·e·dae·mo·ni·an** (las'ə di mō'nē ən), *adj., n.*

lac·er·ate (las'ə rāt') *v.t.*, **lac·er·at·ed, lac·er·at·ing. 1.** to tear roughly or severely; mangle: *The sharp stones lacerated the boy's arm when he fell.* **2.** to hurt or distress; wound: *His harsh comment lacerated his friend's feelings.*

lac·er·a·tion (las'ə rā'shən) *n.* **1.** the act of lacerating. **2.** a rough, jagged tear.

lace·wing (lās'wing') *n.* any of a group of brown or green insects having four long wings veined in a lacy pattern.

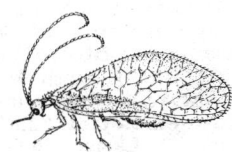
Lacewing

lach·ry·mal (lak'rə məl) *also,* **lac·ri·mal.** *adj.* of or relating to tears or to the shedding of tears.

lach·ry·mose (lak'rə mōs') *adj.* shedding tears or causing the shedding of tears; tearful or sad: *a lachrymose story.* —**lach'ry·mose'ly,** *adv.*

lack (lak) *v.t.* **1.** to be without or have too little of; need: *That poor family lacks food. He lacks sympathy for the problems of others.* **2.** to be missing or short of: *John lacks an inch of being six feet tall.* —*v.i.* to be missing or needing: *What that football player lacks in size, he makes up in speed.* —*n.* **1.** the state of being without or having too little: *The poor harvest was caused by a lack of rain.* **2.** something that is needed: *The most serious lack in his diet is vitamin A.*

lack·a·dai·si·cal (lak'ə dā'zi kəl) *adj.* lacking interest or energy; listless. —**lack'a·dai'si·cal·ly,** *adv.*

lack·ey (lak'ē) *n. pl.,* **lack·eys. 1.** a person who follows or takes orders from another in a fawning, servile manner; flunky. **2.** a male servant, especially a footman.

lack·lus·ter (lak'lus'tər) *also, British,* **lack·lus·tre.** *adj.* that lacks brightness, brilliance, or spirit; dull: *a lackluster performance.*

la·con·ic (lə kon'ik) *adj.* using few words to express much; terse; concise. [Latin *Lacōnicus* relating to the people of Laconia (an ancient region of Greece); because these people were noted for their concise speech.]

lac·quer (lak'ər) *n.* **1.** a fast-drying varnish containing manufactured and natural ingredients, used to protect and decorate objects of wood, metal, and the like with a glossy coating. **2.** a varnish made from the sap of an oriental sumac tree. **3.** wooden articles or decorative work covered with such varnish. —*v.t.* to coat with lacquer.

la·crosse (lə krôs') *n.* a game played with a ball by two teams having ten players each, using a special racket with a net on the end for catching, carrying, or throwing the ball. The object of the game is to get the ball into the opponent's goal.

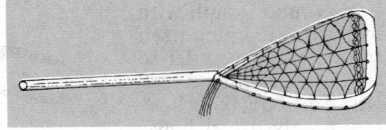
Lacrosse racket

lac·tase (lak'tās) *n.* an enzyme found in yeast and in the digestive juices in the intestines of animals. Lactase aids in the splitting of lactose into two simpler sugars.

lac·tic (lak'tik) *adj.* of, relating to, or obtained from milk.

lactic acid, an acid formed in sour milk, in fermenting molasses, and in other foods.

lac·tose (lak'tōs) *n.* a white sugar present in milk. Also, **milk sugar.**

la·cu·na (lə kyōō'nə) *n. pl.,* **la·cu·nas** or **la·cu·nae** (lə-kyōō'nē). **1.** a space in which something has been left out; gap. **2.** a small cavity in bone or tissue.

lac·y (lā'sē) *adj.,* **lac·i·er, lac·i·est.** of or resembling lace. —**lac'i·ness,** *n.*

lad (lad) *n.* **1.** a young fellow; boy. **2.** *Informal.* a fellow; man.

lad·der (lad'ər) *n.* **1.** a structure made of two long side pieces joined by a series of crosspieces or rungs, used for climbing. **2.** any means of rising from one step or stage to another: *Carl started in the business at the bottom of the ladder as a clerk, but he later became the manager.*

lad·die (lad'ē) *n. Scottish.* a lad.

lade (lād) *v.,* **lad·ed, lad·ed** or **lad·en, lad·ing.** —*v.t.* **1.** to load (something, especially cargo). **2.** to ladle. —*v.i.* **1.** to take on a load, as of cargo. **2.** to ladle liquid.

lad·en (lād'ən) *v.* a past participle of **lade.** —*adj.* **1.** loaded: *The ship was laden with riches.* **2.** weighed down; burdened: *The snow was falling from the laden branches of the pines* (Ernest Hemingway).

lad·ing (lā'ding) *n.* **1.** the act of loading. **2.** something that is loaded; freight; cargo.

la·dle (lād'əl) *n.* a long-handled spoon with a bowl shaped like a cup, used for dipping liquids. —*v.t.,* **la·dled, la·dling.** to dip out with or carry in a ladle. —**la'dler,** *n.*

La·do·ga, Lake (lä'də gä') the largest freshwater lake in Europe, in the northwestern Soviet Union.

la·dy (lā'dē) *n. pl.,* **la·dies. 1.** a polite term for a woman. **2.** the mistress of a household. **3.** a girl or woman of good family or breeding. **4.** a girl or woman who has good manners and good taste. **5. Lady.** in Great Britain, a woman of noble rank by birth, or the wife of a man holding the title of Lord. [Old English *hlǣfdīge* a woman, mistress of a household, wife; possibly having the literal meaning, a maker of bread.]

la·dy·bug (lā'dē bug') *n.* any of a group of beetles having a round, humped body that is often bright red or orange with black spots. It feeds on aphids and other insect pests. Also, **la·dy·bird** (lā'dē-burd').

la·dy·fin·ger (lā'dē fing'gər) *n.* a small sponge cake like a finger in shape.

la·dy·in·wait·ing (lā'dē in wā'-ting) *n. pl.,* **la·dies·in·wait·ing.** a lady who is an attendant of a queen or princess.

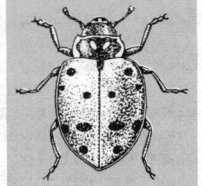
Ladybug

la·dy·like (lā'dē līk') *adj.* like or suitable for a lady.

la·dy·ship (lā'dē ship') *n.* **1.** the rank, status, or position of a lady. **2. Ladyship.** the title or form of address used in speaking or referring to a Lady, usually preceded by *Her* or *Your.*

---

at; āpe; cär; end; mē; it; īce; hot; ōld; fôrk; wood; fōōl; oil; out; up; turn; sing; thin; <u>th</u>is; hw in white; zh in treasure. The symbol ə stands for the sound of **a** in about, **e** in taken, **i** in pencil, **o** in lemon, and **u** in circus.

L

la·dy's-slip·per (lā′dēz slip′ər) *also,* **lady slipper**. *n.* an orchid that bears flowers with a lower petal or lip resembling a shoe. Also, **moccasin flower.**

La·fa·yette, Marquis de (laf′ē et′, lä′fē et′) 1757–1834, French general and statesman.

lag (lag) *v.i.,* **lagged, lag·ging. 1.** to fail to keep up or keep pace: *The little girl lagged behind her brothers, who walked faster.* **2.** to drop or fall off; decline; slump: *His interest lagged after reading a few pages of the book.* —*n.* the act of lagging. —**lag′ger,** *n.*

la·ger (lä′gər) *n.* a light-bodied beer that is made by slow fermentation at low temperature, and is aged for months before being used.

lag·gard (lag′ərd) *n.* a person or thing that lags. —*adj.* that lags; slow; backward: *a laggard person.*

la·goon (lə gōōn′) *n.* **1.** a shallow body of water partly or completely surrounded by a coral island or islands. **2.** a shallow body of sea water partly cut off from the sea by a narrow strip of land.

La·gos (lä′gōs, lā′gos) *n.* the capital and chief port of Nigeria, in the southwestern part of the country. Pop. (1970 est.), 875,000.

La·hore (lə hôr′) *n.* a city in Pakistan, in the eastern part of the country on the Indian border. Pop. (1970 est.), 2,000,000.

laid (lād) the past tense and past participle of **lay¹.**

lain (lān) the past participle of **lie².**

lair (ler) *n.* a home or resting place, especially of a wild animal.

laird (lerd) *n. Scottish.* an owner of a large estate; lord.

lais·sez faire (les′ā fer′, lā′zā fer′) the economic theory that commerce, business, and labor should be left alone or have as little interference or regulation by a government as possible. [French *laissez faire* allow (people) to do (what they please).] —**lais′sez-faire′,** *adj.*

la·i·ty (lā′ə tē) *n. pl.,* **la·i·ties. 1.** all persons who are members of a church but are not ordained for religious work. **2.** those who are not members of a certain profession or who are not trained in a certain field: *Lawyers use many legal words not familiar to the laity.*

lake (lāk) *n.* a large inland body of salt or fresh water, usually entirely surrounded by land.

Lake. Lakes are entered in the dictionary under their proper names. For example, **Lake Huron** is listed in the **H's.**

Lake Charles, a city in southwestern Louisiana. Pop. (1970), 77,998.

Lake District, a region in northwestern England, noted for its scenic mountains and lakes. Also, **Lake Country.**

lake dweller, a member of a prehistoric people who lived in lake dwellings.

lake dwelling, in prehistoric times, a hut built on a platform supported by piles over water or marshland.

lake trout, a large trout that is grayish-green with pale spots, found in lakes of North America.

Lake·wood (lāk′wood′) *n.* a city in southern California, near Los Angeles. Pop. (1970), 82,973.

la·ma (lä′mə) *n.* a Buddhist priest or monk in Tibet.

lamb (lam) *n.* **1.** a young sheep. **2.** the meat from a lamb, used as food. **3.** the skin of a lamb. **4. the Lamb.** Jesus. **5.** a person who is gentle, weak, or innocent. —*v.i.* to give birth to a lamb.

Lamb, Charles (lam) 1775–1834, English essayist and critic.

lam·baste (lam bāst′, lam bast′) *v.t.,* **lam·bast·ed, lam·bast·ing.** *Slang.* **1.** to beat or thrash. **2.** to abuse with words.

lamb·da (lam′də) *n.* the eleventh letter (Λ, λ) of the Greek alphabet, corresponding to the English letter *L, l.*

lam·bent (lam′bənt) *adj.* **1.** shining with a soft glow: *lambent eyes, the lambent light of early morning.* **2.** (of a flame) flickering lightly over or on a surface. **3.** having lightness and brilliance: *a lambent wit.*

lamb·kin (lam′kin) *n.* **1.** a little lamb. **2.** a person who is dearly loved, especially a young child.

lamb·skin (lam′skin′) *n.* **1.** the skin of a lamb, especially when prepared with the wool left on it and used for clothing. **2.** leather made from the skin of a lamb. **3.** parchment made from this leather.

lame (lām) *adj.,* **lam·er, lam·est. 1.** unable to walk easily or properly: *He is lame and has to walk with a cane.* **2.** stiff and painful: *a lame back.* **3.** poor or weak: *He offered a lame excuse for being late.* —*v.t.,* **lamed, lam·ing.** to make lame. —**lame′ly,** *adv.* —**lame′ness,** *n.*

la·mé (la mā′) *n.* a fabric woven with metallic threads.

lame duck 1. a person holding a public office, who has not been reelected but continues to hold office for a time after his defeat. **2.** a person who is weak or useless.

la·ment (lə ment′) *v.t.* to feel or express sorrow, grief, or regret for or about: *He lamented the loss of his parents.* —*v.i.* to feel or express sorrow, grief, or regret. —*n.* **1.** an expression of sorrow, grief, or regret. **2.** a song or poem that expresses sorrow or grief.

lam·en·ta·ble (lam′ən tə bəl, lə men′tə bəl) *adj.* that is to be lamented: *a lamentable tragedy, a lamentable mistake.* —**lam′en·ta·bly,** *adv.*

lam·en·ta·tion (lam′ən tā′shən) *n.* **1.** the act of lamenting. **2. Lamentations.** the book of the Old Testament thought to have been written by Jeremiah.

lam·i·na (lam′ə nə) *n. pl.,* **lam·i·nae** (lam′ə nē) or **lam·i·nas. 1.** a thin plate, scale, or layer. **2.** *Botany.* the flat part of a leaf or petal.

lam·i·nate (*v.,* lam′ə nāt′; *n.,* lam′ə nit, lam′ə nāt′) *v.t.,* **lam·i·nat·ed, lam·i·nat·ing. 1.** to make by binding together different layers, as with glue or heat. **2.** to beat or roll (metal) into thin plates. —*n.* something made by laminating, such as safety glass or plywood. —**lam′i·na′tor,** *n.*

lam·i·na·tion (lam′ə nā′shən) *n.* **1.** the process of laminating or the state of being laminated. **2.** a thin layer: *A lamination of plastic made the counter more durable.*

lamp (lamp) *n.* **1.** a device for making light, as by using an electric light bulb or by burning oil, kerosene, or gas. **2.** a light bulb. Also, **incandescent lamp. 3.** a device that gives off heat or other radiation, such as a sunlamp.

lamp·black (lamp′blak′) *n.* a black pigment consisting of almost pure carbon soot, made by burning oil or gas.

lamp·light (lamp′līt′) *n.* the light from a lamp or lamps.

lamp·light·er (lamp′lī′tər) *n.* formerly, a person whose job was to light gas or oil street lights at night.

lam·poon (lam pōōn′) *n.* a piece of writing that attacks and makes fun of someone or something. —*v.t.* to attack and make fun of in a lampoon. —**lam·poon′er,** *n.*

lamp·post (lamp′pōst′) *n.* a post supporting a lamp, as in a street or a park.

lam·prey (lam′prē) *n. pl.,* **lam·preys.** any of a group of primitive saltwater and freshwater fish that look like eels. The lamprey has a round mouth with teeth for attaching itself to other fish in order to feed on their blood.

Lamprey

Lan·cas·ter (lang′kəs tər) *n.* the royal house to which three kings who ruled England in the fifteenth century belonged. They were Henry IV, Henry V, and Henry VI.

Lan·cas·tri·an (lang kas′trē ən) *adj.* of or relating to the house of Lancaster. —*n.* a member or supporter of the house of Lancaster.

lance (lans) *n.* **1.** a long spear, usually having a wooden shaft with a sharp metal head. **2.** any spearlike weapon or instrument. **3.** a soldier armed with a lance. —*v.t.,* **lanced, lanc·ing. 1.** to pierce with a lance. **2.** to open with a lancet: *The doctor lanced the boil.*

lance corporal, an enlisted person in the U.S. Marine Corps, ranking above a private first class and below a corporal.

Lan·ce·lot (lan′sə lot′) *n.* in the legends of King Arthur, the bravest knight of the Round Table.

lanc·er (lan′sər) *n.* a cavalry soldier armed with a lance.

lanc·ers (lan′sərz) *n., pl.* **1.** a dance that is a form of the quadrille. **2.** the music for such a dance.

lan·cet (lan′sit) *n.* a short surgical knife having two sharp edges.

lance·wood (lans′wood′) *n.* **1.** a tough wood, used mainly for fishing rods and billiard cues. **2.** any of various tropical trees yielding this wood.

Lan·chow (län′jō′) *n.* a city in northwestern China. Pop. (1959 est.), 732,000. Also, **Lan·zhou.**

land (land) *n.* **1.** the part of the surface of the earth that is not under water: *The sailors sighted land after many days at sea.* **2.** ground or soil: *The land around the old house is low and swampy.* **3.** an area marked off by political, cultural, or other boundaries; country or region. **4.** the people who live in a country or region. **5.** real estate; property: *Mr. Brown invested in land.* —*v.i.* **1.** to come down from the air and alight on a surface: *The plane landed at the airport.* **2.** to come to land or shore: *The ship landed safely in the harbor.* **3.** to come ashore from a ship: *The troops have landed.* **4.** to come to rest: *Mary threw her glove, and it landed on the table.* **5.** to end up: *The thief landed in jail.* —*v.t.* **1.** to bring down from the air onto a surface: *The pilot landed the plane carefully.* **2.** to set ashore from a ship or other vessel; unload onto land: *to land a cargo, to land passengers.* **3.** to cause to end up: *Fishing without a license will land you in trouble.* **4.** to bring (a fish) to land or into a boat. **5.** *Informal.* to win; get: *Tim landed a good job.*

lan·dau (lan′dou, lan′dô) *n.* a carriage with four wheels, two seats, and a top that opens in the center and folds down in the back and front.

Landau

land breeze, a breeze blowing toward the sea from the land.

land·ed (lan′did) *adj.* **1.** owning land: *landed gentry.* **2.** consisting of land: *landed property.*

land·fall (land′fôl′) *n.* **1.** the act or instance of reaching or sighting land, as after a long voyage. **2.** the land so reached or sighted.

land·form (land′form′) *n.* a feature on the surface of the earth, such as a valley or mountain range.

land grant, a gift of public land by the government for a public purpose, such as for the establishment of a college.

land·hold·er (land′hōl′dər) *n.* a person who owns land.

land·ing (lan′ding) *n.* **1.** the act or process of coming to the earth or land, or coming ashore. **2.** the space on a dock or pier for coming ashore or for unloading a ship. **3.** a platform at the end of or between flights of stairs.

landing field, an area of land for the takeoff and landing of aircraft.

landing gear, the wheels and other structures on which an aircraft lands.

landing stage, a floating platform for loading and unloading people and goods at a wharf or pier.

landing strip, a long, narrow area for the takeoff and landing of aircraft.

land·la·dy (land′lā′dē) *n. pl.,* **land·la·dies.** a woman landlord.

land·less (land′lis) *adj.* owning no land.

land·locked (land′lokt′) *adj.* **1.** entirely or almost entirely surrounded by land: *a landlocked country.* **2.** living entirely in fresh water: *landlocked salmon.*

land·lord (land′lôrd′) *n.* **1.** a person who owns houses or apartments occupied by tenants. **2.** a person who runs an inn, boarding house, or lodging house.

land·lub·ber (land′lub′ər) *n.* a person who has had little or no experience on board a ship.

land·mark (land′märk′) *n.* **1.** an object in a landscape that is familiar or striking and serves as a guide. **2.** an important building or site: *The Civil War battlefield was declared a national landmark.* **3.** an important fact or event: *The development of the laser was a landmark of modern science.* **4.** an object that serves to mark a boundary line.

land·mass (land′mas′) *n.* a large area of land.

land mine, a small explosive device put underground and set to go off when soldiers or motor vehicles pass over or near it.

land·own·er (land′ō′nər) *n.* a person who owns land. —**land′own′ing,** *adj.*

land-poor (land′poor′) *adj.* owning much land, but not earning enough income from it to pay taxes or other expenses.

land·scape (land′skāp′) *n.* **1.** a stretch or expanse of scenery that can be viewed from one point or place. **2.** a painting, photograph, or other picture showing such a stretch of scenery. —*v.,* **land·scaped, land·scap·ing.** —*v.t.* to beautify or improve (a piece of land) by planting trees and other plants and designing gardens. —*v.i.* to do landscape gardening.

landscape gardener, a person whose work is landscape gardening.

landscape gardening, the art or process of beautifying land, such as the grounds around a house, by planting trees and other plants and designing gardens.

land·slide (land′slīd′) *n.* **1.** the sliding or falling down of a mass of soil or rock: *a landslide down a mountain slope.* **2.** a mass of soil or rock that slides down. **3.** an overwhelming victory in an election.

lands·man (landz′mən) *n. pl.,* **lands·men** (landz′mən). a person who lives or works on land.

land·ward (land′wərd) *adj.* lying or going toward the land. —*adv. also,* **landwards.** toward the land.

lane (lān) *n.* **1.** a narrow way or road: *The boy walked down the country lane.* **2.** a course or route bounded by definite lines: *a shipping lane, a traffic lane.* **3.** a narrow passage of wood on which bowling balls are rolled; bowling alley.

lan·guage (lang′gwij) *n.* **1.** an organized system of spoken sounds by which people communicate their thoughts

at; āpe; cär; end; mē; it; īce; hot; ōld; fôrk; wood; fōōl; oil; out; up; turn; sing; thin; this; hw in white; zh in treasure. The symbol ə stands for the sound of a in about, e in taken, i in pencil, o in lemon, and u in circus.

L

and feelings to each other; human speech. **2.** a group of written symbols representing these spoken sounds. **3.** all the spoken sounds, and the written symbols representing them, that make up a system by which the members of a nation, tribe, or other group communicate with each other: *the Spanish language, the languages of the American Indians.* **4.** any means of communication or expression, as by gestures, signs, or symbols: *computer language. Algebra is a language of mathematics.* **5.** the special words used by a particular profession: *military language, legal language.* **6.** words or wording: *the language of a legal contract.* **7.** a means of communication used by animals: *the language of dolphins.* **8.** the study of language; linguistics.

● The ability to use **language** is a quality that only human beings have. They have been defined as "the language-using animals," and there is a belief that the use of language is the only important characteristic that humans do not share with any other animal. It is language, then, that makes people what they are and that makes all forms of human thought and activity possible.

Until very recently, language scholars believed that children learned how to use language by listening to their parents and other older people speak and then imitating them. Then Noam Chomsky, an American *linguist,* or expert in the science of language, put forth the theory that people are born with a special quality that gives them the ability to use language. He maintained that people do not acquire this language ability entirely through experience.

To support this theory, Chomsky called attention to the way young children learn to talk. He observed that children could make up thousands of new sentences that they had never heard before, but which were entirely understandable to other people. These sentences consistently followed the correct grammatical pattern of English, even though the children obviously had not yet learned anything about the rules of grammar. A child would not say "Want I ball the red" for "I want the red ball." From these observations, Chomsky concluded that the children's ability to form completely new sentences in a correct way was much too creative and sophisticated a skill to be considered as simply the result of an imitation of the speech of older people.

Chomsky then proceeded from this conclusion to a second important theory. There are thousands of languages spoken by man, and there does not seem to be any feature that all of them share. But Chomsky theorized that there is, at a certain level, a way in which all languages are the same. He believes that certain principles of grammar govern all of them. It is known that any child will learn equally well whatever language he or she is first exposed to. Therefore it must follow that if each child is born with a special ability to learn language, all languages must have something in common, or else the child could not use this special ability for different languages.

If Chomsky's theories are correct and people really are born with an innate ability to learn language, this would have great implications for many fields of thought other than the study of language. Biologists can learn about the nature of the brain by studying how a child learns language. In psychology, Chomsky's theories dispute the conclusion that people's actions and behavior are entirely determined by their experiences, as many psychologists now believe. In philosophy, his theories run directly counter to the widely-held modern belief that people are not born with any innate knowledge, but learn all that they know through experience.

lan·guid (lang′gwid) *adj.* showing a lack of energy or force; weak; sluggish: *The languid youth idled away the hours in a hammock.* —**lan′guid·ly,** *adv.*

lan·guish (lang′gwish) *v.i.* **1.** to grow weak or feeble; lose health or vitality: *The farmer's crops languished from neglect.* **2.** to live under unpleasant conditions that cause a loss of health or vitality: *The people languished under the dictator's rule.* **3.** to suffer with desire or longing; pine.

lan·guor (lang′gər) *n.* **1.** lack of vigor; weakness; fatigue: *His languor was caused by the hot, humid weather.* **2.** tenderness or softness of mood or feeling: *The beautiful music brought on a feeling of languor.* —**lan′guor·ous,** *adj.*

lank (langk) *adj.* **1.** long and lean; slender: *The basketball player was tall and lank.* **2.** (of hair) limp and straight.

lank·y (lang′kē) *adj.,* **lank·i·er, lank·i·est.** ungracefully tall and thin; gangling. —**lank′i·ly,** *adv.* —**lank′i·ness,** *n.*

lan·o·lin (lan′əl in) *also,* **lan·o·line** (lan′əl in, lan′-əl ēn′). *n.* a fatty substance obtained from the wool of sheep, used in various ointments, cosmetics, and soaps.

Lan·sing (lan′sing) *n.* the capital of Michigan, in the south-central part of the state. Pop. (1970), 131,546.

lan·tern (lan′tərn) *n.* **1.** a casing or covering for a light, usually made to be carried: *a kerosene lantern.* **2.** the chamber at the top of a lighthouse in which the light is placed. **3.** a structure on the top of a roof, with windows or openings to admit light and air.

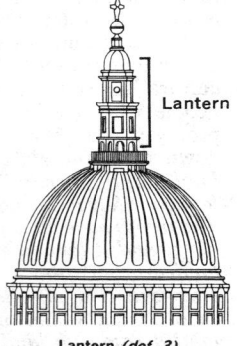

Lantern

Lantern *(def. 3)*

lan·tha·num (lan′thə nəm) *n.* a soft, white metallic element belonging to the rare-earth group, used especially in making electronic devices. Symbol: **La**

lan·yard (lan′yərd) *n.* **1.** a short rope or cord used on ships to fasten or tighten things, such as the supports for the masts. **2.** a cord worn around the neck, used to hang a knife or whistle from. **3.** a cord with a small hook at one end, used in firing certain types of cannon.

Lan·zhou (län′ jō′) another spelling of **Lanchow.**

La·oc·o·ön (lā ok′ō on′) *n. Greek Legend.* a Trojan priest who was killed with his sons by two sea serpents after he warned the Trojans against the large wooden horse left by the Greeks.

La·os (lä′ōs, lā′os) *n.* a country in southeastern Asia, between Thailand and northern Vietnam. Capital, Vientiane. Area, 91,428 sq. mi. Pop. (1980), 3,721,000.

La·o·tian (lā ō′shən) *n.* a person who was born or is living in Laos. —*adj.* of or relating to Laos, its people, or their language.

lap¹ (lap) *n.* **1.** the area in front between the waist and the knees of a seated person. **2.** the clothing that covers this area. **3.** responsibility or control: *She left all her problems in his lap.* **4.** the place or condition in which someone is cared for: *The fortunate girl lives in the lap of luxury.* [Old English *læppa* a flap of a garment.]

lap² (lap) *v.,* **lapped, lap·ping.** —*v.i.* **1.** to lie partly over or beside another; overlap: *The insect's wings lapped over one another.* **2.** to extend beyond something in space or time: *The morning meeting lapped over into the lunch hour.* **3.** to wind, wrap, or fold: *The long scarf lapped around her neck twice.* —*v.t.* **1.** to wind, wrap, or fold about: *The mother lapped the child in a blanket.* **2.** to lay (something) partly over or beside another: *to lap one shingle over another.* **3.** to get ahead of by one length or circuit of something, as a racetrack: *The runner lapped his opponents in* *the race.* —*n.* **1.** the act of lapping over. **2.** the part that lies partly over another. **3.** one length or circuit of something, such as a racetrack. [Probably from *lap¹.*]

lap³ (lap) *v.,* **lapped, lap·ping.** —*v.t.* **1.** to drink (a liquid) by lifting it into the mouth with the tongue: *The cat lapped its milk.* **2.** to move or wash gently against with a splashing sound: *Waves lapped the dock.* —*v.i.* to move or wash something gently with a splashing sound: *The waves lapped against the rocks.* —*n.* **1.** the act of lapping. **2.** a gentle, splashing sound. [Old English *lapian.*]

La Paz (lä päs′) a city in western Bolivia, in the Andes Mountains, the seat of the government and unofficial capital of the country. Pop. (1976), 654,713.

lap dog, a pet dog that is small enough to be held easily on the lap.

la·pel (lə pel′) *n.* the part of the front of a coat or jacket that is folded back and forms a continuation of the collar.

lap·i·dar·y (lap′ə der′ē) *n. pl.,* **lap·i·dar·ies.** a person who engraves, cuts, or polishes precious stones. —*adj.* of or relating to the cutting or engraving of precious stones.

lap·is laz·u·li (lap′is laz′ə lē) a semiprecious stone used for carvings or jewelry, usually deep blue or violet-blue.

Lap·land (lap′land′) *n.* a region in northern Europe, including the northernmost sections of Norway, Sweden, and Finland, and the northwestern Soviet Union.

Lap·land·er (lap′lan′dər) *n.* see **Lapp** (*def. 1*).

La Pla·ta (lä plä′tə) a port city in eastern Argentina. Pop. (1970), 408,300.

Lapp (lap) *n.* **1.** a person who was born or is living in Lapland. **2.** the language of the Lapps.

lap robe, a fur robe or blanket used to protect the legs from the cold, as when riding in an open carriage or sleigh.

lapse (laps) *n.* **1.** a mistake or error, especially a small or unimportant one: *a spelling lapse, a memory lapse.* **2.** a period or interval: *The wanderer returned after a lapse of ten years.* **3.** a slipping back, as from a moral standard: *a lapse into bad habits.* **4.** a gradual ending or falling into disuse: *a lapse of a conversation, a lapse of an insurance policy.* —*v.i.,* **lapsed, laps·ing. 1.** to slip back, as from a moral standard. **2.** to slip or fall: *The building lapsed into ruin.* **3.** to end or fall into disuse: *The contract lapsed.*

lap·wing (lap′wing′) *n.* a bird noted for its slow, irregular wing beat and a shrill, wailing cry.

lar·board (lär′bôrd′, lär′bərd) *n., adj.* another word for **port².**

lar·ce·ny (lär′sə nē) *n. pl.,* **lar·ce·nies.** the crime of unlawfully taking away another person's property; theft. —**lar′ce·nous,** *adj.*

larch (lärch) *n. pl.,* **larch·es. 1.** a tall tree related to the pine, bearing needle-shaped leaves that are shed each year. **2.** the hard, strong, durable wood of this tree.

lard (lärd) *n.* a soft, white fat made from the fatty tissue of a hog, used in cooking. —*v.t.* **1.** to add lard to or cover with lard. **2.** to stuff with pieces of fat before cooking. **3.** to add extra material to (speech or writing): *to lard a passage with quotations.*

lar·der (lär′dər) *n.* **1.** a place where food is kept; pantry. **2.** a stock of food.

lar·es and pe·na·tes (ler′ēz; pə nā′tēz) **1.** the household gods of the ancient Romans. **2.** the treasured possessions of a family or household.

large (lärj) *adj.,* **larg·er, larg·est. 1.** of great size, amount, or number, especially in comparison with others of the same kind: *Tom's room is large. Toby has a large collection of stamps.* **2.** wide in range or capacity: *The ruler's powers are large.* —**large′ness,** *n.*
  at large. a. at liberty; free: *The suspect is still at large.* **b.** of, relating to, or representing an entire area: *a councilman at large.*

large calorie, see **calorie** (*def. 1b*).

large-heart·ed (lärj′här′tid) *adj.* generous; liberal; kindly. —**large′-heart′ed·ness,** *n.*

large intestine, the lower part of the intestines, between the small intestine and the anus.

large·ly (lärj′lē) *adv.* to a great extent; mostly; mainly: *The buildings in town are largely made of brick.*

large-scale (lärj′skāl′) *adj.* **1.** of a wide range; extensive: *a large-scale strike.* **2.** drawn or made to a large scale.

lar·gess (lär jes′, lär′jis) *also,* **lar·gesse.** *n.* **1.** generous giving. **2.** a generous gift or gifts.

lar·go (lär′gō) *adj., adv. Music.* very slow and dignified; stately. —*n. pl.,* **lar·gos.** a slow and dignified musical composition.

lar·i·at (lar′ē ət) *n.* a long rope with a loop at one end, used for roping livestock; lasso.

lark¹ (lärk) *n.* **1.** any of a group of small songbirds, usually having gray-brown feathers. **2.** any of a group of similar but unrelated birds, such as the meadowlark. [Old English *lāwerce.*]

lark² (lärk) *n.* something done just for fun; adventure or antic: *John jumped in the fountain for a lark.* —*v.i.* to do things just for fun. [Of uncertain origin.]

lark·spur (lärk′spur′) *n.* another word for **delphinium.**

lar·va (lär′və) *n. pl.,* **lar·vae** (lär′vē). **1.** an insect in the early, usually wormlike, stage of complete metamorphosis after hatching from an egg, coming before the pupa stage. The caterpillar is the larva of a butterfly. **2.** the early form of an animal. The tadpole is the larva of a frog.

lar·yn·gi·tis (lar′ən jī′tis) *n.* an inflammation of the larynx, often characterized by hoarseness of the voice.

lar·ynx (lar′ingks) *n. pl.,* **la·ryn·ges** (lə rin′jēz) or **lar·ynx·es.** the boxlike chamber at the upper end of the windpipe, containing the vocal cords and serving as the organ of speech.

La·sa (lä′sə, las′ə) another spelling of **Lhasa.**

la·sa·gne (lə zän′yə) *n.* **1.** a baked dish usually with layers of wide noodles, chopped meat, tomato sauce, and cheese. **2.** a broad, flat noodle.

La·Salle, Re·ne Ro·bert Ca·ve·lier, Sieur de (lə sal′; rə nā′ rō·ber′ kä vəl yā′; sur′də) 1643–1687, French explorer of Canada.

las·civ·i·ous (lə siv′ē əs) *adj.* **1.** feeling, showing, or characterized by lust. **2.** tending to cause or arouse lust. —**las·civ′i·ous·ly,** *adv.* —**las·civ′i·ous·ness,** *n.*

Lapels

Lapwing

Larynx

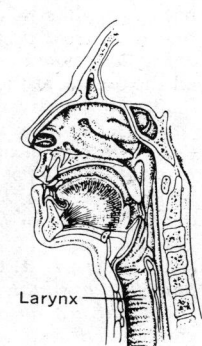

at; āpe; cär; end; mē; it; īce; hot; ōld; fôrk; wood; fōōl; oil; out; up; turn; sing; thin; this; hw in white; zh in treasure. The symbol ə stands for the sound of a in about, e in taken, i in pencil, o in lemon, and u in circus.

L

la·ser (lā′zər) *n.* a device that produces an extremely powerful beam of light consisting of light waves that are of the same wavelength and are in phase. The laser has many possible uses in medicine, communications, and warfare. [Abbreviation of *(l)*ight *(a)*mplification by *(s)*timulated *(e)*mission of *(r)*adiation.]

lash¹ (lash) *n. pl.,* **lash·es. 1.** a stroke or blow with a whip: *The sailor was given ten lashes.* **2.** the flexible, often braided, part of a whip. **3.** see **eyelash. 4.** a movement like that of a whip: *the lash of an animal's tail.* —*v.t.* **1.** to beat or strike with a whip: *The man lashed his horse.* **2.** to beat or strike forcefully or violently; dash against: *The hurricane winds lashed the boats in the harbor.* **3.** to wave or move to and fro like a whip; switch angrily: *The tiger lashed its tail.* **4.** to attack or scold sharply: *The newspaper article lashed the dishonest politician.* —*v.i.* **1.** to dash violently: *The waves lashed against the rocks.* **2.** to beat or strike with or as if with a whip. **3.** to strike out with sudden violence or abuse: *The writer lashed out against his critics.* [Middle English *lashen* to strike.] —**lash′er,** *n.*

lash² (lash) *v.t.* to tie or fasten with a rope or cord: *The boys lashed logs together to make a raft.* [Old French *lachier, lacier* to lace.]

Las Pal·mas (läs päl′mäs) a port city in the Canary Islands. Pop. (1970), 548,984.

lass (las) *n. pl.,* **lass·es.** a young woman; girl.

las·sie (las′ē) *n.* a young girl; lass.

las·si·tude (las′ə tōōd′, las′ə tyōōd′) *n.* a tired feeling; weariness; exhaustion.

las·so (las′ō, la sōō′) *n. pl.,* **las·sos** or **las·soes.** a long rope with a loop, used for roping livestock. —*v.t.,* **las·soed, las·so·ing.** to rope with a lasso: *The cowboy lassoed the steer.*

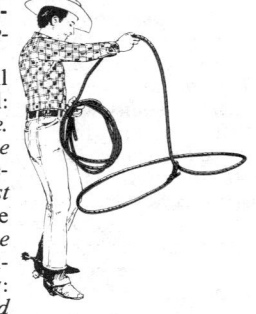

Lasso

last¹ (last) *adj.* **1.** following all others, as in order or time; final: *Fred was the last one in line. December is the last month of the year.* **2.** being the only one remaining: *The boy delivered his last newspaper.* **3.** next before the present; most recent; latest: *She saw a movie last night.* **4.** least expected or likely; most unlikely: *She is the last person you would expect to see there.* —*adv.* **1.** after all the others; at the end: *Cake and coffee were served last.* **2.** at a time nearest the present; most recently: *When did you last write your uncle?* **3.** in conclusion; finally. —*n.* **1.** a person or thing that is last: *He was the last to learn of what happened.* **2.** the end; conclusion: *When will we hear the last of her troubles?* [Old English *latost, lætest,* the superlative of *læt* slow, tardy.]
at last. finally.

last² (last) *v.i.* **1.** to go on; continue: *The visit lasted for only fifteen minutes.* **2.** to stay in good condition: *These shoes will last longer if you take care of them.* **3.** to be enough: *The milk should last until morning.* [Old English *læstan* to follow, continue.]

last³ (last) *n.* a wood or metal form, shaped like a human foot, on which shoes are made or repaired. —*v.t.* to form (shoes) on a last. [Old English *læste.*]

last·ing (las′ting) *adj.* that lasts; permanent; enduring: *lasting fame.* —**last′ing·ly,** *adv.*

Last Judgment, another term for **Judgment Day.**

last·ly (last′lē) *adv.* in the last place; in conclusion.

last quarter, the half moon that follows a full moon.

last straw, a thing that finally makes something impossible to bear or endure.

Last Supper, the final meal of Jesus and the Apostles on the night before His Crucifixion.

Las Ve·gas (läs vā′gəs) a city in southeastern Nevada, noted as a gambling center. Pop. (1970), 125,787.

lat., latitude.

Lat., Latin.

latch (lach) *n. pl.,* **latch·es.** any device for keeping a door, window, or gate closed. A latch is usually made of a bar that falls or slides into a notch, hole, or groove. —*v.t.* to fasten the latch of (something). —*v.i.* to close with a latch: *Do the cabinet doors latch?*
  to latch onto. *Informal.* **a.** to attach oneself to; stick close to. **b.** to grasp or get.

Latch

latch·key (lach′kē′) *n.* a key for opening the latch of a door or gate.

latch·string (lach′string′) *n.* a string passing through a hole in a door, used to open a latch.

late (lāt) *adj.,* **lat·er, lat·est. 1.** coming after the proper or expected time: *I was late for school this morning.* **2.** coming after the usual time: *Tom had a late lunch today.* **3.** beginning or taking place at an advanced time, especially at night: *He telephoned at a late hour. We watched the late show on television.* **4.** of or relating to an advanced stage of history or development: *the late Middle Ages, a late model automobile.* **5.** most recent: *the latest developments.* **6.** recently dead: *His late uncle was a judge.* —*adv.,* **lat·er, lat·est. 1.** after the proper, expected, or usual time: *Wendy arrived late at the party.* **2.** at or until an advanced time, especially at night: *The children stayed up late.* —**late′ness,** *n.*
  of late. lately; recently: *He has been acting rather strangely of late.*

late·com·er (lāt′kum′ər) *n.* **1.** a person who arrives late. **2.** a person or thing that has recently arrived.

la·teen (la tēn′) *adj.* relating to or having a sailing rig with a triangular sail hung from a long slanting rod or yard, and extending both fore and aft of the mast.

Late Greek, a form of the Greek language used from about A.D. 300 to 600.

Late Latin, a form of the Latin language used from about A.D. 300 to 600.

Lateen sails

late·ly (lāt′lē) *adv.* not long ago; recently: *Have you seen her lately? He hasn't been feeling well lately.*

la·tent (lāt′ənt) *adj.* present but not active or seen; hidden: *the latent talents of a child.* —**la′ten·cy,** *n.*

lat·er (lā′tər) the comparative of **late.**

lat·er·al (lat′ər əl) *adj.* of, from, or toward the side: *a lateral doorway, a lateral shoot on the stem of a plant, a lateral pass in football.* —**lat′er·al·ly,** *adv.*

lat·est (lā′tist) the superlative of **late.**

la·tex (lā′teks) *n. pl.,* **la·tex·es** or **lat·i·ces. 1.** a milky liquid that comes from a rubber tree, and is made of small globules of pure rubber suspended in water. **2.** a similar milky liquid found in some other plants, such as milkweeds and poppies. **3.** a similar man-made liquid, used as a base for certain paints.

lath (lath) *n.* any of the thin, narrow strips of wood or metal used to form a lining or a base for a coat of plaster or for tiles or slates, as on a roof. —*v.t.* to build or line with laths.

lathe (lāth) *n.* a machine that holds a long piece of wood, metal, or other material at both ends, and turns it for shaping by a cutting tool.

lath·er (lath'ər) *n.* **1.** foam, froth, or suds made especially from soap moistened with water. **2.** foam caused by sweating, as on a horse. —*v.i.* to form a lather. —*v.t.* to cover with lather: *He lathered his face before shaving.*

lat·i·ces (lat'ə sēz') a plural of **latex.**

Lat·in (lat'in) *n.* **1.** the language of the ancient Romans. **2.** a member of any of the peoples, such as the Italians, Spanish, or Portuguese, whose languages are derived from Latin. **3.** a person who lived in ancient Rome. —*adj.* **1.** of, relating to, or written in Latin. **2.** of or relating to the people or countries that use languages derived from Latin. **3.** of or relating to ancient Rome or its people.

● Several hundred years ago, people in Western Europe believed that **Latin** should be the model for all other languages. The languages that they knew were all related to Latin, and a knowledge of Latin was the mark of an educated person. Much of the literature of the time was written in Latin. The languages spoken by the common people, such as English or French, were thought to be inferior to Latin. People wrote rules of grammar for English that were patterned after rules of Latin grammar, and some English writers even translated their poetry into Latin to see if it was grammatically correct.

Today we know that there are hundreds of languages in the world that have no relation to Latin, and the belief that Latin should be a model for all languages is no longer held. No language can be judged in terms of another, since no two languages are the same. It is now known that Latin is not "better" than English, only different, and that the rules of English grammar must be based on English, not on Latin.

The study of Latin is still very helpful in understanding English, however, because so many English words come from Latin. For example, *dictionary, language, definition, pronunciation,* and *synonym* all go back to Latin.

Latin America, the countries in the Western Hemisphere south of the United States, in which the languages, such as Spanish or Portuguese, are of Latin origin. —**Latin American.**

Lat·in-A·mer·i·can (lat'in ə mer'i kən) *adj.* of or relating to Latin America.

Latin cross, a cross formed by one short horizontal bar that intersects a longer vertical bar near the top. It is used as a sacred symbol, especially in certain Christian religions.

lat·i·tude (lat'ə tōōd, lat'ə tyōōd') *n.* **1.** the distance north or south of the equator, expressed as degrees measured from the earth's center. All points of a given latitude form a circle running east and west and parallel to the equator. **2.** freedom from narrow restrictions: *The students were given great latitude in selecting topics for their essays.*

North Pole
60° N ... 60° N
30° N ... 30° N
0° ... 0°
30° S ... 30° S
60° S ... 60° S
South Pole
Lines of latitude

lat·i·tu·di·nal (lat'ə tōōd'ən əl, lat'ə tyōōd'ən əl) *adj.* of or relating to latitude.

la·trine (lə trēn') *n.* a toilet for the use of a large number of people, especially in an army camp.

lat·ter (lat'ər) *adj.* **1.** the second of two mentioned: *Of swimming and tennis, I much prefer the latter one.* ▲ See **former** for usage note. **2.** nearer to the end: *Fred spent the latter part of the evening with friends.*

Lat·ter-day Saint (lat'ər dā') a member of the Church of Jesus Christ of Latter-day Saints; Mormon.

lat·ter·ly (lat'ər lē) *adv.* at a recent time; recently; lately.

lat·tice (lat'is) *n.* **1.** a structure of crossed or interlaced strips, as of wood or metal, spaced to form a regular pattern of openings. **2.** something having this structure, such as a window. —*v.t.,* **lat·ticed, lat·tic·ing. 1.** to form into or arrange like a lattice. **2.** to furnish with a lattice.

lat·tice·work (lat'is wurk') *n.* **1.** a lattice. **2.** lattices, or something made of lattices.

Lat·vi·a (lat'vē ə) *n.* a republic of the Soviet Union, in the European part of the country, on the Baltic Sea. Area, approx. 24,600 sq. mi. Pop. (1979), 2,521,000.

Lattice window

Lat·vi·an (lat'vē ən) *n.* **1.** a person who was born or is living in Latvia. **2.** the language of the Latvians. —*adj.* of or relating to Latvia, its people, their language, or their culture.

laud (lôd) *v.t.* to praise. —*n.* a hymn or song of praise.

laud·a·ble (lô'də bəl) *adj.* worthy of praise; commendable: *Her work with the sick and aged is very laudable.* —**laud·a·bil·i·ty,** *n.* —**laud·a·bly,** *adv.*

lau·da·num (lôd'ən əm) *n.* a medicinal solution of opium in alcohol.

laud·a·to·ry (lô'də tôr'ē) *adj.* containing or expressing praise.

laugh (laf) *v.i.* **1.** to make the sounds and the facial movements that show amusement, joy, scorn, or other emotions. **2.** to feel amusement or joy; be happy. —*v.t.* to produce an effect upon by laughing: *He tried to laugh his troubles away.* —*n.* the act, sound, or manner of laughing: *His laugh is rather loud.* —**laugh'er,** *n.*
  to laugh off. to dismiss lightly: *The boy received a bad bruise when he fell, but he just laughed it off.*

laugh·a·ble (laf'ə bəl) *adj.* causing laughter or scorn. —**laugh'a·ble·ness,** *n.* —**laugh'a·bly,** *adv.*

laugh·ing (laf'ing) *adj.* **1.** that laughs or seems to laugh: *a laughing brook.* **2.** laughable: *Your mistake is no laughing matter.* —*n.* laughter. —**laugh'ing·ly,** *adv.*

laughing gas, another term for **nitrous oxide.**

laugh·ing·stock (laf'ing stok') *n.* an object of ridicule.

laugh·ter (laf'tər) *n.* the action or sound of laughing.

launch¹ (lônch) *v.t.* **1.** to put (a boat or ship) into the water. **2.** to push or propel by force into the air: *to launch a spear, to launch a rocket.* **3.** to start (someone or something) on a course or career: *to launch a political career.* —*v.i.* **1.** to start something with enthusiasm. **2.** to move outward into the water or air. —*n. pl.,* **launch·es.** the act

at; āpe; cär; end; mē; it; īce; hot; ōld; fôrk; wood; fōōl; oil; out; up; turn; sing; thin; this; hw in white; zh in treasure. The symbol ə stands for the sound of a in about, e in taken, i in pencil, o in lemon, and u in circus.

L

of launching. [Old French *lancier* to throw, from *lance* a spear.] —**launch'er**, *n.*

launch² (lônch) *n. pl.,* **launch·es. 1.** an open motorboat. **2.** the largest boat carried by a warship. [Spanish *lancha* a type of ship's boat.]

launching pad, an area or structure from which a rocket or missile is launched. Also, **launch pad.**

laun·der (lôn'dər) *v.t., v.i.* to wash or wash and iron (clothes or linens). —**laun'der·er**, *n.*

Laun·dro·mat (lôn'drə mat') *n. Trademark.* a self-service laundry with coin-operated washing machines and dryers.

laun·dress (lôn'dris) *n. pl.,* **laun·dress·es.** a woman who is employed to do laundering, or who works in a laundry.

laun·dry (lôn'drē) *n. pl.,* **laun·dries. 1.** things that have been, are, or will be laundered. **2.** a place where laundering is done.

laun·dry·man (lôn'drē mən) *n. pl.,* **laun·dry·men** (lôn'drē mən). **1.** a man who works in a laundry. **2.** a man who collects and delivers laundry.

lau·re·ate (lôr'ē it) *n.* **1.** a person given a special honor: *a Nobel laureate.* **2.** see **poet laureate.** [Latin *laureātus* crowned with laurel; referring to the ancient Roman custom of honoring poets, victorious athletes, and other heroes by crowning them with a laurel wreath.]

lau·rel (lôr'əl) *n.* **1.** a medium-sized evergreen tree bearing spicy, lance-shaped leaves and clusters of tiny yellow flowers. **2.** any of a group of related trees or shrubs, such as the mountain laurel. **3. laurels.** an honor; distinction.
  to rest on one's laurels. to be satisfied with what one has already done.

Laurel flower and leaves

Lau·ren·tian Mountains (lô ren'shən) a low mountain range in eastern Canada, between Hudson Bay and the St. Lawrence River.

Lau·sanne (lō zan') *n.* a city in western Switzerland, on Lake Geneva. Pop. (1977 est.), 132,800.

la·va (lä'və, lav'ə) *n.* **1.** hot liquid rock from a volcano or an opening in the earth's surface. **2.** volcanic rock that has been formed by the cooling of such molten material.

La·val (lə val', lə väl') *n.* a city in southern Quebec, Canada, near Montreal. Pop. (1976), 246,243.

lav·a·to·ry (lav'ə tôr'ē) *n. pl.,* **lav·a·to·ries. 1.** a room with sinks for washing the hands and face. **2.** a toilet. **3.** a sink for washing.

lave (lāv) *v.,* **laved, lav·ing.** —*v.t.* to wash or bathe (someone or something). —*v.i.* to wash or bathe.

lav·en·der (lav'ən dər) *n.* **1.** a pale reddish-purple color. **2.** any of a group of plants and shrubs related to the mint, having narrow grayish leaves and spikes of fragrant pale-purple flowers that yield an oil used in perfumes. **3.** the dried leaves and flowers of this plant, used mainly to give a pleasant fragrance to clothes or linen. —*adj.* **1.** having the color lavender; pale-reddish purple. **2.** having the fragrance of lavender.

lav·ish (lav'ish) *adj.* **1.** giving or spending in great or wasteful amounts: *Jeff is much too lavish with his money.* **2.** given in great amounts; more than necessary: *The hostess served lavish amounts of whipped cream on the dessert.* —*v.t.* to give in great amounts: *The old couple lavished gifts on their grandchildren.* —**lav'ish·ly**, *adv.* —**lav'ish·ness**, *n.*

law (lô) *n.* **1.** a rule that allows or prevents certain conduct or activities, fixed by custom or made by a group of people with authority, such as a legislature or court, and applied to an entire community, state, or country. **2.** a particular set of such rules: *international law, the law of the land.* **3.** the governing of people according to such rules: *respect for law and order.* **4.** an agent or agency, especially the police, that applies or enforces such rules: *The law captured the escaped convict.* **5.** legal action: *to resort to law.* **6.** the study of such rules: *a student of law.* **7.** the profession of being a lawyer: *to practice law.* **8.** a rule or custom: *the laws of grammar.* **9.** a statement in science or mathematics about what always happens whenever certain events take place or certain conditions exist.
  to lay down the law. to command or order something with authority.

law·a·bid·ing (lô'ə bī'ding) *adj.* obedient to the law.

law·break·er (lô'brā'kər) *n.* a person who breaks the law.

law·ful (lô'fəl) *adj.* **1.** allowed by law: *lawful acts.* **2.** according to law: *a lawful marriage.* —**law'ful·ly**, *adv.* —**law'ful·ness**, *n.*

law·giv·er (lô'giv'ər) *n.* a person who makes a law or code of laws for a country or people.

law·less (lô'lis) *adj.* **1.** not obeying the law: *a lawless act, a lawless person.* **2.** not controlled by law: *a lawless frontier town.* —**law'less·ly**, *adv.* —**law'less·ness**, *n.*

law·mak·er (lô'mā'kər) *n.* a person who makes laws; legislator.

law·mak·ing (lô'mā'king) *n.* the making of laws. —*adj.* that makes laws: *a lawmaking body.*

lawn¹ (lôn) *n.* a grassy area that is kept closely mowed, especially around a house. [Old French *launde* grassy land; heath.]

lawn² (lôn) *n.* a lightweight, sheer cotton fabric, used for blouses and handkerchiefs. [From *Laon*, a French town noted for the manufacture of linen.]

lawn bowling, another term for **bowls.**

lawn mower, any of various machines with revolving blades used for cutting grass.

lawn tennis, see **tennis** *(def. 1).*

Law·rence (lôr'əns) **1.** D(avid) H(erbert). 1885–1930, English writer and poet. **2.** T(homas) E(dward). 1888–1935, English soldier, adventurer, and author, known as **Lawrence of Arabia.**

law·ren·ci·um (lô ren'sē əm) *n.* a radioactive element produced by bombarding californium with boron ions. Symbol: **Lr** [From E. O. *Lawrence,* 1901–1958, U.S. physicist who invented the cyclotron.]

law·suit (lô'sōōt') *n.* a legal action begun in a court of law to settle a claim.

law·yer (lô'yər) *n.* a person whose profession is representing clients in lawsuits and advising them in legal matters; attorney.

lax (laks) *adj.* **1.** not careful or strict; not exact; negligent: *lax discipline.* **2.** not rigid or firm; slack: *a lax cord.* —**lax'ly**, *adv.* —**lax'ness**, *n.*

lax·a·tive (lak'sə tiv) *n.* a medicine that stimulates the emptying of the bowels.

lax·i·ty (lak'sə tē) *n.* the state or quality of being lax.

lay¹ (lā) *v.,* **laid, lay·ing.** —*v.t.* **1.** to place or put down on something; cause to lie: *Martha laid the plate on the table.* **2.** to make ready; prepare: *Mary laid the table. John laid plans for the coming holiday.* **3.** to put down and fasten in place: *He laid the carpet.* **4.** to make and deposit (an egg or eggs). **5.** to consider as caused by or resulting from something: *The farmer laid the poor crops to lack of rain.* **6.** to put: *The teacher laid much stress on good study* *habits.* **7.** to offer or present: *She laid claim to the land.* **8.** to fix or set in a particular way or state: *Ann laid aside her knitting. The minister laid her fears at rest.* **9.** to bet: *He laid twenty dollars on the winning team.* **10.** to place in a particular setting or location: *The novel is laid in colonial America.* —*v.i.* to lay an egg or eggs. —*n.* the way something lies or is arranged: *the lay of the land.* [Old English *lecgan* to put, place.]

to lay aside or **to lay away** or **to lay by.** to put away or save for future use; reserve.

to lay bare. to expose or make known: *All the facts are laid bare in the report.*

to lay down. a. to assert or declare: *The father laid down the law.* **b.** to give up; sacrifice: *He laid down his life for his friend.*

to lay into. *Informal.* to make a vigorous physical or verbal attack on.

to lay off. a. to mark off; fix: *to lay off boundaries.* **b.** to dismiss from employment: *to lay off workers.* **c.** *Slang.* to stop: *Alice told the boys to lay off teasing her kid brother.*

to lay out. a. to spread out and arrange: *to lay out one's clothes for packing.* **b.** *Slang.* to spend: *She laid out twenty dollars for the gift.*

to lay over. to stop for a short time: *We laid over in Birmingham on our way to New Orleans.*

to lay to. a. to engage in or do with vigor or enthusiasm. **b.** to bring a boat or ship into the wind and keep it from moving.

to lay up. a. to store or put aside for future use. **b.** to keep indoors because of illness or injury; confine: *Joe was laid up with the flu.*

lay² (lā) the past tense of **lie².**

lay³ (lā) *adj.* **1.** of or relating to those who are not members of the clergy. **2.** of or relating to those not in a certain profession, such as medicine or law. [Old French *lai,* going back to Greek *lāos* the people.]

lay⁴ (lā) *n.* **1.** a short poem originally meant to be sung. **2.** a melody; song. [Old French *lai.*]

lay·er (lā′ər) *n.* **1.** a single thickness laid on or over something: *There is a layer of ice on the street.* **2.** a chicken that lays eggs.

lay·ette (lā et′) *n.* a complete outfit for a newborn baby, including clothes, toilet articles, and bedding.

lay·man (lā′mən) *n. pl.,* **lay·men** (lā′mən). **1.** a person who does not belong to a certain profession. **2.** a person who is not a member of the clergy.

lay·off (lā′ôf′) *n.* **1.** the act of firing or dismissing employees. **2.** a period of unemployment.

lay·out (lā′out′) *n.* **1.** the act or process of laying out. **2.** the way in which the various parts of something are located or arranged; design: *the layout of a building, the layout of a book.* **3.** a thing having or showing such a design.

lay·o·ver (lā′ō′vər) *n.* a stop in the course of a trip.

Laz·a·rus (laz′ər əs) *n.* in the New Testament, a man that Jesus brought back to life after he had died.

laze (lāz) *v.i.,* **lazed, laz·ing.** to be lazy; loaf: *She enjoyed lazing in the sun during her holiday.*

la·zy (lā′zē) *adj.,* **la·zi·er, la·zi·est. 1.** not willing to work or make an effort to do anything: *The boy was very lazy and would not clean up his room.* **2.** moving slowly; sluggish: *a lazy river.* **3.** causing laziness: *a lazy summer day.* —**la′zi·ly,** *adv.* —**la′zi·ness,** *n.*

lb., pound; pounds. [Abbreviation of Latin *libra.*]

lbs., pounds.

l.c., lower case.

-le *suffix* (used to form verbs) repeatedly: *fizzle.*

lea (lē) *n.* a meadow; pasture.

leach (lēch) *v.t.* **1.** to drain or wash by filtering with water or other liquid. **2.** to dissolve or remove loose parts from (ashes, soils, ores, or other materials) by filtration with water or other liquid. —*n. pl.,* **leach·es. 1.** a material or container used to leach. **2.** the act, instance, or result of leaching.

lead¹ (lēd) *v.,* **led, lead·ing.** —*v.t.* **1.** to show the way, especially by going first: *Our guide led us down the trail.* **2.** to conduct or guide, as by pulling or holding by the hand: *The dog led the blind man across the street.* **3.** to be or show a route or way for: *This road will lead you into town.* **4.** to be ahead of or first in: *Jerry led his opponents in the race.* **5.** to be the head of; control or direct: *Pete led the dance committee. The officer led the troops.* **6.** to cause to arrive at a particular opinion or to do a particular thing: *What led you to that conclusion? His doctor's advice led him to stop smoking.* **7.** to have or experience; live: *She led a life of ease.* —*v.i.* **1.** to go or be first; be ahead of all others: *The home team leads seven to three.* **2.** to show the way; be a guide. **3.** to be a route or way: *This hall leads to the bedrooms.* —*n.* **1.** the state or position of being ahead of all others: *Hank took the lead in the race.* **2.** the extent of being ahead: *a seven-yard lead.* **3.** an example or direction: *Helen sat down, and the others followed her lead.* **4.** a piece of information that serves as a guide; clue: *The detective had several good leads on the crime.* **5.** the main role in a play, motion picture, or the like. **6.** a person who has such a role. **7.** an opening or introductory paragraph in a news story. —*adj.* that is first; leading: *a lead article in a magazine, a lead runner in a race.* [Old English *lædan* to conduct, guide.]

to lead off. to begin; open: *The speaker led off his talk with jokes.*

to lead on. to draw or entice into foolish action or mistaken opinion: *She led the boy on, causing him to think she liked him.*

to lead up to. to prepare the way for gradually: *The series of meetings and conferences led up to the trade agreement.*

lead² (led) *n.* **1.** a heavy, soft, dull-gray metallic element. Symbol: **Pb 2.** a thin stick of graphite mixed with clay in a pencil. **3.** a weight attached to a line used to determine the depth of water. **4.** bullets; shot. **5. leads.** frames made of metal, in which panes of glass are placed. —*v.t.* to cover, join, weight, or mix with lead. [Old English *lēad* this metal.]

lead·en (led′ən) *adj.* **1.** made of lead: *a leaden bucket.* **2.** dull-gray like lead: *a leaden sky.* **3.** difficult to move; heavy.

lead·er (lē′dər) *n.* **1.** a person who leads: *He was the leader of the gang. Mr. Smith is the leader of the band.* **2.** a short length of material, connecting the lure or hook to a fish line. —**lead′er·less,** *adj.*

lead·er·ship (lē′dər ship′) *n.* **1.** the position or function of a leader. **2.** the ability to lead or guide others. **3.** leaders as a group: *the union leadership.*

lead·ing (lē′ding) *adj.* **1.** that is chief or principal: *a leading cause of disease.* **2.** that goes or is first: *a leading horse in a race.* **3.** that plays a lead: *Tim is the leading man in the school play.*

---

at; āpe; cär; end; mē; it; īce; hot; ōld; fôrk; wood; fōol; oil; out; up; turn; sing; thin; this; hw in white; zh in treasure. The symbol ə stands for the sound of a in about, e in taken, i in pencil, o in lemon, and u in circus.

L

leaf (lēf) *n. pl.,* **leaves. 1.** the flat, usually green part of a plant, growing from a stem and serving to make food by means of photosynthesis. **2.** a sheet of paper in a book. **3.** a very thin sheet of metal, especially gold, used for decoration. **4.** an extra piece of wood for making a table larger. —*v.i.* **1.** to put forth leaves: *The trees leaf in the spring.* **2.** to turn and glance at the pages of something, as a book or magazine. —**leaf'like'**, *adj.*
to turn over a new leaf. to act in a different and better way: *He vowed to turn over a new leaf and study Latin two hours every day.*

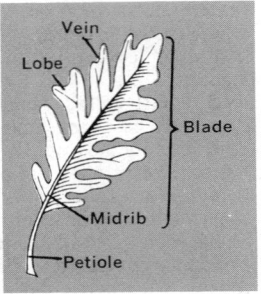

Vein
Lobe
Blade
Midrib
Petiole

Parts of a leaf

leaf·less (lēf'lis) *adj.* without leaves.
leaf·let (lēf'lit) *n.* **1.** a single sheet of printed matter, used to advertise or announce something; handbill; flyer. **2.** a small, unbound book; booklet: *This leaflet contains the instructions for operating the appliance.* **3.** a small or young leaf. **4.** *Botany.* one of the separate blades or divisions of a compound leaf.
leaf·stalk (lēf'stôk') *n.* another word for **petiole.**
leaf·y (lē'fē) *adj.,* **leaf·i·er, leaf·i·est.** covered with or resembling leaves. —**leaf'i·ness,** *n.*
league¹ (lēg) *n.* **1.** an association of people or countries formed to promote their common interests. **2.** an association of athletic teams that compete regularly with each other: *a basketball league.* —*v.i.,* **leagued, lea·guing.** to band together into a league. [French *ligue,* going back to Latin *ligāre* to bind.]
in league. associated together; working together.
league² (lēg) *n.* a measure of distance equal to three miles. [Late Latin *leuga* a measure of distance.]
League of Nations, an association of nations formed in 1920 to settle international disputes and to promote world peace. The League of Nations was disbanded in 1946 and replaced by the United Nations.
lea·guer (lē'gər) *n.* a member of a league.
Le·ah (lē'ə) *n.* in the Old Testament, Jacob's first wife.
leak (lēk) *n.* **1.** an accidental passage of something, such as water, air, or light, through a hole or other small opening: *The tire went flat because of a slow leak.* **2.** the hole itself: *Jack patched the leak in his rowboat.* **3.** the making known of secret information. —*v.i.* **1.** to have a leak: *The water pipes leak.* **2.** to pass through a hole or other small opening: *All the gasoline leaked out of the gas tank during the night.* **3.** to become known: *News of the plot leaked out.* —*v.t.* **1.** to pass or cause (something) to pass through a hole or other opening. **2.** to allow (secret information) to become known: *He leaked the testimony to the newspapers.*
leak·age (lē'kij) *n.* **1.** the act, process, or instance of leaking. **2.** the amount that leaks.
leak·y (lē'kē) *adj.,* **leak·i·er, leak·i·est.** having a leak or leaks. —**leak'i·ness,** *n.*
lean¹ (lēn) *v.,* **leaned** or **leant, lean·ing.** —*v.i.* **1.** to be at an angle from a straight, upright position: *The walls of the old shed lean outward.* **2.** to bend the body: *The customer leaned over the counter.* **3.** to rest on or against something for support: *Lean on my arm.* **4.** to depend on or use: *He leans on his older brother for encouragement.* **5.** to tend, as in opinion; be favorably inclined: *His taste in music leans toward jazz.* —*v.t.* **1.** to cause to bend: *to lean one's body over a railing.* **2.** to cause to be at an angle from a straight, upright position. —*n.* the act or state of leaning. [Old English *hleonian* to incline, bend, lie.]

lean² (lēn) *adj.* **1.** with little or no fat: *The star basketball player is tall and lean.* **2.** (of meat) containing little or no fat. **3.** not having or producing enough; meager; poor: *That was a lean year for farmers.* —*n.* a part of meat with little or no fat. [Old English *hlǣne.*] —**lean'ness,** *n.*
lean·ing (lē'ning) *n.* a tendency to favor one thing over another; inclination.
leant (lent) a past tense and past participle of **lean¹.**
lean-to (lēn'tōo') *n. pl.,* **lean-tos. 1.** a shed or building having a roof that slopes in one direction, supported by the wall of a building against which it is built. **2.** a crude, usually open shelter, with a sloping roof formed of branches, twigs, and the like.

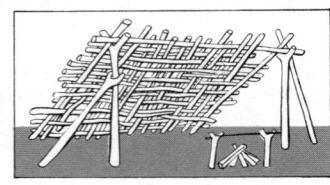

Lean-to

leap (lēp) *v.,* **leaped** or **leapt, leap·ing.** —*v.i.* **1.** to make a big jump: *The dancer leaped into the air.* **2.** to move eagerly or quickly: *The warriors leaped into battle.* —*v.t.* **1.** to make a big jump over: *The horse leaped a wall.* **2.** to cause to make a big jump: *The rider leaped the horse.* —*n.* **1.** a big jump: *The lion made a leap through a burning hoop.* **2.** the distance covered in a leap.
leap·frog (lēp'frôg', lēp'frog') *n.* a game in which players take turns jumping over the backs of the other players. —*v.t.* **leap·frogged, leap·frog·ging.** to leap over in a game of leapfrog.
leapt (lept, lēpt) a past tense and past participle of **leap.**
leap year, a year containing an extra day, February 29. Leap year occurs every four years.
Lear (lēr) *n.* a legendary king of Britain, the hero of Shakespeare's tragedy *King Lear.*
learn (lurn) *v.,* **learned** or **learnt, learn·ing.** —*v.t.* **1.** to gain knowledge of or skill in (something) by study or experience: *Jack is learning algebra. Alice learned to sew.* **2.** to memorize: *He can't learn the lines in the play.* **3.** to find out about: *At last we've learned the truth!* —*v.i.* **1.** to gain knowledge or skill: *Different children learn at different rates.* **2.** to find out: *She was surprised to learn of their marriage.* —**learn'er,** *n.*
learn·ed (lur'nid) *adj.* **1.** having or showing much knowledge: *a learned person.* **2.** produced by someone with much knowledge: *a learned study.* —**learn'ed·ly,** *adv.*
learn·ing (lur'ning) *n.* **1.** the act of gaining knowledge or skill. **2.** knowledge gained by careful study.
learnt (lurnt) a past tense and past participle of **learn.**
lease (lēs) *n.* **1.** a written agreement for the use of property for a specified period of time: *Dad signed the lease for the apartment.* **2.** a period of time specified in such a contract: *The lease expires in two years.* —*v.t.,* **leased, leas·ing. 1.** to take or hold a lease on: *to lease an automobile.* **2.** to allow to have or use with a lease: *The Smith family leased the property to them.*
leash (lēsh) *n. pl.,* **leash·es.** a strap, chain, or other line fastened to a dog or other animal to control or hold it. —*v.t.* to control or hold with a leash: *She leashed the dog to the post.*
least (lēst) *adj.* smallest in size, degree, amount, or importance: *He did the least work of all.* —*n.* something that is least: *That is the least he can do.* —*adv.* in the smallest or lowest degree: *He is the least friendly boy in class.*
at least. a. at the very minimum: *At least twenty people will come to the party.* **b.** at any rate; in any event: *Toby should at least let us know where he is.*
in the least. at all: *I am not in the least interested.*

least common denominator, the smallest number that can be divided by each of the denominators of a given group of fractions without leaving a remainder.

least common multiple, the smallest number that is an exact multiple of two or more given quantities. The least common multiple of 2, 3, and 4 is 12.

least·wise (lēst′wīz′) *also,* **least·ways** (lēst′wāz′). *adv. Informal.* at least; at any rate.

leath·er (leth′ər) *n.* material from an animal skin or hide, prepared for use by tanning. —*adj.* of or made of leather: *leather shoes.*

Leath·er·ette (leth′ə ret′) *n. Trademark.* any of various plastics or fabrics that resemble leather in appearance.

leath·ern (leth′ərn) *adj.* **1.** made of leather. **2.** resembling leather.

leath·er·neck (leth′ər nek′) *n. Slang.* a member of the U.S. Marines. [From the *leather neck* (bands) that used to be part of U.S. Marine uniforms.]

leath·er·y (leth′ər ē) *adj.* resembling leather: *The old man has leathery skin.* —**leath′er·i·ness,** *n.*

leave¹ (lēv) *v.,* **left, leav·ing.** —*v.i.* **1.** to go to another place; go away: *He finally left after visiting us for several days.* **2.** to depart or set out: *The plane leaves at 10:00.* —*v.t.* **1.** to go away from: *Alice left the table after dinner.* **2.** to withdraw or depart from; quit: *John left his job for a better one.* **3.** to neglect to take along or remove; forget to bring: *Someone left his keys on the table.* **4.** to allow to be or remain in a particular state or condition: *He left his work unfinished and went swimming. We leave him alone when he is in a bad mood.* **5.** to let remain; not use: *The food was left on Joan's plate.* **6.** to entrust, refer, or commit: *His future was left to fate.* **7.** to give by will; bequeath: *He left his property to the family.* **8.** to have remaining after subtraction: *10 minus 3 leaves 7.* [Old English *læfan* to allow to remain, bequeath.]

   to leave off. to stop: *Where did we leave off in our discussion?*

   to leave out. to omit or exclude: *In making the stew, she left out onions.*

leave² (lēv) *n.* **1.** permission to do something. **2.** permission to be absent, especially from military duty. Also, **leave of absence. 3.** the period that such permission lasts. [Old English *lēaf* permission.]

   on leave. absent from duty with permission.

   to take leave of. to bid farewell to or leave behind.

leave³ (lēv) *v.i.,* **leaved, leav·ing.** to put forth leaves; leaf. [Middle English *leven,* from *lef* leaf.]

leav·en (lev′ən) *n.* **1.** a substance, such as yeast or baking powder, that causes dough to rise. **2.** an influence that changes something, as by making it lighter or more active: *Without the leaven of wit, his speech would have been dull.* —*v.t.* **1.** to cause (dough) to rise by adding a leaven. **2.** to spread through and change.

leav·en·ing (lev′ə ning) *n.* something that leavens.

leaves (lēvz) the plural of **leaf.**

leave-tak·ing (lēv′tā′king) *n.* the act of taking leave; bidding farewell.

leav·ings (lē′vingz) *n., pl.* something that remains unused: *The dogs ate the leavings from the table.*

Leb·a·non (leb′ə nən) *n.* a country in southwestern Asia, on the eastern shore of the Mediterranean Sea. Capital, Beirut. Area, 4000 sq. mi. Pop. (1971 est.), 2,870,000. —**Leb·a·nese** (leb′ə nēz′), *adj., n.*

lech·er·ous (lech′ər əs) *adj.* given to, characterized by, or showing lechery. —**lech′er·ous·ly,** *adv.* —**lech′er·ous·ness,** *n.*

lech·er·y (lech′ər ē) *n.* too much sexual desire or activity.

lec·tern (lek′tərn) *n.* **1.** a stand with a sloping top for holding the written speech or other papers of a speaker. **2.** a reading desk in a church, especially one from which scripture lessons are read during services.

lec·ture (lek′chər) *n.* **1.** a prepared talk on a particular subject, given before an audience for the purpose of instruction: *The teacher's lecture was about English literature.* **2.** a lengthy scolding: *Father gave Pete a lecture for driving too fast.* —*v.,* **lec·tured, lec·tur·ing.** —*v.i.* to give a lecture or lectures: *to lecture at a university.* —*v.t.* **1.** to give a lecture to; instruct by means of a lecture. **2.** to scold.

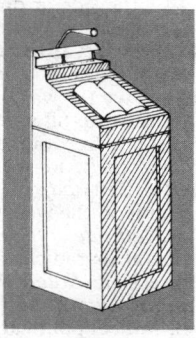

Lectern

lec·tur·er (lek′chər ər) *n.* a person who lectures.

led (led) the past tense and past participle of **lead¹.**

Le·da (lē′də) *n. Greek Mythology.* the mother of two mortals, Castor and Clytemnestra, and of two immortals, Pollux and Helen of Troy.

ledge (lej) *n.* **1.** a narrow shelf or similar flat surface, such as one jutting out from the wall of a building. **2.** a narrow, flat surface jutting out from the side of a mountain or other natural formation.

ledg·er (lej′ər) *n.* an account book in which all the financial transactions of a business are recorded.

ledger line, a short line added above or below a musical staff for notes too high or too low to be put on the staff.

lee (lē) *n.* **1.** a shelter or protection. **2.** a side or part, especially of a ship, sheltered or turned away from the wind. —*adj.* sheltered from the wind: *the lee side of a ship.*

Lee, Robert E. (lē) 1807–1870, Confederate general in the Civil War.

leech (lēch) *n. pl.,* **leech·es. 1.** any of a group of bloodsucking worms found in salt water, fresh water, and damp soil, which suck the blood of animals. Doctors once used leeches to bleed their patients. **2.** a person who clings to another or others for his own personal gain. **3.** *Archaic.* a doctor; physician.

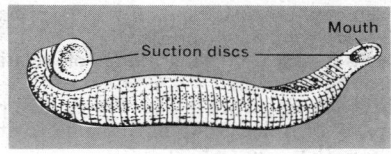

Mouth — Suction discs

Leech

Leeds (lēdz) *n.* a city in north-central England. Pop. (1971), 494,971.

leek (lēk) *n.* **1.** the leaves and stalk of a plant related to the lily, eaten as a vegetable. **2.** the plant itself, growing from a slender underground bulb.

leer (lēr) *n.* a sly look or sidelong glance expressing cunning, lust, or evil intent. —*v.i.* to look with a leer.

leer·y (lēr′ē) *adj. Informal.* suspicious; wary: *She is always somewhat leery of strangers.*

lee shore, the shore lying off the leeward side of a boat or ship, toward which the boat or ship may be driven by the wind.

at; āpe; cär; end; mē; it; īce; hot; ōld; fôrk; wood; fōol; oil; out; up; turn; sing; thin; this; hw in white; zh in treasure. The symbol ə stands for the sound of **a** in about, **e** in taken, **i** in pencil, **o** in lemon, and **u** in circus.

L

lee·ward (lē′wərd, lōō′ərd) *adj.* located on or moving toward the side toward which the wind is blowing. —*n.* the side or direction toward which the wind is blowing; lee. —*adv.* toward the lee.

Lee·ward Islands (lē′wərd) a Caribbean island group forming the northern part of the Lesser Antilles.

lee·way (lē′wā′) *n.* **1.** the sideways drift of a boat or ship to leeward, off its course. **2.** extra time, space, or the like, making freedom of action or movement possible: *If we leave early, we will give ourselves plenty of leeway.*

left¹ (left) *adj.* **1.** of, on, or toward the side of the body that is to the west when one is facing north: *the left hand, the left side of the road.* **2.** *also,* **Left.** relating to or having liberal or radical political views. —*n.* **1.** the left side or direction: *Stuart was seated on my left. The car skidded to the left.* **2.** *also,* **Left.** a party or group having liberal or radical political views. Also, **left wing. 3.** a blow delivered with the left hand, as in boxing. —*adv.* to or toward the left: *Turn left at the next corner.* [Old English *lyft* weak.]

left² (left) the past tense and past participle of **leave**¹.

left field *Baseball.* **1.** the left section of the outfield when viewed from home plate. **2.** the position of the player stationed in this area.

left-hand (left′hand′) *adj.* **1.** on or toward the left: *a left-hand drawer of a desk.* **2.** of, for, relating to, or with the left hand: *a left-hand glove.*

left-hand·ed (left′han′did) *adj.* **1.** using the left hand naturally and more easily than the right: *a left-handed hitter in baseball.* **2.** done with the left hand. **3.** made to be held in or used by the left hand, as a tool. **4.** turning or moving from right to left; counterclockwise. **5.** doubtful, ironic, or insincere: *a left-handed compliment.* —*adv.* with the left hand.

left·ist (lef′tist) *n.* a person who has liberal or radical political views. —*adj.* of, relating to, or characterized by liberal or radical political views.

left·o·ver (left′ō′vər) *n. also,* **leftovers.** something that remains unused, especially food remaining after a meal. —*adj.* remaining; unused.

left-wing (left′wing′) *adj.* of, relating to, or belonging to the left wing.

left wing 1. see **left** (*n. def.* 2). **2.** a portion of a political party or other group having a more liberal or radical outlook than the rest.

leg (leg) *n.* **1.** one of the limbs of human beings and animals used chiefly for supporting the body and for walking. **2.** something like a leg in shape, position, or function: *the leg of a chair.* **3.** the part of a garment, especially of trousers, that covers a leg. **4.** a distinct part or stage of a journey or course: *The first leg of the voyage took them to Australia.* **5.** either of the sides of a triangle other than the base. —*v.i.* **legged, leg·ging.** *Informal.* to walk or run: *We legged it home when the rain started.*

  on one's last legs. *Informal.* close to death, collapse, or failure.

  to pull one's leg. *Informal.* to trick or tease; deceive: *Gail was only pulling your leg when she told you that story.*

leg·a·cy (leg′ə sē) *n. pl.,* **leg·a·cies. 1.** money or property left to someone by a will: *His uncle left Andrew a legacy of $5000.* **2.** something handed down from previous generations or from the past; heritage.

le·gal (lē′gəl) *adj.* **1.** of, relating to, or concerned with law: *legal advice.* **2.** according to or permitted by law; lawful: *a person's legal rights, the legal owner of the property.* **3.** of, relating to, or characteristic of lawyers or the practice of law: *a legal mind.* —**le′gal·ly,** *adv.*

le·gal·i·ty (li gal′ə tē) *n. pl.,* **le·gal·i·ties.** the state or quality of being legal; lawfulness.

le·gal·ize (lē′gə līz′) *v.t.,* **le·gal·ized, le·gal·iz·ing.** to make legal or lawful. —**le′gal·i·za′tion,** *n.*

legal tender, the coin or currency that, by law, must be accepted in payment of debts.

leg·ate (leg′it) *n.* an official representative, especially a person who represents the Pope.

leg·a·tee (leg′ə tē′) *n.* a person to whom a legacy is left.

le·ga·tion (li gā′shən) *n.* **1.** a diplomatic representative below the rank of ambassador, and his staff. **2.** the official residence and offices of such a representative and staff in a foreign country.

le·ga·to (lə gä′tō) *Music. adj.* smooth and even, with no breaks between tones. —*adv.* in a legato manner.

leg·end (lej′ənd) *n.* **1.** a story passed down through the years that is not regarded as historically true, but is usually based on some facts, and is popularly thought of as true: *There are many legends about the adventures of Robin Hood.* **2.** such stories as a group, especially of a nation or culture: *Paul Bunyan is a character in American legend.* **3.** a legendary figure: *The general became a legend in his own time.* **4.** an inscription or motto, especially on a coin, medal, or coat of arms. **5.** an explanatory description accompanying a chart, map, or other illustration.

leg·end·ar·y (lej′ən der′ē) *adj.* **1.** of, relating to, or characteristic of a legend or legends: *a legendary account of a battle.* **2.** celebrated or described in legend: *a legendary queen.*

leg·er·de·main (lej′ər də mān′) *n.* **1.** skill in using the hands, especially in performing tricks; sleight of hand. **2.** artful trickery; deception.

leg·ged (leg′id, legd) *adj.* having a certain kind or number of legs. ▲ used in combination: *a bowlegged man, a four-legged animal.*

leg·gings (leg′ingz) *n., pl.* coverings of cloth or leather for the legs, usually reaching to the ankle.

leg·gy (leg′ē) *adj.,* **leg·gi·er, leg·gi·est. 1.** having awkwardly long legs. **2.** having attractive legs.

Leg·horn (leg′hôrn′, *defs. 2 and 3 also* leg′ərn) *n.* **1.** any of a breed of small, hardy domestic fowl, raised chiefly for their white-shelled eggs. **2. leghorn.** a fine, braided wheat straw used in the manufacture of hats. **3.** a hat made of this straw.

leg·i·ble (lej′ə bəl) *adj.* easily read: *The address on the envelope was not legible.* —**leg′i·bil′i·ty,** *n.* —**leg′i·bly,** *adv.*

le·gion (lē′jən) *n.* **1.** a military unit in the army of ancient Rome, having from 3000 to 6000 infantrymen and from 300 to 700 cavalrymen. **2.** any large military unit; army. **3.** a vast number of persons or things; multitude: *a legion of stars in the sky.* **4.** any of various military or honorary organizations, such as the American Legion.

le·gion·ar·y (lē′jə ner′ē) *adj.* of or relating to a legion. —*n. pl.,* **le·gion·ar·ies.** a soldier or member of a legion.

le·gion·naire (lē′jə ner′) *n.* a member of a legion.

leg·is·late (lej′is lāt′) *v.,* **leg·is·lat·ed, leg·is·lat·ing.** —*v.i.* to make or pass a law or laws: *Parliament legislates for the United Kingdom.* —*v.t.* to cause, regulate, or bring about by passing laws: *Congress legislated increased benefits for veterans.*

leg·is·la·tion (lej′is lā′shən) *n.* **1.** the making or passing of laws. **2.** the laws made or passed: *to enact new legislation.*

leg·is·la·tive (lej′is lā′tiv) *adj.* **1.** of or relating to legislation: *legislative powers.* **2.** having the power to make or pass laws: *Congress is a legislative body.* **3.** of or relating to a legislature.

leg·is·la·tor (lej′is lā′tər) *n.* a member of a legislative body, especially a member of a state legislature or of Congress.

leg·is·la·ture (lej′is lā′chər) *n.* a governmental body made up of a group of persons having the power to make or pass laws for a state or country.

le·git·i·ma·cy (li jit′ə mə sē) *n.* the state or quality of being legitimate.

le·git·i·mate (li jit′ə mit) *adj.* **1.** according to law; lawful; rightful: *The judge ruled that the woman's claim was legitimate.* **2.** logically correct or valid: *a legitimate argument.* **3.** genuine or reasonable: *a legitimate complaint.* **4.** born of parents who are legally married to each other: *a legitimate child.* —**le·git′i·mate·ly,** *adv.*

le·git·i·mize (li jit′ə mīz′) *v.t.,* **le·git·i·mized, le·git·i·miz·ing.** to make legitimate.

leg·ume (leg′yoom, li gyoom′) *n.* **1.** any of a large group of plants that bear pods, including peas, beans, peanuts, and alfalfa. Legumes are grown as food crops, as fodder, and as natural fertilizers. **2.** a seed pod of such a plant, usually having the seeds in rows along the pod.

le·gu·mi·nous (li gyoo′mə nəs) *adj.* of or relating to legumes: *leguminous crops, leguminous vegetables.*

Le Ha·vre (lə hä′vrə) a port city in northern France, at the mouth of the Seine. Pop. (1968), 199,509. Also, **Havre.**

lei (lā) *n. pl.,* **leis.** a wreath of flowers, leaves, or other material, often worn around the neck in Hawaii.

Leices·ter (les′tər) *n.* a city in central England. Pop. (1971 est.), 282,000.

Leip·zig (līp′sig) *n.* a city in southern East Germany. Pop. (1971), 583,311.

lei·sure (lē′zhər, lezh′ər) *n.* **1.** the time that a person can spend as he pleases; free or unoccupied time: *After he retired, grandfather had the leisure to travel.* **2.** freedom from the demands of work or duty: *Most people dream of living a life of leisure.* —*adj.* free or unoccupied: *Kathie spent her leisure hours playing the piano.*

at one's leisure. when a person has free time; at a person's convenience: *Visit us at your leisure.*

lei·sure·ly (lē′zhər lē, lezh′ər lē) *adj.* characterized by leisure; unhurried; relaxed: *He went for a leisurely walk.*

lem·ming (lem′ing) *n.* an arctic rodent having a stout body and long, chiefly yellow-ish-brown fur. Some lemmings migrate in large numbers across the land and drown when they reach the sea.

Lemming

lem·on (lem′ən) *n.* **1.** an oval fruit of a citrus tree, having a thick yellow rind and a juicy, sour pulp that can be eaten. **2.** the thorny evergreen tree bearing this fruit. **3.** a clear, bright yellow color. **4.** *Slang.* a person or thing that is unsatisfactory or worthless: *His car is a real lemon.* —*adj.* **1.** having the color lemon. **2.** made from or flavored with lemon: *lemon juice.*

lem·on·ade (lem′ə nād′) *n.* a drink made of lemon juice, water, and sugar.

le·mur (lē′mər) *n.* a small animal related to the monkey, found chiefly in Madagascar. A lemur has soft, woolly fur, a face like that of a fox, and a long tail. [Modern Latin *lemur,* from Latin *lemurēs* ghosts; because this animal is active at night.]

Lemur

lend (lend) *v.,* **lent, lending.** —*v.t.* **1.** to grant the use of (something) with the understanding that it will be returned: *I'll lend you my records for the party.*

2. to give the temporary use of (money) on condition of repayment and at a set rate of interest. **3.** to provide or give: *The darkness lent an air of mystery to the old house.* **4.** to make available for aid or support: *to lend assistance to someone in trouble.* —*v.i.* to make a loan or loans. —**lend′er,** *n.*

lending library, another term for **circulating library.**

length (lengkth, length) *n.* **1.** the extent of anything from end to end: *The length of the football field is one hundred yards.* **2.** the extent from beginning to end: *the length of a vacation, the length of a book.* **3.** the state, quality, or fact of being long: *The length of the climb exhausted the climbers.* **4.** the measurement of anything considered as a unit: *Dad parked one car's length away from the fire hydrant.* **5.** a piece or portion of anything, usually of a certain or standard size: *a length of rope, a length of pipe.*

at length. a. in full; in detail. **b.** after a time; finally.

length·en (lengk′thən, length′ən) *v.t., v.i.* to make or become longer: *Mother lengthened Sally's dress.*

length·wise (lengkth′wīz′, length′wīz′) *also,* **length·ways** (lengkth′wāz′, length′wāz′). *adj., adv.* in the direction of the length.

length·y (lengk′thē, leng′thē) *adj.,* **length·i·er, length·i·est.** much too long: *The crowd was bored by the lengthy speech.* —**length′i·ly,** *adv.* —**length′i·ness,** *n.*

len·i·en·cy (lē′nē ən sē, lēn′yən sē) *n.* the state or quality of being lenient. Also, **len·i·ence** (lē′nē əns, lēn′yəns).

len·i·ent (lē′nē ənt, lēn′yənt) *adj.* not severe or harsh; merciful; tolerant: *a lenient judge.* —**len′i·ent·ly,** *adv.*

Len·in, Vlad·i·mir Il·yich (len′in; vlad′ə mēr il′-yich) 1870–1924, Russian revolutionary leader and founder of the Soviet Union; also called **Nikolai Lenin.**

Len·in·grad (len′in grad′) *n.* the former capital of Russia, in the northwestern Soviet Union, on an inlet of the Baltic Sea. It was formerly known as St. Petersburg, and later as Petrograd. Pop. (1970 est.), 3,513,000.

lens (lenz) *n. pl.,* **lens·es. 1.** a piece of glass or other transparent material, having one or both surfaces curved, which cause the light rays passing through them to either move apart or come together. Lenses are used in eyeglasses, cameras, microscopes, and the like. **2.** any combination of such lenses. **3.** the colorless, transparent part of the eye that focuses the image on the retina.

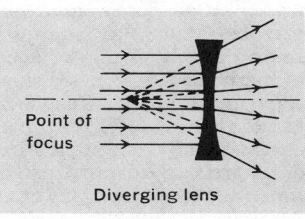
Converging lens

Diverging lens

Lenses

lent (lent) the past tense and past participle of **lend.**

Lent (lent) *n.* the period of penitence and prayer observed in Christian churches beginning on Ash Wednesday and continuing for the forty weekdays before Easter.

at; āpe; cär; end; mē; it; īce; hot; ōld; fôrk; wood; fool; oil; out; up; turn; sing; thin; this; hw in white; zh in treasure. The symbol ə stands for the sound of **a** in about, **e** in taken, **i** in pencil, **o** in lemon, and **u** in circus.

L

Lent·en (lent′ən) *also,* **lent·en.** *adj.* of, relating to, or suitable for Lent: *a Lenten diet.*

len·til (len′til) *n.* **1.** a seed of a plant related to the pea, cooked and eaten as a vegetable, especially in soups and stews. **2.** the plant itself, having broad pods containing two seeds.

Le·o (lē′ō) *n.* **1.** a constellation in the northern sky, thought to resemble a lion in shape. **2.** the fifth sign of the zodiac.

Le·ón (lā ōn′) *n.* a city in central Mexico. Pop. (1976 est.), 525,900.

Le·o·nar·do da Vin·ci (lā′ə när′dō   də vin′chē) 1452–1519, Italian artist and scientist.

le·o·nine (lē′ə nīn′) *adj.* relating to, characteristic of, or resembling a lion: *leonine courage.*

leop·ard (lep′ərd) *n.* a meat-eating animal of the cat family which is found in Africa, India, and eastern Asia. It has either a brownish-yellow coat marked with black spots or a solid black coat. [Old French *leopard,* from Late Latin *leopardus,* from Late Greek *leopardos,* going back to Greek *leōn* lion + *pardos* panther; because it was once believed to be the offspring of a lion and a panther.] —**leop′ard·ess,** *n.*

Leopard

Le·o·pold·ville (lē′ə pōld vil′) *n.* see **Kinshasa.**

le·o·tard (lē′ə tärd′) *also,* **le·o·tards.** *n.* a close-fitting, one-piece garment extending from the neck or waist to the feet. [From Jules *Léotard,* a nineteenth-century French acrobat who made this garment popular.]

lep·er (lep′ər) *n.* a person who has leprosy.

lep·re·chaun (lep′rə kon′, lep′rə kôn′) *n.* in Irish folklore, a mischievous elf resembling a little old man.

lep·ro·sy (lep′rə sē) *n.* an infectious disease caused by a bacterium and affecting the body tissues, especially the skin, nerves, and mucous membranes.

lep·rous (lep′rəs) *adj.* **1.** having leprosy. **2.** of, relating to, or characteristic of leprosy.

les·bi·an (lez′bē ən) *n.* a female homosexual. —*adj.* of or relating to homosexuality between women. [From the reputed homosexuality of the poet Sappho and her friends, who lived on *Lesbos,* a Greek island.]

le·sion (lē′zhən) *n.* an injury; wound.

Le·so·tho (lə sō′tō) *n.* a country in southern Africa, formerly the British possession of Basutoland. It is entirely surrounded by the Republic of South Africa. Capital, Maseru. Area, 11,716 sq. mi. Pop. (1980), 1,341,000.

less (les) *adj.* a comparative of **little. 1.** not as much or as great in quantity, extent, or degree: *less food, less time, less money.* **2.** lower in rank or importance: *No less a person than the principal gave the order.* —*adv.* to a smaller extent or degree: *The movie was less funny than the book.* —*n.* a smaller amount or quantity: *I finished less of the work than I had planned.* —*prep.* with the subtraction of; minus: *Ten less seven is three.*

▲ **Less** and **fewer** both can mean "smaller in number." **Less** is used more often for things that cannot actually be counted: *The doctor advised her to eat less food.* **Fewer** is used more often for things that can be counted: *The doctor advised her to eat fewer calories by cutting out desserts.*

-less *suffix* **1.** (used to form adjectives from nouns) without; having no: *hopeless.* **2.** (used to form adjectives from verbs) that does not: *tireless.* **3.** (used to form adjectives from verbs) that cannot be: *countless.*

les·see (le sē′) *n.* a person to whom a lease is granted.

less·en (les′ən) *v.i.* to become less; decrease: *The pain lessened.* —*v.t.* to make less; reduce; diminish.

less·er (les′ər) *adj.* smaller or less: *to choose the lesser of two evils.*

Lesser Antilles, an island group of the West Indies southeast of Puerto Rico, consisting of the Leeward Islands, the Windward Islands, Barbados, Trinidad, Tobago, the Virgin Islands, and the small islands north of Venezuela.

lesser panda, see **panda** *(def. 2).*

les·son (les′ən) *n.* **1.** a period of time given to the instruction of a particular subject or skill: *a French lesson, a skiing lesson.* **2.** something learned or studied, especially material assigned, presented, or learned at one time: *He didn't understand today's math lesson.* **3.** an event or experience serving to guide or warn: *This experience has taught me a lesson I'll never forget.* **4.** a selection from the Scriptures as part of a church service.

les·sor (les′ôr) *n.* a person who grants a lease.

lest (lest) *conj.* **1.** for fear that: *We came in through the back door lest someone should see us.* **2.** that. ▲ used after words expressing fear or worry: *I feared lest he would lose his way in the forest.*

let[1] (let) *v.,* **let, let·ting.** —*v.t.* **1.** to give permission or opportunity to; permit; allow: *Father let her drive the car.* **2.** to allow to pass, go, or come: *She opened the cage door and let the bird out.* **3.** to cause; make: *I'll let you know my decision.* **4.** to rent or lease: *to let a cottage.* ▲ **Let** is also used as an auxiliary verb, usually in the imperative, to indicate: **a.** a suggestion, command, or warning: *Let's take a walk. Let's go! Just let him try to stop me!* **b.** something that is assumed or supposed: *Let x = 3.* —*v.i.* to be rented: *The apartment lets on a yearly basis.* [Old English *lætan* to allow, leave behind.]

> **to let be.** to leave undisturbed; not interfere with or bother: *Let him be.*
>
> **to let down. a.** to allow to fall or descend; lower. **b.** to fail to fulfill the hopes or expectations of; disappoint: *When I needed her help, she let me down.*
>
> **to let off. a.** to excuse from a duty or service. **b.** to give little or no punishment to; treat leniently: *The judge let him off with a warning.*
>
> **to let on.** *Informal.* to allow something to be known: *Did you let on that you knew the answer?*
>
> **to let out. a.** to give forth; release: *to let out a scream.* **b.** to enlarge or extend (a garment or the like): *When she gained weight, she had to let out the dress.*
>
> **to let up.** *Informal.* to stop or lessen in intensity: *We thought the storm would never let up.*

let[2] (let) *n.* **1.** in tennis, volleyball, and similar games, a stroke that must be repeated because of interference, especially a served ball that touches the net. **2.** *Archaic.* a hindrance; obstacle; obstruction. [Old English *lettan* to hinder.]

-let *suffix* (used to form nouns) **1.** little: *booklet.* **2.** an article worn on or around (a part of the body): *anklet.*

let·down (let′doun′) *n.* **1.** a disappointment; disillusionment: *It was a real letdown when our plan failed.* **2.** a lessening or slowing up.

le·thal (lē′thəl) *adj.* causing or capable of causing death; deadly: *a lethal wound, a lethal poison.*

le·thar·gic (li thär′jik) *adj.* **1.** feeling or showing lethargy; sluggish. **2.** causing lethargy: *lethargic summer heat.* —**le·thar′gi·cal·ly,** *adv.*

leth·ar·gy (leth′ər jē) *n. pl.,* **leth·ar·gies. 1.** the state or quality of being without strength, energy, or alertness; sluggishness. **2.** an abnormal condition characterized by excessive drowsiness or by prolonged deep sleep.

Le·the (lē′thē) *n.* **1.** *Greek and Roman Mythology.* a river in Hades whose water, when drunk, caused a person to forget the past. **2.** forgetfulness; oblivion.

let's (lets) let us.

let·ter (let′ər) *n.* **1.** a mark or character, usually printed or written, that stands for one or more speech sounds; character of an alphabet: *There are three letters in the name "Jim."* **2.** a written or printed message sent by one person to another: *to mail a letter.* **3.** an official or legal document granting a specific right, authority, or privilege to a person: *a letter of credit.* **4.** the literal meaning or exact wording of something, as opposed to a more general meaning or interpretation: *the letter of the law.* **5. letters.** literary culture; literature: *a man of letters.* **6.** the initial of a school or college given as an award: *The athlete was given a letter for being on the basketball team.* —*v.t.* **1.** to mark or write with letters: *to letter a sign.* **2.** to write (a word or words) in letters: *The word "exit" was lettered on the door.* —**let′ter·er,** *n.*

to the letter. exactly as written or spoken; precisely: *He followed the instructions to the letter.*

let·ter·head (let′ər hed′) *n.* **1.** information printed at the top of a sheet of paper, usually the name and address of the sender. **2.** a sheet of paper with such a heading.

let·ter·ing (let′ər ing) *n.* **1.** the act or art of forming or drawing letters. **2.** letters so formed or drawn.

let·ter-per·fect (let′ər pur′fikt) *adj.* correct in every detail; completely accurate.

let·tuce (let′is) *n.* **1.** the large green leaves of any of several plants, forming a round, oval, or long head, eaten mainly as a raw vegetable in salads. **2.** a plant bearing these leaves.

let·up (let′up′) *n. Informal.* a lessening or slackening: *It snowed all day without any letup.*

leu·ke·mi·a (lōō kē′mē ə) *n.* a disease characterized by the formation of abnormal numbers of white blood cells.

leu·ko·cyte (lōō′kə sīt′) *also,* **leu·co·cyte.** *n.* another word for **white blood cell.**

Le·vant (lə vant′) *n.* the region bordering the eastern shore of the Mediterranean Sea, including the present nations of Greece, Turkey, Syria, Lebanon, Israel, and Egypt.

Le·van·tine (lev′ən tīn′, lev′ən tēn′) *n.* a person who was born or is living in the Levant. —*adj.* of, relating to, or characteristic of the Levant.

lev·ee (lev′ē) *n.* **1.** a wall of earth and other materials built along the banks of a river to prevent flooding. **2.** a landing place, especially on a river; pier; quay.

lev·el (lev′əl) *adj.* **1.** having no part higher than another; flat; even: *The steamroller made the ground level.* **2.** parallel to the plane of the horizon; horizontal. **3.** being or placed at the same height

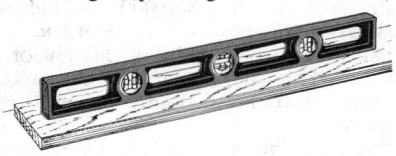

Level (def. 5)

or on the same plane as something else: *The two paintings were level with the window.* **4.** *Informal.* mentally well-balanced; sensible: *a level head.* —*n.* **1.** the relative position or degree of something in any scale or order: *a low level of economic development.* **2.** a horizontal surface, plane, or line from which the height of something is measured: *The town is situated 200 feet above sea level.* **3.** height; depth; altitude: *The stream rose to a level of three feet.* **4.** a floor or story of a structure: *The car is parked on the lower level of the garage.* **5.** any of various devices used to determine whether a surface is horizontal, as in surveying or carpentry. —*v.,* **lev·eled, lev·el·ing;** *also, British,* **lev·elled, lev·el·ling.** —*v.t.* **1.** to make even, flat, or

smooth: *The bulldozer leveled the mound of earth.* **2.** to bring to the level of the ground; destroy; raze: *Fire leveled the house.* **3.** to bring to equality, as in degree, importance, or rank; equalize: *to level the classes of society.* **4.** to bring to a horizontal position and aim or point: *to level a gun at a target.* —*v.i. Slang.* to be frank and honest: *Good friends usually level with each other.* —**lev′el·er,** *n.* —**lev′el·ness,** *n.* —**lev′el·ly,** *adv.*

one's level best. *Informal.* a person's very best; the best a person can do.

on the level. *Informal.* honest; upright; fair: *Is that businessman on the level?*

lev·el·head·ed (lev′əl hed′id) *adj.* having or showing common sense and good judgment; sensible.

lev·er (lev′ər, lē′vər) *n.* **1.** a device made of a rigid rod or bar that transmits force or motion from one point to another as it rotates about a fixed point, or fulcrum. A lever is used to lift weights and pry things loose. **2.** anything that operates in this way, such as a crowbar. **3.** a projecting bar, handle, or piece that is moved to operate, control, or adjust a mechanism.

lev·er·age (lev′ər ij, lē′vər ij) *n.* **1.** the action of a lever. **2.** the mechanical force or motion gained by use of a lever. **3.** an increased power to act or influence: *political leverage.*

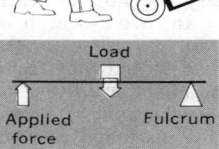

Lever

Le·vi (lē′vī) *n.* in the Old Testament, a son of Jacob and the ancestor of the Levites.

le·vi·a·than (li vī′ə thən) *n.* **1.** in the Old Testament, a huge sea monster, thought to be either a whale or crocodile. **2.** anything of huge size.

Le·vite (lē′vīt) *n.* a member of the tribe of Levi.

Le·vit·i·cus (li vit′i kəs) *n.* the third book of the Old Testament, containing the laws for the priests and Levites and the Jewish ceremonial laws.

lev·i·ty (lev′ə tē) *n. pl.,* **lev·i·ties.** a lack of seriousness in attitude or behavior.

lev·y (lev′ē) *v.t.,* **lev·ied, lev·y·ing. 1.** to impose or collect by force or authority: *to levy taxes.* **2.** to draft or enlist (men) for military service. **3.** to prepare for, start, or wage (war). —*n. pl.,* **lev·ies. 1.** anything collected by authority, such as troops or taxes. **2.** the act of levying.

lewd (lōōd) *adj.* obscene; indecent; vulgar. [Old English *lǣwede* not of the clergy; possibly because people not belonging to the clergy were considered vulgar and wicked.]

Lew·is (lōō′is) **1. John L(lewellyn).** 1880–1969, U.S. labor leader. **2. Mer·i·weth·er** (mer′ē weth′ər). 1774–1809, U.S. explorer who led an expedition to the Pacific Northwest with William Clark. **3. Sinclair.** 1885–1951, U.S. novelist.

lex·i·cog·ra·pher (lek′sə kog′rə fər) *n.* a person whose profession is writing or compiling a dictionary.

lex·i·cog·ra·phy (lek′sə kog′rə fē) *n.* the act or work of writing or compiling a dictionary.

at; āpe; cär; end; mē; it; īce; hot; ōld; fôrk; wood; fōōl; oil; out; up; turn; sing; thin; this; hw in white; zh in treasure. The symbol ə stands for the sound of a in about, e in taken, i in pencil, o in lemon, and u in circus.

L

● **Lexicography** is the making of a dictionary, and people who write dictionaries are called *lexicographers*. The first English dictionaries were produced in the seventeenth century, before scholars had begun to study language scientifically. Early lexicographers often had to rely on guesswork rather than definite evidence about words. These dictionary makers gave their opinions as to the correct spelling, meaning, and usage of words, and they felt that people should speak and write according to these opinions. But they often limited their examination of language to an analysis of the way they and their friends spoke and wrote, and a reading of the works of a few famous writers. So their dictionaries often did not reflect the way a great majority of people actually used language.

Today lexicographers know that it is not their proper role to make personal judgments about words. Their responsibility is to record the way language is really used, not to express opinions as to how it should be used. They base their work on a careful study of English as it is spoken and written at the present time. Lexicographers continually examine a wide range of current books, magazines, newspapers, and other publications to determine what words are in use, and how they are being used. They also listen carefully to the way people speak. From these observations, they decide what words to include in their dictionary and how to describe them.

In their research lexicographers may come across certain words or expressions that they themselves do not use or that they feel are not proper to use. Nevertheless, if a significantly large number of people use such words, lexicographers must include the words in a dictionary. Just as mapmakers cannot leave a country off the map because they do not approve of its government or its policies, lexicographers cannot leave out a word because they do not approve of it. If lexicographers were to leave out such a word, they would not be giving an accurate and complete record of language.

lex·i·con (lek′sə kən, lek′sə kon′) *n.* **1.** a dictionary, especially of Greek, Hebrew, Latin, or another ancient language. **2.** a list of words belonging to a particular field, profession, activity, or the like.

Lex·ing·ton (lek′sing tən) *n.* **1.** a town in northeastern Massachusetts, the site of the first battle of the American Revolution, on April 19, 1775. **2.** a city in north-central Kentucky. Pop. (1970), 108,137.

Ley·den jar (līd′ən) a device for storing an electric charge, consisting of a glass jar that is coated almost to the top with metal foil inside and outside. The two coatings are equivalent to the two plates of a capacitor.

Lha·sa (lä′sə, las′ə) *n.* the capital of Tibet. Pop. (1958 est.), 70,000. Also, **La·sa.**

Li, the symbol for lithium.

li·a·bil·i·ty (lī′ə bil′ə tē) *n. pl.,* **li·a·bil·i·ties. 1.** the state or condition of being liable. **2.** something for which one is liable, especially a financial obligation or debt. **3.** something that works to one's disadvantage; handicap: *His lack of a high school education was a liability to him in getting a job.* **4. liabilities.** in accounting, all the debts or financial commitments of a business.

li·a·ble (lī′ə bəl) *adj.* **1.** legally responsible; obligated by law: *The owner of the car was liable for damages done to the other car.* **2.** subject or susceptible: *He is liable to heart*

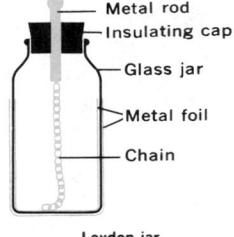

Metal rod
Insulating cap
Glass jar
Metal foil
Chain

Leyden jar

trouble. **3.** *Informal.* apt; likely: *You are liable to fall on the icy sidewalk if you do not watch your step.*

li·ai·son (lē′ə zon′, lē ā′zon′) *n.* a line of communication between parts of an organization, such as military units, used to make sure that actions are properly coordinated.

li·ar (lī′ər) *n.* a person who tells lies.

li·ba·tion (lī bā′shən) *n.* **1.** the pouring out of wine or other liquid as an offering to a god. **2.** a liquid offered in this way.

li·bel (lī′bəl) *n.* **1.** the act or crime of damaging a person's reputation by printing, writing, or representing in a picture false or malicious information about him or her. **2.** any false or malicious statement or picture. —*v.t.,* **li·beled, li·bel·ing;** *also, British,* **li·belled, li·bel·ling.** to write or publish a libel about. —**li′bel·er;** *also, British,* **li′bel·ler,** *n.*

li·bel·ous (lī′bə ləs) *adj.* containing a libel: *a libelous accusation.*

lib·er·al (lib′ər əl) *adj.* **1.** characterized by or tending toward opinions favoring progress and reform, as in politics or religion. **2.** *also,* **Liberal.** of or belonging to a political party that favors progress and reform. **3.** free from prejudice; broad-minded; tolerant: *to be liberal in one's ideas.* **4.** characterized by generosity; generous; bountiful: *Dad is liberal with his money.* **5.** plentiful; abundant: *a liberal supply.* **6.** not literal or strict: *a liberal interpretation of the law.* —*n.* **1.** a person who favors or supports progress and reform, as in politics. **2.** *also,* **Liberal.** a member of a liberal political party. —**lib′er·al·ly,** *adv.* —**lib′er·al·ness,** *n.*

liberal arts, subjects studied mainly for their cultural value rather than their immediate practical use, such as literature, languages, history, and philosophy.

lib·er·al·ism (lib′ər ə liz′əm) *n.* liberal principles and ideals; belief in progress and reform.

lib·er·al·i·ty (lib′ə ral′ə tē) *n. pl.,* **lib·er·al·i·ties. 1.** generosity. **2.** a tolerant attitude or beliefs; broadmindedness. **3.** a generous gift.

lib·er·al·ize (lib′ər ə līz′) *v.t., v.i.,* **lib·er·al·ized, lib·er·al·iz·ing.** to make or become liberal. —**lib′er·al·i·za′tion,** *n.*

lib·er·ate (lib′ə rāt) *v.t.,* **lib·er·at·ed, lib·er·at·ing. 1.** to set free; release: *to liberate slaves.* **2.** *Chemistry.* to free (a gas) from combination, as by heating. —**lib′er·a′tion,** *n.* —**lib′er·a′tor,** *n.*

Li·be·ri·a (lī bēr′ē ə) *n.* a country on the west coast of Africa, first settled in 1822 by freed black slaves from the United States. Capital, Monrovia. Area, 43,000 sq. mi. Pop. (1980), 1,860,000. —**Li·be′ri·an,** *adj., n.*

lib·er·tar·i·an (lib′ər ter′ē ən) *n.* a person who advocates liberty, especially of thought or conduct.

lib·er·tine (lib′ər tēn′) *n.* a person who is lacking in moral restraint; dissolute person. —*adj.* dissolute; immoral.

lib·er·ty (lib′ər tē) *n. pl.,* **lib·er·ties. 1.** freedom from tyranny or foreign domination; political independence: *England was forced to grant the American colonies their liberty.* **2.** freedom from imprisonment, captivity, or other physical restraint: *The prisoner was finally given his liberty.* **3.** the ability to act as one pleases; freedom of choice: *You have the liberty to say what you want.* **4.** the freedom of thought and action possessed by the people of a state or nation: *Freedom of speech is an important liberty.* **5.** an action or speech that is too free or too familiar. **6.** freedom to move within certain limits: *The dog had the liberty of the entire house.* **7.** in the navy, time granted to a sailor to go ashore.

at liberty. a. free. **b.** permitted; allowed: *I am not at liberty to tell you.* **c.** not busy or occupied.

Liberty Bell, the bell rung on July 8, 1776, in Philadelphia to proclaim the signing of the Declaration of Independence by the Continental Congress.

Li·bra (līʹbrə, lēʹbrə) *n.* **1.** a small, dim constellation in the southern sky just south of the celestial equator, thought to resemble a pair of scales. **2.** the seventh sign of the zodiac.

li·brar·i·an (lī brerʹē ən) *n.* **1.** a person who is in charge of a library. **2.** a person who is trained for work in a library.

li·brar·y (līʹbrer ē) *n. pl.,* **li·brar·ies. 1.** a collection of books or other literary, artistic, or reference material. **2.** a room or building containing such a collection. **3.** a public or private institution that maintains and circulates such a collection.

li·bret·tist (li bretʹist) *n.* a writer of a libretto.

li·bret·to (li bretʹō) *n. pl.,* **li·bret·tos** or **li·bret·ti** (li bretʹē). **1.** the text or words of an opera or other long composition. **2.** a book or pamphlet containing such a text.

Li·bre·ville (lēʹbrə vil) *n.* the capital and largest city of Gabon, on the northwestern coast of the country. Pop. (1970 est.), 73,000.

Lib·y·a (libʹē ə) *n.* a country on the Mediterranean coast of northern Africa. Capitals, Tripoli and Benghazi. Area, 679,362 sq. mi. Pop. (1971 est.), 2,010,000. —**Libʹy·an,** *adj., n.*

lice (līs) the plural of **louse.**

li·cense (līʹsəns) *n.* **1.** a document, certificate, or metal object that shows that the holder has official permission to do something, as to drive a car, or to own something, as a dog. **2.** permission given by law or authority to do something: *a license to hunt.* **3.** too much or undisciplined freedom. **4.** the freedom to break or ignore certain rules or standards in order to achieve an effect: *The writer allowed himself license in changing historical facts in his novel.* —*v.t.,* **li·censed, li·cens·ing.** to give a license to or for.

li·cen·see (līʹsən sēʹ) *also,* **li·cen·cee.** *n.* a person to whom a license has been granted.

li·cen·tious (li senʹshəs) *adj.* lacking moral restraint; immoral; lewd. —**li·cenʹtious·ly,** *adv.* —**li·cenʹtious·ness,** *n.*

li·chee (lēʹchē) another spelling of **litchi.**

li·chen (līʹkən) *n.* any of a large group of plants without flowers found in all parts of the world, usually growing on tree trunks, rocks, or the ground. Lichens consist of a fungus and an alga growing together.

lick (lik) *v.t.* **1.** to move the tongue over the surface of: *The kitten licked its paw.* **2.** to taste, eat, or remove by moving the tongue over: *to lick an ice-cream cone.* **3.** to move over or touch lightly or quickly: *Flames licked the logs in the fireplace.* **4.** *Informal.* to hit forcefully; thrash: *The little boy was licked for being naughty.* **5.** *Informal.* to gain a victory over; defeat; overcome: *to lick an opponent, to lick a difficult problem.* —*n.* **1.** a stroke of the tongue over the surface of something: *to give a lollipop a lick.* **2.** a small quantity; bit: *The boy was too lazy to do even a lick of work.* **3.** see **salt lick. 4.** *Informal.* a sharp blow.

lic·o·rice (likʹər is, likʹər ish) *n.* **1.** a sweet juice or extract obtained from the root of a plant, used as a flavoring in candy, medicine, and tobacco. **2.** the plant whose root yields this juice or extract. **3.** a candy flavored with licorice.

lid (lid) *n.* **1.** a hinged or removable cover placed over the opening of a container, box, pot, or other receptacle: *Put the lid on the garbage can.* **2.** see **eyelid.**

lie¹ (lī) *n.* a false statement made with the purpose of deceiving; falsehood. —*v.i.,* **lied, ly·ing. 1.** to make a false statement or statements with the purpose of deceiving: *She always lies about her age.* **2.** to give a false impression: *Mirrors don't lie.* [Old English *lēogan.*]

lie² (lī) *v.i.,* **lay, lain, ly·ing. 1.** to be or place oneself in a flat or reclining position: *to lie in the grass, to lie down on a couch.* **2.** to be or rest on a surface: *The blanket is lying on the bed.* **3.** to remain in a particular state or condition: *The treasure lay hidden in the forest.* **4.** to be located or placed: *Mexico lies south of Texas.* **5.** to continue in a specific direction: *The long highway lay in front of us. A great future lies before him.* **6.** to be; be found; exist: *His fate lies in the hands of the jury.* **7.** to be buried, as in a grave or tomb. —*n.* the matter, direction, or position in which something lies: *the lie of the land.* [Old English *licgan.*]

Liech·ten·stein (likʹtən stīn) *n.* a small country in central Europe, between Austria and Switzerland. Capital, Vaduz. Area, 61 sq. mi. Pop. (1971 est.), 20,000.

lie detector, an instrument that detects certain bodily changes that are assumed to occur when a person lies in answering questions.

lief (lēf) *adv.* willingly; gladly: *We would as lief go there as anywhere else.*

liege (lēj) *n.* **1.** a feudal lord or ruler having the right to the allegiance and service of his vassals or subjects. **2.** a vassal or subject bound to give allegiance and service to a feudal lord or ruler. —*adj.* **1.** having the right to the allegiance and service of vassals or subjects. **2.** bound to give allegiance and service to a feudal lord or ruler.

liege·man (lējʹmən) *n. pl.,* **liege·men** (lējʹmən). **1.** a vassal. **2.** a faithful follower or subject.

lien (lēn) *n.* a legal claim placed on the property of another for payment of a debt.

lieu (lōō) *n.* **in lieu of,** in place of; instead of: *The salesman received commissions in lieu of salary.*

Lieut., Lieutenant.

lieu·ten·an·cy (lōō tenʹən sē) *n. pl.,* **lieu·ten·an·cies.** the rank, status, or commission of a lieutenant.

lieu·ten·ant (lōō tenʹənt) *n.* **1.** in the U.S. Army, Air Force, or Marine Corps, a first lieutenant or a second lieutenant. **2.** in the U.S. Navy or Coast Guard, an officer ranking next below a lieutenant commander and next above a lieutenant junior grade. **3.** a person who acts in the place of a superior; deputy.

lieutenant colonel, in the U.S. Army, Air Force, and Marine Corps, an officer ranking next below a colonel and next above a major.

lieutenant commander, in the U.S. Navy or Coast Guard, an officer ranking next below a commander and next above a lieutenant.

lieutenant general, in the U.S. Army, Air Force, and Marine Corps, an officer ranking next below a general and next above a major general.

lieutenant governor, in most U.S. states, the second-ranking executive officer who takes over the governorship in case of the governor's death or absence.

lieutenant junior grade, in the U.S. Navy or Coast Guard, an officer ranking next below a lieutenant and next above an ensign.

life (līf) *n. pl.,* **lives. 1.** the quality that distinguishes

at; āpe; cär; end; mē; it; īce; hot; ōld; fôrk; wood; fōōl; oil; out; up; turn; sing; thin; this; hw in white; zh in treasure. The symbol ə stands for the sound of **a** in about, **e** in taken, **i** in pencil, **o** in lemon, and **u** in circus.

L

543

animals and plants from rocks or other inorganic matter or a dead organism, and makes it possible for them to grow, reproduce, and adapt to their environment. **2.** the state or fact of possessing this quality: *He nearly lost his life in the fire.* **3.** a spiritual existence coming after physical death: *Some people believe in life after death.* **4.** living organisms: *plant life. No life has been found on the moon.* **5.** a living being; person: *The firemen helped to save many lives.* **6.** the period from birth to death: *His grandmother had a long and happy life.* **7.** the period during which something lasts or remains useful or effective: *Minor accidents can shorten the life of a car.* **8.** way of living: *military life, city life.* **9.** a written account of a person's life; biography: *a life of George Washington.* **10.** vitality; liveliness; spirit: *He is always full of life.*

life belt, a life preserver made like a belt.

life·blood (līf′blud′) *n.* **1.** the blood necessary to life. **2.** something that gives strength or energy: *Freedom of speech is the lifeblood of democracy.*

life·boat (līf′bōt′) *n.* a strong boat, usually carried on a larger ship, equipped for saving lives at sea in case of shipwreck or other emergency.

life buoy, a life preserver, often ring-shaped, used to keep a person afloat.

life cycle *Biology.* the series of changes through which an organism passes from a particular stage in one generation to the development of the same stage in the next generation.

life·guard (līf′gärd′) *n.* a person employed at a beach or a swimming pool to protect and aid swimmers.

life insurance **1.** a contract between an individual and an insurance company by which a person pays small sums of money regularly over a specified period of time in return for a large sum of money to be paid to his family or heirs at his death. **2.** the sum of money specified in such a contract.

life jacket, a life preserver in the form of a jacket or vest.

life·less (līf′lis) *adj.* **1.** not having life. **2.** no longer alive; dead. **3.** not lively; dull. **4.** without living organisms: *a lifeless desert.* **—life′less·ly,** *adv.* **—life′less·ness,** *n.*

life·like (līf′līk′) *adj.* resembling or imitating real life: *The doll was amazingly lifelike.*

life·line (līf′līn′) *n.* **1.** a rope used for rescue, especially one attached to a life preserver and thrown to a person in the water. **2.** a line by which a diver is raised or lowered, and used by him for signaling. **3.** a route that is the only one over which vital supplies are transported to a place.

life·long (līf′lông′) *adj.* lasting or continuing through a lifetime: *a lifelong struggle, lifelong friends.*

life preserver, a device used by a person to keep afloat, usually in the form of a belt, jacket, or circular tube that is inflated with air or filled with cork or other buoyant material.

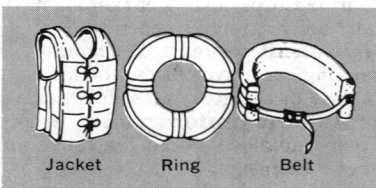

Jacket　Ring　Belt

Life preservers

life raft, a wooden or inflatable rubber raft or boat, used in emergencies to rescue people from the water.

life·sav·er (līf′sā′vər) *n.* **1.** a person who saves another from death, as a lifeguard. **2.** *Informal.* a person or thing that provides help in a time of need or crisis. **3.** a life preserver in the form of a ring.

life-size (līf′sīz′) *also,* **life-sized.** *adj.* of the same size as the thing portrayed: *a life-size portrait of a person.*

life·time (līf′tīm′) *n.* the period of time that a person lives or a thing lasts: *a lifetime devoted to science, the lifetime of a television set.* **—adj.** lasting for such a period: *a lifetime interest in collecting stamps.*

life·work (līf′wurk′) *n.* the main or entire work of a lifetime: *She chose medical research as her lifework.*

lift (lift) *v.t.* **1.** to raise into the air; pick up; elevate: *to lift a heavy suitcase.* **2.** to raise in rank, condition, or estimation; exalt: *The victory lifted the team's spirits.* **3.** to revoke or remove; cancel: *The ban on parking was lifted temporarily.* **4.** *Informal.* to steal: *The burglars lifted three radios.* **—v.i.** **1.** to be or become raised: *This box is too heavy to lift.* **2.** to rise or seem to rise; disappear: *The fog lifted.* **—n.** **1.** the act of lifting. **2.** the distance or height to which a thing is lifted or raised. **3.** the amount that can be lifted at one time. **4.** a free ride given to a person: *The hitchhiker was given a lift into town.* **5.** an elevating influence or effect, especially a happy feeling: *The compliment gave her a lift.* **6.** *British.* see **elevator** *(def.1).* **7.** one of the layers of leather, rubber, or plastic at the bottom of the heel of a shoe. **—lift′er,** *n.*

lift-off (lift′ôf′) *n.* the action of a rocket or spacecraft as it rises from its launching pad.

lig·a·ment (lig′ə mənt) *n.* a band of strong tissue that connects two bones or cartilages or holds an organ of the body in place.

lig·a·ture (lig′ə choor′, lig′ə chər) *n.* **1.** something that is used to bind or tie. **2.** a thread, wire, or string used in surgery to tie off a blood vessel to stop bleeding. **3.** *Printing.* two or more letters joined together to form one character. æ is a ligature.

light¹ (līt) *n.* **1.** a form of radiation that can be detected by the human eye and that travels at a speed of about 186,000 miles per second. **2.** a form of radiation similar to this but invisible to the human eye, especially ultraviolet or infrared radiation. **3.** the condition that makes seeing possible; illumination: *We walked slowly because there was almost no light in the tunnel.* **4.** a particular instance of such illumination: *a strong light, a bright light.* **5.** the sensation produced by stimulation of the organs of sight: *The light hurt his eyes when he walked from the dark house into the street.* **6.** a source of illumination or brightness, such as a lamp or candle: *Turn off the lights when you leave.* **7.** the illumination that comes from the sun; daylight: *Plants grow rapidly when exposed to light.* **8.** dawn; daybreak. **9.** something, such as a flame or spark, used to ignite or set fire to a substance: *Give me a light for my cigarette.* **10.** knowledge or information; understanding: *The investigation shed new light on the mystery.* **11.** public knowledge: *That political scandal has recently come to light.* **12.** the way in which something is seen or judged: *Once he had graduated from college, his parents saw him in a new light.* **13.** an outstanding or well-known person: *He is one of the leading lights in the field of medicine.* **—adj.** **1.** having light; bright; not dark: *The room was lighter in the morning than in the afternoon.* **2.** pale or whitish in color: *a light pink, a light complexion.* **—v., light·ed** *or* **lit, light·ing.** **—v.t.** **1.** to cause to catch fire; kindle; ignite: *to light a candle.* **2.** to cause to give off light: *to light a lamp.* **3.** to give light to; illuminate: *One large bulb lighted the whole room.* **4.** to make bright or lively. **5.** to show the way to by means of a light or lights. **—v.i.** **1.** to take fire; become ignited: *Wet wood will not light easily.* **2.** to become bright or radiant: *Her face lighted up when she heard the good news.* [Old English *lēoht.*]

in the light of. because of: *In the light of this new evidence, the defendant must be found not guilty.*

to see the light. to come to understand something: *She explained the problem several times before I saw the light.*

light² (līt) *adj.* **1.** having little weight; not heavy: *a light suitcase.* **2.** having little weight in proportion to its size or bulk: *Foam rubber is light.* **3.** low in density, amount, force, or degree: *a light wind, a light rain.* **4.** easy to do or bear; not difficult: *light housework, light punishment.* **5.** moving easily; nimble; graceful; agile: *a light step, to be light on one's feet.* **6.** graceful in form or appearance; delicate: *The church had a small, light spire.* **7.** happy, cheerful; carefree: *light laughter, a light heart.* **8.** meant to entertain; not serious: *light reading, light comedy.* **9.** few or slight: *The army suffered light casualties.* **10.** not rich or fatty: *a diet of light foods.* **11.** having an airy or spongy consistency: *The cake is moist and light.* —*adv.* lightly, especially without unnecessary equipment: *to travel light.* [Old English *lēoht, līht.*]

light³ (līt) *v.i.,* **light·ed** or **lit, light·ing. 1.** to get down or descend; alight: *to light from a carriage.* **2.** to settle or come to rest, especially from flight: *A bee lighted on his hand.* **3.** to come by chance; happen: *He lighted on the solution to the problem.* **4.** to fall or strike suddenly: *The blow lighted on his chin.* [Old English *līhtan* to descend.]
  to light into. *Informal.* to attack.
  to light out. *Slang.* to leave suddenly and hastily.

light·en¹ (līt'ən) *v.t.* to make lighter or brighter: *The painter lightened the color by adding white.* —*v.i.* **1.** to become light or bright: *The sky lightened after the storm.* **2.** to flash with lightning. [*Light¹* + *-en¹.*]

light·en² (līt'ən) *v.t.* **1.** to reduce the weight or load of; make less heavy: *to lighten a burden.* **2.** to make less harsh or burdensome: *Machines lighten the work of laborers.* **3.** to make more cheerful; gladden; ease: *to lighten a person's spirits.* [*Light²* + *-en¹.*]

light·er¹ (lī'tər) *n.* a person or thing that causes something to ignite, especially a mechanical device used to light cigarettes, cigars, or the like. [*Light¹* + *-er¹.*]

light·er² (lī'tər) *n.* a flat-bottomed barge usually used in a harbor for loading and unloading ships or for transporting goods short distances. —*v.t.* to transport (goods) in a lighter. [Dutch *lichter.*]

light·face (līt'fās') *n. Printing.* a type whose characters have thin, light lines.

light-foot·ed (līt'foot'id) *adj.* having a light and graceful step.

light-head·ed (līt'hed'id) *adj.* **1.** somewhat faint or delirious; dizzy. **2.** not serious or sensible in attitude or behavior; flighty. —**light'-head'ed·ly,** *adv.* —**light'-head'ed·ness,** *n.*

light-heart·ed (līt'här'tid) *adj.* free from care or anxiety; cheerful; gay. —**light'-heart'ed·ly,** *adv.* —**light'-heart'ed·ness,** *n.*

light·house (līt'hous') *n. pl.,* **light·hous·es** (līt'hou'ziz). a tower or similar structure equipped with a powerful light, built as a warning and guide to ships near a place dangerous to navigation.

Lighthouse

light·ing (lī'ting) *n.* **1.** the act of lighting or the state of being lighted; illumination. **2.** an arrangement or system of lights: *the lighting of a stage in a theater.*

light·ly (līt'lē) *adv.* **1.** with little weight or force; not heavily: *She stroked the cat lightly.* **2.** in a small degree or amount: *to season food lightly.* **3.** with a light or easy motion: *The leaf floated lightly down the stream.* **4.** nimbly: *to step lightly.* **5.** in a carefree manner; cheerfully: *The team ac-* cepted its defeat lightly. *This is too serious a matter to be taken lightly.*

light meter *Photography.* a device used to measure the intensity of light in a certain place and thus determine the correct exposure. Also, **exposure meter.**

light-mind·ed (līt'mīn'did) *adj.* characterized by a lack of seriousness; frivolous.

light·ness¹ (līt'nis) *n.* **1.** the quality or the state of being light; brightness. **2.** paleness of color. [Old English *līhtnes.*]

light·ness² (līt'nis) *n.* **1.** the quality or the state of having relatively little weight, heaviness, force, or the like. **2.** the quality of being nimble or graceful; agility: *The dancer's lightness makes her perfect for the role of the fairy.* **3.** lack of seriousness; frivolity. [*Light²* + *-ness.*]

light·ning (līt'ning) *n.* a flash of light in the sky, caused by an electrical discharge between clouds or between a cloud and the ground.

lightning bug, another term for **firefly.**

lightning rod, a metal rod that is used to protect a building from damage by lightning by conducting the electricity to the ground.

light·ship (līt'ship') *n.* a ship having lights and signals, moored at a place that is dangerous to navigation as a warning and guide to ships.

light·weight (līt'wāt') *n.* **1.** a person or thing of less than average weight. **2.** a boxer weighing between 127 and 135 pounds. —*adj.* **1.** light in weight. **2.** of or relating to a lightweight.

light-year (līt'yēr') *n.* an astronomical unit of distance equal to the distance that light travels through space in one year, or approximately 5.878 trillion miles.

lig·nite (lig'nīt) *n.* a brownish-black, low-quality coal in which the texture of the original wood can be seen.

lik·a·ble (lī'kə bəl) *also,* **like·a·ble.** *adj.* pleasing; agreeable: *She was a likable young woman.* —**lik'a·ble·ness,** *n.*

like¹ (līk) *prep.* **1.** having a close resemblance to; similar to: *She looks like her sister.* **2.** in the same way as; similarly to: *You're acting like a baby!* **3.** characteristic or typical of: *It was just like him to forget her birthday.* **4.** such as: *He does well in subjects like math and science.* **5.** inclined to; desirous of: *Do you feel like going for a walk?* **6.** giving promise or indication of: *It looks like a long, cold winter.* —*adj.* **1.** having identical or similar form, appearance, or characteristics; similar: *The two sisters wore like dresses.* **2.** equal or equivalent: *to donate a like amount.* —*adv. Informal.* probably; likely: *Like enough she'll arrive today.* —*n.* **1.** a person or thing that is considered equal, as in qualities or values, to another; match: *I shall not look upon his like again* (Shakespeare, *Hamlet*). **2.** something of a similar nature: *We bought tomatoes, lettuce, cucumbers, and the like.* —*conj. Informal.* **1.** in the way that; as: *This soup doesn't taste like it should.* **2.** as if; as though: *It looks like it will rain today.* [Old English *līc, gelīc.*]

like² (līk) *v.,* **liked, lik·ing.** —*v.t.* **1.** to take pleasure in; enjoy: *He likes football and baseball.* **2.** to feel affection, tenderness, or fondness for: *I like her more now that I know her better.* **3.** to wish or desire; prefer: *Would you like another piece of cake?* —*v.i.* to have a desire or wish; choose; prefer: *Come whenever you like.* —*n.* usually,

at; āpe; cär; end; mē; it; īce; hot; ōld; fôrk; wood; fōol; oil; out; up; turn; sing; thin; this; hw in white; zh in treasure. The symbol ə stands for the sound of **a** in about, **e** in taken, **i** in pencil, **o** in lemon, and **u** in circus.

L

likes. preference; taste: *She has strange likes and dislikes.* [Old English *līcian* to please.]

-like *suffix* (used to form adjectives from nouns) **1.** resembling or similar to; having the characteristics of: *catlike, childlike.* **2.** appropriate or fit for; suited to: *businesslike, ladylike.*

like·a·ble (līʹkə bəl) *adj.* another spelling of **likable.** —**likeʹa·ble·ness,** *n.*

like·li·hood (līkʹlē hood′) *n.* probability: *In all likelihood, I will leave tomorrow.*

like·ly (līkʹlē) *adj.,* **like·li·er, like·li·est. 1.** apparently true; probably: *a likely cause.* **2.** having or showing a tendency or possibility: *It is likely to rain tomorrow.* **3.** suitable, appropriate: *a likely spot to build a house.* **4.** promising: *a likely candidate.* —*adv.* probably: *She's most likely very intelligent.*

lik·en (līʹkən) *v.t.* to represent as like; compare: *He likened her eyes to stars.*

like·ness (līkʹnis) *n. pl.,* **like·ness·es. 1.** the state or quality of being alike; resemblance: *The two brothers' likeness was very noticeable.* **2.** a picture or other representation. **3.** appearance; form; guise: *The Greek god Zeus often took on the likeness of an animal.*

like·wise (līkʹwīz′) *adv.* **1.** in a like manner; similarly: *I became angry, and he reacted likewise.* **2.** in addition; also.

lik·ing (līʹking) *n.* a preference or fondness.

li·lac (līʹlək) *n.* **1.** a purple, pink, or white flower cluster made up of tiny, fragrant, tube-shaped flowers. **2.** the shrub or small tree that bears this flower. **3.** a pale pinkish-purple color. —*adj.* having the color lilac.

Lilac

Li·long·we (li lông′wā′) *n.* the capital of Malawi, in the west-central part of the country. Pop. (1975 est.), 102,000.

lilt (lilt) *v.t., v.i.* to sing or play (music) with a light, graceful rhythm. —*n.* **1.** a lively song or tune with a light, graceful rhythm. **2.** a lively and rhythmic quality.

lil·y (lilʹē) *n. pl.,* **lil·ies. 1.** a showy, trumpet-shaped flower growing singly or in clusters. **2.** the plant bearing this flower, growing directly from an underground bulb and bearing narrow leaves. **3.** any of various other plants, such as the water lily. —*adj.* like a lily, as in whiteness, delicacy, or beauty. —**lilʹy·like′,** *adj.*

Lily

lily of the valley *pl.,* **lilies of the valley. 1.** a long cluster of small, fragrant, usually white, bell-shaped flowers that grow down one side of a stalk of a plant related to the lily. **2.** the plant bearing this flower, having long, oval leaves.

Li·ma (lēʹmə) *n.* the capital of Peru, in the west-central part of the country. Pop. (1970 est.), 1,800,000.

li·ma bean (līʹmə) **1.** the pale green, kidney-shaped seed of a plant related to the pea, cooked and eaten as a vegetable. **2.** the plant bearing this seed.

limb (lim) *n.* **1.** a part of the body of an animal or human other than the head and torso; an arm, leg, wing, or flipper. **2.** one of the large branches of a tree.

lim·ber (limʹbər) *adj.* bending or moving easily; flexible: *She kept herself limber by exercising.* —*v.t.* to make limber: *He limbered up his arm before the game.* —*v.i.* to become limber, especially by exercising. —**limʹber·ness,** *n.*

lim·bo (limʹbō) *n. pl.,* **lim·bos. 1.** *also,* **Limbo.** in Roman Catholic theology, the abode of souls not entitled to enter Heaven, but not condemned to the punishment of Hell, especially those of infants who died before being baptized. **2.** a place or condition of oblivion or neglect for unwanted, useless, or forgotten people or things.

Lim·burg·er (limʹbur′gər) *n.* a semisoft, white cheese having a strong smell. [From *Limburg,* a province in Belgium where it was first made.]

lime¹ (līm) *n.* a white, powdery compound of calcium and oxygen, usually prepared by burning limestone. It is used in making cement and as a fertilizer. Also, **quicklime.** —*v.t.,* **limed, lim·ing.** to treat with lime; apply lime to. [Old English *līm.*]

lime² (līm) *n.* **1.** a small, yellowish-green, oval or round citrus fruit having a thin rind and a juicy, tart pulp. **2.** the thorny evergreen tree bearing this fruit. [French *lime.*]

lime³ (līm) another word for **linden.**

lime·light (līmʹlīt′) *n.* **1.** a strong light used in the theater to cast light upon a performer, part of the stage, or the like, originally produced by heating lime. **2.** a prominent position before the public; center of interest: *The election victory put the candidate's family in the limelight.*

lim·er·ick (limʹər ik) *n.* a humorous verse form of five lines. For example: *There was an old lady of Reading/Who never knew where she was heading./She'd start to the east/On her way to a feast,/And end in the north at a wedding.* [From *Limerick,* a county in Ireland; said to be from a chorus "Will you come up to *Limerick?*", which followed nonsense verse.]

lime·stone (līmʹstōn′) *n.* a rock consisting chiefly of calcium carbonate, used for building, and for making lime.

lime·wa·ter (līmʹwô′tər) *n.* a solution of lime and water, used as an antacid and to test for the presence of carbon dioxide.

lim·it (limʹit) *n.* **1.** the furthest range, extent, or boundary; point at which something ends or must end: *to exceed the speed limit, to reach the limit of one's patience.* **2.** *also,* **limits.** boundary: *Do not drive beyond the city limits.* **3.** the greatest amount or quantity allowed: *The fisherman caught more than the limit of trout.* —*v.t.* to keep within a bound or bounds; restrict; confine: *to limit spending.*

lim·i·ta·tion (lim′ə tā′shən) *n.* **1.** something that limits; limiting condition or circumstance: *His lack of coordination is a serious limitation in sports.* **2.** the act of limiting or the state of being limited.

lim·it·ed (lim′ə tid) *adj.* **1.** kept within a limit or limits; restricted: *The offer is good for a limited time only.* **2.** lacking imagination, independence, or originality; narrow: *She is a limited person with few interests.* **3.** (of trains, buses, or other public conveyances) making only a small number of stops and carrying few passengers. **4.** restricted in liability to the amount of capital invested by stockholders: *a limited company.* —*n.* a limited train, bus, or other public conveyance.

limn (lim) *v.t.* **1.** to paint or draw. **2.** to portray in words.

lim·ou·sine (lim′ə zēn′, lim′ə zēn′) *n.* **1.** a large sedan with a glass partition between the front and back seats, often driven by a chauffeur. **2.** a large automobile used as a commercial passenger vehicle: *an airport limousine.*

limp¹ (limp) *v.i.* **1.** to walk lamely. **2.** to move or proceed slowly or with difficulty: *The old car limped along the dirt road.* —*n.* a lame walk or movement. [Probably related to Old English *lemphealt* lame.]

limp² (limp) *adj.* **1.** lacking stiffness or firmness; wilted: *After three days the flowers became limp.* **2.** without force or vigor; weak: *a limp argument.* [Possibly of Scandinavian origin.] —**limp′ly,** *adv.* —**limp′ness,** *n.*

lim·pet (lim′pit) *n.* a brownish-green, saltwater shellfish that has a cone-shaped shell and clings to rocks.

lim·pid (lim′pid) *adj.* clear or transparent: *a limpid pool of water.* —**lim·pid′i·ty,** *n.* —**lim′pid·ly,** *adv.*

lim·y (lī′mē) *adj.,* **lim·i·er, lim·i·est.** of, containing, or like lime.

linch·pin (linch′pin′) *n.* a pin that passes through the end of an axle to keep the wheel in place.

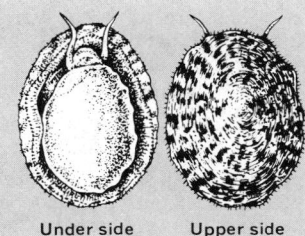

Under side   Upper side

Limpet

Lin·coln (ling′kən) *n.* **1. Abraham.** 1809–1865, the sixteenth president of the United States, from 1861 to 1865. **2.** the capital of Nebraska, in the southeastern part of the state. Pop. (1970), 149,518.

Lind·bergh, Charles A(ugustus) (lind′burg′) 1902–1974, the U.S. aviator who made the first solo, nonstop airplane flight across the Atlantic, in 1927.

lin·den (lin′dən) *n.* any of a large group of tall trees bearing broad, usually heart-shaped, leaves and drooping clusters of small, fragrant, pale yellow flowers.

line¹ (līn) *n.* **1.** a long, narrow mark or stroke, as that made by a pen, pencil, or tool: *White lines divided the lanes of the highway.* **2.** anything resembling such a mark: *Her brow was creased with lines of worry.* **3.** an outline, contour, or profile: *the sleek lines of a sports car.* **4.** a limit or boundary, as between two areas; border: *The town is two miles from the state line.* **5.** a division or separation between contrasting ideas, qualities, conditions, or the like: *the line between fantasy and reality.* **6.** a number of persons or things arranged in one continuous series; row: *We waited in a long line outside the movie theater.* **7.** a continuous series of persons or things following one another in time: *Elizabeth I was the last ruler of the Tudor line.* **8.** a row of words or letters printed or written between the margins of a page or column. **9.** a short letter; note: *She dropped me a line thanking me for the gift.* **10.** a series of words forming a single verse of poetry: *There are six lines in each stanza of the poem.* **11. lines.** the spoken words of a theatrical presentation, especially those for a single performer: *The actor forgot his lines.* **12.** a course or direction of progress or movement: *An innocent bystander was caught in the line of fire.* **13.** a course of action, conduct, or thought; method: *I had trouble understanding the author's line of reasoning.* **14.** *also,* **lines.** a general plan, as of construction, action, or procedure: *The house was designed along very simple lines.* **15.** an area or range of interest, activity, or ability: *Cooking is my line.* **16.** a particular business or activity: *He is in the banking line.* **17.** a kind of goods or merchandise: *The store is selling a new line of bicycles.* **18.** a wire or series of wires connecting points or stations in a telegraph or telephone system. **19.** a connection or contact made between two points in such a system: *Her line is busy.* **20.** a system of transportation consisting of public conveyances traveling regularly over an established route: *a steamship line, a bus line.* **21.** one branch of such a system of transportation. **22.** a track of a railroad: *The workers laid down a new line over the mountains.* **23.** a cord, rope, wire, cable, or the like designed or used for a specific purpose: *a fishing line, to hang wet clothes on a line.* **24.** a channel, wire, or pipe that carries gas, water, or electricity, or the like, from one point to another. **25.** *Mathematics.* the path traced by a moving point thought of as having length but no thickness.

A line may be straight or curved. **26.** *Football.* **a.** see **line of scrimmage.** **b.** the row of players arranged along the line of scrimmage at the beginning of a play. **27. lines.** the arrangement of troops in closest contact with opposing troops: *He was captured behind enemy lines.* **28.** *Informal.* glib, often insincere talk. —*v.,* **lined, lin·ing.** —*v.t.* **1.** to mark or cover with lines: *to line paper. Age lined her face.* **2.** to place or arrange in a line: *The teacher lined the children up according to height.* **3.** to arrange or form a line along; border: *Trees lined the edge of the road.* —*v.i.* to form a line: *People lined up in front of the theater.* [A combination of Old French *ligne* string, cord and Old English *līne* cord, rope.]

all along the line. at every point; in every way.

in line. a. in a line or row. **b.** in agreement: *Most of the speaker's ideas were in line with my own.*

in line for. due for or deserving of: *He is in line for a promotion.*

on a line. even; level.

out of line. not in agreement.

to draw the line. to set the limit.

to hold the line. to maintain a firm position: *The government tried to hold the line against inflation.*

to line up. to gather, get, or arrange for: *to line up support for a proposed law.*

to read between the lines. to understand a hidden meaning.

line² (līn) *v.t.,* **lined, lin·ing. 1.** to cover the inner surface of: *The tailor lined the jacket with silk.* **2.** to supply or fill: *The shelves were lined with books.* **3.** to be used as a lining or covering for: *Portraits lined the walls.* [Middle English *linen* originally, to cover with flax.]

lin·e·age (lin′ē ij) *n.* **1.** a line of direct descent from an ancestor. **2.** those descended from a common ancestor; family.

lin·e·al (lin′ē əl) *adj.* **1.** in the direct line of descent: *The king's grandchild is a lineal heir to the throne.* **2.** of or based upon direct descent; hereditary: *a lineal right to a title.* **3.** of or like a line; linear. —**lin′e·al·ly,** *adv.*

lin·e·a·ment (lin′ē ə mənt) *n.* a feature, detail, or outline of a body or figure, especially of the face.

lin·e·ar (lin′ē ər) *adj.* **1.** of or relating to a line or lines. **2.** consisting of or making use of lines: *a linear drawing.* **3.** along a line or lines: *linear motion.* **4.** relating to length: *the linear dimension of a room.* **5.** like a line; long and narrow: *a linear leaf.* —**lin′e·ar·ly,** *adv.*

linear equation *Mathematics.* an algebraic equation whose graph is a straight line.

linear measure 1. measurement by length. **2.** a unit or system of units for measuring length.

line·back·er (līn′bak′ər) *n.* a defensive player in football, whose position is directly behind the line.

line drive *Baseball.* a strongly hit ball that travels close to the ground in a nearly straight line.

line·man (līn′mən) *n. pl.,* **line·men** (līn′mən). **1.** *also,* **linesman.** a person who installs or repairs telegraph, telephone, or electric wires. **2.** a person who inspects railroad tracks. **3.** *Football.* any of the players in the line.

lin·en (lin′ən) *n.* **1.** a strong cloth woven from flax fibers, used for dresses, suits, and tablecloths. **2.** *also,* **linens.**

at; āpe; cär; end; mē; it; īce; hot; ōld; fôrk; wood; fool; oil; out; up; turn; sing; thin; this; hw in white; zh in treasure. The symbol ə stands for the sound of **a** in about, **e** in taken, **i** in pencil, **o** in lemon, and **u** in circus.

L

household articles, such as sheets, tablecloths, towels, and napkins, made of linen or similar cloth. —*adj.* made of linen: *linen napkins.*

line of force *Physics.* an imaginary line in a field of electric or magnetic force, showing the direction of force of the field.

line of scrimmage, an imaginary line running across a football field parallel to the goal lines, on which the ball is placed by the referee. A new line is established wherever the ball is ruled dead at the end of a play.

lin·er[1] (līʹnər) *n.* **1.** a ship or airplane operated by a transportation line, especially an oceangoing passenger ship. **2.** a person or thing that makes lines. [*Line*[1] +*-er*[1].]

lin·er[2] (līʹnər) *n.* **1.** something serving as a lining: *a trash can liner.* **2.** a person who lines or fits a lining to something. [*Line*[2] + *-er*[1].]

line segment, the part of a line made up of two given points and all the points between them.

lines·man (līnzʹmən) *n. pl.,* **lines·men** (līnzʹmən). **1.** an official who assists the referee in football, tennis, hockey, and other sports. **2.** see **lineman** *(def. 1).*

line·up (līnʹup′) *also,* **line-up.** *n.* **1.** an arrangement of persons or things in a line or row. **2.** a number of people lined up by the police so that a criminal suspect can be identified by a victim or witness. **3.a.** the players on a team actually participating in play at any given time during a game. **b.** a list of such players.

-ling *suffix* (used to form nouns) **1.** little; unimportant: *duckling.* **2.** a person or thing that is related to, characterized by, or concerned with: *earthling.*

lin·ger (lingʹgər) *v.i.* **1.** to stay on as if reluctant to leave; delay leaving: *The fans lingered outside the locker room after the game was over.* **2.** to go or act at a slow pace; dawdle: *Mother told him not to linger on the way home.*

lin·ge·rie (län′zhə rā′, lan′zhə rē′) *n.* women's underwear, nightgowns, robes, and similar garments.

lin·go (lingʹgō) *n. pl.,* **lin·goes.** language or speech that is strange or hard to understand to a person who is unfamiliar with it: *medical lingo, sports lingo.*

lin·gual (lingʹgwəl) *adj.* **1.** of or relating to the tongue. **2.** (of speech sounds) formed chiefly with the tongue, as the letter *t.* **3.** of language or languages.

lin·guist (lingʹgwist) *n.* **1.** an expert in linguistics. **2.** a person who can speak or is skilled in several languages.

lin·guis·tic (ling gwisʹtik) *adj.* of or relating to language or linguistics. —**lin·guis·ti·cal·ly,** *adv.*

lin·guis·tics (ling gwisʹtiks) *n., pl.* **1.** the scientific study of language. **2.** the study of the development and structure of a particular language. ▲ used with a singular verb.

● The science of **linguistics** has developed fairly recently. People have thought about language since ancient times; Hebrew, Greek, and Hindu scholars all studied language more than two thousand years ago. But it was not really until the nineteenth century that *linguists* began to examine language scientifically, by carefully and systematically studying the characteristics of many different languages. These linguists concentrated on comparing languages to determine their similarities. They learned that an ancient language no longer in existence, called *Indo-European,* was the basis for almost all the languages spoken in Europe, such as Greek, Spanish, Russian, and English.

In the twentieth century, linguists set out to study non-European languages that were currently being spoken, rather than examining past languages or those spoken only in Europe. They concentrated especially on the languages of the American Indians. From their research, they learned that many characteristics of European languages, which had been assumed to be true of all language, were

not found at all in some non-European tongues. For example, one American Indian language has present, past, and future tenses for nouns, just as English does for verbs. That is, it has three different words for our word *house*—one for a house that now exists, a second for a house that once was built but no longer exists, and a third for a house that will be built. On the other hand, another Indian language has no nouns at all.

The most important thing that linguists learned from these studies is that the languages of so-called "primitive" peoples are just as complicated as those of "civilized" people. Previously, it had been thought that groups of people that were not as "advanced" as Europeans or Americans spoke much simpler languages, with a very small vocabulary and a less complex system of grammar. Linguists discovered that each language fulfills the needs of the people who speak it. The Eskimo language may have no words for *laser* or *microscope,* because these things are not important in Eskimo culture. But while English has one word for *snow,* Eskimo has several, because snow is such an important part of the life of the Eskimos that they need various words to describe different kinds of snow.

The conclusion that linguists drew from their findings is that all languages are basically equal. French and German are not "better" than native African languages because they have a different vocabulary, including more scientific and literary terms. All languages exist in order to enable the members of a group of people to communicate information, thoughts, and feelings to one another, and these things differ according to each group's way of life. The differences between languages are only reflections of the different ways that various groups of people live.

See the note under **language** for further information.

---

lin·i·ment (linʹə mənt) *n.* a liquid rubbed on the skin to relieve pain or stiffness, as from a bruise, sore muscle, or sprain.

lin·ing (līʹning) *n.* **1.** the surface, layer, or coating covering the inside of something: *the stomach lining, the silk lining of a jacket.* **2.** a material used for this purpose.

link (lingk) *n.* **1.** one of the rings or loops of a chain. **2.** something like a link in a chain: *links of sausage.* **3.** anything that joins or connects: *a link with the past.* —*v.t.* to join by a link or links; unite; connect: *Everyone linked arms and formed a circle.* —*v.i.* to be joined by or as if by a link or links.

link·age (lingʹkij) *n.* **1.** the act of linking or the state of being linked. **2.** a system or series of links.

linking verb, a verb that connects a subject with a predicate adjective or noun without expressing action. In the sentence *Her eyes are lovely,* the word *are* is a linking verb. *Appear, be,* and *seem* are linking verbs.

links (lingks) *n., pl.* another word for **golf course.**

lin·net (linʹit) *n.* a small songbird of Europe and Asia.

li·no·le·um (li nōʹlē əm) *n.* a floor covering made by putting a mixture of linseed oil, finely ground cork or wood, resins, and pigments on a backing of burlap or canvas.

li·no·type (līʹnə tīp′) *n. Trademark.* in printing, a machine for setting type, operated by a keyboard, that sets and casts a line of type in one piece of metal.

lin·seed (linʹsēd′) *n.* the seed of flax, the source of linseed oil.

linseed oil, a yellow or brown oil obtained from the seed of certain flax plants, used in making paints, varnish, printing ink, patent leather, and linoleum.

lin·sey-wool·sey (linʹzē woolʹzē) *n. pl.,* **lin·sey-woolseys.** a strong, coarse, loosely woven fabric of wool and linen or cotton.

lint (lint) *n.* **1.** tiny bits of thread or fluff: *Lint collects easily on a dark fabric.* **2.** a soft, downy, or fleecy material obtained by scraping linen fibers, formerly used as a dressing for wounds.

lin·tel (lint′əl) *n.* a horizontal part or piece set above an opening, as of a door or window, to support the structure above it.

li·on (lī′ən) *n.* **1.** a large animal of the cat family, native to Africa and southern Asia, having a tawny coat of short, coarse hair and a tufted tail. The male has a shaggy mane around the neck, head, and shoulders. **2.** a man of great strength or courage. **3.** a famous person; celebrity.

Lion

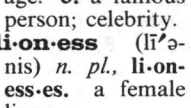
Lioness

Lion and lioness

li·on·ess (lī′ə·nis) *n. pl.,* **li·on·ess·es.** a female lion.

li·on·heart·ed (lī′ən härt′id) *adj.* brave; courageous.

li·on·ize (lī′ə nīz′) *v.t.,* **li·on·ized, li·on·iz·ing.** to treat as very important.

lip (lip) *n.* **1.** either of the two fleshy folds forming the opening of the mouth. **2.** the edge or rim of an opening or cavity: *the lip of a crater, the lip of a pitcher.* **3.** *Botany.* the protruding part in certain plants where the calyx or corolla is divided into unequal parts, as in a snapdragon or orchid. —**lip′like′,** *adj.*

 to keep a stiff upper lip. to face misfortune with courage.

li·pase (lī′pās, lip′ās) *n.* an enzyme that aids in the breaking down of fats into glycerin and fatty acids.

lip-read (lip′rēd′) *v.i.,* **lip-read** (lip′red′), **lip-read·ing.** to engage in lip reading. —**lip′-read′er,** *n.*

lip reading, the act or skill of understanding what someone is saying by watching the movements of his lips, used especially by people who are deaf.

lip·stick (lip′stik′) *n.* a stick of waxlike cosmetic used to color the lips, usually in a small case.

liq·ue·fac·tion (lik′wə fak′shən) *n.* the act of liquefying or the state of being liquefied.

liq·ue·fy (lik′wə fī′) *v.t., v.i.,* **liq·ue·fied, liq·ue·fy·ing.** to change into a liquid. —**liq′ue·fi′er,** *n.*

li·queur (li kur′) *n.* a strong, sweet-flavored alcoholic beverage. Also, **cordial.**

liq·uid (lik′wid) *n.* a form of matter that is not solid or gaseous, characterized by the ability of its atoms or molecules to move about freely within a given area, but not completely independently of the other atoms or molecules. A liquid can take on the shape of its container, but will not necessarily fill it. —*adj.* **1.** in the form of, or having the properties of, a liquid; capable of flowing or being poured: *The medicine comes in liquid form.* **2.** clear or transparent; shining: *liquid eyes.* **3.** gracefully flowing and smooth: *the liquid motion of the ballerina's arms.* **4.** consisting of, or easily changed into, cash: *Bonds are among the liquid assets he owns.*

liquid air, a bluish, transparent or milky liquid formed when air is put under great pressure and then cooled, used as a refrigerant.

liq·ui·date (lik′wə dāt′) *v.t.,* **liq·ui·dat·ed, liq·ui·dat·ing.** **1.** to pay off or settle (a debt). **2.** to settle the accounts of (a business). **3.** to do away with; get rid of. **4.** to murder: *The gangster was liquidated by a rival mob.* —**liq′ui·da′tion,** *n.*

li·quid·i·ty (li kwid′ə tē) *n.* the state or quality of being liquid.

liquid measure, a unit or system of units for measuring the volume of liquids.

liquid oxygen, an extremely cold liquid obtained by putting oxygen under very great pressure and then cooling it, used as fuel in rocket engines.

liq·uor (lik′ər) *n.* **1.** an alcoholic drink that is produced by distillation, as whiskey, rather than by fermentation, as beer. **2.** any liquid, especially a liquid in which food has been cooked.

li·ra (lēr′ə) *n. pl.,* **li·re** (lēr′ā) or **li·ras.** the monetary unit of Italy.

Lis·bon (liz′bən) *n.* the capital, largest city, and chief seaport of Portugal, in the western part of the country. Pop. (1969 est.), 830,600.

lisle (līl) *n.* **1.** a fine, strong thread, usually made of cotton fibers that have been tightly twisted and given a smooth finish, used chiefly for socks, underwear, and gloves. **2.** a knit fabric made of this thread.

lisp (lisp) *n.* a speech defect in which the sounds of *s* and *z* are mispronounced, usually in such a way that they sound like the *th* in *think* and *them,* respectively. —*v.i., v.t.* to speak with a lisp.

lis·some (lis′əm) *also,* **lis·som.** *adj.* bending or moving easily; limber; supple.

list¹ (list) *n.* a series of names, numbers, words, or other items, set down in a certain order or grouping; catalog; roll: *Make a list of the groceries we need.* —*v.t.* **1.** to make a list of: *She listed the items alphabetically.* **2.** to enter or include in a list: *Her name is listed in the telephone directory.* [French *liste.*]

list² (list) *n.* a tilt or leaning to one side. —*v.i.* to tilt to one side: *The ship listed sharply in the storm.* [Of uncertain origin.]

list³ (list) *Archaic. v.i.* to listen. —*v.t.* to listen to; hear. [Old English *hlystan.*]

lis·ten (lis′ən) *v.i.* **1.** to give attention for the purpose of hearing; try to hear: *We listened for the sound of the bell.* **2.** to pay attention: *The child refused to listen to his mother and did as he pleased.* —**lis′ten·er,** *n.*

Lis·ter, Joseph (lis′tər) 1827–1912, English surgeon who developed antiseptic techniques in performing surgery.

list·ing (lis′ting) *n.* **1.** the act of making or entering in a list. **2.** an entry in a list: *a new listing in the telephone directory.*

list·less (list′lis) *adj.* feeling or showing little interest in anything; lacking energy and a desire to do anything: *She felt dull and listless.* —**list′less·ly,** *adv.* —**list′less·ness,** *n.*

list price, the price of an item, as published in a catalog or price list, often subject to discounts.

lists (lists) *n., pl.* **1.** the field or area in which knights fought tournaments. **2.** any area or place of combat, dispute, or competition.

Liszt, Franz (list; fränts) 1811–1886, Hungarian composer and pianist.

at; āpe; cär; end; mē; it; īce; hot; ōld; fôrk; wood; fōōl; oil; out; up; turn; sing; thin; this; hw in white; zh in treasure. The symbol ə stands for the sound of **a** in about, **e** in taken, **i** in pencil, **o** in lemon, and **u** in circus.

L

lit (lit) a past tense and past participle of **light**¹ and **light**³.

lit. 1. liter. 2. literary; literature.

lit·a·ny (lit′ən ē) *n. pl.,* **lit·a·nies.** 1. a form of prayer consisting of a series of requests spoken by the minister to which the choir or the congregation make fixed responses. 2. any long or repetitious series: *a litany of woes.*

li·tchi (lē′chē) *also,* **li·chee.** *n. pl.,* **li·tchis.** 1. a small, round fruit of a tree that is widely grown in China, having a brittle, red outer shell and juicy white flesh that can be eaten. Also, **litchi nut.** 2. the tree bearing this fruit.

li·ter (lē′tər) *also, British,* **li·tre.** *n.* a unit of capacity in the metric system, equal to one cubic decimeter, 1.05668 U.S. liquid quarts, or about 0.9080 U.S. dry quarts.

lit·er·a·cy (lit′ər ə sē) *n.* the ability to read and write: *Proof of literacy was a requirement for voting.*

lit·er·al (lit′ər əl) *adj.* 1. following the exact words of the original; word for word: *The student prepared a literal translation of the Spanish poem.* 2. based on, following, or giving the usual meaning. The literal meaning of the idiom "to pull one's leg" is to tug on somebody's leg. 3. tending to take what is said in an exact manner; using little imagination: *a literal mind.* 4. according to the facts; not exaggerated: *a literal description.* —**lit′er·al·ness,** *n.*

lit·er·al·ly (lit′ər ə lē) *adv.* 1. in a literal manner: *He translated the story literally.* 2. actually; really: *The city was literally destroyed by the earthquake.*

lit·er·a·ry (lit′ə rer′ē) *adj.* 1. of or relating to literature: *literary history, a literary style.* 2. knowing much about or occupied with literature: *a literary family.*

lit·er·ate (lit′ər it) *adj.* 1. able to read and write. 2. knowing much about literature and culture; well-read: *The professor was a highly literate man.* —*n.* 1. a person who can read and write. 2. a person who is well-educated.

lit·er·a·ture (lit′ər ə chər, lit′ər ə choor′) *n.* 1. works of art composed of written words; writings considered to have artistic value. 2. all the writings dealing with a particular subject: *medical literature.* 3. the activity or profession of writing: *to pursue a career in literature.* 4. printed matter of any kind: *The automobile salesman gave us some literature on the latest model.*

lithe (līth) *adj.* easily bent; flexible; pliant. —**lithe′ly,** *adv.* —**lithe′ness,** *n.*

lith·i·um (lith′ē əm) *n.* a soft, silvery metallic element, the lightest of all metals. Symbol: Li

lith·o·graph (lith′ə graf′) *n.* a print made by lithography. —*v.t.* to produce or copy by lithography. —**lith′o·graph′ic,** *adj.*

li·thog·ra·phy (li thog′rə fē) *n.* the art or process of printing from a smooth stone or other flat surface on which a design has been drawn with a special grease crayon. Water and then ink are applied to the surface, and prints are made as the ink sticks to the crayon image, but not to the moist areas. —**li·thog′ra·pher,** *n.*

lith·o·sphere (lith′ə sfēr′) *n.* the crust of the earth.

Lith·u·a·nia (lith′oo ā′nē ə) *n.* a republic of the Soviet Union, in the northwestern part of the country, on the Baltic Sea. Official name: **Lithuanian Soviet Socialist Republic.** Area, 25,200 sq. mi. Pop. (1970), 3,128,000.

Lith·u·a·ni·an (lith′oo ā′nē ən) *n.* 1. a person who was born or is living in Lithuania. 2. the language of Lithuania. —*adj.* of or relating to Lithuania, its people, or their language.

lit·i·gant (lit′i gənt) *n.* a person carrying on a lawsuit.

lit·i·gate (lit′ə gāt′) *v.t.* to make the subject of a lawsuit: *The tenants litigated their complaints against the landlord.* —*v.i.* to carry on a lawsuit. —**lit′i·ga′tor,** *n.*

lit·i·ga·tion (lit′ə gā′shən) *n.* 1. the act or process of carrying on a lawsuit. 2. a lawsuit.

lit·mus (lit′məs) *n.* a dye obtained from any of various lichens, that turns blue in alkaline solutions and red in acid solutions.

litmus paper, a paper stained with litmus, used to determine whether something is acid or alkaline.

li·tre (lē′tər) *British.* another spelling of **liter.**

lit·ter (lit′ər) *n.* 1. bits or scraps of paper or other rubbish scattered about carelessly; mess: *Broken bottles and other litter filled the empty lot.* 2. young animals born at one time: *a litter of kittens.* 3. loose straw, hay, or similar material used as bedding for animals. 4. a vehicle made up of a couch usually enclosed by curtains and carried on men's shoulders or by animals: *Four attendants carried the queen's litter in the procession.* 5. a stretcher for carrying a sick or injured person. —*v.t.* 1. to make disordered or untidy by scattering bits of rubbish about carelessly: *to litter a street with trash.* 2. to give birth to (young). 3. to provide (animals) with litter for bedding. —*v.i.* 1. to scatter bits of rubbish about carelessly: *Littering is against the law.* 2. to give birth to young.

Litter *(def. 4)*

lit·ter·bug (lit′ər bug′) *n. Informal.* a person who litters public places.

lit·tle (lit′əl) *adj.,* **less** or **less·er** or **lit·tler,** **least** or **lit·tlest.** 1. small in size: *A pebble is a little stone.* 2. short in time or distance; brief: *a little while, a little walk.* 3. small in amount or degree; not much: *Add a little water to the mixture.* 4. small in importance or interest; trivial: *a little problem.* 5. small in nature, mind, or spirit; mean; narrow: *She has a nasty little mind.* —*adv.,* **less, least.** to a small extent; not much; slightly: *That poet is little known outside his own country.* —*n.* 1. a small amount: *I ate only a little.* 2. a short time or distance: *Step back a little.* —**lit′tle·ness,** *n.*

little by little. by slow degrees; gradually.

to make little of. to treat as unimportant.

to think little of. to have a low opinion of; consider to be unimportant or worthless.

Little Bear, another term for **Ursa Minor.**

Little Bighorn, a river in northern Wyoming and southern Montana, near the site of the battle in which General George Custer and his entire body of troops were killed by Indians in 1876.

Little Dipper, a group of stars in the constellation Ursa Minor, that forms the outline of a dipper.

Little League, a baseball league for boys under thirteen years of age.

Little Rock, the capital and largest city of Arkansas, in the central part of the state. Pop. (1970), 132,483.

little slam *Bridge.* the winning of twelve tricks in a round of play.

li·tur·gi·cal (li tur′ji kəl) *adj.* of or relating to liturgies. Also, **li·tur·gic** (li tur′jik). —**li·tur′gi·cal·ly,** *adv.*

lit·ur·gy (lit′ər jē) *n. pl.,* **lit·ur·gies.** in various churches, the set form of public worship.

liv·a·ble (liv′ə bəl) *also,* **live·a·ble.** *adj.* 1. fit to live in; habitable: *The old house was not livable.* 2. worth living; endurable: *He felt that life would not be livable as a slave.*

live¹ (liv) *v.,* **lived, liv·ing.** —*v.i.* 1. to be alive; have life: *His grandfather lived before the turn of the century.* 2. to continue to exist; remain alive: *He lived for one hundred years.* 3. to support oneself: *That family lives on a small income.* 4. to feed; subsist: *Some birds live on bugs and worms.* 5. to make one's home; dwell: *We live on the* *east side of town.* **6.** to pass or spend one's life: *to live happily.* **7.** to get the fullest enjoyment from life: *After his twenty-first birthday, he really began to live.* —*v.t.* **1.** to pass or spend (one's life): *The young heiress lived a life of luxury.* **2.** to practice or express in one's life: *to live a lie.* [Old English *lifian, libban.*]

   to live down. to live in such a way that (a past mistake, such as a crime) is forgotten or forgiven.

   to live up to. to abide by or fulfill: *He will live up to his end of the bargain.*

   to live with. to bear with; endure: *to live with one's mistakes.*

live² (līv) *adj.* **1.** having life; living: *The hunter brought back a live elephant.* **2.** filled with life; energetic; lively: *a live personality.* **3.** of present interest or importance; current: *a live topic.* **4.** burning: *a live coal.* **5.** containing an explosive charge: *live ammunition.* **6.** carrying electrical current. **7.** seen or presented while actually happening, as on the stage, or on radio or television: *a live performance, a live broadcast.* [Short for *alive.*]

live·a·ble (līv'ə bəl) another spelling of **livable.**

live·li·hood (līv'lē hood') *n.* the means of staying alive or supporting life: *Selling newspapers is his livelihood.*

live·long (līv'lông') *adj.* whole; entire: *She worked the livelong day.*

live·ly (līv'lē) *adj.,* **live·li·er, live·li·est. 1.** full of life, energy, or movement; vigorous; active: *a lively walk.* **2.** gay; cheerful: *a lively tune.* **3.** stimulating; exciting: *a lively debate.* **4.** inventive or creative: *a lively imagination.* **5.** striking; vivid: *lively colors.* **6.** springing back quickly: *a lively tennis ball.* —*adv.* in a lively manner; energetically; vigorously: *to step lively.* —**live'li·ness,** *n.*

liv·en (lī'vən) *v.t.* to make more cheerful, active, or exciting: *Their arrival livened up the party.* —*v.i.* to become more cheerful; brighter: *He livened up after taking a cold shower.*

live oak (līv) an evergreen oak tree found in the southeastern United States.

liv·er¹ (liv'ər) *n.* **1.** a large, reddish-brown gland that produces bile, stores carbohydrates, and performs various other body functions. It is the largest gland in the human body. **2.** the liver of certain animals, used as food. [Old English *lifer.*]

liv·er² (liv'ər) *n.* a person who lives in a certain manner: *an easy liver.* [*Live¹* + *-er¹.*]

liv·er·ied (liv'ər ēd) *adj.* dressed in livery: *liveried servants.*

Liv·er·pool (liv'ər pool') *n.* a port city in western England. Pop. (1971 est.), 603,210.

liv·er·wort (liv'ər wurt') *n.* any of various plants similar to mosses, found throughout the world and growing mostly in damp, shady areas.

liv·er·wurst (liv'ər wurst') *n.* a sausage made mostly of liver, especially pork liver.

liv·er·y (liv'ər ē) *n. pl.,* **liv·er·ies. 1.** a uniform provided for servants: *a doorman in livery.* **2.** any distinctive dress or uniform worn by members of a group or profession. **3.** the stabling and feeding of horses for pay. **4.** see **livery stable.**

livery stable, a stable where horses are cared for and let out for hire, with or without vehicles.

lives (līvz) the plural of **life.**

live·stock (līv'stok') *n.* domestic animals, such as cattle, horses, sheep, or pigs.

live wire (līv) **1.** a wire carrying an electrical current. **2.** *Informal.* an energetic, alert person.

Diaphragm

Liver   *Small*   *Stomach*

Small intestine

Liver¹

liv·id (liv'id) *adj.* **1.** having a pale, usually bluish, color: *His face was livid with rage.* **2.** furious; enraged. **3.** having a grayish-blue color from a bruise. —**liv'id·ly,** *adv.* —**liv'id·ness,** *n.*

liv·ing (liv'ing) *adj.* **1.** having life; being alive: *a living creature.* **2.** of or relating to life, or suitable for life: *Living conditions in the slums are sometimes unbearable.* **3.** still active or in use: *a living language.* **4.** sufficient for living: *a living wage.* **5.** true to life; lifelike: *The portrait was the living image of her.* —*n.* **1.** the fact or state of being alive. **2.** livelihood: *He earns his living as a carpenter.* **3.** a manner of life: *clean living, plain living.*

living room, a room in a home for general family use or for entertaining guests.

Liv·ing·stone, David (liv'ing stən) 1813–1873, Scottish missionary and explorer in Africa.

Li·vo·ni·a (li vō'nē ə) *n.* a city in southeastern Michigan, a suburb of Detroit. Pop. (1970), 110,109.

liz·ard (liz'ərd) *n.* any of a group of scaly reptiles usually having a long, narrow body, four legs, and a tapering tail. Lizards are found in tropical and temperate regions. The chameleon and horned toad are lizards.

lla·ma (lä'mə) *n. pl.,* **lla·mas** or **lla·ma.** a cud-chewing animal of South America that is related to the camel, having a thick, woolly coat and used as a pack animal.

lla·no (lä'nō) *n. pl.,* **lla·nos.** a level grassland or plain, found especially in South America.

lo (lō) *interj.* look; see: *Lo and behold!*

load (lōd) *n.* **1.** something that is carried by a vehicle, as a truck, or by a man or animal: *Each wagon is carrying a load of dirt.*

Llama

2. the amount or quantity than can be carried: *to order a load of bricks.* **3.** something that burdens, wearies, or oppresses: *a load of sorrow, a load of guilt.* **4.** the amount of work a person or machine is expected to do: *The secretary's typing load was twenty letters a day.* **5.** the weight or pressure supported by a structure or part. **6.** a charge or amount of gunpowder or ammunition for a firearm. **7.** external resistance overcome by an engine or other power source. **8.** loads. *Informal.* a great quantity or number: *My sister has loads of friends.* —*v.t.* **1.** to put a load on or in: *to load a shelf with books.* **2.** to place (something) on or in something for carrying: *to load cattle in a boxcar.* **3.** to weigh down; oppress: *The city council loaded the community with taxes.* **4.** to supply abundantly: *Relatives loaded him with gifts when he graduated.* **5.** to slant so as to prejudice the response or outcome: *to load a question.* **6.** to place something needed to begin operation into (an apparatus): *to load a camera, to load a tape recorder.* **7.** to place (something) into an apparatus: *He loaded the film into the camera.* **8.** to place a charge in (a firearm). —*v.i.* **1.** to put on or receive a load. **2.** to place a charge in a firearm. —**load'er,** *n.*

at; āpe; cär; end; mē; it; īce; hot; ōld; fôrk; wood; fo͞ol; oil; out; up; turn; sing; thin; this; hw in white; zh in treasure. The symbol ə stands for the sound of **a** in about, **e** in taken, **i** in pencil, **o** in lemon, and **u** in circus.

L

load·ed (lō′did) *adj.* **1.** carrying a load: *The cart was loaded with fruit.* **2.** slanted so as to prejudice the response or outcome: *a loaded question.* **3.** *Slang.* drunk. **4.** *Slang.* very wealthy.

load·star (lōd′stär′) another spelling of **lodestar.**

load·stone (lōd′stōn′) another spelling of **lodestone.**

loaf¹ (lōf) *n. pl.,* **loaves. 1.** bread molded and baked as one mass. **2.** any molded mass of food: *a meat loaf.* [Old English *hlāf.*]

loaf² (lōf) *v.i.* to spend time doing little or nothing; idle: *My lazy brother loafs all day.* —*v.t.* to spend (time) doing nothing. [Possibly from *loafer.*]

loaf·er (lō′fər) *n.* **1.** a person who loafs; lazy person. **2.** a shoe for informal wear, resembling a moccasin.

loam (lōm) *n.* soil that is a mixture of clay, sand, and silt, often containing decaying leaves and plants. —**loam′y,** *adj.*

loan (lōn) *n.* **1.** the act of lending. **2.** something lent, especially a sum of money lent at interest. —*v.t.* to lend: *The bank loaned them the money for a new car.*

loath (lōth) *also,* **loth.** *adj.* reluctant; unwilling: *I'm loath to go to the dentist for a checkup.*

loathe (lōth) *v.t.,* **loathed, loath·ing.** to feel disgust or strong dislike for; abhor; detest: *to loathe city life.*

loath·ing (lō′thing) *n.* disgust or strong dislike: *to have a loathing for snakes.* —**loath′ing·ly,** *adv.*

loath·some (lōth′səm) *adj.* extremely disgusting or hateful. —**loath′some·ly,** *adv.* —**loath′some·ness,** *n.*

loaves (lōvz) the plural of **loaf¹.**

lob (lob) *v.t.,* **lobbed, lob·bing.** to hit or throw (a ball) in a high, slow arc. —*n.* a ball hit in such a manner.

lob·by (lob′ē) *n. pl.,* **lob·bies. 1.** an entrance hall or large public room, as in an apartment house, hotel, or theater. **2.** a person or group that tries to influence legislators to vote in a certain way. —*v.,* **lob·bied, lob·by·ing.** —*v.i.* to try to influence legislators in their voting to favor some special group or interest. —*v.t.* to promote the passage of (a law) by lobbying.

lob·by·ist (lob′ē ist) *n.* a person who tries to influence legislators to favor a special group or interest.

lobe (lōb) *n.* a rounded projecting part of something: *a lobe of a leaf, the lobe of the ear.*

lobed (lōbd) *adj.* having a lobe or lobes: *a lobed leaf.*

lo·bel·ia (lō bēl′yə) *n.* any of a large group of plants found in many parts of the world, having blue, red, white, or yellow flowers.

lob·lol·ly pine (lob′lol′ē) **1.** a pine tree of the southern United States, having a coarse bark. **2.** the wood of this tree.

lob·ster (lob′stər) *n.* **1.** a saltwater animal having five pairs of legs, including one pair with large pincer claws. Its body is enclosed in a hard, mottled, dark-green shell that turns red when boiled. **2.** its flesh, used as food.

lobster pot, a slatted wooden trap used to catch lobsters.

lo·cal (lō′kəl) *adj.* **1.** of or relating to a particular place: *a local newspaper, local politics.* **2.** limited or restricted; narrow: *The writer's fame is local rather than national.* **3.** stopping at all stations: *a local train.* **4.** relating to or affecting only a particular part or organ of the body: *a local inflammation, a local anesthetic.* —*n.* **1.** a train, bus, or other means of public transportation that stops at all the stations along its route. **2.** a branch or chapter of

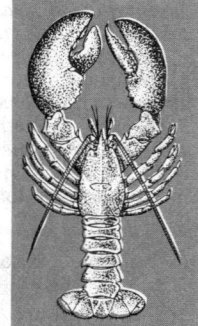
Lobster

an organization, especially a labor union. —**lo′cal·ly,** *adv.*

lo·cale (lō kal′) *n.* a particular place, especially with reference to events or circumstances connected with it; setting: *The play's locale is London during World War II.*

lo·cal·ism (lō′kə liz′əm) *n.* a word, expression, or custom peculiar to a particular place.

lo·cal·i·ty (lō kal′ə tē) *n. pl.,* **lo·cal·i·ties.** a place, region, or district and its surroundings.

lo·cal·ize (lō′kə līz′) *v.t.,* **lo·cal·ized, lo·cal·iz·ing.** to keep within or restrict to a particular place: *The infection was localized in the finger.* —**lo′cal·i·za′tion,** *n.*

lo·cate (lō′kāt) *v.,* **lo·cat·ed, lo·cat·ing.** —*v.t.* **1.** to discover the exact place of: *The police were able to locate the lost child.* **2.** to fix the position of: *The captain located the ship's position on the chart.* **3.** to establish in a particular place; settle: *The company located its branch store in the suburbs.* —*v.i.* to establish oneself in a particular place.

lo·ca·tion (lō kā′shən) *n.* **1.** the act of locating or the state of being located. **2.** an exact position; place: *The police discovered the location of the thief's hideout.* **3.** the place where something, as a store, factory, or home, is or might be established; site: *That busy corner is a perfect location for a drugstore.* **4.** a place away from a motion-picture studio, used in filming.

loch (lok) *n. Scottish.* **1.** a lake. **2.** a narrow arm of the sea, especially one that is partly landlocked.

lo·ci (lō′sī) the plural of **locus.**

lock¹ (lok) *n.* **1.** a mechanical device used to fasten something, as a door, usually consisting of a bolt that is opened by a key having a special shape. **2.** an enclosure in a canal or other waterway, with gates at each end, in which the water level can be changed to raise or lower ships. **3.** the mechanism in a gun that explodes the charge. **4.** any of several holds in wrestling. —*v.t.* **1.** to fasten with a lock or locks: *Don't forget to lock the door.* **2.** to shut up or confine securely: *The guards locked the prisoners up.* **3.** to join or link together firmly: *He locked his arm in hers.* —*v.i.* **1.** to become fastened with a lock or locks: *This door locks automatically when it is closed.* **2.** to become joined or linked together firmly: *The bumpers of the two cars locked.* [Old English *loc.*]

lock² (lok) *n.* **1.** a tuft or strand of hair. **2. locks.** the hair of the head. **3.** a tuft of wool, cotton, or flax. [Old English *locc.*]

lock·er (lok′ər) *n.* **1.** a compartment, as a metal chest or cabinet, that can be locked. **2.** a refrigerated compartment used to store frozen foods.

lock·et (lok′it) *n.* a small ornamental case with a hinged cover, for holding a picture, a lock of hair, or other keepsake. It is usually worn on a chain.

lock·jaw (lok′jô′) *n.* another word for **tetanus.**

lock·out (lok′out′) *n.* the closing of a plant or a business by an employer until certain conditions are met by employees, used to force employees to accept an employer's terms.

lock·smith (lok′smith′) *n.* a person who makes, installs, or repairs locks.

lo·co·mo·tion (lō′kə mō′shən) *n.* the act or power of moving from place to place.

lo·co·mo·tive (lō′kə mō′tiv) *n.* an engine that moves on its own power, used to haul railroad cars. —*adj.* of, relating to, or capable of locomotion.

lo·co·weed (lō′kō wēd′) *n.* a plant of the western United States, containing a poison that is harmful to cattle, sheep, and horses.

lo·cus (lō′kəs) *n. pl.,* **lo·ci. 1.** a place; locality. **2.** *Mathematics.* any set of points that satisfies one or more specified conditions. The locus of all the points in a plane that are equidistant from a given point is a circle.

lo·cust (lō′kəst) *n.* **1.** any of several grasshoppers having short feelers. Locusts travel in huge swarms, destroying the crops in their path. **2.** any of certain cicadas. **3.** any of a group of North American shrubs and trees having clusters of white flowers.

lo·cu·tion (lō kyōō′shən) *n.* **1.** a particular form of expression; phrase. **2.** a style or manner of speech.

lode (lōd) *n.* a deposit or vein containing valuable minerals: *a silver lode.*

lode·star (lōd′stär′) *also,* **load·star.** *n.* a star that serves as a guide to navigators, especially Polaris.

lode·stone (lōd′stōn′) *also,* **load·stone.** *n.* a piece of magnetite that has the properties of a magnet.

lodge (loj) *n.* **1.** a small house, cabin, or hut, especially one used as a place to stay temporarily during a vacation: *a hunting lodge, a ski lodge.* **2.** a branch of an organization, as a fraternity or secret society. **3.** a meeting place for such a branch. **4.** the hut or dwelling of certain North American Indians. **5.** the den of certain wild animals, especially beavers. —*v.,* **lodged, lodg·ing.** —*v.t.* **1.** to provide with a place to stay temporarily, as for the night: *The hurricane victims were lodged in the high school gym.* **2.** to rent a room or rooms to: *The widow lodged students in her home.* **3.** to bring formally to an authority: *to lodge a complaint with the police.* **4.** to put or settle in a particular place or position; fix; embed: *The force of the shot lodged the arrow in a tree.* —*v.i.* **1.** to have a place to stay temporarily: *He lodged with friends for the night.* **2.** to occupy a rented room or rooms. **3.** to be fixed, caught, or embedded: *A pebble lodged in his shoe.*

lodge·ment (loj′mənt) another spelling of **lodgment.**

lodg·er (loj′ər) *n.* a person who rents a room or rooms, as in a private home.

lodg·ing (loj′ing) *n.* **1.** a place to stay temporarily, as for the night: *The couple sought lodging for the night after their car broke down.* **2. lodgings.** a rented room or rooms, as in a private home.

lodg·ment (loj′mənt) *also,* **lodge·ment.** *n.* **1.** the act of lodging or the state of being lodged. **2.** something that is lodged.

Łódź (looj) *n.* a city in central Poland, southwest of Warsaw. Pop. (1970), 761,700.

loess (les, lō′əs) *n.* a yellowish-brown, very fine-grained deposit of silt, commonly found in river valleys.

loft (lôft) *n.* **1.** the upper story of a building, as a warehouse, often used as a storeroom or workroom. **2.** a room or space directly beneath a roof; attic. **3.** a gallery in a hall or church: *a choir loft.* **4.** see **hayloft.** —*v.t.* to hit (a ball) so that it rises in an arc: *The golfer lofted the ball high into the air.*

loft·y (lôf′tē) *adj.,* **loft·i·er, loft·i·est. 1.** extending high in the air; towering: *lofty mountain tops.* **2.** exalted or noble in dignity, rank, character, or quality; elevated: *lofty ideals.* **3.** too proud; haughty: *a lofty manner.* —**loft′i·ly,** *adv.* —**loft′i·ness,** *n.*

log¹ (lôg, log) *n.* **1.** a piece of wood cut from a trunk or limb of a tree, stripped of branches and ready to be sawed. **2.** the record of the voyage of a ship or the flight of an aircraft. **3.** the book in which such records are kept. Also, **logbook. 4.** a device for measuring the speed of a ship. —*v.,* **logged, log·ging.** —*v.t.* **1.** to cut down trees on (an area of land). **2.** to cut (trees) into logs. **3.** to record in a log. **4.** to cover (a certain distance) in a ship or aircraft: *to log 150 miles in three days.* —*v.i.* to cut down trees, cut them into logs, and transport the logs to a sawmill. —*adj.* made of logs: *a log cabin.*

log² (lôg, log) *n.* see **logarithm.**

lo·gan·ber·ry (lō′gən ber′ē) *n. pl.,* **lo·gan·ber·ries. 1.** the tart, reddish-purple fruit of a shrub grown in the

United States. **2.** the thorny shrub bearing this fruit. [From James H. *Logan,* 1841–1928, who first grew this shrub.]

log·a·rithm (lô′gə rith′əm, log′ə rith′əm) *n.* the power to which a fixed number or base must be raised in order to produce a given number. The logarithm of 9 to the base 3 is 2.

log·a·rith·mic (lô′gə rith′mik, log′ə rith′mik) *adj.* of or relating to a logarithm or logarithms: *logarithmic tables.*

log·book (lôg′book′, log′book′) *n.* see **log¹** *(def. 3).*

loge (lōzh) *n.* **1.** a seating area in a theater, made up of the first few rows of the lowest balcony. **2.** a box in a theater.

log·ger (lô′gər, log′ər) *n.* **1.** a person who logs; lumberjack. **2.** a machine for handling logs.

log·ger·head (lô′gər hed′, log′ər hed′) *n.* **1.** a saltwater turtle having a large head, whose flesh and eggs are valued as food. It may weigh as much as 850 pounds. **2.** a stupid person; blockhead.

at loggerheads. taking part in a dispute; quarreling.

log·gia (loj′ə) *n.* an open gallery whose roof is supported by an arcade or colonnade.

log·ging (lô′ging, log′ing) *n.* the work of chopping down trees, cutting them into logs, and transporting the logs to a sawmill.

Loggia

log·ic (loj′ik) *n.* **1.** the science dealing with the rules of correct reasoning and with proof by reasoning; science of correct reasoning. **2.** a system or method of reasoning: *I can't follow your logic.* **3.** sound thinking; reason: *There is much logic in his arguments.*

log·i·cal (loj′i kəl) *adj.* **1.** of, relating to, or in agreement with logic: *a logical explanation.* **2.** following as a natural consequence; reasonably expected: *a logical result.* **3.** capable of reasoning correctly: *a logical mind.* —**log′i·cal·ly,** *adv.*

lo·gi·cian (lō jish′ən) *n.* a person, especially a philosopher, who is skilled in logic.

lo·gis·tic (lō jis′tik) *adj.* of or relating to logistics.

lo·gis·tics (lō jis′tiks) *n., pl.* the branch of military science dealing with the movement, supply, and maintenance of equipment and troops. ▲ used with a singular verb.

log·roll·ing (lôg′rō′ling, log′rō′ling) *n.* **1.** political bargaining among legislators, whereby political aid is given in return for a similar favor. **2.** a sport in which two men stand on a floating log, each trying to get the other off balance and into the water by spinning the log with his feet.

lo·gy (lō′gē) *adj.,* **lo·gi·er, lo·gi·est.** acting or moving slowly; heavy; sluggish.

-logy *combining form* the study or science of: *astrology, theology.*

---

at; āpe; cär; end; mē; it; īce; hot; ōld; fôrk; wood; fōōl; oil; out; up; turn; sing; thin; **th**is; hw in white; zh in treasure. The symbol ə stands for the sound of **a** in about, **e** in taken, **i** in pencil, **o** in lemon, and **u** in circus.

L

loin (loin) *n.* **1.** *usually,* **loins.** in humans and four-legged animals, the part of the body on each side of the backbone, between the hipbone and the lower ribs. **2.** a cut of meat from this part.

loin·cloth (loin′klôth′) *n.* a piece of cloth worn around the hips and loins.

Loire (lwär) *n.* the longest river of France, flowing south into the Bay of Biscay.

loi·ter (loi′tər) *v.i.* **1.** to linger idly or aimlessly about a place: *A group of boys loitered on the corner near the drugstore.* **2.** to move slowly or with frequent pauses: *I always loiter on my way to the dentist.* —*v.t.* to waste (time); dawdle. —**loi′ter·er,** *n.*

loll (lol) *v.i.* **1.** to recline or lean in a careless, lazy, or relaxed manner: *The children lolled about on the lawn.* **2.** to hang down loosely; droop: *The tired dog's tongue lolled out.* —*v.t.* to allow to hang down; let droop.

lol·li·pop (lol′ē pop′) *also,* **lol·ly·pop.** *n.* a piece of candy, especially hard sugar candy, placed on the end of a stick.

Lom·bar·dy (lom′bər dē) *n.* a region of northern Italy.

Lo·mé (lō mā′) *n.* the capital and largest city of Togo. Pop. (1977 est.), 229,400.

Lo·mond, Loch (lō′mənd) a lake in central Scotland.

Lon·don (lun′dən) *n.* **1.** the capital of the United Kingdom and leading city of the Commonwealth of Nations, in southeastern England on the Thames River. Pop. (1978 est.), 6,918,000. **2. City of.** the section of this city that is its financial and commercial center, located on the north bank of the Thames. Area, approx. 1 sq. mi. **3.** a city in southeastern Canada, in Ontario. Pop. (1976), 240,392. **4. Jack.** 1876–1916, U. S. novelist.

Lon·don·der·ry (lun′dən der′ē) *n.* a port city in northwestern Northern Ireland. Pop. (1971), 66,645.

Lon·don·er (lun′də nər) *n.* a person who was born or is living in London.

lone (lōn) *adj.* **1.** without companions; alone; solitary: *a lone traveler.* **2.** standing apart from others; isolated: *a lone tree.* **3.** only; sole: *the lone survivor of a wreck.*

lone·ly (lōn′lē) *adj.,* **lone·li·er, lone·li·est. 1.** solitary; lone: *a lonely hill.* **2.** unhappy from a lack of friendship or companionship; lonesome: *The coming of the dark always made him feel lonely* (Ernest Hemingway). **3.** causing such unhappiness: *a lonely room, a lonely evening.* **4.** not often visited by people; isolated; deserted: *a lonely stretch of highway.* —**lone′li·ness,** *n.*

lone·some (lōn′səm) *adj.* **1.** feeling unhappy because of a lack of friendship or companionship. **2.** causing such unhappiness: *a lonesome journey.* **3.** not often visited by people; deserted: *a lonesome road.*

long[1] (lông) *adj.,* **long·er, long·est. 1.** having great extent in space or time from end to end; not short: *a long highway, a long wait.* **2.** having a specified length: *The road is only two blocks long. The program was an hour long.* **3.** containing many items or entries: *a long grocery list.* **4.** (of vowels) taking more time to pronounce than other sounds. The *e* in *be* is long. —*adv.* **1.** for a great extent of space or time: *He did not stay long.* **2.** throughout the length of: *The phone rang all day long.* **3.** far from the time indicated: *long after, long ago.* —*n.* a long time: *They should be back before long.* [Old English *lang, long.*]

long[2] (lông) *v.i.* to have a strong or restless desire; yearn: *He longed to see his old school friends again.* [Old English *langian.*]

long., longitude.

Long Beach, a city in southwestern California, bordering Los Angeles. Pop. (1970 est.), 358,633.

long·boat (lông′bōt′) *n.* the largest boat carried by a sailing ship.

long·bow (lông′bō′) *n.* a large bow drawn by hand, used during the Middle Ages as a military weapon.

long-dis·tance (lông′dis′təns) *adj.* **1.** covering or capable of covering a long distance: *a long-distance runner.* **2.** connecting distant locations: *a long-distance telephone call.* —*adv.* by long-distance telephone: *to call long-distance.*

long distance, an operator or exchange that handles long-distance telephone calls.

lon·gev·i·ty (lon jev′ə tē) *n.* long life.

Long·fel·low, Henry Wadsworth (lông′fel′ō) 1807–1882, U.S. poet.

long·hand (lông′hand′) *n.* ordinary writing by hand in which the words are written out in full.

long·horn (lông′hôrn′) *n.* one of a breed of cattle having very long horns, formerly widely raised in the southwestern United States.

long house, among the Iroquois and certain other Indian tribes, a long, covered framework used as a dwelling in which many families lived together.

long·ing (lông′ing) *n.* a strong or restless desire; yearning: *to have a longing to travel.* —*adj.* feeling or expressing such a desire: *The hungry children cast longing glances at the cookies.* —**long′ing·ly,** *adv.*

Long Island, a long, narrow island in southeastern New York, south of Connecticut.

Long Island Sound, an arm of the Atlantic Ocean separating Connecticut from Long Island.

lon·gi·tude (lon′jə tōod′, lon′jə tyōod′) *n.* distance on the earth's surface, measured in degrees east and west of the prime meridian, and shown on maps and globes by imaginary lines from the North Pole to the South Pole.

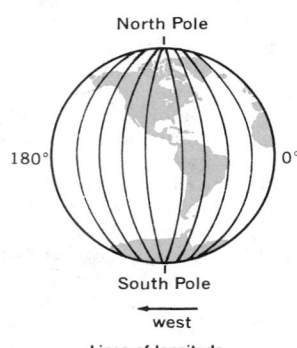

Lines of longitude

lon·gi·tu·di·nal (lon′jə tōod′ən əl, lon′jə tyōod′ən əl) *adj.* **1.** of or relating to longitude. **2.** running lengthwise: *The diagram showed a longitudinal cross section of the boat.* —**lon·gi·tu′di·nal·ly,** *adv.*

long jump, another term for **broad jump.**

long-lived (lông′līvd′, lông′livd′) *adj.* living or lasting a long time: *a long-lived friendship.*

long-play·ing (lông′plā′ing) *adj.* of or relating to a phonograph record played at 33⅓ revolutions per minute.

long-range (lông′rānj′) *adj.* **1.** for or involving the future: *long-range plans.* **2.** capable of firing or traveling over long distances: *long-range guns, a long-range missile.*

long·shore·man (lông′shôr′mən) *n. pl.,* **long·shore·men.** a man whose work is loading or unloading ships.

long shot 1. an entry in a contest or race considered to have little chance of winning. **2.** a venture promising great rewards but having little chance of success.

long-stand·ing (lông′stan′ding) *adj.* lasting a long time: *a long-standing friendship.*

long-suf·fer·ing (lông′suf′ər ing) *adj.* bearing wrongs, trouble, or pain patiently for a long time.

long-term (lông′turm′) *adj.* **1.** planned for or involving a long period of time: *a long-term project, long-term plans.* **2.** requiring payment after a long period of time: *a long-term loan.*

long-wind·ed (lông′win′did) *adj.* **1.** speaking or writing at great length: *a long-winded speaker.* **2.** long and wordy in a very boring way: *a long-winded speech.* —**long'-wind·ed·ly,** *adv.* —**long'-wind'ed·ness,** *n.*

look (look) *v.i.* **1.** to make use of the power of sight; use one's eyes; see: *Look carefully before you cross the street.* **2.** to direct one's eyes: *Susan looked toward the door when she heard footsteps.* **3.** to make a search or examination: *We helped him look for his wallet.* **4.** to give the impression of being; seem: *She looks tired.* **5.** to turn one's attention or regard; take notice: *We look at this situation in a different light now.* **6.** to face in a certain direction or have a certain view: *The windows looked north.* —*v.t.* **1.** to have an appearance appropriate to; appear to be: *She doesn't look her age.* **2.** to direct one's eyes upon or toward: *He looked me straight in the face.* —*n.* **1.** the act or instance of looking; glance: *Take a look at that new car.* **2.** an air or appearance: *He has a cheerful look.* **3. looks.** outward appearance: *The baby has her mother's good looks.* —**look'er,** *n.*

to look after. to take care of: *We looked after our neighbors' dog while they were away.*

to look back on. to recall or think about (what happened in the past).

to look down on. to have contempt for; scorn.

to look forward to. to wait for or anticipate happily or eagerly.

to look into. to examine; investigate.

to look on. a. to be a spectator; watch: *A large crowd looked on as the firemen battled the blaze.* **b.** to regard; consider: *I look on her as my best friend.*

to look out. to take care; watch out.

to look out for. to protect: *She is always looking out for her own interests.*

to look over. to examine, especially hastily.

to look to. a. to attend to; take care of. **b.** to depend upon; rely on.

to look up. a. to locate: *The librarian looked up the date for us in the encyclopedia.* **b.** to pay a visit to: *He looked her up when he got into town.* **c.** *Informal.* to get better; improve: *Business is looking up.*

to look up to. to respect or admire greatly.

looking glass, another term for **mirror.**

look·out (look'out') *n.* **1.** an alert or careful watch, as for someone that may come or something that may happen: *Be on the lookout for her letter.* **2.** a place, often a high place, where a watch is kept. **3.** a person or group that keeps watch: *The lookout warned the robbers that the police were coming.* **4.** *Informal.* a matter of interest or concern: *How he solves the problem is his own lookout.*

loom¹ (loom) *n.* a machine for weaving thread into cloth. [Old English *gelōma* a tool.]

loom² (loom) *v.i.* **1.** to appear indistinctly as a large, threatening shape: *An iceberg loomed in the distance through the fog.* **2.** to appear to the mind as large or ominous: *His final examinations loomed ahead.* [Of uncertain origin.]

loon¹ (loon) *n.* a web-footed diving bird having a slender pointed bill, small pointed wings, and short legs. The loon is noted for its laughing call. [A form of earlier *loom;* of Scandinavian origin.]

Loon¹

loon² (loon) *n.* a crazy or foolish person. [Of uncertain origin.]

loon·y (loo'nē) *Informal. adj.,* **loon·i·er, loon·i·est.** insane; crazy; foolish. —*n. pl.,* **loon·ies.** a crazy or foolish person.

loop (loop) *n.* **1.** a portion of a string, wire, or other similar material that is doubled over itself, forming a circular shape with an opening between the parts. **2.** anything resembling this: *the loops of the letter "g."* **3.** a round or bent piece of material, such as metal or cord, serving as a hook or ornament: *a belt loop.* **4.** a maneuver in which an aircraft makes a complete circle in a vertical plane. **5.** a closed electrical circuit. —*v.t.* **1.** to form into a loop or loops: *to loop a rope.* **2.** to fasten with a loop or loops. **3.** to encircle with a loop: *He looped his finger with a string.* **4.** to fly (an aircraft) in a loop or loops. —*v.i.* to form a loop or loops.

loop·hole (loop'hōl') *n.* **1.** a small opening in a wall, especially of a fort, to look or shoot through. **2.** a means of escape, especially a way of getting around a law or contract because of something that is unclear or left out.

loose (loos) *adj.,* **loos·er, loos·est. 1.** not firmly attached, fastened, or fixed: *There were several loose pages in the book.* **2.** not confined; free: *The dog was loose in the fields.* **3.** not fitting tightly or snugly: *loose clothing.* **4.** not taut; slack: *loose reins.* **5.** not tied or joined together: *loose keys.* **6.** not contained in something, as a package: *loose candy.* **7.** not compact: *loose gravel, cloth with a loose texture.* **8.** not careful, accurate, or precise: *loose reasoning, a loose translation.* **9.** lacking in moral restraint: *loose behavior, a loose person.* —*adv.* in a loose manner: *to let something hang loose.* —*v.t.,* **loosed, loos·ing. 1.** to set free: *to loose a bird from a cage.* **2.** to untie; unfasten: *to loose a knot.* **3.** to make less tight; loosen. **4.** to shoot or let fly: *to loose a dart.* —**loose'ly,** *adv.* —**loose'ness,** *n.*

to break loose. to run away or get away: *The prisoner broke loose from the guard.*

to let loose or **to set loose** or **to turn loose.** to set free; release.

loose-joint·ed (loos'join'tid) *adj.* **1.** having joints that are loosely formed. **2.** capable of relaxed or limber movement: *a loose-jointed dancer.*

loose-leaf (loos'lēf') *adj.* holding or made to hold pages with holes for easy removal: *a loose-leaf notebook.*

loos·en (loo'sən) *v.t.* **1.** to make loose or looser: *to loosen a necktie.* **2.** to set free or release: *He loosened the dog from the rope.* **3.** to make less severe or strict: *to loosen discipline.* —*v.i.* to become loose or looser. —**loos'en·er,** *n.*

loot (loot) *n.* **1.** things taken by thieves in a robbery. **2.** things taken by force from an enemy during a war; booty; plunder. —*v.t.* to rob or plunder: *The soldiers looted the town. The burglars looted the store.* —*v.i.* to take booty; plunder. —**loot'er,** *n.*

lop¹ (lop) *v.t.,* **lopped, lop·ping. 1.** to cut off or remove as unnecessary: *The woodsman lopped the dead branches from the trees.* **2.** to cut off parts from: *to lop trees.* [Of uncertain origin.]

lop² (lop) *v.i.,* **lopped, lop·ping.** to hang loosely; droop. [Of uncertain origin.]

lope (lōp) *v.,* **loped, lop·ing.** —*v.i.* to run with a long, easy, often bounding stride: *The dog loped through the park.* —*v.t.* to cause to run with such a stride: *to lope a horse.* —*n.* a long, easy, often bounding stride.

lop-eared (lop'ērd') *adj.* having ears that hang down loosely: *a lop-eared hound.*

lop·sid·ed (lop'sī'did) *adj.* larger or heavier on one side

at; āpe; cär; end; mē; it; īce; hot; ōld; fôrk; wood; fool; oil; out; up; turn; sing; thin; **th**is; **hw** in white; **zh** in treasure. The symbol ə stands for the sound of **a** in about, **e** in taken, **i** in pencil, **o** in lemon, and **u** in circus.

L

than on the other; leaning or slanting to one side. —**lop′sid·ed·ly**, *adv.* —**lop′sid·ed·ness**, *n.*

lo·qua·cious (lō kwā′shəs) *adj.* tending to talk too much; talkative. —**lo·qua′cious·ly**, *adv.* —**lo·qua′cious·ness**, *n.*

lo·quac·i·ty (lō kwas′ə tē) *n.* the tendency to talk too much.

lo·quat (lō′kwot, lō′kwat) *n.* **1.** a yellow or orange fruit that resembles a plum and has a slightly acid taste. Loquats are used especially in preserves. **2.** the small evergreen tree that bears this fruit.

Lo·rain (lə rān′) *n.* a port city in northern Ohio, on Lake Erie. Pop. (1970), 78,185.

lo·ran (lor′ən) *n.* a navigational system in which the geographical position of a ship or aircraft can be determined by using signals transmitted by three fixed radio stations. [Abbreviation of *lo*(ng)-*ra*(nge) *n*(avigation).]

lord (lôrd) *n.* **1.** a person who has power or authority over others, such as a feudal ruler. **2.** *British.* a titled nobleman or peer belonging to the House of Lords. **3. Lord.** *British.* **a.** the title or form of address for any of various noblemen or peers. The *Earl of Arran* would be referred to informally as *Lord Arran*. **b.** the title or form of address for certain high officials or churchmen: *the Lord Mayor of London.* **4. Lords.** see **House of Lords. 5. the Lord. a.** God. **b.** Christ.

　to lord it over. to behave in a haughty or domineering manner toward: *He lorded it over everyone when he was made captain of the team.*

lord·ly (lôrd′lē) *adj.*, **lord·li·er, lord·li·est. 1.** of, relating to, or suited for a lord: *a lordly estate.* **2.** haughty or domineering: *His lordly manner caused most people to dislike him instantly.* —**lord′li·ness**, *n.*

lord·ship (lôrd′ship′) *n.* **1. Lordship.** *British.* the title or form of address used in speaking or referring to a Lord, usually preceded by *His* or *Your.* **2.** the rank, power, or authority of a lord.

Lord's Prayer, a prayer given by Jesus to His Apostles, which begins with the words "Our Father." Also, **paternoster.**

lore (lôr) *n.* **1.** the body of traditional or popular facts or beliefs on a particular subject: *nature lore.* **2.** learning; knowledge.

lor·gnette (lôrn yet′) *n.* a pair of eyeglasses or opera glasses held by a short, usually decorated handle.

lorn (lôrn) *adj. Archaic.* abandoned; lonely.

Lor·raine (lə rān′) *n.* a region and former province in northeastern France, bordering on Belgium, Luxembourg, and West Germany.

lor·ry (lôr′ē, lor′ē) *n. pl.,* **lor·ries. 1.** a long flat wagon without sides, drawn by a horse. **2.** *British.* a truck.

Los An·ge·les (lôs an′jə ləs, lôs an′jə lēz, lôs ang′gə-ləs) the largest city of California, in the southwestern part of the state. Pop. (1970 est.), 2,816,061.

lose (lōōz) *v.,* **lost, los·ing.** —*v.t.* **1.** to have no longer because of some act or accident: *The family lost everything they owned in the fire.* **2.** to put in a place afterward forgotten; misplace: *She lost her keys somewhere in her apartment.* **3.** to fail to win: *Our team lost the game.* **4.** to fail to keep, preserve, or maintain: *He loses his temper easily. She lost her balance on the icy sidewalk.* **5.** to let pass without using; fail to take advantage of: *to lose one's chance. We lost valuable time waiting for him.* **6.** to fail to keep up with, especially in order to understand or see: *I lost the sense of what he was saying.* **7.** to wander or stray from: *The hikers lost their way in the darkness.* **8.** to let (oneself) be absorbed: *She lost herself in her reading.* **9.** to cause the loss of: *The young man's laziness lost him his job.* —*v.i.* **1.** to suffer loss: *He lost heavily on the stock*

market. **2.** to be defeated: *I usually lose when I play chess.* —**los′er**, *n.*

　to lose out. to fail to get or achieve something.

　to lose out on. to fail to win, get, or take advantage of: *to lose out on an opportunity.*

los·ing (lōō′zing) *adj.* **1.** causing loss: *a losing battle.* **2.** that is defeated: *the losing team.* —*n., pl.* **losings.** an amount lost, especially money lost in gambling.

loss (lôs) *n. pl.,* **loss·es. 1.** the act of losing or the state of being lost: *the loss of a race, a loss of memory.* **2.** a person, thing, or amount that is lost: *a financial loss.* **3.** the damage or disadvantage that results from losing something: *The closing of the factory was a great loss to the town.* **4. losses.** soldiers wounded, killed, or captured in action.

　at a loss. puzzled; confused; perplexed: *Her sudden rudeness left me completely at a loss.*

lost (lôst) *v.* the past tense and past participle of **lose.** —*adj.* **1.** that cannot be found; misplaced or missing: *a lost dog.* **2.** no longer possessed or used: *a lost fortune.* **3.** not won; defeated: *a lost cause.* **4.** not used to good purpose; wasted: *a lost opportunity.* **5.** having gone astray: *We were lost in the woods.* **6.** destroyed; ruined: *a lost reputation.* **7.** absorbed; preoccupied: *to be lost in thought.*

lot (lot) *n.* **1.** one of a set of objects, as bits of paper, wood, or straw, used to decide something by chance: *The boys drew lots to decide who would have the first turn.* **2.** the casting or drawing of such objects as a means of deciding something: *They chose the captain of the team by lot.* **3.** a decision or choice made in this way: *The lot fell to her brother to tell her the bad news.* **4.** something that one gets in this way; portion or share. **5.** a portion or plot of land: *The boys played baseball on an empty lot.* **6.** a motion picture studio and its property. **7.** fortune or fate in life: *The lot of the poor is a hard one.* **8.** a number of persons or things considered as a unit or group: *They were a lazy lot of workers.* **9.** also, **lots.** *Informal.* a great many; a great deal: *a lot of cars, lots of candy.* —*adv.* also, **lots.** a great deal; much: *He is a lot taller than his brother.*

Lot (lot) *n.* in the Old Testament, a nephew of Abraham who was allowed to escape from Sodom before God destroyed it. His wife, ignoring a warning, looked back at the destruction of the city and was changed into a pillar of salt.

loth (lōth) another spelling of **loath.**

lo·tion (lō′shən) *n.* a liquid preparation used on the skin to heal, soothe, soften, or cleanse.

lot·ter·y (lot′ər ē) *n. pl.,* **lot·ter·ies.** a way of raising money in which chances or numbered tickets are sold. Winning tickets are then drawn by lot and prizes are awarded to the winners.

lo·tus (lō′təs) *n. pl.,* **lo·tus·es. 1.** the large flower of a plant related to the water lily. **2.** the plant bearing this flower, having leaves that float on the surface of water. **3.** a shrubby plant related to the pea, having red, white, or pink flowers. **4.** *Greek Legend.* a fruit supposed to cause a dreamy, contented forgetfulness in those who ate it.

Lotus

loud (loud) *adj.* **1.** having a strong and powerful sound: *a loud cry, a loud noise.* **2.** producing such sound: *loud cymbals.* **3.** vehement or insistent: *loud demands.* **4.** tastelessly bright; flashy: *a loud red tie.* **5.** tending to be offensive in appearance or manner: *a loud, vulgar person.* —*adv.* in a loud manner. —**loud′ly**, *adv.* —**loud′ness**, *n.*

loud·speak·er (loud′spē′kər) *also,* **loud-speak·er.** *n.* a device that transforms an electrical signal into sound and amplifies the sound to the desired volume.

Lou·is XIV (lōō′ē, lōō′is) 1638–1715, the king of France from 1643 to 1715. Also, **Louis the Great.**

Louis XVI, 1754–1793, the king of France from 1774 to 1792. He was beheaded during the French Revolution.

Lou·i·si·an·a (lōō ē′zē an′ə, lōō′ə zē an′ə) *n.* a state in the southern United States, on the Gulf of Mexico and the Mississippi River. Capital, Baton Rouge. Area, 48,523 sq. mi. Pop. (1970), 3,643,180. Abbreviation, **La.** —**Lou·i′si·an′an, Lou·i′si·an′i·an,** *adj., n.*

• **Louisiana** comes from the name a French explorer gave to the Mississippi valley in honor of Louis XIV, then the king of France.

Louisiana Purchase, the territory purchased by the United States from France in 1803, extending from the Mississippi River to the Rocky Mountains and from Canada to the Gulf of Mexico.

Lou·is·ville (lōō′ē vil′) *n.* the largest city in Kentucky, in the northern part of the state, on the Ohio River. Pop. (1970), 361,472.

lounge (lounj) *v.,* **lounged, loung·ing.** —*v.i.* **1.** to lean, sit, or lie lazily; loll: *He lounged on the sofa and watched television.* **2.** to move lazily, listlessly, or unhurriedly: *The bored children lounged about the yard.* —*v.t.* to pass (time) by lounging. —*n.* **1.** a public room where one may lounge, smoke, relax, or wait, as in a hotel, restaurant, or club. **2.** a sofa; couch.

lour (lour) another spelling of **lower**².

louse (lous) *n. pl.,* (*def. 1*) **lice** or (*def. 2*) **lous·es.** **1.** any of a large number of tiny wingless insects that live as parasites on man and animals. **2.** *Slang.* a low, contemptible person.

lous·y (lou′zē) *adj.,* **lous·i·er, lous·i·est.** **1.** infested with lice. **2.** *Slang.* disgusting; contemptible: *a lousy trick.* **3.** *Slang.* of wretched quality; terrible: *That was a lousy movie.* —**lous′i·ly,** *adv.* —**lous′i·ness,** *n.*

lout (lout) *n.* an awkward, stupid person; oaf.

lout·ish (lou′tish) *adj.* like a lout; awkward; clumsy. —**lout′ish·ly,** *adv.* —**lout′ish·ness,** *n.*

lou·ver (lōō′vər) *n.* one of a series of horizontal, overlapping slats fitted in a window or other opening, slanted to keep out rain while letting in light and air.

Lou·vre (lōō′vrə) *n.* an art museum in Paris.

lov·a·ble (luv′ə bəl) *also,* **love·a·ble.** *adj.* having qualities that tend to make one loved; worthy of being loved: *a lovable puppy.* —**lov′a·bly,** *adv.*

love (luv) *n.* **1.** a strong feeling of affection, devotion, and concern for another: *love for one's children.* **2.** a strong liking for something: *a love of music.* **3.** a beloved person; sweetheart. **4.** a thing that is loved or greatly liked: *Skiing is his great love.* **5.** in tennis, a score of zero. —*v.,* **loved, lov·ing.** —*v.t.* **1.** to have a deep affection for: *He loves his wife and child.* **2.** to have a strong liking for: *She loves good books.* —*v.i.* to be in love.

  in love. feeling love.

  to fall in love. to begin to love.

  to make love. to caress or embrace.

love·a·ble (luv′ə bəl) another spelling of **lovable.**

love·bird (luv′burd′) *n.* a small parrot, often kept in a cage as a pet. It is noted for showing great affection toward its mate.

Louver

love·less (luv′lis) *adj.* without love: *The couple had a loveless marriage.*

love·lorn (luv′lôrn′) *adj.* abandoned by one's lover; miserable because of love.

love·ly (luv′lē) *adj.,* **love·li·er, love·li·est.** **1.** having beautiful qualities, as of appearance or personality. **2.** *Informal.* very delightful; enjoyable; pleasing: *We had a lovely time!* —**love′li·ness,** *n.*

lov·er (luv′ər) *n.* **1.** a person who loves another. **2.** a person who has a strong liking for something: *a lover of art.*

love seat, a small sofa seating two persons.

love·sick (luv′sik′) *adj.* pining or languishing because of love.

lov·ing (luv′ing) *adj.* feeling or showing love; affectionate; fond. —**lov′ing·ly,** *adv.*

loving cup, a large cup, usually with handles, presented as a prize or trophy and often bearing an inscription.

lov·ing-kind·ness (luv′ing kīnd′nis) *n.* affectionate tenderness and thoughtfulness coming from love.

low¹ (lō) *adj.* **1.** rising only slightly above the surface; not high or tall: *A low hedge surrounds the yard.* **2.** close to the ground: *a low leap, the low branches of a tree.* **3.** below the average or natural level of the ground: *a low valley.* **4.** below the usual or desired level: *The river was low after the drought.* **5.** below what is usual or desired, as in amount, force, or degree: *Food prices were low last summer.* **6.** below or inferior to others, as in rank or position: *a low grade of oil, low intelligence, low marks.* **7.** mean; vulgar; corrupt: *a low person, low language.* **8.** disapproving; critical; unfavorable: *She has a low opinion of him.* **9.** not having an adequate supply: *The store is low on canned goods.* **10.** not loud; soft: *a low whisper.* **11.** deep in pitch: *a low note.* **12.** depressed; gloomy: *Failing the test made him feel low.* **13.** feeble; weak; poor: *The patient's condition is very low.* —*adv.* **1.** near the ground or floor: *The plane flew very low.* **2.** to, in, or at a low point, degree, or level: *Prices sank low.* —*n.* **1.** a low level, place, or position: *The temperature reached a new low for this time of year.* **2.** the arrangement of gears, as in a car, that produces the lowest speed and the greatest power. **3.** an area of low barometric pressure. [Old Norse *lāgr* not high, humble.] —**low′ness,** *n.*

  to lie low. *Informal.* to stay in hiding: *The holdup men decided to lie low after the robbery.*

low² (lō) *v.t., v.i.* to make the bellowing sound characteristic of cattle; moo. —*n.* such a sound. [Old English *hlō-wan.*]

low·boy (lō′boi′) *n.* a low chest of drawers on short legs.

low·brow (lō′brou′) *Informal.* *n.* a person who lacks culture or intellectual interests. —*adj.* of, relating to, or suitable for a lowbrow.

Low Countries, a region of northwestern Europe consisting of the Netherlands, Belgium, and Luxembourg.

low·down (*n.,* lō′doun′; *adj.,* lō′doun′) *also,* **low·down.** *n. Slang.* the bare facts; actual truth: *The reporter tried to get the low-down on the mayor's past.* —*adj. Informal.* mean; disgusting; contemptible: *a low-down trick.*

Low·ell (lō′əl) *n.* a city in northeastern Massachusetts. Pop. (1970), 94,239.

L

low·er¹ (lō′ər) *adj.* the comparative of **low¹**. —*v.t.* **1.** to take or bring down; let down: *to lower the flag, to lower a bucket into a well.* **2.** to reduce, as in height, amount, value, or degree: *to lower prices, to lower the water level in a pool.* **3.** to lessen the intensity or volume of: *Lower your voice.* **4.** to bring down in value or estimation: *He would be lowering himself if he lied.* **5.** to lessen the force or effectiveness of; weaken: *Not eating properly will lower your resistance to illness.* —*v.i.* to become lower. [*Low¹* + *-er².*]

low·er² (lou′ər) *also,* **lour.** *v.i.* **1.** to frown; scowl. **2.** to appear dark, gloomy, or threatening. —*n.* **1.** a frown; scowl. **2.** a dark, gloomy, or threatening appearance, as of the sky. [Middle English *louren, luren* to frown, lie in wait.]

Lower California, a long narrow peninsula in northwestern Mexico, separating the Gulf of California from the Pacific Ocean. Also, **Baja California.**

low·er-case (lō′ər kās′) *adj.* of, relating to, or printed in small letters. —*v.t.,* **low·er-cased, low·er-cas·ing.** to set in or print with small letters.

lower case, another term for **small letters.**

low·er-class (lō′ər klas′) *adj.* of or relating to the lower class.

lower class, the portion of society, including the working class and the very poor, occupying a social and economic position below that of the middle class.

lower house, *also,* **Lower House.** in a legislature having two branches, the larger and more representative branch, such as the House of Representatives in the U.S. Congress.

low·er·most (lō′ər mōst′) *adj.* lowest.

lower world, the abode of the dead; Hades.

low frequency, any radio frequency between 30 and 300 kilocycles per second.

Low German **1.** a form of the German language spoken predominantly in the lowlands of northern Germany. **2.** a group of Germanic languages, including Dutch and Flemish, spoken predominantly in the Low Countries.

low-keyed (lō′kēd′) *adj.* characterized by restraint or subtlety; quiet.

low·land (lō′lənd) *n.* **1.** land that is on a lower level than the surrounding land. **2. Lowlands.** a low region of central Scotland. —*adj.* of, relating to, or characteristic of such land.

low·land·er (lō′lən dər) *n.* **1.** a person who was born or is living in a lowland. **2. Lowlander.** a person who was born or is living in the Lowlands of Scotland.

low·ly (lō′lē) *adj.,* **low·li·er, low·li·est. 1.** humble in condition or quality; low in rank or importance: *a lowly cottage.* **2.** humble in manner or spirit; meek. —*adv.* in a humble manner; humbly; meekly. —**low′li·ness,** *n.*

low-pitched (lō′picht′) *adj.* **1.** having a low tone. **2.** (of a roof) having little slope.

low-pres·sure (lō′presh′ər) *adj.* **1.** having, using, or indicating a low degree of pressure: *low-pressure tires.* **2.** having low atmospheric pressure: *a low-pressure center.* **3.** calm and unhurried; relaxed: *a low-pressure sales technique.*

low relief, another term for **bas-relief.**

low-spir·it·ed (lō′spir′i tid) *adj.* sad; depressed.

low tide **1.** the tide at its lowest level. **2.** the time when this level is reached.

lox (loks) *n.* a kind of smoked salmon.

loy·al (loi′əl) *adj.* **1.** faithful in one's friendship, devotion, or regard: *He is a loyal friend.* **2.** faithful in one's allegiance to one's king, government, or country. **3.** characterized by or showing loyalty: *a loyal declaration.* —**loy′al·ly,** *adv.*

loy·al·ist (loi′ə list) *n.* **1.** a person who supports the existing king or government, especially during times of war or revolution. **2.** *also,* **Loyalist.** a colonist who remained loyal to the British government during the American Revolution.

loy·al·ty (loi′əl tē) *n. pl.,* **loy·al·ties.** constant devotion or allegiance; faithfulness: *loyalty to one's country.*

Loy·o·la, Ignatius (loi ō′lə) see **Ignatius of Loyola.**

loz·enge (loz′inj) *n.* **1.** a small tablet of sugar and other flavoring, often containing medicine. **2.** a figure shaped like a diamond.

LP *n. pl.,* **LPs** or **LP's.** *Trademark.* a long-playing record.

LSD, a psychedelic drug that produces hallucinations and temporary changes in personality. [Abbreviation of *l*(y)-s(ergic acid) *d*(iethylamide).]

Lt., Lieutenant.

Ltd., ltd. *British.* limited.

Lu, the symbol for lutetium.

Lu·an·da (lōō an′də) *n.* the capital and largest city of Angola. Pop. (1970), 475,328.

lu·au (lōō′ou′) *n.* a feast of Hawaiian food.

lub·ber (lub′ər) *n.* **1.** a heavy, clumsy, stupid person. **2.** an awkward or inexperienced sailor; landlubber.

Lub·bock (lub′ək) *n.* a city in northwestern Texas. Pop. (1970), 149,101.

Lü·beck (lōō′bek) *n.* a port city in northeastern West Germany. Pop. (1969 est.), 242,200.

Lu·blin (lōō′blin, lōō′blēn) *n.* a city in eastern Poland. Pop. (1970), 235,900.

lu·bri·cant (lōō′brə kənt) *n.* any substance, as oil or grease, used to reduce friction between the moving parts of a machine.

lu·bri·cate (lōō′brə kāt′) *v.,* **lu·bri·cat·ed, lu·bri·cat·ing.** —*v.t.* **1.** to apply oil, grease, or other lubricant to (the moving parts of a machine) in order to reduce friction. **2.** to make slippery or smooth: *to lubricate the skin with lotion.* —*v.i.* to act as a lubricant. —**lu′bri·ca′tion,** *n.* —**lu′bri·ca′tor,** *n.*

Lu·bum·ba·shi (lōō′bōōm bä′shē) *n.* a city in the southeastern part of the Democratic Republic of the Congo. Pop. (1970), 318,000.

lu·cent (lōō′sənt) *adj.* **1.** shining; bright; luminous. **2.** clear; translucent.

lu·cid (lōō′sid) *adj.* **1.** easily understood; clear: *a lucid explanation.* **2.** showing clear thinking or mental soundness; rational; sane: *a lucid person, lucid reasoning.* **3.** clear; transparent: *the pure and lucid mountain air.* **4.** shining; bright; luminous. —**lu′cid·ly,** *adv.* —**lu′cid·ness,** *n.*

lu·cid·i·ty (lōō sid′ə tē) *n.* the state or quality of being lucid.

Lu·ci·fer (lōō′sə fər) *n.* the rebellious archangel who was cast out of heaven with his followers; Satan.

Lu·cite (lōō′sīt) *n. Trademark.* a transparent, acrylic resin available in solid or liquid form and having many uses, as in light fixtures.

luck (luk) *n.* **1.** the force or factor that seems to influence events or circumstances of a person's life for good or ill: *Luck alone won't get you a job—you'll have to look harder.* **2.** the events or circumstances so influenced: *His life has been filled with bad luck.* **3.** good fortune; success: *She had no luck in finding her glasses.*

　to be down on one's luck. *Informal.* to have bad luck.

　to be in luck. to have good luck.

　to be out of luck. to have bad luck.

luck·i·ly (luk′ə lē) *adv.* with or by a stroke of good luck; fortunately.

luck·less (luk′lis) *adj.* not having good luck; unlucky. —**luck′less·ly,** *adv.* —**luck′less·ness,** *n.*

Luck·now (luk′nou) *n.* a city in north-central India. Pop. (1976 est.), 749,239.

luck·y (luk′ē) *adj.,* **luck·i·er, luck·i·est. 1.** having good luck; fortunate. **2.** happening happily or fortunately: *a lucky meeting.* **3.** thought to bring good luck: *a lucky rabbit's foot.* —**luck′i·ness,** *n.*

lu·cra·tive (lōō′krə tiv) *adj.* bringing money or profit; profitable: *a lucrative business.* —**lu′cra·tive·ly,** *adv.*

lu·cre (lōō′kər) *n.* money or riches, especially when thought of as evil: *filthy lucre.*

Lü·da (lōō′dä′) *n.* a municipality in southern Manchuria that includes the cities of Port Arthur and Dairen. Pop. (1958 est.), 1,590,000.

lu·di·crous (lōō′də krəs) *adj.* laughably absurd; ridiculous: *The little girl looked ludicrous as she wobbled about in her mother's shoes.* —**lu′di·crous·ly,** *adv.*

luff (luf) *n.* **1.** the act of sailing a ship toward the wind. **2.** the forward edge of a fore-and-aft sail. —*v.i.* to turn the bow of a ship toward the wind.

lug¹ (lug) *v.t.,* **lugged, lug·ging.** to pull or carry with effort: *He lugged the heavy trunk down the stairs.* [Probably of Scandinavian origin.]

lug² (lug) *n.* **1.** the projecting part by which something is gripped or held. **2.** *Slang.* a clumsy or stupid person. [Of uncertain origin.]

lug³ (lug) *n.* see **lugsail.**

lug·gage (lug′ij) *n.* the bags, boxes, trunks, or suitcases used by a traveler for carrying belongings; baggage.

lug·ger (lug′ər) *n.* a small boat having two or three masts and rigged with lugsails.

lug·sail (lug′sāl′, lug′səl) *n.* a four-sided sail without a boom, held by a yard that hangs slantwise across the mast. Also, **lug.**

Lugger

lu·gu·bri·ous (loo gōō′brē-əs, loo gyōō′brē əs) *adj.* very mournful or sorrowful: *The boy had a lugubrious look when he found out he couldn't go to the party.* —**lu·gu′bri·ous·ly,** *adv.* —**lu·gu′bri·ous·ness,** *n.*

lug·worm (lug′wurm′) *n.* a worm that burrows in the sand along the seashore, used as bait for fishing.

Luke (lōōk) *n.* **1.** one of the four Evangelists, thought to be the author of Acts. **2.** the third Gospel of the New Testament, thought to have been written by him.

luke·warm (lōōk′wôrm′) *adj.* **1.** slightly warm; tepid: *lukewarm bath water.* **2.** having or showing little warmth or enthusiasm; indifferent: *a lukewarm welcome.* —**luke′-warm′ly,** *adv.* —**luke′warm′ness,** *n.*

lull (lul) *v.t.* to calm with soothing sounds or caresses. —*v.i.* to become calm: *The storm lulled.*

lul·la·by (lul′ə bī′) *n. pl.,* **lul·la·bies.** a soothing song sung to lull a child to sleep.

lum·ba·go (lum bā′gō) *n.* a pain in the lower back between the chest and the pelvis.

lum·bar (lum′bər) *adj.* of, relating to, or near the lower back or loins.

lumb·er¹ (lum′bər) *n.* timber cut as planks and boards. —*v.i.* to cut timber into lumber and get it ready for use. [Possibly from obsolete *lumber* or *lumber-house* a pawnshop. The original meaning of lumber was "useless furniture and other articles; odds and ends" which were often left in pawnshops.]

lum·ber² (lum′bər) *v.i.* to move in a clumsy or noisy manner: *The old wagon lumbered down the dirt road.* [Middle English *lomeren.*]

lum·ber·ing (lum′bər ing) *n.* the business of cutting and preparing timber.

lum·ber·jack (lum′bər jak′) *n.* a person who cuts down trees and gets logs ready for transportation to the sawmill.

lum·ber·man (lum′bər mən) *n. pl.,* **lum·ber·men** (lum′bər mən). **1.** another word for **lumberjack. 2.** a person who works in or manages a lumberyard.

lum·ber·yard (lum′bər yärd′) *n.* a place where lumber is stored and sold.

lu·men (lōō′mən) *n.* a unit of luminous flux equal to the amount of light falling on one square unit of surface area, of which each point is at a distance of one unit from a light source with an intensity of one candle.

lu·mi·nar·y (lōō′mə ner′ē) *n. pl.,* **lu·mi·nar·ies. 1.** a person who is recognized or noted for high achievement in his field: *A group of luminaries discussed the future of space science.* **2.** a light-giving body, especially the sun or the moon.

lu·mi·nes·cence (lōō′mə nes′əns) *n.* the sending out of visible light without heat. Phosphorescence and fluorescence are two forms of luminescence. —**lu′mi·nes′cent,** *adj.*

lu·mi·nos·i·ty (lōō′mə nos′ə tē) *n. pl.,* **lu·mi·nos·i·ties. 1.** the quality or condition of being luminous. **2.** something luminous.

lu·mi·nous (lōō′mə nəs) *adj.* **1.** sending out light of its own; shining: *luminous flames.* **2.** full of light; bright. **3.** clear to the mind; easily understood. —**lu′mi·nous·ly,** *adv.* —**lu′mi·nous·ness,** *n.*

lump (lump) *n.* **1.** a solid, usually shapeless piece or mass: *a lump of iron ore, a lump of clay.* **2.** a small cube: *a lump of sugar.* **3.** a swelling: *He had a lump on his head where the baseball had hit him.* —*adj.* formed in a lump or lumps: *lump sugar.* —*v.t.* to put, bring, or deal with together: *The campers lumped their expenses.* —*v.i.* to form into a lump or lumps; become lumpy: *The oatmeal lumped when it cooled.*

lump·ish (lum′pish) *adj.* **1.** like a lump. **2.** heavy and awkward. **3.** stupid; dull.

lump·y (lum′pē) *adj.,* **lump·i·er, lump·i·est. 1.** covered or filled with lumps: *lumpy oatmeal.* **2.** heavy and awkward; lumpish. —**lump′i·ness,** *n.*

Lu·na (lōō′nə) *n. Roman Mythology.* the goddess of the moon. In Greek mythology she was called Selene.

lu·na·cy (lōō′nə sē) *n. pl.,* **lu·na·cies. 1.** madness; insanity. **2.** senseless or reckless conduct.

lu·na moth (lōō′nə) a large green moth having wings with transparent spots.

lu·nar (lōō′nər) *adj.* of or relating to the moon: *the lunar orbit.*

lunar eclipse, a partial or total darkening of the moon when the earth moves between the moon and the sun.

lunar month, see **month** *(def. 4).*

lunar year, see **year** *(def. 3).*

lu·na·tic (lōō′nə tik) *n.* **1.** an insane person. **2.** a senseless or reckless person. —*adj.* **1.** insane; crazy. **2.** of or for insane

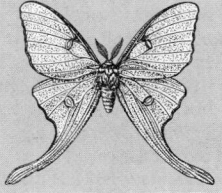

Luna moth

at; āpe; cär; end; mē; it; īce; hot; ōld; fôrk; wood; fōōl; oil; out; up; turn; sing; thin; **th**is; hw in white; zh in treasure. The symbol ə stands for the sound of **a** in about, **e** in taken, **i** in pencil, **o** in lemon, and **u** in circus.

L

people: *a lunatic asylum.* **3.** extremely senseless or reckless. [Late Latin *lūnāticus;* from Latin *lūna* moon; referring to the earlier belief that a form of insanity was related to or caused by the apparent changes in the shape of the moon.]

lunch (lunch) *n. pl.,* **lunch·es. 1.** a light meal between breakfast and dinner, usually eaten around noon. **2.** the food prepared for such a meal. —*v.i.* to eat lunch. —**lunch'er,** *n.*

lunch counter, an area where light meals are served, consisting of a counter and a row of stools.

lunch·eon (lun'chən) *n.* a lunch, especially a formal one.

lunch·eon·ette (lun'chə net') *n.* a small restaurant or lunch counter where light meals, especially breakfast and lunch, are served.

lunch·room (lunch'rōōm', lunch'room') *n.* a place where light meals are served, especially a cafeteria in a school or factory.

lung (lung) *n.* in human beings and many other animals, one of a pair of spongy organs for breathing that supply the blood with oxygen and rid the blood of carbon dioxide.

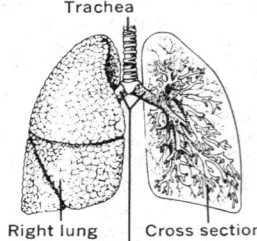

Trachea

Right lung   Cross section of left lung

Bronchial tubes

Lungs (exterior and interior)

lunge (lunj) *n.* **1.** any sudden forward movement: *The catcher made a lunge for the ball.* **2.** a sudden forward thrust, as with a sword. —*v.i.,* **lunged, lung·ing.** to make a sudden forward movement: *We lunged for the falling platter.* —**lung'er,** *n.*

lung·fish (lung'fish') *n. pl.,* **lung·fish** or **lung·fish·es.** any of several fish that have lungs as well as gills, enabling them to breathe in or out of water. Lungfish live in freshwater swamps and marshes in Africa, South America, and Australia.

lu·pine (lōō'pin) *n.* a plant related to the pea, bearing spikes of white, yellow, blue, or purple flowers.

lurch¹ (lurch) *n. pl.,* **lurch·es.** a sudden rolling or swaying to one side or from side to side: *The ship gave a lurch in the choppy water.* —*v.i.* **1.** to move jerkily and unsteadily; stagger: *The boxer lurched to his feet after his opponent knocked him down.* **2.** to roll or sway suddenly to one side or from side to side. [Of uncertain origin.]

lurch² (lurch) *n.* **to leave in the lurch.** to leave (someone) in a difficult or embarrassing situation. [French *lourche* a game no longer known that was thought to resemble backgammon.]

lure (loor) *n.* **1.** a powerful attraction: *the lure of a swim in the ocean on a hot day.* **2.** a bait, as an artificial fly used in fishing. —*v.t.,* **lured, lur·ing.** to attract powerfully; tempt: *The hungry boy was lured to the kitchen by the smell of baking cookies.*

lu·rid (loor'id) *adj.* **1.** terrible; sensational; shocking: *a lurid crime.* **2.** shining with a reddish glow or fiery glare: *a lurid fire.* —**lu'rid·ness,** *n.*

lurk (lurk) *v.i.* **1.** to lie hidden: *A lion lurked in the underbrush.* **2.** to move about in a sneaky manner.

Lu·sa·ka (lōō sä'kə) *n.* the capital and largest city of Zambia, in the south-central part of the country. Pop. (1978 est.), 559,000.

lus·cious (lush'əs) *adj.* **1.** sweet and pleasing to the taste or smell; delicious: *ripe, luscious pears.* **2.** pleasing to the mind or to the senses: *luscious music.* —**lus'cious·ly,** *adv.* —**lus'cious·ness,** *n.*

lush (lush) *adj.* **1.** rich and abundant; luxuriant: *a lush growth of ferns.* **2.** characterized by or covered with luxuri-

ant growth: *lush forests.* **3.** luxurious; rich: *The room had a thick, lush rug.* —**lush'ly,** *adv.* —**lush'ness,** *n.*

Lü·shun (lōō'shoon'), see **Port Arthur.**

lust (lust) *n.* **1.** strong sexual desire. **2.** any strong desire: *The miser had a lust for money.* —*v.i.* to have a strong desire: *The dictator lusted after power.*

lus·ter (lus'tər) *also, British,* **lus·tre.** *n.* **1.** the quality of shining by reflected light; luminous glow; sheen: *The wax gave the kitchen floor a bright luster.* **2.** radiance; brightness: *His eyes lost their luster when he found he could not go to the circus.* **3.** splendor; glory; renown: *His brave deeds add much luster to his reputation.* **4.** a shiny, often iridescent, glazed surface on pottery.

lus·ter·ware (lus'tər wer') *n.* pottery having a shiny, often iridescent, glazed surface.

lust·ful (lust'fəl) *adj.* full of or characterized by lust. —**lust'ful·ly,** *adv.* —**lust'ful·ness,** *n.*

lus·tre (lus'tər) another spelling of **luster.**

lus·trous (lus'trəs) *adj.* having a shining surface: *The girl had long lustrous hair. Satin is a lustrous fabric.* —**lus'trous·ly,** *adv.*

lust·y (lus'tē) *adj.,* **lust·i·er, lust·i·est.** full of strength and vigor; healthy: *a lusty young man.* —**lust'i·ly,** *adv.*

lute (lōōt) *n.* a stringed musical instrument having a pear-shaped body, played by plucking with the fingers or a plectrum.

lu·te·ti·um (lōō tē'shē əm) *n.* a heavy, silvery-white metallic element, one of the rare-earth elements. Symbol: **Lu**

Lu·ther, Martin (lōō'thər) 1483–1546, German theologian, the leader of the Protestant Reformation.

Lu·ther·an (lōō'thər ən) *adj.* of or relating to Luther, his doctrines, or one of the Protestant churches named after him. —*n.* a member of a Lutheran Church.

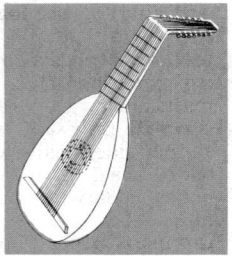

Lute

Lux·em·bourg (luk'səm burg') *also,* **Lux·em·burg.** *n.* **1.** a small country in western Europe, surrounded by France, Belgium, and West Germany. Capital, Luxembourg. Area, 998 sq. mi. Pop. (1980 est.), 358,000. **2.** the capital and chief city of Luxembourg, in the south-central part of the country. Pop. (1974), 78,400.

lux·u·ri·ant (lug zhoor'ē ənt, luk shoor'ē ənt) *adj.* **1.** thick or abundant: *a luxuriant growth of rose bushes.* **2.** rich in ornamentation: *a luxuriant imagination, luxuriant decoration.* **3.** producing in great abundance: *luxuriant soil.* —**lux·u'ri·ance,** *n.* —**lux·u'ri·ant·ly,** *adv.*

lux·u·ri·ate (lug zhoor'ē āt', luk shoor'ē āt') *v.i.,* **lux·u·ri·at·ed, lux·u·ri·at·ing. 1.** to indulge oneself in pleasure or luxury; live luxuriously. **2.** to take great delight: *The dictator luxuriated in his power over the people.* **3.** to grow in great abundance: *The plants luxuriated in the warm, moist climate.*

lux·u·ri·ous (lug zhoor'ē əs, luk shoor'ē əs) *adj.* **1.** given to or liking pleasure or luxury: *His tastes were luxurious but his income was too small.* **2.** characterized by luxury: *a luxurious mansion.* —**lux·u'ri·ous·ly,** *adv.* —**lux·u'ri·ous·ness,** *n.*

lux·u·ry (luk'shər ē, lug'zhər ē) *n. pl.,* **lux·u·ries. 1.** something that adds to a person's comfort or pleasure in life but is not really necessary: *A mink coat is a luxury.* **2.** a way of life that gives great comfort or pleasure: *He lived in luxury on the tropical island.* —*adj.* providing luxury: *a luxury hotel.*

Lu·zon (lōō zon') *n.* the largest and northernmost island of the Philippines.

Lvov (lə vôf′) *n.* a city in the southwestern part of the Soviet Union in the Ukraine. Pop. (1970), 553,000.

-ly¹ *suffix* (used to form adverbs) **1.** in a particular manner or to a particular extent: *gladly, greatly.* **2.** in a particular position or at a particular time: *secondly, hourly.* [Old English *-līce.*]

-ly² *suffix* (used to form adjectives) **1.** like, of the nature of, or suited to: *brotherly, princely.* **2.** happening at specified periods of time: *weekly.* [Old English *-lic.*]

ly·ce·um (lī sē′əm, lī′sē əm) *n.* **1.** a public hall in which educational programs, as concerts or lectures, are presented. **2.** an organization devoted to such educational programs. [Latin *Lycēum* a school near Athens where Aristotle taught.]

Lyd·i·a (lid′ē ə) *n.* an ancient country in western Asia Minor. —**Lyd′i·an,** *adj., n.*

lye (lī) *n.* **1.** sodium hydroxide, used to make soap and detergents. **2.** a strong solution obtained from wood ashes, used in making soap.

ly·ing¹ (lī′ing) *v.* the present participle of **lie¹.** —*n.* the act of telling lies. —*adj.* untruthful or deceitful: *a lying person.*

ly·ing² (lī′ing) the present participle of **lie².**

lymph (limf) *n.* a clear, colorless fluid, similar to blood in composition, that bathes the body cells, bringing nourishment and oxygen to the cells and carrying away waste products.

lym·phat·ic (lim fat′ik) *adj.* **1.** of, relating to, or carrying lymph: *lymphatic vessels.* **2.** dull; sluggish.

lymph gland, any of the small nodes or bodies in the lymphatic vessels that filter out harmful substances and produce lymphocytes. Also, **lymph node.**

lym·pho·cyte (lim′fə sīt′) *n.* one of the white blood cells formed in the lymph glands.

lym·phoid (lim′foid) *adj.* of, relating to, or resembling lymph or the tissue of the lymph glands.

lynch (linch) *v.t.* to seize by mob action and put to death, usually by hanging, without due process of law: *The townspeople lynched the suspected murderer.* —**lynch′er,** *n.*

Lynn (lin) *n.* a port city in eastern Massachusetts, a suburb of Boston. Pop. (1970), 90,293.

lynx (lingks) *n. pl.,* **lynx** or **lynx·es.** a wildcat having long legs, a short tail, and tufted ears.

lynx-eyed (lingks′īd′) *adj.* having sharp vision.

Ly·on (lē ôn′; *French* lyôn) *n.* a city in east-central France. Pop. (1968), 527,800. Also, **Ly·ons** (lī′ənz).

ly·on·naise (lī′ə naz′) *adj.* cooked with finely chopped onions: *lyonnaise potatoes.*

Lynx

Ly·ra (lī′rə) *n.* a constellation in the northern sky, thought to resemble a lyre in shape. It contains the bright star Vega.

lyre (līr) *n.* a stringed musical instrument, used by the ancient Greeks to accompany singing and recitation.

lyre·bird (līr′burd′) *n.* an Australian bird, having brown feathers. The male has a long tail that is lyre-shaped when spread.

lyr·ic (lir′ik) *adj.* of or relating to poetry that expresses strong personal emotion. Also, **lyr·i·cal** (lir′ik əl). —*n.* **1.** a lyric poem or lyric poetry. **2.** **lyrics.** the words written for a song: *That popular song has very clever lyrics.* —**lyr′i·cal·ly,** *adv.*

ly·sin (lī′sin) *n.* any antibody that is capable of bringing about the destruction of tissues, bacteria, or cells, especially red blood cells.

Lyrebird

at; āpe; cär; end; mē; it; īce; hot; ōld; fôrk; wood; fōol; oil; out; up; turn; sing; thin; this; hw in white; zh in treasure. The symbol ə stands for the sound of **a** in about, **e** in taken, **i** in pencil, **o** in lemon, and **u** in circus.

L

1. Egyptian Hieroglyphics	4. Early Hebrew
2. Semitic	5. Greek Ninth Century B.C.
3. Early Phoenician	6. English

M is the thirteenth letter of the English alphabet. The way we write the capital letter **M** today is very much like the way it was written in the time of the earliest alphabets. An Egyptian hieroglyphic (1) depicting an owl was probably the ancestor of the ancient Semitic letter *mem* (2), meaning "water." The design of the early forms of *mem* looks something like waves on the surface of water. The shape of *mem* was altered in the early Phoenician (3) and early Hebrew (4) alphabets by being made angular. The early Greeks (5) borrowed this angular form of *mem* and called it *mu*. In writing *mu*, the Greeks altered the older angular forms by making the first and last strokes of the letter nearly vertical. This form was only slightly altered in the following centuries and looks almost like our modern capital letter **M** (6).

m, M (em) *n. pl.,* **m's, M's. 1.** the thirteenth letter of the English alphabet. **2.** the Roman numeral for 1000.

m. 1. mile; miles. **2.** meter; meters. **3.** minute; minutes. **4.** month. **5.** meridian.

M. 1. Monday. **2.** Master. **3.** Monsieur.

ma (mä) *n. Informal.* mother.

M.A., Master of Arts.

ma'am (mam) *n. Informal.* madam.

ma·ca·bre (mə kä′brə, mə kä′bər) *adj.* suggesting or dealing with death in a frightening way; gruesome; ghastly: *a macabre tale of a haunted cemetery.*

mac·ad·am (mə kad′əm) *n.* a pavement or road made largely or entirely of layers of crushed stone. [From John L. *McAdam,* 1756–1836, a Scottish engineer who developed such a pavement.]

mac·ad·am·ize (mə kad′ə mīz′) *v.t.,* **mac·ad·am·ized, mac·ad·am·iz·ing.** to construct or pave (a road) with macadam. —**mac·ad′am·i·za′tion,** *n.*

Ma·cao (mə kou′) *n.* **1.** a Portuguese province on a peninsula on the southern coast of China. Area, 6 sq. mi. Pop. (1971 est.), 320,000. **2.** a seaport on this peninsula. Pop. (1970), 226,710.

ma·caque (mə kak′, mə käk′) *n.* any of various short-tailed monkeys of Asia and northern Africa having cheek pouches.

mac·a·ro·ni (mak′ə rō′nē) *n. pl.,* **mac·a·ro·nis** or **mac·a·ro·nies.** a food made from flour paste or dough, usually in the shape of short, hollow tubes. Macaroni is prepared for eating by boiling.

mac·a·roon (mak′ə rōōn′) *n.* a small cake or cookie made of ground almonds or coconut, egg whites, and sugar.

Mac·Ar·thur, Douglas (mə kär′thər) 1880–1964, U.S. general.

Ma·cau·lay, Thomas Bab·ing·ton (mə kô′lē; bab′ing tən) 1800–1859, English historian.

ma·caw (mə kô′) *n.* any of several long-tailed, brilliantly colored parrots of Central and South America.

Mac·beth (mək beth′) *n.* the main character in William Shakespeare's play *Macbeth.*

mace¹ (mās) *n.* **1.** a heavy club, usually having a spiked metal head, used as a weapon in the Middle Ages. **2.** an ornamental staff shaped like such a club, used as a ceremonial symbol of office or authority. [Old French *mace.*]

mace² (mās) *n.* a spice made by grinding the dried outer covering of the seed of the nutmeg. [French *macis.*]

mace³ (mās) *n.* a chemical mixture containing tear gas. [From the trademark *Chemical Mace,* from *mace¹.*]

Macaw

Mac·e·do·ni·a (mas′ə dō′nē ə) *n.* **1.** an ancient country north of Greece, the center of the empire created by Alexander the Great. Also, **Mac·e·don** (mas′ə don′). **2.** a historic region in southeastern Europe, including parts of Greece, Yugoslavia, and Bulgaria. —**Mac′e·do′ni·an,** *adj., n.*

mac·er·ate (mas′ə rāt′) *v.,* **mac·er·at·ed, mac·er·at·ing.** —*v.t.* **1.** to soften or separate into parts by soaking in liquid. **2.** to cause (the body) to waste away or grow thin. —*v.i.* to become macerated. —**mac′er·a′tion,** *n.*

ma·chet·e (mə shet′ē, mə chet′ē) *n.* a broad, heavy knife used as a tool and weapon, especially in Latin America.

Mach·i·a·vel·li, Nic·co·lo (mak′ē ə vel′ē; nē′kō lō′) 1469–1527, Italian statesman and political scientist.

Mach·i·a·vel·li·an (mak′ē ə vel′ē ən) *adj.* **1.** acting according to the political theories of Machiavelli, who wrote that a ruler could use any evil means to keep his power and achieve his goals. **2.** of or relating to Machiavelli or his political theories. —*n.* a follower of the political theories of Machiavelli.

mach·i·nate (mak'ə nāt') *v.i.,* **mach·i·nat·ed, mach·i·nat·ing.** to scheme or plot slyly or secretly: *The rebels machinated to overthrow the king.*

mach·i·na·tion (mak'ə nā'shən) *n.* a sly, secret, or elaborate plot or scheme.

ma·chine (mə shēn') *n.* **1.** an apparatus consisting of a number of fixed or moving parts, used to do work: *a drying machine for clothes.* **2.** a device that is used to transmit, redirect, or concentrate an applied physical force. The lever, pulley, screw, and inclined plane are among the simple machines. **3.** a group that controls an organization: *a political machine.* **4.** a person who acts in a mechanical way without thought, emotion, or will. —*v.t.,* **ma·chined, ma·chin·ing.** to make, shape, or finish with a machine.

ma·chine-gun (mə shēn'gun') *v.t.,* **ma·chine-gunned, ma·chine-gun·ning.** to fire at or shoot with a machine gun.

machine gun, an automatic weapon that keeps firing as long as the trigger is pressed.

ma·chin·er·y (mə shē'nər ē) *n. pl.,* **ma·chin·er·ies.**
1. machines or machine parts: *The factory is equipped with the latest machinery.* **2.** the working parts of a particular machine: *The mechanics repaired the machinery of the elevator.* **3.** the means or working parts by which something is kept going or a desired result is obtained: *the machinery of government, the machinery of the courts.*

machine shop, a workshop where metal or other material is cut, shaped, and finished with machine tools.

machine tool, a power-driven tool used to cut or shape metal.

ma·chin·ist (mə shē'nist) *n.* **1.** a person who is skilled in using machine tools. **2.** a person who designs, assembles, installs, or repairs machinery.

ma·chis·mo (mä chēz'mō) *n.* a strong or exaggerated concept of masculinity, characterized by aggressiveness and a sense of male superiority. Also, **macho.**

Mach·me·ter (mäk'mē'tər) *n.* a device that measures and shows the speed of an aircraft in relation to the speed of sound.

Mach number (mäk) *also,* **mach number.** a number expressing the ratio of the speed of a moving body in a given atmosphere to the speed of sound in the same atmosphere. If the speed of sound in a given atmosphere is 700 miles per hour, an airplane traveling at the same speed is traveling at a Mach number of 1. If the airplane is flying twice the speed of sound in a given atmosphere, its Mach number is 2. [From Ernst *Mach,* 1838–1916, an Austrian physicist.]

ma·cho (mä'chō) *n. pl.,* **ma·chos. 1.** another word for **machismo. 2.** in Spanish cultures, a strong, brave, and virile man.

Mac·ken·zie (mə ken'zē) *n.* a river in northwestern Canada, flowing into the Arctic Ocean.

mack·er·el (mak'ər əl) *n. pl.,* **mack·er·els** or **mack·er·el.** a food and game fish related to the tuna, having a silvery body that is marked in metallic blue on its upper surface.

mackerel sky, a sky covered with rows of small, white, fleecy clouds resembling the patterns on the back of a mackerel.

Mack·i·nac, Straits of (mak'ə nô', mak'ə nak') a strait connecting Lake Michigan and Lake Huron.

mack·i·naw (mak'ə nô') *n.* **1.** a short coat made of a heavy woolen fabric that is usually woven in a plaid. **2.** a thick blanket made of a heavy woolen fabric, often woven in wide bands of different colors.

mack·in·tosh (mak'in tosh') *n., pl.* **mack·in·tosh·es.** a raincoat, especially one made of a waterproof, rubberized

cloth. [From Charles *Macintosh,* 1766–1843, Scottish chemist who invented this cloth.]

Ma·con (mā'kən) *n.* a city in central Georgia. Pop. (1970), 122,423.

mac·ra·mé (mak'rə mā') *n.* a coarse lacework made by knotting thread or cord, often in geometric patterns.

mac·ro·cosm (mak'rə koz'əm) *n.* the whole world or universe.

ma·cron (mā'kron) *n.* a short horizontal line (¯) placed over a vowel to show that it has a long sound.

mac·ro·nu·cle·us (mak'rō nōō'klē əs, mak'rō nyōō'klē əs) *n.* the larger of the two types of nuclei present in various protozoans, believed to control processes of nutrition.

mad (mad) *adj.,* **mad·der, mad·dest.**
1. feeling or showing great anger, resentment, or irritation: *The boy was very mad because his parents made him stay home from the party to study.* **2.** out of one's mind; crazy; insane. **3.** wildly foolish or reckless; rash: *The two girls had a mad plan to run away from home and go to Africa.* **4.** very enthusiastic: *Jane is mad about football.* **5.** wildly or frantically confused: *There was a mad rush for tickets to the World Series.* **6.** having rabies: *a mad dog.* —**mad'ly,** *adv.* —**mad'ness,** *n.*

Mad·a·gas·car (mad'ə gas'kər) *n.* an island country in the Indian Ocean, east of southern Africa, formerly known as the Malagasy Republic. Capital, Antananarivo. Pop. (1980), 8,472,000.

mad·am (mad'əm) *n. pl.,* **mad·ams** or **mes·dames.** lady; mistress. ▲ used as a form of respectful or polite address to a woman.

mad·ame (ma dam', mad'əm) *n. pl.,* **mes·dames.** Mrs. ▲ A French form of address for a married woman.

mad·cap (mad'kap') *adj.* wildly reckless or foolish: *The men had the madcap idea of climbing the mountain in the snowstorm.* —*n.* a person who is madcap.

mad·den (mad'ən) *v.t.* to make very angry: *The lazy boy's refusal to help maddened his friends.* —*v.i.* to become maddened.

mad·den·ing (mad'ən ing) *adj.* causing anger, resentment, or irritation: *a maddening delay, a maddening traffic jam.* —**mad'den·ing·ly,** *adv.*

mad·der[1] (mad'ər) *n.* **1.** a climbing plant of Asia and southern Europe, having long, fleshy red roots. **2.** a red dye made from the roots of this plant. **3.** a brilliant red color. [Old English *mædere.*]

mad·der[2] (mad'ər) the comparative of **mad.**

mad·dest (mad'ist) the superlative of **mad.**

mad·ding (mad'ing) *adj. Archaic.* acting as if mad: *Far from the madding crowd's ignoble strife* (Thomas Gray).

made (mād) *v.* the past tense and past participle of **make.** —*adj.* produced, built, or shaped. ▲ often used in combination: *a well-made chair, a handmade sweater.*

Ma·dei·ra (mə dēr'ə) *n.* **1.** a Portuguese island group in the north Atlantic, off the coast of Morocco. Also, **Madeira Islands. 2.** the largest island in this group.

Macramé

at; āpe; cär; end; mē; it; īce; hot; ōld; fôrk; wood; fōōl; oil; out; up; turn; sing; thin; this; hw in white; zh in treasure. The symbol ə stands for the sound of a in about, e in taken, i in pencil, o in lemon, and u in circus.

M

3. a sweet, amber-colored wine originally made on the island of Madeira.

mad·e·moi·selle (mad′ə mə zel′, mad′mwə zel′) *n.* *pl.,* **mes·de·moi·selles** or **mad·e·moi·selles.** miss. ▲ A French form of address for an unmarried girl or woman.

made-up (mād′up′) *adj.* **1.** not real or true; fictitious: *a made-up name.* **2.** having cosmetics or make-up on.

mad·house (mad′hous′) *n.* *pl.,* **mad·hous·es** (mad′hou′-ziz). **1.** formerly, a hospital or asylum for the mentally ill. **2.** a place or scene of wild uproar or confusion: *After our football team won, the locker room was a madhouse.*

Mad·i·son (mad′ə sən) *n.* **1. James.** 1751–1836, the fourth president of the United States, from 1809 to 1817. **2.** the capital of Wisconsin, in the south-central part of the state. Pop. (1970), 173,258.

Madison Avenue 1. a street in New York City where the offices of many advertising firms are located. **2.** the U.S. advertising industry as a whole.

mad·man (mad′man′, mad′mən) *n.* *pl.,* **mad·men** (mad′men′, mad′mən). a man who is or seems to be insane.

Ma·don·na (mə don′ə) *n.* **1.** the Virgin Mary. **2.** a picture or statue of the Virgin Mary.

Ma·dras (mə dras′) *n.* a port city in southeastern India. Pop. (1971), 2,470,288.

mad·ras (mad′rəs, mə dras′) *n.* a cotton fabric usually having a plaid, checked, or striped pattern. [From *Madras,* where it was first made.]

Ma·drid (mə drid′) *n.* the capital and largest city of Spain, in the central part of the country. Pop. (1971 est.), 3,200,000.

mad·ri·gal (mad′ri gəl) *n.* **1.** a short, lyric medieval poem that can be set to music. **2.** a song with parts for several voices, sung without the accompaniment of instruments.

mael·strom (māl′strəm) *n.* **1.** a large, violent or turbulent whirlpool. **2.** something like such a whirlpool in intensity, violence, or destructive force: *the maelstrom of war.* **3. Maelstrom.** a dangerous whirlpool located in a strait off the northwestern coast of Norway.

maes·tro (mīs′trō) *n.* *pl.,* **maes·tros.** any noted conductor, composer, or teacher of music.

Ma·fi·a (mä′fē ə) *n.* **1.** a secret criminal society in Sicily. **2.** an alleged secret criminal organization said to be related to this society, thought to be active in the United States and other countries.

mag·a·zine (mag′ə zēn′, mag′ə zēn′) *n.* **1.** a publication issued weekly or monthly, usually bound in a paper cover and containing articles, stories, pictures, or other features. **2.** a building or room for storing ammunition and explosives, as in a ship or fort. **3.** a metal container for holding bullets or cartridges so that they can be fed into the chamber of a gun for firing.

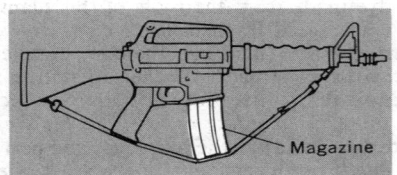

Magazine

Mag·de·burg (mag′də burg′) *n.* a port city in west-central East Germany, on the Elbe River. Pop. (1971), 270,503.

Ma·gel·lan (mə jel′ən) *n.* **1. Ferdinand.** 1480?–1521, Portuguese explorer and navigator. **2. Strait of.** a strait at the southern tip of South America, linking the Atlantic and the Pacific Oceans.

ma·gen·ta (mə jen′tə) *n.* a purplish-red color. —*adj.* having the color magenta.

mag·got (mag′ət) *n.* the wormlike larva of a fly, having a thick body and no legs.

Ma·gi (mā′jī, maj′ī) *n.,pl.* in the New Testament, the three wise men from the East who brought gifts to the infant Jesus.

mag·ic (maj′ik) *n.* **1.** the art or practice of pretending to know how to summon and use supernatural forces

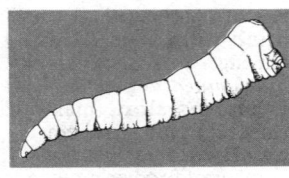

Maggot

with spells, charms, rituals, and the like. **2.** the art or skill of doing tricks or producing baffling effects or illusions, especially for entertainment: *The children loved to see magic performed at parties.* **3.** an enchanting influence; mysterious charm: *The magic of her smile made him fall in love with her.* —*adj.* relating to, done by, or used in magic: *a magic act, a magic trick, a magic wand.*

mag·i·cal (maj′i kəl) *adj.* of, relating to, or done by magic. —**mag·i·cal·ly,** *adv.*

ma·gi·cian (mə jish′ən) *n.* **1.** an entertainer who does tricks or sleight of hand: *The audience applauded when the magician pulled two rabbits from his hat.* **2.** a person who is skilled in the use of magic; sorcerer; wizard.

magic lantern, an early kind of projector for showing slides on a screen or wall.

mag·is·te·ri·al (maj′is tēr′ē əl) *adj.* **1.** of, relating to, or suiting a person in a position of authority; commanding: *a magisterial manner.* **2.** domineering; dictatorial. **3.** of or relating to a magistrate, his office, or his duties. —**mag·is·te·ri·al·ly,** *adv.*

mag·is·tra·cy (maj′is trə sē) *n.* *pl.,* **mag·is·tra·cies. 1.** the office, duties, or term of a magistrate. **2.** magistrates as a group. **3.** the district of a magistrate.

mag·is·trate (maj′is trāt′) *n.* **1.** a government officer who has the power to apply and enforce the law. **2.** a judge having limited power, such as a justice of the peace.

mag·ma (mag′mə) *n.* molten rock beneath the surface of the earth, from which lava and igneous rocks are formed.

Mag·na Car·ta (mag′nə kär′tə) *also,* **Mag·na Char·ta.** the charter that King John of England was forced to grant to his barons at Runnymede on June 15, 1215. The Magna Carta guaranteed certain civil rights and liberties to the barons, merchants, and clergymen of England by limiting the power of the king.

mag·na cum lau·de (mag′nə koom lou′də, mag′nə kum lô′dē) with high honors or praise. ▲ used to show graduation with high honors from a college or university.

mag·na·nim·i·ty (mag′nə nim′ə tē) *n.* *pl.,* **mag·na·nim·i·ties. 1.** the quality of being magnanimous. **2.** a magnanimous act.

mag·nan·i·mous (mag nan′ə məs) *adj.* generous and noble of mind and heart, especially in overlooking insults or grievances; free from pettiness: *The winning candidate was magnanimous toward his opponent.* —**mag·nan′i·mous·ly,** *adv.* —**mag·nan·i·mous·ness,** *n.*

mag·nate (mag′nāt) *n.* a person of great power, importance, or wealth in a field of activity: *a railroad magnate, a shipping magnate.*

mag·ne·sia (mag nē′shə, mag nē′zhə) *n.* a white powder compound used especially in laxatives.

mag·ne·si·um (mag nē′zē əm, mag nē′zhəm) *n.* a tough, very light, silver-white metallic element used especially in the making of lightweight alloys. Symbol: **Mg**

mag·net (mag′nit) *n.* **1.** a piece of stone, metal, or ore, usually shaped like a bar or horseshoe, that has the property of attracting or repelling iron or steel. **2.** a person or thing that attracts.

mag·net·ic (mag net′ik) *adj.* **1.** having the properties of a magnet; able to exert magnetism. **2.** of, relating to, producing, or caused by magnetism. **3.** of or relating to the magnetism of the earth. **4.** having the power to attract followers, supporters, or listeners: *The senator was a magnetic speaker.* —**mag·net′i·cal·ly,** *adv.*

magnetic field, the region around a magnet or an electric current, in which a magnetic force can be detected.

magnetic flux, the total number of lines of force in a magnetic field. Also, **flux.**

magnetic needle, a slender bar of magnetized steel, as in a compass, that points approximately toward the earth's north and south magnetic poles.

magnetic north, the direction toward which the end of a compass needle points, usually differing from true north.

magnetic pole 1. either of the two points of a magnet where its magnetic force seems to be greatest. **2.** either of two points on the earth's surface that are the poles of the earth's magnetic field, and toward which a compass needle points. The north magnetic pole is at approximately 75 degrees north latitude and 101 degrees west longitude. The south magnetic pole is at approximately 69 degrees south latitude and 14 degrees east longitude.

magnetic tape, a thin tape coated with magnetically sensitive material, used to record sound.

mag·net·ism (mag′nə tiz′əm) *n.* **1.** the quality of certain materials and of all electric currents that makes it possible for them to produce a magnetic field outside themselves, and to attract iron, steel, and other materials. **2.** the branch of physics dealing with magnets, their fields of force, and their magnetic qualities. **3.** a strong power to attract, influence, or charm.

mag·net·ite (mag′nə tīt′) *n.* a black magnetic iron ore often found in igneous and metamorphic rocks.

mag·net·ize (mag′nə tīz′) *v.t.,* **mag·net·ized, mag·net·iz·ing. 1.** to give magnetic qualities to; make into a magnet. **2.** to attract as if by a magnet; fascinate; charm. —**mag′net·i·za′tion,** *n.* —**mag′net·iz′er,** *n.*

mag·ne·to (mag nē′tō) *n. pl.,* **mag·ne·tos.** a small generator of alternating current, using permanent magnets rather than electromagnets.

magni- *combining form* great; large: *magnify.*

mag·ni·fi·ca·tion (mag′nə fi kā′shən) *n.* **1.** the act, process, or degree of magnifying. **2.** the state of being magnified. **3.** something that has been magnified.

mag·nif·i·cence (mag nif′ə səns) *n.* the state or quality of being magnificent.

mag·nif·i·cent (mag nif′ə sənt) *adj.* **1.** very beautiful or splendid: *The house on the top of the hill has a magnificent view of the valley.* **2.** very good; exceptional; outstanding. —**mag·nif′i·cent·ly,** *adv.*

mag·ni·fy (mag′nə fī′) *v.,* **mag·ni·fied, mag·ni·fy·ing.** —*v.t.* **1.** to cause to look larger than the real size: *This microscope magnifies objects 1000 times.* **2.** to cause to seem greater or more important; exaggerate: *Some people magnify the dangers involved in traveling by airplane.* —*v.i.* to increase or have the power to increase the apparent size of an object: *The lens in his camera magnifies well.* —**mag′ni·fi′er,** *n.*

magnifying glass, a lens or combination of lenses that causes something to look larger than it really is.

mag·ni·tude (mag′nə tōōd′, mag′nə tyōōd′) *n.* **1.** size or extent, especially greatness of size or extent: *the magnitude of a problem, the magnitude of an angle.* **2.** importance; significance: *The splitting of the atom was an achievement of great magnitude.* **3.** the relative brightness of a star or other heavenly body as measured on a numerical scale.

mag·no·lia (mag nōl′yə) *n.* **1.** any of a group of ornamental trees and tall shrubs having large, fragrant flowers. **2.** the flower itself, growing in white, rose, purple, or yellow. [Modern Latin *Magnolia,* from Pierre *Magnol,* 1638–1715, a French botanist.]

Magnolia

mag·pie (mag′pī) *n.* **1.** a noisy, long-tailed bird having a stout black-and-white bill. **2.** a person who chatters or talks constantly.

mag·uey (mag′wā) *n.* **1.** a Mexican plant that yields long, tough fibers used for making cord and rope. **2.** the fiber obtained from such a plant.

Mag·yar (mag′yär) *n.* **1.** a member of a people who settled in Hungary in the ninth century. **2.** the language of the Magyars; Hungarian. —*adj.* of or relating to the Magyars or their language; Hungarian.

ma·ha·ra·jah (mä′hə rä′jə) *also,* **ma·ha·ra·ja.** *n.* a former ruling prince of India.

ma·ha·ra·ni (mä′hə rä′nē) *also,* **ma·ha·ra·nee.** *n.* **1.** the wife of a maharajah. **2.** a former ruling princess of India.

ma·hat·ma (mə hät′mə) *n.* a wise and holy person. ▲ often used as a Hindu title of reverence for a spiritual leader: *Mahatma Gandhi.*

Ma·hi·can (mə hē′kən) *n. pl.,* **Ma·hi·cans** or **Ma·hi·can.** a member of a tribe of North American Indians, formerly living in the area of the upper Hudson River. Also, **Mohican.**

mah jongg (mä′ jong′) *also,* **mah-jongg, mah-jong.** a game of Chinese origin for two to four players, played with 152 decorated tiles. The object of the game is to obtain any of various winning combinations of tiles.

ma·hog·a·ny (mə hog′ə nē) *n. pl.,* **ma·hog·a·nies. 1.** a strong, hard, reddish-brown or yellowish wood of a tropical evergreen tree, widely used for making furniture and musical instruments. **2.** the tree yielding this wood. **3.** a rich reddish-brown color. —*adj.* having the color mahogany; reddish-brown.

Ma·hom·et (mə hom′it) another name for **Muhammad.**

Ma·hom·et·an (mə hom′ət ən) another name for **Muslim.**

ma·hout (mə hout′) *n.* an elephant driver or trainer.

maid (mād) *n.* **1.** a female servant. **2.** a girl or young unmarried woman.

maid·en (mād′ən) *n.* a girl or young unmarried woman. —*adj.* **1.** of, relating to, or like a maiden. **2.** unmarried: *a maiden lady.* **3.** first or earliest: *a ship's maiden voyage.*

maid·en·hair (mād′ən her′) *n.* any of a large group of delicate ferns, having slender stems and feathery fronds.

maid·en·ly (mād′ən lē) *adj.* characteristic of or suited to a maiden: *maidenly modesty.* —**mai′den·li·ness,** *n.*

maiden name, a woman's last name before she is married.

maid-in-wait·ing (mād′in wā′ting) *n. pl.,* **maids-in-wait·ing.** an unmarried woman, especially a noblewoman, who attends a queen or princess.

---

at; āpe; cär; end; mē; it; īce; hot; ōld; fôrk; wood; fōōl; oil; out; up; turn; sing; thin; this; hw in white; zh in treasure. The symbol ə stands for the sound of **a** in about, **e** in taken, **i** in pencil, **o** in lemon, and **u** in circus.

maid of honor *pl.,* **maids of honor. 1.** the chief unmarried female attendant of the bride at a wedding. **2.** a maid-in-waiting.

maid·ser·vant (mād′sur′vənt) *n.* a female servant.

mail¹ (māl) *n.* **1.** letters and packages sent or received by post. **2.** a collection of such material sent or delivered at a specific time: *His check should arrive in today's mail.* **3.** *also,* **mails.** the system by which mail is collected, transported, and delivered, usually operated by the national government; postal system. —*v.t.* to send by mail: *to mail a package.* [Old French *male* a bag, pouch; originally referring to the pouch in which letters were carried.]

mail² (māl) *n.* flexible armor for protecting the body, made of interlinked rings of metal. —*v.t.* to cover or protect with mail. [Old French *maille.*]

mail·box (māl′boks′) *n. pl.,* **mail·box·es. 1.** a box into which mail is deposited for collection by the post office. **2.** a box into which mail is delivered, as at a person's home.

mail carrier, a person who carries and delivers mail.

mail·gram (māl′gram′) *n.* a letter sent by telegraph to a local post office from which it is delivered together with regular mail.

mail·man (māl′man′) *n. pl.,* **mail·men** (māl′men′). a person who carries and delivers mail. Also, **postman.**

mail order, an order for merchandise that is received and filled by mail. —**mail′·or′der,** *adj.*

maim (mām) *v.t.* to injure or disfigure seriously and horribly, especially to deprive of a limb; cripple; mutilate.

main (mān) *adj.* greatest or foremost in size, extent, or importance; principal: *the main branch of a library.* —*n.* **1.** a principal pipe, duct, conduit, or cable for the passage of water, gas, sewage, or electricity. **2.** the open sea.

main clause, another term for **independent clause.**

Maine (mān) *n.* a state in the northeastern United States, on the Atlantic. Capital, Augusta. Area, 33,215 sq. mi. Pop. (1970), 992,048. Abbreviation, **Me.**

● The name **Maine** comes from the term "the main" (also spelled "the maine") which means "the mainland." It was used by explorers of the coast of New England to distinguish the mainland from the many islands along the coast.

main·land (mān′land′, mān′lənd) *n.* the body of land forming the principal or largest land mass of a region, country, or continent, as distinguished from an island or peninsula: *the mainland of Greece.*

main·line (mān′līn′) *v.t., v.i.,* **main·lined, main·lin·ing.** *Slang.* to inject (a narcotic or other illegal drug) directly into a vein. —**main′lin′er,** *n.*

main·ly (mān′lē) *adv.* for the most part; chiefly: *He is interested mainly in automobiles.*

main·mast (mān′mast′, mān′məst) *n.* the principal mast of a ship.

main·sail (mān′sāl′, mān′səl) *n.* the principal sail of a ship, set on the mainmast.

main·sheet (mān′shēt′) *n.* a rope used to set the mainsail at the proper angle to the wind.

main·spring (mān′spring′) *n.* **1.** the principal spring in a mechanism, especially in a watch or clock. **2.** the main purpose, motive, or cause: *The mainspring of his life was his desire for success.*

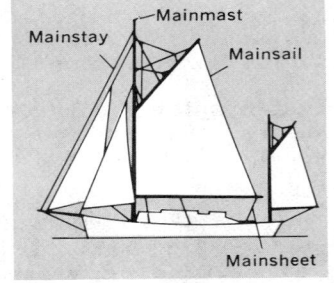

Mainstay
Mainmast
Mainsail
Mainsheet

Mainmast

main·stay (mān′stā′) *n.* **1.** a rope that supports or steadies the mast of a sailing ship. **2.** a person or thing that is the main support of something: *Joe is the mainstay of the football team.*

main·stream (mān′strēm′) *n.* the main direction or trend of development: *That senator's political beliefs are in the mainstream of American politics.*

main·tain (mān tān′) *v.t.* **1.** to go on with; continue: *He maintained a high speed on the expressway, but slowed down as he approached the exit.* **2.** to keep in force, operation, or proper condition: *The city maintains the streets.* **3.** to keep or hold on to: *It was hard for him to maintain his balance on the icy path. The senator maintained his position on a tax increase.* **4.** to state positively or firmly: *No matter what others may think, I still maintain that he is the best man for the job.* **5.** to provide for the support or upkeep of: *He tries to maintain a large family on a small income.* [Old French *maintenir* to carry on with, support, from Latin *manū tenēre* literally, to hold in the hand.]

main·te·nance (mān′tə nəns) *n.* **1.** the act of maintaining or the state of being maintained. **2.** means of support or upkeep.

main·top (mān′top′) *n.* a platform at the head of the lower section of a mainmast.

main yard, the lower yard on the mainmast of a sailing ship.

maize (māz) *n.* **1.** see **corn** *(defs. 1, 2).* **2.** the color of ripe corn; deep yellow. —*adj.* having the color maize; deep yellow.

maj., major.

ma·jes·tic (mə jes′tik) *adj.* having or showing majesty: *a majestic mountain.* Also, **ma·jes·ti·cal** (mə jes′ti kəl). —**ma·jes′ti·cal·ly,** *adv.*

maj·es·ty (maj′is tē) *n. pl.,* **maj·es·ties. 1.** very great dignity, splendor, or grandeur: *The queen was seated on the throne in all her majesty.* **2.** supreme authority or power: *the majesty of the law.* **3.** the form of address used when speaking to or about a sovereign, preceded by *His, Her,* or *Your.*

ma·jor (mā′jər) *adj.* **1.** greater in size, amount, value, importance, or rank: *The Rockies are a major mountain system in America. He is a major player on the basketball team. Mr. Smith's partner takes the major credit for the success of the business.* **2.** *Music.* of, relating to, or based on a major scale: *a major chord, a major key.* —*n.* **1.** in the U.S. Army, Air Force, and Marine Corps, an officer ranking below a lieutenant colonel and above a captain. **2.** the main subject studied at a college or university: *Bill's major is physics.* **3.** **majors.** see **major league.** —*v.i.* to study or specialize in a major subject or field: *Joe majored in English.*

Ma·jor·ca (mə jôr′kə, mə yôr′kə) *n.* the largest of the Balearic Islands in the western Mediterranean. —**Major′can,** *adj., n.*

ma·jor·do·mo (mā′jər dō′mō) *n. pl.,* **ma·jor·do·mos. 1.** the chief steward in a royal, noble, or great household. **2.** a butler; steward.

ma·jor·ette (mā′jə ret′) *n.* another word for **drum majorette.**

major general, in the U.S. Army, Air Force, and Marine Corps, an officer ranking below a lieutenant general and above a brigadier general.

ma·jor·i·ty (mə jôr′ə tē, mə jor′ə tē) *n. pl.,* **ma·jor·i·ties. 1.** the larger number or part of a whole; more than half: *The majority of the students voted to have a dance.* **2.** the amount by which a larger number exceeds a smaller number; margin. **3.** the age at which a person is said to have full legal rights and responsibilities, usually twenty-one.

▲ **Majority** and **plurality** both refer to a winning number of votes. A **majority** is more than half the total number of votes cast. A **plurality** is the number of votes that the winning candidate receives over the highest total of another candidate. If, in a school election in which 100 votes were cast, Betty had 46 votes, John 29 votes, and Joe 25 votes, Betty would lack a majority, but would have a plurality of 17 votes over John.

major league **1.** either of the two main groups of professional baseball teams in the United States. **2.** any league of principal importance in certain other professional sports, such as ice hockey. —**ma′jor-league′**, *adj.*

major scale, a musical scale consisting of eight tones, having half steps instead of whole steps after the third and seventh notes.

make (māk) *v.,* **made, mak·ing.** —*v.t.* **1.** to form or bring into being; construct: *The birds made a nest in the tree.* **2.** to cause to be or occur; bring about: *The slamming door made a loud noise. They made a change in their plans. The two countries made peace.* **3.** to put in a certain condition; cause to become: *The smell of food made him hungry.* **4.** to cause to act or behave in a particular manner: *Peeling the onions made my eyes water.* **5.** to cause to seem or appear: *That dress makes her look thin.* **6.** to force or compel (a person) to do something: *The police could not make the prisoner confess.* **7.** to fashion or reach in one's mind: *to make plans, to make a decision.* **8.** to perform (an action); do: *to make a phone call, to make a speech.* **9.** to earn or gain: *He makes $3.50 an hour.* **10.** to prepare or arrange for use: *to make breakfast, to make a bed.* **11.** to amount to; add up to: *Five and five make ten. Twelve inches make one foot.* **12.** to bring about or make certain the success of: *Her singing made the show.* **13.** *Informal.* to succeed in winning a place or position on: *She made the cheerleading squad.* **14.** to arrive at; reach: *They barely made the train.* —*v.i.* **1.** to move or set out; head: *The ship made for the nearest harbor.* **2.** to put oneself in a certain condition: *The team made ready for the game.* **3.** to act or behave in a certain manner: *to make merry.* —*n.* **1.** a particular style or type of manufactured article; brand. **2.** the way in which a thing is made.

to make after. to chase; pursue.

to make away with. a. to steal. **b.** to kill. **c.** to get rid of or consume.

to make for. a. to be favorable to; help: *The sunny weather made for a pleasant weekend at the beach.* **b.** to provide: *This book makes for very enjoyable reading.*

to make it. *Informal.* to succeed: *That actor has really made it in the movies.*

to make off with. to carry off; steal.

to make out. a. to write out or fill out: *to make out a shopping list, to make out a check.* **b.** to manage to see or read clearly: *I can't make out his handwriting.* **c.** to get along; succeed: *How did you make out at the job interview?*

to make over. a. to change or redo: *The tailor made over Tom's jacket because it was too large.* **b.** to transfer ownership of.

to make up. a. to be the parts of; constitute: *Nine players make up a baseball team.* **b.** to become friendly or loving again: *The two friends quarreled, but now they have made up.* **c.** to invent or create in the mind: *He made up an excuse for being late.* **d.** to put cosmetics on (the face): *Her eyes were very heavily made up.*

make-be·lieve (māk′bi lēv′) *n.* an imagining or acting out in play; fantasy: *The story about ghosts in the house is only make-believe.* —*adj.* imaginary: *The cardboard box became a make-believe rocket ship.*

mak·er (mā′kər) *n.* **1.** a person or thing that makes something. ▲ often used in combination: *noisemaker, shoemaker, troublemaker.* **2. Maker.** God.

make·shift (māk′shift′) *n.* something used temporarily in place of the proper or usual thing: *He used a carton as a makeshift for a table.* —*adj.* of, like, or used as a makeshift: *The sofa was a makeshift bed.*

make·up (māk′up′) *also,* **make·up.** *n.* **1.** cosmetics put on the face. Rouge, lipstick, eyeshadow, and mascara are kinds of make-up. **2.** the cosmetics, wigs, or other articles used by a performer for his or her role. **3.** the way in which something is put together. **4.** physical, mental, or moral nature: *It isn't in his make-up to be rude to people.* **5.** an examination taken by a student for an earlier examination that he or she has missed or failed.

mal- *prefix* bad or badly; wrong or wrongly: *malpractice, malnutrition.*

Ma·la·bo (mä lä′bō) *n.* the capital of Equatorial Guinea, formerly known as Santa Isabel. Pop. (1970), 17,500.

Mal·a·chi (mal′ə kī′) *n.* **1.** a Hebrew prophet of the fifth century B.C. **2.** the last book of the Protestant Old Testament, believed to have been written by him.

mal·a·chite (mal′ə kīt′) *n.* a bright-green copper ore used for making ornaments and jewelry.

mal·ad·just·ed (mal′ə jus′tid) *adj.* poorly adjusted, especially to one's surroundings or circumstances.

mal·ad·just·ment (mal′ə just′mənt) *n.* poor adjustment.

mal·a·droit (mal′ə droit′) *adj.* lacking in skill; awkward; clumsy: *His maladroit motions on the dance floor caused him to step on his partner's foot.* —**mal′a·droit′ly,** *adv.* —**mal′a·droit′ness,** *n.*

mal·a·dy (mal′ə dē) *n. pl.,* **mal·a·dies.** **1.** a sickness or disease. **2.** any disturbed or unwholesome condition: *social maladies.*

Mál·a·ga (mal′ə gə, mä′lə gə) *n.* a port city in southern Spain. Pop. (1976 est.), 443,823.

Mal·a·gas·y Republic (mal′ə gas′ē) see **Madagascar.**

mal·a·prop·ism (mal′ə prop iz′əm) *n.* a funny or silly misuse of words, especially the use of one word for another having a similar sound but a different meaning. For example: *What are you incinerating* (insinuating) *by that last remark?* or *The police learned of the crime by means of a unanimous* (anonymous) *telephone call.* [From Mrs. *Malaprop,* a character in the play *The Rivals* (1775) by Richard Brinsley Sheridan, who was noted for her misuse of words.]

ma·lar·i·a (mə ler′ē ə) *n.* a disease characterized by chills, high fever, and sweating. Malaria is caused by microscopic parasites introduced into the bloodstream by the bite of certain mosquitoes. [Italian *mal′aria,* from *mala aria* bad air; because it was once believed that foul air coming from swamps caused this disease.]

ma·lar·i·al (mə ler′ē əl) *adj.* **1.** relating to or caused by malaria. **2.** having malaria.

Ma·la·wi (mə lä′wē) *n.* a country in southeastern Africa, formerly the British protectorate of Nyasaland. Capital, Lilongwe. Area, 45,483 sq. mi. Pop. (1980), 6,162,000.

Ma·lay (mā′lā) *n.* **1.** a member of a people of southeast-

at; āpe; cär; end; mē; it; īce; hot; ōld; fôrk; wood; fōōl; oil; out; up; turn; sing; thin; **this**; hw in white; zh in treasure. The symbol ə stands for the sound of a in about, e in taken, i in pencil, o in lemon, and u in circus.

M

ern Asia living in the Malay Peninsula, eastern Sumatra, parts of Borneo, Singapore, and some nearby islands. **2.** the language of the Malays. —*adj.* of or relating to the Malays, their language, or their culture.

Ma·lay·a (mə lā′ə) *n.* a region of southeastern Asia on the Malay Peninsula. Malaya is a part of Malaysia and is known as West Malaysia.

Ma·lay·an (mə lā′ən) *adj., n.* another word for **Malay.**

Malay Archipelago, a large island group in the Pacific Ocean, between Australia and southeastern Asia. Also, **East Indies.**

Malay Peninsula, a long, narrow peninsula in southeastern Asia, including Malaya and part of Thailand.

Ma·lay·sia (mə lā′zhə) *n.* **1.** a country in southeastern Asia, divided by the South China Sea, comprising Malaya on the west and Sarawak and Sabah on the east. Capital, Kuala Lumpur. Land area, 128,430 sq. mi. Pop. (1980), 13,640,000. **2.** another name for the **Malay Archipelago.** —**Mal·lay′sian,** *adj., n.*

mal·con·tent (mal′kən tent′) *adj.* unhappy or dissatisfied. —*n.* a person who is malcontent.

Mal·dives (mal′dīvz) an island country in the Indian Ocean. Capital, Male. Land area, 115 sq. mi. Pop. (1980 est.), 148,000.

male (māl) *adj.* **1.** of or relating to the sex that can be the father of young. **2.** see **masculine** (*def. 1*). **3.** of or relating to a plant that bears stamens. **4.** (of an object or device) having a part designed to be inserted into a corresponding hollow part: *a male electric plug.* —*n.* a male person, animal, or plant. —**male′ness,** *n.*

Ma·le (mä′lē) *n.* the capital of Maldives. Pop. (1978), 29,555.

mal·e·dic·tion (mal′ə dik′shən) *n.* **1.** a curse. **2.** malicious talk; slander.

mal·e·fac·tor (mal′ə fak′tər) *n.* **1.** a person who commits a crime; criminal. **2.** an evildoer. —**mal′e·fac′-tress,** *n.*

ma·lev·o·lence (mə lev′ə ləns) *n.* the wish for evil or harm to happen to others.

ma·lev·o·lent (mə lev′ə lənt) *adj.* doing or desiring to do evil or harm to others. —**ma·lev′o·lent·ly,** *adv.*

mal·fea·sance (mal fē′zəns) *n.* *Law.* wrongdoing, especially by a public official: *Police officers are guilty of malfeasance if they accept bribes.*

mal·for·ma·tion (mal′fôr mā′shən) *n.* an abnormal or faulty formation or structure, especially in a part of the body.

mal·formed (mal′fôrmd′) *adj.* having an abnormal or faulty structure or formation; misshapen: *Surgery was employed to repair the patient's malformed foot.*

mal·func·tion (mal′fungk′shən) *n.* the failure to function or work properly: *A malfunction in the carburetor caused the car to stall.* —*v.i.* to fail to function or work properly.

Ma·li (mä′lē) *n.* a country in western Africa. Capital, Bamako. Area, 463,950 sq. mi. Pop. (1980), 6,646,000.

mal·ice (mal′is) *n.* the wish to cause harm, injury, or pain to another; spite: *With malice toward none; with charity for all* (Abraham Lincoln).

ma·li·cious (mə lish′əs) *adj.* characterized by, showing, or resulting from malice: *a malicious person, malicious gossip.* —**ma·li′cious·ly,** *adv.* —**ma·li′cious·ness,** *n.*

ma·lign (mə līn′) *v.t.* to tell damaging lies about; speak ill of; slander: *to malign someone's character.* —*adj.* harmful or injurious.

ma·lig·nan·cy (mə lig′nən sē) *n.* *pl.,* **ma·lig·nan·cies.** **1.** the state or quality of being malignant. Also, **ma·lig·nance** (mə lig′nəns). **2.** any malignant disease or condition, especially a cancerous tumor.

ma·lig·nant (mə lig′nənt) *adj.* **1.** tending to spread through the body and eventually cause death: *a malignant tumor.* **2.** evil or harmful; malicious: *malignant lies that hurt a person's reputation.* —**ma·lig′nant·ly,** *adv.*

ma·lig·ni·ty (mə lig′nə tē) *n.* *pl.,* **ma·lig·ni·ties.** **1.** the state or quality of being malign. **2.** something evil or harmful.

ma·lin·ger (mə ling′gər) *v.i.* to try to avoid work or duty, especially by pretending to be sick or injured. —**ma·lin′ger·er,** *n.*

mall (môl) *n.* **1.** a public walk or promenade that is often lined with trees. **2.** a shopping area closed off to vehicles.

mal·lard (mal′ərd) *n.* *pl.,* **mal·lards** or **mal·lard.** a common wild duck, the male of which has a green head, a white band around the neck, a reddish-brown breast, and a grayish back.

Mallard

mal·le·a·ble (mal′ē ə bəl) *adj.* **1.** that can be hammered, pressed, or beaten into various shapes without breaking. **2.** easy to change or influence: *That young child has a malleable personality.* —**mal·le·a·bil·i·ty** (mal′ē ə bil′ə tē), *n.*

mal·let (mal′it) *n.* **1.** a short-handled hammer with a heavy, usually wooden, head. **2.** a long-handled wooden hammer used to strike the ball in certain games, such as croquet or polo.

mal·le·us (mal′ē əs) *n.* *pl.,* **mal·le·i** (mal′ē ī′). one of the three bones of the middle ear; hammer.

mal·low (mal′ō) *n.* any of various plants having pink or white flowers.

malm·sey (mäm′zē) *n.* a sweet white wine.

mal·nu·tri·tion (mal′nōō trish′ən, mal′nyōō trish′ən) *n.* a condition caused by a lack of enough food or of the right kinds of food.

mal·oc·clu·sion (mal′ə klōō′zhən) *n.* a condition in which the teeth of the upper and lower jaws do not meet properly.

mal·o·dor·ous (mal ō′dər əs) *adj.* having a bad odor. —**mal·o′dor·ous·ly,** *adv.* —**mal·o′dor·ous·ness,** *n.*

mal·prac·tice (mal prak′tis) *n.* **1.** the improper or harmful treatment of a patient by a doctor. **2.** improper or wrong conduct in any professional or official position.

malt (môlt) *n.* **1.** a cereal grain, especially barley, steeped in warm water until it sprouts and then dried. Malt is used chiefly in brewing and distilling. **2.** an alcoholic beverage or liquor brewed from malt, such as beer or ale. —*v.t.* **1.** to cause (grain) to become malt. **2.** to treat or mix with malt.

Mal·ta (môl′tə) *n.* **1.** a country consisting of an island group in the Mediterranean, south of Sicily. Capital, Valletta. Land area, 122 sq. mi. Pop. (1980), 340,000. Also, **Maltese Islands. 2.** the chief island of this country.

malted milk 1. a powdered preparation consisting chiefly of dried milk and malted cereals. **2.** *also,* **malted.** a drink made by mixing this preparation with milk and sometimes ice cream.

Mal·tese (môl tēz′) *n.* *pl.,* **Mal·tese. 1.** a person who was born or is living in Malta. **2.** the language of Malta. —*adj.* of or relating to Malta, its people, or their language.

Maltese cat, a short-haired, bluish-gray domestic cat.

Maltese cross, a cross with four arms that resemble arrowheads.

malt·ose (môl′tōs) *n.* a colorless compound formed by the action of an enzyme on starch. It is used as a foodstuff and as a sweetener.

mal·treat (mal trēt') *v.t.* to treat badly or cruelly; abuse: *to maltreat an animal.* —**mal·treat'ment,** *n.*

ma·ma (mä'mə) *also,* **mam·ma.** *n. Informal.* mother.

mam·bo (mäm'bō) *n. pl.,* **mam·bos.** 1. a Latin American dance. 2. the music for this dance. —*v.i.* to dance the mambo.

mam·mal (mam'əl) *n.* any of a class of warm-blooded animals with backbones, the females of which have mammary glands. Human beings, dogs, elephants, porcupines, bats, cows, and whales are all mammals. —**mam·ma·li·an** (mə mā'lē ən), *adj., n.*

mam·ma·ry gland (mam'ər ē) a gland that produces milk, with which female mammals nourish their young.

Mam·mon (mam'ən) *n.* 1. the personification of riches and worldy gain. 2. *usually,* **mammon.** riches regarded as an evil influence or as an object of greed.

mam·moth (mam'əth) *n.* an extinct prehistoric elephant that had long, upward-curving tusks and shaggy, black hair. —*adj.* of immense size; huge; gigantic.

Mammoth

mam·my (mam'ē) *n. pl.,* **mam·mies.** *Informal.* mother.

man (man) *n. pl.,* **men.** 1. an adult male human being. 2. a member of the human race; human being; person: *All men are created equal.* 3. human beings; the human race; mankind: *the study of man through the ages.* 4. a male human being thought to have strength, courage, and the like. 5. a male worker or servant. 6. one of the pieces used to play certain games, such as chess and checkers. —*v.t.,* **manned, man·ning.** 1. to supply with people, as for work or defense: *Soldiers manned the fort.* 2. to take one's place or station at: *Man the torpedoes.*

Man, Isle of (man) an island in the Irish Sea, administered by the United Kingdom.

man·a·cle (man'ə kəl) *n.* 1. *usually,* **manacles.** handcuffs. 2. anything that restrains or binds. —*v.t.,* **man·a·cled, man·a·cling.** 1. to put manacles on: *Guards manacled the prisoners.* 2. to restrain or bind; hamper.

man·age (man'ij) *v.,* **man·aged, man·ag·ing.** —*v.t.* 1. to direct or guide the affairs or operation of: *to manage a department store, to manage a political campaign.* 2. to succeed in doing: *I'll manage to visit you before I leave.* 3. to control or train; handle: *The cowboy managed the wild horse well.* —*v.i.* to be able to succeed or get along: *I don't know how the team will manage without him.*

man·age·a·ble (man'i jə bəl) *adj.* that can be managed: *a manageable horse.* —**man'age·a·bil'i·ty,** *n.* —**man'age·a·bly,** *adv.*

man·age·ment (man'ij mənt) *n.* 1. the act, art, or practice of managing: *The store went out of business because of bad management.* 2. the person or persons who manage a business, institution, or the like: *She complained to the management of the hotel about the poor service.*

man·ag·er (man'i jər) *n.* 1. a person who directs, guides, or controls: *the manager of a store, the manager of a baseball team.* 2. a person who is skilled in managing: *She is a good manager and lives thriftily.* —**man'ag·er·ship',** *n.*

man·a·ge·ri·al (man'ə jēr'ē əl) *adj.* of or relating to a manager or management: *managerial duties.*

Ma·na·gua (mə nä'gwə) *n.* the capital and largest city of Nicaragua, in the southwestern part of the country. Pop. (1971), 398,514.

Ma·na·ma (mə nam'ə) *n.* the capital of Bahrain. Pop. (1971), 89,112.

ma·ña·na (mä nyä'nä) *Spanish. adv.* 1. tomorrow. 2. at some future time. —*n.* some future time.

man-at-arms (man'ət ärmz') *n. pl.,* **men-at-arms.** a soldier in the Middle Ages.

man·a·tee (man'ə tē') *n.* a sea animal having two broad front flippers and a tail shaped like a paddle. The manatee is found in the warm coastal waters of the Atlantic Ocean.

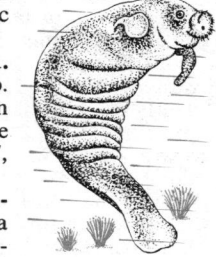
Manatee

Man·ches·ter (man'ches'tər) *n.* 1. a city in northwestern England. Pop. (1978 est.), 489,300. 2. a city in southern New Hampshire, on the Merrimack River. Pop. (1970), 87,754.

Man·chu (man'choo) *n. pl.,* **Man·chus** or **Man·chu.** 1. a member of a Mongolian people living in Manchuria, who conquered China in 1644 and established a dynasty that ruled until 1912. 2. the language of the Manchus. —*adj.* of or relating to the Manchus or to their dynasty, language, or culture.

Man·chu·ri·a (man choor'ē ə) *n.* a region in northeastern China. —**Man·chu'ri·an,** *adj., n.*

man·da·rin (man'dər in) *n.* 1. a member of any of the nine ranks of high public officials under the Chinese empire. 2. **Mandarin.** the principal dialect of the Chinese language. It is the official language of the People's Republic of China. 3. see **mandarin orange.** —*adj.* of, relating to, or characteristic of a mandarin.

mandarin orange, a small, sweet orange having a thin rind that is easy to peel.

man·date (man'dāt) *n.* 1. instruction or support given by voters to their representatives in government, expressed by the results of an election or vote. 2. an official command, order, or charge. 3. a commission given by the League of Nations to a member nation for the administration of a former German colony or other conquered territory. 4. a territory so administered. —*v.t.,* **man·dat·ed, man·dat·ing.** to administer (a territory) under a mandate.

man·da·to·ry (man'də tôr'ē) *adj.* 1. contained in or required by a mandate or rule: *Fastening your seat belt when the plane takes off is mandatory.* 2. of or relating to a mandate.

man·di·ble (man'də bəl) *n.* 1. the bone of the lower jaw. 2. the upper or lower part of a bird's beak. 3. one of a pair of jawlike parts used for seizing and biting, on either side of the mouth opening in insects.

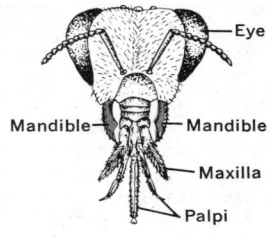
Mandible *(def. 3)*

man·do·lin (mand'əl in') *n.* a musical instrument hav-

at; āpe; cär; end; mē; it; īce; hot; ōld; fôrk; wood; fōōl; oil; out; up; turn; sing; thin; this; hw in white; zh in treasure. The symbol ə stands for the sound of a in about, e in taken, i in pencil, o in lemon, and u in circus.

ing a pear-shaped body that is flat on one side, and metal strings, usually played by plucking with a plectrum.

man·drake (man′drāk′) *n.* **1.** a low-growing plant having thick fleshy roots, oval leaves, and cup-shaped flowers. **2.** the root of this plant, formerly believed to have magical powers.

man·drel (man′dril) *n.* **1.** a shaft, spindle, or similar piece for holding material to be shaped or worked, as on a lathe. **2.** a metal rod or core around which material may be shaped, cast, or bent.

man·drill (man′dril) *n.* a large ground-dwelling baboon of tropical western Africa. The male has brilliantly colored markings on the face and rump.

Mandrake

mane (mān) *n.* long, heavy hair along the back and around the neck of certain animals, such as the horse and lion.

ma·neu·ver (mə nōō′vər) *also, British,* **ma·noeu·vre.** *n.* **1.** a planned and strategic movement of troops or ships. **2.** *usually,* **maneuvers.** military exercises, used for training purposes: *The new troops were sent out on maneuvers.* **3.** any skillful or clever move or plan: *The politician used many maneuvers to gain the party's nomination for governor.* —*v.t.* **1.** to cause troops or ships to perform a maneuver or maneuvers: *The captain maneuvered his men into a position for attacking the enemy.* **2.** to move or manage skillfully or cleverly: *I maneuvered my way through the crowd at the entrance to the theater.* —*v.i.* **1.** to perform a maneuver or maneuvers. **2.** to use skillful or clever moves or plans. —**ma·neu′ver·er,** *n.*

ma·neu·ver·a·ble (mə nōō′vər ə bəl) *adj.* that can be maneuvered, especially easily: *That small airplane is very maneuverable.* —**ma·neu′ver·a·bil′i·ty,** *n.*

man Friday **1.** a dependable, faithful servant, aide, or follower. **2.** a male employee, especially in an office, with many kinds of duties. [From *Friday,* the faithful servant and companion in the novel *Robinson Crusoe* (1719) by Daniel Defoe.]

man·ful (man′fəl) *adj.* having or showing a manly spirit; brave; resolute. —**man′ful·ly,** *adv.* —**man′ful·ness,** *n.*

man·ga·nese (mang′gə nēz′) *n.* a brittle, silver-gray, metallic element, used especially in the production of steel. Symbol: **Mn**

mange (mānj) *n.* a contagious skin disease of cattle, horses, dogs, and other domestic animals. Mange is caused by certain mites, and is characterized by scaly pimples and often by a loss of hair.

man·ger (mān′jər) *n.* a box or trough used to hold feed for horses or cattle.

man·gle¹ (mang′gəl) *v.t.,* **man·gled, man·gling. 1.** to spoil or destroy, as by tearing or crushing; mutilate; disfigure: *The dog mangled the rubber toy by chewing on it.* **2.** to make imperfect or mar; ruin; botch: *The girl's bad piano playing mangled the entire concert.* [Anglo-Norman *mangler* to mutilate, maim, from Old French *mahaignier* to mutilate, maim.]

man·gle² (mang′gəl) *n.* a machine for pressing and smoothing cloth by passing it between rollers. —*v.t.,* **man·gled, man·gling.** to press or smooth with a mangle: *to mangle sheets.* [Dutch *mangel,* possibly short for *mangelstok* a rolling pin.]

man·go (mang′gō) *n. pl.,* **man·goes** or **man·gos. 1.** a yellowish-red, oval, edible fruit of a tree of the cashew family. The mango has a sweet, spicy taste. **2.** the tropical evergreen tree bearing this fruit.

man·grove (man′grōv′) *n.* any of several tropical evergreen trees found in marshy and coastal regions. Some mangroves have branches that send down roots resembling tree trunks.

Mangrove

man·gy (mān′jē) *adj.,* **man·gi·er, man·gi·est. 1.** having, resembling, or caused by mange: *a mangy old cat.* **2.** worn, dirty, and shabby; seedy: *The tramp wore a mangy old coat.* —**man′gi·ly,** *adv.* —**man′gi·ness,** *n.*

man·han·dle (man′hand′əl) *v.t.,* **man·han·dled, man·han·dling.** to handle or treat roughly: *The prisoner charged that the guards had manhandled him.*

Man·hat·tan (man hat′ən) *n.* an island and borough of New York City, in southeastern New York. Area, 22.6 sq. mi. Pop. (1970), 1,524,541.

man·hole (man′hōl′) *n.* an opening, usually with a removable cover, through which a sewer, steam boiler, or other structure may be entered for inspection or repair.

man·hood (man′hood′) *n.* **1.** the state of being an adult male human being: *to reach manhood.* **2.** character or qualities, such as strength and courage, considered to be manly. **3.** men as a group.

man-hour (man′our′) *n.* the amount of work that can be done by one man in one hour, used as a unit or standard of measurement in industry.

man·hunt (man′hunt′) *n.* an intensive search for someone: *a manhunt for an escaped prisoner.*

ma·ni·a (mā′nē ə) *n.* **1.** great enthusiasm or desire: *The boy has a mania for popular music.* **2.** a form of insanity characterized by great excitability and often violent behavior.

ma·ni·ac (mā′nē ak′) *n.* a person who is or seems wildly or violently insane; madman. —*adj.* wildly or violently insane.

ma·ni·a·cal (mə nī′ə kəl) *adj.* of, relating to, or characteristic of mania or a maniac: *maniacal laughter.* —**ma·ni′a·cal·ly,** *adv.*

man·ic (man′ik) *adj.* relating to, resembling, or affected by mania: *a manic personality, a manic mood.*

man·i·cure (man′ə kyoor′) *n.* the cleaning, shaping, and polishing of the fingernails. —*v.t.,* **man·i·cured, man·i·cur·ing. 1.** to give a manicure to. **2.** *Informal.* to trim evenly, closely, or elaborately: *The gardener manicured the lawns of the park.* —**man′i·cur′ist,** *n.*

man·i·fest (man′ə fest′) *v.t.* **1.** to make obvious or clear; show plainly: *He manifested his approval of the plan by nodding.* **2.** to be evidence of; prove: *The fireman's daring rescue of the children from the burning house manifested his courage.* —*adj.* plainly apparent; evident; obvious. —*n.* a list of cargo or passengers for a ship or plane.

man·i·fes·ta·tion (man′ə fes tā′shən) *n.* **1.** the act of manifesting or the state of being manifested. **2.** something that manifests; indication; sign.

man·i·fes·to (man′ə fes′tō) *n. pl.,* **man·i·fes·toes** or **man·i·fes·tos.** a public declaration or proclamation of principles or goals.

man·i·fold (man′ə fōld′) *adj.* **1.** of many kinds or varieties; multiple; diverse: *Her new job has manifold duties.* **2.** having many parts or features: *The novel is a manifold portrait of society.* —*n.* a pipe fitting having several openings for connecting one pipe with others. The exhaust manifold of a car conducts exhausts from each cylinder of the engine to a single exhaust pipe.

man·i·kin (man′ə kin) *also,* **man·ni·kin.** *n.* **1.** a little man; dwarf. **2.** an anatomical model of the human body, such as one used for teaching anatomy. **3.** another spelling of **mannequin.**

ma·nil·a (mə nil′ə) *n.* **1.** see **Manila hemp. 2.** see **Manila paper.** —*adj.* made of Manila paper: *a manila envelope.*

Ma·nil·a (mə nil′ə) *n.* the largest city of the Philippines, on the island of Luzon. Pop. (1970), 1,310,600.

Manila hemp, a fiber obtained from the leaves of the abaca, widely used in the manufacture of rope, cord, and paper.

Manila paper, a strong, brown or yellow paper originally made from Manila hemp, used especially for bags, envelopes, and file folders.

man·i·oc (man′ē ok′) *n.* another word for **cassava** (*def. 1*).

ma·nip·u·late (mə nip′yə lāt′) *v.t.,* **ma·nip·u·lat·ed, ma·nip·u·lat·ing. 1.** to try to influence, adapt, or manage to one's own advantage: *He manipulated other people to do what he wanted.* **2.** to manage or work with the hands, especially in a skillful manner: *By manipulating a few wires, he repaired the lamp.* **3.** to change, falsify, or tamper with for one's own purpose or profit: *The cashier manipulated bank funds so that his theft would not be discovered.* —**ma·nip′u·la′tive,** *adj.* —**ma·nip′u·la′tor,** *n.*

ma·nip·u·la·tion (mə nip′yə lā′shən) *n.* the act of manipulating or the state of being manipulated.

Man·i·to·ba (man′ə tō′bə) *n.* a province in south-central Canada. Area, 251,000 sq. mi. Pop. (1971), 988,247. —**Man′i·to′ban,** *adj., n.*

man·i·tou (man′ə tōō′) *also,* **man·i·to, man·i·tu.** *n.* among the Algonquian Indians, a spirit or god that controls nature.

man·kind (*def. 1* man′kīnd′, *def. 2* man′kīnd′) *n.* **1.** human beings as a group; the human race. **2.** men as a group.

man·like (man′līk′) *adj.* **1.** suitable for a man; manly: *manlike bravery.* **2.** like a man: *manlike apes.*

man·ly (man′lē) *adj.,* **man·li·er, man·li·est. 1.** having the qualities thought of as characteristic of a man. **2.** relating to or suitable for a man: *Football is a manly sport.* —**man′li·ness,** *n.*

man-made (man′mād′) *adj.* made by man, rather than formed by nature; synthetic; artificial: *There was man-made snow on the ski slope.*

Mann (*def. 1* man, *def. 2* män) **1. Horace.** 1796–1859, U.S. educator. **2. Thomas.** 1875–1955, German author.

man·na (man′ə) *n.* **1.** in the Old Testament, the food miraculously supplied to the Israelites during their flight from Egypt. **2.** anything that is badly needed and is unexpected: *The praise of his classmates was manna to the shy boy.*

man·ne·quin (man′i kin) *also,* **man·i·kin.** *n.* **1.** a full-sized, usually jointed model of a human figure, used especially for displaying clothes. **2.** a woman who models clothes.

man·ner (man′ər) *n.* **1.** the way in which something is done: *Please put a heading on your paper in the usual manner.* **2.** a way of acting or behaving: *The man's gruff manner frightened the children.* **3. manners.** polite ways of behaving or acting: *He has very poor table manners.* **4.** kind or sort: *What manner of person is she?* —**man′ner·less,** *adj.*

man·nered (man′ərd) *adj.* **1.** having (a specified kind of) manner or manners. ▲ used in combination: *well-mannered.* **2.** having mannerisms; stilted: *The actor gave a mannered performance.*

man·ner·ism (man′ə riz′əm) *n.* **1.** a peculiar trait or way of acting: *He has the mannerism of rubbing his nose when he is talking.* **2.** an affected or exaggerated use of a particular manner or style: *The senator's speech was full of mannerisms.*

man·ner·ly (man′ər lē) *adj.* having or showing good manners; polite. —*adv.* with good manners; politely. —**man′ner·li·ness,** *n.*

Mann·heim (män′hīm′) *n.* a port city in south-central West Germany, on the Rhine. Pop. (1969 est.), 330,900.

man·ni·kin (man′i kin) another spelling of **manikin** (*defs. 1 and 2*).

man·nish (man′ish) *adj.* **1.** of, for, or characteristic of a man: *The library has a mannish atmosphere.* **2.** like a man: *She dresses in a mannish way.* —**man′nish·ly,** *adv.* —**man′nish·ness,** *n.*

ma·noeu·vre (mə nōō′vər) *British. n., v.t., v.i.,* **ma·noeu·vred, ma·noeu·vring.** another spelling of **maneuver.**

man-of-war (man′əv wôr′) *n. pl.,* **men-of-war.** a warship.

man·or (man′ər) *n.* **1.** under the feudal system, an estate granted to a lord, in which part of the land was divided among serfs who paid rent to the lord in labor and goods. **2.** land largely farmed by tenants who pay rent to the owner. **3.** a mansion, especially the main house on an estate or manor. —**ma·no·ri·al** (mə nôr′ē əl), *adj.*

man·pow·er (man′pou′ər) *n.* **1.** the total number of persons available for work, as in industry or the armed forces: *the manpower of the automobile industry.* **2.** power or force supplied by the physical work of man.

man·sard (man′särd) *n.* **1.** a roof having two slopes on all sides, with the lower slope almost vertical and the upper slope almost horizontal. **2.** the room or story under such a roof.

manse (mans) *n.* the home of a minister, especially of a Presbyterian minister; parsonage.

man·serv·ant (man′sur′vənt) *n. pl.,* **men·serv·ants.** a male servant.

man·sion (man′shən) *n.* a very large, stately, or imposing house.

man·slaugh·ter (man′slô′tər) *n.* **1.** the unlawful killing of a human being by another, without cold-blooded intent. **2.** the slaying of a human being by another.

man·ta (man′tə) *n.* a fish related to the shark, having a flat body and fins resembling wings. The manta may weigh more than 3000 pounds. Also, **manta ray, devilfish.**

man·tel (mant′əl) *n.* **1.** a structure of stone, brick, or other material, around the opening of a fireplace. **2.** the shelf above a fireplace. Also (*def. 2*), **man·tel·piece** (mant′əl pēs′).

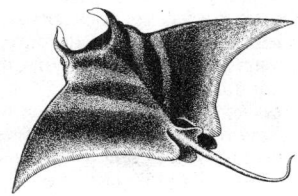

Manta

man·til·la (man til′ə, man tē′ə) *n.* a covering for the head worn by women, especially in Spain and Latin America. The mantilla is usually made of black or white lace.

man·tis (man′tis) *n. pl.,* **man·tis·es** or **man·tes** (man′tēz). see **praying mantis.**

at; āpe; cär; end; mē; it; īce; hot; ōld; fôrk; wood; fōōl; oil; out; up; turn; sing; thin; this; hw in white; zh in treasure. The symbol ə stands for the sound of **a** in about, **e** in taken, **i** in pencil, **o** in lemon, and **u** in circus.

man·tle (mant′əl) *n.* **1.** a loose cloak, usually without sleeves. **2.** something that covers, conceals, or envelops: *the mantle of night.* **3.** the layer of the earth's interior between the crust and the core. **4.** in mollusks, a fleshy fold of tissue that encloses the internal organs and secretes the shell. **5.** the feathers on the back and wings of a bird. —*v.t.,* **man·tled, man·tling.** to cover with or as if with a mantle; conceal; envelop: *The snow mantled the whole countryside in white.*

man·u·al (man′yoō əl) *adj.* **1.** relating to, done by, or involving the use of the hands: *manual crafts, manual labor.* **2.** operated by hand: *a manual control.* —*n.* a book of basic instructions or other information on a particular subject; handbook. —**man′u·al·ly,** *adv.*

manual alphabet, an alphabet used to communicate with the deaf, consisting of a series of signs made with the fingers, each sign representing a letter of the written alphabet.

manual training, practical training in work involving the use of the hands, such as woodworking.

man·u·fac·ture (man′yə fak′chər) *v.t.,* **man·u·fac·tured, man·u·fac·tur·ing.** **1.** to make or produce (a product), especially on a large scale by means of machinery. **2.** to make or process (a raw material) into a form or product suitable for use: *to manufacture wool into cloth.* **3.** to make up; invent: *to manufacture an excuse.* —*n.* **1.** the act or process of manufacturing. **2.** something manufactured; product.

man·u·fac·tur·er (man′yə fak′chər ər) *n.* a person or company whose business is manufacturing.

ma·nure (mə noor′, mə nyoor′) *n.* a natural substance, especially the waste matter of domestic animals, used as fertilizer. —*v.t.,* **ma·nured, ma·nur·ing.** to put manure in or on.

man·u·script (man′yə skript′) *n.* **1.** the typewritten or handwritten version of a book, article, or other work, prepared for a publisher or printer. **2.** a book or document written by hand, especially one written before the invention of printing.

Manx (mangks) *n.* **1. the Manx.** the people of the Isle of Man. **2.** the language spoken on the Isle of Man. —*adj.* of or relating to the Isle of Man, its people, or their language.

Manx cat, a short-haired domestic cat having long hind legs, a high, rounded rump, and, usually, no tail.

man·y (men′ē) *adj.,* **more, most.** consisting of or amounting to a large number; numerous: *The library has many books on history.* —*n.* **1.** a large number: *Many of the club members were not at the meeting.* **2. the many.** the majority of people. —*pron.* a large number of persons or things: *Many were late for the party because of the bad weather.*

Mao·ism (mou′iz′əm) *n.* the political theories, principles, and practices of Mao Tse-tung.

Mao·ist (mou′ist) *n.* a person who believes in or supports Maoism.

Ma·o·ri (mou′rē) *n. pl.,* **Ma·o·ris.** **1.** a member of a Polynesian people living in New Zealand. **2.** the language of these people. —*adj.* of or relating to the Maoris or their language.

Mao Tse-tung (mou′tsə toong′, mou′dzu doong′), *also,* **Mao Ze·dong,** 1893–1976, Chinese Communist leader.

map (map) *n.* **1.** a drawing or other representation of all or part of the earth's surface, usually showing cities, rivers, oceans, mountains, and other features. **2.** a drawing or representation of all or part of the sky, usually showing the position of the stars and planets. —*v.t.,* **mapped, map·ping. 1.** to make a map of; represent on a map.

2. to plan in detail: *His family mapped out his future.*
off the map. out of existence: *The enemy threatened to wipe the region off the map.*
to put on the map. *Informal.* to make well-known: *The discovery of oil in the area put the town on the map.*

ma·ple (mā′pəl) *n.* **1.** any of a large group of trees growing throughout the Northern Hemisphere, having lobed leaves and small two-winged fruits. **2.** the wood of these trees, used in the manufacture of furniture. **3.** the flavor of maple syrup or of maple sugar.

maple sugar, a sugar made by boiling down maple syrup.

maple syrup, a syrup made by boiling and concentrating the sap of the sugar maple or of any other maple tree.

Ma·pu·to (mä poō′tō) *n.* the capital of Mozambique. Pop. (1970), 383,775.

mar (mär) *v.t,* **marred, mar·ring. 1.** to spoil the appearance of; damage: *Water stains marred the table top.* **2.** to damage the quality or character of; impair: *His rude behavior marred an otherwise enjoyable evening.*

Mar., March.

mar·a·bou (mar′ə boō′) *n.* **1.** any of several storks of Africa, India, and southeastern Asia, having white, black, and gray feathers. **2.** the soft, downy feathers of this bird, often used in trimming hats. **3.** the trimming or material made from such feathers.

ma·ra·ca (mə rä′kə) *n.* a musical instrument made of a dried gourd or gourd-shaped rattle that contains seeds or pebbles, often played in pairs.

Marabou

Mar·a·cai·bo (mar′ə kī′bō) *n.* **1.** a port city in northwestern Venezuela, near the Caribbean Sea. Pop. (1971), 651,574. **2. Lake.** a lake in northwestern Venezuela.

mar·a·schi·no cherry (mar′ə skē′nō, mar′ə shē′nō) a cherry preserved in a sweet syrup, often used in drinks.

Ma·rat, Jean Paul (mä rä′; zhän) 1743–1793, French revolutionary leader.

Mar·a·thon (mar′ə thon′) *n.* the plain in Attica, Greece, where the Athenians defeated the Persians in battle in 490 B.C.

mar·a·thon (mar′ə thon′) *n.* **1.** a foot race of 26 miles and 385 yards, run over an open course. **2.** any long race or other competition testing the endurance of the participants; endurance contest: *a dance marathon.* [From *Marathon;* from the legend that a Greek messenger ran 26 miles from Marathon to Athens to announce the Athenian victory over the Persians.]

ma·raud (mə rôd′) *v.i.* to roam or wander in search of plunder; make raids for booty. —*v.t.* to plunder; raid.

ma·raud·er (mə rô′dər) *n.* a person who roams in search of booty or plunder.

mar·ble (mär′bəl) *n.* **1.** a hard stone formed of crystalized limestone, usually mottled or streaked with swirls of different colors, widely used in architecture and sculpture. **2.** a piece, block, or slab of marble. **3.** something made of or resembling marble. **4.** a small hard ball of glass or other material used in children's games. **5. marbles.** any of various games played with a number of these balls. ▲ used with a singular verb. —*adj.* made of or resembling marble. —*v.t.,* **mar·bled, mar·bling.** to color or streak in imitation of marble.

march¹ (märch) *v.i.* **1.** to walk with regular, measured steps, especially in an orderly group or formation: *The soldiers marched down the avenue.* **2.** to move in a steady, deliberate, or solemn manner. **3.** to go or move forward steadily: *Time marches on.* —*v.t.* to cause (someone) to march: *The sergeant marched the troops up and down the field.* —*n. pl.,* **march·es. 1.** the act of marching. **2.** the distance covered by a march: *a twenty-mile march.* **3.** a steady forward movement: *the march of time.* **4.** a regular measured step. **5.** a musical composition having a strong, steady beat and suitable for marching. [French *marcher* to walk.] —**march·er,** *n.*

march² (märch) *n. pl.,* **march·es.** *usually,* **marches.** a region along the border of a country; frontier. [Old French *marche* frontier, boundary.]

March (märch) *n. pl.,* **March·es.** the third month of the year, having thirty-one days. [Old French *march,* from Latin *Martius (mēnsis)* (month) of *Mars,* the Roman god of war.]

mar·chion·ess (mär′shə nis) *n. pl.,* **mar·chion·ess·es.** *British.* another word for **marquise.**

Mar·co·ni, Gu·gliel·mo (mär kō′nē; gō̅ōl yel′mō) 1874–1937, Italian electrical engineer who helped develop the wireless telegraph.

Mar·co Po·lo (mär′kō pō′lō) see **Polo, Marco.**

Mar·cus Au·re·li·us (mär′kəs ô rē′lē əs) A.D. 121–180, Roman emperor and philosopher.

Mar·di Gras (mär′dē grä′) **1.** the last day before Lent. Also, **Shrove Tuesday. 2.** the celebration held in honor of this day, marked by parades and festivities.

mare¹ (mer) *n.* the female of certain animals, such as the horse, donkey, or zebra. [Old English *mere.*]

ma·re² (mär′ā) *n. pl.,* **ma·ri·a.** any of various dark, smooth lowlands on the moon's surface. [Modern Latin *mare,* from Latin *mare* sea; so named by the Italian scientist Galileo, 1564–1642, because he thought these lowlands were seas.]

mar·ga·rine (mär′jər in, mär′jə rēn) *also,* **mar·ga·rin** (mär′jər in). *n.* a food product made from animal or vegetable oil, milk, water, and salt, used as a substitute for butter. Also, **oleomargarine.**

mar·gin (mär′jin) *n.* **1.** the blank space around the written or printed matter on a page. **2.** the amount allowed or available in addition to what is necessary or needed: *In this rainy weather, allow a margin of fifteen minutes for driving home.* **3.** the amount or degree of difference: *We won the game by a narrow margin.* **4.** an edge or border: *the margin of a river.* **5.** the difference between the cost and selling price of merchandise. **6.** the percentage of the total purchase price of stocks and bonds that the purchaser has to pay in cash. —*v.t.* to provide with a margin; border.

mar·gin·al (mär′jin əl) *adj.* **1.** written or printed in the margin of a page: *marginal notes.* **2.** relating to, forming, or located near an edge or border: *the marginal territories of an empire.* **3.** barely enough: *marginal ability.* **4.** making very little profit. —**mar′gin·al·ly,** *adv.*

mar·gue·rite (mär′gə rēt′) *n.* **1.** a daisy having white petals and a yellow center. **2.** any of several other plants bearing flowers that resemble daisies.

ma·ri·a (mär′ē ə) the plural of **mare².**

Mar·i·an·a Islands (mar′ē an′ə) a volcanic island group in the western Pacific Ocean, administered by the United States. Also, **Mar·i·an·as** (mar′ē an′əz).

Ma·rie An·toi·nette (mə rē′ an′twə net′) 1755–1793, the queen of France from 1774 to 1792.

mar·i·gold (mar′ə gōld′) *n.* **1.** a fragrant yellow, orange, or red flower of any of a group of plants. **2.** the plant bearing this flower. **3.** any of various other plants, such as the pot marigold and the marsh marigold.

mar·i·jua·na (mar′ə wä′nə) *also,* **mar·i·hua·na.** *n.* **1.** a drug obtained from the dried flowering tops of the hemp plant. **2.** the hemp plant.

ma·rim·ba (mə rim′bə) *n.* a musical instrument resembling a large xylophone. The marimba is made up of a series of tuned wooden bars and is played by striking the bars with hand-held hammers.

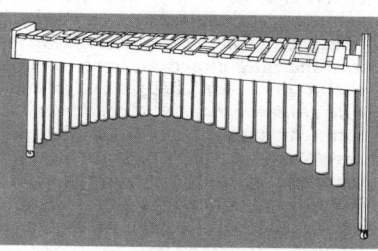

Marimba

ma·ri·na (mə rē′nə) *n.* a dock or basin for mooring and, often, supplying small boats.

mar·i·nade (mar′ə nād′) *n.* a mixture containing vinegar or wine and various spices, in which food is soaked before cooking. —*v.t.,* **mar·i·nad·ed, mar·i·nad·ing.** to marinate.

mar·i·nate (mar′ə nāt′) *v.t.,* **mar·i·nat·ed, mar·i·nat·ing.** to soak (food) in a marinade.

ma·rine (mə rēn′) *adj.* **1.** of or relating to the sea: *marine biology.* **2.** living in the sea: *marine life.* **3.** of, relating to, or used in sea navigation; nautical: *a marine barometer.* **4.** of or relating to commerce or shipping on the sea; maritime. **5.** of or relating to the navy or naval affairs. —*n.* **1. Marine.** a member of the U.S. Marine Corps. **2.** a soldier serving on a ship.

Marine Corps, a branch of the armed forces of the United States, under the Department of the Navy, that specially trains men for overseas landing operations.

mar·i·ner (mar′ə nər) *n.* a person who navigates or assists in navigating a ship; sailor.

mar·i·o·nette (mar′ē ə net′) *n.* a small jointed figure, often of wood, moved by strings, wires, or rods held from above.

mar·i·tal (mar′it əl) *adj.* of or relating to marriage: *marital vows, marital problems.* —**mar′i·tal·ly,** *adv.*

mar·i·time (mar′ə tīm′) *adj.* **1.** bordering on, close to, or living near the sea: *a maritime town, a maritime people.* **2.** of or relating to the sea or to navigation, commerce, or shipping: *maritime law.*

Maritime Provinces, the Canadian provinces of New Brunswick, Nova Scotia, and Prince Edward Island, on the Atlantic Ocean.

Marionette

mar·jo·ram (mär′jər əm) *n.* **1.** an herb related to mint. Marjoram is used for seasoning and, sometimes, as medicine. **2.** the dried leaves of this herb, used as a spice.

mark¹ (märk) *n.* **1.** any visible trace, such as a line, spot, scratch, or stain, left by an object when it comes into contact with the surface of another object. **2.** a sign, symbol, label, inscription, or the like: *a mark of punctuation, an identification mark.* **3.** a number or letter used to show the level or quality of a person's work: *John always got high marks in arithmetic.* **4.** an indication of some quality;

at; āpe; cär; end; mē; it; īce; hot; ōld; fôrk; wood; fōōl; oil; out; up; turn; sing; thin; **th**is; hw in white; zh in treasure. The symbol ə stands for the sound of **a** in about, **e** in taken, **i** in pencil, **o** in lemon, and **u** in circus.

feature or characteristic; trait: *The delicate carving on the bench is a mark of good craftsmanship.* **5.** something, as a line or object, used as a guide, indicator, or point of reference: *The racers have reached the halfway mark.* **6.** something aimed at; target or goal: *The archer missed the mark.* —*v.t.* **1.** to make or put a mark or marks on: *The children marked the sidewalk with chalk.* **2.** to trace, form, or show the limits or boundaries of: *A stone wall marks the end of our property.* **3.** to write down, show, or represent by marks: *I marked my initials on the package.* **4.** to be a feature or characteristic of: *Formality marked the occasion.* **5.** to give or assign a mark to; grade: *The teacher marked the tests.* **6.** to pay attention to; heed: *Mark my words or you will be sorry.* [Old English *mearc* a boundary, trace, sign.]

beside the mark or **wide of the mark. a.** missing what is aimed at. **b.** not to the point; not relevant.

to hit the mark. a. to be accurate; be right. **b.** to attain one's goal; be successful.

to make one's mark. to become famous or successful.

to mark down. to reduce the price of.

to mark time. a. to move the feet as in marching, but without going forward. **b.** to perform the motions or actions of something without really accomplishing anything.

to mark up. to increase the price of.

to miss the mark. a. to fail to attain one's goal; be unsuccessful. **b.** to be inaccurate; be wrong.

mark² (märk) *n.* **1.** see **deutsche mark. 2.** see **ostmark.** [German *Mark.*]

Mark (märk) *n.* **1.** one of the four Evangelists, a disciple of the Apostles Peter and Paul. **2.** one of the four Gospels, the second book of the New Testament.

mark·down (märk′doun′) *n.* a reduction in the selling price of an item.

marked (märkt) *adj.* **1.** very noticeable; obvious: *There is a marked similarity between the two dresses.* **2.** singled out, as for vengeance, punishment, or death: *a marked man.* **3.** having a mark or marks.

mark·ed·ly (mär′kid lē) *adv.* in a marked manner; clearly; obviously.

mark·er (mär′kər) *n.* **1.** a person who marks. **2.** something that marks a place, as a bookmark or gravestone.

mar·ket (mär′kit) *n.* **1.** an open space or building where food products or goods are bought and sold; marketplace: *The farmer took his vegetables to the market every week.* **2.** a shop or store where food products are sold: *a fish market.* **3.** a region or country where goods can be bought and sold: *The company manufactures leather goods for many foreign markets.* **4.** trade and commerce in a service or commodity: *the grain market.* **5.** demand for something: *There is very little market for buggy whips today.* **6.** the available supply of a service or commodity: *a large labor market.* **7.** see **stock market.** —*v.i.* to buy food products and other household items in a market: *Mother goes marketing every Thursday.* —*v.t.* to sell or offer for sale: *The farmer markets his vegetables in town.*

on the market. available for purchase: *That company makes the best television sets on the market.*

to be in the market for. to be interested in buying.

mar·ket·a·ble (mär′ki tə bəl) *adj.* fit for sale; salable. —**mar′ket·a·bil′i·ty,** *n.*

mar·ket·place (mär′kit plās′) *n.* **1.** a place where food products or goods are bought and sold. **2.** business and business activities in general.

mark·ing (mär′king) *n.* **1.** a mark or marks. **2.** *also,* **markings.** the arrangement of marks and colors on a plant or animal: *a bird with red markings.* **3.** the act of making a mark or marks on something.

marks·man (märks′mən) *n. pl.,* **marks·men** (märks′-mən). a person skilled in shooting a gun or other weapon.

marks·man·ship (märks′mən ship′) *n.* skill in shooting a gun or other weapon.

mark·up (märk′up′) *n.* an increase in the selling price of an item.

marl (märl) *n.* a clay containing calcium carbonate and, often, fragments of shells, used in making portland cement and as a fertilizer.

Marl·bor·ough, Duke of (märl′bur′ō) 1650–1722, English general.

mar·lin (mär′lin) *n. pl.,* **mar·lins** or **mar·lin.** a saltwater game fish related to the sailfish and having a long, spear-shaped bill.

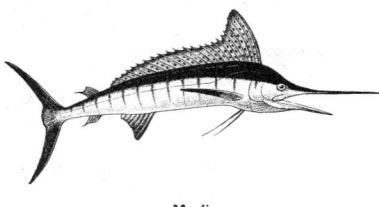

Marlin

mar·line (mär′-lin) *n.* a small cord of two strands loosely twisted together, used for winding around the ends of ropes or cables to prevent fraying.

mar·line·spike (mär′lin spīk′) *also,* **mar·lin·spike.** *n.* a pointed iron pin used to separate strands of rope, as in splicing.

Mar·lowe, Christopher (mär′lō) 1564–1593, English dramatist and poet.

mar·ma·lade (mär′mə lād′) *n.* a jam made by boiling the peel and flesh of fruit, usually citrus fruit, with sugar.

Mar·ma·ra, Sea of (mär′mər ə) a sea between the European and Asian parts of Turkey, connected with the Black Sea by the Bosporus and with the Mediterranean Sea by the Dardanelles.

mar·mo·set (mär′mə zet′) *n.* a monkey of Central and South America, having shaggy or soft and fine fur, long curved claws except on the big toe, and a long tail.

mar·mot (mär′mət) *n.* a plump, short-legged rodent having a gray or brown, thick, coarse coat and a short, bushy tail.

Marmoset

Marne (märn) *n.* a river in east-central France.

ma·roon¹ (mə rōōn′) *n.* a dark brownish-red color. —*adj.* having the color maroon. [French *marron.*]

ma·roon² (mə rōōn′) *v.t.* **1.** to put ashore and leave on a desolate island or coast. **2.** to leave helpless and alone. [French *marron* originally, a runaway slave living in the mountains and forests of the West Indies and Dutch Guiana in the seventeenth and eighteenth centuries.]

mar·quee (mär kē′) *n.* a structure placed over the entrance to a theater, hotel, or other building.

mar·quess (mär′kwis) *n. pl.,* **mar·quess·es.** *British.* another spelling of **marquis.**

Mar·quette, Father Jacques (mär ket′; zhäk) 1637–1675, French missionary who explored the Mississippi River.

mar·quis (mär′kwis, mär kē′) *also, British,* **mar·quess.** *n. pl.,* **mar·quis·es** or **mar·quis** (mär kēz′). a nobleman ranking next below a duke and above an earl or count.

mar·quise (mär kēz′) *n.* **1.** the wife or widow of a marquis. **2.** a woman holding in her own right the rank equal to that of a marquis.

Mar·ra·kesh (mə rä′kish, mar′ə kesh′) *also,* **Mar·ra·kech.** *n.* a city in central Morocco. Pop. (1970 est.), 305,000.

mar·riage (mar'ij) *n.* **1.** the state of being married; wedlock: *a happy marriage.* **2.** the act of marrying. **3.** the ceremony accompanying this. **4.** a close union: *the marriage of minds.*

mar·riage·a·ble (mar'i jə bəl) *adj.* suitable for marriage.

mar·ried (mar'ēd) *adj.* **1.** joined in marriage: *a married couple.* **2.** having a husband or wife. **3.** of or relating to marriage or married persons: *married life.*

mar·row (mar'ō) *n.* **1.** a soft tissue that fills the cavities and spongy parts of bones. **2.** the best or most important part.

mar·row·bone (mar'ō bōn') *n.* a bone containing marrow that can be eaten, used for making soups and stews.

mar·ry[1] (mar'ē) *v.,* **mar·ried, mar·ry·ing.** —*v.t.* **1.** to take as a husband or wife; wed. **2.** to join as husband and wife; unite in wedlock: *The judge will marry the couple in his office.* —*v.i.* to take a husband or wife; enter into marriage: *She married at a young age.* [Old French *marier* to wed.]

mar·ry[2] (mar'ē) *interj. Archaic.* an exclamation of anger, surprise, or indignation. [From the Virgin *Mary.*]

Mars (märz) *n.* **1.** *Roman Mythology.* the god of war. In Greek mythology he was called Ares. **2.** the seventh largest planet of the solar system and fourth in order of distance from the sun, having two moons.

Mar·seilles (mär sā', mär sālz') *also,* **Mar·seille.** *n.* the chief seaport of France, on the Mediterranean Sea. Pop. (1968), 889,029.

marsh (märsh) *n. pl.,* **marsh·es.** an area of low, wet land covered with grasses or similar plants, such as reeds.

mar·shal (mär'shəl) *n.* **1.** an officer of a federal court who is appointed to a judicial district to perform duties similar to those of a sheriff. **2.** in some states, a law officer of a city or borough having powers similar to those of a sheriff. **3.** the head of a city police or fire department. **4.** see **field marshal. 5.** a person in charge of arranging ceremonies and processions, such as parades. —*v.t.,* **marshaled, mar·shal·ing;** *also, British,* **mar·shalled, mar·shal·ling. 1.** to arrange in proper or logical order: *He marshaled his arguments for the debate.* **2.** to organize or place (soldiers) in proper order: *The general marshaled his troops for battle.*

Mar·shall (mär'shəl) **1. George Cat·lett** (kat'lət). 1880–1959, U.S. general and statesman. **2. John.** 1755–1835, the chief justice of the Supreme Court from 1801 to 1835.

Marshall Plan, a U.S. plan for economic aid to Western Europe after World War II. [From George C. *Marshall,* who introduced it.]

marsh gas, another term for **methane.**

marsh·mal·low (märsh'mel'ō, märsh'mal'ō) *n.* a soft, usually white, spongy candy made from starch, sugar, gelatin, and corn syrup and covered with powdered sugar. [This candy was once made from the root of the *marsh mallow.*]

marsh mallow, a tall, leafy plant growing wild in eastern Europe and the eastern United States, bearing downy, oval or heart-shaped leaves and pink flowers.

marsh marigold, any of several plants that grow in damp areas, bearing large heart- or kidney-shaped leaves and flowers resembling buttercups; cowslip.

marsh·y (mär'shē) *adj.,* **marsh·i·er, marsh·i·est.** relating to, containing, or like a marsh or marshes: *marshy land.* —**marsh'i·ness,** *n.*

mar·su·pi·al (mär soo'pē əl) *n.* any of various animals, such as kangaroos, wombats, and opossums, the female of which has a pouch in which the young are carried after birth. —*adj.* of or relating to a marsupial.

mart (märt) *n.* a trading center; market: *a new food mart.*

mar·ten (märt'ən) *n. pl.,* **mar·tens** or **mar·ten. 1.** an animal resembling the weasel, having thick, soft, golden or dark-brown fur. **2.** the fur of this animal, made into coats, stoles, and trimmings; sable.

Marten

Martha's Vineyard, an island off the Massachusetts coast.

mar·tial (mär'shəl) *adj.* **1.** of, relating to, or suitable for war or military life: *martial music.* **2.** of or characteristic of a warrior; warlike: *a martial spirit.*

martial art, any of the Oriental methods of unarmed combat or self-defense, as karate or jujitsu.

martial law, military rule or authority imposed on a civilian population during a time of war or other emergency.

Mar·tian (mär'shən) *adj.* of or relating to the planet Mars. —*n.* a supposed inhabitant of the planet Mars.

mar·tin (märt'ən) *n.* any of various dark-colored swallows found throughout the world.

mar·ti·net (märt'ən et') *n.* a person who demands strict discipline: *The drillmaster was a martinet.*

mar·tin·gale (märt'ən gāl') *n.* a strap of a horse's harness attached under the belly and secured to the head. It prevents the horse from rearing or throwing back its head.

mar·ti·ni (mär tē'nē) *n.* a cocktail made with gin or vodka and dry vermouth.

Mar·ti·nique (mär'ti nēk') *n.* a French island in the Caribbean. Land area, 425 sq. mi. Pop. (1980 est.), 327,000.

mar·tyr (mär'tər) *n.* **1.** a person who suffers death rather than give up his or her religious faith. **2.** a person who dies, suffers greatly, or sacrifices all for a belief, principle, or cause. **3.** a person who willingly suffers greatly or sacrifices much. —*v.t.* **1.** to make a martyr of. **2.** to cause to suffer greatly; torture or persecute.

mar·tyr·dom (mär'tər dəm) *n.* **1.** the state or condition of being a martyr. **2.** the death or suffering of a martyr. **3.** extreme pain or suffering; torture; torment.

mar·vel (mär'vəl) *n.* a wonderful or astonishing thing: *Penicillin is one of the marvels of modern medicine.* —*v.i.,* **mar·veled, mar·vel·ing;** *also, British,* **mar·velled, mar·vel·ling.** to be or become filled with wonder or astonishment: *We marveled at the acrobat's skill.*

mar·vel·ous (mär'və ləs) *also, British,* **mar·vel·lous.** *adj.* **1.** causing or exciting wonder or astonishment: *a marvelous invention.* **2.** very good: *We had a marvelous vacation.*

Marx, Karl (märks; kärl) 1818–1883, German economist and philosopher whose theories formed the foundation for modern socialism and communism.

Marx·ism (märk'siz'əm) *n.* the theories of Karl Marx.

Marx·ist (märk'sist) *n.* a person who believes in or supports Marxism. —*adj.* of or relating to Karl Marx or Marxism. Also, **Marx·i·an** (märk'sē ən).

Mar·y (mer'ē) *n.* in the New Testament, the mother of Jesus. Also, **Blessed Virgin, Virgin Mary.**

at; āpe; cär; end; mē; it; īce; hot; ōld; fôrk; wood; fōol; oil; out; up; turn; sing; thin; this; hw in white; zh in treasure. The symbol ə stands for the sound of **a** in about, **e** in taken, **i** in pencil, **o** in lemon, and **u** in circus.

Mary I, 1516–1558, the queen of England from 1553 to 1558 and wife of Philip II of Spain.

Mar·y·land (mer′ə lənd) *n.* a state in the eastern United States. Capital, Annapolis. Area, 10,577 sq. mi. Pop. (1970), 3,922,399. Abbreviation, **Md.**

• **Maryland** was named for Queen Henrietta Maria of England. She was the wife of King Charles I, from whom the father of Maryland's founder received a grant for the land.

Mary Mag·da·lene (mag′də lēn′) in the New Testament, a woman from whom Jesus cast out seven devils. She is often identified with the repentant sinner who anointed Jesus' feet.

Mary, Queen of Scots, 1542–1587, the queen of Scotland from 1542 to 1567.

masc., masculine.

mas·car·a (mas kar′ə) *n.* a cosmetic preparation used to color the eyelashes.

mas·cot (mas′kot) *n.* an animal, person, or thing kept to bring good luck, especially a pet animal kept by an athletic team: *The school mascot was a bulldog.*

mas·cu·line (mas′kyə lin) *adj.* **1.** of, relating to, or characteristic of a man: *masculine interests.* **2.** having qualities or characteristics regarded as manly. **3.** (of a woman) mannish. **4.** *Grammar.* of or designating one of the genders or classes of words. In English, words of masculine gender apply to persons or things assumed to be male.

mas·cu·lin·i·ty (mas′kyə lin′ə tē) *n.* the state or quality of being masculine.

ma·ser (mā′zər) *n.* an electronic device that produces or amplifies electromagnetic waves.

Mas·e·ru (maz′ə rōō′) *n.* the capital of Lesotho. Pop. (1972), 14,000.

mash (mash) *n. pl.,* **mash·es. 1.** a feed that consists of a mixture of ground grains. Mash is fed either wet or dry to livestock or poultry. **2.** ground or crushed malt or meal combined with water, used to make beer. **3.** any soft, pulpy mass or mixture. —*v.t.* **1.** to make into a soft, pulpy mass or mixture: *to mash potatoes.* **2.** to mix (ground barley malt) with hot water in making beer. **3.** to cause to be crushed or squeezed. —**mash′er,** *n.*

mask (mask) *n.* **1.** a covering worn over all or part of the face, used to hide or disguise one's identity: *Everyone at the costume party wore a mask.* **2.** a covering of metal, plastic, wire, or other material, worn on the face for protection, as in certain sports or occupations: *Baseball catchers wear masks.* **3.** a molded or sculptured likeness of a face, often made of plaster or clay. **4.** anything that hides, disguises, or conceals. **5.** see **gas mask.** —*v.t.* **1.** to cover with a mask: *The children masked their faces for the Halloween party.* **2.** to hide, disguise, or conceal: *A high stone wall masked the house from the road. A smile masked his true feeling of disappointment.*

Roman mask   American Indian mask

Masks

mas·o·chism (mas′ə kiz′əm) *n.* an abnormal tendency to derive pleasure from being hurt, punished, or embarrassed. [From Leopold von Sacher-*Masoch,* 1836–1895, an Austrian novelist who described it.]

ma·son (mā′sən) *n.* **1.** a person whose occupation is building with stone, brick, or concrete. **2. Mason.** see **Freemason.**

Ma·son-Dix·on line (mā′sən dik′sən) the boundary line between Maryland and Pennsylvania, regarded as the boundary line between the North and South.

Ma·son·ic (mə son′ik) *adj.* of, relating to, or characteristic of Freemasons or Freemasonry.

ma·son·ry (mā′sən rē) *n. pl.,* **ma·son·ries. 1.** something built by a mason, especially in stone. **2.** the art, skill, or occupation of a mason. **3. Masonry.** see **Freemasonry.**

masque (mask) *n.* **1.** an elaborate form of dramatic entertainment popular in the sixteenth and seventeenth centuries, in which the performers often wore masks. **2.** see **masquerade** *(def. 1).*

mas·quer·ade (mas′kə rād′) *n.* **1.** a social gathering at which masks and costumes are worn. **2.** a false outward show; pretense. —*v.i.,* **mas·quer·ad·ed, mas·quer·ad·ing. 1.** to take part in a masquerade. **2.** to assume a false appearance or identity; disguise oneself; pose: *The poor girl masqueraded as an heiress.* —**mas′quer·ad′er,** *n.*

mass (mas) *n. pl.,* **mass·es. 1.** a body of matter holding or sticking together without a particular shape: *a mass of snow.* **2.** a large quantity, amount, or number: *a mass of people.* **3.** size or bulk: *The hippopotamus has great mass.* **4.** the main or greater part; majority: *The mass of parents attended the meeting of the school board.* **5.** *Physics.* a property of matter, used as a measure of the quantity of matter a body contains. **6. the masses.** the common people. —*v.t., v.i.* to gather or form into a mass; assemble: *The police massed the crowd behind the barricades. The people massed together in front of the theater.*

Mass (mas) *also,* **mass.** *n. pl.,* **Mass·es. 1.** the main ceremony of worship in the Roman Catholic and certain Anglican churches. **2.** music written for certain parts of this service.

Mass., Massachusetts.

Mas·sa·chu·setts (mas′ə chōō′sits) *n.* a state in the northeastern United States. Capital, Boston. Area, 8257 sq. mi. Pop. (1970), 5,689,170. Abbreviation, **Mass.**

• The name **Massachusetts** comes from an Algonquian word meaning "at the big hill," referring to the Blue Hills near Boston. It was originally the name of an Indian village located in this area. The English applied it also to the tribe living in this village and, later, to the colony and the state.

---

mas·sa·cre (mas′ə kər) *n.* a brutal, wholesale slaughter of people or animals. —*v.t.,* **mas·sa·cred, mas·sa·cring.** to kill brutally and in large numbers.

mas·sage (mə säzh′) *n.* the rubbing or kneading of parts of the body to increase circulation or relax muscles. —*v.t.,* **mas·saged, mas·sag·ing.** to give a massage to.

Mas·sa·soit (mas′ə soit′) 1580?–1661, American Indian chief who helped the Pilgrims.

mass-en·er·gy equation (mas′en′ər jē) an equation, $E = mc^2$, expressing the relation of mass and energy. In the equation, E = energy, m = mass, c = the velocity of light.

mas·seur (mə sur′) *n.* a man whose occupation is giving massages.

mas·seuse (mə sōōz′) *n.* a woman whose occupation is giving massages.

mas·sive (mas′iv) *adj.* **1.** consisting of or forming a large mass; having great size and weight: *The vault had massive steel doors.* **2.** imposing or exceedingly large, as in scope, size, degree, or intensity: *a massive bombing raid.* —**mas′sive·ly,** *adv.* —**mas′sive·ness,** *n.*

mass meeting, a large public gathering of people to discuss, listen to discussion of, or act on some matter of common interest.

mass noun, a noun that names a general thing or idea

that cannot be counted. *Mud* and *snow* are mass nouns; *hat, car,* and *dog* are not.

mass number, the total number of protons and neutrons in the nucleus of an atom.

mass-pro·duce (mas′prə dōōs′, mas′prə dyōōs′) *v.t.,* **mass-pro·duced, mass-pro·duc·ing.** to manufacture or produce (goods) in large quantities, especially by the use of machinery and assembly lines.

mass production, the act or process of mass-producing.

mast (mast) *n.* **1.** an upright pole in a sailing boat or ship to support the yards, sails, and rigging. **2.** any upright pole, as of a crane.

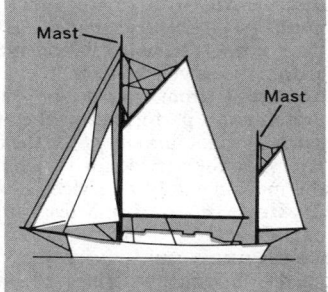
Mast

Mast

mas·ter (mas′tər) *n.* **1.** a person who is in possession of or has power, control, or authority over someone or something: *The dog obeyed his master.* **2.** a person who has great skill, ability, or knowledge in something; expert: *That author is a master of the short story.* **3.** a skilled craftsman or worker qualified to practice his craft or trade independently and to train apprentices. **4.** a male teacher, especially in a private school. **5.** the captain of a merchant ship. **6. Master.** a form of address used before the name of a youth or boy not considered old enough to be addressed as *Mister.* —*adj.* **1.** being a master in one's craft or trade: *a master plumber.* **2.** main; principal: *a master bedroom.* **3.** of, relating to, or characteristic of a master; skilled. **4.** referring to a device or mechanism that controls, operates, or fits any of various similar devices or mechanisms: *a master switch.* —*v.t.* **1.** to gain control over; overcome; defeat: *to master one's fears.* **2.** to acquire complete knowledge or understanding of; become expert in: *to master French, to master a trade.*

mas·ter·ful (mas′tər fəl) *adj.* **1.** forceful or authoritative; domineering. **2.** having or showing mastery; skillful: *a masterful performance.* —**mas′ter·ful·ly,** *adv.*

master key, a key designed to open all the locks of a certain type. Also, **passkey.**

mas·ter·ly (mas′tər lē) *adj.* characteristic of a master; expert. —*adv.* in a masterly manner. —**mas′ter·li·ness,** *n.*

mas·ter·mind (mas′tər mīnd′) *n.* a person who has or shows great intelligence, skill, and ability, especially in planning or directing a course of action. —*v.t.* to plan or direct a course of action for: *to mastermind a robbery.*

Master of Arts, a master's degree given to a person who has completed an advanced course of study in the arts or social sciences.

master of ceremonies, a person who is in charge of a formal gathering or entertainment and introduces the speakers or performers.

Master of Science, a master's degree given to a person who has completed an advanced course of study in science or mathematics.

mas·ter·piece (mas′tər pēs′) *n.* **1.** something, such as a work of art, done with supreme skill or craftsmanship. **2.** something thought of as a person's greatest achievement.

master's degree, a graduate degree usually given to a person who has completed a course of study beyond the bachelor's degree.

master sergeant, a noncommissioned officer of the second highest rank in the U.S. Army and Marine Corps, and of the third highest rank in the U.S. Air Force.

mas·ter·y (mas′tər ē) *n. pl.,* **mas·ter·ies. 1.** the state of being master; rule; control. **2.** expert skill or knowledge: *Susan's mastery of French helped her when she studied in Paris.* **3.** the act of mastering something.

mast·head (mast′hed′) *n.* **1.** the head or top of a ship's mast. **2.** a notice printed in a newspaper or magazine giving the title, publisher's name, and other information.

mas·ti·cate (mas′tə kāt′) *v.t.,* **mas·ti·cat·ed, mas·ti·cat·ing.** to chew. —**mas′ti·ca′tion,** *n.*

mas·tiff (mas′tif) *n.* a large dog having a heavy head, a light-brown, short-haired coat, dark ears and muzzle, and a long, tapering tail.

mas·to·don (mas′tə don′) *n.* any of various extinct animals that resembled elephants and lived in the Northern Hemisphere and South America.

mas·toid (mas′toid) *n.* the part of the skull behind and below each ear. —*adj.* of, relating to, or near the mastoid.

Mastiff

mat¹ (mat) *n.* **1.** a small, flat piece of material, such as rubber or woven straw, used as a floor covering or placed in front of a door. **2.** a small, flat piece of material placed on a table under a vase, dish, or other object for protection or decoration. **3.** a large, thick pad or covering placed on the floor to protect wrestlers, boxers, or gymnasts. **4.** any thick, tangled mass: *a mat of hair.* —*v.,* **mat·ted, mat·ting.** —*v.t.* **1.** to cover with a mat or mats. **2.** to entangle or entwine into a thick mass. —*v.i.* to become entangled into a thick mass. [Old English *matt.*]

mat² (mat) *n.* a piece of cardboard or other material serving as a mount or frame for a picture, or as a border between a picture and its frame. —*v.t.,* **mat·ted, mat·ting.** to provide (a picture) with a mat. [French *mat* a dull color.]

mat·a·dor (mat′ə dôr′) *n.* the man who kills the bull in a bullfight. [Spanish *matador.*]

match¹ (mach) *n. pl.,* **match·es. 1.** a short piece of wood, cardboard, or other material coated on one end with a chemical substance that easily catches fire when rubbed or struck against something. **2.** a wick prepared to burn at an even rate, formerly used to fire guns and cannon. [Old French *mesche* the wick of a candle or lamp.]

match² (mach) *n. pl.,* **match·es. 1.** a person or thing that is exactly equal to or like another; counterpart. **2.** a person or thing that can compete with or oppose another as an equal: *John has yet to meet his match in chess.* **3.** two persons or things that are like, or suitable for, each other: *The blue coat and the blue dress are a good match.* **4.** a game or contest between two or more persons, animals, or teams: *a wrestling match.* **5.** a marriage. —*v.t.* **1.** to be like, suitable for, or equal to: *The pattern on the drapes matches that of the sofa.* **2.** to find, select, or produce (things) that are exactly equal to or like one another: *to*

at; āpe; cär; end; mē; it; īce; hot; ōld; fôrk; wood; fōōl; oil; out; up; turn; sing; thin; **th**is; hw in white; zh in treasure. The symbol ə stands for the sound of a in about, e in taken, i in pencil, o in lemon, and u in circus.

match socks. **3.** to compete with or oppose as an equal; be a match for: *No one can match him in tennis.* **4.** to place in competition or opposition, as in a game or contest: *They matched the fighters according to weight.* —*v.i.* to be exactly equal or alike: *These gloves do not match.* [Old English *mæcca, gemæcca* a companion, mate.]

match·less (mach′lis) *adj.* having no equal; peerless; unrivaled. —**match′less·ly,** *adv.*

match·lock (mach′lok′) *n.* formerly, a type of gun fired by igniting the powder with a slow-burning wick.

match·mak·er (mach′māk′ər) *n.* **1.** a person who arranges marriages for others. **2.** a person who arranges sports contests, such as boxing matches.

mate (māt) *n.* **1.** one of a pair: *Where is the mate to this sock?* **2.** a husband or wife. **3.** the male or female of a pair of animals that have paired or been paired for breeding. **4.** an officer on a merchant ship, ranking next below the captain. **5.** an assistant to a warrant officer in the U.S. Navy. **6.** a close associate; companion. —*v.,* **mat·ed, mat·ing.** —*v.t.* **1.** to join together or match. **2.** to cause (animals) to produce offspring; pair. **3.** to join in marriage. —*v.i.* **1.** (of animals) to pair for breeding: *Birds mate in the spring.* **2.** to become joined in marriage.

ma·té (mä′tā) *n.* **1.** a greenish beverage resembling tea, made from the dried leaves and shoots of an evergreen shrub of the holly family. **2.** the leaves and shoots used to make this beverage. **3.** the shrub bearing these leaves and shoots, found in South America.

ma·ter (mā′tər) *n.* mother. [Latin *māter.*]

ma·te·ri·al (mə tēr′ē əl) *n.* **1.** the substance of which something is or may be made or composed. **2.** something made by weaving, knitting, or otherwise arranging textile fibers; cloth; fabric. **3.** something that may be used, developed, or elaborated on, especially in making something: *material for a new novel.* **4. materials.** things needed to make or do something: *The store sells paints, canvases, and other materials for artists.* —*adj.* **1.** of, relating to, or consisting of matter; physical: *a material object.* **2.** of or relating to the body or physical well-being: *material needs.* **3.** overly or solely concerned with the physical rather than the intellectual or spiritual things of life; materialistic.

ma·te·ri·al·ism (mə tēr′ē ə liz′əm) *n.* **1.** the philosophical doctrine that everything that exists is either composed of matter or depends on matter for its existence. **2.** a tendency to be overly or solely concerned with material rather than intellectual or spiritual things of life.

ma·te·ri·al·ist (mə tēr′ē ə list) *n.* **1.** a believer in philosophical materialism. **2.** a person who is overly or solely concerned with material rather than intellectual or spiritual things of life.

ma·te·ri·al·is·tic (mə tēr′ē ə lis′tik) *adj.* relating to materialism or materialists. —**ma·te′ri·al·is′ti·cal·ly,** *adv.*

ma·te·ri·al·ize (mə tēr′ē ə līz′) *v.,* **ma·te·ri·al·ized, ma·te·ri·al·iz·ing.** —*v.i.* **1.** to come into being; become actual fact; be realized: *His dreams of success failed to materialize.* **2.** to assume or appear in bodily or visible form: *Spirits seemed to materialize before my eyes.* —*v.t.* to give material form or character to. —**ma·te′ri·al·i·za′tion,** *n.*

ma·te·ri·al·ly (mə tēr′ē ə lē) *adv.* **1.** with regard to material or physical things: *He was well-off materially.* **2.** to a great degree; considerably: *The patient's condition did not improve materially.*

ma·té·ri·el (mə tēr′ē el′) *n.* the equipment and supplies of an organized body, especially a military force.

ma·ter·nal (mə turn′əl) *adj.* **1.** of, relating to, or like a mother; motherly: *maternal love.* **2.** inherited or derived from one's mother. **3.** related through one's mother: *a maternal aunt.* —**ma·ter′nal·ly,** *adv.*

ma·ter·ni·ty (mə tur′nə tē) *adj.* **1.** for pregnant women: *a maternity dress.* **2.** designed for the care of newborn babies and women during and after childbirth: *a maternity ward.* —*n.* **1.** the state of being a mother; motherhood. **2.** the qualities or characteristics of a mother; motherliness.

math (math) *n.* see **mathematics.**

math·e·mat·i·cal (math′ə mat′i kəl) *adj.* **1.** of, relating to, like, or concerned with mathematics. **2.** extremely exact; precise: *mathematical certainty.* —**math′e·mat′i·cal·ly,** *adv.*

math·e·ma·ti·cian (math′ə mə tish′ən) *n.* a student of or an expert in mathematics.

math·e·mat·ics (math′ə mat′iks) *n.,pl.* the study of numbers, quantities, shapes, sets, and operations, and of their properties and relationships. Mathematics includes arithmetic, algebra, geometry, and calculus.

mat·i·nee (mat′ən ā′) *also,* **mat·i·née.** *n.* a theatrical presentation performed in the afternoon.

ma·tins (mat′inz) *n., pl.* **1.** the first of the seven canonical hours, or the service for it. **2.** in the Church of England, the morning prayer service.

Ma·tisse, Hen·ri (mä tēs′; än rē′) 1869–1954, French painter.

ma·tri·arch (mā′trē ärk′) *n.* **1.** a woman who is the head of a family or tribe. **2.** a woman who dominates or has great authority in any group.

ma·tri·ar·chal (mā′trē är′kəl) *adj.* **1.** relating to, like, or based on a matriarchy: *a matriarchal culture.* **2.** of or relating to a matriarch.

ma·tri·ar·chy (mā′trē är′kē) *n. pl.,* **ma·tri·ar·chies.** a form of society in which the woman is the head of a family or tribe, and descent is traced through the maternal line.

ma·tri·ces (mā′trə sēz′, mat′rə sēz′) a plural of **matrix.**

mat·ri·cide¹ (mat′rə sīd′, mā′trə sīd′) *n.* the act of killing one's mother. [Latin *mātricīdium,* from *māter* mother + *-cīdium* a killing.]

mat·ri·cide² (mat′rə sīd′, mā′trə sīd′) *n.* a person who kills his mother. [Latin *mātricīda,* from *māter* mother + *-cīda* a killer.]

ma·tric·u·late (mə trik′yə lāt′) *v.,* **ma·tric·u·lat·ed, ma·tric·u·lat·ing.** —*v.i.* to enroll in a college or university as a candidate for a degree: *Jerry matriculated last fall.* —*v.t.* to admit to a college or university as a candidate for a degree. —**ma·tric′u·la′tion,** *n.*

mat·ri·mo·ni·al (mat′rə mō′nē əl) *adj.* of or relating to marriage. —**mat′ri·mo′ni·al·ly,** *adv.*

mat·ri·mo·ny (mat′rə mō′nē) *n. pl.,* **mat·ri·mo·nies.** **1.** the state of being married. **2.** the rite or ceremony of marriage.

ma·trix (mā′triks, mat′riks) *n. pl.,* **ma·tri·ces** or **ma·trix·es.** the place or thing in which something originates, develops, forms, or is contained. A mold for casting metal is a matrix.

ma·tron (mā′trən) *n.* **1.** a married woman, especially one who is mature in age and manner. **2.** a woman who supervises or guards the inmates of an institution, such as a hospital or jail.

ma·tron·ly (mā′trən lē) *adj.* characteristic of, suitable for, or like a matron.

matron of honor, a married woman who is the chief attendant of the bride at a wedding.

Matt., Matthew.

matte (mat) *adj.* not bright or shiny; dull: *a matte finish.* —*n.* a dull finish or surface, as on glass or paper.

mat·ted (mat′id) *adj.* **1.** entangled or entwined in a thick mass: *Her wet hair was matted.* **2.** covered with or made of matting.

mat·ter (mat′ər) *n.* **1.** anything that occupies space and has weight. The three common states of matter are solid, liquid, and gaseous. **2.** a particular kind or form of substance: *A plant is organic matter.* **3.** something that is the subject of discussion, concern, feeling, or action: *a legal matter, a business matter.* **4.** a difficult, unpleasant, or unsatisfactory condition or circumstance; trouble; problem: *What is the matter with my report?* **5.** importance; significance: *It's of no matter to me what you do.* **6.** written or printed material: *reading matter.* **7.** the content of something that is written or spoken: *the matter of a speech.* **8.** an amount, quantity, or extent: *It is only a matter of minutes before he arrives.* **9.** a substance given off by the body, as from a wound or abscess; pus. —*v.i.* to be of importance: *It does not matter to me what you want.*

as a matter of course. as something to be expected.

as a matter of fact. in truth; actually; truthfully: *As a matter of fact, I do know her.*

no matter. regardless of; despite: *No matter what you say, I still disagree with you.*

Mat·ter·horn (mat′ər hôrn′) *n.* a steep, jagged mountain peak in the Alps, on the border between Switzerland and Italy.

mat·ter-of-fact (mat′ər əv fakt′) *adj.* **1.** dealing with facts; unimaginative; practical: *a matter-of-fact description.* **2.** having or showing no emotion or feeling; disinterested: *a matter-of-fact way of speaking.* —**mat′ter-of-fact′ly,** *adv.*

Mat·thew (math′yoo) *n.* **1.** one of the four Evangelists, chosen by Jesus as one of the twelve Apostles. **2.** the first book of the New Testament, believed to have been written by Matthew.

mat·ting (mat′ing) *n.* **1.** a coarse, woven fabric of grass, straw, hemp, or other fiber, used for making floor coverings and as a packing material. **2.** mats as a group.

mat·tock (mat′ək) *n.* a tool with a handle and a two-bladed head, used for loosening soil and cutting roots.

mat·tress (mat′ris) *n. pl.,* **mat·tress·es.** a pad covered with strong cloth or other material, often stuffed with hair, cotton, or rubber, and designed to fit on the frame of a bed, especially on top of a box spring.

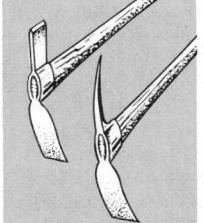

Mattocks

ma·ture (mə choor′, mə toor′, mə tyoor′) *adj.* **1.** having reached full growth or development: *mature fruit, a physically mature person.* **2.** showing the qualities or characteristics of a person who has reached full physical and mental development: *mature behavior, a mature attitude.* **3.** fully developed or thought out: *a mature plan.* **4.** due for payment, as a loan or bond. —*v.,* **ma·tured, ma·tur·ing.** —*v.i.* **1.** to become fully grown or developed; reach maturity. **2.** to become due for payment: *This savings bond matures in seven years.* —*v.t.* to bring to full growth or development: *The difficult experience helped to mature him.* —**ma·ture′ly,** *adv.*

ma·tu·ri·ty (mə choor′ə tē, mə toor′ə tē, mə tyoor′ə tē) *n. pl.,* **ma·tu·ri·ties.** **1.** the state or quality of being mature. **2.** the time at which something, such as a loan or bond is due for payment.

mat·zoh (mät′sə) *also,* **mat·zo.** *n.* a thin, flat piece of unleavened bread, traditionally eaten at Passover. [Hebrew *matztzāh.*]

maud·lin (môd′lin) *adj.* very sentimental.

Maugham, (William) Som·er·set (môm; sum′ər set′) 1874–1965, English writer.

Mau·i (mou′ē) *n.* the second largest island of Hawaii.

maul (môl) *n.* a heavy mallet or hammer used for driving wedges, stakes, and piles. —*v.t.* **1.** to injure, as by beating, bruising, or knocking about: *The angry lion mauled the trainer.* **2.** to handle roughly or clumsily; abuse.

Mau·na Lo·a (mou′nə lō′ə) the largest known active volcano in the world, on the island of Hawaii.

maun·der (môn′dər) *v.i.* **1.** to talk in a rambling, confused manner. **2.** to move or act in an aimless, dreamy, and confused manner.

Mau·pas·sant, Guy de (mō pä sän′; gē′ də) 1850–1893, French short story writer and novelist.

Mau·ri·ta·ni·a (môr′ə tā′nē ə) *n.* a country on the northwestern coast of Africa. Capital, Nouakchott. Area, 397,955 sq. mi. Pop. (1971 est.), 1,200,000.

Mau·ri·tius (mô rish′əs) *n.* a small island country in the western Indian Ocean, east of Madagascar. Mauritius was formerly a British possession. Capital, Port Louis. Area, 720 sq. mi. Pop. (1971 est.), 820,000.

mau·so·le·um (mô′sə lē′əm) *n. pl.,* **mau·so·le·ums** or **mau·so·le·a** (mô′sə lē′ə). a stately, often large, building housing a tomb or tombs.

mauve (mōv) *n.* any of various pale, purplish-blue or rose colors. —*adj.* having the color mauve.

mav·er·ick (mav′ər ik) *n.* **1.** an unbranded animal, especially a calf, traditionally belonging to the first person to find and brand it. **2.** *Informal.* a person whose views, especially in politics, are different from those of the group to which he belongs. [From Samuel A. *Maverick,* 1803–1870, a Texas rancher who did not brand his calves.]

ma·vis (mā′vis) *n. pl.,* **ma·vis·es.** another word for **song thrush.**

maw (mô) *n.* the jaws, mouth, throat, gullet, or stomach of an animal.

mawk·ish (mô′kish) *adj.* overly sentimental. —**mawk′ish·ly,** *adv.* —**mawk′ish·ness,** *n.*

max., maximum.

max·il·la (mak sil′ə) *n. pl.,* **max·il·lae** (mak sil′ē). **1.** the bone of the upper jaw. **2.** either of a pair of appendages located just behind the mandibles in insects, crabs, spiders, and other related animals.

max·il·lar·y (mak′sə ler′ē) *adj.* of, relating to, or situated near the bone of the upper jaw: *maxillary artery.* —*n. pl.,* **max·i·lar·ies.** see **maxilla** *(def. 1).*

max·im (mak′sim) *n.* a short statement expressing a general truth or doctrine; precept. For example: *Haste makes waste* is a maxim.

Max·i·mil·ian (mak′sə mil′yən) 1832–1867, archduke of Austria; the emperor of Mexico from 1864 to 1867.

max·i·mize (mak′sə mīz′) *v.t.,* **max·i·mized, max·i·miz·ing.** to make as great as possible; increase to the maximum.

max·i·mum (mak′sə məm) *n. pl.,* **max·i·mums** or **max·i·ma** (mak′sə mə). **1.** the greatest possible amount, degree, or quantity: *It will take a maximum of three hours to drive home.* **2.** the highest point, degree, or number reached or recorded: *The temperature reached a maximum of 90° yesterday.* —*adj.* greatest possible; highest: *The maximum speed on the road is sixty miles per hour.*

may (mā) *auxiliary verb.* Present tense: *sing.,* first person, **may;** second, **may** or *(archaic)* **mayst;** third, **may;** *pl.,* **may.** Past tense: **might.** **1.** used to ask for or express permission:

at; āpe; cär; end; mē; it; īce; hot; ōld; fôrk; wood; fool; oil; out; up; turn; sing; thin; **th**is; hw in white; zh in treasure. The symbol ə stands for the sound of **a** in about, **e** in taken, **i** in pencil, **o** in lemon, and **u** in circus.

M

May I leave the table? Yes, you may. **2.** used to express possibility or likelihood: *It may snow.* **3.** used to express desire, hope, or a wish: *May you have a happy life.* **4.** used to express opportunity or chance: *He is willing to pay all the expenses so that we may all go on the trip.* ▲ See **can¹** for usage note.

May (mā) *n.* the fifth month of the year, having thirty-one days. [Old French *Mai,* from Latin *Māius (mēnsis)* (month) of Maia, the Roman goddess of the earth and fertility, who was honored in this month.]

Ma·ya (mä′yə) *n. pl.,* **Ma·yas** or **Ma·ya.** **1.** a member of a tribe of highly civilized American Indians who lived in southern Mexico and parts of Central America. They were conquered by the Spanish in the sixteenth century. **2.** the language of the Mayas. —*adj.* of or relating to the Mayas, their language, or their culture.

Ma·yan (mä′yən) *adj., n.* another word for **Maya.**

may·be (mā′bē) *adv.* possibly; perhaps.

May·day (mā′dā′) *n.* an international signal used by ships or aircraft as a call for help. [French *m'aidez* help me.]

May Day, a holiday traditionally celebrated as a spring festival. Some countries pay homage to working people on this day with parades and other demonstrations. It falls on May 1.

may·flow·er (mā′flou′ər) *n.* **1.** any of various plants whose flowers blossom in May, such as the trailing arbutus. **2. Mayflower.** the ship on which the Pilgrims came to America in 1620.

may·fly (mā′flī′) *n. pl.,* **may·flies.** an insect having two pairs of finely veined wings and two or three long filaments attached to the end of the body.

may·hem (mā′həm) *n.* **1.** the crime of violently and unlawfully injuring or maiming a person. **2.** a state of confusion and disorder.

may·n't (mā′ənt) may not.

may·on·naise (mā′ə nāz′) *n.* a thick, creamy sauce made of egg yolks, oil, vinegar or lemon juice, and seasoning.

may·or (mā′ər) *n.* the official head of a city or town government. —**may′or·al,** *adj.*

may·or·al·ty (mā′ər əl tē) *n. pl.,* **may·or·al·ties.** the position or term of office of a mayor.

May·pole (mā′pōl′) *also,* **may·pole.** *n.* a pole decorated with flowers and ribbons, around which people dance on May Day.

mayst (māst) *Archaic.* the present indicative, second person singular of **may.**

maze (māz) *n.* **1.** a confusing network of paths or passageways, usually bordered by high walls or shrubs, through which a person may have difficulty finding his way. **2.** a state of bewilderment, confusion, or doubt.

ma·zur·ka (mə zur′kə, mə zoor′kə) *also,* **ma·zour·ka.** *n.* **1.** a lively Polish dance resembling the polka. **2.** the music for such a dance.

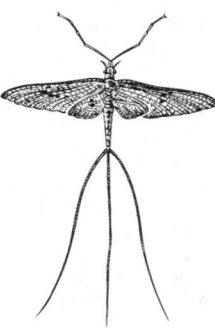

Mayfly

Maze

maz·y (mā′zē) *adj.,* **maz·i·er, maz·i·est.** like a maze; intricate or confusing.

Mba·ba·ne (əm bä bä′nā) *n.* the capital of Swaziland, in the western part of the country. Pop. (1968 est.), 13,800.

M.C., Master of Ceremonies.

Mc·Clel·lan, George B. (mə klel′ən) 1826–1885, Union general in the Civil War.

Mc·Kin·ley (mə kin′lē) *n.* **1. William.** 1843–1901, the twenty-fifth president of the United States, from 1897 to 1901. **2. Mount.** the highest mountain in North America, in south-central Alaska.

Md, the symbol for mendelevium.

Md., Maryland.

M.D., Doctor of Medicine.

mdse., merchandise.

me (mē) *pron.* the objective case of **I.** ▲ According to the rules of traditional grammar, **I,** rather than **me,** should be used after the verb *to be.* However, **me** is often used in conversation by many good speakers and writers when they think **I** would sound too formal: *Who's there? It's only me.*

Me., Maine.

mead¹ (mēd) *n.* an alcoholic drink made from fermented honey and water, and flavored with herbs. [Old English *meodu.*]

mead² (mēd) *n. Archaic.* a meadow. [Old English *mǣd* meadow.]

mead·ow (med′ō) *n.* a piece of grassy land, often used as a pasture or for growing hay.

mead·ow·lark (med′ō lärk′) *n.* a North American songbird having a pointed, coneshaped bill and a yellow breast with a black crescent across it.

mea·ger (mē′gər) *also,* **mea·gre.** *adj.* **1.** barely adequate in amount or quantity; scanty: *He had a meager meal of bread and tea.* **2.** thin; lean: *a meager figure.* —**mea′ger·ly,** *adv.* —**mea′ger·ness,** *n.*

meal¹ (mēl) *n.* **1.** the food served or eaten at one particular time. **2.** the time or occasion during which such food is regularly served or eaten: *The patient took one pill before each meal.* [Old English *mǣl.*]

Meadowlark

meal² (mēl) *n.* **1.** a coarsely ground and unsifted grain. **2.** any similar ground substance. [Old English *melu.*]

meal·time (mēl′tīm′) *n.* the usual time for a meal.

meal·y (mē′lē) *adj.,* **meal·i·er, meal·i·est.** **1.** like meal; dry and grainy: *mealy potatoes.* **2.** of or containing meal. **3.** sprinkled or covered with meal. **4.** pale or sickly: *a mealy complexion.* —**meal′i·ness,** *n.*

meal·y-mouthed (mē′lē mouthd′, mē′lē moutht′) *adj.* unwilling to say plainly what one means; not outspoken; insincere.

mean¹ (mēn) *v.,* **meant, mean·ing.** —*v.t.* **1.** to have in mind as a purpose or intention: *He did not mean to hurt you.* **2.** to intend to express or indicate: *I do not know what you mean by that remark.* **3.** to have as a particular sense; be defined as: *"Do not" and "don't" mean the same thing.* **4.** to intend or design for a particular person, purpose, or use: *He meant that gift for you. She was meant to be an actress.* **5.** to be or serve as an indication or sign of: *Smoke usually means fire.* **6.** to bring about or have as a result: *Her promotion means a raise in salary.* —*v.i.* **1.** to have importance or value: *His friendship means a lot to her.* **2.** to have intentions of a particular kind; be disposed: *to mean well.* [Old English *mǣnan* to have in mind, intend, tell.]

mean² (mēn) *adj.* **1.** lacking in kindness, compassion, or understanding: *She apologized for having been so mean to us.* **2.** full of or showing spite; malicious: *a mean look.*

3. of low birth, rank, or social position. **4.** *Informal.* hard to deal with; difficult: *There is a mean curve in the road just ahead.* **5.** *Slang.* expert; excellent: *Harry plays a mean game of golf.* [Old English *mǣne, gemǣne* common.] —**mean′ly,** *adv.*

mean³ (mēn) *n.* **1.** a point, state, or course of action that is halfway between two extremes. **2. means. a.** the way that something is or may be done: *He got the money by dishonest means.* **b.** money, property, or other resources; wealth: *He is a man of means.* **3.** *Mathematics.* either the second or third term of a mathematical proportion of four terms. In $a/b = c/d$, b and c are the means. —*adj.* **1.** halfway between two extremes. **2.** average, as in size, quality, or degree: *The mean temperature for the month of May was 60°.* [Old French *meien* middle.]

by all means. without fail or hesitation.

by means of. with the help or use of: *He crossed the river by means of the bridge.*

by no means. a. in no way; not at all. **b.** on no account: *By no means should he be left alone.*

not by any means. not at all.

me·an·der (mē an′dər) *v.i.* **1.** to follow a winding course: *The stream meandered through the woods.* **2.** to wander aimlessly or idly: *I meandered through the gardens.*

mean·ing (mē′ning) *n.* **1.** something that is meant as a goal or purpose: *The philosopher tried to find the meaning of life.* **2.** something that is meant to be expressed or understood, as by language; sense: *He didn't understand the meaning of the word.* **3.** expressiveness; suggestiveness: *She gave a glance that was full of meaning.* —*adj.* having meaning; expressive; significant: *a meaning smile.* —**mean′ing·ly,** *adv.*

● Words have no absolute meaning. In fact, word meaning can often be quite fluid. But, in spite of this fluidity, we can establish certain general boundaries for the meanings of words. Consider, for example, the word *beautiful* in *That's a beautiful painting.* Individual members of a language community may agree or disagree as to whether a particular painting is beautiful, but they would agree on certain features of the word *beautiful.* For instance, they would agree that *beautiful* is a term of approval rather than of disapproval and that it is applied to things that produce a sense of delight. Features like these make up the common ground—the generally used and understood meaning—of *beautiful.*

Words also have no fixed meaning. As time passes, the meaning of words can change, sometimes quite drastically. But change of meaning, though sometimes difficult to predict, follows certain observable patterns. Four of the most common patterns of change are: broadening, narrowing, downgrading, and upgrading of meaning.

When the meaning of a word is broadened, its scope is increased. The word *barn,* for example, used to mean "a storehouse for barley." Today the scope of its meaning has been increased to mean "a storehouse for any kind of grain or a place for livestock." The opposite of broadening is narrowing. When the meaning of a word is narrowed, its scope is decreased. The word *starve* used to mean "to die," now it means "to die of hunger." Sometimes words come to mean something worse than what they had previously meant. This is called downgrading. The word *silly* once meant "blessed" or "happy," now it means "stupid." The opposite of downgrading is upgrading; that is, words can come to mean something better than what they had previously meant. *Praise* once meant "to put a value on," now it means "to value highly."

When changes in meaning occur, they occur gradually, so gradually, in fact, that most people do not even realize

that a change has occurred. It is the job of dictionary makers to observe changes in meaning, and then to record them. The dictionaries which result from this work show what words mean at a particular time.

mean·ing·ful (mē′ning fəl) *adj.* full of meaning; significant. —**mean′ing·ful·ly,** *adv.*

mean·ing·less (mē′ning lis) *adj.* without meaning; senseless: *a meaningless statement.* —**mean′ing·less·ly,** *adv.* —**mean′ing·less·ness,** *n.*

mean·ness (mēn′nis) *n.* **1.** the state or quality of being mean. **2.** a mean or spiteful act.

meant (ment) the past tense and past participle of **mean¹.**

mean·time (mēn′tīm′) *n.* the time between: *I'll be gone for an hour; in the meantime, please behave.* —*adv.* **1.** in or during the time between. **2.** at the same time.

mean·while (mēn′hwīl′, mēn′wīl′) *adv.* **1.** in or during the time between: *The train doesn't leave for an hour; meanwhile, I'm going to take a nap.* **2.** at the same time: *Mother went shopping; meanwhile, I cleaned the house.* —*n.* the time between.

mea·sles (mē′zəlz) *n., pl.* **1.** a highly contagious virus disease characterized by cold symptoms, fever, and a rash. **2.** see **German measles.**

mea·sly (mēz′lē) *adj.,* **mea·sli·er, mea·sli·est. 1.** of, like, or having measles. **2.** *Slang.* scanty or worthless: *He gave me a measly fifty cents for mowing the lawn.*

meas·ur·a·ble (mezh′ər ə bəl) *adj.* that can be measured: *a measurable distance.* —**meas′ur·a·bly,** *adv.*

meas·ure (mezh′ər) *v.,* **meas·ured, meas·ur·ing.** —*v.t.* **1.** to find the dimensions, weight, extent, quantity, or capacity of: *to measure a person's height, to measure a room.* **2.** to mark off, set apart, or allot by measuring: *to measure out two cups of flour.* **3.** to serve as a standard or unit of measurement for: *Degrees measure temperature.* **4.** to think over carefully and choose: *to measure one's words.* —*v.i.* **1.** to have a specific measurement: *The room measures ten feet by twelve feet.* **2.** to take measurements: *A carpenter must measure accurately.* —*n.* **1.** the dimensions, weight, extent, quantity, or capacity of something as found by measuring. **2.** a standard or unit of measurement, such as an inch, quart, or mile. **3.** any standard or basis of comparison, estimation, or judgment: *Marks in school are not always a true measure of a person's intelligence.* **4.** a system of measurement. **5.** an instrument, container, or other device used for measuring: *a gallon measure.* **6.** an amount or degree that should not be exceeded; limit: *Her generosity knows no measure.* **7.** an amount, degree, or proportion: *Our success was due in large measure to your help.* **8.** *also,* **measures.** a course of action or procedure used as a means to an end: *to take drastic measures.* **9.** a legislative act or bill: *The measure passed both houses of Congress.* **10.** *Poetry.* **a.** rhythm; meter. **b.** a metrical unit; foot. **11.** *Music.* the music contained between two bar lines; bar.

for good measure. as something extra.

to measure up. to have the needed qualifications: *Does he measure up for the job?*

to measure up to. to fulfill or meet: *The movie didn't measure up to what we had expected.*

---

at; āpe; cär; end; mē; it; īce; hot; ōld; fôrk; wood; fōol; oil; out; up; turn; sing; thin; this; hw in white; zh in treasure. The symbol ə stands for the sound of **a** in about, **e** in taken, **i** in pencil, **o** in lemon, and **u** in circus.

meas·ure·less (mezh'ər lis) *adj.* that cannot be measured.

meas·ure·ment (mezh'ər mənt) *n.* **1.** the act or process of measuring. **2.** something found or determined by measuring, such as dimensions or quantity: *He made a mistake in his measurements for the shelf.* **3.** a system of measuring.

measuring worm, another term for **inchworm.**

meat (mēt) *n.* **1.** the parts of an animal used as food, especially the flesh of a cow or pig. **2.** the fleshy part of anything that can be eaten: *the meat of a coconut.* **3.** the main idea or most important part; substance: *the meat of a book.* **4.** anything eaten for nourishment; food: *meat and drink.*

meat·y (mē'tē) *adj.,* **meat·i·er, meat·i·est. 1.** of, relating to, or like meat: *a meaty taste.* **2.** full of meat; fleshy; plump. **3.** full of substance or significance: *a meaty discussion.*

Mec·ca (mek'ə) *n.* **1.** the birthplace of Muhammad and the holiest city of Islam, in western Saudi Arabia, near the Red Sea. Muslims face Mecca when praying and travel there on pilgrimages. Pop. (1970 est.), 250,000. **2.** *also,* **mecca.** any place that is visited by many people or has a special attraction.

me·chan·ic (mi kan'ik) *n.* a person skilled in designing, repairing, or operating machinery: *an automobile mechanic.*

me·chan·i·cal (mi kan'i kəl) *adj.* **1.** of, relating to, or involving machinery or tools: *a mechanical part, mechanical skills.* **2.** produced or operated by a machine: *a mechanical toy.* **3.** like or suitable for a machine; without thought or feeling; automatic: *a mechanical task.* **4.** of or relating to the science of mechanics. —**me·chan'i·cal·ly,** *adv.*

mechanical drawing 1. a drawing, usually of machinery or mechanical parts, done with the aid of rulers, scales, compasses, and similar instruments. **2.** the art or process of making such a drawing.

me·chan·ics (mi kan'iks) *n., pl.* **1.** the branch of physics that deals with the conditions under which bodies and fluids move or remain at rest. **2.** the body of knowledge dealing with the design, construction, operation, and care of machinery. ▲ used with a singular verb in definitions 1 and 2. **3.** the mechanical or technical aspects of anything: *the mechanics of painting.* ▲ used with a plural verb in definition 3.

mech·a·nism (mek'ə niz'əm) *n.* **1.** the working parts, or arrangement of parts, of a machine: *The jeweler fixed the mechanism of my watch.* **2.** a system of parts resembling those of a machine: *the mechanism of the nervous system, the mechanism of government.* **3.** the way, means, or process by which something is done.

mech·a·nize (mek'ə nīz') *v.t.,* **mech·a·nized, mech·a·niz·ing. 1.** to equip with or convert to machinery as a means of production: *Much industry has been mechanized.* **2.** to equip (a military unit or army) with tanks, armored personnel carriers, and other vehicles. —**mech'a·ni·za'-tion,** *n.*

med. 1. medical. **2.** medicine. **3.** medium.

med·al (med'əl) *n.* a flat piece of metal bearing a design or inscription, often given as an award.

med·al·ist (med'əl ist) *n.* **1.** a person who engraves, designs, or makes medals. **2.** a person who has been awarded a medal: *an Olympic gold medalist.*

me·dal·lion (mi dal'yən) *n.* **1.** a large medal. **2.** anything resembling this, such as a round or ornamental object or design.

med·dle (med'əl) *v.i.,* **med·dled, med·dling. 1.** to concern oneself with or interfere in the affairs of others without having been asked. **2.** to handle or change something without permission; tamper: *Someone has meddled with the lock on this door.* —**med'dler,** *n.*

med·dle·some (med'əl səm) *adj.* tending to meddle. —**med'dle·some·ness,** *n.*

Mede (mēd) *n.* a person who lived in ancient Media.

Me·de·a (mi dē'ə) *n. Greek Legend.* an enchantress who helped Jason get the Golden Fleece in return for his marrying her.

Me·del·lin (med'əl ēn') *n.* a city in west-central Colombia. Pop. (1971 est.), 967,825.

me·di·a (mē'dē ə) a plural of **medium.**

Me·di·a (mē'dē ə) *n.* an ancient kingdom in northwestern Persia.

me·di·ae·val (mē'dē ē'vəl, mid ē'vəl) another spelling of **medieval.**

me·di·al (mē'dē əl) *adj.* **1.** of, relating to, or situated in the middle. **2.** of, relating to, or being the middle number in a set or series; average.

me·di·an (mē'dē ən) *n.* the middle number in a set of numbers or, where there is no middle number, the average of the two middle numbers. In the set *2, 4, 6, 8, 10,* the median is *6.* In the set *11, 25, 41, 65,* the median is *33.* —*adj.* of, relating to, or situated in the middle; medial.

me·di·ate (*v.,* mē'dē āt'; *adj.,* mē'dē it) *v.,* **me·di·at·ed, me·di·at·ing.** —*v.t.* **1.** to bring about by coming between disagreeing or opposing parties: *He mediated a settlement between the union and the owner of the factory.* **2.** to settle (differences) by coming between disagreeing or opposing parties. —*v.i.* to act as a mediator in order to bring about an agreement or settlement. —*adj.* acting through or involving another person or thing; indirect. —**me'di·a'-tion,** *n.*

me·di·a·tor (mē'dē ā'tər) *n.* a person or group that mediates.

med·ic (med'ik) *n. Informal.* **1.** a physician. **2.** a medical student or intern. **3.** in the armed services, an enlisted man trained to give medical assistance.

med·i·cal (med'i kəl) *adj.* of or relating to doctors, medicine, or the study or practice of medicine. —**med'i·cal·ly,** *adv.*

me·dic·a·ment (mi dik'ə mənt) *n.* a substance used to treat disease or relieve pain; medicine.

med·i·cate (med'i kāt') *v.t.,* **med·i·cat·ed, med·i·cat·ing. 1.** to treat with medicine. **2.** to fill with medicine; put medicine on or in: *to medicate an ointment.*

med·i·ca·tion (med'i kā'shən) *n.* **1.** a substance used to treat disease or relieve pain; medicine. **2.** the act of medicating or the state of being medicated.

Med·i·ci (med'i chē) **1. Catherine de'.** 1519?–1589, the queen of France from 1547 to 1559. **2. Co·si·mo de'** (kō'zē mō). 1389–1464, ruler of Florence and the first great patron of arts and letters of the Italian Renaissance. **3. Lo·ren·zo de'** (lô ren'zō). 1449–1492, ruler of Florence and patron of the arts.

me·dic·i·nal (mə dis'ən əl) *adj.* **1.** able to heal, cure, or relieve: *a medicinal substance.* **2.** characteristic of or like medicine: *The hospital room had a medicinal smell.* —**me·dic'i·nal·ly,** *adv.*

med·i·cine (med'ə sin) *n.* **1.** a drug or other substance used to treat disease or relieve pain. **2.** the science that deals with the cause, prevention, and treatment of disease and the preservation of health. **3.** the medical profession. **4.** among North American Indians, any object or ceremony thought to have magical, healing, or curing powers.

medicine ball, a large, heavy stuffed ball thrown from one person to another for exercise.

medicine man, among North American Indians, a person believed to have magical powers; shaman.

me·di·e·val (mē'dē ē'vəl, mid ē'vəl) *also,* **me·di·ae·val.**

adj. of, relating to, belonging to, or characteristic of the Middle Ages.

Medieval Latin, Latin, especially as a literary language, from the eighth to the fifteenth centuries A.D. Also, **Middle Latin.**

Me·di·na (mə dē′nə) *n.* one of the holiest cities of Islam, site of Muhammad's tomb, in western Saudi Arabia.

me·di·o·cre (mē′dē ō′kər) *adj.* not exceptional; ordinary; commonplace. [French *médiocre,* from Latin *mediocris* literally, halfway up a mountain.]

me·di·oc·ri·ty (mē′dē ok′rə tē) *n. pl.,* **me·di·oc·ri·ties.** **1.** the state or quality of being mediocre. **2.** mediocre ability, accomplishment, or performance. **3.** a person who has mediocre talents or ability.

med·i·tate (med′ə tāt′) *v.,* **med·i·tat·ed, med·i·tat·ing.** —*v.i.* to think seriously and carefully; reflect: *to meditate on the problems of the world.* —*v.t.* to consider; plan: *The angry man meditated his revenge.*

med·i·ta·tion (med′ə tā′shən) *n.* serious and careful thought.

med·i·ta·tive (med′ə tā′tiv) *adj.* given to, showing, or characterized by meditation: *a meditative man, a meditative mood.* —**med′i·ta′tive·ly,** *adv.*

Med·i·ter·ra·ne·an (med′ə tə rā′nē ən) *n.* **1.** a large sea between southern Europe, western Asia, and northern Africa. Also, **Mediterranean Sea. 2. the Mediterranean.** a region consisting of this sea and those countries in and around it. —*adj.* of, relating to, or characteristic of the Mediterranean or the nearby countries and their people.

me·di·um (mē′dē əm) *n. pl.,* **me·di·ums** or *(especially for def. 3)* **me·di·a.** **1.** something occupying a position between two extremes; mean: *to find a happy medium between too much work and idleness.* **2.** the substance in which something exists or functions; environment: *Most bacteria grow best in a slightly acid medium.* **3.** a means or form of communication or expression: *Television, radio, newspapers, and magazines are media that reach a large audience in this country.* **4.** a substance or means through, in, or by which something may act or be carried: *The atmosphere is a medium for sound waves.* **5.** a person through whom the spirits of the dead supposedly communicate with the living. **6.** a material or technique used for artistic expression: *That artist's medium is watercolor.* —*adj.* intermediate, as in quantity, amount, or degree: *a dress of medium blue, a girl of medium height.*

med·ley (med′lē) *n. pl.,* **med·leys. 1.** a confused and disordered mixture of things; jumble. **2.** a musical composition made up of various tunes or parts from other compositions.

me·dul·la (mi dul′ə) *n. pl.,* **me·dul·lae** (mi dul′ē). **1.** see **medulla oblongata. 2.** the inner substance of an organ or part.

medulla ob·lon·ga·ta (ob′lông gä′tə) the lowest part of the brain, connected with the top of the spinal cord. It controls breathing and other involuntary functions.

Me·du·sa (mi dōō′sə, mi dyōō′sə) *n. pl.,* **Me·du·sas.** *Greek Mythology.* one of the three Gorgons, who was slain by Perseus.

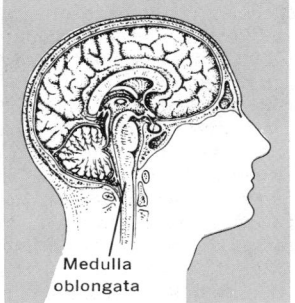
Medulla oblongata

meek (mēk) *adj.* **1.** patient and mild in manner or disposition; gentle. **2.** giving in or yielding easily; lacking spirit: *Tony is too meek to insist on a raise.* —**meek′ly,** *adv.* —**meek′ness,** *n.*

meer·schaum (mēr′shəm) *n.* **1.** a soft, light, white clay mineral that is heat-resistant, used to make tobacco pipes. **2.** a tobacco pipe that has a bowl made of meerschaum. [German *Meerschaum* this mineral; literally, sea foam; because it was originally found along the seashore and was thought to be the foam of the sea hardened into stone.]

meet[1] (mēt) *v.,* **met, meet·ing.** —*v.t.* **1.** to come face to face with; come upon or across: *I met her just as I was leaving.* **2.** to make the acquaintance of; be introduced to: *Haven't I met you before?* **3.** to keep an appointment with: *I'm going to meet him in front of his house.* **4.** to satisfy, fulfill, or comply with: *He didn't meet the qualifications for the job.* **5.** to come into contact with: *The Hudson River meets the ocean at New York City.* **6.** to pay: *I couldn't meet my bills this month.* **7.** to oppose or fight with, as in battle: *The army met the enemy in the valley.* **8.** to come into the observation or notice of: *There is more work involved in this job than meets the eye.* **9.** to deal or cope with effectively; confront: *He met their criticism with indifference.* —*v.i.* **1.** to come face to face: *After avoiding each other all morning, we met in the elevator.* **2.** to be introduced; become acquainted: *That couple met at a party.* **3.** to come into contact or union; join: *Oh, East is East, and West is West, and never the twain shall meet* (Rudyard Kipling). **4.** to come together, as for business or worship: *The committee was scheduled to meet for at least five hours each day.* —*n.* an assembly or gathering, as for an athletic contest: *a swimming meet.* [Old English *mētan* to find, assemble.]

to meet with. a. to receive: *Elizabeth's suggestion met with approval.* **b.** to experience; undergo: *The explorers met with difficulty in the jungle.*

meet[2] (mēt) *adj. Archaic.* suitable; proper. [Old English *mǣte, gemǣte.*]

meet·ing (mē′ting) *n.* **1.** a gathering or assembly of people: *The chairman of the committee presided at the meeting.* **2.** the persons so gathered. **3.** the act of coming together: *a meeting of two minds.* **4.** the place or point where things come together; junction: *the meeting of two rivers.* **5.** a gathering or assembly of people, especially Quakers, for religious worship.

meeting house, a building used for religious worship, especially by Quakers.

mega- *combining form* **1.** large; great: *megaphone.* **2.** multiplied by a million; one million of (a specified unit): *megacycle.*

meg·a·cy·cle (meg′ə sī′kəl) *n.* **1.** one million cycles per second, used especially in measuring frequency of radio waves and other electromagnetic radiation. **2.** one million cycles.

meg·a·lith (meg′ə lith′) *n.* a huge stone, especially one used in prehistoric monuments.

meg·a·lo·ma·ni·a (meg′ə lō mā′nē ə) *n.* a mental disorder characterized by delusions of greatness, power, or wealth.

meg·a·lo·ma·ni·ac (meg′ə lō mā′nē ak′) *n.* a person suffering from megalomania.

meg·a·lop·o·lis (meg′ə lop′ə lis) *n. pl.,* **meg·a·lop·o·lis·es.** a densely populated urban area made up of a number of adjoining cities.

at; āpe; cär; end; mē; it; īce; hot; ōld; fôrk; wood; fōōl; oil; out; up; turn; sing; thin; **this**; hw in white; zh in treasure. The symbol ə stands for the sound of **a** in about, **e** in taken, **i** in pencil, **o** in lemon, and **u** in circus.

meg·a·phone (meg′ə fōn′) *n.* a funnel-shaped device used to increase or direct the sound of the voice.

meg·a·ton (meg′ə tun′) *n.* a unit used to measure the explosive force of nuclear bombs, equal to the force produced by the explosion of one million tons of TNT.

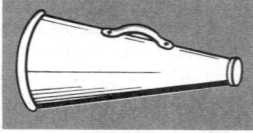
Megaphone

mei·o·sis (mī ō′sis) *n.* in living things that reproduce sexually, the process of cell division by which the number of chromosomes in a sex cell are reduced by half.

Mek·nès (mek nes′) *n.* a city in northwestern Morocco. Pop. (1970 est.), 245,000.

Me·kong (mā′kong′) *n.* a river in southeastern Asia, flowing southeastward from western China into the South China Sea.

mel·an·cho·li·a (mel′ən kō′lē ə) *n.* a mental disorder characterized by severe depression and self-criticism.

mel·an·chol·ic (mel′ən kol′ik) *adj.* **1.** melancholy; sad; depressed. **2.** of, relating to, or suffering from melancholia.

mel·an·chol·y (mel′ən kol′ē) *adj.* **1.** low in spirits; sad; depressed. **2.** suggestive of or causing sadness: *melancholy music.* —*n. pl.,* **mel·an·chol·ies.** a gloomy or depressed state of mind; sadness.

Mel·a·ne·sia (mel′ə nē′zhə) *n.* a group of islands in the Pacific Ocean, east of Australia.

Mel·a·ne·sian (mel′ə nē′zhən) *n.* **1.** a member of a Negroid people living in Melanesia. **2.** any of the languages spoken in Melanesia. —*adj.* of or relating to Melanesia, its people, or their languages.

mé·lange (mā länzh′) *n.* a mixture; medley: *a mélange of antique and modern furniture.* [French *mélange.*]

mel·a·nin (mel′ə nin) *n.* a dark brown pigment present in skin, hair, and other animal tissues. It helps to determine the color of the skin, hair, and eyes.

Mel·ba toast (mel′bə) very thin, dry slices of toast.

Mel·bourne (mel′bərn) *n.* a port city in southeastern Australia, capital of Victoria. Pop. (1971), 2,497,993.

meld (meld) *v.t., v.i.* in card games, to place (one or more cards) on the table in a set or on another set. —*n.* **1.** the act of melding. **2.** the cards melded.

me·lee (mā′lā′, mā lā′) *also,* **mê·lée.** *n.* a confused fight involving a number of people.

mel·lif·lu·ous (me lif′lōō əs) *adj.* sweetly or smoothly flowing: *a mellifluous voice.* —**mel·lif′lu·ous·ly,** *adv.*

mel·low (mel′ō) *adj.* **1.** (of fruit) soft, sweet, and juicy from ripeness. **2.** (of cheese and wine) rich, delicate, and fully aged. **3.** softened and made wise, gentle, and understanding by age and experience. **4.** full, rich, and soft: *a mellow color, a mellow tone.* —*v.t., v.i.* to make or become mellow. —**mel′low·ly,** *adv.* —**mel′low·ness,** *n.*

me·lod·ic (mə lod′ik) *adj.* **1.** relating to or containing melody. **2.** melodious; musical. —**me·lod′i·cal·ly,** *adv.*

me·lo·di·ous (mə lō′dē əs) *adj.* **1.** pleasant to hear; musical: *a melodious voice.* **2.** of, relating to, or producing melody. —**me·lo′di·ous·ly,** *adv.* —**me·lo′di·ous·ness,** *n.*

mel·o·dra·ma (mel′ə drä′mə, mel′ə dram′ə) *n.* **1.** a dramatic performance or play characterized by exaggerated emotions, sensational or overly sentimental incidents, and usually having a happy ending. **2.** such plays as a group. **3.** sensational or overly emotional writing, speech, or behavior.

mel·o·dra·mat·ic (mel′ə drə mat′ik) *adj.* of, relating to, or characteristic of melodrama: *a melodramatic story.* —**mel′o·dra·mat′i·cal·ly,** *adv.*

mel·o·dy (mel′ə dē) *n. pl.,* **mel·o·dies.** **1.** a pleasing arrangement or series of sounds. **2.** *Music.* **a.** a series of notes that makes up a complete phrase or idea; tune. **b.** the main part in a harmonized composition.

mel·on (mel′ən) *n.* a large fruit of any of several leafy vines, having a sweet, soft, juicy pulp that can be eaten. Watermelons, cantaloupes, and casabas are melons.

Mel·pom·e·ne (mel pom′ə nē) *n. Greek Mythology.* the Muse of tragedy.

melt (melt) *v.,* **melt·ed, melt·ed** or *(archaic)* **mol·ten, melt·ing.** —*v.i.* **1.** to be changed from a solid to a liquid state, especially by heating: *By the end of winter the ice on the pond had melted.* **2.** to dissolve, as in water. **3.** to disappear gradually; disperse. **4.** to pass or change by gradual degrees; blend: *The blue of the sky melted into the green landscape.* **5.** to become gentle, tender, or more understanding; soften: *His heart melted when the child began to cry.* —*v.t.* **1.** to change (something) from a solid to a liquid state, especially by heating. **2.** to dissolve (something), as in water: *to melt sugar in lemonade.* **3.** to make gentle, tender, or more understanding. —**melt′er,** *n.*

melting point, the temperature at which a given solid changes into a liquid. The melting point of a solid is identical to its freezing point. Thirty-two degrees Fahrenheit is the melting point of ice.

melting pot, a country, city, or region in which people of various races and nationalities become part of an existing culture.

Mel·ville, Herman (mel′vil) 1819–1891, U.S. novelist.

mem·ber (mem′bər) *n.* **1.** a person, animal, or thing belonging to a group: *The club has 200 members. The wolf is a member of the canine family.* **2.** *also,* **Member.** a representative of a legislative body: *a member of Congress.* **3.** *Mathematics.* **a.** either of the sides of an algebraic equation. **b.** one of the collection of objects that make up a set; element. **4.** a part of a human or animal body, especially a limb.

mem·ber·ship (mem′bər ship′) *n.* **1.** the state or condition of being a member of a group. **2.** the members of a group or organization as a whole: *The union membership voted to strike.* **3.** the number of members in a group or organization: *The club's membership rose this year.*

mem·brane (mem′brān) *n.* a thin layer of tissue that lines a cavity or passage in the body or covers a body surface.

mem·bra·nous (mem′brə nəs) *adj.* **1.** of, relating to, or resembling a membrane. **2.** forming a membrane.

me·men·to (mə men′tō) *n. pl.,* **me·men·tos** or **me·men·toes.** anything serving as a reminder of someone or something; keepsake; souvenir: *The pennant was a memento of his high school days.*

mem·o (mem′ō) *n. pl.,* **mem·os.** see **memorandum.**

mem·oir (mem′wär) *n.* **1.** *usually,* **memoirs. a.** a record of facts and events having to do with a particular subject or period, usually written from the writer's personal knowledge, experiences, and observations. **b.** a written account of the incidents and experiences of one's life; autobiography. **2.** an account of a person's life; biography. **3. memoirs.** a report of the proceedings of an organization or society.

mem·o·ra·bil·i·a (mem′ər ə bil′ē ə) *n., pl.* things that are worth being remembered or recorded.

mem·o·ra·ble (mem′ər ə bəl) *adj.* not to be forgotten; worthy of remembrance; notable: *a memorable event in history.* —**mem′o·ra·bly,** *adv.*

mem·o·ran·dum (mem′ə ran′dəm) *n. pl.,* **mem·o·ran·dums** or **mem·o·ran·da** (mem′ə ran′də). **1.** a brief note written as a reminder. **2.** an informal letter or communication, as that sent between departments in a business office. **3.** a short document stating the terms of a legal or business agreement or transaction.

me·mo·ri·al (mə môr′ē əl) *n.* **1.** something serving as a remembrance of some person or event, such as a monument or plaque: *The town built a memorial to honor men who had died in the war.* **2.** a written request or statement of facts sent to a government, legislative body, or other group in authority. —*adj.* serving as a memorial; commemorative: *a memorial plaque.*

Memorial Day, a legal holiday in memory of servicemen killed in all American wars. It was originally celebrated on May 30, and is now usually celebrated on the last Monday in May. Also, **Decoration Day.**

me·mo·ri·al·ize (mə môr′ē ə līz′) *v.t.,* **me·mo·ri·al·ized, me·mo·ri·al·iz·ing. 1.** to preserve or honor the memory of. **2.** to submit a memorial to; petition.

mem·o·rize (mem′ə rīz′) *v.t.,* **mem·o·rized, mem·o·riz·ing.** to learn by heart; commit to memory. —**mem′o·ri·za′tion,** *n.* —**mem′o·riz′er,** *n.*

mem·o·ry (mem′ər ē) *n. pl.,* **mem·o·ries. 1.** the mental power or ability to recall past experiences. **2.** all that one can or does recall: *I can recite the poem from memory.* **3.** someone or something remembered: *The accident is an unpleasant memory for him.* **4.** something that is remembered of a person or thing: *to honor the memory of those who died in war.* **5.** the act of remembering or the state of being remembered. **6.** the component in an electronic computer in which information is stored.

Mem·phis (mem′fis) *n.* **1.** the largest city in Tennessee, in the southwestern part of the state. Pop. (1970), 623,530. **2.** a city in ancient Egypt, on the west bank of the Nile.

men (men) the plural of **man.**

men·ace (men′is) *n.* **1.** a person or thing that is a threat; danger: *The underwater reefs are a menace to ships entering the harbor.* **2.** a very annoying or troublesome person. —*v.t.,* **men·aced, men·ac·ing.** to put in danger; threaten; endanger: *The storm menaced the small ship.* —**men′ac·ing·ly,** *adv.*

me·nag·er·ie (mə naj′ər ē) *n.* **1.** a collection of wild or unusual animals kept in cages or other enclosures, usually for exhibition. **2.** the enclosure where such animals are kept.

mend (mend) *v.t.* **1.** to return to good condition or working order: *to mend a broken vase, to mend a torn curtain.* **2.** to reform, correct, or improve (something): *The boy was warned to mend his mischievous ways.* —*v.i.* **1.** to knit, as a broken bone; heal. **2.** to regain one's health; recover. —*n.* a mended place: *a mend in the heel of a sock.*

   on the mend. getting better, especially in health; improving.

men·da·cious (men dā′shəs) *adj.* **1.** given to lying; untruthful: *a mendacious person.* **2.** false; untrue: *mendacious rumors.* —**men·da′cious·ly,** *adv.*

men·dac·i·ty (men das′ə tē) *n. pl.,* **men·dac·i·ties. 1.** the quality of being mendacious; untruthfulness. **2.** a falsehood; lie.

Men·del, Gre·gor (mend′əl; greg′ôr) 1822–1884, Austrian monk and botanist whose experiments in heredity were the foundation for the science of genetics.

men·de·le·vi·um (mend′əl ē′vē əm) *n.* a radioactive, metallic element that does not occur in nature. It is produced by bombarding an isotope of einsteinium with helium ions. Symbol: **Mv** [Modern Latin *mendelevium,* from Dmitri Ivanovich *Mendeleev,* 1834–1907, a Russian chemist.]

Men·dels·sohn, Felix (mend′əl sən) 1808–1847, German composer.

men·di·cant (men′di kənt) *adj.* given to or characterized by begging; living on alms. —*n.* a person who lives on alms; beggar.

Men·e·la·us (men′əl ā′əs) *n. Greek Legend.* the king of

Sparta whose wife, Helen, was carried off to Troy by Paris.

men·folk (men′fōk′) *also,* **men·folks.** *n., pl. Informal.* males as a group, especially all the male members of a family or other group.

men·ha·den (men hād′ən) *n. pl.,* **men·ha·den.** a saltwater fish related to the herring, found in the western Atlantic. It is used as a source of animal feed, fertilizer, and oil.

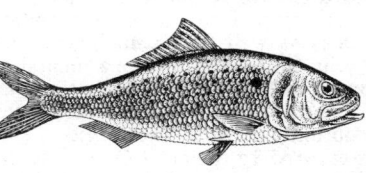
Menhaden

me·ni·al (mē′nē əl) *adj.* **1.** degrading; lowly: *a menial task.* **2.** of, relating to, or suitable for a servant. —*n.* a servant who performs very lowly or humble tasks. —**me′ni·al·ly,** *adv.*

me·nin·ges (mi nin′jēz) *n.,pl. sing.,* **me·ninx** (mē′ningks).** the three membranes that enclose and protect the brain and spinal cord.

men·in·gi·tis (men′in jī′tis) *n.* a serious illness characterized by inflammation of the meninges.

me·nis·cus (mi nis′kəs) *n. pl.,* **me·nis·cus·es** or **me·nis·ci** (mi nis′ī). **1.** a crescent or crescent-shaped body. **2.** the curved upper surface of a liquid in a container. The surface is concave if the liquid wets the walls of the container and convex if it does not. **3.** a lens that is convex on one side and concave on the other.

Men·non·ite (men′ə nīt′) *n.* a member of a Protestant sect founded in Holland in the sixteenth century, that rejects infant baptism, the taking of oaths, the holding of public office, and military service. [From *Menno* Simons, 1492–1559, a Dutch religious reformer who founded this sect.]

men-of-war (men′əv wôr′) the plural of **man-of-war.**

men·o·pause (men′ə pôz′) *n.* the time at which menstruation permanently ceases to occur.

men·ser·vants (men′sur′vənts) the plural of **manservant.**

men·ses (men′sēz) *n., pl.* another word for **menstruation.**

men·stru·al (men′strōō əl) *adj.* of or relating to menstruation.

men·stru·ate (men′strōō āt′) *v.i.,* **men·stru·at·ed, men·stru·at·ing.** to undergo menstruation. [Late Latin *mēnstruātus,* going back to Latin *mēnsis* month; because women usually menstruate once a month.]

men·stru·a·tion (men′strōō ā′shən) *n.* **1.** the periodic discharge of blood and bloody fluid from the uterus through the female genital tract, usually occurring every twenty-eight days. **2.** an instance of this.

men·su·ra·tion (men′shə rā′shən) *n.* **1.** the act or process of measuring. **2.** the branch of mathematics dealing with the determination of lengths, areas, and volumes.

-ment *suffix* (used to form nouns) **1.** the act or process of: *accomplishment, development.* **2.** the state or condition of being: *involvement, amazement.* **3.** the product or result of: *pavement, improvement.* **4.** the means or instrument of: *inducement.*

at; āpe; cär; end; mē; it; īce; hot; ōld; fôrk; wood; fōōl; oil; out; up; turn; sing; thin; <u>th</u>is; hw in white; zh in treasure. The symbol ə stands for the sound of **a** in about, **e** in taken, **i** in pencil, **o** in lemon, and **u** in circus.

men·tal (ment′əl) *adj.* **1.** of or relating to the mind: *mental development, mental awareness.* **2.** carried on in or performed by the mind: *mental arithmetic.* **3.** mentally ill: *a mental patient.* **4.** for the care of the mentally ill: *a mental hospital.*

mental age, the level of mental development as measured by performance on an intelligence test. A child who does as well on an intelligence test as an average ten-year-old is said to have a mental age of ten.

men·tal·i·ty (men tal′ə tē) *n. pl.,* **men·tal·i·ties.** **1.** mental ability or power. **2.** a manner or way of thinking; outlook: *a British mentality.*

men·tal·ly (ment′əl ē) *adv.* **1.** with regard to the mind: *to be mentally ill.* **2.** in or with the mind: *to add or subtract mentally.*

mental retardation, a condition in which there is a poor or incomplete development of intelligence, characterized by difficulty in learning.

men·thol (men′thôl) *n.* a white, crystalline substance obtained from peppermint oil by freezing.

men·tion (men′shən) *v.t.* to speak about or refer to briefly: *David mentioned you in his last letter.* —*n.* a brief remark or reference: *There was no mention of the robbery in today's newspaper.*

Men·tor (men′tər) *n.* **1.** *Greek Mythology.* a loyal friend of Ulysses who was left in charge of his household and son. **2. mentor.** any wise and trusted counselor.

men·u (men′yōō) *n.* **1.** a list of the food served or available in a restaurant or other eating place. **2.** the food served or available.

me·ow (mē ou′) *also,* **mi·aow.** *n.* the cry of a cat. —*v.i.* to make such a sound.

Meph·i·stoph·e·les (mef′ə stof′ə lēz′) *n.* **1.** *German Legend.* the devil to whom Faust sold his soul. **2.** any crafty, evil person.

mer·can·tile (mur′kən tēl′, mur′kən tīl′) *adj.* **1.** of, relating to, or characteristic of merchants or commerce; commercial. **2.** of or relating to mercantilism.

mer·can·til·ism (mur′kən tī liz′əm) *n.* an economic system developed in France and England in the sixteenth and seventeenth centuries that stressed strict government control of the national economy and believed that having more exports than imports was good because it brought in gold and silver from other countries.

Mercator projection (mər kā′tər) a map projection developed in the sixteenth century, in which the distances between parallels of latitude gradually increase, moving to the north and south away from the equator. Though the relative sizes of areas in the higher latitudes are distorted, the Mercator projection shows compass directions as straight lines and so is ideal for navigation over small areas. [From Gerhardus *Mercator,* 1512–1594, a Flemish geographer and map maker.]

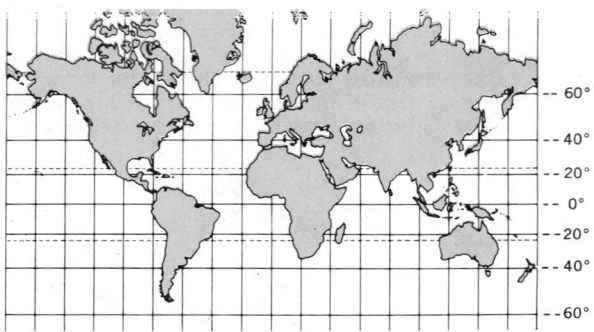

Mercator projection

mer·ce·nar·y (mur′sə ner′ē) *adj.* **1.** working or acting only out of a desire for money or material gain. **2.** (of a soldier) serving in a foreign army for pay. —*n. pl.,* **mer·ce·nar·ies.** a mercenary soldier.

mer·cer·ize (mur′sə rīz′) *v.t.,* **mer·cer·ized, mer·cer·iz·ing.** to treat (cotton thread or fabric) with a caustic soda solution to give it more luster, strength, and absorbency and make it easier to dye. [From John *Mercer,* 1791–1866, the English inventor of this process.]

mer·chan·dise (*v.,* mur′chən dīz′; *n.,* mur′chən dīz′, mur′chən dīs′) *n.* articles bought and sold; commodities; wares. —*v.,* **mer·chan·dised, mer·chan·dis·ing.** —*v.t.* **1.** to buy and sell; trade. **2.** to promote the sale of, as through advertising. —*v.i.* to carry on commerce; trade. —**mer′chan·dis′er,** *n.*

mer·chant (mur′chənt) *n.* **1.** a person whose business is buying and selling merchandise for profit. **2.** a person who owns or runs a retail store; storekeeper. —*adj.* **1.** of or relating to merchants or commerce. **2.** of or relating to the merchant marine.

mer·chant·man (mur′chənt mən) *n. pl.,* **mer·chant·men** (mur′chənt mən). a ship used in commerce.

merchant marine 1. the commercial or trading ships of a nation as a group. **2.** the officers and crews of such ships.

mer·ci·ful (mur′si fəl) *adj.* feeling, showing, or characterized by mercy. —**mer′ci·ful·ly,** *adv.* —**mer′ci·ful·ness,** *n.*

mer·ci·less (mur′si lis) *adj.* without mercy; pitiless. —**mer′ci·less·ly,** *adv.* —**mer′ci·less·ness,** *n.*

mer·cu·ri·al (mər kyoor′ē əl) *adj.* **1.** likely or tending to change, changeable; erratic: *a mercurial personality, mercurial moods.* **2.** of, relating to, containing, or caused by the action of mercury: *mercurial compounds, mercurial poisoning.* **3.** lively; quick. —**mer·cu′ri·al·ly,** *adv.*

Mer·cu·ro·chrome (mər kyoor′ə krōm′) *n. Trademark.* a red antiseptic liquid solution that contains mercury.

Mer·cu·ry (mur′kyər ē) *n.* **1.** *Roman Mythology.* the messenger of the gods and patron of commerce. In Greek mythology he was called Hermes. **2.** the smallest planet of the solar system and closest to the sun. It is the fastest-moving planet, completing a full revolution in eighty-eight days.

mer·cu·ry (mur′kyər ē) *n. pl.,* **mer·cu·ries.** **1.** a heavy, shiny, silver-colored, poisonous metallic element. Mercury is used especially in thermometers and barometers. Symbol: **Hg** Also, **quicksilver.** **2.** a column of mercury in a thermometer or barometer, used as an indication of temperature: *The weather bureau reported that the mercury rose to 90° yesterday.* [From *Mercury* the Roman messenger of the gods; probably because this active metal was compared to the swift messenger.]

mer·cy (mur′sē) *n. pl.,* **mer·cies.** **1.** kindness, forgiveness, or compassion toward another or others where harshness is expected or deserved; leniency: *The guilty man begged the judge for mercy.* **2.** the disposition or power to be kind or forgiving: *The convicted man threw himself on the mercy of the court.* **3.** something to be thankful for; blessing: *His help was a real mercy.*
  at the mercy of. completely in the power of: *We were at the mercy of the enemy.*

mere (mēr) *adj. superlative,* **mer·est.** being nothing more or other than what is specified; only: *a mere trifle, a mere child.*

Mer·e·dith, George (mer′ə dith) 1828–1909, English novelist and poet.

mere·ly (mēr′lē) *adv.* and nothing more; only: *His explanations were merely poor excuses.*

mer·e·tri·cious (mer′ə trish′əs) *adj.* attractive in a vulgar or deceitful way. —**mer′e·tri′cious·ly,** *adv.*

mer·gan·ser (mər gan′sər) *n. pl.,* **mer·gan·sers** or **mer·gan·ser.** a diving duck having a long, slender bill with saw-toothed edges and usually a crested head.

merge (murj) *v.,* **merged, merg·ing.** —*v.i.* to be united so as to become one: *The two paths merge just ahead. The two companies merged.* —*v.t.* to unite so as to become one: *The library merged the two rare book collections.*

merg·er (mur′jər) *n.* the act of merging, especially the union of two or more corporations: *the merger of two advertising companies.*

Mé·ri·da (mer′i də) *n.* a city in southeastern Mexico, on the Yucatán Peninsula. Pop. (1976 est.), 244,700.

me·rid·i·an (mə rid′ē ən) *n.* **1.** an imaginary great circle on the earth's surface passing through the North and South poles. **2.** one half of such a circle extending from pole to pole; a line or parallel of longitude. **3.** a great circle on the celestial sphere passing through the north and south celestial poles. **4.** the highest point; zenith: *the moment at which the fortunes of Montague reached the meridian* (Thomas Macaulay).

me·ringue (mə rang′) *n.* **1.** a mixture of stiffly beaten egg whites and sugar, usually baked and used as a topping, as on cakes or pies. **2.** a small cake or pastry shell made of this mixture.

me·ri·no (mə rē′nō) *n. pl.,* **me·ri·nos. 1.** a sheep of a breed originally developed in Spain, having a light-colored fleece and a white face. It is raised for its wool. **2.** a fine, soft yarn or fabric made from the wool of this sheep, used for such items as suits or dresses. **3.** a knitted fabric woven from a blend of cotton and wool fibers, used for such items as hosiery and underwear.

Merino

mer·it (mer′it) *n.* **1.** quality, worth, or excellence: *The author's latest book has great merit.* **2.** *also,* **merits.** something deserving praise or reward; good quality. **3. merits.** the actual facts of a matter under consideration, whether good or bad: *The judge will decide the case on its merits.* —*v.t.* to be deserving of: *Steve feels that he merits a raise in pay.*

mer·i·to·ri·ous (mer′ə tôr′ē əs) *adj.* worthy of reward or praise; having merit: *The soldier was given a medal for meritorious service.* —**mer′i·to·ri·ous·ly,** *adv.* —**mer′i·to′ri·ous·ness,** *n.*

merle (murl) *also,* **merl.** *n.* a European blackbird.

Mer·lin (mur′lin) *n.* in the legends of King Arthur, the wise magician who protected and counseled the young King Arthur.

mer·maid (mur′mād′) *n.* in folklore, a sea creature having the head and body of a beautiful woman and the tail of a fish instead of legs.

mer·man (mur′man′) *n. pl.,* **mer·men** (mur′men′). in folklore, a sea creature having the head and body of a man and the tail of a fish instead of legs.

Mer·ri·mac (mer′i mak′) *also,* **Mer·ri·mack.** *n.* a U.S. steam-driven wooden frigate converted to an ironclad by the Confederates and renamed the *Virginia.* It engaged in a historic battle with the *Monitor* at Hampton Roads, Virginia, on March 9, 1862.

mer·ri·ment (mer′i mənt) *n.* playfulness and gaiety; fun.

mer·ry (mer′ē) *adj.,* **mer·ri·er, mer·ri·est. 1.** festive and cheerful; full of merriment: *a merry group of people.*

2. characterized by festivity and rejoicing; joyous: *a merry song.* —**mer′ri·ly,** *adv.*

to make merry. to be festive and jovial; celebrate.

mer·ry-an·drew (mer′ē an′drōō) *n.* a clown; buffoon.

mer·ry-go-round (mer′ē gō round′) *n.* **1.** a revolving circular platform equipped with wooden animals, especially horses, and often having seats. It is ridden for amusement. Also, **carousel. 2.** a circular platform that revolves when pushed, found in playgrounds. **3.** a rapid round; whirl: *She went to a merry-go-round of parties during the Christmas holidays.*

mer·ry·mak·ing (mer′ē mā′king) *n.* **1.** the act of engaging in or having fun; making merry. **2.** boisterous or gay festivity: *The merrymaking after the wedding went on until very late at night.* —*adj.* full of joy and fun; gay and festive. —**mer′ry·mak′er,** *n.*

me·sa (mā′sə) *n.* a flat-topped hill or mountain with steep sides descending to the plain below; high plateau. [Spanish *mesa* table.]

mes·ca·line (mes′kə lēn′) *n.* a crystalline drug that produces hallucinations, derived from the dried tops of certain cactuses.

mes·dames (mā däm′) the plural of **madame.**

mes·de·moi·selles (mād mwä zel′) a plural of **mademoiselle.**

mesh (mesh) *n. pl.,* **mesh·es. 1.** one of the open spaces between the cords, threads, or wires of a net or netting. **2.** an open network consisting of interlaced cords, threads, or wires; netting. **3.** any of various fabrics consisting of an open network of interlaced threads. **4.** *also,* **meshes.** anything that entangles or traps: *She was caught in the mesh of her lies.* **5.** the interlocking or engagement of the teeth of a gear. —*v.i.* to become engaged, as the teeth of a gear; interlock.

in mesh. in gear; interlocked.

Me·shed (mə shed′) *n.* a city in northeastern Iran. Pop. (1976), 680,180.

mes·mer·ism (mez′mə riz′əm, mes′mə riz′əm) *n.* another word for **hypnotism.** [From F. A. *Mesmer,* 1734–1815, an Austrian doctor who practiced hypnotism.]

mes·mer·ize (mez′mə rīz′, mes′mə rīz′) *v.t.,* **mes·mer·ized, mes·mer·iz·ing. 1.** to put in a hypnotic trance; hypnotize. **2.** to affect as deeply as by a trance: *He was mesmerized by the dazzling painting.* —**mes′mer·i·za′tion,** *n.* —**mes′mer·iz′er,** *n.*

mes·on (mez′on, mes′on) *n.* any of a group of subatomic particles whose mass is greater than that of an electron but less than that of a proton.

Mes·o·po·ta·mi·a (mes′ə pə tā′mē ə) *n.* a historic region in southwestern Asia, between the Tigris and Euphrates Rivers, forming the eastern part of the area known as the Fertile Crescent. It was an ancient center of civilization. —**Mes′o·po·ta′mi·an,** *adj., n.*

mes·o·sphere (mes′ə sfēr′) *n.* the layer of the atmosphere above the stratosphere, from about thirty to about sixty miles above the earth's surface.

Mes·o·zo·ic (mes′ə zō′ik) *n.* one of the major geological eras, comprising the Cretaceous, Jurassic, and Triassic periods; age of reptiles. —*adj.* of, relating to, or characteristic of this era.

at; āpe; cär; end; mē; it; īce; hot; ōld; fôrk; wood; fōōl; oil; out; up; turn; sing; thin; this; hw in white; zh in treasure. The symbol ə stands for the sound of **a** in about, e in taken, i in pencil, o in lemon, and u in circus.

mes·quite (mes kēt′) *n.* a small thorny tree that grows in desert regions from the southwestern United States to Chile, bearing small flowers, and slender seedpods containing beans used as feed for livestock.

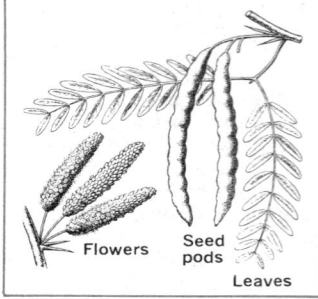
Flowers
Seed pods
Leaves
Mesquite

mess (mes) *n. pl.,* **mess·es.** **1.** an untidy, disorderly, or dirty state or condition: *The closet is in a mess.* **2.** a person or thing that is in such a state or condition: *The room was a mess after the party.* **3.** an unpleasant, difficult, or confusing situation: *He made a mess of his life.* **4.** *Informal.* an indefinite amount: *to catch a mess of fish.* **5. a.** a group of people who take meals together regularly, especially in the army or navy. **b.** the meal eaten by such a group. **c.** the place where such a meal is eaten; mess hall. —*v.t.* **1.** to make dirty or untidy: *to mess up a room.* **2.** to confuse or spoil: *Her late arrival messed up our plans.* —*v.i.* **1.** to interfere or tamper: *Don't mess with my typewriter.* **2.** to take one's meals in a mess hall.

mes·sage (mes′ij) *n.* **1.** a communication sent from one person or group to another. **2.** a formal or official communication: *the President's message to Congress.* **3.** the point of view or idea meant to be communicated: *The movie's message was that crime doesn't pay.*

mes·sen·ger (mes′ən jər) *n.* **1.** a person who picks up and delivers messages or runs errands. **2.** a person employed to deliver telegrams, letters, or parcels. **3.** a person whose work is carrying official dispatches. **4.** a sign of something to come; harbinger; forerunner: *The flowers were a messenger of the coming spring.*

messenger RNA, see **RNA.**

mess hall, a place where a group of people take meals together regularly, especially in the army or navy.

Mes·si·ah (mə sī′ə) *n.* **1.** in Judaism, the expected savior of the Jews promised by God. **2.** in Christianity, Jesus, regarded as the savior of mankind. **3.** *also,* **messiah.** any savior or deliverer.

mes·sieurs (mes′ərz) the plural of **monsieur.**

Mes·si·na (mə sē′nə) *n.* **1.** a port city in northeastern Sicily. Pop. (1970 est.), 274,740. **2. Strait of.** a narrow strait between Italy and Sicily.

mess kit, a compact kit consisting of eating utensils and a metal container that opens to make two separate compartments for holding food, used by a soldier or camper.

mess·mate (mes′māt′) *n.* a regular companion at meals, especially in a ship's mess.

Messrs. (mes′ərz) **1.** Messieurs. **2.** the plural of **Mr.**: *Messrs. Holmes and Watson.*

mess·y (mes′ē) *adj.,* **mess·i·er, mess·i·est.** **1.** being in a mess; untidy: *a messy room.* **2.** causing a mess; unpleasant or difficult: *She got the messy job of cleaning the oven.* —**mess′i·ly,** *adv.* —**mess′i·ness,** *n.*

mes·ti·zo (mes tē′zō) *n. pl.,* **mes·ti·zos** or **mes·ti·zoes.** a person of mixed racial ancestry, especially a person of Spanish and American Indian descent.

met (met) the past tense and past participle of **meet**[1].

met·a·bol·ic (met′ə bol′ik) *adj.* of, relating to, involving, or characterized by metabolism: *metabolic changes.*

me·tab·o·lism (mə tab′ə liz′əm) *n.* the total of all the biological and chemical processes that occur in a living thing. Metabolism is the means by which food is converted into protoplasm and by which the necessary energy is provided to carry on all basic life processes, such as respiration, digestion, and cell division.

met·a·car·pal (met′ə kar′pəl) *adj.* of or relating to the metacarpus. —*n.* one of the bones of the metacarpus. See **hand** for illustration.

met·a·car·pus (met′ə kär′pəs) *n. pl.,* **met·a·car·pi** (met′ə kär′pī). **1.** the part of the hand between the wrist and the fingers, having five bones. **2.** a similar part of the forelimb of an animal.

met·al (met′əl) *n.* **1.** any of a class of chemical elements, such as iron, silver, copper, or lead, that have a shiny surface, can be melted, conduct heat and electricity, and usually can be hammered into thin sheets or drawn out into wires. **2.** a mixture of such elements, as brass or bronze; alloy. **3.** a basic quality or substance; mettle.

me·tal·lic (mə tal′ik) *adj.* **1.** of or having the properties of metal. **2.** containing or yielding metal. **3.** resembling, characteristic of, or suggestive of metal: *a metallic sound.*

met·al·loid (met′əl oid′) *n.* any of a class of chemical elements that have both metallic and nonmetallic properties. —*adj.* **1.** of, relating to, or having the properties of a metalloid. **2.** resembling a metal.

met·al·lur·gy (met′əl ur′jē) *n.* the science and technology of separating metals from ores and preparing them for use, as by refining. —**met′al·lur′gi·cal,** *adj.* —**met′al·lur′gist,** *n.*

met·al·work (met′əl wurk′) *n.* **1.** objects or structures made of metal. **2.** metalworking.

met·al·work·ing (met′əl wur′king) *n.* the act or process of making metal objects or structures. —**met′al·work′er,** *n.*

met·a·mor·phic (met′ə môr′fik) *adj.* **1.** of, relating to, or characterized by metamorphosis. **2.** *Geology.* of, relating to, or produced by metamorphism.

met·a·mor·phism (met′ə môr′fiz əm) *n.* **1.** the change in the texture, structure, and mineral composition of rock caused by processes operating beneath the surface of the earth. **2.** another word for **metamorphosis.**

met·a·mor·phose (met′ə môr′fōz) *v.,* **met·a·mor·phosed, met·a·mor·phos·ing.** —*v.t.* to cause to undergo metamorphosis or metamorphism. —*v.i.* to undergo metamorphosis or metamorphism.

met·a·mor·pho·sis (met′ə môr′fə sis) *n. pl.,* **met·a·mor·pho·ses** (met′ə môr′fə sēz′). **1.** the process by which certain animals go through changes in form, structure, or function as they develop from an immature form at birth or hatching to an adult. Caterpillars become butterflies and tadpoles become frogs through the process of metamorphosis. **2.** any complete or great change, as in form, appearance, character, or condition.

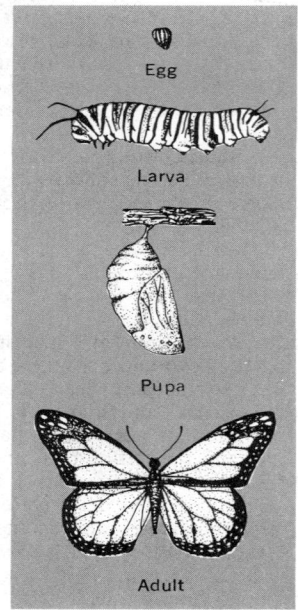
Egg
Larva
Pupa
Adult
Metamorphosis of a butterfly

met·a·phor (met′ə fôr′) *n.* a figure of speech in which one object or idea is compared or identified with another in order to suggest a similarity between the two. For example: *The hockey star is a pillar of strength.*

● **Metaphor** is one of the most common figures of speech. We most often think of it as it is used in poetry and other creative writing. Poets use metaphor to give their writing a fresh, concrete quality and to surprise us by comparing one thing with another to which it is not normally related. For example, when Shakespeare wrote "All the world's a stage and all the men and women merely players," he was comparing life to a play acted in a theater and comparing people in general to actors. Other examples of metaphors that you probably know, but have not thought of as metaphors, are "The Lord is my shepherd," from the Twenty-third Psalm and "We are his people, and the sheep of his pasture," from the Hundredth Psalm. In this metaphor, which appears many times in the Bible, God is seen as protecting and guiding people as a shepherd would his sheep.

We all use metaphor in our everyday speaking and writing. In fact, any new meaning of a word is a kind of metaphor. This means that from the original meaning of a word, new meanings are developed as they are used to compare different things to the original meaning. An example of this type of metaphor is our using the word "leg" to describe one of the supports of a table. If people made up a new word to describe every new thought that they had, it would be almost impossible for them to communicate with each other. Using old words to describe new ideas makes it easier for people to understand the new ideas. Because the word "memory" has been applied to the part of a computer that stores information, we can understand its function, even though a new definition of "memory" is being used. Our language has grown far more from the adoption of metaphorical meanings of existing words than it has from the creation of new words.

met·a·phor·i·cal (met′ə fôr′ik əl) *adj.* relating to or containing metaphors. —**met′a·phor′i·cal·ly,** *adv.*

met·a·phys·i·cal (met′ə fiz′i kəl) *adj.* **1.** of, relating to, or characteristic of metaphysics. **2.** hard to understand; highly abstract. —**met′a·phys′i·cal·ly,** *adv.*

met·a·phy·si·cian (met′ə fi zish′ən) *n.* a student of or an expert in metaphysics.

met·a·phys·ics (met′ə fiz′iks) *n., pl.* the branch of philosophy that deals with the nature and meaning of reality. ▲ used with a singular verb.

me·tas·ta·sis (mə tas′tə sis) *n. pl.,* **me·tas·ta·ses** (mə-tas′tə sēz′). the spread of a disease, especially a cancerous growth, from one part of the body to another.

met·a·tar·sal (met′ə tär′səl) *adj.* of or relating to the metatarsus. —*n.* one of the bones of the metatarsus.

met·a·tar·sus (met′ə tär′səs) *n. pl.,* **met·a·tar·si** (met′ə-tär′sī). **1.** the part of the foot between the ankle and the toes, consisting of five bones. **2.** a similar part of the hind foot of a four-legged animal, or the foot of a bird.

met·a·zo·an (met′ə zō′ən) *n.* any animal whose body is composed of specialized cells grouped to form tissues and organs. All animals are metazoans except the protozoans and the sponges. —*adj.* of, relating to, or characteristic of the metazoans.

mete (mēt) *v.t.,* **met·ed, met·ing.** to distribute by or as if by measuring; allot: *to mete out punishment.*

me·te·or (mē′tē ər) *n.* matter from space that enters the earth's atmosphere, where it is heated by friction until it burns with a bright light during its fall. Also, **shooting star.**

me·te·or·ic (mē′tē ôr′ik) *adj.* **1.** of, relating to, or containing meteors. **2.** resembling a meteor; brilliant and swift: *The young senator had a meteoric rise in politics.* **3.** of, relating to, or occurring in the earth's atmosphere: *Hurricanes are meteoric phenomena.*

me·te·or·ite (mē′tē ə rīt′) *n.* a meteor that has fallen to earth.

me·te·or·oid (mē′tē ə roid′) *n.* a meteor while it is still in space, before it enters the earth's atmosphere.

me·te·or·o·log·i·cal (mē′tē ər ə loj′ik əl) *adj.* of or relating to meteorology. —**me′te·or·o·log′i·cal·ly,** *adv.*

me·te·or·ol·o·gist (mē′tē ə rol′ə jist) *n.* a student of or an expert in meteorology.

me·te·or·ol·o·gy (mē′tē ə rol′ə jē) *n.* the science dealing with the study of the atmosphere and the changes that take place within it. One important branch of meteorology is the study of weather.

me·ter¹ (mē′tər) *also, British,* **me·tre.** *n.* the fundamental unit of length in the metric system, equivalent to 3.28 feet. [French *mètre,* from Greek *metron.*]

me·ter² (mē′tər) *also, British,* **me·tre.** *n.* **1.** the rhythmic arrangement of accented and unaccented or short and long syllables in a line of poetry. **2.** the basic rhythmic pattern of accented notes or beats in a musical composition: *Waltzes are written in triple meter.* [Old English *méter* and Old French *metre.*]

me·ter³ (mē′tər) *n.* **1.** an instrument or device for measuring and recording the amount of gas, water, or electricity used or the rate of flow. **2.** any of various similar instruments or devices for measuring and recording time, speed, distance, or degree of intensity. —*v.t.* to measure or record by means of a meter. [*Mete + -er¹.*]

-meter *combining form* **1.** a device for measuring: *speedometer.* **2.** having a specified amount of meters: *kilometer.* **3.** having a specified number of poetic feet: *pentameter.*

me·ter-kil·o·gram-sec·ond (mē′tər kil′ə gram′sek′-ənd) *adj.* of, relating to, or being a system of measurement in which the meter is the unit of length, the kilogram is the unit of mass, and the second is the unit of time.

meth·a·done (meth′ə dōn′) *n.* a synthetic narcotic drug used as a pain-killer and as a substitute for heroin in the treatment of heroin addiction.

meth·ane (meth′ān) *n.* a colorless, odorless, highly flammable gas that is the simplest compound of carbon and hydrogen. It is the main constituent of natural gas.

meth·a·nol (meth′ə nôl′) *n.* a clear, poisonous, liquid alcohol compound, used in antifreeze, shellac, and rocket fuel. Also, **methyl alcohol, wood alcohol.**

me·thinks (mi thingks′) *v. Archaic.* it seems to me.

meth·od (meth′əd) *n.* **1.** a way, means, or manner of doing something, especially so as to be systematic or orderly. **2.** orderliness and regularity in thought, action, or activity: *The secretary's filing system lacked method.*

me·thod·i·cal (mə thod′i kəl) *adj.* **1.** performed, arranged, or carried on in a systematic or orderly manner: *The police made a methodical search of the house.* **2.** characterized by systematic or orderly habits or behavior: *Mother is a very methodical housekeeper.* —**me·thod′i·cal·ly,** *adv.* —**me·thod′i·cal·ness,** *n.*

Meth·od·ism (meth′ə diz′əm) *n.* the faith, doctrines, and practices of the Methodists.

Meth·od·ist (meth′ə dist) *n.* a member of any of several branches of a Protestant denomination that had its origin in the teachings and work of John Wesley. —*adj.* of, relating to, or characteristic of the Methodists or Methodism.

at; āpe; cär; end; mē; it; īce; hot; ōld; fôrk; wood; fo͞ol; oil; out; up; turn; sing; thin; **th**is; **hw** in white; **zh** in treasure. The symbol ə stands for the sound of **a** in about, **e** in taken, **i** in pencil, **o** in lemon, and **u** in circus.

meth·od·ol·o·gy (meth′ə dol′ə jē) *n. pl.,* **meth·od·ol·o·gies.** an orderly system of principles and methods used in a particular field.

me·thought (mi thôt′) the past tense of **methinks.**

Me·thu·se·lah (mə thōō′zə lə) *n.* **1.** in the Bible, a patriarch who lived 969 years. **2.** any very old man.

meth·yl alcohol (meth′əl) another term for **methanol.**

me·tic·u·lous (mə tik′yə ləs) *adj.* characterized by or showing extreme or excessive concern about details. —**me·tic′u·lous·ly,** *adv.* —**me·tic′u·lous·ness,** *n.*

me·tre[1] (mē′tər) *British.* another spelling of **meter**[1].

me·tre[2] (mē′tər) *British.* another spelling of **meter**[2].

met·ric[1] (met′rik) *adj.* of, relating to, or designating the metric system: *metric measurement.* [French *métrique.*]

met·ric[2] (met′rik) *adj.* another word for **metrical.** [Latin *metricus.*]

met·ri·cal (met′ri kəl) *adj.* **1.** of, relating to, or composed in poetic meter. **2.** of, relating to, or used in measurement. —**met′ri·cal·ly,** *adv.*

met·ri·cate (met′ri kāt′) *v.t.* **met·ri·cat·ed, met·ri·cat·ing.** to change to the metric system: *The government has metricated some highway signs.* —**met′ri·ca′tion,** *n.*

metric system, a decimal system of measurement in which the meter is the fundamental unit of length, the kilogram is the fundamental unit of mass, and the second is the fundamental unit of time.

metric ton, a measure of weight equal to 1000 kilograms or 2204.62 pounds avoirdupois.

met·ro·nome (met′rə nōm′) *n.* a mechanical device used for indicating the exact tempo to be maintained in music. It usually has a reverse pendulum that can be adjusted to produce clicks at different tempos.

me·trop·o·lis (mə trop′ə lis) *n.* **1.** a large city, especially one that is an important center of commerce or culture. **2.** the principal city of a particular country, state, or region. [Late Latin *metropolis* mother city.]

met·ro·pol·i·tan (met′rə pol′ə tən) *adj.* **1.** relating to, resembling, or belonging to a metropolis: *a metropolitan police force.* **2.** consisting of or making up a metropolis and its surrounding regions: *The New York metropolitan area.* —*n.* in the Roman Catholic Church and certain Anglican and Orthodox churches, an archbishop who is head of a church province.

Metronome

-metry *combining form* the art, science, or process of measuring: *geometry, optometry.*

Met·ter·nich, Prince von (met′ər nik) 1773–1859, Austrian statesman.

met·tle (met′əl) *n.* **1.** spirit and courage. **2.** the basic quality or substance, as of a person's character.

Mev (mev) *n.* one million electron volts.

mew[1] (myōō) *n.* the cry of a cat; meow. —*v.t.* to make such a sound. [Imitative of this sound.]

mew[2] (myōō) *n.* a gull, especially of Europe. Also, **sea mew.** [Old English *mǣw.*]

mewl (myōōl) *v.i.* to cry feebly like a baby; whimper.

mews (myōōz) *n., pl.* **1.** stables built around a court or alley. **2.** a narrow street or alley, usually having houses that have been converted from stables.

Mex. 1. Mexico. **2.** Mexican.

Mex·i·can (mek′si kən) *n.* a person who was born or is living in Mexico. —*adj.* of or relating to Mexico, its people, their language, or their culture.

Mexican jumping bean, see **jumping bean.**

Mexican War, the war fought between the United States and Mexico from 1846 to 1848.

Mex·i·co (mek′si kō′) *n.* **1.** a country in North America, bordering the southwestern United States. Capital, Mexico City. Area, 761,604 sq. mi. Pop. (1980), 70,000,000. **2. Gulf of.** an arm of the Atlantic Ocean, between the United States and Mexico.

Mexico City, the capital and largest city of Mexico, in the southern part of the country. Pop. (1976), 8,628,000.

me·zu·zah (mə zooz′ə) *also,* **me·zu·za.** *n. pl.,* **me·zu·zahs** or **me·zu·soth** (mə zooz′ōt). in Judaism, a small container shaped like a tube, containing parchment inscribed with Biblical passages. It is usually attached to a doorpost or worn around the neck.

mez·za·nine (mez′ə nēn′) *n.* **1.** a floor or story between two main floors of a building, usually just above the ground floor. **2.** the lowest balcony in a theater or the first few rows of the balcony.

mez·zo (met′sō) *Music. adj.* half; medium; moderate. —*adv.* moderately.

mez·zo·so·pran·o (met′sō sə pran′ō) *n. pl.,* **mez·zo·so·pran·os. 1.** a female voice lower than soprano and higher than alto. **2.** a singer who has such a voice. **3.** a musical part for such a voice. —*adj.* **1.** able to sing the mezzo-soprano. **2.** for the mezzo-soprano.

Mg, the symbol for magnesium.

mg., milligram; milligrams.

Mgr. 1. Manager. **2.** Monseigneur. **3.** Monsignor.

MHG, M.H.G., Middle High German.

mi (mē) *n. Music.* **1.** the third note of the major scale. **2.** the note E.

mi., mile; miles.

Mi·am·i (mī am′ē) *n.* the largest city in Florida, in the southeastern part of the state. Pop. (1970), 334,859.

Miami Beach, a city in southeastern Florida, just east of Miami. Pop. (1970), 87,072.

mi·aow (mē ou′) another spelling of **meow.**

mi·as·ma (mī az′mə) *n. pl.,* **mi·as·mas** or **mi·as·ma·ta** (mī az′mə tə). **1.** a poisonous vapor formerly believed to rise from the earth and decaying matter and pollute the air. **2.** any harmful influence, effect, or atmosphere.

mi·ca (mī′kə) *n.* any of a group of minerals that look like transparent or cloudy glass and can be separated into thin sheets, often used as insulators in electrical devices. Also, **isinglass.**

Mi·cah (mī′kə) *n.* **1.** in the Old Testament, a Hebrew prophet of the eighth century B.C. **2.** the book of the Old Testament thought to have been written by him.

mice (mīs) the plural of **mouse.**

Mich., Michigan.

Mi·chael, Saint (mī′kəl) in the Bible, the archangel who cast Satan out of heaven.

Mich·ael·mas (mik′əl məs) *n.* the church feast in honor of the archangel Michael. It falls on September 29.

Mi·chel·an·ge·lo (mī′kəl an′jə lō′) 1475–1564, Italian sculptor and painter; full name, Michelangelo Buonarroti.

Mich·i·gan (mish′ə gən) *n.* **1.** a state in the north-central United States. Capital, Lansing. Area, 58,216 sq. mi. Pop. (1970), 8,875,083. Abbreviation, **Mich. 2. Lake.** the third largest of the Great Lakes. It lies between Michigan and Wisconsin.

● **Michigan** is the French version of two Algonquian words that meant "great water," and referred to Lake Michigan.

mi·cra (mī′krə) a plural of **micron.**

micro- *combining form* **1.** very small; minute: *microorganism.* **2.** enlarging, magnifying, or amplifying: *microscope.* **3.** one millionth of (a specified unit): *micron.*

mi·crobe (mī′krōb) *n.* a microscopic living thing, especially one that causes disease.

mi·cro·bi·ol·o·gy (mī′krō bī ol′ə jē) *n.* the branch of biology that studies microorganisms. —**mi′cro·bi′o·log′-i·cal,** *adj.* —**mi′cro·bi·ol′o·gist,** *n.*

mi·cro·coc·cus (mī′krō kok′əs) *n. pl.,* **mi·cro·coc·ci** (mī′krō kok′sī). any of several varieties of bacteria that are spherical or egg-shaped.

mi·cro·cop·y (mī′krə kop′ē) *n. pl.,* **mi·cro·cop·ies.** a photographic copy, as of a manuscript, picture, or letter, that has been reduced in size.

mi·cro·cosm (mī′krə koz′əm) *n.* **1.** a little world; universe in miniature. **2.** anything thought of as being a miniature representation of something: *The small town was a microcosm of all of society.*

mi·cro·film (mī′krə film′) *n.* **1.** a photographic film, usually thirty-five or sixteen millimeters wide, on which a newspaper or other printed matter is reproduced in miniature. **2.** a reproduction made on such film. —*v.t.* to make a microfilm of.

mi·cro·me·te·or·ite (mī′krō mē′tē ə rīt′) *n.* a tiny meteorite that, because of its size, encounters no air resistance in falling to earth.

mi·crom·e·ter (mī krom′ə tər) *n.* **1.** any of a group of instruments that measure very small dimensions, distances, or angles to a high degree of precision. **2.** see micrometer caliper.

micrometer caliper, a caliper having two jaws, one of which can be moved by turning a screw. It is used for making precise measurements.

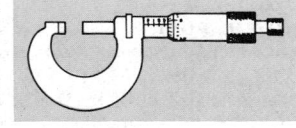

Micrometer caliper

mi·cron (mī′kron) *n. pl.,* **mi·crons** or **mi·cra.** a unit of length equal to one-millionth of a meter.

Mi·cro·ne·sia (mī′krə nē′zhə) *n.* a group of islands in the Pacific Ocean, north of Melanesia.

Mi·cro·ne·sian (mī′krə nē′zhən) *n.* **1.** a person who was born or is living in Micronesia. **2.** any of the languages spoken in Micronesia. —*adj.* of or relating to Micronesia, its people, or their languages.

mi·cro·nu·cle·us (mī′krō nōō′klē əs, mī′krō nyōō′klē əs) *n.* the smaller of the two types of nuclei present in various protozoans, believed to control reproduction.

mi·cro·or·gan·ism (mī′krō ôr′gə niz′əm) *n.* a living thing, such as a virus, that is too small to be seen with the naked eye.

mi·cro·phone (mī′krə fōn′) *n.* a device that converts sound waves to an electrical signal, used to record, transmit, or amplify sound.

mi·cro·scope (mī′krə skōp′) *n.* an instrument with a lens or combination of lenses that gives a clear magnified image of a small object viewed through it.

mi·cro·scop·ic (mī′krə skop′ik) *adj.* **1.** too small to be seen with the naked eye: *microscopic animals.* **2.** extremely small; minute. **3.** of, relating to, or done with a microscope: *a microscopic lens, a microscopic observation of cells.* **4.** resembling or acting like a microscope; very detailed; thorough: *The jury made a microscopic examination of the evidence.* —**mi′cro·scop′i·cal·ly,** *adv.*

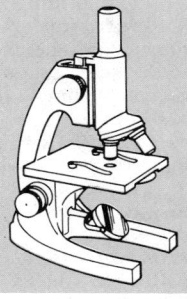

Microscope

mi·cros·co·py (mī kros′kə pē) *n.*

1. the process or technique of using a microscope. **2.** an investigation with a microscope.

mi·cro·wave (mī′krə wāv′) *n.* a high-frequency electromagnetic wave having a wavelength ranging from about one millimeter to thirty centimeters. It is used in radar and for such purposes as long-distance transmission of television signals through the air.

microwave oven, an oven in which food is quickly cooked with the heat produced by the action of microwaves entering the food.

mid¹ (mid) *adj.* being at or near the middle. [Old English *midd.*]

mid² (mid) *also,* **'mid.** *prep. Archaic.* amid.

mid- *combining form* **1.** the middle part of: *midsummer, midweek.* **2.** being in the middle or center: *midpoint.*

mid·air (mid′er′) *n.* a point or region high in the air above the ground: *The acrobat did a flip in midair.*

Mi·das (mī′dəs) *n. Greek Legend.* a king who was given the power of turning everything he touched to gold.

mid·brain (mid′brān′) *n.* the middle part of the brain.

mid·day (mid′dā′) *n.* the middle of the day; noon. —*adj.* of, relating to, or occurring during the middle part of the day: *midday heat, a midday meal.*

mid·dle (mid′əl) *adj.* **1.** equally distant from the sides, ends, or outer points: *We sat in the middle row.* **2.** being or happening halfway between two things: *He is the middle child in the family.* **3.** average; medium: *She is of middle height.* —*n.* **1.** a point, part, or area equally distant from the sides, ends, or outer points: *the middle of the street.* **2.** a part or portion approximately halfway between the beginning and the end: *We left in the middle of his speech.* **3.** the middle part of the body; waist.

middle age, the time of life between youth and old age, usually thought of as being between forty and sixty.

mid·dle-aged (mid′əl ājd′) *adj.* **1.** in or of middle age. **2.** of or relating to persons of middle age.

Middle Ages, the period of European history between the fall of the Western Roman Empire and the beginning of the Renaissance, from about the fifth century to the middle of the fifteenth century.

middle C *Music.* **1.** the note written on the first line below the staff in the treble clef and the first line above the staff in the bass clef. **2.** the tone or key represented by this note.

mid·dle-class (mid′əl klas′) *adj.* of, relating to, or characteristic of the middle class.

middle class, the part of society socially and economically above the lower class and below the upper class.

Middle Dutch, the Dutch language from the twelfth to the sixteenth centuries.

middle ear, the cavity between the eardrum and the inner ear, containing, in humans, the hammer, anvil, and stirrup. Also, **tympanum.**

Middle East, a region consisting of the northeastern coast of Africa, southwestern Asia, the Arabian Peninsula and Asia Minor, including Israel, Egypt, Syria, Turkey, and Iran. Also, **Mideast.** —**Middle Eastern.**

Middle English, the English language from the twelfth to the sixteenth centuries. See **Old English** for further information.

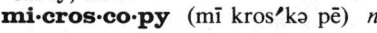

at; āpe; cär; end; mē; it; īce; hot; ōld; fôrk; wood; fōōl; oil; out; up; turn; sing; thin; this; hw in white; zh in treasure. The symbol ə stands for the sound of **a** in about, **e** in taken, **i** in pencil, **o** in lemon, and **u** in circus.

M

Middle French, the French language from the fourteenth to the sixteenth centuries.

Middle High German, High German from the twelfth to the sixteenth centuries.

Middle Latin, another name for **Medieval Latin.**

Middle Low German, Low German from the twelfth to the sixteenth centuries.

mid·dle·man (mid′əl man′) *n. pl.,* **mid·dle·men** (mid′əl men′). **1.** a person who buys goods from the producer and sells them to the retailer or consumer. **2.** a go-between; intermediary.

mid·dle-of-the-road (mid′əl əv thə rōd′) *adj.* not taking or supporting any extreme position or side; moderate: *a middle-of-the-road politician.*

Mid·dles·brough (mid′əlz brə) *n.* a city in northeastern England. Pop. (1971), 395,477.

mid·dle·weight (mid′əl wāt′) *n.* **1.** a boxer, wrestler, or weight lifter weighing between 147 and 160 pounds. **2.** a person or animal of average weight.

Middle West, a region of the north-central United States. Also, **Midwest.** —**Middle Western.**

mid·dy (mid′ē) *n. pl.,* **mid·dies. 1.** *Informal.* a midshipman. **2.** see **middy blouse.**

middy blouse, a loosely fitting blouse designed to resemble a sailor's blouse.

Mid·east (mid′ēst′) *n.* another word for **Middle East.**

midge (mij) *n.* any of various tiny flies.

midg·et (mij′it) *n.* **1.** a very small but normally-proportioned person. **2.** anything that is very small of its kind; dwarf. —*adj.* very small.

Middy blouse

mid·land (mid′lənd) *n.* the central or interior part of a region or country. —*adj.* of or situated in the midland: *a midland village.*

mid·most (mid′mōst′) *adj.* being exactly in or nearest to the middle. —*adv.* in the middle or midst.

mid·night (mid′nīt′) *n.* twelve o'clock at night; the middle of the night. —*adj.* **1.** of, relating to, or occurring at midnight: *a midnight train.* **2.** resembling midnight; very dark: *The dress was midnight blue.*

to burn the midnight oil. to study or work late into the night.

midnight sun, the sun seen at midnight or late at night during summer in the arctic and antarctic regions.

mid·point (mid′point′) *n.* a point that is exactly in the middle of something, as a line.

mid·rib (mid′rib′) *n. Botany.* the central vein of a leaf.

mid·riff (mid′rif′) *n.* **1.** the part of the body below the breast and above the waist. **2.** the part of a woman's garment that covers this part of the body. **3.** a woman's blouse or similar garment that exposes this part of the body. **4.** see **diaphragm** *(def. 1).*

mid·ship (mid′ship′) *adj.* of, relating to, or situated in or near the middle of a ship.

mid·ship·man (mid′ship′mən) *n. pl.,* **mid·ship·men** (mid′ship′mən). **1.** in the U.S. Navy, a student in training at the U.S. Naval Academy for commission as an officer. **2.** *British.* a second-year student in training on board ship for commission as an officer.

mid·ships (mid′ships′) *adv.* another word for **amidships.**

midst[1] (midst) *n.* **1.** the condition or position of being surrounded by or involved in something: *in the midst of a crowd, in the midst of trouble.* **2.** a gathering or association of people; company: *There is a traitor in our midst.* **3.** the central or middle part. [Middle English *middest.*]

midst[2] (midst) *also,* **'midst.** *prep.* amid; amidst.

mid·sum·mer (mid′sum′ər) *n.* **1.** the middle of summer. **2.** the summer solstice, occurring about June 21. —*adj.* of, relating to, or occurring in the middle of summer.

mid·term (mid′turm′) *n.* **1.** the middle of a school term or semester. **2.** a test taken during the middle of a school term or semester. —*adj.* taking place during the middle of a school term or semester: *a midterm examination.*

mid·town (mid′toun′) *n.* the central part of a city or town. —*adj.* relating to or located in midtown.

mid·way (mid′wā′) *adj.* in the middle of the way or distance: *We have reached the midway point of our journey.* —*adv.* in or to the middle of the way or distance; halfway: *Bobby's house is midway between my house and the school.* —*n.* a place where sideshows and other amusements are located, as at a carnival, circus, or fair.

mid·week (mid′wēk′) *n.* the middle of the week. —*adj.* in the middle of the week.

Mid·west (mid′west′) *n.* another word for **Middle West.** —**Mid′west′ern,** *adj.* —**Mid′west′ern·er,** *n.*

mid·wife (mid′wīf′) *n. pl.,* **mid·wives** (mid′wīvz′). a woman who assists women in childbirth.

mid·win·ter (mid′win′tər) *n.* **1.** the middle of winter. **2.** the winter solstice, occurring about December 22. —*adj.* of, relating to, or occurring in the middle of winter.

mid·year (mid′yēr′) *n.* the middle of the year. —*adj.* taking place during the middle of a year.

mien (mēn) *n.* a person's manner or appearance, especially as showing character or mood; bearing: *a man of gentle mien.*

miff (mif) *v.t. Informal.* to cause to be offended or annoyed: *The stranger's rudeness miffed Helen.*

MIG (mig) *also,* **Mig.** *n.* any of various jet fighter planes designed and built by the Soviet Union.

might[1] (mīt) the past tense of **may.**

might[2] (mīt) *n.* **1.** great power, force, or influence: *the might of a nation.* **2.** physical power or strength: *He slammed the door with all his might.* **3.** the power or ability to do or accomplish something: *She tried with all her might not to cry.* [Old English *miht.*]

might·i·ly (mī′tə lē) *adv.* **1.** with great force, power, or strength. **2.** to a great degree; very much; greatly.

might·y (mī′tē) *adj.,* **might·i·er, might·i·est. 1.** having or showing great power, strength, or ability: *a mighty foe.* **2.** very great in amount, degree, intensity, or extent: *a mighty task.* —*adv. Informal.* very; greatly: *It was mighty nice of her to call me.* —**might′i·ness,** *n.*

mi·gnon·ette (min′yə net′) *n.* any of various plants that have narrow spoon-shaped leaves and tiny yellowish-white or greenish-yellow flowers in long spikes or clusters.

mi·graine (mī′grān) *n.* a severe headache, usually affecting only one side of the head and tending to recur periodically.

mi·grant (mī′grənt) *n.* a person or thing that migrates. —*adj.* migrating; migratory: *a migrant worker.*

mi·grate (mī′grāt) *v.i.,* **mi·grat·ed, mi·grat·ing. 1.** to move from one country or region to another in order to settle there. **2.** to move seasonally or periodically from one region or climate to another: *Many birds migrate south in the fall.*

mi·gra·tion (mī grā′shən) *n.* **1.** the act or instance of migrating. **2.** a group, as of people, animals, or fish, that migrate together.

mi·gra·to·ry (mī′grə tôr′ē) *adj.* **1.** characterized by or given to migration; migrating: *migratory birds, migratory farm workers.* **2.** of or relating to migration.

mi·ka·do (mi kä′dō) *also,* **Mi·ka·do.** *n. pl.,* **mi·ka·dos.** the emperor of Japan.

mike (mīk) *n. Informal.* see **microphone.**

mil (mil) *n.* a unit of length equal to one-thousandth of an inch, used in measuring the diameter of wires.

mi·la·dy (mi lā′dē) *also,* **mi·la·di.** *n. pl.,* **mi·la·dies.** my lady. ▲ used in speaking or referring to an English gentlewoman or noblewoman.

Mi·lan (mi lan′) *n.* a city in northern Italy. Pop. (1971 est.), 1,701,612.

milch (milch) *adj.* (of a cow) giving milk.

mild (mīld) *adj.* 1. not extreme, harsh, or severe; moderate: *a mild winter, a mild headache.* 2. not sharp, strong, or bitter in taste or odor: *a mild cheese.* 3. gentle or kind in disposition, manners, or behavior. —**mild′ly,** *adv.* —**mild′ness,** *n.*

mil·dew (mil′dōō′) *n.* 1. any of various fungi that attack crop plants, appearing as a fine powder or fuzzy down. Mildew causes dwarfing, deformation, and loss of the affected parts of the plant. 2. any of various fungi that appear as discolored areas on leather or other materials. —*v.t.* to cause to have mildew: *The dampness in the basement mildewed the books.* —*v.i.* to have mildew.

mile (mīl) *n.* a unit of linear measure equal to 5280 feet or 1760 yards. [Going back to Latin *mīlia passuum* literally, a thousand paces.]

mile·age (mī′lij) *also,* **mil·age.** *n.* 1. the total number of miles covered or traveled in a specified period of time: *We put a lot of mileage on the car during our vacation.* 2. the number of miles traveled, as by an automobile, on a certain amount of fuel: *Twenty miles per gallon is good mileage.* 3. the amount of use, service, or wear yielded by something: *to get good mileage from a set of tires.*

mile·post (mīl′pōst′) *n.* a post set up, as on a highway, to mark the distance in miles to a place.

mile·stone (mīl′stōn′) *n.* 1. a stone set up, as on a highway, to mark the distance in miles to a place. 2. an important event or development: *The invention of the telephone was a milestone in the history of communications.*

mi·lieu (mil yoo′, mil yoo′) *n.* surroundings or environment: *That university has an intellectual milieu.*

mil·i·tant (mil′ə tənt) *adj.* 1. active or aggressive in support of a cause: *The militant protesters refused to leave the building.* 2. engaged in war or fighting: *militant nations.* —*n.* a militant person. —**mil′i·tan·cy,** *n.* —**mil′i·tant·ly,** *adv.*

mil·i·ta·rism (mil′ə tə riz′əm) *n.* 1. the glorification of war, and of the military class, its ideals, and its policies. 2. a national policy of developing and supporting a strong military force.

mil·i·ta·rist (mil′i tər ist) *n.* a person who supports or upholds militarism. —**mil′i·ta·ris′tic,** *adj.*

mil·i·ta·rize (mil′ə tə rīz′) *v.t.,* **mil·i·ta·rized, mil·i·ta·riz·ing.** 1. to train and equip for war. 2. to fill with militarism. —**mil′i·ta·ri·za′tion,** *n.*

mil·i·tar·y (mil′ə ter′ē) *adj.* 1. of, relating to, or involving armed forces, soldiers, or war: *military tactics, a military career.* 2. made of or for members of the armed forces: *a military unit, a military uniform.* —*n.* the military forces of a country; armed forces. —**mil′i·tar′i·ly,** *adv.*

military police, the members of the army assigned to police duties.

mil·i·tate (mil′ə tāt′) *v.i.,* **mil·i·tat·ed, mil·i·tat·ing.** to act, operate, or have influence: *The wrong that he did militated against his good reputation.*

mi·li·tia (mi lish′ə) *n.* a military force that is not professional, such as the National Guard, and is called for service in time of emergency.

mi·li·tia·man (mi lish′ə mən) *n. pl.,* **mi·li·tia·men** (mi lish′ə mən). a member of a militia.

milk (milk) *n.* 1. a white liquid produced by female mammals for the nourishment of their young. 2. this liquid, especially as produced by cows, used as food by human beings. 3. any liquid resembling this: *coconut milk.* —*v.t.* 1. to draw milk from (a cow, goat, or other female mammal). 2. to extract or take (something): *to milk information from someone.* 3. to extract or take from: *The blackmailer milked him for every penny he had.* —*v.i.* to draw milk from a cow, goat, or other female mammal.

milk·er (mil′kər) *n.* 1. a person or machine that milks cows. 2. a cow or other animal that gives milk.

milk·maid (milk′mād′) *n.* a woman or girl who milks cows or works in a dairy.

milk·man (milk′man′) *n. pl.,* **milk·men** (milk′men′). a man who sells or delivers milk.

milk of magnesia, a milky white liquid consisting mainly of magnesia in water, used to settle the stomach or to loosen the bowels.

milk shake, a frothy, cold drink made of milk, flavoring, and sometimes ice cream, shaken or whipped together.

milk·sop (milk′sop′) *n.* an unmanly or cowardly man or boy; sissy.

milk sugar, another term for **lactose.**

milk tooth, in man and other mammals, one of the temporary teeth that fall out and are replaced by permanent teeth.

milk·weed (milk′wēd′) *n.* a plant containing a milky juice, and having large leaves and long, green pods with many seeds.

milk·white (milk′hwīt′, milk′wīt′) *adj.* having the white or bluish-white color of milk.

milk·y (mil′kē) *adj.,* **milk·i·er, milk·i·est.** 1. resembling milk, especially in color. 2. containing or yielding milk or a substance like milk. —**milk′i·ness,** *n.*

Milky Way, a galaxy made up of more than 100 billion stars, appearing as a bright white path across the heavens. Our solar system is part of the Milky Way. Also, **Galaxy.**

Milkweed

mill¹ (mil) *n.* 1. a building or business containing machinery for grinding or crushing grain: *a flour mill, a corn mill.* 2. a machine or device that grinds or crushes grain. 3. any of various machines or devices for grinding or crushing something: *a pepper mill, a coffee mill.* 4. a building or group of buildings containing machinery for manufacturing or processing materials: *a paper mill, a steel mill.* —*v.t.* 1. to grind or crush: *to mill grain.* 2. to stamp or cut a series of notches or ridges around the edge of (a coin or other piece of metal). —*v.i.* to move in an aimless or confused manner. [Old English *mylen.*]

mill² (mil) *n.* a unit of monetary value, equal to 1/10 of a cent. [Short for Latin *mīllesīmus* a thousandth.]

Mill, John Stuart (mil) 1806–1873, English philosopher and economist.

Mil·lay, Edna St. Vincent (mi lā′) 1892–1950, U.S. poet.

mill·dam (mil′dam′) *n.* a dam built across a stream to raise the water level in order to supply water power for a mill.

at; āpe; cär; end; mē; it; īce; hot; ōld; fôrk; wood; fōōl; oil; out; up; turn; sing; thin; **th**is; hw in white; zh in treasure. The symbol ə stands for the sound of **a** in about, **e** in taken, **i** in pencil, **o** in lemon, and **u** in circus.

593 **M**

mil·len·ni·al (mi len′ē əl) *adj.* **1.** of or relating to a thousand years. **2.** of or relating to the millennium.

mil·len·ni·um (mi len′ē əm) *n. pl.,* **mil·len·ni·ums** or **mil·len·ni·a** (mi len′ē ə). **1.** a period of a thousand years. **2.** according to the New Testament, the period of a thousand years during which Christ will reign on earth. **3.** a period of happiness, peace, and prosperity.

mill·er (mil′ər) *n.* **1.** a person who owns or operates a mill for grinding grain. **2.** any white or grayish moth whose wings look as if they were powdered with flour.

mil·let (mil′it) *n.* **1.** a grass that is like wheat and is widely raised for its small, edible grains. **2.** the small grain of this grass.

Mil·let, Jean Fran·cois (mi lā′; zhän′ frän swä′) 1814–1875, French painter and etcher.

milli- *combining form* one-thousandth of (a specified unit): *milligram.*

mil·li·bar (mil′ə bär′) *n.* a unit of measuring atmospheric pressure, equal to 1000 dynes per square centimeter.

mil·li·gram (mil′ə gram′) *also, British,* **mil·li·gramme.** *n.* a metric unit of weight, equal to one-thousandth of a gram.

mil·li·li·ter (mil′ə lē′tər) *also, British,* **mil·li·li·tre.** *n.* a metric measure of capacity, equal to one-thousandth of a liter.

mil·li·me·ter (mil′ə mē′tər) *also, British,* **mil·li·me·tre.** *n.* a metric measure of length, equal to one-thousandth of a meter, or .03937 inch.

Millet grain

mil·li·ner (mil′ə nər) *n.* a person who designs, makes, trims, or sells women's hats.

mil·li·ner·y (mil′ə ner′ē) *n.* **1.** the articles, especially hats, sold by a milliner. **2.** the business of a milliner.

mill·ing (mil′ing) *n.* **1.** the act or process of grinding or crushing grain or some other material by a mill. **2.** the process of stamping or cutting notches or ridges around the edge of a piece of metal, such as a coin. **3.** the notches or ridges produced by this.

mil·lion (mil′yən) *n.* **1.** the cardinal number that is one thousand times one thousand. **2.** a symbol representing this number, such as 1,000,000. **3.** an indefinitely large number: *She has millions of hats.* —*adj.* numbering one million: *a million dollars.*

mil·lion·aire (mil′yə ner′) *n.* a person who has a million or more dollars, pounds, or other unit of currency.

mil·lionth (mil′yənth) *adj.* **1.** (the ordinal of million) being last in a series of one million. **2.** being one of a million equal parts. —*n.* **1.** something that is last in a series of one million. **2.** one of a million equal parts.

mil·li·pede (mil′ə pēd′) *also,* **mil·li·ped.** *n.* an animal having as many as one hundred legs, and feeding mainly on decayed plant matter. [Latin *millepeda* literally, one thousand feet.]

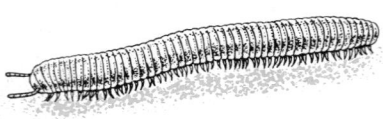

Millipede

mill·pond (mil′pond′) *n.* a pond, usually formed by a dam, for supplying water power to a mill.

mill·race (mil′rās′) *n.* **1.** a current of water leading into and driving a mill wheel. **2.** the channel through which such a current runs.

mill·stone (mil′stōn′) *n.* **1.** either of a pair of circular stones between which grain or similar substances are placed for grinding. **2.** a heavy burden: *a millstone of debt.*

mill·stream (mil′strēm′) *n.* **1.** a stream whose water is used to run a mill. **2.** the water in a millrace.

mill wheel, a large wheel, usually turned by the force of falling water, that supplies mechanical power to run the machinery of a mill.

mi·lord (mi lôrd′) *n.* my lord. ▲ used in speaking or referring to an English gentleman or nobleman.

milque·toast (milk′tōst′) *n.* a weak, timid, apologetic person.

milt (milt) *n.* in the male fish, the sperm cells and the milky fluid containing them.

Mil·ton, John (milt′ən) 1608–1674, English poet.

Mil·wau·kee (mil wô′kē) *n.* a city in southeastern Wisconsin, on Lake Michigan. Pop. (1970), 717,099.

mime (mīm) *n.* **1.** a performer who portrays characters or conveys an idea or story by body movements, facial expressions, and gestures rather than by the use of speech. **2.** the art of pantomime. **3.** a drama popular among the ancient Greeks and Romans that made fun of actual persons and events. **4.** an actor in such a drama. —*v.,* **mimed, mim·ing.** —*v.t.* to act out in pantomime. —*v.i.* to act or perform as a mime. —**mim′er,** *n.*

mim·e·o·graph (mim′ē ə graf′) *n.* **1.** a machine for printing copies of material written, typed, or drawn on a stencil. Trademark: **Mimeograph. 2.** the copy made by such a machine. —*v.t.* to reproduce on a mimeograph: *to mimeograph a financial report.*

mim·ic (mim′ik) *v.t.,* **mim·icked, mim·ick·ing. 1.** to imitate the speech, manners, or gestures of, especially so as to make fun of: *He hurt her feelings by mimicking her.* **2.** to copy closely or reproduce: *He could mimic the style of several famous painters.* —*n.* **1.** a person who mimics, especially a performer skilled in pantomine. **2.** something that is a copy; imitation. —*adj.* **1.** of, like, or characterized by mimicry; imitative. **2.** make-believe; pretend; mock: *a mimic battle.*

mim·ic·ry (mim′ik rē) *n. pl.,* **mim·ic·ries. 1.** the act, practice, or art of mimicking. **2.** the close outward resemblance of one kind of animal to another or to an object in its natural environment. Mimicry helps to protect or conceal an animal.

mi·mo·sa (mi mō′sə) *n.* a plant related to the pea, having leaves that resemble ferns and small white, pink, or purple flowers.

min. 1. minute; minutes. **2.** minimum.

min·a·ret (min′ə ret′) *n.* a tall, slender tower attached to a mosque. A crier summons worshipers to prayer from a balcony near its top.

mince (mins) *v.,* **minced, minc·ing.** —*v.t.* **1.** to cut or chop into very small, fine pieces: *The cook minced the potato.* **2.** to say or speak in a restrained or refined manner: *She doesn't mince words.* —*v.i.* to walk in a dainty way with very short steps. —*n.* see **mincemeat.**

mince·meat (mins′mēt′) *n.* a mixture of finely chopped apples, suet, raisins, currants, sugar, spices, and sometimes meat, used for pies.

mince pie, a pie made with mincemeat.

Minaret

minc·ing (min′sing) *adj.* dainty or refined in speech or manners. —**minc′ing·ly,** *adv.*

mind (mīnd) *n.* **1.** the part of the body where thought takes place; the center of memory, learning, and the emotions. **2.** the power or ability to know, understand, and reason: *Ann has a good mind and learns things quickly.*

3. a healthy mental state; sanity: *He lost his mind.*
4. a way of thinking or feeling; disposition: *Henry has an open mind on most issues.* **5.** memory; remembrance: *I'll keep it in mind for future reference.* **6.** attention: *I can't keep my mind on what I'm doing.* **7.** desire, intention, or wish: *I have a mind to visit them next week.* —*v.t.* **1.** to pay attention to; be concerned or careful about: *Don't mind what he says, he's just upset.* **2.** to take care of; look after; tend: *The babysitter will mind the children.* **3.** to obey: *The children always mind their mother.* **4.** to object to: *She doesn't mind eating alone.* **5.** to look or watch out for: *Mind the broken chair.* —*v.i.* **1.** to object or care: *Do you mind if I borrow your book?* **2.** to be obedient.

a piece of one's mind. a severe scolding.

never mind. disregard or forget: *Never mind what he says.*

on one's mind. in one's thoughts.

to bear in mind or **to keep in mind.** to remember.

to be of one mind. to be in agreement.

to call to mind. to serve as a reminder of: *His story calls to mind a funny thing that happened to me.*

to make up one's mind. to come to a decision; decide: *Phil made up his mind to go to the party.*

Min·da·na·o (min′də nä′ō) *n.* the second-largest island of the Philippines.

mind·ed (mīn′did) *adj.* **1.** favorably disposed; inclined. **2.** having a certain kind of mind. ▲ used in combination: *fair-minded, open-minded.*

mind·ful (mīnd′fəl) *adj.* conscious; aware: *Is he mindful of the risks involved?* —**mind′ful·ly,** *adv.* —**mind′ful·ness,** *n.*

mind·less (mīnd′lis) *adj.* **1.** lacking intelligence; stupid or foolish. **2.** without thought; heedless. —**mind′less·ly,** *adv.*

mine¹ (mīn) *pron.* the one or ones that belong or relate to me: *The brown coat is mine.* —*adj. Archaic.* my. ▲ used before a word beginning with a vowel or *h*, or after a noun: *mine eyes, mine heart, mother mine.* [Old English *mīn.*]

mine² (mīn) *n.* **1.** a large area dug under the ground, from which coal, mineral ores, or other materials are taken. **2.** a deposit of coal, mineral ore, or other material that may be taken from the earth. **3.** any abundant source or supply: *That book is a mine of information.* **4.** an explosive charge placed underground or in water, used to destroy enemy troops, equipment, or ships. —*v.,* **mined, min·ing.** —*v.t.* **1.** to take from the earth: *to mine diamonds.* **2.** to dig in (the earth) for coal, mineral ores, or other materials. **3.** to place explosive mines in or under: *The enemy mined the harbor.* —*v.i.* **1.** to dig in the earth; dig a mine: *to mine for coal.* **2.** to work in a mine. [Old French *miner.*]

mine field, an area in which explosive mines have been laid.

min·er (mī′nər) *n.* a person who mines, especially a person whose occupation is digging in the earth for coal, mineral ores, or other materials.

min·er·al (min′ər əl) *n.* **1.** any substance that is neither animal nor vegetable, and that occurs in nature and has a definite chemical composition. **2.** any of various natural substances, such as water, salt, coal, petroleum, gold, and copper ore, obtained by digging in the earth. —*adj.* of, relating to, or containing a mineral or minerals: *a mineral deposit, mineral ores, mineral water.*

min·er·al·o·gist (min′ə rol′ə jist) *n.* a student of or an expert in mineralogy.

min·er·al·o·gy (min′ə rol′ə jē) *n.* the science or study of minerals. —**min·er·a·log·i·cal** (min′ər ə loj′i kəl), *adj.* —**min′er·a·log′i·cal·ly,** *adv.*

mineral oil, a colorless, nearly odorless, and tasteless oil obtained as a by-product of petroleum refining. Mineral oil is often used as a laxative.

Mi·ner·va (mi nur′və) *n. Roman Mythology.* the goddess of wisdom, arts, and crafts. In Greek mythology she was called Athena.

min·e·stro·ne (min′ə strō′nē) *n.* a thick soup containing vegetables, noodles, barley, and seasonings.

mine sweeper, a ship or device used to find, remove, or destroy mines.

Ming (ming) *n.* the Chinese dynasty that ruled from 1368 to 1644. —*adj.* of or relating to this dynasty or to the art of this period: *a Ming vase.*

min·gle (ming′gəl) *v.,* **min·gled, min·gling.** —*v.i.* **1.** to be or become mixed or joined together. **2.** to move about among others; associate freely: *We mingled with the party guests.* —*v.t.* to mix or join (something) together.

mini- *combining form* smaller or shorter than usual: *miniskirt.*

min·i·a·ture (min′ē ə chər, min′ə chər) *adj.* greatly reduced in size; very small: *a miniature rose. Greg builds miniature automobiles.* —*n.* **1.** a copy on a small scale: *a miniature of the Eiffel Tower.* **2.** a painting done on a very small scale and in much detail: *An artist painted a miniature of Gene's mother.*

min·i·a·tur·ize (min′ē ə chə rīz′, min′ə chə rīz′) *v.t.,* **min·i·a·tur·ized, min·i·a·tur·iz·ing.** to make or design on a very small scale. —**min′i·a·tur·i·za′tion,** *n.*

min·i·com·pu·ter (min ē′kəm pyōō′tər) *n.* a very small computer.

min·i·ma (min′ə mə) a plural of **minimum.**

min·i·mal (min′ə məl) *adj.* of the smallest amount or degree; very small. —**min′i·mal·ly,** *adv.*

min·i·mize (min′ə mīz′) *v.t.,* **min·i·mized, min·i·miz·ing.** **1.** to reduce to the smallest or least possible amount or degree; make as small as possible: *The diplomats from the two countries met to minimize chances of war.* **2.** to treat as being of little importance or value: *Eric minimized his own contribution to the project.* —**min′i·mi·za′tion,** *n.* —**min′i·miz′er,** *n.*

min·i·mum (min′ə məm) *n. pl.,* **min·i·mums** or **min·i·ma.** **1.** the least possible or smallest amount or degree: *The repairman will need a minimum of one week to do the job.* **2.** the lowest point, degree, or number reached or recorded: *The temperature was at its minimum for the day at six o'clock this morning.* —*adj.* least possible; lowest; smallest: *Tom was paid the minimum salary when he started his new job.*

minimum wage, the lowest wage that an employer may pay an employee.

min·ing (mī′ning) *n.* **1.** the act, process, or business of digging mines for coal, ores, gems, or other materials. **2.** the act or process of laying explosive mines.

min·ion (min′yən) *n.* a favorite, follower, or servant, especially one who acts in a slavish manner.

min·i·skirt (min′ē skurt′) *n.* a short skirt, usually ending several inches above the knee.

min·is·ter (min′is tər) *n.* **1.** a person who is ordained for religious service in a church, especially a Protestant church; pastor. **2.** a person who is the head of an important governmental department: *the minister of finance.* **3.** a diplomat ranking below ambassador and acting as his or her nation's chief representative in a foreign country.

---

at; āpe; cär; end; mē; it; īce; hot; ōld; fôrk;
wood; fōol; oil; out; up; turn; sing; thin; this;
hw in white; zh in treasure. The symbol ə
stands for the sound of **a** in about, **e** in taken,
i in pencil, **o** in lemon, and **u** in circus.

M

595

to which an ambassador is not sent. —*v.t.* to give aid, care, or attention: *The nurse ministered to her patient's needs.*

min·is·te·ri·al (min′is tēr′ē əl) *adj.* **1.** of, relating to, or characteristic of religion or the ministry: *a ministerial student.* **2.** of, relating to, or characteristic of a minister of a government department. —**min′is·te′ri·al·ly,** *adv.*

min·is·trant (min′is trənt) *adj.* serving as a minister. —*n.* a person who ministers.

min·is·tra·tion (min′is trā′shən) *n.* **1.** the act, process, or instance of giving aid. **2.** the act of serving as a minister of religion.

min·is·try (min′is trē) *n. pl.,* **min·is·tries. 1.** the profession or work of a minister of religion. **2.** ministers of religion as a group; the clergy. **3.** a governmental department headed by a minister. **4.** the act of ministering.

mink (mingk) *n. pl.,* **minks** or **mink. 1.** an animal resembling a weasel, having soft, lustrous brown fur, and living in woodlands near water. **2.** the valuable fur of this animal.

Mink

Minn., Minnesota.

Min·ne·ap·o·lis (min′ē ap′ə lis) *n.* the largest city in Minnesota, in the southeastern part of the state. Pop. (1970), 434,400.

Min·ne·so·ta (min′ə sō′tə) *n.* a state in the north-central United States. Capital, St. Paul. Area, 84,068 sq. mi. Pop. (1970), 3,805,069. Abbreviation, **Minn.** —**Min′ne·so′tan,** *adj., n.*

• **Minnesota** was the Siouan name for the Minnesota River and meant "sky-tinted water" or "cloudy water." Congress applied the name to the territory in 1847.

min·now (min′ō) *n.* **1.** any of a group of freshwater fish widely used as bait. **2.** any very small fish.

Mi·no·an (mi nō′ən) *adj.* of or relating to the civilization of Crete from about 2500 B.C. to about 1100 B.C. —*n.* a person who lived in Crete during this period.

mi·nor (mī′nər) *adj.* **1.** of lesser importance or rank: *minor details, a minor subject in college, a minor writer.* **2.** of lesser seriousness or danger: *minor errors, a minor risk.* **3.** lesser or limited, as in size or degree. **4.** under legal age. **5.** *Music.* **a.** of or relating to an interval that is a half tone less than a major interval: *C to D is a major second, and C to D♭ is a minor second.* **b.** based on a minor scale: *a minor chord, a minor key.* —*n.* **1.** a person who is under legal age. **2.** at a college or university, a subject in which a student specializes, but upon which he spends less time than on his major: *Alice's major is English, and her minor is history.* **3.** *Music.* a minor scale, key, or interval. **4.** *Sports.* **a.** a minor league. **b. minors.** the minor leagues as a group. —*v.i.* to take courses in a particular academic minor: *Henry minored in art.*

Mi·nor·ca (mi nôr′kə) *n.* the second largest of the Balearic Islands.

mi·nor·i·ty (mə nôr′ə tē, mə nor′ə tē, mī nôr′ə tē) *n. pl.,* **mi·nor·i·ties. 1.** the smaller part of a group or whole: *Only a minority of the students voted.* **2.** a racial, religious, political, or other group that is different from the larger group of which it is a part. **3.** the state or time of being under legal age.

minor league, any league of professional sports clubs, other than the major league or leagues, as in baseball or ice hockey. —**mi′nor-league′,** *adj.*

minor scale, any of three musical scales, consisting of eight tones, having half steps instead of whole steps after the second and fifth, second and seventh, and second, fifth, and seventh tones ascending the scale, and after the sixth and third and eighth, sixth, and third tones descending the scale.

Mi·nos (mī′nəs) *n. Greek Legend.* **1.** a king of Crete who became a judge of the dead in Hades. **2.** the grandson of this king, and also king of Crete, who kept the Minotaur in the Labyrinth.

Min·o·taur (min′ə tôr′) *n. Greek Legend.* a monster that was half bull and half man. It was confined by Minos in the Labyrinth until killed by Theseus.

Minsk (minsk) *n.* a city in the Soviet Union, the capital and largest city of Byelorussia. Pop. (1971 est.), 945,000.

min·ster (min′stər) *n.* **1.** a church attached to a monastery. **2.** a cathedral or other important church.

min·strel (min′strəl) *n.* **1.** in the Middle Ages, a traveling musician who sang or recited poems. **2.** a performer in a minstrel show.

minstrel show, a variety show in which white performers made up to look like Negroes sing songs, dance, tell jokes, and act in humorous skits. It was popular in the United States during the nineteenth and early twentieth centuries.

min·strel·sy (min′strəl sē) *n. pl.,* **min·strel·sies. 1.** the art of a minstrel. **2.** a collection of songs, lyrics, and ballads, such as those sung by minstrels.

mint¹ (mint) *n.* **1.** any of a group of plants, such as the peppermint or spearmint, used as a flavoring or scent. **2.** a piece of candy flavored with mint. [Old English *minte.*] —**mint′y,** *adj.*

mint² (mint) *n.* **1.** a place where money is coined by the government. **2.** *Informal.* a very large amount of money: *Steve spent a mint getting his car repaired.* —*adj.* unused: *in mint condition, a mint stamp.* —*v.t.* **1.** to coin (money). **2.** to create or invent (a phrase or word). [Old English *mynet* a coin.]

mint·age (min′tij) *n.* **1.** the act or process of coining money. **2.** the money coined by a mint. **3.** the cost of minting. **4.** an impression stamped on a coin.

min·u·end (min′yoo end′) *n.* the number from which another is to be subtracted. In $31 - 7 = 24$, the minuend is 31.

min·u·et (min′yoo et′) *n.* **1.** a stately, slow, and graceful dance for couples, introduced in seventeenth-century France. **2.** music for, or in the rhythm of, this dance.

mi·nus (mī′nəs) *prep.* **1.** decreased by; less: *Ten minus seven is three.* **2.** without; lacking: *The dog was minus a leg because of the accident.* —*adj.* **1.** less than zero; negative. **2.** somewhat lower than; less than: *a grade of A minus.* **3.** showing subtraction or a negative quantity: *a minus sign.* —*n. pl.,* **mi·nus·es. 1.** a sign $(-)$ showing subtraction or a negative quantity. Also, **minus sign. 2.** a negative quantity.

mi·nus·cule (min′əs kyool′, mi nus′kyool) *adj.* very small; tiny: *a minuscule amount.*

min·ute¹ (min′it) *n.* **1.** a unit of time equal to ¹⁄₆₀ of an hour; sixty seconds. **2.** a short period of time; moment: *Can I speak to you for a minute?* **3.** a particular moment or point in time; instant: *I recognized her the minute she entered the room.* **4.** a unit of angular measurement equal to ¹⁄₆₀ of a degree. **5. minutes.** a written record of what was said and done at a meeting or conference. [Old French *minute.*]

mi·nute² (mī noot′, mī nyoot′) *adj.* **1.** very small; tiny: *A minute particle of dirt blew into my eye.* **2.** of small importance; trifling: *minute details.* **3.** characterized by close attention to details: *The detective made a minute* *examination of the room for clues.* [Latin *minūtus* small.] —**mi·nute′ly,** *adv.* —**mi·nute′ness,** *n.*

min·ute·man (min′it man′) *also,* **Min·ute·man.** *n. pl.,* **min·ute·men** (min′it men′). during the American Revolution, a volunteer soldier or armed citizen ready to fight at a minute's notice.

mi·nu·ti·ae (mi noō′shē ē′, mi nyoō′shē ē′) *n., pl. sing.,* **mi·nu·ti·a** (mi noō′shē ə, mi nyoō shē ə). small or unimportant details.

minx (mingks) *n. pl.,* **minx·es.** a bold, forward girl.

Mi·o·cene (mī′ə sēn′) *n.* **1.** the fourth geological epoch of the Tertiary period of the Cenozoic era. During the Miocene, early forms of horses, pigs, giraffes, elephants, and other modern animals flourished. **2.** the strata formed in this epoch. —*adj.* of, relating to, or characteristic of this epoch.

mir·a·cle (mir′ə kəl) *n.* **1.** a remarkable event thought to have been brought about by a divine or supernatural power: *Jesus performed the miracle of turning water into wine.* **2.** an amazing or marvelous happening or thing: *the miracle of childbirth.*

miracle play, a religious drama popular in the Middle Ages, based on legends and stories about the saints.

mi·rac·u·lous (mi rak′yə ləs) *adj.* **1.** brought about by a divine or supernatural power; of the nature of a miracle. **2.** amazing; extraordinary; incredible: *a miraculous escape.* **3.** working or having the power to work wonders: *a miraculous medicine.* —**mi·rac′u·lous·ly,** *adv.* —**mi·rac′u·lous·ness,** *n.*

mi·rage (mi räzh′) *n.* an optical illusion caused by the bending of light rays by layers of air having different densities and temperatures. A common mirage is a sheet of water that is seen on a highway during a hot summer day.

mire (mīr) *n.* **1.** an area of wet, soft ground; bog. **2.** deep, soft mud; muck. —*v.,* **mired, mir·ing.** —*v.t.* **1.** to cause to sink or get stuck in mire. **2.** to make dirty with mud or muck. —*v.i.* to sink or get stuck in mire.

mir·ror (mir′ər) *n.* **1.** a smooth surface that forms images by reflecting light, especially such a surface made of glass that is coated on the back with silver or a similar material. **2.** something that gives a true picture: *The novel is a mirror of life in medieval England.* —*v.t.* to reflect or picture.

mirth (murth) *n.* merriment or gaiety.

mirth·ful (murth′fəl) *adj.* full of or expressing mirth; merry. —**mirth′ful·ly,** *adv.* —**mirth′ful·ness,** *n.*

mirth·less (murth′lis) *adj.* without mirth; joyless. —**mirth′less·ly,** *adv.* —**mirth′less·ness,** *n.*

mir·y (mīr′ē) *adj.,* **mir·i·er, mir·i·est.** like a mire; muddy or boggy. —**mir′i·ness,** *n.*

mis- *prefix* **1.** bad or wrong: *misconduct, misconception.* **2.** badly or wrongly: *mismanage, misquote.* **3.** lack of: *mistrust.*

mis·ad·ven·ture (mis′əd ven′chər) *n.* a mishap; misfortune.

mis·al·li·ance (mis′ə lī′əns) *n.* an association or alliance, especially a marriage, that is not proper or suitable.

mis·an·thrope (mis′ən thrōp′) *n.* a person who hates or distrusts mankind. —**mis·an·throp·ic** (mis′ən throp′ ik), *adj.*

mis·an·thro·py (mis an′thrə pē) *n.* the hatred or distrust of mankind.

mis·ap·ply (mis′ə plī′) *v.t.,* **mis·ap·plied, mis·ap·ply·ing.** to apply or use badly or wrongly: *to misapply one's abilities, to misapply public funds.* —**mis·ap·pli·ca·tion** (mis′ap lə kā′shən), *n.*

mis·ap·pre·hend (mis′ap ri hend′) *v.t.* to fail to understand; misunderstand.

mis·ap·pre·hen·sion (mis′ap ri hen′shən) *n.* a misunderstanding.

mis·ap·pro·pri·ate (mis′ə prō′prē āt′) *v.t.,* **mis·ap·pro·pri·at·ed, mis·ap·pro·pri·at·ing.** to take or use wrongly or dishonestly: *The politician misappropriated money from the city treasury.* —**mis′ap·pro′pri·a′tion,** *n.*

mis·be·got·ten (mis′bi got′ən) *adj.* born to a woman who is not married; illegitimate.

mis·be·have (mis′bi hāv′) *v.,* **mis·be·haved, mis·be·hav·ing.** —*v.i.* to behave badly: *The child misbehaved by writing on the wall.* —*v.t.* to conduct (oneself) badly.

mis·be·hav·ior (mis′bi hāv′yər) *also, British,* **mis·be·hav·iour.** *n.* bad or improper behavior.

mis·be·lief (mis′bi lēf′) *n.* a false or erroneous belief or opinion.

misc. **1.** miscellaneous. **2.** miscellany.

mis·cal·cu·late (mis kal′kyə lāt′) *v.t., v.i.,* **mis·cal·cu·lat·ed, mis·cal·cu·lat·ing.** to figure, plan, or judge wrongly: *The general miscalculated the number of men in the opposing army.* —**mis′cal·cu·la′tion,** *n.*

mis·call (mis kôl′) *v.t.* to call by a wrong name; misname.

mis·car·riage (mis kar′ij) *n.* **1.** a failure to achieve the intended result: *Imprisoning an innocent person is a miscarriage of justice.* **2.** the birth of an undeveloped baby that cannot live.

mis·car·ry (mis kar′ē) *v.i.,* **mis·car·ried, mis·car·ry·ing.** **1.** to fail to achieve the intended result; be unsuccessful: *The plans miscarried.* **2.** to give birth to an undeveloped baby that cannot live.

mis·cast (mis kast′) *v.t.,* **mis·cast, mis·cast·ing.** to cast (an actor or actress) in a role not suited to him or her.

mis·ce·ge·na·tion (mis′ə jə nā′shən) *n.* marriage between people of different races.

mis·cel·la·ne·ous (mis′ə lā′nē əs) *adj.* **1.** of different kinds: *Miscellaneous items were scattered all over the floor.* **2.** made up of different things; varied: *He bought a miscellaneous assortment of ties, shirts, and socks.* —**mis′cel·la′ne·ous·ly,** *adv.* —**mis′cel·la·ne·ous·ness,** *n.*

mis·cel·la·ny (mis′ə lā′nē) *n. pl.,* **mis·cel·la·nies.** **1.** a mixture of different things: *The boy's pockets held a miscellany of string, bottle tops, and candy wrappers.* **2.** a book containing different writings on various subjects.

mis·chance (mis chans′) *n.* **1.** bad luck. **2.** an unfortunate event; mishap.

mis·chief (mis′chif) *n.* **1.** an act or conduct that is often playful but causes annoyance or harm. **2.** an inclination to tease or play pranks; teasing playfulness: *The little boy is full of mischief.* **3.** harm or damage.

mis·chie·vous (mis′chə vəs) *adj.* **1.** full of mischief; playful or naughty: *He is a mischievous child.* **2.** showing or suggesting mischief: *She has a mischievous smile.* **3.** annoying, harmful, or damaging: *Mischievous rumors were spread about her.* —**mis′chie·vous·ly,** *adv.* —**mis′chie·vous·ness,** *n.*

mis·ci·ble (mis′ə bəl) *adj.* capable of being mixed: *Oil and water are not miscible.* —**mis′ci·bil′i·ty,** *n.*

mis·con·ceive (mis′kən sēv′) *v.t.,* **mis·con·ceived, mis·con·ceiv·ing.** to fail to understand; have a false or mistaken idea about; misunderstand.

mis·con·cep·tion (mis′kən sep′shən) *n.* a false or mistaken idea.

mis·con·duct (mis kon′dukt) *n.* bad behavior.

at; āpe; cär; end; mē; it; īce; hot; ōld; fôrk; wood; fōōl; oil; out; up; turn; sing; thin; **th**is; **hw** in white; **zh** in treasure. The symbol ə stands for the sound of **a** in about, **e** in taken, **i** in pencil, **o** in lemon, and **u** in circus.

mis·con·strue (mis′kən strōō′) *v.t.,* **mis·con·strued, mis·con·stru·ing.** to mistake the meaning of; misinterpret: *He misconstrued my remark.*

mis·count (*v.,* mis kount′; *n.,* mis′kount′) *v.t.* to count incorrectly. —*n.* an incorrect count.

mis·cre·ant (mis′krē ənt) *n.* a wicked person; evil doer; villain. —*adj.* villainous.

mis·deal (*v.,* mis dēl′; *n.,* mis′dēl′) *v.t., v.i.,* **mis·dealt** (mis delt′), **mis·deal·ing.** to deal cards incorrectly. —*n.* an incorrect deal.

mis·deed (mis dēd′) *n.* a wicked act.

mis·de·mean·or (mis′di mē′nər) *also, British,* **mis·de·mean·our.** *n.* a crime less serious than a felony, usually punishable by a fine or a short term of imprisonment.

mis·di·rect (mis′di rekt′, mis′dī rekt′) *v.t.* to direct wrongly or badly. —**mis′di·rec′tion,** *n.*

mi·ser (mī′zər) *n.* a stingy person who hoards money.

mis·er·a·ble (miz′ər ə bəl) *adj.* **1.** very unhappy; wretched: *The girl felt so miserable she wanted to cry.* **2.** causing or marked by great discomfort or unhappiness: *miserable weather, a miserable toothache.* **3.** of little or no value; of very poor quality: *The actor gave a miserable performance.* —**mis′er·a·ble·ness,** *n.* —**mis′er·a·bly,** *adv.*

mi·ser·ly (mī′zər lē) *adj.* like or characteristic of a miser; stingy. —**mi′ser·li·ness,** *n.*

mis·er·y (miz′ər ē) *n. pl.,* **mis·er·ies. 1.** a state or condition of great unhappiness or distress: *Her constant ill health brought her much misery.* **2.** the cause or source of this: *His broken arm was a misery to him.* **3.** wretched living conditions: *The poor family lived in misery in an old shack.*

mis·fire (mis fīr′) *v.i.,* **mis·fired, mis·fir·ing. 1.** to fail to fire or ignite at the proper time: *The engine misfired. The gun misfired.* **2.** to fail to have the desired effect or result: *All their plans for the trip misfired.* —*n.* the failure to fire or ignite at the proper time.

mis·fit (mis′fit′) *n.* **1.** something that does not fit properly, such as a garment of the wrong size. **2.** a person who is not able to fit in with others around him or with his surroundings.

mis·for·tune (mis fôr′chən) *n.* **1.** bad luck; ill fortune: *It was Jack's misfortune to lose his wallet.* **2.** an instance of this; unlucky accident; mishap: *The train crash was a misfortune.*

mis·giv·ing (mis giv′ing) *n.* a feeling of doubt or uneasiness: *Carol had misgivings about making the long trip with so little money.*

mis·gov·ern (mis guv′ərn) *v.t.* to govern or manage badly. —**mis·gov′ern·ment,** *n.*

mis·guide (mis gīd′) *v.t.,* **mis·guid·ed, mis·guid·ing.** to guide or influence wrongly; lead astray. —**mis·guid·ance** (mis gī′dəns), *n.*

mis·guid·ed (mis gī′did) *adj.* guided or influenced wrongly; led astray; misled. —**mis·guid′ed·ly,** *adv.*

mis·han·dle (mis hand′əl) *v.t.,* **mis·han·dled, mis·han·dling.** to handle, treat, or manage badly.

mis·hap (mis′hap) *n.* an unfortunate accident: *We had a mishap on the highway and lost a hubcap.*

mish·mash (mish′mash′) *n. pl.,* **mish·mash·es.** a confused mixture; jumble.

mis·in·form (mis′in fôrm′) *v.t.* to give false information to: *The suspect misinformed the police of his whereabouts on the night of the crime.* —**mis′in·for·ma′tion,** *n.*

mis·in·ter·pret (mis′in tur′prit) *v.t.* to interpret wrongly. —**mis′in·ter′pre·ta′tion,** *n.*

mis·judge (mis juj′) *v.t., v.i.,* **mis·judged, mis·judg·ing.** to judge wrongly or unfairly: *We misjudged his character.* —**mis·judg′ment;** *also,* **mis·judge′ment,** *n.*

mis·lay (mis lā′) *v.t.,* **mis·laid, mis·lay·ing. 1.** to put in a place that is later forgotten; lose: *Ann mislaid her purse.* **2.** to lay or put down wrongly: *He mislaid the carpet.*

mis·lead (mis lēd′) *v.t.,* **mis·led, mis·lead·ing. 1.** to lead or guide in the wrong direction. **2.** to lead into a mistaken or wrong thought or action: *The advertisements for the product misled us.*

mis·lead·ing (mis lē′ding) *adj.* causing or tending to cause a mistaken or wrong thought or action: *a misleading speech, misleading instructions.* —**mis·lead′ing·ly,** *adv.*

mis·man·age (mis man′ij) *v.t.,* **mis·man·aged, mis·man·ag·ing.** to manage or handle badly: *to mismanage one's money, to mismanage a business.* —**mis·man′age·ment,** *n.*

mis·match (mis mach′) *v.t.* to match or join together unwisely or unsuitably: *The two boxers were mismatched. His socks are mismatched.* —*n. pl.,* **mis·match·es.** an unwise or unsuitable match.

mis·name (mis nām′) *v.t.,* **mis·named, mis·nam·ing.** to call by a wrong name.

mis·no·mer (mis nō′mər) *n.* a name that is not fitting or suitable: *"Yacht" was a misnomer for the small boat.*

mis·place (mis plās′) *v.t.,* **mis·placed, mis·plac·ing. 1.** to mislay; lose: *Gene misplaced his keys.* **2.** to put or locate in a wrong place. **3.** to place improperly or unwisely: *We misplaced our trust in him.*

mis·play (mis plā′) *v.t.* to play badly or wrongly in a game or sport: *to misplay a hand of cards.* —*n.* a bad or wrong play in a game or sport.

mis·print (*n.,* mis′print′; *v.,* mis print′) *n.* an error in printing. —*v.t.* to print incorrectly.

mis·pro·nounce (mis′prə nouns′) *v.t.,* **mis·pro·nounced, mis·pro·nounc·ing.** to pronounce (words or sounds) incorrectly, or in a way that is thought of as incorrect. —**mis·pro·nun·ci·a·tion** (mis′prə nun′sē ā′shən), *n.*

mis·quote (mis kwōt′) *v.t.,* **mis·quot·ed, mis·quot·ing.** to quote incorrectly. —**mis′quo·ta′tion,** *n.*

mis·read (mis rēd′) *v.t.,* **mis·read** (mis red′), **mis·read·ing.** to read or understand incorrectly: *to misread a sign.*

mis·rep·re·sent (mis′rep ri zent′) *v.t.* to give a false or misleading impression of; represent falsely: *The company misrepresented its product.* —**mis′rep·re·sen·ta′tion,** *n.*

mis·rule (mis rōōl′) *n.* bad, unjust, or unwise rule or government. —*v.t.,* **mis·ruled, mis·rul·ing.** to rule or govern badly, unjustly, or unwisely.

miss¹ (mis) *v.t.* **1.** to fail to hit or reach: *The batter missed the ball.* **2.** to fail to catch, meet, or get: *He missed his bus.* **3.** to fail to notice or find: *The driver missed the exit on the highway.* **4.** to fail to do or accomplish: *The golfer missed a short putt.* **5.** to fail to attend or be present for: *Jerry missed an appointment with the dentist.* **6.** to fail to understand: *He missed the point of the lecture.* **7.** to be sad over the absence or loss of: *The mother missed her daughter, who was away at college.* **8.** to discover the absence or loss of: *It was a long time before the lady missed her necklace.* **9.** to fail to take advantage of; let slip by: *Tim has missed a good opportunity.* **10.** to escape: *The mountain climber just missed being struck by falling rocks.* **11.** to be without; lack: *This coat is missing a button.* **12.** to do or answer wrongly: *She missed the question on the test.* —*v.i.* **1.** to fail to hit something: *Several arrows were shot at the target, but they all missed.* **2.** to be unsuccessful; fail: *Your plan can't miss.* **3.** to misfire. —*n. pl.,* **miss·es.** the failure to hit. [Old English *missan.*]

miss² (mis) *n. pl.,* **miss·es. 1. Miss.** a form of address used before the name of a girl or unmarried woman: *Miss Simpson.* **2.** a form of address used in place of the name of a girl or unmarried woman: *May I help you, Miss?* **3.** a girl or young unmarried woman. [Short for *Mistress.*]

Miss., Mississippi.

mis·sal (mis′əl) *n.* a book containing the prayers for celebrating Mass throughout the year.

mis·shape (mis shāp′) *v.t.*, **mis·shaped, mis·shaped** or **mis·shap·en, mis·shap·ing.** to shape badly; deform.

mis·shap·en (mis shā′pən) *adj.* badly shaped; deformed.

mis·sile (mis′əl) *n.* **1.** an object that is thrown or shot in the air, such as a stone, arrow, or bullet. **2.** see **guided missile. 3.** see **ballistic missile.**

miss·ing (mis′ing) *adj.* **1.** not to be found; lost: *The detective's job was tracing missing persons.* **2.** absent or lacking: *This jigsaw puzzle has a missing piece.*

mis·sion (mish′ən) *n.* **1.** a group of persons sent to perform a task or service: *Four men formed a rescue mission to reach the injured mountain climber.* **2.** the task or service that a person or group of persons is sent to perform; assignment: *The spy was sent on a secret mission.* **3.** the task or goal of a military force. **4.** a team of diplomats assigned to a foreign country. **5.** a group of missionaries sent to do religious, humanitarian, or educational work, especially in a foreign country. **6.** a church or other place used by missionaries in their work. **7. missions.** organized missionary work or activities. **8.** the duty or task in life that a person feels he or she is destined to perform.

mis·sion·ar·y (mish′ə ner′ē) *n. pl.,* **mis·sion·ar·ies. 1.** a person who is sent by his or her church to spread that religion among nonbelievers, especially in a foreign country: *Mr. Brown is a Protestant missionary in India.* **2.** a person who goes or is sent to do humanitarian or educational work, especially in a foreign country: *Albert Schweitzer served as a medical missionary in Africa.* —*adj.* of, relating to, or characteristic of missionaries or religious missions: *missionary zeal.*

Mis·sis·sip·pi (mis′ə sip′ē) *n.* **1.** the principal river of the United States, flowing from northern Minnesota to the Gulf of Mexico. **2.** a state in the southern United States. Capital, Jackson. Area, 47,716 sq. mi. Pop. (1970), 2,216,912. Abbreviation, **Miss.** —**Mis′sis·sip′pi·an,** *adj., n.*

● **Mississippi** comes from two Algonquian words meaning "big river," "great water," or "father of the waters." French explorers carried the name from the Great Lakes region to the mouth of the Mississippi River. In 1798, Congress applied it to the territory established there, and the state kept the name of the territory.

mis·sive (mis′iv) *n.* a written message; letter.

Mis·sou·ri (mi zoor′ē, mi zoor′ə) *n.* **1.** the longest river in the United States, flowing from Montana to the Mississippi River. **2.** a state in the central United States. Capital, Jefferson City. Area, 69,686 sq. mi. Pop. (1970), 4,677,399. Abbreviation, **Mo.** —**Mis·sou′ri·an,** *adj., n.*

● The name **Missouri** is an Algonquian word meaning "people of the big canoes." It was the name of a Sioux tribe living near the mouth of the Missouri River at the time of French exploration. The name was transferred from the tribe to the river, and eventually to the territory and the state.

mis·spell (mis spel′) *v.t.*, **mis·spelled** or **mis·spelt** (mis-spelt′), **mis·spell·ing.** to spell (a word) incorrectly.

mis·spend (mis spend′) *v.t.*, **mis·spent** (mis spent′), **mis·spend·ing.** to spend or use wrongly or wastefully.

mis·state (mis stāt′) *v.t.*, **mis·stat·ed, mis·stat·ing.** to state incorrectly or falsely. —**mis·state′ment,** *n.*

mis·step (mis step′) *n.* **1.** a wrong or careless step. **2.** a mistake in conduct; improper act.

miss·y (mis′ē) *n. pl.,* **miss·ies.** *Informal.* miss.

mist (mist) *n.* **1.** a mass or cloud of tiny droplets of water suspended in the air. **2.** something resembling mist, as a thin cloud of smoke or a fine spray from a pressurized can. **3.** cloudiness or filminess that blurs the vision. **4.** something that dims or clouds: *The hero's true deeds were lost in the mist of legend.* —*v.i.* **1.** to be or become covered with or clouded by mist: *The young girl's eyes misted over with tears.* **2.** to rain in very fine drops; drizzle. —*v.t.* to cover or cloud with mist.

mis·take (mis tāk′) *n.* something incorrectly done, thought, or said; error: *Jack made a mistake on the test.* —*v.t.*, **mis·took, mis·tak·en, mis·tak·ing. 1.** to identify (a person or thing) incorrectly: *Janet mistook Pete for his twin brother.* **2.** to make an error about (something).

mis·tak·en (mis tā′kən) *adj.* based on error; wrong: *a mistaken belief.* —**mis·tak′en·ly,** *adv.*

mis·ter (mis′tər) *n.* **1. Mister.** a form of address used before the name or title of a man, usually written *Mr.*: *Mr. Smith, Mr. Chairman.* **2.** *also,* **Mister.** a form of address used in place of a man's name: *Can you help me, Mister?*

mis·tle·toe (mis′əl tō′) *n.* **1.** a plant that lives as a parasite on the branches of various trees and has yellowish-green leaves and small, round fruit. **2.** a sprig of this plant, often used as a Christmas decoration.

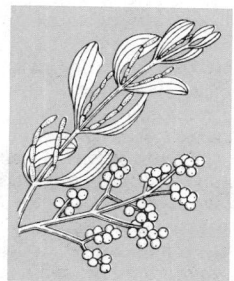

Mistletoe

mis·took (mis took′) the past tense of **mistake.**

mis·treat (mis trēt′) *v.t.* to treat badly: *The child mistreated the kitten by pulling its tail.* —**mis·treat′ment,** *n.*

mis·tress (mis′tris) *n. pl.,* **mis·tress·es. 1.** a woman who has control of a household or estate. **2.** a woman owner of an animal. **3.** *also,* **Mistress.** something that is thought of as female and has control over something else: *England's navy made her mistress of the high seas.* **4.** a woman who lives with or is supported by a man to whom she is not married. **5. Mistress.** *Archaic.* a title of address used before the name of a woman.

mis·tri·al (mis trī′əl) *n. Law.* **1.** a trial that is declared to be without legal force because of some error in the proceedings. **2.** a trial in which the jury fails to agree on a verdict.

mis·trust (mis trust′) *n.* a lack of trust or confidence. —*v.t.* to regard with suspicion or doubt. —**mis·trust′ful,** *adj.*

mist·y (mis′tē) *adj.*, **mist·i·er, mist·i·est. 1.** of, resembling, or clouded by mist: *a misty fog, a misty spring morning.* **2.** blurred or clouded with a mist of tears; tearful: *Sally's eyes were misty.* **3.** vague; indistinct: *She had a misty recollection of what happened.* —**mist′i·ly,** *adv.* —**mist′i·ness,** *n.*

mis·un·der·stand (mis′un dər stand′) *v.t., v.i.*, **mis·un·der·stood** (mis′un dər stood′), **mis·un·der·stand·ing.** to understand (someone or something) incorrectly: *She misunderstood the instructions. He misunderstood when I told him how to operate the lawn mower.*

at; āpe; cär; end; mē; it; īce; hot; ōld; fôrk; wood; fŌol; oil; out; up; turn; sing; thin; this; hw in white; zh in treasure. The symbol ə stands for the sound of a in about, e in taken, i in pencil, o in lemon, and u in circus.

mis·un·der·stand·ing (mis'un dər stan'ding) *n.*
1. the failure to understand correctly. **2.** a disagreement;
quarrel: *The two friends had a slight misunderstanding.*

mis·use (*n.*, mis yōōs'; *v.*, mis yōōz') *n.* a wrong use: *the
misuse of government funds.* —*v.t.*, **mis·used, mis·us·ing.**
1. to use wrongly; misapply. **2.** to treat badly.

mite[1] (mīt) *n.* any of a group of tiny animals related to
spiders, having piercing, sucking mouth parts. Mites often
damage stored foods and live on plants and animals.
[Old English *mīte* any tiny insect.]

mite[2] (mīt) *n.* **1.** a very small thing or creature.
2. a coin of very small value. **3.** a very small amount or
sum: *There was a mite of dust on the floor.* [Middle Dutch
mīte.]

mi·ter (mī'tər) *also,* **mi·tre.** *n.* **1.** a headdress worn by
bishops and other high-ranking church-
men, consisting of a tall, peaked cap that
can be folded flat, with two fringed strips
of material hanging from the back.
2. see **miter joint. 3.** the slanted edge on
either of the pieces used to form a miter
joint. —*v.t.* **1.** to join with a miter joint.
2. to cut or shape for forming a miter
joint.

Miter

miter box, a device with slotted sides
used to guide a saw, as when making
miter joints.

miter joint, a joint formed by cutting
the ends of two pieces of wood or other material at a slant
and fitting them together. Picture frames are usually made
with miter joints at the corners.

mit·i·gate (mit'ə gāt') *v.t.*, **mit·i·gat·ed, mit·i·gat·ing.**
to make milder or less severe or painful: *The nurse tried
to mitigate the suffering of the injured man.* —**mit·i·ga·ble**
(mit'i gə bəl), *adj.* —**mit'i·ga'tion,** *n.* —**mit'i·ga'tor,** *n.*

mi·to·chon·dri·a (mī'tə kon'drē ə, mit'ə kon'drē ə)
n., pl. sing., **mi·to·chon·dri·on** (mī'tə kon'drē ən). very
tiny rods, filaments, or granules found in the cytoplasm
of nearly all cells. They serve as centers of respiration
and as the site of energy production within the cells.

mi·to·sis (mī tō'sis) *n.* a process of cell division in which
the nucleus of a cell divides into two identical nuclei, and
the cell itself divides equally, forming two new cells, each
with the same number of chromosomes as the parent cell.

mi·tre (mī'tər) *n., v.t.,* **mi·tred, mi·tring.** another spelling
of **miter.**

mitt (mit) *n.* **1.** a baseball glove, especially that worn by
the catcher or first baseman. **2.** see **mitten** *(def. 1).*
3. a woman's glove that does not cover the fingers.

mit·ten (mit'ən) *n.* **1.** a covering for the hand that holds
the four fingers together in one part and the thumb separately in another part. **2.** see **mitt** *(def. 3).*

mix (miks) *v.*, **mixed** or **mixt** (mikst), **mix·ing.** —*v.t.*
1. to put together into one mass; combine thoroughly;
blend: *She mixed lemon juice, sugar, and water to make
lemonade.* **2.** to make or prepare by combining ingredients
thoroughly: *Mother mixed some pancake batter.* **3.** to join
or bring together: *The florist mixed red and yellow roses
in a bouquet.* —*v.i.* **1.** to become mixed or be capable of
being mixed: *Oil and water will not mix.* **2.** to go or belong
together. **3.** to associate or get along: *The young writer
wanted to mix with people from all walks of life.* —*n. pl.,*
mix·es. 1. the act, result, or product of mixing; mixture.
2. a mixture of ingredients prepared and sold commercially: *a cake mix.*

　to mix up. a. to confuse or disorder: *The boy is mixed
　up and needs help.* **b.** to involve: *We suspect that he was
　mixed up in the crime.*

mixed (mikst) *adj.* **1.** put together by mixing: *mixed*

ingredients, mixed fruits. **2.** of or formed of different parts
or qualities: *to have mixed feelings about something.*
3. made up of or involving persons of both sexes: *a mixed
class.* **4.** made up of or involving persons of different races,
religions, or national origins: *a mixed marriage.*

mixed number, a number consisting of a whole number and a fraction. The number 4⅞ is a mixed number.

mix·er (mik'sər) *n.* **1.** a person or thing that mixes, especially a machine or device for mixing. **2.** a person who gets
along well with others: *Dan is a good mixer at parties.*
3. a dance, party, or other social gathering for the purpose
of getting people acquainted.

mix·ture (miks'chər) *n.* **1.** a product or result of mixing;
combination; blend: *This batter is a mixture of milk, eggs,
and flour.* **2.** the act or process of mixing: *The mixture of
oil and vinegar makes a salad dressing.* **3.** Chemistry.
two or more substances that, when put together, keep their
individual properties, and are not chemically combined.

mix-up (miks'up') *n.* a state or instance of confusion.

miz·zen (miz'ən) *also,* **miz·en.** *n.* **1.** a fore-and-aft sail
set on the mizzenmast.
2. see **mizzenmast.**
—*adj.* of or relating to
the mizzenmast.

miz·zen·mast (miz'-
ən mast', miz'ən məst)
also, **miz·en·mast.** *n.*
1. the mast nearest the
stern in a ship having
two or three masts.
2. the third mast from
the forward end of a ship
having more than three
masts.

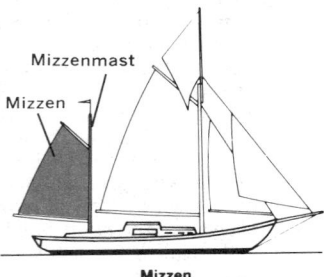

mks, meter-kilogram-second. Also, **MKS, m.k.s., M.K.S.**

ml., milliliter; milliliters.

Mlle., Mademoiselle.

Mlles., Mesdemoiselles.

mm., millimeter; millimeters.

MM., Messieurs.

Mme., Madame.

Mmes., Mesdames.

Mn, the symbol for manganese.

mne·mon·ic (ni mon'ik) *adj.* **1.** helping or intended to
help the memory. **2.** of or relating to memory. —*n.* something, such as a formula or phrase, that helps a person
remember. —**mne·mon'i·cal·ly,** *adv.*

Mo, the symbol for molybdenum.

mo., month.

Mo., Missouri.

M.O. 1. Medical Officer. **2.** money order. Also, **m.o.**

mo·a (mō'ə) *n.* an extinct bird that could not fly, resembling the ostrich. It was once nu-
merous in New Zealand.

moan (mōn) *n.* **1.** a low mournful
sound, usually expressing grief or
pain. **2.** any sound resembling
this: *the wind's eerie moan in the
night.* —*v.i.* to make a moan or
moans: *The injured man moaned
all night.* —*v.t.* to express or say
with a moan or moans: *"I failed
the test," he moaned.*

moat (mōt) *n.* a deep, wide ditch,
usually filled with water, surrounding a castle, fortress, or
town as protection. —*v.t.* to surround with a moat.

Moa

mob (mob) *n.* **1.** a disorderly crowd or throng: *An* *angry mob gathered in front of the courthouse.* **2.** any crowd: *A mob of children came out of the school.* **3. the mob.** common people as a group; the masses. **4.** *Informal.* an organized group of gangsters. —*v.t.,* **mobbed, mobbing. 1.** to crowd around excitedly: *Fans mobbed the actor wherever he went.* **2.** to crowd to capacity: *Shoppers mobbed the store during the big sale.*

mo·bile (*adj.,* mō′bəl, mō′bēl; *n.,* mō′bēl) *adj.* **1.** capable of moving or being moved: *a mobile cannon, a mobile home.* **2.** changing expression freely and quickly: *the clown's mobile features.* **3.** moving or allowing movement from one social class or group to a higher one: *a mobile society.* —*n.* a sculpture of metal, plastic, cardboard, or other material, having parts that are hung from thin wires and set in motion by air currents. —**mo·bil·i·ty** (mō bil′-ə tē), *n.*

Mo·bile (mō′bēl, mō bēl′) *n.* a port city in southwestern Alabama, on Mobile Bay. Pop. (1970), 190,026.

Mobile Bay, a shallow arm of the Gulf of Mexico, extending into southwestern Alabama.

mo·bi·lize (mō′bə līz′) *v.,* **mo·bi·lized, mo·bi·liz·ing.** —*v.t.* to organize or prepare, as for war or an emergency: *The government mobilized the army.* —*v.i.* to become organized or prepared, as for war or an emergency. —**mo·bi·li·za′tion,** *n.*

Mö·bi·us strip (moo′bē əs) *Mathematics.* a continuous surface having only one side and one edge, formed by turning one end of a rectangular strip 180 degrees and then attaching it to the other end. [From A. F. *Möbius,* 1790–1868, a German mathematician who invented it.]

mob·ster (mob′stər) *n. Slang.* a criminal, especially one who is a member of an organized gang; gangster.

moc·ca·sin (mok′ə sin) *n.* **1.** a shoe having a soft sole and no heel, usually made from one piece of leather. Moccasins were originally worn by American Indians. **2.** any similar shoe or slipper. **3.** see **water moccasin.**

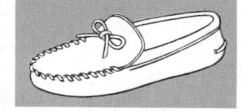

Moccasin

moccasin flower, another name for **lady's-slipper.**

mo·cha (mō′kə) *n.* **1.** a choice coffee originally grown in Arabia. **2.** a flavoring made from coffee and chocolate. —*adj.* flavored with coffee or with a mixture of coffee and chocolate.

mock (mok) *v.t.* **1.** to speak to or treat with contempt; deride: *The writer mocked the policies of the government.* **2.** to imitate or mimic jokingly or rudely: *The rude boy mocked the foreigner's accent.* **3.** to scoff at or defy: *The criminal mocked the law.* —*v.i.* to express contempt; scoff. —*adj.* not real; pretended; sham: *mock humility.* —*n.* **1.** an act of mocking or an expression of mockery. **2.** a person or thing that is mocked. —**mock′er,** *n.*

mock·er·y (mok′ər ē) *n. pl.,* **mock·er·ies. 1.** the act of mocking or a speech or action that mocks; ridicule; derision. **2.** a person or thing that is mocked. **3.** a false or ridiculous imitation: *The trial was a mockery of justice.*

mock·ing·bird (mok′ing burd′) *n.* any of several North and South American birds that can imitate the calls of other birds.

mock orange, a shrub that has showy, creamy white flowers. Also, **syringa.**

Mockingbird

mock-up (mok′up′) also, **mock·up.** *n.* a full-scale model of something, such as an airplane or machine, used for testing, display, or study.

mod (mod) *also,* **Mod.** *adj. Informal.* relating to a style that is fashionable and up-to-date, especially in an unconventional way: *mod clothing.* [Short for *modern.*]

mo·dal auxiliary (mōd əl), a verb used to indicate the mood of the verb with which it is used. *May, must,* and *would* are modal auxiliaries.

mode¹ (mōd) *n.* **1.** a way or method of doing something: *Automobiles are a popular mode of transportation.* **2.** see **mood².** [Latin *modus* measure, manner.]

mode² (mōd) *n.* a current style or fashion, as of dress. [French *mode* style, fashion.]

mod·el (mod′əl) *n.* **1.** a copy of something, usually built on a smaller scale than the original: *Johnny made airplane models from kits.* **2.** a person or thing that serves as an example or standard for imitation or comparison: *The U.S. Constitution is used as a model by many new governments.* **3.** a person who serves as the subject for an artist, photographer, or writer: *The author's wife was the model for the leading female character in his novel.* **4.** a person who is employed to display merchandise, especially clothing. **5.** a style, design, or type: *The car was a very old model.* —*v.,* **mod·eled, mod·el·ing;** *also, British,* **mod·elled, mod·el·ling.** —*v.t.* **1.** to make or fashion after a particular pattern or model: *The painter modeled his style after that of Pablo Picasso.* **2.** to make or form: *Steve modeled a unicorn in wax.* **3.** to serve as a model of: *Ann models dresses.* —*v.i.* **1.** to make a model or models: *The art students are modeling in plaster.* **2.** to serve as a model: *Ellen modeled at a fashion show.* —*adj.* **1.** designed as a copy of something: *He built a model airplane.* **2.** designed as a display of things for sale or study: *The store has a model kitchen.* **3.** worthy of serving as a model: *a model teacher.* —**mod′el·er;** *also, British,* **mod′el·ler,** *n.*

mod·el·ing (mod′əl ing) *also,* **mod·el·ling.** *n.* **1.** the act or art of making a model or models. **2.** the act or occupation of serving as a model: *a career in modeling.*

mod·er·ate (*adj., n.,* mod′ər it; *v.,* mod′ə rāt′) *adj.* **1.** kept within reasonable limits; not going to extremes: *The price of the coat is moderate.* **2.** of medium or average amount, degree, or quality: *There is only moderate traffic on the highway.* **3.** not violent or intense; mild; calm: *moderate weather.* **4.** not radical or extreme: *He holds moderate political opinions.* —*n.* a person who holds moderate views, especially in politics. —*v.,* **mod·er·at·ed, mod·er·at·ing.** —*v.t.* **1.** to keep within reasonable limits; make less extreme: *The student moderated his political beliefs.* **2.** to preside over: *The professor moderated the discussion.* —*v.i.* **1.** to become less excessive, extreme, violent, or intense. **2.** to act as a moderator; preside. —**mod′er·ate·ly,** *adv.* —**mod′er·ate·ness,** *n.*

mod·er·a·tion (mod′ə rā′shən) *n.* **1.** the state or quality of being moderate. **2.** the act of moderating.

mod·e·ra·to (mod′ə rä′tō) *Music. adj.* in moderate tempo. —*adv.* at a moderate tempo. —*n.* a moderato passage or movement.

mod·er·a·tor (mod′ə rā′tər) *n.* a person or thing that moderates, especially a person who presides over a meeting or discussion.

mod·ern (mod′ərn) *adj.* **1.** of or relating to the present or recent time: *I prefer modern art.* **2.** of or relating to the

at; āpe; cär; end; mē; it; īce; hot; ōld; fôrk; wood; fōōl; oil; out; up; turn; sing; thin; **this;** hw in white; zh in treasure. The symbol ə stands for the sound of **a** in about, **e** in taken, **i** in pencil, **o** in lemon, and **u** in circus.

period since about 1400: *modern history.* **3.** up-to-date; not old-fashioned: *The kitchen has modern appliances.* —*n.* a person who has modern views or standards. —**mod′ern·ly,** *adv.* —**mod′ern·ness,** *n.*

Modern English, the English language as it has been spoken and written since about the year 1500. See **Old English** for further information.

mod·ern·ism (mod′ər niz′əm) *n.* something characteristic of modern times, such as a word or practice. —**mod′ern·ist,** *n.* —**mod′ern·is′tic,** *adj.*

mod·ern·ize (mod′ər nīz′) *v.,* **mod·ern·ized, mod·ern·iz·ing.** —*v.t.* to make modern; change to suit present needs: *The town modernized its hospital by installing new equipment.* —*v.i.* to become modern; adopt modern ways. —**mod′ern·i·za′tion,** *n.*

Modern Latin, the Latin language as it has been used since about the year 1500.

mod·est (mod′ist) *adj.* **1.** not boastful or forward: *Tom is modest and does not brag about his accomplishments.* **2.** retiring; reserved: *She is a quiet, modest person.* **3.** having or showing a sense of what is good or proper: *The woman wore a modest dress.* **4.** not grand or showy; simple: *The apartment has modest furnishings.* **5.** within reasonable limits; not extreme; moderate: *We spent only a modest sum of money on our trip.* —**mod′est·ly,** *adv.*

mod·es·ty (mod′is tē) *n.* the state or quality of being modest.

mod·i·cum (mod′i kəm) *n.* a small or moderate amount: *He has only a modicum of talent as an actor.*

mod·i·fi·ca·tion (mod′ə fi kā′shən) *n.* **1.** the act of modifying or the state of being modified. **2.** a change or alteration: *After a few slight modifications, the plan was ready to be put into effect.* **3.** the result of modifying; a modified form.

mod·i·fi·er (mod′ə fī′ər) *n.* **1.** a person or thing that modifies. **2.** *Grammar.* a word, phrase, or clause that limits the meaning of another word or group of words. Adjectives and adverbs are modifiers.

mod·i·fy (mod′ə fī′) *v.t.,* **mod·i·fied, mod·i·fy·ing. 1.** to change or alter: *The inventor modified his original design to make the machine more efficient.* **2.** *Grammar.* to limit the meaning of. In the phrase *a quiet evening,* the adjective *quiet* modifies the noun *evening.* —**mod′i·fi′a·ble,** *adj.*

mod·ish (mō′dish) *adj.* that follows a current style or fashion; fashionable. —**mod′ish·ly,** *adv.* —**mod′ish·ness,** *n.*

mod·u·late (moj′ə lāt′) *v.,* **mod·u·lat·ed, mod·u·lat·ing.** —*v.t.* **1.** to change or vary the tone, volume, or pitch of: *to modulate the voice.* **2.** to adjust or regulate. **3.** to vary the amplitude, frequency, or other characteristic of (a carrier wave) for the transmission of a signal. —*v.i. Music.* to pass from one key to another. —**mod′u la′tor,** *n.* —**mod·u·la·to·ry** (moj′ə lə tôr′ē), *adj.*

mod·u·la·tion (moj′ə lā′shən) *n.* **1.** the act of modulating or the state of being modulated. **2.** *Music.* the passing from one key to another. **3.** the process of varying the amplitude, frequency, or other characteristic of a carrier wave for the transmission of a signal.

mod·ule (moj′ōōl, mod′yōōl) *n.* **1.** a standard or unit of measurement. **2.** a self-contained unit or part of a spacecraft, having a specific function: *a command module.*

Mo·ga·di·shu (mō′gə də′shōō) *n.* the capital of Somalia, in the southeastern part of the country, on the Indian Ocean. Pop. (1972 est.), 230,000.

Mo·gul (mō′gul) *n.* **1.** a member or descendant of the Mongol conquerors of India. **2.** a Mongol or Mongolian. **3. mogul.** a powerful or important person: *The president of the studio was a mogul of the movie industry.*

mo·hair (mō′her′) *n.* **1.** the long, silky hair of the Angora goat. **2.** a woven fabric made of this hair.

Mo·ham·med (mō ham′id) another spelling of **Muhammad.**

Mo·ham·med·an (mō ham′id ən) *adj., n.* another word for **Muslim.**

Mo·ham·med·an·ism (mō ham′id ən iz′əm) *n.* see **Islam** *(def. 1).*

Mohave Desert, another spelling of **Mojave Desert.**

Mo·hawk (mō′hôk) *n. pl.,* **Mo·hawks** or **Mo·hawk. 1.** a river in central New York state. **2.** a member of a tribe of Iroquois Indians formerly living along this river.

Mo·hi·can (mō hē′kən) *n. pl.,* **Mo·hi·cans** or **Mo·hi·can.** another spelling of **Mahican.**

Mohs scale (mōz) a scale for judging the hardness of minerals. The scale consists of ten standard minerals arranged in order of increasing hardness from talc, with a value of 1, to diamond, with a value of 10. The hardness of a mineral is determined by finding which mineral on the scale it can scratch, and then which mineral on the scale can scratch it. [From Friedrich *Mohs,* 1773–1839, a German mineralogist who devised it.]

moi·e·ty (moi′ə tē) *n. pl.,* **moi·e·ties. 1.** a half. **2.** a portion; part; share.

moist (moist) *adj.* **1.** slightly wet; damp: *a moist cloth.* **2.** containing moisture; humid: *moist air.* —**moist′ly,** *adv.* —**moist′ness,** *n.*

moist·en (moi′sən) *v.t., v.i.* to make or become moist.

mois·ture (mois′chər) *n.* **1.** water or other liquid in the air or on a surface. **2.** dampness; slight wetness.

Mo·ja·ve Desert (mō hä′vē) a large desert in southeastern California, covering about 15,000 square miles.

mo·lar (mō′lər) *n.* in humans and most other mammals, any of the largest teeth at the back of the jaws, which have broad, irregular surfaces for grinding food. In humans there are twelve molars.

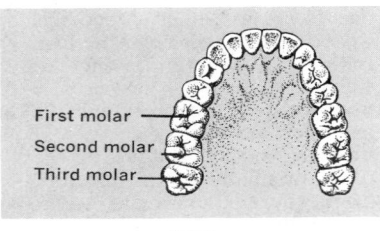

First molar
Second molar
Third molar

Molar

mo·las·ses (mə·las′iz) *n.* a sweet, thick, yellowish-brown syrup that is obtained from sugar cane as the sugar is being refined.

mold¹ (mōld) *n.* **1.** a hollow form for giving a particular shape to something in a fluid or plastic state: *He poured the liquid plaster into the mold to harden.* **2.** something formed or made in a mold: *She served gelatin molds for dessert.* **3.** the general form; shape: *the mold of her face.* **4.** a distinctive character or type: *The pioneers were men of rugged mold.* —*v.t.* **1.** to work into a particular shape; form: *The children molded clay with their hands.* **2.** to form or make with a mold. **3.** to determine the form or nature of; influence or direct: *His parents helped to mold his personality.* [Old French *modle.*] —**mold′er,** *n.*

mold² (mōld) *n.* **1.** any of various woolly or furry growths that form on food and on damp or decaying animal or plant matter. **2.** any of a number of fungus plants that cause such a growth. —*v.i.* to become covered with mold; grow moldy. [Possibly influenced by *mold³,* a form of Middle English *mouled.*]

mold³ (mōld) *n.* a loose soil that is rich in decaying animal or plant matter. [Old English *molde* soil, earth.]

Mol·da·vi·a (mol dā′vē ə) *n.* **1.** a historic region of northeastern Romania. **2.** a republic of the Soviet Union, in the European part of the country, bordering Romania. Official name: **Moldavian Soviet Socialist Republic.** Area,

13,000 sq. mi. Pop. (1970 est.), 3,569,000. —**Mol·da'-vi·an,** *adj., n.*

mold·board (mōld'bôrd') *n.* a curved metal plate or board in a plow that turns over the soil as it is plowed.

mold·er (mōl'dər) *v.i.* to crumble or decay; turn to dust: *The old wooden fence around the field moldered in the dense grass.* —*v.t.* to cause to crumble or decay.

mold·ing (mōl'ding) *n.* **1.** the act or process of forming or making something. **2.** something formed or made by molding; molded object. **3.** a shaped strip of wood, plaster, or other material that serves as a decorative edge, as on a wall or other surface.

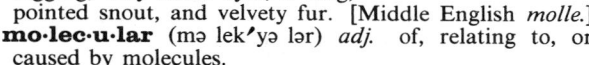

Moldings

mold·y (mōl'dē) *adj.,* **mold·i·er, mold·i·est. 1.** covered with or containing fungus mold: *There was a box of old, moldy biscuits in the cupboard.* **2.** damp or stale; musty: *We noticed a moldy odor in the old house.* —**mold'i·ness,** *n.*

mole[1] (mōl) *n.* a brownish spot on the skin. [Old English *māl* spot, blemish.]

mole[2] (mōl) *n.* an animal that lives in underground burrows. Moles have long claws used for digging, very small eyes, a long, pointed snout, and velvety fur. [Middle English *molle.*]

mo·lec·u·lar (mə lek'yə lər) *adj.* of, relating to, or caused by molecules.

molecular weight, the sum of the atomic weights of the atoms in a molecule.

mol·e·cule (mol'ə kyool') *n.* **1.** a particle of matter made up of two or more atoms joined by a pair of shared electrons. The molecule is the smallest unit of an element or compound that can exist without losing the chemical properties of the element or compound. **2.** any very small particle or bit: *There wasn't even a molecule of truth in the rumor.*

mole·hill (mōl'hil') *n.* a small mound or ridge of earth formed by a mole burrowing under the ground.

to make a mountain out of a molehill. to give too much importance or emphasis to something that is unimportant: *Worrying about the silly argument was making a mountain out of a molehill.*

mo·lest (mə lest') *v.t.* to annoy or disturb; bother. —**mo·les·ta·tion** (mō'les tā'shən), *n.* —**mo·lest'er,** *n.*

Mo·lière (mōl yer') 1622–1673, French dramatist.

moll (mol) *n. Slang.* a female companion of a gangster.

mol·lie (mol'ē) *also,* **mol·ly.** *n. pl.,* **mol·lies.** any of a group of tropical fish that bear their young alive.

mol·li·fy (mol'ə fī') *v.t.,* **mol·li·fied, mol·li·fy·ing.** to reduce the anger or strong feelings of; soothe: *She tried to mollify the two angry boys.* —**mol'li·fi·ca'tion,** *n.*

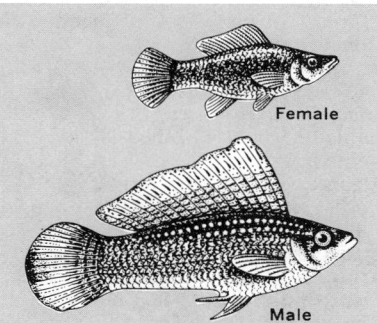

Female

Male

Mollies

mol·lusk (mol'əsk) *also,* **mol·lusc.** *n.* any of a large group of animals without backbones, found mainly in salt water, and including clams, oysters, and snails. Most mollusks have a hard outer shell protecting a soft body, but some mollusks, such as the squid and octopus, lack this type of shell.

mol·ly·cod·dle (mol'ē kod'əl) *n.* a weak-willed, pampered man or boy. —*v.t.,* **mol·ly·cod·dled, mol·ly·cod·dling.** to pamper; overprotect.

Mo·loch (mō'lok) *n.* in the Old Testament, a pagan god to whom parents sacrificed their children by fire.

Mo·lo·kai (mō'lō kī') *n.* one of the major islands of Hawaii, east of Oahu.

Mo·lo·tov (mol'ə tôf') **1. Vya·che·slav Mi·khai·lo·vich** (vyä'che släf' mi hī'lə vich). 1890—, Soviet statesman and diplomat. **2.** see **Perm.**

Molotov cocktail, a makeshift bomb consisting of a bottle filled with gasoline or other flammable liquid and a wick made of cloth or other material.

molt (mōlt) *v.i.* to shed the hair, feathers, skin, or shell and replace with a new growth. —*v.t.* to shed (an outer covering). —*n.* the act or process of molting: *The bird was in molt.*

mol·ten (mōlt'ən) *v. Archaic.* the past participle of **melt.** —*adj.* melted by heat: *Lava is molten rock.*

mol·to (mōl'tō) *adv. Music.* much; very.

Mo·luc·cas (mə luk'əz) *n., pl.* an island group of Indonesia, west of New Guinea. Also, **Molucca Islands.**

mo·lyb·de·num (mə lib'də nəm) *n.* a heavy, very hard, gray or black metallic element, used especially to make high-strength alloys for hardening steel. Symbol: **Mo**

mom (mom) *n. Informal.* mother.

Mom·ba·sa (mom bä'sə) *n.* the principal port city of Kenya, on the Indian Ocean. Pop. (1970 est.), 255,400.

mo·ment (mō'mənt) *n.* **1.** a short period of time: *I'll be back in a moment.* **2.** a particular point in time, especially the present time: *The moment he spoke we recognized his voice.* **3.** importance; significance: *This is a question of great moment.*

mo·men·ta (mō men'tə) a plural of **momentum.**

mo·men·tar·i·ly (mō'mən ter'ə lē) *adv.* **1.** for a moment: *Our train was momentarily delayed.* **2.** at any moment; very soon: *An announcement is expected momentarily.* **3.** from moment to moment: *The swelling from the bruise grew less and less momentarily.*

mo·men·tar·y (mō'mən ter'ē) *adj.* **1.** lasting only a very short time: *There was a momentary lull in the storm.* **2.** occurring at every moment. **3.** occurring at any moment. —**mo'men·tar'i·ness,** *n.*

mo·men·tous (mō men'təs) *adj.* of great importance: *a momentous event.* —**mo·men'tous·ly,** *adv.* —**mo·men'·tous·ness,** *n.*

mo·men·tum (mō men'təm) *n. pl.,* **mo·men·ta** or **mo·men·tums. 1.** *Physics.* the property of a moving body, measured by multiplying its mass by its velocity. **2.** the force or speed resulting from motion; impetus: *The rock gained momentum as it rolled down the hill.*

Mon., Monday.

Mon·a·co (mon'ə kō, mə nä'kō) *n.* **1.** a small country in southwestern Europe, on the Mediterranean Sea. Capital, Monaco. Area, ⅗ sq. mi. Pop. (1971 est.), 20,000. **2.** the capital of this country.

at; āpe; cär; end; mē; it; īce; hot; ōld; fôrk; wood; fool; oil; out; up; turn; sing; thin; this; hw in white; zh in treasure. The symbol ə stands for the sound of **a** in about, **e** in taken, **i** in pencil, **o** in lemon, and **u** in circus.

mon·arch (mon'ərk) *n.* **1.** a hereditary ruler of a state or country, such as a king or queen. **2.** a large orange and black butterfly found in North America.

mo·nar·chi·cal (mə när'ki kəl) *adj.* **1.** of, relating to, or characteristic of a monarch or monarchy. **2.** ruled by or favoring a monarch or monarchy.

Monarch

mon·ar·chism (mon'ər kiz'əm) *n.* **1.** the principles of monarchy. **2.** belief in or support of monarchy as a form of government. **—mon'·arch·ist,** *n.*

mon·ar·chy (mon'ər kē) *n. pl.,* **mon·ar·chies. 1.** government by a monarch: *Some countries have a monarchy as their form of government.* **2.** a nation or state ruled by a monarch.

mon·as·ter·y (mon'əs ter'ē) *n. pl.,* **mon·as·ter·ies. 1.** a place of residence occupied by persons living together in a religious community, especially monks. **2.** the persons living in such a place.

mo·nas·tic (mə nas'tik) *adj.* of, relating to, or characteristic of a monastery, monks, or their way of life: *monastic seclusion, monastic vows.* **—n.** a monk or other member of a religious order. **—mon·as·ti·cism** (mə nas'tə siz'əm), *n.*

mon·au·ral (mon ôr'əl) *adj.* of or relating to a system of sound reproduction in which the sound is heard from a single source.

Mon·day (mun'dē, mun'dā) *n.* the second day of the week. [Old English *mōnandæg* literally, moon's day.]

Mo·net, Claude (mō nā'; klôd) 1840–1926, French impressionist painter.

mon·e·tar·y (mon'ə ter'ē) *adj.* **1.** of or relating to the currency or coinage used by a country: *The franc is the monetary unit of France.* **2.** of or relating to money: *a monetary gift.*

mon·ey (mun'ē) *n. pl.,* **mon·eys** or **mon·ies. 1.** the coins and paper currency issued by a government for payment of debts and for purchase of goods and services; legal tender. **2.** anything used or serving as money. **3.** payment, gain, profit, or loss in terms of money: *The company made money on that deal.* **4.** wealth measured in terms of money: *She tried to give the impression that her family had money.* **5. moneys.** funds collected or stored, as by a government.

mon·ey·bag (mun'ē bag') *n.* **1.** a bag for holding money. **2. moneybags.** *Informal.* a wealthy, often miserly person.

mon·ey·chang·er (mun'ē chān'jər) *n.* a person who exchanges money, usually the money of one country for that of another.

mon·eyed (mun'ēd) *also,* **mon·ied.** *adj.* **1.** having much money; wealthy: *a moneyed family.* **2.** representing or derived from money or wealth: *moneyed influence.*

mon·ey·lend·er (mun'ē len'dər) *n.* a person who lends money at interest.

money order, an order for the payment of a sum of money, especially one issued by a bank or post office.

Mon·gol (mong'gəl) *n.* **1.** a member of one of the nomadic peoples now living in Mongolia. **2.** see **Mongolian.** **—adj.** Mongolian.

Mon·go·li·a (mong gō'lē ə) *n.* **1.** a vast area in east-central Asia, extending from northern China to Siberia. **2.** see **Mongolian People's Republic.**

Mon·go·li·an (mong gō'lē ən) *n.* **1.** a person who was born or is living in Mongolia. **2.** a member of the Mongoloid division of the human race. **3.** a language spoken in Mongolia and central Asia. **—adj.** of or relating to Mongolia.

Mongolian People's Republic, a country in central Asia, bordered by the Soviet Union and China. Capital, Ulan Bator. Area, 604,250 sq. mi. Pop. (1971), 1,300,000.

mon·gol·ism (mong'gə liz'əm) *n.* a birth defect in which a child is mentally deficient and has a broad, flat skull and slanting eyes.

Mon·gol·oid (mong'gə loid') *adj.* **1.** of or relating to one of the major divisions of the human race, whose members have yellowish skin, brown, slanted eyes, and straight, dark hair. The Mongoloid division includes the peoples of eastern Asia and Japan, the Eskimos, and the North American Indians. **2.** of, resembling, or characteristic of Mongols or Mongolians. **3. mongoloid.** having mongolism. **—n. 1.** a member of the Mongoloid division of the human race. **2. mongoloid.** a person having mongolism.

mon·goose (mong'gōos') *n. pl.,* **mon·goos·es.** a slender, flesh-eating animal having a pointed face, a long tail, and rough, shaggy fur. The mongoose is noted for its ability to kill certain poisonous snakes, especially cobras.

Mongoose

mon·grel (mung'grəl, mong'grəl) *n.* **1.** an animal, especially a dog, of mixed breed. **2.** a person or thing that is a mixture of different elements. **—adj.** of mixed breed.

mon·ied (mun'ēd) another spelling of **moneyed.**

mon·ies (mun'ēz) a plural of **money.**

mon·i·tor (mon'ə tər) *n.* **1.** a student in school given a special duty or responsibility, such as keeping order or taking attendance. **2.** a receiver used for checking, watching, or listening to television or radio transmissions. **3. Monitor.** a Union ironclad warship that fought the Merrimack at Hampton Roads, Virginia, in a historic Civil War battle. **4.** a person or thing that warns, advises, or reminds. **—v.t. 1.** to check, watch, or listen to (television or radio transmission). **2.** to watch over or supervise; oversee. **—v.i.** to serve as a monitor.

mon·i·to·ry (mon'ə tôr'ē) *adj.* serving to warn: *A monitory look from the teacher made the class quiet down.*

monk (mungk) *n.* a man who has entered a religious order and is bound by religious vows.

mon·key (mung'kē) *n., pl.* **mon·keys. 1.** any of a group of animals having long limbs, and hands and feet adapted for grasping and climbing. **2.** a person who resembles a monkey in behavior or appearance, especially a mischievous or playful child. **—v.i.,** **mon·keyed, mon·key·ing.** *Informal.* to play, fool, or meddle: *Don't monkey with the machinery.*

monkey wrench, a wrench with one jaw that can be adjusted and one jaw that is fixed, used on nuts and bolts of different sizes.

monk·ish (mung'kish) *adj.* of, relating to, or like a monk or monks.

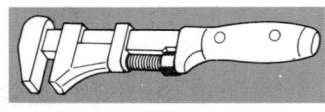
Monkey wrench

monks·hood (mungks'hood') *n.* see **aconite** *(def. 1).*

mon·o (mon'ō) *n. Informal.* infectious mononucleosis.

mon·o·chro·mat·ic (mon'ə krō mat'ik) *adj.* **1.** of or having only one color: *a monochromatic painting.* **2.** consisting of light of one wave length.

mon·o·chrome (mon'ə krōm') *n.* a painting or drawing done in a single color.

mon·o·cle (mon′ə kəl) *n.* an eyeglass worn on one eye.

mon·o·cled (mon′ə kəld) *adj.* wearing a monocle.

mon·o·cot·y·le·don (mon′ə kot′əl ēd′-ən) *n.* a plant that has one cotyledon, or seed leaf, in the embryo. Monocotyledons make up one of the two classes of flowering plants. Also, **mon·o·cot** (mon′ə kot′). —**mon′o·cot′y·le′don·ous**, *adj.*

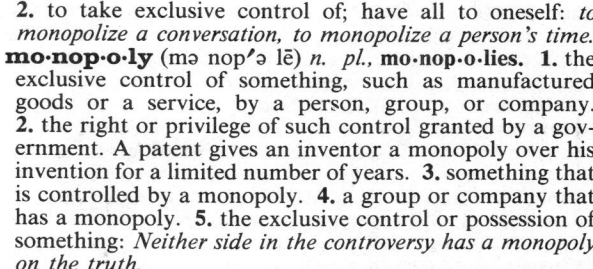

Monocle

mo·noc·u·lar (mə nok′yə lər) *adj.* **1.** having only one eye. **2.** using or for use by one eye: *a monocular microscope.*

mo·nog·a·mist (mə nog′ə mist) *n.* a person who practices or believes in monogamy.

mo·nog·a·mous (mə nog′ə məs) *adj.* of, relating to, or practicing monogamy.

mo·nog·a·my (mə nog′ə mē) *n.* the condition or practice of being married to only one person at a time.

mon·o·gram (mon′ə gram′) *n.* a design made by combining or interlacing two or more letters, especially the initials of one's name, used on clothing, stationery, and other items. —*v.t.,* **mon·o·gramed** or **mon·o·grammed**, **mon·o·gram·ing** or **mon·o·gram·ming**. to mark with a monogram.

mon·o·graph (mon′ə graf′) *n.* a scholarly book, treatise, or article written on a single subject or on a particular aspect of a subject.

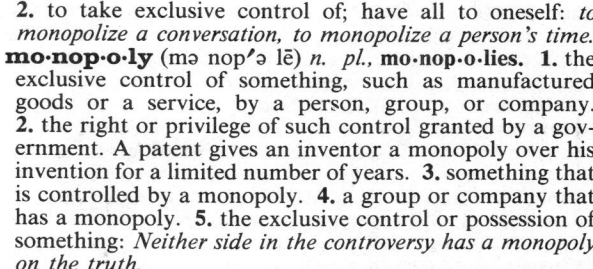

Monogram

mon·o·lith (mon′ə lith′) *n.* **1.** a single, usually very large block of stone, used in architecture and sculpture. **2.** a monument or other structure formed of such a block of stone.

mon·o·lith·ic (mon′ə lith′ik) *adj.* **1.** formed of, relating to, or resembling a monolith: *a monolithic pillar.* **2.** of the nature of a monolith; massive or uniform.

mo·nol·o·gist (mə nol′ə jist) *n.* a person who gives a monologue.

mon·o·logue (mon′ə lôg′, mon′ə log′) *also,* **mon·o·log**. *n.* **1.** a long speech made by one person. **2.** a dramatic or literary composition involving or performed by only one speaker. **3.** a series of jokes or humorous stories presented by a single speaker: *The comedian's monologue was well received by the audience.*

mon·o·ma·ni·a (mon′ə mā′nē ə) *n.* **1.** a mental disorder in which a person has an obsession with one idea but otherwise appears sane. **2.** an excessive preoccupation with or enthusiasm for one idea or subject. —**mon·o·ma·ni·ac** (mon′ə mā′nē ak′), *n.* —**mon·o·ma·ni·a·cal** (mon′ə mə nī′ə kəl), *adj.*

mo·no·mi·al (mo nō′mē əl) *adj.* consisting of a single term or word. —*n.* a monomial expression, quantity, or name.

Mo·non·ga·he·la (mə nong′gə hē′lə) *n.* a river in northern West Virginia and southwestern Pennsylvania joining the Allegheny at Pittsburgh to form the Ohio River.

mon·o·nu·cle·o·sis (mon′ə noō′klē ō′sis, mon′ə nyoō′-klē ō′sis) *n.* see **infectious mononucleosis**.

mon·o·phon·ic (mon′ə fon′ik) *adj.* **1.** *Music.* having a single melodic line with no accompaniment. **2.** another word for **monaural**.

mon·o·plane (mon′ə plān′) *n.* an airplane with only one pair of wings.

mo·nop·o·list (mə nop′ə list) *n.* a person who has a monopoly or favors monopoly. —**mo·nop′o·lis′tic**, *adj.*

mo·nop·o·lize (mə nop′ə līz′) *v.t.,* **mo·nop·o·lized**, **mo·nop·o·liz·ing**. **1.** to obtain or have a monopoly of: *That company is attempting to monopolize the textile industry.*

2. to take exclusive control of; have all to oneself: *to monopolize a conversation, to monopolize a person's time.*

mo·nop·o·ly (mə nop′ə lē) *n. pl.,* **mo·nop·o·lies**. **1.** the exclusive control of something, such as manufactured goods or a service, by a person, group, or company. **2.** the right or privilege of such control granted by a government. A patent gives an inventor a monopoly over his invention for a limited number of years. **3.** something that is controlled by a monopoly. **4.** a group or company that has a monopoly. **5.** the exclusive control or possession of something: *Neither side in the controversy has a monopoly on the truth.*

mon·o·rail (mon′ə rāl′) *n.* **1.** a railway system of public transportation in which the cars ride on a single rail, usually elevated above ground traffic. Cars either ride upon the rail or are suspended beneath it. **2.** the single rail for such a system.

mon·o·syl·lab·ic (mon′ə si lab′ik) *adj.* **1.** having only one syllable: *a monosyllabic name.* **2.** consisting of or using a word or words of one syllable: *a curt, monosyllabic reply.* —**mon′o·syl·lab′i·cal·ly**, *adv.*

mon·o·syl·la·ble (mon′ə sil′ə bəl) *n.* a word of one syllable.

mon·o·the·ism (mon′ə thē iz′əm) *n.* the doctrine or belief that there is only one God. —**mon′o·the′ist**, *n.* —**mon′o·the·is′tic**, *adj.*

mon·o·tone (mon′ə tōn′) *n.* **1.** the saying or uttering of words or sounds with no change in pitch; a single, unchanging tone in speaking: *The lecturer spoke in a dull monotone.* **2.** sameness of style, manner, or color.

mo·not·o·nous (mə not′ən əs) *adj.* **1.** not changing, as in tone, sound, or beat: *a monotonous voice, a monotonous rhythm.* **2.** tiresome or uninteresting because of a lack of variety: *He quickly became bored with the monotonous job.* —**mo·not′o·nous·ly**, *adv.* —**mo·not′o·nous·ness**, *n.*

mo·not·o·ny (mə not′ən ē) *n.* **1.** a tiresome sameness; lack of variety: *the monotony of prison life.* **2.** a lack of change, as in tone, sound, or beat.

mon·ox·ide (mon ok′sīd, mə nok′sīd) *n.* an oxide containing only one atom of oxygen in each molecule.

Mon·roe, James (mən rō′) 1758–1831, the fifth president of the United States, from 1817 to 1825.

Monroe Doctrine, a declaration of U.S. foreign policy made by President Monroe in 1823, opposing further European colonization or interference in the Western Hemisphere.

Mon·ro·vi·a (mon rō′vē ə) *n.* the capital and largest city of Liberia, on the Atlantic Ocean. Pop. (1970 est.), 100,000.

Mon·sei·gneur (mōn se nyoor′) *n. pl.,* **Mes·sei·gneurs** (mā sen yoor′). **1.** a French title of honor given to men of high rank, such as members of the higher nobility, bishops, and cardinals. **2.** *also,* **monseigneur**. a person who bears this title.

mon·sieur (mə syur′) *n. pl.,* **mes·sieurs**. mister; sir. ▲ A French form of respectful or polite address for a man.

Mon·si·gnor (mōn sēn′yər) *n. pl.,* **Mon·si·gnors** or **Mon·si·gno·ri** (mon′sēn yôr′ē). **1.** a title given to certain Roman Catholic dignitaries. **2.** *also,* **monsignor**. a person who bears this title.

at; āpe; cär; end; mē; it; īce; hot; ōld; fôrk; wood; fōol; oil; out; up; turn; sing; thin; this; hw in white; zh in treasure. The symbol ə stands for the sound of a in about, e in taken, i in pencil, o in lemon, and u in circus.

mon·soon (mon sōōn′) *n.* **1.** a seasonal wind of the Indian Ocean and southern Asia, which blows from the southwest towards the land in summer and from the northeast towards the ocean in winter. **2.** the season of the summer monsoon, characterized by heavy rains.

mon·ster (mon′stər) *n.* **1.** an imaginary creature that is large and frightening, and has an abnormal, grotesque, or horrible shape. **2.** *Biology.* an animal or plant that is abnormal in structure or appearance: *A two-headed turtle is a monster.* **3.** an imaginary creature that combines various animal and human features, such as a centaur or griffin. **4.** a person whose behavior is inhumanly wicked, cruel, or immoral: *Hitler is a monster of wickedness, insatiable in his lust for blood* (Winston Churchill). —*adj.* enormous; gigantic: *a monster whale.*

mon·stros·i·ty (mon stros′ə tē) *n. pl.,* **mon·stros·i·ties.** **1.** a monstrous person or thing. **2.** the quality or condition of being monstrous: *the monstrosity of a crime.*

mon·strous (mon′strəs) *adj.* **1.** abnormal, grotesque, or horrible in shape or character: *The dragon was a monstrous creature.* **2.** unusually large; enormous: *an error of monstrous proportions.* **3.** shocking, as in wickedness; horrible. —**mon′strous·ly,** *adv.* —**mon′strous·ness,** *n.*

Mont., Montana.

mon·tage (mon täzh′) *n.* **1.** a picture made by combining several different pictures or parts of pictures. **2.** the art or process of making such pictures.

Mon·tan·a (mon tan′ə) *n.* a state in the northwestern United States. Capital, Helena. Area, 147,138 sq. mi. Pop. (1970), 694,409. Abbreviation, **Mont.** —**Mon·tan′an,** *adj., n.*

● **Montana,** either from Latin "mountainous" or from Spanish "mountain," was originally the name of a town in the area of Pikes Peak. The name was first suggested for the mountainous territory of Idaho but was rejected. It was then adopted for Montana, although that state lies mostly in the Great Plains.

Mont Blanc (mont blangk′) the highest mountain in the Alps, between France and Italy.

Mon·te Car·lo (mon′tē kär′lō) a resort in Monaco, on the Mediterranean, the site of a world-famous gambling casino.

Mon·te·ne·gro (mon′tə nē′grō) *n.* a republic of Yugoslavia, on the Adriatic Sea. It was formerly an independent kingdom.

Mon·ter·rey (mon′tə rā′) *n.* a city in northeastern Mexico. Pop. (1970), 858,107.

Mon·tes·so·ri, Maria (mon′tə sôr′ē) 1870–1952, Italian physician and educator.

Montessori method, a system of education for young children developed by Maria Montessori, emphasizing training of the child's senses through independent activity in a carefully structured classroom, so as to encourage the development of individual expression, self-discipline, and independence.

Mon·te·vi·de·o (mon′tə vi dā′ō) *n.* the capital of Uruguay, in the southern part of the country. Pop. (1971 est.), 1,348,000.

Mon·te·zu·ma II (mon′tə zōō′mə) 1480?–1520, emperor of the Aztecs in Mexico.

Mont·gom·er·y (mont gum′ər ē) *n.* the capital of Alabama, in the central part of the state. Pop. (1970), 133,386.

month (munth) *n.* **1.** one of the twelve parts into which the calendar year is divided. Also, **calendar month.** **2.** the time from any day of one calendar month to the corresponding day of the next month. **3.** a period of about four weeks or thirty days. **4.** the period of a complete revolution of the moon around the earth. Also *(def. 4),* **lunar month.**

month·ly (munth′lē) *adj.* **1.** done, happening, or appearing once a month: *the monthly bills, a monthly magazine.* **2.** of or relating to a month: *monthly rainfall.* **3.** continuing or lasting a month. —*adv.* once a month; every month. —*n. pl.,* **month·lies.** a magazine that is published once a month.

Mont·pel·ier (mont pēl′yər) *n.* the capital of Vermont, in the central part of the state. Pop. (1970), 8609.

Mont·re·al (mon′trē ôl′) *n.* the largest city of Canada, on the St. Lawrence River in southern Quebec. Pop. (1971 est.), 2,570,000.

mon·u·ment (mon′yə mənt) *n.* **1.** a building, statue, arch, or other structure set up or constructed in memory of a person or event. **2.** a memorial stone or marker placed at a grave; tombstone. **3.** a work or achievement of lasting significance: *The discovery of penicillin was a monument in medical research.* **4.** an area or site of special importance or of great natural beauty set aside and preserved by a government.

mon·u·men·tal (mon′yə ment′əl) *adj.* **1.** of lasting significance; notable: *a monumental decision of the U.S. Supreme Court.* **2.** of great size or scope; huge; colossal: *a monumental mistake.* **3.** of, like, or serving as a monument: *A monumental work of sculpture was placed over the hero's grave.* —**mon′u·men′tal·ly,** *adv.*

moo (mōō) *n. pl.,* **moos.** the sound made by a cow. —*v.i.,* **mooed, moo·ing.** to make such a sound.

mood[1] (mōōd) *n.* **1.** a state of mind or feeling at a particular time: *The good news put him in a happy mood.* **2.** a special quality or atmosphere, as of a place or work of art: *the restful mood of a landscape painting.* [Old English *mōd* mind, heart, courage.]

mood[2] (mōōd) *n. Grammar.* the form of a verb that shows whether the statement refers to a fact, command, wish, or possibility. There are three moods in English: indicative, imperative, and subjunctive. Also, **mode.** [Influenced by *mood*[1], a form of *mode*[1].]

mood·y (mōō′dē) *adj.,* **mood·i·er, mood·i·est.** **1.** tending to have changing moods, especially gloomy or sullen moods: *Pete has a moody nature.* **2.** showing or expressing a gloomy mood: *a moody answer.* —**mood′i·ly,** *adv.* —**mood′i·ness,** *n.*

moon (mōōn) *n.* **1.** the earth's natural satellite, visible by the sun's reflected light. The moon orbits the earth from west to east once in about 29½ days. **2.** anything resembling the moon in any of its phases, such as a crescent-shaped object or design. **3.** a satellite of any other planet: *Mars has two small moons.* **4.** a month, especially a lunar month. **5.** moonlight. —*v.i.* to move or look about dreamily or aimlessly.

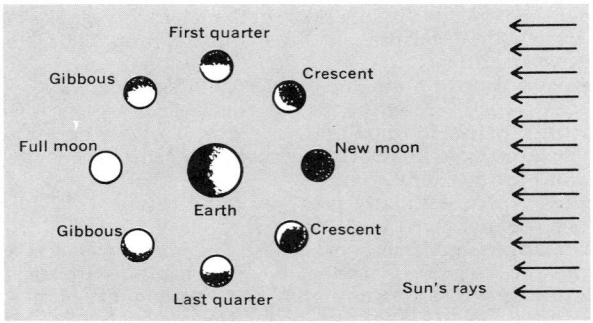

Phases of the moon

moon·beam (mo͞on′bēm′) *n.* a ray of light from the moon.

moon·light (mo͞on′līt′) *n.* the light shining from the moon. —*adj.* **1.** lighted by the moon; moonlit. **2.** happening or done by the light of the moon: *a moonlight ride.* —*v.i.* to work at a second job, especially at night, in addition to one's regular job: *The policeman moonlighted as a taxi driver.* —**moon′light′er,** *n.*

moon·lit (mo͞on′lit′) *adj.* lighted by the moon: *a moonlit night.*

moon·scape (mo͞on′skāp′) *n.* a picture or view of the moon's surface.

moon·shine (mo͞on′shīn′) *n.* **1.** the light shining from the moon; moonlight. **2.** empty talk or ideas; nonsense. **3.** *Informal.* liquor distilled illegally. —*v.t., v.i.,* **moon·shined, moon·shin·ing.** *Informal.* to distill liquor illegally. —**moon′shin′er,** *n.*

moon·stone (mo͞on′stōn′) *n.* a pearly gemstone, a variety of feldspar.

moon·struck (mo͞on′struk′) *adj.* romantically dazed or slightly crazy because of the supposed influence of the moon.

moor[1] (moor) *v.t.* to secure (a ship or other craft) in place with lines or anchors, as at a dock. —*v.i.* **1.** to secure a ship or other craft: *The ship moored at the harbor to take on cargo.* **2.** to be secured, as by ropes and anchors. [Late Middle English *moren.*]

moor[2] (moor) *n.* an area of open, rolling, wild land, often covered with heather and having bogs and marshes. [Old English *mōr.*]

Moor (moor) *n.* a member of a people of mixed Arab and Berber descent living in northern Africa. The Moors invaded and conquered Spain in the eighth century A.D.

moor·age (moor′ij) *n.* **1.** a place for mooring. **2.** the act of mooring or the state of being moored. **3.** a charge for the use of moorings.

Moore, Thomas (moor, môr) 1779–1852, Irish poet.

moor·ing (moor′ing) *n.* **1.** the act of a person or thing that moors. **2.** a device, such as a cable, rope, or anchor, by which a ship is moored. **3.** a place where a boat or a ship can be moored.

Moor·ish (moor′ish) *adj.* of or relating to the Moors.

moose (mo͞os) *n. pl.,* **moose.** a large, heavy animal, the largest member of the deer family, native to the forests of northern North America, having a large head, a short neck, and a blackish-brown coat with gray markings. The male has enormous, broad antlers.

Moose

moot (mo͞ot) *adj.* open to dispute or discussion; debatable: *a moot point in an argument.*

mop (mop) *n.* **1.** a cleaning device that has a bundle of coarse yarn, cloth, sponge, or other absorbent material, fastened at the end of a long handle. **2.** any thick, tangled mass resembling this, such as a bushy head of hair. —*v.t.,* **mopped, mop·ping.** to clean with a mop.
  to mop up. a. to finish a task. **b.** to clear out remaining enemy troops from a captured area.

mope (mōp) *v.i.,* **moped, mop·ing.** to be gloomy and sad.

mo·ped (mō′ped) *n.* a heavy bicycle which has a small engine that the rider can use for additional power.

mop·pet (mop′it) *n.* a little child.

mo·raine (mə rān′) *n.* a mass of rock deposited by a melting glacier.

mor·al (môr′əl, mor′əl) *adj.* **1.** good or virtuous in behavior or character according to a standard of right and wrong: *a moral person, a moral act.* **2.** of, relating to, or concerned with a standard of right and wrong; ethical: *a moral question.* **3.** that promotes or aids right conduct: *moral teachings.* **4.** that can judge between right and wrong: *People are moral beings.* —*n.* **1.** the lesson taught by a fable, story, or event. **2. morals.** principles or standards of right and wrong. —**mor′al·ly,** *adv.*

mo·rale (mə ral′) *n.* the attitude or spirit of a person or group: *Morale was low among the players after the team lost eight games in a row.*

mor·al·ist (môr′ə list, mor′ə list) *n.* **1.** a person who teaches or writes about morals. **2.** a moralistic person.

mor·al·is·tic (môr′ə lis′tik, mor ə lis′tik) *adj.* concerned with morals, especially tending to promote or aid right conduct: *a moralistic person, moralistic teaching.*

mo·ral·i·ty (mə ral′ə tē) *n. pl.,* **mo·ral·i·ties. 1.** the moral rightness or wrongness of an act. **2.** moral conduct; virtue. **3.** a system of morals; ethics.

mor·al·ize (môr′ə līz′, mor′ə līz′) *v.,* **mor·al·ized, mor·al·iz·ing.** —*v.i.* to make judgments on matters of right and wrong, especially to tell people what to do in a self-righteous way. —*v.t.* **1.** to explain or interpret the lesson or moral of. **2.** to view in moral terms; regard as a question of right and wrong.

mo·rass (mə ras′) *n. pl.,* **mo·rass·es.** an area of low, soft, wet ground; marsh; swamp.

mor·a·to·ri·um (môr′ə tôr′ē əm) *n. pl.,* **mor·a·to·ri·ums** or **mor·a·to·ri·a** (môr′ə tôr′ē ə). **1.** the postponing of a legal obligation, such as the paying of a debt. **2.** the period of such a postponement. **3.** a temporary delaying or stopping of some activity: *The nations agreed to a moratorium on testing nuclear weapons.*

Mo·ra·vi·a (mô rā′vē ə) *n.* a historic region in central Czechoslovakia. —**Mo·ra′vi·an,** *adj., n.*

mo·ray (môr′ā) *n.* a brilliantly colored saltwater eel found in warm waters and feared by divers because of its vicious bite. Also, **moray eel.**

mor·bid (môr′bid) *adj.* **1.** overly concerned with or interested in death, disease, decay, or the like: *He has a morbid sense of humor.* **2.** of or relating to death, disease, decay, or the like; gruesome; grisly: *a morbid graveyard scene.* **3.** relating to, caused by, or characteristic of disease: *a morbid condition of the liver.* —**mor′bid·ly,** *adv.* —**mor′bid·ness,** *n.*

mor·bid·i·ty (môr bid′ə tē) *n.* **1.** the quality or state of being morbid. **2.** the rate of disease or proportion of diseased persons in a place.

mor·dant (môrd′ənt) *adj.* biting or sarcastic; cutting: *a mordant wit, a mordant remark.* —*n.* **1.** any substance that serves to fix the color of a dye in cloth. **2.** an acid or other substance used in etching to eat into metal. —**mor′dan·cy,** *n.* —**mor′dant·ly,** *adv.*

more (môr) *adj.* the comparative of **much** and **many. 1.** greater in number, quantity, intensity, or degree: *There are more cars in this country now than there were ten years ago. She needed more sugar for the recipe.* **2.** being an

at; āpe; cär; end; mē; it; īce; hot; ōld; fôrk; wood; fo͞ol; oil; out; up; turn; sing; thin; this; hw in white; zh in treasure. The symbol ə stands for the sound of **a** in about, **e** in taken, **i** in pencil, **o** in lemon, and **u** in circus.

M

additional amount; further: *Please repeat that one more time. I'll need an hour more to finish.* —*adv.* the comparative of **much. 1.** in or to a greater extent or degree: *Be more careful. He exercises more regularly than I do.* **2.** in addition; further; again: *She got up and then fell once more.* —*n.* an additional amount: *He wants more to eat. Say no more.*

  more or less. a. to an indefinite degree; somewhat: *The patient's condition has more or less improved.* **b.** just about; approximately: *We arrived more or less on time.*

More, Sir Thomas (môr) 1478–1535, English statesman and writer. He was made a saint in 1935.

more·o·ver (môr ō′vər) *adv.* in addition to what has been said; also: *The day was dark and cold, and moreover it was raining.*

mo·res (môr′āz) *n., pl.* the established customs of a particular group or society.

Mor·gan (môr′gən) **1. Sir Henry.** 1635?–1688, English pirate. **2. J(ohn) P(ier·pont)** (pēr′pont). 1837–1913, U.S. financier.

morgue (môrg) *n.* **1.** a place in which the bodies of persons found dead are kept for identification. **2.** a reference library in a newspaper office in which old issues, clippings, and other sources of information are stored.

mor·i·bund (môr′ə bund′, mor′ə bund′) *adj.* in a dying state; almost lifeless.

Mor·mon (môr′mən) *n.* a member of the Church of Jesus Christ of Latter-day Saints, a religious sect founded in 1830 by Joseph Smith. —*adj.* of or relating to the Mormons or their religion.

morn (môrn) *n.* see **morning.**

morn·ing (môr′ning) *n.* **1.** the first part of the day, beginning at midnight or daybreak and ending at noon. **2.** dawn. —*adj.* of, relating to, or occurring in the morning: *a morning newspaper, a morning appointment.*

morning glory 1. a trumpet-shaped flower growing mainly in purple, pink, yellow, or white, and generally open only in the early morning. **2.** any of various plants bearing this flower, especially a twining vine widely grown in gardens and having oval or heart-shaped leaves.

morning star, a planet, especially Venus, visible in the eastern sky before sunrise.

Morning glory

mo·roc·co (mə rok′ō) *n. pl.,* **mo·roc·cos.** leather that originally came from Morocco, made from goatskin and used for the bindings of fine books.

Mo·roc·co (mə rok′ō) *n.* a country in northwestern Africa, on the Atlantic and the Mediterranean, formerly governed by France and Spain. Capital, Rabat. Area, 171,835 sq. mi. Pop. (1971 est.), 15,230,000. —**Mo·roc′can,** *adj., n.*

mo·ron (môr′on) *n.* **1.** a person who is mentally retarded, having a mental age of up to 12 years. **2.** *Informal.* a very foolish or stupid person. —**mo·ron·ic** (mə ron′ik) *adj.*

mo·rose (mə rōs′) *adj.* bad-tempered, gloomy, or sullen. —**mo·rose′ly,** *adv.* —**mo·rose′ness,** *n.*

mor·pheme (môr′fēm) *n.* the smallest unit of language that has meaning.

●A **morpheme** is not the same thing as a word. It may be a word, such as *run, fat, cow,* or *sleep.* But it also can be something smaller than a word—a letter or group of letters that cannot be used alone the way a word can, but that can give a different meaning to a word if attached to it. Examples of this kind of morpheme are prefixes, such as

un- in *unwise,* and suffixes, such as *-er* in *jumper.* Another example is *inflected forms* (word endings that show a change in the meaning of the word), such as *-s* in *boys* or *-ed* in *walked.*

  People who study language use the term *morpheme* because it is much easier to determine scientifically what a morpheme is than what a word is. For example, the word *houseplant* also appears very often as two words, *house plant.* Either way, however, it clearly consists of two morphemes, *house* and *plant.*

Mor·phe·us (môr′fē əs, môr′fyōōs) *n. Greek Mythology.* the god of dreams.

mor·phine (môr′fēn) *n.* a powerful, habit-forming drug made from opium. Morphine is used to relieve pain. [From *Morpheus,* because this drug is used to cause sleep.]

mor·pho·log·i·cal (môr′fə loj′i kəl) *adj.* of or relating to morphology. Also, **mor·pho·log·ic** (môr′fə loj′ik).

mor·phol·o·gy (môr fol′ə jē) *n.* **1.** the biological study of the structure of animals and plants. **2.** the structure of an organism. **3.** the branch of linguistics that studies how groups of sounds are joined together to make words.

mor·row (môr′ō, mor′ō) *n.* **1.** the next day; tomorrow: *I shall say good night till it be morrow* (Shakespeare, *Romeo and Juliet*). **2.** *Archaic.* morning.

Morse, Samuel F(inley) B(reese) (môrs) 1791–1872, U.S. inventor and artist.

Morse code, a code used in telegraphy in which combinations of short and long signals, or dots and dashes, are used to represent the letters of the alphabet, numerals, and punctuation marks. It was invented by Samuel F.B. Morse.

mor·sel (môr′səl) *n.* **1.** a small bite or portion of food. **2.** a small quantity or piece; fragment.

mor·tal (môrt′əl) *adj.* **1.** subject to death; certain to die: *All things that live are mortal.* **2.** causing death; fatal: *a mortal blow, a mortal wound.* **3.** fought to the death: *mortal combat.* **4.** relentless; irreconcilable: *mortal enemies.* **5.** very great or intense: *mortal fear.* **6.** of or characteristic of human beings; earthly: *a mortal weakness.* **7.** (of sin) causing spiritual death. —*n.* a human being; person. —**mor′tal·ly,** *adv.*

mor·tal·i·ty (môr tal′ə tē) *n.* **1.** the state or condition of being subject to death. **2.** the number of deaths in a given time in a given place; death rate. **3.** large-scale death or destruction, as from war.

mor·tar[1] (môr′tər) *n.* a building material made of a mixture of sand and water with lime that hardens as it dries, used especially for binding bricks or stones together in a wall or other structure. [Middle English *morter,* from Old English *mortere* and Old French *mortier.*]

mor·tar[2] (môr′tər) *n.* **1.** a thick bowl of marble or other hard material in which substances are crushed to a powder by means of a pestle. **2.** a short cannon for firing shells at high angles. [French *mortier.*]

Mortar[2]

mor·tar·board (môr′tər bôrd′) *n.* **1.** a square, flat plate of wood or metal with a centered handle, used by masons to hold mortar. **2.** a cap attached to a square cloth-covered piece of wood or cardboard, worn by teachers and students at graduations and other academic exercises.

mort·gage (môr′gij) *n.* **1.** a pledge of property, given as security for the payment of a debt. **2.** a document indicating the terms of such a pledge and the manner in which the debt is to be paid. —*v.t.,* **mort·gaged, mort·gag·ing. 1.** to pledge (property) as security for the payment of a debt: *Mr. Brown mortgaged his farm to the bank in* *return for a loan.* **2.** to give up or pledge in advance. [Old French *morgage, mortgage* literally, dead pledge; because if a person did not pay off his mortgage when it was due, he lost the property (the property was "dead" to him).]

mort·ga·gee (môr′gi jē′) *n.* a person to whom property is mortgaged.

mort·ga·gor (môr′gi jər) *also,* **mort·gag·er.** *n.* a person who mortgages his property.

mor·tice (môr′tis) *n., v.t.,* **mor·ticed, mor·tic·ing.** another spelling of **mortise.**

mor·ti·cian (môr tish′ən) *n.* see **undertaker** *(def. 1).*

mor·ti·fi·ca·tion (môr′tə fi kā′shən) *n.* **1.** a feeling of shame, humiliation, or embarrassment. **2.** anything causing such feelings. **3.** the practice of suppressing desires and passions by strict self-discipline. **4.** the death and decay of a part of the body; gangrene.

mor·ti·fy (môr′tə fī′) *v.,* **mor·ti·fied, mor·ti·fy·ing.** —*v.t.* **1.** to cause to feel shame, humiliation, or embarrassment: *The thought of her younger brother reading her diary mortified her.* **2.** to subject to mortification. —*v.i.* to become affected with gangrene; decay. —**mor′ti·fi′er,** *n.*

mor·tise (môr′tis) *also,* **mor·tice.** *n.* a hole, as in a piece of wood, shaped to receive a tenon, or projecting part, of a second piece in order to form a strong joint. —*v.t.,* **mortised, mor·tis·ing. 1.** to join or fasten securely by means of a tenon and mortise: *to mortise two pieces of lumber.* **2.** to cut or make a mortise in.

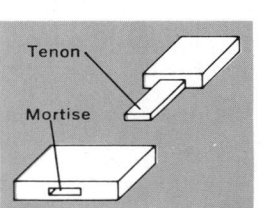

Mortise

mor·tu·ar·y (môr′chōō er′ē) *n. pl.,* **mor·tu·ar·ies.** a place where corpses are prepared or kept until burial or cremation. —*adj.* of or relating to death or burial.

mos., months.

mo·sa·ic (mō zā′ik) *n.* **1.** a picture or design made by fitting together variously colored bits of stone, glass, or other hard material. **2.** the technique or process of making such designs.

Mo·sa·ic (mō zā′ik) *adj.* of or relating to Moses or the writings or laws attributed to him.

Mos·cow (mos′kou, mos′kō) *n.* the capital and leading city of the Soviet Union, in the western part of the country. Pop. (1971 est.), 7,040,000.

Mo·ses (mō′ziz) *n.* in the Old Testament, the great prophet and lawgiver of the Israelites who led them out of Egypt. Moses is regarded as the founder of Judaism.

Mos·lem (moz′ləm) *adj., n. pl.,* **Mos·lems.** another spelling of **Muslim.**

mosque (mosk) *n.* a Muslim temple or place of worship.

mos·qui·to (məs kē′tō) *n. pl.,* **mos·qui·toes** or **mos·qui·tos.** any of a group of two-winged insects, the females of which can pierce the skin of man and animals and suck their blood. The bite of some mosquitoes can transmit such diseases as malaria and yellow fever.

Mosque

mosquito net, a screen or covering resembling gauze, used to keep out mosquitoes and other insects, as from a tent.

moss (môs) *n. pl.,* **moss·es. 1.** any of a large group of nonflowering plants growing in clusters and often forming soft, dense mats. Mosses grow mostly in damp, shady places, as on rocks, next to streams, on tree trunks, and on the ground. **2.** any of various other plants that resemble moss.

moss·y (mô′sē) *adj.,* **moss·i·er, moss·i·est. 1.** covered with moss. **2.** resembling moss.

most (mōst) *adj.* the superlative of **much** and **many. 1.** greatest in number, quantity, or degree: *Which candidate received the most votes?* **2.** the greatest part or number of; majority of: *Most young children like to play games.* —*n.* **1.** the greatest number, quantity, or degree: *That is the most I can give you.* **2.** the greatest part or number of persons: *James did more to help than most would.* —*adv.* the superlative of **much. 1.** very: *She is a most unusual person.* **2.** in or to the greatest extent or degree: *That is the most interesting book I have ever read.*
> **at most** or **at the most.** at the maximum: *At most, you'll get $650 for your car.*
> **for the most part.** in general; mainly.
> **to make the most of.** to use to the best advantage: *Elizabeth makes the most of her free time.*

-most *suffix* (used to form adjectives and adverbs in the superlative degree) most or closest to: *topmost, uppermost.*

most·ly (mōst′lē) *adv.* for the most part; mainly; chiefly: *The weather has been mostly cloudy.*

mote (mōt) *n.* a particle or speck, as of dust.

mo·tel (mō tel′) *n.* a hotel for motorists, usually located near a main road or highway. [A combination of *mo*(tor) and (ho)*tel*.]

moth (môth) *n. pl.,* **moths** (môthz, môths). **1.** any of a group of broad-winged insects resembling butterflies but different from them in flying mostly at night, in being less brightly colored, and in having stouter bodies. **2.** see **clothes moth.**

moth·ball (môth′bôl′) *n.* a small ball of naphthalene or camphor, used to repel clothes moths from fabrics and furs.

moth-eat·en (môth′ēt′ən) *adj.* **1.** eaten away or damaged by clothes moths. **2.** worn-out or old-fashioned: *a moth-eaten superstition.*

moth·er[1] (muth′ər) *n.* **1.** a female parent. **2.** a woman who acts or is thought of as a female parent; guardian or provider. **3.** a source or origin: *The state of Virginia has been called "the Mother of Presidents."* **4.** see **mother superior.** —*adj.* **1.** that is a mother: *a mother hen.* **2.** relating to or characteristic of a mother: *mother love.* **3.** native: *one's mother country.* **4.** giving love or protection like a mother: *the mother church.* —*v.t.* **1.** to give birth to; be the mother of. **2.** to treat in a motherly way, especially by being too protective. [Old English *mōdor.*] —**moth′er·less,** *adj.*

moth·er[2] (muth′ər) *n.* a filmy layer on the surface of fermenting vinegar, wine, or cider, formed of yeast cells and bacteria. [From *mother*[1]; probably because *mother* cells of fermenting vinegar, wine, or cider produce other cells.]

Mother Goose, the imaginary author of a collection of fairy tales and nursery rhymes.

---

at; āpe; cär; end; mē; it; īce; hot; ōld; fôrk; wood; fōōl; oil; out; up; turn; sing; thin; this; hw in white; zh in treasure. The symbol ə stands for the sound of a in about, e in taken, i in pencil, o in lemon, and u in circus.

moth·er·hood (muth′ər hood′) *n.* **1.** the state or role of being a mother. **2.** mothers as a group.

moth·er-in-law (muth′ər in lô′) *n. pl.,* **moth·ers-in-law.** the mother of one's husband or wife.

moth·er·land (muth′ər land′) *n.* **1.** a person's native country. **2.** the country of one's ancestors.

moth·er·ly (muth′ər lē) *adj.* of, like, or characteristic of a mother: *motherly love.* —*adv.* in the manner of a mother. —**moth′er·li·ness,** *n.*

moth·er-of-pearl (muth′ər əv purl′) *n.* a hard, rainbow-colored layer lining the shells of pearl oysters and certain other shells. It is used for making buttons and ornaments. Also, **nacre.**

mother of vinegar, see **mother².**

Mother's Day, a day set aside in honor of mothers, observed annually on the second Sunday of May.

mother superior, a nun who is head of a religious community of women.

mother tongue 1. a person's native language. **2.** a language from which other languages are derived: *Latin is the mother tongue of French and Spanish.*

mo·tif (mō tēf′) *n.* **1.** a recurring idea, situation, problem, or theme in a work of art, literature, or drama. **2.** a distinctive, usually repeated figure, design, or color, as in a decoration or printed pattern: *The wallpaper had a floral motif.* **3.** *Music.* a short and easily recognizable fragment of music that may be associated with a particular character or idea.

mo·tile (mōt′əl) *adj. Biology.* having the power to move itself. —**mo·til·i·ty** (mō til′ə tē), *n.*

mo·tion (mō′shən) *n.* **1.** the fact or process of changing position or place; not staying still: *the endless motion of the sea, the forward motion of a car.* **2.** the act of moving the body or one of its parts: *The policeman signaled with a motion of his hand.* **3.** a formal proposal or suggestion made in a court of law or other meeting or assembly: *John made a motion to take a vote.* —*v.i.* to make a movement of the hand or other part of the body to express one's meaning. —*v.t.* to direct with a movement or gesture: *The hostess motioned me to a seat.*

mo·tion·less (mō′shən lis) *adj.* that does not or cannot move; not moving.

motion picture 1. a presentation or show created by projecting a series of still photographs onto a white screen or the like at high speed, thus producing the illusion of movement or reproducing the movement originally photographed. Also, **moving picture. 2.** a story or other subject matter photographed as a motion picture. —**mo′tion-pic′ture,** *adj.*

mo·ti·vate (mō′tə vāt′) *v.t.,* **mo·ti·vat·ed, mo·ti·vat·ing.** to provide with a motive; move to effort or action.

mo·ti·va·tion (mō′tə vā′shən) *n.* **1.** the act of motivating or the state of being motivated. **2.** something that motivates.

mo·tive (mō′tiv) *n.* **1.** a mental state, inner need, or outward goal that causes a person to act; motivation: *The police were unable to determine the motive for the crime.* **2.** see **motif** *(def. 3).* —*adj.* of, relating to, or producing motion: *Wind is a motive power.*

mot·ley (mot′lē) *adj.* **1.** made up of different kinds; diverse: *a motley blend of images, a motley group of people.* **2.** of different colors: *motley autumn leaves.* —*n.* a suit or costume of many different colors, especially one worn by a clown or court jester.

mo·tor (mō′tər) *n.* **1.** a machine that converts electrical energy into mechanical energy: *the motor of a fan.* **2.** any engine, especially an internal-combustion engine. **3.** *British.* an automobile. —*adj.* **1.** of, for, or relating to a motor or motor vehicle: *motor oil, a motor trip.*

2. equipped with or driven by a motor. **3.** of or relating to that part of the nervous system that sends out impulses to the various muscles in the body: *a motor nerve.* —*v.i.* to travel by automobile.

mo·tor·bike (mō′tər bīk′) *n.* **1.** a bicycle powered by a small motor. **2.** a light or small motorcycle.

mo·tor·boat (mō′tər bōt′) *n.* a boat powered by a motor, especially a small, open boat with an outboard motor.

mo·tor·cade (mō′tər kād′) *n.* a procession of automobiles.

mo·tor·car (mō′tər kär′) *n.* an automobile; car.

mo·tor·cy·cle (mō′tər sī′kəl) *n.* a two-wheeled vehicle that is built like a bicycle but is larger and heavier and is propelled by an internal-combustion engine. —*v.i.,* **mo·tor·cy·cled, mo·tor·cy·cling.** to ride a motorcycle; travel by motorcycle. —**mo′tor·cy′clist,** *n.*

Motorcycle

mo·tor·ist (mō′tər ist) *n.* a person who drives a car.

mo·tor·ize (mō′tə rīz′) *v.t.,* **mo·tor·ized, mo·tor·iz·ing. 1.** to equip or furnish with a motor: *to motorize a wheelchair.* **2.** to supply with motor-driven vehicles: *to motorize farms.* —**mo′tor·i·za′tion,** *n.*

mo·tor·man (mō′tər mən) *n. pl.,* **mo·tor·men** (mō′tər-mən). a person who drives or operates a subway train, streetcar, or similar vehicle.

motor scooter, a two-wheeled motorized vehicle similar in appearance to a child's scooter.

motor vehicle, any vehicle powered by a motor for use on roads and highways, such as an automobile, truck, bus, or motorcycle.

mot·tle (mot′əl) *v.t.,* **mot·tled, mot·tling.** to mark or cover with irregular spots or streaks of different colors. —*n.* a mottled coloring or pattern.

mot·to (mot′ō) *n. pl.,* **mot·toes** or **mot·tos. 1.** a brief saying that expresses a guiding idea or principle: *His motto is "Haste makes waste." * **2.** a short, appropriate statement added to something to express or symbolize its content or nature, such as a phrase inscribed on a coin, document, or monument.

mould (mōld) *British.* another spelling of **mold.**

mould·er (mōl′dər) *British.* another spelling of **molder.**

mould·ing (mōl′ding) *British.* another spelling of **molding.**

mould·y (mōl′dē) *adj.,* **mould·i·er, mould·i·est.** *British.* another spelling of **moldy.** —**mould′i·ness,** *n.*

moult (mōlt) *British.* another spelling of **molt.**

mound (mound) *n.* **1.** a bank or heap of earth or stones. **2.** any heap or pile: *a mound of garbage.* **3.** a small hill. **4.** *Baseball.* the slightly raised area in the center of the diamond from which the pitcher pitches. —*v.t.* to heap up in a mound.

mount¹ (mount) *v.t.* **1.** to go up; climb: *to mount stairs.* **2.** to get up on top of: *to mount a horse.* **3.** to place on or attach to a support or stand: *to mount a camera on a tripod.* **4.** to set in place, as for display: *to mount stamps in an album.* **5.** to prepare and begin to carry out: *to mount an attack.* **6.** to provide (a theatrical presentation) with scenery, costumes, and lighting. **7.** to furnish with a horse or other animal for riding. —*v.i.* **1.** to increase or build up: *Tension mounted as the tied game neared its end.* **2.** to get up on something, as the back of a horse: *The* *cowboys mounted and rode off.* **3.** to rise; ascend. —*n.* **1.** a horse or other animal for riding. **2.** an album, frame, or the like, in which something is set in place, as for display. **3.** something used as a support or stand: *a mount for a microscope.* [Old French *monter* to go up, climb.]

mount² (mount) *n.* mountain. ▲ usually used before a proper name: *Mount Everest.* [Old French *mont* and Old English *munt.*]

Mount. Mountains are entered in the dictionary under their proper names. For example, **Mount Everest** is listed in the E's.

moun·tain (mount′ən) *n.* **1.** a mass of land rising steeply to a great height above the surrounding country. **2.** a huge heap or pile; towering mass: *a mountain of garbage.* **3.** a great quantity or amount: *a mountain of trouble.*

mountain chain, a series of connected mountains.

moun·tain·eer (mount′ən ēr′) *n.* **1.** a person who lives in a mountainous region. **2.** a person who is skilled at mountain climbing.

mountain goat, see **Rocky Mountain goat.**

mountain laurel, an evergreen shrub having glossy, oblong leaves and large clusters of flowers.

mountain lion, another term for **cougar.**

moun·tain·ous (mount′ən-əs) *adj.* **1.** having many mountains: *a mountainous island.* **2.** enormous; huge: *a mountainous pile of old newspapers.*

mountain range, a ridge or series of ridges of mountains, usually alike in origin,

Mountain laurel

geological age, and form. The Rockies are a North American mountain range.

moun·tain·side (mount′ən sīd′) *n.* the side or slope of a mountain: *The cabin was built on the mountainside.*

Mountain Standard Time, the local time used in the west-central United States. It is seven hours behind Greenwich Time.

moun·tain·top (mount′ən top′) *n.* the top of a mountain.

moun·te·bank (moun′tə bank′) *n.* **1.** a person who peddles quack medicines. **2.** a person who is deceitful; trickster; charlatan.

Moun·tie (moun′tē) *n. Informal.* a member of the Royal Canadian Mounted Police.

mount·ing (moun′ting) *n.* **1.** a support or setting: *The rifle is in its mounting on the wall.* **2.** the act of a person or thing that mounts.

Mount Ver·non (vur′nən) the home and burial place of George Washington, in Virginia, on the Potomac River near Washington, D.C.

mourn (môrn) *v.i.* **1.** to feel or express sorrow or grief. **2.** to lament the death of someone: *The mother mourned for her dead son.* —*v.t.* **1.** to feel or express sorrow or grief over: *The people mourned the general's death.* **2.** to complain about or lament: *He mourned his great misfortunes.*

mourn·er (môr′nər) *n.* a person who mourns, especially a person attending a funeral.

mourn·ful (môrn′fəl) *adj.* feeling, expressing, or filled with grief or sorrow: *a mournful widow, a mournful song.* —**mourn′ful·ly,** *adv.* —**mourn′ful·ness,** *n.*

mourn·ing (môr′ning) *n.* **1.** the act of a person who mourns. **2.** the state of feeling sorrow or grief. **3.** a display of sorrow over a person's death, especially the wearing of black. **4.** the customary clothes, draperies, and other furnishings worn or used to express such sorrow. **5.** the period during which such expression of sorrow continues.

mourning dove, a wild North American pigeon, having a mournful, cooing call.

mouse (*n.,* mous; *v.,* mouz) *n. pl.,* **mice.** **1.** a small rodent usually having a pointed snout, relatively small ears, and a thin tail. **2.** a quiet or timid person. —*v.i.,* **moused, mous·ing.** to hunt for or catch mice.

Mourning dove

mous·er (mou′zər) *n.* an animal, especially a cat, that catches mice.

mouse·trap (mous′trap′) *n.* a trap for catching mice.

mousse (mo͞os) *n.* a chilled dessert consisting of whipped cream or beaten egg whites combined with a flavoring.

mous·tache (məs tash′, mus′tash) another spelling of **mustache.**

mous·y (mou′sē) *adj.,* **mous·i·er, mous·i·est.** **1.** of, resembling, or suggesting a mouse, especially in color: *mousy brown hair.* **2.** timid and quiet as a mouse. **3.** infested with mice.

mouth (*n.,* mouth; *v.,* mou̲th) *n. pl.,* **mouths** (mou̲thz). **1.** an opening through which a person or animal takes in food and through which sounds are uttered. **2.** an opening resembling a mouth: *the mouth of a jar, the mouth of a volcano.* **3.** the part of a river where it empties into another body of water. —*v.t.* **1.** to pronounce or speak without believing or understanding; say or repeat automatically: *to mouth someone else's opinions.* **2.** to speak or say words in a pompous affected manner.

　down at the mouth. *Informal.* unhappy; sad.

mouth·ful (mouth′fool′) *n. pl.,* **mouth·fuls.** **1.** an amount of food that is or can be held in the mouth at one time. **2.** a word or phrase that is difficult to pronounce: *That name is quite a mouthful.*

mouth organ, another term for **harmonica.**

mouth·piece (mouth′pēs′) *n.* **1.** a piece or part, as of a musical instrument, telephone, or cigarette, that is placed between or close to the lips. **2.** *Informal.* a person who acts as spokesman for a person or group.

mouth·wash (mouth′wôsh′, mouth′wosh′) *n.* a liquid used to clean the mouth or to sweeten the breath.

mov·a·ble (mo͞o′və bəl) *also,* **move·a·ble.** *adj.* **1.** that can be moved. **2.** that changes from one date to another in different years: *Thanksgiving is a movable holiday.* —*n.* any furnishing or piece of furniture that can be moved.

move (mo͞ov) *v.,* **moved, mov·ing.** —*v.i.* **1.** to change place, position, or direction: *to move to a different seat.* **2.** to change the location of a home or business: *to move to another city.* **3.** to go forward; advance; progress: *Time moves quickly when you're having a good time.* **4.** to live or circulate; be active: *The society columnist moved in a world of banquets, parties, and receptions.* **5.** to make a formal motion, as in a court or legislative assembly: *to move for adjournment.* **6.** in games such as chess and checkers, to change the position of a playing piece. —*v.t.* **1.** to change the location, position, or direction of: *Move the chair away from the door.* **2.** to put or keep in motion: *Wind moves the windmill.* **3.** to cause or urge: *He was moved by curiosity to open the package.* **4.** to affect

at; āpe; cär; end; mē; it; īce; hot; ōld; fôrk; wood; fo͞ol; oil; out; up; turn; sing; thin; **th**is; hw in white; zh in treasure. The symbol ə stands for the sound of **a** in about, **e** in taken, **i** in pencil, **o** in lemon, and **u** in circus.

M

with emotion; stir the feelings of: *The plea for mercy moved us deeply.* —*n.* **1.** an action planned to bring about a result; piece of strategy: *Buying those stocks when he did was a wise move.* **2.** in games such as chess and checkers, the act of moving a playing piece, or a turn to move a piece. **3.** the act of moving; movement or motion: *He was so frightened that he couldn't make a move.*

move·a·ble (mōō′və bəl) another spelling of **movable.**

move·ment (mōōv′mənt) *n.* **1.** the act or process of moving. **2.** a mechanism consisting of many closely associated moving parts, as in a watch. **3.** the efforts or actions of a group of people to achieve some goal: *a civil rights movement, the labor movement.* **4.** a course or tendency; trend: *a movement toward a casual, informal life style.* **5.** *Music.* **a.** one of the main divisions or sections of a sonata, symphony, or other long musical composition. **b.** see **tempo** *(def. 1).* **c.** rhythm.

mov·er (mōō′vər) *n.* **1.** a person or thing that moves. **2.** a person whose work is moving the furniture and belongings of others, especially from one house or office to another.

mov·ie (mōō′vē) *n.* **1.** a motion picture. **2.** *usually,* **movies.** a motion-picture theater. **3. movies.** the motion-picture industry.

mov·ing (mōō′ving) *adj.* **1.** that moves: *a moving target.* **2.** that causes or produces action or motion: *Jim was the moving force behind the charity drive at school.* **3.** stirring or affecting the emotions; touching: *The mother made a moving plea for her son's life.* **4.** used or hired to move furniture and belongings: *a moving van, a moving company.* —**mov′ing·ly,** *adv.*

moving picture, another term for **motion picture.**

mow¹ (mō) *v.,* **mowed, mowed** or **mown, mow·ing.** —*v.t.* **1.** to cut (grass, grain, hay, or the like) with a scythe or machine. **2.** to cut the grass, grain, or hay from: *to mow a lawn.* —*v.i.* to cut grass, grain, hay, or the like. [Old English *māwan.*] —**mow′er,** *n.*

mow² (mou) *n.* **1.** the part of a barn where hay and grain are stored. **2.** a pile or stack of hay or grain. [Old English *mūga, mūha, mūwa* heap, pile.]

Mo·zam·bique (mō′zəm bēk′) *n.* a country in southeastern Africa, formerly a Portuguese possession. Capital, Maputo. Area, 302,330 sq. mi. Pop. (1980), 10, 470,000.

Mo·zart, Wolf·gang A·ma·de·us (mōt′särt; woolf′-gang ä′mə dā′əs) 1756–1791, Austrian composer.

moz·za·rel·la (mot′sə rel′ə, mōt′sə rel′ə) *n.* a soft, white cheese with a slightly acid, walnut flavor.

MP 1. Military Police. **2.** Member of Parliament.

mph, miles per hour.

Mr. (mis′tər) *pl.,* **Messrs.** Mister. ▲ a form of address used before a man's name: *Mr. Simpson.*

Mrs. (mis′iz) *pl.,* **Mmes.** ▲ a form of address used before a married woman's name: *Mrs. Simpson.*

MS *pl.,* **MSS.** manuscript.

Ms. (miz, em′es′) *pl.,* **Mses.** ▲ a form of address used before a woman's name: *Ms. Simpson.*

M.S. *also,* **M.Sc.** Master of Science.

Msgr., Monsignor.

MST., Mountain Standard Time.

Mt. 1. Mount. **2.** mountain.

much (much) *adj.,* **more, most.** great in quantity, amount, or degree: *much money, much rain, much fun, much trouble.* —*adv.,* **more, most. 1.** to a great extent or degree: *He was much disturbed by her behavior.* **2.** just about; nearly; largely: *We feel much the same as you do.* —*n.* **1.** a great amount or quantity: *Much has been written on that subject.* **2.** anything noteworthy or important: *He's not much of a tennis player.*

mu·ci·lage (myōō′sə lij) *n.* **1.** a clear, brownish glue used especially on paper and cardboard. **2.** any of several gluey substances produced by certain plants.

muck (muk) *n.* **1.** any dirty, moist, sticky, or slimy substance, such as mud or manure. **2.** *Informal.* anything messy or disgusting. **3.** a black soil consisting chiefly of decayed plant matter.

muck·rake (muk′rāk′) *v.i.,* **muck·raked, muck·rak·ing.** to search for and expose corruption in government or society. —**muck′rak′er,** *n.*

mu·cous (myōō′kəs) *adj.* **1.** containing or secreting mucus. **2.** of or like mucus: *a mucous secretion.*

mucous membrane, a membrane that secretes mucus and that lines the mouth, throat, and other body passages and cavities open to the outside. The respiratory and digestive tracts are lined with mucous membranes.

mu·cus (myōō′kəs) *n.* a slimy fluid secreted by the mucous membranes, serving to coat and protect the inner surfaces of the mouth, throat, and other body passages and cavities.

mud (mud) *n.* **1.** soft, wet, sticky earth or dirt. **2.** this earth or dirt after it has dried and hardened: *a house of mud and straw.*

mud·dle (mud′əl) *n.* a state of confusion; mess: *He made a muddle of his financial affairs.* —*v.,* **mud·dled, mud·dling.** —*v.t.* to bring to a state of confusion; mix up: *to muddle the issues in a debate.* —*v.i.* to think or act in a confused or bungling manner: *to muddle through a problem.*

mud·dle·head·ed (mud′əl hed′id) *adj.* confused or bungling.

mud·dy (mud′ē) *adj.,* **mud·di·er, mud·di·est. 1.** covered or spattered with mud; full of mud: *a muddy road, a muddy raincoat.* **2.** clouded or dull with mud; not clear or pure: *a muddy pond.* **3.** vague or unclear; muddled: *a muddy style of writing.* —*v.t.,* **mud·died, mud·dy·ing. 1.** to cover or spatter with mud; get mud on: *Don't muddy your new shoes.* **2.** to make cloudy or dull: *to muddy the waters of a stream.* **3.** to make vague or unclear: *to muddy an issue.* —**mud′di·ness,** *n.*

mud puppy, a salamander found in fresh waters of North America, having three pairs of red, external gills.

mud·sling·ing (mud′sling′ing) *n.* the practice of making malicious charges against an opponent, especially against a political rival. —**mud′sling′er,** *n.*

mu·ez·zin (myōō ez′in) *n.* in Muslim communities, the public crier who calls the people to prayer.

muff (muf) *n.* **1.** a fluffy cylinder of fur or other material, designed so that one hand can be slipped in at each end for warmth. **2.** a mistake or missed opportunity. —*v.t.* to fail at or miss: *He had his chance, and he muffed it.* —*v.i.* to make a mistake or miss an opportunity.

muf·fin (muf′in) *n.* **1.** a light bread made of batter containing eggs, baked in individual portions, and usually served with butter. **2.** see **English muffin.**

muf·fle (muf′əl) *v.t.,* **muf·fled, muf·fling. 1.** to deaden or soften (a sound): *She muffled her sobs behind a handkerchief.* **2.** to wrap or cover so as to deaden or soften the sound of (something): *to muffle a hammer with a towel.* **3.** to wrap up or cover for protection or warmth; bundle: *The child was all muffled up in a sweater, scarf, and heavy blanket.*

—Muff

Muff

muf·fler (muf′lər) *n.* **1.** a scarf of wool or other material, worn around the neck for warmth. **2.** a device that reduces the noise from an engine exhaust, as in an automobile.

muf·ti (muf′tē) *n.* street dress or plain clothes, especially when worn by a person who usually wears a uniform.

mug (mug) *n.* **1.** a large, heavy drinking cup. **2.** the contents of a mug; as much as a mug holds: *to drink a mug of beer.* **3.** *Slang.* a person's mouth or face. —*v.t.*, **mugged, mug·ging.** to assault (a person) with intent to rob. —**mug′ger,** *n.*

mug·ging (mug′ing) *n.* a crime in which someone is assaulted and robbed.

mug·gy (mug′ē) *adj.,* **mug·gi·er, mug·gi·est.** warm, humid, and stifling: *a hot, muggy day with no breeze.* —**mug′gi·ness,** *n.*

mug·wump (mug′wump′) *n.* a person who is independent in politics.

Mu·ham·mad (moo ham′əd) *also,* **Mo·ham·med, Ma·hom·et.** 570?–632, Arab prophet and religious leader, the founder of Islam.

Muk·den (mook′dən) *n.* a city in northeastern China. Pop. (1965 est.), 4,000,000.

mu·lat·to (mə lat′ō) *n. pl.,* **mu·lat·toes. 1.** a person who is of mixed white and Negro ancestry. **2.** a person who has one white parent and one Negro parent.

mul·ber·ry (mul′ber′ē) *n. pl.,* **mul·ber·ries. 1.** any of various trees bearing sweet, edible fruit similar to the blackberry. The leaves of some mulberries are fed to silkworms. **2.** the fruit of any of these trees. **3.** a dark reddish-purple color. —*adj.* having the color mulberry; dark reddish-purple.

mulch (mulch) *n. pl.,* **mulch·es.** any of various loose, porous materials, such as straw, leaves, grass, or manure, spread around plants to protect them against loss of moisture or sharp changes in temperature, to help prevent soil erosion, and to slow the growth of weeds. —*v.t.* to cover with mulch.

mulct (mulkt) *v.t.* **1.** to punish by a fine or penalty. **2.** to swindle (someone) out of something: *He mulcted the old man of his savings.* —*n.* any fine or penalty.

mule[1] (myōōl) *n.* **1.** a large-eared animal produced by crossbreeding a female horse with a male donkey. Mules are frequently used as pack animals and for farm work. **2.** *Informal.* a person who is very stubborn. **3.** a machine that spins fiber into yarn and winds it on spindles. [Old French *mul.*]

mule[2] (myōōl) *n.* a slipper that leaves the back of the heel uncovered. [Middle French *mule.*]

Mule[1]

mule deer, a deer of North America having a tawny-gray coat and large ears.

mule skinner *Informal.* a person who drives mules.

mu·le·teer (myōō′lə tēr′) *n.* a person who is in charge of mules.

mul·ish (myōō′lish) *adj.* stubborn; obstinate. —**mul′ish·ly,** *adv.* —**mul′ish·ness,** *n.*

mull[1] (mul) *v.t.* to think about at length; ponder: *The witness mulled the question over in his mind before answering.* [Probably from Middle English *mullen* to grind to a powder or dust.]

mull[2] (mul) *v.t.* to sweeten, heat, and add spices to (wine, cider, or other beverage). [Of uncertain origin.]

mul·lah (mul′ə, mool′ə) *n.* a Muslim religious leader, especially one versed in religious law.

mul·lein (mul′ən) *also,* **mul·len.** *n.* a tall plant having coarse, woolly leaves and yellow flowers.

mul·let (mul′it) *n. pl.,* **mul·lets** or **mul·let.** any of a group of saltwater and freshwater food fish having a gray, red, or striped torpedo-shaped body.

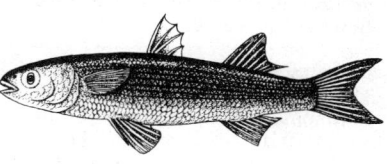

Mullet

multi- *prefix* **1.** more than one or two; many: *multicolored.* **2.** many times over: *multimillionaire.*

mul·ti·col·ored (mul′ti kul′ərd) *adj.* of many or various colors: *a multicolored shirt.*

mul·ti·far·i·ous (mul′tə fer′ē əs) *adj.* having much variety; diverse: *The students in our class have multifarious interests and hobbies.*

mul·ti·form (mul′tə fôrm′) *adj.* having many different forms or appearances.

mul·ti·lat·er·al (mul′ti lat′ər əl) *adj.* **1.** involving or participated in by three or more nations or governments: *a multilateral treaty.* **2.** having many sides; many-sided.

mul·ti·mil·lion·aire (mul′ti mil′yə ner′) *n.* a person who has several millions of some unit of currency, especially dollars.

mul·ti·ple (mul′tə pəl) *adj.* made up of or involving many or more than one: *multiple fractures.* —*n.* a number that is a product of a given number and an integer. The numbers 8, 12, and 16 are multiples of 4.

● Many of the words in this dictionary have **multiple meanings.** The ability of a word to convey more than one meaning is one of the basic and most important characteristics of language. Every word in our language originally had only one meaning. The problem of the need to define new concepts, objects, and actions, which a growing and changing civilization produces, is solved by borrowing words from other languages, by coining new words, or by creating new meanings for existing words. A foreign word or new word would not be immediately understood by most people. A new meaning of an existing word would be clearer because the word itself is familiar and because our knowledge of the original meaning would give us a clue as to what the new meaning describes. For instance, the original meaning of the word *arm* is "the upper limb of the human body." All the other meanings of *arm* in our language developed from this meaning, such as *the arm of a monkey, the arm of a dress, the arm of a chair, an arm of the sea,* and *an arm of the government.*

Some basic words may have several hundred meanings. The word *run* is an example of a basic word whose original meaning has been extended to stand for a very large number of new meanings. The *Oxford English Dictionary,* which is the most complete dictionary of our language, lists over 450 definitions of *run,* including nouns, verbs, idioms, and adjectives. One typical modern dictionary gives 172 separate definitions of the word *run.* If you look up the word *run* in this dictionary, you will see that we have included 83 meanings, omitting those definitions that are rare, highly technical, or obsolete.

The process of adding new meanings to existing words

at; āpe; cär; end; mē; it; īce; hot; ōld; fôrk; wood; fōōl; oil; out; up; turn; sing; thin; this; hw in white; zh in treasure. The symbol ə stands for the sound of a in about, e in taken, i in pencil, o in lemon, and u in circus.

has allowed the scope of our language to grow continually, while limiting the confusion that the addition of entirely new words would cause.

multiple sclerosis, a disease of the nervous system characterized by the destruction of small areas of the brain and spinal cord, leading to eventual paralysis.

mul·ti·pli·cand (mul'tə plə kand') *n.* a number or algebraic expression that is to be multiplied by another.

mul·ti·pli·ca·tion (mul'tə pli kā'shən) *n.* **1.** the process of adding a number to itself a certain number of times. **2.** the act or process of multiplying or increasing. —**mul'ti·pli·ca'tive,** *adj.*

mul·ti·plic·i·ty (mul'tə plis'ə tē) *n. pl.,* **mul·ti·plic·i·ties.** a great number or variety.

mul·ti·pli·er (mul'tə plī'ər) *n.* **1.** a number or algebraic expression by which another is to be multiplied. **2.** a person or thing that multiplies or causes an increase.

mul·ti·ply (mul'tə plī') *v.,* **mul·ti·plied, mul·ti·ply·ing.** —*v.i.* **1.** to perform multiplication. **2.** to grow in number or quantity, as by reproduction: *Rabbits multiply rapidly.* —*v.t.* **1.** to perform multiplication with (numbers or algebraic expressions). **2.** to cause to increase in number or quantity.

mul·ti·tude (mul'tə tōōd', mul'tə tyōōd') *n.* a great number of people or things: *The prophet had a multitude of followers. She has a multitude of problems.*

mul·ti·tu·di·nous (mul'tə tōōd'ən əs, mul'tə tyōōd'ən əs) *adj.* of, like, or forming a multitude. —**mul'ti·tu'di·nous·ly,** *adv.*

mum (mum) *adj.* silent; quiet: *Keep mum about this.* **mum's the word.** keep silent.

mum·ble (mum'bəl) *v.,* **mum·bled, mum·bling.** —*v.t.* to speak (words) low and indistinctly with or as if with the mouth partly closed: *The shy boy mumbled his name.* —*v.i.* to speak low and indistinctly: *to mumble to oneself.* —*n.* a low, indistinct sound or utterance. —**mum'bler,** *n.* —**mum'bling,** *n.*

mum·ble·ty·peg (mum'bəl tē peg') *also,* **mum·ble·dy·peg** (mum'bəl dē peg'). *n.* a game in which one or more players throw or drop a knife from various positions in such a way that it sticks in the ground. Also, **mum·bly·peg** (mum'blē peg').

mum·mer (mum'ər) *n.* **1.** a person who wears a mask or costume, as for a parade or celebration. **2.** an actor.

mum·mi·fy (mum'ə fī') *v.,* **mum·mi·fied, mum·mi·fy·ing.** —*v.t.* to make into a mummy by embalming. —*v.i.* to dry, shrivel up, or become lifeless like a mummy. —**mum'mi·fi·ca'tion,** *n.*

mum·my (mum'ē) *n. pl.,* **mum·mies.** a dead body embalmed and dried for preservation, especially in the manner of the ancient Egyptians.

mumps (mumps) *n.* a contagious disease caused by a virus, characterized by painful swelling of the salivary glands at the sides of the face.

munch (munch) *v.t., v.i.* to chew or eat noisily: *to munch a carrot, to munch on a sandwich.*

mun·dane (mun dān', mun'dān) *adj.* **1.** of or relating to what is practical, common, or ordinary: *the mundane problem of earning a living. He was bored by the mundane life he led.* **2.** of this world; earthly.

Mu·nich (myōō'nik) *n.* a city in southern West Germany. Pop. (1970), 1,293,600.

mu·nic·i·pal (myōō nis'ə pəl) *adj.* of or relating to the local government or affairs of a city, town, or other community: *a municipal election.* —**mu·nic'i·pal·ly,** *adv.*

mu·nic·i·pal·i·ty (myōō nis'ə pal'ə tē) *n. pl.,* **mu·nic·i·pal·i·ties.** a city, town, or other community having local self-government.

mu·nif·i·cent (myōō nif'ə sənt) *adj.* very generous: *a munificent gift, a munificent person.* —**mu·nif'i·cence,** *n.* —**mu·nif'i·cent·ly,** *adv.*

mu·ni·tion (myōō nish'ən) *n. usually,* **munitions.** military supplies, such as guns, ammunition, or bombs. —*v.t.* to provide with munitions.

Mün·ster (moon'stər) *n.* a city in northwestern West Germany. Pop. (1969 est.), 204,600.

mu·ral (myoor'əl) *n.* a picture painted directly on a wall or ceiling. —*adj.* **1.** placed, fixed, or done on a wall or ceiling. **2.** of, relating to, or resembling a wall.

mur·der (mur'dər) *n.* **1.** the unlawful and intentional killing of a human being. **2.** *Informal.* a person or thing that is very difficult, trying, or dangerous: *It was murder to travel on the overcrowded train.* —*v.t.* **1.** to kill (a human being) unlawfully and intentionally. **2.** to abuse, mangle, or mar: *to murder the English language.* —*v.i.* to commit murder. —**mur'der·er, mur'der·ess,** *n.*

mur·der·ous (mur'dər əs) *adj.* **1.** of, relating to, or characterized by murder: *a murderous attack.* **2.** capable of or threatening murder: *There was a murderous gleam in the criminal's eyes.* **3.** very difficult, trying, or dangerous: *The mountain climber undertook the murderous descent to the valley below. The teacher gave a murderous history test.* —**mur'der·ous·ly,** *adv.*

murk (murk) *n.* darkness or gloom.

murk·y (mur'kē) *adj.,* **murk·i·er, murk·i·est.** dark, gloomy, or cloudy: *the murky waters of the muddy river.* —**murk'i·ness,** *n.*

mur·mur (mur'mər) *n.* **1.** a low, continuous sound: *the murmur of the wind in the trees.* **2.** a soft, low voice or spoken sound: *She gave a murmur of approval.* **3.** a faint sound of discontent or protest; grumble: *to accept a punishment without a murmur.* —*v.i.* **1.** to make a murmur. **2.** to make a faint sound of discontent or protest. —*v.t.* to say in a soft, low voice: *The boy murmured his apologies.* —**mur'mur·er,** *n.*

mur·rain (mur'in) *n.* an infectious disease of cattle, usually fatal, that is caused by a tick.

Mus·cat (mus'kat) *n.* the capital of Oman, in the northern part of the country. Pop. (1973 est.), 6500.

Muscat and Oman, see **Oman.**

mus·cle (mus'əl) *n.* **1.** a body tissue made up of fibers that are capable of contracting to produce motion or apply force. **2.** one of the organs of the body composed of these tissues, especially one that is attached by tendons to bones and that functions to move part of the body. **3.** strength or force, especially bodily strength: *He lacks the muscle to do that heavy work.*

mus·cle·bound (mus'əl·bound') *adj.* having tight or overdeveloped muscles, as from too much exercise.

Mus·co·vite (mus'kə vīt') *n.* a person who was born or is living in Moscow or, formerly, in Russia.

Mus·co·vy (mus'kə vē) *n.* a former name for **Russia.**

mus·cu·lar (mus'kyə lər) *adj.* **1.** of, relating to, or involving muscles: *muscular coordination.* **2.** having well-developed muscles; strong: *a muscular young man.* **3.** composed or consisting of muscle: *the muscular system.* —**mus·cu·lar·i·ty** (mus'kyə lar'ə tē), *n.*

Striated

Smooth

Cardiac

Types of muscles

muscular dys·tro·phy (dis′trə fē) a disease that is characterized by a gradual weakening and wasting away of the muscles. It usually begins in early childhood and is usually fatal.

mus·cu·la·ture (mus′kyə lə chər) *n.* the arrangement of the muscles in the body or in a particular part of the body.

muse (myōōz) *v.i.*, **mused, mus·ing.** to think, reflect, or meditate: *to muse on the events of the day.*

Muse (myōōz) *n.* **1.** *Greek Mythology.* any of the nine goddesses of the arts and sciences. **2. muse.** a spirit or other source of genius or inspiration.

mu·se·um (myōō zē′əm) *n.* a building or place where objects of value or interest, as in the fields of art, science, history, or natural history, are preserved and displayed.

mush¹ (mush) *n.* **1.** a thick porridge made by boiling corn meal. **2.** any soft, thick mass. **3.** *Informal.* anything overly sentimental or romantic. [Probably a form of *mash.*]

mush² (mush) *interj.* go or go faster. ▲ said as an order to a team of dogs pulling a sled. —*v.i.* to travel by dog sled. [Possibly from French *marche* go.] —**mush′er,** *n.*

mush·room (mush′rōōm′, mush′room′) *n.* any of various fungus plants usually shaped like an umbrella. Some mushrooms can be eaten; others are poisonous. —*v.i.* **1.** to spring up or grow suddenly and rapidly: *Buildings mushroomed all over the area.* **2.** to spread out into the shape of a mushroom: *The cloud of smoke from the explosion mushroomed in the sky.*

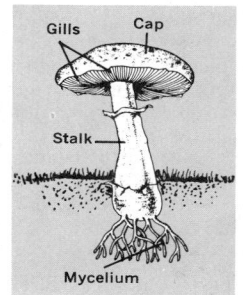

Mushroom

mush·y (mush′ē) *adj.*, **mush·i·er, mush·i·est. 1.** like mush in consistency; soft and thick. **2.** *Informal.* overly sentimental or romantic. —**mush′i·ness,** *n.*

mu·sic (myōō′zik) *n.* **1.** a pleasing or harmonious combination of sounds. **2.** the art of producing and arranging pleasing and expressive combinations of sounds, usually according to principles of rhythm, melody, harmony, and the like. **3.** a musical composition: *Does the pianist know the music to that song?* **4.** the written or printed score of a musical composition: *Jim can read music.* **5.** any pleasant sound or series of sounds: *Her words of welcome were music to his ear.*

mu·si·cal (myōō′zi kəl) *adj.* **1.** of, relating to, or producing music: *a musical instrument.* **2.** set to or accompanied by music: *the musical show.* **3.** pleasant to hear: *the musical sounds of children's laughter.* **4.** fond of or skilled in the performance of music. —*n.* a musical comedy or other musical play. —**mu′si·cal·ly,** *adv.*

musical comedy, a show or play made up of songs, dances, and spoken dialogue.

mu·si·cale (myōō′zi kal′) *n.* a party or other social gathering featuring musical entertainment.

music box, a box or case containing a device that produces a tune mechanically.

music hall, an auditorium or hall for musical performances.

mu·si·cian (myōō zish′ən) *n.* a person skilled in or professionally engaged in the performance or composition of music. —**mu·si′cian·ship′,** *n.*

mu·si·col·o·gy (myōō′zi kol′ə jē) *n.* the study of the history, theory, and forms of music. —**mu′si·col′o·gist,** *n.*

musk (musk) *n.* **1.** an oily, strong-smelling substance obtained from a gland of the male musk deer. Musk is used in making perfumes, medicine, and soaps. **2.** any similar substance made by man or obtained from certain other animals, such as the muskrat or civet cat. **3.** the odor of musk.

musk deer, a hornless deer of central and eastern Asia, the male of which has a gland that secretes musk.

mus·kel·lunge (mus′kə lunj′) *n. pl.*, **mus·kel·lunge.** a large, greenish-brown freshwater game fish related to the pike, found especially in the Great Lakes.

Muskellunge

mus·ket (mus′kit) *n.* a long-barreled gun fired from the shoulder, used before rifles were invented.

mus·ket·eer (mus′ki tēr′) *n.* **1.** a soldier armed with a musket. **2.** a member of the king's guard in seventeenth-century France.

mus·ket·ry (mus′ki trē) *n.* the art or skill of firing muskets or rifles.

musk·mel·on (musk′mel′ən) *n.* **1.** any of several large fruits that can be eaten, such as the cantaloupe, having a hard rind, sweet juicy flesh, and small flat seeds in the center. **2.** any trailing or climbing vine bearing such a fruit.

musk ox, an animal somewhat like a buffalo, native to northern Canada and Greenland, and having a shaggy, dark brown or black coat. It gives off a musky odor during the mating season.

Musk ox

musk·rat (musk′rat′) *n. pl.*, **musk·rat** or **musk·rats. 1.** a North American water rodent having webbed hind feet, a flat tail, a musky odor, and a coat of glossy, dark brown fur. **2.** the fur of this animal.

musk·y (mus′kē) *adj.*, **musk·i·er, musk·i·est.** smelling like musk: *a musky odor.* —**musk′i·ness,** *n.*

Mus·lim (muz′lim, mooz′lim, moos′lim) *also,* **Mus·lem, Mos·lem.** *adj.* of, relating to, or characteristic of Islam or its culture. —*n.* a follower of Islam. Also, **Mohammedan, Mahometan.**

mus·lin (muz′lin) *n.* any of a large group of cotton fabrics, varying from lightweight, sheer materials used for such items as blouses, to heavyweight materials used for sheets and pillowcases.

muss (mus) *Informal. v.t.* to make disordered or untidy; mess: *The sudden gust of wind mussed his hair.* —*n.* a disorder; mess.

mus·sel (mus′əl) *n.* **1.** a saltwater animal related to the clam, having a soft body protected by a bluish-black shell of two hinged parts. **2.** a freshwater animal related to the clam, found in lakes and streams of the central United States.

at; āpe; cär; end; mē; it; īce; hot; ōld; fôrk; wood; fōōl; oil; out; up; turn; sing; thin; this; hw in white; zh in treasure. The symbol ə stands for the sound of **a** in about, **e** in taken, **i** in pencil, **o** in lemon, and **u** in circus.

M

Mus·so·li·ni, Be·ni·to (moos′ə lē′nē, mōō′sə lē′nē; bə nē′tō) 1883–1945, the Fascist dictator of Italy from 1922 to 1943.

Mus·sul·man (mus′əl mən) *n. pl.,* **Mus·sul·mans.** *Archaic.* another word for **Muslim.**

muss·y (mus′ē) *adj.,* **muss·i·er, muss·i·est.** *Informal.* disordered or untidy; messy: *mussy hair.*

must (must) *auxiliary verb* **1.** to be obliged or bound: *I must return the book I borrowed from him.* **2.** to be forced or required, as by necessity: *A person must eat to survive.* **3.** to be likely or certain to: *He must have forgotten about the meeting.* —*n. Informal.* anything necessary or essential: *Gloves are a must in that icy climate.*

mus·tache (mus′tash, məs tash′) *also,* **mous·tache.** *n.* a growth of hair on the upper lip.

mus·ta·chio (məs tash′ō) *n. pl.,* **mus·ta·chios.** another word for **mustache.**

mus·tang (mus′tang) *n.* a wild horse of the American plains.

mus·tard (mus′tərd) *n.* **1.** a pungent, yellowish paste or powder made from the seeds of a plant and used as a seasoning. **2.** the plant itself, bearing yellow flowers. —*adj.* designating a family of plants growing in temperate parts of the world, including many common vegetables, such as broccoli, cabbage, and turnip.

mus·ter (mus′tər) *v.t.* **1.** to call forth from within oneself; collect or summon: *to muster up one's strength.* **2.** to gather or call together; assemble: *to muster troops.* **3.** to dismiss or discharge (someone), especially from military service. —*n.* **1.** the act of gathering or calling troops together for military inspection or service. **2.** the list of those so gathered together.

must·n't (mus′ənt) must not.

mus·ty (mus′tē) *adj.,* **mus·ti·er, mus·ti·est.** **1.** having a stale or moldy odor or taste: *The damp cellar smelled musty.* **2.** out-of-date; old-fashioned: *a musty law, musty beliefs.* —**mus′ti·ness,** *n.*

mu·ta·ble (myōō′tə bəl) *adj.* liable or likely to change; variable; changeable. —**mu′ta·bil′i·ty,** *n.*

mu·tant (myōōt′ənt) *n.* see **mutation** *(def. 2).*

mu·tate (myōō′tāt) *v.t., v.i.,* **mu·tat·ed, mu·tat·ing.** to undergo or cause to undergo change, especially by mutation.

mu·ta·tion (myōō tā′shən) *n.* **1.** a sudden change in a gene that affects the offspring and is inheritable. **2.** a new variety of animal or plant produced by such a change. **3.** a change; variation.

mute (myōōt) *adj.* **1.** unable to speak as a result of a birth defect or an injury. **2.** refusing to speak; not speaking; silent: *The accused man sat mute, offering nothing in his own defense.* **3.** *Language.* not pronounced; silent. The *b* in *lamb* is mute. —*n.* **1.** a person who is unable to speak. **2.** a device inserted in or put on a musical instrument to muffle or soften the tone. —*v.t.,* **mut·ed, mut·ing.** to muffle or soften the sound of (a musical instrument): *to mute a trumpet.* —**mute′ly,** *adv.* —**mute′ness,** *n.*

mu·ti·late (myōōt′əl āt′) *v.t.,* **mu·ti·lat·ed, mu·ti·lat·ing.** **1.** to deform or injure seriously, as by removing a limb; maim. **2.** to damage or disfigure; mar: *The desk was mutilated by deep scratches.* **3.** to make incomplete, imperfect, or less effective by removing an important part or parts: *The censors mutilated the film by cutting out important scenes.* —**mu′ti·la′tion,** *n.*

mu·ti·neer (myōō′tə nēr′) *n.* a person who is guilty of mutiny.

mu·ti·nous (myōōt′ə nəs) *adj.* **1.** engaged in or planning to engage in mutiny: *The mutinous sailors were thrown into the brig.* **2.** rebellious: *a mutinous spirit.* —**mu′ti·nous′ly,** *adv.*

mu·ti·ny (myōō′tə nē) *n. pl.,* **mu·ti·nies.** an open rebellion against authority, especially by sailors or soldiers against their commanding officers. —*v.i.,* **mu·ti·nied, mu·ti·ny·ing.** to engage in a mutiny; revolt against one's leaders: *Working conditions were so bad that the crew mutinied.*

mutt (mut) *n. Informal.* a dog, especially a mongrel.

mut·ter (mut′ər) *v.i.* **1.** to speak in low, unclear tones with the mouth nearly closed: *The worker muttered complaints about his boss as he completed the unpleasant job.* **2.** to complain; grumble. —*v.t.* to utter (words) in low, unclear tones. —*n.* a low, unclear sound or utterance.

mut·ton (mut′ən) *n.* the flesh from a sheep, especially one between one and two years old, used as food.

mu·tu·al (myōō′chōō əl) *adj.* **1.** done, felt, or expressed by each of two toward the other; reciprocal: *mutual defense, a mutual feeling.* **2.** of or having the same relationship toward each other: *mutual enemies.* **3.** shared; common: *They met each other through a mutual friend.* —**mu′tu·al·ly,** *adv.*

mutual fund, an investment company that sells an unlimited number of shares to the public and invests the money of its shareholders in securities.

muz·zle (muz′əl) *n.* **1.** the projecting part of the head of an animal, including the nose, mouth, and jaws; snout. **2.** a device, usually made of straps or wires, put over an animal's mouth to keep it from biting or eating. **3.** the opening at the front end of a gun, out of which the bullet or other projectile leaves the weapon. —*v.t.,* **muz·zled, muz·zling.** **1.** to put a muzzle on. **2.** to restrain or discourage (someone) from speaking; silence.

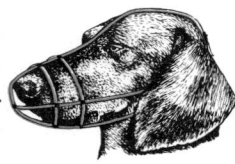

Muzzle

MVP, most valuable player: *Pat was voted our school's MVP of the year.*

my (mī) *adj.* of, belonging to, or done by me: *my brother, my raincoat, my work.*

my·ce·li·um (mī sē′lē əm) *n. pl.,* **my·ce·li·a** (mī sē′lē ə). a part of a fungus, consisting of a network of many thin, threadlike fibers.

my·col·o·gy (mī kol′ə jē) *n.* the branch of botany that studies fungi.

my·e·lin (mī′ə lin) *n.* the white, fatty substance forming a sheath around certain nerve fibers.

my·na (mī′nə) *also,* **my·nah.** *n.* any of several black or brown starlings native to Asia. Some mynas are very skillful at imitating the human voice.

my·o·pi·a (mī ō′pē ə) *n.* the inability to see things that are far away; nearsightedness. —**my·op·ic** (mī op′ik), *adj.*

myr·i·ad (mir′ē əd) *n.* a great or countless number: *Myriads of tiny creatures lived in the swampy water.* —*adj.* too numerous to count; countless.

myrrh (mur) *n.* a fragrant, yellowish-brown resin obtained from any of several tropical trees. Myrrh is used in making perfumes and products for cleaning the teeth.

myr·tle (murt′əl) *n.* **1.** any of a group of fragrant evergreen shrubs and trees bearing shiny leaves and white or pink flowers. **2.** see **periwinkle¹.**

my·self (mī self′) *pron. pl.,* **our·selves.** **1.** the form of **I** or **me** used to give emphasis: *I will do this myself.* **2.** the form used to refer back to **I** or **me** in a sentence: *I cut myself.* **3.** my usual, normal, or true self: *I haven't been myself since the accident.* ▲ **Myself** should not be used as the subject or

Myrtle

object of a sentence; **I** or **me** should be used instead: *You and I* (not *myself*) *will sing. They invited Gail and me* (not *myself*).

mys·te·ri·ous (mis tēr′ē əs) *adj.* full of, surrounded by, or suggesting mystery; difficult or impossible to explain or understand; puzzling: *There is nothing mysterious to a seaman unless it be the sea itself* (Joseph Conrad). *Mysterious happenings had been reported at the old house.* —**mys·te′ri·ous·ly,** *adv.* —**mys·te′ri·ous·ness,** *n.*

mys·ter·y (mis′tər ē) *n. pl.,* **mys·ter·ies. 1.** something that is not or cannot be known, explained, or understood: *The identity of the thief is still a mystery.* **2.** a thing or event that arouses curiosity or suspense because it is not fully explained or revealed: *It is a mystery to me how he can live so well on such a small salary.* **3.** a book, play, motion picture, or the like involving a puzzling crime, with a plot that gradually leads to the discovery of the criminal. **4.** a puzzling or secret character or quality: *An air of mystery surrounded the accident.*

mystery play, a medieval religious drama based on events in the Bible, especially in the life of Christ.

mys·tic (mis′tik) *adj.* **1.** of or relating to beliefs or practices that have hidden or secret meanings: *mystic rites.* **2.** having a hidden or secret meaning or character; mysterious: *the mystic prophecies of an oracle.* **3.** of or relating to mystics or mysticism. **4.** see **mystical** *(def. 1).* —*n.* a person who believes in or practices mysticism.

mys·ti·cal (mis′ti kəl) *adj.* **1.** having a spiritual meaning that is beyond human knowledge or understanding. **2.** of or relating to mystics or mysticism. —**mys′ti·cal·ly,** *adv.*

mys·ti·cism (mis′tə siz′əm) *n.* **1.** the doctrines, beliefs, or ideas of mystics. **2.** the doctrine that knowledge of God or absolute truth may be gained though personal spiritual experience, especially by contemplation.

mys·ti·fy (mis′tə fī′) *v.t.,* **mys·ti·fied, mys·ti·fy·ing.** to bewilder or confuse; puzzle: *The criminal's escape mystified the police.* —**mys′ti·fi·ca′tion,** *n.*

myth (mith) *n.* **1.** a traditional story that expresses a belief of a particular people, usually involving gods and heroes. A myth is an attempt to explain a natural phenomenon, a historical event, or the origin of some custom, practice, or religious belief. **2.** such accounts or stories as a group; mythology. **3.** any imaginary or fictitious person, story, or thing: *The unicorn is a myth.* **4.** an opinion, belief, or ideal that has little or no basis in truth or fact.

myth·i·cal (mith′i kəl) *adj.* **1.** of, based on, or existing only in myths: *a mythical hero, a mythical animal.* **2.** imaginary or fictitious: *The story gave a purely mythical account of the author's early life.* —**myth′i·cal·ly,** *adv.*

myth·o·log·i·cal (mith′ə loj′i kəl) *adj.* of, relating to, or found in mythology: *a mythological tale, a mythological creature.* —**myth′o·log′i·cal·ly,** *adv.*

my·thol·o·gy (mi thol′ə jē) *n. pl.,* **my·thol·o·gies. 1.** myths and legends as a group, especially a body of myths belonging to a particular ancient religion or culture: *Greek mythology.* **2.** the study of myths.

---

at; āpe; cär; end; mē; it; īce; hot; ōld; fôrk; wood; fo͞ol; oil; out; up; turn; sing; thin; **this**; hw in white; zh in treasure. The symbol ə stands for the sound of **a** in about, **e** in taken, **i** in pencil, **o** in lemon, and **u** in circus.

1. **Egyptian Hieroglyphics** ~~~

2. **Semitic** 彡乚

3. **Greek Ninth Century B.C.** 𐤍 𐤍

4. **Greek Classical Capitals** N

5. **Latin Fourth Century B.C. Capitals** Ν

6. **English** N

N is the fourteenth letter of the English alphabet. The earliest form of **N** was an Egyptian hieroglyphic (1) that was a wavy line representing water. In the ancient Semitic alphabet (2), this hieroglyphic was adapted for the letter *nun*, meaning "fish." The early Greeks borrowed *nun* and called it *nu* (3). The shape of *nu* differed from earlier forms in that the crossbar of the letter was drawn on a slant so that it connected the bottom of the first vertical stroke with the top of the second. By about the fifth century B.C., the direction of the slant of the crossbar had been reversed (4). This altered form of *nu* was simplified by the Romans (5) who, by the fourth century B.C., were writing it almost exactly as we write the capital letter **N** today (6).

n, N (en) *n. pl.,* **n's, N's.** the fourteenth letter of the English alphabet.

n (en) *n. Mathematics.* any indefinite number.

N **1.** the symbol for nitrogen. **2.** North. **3.** Northern.

n. **1.** name. **2.** noun. **3.** north. **4.** northern. **5.** noon. **6.** number.

N. **1.** North. **2.** Northern. **3.** Navy.

Na, sodium. [Modern Latin *natrium*.]

N.A., North America.

NAACP, National Association for the Advancement of Colored People.

nab (nab) *v.t.,* **nabbed, nab·bing.** *Informal.* **1.** to capture or arrest: *The police nabbed the thief before he could escape.* **2.** to snatch or steal: *The thief nabbed her purse.*

na·bob (nā′bob) *n.* a rich person.

na·celle (nə sel′) *n.* an enclosed part of an aircraft that carries the engines and sometimes the crew.

na·cre (nā′kər) *n.* another word for **mother-of-pearl.** —**na·cre·ous** (nā′krē əs), *adj.*

na·dir (nā′dər) *n.* **1.** a point in the heavens directly below the place where one stands. **2.** the lowest point: *the nadir of a career.*

nag¹ (nag) *v.,* **nagged, nag·ging.** —*v.t.* **1.** to annoy with ill-tempered scolding or complaining: *His mother was constantly nagging him about his homework.* **2.** to worry or trouble: *His conscience nagged him.* —*v.i.* **1.** to annoy with ill-tempered scolding or complaining. **2.** to be a source of worry. —*n.* a person who nags. [Probably of Scandinavian origin.] —**nag′ger,** *n.*

nag² (nag) *n.* **1.** an old, broken-down horse. **2.** *Informal.* any horse. [Middle English *nagge* pony.]

Na·ga·sa·ki (nä gə sä′kē) *n.* a city on the western coast of Kyushu, Japan. On August 9, 1945, the second atomic bomb used in warfare was dropped on this city. Pop. (1970), 421,114.

Na·go·ya (nä gô′yə) *n.* a city in Japan, on the southern coast of central Honshu. Pop. (1971 est.), 2,035,000.

Nag·pur (näg′poor) *n.* a city in central India. Pop. (1969), 876,020.

Na·hua·tl (nä′wät′əl) *n.* the language spoken by the Aztecs and various other Indian tribes in central Mexico and parts of Central America.

Na·hum (nā′əm, nā′həm) *n.* **1.** in the Old Testament, a Hebrew prophet of the seventh century B.C. **2.** a book of the Old Testament containing his prophecies.

nai·ad (nā′ad) *n. pl.,* **nai·ads** or **nai·a·des** (nā′ə dēz′). *Greek and Roman Mythology.* any of the water nymphs who were believed to live in a fountain, spring, or brook.

nail (nāl) *n.* **1.** a slender piece of metal, usually pointed at one end and enlarged and flattened at the other, used to hold or fasten wood and other materials together. **2.** the thin, hard layer that grows on the upper side of the end of a finger or toe. **3.** any similar part, such as a claw or talon. —*v.t.* **1.** to hold or fasten with a nail or nails. **2.** to hold fast or keep fixed as if with a nail: *Fear nailed him to the spot.* **3.** *Informal.* to catch or capture: *The police nailed the thief as he was about to break into a parked car.*

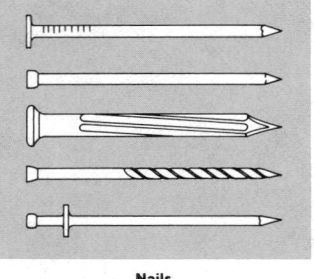

Nails

to hit the nail on the head. to say or do something exactly right.

to nail down. to make certain of; secure: *to nail down a job.*

nain·sook (nān′sook) *n.* a soft, lightweight cotton fabric.

Nai·ro·bi (nī rō′bē) *n.* the capital of Kenya, in the southern part of the country. Pop. (1970 est.), 535,200.

na·ive (nä ēv′) *also,* **na·ïve.** *adj.* simple and childlike; innocent: *He was so naive that he believed everything people told him.* —**na·ive′ly;** *also,* **na·ïve′ly,** *adv.* —**na·ive′ness;** *also,* **na·ïve′ness,** *n.*

na·ive·té (nä ēv′tā′) *also,* **na·ïve·té.** *n.* **1.** the quality or condition of being naive. **2.** a naive remark or action.

na·ked (nā′kid) *adj.* **1.** without clothing or covering; nude. **2.** stripped, as of vegetation, furnishings, or decoration; bare: *a naked room, a naked branch.* **3.** not covered or enclosed; exposed: *a naked light bulb, a naked wire.* **4.** without anything added; plain: *the naked truth.* —**na′ked·ly,** *adv.* —**na′ked·ness,** *n.*

naked eye, the eye unaided by a magnifying glass, telescope, or microscope: *The planet Pluto is not visible to the naked eye.*

nam·a·ble (nā′mə bəl) another spelling of **nameable.**

nam·by-pam·by (nam′bē pam′bē) *adj.* foolishly sentimental. —*n. pl.,* **nam·by-pam·bies.** a namby-pamby person.

name (nām) *n.* **1.** a word or words by which a person, animal, place, or thing is known or referred to. **2.** a word or phrase, usually bad, used to describe a person or thing: *The bully called him names.* **3.** reputation; character: *His constant lying has given him a bad name.* —*v.t.,* **named, nam·ing. 1.** to give a name or names to: *The young couple named their first son Anthony. The islands were named after the man who discovered them.* **2.** to mention by name; refer to by name: *The newspaper article named the people who won the awards.* **3.** to speak of; mention: *Name a few things you'd like for Christmas.* **4.** to nominate, appoint, or assign: *The President named Senator Brown to head the commission.* —**nam′er,** *n.*

　in the name of. a. on behalf of. **b.** by the authority of: *The prime minister spoke in the name of the king.*
　to one's name. belonging to one: *I don't have a cent to my name.*

name·a·ble (nā′mə bəl) *also,* **nam·a·ble.** *adj.* **1.** that can be named. **2.** worthy of being mentioned; memorable.

name·less (nām′lis) *adj.* **1.** without a name: *The newborn baby was still nameless.* **2.** not known or mentioned by name; anonymous: *a nameless author.* **3.** that cannot be identified: *nameless fears.* **4.** too terrible to be mentioned: *nameless atrocities.* —**name′less·ly,** *adv.*

name·ly (nām′lē) *adv.* that is to say; specifically: *We visited two southern states, namely Florida and Georgia.*

name·sake (nām′sāk′) *n.* a person named after or having the same name as another.

Na·mi·bi·a (nä mib′ē ə) another name for South-West Africa.

Nan·king (nan′king′), *also* **Nan·jing** (nan′jing′) *n.* a city in eastern China, on the Yangtze River, formerly the capital of the country. Pop. (1958 est.), 1,455,000.

nan·ny goat (nan′ē) *Informal.* a female goat.

Nantes (nants, nänt) *n.* a port city in western France, on the Loire River. Pop. (1978 est.), 256,693.

Na·o·mi (nā ō′mē) *n.* in the Old Testament, the mother-in-law of Ruth.

nap¹ (nap) *n.* a short sleep. —*v.i.,* **napped, nap·ping. 1.** to sleep for a short while. **2.** to be off guard or unprepared: *The teacher's question caught him napping.* [Old English *hnappian.*]

nap² (nap) *n.* a soft, fuzzy finish on cloth, formed by short fibers raised on the surface. [Middle Dutch *noppe.*]

na·palm (nā′päm) *n.* **1.** a compound used to thicken and jell gasoline. **2.** gasoline that has been thickened and jelled with this, used in incendiary bombs that break on impact and spread the flaming contents in all directions. —*v.t.* to attack with napalm.

nape (nāp, nap) *n.* the back of the neck.

na·per·y (nā′pər ē) *n.* household linens, especially tablecloths and napkins.

Naph·ta·li (naf′tə lī′) *n.* **1.** in the Old Testament, a son of Jacob. **2.** one of the twelve tribes of Israel descended from him.

naph·tha (naf′thə, nap′thə) *n.* any of several liquids made from petroleum or coal tar. Naphtha is used in cleaning fluid, fuel mixtures, and solvents, and in the manufacture of rubber, paints, and varnishes.

naph·tha·lene (naf′thə lēn′, nap′thə lēn′) *n.* a white, crystalline compound made from petroleum or coal tar, used in making moth balls.

nap·kin (nap′kin) *n.* a piece of cloth or paper, used at meals for protecting clothing or for wiping the lips, hands, or fingers.

Na·ples (nā′pəlz) *n.* **1.** a port city in southern Italy, on the Bay of Naples. Pop. (1978 est.), 1,225,377. **2. Bay of.** an inlet of the Tyrrhenian Sea, on the southwestern coast of Italy.

na·po·le·on (nə pō′lē ən) *n.* a rich, usually rectangular, pastry having cream or custard between crisp layers of pastry dough.

Na·po·le·on I (nə pō′lē ən) 1769–1821, French military leader, the emperor of France from 1804 to 1815; full name, Napoleon Bonaparte.

Napoleon III, 1808–1873, the emperor of France from 1852 to 1870, and nephew of Napoleon I; born Charles Louis Napoleon Bonaparte.

Na·po·le·on·ic (nə pō′lē on′ik) *adj.* of, relating to, or characteristic of Napoleon I or of his reign.

nar·cis·sism (när′si siz′əm) *n.* too much admiration for or love of oneself; self-love. [From *Narcissus.*]

Nar·cis·sus (när sis′əs) *n. Greek Mythology.* a handsome youth who fell in love with his own reflection in a pool. He finally died and was changed into the flower narcissus.

nar·cis·sus (när sis′əs) *n. pl.,* **nar·cis·sus·es** or **nar·cis·si** (när sis′ī). **1.** a showy yellow or white flower. **2.** a plant bearing this flower, having long, slender leaves that grow directly from an underground bulb.

nar·cot·ic (när kot′ik) *n.* a drug that dulls the senses, produces sleep, and relieves pain when used in small doses. Opium and morphine are narcotics. —*adj.* of, relating to, or caused by a narcotic or narcotics: *narcotic addiction, a narcotic stupor.*

nar·rate (nar′āt, na rāt′) *v.t.,* **nar·rat·ed, nar·rat·ing.** to tell or relate: *My friend narrated an interesting story.* —**nar′ra·tor;** *also,* **nar′rat·er,** *n.*

nar·ra·tion (na rā′shən) *n.* **1.** the act of narrating. **2.** something that is narrated, such as a story; narrative.

nar·ra·tive (nar′ə tiv) *n.* **1.** a story or account, as of an experience. **2.** the act of narrating. —*adj.* of, relating to, or containing narration: *a narrative poem.*

nar·row (nar′ō) *adj.* **1.** having little width; not broad: *We jumped across the narrow stream.* **2.** limited in extent: *He has a narrow range of interests.* **3.** barely successful; with little margin: *That was a narrow escape!* —*v.t.* to make smaller in width or extent: *The workmen narrowed the sidewalk. We've narrowed the choices down to three.* —*v.i.* to become smaller in width or extent: *The river nar-*

---

at; āpe; cär; end; mē; it; īce; hot; ōld; fôrk; wood; fōōl; oil; out; up; turn; sing; thin; this; hw in white; zh in treasure. The symbol ə stands for the sound of **a** in about, **e** in taken, **i** in pencil, **o** in lemon, and **u** in circus.

rows at the bridge. —*n. also,* **narrows.** a narrow part, as of a body of water, or a strait between two bodies of water: *A bridge was built across the narrows.* —**nar′row·ly,** *adv.* —**nar′row·ness,** *n.*

nar·row-mind·ed (nar′ō mīn′did) *adj.* having or showing a limited or prejudiced outlook; not liberal. —**nar′row-mind′ed·ly,** *adv.* —**nar′row-mind′ed·ness,** *n.*

nar·whal (när′wəl) *n.* a small toothed whale native to arctic seas. The male has a long, twisted tusk.

nar·y (ner′ē) *adj. Informal.* not one: *There's nary a hope that the sunken ship will be found.*

Narwhal

NASA (nas′ə) National Aeronautics and Space Administration.

na·sal (nā′zəl) *adj.* **1.** of, from, or relating to the nose: *nasal passage.* **2.** *Phonetics.* pronounced with the sound passing through the nose, such as the letters *m, n,* and *ng.* —*n.* a nasal sound or letter. —**na′sal·ly,** *adv.*

nas·cent (nas′ənt, nā′sənt) *adj.* in the process of coming into being; beginning to exist or develop. —**nas′cence, nas′cen·cy,** *n.*

Nash·ville (nash′vil′) *n.* the capital of Tennessee, in the central part of the state. Pop. (1970), 447,877.

Nas·sau (nas′ô) *n.* the capital and largest city of the Bahamas. Pop. (1970), 101,182.

Nas·ser, Ga·mal Ab·del (nä′sər, nas′ər; gə mäl′ab′del) 1918–1970, president of Egypt from 1956 to 1970.

na·stur·tium (nə stur′shəm) *n.* **1.** a yellow, orange, or red flower that has sharp-tasting buds and seeds sometimes used in pickling. **2.** the climbing plant bearing this flower.

nas·ty (nas′tē) *adj.,* **nas·ti·er, nas·ti·est. 1.** resulting from hate or spite; spiteful: *a nasty rumor.* **2.** disagreeable or annoying; unpleasant: *nasty weather.* **3.** seriously harmful; severe: *a nasty fall.* **4.** morally bad; indecent: *nasty language.* —**nas′ti·ly,** *adv.* —**nas′ti·ness,** *n.*

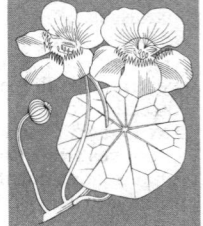

Nasturtium

na·tal (nāt′əl) *adj.* of, relating to, or dating from one's birth: *natal defects.*

na·tion (nā′shən) *n.* **1.** the people living in a particular land under one government, and sharing the same language, culture, and history. **2.** the land where such a people live; country: *The candidate campaigned throughout the nation.* **3.** a tribe or group of tribes of North American Indians.

na·tion·al (nash′ən əl) *adj.* of, belonging to, or characteristic of a nation as a whole: *a national political convention, a national costume.* —*n.* a person who is a member of a nation; citizen or subject. —**na′tion·al·ly,** *adv.*

National Guard, a reserve military force supported by each state of the United States. It is under the control of the governor, but may be put under federal control by the President in time of war or national emergency.

na·tion·al·ism (nash′ən əl iz′əm) *n.* **1.** patriotic devotion to one's nation. **2.** a desire or movement for national independence.

na·tion·al·ist (nash′ən əl ist) *adj.* favoring or supporting nationalism. Also, **na·tion·al·is·tic** (nash′ən əl is′tik). —*n.* a person who favors or supports nationalism. —**na′tion·al·is′ti·cal·ly,** *adv.*

Nationalist China, see **China** *(def. 2).*

na·tion·al·i·ty (nash′ə nal′ə tē) *n. pl.,* **na·tion·al·i·ties. 1.** the fact or state of belonging to a particular nation: *His nationality is Australian.* **2.** a group of people sharing the same language, culture, and history. **3.** the condition of being a politically independent nation.

na·tion·al·ize (nash′ən əl īz′) *v.t.,* **na·tion·al·ized, na·tion·al·iz·ing. 1.** to place under the control or ownership of a national government: *to nationalize an industry.* **2.** to extend throughout a nation; make nationwide: *The broadcasting company nationalized the television network.* —**na′tion·al·i·za′tion,** *n.*

national park, an area of land, usually with great natural beauty or historical importance, maintained by the government for public use.

National Socialism, another term for **Naziism.**

na·tion·wide (nā′shən wīd′) *also,* **na·tion-wide.** *adj.* extending throughout the nation.

na·tive (nā′tiv) *n.* **1.** a person who was born in a particular place or country: *a native of France.* **2.** an original inhabitant of a region or country. **3.** an animal or plant living or growing in a particular place: *That bird is a native of South Carolina.* —*adj.* **1.** belonging to a particular place or country: *Tom is a native New Yorker.* **2.** connected with or belonging to a person by birth: *His native language is French.* **3.** possessed from birth; natural: *She has much native intelligence.* **4.** living or growing in a particular place: *Cactus is native to desert regions.* **5.** of, relating to, or characteristic of the original inhabitants of a region or country: *She studied native tribal dances in Brazil.* **6.** occurring or found in nature in a pure state: *Native silver is very soft.* —**na′tive·ly,** *adv.*

na·tive-born (nā′tiv bôrn′) *adj.* born in the place or country indicated: *a native-born American.*

na·tiv·i·ty (nə tiv′ə tē) *n. pl.,* **na·tiv·i·ties. 1. Nativity. a.** the birth of Christ. **b.** a representation of the birth of Christ, as in painting. **c.** Christmas. **2.** birth.

natl., national.

NATO (nā′tō) North Atlantic Treaty Organization, a military alliance of fifteen Western nations, formed in 1949.

nat·ty (nat′ē) *adj.,* **nat·ti·er, nat·ti·est.** neat, trim, and stylish: *a natty new uniform.* —**nat′ti·ly,** *adv.* —**nat′ti·ness,** *n.*

nat·u·ral (nach′ər əl) *adj.* **1.** found or produced in nature; not manufactured: *a natural metal, natural rock formations.* **2.** of or relating to nature: *The professor is a natural scientist.* **3.** belonging to from birth; innate: *She has natural beauty. She is a natural athlete.* **4.** happening in the normal course of things: *The old man died from natural causes.* **5.** closely following nature; realistic; lifelike: *The portrait of his mother is very natural.* **6.** free from affectation; not forced or contrived: *He spoke in a natural voice. She has an open and natural manner.* **7.** *Music.* neither sharp nor flat. —*n.* **1.** *Music.* the sign (♮) used to cancel the effect of a preceding sharp or flat. **2.** *Informal.* a person who seems well-qualified because of special talents or other abilities: *He is a natural as an athlete.* —**nat′u·ral·ness,** *n.*

natural gas, a colorless, odorless, highly flammable gas, occurring naturally in the earth. It consists mainly of methane and is used as a fuel.

natural history, the study of things in nature, such as animals, plants, and minerals.

nat·u·ral·ist (nach′ər ə list) *n.* a person who studies natural science, especially a botanist or zoologist.

nat·u·ral·is·tic (nach′ər ə lis′tik) *adj.* closely resembling nature.

nat·u·ral·ize (nach′ər ə līz′) *v.t.,* **nat·u·ral·ized, nat·u·ral·iz·ing. 1.** to make a citizen of (a person born in a foreign country); grant citizenship to. **2.** to take in or adopt (a foreign custom or word). **3.** to adapt (an animal or plant) to another place or country. —**nat′u·ral·i·za′tion,** *n.*

nat·u·ral·ly (nach′ər ə lē) *adv.* **1.** as would be expected; of course: *Naturally I'll help you.* **2.** by nature: *She was naturally shy.* **3.** in a natural manner; without affectation: *She was too nervous to act naturally.*

natural number, the number 1 or any number produced by repeatedly adding 1 to it. The numbers 4, 37, and 592 are natural numbers.

natural resources, materials found in nature that are useful to man or necessary for his survival, such as water, forests, and minerals.

natural science, any of the sciences concerned with nature, including biology, physics, chemistry, and geology.

natural selection, the process by which animals and plants having characteristics best suited to their environment tend to survive and pass those characteristics on to their offspring.

na·ture (nā′chər) *n.* **1.** the essential character and qualities of a thing: *It is the nature of fire to be hot.* **2.** *also,* **Nature.** the forces that create and control all things in the universe: *the laws of Nature.* **3.** the entire physical universe. **4.** the disposition or temperament of a person: *He has a kindly nature.* **5.** sort; kind; variety: *She does not enjoy a book of that nature.* **6.** natural plant and animal life: *We took a walk through the woods to observe nature.*

naught (nôt) *also,* **nought.** *n.* **1.** nothing: *All our plans came to naught.* **2.** zero: *Five plus naught equals five.*

naugh·ty (nô′tē) *adj.,* **naugh·ti·er, naugh·ti·est. 1.** mischievous; disobedient: *a naughty child.* **2.** in bad taste; improper: *a naughty word.* —**naugh′ti·ly,** *adv.* —**naugh′ti·ness,** *n.*

nau·sea (nô′zē ə, nô′shə) *n.* **1.** a sick feeling in the stomach; the feeling that one is going to vomit. **2.** extreme disgust; loathing.

nau·se·ate (nô′zē āt′, nô′shē āt′) *v.,* **nau·se·at·ed, nau·se·at·ing.** —*v.t.* to produce nausea in: *The rolling of the ship nauseated the passengers.* —*v.i.* to feel nausea. —**nau′se·at′ing·ly,** *adv.* —**nau′se·a′tion,** *n.*

nau·seous (nô′shəs, nô′zē əs) *adj.* **1.** sickened; nauseated: *The child felt nauseous during the long automobile ride.* **2.** causing nausea: *a nauseous smell.* **3.** disgusting; loathsome. —**nau′seous·ly,** *adv.* —**nau′seous·ness,** *n.*

nau·ti·cal (nô′ti kəl) *adj.* of or relating to ships, seamen, or navigation. —**nau′ti·cal·ly,** *adv.*

nautical mile, a unit of distance equal to 6076.115 feet.

nau·ti·lus (nôt′əl əs) *n. pl.,* **nau·ti·lus·es** or **nau·ti·li** (nôt′əl ī′). **1.** a saltwater animal found in tropical waters, having a flattened spiral shell divided into chambers. The nautilus lives in the outermost chamber of its shell. **2.** a saltwater animal related to the octopus, the female of which has a very thin, delicate shell. Also *(def. 2),* **paper nautilus.**

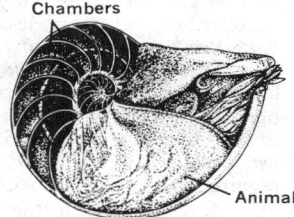

Chambers

Animal

Cutaway view of a nautilus

Nav·a·ho (nav′ə hō′) *n. pl.,* **Nav·a·hos** or **Nav·a·hoes** or **Nav·a·ho.** a member of a tribe of North American Indians living in New Mexico, Arizona, and Utah.

Nav·a·jo (nav′ə hō′) *n. pl.,* **Nav·a·jos** or **Nav·a·joes** or **Nav·a·jo.** another spelling of **Navaho.**

na·val (nā′vəl) *adj.* **1.** of or relating to a navy: *naval supplies.* **2.** having a navy: *That country was once a great naval power.* —**na′val·ly,** *adv.*

nave (nāv) *n.* the main part of a church, located between the side aisles.

na·vel (nā′vəl) *n.* a rounded scar in the middle of the abdomen that remains after the umbilical cord is cut.

navel orange, a large, seedless, sweet orange, having a mark resembling a navel.

nav·i·ga·ble (nav′i gə bəl) *adj.* **1.** able to be sailed on or through by boats or ships: *a navigable river.* **2.** capable of being steered. —**nav′i·ga·bil′i·ty,** *n.*

nav·i·gate (nav′i gāt′) *v.,* **nav·i·gat·ed, nav·i·gat·ing.** —*v.t.* **1.** to direct the course of (a boat, ship, or aircraft); pilot. **2.** to plan or direct the course of (a voyage, flight, or the like). **3.** to sail on or across (a body of water). —*v.i.* to direct the course of a boat, ship, or aircraft.

nav·i·ga·tion (nav′i gā′shən) *n.* **1.** the act or practice of navigating a boat, ship, or aircraft. **2.** the art or science of determining the position and directing the course of boats, ships, and aircraft. —**nav′i·ga′tion·al,** *adj.*

nav·i·ga·tor (nav′i gā′tər) *n.* **1.** a person who navigates. **2.** a person who has skill in or practices navigation.

na·vy (nā′vē) *n. pl.,* **na·vies. 1.** all the warships of a country. **2.** *also,* **Navy. a.** the entire military sea force of a country, including ships, land bases, equipment, and personnel. **b.** the department of government in charge of this. **3.** see **navy blue.**

navy bean, a small, dried, white bean.

navy blue, a very dark-blue color.

navy yard, a base on land used for building or repairing naval vessels.

nay (nā) *adv.* **1.** *Archaic.* no. **2.** not only that, but even: *She was disappointed, nay, heartbroken by the news.* —*n.* **1.** a negative vote or voter. **2.** a refusal or denial; no.

Naz·a·rene (naz′ə rēn′, naz′ə rēn′) *n.* **1.** a person who was born or is living in Nazareth. **2.** a member of a sect of early Christians. **3. the Nazarene.** Jesus.

Naz·a·reth (naz′ər əth) *n.* a town in Galilee, in northern Israel, where Jesus spent his youth.

Na·zi (nät′sē, nat′sē) *n. pl.,* **Na·zis. 1.** a member or follower of the fascist political party that controlled Germany under the leadership of Adolf Hitler from 1933 to 1945. **2.** a person holding views similar to those of the Nazis.

Na·zi·ism (nät′sē iz′əm, nat′sē iz′əm) *also,* **Na·zism** (nät′siz əm, nat′siz əm). *n.* the political doctrines and practices of the Nazis, including a belief in the superiority or inferiority of various racial groups, total government control of the lives of citizens, and an aggressive foreign policy. Also, **National Socialism.**

Nb, the symbol for niobium.

N.B. 1. note well. [Latin *notā bene.*] **2.** New Brunswick.

N.C., North Carolina.

Nd, the symbol for neodymium.

N. Dak., North Dakota. Also, **N.D.**

Ndja·me·na (en jä′mə nə) *n.* the capital of Chad. Pop. (1975 est.), 224,000.

Ne, the symbol for neon.

[diagram labeled: Chancel, Transept, Nave, Nave]

NE 1. northeast. 2. northeastern.

N.E., New England.

Ne·an·der·thal (nē an′dər thôl′, nē an′dər täl′) *adj.* of, relating to, or characteristic of Neanderthal man. —*n.* see **Neanderthal man.**

Neanderthal man, any of an extinct species of prehistoric man that lived in caves in Europe, North Africa, and parts of Asia during the early Stone Age.

Ne·a·pol·i·tan (nē′ə pol′it ən) *n.* a person who was born or is living in Naples. —*adj.* of or relating to Naples.

neap tide (nēp) the tide occurring at the first and third quarters of the moon, when there is the least difference between the levels of high and low tide.

near (nēr) *adv.* 1. not far in time, place, or degree: *Night is drawing near.* 2. almost; nearly: *We were near frantic with worry.* —*adj.* 1. not distant in time, place, or degree: *Will I see you in the near future?* 2. done or missed by only a slight margin: *We had a near escape from the fire.* 3. closely related or associated: *John is a near relative of ours.* —*prep.* close to or by: *They lived in a house near the beach.* —*v.t.* to come or draw near to; approach: *The airplane neared the landing field.* —*v.i.* to come or draw near or nearer. —**near′ness,** *n.*

near·by (nēr′bī′) *adj.* a short distance away; close: *a nearby town.* —*adv.* not far off: *They go to school nearby.*

Near East, a region usually regarded as including the countries of southwestern Asia, northeastern Africa, and sometimes the Balkans.

near·ly (nēr′lē) *adv.* 1. all but; practically: *I nearly forgot your birthday. It is nearly midnight.* 2. closely: *The two boys are nearly related.*

near·sight·ed (nēr′sī′tid) *adj.* able to see close objects more clearly than those that are distant; myopic. —**near′sight′ed·ly,** *adv.* —**near′sight′ed·ness,** *n.*

neat (nēt) *adj.* 1. clean and orderly; tidy: *a neat room, a neat person, neat work.* 2. attractive or pleasing in appearance: *a neat dress.* 3. done in a clever or skillful way: *That was a neat trick.* 4. *Informal.* wonderful; fine: *We had a neat time at the party.* —**neat′ly,** *adv.* —**neat′ness,** *n.*

neath (nēth) *also,* **'neath.** *prep. Archaic.* another word for **beneath.**

Nebr., Nebraska. *Also,* **Neb.**

Ne·bras·ka (ni bras′kə) *n.* a state in the central United States. Capital, Lincoln. Area, 77,227 sq. mi. Pop. (1970), 1,483,791. Abbreviations, **Nebr., Neb.** —**Ne·bras′kan,** *adj., n.*

● **Nebraska,** meaning "flat water," was the Siouan name for the Platte River. Although the river's name was changed, the Indian name survived as that of the territory and then the state.

Neb·u·chad·nez·zar (neb′ə kəd nez′ər, neb′yə kədnez′ər) died 562 B.C., the king of Babylon from 605 to 562 B.C.

neb·u·la (neb′yə lə) *n. pl.,* **neb·u·lae** (neb′yə lē′) or **neb·u·las.** a bright, cloudlike mass, composed of stars or of dust and gases, visible in the night sky. —**neb′u·lar,** *adj.*

neb·u·lous (neb′yə ləs) *adj.* 1. vague or confused; unclear: *a nebulous answer, nebulous outlines.* 2. of or relating to a nebula or nebulae. —**neb′u·lous·ly,** *adv.* —**neb′u·lous·ness,** *n.*

nec·es·sar·i·ly (nes′ə ser′ə lē) *adv.* as an inevitable result: *Tall people are not necessarily good basketball players.*

nec·es·sar·y (nes′ə ser′ē) *adj.* 1. that cannot be done without; needed; required: *Proper food and rest are necessary for good health.* 2. that cannot be avoided; certain; inevitable: *Failure was a necessary result of their poor work.* —*n. pl.,* **nec·es·sar·ies.** something that cannot be done without; necessity; essential: *the necessaries for a camping trip.*

ne·ces·si·tate (ni ses′ə tāt′) *v.t.,* **ne·ces·si·tat·ed, ne·ces·si·tat·ing.** to cause (something) to be needed or done; make necessary: *His refusal to go necessitated a change of plans.* —**ne·ces′si·ta′tion,** *n.*

ne·ces·si·ty (ni ses′ə tē) *n. pl.,* **ne·ces·si·ties.** 1. something that cannot be done without; requirement: *The poor family could afford only the basic necessities, such as food and shelter.* 2. the fact or condition of being necessary: *He realized the necessity of completing school.* 3. the fact or condition of great need.

neck (nek) *n.* 1. the part of the body of a man or animal connecting the head and the trunk. 2. the part of a garment that fits around the neck. 3. the narrow, upper part of a bottle, vase, or other container. 4. a narrow strip of land, such as an isthmus or cape. 5. the narrow part of a stringed musical instrument, such as a violin or guitar.

neck and neck. at an equal pace; even: *The two horses were running neck and neck in the race.*

to stick one's neck out. *Informal.* to take a chance or risk: *I stuck my neck out and volunteered for the task.*

neck·er·chief (nek′ər chif) *n.* a scarf or kerchief worn around the neck.

neck·lace (nek′lis) *n.* an ornament worn around the neck, such as a string or chain of beads or gems.

neck·line (nek′līn′) *n.* the upper edge of a garment at or near the neck.

neck·tie (nek′tī′) *n.* a strip of fabric worn around the neck, usually under the collar, and knotted in front. *Also,* **tie.**

neck·wear (nek′wer′) *n.* any of various articles that are worn around the neck, such as scarfs and neckties.

Neckerchief

nec·ro·man·cy (nek′rə man′sē) *n.* 1. the act of predicting the future by supposedly communicating with the dead. 2. black magic; sorcery. —**nec′ro·man′cer,** *n.*

nec·tar (nek′tər) *n.* 1. *Greek Mythology.* the drink of the gods that made all who drank it immortal. 2. any sweet and delicious drink. 3. a sweet liquid formed in many flowers, used by bees in the making of honey. —**nec′tar·ous,** *adj.*

nec·tar·ine (nek′tə rēn′) *n.* 1. a variety of peach having a smooth skin. 2. the tree that bears this fruit.

née (nā) *also,* **nee.** *adj. French.* born. ▲ used chiefly to show the maiden name of a married woman: *Mrs. Thomas Brown, née Smith.*

need (nēd) *n.* 1. the lack of something necessary, useful, or desired: *The team's defeat showed need of practice.* 2. something necessary, useful, or desired: *What are your basic needs for the camping trip?* 3. a necessity or obligation: *There is no need to stay any longer.* 4. a great desire for something: *The young painter had a need for recognition.* 5. poverty or hardship: *His great need caused him to beg.* 6. a time or condition of difficulty or trouble: *He was truly a friend in need.* —*v.t.* to have need of; lack; require: *to need new shoes, to need a room for the night.* —*v.i.* to be obligated; must. ▲ used as a helping verb in questions and in the negative: *Need she wait for him? No, she need not wait.*

if need be. if necessary.

need·ful (nēd′fəl) *adj.* needed; required; necessary: *She gave her brother needful advice.* —**need′ful·ly,** *adv.* —**need′ful·ness,** *n.*

need·i·ness (nē′dē nis) *n.* the quality or condition of being needy.

nee·dle (nēd′əl) *n.* 1. a thin, pointed steel instrument with a hole at one end through which thread is passed, used in sewing. **2.** a pointer, as on a compass or dial. **3.** the sharp, hollow tube at the end of a hypodermic syringe. **4.** a slender rod tapered at one or both ends, used in knitting. **5.** a slender instrument of metal, usually tipped with diamond, sapphire, or other hard material, mounted in a cartridge and used to transmit sound vibrations from phonograph records. **6.** something resembling a needle in shape, such as an obelisk or pinnacle. **7.** *Botany.* the needle-shaped leaf of a fir tree or pine tree. —*v.t.,* **nee·dled, nee·dling.** *Informal.* to annoy, as by constant teasing: *His friends were needling him about his girlfriend.* —**nee′dle·like′,** *adj.*

nee·dle·point (nēd′əl point′) *n.* embroidery done on canvas, usually with wool yarn.

need·less (nēd′lis) *adj.* not needed; unnecessary: *a needless expense, a needless remark.* —**need′less·ly,** *adv.* —**need′less·ness,** *n.*

nee·dle·work (nēd′əl wurk′) *n.* work done with a needle, such as embroidery.

need·n't (nēd′ənt) need not.

need·y (nē′dē) *adj.,* **need·i·er, need·i·est.** being in need or poverty: *She gave her old clothes to a needy family.*

ne'er (ner) *adv. Archaic.* another word for **never.**

ne'er-do-well (ner′dōō wel′) *n.* a worthless person; good-for-nothing. —*adj.* worthless; good-for-nothing.

ne·far·i·ous (ni fer′ē əs) *adj.* wicked; evil: *nefarious deeds, a nefarious scoundrel.* —**ne·far′i·ous·ly,** *adv.* —**ne·far′i·ous·ness,** *n.*

ne·gate (ni gāt′) *v.t.,* **ne·gat·ed, ne·gat·ing.** **1.** to keep from being effective; make ineffective; nullify: *That one mistake negated all his efforts.* **2.** to deny: *The new evidence negates the prisoner's claim of innocence.*

ne·ga·tion (ni gā′shən) *n.* **1.** the act of negating. **2.** something that negates; denial. **3.** the absence or opposite of something positive: *A lie is the negation of truth.*

neg·a·tive (neg′ə tiv) *adj.* **1.** expressing or implying denial or refusal: *His answer was negative. He gave a negative shake of his head in reply to our question.* **2.** not helpful or constructive: *She gave only negative criticism. He has a negative attitude.* **3.** less than zero: *−3 is a negative number.* **4.** *Electricity.* having more electrons than protons: *a negative charge.* **5.** *Photography.* having the areas that were light in the original subject dark, and those that were dark, light. **6.** not showing a given condition, disease, or the like: *The tests for tuberculosis were negative.* —*n.* **1.** a negative image on a photographic plate or film from which prints can be made. **2.** a word or phrase that expresses denial or refusal. "No" and "not" are negatives. **3.** the side that argues against the proposition in a debate. **4.** a negative number. —**neg′a·tive·ly,** *adv.* —**neg′a·tive·ness,** *n.*

in the negative. in a way that expresses refusal or denial: *to answer in the negative.*

Neg·ev (neg′ev) *n.* a desert region of southern Israel.

neg·lect (ni glekt′) *v.t.* **1.** to fail to give proper attention or care to: *He neglected his work. The children neglected their pets.* **2.** to fail to do; leave undone, especially through carelessness: *She cleaned the house but neglected making the beds.* —*n.* **1.** the act or instance of neglecting; negligence: *His neglect of the business caused its bankruptcy.* **2.** the condition of being neglected: *The old house had fallen into neglect.* —**neg·lect′er,** *n.*

neg·lect·ful (ni glekt′fəl) *adj.* characterized by or showing neglect: *She was neglectful of her homework.* —**neg·lect′ful·ly,** *adv.* —**neg·lect′ful·ness,** *n.*

neg·li·gee (neg′lə zhā′) *n.* a woman's loose, flowing dressing gown.

neg·li·gence (neg′li jəns) *n.* **1.** the state or quality of being negligent. **2.** an act or instance of being negligent.

neg·li·gent (neg′li jənt) *adj.* **1.** habitually neglecting to do what ought to be done; neglectful: *a negligent driver.* **2.** showing carelessness: *negligent dress.* —**neg′li·gent·ly,** *adv.*

neg·li·gi·ble (neg′li jə bəl) *adj.* not worth considering: *His contribution to the project was negligible.* —**neg′li·gi·bil′i·ty,** *n.* —**neg′li·gi·bly,** *adv.*

ne·go·tia·ble (ni gō′shə bəl) *adj.* **1.** that can be sold or transferred, as a bond. **2.** open to discussion: *a negotiable demand.* **3.** that can be gone or passed over: *a negotiable road.* —**ne·go′tia·bil′i·ty,** *n.*

ne·go·ti·ate (ni gō′shē āt′) *v.,* **ne·go·ti·at·ed, ne·go·ti·at·ing.** —*v.t.* **1.** to bring about or arrange the terms of: *The factory owners met with union leaders to negotiate a settlement of the strike.* **2.** to sell or transfer: *to negotiate securities.* **3.** to succeed in going or passing over: *The car was unable to negotiate the icy road.* —*v.i.* to have a discussion in order to bring about an agreement: *The two countries refused to negotiate.* —**ne·go′ti·a′tor,** *n.*

ne·go·ti·a·tion (ni gō′shē ā′shən) *n.* **1.** the act of negotiating. **2.** a discussion for the purpose of bringing about an agreement or sale.

Ne·gro (nē′grō) *n. pl.,* **Ne·groes.** a member of the Negroid division of the human race, including the native peoples of southern and central Africa. —*adj.* of or relating to a Negro or Negroes.

Ne·groid (nē′groid) *adj.* of or relating to one of the major divisions of the human race, whose members are characterized by dark skin, tightly curled hair, and broad features. —*n.* a member of the Negroid race.

Ne·he·mi·ah (nē′ə mī′ə) *n.* **1.** a Hebrew leader of the fifth century B.C. who rebuilt the walls of Jerusalem. **2.** the book of the Old Testament that tells his story.

Neh·ru, Ja·wa·har·lal (nä′rōō; jə wä′hər läl′) 1889–1964, Indian statesman.

neigh (nā) *n.* the characteristic cry of a horse. —*v.i.* to utter a neigh; whinny.

neigh·bor (nā′bər) *also, British,* **neigh·bour.** *n.* **1.** a person who lives near another, especially a person who lives in the house next to or near one's own. **2.** a person, place, or thing located next to another: *Mexico is a neighbor of the United States.* **3.** a fellow human being; brother: *Thou shalt love thy neighbor as thyself* (Mark 12:31).

neigh·bor·hood (nā′bər hood′) *n.* **1.** a small area or district in a town or city where people live: *an Irish-American neighborhood, a tough neighborhood.* **2.** people living in the same district: *The whole neighborhood is talking about the fire.*

in the **neighborhood of.** somewhere near; about; approximately: *Tickets to the game cost in the neighborhood of two dollars.*

neigh·bor·ing (nā′bər ing) *adj.* being next to or near; located or living nearby: *My friend comes from a neighboring town.*

neigh·bor·ly (nā′bər lē) *adj.* characteristic of a good neighbor; friendly; sociable. —**neigh′bor·li·ness,** *n.*

neigh·bour (nā′bər) *British.* another spelling of **neighbor.**

nei·ther (nē′thər, nī′thər) *conj.* **1.** not either: *When I was sick, I could neither eat nor drink.* ▲ used with **nor** before

at; āpe; cär; end; mē; it; īce; hot; ōld; fôrk; wood; fōōl; oil; out; up; turn; sing; thin; this; hw in white; zh in treasure. The symbol ə stands for the sound of **a** in about, **e** in taken, **i** in pencil, **o** in lemon, and **u** in circus.

the first of two or more negative possibilities. **2.** nor: *He doesn't want to go; neither do I.* —*adj.* not the one nor the other; not either: *Neither team played well in the game.* —*pron.* not either one: *She tried on two dresses, but neither fit her.*

Nel·son, Ho·ra·ti·o (nel'sən; hə rā'shē ō') 1758–1805, English admiral.

nem·a·tode (nem'ə tōd') *adj.* of or relating to a large group of worms having a long, round body tapering to a point at each end. —*n.* a nematode worm. Nematodes include many crop pests and parasites, such as the hookworm.

Nem·e·sis (nem'ə sis) *n. pl.,* **Nem·e·ses** (nem'ə sēz). **1.** *Greek Mythology.* the goddess of vengeance. **2. nemesis. a.** a person or thing that punishes wrongdoing. **b.** just punishment for wrongdoing.

ne·o·dym·i·um (nē'ō dim'ē əm) *n.* a yellowish metallic element of the rare-earth group. Symbol: **Nd**

ne·o·lith·ic (nē'ə lith'ik) *adj.* of, relating to, or characteristic of the last period of the Stone Age, when people developed agriculture, tamed animals, and used tools and weapons made from stone.

ne·ol·o·gism (nē ol'ə jiz'əm) *n.* a new word or a new meaning of an existing word.

ne·on (nē'on) *n.* a colorless, odorless, non-metallic element that makes up a very small part of the air. Gaseous neon is used in lights, and liquid neon is used as a cooling substance. Symbol: **Ne**

ne·o·phyte (nē'ə fīt') *n.* **1.** a new convert to a religion or denomination. **2.** a beginner; novice.

Ne·pal (nə pôl') *n.* a country in central Asia, bounded by India and Tibet. Capital, Katmandu. Area, 54,000 sq. mi. Pop. (1980 est.), 14,260,000.

neph·ew (nef'yōō) *n.* **1.** the son of a person's brother or sister. **2.** the son of a person's brother-in-law or sister-in-law.

ne·phri·tis (ni frī'tis) *n.* inflammation of the kidneys.

nep·o·tism (nep'ə tiz'əm) *n.* the giving of special favors or jobs to relatives by a person in a high or official position.

Nep·tune (nep'tōōn, nep'tyōōn) *n.* **1.** *Roman Mythology.* the god of the sea and brother of Jupiter. In Greek mythology he was called Poseidon. **2.** the fourth largest planet of the solar system and eighth in order of distance from the sun. It is invisible to the naked eye, but appears green when viewed through a telescope. Neptune has two known moons.

nep·tu·ni·um (nep tōō'nē əm, nep tyōō'nē əm) *n.* a radioactive metallic element similar to uranium, produced by bombarding uranium with neutrons. Symbol: **Np**

Ne·ro (nēr'ō) A.D. 37–68, the emperor of Rome from A.D. 54 to 68.

nerve (nurv) *n.* **1.** a bundle of fibers carrying impulses between the brain and spinal cord and other parts of the body. **2.** courage; bravery: *The little boy did not have the nerve to jump off the high diving board.* **3. nerves.** the nervous system thought of as the source of a person's state of mind: *He has unsteady nerves.* **4.** *Informal.* impudence; boldness: *You've got a lot of nerve to ask such a personal question.* **5. nerves.** emotional or physical tension; nervousness: *I always have a bad case of nerves before an exam.* —*v.t.,* **nerved, nerv·ing.** to give courage or strength to: *The boxer nerved himself for the fight.*
   to get on one's nerves. to annoy or irritate one: *His constant bragging gets on my nerves.*

nerve cell, another term for **neuron.**

nerve fiber, any of the threadlike fibers that make up neurons; an axon or dendrite.

nerve·less (nurv'lis) *adj.* **1.** lacking strength; feeble;

weak. **2.** controlled and calm; poised. **3.** *Anatomy.* having no nerves. —**nerve'less·ly,** *adv.* —**nerve'less·ness,** *n.*

nerve-rack·ing (nurv'rak'ing) *also,* **nerve-wrack·ing.** *adj.* very irritating, upsetting, or frustrating: *a nerve-racking experience.*

nerv·ous (nur'vəs) *adj.* **1.** having or showing restlessness, tension, or strain; jittery; jumpy: *Loud noises make her nervous. He is a nervous person.* **2.** fearful or timid: *I am very nervous about taking that exam.* **3.** of or relating to the nerves or nervous system: *a nervous disorder.* —**nerv'ous·ly,** *adv.* —**nerv'ous·ness,** *n.*

nervous breakdown, any severe mental or emotional disturbance.

nervous system, the system that includes the brain, spinal cord, and nerves. The nervous system controls and coordinates all the activities of the body.

nerv·y (nur'vē) *adj.,* **nerv·i·er, nerv·i·est.** *Informal.* bold and rude; sassy; impudent. —**nerv'i·ness,** *n.*

-ness *suffix* **1.** the quality, state, or condition of being: *wildness, lightness.* **2.** an act or instance of being: *kindness.*

nest (nest) *n.* **1.** a place or structure built by a bird for holding its eggs and raising its young. **2.** a place or structure used by insects, fish, turtles, or other animals for laying eggs or raising young: *a hornet's nest.* **3.** a group of birds, animals, insects, or other animals living in a nest. **4.** a cozy place or shelter. **5.** a place where something dangerous, bad, or illegal takes place: *a smuggler's nest.* **6.** a set of

Bird's nest   Wasp's nest

Nests

similar objects made so that each fits into the next largest one. —*v.i.* to build or live in a nest: *The robins nested in the oak tree.* —*v.t.* **1.** to place in a nest. **2.** to arrange (objects) in a stack with each fitting into the next largest one.

nest egg 1. a natural or artificial egg left in a nest to persuade or encourage a hen to continue laying eggs in the nest. **2.** money saved for an emergency or some future need.

nes·tle (nes'əl) *v.,* **nes·tled, nes·tling.** —*v.i.* **1.** to press or lie close; snuggle; cuddle: *The foal nestled up to its mother.* **2.** to settle oneself snugly and cozily: *We nestled by the fire.* **3.** to be located in a snug and sheltered spot: *The cabin nestled among the trees.* —*v.t.* to hold or press closely; snuggle: *She nestled the kitten in her arms.* —**nes'tler,** *n.*

nest·ling (nest'ling) *n.* a bird too young to leave the nest.

Nes·tor (nes'tər) *n. Greek Mythology.* the oldest and wisest of the Greek chieftains in the Trojan War.

net¹ (net) *n.* **1.** any of various fabrics made of threads, cords, or ropes that are knotted, twisted, or woven into an open, crisscross pattern. **2.** something made of such fabric, used to catch, hold, or protect: *a badminton net, a butterfly net.* **3.** a fine, openwork fabric, as that used for veils. **4.** something that captures or entangles like a net: *a net of lies.* —*v.t.,* **net·ted, net·ting. 1.** to catch with a net: *to net a fish.* **2.** to make into net: *to net string.* **3.** to hold or protect with a net. [Old English *net, nett.*] —**net'like',** *adj.*

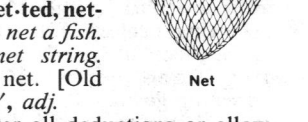

Net

net² (net) *adj.* remaining after all deductions or allowances have been made: *net income, net profit, net weight.*

—*v.t.,* **net·ted, net·ting.** to produce or earn as a final yield or profit: *After taxes John nets $7500 per year.* —*n.* something that remains after all deductions or allowances have been made: *The business produced a yearly net of $50,000.* [Middle French *net* pure, clean.]

neth·er (ne<u>th</u>′ər) *adj.* lying below; lower: *the nether world.*

Neth·er·lands, the (ne<u>th</u>′ər ləndz) *n.* a country in northwestern Europe, on the North Sea. Capital, Amsterdam. Seat of government, The Hague. Area, 12,950 sq. mi. Pop. (1971 est.), 13,119,430. Also, **Holland.** —**Neth·er·land·er** (ne<u>th</u>′ər lan′dər), *n.*

Netherlands Antilles, a Dutch island group in the southern Caribbean Sea.

Netherlands East Indies, a group of islands off the southeastern coast of Asia, formerly controlled by the Netherlands, now part of Indonesia.

Netherlands Guiana, see **Surinam.**

Netherlands New Guinea, see **West Irian.**

neth·er·most (ne<u>th</u>′ər mōst′) *adj.* lowest.

net·ting (net′ing) *n.* netted material, such as fabric or wire mesh.

net·tle (net′əl) *n.* any of a group of weedy plants whose leaves are covered with tiny hairs that sting the skin when touched. —*v.t.,* **net·tled, net·tling.** to cause annoyance to; irritate; rile.

net·work (net′wurk′) *n.* **1.** any system of lines or structures that cross: *a network of wires, a network of highways.* **2.** openwork material; net; netting. **3.** a group of radio or television stations connected so that they may all broadcast the same program.

neu·ral (noor′əl, nyoor′əl) *adj.* of or relating to a nerve, neuron, or nervous system.

neu·ral·gia (noo ral′jə, nyoo ral′jə) *n.* a sharp pain along the path of a nerve. —**neu·ral′gic,** *adj.*

neu·ri·tis (noo rī′tis, nyoo rī′tis) *n.* an inflammation of a nerve or nerves.

neu·rol·o·gist (noo rol′ə jist, nyoo rol′ə jist) *n.* a student of or an expert in neurology.

neu·rol·o·gy (noo rol′ə jē, nyoo rol′ə jē) *n.* the branch of medicine concerned with the nervous system and its disorders.

neu·ron (noor′on, nyoor′on) *also,* **neu·rone** (noor′ōn, nyoor′ōn). *n.* the basic unit of the nervous system, consisting of a cell body and its fibers. The neuron receives nerve impulses and sends them to other cells. Also, **nerve cell.**

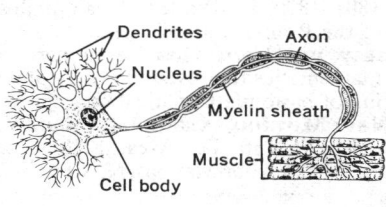

Dendrites Axon Nucleus Myelin sheath Muscle Cell body Neuron

neu·ro·sis (noo rō′sis, nyoo rō′sis) *n. pl.,* **neu·ro·ses** (noo rō′sēz, nyoo rō′sēz). an emotional disorder brought on and characterized by feelings of frustration, anxiety, fear, or the like.

neu·rot·ic (noo rot′ik, nyoo rot′ik) *adj.* having or characteristic of neurosis: *neurotic symptoms, a neurotic person.* —*n.* a person who is neurotic: *The doctor treated many neurotics.* —**neu·rot′i·cal·ly,** *adv.*

neut., neuter.

neu·ter (noo′tər, nyoo′tər) *adj.* **1.** *Grammar.* of or relating to the gender that is neither masculine nor feminine. **2.** having no sex organs or having undeveloped sex organs. —*n.* **1.** a neuter animal or plant. **2.** the neuter gender. **3.** a word belonging to the neuter gender.

neu·tral (noo′trəl, nyoo′trəl) *adj.* **1.** not taking either side in a conflict: *Switzerland was neutral during World War II.* **2.** belonging to neither side in a conflict: *a neutral zone.* **3.** having no particular shade or tint: *Gray is a neutral color.* **4.** *Chemistry.* neither acid nor base. **5.** *Electricity.* neither positive nor negative. —*n.* **1.** a person or thing that is neutral. **2.** a position of gears in which they are not interlocked and do not pass along motion from the engine to the wheels, as in an automobile. —**neu′tral·ly,** *adv.*

neu·tral·ism (noo′trə liz′əm, nyoo′trə liz′əm) *n.* a policy of remaining neutral, especially in foreign affairs. —**neu′tral·ist,** *adj., n.*

neu·tral·i·ty (noo tral′ə tē, nyoo tral′ə tē) *n.* the quality or state of being neutral: *The country maintained its neutrality throughout the war.*

neu·tral·ize (noo′trə līz′, nyoo′trə līz′) *v.t.,* **neu·tral·ized, neu·tral·iz·ing. 1.** to act against the effect or force of; counteract: *to neutralize an enemy's strength, to neutralize an argument.* **2.** to keep (a country or territory) from entering into a conflict; declare neutral. **3.** *Chemistry.* to make neutral. An acid and a base neutralize each other and form a salt and water. **4.** *Electricity.* to make neutral by balancing the positive and negative charges. —**neu′tral·i·za′tion,** *n.* —**neu′tral·iz′er,** *n.*

neutral vowel, another term for **schwa.**

neu·tri·no (noo trē′nō, nyoo trē′nō) *n. pl.,* **neu·tri·nos.** either of two stable subatomic particles having no mass or electric charge.

neu·tron (noo′tron, nyoo′tron) *n.* a particle that forms part of the nucleus of an atom, and carries no electric charge.

Nev., Nevada.

Ne·vad·a (nə vad′ə, nə vä′də) *n.* a state in the western United States. Capital, Carson City. Area, 110,540 sq. mi. Pop. (1970), 488,738. Abbreviation, **Nev.** —**Ne·vad′an,** *adj., n.*

● The name **Nevada** comes from a mountain range in eastern California and in the very southwestern corner of Nevada itself. The Spaniards named these mountains "Sierra Nevada," which means "snowy mountain range."

nev·er (nev′ər) *adv.* **1.** at no time; not ever: *He has never been to Australia.* **2.** in no way or degree; not at all: *This kind of behavior will never do.*

nev·er·more (nev′ər môr′) *adv.* never again.

nev·er·the·less (nev′ər <u>th</u>ə les′) *conj.* in spite of all; however; yet: *It was cloudy; nevertheless, we went to the beach.* —*adv.* anyway; in any case: *He had little money in the bank, but he bought the car nevertheless.*

new (noo, nyoo) *adj.* **1.** having existed only a short time; recently grown or made: *The tree has new buds. Have you heard the new school song?* **2.** seen, known, or thought of for the first time: *John found a new rock for his collection.* **3.** unfamiliar; strange: *There were many new faces in his class.* **4.** not yet accustomed or experienced: *He was still new to the job.* **5.** having recently come into a certain state, relationship, or position: *She made many new friends.* **6.** not yet worn or used: *He needs a new pair of shoes. The store sells both new and used furniture.* **7.** coming or begin-

at; āpe; cär; end; mē; it; īce; hot; ōld; fôrk; wood; fōōl; oil; out; up; turn; sing; thin; <u>th</u>is; hw in white; zh in treasure. The symbol ə stands for the sound of **a** in about, **e** in taken, **i** in pencil, **o** in lemon, and **u** in circus.

ning again: *a new dawn*. **8.** changed, especially for the better: *After his vacation, he felt like a new man.* —*adv.* newly; recently; freshly. ▲ usually used in combination: *new-fallen snow, a new-found friend.* —*n.* something that is new. —**new′ness,** *n.*

● **New words** are constantly being added to our language. As new concepts, actions, and objects are introduced, new words or meanings that describe them must be developed. The continual development of slang words also adds to our vocabulary. Sometimes, particularly in the case of slang, these words do not become a permanent part of our language. Other words do become part of our vocabulary and so are defined in the dictionary.

New words are coming into our language at a faster rate now than they have at any other time. This is caused by the increased communication that modern technology has produced. Television, radio, movies, and other media spread new words to a vast audience. For example, the word *A-OK* was first widely heard in 1961 during the first American manned space flight. Millions of people heard this term and it quickly became part of our language. Within less than a day this word, which hardly anyone had ever heard or seen before, was being used in newspaper headlines.

Among the most common sources of new words are advertisements, government officials, athletes, and the military, because we are in contact with them through the media. Many slang words in particular, which normally would not be used by the general public, are accepted because people hear them being used by other persons whom they respect.

New Amsterdam, a Dutch colonial town on the lower tip of Manhattan, taken by the British in 1664 and renamed New York.

New·ark (nook′ərk, nyook′ərk) *n.* a city in northeastern New Jersey, near New York City. Pop. (1970), 382,417.

New Bed·ford (bed′fərd) a port city in southeastern Massachusetts. Pop. (1970), 101,777.

new·born (nook′bôrn′, nyook′bôrn′) *adj.* **1.** born very recently: *A newborn baby sleeps most of the time.* **2.** born again: *newborn faith.*

New Britain 1. the largest island in the Bismarck Archipelago. **2.** a city in central Connecticut. Pop. (1970), 83,441.

New Bruns·wick (brunz′wik) a province of Canada, in the eastern part of the country. Area, 28,354 sq. mi. Pop. (1971), 634,557.

New·cas·tle (nook′kas′əl, nyook′kas′əl) *n.* a port city in northeastern England. Pop. (1978 est.), 291,600.

new·com·er (nook′kum′ər, nyook′kum′ər) *n.* a person who has recently arrived: *She is a newcomer in town and hasn't made many friends yet.*

New Deal, the domestic program of President Franklin D. Roosevelt during the 1930s that included social and economic reforms.

New Del·hi (del′ē) the capital of India, in the north-central part of the country. Pop. (1971), 301,801.

new·el (nook′əl, nyook′əl) *n.* **1.** the post at the head or foot of a flight of stairs supporting the handrail. Also, **newel post. 2.** the central, upright pillar of a spiral staircase.

New England, a region of the northeastern United States that includes Maine, New Hampshire, Vermont, Massachusetts, Rhode Island, and Connecticut. —**New Englander.**

new·fan·gled (nook′fang′gəld, nyook′fang′gəld) *adj.* recently come into fashion; modern: *a newfangled invention.*

New·found·land (nook′fənd lənd, nyook′fənd lənd) *n.* **1.** an island off the east coast of Canada. **2.** see **Newfoundland and Labrador. 3.** a large, heavily built dog of a breed developed in Newfoundland for pulling sleds and carrying loads, having a dense, usually black coat.

Newfoundland

Newfoundland and Labrador, the easternmost province of Canada, composed of Newfoundland and Labrador. Area, 156,185 sq. mi. Pop. (1971), 522,104.

New Guin·ea (gin′ē) **1.** the second largest island in the world, north of Australia. **2. Territory of.** a former Australian trust territory including northeastern New Guinea, the Bismarck Archipelago, and the Solomon Islands.

New Hamp·shire (hamp′shər) a state in the northeastern United States. Capital, Concord. Area, 9304 sq. mi. Pop. (1970), 737,681. Abbreviation, **N.H.** —**New Hamp·shir·ite** (hamp′shə rīt′).

● One of the founders of **New Hampshire** named the colony after his home county, Hampshire, England.

New Ha·ven (hā′vən) a city in southern Connecticut. Pop. (1970), 137,707.

New Jer·sey (jur′zē′) a state in the eastern United States. Capital, Trenton. Area, 7836 sq. mi. Pop. (1970), 7,168,164. Abbreviation, **N.J.** —**New Jer·sey·ite** (jur′zē īt′).

● **New Jersey** was named after Jersey, a British island in the English Channel which was the birthplace of one of the colony's co-owners.

new·ly (nook′lē, nyook′lē) *adv.* **1.** lately; recently: *He is the newly elected senator.* **2.** again; once more.

new·ly·wed (nook′lē wed′, nyook′lē wed′) *n.* a person who has recently been married.

New·man, John Henry (nook′mən, nyook′mən) 1801–1890, English theologian, philosopher, and cardinal of the Roman Catholic Church.

new mathematics, a modern method of teaching mathematics that uses set theory and stresses understanding of basic mathematical concepts.

New Mexico, a state in the southwestern United States. Capital, Santa Fe. Area, 121,666 sq. mi. Pop. (1970), 1,014,979. Abbreviations, **N. Mex., N.M.** —**New Mexican.**

● **New Mexico** was first called *Nuevo Mejico* by a Spanish explorer. The name *Mexico* was derived from the name of an Aztec God. *New Mexico* is an exact translation of the Spanish name.

new moon 1. a moon when it is not visible or when it is a thin crescent with the hollow side on the right. **2.** the period during which the new moon appears.

New Netherland, a former Dutch colony in North America from 1624 to 1664, that was captured by the English in 1664 and made into the colonies of New York and New Jersey.

New Or·le·ans (ôr′lē ənz, ôr′lənz, ôr lēnz′) a city in southeastern Louisiana, on the Mississippi River. Pop. (1970), 593,471.

Newport News, a port city in southeastern Virginia. Pop. (1970), 138,177.

news (nōōz, nyōōz) *n.* **1.** report or information of a recent event or events: *There's no news from home.* **2.** a recent event or events: *We heard a report of the news on the radio.*

news·boy (nōōz′boi′, nyōōz′boi′) *n.* a person who sells or delivers newspapers.

news·cast (nōōz′kast′, nyōōz′kast′) *n.* a radio or television program on which news is presented. —**news′-cast′er**, *n.*

news·deal·er (nōōz′dē′lər, nyōōz′dē′lər) *n.* a person who sells newspapers and magazines.

news·let·ter (nōōz′let′ər, nyōōz′let′ər) *n.* a printed report of news, usually sent out at regular periods of time.

news·man (nōōz′man′, nyōōz′man′) *n. pl.,* **news·men** (nōōz′men′, nyōōz′men′). a person who reports news, as for a newspaper or radio or television station. —**news′-wom′an**, *n.*

New South Wales, a political subdivision of Australia, in the southeastern part of the country. Area, 309,433 sq. mi. Pop. (1978 est.), 5,011,800.

news·pa·per (nōōz′pā′pər, nyōōz′pā′pər) *n.* a publication printed on sheets of paper that are folded but not bound, containing news, editorials, feature articles, and advertising, and issued regularly, especially every day or every week.

news·pa·per·man (nōōz′pā′pər man′, nyōōz′pā′-pər man′) *n. pl.,* **news·pa·per·men** (nōōz′pā′pər men′, nyōōz′pā′pər men′). a person who works for or owns a newspaper, especially a reporter or editor. —**news′pa′per·wom′an**, *n.*

news·print (nōōz′print′, nyōōz′print′) *n.* a thin paper made chiefly from wood pulp, on which newspapers are usually printed.

news·reel (nōōz′rēl′, nyōōz′rēl′) *n.* a short motion picture dealing with recent events, usually shown in a motion picture theater.

news·stand (nōōz′stand′, nyōōz′stand′) *n.* a stand where newspapers, magazines, and books are sold.

news·wor·thy (nōōz′wur′t͟hē, nyōōz′wur′t͟hē) *adj.* important or interesting enough to be reported in a newscast or newspaper.

news·y (nōō′zē, nyōō′zē) *adj.,* **news·i·er, news·i·est.** *Informal.* chatty and full of news; gossipy: *a newsy letter.*

newt (nōōt, nyōōt) *n.* any of various small, brightly colored salamanders found living in or around water.

New Testament, the second part of the Bible, containing the life and teachings of Christ and His disciples.

Newt

new·ton (nōōt′ən, nyōōt′-ən) *n.* the basic unit of force equal to the amount of force that must be applied to a mass of one kilogram to accelerate it one meter per second per second. [From Sir Isaac *Newton.*]

New·ton, Sir Isaac (nōōt′ən, nyōōt′ən) 1642–1727, English physicist and mathematician.

New·to·ni·an (nōō tō′nē ən, nyōō tō′nē ən) *adj.* of or relating to Sir Isaac Newton or his theories or discoveries.

New World, the Western Hemisphere.

New Year's Day, the first day of the year. It falls on January 1. Also, **New Year, New Year's.**

New York 1. a state in the eastern United States. Capital, Albany. Area, 49,576 sq. mi. Pop. (1970), 18,190,740. Abbreviation, **N.Y.** Also, **New York State. 2.** the largest city of the United States, in southeastern New York, at the mouth of the Hudson River. Pop. (1970), 7,867,760. Also, **New York City.**

●**New York** was named after James, Duke of York and Albany, later King James II of England. The Duke of York was given this colony by his brother, King Charles II.

New York Bay, a bay of the Atlantic Ocean, south of New York City, at the mouth of the Hudson River.

New York·er (yôr′kər) a person who was born or is living in New York, especially New York City.

New Zea·land (zē′lənd) an island country in the South Pacific, east of Australia. Capital, Wellington. Land area, 103,736 sq. mi. Pop. (1978 est.), 3,145,900. —**New Zea′-land·er.**

next (nekst) *adj.* following immediately in time, space, or order: *I'll see you next week. My friend lives in the next house.* —*adv.* **1.** immediately afterward: *The children's choir will sing next.* **2.** on the first time after this one: *Visit us when you are next in town.*

next door. in, at, or to a building, house, apartment, or the like that is nearest: *He lives next door to me.*

next to. a. almost; nearly: *Fixing the toaster was next to impossible.* **b.** beside: *I was standing next to him.*

next-door (nekst′dôr′) *adj.* in or at the nearest building, house, apartment, or the like: *Our next-door neighbors share a driveway with us.*

Nfld., Newfoundland.

N.G. 1. New Guinea. **2.** National Guard.

N.H., New Hampshire.

Ni, the symbol for nickel.

ni·a·cin (nī′ə sin) *n.* a vitamin of the vitamin B complex, found in liver, yeast, beans, and grains, that helps to prevent and cure pellagra. Also, **nicotinic acid.**

Ni·ag·a·ra (nī ag′ər ə, nī ag′rə) *n.* **1.** a short river on which the Niagara Falls is located, flowing from Lake Erie into Lake Ontario. **2.** see **Niagara Falls.**

Niagara Falls 1. a waterfall on the Niagara River between the United States and Canada. **2.** a city in western New York. Pop. (1970), 85,615. **3.** a city in southern Ontario, Canada, opposite Niagara Falls, New York. Pop. (1971), 65,271.

Nia·mey (nyä′mā) *n.* the capital and largest city of Niger. Pop. (1975 est.), 130,300.

nib (nib) *n.* **1.** the tip or point of a pen, especially a fountain pen. **2.** the projecting point of anything. **3.** a bird's bill or beak.

nib·ble (nib′əl) *v.,* **nib·bled, nib·bling.** —*v.t.* **1.** to eat by taking small, quick bites: *The mouse nibbled the cheese.* **2.** to take small, gentle bites on; bite softly: *A fish nibbled our bait.* —*v.i.* **1.** to eat with small, quick bites: *He nibbled on the apple.* **2.** to take small, gentle bites: *He nibbled on the end of his pencil.* —*n.* **1.** a small, quick bite, as that taken by a fish at bait. **2.** a small piece; morsel: *There's not even a nibble of the cake left.* —**nib′bler**, *n.*

Nic·a·ra·gua (nik′ə rä′gwə) *n.* the largest country of Central America. Capital, Managua. Area, 50,193 sq. mi. Pop. (1980), 2,737,000. —**Nic′a·ra′guan**, *adj., n.*

nice (nīs) *adj.,* **nic·er, nic·est. 1.** that is agreeable or pleasant: *The weather was nice yesterday.* **2.** kind; considerate: *It was nice of her to ask us to the party.* **3.** highly satisfac-

at; āpe; cär; end; mē; it; īce; hot; ōld; fôrk; wood; fōōl; oil; out; up; turn; sing; thin; this; hw in white; zh in treasure. The symbol ə stands for the sound of a in about, e in taken, i in pencil, o in lemon, and u in circus.

tory; good: *a nice piece of work.* **4.** showing or requiring accuracy, skill, or delicacy: *That artist makes nice distinctions in color.* **5.** respectable or well-bred: *a nice manner, a nice family.* [Old French *nice* ignorant, foolish.] —**nice′ly,** *adv.* —**nice′ness,** *n.*

nice and. very: *The test was nice and easy.*

Nice (nēs) *n.* a resort city in southeastern France, on the Mediterranean Sea. Pop. (1978 est.), 344,481.

ni·ce·ty (nī′sə tē) *n. pl.,* **ni·ce·ties. 1.** *also,* **niceties.** something that is elegant or refined: *the niceties of life.* **2.** *also,* **niceties.** a small or subtle detail; fine point. **3.** the quality or state of requiring delicacy, subtlety, or accuracy.

niche (nich) *n.* **1.** a decorative, usually arch-shaped recess or hollow in a wall, often used as a setting for statues or other ornaments, such as vases or glassware. **2.** a place, position, or situation for which a person is especially suited: *Tom quickly found his niche in the new school.*

Niche

Nich·o·las, Saint (nik′ə ləs) a bishop in Asia Minor in the fourth century A.D., the patron saint of children. Saint Nicholas is often identified with Santa Claus.

Nicholas II, 1868–1918, the last czar of Russia, from 1894 to 1917.

nick (nik) *n.* a place on a surface or edge that has been cut or chipped: *The razor made a nick on Dad's skin. The table top was full of nicks.* —*v.t.* to make a nick or nicks in or on.

in the nick of time. at the last moment; just in time.

nick·el (nik′əl) *n.* **1.** a hard, silvery, metallic element, used especially in alloys because of its strength and resistance to corrosion. Symbol: **Ni 2.** a coin of the United States equal to five cents, or one-twentieth of a dollar.

nickel silver, any of a group of silver-colored alloys of copper, nickel, and zinc that have good resistance to corrosion. Also, **German silver.**

nick·nack (nik′nak′) another spelling of **knickknack.**

nick·name (nik′nām′) *n.* **1.** a word or phrase, especially one that describes in some way, used in addition to or instead of a name: *Walter's nickname is "Butch."* **2.** a familiar, usually shortened form of a name: *"Dan" is a nickname for Daniel.* —*v.t.,* **nick·named, nick·nam·ing.** to give a nickname to.

Nic·o·si·a (nik′ə sē′ə) *n.* the capital of Cyprus, in the north-central part of the country. Pop. (1974 est.), 51,000.

nic·o·tine (nik′ə tēn′) *n.* a poisonous, oily substance found in the leaves, roots, and seeds of the tobacco plant.

nic·o·tin·ic acid (nik′ə tin′ik) another term for **niacin.**

niece (nēs) *n.* **1.** the daughter of one's brother or sister. **2.** the daughter of one's brother-in-law or sister-in-law.

Nie·tzsche, Frie·drich Wil·helm (nē′chə, nē′chē; frē′drik vil′helm) 1844–1900, German philosopher.

nif·ty (nif′tē) *adj.,* **nif·ti·er, nif·ti·est.** *Informal.* fine, dandy, or stylish: *a nifty idea, a nifty party.*

Ni·ger (nī′jər) *n.* **1.** a country in western Africa. Capital, Niamey. Area, 489,190 sq. mi. Pop. (1980), 5,305,000. **2.** a river flowing from western Africa into the Gulf of Guinea.

Ni·ge·ri·a (nī jēr′ē ə) *n.* a country in western Africa, on the Gulf of Guinea. Capital, Lagos. Area, 356,669 sq. mi. Pop. (1980), 77,100,000. —**Ni·ge′ri·an,** *adj., n.*

nig·gard (nig′ərd) *n.* a stingy person; miser. —*adj.* another word for **niggardly.**

nig·gard·ly (nig′ərd lē) *adj.* **1.** stingy; miserly. **2.** scanty; meager: *a niggardly amount.* —*adv.* in a niggardly manner; stingily. —**nig′gard·li·ness,** *n.*

nigh (nī) *Archaic. adv.* **1.** near; close: *The carriage drew nigh.* **2.** practically; almost: *It's nigh unto midnight.* —*adj.,* **nigh·er, nigh·est** or **next.** near; close: *Christmas day is nigh.* —*prep.* near; close to.

night (nīt) *n.* **1.** the period of darkness between the setting and the rising of the sun; time from sunset to sunrise. **2.** the beginning of night; nightfall. **3.** the darkness of night; the dark; darkness. **4.** a state or time of mental, emotional, or spiritual darkness: *In the real dark night of the soul it is always three o'clock in the morning* (F. Scott Fitzgerald).

night blindness, an inability to see normally in dim light. Night blindness is often caused by not having enough vitamin A.

night·cap (nīt′kap′) *n.* **1.** a soft, cloth cap worn in bed. **2.** *Informal.* an alcoholic drink taken before going to bed.

night·clothes (nīt′klōz′, nīt′klōᵺz) *n., pl.* clothes worn in bed, such as pajamas.

night·club (nīt′klub′) *also,* **night club.** *n.* a place of entertainment open until late at night, usually offering food, drink, and entertainment.

night crawler, any large earthworm, especially one that appears at night.

night·fall (nīt′fôl′) *n.* the end of the day; beginning of night: *Mother told us to come home before nightfall.*

night·gown (nīt′goun′) *n.* a loose gown worn in bed by women or children.

night·hawk (nīt′hôk′) *n.* **1.** an American bird resembling the whippoorwill, having mostly gray feathers. **2.** another word for **night owl.**

night·in·gale (nīt′ən gāl′, nī′ting gāl′) *n.* a small European thrush having mostly reddish-brown feathers and a whitish breast. Nightingales are noted for the beautiful song that the male sings.

Night·in·gale, Florence (nīt′ən gāl′, nī′ting gāl′) 1820–1910, English nurse considered the founder of modern nursing.

Nightingale

night·ly (nīt′lē) *adj.* done, happening, or appearing at night or every night: *to watch a nightly news broadcast.* —*adv.* at night or every night: *to call home nightly.*

night·mare (nīt′mer′) *n.* **1.** a bad dream that causes feelings of great nervousness or fear. **2.** any experience or condition resembling a nightmare; something horrible or frightening: *Being lost in the big city was a nightmare.* —**night′mar·ish,** *adj.*

night owl *Informal.* a person who often stays up late.

night·shade (nīt′shād′) *n.* a plant related to the tomato and the potato, having small flowers and black or red berries which may be poisonous.

night·shirt (nīt′shurt′) *n.* a long shirt worn in bed by a man or boy.

night·stick (nīt′stik′) *n.* a long, slender club carried by a police officer. Also, **billy, billy club.**

night·time (nīt′tīme′) *n.* the period of time between dusk and dawn.

ni·hil·ism (nī′ə liz′əm) *n.* **1.** a total rejection of all existing political and social institutions, and traditional religious and moral values. **2.** any violent revolutionary movement that advocates terrorism or anarchy. —**ni′hil·ist,** *n.* —**ni′hil·is′tic,** *adj.*

Ni·jin·sky, Vas·lav (ni jin′skē; väts läf′) 1890–1950, Russian ballet dancer.

Ni·ke (nī′kē) *n. Greek Mythology.* the goddess of victory, usually represented as a winged figure.

nil (nil) *n.* nothing; zero.

Nile (nīl) *n.* the longest river in the world, in east-central and northeastern Africa, flowing about 4150 miles to the Mediterranean Sea.

nim·ble (nim′bəl) *adj.,* **nim·bler, nim·blest. 1.** light and quick in movement: *a nimble dancer.* **2.** quick to understand or respond: *a nimble mind.* —**nim′ble·ness,** *n.* —**nim′bly,** *adv.*

nim·bo·stra·tus (nim′bō strā′təs, nim′bō strat′əs) *n.* a low, dark gray cloud layer, usually bringing rain or snow.

nim·bus (nim′bəs) *n. pl.,* **nim·bus·es** or **nim·bi** (nim′bī). **1.** a disk or ring of light surrounding the head of a god, saint, or other holy person in a painting. **2.** a feeling of splendor or glory surrounding a person or thing. **3.** see **nimbostratus.**

Nim·rod (nim′rod) *n.* in the Old Testament, a mighty hunter, the great-grandson of Noah.

nin·com·poop (nin′kəm pōōp′, ning′kəm pōōp′) *n. Informal.* a silly or stupid person; fool.

nine (nīn) *n.* **1.** the cardinal number that is one more than eight. **2.** a symbol representing this number, such as 9 or IX. **3.** something having this many units or things, such as a playing card or a baseball team. —*adj.* numbering one more than eight.

nine·fold (nīn′fōld′) *adj.* **1.** nine times as great or numerous. **2.** having or consisting of nine parts. —*adv.* so as to be nine times greater or more numerous.

nine·teen (nīn′tēn′) *n.* **1.** the cardinal number that is nine more than ten. **2.** a symbol representing this number, such as 19 or XIX. **3.** something having this many units or things. —*adj.* numbering nine more than ten.

nine·teenth (nīn′tēnth′) *adj.* **1.** (the ordinal of nineteen) next after the eighteenth. **2.** being one of nineteen equal parts. —*n.* **1.** something that is next after the eighteenth. **2.** one of nineteen equal parts; 1/19.

nine·ti·eth (nīn′tē ith) *adj.* **1.** (the ordinal of ninety) next after the eighty-ninth. **2.** being one of ninety equal parts. —*n.* **1.** something that is next after the eighty-ninth. **2.** one of ninety equal parts; 1/90.

nine·ty (nīn′tē) *n. pl.,* **nine·ties. 1.** the cardinal number that is nine times ten. **2.** a symbol representing this number, such as 90 or XC. —*adj.* numbering nine times ten.

Nin·e·veh (nin′ə və) *n.* the capital of the ancient Assyrian empire. It lay on the east bank of the Tigris River, in what is now northern Iraq.

nin·ny (nin′ē) *n. pl.,* **nin·nies.** a fool; simpleton.

ninth (nīnth) *adj.* **1.** (the ordinal of nine) next after the eighth. **2.** being one of nine equal parts. —*n.* **1.** something that is next after the eighth. **2.** one of nine equal parts; 1/9. —*adv.* in the ninth place.

ni·o·bi·um (nī ō′bē əm) *n.* a steel gray or silvery-white metallic element that is used in various alloys. Symbol: **Nb**

nip¹ (nip) *v.t.,* **nipped, nip·ping. 1.** to seize, as between two surfaces, and pinch or bite: *The parrot nipped the girl's finger.* **2.** to sever by pinching, cutting, or biting: *The gardener nipped the dead leaves off the bush.* **3.** to cause (something) to smart or sting: *The cold night air nipped his fingers.* **4.** to stop or destroy the growth of: *The late frost nipped the fruit trees.* —*n.* **1.** the act of nipping. **2.** a small portion or quantity; little bit. **3.** a sharp, biting cold; chill: *There is a nip in the air today.* **4.** a sharp or pungent flavor; tang. [Middle English *nippen.*]

   nip and tuck. *Informal.* so close or even as to leave the outcome in doubt: *The game was nip and tuck until the last inning.*

nip² (nip) *n.* a little drink; sip: *a nip of brandy.* [Probably short for obsolete *nipperkin* a small vessel for measuring liquor.]

nip·per (nip′ər) *n.* **1.** a person or thing that nips. **2. nippers.** any of various tools that grab and hold or cut,

as pincers or pliers. **3.** one of the large claws of a lobster or similar animal. **4.** *Informal.* a small boy.

nip·ple (nip′əl) *n.* **1.** a small pointed or rounded projection at the center of the breast or udder that, in a female mammal, contains the opening of the milk ducts. **2.** the rubber mouthpiece of a baby's bottle. **3.** anything like a nipple in shape or use, such as a short piece of pipe threaded at each end for use as a coupling.

Nip·pon (ni pon′, nip′on) *n.* another name for **Japan.**

Nip·pon·ese (nip′ə nēz′) *n. pl.,* **Nip·pon·ese.** another name for **Japanese.** —*adj.* of or relating to Japan, its people, their language, or their culture.

nip·py (nip′ē) *adj.,* **nip·pi·er, nip·pi·est. 1.** cold or chilling in a sharp, biting way: *The air is often a bit nippy in November.* **2.** tending or likely to nip.

nir·va·na (nir vä′nə) *also,* **Nir·va·na.** *n.* **1.** the highest state of bliss in Buddhism, in which all desire and suffering are extinguished, and the soul becomes a part of the supreme universal soul. **2.** any place or condition free from care or pain.

Ni·sei (nē′sā′) *n. pl.,* **Ni·sei.** a person who was born and educated in the United States or Canada and whose parents were immigrants from Japan.

nit (nit) *n.* the egg or young of any of various insects, such as a louse.

ni·ter (nī′tər) *also,* **ni·tre.** *n.* **1.** another word for **potassium nitrate. 2.** another word for **sodium nitrate.**

ni·trate (nī′trāt) *n.* **1.** a salt or ester of nitric acid. **2.** sodium nitrate or potassium nitrate used as a fertilizer. —*v.t.,* **ni·trat·ed, ni·trat·ing.** to treat or combine with nitric acid or a nitrate.

ni·tric (nī′trik) *adj.* of or containing nitrogen, especially of a higher valence.

nitric acid, a colorless, highly corrosive, liquid compound that is one of the strongest known oxidizing agents, used in the manufacturing of explosives, nitrate fertilizers, and dyes.

ni·tro·cel·lu·lose (nī′trə sel′yə lōs′) *n.* any of a number of flammable compounds made by adding a mixture of concentrated sulfuric and nitric acids to cellulose. Nitrocellulose is used in making plastics, lacquers, and explosives. Also, **cellulose nitrate.**

ni·tro·gen (nī′trə jən) *n.* a colorless, odorless, nonmetallic element that makes up about 78 percent of the volume of the atmosphere. Symbol: **N** —**ni·trog·e·nous** (nī-troj′ə nəs), *adj.*

nitrogen cycle, a continuous series of chemical changes by which nitrogen circulates between air, soil, and living things. Free nitrogen in the air passes into the soil, where it is converted by bacteria into compounds that can be used by plants and animals. When the plant and animal matter decays, nitrogen is released to the air, completing the cycle.

nitrogen fixation, conversion of free nitrogen that has entered the soil into compounds that can be used by plants and animals.

ni·tro·glyc·er·in (nī′trə glis′ər in) *also,* **ni·tro·glyc·er·ine.** *n.* a colorless, oily, liquid compound that is poisonous and very explosive. Weak alcohol solutions of nitroglycerin are used to treat heart disease.

at; āpe; cär; end; mē; it; īce; hot; ōld; fôrk; wood; fōōl; oil; out; up; turn; sing; thin; **th**is; hw in white; zh in treasure. The symbol ə stands for the sound of **a** in about, **e** in taken, **i** in pencil, **o** in lemon, and **u** in circus.

ni·trous (nī′trəs) *adj.* **1.** of or containing nitrogen, especially of a lower valence. **2.** of or containing niter.

nitrous acid, an unstable compound of nitrogen, occurring only in solution or in the form of its salts.

nitrous oxide, a gas with a sweetish odor and taste that produces an intoxicating effect when breathed in small amounts. It is used by dentists as an anesthetic. Also, **laughing gas.**

nit·wit (nit′wit′) *n.* a stupid person.

nix (niks) *Slang. n.* nothing. —*adv.* no. —*interj.* watch out; stop. —*v.t.* to reject or put a stop to: *The teacher nixed their plans.*

Nix·on, Richard Mil·hous (nik′sən; mil′hous′) 1913—, the thirty-seventh president of the United States, from 1969 to 1974.

N.J., New Jersey.

NLRB, National Labor Relations Board.

N. Mex., also, **N.M.** New Mexico.

no[1] (nō) *adv.* **1.** certainly not; not so. ▲ used to show denial, disagreement, or refusal. The word "no" sometimes makes a negative statement more emphatic: *No, I don't want to do it. No, that's not right.* **2.** not at all. ▲ used with the comparative form of an adjective: *He is no worse than the others.* **3.** not: *whether or no.* —*interj.* used to express surprise, bewilderment, or disbelief. —*n. pl.,* **noes. 1.** the saying of the word "no"; refusal; denial. **2.** a negative vote or voter. [Old English *nā, nō.*]

no[2] (nō) *adj.* **1.** not any: *There were no mistakes in your spelling test. They've had no food all day.* **2.** not a: *He is no great baseball player.* [Old English *nān.*]

No, the symbol for nobelium.

No., no. 1. north. **2.** northern. **3.** number.

No·ah (nō′ə) *n.* in the Old Testament, a patriarch chosen by God to build an ark, in which he, his family, and a pair of every kind of animal survived the Flood.

No·bel, Alfred Bern·hard (nō bel′; ber′närd) 1833–1896, Swedish chemist and industrialist who invented dynamite. He established the Nobel prizes.

no·be·li·um (nō bē′lē əm) *n.* a man-made, radioactive metallic element produced by bombarding curium. Symbol: **No** [Modern Latin *nobelium,* from Alfred *Nobel.*]

Nobel prize, any of the prizes established by Alfred Nobel to be awarded each year for accomplishments in the fields of physics, chemistry, medicine, economics, and literature, and for the promotion of peace.

no·bil·i·ty (nō bil′ə tē) *n. pl.,* **no·bil·i·ties. 1.** a class of people in a society having high birth, rank, or title. Dukes, duchesses, earls, and countesses are among the members of the British nobility. **2.** the state or quality of being distinguished by high birth, rank, or title. **3.** the state or quality of showing greatness in character or superior merit.

no·ble (nō′bəl) *adj.,* **no·bler, no·blest. 1.** distinguished by high birth, rank, or title; aristocratic. **2.** having or showing greatness of character or superior merit; worthy: *noble sentiments, a noble cause, noble conduct.* **3.** impressive in appearance; splendid; magnificent: *a noble oak tree.* —*n.* a nobleman or noblewoman. —**no′ble·ness,** *n.* —**no′bly,** *adv.*

no·ble·man (nō′bəl mən) *n. pl.,* **no·ble·men** (nō′bəlmən). a man of noble birth, rank, or title.

no·ble·wom·an (nō′bəl woom′ən) *n. pl.,* **no·ble·wom·en** (nō′bəl wim′ən). a woman of noble birth, rank, or title.

no·bod·y (nō′bod′ē) *pron.* no person; no one: *Nobody was late.* —*n. pl.,* **no·bod·ies.** a person of no importance, authority, or position.

▲ In formal usage, **nobody** is used with a singular pronoun: *Nobody raised his voice.* In informal usage, it is sometimes used with a plural pronoun: *Nobody called while I was out, did they?*

nock (nok) *n.* **1.** a notch at either end of a bow that holds the bowstring. **2.** a notch at the end of an arrow for receiving the bowstring. —*v.t.* **1.** to put a notch in (an arrow or bow). **2.** to fit (an arrow) to the bowstring for shooting.

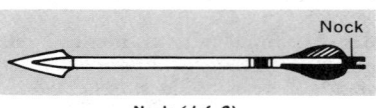

Nock (def. 2)

noc·tur·nal (nok turn′əl) *adj.* **1.** of or happening at night: *nocturnal sounds, a nocturnal walk.* **2.** active at night: *The raccoon is a nocturnal animal.* **3.** (of a flower) opening at night and closing during the day. —**noc·tur′nal·ly,** *adv.*

noc·turne (nok′turn′) *n.* **1.** a musical composition of a dreamy, thoughtful, or romantic character that is suitable for the evening. **2.** a painting of a night scene.

nod (nod) *v.,* **nod·ded, nod·ding.** —*v.i.* **1.** to lower briefly and then raise the head, as in greeting or agreement. **2.** to let the head fall forward with a quick motion, as when sleepy: *The student sat nodding over the dull book.* **3.** to bend forward with a swaying motion: *The grasses nodded as the breeze swept over the field.* —*v.t.* **1.** to lower briefly and then raise (the head), as in greeting or agreement. **2.** to show or express by nodding: *He nodded approval of our request.* —*n.* a lowering and raising of the head, as in greeting or agreement. —**nod′der,** *n.*

node (nōd) *n.* **1.** a knot, knob, or swelling. **2.** a point on a stem from which a leaf or branch grows. —**nod′al,** *adj.*

nod·ule (noj′ool) *n.* **1.** a small knot, swelling, or growth, as on plant or animal tissue. **2.** a small, rounded mass or lump, as of some mineral. —**nod·u·lar** (noj′ə lər), *adj.*

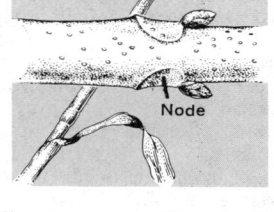

Node

no·ël (nō el′) *n.* **1.** a Christmas carol. **2. Noël.** Christmas.

nog·gin (nog′in) *n.* **1.** a small mug or cup. **2.** a small quantity of drink, especially liquor, equal to about one-fourth of a pint. **3.** *Informal.* a person's head.

noise (noiz) *n.* **1.** a sound that is loud, harsh, or unpleasant: *The noise of the traffic made it difficult to sleep.* **2.** any sound: *I heard a noise outside the window.* —*v.t.,* **noised, nois·ing.** to spread by rumor or report: *It was noised about that the coach intended to resign.*

noise·less (noiz′lis) *adj.* making no noise; silent; quiet: *noiseless movements, a noiseless fan.* —**noise′less·ly,** *adv.* —**noise′less·ness,** *n.*

noise·mak·er (noiz′mā′kər) *n.* something that makes noise, especially a horn, rattle, or other device used to make noise at a celebration or party.

noi·some (noi′səm) *adj.* **1.** offensive or bad to the smell; disgusting: *a noisome odor.* **2.** harmful; injurious: *noisome fumes in the air.* —**noi′some·ly,** *adv.* —**noi′some·ness,** *n.*

nois·y (noi′zē) *adj.,* **nois·i·er, nois·i·est. 1.** making noise: *noisy children.* **2.** full of or characterized by noise: *a noisy argument.* —**nois′i·ly,** *adv.* —**nois′i·ness,** *n.*

no·mad (nō′mad) *n.* **1.** a member of a group or tribe that has no permanent home and moves from place to place in search of food or land on which to graze their animals. **2.** any person who wanders from place to place.

no·mad·ic (nō mad′ik) *adj.* of, or relating to nomads; wandering: *a nomadic tribe.* —**no·mad′i·cal·ly,** *adv.*

no man's land, the land between two opposing armies, not controlled by either one.

nom de plume (nom′də plōōm′) pen name. [A translation of English *pen name* into French.]

no·men·cla·ture (nō′mən klā′chər) *n.* a system of names or special terms, especially in an art or science: *the nomenclature of biology.*

nom·i·nal (nom′ən əl) *adj.* **1.** being so in name but not in fact; not real or actual: *The king is the nominal ruler, while the prime minister has real power.* **2.** small compared with the actual value: *a nominal cost.* **3.** *Grammar.* of, relating to, or used as a noun: *a nominal adjective.* —**nom′i·nal·ly,** *adv.*

nom·i·nate (nom′ə nāt′) *v.t.,* **nom·i·nat·ed, nom·i·nat·ing. 1.** to propose as a candidate for an office or honor: *The Democrats nominated Jimmy Carter for the Presidency in 1980.* **2.** to appoint to an office or duty: *The mayor nominated Pat Smith as police chief.*

nom·i·na·tion (nom′ə nā′shən) *n.* the act of nominating or the state of being nominated.

nom·i·na·tive (nom′ə nə tiv) *Grammar. adj.* of, relating to, or designating the case of the subject of a verb, or of words agreeing with the subject. —*n.* **1.** the nominative case. **2.** a word in the nominative case. *I, they,* and *who* are nominatives.

nom·i·nee (nom′ə nē′) *n.* a person who is nominated, especially as a candidate for office.

non- *prefix* opposite or lack of; not: *nonprofit, nonviolence, nonsense.*

●To understand the meaning of a word that begins with **non-** but is not defined in this dictionary, add the word "not" to the meaning of the basic word. For example, *nonliving* means "not living" and *noncommunist* means "not communist." For some nouns, it is clearer to add the phrase "the opposite of." For example, **noninvolvement** means "the opposite of involvement" and *nonbeliever* means "the opposite of (a) believer." For any important *non-* word that has a special meaning, there is an entry in this dictionary.

---

non·a·ge·nar·i·an (non′ə jə ner′ē ən) *n.* a person who is ninety years old or between ninety and one hundred years old. —*adj.* being ninety years old or between ninety and one hundred years old.

non·a·gon (non′ə gon′) *n.* a polygon with nine sides and nine angles.

nonce (nons) *n.* a particular purpose or occasion. ▲ used chiefly in the phrase *for the nonce.*

nonce word, a word made up and used for a particular purpose or occasion.

non·cha·lance (non′shə läns′) *n.* the state of being nonchalant.

non·cha·lant (non′shə länt′) *adj.* marked by or showing a lack of interest or enthusiasm; casually indifferent. —**non′cha·lant′ly,** *adv.*

non·com (non′kom′) *n. Informal.* a noncommissioned officer.

non·com·bat·ant (non′kəm bat′ənt, non kom′bət ənt) *n.* **1.** a member of the armed forces, such as a doctor or chaplain, whose normal duties do not include fighting. **2.** a civilian in wartime.

non·com·mis·sioned officer (non′kə mish′ənd) an enlisted person of the armed forces who has been promoted to a rank above other enlisted people, but who has not received a commission from the President. A sergeant and a corporal are noncommissioned officers.

non·com·mit·tal (non′kə mit′əl) *adj.* not involving or showing commitment to a particular opinion, view, or course of action: *a noncommittal statement.* —**non′com·mit′tal·ly,** *adv.*

non·com·pli·ance (non′kəm plī′əns) *n.* failure or refusal to comply.

non·con·duc·tor (non′kən duk′tər) *n.* a substance that does not easily conduct some form of energy. Most plastics are nonconductors of heat and electricity.

non·con·form·ist (non′kən fôr′mist) *n.* **1.** a person who does not hold or conform to the thoughts, actions, or beliefs held or approved by most people; unconventional person. **2.** *also,* **Nonconformist.** in English history, any Protestant who was not a member of the Church of England.

non·con·form·i·ty (non′kən fôr′mə tē) *n.* lack of conformity.

non·de·script (non′di skript′) *adj.* without interesting or striking characteristics or features; not distinctive.

none (nun) *pron.* **1.** no one; not one: *Several senators criticized the bill, but none voted against it.* **2.** not any: *None of the stolen money was ever recovered.* **3.** no part; nothing: *He has none of his brother's sense of humor.* ▲ In the past, **none** was used only or mainly with a singular verb: *None of his friends has ever been to Paris.* In current usage, **none** is also used with a plural verb: *None of the passengers were aware of the danger.* —*adv.* by no means; not at all: *Help came none too soon.*

non·en·ti·ty (non en′tə tē) *n. pl.,* **non·en·ti·ties.** a person or thing of little or no importance.

none·the·less (nun′thə les′) *adv.* nevertheless; however.

non·ex·ist·ent (non′ig zis′tənt) *adj.* not existing in reality; unreal. —**non′ex·ist′ence,** *n.*

non·fat (non′fat′) *adj.* (of food) having fat or fat solids removed; containing no fats: *nonfat dry milk.*

non·fic·tion (non fik′shən) *n.* prose literature other than fiction that deals with real situations, persons, or events. Essays and biographies are examples of nonfiction. —**non·fic′tion·al,** *adj.*

non·flam·ma·ble (non flam′ə bəl) *adj.* not likely to catch fire easily; not flammable.

non·met·al (non met′əl) *n.* a chemical element not having the character of a metal, especially an element that tends to gain electrons and form negatively charged ions.

non·me·tal·lic (non′mi tal′ik) *adj.* **1.** not of or like metal. **2.** *Chemistry.* of or relating to a nonmetal.

non·pa·reil (non′pə rel′) *adj.* having no equal; matchless. —*n.* a person or thing that has no equal.

non·par·ti·san (non pär′ti zən) *also,* **non·par·ti·zan.** *adj.* not supporting, belonging to, or influenced by any political party or its interests.

non·plus (non plus′) *v.t.,* **non·plused, non·plus·ing;** *also, British,* **non·plussed, non·plus·sing.** to make unable to say or do more; put at a loss; perplex; bewilder.

non·pro·duc·tive (non′prə duk′tiv) *adj.* **1.** not involved directly in the production of goods: *nonproductive sales personnel.* **2.** producing or yielding little or nothing: *nonproductive soil.* —**non′pro·duc′tive·ly,** *adv.* —**non′pro·duc′tive·ness,** *n.*

non·prof·it (non prof′it) *adj.* not operated for profit.

non·res·i·dent (non rez′ə dənt) *adj.* not living in a particular place, especially not living permanently where one works, attends school, or owns property. —*n.* a nonresident person.

non·re·stric·tive (non′ri strik′tiv) *adj. Grammar.*

---

at; āpe; cär; end; mē; it; īce; hot; ōld; fôrk; wood; fō̇ol; oil; out; up; turn; sing; thin; this; hw in white; zh in treasure. The symbol ə stands for the sound of a in about, e in taken, i in pencil, o in lemon, and u in circus.

designating a word, clause, or phrase that describes a noun without limiting or changing the basic meaning of the sentence, and that is set off by commas. In the sentence *Mr. Bridges, who is a captain in the army, was sent to Japan,* the clause *who is a captain in the army* is nonrestrictive.

non·sec·tar·i·an (non′sek ter′ē ən) *adj.* not restricted or belonging to any particular sect or religion: *a nonsectarian church service.*

non·sense (non′sens) *n.* **1.** language or behavior that is silly or makes no sense: *The little baby babbled nonsense.* **2.** language or behavior that is annoying or lacking in good sense: *Mother said that she would not put up with any more nonsense from the children.* **3.** things of no importance or value; trifles.

non·sen·si·cal (non sen′si kəl) *adj.* making no sense; foolish; absurd: *a nonsensical statement.* —**non·sen′si·cal·ly,** *adv.*

non se·qui·tur (non sek′wi tər) a statement or conclusion that does not follow logically from the statements already made or facts given. For example: *We are tired of our team losing; therefore, our team will win the next game.* [Latin *nōn sequitur* it does not follow.]

non·stan·dard (non stan′dərd) *adj.* **1.** of or relating to usage or language that is not considered acceptable by educated users of the language. **2.** not standard.

non·stop (non′stop′) *adj.* not making any stops: *a nonstop flight.* —*adv.* without stops: *We flew nonstop to Rome.*

non·un·ion (non yōōn′yən) *adj.* **1.** employing people who are not union members: *a nonunion barber shop.* **2.** not belonging to a trade or labor union.

non·vi·o·lence (non vī′ə ləns) *n.* the philosophy or practice of opposing the use of all physical force or violence. —**non·vi′o·lent,** *adj.* —**non·vi′o·lent·ly,** *adv.*

non·white (non hwīt′, non wīt′) *adj.* not white; not belonging to the white race. —*n.* a person who is not white.

noo·dle[1] (nōōd′əl) *n.* a narrow tubelike or flat strip of dried dough made from a mixture of flour, water, and eggs. [German *Nudel.*]

noo·dle[2] (nōōd′əl) *n.* **1.** a silly or stupid person; fool. **2.** *Slang.* the head. [Of uncertain origin.]

nook (nook) *n.* **1.** any small recess or corner. **2.** a secluded or sheltered place: *He found a shady nook in the woods.*

noon (nōōn) *n.* **1.** twelve o'clock in the daytime; the middle of the day. **2.** the highest point: *In the bright wisdom of youth's breathless noon* (Percy Shelley).

noon·day (nōōn′dā′) *n.* see **noon** *(def. 1).* —*adj.* of or occurring at noon: *a noonday meal.*

no one, nobody.

noon·time (nōōn′tīm′) *n.* see **noon** *(def. 1).* Also, **noon·tide** (nōōn′tīd′).

noose (nōōs) *n.* **1.** a loop of rope with a slip knot that allows the loop to tighten when the end of the rope is pulled. **2.** a trap or snare. —*v.t.,* **noosed, noos·ing.** to capture with a noose; entrap.

nor (nôr) *conj.* **1.** used with *neither* or another negative word to introduce another element in a series: *Neither she nor I have seen it.* **2.** used in place of *and . . . not* to continue a negative idea: *He was not at work today, nor will he be there tomorrow.*

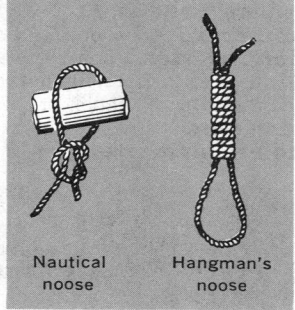

Nautical noose

Hangman's noose

Nooses

▲ *Or* is generally used instead of *nor* to introduce an-

other negative idea if it is clear that the idea is negative: *He would not go on a vacation from work, or even take one day off.*

Nor. **1.** Norman. **2.** North. **3.** Norway; Norwegian.

Nor·dic (nôr′dik) *adj.* of or relating to a people living mainly in northern Europe, especially Scandinavia, characterized by tall stature, long heads, fair skin, and blond hair. —*n.* a member of the Nordic people.

Nor·folk (nôr′fək) *n.* the largest city in Virginia, in the southeastern part of the state. Pop. (1970), 307,951.

norm (nôrm) *n.* **1.** a rule, standard, or pattern, as of behavior. **2.** an average: *statistical norms.*

nor·mal (nôr′məl) *adj.* **1.** conforming to an accepted standard, model, or pattern; usual; standard: *Heavy traffic is normal during rush hour.* **2.** having or showing average mental, physical, or emotional development, as at a particular age: *According to various tests, he has normal intelligence.* —*n.* a usual or standard condition or level: *His temperature was two degrees above normal.*

nor·mal·cy (nôr′məl sē) *n.* another word for **normality.**

nor·mal·i·ty (nôr mal′ə tē) *n.* the state or quality of being normal.

nor·mal·ize (nôr′mə līz′) *v.t.,* **nor·mal·ized, nor·mal·iz·ing.** to make normal: *The diplomats sought to normalize relations between the two hostile countries.* —**nor′mal·i·za′tion,** *n.*

nor·mal·ly (nôr′mə lē) *adv.* **1.** under normal circumstances; ordinarily; usually: *Normally the train takes twenty minutes to reach the next town.* **2.** in a normal manner: *to behave normally.*

normal school, a school that trains high school graduates to be teachers.

Nor·man (nôr′mən) *n.* **1.** a member of the Scandinavian people who invaded and conquered Normandy in the tenth century A.D. **2.** one of the descendants of these people and the French, who conquered England in 1066. **3.** a native or inhabitant of Normandy. **4.** see **Norman French.** —*adj.* of or relating to Normandy or the Normans.

Norman Conquest, the conquest of England by the Normans under William the Conqueror, in 1066.

Nor·man·dy (nôr′mən dē) *n.* a historic region and former province in northwestern France, bordering the English Channel.

Norman French, a dialect of French spoken by the people of Normandy in the Middle Ages.

Norse (nôrs) *adj.* **1.** of or relating to ancient Scandinavia, its people, or their language. **2.** another word for **Norwegian.** —*n.* **1. the Norse. a.** the ancient Scandinavians. **b.** the Norwegians. **2.** the language of Norway; Norwegian.

Norse·man (nôrs′mən) *n. pl.,* **Norse·men** (nôrs′mən). a member of the people of ancient Scandinavia.

north (nôrth) *n.* **1.** the direction to one's right as one faces the sunset. North is one of the four main points of the compass, located directly opposite south and at zero degrees. **2.** *also,* **North.** any region or place lying in this direction. **3. the North.** a region of the United States north of Maryland, the Ohio River, and Missouri, especially the Northern states that fought against the Confederacy in the Civil War. —*adj.* **1.** toward or in the north. **2.** from the north: *the north wind.* —*adv.* toward the north: *He walked north.*

North America, the third largest continent, comprising all the land between the Atlantic and Pacific oceans north of the Panama-Colombia border, including Mexico, the continental United States, and Canada. Area, approx. 9,362,000 sq. mi. Pop. (1971 est.), 327,000,000. —**North American.**

north·bound (north′bound′) *adj.* going north: *northbound traffic.*

North Carolina, a state in the southeastern United States, on the Atlantic Ocean. Capital, Raleigh. Area, 52,712 sq. mi. Pop. (1970), 5,082,059. Abbreviation, **N.C.** —**North Car·o·lin·i·an** (kar′ə lin′ē ən).

● **North Carolina** was formed from the northern part of the colony of Carolina. King Charles I named the colony *Carolana,* meaning "of Charles." The spelling was later changed to Carolina by King Charles II when he granted the unsettled colony to a group of noblemen.

North Dakota, a state in the north-central United States. Capital, Bismarck. Area, 70,665 sq. mi. Pop. (1970), 617,761. Abbreviations, **N. Dak., N.D.** —**North Dakotan.**

● **North Dakota** was once the northern section of the Dakota Territory, which derived its name from the Dakota Indians. The Dakotas were a western branch of the Sioux, and the name Dakota is a Siouan word meaning "allied tribes."

north·east (nôrth′ēst′) *n.* **1.** the direction halfway between north and east. **2.** the point of the compass indicating this direction. **3.** a region or place in this direction. **4. the Northeast.** the northeastern part of the United States, especially New England and New York. —*adj.* **1.** toward or in the northeast; northeastern. **2.** from the northeast. —*adv.* toward the northeast.

north·east·er (nôrth′ēs′tər) *n.* a strong wind or storm from the northeast.

north·east·er·ly (nôrth′ēs′tər lē) *adj., adv.* **1.** toward the northeast. **2.** from the northeast: *northeasterly winds.*

north·east·ern (nôrth′ēs′tərn) *adj.* **1.** toward or in the northeast. **2.** of, relating to, or characteristic of the northeast or Northeast. **3.** coming from the northeast.

north·east·ward (nôrth′ēst′wərd) *adv. also,* **north·east·wards.** toward the northeast. —*adj.* toward or in the northeast. —*n.* a northeastward direction, point, or place.

north·er·ly (nôr′thər lē) *adj., adv.* **1.** toward the north. **2.** from the north.

north·ern (nôr′thərn) *adj.* **1.** toward or in the north. **2.** *also,* **Northern.** of, relating to, or characteristic of the north or North. **3.** from the north.

north·ern·er (nôr′thər nər) *n.* **1.** a person who was born or is living in the north. **2.** *usually,* **Northerner.** a person who was born or is living in the northern part of the United States.

Northern Hemisphere, the half of the earth north of the equator.

Northern Ireland, a political division of the United Kingdom, occupying the northeast corner of the island of Ireland. Capital, Belfast. Area, approx. 5459 sq. mi. Pop. (1978 est.), 1,538,800.

northern lights, another term for **aurora borealis.**

north·ern·most (nôr′thərn mōst′) *adj.* farthest north.

Northern Rhodesia, see **Zambia.**

North Island, the smaller of the two main islands of New Zealand.

North Korea, a country occupying the northern part of the Korean peninsula. Capital, Pyongyang. Area, 46,540 sq. mi. Pop. (1980), 17,910,000.

north·land (nôrth′lənd) *n. also,* **Northland. 1.** the land in the north, such as the northern region of a country. **2.** another name for **Scandinavia.**

North·man (nôrth′mən) *n. pl.,* **North·men** (nôrth′mən). another name for **Norseman.**

north-north·east (nôrth′nôrth′ēst′) *n.* a point on the compass halfway between north and northeast. —*adj., adv.* toward the north-northeast.

north-north·west (nôrth′nôrth′west′) *n.* a point on the compass halfway between north and northwest. —*adj., adv.* toward the north-northwest.

North Pole 1. the northernmost point on earth; the northern end of the earth's axis. **2. north pole.** the pole of a magnet that points to the north when the magnet swings freely.

North Sea, a large arm of the Atlantic Ocean, between Great Britain and Europe.

North Star, another term for **Polaris.**

North·um·bri·a (nôr thum′brē ə) *n.* an ancient kingdom founded by the Angles in northern England.

North Vietnam, see **Vietnam.**

north·ward (nôrth′wərd) *adv. also,* **north·wards.** toward the north. —*adj.* toward or in the north. —*n.* a northward direction, point, or place.

north·west (nôrth′west′) *n.* **1.** the direction halfway between north and west. **2.** the point of the compass indicating this direction. **3.** a region or place in this direction. **4. the Northwest.** the northwestern part of the United States, especially Idaho, Oregon, and Washington. —*adj.* **1.** toward or in the northwest; northwestern. **2.** from the northwest: *the northwest wind.* —*adv.* toward the northwest.

north·west·er (nôrth′wes′tər) *n.* a strong wind or storm from the northwest.

north·west·er·ly (nôrth′wes′tər lē) *adj., adv.* **1.** toward the northwest. **2.** from the northwest.

north·west·ern (nôrth′wes′tərn) *adj.* **1.** toward or in the northwest. **2.** of, relating to, or characteristic of the northwest or Northwest. **3.** coming from the northwest.

Northwest Passage, a supposed sea route along the north coast of North America connecting the Atlantic and Pacific Oceans.

Northwest Territories, a division of Canada, in the northern part of the country. Area, 1,304,903 sq. mi. Pop. (1971), 34,807.

Northwest Territory, a territory organized in 1787, consisting of land between the Ohio and Mississippi Rivers that now forms the states of Illinois, Indiana, Michigan, Ohio, Wisconsin, and part of Minnesota. It was the first nationally organized United States territory.

north·west·ward (nôrth′west′wərd) *adv. also,* **north·west·wards.** toward the northwest. —*adj.* toward or in the northwest. —*n.* a northwestward direction, point, or place.

Nor·walk (nôr′wôk′) *n.* **1.** a city in southern California, near Los Angeles. Pop. (1970), 91,827. **2.** a city in southwestern Connecticut. Pop. (1970), 79,113.

Nor·way (nôr′wā′) *n.* a country in northern Europe occupying the western side of the Scandinavian peninsula. Capital, Oslo. Area, 125,181 sq. mi. Pop. (1980), 4,075,000.

Nor·we·gian (nôr wē′jən) *n.* **1.** a person who was born or is living in Norway. **2.** the Germanic language of Norway. —*adj.* of or relating to Norway, its people, their language, or their culture.

at; āpe; cär; end; mē; it; īce; hot; ōld; fôrk; wood; fōōl; oil; out; up; turn; sing; thin; this; hw in white; zh in treasure. The symbol ə stands for the sound of a in about, e in taken, i in pencil, o in lemon, and u in circus.

nose (nōz) *n.* **1.** the part of the human face that contains the organ of smell and the breathing passages. **2.** the corresponding part of the head in other animals. **3.** the sense of smell: *Cats have good noses.* **4.** a prominent or projecting part of something, such as a ship or airplane. **5.** the ability to discover or learn: *That columnist has a nose for news.* —*v.,* **nosed, nosing.** —*v.t.* **1.** to discover or notice by smell: *The dog nosed out the rabbit.* **2.** to touch or rub with the nose; nuzzle. **3.** to push slowly or gently with or as if with the nose: *Tugboats nosed the ship into the dock.* —*v.i.* **1.** to sniff: *The puppy nosed at my arm.* **2.** to move forward, especially with caution. **3.** to pry or meddle: *to nose around for information.*

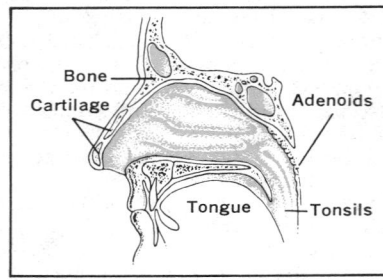

Nose

  by a nose. by a small margin: *He won the race by a nose.*
  to look down one's nose at. to have a superior attitude toward; disdain.
  to turn up one's nose at. to show scorn or contempt for.
  under one's nose. plainly or clearly visible.

nose·bleed (nōz′blēd′) *n.* a bleeding from the nose.
nose cone, the cone-shaped front section of a rocket, often equipped with a heat shield.
nose·dive (nōz′dīv′) *v.i.,* **nose·dived, nose·div·ing.** to make a nose dive.
nose dive **1.** a rapid or sudden plunge downward by an aircraft, with the nose pointing toward the earth. **2.** any rapid or sudden plunge downward: *Prices on the stock market took a nose dive.*
nose·gay (nōz′gā′) *n.* a small bunch of flowers; bouquet.
nos·tal·gia (nos tal′jə) *n.* **1.** a sentimental longing for what is past or far away: *The faded mementos of her youth filled the old woman with nostalgia.* **2.** a longing for one's home and family; homesickness. —**nos·tal′gic,** *adj.* —**nos·tal′gi·cal·ly,** *adv.*

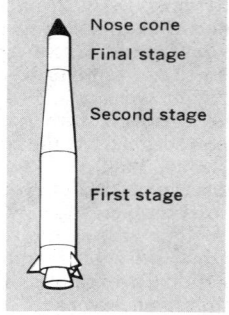

Nose cone of a rocket

Nose cone
Final stage

Second stage

First stage

nos·tril (nos′trəl) *n.* either of the two outer openings of the nose.
nos·trum (nos′trəm) *n.* **1.** a patent medicine, especially one that is a quack remedy. **2.** a favorite scheme or remedy, as for curing social problems.
nos·y (nō′zē) also, **nos·ey.** *adj.,* **nos·i·er, nos·i·est.** *Informal.* overly curious about other people's business; prying. —**nos′i·ly,** *adv.* —**nos′i·ness,** *n.*
not (not) *adv.* at no time; in no way. ▲ used to form negative statements: *She is not home. You may not go.*
no·ta·ble (nō′tə bəl) *adj.* worthy of notice; noteworthy; remarkable: *The novelist's first book was a notable success.* —*n.* a person who is worthy of notice. —**no′ta·bly,** *adv.*
no·ta·rize (nō′tə rīz′) *v.t.,* **no·ta·rized, no·ta·riz·ing.** to witness and certify (a document) to be authentic: *The notary public notarized the will.* —**no′ta·ri·za′tion,** *n.*
no·ta·ry (nō′tər ē) *n. pl.,* **no·ta·ries.** see **notary public.**
notary public, a person authorized to administer oaths and certify documents as authentic.

no·ta·tion (nō tā′shən) *n.* **1.** a system of signs or symbols used to represent values, quantities, or other facts or information: *musical notations.* **2.** the act or process of using such signs or symbols. **3.** a brief note, as in the margin of a book. **4.** the act of writing notes. —**no·ta′tion·al,** *adj.*
notch (noch) *n. pl.,* **notch·es.** **1.** a wedge-shaped nick or other indentation cut into the surface or along the edge of something. **2.** a narrow pass between mountains. **3.** *Informal.* a step or degree. —*v.t.* **1.** to cut a notch or notches in. **2.** to keep count of by or as if by cutting notches.
note (nōt) *n.* **1.** *usually,* **notes.** a brief record, as of a lecture, written down to help the memory: *Lawrence took notes in class. The lecturer spoke without notes.* **2.** a comment that explains or criticizes, added to a text, as at the bottom of a page. **3.** a brief message or letter: *The teacher sent a note to the boy's mother.* **4.** careful notice; regard: *John's opinions are worthy of note.* **5.** distinction or importance; significance: *The judge is a man of note.* **6.** an indication or suggestion, as of an emotion: *He detected a note of bitterness in her voice.* **7.** see **promissory note. 8.** a piece of paper money or a certificate of payment issued by a government or bank. **9.** *Music.* **a.** a tone of definite pitch. **b.** a sign representing such a tone and showing its pitch and duration. **c.** the key of a piano or other similar instrument. —*v.t.,* **not·ed, not·ing. 1.** to set down in writing; make a note of: *He noted her telephone number in his address book.* **2.** to take careful notice of; regard: *Please note the enclosed instructions.* **3.** to mention specially; remark about: *The critic noted several of her poems.*
  to compare notes. to exchange points of view or ideas.

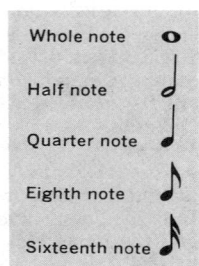

Whole note	○
Half note	♩
Quarter note	♩
Eighth note	♪
Sixteenth note	♬

Musical notes

note·book (nōt′book′) *n.* a book with pages for notes.
not·ed (nō′tid) *adj.* well-known or celebrated; famous; distinguished: *Several noted authors wrote for the paper.*
note·wor·thy (nōt′wur′thē) *adj.* worthy of notice or special attention: *a noteworthy accomplishment.* —**note′wor′thi·ly,** *adv.* —**note′wor′thi·ness,** *n.*
noth·ing (nuth′ing) *n.* **1.** no thing; not anything: *He had nothing to say about the matter. We bought nothing at the store.* **2.** no part or share: *His uncle left him nothing in his will.* **3.** a person or thing that is of no value or importance. **4.** zero: *The final score in the game was two to nothing.* —*adv.* in no way; not at all: *You look nothing like your sister.*
noth·ing·ness (nuth′ing nis) *n.* **1.** the absence of matter; empty space; emptiness. **2.** the absence of existence.
no·tice (nō′tis) *n.* **1.** the act of observing or the state of being observed: *to escape notice, to bring something to notice.* **2.** an announcement or warning: *to attack without notice.* **3.** a printed announcement: *There were notices about the circus posted all over town.* **4.** a formal announcement, as of the end of an agreement: *Steve gave his employer two weeks' notice before leaving for another job.* **5.** a critical review: *The play received very poor notices.* —*v.t.,* **no·ticed, no·tic·ing.** to become aware of; take notice of; observe: *I noticed Fred's car parked outside.*
no·tice·a·ble (nō′ti sə bəl) *adj.* easily noticed: *There is a noticeable difference in her appearance today.* —**no′tice·a·bly,** *adv.*
no·ti·fi·ca·tion (nō′tə fi kā′shən) *n.* **1.** the act of notifying or the state of being notified. **2.** a written or printed notice.
no·ti·fy (nō′tə fī′) *v.t.,* **no·ti·fied, no·ti·fy·ing.** to give notice to; inform: *to notify the police of an accident, to notify customers of a sale.* —**no′ti·fi′er,** *n.*

no·tion (nō′shən) *n.* **1.** mental image; idea: *I haven't the slightest notion of what he meant by that remark.* **2.** a theory, belief, or opinion: *a superstitious notion.* **3.** an intention or whim; desire: *He had a sudden notion to leave.* **4. notions.** small useful items, such as ribbons, pins, needles, and thread.

no·to·chord (nō′tə kôrd′) *n.* a stiff, supporting, rodlike structure that extends lengthwise below the spinal cord in primitive animals with backbones, and is present during the early, or embryonic stage in the development of higher animals with backbones.

no·to·ri·e·ty (nō′tə rī′ə tē) *n. pl.,* **no·to·ri·e·ties.** the quality or state of being notorious.

no·to·ri·ous (nō tôr′ē əs) *adj.* well-known for something bad; widely and unfavorably known: *a notorious criminal, a notorious liar.* —**no·to′ri·ous·ly,** *adv.* —**no·to′ri·ous·ness,** *n.*

Not·ting·ham (not′ing əm) *n.* a city in central England. Pop. (1971), 299,758.

not·with·stand·ing (not′with stan′ding, not′with-stan′ding) *prep.* in spite of: *The game was completed notwithstanding the bad weather.* —*adv.* all the same; nevertheless: *The children were sleepy, but stayed up notwithstanding.* —*conj.* in spite of the fact that; although.

Nouak·chott (nwäk shot′) *n.* the capital of Mauritania, in the western part of the country. Pop. (1971 est.), 35,000.

nou·gat (nōō′gət) *n.* a candy made mainly of sugar or honey and nuts.

nought (nôt) another spelling of **naught.**

noun (noun) *n.* a word that names or denotes something, such as a person, animal, place, thing, action, or quality, and that functions as the subject or object of a verb, or the object of a preposition. Most English nouns have a plural formed by adding -s or -es, and many have a possessive formed by adding -'s.

nour·ish (nur′ish) *v.t.* **1.** to furnish with food and other substances necessary to life and growth. **2.** to promote the development of; foster.

nour·ish·ment (nur′ish mənt) *n.* **1.** something that nourishes; sustenance. **2.** the act of nourishing or the state of being nourished.

Nov., November.

no·va (nō′və) *n. pl.,* **no·vae** (nō′vē) or **no·vas.** a star that rapidly increases in brightness and then gradually fades to its original brightness.

No·va Sco·tia (nō′və skō′shə) a province of Canada, in the southeastern part of the country. Area, 21,425 sq. mi. Pop. (1971), 788,960.

nov·el[1] (nov′əl) *n.* a fictional story written in prose, usually fairly long and having a detailed plot. [Old French *novelle,* from Latin *novella* new things.]

nov·el[2] (nov′əl) *adj.* new and unusual: *a novel idea, a novel technique.* [Old French *novel, nouvel.*]

nov·el·ette (nov′ə let′) *n.* a short novel.

nov·el·ist (nov′ə list) *n.* a person who writes novels.

nov·el·ty (nov′əl tē) *n. pl.,* **nov·el·ties.** **1.** the quality of being new; newness. **2.** something that is new or unusual, such as a thing or event. **3. novelties.** small, inexpensive, manufactured articles, such as ornaments or toys.

No·vem·ber (nō vem′bər) *n.* the eleventh month of the year, having thirty days. [Latin *November (mēnsis)* the ninth (month of the Roman calendar), from *novem* nine.]

no·ve·na (nō vē′nə) *n. pl.,* **no·ve·nas** or **no·ve·nae** (nō-vē′nē). a Roman Catholic devotion consisting of prayers said for a period of nine days.

nov·ice (nov′is) *n.* **1.** a person who is new to an occupation, activity, or the like; beginner. **2.** a person who is admitted into a religious order for a specified period before taking vows.

no·vi·ti·ate (nō vish′ē it) *also,* **no·vi·ci·ate.** *n.* **1.** the state or period of being a novice. **2.** a novice; beginner. **3.** the quarters housing novices in a religious order.

No·vo·cain (nō′və kān′) *n. Trademark.* a drug used as a local anesthetic, especially by dentists; procaine.

No·vo·si·birsk (nō′və si bērsk′) *n.* a city in the south-central Soviet Union, in the Russian Republic. Pop. (1971 est.), 1,180,000.

now (nou) *adv.* **1.** at the present time: *He is now living in London. I am busy now.* **2.** without delay; at once; immediately: *She must leave now.* **3.** a very short while ago: *He arrived just now, while you were out.* **4.** under the present conditions or circumstances: *Since Helen lost her keys, she must now wait until her brother comes home.* **5.** at the point of time referred to; then: *The war was now over, and the soldier could return to his family.* —*conj.* since: *Now that we are alone, we can speak freely.* —*n.* the present time; present: *The time to act is now.* —*interj.* used to express warning, sympathy, or reproach. *Now, watch it!*

now and again or **now and then.** from time to time; occasionally.

now·a·days (nou′ə dāz′) *adv.* at the present time.

no·way (nō′wā′) *also,* **no·ways.** *adv.* in no way; not at all.

no·where (nō′hwer′, nō′wer′) *adv.* to, in, or at no place; not anywhere. —*n.* **1.** no place. **2.** a place or state of obscurity: *Mr. Thompson rose from nowhere to become president of the company.*

no·wise (nō′wīz′) *adv.* in no way; noway.

nox·ious (nok′shəs) *adj.* **1.** very harmful to the health: *noxious gases.* **2.** morally harmful. —**nox′ious·ly,** *adv.* —**nox′ious·ness,** *n.*

noz·zle (noz′əl) *n.* a spout at the end of a hose, pipe, or the like that serves as an outlet for a liquid or gas.

Np, the symbol for neptunium.

N.S., Nova Scotia.

N.T., New Testament.

nth (enth) *adj.* relating to or denoting an indefinitely large or small number or value: *a number raised to the nth power.*

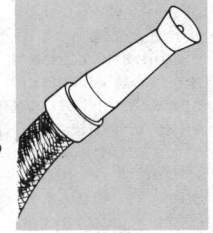

Nozzle

to the nth degree. to the greatest extreme; to the utmost.

nt. wt., net weight.

nu·ance (nōō′äns, nyōō′äns, nōō-äns′, nyōō äns′) *n.* a slight or delicate shade, as of tone, expression, or meaning.

nub (nub) *n.* **1.** a knob or bump. **2.** a small piece or lump: *a nub of a pencil, a nub of coal.* **3.** *Informal.* the main part or point, as of a story.

nub·bin (nub′in) *n.* **1.** a small or imperfect ear of corn. **2.** any small or imperfect fruit.

nub·by (nub′ē) *adj.,* **nub·bi·er, nub·bi·est.** having a rough, lumpy texture: *a nubby fabric, a nubby sweater.*

nu·bile (nōō′bil, nyōō′bil) *adj.* of an age suitable for marriage; marriageable. —**nu·bil′i·ty,** *n.*

nu·cle·ar (nōō′klē ər, nyōō′klē ər) *adj.* **1.** of, relating to, or forming a nucleus. **2.** of, relating to, or involving atomic nuclei or energy derived from atomic nuclei: *a nuclear*

at; āpe; cär; end; mē; it; īce; hot; ōld; fôrk; wood; fōōl; oil; out; up; turn; sing; thin; this; hw in white; zh in treasure. The symbol ə stands for the sound of **a** in about, **e** in taken, **i** in pencil, **o** in lemon, and **u** in circus.

chain reaction, a nuclear weapon. **3.** of, relating to, or having atomic weapons: *a nuclear power.*

nuclear energy, energy obtained from the nucleus of the atom. Also, **atomic energy.**

nuclear fission, see fission *(def. 2).*

nuclear fusion, see fusion *(def. 5).*

nuclear physics, a branch of physics that deals with the structure and properties of atomic nuclei.

nuclear reactor, a device in which a nuclear chain reaction can be begun, continued, and controlled. It is used for generating heat or producing useful radiation.

nu·cle·i (noō′klē ī′, nyoō′klē ī′) a plural of **nucleus.**

nu·cle·ic acid (noō klē′ik, nyoō klē′ik) a group of complex organic compounds found in all living cells, that determine and transmit the inherited traits of all living things. The two main types are DNA and RNA.

nu·cle·o·lus (noō klē′ə ləs, nyoō klē′ə ləs) *n. pl.,* **nu·cle·o·li** (noō klē′ə lī′, nyoō klē′ə lī′). a small round body in the nucleus of a cell.

nu·cle·on (noō′klē on′, nyoō′klē on′) *n.* a proton or neutron, especially one that is a part of the atomic nucleus.

nu·cle·us (noō′klē əs, nyoō′klē əs) *n. pl.,* **nu·cle·i** or **nu·cle·us·es. 1.** a central or necessary part around which other parts are grouped or collected; core: *The nucleus of the building is a large vaulted room. These books form the nucleus of a fine library.* **2.** a small, dense, usually round or oval body located near the center of a plant or animal cell, surrounded by a delicate membrane and containing most of the cell's hereditary material. The nucleus is necessary for growth, reproduction, metabolism, and other vital activities. **3.** the positively charged central portion of an atom, containing most of the atom's mass and consisting of protons and neutrons, except in hydrogen, which consists of only one proton.

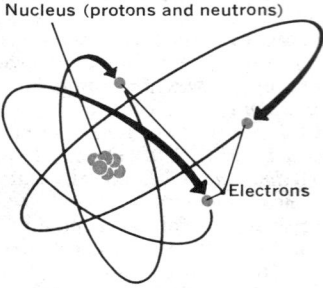

Nucleus (protons and neutrons)

Electrons

Nucleus of an atom

nude (noōd, nyoōd) *adj.* without clothing or other covering; unclothed; bare. —*n.* **1.** an unclothed human figure, especially one represented in a painting or other work of art. **2.** the state of being unclothed. —**nude′ly,** *adv.* —**nude′ness,** *n.*

nudge (nuj) *v.t.,* **nudged, nudg·ing.** to push gently or touch, especially in order to attract attention: *Michael nudged me with his elbow when the teacher called my name.* —*n.* a gentle push or touch.

nu·di·ty (noō′də tē, nyoō′də tē) *n. pl.,* **nu·di·ties.** the state of being nude; nakedness.

nug·get (nug′it) *n.* a lump, especially a lump of gold as it is found in nature.

nui·sance (noō′səns, nyoō′səns) *n.* a person, thing, or action that annoys or offends: *The little boy next door is a nuisance with his water pistol.*

Nu·ku·a·lo·fa (noō′koō ə lō′fə) *n.* the capital and chief port of Tonga. Pop. (1966), 15,545.

null (nul) *adj.* **1.** without force or authority; invalid; ineffective: *He based his argument on theories that were considered null.* **2.** amounting to nothing; nonexistent: *His knowledge of classical music is null.* **3.** *Mathematics.* of or relating to a set that contains no elements or members.

null and void. without legal force; invalid: *After one year, this contract will be null and void.*

nul·li·fi·ca·tion (nul′ə fi kā′shən) *n.* the act of nullifying or the state of being nullified.

nul·li·fy (nul′ə fī′) *v.t.,* **nul·li·fied, nul·li·fy·ing. 1.** to make void; declare invalid; annul: *to nullify a law.* **2.** to cause to amount to nothing; make null: *His mistake was so serious that it nullified all the good work he had done.* —**nul′li·fi·er,** *n.*

numb (num) *adj.* lacking or having lost feeling or movement: *to be numb with cold, to be numb with fear.* —*v.t.* to make numb. —**numb′ly,** *adv.* —**numb′ness,** *n.*

num·ber (num′bər) *n.* **1.** a mathematical idea that shows how many units or objects are contained in a certain group; something that tells how many members there are in a set. **2.** a word or symbol, or group of words or symbols, representing such an idea; numeral. **3.** a specified amount, as of persons or things; total; sum: *The hostess increased the number of invited guests to thirty.* **4.** an unspecified amount, as of persons or things; quantity: *A number of people gathered in front of the store.* **5.** a numeral given to or identifying a person or thing: *What is the number of his room?* **6.** one of the songs or other musical compositions on a program. **7.** a single issue of a magazine. **8.** *Grammar.* a form or property of a word that indicates whether the word is singular or plural. **9. numbers.** strength based on size or amount: *The army overpowered the invaders by force of numbers.* **10. numbers.** arithmetic. —*v.t.* **1.** to find out the number of; count. **2.** to give a number or numbers to. **3.** to amount to or include: *The freshman class numbers over a thousand students.* **4.** to limit the number of: *The days are numbered before summer vacation ends.* —*v.i.* **1.** to amount to a group or total: *The contest winners numbered in the hundreds.* **2.** to list or recite numbers. —**num′ber·er,** *n.* ▲ See **amount** for usage note.

num·ber·less (num′bər lis) *adj.* **1.** too many to be counted; innumerable. **2.** without a number.

number line, a line on which points are identified with real numbers.

Num·bers (num′bərz) *n.* the fourth book of the Old Testament.

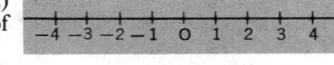

Number line

numb·skull (num′skul′) see **numskull.**

nu·mer·a·ble (noō′mər ə bəl, nyoō′mər ə bəl) *adj.* capable of being counted.

nu·mer·al (noō′mər əl, nyoō′mər əl) *n.* **1.** a symbol or a group of symbols representing a number, such as 7 or VII. **2.** a word standing for such a symbol, such as *seven.* —*adj.* of, relating to, or representing a number or numbers.

nu·mer·ate (noō′mə rāt′, nyoō′mə rāt′) *v.i.,* **nu·mer·at·ed, nu·mer·at·ing.** to number; count. —**nu′mer·a′tion,** *n.*

nu·mer·a·tor (noō′mə rā′tər, nyoō′mə rā′tər) *n.* the number above or to the left of the line in a fraction, indicating the number of equal parts being considered; dividend. In the fraction ½, 1 is the numerator.

nu·mer·i·cal (noō mer′i kəl, nyoō mer′i kəl) *adj.* of, relating to, or represented by a number or numbers. —**nu·mer′i·cal·ly,** *adv.*

nu·mer·ous (noō′mər əs, nyoō′mər əs) *adj.* **1.** forming a large number; many: *We visited them on numerous occasions.* **2.** containing a large number; large: *She has a numerous collection of antiques.* —**nu′mer·ous·ly,** *adv.* —**nu′mer·ous·ness,** *n.*

nu·mis·mat·ics (noō′miz mat′iks, nyoō′miz mat′iks) *n., pl.* the collecting or study of coins, paper money, or medals. —**nu′mis·mat′ic,** *adj.* —**nu·mis·ma·tist** (noō·miz′mə tist, nyoō miz′mə tist), *n.*

num·skull (num′skul′) *also,* **numb·skull.** *n.* a stupid person; blockhead.

nun (nun) *n.* a member of a religious order for women, living under vows in a convent and leading a life of prayer and good works.

nun·ci·o (nun′shē ō′) *n. pl.,* **nun·ci·os.** a permanent ambassador representing the pope in a foreign country.

nun·ner·y (nun′ər ē) *n. pl.,* **nun·ner·ies.** the residence of a group of nuns; convent.

nup·tial (nup′shəl) *adj.* of or relating to marriage or the marriage ceremony: *nuptial bliss, the nuptial feast.* —*n. usually,* **nuptials.** the marriage ceremony; wedding.

Nu·rem·berg (noor′əm burg′, nyoor′əm burg′) *n.* a city in southern West Germany, where many Nazi leaders were placed on trial after World War II. Pop. (1977 est.), 488,755. Also, *German,* **Nürn·berg** (noorn′berk′).

nurse (nurs) *n.* **1.** a person who is trained to attend the sick or injured, usually under the direction of a doctor. **2.** a woman hired to take care of children; nursemaid. —*v.,* **nursed, nurs·ing.** —*v.t.* **1.** to take care of (the sick or injured); act as a nurse for. **2.** to feed (a baby) from the breast; suckle. **3.** to try to cure or heal (an illness or injury). **4.** to handle or use with care: *He nursed his weak knee by limping slightly.* **5.** to aid in the growth or development of; foster: *to nurse a small tree, to nurse a talent.* —*v.i.* **1.** to work as a nurse. **2.** to suckle a baby. **3.** to be fed from the breast.

nurse·maid (nurs′mād′) *n.* a woman hired to take care of children.

nurs·er·y (nur′sər ē) *n. pl.,* **nurs·er·ies. 1.** a room set apart for small children, especially a baby's bedroom. **2.** a place where plants, especially trees and shrubs, are raised for sale.

nurs·er·y·man (nur′sər ē mən) *n. pl.,* **nurs·er·y·men** (nur′sər ē mən). a person who owns or works in a nursery that raises and sells plants.

nursery rhyme, a short, rhymed poem or jingle for young children.

nursery school, a school for children too young for kindergarten.

nurs·ling (nurs′ling) *n.* **1.** a person who is nursed, such as a baby. **2.** a person or thing that receives careful and loving attention.

nur·ture (nur′chər) *v.t.,* **nur·tured, nur·tur·ing. 1.** to take care of; nourish; feed. **2.** to educate, develop, or foster: *to nurture a talent.* —*n.* **1.** something that nourishes; food. **2.** the act or instance of educating, developing, or fostering. —**nur′tur·er,** *n.*

nut (nut) *n.* **1.** the dry fruit of a plant, containing one or more kernels, and having a hard, woody shell. **2.** the kernel of such a fruit. **3.** a block of metal or wood with a screw thread around an opening in the center, into which the threaded end of a bolt fits. **4.** *Slang.* a strange or crazy person. **5.** *Slang.* an enthusiast; devotee; buff: *a jazz nut.* —*v.i.,* **nut·ted, nut·ting.** to hunt for or gather nuts. —**nut′like′,** *adj.*

nut·crack·er (nut′krak′ər) *n.* **1.** a device for cracking nuts. **2.** a bird related to the crow, having a long, pointed bill. Nutcrackers feed on pine seeds and nuts.

nut·hatch (nut′hach′) *n. pl.,* **nut·hatch·es.** any of various small, lively birds related to the titmouse that can run up and down tree trunks and walk upside down on branches.

nut·meat (nut′mēt′) *n.* the edible part of a nut.

Nutcracker

nut·meg (nut′meg′) *n.* **1.** a hard, aromatic seed of an evergreen tree, dried and ground or grated and used as a spice. **2.** the tree bearing this seed, having light-green or yellowish-green leaves and yellow flowers.

nu·tri·a (noo′trē ə, nyoo′trē ə) *n.* **1.** another word for **coypu. 2.** the soft, thick, velvety fur of the coypu, often dyed to look like beaver.

nu·tri·ent (noo′trē ənt, nyoo′trē ənt) *adj.* giving nourishment; nutritious. —*n.* a nutritious substance that is needed by the body. Proteins, fats, carbohydrates, minerals, and vitamins are all sources of nutrients.

nu·tri·ment (noo′trə mənt, nyoo′trə mənt) *n.* anything that nourishes; food.

nu·tri·tion (noo trish′ən, nyoo trish′ən) *n.* **1.** the process by which nutrients are taken and absorbed into body tissues. **2.** nourishment: *The poor child was sick because he had not had proper nutrition.* —**nu·tri′tion·al,** *adj.* —**nu·tri′tion·al·ly,** *adv.*

nu·tri·tious (noo trish′əs, nyoo trish′əs) *adj.* containing or giving nourishment; nourishing: *George was careful to eat only nutritious food.* —**nu·tri′tious·ly,** *adv.* —**nu·tri′tious·ness,** *n.*

nu·tri·tive (noo′tri tiv, nyoo′tri tiv) *adj.* **1.** giving nourishment; nutritious: *a nutritive diet.* **2.** of or relating to nutrition. —**nu′tri·tive·ly,** *adv.*

nuts (nuts) *adj. Slang.* **1.** eccentric or crazy. **2.** in love with or very enthusiastic about something.

nut·shell (nut′shel′) *n.* the hard shell of a nut.
in a nutshell. in a few words: *The book review gave the author's ideas in a nutshell.*

nut·ty (nut′ē) *adj.,* **nut·ti·er, nut·ti·est. 1.** filled with or producing nuts. **2.** having the flavor of nuts. **3.** *Slang.* strange or crazy; nuts: *They must be really nutty to have done such a thing.* —**nut′ti·ly,** *adv.* —**nut′ti·ness,** *n.*

nuz·zle (nuz′əl) *v.,* **nuz·zled, nuz·zling.** —*v.t.* to touch or rub with the nose: *The dog nuzzled his master.* —*v.i.* to press or lie close; nestle; cuddle: *The little girl nuzzled against her mother's shoulder.*

NW, northwest; northwestern.

N.W.T., Northwest Territories.

N.Y., New York.

Ny·as·a, Lake (nyä′sə, nī as′ə) a large lake in southeastern Africa.

Ny·as·a·land (nyä′sə land′, nī as′ə land′) *n.* see **Malawi.**

N.Y.C., New York City.

ny·lon (nī′lon) *n.* **1.** any of a group of strong, synthetic substances that are used to make thread for fabric, bristles for brushes, tires for automobiles, handles for tools, and other products. **2.** a fabric woven with threads made from this substance. **3. nylons.** stockings that are made of nylon.

nymph (nimf) *n.* **1.** *Greek and Roman Mythology.* any of various goddesses that were believed to live in forests, hills, or rivers, and usually represented as beautiful maidens. **2.** a beautiful young woman. **3.** the larva of any of various insects, such as the dragonfly and cicada, that go through gradual changes to reach the adult stage. —**nymph′like′,** *adj.*

N.Z., New Zealand.

at; āpe; cär; end; mē; it; īce; hot; ōld; fôrk; wood; fool; oil; out; up; turn; sing; thin; this; hw in white; zh in treasure. The symbol ə stands for the sound of a in about, e in taken, i in pencil, o in lemon, and u in circus.

O

1. Semitic ○	4. Greek Ninth Century B.C. ○ ▱
2. Early Phoenician ◇	5. Latin Fourth Century B.C. Capitals ○
3. Early Hebrew ○	6. English ○

O is the fifteenth letter of the English alphabet. It is one of the very few letters whose written form has remained almost unchanged throughout the history of the alphabet. The earliest form of the letter **O** was the ancient Semitic letter *ayin* (1), which stood for a breathing sound. A similar, although more oval, letter appeared in the early Phoenician (2) and early Hebrew (3) alphabets. When the Greeks adapted *ayin* for their own alphabet, they used it to represent the short *o* sound and called it *omicron* (4). In Greek, *omicron* literally meant "small *o.*" The Greek letter for the long *o* sound was called *omega,* meaning "great *o.*" The Romans (5) borrowed *omicron* from the Greeks and by the fourth century B.C. were writing it almost exactly the way we write the capital letter **O** today (6).

o, O (ō) *n. pl.,* **o's, O's. 1.** the fifteenth letter of the English alphabet. **2.** something having the shape of this letter. **3.** zero.

O (ō) *interj.* **1.** used in formal address: *O heart, how fares it with thee now?* (Alfred, Lord Tennyson). **2.** another spelling of **oh.**

O, the symbol for oxygen.

o' (ə, ō) *prep.* of: *will-o'-the wisp.*

oaf (ōf) *n.* a stupid, clumsy person. —**oaf'ish,** *adj.*

O·a·hu (ō ä'hōō) *n.* the third largest island of Hawaii, on which Honolulu is located.

oak (ōk) *n.* **1.** any of a large group of trees or shrubs bearing acorns and found especially in northern temperate regions. **2.** the hard, strong wood of this tree, used for making furniture, floorings, and boats.

oak·en (ō'kən) *adj.* made of oak: *an oaken chair.*

Oak·land (ōk'lənd) *n.* a port city in western California, on San Francisco Bay. Pop. (1970), 361,561.

Oak Ridge, a city in eastern Tennessee, a major atomic research center.

oa·kum (ō'kəm) *n.* a loose fiber obtained by untwisting and picking apart old ropes. It is often used for filling up seams and cracks in a wooden boat or ship.

oar (ôr) *n.* **1.** a long, usually wooden pole with a flat or curved blade at one end, used to row or steer a boat. **2.** a person who rows a boat; oarsman. —*v.t.* to propel with oars; row. —*v.i.* to move by rowing.

oar·lock (ôr'lok') *n.* a device, usually U-shaped, for holding an oar in place while rowing. Also, **rowlock.**

oars·man (ôrz'mən) *n. pl.,* **oars·men** (ôrz'mən). a person who rows a boat.

OAS, Organization of American States.

o·a·sis (ō ā'sis) *n. pl.,* **o·a·ses** (ō ā'sēz). **1.** a place in a desert that is fertile because it has a supply of water. **2.** any place or condition that provides refreshment or relief: *The library was an oasis of quiet in the noisy school.*

oat (ōt) *n.* **1.** *also,* **oats.** the cereal grain of a plant of the grass family. It is used as food and as fodder for horses. **2.** *also,* **oats.** the plant bearing this grain, having slender, flat, bluish-green leaves.

oat·en (ōt'ən) *adj.* relating to, containing, or made of oats, oatmeal, or oat straw.

oath (ōth) *n. pl.,* **oaths** (ōthz, ōths). **1.** a formal declaration that is made with an appeal to God or to an honored or sacred person or thing to witness the fact that one will tell the truth or keep a promise. **2.** the use of the name of God or an honored or sacred person or thing to add emphasis or express anger. **3.** a word used in swearing; curse.

under oath. bound by an oath to tell the truth.

Oat

oat·meal (ōt'mēl') *n.* **1.** a meal made by grinding or rolling oats. **2.** a cooked cereal prepared from this.

O·ba·di·ah (ō'bə dī'ə) *n.* **1.** a Hebrew prophet of the sixth century B.C. **2.** a book of the Old Testament containing prophecies attributed to him.

ob·bli·ga·to (ob'li gä'tō) *Music. adj.* (of an accompaniment or part) necessary for the performance of a composition. —*n. pl.,* **ob·bli·ga·tos.** an obbligato accompaniment or part.

ob·du·ra·cy (ob'dər ə sē, ob'dyər ə sē) *n.* the state or quality of being obdurate.

ob·du·rate (ob'dər it, ob'dyər it) *adj.* **1.** not yielding; stubborn; obstinate: *His obdurate denial of the truth made us very angry.* **2.** unmoved by feelings of pity or regret; hard-hearted: *an obdurate attitude.* —**ob'du·rate·ly,** *adv.* —**ob'du·rate·ness,** *n.*

o·be·di·ence (ō bē′dē əns) *n.* the act of obeying or the state of being obedient.

o·be·di·ent (ō bē′dē ənt) *adj.* tending or willing to obey or submit to something, such as a rule, order, or law: *an obedient dog, an obedient child.* —**o·be′di·ent·ly,** *adv.*

o·bei·sance (ō bā′səns, ō bē′səns) *n.* **1.** a movement or gesture of the body showing obedience or respect, such as a bow or curtsy. **2.** deference, respect, or regard given or shown; homage: *to pay obeisance to an important person.*

ob·e·lisk (ob′ə lisk′) *n.* a four-sided stone pillar that narrows as it rises and is shaped like a pyramid at the top. It was often used as a monument in ancient Egypt.

O·ber·hau·sen (ō′bər hou′sən) *n.* a city in northwestern West Germany. Pop. (1969 est.), 249,000.

O·ber·on (ō′bə ron′) *n. Medieval Legend.* the king of the Fairies.

o·bese (ō bēs′) *adj.* extremely fat or fleshy. —**o·bese′ness,** *n.*

o·bes·i·ty (ō bē′sə tē) *n.* the condition of being obese.

o·bey (ō bā′) *v.t.* **1.** to carry out the orders, requests, or instructions of: *The boy obeyed his parents and came home before dark.*

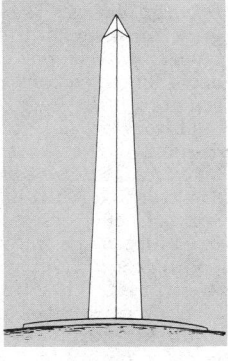

Obelisk

2. to carry out or comply with: *to obey the law, to obey orders.* **3.** to be guided or controlled by: *She obeyed her conscience and did not lie.* —*v.i.* to be obedient.

o·bi (ō′bē) *n. pl.,* **o·bis.** a broad sash worn with a Japanese kimono.

o·bit·u·ar·y (ō bich′ōō er′ē) *n. pl.,* **o·bit·u·ar·ies.** a notice of a person's death, especially in a newspaper, often including a short biography. —*adj.* relating to or recording a death.

obj. 1. object. **2.** objection. **3.** objective.

ob·ject (*n.,* ob′jikt; *v.,* əb jekt′) *n.* **1.** anything that can be seen or touched; material thing: *She held a large round object in her hand.* **2.** a person or thing toward which feeling, thought, or action is directed: *The scientist's theory was the object of much criticism.* **3.** a thing desired or aimed at; pur-

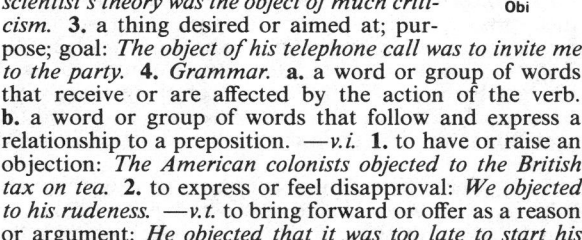

Obi

pose; goal: *The object of his telephone call was to invite me to the party.* **4.** *Grammar.* **a.** a word or group of words that receive or are affected by the action of the verb. **b.** a word or group of words that follow and express a relationship to a preposition. —*v.i.* **1.** to have or raise an objection: *The American colonists objected to the British tax on tea.* **2.** to express or feel disapproval: *We objected to his rudeness.* —*v.t.* to bring forward or offer as a reason or argument: *He objected that it was too late to start his homework.* —**ob·jec′tor,** *n.*

ob·jec·tion (əb jek′shən) *n.* **1.** a cause or reason for opposing, disliking, or disapproving of something: *Mother's objection to our going out was that it was too late.* **2.** a feeling of opposition, dislike, or disapproval: *He showed his objection to our presence by stalking out of the room.*

ob·jec·tion·a·ble (əb jek′shə nə bəl) *adj.* deserving of or causing dislike or disapproval; offensive: *objectionable behavior.* —**ob·jec′tion·a·bly,** *adv.*

ob·jec·tive (əb jek′tiv) *adj.* **1.** not affected or influenced by personal feelings or opinions; without bias; detached: *The reporter tried to be as objective as possible in writing about the election.* **2.** having actual existence independent

of the mind; real: *His fear of the dark had no basis in objective fact.* **3.** *Grammar.* designating the case of the object of a verb or preposition. —*n.* **1.** something toward which effort is directed. **2.** *Grammar.* **a.** the objective case. **b.** a word in this case; object. **3.** a lense or lenses nearest to the object being observed through an optical instrument, such as a telescope, microscope, or camera. —**ob·jec′tive·ly,** *adv.* —**ob·jec′tive·ness,** *n.*

ob·jec·tiv·i·ty (ob′jek tiv′ə tē) *n.* the state or quality of being objective.

object lesson, a practical illustration of some principle or truth.

ob·jet d'art (ōb zhä där′) *n. pl.,* **ob·jets d'art** (ōb zhä-där′). *French.* an object, such as a vase, that has artistic value.

ob·li·gate (ob′lə gāt′) *v.t.,* **ob·li·gat·ed, ob·li·gat·ing.** to bind morally or legally, as by a contract, promise, or sense of duty: *A driver is obligated to obey the traffic laws.*

ob·li·ga·tion (ob′lə gā′shən) *n.* **1.** a binding power, as of a law, promise, or sense of duty: *We are under an obligation to him for lending us the money.* **2.** something that one is morally or legally bound to do: *It is the obligation of all citizens to vote.* **3.** the fact or condition of being grateful or indebted to another for something received: *He feels a deep sense of obligation toward his parents.* **4.** something by which one is bound, such as a promise or sense of duty or responsibility: *He felt an obligation to repay the money his friend gave him.*

ob·lig·a·to·ry (ə blig′ə tôr′ē) *adj.* of the nature of or being an obligation; compulsory.

o·blige (ə blīj′) *v.t.,* **o·bliged, o·blig·ing. 1.** to bind or compel, as by moral or legal force: *Mr. Jones was obliged to pay for the window his son broke.* **2.** to place under an obligation, as for a favor or service; make indebted or grateful: *I am obliged to you for the help you have given me.* **3.** to do a favor or service for: *Please oblige me by returning this book to the library.*

o·blig·ing (ə blī′jing) *adj.* willing to do favors or to be of service; helpful. —**o·blig′ing·ly,** *adv.*

o·blique (ə blēk′) *adj.* **1.** having a slanting or sloping direction, position, or course; inclined: *an oblique line.* **2.** not straightforward or direct: *She gave an oblique answer to my question.* —*n.* something that is oblique, as a line. —**ob·lique′ly,** *adv.*

oblique angle, any angle that is not a right angle; acute angle or obtuse angle.

ob·lit·er·ate (ə blit′ə rāt′) *v.t.,* **ob·lit·er·at·ed, ob·lit·er·at·ing. 1.** to destroy completely; remove all traces of: *The heavy rains obliterated the footprints on the path.* **2.** to blot or rub out, as writing; erase. —**ob·lit′er·a′tion,** *n.*

ob·liv·i·on (ə bliv′ē ən) *n.* **1.** the state or condition of being entirely forgotten: *That author's works have passed into oblivion.* **2.** the state or condition of forgetting completely; forgetfulness.

ob·liv·i·ous (ə bliv′ē əs) *adj.* not aware or conscious; unmindful: *She was oblivious to the noise around her.* —**ob·liv′i·ous·ly,** *adv.* —**ob·liv′i·ous·ness,** *n.*

ob·long (ob′lông′) *adj.* having greater length than width, such as an ellipse and certain rectangles. —*n.* an oblong figure.

at; āpe; cär; end; mē; it; īce; hot; ōld; fôrk; wood; fōōl; oil; out; up; turn; sing; thin; **th**is; hw in white; zh in treasure. The symbol ə stands for the sound of **a** in about, **e** in taken, **i** in pencil, **o** in lemon, and **u** in circus.

ob·lo·quy (ob′lə kwē) *n. pl.,* **ob·lo·quies. 1.** abusive, slanderous language addressed to or aimed at another, especially by a large number of people. **2.** the disgrace or shame resulting from such abuse.

ob·nox·ious (ob nok′shəs) *adj.* extremely annoying, disagreeable, or offensive: *That bully is an obnoxious person.* —**ob·nox′ious·ly,** *adv.* —**ob·nox′ious·ness,** *n.*

o·boe (ō′bō) *n.* a woodwind instrument having a double reed and a high, penetrating tone.

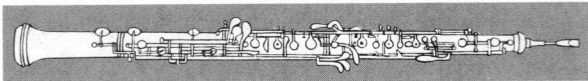

Oboe

ob·scene (əb sēn′) *adj.* offensive to modesty or decency; indecent. —**ob·scene′ly,** *adv.*

ob·scen·i·ty (əb sen′ə tē) *n. pl.,* **ob·scen·i·ties. 1.** the state or quality of being obscene; indecency. **2.** something that is obscene, as an act, expression, or word.

ob·scure (əb skyoor′) *adj.,* **ob·scur·er, ob·scur·est. 1.** not clearly expressed; difficult to understand: *an obscure explanation.* **2.** barely perceived by the senses; not clear or distinct: *She could not recognize the obscure figure in the background of the photograph.* **3.** not well known; undistinguished: *an obscure writer.* **4.** not easily noticed or discovered; remote; hidden: *an obscure mountain village.* **5.** having little or no light; dark; dim: *She hid her diary in an obscure corner of the attic.* —*v.t.,* **ob·scured, ob·scur·ing. 1.** to hide from view; darken or conceal: *Fog obscured the sun.* **2.** to make difficult to understand: *The speaker's frequent use of unfamiliar words obscured his meaning.* —**ob·scure′ly,** *adv.* —**ob·scure′ness,** *n.*

ob·scu·ri·ty (əb skyoor′ə tē) *n. pl.,* **ob·scu·ri·ties. 1.** the state or quality of being obscure. **2.** a person or thing that is obscure.

ob·se·quies (ob′sə kwēz) *n.,pl. sing.,* **ob·se·quy** (ob′sə-kwē). funeral rites or services.

ob·se·qui·ous (əb sē′kwē əs) *adj.* too willing or eager to serve, please, or obey; fawning. —**ob·se′qui·ous·ly,** *adv.* —**ob·se′qui·ous·ness,** *n.*

ob·serv·a·ble (əb zur′və bəl) *adj.* **1.** that can be observed; noticeable: *There was an observable change in temperature.* **2.** that may or must be observed, celebrated, followed, or kept: *Certain formalities are observable in a court of law.* —**ob·serv′a·bly,** *adv.*

ob·serv·ance (əb zur′vəns) *n.* **1.** the act or practice of following, keeping to, or complying with something, such as a rule or law: *State police enforce the observance of the speed limit on the highways.* **2.** the act or practice of keeping or celebrating a customary rite, ceremony, or holiday: *the observance of Easter.* **3.** a customary rite, ceremony, or celebration: *Birthdays are annual observances.* **4.** the act of noticing or perceiving; observation.

ob·serv·ant (əb zur′vənt) *adj.* **1.** quick to notice or perceive; alert: *An observant reader found a misspelling in the book.* **2.** careful in observing anything required, as a rule, law, or custom: *A good citizen must be observant of the laws.* —**ob·serv′ant·ly,** *adv.*

ob·ser·va·tion (ob′zər vā′shən) *n.* **1.** the act, practice, or power of seeing and noticing: *The detective's careful observation helped him to solve the crime.* **2.** the fact or condition of being observed; notice: *The thief escaped observation.* **3.** the act of examining, noting, and recording facts or occurrences, especially for scientific study: *Meteorological observations help us to make weather predictions.* **4.** a remark or comment: *The reporter made some clever observations about the baseball game.* —**ob′ser·va′tion·al,** *adj.*

ob·serv·a·to·ry (əb zur′və tôr′ē) *n. pl.,* **ob·serv·a·to·ries. 1.** a place or building furnished with telescopes and other equipment for observing, studying, and collecting information on the moon, planets, or stars. **2.** a building or place equipped for observing the weather. **3.** any place or building providing a wide view.

ob·serve (əb zurv′) *v.t.,* **ob·served, ob·serv·ing. 1.** to see or notice: *She observed a man entering the neighbor's house.* **2.** to watch carefully; regard with attention: *Observe how much sugar I add to the cake batter.* **3.** to make a careful observation of, especially for a scientific purpose: *The scientist observed the behavior of the mice after they were given the drug.* **4.** to follow or comply with, as a rule or law: *to observe the speed limit.* **5.** to keep or celebrate according to custom: *to observe Christmas.* **6.** to comment; remark: *"It's going to rain this evening," he observed.* —**ob·serv′er,** *n.*

ob·sess (əb ses′) *v.t.* to occupy or trouble the mind of: *The idea that someone was following him obsessed him.*

ob·ses·sion (əb sesh′ən) *n.* **1.** the act of obsessing or the state of being obsessed. **2.** something that obsesses, as a fixed idea or desire: *Making a great deal of money is an obsession with him.*

ob·sid·i·an (ob sid′ē ən) *n.* a hard, glassy rock, usually black, formed when molten lava cools.

ob·so·les·cent (ob′sə les′ənt) *adj.* going out of use; becoming out of date or obsolete: *an obsolescent word.* —**ob′so·les′cence,** *n.*

ob·so·lete (ob′sə lēt′, ob′sə lēt′) *adj.* **1.** no longer in use or practice: *Stagecoaches are obsolete.* **2.** out-of-date; old-fashioned; outmoded.

● **Obsolete** words are words that at one time were part of the standard English vocabulary but are no longer used. There are various reasons why words become obsolete. Over a period of time, a concept or idea can become obsolete. When this happens, the words that relate to such a concept or idea will most likely become obsolete, too. For example, many words that referred to knighthood are no longer used today. Words also can become obsolete because their use is not widespread. For instance, in our own language the large-scale borrowing of Greek and Latin words in the fifteenth and sixteenth centuries brought words into English that were rarely used. A number of these words were considered obsolete as early as the middle of the seventeenth century. Duplication of words also can cause a word to become obsolete. Many words in Old English became obsolete after the Norman conquest brought French words to England. In many cases, when both an Old English word and a French word meant the same thing, the Old English word was dropped from the vocabulary.

Slang words become obsolete more quickly than any other type of word. Unlike most words that are part of standard English, slang words lack a secure position in the language, and one that is fashionable for a time may quickly fall into disuse. Very few slang words ever become a permanent part of our language. Although a large number of the words that have at some time been a part of our language are now obsolete, constant coining and borrowing of new words have more than offset this process, and the English vocabulary is larger now than at any other time in its history.

ob·sta·cle (ob′stə kəl) *n.* a person or thing that opposes, stands in the way, or blocks progress: *The heavy snow was an obstacle to traffic.*

ob·stet·ric (ob stet′rik) *adj.* of or relating to obstetrics and childbirth. Also, **ob·stet·ri·cal** (ob stet′ri kəl).

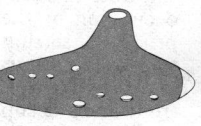

O

ob·ste·tri·cian (ob'stə trish'ən) *n.* a physician specializing in obstetrics.

ob·stet·rics (ob stet'riks) *n.,pl.* the branch of medicine that deals with the care of women from the first sign of pregnancy until a few weeks after the baby is born. ▲ used with a singular verb.

ob·sti·na·cy (ob'stə nə sē) *n. pl.,* **ob·sti·na·cies.** **1.** the state or quality of being obstinate; stubbornness. **2.** an act or instance of this.

ob·sti·nate (ob'stə nit) *adj.* **1.** not yielding to argument, persuasion, or reason; stubborn; inflexible: *It is very difficult to make an obstinate person change his mind.* **2.** difficult to overcome, control, or cure: *an obstinate cough.* —**ob'sti·nate·ly,** *adv.*

ob·strep·er·ous (əb strep'ər əs) *adj.* noisy, boisterous, or unruly: *The speaker could not quiet the obstreperous heckler.* —**ob·strep'er·ous·ly,** *adv.* —**ob·strep'er·ous·ness,** *n.*

ob·struct (əb strukt') *v.t.* **1.** to block or fill with obstacles that prevent passage: *Large boulders obstructed the entrance to the cave.* **2.** to be or come in the way of: *The woman's hat obstructed my view of the stage.* **3.** to interrupt, interfere with, or delay the progress of: *The lawyer tried to obstruct justice by offering the judge a bribe.* —**ob·struc'tive,** *adj.*

ob·struc·tion (əb struk'shən) *n.* **1.** something that obstructs: *The soldiers set up blockades and other obstructions on the road to the city.* **2.** the act of obstructing or the state of being obstructed.

ob·struc·tion·ism (əb struk'shə niz'əm) *n.* the act or practice of obstructing work or progress, especially in a meeting or legislature. —**ob·struc'tion·ist,** *n.*

ob·tain (əb tān') *v.t.* to get as one's own, especially as a result of effort; gain possession of; acquire: *In order to obtain the information I needed, I had to go to the library.* —*v.i.* to be widespread, established, or customary: *The custom of holding family reunions still obtains in many parts of the country.* —**ob·tain'a·ble,** *adj.*

ob·trude (əb trood') *v.,* **ob·trud·ed, ob·trud·ing.** —*v.t.* **1.** to force or thrust upon another or others in a rude or bold manner: *He obtruded his opinions on everyone he met.* **2.** to push out; thrust forward. —*v.i.* to force oneself upon another or others.

ob·tru·sion (əb troo'zhən) *n.* **1.** the act of obtruding. **2.** something obtruded.

ob·tru·sive (əb troo'siv) *adj.* tending to obtrude; forward. —**ob·tru'sive·ly,** *adv.* —**ob·tru'sive·ness,** *n.*

ob·tuse (əb toos', əb tyoos') *adj.* **1.** slow in understanding or sensing; dull or stupid. **2.** not sharp or pointed; blunt. —**ob·tuse'ly,** *adv.* —**ob·tuse'ness,** *n.*

obtuse angle, an angle that is greater than 90 degrees but less than 180 degrees.

ob·verse (*n.,* ob'vurs; *adj.,* ob vurs') *n.* **1.** the side of a coin or medal that bears the main design. **2.** the front or main side of anything. —*adj.* turned toward or facing the observer. —**ob·verse'ly,** *adv.*

Right angle   Obtuse angle

Obtuse angle

ob·vi·ate (ob'vē āt') *v.t.,* **ob·vi·at·ed, ob·vi·at·ing.** to anticipate and prevent or remove; take care of beforehand: *to obviate the risks involved in shipping explosives.*

ob·vi·ous (ob'vē əs) *adj.* **1.** easily seen or understood; clearly evident: *She made it obvious that she didn't want to go.* **2.** not trying to hide one's feelings; without pretense: *He was very obvious about his distrust of us.* —**ob'vi·ous·ly,** *adv.* —**ob'vi·ous·ness,** *n.*

oc·a·ri·na (ok'ə rē'nə) *n.* a musical wind instrument that has ten finger holes and produces a soft tone like that of a whistle when air is blown through the mouthpiece.

Ocarina

O'Ca·sey, Sean (ō kā'sē; shôn) 1880–1964, Irish dramatist.

oc·ca·sion (ə kā'zhən) *n.* **1.** the particular time at which something occurs: *I cannot remember the occasion, but I have met her before.* **2.** an event or occurrence: *I congratulated her on the occasion of her graduation.* **3.** an event or function thought of as being special or important: *The baby's first birthday was an occasion.* **4.** a favorable or suitable time; opportunity: *I don't have many occasions to talk to him.* **5.** an immediate cause or reason: *His departure was the occasion of much sadness.* —*v.t.* to be the cause of; bring about: *His rude behavior occasioned a quarrel.*

on occasion. once in a while; at times; occasionally: *We see them on occasion.*

oc·ca·sion·al (ə kā'zhən əl) *adj.* **1.** happening or appearing now and then; not frequent: *There will be occasional showers today.* **2.** produced or used for some special occasion or event: *His friend wrote an occasional song for his graduation.* **3.** (of furniture) not part of a set: *an occasional chair.*

oc·ca·sion·al·ly (ə kā'zhən əl ē) *adv.* once in a while; at times.

Oc·ci·dent (ok'sə dənt) *n.* the countries of Europe and the Western Hemisphere.

Oc·ci·den·tal (ok'sə dent'əl) *also,* **oc·ci·den·tal.** *adj.* of, relating to, or characteristic of the Occident. —*n.* a member of a people native to the Occident.

oc·cip·i·tal (ok sip'ət əl) *adj.* of or relating to the back part of the head or skull. —*n.* see **occipital bone.**

occipital bone, the bone located at the back of the skull.

oc·clude (ə klood') *v.,* **oc·clud·ed, oc·clud·ing.** —*v.t.* **1.** to stop up, close, or block, as a passage or pore. **2.** to shut in, out, or off. **3.** of a chemical compound, to absorb and retain (another compound). **4.** of a mass of cold air, to force (warm air) upward from the surface of the earth. —*v.i.* of the teeth in the upper and lower jaws, to meet closely.

oc·clu·sion (ə kloo'zhən) *n.* the act of occluding or the state of being occluded.

oc·cult (ə kult', ok'ult) *adj.* **1.** of, relating to, or concerned with certain mystical arts or practices, as astrology or alchemy. **2.** beyond the range of human understanding; mysterious.

oc·cult·ism (ə kul'tiz əm, ok'əl tiz'əm) *n.* **1.** a belief in the existence of mysterious or hidden spiritual powers. **2.** the study or practice of occult arts.

oc·cu·pan·cy (ok'yə pən sē) *n. pl.,* **oc·cu·pan·cies.** **1.** the act of occupying or the state of being occupied. **2.** a period of time during which something is occupied: *The cabin was rented for a one-year occupancy.*

oc·cu·pant (ok'yə pənt) *n.* **1.** a person who occupies a place or position. **2.** a person having legal control or possession of a property, such as a house, office building, or apartment.

at; āpe; cär; end; mē; it; īce; hot; ōld; fôrk; wood; fool; oil; out; up; turn; sing; thin; **this;** hw in white; zh in treasure. The symbol ə stands for the sound of **a** in about, **e** in taken, **i** in pencil, **o** in lemon, and **u** in circus.

oc·cu·pa·tion (ok'yə pā'shən) *n.* **1.** the work that a person does to earn a living; profession; trade. **2.** the act of occupying or the state of being occupied. **3.** the act or process of seizing and maintaining control of enemy territory by a military force.

oc·cu·pa·tion·al (ok'yə pā'shən əl) *adj.* of or resulting from one's occupation: *an occupational disease.*

oc·cu·py (ok'yə pī') *v.t.,* **oc·cu·pied, oc·cu·py·ing. 1.** to take up (time or space): *Running errands for his mother occupied most of the morning.* **2.** to seize and maintain control of by military force: *Enemy troops occupied the town.* **3.** to live in; inhabit: *The family occupied a house.* **4.** to keep busy or engage: *The boy occupied himself by working on his model airplane.* **5.** to have and keep possession of: *Her father occupies a high government position.* —**oc'cu·pi'er,** *n.*

oc·cur (ə kur') *v.i.,* **oc·curred, oc·cur·ring. 1.** to take place; come to pass: *The explosion occurred at noon.* **2.** to appear or be found: *The same theme occurs in much of his writing.* **3.** to come to mind; suggest itself: *It did not occur to me to take my umbrella.*

oc·cur·rence (ə kur'əns) *n.* **1.** the act or fact of occurring. **2.** something that occurs; incident.

o·cean (ō'shən) *n.* **1.** the whole body of salt water that covers nearly three-fourths of the earth's surface. **2.** any one of the four major subdivisions of this body of water; the Atlantic, Pacific, Indian, or Arctic Ocean.

O·ce·an·i·a (ō'shē an'ē ə) *n.* the islands of the Pacific Ocean, including Melanesia, Micronesia, and Polynesia, and sometimes including Australia, New Zealand, and the Malay Archipelago. —**O'ce·an'i·an,** *adj.,* *n.*

o·ce·an·ic (ō'shē an'ik) *adj.* of, relating to, or living in the ocean: *oceanic fish.*

o·cean·og·ra·phy (ō'shə nog'rə fē) *n.* the science of the oceans, dealing with the structure of the ocean basins, composition and movement of the waters, and oceanic life. —**o'cean·og'ra·pher,** *n.* —**o·cean·o·graph·ic** (ō'shə nə graf'ik), *adj.*

o·cel·lus (ō sel'əs) *n. pl.,* **o·cel·li** (ō sel'ī). a simple kind of eye in insects and certain other animals without backbones, used to distinguish between light and dark.

o·ce·lot (os'ə lot', ō'sə lot') *n.* a wildcat native to Central and South America, having a yellowish coat marked with black spots, rings, and stripes.

o·cher (ō'kər) *also,* **o·chre.** *n.* **1.** a mixture of clay and iron oxides ranging in color from yellow to red, used as a pigment. **2.** a reddish- or brownish-yellow color. —*adj.* having the color ocher.

Ocelot

o'clock (ə klok') *adv.* of or according to the clock: *They will meet us at two o'clock.* [Contraction of *of the clock.*]

Oct., October.

octa- *combining form* eight: *octagon.*

oc·ta·gon (ok'tə gon') *n.* a polygon having eight sides and eight angles.

oc·tag·o·nal (ok tag'ən əl) *adj.* having the shape of an octagon. —**oc·tag'o·nal·ly,** *adv.*

oc·tane (ok'tān) *n.* a colorless, liquid hydrocarbon found in petroleum.

octane number, a number indicating the extent to which a motor fuel resists engine knocking. A high octane number produces less knocking.

oc·tave (ok'tiv, ok'tāv) *n.* **1.** *Music.* **a.** the interval between the first and eighth tones or notes of the major scale.

b. a tone or note having twice or half as many vibrations per second as the one below or above it at this interval. **c.** a combination of two tones or notes at this interval sounded together. **d.** a series of tones or notes or of keys of an instrument contained within this interval: *The singer's range is two octaves.* **2.** any group of eight.

oc·ta·vo (ok tā'vō) *n. pl.,* **oc·ta·vos. 1.** a page or paper size, as of a book, usually measuring from 5 by 8 inches to 6 by 9½ inches, formerly ⅛ of a whole printer's sheet. **2.** a book having pages this size.

oc·tet (ok tet') *n.* **1.** *Music.* **a.** a composition for eight voices or instruments. **b.** a group of eight performers. **2.** any group of eight.

Oc·to·ber (ok tō'bər) *n.* the tenth month of the year, having thirty-one days. [Latin *Octōber* the eighth month of the early Roman calendar, in which March was the first month, from *octō* eight.]

oc·to·ge·nar·i·an (ok'tə jə ner'ē ən) *n.* a person who is eighty years old or between eighty and ninety years old. —*adj.* being eighty or between eighty and ninety years old.

oc·to·pus (ok'tə pəs) *n. pl.,* **oc·to·pus·es** or **oc·to·pi** (ok'-tə pī'). a saltwater animal having a soft, rounded body and eight arms, or tentacles, on which there are suckers that help it to move along the ocean bottom and to capture prey.

Octopus diagram labeled: Head, Eye, Siphon, Trunk, Suckers, Tentacles.

Octopus

oc·u·lar (ok'yə lər) *adj.* **1.** of, relating to, or similar to the eye or eyesight. **2.** seen by the eye; visual.

oc·u·list (ok'yə list) *n.* a doctor who specializes in the treatment of diseases and disorders of the eye; ophthalmologist.

odd (od) *adj.* **1.** differing from the usual or ordinary; strange; peculiar: *an odd remark, an odd way of dressing. It is odd that he never answered my letter.* **2.** being what remains of a pair or set: *an odd shoe, an odd dish.* **3.** irregular; occasional: *He does odd jobs after school.* **4.** leaving a remainder of one when divided by two: *5, 7, and 187 are odd numbers.* **5.** with an indefinite amount in addition to a certain round number. ▲ often connected to a numeral by a hyphen: *I have forty-odd dollars in the bank.* **6.** left over; extra: *He was the odd man on the team.* —**odd'ly,** *adv.* —**odd'ness,** *n.*

odd·i·ty (od'ə tē) *n. pl.,* **odd·i·ties. 1.** a person or thing that is odd or peculiar: *His collection of snakes was an oddity.* **2.** the state or quality of being odd; strangeness.

odds (odz) *n.,pl.* **1.** the difference in favor of or against something being true or happening, often stated in the form of a ratio: *The odds are ten to one against that horse's winning the race.* **2.** an allowance or advantage given to the weaker opponent in a contest. **3.** a difference that favors one side and is against another; advantage: *In a contest where strength is important, the odds are with him.* **at odds.** in disagreement; quarreling.

odds and ends, miscellaneous or leftover items: *I bought a few odds and ends at the hardware store.*

ode (ōd) *n.* a dignified and lofty lyric poem, usually rhymed and often addressed to a person or thing.

O·der (ō'dər) *n.* a river flowing into the Baltic Sea, forming part of the boundary between Poland and East Germany.

O·des·sa (ō des'ə) *n.* **1.** a city in western Texas. Pop.

(1970), 78,380. **2.** a port city in the southwestern Soviet Union, on the Black Sea. Pop. (1970 est.), 892,000.

O·din (ō′din) *n. Norse Mythology.* the king of the gods and god of wisdom and war. In Teutonic mythology he was called Woden.

o·di·ous (ō′dē əs) *adj.* causing hate, disgust, or repugnance; detestable: *an odious crime.* —**o′di·ous·ly,** *adv.* —**o′di·ous·ness,** *n.*

o·di·um (ō′dē əm) *n.* **1.** extreme hatred, disgust, or repugnance, detestation: *We view cruelty to animals with odium.* **2.** shame or disgrace: *the odium of being disloyal.*

o·dom·e·ter (ō dom′ə tər) *n.* a device for measuring the distance traveled by a vehicle.

o·dor (ō′dər) *n.* **1.** the quality of a thing or substance that affects the sense of smell; scent. **2.** reputation or estimation. —**o′dor·less,** *adj.*

o·dor·if·er·ous (ō′də rif′ər əs) *adj.* having or giving off an odor, especially a pleasant one. —**o′dor·if′er·ous·ly,** *adv.* —**o′dor·if′er·ous·ness,** *n.*

o·dor·ous (ō′dər əs) *adj.* another word for **odoriferous.** —**o′dor·ous·ly,** *adv.* —**o′dor·ous·ness,** *n.*

O·dys·se·us (ō dis′ē əs) *n.* another name for **Ulysses.**

Od·ys·sey (od′ə sē) *n. pl.,* **Od·ys·seys. 1.** an ancient Greek epic poem describing the adventures of Odysseus after the Trojan War. It is thought to have been written by Homer. **2. odyssey.** any long, adventurous journey.

O. E. D., Oxford English Dictionary. See **Oxford.**

Oed·i·pus (ed′ə pəs, ē′də pəs) *n. Greek Legend.* a king who fulfilled a prophecy by unknowingly killing his father and marrying his mother.

o′er (ôr) *prep., adv.* over. ▲ used in literature.

of (ov, uv; *unstressed* əv) *prep.* **1.** belonging to: *the cover of a book, the leg of a chair.* **2.** descended or coming from: *a citizen of France.* **3.** away or at a distance from: *He fell within a yard of the finish line. We met at five minutes of twelve.* **4.** that is or is called; named: *the city of New York.* **5.** having as a quality; characterized by: *a man of honor.* **6.** in or with regard to; concerning: *to be innocent of a crime.* **7.** as a result of; caused by: *to die of suffocation.* **8.** having; possessing: *a family of wealth.* **9.** filled with or containing: *a glass of water, a book of poetry.* **10.** from the whole number, amount, or group making up: *Three members of the class were absent.* **11.** made, created, or produced by: *the novels of Dickens, the sweet fragrance of flowers.* **12.** made from or with: *a house of stone.*

off (ôf) *prep.* **1.** so as to be no longer on or connected with; away from: *to take a book off a shelf, to jump off a horse.* **2.** not engaged in or occupied with; free from: *to be off duty.* **3.** differing from or less than the usual or normal: *He fell because he was off balance.* **4.** *Informal.* no longer using or eating: *He's been off cake and candy since his illness.* **5.** seaward of: *The submarine was a mile off the coast.* —*adv.* **1.** so as to be no longer connected, attached, or on: *to break off a piece of bread, to take off one's coat.* **2.** so as to be no longer working, continuing, or taking place: *to call off a party, to turn a motor off.* **3.** at or to a distance: *The dog scared off the stranger.* **4.** so as to be away from work or duty: *to take the day off.* **5.** so as to divide, set apart, or form: *to mark off an area on a map.* **6.** on the way: *to start off on a trip.* —*adj.* **1.** no longer working, continuing, or taking place: *The electricity is off.* **2.** not engaged in or occupied with work or duty: *She was off for the holidays.* **3.** in a specified state or condition: *to be well off financially.* **4.** not accurate or correct: *His addition of the bill was off by three cents.* **5.** on the way; going: *The children are off to bed.* **6.** not up to the usual or normal level or standard; below average: *an off year.*

off and on. now and then; at times.

off with. take off; remove: *Off with their heads!*

of·fal (ô′fəl) *n.* **1.** the waste parts of a butchered animal. **2.** garbage; refuse.

off-beat (ôf′bēt′) *n. Music.* any weak or unaccented beat in a measure. —*adj. Informal.* differing from the usual or ordinary; strange; unconventional: *an off-beat movie.*

off-col·or (ôf′kul′ər) *adj.* **1.** slightly improper; not decent: *an off-color joke.* **2.** without the usual color.

Of·fen·bach, Jacques Le·vy (ô′fən bäk′; zhäk·lā vē′) 1819–1880, French composer, born in Germany.

of·fence (ə fens′) *British.* another spelling of **offense.**

of·fend (ə fend′) *v.t.* **1.** to cause or arouse resentment, anger, or displeasure; insult: *Your remarks offended her.* **2.** to be displeasing or disagreeable to. —*v.i.* to commit an offense; do wrong. —**of·fend′er,** *n.*

of·fense (*defs. 1–4* ə fens′; *def. 5* ô′fens) *also, British,* **offence.** *n.* **1.** the act of breaking or violating the law or a rule. **2.** the act of causing or arousing resentment, anger, or displeasure: *He meant no offense by that remark.* **3.** something that offends: *His behavior was an offense to me.* **4.** the act of attacking or assaulting: *A knife may be used for offense.* **5.** *Sports.* the side, team, or players having possession of the ball or puck and trying to score, as in football, basketball, or hockey.

to give offense. to offend.

to take offense. to be offended.

of·fen·sive (ə fen′siv) *adj.* **1.** causing resentment, anger, or displeasure; giving offense: *offensive behavior.* **2.** unpleasant to the senses; disagreeable: *an offensive smell.* **3.** relating to or used for attack: *an offensive weapon, offensive tactics.* **4.** *Sports.* of or relating to the offense. —*n.* a position, attitude, or course of attack: *The enemy took the offensive and attacked the fort.* —**of·fen′sive·ly,** *adv.* —**of·fen′sive·ness,** *n.*

of·fer (ô′fər) *v.t.* **1.** to present for acceptance or refusal: *to offer an apology.* **2.** to express one's willingness or readiness (to do or give something); volunteer: *She offered to help.* **3.** to put forth or propose for consideration: *to offer an opinion.* **4.** to attempt or make a show of: *The enemy offered little resistance.* **5.** to suggest or propose as a price: *We offered ten dollars for the book.* **6.** to present as an act of religious worship or devotion: *to offer up prayers in thanksgiving.* —*v.i.* **1.** to present itself; occur: *He will visit us whenever the opportunity offers.* **2.** to make an offering in religious worship or devotion. —*n.* **1.** the act of offering. **2.** something that is offered.

of·fer·ing (ô′fər ing) *n.* **1.** something that is offered, such as a contribution at a religious service. **2.** the act of making an offer.

of·fer·to·ry (ô′fər tôr′ē) *n. pl.,* **of·fer·to·ries. 1.** the part of the Mass or Communion service at which the unconsecrated bread and wine are offered to God. **2.** the collection of the congregation's offerings at a religious service. **3.** the verses said or the music sung by the choir during the offerings at Mass or other religious services.

off·hand (ôf′hand′) *adv.* without previous thought or preparation: *She could not say offhand when she would arrive.* —*adj.* **1.** done, made, or said offhand: *offhand comments.* **2.** casual; informal: *an offhand manner.*

off·hand·ed (ôf′han′did) *adj.* done, made, or said offhand. —**off′hand′ed·ly,** *adv.* —**off′hand′ed·ness,** *n.*

at; āpe; cär; end; mē; it; īce; hot; ōld; fôrk; wood; fōōl; oil; out; up; turn; sing; thin; this; hw in white; zh in treasure. The symbol ə stands for the sound of a in about, e in taken, i in pencil, o in lemon, and u in circus.

of·fice (ô′fis) *n.* **1.** a place in which business, professional services, or clerical duties are carried on. **2.** all the people who work in such a place: *The office is having a Christmas party.* **3.** a position or post of authority, trust, or responsibility, especially in a government or corporation: *the office of vice-president.* **4.** a duty, service, or responsibility of one's position or post: *He exercises the offices of teacher and counselor.* **5.** *also,* **Office.** an administrative unit or branch of a government. **6.** *also,* **offices.** something done for another; kindness, service, or favor. **7.** *also,* **Office.** a religious ceremony for a particular occasion or purpose.

of·fice·hold·er (ô′fis hōl′dər) *n.* a person who holds a public office.

of·fi·cer (ô′fə sər) *n.* **1.** a person appointed to a particular rank and position of authority in a military service, especially one holding a commission, as a general or captain. **2.** a person who holds an office or position, as in a club or business. **3.** the captain or any of the captain's chief assistants on a boat or ship. **4.** a member of the police.

of·fi·cial (ə fish′əl) *n.* a person who holds an office or position. *—adj.* **1.** of or relating to an office or position of authority: *official duties.* **2.** coming from or authorized by a proper authority: *The President made an official statement to the press.* **3.** authorized to carry out some specific function: *an official scorekeeper.* **4.** characteristic of or suitable for a person of authority; formal: *There was an official reception for the visiting king.* —**of·fi′cial·ly,** *adv.*

of·fi·ci·ate (ə fish′ē āt′) *v.i.,* **of·fi·ci·at·ed, of·fi·ci·at·ing.** to perform the duties and functions of an office or position: *The governor officiated at the opening of the new school.*

of·fi·cious (ə fish′əs) *adj.* too forward in offering services or advice to others; meddlesome: *an officious neighbor.* —**of·fi′cious·ly,** *adv.* —**of·fi′cious·ness,** *n.*

off·ing (ô′fing) *n.* that part of the sea that can be seen lying between the shore and the horizon.
  in the offing. in the near future: *Their wedding is in the offing.*

off·set (*v.,* ôf′set′; *n.,* ôf′set′) *v.t.,* **off·set, off·set·ting. 1.** to balance or make up for: *Her virtues offset her faults.* **2.** to reproduce (something) by offset printing. *—n.* **1.** something that balances or makes up for something else; compensation. **2.** a shoot or branch that grows from a root or main stem near the ground and can take root as a new plant. **3.** see **offset printing.**

offset printing, a printing process in which an inked impression is transferred from a coated zinc or aluminum plate to a cylinder covered with rubber, which in turn transfers it onto paper.

off·shoot (ôf′shoot′) *n.* **1.** a shoot or branch that grows from the main stem of a plant. **2.** anything that develops, grows, or branches off from something else.

off·shore (ôf′shôr′) *adj.* **1.** moving or directed away from the shore: *an offshore storm.* **2.** at a distance from the shore: *offshore fishing.* *—adv.* **1.** in a direction away from the shore. **2.** at a distance from the shore: *to anchor a ship offshore.*

off·side (ôf′sīd′) *also,* **off side.** *adj.* **1.** in football, illegally ahead of the ball before a play begins. **2.** in certain games, especially hockey, illegally ahead of the puck or ball in an attacking zone or area. *—adv.* in or to a position that is offside.

off·spring (ôf′spring′) *n. pl.,* **off·spring** or **off·springs.** the young of a person, animal, or plant.

off·stage (ôf′stāj′) *adj.* in or from that part of the stage that cannot be seen by the audience. *—adv.* away from that part of the stage that can be seen by the audience.

oft (ôft) *adv. Archaic.* often.

of·ten (ô′fən) *adv.* many times; repeatedly; frequently.

of·ten·times (ô′fən tīmz′) *adv.* frequently; often. Also, **oft·times** (ôft′tīmz′).

o·gle (ō′gəl) *v.t.,* **o·gled, o·gling.** to look or stare at in a leering or amorous way. *—n.* a leering or amorous look. —**o′gler,** *n.*

o·gre (ō′gər) *n.* **1.** in fairy tales and legends, a fearsome man-eating giant or monster. **2.** any person or thing that is cruel, brutal, or dreaded.

oh (ō) *also,* **O.** *interj.* used to express an emotion or feeling, as of surprise, joy, grief, or pain.

O. Hen·ry (ō hen′rē) 1862–1910, U.S. short story writer; born William Sidney Porter.

O·hi·o (ō hī′ō) *n.* **1.** a state in the north-central United States. Capital, Columbus. Area, 41,222 sq. mi. Pop. (1970), 10,652,017. **2.** a river in the east-central United States, flowing from Pittsburgh southwest into the Mississippi. —**O·hi′o·an,** *adj., n.*

● **Ohio** was an Iroquoian name meaning "fine, great, beautiful river." Settlers used the name for the district around the Ohio River. It was later given to the territory and the state.

ohm (ōm) *n.* a unit of electrical resistance equal to the resistance of a conductor in which a potential difference of one volt produces a current of one ampere. [From Georg S. *Ohm,* 1787–1854, a German physicist.]

-oid *suffix* (used to form adjectives from nouns) having the form, nature, or appearance of: *spheroid.*

oil (oil) *n.* **1.** any of a large group of greasy substances that will dissolve in alcohol but not in water. Oils are liquid at normal temperatures or liquefy readily when warmed. Oil is obtained from animals, as whale oil, from vegetables, as linseed oil, and from minerals, as kerosene. **2.** another word for **petroleum. 3.** see **oil paint. 4.** see **oil painting.** *—v.t.* to cover, smear, grease, supply, or polish with oil: *to oil a hinge, to oil furniture.* —**oil′er,** *n.*

oil burner, a furnace or heating unit that burns fuel oil.

oil·cloth (oil′klôth′) *n.* a waterproof fabric made by coating cloth with oil or a similar substance. It is used for tablecloths, shelf lining, cushion covers, and the like.

oil color, another term for **oil paint.**

oil of vitriol, another term for **sulfuric acid.**

oil paint, paint that is made of pigment ground in linseed or other oil.

oil painting 1. a painting done in oil paints. **2.** the art of painting in oil paints.

oil·skin (oil′skin′) *n.* **1.** a fabric that has been treated with oil or a similar substance to make it waterproof. It is used especially for rainwear. **2.** a garment made of this fabric.

oil well, a well that is dug or drilled in the earth to obtain petroleum.

oil·y (oi′lē) *adj.,* **oil·i·er, oil·i·est. 1.** of, containing, or like oil: *an oily taste.* **2.** covered, smeared, or soaked with oil; greasy: *an oily rag.* **3.** too smooth or polished in speech or manner: *an oily salesman.* —**oil′i·ness,** *n.*

oint·ment (oint′mənt) *n.* a soft, usually greasy, substance, often medicated, applied to the skin to soothe, protect, or heal it; salve.

O·jib·wa (ō jib′wä′) *n. pl.,* **O·jib·wa** or **O·jib·was. 1.** a member of a large tribe of North American Indians formerly living in the Great Lakes region, now living mainly in Minnesota, Wisconsin, and North Dakota. **2.** the language of this tribe. Also, **Chippewa.**

OK (ō′kā′) *also,* **o·kay.** *Informal. adj., adv., interj.* all right: *Is it OK if I borrow your book?* *—n. pl.,* **OK's.** agreement or approval: *We need the treasurer's OK before we can spend more money.* *—v.t.,* **OK'd, OK'ing.** to ap-

O

prove or agree to: *to OK a plan.* [Probably made popular as a slogan of the *O. K. Club* of the Democratic Party in 1840. The club name was an abbreviation of *Old Kinderhook,* the nickname of the Democratic candidate, Martin Van Buren, who was born in Kinderhook, New York. *OK* was in use before 1840, but its origin is not known.]

o·ka·pi (ō kä′pē) *n. pl.,* **o·ka·pis** or **o·ka·pi.** an African animal related to the giraffe, having a dark purplish-brown coat and black and white stripes resembling those of a zebra on the upper legs and hindquarters.

Okapi

o·kay (ō′kā′) *Informal. adj., adv., interj., n. pl.,* **o·kays,** *v.t.,* **o·kayed, o·kay·ing.** another spelling of **OK.**

O·khotsk, Sea of (ō kotsk′) an arm of the Pacific Ocean, off the eastern coast of Siberia.

O·kie (ō′kē) *n. Informal.* a migrant farm worker. [From *Oklahoma;* because poor farming conditions forced Oklahoma farmers to migrate during the depression of the 1930s.]

O·ki·na·wa (ō′kə nä′wə) *n.* an island in the Pacific Ocean, south of Japan, administered by the United States from 1945 to 1972, and now administered by Japan. It was the site of a major battle of World War II in 1945.

Okla., Oklahoma.

O·kla·ho·ma (ō′klə hō′mə) *n.* a state in the south-central United States. Capital, Oklahoma City. Area, 69,919 sq. mi. Pop. (1970), 2,559,253. Abbreviation, **Okla.** —**O′kla·ho′man,** *adj., n.*

● In an Indian treaty of 1866, the Choctaws used **Oklahoma,** meaning "red people," to designate their lands. The name was borrowed for a railroad station at the present site of Oklahoma City, and was adopted later for the territory and the state.

Oklahoma City, the capital of Oklahoma, in the central part of the state. Pop. (1970), 366,481.

o·kra (ō′krə) *n.* **1.** the soft, sticky pods of a plant, used in soups and eaten as a vegetable. **2.** the plant bearing these pods. Also, **gumbo.**

O·laf V (ō′läf) 1903—, the king of Norway since 1957.

old (ōld) *adj.,* **old·er** or **eld·er, old·est** or **eld·est. 1.** having lived or existed for a long period of time: *an old man.* **2.** of a certain age: *Our car is three years old.* **3.** not new, recent, or current: *an old song, an old joke.* **4.** known or used in the past or for a long time; familiar: *We are old friends.* **5.** of or belonging to the ancient or remote past. **6.** former: *an old boyfriend.* **7.** worn with age or use; worn-out: *We gave all our old clothes to charity.* —*n.* former times: *knights of old.*

old country, a country from which a person has emigrated.

Old Delhi, another name for **Delhi.**

old·en (ōld′ən) *adj.* old; ancient: *stories of olden days.*

Old English 1. the English language as it was spoken until about the year 1100. Also, **Anglo-Saxon. 2.** a style of printing characterized by elaborate, angular letters, used especially in printing formal documents or invitations. It is the style that was used by the first printers of books.

𝕬𝕭𝕮𝕯𝕰𝕱𝕲𝕳
𝖓𝖔𝖕𝖖𝖗𝖘𝖙𝖚𝖛𝖜𝖝𝖞𝖟

Old English letters

● **Old English** is the earliest form of the English language. It was brought to England by Germanic tribes of Angles, Saxons, and Jutes from northwestern Europe who invaded the island in the fifth century A.D. Because these tribes were conquerors, they soon made their language, which is also called *Anglo-Saxon,* the common language of England. Old English would seem like a completely foreign language to you if you were to hear or see it today, even though approximately one-fifth of our modern vocabulary comes from it. Unlike modern English, it is a highly *inflected* language. This means that the case, number, and tense of a word are indicated by a change within the word itself, rather than by the use of a preposition, such as *of, to,* or *for,* before a noun, or an auxiliary verb, such as *will, have,* or *had,* before a verb. Nouns in Old English are considered to be of the masculine, feminine, or neuter gender. The ending of an adjective or the definite article is changed to agree with the gender and case of a noun.

The invasion and conquest of England in 1066 by French-speaking Normans had a great effect on the English language. Old English had been slowly changing during the previous centuries. These natural changes combined with the introduction of French to produce a new form of the language, which is called **Middle English.** English vocabulary was greatly enriched by the addition of French words and, because French developed as a dialect of Latin, a large number of Latin words. Over a period of hundreds of years, Old English had tended to lose some of its inflections. This trend continued in Middle English, and, by the fourteenth century, English grammar had been greatly changed. It is much less difficult to understand written or spoken Middle English than Old English because the vocabulary, pronunciation, and grammar of Middle English are not that different from Modern English.

The beginnings of **Modern English** are in the fifteenth and sixteenth centuries, during which there was a revival of interest in classical learning. Many words from Latin, the language which has contributed the largest number of words to our modern vocabulary, were borrowed at this time. Greek words, especially those that related to art and science, were also borrowed. At the same time, the pronunciation of English, particularly of vowel sounds, changed. These changes produced the pronunciation that we give to most words today. Only the spelling of early Modern English, which was similar to the spelling of Old English and Middle English, would be difficult for a modern reader to understand. English spelling was not standardized until the eighteenth century. At that time, a growing interest in standardizing written and spoken English developed. This interest caused scholars to write dictionaries which were responsible for providing most of the standards of spelling that we follow today. From the eighteenth century to the present time, our language has changed very little, except in vocabulary. Industrial and technological advances have made it necessary to create thousands of new terms. The tremendous increase in foreign trade and travel have also brought many words into our language.

at; āpe; cär; end; mē; it; īce; hot; ōld; fôrk; wood; fo͝ol; oil; out; up; turn; sing; thin; this; hw in white; zh in treasure. The symbol ə stands for the sound of a in about, e in taken, i in pencil, o in lemon, and u in circus.

Old English sheepdog, a large dog having a long, shaggy, gray or bluish-gray coat with white markings.

old·fash·ioned (ōld′fash′ənd) *adj.* **1.** keeping to or favoring old ways, ideas, or customs: *My aunt is very old-fashioned about many things.* **2.** of, relating to, or characteristic of former times; out-of-date: *an old-fashioned hat, an old-fashioned idea.*

Old French, the French language from the ninth to the thirteenth centuries A.D.

Old Glory, the flag of the United States.

Old High German, the form of the German language spoken in southern Germany from the eighth to the twelfth centuries A.D. Modern German is descended from Old High German.

Old Icelandic, the Icelandic language from the ninth to the thirteenth centuries A.D.

old·ish (ōl′dish) *adj.* somewhat old.

Old Latin, the Latin language before the second century B.C.

old maid **1.** an older woman who has never been married. **2.** *Informal.* a person who is prim, fussy, and prudish. **3.** a simple card game in which the player holding the odd queen at the end is the loser.

Old Norse, the language of Scandinavia from the eighth to the fourteenth centuries A.D., especially in its Norwegian and Icelandic forms.

old·ster (ōld′stər) *n. Informal.* a person who is old or elderly.

Old Testament, the collection of writings that makes up the Jewish Bible and the first part of the Christian Bible. It contains an account of the Creation and early man, the sacred agreements between God and the Hebrews, and the laws, prophecies, and religious literature of the Hebrew nation up to the second century B.C.

old·time (ōld′tīm′) *adj.* of, belonging to, or characteristic of former times: *old-time movies.*

old·tim·er (ōld′tī′mər) *n. Informal.* **1.** a person who has been a member of a group or organization for a long time. **2.** a person who is old or elderly.

Old-World (ōld′wurld′) *adj.* **1.** of, relating to, or belonging to the Old World: *Old-World customs, Old-World monkeys.* **2.** old-world. belonging to or characteristic of former times: *old-world politeness.*

Old World, the Eastern Hemisphere, including Europe, Asia, and Africa: *Columbus sailed from the Old World.*

o·le·an·der (ō′lē an′dər) *n.* a very poisonous evergreen shrub, having narrow, lance-shaped leaves and clusters of fragrant, funnel-shaped flowers that are red, purple, or white.

Flower   Fruit

Oleander

o·le·o·mar·ga·rine (ō′lē ō-mär′jər in) *also,* **o·le·o·mar·ga·rin.** *n.* see **margarine.** Also, **o·le·o** (ō′lē ō′).

ol·fac·to·ry (ol fak′tər ē) *adj.* of or relating to the sense of smell: *an olfactory nerve.* —*n. pl.,* **ol·fac·to·ries.** an olfactory organ.

ol·i·garch (ol′ə gärk′) *n.* any of the rulers in an oligarchy.

ol·i·gar·chic (ol′ə gär′kik) *adj.* of, relating to, or ruled by an oligarchy. Also, **ol·i·gar·chi·cal** (ol′ə gär′ki kəl).

ol·i·gar·chy (ol′ə gär′kē) *n. pl.,* **ol·i·gar·chies.** **1.** a form of government in which power is held by only a few people.

2. a state having such a government. **3.** the body of persons making up such a government.

Ol·i·go·cene (ol′ə gō sēn′) *n.* the third geological epoch of the Tertiary period, when the first monkeys and apes appeared. —*adj.* of, relating to, or characteristic of this epoch.

ol·ive (ol′iv) *n.* **1.** a small, oily fruit of any of a group of evergreen shrubs and trees, having a single hard seed and firm flesh. It is often eaten pickled and is widely used as a source of olive oil. **2.** a shrub or tree bearing this fruit. **3.** a dull yellowish-green color. Also, **olive green.** —*adj.* having the color olive.

olive branch **1.** a branch of the olive tree thought of as a symbol of peace. **2.** anything offered as a sign or token of peace or good will.

olive drab **1.** a dull greenish-brown color. **2.** a woolen fabric of this color. **3.** *also,* **olive drabs.** a military uniform made of this fabric.

olive oil, a clear yellow or greenish-yellow oil obtained by pressing olives, used as a salad and cooking oil.

Ol·ives, Mount of (ol′ivz) a ridge of hills east of Jerusalem, thought to be the site of Jesus' Ascension.

O·lym·pi·a (ō lim′pē ə) *n.* **1.** the capital of Washington, in the western part of the state. Pop. (1970), 23,111. **2.** a plain in the northwestern Peloponnesus, the site of the Olympic games in ancient Greece.

O·lym·pi·ad (ō lim′pē ad′) *n.* **1.** a period of four years from one celebration of the Olympic games to another, by which the ancient Greeks reckoned time. **2.** a celebration of the modern Olympic games.

O·lym·pi·an (ō lim′pē ən) *adj.* **1.** of or relating to Mount Olympus or the gods who, in Greek mythology, lived there. **2.** of or relating to the plain of Olympia. **3.** like a god; majestic; exalted: *Olympian beauty.* —*n.* **1.** one of the twelve major Greek gods who lived on Mount Olympus. **2.** a person who competes in the Olympic games.

O·lym·pic (ō lim′pik) *adj.* **1.** of or relating to Mount Olympus or to the plain of Olympia. **2.** of or relating to the Olympic games. —*n.* **Olympics.** see **Olympic games.**

Olympic games **1.** in ancient Greece, a festival consisting of a series of competitions in athletics, poetry, music, and oratory. It was held every four years at Olympia in honor of Zeus. **2.** modern international athletic contests modeled on the ancient athletic games, held every four years in a different country.

O·lym·pus, Mount (ō lim′pəs) a mountain in northeastern Greece that, in Greek mythology, was the home of the twelve major gods.

O·ma·ha (ō′mə hô′, ō′mə hä′) *n.* a city in eastern Nebraska. Pop. (1970), 347,328.

O·man (ō män′) *n.* a country on the southeastern coast of the Arabian peninsula, formerly known as **Muscat and Oman.** Capital, Muscat. Area, 82,000 sq. mi. Pop. (1978 est.), 840,000.

O·mar Khay·yám (ō′mär kī yäm′) died 1123?, Persian poet, astronomer, and mathematician.

om·buds·man (om′budz mən) *n. pl.,* **om·buds·men** (om-budz′mən). an official who investigates complaints made by private citizens against government officials and agencies.

o·meg·a (ō meg′ə, ō mē′gə) *n.* **1.** the twenty-fourth and last letter of the Greek alphabet (Ω, ω), corresponding to the English long *o.* **2.** the last in a group or series; end.

om·e·let (om′ə lit, om′lit) *also,* **om·e·lette.** *n.* a dish made of beaten eggs that have been cooked in a pan and then folded over. It often has a filling of cheese or meat.

o·men (ō′mən) *n.* a sign or event that is supposed to foretell good or bad luck.

om·i·nous (om′ə nəs) *adj.* foretelling trouble or misfortune; threatening: *ominous black clouds coming in from the sea.* —**om′i·nous·ly,** *adv.* —**om′i·nous·ness,** *n.*

o·mis·sion (ō mish′ən) *n.* **1.** the act of omitting or the state of being omitted. **2.** something that is omitted.

o·mit (ō mit′) *v.t.,* **o·mit·ted, o·mit·ting. 1.** to leave out; fail to include: *to omit an item on a shopping list.* **2.** to fail to do or perform; neglect: *He omitted putting his bicycle away.*

om·ni·bus (om′nə bus′) *n. pl.,* **om·ni·bus·es. 1.** see **bus.** **2.** a collection of works written by the same author or of writings relating to the same subject: *an omnibus of ghost stories.* —*adj.* including or covering a number of different items, cases, or instances: *The legislature passed an omnibus bill.*

om·nip·o·tence (om nip′ət əns) *n.* unlimited power or authority: *the omnipotence of a dictator.*

om·nip·o·tent (om nip′ət ənt) *adj.* having unlimited power or authority; all-powerful. —*n.* **the Omnipotent.** God. —**om·nip′o·tent·ly,** *adv.*

om·ni·pres·ent (om′nə prez′ənt) *adj.* present in all places at the same time: *an omnipresent god.* —**om′ni·pres′ence,** *n.*

om·nis·cient (om nish′ənt) *adj.* having unlimited knowledge; knowing everything. —*n.* **the Omniscient.** God. —**om·nis′cience,** *n.* —**om·nis′cient·ly,** *adv.*

om·niv·o·rous (om niv′ər əs) *adj.* **1.** eating both animal and vegetable food: *Bears are omnivorous.* **2.** eating all kinds of food. **3.** taking in everything: *an omnivorous reader.* —**om·niv′o·rous·ly,** *adv.* —**om·niv′o·rous·ness,** *n.*

Omsk (omsk) *n.* a city in the central Soviet Union. Pop. (1970 est.), 821,000.

on (ôn, on) *prep.* **1.** in a position above and supported by; above and in contact with: *The coats are on the bed.* **2.** so as to be in contact with a surface: *He put the ring on her finger. Please put butter on both sides of the bread.* **3.** fastened to or suspended from: *a watch on a chain.* **4.** in a position at, near, or next to: *Their cabin is on the lake.* **5.** in the direction of; toward; to: *Our house is on the left.* **6.** directed toward, especially in the way of attack; against: *to make war on one's enemies.* **7.** in the state, condition, or process of: *I bought the dress on sale. The guard was on duty.* **8.** in regard to; about; concerning: *The lecture was on the fall of the Roman Empire.* **9.** during the time, course, or occasion of: *We left on Thursday.* **10.** connected or associated with as a member: *Harry is on the football team.* **11.** by means or use of: *We went for a ride on our bicycles.* —*adv.* **1.** in or into a position in contact with, supported by, or covering something: *to put one's shoes on.* **2.** forward in time or space; onward: *Please move on. Time marches on.* **3.** in or into action, operation, or movement: *to turn the water on.* **4.** in or at the present place or position: *If you don't hang on, you'll fall.* —*adj.* **1.** taking place; happening: *The war is still on.* **2.** in operation or movement: *The radio is on.*

  and so on. and more of the same; and so forth.
  on and off. from time to time; occasionally.
  on and on. without stopping; continuously.

once (wuns) *adv.* **1.** one time: *He has a piano lesson once a week.* **2.** in time past; previously: *She was once a beautiful woman.* **3.** at any time; ever: *If our dog once gets loose, he'll be gone for the rest of the day.* —*n.* one single time: *Once should be enough.* —*conj.* as soon as; when; whenever: *That game is easy, once you learn the basic rules.*

  all at once. all at the same time: *He tried to do everything all at once.*
  at once. a. without delay; immediately: *Come here at once.* **b.** at the same time.

once and for all. finally or for the last time.
once in a while. from time to time; occasionally.
once upon a time. at some time in the past; long ago.

on·com·ing (ôn′kum′ing, on′kum′ing) *adj.* approaching: *an oncoming train.* —*n.* approach: *the oncoming of summer.*

one (wun) *n.* **1.** the first and lowest cardinal number. **2.** a symbol representing this number, such as 1 or I. **3.** a single person or thing: *There is only one left in the box.* —*adj.* **1.** being a single person or thing: *one girl, one pencil, one loaf of bread.* **2.** being a specific person, thing, or group: *The child ran from one side of the yard to the other.* **3.** some: *His quick temper will get him in trouble one day.* **4.** a certain: *The winner was one Bill Jones.* —*pron.* **1.** a specific person or thing: *One of the boys was left behind.* **2.** any person or thing: *One could see that he was very upset.*

  at one. in harmony, unity, or agreement.
  one and all. everyone.
  one another. each other: *They loved one another.*
  one by one. one at a time in succession.

O·nei·da (ō nī′də) *n. pl.,* **O·nei·das** or **O·nei·da. 1.** a member of a tribe of Iroquois Indians of central New York State. **2.** the language of this tribe.

O′Neill, Eugene (ō nēl′) 1888–1953, U.S. dramatist.

one·ness (wun′nis) *n.* the state or quality of being one; singleness or sameness.

one·self (wun self′) *also,* **one's self.** *pron.* **1.** one's own self: *Seeing oneself on television is exciting.* **2.** one's usual or normal self.

one·sid·ed (wun′sī′did) *adj.* **1.** favoring or presenting only one side; biased; partial: *The reporter wrote a very one-sided account of the trial.* **2.** unequal or uneven: *a one-sided game.* **3.** having or on one side only.

one·time (wun′tīm′) *adj.* former: *a one-time actor.*

one-to-one (wun′tə wun′) *adj.* **1.** equal on both sides: *a one-to-one exchange of letters.* **2.** *Mathematics.* relating to a rule of correspondence that pairs each element of one set with one and only one element from another set.

one·track (wun′trak′) *adj.* limited to only one idea or purpose at a time; narrow: *a one-track mind.*

one·way (wun′wā′) *adj.* **1.** moving or allowing movement in one direction only: *one-way traffic, a one-way street.* **2.** allowing travel in one direction only: *a one-way ticket.* **3.** one-sided: *a one-way conversation.*

on·go·ing (ôn′gō′ing, on′gō′ing) *adj.* continuing: *Building new housing is an ongoing program of the city.*

on·ion (un′yən) *n.* **1.** a plant bulb having a strong taste and smell, eaten as a vegetable either raw or cooked. **2.** the plant bearing this bulb. —**on′-ion·like′,** *adj.*

on·ion·skin (un′yən skin′) *n.* a thin, strong, translucent paper.

on·look·er (ôn′look′ər, on′-look′ər) *n.* a person who looks on without taking part; spectator.

on·ly (ōn′lē) *adj.* **1.** alone of its kind or class; without oth-

Onions

ers; solitary: *Tom is an only child.* **2.** most suitable or excellent of all; best: *She is the only person for the job.* —*adv.* **1.** no more than; nothing but: *I have only two dollars.* **2.** no one or nothing other than: *Only Jan remembered that it was my birthday.* **3.** exclusively; solely: *This bus runs only on weekends.* —*conj.* except that; but: *I would have gone, only it was raining.*

  only too. very: *He was only too glad to help us plan the party.*

on·o·mat·o·poe·ia (on′ə mat′ə pē′ə, on′ə mä′tə-pē′ə) *n.* **1.** the forming of a name or word by imitating the natural sound associated with the thing indicated. **2.** a word formed in this way. **3.** the use of such words, as in poetry.

● **Onomatopoeia** is one of the ways in which new words are created. Throughout the history of our language, onomatopoetic words have been coined when a word is needed to describe a natural sound or the sound made by an object or action. Many of these words, such as *buzz, hiss, clang,* and *meow,* have become a part of the standard English vocabulary. Other onomatopoetic words are *nonce words,* or words that are made up for a special purpose and are not a permanent part of our language. A person reading or hearing such a word will easily understand its meaning because the word clearly imitates a sound. For example, in the sentence "The stone fell ker-plunk into the lake," you can imagine what the word *ker-plunk* means even though it is not a real English word.

  In Greek, the word *onomatopoeia* means literally "to make names." Some scholars believe that "making names" by coining onomatopoetic words is the way language first developed. Early language may have been the attempt of people to imitate the natural sounds that they heard around them.

  One of the most interesting features of onomatopoeia is the comparison of related words among various languages. Because we hear the same sounds, the words are very often similar. For instance, in English we use the word *cock-a-doodle-doo* to describe the sound a rooster makes. In French the equivalent word is *cocorico,* in Spanish it is *quiquiriquí,* in German it is *kikeriki,* and in Japanese it is *kokke-kokko.*

---

on·o·mat·o·po·et·ic (on′ə mat′ə pō et′ik, on′ə mä′tə pō et′ik) *adj.* relating to or of the nature of onomatopoeia.

On·on·da·ga (on′ən dô′ga) *n. pl.,* **On·on·da·gas** or **On·on·da·ga. 1.** a member of a tribe of Iroquois Indians formerly living in central New York state, now living mainly in Canada. **2.** the language of this tribe.

on·rush (ôn′rush′, on′rush′) *n.* a rapid or violent forward flow or rush: *The house was swept from its foundations by the onrush of floodwaters.*

on·set (ôn′set′, on′set′) *n.* **1.** the beginning; start: *the onset of summer.* **2.** an attack; assault.

on·shore (ôn′shôr′, on′shôr′) *adv., adj.* on or toward the shore.

on·side (ôn′sīd′, on′sīd′) *adj., adv.* in various sports, not offside.

on·slaught (ôn′slôt′, on′slôt′) *n.* a vigorous or destructive attack or assault: *The onslaught of the storm took the campers by surprise.*

Ont., Ontario.

On·tar·i·o (on ter′ē ō′) *n.* **1.** Lake. the smallest and easternmost of the five Great Lakes, between New York and Canada. **2.** a province of Canada, in the southeastern part of the country, north of the Great Lakes. Area, 412,582 sq. mi. Pop. (1971), 7,703,106. —**On·tar′i·an,** *adj., n.*

on·to (ôn′tōō, on′tōō) *prep.* **1.** to a position on: *The door opens onto the street. The actress walked onto the stage.* **2.** *Informal.* aware of: *I'm onto your tricks.*

o·nus (ō′nəs) *n. pl.,* **o·nus·es.** a burden; responsibility: *The onus of caring for her aging parents fell upon the oldest daughter.*

on·ward (ôn′wərd, on′wərd) *adv. also,* **on·wards.** toward a position that is ahead or in front: *They climbed onward toward the top of the mountain.* —*adj.* moving or directed toward a point in front; forward: *the onward rush of flood waters.*

on·yx (on′iks) *n. pl.,* **on·yx·es.** a variety of quartz consisting of different colored layers that are usually white, yellow, black, or red.

oo·dles (ōōd′əlz) *n., pl. Informal.* a large amount; a lot.

ooze¹ (ōōz) *v.,* **oozed, ooz·ing.** —*v.i.* **1.** to leak out slowly through small openings; seep: *Blood oozed from the scrape on the little boy's knee.* **2.** to disappear gradually as if by slowly leaking out: *Tom's enthusiasm for the plan oozed away when he realized how much work he would have to do.* —*v.t.* to give off slowly or gradually. [Old English *wās* juice, sap.]

ooze² (ōōz) *n.* soft, wet mud or slime, especially at the bottom of a body of water, such as a pond. [Old English *wāse.*]

oo·zy¹ (ōō′zē) *adj.,* **oo·zi·er, oo·zi·est.** slowly leaking; dripping. [*Ooze¹* + -*y¹*.]

oo·zy² (ōō′zē) *adj.,* **oo·zi·er, oo·zi·est.** of or like ooze; slimy: *There was oozy mud at the bottom of the lake.* [*Ooze²* + -*y¹*.] —**oo′zi·ness,** *n.*

op., opus.

o·pac·i·ty (ō pas′ə tē) *n.* the state or quality of being opaque.

o·pal (ō′pəl) *n.* any of various forms of silica which are used as gems. Opals show delicate changes of iridescent colors when they are moved in the light.

o·pal·es·cence (ō′pə les′əns) *n.* iridescent changes of colors like that of the opal.

o·pal·es·cent (ō′pə les′ənt) *adj.* showing delicate changes of iridescent colors like an opal.

o·paque (ō pāk′) *adj.* **1.** not letting light through; not transparent or translucent: *The opaque shades kept the sunlight out of the room.* **2.** not shining or lustrous; dull: *The table had an opaque finish.* **3.** hard to understand; obscure. —**o·paque′ly,** *adv.* —**o·paque′ness,** *n.*

ope (ōp) *v.t., v.i.,* **oped, op·ing.** *Archaic.* to open.

o·pen (ō′pən) *adj.* **1.** allowing free passage in and out; not shut: *an open door, an open window, an open lane on a highway.* **2.** not having its lid, door, or other cover closed: *an open box, an open closet, an open bottle.* **3.** not closed in; having no surrounding barriers: *open country, an open meadow.* **4.** having spaces, holes, or gaps: *cloth with an open weave, an open formation of troops.* **5.** not protected; exposed: *open to attack. The boys built an open fire on the beach.* **6.** that can be used; not taken or reserved; available: *The job of school secretary is still open.* **7.** able or ready to receive new ideas, facts, or views without prejudice: *Tom is always open to suggestions. Donald has an open mind.* **8.** outspoken; frank; candid: *She was very open with me about her troubles.* **9.** free or accessible to the general public: *an open meeting of the city council.* **10.** not settled or determined: *Where we will go on our vacation is an open question.* **11.** ready to do business: *That store is not open on Saturdays.* —*v.t.* **1.** to cause to be open: *to open a drawer, to open a letter, to open one's mouth.* **2.** to take off a lid or other covering from: *to open a jar.* **3.** to spread out; unfold: *The captain opened the map.* **4.** to make available or accessible: *The school board opened the meeting to the whole town.* **5.** to set into operation: *to open a new* movie theater. **6.** to begin; start: *He opened the meeting with a prayer.* —*v.i.* **1.** to become open: *The old door creaked as it opened.* **2.** to have an opening: *The room opened onto a terrace.* **3.** to become ready to do business: *The new store opens next week.* **4.** to begin: *The exhibition opens tomorrow.* **5.** to spread out; unfold: *The buds on the bush opened in the spring.* —*n.* **1.** an athletic contest, such as a golf tournament, in which both amateurs and professionals may take part. **2.** the open. **a.** any clear or unenclosed space or area. **b.** public or general knowledge: *Her secret is now in the open.* —**o′pen·ly,** *adv.* —**o′pen·ness,** *n.*

o·pen-air (ō′pən er′) *adj.* outdoor: *The play was performed in an open-air theater.*

open air, outdoors.

o·pen-and-shut (ō′pen ən shut′) *adj.* that can be easily settled or decided: *The jury felt that it was an open-and-shut case.*

o·pen·er (ō′pə nər) *n.* **1.** an instrument or device for opening closed or sealed containers, such as cans and bottles. **2.** the first item or part in any series: *Their baseball team won the opener.* **3.** a person or thing that opens.

o·pen-eyed (ō′pən īd′) *adj.* **1.** having the eyes wide open, as in amazement or surprise. **2.** very watchful; alert.

o·pen·hand·ed (ō′pən han′did) *adj.* generous in giving. —**o′pen·hand′ed·ly,** *adv.* —**o′pen·hand′ed·ness,** *n.*

o·pen·heart·ed (ō′pən här′tid) *adj.* **1.** frank; candid. **2.** generous. —**o′pen·heart′ed·ly,** *adv.* —**o′pen·heart′ed·ness,** *n.*

o·pen-hearth (ō′pən härth′) *adj.* relating to or used in a process for making steel, in which a furnace reflects heat from a low roof onto the raw material and brickwork on either side of the furnace keeps in the heat so that it can be reused.

open house 1. a party that is open to all who wish to come. **2.** an occasion when an institution, school, or the like is open to visitors.

o·pen·ing (ō′pə ning) *n.* **1.** a vacant or empty space: *an opening in a forest, an opening in a fence.* **2.** the first steps or stage; beginning: *the opening of a book.* **3.** an unfilled job; vacancy: *There is an opening for a delivery boy at the grocery store.* **4.** the first performance or occasion: *the opening of a play.* **5.** the act of becoming open. **6.** a favorable opportunity or chance.

open letter, a statement of protest, appeal, or belief written in the form of a personal letter but meant for the public. An open letter is usually published in a newspaper or magazine.

o·pen-mind·ed (ō′pən mīn′did) *adj.* ready and able to accept new facts, ideas, views, or beliefs; unprejudiced. —**o′pen-mind′ed·ly,** *adv.* —**o′pen-mind′ed·ness,** *n.*

open sesame, any miraculous, swift, or unfailing means of reaching a desired result or goal: *He believed that money was the open sesame to happiness.* [From the magic words used to open the door of the robbers' cave in a story in the *Arabian Nights.*]

open shop, a factory or business in which belonging to or becoming a member of a union is not a requirement for employment.

o·pen-work (ō′pen wurk′) *n.* any ornamental material containing numerous small openings.

op·e·ra¹ (op′ər ə) *n.* a play having all or most of its words sung, usually performed by solo voices, chorus, and orchestra. It is presented with costumes, scenery, acting, and, sometimes, dancing. [Italian *opera.*]

op·e·ra² (ō′pər ə, op′ər ə) a plural of **opus.**

op·er·a·ble (op′ər ə bəl) *adj.* **1.** that can be done, carried out, or used: *Bill had a very old but operable automobile.* **2.** that can be treated by surgery.

opera glasses, small, low-power binoculars for use at operas, plays, or concerts.

opera house, a theater especially designed for the performance of operas.

Opera glasses

op·er·ate (op′ə rāt′) *v.,* **op·er·at·ed, op·er·at·ing.** —*v.i.* **1.** to perform or function; work: *The car's motor operates well.* **2.** to produce the intended or proper effect: *The pills operated at once to make him feel better.* **3.** to perform a surgical operation: *The surgeon operated on Bob to remove his appendix.* **4.** to carry on military activities: *The guerrillas operated behind enemy lines.* —*v.t.* **1.** to cause to work: *to operate a machine, to operate an elevator.* **2.** to manage or direct the affairs of: *to operate a business.*

op·er·at·ic (op′ə rat′ik) *adj.* of, relating to, or like the opera: *operatic music.* —**op′er·at′i·cal·ly,** *adv.*

op·er·a·tion (op′ə rā′shən) *n.* **1.** the act or way of performing, directing, or working: *The operation of a large business is a full-time job.* **2.** the state of being at work: *The machine is in operation.* **3.** surgical treatment performed on the body to cure a physical ailment or repair an injured part: *Bill had an operation to remove his tonsils.* **4.** *Mathematics.* something done to one or more numbers or algebraic expressions to produce a single number or algebraic expression. Addition, subtraction, multiplication, and division are the four most common operations.

op·er·a·tive (op′ər ə tiv) *adj.* **1.** in operation; in force; functioning: *That law is no longer operative in this state.* **2.** relating to physical or mechanical work: *the operative part of an automobile factory.* **3.** resulting from or relating to a surgical operation: *operative techniques.* —*n.* a private or secret agent or investigator.

op·er·a·tor (op′ə rā′tər) *n.* **1.** a person who operates a machine or other mechanical device: *an elevator operator, a telephone operator.* **2.** a person who owns or runs a business or factory. **3.** *Informal.* a person who is shrewd, crafty, and often dishonest in getting what he wants.

op·er·et·ta (op′ə ret′ə) *n. pl.,* **op·er·et·tas.** a light and amusing short opera in which music and song are combined with spoken dialogue and dancing.

oph·thal·mol·o·gist (of′thal mol′ə jist) *n.* a doctor who specializes in ophthalmology.

oph·thal·mol·o·gy (of′thal mol′ə jē) *n.* the branch of medicine that deals with the treatment of diseases and disorders of the eye and includes eye surgery.

o·pi·ate (ō′pē it, ō′pē āt′) *n.* **1.** a drug that contains opium, used to lessen pain and bring sleep. **2.** anything that soothes or quiets: *The comfort of his mother's arms was an opiate to the injured child.* —*adj.* **1.** made with or containing opium. **2.** bringing sleep or relaxation.

o·pine (ō pīn′) *v.t., v.i.,* **o·pined, o·pin·ing.** to hold or express as an opinion; think.

o·pin·ion (ə pin′yən) *n.* **1.** a belief or conclusion based on a person's judgment rather than on what is proven or known to be true: *It is my opinion that he will win the election.* **2.** an impression or estimation of the worth, excellence, or quality of a person or thing: *What is your*

at; āpe; cär; end; mē; it; īce; hot; ōld; fôrk; wood; fōol; oil; out; up; turn; sing; thin; this; hw in white; zh in treasure. The symbol ə stands for the sound of a in about, e in taken, i in pencil, o in lemon, and u in circus.

opinion of that book? **3.** a formal estimation or judgment given by an expert: *The judge wrote an opinion on the case.*

o·pin·ion·at·ed (ə pin′yə nā′tid) *adj.* stubbornly holding to one's opinions; dogmatic: *He's too opinionated to listen to someone else's point of view.*

o·pi·um (ō′pē əm) *n.* a powerful, habit-forming drug made from a white fluid contained in the unripe seed capsules of a poppy, used for relieving pain and causing sleep. Opium is the source of morphine and codeine.

O·por·to (ō pôr′tō) *n.* a port city in northwestern Portugal. Pop. (1969 est.), 325,400.

o·pos·sum (ə pos′əm) *n.* a small, furry animal that lives in trees and carries its young in a pouch. When frightened, the opossum lies still as if it were dead.

Opossum

op·po·nent (ə pō′nənt) *n.* a person who opposes, fights, or competes with another, as in a game or discussion: *an opponent of injustice.* —*adj.* acting or behaving in opposition; opposing: *The colors of the opponent team were blue and red.*

op·por·tune (op′ər tōōn′, op′ər tyōōn′) *adj.* **1.** suitable or appropriate for a particular purpose: *Bill came at an opportune time, because his friend needed help to move the desk.* **2.** well-timed; timely. —**op′por·tune′ly,** *adv.* —**op′por·tune′ness,** *n.*

op·por·tun·ist (op′ər tōō′nist, op′ər tyōō′nist) *n.* a person who takes advantage of every opportunity to get what he wants, regardless of right or wrong. —**op′por·tun′ism,** *n.* —**op′por·tun·is′tic,** *adj.*

op·por·tu·ni·ty (op′ər tōō′nə tē, op′ər tyōō′nə tē) *n. pl.,* **op·por·tu·ni·ties.** **1.** a time or circumstance that is favorable or suitable for a particular purpose: *When the pond froze, we had a good opportunity to go ice skating.* **2.** a good chance, as to advance oneself.

op·pose (ə pōz′) *v.t.,* **op·posed, op·pos·ing.** **1.** to be against; struggle against; offer resistance to: *The older members were opposed to changing the club's membership rules.* **2.** to put in opposition; contrast: *Good is opposed to evil.* —**op·pos′er,** *n.*

op·po·site (op′ə zit) *adj.* **1.** placed face to face with; on the other side of or across from another person or thing; facing: *She lives on the opposite side of the street.* **2.** turned or moving the other way: *The two cars were traveling in opposite directions.* **3.** completely and entirely different: *Hot is opposite to cold.* —*n.* a person or thing that is opposite or contrary to another: *Summer and winter are opposites.* —*prep.* across from: *Meet me opposite the drugstore.* —**op′po·site·ly,** *adv.* —**op′po·site·ness,** *n.*

op·po·si·tion (op′ə zish′ən) *n.* **1.** the act of opposing or the state of being opposed: *His opposition to the plan surprised his friends. The manager was in opposition to a raise in wages for the workers.* **2.** contrary or opposing action or feeling: *The plan for higher taxes met with opposition.* **3.** a position that is opposite to another. **4.** also, **Opposition.** a political party opposed to the party in power.

op·press (ə pres′) *v.t.* **1.** to control or govern by cruel and unjust use of force or authority; tyrannize: *The dictator's secret police oppressed the people.* **2.** to weigh heavily on so as to depress or trouble: *Bill's failure on the test oppressed him.* —**op·pres′sor,** *n.*

op·pres·sion (ə presh′ən) *n.* **1.** the act of oppressing or the state of being oppressed. **2.** something that causes difficulty, pain, or suffering; hardship; burden: *the oppression of having many debts.* **3.** the feeling of being mentally or physically weighed down.

op·pres·sive (ə pres′iv) *adj.* **1.** cruel and unjust; tyrannical: *an oppressive law.* **2.** causing a state or feeling of oppression: *The hot, muggy day was oppressive.* —**op·pres′sive·ly,** *adv.* —**op·pres′sive·ness,** *n.*

op·pro·bri·ous (ə prō′brē əs) *adj.* **1.** expressing reproach, disapproval, or disgrace; abusive: *Calling a person a coward is an opprobrious remark.* **2.** deserving reproach or disapproval; disgraceful: *opprobrious conduct.* —**op·pro′bri·ous·ly,** *adv.* —**op·pro′bri·ous·ness,** *n.*

op·pro·bri·um (ə prō′brē əm) *n.* **1.** a disgrace or reproach caused by shameful conduct. **2.** a cause of disgrace or reproach.

opt (opt) *v.i.* to make a choice; choose: *I opt to have the picnic at the seashore instead of at the lake.*

op·tic (op′tik) *adj.* of or relating to the eye or to the sense of sight.

op·ti·cal (op′ti kəl) *adj.* **1.** of or relating to the sense of sight: *A mirage is an optical illusion.* **2.** designed to aid sight: *A microscope is an optical instrument.* **3.** of or relating to the science of optics. —**op′ti·cal·ly,** *adv.*

op·ti·cian (op tish′ən) *n.* a person who makes or sells eyeglasses and other optical instruments.

optic nerve, the nerve that carries impulses from the eye to the brain.

op·tics (op′tiks) *n.,pl.* the branch of physics dealing with the nature and behavior of light. ▲ used with a singular verb.

op·ti·mal (op′tə məl) *adj.* best or most favorable: *The astronauts had optimal conditions for the beginning of their mission.*

op·ti·mism (op′tə miz′əm) *n.* **1.** a belief that things will turn out for the best: *There was great optimism that the railroad strike would soon end.* **2.** a tendency to hope for or expect the best, or to look on the bright side of things: *She is always cheerful and full of optimism.*

op·ti·mist (op′tə mist) *n.* a person who expects the best or looks on the bright side of things.

op·ti·mis·tic (op′tə mis′tik) *adj.* **1.** inclined to look on the bright side of things and believe that everything will turn out for the best: *Steve was very optimistic about his chances of getting a summer job.* **2.** of or relating to optimism. —**op′ti·mis′ti·cal·ly,** *adv.*

op·ti·mum (op′tə məm) *n. pl.,* **op·ti·mums** or **op·ti·ma** (op′tə mə). the best, highest possible, or most favorable point or level: *Business profits are at an optimum.* —*adj.* best, highest possible, or most favorable.

op·tion (op′shən) *n.* **1.** the right or opportunity to choose. **2.** the act of choosing or the course of action chosen: *My option is to stay home and watch television.* **3.** something chosen or available for choosing. **4.** the right to buy, sell, rent, or use something for a specified price within a stated period of time.

op·tion·al (op′shən əl) *adj.* left to one's choice; not required or automatic: *Attendance at tonight's club meeting is optional.* —**op′tion·al·ly,** *adv.*

op·tom·e·trist (op tom′ə trist′) *n.* a person licensed to practice optometry.

op·tom·e·try (op tom′ə trē) *n.* the practice or profession of testing the eyes for defects of vision and prescribing corrective lenses.

op·u·lent (op′yə lənt) *adj.* **1.** having much wealth; affluent: *an opulent business executive.* **2.** showing wealth or affluence: *an opulent gift, an opulent apartment.* **3.** plentiful; abundant; luxuriant: *the opulent vegetation of the jungle.* —**op′u·lence,** *n.*

o·pus (ō′pəs) *n. pl.,* **op·er·a** or **o·pus·es.** a musical or literary work or composition. ▲ often followed by a number to identify a composer's works by the order in which they were composed or published.

or (ôr) *conj.* **1.** used to introduce an alternative of two or more: *Is the water warm or cold? You may use red, blue, or green ink.* **2.** used to introduce the second of two alternatives when the first is introduced by *either* or *whether:* *Either write or phone me. We didn't know whether to stay or leave.* **3.** used to introduce a word or phrase meaning the same thing: *aeronautics, or the science of flight.* **4.** otherwise: *You should eat lunch or you will be hungry.* ▲ See **nor** for usage note.

-or *suffix* **1.** (used to form nouns from verbs) a person or thing that performs the action of: *inventor, governor, elevator.* **2.** (used to form nouns) a state, condition, or quality: *stupor, color, tremor.*

or·a·cle (ôr′ə kəl, or′ə kəl) *n.* **1.** a priest or priestess through whom certain ancient gods, such as Apollo, answered the questions of their worshipers. **2.** a shrine or temple of a god, such as that at Delphi, where answers were given. **3.** an answer given by a priest or priestess at such a shrine, often having a vague or hidden meaning. **4.** a person or thing that is believed to have great wisdom or authority.

o·rac·u·lar (ô rak′yə lər) *adj.* **1.** of, relating to, or like an oracle. **2.** with vague or hidden meaning: *an author whose writings are mysterious and oracular.* —**o·rac′u·lar·ly,** *adv.*

o·ral (ôr′əl) *adj.* **1.** not written; using speech; spoken: *Each student had to prepare an oral report on the book he read.* **2.** of or relating to the mouth: *oral hygiene.* **3.** taken into the body through the mouth: *an oral vaccine.* —**o′ral·ly,** *adv.*

O·ran (ô ran′) *n.* a port city in northwestern Algeria, on the Mediterranean Sea. Pop. (1966), 328,257.

or·ange (ôr′inj, or′inj) *n.* **1.** a round citrus fruit having a thick orange or yellow rind and a juicy, sweetish or acid pulp. **2.** a tropical evergreen tree bearing this fruit, having waxy white flowers. **3.** a reddish-yellow color. —*adj.* **1.** having the color orange. **2.** made from or flavored with oranges: *orange juice.*

Or·ange (ôr′inj, or′inj) *n.* a city in southern California, near Los Angeles. Pop. (1970), 77,374.

or·ange·ade (ôr′in jād′, or′in jād′) *n.* a drink made of orange juice and water and sweetened with sugar.

o·rang·u·tan (ô rang′oo tan′) *also,* **o·rang·u·tang, o·rang·ou·tang** (ô rang′oo-tang′). *n.* a large tree-dwelling ape of the forests of Borneo and Sumatra, having very long powerful arms, short legs, and a shaggy coat of reddish-brown hair.

Orangutan

o·rate (ô rāt′) *v.i.,* **o·rat·ed, o·rat·ing.** to speak in a grand, pompous, or formal manner.

o·ra·tion (ô rā′shən) *n.* a long, elaborate, formal speech, especially one given on a special occasion before a large audience.

or·a·tor (ôr′ə tər, or′ə tər) *n.* **1.** a person who delivers orations or an oration. **2.** any skilled public speaker.

or·a·tor·i·cal (ôr′ə tôr′i kəl, or′ə tôr′i kəl) *adj.* of, relating to, or characteristic of orators or oratory. —**or′a·tor′i·cal·ly,** *adv.*

or·a·to·ri·o (ôr′ə tôr′ē ō′, or′ə tôr′ē ō′) *n. pl.,* **or·a·to·ri·os.** a dramatic musical composition, usually set to a religious text and performed by solo voices, chorus, and orchestra, without action, costumes, or scenery.

or·a·to·ry¹ (ôr′ə tôr′ē, or′ə tôr′ē) *n.* **1.** eloquence or skill in public speaking: *The candidate was a master of campaign oratory.* **2.** the art of public speaking. [Latin *(ars) ōrātōria* (the art) of public speaking.]

or·a·to·ry² (ôr′ə tôr′ē, or′ə tôr′ē) *n. pl.,* **or·a·to·ries.** a place set aside for prayer, as a room in a convent. [Church Latin *ōrātōrium* a place of prayer.]

orb (ôrb) *n.* **1.** something round, such as a sphere or globe. **2.** the sun, moon, or any other heavenly body. **3.** the eye or eyeball. ▲ used in literature. **4.** a small globe having a cross on the top, used as a symbol of royal power.

or·bit (ôr′bit) *n.* **1.** the path of a heavenly body as it revolves in a closed curve about another body: *the orbit of the earth around the sun.* **2.** one complete trip of a spacecraft or artificial satellite along such a path. **3.** a range of activity, influence, or knowledge. **4.** either of the bony hollows or cavities in the skull in which the eyeballs are located; eye socket. —*v.t.* **1.** to move in an orbit around: *the planet Mercury orbits the sun.* **2.** to put (a spacecraft or satellite) into an orbit. —*v.i.* to move in an orbit.

or·bit·al (ôr′bit əl) *adj.* of or relating to an orbit: *the orbital velocity of a spacecraft.*

or·chard (ôr′chərd) *n.* **1.** an area where fruit or nut trees are grown. **2.** a group of such trees.

or·ches·tra (ôr′kis trə) *n.* **1.** a group of musicians playing together on various instruments, usually including strings, woodwinds, brasses, and percussion instruments. **2.** the instruments played by such a group. **3.** the main floor of a theater. **4.** a usually lowered or sunken area just in front of a stage, in which the orchestra plays at the performance of an opera, ballet, or other musical show.

or·ches·tral (ôr kes′trəl) *adj.* of, relating to, composed for, or performed by an orchestra: *orchestral music.* —**or·ches′tral·ly,** *adv.*

or·ches·trate (ôr′kis trāt′) *v.t.,* **or·ches·trat·ed, or·ches·trat·ing.** to compose or arrange (music) for an orchestra. —**or′ches·tra′tion,** *n.* —**or′ches·tra′tor,** *n.*

or·chid (ôr′kid) *n.* **1.** any of various irregularly shaped flowers, often pale purple or white. **2.** a plant bearing this flower. **3.** a bluish-purple color. —*adj.* having the color orchid; bluish-purple.

Orchid

or·dain (ôr dān′) *v.t.* **1.** to fix, decide, or command by decree or authority: *The law ordains the punishment of a convicted criminal.* **2.** to appoint formally to the ministry or another religious office.

or·deal (ôr dēl′, ôr′dēl) *n.* **1.** a very difficult test or painful experience: *His first day of combat was an ordeal for the young soldier.* **2.** in former times, a way of deciding whether an accused person was guilty or innocent of a crime by making him undergo a dangerous or painful test. If the person was unharmed, it was believed to be proof of his innocence.

or·der (ôr′dər) *n.* **1.** a direction or command to do something: *A soldier must obey orders. The lawyer got a court order to release the prisoner on bail.* **2.** an arrangement of things; position in a series: *Arrange the names in alphabeti-*

at; āpe; cär; end; mē; it; īce; hot; ōld; fôrk; wood; fōōl; oil; out; up; turn; sing; thin; **th**is; hw in white; zh in treasure. The symbol ə stands for the sound of **a** in about, **e** in taken, **i** in pencil, **o** in lemon, and **u** in circus.

cal order. **3.** any fixed system or condition: *the order of the universe.* **4.** a condition in which laws and rules are obeyed: *Police restored order after the riot.* **5.** clean, neat, or proper condition: *Tom kept his room in order.* **6.** a request for goods: *a grocery order.* **7.** the goods requested or supplied: *The company shipped the order by railway express.* **8.** a single portion of food: *an order of pie.* **9.** kind; sort: *He has intelligence of a high order.* **10.** a category in the classification of plants and animals that ranks higher than a family but lower than a class. **11.** a grade or rank of the clergy: *He was a member of the order of deacons.* **12.** a group of persons living under the same rules, especially a religious group: *an order of monks.* **13.** a society into which a person is admitted as an honor. **14.** a fraternal organization: *the Masonic order.* **15.** any one of the three major styles of classical Greek architecture: Doric, Ionic, or Corinthian. —*v.t.* **1.** to command or direct; give an order to: *The policeman ordered the suspect to put up his hands.* **2.** to place an order for; request: *to order eggs and milk from the grocery store.* **3.** to put into proper order; give order to: *He ordered his business affairs before he left on his vacation.* —*v.i.* to place or give an order or orders.

by order or **by order of.** according to an order given by a person with the proper authority.

in order. a. in the right or proper position or condition: *The books were in order on the shelf.* **b.** in working condition. **c.** according to the rules: *Nominations for class president are now in order.*

in order that. for the purpose that; so that.

in order to. so as to: *He stood on a chair in order to see.*

in short order. without delay; quickly.

on order. having been ordered but not yet delivered: *My father has a new car on order.*

on the order of. similar to; like.

out of order. a. not working properly: *The telephone is out of order.* **b.** against the rules: *The chairman ruled that his proposal was out of order.*

to call to order. to ask to be quiet and pay attention: *The chairman called the meeting to order.*

to order. according to the wishes of the buyer: *to have a suit made to order.*

to take orders. to become ordained as a member of the clergy.

ordered pair *Mathematics.* a pair of numbers or elements in which one of the pair is considered the first and the other the second.

or·der·ly (ôr′dər lē) *adj.* **1.** that is in a certain order or has order: *to march in an orderly line, an orderly room.* **2.** free from disturbances, trouble, or violence: *an orderly demonstration, an orderly crowd.* —*n. pl.,* **or·der·lies. 1.** a soldier assigned to an officer or officers for the purpose of carrying messages and doing various other tasks. **2.** a male hospital attendant. —**or′der·li·ness,** *n.*

Order of the Garter, the oldest and most important order of knighthood in England, founded about 1350.

or·di·nal (ôrd′ən əl) *adj.* of, relating to, or indicating order or position in a series. —*n.* see **ordinal number.**

ordinal number, a number that shows sequence or position in a set or collection, as first, second, third, and so forth. ▲ See **cardinal number** for usage note.

or·di·nance (ôrd′ən əns) *n.* a regulation or law, especially one made by the government of a city or town: *Our city has an ordinance that prohibits littering.*

or·di·nar·i·ly (ôrd′ən er′ə lē) *adv.* **1.** in most cases; usually; commonly: *Ordinarily, the museum is open on Sundays.* **2.** in a usual or normal way.

or·di·nar·y (ôrd′ən er′ē) *adj.* **1.** commonly used; habitual or regular; usual: *Betsy's ordinary tone of voice is*

very soft. **2.** not distinguished in any way from others; average; everyday: *The author's first book was a very ordinary novel.* —**or′di·nar′i·ness,** *n.*

out of the ordinary. unusual; exceptional: *Such hot weather is out of the ordinary this time of year.*

or·di·nate (ôrd′ən it, ôrd′ən āt′) *n.* **1.** on a line graph, the distance of a point from the horizontal axis measured parallel to the vertical axis. It is used to define the point in the system of Cartesian coordinates. See **abscissa** for illustration. **2.** a line, number, or algebraic expression representing this distance.

or·di·na·tion (ôrd′ən ā′shən) *n.* **1.** the ceremony of ordaining. **2.** the state of being ordained.

ord·nance (ôrd′nəns) *n.* **1.** military weapons and equipment. **2.** the branch of a military service that obtains, stores, and issues ordnance.

Or·do·vi·cian (ôr′də vish′ən) *n.* the second geological period of the Paleozoic era, when fish, the first animals with backbones, appeared. —*adj.* of, relating to, or characteristic of this period.

ore (ôr) *n.* a rock or other mineral substance in the earth containing enough of a metal or of a useful mineral to make mining it profitable.

Ore., Oregon.

Oreg., Oregon.

o·reg·a·no (ə reg′ə nō′) *n.* any of various plants related to the mint, having fragrant leaves that are used for seasoning.

Or·e·gon (ôr′ə gon′, ôr′ə gən, or′ə gon′, or′ə gən) *n.* a state in the northwestern United States, on the Pacific Ocean. Capital, Salem. Area, 96,981 sq. mi. Pop. (1970), 2,091,385. Abbreviations, **Oreg., Ore.** —**Or·e·go·ni·an** (ôr′ə gō′nē ən, or′ə gō′nē ən), *adj., n.*

● The origin of the name **Oregon** is not definitely known. One theory is that it came from a mistake made by a French mapmaker. He wrote the word *Ouisconsink* (the Indian name for the Wisconsin River) as *Ouariconsint,* with *Ouaricon* on one line and *sint* on the next. According to the theory, the first part of the name, *Ouaricon,* then became associated with a legendary river flowing into the Pacific Ocean. The name for this river changed several times until it became *Oregon.* The explorers who discovered what is now called the Columbia River thought that it was the legendary Oregon River. Oregon later became the name of the state bordering on this river.

O·res·tes (ō res′tēz) *n. Greek Mythology.* the son of Agamemnon and Clytemnestra, who killed his mother and her lover because they had murdered his father.

or·gan (ôr′gən) *n.* **1.** a musical instrument consisting of pipes of different lengths which are sounded by air blown from a bellows. It is played by means of one or more keyboards. **2.** a similar instrument whose tones are produced and amplified electrically. **3.** any of various other musical instruments, such as the reed organ. **4.** a part of an animal or plant that is composed of several kinds of tissues and that performs a specific function or functions. The heart, liver, and eyes are organs of the body. **5.** a newspaper, newsletter, or magazine published by a political party, business, or some other group or organization. **6.** a means of getting something done: *The city council is an organ of local government.*

or·gan·dy (ôr′gən dē) *also,* **or·gan·die.** *n. pl.,* **or·gan·dies.** a sheer, lightweight fabric, usually made of cotton and given a crisp finish. It is used especially for dresses and curtains.

organ grinder, a street musician who plays a hand organ.

or·gan·ic (ôr gan′ik) *adj.* **1.** relating to, deriving from, or including living things: *Decaying leaves, grass, vegetables, and other organic matter are used to enrich soil.* **2.** of or relating to a body organ: *an organic disease.* **3.** of, using, or grown by farming or gardening methods in which chemical fertilizers or insecticides are not used: *organic farming, organic foods.* **4.** made up of related parts: *an organic whole.* **5.** of, relating to, or belonging to a class of chemical compounds including most of the compounds of carbon. Starches and proteins are organic compounds. —**or·gan′i·cal·ly,** *adv.*

organic chemistry, the branch of chemistry that deals with organic compounds.

or·gan·ism (ôr′gə niz′əm) *n.* **1.** a living animal or plant; any living thing. **2.** something having parts that work together to form a whole: *the economic organism.*

or·gan·ist (ôr′gə nist) *n.* a person who plays the organ.

or·gan·i·za·tion (ôr′gə ni zā′shən) *n.* **1.** the act or process of organizing: *The class president was in charge of the organization of the school dance.* **2.** the state or manner of being organized: *In our library the organization of books is by author.* **3.** a group of persons united or organized for a particular purpose: *a labor organization.*

Organization of American States, an organization of twenty-two Latin American countries and the United States, formed in 1948 to provide collective security, economic cooperation, and peaceful settlement of disputes.

or·gan·ize (ôr′gə nīz′) *v.,* **or·gan·ized, or·gan·iz·ing.** —*v.t.* **1.** to arrange in an orderly, systematic way: *He organized the coins in his collection according to what country they were from.* **2.** to put or bring together; bring into being: *to organize an amateur theater group.* **3.** to cause (employees) to form or join a labor union: *to organize steel workers.* **4.** to cause employees of (a business or an industry) to form or join a labor union. —*v.i.* to form or join a labor union or other organization. —**or′gan·iz′a·ble,** *adj.* —**or′gan·iz′er,** *n.*

organized labor, all the members of labor unions as a group.

or·gan·za (ôr gan′zə) *n.* a transparent, lightweight fabric that looks like organdy.

or·gy (ôr′jē) *n. pl.,* **or·gies. 1.** a wild, drunken, unrestrained revelry or party. **2. orgies.** in ancient Greece and Rome, secret rites or ceremonies that were dedicated to certain gods, such as Bacchus, and were accompanied by drunkenness and wild dancing and singing.

o·ri·el (ôr′ē əl) *n.* a bay window built out from a wall.

o·ri·ent (*n.,* ôr′ē ənt; *v.,* ôr′ē ent′) *n.* **Orient.** the countries of Asia, especially the Far East. —*v.t.* **1.** to make familiar with new surroundings or circumstances or a situation: *It took a while for the new student to orient himself.* **2.** to get or fix the location or bearings of: *The lost explorer climbed a tree in order to orient himself by the North Star.* **3.** to fix so as to be pointed or directed: *to orient a tennis court north and south, to orient fashions toward youthful buyers.*

O·ri·en·tal (ôr′ē ent′əl) also, **o·ri·en·tal.** *adj.* of, relating to, or characteristic of the Orient. —*n.* **1.** a person who was born or is living in the Orient. **2.** a person who is descended from one of the native peoples of the Orient.

o·ri·en·tate (ôr′ē ən tāt′) *v.t., v.i.,* **o·ri·en·tat·ed, o·ri·en·tat·ing.** to orient or become oriented.

o·ri·en·ta·tion (ôr′ē ən tā′shən) *n.* **1.** the act of orienting or the state of being oriented. **2.** an introduction to

Oriel

familiarize people with new surroundings or circumstances: *The college gave an orientation for the new freshman class.* **3.** one's awareness of one's surroundings and environment, and of other people in relation to oneself.

or·i·fice (ôr′ə fis, or′ə fis) *n.* a passage or opening, especially in the body, such as the ears, nose, and mouth.

or·i·ga·mi (ôr′i gä′mē) *n.* the Japanese art of folding paper into the form of an animal, flower, or other object.

or·i·gin (ôr′ə jin, or′ə jin) *n.* **1.** the source from which something begins or comes; root or cause: *The basement was the place of origin of the fire. What is the origin of that rumor?* **2.** parentage; ancestry: *Brian is of Irish origin.* **3.** *Mathematics.* the point of intersection of the x-axis and the y-axis of a Cartesian coordinate system.

o·rig·i·nal (ə rij′ən əl) *adj.* **1.** that has not been made, done, thought of, or used before; new or unusual: *an original suggestion, original research.* **2.** able to produce, do, or think of something new or unusual; inventive; creative: *an original thinker.* **3.** of, relating to, or belonging to the origin or beginning of something; first; starting: *The original owner of the house still lives there.* **4.** that is not a copy, imitation, or translation: *an original painting by Van Gogh.* —*n.* something that is not a print, copy, imitation, or translation; something original.

o·rig·i·nal·i·ty (ə rij′ə nal′ə tē) *n.* **1.** the quality of being original. **2.** the ability to be inventive or creative.

o·rig·i·nal·ly (ə rij′ən əl ē) *adv.* **1.** at or from the start; at first; initially: *Basketball was originally played in the United States.* **2.** in a new, fresh, or unusual manner.

o·rig·i·nate (ə rij′ə nāt′) *v.,* **o·rig·i·nat·ed, o·rig·i·nat·ing.** —*v.t.* to start or bring into existence: *to originate a new card game.* —*v.i.* to come into existence; begin: *an airplane flight that originates in Boston.* —**o·rig′i·na′tion,** *n.* —**o·rig′i·na′tor,** *n.*

O·ri·no·co (ôr′ə nō′kō) *n.* a large river in South America, flowing through Venezuela into the Atlantic.

o·ri·ole (ôr′ē ōl′) *n.* **1.** any of various songbirds related to the crow, found from Europe to Australia. The male is usually bright orange or yellow and has black markings on the head, wings, and tail, while the female is dull greenish yellow. **2.** any of various similar American songbirds, such as the Baltimore oriole.

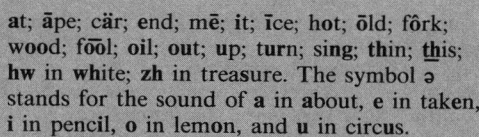
Oriole

O·ri·on (ô rī′ən) *n.* a constellation on the celestial equator, thought to resemble a hunter wearing a belt with a sword attached at the side.

o·ri·son (ôr′i zən, or′i zən) *n. Archaic.* a prayer.

Ork·ney Islands (ôrk′nē) a group of islands off the northeast coast of Scotland.

Or·lan·do (ôr lan′dō) *n.* a city in east-central Florida. Pop. (1970), 99,006.

Or·lé·ans (ôr′lē ənz) *n.* a historic city in north-central France that was saved by Joan of Arc from an English siege in 1429.

Or·lon (ôr′lon) *n. Trademark.* a synthetic fiber that is widely used in making clothing, bedding, and other textile products.

---

at; āpe; cär; end; mē; it; īce; hot; ōld; fôrk; wood; fōol; oil; out; up; turn; sing; thin; this; hw in white; zh in treasure. The symbol ə stands for the sound of a in about, e in taken, i in pencil, o in lemon, and u in circus.

or·na·ment (*n.,* ôr′nə mənt; *v.,* ôr′nə ment′) *n.* **1.** a small, often brightly colored or shiny, decorative object: *The Christmas tree was hung with ornaments.* **2.** anything used to decorate or beautify. —*v.t.* to add an ornament or ornaments to: *to ornament a dress with silver buttons.* —**or′na·men·ta′tion,** *n.*

or·na·men·tal (ôr′nə ment′əl) *adj.* relating to or being an ornament: *an ornamental design on a blouse.* —**or′na·men′tal·ly,** *adv.*

or·nate (ôr nāt′) *adj.* having much ornamentation: *The palace was furnished with ornate furniture.* —**or·nate′ly,** *adv.* —**or·nate′ness,** *n.*

or·ner·y (ôr′nər ē) *adj.,* **or·ner·i·er, or·ner·i·est. 1.** stubborn and difficult to manage; unruly: *an ornery mule.* **2.** mean or ugly: *The man was in an ornery mood.* —**or′ner·i·ness,** *n.*

or·ni·thol·o·gist (ôr′nə thol′ə jist) *n.* a student of or an expert in ornithology.

or·ni·thol·o·gy (ôr′nə thol′ə jē) *n.* the branch of zoology that deals with the study of birds. —**or·ni·tho·log·i·cal** (ôr′ni thə loj′i kəl), *adj.*

o·ro·tund (ôr′ə tund′) *adj.* **1.** (of the voice) strong, resonant, and mellow. **2.** pompous; bombastic: *an orotund speech.*

or·phan (ôr′fən) *n.* a child whose natural parents are absent or dead and who must be brought up in an orphanage or by foster parents. —*v.t.* to make an orphan of: *The war orphaned hundreds of children.*

or·phan·age (ôr′fə nij) *n.* an institution that takes in and cares for orphans.

Or·phe·us (ôr′fē əs) *n. Greek Mythology.* a musician renowned for the beautiful way in which he played the lyre. His playing enchanted trees and stones and tamed wild beasts.

or·ris (ôr′is, or′is) *n.* any of several varieties of iris having a fragrant root.

or·ris·root (ôr′is rōot′, ôr′is root′, or′is rōot′, or′is-root′) *n.* the violet-scented root of the orris. It is dried and powdered for use in perfume, sachets, and tooth powder.

or·tho·clase (ôr′thə klās′, ôr′thə klāz′) *n.* a hard mineral that is a type of feldspar and is found mainly in igneous rock.

or·tho·don·tics (ôr′thə don′tiks) *n., pl.* the branch of dentistry that deals with the straightening of the teeth. ▲ used with a singular verb. Also, **or·tho·don·tia** (ôr′thə-don′chə).

or·tho·don·tist (ôr′thə don′tist) *n.* a dentist who specializes in orthodontics.

or·tho·dox (ôr′thə doks′) *adj.* **1.** established or accepted: *orthodox political views.* **2.** following widely used or proven methods: *an orthodox approach to education.* **3. Orthodox. a.** of, relating to, or characteristic of the Orthodox Church. **b.** of, relating to, or designating the branch of Judaism that adheres to a strict interpretation and observance of the Torah.

Orthodox Church, a group of Christian churches that developed from the church of the Byzantine Empire. The Orthodox Church does not recognize the supremacy of the Pope. Also, **Eastern Church, Eastern Orthodox Church, Greek Orthodox Church.**

or·tho·dox·y (ôr′thə dok′sē) *n. pl.,* **or·tho·dox·ies. 1.** the quality or character of being orthodox. **2.** an orthodox belief or opinion.

or·tho·graph·ic (ôr′thə graf′ik) *adj.* **1.** of or relating to orthography. **2.** correct in spelling. Also, **or·tho·graph·i·cal** (ôr′thə graf′i kəl). —**or′tho·graph′i·cal·ly,** *adv.*

or·thog·ra·phy (ôr thog′rə fē) *n. pl.,* **or·thog·ra·phies. 1.** the way of representing the sounds of a language by written or printed symbols. **2.** the correct spelling of words. **3.** the study of letters and spelling.

or·tho·pe·dic (ôr′thə pē′dik) *adj.* of, relating to, or used in orthopedics.

or·tho·pe·dics (ôr′thə pē′diks) *n., pl.* the branch of medicine that deals with injuries, deformities, and diseases of the bones, tendons, ligaments, muscles, and joints. ▲ used with a singular verb.

or·tho·pe·dist (ôr′thə pē′dist) *n.* a physician who specializes in orthopedics.

Or·well, George (ôr′wel) 1903–1950, English novelist and essayist, born in India. His real name was Eric Blair.

Or·well·i·an (ôr wel′ē ən) *adj.* of or relating to George Orwell or his writings.

-ory *suffix* **1.** (used to form adjectives from verbs or from nouns) **a.** of, relating to, or doing: *contradictory.* **b.** serving to or characterized by: *compulsory, contributory.* **2.** (used to form nouns from verbs or from other nouns) a place or instrument for: *observatory.*

o·ryx (ôr′iks) *n. pl.,* **o·ryx·es** or **o·ryx.** an antelope found in desert regions of Africa and Arabia, having a gray or brown coat with black or brown markings and long, nearly straight horns.

Os, the symbol for osmium.

O·sage (ō′sāj, ō sāj′) *n.* **1.** a member of a tribe of North American Indians, originally living in parts of Kansas, Missouri, and Illinois, now living in Oklahoma. **2.** the language of this tribe. —*adj.* of or relating to these people or their language.

O·sa·ka (ō sä′kə) *n.* a port city in southwestern Japan. Pop. (1971 est.), 2,909,000.

os·cil·late (os′ə lāt′) *v.i.,* **os·cil·lat·ed, os·cil·lat·ing. 1.** to vibrate or swing back and forth between two points: *The flame of the candle oscillated because of the draft from the window.* **2.** *Physics.* to produce oscillation.

os·cil·la·tion (os′ə lā′shən) *n.* **1.** the act or process of oscillating. **2.** a single movement from one point, limit, or extreme to another: *an oscillation of a pendulum.* **3.** *Physics.* the periodic fluctuation between two extremes of a quantity, such as voltage, or two extreme positions, as in a vibrating tuning fork.

os·cil·la·tor (os′ə lā′tər) *n.* **1.** a person or thing that oscillates. **2.** a device that produces electrical oscillations, or alternating current, used in radio and television transmitters and receivers. —**os·cil·la·to·ry** (ôs′ə lə tôr′ē), *adj.*

os·cil·lo·scope (ə sil′ə skōp′) *n.* an electronic instrument that produces a visible wave pattern on the fluorescent screen of a cathode-ray tube corresponding to the electric signals fed into it.

os·cu·late (os′kyə lāt′) *v.i., v.t.,* **os·cu·lat·ed, os·cu·lat·ing.** to kiss. —**os′cu·la′tion,** *n.*

-ose¹ *suffix* (used to form adjectives) full of, given to, or like: *grandiose, verbose.* [Latin *-ōsus* full of.]

-ose² *suffix* used in chemistry to indicate a carbohydrate: *dextrose.* [From *glucose.*]

o·sier (ō′zhər) *n.* **1.** any of various species of willow, having flexible twigs and branches that are used in making baskets and wicker furniture. **2.** a twig of such a willow.

O·si·ris (ō sī′ris) *n. Egyptian Mythology.* the god of the lower world and judge of the dead.

Os·lo (os′lō, oz′lō) *n.* the capital of Norway, in the southeastern part of the country. Pop. (1971 est.), 481,204.

os·mi·um (oz′mē əm) *n.* a very hard, heavy, bluish-white metallic element. Symbol: **Os**

os·mo·sis (oz mō′sis, os mō′sis) *n.* **1.** the movement through a membrane, such as a plant or animal cell membrane, of a more concentrated solution toward a less concentrated one. This equalizes the pressure on both sides of the membrane. **2.** any gradual process of absorbing that seems to happen without conscious effort: *Young children learn the customs and the language of their native land by osmosis.* **—os·mot·ic** (oz mot′ik, os mot′ik), *adj.*

os·prey (os′prē) *n. pl.,* **os·preys.** a fish-eating hawk having brownish-black feathers with a white head and undersides. Also, **fish hawk.**

os·si·fi·ca·tion (os′ə fi·kā′shən) *n.* **1.** the process of changing into bone. **2.** a part that has become changed into bone.

os·si·fy (os′ə fī′) *v.t., v.i.,* **os·si·fied, os·si·fy·ing.** to change into bone.

Osprey

os·ten·si·ble (os ten′sə bəl) *adj.* put forth as actual; apparent: *His ostensible reason for missing school was that he was sick, but actually he wanted to watch a baseball game on television.* **—os·ten′si·bly,** *adv.*

os·ten·ta·tion (os′tən tā′shən) *n.* a showy display meant to impress others or attract attention: *Although she is very wealthy, she lives without ostentation.*

os·ten·ta·tious (os′tən tā′shəs) *adj.* **1.** done to impress others or attract attention; showy: *He made an ostentatious tour of the neighborhood in his expensive new sports car.* **2.** characterized by or showing ostentation. **—os′ten·ta′tious·ly,** *adv.* **—os′ten·ta′tious·ness,** *n.*

os·te·o·path (os′tē ə path′) *n.* a person who is trained to practice osteopathy.

os·te·o·pa·thy (os′tē op′ə thē) *n.* the method of treating diseases by manipulating the bones and muscles. Osteopathy also includes other methods of medical treatment, such as the use of drugs and surgery.

os·tler (os′lər) another spelling of **hostler.**

ost·mark (ost′märk′) *n.* the monetary unit of East Germany, equal to 100 pfennigs.

os·tra·cism (os′trə siz′əm) *n.* **1.** the act of ostracizing or the state of being ostracized. **2.** in ancient Greece, temporary banishment by vote of the people.

os·tra·cize (os′trə sīz′) *v.t.,* **os·tra·cized, os·tra·ciz·ing. 1.** to cut off or exclude from a group or from society: *His classmates ostracized him when they discovered he had cheated on the test.* **2.** in ancient Greece, to banish temporarily by vote of the people. [Greek *ostrakezein,* from *ostrakon* a piece of pottery or tile. In ancient Greece, votes to banish a person were cast on pieces of pottery or tile.]

os·trich (ôs′trich, os′trich) *n.* a two-toed bird of central Africa, the largest of all living birds. It has a long neck, long, powerful legs, a small, flat head, and, in the male, large, white plumes on the wings and tail that are used for ornaments. The ostrich cannot fly, but it can run very swiftly.

Os·tro·goth (os′trə goth′) *n.* a member of the eastern branch of the Goths, who controlled Italy from A.D. 493 to 554. **—Os′tro·goth′ic,** *adj.*

O.T., Old Testament.

O·thel·lo (ə thel′ō) *n.* the main character of Shakespeare's tragedy *Othello,* who, driven to suspicion and jealousy, murders his faithful wife.

oth·er (uth′ər) *adj.* **1.** different from the one or ones already mentioned; not the same: *If he doesn't accept the*

Ostrich

job, some other person will. **2.** remaining: *The other guests have not arrived yet.* **3.** additional; further: *The thief had no other choice but to surrender.* **4.** recently past: *the other morning, the other night.* **—pron. 1.** a different or additional person or thing. **2.** the remaining one or ones: *The others will join us later.* **—adv.** otherwise: *I could not feel other than surprised.*

every other. every second or alternate: *The team has practice every other day.*

oth·er·wise (uth′ər wīz′) *adv.* **1.** apart from that; in other respects: *The food ran out early, but otherwise the party was a success.* **2.** under any different circumstances; if not for that: *Fortunately the shipwrecked sailors had a life raft; otherwise they would have drowned.* **3.** in a different way or in any other way: *I cannot believe otherwise but that we shall succeed.* **—adj.** different; other: *His account of what happened sounds reasonable, but the facts are otherwise.* **—conj.** because if not; or else: *The shingles must be fixed; otherwise, the roof will leak.*

Ot·ta·wa (ot′ə wə) *n.* **1.** the capital of Canada, in the southeastern part of the country, in Ontario. Pop. (1971), 298,087. **2.** a member of a tribe of Algonquian Indians who lived near the Great Lakes in what is now Michigan.

ot·ter (ot′ər) *n. pl.,* **ot·ters** or **ot·ter. 1.** a web-footed, water animal related to and resembling the weasel and mink. It has a long, slightly flattened tail. **2.** the valuable, brown, glossy fur of this animal.

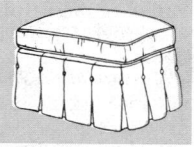
Otter

Ot·to I (ot′ō) A.D. 912–973, emperor of the Holy Roman Empire from A.D. 962 to 973. Also, **Otto the Great.**

Ot·to·man (ot′ə mən) *n. pl.,* **Ot·to·mans. 1.** another name for **Turk. 2. ottoman.** a low, boxlike, upholstered seat or footstool. **—adj.** another word for **Turkish.**

Ottoman Empire, a Turkish empire that lasted from 1289 to 1922 and included part of eastern Europe, the Near East, Asia Minor, northern Africa, and the eastern Mediterranean.

Ottoman

Oua·ga·dou·gou (wä′gə dōō′gōō) *n.* the capital of Upper Volta, in the central part of the country. Pop. (1970 est.), 110,000.

ouch (ouch) *interj.* used to express sudden pain.

ought¹ (ôt) *auxiliary verb* **1.** to be bound by a promise or duty: *You ought to obey the law.* **2.** to be expected or likely: *I put in new batteries, so the radio ought to work.* **3.** to be sensible or wise: *You ought to take care of your cold.* [Old English *āhte.*]

ought² (ôt) another spelling of **aught¹.**

ounce¹ (ouns) *n.* **1.** a unit of weight equal to 1/16 pound avoirdupois, or 1/12 pound troy. **2.** in liquid measure, a fluid ounce. **3.** a small quantity: *The climbers didn't have an ounce of energy left when they reached the peak of the mountain.* [Old French *unce.*]

at; āpe; cär; end; mē; it; īce; hot; ōld; fôrk; wood; fōōl; oil; out; up; turn; sing; thin; this; hw in white; zh in treasure. The symbol ə stands for the sound of **a** in about, **e** in taken, **i** in pencil, **o** in lemon, and **u** in circus.

ounce² (ouns) *n.* another word for **snow leopard.** [Old French *once.*]

our (our) *adj.* of or belonging to us: *Our house is on Oak Street.*

ours (ourz) *pron.* the one or ones belonging to us: *Their dog is larger than ours. Ours is a miniature poodle.*

our·selves (our selvz′) *pron., pl.* **1.** the form of **we** or **us** used to give emphasis to the word it goes with: *We ourselves made the decision.* **2.** the form of **we** or **us** used to show that the subject and direct object of a verb are the same: *We took it upon ourselves to tell you.* **3.** our usual or normal selves.

-ous *suffix* (used to form adjectives from nouns) of, full of, characterized by, or like: *religious, dangerous, famous, clamorous.*

oust (oust) *v.t.* to force or drive out; expel; dispossess: *The player was ousted from the game when he argued with the umpire.*

oust·er (ous′tər) *n.* the act or an instance of ousting: *The discovery that funds were missing caused the ouster of a dishonest bank clerk.*

out (out) *adv.* **1.** from within or the inside; away from the center: *The water rushed out.* **2.** away from one's home or business: *The doctor went out on a call.* **3.** into the open air; outdoors: *The children went out to play.* **4.** from a source or container: *to draw out a sword, to pour out wine.* **5.** so as to project or extend: *The rocks jutted out into the sea.* **6.** to an end or conclusion: *to fight it out, to hear someone out.* **7.** into a condition of inactivity or extinction: *The firemen put out the flames.* **8.** so as to be exhausted or consumed: *The supplies gave out.* **9.** into or within view, public notice, or circulation: *The sun came out. The book came out last week.* **10.** *Baseball.* so as to be unsuccessful in reaching a base. —*adj.* **1.** not in control or power: *the out political party.* **2.** not in working order or condition: *That road is out because of the flood.* **3.** directed outward: *an out train.* **4.** outlying: *out islands.* **5.** *Baseball.* (of a batter or base runner) unsuccessful in reaching a base. —*prep.* **1.** from within; out from: *She looked out the window.* **2.** outward on; out along: *Drive out the dirt road until you come to the highway.* —*n.* **1.** *usually,* **outs.** the people not in office or in power. **2.** a way or means of escaping or avoiding: *She didn't want to go, but she couldn't think of an out.* **3.** *Baseball.* the act of putting out a batter or base runner. —*v.i.* to be revealed; come out: *The truth will out.* —*interj.* away; begone.

   on the outs or **at outs.** in disagreement; not friendly: *They have been on the outs since their fight.*

   out for. trying hard to get or do: *He is out for a raise in salary.*

   out of. a. from within: *He looked out of the window.* **b.** beyond the limits, reach, or range of: *The airplane flew out of sight. He was out of hearing.* **c.** without: *The swimmer was out of breath. I'm out of butter.* **d.** from, as material: *That house is built out of brick.* **e.** from among: *to choose one out of three.* **f.** because of; as a result of: *He did it out of kindness.*

   out to. trying hard to: *He is out to earn a lot of money this summer.*

out- *prefix* **1.** outside or outward: *outline, outcry.* **2.** more than or better than: *outgrow, outshine, outshoot.*

out-and-out (out′ən out′) *adj.* thorough; complete: *an out-and-out liar.*

out·back (out′bak′) *n.* a wild, undeveloped part of Australia.

out·bid (out′bid′) *v.t.,* **out·bid, out·bid** or **out·bid·den, out·bid·ding.** to offer a higher price than (someone else).

out·board (out′bôrd′) *adj.* outside the hull or farther away from the center of a ship or boat.

outboard motor, a gasoline engine with a shaft that has a propeller at the end and is attached to the outside of the stern of a small boat.

Outboard motor

out·bound (out′bound′) *adj.* outward bound: *an outbound flight.*

out·break (out′brāk′) *n.* a sudden occurrence or outburst: *an outbreak of flu, the outbreak of World War II.*

out·build·ing (out′bil′ding) *n.* a building, such as a woodshed, barn, or garage, that is separate from a main building.

out·burst (out′burst′) *n.* an outpouring or explosion: *an outburst of flames. We were surprised at his sudden outburst of temper.*

out·cast (out′kast′) *n.* a person who is rejected or forced out of a group: *The traitor was an outcast.* —*adj.* forced out or rejected: *an outcast criminal.*

out·class (out′klas′) *v.t.* to be better or higher than in rank or quality; surpass: *Tom outclassed the other students in arithmetic.*

out·come (out′kum′) *n.* a result or consequence: *We are waiting to hear the outcome of the election.*

out·crop (*n.,* out′krop′; *v.,* out′krop′) *n.* the part of a rock layer that comes out to the surface of the ground so as to be seen or easily mined: *an outcrop of ore.* —*v.i.,* **out·cropped, out·crop·ping.** to come to the surface of the ground.

out·cry (out′krī′) *n. pl.,* **out·cries. 1.** a strong objection or protest: *The proposed tax caused an outcry.* **2.** a cry; shout.

out·dat·ed (out′dā′tid) *adj.* out-of-date; old-fashioned.

out·dis·tance (out′dis′təns) *v.t.,* **out·dis·tanced, out·dis·tanc·ing.** to leave behind, as in a race: *Jim easily outdistanced the other runners.*

out·do (out′doo′) *v.t.,* **out·did** (out′did′), **out·done** (out′-dun′), **out·do·ing.** to do better than; exceed: *Jane outdoes the rest of the class in geography.*

out·door (out′dôr′) *adj.* done, being, or used out in the open rather than inside a house or other building: *outdoor furniture, an outdoor game.*

out·doors (out′dôrz′) *adv.* not in a house or other building; out under the sky: *to take a walk outdoors, to eat outdoors.* —*n.* the world that is outside houses or other buildings; the open air.

out·er (ou′tər) *adj.* **1.** on the outside: *I wear warm outer clothes in winter.* **2.** far away from the center: *the outer reaches of the universe.*

outer ear, another term for **external ear.**

out·er·most (ou′tər mōst′) *adj.* most distant or farthest out.

outer space 1. the space beyond the earth's atmosphere: *Mars is in outer space.* **2.** the space between the planets or between the stars.

out·field (out′fēld′) *n.* **1.** the part of a baseball field beyond the infield and between the foul lines. **2.** the players who play in this area.

out·field·er (out′fēl′dər) *n.* a baseball player who plays a position in the outfield.

out·fit (out′fit′) *n.* **1.** a set of different articles or equipment for doing something: *a camping outfit.* **2.** a set of clothes; ensemble: *She wore a red outfit.* **3.** *Informal.* any group, such as a team or military outfit. —*v.t.,* **out·fit·ted, out·fit·ting.** to provide with articles or equipment: *to outfit an expedition of explorers going to the North Pole.* —**out′·fit·ter,** *n.*

O

out·flank (out′flangk′) *v.t.* **1.** to outmaneuver (an opposing army or other force) by getting around its side. **2.** to get the better of (an opponent), especially by avoiding a direct assault.

out·flow (out′flō′) *n.* **1.** the act of flowing out. **2.** something that flows out: *an outflow of lava from a volcano.*

out·go (out′gō′) *n. pl.,* **out·goes.** something that goes out, especially money spent.

out·go·ing (out′gō′ing) *adj.* **1.** sociable, open, and talkative; not withdrawn or private: *An outgoing person makes friends quickly.* **2.** going out or departing: *an outgoing President.*

out·grow (out′grō′) *v.t.,* **out·grew, out·grown, out·grow·ing. 1.** to grow too large for: *to outgrow one's clothing.* **2.** to leave behind or lose as one grows older: *to outgrow a fear of the dark.* **3.** to grow taller than: *James outgrew his older brother by four inches.*

out·growth (out′grōth′) *n.* **1.** something that develops or results from something else: *Bill's interest in learning to speak Spanish is an outgrowth of his visit to Spain.* **2.** something that grows out; growth.

out·guess (out′ges′) *v.t.* to guess correctly the plans of; be smarter or more clever than; outwit.

out·house (out′hous′) *n. pl.,* **out·hous·es** (out′hou′ziz). **1.** a small shed or stall outdoors that is used as a toilet. **2.** another word for **outbuilding.**

out·ing (ou′ting) *n.* a short pleasure trip; excursion: *The students all enjoyed the school outing.*

out·land·ish (out lan′dish) *adj.* strange, unfamiliar, or odd: *The girl wore outlandish clothes.*

out·last (out′last′) *v.t.* to last longer than.

out·law (out′lô′) *n.* **1.** a person who habitually breaks or defies the law; criminal. **2.** formerly, a person who was excluded from the benefits and protection of the law; fugitive or exile. —*v.t.* **1.** to make illegal; prohibit: *to outlaw the sale of certain drugs.* **2.** to declare (someone) an outlaw.

out·lay (out′lā′) *n.* an investment or expenditure of money.

out·let (out′let) *n.* **1.** a place at which something escapes or comes out: *Leaves clogged the outlets of the swimming pool.* **2.** a means of expression or release: *Sports are a good outlet for a young boy's energy.* **3.** a place in an electrical wiring system where appliances can be plugged in. **4.** a place where products are sold, especially a store that sells the goods of a single manufacturer.

out·line (out′līn′) *n.* **1.** the shape or contour of an object formed by following or tracing along its outer edges: *Through the fog they saw the outline of a passing ship.* **2.** a summary or general description, especially one that organizes the contents of a story, composition, or speech. **3.** a style of drawing in which an object or scene is represented merely by its outer lines with no shading. —*v.t.,* **out·lined, out·lin·ing. 1.** to set off or make visible: *Skyscrapers were outlined against the sky.* **2.** to summarize or give a general description of: *to outline a plan of action.* **3.** to draw the outline of.

out·live (out′liv′) *v.t.,* **out·lived, out·liv·ing.** to live or last longer than.

out·look (out′look′) *n.* **1.** a view into the future; expectation: *The weather outlook for tomorrow is not good.* **2.** a point of view or set of opinions: *He has an optimistic outlook on life.* **3.** a place from which a view is obtained; lookout. **4.** the view from such a place.

out·ly·ing (out′lī′ing) *adj.* located far from the center of something: *The zoo is located in an outlying district of the city.*

out·ma·neu·ver (out′mə nōō′vər) *v.t.* to maneuver better than or defeat by maneuvering.

out·mod·ed (out′mō′did) *adj.* no longer in style, suitable, or useful: *an outmoded machine.*

out·most (out′mōst′) *adj.* farthest out; outermost.

out·num·ber (out′num′bər) *v.t.* to exceed in number; be greater in number than: *The soldiers were greatly outnumbered by the enemy.*

out-of-bounds (out′əv boundz′) *adv.* in sports, outside the legal area of play: *The ball was thrown out-of-bounds.* —*adj.* being outside the legal area of play.

out-of-date (out′əv dāt′) *adj.* no longer in style or use; outmoded: *an out-of-date manner of dress.*

out-of-doors (out′əv dôrz′) *adj.* also, **out-of-door.** another term for **outdoor.** —*n., adv.* another term for **outdoors.**

out-of-the-way (out′əv thə wā′) *adj.* **1.** remote; secluded: *an out-of-the-way spot.* **2.** not usually met with; little known or unusual.

out·pa·tient (out′pā′shənt) *n.* a patient who receives care or treatment from a hospital, clinic, or similar institution without staying there.

out·play (out′plā′) *v.t.* to play better than.

out·post (out′pōst′) *n.* **1.** a small military station, usually at some distance from the main force, established to keep control over an area and to guard against attack. **2.** the soldiers assigned to such a station. **3.** a remote settlement, as on a frontier.

out·put (out′poot′) *n.* **1.** the amount of something produced: *electrical output, work output.* **2.** the information made available by a computer.

out·rage (out′rāj′) *n.* **1.** an act of extreme violence, viciousness, or cruelty: *The murder of the hostages was an outrage against humanity.* **2.** great anger or rage: *The peasants felt outrage at the attacks on their villages.* **3.** a great insult or offense: *Such behavior in public is an outrage.* —*v.t.,* **out·raged, out·rag·ing. 1.** to cause great anger in: *The newspaper's editorial outraged the senator.* **2.** to subject to an outrage; abuse or injure greatly.

out·ra·geous (out rā′jəs) *adj.* **1.** going beyond proper limits: *an outrageous price, an outrageous demand.* **2.** shameful; offensive; shocking: *outrageous behavior.* —**out·ra′geous·ly,** *adv.*

out·rank (out′rangk′) *v.t.* to be of a higher rank than: *A major outranks a captain.*

out·rig·ger (out′rig′ər) *n.* an extra float and its supporting frame that can be attached to the side of a canoe to extend out into the water and prevent the boat from capsizing.

out·right (out′rīt′) *adj.* complete; total; thorough: *an outright lie.* —*adv.* **1.** in a direct or straightforward way; openly: *Please say outright what you mean.* **2.** completely and all at once: *to pay for a house outright.* **3.** at once; immediately.

out·run (out′run′) *v.t.,* **out·ran** (out′-ran′), **out·run, out·run·ning. 1.** to run farther or faster than: *Our horse outran all the others in the race.* **2.** to go beyond; exceed: *The demand for the new book outran the store's supply.*

Spar

Float

Outrigger

at; āpe; cär; end; mē; it; īce; hot; ōld; fôrk; wood; fōōl; oil; out; up; turn; sing; thin; this; hw in white; zh in treasure. The symbol ə stands for the sound of a in about, e in taken, i in pencil, o in lemon, and u in circus.

out·sell (out′sel′) *v.t.,* **out·sold** (out′sōld′), **out·sel·ling.**
1. to sell more merchandise than: *Peter outsold the other salesmen.* **2.** to be sold in greater quantities than.

out·set (out′set′) *n.* the beginning; start: *the outset of a journey.*

out·shine (out′shīn′) *v.t.,* **out·shone, out·shin·ing.**
1. to shine more brightly than. **2.** to be better than; excel.

out·side (out′sīd′, out′sīd′) *n.* the outer side, surface, or part; exterior: *The outside of the house was painted white.* —*adj.* **1.** situated on the outside; outer: *The outside layer of paint was peeling.* **2.** coming from or acting from without: *The revolution was encouraged by outside influences.* **3.** extremely slight; remote: *There is only an outside chance that we will be able to come to the party.* **4.** reaching the utmost limit possible: *an outside estimate of expenses.* —*adv.* on, to, or toward the outside; outdoors: *Do you want to go outside for a while? The children played outside all day.* —*prep.* **1.** beyond the walls, surfaces, or boundaries of: *They live just outside Philadelphia.* **2.** beyond the range or limits of: *The matter falls outside the jurisdiction of this court.*
at the outside. at most: *The repairman guessed the job would take two hours at the outside.*
outside of. a. outside. **b.** with the exception of.

out·sid·er (out′sī′dər) *n.* a person who is not a member of a certain group, society, or organization.

out·skirts (out′skurts′) *n., pl.* the regions or sections surrounding a or at the edge of a specified area, as a city.

out·smart (out′smärt′) *v.t.* to outwit.

out·spo·ken (out′spō′kən) *adj.* **1.** open or frank in speech: *The senator was very outspoken in his criticism of the President.* **2.** expressed frankly or boldly: *outspoken disapproval.* —**out′spo′ken·ly,** *adv.* —**out′spo′ken·ness,** *n.*

out·spread (out′spred′) *adj.* spread out; extended.

out·stand·ing (out′stan′ding) *adj.* **1.** so excellent as to stand out from others of its kind: *an outstanding athlete, an outstanding example of Greek architecture.* **2.** that remains to be done, settled, or paid: *an outstanding debt.* —**out′stand′ing·ly,** *adv.*

out·stay (out′stā′) *v.t.* to remain longer than or beyond the time of: *to outstay one's welcome.*

out·strip (out′strip′) *v.t.,* **out·stripped, out·strip·ping.**
1. to surpass; excel: *That country outstrips all other nations in coal production.* **2.** to run farther or faster than, as in a race.

out·ward (out′wərd) *also,* **out·wards.** *adv.* to or toward the outside; away; out: *The door opens outward.* —*adj.* **1.** toward the outside. **2.** relating to the outside, the visible, or the external: *There were outward changes, but the city remained essentially the same.* —**out′ward·ness,** *n.*

out·ward·ly (out′wərd lē) *adv.* **1.** on or toward the outside. **2.** in appearance; seemingly: *outwardly happy.*

out·wear (out′wer′) *v.t.,* **out·wore** (out′wôr′), **out·worn** (out′wôrn′), **out·wear·ing. 1.** to last longer or wear better than: *This fabric outwears most other materials.* **2.** to wear out or exhaust.

out·weigh (out′wā′) *v.t.* **1.** to be greater in weight than: *You outweigh me by at least ten pounds.* **2.** to be more important than: *The advantages of the new system outweigh the disadvantages.*

out·wit (out′wit′) *v.t.,* **out·wit·ted, out·wit·ting.** to get the better of (someone) by cunning or cleverness.

out·work (out′wurk′) *v.t.* to work better or faster than; outdo in working.

out·worn (out′wôrn′) *adj.* **1.** worn out: *an outworn coat.* **2.** no longer in use; out-of-date.

o·va (ō′və) the plural of **ovum.**

o·val (ō′vəl) *adj.* **1.** shaped like an egg. **2.** shaped like an ellipse. —*n.* something having an oval shape.

o·va·ry (ō′vər ē) *n. pl.,* **o·va·ries. 1.** the female reproductive organ that produces eggs. **2.** *Botany.* the part of a plant in which the seeds are formed.

o·vate (ō′vāt) *adj.* having an oval shape: *an ovate leaf.*

o·va·tion (ō vā′shən) *n.* an enthusiastic burst of applause or other demonstration of public approval: *The pianist received a standing ovation.*

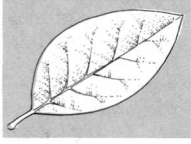
Ovate leaf

ov·en (uv′ən) *n.* an enclosed chamber, as in a stove, that is used to heat, bake, roast, or dry objects that are placed inside.

ov·en·bird (uv′ən burd′) *n.* a North American bird with brownish feathers, that builds a dome-shaped nest on the ground.

o·ver (ō′vər) *prep.* **1.** in a place or position higher than; above: *Clouds hung over the lake.* **2.** upon so as to cover or close: *The woman put a blanket over her sleeping child.* **3.** on the surface of: *to spread butter over bread.* **4.** to the other side of; across: *The horse jumped over the fence.* **5.** forward and down from: *to fall over a cliff.* **6.** from one end of to the other; along: *to drive over a new road.* **7.** on the other side of; beyond: *The town is over the next hill.* **8.** during; throughout: *School is closed over the holidays.* **9.** above in authority, power, or rank: *Those soldiers need a strong leader over them.* **10.** more than: *She spent over twenty dollars on groceries.* **11.** in preference to: *Carol was chosen over ten other candidates.* **12.** with reference to; concerning; about: *Don't get so upset over minor details.* —*adv.* **1.** above: *We could hear a plane flying over.* **2.** down or forward and down: *The ball rolled to the edge of the cliff and fell over.* **3.** above and beyond the top, brim, or edge: *The water boiled over.* **4.** from an erect or upright position: *The cat knocked the vase over.* **5.** so as to cover or be covered: *The lake froze over.* **6.** from one side or place to the other: *Come over for dinner tonight.* **7.** once more; again: *If you don't do the job right, you'll have to do it over.* **8.** in repetition or succession: *three times over.* **9.** in excess; in addition; remaining: *Four goes into ten twice with two left over.* —*adj.* **1.** ended; finished: *The war was soon over.* **2.** higher or upper; in excess: *Our estimate was two dollars over.*
over again. once more: *Please tell me that story over again.*
over and above. in addition; besides.
over and over. again and again; repeatedly.

over- *prefix* **1.** too much, too highly, or too: *overload, overrate, overanxious.* **2.** above; higher: *overhead.* **3.** around, covering, or on top: *overgrowth, overcoat, overshoe.* **4.** from above to below; down: *overthrow, overturn.*

⏺ To understand the meaning of a word that begins with **over-** but is not defined in this dictionary, add the words "too much" or "too" to the meaning of the basic word. For example, *overcooked* means "cooked too much" and *overambitious* means "too ambitious." For any important *over-* word that has a special meaning, there is an entry in the dictionary.

o·ver·act (ō′vər akt′) *v.i., v.t.* to act (a role or part) in an exaggerated or unrealistic way; overdo in acting.

o·ver·ac·tive (ō′vər ak′tiv) *adj.* too active: *an overactive child.* —**o′ver·ac′tive·ly,** *adv.*

o·ver·all (ō′vər ôl′) *adj.* **1.** general or total: *My overall impression of him was favorable.* **2.** from one end to the other: *The overall length of the car is twelve feet.*

o·ver·alls (ō′vər ôlz′) *n., pl.* loose-fitting trousers usually having a piece that covers the chest with suspenders attached.

o·ver·anx·ious (ō′vər angk′shəs) *adj.* too anxious.

o·ver·ate (ō′vər āt′) the past tense of **overeat**.

o·ver·awe (ō′vər ô′) *v.t.,* **o·ver·awed, o·ver·aw·ing.** to overcome or restrain by inspiring awe.

o·ver·bal·ance (ō′vər bal′əns) *v.t.,* **o·ver·bal·anced, o·ver·bal·anc·ing.** 1. to cause to lose balance. 2. to be greater than in weight or importance.

o·ver·bear (ō′vər ber′) *v.t.,* **o·ver·bore** (ō′vər bôr′), **o·ver·borne** (ō′vər bôrn′), **o·ver·bear·ing.** to overcome or drive down, as by weight or power.

o·ver·bear·ing (ō′vər ber′ing) *adj.* arrogantly superior in manner; domineering. —**o′ver·bear′ing·ly,** *adv.*

o·ver·board (ō′vər bôrd′) *adv.* over the side of a ship into the water: *The sailor slipped and fell overboard.*
  to go overboard. to go to extremes, especially because of enthusiasm or affection.

o·ver·bur·den (ō′vər burd′ən) *v.t.* to put too great a weight or burden on; overload.

o·ver·came (ō′vər kām′) the past tense of **overcome**.

o·ver·cast (ō′vər kast′) *adj.* clouded over; cloudy; dark; gloomy: *an overcast sky.* —*v.t.,* **o·ver·cast, o·ver·cast·ing.** 1. to cover with clouds or darkness. 2. to sew (the edge of fabric) over and over with long stitches to prevent raveling. —*n.* 1. a covering of clouds. 2. a stitch sewn by overcasting.

o·ver·cau·tious (ō′vər kô′shəs) *adj.* too cautious.

o·ver·charge (*v.,* ō′vər chärj′; *n.,* ō′vər chärj′) *v.t.,* **o·ver·charged, o·ver·charg·ing.** 1. to charge (someone) too high a price: *The salesclerk overcharged me on that purchase.* 2. to load or supply with too great a charge: *to overcharge an electric battery.* —*n.* a charge that is too great.

o·ver·cloud (ō′vər kloud′) *v.t.* to cover with clouds.

o·ver·coat (ō′vər kōt′) *n.* a heavy outer coat worn over other clothing for added warmth.

o·ver·come (ō′vər kum′) *v.,* **o·ver·came, o·ver·come, o·ver·com·ing** —*v.t.* 1. to get the better of, as in a contest or conflict; conquer: *The army overcame all opposition.* 2. to rise above or get over: *He overcame his fear of heights.* 3. to exhaust, overwhelm, or make helpless: *Many people in the crowd were overcome by the heat.* —*v.i.* to be victorious; conquer.

o·ver·con·fi·dent (ō′vər kon′fə dənt) *adj.* too confident. —**o′ver·con′fi·dence,** *n.*

o·ver·crowd (ō′vər kroud′) *v.t.* to put too many people or things in: *The small apartment was overcrowded by the large family.*

o·ver·de·vel·op (ō′vər di vel′əp) *v.t.* 1. to develop too much. 2. to submerge (a photographic film or plate) in developing solution too long, so that it becomes too dark.

o·ver·do (ō′vər dōō′) *v.,* **o·ver·did** (ō′vər did′), **o·ver·done** (ō′vər dun′), **o·ver·do·ing.** —*v.t.* 1. to do or use too much; carry too far. 2. to cook (food) too much. —*v.i.* to do too much or go too far.

o·ver·dose (ō′vər dōs′) *n.* too large a dose, as of a drug. —*v.t.,* **o·ver·dosed, o·ver·dos·ing.** to give too large a dose to.

o·ver·draft (ō′vər draft′) *n.* 1. an overdrawing of a bank account. 2. the amount overdrawn: *The bank informed him that his overdraft was fifty dollars.*

Overalls

o·ver·draw (ō′vər drô′) *v.t.,* **o·ver·drew** (ō′vər drōō′), **o·ver·drawn, o·ver·draw·ing.** 1. to write a check against (a bank account) that is larger than the account's balance or credit. 2. to exaggerate: *The fisherman's description of the size of the fish he caught was overdrawn.*

o·ver·dress (ō′vər dres′) *v.i., v.t.* to dress in clothes that are too formal or fancy for the occasion.

o·ver·due (ō′vər dōō′, ō′vər dyōō′) *adj.* 1. remaining unpaid past the assigned date of payment: *The rent is overdue.* 2. that has not yet happened or arrived, though the expected or scheduled time is past: *The birth of her baby is overdue.* 3. that should have happened sooner: *An apology from him is long overdue.*

o·ver·eat (ō′vər ēt′) *v.i.,* **o·ver·ate, o·ver·eat·en, o·ver·eat·ing.** to eat too much.

o·ver·em·pha·size (ō′vər em′fə sīz′) *v.t.,* **o·ver·em·pha·sized, o·ver·em·pha·siz·ing.** to place too much emphasis on; stress too much. —**o′ver·em′pha·sis,** *n.*

o·ver·es·ti·mate (*v.,* ō′vər es′tə māt′; *n.,* ō′vər es′tə·mit) *v.t.,* **o·ver·es·ti·mat·ed, o·ver·es·ti·mat·ing.** to make too high an estimate of: *to overestimate a person's ability.* —*n.* an estimate that is too high. —**o′ver·es′ti·ma′·tion,** *n.*

o·ver·ex·pose (ō′vər eks pōz′) *v.t.,* **o·ver·ex·posed, o·ver·ex·pos·ing.** 1. to display or expose (someone or something) too much. 2. to expose (a photographic film or plate) for too long a time. —**o′ver·ex·po′sure,** *n.*

o·ver·feed (ō′vər fēd′) *v.t.,* **o·ver·fed** (ō′vər fed′), **o·ver·feed·ing.** to feed too much.

o·ver·flow (*v.,* ō′vər flō′; *n.,* ō′vər flō′) *v.,* **o·ver·flowed, o·ver·flown, o·ver·flow·ing.** —*v.i.* 1. to flow beyond the usual limits: *Water from the kitchen sink overflowed onto the floor.* 2. to be so full that the contents flow over: *The bathtub overflowed.* 3. to be very full: *Her heart overflowed with love for the child.* —*v.t.* 1. to flow over the top edge or rim of: *The river overflowed its banks.* 2. to flow or spread over; flood: *When the dam burst, water overflowed the town.* —*n.* 1. the act of overflowing. 2. something that overflows. 3. an outlet for excess liquid.

o·ver·grow (ō′vər grō′) *v.,* **o·ver·grew** (ō′vər grōō′), **o·ver·grown, o·ver·grow·ing.** —*v.t.* 1. to cover with growth; grow over: *Weeds overgrew the yard.* 2. to grow too large for; outgrow. —*v.i.* to grow too much or too fast.

o·ver·grown (ō′vər grōn′) *adj.* 1. grown too large or beyond normal size. 2. covered with weeds, vines, or other growth.

o·ver·growth (ō′vər grōth′) *n.* 1. excessive growth. 2. growth spreading over or covering something.

o·ver·hand (ō′vər hand′) *adj.* performed with the hand raised above the elbow or the arm raised above the shoulder: *an overhand pitch.* —*adv. also,* **o′ver·hand′ed.** in an overhand style or manner: *to throw overhand.*

o·ver·hang (*v.,* ō′vər hang′; *n.,* ō′vər hang′) *v.,* **o·ver·hung** (ō′vər hung′), **o·ver·hang·ing.** —*v.t.* to hang out over (something): *a smooth broad highway overhung by the dark cloud of a mountain ridge* (John Updike). —*v.i.* to hang or project over something. —*n.* a part or section that overhangs; projection.

o·ver·haul (ō′vər hôl′) *v.t.* 1. to examine thoroughly and make needed repairs or adjustments: *to overhaul an*

at; āpe; cär; end; mē; it; īce; hot; ōld; fôrk; wood; fōol; oil; out; up; turn; sing; thin; this; hw in white; zh in treasure. The symbol ə stands for the sound of **a** in about, **e** in taken, **i** in pencil, **o** in lemon, and **u** in circus.

automobile engine. **2.** to make far-reaching changes in: *The governor introduced legislation designed to overhaul the prison system.* **3.** to catch up with; overtake: *The coast guard cutter quickly overhauled the fishing boat.* —*n.* the act of overhauling: *The engine needs a complete overhaul.*

o·ver·head (*adv.*, ō′vər hed′; *n., adj.*, ō′vər hed′) *adv.* above the level of the head: *a light burning overhead, birds flying overhead.* —*n.* the general operating expenses of a business, such as rent, taxes, heating, lighting, and repair, as opposed to costs of materials, supplies, and labor. —*adj.* situated, operating, or moving overhead: *overhead lights.*

o·ver·hear (ō′vər hēr′) *v.t.*, **o·ver·heard** (ō′vər hurd′), **o·ver·hear·ing.** to hear without the speaker's intention or knowledge: *to overhear a private conversation.*

o·ver·heat (ō′vər hēt′) *v.i., v.t.* to become or cause to become too hot: *The car's engine overheated.*

o·ver·in·dulge (ō′vər in dulj′) *v.t., v.i.*, **o·ver·in·dulged, o·ver·in·dulg·ing.** to indulge too much. —**o′ver·in·dul′-gence,** *n.*

o·ver·joy (ō′vər joi′) *v.t.* to make very joyful: *We were overjoyed by the news of the team's victory.*

o·ver·kill (ō′vər kil′) *n.* the ability to destroy more of an enemy or opponents or inflict greater damage than is necessary for victory.

o·ver·land (ō′vər land′) *adv.* by, on, or across land: *to travel overland.* —*adj.* over or across land: *an overland mail route.*

o·ver·lap (*v.*, ō′vər lap′; *n.*, ō′vər lap′) *v.*, **o·ver·lapped, o·ver·lap·ping.** —*v.t.* **1.** to rest on top of (something) and partially cover it up: *One feather overlaps another on a bird's wing.* **2.** to coincide partly with or have something in common: *Our study of English literature overlapped our study of English history.* —*v.i.* **1.** to rest on top of something, partially covering it. **2.** to coincide in part. —*n.* **1.** an instance of overlapping. **2.** a part that overlaps. **3.** the extent or amount of overlapping.

o·ver·lay (*v.*, ō′vər lā′; *n.*, ō′vər lā′) *v.t.*, **o·ver·laid, o·ver·lay·ing.** **1.** to place over or on each other: *to overlay shingles on a roof.* **2.** to cover or spread with something, such as a layer of protective or decorative material: *to overlay painted wood with shellac.* —*n.* **1.** a decorative or protective layer: *There was an overlay of gold on the rim of the mirror.* **2.** any added surface, front, or veneer: *An overlay of friendliness covered his anger.*

o·ver·load (*v.*, ō′vər lōd′; *n.*, ō′vər lōd′) *v.t.* to put too great a load or burden in or upon: *to overload a car, to overload an electrical system.* —*n.* a load or burden that is too great.

o·ver·look (ō′vər look′) *v.t.* **1.** to fail to see, notice, or think of: *The visitors overlooked the possibility that the family might be away.* **2.** to disregard; ignore: *to overlook an insult. He had so many good points that she was willing to overlook his faults.* **3.** to look over or down upon from a higher place or position: *From the tower we overlooked the whole valley.* **4.** to provide a view of: *The house on the hill overlooks a river.*

o·ver·lord (ō′vər lôrd′) *n.* a person who is the lord of other lords or rulers.

o·ver·ly (ō′vər lē) *adv.* excessively; too: *overly generous, overly careful.*

o·ver·much (ō′vər much′) *adj., adv., n.* too much.

o·ver·night (ō′vər nīt′) *adv.* **1.** during or through the night: *to keep watch overnight.* **2.** very quickly; suddenly: *A person's character does not change overnight.* —*adj.* **1.** for one night: *an overnight guest.* **2.** of, lasting through, or occurring during the night: *an overnight airplane ride, an overnight storm.* **3.** suitable, used, or made for short trips: *an overnight bag.*

o·ver·pass (ō′vər pas′) *n. pl.*, **o·ver·pass·es.** a bridge, road, or other passage that crosses above another roadway.

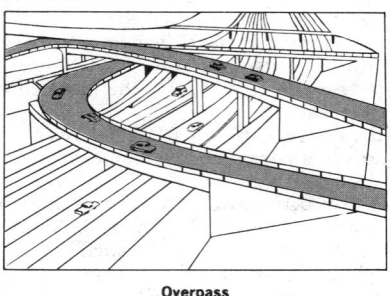
Overpass

o·ver·pay (ō′vər pā′) *v.*, **o·ver·paid, o·ver·pay·ing.** —*v.t.* **1.** to pay (someone) too much. **2.** to pay more than what is required or due. —*v.i.* to pay too much. —**o′ver·pay′ment,** *n.*

o·ver·play (ō′vər plā′) *v.t.* to play (a part or role) in an exaggerated manner; overact.

o·ver·pop·u·late (ō′vər pop′yə lāt′) *v.t.*, **o·ver·pop·u·lat·ed, o·ver·pop·u·lat·ing.** to fill with too many people. —**o′ver·pop′u·la′tion,** *n.*

o·ver·pow·er (ō′vər pou′ər) *v.t.* **1.** to overcome by greater strength or power: *My friend overpowered me at wrestling, and I lost the match.* **2.** to make helpless or ineffective; overcome: *He was overpowered by sadness.*

o·ver·price (ō′vər prīs′) *v.t.*, **o·ver·priced, o·ver·pric·ing.** to set too high a price on.

o·ver·pro·duce (ō′vər prə dōos′, ō′vər prə dyōos′) *v.t.*, **o·ver·pro·duced, o·ver·pro·duc·ing.** to produce more (goods) than is necessary. —**o′ver·pro·duc′tion,** *n.*

o·ver·pro·tect (ō′vər prə tekt′) *v.t.* to protect or shelter too much or to a great degree. —**o′ver·pro·tec′tive,** *adj.*

o·ver·ran (ō′vər ran′) the past tense of **overrun.**

o·ver·rate (ō′vər rāt′) *v.t.*, **o·ver·rat·ed, o·ver·rat·ing.** to rate, value, or estimate too highly.

o·ver·reach (ō′vər rēch′) *v.t.* to reach or extend over or beyond. —*v.i.* to reach too far. —**o′ver·reach′er,** *n.*

to overreach oneself. to fail by trying to do too much.

o·ver·ride (ō′vər rīd′) *v.t.*, **o·ver·rode** (ō′vər rōd′), **o·ver·rid·den** (ō′vər rid′ən), **o·ver·rid·ing.** **1.** to set aside (an action or decision) by superior authority; cancel: *The legislature overrode the governor's veto.* **2.** to prevail over; supersede: *This problem overrides all other matters.*

o·ver·rule (ō′vər rōol′) *v.t.*, **o·ver·ruled, o·ver·rul·ing.** **1.** to set aside or rule against by higher authority: *The Supreme Court overruled the decision of the lower court.* **2.** to decide against or prevail over: *Albert said we should stay, but the rest of the group overruled him.*

o·ver·run (ō′vər run′) *v.t.*, **o·ver·ran, o·ver·run, o·ver·run·ning.** **1.** to swarm or spread over or throughout: *The invading army overran the countryside.* **2.** to flow over: *The river overran its banks.* **3.** to run beyond: *The player overran second base.*

o·ver·seas (ō′vər sēz′) *also*, **o·ver·sea.** *adv.* over, across, or beyond the sea; abroad: *to travel overseas.* —*adj.* **1.** employed, situated, or serving overseas: *a company's overseas representative.* **2.** of or relating to countries across the sea; foreign: *overseas trade.*

o·ver·see (ō′vər sē′) *v.t.*, **o·ver·saw** (ō′vər sô′), **o·ver·seen, o·ver·see·ing.** to watch over and manage; have charge of; direct: *to oversee the building of a canal.*

o·ver·se·er (ō′vər sē′ər) *n.* a person who oversees, especially a person who directs the work of laborers.

o·ver·shad·ow (ō′vər shad′ō) *v.t.* **1.** to be more important or significant than: *War overshadowed all the country's other problems.* **2.** to cast a shadow over; obscure; darken.

o·ver·shoe (ō′vər shōo′) *n.* a shoe or boot, usually made of rubber, worn over an ordinary shoe to protect against cold, snow, water, or mud.

o·ver·shoot (ō′vər shoot′) v., o·ver·shot, o·ver·shoot·ing. —v.t. 1. to go or pass over, above, or beyond (a target, mark, or goal): *The aircraft overshot the landing field.* 2. to shoot or project (something) over or beyond a target or goal. —v.i. to shoot or go too far beyond.

o·ver·shot (ō′vər shot′) adj. 1. having the upper jaw projecting beyond the lower jaw. 2. (of a water wheel) driven by water falling down from above, rather than by water flowing past.

Overshot water wheel

o·ver·sight (ō′vər sīt′) n. a careless, unintentional mistake: *The omission of her name from the guest list was an oversight.*

o·ver·sim·pli·fy (ō′vər sim′plə fī′) v.t., o·ver·sim·pli·fied, o·ver·sim·pli·fy·ing. to make (something) appear to be much simpler than it really is. —o′ver·sim′pli·fi·ca′tion, n.

o·ver·size (ō′vər sīz′) also, o·ver·sized. adj. larger than the normal or usual size.

o·ver·sleep (ō′vər slēp′) v.i., o·ver·slept (ō′vər slept′), o·ver·sleep·ing. to sleep beyond one's intended or usual time for waking up.

o·ver·state (ō′vər stāt′) v.t., o·ver·stat·ed, o·ver·stat·ing. to state too strongly; exaggerate. —o′ver·state′ment, n.

o·ver·stay (o′vər stā′) v.t. to stay beyond the time or limit of: *to overstay one's welcome.*

o·ver·step (ō′vər step′) v.t., o·ver·stepped, o·ver·step·ping. to go over or beyond (a limit); exceed: *to overstep one's authority.*

o·ver·stock (ō′vər stock′) v.t. to supply with more than is needed. —n. a stock or supply that is too large.

o·ver·stuffed (ō′vər stuft′) adj. 1. stuffed to excess. 2. (of furniture) having the frame covered over with a thick padding or large amount of stuffing.

o·vert (ō vurt′, ō′vurt′) adj. not hidden, concealed, or secret; easily observed: *The invasion of the neutral country was an overt act of aggression.* —o·vert′ly, adv.

o·ver·take (ō′vər tāk′) v.t., o·ver·took (ō′vər took′), o·ver·tak·en, o·ver·tak·ing. 1. to catch up with: *The police car overtook the speeding driver.* 2. to catch up with and then pass: *Japan has overtaken West Germany in industrial production.* 3. to come upon unexpectedly or suddenly.

o·ver·tax (ō′vər taks′) v.t. 1. to place too heavy a burden on or draw too much from: *Years of war had overtaxed the country's resources.* 2. to charge too great a tax on.

o·ver·throw (v., ō′vər thrō′; n., ō′vər thrō′) v.t., o·ver·threw (ō′vər throo′), o·ver·thrown, o·ver·throw·ing. 1. to remove from a position of power or dominance, especially by force or struggle: *The rebels overthrew the government.* 2. to throw or knock down; overturn; upset: *to overthrow a table in rage.* 3. to throw something, as a baseball, beyond (the intended place). —n. 1. the act of overthrowing or the state of being overthrown. 2. a throw that goes beyond the intended place.

o·ver·time (ō′vər tīm′) n. 1. time worked beyond the regular working hours. 2. the pay for such extra time worked. 3. *Sports.* an extra period of play to decide the winner of a contest that has ended in a tie. —adv. beyond regular hours: *to work overtime.* —adj. of or for overtime.

o·ver·tone (ō′vər tōn′) n. 1. a fainter and higher tone that occurs with the fundamental tone produced by a musical instrument. Also, **harmonic.** 2. a secondary or implied meaning or quality; suggestion; hint: *His congratulations to his friend for winning the prize carried an overtone of jealousy.*

o·ver·ture (ō′vər chər) n. 1. an orchestral musical composition that introduces a larger musical work, such as an opera. 2. a suggestion or proposal meant to lead to some new action; offer to begin something: *Joan made overtures of friendship to the new girl.*

o·ver·turn (ō′vər turn′) v.t. 1. to turn or throw over; upset: *Heavy winds overturned the sailboat.* 2. to overthrow, defeat, or destroy. —v.i. to be or become turned over: *The speeding car overturned on the sharp curve.*

o·ver·use (v., ō′vər yooz′; n., ō′vər yoos′) v.t., o·ver·used, o·ver·us·ing. to use too much. —n. too much or too frequent use.

o·ver·view (ō′vər vyoo′) n. a broad, general view or survey.

o·ver·ween·ing (ō′vər wē′ning) adj. having or showing great arrogance, conceit, or self-importance.

o·ver·weight (ō′vər wāt′) adj. above the normal, desirable, or allowed weight. —n. more weight than is normal, desirable, or allowed.

o·ver·whelm (ō′vər hwelm′, ō′vər welm′) v.t. 1. to overcome completely; overpower or crush: *Enemy forces overwhelmed the outpost. He was overwhelmed by the death of his father.* 2. to cover or bury completely. —o′ver·whelm′ing·ly, adv.

o·ver·work (v., ō′vər wurk′; n., ō′vər wurk′) v.t. to cause to work too hard; tire or exhaust with work: *The farmer overworked his mule.* —n. more work than one should do or can be expected to do.

o·ver·wrought (ō′vər rôt′) adj. 1. worked up to a state of excessive excitement or nervousness. 2. too elaborate or fancy; overdone.

Ov·id (ov′id) 43 B.C.–A.D. 17?, Roman poet.

o·vi·duct (ō′və dukt′) n. in animals, the tube through which the egg cell passes from the ovary.

o·vip·a·rous (ō vip′ər əs) adj. producing eggs that hatch after they have left the body of the female. All birds and most fish and reptiles are oviparous.

o·vi·pos·i·tor (ō′və poz′i tər) n. an organ at the end of the abdomen of the female of certain insects, by which eggs are deposited.

o·void (ō′void) adj. having the shape of an egg; egg-shaped. —n. something shaped like an egg.

o·vo·vi·vip·a·rous (ō′vō vī vip′ər əs) adj. producing eggs that develop inside the body of the female and hatch either inside the mother or soon after they are laid. Certain reptiles and fish and many insects are ovoviviparous.

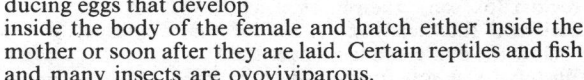

Ovipositor

o·vu·late (ō′vyə lāt′) v.i., o·vu·lat·ed, o·vu·lat·ing. to produce egg cells or discharge them from the ovary. —o′vu·la′tion, n.

o·vule (ō′vyool) n. 1. a small egg, especially one in an

at; āpe; cär; end; mē; it; īce; hot; ōld; fôrk; wood; fool; oil; out; up; turn; sing; thin; this; hw in white; zh in treasure. The symbol ə stands for the sound of **a** in about, **e** in taken, **i** in pencil, **o** in lemon, and **u** in circus.

early stage of growth. **2.** a part of a plant that develops into a seed after fertilization.

o·vum (ō′vəm) *n. pl.,* **o·va.** see **egg**[1] *(def. 4).*

owe (ō) *v.,* **owed, ow·ing.** —*v.t.* **1.** to be under obligation to pay or repay (money): *to owe ten dollars to a friend, to owe the landlord two months' rent.* **2.** to be under obligation to offer or give: *I think we owe her an apology.* **3.** to be obliged or indebted for: *Modern physics owes a great deal to Einstein.* —*v.i.* to be in debt.

ow·ing (ō′ing) *adj.* due to be paid; unpaid; owed.

   owing to. because of: *Owing to bad weather, I didn't go.*

owl (oul) *n.* any of various birds of prey having a rounded head with large staring eyes and a hooked bill, a short, square tail, rounded wings, and soft, downy feathers. Owls usually hunt at night and feed chiefly on rodents and other small mammals.

Owl

owl·et (ou′lit) *n.* a young or small owl.

owl·ish (ou′lish) *adj.* like or resembling an owl.

own (ōn) *adj.* of, relating to, or belonging to oneself or itself: *The accident was her own fault. His own brother testified against him.* —*n.* something that belongs to oneself or itself: *Jim's idea was better than my own.* —*v.t.* **1.** to have as one's property; have ownership of: *He owns all the land between here and the river.* **2.** to acknowledge or admit: *I own that the mistake was mine.*

   of one's own. belonging exclusively to oneself: *She has never had a pet of her own.*

   on one's own. a. relying only on oneself for support or success: *Since his parents died, he has been on his own.* **b.** through one's personal efforts.

   to come into one's own. to receive the success or recognition one deserves: *The man had been an artist for many years before he finally came into his own.*

   to hold one's own. to maintain one's position or standing, as against opposition or competition.

   to own up. to confess frankly and fully.

own·er (ō′nər) *n.* a person who owns something.

own·er·ship (ō′nər ship′) *n.* the state of being an owner; right of possession.

ox (oks) *n. pl.,* **ox·en. 1.** the adult castrated male of domestic cattle, used as a work animal or for beef. **2.** any of various related animals, such as the buffalo, bison, or yak.

ox·blood (oks′blud′) *n.* a deep red color. —*adj.* having the color oxblood; deep red.

ox·bow (oks′bō′) *n.* **1.** the wooden, U-shaped part of a yoke, placed as a collar under and around the neck of an ox. **2.** a U-shaped bend in a river.

ox·cart (oks′kärt′) *n.* a cart pulled by an ox or oxen.

ox·en (ok′sən) the plural of **ox.**

ox·ford (oks′fərd) *n.* **1.** a shoe that comes up to just below the ankle and laces over the instep. **2.** a soft, medium-weight cotton fabric, used chiefly for shirts and blouses. Also *(def. 2),* **oxford cloth.**

Oxfords

Ox·ford (oks′fərd) *n.* **1.** a city in south-central England, on the Thames. Pop. (1978 est.), 123,700. **2.** a noted university located there, established in the twelfth century. It is the oldest university in Great Britain.

●The **Oxford English Dictionary** is the largest and most informative dictionary ever written in any language. It contains over 600,000 entries, 16,000 pages, and about two million quotations, and it gives the history of every word to appear in written English since the seventh century. The *O.E.D.* has twelve volumes, and there are also two supplementary volumes, with two more to be issued by 1980. It was begun in 1857, and the final volume was not completed until 1928.

The *Oxford English Dictionary* gets its name from Oxford University, where the dictionary was written. The *O.E.D.* is an invaluable source of knowledge for people who study English, since it provides a complete picture of the way our language has changed and developed over the centuries. Some of the quotations in the book go back to the year 600, and the most recent supplement includes many words that are less than ten years old.

Oxford gray, a very dark gray color.

ox·i·da·tion (ok′sə dā′shən) *n.* the act of oxidizing or the state of being oxidized.

ox·ide (ok′sīd) *n.* a compound of oxygen and one other element.

ox·i·dize (ok′sə dīz′) *v.,* **ox·i·dized, ox·i·diz·ing.** —*v.t.* to combine (a chemical substance) with oxygen; make into an oxide. —*v.i.* to become oxidized.

ox·i·diz·er (ok′sə dī′zər) *n.* **1.** a substance that yields oxygen for the burning of rocket fuel or a propellant. **2.** any substance that causes oxidation.

ox·y·a·cet·y·lene torch (ok′sē ə set′əl ēn′) a metal torch used for cutting and welding. It burns a mixture of oxygen and acetylene.

ox·y·gen (ok′sə jən) *n.* a colorless, odorless, gaseous element that makes up about one-fifth of the air. Oxygen is essential to life. Symbol: **O**

ox·y·gen·ate (ok′sə jə nāt′) *v.t.,* **ox·y·gen·at·ed, ox·y·gen·at·ing.** to treat, supply with, or mix with oxygen. —**ox′y·gen·a′tion,** *n.*

oxygen mask, a device worn over the nose and mouth, through which oxygen is supplied from a storage container.

oxygen tent, a structure resembling a tent, usually made of a clear plastic material. It is placed over a patient's head and supplied with a flow of oxygen to aid breathing.

ox·y·he·mo·glo·bin (ok′sē hē′mə glō′bin) *n.* a bright red substance consisting of hemoglobin combined with oxygen. It is carried to the tissues by the arteries.

o·yez (ō′yes, ō′yez) *interj.* hear ye! ▲ used to announce that court is in session and to ask for silence.

oys·ter (ois′tər) *n.* any of a group of shellfish found in shallow coastal waters, having a soft body enclosed in two irregular ear-shaped shells hinged at the narrow end. Some oysters are highly valued as food, while others are raised for the fine pearls they produce.

Valve
Mantle
Heart
Stomach
Gills
Mouth

Oyster

oyster bed, an area on the bottom of shallow coastal waters where oysters breed or are cultivated.

oz. *pl.,* **ozs.** ounce.

O·zark Mountains (ō′zärk) a low, hilly area in southern Missouri, northern Arkansas, and northeastern Oklahoma. Also, **O·zarks** (ō′zärks).

o·zone (ō′zōn) *n.* a form of oxygen that is a pale blue gas with a distinctive odor, formed when an electric discharge passes through the air. It is used as a bleach, disinfectant, and deodorant.

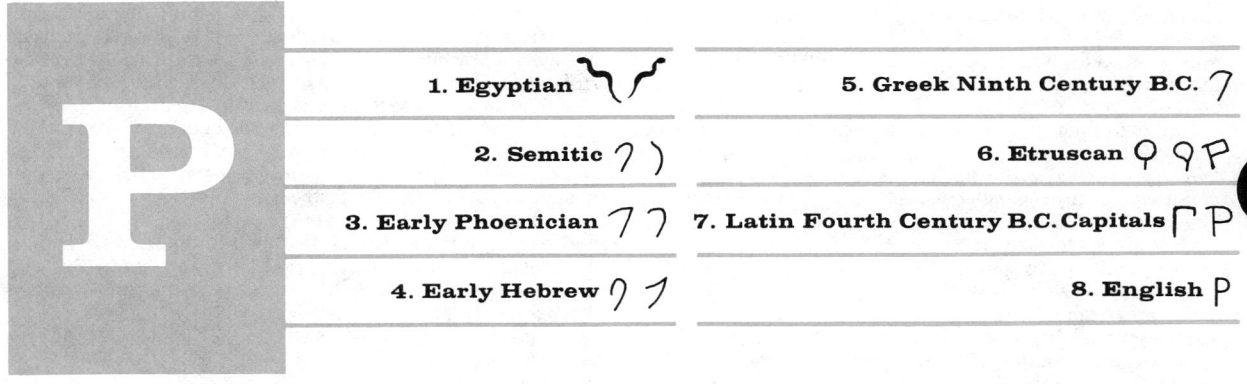

1. Egyptian	5. Greek Ninth Century B.C.
2. Semitic	6. Etruscan
3. Early Phoenician	7. Latin Fourth Century B.C. Capitals
4. Early Hebrew	8. English

P

P is the sixteenth letter of the English alphabet. The earliest ancestor of our modern letter **P** was an Egyptian hieroglyphic (1) which represented a mouth. The ancient Semitic (2) form of **P**, which looked like a hook, was a simplified version of the Egyptian symbol. This hook-shaped letter, which was called *pe*, was used, with only slight changes, in the early Phoenician (3) and early Hebrew (4) alphabets. The ancient Greeks borrowed *pe* and called it *pi* (5), writing it very much as it had been written in the preceding alphabets. When the Etruscans (6) borrowed *pi* for use in their own alphabet, they changed its shape by adding a closed loop at the top of the letter. The Romans (7), who originally adopted both the Greek and the Etruscan forms of *pi*, eventually used only the Etruscan form. By about 2300 years ago, the Romans were writing this form of *pi* exactly as we write the capital letter **P** today (8).

p, P (pē) *n. pl.,* **p's, P's.** the sixteenth letter of the English alphabet.

p 1. *Music.* piano. **2.** *Baseball.* pitcher.

P, the symbol for phosphorus.

p. 1. page. **2.** part. **3.** participle. **4.** pint.

pa (pä) *n. Informal.* father; papa.

Pa, the symbol for protactinium.

Pa., Pennsylvania.

PA, public-address system.

pace (pās) *n.* **1.** a single step. **2.** the distance covered in a step, often used as a measure of length averaging from 2½ to 3½ feet. **3.** the rate of speed in walking, running, or other activity: *He quickened his pace as he neared home. Ed worked at a hectic pace to finish his report.* **4.** a gait of a horse in which both feet on the same side are lifted and put down together. —*v.,* **paced, pac·ing.** —*v.t.,* **1.** to walk back and forth across: *Jan paced the room while she waited.* **2.** to measure by paces: *He paced off twenty feet from wall to wall.* **3.** to set the rate of speed for: *The coach paced the runner.* —*v.i.* **1.** to walk with slow, steady steps. **2.** (of a horse) to move at a pace.

  to keep pace with. a. to keep the same speed of movement as. **b.** to maintain the same rate of progress or development as.

  to set the pace. a. to set the speed for others to keep up with or go beyond. **b.** to be an example for others to follow.

pace·mak·er (pās′mā′kər) *n.* **1.** a person who sets the pace in a race. **2.** a person who leads a trend or sets an example for others. **3.** an electronic device implanted in the body to control the rhythm of the heart, used in the treatment of heart disorders.

pac·er (pā′sər) *n.* **1.** a person who paces. **2.** a horse that paces.

pach·y·derm (pak′ə durm′) *n.* any of several large,

thick-skinned, hoofed animals, such as the elephant, hippopotamus, or rhinoceros.

pa·cif·ic (pə sif′ik) *adj.* **1.** making or tending to make peace: *pacific efforts.* **2.** of a peaceful nature; calm; tranquil: *pacific waters.* —**pa·cif′i·cal·ly,** *adv.*

Pa·cif·ic (pə sif′ik) *n.* the ocean separating North and South America from Asia and Australia. It is the largest body of water in the world. Also, **Pacific Ocean.** —*adj.* **1.** of or relating to the Pacific. **2.** on, along, or near the coast of the Pacific.

pac·i·fi·ca·tion (pas′ə fi kā′shən) *n.* the act of pacifying or the state of being pacified.

Pacific Standard Time, the standard time used in the western United States. It is eight hours earlier than Greenwich Time.

pac·i·fi·er (pas′ə fī′ər) *n.* **1.** a person or thing that pacifies. **2.** a rubber nipple or similar object for babies to suck on.

pac·i·fism (pas′ə fiz′əm) *n.* the principle of opposition to war or other violence, and the belief that peaceful means should be used to settle differences between countries.

pac·i·fist (pas′ə fist) *n.* a person who opposes war or other violence. —**pac′i·fis′tic,** *adj.*

pac·i·fy (pas′ə fī′) *v.t.,* **pac·i·fied, pac·i·fy·ing. 1.** to make calm or quiet: *The mayor tried to pacify the angry crowd.* **2.** to make peaceful; bring peace to.

pack¹ (pak) *n.* **1.** a collection of things wrapped or tied together, especially for carrying on the back: *The camper's pack was heavy.* **2.** a package containing a certain number of similar things: *Do you have a pack of matches? He bought a pack of gum.* **3.** a set or group of similar things: *a pack of cards.* **4.** a group of animals living or hunting together: *a pack of wolves.* **5.** a large quantity or amount: *He told a pack of lies.* **6.** something soaked in water or medicine and applied to a part of the body as a treatment.

—*v.t.* **1.** to place in something for storing or carrying: *We packed the books in boxes.* **2.** to fill (something) with objects: *She packed her suitcase for the trip.* **3.** to crowd closely together: *The child packed the sand down with his shovel.* **4.** to fill by crowding or pressing together: *A large crowd packed the ball park.* **5.** *Informal.* to carry or wear on one's person regularly: *The detective packs a gun.* —*v.i.* **1.** to place articles in something, such as a box or suitcase, for carrying or storing: *Have you packed for the trip yet?* **2.** to become packed or compressed: *This suit packs easily.* **3.** to press together tightly; crowd together: *People packed into the subway car.* [Middle Dutch and Middle Low German *pak.*]

pack² (pak) *v.t.* to select, arrange, or manipulate dishonestly or to one's own advantage: *to pack a jury.* [Possibly from either *pack¹* or *pact.*]

pack·age (pak'ij) *n.* **1.** a thing or group of things packed, wrapped up, or bound together; parcel. **2.** a box, case, or the like in which things may be packed. —*v.t.,* **pack·aged, pack·ag·ing.** to make or put into a package.

pack animal, an animal used for carrying loads, such as a horse or mule.

pack·er (pak'ər) *n.* a person or thing that packs, especially a person who owns or is employed in a business where items are packaged for sale: *a meat packer.*

pack·et (pak'it) *n.* **1.** a small package or parcel: *a packet of letters.* **2.** see **packet boat.**

packet boat, a boat that carries mail, passengers, and freight at scheduled times over a regular route, especially along a coast or river.

pack ice, a large layer of floating ice formed by pieces of ice that are pressed together and frozen into a single mass. Also, **ice pack.**

packing house, a place where items to be sold are packaged for sale. Also, **packing plant.**

pack rat, a North American rat noted for its habit of collecting small shiny objects and leaving other objects, such as nuts or pine cones, in their place.

pack·sad·dle (pak'sad'əl) *n.* a saddle for carrying the load on a pack animal.

Pack rat

pact (pakt) *n.* an agreement between persons or countries, such as a treaty: *The two warring nations signed a peace pact.*

pad¹ (pad) *n.* **1.** a cushion or soft piece of thick material, used as a stuffing for protection or comfort. **2.** a number of sheets of paper fastened together along one edge; tablet: *a note pad, an artist's sketch pad.* **3.** one of the cushionlike parts on the underside of the toes of dogs, foxes, and certain other animals. **4.** the foot of a dog, fox, and certain other animals. **5.** a small ink-soaked block of cloth or other material, used to ink a rubber stamp. **6.** a large floating leaf of a water lily or other water plant. **7.** see **launching pad.** **8.** *Slang.* the place where a person lives, such as a room or apartment. —*v.t.,* **pad·ded, pad·ding. 1.** to cover, stuff, or line with a pad or padding. **2.** to lengthen by adding unnecessary material: *to pad an essay with quotations.* **3.** to add to dishonestly: *to pad an expense account with false expenditures.* [Possibly of Low German origin.]

pad² (pad) *v.i.,* **pad·ded, pad·ding.** to move with soft or almost silent steps: *We took our shoes off and padded across the room.* —*n.* a soft sound, as of a footstep. [Possibly imitative of the sound of this movement.]

pad·ding (pad'ing) *n.* **1.** a material, such as cotton or foam rubber, used to make a pad. **2.** unnecessary material used to lengthen a speech or written material.

pad·dle¹ (pad'əl) *n.* **1.** a short oar with a blade at one or both ends, used to propel a canoe or other small boat. **2.** a round or rectangular board with a short handle, used to strike the ball in table tennis and similar games. **3.** any of various flat, wooden tools used for beating, stirring, or mixing. **4.** one of the broad boards set in a paddle wheel or water wheel. —*v.,* **pad·dled, pad·dling.** —*v.t.* **1.** to propel (a canoe or other small boat) by means of a paddle or paddles. **2.** to strike or punish, as with a paddle; spank. —*v.i.* to propel a canoe or other small boat by means of a paddle. [Of uncertain origin.] —**pad'dle·like',** *adj.* —**pad'dler,** *n.*

pad·dle² (pad'əl) *v.i.,* **pad·dled, pad·dling.** to move about or splash in shallow water. [Possibly from *pad².*]

pad·dle·fish (pad'əl fish') *n. pl.,* **pad·dle·fish** or **pad·dle·fish·es.** any of several large, grayish fish, having a long, paddlelike snout.

Paddlefish

paddle wheel, a wheel having projecting paddles set at right angles, used to propel a water vehicle, as a steamboat.

pad·dock (pad'ək) *n.* **1.** a small field or enclosure in which an animal can graze and exercise. **2.** an area at a racetrack where the horses are saddled and mounted.

pad·dy (pad'ē) *n. pl.,* **pad·dies. 1.** rice in the husk. **2.** a field where rice is grown.

Pad·e·rew·ski, Ig·nace Jan (pad'ə ref'skē; ēn yäs' yän) 1860–1941, Polish pianist, composer, and statesman.

pad·lock (pad'lok') *n.* a detachable lock with a curved bar that is passed through an opening. —*v.t.* to fasten with a padlock.

pa·dre (pä'drā) *n.* father. ▲ used in addressing or referring to a priest in Italy, Spain, Portugal, and Latin America.

Pad·u·a (paj'ōō ə, pad'yōō ə) *n.* a city in northeastern Italy. Pop. (1978 est.), 242,816.

pae·an (pē'ən) *also,* **pe·an.** *n.* a song of praise or thanksgiving.

pa·gan (pā'gən) *n.* **1.** a person who is not a Christian, Jew, or Muslim, especially a person who worships many gods. The ancient Greeks and Romans were pagans. **2.** a person who has no religion. —*adj.* of or relating to pagans or paganism. [Late Latin *pāgānus* a person who lives in the country; also, a civilian. The early Christians, who lived mainly in cities, thought of themselves as soldiers of Christ. Non-Christians, who usually lived in rural areas, were thought of as "civilians," people who were not soldiers of Christ.]

Pag·a·ni·ni, Ni·co·lò (pag'ə nē'nē; nē'kō lō') 1782–1840, Italian violinist and composer.

pa·gan·ism (pā'gə niz'əm) *n.* **1.** the beliefs, practices, and customs of pagans. **2.** the state of being a pagan.

page¹ (pāj) *n.* **1.** one side of a leaf of a book or letter. **2.** the print, writing, or type used on one side of a leaf. **3.** an event or events worthy of recording: *The Civil War was a tragic page in American history.* —*v.t.,* **paged, paging.** to number the pages of. [Old French *page* one side of a leaf of a book.]

page² (pāj) *n.* **1.** a male servant or attendant, especially a boy who attends a person of rank. **2.** a young person employed to serve as an attendant to members of Congress or other legislative bodies. **3.** a person employed to run errands or carry messages, as in a hotel. **4.** formerly, a boy in training for knighthood. —*v.t.,* **paged, paging.** to summon or try to find (someone) by calling out the name.

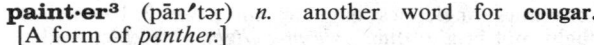

[Old French *page* a boy who attends a person of rank.]
pag·eant (paj′ənt) *n.* **1.** a theatrical presentation that is based on or dramatizes events in history or legend. **2.** an elaborate spectacle, procession, or parade.

pag·eant·ry (paj′ən trē) *n. pl.,* **pag·eant·ries. 1.** pageants as a group. **2.** an elaborate or spectacular display: *She enjoyed the pageantry of the king's coronation.*

pa·go·da (pə gō′də) *n.* in the Far East, a temple or memorial tower of several stories, often with a series of projecting roofs that curve upward from each story.

Pa·go Pa·go (päng′ō päng′ō, pä′gō pä′gō) the capital of American Samoa. Pop. (1970), 2451.

paid (pād) the past tense and past participle of **pay¹.**

pail (pāl) *n.* **1.** a round, open container, usually with a handle, used for carrying water, sand, or other materials. **2.** the amount that a pail holds; pailful.

pail·ful (pāl′fool′) *n. pl.,* **pail·fuls.** the amount that a pail holds.

pain (pān) *n.* **1.** a feeling of great discomfort, usually in a particular part of the body; physical distress or suffering: *He has a pain in his knee.* **2.** emotional or mental distress or suffering; anxiety; grief: *the pain of loneliness.* **3. pains.** care or effort: *The boy took great pains to assemble the model airplane neatly.* —*v.t.* to cause pain to; make suffer: *My knee pains me on damp days. The old man's poverty pained him.*

on pain of or **under pain of.** at the risk of (punishment or death).

Paine, Thomas (pān) 1737–1809, U.S. patriot and political writer, born in England.

pained (pānd) *adj.* **1.** suffering from pain; hurt or distressed. **2.** showing pain: *He had a pained expression on his face.*

pain·ful (pān′fəl) *adj.* **1.** causing physical or mental pain; distressing: *a painful wound, a painful subject.* **2.** requiring effort or care: *a painful decision.* —**pain′ful·ly,** *adv.* —**pain′ful·ness,** *n.*

pain·less (pān′lis) *adj.* free from pain; causing no pain. —**pain′less·ly,** *adv.* —**pain′less·ness,** *n.*

pains·tak·ing (pānz′tā′king) *adj.* that needs or shows close, careful work or attention: *a painstaking job, a painstaking workman.* —**pains′tak′ing·ly,** *adv.*

paint (pānt) *n.* **1.** a coloring material made of a pigment mixed with a liquid, such as oil or water. Paint is applied to surfaces as a protective or decorative coating. **2.** a layer or coating of such a material. **3.** a cosmetic, such as rouge, used to add color. —*v.t.* **1.** to represent on a surface with paints: *The artist painted a landscape on his canvas.* **2.** to coat or cover the surface of with paint: *The workmen painted the house.* **3.** to describe vividly in words. **4.** to put on or apply with a brush or swab: *to paint a wound with antiseptic.* **5.** to color with cosmetics; apply cosmetics to: *She painted her face with rouge.* —*v.i.* **1.** to practice the art of painting; make pictures: *He paints well.* **2.** to use paint.

paint·brush (pānt′brush′) *n. pl.,* **paint·brush·es.** a brush for applying paint.

paint·er¹ (pān′tər) *n.* **1.** an artist who paints pictures. **2.** a person whose work is painting walls or other surfaces. [Old French *peintour, peintor.*]

paint·er² (pān′tər) *n.* a rope attached to the bow of a boat for tying it up to something. [Possibly from Old French *pentoir, pentour* a rope on which things were hung.]

paint·er³ (pān′tər) *n.* another word for **cougar.** [A form of *panther.*]

paint·ing (pān′ting) *n.* **1.** the act or art of applying paints to a surface: *to study painting.* **2.** a picture produced in this way.

pair (per) *n. pl.,* **pairs** or **pair. 1.** a set of two things meant to be used together: *a pair of slippers, a pair of oars.* **2.** a single thing made up of two parts: *a pair of pliers, a pair of glasses.* **3.** two persons or animals associated or working together: *a pair of policemen, a pair of horses.* **4.** a married or engaged couple. **5.** two animals mated together. —*v.t.* to join or match (two persons or things) in a pair: *They paired the two tallest boys to lead the march.* —*v.i.* to form a pair or pairs.

to pair off. to join in a pair; form a pair.

pais·ley (pāz′lē) *n.* a colorful design with curved forms on a patterned background. —*adj.* having such a design: *a paisley shirt.* [From *Paisley,* a city in Scotland, where wool shawls having this design were first made.]

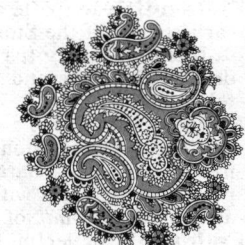

pa·ja·mas (pə jä′məz, pə jam′əz) *also, British,* **py·ja·mas.** *n.,pl.* a garment for sleeping or informal wear, consisting of a top and trousers.

Pak·i·stan (pak′i stan′) *n.* a country in southern Asia. Capital, Islamabad. Area, approx. 311,000 sq. mi. Pop. (1972 est.), 56,040,000.

Paisley design

Pak·i·stan·i (pak′i stan′ē) *n. pl.,* **Pak·i·stan·i** or **Pak·i·stan·is.** a person who was born or is living in Pakistan. —*adj.* of or relating to Pakistan or its people.

pal (pal) *Informal. n.* a close friend. —*v.i.,* **palled, palling.** to associate as close friends.

pal·ace (pal′is) *n.* **1.** the official residence of a king, emperor, or other ruler. **2.** any large, grand residence or building.

pal·an·quin (pal′ən kēn′) *also,* **pal·an·keen.** *n.* a covered vehicle for one person, carried on the shoulders of two or more men by means of poles, used especially in Eastern countries.

pal·at·a·ble (pal′ə tə bəl) *adj.* **1.** pleasant to the taste; pleasing in flavor. **2.** agreeable to the mind or feelings; acceptable: *a palatable solution to a problem.* —**pal′at·a·bil′i·ty,** *n.* —**pal′at·a·bly,** *adv.*

pal·ate (pal′it) *n.* **1.** the roof of the mouth. The bony part in the front is the hard palate, and the fleshy part in the back is the soft palate. **2.** the sense of taste: *food that is pleasing to the palate.*

pa·la·tial (pə lā′shəl) *adj.* of or like a palace: *a palatial home.* —**pa·la′tial·ly,** *adv.*

pal·a·tine (pal′ə tīn′) *adj.* formerly, having royal privileges and rights in one's own territory: *a count palatine.*

pa·lav·er (pə lav′ər) *n.* **1.** idle talk; chatter. **2.** a parley or conference, especially between explorers or traders and native inhabitants. —*v.i.* to talk idly.

pale¹ (pāl) *adj.,* **pal·er, pal·est. 1.** without a natural or healthy color; ashen; pallid: *a pale complexion.* **2.** without

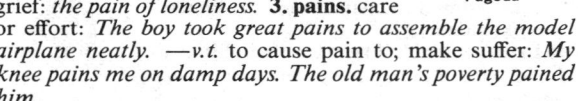

Pagoda

at; āpe; cär; end; mē; it; īce; hot; ōld; fôrk; wood; fool; oil; out; up; turn; sing; thin; this; hw in white; zh in treasure. The symbol ə stands for the sound of **a** in about, **e** in taken, **i** in pencil, **o** in lemon, and **u** in circus.

brightness or richness of color: *pale green.* **3.** having little light; not bright; dim: *pale moonlight.* **4.** feeble; weak: *a pale imitation.* —*v.,* **paled, pal·ing.** —*v.i.* to turn pale: *He paled when he heard the scream.* —*v.t.* to make pale. [Old French *pale.*] —**pale′ly,** *adv.* —**pale′ness,** *n.*

pale² (pāl) *n.* **1.** a narrow, pointed piece of wood, used for fences; stake; picket. **2.** any boundary, barrier, or limit: *His behavior is beyond the pale of what is right or proper.* —*v.t.,* **paled, pal·ing.** to enclose with pales; fence in. [Middle French *pal.*]

pale·face (pāl′fās′) *n.* a white person. ▲ supposedly first used by North American Indians.

Pa·le·o·cene (pā′lē ə sēn′) *n.* the earliest geological epoch of the Tertiary period of the Cenozoic era, characterized by the development of many primitive mammals. —*adj.* of or relating to this epoch.

Pa·le·o·lith·ic (pā′lē ə lith′ik) *adj.* of or relating to the earliest part of the Stone Age.

pa·le·on·tol·o·gy (pā′lē ən tol′ə jē) *n.* the science that deals with fossils and extinct forms of life. —**pa′le·on·tol′o·gist,** *n.*

Pa·le·o·zo·ic (pā′lē ə zō′ik) *n.* a geological era that began about 600 million years ago and ended about 220 million years ago, characterized by the appearance of land plants, sea animals without backbones, fish, amphibians, and reptiles. —*adj.* of or relating to this era.

Pa·ler·mo (pə ler′mō) *n.* the capital and largest city of Sicily, a port in the northwestern part of the island. Pop. (1970 est.), 1,177,203.

Pal·es·tine (pal′is tīn′) *n.* **1.** a region in southwestern Asia between the Mediterranean Sea and the Jordan River. In Biblical times it was the land of the Jews. Also, **Holy Land. 2.** a former country in this region, under a British mandate following World War I, divided into the country of Israel and a part of the country of Jordan in 1947. Israel has occupied the Jordanian part of Palestine since 1967. —**Pal·es·tin·i·an** (pal′is tin′ē ən), *adj., n.*

pal·ette (pal′it) *n.* a thin board or tablet, usually having a hole for the thumb, on which artists place and mix their paints.

pal·frey (pôl′frē) *n. pl.,* **pal·freys.** *Archaic.* a saddle horse, especially for a woman.

pal·ing (pā′ling) *n.* **1.** a fence made of pales. **2.** pales as a group. **3.** one of the pales forming a fence.

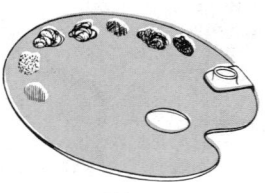

Palette

pal·i·sade (pal′i sād′) *n.* **1.** a fence of strong, pointed stakes placed closely together and set firmly in the ground, used for defense or protection. **2.** one of the stakes used in such a fence. **3. palisades.** a line of steep cliffs, usually rising along a river. —*v.t.,* **pal·i·sad·ed, pal·i·sad·ing.** to enclose or fortify with a palisade.

pall¹ (pôl) *n.* **1.** a heavy covering of black or purple cloth laid over a coffin, hearse, or tomb. **2.** something that covers with darkness and gloom: *A pall fell over the room when the news of the accident was announced.* —*v.t.* to cover with a pall. [Old English *pæll* a robe, cloak.]

pall² (pôl) *v.i.* to become dull or boring: *After ten minutes the television program began to pall.* [Middle English *pallen.*]

pal·la·di·um (pə lā′dē əm) *n.* a silver-white metallic element of the platinum family, used as an alloy with certain metals, such as platinum and copper. Symbol: **Pd**

Pal·las (pal′əs) *n. Greek Mythology.* another name for **Athena.** Also, **Pallas Athena.**

pall·bear·er (pôl′ber′ər) *n.* one of the persons who carry the coffin at a funeral.

pal·let (pal′it) *n.* **1.** a straw bed or mattress. **2.** any small, hard, or temporary bed, often on the floor.

pal·li·ate (pal′ē āt′) *v.t.,* **pal·li·at·ed, pal·li·at·ing. 1.** to make (an offense or fault) appear less serious. **2.** to lessen the pain or effects of (a disease or illness) without curing it. —**pal′li·a′tion,** *n.*

pal·li·a·tive (pal′ē ā′tiv) *adj.* serving to palliate: *palliative drugs.* —*n.* something that palliates.

pal·lid (pal′id) *adj.* lacking color; pale.

pal·lor (pal′ər) *n.* lack of color; paleness: *The boy's pallor was due to lack of sleep.*

palm¹ (päm) *n.* **1.** the inner surface of the hand from the wrist to the base of the fingers. **2.** a measure of length equal to the width of a hand, or about three to four inches. **3.** the part of a glove or mitten covering the palm. —*v.t.* to hold or hide in the palm or hand: *to palm cards.* [Old French *palme, paume.*]

to palm off. to pass off by deceit or fraud.

palm² (päm) *n.* **1.** any of a group of tropical and subtropical trees or shrubs usually having large, featherlike or fan-shaped leaves growing in a cluster at the top of a tall trunk. **2.** a leaf of such a tree, used as a symbol of victory or success. [Old English *palm,* from Latin *palma* palm tree; originally also palm of the hand; because the flat leaves of this tree were thought to resemble the palm of the hand when the fingers are extended.]

pal·mate (pal′māt) *adj.* resembling a hand with the fingers spread out: *a palmate leaf.*

pal·met·to (pal met′ō) *n. pl.,* **pal·met·tos** or **pal·met·toes.** a palm tree grown in the southern United States.

palm·ist (pä′mist) *n.* a person who practices palmistry.

palm·is·try (pä′mis trē) *n.* the art or practice of telling a person's fortune by studying the pattern of the lines in the palm of the hand.

Palm tree

Palm Sunday, the Sunday before Easter Sunday, commemorating Christ's entry into Jerusalem, when people spread palm branches before Him.

palm·y (pä′mē) *adj.,* **palm·i·er, palm·i·est. 1.** full of palm trees. **2.** flourishing; prosperous: *The old man often thought of the palmy days of his life.*

pal·o·mi·no (pal′ə mē′nō) *n. pl.,* **pal·o·mi·nos.** a light tan horse having a cream-colored or white mane and tail.

pal·pa·ble (pal′pə bəl) *adj.* **1.** capable of being touched or felt; tangible. **2.** easily perceived by the senses or mind; obvious; noticeable: *a palpable lie, a palpable error.* —**pal′pa·bil′i·ty,** *n.* —**pal′pa·bly,** *adv.*

pal·pi·tate (pal′pə tāt′) *v.i.,* **pal·pi·tat·ed, pal·pi·tat·ing. 1.** to beat at a rapid rate: *His heart palpitated from excitement.* **2.** to quiver or tremble. —**pal′pi·ta′tion,** *n.*

pal·sied (pôl′zēd) *adj.* affected with palsy; trembling; shaking.

pal·sy (pôl′zē) *n. pl.,* **pal·sies.** weakness or paralysis of a muscle, usually characterized by trembling. —*v.t.,* **palsied, pal·sy·ing.** to affect with palsy; cause to tremble.

pal·try (pôl′trē) *adj.,* **pal·tri·er, pal·tri·est.** having little or no value: *He gave the waiter a paltry amount of money as a tip.* —**pal′tri·ness,** *n.*

pam·pas (pam′pəz) *also,* **pam·pa.** *n.,pl.* vast, treeless plains extending from the Atlantic Ocean to the Andes Mountains in Argentina and some other areas of South America.

pam·per (pam′pər) *v.t.* to treat too well; indulge or cater to; coddle: *Ann pampers her son.* —**pam′per·er,** *n.*

pam·phlet (pam′flit) *n.* a short book, usually having a paper cover: *a political pamphlet.*

pam·phlet·eer (pam′fli tēr′) *n.* a person who writes or publishes pamphlets.

pan[1] (pan) *n.* **1.** a dish or container of metal, usually broad, shallow, and without a cover, used especially for cooking or baking. **2.** something like this, such as the container used to separate precious minerals from gravel by washing with water. **3.** a layer of hard earth underneath soft soil; hardpan. —*v.,* **panned, pan·ning.** —*v.t.* **1.** to cook in a pan. **2.** *Informal.* to criticize harshly: *The critics panned the movie.* **3.** to separate (gold or other precious minerals) from gravel by washing in a pan. —*v.i.* to wash earth or gravel in a pan in search of gold or other precious minerals: *The prospector panned for gold.* [Old English *panne.*]

   to pan out. *Informal.* to turn out well; succeed.

pan[2] (pan) *v.,* **panned, pan·ning.** —*v.t.* to move (a movie or television camera) in order to take in a wide area or follow a moving object. —*v.i.* to move a movie or television camera in this way. [From *panorama.*]

Pan (pan) *n. Greek Mythology.* the god of forests, fields, flocks, and shepherds, represented as a man with the horns, ears, legs, and tail of a goat.

pan- *combining form* **1.** all; every: *panchromatic.* **2.** *usually,* **Pan-.** of or relating to all members of a specified group or area: *Pan-American.*

pan·a·ce·a (pan′ə sē′ə) *n.* something that will cure all diseases or evils; cure-all.

pan·a·ma (pan′ə mä′) *also,* **Pan·a·ma.** *n.* a hat for men made from the young leaves of a tropical American plant.

Pan·a·ma (pan′ə mä′) *n.* **1. Isthmus of.** a narrow strip of land connecting North and South America. **2.** a country on the Isthmus of Panama, on either side of the Canal Zone. Capital, Panama City. Area, 29,209 sq. mi. Pop. (1971 est.), 1,480,000. **3.** the capital of this country, on the Pacific coast. Pop. (1970), 348,704. Also *(def. 3),* **Panama City.**

Panama Canal, a canal for ships across the Isthmus of Panama, connecting the Atlantic and Pacific Oceans, built and administered by the United States.

Panama Canal Zone, see **Canal Zone.**

Pan·a·ma·ni·an (pan′ə mā′nē ən) *n.* a person who was born or is living in Panama. —*adj.* of or relating to Panama or its people.

Pan-A·mer·i·can (pan′ə mer′i kən) *adj.* relating to the countries or people of North, Central, and South America.

pan·cake (pan′kāk′) *n.* a flat cake of batter, cooked in a pan or on a griddle; griddlecake; flapjack.

pan·chro·mat·ic (pan′krō mat′ik) *adj.* sensitive to light of all colors, as a photographic film.

pan·cre·as (pan′krē əs) *n.* a long, narrow gland below the stomach that sends digestive juices into the small intestine and the hormone insulin into the bloodstream. —**pan·cre·at·ic** (pan′krē at′ik), *adj.*

pan·da (pan′də) *n.* **1.** a bearlike animal native to the bamboo forests of southwestern China, having a shaggy white coat with black markings. Also, **giant panda. 2.** a reddish-brown animal native to the Himalayas, having short legs, a long, bushy, ringed tail, and a white face. Also, **lesser panda.**

Panda

pan·de·mo·ni·um (pan′də mō′nē əm) *n.* **1.** wild disorder or uproar. **2.** a place of wild disorder or uproar.

pan·der (pan′dər) *n.* a person who takes advantage of or makes money from the weaknesses or vices of others. —*v.i.* to act as a pander: *That writer panders to the public taste for violence in his stories.*

Pan·do·ra (pan dôr′ə) *n. Greek Mythology.* the first woman, whose curiosity led her to open a box into which Zeus had put all human evils and miseries, thus allowing them to escape into the world.

pane (pān) *n.* a sheet of glass or similar material placed in a window or door.

pan·e·gyr·ic (pan′ə jir′ik) *n.* **1.** a formal speech or writing praising a person or thing. **2.** lofty praise.

pan·el (pan′əl) *n.* **1.** a section of a door, cabinet, or other surface, set off from the surrounding surface by being raised, recessed, or bordered. **2.** a flat piece of material, as of wood or plastic, made to be joined with others. **3.** a section of fabric in a garment, as a skirt. **4.** a thin wooden board used as the surface for an oil painting. **5.** a board on which dials or other controls are mounted, as in an automobile or airplane. **6.** a group of persons to discuss or judge something: *a panel of experts.* **7.** a list of persons called for jury duty. —*v.t.* to furnish or decorate with panels: *The walls of the living room were paneled in walnut.*

pan·el·ing (pan′əl ing) *n.* **1.** wood or other material used to make panels. **2.** panels as a group.

pan·el·ist (pan′əl ist) *n.* a person who serves on a panel.

pang (pang) *n.* **1.** a sudden, sharp feeling of discomfort or pain: *pangs of hunger.* **2.** a sharp feeling of mental distress: *The boy felt pangs of guilt after lying to his friend.*

pan·go·lin (pang gō′lin) *n.* a scale-covered animal having sharp claws, a long tongue, and usually a long tail. Also, **scaly anteater.**

pan·han·dle (pan′hand′əl) *n.* **1.** the handle of a pan. **2.** *also,* **Panhandle.** a narrow strip of land attached to a larger area of land and resembling the handle of a pan: *the Texas Panhandle.*

pan·ic (pan′ik) *n.* **1.** a terrible, often uncontrollable fear that can spread suddenly through a crowd: *When the school caught fire there was a panic.* **2.** a wide-spread financial crisis caused by a loss of public confidence in stocks or other investments. —*v.,* **pan·icked, pan·ick·ing.** —*v.i.* to become affected with panic: *The children panicked when they realized they were lost.* —*v.t.* to affect with panic: *Harry was afraid that the storm would panic the horses.* [Going back to Greek *pānikos* relating to *Pan;* because it was believed that this god inspired a terrible fear.] —**pan′ick·y,** *adj.*

pan·ic-strick·en (pan′ik strik′ən) *adj.* overcome by panic.

pan·ni·er (pan′ē ər) *n.* a large basket for carrying goods, especially one of two baskets to be slung across the back of a pack animal.

pan·o·ply (pan′ə plē) *n. pl.,* **pan·o·plies. 1.** a complete suit of armor. **2.** any magnificent covering or display: *a panoply of jewels.*

pan·o·ram·a (pan′ə ram′ə) *n.* **1.** a wide or complete view of an area: *From the mountaintop we could see the vast panorama of the valley below us.* **2.** a complete survey or presentation of a subject. **3.** a picture or series of pic-

at; āpe; cär; end; mē; it; īce; hot; ōld; fôrk; wood; fōol; oil; out; up; turn; sing; thin; this; hw in white; zh in treasure. The symbol ə stands for the sound of **a** in about, **e** in taken, **i** in pencil, **o** in lemon, and **u** in circus.

tures unrolled and passed before the viewers, showing a continuous scene.

pan·o·ram·ic (pan′ə ram′ik, pan′ə rä′mik) *adj.* of or like a panorama. —**pan′o·ram′i·cal·ly,** *adv.*

pan·pipe (pan′pīp′) *also,* **Pan·pipe.** *n.* a primitive musical instrument made of a series of reeds or tubes bound together.

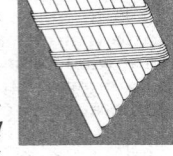
Panpipe

pan·sy (pan′zē) *n. pl.,* **pan·sies. 1.** a flower having five flat overlapping petals and growing in a variety of colors. **2.** the plant bearing this flower.

pant (pant) *v.i.* **1.** to breathe quickly or heavily; gasp for breath: *Jerry panted after running up the stairs.* **2.** to long eagerly; yearn: *to pant for success.* —*v.t.* to say breathlessly: *The injured man panted, "Help me!"* —*n.* a short labored breath; gasp.

pan·ta·lets (pant′əl ets′) *also,* **pan·ta·lettes.** *n.,pl.* long ruffled drawers formerly worn by women and girls.

pan·ta·loon (pant′əl ōōn′) *n.* **1.** **pantaloons.** tight-fitting trousers formerly worn by men. **2.** **Pantaloon.** a comic character in pantomime, usually a foolish old man wearing pantaloons and slippers.

pan·the·ism (pan′thē iz′əm) *n.* the religious belief that everything in nature is part of God and that God is in everything.

pan·the·ist (pan′thē ist) *n.* a person who believes in pantheism. —**pan′the·is′tic,** *adj.* —**pan′the·is′ti·cal·ly,** *adv.*

pan·the·on (pan′thē on′) *n.* **1.** **Pantheon.** a round, domed temple built at Rome for all the gods, later used as a Christian church. **2.** all the gods worshiped by a people. **3.** a public building serving as a memorial or mausoleum for the famous people of a country.

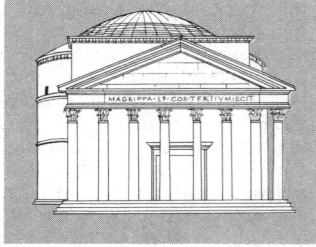
Pantheon

pan·ther (pan′thər) *n. pl.,* **pan·thers** or **pan·ther. 1.** a large leopard having a black coat. **2.** another word for **cougar. 3.** another word for **jaguar.**

pant·ies (pan′tēz) *n.,pl.* short underpants worn by girls and women.

pan·to·mime (pan′tə mīm′) *n.* **1.** the telling of a story without speech, through the use of gestures, body movements, and facial expressions. **2.** a dramatic performance acted in this way. —*v.,* **pan·to·mimed, pan·to·mim·ing.** —*v.t.* to express in pantomime. —*v.i.* to act in pantomime. —**pan′to·mim′ist,** *n.*

pan·try (pan′trē) *n. pl.,* **pan·tries.** a room or closet for storing food, utensils, china, and the like.

pants (pants) *n.,pl.* **1.** another word for **trousers. 2.** another word for **underpants.**

pant·suit (pant′sōōt′) *also,* **pants suit.** *n.* a woman's outfit consisting of matching jacket and slacks.

pap (pap) *n.* soft food for babies or sick people.

pa·pa (pä′pə) *n.* father; daddy.

pa·pa·cy (pä′pə sē) *n. pl.,* **pa·pa·cies. 1.** the office or authority of the pope. **2.** the period of a pope's reign. **3.** popes as a group. **4.** the government of the Roman Catholic Church by the pope as the supreme ruler.

pa·pal (pä′pəl) *adj.* **1.** of or relating to the pope or the papacy: *papal influence, papal reforms.* **2.** of or relating to the Roman Catholic Church.

pa·paw (pô′pô) *also,* **paw·paw.** *n.* **1.** a fruit having yellow flesh and a taste like that of a banana. **2.** the tree bearing this fruit, growing mainly in the central United States.

pa·pa·ya (pə pä′yə) *n.* **1.** a yellowish-orange fruit having a thick rind, many small black seeds, and a fleshy pulp with a sweet flavor. **2.** the tropical American tree bearing this fruit.

pa·per (pä′pər) *n.* **1.** a material made from wood pulp, rags, or certain grasses, usually formed in thin sheets. Paper is used for writing, printing, wrapping, and many other purposes. **2.** a piece or sheet of this material: *She wrote her name at the top of the paper.* **3.** a written report or essay: *Her history paper is due tomorrow. The scientist presented a paper on space travel.* **4.** a newspaper: *Has the paper been delivered yet?* **5.** **papers.** a collection of letters, journals, or other writings, especially by one person: *the Churchill papers.* **6.** **papers.** a collection of documents that identify a person. **7.** see **wallpaper.** —*v.t.* to cover or decorate with paper, especially wallpaper: *to paper a room.* —*adj.* made of paper: *paper flowers.* —**pa′per·er,** *n.* —**pa′per·y,** *adj.*
on paper. a. in written or printed form. **b.** in theory: *The idea looked good on paper, but it never worked out.*

Papaya tree

pa·per·back (pä′pər bak′) *n.* a book bound in a paper cover. —*adj.* bound in a paper cover.

paper boy, a person who sells or delivers newspapers.

paper clip, a device made of bent wire that holds sheets of paper together.

pa·per·hang·er (pä′pər hang′ər) *n.* a person whose work is hanging wallpaper.

paper money, currency printed on paper.

paper nautilus, see **nautilus** *(def. 2).*

pa·per·weight (pä′pər wāt′) *n.* a small, heavy object placed on top of loose sheets of paper to hold them down.

pa·pier-mâ·ché (pä′pər mə shā′) *n.* a substance made of shreds of paper mixed with glue and other materials. It can be molded when wet and hardens when dry.

pa·pil·la (pə pil′ə) *n. pl.,* **pa·pil·lae** (pə pil′ē). **1.** a small knoblike projection of skin containing tiny blood vessels that nourish the root of a hair. **2.** any of certain other small projections, as on the surface of the tongue.

pa·poose (pa pōōs′) *also,* **pap·poose.** *n.* a North American Indian baby or small child.

pap·ri·ka (pa prē′kə, pap′ri kə) *n.* a reddish-orange spice made from the powdered pods of a sweet red pepper.

Papua New Guinea, a country in the southwestern Pacific, formerly administered by Australia. Capital, Port Moresby. Pop. (1980), 3,082,000.

pa·py·rus (pə pī′rəs) *n. pl.,* **pa·py·ri** (pə pī′rī). **1.** a plant found growing in swamps and along rivers in northern Africa and southern Europe, having dark-green hollow stalks. **2.** a writing material made from the stems of this plant by the ancient Egyptians and other peoples. **3.** an ancient manuscript or document written on this.

par (pär) *n.* **1.** an average or normal amount, condition, or degree: *Her work is above par.* **2.** an equal level: *Her work is on a par with his.* **3.** the value of a stock printed on the stock certificate. **4.** *Golf.* the number of strokes set as a standard for playing a hole or course. —*adj.* **1.** average or normal. **2.** of or at par: *the par value of a bond.*

par. **1.** paragraph. **2.** parallel.

para-¹ *prefix* **1.** beside; near: *parallel, paraphrase.* **2.** beyond: *paradox.* **3.** disordered; abnormal: *paranoia.* **4.** subsidiary: *paramedic.* [Greek *para*.]

para-² *combining form* **1.** protection against: *parachute, parasol.* **2.** using a parachute: *paratroops.* [French *para-*.]

par·a·ble (par′ə bəl) *n.* a short story that teaches some truth or moral lesson.

pa·rab·o·la (pə rab′ə lə) *n.* an open curve consisting of a set of points in a plane that lie at equal distances from a fixed point and a fixed line. A parabola is formed by the intersection of a cone and a plane parallel to a side of the cone.

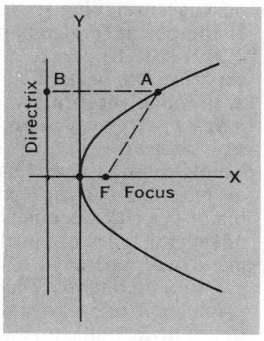

Parabola

par·a·chute (par′ə shoot′) *n.* a device resembling an umbrella, used for slowing the speed of a body falling through the air. Parachutes are employed mainly to drop a person or object safely to the ground from an aircraft. —*v.,* **par·a·chut·ed, par·a·chut·ing.** —*v.i.* to descend by parachute: *The pilot parachuted from the burning plane.* —*v.t.* to drop (something, such as troops or supplies) by parachute: *They parachuted medical supplies to the troops who were surrounded by the enemy.*

par·a·chut·ist (par′ə shoo′tist) *n.* a person who uses a parachute or is skilled in parachuting.

pa·rade (pə rād′) *n.* **1.** a march or procession in honor of a person or event: *We went to the parade held for the astronauts.* **2.** a showy display; exhibition: *He made a parade of his wealth.* **3.** a public place where people stroll. **4.** a procession of troops for display or review. —*v.,* **pa·rad·ed, pa·rad·ing.** —*v.i.* **1.** to march publicly in a procession: *The soldiers paraded through town.* **2.** to walk about to show oneself off. —*v.t.* **1.** to display in a showy manner; make a show of: *He liked to parade his knowledge before everyone he met.* **2.** to cause (troops) to march in review. —**pa·rad′er,** *n.*

par·a·digm (par′ə dīm′, par′ə dim′) *n.* **1.** a pattern or example. **2.** *Grammar.* a list of all the inflected forms of a word, used as a pattern for other words of the same class.

par·a·dise (par′ə dīs′) *n.* **1.** the dwelling place of God, the angels, and those who are saved; heaven. **2.** any place of great beauty or delight. **3.** a state of supreme happiness or bliss. **4. Paradise.** the garden of Eden.

par·a·dox (par′ə doks′) *n. pl.,* **par·a·dox·es. 1.** a statement that seems to be contradictory, but in fact may be true. The statement "Liberty is the only thing you cannot have unless you are willing to give it to others," is a paradox. **2.** a statement that contradicts itself and is therefore unclear, meaningless, or untrue: *John puzzled his friends with this paradox: "All that I say is false, including this statement."* **3.** any person or thing that seems to be contradictory. —**par′a·dox′i·cal,** *adj.* —**par′a·dox′i·cal·ly,** *adv.*

par·af·fin (par′ə fin) *n.* a waxy, white substance obtained from petroleum and used for making candles, waxed paper, and for sealing jars of preserves.

par·a·gon (par′ə gon′) *n.* an excellent or perfect model or pattern: *She is a paragon of virtue.*

par·a·graph (par′ə graf′) *n.* **1.** a distinct part of something written, consisting of one or more sentences on one particular subject or idea, and beginning on a new, usually indented, line. **2.** a brief article or item, as in a newspaper. **3.** a mark (¶) used in printing and writing to indicate the beginning of a new paragraph. —*v.t.* to arrange in or divide into paragraphs: *The editor paragraphed the news story.* —**par′a·graph′er,** *n.*

Par·a·guay (par′ə gwā′, par′ə gwī′) *n.* a country in south-central South America. Capital, Asunción. Area, 157,048 sq. mi. Pop. (1980 est.), 3,067,000. —**Par′a·guay′an,** *adj., n.*

par·a·keet (par′ə kēt′) *also,* **par·ra·keet.** *n.* any of a group of small parrots, usually having brightly colored feathers, often kept as cage birds.

par·al·lax (par′ə laks′) *n.* the apparent change in the position of an object that occurs when the observer changes his position. In astronomy parallax is used to find the distance of a star from the observer.

par·al·lel (par′ə lel′) *adj.* **1.** going in the same direction and always being the same distance apart at every point, so as never to meet: *The rails of a railroad track are parallel.* **2.** closely similar or corresponding: *parallel opinions, parallel wording.* **3.** of or relating to an electric circuit connected in parallel. —*n.* **1.** a parallel line, plane, or surface. **2.** a close similarity or correspondence: *The explorer found many parallels in the customs of the two tribes.* **3.** any of the imaginary lines that circle the earth parallel to the equator and show degrees of latitude. —*v.t.,* **par·al·leled, par·al·lel·ing;** *also,* British, **par·al·lelled, par·al·lel·ling. 1.** to be or lie in a direction parallel to: *The railroad tracks paralleled the highway.* **2.** to be similar or correspond to: *The growth of the town paralleled that of the county.* —*adv.* in a parallel manner or direction: *The highway runs parallel with the river.*

Parakeet

in parallel. of an electric circuit, connected so as to form separate paths between the positive and negative terminals of the current source of each object, as each light, in the circuit.

parallel bars, two poles set parallel to each other and raised above the floor, used in gymnastics.

par·al·lel·e·pi·ped (par′ə lel′ə pī′ped) *n.* a solid form with six faces that are all parallelograms.

par·al·lel·ism (par′ə le liz′əm) *n.* **1.** the state or condition of being parallel. **2.** a close similarity or correspondence.

par·al·lel·o·gram (par′ə lel′ə gram′) *n.* a plane figure with four sides whose opposite sides are parallel and equal in length.

pa·ral·y·sis (pə ral′ə sis) *n. pl.,* **pa·ral·y·ses** (pə ral′ə sēz′). **1.** the loss of the power of motion or feeling in a part of the body. **2.** the stopping of normal activity or movement.

par·a·lyt·ic (par′ə lit′ik) *adj.* **1.** of, relating to, or characteristic of paralysis. **2.** having paralysis. —*n.* a person who has paralysis.

par·a·lyze (par′ə līz′) *v.t.,* **par·a·lyzed, par·a·lyz·ing. 1.** to affect with paralysis; make paralytic. **2.** to make helpless, powerless, or inactive: *The bus strike paralyzed the city.*

Par·a·mar·i·bo (par′ə mar′ə bō′) *n.* the capital of Suriname, a port city in the northern part of the territory. Pop. (1971), 175,000.

at; āpe; cär; end; mē; it; īce; hot; ōld; fôrk; wood; fool; oil; out; up; turn; sing; thin; this; hw in white; zh in treasure. The symbol ə stands for the sound of **a** in about, **e** in taken, **i** in pencil, **o** in lemon, and **u** in circus.

par·a·me·ci·um (par′ə mē′shē əm) *n. pl.,* **par·a·me·ci·a**
(par′ə mē′shē ə).
a freshwater ani-
mal consisting of
a single cell. It is
so small that it
can be seen only
through a micro-
scope. The para-
mecium has very
small hairlike
structures, called

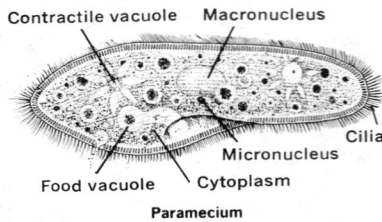

Contractile vacuole Macronucleus
Cilia
Micronucleus
Food vacuole Cytoplasm
Paramecium

cilia, that enable it to swim about and help it to sweep food
into its mouth.

par·a·med·ic (par′ə med′ik) *n.* a person who is specially
trained to assist a doctor, and to give first aid at the scene
of an emergency.

par·a·mount (par′ə mount′) *adj.* above all others, as
in influence or importance; supreme.

par·a·mour (par′ə moor′) *n.* a lover, especially of a
person who is married to someone else.

par·a·noi·a (par′ə noi′ə) *n.* **1.** a mental illness marked
by feelings of grandeur or persecution. **2.** a tendency to
distrust others and to look on everyone as an enemy.

par·a·noid (par′ə noid′) *adj.* relating to, characteristic
of, or affected with paranoia. —*n.* a person who is affected
with paranoia. Also, **par·a·noi·ac** (par′ə noi′ak).

par·a·pet (par′ə pet′) *n.* **1.** a low wall of earth or stone
to protect troops from being fired
upon. **2.** a low wall or railing
around the edge of a balcony, roof,
or other structure. —**par′a-
pet′ed,** *adj.*

par·a·pher·nal·ia (par′ə fər-
nāl′yə) *n.,pl.* **1.** personal belongings. **2.** any equipment used for a
particular purpose or activity;
gear: *fishing paraphernalia.*

par·a·phrase (par′ə frāz′) *n.*
the use of different words to express the same meaning; restate-
ment of the meaning of a work or
passage. —*v.t.,* **par·a·phrased,
par·a·phras·ing.** to express in a
paraphrase: *The speaker paraphrased the author's words.*

Parapet

par·a·pro·fes·sion·al (par′ə prə fesh′ən əl) *n.* a person who works with and helps a teacher, nurse, or other
professional.

par·a·site (par′ə sīt′) *n.* **1.** an animal or plant that lives
on or in another animal or plant of a different species, from
which it gets all or part of its food. Fleas, tapeworms, and
mistletoe are parasites. **2.** a person who lives off another
or who associates with another for his or her own gain
while giving nothing in return.

par·a·sit·ic (par′ə sit′ik) *adj.* **1.** of or like a parasite.
2. caused by a parasite: *Trichinosis is a parasitic disease.*
Also, **par·a·sit·i·cal** (par′ə sit′i kəl).

par·a·sol (par′ə sôl′) *n.* a small, light umbrella, used
especially by women for protection from the sun.

par·a·thy·roid glands (par′ə thī′roid) the small endocrine glands behind the thyroid glands, secreting a hormone that regulates the amounts of calcium and
phosphorus in the blood.

par·a·troop·er (par′ə trōo′pər) *n.* a member of the
paratroops.

par·a·troops (par′ə trōops′) *n.,pl.* a group of soldiers
trained to parachute from airplanes into an area of battle.

par·boil (pär′boil′) *v.t.* to cook partially by boiling, usually for a short time.

par·cel (pär′səl) *n.* **1.** a thing or group of things packed
together; package; bundle: *The mailman delivered a parcel
of books.* **2.** a section or part, as of land. **3.** a group of
similar persons or things; pack; bunch. —*v.t.* to divide into
sections or parts: *to parcel land, to parcel out supplies.*

parcel post **1.** a class of mail made up primarily of
packages weighing sixteen ounces or more. **2.** the branch
of the postal service handling such mail.

parch (pärch) *v.t.* **1.** to make very dry or shriveled, as by
exposure to heat: *The summer sun parched the lawn.*
2. to make very thirsty. **3.** to dry by roasting slightly: *to
parch nuts.* —*v.i.* to become very dry or hot, as by exposure to heat.

parch·ment (pärch′mənt) *n.* **1.** the skin of sheep, goats,
or other animals, prepared as a writing material. **2.** a
manuscript or document written on this material. **3.** any
of several types of paper made to resemble this material.

par·don (pärd′ən) *v.t.* **1.** to free (a person) from punishment for an offense: *The governor pardoned the condemned
prisoner.* **2.** to pass over (an offense) without placing blame
or requiring punishment; forgive. **3.** to excuse or overlook:
Please pardon my questions. —*n.* **1.** a freeing from punishment for an offense. **2.** a passing over an offense without
placing blame or requiring punishment; forgiveness.
3. polite excuse or toleration: *I beg your pardon if I bumped
you.* —**par′don·a·ble,** *adj.* —**par′don·a·bly,** *adv.* —**par′-
don·er,** *n.*

pare (per) *v.t.,* **pared, par·ing. 1.** to cut or peel off the
outer layer or skin of: *He pared the apple with his knife.*
2. to cut or peel off (an outer layer or part): *to pare the
bark from a twig.* **3.** to reduce or make less as if by cutting:
He pared down his essay. She tried to pare expenses.

par·e·gor·ic (par′ə gôr′ik) *n.* a medicine containing
opium and camphor, used to relieve pain and coughing and
to treat diarrhea.

pa·ren·chy·ma (pə reng′kə mə) *n.* **1.** the tissue in
plants made up of thin-walled cells that serve for storage,
as in leaves and fruit. **2.** the tissue of an animal organ, as
distinguished from the connective tissue that supports the
organ.

par·ent (per′ənt) *n.* **1.** a person who is a father or mother.
2. a person who serves as a father or mother. **3.** any
organism that produces offspring. **4.** a cause, origin, or
source. —*adj.* of, relating to, or like a parent or parents:
a parent organization.

par·ent·age (per′ən tij) *n.* descent from parents.

pa·ren·tal (pə rent′əl) *adj.* of, relating to, or characteristic of a parent: *parental duties.* —**pa·ren′tal·ly,** *adv.*

pa·ren·the·sis (pə ren′thə sis) *n. pl.,* **pa·ren·the·ses** (pə-
ren′thə sēz′). **1.** an additional word or phrase placed in
a sentence to explain or modify what is said, usually set
off by curved marks. **2.** either of the curved marks ( ) used
to set off such a word or phrase, or to enclose symbols or
numbers.

par·en·thet·i·cal (par′ən thet′i kəl) *adj.* **1.** placed
within parentheses: *Each foreign word was followed by a
parenthetical translation.* **2.** briefly explaining or modifying what is said. Also, **par·en·thet·ic** (par′ən thet′ik).
—**par′en·thet′i·cal·ly,** *adv.*

par·ent·hood (per′ənt hood′) *n.* the state of being a
parent.

par·fait (pär fā′) *n.* **1.** a dessert made of layers of ice
cream, syrup, and sometimes fruit. It is usually served in
a tall slender glass. **2.** a dessert made of custard or
whipped cream and syrup frozen together.

pa·ri·ah (pə rī′ə) *n.* a person who is rejected or avoided
by others; outcast.

par·ing (per′ing) *n.* something pared off.

Par·is (par′is) *n.* the capital and largest city of France, in the north-central part of the country, on the Seine River. Pop. (1971 est.), 2,488,600.

Par·is (par′is) *n. Greek Legend.* the son of Priam, King of Troy, who carried off Helen, Queen of Sparta, and by this act brought on the Trojan War.

par·ish (par′ish) *n. pl.*, **par·ish·es.** **1.** a church district with its own church and one or more clergymen. **2.** in Louisiana, a district corresponding to a county in other states. **3.** the people of a parish.

pa·rish·ion·er (pə rish′ə nər) *n.* a member of a parish.

Pa·ri·sian (pə rē′zhən, pə rizh′ən) *n.* a person who was born or is living in Paris. —*adj.* of or relating to Paris or its people.

par·i·ty (par′ə tē) *n.* the state or quality of being equal: *The two countries reached parity in military strength.*

park (pärk) *n.* **1.** an area of land set apart for the pleasure and use of the public, such as a small area in a city with paths, benches, and playgrounds. **2.** a large area of scenic land kept in its natural state. **3.** the grounds of a country estate, often having woods, lakes, and fields. —*v.t.* **1.** to leave (an automobile or other vehicle) in a certain place where it may remain for a time: *He parked his car near the house.* **2.** *Informal.* to place or leave: *Park your coat in the closet.* —*v.i.* to leave an automobile or other vehicle for a time: *Mr. Johnson parked too close to the fire hydrant.*

par·ka (pär′kə) *n.* **1.** a hooded fur outer garment worn by Eskimos. **2.** any hooded jacket for outdoor wear.

parking lot, an area set aside for cars to be parked.

parking meter, a timer mounted on a pole, into which coins are inserted to pay for the use of a parking space for a limited period of time.

park·way (pärk′wā′) *n.* a highway or wide thoroughfare divided by or bordered with landscaped trees, bushes, or grass.

par·lance (pär′ləns) *n.* a manner of speech; type of language: *medical parlance.*

Parka *(def. 2)*

par·lay (pär′lā, pär′lē) *v.t.* **1.** to bet (the money from a first bet plus the winnings) on one or more succeeding races or contests. **2.** to increase (money or talent) successfully: *He parlayed his small inheritance into a fortune.* —*n.* a bet made by parlaying.

par·ley (pär′lē) *n. pl.*, **par·leys.** a conference, especially one between enemies to decide the terms of a truce or agreement. —*v.i.* to hold a parley.

par·lia·ment (pär′lə mənt) *n.* **1.** an assembly that makes the laws of a country. **2. Parliament.** the legislature of Great Britain, made up of the House of Commons and the House of Lords.

par·lia·men·tar·i·an (pär′lə men ter′ē ən) *n.* a person who is expert in parliamentary procedure or debate.

par·lia·men·ta·ry (pär′lə men′tər ē) *adj.* **1.** of, relating to, or having a parliament: *a parliamentary government.* **2.** according to the rules of a parliament or other lawmaking assembly: *parliamentary procedure.* **3.** enacted by a parliament: *a parliamentary act.*

par·lor (pär′lər) *also, British,* **par·lour.** *n.* **1.** a room in a home in which visitors are received and entertained. **2.** a room or group of rooms equipped for a special purpose or business: *an ice-cream parlor.*

parlor car, a railroad passenger car with individual chairs.

Par·ma (pär′mə) *n.* a city in northeastern Ohio. Pop. (1970), 100,216.

Par·me·san cheese (pär′mə zän′) a pale-yellow, hard, dry Italian cheese, usually grated.

Par·nas·sus, Mount (pär nas′əs) a mountain in southern Greece, thought to be sacred to Apollo and the Muses in ancient times.

pa·ro·chi·al (pə rō′kē əl) *adj.* **1.** of, relating to, or supported by a parish: *Tom attended a parochial school.* **2.** limited in point of view; narrow: *parochial ideas.* —**pa·ro′chi·al·ly,** *adv.*

pa·ro·chi·al·ism (pə rō′kē ə liz′əm) *n.* the quality of being parochial in thinking.

parochial school, a school supported and run by a church or other religious organization.

par·o·dy (par′ə dē) *n. pl.*, **par·o·dies.** a humorous imitation of something serious, such as a literary or artistic work. —*v.t.*, **par·o·died, par·o·dy·ing.** to make a parody of: *The film parodied old silent movies.*

pa·role (pə rōl′) *n.* the conditional release of a prisoner before his full sentence is served. —*v.t.*, **pa·roled, pa·rol·ing.** to release (a prisoner) from prison before his full sentence is served: *The prisoner was paroled for good behavior.*

par·ox·ysm (par′ək siz′əm) *n.* **1.** a sudden outburst or fit: *a paroxysm of laughter.* **2.** a sudden attack of a disease, usually of a recurring nature: *He suffers paroxysms of malaria every few years.*

par·quet (pär kā′, pär ket′) *n.* **1.** flooring made of pieces of wood fitted together in a decorative pattern. **2.** the main floor of a theater; orchestra. —*adj.* made of parquet: *parquet floors.*

par·quet·ry (pär′ki trē) *n. pl.*, **par·quet·ries.** a decorative pattern formed by pieces of wood fitted together, used for floors.

par·ra·keet (par′ə kēt′) another spelling of **parakeet.**

par·ri·cide[1] (par′ə sīd′) *n.* the murder of a parent or other close relative. [French *parricide* such a murder, from Latin *pārricīdium.*] —**par′ri·cid′al,** *adj.*

par·ri·cide[2] (par′ə sīd′) *n.* a person who murders a parent or other close relative. [French *parricide* such a murderer, from Latin *parricīda.*]

par·rot (par′ət) *n.* **1.** any of a number of tropical birds having a hooked bill, large head, and glossy, usually brightly colored feathers. Some parrots can imitate speech and other sounds, and are popular as pets. **2.** a person who repeats or imitates the words or actions of others without thinking or understanding. —*v.t.* to repeat or imitate without thinking or understanding: *His friend parroted everything he said about the plan.* —**par′rot·like′,** *adj.*

Parrot

par·ry (par′ē) *v.t.*, **par·ried, par·ry·ing.** **1.** to ward off; deflect: *The boxer parried his opponent's blows.* **2.** to turn aside; evade: *The speaker parried the questions from the audience with his clever replies.* —*n. pl.*, **par·ries.** the act of parrying.

parse (pärs) *v.t.*, **parsed, pars·ing.** **1.** to analyze (a sentence) grammatically, naming the parts of speech and their uses in the sentence. **2.** to analyze (a

at; āpe; cär; end; mē; it; īce; hot; ōld; fôrk; wood; fōōl; oil; out; up; turn; sing; thin; this; hw in white; zh in treasure. The symbol ə stands for the sound of **a** in about, **e** in taken, **i** in pencil, **o** in lemon, and **u** in circus.

word in a sentence) by naming its part of speech and its use in a sentence.

Par·see (pär′sē) *also,* **Par·si.** *n.* a member of a Zoroastrian sect in India, descended from Persians who fled from Muslim persecution in the eighth century A.D.

par·si·mo·ni·ous (pär′sə mō′nē əs) *adj.* too careful in spending money; stingy. —**par′si·mo′ni·ous·ly,** *adv.* —**par′si·mo′ni·ous·ness,** *n.*

par·si·mo·ny (pär′sə mō′nē) *n.* too much care in spending money; stinginess.

pars·ley (pärs′lē) *n. pl.,* **pars·leys.** a plant related to the carrot, having finely divided, fragrant leaves used to flavor and decorate food. —*adj.* designating a family of plants grown throughout most parts of the world, including such vegetables as celery, carrots, and parsnips, and many herbs.

pars·nip (pärs′nip) *n.* **1.** the thick, white root of a plant of the parsley family, cooked and eaten as a vegetable. **2.** the plant bearing this root, having clusters of greenish flowers.

par·son (pär′sən) *n.* **1.** a clergyman in charge of a parish; pastor. **2.** any clergyman, especially a Protestant minister.

par·son·age (pär′sə nij) *n.* the house of a parson or clergyman, usually provided by the church.

part (pärt) *n.* **1.** something less than the whole: *Jim ate only part of his dinner. The last part of the movie is very exciting.* **2.** one of several equal portions or quantities into which a whole may be divided: *An inch is a twelfth part of a foot.* **3.** a separate piece that together with other pieces makes up a whole, as in a machine: *the parts of a television set.* **4.** a share, as of responsibility, work, or concern: *They all did their part to make the picnic a success.* **5.** one of the sides in a contest, dispute, or question. **6.** a line made when combing one's hair: *She always wears a center part.* **7.** *usually,* **parts.** a region, place, or district: *He is going to travel in foreign parts this summer.* **8. parts.** ability; talent: *a man of many parts.* **9.** a character or role in a motion picture, play, or opera: *He played the part of a cowboy in the movie.* **10.** the lines of a character in a motion picture, play, or opera. **11.** one of the voices or instruments in a piece of music: *the soprano part, the piano part.* **12.** the music for one of the voices or instruments in a piece of music. —*v.t.* **1.** to separate by coming between; force, draw, or hold apart: *The referee parted the boxers.* **2.** to comb (the hair) so as to make a part. **3.** to divide into two or more portions or sections: *to part a pie with a knife.* —*v.i.* **1.** to become separated or divided into two or more pieces: *The shirt parted at the seams.* **2.** to go in different directions; go apart from one another: *They parted at the corner.* —*adv.* in part; partly. —*adj.* not full or complete; partial: *He is part owner of the store.*

  for one's part. as far as one is concerned.
  for the most part. mostly; generally.
  in part. partly.
  part and parcel. a part that is necessary.
  to part from. to go away from; leave.
  to part with. to give up: *to part with one's money.*
  to take part. to take or have a share: *He took part in school sports.*

part. **1.** participle. **2.** particular.

par·take (pär tāk′) *v.i.,* **par·took, par·tak·en, par·tak·ing.** to take part; participate: *She partook in the festivities.* —**par·tak′er,** *n.*

  to partake of. a. to take or have a portion of: *to partake of dinner.* **b.** to have the character or quality of; resemble: *His wild acts partake of madness.*

par·the·no·gen·e·sis (pär′thə nō jen′ə sis) *n.* reproduction in which a new organism develops from an egg cell without fertilization.

Par·the·non (pär′thə non′) *n.* the temple of Athena on the Acropolis in Athens, built in the fifth century B.C. It is considered the finest existing example of Greek Doric architecture.

Parthenon

par·tial (pär′shəl) *adj.* **1.** not complete or total: *a partial recovery.* **2.** favoring one side, person, or group more than another; prejudiced; biased: *The umpire was partial to one of the teams.* **3.** having a strong liking for someone or something: *Our whole family is partial to candy.* —**par′tial·ly,** *adv.*

par·ti·al·i·ty (pär′shē al′ə tē) *n. pl.,* **par·ti·al·i·ties.** **1.** the state or quality of favoring one side, person, or group more than another; bias; prejudice: *The jury considered the case without partiality.* **2.** a strong liking or fondness: *He has a partiality for water sports.*

par·tic·i·pant (pär tis′ə pənt) *n.* a person who participates. —*adj.* taking part; participating.

par·tic·i·pate (pär tis′ə pāt′) *v.i.,* **par·tic·i·pat·ed, par·tic·i·pat·ing.** to take part or have a share with others, as in an activity or quality. —**par·tic′i·pa′tion,** *n.*

par·ti·cip·i·al (pär′tə sip′ē əl) *adj.* of, based on, or used as a participle: *a participial phrase.*

par·ti·ci·ple (pär′tə sip′əl) *n.* a verb form that is used with auxiliary verbs to form certain tenses, and that sometimes can function as an adjective or noun.

par·ti·cle (pär′ti kəl) *n.* **1.** a very small bit or minute amount; trace; speck: *a particle of soot, a particle of truth.* **2.** see **subatomic particle.** **3.** a short part of speech, as a preposition, conjunction, or article. **4.** a prefix or suffix.

particle accelerator, see **accelerator** *(def. 2).*

par·ti·col·ored (pär′ti kul′ərd) *adj.* having different colors in different parts: *a parti-colored flower.*

par·tic·u·lar (pər tik′yə lər) *adj.* **1.** apart or distinct from others: *This particular suitcase is too small for such a long trip.* **2.** belonging to or characteristic of a single person or thing: *His particular hobby is collecting stamps.* **3.** unusual in some way; special; noteworthy: *That book is of particular interest to sports fans.* **4.** very careful about details; demanding; fussy: *She is very particular about keeping her room neat.* —*n.* a single and distinct fact or part; item: *The article included the particulars of the scandal.*

  in particular. especially: *I like all kinds of ice cream, but I like chocolate in particular.*

par·tic·u·lar·i·ty (pər tik′yə lar′ə tē) *n. pl.,* **par·tic·u·lar·i·ties.** **1.** the quality of being distinct from others. **2.** carefulness about details. **3.** a distinctive characteristic or trait. **4.** a particular item or detail.

par·tic·u·lar·ize (pər tik′yə lə rīz′) *v.,* **par·tic·u·lar·ized, par·tic·u·lar·iz·ing.** —*v.t.* to mention in detail; treat individually; specify. —*v.i.* to give particulars; go into detail. —**par·tic′u·lar·i·za′tion,** *n.*

par·tic·u·lar·ly (pər tik′yə lər lē) *adv.* **1.** to an unusual degree; especially: *He is particularly clever.* **2.** in a detailed manner; item by item: *to discuss a problem particularly.*

part·ing (pär′ting) *n.* **1.** the act of taking leave; departure: *The mother cried at her son's parting.* **2.** a separation or division: *a parting of one's hair.* —*adj.* **1.** given, spoken, or done at parting: *a parting warning, a parting request.* **2.** leaving; departing.

par·ti·san (pär′tə zən) *also,* **par·ti·zan.** *n.* **1.** a person who strongly supports a person, idea, cause, or side: *The senator is a partisan of tax reform.* **2.** a member of a group of resistance fighters; guerrilla. —*adj.* of, relating to, or characteristic of a partisan or partisans: *partisan politics, an attack of partisan troops.*

par·ti·tion (pär tish′ən) *n.* **1.** a division into shares or distinct parts: *the partition of territory between rival states.* **2.** something that divides, especially a movable structure that separates parts of a room. —*v.t.* **1.** to divide into shares or distinct parts: *to partition land for sale.* **2.** to separate by a partition: *to partition off a place to sleep.*

par·ti·zan (pär′tə zən) another spelling of **partisan.**

part·ly (pärt′lē) *adv.* in part; in some degree; not wholly or completely: *He is only partly responsible for the damage.*

part·ner (pärt′nər) *n.* **1.** a person who shares or joins with another: *partners in crime.* **2.** a person associated with another or others in a business: *He is a partner in a large law firm.* **3.** a person with whom one plays a game, usually on the same side: *a bridge partner.* **4.** either of two persons dancing together. **5.** a wife or husband.

part·ner·ship (pärt′nər ship′) *n.* **1.** the state of being a partner; association: *Tom started a paper route in partnership with a friend.* **2.** a business organization in which two or more persons are associated, usually sharing the profits and losses.

part of speech, any of the major grammatical classes into which the words of a language can be divided. The traditional parts of speech for English are noun, pronoun, adjective, verb, adverb, preposition, conjunction, and interjection.

● In recent years, many language scholars have been critical of the traditional method used in classifying English words according to **parts of speech.** They have pointed out that the eight traditional parts of speech are based on Greek and Latin grammar, rather than on English. In former times, it was believed that all languages should be modeled on Latin and Greek. However, scholars know now that there are many languages in the world, including English, that cannot be classified according to the parts of speech of Greek and Latin.

Modern scholars have done a great deal of research in an attempt to develop a system of parts of speech that truly reflects the nature of English. Although all grammarians now agree that the traditional parts of speech are not entirely adequate, there is at present no agreement as to what new system is suitable to replace the traditional one. Several different possibilities have been advanced, but none has yet been generally accepted as completely satisfactory.

For this reason, this dictionary uses the traditional parts of speech in classifying words. This is the only method that is familiar to all students, and it does not require learning any new rules or terms. A dictionary must reflect the language as it is being used, and until any new system of parts of speech becomes universally accepted, dictionaries will continue to employ the traditional classes.

---

par·took (pär took′) the past tense of **partake.**

par·tridge (pär′trij) *n. pl.,* **par·tridg·es** or **par·tridge.** **1.** any of several plump game birds of Europe, Asia, and Africa, having gray, brown, and white feathers. **2.** any of various similar or related birds of the United States, such as the ruffed grouse and the bob-white.

Partridge

part-time (pärt′tīm′) *adj.* for or during only part of the normal working time: *a part-time job.* —*adv.* on a part-time basis: *Jack works part-time as a clerk in a supermarket.*

par·tu·ri·tion (pär′tə rish′ən, pär′chə rish′ən) *n.* the act of giving birth; childbirth.

par·ty (pär′tē) *n. pl.,* **par·ties. 1.** a gathering of people for pleasure or entertainment: *Everyone had a good time at the birthday party.* **2.** a group of people gathered together for some common purpose: *A search party was organized to find the lost child.* **3.** a group of people organized to gain political influence or control: *Each political party selected its candidate for the office of President.* **4.** a person who takes part in an action or plan: *He refused to be a party to such underhanded schemes.* **5.** a person or organization involved in a lawsuit or other legal matter. **6.** *Informal.* a person: *A certain party telephoned you twice this evening.*

party line 1. a single telephone circuit with two or more subscribers on it. **2.** the official views and policies of a political party, especially the Communist Party.

par·ve·nu (pär′və nōō′, pär′və nyōō′) *n.* a person who has recently or suddenly risen to a position of wealth or importance for which he is not fit; upstart. [French *parvenu,* the past participle of *parvenir* to arrive at, succeed.]

Pas·a·de·na (pas′ə dē′nə) *n.* **1.** a city in southern California, near Los Angeles. Pop. (1970), 113,327. **2.** a city in southeastern Texas, a suburb of Houston. Pop. (1970), 89,277.

Pas·cal, Blaise (pas kal′; blez) 1623–1662, French philosopher, mathematician, physicist, and inventor.

pas·chal (pas′kəl) *adj.* **1.** of or relating to Passover. **2.** of or relating to Easter.

pa·sha (pə shä′) *n.* the title formerly placed after the name of a high-ranking Turkish civil or military official.

pass (pas) *v.i.* **1.** to go or move; proceed: *The waitress passed from table to table. Several thoughts passed through my mind.* **2.** to go or move by: *A flock of birds passed overhead. The hours passed slowly.* **3.** to extend; run: *The new subway passes under the park.* **4.** to get away or get by without notice: *You let a good opportunity pass.* **5.** to come to an end; cease: *As time went on, his sorrow passed.* **6.** to complete an examination, trial, or course of study successfully or satisfactorily: *The student passed after taking the test over again.* **7.** to be approved or ratified: *The bill passed easily in the Senate.* **8.** to take place; happen; occur: *We had no idea of what had passed at the meeting.* **9.** *Sports.* to transfer the ball or puck to a teammate. **10.** to decline to bid, play, or bet in a card game. —*v.t.* **1.** to go or move by (something): *I pass the park on my way to school.* **2.** to complete (an examination, trial, or course of study) successfully or satisfactorily. **3.** to hand about or over, or spread from one person or place to another: *Please pass the salt. Did you pass the word?* **4.** to cause or allow (something) to move or go in a particular way: *to pass thread through the eye of a needle.* **5.** to go beyond; exceed; surpass: *This year's attendance may pass that of last year.* **6.** to go through, across, or over. **7.** to cause or allow to elapse; spend: *She passed the summer traveling.* **8.** to approve or ratify: *Congress passed the resolution.* **9.** to be approved or ratified by: *The bill passed the Senate.* **10.** to pronounce or express: *The judge passed sentence.* **11.** *Sports.* to transfer (the ball or puck) to a

at; āpe; cär; end; mē; it; īce; hot; ōld; fôrk; wood; fōōl; oil; out; up; turn; sing; thin; this; hw in white; zh in treasure. The symbol ə stands for the sound of **a** in about, **e** in taken, **i** in pencil, **o** in lemon, and **u** in circus.

teammate. —*n. pl.,* **pass·es. 1.** a permit or written authorization to come, go, or move about freely: *No one was allowed to enter the building without showing a pass.* **2.** a ticket, usually free, entitling the holder to admission or transportation: *Tom's employer gave him two passes to the baseball game.* **3.** a way or opening through which one can go or move, especially a narrow gap in or passage through a mountain range or ridge. **4.** a condition or situation; state of affairs: *Events had come to a critical pass.* **5.** a movement or motion of the hand or hands: *The magician made a pass over his hat and then pulled out a rabbit.* **6.** *Sports.* a transfer of the ball or puck to a teammate. —**pas′ser,** *n.*

to bring to pass. to cause to happen.
to come to pass. to happen.
to pass away. to die.
to pass off. to cause to be accepted as genuine: *The crook tried to pass the rabbit fur off as mink.*
to pass out. a. to give out: *to pass out pamphlets.* **b.** to lose consciousness; faint.
to pass over. to overlook or ignore.
to pass up. to fail to take advantage of; refuse: *Tom passed up an offer for a summer job.*

pass·a·ble (pas′ə bəl) *adj.* **1.** fairly good; adequate; acceptable: *She speaks passable French.* **2.** that can be traveled through or across: *The dense jungle was barely passable.*

pass·a·bly (pas′ə blē) *adv.* fairly well; adequately: *He plays the piano passably.*

pas·sage (pas′ij) *n.* **1.** a portion, usually short, of a written work or speech: *The author read a passage from his latest novel to the class.* **2.** a short section of a musical composition. **3.** a route, path, or other way by which a person or thing can pass: *air passages in a mine, a mountain passage.* **4.** a hall or passageway in a building; corridor. **5.** the right, permission, or freedom to pass, go, or travel: *The king granted them passage through his realm.* **6.** a journey or voyage, especially by sea or air: *Her passage across the Pacific was rough.* **7.** passenger accommodations: *Elizabeth wrote months in advance to book passage on an ocean liner.* **8.** course, progress, or advance: *the passage of time.* **9.** approval or enactment by a legislative body: *Congressional passage of such a resolution seemed unlikely.*

pas·sage·way (pas′ij wā′) *n.* a way by which a person or thing can pass, as a corridor or alley.

pass·book (pas′book′) *n.* another word for **bankbook.**

pas·sé (pa sā′) *adj.* no longer in style; out-of-date.

passed ball *Baseball.* a pitch that gets away from the catcher even though it was within his reach, allowing one or more base runners to advance.

pas·sen·ger (pas′ən jər) *n.* a person who travels in an automobile, train, airplane, or other conveyance.

passenger pigeon, an extinct wild pigeon of North America.

pass·er·by (pas′ər bī′) *n. pl.,* **pass·ers·by.** a person who passes or goes by: *A passerby saw the accident and described it to the police.*

pas·ser·ine (pas′ər in, pas′ə rīn′) *adj.* of or belonging to a group of perching birds, including all songbirds. More than half of all living birds belong to this group. —*n.* a passerine bird.

pass·ing (pas′ing) *adj.* **1.** going or moving by: *The boy watched the passing circus parade. She grew more beautiful with the passing years.* **2.** not lasting; brief: *Tom*

Passenger pigeon

had a passing fancy for collecting miniature cars. **3.** given or done casually or in passing. **4.** allowing one to pass an examination, trial, or course of study; satisfactory: *a passing grade.* —*n.* **1.** the act of a person or thing that passes: *the passing of the days.* **2.** a means or place of passing or crossing, as a ford.

in passing. incidentally: *The speaker remarked in passing that he was glad to be here.*

pas·sion (pash′ən) *n.* **1.** a strong or intense feeling, such as love, hate, or anger. **2.** a strong liking, desire, or enthusiasm: *Tom has a passion for baseball.* **3.** the object of strong feeling, liking, desire, or enthusiasm: *Painting was the artist's only passion.* **4.** strong love between a man and a woman. **5.** an outburst or fit of rage. **6. Passion. a.** the sufferings of Jesus Christ following the Last Supper and ending with the Crucifixion. **b.** the chapters in the Gospels that tell of these sufferings.

pas·sion·ate (pash′ə nit) *adj.* **1.** characterized by or showing strong or intense feeling; ardent: *The young man was a passionate defender of freedom of speech.* **2.** showing or coming from strong or intense feeling: *The lawyer made a passionate plea for his client's life.* **3.** easily angered; hot-tempered. —**pas′sion·ate·ly,** *adv.*

pas·sion·flow·er (pash′ən flou′ər) *n.* **1.** a large showy flower of any of a group of climbing vines. **2.** a vine that bears this flower.

pas·sion·less (pash′ən lis) *adj.* without strong feeling.

Passion play *also,* **passion play.** a play representing the Passion, death, and Resurrection of Jesus Christ.

pas·sive (pas′iv) *adj.* **1.** acted upon without responding or acting back: *He played a passive role in the student protest.* **2.** giving in without opposition or resistance; submissive: *The prisoner was passive as the judge pronounced his sentence.* **3.** *Grammar.* relating to or designating the voice of a verb whose subject receives the action expressed by the verb. In the sentence *The boy was struck by an automobile, was struck* is in the passive voice. —*n.* **1.** the passive voice. **2.** a verb form in this voice. —**pas′sive·ly,** *adv.* —**pas′sive·ness,** *n.*

Passionflower

passive resistance, a method of resisting authority or protesting against some law or act by nonviolent means, as by refusing to obey.

pas·siv·i·ty (pa siv′ə tē) *n.* the state or condition of being passive.

pass·key (pas′kē′) *n.* **1.** another word for **master key. 2.** any of various other keys, as a skeleton key or latchkey.

Pass·o·ver (pas′ō′vər) *n.* the annual Jewish feast commemorating the Exodus of the Jews from Egypt. [From the phrase *to pass over;* referring to the story in the Bible in which the Jews were in captivity in Egypt and God *passed over* their homes when He killed the first-born sons of the Egyptians.]

pass·port (pas′pôrt′) *n.* **1.** a document issued by the government of a citizen's own country giving him official permission to travel abroad. **2.** anything that gives a person acceptance or admission: *A clever mind was his passport to success.*

pass·word (pas′wurd′) *n.* a secret word or phrase that identifies the speaker or allows him to pass a guard.

past (past) *adj.* **1.** gone by; ended; over: *The days of his youth are past.* **2.** having happened or existed in time gone by: *to study the past events in the history of a country.* **3.** gone by just before the present time: *She has been on the telephone for the past hour.* **4.** having served formerly:

a past mayor. **5.** *Grammar.* indicating a state or action in time gone by. —*n.* **1.** a time that has gone by: *Dinosaurs lived in the distant past.* **2.** something that was done or has happened in the past. **3.** *Grammar.* the past tense or a verb in the past tense. —*prep.* **1.** beyond in place; farther than: *John threw the ball past the catcher.* **2.** beyond in time; after: *It is past my bedtime.* **3.** beyond the power, scope, or limits of: *His poetry is past understanding.* **4.** beyond in amount, number, or degree: *The old man is past ninety.* —*adv.* so as to pass or go by: *We watched the train rumble past.*

pas·ta (päs′tə) *n.* **1.** a paste or dough made with flour, used to make macaroni, ravioli, and similar food. **2.** a dish of cooked pasta.

paste (pāst) *n.* **1.** a mixture, as of flour and water, used to stick things together. **2.** any soft, smooth, often moist, mixture: *anchovy paste.* **3.** a dough used for pastry. **4.** a hard, glasslike material used to make artificial or imitation gems. —*v.t.,* **past·ed, past·ing. 1.** to stick with paste: *She pasted the photographs in her album.* **2.** to cover with something that is pasted on: *Jimmy pasted the walls of his room with posters.* **3.** *Slang.* to strike with a hard blow; punch.

paste·board (pāst′bôrd′) *n.* a stiff material made of sheets of paper pasted together or of paper pulp pressed together. —*adj.* made of pasteboard: *a pasteboard box.*

pas·tel (pas tel′) *n.* **1.** a chalklike crayon used in drawing. **2.** a picture drawn with such crayons. **3.** a pale, soft shade of a color. —*adj.* **1.** of, relating to, or drawn with pastels. **2.** having a pale, soft shade: *Margo wanted a dress in pastel blue.*

pas·tern (pas′tərn) *n.* the part of a horse's foot between the fetlock and the hoof.

Pas·teur, Lou·is (pas tur′; lōō′ē) 1822–1895, French chemist and bacteriologist.

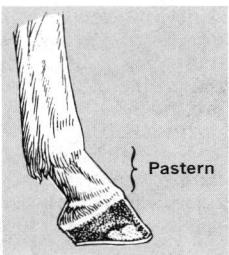

Pastern

pas·teur·ize (pas′chə rīz′) *v.t.,* **pas·teur·ized, pas·teur·iz·ing.** to heat (milk or other food) to a temperature high enough to destroy disease-producing bacteria and organisms that cause food spoilage. [From Louis *Pasteur,* who invented this process.] —**pas′teur·i·za′tion,** *n.*

pas·time (pas′tīm′) *n.* something that makes time pass pleasantly and happily: *Playing baseball is a favorite pastime for many boys.*

pas·tor (pas′tər) *n.* a clergyman in charge of a parish or congregation. [Going back to Latin *pāstor* shepherd; because this clergyman was thought of as the shepherd of his flock, or congregation.]

pas·tor·al (pas′tər əl) *adj.* **1.** of, relating to, or describing shepherds or country life: *pastoral poetry.* **2.** having the simplicity, peacefulness, charm, and other qualities usually associated with country life: *pastoral scenery.* **3.** of or relating to a pastor or his duties. —*n.* a poem, play, or picture that deals with shepherds or country life. —**pas′tor·al·ly,** *adv.*

pas·tor·ate (pas′tər it) *n.* **1.** the office, position, or jurisdiction of a pastor. **2.** the term or length of service of a pastor with one parish or congregation. **3.** pastors as a group.

past participle, a participle expressing a past action or state, used with auxiliary verbs to form perfect tenses of the active voice and all tenses of the passive voice. In the sentence *He has studied all day,* the word *studied* is a past participle.

past perfect 1. a verb tense expressing past action com-

pleted before another past action or before a specified past time. In the sentence *He had returned by the time his guests began to arrive,* the phrase *had returned* is in the past perfect. **2.** a verb in this tense. Also, **pluperfect.**

pas·tra·mi (pəs trä′mē) *n.* a cut of beef, especially a shoulder cut, smoked and highly seasoned.

pas·try (pās′trē) *n. pl.,* **pas·tries. 1.** any of several flour doughs used in making pie crusts, tarts, and other baked goods. **2.** baked foods made with such a dough. **3.** any sweet, baked food.

past tense 1. a verb tense expressing an action or state that happened or existed in the past. In the sentence *The bird flew away,* the word *flew* is in the past tense. **2.** a verb in this tense.

pas·tur·age (pas′chər ij) *n.* **1.** growing grass and other plants that livestock feed on. **2.** land used or suitable for grazing livestock.

pas·ture (pas′chər) *n.* **1.** a field or other tract of land used for the grazing of cattle, sheep, or other animals. **2.** grass and other growing plants that livestock feed on. —*v.,* **pas·tured, pas·tur·ing.** —*v.t.* to put (animals) in a pasture to graze. —*v.i.* to graze.

past·y¹ (pās′tē) *adj.,* **past·i·er, past·i·est. 1.** like paste: *a pasty mixture.* **2.** pale and sickly: *a pasty complexion.* [*Paste* + *-y¹.*] —**past′i·ness,** *n.*

pas·ty² (pas′tē) *n. pl.,* **pas·ties.** a small pie with a filling, usually of meat. [Old French *paste.*]

pat¹ (pat) *v.t.,* **pat·ted, pat·ting. 1.** to stroke or tap gently, usually with the hand, especially in affection or approval: *She patted the dog.* **2.** to shape or smooth by striking gently with something flat. —*n.* **1.** a gentle tap or stroke. **2.** the sound made by such a tap or stroke. **3.** a small slice or molded mass: *a pat of butter.* [Imitative of this sound.] **pat on the back.** *Informal.* praise or approval.

pat² (pat) *adj.* exactly suitable for the purpose or occasion; fitting: *He had a pat answer to every question.* —*adv.* aptly; suitably. [From *pat¹.*] **to have down pat** or **to know pat.** to know perfectly or thoroughly. **to stand pat.** to stay firm without changing.

pat., patent; patented.

Pat·a·go·ni·a (pat′ə gō′nē ə) *n.* a region in southern Argentina, between the Andes and the Atlantic Ocean. —**Pat′a·go′ni·an,** *adj., n.*

patch (pach) *n. pl.,* **patch·es. 1.** a piece of material used to mend or cover a hole, strengthen a worn spot, or decorate a garment. **2.** a pad, piece of cloth, or other covering worn or put over a wound or injured part for protection: *an eye patch.* **3.** any of the pieces of material used in making patchwork. **4.** a small area, as of a surface, that differs or stands out from the rest: *Nothing showed on the surface of the water but some patches of yellow weed* (Ernest Hemingway). **5.** a small piece of ground: *a lettuce patch.* —*v.t.* **1.** to mend, cover, strengthen, or decorate with a patch or patches: *to patch up a torn pair of dungarees.* **2.** to fix, repair, or put together, especially in a hasty or makeshift way: *The man patched up the roof before the rain could leak in.* **3.** to make by joining pieces together: *to patch a quilt.* **to patch up.** to smooth over; settle: *to patch up a quarrel.*

at; āpe; cär; end; mē; it; īce; hot; ōld; fôrk; wood; fōōl; oil; out; up; turn; sing; thin; this; hw in white; zh in treasure. The symbol ə stands for the sound of **a** in about, **e** in taken, **i** in pencil, **o** in lemon, and **u** in circus.

patch·work (pach′wurk′) *n.* **1.** needlework consisting of pieces of material, usually of various colors or shapes, that are sewed together. **2.** anything like this: *Joe's composition was a patchwork of many unrelated facts.*

Patchwork

patch·y (pach′ē) *adj.,* **patch·i·er, patch·i·est.** made up of, like, or occurring in patches. —**patch′i·ly,** *adv.* —**patch′i·ness,** *n.*

patd., patented.

pate (pāt) *n.* the head, especially the crown of the head.

pâ·té (pä tā′) *n. French.* a meat paste.

pa·tel·la (pə tel′ə) *n. pl.,* **pa·tel·lae** (pə tel′ē) or **pa·tel·las.** another word for **kneecap.**

pat·ent (pat′ənt) *n.* **1.** a government grant that gives a person or company the exclusive right of making, using, or selling a new invention for a certain period of time. **2.** an invention that is protected by such a grant. **3.** an official document granting a right or privilege: *a patent of nobility.* —*adj.* **1.** protected by a patent. **2.** obvious; evident; clear: *He told a patent lie.* —*v.t.* to get a patent for; protect with a patent. —**pat′ent·a·ble,** *adj.* —**pat′ent·ly,** *adv.*

pat·ent·ee (pat′ən tē′) *n.* a person to whom a patent is granted.

patent leather, a smooth, soft leather that is finished to a very high gloss.

patent medicine, any medicine that is patented and can be purchased without a prescription.

pa·ter (pā′tər) *n.* father. [Latin *pater.*]

pa·ter·nal (pə turn′əl) *adj.* **1.** of, relating to, or like a father; fatherly: *paternal affection.* **2.** related through one's father: *a paternal grandmother.* **3.** inherited or derived from one's father: *a paternal fortune.* —**pa·ter′nal·ly,** *adv.*

pa·ter·nal·ism (pə turn′əl iz′əm) *n.* the principle or practice of regulating the life and supplying the needs of a group of people in a way suggestive of a father handling his children. —**pa·ter′nal·is′tic,** *adj.*

pa·ter·ni·ty (pə tur′nə tē) *n.* **1.** the state of being a father; fatherhood. **2.** paternal origin: *The paternity of the orphan was unknown.*

pat·er·nos·ter (pā′tər nos′tər, pat′ər nos′tər) *n.* the Lord's Prayer, especially the Latin version. [Latin *pater noster* our father; referring to the first two words of the Latin version of this prayer.]

Pat·er·son (pat′ər sən) *n.* a city in northeastern New Jersey. Pop. (1970), 144,824.

path (path) *n. pl.,* **paths** (path̲z, paths). **1.** a trail or way that has been made or worn by footsteps, as through a forest. **2.** a way or road made for a specific purpose: *to shovel a path through the snow.* **3.** a course or route along which a person or thing travels: *The scientists traced the path of the rocket. A black cat crossed his path.* **4.** a way or line of action or behavior: *Peter seemed to be on the path to success.*

path., pathology; pathological.

pa·thet·ic (pə thet′ik) *adj.* **1.** arousing pity, sadness, or sympathy: *An abandoned child is a pathetic sight.* **2.** pitifully unsuccessful or inadequate: *a pathetic attempt.* —**pa·thet′i·cal·ly,** *adv.*

path·find·er (path′fīn′dər) *n.* a person who discovers or leads the way: *a pathfinder in space science.*

path·o·gen (path′ə jən) *n.* any microorganism that causes disease.

path·o·gen·ic (path′ə jen′ik) *adj.* that can cause disease: *a pathogenic organism.*

pathol., pathology; pathological.

path·o·log·i·cal (path′ə loj′i kəl) *adj.* **1.** of, relating to, or concerned with pathology: *a pathological study of blood cells.* **2.** characteristic of, caused by, or accompanying disease: *a pathological condition of the heart.* Also, **path·o·log·ic** (path′ə loj′ik). —**path′o·log′i·cal·ly,** *adv.*

pa·thol·o·gist (pə thol′ə jist) *n.* a doctor who specializes in pathology.

pa·thol·o·gy (pə thol′ə jē) *n. pl.,* **pa·thol·o·gies. 1.** the science that deals with the nature, cause, and development of disease. **2.** the abnormal condition and bodily changes resulting from a disease.

pa·thos (pā′thos) *n.* a quality in an event or work of art or literature that arouses a feeling of pity, sadness, or sympathy.

path·way (path′wā′) *n.* a path or course.

pa·tience (pā′shəns) *n.* **1.** the quality or fact of being patient: *The crowd showed great patience as they waited in line for tickets to the game.* **2.** see **solitaire** *(def. 1).*

pa·tient (pā′shənt) *adj.* **1.** able to put up with hardship, pain, trouble, or delay calmly and without complaint or anger: *The boy was very patient when they put the cast on his broken leg.* **2.** showing or characterized by the ability to wait or put up with calmly and without anger: *Margaret gave the two children a patient smile.* —*n.* a person who is under the care or treatment of a doctor. —**pa′tient·ly,** *adv.*

pa·ti·o (pat′ē ō′) *n. pl.,* **pat·i·os. 1.** a terrace for outdoor cooking, eating, and lounging. **2.** an inner court open to the sky, as in a Spanish or Spanish-American house.

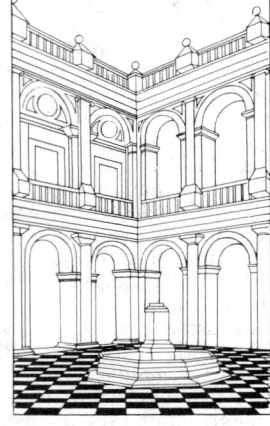

Patio *(def. 2)*

pat·ois (pat′wä) *n. pl.,* **pat·ois** (pat′wäz). a dialect spoken by the people of a region.

pat. pend., patent pending.

pa·tri·arch (pā′trē ärk′) *n.* **1.** the father and head of a family or tribe. Abraham, Isaac, and Jacob were Hebrew patriarchs. **2.** an old man who is respected and honored. **3.** in the Roman Catholic, Orthodox, and various other Christian churches, a high-ranking bishop.

pa·tri·ar·chal (pā′trē är′kəl) *adj.* **1.** of, relating to, or characteristic of a patriarch: *patriarchal authority, a patriarchal form of government.* **2.** ruled by a patriarch: *a patriarchal tribe.*

pa·tri·cian (pə trish′ən) *n.* **1.** a member of one of the aristocratic families in ancient Rome. **2.** a person who is of high birth or social status; aristocrat. —*adj.* **1.** of or relating to the aristocracy, especially of ancient Rome. **2.** aristocratic; noble.

pat·ri·cide¹ (pat′rə sīd′) *n.* the act of killing one's father. [Latin *pater* father + *-cīdium* a killing.]

pat·ri·cide² (pat′rə sīd′) *n.* a person who kills his father. [Latin *pater* father + *-cīda* a killer.]

Pat·rick, Saint (pat′rik) A.D. 389?–461?, Christian missionary; the patron saint of Ireland.

pat·ri·mo·ny (pat′rə mō′nē) *n. pl.,* **pat·ri·mo·nies. 1.** property inherited or handed down from one's father or ancestors. **2.** anything inherited; heritage: *Americans enjoy a patrimony of freedom of speech.* **3.** the property or endowment of a church or other religious institution.

pa·tri·ot (pā′trē ət) *n.* a person who loves and enthusiastically and loyally supports his or her country.

pa·tri·ot·ic (pā′trē ot′ik) *adj.* characterized by or showing patriotism: a *patriotic holiday.* —**pa′tri·ot′i·cal·ly,** *adv.*

pa·tri·ot·ism (pā′trē ə tiz′əm) *n.* a love for and enthusiastic and loyal support of one's country.

pa·trol (pə trōl′) *v.,* **pa·trolled, pa·trol·ling.** —*v.t.* to go through or around (an area or place) for the purpose of guarding or inspecting: *The commissioner ordered additional police cars to patrol the neighborhood.* —*v.i.* to go through or around an area or place for the purpose of guarding or inspecting. —*n.* **1.** one or more persons who patrol or are assigned to patrol. **2.** a group of soldiers, ships, or airplanes sent out for combat or to find out about the enemy's position. **3.** the act of patrolling. **4.** a unit of a Boy or Girl Scout troop, usually consisting of eight scouts. [French *patrouiller* originally, to trample in the mud; because sentries often had to walk in mud when they patrolled.]

patrol car, a police car assigned to patrol a particular area. Also, **squad car.**

pa·trol·man (pə trōl′mən) *n. pl.,* **pa·trol·men** (pə trōl′mən).** a police officer assigned to patrol a particular area.

patrol wagon, a specially equipped truck used by the police for carrying prisoners.

pa·tron (pā′trən) *n.* **1.** a person who supports, assists, or protects a person, cause, organization, or undertaking by the use of his or her money or influence: *a patron of the arts.* **2.** a regular customer: *a patron of a restaurant.*

pa·tron·age (pā′trə nij, pat′rə nij) *n.* **1.** the support or assistance given by a patron. **2.** the support given to a store, restaurant, or other business establishment by customers. **3.** a condescending manner or treatment. **4.** the power or system of giving out jobs, government contracts, or other political favors: *the patronage of a senator.* **5.** the political jobs or favors given out.

pa·tron·ize (pā′trə nīz′, pat′rə nīz′) *v.t.,* **pa·tron·ized, pa·tron·iz·ing. 1.** to be a customer of (a store, restaurant, or other business establishment), especially on a regular basis. **2.** to treat in a condescending manner: *Bill always patronized his little brother.* **3.** to give support or assistance to; act as a patron toward.

patron saint, a saint looked on as the special guardian or protector of a person, place, or group.

pa·troon (pə trōōn′) *n.* under Dutch colonial rule in New York and New Jersey, a person who owned a large amount of land and was given certain rights and privileges.

pat·ter¹ (pat′ər) *v.i.* **1.** to make soft, rapid taps: *She heard the sound of raindrops as they pattered on the roof.* **2.** to move with soft, rapid steps: *We heard the children pattering down the stairs.* —*n.* a series of soft, rapid taps. [*Pat¹* + *-er* repeatedly.]

pat·ter² (pat′ər) *n.* rapid speech, especially the fast, glib talk of a salesperson or the like. [Middle English *patren, patteren* originally, to recite pater nosters rapidly.]

pat·tern (pat′ərn) *n.* **1.** an arrangement or design of colors, shapes or lines: *The wallpaper was printed with a pretty flower pattern.* **2.** a guide or model used in making something: *Betty made the dress according to a pattern.* **3.** an example or model worthy of being followed or copied: *Tom was the pattern of politeness.* **4.** a set of actions or characteristics that does not change: *The scientist studied the pattern of the monkey's behavior.* —*v.t.* to make according to a pattern or example: *The author patterned his novel after a famous legend.*

pat·ty (pat′ē) *n. pl.,* **pat·ties. 1.** a small, round, flat piece of food: *a hamburger patty.* **2.** a small, flat piece of candy.

pau·ci·ty (pô′sə tē) *n.* **1.** a small number: *There was a*

paucity of people in the stadium. **2.** a scarcity; insufficiency: *That country has a paucity of land fit for farming.*

Paul, Saint (pôl) died A.D. 68?, the Christian Apostle to the Gentiles, who wrote several books of the New Testament.

Paul VI, 1897–1978, the pope from 1963 to 1978.

Paul Bunyan, in American folklore, a giant lumberjack known for his superhuman strength and courage.

paunch (pônch) *n. pl.,* **paunch·es.** the belly or stomach, especially when large and sticking out.

paunch·y (pôn′chē) *adj.,* **paunch·i·er, paunch·i·est.** having a large belly. —**paunch′i·ness,** *n.*

pau·per (pô′pər) *n.* a very poor person, especially one supported by charity.

pau·per·ism (pô′pə riz′əm) *n.* the state of being very poor; poverty.

pause (pôz) *v.i.* to stop for a short time: *The rider paused to let his horse rest.* —*n.* **1.** a short stop: *After a pause because of rain, the game continued.* **2.** a short stop or break in speaking, reading, or writing: *The speaker continued his speech, after a pause for applause.* **3.** *Music.* a sign (⌒ or ⌣) placed above or below a note or rest to show that it is to be held longer.

pa·vane (pə vän′, pə van′) *n.* **1.** a slow, stately dance of the sixteenth century. **2.** the music for this dance.

pave (pāv) *v.t.,* **paved, pav·ing.** to cover (a road or other surface) with pavement: *It took the men three days to pave the driveway.*

to pave the way. to prepare or lead the way; make progress easier: *His research paved the way for the discoveries of later scientists.*

pave·ment (pāv′mənt) *n.* **1.** a covering or surface of concrete, asphalt, brick, or similar material, as for a street, road, or sidewalk. **2.** the material used to make such a covering or surface. **3.** a sidewalk.

pa·vil·ion (pə vil′yən) *n.* **1.** an ornamental, often open building used for exhibition, entertainment, recreation, or shelter, as in a park or at a fair: *They went to a concert in the pavilion.* **2.** a large tent, often with a pointed top. **3.** one of a group of related buildings, as of a hospital. **4.** a projecting part of a building, often elaborately decorated.

pav·ing (pā′ving) *n.* **1.** a paved surface; pavement. **2.** the material used for pavement.

Pav·lov, Ivan (pav′lov) 1849–1936, Russian physiologist.

Pav·lo·va, Anna (pav lō′və) 1882–1931, Russian ballerina.

paw (pô) *n.* the foot of a four-footed animal having nails or claws. —*v.t.* **1.** to strike or scrape (something) with the paws or hooves: *The angry bull pawed the ground.* **2.** to touch or handle roughly, clumsily, or in too familiar a manner.

pawl (pôl) *n.* a catch or bar on a pivot that catches the teeth of a ratchet wheel, allowing the wheel to revolve in only one direction.

pawn¹ (pôn) *v.t.* to leave (something valuable) with a lender, especially a pawnbroker, as a pledge to repay a loan. —*n.* something left as a pledge to repay a loan. [Old French *pan* a piece of cloth; later, a pledge, security.]

at; āpe; cär; end; mē; it; īce; hot; ōld; fôrk; wood; fōōl; oil; out; up; turn; sing; thin; **this**; hw in white; zh in treasure. The symbol ə stands for the sound of **a** in about, e in taken, i in pencil, o in lemon, and u in circus.

pawn² (pôn) *n.* **1.** *Chess.* any of the sixteen chess pieces of lowest value, eight to each player. A pawn is able to move only one square forward at a time (or two squares on its first move) and captures by moving one square diagonally. **2.** a person or thing used by someone for personal gain or advantage: *His friends were only pawns for his ambition to become rich.* [Old French *paon, peon.*]

Pawn²

pawn·bro·ker (pôn′brō′kər) *n.* a person whose business is lending money at interest in exchange for articles of personal property left as security.

Paw·nee (pô nē′) *n. pl.,* **Paw·nees** or **Paw·nee. 1.** a member of any of a group of North American Indian tribes formerly living in Nebraska, now living in Oklahoma. **2.** the language of the Pawnees.

pawn·shop (pôn′shop′) *n.* a pawnbroker's shop.

paw·paw (pô′pô) another spelling of **papaw.**

Paw·tuck·et (pô tuk′it) *n.* a city in northeastern Rhode Island. Pop. (1970), 76,984.

pay (pā) *v.,* **paid** or *(def. 7)* **payed, pay·ing.** —*v.t.* **1.** to give (money) in return for services or goods: *We paid fifteen dollars to have the radio fixed.* **2.** to give money to in return for services or goods: *I paid the saleslady for the dress.* **3.** to give money in order to settle: *to pay a bill, to pay a fine.* **4.** to give as a return: *This job pays ninety dollars a week.* **5.** to be profitable to or worthwhile for: *It will pay him to plan now for the future.* **6.** to give or make: *to pay a compliment. John paid a visit to his great aunt.* **7.** to slacken or let out (a rope or line). —*v.i.* **1.** to give something in making a purchase or settling a debt; make payment. **2.** to be profitable or worthwhile: *It pays to eat a balanced diet.* —*n.* something given in return for services or goods: *The workers threatened to strike if the company did not meet their demands for higher pay.* —*adj.* operated by or made available for use by the deposit of a coin or coins: *Joan asked where she could find the nearest pay telephone.*

to pay back. to return or repay: *Fred paid back the money Jim had lent him.*

to pay off. a. to pay all that is owed; pay in full: *to pay off a debt.* **b.** to get even with.

to pay up. to pay all that is owed.

pay·a·ble (pā′ə bəl) *adj.* **1.** to be paid; due: *The bill is payable within ninety days.* **2.** that can be paid: *He made the check payable to the owner of the store.*

pay·day (pā′dā′) *n.* the day on which wages are paid: *Payday in that company is every other Friday.*

pay·ee (pā ē′) *n.* a person to whom money has been or is to be paid.

pay·er (pā′ər) *n.* a person who pays or is responsible for paying something, as a bill.

pay·load (pā′lōd′) *n.* **1.** a cargo or part of a cargo that produces profit. **2.** in a rocket, aircraft, or spacecraft, anything carried in addition to what is essential to the operation of the craft: *The rocket carried a payload of scientific instruments for collecting data.* **3.** the warhead of a guided or ballistic missile.

pay·mas·ter (pā′mas′tər) *n.* a person in charge of paying wages or salaries.

pay·ment (pā′mənt) *n.* **1.** the act of paying: *The company required that payment be made on time.* **2.** something that is paid: *The man received little payment for his work.* **3.** a reward or punishment: *The harsh sentence was just payment for his crime.*

pay·off (pā′ôf′) *n.* **1.** a payment, as of wages. **2.** a reward or punishment. **3.** *Informal.* a climax or outcome, as of a story or series of events.

pay·roll (pā′rōl′) *also,* **pay roll.** *n.* **1.** a list of employees to be paid, with the amount that each is to receive. **2.** the total amount of money to be paid to employees.

Pb, the symbol for lead. [Latin *plumbum.*]

p.c. 1. percent. **2.** post card. **3.** petty cash.

pct., percent.

pd., paid.

Pd, the symbol for palladium.

P.D., Police Department.

pea (pē) *n. pl.,* **peas** or *(archaic)* **pease. 1.** the round, usually green seed of a pod-bearing plant, eaten as a vegetable. **2.** the plant bearing this seed.

peace (pēs) *n.* **1.** freedom from war: *a time of peace.* **2.** an agreement, treaty, or settlement to end a war or hostilities. **3.** freedom from lawlessness or other strife; public order: *Law officers were assigned to keep the peace.* **4.** calmness; tranquility: *the peace and quiet of the country.* **5.** freedom from fear or worry: *peace of mind.*

at peace. free from war or other strife.

to hold one's peace or **to keep one's peace.** to be or keep silent.

peace·a·ble (pē′sə bəl) *adj.* **1.** liking peace; avoiding strife and disturbance. **2.** characterized by peace; peaceful: *The king had a long and peaceable reign.* —**peace′a·ble·ness,** *n.* —**peace′a·bly,** *adv.*

Peace Corps, a U.S. government agency that trains and sends volunteer workers to aid emerging countries.

peace·ful (pēs′fəl) *adj.* **1.** free from war, strife, or other disturbance. **2.** not warlike or quarrelsome: *to decide a dispute by peaceful means.* **3.** calm; tranquil; serene: *a peaceful atmosphere.* —**peace′ful·ly,** *adv.* —**peace′ful·ness,** *n.*

peace·mak·er (pēs′mā′kər) *n.* a person who brings about or tries to bring about peace between others.

peace pipe, a tobacco pipe with a long decorated stem, used by North American Indians on ceremonial occasions as a symbol of peace. Also, **calumet.**

peace·time (pēs′tīm′) *n.* a period when a nation is not at war. —*adj.* of, for, or characteristic of such a period: *a peacetime army.*

peach (pēch) *n. pl.,* **peach·es. 1.** a sweet, juicy fruit, having a large rough stone or pit and a velvety yellow or yellow-red skin. **2.** the tree bearing this fruit, having pink flowers. **3.** a yellowish-pink color. —*adj.* having the color peach. —**peach′like′,** *adj.*

pea·cock (pē′kok′) *n. pl.,* **pea·cocks** or **pea·cock. 1.** the male of the peafowl, having a fan-shaped crest, shiny blue feathers on the head, neck, and body, and a train of bright green feathers covered with large eye-like spots. When the train is raised and spread, it is fan-shaped. **2.** any peafowl. **3.** a vain and showy person.

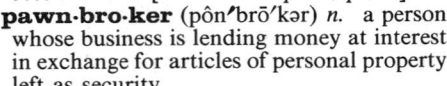

Peacock

peacock blue, a bright greenish-blue color.

pea·fowl (pē′foul′) *n. pl.,* **pea·fowls** or **pea·fowl.** a pheasant of Asia and Africa, noted for the brilliant ornamental feathers of the male.

pea·hen (pē′hen′) *n.* a female peafowl.

pea jacket, a short, double-breasted coat of thick woolen cloth, worn especially by sailors.

peak (pēk) *n.* **1.** the pointed top of a mountain or hill. **2.** a mountain having a pointed top, usually standing alone. **3.** a sharp, tapering, or projecting point or end. **4.** the highest point or greatest level: *Traffic reaches its peak during rush hour. He was at the peak of his career.* **5.** the brim of a cap that sticks out.

peaked¹ (pēkt) *adj.* having or ending in a peak; pointed: *a peaked roof.* [*Peak* + *-ed².*]

peak·ed² (pē′kid) *adj.* pale and thin; sickly: *He looked rather peaked after his illness.* [Of uncertain origin.]

peal (pēl) *n.* **1.** a loud, long sound or series of sounds: *a peal of thunder, a peal of laughter.* **2.** a set of bells tuned to one another. —*v.i., v.t.* to sound or ring out in a peal or peals: *The church bells pealed on Sunday morning.*

pea·nut (pē′nut′) *n.* **1.** the nutlike seed of a plant related to the pea, that develops in an underground pod and has a thin brownish skin. **2.** such a pod, usually containing two of these seeds. **3.** the plant bearing this pod.

peanut butter, a soft, creamy spread made from ground, roasted peanuts.

peanut oil, an oil pressed from peanuts, used in cooking and in the manufacture of margarine.

Peanut plant

pear (per) *n.* **1.** a bell-shaped fruit having a firm, sweet, juicy flesh and a smooth yellow, brown, or reddish skin. **2.** the tree bearing this fruit.

pearl (purl) *n.* **1.** a rounded, lustrous, usually white or cream-colored, gem. Pearls are formed inside the shells of certain kinds of oysters or other similar shellfish. **2.** something that looks like a pearl. **3.** a person or thing like a pearl in value: *pearls of wisdom.* **4.** see **mother-of-pearl.** **5.** see **pearl gray.** —*adj.* **1.** of, relating to, or like a pearl or pearls. **2.** having the color pearl gray.

pearl gray, a clear, pale, bluish-gray color.

Pearl Harbor, the principal U.S. naval base in the Pacific, near Honolulu on the island of Oahu, Hawaii. It was bombed by the Japanese on December 7, 1941.

pearl·y (pur′lē) *adj.,* **pearl·i·er, pearl·i·est. 1.** resembling a pearl or pearls: *pearly teeth.* **2.** adorned with pearls or mother-of-pearl.

Pea·ry, Robert Edwin (pēr′ē) 1856–1920, U.S. Arctic explorer.

peas·ant (pez′ənt) *n.* a member of a class of small farmers or farm laborers.

peas·ant·ry (pez′ən trē) *n.* peasants as a group.

pease (pēz) *Archaic.* a plural of **pea.**

peat (pēt) *n.* rotted plant matter found in bogs and swamps. Peat is used as a fertilizer and is burned as fuel.

peat moss, a pale green moss that grows in swamps and bogs and is the major source of peat.

peb·ble (peb′əl) *n.* a small, usually round, stone that is worn smooth by water or sand. —*v.t.,* **peb·bled, peb·bling. 1.** to cover with pebbles: *to pebble a walk.* **2.** to give a rough, uneven surface to (leather or paper). —**peb′bly,** *adj.*

pe·can (pi kän′, pi kan′) *n.* **1.** a sweet nut having a thin, brittle shell. **2.** the large tree bearing this nut.

pec·ca·dil·lo (pek′ə dil′ō) *n. pl.,* **pec·ca·dil·loes** or **pec·ca·dil·los.** a slight fault or sin.

pec·ca·ry (pek′ər ē) *n. pl.,* **pec·ca·ries.** a wild, piglike animal found from the southern United States to Argentina, having coarse, bristly hair and straight tusks that point downward.

Peccary

peck¹ (pek) *n.* **1.** a unit of measure for fruit, vegetables, grain, and other dry things, equal to eight quarts or one-fourth of a bushel. **2.** a container holding or measuring a peck. **3.** *Informal.* a great

deal: *The boy got into a peck of trouble when he broke the window.* [Old French *pek.*]

peck² (pek) *v.t.* **1.** to strike (something) with the beak in a short, rapid movement: *The parakeet pecked the bars of its cage.* **2.** to make by striking with the beak or a pointed tool: *The chick pecked a hole through the box.* **3.** to strike at and pick up with the beak: *The hen pecked the grains of corn.* —*v.i.* to strike or try to strike with the beak in a short, rapid movement: *The parrot pecked at my finger.* —*n.* **1.** a short, rapid stroke made with the beak or a pointed tool. **2.** a hole or mark made by such a stroke. **3.** *Informal.* a quick, light kiss: *He greeted her with a peck on the cheek.* [Possibly a form of *pick¹.*]

pecking order 1. a pattern of social organization in a group of birds, especially poultry, in which each bird has a definite rank determined by aggressiveness. Each bird pecks at those birds that are weaker than it is, and is pecked at by those birds that are stronger. **2.** any human social organization having definite levels of rank, especially one in which rank is determined by aggressive behavior.

pec·tin (pek′tin) *n.* any of several substances that cause jams and jellies to set, found especially in certain ripe fruits.

pec·to·ral (pek′tər əl) *adj.* of, in, or on the chest. —*n.* a pectoral organ, such as a muscle.

pe·cu·liar (pi kyōōl′yər) *adj.* **1.** strange or unusual; odd: *She has many peculiar habits.* **2.** belonging to a certain person, group, place, or thing: *The koala bear is peculiar to Australia.* —**pe·cu′liar·ly,** *adv.*

pe·cu·li·ar·i·ty (pi kyōō′lē ar′ə tē) *n. pl.,* **pe·cu·li·ar·i·ties. 1.** a strange or unusual feature or characteristic. **2.** a special or particular characteristic: *A long tail is a peculiarity of that breed of dog.* **3.** the state or quality of being peculiar: *The peculiarity of her answer puzzled them.*

pe·cu·ni·ar·y (pi kyōō′nē er′ē) *adj.* of, relating to, or consisting of money: *a pecuniary reward.*

ped·a·gog·ic (ped′ə goj′ik) *adj.* of, relating to, or characteristic of a pedagogue or pedagogy. Also, **ped·a·gog·i·cal** (ped′ə goj′i kəl). —**ped′a·gog′i·cal·ly,** *adv.*

ped·a·gogue (ped′ə gog′) *also,* **ped·a·gog.** *n.* **1.** any teacher. **2.** a teacher who is pedantic and narrow-minded.

ped·a·go·gy (ped′ə goj′ē, ped′ə gō′jē) *n.* the art, science, or profession of teaching.

ped·al (ped′əl) *n.* **1.** a foot-operated part or lever that operates, moves, or controls a machine or part of a machine, as in a bicycle or automobile. **2.** a similar part or lever worked by the foot, that changes the sound of a musical instrument, as a piano. —*v.,* **ped·aled, ped·al·ing;** *also, British,* **ped·alled, ped·al·ling.** —*v.t.,* to work the pedals of; operate by working pedals: *to pedal a bicycle.* —*v.i.* to work or use a pedal or pedals: *to pedal slowly.* —*adj.* **1.** of or relating to a foot or the feet. **2.** of, relating to, or operated by a pedal or pedals.

ped·ant (ped′ənt) *n.* a person who presents his knowledge in a showy or dull manner, often placing too much emphasis on unimportant details and formal rules.

pe·dan·tic (pi dan′tik) *adj.* of, like, or characteristic of a pedant or pedantry: *a pedantic lecturer.* —**pe·dan′ti·cal·ly,** *adv.*

ped·ant·ry (ped′ən trē) *n. pl.,* **ped·ant·ries. 1.** a showy

at; āpe; cär; end; mē; it; īce; hot; ōld; fôrk; wood; fōōl; oil; out; up; turn; sing; thin; this; hw in white; zh in treasure. The symbol ə stands for the sound of a in about, e in taken, i in pencil, o in lemon, and u in circus.

display of knowledge or too much emphasis on unimportant details and formal rules. **2.** an instance of being pedantic.

ped·dle (ped′əl) *v.*, **ped·dled, ped·dling.** —*v.t.*, **1.** to sell (goods), usually in small quantities, by traveling from place to place: *The boy peddled vegetables from door to door.* **2.** to deal out or distribute: *to peddle rumors.* —*v.i.* to travel from place to place offering goods for sale.

ped·dler (ped′lər) *also,* **ped·lar.** *n.* a person who peddles goods.

-pede *combining form* foot; feet: *centipede.*

ped·es·tal (ped′əs təl) *n.* **1.** a support at the base of a column, statue, or similar upright structure. **2.** any base or supporting structure, as for a tall lamp or vase.

   on a pedestal. in a position or condition of high, often exaggerated, regard or admiration: *The little boy put his father on a pedestal.*

ped·es·tri·an (pə des′trē ən) *n.* a person who travels on foot; walker. —*adj.* **1.** of or for people traveling on foot: *a pedestrian path.* **2.** lacking originality, imagination, or excitement; commonplace or dull: *a pedestrian style of writing.*

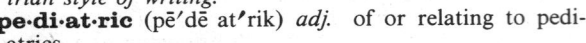

Pedestal

pe·di·at·ric (pē′dē at′rik) *adj.* of or relating to pediatrics.

pe·di·a·tri·cian (pē′dē ə trish′ən) *n.* a doctor who specializes in pediatrics.

pe·di·at·rics (pē′dē at′riks) *n.,pl.* the branch of medicine that deals with the care of babies and children and the treatment of their diseases. ▲ used with a singular verb.

ped·i·cel (ped′i səl) *also,* **ped·i·cle** (ped′i kəl). *n.* a small stem, especially one supporting a single flower in a flower cluster.

ped·i·cure (ped′i kyoor′) *n.* a beauty treatment of the feet, especially a trimming and polishing of the toenails.

ped·i·gree (ped′ə grē′) *n.* **1.** a line of ancestors; descent; lineage. **2.** a detailed record or list of ancestry or descent, especially of an animal: *the pedigree of a champion dog.*

ped·i·greed (ped′ə grēd′) *adj.* having a recorded or known pedigree: *a pedigreed cat.*

ped·i·ment (ped′ə mənt) *n.* **1.** a triangular part on the front of a building in the Greek architectural style. **2.** a similar ornamental part, as over a door, mantel, or window.

ped·lar (ped′lər) another spelling of **peddler.**

pe·dom·e·ter (pi dom′ə tər) *n.* an instrument that measures the distance covered in walking by counting the number of steps taken and multiplying by the length of a single step.

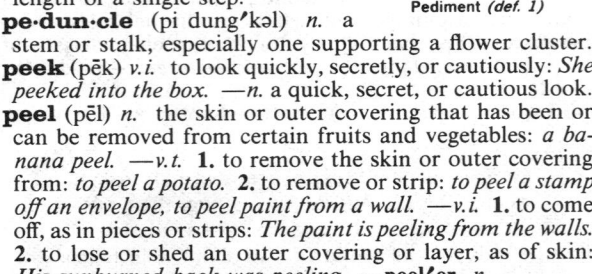

Pediment *(def. 1)*

pe·dun·cle (pi dung′kəl) *n.* a stem or stalk, especially one supporting a flower cluster.

peek (pēk) *v.i.* to look quickly, secretly, or cautiously: *She peeked into the box.* —*n.* a quick, secret, or cautious look.

peel (pēl) *n.* the skin or outer covering that has been or can be removed from certain fruits and vegetables: *a banana peel.* —*v.t.* **1.** to remove the skin or outer covering from: *to peel a potato.* **2.** to remove or strip: *to peel a stamp off an envelope, to peel paint from a wall.* —*v.i.* **1.** to come off, as in pieces or strips: *The paint is peeling from the walls.* **2.** to lose or shed an outer covering or layer, as of skin: *His sunburned back was peeling.* —**peel′er,** *n.*

   to keep one's eyes peeled. *Informal.* to be watchful; keep alert.

peep¹ (pēp) *v.i.* **1.** to look secretly, cautiously, or quickly, as through a narrow opening or from a hiding place; peek: *to peep through a crack in a wall.* **2.** to come slowly or partly into view: *The moon peeped through the clouds.* —*n.* **1.** a secret, cautious, or quick look. **2.** the first appearance: *the peep of dawn.* [Possibly a form of *peek.*]

peep² (pēp) *n.* **1.** a short, sharp sound, such as that made by a young bird; cheep. **2.** any sound; utterance: *Not another peep out of you!* —*v.i.* to utter a peep. [Imitative of this sound.]

peep·er¹ (pē′pər) *n.* **1.** a person who peeps or spies. **2.** *Informal.* an eye. [*Peep¹* + *-er¹.*]

peep·er² (pē′pər) *n.* any of several tree frogs that make a shrill, peeping noise. [*Peep²* + *-er¹.*]

peep·hole (pēp′hōl′) *n.* a small hole or opening, especially in a door, through which one may look.

peer¹ (pēr) *n.* a person who is equal to another, as in status, social class, age, or ability; equal: *He will be tried by a jury of his peers. As a pitcher, he has few peers.* **2.** in Great Britain, a member of one of the five degrees of nobility: duke, marquis, earl, viscount, or baron. **3.** any titled member of the nobility. [Old French *per.*]

peer² (pēr) *v.i.* **1.** to look closely or searchingly, as in an effort to see clearly: *We tried to peer through the darkness.* **2.** to come into view; be partly visible: *The sun peered over the mountain.* [Possibly a form of *appear.*]

peer·age (pēr′ij) *n.* **1.** the rank or dignity of a peer. **2.** the peers of a country thought of as a group. **3.** a book listing the peers of a country and their genealogies.

peer·ess (pēr′is) *n. pl.*, **peer·ess·es. 1.** the wife or widow of a peer. **2.** a woman who holds the rank of a peer in her own right.

peer·less (pēr′lis) *adj.* without equal; matchless: *a peerless performance.* —**peer′less·ly,** *adv.* —**peer′less·ness,** *n.*

peeve (pēv) *v.t.*, **peeved, peev·ing.** to annoy; irritate; vex. —*n.* a cause of annoyance; grievance: *Rude people are one of my biggest peeves.*

pee·vish (pē′vish) *adj.* **1.** irritable and ill-tempered; cranky: *The baby always gets very peevish when he does not feel well.* **2.** showing or marked by annoyance or irritation: *a peevish look.* —**pee′vish·ly,** *adv.* —**pee′vish·ness,** *n.*

peg (peg) *n.* **1.** a piece of wood, metal, or another hard substance that can be fitted or driven into a surface, as to fasten parts together, hang something on, or serve as a marker. **2.** a wooden, plastic, or metal pin in a stringed musical instrument that fastens and controls the tension of a string. **3.** a step or degree: *Ever since he lied to me, he has come down a peg in my estimation.* **4.** *Informal.* a throw, as in baseball. —*v.t.*, **pegged, peg·ging. 1.** to fasten or mark with a peg or pegs. **2.** *Informal.* to throw. **3.** *Informal.* to recognize or classify; identify: *I pegged him as a cheat from the very beginning.*

Peg·a·sus (peg′ə səs) *n. Greek Mythology.* a winged horse, the steed of the Muses.

P.E.I., Prince Edward Island.

Pei·ping (pā′ping′, bā′ping′) *n.* see **Peking.**

pe·jo·ra·tive (pi jôr′ə tiv, pi jor′ə tiv, pej′ə rā′tiv) *adj.* having an unfavorable meaning or effect; disparaging: *to use a word in a pejorative sense.*

Pe·kin·ese (pē′kə nēz′) *n. pl.*, **Pe·kin·ese.** another spelling of **Pekingese.**

Pe·king (pē′king′) *n.* the capital of the People's Republic of China, in the northeastern part of the country, formerly known as Peiping. Pop. (1968 est.), 7,000,000. Also, **Beijing.**

Pe·king·ese (pē′kə nēz′, pē′king ēz′) *also,* **Pe·kin·ese.** *n. pl.*, **Pe·king·ese. 1.** a small dog having a wrinkled, flat face, bulging eyes, and a long, silky coat. **2.** a person who was born or is living in Peking. **3.** the Chinese dialect spoken in Peking. —*adj.* of or relating to Peking or its people.

Peking man, an extinct primitive man whose fossil remains were found near Peking, China.

pe·koe (pē′kō) *n.* a superior grade of black tea from India, Ceylon, and Java, made from the smallest tea leaves.

pelf (pelf) *n.* money or wealth, especially if dishonestly obtained.

pel·i·can (pel′i kən) *n.* any of various web-footed water birds having a large pouch beneath the bill that is used for storing fish. Most pelicans have chiefly white feathers.

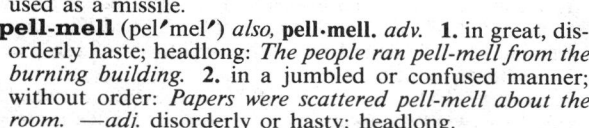

Pelican

pel·la·gra (pə lag′rə) *n.* a disease caused by a lack of niacin in the diet, characterized by diarrhea, skin eruptions, and nervous disorders.

pel·let (pel′it) *n.* **1.** a small ball, as of food, medicine, or paper. **2.** a bullet or piece of shot. **3.** a ball, usually of stone, formerly used as a missile.

pell-mell (pel′mel′) *also,* **pell·mell.** *adv.* **1.** in great, disorderly haste; headlong: *The people ran pell-mell from the burning building.* **2.** in a jumbled or confused manner; without order: *Papers were scattered pell-mell about the room.* —*adj.* disorderly or hasty; headlong.

pel·lu·cid (pə lōō′sid) *adj.* **1.** clear, as glass; transparent: *a pellucid stream.* **2.** easy to understand; lucid: *a pellucid writing style.*

Pel·o·pon·ne·sian War (pel′ə pə nē′zhən) the war between Athens and Sparta from 431 to 404 B.C., ending in victory for Sparta.

Pel·o·pon·ne·sus (pel′ə pə nē′səs) *n.* a peninsula in southern Greece between the Ionian and Aegean Seas. —**Pel′o·pon·ne′sian,** *adj., n.*

pelt[1] (pelt) *v.t.* **1.** to attack or strike repeatedly: *The children pelted each other with snowballs.* **2.** to beat against continuously or repeatedly: *Hail pelted the roof.* **3.** to throw or hurl: *The boys pelted stones against the wall.* —*v.i.* to beat or strike heavily or continuously: *The rain pelted against the windows.* —*n.* a hard blow, as from something thrown. [Of uncertain origin.]

pelt[2] (pelt) *n.* a skin of an animal with its fur or hair, especially when removed to be used for making garments or other items. [Possibly from earlier *peltry*.]

pel·vic (pel′vik) *adj.* of or relating to the pelvis.

pel·vis (pel′vis) *n. pl.,* **pel·vis·es** or **pel·ves** (pel′vēz). **1.** the large, basin-shaped ring of bone that protects and supports the organs in the lower part of the human body, consisting of the sacrum, the coccyx, and the hipbones. **2.** a similar structure in other animals. [Latin *pēlvis* basin; referring to the resemblance of this bone to a basin.]

Ilium

Ischium   Pubis

Pelvis

pem·mi·can (pem′i kən) *also,* **pem·i·can.** *n.* lean meat that is dried, pounded, and mixed with melted fat to form a paste and pressed into cakes.

pen[1] (pen) *n.* **1.** any of various instruments for writing or drawing with ink, such as a fountain pen or a ball-point pen. **2.** writing style or ability: *That author has a satiric pen.* —*v.t.,* **penned, pen·ning.** to write with a pen: *to pen a letter.* [Old French *penne* a quill, from Latin *penna* feather; because the first pens were made from feathers.]

pen[2] (pen) *n.* **1.** a small enclosed area used to confine animals. **2.** the animals confined to such an area. **3.** any of various small enclosed areas, as a playpen or a bull pen. —*v.t.,* **penned** or **pent, pen·ning.** to confine in a pen or other small area. [Old English *penn.*]

pen[3] (pen) *n. Slang.* see **penitentiary.**

pe·nal (pēn′əl) *adj.* **1.** of or relating to punishment, especially legal punishment: *penal laws.* **2.** being or serving as punishment: *penal labor.* **3.** punishable: *a penal offense.*

pe·nal·ize (pēn′əl īz′) *v.t.,* **pe·nal·ized, pe·nal·iz·ing.** to subject to a penalty or punishment.

pen·al·ty (pen′əl tē) *n. pl.,* **pen·al·ties.** **1.** a punishment established or imposed for violating a law or regulation. **2.** an unpleasant or painful result of an action or condition. **3.** *Sports.* a disadvantage or punishment imposed on a player or team for breaking the rules.

penalty box, an area alongside a hockey rink where a player must sit for a certain amount of time as a penalty for breaking a rule.

pen·ance (pen′əns) *n.* **1.** a punishment, usually self-imposed, undergone to show or express sorrow and obtain forgiveness for a sin or offense. **2.** in some Christian churches, a sacrament that includes sorrow for and confession of sin, acceptance of punishment, and absolution.

Pe·nang (pi nang′) *n.* **1.** an island off the western coast of the Malay Peninsula. **2.** a port city on this island, formerly known as George Town. Pop. (1970), 270,019.

pence (pens) *British.* the plural of **penny.**

pen·chant (pen′chənt) *n.* a strong liking or inclination: *Bill has a penchant for gardening.*

pen·cil (pen′səl) *n.* **1.** a marking, drawing, or writing implement, usually consisting of a stick of graphite, chalk, or similar substance enclosed in a case of wood, metal, or plastic. **2.** something like a pencil in shape or use, especially an implement having a cosmetic or medicinal use. —*v.t.,* **pen·ciled, pen·cil·ing;** *also, British,* **pen·cilled, pen·cil·ling.** to write, draw, mark, or color with a pencil.

pend·ant (pen′dənt) *n.* an ornamental object, such as a jewel, that hangs from something else. —*adj.* another spelling of **pendent.**

pend·ent (pen′dənt) *adj.* **1.** suspended; hanging: *pendent glass beads.* **2.** jutting out; overhanging. **3.** undecided or unsettled; pending. —*n.* another spelling of **pendant.**

pend·ing (pen′ding) *adj.* **1.** not yet decided or settled; unresolved: *The decision on that question is still pending.* **2.** about to happen; impending; imminent: *a pending disaster.* —*prep.* while awaiting; until: *We postponed our picnic pending a change in the weather.*

pen·du·lous (pen′jə ləs) *adj.* **1.** hanging, especially in a loose or drooping manner: *a pendulous branch of a tree.* **2.** swinging: *a pendulous motion.*

pen·du·lum (pen′jə ləm) *n.* a suspended weight or other body that can be set in motion to swing back and forth from a fixed point, often used to regulate the movement of a clock.

Pe·nel·o·pe (pə nel′ə pē) *n. Greek and Roman Legend.* the wife of Ulysses, noted for her faithfulness during her husband's long absence.

at; āpe; cär; end; mē; it; īce; hot; ōld; fôrk; wood; fōōl; oil; out; up; turn; sing; thin; this; hw in white; zh in treasure. The symbol ə stands for the sound of **a** in about, **e** in taken, **i** in pencil, **o** in lemon, and **u** in circus.

P

pen·e·tra·ble (pen′ə trə bəl) *adj.* that can be penetrated. —**pen′e·tra·bil′i·ty,** *n.*

pen·e·trate (pen′ə trāt′) *v.,* **pen·e·trat·ed, pen·e·trat·ing.** —*v.t.* **1.** to pass into or through, especially by force or with difficulty: *The lance penetrated the knight's shield.* **2.** to seep or spread through: *The rain penetrated my jacket.* **3.** to discover the meaning of; understand: *Science attempts to penetrate the mysteries of nature.* —*v.i.* to pass or force a way into or through something.

pen·e·tra·tion (pen′ə trā′shən) *n.* **1.** the act or power of penetrating. **2.** the degree or extent to which something penetrates. **3.** keenness of mind; insight; discernment.

pen·guin (pen′gwin, peng′gwin) *n.* a sea bird that cannot fly, native to Antarctica and to the coastlines of southern continents. Penguins have webbed feet, dense feathers that are usually black or gray on the back and white on the chest, stomach, and legs, and wings that resemble flippers and are used for swimming.

pen·i·cil·lin (pen′ə sil′in) *n.* a powerful antibiotic made from certain penicillium molds, used in the treatment of a wide variety of bacterial infections.

pen·i·cil·li·um (pen′ə sil′ē əm) *n. pl.,* **pen·i·cil·li·ums** or **pen·i·cil·li·a** (pen′ə sil′ē ə). any of a group of fungi commonly found as a blue-green mold on bread, cheese, and other foods.

Penguin

pen·in·su·la (pə nin′sə lə, pə nin′syə lə) *n.* a body of land almost entirely surrounded by water, that projects out from a larger land mass. Italy is a peninsula.

pen·in·su·lar (pə nin′sə lər, pə nin′syə lər) *adj.* of, relating to, or like a peninsula.

pe·nis (pē′nis) *n. pl.,* **pe·nis·es** or **pe·nes** (pē′nēz). the male organ of urination and sex.

pen·i·tence (pen′ə təns) *n.* the state of being penitent; repentance.

pen·i·tent (pen′ə tənt) *adj.* feeling or showing sorrow or regret for sin or wrongdoing; repentant: *He wrote a penitent letter apologizing for his rudeness.* —*n.* a person who is penitent, especially one who confesses his sin and receives the sacrament of penance. —**pen′i·tent·ly,** *adv.*

pen·i·ten·tial (pen′ə ten′shəl) *adj.* **1.** relating to or showing penitence or repentance. **2.** relating to penance.

pen·i·ten·tia·ry (pen′ə ten′shər ē) *n. pl.,* **pen·i·ten·tia·ries.** a prison, especially a state or federal prison, for persons convicted of major crimes. —*adj.* **1.** punishable by imprisonment in a penitentiary: *a penitentiary offense.* **2.** of or relating to penance.

pen·knife (pen′nīf′) *n. pl.,* **pen·knives** (pen′nīvz′). a small pocketknife, originally used for making or sharpening quill pens.

pen·man (pen′mən) *n. pl.,* **pen·men** (pen′mən). **1.** a writer; author. **2.** a person skilled in penmanship.

pen·man·ship (pen′mən ship′) *n.* **1.** the style or quality of handwriting. **2.** the art or skill of handwriting.

Penn, William (pen) 1644–1718, English Quaker leader and the founder of Pennsylvania.

Penn., Pennsylvania. Also, **Pa.**

pen name, a fictitious name under which an author writes; pseudonym.

pen·nant (pen′ənt) *n.* **1.** a long, usually triangular, flag, used especially as a school or team emblem or, on a ship, for signaling or identification. **2.** such a flag symbolizing a victory or championship, especially in professional baseball.

pen·ni·less (pen′ē lis) *adj.* having no money; very poor.

pen·non (pen′ən) *n.* **1.** a long, usually triangular, flag or streamer carried on the head of a knight's lance in the Middle Ages. **2.** any flag or banner.

Penn·syl·va·nia (pen′səl vān′yə) *n.* a state in the eastern United States. Capital, Harrisburg. Area, 45,333 sq. mi. Pop. (1970), 11,793,909. Abbreviations, **Pa., Penn.** —**Penn′syl·va′ni·an,** *adj., n.*

● **Pennsylvania,** usually translated "Penn's wood," is a combination of the Latin word for wooded land and the family name "Penn." King Charles II of England gave this name to the colony when he granted the land to William Penn.

Pennsylvania Dutch 1. the descendants of German immigrants who settled in Pennsylvania in the seventeenth and eighteenth centuries. **2.** a German dialect heavily mixed with English, spoken by these people.

pen·ny (pen′ē) *n. pl.,* **pen·nies** or *(def. 2)* **pence. 1.** a coin of the United States and Canada, equal to one cent or ¹/₁₀₀ of a dollar. **2.** a coin of the United Kingdom, equal to ¹/₁₀₀ of a pound, formerly equal to ¹/₁₂ of a shilling. **3.** a sum of money.

pen·ny·weight (pen′ē wāt′) *n.* a measure of weight equal to twenty-four grains or ¹/₂₀ of an ounce in troy weight.

pen·ny·wise (pen′ē wīz′) *adj.* cautious or thrifty in small matters.

to be penny-wise and pound-foolish. to be cautious or thrifty in small matters but wasteful in large ones.

pen·ny·worth (pen′ē wurth′) *n.* **1.** as much as can be bought for a penny. **2.** a small amount of anything.

pe·nol·o·gy (pē nol′ə jē) *n.* the study of the punishment and rehabilitation of criminals and the management of prisons.

pen·sion (pen′shən) *n.* a sum of money, other than wages, paid regularly by a former employer to a retired or disabled person who has fulfilled certain requirements or conditions. —*v.t.* **1.** to give a pension to. **2.** to retire or dismiss with a pension: *The company pensioned off employees at the age of sixty-five.*

pen·sion·er (pen′shə nər) *n.* a person who receives a pension.

pen·sive (pen′siv) *adj.* **1.** in deep and serious thought, often about matters of a sad nature: *The pensive man sat silently on the bench.* **2.** characterized by or showing deep, often sad, thoughtfulness: *a pensive look, a pensive mood.* —**pen′sive·ly,** *adv.* —**pen′sive·ness,** *n.*

pent (pent) *v.* a past tense and past participle of **pen².** —*adj.* closely confined; shut up.

penta- *combining form* five: pentagon.

pen·ta·gon (pen′tə gon′) *n.* **1.** a polygon with five sides and five angles. **2. the Pentagon.** a five-sided building in Arlington, Virginia, that is the headquarters of the U.S. Department of Defense.

pen·tag·o·nal (pen tag′ən əl) *adj.* having five sides and five angles; like a pentagon.

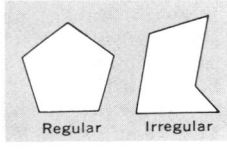

Regular   Irregular

Pentagons

pen·tam·e·ter (pen tam′ə tər) *n.* **1.** a line of verse consisting of five metrical feet. **2.** a verse composed of such lines. —*adj.* containing five metrical feet.

Pen·ta·teuch (pen′tə tōōk′, pen′tə tyōōk′) *n.* the first five books of the Old Testament.

pen·tath·lon (pen tath'lən) *n.* an athletic contest in which each contestant participates in five different events.

Pen·te·cost (pen'tə kôst') *n.* **1.** a Christian feast observed on the seventh Sunday after Easter, commemorating the descent of the Holy Ghost upon the Apostles. Also, **Whitsunday. 2.** another word for **Shavuoth.**

pent·house (pent'hous') *n. pl.,* **pent·hous·es** (pent'hou'-ziz). an apartment or other dwelling built on the roof of a building.

pent-up (pent'up') *adj.* not expressed or released; held in; restrained: *pent-up feelings, pent-up hostility.*

pe·nult (pē'nult, pi nult') *n.* the next to last syllable in a word.

pe·nul·ti·mate (pi nul'tə mit) *adj.* **1.** next to the last. **2.** of, relating to, or occurring on the penult of a word: *a penultimate stress.* —*n.* the next to last.

pe·num·bra (pi num'brə) *n. pl.,* **pe·num·brae** (pi num'-brē) or **pe·num·bras. 1.** in an eclipse, the partial shadow between the area of total eclipse and the area of complete illumination. **2.** the grayish fringe around the dark central portion of a sunspot. **3.** the partially darkened area surrounding the completely dark central region of a shadow.

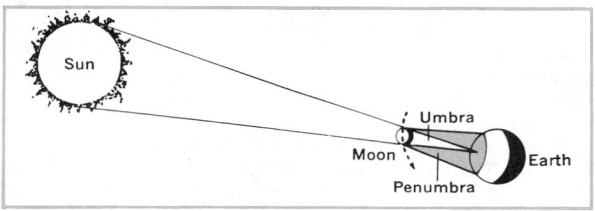

Penumbra

pe·nu·ri·ous (pi noor'ē əs, pi nyoor'ē əs) *adj.* **1.** greatly reluctant to spend or part with money; stingy; miserly. **2.** very poor; poverty-stricken: *a penurious existence.* —**pe·nu'ri·ous·ly,** *adv.* —**pe·nu'ri·ous·ness,** *n.*

pen·u·ry (pen'yər ē) *n.* extreme poverty.

pe·on (pē'on) *n.* an unskilled worker or farm laborer in Latin America or the southwestern United States, especially one who is forced to work in exchange for the payment of debts.

pe·on·age (pē'ə nij) *n.* **1.** the condition of being a peon. **2.** the system or practice of forcing people to work in exchange for the payment of debts.

pe·o·ny (pē'ə nē) *n. pl.,* **pe·o·nies. 1.** a large, showy, pink, red, or white flower of any of a group of hardy plants. **2.** the plant bearing this flower, widely grown in gardens.

peo·ple (pē'pəl) *n. pl.,* **peo·ple** or *(def. 2)* **peo·ples. 1.** men, women, and children; persons: *This theater can seat 500 people.* **2.** the body of persons making up a nation, race, tribe, or group: *the Israeli people, primitive peoples, the peoples of Europe.* **3.** the body of citizens of a state or other political unit: *Congressmen are elected by the people.* **4.** the body or mass of common persons. **5.** persons in relation to a superior, such as the subjects of a ruler: *The king loved his people.* **6.** human beings as distinguished from animals: *Distemper is not a disease that affects people.* **7.** *Informal.* one's family; relatives. —*v.t.,* **peo·pled, peo·pling.** to fill with people; inhabit; populate: *A great number of human beings people the earth.*

Pe·o·ri·a (pē ôr'ē ə) *n.* a city in north-central Illinois. Pop. (1970), 126,963.

pep (pep) *n.* liveliness and high spirits; energy: *She is always full of pep in the morning.* —*v.t.,* **pepped, pep·ping.** to make lively or cheerful; fill with energy: *The good news pepped him up.* [Short for *pepper.*]

pep·per (pep'ər) *n.* **1.** a hot, pungent spice consisting of berries, either whole or ground, of a tropical American plant. Black pepper is made from whole dried berries that are ground. White pepper is made from the dried, ground seeds of the berries with the outer coat and pulp removed. **2.** the plant bearing these berries. **3.** the red or green, sweet or hot fruit of any of a group of plants. Peppers may be eaten either raw or cooked or may be ground into spices. **4.** the plant bearing this fruit. **5.** a hot spice made from hot red peppers; cayenne. —*v.t.* **1.** to sprinkle or season with pepper. **2.** to cover or sprinkle: *The tweed fabric was peppered with flecks of red and blue.* **3.** to shower or pelt with bullets or other small objects.

pep·per·corn (pep'ər kôrn') *n.* the dried fruit of the black pepper, used as a spice, either whole or ground.

pepper mill, a utensil used to grind peppercorns.

pep·per·mint (pep'ər mint') *n.* **1.** a fragrant plant related to the mint, having small purple or white flowers and tooth-edged leaves. **2.** the oil obtained from this plant, having a minty aroma and taste and used as a flavoring, especially in candy, chewing gum, and toothpaste. **3.** a candy or lozenge flavored with peppermint oil.

pep·per·y (pep'ər ē) *adj.* **1.** of, like, or relating to pepper; pungent: *a peppery taste.* **2.** sharp or fiery; stinging: *a peppery speech, peppery writing.* **3.** hot-tempered; testy. —**pep'per·i·ness,** *n.*

pep·py (pep'ē) *adj.,* **pep·pi·er, pep·pi·est.** *Informal.* full of pep or energy; lively. —**pep'pi·ness,** *n.*

Peppermint plant

pep·sin (pep'sin) *n.* **1.** an enzyme that is produced in the stomach and aids in the digestion of eggs, fish, meat, and other proteins. **2.** a medicine used to relieve indigestion, containing pepsin taken from the stomach of certain animals.

pep talk, a speech given for the purpose of increasing enthusiasm or confidence or boosting morale: *The coach gave the team a pep talk before the big game.*

pep·tic (pep'tik) *adj.* **1.** of, relating to, or aiding digestion. **2.** of or relating to pepsin or other digestive secretions, or resulting from their action: *a peptic ulcer.*

per (pur; *unstressed* pər) *prep.* **1.** for each: *He earns $120 per week.* **2.** by means of; through. **3.** according to: *per instructions.*

per·ad·ven·ture (pur'əd ven'chər) *adv. Archaic.* perhaps; maybe.

per·am·bu·late (pər am'byə lāt') *v.,* **per·am·bu·lat·ed, per·am·bu·lat·ing.** —*v.t.* to walk through, around, or about (a place), especially so as to survey, inspect, or examine: *The tourists perambulated the estate.* —*v.i.* to walk about; stroll. —**per·am'bu·la'tion,** *n.*

per·am·bu·la·tor (pər am'byə lā'tər) *n.* a baby carriage.

per an·num (pər an'əm) for each year; per year; annually: *His income is over $12,000 per annum.* [Latin *per annum.*]

---

at; āpe; cär; end; mē; it; īce; hot; ōld; fôrk; wood; fōōl; oil; out; up; turn; sing; thin; this; hw in white; zh in treasure. The symbol ə stands for the sound of a in about, e in taken, i in pencil, o in lemon, and u in circus.

per·cale (pər kāl′) *n.* a closely woven, lightweight cotton fabric with a smooth, dull finish, used especially for sheets, pajamas, and shirts.

per ca·pi·ta (pər kap′i tə) for, from, or by each person: *per capita income.* [Latin *per capita* literally, by heads.]

per·ceive (pər sēv′) *v.t.,* **per·ceived, per·ceiv·ing. 1.** to be or become aware of through the senses; see, hear, taste, smell, or feel: *to perceive a change in the temperature.* **2.** to take in or grasp mentally; comprehend: *I perceived that he was angry with us.*

per·cent (pər sent′) *also,* **per cent.** *n.* the number of parts in or to every hundred. Two percent of 50 is ²/₁₀₀ x 50, or 1. ▲ the symbol for percent (%) is often used with figures, as in *6% interest.*

per·cent·age (pər sen′tij) *n.* **1.** the rate or proportion of something to every hundred: *What percentage of registered voters actually voted?* **2.** a part of a whole; portion: *A large percentage of the students ride the bus to school.*

per·cen·tile (pər sen′tīl) *n.* any value in a series of values on a scale found by dividing a group into a hundred equal parts. A person with a percentile of eighty on a test has done as well as or better than eighty percent of the people taking the test.

per·cep·ti·ble (pər sep′tə bəl) *adj.* that can be perceived; noticeable: *There has been a perceptible change in his behavior lately.* —**per·cep′ti·bil′i·ty,** *n.* —**per·cep′ti·bly,** *adv.*

per·cep·tion (pər sep′shən) *n.* **1.** the act or process of perceiving. **2.** the power or faculty of perceiving: *His perception of colors is poor.* **3.** the result of perceiving; observation. **4.** depth of understanding; insight; perceptiveness: *He is a person of great perception.*

per·cep·tive (pər sep′tive) *adj.* capable of or characterized by keen perception: *a perceptive judge of human nature.* —**per·cep′tive·ly,** *adv.* —**per·cep′tive·ness,** *n.*

perch¹ (purch) *n. pl.,* **perch·es. 1.** anything on which a bird can come to rest, such as a horizontal bar or branch. **2.** any raised place for sitting or standing: *The lifeguard watched the swimmers from his perch above the pool.* —*v.i.* to rest on; sit on a perch; settle: *The blue jay perched on the lowest branch of the tree.* —*v.t.* to set or place on a perch: *The cat perched himself on the bookcase.* [Old French *perche* a horizontal bar, from Latin *pertica* a pole.]

perch² (purch) *n. pl.,* **perch·es** or **perch.** any of a large group of fresh-water food and game fish found throughout North America and in most of Europe. [Old French *perche,* from Latin *perca.*]

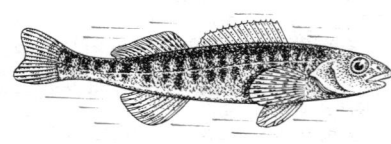
Perch²

per·chance (pər chans′) *adv.* by chance; possibly; perhaps.

per·co·late (pur′kə lāt′) *v.,* **per·co·lat·ed, per·co·lat·ing.** —*v.t.* **1.** to prepare in a percolator: *to percolate coffee.* **2.** to cause (a liquid) to drip through tiny spaces or holes. —*v.i.* to drip through tiny spaces or holes. —**per′co·la′tion,** *n.*

per·co·la·tor (pur′kə lā′tər) *n.* a kind of coffee pot in which boiling water rises through a tube to a perforated basket containing ground coffee, and then drips back down to the bottom.

per·cus·sion (pər kush′ən) *n.* **1.** the striking of one body against another with great force; collision. **2.** the sound or vibration resulting from such a collision. **3.** the striking of sound waves upon the ear. **4.** *Medicine.* the tapping of a part of the body in order to find out about its condition from the sounds produced. **5.** musical percussion instruments as a group.

percussion cap, a device that contains a small amount of explosive powder and is covered with a layer of tinfoil and sealed with shellac. It explodes to set off a larger charge when it is struck, as by the hammer of a gun.

percussion instrument, any of various musical instruments in which tones are produced by striking one thing against another. The drum, cymbal, xylophone, and piano are percussion instruments.

per di·em (pər dē′əm) for each day; per day; daily. [Latin *per diem* daily.]

per·di·tion (pər dish′ən) *n.* **1.** the loss of one's soul; loss of heavenly salvation; eternal damnation. **2.** another word for **hell. 3.** complete loss or destruction.

per·e·grine (per′ə grin) *n.* a falcon having predominantly bluish-gray feathers, formerly much used in falconry. Also, **peregrine falcon.**

per·emp·to·ry (pə remp′tər ē) *adj.* **1.** absolutely settled or determined; unconditional; final: *a peremptory court decision.* **2.** not to be disobeyed, refused, or questioned; imperative: *the king's peremptory orders.* **3.** imperious; dictatorial; dogmatic: *a peremptory manner.* —**per·emp′to·ri·ly,** *adv.* —**per·emp′to·ri·ness,** *n.*

per·en·ni·al (pə ren′ē əl) *adj.* **1.** lasting or existing through the year or many years: *a perennial stream that doesn't dry up during the summer.* **2.** lasting for a long time; enduring: *the perennial optimism of youth.* **3.** *Botany.* living more than two years: *perennial plants.* —*n.* a perennial plant. —**per·en′ni·al·ly,** *adv.*

Peregrine

per·fect (*adj., n.,* pur′fikt; *v.,* pər fekt′) *adj.* **1.** free from any defect or imperfection; faultless: *Her examination paper was perfect, without even one spelling mistake.* **2.** fully developed, formed, or done; complete: *She drew a perfect circle.* **3.** corresponding exactly to the original; accurate; correct: *That painted portrait is a perfect likeness of her.* **4.** very great; absolute; utter: *He made a perfect fool of himself!* **5.** *Grammar.* of, relating to, or designating the tenses of a verb that express action completed in the past. There are three perfect tenses in English: the present perfect, the past perfect (or pluperfect), and the future perfect. —*n. Grammar.* **1.** a perfect tense. **2.** a verb form in such a tense. —*v.t.* **1.** to make perfect or flawless. **2.** to bring to completion; complete: *The scientists finally perfected a system for space travel.*

per·fect·i·ble (pər fek′tə bəl) *adj.* that can be made perfect. —**per·fect′i·bil′i·ty,** *n.*

per·fec·tion (pər fek′shən) *n.* **1.** the state or quality of being perfect or faultless; excellence; flawlessness: *He always strives for perfection in his work.* **2.** a person or thing that is regarded as being perfect or excellent: *The performance of the symphony orchestra was perfection.* **3.** the act or process of perfecting: *the perfection of a style.*

per·fec·tion·ist (pər fek′shə nist) *n.* a person who sets extremely high standards and goals for himself and others; person who demands perfection.

per·fect·ly (pur′fikt lē) *adv.* **1.** in a perfect manner; faultlessly: *This dress fits perfectly.* **2.** completely; entirely: *Today was a perfectly awful day.*

perfect number, a number that is equal to the sum of its divisors, not including the number itself. The number 28, which can be divided by 1, 2, 4, 7, and 14, is a perfect number.

per·fid·i·ous (pər fid′ē əs) *adj.* given to or characterized by perfidy; not faithful; treacherous: *a perfidious companion.* —**per·fid′i·ous·ly,** *adv.* —**per·fid′i·ous·ness,** *n.*

per·fi·dy (pur′fi dē) *n. pl.,* **per·fi·dies.** a deliberate breaking of faith; faithlessness; disloyalty.

per·fo·rate (pur′fə rāt′) *v.t.,* **per·fo·rat·ed, per·fo·rat·ing. 1.** to make a hole or holes through; pierce: *Jan had perforated the carton with a knife so that the kittens could breathe.* **2.** to make a row of small holes through: *The edge of the order blank in the catalog was perforated so that it could be torn out easily.*

per·fo·ra·tion (pur′fə rā′shən) *n.* **1.** the act of perforating or the state of being perforated. **2.** a hole made by boring or piercing through something: *perforations in a sheet of postage stamps.*

per·force (pər fôrs′) *adv. Archaic.* of or by necessity; necessarily.

per·form (pər fôrm′) *v.t.* **1.** to begin and carry out to completion; execute; do: *to perform a job, to perform an operation.* **2.** to meet or satisfy; fulfill; discharge: *to perform one's duty.* **3.** to give a performance of: *to perform a play by Shakespeare.* —*v.i.* **1.** to carry out a job, duty, task, or the like; function: *He performs well under pressure.* **2.** to give a performance: *The singer performed in New York.*

per·for·mance (pər fôr′məns) *n.* **1.** a public presentation, as of a play, musical program, or other entertainment: *The show closed after ten performances.* **2.** the act of performing or the state of being performed: *the performance of an operation.* **3.** the way in which someone or something performs; manner of performing: *The driver wanted to test the car's performance on rough roads.* **4.** something performed; accomplishment; deed: *Climbing the cliff was a daring performance.*

per·form·er (pər fôr′mər) *n.* a person who performs, especially a person who gives or takes part in public entertainment.

per·fume (*n.,* pur′fyoom, pər fyoom′; *v.,* pər fyoom′) *n.* **1.** a liquid with a pleasing fragrance, used for personal adornment and to give a pleasing odor to various products. **2.** a sweet or pleasant odor; fragrance: *the perfume of a flower garden.* —*v.t.,* **per·fumed, per·fum·ing.** to fill or scent with a sweet or pleasant odor: *Gardenias perfumed the air.*

per·fum·er·y (pər fyoo′mər ē) *n. pl.,* **per·fum·er·ies. 1.** the art of making perfumes or the business of selling them. **2.** a place where perfumes are made or sold. **3.** perfume or perfumes.

per·func·to·ry (pər fungk′tər ē) *adj.* **1.** done hurriedly and as a matter of routine; mechanical; superficial: *He did his work in a perfunctory manner. She gave a perfunctory greeting.* **2.** acting in such a manner; half-hearted; indifferent: *a perfunctory salesman.* —**per·func′to·ri·ly,** *adv.*

per·haps (pər haps′) *adv.* possibly but not certainly; maybe: *Perhaps your friend would like to join us.*

per·i·car·di·um (per′ə kär′dē əm) *n. pl.,* **per·i·car·di·a** (per′ə kär′dē ə). the thin membranous sac that surrounds and protects the heart.

Per·i·cles (per′ə klēz′) 495?–429 B.C., Athenian statesman, orator, and general.

per·i·gee (per′ə jē) *n.* the point in the orbit of the moon or an artificial satellite at which it is closest to the earth.

per·i·he·li·on (per′ə hē′lē ən) *n. pl.,* **per·i·he·li·a** (per′ə hē′lē ə). the point in the orbit of a planet or other heavenly body at which it is closest to the sun.

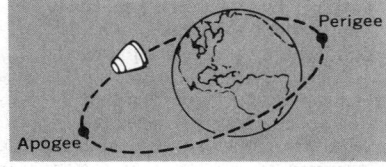

Perigee

per·il (per′əl) *n.* **1.** a chance or risk of injury, loss, or destruction; danger: *The general led the army well during a time of great peril.* **2.** something that may cause injury or damage: *Icy roads are a peril to motorists.* —*v.t.,* **per·iled, per·il·ing;** *also, British,* **per·illed, per·il·ling.** to expose to danger; imperil.

per·il·ous (per′ə ləs) *adj.* full of or involving peril; hazardous; dangerous: *a perilous journey.* —**per′il·ous·ly,** *adv.* —**per′il·ous·ness,** *n.*

pe·rim·e·ter (pə rim′ə tər) *n.* **1.** the boundary of an area or a closed plane figure: *the perimeter of a yard, the perimeter of a square.* **2.** the length of such a boundary.

pe·ri·od (pēr′ē əd) *n.* **1.** a portion of time of a given length or marked by certain conditions or events: *He went to Europe for a period of three months. During November we had a period of relatively mild weather.* **2.** a span of historical time; era: *the colonial period in America.* **3.** a portion of time marked off by the repeated occurrence of some action or event; cycle: *The period of a day is divided into twenty-four hours.* **4.** the time that it takes a planet or satellite to make one complete revolution. **5.** a timed portion of certain games and sports: *The goal was scored in the second period of the hockey game.* **6.** one of the divisions of time in a school day: *His English class meets during the first period in the morning.* **7.** one of the divisions of geological time, a major subdivision of an era. It is characterized by certain kinds of rock formations and usually named for the place where such formations were discovered or are particularly prominent. **8.** a mark of punctuation (.) indicating the end of a sentence or an abbreviation. —*adj.* of or relating to a certain past era or time: *The actors in the Shakespearean play were all dressed in period costumes.*

pe·ri·od·ic (pēr′ē od′ik) *adj.* **1.** happening on occasion: *The team has lost most of its games, but has had periodic wins. She makes periodic purchases of new shoes.* **2.** appearing or occurring at regular intervals: *the periodic rise and fall of the tide. The state law requires the periodic inspection of cars.* —**pe′ri·od′i·cal·ly,** *adv.*

pe·ri·od·i·cal (pēr′ē od′i kəl) *n.* a publication issued at regular intervals, usually every two weeks or every month. —*adj.* **1.** of or relating to periodicals. **2.** another word for **periodic.**

periodic law, a statement that the properties of the chemical elements vary at regular intervals with their atomic numbers.

periodic table, a table in which the chemical elements are arranged in order of increasing atomic numbers, with elements having similar properties arranged in vertical columns.

per·i·pa·tet·ic (per′ə pə tet′ik) *adj.* walking or traveling from place to place: *a peripatetic peddler.*

pe·riph·er·al (pə rif′ər əl) *adj.* relating to, located at, or forming the outermost part: *peripheral vision, the peripheral areas of a park.* —**pe·riph′er·al·ly,** *adv.*

pe·riph·er·y (pə rif′ər ē) *n. pl.,* **pe·riph·er·ies. 1.** the outermost part of an area: *the periphery of an empire, the periphery of one's field of vision.* **2.** the limit or boundary of an area or surface: *the periphery of a circle.* **3.** the area just beyond a boundary; environs.

at; āpe; cär; end; mē; it; īce; hot; ōld; fôrk; wood; fool; oil; out; up; turn; sing; thin; this; hw in white; zh in treasure. The symbol ə stands for the sound of a in about, e in taken, i in pencil, o in lemon, and u in circus.

per·i·scope (per′ə skōp′) *n.* an instrument, as in a submarine or tank, for seeing objects not directly in the observer's line of sight. It is made up of a tube with an arrangement of prisms or mirrors that reflect the image through the tube to the eye of the observer.

per·ish (per′ish) *v.i.* **1.** to die, especially in a tragic or violent way: *Many people perished when the ship sank.* **2.** to pass from existence; disappear; vanish: *Government of the people, by the people, and for the people, shall not perish from the earth* (Abraham Lincoln).

per·ish·a·ble (per′i shə bəl) *adj.* likely to spoil or decay quickly: *Perishable foods, such as milk or butter, should be refrigerated.* —*n. usually,* **perishables.** foods that are likely to spoil or decay. —**per′ish·a·bil′i·ty, per′ish·a·ble·ness,** *n.*

per·i·stal·sis (per′ə stal′sis) *n. pl.,* **per·i·stal·ses** (per′ə stal′sēz). the successive waves of contractions in the walls of the intestine or another tubular organ, that force the contents of the organ to move through it.

per·i·to·ne·um (per′i tə nē′əm) *also,* **per·i·to·nae·um.** *n. pl.,* **per·i·to·ne·a** or **per·i·to·nae·a** (per′i tə nē′ə). the transparent membrane that lines the walls of the abdomen and covers the organs in it.

per·i·to·ni·tis (per′i tə nī′tis) *n.* inflammation of the peritoneum.

per·i·wig (per′i wig′) *n.* a large wig, either powdered or in natural color, worn in the late seventeenth and eighteenth centuries.

per·i·win·kle¹ (per′i wing′kəl) *n.* an erect trailing plant having shiny leaves and small trumpet-shaped flowers. [Old English *perwince.*]

per·i·win·kle² (per′i wing′kəl) *n.* a sea snail having a cone-shaped spiral shell. [Old English *pīnewincle.*]

Periwinkle²

per·jure (pur′jər) *v.t.,* **per·jured, per·jur·ing.** to make (oneself) guilty of perjury: *The district attorney proved that the witness had perjured himself.* —**per′jur·er,** *n.*

per·ju·ry (pur′jər ē) *n. pl.,* **per·ju·ries.** the act of swearing under oath to the truth of something that one knows to be untrue.

perk (purk) *v.i.* to recover one's liveliness and vigor: *My sick friend perked up when he got the box of candy.* —*v.t.* to raise smartly or briskly: *The fox perked up its ears.*

perk·y (pur′kē) *adj.,* **perk·i·er, perk·i·est.** full of liveliness and vigor; brisk and lively: *a perky puppy.* —**perk′i·ly,** *adv.* —**perk′i·ness,** *n.*

Perm (perm) *n.* a city in the west-central Soviet Union, in the Russian Republic, formerly known as Molotov. Pop. (1976 est.), 957,000.

per·ma·frost (pur′mə frôst′) *n.* a layer of earth that is frozen permanently in very cold regions of the world.

per·ma·nence (pur′mə nəns) *n.* the state or quality of being permanent; durability; endurance.

per·ma·nen·cy (pur′mə nən sē) *n. pl.,* **per·ma·nen·cies. 1.** another word for **permanence. 2.** something permanent.

per·ma·nent (pur′mə nənt) *adj.* lasting or intended to last indefinitely without change; enduring. —*n.* see **permanent wave.** —**per′ma·nent·ly,** *adv.*

permanent press, (of a fabric or garment) having such a finish that little or no ironing is required after washing.

permanent wave, a curl lasting several months, set in the hair with a chemical solution or with heat.

per·me·a·bil·i·ty (pur′mē ə bil′ə tē) *n.* the state or quality of allowing something, especially a liquid, to pass through: *the permeability of a fabric.*

per·me·a·ble (pur′mē ə bəl) *adj.* that allows something to pass through; capable of being permeated: *This material is permeable by water. The enemy's defenses were permeable at several points.*

per·me·ate (pur′mē āt′) *v.,* **per·me·at·ed, per·me·at·ing.** —*v.t.* **1.** to pass through the holes, pores, or openings of: *Water will not permeate this fabric.* **2.** to spread throughout; pervade: *The smells from the refinery permeated the town.* —*v.i.* to spread itself: *Fear permeated throughout the entire community.* —**per′me·a′tion,** *n.*

Per·mi·an (pur′mē ən) *n.* the seventh and last geological period of the Paleozoic era, when the reptile ancestors of mammals and the ancestors of coniferous trees appeared. —*adj.* of, relating to, or characteristic of this period.

per·mis·si·ble (pər mis′ə bəl) *adj.* that may be permitted; allowable. —**per·mis′si·bly,** *adv.*

per·mis·sion (pər mish′ən) *n.* **1.** the act of permitting. **2.** a formal consent or authorization; leave: *Do I have your permission to go?*

per·mis·sive (pər mis′iv) *adj.* **1.** allowing much freedom; not strict; lenient: *a permissive parent.* **2.** granting permission; permitting; allowing: *a permissive proclamation.* —**per·mis′sive·ly,** *adv.* —**per·mis′sive·ness,** *n.*

per·mit (*v.,* pər mit′; *n.,* pur′mit, pər mit′) *v.,* **per·mit·ted, per·mit·ting.** —*v.t.* **1.** to allow (a person) to do something; give leave to: *Permit me to be of assistance to you.* **2.** to allow (something) to be done; give consent to: *The county permits the sale of alcoholic beverages.* **3.** to give an opportunity for; admit of: *The large window permitted a good view of the mountain.* —*v.i.* to give an opportunity; allow: *I'll call you today if time permits.* —*n.* a written order or license granting permission to perform some action: *The game warden asked to see their fishing permits.*

per·mu·ta·tion (pur′myŏŏ tā′shən) *n.* **1.** the act of rearranging; alteration. **2.** *Mathematics.* **a.** a change in the sequence of the elements of a set. **b.** any ordered arrangement of the elements of a set of objects. The sequences *abc, acb, bac,* and *cab* are permutations of the set containing *a, b,* and *c.*

per·ni·cious (pər nish′əs) *adj.* **1.** causing great harm or destruction; malicious: *Pernicious gossip ruined his reputation.* **2.** causing serious injury or death; severe or fatal: *a pernicious disease.* —**per·ni′cious·ly,** *adv.* —**per·ni′cious·ness,** *n.*

per·nick·e·ty (pər nik′ə tē) another spelling of **persnickety.**

per·o·ra·tion (per′ə rā′shən) *n.* the final part of a speech or oration, summing up what has been said.

per·ox·ide (pə rok′sīd) *n.* **1.** a compound of a metal and oxygen, in which the oxygen atoms form a weak bond with each other. **2.** an oxide containing the highest possible proportion of oxygen. **3.** see **hydrogen peroxide.** —*v.t.,* **per·ox·id·ed, per·ox·id·ing.** to bleach (hair) by using hydrogen peroxide.

per·pen·dic·u·lar (pur′pən dik′yə lər) *adj.* **1.** straight up and down; upright; vertical: *a perpendicular pole.* **2.** *Mathematics.* at right angles to a given line, plane, or surface. The sides of a square are perpendicular to the base. —*n.* **1.** a perpendicular line or plane. **2.** a perpendicular position.

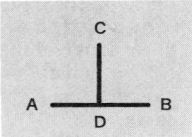

Perpendicular lines

per·pe·trate (pur′pə trāt′) *v.t.,* **per·pe·trat·ed, per·pe·trat·ing.** to commit or perform (a crime, trick, or the like): *The boys perpetrated a hoax that fooled everyone.* —**per′pe·tra′tion,** *n.* —**per′pe·tra′tor,** *n.*

per·pet·u·al (pər pech′ŏŏ əl) *adj.* **1.** lasting or enduring for a very long time or forever: *a mountaintop covered by perpetual snow.* **2.** continuing throughout one's lifetime; permanent: *perpetual ownership.* **3.** continuing without interruption; unceasing: *the perpetual ebb and flow of the tide.* —**per·pet′u·al·ly,** *adv.*

per·pet·u·ate (pər pech′ōō āt′) *v.t.,* **per·pet·u·at·ed, per·pet·u·at·ing.** to preserve in fact or existence; keep alive, active, or current: *The monument perpetuates the memory of those who fought in the war.* —**per·pet′u·a′tion,** *n.*

per·pe·tu·i·ty (pur′pə tōō′ə tē, pur′pə tyōō′ə tē) *n. pl.,* **per·pe·tu·i·ties. 1.** the state or quality of being perpetual; endless existence or duration. **2.** something perpetual.

in perpetuity. forever.

per·plex (pər pleks′) *v.t.* to fill with uncertainty; confuse; bewilder: *His strange behavior perplexed us.*

per·plex·i·ty (pər plek′sə tē) *n. pl.,* **per·plex·i·ties. 1.** the state or condition of being perplexed; bewilderment; confusion. **2.** something that perplexes; puzzling situation or circumstances.

per·qui·site (pur′kwə zit) *n.* an additional profit or benefit received for work besides a salary: *Free health insurance was one of the perquisites of the job.*

Per·ry (per′ē) **1.** Oliver Haz·ard (haz′ərd). 1785–1819, U.S. naval commander. **2.** Matthew Cal·braith (kal′-brāth). 1794–1858, his brother; U.S. naval officer.

per se (pər sā′) *Latin.* by or in itself; intrinsically.

per·se·cute (pur′sə kyōōt′) *v.t.,* **per·se·cut·ed, per·se·cut·ing. 1.** to subject continually to cruel, harmful, or unjust treatment: *Many minority groups have been persecuted over the years. The heretic was persecuted for his beliefs.* **2.** to harass, vex, or annoy constantly: *A salesman persecuted her with telephone calls.* —**per′se·cu′tor,** *n.*

▲ **Persecute** and **prosecute** should not be confused, even though they look somewhat alike. **Persecute** generally means to treat a person or group cruelly or unjustly: *The early Christians were persecuted for their religious beliefs.* **Prosecute** usually refers to bringing a case before a court of law for trial: *Mr. Smith's lawyer is prosecuting a suit against Mr. Brown.*

per·se·cu·tion (pur′sə kyōō′shən) *n.* the act of persecuting or the state of being persecuted.

Per·seph·o·ne (pər sef′ə nē) *n. Greek Mythology.* the goddess of vegetation and of death. She was the daughter of Zeus and Demeter and the wife of Hades, god of the underworld. In Roman mythology she was called Proserpina.

Per·se·us (pur′sē əs) *n.* **1.** *Greek Mythology.* the hero who killed Medusa and rescued Andromeda from a sea monster. **2.** a constellation in the northern sky, between Taurus and Cassiopeia.

per·se·ver·ance (pur′sə vēr′əns) *n.* the act or quality of persevering; persistence.

per·se·vere (pur′sə vēr′) *v.i.,* **per·se·vered, per·se·ver·ing.** to continue steadily in a course of action or purpose in spite of difficulties or obstacles; persist: *Despite the failure of his early experiments, the scientist persevered in his research.*

Per·shing, John Joseph (pur′shing) 1860–1948, U.S. general who commanded the U.S. Army in World War I.

Per·sia (pur′zhə) *n.* **1.** a great ancient empire of southwestern Asia, extending at its height from Egypt to the Indus River. It was conquered by Alexander the Great in the fourth century B.C. **2.** see **Iran.**

Per·sian (pur′zhən) *adj.* of or relating to Persia, its people, their language, or their culture. —*n.* **1.** a person who was born or is living in Iran. **2.** a person who lived in ancient Persia. **3.** the language of ancient Persia or modern Iran.

Persian cat, a cat of a breed having a round head and long, silky fur.

Persian Gulf, a shallow body of water between Iran and Arabia.

Persian lamb, the tightly curled fur from newborn karakul lambs.

per·si·flage (pur′sə fläzh′) *n.* light, playful speech or writing; banter.

per·sim·mon (pər sim′ən) *n.* **1.** the fleshy fruit of any of a group of trees and shrubs, having thin orange or yellow skin and containing from one to ten flat seeds. Persimmons are sweet when they are fully ripe and may be eaten either fresh or dried. **2.** the tropical tree or shrub bearing this fruit.

Fruit and leaves
Halved fruit
Persimmons

per·sist (pər sist′) *v.i.* **1.** to continue firmly and steadily in spite of opposition or difficulty; persevere: *If she persists in misbehaving, she will be punished.* **2.** to continue to exist; endure: *The bad weather persisted all week.*

per·sist·ence (pər sis′təns) *n.* **1.** the act of persisting: *The salesclerk's persistence made the customer angry.* **2.** the state or quality of being persistent: *He was known for his persistence.* **3.** the power or condition of lasting; continued existence: *the persistence of a backache.* Also, **per·sist·en·cy** (pər sis′tən sē).

per·sist·ent (pər sis′tənt) *adj.* **1.** continuing firmly and steadily in spite of opposition or difficulty; persevering: *a persistent salesman.* **2.** lasting; continuing: *a persistent cough, persistent interruptions.* —**per·sist′ent·ly,** *adv.*

per·snick·e·ty (pər snik′ə tē) *also,* **per·nick·e·ty.** *adj. Informal.* very fussy about trivial matters or details.

per·son (pur′sən) *n.* **1.** a man, woman, or child; human being; individual. **2.** the living body of a human being. **3.** bodily appearance: *Mother was always very neat about her person.* **4.** *Grammar.* any of three classes of personal pronouns and verb forms indicating the person speaking (the first person), the person spoken to (the second person), or the person or thing spoken of (the third person).

in person. in the flesh; physically present: *The movie star looked old when I saw him in person.*

per·son·a·ble (pur′sə nə bəl) *adj.* having a pleasing or attractive appearance and manner: *John is a personable young man.* —**per′son·a·ble·ness,** *n.* —**per′son·a·bly,** *adv.*

per·son·age (pur′sə nij) *n.* **1.** a person of distinction or importance. **2.** any person; individual. **3.** a character in a play, novel, or the like.

per·son·al (pur′sən əl) *adj.* **1.** of or relating to a particular person; private: *His problems are a personal matter that shouldn't be discussed in public.* **2.** done, made, or performed in person: *The famous actress made a personal appearance on a television program.* **3.** of or relating to a person's body or physical appearance: *personal hygiene, personal adornments.* **4.** asking or making remarks about private matters: *The reporter became very personal in his questions.* **5.** directed to a particular person or persons,

at; āpe; cär; end; mē; it; īce; hot; ōld; fôrk; wood; fōōl; oil; out; up; turn; sing; thin; this; hw in white; zh in treasure. The symbol ə stands for the sound of **a** in **about, e** in **taken, i** in **pencil, o** in **lemon,** and **u** in **circus.**

especially in a rude or offensive way: *a personal insult, a personal attack.* —*n.* a short paragraph or item in a newspaper relating to a particular person or persons or to a private matter.

personal foul, any of various violations of the rules in certain team sports, such as basketball, usually involving body contact.

per·son·al·i·ty (pur′sə nal′ə tē) *n. pl.,* **per·son·al·i·ties.** **1.** the sum of the traits, habits, attitudes, and behavior of a person that makes him or her different from all others. **2.** attractive personal qualities: *She was popular at school because of her personality.* **3.** a person, especially one who is well-known or distinguished: *He is a famous television personality.*

per·son·al·ize (pur′sən əl īz′) *v.t.,* **per·son·al·ized, per·son·al·iz·ing. 1.** to be an example or type of; personify. **2.** to mark (property or possessions) with the name or initials of a person: *Vera's stationery was personalized with her initials.*

per·son·al·ly (pur′sən əl ē) *adv.* **1.** not by the aid of or through others; by oneself; in person: *The senator answered my letter personally.* **2.** as far as oneself is concerned; for oneself: *Personally, I am in favor of going on a camping trip.* **3.** as an individual: *He is a friend of the family, but I don't like him personally.* **4.** as though directed toward or meant for one as a person: *Bill took her remarks personally and felt insulted.*

personal name, a name given to a person or by which a person is known.

● Most of the **personal names** that English-speaking people use today can be traced back to five languages: Hebrew, Teutonic, Celtic, Latin, and Greek. At first people had only one name, the equivalent of our "given" or "Christian" name, which they received at birth or shortly afterward. All early names had meanings, and much importance was attached to naming because people believed that a name would affect a person's character and success in life.

Originally any word or group of words could be used as a name. Then the early Christian church declared that Christians could use only the names of saints and martyrs. Given at baptism, these names were known as *christened* names, from which our term *Christian name* comes. As Christianity spread throughout Europe and the British Isles, many of the early "pagan" names were discarded, greatly limiting the choice of names. There were so many people with the same name, often several in one family, that there developed the need for some additional way of distinguishing them from one another. The use of *surnames* then became common. These added names had been developed in families where father and son, or grandfather and grandson, had the same name. The common practice was to give an additional name after a person was older, and the names usually described some particular characteristic of the person, or some circumstance of his life. Especially common were names describing a person's complexion or hair color, such as "the Red." In many places it was customary to derive the surname from the father's name. For example, the Scottish word *Mac,* meant "son of" or sometimes "grandson or descendant of" and was added to the father's or ancestor's name to produce names such as *MacDonald.* Scandinavians often added *-son* at the end of the father's name to produce names such as *Johnson.*

The other two most common sources for surnames were a person's profession, such as *Miller* or *Smith,* and the locality in which he lived. Names derived from locality are the most numerous and come in large part from the laws passed by many rulers in the Middle Ages demanding that

their subjects choose permanent or hereditary surnames to be passed from one generation to the next. It became common practice to take the name from one's estate, town, county, or some natural feature near one's home.

An interesting development, particularly in modern times, has been the derivation of common vocabulary words from personal names. *Silhouette, boycott, pasteurize, maverick* and *chauvinist* are all words that were developed from people's surnames.

---

personal pronoun, one of a group of pronouns indicating the speaker, the person or persons addressed, or any other persons, places, or things spoken about. *I, you, she, it,* and *they* are personal pronouns.

per·so·na non gra·ta (pər sō′nə non grä′tə, pər sō′-nə non grat′ə) a person who is not acceptable or welcome. [Latin *persōna nōn grāta.*]

per·son·i·fi·ca·tion (pər son′ə fi kā′shən) *n.* **1.** a figure of speech in which human characteristics are given to an animal, thing, idea, or quality. For example: *A pity beyond all telling is hid in the heart of love* (William Butler Yeats). *The sun smiled down on the green meadows.* **2.** a person or thing that typifies a quality; embodiment: *The hero is the personification of bravery.* **3.** an imaginary or ideal person thought of as representing a thing or idea: *In Greek mythology, Poseidon was the personification of the sea.*

per·son·i·fy (pər son′ə fī′) *v.t.,* **per·son·i·fied, per·son·i·fy·ing. 1.** to regard or represent as having human characteristics: *to personify purity as an innocent child.* **2.** to typify in one's own person; be the embodiment of: *That dictator personifies evil.*

per·son·nel (pur′sə nel′) *n.* the persons working in a business or other place of employment: *The hospital personnel includes doctors and nurses.*

per·spec·tive (pər spek′tiv) *n.* **1.** the art or theory of representing objects on a flat surface in such a way as to give the appearance of three dimensions, depth, and distance. **2.** a picture that represents objects in this way. **3.** a scene or view from a distance;

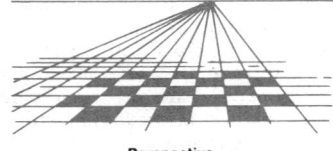

Perspective

vista: *You can get an interesting perspective of the town from the church tower.* **4.** the effect of distance on the way something looks. **5.** a point of view: *Let's try and think about the problem from a different perspective.* **6.** the relation of events, ideas, facts, or the like, to one another: *If you keep things in their proper perspective, you won't worry about what is unimportant.* —*adj.* of, relating to, or represented in perspective: *a perspective drawing.*

per·spi·ca·cious (pur′spə kā′shəs) *adj.* having keen powers of observation and judgment; discerning. —**per′-spi·ca′cious·ly,** *adv.*

per·spi·cac·i·ty (pur′spə kas′ə tē) *n.* keenness of observation and judgment; discernment.

per·spi·ra·tion (pur′spə rā′shən) *n.* **1.** moisture given off through the pores of the skin by the sweat glands; sweat: *There were beads of perspiration on the runner's brow.* **2.** the act or process of perspiring.

per·spire (pər spīr′) *v.i.,* **per·spired, per·spir·ing.** to give off perspiration; sweat.

per·suade (pər swād′) *v.t.,* **per·suad·ed, per·suad·ing.** to cause (someone) to do or believe something, as by argument; convince: *The salesman persuaded us to buy the car.* —**per·suad′er,** *n.*

per·sua·sion (pər swā′zhən) *n.* **1.** the act of persuading.

2. the power or ability to persuade; persuasiveness. **3.** a firm belief; conviction: *The two friends are of different political persuasions.* **4.** a religious belief, sect, or denomination: *a clergyman of the Lutheran persuasion.*

per·sua·sive (pər swā′siv) *adj.* able or tending to persuade: *The lawyer presented a persuasive argument in defense of his client.* —**per·sua′sive·ly,** *adv.* —**per·sua′sive·ness,** *n.*

pert (purt) *adj.* **1.** showing disrespect in speech or behavior; saucy; impudent: *The girl made a pert reply to the woman's question.* **2.** spirited; lively. **3.** trim and smart-looking: *a pert hat.* —**pert′ly,** *adv.* —**pert′ness,** *n.*

per·tain (pər tān′) *v.i.* **1.** to have reference; refer; relate: *The President and his advisors discussed matters that pertained to the economy.* **2.** to belong or be connected: *The duke's son inherits his title and all that pertains to it.*

Perth (purth) *n.* a city in southwestern Australia, near the Indian Ocean. Pop. (1971), 97,242.

per·ti·na·cious (purt′ən ā′shəs) *adj.* holding firmly to a purpose, action, or opinion; stubbornly persistent. —**per′ti·na′cious·ly,** *adv.*

per·ti·nac·i·ty (purt′ən as′ə tē) *n.* the quality of being pertinacious; stubborn persistence.

per·ti·nence (purt′ən əns) *n.* the quality of being pertinent; relevance.

per·ti·nent (purt′ən ənt) *adj.* relating to the matter at hand; relevant: *Jim made a number of pertinent remarks on the subject we were discussing.* —**per′ti·nent·ly,** *adv.*

per·turb (pər turb′) *v.t.* to disturb greatly; make uneasy or anxious; trouble: *He was perturbed by his friend's foolish behavior.* —**per′tur·ba′tion,** *n.*

Pe·ru (pə rōō′) *n.* a country on the western coast of South America. Capital, Lima. Area, 496,224 sq. mi. Pop. (1971 est.), 14,010,000.

pe·ruke (pə rōōk′) *n.* a wig, especially of the type worn by men in the seventeenth and eighteenth centuries.

pe·rus·al (pə rōō′zəl) *n.* the act of reading through or examining, especially with great care: *A careful perusal of the documents revealed several errors.*

pe·ruse (pə rōōz′) *v.t.,* **pe·rused, pe·rus·ing.** to read through or examine, especially with great care: *to peruse a letter.*

Pe·ru·vi·an (pə rōō′vē ən) *n.* a person who was born or is living in Peru. —*adj.* of or relating to Peru, its people, their language, or culture.

Peruvian bark, see **cinchona** (def. 2).

per·vade (pər vād′) *v.t.,* **per·vad·ed, per·vad·ing.** to spread through or be present in every part of: *The scent of her perfume pervaded the room. A strong sense of humor pervades the author's writings.* —**per·va·sion** (pər vā′zhən), *n.*

per·verse (pər vurs′) *adj.* **1.** willfully going against what is right, reasonable, or required; wrong: *a perverse opinion, perverse behavior.* **2.** determined to do as one pleases; stubborn; obstinate: *He was a perverse little boy who refused to obey anyone.* **3.** morally wrong or corrupt; wicked: *O faithless and perverse generation* (Matthew 17:17). —**per·verse′ly,** *adv.* —**per·verse′ness,** *n.*

per·ver·sion (pər vur′zhən) *n.* **1.** the act of perverting or the state of being perverted: *a perversion of facts.* **2.** any abnormal sexual act or practice.

per·ver·si·ty (pər vur′sə tē) *n. pl.,* **per·ver·si·ties. 1.** the state or quality of being perverse. **2.** an instance of this; a wrong or wicked act, habit, or thing.

per·vert (*v.,* pər vurt′; *n.,* pur′vurt) *v.t.* **1.** to lead or turn from what is considered right or moral; lead astray; corrupt: *Socrates was accused of perverting the young.* **2.** to distort the meaning of: *to pervert the truth.* **3.** to use wrongly; misuse: *to pervert one's skills.* —*n.* a person who

is perverted or given to perversion, especially sexual perversion.

pes·ky (pes′kē) *adj.,* **pes·ki·er, pes·ki·est.** *Informal.* troublesome; annoying. —**pes′ki·ly,** *adv.* —**pes′ki·ness,** *n.*

pe·so (pā′sō) *n. pl.,* **pe·sos.** the monetary unit of Mexico, several South and Central American countries, Cuba, the Dominican Republic, and the Philippines.

pes·si·mism (pes′ə miz′əm) *n.* **1.** the tendency to take a gloomy view of life or to see only the bad side of things. **2.** the belief that the world is evil.

pes·si·mist (pes′ə mist) *n.* a person who expects the worst or takes a gloomy view of life. —**pes′si·mis′tic,** *adj.* —**pes′si·mis′ti·cal·ly,** *adv.*

pest (pest) *n.* a person or thing that is troublesome, annoying, or destructive; nuisance: *Locusts, gnats, and mosquitos are insect pests.*

pes·ter (pes′tər) *v.t.* to trouble or bother; annoy: *The little boy pestered his older sister with his frequent demands for candy.*

pes·ti·cide (pes′tə sīd′) *n.* a chemical or other substance used to destroy harmful plants or animals.

pes·tif·er·ous (pes tif′ər əs) *adj.* producing or carrying disease: *a pestiferous swamp.*

pes·ti·lence (pes′tə ləns) *n.* any highly infectious, epidemic disease, especially bubonic plague.

pes·ti·lent (pes′tə lənt) *adj.* **1.** causing or tending to cause disease or death. **2.** harmful or destructive to peace, morals, or society.

pes·ti·len·tial (pes′tə len′shəl) *adj.* **1.** of, relating to, or causing a pestilence. **2.** harmful; destructive.

pes·tle (pes′əl, pest′əl) *n.* a blunt tool for pounding, grinding, or mixing substances in a mortar. See **mortar** for illustration.

pet¹ (pet) *n.* **1.** a tame animal, such as a cat or dog, that is kept chiefly for amusement and companionship. **2.** any person who is treated with special favor or kindness; favorite: *That boy is the teacher's pet.* —*adj.* **1.** kept or treated as a pet: *a pet frog.* **2.** expressing fondness or familiarity; affectionate: *a pet name.* **3.** favorite; cherished: *Getting his old car to run is his pet project.* —*v.t.,* **pet·ted, pet·ting.** to stroke, pat, or caress: *The cat purred when she was petted.* [Of uncertain origin.]

pet² (pet) *n.* a fit of peevishness or ill humor; discontent. [Of uncertain origin.]

pet·al (pet′əl) *n.* one of the divisions or parts, usually colored, of a flower. —**pet′aled;** *also,* **pet′alled,** *adj.* —**pet′al·like′,** *adj.*

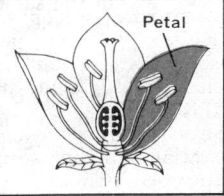
Petal

pet·cock (pet′kok′) *n.* a small valve or faucet.

pe·ter (pē′tər) *v.i. Informal.* to diminish gradually and disappear: *The tennis player's strength petered out toward the end of the game.*

Pe·ter (pē′tər) *n.* **1. Saint.** died A.D. 67?, one of the twelve Apostles. Also, **Simon Peter. 2.** either of two Epistles of the New Testament thought to have been written by him.

at; āpe; cär; end; mē; it; īce; hot; ōld; fôrk; wood; fōol; oil; out; up; turn; sing; thin; **th**is; hw in white; zh in treasure. The symbol ə stands for the sound of **a** in about, **e** in taken, **i** in pencil, **o** in lemon, and **u** in circus.

Peter I, 1672–1725, the czar of Russia from 1682 to 1725. Also, **Peter the Great.**

pet·i·ole (pet′ē ōl′) *n.* the slender stalk by which a leaf is attached to a stem. Also, **leafstalk.**

pe·tite (pə tēt′) *adj.* (of a woman or girl) of small size; little; tiny.

pe·ti·tion (pə tish′ən) *n.* **1.** a formal request made to a person in a position of authority: *The students signed a petition asking the principal to open the school library on weekends.* **2.** a prayer or entreaty. —*v.t.* to make a petition to: *to petition the government.* —*v.i.* to make a petition. —**pe·ti′tion·er,** *n.*

pet·it jury (pet′ē) a jury, usually of twelve persons, selected to hear a civil or criminal case in a court of law.

Pe·trarch (pē′trärk) 1304–1374, Italian poet and scholar.

pet·rel (pet′rəl) *n.* a hook-billed sea bird usually having blackish or brownish feathers with white markings.

pet·ri·fac·tion (pet′rə fak′shən) *n.* **1.** the act of petrifying or the state of being petrified. **2.** something that is petrified. Also, **pet·ri·fi·ca·tion** (pet′rə fi kā′shən).

pet·ri·fy (pet′rə fī′) *v.,* **pet·ri·fied, pet·ri·fy·ing.** —*v.t.* **1.** to convert (organic material) into stone or a stony substance. **2.** to paralyze with fear, astonishment, or horror: *The child was petrified by his father's angry shouting.* —*v.i.* to become stone or like stone.

Pet·ro·grad (pet′rə grad′) *n.* see **Leningrad.**

pet·rol (pet′rəl) *n. British.* another word for **gasoline.**

pe·tro·le·um (pə trō′lē əm) *n.* an oily, flammable liquid made up of a mixture of hydrocarbons, usually found beneath the earth's surface. Petroleum yields such products as gasoline, diesel fuel, and lubricants.

pet·ti·coat (pet′ē kōt′) *n.* a skirt or slip worn as an undergarment.

pet·tish (pet′ish) *adj.* ill-tempered; cross; peevish. —**pet′tish·ly,** *adv.*

pet·ty (pet′ē) *adj.,* **pet·ti·er, pet·ti·est. 1.** of little value or importance; insignificant: *a petty complaint.* **2.** mean, spiteful, or narrow-minded: *He is a petty person who only thinks of himself.* **3.** minor; inferior; subordinate: *a petty government official.* —**pet′ti·ly,** *adv.* —**pet′ti·ness,** *n.*

petty cash, a small amount of cash kept on hand to pay minor incidental expenses, as in a business office.

petty officer, a noncommissioned officer in the U.S. Navy or Coast Guard.

pet·u·lant (pech′ə lənt) *adj.* ill-humored; peevish. —**pet′u·lance,** *n.* —**pet′u·lant·ly,** *adv.*

pe·tu·nia (pə tōōn′yə, pə tyōōn′yə) *n.* **1.** a funnel-shaped white, pink, or purple flower sometimes having fringed or ruffled petals. **2.** the plant bearing this flower.

Petunias

pew (pyōō) *n.* a long bench for seating worshipers in a church.

pe·wee (pē′wē′) *n.* a small American bird having dull olive-brown or gray feathers.

pew·ter (pyōō′tər) *n.* **1.** an alloy, formerly made of tin, lead, and copper, now made of tin, copper, and antimony. It is used to make tableware, utensils, and ornamental objects. **2.** articles made of this alloy. —*adj.* made of pewter: *a pewter mug.*

pey·o·te (pā ō′tē) *n.* **1.** a small cactus grown in dry regions from Texas to Central America. Also, **mescal. 2.** a drug that produces hallucinations, derived from this cactus; mescaline.

Pfc., private first class.

pha·e·ton (fā′ət ən) *n.* **1.** a light, low, open, four-wheeled carriage. **2.** an open automobile whose body resembles that of such a carriage.

Phaeton *(def. 1)*

phag·o·cyte (fag′ə sīt′) *n.* any cell, especially a white blood cell, or leucocyte, that can absorb and destroy bacteria and other harmful material in the body.

pha·lanx (fā′langks) *n. pl.,* **pha·lanx·es** or **pha·lan·ges** (fə lan′jēz). **1.** in ancient Greek and Macedonian armies, a battle formation of infantry standing in close ranks with their shields and long spears overlapping each other. **2.** a compact body of persons, animals, or things massed together, as for attack or for defense: *A phalanx of police held back the crowd.* **3.** a number of persons united for a common purpose. **4.** any of the bones in the fingers or toes. See **hand** for illustration.

phan·tasm (fan′taz əm) *n.* **1.** something seen in the imagination; unreal or fantastic idea or fancy: *the bizarre phantasms of a nightmare.* **2.** a ghost; phantom. —**phan·tas′mal,** *adj.*

phan·ta·sy (fan′tə sē) *n. pl.,* **phan·ta·sies.** another spelling of **fantasy.**

phan·tom (fan′təm) *n.* **1.** something that appears to be real but is not; ghost; apparition. **2.** something existing only as an image in the mind; illusion. —*adj.* of the nature of a phantom; ghostly: *a tale of a phantom ship.*

Phar·aoh (fer′ō) *n.* the title of the kings of ancient Egypt.

Phar·i·see (fer′ə sē) *n.* **1.** a member of an ancient Jewish sect that was very strict in observing both the written law and the oral tradition of Judaism. **2.** pharisee. a self-righteous or hypocritical person.

phar·ma·ceu·ti·cal (fär′mə sōō′ti kəl) *adj.* of or relating to a pharmacy or pharmacist. Also, **phar·ma·ceu·tic** (fär′mə sōō′tik). —*n.* a medicinal product; drug.

phar·ma·cist (fär′mə sist) *n.* a person who is licensed to prepare drugs and fill prescriptions.

phar·ma·col·o·gy (fär′mə kol′ə jē) *n.* the branch of science that deals with the preparation, uses, and effects of drugs.

phar·ma·cy (fär′mə sē) *n. pl.,* **phar·ma·cies. 1.** another word for **drugstore. 2.** the science, practice, or profession of preparing and giving out or selling drugs.

Phar·os (fār′os) *n.* a huge lighthouse constructed on an island in the harbor of Alexandria, Egypt, in the third century B.C.

phar·ynx (far′ingks) *n. pl.,* **phar·ynx·es** or **pha·ryn·ges** (fə rin′jēz). the upper part of the digestive tract, made up of a short, muscular tube that connects the mouth and nasal cavity with the esophagus and windpipe.

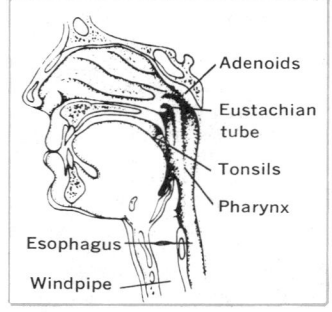

Adenoids

Eustachian tube

Tonsils

Pharynx

Esophagus

Windpipe

Pharynx

phase (fāz) *n.* **1.** a stage of development of a person or thing: *an early phase of a disease. The child went through a phase during which he was ill-tempered and stubborn.* **2.** one side, view, or aspect: *He was interested in all phases of stamp*

690

collecting. **3.** *Astronomy.* the appearance of the moon or a planet at a particular time, depending on how much of its lighted side can be seen from the earth.

to phase out. to eliminate in stages: *The army plans to phase out the old equipment as more modern equipment becomes available.*

Ph.D., Doctor of Philosophy.

pheas·ant (fez′ənt) *n. pl.,* **pheas·ants** or **pheas·ant.** any of various long-tailed birds originally native to Asia and now found in most parts of the world, the male of which often has brilliantly colored feathers.

phe·nol (fē′nôl) *n.* a poisonous crystalline compound used in plastics, explosives, weed killers, and drugs. It was formerly used as an antiseptic and disinfectant. Also, **carbolic acid.**

phe·nom·e·nal (fə nom′ən əl) *adj.* **1.** of or relating to a phenomenon or phenomena. **2.** extraordinary or remarkable: *He has phenomenal strength.* —**phe·nom′e·nal·ly,** *adv.*

phe·nom·e·non (fə nom′ə non′) *n. pl.,* **phe·nom·e·na** (fə nom′ə nə) or **phe·nom·e·nons. 1.** a fact, event, or condition that can be observed or perceived: *Rain and snow are phenomena of the weather.* **2.** a person or thing that is extraordinary or remarkable: *The young woman's rapid success made her a phenomenon in the business world.*

phi·al (fī′əl) another spelling of **vial.**

Phid·i·as (fid′ē əs) 490?–432? B.C., Greek sculptor.

Phil·a·del·phi·a (fil′ə del′fē ə) *n.* a city in southeastern Pennsylvania, on the Delaware River. Pop. (1970), 1,948,609.

phil·an·throp·ic (fil′ən throp′ik) *n.* relating to, characterized by, or engaged in philanthropy; charitable. Also, **philanthropical.** —**phil·an·throp′i·cal·ly,** *adv.*

phil·an·thro·pist (fi lan′thrə pist) *n.* a person who gives his or her money or time to good causes.

phil·an·thro·py (fi lan′thrə pē) *n. pl.,* **phi·lan·thro·pies. 1.** a love of mankind expressed by the giving of money or time to good causes. **2.** a charitable action, service, or institution.

phi·lat·e·list (fə lat′əl ist) *n.* a person who collects and studies postage stamps and related items.

phi·lat·e·ly (fə lat′əl ē) *n.* the collecting and study of postage stamps and related items. —**phil·a·tel·ic** (fil′ə tel′ik), *adj.*

Phi·le·mon (fi lē′mən) *n.* the New Testament Epistle written by Paul.

phil·har·mon·ic (fil′här mon′ik) *adj.* **1.** fond of or devoted to music. **2.** of, relating to, or presented by a musical society or an orchestra, especially a symphony orchestra: *a philharmonic concert.* —*n.* a philharmonic orchestra, concert, or society.

Phil·ip (fil′əp) *n.* one of the twelve Apostles of Christ.

Philip II 1. 382–336 B.C., the king of Macedonia from 359 to 336 B.C. and the father of Alexander the Great; known as Philip of Macedon. **2.** 1527–1598, the king of Spain, from 1556 to 1598.

Phil·ip·pine (fil′ə pēn′) *adj.* of or relating to the Philippines or their inhabitants. Also, **Filipino.**

Phil·ip·pines (fil′ə pēnz′) *n.* an island country in the western Pacific Ocean, southeast of China. Capital, Quezon City. Land area, 115,831 sq. mi. Pop. (1971 est.), 37,960,000. Also, **Philippine Islands.**

Phil·is·tine (fil′is tēn′, fi lis′tin) *n.* **1.** in the Bible, a member of an ancient people of southwestern Palestine often mentioned in the Old Testament as enemies of the Israelites. **2.** *also,* **philistine.** a person who is uncultured or narrow-minded in his ideas and tastes. —*adj.* **1.** of or relating to the Philistines. **2.** *also,* **philistine.** uncultured or narrow-minded in ideas and tastes.

phil·o·den·dron (fil′ə den′drən) *n.* a tropical American plant often having heart-shaped, glossy leaves, commonly grown as a house plant.

phi·lol·o·gist (fi lol′ə jist) *n.* a student of or an expert in philology.

phi·lol·o·gy (fi lol′ə jē) *n.* the study of languages, especially of their history and development. —**phil·o·log·i·cal** (fil′ə loj′i kəl), *adj.*

phi·los·o·pher (fə los′ə fər) *n.* **1.** a student of or an expert in philosophy. **2.** a person who develops a system of philosophy. **3.** a person who accepts life and its problems with calmness and understanding.

phil·o·soph·i·cal (fil′ə sof′i kəl) *adj.* **1.** of or relating to philosophy: *a philosophical essay.* **2.** of or relating to a philosopher: *philosophical thought.* **3.** accepting life and its problems with calmness and understanding. Also, **phil·o·soph·ic** (fil′ə sof′ik). —**phil′o·soph′i·cal·ly,** *adv.*

phi·los·o·phize (fi los′ə fīz′) *v.i.,* **phi·los·o·phized, phi·los·o·phiz·ing.** to think as a philosopher does: *to philosophize about the meaning of life.* —**phi·los′o·phiz′er,** *n.*

phi·los·o·phy (fə los′ə fē) *n. pl.,* **phi·los·o·phies. 1.** the study of the basic nature and purpose of humanity, the universe, and life itself. **2.** the system of thought of a particular school or philosopher: *the philosophy of Plato.* **3.** the study of the basic principles of a branch of knowledge or of an activity: *the philosophy of history.* **4.** a person's principles and beliefs: *His philosophy is "live and let live."*

phil·ter (fil′tər) *n.* a magic drug or potion, especially one that is supposed to make a person fall in love.

phlegm (flem) *n.* mucus, especially in the nose or throat.

phleg·mat·ic (fleg mat′ik) *adj.* sluggish in disposition; indifferent. [Old French *fluematique,* going back to Greek *phlegmatikos* full of phlegm; referring to the ancient belief that phlegm was one of the four humors and that too much of it in the body made a person sluggish.] —**phleg·mat′i·cal·ly,** *adv.*

phlo·em (flō′em) *n.* a layer of plant tissue that conducts food made in the leaves down to the other parts of the plant. In woody plants, it lies just under the hard, outer bark. Also, **bast.**

phlox (floks) *n. pl.,* **phlox·es.** an erect or trailing plant bearing showy clusters of small flowers that are white, red, pink, violet, or blue.

Phlox

Phnom Penh (pə nôm′ pen′) also, **Pnom·penh.** the capital and largest city of Cambodia, in the south-central part of the country. Pop. (1969 est.), 650,000.

pho·bi·a (fō′bē ə) *n.* a strong dread or fear of something: *a phobia about the dark.*

phoe·be (fē′bē) *n.* a small bird having gray-brown feathers with white underparts, named for the sound of its two-noted song.

Phoe·be (fē′bē) *n. Greek Mythology.* another name for Artemis as goddess of the moon.

Phoe·bus (fē′bəs) *n. Greek Mythology.* another name for Apollo as god of the sun. Also, **Phoebus Apollo.**

at; āpe; cär; end; mē; it; īce; hot; ōld; fôrk; wood; fōōl; oil; out; up; turn; sing; thin; **th**is; **hw** in white; **zh** in treasure. The symbol ə stands for the sound of **a** in about, **e** in taken, **i** in pencil, **o** in lemon, and **u** in circus.

Phoe·ni·cia (fə nish′ə) *n.* an ancient country on the eastern coast of the Mediterranean Sea.

Phoe·ni·cian (fə nish′ən) *adj.* of or relating to Phoenicia, its people, their language, or culture. —*n.* **1.** a person who lived in Phoenicia. **2.** the ancient language of Phoenicia.

phoe·nix (fē′niks) *n. pl.,* **phoe·nix·es.** *Egyptian and Greek Mythology.* a miraculous bird thought to live for 500 years and to die in the flames of a funeral pyre, and then to rise again from its own ashes.

Phoe·nix (fē′niks) *n.* the capital and largest city of Arizona, in the south-central part of the state. Pop. (1970), 581,562.

phone (fōn) *Informal. n.,v.,* **phoned, phon·ing.** see **tele·phone.**

pho·neme (fō′nēm) *n.* the smallest unit of speech sound that can distinguish one word from another. The words *hat* and *rat* are distinguished by the different phonemes *h* and *r.*

pho·nem·ic (fə nēm′ik) *adj.* of or relating to a phoneme or phonemes.

pho·net·ic (fə net′ik) *adj.* **1.** of or relating to speech sounds or phonetics. **2.** representing speech sounds with a set of symbols, each of which stands for a single speech sound: *a phonetic alphabet, the phonetic spelling of a word.* —**pho·net′i·cal·ly,** *adv.*

pho·ne·ti·cian (fō′nə tish′ən) *n.* a student of or an expert in phonetics.

pho·net·ics (fə net′iks) *n.,pl.* the science or study of speech sounds and their representation by symbols. ▲ used with a singular verb.

phon·ic (fon′ik) *adj.* of, relating to, or of the nature of sound, especially speech sound.

phon·ics (fon′iks) *n.,pl.* any of various methods of teaching reading by explaining how letters and groups of letters are pronounced. ▲ used with a singular verb.

pho·no·graph (fō′nə graf′) *n.* a device that reproduces sounds recorded on a disk of plastic or other material.

pho·no·graph·ic (fō′nə graf′ik) *adj.* of, relating to, or produced by a phonograph.

pho·ny (fō′nē) *Informal. adj.,* **pho·ni·er, pho·ni·est.** not genuine; counterfeit; fake: *a phony diamond.* —*n. pl.,* **pho·nies. 1.** something that is not genuine; fake: *The painting was a phony.* **2.** a person who tries to be what he is not. —**pho′ni·ness,** *n.*

phos·phate (fos′fāt) *n.* **1.** a salt of phosphoric acid. **2.** a fertilizer having a high phosphorus content. **3.** a beverage made with carbonated water and flavored syrup.

phos·phor (fos′fər) *n.* a substance that gives off light when affected by a form of radiant energy, such as ultraviolet light.

phos·pho·res·cence (fos′fə res′əns) *n.* **1.** the giving off of light from a substance that has absorbed radiant energy, continuing after the source of energy is removed. **2.** a light so produced. —**phos′pho·res′cent,** *adj.*

phos·phor·ic (fos fôr′ik) *adj.* of, relating to, or containing phosphorus.

phosphoric acid, any of three acids containing phosphorus.

phos·pho·rous (fos′fər əs) *adj.* of, relating to, or containing phosphorus.

phos·pho·rus (fos′fər əs) *n.* a nonmetallic element that exists in three forms. Yellow phosphorus is a poisonous, waxy solid that glows faintly in the dark. Red phosphorus is a less reactive, reddish-brown crystalline powder. Black phosphorus is prepared by heating yellow phosphorus under very high pressure. Symbol: **P**

pho·to (fō′tō) *n. pl.,* **pho·tos.** *Informal.* see **photograph.**

photo- *combining form* **1.** of, relating to, or produced by

light: *photosynthesis.* **2.** of, relating to, or produced by photography; photographic: *photocopy.*

pho·to·cop·y (fō′tə kop′ē) *v.t.,* **pho·to·cop·ied, pho·to·cop·y·ing.** to make a copy or copies of (printed matter or the like) by a photographic process. —*n. pl.,* **pho·to·cop·ies.** a copy produced by such a process.

pho·to·e·lec·tric cell (fō′tō i lek′trik) an electric device that is sensitive to light or other electromagnetic radiation, used especially in electric eyes, television cameras, and light meters. Also, **pho·to·cell** (fō′tō sel′).

photo finish, the finish of a race that is so close that a photograph is needed to decide the winner.

pho·to·gen·ic (fō′tə jen′ik) *adj.* that is a good subject for a photograph; that photographs well: *Sharon has a very photogenic face.*

pho·to·graph (fō′tə graf′) *n.* a picture or reproduction made by photography. —*v.t.* to take a photograph of. —*v.i.* to appear or look in a photograph: *That actress always photographs well.*

pho·tog·ra·pher (fə tog′rə fər) *n.* a person who takes photographs, especially as a profession.

pho·to·graph·ic (fō′tə graf′ik) *adj.* **1.** relating to, used in, or produced by photography: *photographic equipment.* **2.** resembling a photograph, as in accuracy: *a photographic memory.* —**pho′to·graph′i·cal·ly,** *adv.*

pho·tog·ra·phy (fə tog′rə fē) *n.* **1.** the technique of recording the image of a given area or object by the action of light on a light-sensitive surface. **2.** the art or practice of taking photographs.

pho·ton (fō′ton) *n.* the basic unit of light or other form of radiant energy, considered as a particle.

pho·to·sphere (fō′tə sfēr′) *n.* **1.** the visible surface of the sun, made up of a layer of hot gases about 250 miles thick. **2.** a similar surface on any star.

Pho·to·stat (fō′tə stat′) *n.* **1.** *Trademark.* a device for making photographic copies directly on specially prepared paper. **2.** *also,* **photostat.** a copy made by Photostat. —*v.t.* **photostat.** to make a photostat.

pho·to·syn·the·sis (fō′tə sin′thə sis) *n.* the process by which green plants make food. In photosynthesis, carbohydrates are manufactured from carbon dioxide and water, using the energy produced when light is absorbed by chlorophyll.

phrase (frāz) *n.* **1.** a group of words expressing a single thought, but not containing a subject and predicate. In the sentence *To achieve success is his goal, To achieve success* is a phrase. **2.** a brief, often striking expression: *"No more war" was the phrase the protesters chanted as they marched.* **3.** *Music.* a group of musical notes that forms a unit of melody. —*v.t.,* **phrased, phras·ing. 1.** to express in a particular way: *The defense attorney phrased his questions very carefully.* **2.** to divide or mark off (a melody, musical composition, or the like) into phrases. —**phras′al,** *adj.*

phra·se·ol·o·gy (frā′zē ol′ə jē) *n. pl.,* **phra·se·ol·o·gies.** a particular style or manner of expression; choice and arrangement of words: *legal phraseology.*

phre·nol·o·gy (fri nol′ə jē) *n.* the system of judging a person's character and intelligence by studying the shape of his or her skull.

phy·lum (fī′ləm) *n. pl.,* **phy·la** (fī′lə). a major subdivision of the animal or plant kingdom.

phys·ic (fiz′ik) *n.* any medicine, especially a laxative.

phys·i·cal (fiz′i kəl) *adj.* **1.** of or relating to the body: *physical strength, physical fitness.* **2.** of, relating to, or containing matter: *physical things.* **3.** of or relating to matter and energy, or to the laws governing them. **4.** of or relating to nature or to natural objects: *a map of the physical features of a country.* —*n.* see **physical examination.** —**phys′i·cal·ly,** *adv.*

physical education, instruction in physical activities and the care of the body.

physical examination, a medical examination to find out a person's general state of health or his fitness for a certain activity.

physical geography, the study of the physical features of the earth, such as land formation, climate, and vegetation.

physical science, any science concerned with matter and energy and with the laws governing them, such as physics, chemistry, or astronomy.

physical therapy, the treatment of disease or injury by physical methods, such as heat, massage, or exercise. Also, **physiotherapy.**

phy·si·cian (fi zish′ən) *n.* a person who is licensed to practice medicine; doctor.

phys·i·cist (fiz′ə sist) *n.* a student of or an expert in physics.

phys·ics (fiz′iks) *n., pl.* the science that deals with matter and energy, and with the laws governing them. ▲ used with a singular verb.

phys·i·og·no·my (fiz′ē og′nə mē) *n. pl.,* **phys·i·og·no·mies.** 1. the features or appearance of the face: *The sailor had a rugged physiognomy.* 2. the art of judging character from the features or appearance of the face. 3. the general appearance of something: *the physiognomy of a mountain.*

phys·i·o·log·i·cal (fiz′ē ə loj′i kəl) *adj.* of or relating to physiology. —**phys′i·o·log′i·cal·ly,** *adv.*

phys·i·ol·o·gy (fiz′ē ol′ə jē) *n.* 1. the science that deals with the functions of living things or any of their parts. 2. the functions of a living thing or of any of its parts: *the physiology of the frog.* —**phys′i·ol′o·gist,** *n.*

phys·i·o·ther·a·py (fiz′ē ō ther′ə pē) *n.* another word for **physical therapy.**

phy·sique (fi zēk′) *n.* the structure, development, or appearance of the body: *a muscular physique.*

pi (pī) *n. pl.,* **pis.** 1. the sixteenth letter of the Greek alphabet (Π, π). 2. the ratio of the circumference of a circle to its diameter, represented by the Greek letter π. Pi is approximately 3.1416.

P.I., Philippine Islands.

pi·a·nis·si·mo (pē′ə nis′i mō′) *Music. adj.* very soft. —*adv.* very softly.

pi·an·ist (pē an′ist, pē′ə nist) *n.* a piano player.

pi·an·o¹ (pē an′ō) *n. pl.,* **pi·an·os.** a musical instrument that produces tones when felt-covered hammers, operated by a keyboard, strike metal strings. Also, **pianoforte.** [Short for *pianoforte.*]

pi·a·no² (pē ä′nō) *Music. adj.* soft. —*adv.* softly. [Italian *piano* softly.]

pi·an·o·for·te (pē an′ə fôr′tē) *n.* another word for **piano¹.**

pi·az·za (pē az′ə, pē ät′sə) *n.* 1. a public square in a town, especially in Italy. 2. a veranda; porch.

pi·ca (pī′kə) *n.* 1. a unit of measure used in printing, equal to about ⅙ inch. 2. a size of type for typewriters, providing ten characters to the inch.

pic·a·dor (pik′ə dôr′) *n.* a horseman in a bullfight who pricks the neck of the bull with a lance in order to weaken the bull's neck muscles.

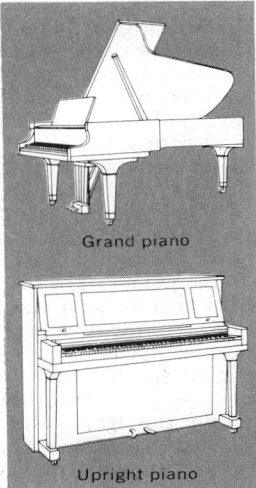

Grand piano

Upright piano

Pianos

Pic·ar·dy (pik′ər dē) *n.* a historic region and former province of northern France.

pic·a·resque (pik′ə resk′) *adj.* of or relating to usually low-born, roguish young men and their adventures, especially as described in fiction.

Pi·cas·so, Pa·blo (pi kä′sō; pä′blō) 1881–1973, Spanish painter and sculptor who lived in France.

pic·a·yune (pik′ə yōōn′) *adj.* 1. of little value or importance; paltry: *a picayune sum of money.* 2. narrow-minded; mean; petty.

Pic·ca·dil·ly (pik′ə dil′ē) *n.* one of the main streets of London.

pic·ca·lil·li (pik′ə lil′ē) *n.* a relish made of chopped vegetables, sugar, hot spices, and vinegar.

pic·co·lo (pik′ə lō′) *n. pl.,* **pic·co·los.** a small flute having a pitch one octave higher than the ordinary flute.

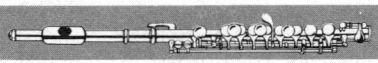

Piccolo

pick¹ (pik) *v.t.* 1. to select from a number; choose: *The city picked a site for the new museum. Have you picked out the book you want to buy?* 2. to gather with the fingers; pluck: *to pick flowers, to pick berries.* 3. to use the fingers or a pointed instrument, such as a toothpick, in order to remove matter from: *to pick one's teeth.* 4. to remove bit by bit with the fingers or an instrument, such as a fork: *to pick the meat from a bone.* 5. to make or form (a hole) with a pointed instrument or tool. 6. to pluck with the fingers or a plectrum: *to pick the strings of a guitar.* 7. to play (a stringed instrument) by plucking the strings with the fingers or a plectrum. 8. to cause deliberately; provoke: *The boy picked a fight with his older brother.* 9. to steal the contents of: *The thief picked the man's pocket.* 10. to open (a lock) with a pointed instrument or wire instead of a key. —*v.i.* 1. to select, especially in a careful manner. 2. to eat in small amounts or without appetite: *to pick at one's food.* —*n.* 1. a choice; selection: *Take your pick of the books on the table.* 2. the best or the choicest part or example: *That puppy is the pick of the litter.* 3. another word for **plectrum.** [Possibly from a blend of Middle French *piquer* to prick, sting and the unknown verb of the Old English noun *picung* a pricking.]

to pick on. *Informal.* to criticize or annoy; harass: *The older boys picked on the new student.*

to pick up. a. to take or lift up: *to pick up pebbles from the ground.* **b.** to take (someone or something) into a vehicle or ship: *to pick up a hitchhiker.* **c.** to get or acquire casually or by chance: *Roy picked up a few dollars by doing odd jobs.* **d.** to learn: *Joan picks up foreign languages easily.* **e.** to go faster; accelerate: *The car picked up speed as it went down the hill.* **f.** *Informal.* to improve; recover: *Business is picking up now that summer is over.* **g.** *Informal.* to take into custody: *Police picked up the criminal as he was boarding a train.*

pick² (pik) *n.* 1. a chipping or breaking tool that has a metal head, usually with one or two tips sharpened to a point, attached to a wooden handle; pickax. 2. any of various pointed instruments or tools without a head, such as an ice pick. [A form of *pike².*]

at; āpe; cär; end; mē; it; īce; hot; ōld; fôrk; wood; fŏŏl; oil; out; up; turn; sing; thin; <u>th</u>is; hw in white; zh in treasure. The symbol ə stands for the sound of **a** in about, **e** in taken, **i** in pencil, **o** in lemon, and **u** in circus.

pick·a·back (pik′ə bak′) *adv., adj.* another word for **piggyback.**

pick·ax (pik′aks′) *also,* **pick·axe.** *n. pl.,* **pick·ax·es.** see **pick²** *(def. 1).*

pick·er·el (pik′ər əl) *n. pl.,* **pick·er·els** or **pick·er·el.** a freshwater game and food fish of North America, having a slender body and a long snout. It is related to the pike.

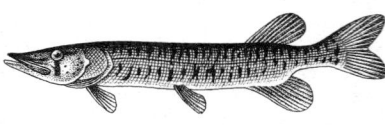
Pickerel

pick·et (pik′it) *n.* **1.** a pointed stake or slat usually driven into the ground to hold something in place or to build something, such as a fence. **2.** a person who stands or walks outside a place of business, government office, or other establishment to protest against something, as in a labor dispute or political demonstration. **3.** *Military.* a guard or body of troops stationed ahead of an army or outside a camp to watch for and give warning of the enemy's approach. —*v.t.* **1.** to act as or station a picket or pickets outside: *to picket an embassy.* **2.** to guard with a picket or pickets. **3.** to post as a picket. **4.** to fasten to a picket, as a horse. —*v.i.* to stand or walk about as a picket.

picket fence, a fence made of a row of pickets.

pick·ing (pik′ing) *n.* **1.** the act of a person who picks. **2. pickings.** something that is left over; scraps.

pick·le (pik′əl) *n.* **1.** any food, especially a cucumber, that has been preserved in a solution of salt water or vinegar. **2.** a solution of salt water or vinegar used to preserve or flavor food. **3.** *Informal.* a difficult or disagreeable situation. —*v.t.,* **pick·led, pick·ling.** to preserve or flavor in a solution of salt water or vinegar.

pick·pock·et (pik′pok′it) *n.* a thief who steals from the pockets or purses of others.

pick·up (pik′up′) *n.* **1.** the act of picking up: *a pickup of mail.* **2.** the capacity for quick acceleration: *The old car doesn't have much pickup.* **3.** a device that holds a phonograph needle and converts its vibrations into a weak electric current; cartridge. **4.** in radio and television, the reception of sound or light waves by the transmitter for conversion into electric waves. **5.** a small truck with an open body. Also, **pickup truck. 6.** *Informal.* an increase or improvement, as in activity or business.

pick·y (pik′ē) *adj.,* **pick·i·er, pick·i·est.** hard to please; fussy: *She is a picky eater.*

pic·nic (pik′nik) *n.* an outing that includes a meal eaten out-of-doors. —*v.i.,* **pic·nicked, pic·nick·ing.** to go on or have a picnic: *We picnicked in the park.* —**pic′nick′er,** *n.*

pi·cot (pē′kō) *n.* one of a series of small loops forming an ornamental edging on a piece of material, such as ribbon or lace. —*v.t.* to finish or ornament with such loops.

Pict (pikt) *n.* a member of an ancient people formerly living in northern and central Scotland.

pic·to·graph (pik′tə graf′) *n.* **1.** a picture that stands for a word or idea in a system of picture writing. **2.** a diagram, graph, or chart using pictures to represent data.

pic·to·ri·al (pik tôr′ē əl) *adj.* **1.** of, relating to, or of the nature of pictures: *pictorial art, pictorial writing.* **2.** illustrated by or containing pictures: *The school library subscribes to several pictorial publications.* **3.** very descriptive; graphic. —**pic·to′ri·al·ly,** *adv.*

Pictograph
meaning
"No bicycle riding"

pic·ture (pik′chər) *n.* **1.** a visual representation of something on a flat surface; drawing, painting, photograph, or the like. **2.** something presented to the eye. as an image on a motion-picture or television screen.

3. a description in words: *The lecturer gave an excellent picture of living conditions in China.* **4.** an impression or idea: *The boy formed a mental picture of life in ancient Greece.* **5.** a typical example; embodiment: *He looks the picture of health.* **6.** see **motion picture. 7.** a situation: *the political picture.* —*v.t.,* **pic·tured, pic·tur·ing. 1.** to represent something visually, as in a drawing or painting; depict: *The artist pictured an old man sitting in a chair.* **2.** to give a description of; describe: *The writer pictured the horror and destruction of war.* **3.** to form an impression or idea of; imagine: *Can you picture him playing football?*

pic·tur·esque (pik′chə resk′) *adj.* **1.** having pleasing qualities suitable for a picture: *A cottage by the sea is a picturesque setting.* **2.** striking or expressive: *picturesque speech.* —**pic′tur·esque′ly,** *adv.* —**pic′tur·esque′ness,** *n.*

picture tube, a cathode-ray tube that serves as the screen of a television receiver. Also, **kinescope.**

pid·dling (pid′ling) *adj.* unimportant or trivial; petty.

pid·gin (pij′ən) *n.* a mixture of two or more languages having a simplified grammar and vocabulary, used for communication between peoples who speak different languages.

pie¹ (pī) *n.* a baked dish made of pastry with a filling of meat, fish, fruit, or other food. [Middle English *pie.*]

pie² (pī) *n.* see **magpie.** [Old French *pie.*]

pie·bald (pī′bôld′) *adj.* having spots or patches, especially of black and white. —*n.* a piebald animal, especially a horse.

piece (pēs) *n.* **1.** a separated part; fragment: *a piece of broken glass.* **2.** a part of something forming a single unit or whole: *a piece of land, a piece of cake.* **3.** a single object belonging to a set or group: *a piece of luggage, a piece of china.* **4.** an artistic composition or production: *a piece of music, a literary piece.* **5.** a particular quantity or amount, as of fabric sold or work done. **6.** an instance; example: *That car is a piece of junk.* **7.** a coin: *a ten-cent piece.* **8.** any of the small objects, such as disks or chessmen, used in playing checkers, chess, or other board games. **9.** a gun or cannon. —*v.t.,* **pieced, piec·ing. 1.** to join the pieces of in order to construct: *to piece a story from scattered information.* **2.** to mend by bringing together or adding a piece or pieces; patch: *to piece a ripped dress.*

to go to pieces. *Informal.* to break down emotionally.

piece·meal (pēs′mēl′) *adv.* **1.** piece by piece; a little at a time: *The book was written piecemeal over a long period of time.* **2.** into pieces or fragments: *to be torn piecemeal.* —*adj.* made or done piece by piece: *a piecemeal effort.*

piece of eight, an obsolete Spanish silver coin.

piece·work (pēs′wurk′) *n.* work done and paid for by the piece rather than by the hour or the day. —**piece′-work′er,** *n.*

pied (pīd) *adj.* having large spots of different colors.

Pied·mont (pēd′mont) *n.* a region of the eastern United States extending from northeastern New Jersey to central Alabama and sloping seaward from the Appalachian Mountains to the Atlantic coastal plain.

pier (pēr) *n.* **1.** a structure built out over the water, used especially as a landing place for boats or ships. **2.** a solid support on which an arch rests, as in a bridge. **3.** the solid part of a wall between openings, as windows.

Pier

pierce (pērs) *v.,* **pierced, pierc·ing.** —*v.t.* **1.** to penetrate or pass into or through, as with a sharp-pointed instrument: *The splinter pierced my skin.* **2.** to make a hole or opening in or through; perforate: *The pick pierced the layer of* *ice.* **3.** to force or break a way into or through: *The enemy's attack pierced our line of defense.* **4.** to perceive with the mind or senses; see into or through; discern: *to pierce a mystery.* **5.** to affect the emotions keenly; touch or move deeply: *The sad tale pierced our hearts.* **6.** to penetrate with a sharp sound: *A shout pierced the stillness of the night.* —*v.i.* to pass into or through; penetrate: *The knife did not pierce very deeply.*

Pierce, Franklin (pērs) 1804–1869, the fourteenth president of the United States, from 1853 to 1857.

pierc·ing (pēr′sing) *adj.* penetrating; sharp: *a piercing scream, a piercing look.* —**pierc′ing·ly,** *adv.*

Pierre (pēr) *n.* the capital of South Dakota, in the central part of the state. Pop. (1970), 9699.

Pie·tà (pē′ä tä′) *also,* **pie·tà.** *n.* a representation in a work of art, such as a painting or sculpture, of the Virgin Mary holding the dead body of Christ.

pi·e·ty (pī′ə tē) *n. pl.,* **pi·e·ties. 1.** reverence for God; religious devoutness; godliness. **2.** loyalty and obedience, as to one's parents. **3.** a pious act or belief.

pig (pig) *n.* **1.** a hoofed animal, especially one of various breeds widely raised for food, having a stout, roundish body, short legs, and a blunt snout. **2.** a young swine. **3.** the flesh of a pig used as food; pork. **4.** *Informal.* a person who is dirty, greedy, or very fat. **5.** an oblong mass of metal, especially iron, cast from a smelting furnace.

pi·geon (pij′ən) *n.* **1.** any of numerous wild or domesticated birds with a stout body, small head, and thick, soft feathers. **2.** a blue and gray bird of this group, commonly found in cities and sometimes raised for food. **3.** *Slang.* a person who is easily cheated or fooled; dupe.

Pigeon

pi·geon·hole (pij′ən hōl′) *n.* **1.** a small compartment, as in a cabinet or desk, for holding papers or other articles. **2.** a small hole or place for pigeons to nest in. —*v.t.,* **pi·geon·holed, pi·geon·hol·ing. 1.** to put in a small compartment; file. **2.** to lay aside or put away and forget: *The committee pigeonholed the proposal.* **3.** to put in a category; classify: *She pigeonholed him as a troublemaker from the very beginning.*

pi·geon·toed (pij′ən tōd′) *adj.* having the toes or feet turned inward.

pig·gish (pig′ish) *adj.* like a pig in habits or manners, especially in being greedy or dirty. —**pig′gish·ly,** *adv.* —**pig′gish·ness,** *n.*

pig·gy·back (pig′ē bak′) *adv., adj.* on the back or shoulders. Also, **pickaback.**

piggy bank, a small bank, often in the shape of a pig, used especially by children for saving coins.

pig·head·ed (pig′hed′id) *adj.* unreasonably stubborn; obstinate. —**pig′-head′ed·ly,** *adv.* —**pig′-head′ed·ness,** *n.*

pig iron, crude iron as it comes from the blast furnace.

pig·ment (pig′mənt) *n.* **1.** a substance used for coloring, especially a powdered substance that is mixed with a liquid to produce a paint or dye. **2.** a substance, such as chlorophyll, that gives color to plant or animal tissues.

pig·men·ta·tion (pig′men tā′shən) *n.* the coloration in plant or animal tissues caused by pigment.

Pig·my (pig′mē) *n. pl.,* **Pig·mies.** another spelling of **Pygmy.**

pig·pen (pig′pen′) *n.* **1.** a pen for pigs. **2.** a dirty place.

pig·skin (pig′skin′) *n.* **1.** the skin of a pig. **2.** leather made of this. **3.** *Informal.* a football.

pig·sty (pig′stī′) *n. pl.,* **pig·sties.** another word for **pigpen.**

pig·tail (pig′tāl′) *n.* a braid of hair hanging down from the back or either side of the head.

pike¹ (pīk) *n.* a weapon consisting of a long wooden shaft with a pointed tip of iron or steel, formerly used by foot soldiers. [Old French *pique.*]

pike² (pīk) *n.* a sharp point, such as the tip of a spear. [Old English *pīc.*]

pike³ (pīk) *n.* a large freshwater fish of Europe, Asia, and northern North America, having a slim, tapering, olive-green body and a duck-billed snout with many sharp teeth. [Possibly from *pike²*; referring to the pointed shape of the head.]

pike⁴ (pīk) *n.* see **turnpike.**

pik·er (pī′kər) *n. Slang.* a person who is stingy, overly cautious, or petty.

Pikes Peak (pīks) a mountain of the Rocky Mountains, in central Colorado.

pike·staff (pīk′staf′) *n. pl.,* **pike·staves** (pīk′stāvz′). **1.** the shaft of a pike. **2.** a walking stick with a metal tip at the lower end.

pi·las·ter (pi las′tər) *n.* a rectangular flat column projecting slightly from a wall.

Pi·late, Pon·tius (pī′lət; pon′shəs) the Roman governor of Judea from A.D. 26 to 36.

pile¹ (pīl) *n.* **1.** a number of things laid or lying one upon another; heap: *a pile of newspapers, a pile of dirt.* **2.** *Informal.* a large amount or quantity: *a pile of money, a pile of troubles.* **3.** see **nuclear reactor.** —*v.,* **piled, pil·ing.** —*v.t.* **1.** to form into a heap or mass: *The gardener piled up fallen leaves in a corner of the yard.* **2.** to accumulate: *to pile up debts.* **3.** to cover or load with a pile: *The man piled his desk with books.* —*v.i.* **1.** to form or rise in a heap or mass: *The snow piled in drifts.* **2.** *Informal.* to move in a confused or disorderly mass; crowd: *The whole family piled into the car.* [Old French *pile* heap.]

Pilasters

pile² (pīl) *n.* a strong, slender beam of wood, steel, or concrete, driven vertically into the ground to support a structure, such as a bridge or wharf. [Old English *pīl* a pointed stake.]

pile³ (pīl) *n.* **1.** the raised cut or uncut loops of yarn that form the surface of a fabric, such as velvet, or of a carpet. **2.** fine, soft hair or fiber. [Latin *pilus* a hair.]

pile driver, a machine for driving piles into the ground, usually consisting of a frame in which a heavy weight is suspended and then dropped on the pile.

pil·fer (pil′fər) *v.t., v.i.* to steal in small quantities. —**pil′fer·age,** *n.*

pil·grim (pil′grəm) *n.* **1.** a person who journeys to a sacred place for a religious purpose, as for penance or devotion. **2.** any traveler. **3. Pilgrim.** one of the group of English Puritans who founded Plymouth Colony in 1620.

pil·grim·age (pil′grə mij) *n.* **1.** a journey to a sacred place for a religious purpose. **2.** any long journey.

at; āpe; cär; end; mē; it; īce; hot; ōld; fôrk; wood; fŏŏl; oil; out; up; turn; sing; thin; **this;** hw in white; zh in treasure. The symbol ə stands for the sound of **a** in about, **e** in taken, **i** in pencil, **o** in lemon, and **u** in circus.

pil·ing (pī′ling) *n.* a number of piles, or a structure made up of a number of piles.

pill (pil) *n.* 1. a pellet of medicine that is swallowed whole or chewed. 2. something that is disagreeable but must be endured: *The loss of the election was a bitter pill for him to swallow.* *Slang.* a disagreeable or boring person.

pil·lage (pil′ij) *v.,* **pil·laged, pil·lag·ing.** —*v.t.* to rob by force, as during a war; plunder: *The soldiers pillaged the town.* —*v.i.* to take booty: *The invading army pillaged throughout the countryside.* —*n.* 1. the act of plundering. 2. something carried off as booty; plunder: *The pillage from the cargo ship made the pirates rich.* —**pil′lag·er,** *n.*

pil·lar (pil′ər) *n.* 1. an upright structure that serves as a support for a building or stands alone as a monument. 2. something resembling a pillar in shape or function. 3. a person who is a chief supporter or important member of something: *a pillar of society.*
   from pillar to post. from one place, person, or situation to another without purpose or aim.

pill·box (pil′boks′) *n. pl.,* **pill·box·es.** 1. a small box for pills. 2. a small, low, concrete structure with guns to defend a coast, border, or the like. 3. a woman's small round hat.

pil·lion (pil′yən) *n.* a pad or cushion behind the saddle of a horse or the seat of a motorcycle for another rider.

pil·lo·ry (pil′ər ē) *n. pl.,* **pil·lo·ries.** a wooden frame fitted with openings to hold the head and hands, formerly used to expose a person to public ridicule as punishment for an offense. —*v.t.,* **pil·lo·ried, pil·lo·ry·ing.** 1. to put in a pillory. 2. to expose to public ridicule or abuse: *The crooked businessman was pilloried by the newspapers.*

Pillory

pil·low (pil′ō) *n.* a bag or casing filled with soft material, such as feathers, down, or foam rubber, used to support the head during sleep, or for decoration. —*v.t.* to rest on or as if on a pillow: *John pillowed his head on his hand.*

pil·low·case (pil′ō kās′) *n.* a removable cloth cover for a pillow. Also, **pil·low·slip** (pil′ō slip′).

pi·lot (pī′lət) *n.* 1. a person who operates the controls of an aircraft or spacecraft. 2. a person who steers a ship, especially into or out of a harbor. 3. any person who guides or leads. 4. see **pilot light.** —*v.t.* 1. to act as the pilot of; steer. 2. to guide. —*adj.* trial or sample: *a pilot study.*

pilot fish, a small fish that usually swims along with sharks or other large fish.

pi·lot·house (pī′lət hous′) *n. pl.,* **pi·lot·hous·es** (pī′lət hou′ziz). a structure on the deck of a ship that shelters the steering equipment and the pilot.

pilot light, a small flame kept burning in order to light a gas burner when it is turned on.

pi·men·to (pi men′tō) *n. pl.,* **pi·men·tos.** 1. an evergreen tree related to the myrtle, from which allspice is obtained. 2. another spelling of **pimiento.**

pi·mien·to (pi myen′tō) *also,* **pi·men·to.** *n. pl.,* **pi·mien·tos.** a mild, sweet red pepper used to stuff olives or to garnish food.

pim·per·nel (pim′pər nel′) *n.* 1. a small scarlet or white flower of a plant related to the primrose. 2. the plant bearing this flower.

pim·ple (pim′pəl) *n.* a small raised blemish on the skin, often red and sore, that contains pus. —**pim′pled, pim′ply,** *adj.*

pin (pin) *n.* 1. a short, straight, stiff piece of wire with a point at one end and a head at the other, used to fasten things together. 2. an ornament or emblem that has a pin or clasp for attaching it to clothing: *a fraternity pin.* 3. anything like a pin in form or use, such as a safety pin, a clothespin, a hairpin, or a bobby pin. 4. a peg of wood, plastic, or metal, used for various purposes, as for fastening things together or hanging something on. 5. *Bowling.* a bottle-shaped piece of wood set up as a target to be knocked down by the ball. 6. *Golf.* the staff of the flag that marks the hole on a green. 7. **pins.** *Informal.* legs. —*v.t.,* **pinned, pin·ning.** 1. to fasten or attach with a pin or pins. 2. to seize and hold fast in one spot or position: *The boxer pinned his opponent against the ropes.* 3. *Slang.* to place the blame for: *The police tried to pin the robbery on him.*
   to be on pins and needles. to be nervous or anxious.

pin·a·fore (pin′ə fôr′) *n.* a garment resembling an apron, covering most of a dress, worn especially by young girls.

pi·ña·ta (pēn yä′tə) *n.* a colorfully decorated container used in Latin American Christmas celebrations. It is filled with fruit, candy, and gifts, and hung from the ceiling to be broken with a stick by a child who is blindfolded.

pince-nez (pans′nā′, pins′nā′) *n. pl.,* **pince-nez.** eye-glasses held on the nose by a spring. [French *pince-nez* literally, pinch-nose.]

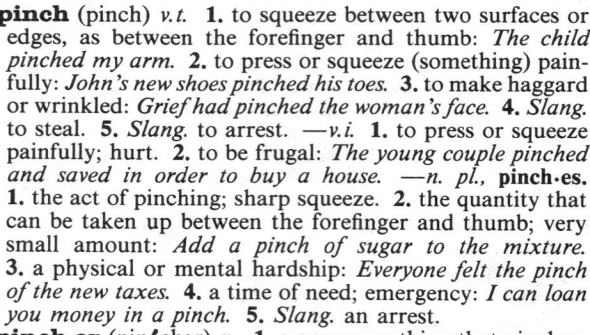

Pinafore

pin·cers (pin′sərz) *also,* **pinch·ers.** *n.,pl.* 1. a gripping instrument having a pair of jaws and handles that are fastened on a pivot. 2. a grasping claw resembling this, such as that of a crab or lobster.

pinch (pinch) *v.t.* 1. to squeeze between two surfaces or edges, as between the forefinger and thumb: *The child pinched my arm.* 2. to press or squeeze (something) painfully: *John's new shoes pinched his toes.* 3. to make haggard or wrinkled: *Grief had pinched the woman's face.* 4. *Slang.* to steal. 5. *Slang.* to arrest. —*v.i.* 1. to press or squeeze painfully; hurt. 2. to be frugal: *The young couple pinched and saved in order to buy a house.* —*n. pl.,* **pinch·es.** 1. the act of pinching; sharp squeeze. 2. the quantity that can be taken up between the forefinger and thumb; very small amount: *Add a pinch of sugar to the mixture.* 3. a physical or mental hardship: *Everyone felt the pinch of the new taxes.* 4. a time of need; emergency: *I can loan you money in a pinch.* 5. *Slang.* an arrest.

pinch·er (pin′chər) *n.* 1. a person or thing that pinches. 2. **pinchers.** another spelling of **pincers.**

pinch-hit (pinch′hit′) *v.i.,* **pinch-hit, pinch-hit·ting.** 1. *Baseball.* to bat in place of another player. 2. to take someone's place; be a substitute.

pinch hitter, a person who pinch-hits.

pin·cush·ion (pin′koosh′ən) *n.* a small cushion into which sewing needles and pins are stuck when they are not being used.

pine[1] (pīn) *n.* 1. any of a large group of evergreen trees bearing cones and needlelike leaves. 2. the wood of any of these trees, widely used in building and as a source of turpentine. [Old English *pīn.*]

pine[2] (pīn) *v.i.,* **pined, pin·ing.** to become weak or unhealthy, as from grief or longing: *After her husband's death, the old woman pined away.* [Old English *pīnian* to torment.]

pin·e·al body (pin′ē əl) a small organ whose function is not fully known, found in the brain of human beings and other animals with backbones. Also, **pineal gland.**

pine·ap·ple (pīn′ap′əl) *n.* **1.** a large, oval fruit having firm, juicy, yellow flesh that can be eaten and a hard, scaly outer covering. **2.** the plant bearing this fruit, having jagged-edged leaves and clusters of reddish or violet flowers.

Pineapple

pine needle, a slender needle-like leaf of a pine tree.

pin·ey (pī′nē) *adj.,* **pin·i·er, pin·i·est.** another spelling of **piny.**

pin·feath·er (pin′feth′ər) *n.* an undeveloped feather that is just beginning to break through the skin of a young bird.

Ping-Pong (ping′pong′) *n. Trademark.* another word for **table tennis.**

pin·hole (pin′hōl′) *n.* a small hole made by or as if by a pin.

pin·ion¹ (pin′yən) *n.* a bird's wing, especially the last segment. —*v.t.* **1.** to prevent (a bird) from flying by clipping or binding the pinions. **2.** to clip or bind (the pinions). **3.** to bind or hold firmly: *The wrestler pinioned his opponent's arms behind him.* [Middle French *pignon.*]

pin·ion² (pin′yən) *n.* a small wheel with cogs that lock into the cogs of a larger wheel or rack. [French *pignon.*]

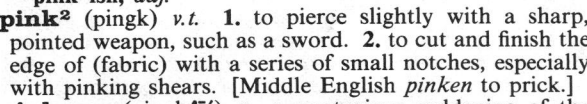

Pinion

Pinion²

pink¹ (pingk) *n.* **1.** a light red color. **2.** the highest degree: *He is in the pink of health.* **3.** a fragrant flower of any of a group of plants having five or more petals, such as the carnation. **4.** a plant bearing this flower, having grayish-green leaves. —*adj.* having the color pink. [Of uncertain origin.] —**pink′ish,** *adj.*

pink² (pingk) *v.t.* **1.** to pierce slightly with a sharp, pointed weapon, such as a sword. **2.** to cut and finish the edge of (fabric) with a series of small notches, especially with pinking shears. [Middle English *pinken* to prick.]

pink·eye (pingk′ī′) *n.* a contagious reddening of the tissue that covers the eyeball and lines the lower and upper eyelids; conjunctivitis.

pink·ie (ping′kē) *also,* **pink·y.** *n. pl.,* **pink·ies.** *Informal.* the smallest finger.

pinking shears, scissors having notched blades, used to pink fabric.

pin money, a small sum of money for minor expenses or purchases, originally an allowance given by a man to his wife for her personal expenses.

pin·na·cle (pin′ə kəl) *n.* **1.** a high, pointed formation, such as a mountain peak. **2.** the highest point; acme: *The scientist achieved the pinnacle of success in his field.* **3.** *Architecture.* a small tower set above a larger structure.

pin·nate (pin′āt) *adj.* resembling a feather in shape or structure: *pinnate leaves.* —**pin′nate·ly,** *adv.*

pi·noch·le (pē′nuk′əl, pē′nok′əl) *also,* **pi·noc·le.** *n.* a game played with a special deck of forty-eight cards having two of the ace, ten, king, queen, jack, and nine in each suit.

pi·ñon (pin′yon, pin′yōn) *n. pl.,* **pi·ñons** or **pi·ño·nes** (pin yō′nēz). **1.** a small pine tree found in the southwestern United States. **2.** the edible nut of this tree.

pin·point (pin′point′) *v.t.* to locate, fix, or identify precisely: *The soldiers pinpointed the camp of the enemy.* —*adj.* strict; exact: *The gunners were able to fire with pinpoint accuracy.* —*n.* **1.** the point of a pin. **2.** something very small or

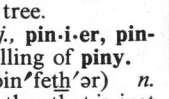

Pinnacle
(def. 3)

unimportant: *In the distance we saw a pinpoint of light.*

pint (pīnt) *n.* **1.** a unit of liquid measure equal to half a quart or one-eighth of a gallon. **2.** a unit of dry measure equal to half a quart or one-sixteenth of a peck.

pin·tail (pin′tāl′) *n. pl.,* **pin·tails** or **pin·tail.** **1.** a long-necked duck, having long, pointed central tail feathers. **2.** a grouse of North America, having a long, pointed tail.

pin·to (pin′tō) *adj.* having spots or patches of two or more colors; mottled. —*n. pl.,* **pin·tos.** a pinto horse or pony.

pin·wheel (pin′hwēl′, pin′wēl′) *n.* a toy made of colored paper or plastic pinned to a stick so as to revolve when spun by hand or blown upon.

pin·worm (pin′wurm′) *n.* a small roundworm found in the lower intestinal tract.

pin·y (pī′nē) *also,* **pine·y.** *adj.,* **pin·i·er, pin·i·est.** **1.** of, relating to, or like pine trees: *a piny fragrance.* **2.** covered with or having many pine trees: *a piny forest.*

Pin·yin (pin′yin′) *n.* a system for spelling Chinese proper names in English. [Chinese *pinyin* transliteration.]

pi·o·neer (pī′ə nēr′) *n.* **1.** a person who is the first or among the first to explore or settle a region. **2.** a person who is the first or among the first to open up or develop an area of thought, research, or activity: *Sigmund Freud was a pioneer in psychology.* —*v.t.* **1.** to explore or settle: *Courageous settlers pioneered the Northwest Territory.* **2.** to open up or develop. —*v.i.* to be a pioneer: *American industry pioneered in the development of mass production.* [French *pionnier* foot soldier; later, pioneer, going back to Latin *pedō* foot soldier, from *pēs* foot; originally referring to a foot soldier who went ahead of an army to prepare the way. (His work included digging ditches and repairing roads.)]

pi·ous (pī′əs) *adj.* **1.** deeply religious: *a pious woman.* **2.** of or relating to religious devotion: *pious writings.* —**pi′ous·ly,** *adv.* —**pi′ous·ness,** *n.*

pip¹ (pip) *n.* **1.** the seed of a fruit, such as an apple or orange. **2.** *Slang.* a person or thing that is remarkable or excellent: *He sure is a pip!* [Short for *pippin.*]

pip² (pip) *n.* a contagious disease of chickens and other birds, characterized by the secretion of thick mucus in the mouth and throat. [Middle Dutch *pippe* mucus.]

pip³ (pip) *n.* any of the spots or marks on dominoes, dice, or playing cards. [Of uncertain origin.]

pipe (pīp) *n.* **1.** a tube of metal, glass, or similar material for carrying a gas or liquid. **2.** a tube with a bowl of briar or clay at one end, used for smoking. **3.** a musical instrument in the form of a tube that is blown into at one end. **4.** one of the tubes in an organ in which tones are produced. **5.** pipes. **a.** a musical instrument made up of a series of tubes bound together; panpipe. **b.** see **bagpipe.** —*v.,* **piped, pip·ing.** —*v.t.* **1.** to convey by means of a pipe or pipes: *The farmer piped water to his fields.* **2.** to supply with pipes: *The builders piped the new house for gas.* **3.** to play (music) on a pipe. **4.** to say or sing in a loud, shrill voice. —*v.i.* **1.** to make a loud, shrill sound. **2.** to play on a pipe. —**pipe′like′,** *adj.*

to pipe down. *Slang.* to be quiet.

pipe dream, a fanciful notion or wish: *The poor student's pipe dream was to live and study in Europe.*

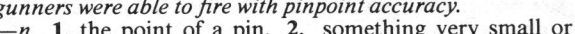

at; āpe; cär; end; mē; it; īce; hot; ōld; fôrk; wood; fōol; oil; out; up; turn; sing; thin; this; hw in white; zh in treasure. The symbol ə stands for the sound of a in about, e in taken, i in pencil, o in lemon, and u in circus.

pipe·line (pīp′līn′) *n.* **1.** a line of pipes for carrying gas or liquid. **2.** a route by which information or supplies are carried: *The businessman has a direct pipeline to the governor's office.*

pip·er (pī′pər) *n.* a person who plays on a pipe, especially on the bagpipes.

to pay the piper. to bear the responsibility of one's actions.

pi·pette (pī pet′) *n.* a slender glass tube for measuring or for transferring measured amounts of liquids.

pip·ing (pī′ping) *n.* **1.** a system of pipes. **2.** the music of a pipe or pipes: *the piping of a flute.* **3.** a loud, shrill sound: *the piping of a bird.* —*adj.* shrill: *a piping voice.*

piping hot. very hot.

pip·it (pip′it) *n.* any of various small birds resembling a sparrow, having a thin bill and brown feathers.

pip·pin (pip′in) *n.* any of various kinds of apples.

pi·quant (pē′kənt) *adj.* **1.** pleasantly sharp to the taste; pungent; tart: *The cook poured a piquant sauce over the meat.* **2.** interesting or stimulating: *The critic made piquant comments about the author's newest book.* —**pi′quan·cy,** *n.* —**pi′quant·ly,** *adv.*

pique (pēk) *n.* resentment caused by having one's feelings hurt or one's pride wounded: *Helen gave back the engagement ring in a fit of pique.* —*v.t.,* **piqued, pi·quing. 1.** to cause a feeling of anger or resentment in; offend: *She was piqued by his thoughtless remark.* **2.** to arouse; excite: *The locked closet piqued my curiosity.*

pi·qué (pi kā′, pē kā′) *n.* a fabric usually made of cotton, woven with narrow, lengthwise ribs.

pi·ra·cy (pī′rə sē) *n. pl.,* **pi·ra·cies. 1.** robbery on the high seas. **2.** the use of another's work, invention, or ideas without permission or in violation of a copyright.

Pi·rae·us (pī rē′əs, pi rā′əs) *n.* the leading industrial center of Greece and port of nearby Athens, in the eastern part of the country. Pop. (1971), 186,223.

pi·ra·nha (pi ran′yə) *n.* a freshwater fish of tropical South America, which travels in schools and feeds on other fish. Piranhas will also attack large animals, including man.

pi·rate (pī′rit) *n.* **1.** a person who robs on the high seas. **2.** a person who uses the work, invention, or ideas of another without permission or in violation of a copyright. —*v.,* **pi·rat·ed, pi·rat·ing. 1.** to rob on the high seas. **2.** to use (another's work, invention, or ideas) without permission or in violation of a copyright. —*v.i.* to practice piracy.

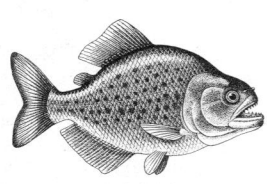

Piranha

pir·ou·ette (pir′ŏŏ et′) *n.* a rapid turning about on the toes, especially in dancing. —*v.i.,* **pir·ou·et·ted, pir·ou·et·ting.** to perform a pirouette.

Pi·sa (pē′zə) *n.* a city in central Italy. Pop. (1970 est.), 103,223.

Pis·ces (pī′sēz, pis′ēz) *n.* **1.** a constellation in the northern sky, thought to resemble two fish in shape. **2.** the twelfth sign of the zodiac.

pis·ta·chi·o (pis tash′ē ō′) *n. pl.,* **pis·ta·chi·os. 1.** a small, edible, greenish nut having a thin purple skin and covered by a hard gray shell. **2.** the small tree bearing this nut. **3.** the flavor of the nut. **4.** a light yellowish-green color. —*adj.* having the color pistachio.

pis·til (pist′əl) *n.* the part of a flower where seeds are produced. It is made up of the ovary, style, and stigma.

pis·til·late (pist′əl āt′) *adj.* having a pistil or pistils, especially having pistils but no stamens.

pis·tol (pist′əl) *n.* a small firearm that is held and fired with one hand.

pis·ton (pis′tən) *n.* **1.** a disk or cylinder that fits closely inside a sleeve or hollow cylinder, where it moves back and forth. **2.** in a brass musical instrument, a sliding valve used to change the pitch of tones.

piston ring, a metal ring that fits into grooves near the top end of the piston and seals off the gap between the piston and the surrounding cylinder.

piston rod, a rod connected to a piston that makes it move, or by which the piston makes another part move.

Piston rings

Cylinder

Piston

Piston rod

Crankshaft

Piston in a
gasoline engine

pit¹ (pit) *n.* **1.** a hole in the ground, either natural or man-made. **2.** a very small scar on a surface, as a pockmark on the skin. **3.** a natural hollow in the body: *the pit of the arm.* **4.** a sunken or enclosed area for fights between animals. **5.** a sunken area in front of the stage of a theater for the orchestra. **6.** hell. —*v.t.,* **pit·ted, pit·ting. 1.** to make small holes in; mark with pits: *Pebbles thrown against the windows pitted the glass.* **2.** to place in opposition; match: *They pitted the challenger against the champion.* [Old English *pytt.*]

pit² (pit) *n.* the hard stone of a fruit, such as a peach or cherry. —*v.t.,* **pit·ted, pit·ting.** to remove stones from (fruit). [Dutch *pit.*]

pit·a·pat (pit′ə pat′) *adv.* with quick beats or taps: *Mary's heart went pitapat.* —*v.i.,* **pit·a·pat·ted, pit·a·pat·ting.** to go pitapat. —*n.* the sound made by this.

pitch¹ (pich) *v.t.* **1.** to throw, hurl, or toss: *to pitch horseshoes, to pitch pennies.* **2.** *Baseball.* to throw (the ball) to the batter. **3.** to set up; erect: *to pitch a camp, to pitch a tent.* **4.** to set on a slope; incline: *to pitch a roof.* **5.** *Music.* to set the key of: *to pitch a guitar, to pitch a tune.* —*v.i.* **1.** to fall or plunge forward: *The painter lost his balance and pitched off the ladder.* **2.** to slope downward. **3.** *Baseball.* to throw the ball to the batter. **4.** to plunge so that the bow and stern rise and fall: *The ship pitched in the rough sea.* —*n. pl.,* **pitch·es. 1.** a throw, hurl, or toss. **2.** a point, degree, or level: *a high pitch of enthusiasm.* **3.** a downward slope: *the pitch of a roof.* **4.** *Baseball.* **a.** the act or manner of pitching the ball to the batter. **b.** the ball that is pitched. **5.** the highness or lowness of a sound or musical tone. **6.** *Slang.* a talk intended to persuade, usually using high-pressure tactics: *a sales pitch.* [Possibly from an unrecorded Old English word.]

pitch² (pich) *n.* **1.** a dark, thick, sticky substance obtained from petroleum, coal tar, or wood tar, used for waterproofing and paving. **2.** a resin obtained from pine trees. —*v.t.* to cover or smear with pitch. [Old English *pic.*] —**pitch′y,** *adv.*

pitch-black (pich′blak′) *adj.* extremely black.

pitch·blende (pich′blend′) *n.* a black, lumpy variety of uraninite.

pitch-dark (pich′därk′) *adj.* extremely dark.

pitched battle, a fierce, closely fought battle.

pitch·er¹ (pich′ər) *n.* **1.** a vessel with a handle and a lip or spout, used chiefly for holding and pouring liquids. **2.** the amount contained by a pitcher. [Old French *pichier.*]

pitch·er² (pich′ər) *n.* a person who pitches, especially the player on a baseball team who throws the ball to the batter. [*Pitch¹* + *-er¹.*]

pitcher plant, a plant having pitcher-shaped leaves that trap insects.

pitch·fork (pich′fôrk′) *n.* a long-handled tool with projecting prongs, used especially to lift and pitch hay.

pitch·out (pich′out′) *n.* **1.** a pitch in baseball thrown high and wide to make it easier for the catcher to throw out a base runner attempting to steal. **2.** a lateral pass in football behind the line of scrimmage, usually from the quarterback to another back.

pitch pipe, a small pipe that has a fixed note, used to give the pitch to a person who sings or plays an instrument.

pit·e·ous (pit′ē əs) *adj.* deserving or arousing pity; pitiable; pathetic. —**pit′e·ous·ly,** *adv.* —**pit′e·ous·ness,** *n.*

Pitchfork

pit·fall (pit′fôl′) *n.* **1.** a pit dug into the ground and covered over, used to catch animals. **2.** any hidden danger or difficulty.

pith (pith) *n.* **1.** soft, spongy tissue in the center of the stems of certain plants. **2.** soft tissue resembling this: *the pith of a grapefruit.* **3.** the important or essential part: *the pith of an essay.*

Pith·e·can·thro·pus (pith′ə kan′thrə pəs) *n. pl.,* **Pith·e·can·thro·pi** (pith′ə kan′thrə pī′). another word for **Java man.**

pith·y (pith′ē) *adj.,* **pith·i·er, pith·i·est. 1.** of, like, or full of pith. **2.** short and full of meaning: *a pithy statement.* —**pith′i·ly,** *adv.* —**pith′i·ness,** *n.*

pit·i·a·ble (pit′ē ə bəl) *adj.* deserving or arousing pity: *He was a pitiable old man.* —**pit′i·a·ble·ness,** *n.* —**pit′i·a·bly,** *adv.*

pit·i·ful (pit′i fəl) *adj.* **1.** arousing pity: *a pitiful look.* **2.** arousing contempt; paltry: *a pitiful excuse.* —**pit′i·ful·ly,** *adv.* —**pit′i·ful·ness,** *n.*

pit·i·less (pit′i lis) *adj.* without pity; showing no mercy: *a pitiless attack.* —**pit′i·less·ly,** *adv.* —**pit′i·less·ness,** *n.*

Pitt (pit) **1. William.** 1708–1778, English statesman. **2. William.** 1759–1806, his son; English statesman; prime minister from 1783 to 1801 and from 1804 to 1806.

pit·tance (pit′əns) *n.* a small or meager amount or allowance, as of money: *He was paid only a pittance for mowing the lawn.*

pit·ter-pat·ter (pit′ər pat′ər) *n.* the sound of quick taps or beats: *the pitter-patter of footsteps.* —*adv.* with quick taps or beats.

Pitts·burgh (pits′burg′) *n.* a city in southwestern Pennsylvania. Pop. (1970), 520,117.

pi·tu·i·tar·y (pi tōō′ə ter′ē, pi tyōō′ə ter′ē) *n.* see **pituitary gland.** —*adj.* of or relating to the pituitary gland.

pituitary gland, a small, oval endocrine gland located beneath the brain. The pituitary gland secretes hormones that regulate body growth and the functions of many other parts of the body.

pit viper, any of several poisonous snakes including the bushmaster, copperhead, and water moccasin, having a deep pit on each side of the head.

pit·y (pit′ē) *n. pl.,* **pit·ies. 1.** a feeling of sorrow and sympathy aroused by the unhappiness or suffering of another or others. **2.** a cause for regret: *What a pity you can't go.* —*v.t.,* **pit·ied, pit·y·ing.** to feel pity for: *We pitied the people who lost their homes in the flood.* —**pit′y·ing·ly,** *adv.*

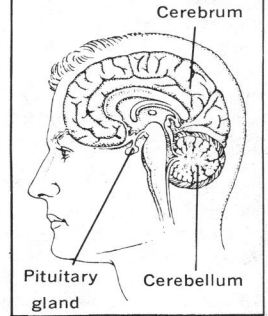

Cerebrum

Pituitary gland

Cerebellum

Pituitary gland

piv·ot (piv′ət) *n.* **1.** a point, shaft, or pin that something turns on. **2.** a person or thing of importance that something depends on. **3.** the act of turning on a pivot or as if on a pivot. —*v.t.* to place on or furnish with a pivot. —*v.i.* to turn on a pivot or as if on a pivot: *He pivoted around to face the person who called his name.*

piv·ot·al (piv′ət əl) *adj.* **1.** of, relating to, or serving as a pivot. **2.** of much importance; crucial: *a pivotal matter.* —**piv′ot·al·ly,** *adv.*

pix·y (pik′sē) *also,* **pix·ie.** *n. pl.,* **pix·ies. 1.** an imaginary small or mischievous being; fairy; elf. **2.** a mischievous child.

Pi·zar·ro, Fran·cis·co (pi zär′ō; fran sis′kō) 1471?–1541, Spanish conqueror of Peru.

piz·za (pēt′sə) *n.* a baked Italian dish made with a flat, crisp crust topped with tomatoes, cheese, and sometimes other ingredients, such as sausages or mushrooms.

piz·ze·ri·a (pēt′sə rē′ə) *n.* a place where pizzas are prepared and sold.

piz·zi·ca·to (pit′si kä′tō) *Music. adj.* played by plucking the strings of an instrument with the finger. —*n. pl.,* **piz·zi·ca·ti** (pit′si kä′tē). a note or passage of music played in this way.

pk. *pl.,* **pks. 1.** pack. **2.** peak. **3.** peck.

pkg. *pl.,* **pkgs.** package.

pl. 1. place. **2.** plate. **3.** plural.

plac·ard (plak′ärd) *n.* a large sign or notice made of paper or cardboard for displaying in a public place. —*v.t.* to display placards on or in: *to placard the wall of the building.*

pla·cate (plā′kāt, plak′āt) *v.t.,* **pla·cat·ed, pla·cat·ing.** to calm the hostility or anger of; pacify: *The salesman tried to placate the indignant woman.* —**pla·cat′er,** *n.* —**pla·ca′tion,** *n.*

place (plās) *n.* **1.** a portion of space; location: *The vase has a place on the shelf. Here is a place to hang your coat.* **2.** an area or locality, such as a town or city: *He visited several interesting places on his trip.* **3.** a building or part of a building: *The town has ten places of worship.* **4.** a house or other residence: *They have a place in the mountains.* **5.** a particular part or spot: *There is a sore place on my arm.* **6.** a particular passage in a book or other writing: *She lost her place when she dropped her book.* **7.** a space or seat for a person: *Save a place for me on the bus.* **8.** a position or standing: *Michelangelo has an important place in the history of art.* **9.** a job: *She found a place as a salesgirl.* **10.** duty or business: *It is not your place to criticize.* **11.** a position in a line, list, or the like. **12.** the position of the horse that finishes second in a race. **13.** a short street or public square. **14.** *Mathematics.* the position of a figure in a series relative to the positions of other figures. In the number .347, 4 is in the second decimal place. —*v.,* **placed, plac·ing.** —*v.t.* **1.** to put or set in a particular place: *Place the napkin beside the plate.* **2.** to identify by connecting with the correct location or time: *Mr. Brown finally placed the other man as a childhood friend.* —*v.i.* to be in a particular position, as in a contest or race: *Helen placed third in the beauty contest.*

 in place. in the original, proper, or natural place: *The books were in place on the shelves.*

at; āpe; cär; end; mē; it; īce; hot; ōld; fôrk; wood; fōōl; oil; out; up; turn; sing; thin; this; hw in white; zh in treasure. The symbol ə stands for the sound of **a** in about, **e** in taken, **i** in pencil, **o** in lemon, and **u** in circus.

in place of. instead of: *Use cream in place of milk in the recipe.*

out of place. a. not in the original, proper, or natural place. **b.** not proper; unsuitable: *Shouting is out of place in a museum.*

to take place. to happen; occur.

pla·ce·bo (plə sē′bō) *n. pl.,* **pla·ce·bos** or **pla·ce·boes.** a preparation having no value as medicine, given to soothe or humor a patient. [Latin *placebō* I shall please.]

place-kick (plās′kik′) *v.t.* to give a place kick to (a football). —*v.i.* to give a place kick.

place kick, a kick in which a football is placed or held nearly upright on the ground, as in attempting a field goal or an extra point.

place mat, a mat laid on a table under each place setting and dish for protection or decoration.

place·ment (plās′mənt) *n.* **1.** the act or instance of putting or setting in a particular place. **2.** the act or function of finding suitable jobs, schools, or living quarters for people. **3.** the placing of the ball in football for a place kick.

pla·cen·ta (plə sen′tə) *n. pl.,* **pla·cen·tae** (plə sen′tē) or **pla·cen·tas.** in many female animals, the organ through which the unborn young, or fetus, receives food and oxygen and gives off waste. —**pla·cen′tal,** *adj.*

plac·er (plas′ər) *n.* a deposit, as of gravel or sand, that contains particles of gold or other valuable minerals.

plac·er mining (plas′ər) mining in which gravel or sand is washed to sort out gold or other valuable minerals.

plac·id (plas′id) *adj.* not easily excited or disturbed; calm or peaceful: *Alice has a placid disposition.* —**pla·cid′i·ty, plac′id·ness,** *n.* —**plac′id·ly,** *adv.*

plack·et (plak′it) *n.* an opening or slit at the top of a garment, as at the neckline or wrists, that makes it easy to put the garment on or take it off.

pla·gia·rism (plā′jə riz′əm) *n.* **1.** the act of copying someone else's work and passing it off as one's own. **2.** the work or ideas of another taken and passed off as one's own. —**pla′gia·rist,** *n.* —**pla′gia·ris′tic,** *adj.*

pla·gia·rize (plā′jə rīz′) *v.,* **pla·gia·rized, pla·gia·riz·ing.** —*v.t.* to take and pass off as one's own (someone else's work or ideas): *The writer plagiarized a passage from Emerson.* —*v.i.* to commit plagiarism. —**pla′gia·riz′er,** *n.*

plague (plāg) *n.* **1.** any serious, often fatal disease that affects a large part of the population of an area. **2.** see **bubonic plague. 3.** a great misfortune or evil: *The land was ravaged by a plague of locusts.* **4.** a cause of trouble or annoyance: *A plague of bills arrived on the first.* —*v.t.,* **plagued, plagu·ing. 1.** to afflict with a serious disease, misfortune, or evil: *After the storm, flooding and traffic breakdowns plagued the countryside.* **2.** to trouble or annoy: *Back-seat instructions plague most drivers.*

plaice (plās) *n. pl.,* **plaic·es** or **plaice. 1.** a European flatfish found in the North Atlantic Ocean. **2.** any of various American flatfish.

plaid (plad) *n.* **1.** a pattern that has narrow and wide stripes of different colors crossing one another at right angles. **2.** a shawl having such a pattern. It is part of the traditional Scottish Highland dress. **3.** a fabric made with such a pattern. —*adj.* having such a pattern.

plain (plān) *adj.* **1.** clearly seen or heard; distinct: *She was in plain sight.* **2.** clearly understood; evident; obvious: *He made it plain that he did not agree.* **3.** downright; sheer: *That's just plain nonsense!* **4.** straightforward or direct; outspoken; frank: *I will be plain with you and tell you the truth.* **5.** without ornament; unadorned: *She wore a plain black dress.* **6.** not rich or highly seasoned: *plain food.* **7.** unsophisticated or ordinary: *plain people.* **8.** not beautiful; homely: *a plain face.* —*n.* an area of level or nearly level land. —**plain′ly,** *adv.* —**plain′ness,** *n.*

plain·clothes man (plān′klōz′, plān′klōthz′) *also,* **plain·clothes·man.** a police officer who wears civilian clothes while on duty.

Plains Indian, a member of any of various American Indian tribes who formerly lived on the Great Plains.

plains·man (plānz′mən) *n. pl.,* **plains·men** (plānz′mən). a person who lives on the plains.

plain·song (plān′sông) *n.* medieval church music having a simple melody. It is sung in unison without accompaniment. Also, **Gregorian chant.**

plain-spo·ken (plān′spō′kən) *adj.* open in speech; outspoken; frank.

plaint (plānt) *n.* **1.** a complaint; grievance. **2.** *Archaic.* a lament.

plain·tiff (plān′tif) *n.* the person who brings a suit in a court of law.

plain·tive (plān′tiv) *adj.* expressing sorrow; mournful; sad: *He has a plaintive expression.* —**plain′tive·ly,** *adj.* —**plain′tive·ness,** *n.*

plait (plāte, plat) *n.* **1.** a braid, as of hair. **2.** another word for **pleat.** —*v.t.* **1.** to braid. **2.** to make by braiding: *The two women plaited a rug.* **3.** another word for **pleat.**

plan (plan) *n.* **1.** a method or way of doing something that has been thought out beforehand: *The general had a plan of attack.* **2.** something that a person intends to do: *I have no plans for this weekend.* **3.** a drawing or diagram that shows how the parts of something are to be arranged: *The architect drew up the plans for the house.* —*v.,* **planned, plan·ning.** —*v.t.* **1.** to prepare beforehand: *The general planned the defense of the city.* **2.** to have in mind; intend: *Mary plans to go shopping tomorrow.* **3.** to make a drawing or diagram of; design: *The architect planned a house for us.* —*v.i.* to make a plan or plans: *The townspeople planned for the celebration.* —**plan′ner,** *n.*

pla·nar·i·an (plə ner′ē ən) *n.* any of a group of flatworms living in freshwater lakes, streams, or ponds.

plane¹ (plān) *n.* **1.** a flat or level surface. **2.** a level or degree: *Sam reached a high plane of achievement in his work.* **3.** see **airplane. 4.** *Geometry.* a flat surface that wholly contains every line connecting any two points on it. —*adj.* **1.** level; flat. **2.** of or relating to a plane or planes, or a figure contained in a plane: *a plane curve.* [Latin *plānum* level ground.]

plane² (plān) *n.* a hand tool with a blade that projects from the bottom, used for smoothing wood. —*v.,* **planed, plan·ing.** —*v.t.* to smooth with a plane. —*v.i.* to work with a plane. [Middle French *plane,* going back to Late Latin *planare* to level, make flat.]

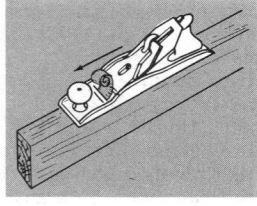

Plane²

plane³ (plān) *n.* see **plane tree.**

plane geometry, the branch of geometry that deals with plane figures.

plan·er (plā′nər) *n.* a person or thing that planes.

plan·et (plan′it) *n.* any one of the nine large bodies that revolve around the sun. The planets in order of their distance from the sun are Mercury, Venus, Earth, Mars, Jupiter, Saturn, Uranus, Neptune, and Pluto.

plan·e·tar·i·um (plan′ə ter′ē əm) *n. pl.,* **plan·e·tar·i·a** (plan′ə ter′ē ə) or **plan·e·tar·i·ums. 1.** an apparatus that shows the positions and motions of stars, planets, and other heavenly bodies by projecting their images on the inside of a dome. **2.** a room or building housing such an apparatus.

plan·e·tar·y (plan′ə ter′ē) *adj.* of, relating to, or resembling a planet.

plan·et·oid (plan′ə toid′) *n.* another word for **asteroid**.

plane tree, any of a group of trees having smooth, brown bark that flakes off in thin layers, and bearing clusters of tiny flowers at the ends of the branches. The plane tree of North America is also called the sycamore.

plank (plangk) *n.* **1.** a long, flat piece of sawed wood. **2.** a statement of a goal or principle forming part of the platform of a political party. —*v.t.* **1.** to cover or lay with planks. **2.** to cook and serve (steak or fish) on a board. **3.** *Informal.* to put down quickly or at once: *John planked down the money to pay his share of the bill.*

  to walk the plank, to walk blindfolded off a plank that sticks out over the water from a ship.

plank·ing (plang′king) *n.* **1.** planks as a group: *the planking on a floor.* **2.** the act of covering or laying with planks.

plank·ton (plangk′tən) *n.* very small plants and animals that drift or float in the sea or another body of water. Plankton is the basic source of food for all animals that live in the sea.

plant (plant) *n.* **1.** any living thing that is not able to move about, lacks sense organs and a nervous system, and has cell walls of cellulose. Those plants that have chlorophyll are able to produce their own food by photosynthesis. **2.** a small plant having a soft stem, as distinguished from a tree or shrub. **3.** a young tree, vine, shrub, or other plant recently planted or ready for planting. **4.** the buildings, machinery, tools, and the like used in manufacturing; factory: *an automobile plant.* **5.** equipment for a particular purpose: *a heating plant for an office building.* **6.** *Slang.* a person or thing placed in a location in order to deceive or trick. —*v.t.* **1.** to set or place in the ground so that it will take root and grow: *to plant seeds, to plant a small tree.* **2.** to furnish (land) with growing plants. **3.** to fix or introduce in the mind; instill. **4.** to place or set firmly in position: *to plant one's feet on the ground.* **5.** *Slang.* to place (someone or something) in order to deceive or trick: *to plant fake evidence.*

Plan·tag·e·net (plan taj′ə nit) *n.* the family that ruled England from 1154 to 1399. The kings from Henry II through Richard II were Plantagenets. —*adj.* of or relating to this royal family or the period of their rule.

plan·tain[1] (plant′ən) *n.* **1.** a large greenish-yellow fruit resembling a banana. **2.** the plant bearing this fruit. [Spanish *plátano, plántano.*]

plan·tain[2] (plant′ən) *n.* a plant found as a common weed, bearing clusters of tiny flowers and large leaves. [Old French *plantain.*]

plan·ta·tion (plan tā′shən) *n.* **1.** a large estate or farm where one crop is grown: *a sugar plantation.* **2.** a group of plants, such as rubber trees, grown as a crop.

plant·er (plant′ər) *n.* **1.** a person or machine that plants. **2.** a person who owns or manages a plantation. **3.** a container for growing plants.

plant louse, another term for **aphid**.

plaque (plak) *n.* a flat plate or slab of hard material, such as porcelain, wood, or metal, that is ornamented or engraved for mounting on a wall.

plash (plash) *v., n. pl.,* **plash·es.** another word for **splash**.

plas·ma (plaz′mə) *n.* a clear yellow liquid that forms the fluid portion of blood, and in which the blood cells are suspended.

plas·ter (plas′tər) *n.* **1.** a mixture of lime, sand, and water that becomes a hard, smooth material when dry, used for coating walls and ceilings. **2.** see **plaster of Paris**. **3.** a medical preparation that is spread on cloth and then applied to the body for healing purposes. —*v.t.* **1.** to cover or coat with plaster. **2.** to cover thoroughly, as if with plaster: *The men plastered the fence with posters.* **3.** to

cause to lie flat: *He plastered his hair down with hair tonic.* —**plas′ter·er,** *n.*

plas·ter·board (plas′tər bôrd′) *n.* a thin, firm board composed of layers of paper and plaster, used for walls or partitions.

plaster cast, a rigid form made of plaster of Paris and gauze, used to hold a leg or arm firmly while a broken bone or badly sprained muscle heals.

plaster of Paris, powdered gypsum that is mixed with water to form a paste which dries rapidly into a hard, solid mass. It is used for making molds, casts, or copies of works of art. [Referring to the fact that it was first made in *Paris.*]

plas·tic (plas′tik) *n.* a man-made material that can be molded or shaped when soft. Cellophane and vinyl are plastics. —*adj.* **1.** capable of being molded or shaped: *Wax is a plastic material.* **2.** of or relating to molding or shaping: *Ceramics is a plastic art.* **3.** made of plastic: *The radio has a plastic cabinet.* —**plas′ti·cal·ly,** *adv.* —**plas·tic·i·ty** (plas tis′ə tē), *n.*

plastic surgery, surgery for repairing or restoring injured or badly formed parts of the body.

plat[1] (plat) *n.* **1.** a small piece of ground; plot. **2.** a map, chart, or plan. [From obsolete *plat* a flat surface.]

plat[2] (plat) *n., v.t.,* **plat·ted, plat·ting.** another word for **plait**.

plate (plāt) *n.* **1.** a flat or shallow dish for holding food to be served or eaten: *Joyce set the plates on the table.* **2.** the food held by such a dish: *Hank was served a plate of fried chicken.* **3.** food for one person at a meal. **4.** a dish passed to take collections, as in a church. **5.** dishes and table utensils made of or coated with a layer of silver or gold. **6.** a flat thin sheet of metal of even thickness and surface: *a plate of steel.* **7.** armor made of such pieces of metal. **8.** a piece of metal on which something is or can be engraved, such as a license plate or a plate used for printing. **9.** a print made from an engraved piece of metal, as an illustration in a book: *The art book has many color plates.* **10.** *Printing.* a cast of a page of type to be printed, such as an electrotype or a stereotype. **11.** *Photography.* a thin sheet of glass, metal, or other material coated with a substance sensitive to light, used to take photographs. **12.** *Baseball.* see **home plate**. **13.** a piece of metal, plastic, or similar material with a set of artificial teeth, fitted to the gums to replace missing teeth. **14.** a thin cut of beef from the lower end of the breast or brisket. —*v.t.,* **plat·ed, plat·ing. 1.** to coat with a layer of metal: *to plate knives, spoons, and forks with silver.* **2.** to cover with metal plates for protection. **3.** *Printing.* to make an electrotype or stereotype from (a page of type). —**plate′like′,** *adj.*

pla·teau (pla tō′) *n. pl.,* **pla·teaus** or **pla·teaux** (pla tōz′). **1.** an area of flat land raised above the surrounding land. **2.** a stage, as in development: *The economy reached a new plateau.*

plate·ful (plāt′fool′) *n. pl.,* **plate·fuls.** as much as a plate will hold, especially a large amount of food.

plate glass, a strong glass used for windowpanes or mirrors.

plate·let (plāt′lit) *n.* any of the tiny round, oval, or

at; āpe; cär; end; mē; it; īce; hot; ōld; fôrk; wood; fool; oil; out; up; turn; sing; thin; this; hw in white; zh in treasure. The symbol ə stands for the sound of **a** in about, **e** in taken, **i** in pencil, **o** in lemon, and **u** in circus.

rod-shaped cell fragments in the blood that aid in blood clotting.

plat·form (plat′fôrm′) *n.* **1.** a raised, flat structure or flooring: *The speaker stood on a platform. We waited on the platform for the train.* **2.** a statement of principles, especially a public statement of the principles and policies of a political party.

platform tennis, a form of tennis that is played with wooden paddles and a rubber ball on a wooden platform surrounded by a high wire fence.

plat·ing (plā′ting) *n.* a thin coating or layer of metal, especially gold or silver.

plat·i·num (plat′ən əm) *n.* a heavy, soft, silvery metallic element that resists tarnishing. Symbol: **Pt**

plat·i·tude (plat′ə tōōd′, plat′ə tyōōd′) *n.* a dull, trite, or commonplace remark, especially one meant to sound original or important.

plat·i·tu·di·nous (plat′ə tōōd′ən əs, plat′ə tyōōd′ən əs) *adj.* **1.** of, relating to, or having the nature of a platitude; trite: *a platitudinous statement.* **2.** given to or full of platitudes. **—plat′i·tu′di·nous·ly,** *adv.*

Pla·to (plā′tō) 428?–347? B.C., Greek philosopher.

Pla·ton·ic (plə ton′ik) *adj.* **1.** of or relating to Plato or his philosophy. **2.** *also,* **platonic.** of or relating to a relationship between a man and woman that is spiritual or intellectual rather than sexual. **—Pla·ton′i·cal·ly,** *adv.*

Pla·to·nism (plāt′ən iz′əm) *n.* the philosophy of Plato or his followers.

pla·toon (plə tōōn′) *n.* **1.** a military unit forming part of a company, usually commanded by a lieutenant. **2.** a group of football players who specialize in either offensive or defensive play and enter or leave the game as a unit.

Platte (plat) *n.* a river flowing from central Nebraska into the Missouri River.

plat·ter (plat′ər) *n.* **1.** a large, oval, flat dish for serving food, especially fish or meat. **2.** food served on a platter: *a platter of roast beef.*

plat·y·pus (plat′ə pəs) *n. pl.,* **plat·y·pus·es** or **plat·y·pi** (plat′ə pī′). an egg-laying mammal found in Australia and Tasmania. It has a flat, wide bill that is very sensitive to touch, webbed feet, and a plump body covered with soft brown fur. Also, **duckbill, duckbilled platypus.**

Platypus

plau·dit (plô′dit) *n. usually,* **plau·dits.** an expression of praise or approval: *The speaker sought the plaudits of the crowd.*

plau·si·ble (plô′zə bəl) *adj.* seeming to be true, honest, or worthy of trust; believable: *What he says is plausible. Her excuse was plausible, but I still had doubts.* **—plau′si·bil′i·ty, plau′si·ble·ness,** *n.* **—plau′si·bly,** *adv.*

play (plā) *n.* **1.** something done for pleasure or amusement; recreation: *The children spent several hours at play.* **2.** the act or manner of carrying on a game: *The play began when the coach blew the whistle.* **3.** a move or turn to move in a game. **4.** a work of literature written to be performed on a stage; drama. **5.** a way of acting or behaving: *Tom is admired for his sense of fair play.* **6.** an action or operation: *The engine was in full play.* **7.** a quick flickering movement: *a play of light across a surface.* **8.** freedom of movement: *The play of the wheel was hindered by the tight bolt.* **—v.i. 1.** to do something for pleasure or amusement; have fun: *The children played in the backyard.* **2.** to act carelessly with something; toy: *Don't play with matches.*

3. to perform in a play, movie, or television program. **4.** to be performed or presented: *What is playing on television tonight?* **5.** to act or behave in a particular way: *He plays rough.* **6.** to perform music or perform on a musical instrument: *The band is playing.* **7.** to give out sound or music: *The phonograph stopped playing.* **8.** to have a quick, flickering movement: *A smile played on her lips.* **9.** to be in a game: *Jack played for three innings.* **—v.t. 1.** to act the part of or behave like: *He played an old sailor in the movie.* **2.** to make believe or pretend to be for pleasure or amusement: *The children played cowboys and Indians.* **3.** to do, especially in fun: *Carl played a trick on Pat.* **4.** to cause to act or operate: *The fireman played a hose on the burning building.* **5.** to perform on (a musical instrument): *Helen plays the clarinet.* **6.** to perform: *The orchestra played a work by Beethoven.* **7.** to cause to give out sound or music: *He played his radio.* **8.** to be in (a game or other activity): *The two boys played tennis.* **9.** to be in a game against; contend against: *Our team played Lincoln High School in basketball.* **10.** to be in (a particular position) in a game: *Gene will play first base.* **—play′a·ble,** *adj.*

in play. *Sports.* being in use or motion: *The ball is in play.*

out of play. *Sports.* no longer in use or motion.

to play into the hands of. to act so that another gets the advantage.

to play off. to play one or more games in order to settle a tie.

to play on. to take advantage of: *to play on a person's sympathies.*

to play up. to treat as of much importance; stress the importance of.

to play up to. *Informal.* to try to gain the favor of.

play·back (plā′bak′) *n.* the act or process of playing a recording again, especially a tape recording that has just been made.

play·bill (plā′bil′) *n.* a program of a play.

play·boy (plā′boi′) *n.* a wealthy man who spends much of his time seeking pleasure.

play·er (plā′ər) *n.* **1.** a person who plays in a sport or game: *a baseball player, a chess player.* **2.** a person who performs on the stage; actor. **3.** a person who performs on a musical instrument; musician: *a piano player.* **4.** a mechanical device or machine for giving out sound or music: *a record player.*

player piano, a piano played by a mechanical device.

play·fel·low (plā′fel′ō) *n.* another word for **playmate.**

play·ful (plā′fəl) *adj.* **1.** full of spirit and play; frolicsome; lively: *a playful puppy.* **2.** humorous; joking: *a playful remark.* **—play′ful·ly,** *adv.* **—play′ful·ness,** *n.*

play·go·er (plā′gō′ər) *n.* a person who goes to the theater regularly or often.

play·ground (plā′ground′) *n.* an area used for outdoor recreation, especially by children.

play·house (plā′hous′) *n. pl.,* **play·hous·es** (plā′hou′ziz). **1.** a place where plays and the like are given; theater. **2.** a small house for children to play in.

playing card, a card used in playing games, especially one of a deck of fifty-two cards divided into four suits (clubs, diamonds, hearts, and spades) and thirteen ranks (jacks, queens, kings, aces, and the numbers from two to ten).

play·mate (plā′māt′) *n.* a companion in games and other amusements.

play·off (plā′ôf′) *n.* **1.** a game played to break a tie. **2.** one or more games played to decide a championship.

play·pen (plā′pen′) *n.* a small pen that is easily folded and moved, used for a baby or small child to play in.

play·room (plā′rōōm′, plā′room′) *n.* a room, usually in a home, for a child or children to play in.

play·thing (plā′thing′) *n.* a thing to play with; toy: *The children's playthings were put neatly away.*

play·wright (plā′rīt′) *n.* a person who writes plays.

pla·za (plä′zə, plaz′ə) *n.* a public square or open space in a city or town.

plea (plē) *n.* **1.** an earnest request or appeal: *a plea for help.* **2.** a reason given as an explanation; excuse. **3.** *Law.* the answer that the accused person makes to the charge against him: *He entered a plea of not guilty.*

plead (plēd) *v.,* **plead·ed** or **pled, plead·ing.** —*v.i.* **1.** to make an earnest request or appeal; beg: *to plead for mercy.* **2.** to argue a case in a court of law: *to plead before a jury.* —*v.t.* **1.** to give as an excuse: *to plead illness.* **2.** to argue (a case or cause) in a court of law. **3.** to give as an answer to a charge in a court of law: *to plead not guilty.*

pleas·ant (plez′ənt) *adj.* **1.** that is pleasing; giving pleasure; agreeable: *pleasant surroundings.* **2.** having or showing pleasing manners or behavior: *a pleasant personality.* —**pleas′ant·ly,** *adv.* —**pleas′ant·ness,** *n.*

pleas·ant·ry (plez′ən trē) *n. pl.,* **pleas·ant·ries. 1.** a pleasant, courteous remark. **2.** a humorous or playful remark or action.

please (plēz) *v.,* **pleased, pleas·ing.** —*v.t.* **1.** to give pleasure to; be agreeable to: *Winning the prize really pleased him. It pleases me to see you so happy.* **2.** to be so kind as to. ▲ used to express a request or command politely: *Please close the door.* **3.** to be the will of: *May it please Your Honor to hear this testimony.* —*v.i.* **1.** to give pleasure; be agreeable: *He is trying very hard to please.* **2.** to have the will or desire; choose: *You may come back to visit whenever you please.*

pleas·ing (plē′zing) *adj.* giving pleasure; agreeable. —**pleas′ing·ly,** *adv.* —**pleas′ing·ness,** *n.*

pleas·ur·a·ble (plezh′ər ə bəl) *adj.* giving pleasure: *a pleasurable experience.* —**pleas′ur·a·ble·ness,** *n.* —**pleas′ur·a·bly,** *adv.*

pleas·ure (plezh′ər) *n.* **1.** an enjoyable or delightful feeling or emotion: *She takes great pleasure in helping other people. The children's pleasure showed in their faces.* **2.** something that gives such a feeling or emotion: *It is a pleasure to be here again.* **3.** amusement that satisfies the senses or appetites. **4.** desire; will: *It is His Majesty's pleasure that you join him.*

pleat (plēt) *n.* a lengthwise, flat fold in cloth or other material, made by doubling the material upon itself and then fastening it into place. —*v.t.* to make a pleat or pleats in; arrange in pleats. Also, **plait.**

plebe (plēb) *n.* a member of the freshman class at the U.S. Military Academy or Naval Academy.

Box pleats   Knife pleats

Pleat

ple·be·ian (pli bē′ən) *n.* **1.** a member of the common people in ancient Rome. **2.** a person who is ordinary, common, or vulgar. —*adj.* **1.** of or relating to the common people of ancient Rome. **2.** ordinary, common, or vulgar: *plebeian tastes in art.*

pleb·i·scite (pleb′ə sīt′) *n.* a direct vote by the people of a country or state on an important question or issue.

plec·trum (plek′trəm) *also,* **plec·tron** (plek′trän). *n. pl.,* **plec·trums** or **plec·tra** (plek′trə). a small, thin piece of horn, plastic, or other material, used for plucking the strings of a guitar or similar instrument. Also, **pick.**

pled (pled) a past tense and past participle of **plead.**

pledge (plej) *n.* **1.** a solemn or formal promise: *The boys made a pledge of secrecy.* **2.** something given or held as security: *He left his watch as a pledge that he would pay the debt.* **3.** the state of being held as security: *He left his money in pledge.* **4.** something given as a token: *She accepted the ring as a pledge of his love.* **5.** an expression of good will made by drinking to a person's health; toast. —*v.t.,* **pledged, pledg·ing. 1.** to guarantee with a pledge; promise solemnly or formally: *He pledged his help. They pledged allegiance to the flag.* **2.** to give (something) as security. **3.** to drink a toast to.

Plei·o·cene (plī′ə sēn′) another spelling of **Pliocene.**

Pleis·to·cene (plīs′tə sēn′) *n.* the first geological epoch of the Quaternary period of the Cenozoic era. During the Pleistocene, glaciers advanced, and then receded, over large areas of North and South America, Europe, and Asia, and man appeared. Also, **Ice Age.** —*adj.* of, relating to, or belonging to this epoch.

ple·na·ry (plē′nər ē, plen′ər ē) *adj.* **1.** attended by everyone who has a right to be there: *The members of Congress attended a plenary session.* **2.** full; complete: *The diplomat was given plenary powers.*

plen·i·po·ten·ti·ar·y (plen′i pə ten′chē er′ē) *n. pl.,* **plen·i·po·ten·ti·ar·ies.** an ambassador or other diplomat having full power in representing his government. —*adj.* having full power.

plen·i·tude (plen′i tōōd′, plen′i tyōōd′) *n.* the quality or state of being abundant; abundance.

plen·te·ous (plen′tē əs) *adj.* in great quantity; plentiful. —**plen′te·ous·ly,** *adv.* —**plen′te·ous·ness,** *n.*

plen·ti·ful (plen′ti fəl) *adj.* **1.** in great quantity; abundant; ample: *Food was plentiful on the prosperous farm.* **2.** providing or yielding an abundance: *a plentiful harvest.* —**plen′ti·ful·ly,** *adv.* —**plen′ti·ful·ness,** *n.*

plen·ty (plen′tē) *n. pl.,* **plen·ties. 1.** a full supply or amount: *There's plenty of milk in the refrigerator.* **2.** more than enough food and material goods; general prosperity: *a time of plenty.* —*adj.* ample; plentiful: *One helping of meat is plenty for me.*

ple·si·o·saur (plē′sē ə sôr′) *n.* an extinct water-dwelling reptile that had a small head, long neck, and four paddlelike limbs. Also, **ple·si·o·saur·us** (plē′sē ə sôr′əs).

pleth·o·ra (pleth′ər ə) *n.* more than is needed; too much; excess.

pleu·ra (ploor′ə) *n. pl.,* **pleu·rae** (ploor′ē). a thin membrane enclosing the lungs and lining the inner walls of the chest cavity. —**pleu′ral,** *adj.*

pleu·ri·sy (ploor′ə sē) *n.* an inflammation of the pleura, often accompanied by fever, difficulty in breathing, and a painful cough. Also, **pleu·ri·tis** (ploo rī′tis).

Plex·i·glas (plek′si glas′) *n. Trademark.* a strong, transparent plastic.

plex·us (plek′səs) *n. pl.,* **plex·us·es** or **plex·us.** a network of fibers, as of nerves or blood vessels.

pli·a·ble (plī′ə bəl) *adj.* **1.** easily molded or bent; flexible: *Clay and wax are pliable.* **2.** easily influenced or persuaded: *a pliable personality.* —**pli′a·bil′i·ty, pli′a·ble·ness,** *n.* —**pli′a·bly,** *adv.*

pli·an·cy (plī′ən sē) *n.* the state or quality of being pliant.

at; āpe; cär; end; mē; it; īce; hot; ōld; fôrk; wood; fŏŏd; oil; out; up; turn; sing; thin; **th**is; **hw** in white; **zh** in treasure. The symbol ə stands for the sound of **a** in about, **e** in taken, **i** in pencil, **o** in lemon, and **u** in circus.

pli·ant (plī′ənt) *adj.* **1.** that can be bent with ease; pliable; supple: *pliant material.* **2.** easily influenced or controlled: *a pliant person.* —**pli′ant·ly,** *adv.*

pli·ers (plī′ərz) *n., pl.* small pincers used chiefly for gripping and bending things.

plight¹ (plīt) *n.* a situation or condition, especially one that is bad: *the terrible plight of flood victims.* [Middle English *plit;* originally, a way of folding something.]

plight² (plīt) *v.t.* to bind by a pledge; promise. [Old English *plihtan* to pledge, from *pliht* danger, risk.]

plink (plingk) *n.* a light, sharp, high sound, such as that made on a piano. —*v.i.* to make such a sound. —*v.t.* to cause to make such a sound: *to plink a banjo.*

plinth (plinth) *n.* a slab, block, stone, or other projecting part on which a column, pedestal, or the like rests.

Plinth

Pli·o·cene (plī′ə sēn′) *also,* **Plei·o·cene.** *n.* the fifth and last geological epoch of the Tertiary period of the Cenozoic era. During the Pliocene, most of the major mountain ranges were formed. —*adj.* of or relating to this epoch.

plod (plod) *v.i.,* **plod·ded, plod·ding. 1.** to walk or move slowly and heavily; trudge: *The tired man silently plodded through the snow.* **2.** to work slowly but steadily: *Henry plodded through the geography book.* —*n.* the act of plodding. —**plod′der,** *n.*

plop (plop) *v.,* **plopped, plop·ping.** —*v.i.* to drop or fall heavily with a sound like that of an object dropping into water. —*v.t.* to drop or let fall so as to make such a sound. —*n.* the act or sound of plopping: *The wet clay fell on the floor with a plop.*

plot (plot) *n.* **1.** a secret plan, especially to bring about an evil or illegal purpose: *The criminals formed a plot to kidnap the banker.* **2.** the main story in a play, novel, or other literary work. **3.** a small piece of ground: *a cemetery plot.* —*v.,* **plot·ted, plot·ting.** —*v.t.* **1.** to make a secret plan for: *The thieves plotted to rob the safe.* **2.** to make a diagram or map of; chart: *The navigator plotted the ship's course.* —*v.i.* to form a plot; scheme. —**plot′ter,** *n.*

plo·ver (pluv′ər, plō′vər) *n.* a bird having a straight, pointed bill.

plow (plou) *also,* **plough.** *n.* **1.** a farm tool for turning over or breaking up the soil for sowing or planting. A plow is usually drawn by animals or by a tractor. **2.** any of various devices resembling a plow in shape or use, such as a snowplow. —*v.t.* **1.** to break and turn up the surface of (soil) with a plow: *The farmer plowed the field.* **2.** to form or make with or as if with a plow: *We plowed our way through the crowd in front of the theater.* —*v.i.* **1.** to break and turn up soil with a plow. **2.** to move forward steadily, forcefully, or with difficulty.

Plover

plow·man (plou′mən) *also,* **plough·man.** *n. pl.,* **plow·men** (plou′mən). **1.** a man who guides or operates a plow. **2.** a farmer or farm worker.

plow·share (plou′sher′) *also,* **plough·share.** *n.* the front edge or blade of a plow, which cuts the soil.

ploy (ploi) *n.* a tricky move or piece of strategy: *Her crying was only a ploy to gain our sympathy.*

pluck (pluk) *v.t.* **1.** to pull out or off; pick: *to pluck the feathers from a chicken.* **2.** to pull out the hair or feathers from: *to pluck one's eyebrows.* **3.** to pull with sudden force or with a jerk; snatch: *He plucked the letter from her*

hands. **4.** to pull on and quickly let go of (the strings of a musical instrument), causing them to sound. —*v.i.* to give a pull; grasp; tug: *The little girl plucked at her mother's skirt.* —*n.* **1.** spirit and courage, especially in the face of danger or difficulty. **2.** the act of pulling; tug; jerk.

pluck·y (pluk′ē) *adj.,* **pluck·i·er, pluck·i·est.** having or showing spirit and courage, especially in the face of danger or difficulty. —**pluck′i·ly,** *adv.* —**pluck′i·ness,** *n.*

plug (plug) *n.* **1.** a piece of wood, rubber, or other material used to close up a hole or fill a gap. **2.** a fitting with two or three prongs, attached to the end of a wire or cable and inserted into an outlet to make an electrical connection. **3.** a cake of pressed or twisted tobacco, or a piece of it cut off for chewing. **4.** see **spark plug** *(def. 1).* **5.** *Informal.* a favorable mention of or piece of publicity about someone or something. **6.** *Slang.* an old or worn-out horse. —*v.,* **plugged, plug·ging.** —*v.t.* **1.** to stop or fill with or as if with a plug: *The coffee grounds plugged up the kitchen drain.* **2.** to insert the plug of (an electric device) into an outlet to make an electrical connection: *She plugged in the toaster.* **3.** *Informal.* to make favorable public mention of; publicize or advertise: *The disc jockey plugged the singer's new record.* —*v.i. Informal.* to work hard or persistently: *Jim kept on plugging until he solved the math problem.* —**plug′ger,** *n.*

plum (plum) *n.* **1.** the round or oval fruit of a tree of the rose family, having a flattened pit, soft, juicy flesh that can be eaten, and smooth reddish-purple or bluish-red skin. **2.** the tree bearing this fruit, having oval leaves and small white or pink flowers. **3.** something very good or desirable, such as a fine job or position. **4.** a reddish-purple or bluish-red color. **5.** a raisin, when added to a pudding or other dish. —*adj.* having the color plum.

plum·age (plo̅o̅′mij) *n.* the feathers of a bird.

plumb (plum) *v.t.* **1.** to test or adjust by a plumb line. **2.** to measure the depth of (a body of water) with a plumb line. **3.** to discover or examine closely the dimensions, nature, or contents of: *to plumb a mystery.* **4.** to make vertical; straighten. —*adj.* **1.** vertical; straight. **2.** *Informal.* complete; total: *That's plumb nonsense.* —*adv.* **1.** in a vertical direction or line; vertically: *The wall must run plumb.* **2.** *Informal.* completely; totally: *She's plumb crazy.* —*n.* see **plumb bob.**

plumb bob, a weight at the end of a plumb line. Also, **plumb, plummet.**

plumb·er (plum′ər) *n.* a person who installs and repairs plumbing.

plumb·ing (plum′ing) *n.* **1.** the pipes and fixtures for bringing water into or taking water and wastes out of a building or other structure. **2.** the work that is done by a plumber.

plumb line, a line from which a weight hangs, used to measure depths, as of bodies of water, or to test whether something is vertical. Also, **plummet.**

plume (plo̅o̅m) *n.* **1.** a large, fluffy, showy feather. **2.** an ornament made up of a plume or cluster of plumes, or of a feathery tuft of fluffy material. **3.** something resembling a plume: *A plume of smoke rose from the fire.* —*v.t.,* **plumed, plum·ing. 1.** to adorn with a plume or plumes. **2.** (of a bird) to smooth (itself) with the beak; preen.

plum·met (plum′it) *v.i.* to fall or drop straight downward; plunge. —*n.* **1.** another word for **plumb bob.** **2.** another word for **plumb line.**

Hat with a plume

plump¹ (plump) *adj.* having a full or rounded form; somewhat fat or well filled out: *a plump* *child, a plump cushion.* —*v.t.* to make plump: *Jean plumped up the pillows on the couch.* —*v.i.* to become plump. [Possibly from Middle Dutch *plomp* blunt, dull.] —**plump′ness,** *n.*

plump² (plump) *v.i.* to fall or drop heavily or suddenly: *Paul plumped down onto the sofa.* —*v.t.* to throw, put, or let fall heavily or suddenly. —*adv.* heavily or suddenly: *John fell plump on the bed.* [Imitative of the sound made by such a fall.]

plum pudding, a boiled or steamed pudding made of flour, suet, eggs, raisins, currants, and spices.

plum·y (plōō′mē) *adj.,* **plum·i·er, plum·i·est. 1.** covered or adorned with feathers or plumes: *a plumy hat.* **2.** like a plume; feathery.

plun·der (plun′dər) *v.t.* **1.** to loot or rob, as during a war: *The Mongols plundered northern China in the 13th century.* **2.** to take illegally or by force; steal: *to plunder goods.* —*v.i.* to take goods or valuables by force. —*n.* **1.** something that is taken by plundering; booty; loot. **2.** the act of plundering. —**plun′der·er,** *n.*

plunge (plunj) *v.,* **plunged, plung·ing.** —*v.t.* **1.** to put forcefully or suddenly; thrust: *to plunge one's hand into water.* **2.** to force or place suddenly into some condition or course of action: *A power failure plunged the room into darkness.* —*v.i.* **1.** to dive, fall, or move suddenly or sharply in a downward direction: *The elevator plunged three stories when the cable snapped.* **2.** to move quickly, suddenly, or with a headlong lunge. **3.** to enter or fall suddenly into some condition or course of action: *The nations plunged into war.* **4.** to go downward suddenly: *The road plunges toward the beach.* —*n.* the act or motion of plunging.

plung·er (plun′jər) *n.* **1.** a device made of a rubber suction cup attached to the end of a long handle, used to clear toilets and drains that are stopped up. **2.** any device or machine that works with a plunging or thrusting motion, especially a piston when it is part of a pump. **3.** a person or thing that plunges.

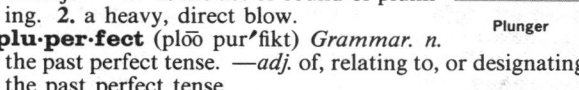

Plunger

plunk (plungk) *Informal. v.t.* **1.** to pluck or strum the strings of (a musical instrument): *to plunk a banjo.* **2.** to throw or put heavily or suddenly: *Richard plunked down all his change.* —*v.i.* **1.** to drop or fall heavily or suddenly: *The stone plunked into the pond.* **2.** to make a twanging sound, as a banjo. —*n.* **1.** the act or sound of plunking. **2.** a heavy, direct blow.

plu·per·fect (plōō pur′fikt) *Grammar. n.* the past perfect tense. —*adj.* of, relating to, or designating the past perfect tense.

plur., plural.

plu·ral (ploor′əl) *adj.* **1.** of, relating to, or containing more than one. **2.** of or relating to a grammatical form showing more than one: *a plural noun, a plural verb.* —*n.* the form of a word showing more than one. *Doors* is the plural of *door,* and *women* is the plural of *woman.* —**plu′ral·ly,** *adv.*

plu·ral·i·ty (ploo ral′ə tē) *n. pl.,* **plu·ral·i·ties. 1.** the number of votes that a winning candidate receives over and above the number cast for his nearest opponent. **2.** the number of votes cast for any one candidate in a contest of more than two candidates, if it is greater than the number received by any other candidate, but not greater than one-half of the total votes cast. **3.** the state or fact of being plural. ▲ See **majority** for usage note.

plus (plus) *prep.* **1.** increased by; added to: *Two plus two is four.* **2.** with the addition of; together with: *The set consists of a table plus chairs.* —*adj.* **1.** somewhat higher

than: *a grade of C plus.* **2.** favorable: *a plus factor.* **3.** more than zero; positive: *a plus four.* **4.** showing addition or a positive quantity: *a plus sign.* —*n. pl.,* **plus·es. 1.** a sign (+) showing addition or a positive quantity. **2.** a favorable factor or quality: *His good record is a plus in his favor.* **3.** a positive quantity.

plush (plush) *adj.* showing or characterized by richness or luxury; luxurious: *a plush hotel.* —*n. pl.,* **plush·es.** a fabric similar to but having a deeper pile than velvet, used especially for upholstery. —**plush′y,** *adj.*

Plu·tarch (plōō′tärk) A.D. 46?–120?, Greek essayist and biographer.

Plu·to (plōō′tō) *n.* **1.** *Greek Mythology.* the god of the dead and ruler of the underworld. Also, **Hades. 2.** the planet that is ninth in order of distance from the sun.

plu·toc·ra·cy (plōō tok′rə sē) *n. pl.,* **plu·toc·ra·cies. 1.** government by the wealthy. **2.** a powerful or influential class of wealthy persons.

plu·to·crat (plōō′tə krat′) *n.* a person who has power or influence because of his wealth.

plu·to·crat·ic (plōō′tə krat′ik) *adj.* relating to plutocrats or plutocracy. —**plu′to·crat′i·cal·ly,** *adv.*

plu·to·ni·um (plōō tō′nē əm) *n.* a silvery, radioactive metallic element. It is important as a fuel in nuclear reactors and as the fission material in atomic bombs. Symbol: **Pu**

plu·vi·al (plōō′vē əl) *adj.* of or relating to rain.

ply¹ (plī) *v.,* **plied, ply·ing.** —*v.t.* **1.** to use or apply; work with: *The carpenter plied his saw and chisel.* **2.** to work at or pursue busily or steadily; practice: *Mr. Jones plied his trade as a carpenter.* **3.** to provide often: *The teacher plied him with good books.* **4.** to travel regularly: *The boat plies the route from the island to the mainland.* —*v.i.* to travel the same course regularly. [Short for *apply.*]

ply² (plī) *n. pl.,* **plies. 1.** a fold or layer, as of cloth or wood. **2.** one of the strands twisted together to make yarn, rope, or similar material. ▲ used in combination to show a certain number of layers or strands: *two-ply tissues, three-ply yarn.* [Old French *pli.*]

Plym·outh (plim′əth) *n.* **1.** a town in southeastern Massachusetts, on the Atlantic Ocean, settled in 1620 by the Pilgrims. **2.** a seaport in southwestern England, on the English Channel. Pop. (1971), 239,314.

Plymouth Colony, the first English settlement in New England, founded by the Pilgrims at Plymouth, Massachusetts, in 1620.

Plymouth Rock 1. a rock at Plymouth, Massachusetts, on which the Pilgrims, according to tradition, first set foot in America in 1620. **2.** one of an American breed of domestic chickens, having white, buff, or blue feathers sometimes striped with gray.

ply·wood (plī′wood′) *n.* a construction material made of a number of thin layers of wood glued together, with the grain of one layer at right angles to the grain of the next.

Pm, the symbol for promethium.

p.m. 1. post meridiem. **2.** post-mortem.

P.M. 1. post meridiem. **2.** Prime Minister. **3.** Postmaster.

pneu·mat·ic (nōō mat′ik, nyōō mat′ik) *adj.* **1.** operated by or using the force of compressed air: *a pneumatic drill.*

at; āpe; cär; end; mē; it; īce; hot; ōld; fôrk; wood; fōōl; oil; out; up; turn; sing; thin; this; hw in white; zh in treasure. The symbol ə stands for the sound of **a** in about, e in taken, i in pencil, o in lemon, and u in circus.

2. containing or filled with air, especially compressed air: *a pneumatic tire.* **3.** of or relating to air or other gases or to pneumatics. —**pneu·mat′i·cal·ly,** *adv.*

pneumatic caisson, a large, boxlike or cylindrical structure for laying underwater foundations, having an airtight work chamber at the bottom. Compressed air is pumped into this chamber to force out the water. Workers enter the chamber through an air lock.

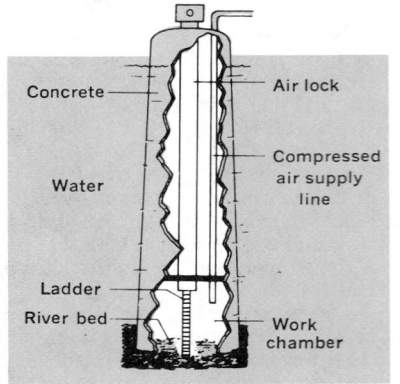

Pneumatic caisson

pneu·mat·ics (nōō mat′iks, nyōō mat′iks) *n., pl.* the branch of physics that deals with the physical properties of air and other gases and with their effect on objects. ▲ used with a singular verb.

pneu·mo·nia (nōō mōn′yə, nyōō mōn′yə) *n.* any of several diseases that cause an inflammation of the lungs, usually caused by a bacterial or viral infection.

Pnom·penh (pə nom′pen′) *also,* **Pnom-Penh.** *n.* another spelling of **Phnom Penh.**

Po (pō) *n.* the largest and longest river in Italy, in the northern part of the country, flowing into the Adriatic Sea.

Po, the symbol for polonium.

P.O., post office.

poach[1] (pōch) *v.t.* **1.** to cook (an egg) in simmering water or in a container placed above simmering water. **2.** to cook in simmering liquid: *to poach fish.* [Middle English *pochen.*]

poach[2] (pōch) *v.i.* **1.** to hunt or fish illegally, as on someone else's property. **2.** to trespass for the purpose of hunting or fishing. —*v.t.* **1.** to take (game or fish) illegally. **2.** to trespass on (property) for the purpose of hunting or fishing. [Middle French *pocher* to stick one's fingers into.] —**poach′er,** *n.*

Po·ca·hon·tas (pō′kə hon′təs) 1595?–1617, an American Indian princess, supposed to have saved the life of Captain John Smith.

pock (pok) *n.* **1.** a swelling on the skin that is filled with pus, caused by such diseases as smallpox and acne. **2.** a scar or pit left by such a swelling. —*v.t.* to mark with pocks.

pock·et (pok′it) *n.* **1.** a pouch sewn into or on a garment, used especially to hold small articles. **2.** something resembling a pocket in shape or function: *There are pockets inside the suitcase for stockings and shoes.* **3.** an isolated, usually small area or group that is different in some way from a surrounding area or group: *A pocket of poverty existed in the middle of the wealthy community.* **4.** any of the pouches at the corners and sides of a pool or billiard table, into which the balls are driven. **5.** see **air pocket. 6.** a hole in the earth containing ore. —*adj.* made small enough or intended to be carried in a pocket: *a pocket radio.* —*v.t.* **1.** to put in a pocket: *Dan pocketed his change and left.* **2.** to take for one's own, especially dishonestly: *The salesclerk pocketed the day's receipts.*

pock·et·book (pok′it book′) *n.* **1.** a bag or case, often made of leather, used by women for carrying small articles. **2.** financial means or interests; money: *Rising food prices*

are a drain on everyone's pocketbook. **3.** *also,* **pocket book.** a book, usually bound in paper, small enough to be carried in a pocket.

pock·et·ful (pok′it fool′) *n. pl.,* **pock·et·fuls.** the amount that a pocket holds.

pock·et·knife (pok′it nīf′) *n. pl.,* **pock·et·knives** (pok′it nīvz′). a small knife with one or more blades that fold into the handle.

pocket veto 1. the power of the President of the United States to veto a bill passed by Congress during the last ten days of a session by simply not signing the bill before Congress adjourns. **2.** a similar power exercised by a chief executive, such as a state governor.

pock·mark (pok′märk′) *n.* a pit or scar left on the skin by a disease, such as smallpox or acne. —*v.t.* to mark with pockmarks.

pod (pod) *n.* **1.** the part of certain plants, such as a pea or bean, that carries the seeds and usually splits along two seams when it is ripe. **2.** a separate enclosed section on an aircraft, usually located beneath a wing, for storing fuel, cargo, weapons, an engine, or the like: *a rocket pod.* —*v.i.,* **pod·ded, pod·ding. 1.** to produce pods. **2.** to swell out into a pod.

po·di·a·trist (pə dī′ə trist) *n.* a person who is trained in and licensed to practice podiatry. Also, **chiropodist.**

po·di·a·try (pə dī′ə trē) *n.* the branch of medicine dealing with the diagnosis, prevention, and treatment of diseases and injuries of the foot. Also, **chiropody.**

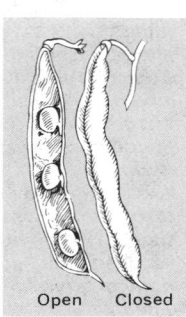

Open   Closed

Pods

po·di·um (pō′dē əm) *n. pl.,* **po·di·a** (pō′dē ə) or **po·di·ums. 1.** a raised platform from which a conductor leads an orchestra. **2.** a place or structure from which to speak to a group; lectern; rostrum.

Poe, Edgar Allan (pō) 1809–1849, U.S. writer, poet, and critic.

po·em (pō′əm) *n.* **1.** a composition expressing emotion or imaginative thought, usually written in some rhythmic pattern in language that is more condensed and vivid than that used in prose writing. Poems often use such devices as rhyme, meter, and metaphor. **2.** anything having the quality or effect of a poem: *The eagle's flight was a poem of graceful motion.*

po·e·sy (pō′ə sē) *n. Archaic.* **1.** poems as a group; poetry. **2.** the art of writing poetry.

po·et (pō′it) *n.* a person who writes poetry.

po·et·ess (pō′i tis) *n.* a woman who writes poetry. ▲ **Poet,** rather than **poetess,** is now generally used for a woman who writes poetry.

po·et·ic (pō et′ik) *adj.* **1.** of or relating to poetry: *poetic genius, poetic works.* **2.** having the quality or effect of poetry: *a poetic description.* **3.** characteristic of or like a poet. Also, **po·et·i·cal** (pō et′i kəl). —**po·et′i·cal·ly,** *adv.*

poetic justice, a suitable reward for goodness or punishment for evil.

poetic license, the freedom to ignore a rule, fact, or the like in order to achieve a desired artistic effect.

po·et·ics (pō et′iks) *n., pl.* the branch of literary criticism that deals with the theory, nature, and forms of poetry.

poet laureate *pl.,* **poets laureate** or **poet laureates.** in Great Britain, a poet appointed for life by the king or queen to be the official poet of the royal household. The poet laureate's duties formerly included writing poems to commemorate state occasions.

po·et·ry (pō′i trē) *n.* **1.** poems as a group: *He published his first volume of poetry at a young age.* **2.** the writing or language typical of poems. **3.** the art of writing poems. **4.** a quality or effect that is like that of poetry: *the poetry of a ballerina's movements.* **5.** something that has such a quality or effect.

po·go stick (pō′gō) a toy that is like a stilt, made of a pole with footrests and a spring at its base, on which a person may propel himself in a series of hops.

po·grom (pō grom′, pō′grəm) *n.* the organized persecution or massacre of a minority group, especially of Jews. [Russian *pogrom* devastation.]

poi (poi) *n.* a Hawaiian food made from a root of the taro plant that has been cooked, pounded into a paste, and fermented.

poign·ant (poin′yənt) *adj.* **1.** bringing out deep emotions, especially sadness; touching: *The magazine printed a poignant story of a son leaving for the war.* **2.** sharply felt; acute: *a poignant sense of loss.* **3.** sharp; penetrating. —**poign′an·cy,** *n.* —**poign′ant·ly,** *adv.*

poin·set·ti·a (poin set′ē ə) *n.* a tropical American shrub bearing oval leaves and small flowers, surrounded by showy red, pink, or white leaves that resemble flower petals.

Poinsettia

point (point) *n.* **1.** a sharp or tapering end: *the point of a pencil, the point of a knife.* **2.** a tapering piece of land that projects into the water: *A lighthouse was built on the point.* **3.** a dot or other small mark used in writing or printing, such as a decimal point or period. **4.** *Mathematics.* something having a position, but no length, width, or height: *to draw a line between two points.* **5.** a particular location; place; spot: *The tourists visited all the points of interest in the city.* **6.** a position on a scale: *The boiling point of water is 100 degrees centigrade.* **7.** a stage in a process: *Natalie worked to the point of exhaustion.* **8.** a particular moment or time: *At that point, Chris got up and left the room.* **9.** the main or most important part or idea: *What is the point of the story?* **10.** an object; purpose: *I don't see any point in going if the party is almost over.* **11.** an item; detail: *The general explained the plan point by point.* **12.** a special or personal quality; characteristic; trait: *Loyalty to his friends is one of his good points.* **13.** a unit of scoring in a game: *A touchdown in football counts as six points.* **14.** *Printing.* a unit for measuring type, approximately 1/72 inch. **15.** one of the thirty-two marks showing direction on a compass. —*v.t.* **1.** to direct or aim: *The soldier pointed the gun at the target.* **2.** to direct attention to: *He pointed her mistakes out to her. The sign pointed the way to the town.* **3.** to give force to; emphasize: *The speaker pointed up his remarks by speaking louder.* —*v.i.* **1.** to direct attention with or as if with the finger: *The child pointed at the toy he wanted.* **2.** to direct the mind or thought in a certain direction: *All the evidence points toward his guilt.* **3.** (of a hunting dog) to show where a bird or animal is by standing still with the nose and the body facing it.

  beside the point. not related to the subject; irrelevant: *What you say is probably true, but it's beside the point.*

  in point. related to the subject; relevant; pertinent: *a case in point.*

  to make a point of. to be determined to; insist upon: *George makes a point of always being on time.*

  to the point. related to the subject; relevant: *The mayor's speech was brief and to the point.*

point-blank (point′blangk′) *adv.* **1.** from a very close range: *Steve fired the gun point-blank at the target.* **2.** plainly and bluntly; flatly: *They asked him point-blank if he had stolen the money.* —*adj.* **1.** pointed or aimed straight at the target, especially from close range: *to be exposed to point-blank fire.* **2.** very close to the target: *point-blank range.* **3.** plain and blunt: *a point-blank refusal.*

point·ed (poin′tid) *adj.* **1.** having or coming to a point or points: *a clown's pointed cap, a pointed stick.* **2.** related to the subject; to the point: *a pointed question.* **3.** clearly aimed at or referring to a person, group, or thing: *a pointed comment.* —**point′ed·ly,** *adv.* —**point′ed·ness,** *n.*

point·er (poin′tər) *n.* **1.** a long stick used to point out things, as on a blackboard, chart, or map. **2.** a short-haired dog having long ears, and a long, tapering tail. Pointers hunt game birds by scent and point to their location. **3.** a needle or similar device, as on a scale or meter, showing a measurement. **4.** *Informal.* a piece of

Pointer

information or advice; hint; suggestion: *The teacher gave me some good pointers on how to write the composition.* **5.** a person or thing that points.

point·less (point′lis) *adj.* **1.** without force, purpose, or result; useless: *a pointless attempt.* **2.** without meaning; senseless: *a pointless remark, a pointless joke.* **3.** without a sharp or tapering end. —**point′less·ly,** *adv.* —**point′less·ness,** *n.*

point of order, a question raised as to whether correct parliamentary procedure is being followed.

point of view **1.** a manner of thinking or feeling about something; attitude. **2.** the position from which something is considered or looked at.

poise (poiz) *n.* **1.** a calm, confident manner; self-assurance and composure. **2.** a state of balance; stability. —*v.,* **poised, pois·ing.** —*v.t.* to place, carry, or hold in balance: *The diver poised himself on the edge of the diving board.* —*v.i.* to be held in balance.

poi·son (poi′zən) *n.* **1.** a substance that causes serious injury, illness, or death by its chemical action on a living thing. **2.** anything that harms, corrupts, or destroys. —*v.t.* **1.** to give poison to; injure or kill with poison. **2.** to put poison in; cause to become harmful or deadly: *Dangerous bacteria poisoned the canned soup.* **3.** to have a harmful, corrupting, or destructive effect on: *She poisoned his mind with ideas of hate and revenge.* —*adj.* that poisons; poisonous. [Going back to Latin *pōtiō* a drink, poisonous drink; originally referring to any drink.] —**poi′son·er,** *n.*

poison ivy **1.** a woody vine of North America, having shiny leaves made up of three jagged oval leaflets. It contains an oil in the stems, leaves, and roots that causes a rash when it comes in contact with the skin. **2.** the rash caused by contact with this plant.

---

at; āpe; cär; end; mē; it; īce; hot; ōld; fôrk; wood; fōōl; oil; out; up; turn; sing; thin; this; hw in white; zh in treasure. The symbol ə stands for the sound of **a** in about, **e** in taken, **i** in pencil, **o** in lemon, and **u** in circus.

poison oak **1.** a slender woody plant related to poison ivy and causing a similar rash. It has leaves made up of three usually oval leaflets. **2.** the rash caused by contact with this plant.

poi·son·ous (poi′zənəs) *adj.* **1.** causing serious injury, illness, or death by poison: *a poisonous snake, a poisonous liquid.* **2.** having a harmful, corrupting, or destructive effect. **3.** full of anger, spite, or ill will: *She gave him a poisonous glance.* —**poi′son·ous·ly,** *adv.* —**poi′son·ous·ness,** *n.*

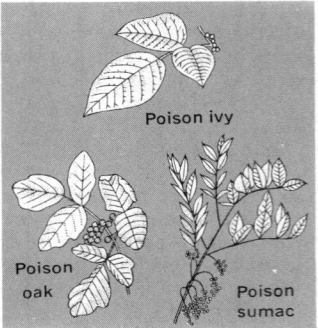

Poison ivy

Poison oak

Poison sumac

poison sumac **1.** a shrub or small tree related to poison ivy and causing a similar rash. It has leaves made up of from seven to thirteen oblong or oval leaflets. **2.** the rash caused by contact with this plant.

poke¹ (pōk) *v.,* **poked, pok·ing.** —*v.t.* **1.** to push into or against, as with something pointed; prod: *Mark poked the frog with a stick to make it jump.* **2.** to push or thrust: *Margie poked her head out of the window.* **3.** to make by pushing or thrusting: *The stick poked a hole in the drum.* —*v.i.* **1.** to make a pushing, thrusting, or prodding motion. **2.** to thrust forward or stick out; protrude: *A large rock poked up out of the water.* **3.** to look, search, or investigate. **4.** to move or go slowly or lazily; dawdle: *We'll be late if you don't stop poking along.* —*n.* a pushing, thrusting, or prodding motion. [Middle English *poken.*]
  to poke fun at. to make fun of; mock.

poke² (pōk) *n.* a bag; sack. [Dialectal Old French *poque.*]

poke bonnet, a bonnet having a large, deep brim that sticks out in front.

pok·er¹ (pō′kər) *n.* **1.** a metal rod for stirring a fire. **2.** a person or thing that pokes. [*Poke¹* + *-er¹.*]

pok·er² (pō′kər) *n.* any of various card games in which the players bet on the value of their hands. [Of uncertain origin.]

pok·y (pō′kē) *also,* **pok·ey.** *adj.,* **pok·i·er, pok·i·est.** extremely slow; dawdling.

Poke bonnet

Po·land (pō′lənd) *n.* a country in central Europe, on the Baltic Sea. Capital, Warsaw. Area, 120,360 sq. mi. Pop. (1980), 35,800,000.

po·lar (pō′lər) *adj.* **1.** of or relating to a pole or poles, as of a magnet, battery, or sphere. **2.** relating to, near, or coming from the North or South Pole: *a polar expedition.* **3.** directly opposite, as in character or tendency.

polar bear, a large white bear, native to arctic regions.

Po·lar·is (pō lar′is) *n.* a star located in the northern sky above the North Pole. It is the outermost star in the handle of the Little Dipper. Also, **North Star, polestar.**

po·lar·i·ty (pō lar′ə tē) *n. pl.,* **po·lar·i·ties.** **1.** the possession of two poles at opposite ends with opposite properties, as in a magnet. **2.** the condition of being directly opposite, as in character or tendency: *political polarity.*

Polar bear

po·lar·ize (pō′lə rīz′) *v.t.,* **po·lar·ized, po·lar·iz·ing.** **1.** to give polarity to. **2.** to cause to separate into opposing groups: *Disagreement over the government's policies threatened to polarize the country.* **3.** to act upon (light or other electromagnetic radiation) so that the vibrations of the waves are confined to a single plane or direction. —*v.i.* to become polarized. —**po′lar·i·za′tion,** *n.*

Po·lar·oid (pō′lə roid′) *n. Trademark.* **1.** a transparent plastic material capable of polarizing light, used especially in lamps and eyeglasses to reduce glare. **2.** a portable camera that produces a finished photograph within seconds. Also *(def. 2),* **Polaroid Land Camera.**

pole¹ (pōl) *n.* a long, slender piece of wood, metal, or other material: *a fishing pole.* —*v.t.,* **poled, pol·ing.** to move, push, or strike with a pole: *to pole a boat down a river.* [Old English *pāl.*]

pole² (pōl) *n.* **1.** either end of the earth's axis; North Pole or South Pole. **2.** see **celestial pole. 3.** either of two regions or parts having forces opposite to one another, as the ends of a magnet or the terminals of an electric battery. **4.** *Biology.* either end of a nucleus, cell, or ovum, at or near which certain parts are symmetrically arranged. **5.** either of two principles, ideas, or the like that are directly opposite, as in character or tendency: *Their political beliefs are at opposite poles.* [Old French *pole.*]

Pole (pōl) *n.* a person who was born or is living in Poland.

pole·cat (pōl′kat′) *n.* **1.** a small, meat-eating European animal closely related to the weasel and ferret, and having long, soft, buff-gray fur. Polecats spray a foul-smelling liquid when attacked or frightened. **2.** a skunk.

po·lem·ic (pə lem′ik) *n.* **1.** an argument or discussion, especially an attack on a particular opinion, doctrine, or theory. **2. polemics.** the art or practice of argument. ▲ used with a singular verb. —*adj. also,* **po·lem·i·cal** (pəlem′i kəl). of or relating to controversy or dispute. —**po·lem′i·cal·ly,** *adv.*

pole·star (pōl′stär′) *n.* another word for **Polaris.**

pole-vault (pōl′vôlt′) *v.i.* to make a pole vault. —**pole′-vault′er,** *n.*

pole vault, an athletic field event in which the contestant vaults over a horizontal bar with the aid of a long pole.

po·lice (pə lēs′) *n.* **1.** an official force established and given power by a government to prevent and detect crime, enforce the law, and keep public order. **2.** the members of such a force as a group. **3.** any group officially given power to enforce regulations or keep order: *campus police.* —*v.t.,* **po·liced, po·lic·ing. 1.** to patrol or keep order in (an area) by means of police. **2.** to make (an area, as in a military camp) clean and tidy.

police dog **1.** another term for **German shepherd. 2.** any dog used to aid police in their work.

po·lice·man (pə lēs′mən) *n. pl.,* **po·lice·men** (pə lēs′mən). a member of the police.

po·lice·wom·an (pə lēs′woom′ən) *n. pl.,* **po·lice·wom·en.** (pə lēs′wim′ən). a female member of the police.

police state, a country or state in which the government seeks to control the lives of its citizens, especially by means of a secret police force.

pol·i·cy¹ (pol′ə sē) *n. pl.,* **pol·i·cies. 1.** a guiding principle that helps determine what decision to make: *The policy of the store was not to make refunds.* **2.** wisdom or shrewdness in the management of affairs; prudence. [Old French *policie* government, administration.]

pol·i·cy² (pol′ə sē) *n. pl.,* **pol·i·cies.** a written contract of insurance between an insurance company and the person or persons insured. [French *police* this contract.]

po·li·o (pō′lē ō′) *n.* see **poliomyelitis.**

po·li·o·my·e·li·tis (pō′lē ō mī′ə lī′tis) *n.* a highly contagious disease caused by a virus and occurring mainly in children. In its mild forms, it causes headache, sore throat, and fever. In its severe forms, it attacks the central nervous system and causes muscular weakness, and paralysis. Also, **infantile paralysis.**

pol·ish (pol′ish) *n. pl.,* **pol·ish·es. 1.** the smoothness or shininess of a surface or finish, such as that produced by rubbing or by applying a special substance; luster: *Henry buffed the floor to a high polish.* **2.** a preparation or substance used to shine, clean, or smooth a surface: *shoe polish.* **3.** smooth elegance of manner or style; refinement: *a sophisticated man with polish and poise.* —*v.t.* **1.** to shine, clean, or smooth, as by rubbing or applying a special substance: *to polish silverware.* **2.** to make more finished or complete; improve or refine: *Polish up that speech a bit.* —*v.i.* to become smooth or glossy. —**pol′ish·er,** *n.*

  to polish off. *Informal.* to finish completely and quickly: *to polish off a meal, to polish off an assignment.*

Pol·ish (pō′lish) *adj.* of or relating to Poland, its people, their language, or their culture. —*n.* the language of Poland.

Po·lit·bu·ro (pə lit′byoor′ō) *n.* the highest policy-making and executive committee of the Communist Party in the Soviet Union.

po·lite (pə līt′) *adj.* **1.** having or showing good manners, consideration for others, and a regard for correct social behavior; courteous. **2.** marked by correct social behavior; refined: *polite society.* —**po·lite′ly,** *adv.* —**po·lite′ness,** *n.*

pol·i·tic (pol′ə tik) *adj.* characterized by or showing good judgment, tact, or shrewdness: *politic advice.*

po·lit·i·cal (pə lit′i kəl) *adj.* **1.** of, relating to, or concerned with the organization or activities of government. **2.** of, relating to, or involved in politics: *a political party.* **3.** of, relating to, or characteristic of politicians. —**po·lit′i·cal·ly,** *adv.*

political science, the study of the origin, organization, principles, and operation of government.

pol·i·ti·cian (pol′ə tish′ən) *n.* **1.** a person who is active in politics, especially a person who holds or seeks public office. **2.** a person who is skilled in shrewd dealings with others.

pol·i·tics (pol′ə tiks) *n.,pl.* **1.** the affairs or activities of a government: *state politics.* **2.** the science or art of government. **3.** general political opinions or convictions: *Mr. Brown is liberal in his politics.* **4.** competition for positions of power within a group: *office politics.*

pol·i·ty (pol′ə tē) *n. pl.,* **pol·i·ties. 1.** a form, system, or method of government. **2.** any community living under some form or system of government.

Polk, James Knox (pōk) 1795–1849, the eleventh president of the United States, from 1845 to 1849.

pol·ka (pōl′kə, pō′kə) *n.* **1.** a lively dance that originated in Central Europe. It is danced in couples, and its basic movement consists of three steps and a hop. **2.** the music for this dance. —*v.i.,* **pol·kaed, pol·ka·ing.** to dance the polka.

pol·ka dot (pō′kə) **1.** one of a series of round dots spaced to form a pattern on fabric or other materials. **2.** a pattern or material with such dots.

poll (pōl) *n.* **1.** a survey of public opinion on a given subject, usually gotten by questioning a sample group of people. **2.** the casting and recording of votes in an election. **3.** the total number of votes cast or recorded. **4. polls.** a place where votes are cast and recorded. **5.** a list of persons, especially those who can vote. **6.** the head, especially that part of it on which the hair grows. —*v.t.* **1.** to receive (a given number of votes) in an election: *The winner polled twice as many votes as his opponent.* **2.** to question (a sample group of people) to get a survey of public opinion. **3.** to record or register the votes of: *to poll*

a district. **4.** to cut off, trim, or crop: *to poll hair, to poll the horns of a cow.*

pol·len (pol′ən) *n.* a fine, yellowish, powdery material produced in the anthers of flowering plants. Grains of pollen are the male reproductive cells, and they fertilize the female reproductive cells, or ovules, to form seeds.

pol·li·nate (pol′ə nāt′) *v.t.,* **pol·li·nat·ed, pol·li·nat·ing.** to carry pollen from an anther to a stigma of (a plant).

pol·li·na·tion (pol′ə nā′shən) *n.* the transfer of pollen from the anther of a flower to the stigma of the same or another flower. The grains of pollen then fertilize the female reproductive cells, or ovules, in the ovary of the flower in order to form seeds.

pol·li·wog (pol′ē wog′) *also,* **pol·ly·wog.** *n.* another word for **tadpole.**

poll·ster (pōl′stər) *n.* a person who questions people to get a survey of public opinion; person who conducts public opinion polls.

poll tax, a tax on persons who are qualified to vote, which in some states formerly had to be paid before voting.

pol·lut·ant (pə loot′ənt) *n.* something that pollutes, especially industrial waste or other material that pollutes air, water, or soil.

pol·lute (pə loot′) *v.t.,* **pol·lut·ed, pol·lut·ing. 1.** to make impure or dirty, as with harmful chemicals, gases, or other wastes: *Oil from the damaged ship polluted the river. Exhaust from automobile engines pollutes the air.* **2.** to destroy the purity of; corrupt.

pol·lu·tion (pə loo′shən) *n.* **1.** the act of polluting or the state of being polluted. **2.** something that pollutes.

Pol·lux (pol′əks) *n.* see **Castor and Pollux.**

pol·ly·wog (pol′ē wog′) *n.* another word for **tadpole.**

po·lo (pō′lō) *n.* **1.** a game played on horseback by two teams of four players, using long-handled mallets with which they attempt to hit a wooden ball through the opponent's goal posts. **2.** see **water polo.**

Po·lo, Mar·co (pō′lō; mär′kō) 1254?–1324, Italian traveler who visited and wrote about China.

pol·o·naise (pol′ə nāz′, pō′lə nāz′) *n.* **1.** a stately dance of Polish origin, in three-quarter time, marked by slow, gliding steps. **2.** the music for this dance. **3.** a woman's dress popular in the eighteenth century, having a fitted bodice and a full skirt, worn over a separate skirt and open in the front so that the sides could be looped up to form three panels.

po·lo·ni·um (pə lō′nē əm) *n.* a heavy, radioactive metallic element, the first radioactive element to be discovered. It occurs naturally when pitchblende, a uranium ore, decays. Symbol: **Po** [Modern Latin *polonium* this element, from *Polônia,* the Latin name of Poland; so named by its discoverers, Pierre and Marie Curie, because Marie Curie was born in Poland.]

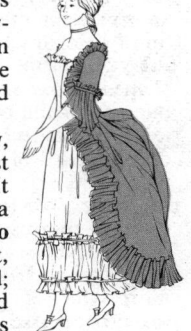

Polonaise

polo shirt, a sport shirt made of knitted cotton, usually close-fitting and having short sleeves.

pol·troon (pol troon′) *n.* a complete coward.

at; āpe; cär; end; mē; it; īce; hot; ōld; fôrk; wood; fool; oil; out; up; turn; sing; thin; this; hw in white; zh in treasure. The symbol ə stands for the sound of **a** in about, **e** in taken, **i** in pencil, **o** in lemon, and **u** in circus.

poly- *combining form* more than one; many; much: *polygamy, polygon.*

pol·y·es·ter (pol′ē es′tər) *n.* any of several light, artificial resins, used especially in making textile fibers.

pol·y·eth·y·lene (pol′ē eth′ə lēn′) *n.* a strong, light plastic used in manufacturing bags, containers, and insulation.

po·lyg·a·mist (pə lig′ə mist) *n.* a person who practices polygamy.

po·lyg·a·mous (pə lig′ə məs) *adj.* of, relating to, or practicing polygamy. —**po·lyg′a·mous·ly,** *adv.*

po·lyg·a·my (pə lig′ə mē) *n.* the practice, custom, or condition of having more than one spouse at a time.

pol·y·glot (pol′ē glot′) *n.* **1.** a person who speaks, understands, or writes several languages. **2.** a mixture or confusion of several languages. —*adj.* **1.** speaking, understanding, or writing several languages. **2.** made up of or expressed in several languages.

pol·y·gon (pol′ē gon′) *n.* a closed figure lying in a plane and having at least three straight sides. A square is a polygon. —**po·lyg·o·nal** (pə lig′ən əl), *adj.*

pol·y·he·dron (pol′ē hē′drən) *n. pl.,* **pol·y·he·drons** or **pol·y·he·dra** (pol′ē hē′drə). a closed solid figure that is the union of plane polygons, each two adjoining polygons having a common edge. —**pol′y·he′dral,** *adj.*

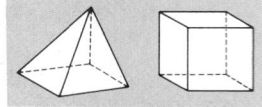
Polyhedrons

pol·y·mer (pol′i mər) *n.* **1.** any large molecule formed of smaller simple molecules linked together in long chains of repeating units. The number of molecules that unite to form a polymer may vary from a few to thousands. **2.** a substance made of polymers.

Pol·y·ne·sia (pol′i nē′zhə) *n.* one of the three main divisions of the Pacific islands, in the central and southern part of the Pacific, east of Melanesia and Micronesia.

Pol·y·ne·sian (pol′i nē′zhən) *n.* **1.** a person who was born or is living in Polynesia. **2.** the sub-family of languages spoken mainly in Polynesia and including Hawaiian, Maori, and Tahitian. —*adj.* of or relating to Polynesia, its people, their languages, or culture.

pol·y·no·mi·al (pol′ē nō′mē əl) *n. Mathematics.* an expression made up of two or more terms. —*adj.* made up of or characterized by two or more terms.

pol·yp (pol′ip) *n.* a small marine animal with a cup-shaped or sac-shaped body, having a mouth opening at one end of the body surrounded by many tentacles.

pol·y·phon·ic (pol′ē fon′ik) *adj. Music.* of, relating to, or composed of two or more separate melodic voices or parts.

pol·y·syl·lab·ic (pol′ē si lab′ik) *adj.* **1.** made up of three or more syllables. **2.** marked by words of three or more syllables: *polysyllabic writing.*

pol·y·syl·la·ble (pol′ē sil′ə bəl) *n.* a word of three or more syllables.

pol·y·tech·nic (pol′ē tek′nik) *adj.* of, relating to, or giving instruction in many crafts and applied sciences: *a polytechnic institute.*

pol·y·the·ism (pol′ē thē iz′əm) *n.* the belief in or worship of more than one god. —**pol′y·the′ist,** *n.* —**pol′y·the·is′tic,** *adj.*

pol·y·un·sat·u·rat·ed (pol′ē un sach′ə rā′tid) *adj.* containing more than two double or triple bonds in a molecule, as certain vegetable and animal fats and oils.

po·made (po mād′) *n.* a perfumed ointment, especially one for dressing the hair. —*v.t.,* **po·mad·ed, po·mad·ing.** to dress (one's hair) with pomade.

pome (pōm) *n.* a fleshy, firm fruit that can be eaten, having several seeds. The apple and pear are pomes.

pome·gran·ate (pom′gran′it) *n.* **1.** the round fruit of a shrub or small tree, having a tough golden-red rind and containing many seeds, each of which is enclosed by a juicy reddish pulp that can be eaten. **2.** the shrub or tree bearing this fruit, having red or orange trumpet-shaped flowers.

Pom·er·a·ni·an (pom′ə rā′nē ən) *n.* a small, long-haired dog having a head like a fox and a bushy tail that lies flat on the back.

Pomeranian

pom·mel (pum′əl, pom′əl) *n.* **1.** the raised front part of a saddle, consisting of a knob that is used chiefly as a grip. **2.** the rounded knob on the hilt of a sword, dagger, or similar weapon. —*v.t.* another spelling of **pummel.**

pomp (pomp) *n.* a stately and splendid ceremony or display; splendor; pageantry: *The newspaper described the pomp and ritual of the Queen's coronation.*

pom·pa·dour (pom′pə dôr′) *n.* **1.** a man's hair style in which the hair is combed up high and back from the forehead. **2.** a woman's hair style in which the hair is combed back from the forehead and puffed high in front, often over a pad. [From the Marquise de *Pompadour,* 1721–1764, the mistress of King Louis XV of France, who wore her hair in this style.]

pom·pa·no (pom′pə nō′) *n. pl.,* **pom·pa·nos.** a fish found in temperate and tropical waters of North and South America. It has a flattened roundish or oval body that is usually silver in color.

Pom·peii (pom pā′) *n.* a partially excavated ancient city in southwestern Italy, near Naples, buried by the eruption of Mount Vesuvius in A.D. 79. —**Pom·pei′an,** *adj., n.*

Pom·pey (pom′pē) 106–48 B.C., Roman general and statesman.

pom·pom (pom′pom′) *also,* **pom·pon** (pom′pon′). *n.* **1.** an ornamental ball or tuft of wool or other material, used especially as a decoration on clothing. **2.** a small, round flower, such as a chrysanthemum.

pom·pos·i·ty (pom pos′ə tē) *n. pl.,* **pom·pos·i·ties.** **1.** the state or quality of being pompous. **2.** a pompous action, remark, or display.

pom·pous (pom′pəs) *adj.* **1.** marked by or showing too much dignity or self-importance. **2.** very lofty or ornate; pretentious. —**pom′pous·ly,** *adv.* —**pom′pous·ness,** *n.*

Ponce de Le·ón, Juan (pons′ də lē′ən; hwän) 1460?–1521, the Spanish explorer who discovered Florida.

pon·cho (pon′chō) *n. pl.,* **pon·chos.** **1.** a garment that is like a cloak, made of a piece of cloth with a slit or hole in the middle so that it can be slipped over the head. **2.** a waterproof garment resembling this, worn chiefly as a raincoat.

pond (pond) *n.* a body of still water, usually smaller than a lake.

pon·der (pon′dər) *v.t.* to consider or think over carefully: *They pondered what they should do next.* —*v.i.* to think carefully; muse; reflect: *to ponder over a problem.*

pon·der·ous (pon′dər əs) *adj.* **1.** having great weight or bulk; heavy; unwieldy: *The ponderous old cart lumbered down the road.* **2.** clumsy and slow: *the ponderous movements of an elephant.* **3.** dull and hard to read: *The law journal was full of ponderous articles.* —**pon′der·ous·ly,** *adv.* —**pon′der·ous·ness,** *n.*

Poncho

pone (pōn) *n.* see **corn pone.**

pon·gee (pon jē′) *n.* a brownish-yellow, thin fabric having an uneven surface, originally hand-woven in China from silk.

pon·iard (pon′yərd) *n.* another word for **dagger**.

pons (ponz) *n. pl.,* **pon·tes** (pon′tēz). a band of nerve fibers in the brain connecting the cerebellum, cerebrum, and medulla oblongata.

Pon·ti·ac (pon′tē ak′) *n.* **1.** 1720?–1769, Ottawa Indian chief. **2.** a city in southeastern Michigan. Pop. (1970), 85,279.

pon·tiff (pon′tif) *n.* **1.** another word for **pope**. **2.** any high priest. **3.** any bishop.

pon·tif·i·cal (pon tif′i kəl) *adj.* of or relating to a pope, high priest, or bishop.

pon·tif·i·cate (*v.,* pon tif′i kāt′; *n.,* pon tif′i kit, pon-tif′i kāt′). *v.i.,* **pon·tif·i·cat·ed, pon·tif·i·cat·ing. 1.** to perform the duties of or act as a pope or bishop. **2.** to speak or act in a pompous manner. —*n.* the office or term of office of a pope or bishop.

pon·toon (pon tōōn′) *n.* **1.** a flat-bottomed boat or similar floating structure used as a support, as in the building of floating bridges over water or in the raising of submerged vessels. **2.** the float of a seaplane.

pontoon bridge, a bridge that is supported in the water by pontoons.

po·ny (pō′nē) *n. pl.,* **po·nies.**
1. a horse of any of various small breeds. **2.** any horse, especially a small one. **3.** *Informal.* a text or aid, especially a literal translation of a work in a foreign language, used by students, usually dishonestly, in doing schoolwork or in preparing for an exam.

Pontoon bridge

pony express, a postal service in which mail was carried in relays by riders on horseback. The pony express ran between Missouri and California from 1860 to 1861.

po·ny·tail (pō′nē tāl′) *also,* **pony tail.** *n.* a hair style in which the hair is drawn back from the face and fastened at the back of the head, so as to hang down like a pony's tail.

pooch (pōōch) *n. pl.,* **pooch·es.** *Slang.* a dog.

poo·dle (pōōd′əl) *n.* a curly-haired dog having a thick, usually solid-colored coat that is often clipped in elaborate styles.

pooh (pōō) *interj.* used to express dislike, contempt, or scorn.

pooh-pooh (pōō′pōō′) *v.t. Informal.* to express contempt or scorn for: *We pooh-poohed their plan to play a practical joke on the teacher.*

pool¹ (pōōl) *n.* **1.** a small body of still, usually fresh, water. **2.** an indoor or outdoor tank designed for swimming. Also, **swimming pool. 3.** a small, shallow amount of liquid on a surface: *a pool of gravy, a pool of oil.* **4.** a still, deep place in a stream or river. [Old English *pōl.*]

pool² (pōōl) *n.* **1.** a game played on a pool table, with the object being to drive balls into pockets by striking them with the cue ball. **2.** a common fund or supply, as of money or skilled people: *a typing pool.* **3.** an arrangement in which a number of people share the use of something: *a car pool.* **4.** the amount that the winner gets in certain gambling games. —*v.t.* to put into a common fund or joint effort: *The members of the football team pooled their money to buy some new equipment.* [French *poule* a stake in a game; originally, hen; possibly because a hen was a prize in a game.]

pool·room (pōōl′rōōm′, pōōl′room′) *n.* a room or place of business where pool or billiards may be played.

pool table, a rectangular table used in playing pool, having a slate surface covered with felt and six pockets, one in each of the four corners and one in the center of both long sides.

Poo·na (pōō′nə) *n.* a city in western India, southeast of Bombay. Pop. (1971), 853,226.

poop (pōōp) *n.* the short deck above the main deck at the stern of a boat or ship, often forming the roof of a cabin. Also, **poop deck.**

poor (poor) *adj.* **1.** having little or no money; needy. **2.** marked by or showing such need: *a poor neighborhood.* **3.** below a standard; inferior; bad: *poor health, poor quality.* **4.** being less than is wanted, needed, or expected; insufficient: *a poor wheat crop.* **5.** lacking skill or ability; not capable or talented: *a poor writer, a poor student.* **6.** deserving pity or compassion; unfortunate: *The poor man has lived alone for years.* —*n.* **the poor.** poor or needy persons as a group. —**poor′ness,** *n.*

poor·house (poor′hous′) *n. pl.,* **poor·hous·es** (poor′-hou′ziz). a place kept at public expense to shelter and aid poor people.

poor·ly (poor′lē) *adv.* in a poor manner; badly: *He has performed rather poorly in school this term.* —*adj. Informal.* somewhat ill: *She's been feeling poorly lately.*

pop¹ (pop) *v.,* **popped, pop·ping.** —*v.i.* **1.** to make a short, sharp, explosive sound: *The champagne cork popped when the bottle was opened.* **2.** to burst open or explode with such a sound: *The corn popped quickly.* **3.** to move, go, appear, or come quickly or suddenly: *She popped in to see us yesterday.* **4.** (of the eyes) to open wide suddenly. **5.** *Baseball.* to hit a pop fly. —*v.t.* **1.** to cause to burst with a short, sharp, explosive sound: *The pin popped the balloon.* **2.** to put or thrust quickly or suddenly: *The boy popped his head out the window.* —*n.* **1.** a short, sharp, explosive sound. **2.** a flavored, nonalcoholic beverage; soda. [Imitative of this sound.]

pop² (pop) *adj. Informal.* of, relating to, or designating popular music: *a pop singer.* [Short for *popular.*]

pop³ (pop) *n. Informal.* another word for **father.** [A form of *papa.*]

pop. 1. population. **2.** popular; popularly.

pop art, art that takes its subjects, themes, and techniques from advertising, comic strips, motion pictures, and other forms of popular culture.

pop·corn (pop′kôrn′) *n.* **1.** a variety of corn having small, hard kernels that burst open when heated and puff out to form white, fluffy masses. **2.** the burst kernels of this corn, eaten as a snack.

pope (pōp) *also,* **Pope.** *n.* the bishop of Rome and supreme head of the Roman Catholic Church.

Pope, Alexander (pōp) 1688–1744, English poet.

pop fly *Baseball.* a high fly ball hit into or near the infield.

pop·gun (pop′gun′) *n.* a toy gun that makes a loud pop when fired, especially one that fires pellets or corks by means of air compressed in the barrel.

pop·in·jay (pop′in jā′) *n.* a vain, silly person who talks too much.

at; āpe; cär; end; mē; it; īce; hot; ōld; fôrk;
wood; fōōl; oil; out; up; turn; sing; thin; **this;**
hw in white; zh in treasure. The symbol ə
stands for the sound of **a** in about, **e** in taken,
i in pencil, **o** in lemon, and **u** in circus.

P

pop·lar (pop′lər) *n.* **1.** any of a small group of fast-growing trees of the willow family, found throughout the Northern Hemisphere, having pale ridged bark and broad leaves. **2.** the soft white wood of such a tree, often used to make shipping boxes and pulp.

Fruit   Leaves

Poplar

pop·lin (pop′lin) *n.* a durable fabric woven with a crosswise rib. It is often made of cotton, and used for shirts, dresses, curtains, and pajamas.

Po·po·cat·e·petl (pō′pō kə tā′pet′əl, pō′pō kat′ə pet′əl) *n.* a volcano in south-central Mexico.

pop·o·ver (pop′ō′vər) *n.* a very light muffin, made of flour, eggs, milk, and shortening, that puffs up and becomes hollow when baked.

pop·py (pop′ē) *n. pl.,* **pop·pies. 1.** a round showy flower often grown as a garden flower. **2.** the plant bearing this flower, containing a milky juice. One species of poppy is the source of the drug opium. **3.** a bright orange-red color. —*adj.* having the color poppy.

pop·py·cock (pop′ē kok′) *n.* completely foolish or empty talk; nonsense.

pop·u·lace (pop′yə lis) *n.* **1.** all the inhabitants of a place; population. **2.** the common people; the masses.

pop·u·lar (pop′yə lər) *adj.* **1.** pleasing to or favored by very many or most people: *a popular actor, a popular restaurant.* **2.** having many friends and acquaintances; well-liked: *My brother was voted the most popular boy in his class.* **3.** of, relating to, or representing the general public: *a popular election, popular government.* **4.** accepted or widespread among the general public; common: *The belief that pencils contain lead is a popular mistake.* **5.** suited to the taste and intelligence of the average person or the general public: *popular music.* **6.** suited to or within the means of ordinary people; moderate: *This model is now available at popular prices.* —**pop′u·lar·ly,** *adv.*

pop·u·lar·i·ty (pop′yə lar′ə tē) *n.* the quality or state of being widely liked, admired, or favored.

pop·u·lar·ize (pop′yə lə rīz′) *v.t.,* **pop·u·lar·ized, pop·u·lar·iz·ing.** to make (something) popular or understandable to the general public. —**pop′u·lar·i·za′tion,** *n.* —**pop′u·lar·iz′er,** *n.*

pop·u·late (pop′yə lāt′) *v.t.,* **pop·u·lat·ed, pop·u·lat·ing. 1.** to live in; inhabit: *The forest is populated by wildlife.* **2.** to furnish with inhabitants, as by colonization.

pop·u·la·tion (pop′yə lā′shən) *n.* **1.** the total number of people living in an area or place: *The population of that town has doubled in the past decade.* **2.** the people themselves: *The entire population of the town came to watch the parade.* **3.** a distinct group of such people: *the French-speaking population of Montreal.* **4.** the act or process of populating; furnishing with inhabitants.

Pop·u·list (pop′yə list) *adj.* of, relating to, or characteristic of the Populist Party. —*n.* a member or supporter of the Populist Party.

Populist Party, a political party active in the United States in the 1890s that favored the farmers and workers.

pop·u·lous (pop′yə ləs) *adj.* having many inhabitants; heavily populated.

por·ce·lain (pôr′sə lin) *n.* **1.** a fine ceramic material that is hard and white. **2.** objects made of this.

porch (pôrch) *n. pl.,* **porch·es. 1.** a roofed, sometimes enclosed area attached to the outside of a house. **2.** a structure forming an entrance to a building.

por·cu·pine (pôr′kyə pīn′) *n.* an animal whose body and tail are covered with sharp spines or quills that serve as protection.

pore¹ (pôr) *n.* a very small opening, as in the skin of an animal or in the surface of a leaf, through which water, air, or the like may pass. [Middle French *pore.*]

pore² (pôr) *v.i.,* **pored, por·ing.** to read or study with great attention or care: *Barbara pored over her notes while waiting for her turn to speak.* [Of uncertain origin.]

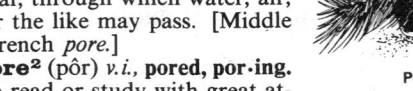

Porcupine

por·gy (pôr′gē) *n. pl.,* **por·gies** or **por·gy.** a food and game fish found chiefly in coastal waters of the Atlantic Ocean.

pork (pôrk) *n.* the meat of a pig or hog used as food.

pork·er (pôr′kər) *n.* a pig or hog, especially one fattened for slaughter.

por·nog·ra·phy (pôr nog′rə fē) *n.* writing or pictures meant to arouse sexual desires. —**por·no·graph·ic** (pôr′nə graf′ik), *adj.*

po·ros·i·ty (pô ros′ə tē) *n. pl.,* **po·ros·i·ties.** the quality or condition of being porous.

po·rous (pôr′əs) *adj.* having or full of pores: *a porous material.* —**po′rous·ness,** *n.*

por·phy·ry (pôr′fər ē) *n. pl.,* **por·phy·ries.** volcanic rock composed of two or more minerals, usually including a feldspar mineral.

por·poise (pôr′pəs) *n. pl.,* **por·pois·es** or **por·poise.** a warm-blooded animal that is closely related to the dolphin and is found in all oceans except those in polar regions. The porpoise has a torpedo-shaped body that is usually black with white undersides.

Porpoise

por·ridge (pôr′ij, por′ij) *n.* a soft food made by boiling oatmeal or other meal in water or milk until thickened, usually served as a breakfast dish.

por·rin·ger (pôr′in jər, por′in jər) *n.* a small, shallow bowl, usually with a short handle, for holding porridge or other food.

port¹ (pôrt) *n.* **1.** a place along a coast or waterway where boats and ships can anchor and be protected from storms; harbor. **2.** a city or town with a harbor. [Old English *port* and Old French *port* harbor.]

port² (pôrt) *n.* the left side of a boat or ship as one faces the bow. —*adj.* of, relating to, or located on the left side of a boat or ship. —*v.t.* to turn or shift to the port side. [From either *port¹* or *port⁴.*]

port³ (pôrt) *n.* a strong, sweet wine, usually dark red in color. [From *Oporto,* a Portuguese city that shipped this wine.]

port⁴ (pôrt) *n.* **1.** see **porthole. 2.** the covering for a porthole. [Old French *porte* gate, door.]

port·a·ble (pôr′tə bəl) *adj.* that can be carried easily, especially by hand: *a portable radio, a portable phonograph.* —*n.* something that is portable, such as a lightweight typewriter.

por·tage (pôr′tij) *n.* **1.** the act of transporting boats or goods overland from one river or other body of water to another. **2.** the route or place over which this is done. **3.** the cost or charge for this. —*v.t., v.i.,* **por·taged, por·tag·ing.** to carry (boats or goods) over a portage.

por·tal (pôr′əl) *n.* a door, gate, or entrance, especially a large and imposing one: *the portal of a cathedral.*

Port Arthur, a port city in southern Manchuria, part of the municipality of Lüda. Also, **Lüshun.**

Port-au-Prince (pôrt′ō prins′) *n.* the capital of Haiti, in the southwestern part of the country, on the Caribbean Sea. Pop. (1975 est.), 745,700.

port·cul·lis (pôrt kul′is) *n. pl.,* **port·cul·lis·es.** a heavy grating built so as to slide up and down in grooves cut in the sides of the gateway of a castle or fortress. It could be lowered quickly as a defense against assault.

Portcullis

Port Elizabeth, a port city on the southern coast of the Republic of South Africa. Pop. (1971 est.), 390,982.

por·tend (pôr tend′) *v.t.* to be a warning, sign, or indication of: *A black sky portended the coming storm.*

por·tent (pôr′tent) *n.* a warning, sign, or indication of what is to come, especially of something very important or disastrous; omen.

por·ten·tous (pôr ten′təs) *adj.* **1.** threatening; ominous. **2.** very remarkable or important: *a portentous era in history.* —**por·ten′tous·ly,** *adv.* —**por·ten′tous·ness,** *n.*

por·ter[1] (pôr′tər) *n.* **1.** a person who is employed to carry baggage, as at a railroad station or in a hotel. **2.** an attendant who helps passengers in a railroad car. [Middle French *porteur* bearer, carrier.]

por·ter[2] (pôr′tər) *n.* a person employed to do cleaning and repair work in a building, as in an apartment house; janitor. [Old French *portier* doorkeeper, gatekeeper.]

por·ter[3] (pôr′tər) *n.* a dark-brown, heavy, bitter beer brewed from partly charred malt.

Por·ter, William Sydney (pôr′tər) see **O. Henry.**

por·ter·house (pôr′tər hous′) *n. pl.,* **por·ter·hous·es** (pôr′tər hou′ziz) a cut of beef taken from the loin, including a large part of the tenderloin. Also, **porterhouse steak.**

port·fo·li·o (pôrt fō′lē ō′) *n. pl.,* **port·fo·li·os.** **1.** a portable case for holding or carrying loose papers, drawings, documents, and similar materials. **2.** the office, position, and duties of a cabinet member or a minister of state in charge of a department. **3.** a list or group of stocks, bonds, and the like, belonging to a bank, investment company, or private investor.

port·hole (pôrt′hōl′) *n.* **1.** a small, usually circular, opening in the side of a boat or ship for letting in air and light. **2.** an opening in a wall, as of a fort, through which a gun can be fired.

por·ti·co (pôr′ti kō′) *n. pl.,* **por·ti·coes** or **por·ti·cos.** a roofed structure supported by columns or piers, and open on at least one side, forming a covered walk and usually attached to a building.

por·tion (pôr′shən) *n.* **1.** a limited amount or part of something: *He spent a portion of the day running errands. I only saw a portion of the movie before I fell asleep.* **2.** a part of a whole that is given to or belongs to one person or group; share: *What is she going to do with her portion of the inheritance?* **3.** a quantity of food

Portico

served to one person: *a portion of potatoes.* —*v.t.* to divide (something) into portions or shares; distribute.

Port·land (pôrt′lənd) *n.* **1.** the largest city of Oregon, in the northwestern part of the state. Pop. (1970), 382,619. **2.** the largest city of Maine, in the southwestern part of the state. Pop. (1970), 65,116.

port·land cement (pôrt′lənd) *also,* **Portland cement.** a bluish-gray cement made up chiefly of silicon and aluminum compounds of calcium. When mixed with sand or gravel, it forms concrete that will harden under water as well as in the air.

Port Louis, the capital of Mauritius, on the northwestern coast of the island. Pop. (1978 est.), 142,853.

port·ly (pôrt′lē) *adj.,* **port·li·er, port·li·est.** having a heavy or stout but usually dignified appearance. —**port′li·ness,** *n.*

port·man·teau (pôrt man′tō) *n. pl.,* **port·man·teaus** or **port·man·teaux** (pôrt man′tōz). a suitcase or traveling bag, especially one made of leather and hinged at the back so as to open like a book into two compartments.

Port Mores·by (môrz′bē) the capital of Papua New Guinea. Pop. (1971), 76,507.

Pôr·to A·le·gre (pôr′tō ə lā′grə) an inland port city in southern Brazil. Pop. (1975 est.), 1,043,964.

Port-of-Spain (pôrt′əv spān′) *also,* **Port of Spain.** *n.* the capital and chief port of Trinidad and Tobago, in the northwestern part of the island of Trinidad. Pop. (1973 est.), 60,450.

Por·to-No·vo (pôr′tō nō′vō) *n.* the capital of Benin, in the southeastern part of the country. Pop. (1975 est.), 104,000.

Por·to Ri·co (pôr′tō rē′kō) see **Puerto Rico.**

por·trait (pôr′trit, pôr′trāt) *n.* **1.** a painting, photograph, or other representation of a person, usually showing only the face and upper part of the body. **2.** a picture or description in words, especially of a person.

por·trait·ist (pôr′tri tist, pôr′trā tist) *n.* a person who makes portraits; portrait painter or photographer.

por·trai·ture (pôr′trə chər) *n.* **1.** the art or practice of making portraits. **2.** a portrait.

por·tray (pôr trā′) *v.t.* **1.** to give a picture of in words; tell or write about; describe: *She portrayed her parents as kind and understanding people in her novel.* **2.** to make a picture or other likeness of: *The artist portrayed the beautiful girl in a painting.* **3.** to play the part of: *The actress portrayed Queen Elizabeth I in the movie.* —**por·tray′er,** *n.*

por·tray·al (pôr trā′əl) *n.* **1.** the act or process of portraying. **2.** something that is portrayed.

Port Sa·id (sä ēd′) a port city in northeastern Egypt, on the Suez Canal near the Mediterranean Sea. Pop. (1976), 262,620.

Ports·mouth (pôrts′məth) *n.* **1.** a port city in southern England, on the English Channel. Pop. (1978 est.), 191,400. **2.** a port city and naval base in southeastern Virginia. Pop. (1970), 110,963.

Por·tu·gal (pôr′chə gəl) *n.* a country in southwestern Europe, in the western part of the Iberian Peninsula, on the Atlantic Ocean. Capital, Lisbon. Area, 35,340 sq. mi. Pop. (1977 est.), 9,773,000.

at; āpe; cär; end; mē; it; īce; hot; ōld; fôrk; wood; fōōl; oil; out; up; turn; sing; thin; this; hw in white; zh in treasure. The symbol ə stands for the sound of a in about, e in taken, i in pencil, o in lemon, and u in circus.

Por·tu·guese (pôr′chə gēz′) *n. pl.,* **Por·tu·guese.**
1. a person who was born or is living in Portugal.
2. the language of Portugal, also spoken in Brazil.
—*adj.* of or relating to Portugal, its people, their language, or their culture.

Portuguese Guinea, a former Portuguese possession on the coast of western Africa, now the country of **Guinea Bissau.**

Portuguese man-of-war, a floating colony of sea animals found in warm waters of the Atlantic Ocean. In each colony there is one animal that forms a gas-filled, floating sac, and other animals that form long tentacles with stinging cells for stunning and capturing prey.

Portuguese
man-of-war

pose (pōz) *n.* **1.** a position of the body, as for a portrait by an artist or photographer. **2.** an attitude or way of behaving assumed for effect; pretense: *His bravery is just a pose.* —*v.,* **posed, pos·ing.** —*v.i.* **1.** to hold a position, as for a portrait. **2.** to assume a false appearance or identity: *The swindler posed as a member of the nobility.* —*v.t.* **1.** to place in a particular position. **2.** to put forward; present: *The reporter posed an interesting question. His refusal to cooperate poses a problem.* —**pos′er,** *n.*

Po·sei·don (pə sīd′ən) *n. Greek Mythology.* the god of the sea and brother of Zeus and Pluto. In Roman mythology he was called Neptune.

posh (posh) *adj. Informal.* fashionable, luxurious, or elegant: *a posh hotel.*

po·si·tion (pə zish′ən) *n.* **1.** the place where a person or thing is: *From his position at the window he could see the entire parade.* **2.** an arrangement of the body or of its parts: *an uncomfortable position.* **3.** the proper or appropriate place: *The members of the team were in position.* **4.** the way in which one looks upon or views a particular issue or subject; point of view: *What is the senator's position on the treaty?* **5.** social standing or rank: *He is a man of high position.* **6.** a place or post of employment; job: *He has held the same position with the company for three years.* —*v.t.* to put in a particular place or arrangement: *We positioned the chairs in a circle.*

pos·i·tive (poz′ə tiv) *adj.* **1.** admitting of no question or doubt; undeniable: *positive proof.* **2.** clearly expressed; definite; emphatic: *He answered my question with a positive "no."* **3.** fully assured; certain; convinced: *Are you positive that you saw him?* **4.** showing, containing, or suggesting approval or acceptance: *a positive reply.* **5.** helpful or practical: *He made a positive contribution to the discussion.* **6.** tending or moving toward an improved condition: *There was a positive change in his behavior.* **7.** *Mathematics.* greater than zero: *a positive number.* **8.** *Medicine.* (of a test) indicating the presence of a particular disease, germ, or other abnormal condition. **9.** *Electricity.* having more protons than electrons. **10.** *Photography.* showing light and shade as they appear in the original subject: *a positive image.* **11.** *Grammar.* designating the form or degree of an adjective or adverb used when no comparison is made. *Fast* is the positive form of the adjective *fast, faster* is the comparative form, and *fastest* is the superlative form. —*n.* **1.** a positive photographic print, image, or picture. **2.** the positive form or degree of an adjective or adverb. —**pos′i·tive·ly,** *adv.* —**pos′i·tive·ness,** *n.*

poss. 1. possessive. **2.** possession.

pos·se (pos′ē) *n.* a group of people summoned by a sheriff for help, as in capturing a criminal.

pos·sess (pə zes′) *v.t.* **1.** to hold as property; own: *He possesses great wealth.* **2.** to have as a quality, characteristic, or attribute: *She possesses much talent.* **3.** to have an overwhelming power or influence over: *What possessed her to buy that hat? A need for revenge possessed him.* —**pos·ses′sor,** *n.*

pos·sessed (pə zest′) *adj.* **1.** in possession of; having: *She is possessed of a quick temper.* **2.** controlled by or as if by a strong emotion or evil spirit: *The rumor was that the house was haunted and its owner possessed.*

pos·ses·sion (pə zesh′ən) *n.* **1.** the act or fact of holding or owning: *He has possession of the property.* **2.** the state of being possessed; ownership: *A large amount of money comes into her possession at the age of twenty-one.* **3.** something that is held or owned: *That poor family has few possessions.* **4.** a territory that is under the rule of a foreign country.

pos·ses·sive (pə zes′iv) *adj.* **1.** characterized by or showing a strong desire to own, keep, or dominate: *He's very possessive about his books.* **2.** *Grammar.* relating to or designating a case of nouns and pronouns that show possession. —*n. Grammar.* the possessive case or a word in the possessive case. In the sentence *I met Karen's brother, Karen's* is a possessive. —**pos·ses′sive·ly,** *adv.* —**pos·ses′sive·ness,** *n.*

possessive adjective, an adjective that shows possession, formed from a personal pronoun. In the sentence *This is your book, your* is a possessive adjective.

possessive pronoun, a pronoun that shows possession, formed from a personal pronoun. In the sentence *This book is mine, mine* is a possessive pronoun.

pos·si·bil·i·ty (pos′ə bil′ə tē) *n. pl.,* **pos·si·bil·i·ties.** **1.** the state or fact of being possible; likelihood: *There is a possibility that she will meet him tonight.* **2.** something possible: *Winning the championship is a possibility for our team.*

pos·si·ble (pos′ə bəl) *adj.* **1.** capable of existing, happening, being done, or being proven true: *It is possible that he is lying. It is not possible to be in two places at the same time.* **2.** that can be used, chosen, or considered; potential: *The senator is a possible candidate for the Presidency.*

pos·si·bly (pos′ə blē) *adv.* **1.** by any possibility: *Our plan can't possibly succeed.* **2.** by some possibility; perhaps: *I'll see you today, or possibly tomorrow.*

pos·sum (pos′əm) *n.* see **opossum.**
to play possum. to pretend to be dead or asleep.

post¹ (pōst) *n.* an upright piece of wood, stone, or other solid material, usually used as a support or marker. —*v.t.* **1.** to put up (an announcement or notice) in a public place. **2.** to announce by or as if by putting up a notice: *The teacher posted the grades on the door. The authorities posted a reward for his arrest.* **3.** to put up signs or notices warning against trespassing on (property): *Mr. Jones posted his land.* [Old English *post* pillar, support, doorpost.]

post² (pōst) *n.* **1.** a place where a soldier, police officer, or the like is stationed or assigned for duty: *The guard was ordered not to leave her post except in an emergency.* **2.** a military area with permanent buildings where soldiers are assigned for work and training; military base. **3.** a position of employment, especially a public office to which one is appointed: *The ambassador has just been assigned a new post.* **4.** see **trading post.** —*v.t.* to station at or assign to a post: *The police posted guards at all exits of the building.* [Middle French *poste.*]

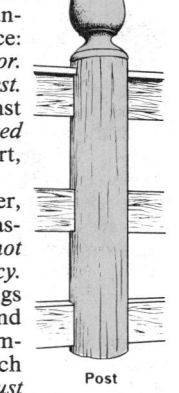

Post

post³ (pōst) *n.* **1.** a system by which mail is collected, carried, and delivered: *to send a letter by post.* **2.** a single delivery of mail: *I received a letter in today's post.* **3.** formerly, one of a series of stations providing relays of men and horses for the carrying and delivery of mail. —*v.t.* **1.** to deposit in a mailbox or at a post office: *to post a letter.* **2.** *Informal.* to supply with information or the latest news; inform: *Keep me posted on what happens while I am away.* [Middle French *poste* a relay station, speedy messenger.]

post- *prefix* coming afterward in time or order: *postwar.*

post·age (pōs′tij) *n.* the amount charged for sending something by mail.

postage stamp, an official stamp issued and sold by a government, to be placed on mail to show payment of postage.

post·al (pōst′əl) *adj.* of, relating to, or concerning mail or its collection and delivery.

post card **1.** a card, usually with a picture on one side, that can be sent through the mail without an envelope. **2.** a card issued and sold by a government and bearing an imprinted stamp. It can be sent through the mail without an envelope. Also, **postal card.**

post chaise, a four-wheeled, horse-drawn carriage, used to carry mail and passengers from station to station.

post·date (pōst′dāt′) *v.t.,* **post·dat·ed, post·dat·ing.** **1.** to date (a check, letter, or the like) with a date that is later than the actual one. **2.** to occur later than; follow in time.

post·er (pōs′tər) *n.* a large printed sign that carries a public notice or advertisement, often with a colorful illustration.

pos·te·ri·or (pos tēr′ē ər, pōs tēr′ē ər) *adj.* **1.** situated at or toward the back; rear. **2.** later in time; subsequent. —*n.* the rear; buttocks.

pos·ter·i·ty (pos ter′ə tē) *n.* **1.** all generations of the future: *Neil Armstrong will be remembered by posterity as the first man to walk on the moon.* **2.** all of one's descendants.

pos·tern (pōs′tərn, pos′tərn) *n.* the back door or gate, as of a castle or fortification.

post exchange, a government store at a military post that sells tax-free goods to soldiers, their families, and to civilian employees.

post·grad·u·ate (pōst′graj′oo it) *adj.* of, relating to, or taking a course of study after graduation from a college or university, especially after receiving a bachelor's degree. —*n.* a postgraduate student.

post·haste (pōst′hāst′) *adv.* as quickly as possible; with the utmost haste.

post·hu·mous (pos′chə məs) *adj.* **1.** published after the death of the author: *a posthumous book.* **2.** coming or happening after one's death: *a posthumous award, posthumous fame.* **3.** (of a child) born after the death of the father. —**post′hu·mous·ly,** *adv.*

pos·til·ion (pōs til′yən, pos til′yən) also, **pos·til·lion.** *n.* a person who guides the team of a horse-drawn carriage by riding the left lead horse.

post·im·pres·sion·ism (pōst′im presh′ə niz′əm) *n.* a period in French painting, beginning in the late nineteenth century and lasting until the early twentieth century, during which such painters as George Seurat, Vincent Van Gogh, and Paul Cezanne were active. —**post′im·pres′sion·ist,** *n., adj.* —**post′im·pres′sion·is′·tic,** *adj.*

post·man (pōst′mən) *n. pl.,* **post·men** (pōst′mən). another word for **mailman** or **mail carrier.**

post·mark (pōst′märk′) *n.* an official mark stamped on mail to cancel the postage stamp and to show the place and date of mailing. —*v.t.* to stamp with a postmark.

post·mas·ter (pōst′mas′tər) *n.* the official in charge of a post office. —**post′mis′tress,** *n.*

postmaster general *pl.,* **postmasters general.** **1.** the head of the postal service of a country. **2.** **Postmaster General.** the head of the postal service of the United States, appointed by the President with the approval of the Senate.

post me·ri·di·em (pōst′mə rid′ē əm) between noon and midnight. Abbreviation, **P.M.** [Latin *post merīdiem* after midday.]

post·mor·tem (pōst′môr′təm) *adj.* taking place or done after a person's death: *a post-mortem examination.* —*n.* the medical examination of a dead body; autopsy.

post·na·tal (pōst′nāt′əl) *adj.* taking place after birth: *postnatal care.*

post office **1.** the department or agency of a national government in charge of handling mail. **2.** the local branch of such a department, responsible for the collection, sorting, and distribution of mail.

post·op·er·a·tive (pōst′op′ər ə tiv) *adj.* done or happening after a surgical operation: *postoperative care.*

post·paid (pōst′pād′) *adj.* having the postage paid by the sender.

post·pone (pōst pōn′) *v.t.,* **post·poned, post·pon·ing.** to put off to a later time. —**post·pone′ment,** *n.*

post road, a road over which mail was carried by riders, with stations along the way that provided horses.

post·script (pōst′skript′) *n.* **1.** a message or note added to a letter after the writer's signature. **2.** any material added to or supplementing a composition or literary work.

pos·tu·late (*n.,* pos′chə lit; *v.,* pos′chə lāt′) *n.* a statement or principle accepted as true without proof; self-evident or universally accepted truth. —*v.t.,* **pos·tu·lat·ed, pos·tu·lat·ing.** **1.** to accept (something) as true without proof; take for granted. **2.** to require, demand, or claim.

pos·ture (pos′chər) *n.* **1.** the way of carrying or holding the head and body; carriage: *That athlete has good posture.* **2.** a position of the body or of parts of the body: *a crouching posture.* —*v.,* **pos·tured, pos·tur·ing.** —*v.i.* to take or assume a certain bodily position, especially for effect. —*v.t.* to put in a certain position; pose. —**pos′tur·al,** *adj.*

post·war (pōst′wôr′) *adj.* after a war.

po·sy (pō′zē) *n. pl.,* **po·sies.** **1.** a single flower. **2.** a bouquet of flowers; nosegay.

pot (pot) *n.* **1.** a container of metal, earthenware, or other material, usually round and having one or two handles, used in cooking, for holding growing plants, and for many other purposes. **2.** the amount contained in a pot: potful: *I made a pot of coffee.* **3.** the amount of money bet on a single hand in a card game, especially poker. **4.** see **lobster pot.** **5.** *Informal.* a large sum of money. —*v.t.,* **pot·ted, pot·ting.** **1.** to put into a flowerpot: *to pot a plant.* **2.** to cook or preserve (food) in a pot or jar: *to pot beef.* **3.** to shoot (game) for food rather than for sport.
  to go to pot. to become ruined or rundown: *The estate went to pot after the baron died.*

po·ta·ble (pō′tə bəl) *adj.* fit or suitable for drinking. —*n. also,* **potables.** something drinkable; drink.

pot·ash (pot′ash′) *n.* any of various compounds that contain potassium, used especially in fertilizers, soaps, and in making glass.

at; āpe; cär; end; mē; it; īce; hot; ōld; fôrk; wood; fool; oil; out; up; turn; sing; thin; this; hw in white; zh in treasure. The symbol ə stands for the sound of a in about, e in taken, i in pencil, o in lemon, and u in circus.

po·tas·si·um (pə tas′ē əm) *n.* a very soft, light, silver-white metallic element whose compounds include fertilizers and industrial chemicals. Symbol: **K**

potassium hydroxide, a caustic, white compound, used especially in making soap.

potassium nitrate, a colorless crystalline compound, used especially in gunpowder and explosives, fertilizers, and medicine. Also, **niter, saltpeter.**

po·ta·to (pə tā′tō) *n. pl.,* **po·ta·toes. 1.** the underground tuber of a leafy, low-growing plant, used as a vegetable. The potato was originally grown in South America. It is a basic food in Europe, America, and other parts of the world, and is used to make a wide variety of products, such as starch, flour, and vodka. **2.** the plant bearing this tuber. **3.** see **sweet potato.**

potato chip, a very thin slice of potato, fried crisp and usually salted.

pot·bel·lied (pot′bel′ēd) *adj.* **1.** having a potbelly. **2.** having the shape of a potbelly: *a potbellied stove.*

pot·bel·ly (pot′bel′ē) *n. pl.,* **pot·bel·lies. 1.** a large bulging belly. **2.** a person who has such a belly.

po·ten·cy (pōt′ən sē) *n.* the state or quality of being potent.

po·tent (pōt′ənt) *adj.* having force, effectiveness, strength, or power: *a potent medicine, a potent argument.* —**po′-tent·ly,** *adv.*

po·ten·tate (pōt′ən tāt′) *n.* a person who has great power or authority, such as a monarch or ruler.

po·ten·tial (pə ten′shəl) *adj.* capable of being or becoming; possible but not actual: *a potential leader, a potential criminal, a potential source of trouble.* —*n.* **1.** a quality or ability capable of being developed or advanced: *a novelist with great potential.* **2.** the amount of electrification of a point in an electric circuit or field in relation to some standard reference point in the same circuit or field. —**po·ten′tial·ly,** *adv.*

Potbellied stove

potential energy, the energy possessed by a body due to its position or structure. A coiled spring has potential energy.

po·ten·ti·al·i·ty (pə ten′shē al′ə tē) *n. pl.,* **po·ten·ti·al·i·ties. 1.** a potential quality or ability. **2.** something potential; possibility.

pot·ful (pot′fool′) *n. pl.,* **pot·fuls.** the amount that a pot can hold: *a potful of tea.*

pot·herb (pot′urb′, pot′hurb′) *n.* any plant whose leaves, stems, or flowers are cooked and eaten as a vegetable, such as spinach, or are used as a seasoning, such as sage or thyme.

pot·hole (pot′hōl′) *n.* **1.** a deep hole worn in the rock bed of a river or stream by stones and gravel whirled around by the force of the current. **2.** any deep hole, especially in the surface of a street or road.

pot·hook (pot′hook′) *n.* **1.** a hook used to hang a pot over an open fire. **2.** an iron rod with a hook at the end, used to lift hot pots, irons, or stove lids.

po·tion (pō′shən) *n.* a drink, especially one believed to have magical powers.

pot·luck (pot′luk′) *n.* whatever food may be available for a meal for which no special preparation was made.

Po·to·mac (pə tō′mək) *n.* a river in the eastern United States, flowing through West Virginia, Virginia, and Maryland.

pot·pie (pot′pī′) *n.* **1.** a pie filled with meat or poultry and usually vegetables. **2.** a meat stew with dumplings.

pot·pour·ri (pō′poo rē′) *n.* **1.** a medley, mixture, or collection: *a potpourri of folk songs.* **2.** a mixture of dried flower petals and spices, kept in a jar and used for fragrance.

pot roast, meat, usually beef, browned in a pot, covered, and cooked slowly in a small amount of water, often with vegetables.

pot·sherd (pot′shurd′) *n.* a fragment of pottery, especially one found at an archaeological site.

pot shot 1. a shot fired at random or without careful aim from close range. **2.** a shot fired to kill game for food, with little or no regard to the rules of sport.

pot·tage (pot′ij) *n.* a thick soup or broth.

pot·ter¹ (pot′ər) *n.* a person who makes pottery.

pot·ter² (pot′ər) another word for **putter¹.**

potter's field, a piece of ground used as a burial place for the poor and the unknown.

potter's wheel, a rotating level disk that is turned by a motor or by pumping with the foot, used by a potter to make objects from soft clay.

pot·ter·y (pot′ər ē) *n. pl.,* **pot·ter·ies. 1.** pots, vases, and other objects made from soft clay and hardened by heat. **2.** the art or technique of making pottery. **3.** a place where pottery is made.

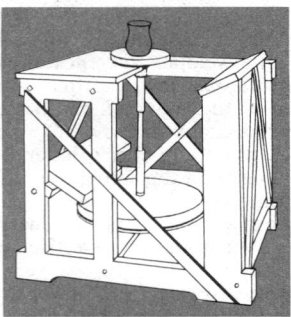

Potter's wheel

pouch (pouch) *n. pl.,* **pouch·es. 1.** a bag or sack made of a flexible material, such as leather or canvas: *The mailman took the letter out of his pouch.* **2.** a baglike part on the belly of the female of certain animals, such as kangaroos and opossums, in which the young are carried after birth. **3.** any baglike part, as under the bill of a pelican.

poul·tice (pōl′tis) *n.* a soft, moist mass of a substance, such as mustard, heated and applied to a part of the body as a medicine for soreness or inflammation. —*v.t.,* **poul·ticed, poul·tic·ing.** to apply a poultice to.

poul·try (pōl′trē) *n.* any domestic fowl, such as chickens, turkeys, geese, and ducks, raised for their meat or eggs.

pounce (pouns) *v.i.,* **pounced, pounc·ing.** to swoop down, spring, or leap suddenly in or as if in attack: *The tiger pounced on its prey.* —*n.* the act of pouncing.

pound¹ (pound) *n. pl.,* **pounds** or **pound. 1.** a unit of weight equal to 16 ounces in avoirdupois weight or 12 ounces in troy weight or 5760 grains in apothecaries' weight. **2.** the basic monetary unit of the United Kingdom, equal to 100 pence, formerly equal to twenty shillings. Also, **pound sterling. 3.** a monetary unit of various other countries, such as Ireland, Egypt, Ghana, and Israel. [Old English *pund* a measure of weight.]

pound² (pound) *v.t.* **1.** to hit with heavy, repeated blows: *John pounded the nail into the wall.* **2.** to make into a powder or pulp by pounding; pulverize: *to pound grain into meal.* —*v.i.* **1.** to strike heavy, repeated blows: *The waves pounded against the rocks.* **2.** to beat heavily: *The runner could feel his heart pounding against his chest.* **3.** to move heavily: *The horses pounded along the road.* —*n.* **1.** a heavy blow. **2.** the sound of this; thump; thud. [Old English *punian* to bruise.]

pound³ (pound) *n.* an enclosed place for confining animals, especially stray dogs. [Old English *pund.*]

Pound, Ezra (pound) 1885–1972, U.S. poet, critic, and translator.

pound·fool·ish (pound′foo͞o′lish) *adj.* unwise or careless about spending large sums of money.

pound sterling, see **pound**¹ *(def. 2).*

pour (pôr) *v.t.* **1.** to cause to flow in a steady stream: *to pour water from a bucket.* **2.** to speak of or reveal freely or openly: *to pour out one's anger.* —*v.i.* **1.** to flow in a steady stream: *The stream poured into the river.* **2.** to rain hard. **3.** to move or come forth in great numbers; swarm: *The people poured out of the stadium.* **4.** to act as a hostess by pouring beverages for guests. —*n.* a heavy rainfall; downpour.

pout (pout) *v.i.* **1.** to thrust out the lips, as in displeasure or sullenness. **2.** to be sullen; sulk. —*n.* **1.** a thrusting out of the lips, as when displeased. **2.** a fit of sullenness: *The little boy was in a pout all day.*

pout·er (pou′tər) *n.* any of a breed of domestic pigeons having an enlarged crop that can be inflated with air and puffed out.

pov·er·ty (pov′ər tē) *n.* **1.** the state or condition of being poor: *to live in poverty.* **2.** the lack of what is needed or desired: *the poverty of the soil in a desert area.* **3.** smallness of amount; scarcity: *His writings show a poverty of imagination.*

pov·er·ty-strick·en (pov′ər tē strik′ən) *adj.* very poor; destitute.

POW, prisoner of war.

pow·der (pou′dər) *n.* **1.** fine, minute particles produced by grinding, crushing, pounding, or crumbling a dry substance. **2.** any of various preparations or substances in such a form: *soap powder.* **3.** see **gunpowder.** —*v.t.* **1.** to make into powder; pulverize. **2.** to sprinkle or cover with powder or something like powder: *She powdered the rolling pin with flour.* **3.** to use powder as a cosmetic on (the face or body). —*v.i.* to become or be made into powder.

powder horn, a horn of a cow or other animal, used for carrying gunpowder.

powder puff, a soft pad for applying powder to the skin.

pow·der·y (pou′dər ē) *adj.* **1.** of or like powder: *powdery snow.* **2.** sprinkled or covered with powder. **3.** easily made into powder.

pow·er (pou′ər) *n.* **1.** the ability to do, act, or bring about a particular result or effect: *It is not in his power to help you. The President has the power to veto bills.* **2.** the ability or right to command, control, or make decisions; authority: *He has no power over you.* **3.** *also,* **powers.** a particular ability or faculty: *the power of speech.* **4.** a person or thing that has or exercises influence, control, or authority over others: *The United States is a major world power.* **5.** the political or military strength of a nation, government, or similar organization. **6.** strength; force: *There was no power behind his punch.* **7.** *Mathematics.* **a.** the number of times, indicated by an exponent, that a given number or algebraic expression is multiplied by itself. The power of 4^3 is 3; the power of y^4 is 4. **b.** the product found by multiplying a number or algebraic expression by itself a given number of times as indicated by an exponent. The second power of 5 is 25 since $5^2 = 5 \times 5 = 25$. **8.** energy or force that can do work, such as electricity. **9.** the rate at which work is done or energy is used. **10.** the capacity of a lens or a combination of lenses to magnify the apparent size of an object. —*v.t.* to provide with power, especially mechanical power.

pow·er·boat (pou′ər bōt′) *n.* another word for **motorboat.**

pow·er·ful (pou′ər fəl) *adj.* having great strength, influence, or authority: *a powerful machine, a powerful athlete, a powerful nation.* —**pow′er·ful·ly,** *adv.*

pow·er·house (pou′ər hous′) *n. pl.,* **pow·er·hous·es** (pou′ər hou′ziz). **1.** another word for **power plant. 2.** *Informal.* a person or thing having a great deal of strength or energy.

pow·er·less (pou′ər lis) *adj.* **1.** lacking the ability or authority to do or act. **2.** lacking power or strength; weak. —**pow′er·less·ly,** *adv.*

power of attorney 1. a written document giving one person the authority to act as the attorney or legal representative for another. **2.** the legal authority granted by such a document.

power plant, a building where electrical power is generated.

Pow·ha·tan (pou′ə tan′) 1550?–1618, Algonquian Indian chief.

pow·wow (pou′wou′) *n.* **1.** a conference of or with North American Indians. **2.** a North American Indian ceremony characterized by feasting, dancing, and rites performed by a medicine man, especially for the cure of disease or success in war or hunting. **3.** *Informal.* any conference or meeting. —*v.i.* to hold a powwow.

pox (poks) *n.* any of several diseases characterized by skin eruptions, such as chicken pox or smallpox.

Poz·nan (pōz′nän) *n.* a city in western Poland. Pop. (1970), 469,000.

pp, pianissimo.

pp. 1. pages. **2.** past participle.

p.p. 1. parcel post. Also, **P.P. 2.** past participle. **3.** postpaid.

ppd. 1. postpaid. **2.** prepaid.

ppr., present participle. Also, **p.pr.**

Pr, the symbol for praseodymium.

pr. 1. pair; pairs. **2.** price.

PR, Public Relations.

P.R., Puerto Rico.

prac·ti·ca·ble (prak′ti kə bəl) *adj.* **1.** that can be put into practice; feasible: *a practicable plan.* **2.** that can be used: *a practicable bridge.* —**prac′ti·ca·bil′i·ty,** *n.* —**prac′ti·ca·bly,** *adv.*

prac·ti·cal (prak′ti kəl) *adj.* **1.** of, relating to, or coming from experience, action, or use rather than from thought or theory: *practical knowledge.* **2.** that can be done, used, or carried out: *a practical method of solving a problem.* **3.** having or showing good judgment or good sense; sensible. **4.** tending or preferring to do things rather than to think or theorize about them: *a practical man.* **5.** to all intents and purposes; virtual: *His behavior toward us was a practical insult.*

prac·ti·cal·i·ty (prak′tə kal′ə tē) *n. pl.,* **prac·ti·cal·i·ties. 1.** the state or quality of being practical. **2.** something practical.

practical joke, a prank, trick, or other joke played on someone, especially in order to cause him embarrassment.

prac·ti·cal·ly (prak′ti kə lē, prak′tik lē) *adv.* **1.** to all intents and purposes; virtually: *They are practically engaged.* **2.** nearly; almost: *The work is practically finished.* **3.** in a practical manner.

practical nurse, a person who has training and experience in performing certain nursing duties, but lacks the training and education of a registered nurse.

at; āpe; cär; end; mē; it; īce; hot; ōld; fôrk; wood; fōol; oil; up; turn; sing; thin; this; hw in white; zh in treasure. The symbol ə stands for the sound of a in about, e in taken, i in pencil, o in lemon, and u in circus.

prac·tice (prak'tis) *also, British,* **prac·tise.** *n.* **1.** the repeated or continuous performance of an action in order to gain knowledge or skill: *Practice makes perfect.* **2.** a period or session during which such an action is performed: *He has football practice every afternoon.* **3.** the condition of being skilled through repeated or continuous performance of an action: *to be out of practice.* **4.** the act or process of doing, using, or carrying out something; execution: *The idea seemed good, but it did not work in practice.* **5.** the usual way of doing something; custom; habit: *He makes a practice of calling whenever he is going to be late.* **6.** the active following of or working at a profession or occupation: *the practice of medicine.* **7.** the business of a doctor or lawyer: *The new doctor has a small practice.* —*v.,* **prac·ticed, prac·tic·ing.** —*v.t.* **1.** to do (something) repeatedly or continuously in order to gain knowledge or skill: *Joe practices the piano every day.* **2.** to carry out in action; put into practice: *Practice what you preach.* **3.** to make a habit or custom of: *to practice caution.* **4.** to work at or follow as a profession or occupation: *to practice law.* —*v.i.* **1.** to perform something repeatedly or continuously in order to gain knowledge or skill. **2.** to work at or follow a profession or occupation.

prac·ticed (prak'tist) *also, British,* **prac·tised.** *adj.* skilled or expert through practice; experienced.

prac·tise (prak'tis) *British. n., v.,* **prac·tised, prac·tis·ing.** another spelling of **practice.**

prac·ti·tion·er (prak tish'ə nər) *n.* a person who practices a profession.

prae·tor (prē'tər) *n.* in ancient Rome, an elected magistrate or judge ranking next below a consul.

prae·to·ri·an (prē tôr'ē ən) *adj.* **1.** of or relating to a praetor. **2. Praetorian.** of or relating to the bodyguard of a Roman emperor or commander. —*n.* **1.** another word for **praetor. 2. Praetorian.** a bodyguard of a Roman emperor or commander.

prag·mat·ic (prag mat'ik) *adj.* **1.** concerned with practical results or values rather than thought or theory. **2.** of or relating to pragmatism. Also, **prag·mat·i·cal** (pragmat'i kəl). —**prag·mat'i·cal·ly,** *adv.*

prag·ma·tism (prag'mə tiz'əm) *n.* a philosophy set forth in the late nineteenth century, holding that the truth of an idea should be evaluated in terms of its practical consequences.

prag·ma·tist (prag'mə tist) *n.* a person who believes in pragmatism.

Prague (präg) *n.* the capital of Czechoslovakia, in the western part of the country. Pop. (1970), 1,078,096.

prai·rie (prer'ē) *n.* a large, level or gently rolling grassland without trees.

prairie chicken, a grouse of the prairies of North America.

prairie dog, a burrowing animal that lives in large colonies in the plains of central North America and has a call like a dog's bark.

prairie schooner, a covered wagon used by pioneers in crossing the prairies westward to the Pacific coast.

prairie wolf, another term for **coyote.**

praise (prāz) *n.* **1.** the expression of admiration or approval. **2.** the worship or glorification of a god, ruler, or hero, especially worship of God when expressed in words or song. —*v.t.,* **praised, prais·ing. 1.** to express admiration or approval of; commend: *The critics praised his latest novel.* **2.** to worship or glorify in words or song: *to praise God.* —**prais'er,** *n.*

Prairie dog

praise·wor·thy (prāz'wur'thē) *adj.* worthy of praise; commendable. —**praise'wor'thi·ly,** *adv.* —**praise'wor'thi·ness,** *n.*

pram (pram) *n. Informal.* a baby carriage; perambulator.

prance (prans) *v.i.,* **pranced, pranc·ing. 1.** to move in a proud, gay way; strut; swagger: *The majorettes pranced across the football field.* **2.** (of a horse) to spring forward from the hind legs. **3.** to ride on a horse that is prancing. **4.** to run, leap, or skip about in play: *The children pranced about in the yard.* —*n.* **1.** the act of prancing. **2.** a prancing movement.

prank (prangk) *n.* a mischievous or playful act.

pra·se·o·dym·i·um (prā'sē ō dim'ē əm) *n.* a soft, slightly yellow, rare-earth metallic element, used in small amounts to color glass, enamel, and man-made emeralds. Symbol: **Pr**

prate (prāt) *v.,* **prat·ed, prat·ing.** —*v.i.* to talk at length in an idle or foolish manner; chatter; babble. —*v.t.* to say in an idle or foolish manner. —*n.* idle or foolish talk; prattle. —**prat'er,** *n.*

prat·tle (prat'əl) *v.,* **prat·tled, prat·tling.** —*v.i.* to talk childishly or foolishly; babble. —*v.t.* to say or tell in a childish or foolish manner. —*n.* **1.** childish or foolish talk. **2.** a sound that is similar to baby talk. —**prat'tler,** *n.*

prawn (prôn) *n.* any of various shellfish resembling shrimp but larger, found in salt and fresh waters.

pray (prā) *v.i.* **1.** to speak to God with adoration, appeal, or thanksgiving. **2.** to ask or request from God: *to pray for divine guidance.* —*v.t.* **1.** to ask of or for earnestly; beg; entreat: *I pray you to stay.* **2.** to get or bring about by praying. **3.** to be so kind or obliging as to; please. ▲ used to express a request or command politely: *Pray be quiet.*

prayer (prer) *n.* **1.** the act of praying to God. **2.** something prayed for: *Their prayers were granted.* **3.** a set form of words used in praying: *a book of prayers.* **4.** also, **prayers.** a form of worship consisting mainly of prayers: *morning prayers.* **5.** an earnest request; entreaty.

prayer·ful (prer'fəl) *adj.* given to prayer; devout. —**prayer'ful·ly,** *adv.* —**prayer'ful·ness,** *n.*

praying mantis, any of a group of brown or green insects related to the grasshopper, found especially in the tropics, having stout, spiny forelegs for grasping its prey. Also, **mantis.** [Because it often holds its forelegs in a position suggesting hands folded in *prayer.*]

pre- *prefix* **1.** before in place, time, or rank: *prewar, prehistoric.* **2.** in preparation for: *preschool.*

Praying mantis

preach (prēch) *v.i.* **1.** to speak publicly on a religious subject; deliver a sermon. **2.** to give advice, especially in a boring way: *She is always preaching to me about saving my allowance.* —*v.t.* **1.** to set forth by preaching: *The missionaries preached the word of God.* **2.** to deliver (a sermon).

preach·er (prē'chər) *n.* a person who preaches, especially a Protestant clergyman.

pre·am·ble (prē'am'bəl) *n.* a preliminary statement or introduction, especially one stating or explaining reasons or purposes: *the preamble of a law.*

pre·ar·range (prē'ə rānj') *v.t.,* **pre·ar·ranged, pre·ar·rang·ing.** to arrange beforehand. —**pre'ar·range'ment,** *n.*

Pre·cam·bri·an (prē kam'brē ən) *n.* the geological era during which the earliest animals appeared, and bacteria

P

and algae were the only forms of plant life. —*adj.* of, relating to, or characteristic of this era.

pre·car·i·ous (pri ker′ē əs) *adj.* **1.** dependent on chance or circumstance; uncertain; insecure: *a precarious investment.* **2.** dangerous; perilous: *The climber was in a precarious position on a cliff.* [Latin *precārius* originally, obtained by begging or prayer; later, uncertain; because it was not certain that a person would receive anything by begging or praying.] —**pre·car′i·ous·ly,** *adv.*

pre·cau·tion (pri kô′shən) *n.* **1.** a measure taken beforehand to avoid danger, failure, loss, or harm: *He took precautions against burglary by installing an alarm.* **2.** caution or care taken beforehand; foresight.

pre·cau·tion·ar·y (pri kô′shə ner′ē) *adj.* relating to, advising, or using precaution: *precautionary advice.*

pre·cede (pri sēd′) *v.,* **pre·ced·ed, pre·ced·ing.** —*v.t.* to go or come before or ahead of, as in time, order, rank, or importance: *She preceded me through the door.* —*v.i.* to be, go, or come before.

prec·e·dence (pres′ə dəns, pri sēd′əns) *n.* **1.** the act or fact of preceding, as in time, rank, or order: *Deciding on a new class treasurer will take precedence over collecting the dues.* **2.** the right to precede others because of superiority of rank or position, especially at ceremonial or formal occasions: *the precedence of a senator over a representative at a state banquet.*

prec·e·dent (*n.,* pres′ə dənt; *adj.,* pri sēd′ənt, pres′ə dənt) *n.* an action that may serve as an example for similar future actions: *Electing class officers by secret ballot for the first time this year will set a precedent.* —*adj.* going or coming before; preceding.

pre·ced·ing (pri sē′ding) *adj.* that precedes; previous: *His signature is on the preceding page.*

pre·cept (prē′sept) *n.* **1.** a rule or principle intended as a guide for behavior or action. **2.** a short statement expressing a general truth or doctrine. For example: *A stitch in time saves nine.*

pre·cep·tor (pri sep′tər) *n.* a teacher; instructor.

pre·ces·sion (prē sesh′ən) *n.* the act or fact of preceding.

pre·cinct (prē′singkt′) *n.* **1.** a subdivision or district of a city or town: *a police precinct, an election precinct.* **2.** a police station in such a district. **3.** *also,* **precincts.** a space or area within fixed limits: *the precincts of a university campus.*

pre·cious (presh′əs) *adj.* **1.** having great cost or value; costly: *Silver is a precious metal. Diamonds are precious stones.* **2.** beloved; dear: *a precious child.* **3.** overly elegant or refined: *precious manners.* **4.** *Informal.* very great. —*adv. Informal.* extremely; very: *The campers had precious little food remaining.* —*n.* loved one; dear; darling. —**pre′cious·ly,** *adv.* —**pre′cious·ness,** *n.*

precious stone, a rare, valuable gem, as a diamond or emerald.

prec·i·pice (pres′ə pis) *n.* a high, steep, often vertical face of rock.

pre·cip·i·tate (*v.,* pri sip′ə tāt′; *n., adj.,* pri sip′ə tit, pri sip′ə tāt′) *v.,* **pre·cip·i·tat·ed, pre·cip·i·tat·ing.** —*v.t.* **1.** to cause to happen before expected, needed, or desired: *His hasty criticism precipitated the argument.* **2.** to throw down violently; hurl downward. **3.** *Chemistry.* to cause (a substance in a solution) to combine to form a solid substance. **4.** to cause (a vapor) to condense and fall as rain, snow, or dew. —*v.i.* **1.** (of vapor) to be condensed and fall in the form of rain, snow, or dew. **2.** *Chemistry.* to be precipitated. **3.** to fall headlong. —*n.* a solid chemical compound formed in a solution by the reaction of ions of a dissolved compound or element with ions of a compound or element added to the solution. —*adj.* **1.** falling or rushing rapidly or headlong. **2.** acting or done in a hasty or rash manner. **3.** coming on suddenly or unexpectedly; abrupt: *a precipitate change in the weather.* —**pre·cip′i·tate·ly,** *adv.*

pre·cip·i·ta·tion (pri sip′ə tā′shən) *n.* **1.** any form of water that falls to earth, such as rain, hail, or snow. **2.** the depositing of such moisture on the earth. **3.** the amount, as of rain or snow, deposited. **4.** the chemical process of forming solid substances in a solution. **5.** the act of precipitating or the state of being precipitated. **6.** rash or sudden haste.

pre·cip·i·tous (pri sip′ə təs) *adj.* **1.** like or having a precipice or precipices; very steep: *precipitous cliffs.* **2.** hasty; rash: *a precipitous decision.* —**pre·cip′i·tous·ly,** *adv.* —**pre·cip′i·tous·ness,** *n.*

pre·cise (pri sīs′) *adj.* **1.** very accurate or definite; exact: *His instructions were not very precise.* **2.** being exactly what is called for or needed; neither more nor less: *She measured out the precise amount of flour for the cake.* **3.** distinguished from others; particular; very: *At that precise moment he entered the room.* **4.** very strict or careful, as in following rules or standards: *a rigid, precise person.* —**pre·cise′ly,** *adv.* —**pre·cise′ness,** *n.*

pre·ci·sion (pri sizh′ən) *n.* the state or quality of being precise; accuracy; exactness. —*adj.* marked by or designed for a high degree of fineness or accuracy: *a precision tool.*

pre·clude (pri klōōd′) *v.t.,* **pre·clud·ed, pre·clud·ing.** to make impossible; prevent: *A lack of money precluded our going to the circus.*

pre·co·cious (pri kō′shəs) *adj.* developed or matured earlier than usual: *a precocious child.* —**pre·co′cious·ly,** *adv.* —**pre·co′cious·ness,** *n.*

pre·coc·i·ty (pri kos′ə tē) *n.* the state or quality of being precocious; early development or maturity.

pre·con·ceive (prē′kən sēv′) *v.t.,* **pre·con·ceived, pre·con·ceiv·ing.** to form an idea or opinion of beforehand: *preconceived notions.*

pre·con·cep·tion (prē′kən sep′shən) *n.* an idea or opinion formed beforehand.

pre·cur·sor (pri kur′sər) *n.* a person or thing that precedes and announces or indicates the approach of another; forerunner.

pred., predicate.

pre·date (prē dāt′) *v.t.,* **pre·dat·ed, pre·dat·ing. 1.** to give a date earlier than the correct one: *to predate a check.* **2.** to be or happen earlier than; precede in time.

pred·a·tor (pred′ə tər) *n.* **1.** an animal, such as a wolf, lion, or hawk, that lives by preying on other animals. **2.** a predatory person.

pred·a·to·ry (pred′ə tôr′ē) *adj.* **1.** living by preying on other animals: *Wolves are predatory animals.* **2.** given to plundering, robbing, or exploiting others: *a predatory pirate and crew.*

pred·e·ces·sor (pred′ə ses′ər) *n.* a person who comes before another person in time, especially in an office or position.

pre·des·ti·na·tion (prē des′tə nā′shən) *n.* **1.** the act of predestining or the state of being predestined. **2.** the doctrine that God has preordained from the beginning the salvation or damnation of each soul.

at; āpe; cär; end; mē; it; īce; hot; ōld; fôrk; wood; fōōl; oil; out; up; turn; sing; thin; this; hw in white; zh in treasure. The symbol ə stands for the sound of **a** in about, e in taken, i in pencil, o in lemon, and u in circus.

pre·des·tine (prē des′tin) *v.t.*, **pre·des·tined, pre·des·tin·ing.** to determine, decree, or decide beforehand; foreordain.

pre·de·ter·mine (prē′di tur′min) *v.t.*, **pre·de·ter·mined, pre·de·ter·min·ing.** to determine, decree, or decide beforehand. —**pre′de·ter′mi·na′tion,** *n.*

pre·dic·a·ment (pri dik′ə mənt) *n.* an unpleasant, trying, or difficult situation.

pred·i·cate (*n., adj.,* pred′i kit; *v.,* pred′i kāt′) *n.* the part of a sentence or clause that expresses what is said about the subject, consisting of the verb with its objects and modifiers. In the sentence *The dog ran home quickly, ran home quickly* is the predicate. —*v.t.,* **pred·i·cat·ed, pred·i·cat·ing. 1.** to found or base (an action, statement, or the like): *to predicate a belief on one's experiences.* **2.** to declare or affirm to be an attribute, quality, or property of something: *to predicate coldness of ice.* **3.** to declare or affirm. —**pred′i·ca′tive·ly,** *adv.*

predicate adjective, an adjective that follows a linking verb and refers to the subject of the verb. In the sentence *The woods are lovely, lovely* is a predicate adjective.

predicate nominative, a noun or pronoun that follows a linking verb and refers to the subject of the verb. In the sentence *He is a student, student* is a predicate nominative.

predicate noun, a noun that is a predicate nominative.

pre·dict (pri dikt′) *v.t.* to announce or declare beforehand; prophesy: *to predict tomorrow's weather.* —*v.i.* to make a prediction. —**pre·dict′a·ble,** *adj.* —**pre·dict′a·bly,** *adv.*

pre·dic·tion (pri dik′shən) *n.* **1.** the act of predicting. **2.** something predicted; prophecy: *His predictions about the election came true.*

pre·di·lec·tion (pred′əl ek′shən, prēd′əl ek′shən) *n.* a preference or particular liking: *She has a predilection for sweets.*

pre·dis·pose (prē′dis pōz′) *v.t.*, **pre·dis·posed, pre·dis·pos·ing. 1.** to make susceptible or subject to: *His poor health predisposes him to colds.* **2.** to give an inclination to; influence: *His honesty predisposed me to like him.*

pre·dis·po·si·tion (prē′dis pə zish′ən) *n.* the state of being predisposed; inclination: *He has a predisposition to suspect everyone of lying.*

pre·dom·i·nance (pri dom′ə nəns) *n.* the state or quality of being predominant: *We were surprised to find a predominance of men at the flower arranging class.*

pre·dom·i·nant (pri dom′ə nənt) *adj.* **1.** having or exerting superior power, authority, or influence over others: *John is the predominant member of his class.* **2.** more frequent, common, or noticeable: *Red is the predominant color in that painting.* —**pre·dom′i·nant·ly,** *adv.*

pre·dom·i·nate (pri dom′ə nāt′) *v.i.*, **pre·dom·i·nat·ed, pre·dom·i·nat·ing. 1.** to have or exert superior power, authority, or influence; have control: *She predominates over her younger sister.* **2.** to be greater than others, as in power or influence; prevail: *Bright colors predominate in this printed fabric.* —**pre·dom′i·na′tion,** *n.*

pre·em·i·nent (prē em′ə nənt) *also,* **pre-em·i·nent.** *adj.* superior to or surpassing others; outstanding: *He is a preeminent surgeon.* —**pre·em′i·nence;** *also,* **pre-em′i·nence,** *n.* —**pre·em′i·nent·ly;** *also,* **pre-em′i·nent·ly,** *adv.*

pre·empt (prē empt′) *also,* **pre-empt.** *v.t.* **1.** to get or take possession of before others: *Father always preempted the morning paper.* **2.** to settle on (public land) with the right to purchase it before or in preference to others. **3.** (of a radio or television program) to be presented in the place of (another): *The football game preempted the regularly scheduled program.* —**pre·emp′tion;** *also,* **pre-emp′tion,** *n.*

preen (prēn) *v.t.* **1.** (of birds) to clean and smooth (feathers) with the beak. **2.** to dress or adorn (oneself) carefully; primp. **3.** to take or show pride or satisfaction in: *He preens himself on having made the honor roll.* —*v.i.* to primp.

pre·ex·ist (prē′ig zist′) *also,* **pre-ex·ist.** *v.i.* to exist beforehand.

pre·ex·ist·ent (prē ig zis′tənt) *also,* **pre-ex·ist·ent.** *adj.* existing beforehand. —**pre′ex·ist′ence;** *also,* **pre′-ex·ist′ence,** *n.*

pre·fab (prē fab′) *n.* a prefabricated house or other building.

pre·fab·ri·cate (prē fab′rə kāt′) *v.t.*, **pre·fab·ri·cat·ed, pre·fab·ri·cat·ing. 1.** to construct or manufacture in standardized parts for easy and rapid assembly: *to prefabricate houses.* **2.** to make up beforehand: *to prefabricate an excuse for being late.* —**pre′fab·ri·ca′tion,** *n.*

pref·ace (pref′is) *n.* an introduction to a speech, book, or similar work, often written by the author. —*v.t.,* **pre·faced, pre·fac·ing. 1.** to introduce or furnish with a preface. **2.** to serve as a preface to: *A short documentary prefaced the featured movie.*

pref·a·to·ry (pref′ə tôr′ē) *adj.* relating to, like, or serving as a preface; introductory: *prefatory remarks.*

pre·fect (prē′fekt) *n.* **1.** in ancient Rome, any of various high-ranking military or civil officials. **2.** the head administrative official of one of the departments of France. **3.** the police chief of Paris.

pre·fer (pri fur′) *v.t.,* **pre·ferred, pre·fer·ring. 1.** to like better; choose above others: *I prefer tea to coffee.* **2.** to put forward or offer for consideration or decision before a court of law or other legal authority: *We didn't prefer charges, since the stolen articles were returned.*

pref·er·a·ble (pref′ər ə bəl) *adj.* worthy of being chosen; more desirable. —**pref′er·a·bly,** *adv.*

pref·er·ence (pref′ər əns) *n.* **1.** the act of choosing one over others. **2.** the right or opportunity of so choosing: *You may have your preference between the two dresses.* **3.** a person or thing that is preferred; first choice. **4.** the granting of rights or privileges to one over others.

pref·er·en·tial (pref′ə ren′chəl) *adj.* showing or giving preference: *preferential treatment.* —**pref′er·en′tial·ly,** *adv.*

pre·fer·ment (pri fur′mənt) *n.* **1.** an advancement, as to higher rank; promotion. **2.** a position or office to which one is advanced.

preferred stock, the stock of a corporation on which dividends must be paid before they can be paid on common stock.

pre·fig·ure (prē fig′yər) *v.t.,* **pre·fig·ured, pre·fig·ur·ing. 1.** to show, indicate, or suggest beforehand; foreshadow: *The dark clouds prefigured a storm.* **2.** to picture or imagine to oneself beforehand. —**pre′fig·ur·a′tion,** *n.*

pre·fix (*n.,* prē′fiks′; *v.,* prē fiks′) *n. pl.,* **pre·fix·es.** a syllable or group of syllables added to the beginning of a word, root, or stem so as to change its meaning or to form a new word. In the word *postwar, post-* is a prefix. —*v.t.* to put before or at the beginning: *He prefixed the title "count" to his name.*

preg·nan·cy (preg′nən sē) *n. pl.,* **preg·nan·cies.** the quality or condition of being pregnant.

preg·nant (preg′nənt) *adj.* **1.** (of a female animal) having one or more unborn offspring in the uterus; being with child or young. **2.** full of meaning or importance: *a pregnant statement.* **3.** filled; abounding: *That remark was pregnant with meaning.*

pre·hen·sile (prē hen′sil) *adj.* adapted for grasping or holding, especially by wrapping around: *A monkey has a prehensile tail.*

pre·his·tor·ic (prē′his tôr′ik, prē′his tor′ik) *adj.* of, relating to, or belonging to the period before recorded history: *prehistoric peoples, prehistoric fish.* Also, **pre·his·tor·i·cal** (prē′his tôr′i kəl, prē′his tor′i kəl). —**pre′his·tor′i·cal·ly,** *adv.*

pre·judge (prē juj′) *v.t.,* **pre·judged, pre·judg·ing.** to judge beforehand or without knowing all the facts. —**pre·judg′ment;** *also,* **pre·judge′ment,** *n.*

prej·u·dice (prej′ə dis) *n.* **1.** an opinion or judgment, especially an unfavorable one, formed beforehand or without knowing all the facts. **2.** hatred or intolerance of a particular group, such as members of a race or religion. **3.** injury or damage resulting from an unfair or hasty judgment: *The new hiring policy worked to the prejudice of the minorities it attempted to protect.* —*v.t.,* **prej·u·diced, prej·u·dic·ing. 1.** to cause to have a prejudice: *A movie's publicity often prejudices the public and affects attendance.* **2.** to damage or injure, as by an unfair action.

prej·u·di·cial (prej′ə dish′əl) *adj.* causing prejudice or injury: *His behavior was prejudicial to others.* —**prej′u·di′cial·ly,** *adv.*

prel·ate (prel′it) *n.* a clergyman of high rank, as a bishop, archbishop, or cardinal.

pre·lim·i·nar·y (pri lim′ə ner′ē) *adj.* coming before and leading up to the main event, subject, or action: *preliminary arrangements for a party.* —*n. pl.,* **pre·lim·i·nar·ies. 1.** a preliminary step or action. **2.** a contest or match coming before the main one. —**pre·lim′i·nar′i·ly,** *adv.*

prel·ude (prel′yo͞od, prā′lo͞od) *n.* **1.** a preliminary or introductory event, action, or performance: *His rudeness was a prelude to the argument.* **2.** *Music.* **a.** a composition or movement introducing another, such as that played before a religious service. **b.** a short, independent composition, often written for a keyboard instrument or an orchestra. —*v.t.,* **prel·ud·ed, prel·ud·ing. 1.** to serve as a prelude to. **2.** to introduce with a prelude. —*v.i.* to serve as a prelude.

pre·ma·ture (prē′mə choor′, prē′mə tyoor′, prē′mə toor′) *adj.* arriving, happening, or existing before the usual or proper time: *a premature baby, a premature decision.* —**pre′ma·ture′ly,** *adv.* —**pre′ma·ture′ness,** *n.*

pre·med (prē′med′) *Informal. adj.* see **premedical.** —*n.* a premedical student.

pre·med·i·cal (prē med′i kəl) *adj.* of, relating to, or preparing for the study of medicine.

pre·med·i·tate (prē med′ə tāt′) *v.t.,* **pre·med·i·tat·ed, pre·med·i·tat·ing.** to consider, think out, or plan beforehand: *They tried to prove that he had premeditated the crime.* —**pre·med′i·ta′tion,** *n.*

pre·mier (pri mēr′) *n.* a prime minister in certain European countries, such as France and Italy. —*adj.* **1.** first in position, rank, or authority; chief: *the premier reason.* **2.** first in order of time; earliest.

pre·miere (pri mēr′, prim yer′) *also,* **pre·mière.** *n.* the first formal public performance or presentation, as of a play or motion picture. —*v.i.,* **pre·miered, pre·mier·ing.** to appear or be presented for the first time: *The movie premiered in August.*

prem·ise (prem′is) *n.* **1.** a statement or principle accepted as true without proof and from which a conclusion is drawn. **2. premises. a.** land and the buildings on it. **b.** a building or part of a building. —*v.t.,* **pre·mised, pre·mis·ing. 1.** to mention beforehand as an introduction or explanation. **2.** to state or assume as a premise in an argument.

pre·mi·um (prē′mē əm) *n.* **1.** something offered free or at a lower price as an inducement to buy. **2.** an amount paid for insurance. **3.** a high or unusual value: *to put a*

premium on honesty. **4.** an amount paid in addition to the regular or usual price, wage, or other fixed amount.
   at a premium. a. in great demand; valuable. **b.** at more than the normal or usual price or value: *He bought his new gold watch at a premium.*

pre·mo·lar (prē mō′lər) *n.* any of eight permanent human teeth, having double-pointed crowns and situated between the molars and the cuspids; bicuspid. —*adj.* of or relating to the premolars.

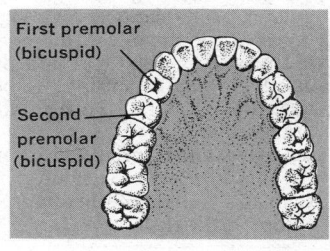

Premolar

pre·mo·ni·tion (prē′mə nish′ən, prem′ə nish′ən) *n.* **1.** a feeling that something is about to happen, especially something bad or harmful. **2.** a warning or sign of something to come; forewarning: *a premonition of danger.*

pre·na·tal (prē nāt′əl) *adj.* of or relating to the period before birth.

pre·oc·cu·pa·tion (prē ok′yə pā′shən) *n.* **1.** the state of being preoccupied; engrossment; absorption. **2.** anything that occupies the mind or attention: *Reading is his main preoccupation.* **3.** the act of occupying beforehand or before others.

pre·oc·cu·pied (prē ok′yə pīd′) *adj.* **1.** absorbed in thought; engrossed. **2.** occupied beforehand or before others.

pre·oc·cu·py (prē ok′yə pī′) *v.t.,* **pre·oc·cu·pied, pre·oc·cu·py·ing. 1.** to take up all the attention of; engross: *Plans for the wedding preoccupied her.* **2.** to occupy or take possession of beforehand or before others.

pre·or·dain (prē′ôr dān′) *v.t.* to decide or determine beforehand; predestine.

prep. 1. preposition. **2.** preparatory.

pre·paid (prē pād′) the past tense and past participle of **prepay.**

prep·a·ra·tion (prep′ə rā′shən) *n.* **1.** the act or process of preparing. **2.** the state of being prepared or in readiness. **3.** an action or measure needed or taken to prepare for something: *preparations for a party.* **4.** something prepared for a specific purpose, as a medicine or food.

pre·par·a·to·ry (pri par′ə tôr′ē, prep′ər ə tôr′ē) *adj.* **1.** serving to prepare; preliminary: *a preparatory course.* **2.** undergoing preparation, as for college: *a preparatory student.*

preparatory school, a school, especially one that is private, that prepares students for college.

pre·pare (pri per′) *v.,* **pre·pared, pre·par·ing.** —*v.t.* **1.** to make ready or fit, as for a particular purpose, event, or undertaking: *He prepared himself for the race by practicing every day.* **2.** to put together by combining various ingredients or parts: *to prepare a meal, to prepare a medicine, to prepare a speech.* —*v.i.* to get ready: *to prepare for college, to prepare for a party.* —**pre·par′er,** *n.*

pre·par·ed·ness (pri per′id nis) *n.* the state of being prepared.

at; āpe; cär; end; mē; it; īce; hot; ōld; fôrk; wood; fo͞ol; oil; out; up; tûrn; sing; thin; this; hw in white; zh in treasure. The symbol ə stands for the sound of a in about, e in taken, i in pencil, o in lemon, and u in circus.

721

pre·pay (prē pā′) *v.t.,* **pre·paid, pre·pay·ing.** to pay or pay for in advance. —**pre·pay′ment,** *n.*

pre·pon·der·ance (pri pon′dər əns) *n.* superiority, as in quantity, weight, power, influence, or importance: *There was a preponderance of adults at the party.* Also, **pre·pon·der·an·cy** (pri pon′dər ən sē).

pre·pon·der·ant (pri pon′dər ənt) *adj.* superior or greater, as in quantity, weight, power, influence, or importance; predominant. —**pre·pon′der·ant·ly,** *adv.*

pre·pon·der·ate (pri pon′də rāt′) *v.i.,* **pre·pon·der·at·ed, pre·pon·der·at·ing.** to be superior or greater, as in quantity, weight, power, influence, or importance; predominate.

prep·o·si·tion (prep′ə zish′ən) *n.* a word that shows the relationship between a noun or pronoun and another word, such as a verb or another noun. *By, into,* and *on* are prepositions in English.

● According to the rules of traditional grammar, it is incorrect to end a sentence with a **preposition.** However, in modern usage, it is often considered acceptable, especially when the sentence would be awkward if the preposition were placed before an object: *What did he ask for?*

prep·o·si·tion·al (prep′ə zish′ən əl) *adj.* relating to, serving as, or having a preposition: *a prepositional phrase.*

pre·pos·sess·ing (prē′pə zes′ing) *adj.* making a favorable impression; pleasing: *He has a prepossessing manner.*

pre·pos·ter·ous (pri pos′tər əs) *adj.* contrary to reason or common sense; absurd; ridiculous: *Driving a car in this storm is preposterous.* —**pre·pos′ter·ous·ly,** *adv.*

pre·req·ui·site (prē rek′wə zit) *n.* something required or necessary beforehand for something that follows. —*adj.* required or necessary beforehand: *a prerequisite course.*

pre·rog·a·tive (pri rog′ə tiv) *n.* a right or privilege belonging to a particular person, class, or group of persons: *Congress has the prerogative of making laws.*

pres., present.

Pres., President.

pres·age (*n.,* pres′ij; *v.,* pres′ij, pri sāj′) *n.* **1.** a sign or warning of a future event; omen; portent. **2.** a feeling that something is about to happen; premonition. —*v.,* **pres·aged, pres·ag·ing.** —*v.t.* **1.** to give or be a sign or warning of; portend: *The violent argument presaged a fist fight between the two men.* **2.** to have a feeling about beforehand. **3.** to give a prophecy of; predict; foretell: *The old woman claimed to be able to presage the future.* —*v.i.* to make a prediction.

pres·by·ter (prez′bə tər) *n.* **1.** in the early Christian church, an elder who belonged to a council that governed a congregation. **2.** a minister in the Presbyterian church or in certain other churches.

Pres·by·te·ri·an (prez′bə tēr′ē ən) *n.* a person who believes in Presbyterianism, especially a member of a Presbyterian church. —*adj.* of, relating to, or belonging to any of various Protestant denominations, especially those of English or Scottish origin, in which church government is by ministers or elders of equal rank.

Pres·by·te·ri·an·ism (prez′bə tēr′ē ə niz′əm) *n.* **1.** a system of church government by ministers or elders of equal rank. **2.** the doctrines, beliefs, and practices of the Presbyterian churches.

pres·by·ter·y (prez′bə ter′ē) *n. pl.,* **pres·by·ter·ies. 1.** in Presbyterianism, a church court having jurisdiction over the congregations in a certain area, made up of all the ministers and certain of the elders of the congregations. **2.** all the congregations under the jurisdiction of such a court. **3.** the part of a church reserved for the clergy.

pre·school (prē′sko͞ol′) *adj.* of, relating to, or for a child younger than school age, usually between the ages of two and five.

pre·sci·ence (prē′shē əns) *n.* knowledge of something before it exists or happens; foreknowledge.

pre·sci·ent (prē′shē ənt) *adj.* having knowledge of something before it exists or happens.

pre·scribe (pri skrīb′) *v.,* **pre·scribed, pre·scrib·ing.** —*v.t.* **1.** to set down or give as a rule or direction to be followed: *The law prescribes a speed limit of sixty miles per hour on this road.* **2.** to order or recommend for use as a remedy or treatment: *The doctor prescribed an ointment for the patients' skin rash.* —*v.i.* **1.** to set down or give rules or directions; dictate. **2.** to give medical advice or a prescription.

pre·scrip·tion (pri skrip′shən) *n.* **1.** an order written by a doctor for the making and use of a medicine or other remedy. **2.** the medicine or remedy ordered. **3.** the act of prescribing. **4.** something that is prescribed; rule or direction.

pre·scrip·tive (pri skrip′tiv) *adj.* **1.** giving or setting down strict rules, laws, or directions. **2.** according to established use or custom. See **descriptive** for further information.

pres·ence (prez′əns) *n.* **1.** the state or fact of being in a specific place at a given time: *The big dog's presence in the room made me uneasy.* **2.** the area immediately surrounding a person or thing: *to sign a contract in the presence of witnesses.* **3.** the appearance or bearing of a person, especially when dignified or impressive: *The Queen has a stately presence.* **4.** something, such as a spirit, ghost, or invisible influence, felt to be present.

presence of mind, the ability to think and act calmly and intelligently in an emergency or other difficult situation: *The boy showed presence of mind by calling the police when he saw the robbery.*

pres·ent[1] (prez′ənt) *adj.* **1.** in a specific place at a given time: *We were not present when Tom arrived.* **2.** existing or going on at this time: *the present generation.* **3.** to be found; existing: *Lead is present in some paints.* **4.** *Grammar.* indicating an action now taking place or a state of being now existing. —*n.* **1.** the present time; time now passing: *He is not working at present.* **2.** *Grammar.* the present tense or a verb in the present tense. [Old French *present.*]

pre·sent[2] (*v.,* pri zent′; *n.,* prez′ənt) *v.t.* **1.** to introduce to another or others; make acquainted: *May I present you to my mother?* **2.** to bring into the presence of another or others or into a particular place: *He presented himself at the principal's office.* **3.** to make a gift, award, offer, or donation of; bestow: *The principal will present the diplomas.* **4.** to give to as a gift: *The author presented me with a copy of his latest book.* **5.** to suggest or bring up for consideration: *My lack of money presents a problem.* **6.** to put before the public; display; show: *The museum will present the works of a new artist.* **7.** to hand or send in; submit: *The milkman presented a bill.* —*n.* something given, as a gift or donation. [Old French *presenter* to introduce, offer.]

pre·sent·a·ble (pri zen′tə bəl) *adj.* **1.** suitable or good enough to be present in company: *He bought a new suit to make himself presentable for the party.* **2.** fit to be seen: *to make a room presentable.* **3.** suitable to be offered or given: *to put a report in presentable form.* —**pre·sent′a·bil′i·ty,** *n.* —**pre·sent′a·bly,** *adv.*

pres·en·ta·tion (prez′ən tā′shən, prē′zən tā′shən) *n.* **1.** the act of presenting or the state of being presented. **2.** an exhibition or showing, as of a play. **3.** something presented, as a gift or donation.

pres·ent-day (prez′ənt dā′) *adj.* of, belonging to, or happening at the present time; current: *present-day events.*

pre·sen·ti·ment (pri zen′tə mənt) *n.* a feeling that something is about to happen, especially something bad; premonition.

pres·ent·ly (prez′ənt lē) *adv.* **1.** in a little while; shortly: *They will arrive presently.* **2.** at the present time; currently: *Our class is presently studying Mexican history.*

pre·sent·ment (pri zent′mənt) *n.* **1.** the act of presenting. **2.** something presented; exhibition; showing.

present participle, a participle expressing a present action or state, formed with the suffix *-ing* and used especially to form the progressive tenses and as an adjective or noun. In the sentence *I am awaiting your reply,* the word *awaiting* is a present participle.

present perfect 1. a verb tense expressing action completed at the time of speaking. In the sentence *Bill has seen that science fiction movie three times,* the phrase *has seen* is in the present perfect. **2.** a verb in this tense.

present tense 1. a verb tense expressing an action or state that is happening or exists at the present time. In the sentence *He plays the bugle well,* the word *plays* is in the present tense. **2.** a verb in this tense.

pre·serv·a·tive (pri zur′və tiv) *n.* anything that preserves, especially a chemical substance added to foods to keep them from spoiling. —*adj.* tending or serving to preserve.

pre·serve (pri zurv′) *v.t.,* **pre·served, pre·serv·ing. 1.** to maintain or keep; make lasting: *to preserve an old house.* **2.** to prepare (food) for future use, as by canning, smoking, or pickling. **3.** to protect from harm or danger; keep in safety; save: *to preserve freedom of speech.* **4.** to keep from spoiling or decaying, as with ice or chemical substances. —*n.* **1.** *usually,* **preserves.** fruit that has been boiled with sugar and stored in airtight containers to keep it from spoiling or fermenting. **2.** an area set aside for the protection of plant and animal life or other natural resources. —**pre·serv′a·ble,** *adj.* —**pres·er·va·tion** (prez′ər vā′shən), *n.* —**pre·serv′er,** *n.*

pre·side (pri zīd′) *v.i.,* **pre·sid·ed, pre·sid·ing. 1.** to act as chairman, as at a meeting. **2.** to have authority or control: *to preside over a business.* —**pre·sid′er,** *n.*

pres·i·den·cy (prez′ə dən sē) *n. pl.,* **pres·i·den·cies. 1.** the office or function of president. **2.** the time during which a president holds office. **3.** *also,* **Presidency.** the office of the President of the United States.

pres·i·dent (prez′ə dənt) *n.* **1.** *also,* **President.** the chief executive of a republic, especially of the United States. **2.** a chief officer, as of a company, college, or organization. —**pres·i·den′tial** (prez′ə den′shəl), *adj.*

pres·i·dent-e·lect (prez′ə dənt i lekt′) *n.* a person who has been elected president but has not yet been inaugurated.

Pre·sid·i·um (pri sid′ē əm) *n.* a permanent committee of the Soviet government that acts when the Supreme Soviet is not in session.

press¹ (pres) *v.t.* **1.** to use steady force or weight on or against: *to press the button of an elevator, to press one's nose against a window.* **2.** to remove (juice or other contents) by squeezing: *to press juice from lemons.* **3.** to remove juice or other contents from (something) by squeezing: *The workers pressed the grapes to make wine.* **4.** to give a particular shape or consistency to by means of pressure: *The artist pressed the clay into a ball.* **5.** to iron: *Nancy pressed her dress after she washed it.* **6.** to hold close; embrace; hug: *The man pressed the crying child to him.* **7.** to urge strongly: *The bank pressed him to pay back the loan.* **8.** to cause difficulties for; harass: *Enemy soldiers pressed our troops from all sides.* —*v.i.* **1.** to use steady force or

weight: *You have to press down on the lever to make the machine work.* **2.** to push or strain forward: *The police pressed through the crowd.* **3.** to demand or seek urgently: *The senator pressed for passage of the civil rights bill.* —*n. pl.,* **press·es. 1.** the act of pressing: *A press of the button started the washing machine.* **2.** any of various tools or machines that exert pressure, as to stamp or compress materials or to get juice from fruits or vegetables. **3.** see **printing press. 4.** a business establishment for printing or publishing. **5.** printed matter, especially newspapers and magazines: *The President's speech was described the next day in the press.* **6.** people who gather, write, or distribute news, as reporters and journalists: *The press came to the opening of the new play.* [Old French *presser* to squeeze, clasp, crush.] —**press′er,** *n.*

press² (pres) *v.t.* to force into military service; impress. [From obsolete *prest* to enlist men as soldiers or sailors by advancing them money. When men were later forced into military service, this word became associated with *press¹.*]

press agent, a person who manages publicity or public relations for a person or organization, such as an actor or motion picture studio.

press conference, an interview given to a gathering of newsmen, as by a public official or celebrity.

press·ing (pres′ing) *adj.* demanding or calling for immediate action or attention: *pressing business, a pressing problem.* —**press′ing·ly,** *adv.*

pres·sure (presh′ər) *n.* **1.** the force exerted by one thing upon another with which it is in contact: *The pressure of the water broke the dam.* **2.** a compelling force or influence: *My parents put pressure on me to study harder.* **3.** urgent demands on one's time or energy: *He works well under pressure.* **4.** a burden or strain, as of something difficult to bear: *the pressure of grief.* **5.** *Physics.* the amount of force exerted on a unit of area. —*v.t.,* **pres·sured, pres·sur·ing.** to compel by force or influence: *The salesman pressured me into buying the more expensive suit.*

pressure cooker, an airtight metal pot that uses steam pressure to cook foods quickly.

pressure suit, an inflatable suit worn, as by an astronaut, to keep normal atmospheric pressure around the body while flying at high altitudes.

pres·sur·ize (presh′ə rīz′) *v.t.,* **pres·sur·ized, pres·sur·iz·ing. 1.** to keep normal atmospheric pressure in the interior of (something, such as an airplane, spacecraft, or diving apparatus). **2.** to keep under high pressure, as the contents of an aerosol can. —**pres′sur·i·za′tion,** *n.*

pres·ti·dig·i·ta·tion (pres′tə dij′ə tā′shən) *n.* sleight of hand. —**pres′ti·dig′i·ta′tor,** *n.*

pres·tige (pres tēzh′) *n.* power, influence, or respect that is based on success, reputation, or achievements: *The scientist's discoveries brought him prestige.*

pres·to (pres′tō) *adv.* **1.** at once; immediately. **2.** *Music.* very quickly. —*adj. Music.* rapid; quick. —*n. Music.* a presto passage, movement, or piece.

pre·sum·a·ble (pri zōō′mə bəl) *adj.* that can be presumed or taken for granted; likely; probable. —**pre·sum′a·bly,** *adv.*

pre·sume (pri zōōm′) *v.,* **pre·sumed, pre·sum·ing.** —*v.t.* **1.** to accept as true until proven to be untrue; take for granted; suppose: *I presume that you know what you are talking about.* **2.** to do or take upon oneself without permission or authority; dare: *Do you presume to tell me how to choose my friends?* —*v.i.* **1.** to be presumptuous; take liberties. **2.** to take unfair advantage: *We will leave after dinner rather than presume on your hospitality.* —**pre·sum·ed·ly** (pri zōō′mid lē), *adv.* —**pre·sum′er,** *n.*

pre·sump·tion (pri zump′shən) *n.* **1.** the act of presuming. **2.** something taken for granted; assumption: *He went to the party on the presumption that we would be there.* **3.** thought or behavior that is too bold or arrogant.

pre·sump·tive (pri zump′tiv) *adj.* **1.** giving a good reason for accepting or believing: *presumptive evidence.* **2.** based on presumption or likelihood; presumed. —**pre·sump′tive·ly,** *adv.*

pre·sump·tu·ous (pri zump′chōō əs) *adj.* too bold or arrogant; forward; impertinent. —**pre·sump′tu·ous·ly,** *adv.* —**pre·sump′tu·ous·ness,** *n.*

pre·sup·pose (prē′sə pōz′) *v.t.,* **pre·sup·posed, pre·sup·pos·ing.** **1.** to take for granted; assume beforehand. **2.** to require as a necessary condition; imply: *A good musical performance presupposes much training and practice.*

pre·sup·po·si·tion (prē′sup ə zish′ən) *n.* **1.** the act of presupposing. **2.** something that is presupposed.

pre·tence (prē′tens, pri tens′) another spelling of **pretense.**

pre·tend (pri tend′) *v.t.* **1.** to claim, especially falsely or insincerely: *He does not pretend to be an expert chess player.* **2.** to give a false appearance of; feign: *to pretend sleep.* **3.** to act out in play; make believe: *The little boy pretended he was a soldier.* —*v.i.* **1.** to act out in play: *Children love to pretend.* **2.** to give a false appearance in order to deceive: *I am not sure if she is sick or only pretending.* **3.** to lay claim: *The duke pretended to the throne of France.*

pre·tend·ed (pri ten′did) *adj.* claimed falsely or insincerely; not genuine; false: *a pretended friend.* —**pre·tend′ed·ly,** *adv.*

pre·tend·er (pri ten′dər) *n.* **1.** a person who makes false or insincere claims or presents a false appearance. **2.** a person who lays claim to something, especially a throne.

pre·tense (prē′tens, pri tens′) *also,* **pre·tence.** *n.* **1.** a false show or appearance, especially for the purpose of deceiving: *The boy used any pretense to avoid going to the dentist.* **2.** a claim, especially one that is false or insincere. **3.** false show or display; affectation: *That is a simple family that lives without pretence.* **4.** acting out in play; fantasy.

pre·ten·sion (pri ten′shən) *n.* **1.** a claim: *pretensions to a throne.* **2.** the act of laying claim to something. **3.** a false show or display; affectation.

pre·ten·tious (pri ten′shəs) *adj.* **1.** making claims to, or presenting a false display of, some distinction or quality: *a talented but pretentious writer.* **2.** intended to show off or attract attention. —**pre·ten′tious·ly,** *adv.* —**pre·ten′-tious·ness,** *n.*

pret·er·it (pret′ər it) *also,* **pret·er·ite.** *Grammar. n.* **1.** the past tense. **2.** a verb in the past tense. —*adj.* expressing past time or action: *the preterit tense.*

pre·ter·nat·u·ral (prē′tər nach′ər əl) *adj.* going beyond or differing from the natural or ordinary; extraordinary or abnormal. —**pre′ter·nat′u·ral·ly,** *adv.*

pre·text (prē′tekst′) *n.* a false reason or excuse given to hide a true reason or motive: *She left the boring party on the pretext of being sick.*

Pre·to·ri·a (pri tôr′ē ə) *n.* the administrative capital of the Republic of South Africa, in the northeastern part of the country. Pop. (1971 est.), 542,200.

pret·ty (prit′ē) *adj.,* **pret·ti·er, pret·ti·est.** **1.** pleasing or attractive, especially in a graceful or dainty way: *a pretty girl, a pretty flower, a pretty poem.* **2.** fine; nice. ▲ usually used ironically: *He certainly got us into a pretty mess this time.* —*adv.* fairly; rather; quite: *It was raining pretty hard when we left.* —**pret′ti·ly,** *adv.* —**pret′ti·ness,** *n.*

pret·zel (pret′səl) *n.* a thin roll of dough that is usually baked in the form of a loose knot or a short stick and salted on the outside.

pre·vail (pri vāl′) *v.i.* **1.** to be greater in power or influence; be victorious; triumph or succeed: *I believe that man will not merely endure; he will prevail* (William Faulkner). **2.** to be widespread; persist: *Crime still prevails in our cities.* **to prevail on** or **to prevail upon.** to use persuasion successfully: *They prevailed on me to stay.*

pre·vail·ing (pri vā′ling) *adj.* **1.** most common or frequent: *prevailing winds.* **2.** having greater power or influence. —**pre·vail′ing·ly,** *adv.*

prev·a·lent (prev′ə lənt) *adj.* commonly or generally happening, used, or accepted; widespread: *a prevalent belief.* —**prev′a·lence,** *n.* —**prev′a·lent·ly,** *adv.*

pre·var·i·cate (pri var′ə kāt′) *v.i.,* **pre·var·i·cat·ed, pre·var·i·cat·ing.** to speak falsely; evade the truth; lie. —**pre·var′i·ca′tion,** *n.* —**pre·var′i·ca′tor,** *n.*

pre·vent (pri vent′) *v.t.* **1.** to keep from happening or developing: *to prevent forest fires.* **2.** to keep from doing something: *The traffic noises prevented me from sleeping.* —**pre·vent′a·ble;** *also,* **pre·vent′i·ble,** *adj.*

pre·ven·tion (pri ven′shən) *n.* **1.** the act of preventing. **2.** something that prevents.

pre·ven·tive (pri ven′tiv) *adj.* serving or intended to prevent something; concerned with prevention: *to take preventive measures against disease.* —*n.* **1.** something that prevents; means of preventing. **2.** a drug or other agent used to prevent disease. Also, **pre·vent·a·tive** (pri ven′-tə′tiv). —**pre·ven′tive·ly,** *adv.* —**pre·ven′tive·ness,** *n.*

pre·view (prē′vyōō) *also,* **pre·vue.** *n.* **1.** an advance showing of a motion picture, play, or exhibition before its public opening. **2.** an advance showing of scenes from a motion picture or television program in order to advertise it. —*v.t.* to present or view in advance.

pre·vi·ous (prē′vē əs) *adj.* coming or made before; earlier: *the previous day, a previous appointment.* —**pre′vi·ous·ly,** *adv.*

previous to. before: *He left previous to her arrival.*

pre·war (prē′wôr′) *adj.* happening or existing before a war.

prey (prā) *n.* **1.** any animal hunted or killed by another animal for food. **2.** a person or thing that is a victim: *The old man was the prey of a mugger.* **3.** the act or habit of hunting or killing for food: *A tiger is a beast of prey.* —*v.i.* **1.** to hunt or kill for food: *Owls prey on mice and other small animals.* **2.** to take advantage of; victimize: *He was preyed upon by a dishonest salesman.* **3.** to have a harmful or wearing effect: *Worry about his examinations preyed on his mind.*

Pri·am (prī′əm) *n. Greek Legend.* the King of Troy during the Trojan War, and the father of Hector and Paris.

price (prīs) *n.* **1.** the amount of money or its equivalent for which something is bought or sold: *The price of milk may go up next year.* **2.** the cost at which something is obtained: *The war was won at the price of many lives.* **3.** a reward offered for the capture or killing of a person: *There was a price on the murderer's head.* **4.** value; worth: *jewels of great price.* —*v.t.,* **priced, pric·ing. 1.** to set a price on; fix the price of: *This meat is priced much too high.* **2.** to find out the price of: *to price a car.*

price·less (prīs′lis) *adj.* **1.** too valuable to be priced; invaluable: *a priceless painting.* **2.** very amusing: *That remark was priceless.*

prick (prik) *v.t.* **1.** to pierce slightly with a sharp point: *She pricked her finger with a pin.* **2.** to cause a sharp pain to; sting: *His conscience pricked him for having told a lie.* —*n.* **1.** the act of pricking. **2.** a mark or opening made by a sharp point; puncture. **3.** a pointed object or instrument, such as a thorn.

  to prick up one's ears. a. to raise the ears to an erect position: *The dog pricked up its ears at the sound.* **b.** to listen closely or with sudden interest: *He pricked up his ears when he heard his name mentioned.*

prick·le (prik'əl) *n.* **1.** a small, sharp point, such as a thorn. **2.** a stinging or tingling sensation, as of being pricked. —*v.,* **prick·led, prick·ling.** —*v.t.* to cause a stinging or tingling sensation in. —*v.i.* to sting or tingle.

prick·ly (prik'lē) *adj.,* **prick·li·er, prick·li·est. 1.** having prickles. **2.** stinging; tingling. **3.** difficult; troublesome: *a prickly situation.* —**prick'li·ness,** *n.*

prickly heat, a skin rash characterized by redness and itching, caused by inflammation of the sweat glands.

prickly pear 1. the red or purple pear-shaped fruit of any of a large group of cacti found in North and South America. **2.** the plant that bears this fruit.

Prickly pear

pride (prīd) *n.* **1.** a sense of one's personal worth or dignity; self-respect: *Despite years of poverty, the man had kept his pride.* **2.** an exaggerated or unreasonable sense of one's worth or importance: *He knew he was wrong, but his foolish pride kept him from apologizing.* **3.** pleasure or satisfaction resulting as from an achievement or possession: *The woodcarver took pride in his work.* **4.** a person or thing that causes such pleasure or satisfaction: *The child was his mother's pride and joy.* **5.** a family or group of lions. —*v.t.,* **prid·ed, prid·ing.** to take pride, pleasure, or satisfaction in (oneself) for: *The woman prided herself on her financial success in business.*

pried (prīd) the past tense and past participle of **pry.**

priest (prēst) *n.* **1.** in certain Christian churches, a member of the clergy or minister. **2.** a person who performs the rites of a deity: *a priest of Apollo.* —**priest'ess,** *n.*

priest·hood (prēst'hood') *n.* **1.** the office or duties of a priest. **2.** priests as a group.

priest·ly (prēst'lē) *adj.,* **priest·li·er, priest·li·est.** of or like a priest.

prig (prig) *n.* a smug, self-righteous person; prude. —**prig'gish,** *adj.* —**prig'gish·ness,** *n.*

prim (prim) *adj.,* **prim·mer, prim·mest.** very formal, neat, or precise; proper. —**prim'ly,** *adv.* —**prim'ness,** *n.*

pri·ma·cy (prī'mə sē) *n. pl.,* **pri·ma·cies. 1.** the state of being first, as in rank or importance. **2.** the rank or dignity of a primate of a Church. **3.** in the Roman Catholic Church, the supreme authority of the pope.

pri·ma don·na (prē'mə don'ə) *pl.,* **pri·ma don·nas. 1.** the leading female singer in an opera company. **2.** a temperamental or vain person. [Italian *prima donna* literally, first lady.]

pri·mal (prī'məl) *adj.* **1.** of or relating to early times; original; first. **2.** of first importance; chief; fundamental.

pri·ma·ri·ly (prī mer'ə lē) *adv.* **1.** chiefly; principally. **2.** in the first place; originally.

pri·ma·ry (prī'mer'ē) *adj.* **1.** first or greatest in importance or degree; principal: *Your safety is my primary concern.* **2.** first in order, as in a series: *primary school.* **3.** first or earliest in time; primitive; elementary: *the primary phase of development.* **4.** basic; fundamental; elemen-

tal. **5.** not derived from something else; original; direct: *We consulted only primary sources in our research.* **6.** relating to the induction circuit, coil, or current in an electrically powered machine. —*n. pl.,* **pri·ma·ries. 1.** an election in which contenders from the same party oppose each other for the party's nomination or for the right to run for office with the party's support. Also, **primary election. 2.** one of the primary colors.

primary accent 1. the main stress in the pronunciation of a word. **2.** the mark (′) used to indicate this stress.

primary colors, any of several groups of colors from which all other colors are considered to be derived. The primary colors produced by directing light through a prism are orange-red, green, and blue; those used in mixing pigments are red, yellow, and blue.

primary school, a school providing instruction for very young pupils, comprising the first three or four grades of elementary school.

pri·mate (prī'māt, prī'mit) *n.* **1.** any member of the highest order of mammals, including human beings, apes, monkeys, and lemurs. **2.** an archbishop of the highest rank in a country or church province.

prime (prīm) *adj.* **1.** first in importance or value; main; chief: *Her happiness was his prime concern.* **2.** first in rank, dignity, influence, or authority: *The king was the prime ruler of the land.* **3.** of the best quality; excellent: *a prime cut of beef.* **4.** *Mathematics.* **a.** relating to or designating a prime number. **b.** having no common divisor except 1. —*n.* **1.** the best or most flourishing stage or condition: *the prime of a person's life. The trees were cut down before they had reached their prime.* **2.** see **prime number.** —*v.t.,* **primed, prim·ing. 1.** to make ready or prepare for use by filling or charging with something: *to prime a car's carburetor with gasoline.* **2.** to pour water into (a pump) so as to make it ready for operation. **3.** to prepare for painting, as by applying a base coat. **4.** to instruct or prepare (a person) beforehand in what he is to say or do: *The lawyer primed the witness.* **5.** to prepare (a gun or mine) for firing by supplying a charge of gunpowder or a primer. [Old English *prīme* the first period of the day in the Christian Church.] —**prime'ness,** *n.*

prime meridian, the meridian that passes through Greenwich, England, designated as zero degrees longitude, and from which longitude east and west is measured.

prime minister, the highest-ranking member of a body of administrators or of a council of ministers, especially in a parliamentary government, as that of Great Britain.

prime number, a number that can be divided without a remainder only by itself and by 1, as 2, 3, 7, 13, 29, or 41.

prim·er¹ (prim'ər) *n.* **1.** an elementary book for teaching children to read. **2.** an elementary or introductory book on any subject. [Going back to Latin *prīmārius* first, chief.]

prim·er² (prī'mər) *n.* **1.** a flat disk or other device that is filled with a small quantity of explosive and used to set off the main charge, as in a cartridge or shell. **2.** a substance put on a surface to prepare it for painting, especially a first coat of paint applied as a base. **3.** a person or thing that primes. [*Prime* + *-er¹.*]

at; āpe; cär; end; mē; it; īce; hot; ōld; fôrk; wood; fool; oil; out; up; turn; sing; thin; this; hw in white; zh in treasure. The symbol ə stands for the sound of a in about, e in taken, i in pencil, o in lemon, and u in circus.

pri·me·val (prī mē′vəl) *adj.* of, relating to, or belonging to the first or earliest age or ages, especially of the world; primitive. —**pri·me′val·ly,** *adv.*

prim·ing (prī′ming) *n.* **1.** powder or other material used to ignite a charge. **2.** a substance put on a surface to prepare it for painting; primer.

prim·i·tive (prim′ə tiv) *adj.* **1.** of, relating to, or characteristic of an early or original stage, especially in the development of something: *The animals that are now on the earth evolved from primitive forms.* **2.** of, relating to, or characteristic of the earlier stages in the development of human civilization or culture: *an exhibit of primitive art.* **3.** crude or simple; unsophisticated: *primitive adobe huts.* —*n.* a member of a primitive people. —**prim′i·tive·ly,** *adv.* —**prim′i·tive·ness,** *n.*

pri·mo·gen·i·ture (prī′mə jen′ə choor′, prī′mə jen′ə-chər) *n.* **1.** the state or fact of being the first-born child. **2.** the right of the eldest son to inherit his father's entire estate.

pri·mor·di·al (prī môr′dē əl) *adj.* **1.** of, relating to, or existing at or from the very beginning. **2.** fundamental; basic. —**pri·mor′di·al·ly,** *adv.*

primp (primp) *v.t., v.i.* to dress, groom, or adorn, especially with excessive vanity.

prim·rose (prim′rōz′) *n.* **1.** a trumpet-shaped flower of any of a large group of plants, grown as a garden flower. **2.** a plant bearing this flower. **3.** a pale greenish-yellow color. —*adj.* having the color primrose.

Primrose

prince (prins) *n.* **1.** any male member of a royal family other than the king. **2.** a male sovereign; monarch. **3.** the ruler of a small state or territory. **4.** a high-ranking nobleman in certain countries. **5.** a person or thing that is outstanding in a group, class, or profession: *He is a prince of artists.*

prince consort, the husband of a female sovereign.

prince·dom (prins′dəm) *n.* **1.** the state or territory ruled by a prince; principality. **2.** the rank or dignity of a prince.

Prince Edward Island, the smallest province of Canada, consisting of an island in the Gulf of St. Lawrence. Area, 2184 sq. mi. Pop. (1976), 118,230.

prince·ly (prins′lē) *adj.,* **prince·li·er, prince·li·est. 1.** of, relating to, resembling, or suitable for a prince. **2.** lavish; magnificent; sumptuous: *The house cost a princely sum.* —**prince′li·ness,** *n.*

Prince of Wales, the male heir apparent to the British throne, a title usually given to the sovereign's eldest son.

prin·cess (prin′sis, prin′ses) *n. pl.,* **prin·cess·es. 1.** any female member of a royal family other than the queen. **2.** the wife of a prince. **3.** a female sovereign.

prin·ci·pal (prin′sə pəl) *adj.* greatest or first, as in importance, rank, or value; chief: *The principal demand of the striking workers was higher pay.* —*n.* **1.** the head of an elementary or secondary school. **2.** a person who takes a leading part or plays the main role in some activity: *She is the principal in that new play.* **3.** an original sum of money borrowed or invested, without interest charged or income earned.

prin·ci·pal·i·ty (prin′sə pal′ə tē) *n. pl.,* **prin·ci·pal·i·ties. 1.** a state or territory ruled by a prince or from which a prince takes his title. **2.** the position or authority of a prince.

principal parts, the forms of a verb from which all other inflected forms can be derived. In English the princi-

pal parts are the present infinitive, the past tense, and the past participle, such as *jump, jumped, jumped* or *throw, threw, thrown.*

prin·ci·ple (prin′sə pəl) *n.* **1.** a basic truth, law, belief, or doctrine: *This government is said to be based on the principle that all men are created equal.* **2.** a rule of personal conduct: *It is my principle to answer letters promptly.* **3.** a sense of right or honorable action; integrity: *His principle kept him from telling a lie.* **4.** a scientific rule or law concerned with or explaining how something acts or operates: *the principle of gravity.*

print (print) *v.t.* **1.** to produce (a text, picture, or design) on a surface, such as paper, by applying inked type, plates, or blocks. **2.** to produce a text, picture, or design on (a surface) by applying inked type, plates, or blocks. **3.** to cause to be printed; publish: *The newspaper printed the story of his political career.* **4.** to write in letters like those made by type: *Please print your name on the application.* **5.** to produce (a photograph) by passing light through a negative onto a sensitized surface. —*v.i.* **1.** to take an impression from type, as in a printing press. **2.** to write in letters like those made by type. **3.** to produce something by the process of printing. —*n.* **1.** printed lettering: *The book was written in large print.* **2.** a mark or indentation made by pressing or stamping: *There were prints where we had walked in the snow.* **3.** something that has been marked or formed by pressing or stamping. **4.** a picture or design printed from a block or plate. **5.** a photograph made from a negative. **6.** a cloth with a design printed on it by means of dyes on engraved rollers, woodblocks, or screens. **7.** something made of such cloth. —**print′a·ble,** *adj.*

in print. a. in a printed form. **b.** still being printed and available for purchase from the publisher.

out of print. no longer available for purchase from the publisher.

printed circuit, an electrical circuit consisting of a pattern of conducting material deposited on a flat plate or base of insulating material, widely used in electronic equipment.

print·er (prin′tər) *n.* **1.** a person or thing that prints, especially a person or company whose business is printing. **2.** the part of a computer that delivers output data in printed form.

printer's devil, see devil *(def. 6).*

print·ing (prin′ting) *n.* **1.** the process, business, or art of producing printed matter, especially by means of a printing press. **2.** something that is printed; printed matter. **3.** all the copies of a book or other matter printed at one time: *The first printing of the book was 20,000 copies.* **4.** writing that resembles that made by type.

printing press, a machine for producing copies by transferring ink from a metal plate, typeface, or similar device, to paper or other material.

print-out (print′out′) *n.* the printed output of a computer.

pri·or[1] (prī′ər) *adj.* earlier or before in time, order, or importance: *She isn't coming to the party because she has a prior engagement.* [Latin *prior* former, superior.]

prior to. before: *Prior to living in New York, she lived in Massachusetts.*

pri·or[2] (prī′ər) *n.* a monk who ranks next below an abbot in a monastery or who is the superior of a priory. [Old English *prior.*]

pri·or·ess (prī′ər is) *n. pl.,* **pri·or·ess·es.** a nun who ranks next below an abbess in an abbey or who is the superior of a priory.

pri·or·i·ty (prī ôr′ə tē, prī or′ə tē) *n. pl.,* **pri·or·i·ties. 1.** the condition of coming before another or others, as in order or importance. **2.** the right to have superior or special treatment: *Military personnel often have priority over civilians during wartime.* **3.** a matter deserving or receiving special emphasis or attention: *Buying a new car was Philip's first priority.*

pri·o·ry (prī′ər ē) *n. pl.*, **pri·o·ries.** a religious house ranking next below an abbey, governed by a prior or prioress.

prism (priz′əm) *n.* **1.** a solid having two congruent and parallel faces, and whose other faces are parallelograms. **2.** a transparent solid having this shape, used for dispersing light or for breaking it up into its component colors.

Prism

pris·mat·ic (priz mat′ik) *adj.* **1.** of, relating to, produced by, or like a prism. **2.** of varied colors; brilliant. —**pris·mat′i·cal·ly,** *adv.*

prismatic colors, the seven colors, red, orange, yellow, green, blue, indigo, and violet, that are produced when white light is passed through a prism.

pris·on (priz′ən) *n.* **1.** a building or institution in which persons convicted or accused of crimes are confined. **2.** any place of confinement.

pris·on·er (priz′ə nər) *n.* **1.** a person confined in a prison. **2.** a person who is arrested or taken into custody. **3.** a person or thing that is restrained, deprived of freedom, or held in captivity. **4.** see **prisoner of war.**

prisoner of war, a person captured or held by the enemy in war.

pris·sy (pris′ē) *adj.*, **pris·si·er, pris·si·est.** very prim, fussy, or prudish.

pris·tine (pris′tēn) *adj.* **1.** of or relating to the earliest time, period, or condition; original; primitive. **2.** not corrupt; pure; unspoiled: *the pristine beauty of freshly fallen snow.*

prith·ee (priṯẖ′ē) *interj. Archaic.* I pray thee; please.

pri·va·cy (prī′və sē) *n. pl.*, **pri·va·cies. 1.** the state or condition of being private, secluded, or isolated: *The writer needed privacy to finish his novel.* **2.** the right to be free from interference with one's private affairs: *Opening someone else's mail is an invasion of privacy.*

pri·vate (prī′vit) *adj.* **1.** belonging or restricted to a particular person or persons: *a private driveway, private property.* **2.** personal; individual: *June told her private thoughts to no one.* **3.** not intended for general or public knowledge; confidential: *a private conversation.* **4.** not holding public office or having an official position: *The former senator retired to private life.* **5.** secluded; isolated: *We had our picnic in a private spot.* —*n.* in the U.S. Army and Marine Corps, an enlisted man of the lowest rank. —**pri′vate·ly,** *adv.* —**pri′vate·ness,** *n.*

   in private. confidentially or secretly; privately.

private detective, a detective who is employed by a private person or group rather than a police force or government agency. Also, **private investigator.**

private enterprise, another term for **free enterprise.**

pri·va·teer (prī′və tēr′) *n.* **1.** a privately owned armed ship commissioned by a government to attack enemy ships, especially merchant ships. **2.** the commander or a member of the crew of such a ship. —*v.i.* to sail on or as a privateer.

private eye *Informal.* a private detective.

private first class 1. in the U.S. Army, an enlisted man ranking below a corporal and above a private. **2.** in the U.S. Marine Corps, an enlisted man ranking below a lance corporal and above a private.

private school, a school that is supported and managed by a private group rather than by the government.

pri·va·tion (prī vā′shən) *n.* **1.** the lack of the comforts or necessities of life or the condition resulting from such a lack. **2.** the act of depriving or the state of being deprived.

priv·et (priv′it) *n.* any of a group of evergreen shrubs or small trees widely used for hedges, usually having white flowers and black berries.

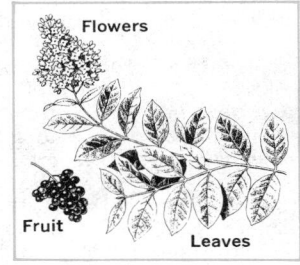

Privet

priv·i·lege (priv′ə lij) *n.* a special right, advantage, or benefit granted to or held by a certain person, group, or class: *The older boys were given the privilege to stay out late.* —*v.t.,* **priv·i·leged, priv·i·leg·ing.** to grant a privilege to.

priv·i·leged (priv′ə lijd) *adj.* **1.** having or enjoying a privilege or privileges: *a privileged group.* **2.** confidential; private; restricted: *privileged information.*

priv·i·ly (priv′ə lē) *adv.* privately; secretly.

priv·y (priv′ē) *adj.* having knowledge of something secret or private: *Only three people were privy to the plot.* —*n. pl.,* **priv·ies.** see **outhouse** *(def. 1).*

Privy Council, an honorary body appointed by the British sovereign, having about 300 members.

prize¹ (prīz) *n.* **1.** something that is offered or won as a reward, especially for winning in a competition or in a game of chance. **2.** anything worth winning; something valuable. —*adj.* **1.** that has won or is likely to win a prize: *a prize painting.* **2.** offered or given as a prize. **3.** worthy of a prize; outstanding. [Old French *pris* price, reward.]

prize² (prīz) *n.* something seized or captured, especially an enemy ship captured at sea during wartime. [Old French *prise* seizure.]

prize³ (prīz) *v.t.,* **prized, priz·ing. 1.** to value or esteem highly: *to prize a friend's advice.* **2.** to estimate the value of; appraise: *He was a man who prized his honor above his life.* [Old French *preisier.*]

prize⁴ (prīz) *v.t.,* **prized, priz·ing.** to raise or force with a lever; pry. —*n.* an instrument used for prying; lever. [From *prize².*]

prize·fight (prīz′fīt′) *n.* a match between professional boxers. —**prize′fight·er,** *n.*

pro¹ (prō) *adv.* in favor of; for. —*n. pl.,* **pros.** a reason, argument, or person in favor of something: *The chairman listed all the pros and cons of the plan.* [Latin *prō.*]

pro² (prō) *adj., n. pl.,* **pros.** *Informal.* professional.

pro-¹ *prefix* **1.** in favor of; supporting; in behalf of: *pro-British.* **2.** forward; forth; out: *proclaim.* **3.** in place of; acting as: *pronoun.* [Latin *prō-.*]

pro-² *prefix* before in time or place: *prognosis.* [Greek *pro-.*]

prob·a·bil·i·ty (prob′ə bil′ə tē) *n. pl.,* **prob·a·bil·i·ties. 1.** the state or quality of being probable; likelihood: *Bad weather increases the probability of highway accidents.* **2.** something probable or likely: *It is a probability that she will come.* **3.** *Mathematics.* the ratio of the number of

at; āpe; cär; end; mē; it; īce; hot; ōld; fôrk; wood; fo͞ol; oil; out; up; turn; sing; thin; ṯẖis; hw in white; zh in treasure. The symbol ə stands for the sound of **a** in about, **e** in taken, **i** in pencil, **o** in lemon, and **u** in circus.

727

chances favoring the occurrence of an event to the total number of possible occurrences.

in all probability. most probably; very likely.

prob·a·ble (prob′ə bəl) *adj.* **1.** likely to occur but not certain; that can reasonably be expected: *The experts agreed on the probable outcome of the boxing match.* **2.** likely to be true; plausible: *She might have forgotten, but it's not probable.*

prob·a·bly (prob′ə blē) *adv.* in all likelihood; most likely.

pro·bate (prō′bāt) *n.* the act or process of legally proving a will. —*adj.* of or relating to the legal proving of a will: *a probate court.* —*v.t.,* **pro·bat·ed, pro·bat·ing.** to establish the authenticity or validity of (a will).

pro·ba·tion (prō bā′shən) *n.* **1.** a testing or trial of the ability, qualifications, or suitability of a person, as a new employee, usually for a specified period of time. **2.** *Law.* **a.** the action or practice of allowing a person convicted of a minor or first offense to go free under close supervision, rather than be put in prison. **b.** the period of being on probation or the status of a person on probation.

pro·ba·tion·er (prō bā′shə nər) *n.* a person who is on probation.

probation officer, an officer appointed to supervise someone who is on probation.

probe (prōb) *n.* **1.** a thorough investigation or examination: *The newspaper article led to a probe into prison conditions.* **2.** a slender surgical tool for exploring a body cavity, wound, or similar opening. **3.** a device, mechanism, or object used for investigation or exploration, especially a space probe. —*v.,* **probed, prob·ing.** —*v.t.* **1.** to investigate, examine, or explore thoroughly: *The police probed all the details of the crime.* **2.** to examine or explore with a surgical probe. —*v.i.* to conduct a thorough investigation or examination: *Scientists probed into the nature of the substance.*

pro·bi·ty (prō′bə tē, prob′ə tē) *n.* moral strength; integrity.

prob·lem (prob′ləm) *n.* **1.** a question, situation, or condition that is difficult, confusing, or not resolved: *Air pollution is a major problem facing our cities.* **2.** a person who is troublesome or causes difficulty: *The oldest boy at camp was a problem to his counselor.* **3.** a question proposed for thinking, discussing, or solving: *an arithmetic problem.* —*adj.* being a problem; difficult to handle: *a problem child.*

prob·lem·at·ic (prob′lə mat′ik) *adj.* being, presenting, or involving a problem; uncertain. Also, **prob·lem·at·i·cal** (prob′lə mat′i kəl). —**prob·lem·at′i·cal·ly,** *adv.*

pro·bos·cis (prō bos′is) *n. pl.,* **pro·bos·cis·es** or **pro·bos·ci·des** (prō bos′i dēz′). **1.** the trunk of an elephant. **2.** a long, flexible snout, as that of a tapir. **3.** the long, tubular mouth parts of certain insects, as mosquitoes and butterflies, adapted for sucking.

pro·caine (prō′kān) *n.* a synthetic drug widely used as a local anesthetic in dentistry and medicine.

pro·ce·dure (prə sē′jər) *n.* **1.** a particular course of action, especially one that follows a definite order of steps: *What is the proper procedure for leaving the building in case of fire?* **2.** the customary or established way of conducting legal, parliamentary, or similar business. **3.** a manner of proceeding or acting. —**pro·ce′du·ral,** *adj.*

pro·ceed (prə sēd′) *v.i.* **1.** to continue, especially after a stop or interruption: *The speaker waited for the applause to die down and then proceeded.* **2.** to begin or undertake some action or process: *The mechanic jacked up the car and then proceeded to change the tire.* **3.** to move on or forward: *The parade proceeded through town.* **4.** to be carried on or put into action: *The experiment is proceeding as planned.*

pro·ceed·ing (prə sē′ding) *n.* **1.** an action or course of action; procedure. **2. proceedings.** a series of actions or events; happenings. **3. proceedings.** a record of business transacted at a meeting of a society or similar organization. **4. proceedings.** *Law.* legal action.

pro·ceeds (prō′sēdz) *n., pl.* the money or profit derived from a commercial undertaking, especially money raised for a particular cause.

proc·ess (pros′es, prō′ses) *n. pl.,* **proc·ess·es. 1.** the series of acts or operations performed in making or doing something: *My grandmother taught me the process of making a dress.* **2.** a series of continuous changes or actions leading to an end: *the process of growth.* **3.** a course or lapse: *In the process of time the job will be done.* **4.** the course of being done or going on: *The novelist is in the process of writing another book.* **5.** *Law.* **a.** a writ or summons by which a person is ordered to appear in court in a legal action. **b.** all of the proceedings in a legal action. **6.** *Biology.* an outgrowth or protruding part: *The animal had a bony process on top of its head.* —*v.t.* **1.** to handle by routine procedures: *The college staff processes new students at the beginning of each year.* **2.** to treat, make, or prepare, as by a special method: *to process cheese.* —*adj.* made or prepared by some special method: *process cheese.*

pro·ces·sion (prə sesh′ən) *n.* **1.** a continuous or steady forward movement or progression, especially in a formal, orderly, or ceremonious manner. **2.** a group of persons or things moving along in this way, often in a long line: *The wedding procession moved slowly down the aisle.* **3.** a continuous course or succession.

pro·ces·sion·al (prə sesh′ən əl) *adj.* of, relating to, or moving in a procession. —*n.* the music accompanying a procession.

pro·claim (prə klām′) *v.t.* **1.** to announce officially; declare publicly: *The enemy nations proclaimed a truce.* **2.** to make clear; reveal: *The boy's tears proclaimed his sorrow.*

proc·la·ma·tion (prok′lə mā′shən) *n.* **1.** something that is proclaimed, especially an official public announcement. **2.** the act of proclaiming.

pro·cliv·i·ty (prō kliv′ə tē) *n. pl.,* **pro·cliv·i·ties.** a tendency or inclination; propensity: *The sickly child showed a proclivity to complain.*

pro·con·sul (prō kon′səl) *n.* the governor or military commander of an ancient Roman province.

pro·cras·ti·nate (prō kras′tə nāt′) *v.i.,* **pro·cras·ti·nat·ed, pro·cras·ti·nat·ing.** to put off doing something until a future time, especially to do this as a habit. —**pro·cras′ti·na′tion,** *n.* —**pro·cras′ti·na′tor,** *n.*

pro·cre·ate (prō′krē āt′) *v.t., v.i.,* **pro·cre·at·ed, pro·cre·at·ing.** to produce offspring. —**pro′cre·a′tion,** *n.*

proc·tor (prok′tər) *n.* a person appointed to keep order and supervise students during an examination at a college or university. —*v.t.* to act as proctor for (an examination).

pro·cure (prə kyoor′) *v.t.,* **pro·cured, pro·cur·ing. 1.** to acquire or get, especially with effort: *The children procured the money to buy the present by cutting grass.* **2.** to bring about; effect; cause. —**pro·cure′ment,** *n.*

prod (prod) *v.t.,* **prod·ded, prod·ding. 1.** to push or jab, as with a pointed instrument. **2.** to stir to action; rouse. —*n.* **1.** a push or jab. **2.** a pointed instrument used for prodding, as a goad. **3.** something that stirs to action. —**prod′der,** *n.*

prod·i·gal (prod′i gəl) *adj.* **1.** foolishly extravagant; wasteful: *The man's prodigal spending habits put him into debt.* **2.** lavish, generous, or profuse; abundant: *prodigal talents.* —*n.* a person who is recklessly extravagant. —**prod·i·gal·i·ty** (prod′ə gal′ə tē), *n.* —**prod′i·gal·ly,** *adv.*

pro·di·gious (prə dij′əs) *adj.* **1.** huge or extraordinary in size, number, or degree; enormous: *The mountains rose to a prodigious height.* **2.** causing amazement; marvelous: *a prodigious feat of strength.* —**pro·di′gious·ly,** *adv.* —**pro·di′gious·ness,** *n.*

prod·i·gy (prod′ə jē) *n. pl.,* **prod·i·gies. 1.** an extremely gifted or talented person, especially a child. **2.** something that causes wonder or amazement; marvel.

pro·duce (*v.,* prə dōōs′, prə dyōōs′; *n.,* prod′ōōs, prod′-yōōs, prō′dōōs, prō′dyōōs) *v.,* **pro·duced, pro·duc·ing.** —*v.t.* **1.** to make or bring into being, especially by means of machinery and on a large scale; manufacture: *That company produces steel.* **2.** to bring forth; yield; bear: *A cow produces milk.* **3.** to bring into existence by mental or artistic effort; create: *Shakespeare produced some of the greatest plays ever written.* **4.** to give rise to; cause: *The song produced a strong reaction from the audience.* **5.** to bring forward or present; show; furnish: *The lawyer could not produce any evidence.* **6.** to prepare (a play, motion picture, or other form of entertainment) for public showing, as by securing financial backing and hiring performers. —*v.i.* to bring forth or make something: *These workers produce at a very fast rate.* —*n.* **1.** something that is produced. **2.** farm products, especially fresh fruit and vegetables.

pro·duc·er (prə dōō′sər, prə dyōō′sər) *n.* **1.** a person or thing that produces. **2.** a person in charge of producing a play, motion picture, or other form of entertainment.

prod·uct (prod′əkt) *n.* **1.** anything that is produced: *dairy products.* **2.** result; consequence: *Ina's good grades were the product of studying.* **3.** a number or algebraic expression obtained by multiplication: *12 is the product of 4 and 3.*

pro·duc·tion (prə duk′shən) *n.* **1.** the act of producing. **2.** the amount produced: *Steel production has increased this year.* **3.** something that is produced, especially a play, motion picture, or other form of entertainment.

pro·duc·tive (prə duk′tiv) *adj.* **1.** producing abundantly; fertile or prolific: *productive land, a productive author.* **2.** having favorable, useful, or positive results; fruitful; effective: *Talks to end the strike had not been very productive.* **3.** yielding some product at a profit: *a productive business.* **4.** producing, tending to produce, or capable of producing: *Our club meeting was productive of good ideas for the picnic.* —**pro·duc′tive·ly,** *adv.* —**pro·duc′-tive·ness,** *n.*

pro·duc·tiv·i·ty (prō′duk tiv′ə tē) *n.* the state or quality of being productive.

Prof., professor.

prof·a·na·tion (prof′ə nā′shən) *n.* the act of profaning.

pro·fane (prō fān′, prə fān′) *adj.* **1.** showing or marked by irreverence, disrespect, or contempt for God or sacred things; blasphemous. **2.** not concerned with or relating to religion or religious matters; secular. **3.** vulgar; coarse; obscene: *profane language.* —*v.t.,* **pro·faned, pro·fan·ing. 1.** to treat (something sacred) with disrespect or contempt; desecrate: *You have been guilty of profaning the Lord's day* (Daniel Defoe). **2.** to put to wrong, degrading, or unworthy use; abuse: *to profane one's precious time.* —**pro·fane′ly,** *adv.* —**pro·fane′ness,** *n.*

pro·fan·i·ty (prō fan′ə tē, prə fan′ə tē) *n. pl.,* **pro·fan·i·ties. 1.** a profane act. **2.** the use of profane or vulgar language. **3.** the state or quality of being profane.

pro·fess (prə fes′) *v.t.* **1.** to claim, especially falsely or insincerely: *Maggie professes to know everything about sculpture.* **2.** to declare openly; affirm: *We profess ourselves to be the slaves of chance* (Shakespeare, *The Winter's Tale*). **3.** to affirm one's faith in: *to profess Judaism.* —*v.i.* to make a declaration or affirmation.

pro·fessed (prə fest′) *adj.* **1.** alleged; pretended: *professed generosity.* **2.** openly declared: *a professed enemy.*

pro·fes·sion (prə fesh′ən) *n.* **1.** an occupation that requires special education and training, such as law or medicine. **2.** a group of persons following such an occupation: *the medical profession.* **3.** any activity considered as a profession: *George chose the acting profession.* **4.** the act or an instance of professing; declaration: *a profession of loyalty.* **5.** the affirming of faith in a religion.

pro·fes·sion·al (prə fesh′ən əl) *adj.* **1.** of or relating to a profession or a person in a profession: *The doctor charged a fee for professional services.* **2.** engaged in a profession: *The meeting was restricted to professional people.* **3.** working for money in an activity or occupation not usually pursued for gain, especially a sport: *a professional golfer.* **4.** engaged in by professionals as opposed to amateurs: *professional basketball.* —*n.* **1.** a person engaged in a profession. **2.** a person working for money in an activity or occupation not usually pursued for gain, especially an athlete. **3.** a person who is skilled or expert in a particular activity or occupation. —**pro·fes′sion·al·ly,** *adv.*

pro·fes·sion·al·ism (prə fesh′ən əl iz′əm) *n.* professional methods, character, or status.

pro·fes·sor (prə fes′ər) *n.* **1.** a teacher of the highest rank in a college, university, or other institution of higher education. **2.** *Informal.* any teacher.

pro·fes·so·ri·al (prō′fə sôr′ē əl, prof′ə sôr′ē əl) *adj.* of, relating to, or characteristic of a professor. —**pro′fes·so′ri·al·ly,** *adv.*

pro·fes·sor·ship (prə fes′ər ship′) *n.* the position or duties of a professor.

prof·fer (prof′ər) *v.t.* to present for acceptance; offer: *He proffered an apology for his lateness.* —*n.* something presented for acceptance; offer.

pro·fi·cien·cy (prə fish′ən sē) *n. pl.,* **pro·fi·cien·cies.** the state or quality of being proficient; skill.

pro·fi·cient (prə fish′ənt) *adj.* highly skilled; expert; adept: *Years of practice had made Steve proficient in playing the flute.* —**pro·fi′cient·ly,** *adv.*

pro·file (prō′fīl) *n.* **1.** a side view, especially of a human face or head. **2.** an outline, drawing, or other representation of this. **3.** any outline or representation of an outline: *The mountain's jagged profile stood out against the sky.* **4.** a brief biographical sketch: *The newspaper printed a profile of the new mayor.* **5.** an analysis, usually shown by means of a graph or diagram, of some person, process, or thing: *a profile of the voters in a district.* —*v.t.,* **pro·filed, pro·fil·ing.** to make, sketch, or write a profile of.

Profile

prof·it (prof′it) *n.* **1.** *also,* **profits.** the amount remaining after all the costs of a business or business transaction have been paid. **2.** *also,* **profits.** financial gain, especially return or income received from investment or property. **3.** a benefit or advantage; gain. —*v.i.* **1.** to get benefit or profit; gain: *to profit from an experience.* **2.** to be of advantage, use, or benefit. —*v.t.* to be of advantage, use, or benefit to.

at; āpe; cär; end; mē; it; īce; hot; ōld; fôrk; wood; fōōl; oil; out; up; turn; sing; thin; <u>th</u>is; hw in white; zh in treasure. The symbol ə stands for the sound of **a** in about, **e** in taken, **i** in pencil, **o** in lemon, and **u** in circus.

prof·it·a·ble (prof′i tə bəl) *adj.* **1.** yielding a financial profit: *a profitable business.* **2.** beneficial; rewarding; useful: *a profitable experience.* —**prof′it·a·ble·ness,** *n.* —**prof′it·a·bly,** *adv.*

prof·it·eer (prof′ə tēr′) *n.* a person who makes or seeks to make excessive profits, especially by selling goods at very high prices during a time of shortage. —*v.i.* to act as a profiteer.

prof·li·gate (prof′lə git) *adj.* **1.** totally corrupt with regard to morals; thoroughly immoral; dissolute. **2.** recklessly extravagant or wasteful. —*n.* a profligate person. —**prof′li·ga·cy,** *n.* —**prof′li·gate·ly,** *adv.*

pro·found (prə found′) *adj.* **1.** showing or characterized by great understanding, knowledge, or insight: *a profound idea, a profound book.* **2.** coming from the depth of one's being; intensely felt: *We felt profound sorrow upon hearing of his death.* **3.** significant; important; extensive: *The doctor's discovery will have a profound influence on mankind.* **4.** absolute; complete; thorough: *There was a profound silence when the President began to speak.* —**pro·found′ly,** *adv.* —**pro·found′ness,** *n.*

pro·fun·di·ty (prə fun′də tē) *n. pl.,* **pro·fun·di·ties.** **1.** the state or quality of being profound; depth. **2.** a profound or complicated statement, idea, or matter.

pro·fuse (prə fyōōs′) *adj.* **1.** great or abundant in amount; plentiful: *profuse foliage, profuse bleeding.* **2.** given or giving freely, often to too great a degree; lavish: *profuse compliments.* —**pro·fuse′ly,** *adv.* —**pro·fuse′ness,** *n.*

pro·fu·sion (prə fyōō′zhən) *n.* **1.** a plentiful amount; abundance. **2.** extravagance; lavishness.

pro·gen·i·tor (prō jen′ə tər) *n.* **1.** an ancestor from whom descent is traced; forefather. **2.** originator: *Sir Isaac Newton was one of the progenitors of modern science.*

prog·e·ny (proj′ə nē) *n. pl.,* **prog·e·nies.** offspring, descendants, or children as a group.

prog·no·sis (prog nō′sis) *n. pl.,* **prog·no·ses** (prog nō′-sēz). **1.** a prediction of the probable course and outcome of a disease. **2.** any prediction or forecast.

prog·nos·tic (prog nos′tik) *adj.* **1.** of, relating to, or serving as a basis for a prognosis. **2.** foretelling; predictive. —*n.* **1.** a sign or indication of some future occurrence. **2.** a prediction or forecast.

prog·nos·ti·cate (prog nos′tə kāt′) *v.t.,* **prog·nos·ti·cat·ed, prog·nos·ti·cat·ing.** **1.** to predict on the basis of present indications; forecast; prophesy. **2.** to foreshadow. —**prog·nos′ti·ca′tion,** *n.* —**prog·nos′ti·ca′tor,** *n.*

pro·gram (prō′gram) *also, British,* **pro·gramme.** *n.* **1.** a list or printed announcement, especially for some public presentation, as a play or concert, usually showing what is to be presented and who will participate. **2.** a presentation or performance, especially a television or radio show. **3.** a schedule or procedure: *The congressman proposed a new program for fighting crime.* **4.** a set of organized activities or other offerings planned by or available at a particular place or institution: *That university has an excellent English program.* **5.** a series of steps specified for the solution of a particular problem, to be coded for use in a computer. **6.** a series of coded instructions used to direct a computer in the solution of a problem. —*v.t.,* **pro-gramed, pro·gram·ing;** *also, British,* **pro·grammed, pro-gram·ming.** **1.** to arrange or include in a program or schedule. **2.** to make up or work out a program for. **3.** to write a program for (a computer).

pro·gram·mer (prō′gram′ər) *also,* **pro·gram·er.** *n.* a person who programs, especially a person who programs computers.

prog·ress (*n.,* prog′res; *v.,* prə gres′) *n.* **1.** a forward movement in space: *Heavy rains slowed the explorer's prog-* *ress through the jungle.* **2.** movement toward a goal or toward completion: *Are you making any progress with your book report?* **3.** development to a better or higher state; improvement: *The patient is making progress toward recovery.* —*v.i.* **1.** to move forward or onward; proceed: *The debater's argument progressed logically from one step to the next.* **2.** to move toward a goal or toward completion: *Construction of the new hospital is progressing according to schedule.*

pro·gres·sion (prə gresh′ən) *n.* **1.** the act of progressing; advance. **2.** *Mathematics.* a sequence of numbers or algebraic expressions in which there is the same relation between each quantity and the one succeeding it; arithmetic or geometric progression. **3.** a sequence or succession, as of events. **4.** *Music.* **a.** the movement from one tone or chord to another. **b.** a succession of tones or chords.

pro·gres·sive (prə gres′iv) *adj.* **1.** moving forward; advancing. **2.** proceeding steadily or step by step. **3.** favoring, supporting, or characterized by progress, reform, or improvement, especially in political or social matters: *The candidate promised progressive leadership if elected.* **4.** *Grammar.* denoting action in progress. —*n.* a person who favors or advocates progress or reform, as in political, social, or educational matters. —**pro·gres′sive·ly,** *adv.* —**pro·gres′sive·ness,** *n.*

pro·hib·it (prō hib′it) *v.t.* **1.** to forbid by authority: *Smoking is prohibited in this building.* **2.** to prevent; hinder: *Poor health prohibited him from traveling.*

pro·hi·bi·tion (prō′ə bish′ən) *n.* **1.** the act of prohibiting. **2.** a law, order, or rule that forbids something. **3.** the forbidding by law of the manufacture, transportation, and sale of alcoholic beverages. **4. Prohibition.** the period from 1920 to 1933 during which alcoholic beverages were prohibited by federal law in the United States.

pro·hi·bi·tion·ist (prō′ə bish′ə nist) *n.* a person who favors the prohibition of alcoholic beverages.

pro·hib·i·tive (prō hib′ə tiv) *adj.* **1.** so high or expensive as to make buying, paying, or using difficult or impossible: *The house was being sold at an almost prohibitive price.* **2.** prohibiting or tending to prohibit: *a prohibitive law.* Also, **pro·hib·i·to·ry** (prō hib′ə tôr′ē).

proj·ect (*n.,* proj′ekt; *v.,* prə jekt′) *n.* **1.** a plan; scheme; proposal. **2.** a task or activity that is to be done; undertaking: *Our town has begun a project to improve the roads.* **3.** housing, usually made up of apartment buildings, especially such housing supported by the government to provide for families with lower incomes. —*v.t.* **1.** to throw, shoot, or hurl forward: *The boy projected stones into the air with a slingshot.* **2.** to cause (a shadow, light, or image) to fall on a surface. **3.** to cause (one's voice) to be heard clearly at a distance. **4.** to visualize or think of by using one's imagination: *to project oneself into the future.* **5.** to predict on the basis of certain given or known information: *to project the winner of an election by using a computer.* —*v.i.* **1.** to stick out; protrude: *A narrow piece of land projected into the sea.* **2.** to cause one's voice to be heard clearly at a distance.

pro·jec·tile (prə jek′til) *n.* an object that is designed to be shot or in some other way projected through space, as a bullet. —*adj.* **1.** capable of being thrown, shot, or hurled forward. **2.** impelling or driving forward: *the projectile force of a weapon.*

pro·jec·tion (prə jek′shən) *n.* **1.** the act of projecting. **2.** something that sticks out or projects; protruding part. **3.** the process of projecting images, as from a film or printed page, onto a screen or other surface. **4.** an image that is so projected. **5.** a prediction based on certain given or known information: *a computer projection of an election's outcome.*

pro·jec·tor (prə jek′tər) *n.* **1.** a device that projects images, as from a film or printed page, onto a screen or other surface. **2.** a person who devises projects or plans.

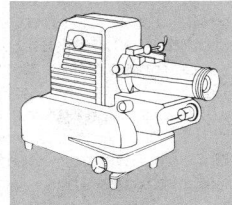

Projector

Pro·kof·iev, Ser·gei Ser·ge·ye·vich (prə kôf′yef; ser gā′ ser gā′yə vich) 1891–1953, Russian composer.

pro·le·tar·i·an (prō′lə ter′ē ən) *adj.* of, relating to, or characteristic of the proletariat. —*n.* a member of the proletariat. [Latin *prōlētārius* Roman citizen of the lowest class, who was so poor that he was considered able to serve the state only by having children.]

pro·le·tar·i·at (prō′lə ter′ē ət) *n.* **1.** the working class, especially the industrial working class. **2.** in ancient Rome, the lowest class of citizens.

pro·lif·er·ate (prō lif′ə rāt′) *v.,* **pro·lif·er·at·ed, pro·lif·er·at·ing.** —*v.i.* to multiply, reproduce, or grow rapidly: *The bacteria proliferated in the laboratory.* —*v.t.* to cause to multiply, reproduce, or grow rapidly. —**pro·lif′er·a′· tion,** *n.*

pro·lif·ic (prə lif′ik) *adj.* **1.** producing abundantly through creative or artistic effort; highly productive: *The prolific novelist had written more than thirty books.* **2.** producing offspring or fruit in abundance; fertile: *a prolific apple tree.* —**pro·lif′i·cal·ly,** *adv.*

pro·lix (prō liks′, prō′liks′) *adj.* **1.** so long and wordy as to be boring: *a prolix sermon.* **2.** inclined to speak or write in a boringly long and wordy manner. —**pro·lix′· i·ty,** *n.*

pro·logue (prō′lôg′, prō′log′) *also,* **pro·log.** *n.* **1.** an introduction to a play, poem, or other literary work. **2.** any introductory or preliminary act or event.

pro·long (prə lông′) *v.t.* to make longer, especially in time; extend: *Judy prolonged the suspense by not telling us what had happened until the next day.*

pro·lon·ga·tion (prō′lông gā′shən) *n.* **1.** the act of prolonging or the state of being prolonged. **2.** something that prolongs or is prolonged.

prom (prom) *n. Informal.* a formal school or college dance.

prom·e·nade (prom′ə nād′, prom′ə näd′) *n.* **1.** a leisurely walk, especially one taken in a public place for pleasure or display. **2.** a place or area for such walking. **3.** a formal dance; ball. **4.** a march of the guests at the opening of a formal dance. **5.** a march of dancers in a square dance. —*v.i.,* **prom·e·nad·ed, prom·e·nad·ing. 1.** to go on a promenade or leisurely walk. **2.** to perform a promenade in a square dance.

Pro·me·the·us (prə mē′thē əs) *n. Greek Mythology.* a Titan who stole fire from the gods and brought it to man. Zeus punished him by chaining him to a rock where an eagle ate away at his liver every day.

pro·me·thi·um (prə mē′thē əm) *n.* a radioactive, metallic element not found in nature. It is one of the rare-earth elements. Symbol: **Pm**

prom·i·nence (prom′ə nəns) *n.* **1.** the state or quality of being prominent: *I was snatched out of virtual oblivion and thrust into sudden prominence* (Tennessee Williams). **2.** something prominent; projection.

prom·i·nent (prom′ə nənt) *adj.* **1.** well-known or important; notable: *a prominent member of the community.* **2.** very noticeable; conspicuous: *One large oak tree was the landscape's only prominent feature.* **3.** sticking out from a surface; projecting: *The cliff had a prominent overhang.* —**prom′i·nent·ly,** *adv.*

prom·is·cu·i·ty (prom′ə skyo͞o′ə tē) *n.* **1.** promiscuous or loose sexual relations or behavior. **2.** the state or quality of being promiscuous.

pro·mis·cu·ous (prə mis′kyo͞o əs) *adj.* **1.** indiscriminate, especially having sexual relations indiscriminately or with many persons. **2.** made up of varied and unrelated things, parts, or individuals. —**pro·mis′cu·ous·ly,** *adv.* —**pro·mis′cu·ous·ness,** *n.*

prom·ise (prom′is) *n.* **1.** an assurance or pledge given that one will or will not do something, or that something will or will not occur: *Joe made a promise that he would keep his room neat.* **2.** an indication of or reason for expecting future excellence, success, or progress: *The new drug shows promise in treating the disease. That young musician shows promise.* **3.** an indication of something that may occur or develop: *There was a promise of spring in the air.* —*v.,* **prom·ised, prom·is·ing.** —*v.t.* **1.** to declare or guarantee with a promise: *Everyone promised to keep the surprise party a secret.* **2.** to make a promise of (something): *The new owner promised improvements that never took place.* **3.** to give reason to expect or anticipate (something): *The clear skies promised a nice day.* —*v.i.* to make or give a promise.

Promised Land 1. in the Old Testament, the land of Canaan, promised by God to Abraham and his descendants. **2. promised land.** any place where final happiness is hoped or expected to be found.

prom·is·ing (prom′i sing) *adj.* showing promise for the future: *The young man's sharp wit made him one of the most promising new playwrights.* —**prom′is·ing·ly,** *adv.*

prom·is·so·ry (prom′i sôr′ē) *adj.* containing or conveying a promise: *a promissory pact.*

promissory note, a written promise to pay a particular sum of money to a certain party at a specified future time or on demand.

prom·on·to·ry (prom′ən tôr′ē) *n. pl.,* **prom·on·to·ries.** a raised portion of land extending out into a body of water.

pro·mote (prə mōt′) *v.t.,* **pro·mot·ed, pro·mot·ing. 1.** to raise in rank, position, or honor: *The private was promoted to the rank of corporal.* **2.** to aid in or contribute to the growth, development, or progress of: *Certain foods promote tooth decay.* **3.** to work for; advocate: *The young senator promoted the passage of the bill.* **4.** to advance (a student) to the next higher grade. **5.** to try to sell, make more popular, or get the necessary money for (a product, business undertaking, or the like), as by advertising.

pro·mot·er (prə mō′tər) *n.* **1.** a person or thing that promotes, advances, or furthers something. **2.** a person who organizes or promotes a business undertaking or commercial enterprise, especially a person who arranges for the presentation of a sports event.

pro·mo·tion (prə mō′shən) *n.* **1.** an advancement in rank, position, honor, or grade. **2.** the furthering of a business undertaking or commercial enterprise. **3.** the act of promoting. —**pro·mo′tion·al,** *adj.*

prompt (prompt) *adj.* **1.** acting or occurring at the proper time; on time; punctual: *Henry is usually prompt in arriving.* **2.** done or given without delay: *This repair shop is known for its prompt service.* **3.** quick to act; ready: *Jane is always prompt to voice some criticism.* —*v.t.* **1.** to move

---

at; āpe; cär; end; mē; it; īce; hot; ōld; fôrk; wood; fo͞ol; oil; out; up; turn; sing; thin; **th**is; hw in white; zh in treasure. The symbol ə stands for the sound of **a** in about, **e** in taken, **i** in pencil, **o** in lemon, and **u** in circus.

to action; incite: *An odd feeling that something was wrong prompted me to return home.* **2.** to give rise to; inspire: *The scandal prompted a Senate investigation.* **3.** to supply (a performer or speaker) with words he has forgotten or a cue he has missed. —**prompt′ly,** *adv.* —**prompt′ness,** *n.*

prompt·er (promp′tər) *n.* a person whose task is to prompt the actors in a theatrical production.

promp·ti·tude (promp′tə tood′, promp′tə tyood′) *n.* the quality of being prompt; promptness.

prom·ul·gate (prom′əl gāt′, prō mul′gāt) *v.t.,* **prom·ul·gat·ed, prom·ul·gat·ing. 1.** to make known or put into effect formally and officially, especially by public declaration; proclaim: *to promulgate a new law.* **2.** to make widespread; spread. —**prom′ul·ga′tion,** *n.* —**prom′ul·ga′tor,** *n.*

pron. 1. pronoun. **2.** pronunciation.

prone (prōn) *adj.* **1.** lying with the face or front downward; prostrate. **2.** naturally inclined; disposed: *She is prone to distrust strangers.* —**prone′ly,** *adv.* —**prone′ness,** *n.*

prong (prông, prong) *n.* **1.** a sharply pointed end of a tool or implement, as of a fork. **2.** any sharply pointed projection, as of an antler.

pronged (prôngd, prongd) *adj.* having prongs.

prong·horn (prông′hôrn′, prong′hôrn′) *n. pl.,* **prong·horns** or **prong·horn.** a cud-chewing animal resembling an antelope, found chiefly on the Rocky Mountain plains, and having slender, pronged horns.

Pronghorn

pro·noun (prō′noun′) *n.* a word used as a substitute for a noun or noun phrase, signifying a person, place, or thing without naming it. *I, you, he, who, what,* and *this* are pronouns.

pro·nounce (prə nouns′) *v.,* **pro·nounced, pro·nounc·ing.** —*v.t.* **1.** to utter (a word or sound). **2.** to utter (a word or sound) in a particular way, especially with a certain accent or according to an accepted standard. **3.** to indicate the correct manner of uttering (a word) with phonetic symbols. **4.** to declare or state, especially officially, formally, or solemnly: *The judge pronounced the man not guilty.* —*v.i.* **1.** to state an opinion, judgment, or decision; make a pronouncement. **2.** to utter or pronounce words. —**pro·nounce′a·ble,** *adj.*

pro·nounced (prə nounst′) *adj.* clearly recognizable; strongly defined; decided.

pro·nounce·ment (prə nouns′mənt) *n.* **1.** a formal or official declaration or statement. **2.** an opinion, judgment, or decision.

pron·to (pron′tō) *adv. Informal.* quickly; promptly.

pro·nun·ci·a·tion (prə nun′sē ā′shən) *n.* **1.** the act or manner of pronouncing words. **2.** an accepted or standard way of pronouncing a word: *There are many words that have more than one pronunciation.* **3.** the phonetic representation of a word, indicating the way it is pronounced.

● There have been considerable changes in the **pronunciation** of the English language from its early forms until the present day. The pronunciation of Old English is very different from Modern English pronunciation. Middle English pronunciation was more like our own, differing mainly in the pronunciation of vowels and in the sounding of vowels and consonants which in Modern English are

silent. Because there are obviously no living speakers of these early forms of our language, language scholars must draw their conclusions about early pronunciation by studying Middle English spelling and rhymes, statements made by writers of the period, and old books about foreign languages, in which foreign sounds are given English equivalents. By using this evidence, scholars have found that there were basic changes in English pronunciation in the fifteenth and sixteenth centuries. The changes that took place during these years, which mark the difference in pronunciation between the Middle English of Geoffrey Chaucer and the Elizabethan English of William Shakespeare, are often called the *Great Vowel Shift.* Although many of the Elizabethan vowel sounds are not the same as modern vowel sounds, they are closer to them than the Middle English vowel sounds were. For example, the Modern English words *bite, about, beet, boot, beat, boat,* and *abate* were pronounced in Middle English as *beet, aboot, bait, boat, bet, bought,* and *abaht.* In Shakespeare's time the vowel sounds had changed so that these words were pronounced *bait, aboat, beet, boot, bate, bote,* and *abet.* The sound of a vowel coming before the letter *r* also changed at this time, so that the Middle English word *derke* was pronounced *dark.* A few Modern English words, such as *Derby* and *clerk,* are pronounced in Great Britain with the *e* sounding like the *a* in *farm,* although Americans do not pronounce them in this way. In Chaucer's time, many letters, such as the *e* in *made* and the *ed* in *named,* were pronounced that are silent in later forms of English. The *l* in *should* and *would,* the *k* before *n* in such words as *knee* and *knight,* and the *g* before *n* in such words as *gnaw,* are other examples of sounds that were once pronounced but are now silent.

The pronunciation of English has been changed by distance as well as time. American English, which has its roots in the English spoken by seventeenth century settlers, is pronounced in a different way from British English. Because the English settlers in America came from various parts of Britain, and later settlers came from all over the world, the pronunciation of American English varies from one part of our country to another. These differences, although noticeable, are small enough so that it is rarely difficult for a person from one part of the United States to communicate with a person from another part.

The many regional pronunciations of American English are all correct and acceptable. In this dictionary you will find more than one pronunciation listed for many words, such as *apricot* and *tomato.* Each of these pronunciations is equally correct. The pronunciation key, which is at the bottom of each right-hand page, will show you how a sound is pronounced in a common word that you know. These common words, such as *at, end,* and *old,* are pronounced differently in different parts of our country. Therefore, the pronunciation key is intended to enable you to pronounce any word in this book according to your own accent, not to make you change your way of speaking to fit a different accent.

Although there is no such thing as a theoretically "correct" way of saying a word, the speakers of a particular language all pronounce its words in a basically similar way. The reason for this is that people use language to communicate, and, if there were too much variation in the way different people pronounced the same word, they would have great difficulty in understanding one another.

proof (proof) *n.* **1.** evidence that establishes a fact or shows something to be true: *The lawyer had proof of his client's innocence.* **2.** a test or trial, as of the truth, quality, or strength of something. **3.** establishment of the truth or validity of something; conclusive demonstration: *The philosopher used simple logic in the proof of his statement.* **4.** the standard alcoholic content and strength of a liquor. **5.** strength with reference to this standard. **6.** *Printing.* a trial impression taken from type, blocks, or plates for the purpose of checking and making corrections or changes before printing. **7.** *Etching and Engraving.* a trial impression taken from an engraved stone, plate, or block for the purpose of examination. **8.** *Photography.* a trial print from a photographic negative.

-proof *combining form* **1.** impervious or resistant to: *waterproof, fireproof.* **2.** safe from; protected against: *foolproof.*

proof·read (prōōf′rēd′) *v.t.,* **proof·read** (prōōf′red′), **proof·read·ing.** to read (written or printed material) for the purpose of finding and correcting errors. —**proof′-read′er,** *n.*

prop¹ (prop) *v.t.,* **propped, prop·ping. 1.** to support, hold up, or hold in place by placing something under or against: *The man propped up the sagging roof with some pieces of lumber.* **2.** to sustain; support; bolster: *The coach propped up the team's spirit after they lost the game.* —*n.* **1.** something that serves to prop up an object or hold something in place; support. **2.** a person or thing that props or sustains. [Possibly from Middle Dutch *proppe* a support.]

prop² (prop) *n.* see **property** *(def. 5).*

prop³ (prop) *n. Informal.* propeller.

prop·a·gan·da (prop′ə gan′də) *n.* **1.** a body of doctrines, ideas, or attitudes of a particular group promoted or spread, often in a distorted or biased form, in order to influence the point of view of others, gain supporters, or damage an opposing group. **2.** the systematic promotion or spreading of such doctrines, ideas, or attitudes.

prop·a·gan·dist (prop′ə gan′dist) *n.* a person who spreads propaganda. —*adj.* of, like, or relating to propaganda.

prop·a·gan·dize (prop′ə gan′dīz) *v.,* **prop·a·gan·dized, prop·a·gan·diz·ing.** —*v.t.* **1.** to spread by means of propaganda. **2.** to subject to propaganda. —*v.i.* to spread or carry on propaganda.

prop·a·gate (prop′ə gāt′) *v.,* **prop·a·gat·ed, prop·a·gat·ing.** —*v.i.* to multiply by reproduction; breed. —*v.t.* **1.** to cause (animals or plants) to reproduce; breed or raise. **2.** to spread or transmit from person to person, as information; disseminate: *to propagate false rumors.*

pro·pane (prō′pān) *n.* a colorless gas found in petroleum and natural gas, widely used as a heating fuel.

pro·pel (prə pel′) *v.t.,* **pro·pelled, pro·pel·ling. 1.** to cause to move forward or onward; put or keep in motion: *to propel an aircraft by jet engines.* **2.** to urge onward: *The explorer was propelled by a desire for fame.*

pro·pel·lant (prə pel′ənt) *also,* **pro·pel·lent.** *n.* a propelling agent or substance, especially a fuel for propelling a rocket.

pro·pel·lent (prə pel′ənt) *adj.* propelling or capable of propelling. —*n.* another spelling of **propellant.**

pro·pel·ler (prə pel′ər) *n.* a device consisting of a hub with blades mounted at an angle. When the hub revolves, the action of the blades creates a driving force that can be used to propel a boat or aircraft.

pro·pen·si·ty (prə pen′sə tē) *n. pl.,* **pro·pen·si·ties.** a natural tendency; inclination: *She has a propensity for overeating.*

prop·er (prop′ər) *adj.* **1.** suitable, appropriate, or correct for a given purpose: *To do good work, a carpenter must have the proper tools.* **2.** conforming to a particular or the accepted standard: *The visiting dignitary was given a proper reception.* **3.** strictly formal, neat, or respectable; prim. **4.** understood or considered in a precise or strict sense:

That area is not really part of the city proper. **5.** *Grammar.* referring to or derived from a particular person, place, or thing.

proper fraction, a fraction in which the numerator is less than the denominator, such as ⅝ or ⅔.

prop·er·ly (prop′ər lē) *adv.* **1.** in a suitable, appropriate, or correct manner: *We were not properly equipped for a fishing trip.* **2.** in accordance with a particular or accepted standard: *to be properly married.* **3.** with precision or accuracy; exactly; strictly: *Properly speaking, that book is not a novel.*

proper noun, a noun that names a particular person, place, or thing and, in English, is always capitalized when written. For example, *Elizabeth, Geneva,* and *Saturday* are proper nouns.

proper subset, a set that contains fewer members than the set of which it is a subset. The proper subsets of the set [a,b] are [a], [b], and [0].

prop·er·ty (prop′ər tē) *n. pl.,* **prop·er·ties. 1.** something that is owned by someone; possession: *The statue was considered town property.* **2.** a piece of real estate: *My uncle purchased some property in Florida.* **3.** the right to the possession, use, or disposal of a thing or things; ownership. **4.** a special attribute or quality of a person or thing: *A resistance to heat is one of the properties of this metal.* **5.** any movable article, except scenery and costumes, used on the set of a theatrical production; prop.

proph·e·cy (prof′ə sē) *n. pl.,* **proph·e·cies. 1.** the act of telling beforehand what is to come; foretelling of the future. **2.** something that is foretold; prediction. **3.** a divinely inspired utterance or revelation. **4.** the power or ability to foretell the future.

proph·e·sy (prof′ə sī′) *v.,* **proph·e·sied, proph·e·sy·ing.** —*v.t.* to tell beforehand (what is to come); foretell; predict: *The seer prophesied that the king would have a long and prosperous reign.* —*v.i.* **1.** to foretell the future; make predictions. **2.** to speak as a prophet.

proph·et (prof′it) *n.* **1.** a person who speaks or claims to speak by divine inspiration or as the interpreter of divine will, especially a religious leader professing or considered to be divinely inspired. **2.** a person who foretells the future. **3.** a spokesman, as for a cause or movement. **4.** the **Prophet.** another name for **Muhammad. 5.** the **Prophets.** those books of the Old Testament either written by prophets or composed mainly of prophecies. —**proph′et·ess,** *n.*

pro·phet·ic (prə fet′ik) *adj.* **1.** containing or of the nature of prophecy: *prophetic words.* **2.** of, relating to, or belonging to a prophet. —**pro·phet′i·cal·ly,** *adv.*

pro·phy·lac·tic (prō′fi lak′tik) *adj.* serving to protect against or prevent something, especially disease. —*n.* a prophylactic device, medicine, or treatment.

pro·pin·qui·ty (prō ping′kwə tē) *n.* **1.** nearness in time or place; proximity. **2.** nearness of relation; kinship.

pro·pi·ti·ate (prə pish′ē āt′) *v.t.,* **pro·pi·ti·at·ed, pro·pi·ti·at·ing.** to win over (someone, especially someone who has been offended); appease; conciliate. —**pro·pi′ti·a′tion,** *n.*

pro·pi·tious (prə pish′əs) *adj.* favorable or suitable; opportune: *It appeared to be a propitious time for our voyage.* —**pro·pi′tious·ly,** *adv.* —**pro·pi′tious·ness,** *n.*

---

at; āpe; cär; end; mē; it; īce; hot; ōld; fôrk; wood; fōōl; oil; out; up; turn; sing; thin; **th**is; hw in white; zh in treasure. The symbol ə stands for the sound of **a** in about, **e** in taken, **i** in pencil, **o** in lemon, and **u** in circus.

pro·po·nent (prə pō′nənt) *n.* **1.** a person who favors or supports something; advocate: *The senator is a leading proponent of the new tax-reform program.* **2.** a person who proposes or propounds something.

pro·por·tion (prə pôr′shən) *n.* **1.** the relation of one thing to another with respect to size, number, amount, or degree; ratio: *the proportion of men to women in a profession.* **2.** a proper or balanced relation, as between parts; harmony; symmetry: *The length and height of the room were in proportion.* **3.** a part or share: *A proportion of the profits was given to each partner in the company.* **4. proportions.** dimensions: *the proportions of a room.* **5.** the relation between two ratios in which the first of four quantities divided by the second is equal to the third divided by the fourth. For example: 8 is to 4 as 6 is to 3. —*v.t.* **1.** to cause to be in a proper or balanced relation: *The architect proportioned the width of the building to its height.* **2.** to form the parts of (a whole) so as to be in a proper or balanced relation: *to proportion a sculpture.*

pro·por·tion·al (prə pôr′shən əl) *adj.* **1.** in or having proportion. **2.** of, relating to, or based on proportion; relative: *a proportional scale of measurements.* **3.** *Mathematics.* having the same or a constant ratio. —**pro·por·tion·al·ly,** *adv.*

pro·por·tion·ate (prə pôr′shə nit) *adj.* in proper proportion; proportional. —**pro·por′tion·ate·ly,** *adv.*

pro·pos·al (prə pō′zəl) *n.* **1.** something put forward for consideration, discussion, or acceptance, as a plan or a course of action: *The committee voted in favor of the chairman's proposal.* **2.** an offer of marriage. **3.** the act of proposing.

pro·pose (prə pōz′) *v.,* **pro·posed, pro·pos·ing.** —*v.t.* **1.** to put forward for consideration, discussion, or acceptance: *The mayor proposed a new plan for settling the strike.* **2.** to suggest or present (someone), as for a position or office. **3.** to intend; plan: *The general proposes to attack the city at dawn.* **4.** to suggest (a toast). —*v.i.* to make an offer of marriage.

prop·o·si·tion (prop′ə zish′ən) *n.* **1.** something that is proposed for consideration, discussion, or acceptance; proposal, offer, or suggestion: *The company rejected the man's business proposition.* **2.** *Informal.* matter, undertaking, or situation: *Finding a buyer for this old car is not an easy proposition.* **3.** a statement or subject to be discussed: *The two teams prepared to debate the given proposition.* **4.** *Mathematics.* a statement of a theorem to be demonstrated or a problem to be solved. **5.** *Informal.* a thought, idea, or possibility: *The proposition of studying all night made me quite unhappy.* —*v.t.* to make a proposal or offer to.

pro·pound (prə pound′) *v.t.* to put forward for consideration; set forth; propose: *The scientist propounded a new theory.* —**pro·pound′er,** *n.*

pro·pri·e·tar·y (prə prī′ə ter′ē) *adj.* **1.** of, relating to, or characteristic of a proprietor or proprietors. **2.** made and sold by exclusive legal right, as a medicine. **3.** privately owned and operated: *a proprietary hospital.* —*n. pl.,* **pro·pri·e·tar·ies.** **1.** another word for **proprietor. 2.** a group of proprietors. **3.** a proprietary medicine.

pro·pri·e·tor (prə prī′ə tər) *n.* **1.** a person who has legal title or right to something, especially property; owner. **2.** an owner or operator of a small business establishment.

pro·pri·e·ty (prə prī′ə tē) *n. pl.,* **pro·pri·e·ties. 1.** the quality of being proper or suitable; suitability. **2.** conformity with what is proper, especially with socially approved standards of manners and conduct.

pro·pul·sion (prə pul′shən) *n.* **1.** the act or process of driving forward or propelling. **2.** something that propels.

pro·rate (prō rāt′, prō′rāt′) *v.t.,* **pro·rat·ed, pro·rat·ing.**

to divide proportionately: *The three friends prorated the expenses for their party.*

pro·sa·ic (prō zā′ik) *adj.* **1.** lacking in uniqueness, freshness, or imagination; unimaginative; commonplace; ordinary: *a prosaic subject, a prosaic person.* **2.** of or like prose. —**pro·sa′i·cal·ly,** *adv.* —**pro·sa′ic·ness,** *n.*

pro·sce·ni·um (prō sē′nē əm) *n. pl.,* **pro·sce·ni·a** (prō-sē′nē ə). **1.** the part of the stage in front of the curtain. **2.** the structure, usually arched, that frames the stage opening. Also, **proscenium arch. 3.** the entire stage in an ancient theater.

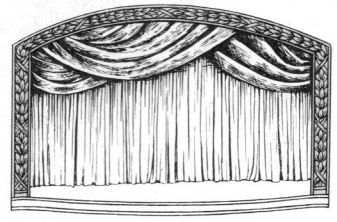

Proscenium

pro·scribe (prō skrīb′) *v.t.,* **pro·scribed, pro·scrib·ing. 1.** to prohibit or condemn (something); forbid. **2.** to outlaw (someone); banish. —**pro·scrib′er,** *n.*

prose (prōz) *n.* everyday written or spoken language that is not like poetry. —*adj.* of, relating to, or written in prose: *a prose narrative.*

pros·e·cute (pros′ə kyōōt′) *v.,* **pros·e·cut·ed, pros·e·cut·ing.** —*v.t.* **1.** to begin and carry on a legal action against (a person, corporation, or institution) in a court of law: *to prosecute someone for theft.* **2.** to seek to obtain or enforce by legal means: *to prosecute a claim for damages.* **3.** to carry out (something), especially to completion: *to prosecute an investigation.* —*v.i.* **1.** to begin and carry on a legal action in a court of law. **2.** to act as prosecutor. ▲ See **persecute** for usage note.

pros·e·cu·tion (pros′ə kyōō′shən) *n.* **1.** the act or process of beginning and carrying on a legal action in a court of law. **2.** the person or group conducting this. **3.** the act of prosecuting.

pros·e·cu·tor (pros′ə kyōō′tər) *n.* **1.** an attorney who represents the government in criminal prosecutions. **2.** a person who begins and carries on a legal action against another.

pros·e·lyte (pros′ə līt′) *n.* a person who has recently been persuaded to accept a faith or doctrine, especially a new convert to a religion. —*v.t., v.i.,* **pros·e·lyt·ed, pros·e·lyt·ing.** to proselytize.

pros·e·lyt·ize (pros′ə li tīz′) *v.t., v.i.,* **pros·e·lyt·ized, pros·e·lyt·iz·ing.** to convert or attempt to convert from one faith or doctrine to another.

Pro·ser·pi·na (prō sur′pə nə) also, **Pro·ser·pi·ne** (prō-sur′pə nē). *n. Roman Mythology.* the daughter of Jupiter and Ceres, who was carried off by Pluto, who made her queen of the underworld. She was allowed to revisit the earth for part of each year, and her return was accompanied by the coming of spring. In Greek mythology she was called Persephone.

pros·o·dy (pros′ə dē) *n. pl.,* **pros·o·dies. 1.** the study or science of poetic form. **2.** a particular system of poetic form.

pros·pect (pros′pekt) *n.* **1.** something looked forward to or expected: *Herb was excited by the prospect of owning his own boat.* **2.** *usually,* **prospects.** a chance for future success. **3.** a person who shows promise of some kind, such as a possible customer or winner in a political or athletic contest. **4.** a scene presented to the eye; view. —*v.i.* to search or explore: *to prospect for gold.* —*v.t.* to explore (a region): *to prospect an area for minerals.*

pro·spec·tive (prə spek′tiv) *adj.* **1.** possible or expected; future: *a prospective buyer, a prospective bride.* **2.** of, relating to, or in the future. —**pro·spec′tive·ly,** *adv.*

pros·pec·tor (pros′pek tər, prə spek′tər) *n.* a person who explores an area for minerals, such as gold.

pro·spec·tus (prə spek′təs) *n.* *pl.*, **pro·spec·tus·es.** a printed statement describing something, such as a proposed undertaking or work.

pros·per (pros′pər) *v.i.* to be prosperous; flourish.

pros·per·i·ty (pros per′ə tē) *n.* the state or condition of being prosperous.

pros·per·ous (pros′pər əs) *adj.* having success, wealth, or good fortune; flourishing: *a prosperous town, a prosperous man.* **—pros′per·ous·ly,** *adv.* **—pros′per·ous·ness,** *n.*

pros·tate (pros′tāt) *n.* a chestnut-shaped gland present in male mammals, lying below the bladder and surrounding the urethra. Also, **prostate gland.** **—adj.** of, relating to, or affecting this gland.

pros·ti·tute (pros′tə tōōt′, pros′tə tyōōt′) *n.* a person who engages in sexual acts for money. **—v.t.,** **pros·ti·tut·ed, pros·ti·tut·ing. 1.** to sell (oneself or another) for sexual purposes. **2.** to put (oneself or one's abilities) to an unworthy use, especially for money: *The great novelist prostituted his talent by writing books in praise of the cruel dictator.*

pros·ti·tu·tion (pros′tə tōō′shən, pros′tə tyōō′shən) *n.* **1.** the act or practice of engaging in sexual acts for money. **2.** the act of putting oneself or one's abilities to an unworthy use.

pros·trate (pros′trāt) *v.t.,* **pros·trat·ed, pros·trat·ing. 1.** to lay or throw (oneself) face downward on the ground, as in humility or submission. **2.** to lay or throw down on the ground; flatten. **3.** to weaken or make helpless: *The disease prostrated him.* **—adj. 1.** lying face downward on the ground. **2.** lying or thrown down. **3.** completely exhausted, helpless, or overcome: *The country was left prostrate by war.*

pros·tra·tion (pros trā′shən) *n.* **1.** the act of prostrating or the state of being prostrated. **2.** extreme exhaustion.

Prot., Protestant.

prot·ac·tin·i·um (prō′tak tin′ē əm) *n.* a rare radioactive metallic element. Symbol: **Pa**

pro·tag·o·nist (prō tag′ə nist) *n.* the leading character in a novel, play, or other work of literature.

pro·te·an (prō′tē ən) *adj.* taking different shapes or forms readily; variable. [From *Proteus.*]

pro·tect (prə tekt′) *v.t.* to defend or keep from harm: *A football player wears a helmet to protect his head.* **—pro·tect′ing·ly,** *adv.*

pro·tec·tion (prə tek′shən) *n.* **1.** the act of protecting or the state of being protected. **2.** a person or thing that protects.

pro·tec·tive (prə tek′tiv) *adj.* protecting or intended to protect: *A turtle has a protective shell.* **—pro·tec′tive·ly,** *adv.* **—pro·tec′tive·ness,** *n.*

protective coloration, the natural coloring of certain animals that allows them to match their natural surroundings and thus escape the notice of their enemies. Also, **protective coloring.**

pro·tec·tor (prə tek′tər) *n.* a person or thing that protects; guardian; defender: *In Greek mythology, a fierce dragon was the protector of the Golden Fleece.*

pro·tec·tor·ate (prə tek′tər it) *n.* **1.** a weak country that is protected and controlled by a strong country. **2.** the relationship between two such countries.

pro·té·gé (prō′tə zhā′) *n.* a person who is under the care, guidance, or patronage of an influential or prominent person.

pro·tein (prō′tēn) *n.* any of a large group of organic compounds that contain nitrogen, carbon, hydrogen, and oxygen, and are present in all living cells.

pro tem (prō tem′) see **pro tempore.**

pro tem·po·re (prō tem′pər ē) *Latin.* for the time being; temporarily.

Prot·er·o·zo·ic (prō′tər ə zō′ik) *n.* a geological division of the Precambrian era, during which the earliest animals appeared, and algae and bacteria were the only forms of plant life. **—adj.** of, relating to, or characteristic of the Proterozoic.

pro·test (*n.*, prō′test; *v.*, prə test′) *n.* **1.** an expression of disapproval or objection: *The demonstration was a protest against the proposed new highway.* **2.** a formal objection, especially one made in writing. **—v.i.** to express disapproval or objection: *The students protested against the closing of the library on weekends.* **—v.t. 1.** to express disapproval of; object to: *He protested the cut in his allowance.* **2.** to declare earnestly; assert: *The accused girl protested that she knew nothing about the missing jewels.* **—pro′test·er,** *n.*

Prot·es·tant (prot′is tənt) *n.* a Christian who does not belong to the Roman Catholic Church or the Orthodox Church. **—adj.** of or relating to Protestants or Protestantism.

Protestant Episcopal Church, a church in the United States that agrees in doctrine, beliefs, and practices with the Church of England.

Prot·es·tant·ism (prot′is tən tiz′əm) *n.* **1.** the doctrines, beliefs, and practices of Protestants. **2.** Protestants or the Protestant churches as a group.

prot·es·ta·tion (prot′is tā′shən, prō′tes tā′shən) *n.* **1.** the act of protesting. **2.** an earnest declaration: *protestations of loyalty.* **3.** an expression of disapproval or objection; protest: *A group of senators filibustered as a protestation against the bill.*

Pro·te·us (prō′tē əs) *n. Greek Mythology.* a sea god who could assume many different shapes.

proto- *combining form* first in time; earliest; original: *protozoan, prototype.*

pro·to·col (prō′tə kôl′, prō′tə kol′) *n.* **1.** the customs and rules of polite behavior and order of rank observed by diplomats; diplomatic etiquette. **2.** the original copy of a treaty or other document.

pro·ton (prō′ton) *n.* a particle found in the nucleus of all atoms, having a positive electric charge equal to the negative charge of an electron. The atomic number of an atom is equal to the number of protons in its nucleus.

pro·to·plasm (prō′tə plaz′əm) *n.* a substance somewhat like jelly that is the living matter of every plant and animal cell. It consists of water, proteins, sugars, fats, acids, and salts.

pro·to·type (prō′tə tīp′) *n.* **1.** the original or model from which something is derived or on which something is based: *the prototype of a new automobile engine.* **2.** the first, early, or typical example: *Sir Lancelot is a prototype of the romantic hero.*

pro·to·zo·an (prō′tə zō′ən) *n.* any of a large group of single-celled microscopic animals, such as the ameba. **—adj.** of or relating to protozoans. [Modern Latin *Protozoa* this group of animals, from Greek *prōtos* first + *zōia* animals.]

pro·tract (prō trakt′) *v.t.* to lengthen in time; prolong: *to protract a speech.* **—pro·trac′tion,** *n.*

at; āpe; cär; end; mē; it; īce; hot; ōld; fôrk; wood; fōōl; oil; out; up; turn; sing; thin; this; hw in white; zh in treasure. The symbol ə stands for the sound of **a** in about, **e** in taken, **i** in pencil, **o** in lemon, and **u** in circus.

pro·trac·tor (prō trak′tər) *n.* an instrument in the form of a semicircle marked off in degrees, used for measuring or drawing angles.

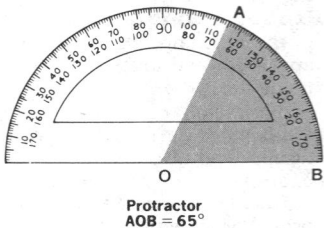

Protractor
AOB = 65°

pro·trude (prō trōōd′) *v.*, **pro·trud·ed, pro·trud·ing.** —*v.i.* to stick out; project: *Rocks protruded from the snow.* —*v.t.* to cause to stick out: *The snail protruded its horns.*

pro·tru·sion (prō trōō′zhən) *n.* **1.** the act of protruding or the state of being protruded. **2.** something that protrudes.

pro·tu·ber·ance (prō tōō′bər əns, prō tyōō′bər əns) *n.* **1.** something that sticks out, as a swelling or bulge. **2.** the state or condition of being protuberant.

pro·tu·ber·ant (prō tōō′bər ənt, prō tyōō′bər ənt) *adj.* sticking out; bulging. —**pro·tu′ber·ant·ly,** *adv.*

proud (proud) *adj.* **1.** taking great personal satisfaction in something or someone: *The boy was proud of his father's achievements.* **2.** having a sense of one's personal worth or dignity: *She was too proud to ask her friends for money.* **3.** having too high an opinion of oneself; conceited; haughty: *He was too proud to admit his mistake.* **4.** causing pleasure or satisfaction: *Winning the award was Ann's proudest moment.* **5.** arising from or caused by pride: *The matador had a proud, haughty look.* —**proud′ly,** *adv.*

Proust, Mar·cel (prōost; mar sel′) 1871–1922, French novelist.

prov., province; provincial.

prove (prōōv) *v.*, **proved, proved** or **prov·en** (prōō′vən), **prov·ing.** —*v.t.* **1.** to show the truth or genuineness of: *The lawyer proved the innocence of his client.* **2.** to show the merits or worth of: *to prove oneself.* **3.** to test the qualities of: *to prove a new rifle.* —*v.i.* to turn out: *The play proved to be very enjoyable.* —**prov′a·ble,** *adj.*

Pro·ven·çal (prō′vən säl′) *n.* **1.** a person who was born or is living in Provence. **2.** the language of Provence. —*adj.* of or relating to Provence, its people, or their language.

Pro·vence (prō väns′) *n.* a historic region and former province in southeastern France, bordering the Mediterranean Sea.

prov·en·der (prov′ən dər) *n.* dry food for livestock.

prov·erb (prov′ərb) *n.* a short, popular saying that expresses a truth. For example: *He who hesitates is lost.*

pro·ver·bi·al (prə vur′bē əl) *adj.* **1.** of, relating to, expressed in, or characteristic of a proverb: *proverbial wisdom.* **2.** commonly spoken of; well-known: *the proverbial courage of American pioneers.* —**pro·ver′bi·al·ly,** *adv.*

Prov·erbs (prov′ərbz) *n., pl.* a book of the Old Testament containing practical advice and moral instruction.

pro·vide (prə vīd′) *v.*, **pro·vid·ed, pro·vid·ing.** —*v.t.* **1.** to give what is needed or desired; supply; furnish: *Tim's parents provided him with equipment for the camping trip.* **2.** to give or yield: *Trees provide shelter from the sun.* **3.** to set as a condition; stipulate: *The law provides that a person is innocent until proven guilty.* —*v.i.* **1.** to make preparation for a future need: *to provide for one's old age.* **2.** to take care of present needs: *He provided for his family by working in a factory.* —**pro·vid′er,** *n.*

pro·vid·ed (prə vī′did) *conj.* on the condition that; if: *I'll lend you the book, provided you return it next week.*

prov·i·dence (prov′ə dəns) *n.* **1.** God's care or guidance. **2.** a regard for the future. **3. Providence.** God.

Prov·i·dence (prov′ə dəns) *n.* the capital of Rhode Island, in the eastern part of the state. Pop. (1970), 179,213.

prov·i·dent (prov′ə dənt) *adj.* **1.** having a regard for the future; showing foresight. **2.** economical; thrifty. —**prov′i·dent·ly,** *adv.*

prov·i·den·tial (prov′ə den′shəl) *adj.* **1.** of, relating to, or proceeding from divine providence. **2.** coming about as if through divine intervention; fortunate: *A providential rain put out the forest fire.* —**prov′i·den′tial·ly,** *adv.*

pro·vid·ing (prə vī′ding) *conj.* provided; if.

prov·ince (prov′ins) *n.* **1.** a political division of a country. Canada is divided into ten provinces that are similar to the states of the United States. **2.** a range or sphere of activity or authority: *Judging the legality of this law is only within the province of the Supreme Court.* **3.** in ancient times, a territory outside Italy ruled by Rome. **4. the provinces.** regions of a country outside the capital or cultural center.

pro·vin·cial (prə vin′shəl) *adj.* **1.** of or relating to a province: *a provincial government.* **2.** characteristic of the inhabitants of a rural province; unsophisticated or unfashionable: *provincial manners.* **3.** having or showing a limited point of view; narrow-minded: *provincial attitudes.* —*n.* **1.** a person who was born or is living in a province. **2.** a narrow-minded person. —**pro·vin′cial·ly,** *adv.*

pro·vin·cial·ism (prə vin′shə liz′əm) *n.* **1.** the state or quality of being provincial, especially in manner, speech, or point of view. **2.** something that is provincial, such as a particular word, expression, or pronunciation.

pro·vi·sion (prə vizh′ən) *n.* **1.** the act of giving or supplying: *The coach supervised the provision of equipment to the players.* **2.** preparation for a future or possible need: *The man had made little provision for his retirement.* **3.** something that is specified as a condition; stipulation: *A provision in the labor agreement called for a pay increase.* **4. provisions.** a supply of food: *The ship had provisions for three weeks.* —*v.t.* to supply with provisions.

pro·vi·sion·al (prə vizh′ən əl) *adj.* for the time being; temporary: *A provisional government ruled the country until elections could be held.* —**pro·vi′sion·al·ly,** *adv.*

pro·vi·so (prə vī′zō) *n. pl.*, **pro·vi·sos** or **pro·vi·soes.** a statement that makes a condition; stipulation: *a proviso in a contract.*

prov·o·ca·tion (prov′ə kā′shən) *n.* **1.** the act of provoking. **2.** something that angers or incites: *Henry often loses his temper without provocation.*

pro·voc·a·tive (prə vok′ə tiv) *adj.* tending to provoke, especially by arousing anger, interest, or desire: *a provocative newspaper editorial.* —**pro·voc′a·tive·ly,** *adv.* —**pro·voc′a·tive·ness,** *n.*

pro·voke (prə vōk′) *v.t.*, **pro·voked, pro·vok·ing.** **1.** to make angry; irritate greatly: *The insulting remark provoked her.* **2.** to stir up (a person); excite: *His rudeness provoked her to anger.* **3.** to cause by inciting; bring about deliberately: *to provoke a fight, to provoke an argument.* **4.** to call forth or bring out; arouse: *to provoke interest, to provoke thought.* —**pro·vok′ing·ly,** *adv.*

prov·ost (prō′vōst) *n.* **1.** a high administrative official in certain colleges or universities. **2.** the chief magistrate of a Scottish town or city. **3.** the head of a cathedral.

prow (prou) *n.* **1.** the forward part of a boat or ship; bow. **2.** something like the prow of a ship, such as the front end of an airplane.

prow·ess (prou′is) *n.* **1.** great bravery or daring, especially in battle. **2.** great ability or skill: *athletic prowess.*

prowl (proul) *v.i.* to move about quietly and secretly, as in search of prey: *The tiger prowled through the jungle.* —*v.t.* to move or roam over or through: *The gang prowled the streets at night.* —*n.* the act of prowling. —**prowl′er,** *n.*

prowl car, another term for **squad car.**

prox·im·i·ty (prok sim′ə tē) *n.* nearness; closeness: *My parents bought this house because of its proximity to the school.*

prox·y (prok′sē) *n. pl.,* **prox·ies. 1.** a person authorized to act for another; substitute. **2.** the act or instance of authorizing such a person: *to vote by proxy.* **3.** a document authorizing a person to act for another.

prude (prōōd) *n.* a person who is too modest or proper in behavior, dress, and speech.

pru·dence (prōōd′əns) *n.* **1.** the quality of being prudent; good judgment. **2.** careful management; economy.

pru·dent (prōōd′ənt) *adj.* **1.** having or showing good judgment or caution; wise; sensible: *a prudent man, a prudent act.* **2.** showing careful management; economical; frugal: *a prudent use of one's money.* —**pru′dent·ly,** *adv.*

pru·den·tial (prōō den′shəl) *adj.* characterized by or using good judgment or caution. —**pru·den′tial·ly,** *adv.*

prud·er·y (prōō′dər ē) *n. pl.,* **prud·er·ies. 1.** extreme modesty. **2.** a prudish act or behavior.

prud·ish (prōō′dish) *adj.* very modest or proper. —**prud′ish·ly,** *adv.* —**prud′ish·ness,** *n.*

prune¹ (prōōn) *n.* a dried plum. [Old French *prune.*]

prune² (prōōn) *v.t.,* **pruned, prun·ing. 1.** to cut off (branches, twigs, or roots). **2.** to cut off unwanted branches, twigs, or roots from (a plant), usually to improve growth or appearance. **3.** to remove unnecessary or unwanted parts from: *The writer pruned his story.* [Old French *proignier* to trim (vines).] —**prun′er,** *n.*

pru·ri·ent (proor′ē ənt) *adj.* characterized by or having indecent thoughts. —**pru′ri·ent·ly,** *adv.*

Prus·sia (prush′ə) *n.* a former state in northern Germany, formally dissolved in 1947 and divided among East and West Germany, Poland, and the Soviet Union. —**Prus′sian,** *adj., n.*

prus·sic acid (prus′ik) another term for **hydrocyanic acid.**

pry¹ (prī) *v.i.,* **pried, pry·ing.** to look closely or curiously: *to pry into another person's affairs.* [Of uncertain origin.]

pry² (prī) *v.t.,* **pried, pry·ing. 1.** to move, raise, or pull by force, as with a lever: *to pry off the top of a box.* **2.** to get with much effort: *to pry information from someone.* —*n. pl.,* **pries.** anything used as a lever for prying, such as a crowbar. [From *prize* a lever, which was mistaken for a plural form of the singular word *pry.*]

pry·ing (prī′ing) *adj.* too curious: *a prying old woman.* —**pry′ing·ly,** *adv.*

Ps., Psalm; Psalms.

P.S. 1. postscript. **2.** public school.

psalm (säm) *n.* **1.** a sacred poem, song, or hymn. **2. Psalm.** any one of the sacred lyric poems that form the Book of Psalms in the Old Testament.

psalm·ist (sä′mist) *n.* a writer or composer of psalms.

Psalms (sämz) *n., pl.* a book of sacred, lyric poetry in the Old Testament. ▲ used with a singular verb.

Psal·ter (sôl′tər) *n.* **1.** the Book of Psalms. **2.** a version of all or part of the Psalms arranged for liturgical or devotional use.

psal·ter·y (sôl′tər ē) *n. pl.,* **psal·ter·ies.** an ancient musical instrument played by plucking its strings.

pseu·do (sōō′dō) *adj.* false; pretended: *a pseudo intellectual.*

pseudo- *combining form* false; pretended: *pseudonym.*

pseu·do·nym (sōōd′ən im) *n.* a fictitious name, especially one used by an author as a pen name: *The novelist wrote books under his real name as well as under a pseudonym.*

pseu·do·pod (sōō′də pod′) *n.* a temporary, tongue-shaped projection sent out from an ameba as a means of moving about and taking in food.

pshaw (shô) *interj.* used to express scorn, impatience, or disapproval.

psit·ta·co·sis (sit′ə kō′sis) *n.* an infectious disease of certain birds, especially parrots, that can be transmitted to man, in whom it produces a form of pneumonia.

pso·ri·a·sis (sə rī′ə sis) *n.* a chronic skin disease characterized by scaly, reddish patches on the skin.

PST, Pacific Standard Time.

Psy·che (sī′kē) *n. Greek and Roman Mythology.* a beautiful princess who fell in love with Eros. She was considered the personification of the human soul.

psy·che (sī′kē) *n.* the human soul or mind. [From *Psyche.*]

psy·che·del·ic (sī′kə del′ik) *adj.* of, characterized by, or causing hallucinations or a state like a trance: *a psychedelic drug.*

psy·chi·at·ric (sī′kē at′rik) *adj.* of or relating to psychiatry. Also, **psy·chi·at·ri·cal** (sī kē at′ri kəl). —**psy′chi·at′ri·cal·ly,** *adv.*

psy·chi·a·trist (si kī′ə trist, sī kī′ə trist) *n.* a physician who specializes in the diagnosis and treatment of emotional and mental disorders.

psy·chi·a·try (si kī′ə trē, sī kī′ə trē) *n.* the branch of medicine that deals with the diagnosis and treatment of emotional and mental disorders.

psy·chic (sī′kik) *adj.* **1.** of or relating to the human soul or mind; spiritual or mental. **2.** of, relating to, or caused by supernatural influences or forces, such as telepathy. **3.** sensitive to such influences or forces. Also, **psy·chi·cal** (sī′ki kəl). —*n.* a person who is sensitive to supernatural influences or forces. —**psy′chi·cal·ly,** *adv.*

psycho- *combining form* the mind or mental processes: *psychology.*

psy·cho·a·nal·y·sis (sī′kō ə nal′ə sis) *n.* **1.** a theory of psychology, developed by Sigmund Freud and others, that tries to explore the unconscious mind. **2.** the methods used to explore the unconscious mind and treat emotional and mental disorders.

psy·cho·an·a·lyst (sī′kō an′əl ist) *n.* a person who practices psychoanalysis. Also, **analyst.**

psy·cho·an·a·lyt·ic (sī′kō an′əl it′ik) *adj.* of or relating to psychoanalysis. Also, **psy′cho·an′a·lyt′i·cal.** —**psy′cho·an′a·lyt′i·cal·ly,** *adv.*

psy·cho·an·a·lyze (sī′kō an′əl īz′) *v.t.,* **psy·cho·an·a·lyzed, psy·cho·an·a·lyz·ing.** to treat by psychoanalysis.

psy·cho·log·i·cal (sī′kə loj′i kəl) *adj.* **1.** of or relating to psychology. **2.** of or relating to the mind or mental processes. Also, **psy·cho·log·ic** (sī′kə loj′ik). —**psy′cho·log′i·cal·ly,** *adv.*

psy·chol·o·gist (sī kol′ə jist) *n.* a person who is trained or who specializes in psychology.

psy·chol·o·gy (sī kol′ə jē) *n. pl.,* **psy·chol·o·gies. 1.** the study of the mind and of mental and emotional processes, and of human behavior. **2.** the mental, emotional, or behavioral processes characteristic of a person or group, or relating to an experience: *the psychology of the criminal, the psychology of defeat.*

psy·cho·neu·ro·sis (sī′kō noo rō′sis, sī′kō nyoo rō′sis) *n. pl.,* **psy·cho·neu·ro·ses** (sī′kō noo rō′sēz, sī′kō′nyoo rō′sēz). see **neurosis.**

at; āpe; cär; end; mē; it; īce; hot; ōld; fôrk; wood; fōōl; oil; out; up; turn; sing; thin; this; hw in white; zh in treasure. The symbol ə stands for the sound of a in about, e in taken, i in pencil, o in lemon, and u in circus.

psy·cho·path (sī′kə path′) *n.* a person who is mentally unbalanced, especially a person who behaves in an antisocial or criminal way. —**psy′cho·path′ic,** *adj.*

psy·chop·a·thy (sī kop′ə thē) *n.* a mental disorder.

psy·cho·sis (sī kō′sis) *n. pl.,* **psy·cho·ses** (sī kō′sēz). a severe mental disorder involving loss of contact with reality.

psy·cho·so·mat·ic (sī′kō sə mat′ik) *adj.* **1.** of or relating to the relation between the mind and body. **2.** of or relating to physical symptoms and changes in the body that are the result of emotional or mental conditions: *a psychosomatic illness, the study of psychosomatic medicine.*

psy·cho·ther·a·py (sī′kō ther′ə pē) *n.* the treatment of emotional or mental disorders by psychological means, as by psychoanalysis and group therapy.

psy·chot·ic (sī kot′ik) *n.* a person afflicted with a psychosis. —*adj.* of, relating to, suffering from, or caused by a psychosis. —**psy·chot′i·cal·ly,** *adv.*

Pt, the symbol for platinum.

pt. **1.** part. **2.** payment. **3.** pint. **4.** point.

PTA, Parent-Teacher Association.

ptar·mi·gan (tär′mi gən) *n. pl.,* **ptar·mi·gans** or **ptar·mi·gan.** any of various grouse of northern regions, having brownish feathers and feathered legs and feet.

PT boat, a small, fast, and highly maneuverable boat armed with torpedoes. [Abbreviation of *p*(atrol) *t*(orpedo) boat.]

pter·id·o·phyte (tə rid′ə fīt′) *n.* any of a group of seedless, flowerless plants, such as club mosses or ferns, that reproduce by means of spores.

pter·o·dac·tyl (ter′ə dak′til) *n.* any of a group of extinct flying reptiles, having greatly enlarged fourth fingers supporting featherless, leathery wing membranes.

Pterodactyl

Ptol·e·ma·ic (tol′ə mā′ik) *adj.* **1.** of or relating to the astronomer Ptolemy. **2.** of or relating to the Ptolemies who ruled Egypt.

Ptolemaic System, a theory named for the astronomer Ptolemy. It maintained that the earth is the center of the universe and that the sun, moon, and all the planets move around it.

Ptol·e·my (tol′ə mē) *n.* **1. Claudius.** Greek astronomer, geographer, and mathematician who lived in the second century A.D. **2.** any member of a Greek dynasty that ruled Egypt from 323 B.C. to 30 B.C.

pto·maine (tō′mān) *also,* **pto·main.** *n.* any of various, often poisonous, substances formed by the decay of food.

pty·a·lin (tī′ə lin) *n.* an enzyme in the saliva that converts starch into dextrin and maltose.

Pu, the symbol for plutonium.

pub (pub) *n. Informal.* a tavern or inn. [Short for *public house.*]

pu·ber·ty (pyōō′bər tē) *n.* the age at which a person becomes physically capable of reproducing offspring, occurring at about fourteen for boys and twelve for girls.

pu·bic (pyōō′bik) *adj.* of, relating to, or near the pubis.

pu·bis (pyōō′bis) *n. pl.,* **pu·bes** (pyōō′bēz). the part of the hipbone that forms the front of the pelvis.

pub·lic (pub′lik) *adj.* **1.** of, relating to, or affecting the people as a whole: *public welfare.* **2.** for the use of all the people; open to all: *a public park, a public lecture.* **3.** of, relating to, or engaged in the affairs or service of a community or country: *a public official.* **4.** generally known: *He made a public denial of the charges against him.* —*n.* **1.** the people as a whole; all the people of a community, state, or country. **2.** a group of people having similar interests or tastes: *the reading public, a movie star's public.*
 in public. not in private; openly: *That singer has appeared in public many times.*

pub·lic-ad·dress system (pub′lik ə dres′) an electrical apparatus with microphones, amplifiers, and loudspeakers, used to amplify sound.

pub·li·can (pub′li kən) *n.* **1.** *British.* the keeper of a public house. **2.** in ancient Rome, a collector of taxes, tolls, and other public monies.

pub·li·ca·tion (pub′li kā′shən) *n.* **1.** the act of publishing: *The novel is ready for publication.* **2.** something that has been published, such as a book or magazine. **3.** public announcement: *Her comments are not for publication.*

public house *British.* a tavern; saloon.

pub·li·cist (pub′lə sist) *n.* **1.** a person who is skilled in or who writes on law or public affairs. **2.** a person who manages publicity or public relations for an individual or organization; press agent.

pub·lic·i·ty (pu blis′ə tē) *n.* **1.** information about a person or thing brought to notice or public attention: *There was a great deal of publicity about the space flight.* **2.** public notice or attention: *The shy novelist didn't like publicity.* **3.** the means used to bring a person or thing to public notice or attention: *She is in charge of the publicity for the school play.*

pub·li·cize (pub′lə sīz′) *v.t.,* **pub·li·cized, pub·li·ciz·ing.** to give publicity to; bring to public attention: *to publicize a new motion picture.*

pub·lic·ly (pub′lik lē) *adv.* **1.** in a public manner: *The senator publicly announced his candidacy for President.* **2.** by or in the name of the public: *That beach is publicly owned.*

public opinion, the opinion of the majority of the people in a country, community, city, or the like.

public relations, the act or method of promoting good will for an individual or organization: *That company has poor public relations.*

public school **1.** a free elementary or secondary school supported by taxes. **2.** in Great Britain, a private boarding school.

public servant, a person who serves the public by holding a government office.

pub·lic-spir·it·ed (pub′lik spir′ə tid) *adj.* working for or showing a concern for the welfare of the community: *a public-spirited citizen.*

public television, television that broadcasts cultural and educational programs for the public. It is supported by donated and public funds rather than by revenues from commercial advertising.

public utility, see **utility** (*def. 2*).

public works, projects built and financed by the government for public use, such as roads, dams, or sewers.

pub·lish (pub′lish) *v.t.* **1.** to produce and offer (printed material, such as a book) for sale to the public. **2.** to make known publicly: *Don't publish all your troubles.*

pub·lish·er (pub′li shər) *n.* a person or company whose business is the publishing of books, magazines, newspapers, and the like.

Puc·ci·ni, Gia·co·mo (pōō chē′nē; jä′kō mō) 1858–1924, Italian composer of operas.

puce (pyōōs) *n.* a purplish-brown or reddish-brown color. —*adj.* having the color puce.

puck[1] (puk) *n.* a black disk of rubber or other hard material, used in playing ice hockey. [From dialectal English *puck* to strike, a form of *poke*[1].]

puck² (puk) *n.* **1.** a mischievous sprite; elf. **2. Puck.** a mischievous fairy or sprite in English folklore. [Old English *pūca.*]

puck·er (puk′ər) *v.t.* to gather into irregular folds or wrinkles: *to pucker the sleeves of a dress in sewing, to pucker the lips.* —*v.i.* to become gathered into wrinkles: *His brows puckered in puzzlement.* —*n.* an irregular fold or wrinkle.

puck·ish (puk′ish) *adj.* mischievous; impish.

pud·ding (pood′ing) *n.* **1.** a sweet, soft dessert that is cooked by being boiled, baked, or steamed. **2.** a similar dish that is unsweetened, served as a part of a main course: *corn pudding.*

pud·dle (pud′əl) *n.* **1.** a small, shallow pool of water, especially of muddy water: *The boy liked to splash in the puddles after a rainstorm.* **2.** a small, shallow pool of any liquid: *a puddle of spilled milk.* **3.** a mixture of clay, sand, and water, used to make something watertight. —*v.t.,* **pud·dled, pud·dling. 1.** to make muddy. **2.** to make (clay, sand, and water) into a watertight mixture. **3.** to convert (pig iron) into wrought iron. —**pud′dly,** *adj.*

pud·dling (pud′ling) *n.* the process of converting pig iron into wrought iron by removing the impurities and excess carbon in a furnace.

pudg·y (puj′ē) *adj.,* **pudg·i·er, pudg·i·est.** short and fat. —**pudg′i·ness,** *n.*

pueb·lo (pweb′lō) *n. pl.,* **pueb·los. 1.** an Indian village consisting of adobe and stone houses joined in groups, found especially in the southwestern United States. **2. Pueblo.** a member of any of several Indian tribes that live in such villages, as the Hopi. [Spanish *pueblo* people, village, from Latin *populus* peoples.]

Pueb·lo (pweb′lō) *n.* a city in south-central Colorado. Pop. (1970), 97,453.

puer·ile (pyoor′il) *adj.* **1.** childish; silly: *puerile pranks.* **2.** of or relating to boyhood or childhood.

Puer·to Ri·co (pwer′tō rē′kō) an island in the West Indies, a commonwealth of the United States. Capital, San Juan. Area, 3435 sq. mi. Pop. (1971 est.), 2,760,000. Also, **Porto Rico.** —**Puerto Rican.**

puff (puf) *n.* **1.** a short, sudden blast, as of air, breath, or smoke: *A puff of wind rippled the pond.* **2.** a drawing in or blowing out of smoke, as from a cigarette or pipe. **3.** something that looks soft and fluffy: *Puffs of clouds filled the sky.* **4.** a small pad for putting powder on the face or body; powder puff. **5.** a light pastry shell having a filling, such as whipped cream. **6.** a slight swelling: *Tom had puffs under his eyes from lack of sleep.* —*v.i.* **1.** to blow with a puff or puffs: *Smoke puffed out of the chimney.* **2.** to breathe hard: *The climbers puffed as they reached the top of the steep hill.* **3.** to give out puffs, as of steam or smoke: *The locomotive puffed.* **4.** to take puffs: *to puff on a cigarette.* **5.** to swell with air or a liquid: *His bruised eye puffed up.* —*v.t.* **1.** to blow or send out in a puff or puffs: *The engine puffed smoke.* **2.** to smoke (a cigar, cigarette, or pipe). **3.** to swell or make fluffy: *The wind puffed the ship's sails.*

puff adder, a very poisonous snake of Africa, that puffs up its body when disturbed. It has a brown or gray body with crescent-shaped yellow markings.

puff·ball (puf′bôl′) *n.* a round fungus similar to a mushroom, that sends out a cloud of spores when ripe.

puff·er (puf′ər) *n.* **1.** a person or thing that puffs. **2.** any of various fish that can expand their bodies with air or water.

puf·fin (puf′in) *n.* a sea bird of northern regions, having a large, brightly striped triangular bill.

puff·y (puf′ē) *adj.,* **puff·i·er, puff·i·est. 1.** puffed up; swollen: *a puffy face.* **2.** blowing in puffs: *a puffy wind.* —**puff′i·ness,** *n.*

pug¹ (pug) *n.* **1.** a short-haired dog having a curled tail and wrinkled face. **2.** see **pug nose.** [Possibly from *puck².*]

pug² (pug) *n. Slang.* see **pugilist.**

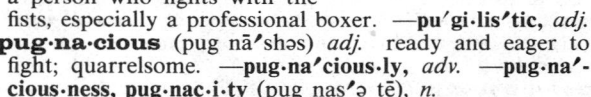

Pu·get Sound (pyōō′jit) an inlet of the Pacific Ocean extending into the northwestern part of the state of Washington.

pu·gi·lism (pyōō′jə liz′əm) *n.* the art or practice of fighting with the fists; boxing.

Pug¹

pu·gi·list (pyōō′jə list) *n.* a person who fights with the fists, especially a professional boxer. —**pu′gi·lis′tic,** *adj.*

pug·na·cious (pug nā′shəs) *adj.* ready and eager to fight; quarrelsome. —**pug·na′cious·ly,** *adv.* —**pug·na′cious·ness, pug·nac·i·ty** (pug nas′ə tē) *n.*

pug nose, a short, broad, turned-up nose. —**pug′nosed′,** *adj.*

puis·sance (pwis′əns, pyōō′i səns) *n.* power; strength.

puis·sant (pwis′ənt, pyōō′i sənt) *adj.* powerful; strong.

puke (pyōōk) *Slang. v.t., v.i.,* **puked, puk·ing.** to vomit. —*n.* vomit.

Pu·las·ki, Count Cas·i·mir (pə las′kē; kaz′ə mir) 1748–1779, Polish nobleman and an American general in the Revolutionary War.

pul·chri·tude (pul′krə tōōd′, pul′krə tyōōd′) *n.* physical beauty: *The girl had great pulchritude.*

pule (pyōōl) *v.i.,* **puled, pul·ing.** to cry in a weak voice; whimper; whine. —**pul′er,** *n.*

Pu·litz·er, Joseph (pool′it sər, pyōō′lit sər) 1847–1911, U.S. newspaper publisher.

pull (pool) *v.t.* **1.** to use force on (something) so as to cause it to move toward the force: *Two horses pulled the wagon. She pulled the closet door open.* **2.** to tug at; yank: *She pulled his sleeve to get his attention.* **3.** to tear away or remove: *to pull a tooth, to pull a branch from a tree.* **4.** to rip or tear: *The puppy pulled the blanket to pieces.* **5.** to injure or weaken by too much stretching; strain: *The baseball player pulled a muscle in his shoulder.* **6.** *Informal.* to carry out; bring about; do: *He was suspected of pulling the robbery.* **7.** *Informal.* to draw or attract: *That new motion picture is pulling crowds.* **8.** *Informal.* to draw out so as to use: *The bandit pulled a gun.* —*v.i.* **1.** to draw or tug: *The jockey pulled on the reins to slow up the horse.* **2.** to go, move, or proceed: *The car pulled into the driveway.* **3.** to row: *They pulled toward the bank of the river.* —*n.* **1.** the act of pulling. **2.** the effort used in pulling: *It was a long, hard pull for them to reach the top of the hill.* **3.** anything used for pulling, such as a handle, knob, or rope. **4.** a drawing or attracting force: *the pull of a magnet.* **5.** *Informal.* influence or advantage: *He got his job through pull, because he knew the boss.* **6.** *Informal.* the ability to attract or appeal: *That star has great pull at the box office.* —**pull′er,** *n.*

to pull for. *Informal.* to hope for the success of: *We are all pulling for our home baseball team.*

to pull off. *Informal.* to accomplish in spite of difficulties.

to pull oneself together. to regain one's self-control.

to pull through. to get through a serious or difficult situation successfully.

to pull up. to halt; stop: *The car pulled up at the curb.*

pul·let (pool'it) *n.* a young hen less than a year old.

pul·ley (pool'ē) *n. pl.,* **pul·leys. 1.** a grooved wheel on which a rope or chain is pulled, used to lift heavy loads or change the direction of an applied force. **2.** a simple machine consisting of such a wheel or set of such wheels mounted in a casing.

Pull·man (pool'mən) *n.* a railroad car with sleeping accommodations. [From George M. *Pullman,* 1831–1897, a U.S. industrialist who designed it.]

pull·o·ver (pool'ō'vər) *n.* a garment, such as a shirt or sweater, that is put on by being pulled over the head.

pul·mo·nar·y (pool'mə ner'ē, pul'mə ner'ē) *adj.* of, relating to, or affecting the lungs: *a pulmonary disease.*

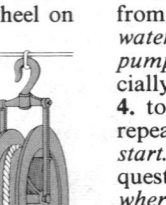

Pulley

pulp (pulp) *n.* **1.** the soft, juicy part of certain fruits and vegetables. **2.** the inner part of a tooth containing soft tissue, blood vessels, and nerves. **3.** any soft, moist, formless mass, such as the mixture of matted fibers of wood used in making paper. **4.** a magazine printed on a cheap grade of paper made from wood pulp, usually containing sensational stories or articles. —*v.t.* to make into pulp.

pul·pit (pool'pit) *n.* **1.** a raised structure from which a minister delivers a sermon. **2.** ministers as a group; the clergy.

pulp·wood (pulp'wood') *n.* wood used to make paper, especially pine, fir, or spruce.

pulp·y (pul'pē) *adj.,* **pulp·i·er, pulp·i·est.** of or like pulp; soft or fleshy. —**pulp'i·ly,** *adv.* —**pulp'i·ness,** *n.*

pul·sar (pul'sär) *n.* any of a number of astronomical objects that send out intense pulses of electromagnetic energy at regular intervals.

pul·sate (pul'sāt) *v.i.,* **pul·sat·ed, pul·sat·ing. 1.** to expand and contract rhythmically: *The heart pulsates.* **2.** to vibrate; quiver.

pul·sa·tion (pul sā'shən) *n.* **1.** the act of pulsating. **2.** a single beat or vibration.

Pulpit

pulse¹ (puls) *n.* **1.** the rhythmic expansion and contraction of the arteries caused by the pulsation of the heart as it pumps blood. **2.** any regular, rhythmical beating or vibrating: *the steady pulse of an engine.* **3.** the feeling or opinion of a group: *the political pulse of the country.* —*v.i.,* **pulsed, puls·ing.** to beat or vibrate; pulsate. [Latin *pulsāre.*]

pulse² (puls) *n.* **1.** the seeds of such plants as peas, beans, or lentils, used as food. **2.** any plant yielding such seeds. [Old French *pols, pous.*]

pul·ver·ize (pul'və rīz') *v.,* **pul·ver·ized, pul·ver·iz·ing.** —*v.t.* **1.** to grind or pound into powder or dust. **2.** to smash or destroy completely: *The enemy bombs almost pulverized the town.* —*v.i.* to become powder or dust. —**pul'ver·i·za'tion,** *n.* —**pul'ver·iz'er,** *n.*

pu·ma (pyōō'mə) *n. pl.,* **pu·mas** or **pu·ma.** another word for **cougar.**

pum·ice (pum'is) *n.* a light, porous volcanic rock used for cleaning, smoothing, or polishing. —*v.t.,* **pum·iced, pum·ic·ing.** to clean, smooth, or polish with pumice.

pum·mel (pum'əl) *also,* **pom·mel.** *v.t.,* **pum·meled, pum-**

mel·ing; *also, British,* **pum·melled, pum·mel·ling.** to strike again and again with the fists: *The two boys pummeled one another.*

pump¹ (pump) *n.* a machine for moving liquids or gases from one place to another. —*v.t.* **1.** to make (a fluid) move from one place to another by means of a pump: *to pump water into a swimming pool.* **2.** to remove fluid from: *to pump out a flooded basement.* **3.** to fill with a gas, especially with air, by means of a pump: *to pump up a flat tire.* **4.** to move by forcing up and down or back and forth repeatedly: *He pumped the gas pedal, but the car would not start.* **5.** to get or try to get information from by close questioning: *The police pumped the suspect to find out where he had been on the day of the crime.* —*v.i.* to make a fluid move from place to place by means of a pump. [Possibly from Middle Dutch *pompe* a pipe used for moving water.] —**pump'er,** *n.*

pump² (pump) *n.* a low-cut shoe without laces or other fasteners. [Of uncertain origin.]

pum·per·nick·el (pum'pər nik'əl) *n.* a coarse dark bread made of unsifted rye flour.

pump·kin (pump'kin, pum'kin, pung'kin) *n.* **1.** a large orange or yellow-orange fruit, having a soft pulp containing many seeds and a firm outer rind. **2.** the trailing vine bearing this fruit.

pun (pun) *n.* a play on words in which a double meaning is applied to one word or to two words having the same sound. —*v.i.,* **punned, pun·ning.** to make a pun or puns.

punch¹ (punch) *v.t.* **1.** to hit (someone or something) with the fist. **2.** to work by pressing: *to punch an elevator button.* **3.** *Informal.* to herd or drive (cattle). —*v.i.* to hit, especially with the fist. —*n. pl.,* **punch·es. 1.** a blow made with the fist. **2.** *Informal.* force; vitality: *The politician put punch in his words.* [Middle English *punchen* to perforate.] —**punch'er,** *n.*

punch² (punch) *n. pl.,* **punch·es.** a tool for making holes in or stamping or pressing a design on a surface. —*v.t.* to make holes in or stamp or press a design on with a punch: *to punch paper for a notebook.* [Short for *puncheon².*]

punch³ (punch) *n. pl.,* **punch·es.** a drink made from various ingredients, usually fruit juices and an alcoholic or carbonated beverage. [Hindi *pānch* five; because this drink was first made from five ingredients.]

Punch (punch) *n.* the ill-tempered, humpbacked hero of the puppet show *Punch and Judy.*

punch card, a card with holes punched in specific positions to provide instructions or information for a data-processing machine.

pun·cheon¹ (pun'chən) *n.* **1.** a large cask of varying capacity, holding from 70 to 120 gallons. **2.** the amount contained in a puncheon. [Old French *poinchon, poinçon* a wine cask.]

pun·cheon² (pun'chən) *n.* **1.** a broad, heavy piece of timber roughly finished on one side. **2.** see **punch².** [Old French *poinchon, poinçon* a pointed tool.]

punching bag, an inflated or stuffed leather or canvas bag, usually suspended, punched for exercise or training in boxing.

punch line, the last sentence or phrase of a joke or story, that gives it humor or meaning.

punch·y (pun'chē) *adj.,* **punch·i·er, punch·i·est.** *Informal.* dizzy or groggy.

punc·til·i·o (pungk til'ē ō') *n. pl.,* **punc·til·i·os. 1.** a fine point of proper or polite behavior. **2.** strict or careful attention to such fine points.

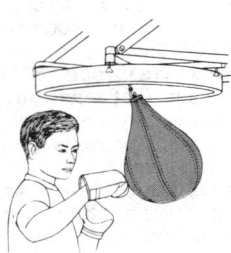

Punching bag

punc·til·i·ous (pungk til′ē əs) *adj.* **1.** strictly or carefully attentive to the fine points of proper or polite behavior: *He had punctilious table manners.* **2.** very careful and exact: *She was punctilious in doing her homework.* —**punc·til′i·ous·ly,** *adv.* —**punc·til′i·ous·ness,** *n.*

punc·tu·al (pungk′chŏŏ əl) *adj.* happening or acting at the correct time; on time; prompt: *The train was punctual.* —**punc·tu·al·i·ty** (pungk′chŏŏ al′ə tē), *n.* —**punc′tu·al·ly,** *adv.*

punc·tu·ate (pungk′chŏŏ āt′) *v.,* **punc·tu·at·ed, punc·tu·at·ing.** —*v.i.* **1.** to mark (written material) with periods, commas, and other marks to make the meaning clear: *He punctuated the paragraph carefully.* **2.** to interrupt from time to time: *The candidate's speech was punctuated by cheers from the enthusiastic crowd.* **3.** to give emphasis to: *He punctuated his remarks by banging on the table.* —*v.i.* to use punctuation marks.

punc·tu·a·tion (pungk′chŏŏ ā′shən) *n.* **1.** the use of periods, commas, and other marks to make the meaning of written material clear and understandable. **2.** a punctuation mark or marks.

● **Punctuation** is used to indicate the division of written language into sentences and sentence parts, and to show the relationship between sentence parts. Punctuation makes the meaning of written language clear in much the same way that pauses, stresses, and the rising and falling of the voice clarify the meaning of spoken language. When punctuation marks are not used, the meaning of what is written can be unclear. There is a story that in ancient Rome some soldiers went to a soothsayer (a person who was thought to be able to predict the future) to find out whether or not they would survive a coming battle. The written answer that they received was "You will go and return not die in battle." The soothsayer had intentionally given the soldiers an answer that, depending upon whether there should be a comma before the word "not" or after it, could mean either survival or death.

The ancient Greeks and Romans used very little punctuation in their writing. The punctuation marks that they used included a dot above the line, indicating a period; a dot below the line, indicating a semicolon; and a dot in the middle of the line, indicating a comma. These marks, however, were not used in a standard or systematic way.

The punctuation in Old English and Middle English manuscripts was also scanty and irregular. The eighth century manuscript of the Anglo-Saxon epic poem *Beowulf* contains almost no punctuation other than a mark at the end of a sentence. In other early writings there were marks that represented our modern comma, semicolon, and period, but the form and use of these marks were not standardized. The invention of movable type in the middle of the fifteenth century and other advances in printing caused a vast increase in available written material. As the written language became more important, people began to see the need for adequate, standardized punctuation. Printers, rather than writers, were responsible for many of the developments in punctuation that occurred at this time. In the following 130 years, they established the modern comma and various other marks. The period, comma, colon, semicolon, exclamation mark, question mark, and parentheses were all used in the First Folio edition of Shakespeare's plays, published in 1623. Writers in the seventeenth and eighteenth centuries began to use punctuation marks, particularly the comma and the semicolon, very frequently. This resulted in a highly complicated style of writing. For instance, in a poem written by John Milton in 1644, two consecutive sentences contained a total of thirty-nine commas and four semicolons.

The use of very heavy punctuation continued up until the nineteenth century. The works of certain nineteenth-century American writers, such as Ralph Waldo Emerson and Henry David Thoreau, show a clearer and simpler style of writing that is punctuated only when necessary. This trend toward simplification has continued until the present. Most modern writing, in comparison to the writing of earlier periods, is characterized by a decrease in the average number of punctuation marks per sentence and by a shortening of the length of the average sentence so that it more closely resembles natural speech. A recent sampling of ten American periodicals showed an average of only 2.1 punctuation marks per sentence.

punctuation mark, any of various marks used to make the meaning of written material clear. Periods, commas, semicolons, and question marks are punctuation marks.

punc·ture (pungk′chər) *v.,* **punc·tured, punc·tur·ing.** —*v.t.* **1.** to make a hole in (something) with a sharp or pointed object; pierce: *to puncture a balloon with a pin.* **2.** to make (a hole) by piercing. **3.** to lessen in importance, spoil, or ruin as if by puncturing: *The bad news punctured her happiness.* —*v.i.* to become punctured. —*n.* **1.** a hole made by a sharp or pointed object. **2.** the act of puncturing.

pun·dit (pun′dit) *n.* **1.** a learned Brahmin, especially one who is an expert in the laws, language, or religion of India. **2.** a very learned person, especially one who is an expert in a particular field.

pun·gent (pun′jənt) *adj.* **1.** sharp and stinging to the taste or smell: *Ammonia is pungent.* **2.** piercing or severe: *The new book received pungent criticism from the reviewers.* —**pun·gen·cy,** *n.* —**pun′gent·ly,** *adv.*

pun·ish (pun′ish) *v.t.* **1.** to cause (someone) to suffer for a crime, offense, or fault: *The mother punished the naughty child.* **2.** to inflict a penalty for (an offense, crime, or fault): *The law punishes robbery. The teacher punishes cheating on a test.* **3.** to treat or handle roughly or severely. —**pun′ish·a·ble,** *adj.* —**pun′ish·er,** *n.*

pun·ish·ment (pun′ish mənt) *n.* **1.** the act of punishing or the state of being punished. **2.** a penalty inflicted for a crime, offense, or fault. **3.** severe treatment; rough handling: *The car took a lot of punishment on the bumpy dirt road.*

pu·ni·tive (pyōō′nə tiv) *adj.* of, relating to, or inflicting punishment; punishing: *a punitive law.* —**pu′ni·tive·ly,** *adv.* —**pu′ni·tive·ness,** *n.*

Pun·jab (pun jäb′, pun′jäb′) *n.* a region and former province in northern India, now divided between India and Pakistan.

punk[1] (pungk) *n.* **1.** a dry substance that burns slowly without a flame, used especially to light fireworks. **2.** dry, decayed wood, used especially as tinder. [Possibly from Algonquian *punk* live ashes.]

punk[2] (pungk) *Slang. n.* a young, worthless, or inexperienced person. —*adj.* of poor quality; worthless. [Of uncertain origin.]

pun·ster (pun′stər) *n.* a person who frequently makes puns.

at; āpe; cär; end; mē; it; īce; hot; ōld; fôrk; wood; fōōl; oil; out; up; turn; sing; thin; this; hw in white; zh in treasure. The symbol ə stands for the sound of **a** in about, **e** in taken, **i** in pencil, **o** in lemon, and **u** in circus.

741

punt¹ (punt) *n.* a flat-bottomed boat with square ends, usually moved by a long pole. —*v.t.* **1.** to move (a boat) with a long pole. **2.** to carry in a punt. —*v.i.* to go or travel in a punt. [Old French *punt.*] —**punt′er**, *n.*

Punt¹

punt² (punt) *n.* a kick in which a football is dropped from the hands and kicked before it reaches the ground. —*v.t., v.i.* to kick (a football) before it reaches the ground. [Of uncertain origin.] —**punt′er**, *n.*

pu·ny (pyōo′nē) *adj.*, **pu·ni·er, pu·ni·est.** inferior in size, strength, or importance: *a puny calf.* —**pu′ni·ness**, *n.*

pup (pup) *n.* **1.** a young dog; puppy. **2.** the young of various other animals, such as the fox, wolf, or seal.

pu·pa (pyōo′pə) *n. pl.*, **pu·pae** (pyōo′pē) or **pu·pas.** an insect in the intermediate stage of development, coming after the larva and before the adult. A caterpillar in its cocoon is a pupa. —**pu′pal**, *adj.*

pu·pil¹ (pyōo′pəl) *n.* a person who studies under the direction of an instructor; student. [Going back to Latin *pūpillus* orphan, ward; literally, little boy.]

pu·pil² (pyōo′pəl) *n.* the opening in the center of the iris through which light enters the eye. [Going back to Latin *pūpilla* little girl; referring to the small images that are reflected in this opening.]

pup·pet (pup′it) *n.* **1.** a small, usually jointed, figure made to look like a person or animal and moved by the hand or by strings, wires, or rods. **2.** a person or thing that is under the complete control of another: *The legislature was only a puppet under the dictator.*

pup·pet·eer (pup′ə tēr′) *n.* a person who operates puppets for entertainment.

pup·pet·ry (pup′i trē) *n.* the art of making puppets or producing puppet shows.

Puppet

pup·py (pup′ē) *n. pl.*, **pup·pies.** a young dog.

pup tent, a small, portable tent for use by two people.

pur·blind (pur′blīnd′) *adj.* **1.** nearly blind. **2.** slow to understand. —**pur′blind′ly**, *adv.* —**pur′blind′ness**, *n.*

pur·chase (pur′chəs) *v.t.*, **pur·chased, pur·chas·ing. 1.** to get by paying money; buy: *Father is going to purchase a new car.* **2.** to get by hardship, sacrifice, or suffering: *The military victory was purchased at great cost of life.* —*n.* **1.** the act of purchasing. **2.** something purchased. **3.** a firm hold or grasp to help in moving something or to keep from slipping. —**pur′chas·er**, *n.*

pure (pyoor) *adj.*, **pur·er, pur·est. 1.** not mixed with anything else; unadulterated: *a scarf of pure silk.* **2.** not stained, spotted, or contaminated; clean: *pure water.* **3.** free from evil or guilt: *a pure heart.* **4.** of unmixed descent: *That cat is pure Siamese.* **5.** nothing but; sheer; utter: *His explanation of what happened is pure nonsense.* **6.** concerned with theory rather than with practical application; abstract: *pure science.* —**pure′ness**, *n.*

pure·bred (pyoor′bred′) *adj.* coming from ancestors of unmixed breed: *That dog is a purebred setter.*

pu·rée (pyoo rā′) *n. pl.*, **pu·rées. 1.** food that is put through a sieve or blender and made into a thick, moist mass. **2.** a smooth, thick soup. —*v.t.*, **pu·réed, pu·rée·ing.** to make (food) into a purée.

pure·ly (pyoor′lē) *adv.* **1.** entirely; simply: *Breaking the dish was purely accidental.* **2.** in a pure manner.

pur·ga·tive (pur′gə tiv) *n.* a medicine that causes the bowels to empty. —*adj.* purging; cleansing.

pur·ga·to·ri·al (pur′gə tôr′ē əl) *adj.* of or relating to purgatory.

pur·ga·to·ry (pur′gə tôr′ē) *n. pl.*, **pur·ga·to·ries. 1.** in Roman Catholic belief, a temporary place of purification, where the souls of those who have died are purged of unrepented minor sins or of major sins that have been forgiven but not wholly punished. **2.** any place or condition of temporary punishment or suffering.

purge (purj) *v.t.*, **purged, purg·ing. 1.** to cleanse or rid of whatever is unclean or undesirable. **2.** to remove undesired or disloyal persons from (a political party, government, or other organization). **3.** to remove (undesired or disloyal persons) from a political party, government, or other organization. **4.** to free of sin or guilt. **5.** to cause (the bowels) to empty. —*n.* **1.** the act or process of purging. **2.** the elimination of undesired or disloyal persons from a political party, government, or other organization. **3.** a medicine that causes the bowels to empty; cathartic.

pu·ri·fi·ca·tion (pyoor′ə fi kā′shən) *n.* the act of purifying or the state of being purified.

pu·ri·fy (pyoor′ə fī′) *v.*, **pu·ri·fied, pu·ri·fy·ing.** —*v.t.* to make pure or clean: *to purify air with filters.* —*v.i.* to become pure. —**pu′ri·fi′er**, *n.*

Pu·rim (poor′im) *n.* an annual Jewish holiday observed in February or March, commemorating the rescue of the Jews by Queen Esther from a plot to massacre them.

pu·rine (pyoor′ēn) *n.* a chemical compound that is the fundamental base of many substances.

pur·ist (pyoor′ist) *n.* a person who is very strict about purity or correctness, especially in language: *The teacher was a purist and did not like his pupils to use slang.*

Pu·ri·tan (pyoor′it ən) *n.* **1.** a member of a sect of English Protestants in the sixteenth and seventeenth centuries who wanted simpler religious ceremonies and high standards of morality. **2. puritan.** a person who is very strict in matters of morality or religion. —*adj.* **1.** of, relating to, or characteristic of the Puritans or Puritanism. **2. puritan.** of, relating to, or characteristic of a puritan.

pu·ri·tan·i·cal (pyoor′i tan′i kəl) *adj.* **1.** very strict in matters of morality or religion: *a puritanical attitude.* **2. Puritanical.** of, relating to, or characteristic of Puritans or Puritanism. Also, **pu·ri·tan·ic** (pyoor′i tan′ik). —**pu′ri·tan′i·cal·ly**, *adv.* —**pu′ri·tan′i·cal·ness**, *n.*

Pu·ri·tan·ism (pyoor′it ən iz′əm) *n.* **1.** the beliefs and practices of the Puritans. **2. puritanism.** great strictness in matters of morality or religion.

pu·ri·ty (pyoor′ə tē) *n.* **1.** the state or quality of being pure. **2.** freedom from evil or guilt. **3.** great strictness about correctness of language.

purl¹ (purl) *v.i.* to flow, ripple, or swirl, especially with a murmuring sound. —*n.* a murmuring sound made by a shallow stream or brook. [Possibly imitative of this sound.]

purl² (purl) *v.t., v.i.* to knit with inverted stitches. [Of uncertain origin.]

pur·loin (pur loin′) *v.t., v.i.* to steal. —**pur·loin′er**, *n.*

pur·ple (pur′pəl) *n.* **1.** the color made by mixing red and blue. **2.** a cloth or robe of this color, especially one worn to show royalty or high rank. **3.** royalty or high rank. —*adj.* having the color purple.

Purple Heart, a U.S. military award given to a member of the armed forces who is wounded while in action against the enemy.

pur·port (*v.,* pər pôrt′; *n.,* pur′pôrt) *v.t.* **1.** to claim or profess, often falsely: *He purports to be an expert on au-*

tomobiles. **2.** to intend; mean. —*n.* meaning or substance: *Her letter gives the purport of our telephone conversation.*

pur·pose (pur′pəs) *n.* **1.** the result or goal that one wants; intention; aim: *His purpose is to go to college.* **2.** the object or reason for which something is made or done; function or use: *What is the purpose of that hook on the kitchen wall?* —*v.t.,* **pur·posed, pur·pos·ing.** to intend, resolve, or aim.

on purpose. not by accident; intentionally.

pur·pose·ful (pur′pəs fəl) *adj.* **1.** having a purpose or meaning; intentional: *a purposeful insult.* **2.** having or showing determination: *a purposeful man.* —**pur′pose·ful·ly,** *adv.* —**pur′pose·ful·ness,** *n.*

pur·pose·less (pur′pəs lis) *adj.* without purpose or meaning. —**pur′pose·less·ly,** *adv.* —**pur′pose·less·ness,** *n.*

pur·pose·ly (pur′pəs lē) *adv.* on purpose; intentionally.

purr (pur) *n.* **1.** a soft, murmuring sound made by a cat when pleased or contented. **2.** any similar sound: *the purr of an engine.* —*v.i.* to make a soft, murmuring sound. —*v.t.* to express by making a soft, murmuring sound: *She purred her thanks.*

purse (purs) *n.* **1.** a woman's handbag. **2.** a small bag, pouch, or case for carrying money. **3.** money; funds. **4.** a sum of money offered as a prize or given as a gift. —*v.t.,* **pursed, purs·ing.** to draw together into wrinkles or folds; pucker: *She pursed her lips in anger.*

purs·er (pur′sər) *n.* the officer who has charge of financial matters on board a ship.

purs·lane (purs′lin, purs′lān) *n.* a trailing plant having bright yellow flowers and fleshy stems and leaves, sometimes used as a salad green.

pur·su·ance (pər soo′əns) *n.* a carrying out: *In pursuance of his plan, he spent the summer camping.*

pur·su·ant (pər soo′ənt) *adj.* going in pursuit; pursuing.

pursuant to. in accordance with: *I loaned him the money, pursuant to our agreement.*

pur·sue (pər soo′) *v.,* **pur·sued, pur·su·ing.** —*v.t.* **1.** to follow in order to overtake, capture, or kill: *The hounds pursued the fox.* **2.** to go along or hold to the course of; follow: *The class pursued their plans for the picnic.* **3.** to strive for; seek: *The boy pursued his goal of being on the baseball team by practicing every day.* **4.** to continue or follow through: *to pursue the study of Spanish.* —*v.i.* to go in pursuit; follow. —**pur·su′er,** *n.*

pur·suit (pər soot′) *n.* **1.** the act of following in order to overtake: *The police were in pursuit of a robber.* **2.** the act of seeking: *the pursuit of wealth.* **3.** any occupation, pastime, or interest: *Collecting stamps was his favorite pursuit.*

pur·vey (pər vā′) *v.t.* to supply food or provisions: *to purvey eggs and milk to troops.* —**pur·vey′ance,** *n.*

pur·vey·or (pər vā′ər) *n.* a person who supplies food or provisions: *a purveyor of fruits.*

pus (pus) *n.* a thick, yellowish fluid that collects in abscesses and other infections in the body, and contains bacteria and dead white blood cells.

Pu·san (poo′sän′) *n.* the chief port of South Korea, on the southeastern coast of the country. Pop. (1970), 1,880,710.

push (poosh) *v.t.* **1.** to press forcefully on or against so as to move: *He pushed the door with his shoulder. She pushed the baby carriage up the hill.* **2.** to urge vigorously: *That senator always pushes reform of city government.* **3.** to put strain or pressure on: *He was pushed for time.* **4.** to make with effort or force: *The campers pushed their way through the bushes.* **5.** to advance or expand by effort: *The settlers pushed the frontier farther west.* **6.** to make an effort to sell: *That grocery store is pushing canned goods*

this week. —*v.i.* **1.** to press forcefully on or against something so as to move it: *If you push against the fence it will give way.* **2.** to move forward with effort: *to push through a crowd.* —*n. pl.,* **push·es. 1.** the act of pushing: *The bully gave Tom a push that knocked him down.* **2.** a forceful effort, attempt, or drive: *The troops made one last push to take the town.*

to push around. *Informal.* to treat roughly.

to push off. *Informal.* to leave; depart.

push·cart (poosh′kärt′) *n.* a small cart pushed by hand, used especially by a peddler.

push·er (poosh′ər) *n.* **1.** a person or thing that pushes. **2.** *Slang.* a person who sells drugs illegally.

Push·kin, Alexander Ser·ge·ye·vich (poosh′kin; ser gā′yə vich) 1799–1837, Russian poet and dramatist.

push·o·ver (poosh′ō′vər) *n. Slang.* **1.** a person who is easily defeated, fooled, or taken advantage of. **2.** anything easily done.

push·up (poosh′up′) *n.* an exercise in which a person lies face down and, keeping his body straight, raises and lowers himself by straightening and bending his arms.

push·y (poosh′ē) *adj.,* **push·i·er, push·i·est.** *Informal.* forward or aggressive in an offensive manner. —**push′i·ly,** *adv.* —**push′i·ness,** *n.*

pu·sil·lan·i·mous (pyoo′sə lan′ə məs) *adj.* lacking courage; faint-hearted; cowardly. —**pu′sil·lan′i·mous·ly,** *adv.*

puss[1] (poos) *n. pl.,* **puss·es.** a cat. [Possibly imitative of the spitting of a cat.]

puss[2] (poos) *n. pl.,* **puss·es.** *Slang.* the face or mouth. [Irish Gaelic *pus* lip, mouth.]

puss·y (poos′ē) *n. pl.,* **puss·ies.** a cat.

puss·y·foot (poos′ē foot′) *v.i.* **1.** to move quietly, cautiously, or secretly. **2.** to act in a cautious or timid manner; be unwilling to commit oneself.

pussy willow, an American shrub or small tree bearing furry silvery-gray catkins.

pus·tule (pus′chool) *n.* **1.** a small, inflamed swelling of the skin containing pus. **2.** any similar swelling.

—Catkin

Pussy willow

put (poot) *v.,* **put, put·ting.** —*v.t.* **1.** to cause to be in a certain place or position; place; set; lay: *Put the package on the table. Tom put another log on the fire.* **2.** to cause to be in a certain condition: *The teacher's warm smile put the shy boy at ease.* **3.** to cause to undergo; subject: *to put a person to a great deal of trouble.* **4.** to set at a certain point or amount; estimate: *He put the value of the car at five hundred dollars.* **5.** to attribute; ascribe; assign: *The report put the blame on him.* **6.** to express; state: *Put your question clearly.* **7.** to throw (the shot) with an overhand, pushing motion. —*v.i.* to go; proceed: *The ship put out to sea.* —*n.* an overhand, pushing throw.

to put aside. to save for later use.

to put away. a. to save for later use. **b.** *Informal.* to eat

at; āpe; cär; end; mē; it; īce; hot; ōld; fôrk; wood; fool; oil; out; up; turn; sing; thin; this; hw in white; zh in treasure. The symbol ə stands for the sound of **a** in about, **e** in taken, **i** in pencil, **o** in lemon, and **u** in circus.

or drink. **c.** to give up; abandon: *to put away childish habits.* **d.** *Informal.* to kill.

to put by. to save for later use.

to put down. a. to put an end to: *to put down the rebellion.* **b.** to write down. **c.** to belittle or snub.

to put forth. a. to send out; sprout; grow: *The tree put forth leaves.* **b.** to exert: *to put forth great effort.*

to put forward. to propose; present.

to put in. a. *Informal.* to spend (time) in a certain way: *to put in a long day at the office.* **b.** (of a ship) to enter (a port). **c.** to make or present a request, offer, claim, or the like: *to put in for a car loan.*

to put off. a. to postpone or delay: *to put off a trip.* **b.** to get rid of by delay or evasion: *He put off the people he owed by false promises to pay.*

to put on. a. to assume or pretend: *He put on a brave front.* **b.** to present or perform: *to put on a play.* **c.** to apply: *The driver put on the brakes.*

to put out. a. to extinguish: *to put out a fire, to put out the lights.* **b.** to annoy or inconvenience. **c.** to publish: *to put out a new book.* **d.** *Baseball.* to cause (a batter or base runner) to be out.

to put over. *Informal.* to carry out with success: *He put over the deal.*

to put through. to carry out with success.

to put up. a. to build: *to put up a new office building.* **b.** to preserve (food). **c.** to get food and lodging: *They put up at a motel.* **d.** to give food and lodging to: *He put up his friend for the night.* **e.** to propose or nominate: *to put up a candidate for office.* **f.** to show: *The lost child put up a brave front.*

to put upon. to take advantage of; treat unfairly.

to put up to. *Informal.* to encourage (a person) to do: *He put the other boys up to that prank.*

to put up with. to bear patiently; endure.

put·down (poot'doun') *n. Slang.* a remark or action meant to belittle or snub someone.

put·on (poot'ôn', poot'on') *adj.* pretended; assumed: *a put-on display of grief.*

put·out (poot'out') *n. Baseball.* the act or instance of putting out a batter or base runner.

pu·tre·fac·tion (pyōō'trə fak'shən) *n.* the act of putrefying or the state of being putrefied.

pu·tre·fy (pyōō'trə fī') *v.,* **pu·tre·fied, pu·tre·fy·ing.** —*v.t.* to cause to decay or rot; make putrid. —*v.i.* to rot.

pu·trid (pyōō'trid) *adj.* **1.** decayed and foul-smelling; rotten: *putrid fish.* **2.** characteristic of or produced by putrefying: *a putrid smell.* —**pu'trid·ly,** *adv.* —**pu'trid·ness,** *n.*

putt (put) *n. Golf.* a light stroke made on a putting green in an attempt to send the ball into the cup. —*v.t.* to hit (a ball) with such a stroke. —*v.i.* to hit a ball with such a stroke.

put·tee (put'ē, pu tē') *n.* a long, narrow strip of cloth wound round the leg from ankle to knee, worn as a protection and support for the leg.

put·ter¹ (put'ər) *also,* **pot·ter.** *v.i.* to work or act in an aimless or useless way: *Tom puttered around all day.* —*v.t.* to waste (time) in puttering. [A form of *potter²,* from Old English *potian* to push.] —**put'ter·er,** *n.*

putt·er² (put'ər) *n.* **1.** a golf club with a short shaft and a metal head, used in putting. **2.** a person who putts. [*Putt* + -*er¹.*]

putting green, see **green** (def. 3).

put·ty (put'ē) *n. pl.,* **put·ties.** a soft, doughlike mixture of powdered chalk and linseed oil, used especially for filling cracks or attaching panes of glass. —*v.t.,* **put·tied, put·ty·ing.** to fill, fasten, or cover with putty.

puz·zle (puz'əl) *n.* **1.** a person or thing that confuses or bewilders: *Algebra is a real puzzle to me.* **2.** a toy or game that presents a problem to solve or a task to be done for fun: *He tried to fit together the pieces of the puzzle.* —*v.,* **puz·zled, puz·zling.** —*v.t.* to confuse or bewilder: *His rude behavior puzzles me.* —*v.i.* to be confused or bewildered: *She puzzled over the arithmetic problem.* —**puz'zler,** *n.*

puz·zle·ment (puz'əl mənt) *n.* the state of being puzzled.

Pvt., Private.

Pyg·ma·lion (pig māl'yən) *n. Greek Legend.* a sculptor and king of Cyprus who fell in love with the statue of a maiden he had carved.

Pyg·my (pig'mē) *also,* **Pig·my.** *n. pl.,* **Pyg·mies. 1.** a member of a dark-skinned people of Africa who are usually less than five feet tall. **2. pygmy.** a very small person or thing. —*adj.* **1.** of or relating to the Pygmies. **2. pygmy.** very small.

py·ja·mas (pə jä'məz, pə jam'əz) *British.* another spelling of **pajamas.**

py·lon (pī'lon) *n.* **1.** a monumental gateway, especially to an ancient Egyptian temple. **2.** a tower for guiding aviators, especially in a race. **3.** a tall steel tower that supports high-tension wires.

py·lo·rus (pī lôr'əs) *n. pl.,* **py·lo·ri** (pī lôr'ī). the opening between the stomach and the duodenum. —**py·lor'ic,** *adj.*

Pyong·yang (pyung'yäng') *n.* the capital of North Korea, in the west-central part of the country. Pop. (1970), 1,500,000.

py·or·rhe·a (pī'ə rē'ə) *also,* **py·or·rhoe·a.** *n.* an inflammation of the gums and other soft tissues that surround the teeth, resulting in the loosening of the teeth.

pyr·a·mid (pir'ə mid') *n.* **1. Pyramids.** the massive stone structures, usually having a square base and four triangular sides that slope upward to an apex, built as tombs by the ancient Egyptians. **2.** a solid figure having a polygon for a base and triangular sides intersecting at a point. **3.** anything resembling a pyramid in form or structure: *The acrobats formed a human pyramid.* —*v.t.* to arrange or raise in the shape of a pyramid. —*v.i.* **1.** to have the shape of a pyramid. **2.** to rise or increase: *The cost of food has pyramided in recent years.*

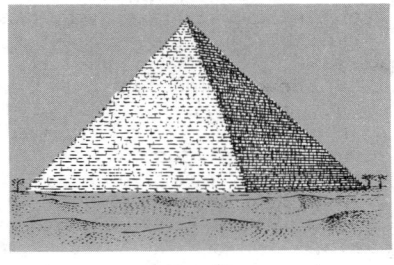

Pyramid

py·ram·i·dal (pi ram'əd əl) *adj.* of, relating to, or like a pyramid. —**py·ram'i·dal·ly,** *adv.*

pyre (pīr) *n.* a pile of wood or other combustible material for burning a dead body.

Pyr·e·nees (pir'ə nēz') *n., pl.* a mountain range in southwestern Europe, extending along the border of France and Spain from the Bay of Biscay to the Mediterranean Sea. —**Pyr'e·ne'an,** *adj.*

Py·rex (pī'reks) *n. Trademark.* a kind of glass that is resistant to heat, used to make cooking utensils and laboratory glassware.

pyr·i·dox·ine (pir'ə dok'sēn) *n.* another word for **vitamin B₆.**

py·rite (pī'rīt) *n.* a hard, shiny, yellow compound of iron and sulfur, often mistaken for gold, used in the manufacture of sulfuric acid; fool's gold.

py·ri·tes (pī rī′tēz, pī′rīts) *n., pl.* any of various compounds of sulfur and a metal.

py·ro·ma·ni·a (pī′rə mā′nē ə) *n.* an uncontrollable desire to set fire to things.

py·ro·ma·ni·ac (pī′rə mā′nē ak) *n.* a person who has an uncontrollable desire to set fire to things. —**py·ro·ma·ni·a·cal** (pi′rō mə nī′ə kəl), *adj.*

py·ro·tech·nic (pī′rə tek′nik) *adj.* **1.** of or relating to fireworks. **2.** like fireworks; brilliant: *a pyrotechnic display of skill on the violin.* Also, **py·ro·tech·ni·cal** (pī′rə tek′ni·kəl). —**py′ro·tech′ni·cal·ly,** *adv.*

py·ro·tech·nics (pī′rə tek′niks) *n., pl.* **1.** the manufacture or use of fireworks. **2.** a display of fireworks. **3.** any brilliant, dazzling, or sensational display.

Pyrrhic victory (pir′ik) a victory won at a huge or ruinous cost. [From *Pyrrhus,* an ancient king who suffered very heavy losses in defeating the Romans in 279 B.C.]

Py·thag·o·ras (pi thag′ər əs) 580?–500? B.C., Greek mathematician and philosopher.

Py·thag·o·re·an (pi thag′ə rē′ən) *adj.* of or relating to Pythagoras, his doctrines, or his followers. —*n.* a follower of Pythagoras.

Pythagorean theorem, the theorem that in a right triangle, the square of the length of the hypotenuse is equal to the sum of the squares of the lengths of the other two sides.

Pyth·i·as (pith′ē əs) *n.* see **Damon.**

py·thon (pī′thon) *n.* any of a group of large, nonpoisonous snakes related to the boas, that are found in Asia, Africa, the East Indies, and Australia. Pythons coil around and suffocate or crush their prey.

P

at; āpe; cär; end; mē; it; īce; hot; ōld; fôrk; wood; fōōl; oil; out; up; turn; sing; thin; this; hw in white; zh in treasure. The symbol ə stands for the sound of a in about, e in taken, i in pencil, o in lemon, and u in circus.

1. Semitic Ϙ	**4. Early Latin** Q
2. Greek Ninth Century B.C. Ϙ	**5. Classical Latin** Q
3. Etruscan Ϙ	**6. English** Q

Q is the seventeenth letter of the English alphabet. It is one of the few letters whose design has remained basically unchanged since the time of the early alphabets. The oldest form of the letter **Q** was the ancient Semitic letter *koph* (1), which represented the head of either a man or a monkey. This letter, which was pronounced like a *k* sound made at the back of the throat, was passed down through various alphabets and adopted by the early Greeks, who called it *koppa* (2). The Greeks made no distinction between the Semitic *k* sound and a hard *k* sound, like the *k* in *king*. Because they used the letter *kappa* to represent the hard *k* sound, *koppa* was not needed and was dropped from later Greek alphabets. When the early Greek alphabet was borrowed by the Etruscans (3), the letters *gamma, kappa,* and *koppa* were adopted, even though they all stood for the same hard *k* sound. The only distinction that the Etruscans made in the use of these letters was in spelling: *gamma,* which became our letter **C,** was used before **E** and **I;** *kappa,* which became our letter **K,** was used before **A;** and *koppa,* which became our letter **Q,** was used before **U.** In early Latin (4), these letters were used in the same way, except that the letter **O,** which the Etruscans did not use, sometimes followed the Latin **Q.** These unnecessary spelling variations were eliminated in classical Latin (5), in which the letter **K** was dropped almost entirely and **Q** was used only in combination with the letter **U,** in order to produce a *kw* sound. Our spelling rule that **Q** is followed by **U** comes from this spelling rule in Latin. By about 2000 years ago, the Romans were writing and pronouncing the letter **Q** almost exactly as we do today (6).

q, Q (kyōo) *n. pl.,* **q's, Q's.** the seventeenth letter of the English alphabet.

q. 1. quart. **2.** quarter; quarterly.

Q., Queen.

Qa·tar (kä′tər) *n.* a country, an independent sheikdom, in southwestern Asia, on the Persian Gulf coast of Arabia. Capital, Doha. Area, 8500 sq. mi. Pop. (1978 est.), 100,000.

Q.E.D., which was to be proved or demonstrated. [An abbreviation of Latin *quod erat demonstrandum.*]

Qing·dao (ching′dou′) another spelling of **Tsingtao.**

qt. 1. quart; quarts. **2.** quantity.

quack¹ (kwak) *n.* the harsh, flat sound made by a duck. —*v.i.* to make such a sound. [Imitative of this sound.]

quack² (kwak) *n.* **1.** a dishonest person who pretends to have skill as a doctor. **2.** a person with little knowledge or skill who poses as an expert; charlatan. —*adj.* relating to or characteristic of a quack or quackery; fake: *a quack doctor.* [Short for earlier *quacksalver;* originally referring to a dishonest peddler of ointments and salves.]

quack·er·y (kwak′ər ē) *n. pl.,* **quack·er·ies.** the practices or methods of a quack; fakery.

quad·ran·gle (kwod′rang′gəl) *n.* **1.** a plane geometric figure having four angles and four sides; quadrilateral. **2.** a square space, especially a courtyard, partly or entirely surrounded by a building or buildings. **3.** the building or buildings surrounding such a space.

quad·rant (kwod′rənt) *n.* **1.** a quarter of a circle, or an arc of 90 degrees. **2.** an instrument consisting of an arc divided into 90 degrees, used in navigation and astronomy for measuring the altitude or angular distance of an object above the horizon. **3.** any of the four parts into which a plane is divided by perpendicular coordinate axes.

quad·ra·phon·ic (kwod′rə fon′ik) *adj.* relating to the transmission, recording, or reproduction of sound by the use of four different transmission channels.

quad·rat·ic (kwo drat′ik) *adj. Algebra.* of, relating to, or involving a quantity or quantities that are squared but none that are raised to a higher power: $x^2 + 4x + 3 = 15$ is a quadratic equation. —*n.* a quadratic equation or expression.

Quadrant *(def. 2)*

quad·ren·ni·al (kwo dren′ē əl) *adj.* **1.** occurring every four years: *a quadrennial election.* **2.** lasting four years.

quad·ri·lat·er·al (kwod′rə lat′ər əl) *adj.* having four sides. —*n.* a polygon with four sides and four angles.

qua·drille (kwo dril′) *n.* **1.** a square dance for four couples that usually has five parts. **2.** the music for such a dance.

quad·ril·lion (kwo dril′yən) *n.* **1.** in the United States and France, the cardinal number that is represented by one followed by fifteen zeros. **2.** in Great Britain and Germany, the cardinal number that is represented by one followed by twenty-four zeros. —*adj.* numbering one quadrillion. —**quad·ril′lionth,** *adj., n.*

quad·ri·no·mi·al (kwod′rə nō′mē əl) *n.* in algebra, an expression with four terms.

quad·ru·ped (kwod′rə ped′) *n.* any animal having four feet. A dog is a quadruped. —*adj.* having four feet.

quad·ru·ple (kwo drōō′pəl) *adj.* **1.** consisting of four parts or members: *a quadruple alliance.* **2.** four times as great or as many: *The value of this land is quadruple what it was a hundred years ago.* —*v.,* **quad·ru·pled, quad·ru·pling.** —*v.i.* to become four times as great or as many: *The value of their farm quadrupled when the new road was built.* —*v.t.* to make four times as great or as many. —*n.* a number or amount four times as great as another.

quad·rup·let (kwo drōō′plit) *n.* **1.** one of four children born at the same birth. **2.** any set or group of four.

quaff (kwäf, kwaf) *v.t.* to drink heartily and with large swallows: *to quaff water.* —*v.i.* to drink with large swallows. —*n.* a hearty drink.

quag·mire (kwag′mīr′, kwog′mīr′) *n.* **1.** soft, muddy ground. **2.** a difficult position or situation: *to be caught in a quagmire of debts.*

qua·hog (kwô′hôg′, kwô′hog′) *n.* a roundish hard-shelled clam, found in shallow waters along the Atlantic coast of North America.

quail¹ (kwāl) *n. pl.,* **quails** or **quail.** any of various game birds, having gray or brown feathers that are often speckled with white. [Old French *quaille.*]

quail² (kwāl) *v.i.* to shrink back in fear: *The small boy quailed when the dog growled.* [Of uncertain origin.]

quaint (kwānt) *adj.* **1.** charming or attractive in an old-fashioned way: *the quaint, narrow streets of an old town.* **2.** pleasingly unusual or odd: *The young man found her French accent quaint.* —**quaint′ly,** *adv.* —**quaint′ness,** *n.*

European quail

quake (kwāk) *v.i.,* **quaked, quak·ing.** to shake; tremble: *to quake with terror. The clap of thunder made the house quake.* —*n.* **1.** a trembling or shaking. **2.** see **earthquake.**

Quak·er (kwā′kər) *n.* a member of the Society of Friends, a Christian sect founded in the seventeenth century. Also, **Friend.**

Quak·er·ism (kwā′kə riz′əm) *n.* the doctrines and practices of the Quakers.

qual·i·fi·ca·tion (kwol′ə fi kā′shən) *n.* **1.** the act of qualifying or the state of being qualified. **2.** any ability, accomplishment, or knowledge that makes a person fit for a certain job, task, or office: *His past teaching experience was a qualification for his position as principal of the school.* **3.** something that limits or restricts: *He is, without qualification, the most intelligent man I've ever known.*

qual·i·fied (kwol′ə fīd′) *adj.* **1.** having the necessary abilities, accomplishments, or requirements: *a qualified voter, a person who is qualified for a job.* **2.** limited; restricted: *The play was at best a qualified success.*

qual·i·fi·er (kwol′ə fī′ər) *n.* **1.** a person or thing that qualifies. **2.** a word that limits or modifies the meaning of another word, such as an adjective or adverb.

qual·i·fy (kwol′ə fī′) *v.,* **qual·i·fied, qual·i·fy·ing.**
—*v.t.* **1.** to make fit, as for a certain job, task, or office: *Her previous experience qualified her for the job.* **2.** to limit or restrict: *Tom should have qualified his statement that boys like sports with the word "usually."* **3.** to limit or modify the meaning of (a word or phrase): *Adjectives qualify nouns.* —*v.i.* to be or become fit.

qual·i·ta·tive (kwol′ə tā′tiv) *adj.* of or relating to quality or kind: *qualitative change.* —**qual′i·ta′tive·ly,** *adv.*

qualitative analysis, a method for finding out the constituents in a chemical substance by tests.

qual·i·ty (kwol′ə tē) *n. pl.,* **qual·i·ties. 1.** something that makes a person or thing what it is: *He has all the qualities of a successful businessman. Lemons have a sour quality.* **2.** basic character; nature: *The quality of that singer's voice is beautiful.* **3.** degree of excellence; grade: *Our butcher sells meat that is of a very high quality.* **4.** excellence; fineness; superiority: *That restaurant prides itself on the quality of its food.* **5.** high rank or social position.

qualm (kwäm) *n.* **1.** a twinge of conscience: *to have qualms about cheating.* **2.** a sudden feeling of uneasiness or doubt; misgiving: *The old lady had some qualms about her first airplane flight.*

quan·da·ry (kwon′dər ē) *n. pl.,* **quan·da·ries.** a state of hesitation or uncertainty; dilemma; predicament.

quan·ta (kwon′tə) the plural of **quantum.**

quan·ti·ta·tive (kwon′tə tā′tiv) *adj.* of or relating to quantity. —**quan′ti·ta′tive·ly,** *adv.*

quantitative analysis, a method for finding out the amounts of each constituent of a chemical substance.

quan·ti·ty (kwon′tə tē) *n. pl.,* **quan·ti·ties. 1.** a number or amount: *The recipe calls for a small quantity of milk.* **2.** a large number or amount: *It is often less expensive to buy goods in quantity.* **3.** the property of a thing that can be determined by measurement, as of volume, length, or weight. **4.** an amount, number, or algebraic expression representing a mathematical value. **5.** the length of a vowel sound or syllable in pronunciation. **6.** *Music.* the length of a note or tone.

quan·tum (kwon′təm) *n. pl.,* **quan·ta.** *Physics.* a separate and indivisible basic unit of energy.

quantum theory, the theory that radiant energy is emitted and absorbed in quanta, rather than in a continuous manner.

quar·an·tine (kwôr′ən tēn′, kwor′ən tēn′) *n.* **1.** the isolation of persons, animals, ships, or goods infected by or exposed to an infectious disease, to prevent the spread of the disease. **2.** the place or length of time of such isolation. **3.** any enforced isolation. —*v.t.,* **quar·an·tined, quar·an·tin·ing.** to keep away from others in order to prevent the spreading of a disease.

quark (kwôrk) one of three hypothetical particles that are thought to be the basic constituents of all known atomic particles. [Named by Murray Gell-Mann, 1929—, American physicist, from a word coined by James Joyce in *Finnegan's Wake.*]

quar·rel (kwôr′əl, kwor′əl) *n.* **1.** an angry dispute or disagreement: *Tom and Betty had a quarrel about whose turn it was to wash the dishes.* **2.** a cause for such a dispute or disagreement: *I have no quarrel with your plan.* —*v.i.,* **quar·reled, quar·rel·ing;** *also, British,* **quar·relled, quar·rel·**

at; āpe; cär; end; mē; it; īce; hot; ōld; fôrk; wood; fōōl; oil; out; up; turn; sing; thin; **th**is; **hw** in white; **zh** in treasure. The symbol ə stands for the sound of **a** in about, **e** in taken, **i** in pencil, **o** in lemon, and **u** in circus.

ling. **1.** to have an angry dispute or disagreement: *The children quarreled about who would ride the bicycle first.* **2.** to find fault: *We quarreled with his methods, not his goals.* —**quar′rel·er,** *n.*

quar·rel·some (kwôr′əl səm, kwor′əl səm) *adj.* prone to quarreling; likely to dispute: *That boy is so quarrelsome that no one likes him.* —**quar′rel·some·ly,** *adv.* —**quar′rel·some·ness,** *n.*

quar·ri·er (kwôr′ē ər, kwor′ē ər) *n.* a person who works in a quarry.

quar·ry¹ (kwôr′ē, kwor′ē) *n. pl.,* **quar·ries.** a place where stone is cut or blasted out for use in building, road construction, or the like. —*v.t.,* **quar·ried, quar·ry·ing. 1.** to cut or blast from a quarry: *to quarry marble.* **2.** to make a quarry in: *to quarry a hillside.* [Old French *quariere* a place where stone is dug.]

quar·ry² (kwôr′ē, kwor′ē) *n. pl.,* **quar·ries.** an animal that is hunted or chased; prey. [Old French *cuiree* prey; originally referring to the parts of a slain animal that were given to the hunting dogs as a reward.]

quart (kwôrt) *n.* **1.** a unit of liquid measure equal to one-fourth of a gallon, or two pints. **2.** a unit of dry measure equal to one-eighth of a peck, or two pints. **3.** a container for holding or measuring a quart.

quar·ter (kwôr′tər) *n.* **1.** one of four equal or corresponding parts; one-fourth: *Mary divided the pie into quarters.* **2.** a coin of the United States and Canada equal to twenty-five cents, or one-quarter of a dollar. **3.** one-fourth of an hour; fifteen minutes. **4.** one-fourth of a year; three months. **5.** a part of a school or college year, usually lasting three months. **6.** a fourth part of the period of the moon's revolution around the earth, lasting about seven days: *The moon is in its first quarter.* **7.** one of the four equal time periods into which certain games, such as football or basketball, are divided. **8.** one of the four principal divisions of the compass. **9.** a section or district, as of a city or town: *Sightseers were delighted with the quaint French quarter of the city.* **10.** a person, place, or group: *The ruling came from the highest quarters.* **11. quarters. a.** a place to live; living accommodations: *the winter quarters of a circus.* **b.** an assigned position or station, as on a warship. **12.** one of the legs of a four-footed animal, with the nearby parts: *a quarter of lamb.* **13.** mercy, especially when granted to a defeated enemy: *The king gave no quarter to the traitor.* —*v.t.* **1.** to divide into four equal parts: *to quarter an apple.* **2.** to provide with living accommodations; lodge: *to quarter troops in tents for the night.* —*adj.* **1.** being one of four equal parts: *He and his three partners each received a quarter part of the profits from the business.* **2.** being equal to one-fourth of a standard unit of measure: *a quarter pound of butter.*

at close quarters. at close range; very close together.

quar·ter·back (kwôr′tər bak′) *n. Football.* a player whose position is directly behind the center, and who directs the team and calls signals for the offense.

quar·ter·deck (kwôr′tər dek′) *n.* the part of the upper deck of a ship between the stern and mainmast, used especially by officers.

quar·ter·ly (kwôr′tər lē) *adj.* happening once every three months: *to figure the quarterly interest on a savings account.* —*n. pl.,* **quar·ter·lies.** a magazine published four times a year, or once every three months. —*adv.* once every three months: *The payments were made quarterly.*

quar·ter·mas·ter (kwôr′tər mas′tər) *n.* **1.** in the U.S. Army, an officer responsible for providing quarters, clothing, food, equipment, and the like for troops. **2.** in the U.S. Navy, a petty officer on a ship who is in charge of navigation and certain equipment, such as compasses and signals.

quarter note *Music.* a note having one-fourth the time value of a whole note.

quar·ter·staff (kwôr′tər staf′) *n. pl.,* **quar·ter·staves** (kwôr′tər stāvz′). a stout pole six to eight feet long, having an iron tip. It was formerly used in England as a weapon.

quar·tet (kwôr tet′) *also,* **quar·tette.** *n.* **1.** a musical composition for four voices or instruments. **2.** a musical group of four performers. **3.** any group or set of four.

quar·to (kwôr′tō) *n. pl.,* **quar·tos. 1.** the page size of a book made up of sheets of paper folded into four leaves, each usually about nine by twelve inches. **2.** a book composed of pages of this size.

quartz (kwôrts) *n.* a very hard form of silica that occurs in crystals or in a single mass, and is colorless and transparent in its pure state. Certain impure colored varieties, as amethyst, are used as semiprecious stones. Quartz is the most common of all minerals and is the main constituent of sand.

quartz·ite (kwôrt′sīt) *n.* a granular metamorphic rock consisting chiefly of quartz.

qua·sar (kwā′sär) *n.* any of various starlike celestial objects that emit extremely powerful radio waves, light, and other electromagnetic radiation.

quash¹ (kwosh) *v.t.* to put down forcibly and quickly: *The dictator was quick to quash the insurrection.* [Middle English *quashen* to put down forcibly and quickly, from Old French *quasser* to break.]

quash² (kwosh) *v.t.* to make void or set aside, as a law, election, or indictment: *The judge quashed the lower court's decision.* [Middle English *quassen* to make void, from Old French *quasser* to make void, break, from Latin *quassāre* to shake violently.]

qua·si (kwā′zī, kwā′sī, kwä′zē, kwä′sē) *adj.* resembling or similar to, but not the same as. —*adv.* seemingly, but not really; almost or somewhat. ▲ usually used in combination: *a quasi-success.*

Qua·ter·na·ry (kwä′tər ner′ē) *n.* the second geological period of the Cenozoic era, including the Pleistocene and Recent epochs. —*adj.* of, relating to, or characteristic of this period.

quat·rain (kwot′rān) *n.* a stanza or poem of four lines, especially one with alternately rhyming lines.

qua·ver (kwā′vər) *v.i.* to tremble or shake: *The little girl's voice quavered with fright.* —*n.* **1.** a shaking or trembling, especially of the voice. **2.** a trill produced or performed in singing or in playing a musicial instrument. —**qua′ver·y,** *adj.*

quay (kē) *n.* a landing place for boats and ships, usually made of stone.

Que., Quebec.

quea·sy (kwē′zē) *adj.,* **quea·si·er, quea·si·est. 1.** sick to one's stomach; nauseated: *The boat trip made her queasy.* **2.** causing or tending to cause nausea. **3.** uneasy; uncomfortable: *She had a queasy feeling that she had failed the test.* **4.** easily troubled, especially as a result of a guilty conscience.

Quay

Que·bec (kwi bek′) *n.* **1.** the largest province of Canada, in the eastern part of the country. Area, 594,860 sq. mi. Pop. (1971), 6,027,764. **2.** the capital of this province, a port city in southeastern Canada, on the St. Lawrence River. Pop. (1971), 182,418.

que·bra·cho (kā brä′chō) *n.* any of several tropical American trees whose bark and hard wood are used in tanning and dyeing.

queen (kwēn) *n.* **1.** the wife or widow of a king. **2.** a female sovereign of a kingdom who rules in her own right. **3.** a woman, or a thing thought of as female, that is very important or outstanding: *That new ocean liner is the queen of the seas.* **4.** a fully developed, mated female in a colony of bees, ants, or termites, who lays eggs. **5.** a playing card bearing a picture of a queen. **6.** *Chess.* the most powerful piece. It can move any number of spaces in any straight or diagonal line. —*v.i.* to reign as or act like a queen. —**queen′like′,** *adj.*

Queen (def. 6)

Queen Anne's lace, a wild species of carrot, having flat lacy clusters of tiny white flowers.

queen consort, the wife of a reigning king.

queen·ly (kwēn′lē) *adj.,* **queen·li·er, queen·li·est.** characteristic of, like, or suitable for a queen. —*adv.* in a queenly manner. —**queen′li·ness,** *n.*

queen mother, the widow of a king who is also the mother of the reigning sovereign.

queen regent, a queen ruling in place of a king who is absent or who is unable or too young to reign.

Queens (kwēnz) *n.* the largest borough of New York City, east of Manhattan. Area, 114.7 sq. mi. Pop. (1970), 1,973,708.

Queen's English, see **King's English.**

Queens·land (kwēnz′lənd) *n.* a state of Australia, in the northeastern part of the country. Area, 667,000 sq. mi. Pop. (1971), 1,823,362.

queer (kwēr) *adj.* different from what is normal or expected; strange; peculiar; unusual: *That was a queer way for her to behave.* —**queer′ly,** *adv.* —**queer′ness,** *n.*

quell (kwel) *v.t.* **1.** to put down; crush; suppress: *The captain quelled the mutiny.* **2.** to put an end to; ease: *Medicine quelled the pain.*

quench (kwench) *v.t.* **1.** to satisfy; slake: *Bill quenched his thirst with a glass of milk.* **2.** to put out or extinguish: *The firemen quenched the fire.* —**quench′a·ble,** *adj.*

quer·u·lous (kwer′ə ləs) *adj.* finding fault; complaining: *The sick child was querulous about everything.* —**quer′u·lous·ly,** *adv.* —**quer′u·lous·ness,** *n.*

que·ry (kwēr′ē) *n. pl.,* **que·ries.** a question; inquiry. —*v.t.,* **que·ried, que·ry·ing. 1.** to ask about; inquire into: *My friend queried my reasons for quitting my job.* **2.** to ask a question or questions of: *The police queried the robbery suspect.* **3.** to feel doubt about the correctness or truth of: *to query a statement in a magazine article.*

quest (kwest) *n.* **1.** a search or pursuit: *The explorer's quest for gold was in vain.* **2.** in the Middle Ages, an expedition or journey made by a knight or knights, especially one made in order to find or achieve something. **3.** a knight or knights on such an expedition or journey. —*v.i.* to go on a quest.

ques·tion (kwes′chən) *n.* **1.** something asked in order to receive a reply or find out something: *Betty could not answer the teacher's questions.* **2.** a matter to be discussed or considered: *The meeting dealt with the question of civil rights.* **3.** a matter of dispute or doubt; controversy: *A question arose as to who owned the land.* **4.** uncertainty; doubt: *Jim is, without question, the smartest boy I know.* **5.** a proposal to be voted on: *After much debate, the members of the legislature were ready for the question.* —*v.t.* **1.** to ask a question or questions of: *The police questioned the suspect.* **2.** to ask questions about; doubt; challenge: *Joe questioned the truth of Tom's account of the accident.* —**ques′tion·er,** *n.*

  beside the question. off the subject: *Your comment is beside the question.*

beyond question. without doubt: *He is, beyond question, the best baseball player in the school.*

in question. under discussion or consideration: *The matter in question was the building of the new gymnasium.*

out of the question. not to be considered or thought of.

to call in question. to raise doubts about; challenge: *He called my honesty in question by hinting that I was lying.*

ques·tion·a·ble (kwes′chə nə bəl) *adj.* **1.** of doubtful character, honesty, respectability, or the like: *questionable behavior.* **2.** open to doubt or dispute; uncertain: *That theory is questionable.* —**ques′tion·a·bly,** *adv.*

ques·tion·ing·ly (kwes′chə ning lē) *adv.* in the manner of one who questions: *He looked at her questioningly.*

question mark, a punctuation mark (?) put at the end of a question. Also, **interrogation point.**

ques·tion·naire (kwes′chə ner′) *n.* a written or printed form consisting of a list of questions, used to get information or a sample of public opinion.

quet·zal (ket säl′) *n.* a Central American bird having shiny green and bright red feathers. The male has a tail of long feathers.

queue (kyōō) *n.* **1.** a braid of hair made at the back of the head. **2.** *also,* **cue.** a line of people, automobiles, or the like. —*v.i.,* **queued, queu·ing.** to form, stand, or wait in a line: *People queued up to buy tickets for the movie.*

Que·zon, Ma·nuel Lu·is (kā′zon; män′wel′ lōō ēs′) 1878–1944, Philippine independence leader and statesman.

Que·zon City (kā′zon) the capital of the Philippines, a suburb of Manila. Pop. (1975), 956,684.

quib·ble (kwib′əl) *v.i.,* **quib·bled, quib·bling.** to make petty or minor objections or criticisms to avoid the truth or main point: *The two lawyers quibbled about the terms of the contract.* —*n.* a petty objection or criticism. —**quib′bler,** *n.*

Quetzal

quick (kwik) *adj.* **1.** done or happening within a very short time; rapid: *a quick glance.* **2.** moving with speed: *That secretary is a quick typist.* **3.** understanding, thinking, learning, or responding easily or rapidly: *He did not have as quick a mind as his little brother.* **4.** easily aroused or stirred: *a quick temper.* —*n.* **1.** tender, sensitive flesh, especially that beneath a fingernail or toenail. **2.** living persons. ▲ used chiefly in the phrase *the quick and the dead.* —*adv.* quickly. —**quick′ness,** *n.*

quick·en (kwik′ən) *v.t.* **1.** to cause to go or move more rapidly; hasten: *He quickened his steps.* **2.** to give new life to; revive: *The camper quickened the fire by adding more wood.* **3.** to excite; stimulate: *The book quickened his interest in American history.* —*v.i.* **1.** to go or move more rapidly. **2.** to return to life; revive. **3.** to begin to show signs of life: *The earth quickened when spring arrived.*

quick-freeze (kwik′frēz′) *v.t.,* **quick-froze** (kwik′frōz′), **quick-fro·zen** (kwik′frō′zən), **quick-freez·ing.** to freeze food so rapidly that it retains its flavor and is able to undergo long storage at low temperatures.

quick·lime (kwik′līm′) *n.* see **lime¹.**

at; āpe; cär; end; mē; it; īce; hot; ōld; fôrk; wood; fōōl; oil; out; up; turn; sing; thin; **this;** hw in white; zh in treasure. The symbol ə stands for the sound of **a** in about, **e** in taken, **i** in pencil, **o** in lemon, and **u** in circus.

Q

quick·ly (kwik′lē) *adv.* with speed or haste; rapidly: *He answered the phone quickly.*

quick·sand (kwik′sand′) *n.* very deep, loose, wet sand that can engulf any heavy object that rests or moves upon it.

quick·sil·ver (kwik′sil′vər) *n.* see **mercury** *(def. 1).*

quick·step (kwik′step′) *n.* **1.** a rapid marching step. **2.** march music with a rapid tempo.

quick-tem·pered (kwik′tem′pərd) *adj.* easily angered or irritated.

quick time, the normal military marching rate, consisting of 120 thirty-inch steps per minute.

quick-wit·ted (kwik′wit′id) *adj.* having or showing a quick or ready mind; mentally alert or keen: *a quick-witted pupil.* —**quick′-wit′ted·ly,** *adv.*

quid¹ (kwid) *n.* a piece of something to be chewed, especially tobacco. [Old English *cwidu* cud.]

quid² (kwid) *n. pl.,* **quid.** *British. Slang.* one pound sterling. [Of uncertain origin.]

qui·es·cent (kwī es′ənt) *adj.* in a state of inactivity or rest: *a quiescent frame of mind.* —**qui·es′cence,** *n.* —**qui·es′cent·ly,** *adv.*

qui·et (kwī′it) *adj.* **1.** making little or no noise: *The children were quiet while the teacher talked.* **2.** with or characterized by little or no noise: *Tom found it easier to study when the room was quiet.* **3.** having little or no motion; still: *a quiet pond.* **4.** free from disturbance; peaceful: *a quiet evening, to lead a quiet life in the country.* **5.** restful or soothing, as to the eye: *The room was decorated in beige and other quiet colors.* —*n.* the quality or state of being quiet: *Mary enjoyed the peace and quiet of the little country town.* —*v.t.* to make quiet: *The mother quieted the crying child.* —*v.i.* to become quiet: *The waves quieted down after the storm passed.* —**qui′et·er,** *n.* —**qui′et·ly,** *adv.* —**qui′et·ness,** *n.*

qui·e·tude (kwī′i tōōd′, kwī′i tyōōd′) *n.* calmness or tranquility: *the quietude of the countryside.*

qui·e·tus (kwī ē′təs) *n.* the final ending or settling of something: *the quietus of death.*

quill (kwil) *n.* **1.** a large, stiff feather. **2.** the hard, hollow stem of a feather. **3.** a pen made from the hollow stem of a feather. **4.** one of the sharp spines of a porcupine or hedgehog.

quilt (kwilt) *n.* a bed covering consisting of two pieces of cloth filled with soft stuffing material, such as feathers or cotton batting, and held together by lines of stitching, usually in a pattern, across the entire surface. —*v.i.* to make a quilt or quilts. —*v.t.* to stitch together with a soft lining: *to quilt a jacket.*

Quill

quilt·ing (kwil′ting) *n.* **1.** the act of making quilts or quilted work. **2.** the material used in making quilts.

quince (kwins) *n.* **1.** a pear-shaped yellow fruit of a small Asian tree, used in preserves. **2.** the tree bearing this fruit, having round white or pale-pink flowers.

Quin·cy (kwin′zē) *n.* a city in eastern Massachusetts. Pop. (1970), 87,966.

qui·nine (kwī′nīn) *n.* a bitter, colorless, crystalline drug made from the bark of the cinchona tree. It is used to treat malaria and other illnesses.

Quince branch

quin·sy (kwin′zē) *n.* a severe inflammation of the tonsils and throat, often accompanied by the formation of an abscess.

quint (kwint) *n. Informal.* see **quintuplet.**

quin·tes·sence (kwin tes′əns) *n.* **1.** the purest part or form of something; pure essence: *This chapter contains the quintessence of the author's thought.* **2.** the most perfect example of something: *His behavior was the quintessence of generosity.*

quin·tet (kwin tet′) *also,* **quin·tette.** *n.* **1.** a musical composition for five voices or instruments. **2.** a musical group of five performers. **3.** any group or set of five.

quin·tu·ple (kwin tōō′pəl, kwin′tə pəl) *adj.* **1.** consisting of five parts or members. **2.** five times as great or as many. —*v.,* **quin·tu·pled, quin·tu·pling.** —*v.i.* to become five times as great or as many. —*v.t.* to make five times as great or as many. —*n.* a number or amount five times as great as another.

quin·tu·plet (kwin tup′lit, kwin′təp lit) *n.* **1.** one of five children born at the same birth. **2.** any set or group of five.

quip (kwip) *n.* **1.** a clever or witty remark or saying, usually made on the spur of the moment. **2.** a sharp or sarcastic remark; taunt; gibe. —*v.i.,* **quipped, quip·ping.** to make a quip or quips.

quire (kwīr) *n.* twenty-four or twenty-five sheets of paper of the same size and quality.

quirk (kwurk) *n.* **1.** a strange mannerism or way of acting. **2.** a sudden or unexpected twist or turn: *a quirk of fate.*

quirt (kwurt) *n.* a flexible riding whip made of knotted rawhide thongs and having a short handle.

quis·ling (kwiz′ling) *n.* a person who betrays his own country by aiding an invading enemy. [From Vidkun *Quisling,* 1887–1945, a Norwegian politician who betrayed his country by collaborating with the invading Germans during World War II.]

Quirt

quit (kwit) *v.,* **quit** or **quit·ted, quit·ting.** —*v.t.* **1.** to stop, cease, or discontinue: *He quit studying to take a walk. It was hard to quit smoking.* **2.** to give up or abandon: *to quit a job.* **3.** to go away from; leave: *The guard did not quit his post all night long.* —*v.i.* **1.** to stop, cease, or discontinue doing something. **2.** to resign from a position: *She quit because her salary was too low.* **3.** to give up or stop trying, as in defeat or discouragement: *He quit when he realized he could not win the race.* —*adj.* free, clear, or rid of: *He is quit of all debts.*

quit·claim (kwit′klām′) *Law. n.* the giving up of one's claim, title, or right of action. —*v.t.* to give up one's claim or title to or right of action on.

quite (kwīt) *adv.* **1.** completely; entirely; wholly: *They left the sulky child quite alone. I believe quite the opposite.* **2.** actually; really: *Climbing that mountain was quite an accomplishment.* **3.** to a considerable extent or degree; rather: *The weather is quite warm for November.*

Qui·to (kē′tō) *n.* the capital of Ecuador, in the north-central part of the country, in the Andes. Pop. (1970 est.), 528,100.

quits (kwits) *adj.* on even terms by means of repayment or revenge: *After he made the last payment on the television set, he was quits with the store.*

to call it quits. to discontinue or stop something: *After Tom studied all morning, he decided to call it quits.*

quit·ter (kwit′ər) *n.* a person who gives up easily.

quiv·er¹ (kwiv′ər) *v.i.* to shake slightly; shiver; tremble: *The child quivered with excitement when he saw his new* bicycle. —*n.* the act or motion of quivering: *the quiver of leaves in a breeze.* [Possibly a form of *quaver.*]

quiv·er² (kwiv′ər) *n.* a case for holding arrows. [Anglo-Norman *quiveir.*]

Qui·xo·te, Don (ki hō′tē, kwik′sət) see **Don Quixote.**

quix·ot·ic (kwik sot′ik) *adj.* ridiculously chivalrous or romantic; too idealistic: *a quixotic young man.* [From *Don Quixote.*] —**quix·ot′i·cal·ly,** *adv.*

quiz (kwiz) *n. pl.,* **quiz·zes.** a short, informal examination: *a history quiz.* —*v.t.,* **quizzed, quiz·zing.** to question; examine: *The police quizzed the suspect. The students were quizzed on last week's work.* —**quiz′zer,** *n.*

quiz show, a radio or television show in which contestants try to answer questions, usually for prizes.

Quiver²

quiz·zi·cal (kwiz′i kəl) *adj.* **1.** questioning; uncertain; puzzled: *The child looked quizzical because he didn't understand the question.* **2.** teasing; mocking: *a quizzical remark.* —**quiz′zi·cal·ly,** *adv.*

quoin (koin, kwoin) *n.* **1.** an outside angle of a wall or building. **2.** one of the stones forming such an angle. **3.** a wedge or wedge-shaped piece of material used in printing to lock type in a galley.

quoit (kwoit) *n.* **1.** **quoits.** a game played by throwing a flattened metal or rope ring in an attempt to encircle or come as close as possible to a peg stuck in the ground. ▲ used with a singular verb. **2.** the flattened metal or rope ring used in this game.

quon·dam (kwon′dəm) *adj.* that once was; former: *a quondam friend.*

Quon·set hut (kwon′sit) *Trademark.* a prefabricated building made of corrugated metal and supported by steel trusses, having a semi-circular roof whose sides curve down to form the walls. [From *Quonset* Point, Rhode Island, where this hut was first built.]

Quonset hut

quo·rum (kwôr′əm) *n.* the minimum number of members of a committee, organization, assembly, or the like, whose presence at a meeting is necessary if the meeting is to make binding or legal decisions.

quot., quotation.

quo·ta (kwō′tə) *n.* **1.** a fixed amount, or a share of a total, due to or required of a person, group, state, or the like: *Each soldier received his daily quota of rations. The salesman failed to sell his quota of shoes.* **2.** a fixed or maximum number or proportion of a certain group or category of people that may be admitted, as to a country.

quot·a·ble (kwō′tə bəl) *adj.* that can be quoted.

quo·ta·tion (kwō tā′shən) *n.* **1.** the act of quoting. **2.** a person's words quoted or repeated exactly by another person: *The book contained quotations from many authors.* **3.** a statement of the current price offered or bid for a stock, bond, or commodity. **4.** the price so stated.

quotation mark, one of a pair of punctuation marks (" ") used chiefly to indicate the beginning and end of a quotation. Single quotation marks (' ') are usually used to indicate a quotation within another quotation.

quote (kwōt) *v.,* **quot·ed, quot·ing.** —*v.t.* **1.** to repeat or reproduce the exact words of: *The newspapers quoted the President's speech. The author frequently quoted Shakespeare.* **2.** to bring forward as an example or evidence: *The driving instructor quoted the statistics on automobile accidents to his pupil.* **3.** to state (a price) for a stock, bond, or commodity. **4.** to enclose in quotation marks. —*v.i.* to repeat or reproduce the exact words of another: *If you're going to quote, give credit to the author.* —*n. Informal.* **1.** see **quotation. 2.** see **quotation mark.** —**quot′er,** *n.*

quoth (kwōth) *v. Archaic.* said or spoke.

quo·tient (kwō′shənt) *n.* a number or algebraic expression obtained by dividing one number or algebraic expression by another. In $12 \div 4 = 3$, 3 is the quotient.

q.v., which see. [Abbreviation of Latin *quod vide.*]

at; āpe; cär; end; mē; it; īce; hot; ōld; fôrk; wood; fōol; oil; out; up; turn; sing; thin; **th**is; **hw** in white; **zh** in treasure. The symbol ə stands for the sound of **a** in about, **e** in taken, **i** in pencil, **o** in lemon, and **u** in circus.

1. Egyptian Hieroglyphics ○ ⟨	**5. Greek Ninth Century B.C.** ⟨
2. Semitic ⟨	**6. Greek Classical Capitals** P
3. Early Phoenician ⟨⟨	**7. Latin Fourth Century B.C. Capitals** ℛℛ
4. Early Hebrew ⟨ ⟨	**8. English** R

R is the eighteenth letter of the English alphabet. The earliest ancestor of **R** was an Egyptian hieroglyphic (1) that represented a mouth. In the ancient Semitic alphabet this symbol became the letter *resh* (2), meaning "head," and looked somewhat like a profile of a human head facing left. *Resh* continued to be written in this way in the early Phoenician (3) and early Hebrew (4) alphabets. The ancient Greeks, who borrowed *resh* and called it *rho* (5), wrote it as it had been written in earlier alphabets. In ancient times, the Greeks wrote from right to left or in alternating rows of right to left and left to right. Later, when they began to write from left to right, the shape of certain letters, including *rho,* was reversed (6). This new form of *rho,* which looked like our modern capital letter **P,** was adopted by the Romans (7). By about 2300 years ago, a stroke was added to the Latin form of *rho,* making it look very much like our modern capital letter **R** (8).

r, R (är) *n. pl.,* **r's, R's.** the eighteenth letter of the English alphabet.

 the three R's. reading, writing, and arithmetic (humorously spelled *reading, 'riting, and 'rithmetic*).

r, roentgen.

R. **1.** river. **2.** Republican. **3.** rabbi. **4.** road.

Ra (rä) *n.* a hawk-headed sun god of ancient Egypt.

Ra, the symbol for radium.

R.A., rear admiral.

Ra·bat (rə bät′) *n.* the capital of Morocco, in the northern part of the country. Pop. (1970), 374,800.

rab·bi (rab′ī) *n. pl.,* **rab·bis** or **rab·bies.** a teacher of the Jewish religion who is usually the leader of a Jewish congregation. [Hebrew *rabbī* my master.]

rab·bin·i·cal (rə bin′i kəl) *adj.* of or relating to rabbis or their views, teachings, or writings.

rab·bit (rab′it) *n.* **1.** any of a group of burrowing animals that have long ears, soft fur, and a short tail. **2.** the fur of this animal.

rab·ble (rab′əl) *n.* **1.** a disorderly crowd; mob. **2. the rabble.** the common people. ▲ used to show contempt: *The Duke refused to associate with the rabble.*

rab·ble-rous·er (rab′əl rou′zər) *n.* a person who tries to stir up people by exciting their fears, prejudices, or passions.

Rab·e·lais, Fran·çois (rab′ə lā′; frän swä′) 1494–1553, French satirist and humorist.

rab·id (rab′id) *adj.* **1.** showing too much zeal or enthusiasm in one's beliefs or actions; fanatical: *a rabid patriot. Roberta and her husband are rabid football fans.* **2.** violent; raging; furious: *rabid with anger.* **3.** of or affected with rabies; mad: *a rabid fox.* —**rab′id·ly,** *adv.* —**rab′id·ness,** *n.*

ra·bies (rā′bēz) *n.* a disease of warm-blooded animals, such as dogs, bats, and humans, that attacks the central nervous system and is usually transmitted by the bite of a rabid animal. Also, **hydrophobia.**

rac·coon (ra kōōn′) *also,* **ra·coon.** *n.* **1.** a small tree-dwelling animal of North and Central America, having brownish-gray fur, black masklike facial markings, and a ringed tail. **2.** the fur of this animal.

Raccoon

race[1] (rās) *n.* **1.** a contest to determine which contestant is fastest: *a running race, an automobile race.* **2.** any contest or competition: *a race for a political office.* —*v.,* **raced, rac·ing.** —*v.i.* **1.** to take part in a contest of speed: *Jack raced on his motorcycle.* **2.** to run, move, or go rapidly: *The boy raced down five flights of stairs.* **3.** (of machinery) to run at high speed. —*v.t.* **1.** to try to go faster than; be in a contest of speed against: *Bill raced his brother to the pool.* **2.** to cause to race: *He will race his sailboat tomorrow. Steve raced the engine of the car.* [Old Norse *rās.*]

race[2] (rās) *n.* **1.** a division of mankind having particular physical characteristics that are passed on from generation to generation: *the Caucasian race.* **2.** a group of persons sharing a common ancestry, history, nationality, or area of origin. **3.** a group of people sharing similar interests or habits. **4.** a group of animals or plants having particular characteristics that are passed on from one generation to another. [Middle French *race.*]

race·course (rās′kôrs′) *n.* another word for **racetrack.**

race·horse (rās′hôrs′) *n.* a horse that is bred and trained for racing.

ra·ceme (rā sēm′, rə sēm′) *n.* a simple arrangement of flowers on a stem, in which each flower grows on its own short stalk.

rac·er (rā′sər) *n.* **1.** a person or thing that races or takes part in a race, or is able to go very fast. **2.** any of a group of swift American snakes, especially the blacksnake.

race·track (rās′trak′) *n.* an area of ground for racing, usually oval in shape. Also, **racecourse.**

Ra·chel (rā′chəl) *n.* in the Old Testament, the second and favorite wife of Jacob and the mother of Joseph and Benjamin.

Rach·ma·ni·noff, Ser·gei (räk mä′ni-nôf′; ser gā′) 1873–1943, Russian composer and pianist.

ra·cial (rā′shəl) *adj.* **1.** of, relating to, or characteristic of a race: *racial characteristics.* **2.** of, relating to, or arising from relations between races: *racial prejudice, racial harmony.* —**ra′cial·ly,** *adv.*

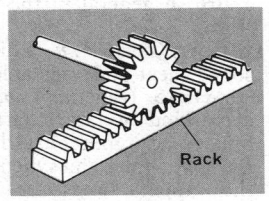

Raceme of a lily of the valley

rac·ism (rā′siz əm) *n.* **1.** a doctrine or belief that one race, especially one's own, is superior to another. **2.** a political policy or social system based on this. Also, **ra·cial·ism** (rā′shə liz′əm).

rac·ist (rā′sist) *n.* a person who believes in or supports racism. —*adj.* of or relating to racism.

rack¹ (rak) *n.* **1.** a framework or stand for hanging, showing, or storing things: *a coat rack, a display rack.* **2.** see **hayrack** *(def. 2).* **3.** an instrument of torture used to stretch a victim's body. **4.** a bar with teeth on one surface that mesh with a toothed gear or wheel. —*v.t.* **1.** to cause to suffer mentally or physically; torment: *The injured man was racked with pain.* **2.** to place in or on a rack. [Possibly from Middle Dutch *recke* framework.]

Rack

Rack¹ *(def. 4)*

rack² (rak) *n.* **to go to rack and ruin.** to deteriorate; fall apart. [A form of *wrack.*]

rack·et¹ (rak′it) *n.* **1.** a loud or confusing noise; clamor. **2.** *Informal.* a dishonest scheme or activity for getting money by the use of bribery, extortion, fraud, or threats of violence. [Possibly imitative of this noise.]

rack·et² (rak′it) *also,* **rac·quet.** *n.* **1.** a round or oval frame strung with a network of gut, nylon, or other material, and having a handle of different lengths, used to strike a ball, as in tennis or squash. **2.** see **paddle¹** *(def. 2).* [Middle French *raquette.*]

rack·et·eer (rak′ə tēr′) *n.* a person who organizes or takes part in a dishonest scheme or activity for getting money. —*v.i.* to organize or take part in a racket.

ra·coon (ra kōōn′) another spelling of **raccoon.**

rac·quet (rak′it) another spelling of **racket².**

rac·quets (rak′its) *n.,pl.* a game like tennis but played in a court enclosed by four walls. ▲ used with a singular verb.

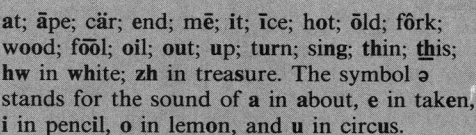

Racket²

rac·y (rā′sē) *adj.,* **rac·i·er, rac·i·est. 1.** somewhat indecent or improper. **2.** full of spirit; spirited; lively: *He has a racy style of writing.* —**rac′i·ly,** *adv.* —**rac′i·ness,** *n.*

ra·dar (rā′där) *n.* a device used to locate and track distant objects by the reflection of radio waves. [Short for *ra*(dio) *d*(etecting) *a*(nd) *r*(anging).]

ra·di·al (rā′dē əl) *adj.* **1.** of, relating to, or arranged like rays or radii. **2.** having parts branching outward from a common center. —**ra′di·al·ly,** *adv.*

ra·di·ance (rā′dē əns) *n.* the quality or state of being radiant. Also, **ra·di·an·cy** (rā′dē ən sē).

ra·di·ant (rā′dē ənt) *adj.* **1.** giving off rays of light or heat; shining brightly: *a radiant lamp.* **2.** beaming with joy, contentment, love, or the like: *a radiant smile, a radiant face.* **3.** made up of, having, or transmitted by radiation: *radiant heat.* —**ra′di·ant·ly,** *adv.*

radiant energy, energy transmitted by waves, especially by electromagnetic waves. X rays, visible light, heat, and radio waves are forms of radiant energy.

ra·di·ate (rā′dē āt′) *v.,* **ra·di·at·ed, ra·di·at·ing.** —*v.i.* **1.** to give off rays of light or heat. **2.** to issue in rays: *Heat radiates from the sun.* **3.** to move or branch outward from a center: *Streets radiated from the town's main square.* —*v.t.* **1.** to give off in rays: *The sun radiates light and heat.* **2.** to show (joy, contentment, love, or the like): *Her face radiates happiness.* —*adj.* **1.** having rays spreading out from a center: *a radiate flower.* **2.** radiating from a center.

ra·di·a·tion (rā′dē ā′shən) *n.* **1.** the process of giving off radiant energy in waves or particles. **2.** radiant energy given off in the form of waves or particles. **3.** the act or process of radiating.

ra·di·a·tor (rā′dē ā′tər) *n.* **1.** a heating device made up of a series of pipes or coils through which steam or hot water is made to circulate. **2.** a cooling device, as in an automobile engine, in which water is cooled and then circulated through ducts in the engine.

rad·i·cal (rad′i kəl) *adj.* **1.** going to the root or origin; fundamental; basic: *He has made a radical change in his study habits.* **2.** favoring or supporting extreme change, especially in political, social, and economic institutions. **3.** of or forming the root of a number or quantity. —*n.* **1.** a person who favors or supports extreme change, as in political, social, and economic institutions. **2.** a group of atoms remaining connected and acting as a unit, often in the form of an ion, in chemical reactions. **3.** *Mathematics.* **a.** a root of a number or quantity. **b.** a radical sign. —**rad′i·cal·ly,** *adv.* —**rad′i·cal·ness,** *n.*

rad·i·cal·ism (rad′i kə liz′əm) *n.* the support of extreme change, as in political, social, and economic institutions.

radical sign *Mathematics.* the sign ($\sqrt{}$) placed above a number or an algebraic expression to show that the root of it is to be found. For example: $\sqrt[3]{8}$ = *the cube root of 8* = 2.

rad·i·cand (rad′i kand′) *n.* the quantity under a radical sign: *9 is the radicand of* $\sqrt{9}.$

ra·di·i (rā′dē ī′) a plural of **radius.**

ra·di·o (rā′dē ō′) *n., pl.* **ra·di·os. 1.** a means of sending sound signals in the form of electromagnetic waves to a receiver. **2.** an apparatus for receiving radio broadcasts or for sending and receiving radio messages. **3.** radio broadcasting as a business or form of entertainment: *He is an announcer in radio.* —*adj.* of or relating to a radio. —*v.,* **ra·di·oed, ra·di·o·ing.** —*v.t.* **1.** to send (a message) by radio. **2.** to send a radio message to. —*v.i.* to send a message by radio: *The pilot radioed for landing instructions.*

at; āpe; cär; end; mē; it; īce; hot; ōld; fôrk; wood; fōōl; oil; out; up; turn; sing; thin; **th**is; hw in white; zh in treasure. The symbol ə stands for the sound of **a** in about, **e** in taken, **i** in pencil, **o** in lemon, and **u** in circus.

ra·di·o·ac·tive (rā′dē ō ak′tiv) *adj.* of, relating to, caused by, or showing radioactivity.

ra·di·o·ac·tiv·i·ty (rā′dē ō ak tiv′ə tē) *n.* the giving off of energy in the form of alpha and beta particles and gamma rays from the nuclei of atoms during a process of disintegration, in which atoms of one element are changed into atoms of another element.

radio astronomy, the branch of astronomy that studies heavenly objects by means of the radio waves that they give off.

ra·di·o·car·bon (rā′dē ō kär′bən) *n.* a radioactive carbon, especially carbon 14.

radio frequency, electromagnetic frequency from about ten kilocycles per second to several thousand megacycles per second, used especially in sending radio and television signals.

ra·di·o·gram (rā′dē ō gram′) *n.* a message sent by a wireless form of telegraphy.

ra·di·o·graph (rā′dē ō graf′) *n.* a picture made on a sensitive surface by radiation other than visible light, especially by X rays. —*v.t.* to make a radiograph of.

ra·di·ol·o·gist (rā′dē ol′ə jist) *n.* a doctor who specializes in radiology.

ra·di·ol·o·gy (rā′dē ol′ə jē) *n.* the science that deals with the use of X rays and other forms of radiant energy in the diagnosis and treatment of diseases.

ra·di·o·sonde (rā′dē ō sond′) *n.* an instrument that is carried into the sky by a balloon to radio back information about meteorological conditions at high altitudes.

ra·di·o·tel·e·phone (rā′dē ō tel′ə fōn′) *n.* a telephone that uses radio waves to send sound.

ra·di·o·tel·e·scope (rā′dē ō tel′ə skōp′) *n.* a telescope that detects radio waves coming from sources both inside and outside the solar system.

radio wave, an electromagnetic wave within radio frequency.

rad·ish (rad′ish) *n. pl.,* **rad·ish·es. 1.** a fleshy, red or white root that has a strong, biting taste and is usually eaten raw. **2.** the plant bearing this root.

ra·di·um (rā′dē əm) *n.* a white, highly radioactive metallic element found in pitchblende and other uranium ores. Symbol: **Ra**

ra·di·us (rā′dē əs) *n. pl.,* **ra·di·i** or **ra·di·us·es. 1.** a line going from the center to the outside of a circle or sphere. **2.** a circular area measured by such a line or by its circumference: *There is no other house within a radius of three miles of here.* **3.** the shorter and thicker of the two bones of the upper arm, extending from the humerus to the wrist on the thumb side of the arm.

ra·don (rā′don) *n.* a colorless, radioactive gaseous element given off in the disintegration of radium, used in the treatment of cancer. Symbol: **Rn**

RAF, Royal Air Force.

raf·fi·a (raf′ē ə) *n.* **1.** a strong fiber obtained from the leaves of a palm tree, used to make matting and baskets. **2.** the tree itself, found in Madagascar.

raf·fle (raf′əl) *n.* a lottery in which chances are sold for a prize. —*v.t.,* **raf·fled, raf·fling.** to sell by a raffle: *The club raffled off a turkey.*

raft (raft) *n.* **1.** a flat platform of logs, planks, or other material fastened together, used for transportation on water. **2.** see **life raft.**

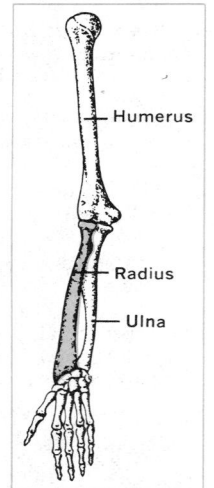

Radius *(def. 3)*

Humerus

Radius

Ulna

raft·er (raf′tər) *n.* one of the sloping beams that supports a roof.

rag¹ (rag) *n.* **1.** a small piece of cloth, especially one that is torn or worn out. **2. rags.** old, worn, tattered clothing. [Old English *ragg.*]

rag² (rag) *v.t.,* **ragged, ragging.** *Slang.* **1.** to tease. **2.** to scold. [Of uncertain origin.]

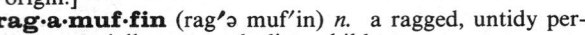

Rafters

rag·a·muf·fin (rag′ə muf′in) *n.* a ragged, untidy person, especially a ragged, dirty child.

rage (rāj) *n.* **1.** violent or uncontrolled anger; fury: *His eyes flashed with rage.* **2.** a fit of violent anger: *He was in a rage.* **3.** great force or violence. **4.** a fad; fashion; craze. —*v.i.,* **raged, rag·ing. 1.** to feel or show violent anger; be in a rage. **2.** to act or move with great force or violence: *The hurricane raged along the coast.*

rag·ged (rag′id) *adj.* **1.** worn into rags; tattered: *a ragged dress.* **2.** wearing tattered clothing: *a ragged beggar.* **3.** shaggy; unkempt: *ragged hair.* **4.** rough or uneven; jagged: *ragged cliffs.* —**rag′ged·ly,** *adv.* —**rag′ged·ness,** *n.*

rag·lan (rag′lən) *n.* a sleeve that extends over the shoulder to the collar. —*adj.* of or having such sleeves: *a raglan coat.* [From Lord *Raglan,* 1788–1855, a British general in the Crimean War.]

ra·gout (ra gōō′) *n.* a highly seasoned meat and vegetable stew.

rag·time (rag′tīm′) *n.* **1.** an early kind of jazz, characterized by a steady, marching rhythm in the lower notes and syncopation in the upper notes or melody. **2.** the syncopated rhythm of such music.

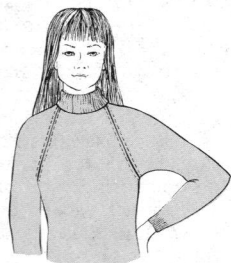

Raglan sleeves on a sweater

rag·weed (rag′wēd′) *n.* any of several coarse weeds whose pollen is one of the major causes of hay fever.

rah (rä) *interj., n.* see **hurrah.**

raid (rād) *n.* **1.** a sudden, surprise entering of a place, as by the police, for the purpose of seizing illegal equipment or stolen goods, and of making arrests. **2.** a sudden attack by a small force of soldiers. —*v.t.* to make a raid on. —*v.i.* to take part in or lead a raid. —**raid′er,** *n.*

rail¹ (rāl) *n.* **1.** a long, narrow bar of wood, metal, or other material, resting horizontally on posts and used as a guard or support. **2.** a fence or railing. **3.** one of a pair of metal bars that make up a railroad track. **4.** a railroad as a means of transportation: *The company sent its products by rail.* —*v.t.* to provide or enclose with a rail or rails. [Old French *reille* a bar, iron rod.]

rail² (rāl) *v.i.* to use scolding, bitter words; complain angrily or bitterly. [Middle French *railler* to mock.]

rail³ (rāl) *n.* a small bird that has short wings, long toes, and a harsh cry, found in marshy areas. [Old French *raale.*]

rail·ing (rā′ling) *n.* **1.** a fence or barrier made of a rail or rails. **2.** rails or the material for making rails.

rail·ler·y (rā′lər ē) *n. pl.,* **rail·ler·ies.** good-natured teasing; banter.

rail·road (rāl′rōd′) *n.* **1.** a permanent road laid with parallel metal rails fixed by ties and pro-

Rail³

viding a track for trains. **2.** an entire transportation system of such roads, including stations, trains, and land. **3.** the company that owns or manages such a system. —*v.t.* **1.** to transport by railroad. **2.** *Informal.* to rush or push through with great haste and without proper consideration: *The senators tried to railroad the bill through Congress.* **3.** *Slang.* to cause to be imprisoned on false charges or without a fair trial.

rail·way (rāl′wā′) *n.* **1.** another word for **railroad.** **2.** any set of rails for wheels.

rai·ment (rā′mənt) *n.* clothing; attire.

rain (rān) *n.* **1.** water condensed from vapor in the atmosphere, falling in drops from the sky to the earth: *Rain came through the window and soaked my book.* **2.** a fall of rain; rainstorm or shower: *She was caught in the rain.* **3.** a heavy or rapid fall of anything: *a rain of missiles.* **4. the rains.** the rainy season, as in tropical climates. —*v.i.* **1.** (of rain) to fall: *It is raining hard.* **2.** to fall like rain: *Bullets rained down on the soldiers.* —*v.t.* to pour or send down like rain: *People rained confetti from windows onto the parade.*

to rain out. to cause (an outdoor event) to be canceled or postponed because of rain.

rain·bow (rān′bō′) *n.* an arc of colored light showing all the colors of the spectrum, seen in the sky opposite the sun, caused by the reflection and refraction of the sun's rays by water droplets in the air.

rain·coat (rān′kōt′) *n.* a waterproof coat for use when it rains.

rain·drop (rān′drop′) *n.* a drop of rain.

rain·fall (rān′fôl′) *n.* **1.** a fall or shower of rain. **2.** the amount of water falling in the form of rain, snow, sleet, or hail in a given area within a given time.

rain forest, a dense, tropical forest in a region having a high annual rainfall.

Rai·nier, Mount (rə nēr′) a mountain in west-central Washington.

rain·proof (rān′proōf′) *adj.* not letting rain in; shedding rain.

rain·storm (rān′stôrm′) *n.* a storm with heavy rain.

rain·y (rā′nē) *adj.,* **rain·i·er, rain·i·est. 1.** characterized by or full of rain: *a rainy night, rainy weather.* **2.** wet with rain: *rainy streets.* —**rain′i·ness,** *n.*

rainy day, a time of need: *to save money for a rainy day.*

raise (rāz) *v.t.,* **raised, rais·ing. 1.** to move or cause to move to a higher position: *The boy raised his arm above his head.* **2.** to cause to rise or appear: *The bee sting raised a bump on my leg.* **3.** to move to a higher rank, position, or dignity: *The young officer was raised to the rank of major.* **4.** to increase, as in amount or volume: *The government raised taxes. He raised his voice in anger.* **5.** to gather together; collect: *The club needs to raise money.* **6.** to breed or grow: *The farmer raises wheat.* **7.** to bring up; rear: *The young couple wants to raise a family.* **8.** to bring up for consideration or discussion: *He raised an important question.* **9.** to stir up; arouse: *The rowdy boys raised a commotion.* **10.** to cause to rise with yeast: *to raise dough.* **11.** to build; construct: *The men raised the barn.* —*n.* **1.** the act of raising. **2.** an increase in amount: *a raise in salary.* —**rais′er,** *n.*

rai·sin (rā′zin) *n.* a sweet dried grape.

ra·jah (rä′jə) also, **ra·ja.** *n.* a ruler or prince in India or the East Indies.

rake¹ (rāk) *n.* a tool having a long handle with teeth or prongs attached at one end, used for gathering together such things as leaves or hay, or for smoothing surfaces, as of the soil. —*v.,* **raked, rak·ing.** —*v.t.* **1.** to gather or smooth with a rake. **2.** to collect in a large amount; amass: *He raked in money.* **3.** to search carefully and thoroughly: *She raked her bureau drawers for the lost key.* **4.** to bring

to attention: *The reporter raked up an old scandal.* **5.** to direct gunfire along the length of. —*v.i.* to use a rake: *Tom has been raking in the yard.* [Old English *raca.*]

rake² (rāk) *n.* an immoral man who seeks only pleasure. [Middle English *rakel* rash, wild.]

rake³ (rāk) *n.* a slope, as of the mast of a ship. [Of uncertain origin.]

rak·ish¹ (rā′kish) *adj.* **1.** dashing or stylish; jaunty: *He wore his hat at a rakish angle.* **2.** suggesting speed; streamlined, as a boat. [*Rake³* + *-ish.*] —**rak′ish·ly,** *adv.* —**rak′-ish·ness,** *n.*

rak·ish² (rā′kish) *adj.* like a rake; immoral and pleasure loving. [*Rake²* + *-ish.*]

Ra·leigh (rô′lē) *n.* **1. Sir Walter.** 1552?–1618, English adventurer and author. **2.** the capital of North Carolina, in the central part of the state. Pop. (1970), 121,577.

ral·ly¹ (ral′ē) *v.,* **ral·lied, ral·ly·ing.** —*v.t.* **1.** to bring together into order again; gather again: *The general rallied his scattered troops.* **2.** to bring together for a common purpose; assemble: *The club president rallied the members for the meeting.* —*v.i.* **1.** to be brought together into order again: *The soldiers quickly rallied.* **2.** to unite or come together for a common purpose. **3.** to come to the aid or support of a cause or person: *The public rallied behind the President.* **4.** to recover strength or energy: *The patient rallied overnight.* **5.** in tennis and similar games, to exchange a series of strokes before a point is made. —*n. pl.,* **ral·lies. 1.** the act of rallying. **2.** a meeting for a common purpose: *a political rally.* **3.** in tennis and similar games, a series of strokes exchanged before a point is made. [French *rallier* to assemble.]

ral·ly² (ral′ē) *v.t., v.i.,* **ral·lied, ral·ly·ing.** to tease goodnaturedly; banter. [French *railler* to mock.]

ram (ram) *n.* **1.** a male sheep. **2.** a device used to batter, crush, or force something, such as a battering ram. —*v.,* **rammed, ram·ming.** —*v.t.* **1.** to batter or strike against with great force; butt against: *The two ships tried to ram each other.* **2.** to force or drive down or into place: *He rammed the stake into the ground.* **3.** to stuff or cram: *The child rammed the food into his mouth.* —*v.i.* to strike against something with great force; collide: *His car rammed into the car ahead.* —**ram′mer,** *n.*

ram·ble (ram′bəl) *v.i.,* **ram·bled, ram·bling. 1.** to go about or move about aimlessly; roam. **2.** to talk or write in a confused and disordered way: *The speaker rambled on and never came to the point.* —*n.* a pleasant stroll or walk.

ram·bler (ram′blər) *n.* **1.** a person or thing that rambles. **2.** any of certain climbing roses.

ram·bunc·tious (ram bungk′shəs) *adj.* wild and boisterous: *a rambunctious child.* —**ram·bunc′tious·ly,** *adv.*

Ram·e·ses (ram′ə sēz) *also,* **Ram·ses.** *n.* any of eleven kings reigning in Egypt from about 1320 B.C. to about 1090 B.C., especially **Rameses II,** who died 1234? B.C., believed to be the pharaoh who oppressed the Hebrews.

ram·i·fi·ca·tion (ram′ə fi kā′shən) *n.* **1.** the act or process of dividing or spreading into branches. **2.** something, such as an effect or consequence, that results from a situation or statement: *What are the ramifications of his plan?*

at; āpe; cär; end; mē; it; īce; hot; ōld; fôrk; wood; fōōl; oil; out; up; turn; sing; thin; this; hw in white; zh in treasure. The symbol ə stands for the sound of **a** in about, **e** in taken, **i** in pencil, **o** in lemon, and **u** in circus.

755

ram·i·fy (ram′ə fī′) *v.i.,* **ram·i·fied, ram·i·fy·ing.** to divide or spread into branches or as if into branches.

ramp (ramp) *n.* **1.** a sloping passageway or roadway connecting different levels. **2.** a movable staircase for entering or leaving an airplane.

ram·page (*n.,* ram′pāj′; *v.,* ram′pāj′, ram pāj′) *n.* a fit of violent or reckless behavior or action: *The bear went on a rampage and knocked over tents at the campsite.* —*v.i.,* **rampaged, ram·pag·ing.** to behave in a violent or reckless way; rage.

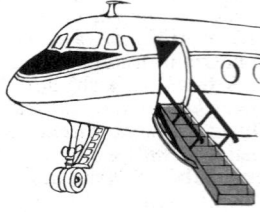
Ramp¹ *(def. 2)*

ramp·ant (ram′pənt) *adj.* **1.** thick or abundant; luxuriant: *a rampant growth of wild flowers.* **2.** acting or spreading without control; unchecked; unrestrained: *Flu was rampant in the town.* **3.** (of an animal on a coat of arms) rearing up on the hind legs and with the head and body in profile: *a lion rampant.* —**ramp′ant·ly,** *adv.*

ram·part (ram′pärt) *n.* **1.** a bank of earth built up around a fort or castle and sometimes supporting a wall, used for defense. **2.** anything that serves as a defense or protection.

ram·rod (ram′rod′) *n.* **1.** a rod used for ramming the charge down the barrel of a gun that is loaded through the muzzle. **2.** a rod used to clean the barrel of a gun.

Ram·ses (ram′sēz) another name for **Rameses.**

ram·shack·le (ram′shak′əl) *adj.* likely to collapse; dilapidated; rickety: *a ramshackle old house.*

ran (ran) the past tense of **run.**

ranch (ranch) *n. pl.,* **ranch·es. 1.** a large farm, especially in the western United States, used to raise large herds of cattle, sheep, or horses. **2.** any farm devoted to raising a particular crop or animal: *a fruit ranch.* —*v.i.* to manage or work on a ranch.

ranch·er (ran′chər) *n.* a person who owns or works on a ranch.

ran·cid (ran′sid) *adj.* having the unpleasant odor or taste of spoiled oil or fat: *rancid butter.* —**ran′cid·ly,** *adv.* —**ran′cid·ness,** *n.*

ran·cor (rang′kər) *n.* deep or bitter resentment; hatred; spite.

ran·cor·ous (rang′kər əs) *adj.* deeply or bitterly resentful; spiteful. —**ran′cor·ous·ly,** *adv.* —**ran′cor·ous·ness,** *n.*

ran·dom (ran′dəm) *adj.* lacking a definite plan or purpose; happening by chance; unplanned; haphazard: *He made a random choice.* —**ran′dom·ly,** *adv.* —**ran′dom·ness,** *n.*

at random. with no definite plan or purpose: *He picked a magazine at random from the pile.*

rang (rang) the past tense of **ring².**

range (rānj) *n.* **1.** the limits between which something varies: *There is a wide range in prices for a television set.* **2.** the area in which something can act or be effective: *The airplane flew beyond his range of vision. The boy's range of knowledge is still limited.* **3.** the greatest distance that a gun, cannon, or other similar weapon can be shot. **4.** the greatest distance that a plane, ship, or land vehicle can travel without refueling. **5.** a place set aside for shooting practice or for testing rockets and missiles. **6.** a large area of open land over which livestock roam and graze. **7.** a row or series, especially of mountains. **8.** a large stove having burners and an oven: *a cooking range.* **9.** a region in which a particular plant or animal normally lives. —*v.,* **ranged, rang·ing.** —*v.t.* **1.** to place in a particular order; arrange: *The librarian ranged the books on the shelf.* **2.** to place in a particular position or group. **3.** to move or wander over (an area): *Cattle ranged the prairie.* —*v.i.* **1.** to vary between certain limits: *The price for that bicycle ranges between forty and sixty dollars in different stores.* **2.** to wander or roam. **3.** to stretch out in a line; extend: *Trees ranged along the road.* **4.** (of plants and animals) to live or grow in a region.

rang·er (rān′jər) *n.* **1.** see **forest ranger. 2.** a member of an armed group that patrols a region to maintain law and order. **3.** a person or thing that ranges.

Ran·goon (rang gōōn′) *n.* the capital and chief port of Burma, in the southern part of the country. Pop. (1977 est.), 2,276,000.

rang·y (rān′jē) *adj.,* **rang·i·er, rang·i·est.** having long legs and a slender body: *a rangy youth.*

rank¹ (rangk) *n.* **1.** relative position or standing: *Carol has a high rank in her class at school.* **2.** position or grade: *He has the rank of captain.* **3.** high position, standing, or class: *The prime minister is a man of rank.* **4.** a line or row of soldiers standing side by side in close order. **5. ranks. a.** the common soldiers or enlisted men of an army. **b.** an army. **6.** *Chess.* any row of squares running across the board. —*v.t.* **1.** to arrange in a row or rows: *to rank soldiers.* **2.** to assign a position to; classify: *to rank students according to their grades.* **3.** to take precedence over; outrank: *Lieutenants rank sergeants.* —*v.i.* to have a certain rank or position: *That student ranks high in his class.* [Old French *ranc* row, line.]

rank² (rangk) *adj.* **1.** growing thickly and unchecked: *a rank growth of grass.* **2.** having a strong, bad smell or taste: *rank pork, rank cigars.* **3.** utter or complete: *a rank liar.* [Old English *ranc* strong, brave.] —**rank′ly,** *adv.* —**rank′ness,** *n.*

rank and file 1. the common soldiers or enlisted people of an army, as distinguished from the officers. **2.** the people who make up a group, as distinguished from the leaders: *the rank and file of organized labor.*

ran·kle (rang′kəl) *v.,* **ran·kled, ran·kling.** —*v.t.* to irritate, hurt, or anger (someone) continuously. —*v.i.* to irritate, hurt, or anger: *Her unkind remark rankled in his mind for many months.*

ran·sack (ran′sak′) *v.t.* **1.** to search thoroughly: *She ransacked her purse looking for change.* **2.** to search through for valuables: *Thieves ransacked the house.*

ran·som (ran′səm) *n.* **1.** the release of a person or property for a price: *to hold someone for ransom.* **2.** the price paid or demanded. —*v.t.* **1.** to obtain the release of by paying a certain price. **2.** to release upon receiving payment of ransom.

rant (rant) *v.i.* to speak in a wild, excited way; rave. —*n.* wild, excited, and loud speech or way of speaking.

rap¹ (rap) *n.* **1.** a quick, sharp, or light knock or tap. **2.** *Slang.* punishment or blame, especially a prison sentence: *The man took the rap for a crime he did not commit.* **3.** *Slang.* a conversation or discussion. —*v.,* **rapped, rapping.** —*v.i.* **1.** to knock or tap sharply: *to rap at a door.* **2.** *Slang.* to talk; converse. —*v.t.* **1.** to knock or tap sharply: *to rap a table with a pencil.* **2.** to say sharply: *to rap out a reply.* [Possibly imitative of the sound of a light, sharp knock.]

rap² (rap) *n. Informal.* the least bit: *He doesn't care a rap about sports.* [Of uncertain origin.]

ra·pa·cious (rə pā′shəs) *adj.* **1.** wanting more than one's share; grasping; greedy: *a rapacious miser.* **2.** (of animals) living on live prey; predatory. **3.** given to taking by force; plundering: *rapacious pirates.* —**ra·pa′cious·ly,** *adv.* —**ra·pa′cious·ness,** *n.*

ra·pac·i·ty (rə pas′ə tē) *n.* the quality of being rapacious.

rape¹ (rāp) *n.* **1.** the crime of forcing a woman to do a sexual act against her will. **2.** a seizing and carrying off by force. —*v.t.,* **raped, rap·ing.** to force to do a sexual act. [Old French *raper* to seize.]

rape² (rāp) *n.* a plant whose leaves are used as fodder and whose seeds yield an oil that is used as a lubricant. [Latin *rāpa.*]

Raph·a·el (raf′ē əl, rā′fē əl) 1483–1520, Italian painter.

rap·id (rap′id) *adj.* moving or acting with great speed; swift: *a rapid pace, rapid development.* —*n.* usually, **rap·ids.** a part of a river where the current is swift, caused by a steep descent of the riverbed. —**rap′id·ly,** *adv.* —**rap′id·ness,** *n.*

rap·id-fire (rap′id fīr′) *adj.* **1.** (of guns) firing shots in rapid succession. **2.** happening quickly, one after another: *rapid-fire questions.*

ra·pid·i·ty (rə pid′ə tē) *n.* the state or quality of being rapid; quickness.

ra·pi·er (rā′pē ər) *n.* a light sword having a sharp point and no cutting edge, used only for thrusting.

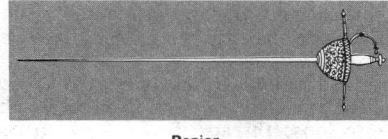
Rapier

rap·ine (rap′in) *n.* the act of seizing and carrying off property belonging to another; plunder; pillage: *the rapine of a town by raiders.*

rap·port (ra pôr′) *n.* a relationship characterized by harmony or close agreement: *The teacher had good rapport with his students.*

rap·proche·ment (ra prōsh män′) *n.* the establishing or renewing of friendly relations, as between nations.

rap·scal·lion (rap skal′yən) *n.* a rascal; rogue; scamp.

rapt (rapt) *adj.* **1.** carried away with joy or delight; enraptured. **2.** deeply absorbed: *He was so rapt in his book that he didn't hear her question.*

rap·ture (rap′chər) *n.* a feeling of great happiness, delight, or joy.

rap·tur·ous (rap′chər əs) *adj.* showing or feeling rapture. —**rap′tur·ous·ly,** *adv.*

rare¹ (rer) *adj.,* **rar·er, rar·est. 1.** seldom happening, seen, or found: *Meeting the astronaut was a rare experience for him.* **2.** unusually fine or valuable: *He has a collection of rare stamps.* **3.** having little density; thin: *The air is rare at high altitudes.* [Latin *rārus* scarce, thin.] —**rare′ness,** *n.*

rare² (rer) *adj.,* **rar·er, rar·est.** (of meat) cooked for a short period of time. [Old English *hrēr* not cooked enough.] —**rare′ness,** *n.*

rare·bit (rer′bit) *n.* see **Welsh rabbit.**

rare-earth element (rer′urth′) any of the metallic elements with atomic numbers from 57 through 71. Also, **rare-earth metal.**

rar·e·fy (rer′ə fī′) *v.,* **rar·e·fied, rar·e·fy·ing.** —*v.t.* **1.** to make thinner or less de̶̶̶̶̶ or purify: *to rarefy one's̶̶̶̶̶̶̶̶ less dense.*

rare·ly (rer′lē) *adv.* to the movies. **2.** un

rar·i·ty (rer′ə tē) that is rare: *Rain̶̶̶̶* fact of being rar̶̶

ras·cal (ras′kəl 2.** a low, mean,

ras·cal·i·ty (ra̶̶ acter or behavi̶̶

ras·cal·ly (ras̶̶ —*adv.* in a ras̶̶

rash¹ (rash) *adj.* too hasty; reckless: *a rash young man, a rash decision.* [Middle English *rasch* quick.] —**rash′ly,** *adv.* —**rash′ness,** *n.*

rash² (rash) *n. pl.,* **rash·es.** a breaking out of red spots on the skin. [Old French *rasche.*]

rash·er (rash′ər) *n.* a slice of bacon for frying or broiling.

rasp (rasp) *v.t.* **1.** to scrape or grate with a rough tool, such as a file. **2.** to grate upon; irritate: *The loud noise rasped his nerves.* **3.** to say in a rough, grating voice: *The policeman rasped a command to the recruits.* —*v.i.* to make a rough, grating sound. —*n.* **1.** a rough, grating sound. **2.** a coarse file with raised, pointed projections, used on wood.

rasp·ber·ry (raz′ber′ē) *n. pl.,* **rasp·ber·ries. 1.** the sweet red fruit of any of several plants of the rose family. **2.** the prickly plant that bears this fruit. **3.** *Slang.* a sound of disapproval or contempt made with the tongue and lips.

Raspberries

rat (rat) *n.* **1.** an animal similar to a mouse but larger, having a long snout, rounded ears, and a long slender tail. Rats are found throughout most of the world. **2.** *Slang.* a sneaky, low person who cannot be trusted. —*v.i.,* **rat·ted, rat·ting. 1.** to hunt for rats. **2.** *Slang.* to tell on; betray.

ra·tan (ra tan′) another spelling of **rattan.**

ratch·et (rach′it) *n.* **1.** a mechanism made up of a wheel whose slanted teeth are caught on a pawl, allowing the wheel to revolve in one direction only. **2.** the pawl or wheel of such a mechanism.

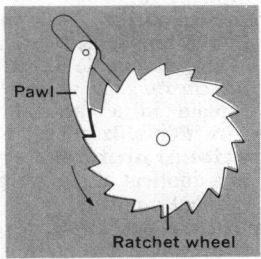
Ratchet

rate (rāt) *n.* **1.** an amount or number in relation to the amount or number of something else: *The car was going at a rate of sixty miles per hour.* **2.** price or charge per unit, as of a service: *telephone rates.* **3.** a certain rank or class: *Her work is of the first rate.* —*v.,* **rat·ed, rat·ing.** —*v.t.* **1.** to estimate or set the value of: *He rated the movie as poor.* **2.** to place in a certain class or rank: *That university is rated first among college football teams.* **3.** to consider; regard: *The students rate Jerry as the best athlete in school.* **4.** *Informal.* to deserve; merit: *The manager thinks that Harry rates a raise.* —*v.i.* to have a certain rank or class.

at any rate. in any case; at least.

rath·er (rath′ər) *adv.* **1.** more readily or willingly: *I would rather stay home than go out tonight.* **2.** more properly; instead: *Jim, rather than Bill, deserved to win.* **3.** more correctly: *The airplane is arriving at noon or, rather, at 12:15 p.m.* **4.** somewhat: *It is rather cold out.* **5.** on the contrary: *He is not happy; rather, he is sad.* —*interj. British.* certainly.

at; āpe; cär; end; mē; it; īce; hot; ōld; fôrk; ̶̶̶wood; fo͞ol; oil; out; up; turn; sing; thin; this; ̶̶̶w in white; zh in treasure. The symbol ə ̶̶̶nds for the sound of a in about, e in taken, ̶̶̶n pencil, o in lemon, and u in circus.

rat·i·fi·ca·tion (rat′ə fi kā′shən) *n.* the act of ratifying or the state of being ratified.

rat·i·fy (rat′ə fī′) *v.t.,* **rat·i·fied, rat·i·fy·ing.** to consent to officially; approve: *Congress ratified the trade agreement.* —**rat′i·fi′er,** *n.*

rat·ing (rā′ting) *n.* **1.** a certain rank or grade: *That television show has a high rating.* **2.** an estimate of the financial position of a person or business.

ra·ti·o (rā′shē ō′) *n. pl.,* **ra·ti·os. 1.** a comparison between two things: *The ratio of girls to boys in the class is four to three.* **2.** *Mathematics.* a comparison between two numbers or algebraic expressions expressed as a quotient. The ratio of 3 to 7 is written 3 : 7 or $\frac{3}{7}$.

ra·tion (rash′ən, rā′shən) *n.* **1.** a fixed portion or share. **2.** the daily amount of food allowed, as for a soldier. **3. rations.** food. —*v.t.* **1.** to give out in portions: *After the flood, food and clothes were rationed to the victims.* **2.** to supply with rations: *to ration an army.* **3.** to limit to fixed portions: *The government rationed meat during the war.*

ra·tion·al (rash′ən əl) *adj.* **1.** based on or conforming to reason; sensible: *He used rational arguments to support his opinions.* **2.** able to think clearly; sane: *The old man was perfectly rational when he made out his will.* **3.** having the ability to reason: *Man is a rational being.* **4.** *Mathematics.* of or relating to a rational number. —**ra′tion·al·ly,** *adv.*

ra·tion·ale (rash′ə nal′) *n.* a rational or logical basis.

ra·tion·al·ism (rash′ən əl iz′əm) *n.* the depending on reason alone as the authority or guide for one's opinion, belief, or conduct.

ra·tion·al·i·ty (rash′ə nal′ə tē) *n.* the quality or state of being rational.

ra·tion·al·ize (rash′ən əl īz′) *v.t.,* **ra·tion·al·ized, ra·tion·al·iz·ing. 1.** to explain (one's behavior) in a way that seems reasonable but is probably untrue: *He rationalized his cheating by saying that everyone else cheated.* **2.** to explain in a rational way. —**ra′tion·al·i·za′tion,** *n.* —**ra′tion·al·iz′er,** *n.*

rational number, a real number that can be expressed as a quotient of two integers or as an integer. ¾ and 5 are rational numbers.

rat·line (rat′lin) *also,* **rat·lin.** *n.* one of the small ropes stretching horizontally across the shrouds of a ship, used as a ladder.

rat·tan (ra tan′) *also,* **ra·tan.** *n.* **1.** the long thin stems of a tropical palm tree, used for mats, baskets, wicker chairs, and other products. **2.** the tree having these stems. **3.** a cane or switch made from these stems.

rat·ter (rat′ər) *n.* an animal, such as a dog or cat, that catches rats.

Ratlines

rat·tle (rat′əl) *v.,* **rat·tled, rat·tling.** —*v.i.* **1.** to make a quick series of short, sharp sounds: *The doors and windows rattled when the wind blew against the house.* **2.** to move with such sounds; clatter: *The old car rattled over the cobblestones.* **3.** to talk quickly and aimlessly; chatter: *The child rattled on.* —*v.t.* **1.** to cause to rattle. **2.** to say quickly: *She rattled off her answers.* **3.** to confuse; embarrass: *He was rattled by his mistake.* —*n.* **1.** a quick series of short, sharp sounds. **2.** an object, especially a baby's toy, that makes a rattling noise when shaken. **3.** a series of rings of horny tissue at the end of a rattlesnake's tail.

rat·tler (rat′lər) *n.* **1.** a person or thing that rattles. **2.** a rattlesnake.

rat·tle·snake (rat′əl snāk′) *n.* any of a group of poisonous American snakes having a series of rings of horny tissue at the end of the tail that rattle when shaken.

Rattlesnake

rau·cous (rô′kəs) *adj.* **1.** harsh; grating: *He has a raucous voice.* **2.** disorderly; rowdy: *The raucous party left the house in shambles.* —**rau′cous·ly,** *adv.* —**rau′cous·ness,** *n.*

rav·age (rav′ij) *v.,* **rav·aged, rav·ag·ing.** —*v.t.* to lay waste to; destroy: *The fire ravaged the town.* —*v.i.* to lay waste; be destructive. —*n.* a destructive action or its result: *The ravages of time left their marks on the old woman's face.* —**rav′ag·er,** *n.*

rave (rāv) *v.i.,* **raved, rav·ing. 1.** to talk in a wild or crazy way. **2.** to talk with much or too much enthusiasm: *He raved about his new car.* —*n.* **1.** the act of raving. **2.** very enthusiastic approval or recommendation. —*adj.* very enthusiastic or approving: *The new television show received rave reviews.*

rav·el (rav′əl) *v.,* **rav·eled, rav·el·ing;** *also, British,* **rav·elled, rav·el·ling.** —*v.t.* to cause (cloth or rope) to separate into loose threads; fray. —*v.i.* to become raveled; fray. —*n.* a loose thread or raveled part.

Rav·el, Mau·rice (rə vel′; mô rēs′) 1875–1937, French composer.

ra·ven (rā′vən) *n.* a bird similar to a crow but larger, having glossy black feathers and a harsh cry. —*adj.* having a glossy black color.

rav·en·ing (rav′ə ning) *adj.* greedy; rapacious.

rav·en·ous (rav′ə nəs) *adj.* **1.** extremely hungry; famished. **2.** greedy; rapacious: *The ravenous mob pillaged the town.* —**rav′en·ous·ly,** *adv.*

Raven

ra·vine (rə vēn′) *n.* a deep, narrow valley, especially one eroded by running water.

rav·ing (rā′ving) *adj.* **1.** wild; frenzied: *a raving lunatic.* **2.** *Informal.* outstanding; extraordinary: *a raving beauty.* —*n.* wild talk: *the ravings of a madman.*

rav·i·o·li (rav′ē ō′lē) *n.,pl.* a food made of dough filled with chopped meat, cheese, or other filling, boiled and served with a tomato sauce.

rav·ish (rav′ish) *v.t.* **1.** to seize and carry off by force. **2.** to rape. **3.** to carry away with joy; enrapture. —**rav′ish·er,** *n.* —**rav′ish·ment,** *n.*

rav·ish·ing (rav′i shing) *adj.* delightful; enchanting. —**rav′ish·ing·ly,** *adv.*

raw (rô) *adj.* **1.** uncooked: *raw meat.* **2.** not refined or processed; in a natural state: *raw cotton, raw milk.* **3.** having the skin rubbed or worn off: *a raw wound.* **4.** having no experience ▮▮▮ing: *a raw recruit.* **5.** damp and cold: *raw weather.* ▮▮▮ fair or harsh: *a raw deal.* —**raw′ly,** *adv.* —**raw▮**

raw·boned (rô′bōn▮▮ ▮▮g little flesh; gaunt.

raw·hide (rô′hīd′) ▮▮▮ed hide of cattle or other animals. **2.** ▮▮▮le of such hide.

raw material, ▮▮▮ed, manufactured, or processed: *Woo▮▮▮▮▮▮l of paper.*

ray¹ (rā) *n.* **1.** a▮▮▮▮ or other radiant energy: *the rays▮▮▮* a group of lines coming from a▮▮▮ething projecting from a commo▮▮▮f a starfish. **4.** a very small am▮▮▮Old French *rai.*]

ray² (rā) *n.* any of a number of flat fish having a skeleton of cartilage rather than of bone. [Old French *raie*.]

ray·on (rā′on) *n.* **1.** a fiber made from cellulose. **2.** cloth or thread made of rayon.

raze (rāz) *v.t.,* **razed, raz·ing.** to tear down; demolish: *The city razed the old buildings to make room for a park.*

ra·zor (rā′zər) *n.* an instrument or device used for shaving off or cutting hair.

razz (raz) *v.t. Slang.* to make fun of; ridicule.

Rb, the symbol for rubidium.

R.C. 1. Red Cross. **2.** Roman Catholic.

Rd., rd., road.

R.D., rural delivery.

re¹ (rā) *n. Music.* **1.** the second note of the major scale. **2.** the note D.

re² (rē) *prep.* about; concerning. [Latin *rē*.]

Re, the symbol for rhenium.

re- *prefix* **1.** again: *re-count.* **2.** back: *repel.* [Old French *rē-* again, back, from Latin *re-* again, back.]

● To understand the meaning of a word that begins with **re-** but is not defined in this dictionary, add the word "again" to the meaning of the basic word. For example, *reheat* means "heat again" and *rediscover* means "discover again."

reach (rēch) *v.t.* **1.** to arrive at; get as far as; come to: *We reached his house after driving for several hours.* **2.** to touch or grasp: *The little girl was not able to reach the dish on the shelf.* **3.** to stretch or extend: *He reached out his arms to greet his friend.* **4.** to get in touch with; contact: *I reached him by telephone.* —*v.i.* **1.** to stretch the arm or hand out: *He reached to touch the ceiling.* **2.** to try to grasp something: *He reached for his wallet.* **3.** to stretch or extend: *The drapes reached from the ceiling to the floor.* —*n. pl.,* **reach·es. 1.** the act of reaching or stretching out. **2.** the extent or distance covered in reaching: *A person would have to have a long reach to touch that ceiling.* **3.** the extent or amount that a person is able to understand or do; range: *Choose a goal within your reach.*

re·act (rē akt′) *v.i.* **1.** to act in response to something; respond: *The kitten reacts to kindness by purring.* **2.** to act in opposition: *He reacted against his parents' strictness.* **3.** to act in return: *His friends' ideas react on his own thinking.* **4.** to undergo a chemical reaction.

re·ac·tion (rē ak′shən) *n.* **1.** an action in response to something: *What was his parents' reaction when they saw his report card?* **2.** a political or social tendency to return to a former condition or state of affairs: *During the period of political reaction, the king was returned to his throne.* **3.** *Chemistry.* a process in which substances are changed chemically into new substances. **4.** *Physics.* a force equal to but opposing the force that produces it.

re·ac·tion·ar·y (rē ak′shə ner′ē) *adj.* of, relating to, or favoring a return to a former political or social condition or state of affairs. —*n. pl.,* **re·ac·tion·ar·ies.** a person who favors political and social reaction.

re·ac·ti·vate (rē ak′tə vāt′) *v.t.,* **re·ac·ti·vat·ed, re·ac·ti·vat·ing.** to make active again. —**re·ac′ti·va′tion,** *n.*

re·ac·tive (rē ak′tiv) *adj.* **1.** tending to react. **2.** relating to or characterized by reaction.

re·ac·tor (rē ak′tər) *n.* see **nuclear reactor.**

read (rēd) *v.,* **read** (red), **read·ing.** —*v.t.* **1.** to look at and understand the meaning of (something written or printed): *Helen read a magazine.* **2.** to say aloud (something written or printed): *The mother read bedtime stories to her children.* **3.** to understand letters or symbols in (a foreign language): *He learned to read French.* **4.** to get the meaning of; understand: *She read his thoughts.* **5.** to give or

register (information): *The speedometer read sixty miles per hour.* **6.** *British.* to study: *to read law.* —*v.i.* **1.** to understand something written or printed: *His little sister hasn't learned to read yet.* **2.** to say aloud something written or printed. **3.** to learn by reading: *I read about the incident in the newspaper.* **4.** to be worded in a particular way: *These two editions of the book read differently.*
to read between the lines. to find another meaning besides the one expressed in the written or spoken words.
to read up on. to study.

read·a·ble (rē′də bəl) *adj.* **1.** easy or interesting to read. **2.** able to be read; legible: *His poor handwriting is barely readable.* —**read′a·bil′i·ty, read′a·ble·ness,** *n.*

read·er (rē′dər) *n.* **1.** a person who reads. **2.** a schoolbook with exercises for learning and practicing reading.

read·i·ly (red′ə lē) *adv.* **1.** in a willing manner; without opposition; willingly: *The boy readily followed his friend's advice.* **2.** without difficulty; easily: *His remark was readily understood by everyone.*

read·i·ness (red′ē nis) *n.* **1.** the quality or state of being ready. **2.** willingness. **3.** ease.

read·ing (rē′ding) *n.* **1.** the act or practice of a person who reads. **2.** the act or instance of saying aloud something written or printed: *The author gave a public reading of his work.* **3.** something read or to be read: *That book is interesting reading.* **4.** a personal interpretation: *The actor gave a fine reading of the role of Hamlet.* **5.** the information given or amount indicated by a meter, dial, or other instrument. —*adj.* **1.** that reads: *the reading public.* **2.** made or used for reading: *reading glasses.*

Read·ing (red′ing) *n.* a city in southeastern Pennsylvania. Pop. (1970), 87,643.

re·ad·just (rē′ə just′) *v.t.* to adjust again. —*v.i.* to become adapted to again: *The former soldier tried to readjust to civilian life.* —**re′ad·just′ment,** *n.*

read·y (red′ē) *adj.,* **read·i·er, read·i·est. 1.** prepared or fit for use or action: *The car is ready for the trip. We are ready to start the game.* **2.** mentally prepared; willing: *He was ready to work hard in order to earn money for a bicycle.* **3.** immediately liable or likely: *The dynamite is ready to explode.* **4.** quick or prompt: *John always has a ready answer.* **5.** immediately available: *He keeps ready cash for emergencies.* —*v.t.,* **read·ied, read·y·ing.** to make ready; prepare: *The plane was readied for takeoff.*

read·y-made (red′ē mād′) *adj.* not made to order.

Rea·gan, Ronald W. (rā′gən) 1911—, the fortieth president of the United States, since 1981.

re·a·gent (rē ā′jənt) *n.* a substance used in a chemical reaction in order to find, analyze, or produce other substances.

re·al¹ (rē′əl, rēl) *adj.* **1.** actual or true; not imagined: *The man's adventures were quite real; he did not make them up.* **2.** not artificial; genuine; authentic: *The flowers are real, not plastic.* **3.** *Law.* relating to or consisting of permanent or immovable things, such as lands or buildings: *real property.* —*adv. Informal.* very; extremely: *I'm real hungry.* [Old French *real* actual.]

re·al² (rā äl′) *n. pl.,* **re·als** or **re·a·les** (rā ä′lās). a former coin and monetary unit of Spain and various Latin American countries. [Spanish *real.*]

at; āpe; cär; end; mē; it; īce; hot; ōld; fôrk; wood; fōōl; oil; out; up; turn; sing; thin; this; hw in white; zh in treasure. The symbol ə stands for the sound of **a** in about, e in taken, i in pencil, o in lemon, and u in circus.

real estate, land together with the buildings, trees, water, or other things on it.

re·al·ism (rē′ə liz′əm) *n.* **1.** concern with what is actual or practical, instead of with what does not or cannot exist. **2.** in art and literature, the showing of people, things, and events as they actually are in everyday life. **3.** a theory in philosophy that the real world exists apart from man's awareness of it and that man's senses give real knowledge of it.

re·al·ist (rē′ə list) *n.* **1.** a person who is concerned with what is actual or practical, instead of with what does not or cannot exist. **2.** an artist or writer whose work is characterized by realism. **3.** a person who believes in or follows realism in philosophy.

re·al·is·tic (rē′ə lis′tik) *adj.* **1.** showing people, things, or events as they actually are in everyday life: *a realistic painting.* **2.** concerned with what is actual or practical: *a realistic person, a realistic attitude.* **3.** of, relating to, or characterized by realism in philosophy. —**re′al·is′ti·cal·ly,** *adv.*

re·al·i·ty (rē al′ə tē) *n. pl.,* **re·al·i·ties. 1.** the state or quality of being real. **2.** a real thing, fact, or event.

re·al·i·za·tion (rē′ə li zā′shən) *n.* **1.** the act of realizing or the state of being realized. **2.** something realized.

re·al·ize (rē′ə līz′) *v.t.,* **re·al·ized, re·al·iz·ing. 1.** to understand completely: *Does he realize what he has done?* **2.** to make real, as an idea or emotion: *His hopes were never realized.* **3.** to gain (a sum of money): *He realized $300 in the sale of his coin collection.*

re·al·ly (rē′ə lē, rē′lē) *adv.* **1.** in fact; actually: *She told us what really happened.* **2.** indeed: *Really, you can't be serious!* **3.** truly; genuinely: *We spent a really pleasant day in the park.*

realm (relm) *n.* **1.** a kingdom. **2.** a field, area, or sphere, as of knowledge or interest: *the realm of science, the realm of fantasy.*

real number *Mathematics.* any rational or irrational number.

re·al·tor (rē′əl tər) *n.* a real estate agent or broker.

re·al·ty (rē′əl tē) *n. pl.,* **re·al·ties.** another word for **real estate.**

ream¹ (rēm) *n.* **1.** a quantity of paper of the same size and quality, varying from 480 to 500 sheets. **2. reams.** a large amount; great quantity: *The clerk had reams of office forms to check over.* [Old French *raime.*]

ream² (rēm) *v.t.* **1.** to create or enlarge (a hole). **2.** to remove with a reamer. [Old English *rȳman.*]

ream·er (rē′mər) *n.* **1.** a steel tool with lengthwise blades or cutting edges, used to enlarge or shape a drilled hole. **2.** a utensil used for removing the juice from oranges, lemons, and other fruit.

reap (rēp) *v.t.* **1.** to cut down (grain). **2.** to gather (a crop) by reaping. **3.** to cut down or harvest the crop from: *to reap fields.* **4.** to receive as a reward: *The child's good behavior reaped praise.*

reap·er (rē′pər) *n.* **1.** a person who reaps. **2.** a machine used to cut and gather grain.

re·ap·pear (rē′ə pēr′) *v.i.* to appear again. —**re′ap·pear′ance,** *n.*

rear¹ (rēr) *n.* **1.** the part that is behind or in the back; back: *the rear of a room, the rear of a bus.* **2.** the part of a military force farthest from the fighting area. —*adj.* relating to or located behind or in the back: *a rear seat.* [Probably short for *arrear,* an old word meaning "the back."]

rear² (rēr) *v.t.* **1.** to help bring to maturity; raise: *to rear children, to rear cattle.* **2.** to construct; build. **3.** to bring to an upright position; lift up. —*v.i.* (of an animal) to rise on the hind legs. [Old English *rǣran.*]

rear admiral, an officer in the U.S. Navy ranking below a vice admiral and above a captain.

re·arm (rē ärm′) *v.t.* to arm again, especially with new or better weapons. —**re·ar·ma·ment** (rē är′mə mənt), *n.*

re·ar·range (rē′ə rānj′) *v.t.,* **re·ar·ranged, re·ar·rang·ing.** to arrange again, especially in a different way. —**re′ar·range′ment,** *n.*

rear·ward (rēr′wərd) *adj.* located in or moving toward the rear. —*adv.* also, **rear·wards.** in, at, or toward the rear.

rea·son (rē′zən) *n.* **1.** a cause or motive: *There is no reason to doubt his word.* **2.** a statement used to justify, prove, or explain: *He could give no reason for hitting his brother.* **3.** the ability to think logically and clearly: *The shock caused him to lose all reason.* —*v.i.* **1.** to think logically and clearly: *The professor's aim was to teach his students to reason.* **2.** to try to persuade or influence someone: *It was useless to reason with him.* —*v.t.* **1.** to think about logically and clearly: *He reasoned the problem out.* **2.** come to an opinion about; conclude: *She reasoned that her friend was innocent.* —**rea′son·er,** *n.*

by reason of. due to the fact that; because of.

in reason or **within reason.** fair; reasonable.

to stand to reason. to be logical or reasonable: *It stands to reason that the air is cleaner in the country than in the city.*

rea·son·a·ble (rē′zə nə bəl, rēz′nə bəl) *adj.* **1.** showing or using good sense or judgment; not foolish; sensible: *a reasonable man.* **2.** moderate; fair: *a reasonable request.* **3.** not too expensive: *The tomatoes are reasonable today.* —**rea′son·a·ble·ness,** *n.* —**rea′son·a·bly,** *adv.*

rea·son·ing (rē′zə ning, rēz′ning) *n.* **1.** the process of drawing conclusions from facts. **2.** arguments or evidence; reasons.

re·as·sem·ble (rē′ə sem′bəl) *v.,* **re·as·sem·bled, re·as·sem·bling.** —*v.t.* to bring or fit together again: *to reassemble a broken toy, to reassemble a group of people.* —*v.i.* to meet or come together again.

re·as·sure (rē′ə shoor′) *v.t.,* **re·as·sured, re·as·sur·ing. 1.** to restore confidence or courage in: *The father reassured the frightened child.* **2.** to assure again. —**re′as·sur′ance,** *n.* —**re′as·sur′ing·ly,** *adv.*

re·bate (rē′bāt, ri bāt′) *n.* a sum of money returned from an amount that has been paid. —*v.t.,* **re·bat·ed, re·bat·ing.** to make a rebate of.

Re·bec·ca (ri bek′ə) *n.* in the Old Testament, the wife of Isaac, and the mother of Esau and Jacob.

reb·el (*n., adj.,* reb′əl; *v.,* ri bel′) *n.* **1.** a person who resists or refuses to obey authority. **2. Rebel.** a person who fought on the side of the Confederacy in the Civil War. —*adj.* of a rebel or rebels: *rebel forces, a rebel victory.* —*v.i.,* **re·belled, re·bel·ling. 1.** to resist or disobey authority. **2.** to feel or show intense dislike: *The boy rebelled against taking the medicine.*

re·bel·lion (ri bel′yən) *n.* **1.** an armed uprising against a legal government. **2.** resistance or defiance against any control or authority.

re·bel·lious (ri bel′yəs) *adj.* **1.** resisting or refusing to obey authority: *rebellious soldiers.* **2.** characteristic of or marked by rebellion: *a rebellious period in the history of a country.* **3.** hard to manage: *a rebellious child.* —**re·bel′lious·ly,** *adv.* —**re·bel′lious·ness,** *n.*

re·birth (rē burth′, rē′burth′) *n.* **1.** a second birth; reincarnation. **2.** revival; renaissance.

re·born (rē bôrn′) *adj.* born again.

re·bound (*v.,* ri bound′; *n.,* rē′bound′, ri bound′) *v.i.* to bound back; spring back. —*n.* the act of springing back: *He tried to catch the ball on the rebound.*

re·buff (ri buf′) *n.* **1.** a blunt or rude rejection, as of a person's offer to help, or a request for something. **2.** a sudden, unexpected check, as to a person's plans; repulse. —*v.t.* **1.** to reject bluntly or rudely. **2.** to check suddenly; repulse.

re·build (rē bild′) *v.,* **re·built** (rē bilt′), **re·build·ing.** —*v.t.* **1.** to build (something) again. **2.** to make changes in; repair or remodel. —*v.i.* to build again.

re·buke (ri byook′) *v.t.,* **re·buked, re·buk·ing.** to scold sharply; reprimand. —*n.* a sharp scolding; reprimand; reproof. —**re·buk′er,** *n.*

re·bus (rē′bəs) *n. pl.,* **re·bus·es.** a representation of a syllable, word, or phrase by pictures or symbols whose names sound like the intended syllable or words. A picture of an eye followed by a picture of the numeral 1 is a rebus for "I won."

re·but (ri but′) *v.t.,* **re·but·ted, re·but·ting.** to disprove; refute. —**re·but′ter,** *n.*

re·but·tal (ri but′əl) *n.* the act of rebutting.

re·cal·ci·trant (ri kal′sə trənt) *adj.* stubborn and hard to manage; obstinate and disobedient: *The recalcitrant boy would not obey his parents.* —*n.* a person who is stubborn and hard to manage. —**re·cal′ci·trance, re·cal′ci·tran·cy,** *n.*

re·call (*v.,* ri kôl′; *n.,* ri kôl′, rē′kôl′) *v.t.* **1.** to call or bring back to mind; remember: *I don't recall his name.* **2.** to call back; summon back: *The auto manufacturer recalled the cars because of defects.* **3.** to take back; revoke: *Permission to make the trip was recalled.* —*n.* **1.** a remembering of someone or something; remembrance: *He had total recall of the book.* **2.** a calling back; summoning back: *the recall of an ambassador.* **3.** the taking back of something granted earlier. **4.** the process of removing an unwanted public official from office before his term is over by a vote of the people.

re·cant (ri kant′) *v.t.* to take back formally or publicly; renounce; retract: *The official recanted his incorrect statements.* —*v.i.* to take back or deny an opinion or belief: *The church authorities made the man recant.* —**re·can·ta·tion** (rē′kan tā′shən), *n.*

re·ca·pit·u·late (rē′kə pich′ə lāt′) *v.t.,* **re·ca·pit·u·lat·ed, re·ca·pit·u·lat·ing.** to restate or go over again briefly; summarize. —**re′ca·pit′u·la′tion,** *n.*

re·cap·ture (rē kap′chər) *v.t.,* **re·cap·tured, re·cap·tur·ing.** **1.** to retake possession of; capture again. **2.** to bring back to mind: *to recapture one's youth.*

re·cast (rē kast′) *v.t.,* **re·cast, re·cast·ing. 1.** to cast again or anew. **2.** to change the form of; remodel; reconstruct: *to recast a statement.*

recd., received. Also, **rec'd.**

re·cede (ri sēd′) *v.i.,* **re·ced·ed, re·ced·ing. 1.** to move back or away: *The waves receded.* **2.** to slope or appear to slope backward: *The man's hairline receded.*

re·ceipt (ri sēt′) *n.* **1.** a written statement that something, such as money, goods, or mail, has been received. **2.** **receipts.** the amount or quantity, especially of money, that has been received: *The store's receipts for the week were over $5000.* **3.** the act of receiving or the state of being received. —*v.t.* **1.** to write a receipt for (money, goods, or mail). **2.** to mark (a bill or account) as paid.

re·ceiv·a·ble (ri sē′və bəl) *adj.* **1.** that can be received; acceptable. **2.** awaiting receipt of payment; due. Accounts receivable are unpaid accounts held by a creditor, rather than a debtor.

re·ceive (ri sēv′) *v.,* **re·ceived, re·ceiv·ing.** —*v.t.* **1.** to take (something) into one's hands or possession; get: *Jan received a watch for her birthday. I received a letter from him today.* **2.** to take in mentally; learn; comprehend: *He is always willing to receive new ideas.* **3.** to meet with; experience: *We received a shock when we heard the news.* **4.** to be subjected to; suffer: *He received a broken arm*

playing football. **5.** to greet or welcome: *The host received his guests at the door.* —*v.i.* **1.** to take, acquire, or get something. **2.** to greet and entertain visitors.

re·ceiv·er (ri sē′vər) *n.* **1.** a person or thing that receives. **2.** a person appointed by a court of law to take charge of and administer the property or business of others until a legal decision has been made, as when a company becomes bankrupt. **3.** a device that receives electrical impulses or radio waves and converts them into pictures or sound, as the part of a telephone held to the ear.

re·ceiv·er·ship (ri sē′vər ship′) *n.* **1.** the condition of being in the hands of a receiver. **2.** the position and functions of a receiver appointed by a court.

re·cent (rē′sənt) *adj.* **1.** done, happening, or made just before the present: *What is the most recent news?* **2.** of or belonging to a period of time not long ago; modern: *a recent period in history.* **3. Recent.** of, relating to, or characteristic of the present geological epoch, the second of the Quaternary period, during which the climate has become warmer, glaciers have melted, and modern man has flourished. Also *(def. 3),* **Holocene.** —*n.* **Recent.** the present geological epoch. Also, **Holocene.** —**re′cent·ly,** *adv.* —**re′cent·ness,** *n.*

re·cep·ta·cle (ri sep′tə kəl) *n.* a container or place used to hold something: *We use a large metal can as a receptacle for garbage.*

re·cep·tion (ri sep′shən) *n.* **1.** the act of receiving or the state of being received. **2.** the way in which a person or thing is accepted or received: *We got a very rude reception from our new neighbors.* **3.** a social gathering, especially one at which guests are formally received: *There will be a reception immediately after the wedding.* **4.** the conversion of radio or television signals into sound or pictures, especially with reference to quality: *We have been getting poor reception from our new television set.*

re·cep·tion·ist (ri sep′shə nist) *n.* a person who is employed in an office to receive callers, make appointments, and give information.

re·cep·tive (ri sep′tiv) *adj.* able or willing to receive suggestions, new ideas, or impressions: *Bill is easy to work with because he has a receptive mind.* —**re·cep′tive·ly,** *adv.* —**re·cep′tive·ness,** *n.*

re·cess (rē′ses, ri ses′) *n. pl.,* **re·cess·es. 1.** a period of time during which work or other activity is temporarily stopped. **2.** a part of a wall that is set back or indented from the rest; niche. **3.** an inner or secret spot or part; hidden place: *the recesses of one's heart.* —*v.t.* **1.** to place in a recess; set back or away. **2.** to make a recess in. —*v.i.* to take a recess: *The court recessed for the afternoon.*

re·ces·sion (ri sesh′ən) *n.* **1.** the act of receding or moving back or away; withdrawal. **2.** a period of decline in business activity, shorter and less severe than a depression.

re·ces·sion·al (ri sesh′ən əl) *adj.* of, relating to, or happening at the end of a church service: *a recessional hymn.* —*n.* **1.** a recessional hymn or music. **2.** a procession at the end of a ceremony, as of the clergy leaving the church.

re·ces·sive (ri ses′iv) *adj.* **1.** tending to go back; receding. **2.** relating to or indicating one of a pair of hereditary characteristics that is dominated by the other when both are present. —*n.* a recessive hereditary characteristic.

at; āpe; cär; end; mē; it; īce; hot; ōld; fôrk; wood; fo͞ol; oil; out; up; turn; sing; thin; **this;** hw in white; zh in treasure. The symbol ə stands for the sound of **a** in about, **e** in taken, **i** in pencil, **o** in lemon, and **u** in circus.

R

re·charge (rē charj′) *v.t.,* **re·charged, re·charg·ing.** to charge with electricity or electrical energy again: *to recharge a battery.*

rec·i·pe (res′ə pē′) *n.* **1.** a list of ingredients and directions for preparing food or drink. **2.** a method or formula for doing or preparing anything: *a recipe for happiness.*

re·cip·i·ent (ri sip′ē ənt) *n.* a person or thing that receives: *the recipient of a gift.* —*adj.* receiving or able to receive; receptive.

re·cip·ro·cal (ri sip′rə kəl) *adj.* **1.** given, felt, or shown by both sides: *reciprocal respect, reciprocal acts of hostility.* **2.** given, felt, or shown in return: *reciprocal aid, a reciprocal vow.* **3.** indicating a pronoun that expresses mutual action or relation. *One another* is a reciprocal pronoun. —*n. Mathematics.* a number or algebraic expression by which a given number or an algebraic expression is multiplied to produce one. The reciprocal of $3/5$ is $5/3$, since $3/5 \times 5/3 = 1$. —**re·cip′ro·cal·ly,** *adv.*

re·cip·ro·cate (ri sip′rə kāt′) *v.,* **re·cip·ro·cat·ed, re·cip·ro·cat·ing.** —*v.t.* **1.** to give, feel, or show in return: *to reciprocate love.* **2.** to give and return in exchange; interchange: *to reciprocate favors.* —*v.i.* to give, feel, or show something in return: *She loved him, but he did not reciprocate.* —**re·cip′ro·ca′tion,** *n.*

rec·i·proc·i·ty (res′ə pros′ə tē) *n. pl.,* **rec·i·proc·i·ties. 1.** the quality or state of being reciprocal. **2.** a mutual interchange between countries, states, or organizations, such as the exchange of trading privileges.

re·cit·al (ri sīt′əl) *n.* **1.** a performance or concert of music or dance, often given by a single performer or devoted to the works of a single composer: *a piano recital.* **2.** the act of repeating or reading something aloud in public: *a poetry recital.*

rec·i·ta·tion (res′ə tā′shən) *n.* **1.** the act of repeating or reading something aloud in public; recital. **2.** the act of reciting a lesson.

rec·i·ta·tive (res′ə tə tēv′) *n.* **1.** a style of music in which words are sung in a manner similar to speaking, found especially in operas. **2.** a passage, part, or composition in this style.

re·cite (ri sīt′) *v.,* **re·cit·ed, re·cit·ing.** —*v.t.* **1.** to repeat from memory: *to recite a poem.* **2.** to give an account of; narrate: *to recite one's life story.* —*v.i.* **1.** to repeat something memorized, especially before an audience. **2.** to repeat a lesson or answer questions in class. —**re·cit′er,** *n.*

reck·less (rek′lis) *adj.* **1.** not careful; heedless: *Reckless of the danger, John skated on the thin ice.* **2.** characterized or distinguished by such heedlessness; irresponsible: *reckless driving.* —**reck′less·ly,** *adv.* —**reck′less·ness,** *n.*

reck·on (rek′ən) *v.t.* **1.** to count or figure; calculate: *Interest on my savings account is reckoned quarterly.* **2.** to suppose to be; consider; regard: *They reckon her a beauty.* **3.** *Informal.* to think; suppose: *I reckon that he'll come.* —*v.i.* **1.** to count, depend, or rely: *You can reckon on our support.* **2.** to make a calculation; count or figure. **3.** *Informal.* to suppose; guess. —**reck′on·er,** *n.*
   to reckon with. to take into consideration.

reck·on·ing (rek′ən ing) *n.* **1.** the act of calculating; calculation. **2.** the settlement of accounts. **3.** a bill, as at an inn or hotel. **4.** see **dead reckoning.**

re·claim (ri klām′) *v.t.* **1.** to bring back to a useful state or condition: *to reclaim land.* **2.** to get or recover from old or waste products: *to reclaim metal from a junkyard.* —**re·claim′a·ble,** *adj.*

rec·la·ma·tion (rek′lə mā′shən) *n.* the act of reclaiming or the state of being reclaimed; restoration.

re·cline (ri klīn′) *v.,* **re·clined, re·clin·ing.** —*v.i.* to lie back or down: *He reclined on his bed.* —*v.t.* to cause to lie back or down.

rec·luse (rek′lōōs, ri klōōs′) *n.* a person who lives alone, away from other people.

rec·og·ni·tion (rek′əg nish′ən) *n.* **1.** the act of recognizing or the state of being recognized. **2.** an acknowledgment of something, especially as being true or valid. **3.** favorable attention or notice; acceptance: *The doctor gained recognition for his work with the poor.*

re·cog·ni·zance (ri kog′nə zəns) *n. Law.* **1.** a bond or obligation by which a person promises to perform a particular act, such as appearing for a hearing or trial. **2.** the amount of money to be forfeited if the act is not performed.

rec·og·nize (rek′əg nīz′) *v.t.,* **rec·og·nized, rec·og·niz·ing. 1.** to know as someone or something previously seen or known; know again: *I recognized her face at once.* **2.** to identify, as from a description or a distinctive feature: *to recognize a bird by its coloring.* **3.** to be aware of or understand clearly; realize: *to recognize a fact.* **4.** to take notice of as having the right to speak, as at a formal meeting: *The chairman recognized the club's treasurer.* **5.** to show or express appreciation of: *The president of the company recognized the employee's long service by giving him a bonus.* **6.** to acknowledge the existence of (another nation), usually by establishing diplomatic relations. —**rec′og·niz′a·ble,** *adj.* —**rec′og·niz′a·bly,** *adv.*

re·coil (*v.,* ri koil′; *n.,* ri koil′, rē′koil′) *v.i.* **1.** to draw or shrink back, as in fear, horror, or surprise: *She recoiled at the sight of the rat.* **2.** to fly back, as from force of impact or discharge; spring back: *The gun recoiled after being fired.* —*n.* **1.** the act of recoiling. **2.** the backward movement of a firearm when discharged.

rec·ol·lect (rek′ə lekt′) *v.t.* to call back to mind; remember: *I cannot recollect her address at the moment.* —*v.i.* to have a recollection; remember.

rec·ol·lec·tion (rek′ə lek′shən) *n.* **1.** the act or power of calling back to mind. **2.** a thing remembered.

rec·om·mend (rek′ə mend′) *v.t.* **1.** to speak of or present favorably: *Can you recommend a good restaurant?* **2.** to advise; suggest: *I recommend that you go to the doctor.* **3.** to make acceptable, pleasing, or attractive: *His ability recommends him for the job.* **4.** to put in the care of.

rec·om·men·da·tion (rek′ə men dā′shən) *n.* **1.** the act of recommending. **2.** anything that recommends, such as a letter.

rec·om·pense (rek′əm pens′) *v.t.,* **rec·om·pensed, rec·om·pens·ing. 1.** to pay or repay (someone), as for something done or given: *We recompensed him for his services.* **2.** to make up for; give compensation for: *His insurance company will recompense him for the damage caused by the fire.* —*n.* **1.** payment, as for something done or given; reward. **2.** compensation, as for loss or injury.

rec·on·cile (rek′ən sīl′) *v.t.,* **rec·on·ciled, rec·on·cil·ing. 1.** to make friendly again, as after an argument or fight: *The quarreling friends are now reconciled.* **2.** to make (someone) happy or content with: *The boy could not reconcile himself to failure.* **3.** to bring to an end; settle: *The referee tried to reconcile the disagreement between the two teams.* **4.** to bring into harmony; make agree: *The policeman tried to reconcile the different accounts of the accident.* —**rec′on·cil′a·ble,** *adj.* —**rec′on·cile′ment,** *n.*

rec·on·cil·i·a·tion (rek′ən sil′ē ā′shən) *n.* the act of reconciling or the state of being reconciled.

rec·on·dite (rek′ən dīt′, ri kon′dīt) *adj.* **1.** hard to understand; profound: *a recondite mathematical theory.* **2.** dealing with difficult or little known matters: *recondite research.*

re·con·nais·sance (ri kon′ə səns) *n.* an examination or survey made in order to obtain information, especially military information about an enemy.

re·con·noi·ter (rē′kə noi′tər, rek′ə noi′tər) *v.t.* to inspect, examine, or survey (an area or position) in order to obtain information, as for military purposes. —*v.i.* to make a reconnaissance.

re·con·noi·tre (rē′kə noi′tər, rek′ə noi′tər) *v.*, **re·con·noi·tred, re·con·noi·tring.** *British.* another spelling of **reconnoiter.**

re·con·sid·er (rē′kən sid′ər) *v.t.* to consider again, especially with the possibility of changing one's mind. —**re′con·sid′er·a′tion,** *n.*

re·con·struct (rē′kən strukt′) *v.t.* **1.** to construct again; rebuild. **2.** to recreate (something that happened or existed) in the mind from available evidence or information: *The detective tried to reconstruct the crime.*

re·con·struc·tion (rē′kən struk′shən) *n.* **1.** the act of reconstructing or the state of being reconstructed. **2.** something reconstructed. **3. Reconstruction. a.** the process of restoring the former Confederate States to the Union after the Civil War. **b.** the period during which this process took place, from 1867 to 1877.

rec·ord (*n., adj.,* rek′ərd; *v.,* ri kôrd′) *n.* **1.** an account in writing or in another permanent form: *The school keeps health records for each student.* **2.** an official written account: *a record of a town meeting.* **3.** the facts about the activities or achievements of a person or group of people: *His school record was outstanding.* **4.** a performance or achievement surpassing all others of its kind, as in sports: *He set a record in the 100-yard dash.* **5.** a disk on which sounds are recorded to be played back on a phonograph. —*adj.* surpassing all others of its kind: *There was a record attendance at the ball game.* —*v.t.* **1.** to set down in permanent form, as in writing, for future use: *to record history.* **2.** to indicate; show; register: *The dial on the left records speed.* **3.** to put (sound) on a phonograph record or magnetic tape. **4.** to make a recording of: *to record a song.*
   off the record. not for publication or quotation: *The candidate's remarks at the banquet were off the record.*
   on record. known publicly or officially.

re·cord·er (ri kôr′dər) *n.* **1.** a person who is employed to take notes and keep records. **2.** a machine that records sounds, as on magnetic tape. **3.** a musical wind instrument having eight finger holes to regulate pitch, and producing a tone similar to a flute's.

re·cord·ing (ri kôr′ding) *n.* **1.** a phonograph record or magnetic tape. **2.** a sound registered on a phonograph record or magnetic tape.

record player, an instrument that reproduces sound from a phonograph record; phonograph.

re·count (ri kount′) *v.t.* to tell in detail; narrate: *Grandfather recounted the experiences of his youth.*

re·count (*v.,* rē′kount′; *n.,* rē′kount′) *v.t.* to count again. —*n.* a second count, especially of votes in an election.

re·coup (ri kōōp′) *v.t.* **1.** to make up for or get back: *The gambler tried to recoup his losses.* **2.** to pay back: *The insurance company recouped the storekeeper for his losses in the fire.*

re·course (rē′kôrs′, ri kôrs′) *n.* **1.** a turning or appealing to a person or thing for help or protection: *Our recourse when a fire breaks out is to call the fire department.* **2.** a person or thing that is turned or appealed to; resort: *His father was his recourse in time of trouble.*

re·cov·er (ri kuv′ər) *v.t.* **1.** to get back (something lost or stolen); regain: *The police recovered the stolen jewelry.* **2.** to make up for: *We took a short cut to recover the time that was spent getting gas.* **3.** to get (oneself) back to a normal position or condition: *He slipped but recovered himself before he fell.* —*v.i.* to get back to a normal position or condition: *She is recovering from the flu.*

re·cov·er (rē′kuv′ər) *v.t.* to cover again.

re·cov·er·y (ri kuv′ər ē) *n. pl.,* **re·cov·er·ies. 1.** the act of recovering or the state of being recovered. **2.** a return to a normal or healthy condition: *Susan had a speedy recovery from the mumps.*

recovery room, a hospital room where patients are taken after an operation for special care and observation.

rec·re·ant (rek′rē ənt) *adj.* **1.** not faithful; disloyal. **2.** not brave; cowardly. —*n.* an unfaithful or cowardly person.

re·cre·ate (rē′krē āt′) *v.t.,* **re·cre·at·ed, re·cre·at·ing.** to create anew.

rec·re·a·tion (rek′rē ā′shən) *n.* **1.** refreshment by means of some form of amusement or relaxation; diversion. **2.** any particular form of amusement or relaxation: *Fishing is my favorite recreation.*

rec·re·a·tion·al (rek′rē ā′shə nəl) *adj.* of or relating to recreation: *recreational activities.*

re·crim·i·nate (ri krim′ə nāt′) *v.i.,* **re·crim·i·nat·ed, re·crim·i·nat·ing.** to answer an accusation by making one in return. —**re·crim′i·na′tion,** *n.*

re·cru·des·cence (rē′krōō des′əns) *n.* a new outbreak, as of a disease. —**re′cru·des′cent,** *adj.*

re·cruit (ri krōōt′) *n.* **1.** a newly enlisted member of the armed forces. **2.** a new member of any group or organization. —*v.t.* **1.** to get (someone) to join the armed forces; enlist (someone) for military service. **2.** to raise or make up by enlisting: *to recruit a new army.* **3.** to hire or get the services of. —**re·cruit′er,** *n.* —**re·cruit′ment,** *n.*

rec·tal (rekt′əl) *adj.* relating to, affecting, or near the rectum.

rec·tan·gle (rek′tang′gəl) *n.* a parallelogram having four right angles.

rec·tan·gu·lar (rek tang′gyə lər) *adj.* shaped like a rectangle: *a rectangular piece of wood.*

rec·ti·fi·er (rek′tə fī′ər) *n.* **1.** a person or thing that rectifies. **2.** *Electronics.* a device for changing alternating current into direct current.

Rectangles

rec·ti·fy (rek′tə fī′) *v.t.,* **rec·ti·fied, rec·ti·fy·ing. 1.** to set or make right; amend; correct: *to rectify a mistake.* **2.** *Electronics.* to change (an alternating current) into a direct current. **3.** *Chemistry.* to refine or purify (liquids) by repeated distillation. —**rec′ti·fi·ca′tion,** *n.*

rec·ti·lin·e·ar (rek′tə lin′ē ər) *adj.* **1.** moving in or forming a straight line. **2.** made up of or bounded by straight lines.

rec·ti·tude (rek′tə tōōd′, rek′tə tyōōd′) *n.* uprightness of moral character or conduct; righteousness.

rec·tor (rek′tər) *n.* **1.** an Anglican or Episcopalian clergyman who has charge of a parish. **2.** a priest in the Roman Catholic Church in charge of a seminary, college, or religious house. **3.** the chief administrator in certain schools, colleges, or universities.

rec·to·ry (rek′tər ē) *n. pl.,* **rec·to·ries.** a rector's house.

rec·tum (rek′təm) *n.* the lowest part of the large intestine, connecting the colon to the anus.

re·cum·bent (ri kum′bənt) *adj.* lying down; reclining: *a painting of a recumbent woman.* —**re·cum′bent·ly,** *adv.*

at; āpe; cär; end; mē; it; īce; hot; ōld; fôrk; wood; fōōl; oil; out; up; turn; sing; thin; **th**is; hw in white; zh in treasure. The symbol ə stands for the sound of **a** in about, **e** in taken, **i** in pencil, **o** in lemon, and **u** in circus.

re·cu·per·ate (ri kōō′pə rāt′, ri kyōō′pə rāt′) *v.i.* **re·cu·per·at·ed, re·cu·per·at·ing.** to gain back health or strength; recover: *He recuperated at home after his illness.* —**re·cu′per·a′tion,** *n.*

re·cur (ri kur′) *v.i.*, **re·curred, re·cur·ring. 1.** to happen or appear again: *His fever recurred after two days.* **2.** to come back or return to the mind or memory: *Thoughts of home and family recurred to the lonely traveler.* **3.** to go back or return in thought or speech: *At the meeting we recurred to the subject we had discussed the week before.* —**re·cur′rence,** *n.*

re·cur·rent (ri kur′ənt) *adj.* happening or appearing again, especially repeatedly or at intervals: *a recurrent nightmare.* —**re·cur′rent·ly,** *adv.*

re·cy·cle (rē sī′kəl) *v.t.*, **re·cy·cled, re·cy·cling.** to make (waste material) suitable for reuse: *to recycle old newspapers.*

red (red) *n.* **1.** the color of fresh blood. **2.** something having this color, such as a dye or paint. **3.** *also,* **Red.** *Informal.* **a.** a communist. **b.** any radical or revolutionary. —*adj.,* **red·der, red·dest. 1.** having the color red. **2.** blushing; flushed: *to be red with embarrassment.* **3.** *also,* **Red.** *Informal.* **a.** communist. **b.** radical or revolutionary. —**red′ness,** *n.*

in the red. losing or owing money.

red·bird (red′burd′) *n.* any of several birds having mainly red feathers, such as the cardinal, bullfinch, or scarlet tanager.

red blood cell, one of the cells found in the blood of man and other animals with backbones, containing hemoglobin, and functioning chiefly to carry oxygen to the cells and tissues, and carbon dioxide back to the respiratory organs.

red·blood·ed (red′blud′id) *adj.* full of vitality; vigorous.

red·breast (red′brest′) *n.* any of various birds having a red breast, especially a robin.

red·cap (red′kap′) *n.* a porter who handles baggage, especially at a railroad station. [From the *red cap* usually worn by this porter.]

Red China, see **China** *(def. 1).*

red·coat (red′kōt′) *n.* a British soldier when the British uniform included a red coat, as during the American Revolution and the War of 1812.

Red Cross 1. an international organization founded in 1864, having as its main purpose the care and relief of victims of war and natural disasters, such as floods, fires, or earthquakes. **2.** any branch of this organization.

red deer, a reddish-brown deer found in Europe and Asia.

red·den (red′ən) *v.t., v.i.* to make or become red.

red·dish (red′ish) *adj.* somewhat red.

re·deem (ri dēm′) *v.t.* **1.** to get or win back; regain; recover: *to redeem a pawned watch.* **2.** to exchange for money or merchandise: *to redeem trading stamps.* **3.** to make up for; compensate for: *His apologies could not redeem his poor manners.* **4.** to set free from or deliver from a sinful state. —**re·deem′a·ble,** *adj.*

re·deem·er (ri dē′mər) *n.* **1.** a person who redeems or rescues another person. **2. The Redeemer.** Jesus Christ.

Red deer

re·demp·tion (ri demp′shən) *n.* **1.** the act of redeeming or the state of being redeemed. **2.** deliverance from sin.

red-hand·ed (red′han′did) *adj.* in the act of doing something wrong: *The police caught the shoplifter red-handed.*

red·head (red′hed′) *n.* a person having red hair.

red·head·ed (red′hed′id) *adj.* having red hair.

red herring 1. a herring dried and smoked to a reddish color. **2.** something intended to draw attention away from the problem at hand.

red-hot (red′hot′) *adj.* **1.** red or glowing with heat; very hot. **2.** marked by or showing great intensity, as of enthusiasm or anger: *a red-hot discussion.* **3.** fresh from a source; new: *red-hot news.*

re·did (rē did′) the past tense of **redo.**

red-let·ter (red′let′ər) *adj.* especially important or happy; memorable: *a red-letter day.* [From the practice of marking religious holidays in *red letters* on church calendars.]

re·do (rē dōō′) *v.t.,* **re·did, re·done, re·do·ing.** to do over or again.

red·o·lent (red′əl ənt) *adj.* **1.** having or giving off a pleasant odor; fragrant. **2.** suggestive; reminiscent: *Not permitting the bridegroom to see the bride before the wedding is a custom redolent of superstition.* —**red′o·lence,** *n.* —**red′o·lent·ly,** *adv.*

re·done (rē dun′) the past participle of **redo.**

re·dou·ble (rē dub′əl) *v.t., v.i.,* **re·dou·bled, re·dou·bling. 1.** to increase greatly. **2.** to double again.

re·doubt (ri dout′) *n.* a small enclosed fortification.

re·doubt·a·ble (ri dou′tə bəl) *adj.* inspiring fear or awe; formidable; awesome: *a redoubtable army.*

re·dound (ri dound′) *v.i.* to be added; contribute: *Her good manners redound to her family's credit.*

red pepper 1. the fruit of any of a group of pepper plants, such as the sweet pepper. **2.** another term for **cayenne.**

re·dress (*v.,* ri dres′; *n.,* rē′dres′, ri dres′) *v.t.* to correct and make up for; set right; remedy: *to redress a wrong.* —*n.* **1.** something given or done to make up for an injury or wrong. **2.** the act of redressing.

Red Sea, the narrow sea between the Arabian peninsula and northeastern Africa, opening into the Gulf of Aden and the Arabian Sea.

red snapper, a food and game fish that is bright red in color, found in the Caribbean Sea and the Gulf of Mexico.

red·start (red′stärt′) *n.* **1.** a small European bird having a reddish tail. **2.** a fly-catching warbler of eastern North America, the male of which is black with orange or red patches.

Redstart

red tape, too much attention to official rules and forms in a business or government office, usually resulting in inaction or delay. [From the *red tape* formerly used to tie official papers of the British government.]

re·duce (ri dōōs′, ri dyōōs′) *v.,* **re·duced, re·duc·ing.** —*v.t.* **1.** to make less or smaller, as in size, number, or degree; decrease; diminish: *to reduce the speed of an automobile, to reduce the price of an item for sale.* **2.** to lower in rank, position, or condition; degrade: *The colonel reduced the sergeant to private for disobeying orders.* **3.** to bring to a particular state, form, or condition: *The fire reduced the forest to ashes.* **4.** to break down or bring to a simpler form or character: *to reduce an argument to its basic points.* **5.** *Mathematics.* to change (an expression) to its simpler form: *to reduce ⁴⁄₈ to ¹⁄₂.* **6.** *Chemistry.*

a. to add electrons to (the atom of an element) so that its oxidation number is decreased. **b.** to remove oxygen from (a compound). —*v.i.* **1.** to lose weight, as by dieting. **2.** to become reduced. —**re·duc′er,** *n.* —**re·duc′i·ble,** *adj.*

re·duc·tion (ri duk′shən) *n.* **1.** the act of reducing or the state of being reduced. **2.** the amount by which something is reduced: *The store is offering a 10 percent reduction on summer clothes.*

re·dun·dan·cy (ri dun′dən sē) *n. pl.,* **re·dun·dan·cies.** **1.** the use of more words than necessary to express an idea; wordiness. **2.** an amount that is more than enough.

re·dun·dant (ri dun′dənt) *adj.* **1.** using more words than necessary; characterized by wordiness. **2.** more than enough; unnecessary; superfluous. —**re·dun′dant·ly,** *adv.*

red-winged blackbird (red′wingd′) an American blackbird, the male of which has a scarlet patch at the shoulder of each wing. Also, **red·wing** (red′wing′).

red·wood (red′wood′) *n.* **1.** a tall evergreen tree having a thick reddish-brown bark, found only along the western coast of North America. Redwoods may grow from 300 to 340 feet tall, and some are probably more than 2000 years old. **2.** the soft, light wood obtained from this tree. Redwood is strong and highly resistant to decay.

reed (rēd) *n.* **1.** a tall grass having long narrow leaves and slender, jointed stems. Reeds grow chiefly around marshes and other wet areas. **2.** the stem of this grass. **3.** a musical pipe made from a reed or from some other hollow stalk or stem. **4.** *Music.* **a.** a thin piece of wood, reed, metal, or plastic, used in the mouthpiece of certain wind instruments and in the pipes of certain organs. A reed produces a musical sound when a current of air passes over it and causes it to vibrate. **b.** *also,* **reed instrument.** a musical wind instrument, such as the clarinet or oboe, whose tone is produced by the vibration of a single or double reed.

Reed, Walter (rēd) 1851–1902, U.S. army surgeon who proved that yellow fever is carried by mosquitoes.

reed·bird (rēd′burd′) *n.* see **bobolink.**

reed organ, a keyboard musical instrument whose tones are produced by currents of air causing small metal reeds to vibrate. Also, **harmonium.**

reed·y (rē′dē) *adj.,* **reed·i·er, reed·i·est. 1.** having a sound like a reed instrument: *reedy voices.* **2.** like a reed or reeds: *reedy legs.* **3.** full of reeds: *reedy marshes.* —**reed′i·ness,** *n.*

reef¹ (rēf) *n.* a ridge of sand, rock, or coral that lies at or near the surface of a sea or other body of water. [Middle Dutch *rif.*]

reef² (rēf) *n.* a portion of a sail that can be rolled up or let out in order to reduce the area of the sail exposed to the wind. —*v.t.* to reduce the area of (a sail) by rolling or folding up a portion and fastening it. [Old Norse *rif.*]

reek (rēk) *v.i.* to give off or be filled with a strong, bad odor; smell strongly and unpleasantly: *The empty lot reeks from the garbage dumped there. The room reeks of stale cigar smoke.* —*n.* a strong, bad odor.

reel¹ (rēl) *n.* **1.** a spool or similar device on which long strips of rope, fish line, motion picture film, tape, or the like can be wound: *a reel of wire.* **2.** the amount of material wound on a reel: *two reels of film.* —*v.t.* **1.** to draw or pull by winding a line on a reel: *to reel in a trout.* **2.** to wind on a reel: *to reel a rope.* [Old English *hrēol.*]

> **to reel off.** to say or write quickly and easily: *He reeled off the answers.*

Reel¹ (fishing reel)

reel² (rēl) *v.i.* **1.** to be thrown off balance, as from a blow; stagger: *John reeled when Sam*

ran into him. **2.** to walk or move unsteadily; totter. **3.** to turn or seem to turn round and round; whirl. —*v.t.* to cause to reel. —*n.* a reeling movement. [Possibly from *reel*¹.]

reel³ (rēl) *n.* **1.** a lively folk dance, performed by two or more couples, in which the dancers form two lines facing each other. **2.** the music for such a dance. [Probably from *reel*².]

re·e·lect (rē′i lekt′) *v.t.* to elect again: *The voters reelected the governor to another term in office.* —**re′e·lec′-tion,** *n.*

re·en·force (rē′en fôrs′) *also,* **re-en·force.** *v.t.,* **re·en·forced, re·en·for·cing.** another spelling of **reinforce.**

re·en·force·ment (rē′en fôrs′mənt) *also,* **re-en·force·ment.** *n.* another spelling of **reinforcement.**

re·en·list (rē′en list′) *also,* **re-en·list.** *v.t., v.i.* to enlist again: *The private reenlisted.* —**re′en·list′ment;** *also,* **re′-en·list′ment,** *n.*

re·en·ter (rē′en′tər) *also,* **re-en·ter.** *v.t.* to enter or go into again.

re·en·try (rē en′trē) *also,* **re-en·try.** *n. pl.,* **re·en·tries. 1.** the act or instance of entering again. **2.** the return of a missile or spacecraft to the earth's atmosphere.

re·es·tab·lish (rē′es tab′lish) *also,* **re-es·tab·lish.** *v.t.* to establish again; restore. —**re′es·tab′lish·ment;** *also,* **re′-es·tab′lish·ment,** *n.*

re·ex·am·ine (rē′ig zam′in) *also,* **re-ex·am·ine.** *v.t.,* **re·ex·am·ined, re·ex·am·in·ing. 1.** to examine again. **2.** *Law.* to question (a witness) again after cross-examination. —**re′ex·am′i·na′tion;** *also,* **re′-ex·am′i·na′tion,** *n.*

re·fec·to·ry (ri fek′tər ē) *n. pl.,* **re·fec·to·ries.** a dining hall, as in a school, monastery, or other institution.

re·fer (ri fur′) *v.,* **re·ferred, re·fer·ring.** —*v.t.* **1.** to send or direct (someone), as for information or aid: *The doctor referred the patient to a surgeon.* **2.** to turn over or submit for consideration or for a recommendation or decision: *The clerk referred the problem to the owner of the store.* —*v.i.* **1.** to call or direct attention; make reference: *He was referring to the party last Friday.* **2.** to use as a source, as of information: *to refer to notes while speaking.*

ref·er·ee (ref′ə rē′) *n.* **1.** an official in certain sports and games, often the chief official, who interprets and enforces the rules. **2.** a person who settles a matter or question in dispute. —*v.,* **ref·er·eed, ref·er·ee·ing.** —*v.t.* to act as a referee in: *to referee a boxing match.* —*v.i.* to act as a referee.

ref·er·ence (ref′ər əns) *n.* **1.** the act of referring. **2.** a statement that calls or directs attention; mention: *The candidate for mayor made a reference to his opponent's past record.* **3.** relation; respect; regard: *Mr. Smith wrote Mr. Jones in reference to his letter of November 5.* **4.** a person or thing that is referred to; a source, as of information or aid: *The encyclopedia was his reference for his report.* **5.** a statement about a person's character or ability: *His references indicate that he is highly qualified for the job.* **6.** a person from whom such a statement may be obtained: *Sara gave Mr. White as her reference.* **7.** a note referring a reader to a source or sources, as of information: *The author has included a table of references at the end of the book.* —*adj.* used for information: *A dictionary is a reference book.*

---

at; āpe; cär; end; mē; it; īce; hot; ōld; fôrk; wood; fōōl; oil; out; up; turn; sing; thin; **this;** hw in white; zh in treasure. The symbol ə stands for the sound of **a** in about, **e** in taken, **i** in pencil, **o** in lemon, and **u** in circus.

ref·er·en·dum (ref′ə ren′dəm) *n. pl.,* **ref·er·en·dums** or **ref·er·en·da** (ref′ə ren′də). **1.** a method of presenting public measures to the vote of the people for approval or rejection. **2.** a direct vote by the people on a public measure.

re·fill (*v.,* rē fil′; *n.,* rē′fil′) *v.t.* to fill again. —*n.* a supply of a product replacing material that filled the original container and has been used up.

re·fine (ri fīn′) *v.t.,* **re·fined, re·fin·ing. 1.** to make fine or pure; free from impure or unwanted matter: *to refine crude oil.* **2.** to make more elegant, cultured, or polished. —**re·fin′er,** *n.*

re·fined (ri fīnd′) *adj.* **1.** free from coarseness and vulgarity; elegant, cultured, or polished: *She has refined taste in music.* **2.** free from impure or unwanted matter.

re·fine·ment (ri fīn′mənt) *n.* **1.** freedom from coarseness and vulgarity. **2.** the act or process of refining. **3.** a change or addition meant to improve; improvement.

re·fin·er·y (ri fī′nər ē) *n. pl.,* **re·fin·er·ies.** a place where some crude substance, such as crude petroleum or sugar, is refined.

re·fit (rē fit′) *v.t., v.i.,* **re·fit·ted, re·fit·ting.** to make or be made fit for use again: *to refit an old ship.*

re·flect (ri flekt′) *v.t.* **1.** to turn or throw back: *Because light-colored fabric reflects heat, it is often used for summer clothes.* **2.** to give back an image of; mirror: *The clear water in the lake reflected our faces.* **3.** to express or represent: *Her clothes reflect her good taste.* **4.** to bring or give back as a result; cast: *His brave deeds reflected honor upon him.* —*v.i.* **1.** to think seriously or carefully; ponder: *He reflected on the question.* **2.** to bring blame or discredit: *His cowardice reflects on his character.*

re·flec·tion (ri flek′shən) *n.* **1.** an image given back by a reflecting surface: *The little girl stared at her reflection in the mirror.* **2.** something reflected or produced by reflection: *The reflection of the sun on the windshield temporarily blinded the driver.* **3.** serious or careful thinking; consideration: *Upon further reflection, he decided to accept the job.* **4.** an observation or statement that results from such thinking. **5.** the turning back of light, heat, or sound waves. **6.** something that expresses or represents something else: *His smile was a reflection of his happiness.* **7.** something that causes or brings blame or discredit. **8.** the act of reflecting or the state of being reflected.

re·flec·tive (ri flek′tiv) *adj.* **1.** given to or showing serious or careful thinking; thoughtful. **2.** that throws back light, heat, or sound waves; reflecting: *Silver has a reflective surface.* —**re·flec′tive·ly,** *adv.*

re·flec·tor (ri flek′tər) *n.* **1.** something that reflects. **2.** a surface or device designed to reflect light, heat, or sound waves. **3.** a telescope that reflects light to form an image.

re·flex (rē′fleks′) *n. pl.,* **re·flex·es. 1.** the response to a stimulus that happens without a person's control or effort. The contraction of a muscle is a reflex. **2. reflexes.** the ability to react with speed and accuracy: *The doctor checked the boy's reflexes.* —*adj.* relating to, produced by, or indicating a response to a stimulus that happens without a person's control or effort. The immediate withdrawal of one's hand from a hot surface is a reflex action.

re·flex·ive (ri flek′siv) *adj. Grammar.* relating to or expressing an action directed back on the subject. In the sentence *He washed himself, himself* is a reflexive pronoun and *washed* is a reflexive verb. —*n.* a reflexive verb or pronoun. —**re·flex′ive·ly,** *adv.*

re·form (ri fôrm′) *v.t.* **1.** to make a change for the better in; correct what is wrong with: *The government tried to reform the postal system.* **2.** to cause (someone) to change for the better; rehabilitate: *to reform a criminal.* —*v.i.* to

become changed for the better. —*n.* a change for the better: *a reform of the prison system.* —*adj.* **1.** of or relating to reform or correction. **2. Reform.** of, relating to, or indicating the branch of Judaism that retains only those traditional laws and rituals considered meaningful in the modern world. —**re·form′er,** *n.*

ref·or·ma·tion (ref′ər mā′shən) *n.* **1.** the act of reforming or the state of being reformed. **2. Reformation.** a religious movement in sixteenth-century Europe, led by Martin Luther, that began as an attempt to reform the Catholic Church and resulted in the establishment of Protestant churches.

re·form·a·to·ry (ri fôr′mə tôr′ē) *n. pl.,* **re·form·a·to·ries.** an institution to which young offenders are sent, and which stresses rehabilitation rather than punishment. —*adj.* serving or intended to reform.

reform school, see **reformatory.**

re·fract (ri frakt′) *v.t.* to cause to undergo refraction.

re·frac·tion (ri frak′shən) *n.* the bending of waves, especially light waves, as they pass from one substance to another substance having a different density, or as they pass through a substance whose density is not uniform.

re·frac·tor (ri frak′tər) *n.* **1.** something that refracts. **2.** a telescope that refracts light to form an image.

re·frac·to·ry (ri frak′tər ē) *adj.* **1.** difficult to control or manage; rebellious; obstinate: *a refractory student.* **2.** resisting treatment, as a disease. **3.** resisting heat or fusion, as certain ores or metals.

re·frain¹ (ri frān′) *v.i.* to hold oneself back; restrain oneself: *She could scarcely refrain from laughing.* [Old French *réfréner.*]

re·frain² (ri frān′) *n.* **1.** a phrase or verse in a song, poem, or the like, that is repeated regularly, especially at the end of each stanza; chorus. **2.** a musical setting for this. [Old French *refrain.*]

re·fresh (ri fresh′) *v.t.* **1.** to restore strength or vitality to; make fresh again; revive: *The weary children refreshed themselves with cold lemonade.* **2.** to cause to remember; prompt (the memory). —**re·fresh′er,** *n.*

re·fresh·ing (ri fresh′ing) *adj.* **1.** that refreshes: *A cold shower on a warm day is refreshing.* **2.** pleasingly different or unusual: *He has a refreshing honesty about himself.* —**re·fresh′ing·ly,** *adv.*

re·fresh·ment (ri fresh′mənt) *n.* **1. refreshments.** food and drink taken as a snack or light meal. **2.** something that refreshes. **3.** the act of refreshing.

re·frig·er·ant (ri frij′ər ənt) *n.* any substance used in cooling or refrigeration.

re·frig·er·ate (ri frij′ə rāt′) *v.t.,* **re·frig·er·at·ed, re·frig·er·at·ing.** to make or keep cool or cold, especially to chill or freeze (food) in order to preserve it. —**re·frig′er·a′tion,** *n.*

re·frig·er·a·tor (ri frij′ə rā′tər) *n.* **1.** a closed, usually box-shaped appliance with a cooling system, used to preserve food and other perishables. **2.** any closed area, such as a room or railroad car, that is kept cool by refrigeration.

re·fu·el (rē fyoo′əl) *v.,* **re·fu·eled, re·fu·el·ing;** *also, British,* **re·fu·elled, re·fu·el·ling** —*v.t.* to supply again with fuel: *to refuel an airplane.* —*v.i.* to take on a fresh supply of fuel.

ref·uge (ref′yooj) *n.* **1.** a shelter or protection, as from danger, trouble, or hardship: *The frightened puppy took refuge under the bed.* **2.** a place providing shelter, protection, or safety; haven: *The abandoned shack was his refuge during the storm.* **3.** a source of aid or relief.

ref·u·gee (ref′yoo jē′) *n.* a person who flees to safety or refuge, especially one who leaves his home or homeland because of persecution, war, or danger, and seeks safety in another place.

re·ful·gent (ri ful′jənt) *adj.* shining brightly; radiant. —**re·ful′gence,** *n.* —**re·ful′gent·ly,** *adv.*

re·fund (*v.,* ri fund′; *n.,* rē′fund) *v.t.* to give or pay back: *The salesman promised to refund Mary's deposit if she should decide not to buy the sofa.* —*n.* **1.** the amount refunded: *a refund of five dollars.* **2.** the act or an instance of refunding.

re·fur·bish (rē fur′bish) *v.t.* to brighten or freshen up: *to refurbish an old brass lamp.*

re·fus·al (ri fyoo′zəl) *n.* **1.** the act of refusing. **2.** the opportunity or privilege of accepting or refusing before others.

re·fuse¹ (ri fyooz′) *v.,* **re·fused, re·fus·ing.** —*v.t.* **1.** to withhold acceptance of; turn down; reject: *to refuse a gift, to refuse an offer.* **2.** to withhold the giving or granting of; deny: *The neutral country refused asylum to the hijackers.* **3.** to be determined not to do (something); be unwilling: *You always refuse to see my point of view. She refuses to see us.* —*v.i.* to be unwilling to do something: *He can't refuse if you ask politely.* [Old French *refuser.*]

ref·use² (ref′yoos) *n.* anything thrown away as useless or worthless; waste; rubbish. [Middle French *refus* rejection, denial.]

ref·u·ta·tion (ref′yoo tā′shən) *n.* **1.** the act of refuting. **2.** something that refutes or disproves, as evidence or an argument.

re·fute (ri fyoot′) *v.t.,* **re·fut·ed, re·fut·ing. 1.** to prove (a statement or argument) to be false or incorrect. **2.** to prove (someone) to be wrong: *The lawyer refuted the witness.* —**re·fut′a·ble,** *adj.* —**re·fut′er,** *n.*

re·gain (rē gān′) *v.t.* **1.** to get possession of again; get back; recover: *to regain one's health.* **2.** to reach again; get back to: *We regained the main highway easily from the side road.*

re·gal (rē′gəl) *adj.* **1.** suitable for or characteristic of a king or other ruler; stately; splendid; dignified: *a regal manner.* **2.** of or belonging to a king or other ruler; royal. —**re′gal·ly,** *adv.*

re·gale (ri gāl′) *v.,* **re·galed, re·gal·ing.** —*v.t.* **1.** to give great pleasure to; delight or entertain: *Grandmother regaled us with stories of her childhood.* **2.** to provide a feast for. —*v.i.* to feast.

re·ga·li·a (ri gā′lē ə) *n.,pl.* **1.** the symbols or emblems of royalty, including crowns, scepters, and ceremonial swords. **2.** the symbols, emblems, or decorations of any rank, office, society, or order. **3.** splendid or fancy clothes; finery.

re·gard (ri gärd′) *v.t.* **1.** to look upon or think of; consider: *He regards Jim as the best man for the job.* **2.** to look at closely: *The guard regarded us with suspicion.* **3.** to show respect or consideration for: *to regard the rights of others.* **4.** to have relation to; have to do with; concern: *Her question regards his future plans.* **5.** to pay attention to; heed: *He did not regard their warnings.* —*n.* **1.** careful thought, notice, or attention; consideration; heed: *He gave no regard to the wishes of his friends.* **2.** respect or affection. **3. regards.** best wishes: *Give my regards to your family.* **4.** a particular point; matter: *I agree with you in that regard.*

re·gard·ful (ri gärd′fəl) *adj.* **1.** heedful; observant; mindful: *He was always regardful of the rights of others.* **2.** respectful.

re·gard·ing (ri gär′ding) *prep.* in reference to; concerning.

re·gard·less (ri gärd′lis) *adj.* having or showing no regard or consideration; heedless; unmindful: *The acrobat was regardless of the risks involved in the difficult stunt.* —*adv.* in spite of everything; anyway: *I am buying the skis, regardless.* —**re·gard′less·ly,** *adv.*

re·gat·ta (ri gat′ə) *n.* a boat race or a series of boat races.

re·gen·cy (rē′jən sē) *n. pl.,* **re·gen·cies. 1.** the office, government, or power of a regent or body of regents. **2.** the period during which a regent or body of regents governs. **3. Regency.** in English history, the period from 1811 to 1820.

re·gen·er·ate (*v.,* ri jen′ə rāt′; *adj.,* ri jen′ər it) *v.,* **re·gen·er·at·ed, re·gen·er·at·ing.** —*v.t.* **1.** to cause to be morally or spiritually renewed. **2.** to give new strength, energy, or life to: *The tennis player's recent victory regenerated his desire to become a professional athlete.* **3.** to reproduce or grow anew in order to replace something lost or damaged: *A lobster can regenerate a claw that has been broken off.* —*v.i.* **1.** to become formed anew; be reproduced. **2.** to be morally or spiritually renewed. —*adj.* **1.** morally or spiritually renewed. **2.** restored to a better state; renewed. —**re·gen′er·a′tion,** *n.*

re·gen·er·a·tive (ri jen′ə rā′tiv) *adj.* **1.** of or relating to regeneration: *regenerative power.* **2.** tending to regenerate: *a regenerative species.*

re·gent (rē′jənt) *n.* **1.** a person who governs in place of a monarch who is absent, disabled, or too young. **2.** a member of a governing board, as of a state college or university or of a state educational system. —*adj.* acting as a regent: *a prince regent.*

re·gime (rə zhēm′, rā zhēm′) *also,* **ré·gime.** *n.* **1.** a system of government: *a dictatorial regime.* **2.** another word for **regimen.**

reg·i·men (rej′ə men′) *n.* a regular schedule, as for diet, exercise, sleep, or study.

reg·i·ment (*n.,* rej′ə mənt; *v.,* rej′ə ment′) *n.* a military unit, usually commanded by a colonel, made up of three battalions and a headquarters, and forming part of a division. —*v.t.* to force to behave in the same strict way; enforce uniformity on: *The military school regiments its students. The company regiments its workers.* —**reg′i·men·ta′tion,** *n.*

reg·i·men·tal (rej′ə ment′əl) *adj.* of or relating to a regiment. —*n.* **regimentals. 1.** the uniform of a regiment. **2.** any military uniform.

Re·gi·na (ri jī′nə) *n.* a city in southern Canada, capital of Saskatchewan. Pop. (1971), 137,759.

re·gion (rē′jən) *n.* **1.** a geographic area having one or more characteristics in common that set it apart from other areas: *a mining region, desert regions.* **2.** a large portion of a territory, space, or area: *the upper regions of the atmosphere.* **3.** a division or part of the body: *the abdominal region.* **4.** a sphere of interest or activity; a field; realm: *the region of philosophy.*

re·gion·al (rē′jən əl) *adj.* of or relating to a particular region. —**re′gion·al·ly,** *adv.*

reg·is·ter (rej′is tər) *n.* **1.** a formal or official record or list, as of names, facts, or events: *a register of marriages, a register of volunteers.* **2.** a book for such records: *a hotel register.* **3.** a machine that automatically records or counts, such as a cash register. **4.** in a heating or ventilating system, a grille or other device over an opening in a wall or floor, that can be opened or closed to regulate the passage of air into a room. **5.** *Music.* **a.** the range of a voice or instrument, or a particular portion of the range.

---

at; āpe; cär; end; mē; it; īce; hot; ōld; fôrk; wood; fool; oil; out; up; turn; sing; thin; this; hw in white; zh in treasure. The symbol ə stands for the sound of **a** in about, **e** in taken, **i** in pencil, **o** in lemon, and **u** in circus.

b. a set of organ pipes controlled by one stop. —*v.t.* **1.** to enter in a register; record: *to register the names of absent students, to register a complaint.* **2.** to enroll formally or officially: *The volunteers registered the new voters.* **3.** to show or record, as on a scale: *The thermometer registered fifty degrees.* **4.** to show or express: *His face registered disappointment.* **5.** to have (mail) officially recorded by paying a fee, so as to insure against loss, theft, or damage. —*v.i.* **1.** to enter one's name in a register: *to register at a hotel.* **2.** to enroll formally or officially: *The students register in September for the fall term.*

registered nurse, a nurse licensed by the state in which he or she practices after completing certain training and education requirements.

reg·is·trar (rej′is trär′) *n.* an official, especially at a college or university, in charge of keeping records.

reg·is·tra·tion (rej′is trā′shən) *n.* **1.** the act of registering or the state of being registered. **2.** a document showing that something has been registered: *an automobile registration.* **3.** an entry in a register. **4.** the number of people registered, especially at a college or university; total enrollment.

reg·is·try (rej′is trē) *n. pl.,* **reg·is·tries. 1.** the act of registering. **2.** a place where a register is kept; office of registration. **3.** see **register** *(def. 1).*

re·gress (ri gres′) *v.i.* to go back or return to an earlier or less advanced form or state; revert. —**re·gres′sion,** *n.*

re·gret (ri gret′) *v.t.,* **re·gret·ted, re·gret·ting. 1.** to feel sorry or distressed about: *I regret the loss of her friendship.* **2.** to remember with a feeling of loss or sadness: *The old man regretted his lost youth.* —*n.* **1.** sorrow or distress: *I feel no regret for my decision.* **2.** a sense of loss or sadness. **3. regrets.** a polite apology, especially for refusing an invitation: *to send one's regrets.* —**re·gret′ta·ble,** *adj.* —**re·gret′ta·bly,** *adv.*

re·gret·ful (ri gret′fəl) *adj.* feeling or showing regret; filled with regret. —**re·gret′ful·ly,** *adv.* —**re·gret′ful·ness,** *n.*

reg·u·lar (reg′yə lər) *adj.* **1.** customary or expected; normal; usual: *Our regular teacher was absent today. Twelve o'clock is our regular lunchtime.* **2.** happening at fixed periods of time or according to a set schedule; unvarying; steady: *a regular summer vacation, regular train departures.* **3.** evenly shaped, spaced, or arranged: *She has regular teeth.* **4.** according to habit or a usual way of doing something: *a regular customer.* **5.** belonging to or making up a permanent or standing armed service: *Many early American statesmen were against establishing a regular army.* **6.** *Grammar.* using the most common inflectional endings, such as *-s* for nouns, *-ed* and *-ing* for verbs, and *-er* and *-est* for adjectives. *Lift* and *cook* are regular verbs. **7.** *Informal.* nice; decent; pleasant: *a regular guy.* —*n.* a soldier belonging to a permanent or standing armed service. [Old French *reguler.*] —**reg′u·lar·ly,** *adv.*

reg·u·lar·i·ty (reg′yə lar′ə tē) *n.* the quality or condition of being regular.

reg·u·late (reg′yə lāt′) *v.t.,* **reg·u·lat·ed, reg·u·lat·ing. 1.** to manage or control according to a set rule, principle, or system: *to regulate the economy.* **2.** to maintain at a certain level or standard; keep constant: *a valve that regulates the intake of fuel in an engine.* **3.** to put or keep in good or proper working order: *to regulate a mechanical part.* —**reg′u·la′tor,** *n.*

reg·u·la·tion (reg′yə lā′shən) *n.* **1.** a law, rule, or order intended to control behavior or procedure; governing rule or law: *school regulations.* **2.** the act of regulating or the state of being regulated. —*adj.* required by or in accordance with regulation: *a regulation size, a regulation uniform.*

re·gur·gi·tate (rē gur′jə tāt′) *v.,* **re·gur·gi·tat·ed, re·gur·gi·tat·ing.** —*v.t.* to vomit. —*v.i.* to rush, pour, or flow back, as liquids, gases, or undigested food.

re·ha·bil·i·tate (rē′hə bil′ə tāt′) *v.t.,* **re·ha·bil·i·tat·ed, re·ha·bil·i·tat·ing. 1.** to restore or bring to a healthy or useful state: *to rehabilitate an injured soldier.* **2.** to restore to a good condition; renovate: *to rehabilitate an abandoned cabin.* **3.** to restore the former rank, privileges, or good name of; reinstate. —**re′ha·bil′i·ta′tion,** *n.*

re·hash (*v.,* rē hash′; *n.,* rē′hash′) *v.t.* to go over or deal with again without making changes or improvements: *The lecturer rehashed the same ideas used by another lecturer yesterday.* —*n.* **1.** work or thought that is not original or creative; something rehashed. **2.** the act of rehashing.

re·hears·al (ri hur′səl) *n.* **1.** a period of practice in preparation for a public or official performance: *a dance rehearsal.* **2.** the act of rehearsing.

re·hearse (ri hurs′) *v.,* **re·hearsed, re·hears·ing.** —*v.t.* **1.** to practice in preparation for a public or official performance: *to rehearse a play.* **2.** to train or improve by practice: *The director rehearsed the actors until they all knew their parts.* —*v.i.* to take part in a rehearsal.

reign (rān) *n.* **1.** the period of rule of a monarch or other ruler: *the reign of Queen Victoria.* **2.** supreme power or rule, as of a monarch; sovereignty. —*v.i.* **1.** to hold or use the power of a monarch or other ruler: *Louis XIV reigned for seventy-two years.* **2.** to have a widespread influence; prevail: *A severe famine reigned throughout the country.*

Reign of Terror, a period of the French Revolution, from about May 1793 to July 1794, during which thousands of persons were imprisoned or guillotined.

re·im·burse (rē′im burs′) *v.t.,* **re·im·bursed, re·im·burs·ing.** to pay back for what has been spent, used, or lost; recompense: *The company reimburses sales personnel for their traveling expenses.* —**re·im·burse′ment,** *n.*

Reims (rēmz) *also,* **Rheims.** *n.* a city in northern France, northeast of Paris. Pop. (1975), 178,381.

rein (rān) *n.* **1.** either of two or more long, narrow straps attached to a bit at either side of a horse's mouth and used to control the movement of a horse. **2.** any means of guidance or control; check: *He kept a tight rein on his temper.* —*v.t.* to guide, control, or check with or as if with reins: *to rein a horse, to rein one's anger.* —*v.i.* to slow down or stop a horse or other animal by means of reins: *to rein in a horse.*

to give rein to or **to give free rein to.** to give complete freedom to: *to give rein to one's imagination.*

re·in·car·nate (rē′in kär′nāt) *v.t.,* **re·in·car·nat·ed, re·in·car·nat·ing.** to cause to undergo reincarnation.

re·in·car·na·tion (rē′in kär nā′shən) *n.* the passage of a soul at death into another body; transmigration.

rein·deer (rān′dēr′) *n. pl.,* **rein·deer.** a large deer found in Lapland, Greenland, and other northern regions, having a white, gray, or brown coat, and branched antlers.

re·in·force (rē′in fôrs′) *also,* **re·en·force, re·en·force.** *v.t.,* **re·in·forced, re·in·forc·ing. 1.** to strengthen by repairing or by adding new or extra parts or materials: *to reinforce a dam with sandbags.* **2.** to strengthen a military or naval force with additional men, supplies, or other equipment: *to reinforce a fort.*

Reindeer

re·in·force·ment (rē′in fôrs′mənt) *also,* **re·en·force-**

ment, re·en·force·ment. n. **1.** the act of reinforcing or the state of being reinforced. **2.** something that reinforces. **3. reinforcements.** additional troops, ships, or other supplies to be used in a military action.

re·in·state (rē′in stāt′) v.t., re·in·stat·ed, re·in·stat·ing. to restore to a former position or condition: *The city official was reinstated after the charges against him were proved untrue.* —**re′in·state′ment,** n.

re·it·er·ate (rē it′ə rāt′) v.t., re·it·er·at·ed, re·it·er·at·ing. to say or do again or repeatedly; repeat: *She reiterated her plea for silence.* —**re·it′er·a′tion,** n.

re·ject (v., ri jekt′; n., rē′jekt) v.t. **1.** to refuse to accept, believe, grant, or approve: *Mr. James rejected Mr. Smith's offer to buy his house.* **2.** to throw away, set aside, or discard as marred or worthless: *She rejected the chipped glasses.* **3.** to be unable to accept; expel: *The patient's body rejected the heart transplant.* —n. a person or thing that is rejected. —**re·jec′tion,** n.

re·joice (ri jois′) v., re·joiced, re·joic·ing. —v.i. to express great joy or be filled with joy: *The soldier's parents rejoiced at the news of his safe return from the war.* —v.t. to fill with joy; gladden.

re·join[1] (rē join′) v.t. **1.** to join the company of again: *He rejoined his friends after class.* **2.** to join together again: *She rejoined the broken parts of the vase with glue.* [Re- + join.]

re·join[2] (ri join′) v.i. to answer; reply: *"It's the best I can do,"* he rejoined sharply to her criticism. [Middle English *rejoinen* to answer a legal charge.]

re·join·der (ri join′dər) n. an answer or reply.

re·ju·ve·nate (ri jōō′və nāt′) v.t., re·ju·ve·nat·ed, re·ju·ve·nat·ing. to make young or vigorous again: *The vacation rejuvenated her.* —**re·ju′ve·na′tion,** n.

re·lapse (n., rē′laps′; v., rē laps′) n. the act of falling or slipping back into a former condition, especially the return of an illness after partial recovery. —v.i., re·lapsed, re·laps·ing. to have a relapse.

re·late (ri lāt′) v., re·lat·ed, re·lat·ing. —v.t. **1.** to report the events or details of; narrate; tell: *The witness related what he had seen.* **2.** to show as having to do with; bring into relation; link: *His teacher related his improved grades to better study habits.* —v.i. **1.** to be connected; apply; pertain: *How does his comment relate to what we are discussing?* **2.** to establish a close or friendly relationship with: *She relates well to children.*

re·lat·ed (ri lā′tid) adj. **1.** having relation; connected: *related problems.* **2.** connected by blood, marriage, or common origin. —**re·lat′ed·ness,** n.

re·la·tion (ri lā′shən) n. **1.** the fact or condition of having to do with another or other things; connection between two or more things: *The doctor stressed the relation between a good diet and a healthy body.* **2.** the position of one person or thing with respect to another: *the relation of parent to child.* **3. relations.** matters or conditions that bring one person or thing in contact with another; affairs; dealings: *business relations.* **4.** a connection formed by blood, marriage, or common origin. **5.** a relative: *He visited his relations in Virginia.* **6.** the act or instance of narrating or telling.

re·la·tion·ship (ri lā′shən ship′) n. **1.** the state or condition of being related; connection; link. **2.** the condition of being connected by blood, marriage, or common origin; kinship.

rel·a·tive (rel′ə tiv) adj. **1.** resulting from or judged by comparison; comparative: *She walked with relative ease after the operation.* **2.** existing or having meaning only in relation to something else, such as the terms *right* and *left*, *big* and *little*. **3.** *Grammar.* modifying or referring to a person or thing previously mentioned. In the sentence *The*

person who called was my uncle, the word *who* is a relative pronoun referring to *uncle.* —n. **1.** a person connected with another by blood or marriage: *Most of her relatives live in California.* **2.** *Grammar.* a relative word or term. —**rel′a·tive·ly,** adv.

relative humidity, see **humidity** (def. 2).

rel·a·tiv·i·ty (rel′ə tiv′ə tē) n. **1.** the quality, state, or fact of being relative. **2.** a theory, developed by Albert Einstein, that deals with the way in which measurements of physical quantities, such as space, time, and energy, differ when made by observers who are in motion relative to one another. It is based on the principle that all motion is relative and on the fact that the speed of light is the same with respect to all observers. The **special theory of relativity** treats the case in which the relative motion of the observers is along a straight line at a constant speed. Among its conclusions are that nothing can move faster than the speed of light and that mass and energy are equivalent. The **general theory of relativity** extends this theory to include all kinds of motion and provides an explanation for the force of gravity.

re·lax (ri laks′) v.t. **1.** to make less rigid or tense; loosen: *The hot bath helped to relax his muscles.* **2.** to make less strict, severe, or harsh: *The club relaxed its rules on accepting new members.* **3.** to provide release from tension or strain: *He needed a vacation to relax him.* —v.i. **1.** to become less rigid or tense. **2.** to become less tense, nervous, or anxious: *She relaxed by watching television.*

re·lax·a·tion (rē′lak sā′shən) n. **1.** the act of relaxing or the state of being relaxed. **2.** something that relaxes.

re·lay (n., rē′lā′; v., rē′lā′, ri lā′) n. **1.** a fresh set or team, as of men or animals, prepared to replace or relieve another. **2.** see **relay race.** **3.** an electric switch that opens or closes in response to mechanical forces or to changes in the condition of an electric current. —v.t. to carry forward or pass along by or as if by relays: *I will relay your message to Mr. Jones.*

relay race, a race between two or more teams in which each team member in turn covers a certain distance and is then relieved by a teammate.

re·lease (ri lēs′) v.t., re·leased, re·leas·ing. **1.** to set free or loose: *to release a hostage.* **2.** to let go or cause to be free from something that holds or fastens: *to release a brake.* **3.** to relieve from duty, responsibility, or obligation: *to release someone from a promise.* **4.** to authorize or permit the publication, circulation, sale, or use of: *to release a motion picture for distribution.* **5.** to give up (a right, privilege, or claim). —n. **1.** the act of releasing or the state of being released. **2.** something that offers freedom or relief, as from work or tension: *Playing golf is his only release.* **3.** a written discharge or authorization: *The warden signed the prisoner's release.* **4.** something that is formally issued or released to the public: *a news release.* **5.** a device, such as a catch or button, that starts or holds a mechanism.

rel·e·gate (rel′ə gāt′) v.t., rel·e·gat·ed, rel·e·gat·ing. **1.** to send away or remove, especially to a lower or less important place or position: *We relegated the old toys to the attic.* **2.** to turn over (a matter or task) to another. —**rel′e·ga′tion,** n.

at; āpe; cär; end; mē; it; īce; hot; ōld; fôrk; wood; fōōl; oil; out; up; turn; sing; thin; **this**; hw in white; zh in treasure. The symbol ə stands for the sound of **a** in about, **e** in taken, **i** in pencil, **o** in lemon, and **u** in circus.

R

re·lent (ri lent′) *v.i.* to become less harsh or severe; soften; yield.

re·lent·less (ri lent′lis) *adj.* **1.** harsh or severe; pitiless; unyielding. **2.** steady and persistent; ceaseless: *The story told of a scientist's long and relentless search for a vaccine.* —**re·lent′less·ly,** *adv.* —**re·lent′less·ness,** *n.*

rel·e·vant (rel′ə vənt) *adj.* connected or having to do with the matter at hand; appropriate; pertinent: *His question about Christopher Columbus was relevant to our discussion of explorers.* —**rel′e·vance, rel′e·van·cy,** *n.*

re·li·a·ble (ri lī′ə bəl) *adj.* that can be depended on with confidence; trustworthy: *a reliable friend, a reliable business firm.* —**re·li·a′bil′i·ty,** *n.* —**re·li′a·bly,** *adv.*

re·li·ance (ri lī′əns) *n.* **1.** the act of relying. **2.** confidence, trust, or dependence. **3.** a person or thing that is relied on.

re·li·ant (ri lī′ənt) *adj.* having or showing reliance.

rel·ic (rel′ik) *n.* **1.** something from the past, such as an object or custom, that has survived the passage of time; remnant: *The archaeologist found relics of Roman civilization.* **2.** the body or part of the body of a saint, martyr, or other holy person, or some object associated with him, often enshrined as a memorial. **3.** something that is kept and cherished for its age or sentimental associations; memento; keepsake: *Dad kept his uniform as a relic of his army days.*

re·lief¹ (ri lēf′) *n.* **1.** the freeing from or lessening of pain, anxiety, discomfort, or the like: *We sought relief from the heat in the air-conditioned room.* **2.** something that stops or lessens discomfort. **3.** financial aid, as from government funds, to those in poverty or need: *to go on relief, relief for flood victims.* **4.** release from a post or duty, as by a person or persons substituting for another. **5.** a person or persons who substitute for another. [Middle French *relief* literally, a raising.]

re·lief² (ri lēf′) *n.* **1.** distinctness or prominence resulting from contrast: *The huge tree stood in bold relief against the clear sky.* **2.** a variation in the height of an area of the earth's surface, especially as shown on a relief map. **3.** a projection of a figure or design from a flat background or other surface, as in sculpture: *The marble block contained figures carved in relief.* **4.** a work of sculpture made with such a projection. **5.** the illusion of depth created in a painting or drawing by the use of line, shading, or color. [French *relief* a projection of a figure or design from a flat surface.]

Relief carving

relief map, a map that shows variations in the height of an area on the earth's surface by means of contour lines, shading, color, or molding.

re·lieve (ri lēv′) *v.t.,* **re·lieved, re·liev·ing. 1.** to free from or lessen (pain, anxiety, discomfort, or the like): *He gargled to relieve his sore throat.* **2.** to free from pain, anxiety, discomfort, or the like: *The good news relieved him.* **3.** to free from a post or duty by providing or serving as a substitute: *The corporal will relieve the sentry in an hour.* **4.** to furnish aid to: *to relieve the poor and needy.*

re·li·gion (ri lij′ən) *n.* **1.** belief in, reverence for, or worship of God or a god or gods, who are thought of as having created or as ruling the universe. **2.** a particular system of such belief and worship: *the Christian religion.* **3.** some-

thing believed in or followed with great devotion or seriousness: *Success was the businessman's religion.*

re·li·gious (ri lij′əs) *adj.* **1.** showing devotion to a religion; devout: *a religious person.* **2.** of or relating to religion: *religious beliefs.* **3.** very careful and exact; conscientious; strict: *The craftsman paid religious attention to details in his work.* **4.** of, relating to, or belonging to an order or community bound by monastic vows. —*n. pl.,* **re·li·gious.** a person bound by monastic vows, as a monk or nun. —**re·li′gious·ly,** *adv.* —**re·li′gious·ness,** *n.*

re·lin·quish (ri ling′kwish) *v.t.* **1.** to give over possession or control of; surrender; yield: *The defeated nation relinquished territory to the conquerors.* **2.** to put aside or give up; abandon: *He relinquished all claim to the money.* **3.** to let go; release: *The child relinquished his hold on his mother's hand.* —**re·lin′quish·ment,** *n.*

rel·ish (rel′ish) *n. pl.,* **rel·ish·es. 1.** a mixture of spices, pickles, olives, chopped vegetables, or the like, used chiefly to flavor other food or as a side dish. **2.** interest or pleasure; enjoyment: *The child opened his birthday presents with great relish.* **3.** anything that lends interest or pleasure to something else. —*v.t.* to take pleasure in; savor; enjoy: *to relish a meal.*

re·live (rē liv′) *v.t.,* **re·lived, re·liv·ing.** to live over again, especially in the mind: *to relive one's childhood.*

re·lo·cate (rē lō′kāt) *v.t., v.i.,* **re·lo·cat·ed, re·lo·cat·ing.** to move to another place: *to relocate a business.*

re·luc·tance (ri luk′təns) *n.* the state of being reluctant; lack of eagerness; hesitation or unwillingness.

re·luc·tant (ri luk′tənt) *adj.* **1.** feeling hesitation or unwillingness; unwilling; averse: *I was reluctant to lend him my books.* **2.** marked by hesitation or unwillingness: *a reluctant apology.* —**re·luc′tant·ly,** *adv.*

re·ly (ri lī′) *v.i.,* **re·lied, re·ly·ing.** to have confidence; trust; depend: *You can rely on him to be prompt.*

re·main (ri mān′) *v.i.* **1.** to continue in the same place; stay behind; abide: *You should have remained at home.* **2.** to continue unchanged; go on being: *We remained friends for years.* **3.** to be left: *All that remains of the ancient city is ruins. If you take three apples from five apples, two remain.*

re·main·der (ri mān′dər) *n.* **1.** something that remains or is left; remaining part: *We played ball for the remainder of the day.* **2.** *Mathematics.* **a.** the number found when one number is subtracted from another. 10 subtracted from 12 leaves a remainder of 2. **b.** the number remaining when one number is divided by another. 7 divided by 3 gives 2 and a remainder of 1.

re·mains (ri mānz′) *n.,pl.* **1.** something that is left: *the remains of ancient Rome.* **2.** a dead body; corpse.

re·make (*n.,* rē′māk′; *v.,* rē māk′) *n.* something made again or anew: *a remake of an old motion picture.* —*v.t.,* **re·made** (rē mād′), **re·mak·ing.** to make again or anew.

re·mand (ri mand′) *v.t.* **1.** to send, call, or order back: *to remand a soldier to his post.* **2.** *Law.* **a.** to return (a prisoner or an accused person) to custody. **b.** to send (a case) back to a lower court for further proceedings. —*n.* the act of remanding or the state of being remanded.

re·mark (ri märk′) *n.* **1.** a spoken or written statement or observation, especially a brief or casual comment. **2.** the act of taking notice or observing; notice. —*v.t.* **1.** to express as an opinion or observation. **2.** to take notice of; observe; perceive. —*v.i.* to make remarks: *He remarked on her new dress.*

re·mark·a·ble (ri märk′ə bəl) *adj.* **1.** having unusual qualities; extraordinary; uncommon: *His intelligence is remarkable.* **2.** worthy of notice or likely to be noticed: *She is a remarkable person.* —**re·mark′a·ble·ness,** *n.* —**re·mark′a·bly,** *adv.*

re·mar·ry (rē mar′ē) *v.*, **re·mar·ried**, **re·mar·ry·ing.** —*v.i.* to marry again after being widowed or divorced. —*v.t.* to marry (a former spouse) again. —**re·mar·riage** (rē mar′ij), *n.*

Rem·brandt (rem′brant) 1606–1669, Dutch painter and etcher.

re·me·di·a·ble (ri mē′dē ə bəl) *adj.* that can be remedied. —**re·me′di·a·bly,** *adv.*

re·me·di·al (ri mē′dē əl) *adj.* providing or intending to provide a remedy or improvement: *The new community center started a remedial reading program.* —**re·me′di·al·ly,** *adv.*

rem·e·dy (rem′ə dē) *n. pl.,* **rem·e·dies. 1.** something that relieves, heals, or improves a disease, disorder, or the like: *a headache remedy.* **2.** something that corrects or gets rid of something bad or harmful: *a remedy for air pollution.* —*v.t.,* **rem·e·died, rem·e·dy·ing. 1.** to relieve, heal, or improve (a disease, disorder, or the like), as by treatment with medicine. **2.** to set or make right; correct: *to remedy conditions in the slums.*

re·mem·ber (ri mem′bər) *v.t.* **1.** to bring back or recall to the mind or memory; recollect: *Do you remember where you put the keys?* **2.** to keep in mind carefully: *to remember an appointment.* **3.** to think of or keep in mind as worthy of affection, regard, or recognition: *I'll always remember you for your kindness.* **4.** to reward or present with a gift: *My grandfather remembered me in his will.* **5.** to send greetings from: *Remember me to your parents.* —*v.i.* to use the memory.

re·mem·brance (ri mem′brəns) *n.* **1.** something that is remembered; recollection: *a remembrance from childhood.* **2.** the act or power of remembering. **3.** the state of being remembered. **4.** an object, such as a gift, serving to bring someone or something to mind; memento; keepsake: *He gave her a bracelet as a remembrance of him.*

re·mind (ri mīnd′) *v.t.* to make (someone) think of something or someone; bring back to mind; cause to remember: *Tony reminded Sue to return the library book. She reminds me of my sister.* —**re·mind′er,** *n.*

rem·i·nisce (rem′ə nis′) *v.i.,* **rem·i·nisced, rem·i·nisc·ing.** to think or tell of past experiences or events: *The two friends reminisced about their school days.*

rem·i·nis·cence (rem′ə nis′əns) *n.* **1.** a thinking of past experiences or events. **2.** *also,* **reminiscences.** a story or account of past experiences or events. **3.** something remembered; memory.

rem·i·nis·cent (rem′ə nis′ənt) *adj.* **1.** reminding or suggestive: *John's manner of speaking is reminiscent of his father.* **2.** marked by or given to reminiscence.

re·miss (ri mis′) *adj.* **1.** careless or negligent, as in one's duty; lax: *He was very remiss, and failed to get his work in on time.* **2.** showing carelessness or negligence: *a remiss way of doing something.* —**re·miss′ly,** *adv.* —**re·miss′ness,** *n.*

re·mis·sion (ri mish′ən) *n.* **1.** the act of remitting or the state of being remitted. **2.** a freeing from penalty or guilt; forgiveness; pardon: *remission from one's sins.* **3.** a temporary lessening of pain or the symptoms of a disease. **4.** a cancellation, as of a debt.

re·mit (ri mit′) *v.,* **re·mit·ted, re·mit·ting.** —*v.t.* **1.** to send (money) in payment. **2.** to free from the penalty or guilt of; forgive; pardon: *to remit a sin.* **3.** to do away with; cancel: *to remit punishment.* **4.** to make less; lessen; reduce: *to remit one's efforts.* **5.** to submit or refer for consideration, decision, or action, especially to someone in authority. **6.** *Law.* to send (a case) back to a lower court for further proceedings. —*v.i.* **1.** to send money in payment. **2.** to become less; abate; diminish: *The fever remitted.* —**re·mit′ter,** *n.*

re·mit·tance (ri mit′əns) *n.* **1.** the sending of money. **2.** the money sent.

rem·nant (rem′nənt) *n.* **1.** a remaining piece or part; remainder: *The remnants of the meal were still on the table. The archaeologist uncovered the remnants of an ancient civilization.* **2.** a piece of cloth left over from the cutting of a larger piece, often sold at a reduced price.

re·mod·el (rē mod′əl) *v.t.,* **re·mod·eled, re·mod·el·ing;** *also, British,* **re·mod·elled, re·mod·el·ling.** to make over or anew; reconstruct; renovate: *The builder remodeled the store for the new owner.*

re·mon·strance (ri mon′strəns) *n.* the act or instance of remonstrating; protest.

re·mon·strate (ri mon′strāt) *v.i.,* **re·mon·strat·ed, re·mon·strat·ing.** to present reasons against something; plead or argue in opposition: *He remonstrated with his friends against going on the trip.*

re·morse (ri môrs′) *n.* a deep, painful feeling of guilt, sorrow, or distress for wrongdoing: *The youth showed remorse for having stolen the watch.* —**re·morse′ful,** *adj.* —**re·morse′ful·ly,** *adv.* —**re·morse′ful·ness,** *n.*

re·morse·less (ri môrs′lis) *adj.* having no pity or remorse; merciless; cruel. —**re·morse′less·ly,** *adv.* —**re·morse′less·ness,** *n.*

re·mote (ri mōt′) *adj.,* **re·mot·er, re·mot·est. 1.** located at a distance; not near: *remote regions.* **2.** located out of the way; secluded: *a remote house.* **3.** far removed from the present; distant in time: *the remote past.* **4.** small in degree; slight; faint: *There was only a remote possibility that our team would win.* **5.** having no close connection or bearing: *His question was remote from the subject of the talk.* —**re·mote′ly,** *adv.* —**re·mote′ness,** *n.*

remote control, control of a machine or apparatus, such as a guided missile or a television receiver, from a distance, especially by means of radio signals.

re·mount (rē mount′) *v.t.* to mount (something) again: *The rider remounted his horse.* —*v.i.* to mount again. —*n.* a fresh horse that takes the place of another.

re·mov·al (ri moo′vəl) *n.* **1.** the act of removing or the state of being removed: *The removal of the books from the shelf took only a few minutes.* **2.** a changing of location, as of a business. **3.** dismissal from an office or position: *the removal of a dishonest mayor.*

re·move (ri moov′) *v.,* **re·moved, re·mov·ing.** —*v.t.* **1.** to take or move away, as from one place or position to another: *to remove dishes from a table.* **2.** to take off or shed: *He removed his coat when he went inside.* **3.** to do away with; eliminate: *to remove all cause for alarm.* **4.** to dismiss from an office or position. —*v.i.* to change one's place of residence or business; move. —*n.* a distance or space separating one person or thing from another. —**re·mov′a·ble,** *adj.* —**re·mov′er,** *n.*

re·moved (ri moovd′) *adj.* **1.** separated by a degree in relationship: *My first cousin's son is my first cousin once removed.* **2.** distant; remote.

re·mu·ner·ate (ri myoo′nə rāt′) *v.t.,* **re·mu·ner·at·ed, re·mu·ner·at·ing. 1.** to pay (someone) for any service, loss, or expense; reward; repay: *He remunerated the boy for mowing the lawn.* **2.** to compensate for. —**re·mu′ner·a′tion,** *n.*

at; āpe; cär; end; mē; it; īce; hot; ōld; fôrk; wood; fool; oil; out; up; turn; sing; thin; **this;** **hw** in white; **zh** in treasure. The symbol ə stands for the sound of **a** in about, **e** in taken, **i** in pencil, **o** in lemon, and **u** in circus.

R

re·mu·ner·a·tive (ri myōō′nə rā′tiv) *adj.* that remunerates; profitable: *a remunerative investment.*

Re·mus (rē′məs) *n.* see **Romulus.**

ren·ais·sance (ren′ə säns′, ren′ə säns′) *n.* **1.** a renewal of activity, interest, or enthusiasm about something; rebirth; revival: *There was a renaissance of the arts in our town.* **2. Renaissance. a.** a revival of art and learning that began in Italy during the fourteenth century, marked by a growth of interest in ancient Greek and Latin literature and art, concern with individualism, and intellectual and scientific activity. **b.** the period of European history during which this occurred, extending from the fourteenth through the sixteenth centuries. **c.** a style of art and architecture developed during this period. —*adj.* of, characteristic of, or in the style of the Renaissance. Also, **renascence.**

re·nal (rēn′əl) *adj.* of, relating to, or near the kidneys.

re·nas·cence (ri nas′əns, ri nā′səns) *n., adj.* another word for **renaissance.**

re·nas·cent (ri nas′ənt, ri nā′sənt) *adj.* showing renewed growth or vigor; being born again.

rend (rend) *v.t.,* **rent** or **rend·ed, rend·ing. 1.** to split or tear apart or into pieces forcibly or violently: *The wind rent the sails of the yacht.* **2.** to divide or split into parts as if by tearing: *Political disagreements rent the community.* **3.** to remove forcibly; wrest: *to rend a weapon from someone's hands.*

ren·der (ren′dər) *v.t.* **1.** to cause to be or become; make: *to render someone helpless.* **2.** to give or pay as something owed or due: *to render an apology, to render homage.* **3.** to give or make available; provide: *to render aid to the needy.* **4.** to represent or show, as in a painting. **5.** to present and interpret in performance: *The pianist rendered the musical composition in a lively manner.* **6.** to deliver or state formally: *The jury rendered a verdict of not guilty.* **7.** to reproduce or express in another language; translate: *The student rendered an English poem into Russian.* **8.** to give up; surrender; yield: *to render one's life for a worthy cause.* **9.** to separate, purify, or extract by melting: *to render fat.*

ren·dez·vous (rän′də vōō′) *n. pl.,* **ren·dez·vous** (rän′də vōōz′). **1.** an appointment to meet at a fixed place or time. **2.** the place chosen for such a meeting. **3.** any meeting or gathering place. —*v.,* **ren·dez·voused** (rän′də vōōd′), **ren·dez·vous·ing** (rän′də vōō′ing). —*v.i.* to meet by arrangement. —*v.t.* to cause to meet by arrangement. [French *rendezvous,* from *rendez-vous* present yourself.]

ren·di·tion (ren dish′ən) *n.* **1.** an interpretation given by a performer to an artistic, dramatic, or musical composition. **2.** an interpretation or version of a text; translation: *He read an English rendition of Homer's Iliad.* **3.** the act of rendering.

ren·e·gade (ren′ə gād′) *n.* a person who abandons, rejects, or turns against his group in favor of another; traitor. —*adj.* that is a renegade: *a renegade soldier.*

re·nege (ri nig′, ri neg′) *v.i.,* **re·neged, re·neg·ing. 1.** to fail to fulfill a promise or commitment: *to renege on a business deal.* **2.** in a card game, to fail to play a card of the suit led when the rules require such a play and the player is able to make it.

re·new (ri nōō′, ri nyōō′) *v.t.* **1.** to make new or as if new again; restore to a previous or good condition: *to renew the finish on a table, to renew one's spirits.* **2.** to begin again or start over; take up again; resume: *to renew a friendship, to renew a discussion.* **3.** to cause to continue for another period of time: *to renew a library book, to renew a subscription.* **4.** to replace with something new of the same sort; fill again; replenish: *The ship renewed its provisions.*

re·new·al (ri nōō′əl, ri nyōō′əl) *n.* **1.** the act of renewing

or the state of being renewed. **2.** something renewed.

ren·net (ren′it) *n.* a substance containing rennin, obtained from the stomachs of young calves, and added to milk in the making of cheese.

ren·nin (ren′in) *n.* an enzyme present in the gastric juice of certain animals, especially young calves, that curdles milk into a pulpy mass.

Re·no (rē′nō) *n.* a city in western Nevada. Pop. (1970), 72,863.

Re·noir, Pierre Au·guste (ren′wär; pyer ō goost′) 1841–1919, French painter.

re·nounce (ri nouns′) *v.t.,* **re·nounced, re·nounc·ing. 1.** to give up or abandon, especially by formal declaration: *to renounce a claim.* **2.** to refuse to recognize or accept as one's own; disown: *The angry father renounced his son.* —**re·nounce′ment,** *n.*

ren·o·vate (ren′ə vāt′) *v.t.,* **ren·o·vat·ed, ren·o·vat·ing.** to make like new; renew: *to renovate a building.* —**ren′·o·va′tion,** *n.* —**ren′o·va′tor,** *n.*

re·nown (ri noun′) *n.* widespread reputation; fame.

re·nowned (ri nound′) *adj.* having renown; famous.

rent[1] (rent) *n.* a payment for the use of property, especially such payment made regularly by a tenant to a landlord or owner. —*v.t.* **1.** to get the right to use (property) in return for the paying of rent: *to rent a car, to rent a house.* **2.** to grant the use of (property) in return for the paying of rent: *The store rents out bicycles.* —*v.i.* to be for rent: *The apartment rents for two hundred dollars a month.* [Old French *rente.*]

for rent. available for use in return for the paying of rent.

rent[2] (rent) *v.* a past tense and past participle of **rend.** —*n.* **1.** an opening or hole made by rending or tearing; gap or slit: *a rent in a dress, a rent in a wall.* **2.** a sharp division or split, as in a group or organization. [Old English *rendan* to tear.]

rent·al (rent′əl) *n.* **1.** an amount charged, paid, or collected as rent. **2.** the act of renting. **3.** property rented or available for renting. —*adj.* of or relating to rent or renting: *a car rental agency.*

re·nun·ci·a·tion (ri nun′sē ā′shən) *n.* the act of renouncing.

re·o·pen (rē ō′pən) *v.t., v.i.* **1.** to open again: *He reopened the bottle of soda. School reopens in September.* **2.** to begin again; resume: *We reopened the discussion.*

re·or·gan·i·za·tion (rē′ôr gə ni zā′shən) *n.* the act of reorganizing or the state of being reorganized.

re·or·gan·ize (rē ôr′gə nīz′) *v.t., v.i.,* **re·or·gan·ized, re·or·gan·iz·ing.** to organize again or anew.

Rep., Republican.

re·paid (ri pād′) the past tense and past participle of **repay.**

re·pair[1] (ri per′) *v.t.* **1.** to restore to a good condition or working order, as by replacing parts or putting together what has broken; fix; mend: *The road crew repaired the highway. Bill repaired the toaster.* **2.** to correct or eliminate by repairing: *The carpenter repaired the broken leg of the table.* **3.** to bring back to a sound and healthy state; renew: *to repair damaged body tissues.* **4.** to make good; set right; remedy: *to repair a wrong.* —*n.* **1.** the act or process of repairing: *The roof is beyond repair.* **2.** the result of repairing. **3.** condition in terms of soundness or need of repairing. [Old French *réparer.*] —**re·pair′er,** *n.*

re·pair[2] (ri per′) *v.i.* to go: *He repairs to his country home every weekend.* [Middle French *repairer, repairier* to return to one's country.]

re·pair·man (ri per′man′) *n. pl.,* **re·pair·men** (ri per′men′). a person whose occupation is making repairs.

rep·a·ra·ble (rep′ər ə bəl) *also,* **re·pair·a·ble** (ri per′ə·bəl). *adj.* capable of being repaired.

rep·a·ra·tion (rep′ə rā′shən) n. **1.** the act of giving satisfaction or making amends, as for a wrong or injury. **2.** something done or given as satisfaction or amends. **3. reparations.** money or material given in compensation for damage or loss in war, especially that given by a defeated nation to a victorious one.

rep·ar·tee (rep′ər tē′) n. **1.** an exchange of quick, witty replies. **2.** skill or quickness in making such replies. **3.** a quick, witty reply.

re·past (ri past′) n. a meal, or the food and drink eaten or provided at a meal.

re·pa·tri·ate (v., rē pā′trē āt′; n., rē pā′trē it) v.t., **re·pa·tri·at·ed, re·pa·tri·at·ing.** to return (someone) to the country in which he was born or is a citizen. —n. a person who has been repatriated. —**re·pa·tri·a′tion,** n.

re·pay (ri pā′) v.t., **re·paid, re·pay·ing. 1.** to pay or give back: to repay a loan. **2.** to pay or give something back to (someone): I'll never be able to repay you for your help. **3.** to give, make, or do in return: to repay a compliment. —**re·pay′a·ble,** adj. —**re·pay′ment,** n.

re·peal (ri pēl′) v.t. to withdraw or cancel formally or officially; revoke: to repeal a law. —n. the act of repealing: the repeal of a constitutional amendment.

re·peat (ri pēt′) v.t. **1.** to say or utter (something already said) again: Joe repeated his question. **2.** to tell to another or others: Don't repeat a word of what I'm about to tell you. **3.** to say again or recite from memory. **4.** to do, make, or perform again: The tennis player repeated the serve. —v.i. to say or do something again. —n. **1.** the act of repeating. **2.** something repeated; repetition. **3.** Music. **a.** a passage, section, or movement that is to be repeated. **b.** any of several signs indicating this, especially double bar lines with two dots placed at the end (:‖) and usually also at the beginning (‖:) of such a passage. —**re·peat′er,** n.

re·peat·ed (ri pē′tid) adj. said, done, or happening again and again. —**re·peat′ed·ly,** adv.

repeating decimal, a decimal in which a particular digit or series of digits is repeated indefinitely. 0.666 . . . and 0.1232323 . . . are repeating decimals.

re·pel (ri pel′) v.t., **re·pelled, re·pel·ling. 1.** to drive back or away: to repel an attack. **2.** to cause to feel dislike or disgust: Violence repelled him. **3.** to withstand the action or effect of; resist: This material will repel heat and moisture. **4.** to refuse to accept or consider; reject: to repel an offer. **5.** to push away or force apart: The negative poles of two magnets will repel each other.

re·pel·lent (ri pel′ənt) adj. **1.** causing dislike or disgust; repugnant. **2.** that resists something. ▲ usually used in combination: a water-repellent coat. **3.** serving or tending to drive away. —n. something that repels: a mosquito repellent.

re·pent (ri pent′) v.i. **1.** to feel sorrow or deep regret for something one has done or failed to do: The sinful man repented. **2.** to change one's mind about or regret something one has done. —v.t. to feel sorrow or deep regret for: He repented his mistakes and resolved to be a better person.

re·pent·ance (ri pent′əns) n. **1.** sorrow or deep regret, as for sin or wrongdoing. **2.** the act or process of repenting.

re·pent·ant (ri pent′ənt) adj. feeling, showing, or marked by repentance; penitent. —**re·pent′ant·ly,** adv.

re·per·cus·sion (rē′pər kush′ən) n. **1.** a result or effect of an action or event; consequence: The firing of the coach caused repercussions throughout the school. **2.** an echo: the repercussions of a loud noise.

rep·er·toire (rep′ər twär′) n. **1.** the artistic works, such as plays, operas, or songs, that a performer or group of performers has learned. **2.** a list of such works.

rep·er·to·ry (rep′ər tôr′ē) n. pl., **rep·er·to·ries. 1.** another word for **repertoire. 2.** a store or collection. **3.** see **repertory theater.**

repertory theater, a theatrical organization in which a permanent acting company repeats the performances of different plays during a season.

rep·e·ti·tion (rep′ə tish′ən) n. **1.** the act of repeating. **2.** something that is repeated.

rep·e·ti·tious (rep′ə tish′əs) adj. full of, marked by, or containing repetition: a repetitious speaker, a repetitious article. —**rep′e·ti′tious·ly,** adv. —**rep′e·ti′tious·ness,** n.

re·pet·i·tive (ri pet′ə tiv) adj. another word for **repetitious.**

re·pine (ri pīn′) v.i., **re·pined, re·pin·ing.** to feel or express discontent or unhappiness; fret; complain.

re·place (ri plās′) v.t., **re·placed, re·plac·ing. 1.** to take or fill the place of: Richard will replace John as club president. **2.** to provide or get a substitute for: The car battery is defective and should be replaced. **3.** to restore or return to the original or proper place; put back: Christine replaced the magazine in the rack.

re·place·ment (ri plās′mənt) n. **1.** a person or thing that replaces. **2.** the act of replacing or the state of being replaced.

re·plen·ish (ri plen′ish) v.t. **1.** to bring back to a state of fullness or completeness, as by replacing what is lacking or has been used: to replenish one's food supplies. **2.** to provide a new supply for: to replenish a cupboard. —**re·plen′ish·ment,** n.

re·plete (ri plēt′) adj. **1.** supplied in abundance; abounding: a garden replete with brightly colored flowers. **2.** filled with food or drink; sated.

re·ple·tion (ri plē′shən) n. **1.** the state or condition of being replete: to eat to repletion. **2.** satisfaction or fulfillment.

rep·li·ca (rep′li kə) n. a close or exact copy, especially one done on a smaller scale than the original: Jim built a replica of a battleship.

re·ply (ri plī′) v., **re·plied, re·ply·ing.** —v.i. **1.** to respond in speech or writing; answer: He did not reply to her question. **2.** to respond by some action; react. —v.t. to say in response; give as a response: She replied that she liked the movie. —n. pl., **re·plies.** something said, written, or done in response.

re·port (ri pôrt′) n. **1.** an account, statement, or announcement: a news and weather report. **2.** an explosive sound or noise, especially that made by a rifle or pistol when fired. **3.** reputation; repute: The judge is a woman of good report. —v.t. **1.** to make or give an account, statement, or announcement of: to report the news. **2.** to bring charges of wrongdoing against; complain about: She reported the rude salesman to the manager. —v.i. **1.** to make a report: The newspaper reported on the election. **2.** to present oneself: Jack reported for work at noon.

report card, a written report of a pupil's grades and conduct.

re·port·ed·ly (ri pôr′tid lē) adv. according to report: The senator is reportedly going to visit Russia.

re·port·er (ri pôr′tər) n. **1.** a person employed to gather and report news for a newspaper or magazine, or for televi-

at; āpe; cär; end; mē; it; īce; hot; ōld; fôrk;
wood; fōōl; oil; out; up; turn; sing; thin; this;
hw in white; zh in treasure. The symbol ə
stands for the sound of a in about, e in taken,
i in pencil, o in lemon, and u in circus.

sion or radio. **2.** a person who takes down and makes a record of what is said in a courtroom during a trial. **3.** any person who reports.

re·pose¹ (ri pōz′) *n.* **1.** relaxation, as after activity; rest; sleep. **2.** peace and quiet; tranquility: *the beauty and repose of the forest.* **3.** calmness or ease, as of manner; composure. —*v.i.,* **re·posed, re·pos·ing. 1.** to lie or be at rest; sleep: *He reposed on the sofa.* **2.** to be supported; rest; lie: *The vase reposes on the table.* **3.** to lie dead. [Old French *reposer* to rest.]

re·pose² (ri pōz′) *v.t.,* **re·posed, re·pos·ing.** to place, as confidence or hope. [*Re-* + *pose¹.*]

re·pos·i·to·ry (ri poz′ə tôr′ē) *n. pl.,* **re·pos·i·to·ries.** a place or receptacle in which something is or may be stored or deposited.

re·pos·sess (rē′pə zes′) *v.t.* **1.** to possess again; regain possession of. **2.** to resume possession of (something bought on installments or credit) because the buyer has failed to make due payment: *The company repossessed the car.* —**re·pos·ses·sion** (rē′pə zesh′ən), *n.*

rep·re·hend (rep′ri hend′) *v.t.* to criticize sharply; reprove; censure.

rep·re·hen·si·ble (rep′ri hen′sə bəl) *adj.* deserving sharp criticism or reproof. —**rep′re·hen′si·bly,** *adv.*

rep·re·hen·sion (rep′ri hen′shən) *n.* the act of reprehending; criticism; reproof.

rep·re·sent (rep′ri zent′) *v.t.* **1.** to serve as a symbol, sign, or expression of; stand for; symbolize: *In this story the witch represents evil.* **2.** to express by some symbol, character, sign, or the like: *to represent speech sounds by letters.* **3.** to speak or act for; serve as the delegate or agent of: *Two senators represent the citizens of each state in Congress.* **4.** to present an image or likeness of, as in painting or sculpture. **5.** to serve as an example or instance of; typify: *The works of Dickens represent the Victorian novel.*

rep·re·sen·ta·tion (rep′ri zen tā′shən, rep′ri zən tā′shən) *n.* **1.** the act of representing or the state of being represented. **2.** an account, statement, or description: *The salesman gave a true representation of the product.* **3.** something that represents, such as a picture or other likeness. **4.** the state, fact, or right of being represented in a legislative or deliberative assembly. **5.** a body or number of representatives. —**rep′re·sen·ta′tion·al,** *adj.*

rep·re·sent·a·tive (rep′ri zen′tə tiv) *n.* **1.** a person who is chosen or authorized to represent another or others; delegate; agent: *The company had a representative in Rome.* **2.** a person or thing serving to typify a group, kind, or class. **3.** an elected member of a legislative assembly, especially a member of the lower house of Congress or of a state legislature. —*adj.* **1.** typifying a group, kind, or class; typical; characteristic: *The museum has a representative collection of modern art.* **2.** acting for or authorized to act for another or others. **3.** composed of representatives or based on political representation: *a representative government.* **4.** serving to represent, portray, or symbolize.

re·press (ri pres′) *v.t.* **1.** to hold back or keep under control; restrain: *to repress a smile.* **2.** to put down or put a stop to, especially by force: *to repress a revolution.* **3.** to prevent the natural development or expression of: *His creative talents have been repressed for too long.* **4.** to keep (painful memories or disturbing desires) in the unconscious mind. —**re·press′er,** *n.*

re·pres·sion (ri presh′ən) *n.* **1.** the act of repressing or the state of being repressed. **2.** an instance of this. **3.** a psychological process by which painful memories or disturbing desires are kept in the unconscious mind.

re·pres·sive (ri pres′iv) *adj.* tending or serving to repress. —**re·pres′sive·ly,** *adv.*

re·prieve (ri prēv′) *n.* **1.** an official postponement of the

carrying out of a sentence, especially a delay in the execution of a condemned person. **2.** a temporary relief or escape, as from something unpleasant or difficult. —*v.t.,* **re·prieved, re·priev·ing. 1.** to grant a reprieve to (someone), especially to delay the execution of (a condemned person). **2.** to free temporarily, as from something unpleasant or difficult.

rep·ri·mand (rep′rə mand′) *v.t.* to reprove sharply or formally. —*n.* a sharp reproof, especially one formally or officially given.

re·print (*n.,* rē′print′; *v.,* rē print′) *n.* a new edition of a work that has already been published. —*v.t.* to print a new edition or copy of; print again.

re·pris·al (ri prī′zəl) *n.* **1.** harm or injury done to an enemy for injuries or losses suffered. **2.** the act or instance of retaliating.

re·prise (ri prīz′, ri prēz′) *n. Music.* the repetition of a song that has been sung previously, or of an earlier section of a composition.

re·proach (ri prōch′) *v.t.* to charge with or blame for a fault or wrongdoing; reprove: *The coach reproached the team members for their poor play.* —*n. pl.,* **re·proach·es. 1.** the act of reproaching; blame; reproof. **2.** an expression of this. **3.** the cause, object, or occasion of blame or disgrace: *Litter in the streets is a reproach to our city.*

re·proach·ful (ri prōch′fəl) *adj.* full of or expressing reproach: *a reproachful look.* —**re·proach′ful·ly,** *adv.*

rep·ro·bate (rep′rə bāt′) *n.* a wicked or immoral person. —*adj.* given to wickedness or immorality; sinful.

rep·ro·ba·tion (rep′rə bā′shən) *n.* condemnation; censure.

re·pro·duce (rē′prə dōōs′, rē′prə dyōōs′) *v.,* **re·pro·duced, re·pro·duc·ing.** —*v.t.* **1.** to produce, form, or bring about again or anew: *The movie reproduced the grandeur of ancient Greece.* **2.** to make a duplicate or representation of: *to reproduce a picture.* **3.** to give rise to or produce (offspring or others of the same kind). —*v.i.* **1.** to give rise to or produce offspring or others of the same kind. **2.** to undergo reproduction: *The photograph reproduced clearly.*

re·pro·duc·tion (rē′prə duk′shən) *n.* **1.** the process by which living things give rise to or produce offspring or others of their kind. **2.** something that is reproduced. **3.** the act of reproducing or the state of being reproduced.

re·pro·duc·tive (rē′prə duk′tiv) *adj.* of, used in, or relating to reproduction. —**re′pro·duc′tive·ly,** *adv.* —**re′pro·duc′tive·ness,** *n.*

re·proof (ri prōōf′) *n.* **1.** the act of reproving. **2.** an expression of criticism; scolding or reprimand.

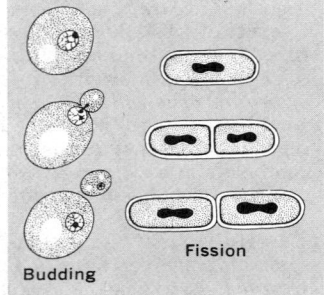
Asexual reproduction

re·prove (ri prōōv′) *v.t.,* **re·proved, re·prov·ing.** to blame or find fault with; scold; rebuke.

rep·tile (rep′təl) *n.* any of a group of cold-blooded animals with backbones, including lizards, snakes, crocodiles, and turtles. Reptiles have dry, usually scaly skin and usually reproduce by laying eggs. —*adj.* another word for **reptilian.**

rep·til·i·an (rep til′ē ən) *adj.* **1.** of, relating to, or characteristic of a reptile or reptiles. **2.** like a reptile in appearance or behavior. —*n.* another word for **reptile.**

Repub. **1.** Republic. **2.** Republican.

re·pub·lic (ri pub′lik) *n.* **1.** a form of government in which the final authority of the state rests with voting citizens and is exercised by elected officials, rather than by a hereditary monarch. **2.** a nation or state that has such a form of government. ▲ See **democracy** for usage note.

re·pub·li·can (ri pub′li kən) *adj.* **1.** of, characteristic of, or like a republic. **2. Republican.** of, relating to, or characteristic of the Republican Party. **3.** supporting or advocating a republic as a form of government. —*n.* **1. Republican.** a member of the Republican Party. **2.** a person who believes in or advocates a republic as a form of government.

Republican Party, one of the two major political parties in the United States.

re·pu·di·ate (ri pyōō′dē āt′) *v.t.,* **re·pu·di·at·ed, re·pu·di·at·ing. 1.** to reject as unjust or untrue: *to repudiate an accusation.* **2.** to refuse to have anything to do with; cast off; disown. **3.** to refuse to acknowledge or pay: *to repudiate a debt.* —**re·pu′di·a′tion,** *n.*

re·pug·nance (ri pug′nəns) *n.* extreme dislike or aversion; disgust.

re·pug·nant (ri pug′nənt) *adj.* causing extreme dislike or aversion; highly distasteful; repulsive.

re·pulse (ri puls′) *v.t.,* **re·pulsed, re·puls·ing. 1.** to beat or drive back: *Our army repulsed the enemy's advance.* **2.** to refuse to accept; reject; rebuff: *She repulsed his attentions.* —*n.* **1.** the act of repulsing or the state of being repulsed. **2.** a rejection; rebuff.

re·pul·sion (ri pul′shən) *n.* **1.** extreme dislike or aversion; disgust. **2.** the act of repelling or the state of being repelled.

re·pul·sive (ri pul′siv) *adj.* **1.** causing extreme dislike or aversion; highly distasteful or offensive. **2.** tending to repel. —**re·pul′sive·ly,** *adv.* —**re·pul′sive·ness,** *n.*

rep·u·ta·ble (rep′yə tə bəl) *adj.* having a good reputation; trustworthy; respectable: *to do business with a reputable company.* —**rep′u·ta·bly,** *adv.*

rep·u·ta·tion (rep′yə tā′shən) *n.* **1.** a general or public estimation of something or someone: *That judge has a reputation for honesty.* **2.** the state of being highly regarded or esteemed: *The scandal ruined his reputation.*

re·pute (ri pyōōt′) *n.* **1.** a general or public estimation of something or someone. **2.** the state of being highly regarded or esteemed. —*v.t.,* **re·put·ed, re·put·ing.** to consider to be; suppose.

re·put·ed (ri pyōō′tid) *adj.* generally considered or supposed: *He is the reputed author of this poem.* —**re·put′ed·ly,** *adv.*

re·quest (ri kwest′) *v.t.* **1.** to express a wish or desire for; ask for: *He requested permission to leave the room.* **2.** to express a wish or desire to; ask: *She requested us to be on time for the party.* —*n.* **1.** the act or instance of requesting. **2.** something that is requested: *to grant a request.* **3.** the state of being so desired or esteemed as to be sought after or in demand.

Req·ui·em (rek′wē əm) *n.* **1.** a Mass offered for the eternal rest of the soul of one or more deceased persons, especially as part of a funeral. **2.** *also,* **requiem.** a musical setting for this. **3. requiem.** any musical composition, hymn, or service in honor of the dead.

re·quire (ri kwīr′) *v.t.,* **re·quired, re·quir·ing. 1.** to have need of: *That cut will require medical attention.* **2.** to have as an obligation or condition: *Knitting requires much patience.* **3.** to order or compel (someone) to do something: *The customs officer required the traveler to unlock his luggage.*

re·quire·ment (ri kwīr′mənt) *n.* **1.** something that is imposed as an obligation or condition: *Good grades are a requirement for getting into this college.* **2.** something that

is needed: *A proper diet is one requirement for good health.*

req·ui·site (rek′wə zit) *adj.* that is required; necessary. —*n.* something that cannot be done without; essential.

req·ui·si·tion (rek′wə zish′ən) *n.* **1.** an official written request or application, as for new equipment. **2.** the act of taking, as through authority: *The army's requisition of food brought hardship to the people.* —*v.t.* **1.** to put through a requisition for: *The secretary requisitioned new supplies.* **2.** to take, as through authority.

re·quit·al (ri kwīt′əl) *n.* **1.** the act of requiting. **2.** something that is given or done in return: *Ellen's sarcastic answer was a proper requital for his insult.*

re·quite (ri kwīt′) *v.t.,* **re·quit·ed, re·quit·ing. 1.** to give or pay back in kind; return: *Dan requited Cindy's love.* **2.** to repay or reward.

re·run (*n.,* rē′run′; *v.,* rē run′) *n.* **1.** the showing of a filmed or taped performance, as a motion picture, after its original showing. **2.** the filmed or taped performance itself. **3.** the act of running again. —*v.t.,* **re·ran** (rē ran′), **re·run·ning. 1.** to show as a rerun. **2.** to run again: *to rerun a race.*

re·sale (rē′sāl′) *n.* the act of selling what one has bought.

re·scind (ri sind′) *v.t.* to make void; annul; cancel: *to rescind a law.*

res·cue (res′kyōō) *v.t.,* **res·cued, res·cu·ing.** to save or free, as from danger: *The lifeguard rescued the drowning woman.* —*n.* the act of rescuing. —**res′cu·er,** *n.*

re·search (ri surch′, rē′surch′) *n. pl.* **re·search·es.** a study or investigation in a particular field, usually for the purpose of learning new facts and making new interpretations. —*v.t.* to do research on or for. —**re·search′er,** *n.*

re·sem·blance (ri zem′bləns) *n.* a similarity, as of physical appearance; likeness: *There is a close resemblance between the two brothers.*

re·sem·ble (ri zem′bəl) *v.t.,* **re·sem·bled, re·sem·bling.** to be similar to, as in appearance or nature.

re·sent (ri zent′) *v.t.* to feel resentment at or toward: *John resented Steve because of his success.*

re·sent·ful (ri zent′fəl) *adj.* characterized by or tending to feel resentment. —**re·sent′ful·ly,** *adv.* —**re·sent′ful·ness,** *n.*

re·sent·ment (ri zent′mənt) *n.* indignation, anger, or bitterness caused by a real or imagined offense or injury.

res·er·va·tion (rez′ər vā′shən) *n.* **1.** an arrangment by which something, such as a theater seat or hotel room, is reserved. **2.** something that is reserved: *Our reservation for dinner is at 8:00.* **3.** land set aside by the U.S. government for a special purpose, as for an Indian tribe to live on or for a wildlife preserve. **4.** doubt; misgiving: *Natalie had some reservations about traveling alone.* **5.** something that limits; restriction; qualification: *They approved the plan without a single reservation.*

re·serve (ri zurv′) *v.t.,* **re·served, re·serv·ing. 1.** to set aside or have set aside for a particular person or purpose or for future use: *Mr. Johnson reserved a table for two.* **2.** to save until a later time: *The athlete reserved his strength for the race.* **3.** to keep for oneself: *I reserve the right to make my own decisions.* —*n.* **1.** something that is set aside, as for a special purpose or future use; store; supply. **2.** the state or condition of being set aside or saved: *There*

at; āpe; cär; end; mē; it; īce; hot; ōld; fôrk; wood; fōōl; oil; out; up; turn; sing; thin; this; hw in white; zh in treasure. The symbol ə stands for the sound of a in about, e in taken, i in pencil, o in lemon, and u in circus.

was food in reserve for emergencies. **3.** land set aside by the government for a special purpose; preserve. **4.** the habit of keeping one's feelings or thoughts to oneself; self-control or restraint. **5.** *Finance.* the amount of capital or gold held back, as from investment, to meet emergencies or special demands. **6.** *also,* **reserves.** the part of the armed forces not on active duty but available for service in an emergency. —*adj.* kept in reserve.

re·served (ri zurvd′) *adj.* **1.** set aside for a particular person or purpose or for future use: *This seat is reserved.* **2.** characterized by reserve in speech and behavior. —**re·serv·ed·ly** (ri zur′vid lē), *adv.*

re·serv·ist (ri zur′vist) *n.* a member of a military reserve.

res·er·voir (rez′ər vwär′) *n.* **1.** a natural or man-made place used for the storage of water. **2.** a receptacle or part used for the storage of a liquid or gas. **3.** a store; supply: *This book contains a reservoir of facts.*

re·side (ri zīd′) *v.i.,* **re·sid·ed, re·sid·ing. 1.** to make one's home permanently or for a time: *The woman resides with her mother.* **2.** to be present: *Much goodness resides in him.* —**re·sid′er,** *n.*

res·i·dence (rez′ə dəns) *n.* **1.** a place where a person resides. **2.** the act or state of residing, especially in order to satisfy legal requirements: *Mrs. Richardson's residence in the town enabled her to vote there.* **3.** a period of time spent residing in a place: *After ten years' residence, he left the community.*

res·i·den·cy (rez′ə dən sē) *n. pl.,* **res·i·den·cies.** the period of time during which a physician receives advanced, specialized training.

res·i·dent (rez′ə dənt) *n.* **1.** a person who resides in a particular place. **2.** a physician serving a residency. —*adj.* **1.** residing in a particular place. **2.** residing in a place in connection with work or duty: *a resident surgeon.*

res·i·den·tial (rez′ə den′shəl) *adj.* **1.** of or relating to residence: *He met the residential requirement for voting.* **2.** characterized by, restricted to, or suitable for residences: *a residential neighborhood.*

re·sid·u·al (ri zij′oo əl) *adj.* of, relating to, or being a residue; remaining. —*n. also,* **residuals.** payments made to a performer for the repeated use or showing of a film in which he appears.

res·i·due (rez′ə doo′, rez′ə dyoo′) *n.* **1.** a substance remaining at the end of a separating process, such as evaporation, combustion, or filtration. **2.** anything that remains, as after a main part is taken away.

re·sign (ri zīn′) *v.i.* to give up voluntarily, as a job, position, or office: *The president of the club resigned today.* —*v.t.* **1.** to give up (a position or responsibility) voluntarily: *The general resigned his commission.* **2.** to make (oneself) accept without protest or complaint: *He resigned himself to the unpleasant situation.*

res·ig·na·tion (rez′ig nā′shən) *n.* **1.** the act of resigning. **2.** a formal, usually written, notice that a person is resigning. **3.** the acceptance of something without protest or complaint; submission: *He suffered the loss with resignation.*

re·signed (ri zīnd′) *adj.* characterized by or showing resignation; submissive: *a resigned look* —**re·sign·ed·ly** (ri zī′nid lē), *adv.*

re·sil·ience (ri zil′yəns, ri zil′ē əns) *n.* the power or quality of being resilient. Also, **re·sil·ien·cy** (ri zil′yən sē, ri zil′ē ən sē).

re·sil·ient (ri zil′yənt, ri zil′ē ənt) *adj.* **1.** capable of springing back to the original size, shape, or position after being bent, compressed, or stretched. **2.** capable of recovering quickly or easily, as from depression or difficulty.

res·in (rez′in) *n.* **1.** any of various translucent yellow or brown sticky substances that come from certain trees, such as pine and balsam, and are used especially to improve paints and plastics and to make linoleum, glue, and rubber. **2.** any of various similar man-made materials that are the basic ingredient of plastics. **3.** see **rosin** *(def. 1).*

res·in·ous (rez′ə nəs) *adj.* **1.** of, relating to, or resembling resin. **2.** obtained from or containing resin.

re·sist (ri zist′) *v.t.* **1.** to keep from yielding to; abstain from: *Peter found it difficult to resist telling me the secret.* **2.** to repel or oppose: *The nation was unable to resist the invasion.* **3.** to withstand the action or effect of: *This metal resists rusting.* —*v.i.* to act in opposition. —**re·sist′er,** *n.*

re·sist·ance (ri zis′təns) *n.* **1.** the act of resisting. **2.** the ability to resist something, especially disease: *Sally caught a cold because her resistance was low.* **3.** a group that works against or opposes an occupying or oppressive army or government, especially by guerrilla tactics. **4.** a force that opposes or hinders the motion of another: *Cars are streamlined to overcome air resistance.* **5.** the characteristic of a substance that opposes the flow of electrical current and produces heat. A good conductor, such as silver, has low resistance.

re·sist·ant (ri zis′tənt) *adj.* offering resistance; resisting.

re·sist·less (ri zist′lis) *adj.* **1.** that cannot be resisted. **2.** that does not or cannot resist.

re·sis·tor (ri zis′tər) *n.* an electric element whose resistance is used in an electric circuit to limit the flow of current or to produce heat, as in a toaster.

res·o·lute (rez′ə loot) *adj.* having or showing strong determination. —**res′o·lute·ly,** *adv.* —**res′o·lute·ness,** *n.*

res·o·lu·tion (rez′ə loo′shən) *n.* **1.** the act or process of resolving or determining. **2.** something that is resolved upon; vow: *She made a New Year's resolution to go on a diet.* **3.** a formal statement of a decision, opinion, or course of action, presented to or adopted by an assembly. **4.** the state or quality of being resolute. **5.** the act or result of settling, explaining, or solving: *the resolution of a problem.* **6.** the act or process of breaking or changing into separate or simpler parts.

re·solve (ri zolv′) *v.,* **re·solved, re·solv·ing.** —*v.t.* **1.** to decide (to do something); determine: *Leslie resolved not to go to the party.* **2.** to settle, explain, or solve: *to resolve a dispute.* **3.** to give a decision or opinion formally by vote, as in a legislative assembly. **4.** to break or change into simpler or separate parts: *The prism resolved the light into the colors of the spectrum.* —*v.i.* **1.** to come to a decision; decide: *Ruth resolved on the blue dress for the party.* **2.** to be broken or changed into simpler or separate parts. —*n.* **1.** strong determination or firmness of purpose. **2.** something resolved upon; resolution.

re·solved (ri zolvd′) *adj.* resolute; determined. —**re·solv·ed·ly** (ri zol′vid lē), *adv.*

res·o·nance (rez′ə nəns) *n.* **1.** the state or quality of being resonant; fullness and richness of sound: *the resonance of a piano.* **2.** *Physics.* **a.** the state of a mechanical or electrical system characterized by a vibration of large amplitude, occurring when an outside force is applied at a frequency equal or nearly equal to one of the natural frequencies of the system. Because of resonance, a swing will rise to a great height if it is given a regular series of pushes at the same frequency at which it swings. **b.** the vibration produced in such a state. **3.** the increasing and prolonging of sound by the similar vibration of another object, as when the tone produced by the strings of a violin is enhanced by vibrations of the instrument's wooden body.

res·o·nant (rez′ə nənt) *adj.* **1.** continuing to sound; echoing. **2.** capable of increasing or prolonging sounds: *the resonant wood of a guitar.* **3.** having a full, rich sound: *a resonant voice.* —**res′o·nant·ly,** *adv.*

re·sort (ri zôrt′) *v.i.* **1.** to make use of or appeal to for aid, relief, protection, or support: *He resorts to lying whenever he's in trouble.* **2.** to go often or by habit, as for recreation. —*n.* **1.** a place where people go, especially for recreation or relaxation: *a ski resort.* **2.** a person or thing that one makes use of or appeals to, as for protection or support: *Lawrence borrowed money from his family only as a last resort.* **3.** the use of or appeal to a person or thing, as for protection or support: *to have resort to friends in an emergency.*

re·sound (ri zound′) *v.i.* **1.** to be filled with sound: *The church resounded with music.* **2.** to produce a loud, echoing, or prolonged sound: *The rocket resounded as it blasted off the launching pad.* **3.** (of sounds) to be echoed; ring: *The shouts resounded in our ears.*

re·source (rē′sôrs, ri sôrs′) *n.* **1.** someone or something that is made use of or appealed to, as for aid or support. **2.** *usually,* **resources.** the actual wealth of a country or its means of producing wealth: *Oil is one of that country's largest natural resources.* **3.** skill and cleverness in dealing with situations: *The prisoner showed great resource in escaping.* **4.** the action or means used in an emergency or a difficult situation: *When caught, the spy's only resource was to lie.*

re·source·ful (ri sôrs′fəl) *adj.* capable of or skilled in dealing with new or difficult situations. —**re·source′ful·ly,** *adv.* —**re·source′ful·ness,** *n.*

re·spect (ri spekt′) *n.* **1.** a regard for or appreciation of the basic worth or value of someone or something: *a respect for life, a respect for the rights of other people.* **2.** a recognition of superiority, as in strength or wisdom: *The chief had the respect of everyone in the village.* **3.** high or courteous regard or consideration: *to show respect for one's elders.* **4.** a specific aspect or manner; particular detail: *In some respects, Kathy is a better student than Louise.* **5.** relation; reference: *John showed an improvement with respect to grades.* **6.** **respects.** courteous expressions of regard and greeting: *Please send my respects to your family.* —*v.t.* **1.** to have or feel respect for: *We respect Arnold's honesty.* **2.** to show consideration for; act so as not to interfere with: *I respect his privacy.* **3.** to relate or refer to; concern.

re·spect·a·bil·i·ty (ri spek′tə bil′ə tē) *n.* the state, quality, or condition of being respectable.

re·spect·a·ble (ri spek′tə bəl) *adj.* **1.** having or showing proper or approved standards of conduct; honest and decent. **2.** fit to be seen or used; presentable: *a respectable suit of clothes.* **3.** better than average; reasonably good: *The amateur drama group put on a respectable performance.* —**re·spect′a·bly,** *adv.*

re·spect·ful (ri spekt′fəl) *adj.* full of, marked by, or showing respect, especially courteousness. —**re·spect′ful·ly,** *adv.* —**re·spect′ful·ness,** *n.*

re·spect·ing (ri spek′ting) *prep.* with respect to; concerning.

re·spec·tive (ri spek′tiv) *adj.* relating or belonging to each of two or more persons or things under consideration; particular: *The committee studied the respective advantages of each plan.*

re·spec·tive·ly (ri spek′tiv lē) *adv.* with respect to each of two or more in the order considered: *Mr. Jones and Mr. Lane are, respectively, producer and director of the film.*

re·spell (rē spel′) *v.t.* **1.** to spell again. **2.** to spell out according to a system of letters or symbols different from ordinary writing, especially a phonetic alphabet.

res·pi·ra·tion (res′pə rā′shən) *n.* **1.** the act of breathing in and out. **2.** all of the physical and chemical processes by which living things get energy from food. These processes include the breathing in and out of gases and a series of chemical reactions occurring within cells.

res·pi·ra·tor (res′pə rā′tər) *n.* **1.** a machine with compressed air or oxygen, used in giving artificial respiration. **2.** a device worn over the mouth, or over the nose and mouth, to prevent the breathing in of fumes, dust, or the like.

res·pi·ra·to·ry (res′pər ə tôr′ē) *adj.* of or relating to respiration or to organs used in respiration: *a respiratory disease.*

re·spire (ri spīr′) *v.i.,* **re·spired, re·spir·ing.** to inhale and exhale; breathe.

Respirator

res·pite (res′pit) *n.* **1.** a brief or temporary period of rest or relief, as from work or unpleasantness: *Having a glass of lemonade was a pleasant respite for the boys while they were mowing the lawn.* **2.** a delay or postponement, as in carrying out a sentence of death.

re·splend·ence (ri splen′dəns) *n.* the state or quality of being full of splendor.

re·splend·ent (ri splen′dənt) *adj.* full of splendor; gleaming; brilliant. —**re·splend′ent·ly,** *adv.*

re·spond (ri spond′) *v.i.* **1.** to give an answer: *He did not respond to my question.* **2.** to act in return; react: *Lily responded to the sudden light by blinking her eyes.* **3.** to be improved or positively affected by: *The patient responded to treatment.*

re·sponse (ri spons′) *n.* **1.** the act of responding. **2.** something said in answer: *What was Jane's response to the question?* **3.** behavior caused by an outward influence or stimulus. **4.** words said or sung by the congregation or choir in answer to a short sentence said or sung by the clergyman.

re·spon·si·bil·i·ty (ri spon′sə bil′ə tē) *n. pl.,* **re·spon·si·bil·i·ties.** **1.** the state, quality, or condition of being responsible. **2.** a job, duty, or area of concern: *Setting the table is your responsibility.*

re·spon·si·ble (ri spon′sə bəl) *adj.* **1.** having as a job, duty, or concern: *The government is responsible for the nation's welfare.* **2.** faithful to duties; trustworthy; reliable: *Alice is a very responsible baby sitter.* **3.** being the main cause: *Careless driving is responsible for many car accidents.* **4.** involving important duties: *a responsible job.* **5.** liable to get the credit or blame for something; accountable: *to be responsible for one's actions.* —**re·spon′si·ble·ness,** *n.* —**re·spon′si·bly,** *adv.*

re·spon·sive (ri spon′siv) *adj.* **1.** readily reacting with sympathy, warmth, or understanding: *Suzanne was responsive to her friend's misery.* **2.** of, relating to, or indicating a response: *A nod of the head is a responsive gesture.* **3.** marked by or made up of responses: *a responsive chant.* —**re·spon′sive·ly,** *adv.* —**re·spon′sive·ness,** *n.*

rest¹ (rest) *n.* **1.** a period of inactivity, relaxation, or refreshment, especially after work or physical activity: *The carpenter took a rest before finishing the job.* **2.** freedom from work, distress, or disturbance; quiet; ease: *Sunday was our day of rest.* **3.** sleep: *Larry does not get enough rest at night.* **4.** the state of being motionless: *The plane came to rest in the field.* **5.** something that serves as a stand or

at; āpe; cär; end; mē; it; īce; hot; ōld; fôrk; wood; fōol; oil; out; up; turn; sing; thin; **th**is; hw in white; zh in treasure. The symbol ə stands for the sound of **a** in about, **e** in taken, **i** in pencil, **o** in lemon, and **u** in circus.

support: *a book rest.* **6.** death: *to go to one's rest.* **7.** *Music.* **a.** an interval of silence between tones, lasting for the same amount of time as a note of the same name: *half rest, whole rest.* **b.** any of the various symbols indicating such a pause. —*v.i.*

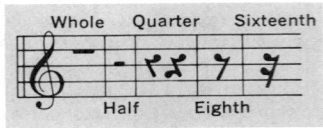

Rest¹ *(def. 7b)*

1. to relax or refresh oneself: *The children rested on the porch after the ball game.* **2.** to be quiet or at ease: *Mrs. Roberts wouldn't rest until she knew that her son was safe.* **3.** to be supported, as by leaning or lying: *Laurie's hands rested in her lap.* **4.** to be fixed or directed: *Herbert's gaze rested on the strange woman.* **5.** to remain without change or further action; stand: *We decided to let the matter rest.* **6.** to lie in death: *May he rest in peace.* **7.** *Law.* to stop presenting evidence in a case voluntarily: *The defense rests.* —*v.t.* **1.** to give rest to: *He rested his horse after the race.* **2.** to put, lay, or lean (something), as for support: *Jim rested his arm on the table.* **3.** *Law.* to stop presenting evidence in (a case) voluntarily. [Old English *rest.*]

rest² (rest) *n.* **1.** that which remains; remainder. **2.** those remaining; others: *The rest will meet us at the theater.* ▲ used with a plural verb in definition 2. —*v.i.* to continue to be; remain: *You may rest assured that I'll be there.* [Old French *reste* remainder.]

res·tau·rant (res′tər ənt) *n.* a place where food is prepared and served to customers at tables by a waiter or waitress.

res·tau·ra·teur (res′tər ə tur′) *n.* a person who owns or manages a restaurant.

rest·ful (rest′fəl) *adj.* **1.** full of or giving rest: *a restful vacation.* **2.** being at rest; quiet; tranquil: *a restful landscape.* —**rest′ful·ly,** *adv.* —**rest′ful·ness,** *n.*

res·ti·tu·tion (res′tə tōō′shən, res′tə tyōō′shən) *n.* **1.** the act of restoring something that has been lost or taken away. **2.** compensation for loss or damage; reparation.

res·tive (res′tiv) *adj.* **1.** unable to rest; restless; fretful. **2.** stubborn and difficult to manage; unruly: *a restive horse.* —**res′tive·ly,** *adv.* —**res′tive·ness,** *n.*

rest·less (rest′lis) *adj.* **1.** nervous or agitated in mind or body; unable to rest: *The restless man paced back and forth.* **2.** characterized by lack of rest; not restful: *The patient spent a restless night.* **3.** constantly in motion; never still: *the restless wind, the restless sea.* **4.** constantly shifting or changing from one thing to another: *a restless mind.* —**rest′less·ly,** *adv.* —**rest′less·ness,** *n.*

res·to·ra·tion (res′tə rā′shən) *n.* **1.** the act of restoring or the state of being restored. **2.** something that is or has been restored. **3. Restoration. a.** the return of the English monarchy in 1660 under King Charles II. **b.** the period following this, including the reign of Charles II, from 1660 to 1685, and sometimes also the reign of James II, from 1685 to 1688.

re·stor·a·tive (ri stôr′ə tiv) *adj.* **1.** capable of restoring. **2.** relating to restoration. —*n.* something that restores.

re·store (ri stôr′) *v.t.,* **re·stored, re·stor·ing. 1.** to bring back; reestablish: *The monarchy was restored ten years after the revolution.* **2.** to bring back to a former or original state or condition: *The cathedral was restored during the early eighteenth century.* **3.** to return (something lost, taken, or stolen): *The police restored the jewels to their rightful owner.* —**re·stor′er,** *n.*

re·strain (ri strān′) *v.t.* **1.** to hold in; keep in check: *Peter tried to restrain his laughter.* **2.** to prevent from acting; hold back: *We restrained the boy from breaking the window.* **3.** to take away the liberty of, as by confinement in prison. —**re·strain′a·ble,** *adj.*

re·straint (ri strānt′) *n.* **1.** the act of restraining or the state of being restrained. **2.** something that restrains. **3.** a holding back; reserve.

restraint of trade, interference with the free movement of goods or services or with free competition.

re·strict (ri strikt′) *v.t.* to keep within specified limits; confine: *Use of the swimming pool is restricted to club members.*

re·stric·tion (ri strik′shən) *n.* **1.** something that restricts. **2.** the act of restricting or the state of being restricted.

re·stric·tive (ri strik′tiv) *adj.* **1.** serving or tending to restrict: *The students felt that the school's rules were too restrictive.* **2.** *Grammar.* designating a word, clause, or phrase that limits the meaning of the word it modifies and is usually not set off by commas. In the sentence *Anyone who stands up to that bully will be a neighborhood hero,* the clause *who stands up to that bully* is restrictive. —**re·stric′tive·ly,** *adv.* —**re·stric′tive·ness,** *n.*

rest room, a toilet in a public building.

re·sult (ri zult′) *n.* something that occurs or is brought about because of an earlier action, process, or condition; effect: *The accident was the result of careless driving.* —*v.i.* **1.** to be a result: *Her low grades result from her poor study habits.* **2.** to have as a result: *The trial resulted in his being found innocent.*

re·sult·ant (ri zul′tənt) *adj.* occurring or brought about as a result. —*n.* **1.** a result. **2.** *Physics.* a force that is the equivalent and result of, and has the same effect as, two or more forces acting together.

re·sume (ri zōōm′) *v.t.,* **re·sumed, re·sum·ing. 1.** to go on after interruption: *The violinist resumed playing after the intermission.* **2.** to take or occupy again: *Mr. O'Brien resumed his former position with the company.*

ré·su·mé (rez′ŏŏ mā′, rez′ŏŏ mā′) *n.* **1.** a statement of one's qualifications and work record, used in applying for work. **2.** a summary: *The professor gave a résumé of the main points of his lecture.*

re·sump·tion (ri zump′shən) *n.* the act or instance of resuming.

re·sur·gence (ri sur′jəns) *n.* a rising again; revival.

re·sur·gent (ri sur′jənt) *adj.* rising or tending to rise again.

res·ur·rect (rez′ə rekt′) *v.t.* **1.** to raise (a person) from the dead; restore to life. **2.** to bring back into use or notice; restore after disuse or neglect: *to resurrect the writings of a forgotten author.* —*v.i.* to rise from the dead.

res·ur·rec·tion (rez′ə rek′shən) *n.* **1.** the act of rising from the dead. **2.** the state of having risen from the dead. **3.** the bringing back of something after disuse or neglect; revival. **4. Resurrection.** the rising again of Christ after His death and burial.

re·sus·ci·tate (ri sus′ə tāt′) *v.t.,* **re·sus·ci·tat·ed, re·sus·ci·tat·ing.** to bring back to life or consciousness. —**re·sus′ci·ta′tion,** *n.*

re·sus·ci·ta·tor (ri sus′ə tā′tər) *n.* **1.** a person or thing that resuscitates. **2.** a machine or other device that resuscitates by forcing oxygen into the lungs.

re·tail (rē′tāl) *n.* the sale of goods or articles individually or in small quantities, directly to the consumer. —*adj.* of, relating to, or engaged in the selling of goods at retail: *a retail store.* —*adv.* in a retail quantity or at a retail price: *to buy a dress retail.* —*v.t.* **1.** to sell (goods or articles) individually or in small quantities, directly to the consumer: *to retail clothing.* **2.** to repeat or retell: *to retail gossip.* —*v.i.* to be sold at retail: *This shirt retails for eight dollars.* [Going back to Old French *retaille* a piece cut off, from *retaillier* to cut off; referring to the sale of goods or articles in small, or "cut off," quantities.]

re·tail·er (rē′tā lər) *n.* a merchant or dealer who sells retail.

re·tain (ri tān′) *v.t.* **1.** to continue to have or hold; maintain or preserve: *She retained ownership of the house after her father's death.* **2.** to hold back or contain: *The cracked jar would not retain water.* **3.** to keep in mind; remember: *to retain facts.* **4.** to employ by the payment of a fee: *Mrs. Judson retained a lawyer to represent her.*

re·tain·er[1] (ri tā′nər) *n.* an attendant or servant. [*Retain* + *-er*[1].]

re·tain·er[2] (ri tā′nər) *n.* a fee paid to obtain services, especially of an attorney. [Middle French *retenir.*]

re·tal·i·ate (ri tal′ē āt′) *v.*, **re·tal·i·at·ed, re·tal·i·at·ing.** —*v.i.* to return or repay in kind, especially to return a wrong or injurious act with a similar one: *Lois retaliated by not inviting Jean to her party.* —*v.t.* to repay (an injury or wrong) with the like. —**re·tal′i·a′tion,** *n.*

re·tal·i·a·to·ry (ri tal′ē ə tôr′ē) *adj.* of, relating to, or serving as retaliation: *a retaliatory action.*

re·tard (ri tärd′) *v.t.* to delay the progress of (an action or process); hinder: *The long and serious illness retarded her growth.* —*v.i.* to be delayed. —**re·tard′er,** *n.*

re·tar·da·tion (rē′tär dā′shən) *n.* **1.** the act of retarding or the state of being retarded. **2.** something that retards; impediment; hindrance. **3.** see **mental retardation.**

re·tard·ed (ri tär′did) *adj.* suffering from or marked by mental retardation.

retch (rech) *v.i.* to make an effort to vomit.

re·ten·tion (ri ten′shən) *n.* **1.** the act of retaining or the state of being retained. **2.** the ability or power to retain. **3.** the ability to remember.

re·ten·tive (ri ten′tiv) *adj.* having the ability or capacity to retain: *She has a very retentive mind.* —**re·ten′tive·ness,** *n.*

ret·i·cence (ret′ə səns) *n.* restraint or reserve, especially in speech: *His reticence in class is due to shyness.*

ret·i·cent (ret′ə sənt) *adj.* restrained or reserved, especially in speech. —**ret′i·cent·ly,** *adv.*

re·tic·u·late (*v.,* ri tik′yə lāt′; *adj.,* ri tik′yə lit, ri tik′yə lāt′) *v.*, **re·tic·u·lat·ed, re·tic·u·lat·ing.** —*v.t.* to form into, cover, or mark with a network. —*v.i.* to form a network. —*adj.* covered with or resembling a network.

ret·i·na (ret′ən ə) *n. pl.,* **ret·i·nas** or **ret·i·nae** (ret′ən ē′). the inner membrane of the eyeball, made up of several layers of cells that are sensitive to light and transmit the images entering the eye to the optic nerve.

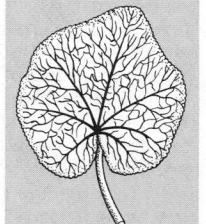

Reticulate leaf

ret·i·nal (ret′ən əl) *adj.* of or relating to the retina.

ret·i·nue (ret′ən ōō′, ret′ən yōō′) *n.* a group of people, such as servants or assistants, who accompany a person of rank or authority.

re·tire (ri tīr′) *v.*, **re·tired, re·tir·ing.** —*v.i.* **1.** to withdraw oneself from business, public life, or active service: *My grandfather retired from his job when he was 65.* **2.** to go to bed: *We retired early last night.* **3.** to go away, as for seclusion or rest: *to retire to the country.* —*v.t.* **1.** to remove from an office, position, or active service. **2.** *Baseball.* to put out (a batter or side). —**re·tire′ment,** *n.*

re·tir·ing (ri tīr′ing) *adj.* avoiding people or publicity; reserved; shy.

re·tort[1] (ri tôrt′) *v.i.* to make a reply, especially in a quick, witty, or sharp manner. —*n.* a quick, witty, or sharp reply. [Latin *retortus,* the past participle of *retorquēre* to twist back.]

re·tort[2] (ri tôrt′) *n.* a container, usually consisting of a glass globe with a long tube extending downward, in which chemists distill or decompose substances by heat. [Going back to Medieval Latin *retorta* a container with a bent neck.]

re·touch (rē tuch′) *v.t.* **1.** to improve, as a painting, by additional touches or slight changes. **2.** to change (a photographic negative or print) by removing or adding details.

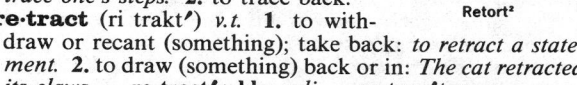

Retort[2]

re·trace (rē trās′) *v.t.*, **re·traced, re·trac·ing.** **1.** to go back over: *to retrace one's steps.* **2.** to trace back.

re·tract (ri trakt′) *v.t.* **1.** to withdraw or recant (something); take back: *to retract a statement.* **2.** to draw (something) back or in: *The cat retracted its claws.* —**re·tract′a·ble,** *adj.* —**re·trac′tor,** *n.*

re·trac·tile (ri trak′til) *adj.* capable of being drawn back or in, as the head of a turtle.

re·trac·tion (ri trak′shən) *n.* **1.** the act of retracting or the state of being retracted. **2.** a statement that retracts: *The newspaper printed a retraction of a previous article.*

re·tread (*v.,* rē tred′; *n.,* rē′tred′) *v.t.*, **re·tread·ed, re·tread·ing.** to put a new tread on (a tire). —*n.* a retreaded tire.

re·treat (ri trēt′) *v.i.* to withdraw, as from battle; draw back: *The defeated army retreated.* —*n.* **1.** the act of retreating. **2.** a place of rest or relaxation: *a summer retreat.* **3.** a signal for a military retreat. **4.** *Military.* **a.** a flag-lowering ceremony at sunset. **b.** a signal, as on a bugle, played at this ceremony.

re·trench (ri trench′) *v.t.* **1.** to cut down: *to retrench expenses.* **2.** to put an end to or remove: *The dictator gradually retrenched the people's freedoms.* —*v.i.* to cut down expenses; economize. —**re·trench′ment,** *n.*

re·tri·al (rē′trī′əl) *n.* a second trial, as of a case in a court.

ret·ri·bu·tion (ret′rə byōō′shən) *n.* **1.** the act of paying back for evil done. **2.** something done or given as punishment for wrongdoing.

re·trib·u·tive (ri trib′yə tiv) *adj.* serving as or characterized by retribution.

re·triev·al (ri trē′vəl) *n.* the act or process of retrieving.

re·trieve (ri trēv′) *v.t.*, **re·trieved, re·triev·ing. 1.** to get back; recover; regain: *He retrieved the golf ball from the lake.* **2.** to bring back to a former condition; restore. **3.** to make amends for; make good: *He attempted to retrieve his debts.* **4.** (of dogs) to locate and fetch (wounded or dead game). —**re·triev′a·ble,** *adj.*

re·triev·er (ri trē′vər) *n.* a dog trained to retrieve game for a hunter.

retro- *prefix* backward, back, or behind: *retrograde.*

ret·ro·ac·tive (ret′rō ak′tiv) *adj.* influencing or affecting something that has taken place in the past.

ret·ro·grade (ret′rə grād′) *adj.* **1.** moving backward; reversed: *Numbers in a countdown are given in retrograde order.* **2.** becoming worse; deteriorating: *There are retrograde conditions in the poorer sections of the city.* —*v.i.,* **ret·ro·grad·ed, ret·ro·grad·ing. 1.** to move backward; reverse. **2.** to become worse; deteriorate.

at; āpe; cär; end; mē; it; īce; hot; ōld; fôrk; wood; fōōl; oil; out; up; turn; sing; thin; <u>th</u>is; hw in white; zh in treasure. The symbol ə stands for the sound of **a** in about, **e** in taken, **i** in pencil, **o** in lemon, and **u** in circus.

R

ret·ro·gress (ret′rə gres′, ret′rə gres′) *v.i.* **1.** to move or go backward. **2.** to go to a worse or a less advanced condition. —**ret′ro·gres′sion,** *n.*

ret·ro·gres·sive (ret′rə gres′iv) *adj.* of or characterized by retrogression. —**ret′ro·gres′sive·ly,** *adv.*

ret·ro·rock·et (ret′rō rok′it) *n.* a rocket engine that produces thrust opposite to the forward motion of a spacecraft in flight in order to reduce speed, to make midcourse corrections, or to separate a section of the spacecraft.

ret·ro·spect (ret′rə spekt′) *n.* a thoughtful review or survey of past events: *In retrospect, we were wrong.*

ret·ro·spec·tion (ret′rə spek′shən) *n.* the act of looking back on or thinking about past events.

ret·ro·spec·tive (ret′rə spek′tiv) *adj.* **1.** looking back on or thinking about past events. **2.** applying to the past; retroactive. —**ret′ro·spec′tive·ly,** *adv.*

re·turn (ri turn′) *v.i.* **1.** to come or go back, as to a former place or condition: *to return to consciousness, to return home.* **2.** to come or go back in thought or speech: *The speaker finally returned to the subject.* **3.** to happen or appear again: *Winter returns every year.* —*v.t.* **1.** to take, bring, send, give, or put back: *She returned the book to the library.* **2.** to give or pay back in the same way: *I returned her visit.* **3.** to report officially: *The jury returned a verdict.* **4.** to yield: *The new tax returned only part of the money needed to build the new school.* —*n.* **1.** a coming or going back: *The man made a return to his home town.* **2.** the act of happening or appearing again: *The return of winter brought hardship to the settlers.* **3.** the act of taking, sending, or putting back: *the return of a book to the library.* **4.** the act of giving or paying back in the same way: *His prompt return of my phone call pleased me.* **5.** an official or formal report: *a tax return, election returns.* **6.** also, **returns.** yield or profit: *The returns from the cake sale were more than fifty dollars.* —*adj.* **1.** of or relating to a return: *a return ticket, a return route.* **2.** given or done in return: *a return visit.* —**re·turn′a·ble,** *adj.*

re·un·ion (rē yōōn′yən) *n.* **1.** the act of reuniting or the state of being reunited. **2.** a social gathering of friends, classmates, or relatives after separation or absence: *His high school class is holding its tenth reunion.*

re·u·nite (rē′yōō nīt′) *v.,* **re·u·nit·ed, re·u·nit·ing.** —*v.t.* to bring together again: *The family was reunited after years of being apart.* —*v.i.* to come together again.

re·use (*v.,* rē yōōz′; *n.,* rē yōōs′) *v.t.,* **re·used, re·us·ing.** to use again. —*n.* the act of using again. —**re·us′a·ble,** *adj.*

rev (rev) *n.* the revolution of an engine or motor. —*v.t.,* **revved, rev·ving.** to increase the speed of: *John revved up the car's engine.*

rev. **1.** revenue. **2.** reverse. **3.** revolution.

Rev. **1.** Reverend. **2.** Revelation.

re·val·u·ate (rē val′yōō āt′) *v.t.,* **re·val·u·at·ed, re·val·u·at·ing.** to make a new valuation of: *to revaluate currency.* —**re·val′u·a′tion,** *n.*

re·vamp (rē vamp′) *v.t.* **1.** to repair or replace the vamp of (a shoe). **2.** to patch up, renovate, or revise: *The author revamped his novel.*

re·veal (ri vēl′) *v.t.* **1.** to make known; divulge: *to reveal a secret.* **2.** to expose to view; display; show: *The open door revealed a large living room.*

rev·eil·le (rev′ə lē) *n.* a signal on a bugle to awaken troops.

rev·el (rev′əl) *v.i.,* **rev·eled, rev·el·ing;** also, British, **rev·elled, rev·el·ling.** **1.** to take great pleasure: *The lottery winners reveled in their unaccustomed wealth.* **2.** to make merry: *The guests at the party reveled all night long.* —*n.* loud merrymaking. —**rev′el·er;** also, British, **rev′el·ler,** *n.*

rev·e·la·tion (rev′ə lā′shən) *n.* **1.** the act of revealing. **2.** something revealed. **3.** a disclosure or communication of divine truth by supernatural means. **4. Revelation.** the last book of the New Testament, believed to have been written by Saint John. Also, **Apocalypse.**

rev·el·ry (rev′əl rē) *n. pl.,* **rev·el·ries.** loud merrymaking.

re·venge (ri venj′) *n.* **1.** injury, harm, or punishment in return for a wrong or offense: *The murdered woman's brother swore to get revenge on those who had killed her.* **2.** a desire for vengeance. —*v.t.,* **re·venged, re·veng·ing. 1.** to inflict injury, harm, or punishment in return for: *to revenge an insult.* **2.** to inflict injury, harm, or punishment on behalf of: *He vowed to revenge his sister.*

re·venge·ful (ri venj′fəl) *adj.* full of or showing revenge. —**re·venge′ful·ly,** *adv.* —**re·venge′ful·ness,** *n.*

rev·e·nue (rev′ə nōō′, rev′ə nyōō′) *n.* **1.** the income from property or other investments. **2.** the annual or current income of a government from taxation and other sources.

re·ver·ber·ate (ri vur′bə rāt′) *v.i.,* **re·ver·ber·at·ed, re·ver·ber·at·ing.** to be echoed; resound: *The sound of footsteps reverberated through the empty house.* —**re·ver′ber·a′tion,** *n.*

re·vere (ri vēr′) *v.t.,* **re·vered, re·ver·ing.** to feel deep respect and affection for: *The children revered their grandfather.*

Re·vere, Paul (ri vēr′) 1735–1818, U.S. patriot.

rev·er·ence (rev′ər əns, rev′rəns) *n.* **1.** a feeling of deepest respect and affection; veneration. **2.** an act or expression of respect, as a bow or curtsy. **3.** the state of being revered. **4. Reverence.** a title or form of address used in referring to a Roman Catholic priest, usually preceded by *Your.* —*v.t.,* **rev·er·enced, rev·er·enc·ing.** to feel reverence for: *to reverence one's parents.*

rev·er·end (rev′ər ənd) *adj.* **1.** worthy of reverence. **2. Reverend.** a form of address used in referring to a clergyman, usually preceded by *the.*

rev·er·ent (rev′ər ənt) *adj.* feeling or showing reverence: *to be reverent in church.* —**rev′er·ent·ly,** *adv.*

rev·er·en·tial (rev′ə ren′shəl) *adj.* feeling or showing reverence; reverent. —**rev′er·en′tial·ly,** *adv.*

rev·er·ie (rev′ər ē) also, **rev·er·y.** *n.* **1.** dreamy thinking or daydreaming of happy, pleasant things. **2.** an instance of this; daydream.

re·ver·sal (ri vur′səl) *n.* the act of reversing or the state of being reversed: *If man does find the solution for world peace, it will be the most revolutionary reversal of his record we have ever known* (George C. Marshall).

re·verse (ri vurs′) *n.* **1.** something that is the direct opposite of something else; contrary: *Tom did the reverse of what he was supposed to do.* **2.** the position of gears in a machine that makes them transmit force or cause movement in a direction opposite to that which is usual. **3.** the back side of something: *the reverse of a phonograph record.* **4.** the side of a coin or medal that does not bear the principal design. **5.** a change of fortune from good to bad; setback: *The man suffered many business reverses.* —*adj.* **1.** opposite, as in position, direction, or order. **2.** moving or causing movement in a direction opposite to that which is usual: *He put the car in reverse gear.* —*v.,* **re·versed, re·vers·ing.** —*v.t.* **1.** to turn (something) around, upside down, or inside out: *to reverse a sock.* **2.** to change to the opposite: *to reverse an opinion.* **3.** to turn or cause to turn or move in a direction opposite to that which is usual. **4.** to set aside, as a judgment; annul; revoke: *The judge reversed the original decision.* —*v.i.* to move or turn in the opposite direction. —**re·verse′ly,** *adv.* —**re·vers′er,** *n.*

re·vers·i·ble (ri vur′sə bəl) *adj.* **1.** that can be reversed. **2.** made so as to be worn or used on either side: *a reversible jacket, a reversible fabric.* —*n.* a garment worn with either side out. —**re·vers′i·bil′i·ty, re·vers′i·ble·ness,** *n.* —**re·vers′i·bly,** *adv.*

re·ver·sion (ri vur′zhən) *n.* **1.** a return, as to a former condition, practice, or belief. **2.** the act of reversing or the state of being reversed.

re·vert (ri vurt′) *v.i.* to return, as to a former condition, practice, or belief: *The old man's thoughts reverted to the days of his youth.*

rev·er·y (rev′ər ē) *n. pl.,* **rev·er·ies.** another spelling of **reverie.**

re·view (ri vyoo′) *v.t.* **1.** to study, go over, or examine again: *John reviewed his notes in preparing for the exam.* **2.** to go over in one's mind; look back on: *Phyllis reviewed the day's events with a smile.* **3.** to write or give a critical summary or discussion of: *A famous critic was asked to review the play for the newspaper.* **4.** to consider or examine (a court action) again. **5.** to make a formal or official inspection of: *The general reviewed the troops.* —*n.* **1.** a studying, going over, or examining again: *a review of one's notes for a test.* **2.** a looking back: *a review of the main events of one's childhood.* **3.** a summary or survey: *The speaker gave a review of recent political developments in the country.* **4.** a critical summary or discussion: *The reviews of the new motion picture are not very good.* **5.** a formal or official inspection: *a review of troops.*

re·view·er (ri vyoo′ər) *n.* **1.** a person whose business is writing articles criticizing books, plays, and the like. **2.** any person who reviews.

re·vile (ri vīl′) *v.,* **re·viled, re·vil·ing.** —*v.t.* to attack with insulting language; call bad names: *The beggar reviled the man who refused to give him money.* —*v.i.* to use insulting language. —**re·vile′ment,** *n.* —**re·vil′er,** *n.*

re·vise (ri vīz′) *v.t.,* **re·vised, re·vis·ing. 1.** to change in order to correct or improve: *to revise a manuscript.* **2.** to make different; alter: *to revise one's opinion.* —**re·vis′er,** *n.*

re·vi·sion (ri vizh′ən) *n.* **1.** the act or process of revising. **2.** something revised: *a revision of a dictionary.*

re·viv·al (ri vī′vəl) *n.* **1.** the act of reviving or the state of being revived. **2.** an awakening or increase of interest in religion in a church, community, or denomination. **3.** a special service held to increase interest in religion.

re·viv·al·ist (ri vī′və list) *n.* a person who holds or promotes religious revivals.

re·vive (ri vīv′) *v.,* **re·vived, re·viv·ing.** —*v.t.* **1.** to bring back to consciousness: *The fireman revived the unconscious child.* **2.** to bring back into existence, use, currency, or awareness: *The old motion picture was revived with great success.* **3.** to give new strength, vitality, or freshness to: *A good meal revived the hungry boy.* —*v.i.* **1.** to come back to consciousness. **2.** to show new strength, vitality, or freshness. —**re·viv′er,** *n.*

rev·o·ca·ble (rev′ə kə bəl) *adj.* that can be revoked.

rev·o·ca·tion (rev′ə kā′shən) *n.* **1.** the act or fact of revoking: *the revocation of a driver's license.* **2.** the state of being revoked.

re·voke (ri vōk′) *v.t.,* **re·voked, re·vok·ing.** to cancel or make no longer valid: *The motor vehicle bureau revoked his driver's license.*

re·volt (ri vōlt′) *n.* an uprising or rebellion against authority: *The farmers took part in the revolt against the government.* —*v.i.* **1.** to rebel against authority. **2.** to be disgusted or repelled. —*v.t.* to disgust or repel: *The idea revolted her.*

re·volt·ing (ri vōl′ting) *adj.* disgusting or repulsive; repellent: *a revolting smell.* —**re·volt′ing·ly,** *adv.*

rev·o·lu·tion (rev′ə loo′shən) *n.* **1.** the overthrow of an existing political system or form of government by those governed, usually through the use of force, and the establishment of a new or different system of government. **2.** any sudden, far-reaching, or very great change: *The development of modern machines brought about a revolution in industry.* **3.** movement in a closed curve around a central point or object. **4.** a spinning or turning around an axis; rotation. **5.** one complete turn of a rotating body: *The crankshaft of this engine makes up to 5000 revolutions per minute.* **6.** the movement of one celestial body in an orbit around another, especially the movement of the planets about the sun. **7.** one complete course of such a body. **8.** such a course considered to be complete when the first body has passed twice over a particular point on the second, rather than when it has completed a circuit in space. **9.** a cycle or series: *the revolution of the seasons.*

rev·o·lu·tion·ar·y (rev′ə loo′shə ner′ē) *adj.* **1.** relating to, of the nature of, or tending to bring a revolution. **2. Revolutionary.** of or relating to the American Revolution. —*n. pl.,* **rev·o·lu·tion·ar·ies.** a person who takes part in or supports a revolution.

Revolutionary War, another term for **American Revolution.**

rev·o·lu·tion·ist (rev′ə loo′shə nist) *n.* a person who takes part in or supports a revolution; revolutionary.

rev·o·lu·tion·ize (rev′ə loo′shə nīz′) *v.t.,* **rev·o·lu·tion·ized, rev·o·lu·tion·iz·ing.** to produce a far-reaching or very great change in: *The development of the airplane revolutionized transportation.*

re·volve (ri volv′) *v.,* **re·volved, re·volv·ing.** —*v.i.* **1.** to move in a circle or orbit around a central point or object: *The planets revolve around the sun.* **2.** to spin or turn around on an axis; rotate: *Wheels revolve when in motion.* **3.** to move or happen in a cycle: *The seasons revolve.* —*v.t.* **1.** to cause to move in a circle or orbit. **2.** to cause to rotate. **3.** to think about; ponder; consider. **4.** to depend upon: *The doctor's whole life revolves around his work.*

re·volv·er (ri vol′vər) *n.* a pistol fitted with a cylinder that holds the bullets and revolves with each shot, thus allowing the weapon to be fired several times without reloading.

Revolver

re·vue (ri vyoo′) *also,* **re·view.** *n.* a theatrical presentation usually consisting of songs, dances, and skits that make fun of people and recent events.

re·vul·sion (ri vul′shən) *n.* **1.** strong disgust; repugnance: *When she saw the slum conditions, she was filled with revulsion.* **2.** the act of drawing back or away; withdrawal.

re·ward (ri wôrd′) *n.* **1.** something given or received in return, as for service or merit: *The student received a medal as a reward for getting the best marks in arithmetic.* **2.** money offered or given for the recovery of lost property or the capture of criminals: *She offered a reward for the return of her lost dog.* —*v.t.* **1.** to give a reward to: *The*

at; āpe; cär; end; mē; it; īce; hot; ōld; fôrk; wood; fool; oil; out; up; turn; sing; thin; this; hw in white; zh in treasure. The symbol ə stands for the sound of **a** in about, **e** in taken, **i** in pencil, **o** in lemon, and **u** in circus.

man rewarded Betty for finding his wallet. **2.** to give a reward for: *Our country rewards bravery.* **3.** to be a reward for: *Success rewarded his efforts.* —**re·ward′er,** *n.*

Rey·kja·vik (rā′kyə vēk′) *n.* the capital and largest city of Iceland, in the southwestern part of the country. Pop. (1978 est.), 83,376.

Reyn·ard (ren′ərd, rā′närd) *n.* in medieval fables, the clever fox who outwits other animals.

Rey·nolds, Sir Joshua (ren′əldz) 1723–1792, English painter.

RFD, R.F.D., Rural Free Delivery.

Rh, the symbol for rhodium.

rhap·sod·ic (rap sod′ik) *adj.* of, relating to, or characteristic of rhapsody; overly emotional or enthusiastic. Also, **rhapsodical.** —**rhap·sod′i·cal·ly,** *adv.*

rhap·so·dy (rap′sə dē) *n. pl.,* **rhap·so·dies. 1.** speech or writing characterized by or expressing too much emotion or enthusiasm: *Betty went into rhapsodies about her new dress.* **2.** an instrumental musical composition that is irregular in form and full of emotion.

rhe·a (rē′ə) *n.* a South American bird that cannot fly, resembling the ostrich, and having brownish feathers.

Rheims (rēmz) see **Reims.**

Rhen·ish (ren′ish) *adj.* of or relating to the Rhine River or the regions bordering it.

rhe·ni·um (rē′nē əm) *n.* a soft, heavy, silver-white metallic element, used especially to make electrical contacts. Symbol: **Re**

rhe·o·stat (rē′ə stat′) *n.* an electrical device for varying the resistance of a circuit, used especially in switches that slowly dim lights.

rhe·sus monkey (rē′səs) a yellowish-brown monkey native to northern India, used widely in biological experiments.

Rhea

rhet·o·ric (ret′ər ik) *n.* **1.** the art or skill of speaking or writing well. **2.** showy, exaggerated, or insincere language in speech or writing: *The politician's speech was mere rhetoric.*

rhe·tor·i·cal (ri tôr′i kəl, ri tor′i kəl) *adj.* **1.** of, like, or relating to rhetoric. **2.** using rhetoric. —**rhe·tor′i·cal·ly,** *adv.* —**rhe·tor′i·cal·ness,** *n.*

rhetorical question, a question asked only for effect, with no answer expected: *The speaker asked the audience the rhetorical question, "Don't we all want peace?"*

rhet·o·ri·cian (ret′ə rish′ən) *n.* **1.** a person who is skilled in or teaches rhetoric. **2.** a person who writes or speaks in a rhetorical manner.

rheum (rōōm) *n.* a watery discharge from mucous membranes, such as those in the nose.

rheu·mat·ic (rōō mat′ik) *adj.* of, relating to, or caused by rheumatism. —*n.* a person who has rheumatism. —**rheu·mat′i·cal·ly,** *adv.*

rheumatic fever, an inflammatory disease of unknown origin, most frequently occurring in childhood, characterized by inflammation in the joints and often serious damage to the heart.

rheu·ma·tism (rōō′mə tiz′əm) *n.* any of several diseases characterized by inflammation, swelling, and stiffness of the muscles and joints.

Rh factor, a substance often found in the blood of humans and certain other mammals. Blood containing this substance, **Rh positive,** often causes severe reactions when combined with blood lacking it, **Rh negative,** as in transfusions. [From the *rh*(esus) monkey; because the substance was first discovered in the blood of this monkey.]

Rhine (rīn) *n.* a river flowing from eastern Switzerland through West Germany and the Netherlands.

Rhine·land (rīn′land′) *n.* a region in the westernmost part of West Germany, along the Rhine River.

rhine·stone (rīn′stōn′) *n.* a colorless, cut gem made of quartz or glass paste, used to imitate diamonds.

rhi·no (rī′nō) *n. pl.,* **rhi·nos.** see **rhinoceros.**

rhi·noc·er·os (rī nos′ər əs) *n. pl.,* **rhi·noc·er·os·es** or **rhi·noc·er·os.** a large, thick-skinned animal of Africa and Asia, having one or two horns rising from the snout.

rhi·zome (rī′zōm) *n.* a fleshy underground stem, usually growing parallel to the surface of the ground, containing stored food materials and bearing many nodes that can give rise to new plants. Also, **rootstock.**

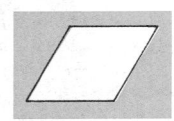

Rhinoceros

Rhode Island (rōd) a state in the northeastern United States, the smallest state in the country. Capital, Providence. Area, 1214 sq. mi. Pop. (1970), 949,723. Abbreviation, **R.I.**

● The name **Rhode Island** comes from the island of Rhodes in the Aegean Sea. An Italian navigator first gave the name to what is now called Block Island, which he thought resembled the Aegean island. Roger Williams, the founder of the colony of Rhode Island, transferred the name to Aquidneck Island, a large island off the coast of the colony. Eventually the name came to include the entire colony, and later the state. It is possible that the name was also influenced by the Dutch *Roodt Eylandt,* which means "red island."

Rhodes (rōdz) *n.* **1.** a Greek island in the southeastern Aegean Sea, off the coast of Turkey. **2.** a port city on this island. The Colossus of Rhodes, one of the Seven Wonders of the World, stood at the entrance to its harbor during the third century B.C.

Rho·de·sia (rō dē′zhə) *n.* see **Zimbabwe.**

rho·di·um (rō′dē əm) *n.* a heavy, silver-white metallic element, often used in alloys with platinum for making high-temperature laboratory equipment. Symbol: **Rh** [Modern Latin *rhodium,* from Greek *rhodon* rose¹; because its salts are rose-colored.]

rho·do·den·dron (rō′də den′drən) *n.* any of a large group of shrubs and trees, bearing clusters of bell-shaped flowers.

rhom·bus (rom′bəs) *n. pl.,* **rhom·bus·es** or **rhom·bi** (rom′bī). a parallelogram with equal sides, having two obtuse angles and two acute angles.

Rhône (rōn) *n.* a river flowing from central Switzerland through southeastern France into the Mediterranean Sea.

rhu·barb (rōō′bärb) *n.* **1.** a plant having reddish leafstalks that have a slightly sour taste. **2.** the leafstalks of this plant, cooked in pies, sauces, and other dishes. **3.** *Slang.* a heated dispute or squabble.

Rhombus

rhyme (rīm) *also,* **rime.** *n.* **1.** the correspondence or repetition of similar or the same sounds at the ends of lines of verse. For example: I must down to the seas again, to the lonely sea and the *sky/* And all I ask is a tall ship and a star to steer her *by* (John Masefield). **2.** a word having a sound that is similar to or the same as another: *"Stale" is a rhyme for "pail."* **3.** verse or poetry whose lines have similar or the same sounds at the end. —v., **rhymed, rhym-ing.** —v.i. **1.** to form or make a rhyme: *"Wide" rhymes with "side."* **2.** to compose rhyme or verse. —v.t. **1.** to put into rhyme. **2.** to use as a rhyme. —**rhym′er,** n.

rhythm (ri<u>th</u>′əm) n. **1.** a regular or orderly repetition of sounds or movements: *the rhythm of drumbeats.* **2.** movement marked by such regular or orderly repetition. **3.** see **meter².** **4.** *Music.* **a.** a repeated pattern of beats, formed by the different lengths of tones and by the way in which the tones are accented. **b.** a particular or characteristic form of this: *That song is written in waltz rhythm.*

rhyth·mi·cal (ri<u>th</u>′mi kəl) adj. of, relating to, or characterized by rhythm. Also, **rhyth·mic** (ri<u>th</u>′mik).

R.I., Rhode Island.

rib (rib) n. **1.** one of the series of curved bones attached in pairs to the backbone and enclosing the chest cavity. **2.** a cut of meat including one or more ribs. **3.** anything like a rib: *the ribs of an umbrella.* **4.** a raised ridge, as in a knitted sweater or sock. **5.** the main vein of a leaf. —v.t., **ribbed, rib·bing. 1.** *Informal.* to poke fun at; tease. **2.** to strengthen or support with ribs. **3.** to make raised ridges in.

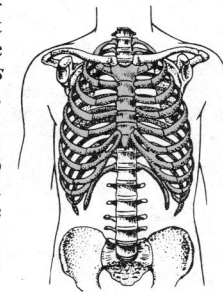
Ribs

rib·ald (rib′əld) adj. vulgar; coarse: *ribald humor.*

rib·ald·ry (rib′əld rē) n. ribald behavior or language.

rib·bon (rib′ən) n. **1.** a band of fabric, paper, or other material used for decoration. **2.** any similar band of a flexible material: *a typewriter ribbon.* **3.** a strip: *The road was a ribbon of concrete across the desert.* **4.** a small strip of cloth used as a military decoration. —**rib′bon·like′,** adj.

ri·bo·fla·vin (rī′bə flā′vin) n. see **vitamin B₂.**

ri·bo·nu·cle·ic acid (rī′bō n<del>oo</del> klē′ik, rī′bō ny<del>oo</del>-klē′ik) see **RNA.**

ri·bose (rī′bōs) n. a simple sugar that is a component of ribonucleic acid.

rice (rīs) n. **1.** the starchy grains of a cereal grass that is an important food in many parts of the world, such as India and China. **2.** the plant bearing these grains. —v.t., **riced, ric·ing.** to reduce to grains resembling rice.

rice·bird (rīs′burd′) n. another word for **bobolink.**

rich (rich) adj. **1.** having great wealth: *a rich man, a rich country.* **2.** well-supplied with something: *The old house was rich in memories.* **3.** productive; fertile: *rich soil, a rich imagination.* **4.** deep and full: *a rich baritone voice, a rich brown color.* **5.** (of foods) having a heavy, strong flavor or containing large amounts of nutritious, sugary, or creamy ingredients: *a rich sauce.* **6.** not thin or diluted: *a rich mixture of fuel.* —**rich′ly,** adv. —**rich′ness,** n.

Rich·ard I (rich′ərd) 1157–1199, the king of England from 1189 to 1199. Also, **Richard the Lion-Hearted.**

Richard II, 1367–1400, the king of England from 1377 to 1399.

Richard III, 1452–1485, the king of England from 1483 to 1485.

Rich·ard·son, Samuel (rich′ərd sən) 1689–1761, English novelist.

Rich·e·lieu, Cardinal (rish′ə l<del>oo</del>′) 1585–1642, French statesman.

rich·es (rich′iz) n., pl. an abundance of money, land, and other valuable possessions; wealth.

Rich·mond (rich′mənd) n. **1.** the capital of Virginia, a port city in the eastern part of the state. Pop. (1970), 249,621. **2.** a port city in western California, on San Francisco Bay. Pop. (1970), 79,043. **3.** a borough of New York

City comprising Staten Island. Area, 60.9 sq. mi. Pop. (1970), 295,443.

Rich·ter scale (rik′tər) a scale for measuring the magnitude of earthquakes, having graded steps from 1 to 10. Each successive number stands for an increase of 10 in the strength of the tremors and an increase of 30 in the amount of energy the earthquake releases. 1.5 stands for a very slight earthquake, 4.5 stands for an earthquake causing slight damage, and 8.5 stands for a very destructive earthquake. [From Charles F. *Richter,* 1900—, American scientist who devised this scale.]

rick (rik) n. a stack of hay, straw, or grain, especially one that has been covered so that rain will run off it. —v.t. to form into a rick or ricks.

rick·ets (rik′its) n. a disease of infants and children, usually caused by a lack of vitamin D, characterized by softening, and sometimes bending, of the bones and enlargement of the liver and spleen.

rick·et·y (rik′ə tē) adj. **1.** liable to fall; shaky: *a rickety old fence.* **2.** having rickets. **3.** feeble in the joints; infirm.

rick·sha (rik′shô′) also, **rick·shaw.** n. a two-wheeled carriage with a hood, drawn by one or two men, originally used in the Orient. Also, **jin-ricksha.**

ric·o·chet (rik′ə shā′) n. the skipping or glancing of an object off a flat surface. —v.i., **ric·o·cheted** (rik′ə shād′), **ric·o·chet·ing** (rik′ə shā′ing). to skip or glance off a flat surface: *The ball ricocheted off the wall.*

Ricksha

rid (rid) v.t., **rid** or **rid·ded, rid·ding.** to clear or free, as from something unpleasant or undesirable.

to be rid of. to be freed from: *to be rid of debts.*

to get rid of. a. to get free from: *to get rid of a cold.* **b.** to do away with: *Poison got rid of the ants in the house.*

rid·dance (rid′əns) n. the act of ridding or the state of being rid.

good riddance. a welcome relief from someone or something undesirable or unpleasant.

rid·den (rid′ən) the past participle of **ride.**

rid·dle¹ (rid′əl) n. **1.** a puzzling problem or question. **2.** a person or thing that is hard to understand. —v., **rid·dled, rid·dling.** —v.i. to speak in riddles. —v.t. to solve or explain (a riddle). [Old English *rædels.*]

rid·dle² (rid′əl) v.t., **rid·dled, rid·dling. 1.** to pierce in many places with holes. **2.** to sift through a coarse sieve. —n. a coarse sieve. [Old English *hriddel.*]

ride (rīd) v., **rode, rid·den, rid·ing.** —v.i. **1.** to sit on and be carried by something in motion, such as a horse or vehicle, while controlling its movement: *He rides to school every day on his bicycle.* **2.** to travel or be carried on or in a vehicle or other conveyance: *We rode through the countryside on the train.* **3.** to proceed or be carried along, as if riding: *The ship rode over the waves.* **4.** to be carried or supported while moving: *The racing car rode on two wheels as it rounded the turn.* **5.** to carry or support a rider

at; āpe; cär; end; mē; it; īce; hot; ōld; fôrk; wood; f<del>oo</del>l; oil; out; up; turn; sing; thin; <u>th</u>is; hw in white; zh in treasure. The symbol ə stands for the sound of **a** in about, **e** in taken, **i** in pencil, **o** in lemon, and **u** in circus.

in a certain manner: *The car rides smoothly.* **6.** to move or work upward out of place: *Her dress rode up at the waist.* **7.** to be moored: *The ship rode at anchor in the harbor.* **8.** *Informal.* to continue unchanged or without interruption: *Let the matter ride until tomorrow.* —*v.t.* **1.** to sit on and be carried by (something) in motion, while controlling its movements: *Can you ride a horse?* **2.** to travel or be carried on or in (something): *to ride a train to Chicago.* **3.** to ride over or along: *The cowboy rode the range.* **4.** *Informal.* to harass or tease: *The youth's friends rode him about his girlfriend.* —*n.* **1.** a short trip on an animal or in a vehicle: *We took a ride in the country.* **2.** any of various vehicles or devices, such as a merry-go-round or ferris wheel, that people can ride on or in for amusement: *We tried all the rides at the amusement park.* **3.** the manner in which a vehicle moves: *a smooth ride.*

rid·er (rī′dər) *n.* **1.** a person or thing that rides. **2.** an amendment or addition, as to a contract or legislative bill.

ridge (rij) *n.* **1.** the long and narrow upper part of something: *the ridge of an animal's back.* **2.** any raised narrow strip, as on fabric: *Corduroy has ridges.* **3.** a long and narrow chain of hills or mountains. **4.** a line formed by the meeting of two sloping sides: *the ridge of a roof.* —*v.t.,* **ridged, ridg·ing. 1.** to form or make into ridges. **2.** to mark or cover with ridges.

ridge·pole (rij′pōl′) *n.* a horizontal timber along the top of a roof or tent to which sloping beams are fastened.

rid·i·cule (rid′ə kyool′) *v.t.,* **rid·i·culed, rid·i·cul·ing.** to make (someone or something) appear foolish; expose to laughter. —*n.* words or actions intended to ridicule someone or something: *His strange behavior often exposes him to ridicule.*

ri·dic·u·lous (ri dik′yə ləs) *adj.* deserving or arousing ridicule; laughable; silly. —**ri·dic′u·lous·ly,** *adv.* —**ri·dic′u·lous·ness,** *n.*

rife (rīf) *adj.* **1.** happening commonly and often; widespread: *Poverty is rife in that area.* **2.** filled; abounding: *The school was rife with rumors that the principal would resign.*

riff·raff (rif′raf′) *n.* **1.** low or worthless persons. **2.** trash; rubbish.

ri·fle¹ (rī′fəl) *n.* a firearm designed to be fired from the shoulder, having spiral grooves cut into its bore to cause the bullet to spin as it is fired. —*v.t.,* **ri·fled, ri·fling.** to cut spiral grooves in (the bore of a firearm). [French *rifler* to file, scrape.]

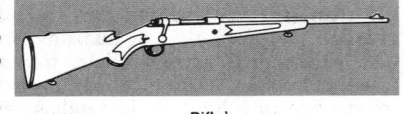

Rifle¹

ri·fle² (rī′fəl) *v.t.,* **ri·fled, ri·fling. 1.** to search through and rob; ransack: *The thief rifled the wall safe.* **2.** to strip (something) bare: *The burglars rifled the house of its contents.* [Old French *rifler.*] —**ri′fler,** *n.*

ri·fle·man (rī′fəl mən) *n. pl.,* **ri·fle·men** (rī′fəl mən). **1.** a soldier armed with a rifle. **2.** a man skilled in the use of a rifle.

ri·fling (rī′fling) *n.* **1.** the act or process of cutting spiral grooves in the bore of a firearm. **2.** the spiral grooves of a firearm.

rift (rift) *n.* **1.** an opening made by splitting; break; fissure: *a rift in a rock.* **2.** a breach in a relationship; quarrel: *a rift between friends.* —*v.t., v.i.* to split; cleave.

rig¹ (rig) *v.t.,* **rigged, rig·ging. 1.** to fit (a boat or ship) with masts, sails, spars, lines, and the like. **2.** to fit out; equip: *Tom rigged his car to carry skis.* **3.** to make or build hurriedly or as a makeshift: *The boy rigged up a hi-fi set from old radio parts.* —*n.* **1.** an arrangement of masts,

sails, spars, lines, and the like on a boat or ship. **2.** apparatus or equipment used for drilling an oil well. **3.** any apparatus or equipment used for a particular purpose: *a fishing rig.* **4.** *Informal.* dress; clothing; costume. [Probably of Scandinavian origin.]

rig² (rig) *v.t.,* **rigged, rig·ging.** to arrange in a dishonest way: *to rig an election.* [Of uncertain origin.]

Ri·ga (rē′gə) *n.* **1.** a port city in the western Soviet Union on the Baltic Sea, the capital of Latvia. Pop. (1971 est.), 743,000. **2. Gulf of.** the arm of the eastern Baltic Sea bordering Estonia and Latvia.

rig·ger (rig′ər) *n.* **1.** a person who rigs. **2.** a person who installs and repairs the rigging and hoisting gear of sailboats or ships.

rig·ging (rig′ing) *n.* **1.** all the lines of a boat or ship, as the ropes, chains, and wires, used for supporting the masts or working the sails. **2.** apparatus or equipment used for a special purpose, such as drilling an oil well.

right (rīt) *adj.* **1.** free from error; correct or true; accurate: *Bill gave the right answer to the arithmetic problem.* **2.** just, moral, or good: *Telling the truth was the right thing to do.* **3.** of, on, or toward the side of the body that is to the east when one is facing north: *the right hand, a right turn on a highway.* **4.** suitable; proper: *She is the right person for the job.* **5.** with or having the side or surface meant to be seen: *the right side of a piece of cloth.* **6.** *also,* **Right.** relating to or having conservative or reactionary political views. —*n.* **1.** something that is just, moral, good, or true: *the triumph of right over wrong.* **2.** *also,* **rights.** a just, legal, or moral claim: *the right to free speech.* **3.** the right side or direction: *to drive on the right.* **4.** *also,* **Right.** a party or group having conservative or reactionary political views. Also, **right wing. 5.** a blow delivered with the right hand, as in boxing. —*adv.* **1.** according to truth, fact, or reason; correctly: *John didn't spell my name right.* **2.** according to that which is just, moral, or good: *to do right.* **3.** in a proper or suitable way: *This telephone doesn't work right.* **4.** exactly; precisely: *Put the book right here on the table.* **5.** without delay; immediately: *Let's leave right after lunch.* **6.** to or toward the right: *Turn right at the foot of the hill.* **7.** very. ▲ used as part of certain formal titles: *The Right Reverend O'Grady.* —*v.t.* **1.** to make good, just, or correct: *to right a wrong.* **2.** to put into a proper or normal position: *The boys righted the capsized boat.* —*v.i.* to get into a proper or normal position: *The boat righted slowly as the wind died down.*

in the right. not wrong, mistaken, or at fault.

right away or **right off.** immediately: *I'll be there right away.*

right angle, an angle of 90 degrees, formed by two lines that are perpendicular to each other.

right-an·gled (rīt′ang′gəld) *adj.* containing one or more right angles.

right·eous (rī′chəs) *adj.* **1.** doing what is right; virtuous. **2.** coming from a sense of what is right; justifiable: *He showed righteous indignation at her insult.* —**right′eous·ly,** *adv.* —**right′eous·ness,** *n.*

right field *Baseball.* **1.** the right section of the outfield when viewed from home plate. **2.** the position of the player stationed in this area.

right·ful (rīt′fəl) *adj.* **1.** having a just, legal or moral claim: *The young prince is the rightful heir to the throne.* **2.** owned or held by such claim: *rightful property.* —**right′-ful·ly,** *adv.* —**right′ful·ness,** *n.*

right-hand (rīt′hand′) *adj.* **1.** on or toward the right: *to drive on the right-hand side of the street.* **2.** of, for, relating to, or with the right hand. **3.** most trusted and useful: *Jim is the coach's right-hand man.*

right-hand·ed (rīt′han′did) *adj.* **1.** using the right hand more often and more easily than the left. **2.** done with the right hand: *a right-handed catch.* **3.** made to be held in or used by the right hand. **4.** turning or moving from left to right: *a right-handed spiral.* —*adv. also,* **right-handedly.** with the right hand: *to pitch right-handed.* —**right′-hand′-ed·ness,** *n.*

right·ist (rī′tist) *n.* a person who has conservative or reactionary political views. —*adj.* of, relating to, or characterized by conservative or reactionary political views.

right·ly (rīt′lē) *adv.* **1.** in a correct way; accurately: *Tom answered the question rightly.* **2.** properly; suitably. **3.** justly or honestly.

right of way **1.** the right of a person or thing to go first or cross in front of another or others: *A pedestrian in a crosswalk has the right of way.* **2.** a legal right to go across property belonging to another. **3.** a strip of land set aside for a specific purpose, as for railroad tracks, public roads, or power lines.

right triangle, a triangle with a right angle.

right-wing (rīt′wing′) *adj.* of, relating to, or belonging to the right wing.

right wing **1.** see **right** (*n., def. 4*). **2.** a portion of a political party or other group having a more conservative or reactionary outlook than the rest.

rig·id (rij′id) *adj.* **1.** not yielding or bending; stiff: *Rigid steel girders made up the frame of the building.* **2.** strict; rigorous: *rigid discipline.* **3.** not changing; inflexible; fixed: *The requirements for membership are rigid.* —**rig′id·ly,** *adv.* —**rig′id·ness,** *n.*

ri·gid·i·ty (ri jid′ə tē) *n.* the state of being rigid.

rig·ma·role (rig′mə rōl′) *n.* **1.** complicated and often foolish or unnecessary action: *He went through a lot of rigmarole to get a check cashed.* **2.** foolish or senseless talk; nonsense.

rig·or (rig′ər) *also, British,* **rig·our.** *n.* **1.** the state or quality of being strict; strictness: *the rigor of the law.* **2.** severity; harshness: *the rigor of winter, the rigors of tyranny.* **3.** exactness; precision: *the rigor of mathematics.*

rig·or mor·tis (rig′ər môr′tis) the temporary stiffening of the muscles that begins shortly after death.

rig·or·ous (rig′ər əs) *adj.* **1.** very strict; inflexible: *rigorous rules.* **2.** severe; harsh: *the rigorous climate of the North Pole.* **3.** very exact; precise. —**rig′or·ous·ly,** *adv.* —**rig′or·ous·ness,** *n.*

rile (rīl) *v.t.,* **riled, ril·ing.** *Informal.* **1.** to irritate or annoy; provoke: *His rudeness really riles me.* **2.** to roil (liquid).

rill (ril) *n.* a tiny stream or brook.

rim (rim) *n.* **1.** the outer edge or border of something: *the rim of a glass.* **2.** a strip of metal on an automobile wheel on which the tire is fastened. —*v.t.,* **rimmed, rim·ming. 1.** to form a rim around: *The mountains rimmed the valley.* **2.** to roll around the rim of (something) without going in: *The basketball rimmed the basket and bounced out.*

rime¹ (rīm) *n., v.,* **rimed, rim·ing.** another spelling of **rhyme.**

rime² (rīm) *n.* frost, especially when it forms a white coating on a surface; hoarfrost. —*v.t.,* **rimed, rim·ing.** to cover with rime. [Old English *hrīm.*]

Rim·ski-Kor·sa·kov, Ni·ko·lai (rim′skē kôr′sə kôf′; nē kə lī′) 1844–1908, Russian composer.

rim·y (rī′mē) *adj.,* **rim·i·er, rim·i·est.** covered with rime; frosty.

rind (rīnd) *n.* a firm outer covering or skin, as of fruit or cheese.

ring¹ (ring) *n.* **1.** a continuous, closed curved line; circle. **2.** a circular band, often of precious metal, worn on the finger. **3.** any circular band, as of metal, wood, or plastic, used especially for holding or carrying something: *a napkin ring, curtain rings.* **4.** a circular course: *The children*

danced in a ring around the campfire. **5.** a group of persons or things forming a circle: *The President was surrounded by a ring of bodyguards.* **6.** a circular, usually enclosed, area used especially for circus performances. **7.** an area used for boxing matches. **8.** a group of persons working together, especially for a criminal purpose: *a ring of car thieves.* **9.** any of a series of concentric layers of wood produced yearly in the trunk of a tree. **10.** *Chemistry.* a closed chain of atoms. —*v.t.* **1.** to put a ring around; enclose with a ring; encircle. **2.** to form into a ring or rings. **3.** in certain games, to throw a horseshoe, ring, or other object over: *Tom ringed the stake.* —*v.i.* to move in a ring or spiral. [Old English *hring.*] —**ring′like′,** *adj.*

ring² (ring) *v.,* **rang, rung, ring·ing,** —*v.i.* **1.** to make a clear, resonant sound, as that made by a bell when struck. **2.** to cause a bell or bells to sound, especially as a signal or summons: *She rang for the maid.* **3.** to resound loudly and clearly; reverberate; echo: *The room rang with laughter.* **4.** to have a sensation, as of an echoing sound or buzzing: *My ears rang from the shrill noise.* —*v.t.* **1.** to cause (something) to ring: *The visitor rang the doorbell.* **2.** to announce or proclaim by the ringing of bells: *The chimes rang the hour.* **3.** to call on the telephone: *Ring me up when you get home.* —*n.* **1.** the act of ringing something, especially a bell. **2.** a clear, resonant sound, as that made by a bell when struck. **3.** a sound expressing a certain quality; tone: *The senator's voice had a ring of sincerity.* **4.** *Informal.* a telephone call: *I'll give you a ring when I get home tonight.* [Old English *hringan.*]

ring·bolt (ring′bōlt′) *n.* a bolt with a ring fitted into an eye in its head.

ring·er¹ (ring′ər) *n.* **1.** a person or thing that rings. **2.** a horseshoe or quoit thrown so as to encircle a stake or pin. [*Ring¹* + *-er¹.*]

ring·er² (ring′ər) *n.* **1.** a person or thing that rings a bell, chime, or the like. **2.** *Slang.* a horse or athlete illegally entered in a contest, as by the falsification of name or age. **3.** *Slang.* a person or thing that closely resembles another: *Bill is a ringer for his uncle.* [*Ring²* + *-er¹.*]

ring·lead·er (ring′lē′dər) *n.* a person who leads others, especially in wrong or unlawful acts.

ring·let (ring′lit) *n.* **1.** a coiled or curved lock of hair. **2.** *Archaic.* a small ring.

Ringbolt

ring·mas·ter (ring′mas′tər) *n.* a person who introduces the acts in a circus.

ring·side (ring′sīd′) *n.* **1.** an area just outside a ring, especially the area containing the first row of seats at a prize fight. **2.** any area where a person can have a close view.

ring·worm (ring′wurm′) *n.* any of several contagious fungus infections of the skin characterized by ring-shaped patches, including athlete's foot.

rink (ringk) *n.* **1.** a building, part of a building, or an area containing a surface for ice skating or roller skating. **2.** the surface itself.

rinse (rins) *v.t.,* **rinsed, rins·ing. 1.** to remove (soap or impurities) by washing with clear water: *He rinsed the soap off his hands.* **2.** to remove soap or impurities from (some-

at; āpe; cär; end; mē; it; īce; hot; ōld; fôrk; wood; fōōl; oil; out; up; turn; sing; thin; **th**is; hw in white; zh in treasure. The symbol ə stands for the sound of **a** in about, **e** in taken, **i** in pencil, **o** in lemon, and **u** in circus.

thing) by washing with clear water: *to rinse clothes.* **3.** to cleanse or wash lightly: *She rinsed her blouse and hung it to dry.* —*n.* **1.** the act of rinsing. **2.** water or other liquid used for rinsing. **3.** a liquid preparation that is applied to the hair to tint or condition it.

Ri·o de Ja·nei·ro (rē′ō dā zhə ner′ō) a port city in southeastern Brazil. Pop. (1970), 4,252,009.

Ri·o Grande (rē′ō grand′, rē′ō gran′dē) a river flowing from southwestern Colorado into the Gulf of Mexico and forming the border between Texas and Mexico.

ri·ot (rī′ət) *n.* **1.** a disorderly, often violent, disturbance or outbreak by a large crowd. **2.** *Law.* a disturbance of the peace by three or more persons acting together. **3.** a bright, lavish display: *The autumn leaves were a riot of color.* **4.** *Slang.* a person or thing that is extremely amusing. —*v.i.* to take part in a disorderly, often violent, disturbance: *The prisoners rioted.* —**ri′ot·er,** *n.*

  to run riot. a. to behave or move wildly and without restraint. **b.** to grow in great amounts or without control: *Weeds ran riot in the garden.*

ri·ot·ous (rī′ə təs) *adj.* **1.** of, relating to, or taking part in a disorderly, often violent, disturbance. **2.** noisy or rowdy; boisterous: *riotous laughter.* —**ri′ot·ous·ly,** *adv.* —**ri′ot·ous·ness,** *n.*

rip[1] (rip) *v.,* **ripped, rip·ping.** —*v.t.* **1.** to tear (something); rend: *The boy ripped his trousers on the fence.* **2.** to make by ripping: *The nail ripped a hole in her dress.* **3.** to tear or cut into pieces: *to rip up a piece of paper.* **4.** to remove (something) by tearing or pulling: *to rip out a seam.* **5.** to saw or split (wood) along the grain. —*v.i.* to become torn apart. —*n.* a torn place; tear: *The little girl had a rip in her dress.* [Of Scandinavian or Low German origin.]

rip[2] (rip) *n.* **1.** a stretch of rough water formed by the meeting of opposing currents. **2.** see **riptide.** [Possibly from *rip*[1].]

rip cord, a cord with a handle that opens a parachute when pulled.

ripe (rīp) *adj.,* **rip·er, rip·est. 1.** fully grown and ready to be gathered and used as food: *The tomatoes were not yet ripe.* **2.** fully developed; mature: *ripe tobacco.* **3.** advanced in years: *My grandmother lived to a ripe old age.* **4.** fully prepared and ready: *The country was ripe for revolution.* **5.** favorable or suitable: *The time is ripe.* —**ripe′ly,** *adv.* —**ripe′ness,** *n.*

rip·en (rī′pən) *v.t., v.i.* to make or become ripe: *to ripen cheese. The tomatoes ripened on the vine.*

ri·poste (ri pōst′) *n.* **1.** *Fencing.* a quick thrust made after successfully parrying an opponent's lunge. **2.** a quick, witty, or sharp reply; retort.

rip·ple (rip′əl) *n.* **1.** a very small wave on the surface of a liquid, such as water: *The breeze made ripples on the surface of the pond.* **2.** anything resembling this: *ripples in a fabric.* **3.** a sound resembling that made by the flowing of very small waves: *a ripple of applause.* —*v.,* **rip·pled, rip·pling.** —*v.i.* **1.** to form or have ripples: *The grass rippled gently in the wind* (Ernest Hemingway). **2.** to make a rippling sound. —*v.t.* to cause ripples on.

rip·saw (rip′sô′) *n.* a handsaw with squared, cutting edges on its teeth, used to cut wood along the grain. See **crosscut saw** for illustration.

rip·tide (rip′tīd′) *n.* a strong current of water flowing rapidly outward from the shore.

Rip Van Win·kle (rip′ van wing′kəl) the hero of a story by Washington Irving. He slept for twenty years and awakened to find his village and country changed completely.

rise (rīz) *v.i.,* **rose, ris·en, ris·ing. 1.** to get up from a sitting, kneeling, or lying position; stand up: *Everyone rose*

when the judge entered the courtroom. **2.** to get out of bed: *That farmer always rises early.* **3.** to move from a lower to a higher place; go upward: *Smoke rose from the chimney.* **4.** (of the sun and other heavenly bodies) to appear above the horizon. **5.** to slope upward: *The hills rise beyond the fields.* **6.** to extend upward: *That tall building rises above all the others.* **7.** to increase, as in amount, value, degree, or force: *The cost of living rose last year.* **8.** to advance, as in rank, position, or influence: *He rose to the presidency of the company.* **9.** to reach a higher level; increase in height: *The river rose two feet.* **10.** to grow larger and become lighter: *The cake will rise.* **11.** to become louder or higher in pitch: *His voice rose with anger.* **12.** to have as an origin; start; begin: *That river rises in the mountains.* **13.** to revolt; rebel: *The people rose against the tyrant.* **14.** to come back from death; return to life. —*n.* **1.** an upward movement; ascent: *the rise of water in a river.* **2.** an increase, as in amount, value, degree, or force: *a rise in temperature, a rise in prices.* **3.** an upward slope or direction: *the rise of a hill.* **4.** a piece of rising ground; hill: *The house was built on a rise above the river.*

  to give rise to. to cause; begin; start: *The depression gave rise to widespread unemployment.*

  to rise to. to be equal to the demands of: *Paul rose to the occasion and scored the winning goal.*

ris·en (riz′ən) the past participle of **rise.**

ris·er (rī′zər) *n.* **1.** a person or thing that rises: *The farmer was an early riser.* **2.** the vertical part of a step.

risk (risk) *n.* a chance of loss or harm; danger: *There is great risk involved in that plan.* —*v.t.* **1.** to expose to loss or harm: *The boy risked his life to save the child from the burning house.* **2.** to take the risk of: *The businessman risked losing all his money with his latest venture.*

Risers

risk·y (ris′kē) *adj.,* **risk·i·er, risk·i·est.** full of risk; dangerous: *Climbing that mountain was risky. Being a race car driver is a risky profession.* —**risk′i·ness,** *n.*

ris·qué (ris kā′) *adj.* slightly improper; suggestive: *a risqué story.*

ri·tar·dan·do (rē′tär dän′dō) *Music. adj.* becoming gradually slower. —*n. pl.,* **ri·tar·dan·dos.** a gradual slowing of tempo.

rite (rīt) *n.* **1.** a formal act or series of acts set by ritual or tradition: *marriage rites.* **2.** a particular form or ceremony for the performance of this: *the rite of baptism.*

rit·u·al (rich′ōō əl) *n.* **1.** a set form or procedure for the performance of a religious or solemn rite. **2.** a system or body of rites. **3.** a routine faithfully followed: *Jim has made a ritual of exercising every morning.* —*adj.* of, relating to, or performed as a ritual. —**rit′u·al·ly,** *adv.*

rit·u·al·ism (rich′ōō ə liz′əm) *n.* **1.** a strict observance of or adherence to ritual. **2.** a study of religious ritual.

ri·val (rī′vəl) *n.* **1.** a person who competes with another to achieve the same thing or tries to equal or do better than another; competitor: *The two boys were rivals for the athletic prize.* **2.** a person or thing that compares favorably with or equals another: *In chess, Bobby has no rival.* —*v.t.,* **ri·valed, ri·val·ing;** *also, British,* **ri·valled, ri·val·ling. 1.** to try to equal or do better than; compete with. **2.** to compare favorably with or be the equal of: *Joan rivals her sister in beauty.* —*adj.* being a rival; competing: *rival football teams.* [Going back to Latin *rīvālis* a person who uses water from the same brook as another; because such people often quarreled about the use of the water.]

ri·val·ry (rī′vəl rē) *n. pl.*, **ri·val·ries.** **1.** the act of rivaling; competition. **2.** the state of being rivals: *There was great rivalry between the two schools in basketball.*

rive (rīv) *v.t.*, **rived, rived** or **riv·en** (riv′ən), **riv·ing.** to split; cleave: *to rive a log with an ax.*

riv·er (riv′ər) *n.* **1.** a large stream of water that flows in a natural channel and empties into a lake, ocean, or another river. **2.** anything resembling a river, as in quantity or flow: *a river of oil.*

river basin, the land area drained by a river and its tributaries.

riv·er·bed (riv′ər bed′) *n.* the bottom of the channel through which a river flows or formerly flowed.

riv·er·head (riv′ər hed′) *n.* the source of a river.

riv·er·side (riv′ər sīd′) *n.* an area beside the edge or bank of a river.

Riv·er·side (riv′ər sīd′) *n.* a city in southwestern California. Pop. (1970), 140,089.

riv·et (riv′it) *n.* a metal bolt used to make permanent fastenings, especially in metalwork and leatherwork. The shaft of the rivet is put through aligned holes in materials to be joined, and the headless end is flattened to make a tight connection. —*v.t.* **1.** to fasten with a rivet or rivets. **2.** to fasten or hold firmly: *John's complete attention was riveted on the football game.* —**riv′et·er,** *n.*

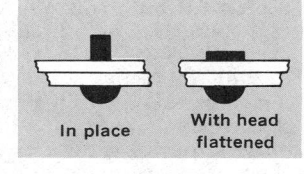

In place | With head flattened

Rivets

Riv·i·er·a (riv′ē er′ə) *n.* a narrow strip of land along the Mediterranean coasts of Italy, France, and Monaco, famous as a resort.

riv·u·let (riv′yə lət) *n.* a tiny stream or brook.

Ri·yadh (rē yäd′) *n.* the capital of Saudi Arabia, in the east-central part of the country. Pop. (1970 est.), 300,000.

rm. 1. room. **2.** ream.

Rn, the symbol for radon.

RN 1. registered nurse. **2.** Royal Navy.

RNA, any of various nucleic acids found in the cytoplasm and nucleus of all living cells, consisting of a long strand made up of alternating units of sugar and phosphate connected by a nitrogen base. One form of this acid, **messenger RNA,** carries the genetic information contained in DNA from the cell nucleus to the cytoplasm. Another form, **transfer RNA,** arranges amino acids so that protein is produced in the manner directed by DNA. [An abbreviation of *r*(ibo)*n*(ucleic) *a*(cid).]

roach[1] (rōch) *n. pl.*, **roach·es.** see **cockroach.**

roach[2] (rōch) *n. pl.*, **roach·es** or **roach.** **1.** a freshwater fish related to the carp and found in lakes and rivers in northern Europe. **2.** any of several similar fish found in North America. [Old French *roche.*]

road (rōd) *n.* **1.** a strip of pavement or cleared ground used for traveling between places; open way for the passage of vehicles, persons, or animals. **2.** any means of going or moving toward a specific goal: *the road to power.* **3.** *often,* **roads.** see **roadstead.** **4.** a railroad.

 on the road. traveling for professional or business reasons.

road agent, formerly, a highwayman who robbed stagecoaches in the western United States.

road·bed (rōd′bed′) *n.* **1.** a foundation or bed for the ties and rails of a railroad. **2.** the foundation or surface of a road.

road·block (rōd′blok′) *n.* **1.** a blockade to stop traffic on a road, as that used by police to stop criminals. **2.** anything that hinders progress.

road hog *Informal.* a driver who obstructs traffic by driving his vehicle in more than one lane of the road.

road·run·ner (rōd′run′ər) *n.* a bird related to the cuckoo, native to southwestern North America. The roadrunner has brownish-black streaked feathers, a long, white-tipped tail, and a shaggy crest. It usually runs very swiftly instead of flying.

Roadrunner

road·side (rōd′sīd′) *n.* an area along the side of a road: *Let's pull up on the roadside and rest.* —*adj.* along the side of a road: *a roadside vegetable stand.*

road·stead (rōd′sted′) *n.* a protected area near the shore where ships may anchor. It is less sheltered than a harbor.

road·ster (rōd′stər) *n.* an open automobile with a single seat for two or more people, often with a rumble seat or luggage compartment in the rear.

road test, a test of a vehicle or any of its parts under actual driving conditions.

road·way (rōd′wā′) *n.* a road, especially that part over which vehicles travel.

road·work (rōd′wurk′) *n.* physical exercise or training consisting of long runs over a road or path.

roam (rōm) *v.i.* to go about without any purpose or destination, especially over a large area; wander: *to roam through the woods.* —*v.t.* to wander over or through (a place): *The wolves roamed the forest in search of food.* —**roam′er,** *n.*

roan (rōn) *adj.* reddish-brown mixed with gray or white. —*n.* **1.** a roan color. **2.** a horse of this color.

Ro·a·noke (rō′ə nōk′) *n.* a city in southwestern Virginia. Pop. (1970), 92,115.

roar (rôr) *v.i.* **1.** to make a loud, deep sound or cry: *The lion roared.* **2.** to resound loudly and deeply: *The motor roared.* **3.** to move with a loud, deep noise: *The plane roared up the runway.* **4.** to laugh loudly: *The audience roared at the comedian's jokes.* —*v.t.* to shout or express in a roar: *He roared his displeasure at being disturbed.* —*n.* **1.** a loud, deep sound or cry. **2.** a loud, resounding noise: *the roar of ocean waves.* —**roar′er,** *n.*

roast (rōst) *v.t.* **1.** to cook in a dry oven or over an open fire or hot coals: *to roast a chicken, to roast chestnuts.* **2.** to dry and brown by heat: *to roast coffee beans.* **3.** *Informal.* to criticize or ridicule severely: *His father roasted him for being late.* **4.** to make very hot. **5.** to heat (ore) with air in a furnace so as to purify, dehydrate, or oxidize. —*v.i.* **1.** to be cooked in a dry oven or over an open fire or hot coals. **2.** to be uncomfortably hot: *I'm roasting in this heavy coat.* —*n.* **1.** a cut of meat that has been roasted or is prepared to be roasted. **2.** an outdoor gathering at which food is cooked over an open fire or hot coals.

roast·er (rōs′tər) *n.* **1.** a pan or appliance used for roasting. **2.** an animal suitable for roasting, especially a chicken or a young pig.

---

at; āpe; cär; end; mē; it; īce; hot; ōld; fôrk;
wood; fōōl; oil; out; up; turn; sing; thin; this;
hw in white; zh in treasure. The symbol ə
stands for the sound of **a** in about, **e** in taken,
i in pencil, **o** in lemon, and **u** in circus.

rob (rob) *v.,* **robbed, rob·bing.** —*v.t.* **1.** to take property from unlawfully by threats or by the use of violence: *They robbed the jewelry store in broad daylight.* **2.** *Informal.* to take away (property) by illegal means; steal: *Someone robbed the pencils from my desk.* **3.** to take away from, especially by unjust or dishonest means: *The gossip robbed him of his reputation.* —*v.i.* to commit robbery: *The poor man robbed to feed his family.*

rob·ber (rob'ər) *n.* a person who robs.

rob·ber·y (rob'ər ē) *n. pl.,* **rob·ber·ies.** the act of unlawfully taking another's property; theft.

robe (rōb) *n.* **1.** a loose outer garment, especially one worn at home or on informal occasions: *a beach robe.* **2.** a garment worn to show office, profession, or rank: *a judge's robe, a clergyman's robe.* **3.** a blanket or other covering, as for use by spectators at outdoor sporting events. —*v.,* **robed, rob·ing.** —*v.t.* to put a robe on. —*v.i.* to put on a robe. [Old French *robe* booty, clothes taken as booty, a loose outer garment; of Germanic origin; originally referring to booty because common people were so poor in the Middle Ages that they often stole clothes, including robes.]

Robes·pierre, Max·i·mi·lien (rōbz'pēr; mäk sē mēl'yän') 1758–1794, one of the leaders of the French Revolution.

rob·in (rob'in) *n.* **1.** a North American thrush having a reddish-orange breast and a black head and tail. **2.** a thrush of Europe and parts of Asia and Africa, having a brown back, a white underside, and a reddish-brown breast.

Robin

Robin Hood *English Legend.* an outlaw who, with his band of men, robbed the rich in order to give help to the poor.

Rob·in·son Cru·soe (rob'in sən krōō'sō) the hero of Daniel Defoe's novel of the same name, published in 1719.

ro·bot (rō'bət) *n.* **1.** a machine somewhat resembling a man, that can perform some human tasks. **2.** a person who works or acts in a mechanical way. [Czech *robotnik* slave, from *robota* forced labor; made popular by Karel Čapek, 1890–1938, a Czech playwright, in his play *R. U. R. (Rossum's Universal Robots).*]

ro·bust (rō bust', rō'bust) *adj.* **1.** having strength and vigor; in good health; hardy: *a robust young athlete.* **2.** requiring strength and vigor: *the robust life of a lumberjack.* **3.** rich and full-bodied: *a robust flavor.*

roc (rok) *n. Arabian Legend.* an enormous and fearsome bird of prey.

Ro·cham·beau, Count de (rō'shäm bō') 1725–1807, commander of the French forces that fought with the American army during the Revolutionary War.

Roch·es·ter (roch'es'tər) *n.* a city in western New York, on Lake Ontario. Pop. (1970), 296,233.

rock¹ (rok) *n.* **1.** a fragment or piece of stone: *The boys threw rocks into the pond.* **2.** a large mass of stone forming a cliff or peak: *The ship was dashed violently against the rocks.* **3.** *Geology.* **a.** an extensive, naturally formed mass of mineral matter that forms part of the crust of the earth. **b.** a particular kind of such matter. Granite, limestone, and slate are rocks. **4.** something resembling a rock in firmness or as a source of strength or support. [Old French *roche.*] —**rock'like',** *adj.*

on the rocks. *Informal.* **a.** in a state of destruction or ruin. **b.** (of a drink) served over ice.

rock² (rok) *v.t.* **1.** to move back and forth or from side to side gently: *The mother rocked the baby in her arms.*

2. to move or shake violently: *The earth tremor rocked the house.* **3.** to upset or unnerve: *The news of the football star's illness rocked the student body.* —*v.i.* **1.** to be moved back and forth or from side to side gently: *The porch chair rocked in the breeze.* **2.** to be shaken violently: *The ship rocked in the squall.* —*n.* **1.** a rocking motion. **2.a.** see **rock 'n' roll. b.** a form of popular music that developed from rock 'n' roll, influenced by folk and country-and-western music. It is characterized especially by the use of instruments that have been electrically amplified and by generally more complex lyrics and arrangements than rock 'n' roll. [Old English *roccian.*]

rock-and-roll (rok'ən rōl') another spelling of **rock 'n' roll.**

rock bottom, the lowest level; very bottom: *The stock market hit rock bottom.* —**rock'-bot'tom,** *adj.*

rock candy, clear, hard crystals of pure sugar.

rock crystal, a clear, colorless variety of quartz, used to make optical devices, jewelry, vases, and other ornaments.

Rock·e·fel·ler (rok'ə fel'ər) **1. John D(avison).** 1839–1937, U.S. industrialist and philanthropist. **2. Nelson A.** 1908–1979, U.S. political leader.

rock·er (rok'ər) *n.* **1.** a rocking chair. **2.** one of the two curved pieces on which a cradle, rocking chair, or other object rocks.

rock·et (rok'it) *n.* **1.** a device that is propelled by a jet of hot gases ejected in a direction opposite to the direction of motion, and that does not require air from the outside for its operation. **2.** a vehicle, missile, or projectile propelled by such a device. —*v.i.* to move or rise swiftly: *The price of food is rocketing upward.*

rock·et·eer (rok'ə tēr') *n.* a person who works with rockets, especially an expert in rocketry.

rock·et·ry (rok'it rē) *n.* the science of rocket design, construction, and flight.

Rock·ford (rok'fərd) *n.* a city in northern Illinois. Pop. (1970), 147,370.

rock garden, a garden arranged with flowers and plants on rocky ground or among rocks.

Rock·ies (rok'ēz) *n.* see **Rocky Mountains.**

rocking chair, a chair mounted on rockers or springs, so that it can rock back and forth.

rocking horse, a toy horse mounted on rockers, large enough for a child to ride. Also, **hobbyhorse.**

Rocking horse

rock lobster, see **spiny lobster.**

rock 'n' roll (rok' ən rōl') *also,* **rock-and-roll.** **1.** a form of popular music derived from blues and jazz, characterized especially by a strong, persistent beat and relatively simple lyrics and arrangements. **2.** a kind of popular dance done to this music.

rock salt, common salt occurring in solid form, especially in large crystals; halite.

rock wool, fibrous, fireproof insulating material made by blowing steam or hot air through a molten mass of rock, as limestone.

rock·y¹ (rok'ē) *adj.,* **rock·i·er, rock·i·est. 1.** full of rocks: *a rocky hill.* **2.** like rock; hard; unyielding. [*Rock¹* + *-y¹.*] —**rock'i·ness,** *n.*

rock·y² (rok'ē) *adj.,* **rock·i·er, rock·i·est. 1.** likely to sway or totter; shaky. **2.** *Informal.* physically weak or unsteady: *The fever made her feel rocky.* [*Rock²* + *-y¹.*] —**rock'i·ness,** *n.*

Rocky Mountain goat, a cud-chewing animal of the mountain ranges of western North America, having black horns and a thick coat of long, white hair. Also, **mountain goat.**

Rocky Mountain goat

Rocky Mountains, a mountain system in the western United States and Canada, extending for more than 3000 miles from central New Mexico to northern Alaska. Also, **Rockies.**

Rocky Mountain sheep, another term for **bighorn.**

Rocky Mountain spotted fever, an infectious disease caused by a microorganism and transmitted by the bite of a tick, characterized by high fever, headache, muscular pain, and a red or purple rash.

ro·co·co (rō kō′kō) *n.* a style of interior decoration, architecture, and painting that originated in France and northern Italy and was much used during the eighteenth century, characterized especially by the use of curved forms based on objects from nature, such as shells, flowers, and leaves. —*adj.* of, relating to, or in this style.

rod (rod) *n.* **1.** a thin, straight, usually cylindrical piece of metal, wood, or other material. **2.** a slender straight stick cut from or growing on a tree or bush. **3.** see **fishing rod. 4.** a stick or bundle of sticks used to beat or punish. **5. the rod.** punishment; discipline: *Spare the rod and spoil the child* (Samuel Butler). **6.** a unit of measurement equal to 5½ yards or 16½ feet. **7.** *Slang.* a pistol or revolver. **8.** one of the rod-shaped cells on the retina of the eye that are sensitive to dim light. —**rod′like′,** *adj.*

rode (rōd) the past tense of **ride.**

ro·dent (rōd′ənt) *n.* any of various animals having a pair of large front teeth used for gnawing. Rats, mice, squirrels, guinea pigs, porcupines, and beavers are rodents. —*adj.* **1.** gnawing: *the rodent teeth of a beaver.* **2.** of, relating to, or characteristic of a rodent.

ro·de·o (rō′dē ō′, rō dā′ō) *n. pl.,* **ro·de·os. 1.** a show in which cowboys compete in various events, such as horseback riding, calf roping, and steer wrestling, often for cash prizes. **2.** a roundup of cattle.

Ro·din, Au·guste (rō dan′; ō goost′) 1840–1917, French sculptor.

roe[1] (rō) *n.* the eggs of fish. [Possibly from Old Norse *hrogn.*]

roe[2] (rō) *n. pl.,* **roes** or **roe.** a small deer native to the forests of Europe and northern Asia, having a coarse, reddish-brown coat with a white patch over the rump. [Old English *rāha.*]

Roe[2]

roe·buck (rō′buk′) *n. pl.,* **roe·bucks** or **roe·buck.** a male roe deer.

roent·gen (rent′gən) *n.* the international unit for measuring the intensity of X rays or gamma rays. [From Wilhelm K. *Roentgen,* 1845–1923, the German scientist who discovered X rays.]

rog·er (roj′ər) *interj.* **1.** in radio communications, message received and understood. **2.** *Informal.* all right or okay.

rogue (rōg) *n.* **1.** a person who is dishonest and deceitful; scoundrel. **2.** a person who is mischievous and playful.

3. a wild animal, especially an elephant, of a dangerous or savage nature, living apart from the herd.

ro·guer·y (rō′gər ē) *n. pl.,* **ro·guer·ies. 1.** dishonest and deceitful actions or behavior. **2.** playfully mischievous actions or behavior.

rogues′ gallery, a collection of photographs of known criminals and suspects kept by police to aid in making identifications.

ro·guish (rō′gish) *adj.* **1.** dishonest and deceitful. **2.** playfully mischievous: *a roguish wink.* —**ro′guish·ly,** *adv.* —**ro′guish·ness,** *n.*

roil (roil) *v.t.* **1.** to make (liquid) muddy or unsettled by stirring up sediment. **2.** to disturb or make angry; vex.

rois·ter (rois′tər) *v.i.* to behave or frolic in a loud or boisterous manner. —**rois′ter·er,** *n.*

Ro·land (rō′lənd) *n.* in French and Italian literature, the hero who fought under Charlemagne and, according to legend, was killed by the Saracens in 778.

role (rōl) *also,* **rôle.** *n.* **1.** a character or part played by an actor. **2.** a part played by anyone or anything; position or function: *He assumed the role of interpreter for the group.* [French *rôle* originally, a roll on which an actor's part was written.]

roll (rōl) *v.i.* **1.** to move by turning over and over: *The ball rolled off the table.* **2.** to move or be moved on rollers or wheels: *The wagon rolled down the street.* **3.** to turn over many times: *The dog rolled in the mud.* **4.** to move or extend in a smooth, rising and falling manner: *The fog rolled in from the water.* **5.** to pass or go: *The years roll on.* **6.** to turn around wholly or partially: *His eyes rolled in amazement.* **7.** to rock or move from side to side; sway: *The ship rolled violently in the storm.* **8.** to make a deep, continuous sound; rumble: *The drums rolled.* **9.** *Informal.* to make progress or start: *Let's get this project rolling.* —*v.t.* **1.** to cause to move by turning over and over: *to roll a hoop.* **2.** to move (something) by means of rollers or wheels: *to roll a bed against the wall.* **3.** to wrap (something) around on itself or on something else; shape into a ball or cylinder: *to roll up a blanket.* **4.** to enclose or wrap in a covering: *She rolled the old clothes in a newspaper.* **5.** to spread out, flatten, or make smooth with a roller: *to roll metal into sheets, to roll dough for cookies.* **6.** to cause to rock from side to side: *The strong winds rolled the boat.* **7.** to pronounce (a speech sound, especially the sound of *r*) with a trill. **8.** to turn (the eyes) around, wholly or partly. **9.** to cast (dice). —*n.* **1.** a ball or cylinder formed by winding something round and round; something rolled up: *a roll of stamps, a roll of wallpaper.* **2.** a list of names of people belonging to a group: *a class roll.* **3.** a mass of something that is rounded or cylindrical. **4.** an individual piece of baked bread dough. **5.** any food, such as meat or cake, that is rolled up. **6.** a rolling or swaying motion: *The roll of the boat was making us dizzy.* **7.** a rapid, continuous series of short sounds, as those made by beating on a drum. **8.** see **roller. 9.** the act of rolling.

roll call, the act of calling a list of names, such as those registered in a class, to find out who is present.

roll·er (rō′lər) *n.* **1.** a cylinder on which something is rolled or wound up: *the roller of a window shade.* **2.** a cylinder that smooths, spreads out, flattens, or crushes: *a*

at; āpe; cär; end; mē; it; īce; hot; ōld; fôrk; wood; fool; oil; out; up; turn; sing; thin; **th**is; hw in white; zh in treasure. The symbol ə stands for the sound of **a** in about, **e** in taken, **i** in pencil, **o** in lemon, and **u** in circus.

paint roller. **3.** a small wheel on which something is rolled: *We had to put the piano on rollers before we could move it.* **4.** a hollow cylinder of wire mesh or plastic on which hair is rolled up. **5.** a long, swelling wave breaking on a shoreline. **6.** a person who rolls.

roller coaster, an amusement ride consisting of a series of open, attached cars that move at high speeds over a track having sharp turns and sudden, steep inclines.

roll·er·skate (rō′lər skāt′) *v.i.,* **roll·er·skat·ed, roll·er·skat·ing.** to skate on roller skates.

roller skate, a skate having small wheels on the bottom, used for skating on a flat surface, such as a sidewalk.

rol·lick (rol′ik) *v.i.* to behave in a carefree, joyous manner; frolic.

rol·lick·ing (rol′i king) *adj.* carefree and joyous; merry; frolicking.

Roller skates

rolling pin, a smooth, usually wooden, cylinder with a handle at each end, used to roll out dough.

rolling stock, locomotives, cars, and other wheeled vehicles of a railroad.

ro·ly-po·ly (rō′lē pō′lē) *adj.* short and plump; pudgy: *a roly-poly child.* —*n. pl.,* **ro·ly-po·lies.** a short, plump person or thing.

Rom. **1.** Roman. **2.** Romans. **3.** Romance (languages).

ro·maine (rō mān′) *n.* **1.** the narrow crisp leaves of a lettuce plant, forming a long loose head. **2.** the plant bearing these leaves.

Ro·man (rō′mən) *adj.* **1.** of or relating to ancient or modern Rome, its people, or their culture. **2.** of or relating to the Roman Catholic Church or its members. **3.** *usually,* **roman.** of or designating the most widely used style of type or lettering, characterized by upright letters. This sentence is in roman type. —*n.* **1.** a person who was born or is living in Rome. **2.** a person who lived in ancient Rome. **3.** *usually,* **roman.** roman type or lettering.

Roman Catholic **1.** of, relating to, or characteristic of the Roman Catholic Church. **2.** a member of the Roman Catholic Church.

Roman Catholic Church, the Christian church that recognizes the pope as its supreme head.

Roman Catholicism, the beliefs, practices, and system of government of the Roman Catholic Church.

ro·mance (rō mans′, rō′mans) *n.* **1.** a love affair. **2.** a quality of love, excitement, mystery, or adventure: *The dim lights gave a sense of romance to the room.* **3.** a story or poem dealing with heroes and their deeds, especially one about knights and chivalry: *the romances of King Arthur and his knights of the Round Table.* **4.** a story about love or adventure in mysterious or faraway places; fanciful or exaggerated story. —*v.,* **ro·manced, ro·manc·ing.** —*v.i.* **1.** to behave or speak in a romantic way. **2.** to make up or tell fanciful stories. —*v.t. Informal.* to make love to; court; woo. —**ro·manc′er,** *n.*

Romance languages, the languages developed from Latin, including French, Italian, Spanish, Portuguese, Romanian, Catalan, and Provençal.

Roman Empire, the empire of ancient Rome, extending from Britain to North Africa to the Persian Gulf. It was begun under the Emperor Augustus in 27 B.C. and lasted until A.D. 395, when it was divided into the Eastern Roman Empire and the Western Roman Empire.

Ro·man·esque (rō′mə nesk′) *adj.* of, relating to, or in the style of architecture that was widely used in western Europe during the eleventh and twelfth centuries, charac-

terized by massive stone construction, rounded arches and vaults, and elaborate ornamentation. —*n.* the Romanesque style of architecture.

Ro·ma·ni·a (rō mā′nē ə) *also,* **Rou·ma·ni·a, Ru·ma·ni·a.** *n.* a country in southeastern Europe, in the northeastern part of the Balkan Peninsula. Capital, Bucharest. Area, 91,700 sq. mi. Pop. (1971 est.), 20,470,000.

Ro·ma·ni·an (rō mā′nē ən) *also,* **Rou·ma·ni·an, Ru·ma·ni·an.** *n.* **1.** a person who was born or is living in Romania. **2.** the language of Romania. —*adj.* of or relating to Romania, its people, or their language.

Roman nose, a nose with a jutting or prominent bridge.

Roman numeral, any of the numerals I, V, X, L, C, D, M, or any combination of these, used in the ancient Roman numbering system. I = 1, V = 5, X = 10, L = 50, C = 100, D = 500, and M = 1000. The value of any combination of numerals is their sum, except when a smaller numeral is placed in front of a larger numeral. In such a case, the smaller is subtracted from the larger. Thus VI = 6, but IV = 4.

Ro·ma·nov (rō′mə nôf′) *also,* **Ro·ma·noff.** *n.* **1.** the dynasty that ruled Russia from 1613 to 1917. **2. Mi·kha·il Feo·do·ro·vich** (mi kī ēl′ fyô′dər ə vich). 1596–1645, the czar of Russia from 1613 to 1645, founder of this dynasty.

Ro·mans (rō′mənz) *n.,pl.* a book of the New Testament, a letter from Saint Paul to the Christians of Rome.

ro·man·tic (rō man′tik) *adj.* **1.** of, relating to, or characterized by romance: *a romantic story.* **2.** having thoughts and feelings of love and adventure: *a romantic person.* **3.** having a quality of adventure, excitement, or mystery: *the romantic life of Robin Hood.* **4.** suitable for love or romance: *The candlelit room created a romantic atmosphere.* **5.** not practical or real; idealized: *The young man had romantic notions about living away from home.* **6.** *also,* **Romantic.** of or relating to romanticism in art, literature, or music. —*n.* **1.** a romantic person. **2.** a romanticist. —**ro·man′ti·cal·ly,** *adv.*

ro·man·ti·cism (rō man′tə siz′əm) *n.* a style of literature, music, and art during the last part of the eighteenth century and the first half of the nineteenth century. It is characterized by strong feeling, love of nature, and freedom of form.

ro·man·ti·cist (rō man′tə sist) *n.* a person who follows the principles of romanticism in literature, music, or art.

ro·man·ti·cize (rō man′tə sīz′) *v.,* **ro·man·ti·cized, ro·man·ti·ciz·ing.** —*v.t.* to give a romantic spirit or character to; make romantic: *to romanticize one's life.* —*v.i.* to act, talk, or think romantically.

Rom·a·ny (rom′ə nē, rō′mə nē) *n. pl.,* **Rom·a·nies.** **1.** a Gypsy. **2.** the language of the Gypsies. —*adj.* of or relating to the Gypsies or their language.

Rome (rōm) *n.* **1.** the capital of Italy, on the Tiber River, the former capital and center of the ancient Roman republic and the Roman Empire. It is the site of Vatican City, the headquarters of the pope and the Roman Catholic Church. Pop. (1970 est.), 2,778,872. **2.** the ancient Roman republic. **3.** the ancient Roman Empire.

Ro·me·o (rō′mē ō′) *n.* the hero of William Shakespeare's play *Romeo and Juliet.*

romp (romp) *v.i.* to play or frolic in a lively or noisy way. —*n.* lively or noisy play; frolic: *The boy and his dog went for a romp in the woods.* —**romp′er,** *n.*

romp·ers (rom′pərz) *n.,pl.* a loose one-piece garment worn by young children.

Rom·u·lus (rom′yə ləs) *n. Roman Mythology.* the founder and first king of the city of Rome. He and his twin brother, Remus, were abandoned as infants and raised by a wolf.

rood (rood) *n.* **1.** a unit of land measure equal to 40 square rods or one-fourth of an acre. **2.** a cross or crucifix, especially a large crucifix over an altar.

roof (roof, roof) *n.* **1.** the outer covering of the top of a building. **2.** something like a roof in position or use: *the roof of the mouth, the roof of a car.* —*v.t.* to provide or cover with a roof: *to roof a house.* —**roof′like′,** *adj.*

roof·er (roo′fər, roof′ər) *n.* a person who builds or repairs roofs.

roof·ing (roo′fing, roof′ing) *n.* the material used to build roofs.

roof·tree (roof′trē′, roof′trē′) *n.* the ridgepole of a roof.

rook[1] (rook) *n.* a European bird that nests in colonies, closely related to and resembling the crow. —*v.t. Informal.* to cheat; swindle. [Old English *hrōc.*]

rook[2] (rook) *n. Chess.* any of the four pieces, two to each player, that may move any number of spaces parallel to the sides of the board. Also, **castle.** [Old French *roc.*]

rook·er·y (rook′ər ē) *n. pl.,* **rook·er·ies. 1.** a breeding place or colony of rooks. **2.** a breeding place or colony of other birds or of animals, such as penguins and seals.

rook·ie (rook′ē) *n. Informal.* **1.** an inexperienced recruit, as on a police force. **2.** an inexperienced athlete, especially a player in his or her first season with a professional sports team. **3.** any beginner; novice.

Rook[2]

room (room, room) *n.* **1.** an area that is or may be occupied by something; space: *There was no room to park the car.* **2.** an area within a house or other building that is separated or set off by walls or partitions: *a house with seven rooms.* **3.** the people in such an area: *The whole room stared as she walked in.* **4.** a suitable chance or opportunity; possibility: *There is room for improvement in his work.* **5. rooms.** living quarters; lodgings: *The student took rooms near the campus.* —*v.i.* to live in a room or rooms; lodge: *Rick and Jack roomed together at college.*

room and board, lodging and meals.

room·er (roo′mər, room′ər) *n.* a person who occupies a rented room or rooms in another's house; lodger.

room·ful (room′fool′, room′fool′) *n. pl.,* **room·fuls. 1.** as much or as many as a room will hold: *a roomful of furniture.* **2.** the people or objects in a room.

rooming house, a house with furnished rooms for rent.

room·mate (room′māt′, room′māt′) *n.* a person or persons with whom one shares a room or rooms.

room·y (roo′mē, room′ē) *adj.,* **room·i·er, room·i·est.** having plenty of room; large; spacious. —**room′i·ness,** *n.*

Roo·se·velt (rō′zə velt′) **1. (Anna) Eleanor.** 1884–1962, U.S. humanitarian, writer, and diplomat; wife of Franklin D. Roosevelt. **2. Franklin Del·a·no** (del′ə nō′). 1882–1945, the thirty-second president of the United States, from 1933 to 1945. **3. Theodore.** 1858–1919, the twenty-sixth president of the United States, from 1901 to 1909.

roost (roost) *n.* **1.** a perch on which birds rest or sleep. **2.** a building or other place for birds to rest or sleep for the night. **3.** a place in which people rest, stay, or gather. —*v.i.* **1.** to rest or sleep on a roost as a bird does. **2.** to rest or stay for the night.

roost·er (roos′tər) *n.* a male domestic fowl. Also, **cock.**

root[1] (root, root) *n.* **1.** the lower part of a plant that grows downward, serving to hold the plant in the soil. Roots absorb water and dissolved minerals from the soil and store food. **2.** any underground part of a plant, such as a tuber. **3.** an attached or embedded part of an organ or body structure: *the root of a tooth, the root of a hair.* **4.** a part from which anything comes or develops; origin; source: *The teacher traced the roots of the Industrial Revolution.*

5. the basic part; base; core: *We must get to the root of the problem.* **6. roots.** the condition or feeling of being settled and belonging to a particular place, society, or tradition: *He had moved so often that he had no roots anywhere.* **7.** a word to which suffixes, prefixes, and combining forms are added to form new words. *Faith* is the root of *faithful, faithless,* and *unfaithful.* **8.** *Mathematics.* a quantity that, when multiplied by itself a specified number of times, produces a given quantity. 3 is the square root of 9 and the cube root of 27. —*v.i.* **1.** to develop roots and begin to grow: *These plants will not root in this poor soil.* **2.** to be or become firmly fixed, settled, or established. —*v.t.* **1.** to fix or establish firmly: *Fear rooted him to the spot.* **2.** to pull, tear, or dig by or as by the roots; remove completely: *to root up a weed, to root out a troublemaker.* [Old Norse *rōt.*] —**root′like′,** *adj.*

  to take root. a. to develop roots and begin to grow. **b.** to become firmly fixed, settled, or established.

root[2] (root, root) *v.i.* **1.** to turn up or dig in the earth with the snout or nose: *The pig rooted about for food.* **2.** to search for something; rummage: *We rooted through the closet for the missing shoe.* [Old English *wrōtan.*]

root[3] (root, root) *v.i.* **1.** to give encouragement to a contestant or team, as by applauding or shouting: *Everyone was rooting for our team to win.* **2.** to wish success to someone or something: *We are all rooting for him to win the scholarship.* [Possibly from *root*[2].] —**root′er,** *n.*

root beer, a soft drink made from the juice of the roots of various plants, such as sarsaparilla or sassafras.

root hair, a thin, hairlike growth on a plant root that absorbs water and dissolved minerals from the soil.

root·less (root′lis, root′lis) *adj.* **1.** without ties to a particular place, society, or tradition. **2.** having no roots.

root·let (root′lit, root′lit) *n.* a small root.

root·stock (root′stok′, root′stok′) *n.* another word for **rhizome.**

Root hairs

rope (rōp) *n.* **1.** a strong cord made of twisted or intertwined strands of fiber, wire, or similar material. **2.** a number of things joined together by twisting, twining, or threading: *a rope of pearls.* **3.** a hangman's noose. **4.** a lasso. **5.** a sticky, stringy mass or thread. —*v.,* **roped, rop·ing.** —*v.t.* **1.** to tie, bind, or fasten with a rope. **2.** to separate or enclose with a rope or ropes: *to rope off a street for a parade.* **3.** to catch with a lasso. —*v.i.* to form sticky, stringy threads. —**rop′er,** *n.*

  to know the ropes. *Informal.* to be familiar with all the details of an operation or activity.

  to learn the ropes. to learn all the details or aspects of an operation or activity.

rop·y (rō′pē) *adj.,* **rop·i·er, rop·i·est. 1.** forming or having sticky, stringy threads: *a ropy syrup.* **2.** like a rope or cord. —**rop′i·ness,** *n.*

Roque·fort cheese (rōk′fərt) a strong, cream-colored cheese having a blue mold running through it. [From *Roquefort,* a village in France where it was first made.]

---

at; āpe; cär; end; mē; it; īce; hot; ōld; fôrk; wood; fool; oil; out; up; turn; sing; thin; this; hw in white; zh in treasure. The symbol ə stands for the sound of **a** in about, **e** in taken, **i** in pencil, **o** in lemon, and **u** in circus.

Ro·sa·ri·o (rō zär′ē ō′) *n.* a port city in east-central Argentina. Pop. (1970), 750,455.

ro·sa·ry (rō′zər ē) *n. pl.*, **ro·sa·ries. 1.** in the Roman Catholic Church, a string of beads used for counting in the saying of prayers. **2.** a series of prayers said with these beads.

rose¹ (rōz) *n.* **1.** the fragrant flower of any of a large group of plants. Roses are usually red, pink, yellow, or white. **2.** the woody plant bearing this flower, having thorny stems. **3.** a pinkish-red color. **4.** something resembling a rose in shape or form, as a rosette. —*adj.* **1.** having the color rose. **2.** designating a large family of flowering plants that grow in temperate parts of the world, many of which are cultivated for their fruit or flowers. [Old English *rose.*]

Tea rose Shrub rose
Hybrid perpetual rose
Roses

rose² (rōz) the past tense of **rise.**

ro·se·ate (rō′zē it, rō′zē āt′) *adj.* **1.** resembling a rose in color; rosy. **2.** full of hope or optimism; cheerful.

rose·bud (rōz′bud′) *n.* the bud of a rose.

rose·bush (rōz′boosh′) *n. pl.*, **rose·bush·es.** a bush or vine bearing roses.

rose·mar·y (rōz′mer′ē) *n. pl.*, **rose·mar·ies. 1.** the fragrant leaves of an evergreen shrub, used as a seasoning. **2.** the shrub bearing these leaves, having pale blue flowers.

ro·sette (rō zet′) *n.* **1.** an ornament, usually made of gathered ribbon in the shape of a rose, used as a decoration or a badge of honor or office. **2.** something shaped like a rose, as a circular carved ornament used in architecture.

rose water, a preparation usually made by mixing oil of roses with water, used in cosmetics and in cooking.

rose window, a circular window, usually made up of stained glass sections that radiate from a center.

rose·wood (rōz′wood′) *n.* **1.** a hard, strongly grained, dark red wood of any of several tropical evergreen trees, widely used to make fine furniture. **2.** the tree yielding this wood.

Rose window

Rosh Ha·sha·nah (rōsh′ hə shä′nə) the Jewish New Year, occurring in September or early October.

ros·in (roz′in) *n.* **1.** a hard, brittle substance obtained by heating crude turpentine and removing the surface oil. It is used in the manufacture of paints and other products, and is rubbed on the surface of certain items, such as violin bows and dancers' shoes, to make them less slippery. **2.** see **resin** (*def. 1*). —*v.t.* to rub or cover with rosin.

Ross, Betsy (rôs) 1752–1836, American woman who is said to have made the first American flag.

Ros·si·ni, Gio·ac·chi·no An·to·nio (rō sē′nē; jō′ä kē′nō än tōn′yō) 1792–1868, Italian composer of operas.

Ross Sea, a large inlet of the Pacific Ocean, on the coast of Antarctica.

ros·ter (ros′tər) *n.* **1.** a list of military officers and men enrolled for duty. **2.** any list of names.

Ros·tov (ros tôf′) *n.* a port city in the southwestern Soviet Union, on the Don River. Pop. (1979), 934,000.

ros·trum (ros′trəm) *n. pl.*, **ros·trums** or **ros·tra** (ros′trə). a raised area, such as a platform or pulpit, used for public speaking.

ros·y (rō′zē) *adj.*, **ros·i·er, ros·i·est. 1.** having the color rose; pinkish-red: *The baby's cheeks were rosy from the cold.* **2.** full of hope or optimism; bright: *a rosy outlook on life.* —**ros′i·ly,** *adv.* —**ros′i·ness,** *n.*

rot (rot) *v.*, **rot·ted, rot·ting.** —*v.i.* **1.** to become rotten; decay: *The apples rotted on the tree.* **2.** to become useless or worthless. —*v.t.* to cause to become rotten; decay: *The damp air in the basement rotted the old wooden chest.* —*n.* **1.** the process of rotting. **2.** something that is rotting or rotted. **3.** a disease of plants caused by any of various fungi or bacteria. **4.** *Informal.* nonsense; rubbish; trash.

ro·ta·ry (rō′tər ē) *adj.* **1.** turning or designed to turn around an axis; rotating. **2.** having a part or parts that rotate: *a rotary plow.* —*n. pl.*, **ro·ta·ries.** another word for **traffic circle.**

rotary engine 1. an internal-combustion engine in which circularly arranged cylinders revolve about a fixed crankshaft. **2.** any engine that produces rotation or torque directly, rather than by back-and-forth movement.

ro·tate (rō′tāt) *v.*, **ro·tat·ed, ro·tat·ing.** —*v.i.* **1.** to turn around on an axis: *The earth rotates from west to east.* **2.** to change in a fixed order; alternate regularly: *The guards will rotate every four hours.* —*v.t.* **1.** to cause to turn on an axis. **2.** to cause to change in a fixed order; alternate (something) regularly: *to rotate crops.*

ro·ta·tion (rō tā′shən) *n.* **1.** the act or process of turning on an axis. **2.** one complete turn of such a movement: *The rotation of the earth takes twenty-four hours.* **3.** a change in a fixed order: *the rotation of crops.*

ro·ta·tor (rō′tā tər) *n.* a person or thing that rotates.

ro·ta·to·ry (rō′tə tôr′ē) *adj.* **1.** of, relating to, or characterized by rotation. **2.** causing rotation: *a rotatory muscle.*

ROTC, Reserve Officers' Training Corps, a U.S. military corps in which college and high school students are trained to become officers in the armed services.

rote (rōt) *n.* a mechanical way of doing something.

by rote. in a mechanical way, without attention to meaning: *to recite a lesson by rote.*

ro·tis·se·rie (rō tis′ər ē) *n.* a cooking device or appliance having a rotating spit on which food is roasted.

ro·to·gra·vure (rō′tə grə vyoor′) *n.* **1.** a printing process in which the image to be printed is reproduced on a copper surface in a pattern of depressions. These depressions are then filled with ink and the pattern is transferred under pressure to the surface to be printed. **2.** a picture or print made by this process. **3.** a section of a newspaper printed by this process.

ro·tor (rō′tər) *n.* **1.** the rotating part of a motor or other machine. **2.** a set of large, revolving blades that lifts and moves an aircraft, as a helicopter.

rot·ten (rot′ən) *adj.* **1.** having undergone decomposition or decay from the action of bacteria; decayed: *That is a rotten apple. This meat is rotten.* **2.** likely to break, crack, or give way; weak: *rotten timbers.* **3.** very bad; disagreeable; contemptible: *a rotten movie, rotten weather.* **4.** corrupt, dishonest, or depraved: *Something is rotten in the state of Denmark* (Shakespeare, *Hamlet*). —**rot′ten·ly,** *adv.* —**rot′ten·ness,** *n.*

Rotor

Rot·ter·dam (rot′ər dam′) *n.* a port city in the southwestern Netherlands, near the North Sea. Pop. (1976 est.), 614,800.

ro·tund (rō tund′) *adj.* **1.** rounded; plump: *a rotund man.* **2.** full-toned; deep: *a rotund voice.* —**ro·tund′ly,** *adv.* —**ro·tund′ness,** *n.*

ro·tun·da (rō tun′də) *n.* a circular building or hall, especially one having a dome.

ro·tun·di·ty (rō tun′də tē) *n. pl.,* **ro·tun·di·ties. 1.** the state or condition of being rotund. **2.** something round.

rou·ble (rōō′bəl) another spelling of **ruble.**

rou·é (rōō ā′) *n.* an immoral man; rake.

Rou·en (rōō än′) *n.* a port city in northern France, on the Seine, the site of Joan of Arc's execution.

rouge (rōōzh) *n.* **1.** any of various red or pink cosmetics used to color the cheeks. **2.** a red, powdery pigment, used to polish metal, gems, and glass. —*v.t.,* **rouged, roug·ing.** to color with rouge.

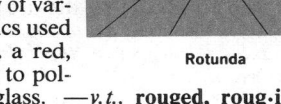

Rotunda

rough (ruf) *adj.* **1.** having an uneven surface; not smooth or level: *the rough bark of a tree, a rough country road.* **2.** characterized by or showing force, violence, or ruggedness: *Ice hockey is a rough game. The little boat battled against the rough seas.* **3.** having or showing a lack of gentleness, refinement, or politeness; harsh; rude: *He has a rough way of dealing with people.* **4.** partly, imperfectly, or hastily made or done: *a rough estimate, a rough sketch.* **5.** in a natural or crude state: *rough, unpolished gems.* **6.** difficult or unpleasant; hard: *He had a rough day at school.* **7.** without luxury, ease, or the usual comforts: *The pioneers in the West led a rough life.* **8.** having a shaggy or uneven texture; coarse: *The dog had a rough coat.* —*v.t.* **1.** to treat violently: *The gang roughed up their hostage before releasing him.* **2.** to plan, shape, or sketch in an incomplete form: *to rough in the details of a drawing, to rough out the plan of a house.* **3.** to make rough; roughen. —*adv.* in a rough manner; roughly. —*n.* **1.** the unmowed part of a golf course surrounding the fairways and greens. **2.** a crude, coarse person; ruffian; rowdy. —**rough′ly,** *adv.* —**rough′ness,** *n.*

  in the rough. in a crude or unfinished condition: *The floor plans for our new house are still in the rough.*

  to rough it. to live without the usual comforts or conveniences: *We plan to rough it on our canoe trip.*

rough·age (ruf′ij) *n.* **1.** coarse food, such as bran or lettuce, that serves to stimulate and aid the movement of food through the intestines. **2.** any rough or coarse material.

rough·en (ruf′ən) *v.t., v.i.* to make or become rough.

rough·hew (ruf′hyōō′) *v.t.,* **rough·hewed, rough·hewed** or **rough·hewn, rough·hew·ing.** to hew (something, as timber or stone) without smoothing or finishing.

rough·house (ruf′hous′) *n.* rough, boisterous play. —*v.i.,* **rough·housed, rough·hous·ing.** to behave or play in a rough, boisterous way.

rough·neck (ruf′nek′) *n. Informal.* a rough, crude person; rowdy.

rough·rid·er (ruf′rī′dər) *n.* a person who breaks in or rides wild horses.

rough·shod (ruf′shod′) *adj.* having horseshoes with calks or other projections to prevent slipping.

  to ride roughshod over. to be cruel or inconsiderate to.

rou·lette (rōō let′) *n.* **1.** a gambling game in which the players bet on which space of a wheel a ball will come to rest in after the wheel has been spun. **2.** a small, toothed wheel, used to make rows of marks, dots, or holes when rolled over a surface.

Rou·ma·ni·a (rōō mā′nē ə) another spelling of **Romania.**

Rou·ma·ni·an (rōō mā′nē ən) another spelling of **Romanian.**

round (round) *adj.* **1.** shaped like a globe or ball: *a round mass of clay, a round grapefruit.* **2.** shaped like a circle; circular, as a tire or hoop: *a round table.* **3.** having a curved surface or outline: *round shoulders.* **4.** not missing any parts; full; complete: *a round dozen.* **5.** full and mellow: *The piano had a rich, round tone.* **6.** pronounced with the lips formed in a nearly oval shape. The *o* in *lone* is a round vowel. —*n.* **1.** something round in shape. **2.** movement in a circle or about an axis; revolution: *the sun's round.* **3. rounds.** a fixed or regular course or route: *a postman's rounds.* **4.** a series of actions or events: *a round of parties.* **5.** a single outburst, as of applause or cheering: *a round of applause.* **6.** any of various periods into which certain sports and games are divided: *a boxing match of ten rounds.* **7.** a complete game: *a round of golf.* **8.** a short song that is sung by three or more voices, each voice beginning the song in turn at a different time. **9.** a single discharge of a gun or other firearm. **10.** a charge of ammunition for a single shot. **11.** a cut of beef just above the hind leg between the leg and the rump. **12.** see **round dance.** —*v.t.* **1.** to make round: *Dad rounded the corners of the table he was making.* **2.** to pass or travel to the other side of; go around: *The car rounded the corner. The ship rounded the tip of the peninsula.* **3.** to express as a round number: *to round 49.8 to 50.* **4.** to make complete; finish or perfect: *We are such stuff as dreams are made on; and our little life is rounded with a sleep* (Shakespeare, *The Tempest*). *That coin rounds out his collection.* **5.** to pronounce with the lips formed in a nearly oval shape. —*v.i.* to become round. —*adv.* around: *The top spun round and round.* —*prep.* around: *The crowd gathered round the speaker.* —**round′ness,** *n.*

  in the round. a. having seats surrounding a central stage: *a theater in the round.* **b.** fully carved or sculptured on all sides, standing free from any background: *a statue in the round.*

  to round up. to drive or gather together: *to round up stray cattle, to round up all the children at a party.*

▲ In the United States, **around** is much more common than **round** as an adverb or a preposition: *They hunted around until they found the still* (William Faulkner). In British use, **round** is generally preferred: *He gripped my wrist and twisted it round* (George Orwell). The two words, however, may be used interchangeably.

round·a·bout (round′ə bout′) *adj.* not straight or direct: *a roundabout route, a roundabout way of saying something.*

round dance 1. a ballroom dance characterized by circular or revolving movements, as the waltz or the polka. **2.** a folk dance in which the dancers move in a circle.

roun·de·lay (round′əl ā′) *n.* **1.** a song in which a section, phrase, or line, especially the first verse, is continually repeated. **2.** a dance performed in a circle.

Round·head (round′hed′) *n.* a member of the Puritan

R

at; āpe; cär; end; mē; it; īce; hot; ōld; fôrk; wood; fōōl; oil; out; up; turn; sing; thin; **this**; hw in white; zh in treasure. The symbol ə stands for the sound of **a** in about, **e** in taken, **i** in pencil, **o** in lemon, and **u** in circus.

or Parliamentary party during the English civil war from 1642 to 1652. [From the short-cropped hair of the members of this party, as distinguished from the long hair of their opponents, the Cavaliers.]

round·house (round'hous') *n.* *pl.,* **round·hous·es** (round'hou'ziz). **1.** a circular building with a large turntable in the center, used for housing, repairing, and turning locomotives around. **2.** a cabin on the rear part of the quarterdeck of a ship.

round·ish (roun'dish) *adj.* somewhat round.

round·ly (round'lē) *adv.* **1.** in a frank, straightforward manner; bluntly: *He refused the offer roundly.* **2.** in a complete manner; fully; thoroughly: *to be beaten roundly.* **3.** in a round form.

round number, a number expressed to the nearest whole number or to a multiple of five or ten. 500 is the round number for 498, and 6 is the round number for 5⅞.

round robin, a tournament, as in tennis, in which each player or team plays every other player or team.

Round Table 1. a table around which King Arthur and his knights sat. It was round to prevent quarrels about the order of seating. **2.** King Arthur and his knights. **3. round table. a.** a group of persons gathered for an informal conference or discussion. **b.** such a conference or discussion.

round trip, a trip to a place and back to the starting point. —**round'-trip'**, *adj.*

round·up (round'up') *n.* **1.** the act of driving scattered cattle together, as for counting, branding, or selling. **2.** the men and horses that do this. **3.** any gathering together, as of people, objects, or facts: *a news roundup, a roundup of criminal suspects.*

round·worm (round'wurm') *n.* any of a large group of worms having thin, round bodies. Roundworms are found living in water and soil or as parasites in the intestines of man and other animals.

rouse (rouz) *v.,* **roused, rous·ing.** —*v.t.* **1.** to awaken from sleep, unconsciousness, rest, or the like: *Sounds of thunder roused us.* **2.** to stir up; excite: *His speech roused the crowd to a frenzy.* —*v.i.* **1.** to awaken from sleep, unconsciousness, or the like. **2.** to become active or excited. —**rous'er,** *n.*

Rous·seau (rōō sō') **1. Hen·ri** (än rē'). 1844–1910, French painter. **2. Jean Jacques** (zhän zhäk). 1712–1778, French philosopher and writer, born in Switzerland.

roust·a·bout (roust'tə bout') *n.* an unskilled laborer, as on a ranch or dock, or in an oil field or circus.

rout[1] (rout) *n.* **1.** an overwhelming or complete defeat. **2.** a disorderly flight or retreat after a defeat. —*v.t.* **1.** to defeat overwhelmingly: *to rout a team in football.* **2.** to put to disorderly flight or retreat: *to rout enemy troops.* [Middle French *route* crowd; literally, a broken group.]

rout[2] (rout) *v.t.* **1.** to uncover or find by searching; bring to view; discover: *He routed out his old baseball glove from his closet.* **2.** to drive or force out; make leave: *The hurricane routed us from our homes.* **3.** to dig up with the snout. —*v.i.* **1.** to dig with the snout: *The pig routed about in the ground.* **2.** to search; rummage. [A form of *root*[2].]

route (rōōt, rout) *n.* **1.** a course, road, or way for travel: *a trade route.* **2.** a regular course or territory covered by a salesman or deliveryman: *a milk route, a newspaper route, a mail route.* —*v.t.,* **rout·ed, rout·ing. 1.** to arrange the route for: *Our travel agent routed us across the country.* **2.** to send by a certain route; dispatch: *The company routes its goods through New York.*

rou·tine (rōō tēn') *n.* **1.** a fixed way or method of doing something; regular procedure: *Shopping for groceries is part of her daily routine.* **2.** sameness of actions or procedures: *The boys were soon bored with the routine of camp life.* **3.** a theatrical act or part of an act, such as a funny

story or a dance number. —*adj.* **1.** according to or using routine; regular; habitual: *routine chores.* **2.** not creative or original; commonplace; dull: *The actor gave a routine performance.* —**rou·tine'ly,** *adv.*

rove (rōv) *v.,* **roved, rov·ing.** —*v.i.* to wander aimlessly from place to place; roam about: *We roved about the park all afternoon.* —*v.t.* to wander over or through.

rov·er[1] (rō'vər) *n.* a person who roves; wanderer. [*Rove*[1] + *-er*[1].]

rov·er[2] (rō'vər) *n.* **1.** a pirate. **2.** a pirate ship. [Middle Dutch *rover* a robber.]

row[1] (rō) *n.* **1.** a series of people or things arranged in a line; line: *a row of trees.* **2.** a line of seats, as in a theater or classroom: *We were seated in the last row.* **3.** a line of houses on a street. **4.** a street lined with buildings on both sides. [Old English *rāw, rǣw.*]

row[2] (rō) *v.i.* to use oars to propel a boat. —*v.t.* **1.** to propel (a boat) by the use of oars. **2.** to carry in a rowboat: *to row a person to shore.* —*n.* a trip in a rowboat: *It is a long row across the lake.* [Old English *rōwan.*] —**row'er,** *n.*

row[3] (rou) *n.* a noisy quarrel, fight, or disturbance; clamor. [Probably from *rouse.*]

row·boat (rō'bōt') *n.* a boat propelled by oars.

row·dy (rou'dē) *n. pl.,* **row·dies.** a rude, boisterous, disorderly person. —*adj.,* **row·di·er, row·di·est.** rude; boisterous; disorderly: *a rowdy crowd.* —**row'di·ness,** *n.*

row·el (rou'əl) *n.* a small wheel with sharp points, as on the end of a rid-er's spur.

row·lock (rō'lok') *n.* another word for **oarlock.**

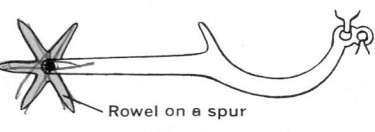
Rowel on a spur

Rowel

roy·al (roi'əl) *adj.* **1.** of or relating to a king or queen: *royal blood, a royal family.* **2.** belonging to or serving a king or queen: *a royal palace, a royal navy.* **3.** coming from or by a king or queen: *a royal command.* **4.** suitable for or characteristic of a king or queen; magnificent; majestic: *a royal banquet, a royal welcome.* —**roy'al·ly,** *adv.*

roy·al·ist (roi'ə list) *n.* **1.** a person who supports a king or queen or a royal government. **2. Royalist.** a supporter of King Charles I in his struggle with Parliament from 1641 to 1649; Cavalier. **3. Royalist.** an American colonist who supported the British in the American Revolution; Tory. —*adj.* of or relating to a royalist.

Royal Oak, a city in southeastern Michigan. Pop. (1970), 85,499.

roy·al·ty (roi'əl tē) *n. pl.,* **roy·al·ties. 1.** a royal person, such as a king, queen, prince, or princess. **2.** royal persons as a group. **3.** the position or power of a king or queen: *A crown is a symbol of royalty.* **4.** a share of the profits from the sale or performance of a work, such as a play or musical composition, paid to the author or composer. **5.** a payment to the owner of a patent for the use of it.

rpm, revolutions per minute.

R.R., railroad.

R.S.F.S.R., Russian Soviet Federated Socialist Republic.

RSVP, please reply. [An abbreviation of French *r*(épondez) *s*('il) *v*(ous) *p*(lâit).]

rte., route

Ru, the symbol for ruthenium.

rub (rub) *v.,* **rubbed, rub·bing.** —*v.t.* **1.** to apply friction or pressure over the surface of: *The swimmer rubbed his leg to ease the cramp.* **2.** to apply or spread (something) with friction or pressure: *He rubbed lotion on his sunburned arm.* **3.** to move (an object or objects) against another or each other: *He rubbed his hands together.*

4. to subject (something) to pressure and friction in order to clean, polish, or make smooth: *She rubbed the silverware until it gleamed.* **5.** to irritate or wear down by friction: *The elastic on my cuff is rubbing my wrist.* **6.** to remove or erase by friction or pressure: *to rub off tarnish, to rub out ink stains.* —*v.i.* **1.** to move with friction or pressure; press: *The cat rubbed gently against his leg.* **2.** to be able to be removed or erased by friction: *This ink rubs out easily.* —*n.* **1.** the act of rubbing. **2.** something that hurts or annoys, as a rude remark. **3.** a difficulty or hindrance: *Aye, there's the rub* (Shakespeare, *Hamlet*).

> **to rub down.** to massage: *to rub down an athlete after a game.*

> **to rub it in.** *Slang.* to keep mentioning a person's failures or mistakes.

> **to rub the wrong way.** *Slang.* to irritate or annoy.

rub·ber¹ (rub′ər) *n.* **1.** a tough, elastic, waterproof substance obtained from the milky liquid in any of several tropical trees. **2.** an overshoe made of this substance. **3.** any of various other articles made of this substance, such as a pencil eraser. **4.** a person or thing that rubs. —*adj.* made of rubber: *a rubber ball.* [*Rub* + *-er¹*; originally referring to a pencil eraser.] —**rub′ber·like′,** *adj.*

rub·ber² (rub′ər) *n.* **1.** in bridge and other games, a series of an odd number of games, usually three, in which the final winner is the side that wins the most games. **2.** any game that breaks a tie and determines the outcome of a series of games. [Of uncertain origin.]

rubber band, an elastic loop of rubber, used to hold things together.

rub·ber·ize (rub′ə rīz′) *v.t.,* **rub·ber·ized, rub·ber·iz·ing.** to coat or treat with rubber.

rubber plant **1.** a tropical evergreen plant, found growing wild in India and Malaya, and widely raised as a houseplant, having a single woody stem, and thick leathery leaves. **2.** any of various plants yielding rubber.

rub·ber-stamp (rub′ər stamp′) *v.t.* **1.** to print or mark with a rubber stamp. **2.** *Informal.* to approve or endorse as a matter of routine: *The state legislature rubber-stamps all the bills proposed by the governor.*

rubber stamp, a hand stamp with a raised message or design made of rubber that can be inked and used to print dates, names, and the like.

rub·ber·y (rub′ər ē) *adj.* like rubber; elastic.

rub·bish (rub′ish) *n.* **1.** useless waste material; refuse; trash. **2.** worthless talk or thoughts; nonsense.

rub·ble (rub′əl) *n.* **1.** rough broken pieces of solid material, as stone or rock: *The rescuers searched through the rubble of the bombed building for survivors.* **2.** masonry made of rough, irregular stones.

rub·down (rub′doun′) *n.* a rubbing of the body; massage.

ru·bel·la (rōō bel′ə) *n.* a contagious disease usually producing a pink, blotchy rash; German measles.

Ru·bens, Peter Paul (rōō′bənz) 1577–1640, Flemish painter.

Ru·bi·con (rōō′bi kon′) *n.* a stream in north-central Italy that formed the northern boundary of the ancient Roman republic. Julius Caesar's crossing of the Rubicon in 49 B.C. began a civil war in Rome that led to his dictatorship.

ru·bi·cund (rōō′bi kənd) *adj.* reddish; ruddy.

ru·bid·i·um (rōō bid′ē əm) *n.* a soft, light, silver-white metallic element similar to potassium and sodium, used in photoelectric cells and electron tubes. Symbol: **Rb**

ru·ble (rōō′bəl) *also,* **rou·ble.** *n.* the monetary unit of the Soviet Union.

ru·bric (rōō′brik) *n.* **1.** the title, chapter heading, or other division in a book or manuscript, printed in red or in a special color or design to set it off from the rest of the text. **2.** a direction or rule for the conducting of a religious ceremony, inserted in a prayer book, missal, or similar book. **3.** any established rule or guide.

ru·by (rōō′bē) *n. pl.,* **ru·bies.** **1.** a transparent red variety of corundum, valued as a precious stone. **2.** a deep red color. —*adj.* having the color ruby.

ruck·sack (ruk′sak′) *n.* a kind of knapsack.

ruck·us (ruk′əs) *n. Slang.* a loud commotion; uproar.

rud·der (rud′ər) *n.* **1.** a broad, flat, movable piece of wood, metal, or similar material, attached vertically at the rear of a boat or ship and used in steering. **2.** a similar piece at the tail of an aircraft.

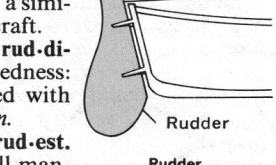

Rudder

rud·dy (rud′ē) *adj.,* **rud·di·er, rud·di·est.** **1.** of or having a healthy redness: *a ruddy complexion.* **2.** tinged with red; reddish. —**rud′di·ness,** *n.*

rude (rōōd) *adj.,* **rud·er, rud·est.** **1.** not polite or courteous; ill-mannered; uncivil: *a rude reply, a rude child.* **2.** roughly made or formed; showing a lack of skill or polish; crude: *People of the Stone Age used rude tools.* **3.** rough or violent; forceful: *a rude shove.* **4.** not developed or advanced; primitive: *a rude culture.* —**rude′ly,** *adv.* —**rude′ness,** *n.*

ru·di·ment (rōō′də mənt) *n.* **1.** *usually,* **rudiments.** the first or basic principle of something: *to learn the rudiments of baseball.* **2.** *usually,* **rudiments.** the beginning or early stage of something: *the rudiments of civilization.* **3.** *Biology.* an organ or part that is not completely developed, especially one that has no function in the adult individual, as the appendix.

ru·di·men·ta·ry (rōō′də men′tər ē) *adj.* **1.** of or having the nature of a first principle; elementary: *rudimentary knowledge.* **2.** in a beginning or early stage of development. **3.** *Biology.* incompletely or imperfectly developed: *A penguin has rudimentary wings.*

rue¹ (rōō) *v.t.,* **rued, ru·ing.** to feel sorrow or remorse for; regret: *He rued the day he left home.* —*n.* sorrow; regret. [Old English *hrēowan* to make sad.]

rue² (rōō) *n.* any of a large family of strong-smelling plants, having yellow flowers. [Old French *rue.*]

rue·ful (rōō′fəl) *adj.* **1.** showing sorrow or regret: *a rueful cry.* **2.** causing sorrow or grief; pitiable: *a rueful sight.* —**rue′ful·ly,** *adv.* —**rue′ful·ness,** *n.*

ruff (ruf) *n.* **1.** a growth of distinctively marked feathers or hairs around the neck of a bird or animal. **2.** a stiff, circular frill, worn as a collar by men and women in the fifteenth, sixteenth, and seventeenth centuries.

ruffed (ruft) *adj.* having a ruff.

ruffed grouse, a North American game bird having brownish feathers and a fan-shaped tail. The male has a tuft of black feathers on each side of the neck.

ruf·fi·an (ruf′ē ən) *n.* a rough, brutal, or violent person. —*adj.* rough, brutal, and violent: *ruffian behavior.*

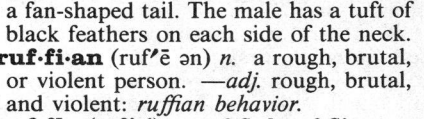

Ruff *(def. 2)*

ruf·fle (ruf′əl) *v.,* **ruf·fled, ruf·fling.** —*v.t.* **1.** to disturb

at; āpe; cär; end; mē; it; īce; hot; ōld; fôrk; wood; fōōl; oil; out; up; turn; sing; thin; this; hw in white; zh in treasure. The symbol ə stands for the sound of a in about, e in taken, i in pencil, o in lemon, and u in circus.

the smoothness or order of: *The wind ruffled the water. The bird ruffled its feathers when it saw the cat beneath the tree.* **2.** to disturb or upset: *Nothing, not even an emergency, could ruffle him.* **3.** to gather (ribbon, lace, or other material) together along one edge. —*v.i.* **1.** to become disordered or uneven. **2.** to become upset. **3.** to rise or become stiff, as in anger or fright: *The bird's feathers ruffled at the sight of the fox.* —*n.* **1.** a strip of ribbon, lace, or other material gathered along one edge, used for trimming or as a border, as on garments or such items as curtains or bedspreads. **2.** a disturbance of a smooth surface.

rug (rug) *n.* **1.** a piece of heavy fabric, used to cover part of a floor. **2.** an animal hide used as a covering: *a bearskin rug.* **3.** another word for **lap robe.**

Rug·by (rug′bē) *also,* **rug·by.** *n.* a form of football played with an oval ball by two fifteen-man teams. The American form of football developed from this game. [From *Rugby,* a school for boys in England where this game was first played.]

rug·ged (rug′id) *adj.* **1.** having a sharp, jagged outline or surface; rough and uneven: *rugged mountain peaks, a rugged coastline.* **2.** able to endure physical hardship; sturdy; robust: *a rugged football team.* **3.** (of the face or its features) strong, lined, or uneven. **4.** difficult to do or endure; harsh; hard: *a rugged life, a rugged test.* —**rug′ged·ly,** *adv.* —**rug′ged·ness,** *n.*

Ruhr (roor) *n.* **1.** a river in northwestern Germany, flowing into the Rhine. **2.** a coal mining and industrial region along this river.

ru·in (roo′in) *n.* **1.** destruction, decay, or collapse: *the ruin of an empire, financial ruin.* **2. ruins.** the remains of something destroyed or decayed: *the ruins of a bombed city.* **3.** something that causes destruction, decay, or collapse. —*v.t.* **1.** to bring to ruin: *The drought ruined the crops. The flood ruined many local businessmen.* **2.** to spoil or harm greatly: *His sprained ankle ruined his chances of winning the race.*

ru·in·a·tion (roo′i nā′shən) *n.* **1.** the act of ruining or the state of being ruined. **2.** something that causes ruin: *His dishonesty was his ruination.*

ru·in·ous (roo′i nəs) *adj.* **1.** bringing or tending to bring to ruin; disastrous; destructive: *a ruinous war.* **2.** fallen to ruin; decayed; destroyed: *The garden is in a ruinous condition.* —**ru′in·ous·ly,** *adv.* —**ru′in·ous·ness,** *n.*

rule (rool) *n.* **1.** a fixed principle or direction regulating behavior, procedure, or action: *the rules of baseball, the rules of etiquette, the rules of logic.* **2.** controlling power or authority; government: *the rule of an emperor.* **3.** a straight-edged instrument used for drawing straight lines or measuring; ruler. **4.** something that usually or normally occurs or is done: *Long hair is the rule among the boys in our town.* —*v.,* **ruled, rul·ing.** —*v.t.* **1.** to have power or authority over; govern; control: *to rule a country.* **2.** to have great influence over; guide: *Fear ruled his actions.* **3.** to declare with authority: *The higher court ruled the law unconstitutional.* **4.** to mark with lines, especially by using a ruler: *He ruled the paper carefully.* —*v.i.* **1.** to have power or authority; govern: *to rule with justice and mercy.* **2.** to make a decision with authority: *The club ruled against accepting new members.*

  as a rule. usually; generally.

  to rule out. to decide to ignore or omit.

rule of thumb, a general principle or guide that is based on experience or practical knowledge instead of on scientific knowledge.

rul·er (roo′lər) *n.* **1.** a person who rules. **2.** a straight-edged strip of wood, plastic, metal, or other material marked off into measuring units, used for drawing straight lines or measuring.

rul·ing (roo′ling) *n.* a decision made with authority, as by a judge or court of law. —*adj.* **1.** having authority; governing: *the ruling class.* **2.** most commonly accepted; widespread; prevalent: *the ruling opinion in the community.*

rum (rum) *n.* **1.** an alcoholic liquor made from fermented juice, syrup, or molasses obtained from sugar cane. **2.** any alcoholic beverage.

Ru·ma·ni·a (roo mā′nē ə) another spelling of **Romania.**

Ru·ma·ni·an (roo mā′nē ən) another spelling of **Romanian.**

rum·ba (rum′bə) *also,* **rhum·ba.** *n.* **1.** a Cuban dance of African origin. **2.** a modern ballroom dance resembling this. **3.** the music for this dance. —*v.i.* to dance the rumba.

rum·ble (rum′bəl) *v.i.,* **rum·bled, rum·bling. 1.** to make a heavy, deep, rolling sound. **2.** to move or advance with such a sound: *The tank rumbled along the road.* —*n.* **1.** a heavy, deep, rolling sound: *the rumble of thunder.* **2.** an area in the back of a carriage used for seating or as a luggage compartment.

rumble seat, an open, folding seat in the back of an automobile, as in a coupe or roadster.

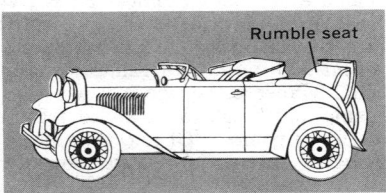
Rumble seat

ru·men (roo′min) *n. pl.,* **ru·mi·na** (roo′mi nə). the first stomach of a cud-chewing animal, such as a cow.

ru·mi·nant (roo′mə nənt) *n.* any of various cud-chewing, hoofed animals that have a stomach consisting of four chambers. Cows, sheep, deer, antelope, giraffes, and camels are ruminants. —*adj.* of or relating to a ruminant.

ru·mi·nate (roo′mə nāt′) *v.i.,* **ru·mi·nat·ed, ru·mi·nat·ing. 1.** to think deeply; meditate: *to ruminate on one's misfortunes.* **2.** to chew the cud, as a cow does. —**ru′mi·na′tion,** *n.*

rum·mage (rum′ij) *v.,* **rum·maged, rum·mag·ing.** —*v.t.* **1.** to search through (something) thoroughly by moving about its contents: *He rummaged the entire attic for his old scrapbook.* **2.** to find or bring forth by searching: *The children rummaged some old suits out of the trunk.* —*v.i.* to search thoroughly by moving about the contents of something: *The child rummaged in the toy box.* —*n.* **1.** a thorough search made by moving things about. **2.** items on sale at a rummage sale.

rummage sale, a sale of miscellaneous items, such as furniture or old clothing, usually held to raise money for some charity.

rum·my (rum′ē) *n.* a card game in which the players try to lay down all the cards in their hands by matching them in sets of three or four cards of the same rank, or in sets of three or more cards of the same suit in sequence.

ru·mor (roo′mər) *n.* **1.** a report or statement passed from person to person as truth without any evidence to support it; unverified story: *Someone started a rumor that the game next Saturday has been canceled.* **2.** general talk; hearsay: *Rumor has it that the star will leave the play next week.* —*v.t.* to spread or tell by rumor.

rump (rump) *n.* **1.** the part of an animal's body where the trunk and legs are joined. **2.** a cut of beef from this part. **3.** in man, the buttocks.

rum·ple (rum′pəl) *v.,* **rum·pled, rum·pling.** —*v.t.* to mess by wrinkling or creasing: *Jane rumpled her jacket by sitting on it.* —*v.i.* to become messed by wrinkling or creasing: *This material rumples easily.* —*n.* an uneven crease; wrinkle.

rum·pus (rum′pəs) *n. Informal.* a noisy disturbance; uproar.

rumpus room, a room for play and informal parties.

run (run) *v.*, **ran, run, run·ning.** —*v.i.* **1.** to move quickly with both legs in the air for an instant during each step; proceed at a pace faster than walking: *He ran to catch the bus.* **2.** to go or move quickly; rush; hasten: *The little boy ran for help when he saw the cat on top of the roof.* **3.** to leave rapidly; flee; escape: *The dog broke loose and ran.* **4.** to make a short or quick trip: *I'm going to run to the store for a loaf of bread.* **5.** to go or travel regularly: *The express runs hourly between Boston and New York.* **6.** to move about or pass freely or easily; go without restraint: *We always let our cats run in the house.* **7.** to take part in a race or other contest: *Seven horses ran in the derby. He plans on running for mayor.* **8.** to extend in a certain direction: *The road runs north for about ten miles.* **9.** (of plants) to grow in a certain direction or area; creep; climb: *The ivy runs up the wall.* **10.** to be in operation; work; function: *The radio runs on batteries. The factory runs day and night.* **11.** to be in effect; last: *The sale will run for one week.* **12.** to pass into a particular state or condition: *If you run into trouble on your trip, call me.* **13.** to have a particular size, quality, or price: *Meat prices are running high.* **14.** to occur to the mind over and over: *The melody ran through his head.* **15.** to be present or common: *Blonde hair runs in her family.* **16.** to flow in a stream: *The water stopped running through the pipes.* **17.** to spread or mingle when exposed to water: *The colors in the shirt ran after the first washing.* **18.** to discharge serum, mucus, or pus: *The sore on his leg was running.* **19.** to have the stitches break at some point and unravel: *Her stockings ran.* **20.** (of fish) to migrate upstream or from the sea for spawning, especially in a school: *The salmon are running.* —*v.t.* **1.** to go or move along by running: *He ran the length of the yard.* **2.** to perform by or as if by running: *to run a race, to run an errand.* **3.** to cause to run: *The rider ran the horse until it was exhausted.* **4.** to bring to a particular place, state, or condition: *The man ran his car off the road.* **5.** to enter in a race or other contest: *The party will run Mr. Edwards for mayor.* **6.** to cause to keep working; operate: *to run a machine.* **7.** to expose oneself to: *She ran the risk of catching a cold by going out in the rain.* **8.** to cause to move, pass, or slide easily: *to run a flag up a pole.* **9.** to be in charge or control of; manage: *The chairman ran the meeting. She runs the local grocery store.* **10.** to cause to flow in a stream: *to run water in a bathtub.* **11.** to cause to extend in a certain direction: *to run a pipe underneath a road.* **12.** to publish, as in a newspaper or magazine: *The company ran an advertisement for the product in today's paper.* **13.** to cause to be presented or shown: *The theater ran the movie for one week.* **14.** to drive, force, or thrust: *The angry man ran his hand through the window glass.* **15.** to suffer from; have: *to run a fever.* **16.** to flow with: *The streets ran with water after the heavy rain.* **17.** to get past or through: *The ship tried to run the blockade in the fog.* —*n.* **1.** the act of running: *to take a run around the block.* **2.** a pace that is faster than a walk: *The children broke into a run when they neared the park.* **3.** a distance covered or time taken by moving at such a pace: *a one-mile run.* **4.** a short or quick trip or visit: *We took a run into town this afternoon.* **5.** a distance traveled regularly between two places, as by a train: *The conductor worked on the run between Baltimore and Washington.* **6.** a journey or trip over this distance: *The train makes four runs daily.* **7.** the freedom to move about or use: *Mrs. Jones gave us the run of the house.* **8.** a continuous series: *We had a run of rainy days during July.* **9.** a period of continuing per-

formance or exhibition: *The play had a six-month run.* **10.** a general direction or tendency; trend: *We were not surprised at the run of events after the scandal became known.* **11.** a period of operation, as of a factory or machine. **12.** a series of sudden demands: *There was a run on the banks.* **13.** a place where stitches have broken and unraveled: *a run in a stocking.* **14.** a flowing movement, as of a liquid: *a run of sap.* **15.** an enclosed area where animals can exercise: *The kennel had a large run for the dogs.* **16.** *Baseball.* **a.** a score made by touching home plate after touching the three bases. **b.** a point scored in this way.

a run for one's money. a. strong competition. **b.** return or satisfaction for money or effort spent.

in the long run. in the end; ultimately.

on the run. a. constantly active or in motion. **b.** in rapid retreat or flight.

to run across. to meet or come upon by chance: *Mary ran across Jane on the way home.*

to run away with. to win or outshine by excelling all others: *He ran away with first prize.*

to run down. a. to make or become weak, as in strength or health. **b.** to chase until caught or killed: *to run down a criminal, to run down an animal.* **c.** to stop operating: *The clock ran down.* **d.** to knock down by colliding with: *Did anyone see the car that ran him down?* **e.** to say mean or bad things about: *The candidate ran down his opponent.* **f.** to find or trace by searching: *The workman ran down the source of the trouble.*

to run for it. to run in order to escape.

to run in. a. to include. **b.** *Slang.* to arrest.

to run into. a. to meet or come upon by chance. **b.** to collide with: *The car ran into a telephone pole.*

to run off. a. to print or make copies of: *We ran off 200 copies of the school newspaper.* **b.** to hold (a final contest or election) in order to break a tie.

to run out. to come to an end; be used up; expire: *The time ran out. His strength ran out.*

to run out of. to use up the supply of: *to run out of sugar.*

to run out on. to desert; forsake.

to run over. a. to ride or drive over: *The car ran over the bicycle in the driveway.* **b.** to go over or examine quickly: *The speaker ran over his notes before the lecture.*

to run through. a. to use up quickly or in a foolish manner: *He ran through his fortune in three years.* **b.** to drive into; pierce. **c.** to go over or examine quickly.

to run up. to allow to accumulate: *We ran up a bill at the grocery last month.*

run·a·bout (run′ə bout′) *n.* **1.** a small motorboat. **2.** a light, open carriage or wagon.

run·a·way (run′ə wā′) *n.* **1.** a person or thing that runs away, such as a fugitive or a horse that has broken out of the driver's control. **2.** the act of running away. —*adj.* **1.** escaping from control; running away; fleeing: *a runaway horse.* **2.** brought about by running away. **3.** rising or expanding rapidly: *runaway prices, runaway inflation.*

run·back (run′bak′) *n.* **1.** a football play in which a player catches a punt or kickoff, or intercepts a pass, and carries it back toward the opposing team's goal. **2.** the distance covered by such a play.

at; āpe; cär; end; mē; it; īce; hot; ōld; fôrk; wood; fōōl; oil; out; up; turn; sing; thin; this; hw in white; zh in treasure. The symbol ə stands for the sound of **a** in about, **e** in taken, **i** in pencil, **o** in lemon, and **u** in circus.

R

run·down (run′doun′) *n.* a summary; résumé: *a rundown of current events.*

run·down (run′doun′) *adj.* **1.** in poor health; tired out; exhausted. **2.** in need of repair; dilapidated: *a run-down old mansion.* **3.** not wound and not working, as a clock or watch.

rune¹ (rōōn) *n.* **1.** a letter or character used in an ancient Germanic system of writing, found mainly in Scandinavia and England. **2.** a similar letter or character

Rune¹

that is supposed to have mysterious or magical power or meaning. [Old English *rūn* mystery, secret; because writing was regarded as a mystery in earlier times when few people could read and write.]

rune² (rōōn) *n.* an ancient Scandinavian poem or song. [Finnish *runo.*]

rung¹ (rung) a past tense and past participle of **ring².**

rung² (rung) *n.* **1.** a crosspiece forming a step of a ladder. **2.** a supporting crosspiece placed between the legs or within the framework of the back of a chair. [Old English *hrung* a pole, staff.]

ru·nic (rōō′nik′) *adj.* of, relating to, or consisting of runes.

run-in (run′in′) *n. Informal.* a disagreement; quarrel: *He had a run-in with his teacher.*

run·let (run′lit) *n.* a small stream or brook; runnel.

run·nel (run′əl) *n.* a small stream or brook.

run·ner (run′ər) *n.* **1.** a person or animal that runs, such as a contestant in a race. **2.** one of the long, narrow parts on which a sled or an ice skate glides. **3.** a person who runs errands or delivers messages. **4.** a long, narrow rug or carpet, used for hallways and staircases. **5.** a narrow strip

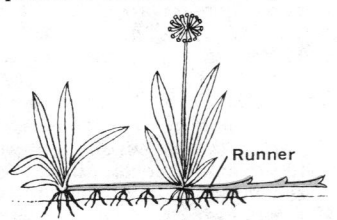

Runner

of cloth used to cover table tops, dressers, and other furniture. **6.** *Botany.* the slender trailing stem of certain plants that gives rise to roots that produce new plants.

run·ner-up (run′ər up′) *n., pl.* **run·ners-up** a contestant or team that finishes in second place.

run·ning (run′ing) *n.* the act of a person or thing that runs. —*adj.* **1.** moving rapidly; proceeding at a run. **2.** flowing: *running water.* **3.** going on continuously: *a running battle.* **4.** done with or during a run: *The outfielder made a running catch.* **5.** in operation, as a machine; working: *the running parts for an engine.* **6.** discharging matter: *a running sore.* —*adv.* in close succession; consecutively: *I had the same dream for six nights running.*

in the running. having a good chance to win or succeed.
out of the running. not likely to win or succeed.

running board, a footboard along the side of certain automobiles.

running knot, a knot made so as to form a noose that tightens as the line is pulled.

running mate, a person who campaigns for office on the same ticket with another, for the lesser of the two offices: *a Presidential candidate and his running mate.*

Run·ny·mede (run′ē mēd′) *n.* a meadow on the Thames, near London, where King John signed the Magna Carta on June 15, 1215.

run-off (run′ôf′) *n.* **1.** rain or snow not absorbed by the soil, which forms surface streams. **2.** a final contest or election held in order to break a tie.

run-of-the-mill (run′əv thə mil′) *adj.* not special or outstanding in any way; ordinary; average.

run-on entry (run′on′, run′on′) an undefined word in a dictionary added at the end of a defined word. It is formed by the addition of a suffix to the defined word, and its meaning can be derived from the meaning of the defined word and the meaning of the suffix. *Ruggedness* is a run-on entry under the word *rugged.*

runt (runt) *n.* a stunted or undersized animal or person.

run-through (run′thrōō′) *n.* a quick rehearsal, review, or examination.

run·way (run′wā′) *n.* **1.** a long, narrow area where an airplane can take off and land. **2.** a ramp extending from a stage in a theater.

ru·pee (rōō pē′) *n.* a monetary unit and coin of India and various other countries.

rup·ture (rup′chər) *n.* **1.** the act of breaking open or bursting: *the rupture of a blood vessel.* **2.** a hernia, especially one in or near the groin. **3.** a break in friendly or diplomatic relations between people or countries. —*v.,* **rup·tured, rup·tur·ing.** —*v.t.* **1.** to break open or apart; burst: *to rupture a blood vessel.* **2.** to end or break off (friendly or diplomatic relations). **3.** to affect with a hernia, especially one in or near the groin. —*v.i.* to suffer a break; burst: *His appendix ruptured.*

ru·ral (roor′əl) *adj.* **1.** of, relating to, or characteristic of the country: *rural areas, rural population.* **2.** of or relating to agriculture: *a rural economy.* —**ru′ral·ly,** *adv.*

rural free delivery, the delivery of mail in rural or farm areas by carriers employed by the government.

ruse (rōōz) *n.* an action or plan intended to deceive; trick: *Her headache was a ruse so that she could stay home.*

rush¹ (rush) *v.i.* **1.** to move, go, or come with speed or haste: *He had to rush to catch the bus. Blood rushed to her head.* **2.** to act quickly and rashly: *He rushed into the campaign without any political experience.* —*v.t.* **1.** to take, send, or cause to move with speed or haste: *The policemen rushed the injured man to the hospital.* **2.** to do or complete hastily: *I can't rush my work without making errors.* **3.** to attack or overcome swiftly and forcefully: *The troops planned to rush the fortress in the morning.* —*n. pl.,* **rush·es.** **1.** the act of rushing; sudden swift movement: *a rush of water.* **2.** a sudden and hasty movement of many people to get to a place: *We left home at ten o'clock to avoid the morning rush.* **3.** bustling activity; being busy; haste: *the rush of a crowded department store during the Christmas season.* **4.** a sudden demand: *a rush for tickets to the championship game.* **5.** a hurried state: *He is always in a rush to leave the house in the morning.* —*adj.* requiring haste; urgent: *a rush job.* [Possibly from Old French *reüser* to cause to retreat, turn away from.]

rush² (rush) *n. pl.,* **rush·es.** **1.** any of several plants resembling reeds or grass, found in marshy areas, having slender, often hollow stems, and clusters of small green or brown flowers. **2.** the stem of any of these plants, often woven into mats, baskets, chair seats, and other products. [Old English *risc.*]

rush hour, the period during a day when traffic is heaviest, and buses, subways, or trains are most crowded.

Rush·more, Mount (rush′môr) a mountain in the Black hills of western South Dakota, on the side of which are carved huge heads of George Washington, Thomas Jefferson, Abraham Lincoln, and Theodore Roosevelt.

rusk (rusk) *n.* **1.** a sweet or plain bread or cake baked in the oven, sliced, and then baked again to make it brown, dry, and crisp. **2.** a light, soft, sweetened biscuit.

Russ. **1.** Russia. **2.** Russian.

Rus·sell, Ber·trand (rus′əl; bur′trənd) 1872–1970, English philosopher and mathematician.

rus·set (rus′it) *n.* **1.** a yellowish-brown or reddish-brown color. **2.** any of various kinds of apples having this color. **3.** a coarse, homespun woolen fabric having this color. —*adj.* having the color russet.

Rus·sia (rush′ə) *n.* **1.** another word for **Soviet Union**. **2.** the former empire in eastern Europe and northern Asia ruled by the czars until the Russian Revolution. **3.** another word for **Russian Soviet Federated Socialist Republic.**

Rus·sian (rush′ən) *n.* **1.** a person who was born or is living in Russia. **2.** the language of Russia. —*adj.* of or relating to Russia, its people, their language, or their culture.

Russian Church, the largest branch of the Orthodox Church, governed by a patriarch and a number of other prelates. It was the official church of imperial Russia. Also, **Russian Orthodox Church.**

Russian dressing, a dressing made of mayonnaise mixed with chili sauce or ketchup, and other ingredients, such as chopped pickles or olives.

Russian Revolution, a revolution in Russia, in 1917, that ended the czarist form of government and later established the Russian government under the leadership of the Bolsheviks headed by Lenin.

Russian Soviet Federated Socialist Republic, the largest republic of the Soviet Union, comprising more than three-quarters of the country's area. Area, 6,592,658 sq. mi. Pop. (1970 est.), 96,034,000. Also, **Russia, Soviet Russia.**

Russian wolfhound, another term for **borzoi.**

rust (rust) *n.* **1.** a reddish-brown or orange coating that forms on the surface of iron when it is exposed to moisture and oxygen. **2.** any of various plant diseases caused by parasitic fungi, characterized by the appearance of reddish-brown or orange spots and streaks on the plants. **3.** any of the parasitic fungi causing such a disease. **4.** a reddish-brown or orange color. —*v.i.* **1.** to corrode by becoming covered with rust. **2.** to become weakened or ruined through lack of use. **3.** (of a plant) to become infected with a rust. —*v.t.* to cause to become covered with rust. —*adj.* having the color rust.

rus·tic (rus′tik) *adj.* **1.** of, relating to, or characteristic of the country: *a rustic scene.* **2.** characteristic of country people or country life; simple; plain: *rustic manners.* **3.** made of rough, untrimmed trees or branches: *rustic furniture.* —*n.* a person who lives in the country, especially one who is simple or awkward. —**rus′ti·cal·ly,** *adv.*

rus·tle (rus′əl) *v.,* **rus·tled, rus·tling.** —*v.i.* **1.** to make a series of soft, fluttering sounds, as that of papers or leaves being rubbed together or stirred about: *The leaves rustled in the wind.* **2.** *Informal.* to steal cattle. —*v.t.* **1.** to cause to make a series of soft, fluttering sounds: *The wind rustled the papers on the desk.* **2.** *Informal.* to steal (cattle). —*n.* a series of soft, fluttering sounds.

rus·tler (rus′lər) *n.* a cattle thief.

rust·y (rus′tē) *adj.,* **rust·i·er, rust·i·est. 1.** covered or affected with rust: *a rusty nail.* **2.** consisting of or made by rust: *rusty spots on a metal chair.* **3.** having the color rust. **4.** weakened or ruined through lack of use: *My French is a bit rusty.* **5.** less skilled through lack of use: *He's gotten rusty in math.* —**rust′i·ly,** *adv.* —**rust′i·ness,** *n.*

rut (rut) *n.* **1.** a groove or track made in the ground by a wheel or by continuous wear. **2.** a fixed way of living, thinking, or acting; boring routine: *He was in a rut, doing the same thing day after day.* —*v.t.,* **rut·ted, rut·ting.** to make a rut in: *The heavy tractors rutted the road.*

ru·ta·ba·ga (rōō′tə bā′gə) *n.* a turnip having a thick yellow root that is used as food.

Ruth (rōōth) *n.* **1.** in the Old Testament, the daughter-in-law of Naomi, to whom she was devoted. **2.** the book of the Old Testament relating her story.

Ruth, Babe (rōōth; bāb) 1895–1948, U.S. baseball player; born George Herman Ruth.

ru·the·ni·um (rōō thē′nē əm) *n.* a hard, silvery metallic element. Symbol: **Ru**

Ruth·er·ford, Lord Ernest (ruth′ər fərd) 1871–1937, English physicist.

ruth·less (rōōth′lis) *adj.* without pity, mercy, or compassion: *a ruthless criminal.* —**ruth′less·ly,** *adv.* —**ruth′less·ness,** *n.*

Rwan·da (rōō än′də) *n.* a country in east-central Africa. Capital, Kigali. Area, 10,169 sq. mi. Pop. (1971 est.), 3,830,000.

-ry, a form of the suffix **-ery,** as in *revelry, jewelry, ministry.*

Ry., railway.

rye (rī) *n.* **1.** the grain of a hardy slender-stemmed plant of the grass family, used chiefly as feed for animals, and in the manufacture of flour, whiskey, gin, and grain alcohol. **2.** the plant bearing this grain, widely cultivated and often used as a winter cover crop to prevent soil erosion.

Ryu·kyu Islands (rē ōō′kyōō′) an island chain in the western Pacific Ocean, extending from Kyushu, Japan, to Taiwan. Land area, 1800 sq. mi. Pop. (1971 est.), 950,000.

Grain head   Plant

Rye

at; āpe; cär; end; mē; it; īce; hot; ōld; fôrk; wood; fōōl; oil; out; up; turn; sing; thin; this; hw in white; zh in treasure. The symbol ə stands for the sound of **a** in about, **e** in taken, **i** in pencil, **o** in lemon, and **u** in circus.

1. Egyptian Hieroglyphics	5. Greek Ninth Century B.C.
2. Semitic	6. Etruscan
3. Early Phoenician	7. Latin Fourth Century B.C. Capitals
4. Early Hebrew	8. English

S is the nineteenth letter of the English alphabet. The earliest forms of S bear no resemblance to our modern letter. The first of these forms was an Egyptian hieroglyphic (1) which pictured teeth. In the ancient Semitic alphabet the Egyptian symbol was adapted for the letter *shin* (2), meaning "tooth." *Shin* and the early Phoenician (3) and early Hebrew (4) versions of it were written very much as we write the letter **W**. Between about 2800 and 2500 years ago, a new form of *shin* appeared in the earliest Greek alphabets. This letter (5), called *sigma,* was adopted by the Etruscans (6). By about 2200 years ago, the Romans (7), who borrowed the Etruscan form of *sigma,* were writing the letter **S** very much as we write it today (8).

s, S (es) *n. pl.,* **s's, S's. 1.** the nineteenth letter of the English alphabet. **2.** something having the shape of this letter.

-s¹, the ending used to form the plural of most nouns: *horses.*

-s², the ending used to form the third person singular of the present indicative of most verbs: *talks, runs, eats.*

's¹, the ending used to form the possessive case of singular nouns, of plural nouns not ending in *s,* and of some pronouns: *a girl's dress, children's toys, anyone's hat.*

's² 1. is: *She's three years old. He's away for the day.* **2.** has: *He's already been there.* **3.** us: *Let's go before it begins to rain.*

s. 1. second. **2.** shilling. **3.** singular.

S, the symbol for sulfur.

S, South; Southern.

S.A. 1. South America. **2.** South Africa. **3.** Salvation Army.

Saar (sär, zär) *n.* **1.** a river flowing from northeastern France into West Germany, where it joins the Moselle River. **2.** see **Saarland.**

Saar·land (sär′land′, zär′land′) *n.* a state in West Germany, in the western part of the country. Area, 991 sq. mi. Pop. (1969 est.), 1,127,400. Also, **Saar.**

Sa·bah (sä′bə) *n.* a state of Malaysia, on the northeastern coast of Borneo. Area, 29,388 sq. mi. Pop. (1970), 654,949.

Sab·bath (sab′əth) *n.* the day of the week for rest and religious worship. Sunday is the Sabbath for most Christians; Saturday is the Sabbath for the Jews and certain Christian denominations.

sab·bat·i·cal (sə bat′i kəl) *n.* a period of leave from one's regular work, especially such a leave granted to a professor or teacher for travel or study. —*adj. also,* **Sabbatical.** of, relating to, or proper for the Sabbath.

sa·ber (sā′bər) *also, British,* **sa·bre.** *n.* **1.** a heavy sword with one cutting edge and a long, usually curved blade. **2.** a light fencing sword with two cutting edges.

sa·ber-toothed tiger (sā′bər tooth′) any of various large extinct animals related to the cat, that had long, curved teeth in the upper jaw. Saber-toothed tigers lived from thirty-five to three million years ago.

Saber-toothed tiger

Sa·bin, Albert Bruce (sā′bin) 1906—, U.S. physician, born in Poland, who developed an oral vaccine against poliomyelitis.

sa·ble (sā′bəl) *n.* **1.** any of several animals that look like weasels, especially such an animal that lives in the northern pine forests of Siberia and Europe and has a bushy tail, round ears, and soft, brown fur. **2.** the valuable fur of this animal, used for making coats. **3.** the color black. **4. sables.** black mourning clothes. —*adj.* having the color sable; black.

sab·ot (sab′ō, sa bō′) *n.* **1.** a shoe carved from a single piece of wood, worn in the Netherlands, Belgium, and France. **2.** a heavy leather sandal or shoe having a thick wooden sole.

sab·o·tage (sab′ə täzh′) *n.* **1.** the deliberate damage or destruction of buildings or other property, or interference with work or other activity, as at a factory, by enemy agents in order to hinder a nation's war or defense efforts. **2.** any deliberate damage or destruction that is done to hinder some activity or effort: *The sabotage of the machinery by the striking workmen forced the owners to close down the factory.* —*v.t.,* **sab·o·taged, sab·o·tag·ing.** to damage or destroy deliberately. [French *sabotage;* going back to *sabot* wooden shoe; supposedly referring to the former practice of damaging an employer's machinery by throwing wooden shoes into it.]

sab·o·teur (sab′ə tur′) *n.* a person who commits or is guilty of sabotage.

sa·bra (sä′brə) *n.* a person who was born in Israel. [Hebrew *sābrāh* such a person; literally, prickly pear; referring to a cactus that is native to Israel.]

sa·bre (sā′bər) *British.* another spelling of **saber.**

sac (sak) *n.* a part in a plant or animal that is shaped like a pouch or bag, and that often contains a liquid.

SAC, Strategic Air Command.

sac·cha·rin (sak′ər in) *n.* a white powder that is a man-made substitute for sugar. It is very sweet but has no calories.

sac·cha·rine (sak′ər in) *adj.* **1.** much too sweet: *a saccharine smile.* **2.** of or like sugar; very sweet. —*n.* another spelling of **saccharin.**

sac·er·do·tal (sas′ər dōt′əl) *adj.* of or relating to a priest or the priesthood; priestly.

sa·chem (sā′chəm) *n.* a chief of certain North American Indian tribes. The sachem inherited his position rather than being chosen for it.

sa·chet (sa shā′) *n.* a small bag or pad containing a perfumed powder or other substance, usually put in a drawer to make clothes, towels, or sheets smell sweet.

sack[1] (sak) *n.* **1.** a large bag made of coarse, strong material: *The clerks sorted the mail and put it into sacks.* **2.** any bag. **3.** a sack and what it holds: *We bought a sack of potatoes at the market.* **4.** a short, loose-fitting jacket for women and children. —*v.t.* **1.** to put into a sack or sacks. **2.** *Slang.* to fire from a job. [Old English *sacc.*]
the sack. *Slang.* **a.** a dismissal from one's job. **b.** bed: *He stayed in the sack all morning.*
to hit the sack. *Slang.* to go to bed.

sack[2] (sak) *v.t.* to steal everything of value or use in a town or city that has been captured in a war; plunder. —*n.* the act of plundering a captured town or city. [French *sac.*]

sack[3] (sak) *n.* **1.** a light-colored sherry. **2.** any of various strong, dry white wines. [French *(vin) sec* dry (wine), from Latin *siccus* dry.]

sack·cloth (sak′klôth′) *n. pl.,* **sack·cloths** (sak′klôths′, sak′klô*th*z′). **1.** a coarse cloth for making sacks; sacking. **2.** a garment of such cloth, worn to show mourning, humility, or penitence.

sack·ful (sak′fool′) *n. pl.,* **sack·fuls.** the amount that a sack holds.

sack·ing (sak′ing) *n.* any coarsely woven cloth, such as burlap, used for making sacks.

sac·ra·ment (sak′rə mənt) *n.* **1.** any of several sacred Christian rites, such as baptism and confirmation. **2.** *also,* **the Sacrament. a.** another term for **Holy Communion. b.** the consecrated bread and wine used in Holy Communion, or the bread alone. —**sac·ra·ment·al** (sak′rə ment′əl), *adj.*

Sac·ra·men·to (sak′rə men′tō) *n.* the capital of California, in the central part of the state. Pop. (1970), 254,413.

sa·cred (sā′krid) *adj.* **1.** associated with, set apart for, or belonging to God or a god: *sacred relics, sacred ground, a sacred name.* **2.** of or relating to religion; having a religious use or purpose: *sacred music.* **3.** deserving respect or reverence: *He made a sacred promise and would not break it.* —**sa′cred·ly,** *adv.* —**sa′cred·ness,** *n.*

sacred cow, a person or thing not to be criticized. [From the Hindu belief that the *cow* is a *sacred* animal.]

sac·ri·fice (sak′rə fīs′) *n.* **1.** the act of offering something, such as an animal or a human life, to a god as an act of worship. **2.** an animal, person, or thing so offered: *The usual sacrifice of the ancient Greeks was an animal, such as a sheep.* **3.** the giving up of something that is valued or wanted, usually for the sake of something else: *The*

parents made many sacrifices in order to save money for their son's college education. **4.** something given up. **5.** a loss of profit when something is sold for less than it is worth. **6.** see **sacrifice hit.** —*v.,* **sac·ri·ficed, sac·ri·fic·ing.** —*v.t.* **1.** to offer as a sacrifice to a god. **2.** to give up or destroy for the sake of something else. **3.** to sell at a loss. **4.** *Baseball.* to advance (a runner or runners) by making a sacrifice hit. —*v.i.* **1.** to offer or make a sacrifice. **2.** *Baseball.* to make a sacrifice hit.

sacrifice fly *Baseball.* a fly ball that enables a base runner to score after the ball is caught by an opposing player.

sacrifice hit *Baseball.* a bunt that enables a base runner or runners to advance, but results in the batter being put out.

sac·ri·fi·cial (sak′rə fish′əl) *adj.* relating to, used in, or like a sacrifice. —**sac·ri·fi′cial·ly,** *adv.*

sac·ri·lege (sak′rə lij) *n.* an act that shows disrespect for or harms something sacred.

sac·ri·le·gious (sak′rə lij′əs) *adj.* of, relating to, or being a sacrilege. —**sac·ri·le′gious·ly,** *adv.* —**sac·ri·le′gious·ness,** *n.*

sac·ris·ty (sak′ris tē) *n. pl.,* **sac·ris·ties.** the room or rooms in a church where the sacred vessels, robes, and other objects used in ceremonies are kept.

sac·ro·sanct (sak′rō sangkt′) *adj.* very sacred.

sad (sad) *adj.,* **sad·der, sad·dest. 1.** feeling or showing unhappiness, sorrow, or gloom: *She was sad when her friend moved away.* **2.** causing or marked by unhappiness, sorrow, or gloom: *A sad memory made her cry. It was a sad day when our team lost the game.* **3.** so bad as to arouse pity; pitiful: *The wet dog was a sad sight.* —**sad′ly,** *adv.* —**sad′ness,** *n.*

sad·den (sad′ən) *v.t., v.i.* to make or become sad.

sad·dle (sad′əl) *n.* **1.** a seat or pad for a rider, used on the back of a horse or similar animal that has to carry a load. **2.** a similar padded seat, as on a motorcycle. **3.** something that looks like a saddle, such as a ridge of land between two mountain peaks. **4.** a cut of meat that comes from the back of an animal: *The cook prepared a saddle of lamb.* —*v.t.,* **sad·dled, sad·dling. 1.** to put a saddle on: *to saddle a horse.* **2.** to load or burden: *She was saddled with the responsibility of caring for her baby brother.*

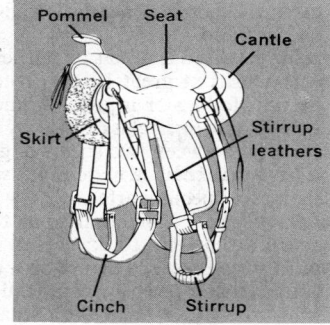

Saddle

sad·dle·bag (sad′əl bag′) *n.* a bag of leather or other material, usually one of a pair that is hung from a saddle.

sad·dler (sad′lər) *n.* a person who makes, repairs, or sells saddles and harnesses.

saddle shoe, a shoe that is usually white with a band of dark color.

at; āpe; cär; end; mē; it; īce; hot; ōld; fôrk; wood; fool; oil; out; up; turn; sing; thin; *th*is; hw in white; zh in treasure. The symbol ə stands for the sound of **a** in about, **e** in taken, **i** in pencil, **o** in lemon, and **u** in circus.

S

saddle soap, a mild soap used to clean, soften, and preserve leather and leather articles.

sa·dism (sā'diz'əm, sad'iz'əm) *n.* the tendency of a person to get pleasure from causing physical or mental pain to others. [French *sadisme,* from the Marquis de *Sade,* 1740–1814, who wrote about this tendency.]

sa·dist (sā'dist, sad'ist) *n.* a person who gets pleasure from causing physical or mental pain to others.

sa·dis·tic (sə dis'tik) *adj.* relating to or showing sadism. —**sa·dis'ti·cal·ly,** *adv.*

sa·fa·ri (sə fär'ē) *n. pl.,* **sa·fa·ris.** a hunting expedition, especially in Africa.

safe (sāf) *adj.,* **saf·er, saf·est. 1.** free from harm or danger: *It's not safe to skate on that thin ice.* **2.** having escaped injury; unharmed: *The soldier arrived safe at headquarters after crossing enemy lines.* **3.** giving protection from harm or danger: *He found a safe place to put the secret document.* **4.** without risk of failure or error: *a safe bet.* **5.** not able to do harm or injury: *The lion is safe in its cage.* **6.** not taking dangerous chances; careful: *He is a safe driver.* **7.** *Baseball.* having reached a base without being put out. —*n.* a strong metal box or other container that can be locked, used for the safekeeping of valuables, such as jewelry and money. —**safe'ly,** *adv.* —**safe'ness,** *n.*

safe·guard (sāf'gärd') *n.* something that protects: *She put a gate across the stairway as a safeguard for her baby. Getting enough sleep is a safeguard against sickness.* —*v.t.* to guard; protect; defend.

safe·keep·ing (sāf'kē'ping) *n.* care or protection; custody: *He left his bicycle in the safekeeping of his friend.*

safe·ty (sāf'tē) *n. pl.,* **safe·ties. 1.** freedom from danger, injury, or risk; being safe. **2.** a device to prevent accident or injury, such as the catch on a gun that prevents it from firing. **3.** *Football.* **a.** a score of two points for the defensive team, resulting from the ball being downed by the offensive team behind its own goal line. **b.** a defensive player who takes the position nearest to his team's goal line. —*adj.* giving safety.

safety belt 1. a belt or harness used to fasten a person who works at great heights to a fixed object in order to prevent falling or injury. **2.** another term for **seat belt.**

safety glass, glass made by putting a layer of plastic material between two sheets of glass to prevent shattering.

safety match, a match that will light only when struck against a special surface.

safety pin, a pin bent so as to form a spring, having a guard at one end to cover and hold the point.

safety valve 1. a device on a container, such as a steam boiler, that opens automatically to let some steam out when the pressure in the container reaches a dangerous point. **2.** something that helps a person get rid of too much energy or emotion: *Hitting the punching bag was a good safety valve for him when he was angry.*

saf·flow·er (saf'lou'ər) *n.* a tall plant that looks like the thistle and has yellowish-orange flowers. The seeds yield an oil used in cooking.

saf·fron (saf'rən) *n.* **1.** a yellow substance that is used as a dye and for flavoring food. It is made from the dried stigmas of the flowers of a kind of crocus. **2.** the plant bearing this substance, having fragrant purple or white flowers. **3.** an orange-yellow color. —*adj.* having the color saffron; orange-yellow.

S. Afr., South Africa; South African.

sag (sag) *v.i.,* **sagged, sag·ging. 1.** to sink or hang down, especially in the middle, as from weight; droop: *The old mattress sags.* **2.** to bend or hang unevenly or loosely: *The rusty gate sagged on its hinges.* **3.** to lose firmness or strength; weaken: *Their courage sagged when they realized help wasn't on the way.* **4.** to slow up or move down;

decline: *Production sagged during the recession.* —*n.* **1.** the act, state, or amount of sagging. **2.** a place where something sags.

sa·ga (sä'gə) *n.* **1.** an adventure story that originated in Iceland during the Middle Ages, usually dealing with heroes and kings of Scandinavia and their deeds. **2.** any long story about adventurous or heroic deeds.

sa·ga·cious (sə gā'shəs) *adj.* very wise: *The judge was a sagacious man.* —**sa·ga'cious·ly,** *adv.* —**sa·ga'cious·ness,** *n.*

sa·gac·i·ty (sə gas'ə tē) *n.* the quality of being sagacious.

sag·a·more (sag'ə môr') *n.* among certain North American Indian tribes, an elected ruler or chief, especially one who had less power than a sachem.

sage¹ (sāj) *n.* a person who is very wise, especially an older man. —*adj.,* **sag·er, sag·est.** having or showing great wisdom and sound judgment: *My grandmother gave me sage advice.* [Old French *sage.*] —**sage'ly,** *adv.* —**sage'ness,** *n.*

sage² (sāj) *n.* **1.** a small plant related to the mint, having fragrant leaves that are used to flavor food. **2.** see **sagebrush.** [Old French *sauge.*]

sage·brush (sāj'brush') *n.* a shrub that grows on the dry plains of western North America. It has silvery white leaves and small yellow or white flowers.

Sag·it·tar·i·us (saj'ə ter'ē əs) *n.* **1.** a constellation in the northern sky, thought to look like an archer with a bow. **2.** the ninth sign of the zodiac.

sa·go (sā'gō) *n. pl.,* **sa·gos. 1.** a grainy or powdered starch obtained from the trunk and stems of various palm trees, used to thicken soups, sauces, and other foods. **2.** see **sago palm.**

Sage leaves

sago palm, a palm tree found in marshy areas of the East Indies. It is the major source of sago.

sa·gua·ro (sə gwär'ō) *n. pl.,* **sa·gua·ros.** *also,* **sa·hua·ro** (sə wär'ō). a very large cactus found in southern Arizona and neighboring regions, having white flowers, branches covered with heavy spines, and fruit that can be eaten.

Sa·har·a (sə har'ə, sə her'ə) *n.* a desert in northern Africa, the largest in the world. Area, approx. 3,000,000 sq. mi.

sa·hib (sä'ib, sä'hib) *n.* sir; master. ▲ formerly used as a title of respect for Europeans in colonial India.

said (sed) the past tense and past participle of **say.**

Sai·gon (sī gon') *n.* a port city in southern Vietnam, formerly the capital of South Vietnam. Pop. (1971 est.), 1,804,900. Also, **Ho Chi Minh City.**

sail (sāl) *n.* **1.** a piece of canvas or other material attached to a boat or ship so that it can catch the wind and cause the vessel to move through the water. **2.** something resembling a sail in shape, position, or use, such as an arm of a windmill. **3.** a trip or ride in a boat or other vessel: *It was a beautiful day for a sail.* —*v.i.* **1.** (of a boat or ship) to move through the water by means of a sail or sails or by means of an engine. **2.** to travel over water in a boat or ship. **3.** to begin a voyage by water: *The ship will sail for Hawaii in two weeks.* **4.** to steer and operate a boat, especially a sailboat. **5.** to move smoothly and without difficulty: *The ballet dancer sailed through the air.* —*v.t.* **1.** to move or travel over or across (a body of water): *This ship sailed the Mediterranean last year.* **2.** to steer, manage, or navigate (a boat or ship).

sail·boat (sāl′bōt′) *n.* a boat that has a sail or sails, by means of which it is moved through the water.

sail·cloth (sāl′klôth′) *n. pl.,* **sail·cloths** (sāl′klôths′, sāl′klôthz′). canvas or other strong material that is used for making sails, tents, or the like.

sail·fish (sāl′fish′) *n. pl.,* **sail·fish** or **sail·fish·es.** a saltwater fish that lives in warm coastal waters. It has a large fin resembling a sail on its back.

sail·ing (sā′ling) *n.* **1.** the art or sport of operating a boat or ship, especially a sailboat. **2.** the act of a person or thing that sails.

sail·or (sā′lər) *n.* **1.** a person whose trade or occupation is sailing or navigating boats and ships; seaman. **2.** a member of a country's navy.

saint (sānt) *n.* **1.** a very holy person, especially one honored after death as being worthy of special reverence, as in the Roman Catholic Church. **2.** a person who is very kind, patient, or unselfish: *The nurse's patients said she was a saint.* —*v.t.* to declare to be a saint; canonize.

Saint. Saints are entered in the dictionary under their proper names. For example, **Saint Peter** is listed in the P's. For places that begin with the word **Saint**, look under **St.** plus the proper name, as in **St. Louis** or **St. Augustine.**

Saint Ber·nard (bər närd′) a large, reddish-brown and white dog having a large head, a long bushy tail, and a very thick coat. The Saint Bernard is famous for rescuing people lost in the snow in the Swiss Alps. [Originally referring to the use of this dog at the Great *St. Bernard* Pass to rescue people lost in the snow.]

Saint Bernard

saint·ed (sān′tid) *adj.* **1.** declared to be a saint; canonized. **2.** of or like a saint; pious; saintly. **3.** thought to be among the saints in heaven; deceased; dead.

saint·hood (sānt′hood′) *n.* **1.** the character or condition of being a saint. **2.** saints as a group.

saint·ly (sānt′lē) *adj.,* **saint·li·er, saint·li·est.** of, relating to, or proper for a saint: *saintly behavior.* —**saint′li·ness,** *n.*

Saint Patrick's Day, the day on which Saint Patrick is honored. It falls on March 17.

Saint Valentine's Day, see **Valentine's Day.**

Saint Vi·tus' dance (vī′tə siz) a disease that affects the nerves, causing the muscles in the face, arms, and legs to twitch. Also, **chorea.** [From *Saint Vitus,* the saint to whom prayers for a cure of this disease were made.]

saith (seth, sā′ith) *Archaic.* the third person singular present indicative of **say.**

sake[1] (sāk) *n.* **1.** good or advantage; benefit: *He moved to a dry climate for the sake of his health.* **2.** purpose; reason: *He took that new job just for the sake of making more money.* [Old English *sacu* strife, lawsuit.]

sa·ke[2] (sä′kē) also, **sa·ki.** *n.* a Japanese liquor that is made from rice. [Japanese *sake.*]

sa·laam (sə läm′) *n.* **1.** in certain Asian countries, a greeting or gesture of respect performed by bowing low and touching the right hand to the forehead. **2.** a greeting meaning "peace," used by Muslims. —*v.i.* to make a salaam. —*v.t.* to greet with a salaam.

sal·a·ble (sā′lə bəl) *also,* **sale·a·ble.** *adj.* that can be sold. —**sal′a·bil′i·ty, sal′a·ble·ness,** *n.*

sa·la·cious (sə lā′shəs) *adj.* not decent; obscene. —**sa·la′cious·ly,** *adv.* —**sa·la′cious·ness,** *n.*

sal·ad (sal′əd) *n.* a cold dish usually made with raw vegetables, such as lettuce and tomato, and served with a dressing. When a salad makes up a whole meal, it often includes meat or fish.

Sal·a·din (sal′ə din) 1138?–1193?, Muslim conqueror and sultan of Egypt and Syria.

sal·a·man·der (sal′ə man′dər) *n.* any of a group of animals that look like small lizards. Salamanders live in and near fresh water, and have smooth, moist skin.

Salamander

sa·la·mi (sə lä′mē) *n. pl.,* **sa·la·mis.** a sausage made of pork or beef and spices.

sal·a·ried (sal′ə rēd) *adj.* getting or paying a salary.

sal·a·ry (sal′ə rē) *n. pl.,* **sal·a·ries.** a fixed sum of money paid to someone at regular intervals for work that is done. [Latin *salārium* pay, allowance; originally, money given to soldiers to buy salt.]

sale (sāl) *n.* **1.** a change of ownership of something from one person or group to another in exchange for money: *the sale of a house.* **2.** the offering or selling of something for less than it usually costs: *The store is having a sale on ski equipment.* **3. sales. a.** an amount sold: *Sales are up at the store.* **b.** the work or department that has to do with selling goods or services: *She is interested in a job in sales.* **for sale.** available for purchase.

sale·a·ble (sā′lə bəl) another spelling of **salable.**

Sa·lem (sā′ləm) *n.* the capital of Oregon, in the northwestern part of the state. Pop. (1970), 68,296.

sales·clerk (sālz′klurk′) *n.* a person who sells merchandise in a store.

sales·man (sālz′mən) *n. pl.,* **sales·men** (sālz′mən). a man who sells merchandise or services.

sales·man·ship (sālz′mən ship′) *n.* skill in selling.

sales·peo·ple (sālz′pē′pəl) *n. pl.,* salespersons.

sales·per·son (sālz′pur′sən) *n.* a person who sells merchandise or services.

sales tax, a tax on goods that are sold. It is usually a percentage of the selling price.

sales·wom·an (sālz′woom′ən) *n. pl.,* **sales·wom·en** (sālz′wim′ən). a woman who sells merchandise or services.

sal·i·cyl·ic acid (sal′ə sil′ik) a white, crystalline organic compound used in the making of aspirin.

sa·li·ent (sā′lē ənt) *adj.* standing out from the rest; most noticeable or important: *The salient feature of the lecture was the description of the tribe.* —*n.* the part of a fortification or line of defense that is closest to the enemy.

sa·line (sā′lēn) *adj.* **1.** of, relating to, or like salt; salty. **2.** containing salt. —*n.* a solution that has a large amount of salt. Such solutions are used in medicine, surgery, and biological experiments.

sa·lin·i·ty (sə lin′ə tē) *n.* **1.** the quality or condition of being saline. **2.** the amount of salt in something.

Salis·bur·y (sôlz′ber′ē) *n.* the capital and largest city of Zimbabwe, in the northeastern part of the country. Pop. (1976 est.), 566,000.

Salisbury steak, ground beef, often mixed with eggs or bread crumbs, that is formed into patties and cooked.

at; āpe; cär; end; mē; it; īce; hot; ōld; fôrk; wood; fōōl; oil; out; up; turn; sing; thin; this; hw in white; zh in treasure. The symbol ə stands for the sound of **a** in about, **e** in taken, **i** in pencil, **o** in lemon, and **u** in circus.

sa·li·va (sə lī′və) *n.* a colorless liquid that is secreted by the glands of the mouth. Saliva keeps the mouth moist, moistens food during chewing, and starts the digestion of starches.

sal·i·var·y (sal′ə ver′ē) *adj.* of, relating to, or secreting saliva: *a salivary gland.*

sal·i·vate (sal′ə vāt′) *v.i.*, **sal·i·vat·ed, sal·i·vat·ing.** to secrete saliva. —**sal′i·va′tion,** *n.*

Salk, Jonas Edward (sôlk, sôk) 1914—, U.S. physician who developed the first successful vaccine against poliomyelitis.

sal·low (sal′ō) *adj.* of a sickly, yellowish color or complexion: *sallow skin.*

sal·ly (sal′ē) *v.i.*, **sal·lied, sal·ly·ing. 1.** to start or go out briskly: *The children sallied forth into the cold night to sing carols.* **2.** to rush suddenly, as into battle: *The soldiers bravely sallied across the field.* —*n. pl.*, **sal·lies. 1.** a sudden rushing forth, especially a charge by soldiers at the enemy. **2.** a quick, witty remark. **3.** a short trip.

salm·on (sam′ən) *n. pl.*, **salm·on** or **salm·ons. 1.** a popular food fish that usually has a large, silver body with a dark back. Some salmon live and spawn in fresh water, but most live in salt water and migrate

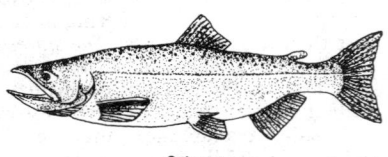
Salmon

to fresh water to spawn. **2.** a yellowish-pink color. —*adj.* having the color salmon; yellowish-pink.

Sa·lo·me (sə lō′mē) *n.* in the New Testament, the stepdaughter of Herod Antipas. As a reward for dancing for Herod on his birthday, Salome was granted the head of John the Baptist.

sa·lon (sə lon′) *n. pl.*, **sa·lons. 1.** an elegant and usually large hall or room for receiving or entertaining guests. **2.** a gathering of guests in such a room. A salon is usually held so that famous people, such as artists or writers, can meet one another. **3.** a stylish shop or store, especially one that provides a special service or product: *a beauty salon.* **4.** a place used to show works of art.

Sa·lo·ni·ka (sə lon′i kə) *n.* a port city in northern Greece. Pop. (1971), 339,496.

sa·loon (sə lōōn′) *n.* **1.** a place where alcoholic drinks are served; bar; tavern. **2.** a large room for public use, especially the main lounge on a passenger ship.

sal soda, another term for **sodium carbonate** *(def. 2).*

salt (sôlt) *n.* **1.** a white compound made up of sodium and chlorine and found in sea water and in mineral deposits in the earth. It is used to season and preserve food. Formula: NaCl Also, **sodium chloride. 2.** in chemistry, any compound formed, along with water, by the reaction of an acid with a base. The salt is made up of the positive ion of the base and the negative ion of the acid. **3. salts. a.** any of various salts used as a laxative, such as Epsom salts. **b.** see **smelling salts. 4.** something that adds flavor or liveliness; zest. **5.** *Informal.* a sailor, especially an old and experienced one. —*adj.* **1.** tasting of or containing salt. **2.** preserved with salt: *salt pork.* **3.** flooded with or growing in or near salt water: *a salt meadow, a salt plant.* —*v.t.* **1.** to sprinkle or season with salt. **2.** to preserve with salt or a salt solution. **3.** to add flavor or zest to; make lively: *Their grandfather salted his conversation with stories of his youth.*

to salt away. *Informal.* to store away; save: *Her uncle salted away a fortune.*

with a grain of salt. with some doubt; not too seriously: *He accepted her excuse for being late with a grain of salt.*

salt·cel·lar (sôlt′sel′ər) *n.* a shaker or dish that holds salt and is used at the table.

salt·ine (sôl tēn′) *n.* a thin, crisp cracker sprinkled with salt.

Salt Lake City, the capital and largest city of Utah, in the northern part of the state. Pop. (1970), 175,885.

salt lick, a natural salt deposit, or a block of salt put out in a field, that animals can lick to get the salt they need.

salt·pe·ter (sôlt′pē′tər) *also,* **salt·pe·tre.** *n.* see **potassium nitrate.**

Saltcellar

salt·shak·er (sôlt′shā′kər) *n.* a container having a top with a hole or holes in it, used for sprinkling salt on food.

salt·wa·ter (sôlt′wô′tər) *adj.* of, relating to, or living in salt water or the sea: *saltwater fish.*

salt·y (sôl′tē) *adj.*, **salt·i·er, salt·i·est. 1.** relating to, containing, or tasting of salt. **2.** of or suggesting the sea or life at sea. **3.** witty or lively, especially in a coarse or earthy way. —**salt′i·ness,** *n.*

sa·lu·bri·ous (sə lōō′brē əs) *adj.* good for a person's health; healthful: *Fresh sea air is thought to be salubrious.* —**sa·lu′bri·ous·ly,** *adv.* —**sa·lu′bri·ous·ness,** *n.*

sal·u·tar·y (sal′yə ter′ē) *adj.* **1.** good for a person's health: *Jogging is a salutary exercise.* **2.** having a good effect; beneficial: *His mother gave him salutary advice about applying for the job.*

sal·u·ta·tion (sal′yə tā′shən) *n.* **1.** the act of greeting, welcoming, or saluting by gestures or words. **2.** gestures or words used in greeting, welcoming, or saluting. **3.** a word or phrase, such as "Dear Sir," that is used to begin a letter.

sal·u·ta·to·ri·an (sə lōō′tə tôr′ē ən) *n.* the student, usually ranking second in his class, who gives the opening speech at graduation.

sa·lu·ta·to·ry (sə lōō′tə tôr′ē) *adj.* of, relating to, or expressing a greeting or salutation: *a salutatory gesture.* —*n. pl.*, **sa·lu·ta·to·ries.** an opening speech, especially one given at a graduation.

sa·lute (sə lōōt′) *v.*, **sa·lut·ed, sa·lut·ing.** —*v.t.* **1.** to show respect for in a particular way, as by raising the right hand to the forehead: *The private saluted his commanding officer.* **2.** to greet with words or gestures of welcome or respect: *Grandfather saluted the ladies by tipping his hat to them.* —*v.i.* to make a gesture of respect, especially by raising the right hand to the forehead: *He saluted when the flag was raised.* —*n.* **1.** the act, gesture, or ceremony of saluting. **2.** the position or attitude taken when one salutes: *to stand at salute.*

Salv., Salvador.

Sal·va·dor (sal′və dôr′) *n.* **1.** see **El Salvador. 2.** a port city on the eastern coast of Brazil, north of Rio de Janeiro. Pop. (1970), 1,007,744.

Sal·va·do·ran (sal′və dôr′ən) *n.* a person who was born or is living in El Salvador. —*adj.* of or relating to El Salvador or its people. Also, **Sal·va·do·ri·an** (sal′və dôr′ē ən).

sal·vage (sal′vij) *v.t.*, **sal·vaged, sal·vag·ing.** to save or rescue from being lost or destroyed: *The owner salvaged only a few pieces of furniture from his burning store.* —*n.* **1.** the act of saving a ship, its crew, or its cargo from being lost or destroyed. **2.** the ship, crew, cargo, or property that is saved. **3.** payment given to those who help save a ship, its crew, or its cargo from being lost or destroyed. **4.** the act of saving any property from being lost or destroyed. —**sal′vage·a·ble,** *adj.* —**sal′vag·er,** *n.*

sal·va·tion (sal vā′shən) *n.* **1.** the saving or freeing from difficulty, danger, destruction, or evil. **2.** a person or thing that saves or frees. **3.** the freeing of the soul from sin and from punishment for sin; redemption.

Salvation Army, an international Protestant organization engaged in preaching Christianity and helping the poor. It was founded by William Booth in 1865.

salve (sav) *n.* **1.** a soft, often medicated substance that is put on the skin to help heal an injury and to stop pain; ointment. **2.** anything that soothes: *His mother's kindness was a salve when he was unhappy.* —*v.t.,* **salved, sal·ving. 1.** to soothe or calm; comfort: *Her words of praise salved his hurt feelings.* **2.** to put salve on: *to salve a burn.*

sal·ver (sal′vər) *n.* a tray, especially one made of metal and used for serving food or drink.

sal·vo (sal′vō) *n. pl.,* **sal·vos** or **sal·voes. 1.** a firing of several guns at the same time, often as a salute. **2.** the dropping at the same time of all the bombs or missiles carried by an airplane. **3.** a sudden outburst, as of cheers.

S. Am., South America; South American.

Sa·ma·ra (sə mär′ə) *n.* see **Kuibyshev.**

Sa·mar·i·a (sə mer′ē ə) *n.* **1.** in the Bible, an ancient region west of the Jordan. **2.** the main city of this region.

Sa·mar·i·tan (sə mar′ət ən) *n.* **1.** a person who lived in Samaria. **2.** see **Good Samaritan.** —*adj.* of or relating to Samaria or its people.

sa·mar·i·um (sə mer′ē əm) *n.* a silvery metallic element used in the production of certain lasers and in nuclear reactors. Symbol: **Sm**

Sam·ar·kand (sam′ər kand′) *n.* a city in the Soviet Union, in central Asia. Pop. (1970 est.), 267,000.

same (sām) *adj.* **1.** resembling another in every way; exactly alike: *The two girls wore the same dress to the dance.* **2.** being the very one; not another; identical: *That is the same man I sat next to on the bus today.* **3.** not changed, as in character: *Ann is the same kind, friendly person that she was years ago.* —*n.* a person or thing that is alike or identical: *He ordered pie, and I asked for the same.*

all the same or **just the same.** nevertheless.

the same. in the same manner: *She feels the same as you do about it.*

same·ness (sām′nis) *n.* **1.** the state or quality of being alike or identical. **2.** lack of variety; monotony.

S. Amer., South America; South American.

Sa·mo·a (sə mō′ə) *n.* an island group in the South Pacific, divided into Western Samoa and American Samoa. —**Sa·mo′an,** *adj., n.*

sam·o·var (sam′ə vär′) *n.* a metal urn that has a spigot. It is used especially in Russia for boiling water for tea.

Sam·o·yed (sam′ə yed′) *n.* a dog having a thick, white coat that forms a ruff around the shoulders. It was first bred in Siberia for pulling sleds and herding reindeer.

sam·pan (sam′pan′) *n.* a small boat with a flat bottom, a large oar at the stern, and often one sail, used in China and Japan.

sam·ple (sam′pəl) *n.* a small part or piece of anything, or one item of a group, that shows the quality, nature, or characteristics of the whole: *Mother*

Samoyed

brought home a sample of the wallpaper. —*v.t.,* **sam·pled, sam·pling.** to test, examine, or judge by taking a sample.

sam·pler¹ (sam′plər) *n.* a decorative piece of cloth embroidered with designs or letters. [Old French *essemplaire* pattern, sample.]

sam·pler² (sam′plər) *n.* a person who samples. [*Sample* + -*er*¹.]

Sam·son (sam′sən) *n.* **1.** in the Old Testament, a Hebrew judge or ruler, famous for his great strength. **2.** any man of great strength.

Sam·u·el (sam′yōō əl) *n.* **1.** in the Old Testament, a Hebrew judge and prophet. **2.** either of two books of the Old Testament, containing Hebrew history from the birth of Samuel to the death of David.

sam·u·rai (sam′oo rī′) *n. pl.,* **sam·u·rai. 1.** in feudal Japan, a member of the warrior class. **2.** this warrior class.

Sa·na (sä nä′) *n.* the capital of Yemen, in the central part of the country. Pop. (1970), 120,800.

San An·to·ni·o (san′ an tō′nē ō′) a city in south-central Texas. Pop. (1970), 654,153.

san·a·to·ri·um (san′ə tôr′ē əm) *n. pl.,* **san·a·to·ri·ums** or **san·a·to·ri·a** (san′ə tôr′ē ə). **1.** an institution for the care and treatment of patients who have tuberculosis or other diseases that require treatment over a long period of time. **2.** a health resort; sanitarium.

San Ber·nar·di·no (san′ bur′nər dē′nō) a city in southern California, east of Los Angeles. Pop. (1970), 104,251.

San·cho Pan·za (sän′chō pän′zə) the peasant squire of Don Quixote.

sanc·ti·fy (sangk′tə fī′) *v.t.,* **sanc·ti·fied, sanc·ti·fy·ing. 1.** to set apart as sacred or holy; reserve for religious use; consecrate: *The priest sanctified the new chapel.* **2.** to make free from sin; purify. **3.** to give religious approval to: *to sanctify marriage.* **4.** to make acceptable or give approval to. —**sanc′ti·fi·ca′tion,** *n.*

sanc·ti·mo·ni·ous (sangk′tə mō′nē əs) *adj.* pretending to be very pious or religious. —**sanc′ti·mo′ni·ous·ly,** *adv.* —**sanc′ti·mo′ni·ous·ness,** *n.*

sanc·tion (sangk′shən) *v.t.* **1.** to give approval, support, or encouragement to: *The owner did not sanction hunting on his property.* **2.** to permit, accept, or approve officially: *The court sanctioned the new law.* —*n.* **1.** official permission, acceptance, or approval. **2.** approval or encouragement that serves to make something acceptable or permissable. **3.** *usually,* **sanctions.** in international law, the action by one or more countries against another country to force it to obey the law.

sanc·ti·ty (sangk′tə tē) *n. pl.,* **sanc·ti·ties. 1.** piety, as of life or character; saintliness. **2.** the state or quality of being holy; sacredness: *the sanctity of a church.* **3.** the state or quality of being regarded with great respect.

sanc·tu·ar·y (sangk′chōō er′ē) *n. pl.,* **sanc·tu·ar·ies. 1.** any place of refuge or protection. **2.** refuge or protection so provided. **3.** a holy or sacred place, such as a church or temple. **4.** the most holy part of a church or temple. **5.** a natural area where birds and animals are protected from hunters.

sanc·tum (sangk′təm) *n. pl.,* **sanc·tums** or **sanc·ta** (sangk′tə). **1.** a holy or sacred place. **2.** a private room or other place where a person can be undisturbed.

sand (sand) *n.* **1.** tiny, loose grains of crushed or worn-down rocks. Sand is formed by the process of erosion. **2.** *usually,* **sands.** a region covered with this material, such as a desert or beach. —*v.t.* **1.** to scrape, smooth, or polish with sand or sandpaper: *to sand a floor.* **2.** to sprinkle or cover with sand: *to sand the roads after a snowfall.*

at; āpe; cär; end; mē; it; īce; hot; ōld; fôrk; wood; fōōl; oil; out; up; turn; sing; thin; this; hw in white; zh in treasure. The symbol ə stands for the sound of **a** in about, **e** in taken, **i** in pencil, **o** in lemon, and **u** in circus.

san·dal (sand′əl) *n.* **1.** a shoe consisting of a sole held to the foot by one or more straps or thongs. **2.** a shoe with an open design on the top part, and usually fastened with a strap or straps, worn especially by children.

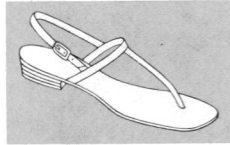
Sandal

san·dal·wood (sand′əl wood′) *n.* **1.** the hard, yellowish, fine-grained wood of an evergreen tree, used for making carved boxes and fans. It also yields a fragrant oil used in perfumes and soaps. **2.** the tree from which this wood comes.

sand·bag (sand′bag′) *n.* **1.** a bag filled with sand, used as ballast in balloons and to build dams or walls for protection when there is danger of a flood or attack. **2.** a small, narrow bag filled with sand and used as a weapon. —*v.t.*, **sand·bagged, sand·bag·ging. 1.** to place sandbags in or around: *to sandbag the banks of a river.* **2.** to hit with a sandbag.

sand·bar (sand′bär′) *also,* **sand bar.** *n.* a ridge of sand in a river or bay or along the shore, built up by the action of waves and currents.

sand·blast (sand′blast′) *v.t.* to clean, grind, or decorate a hard surface, such as glass, metal, or brick, with a high-speed stream of sand. —*n.* a high-speed stream of sand.

sand·box (sand′boks′) *n. pl.,* **sand·box·es.** a large, low box filled with sand for children to play in.

Sand·burg, Carl (sand′burg′) 1878–1967, U.S. poet.

sand dollar, a round, flat, spiny animal that lives in the sandy bottom of shallow ocean waters throughout the world.

sand·er (san′-dər) *n.* **1.** a machine that has a disc or belt of sandpaper, used to sand floors or woodwork. **2.** a person who sands.

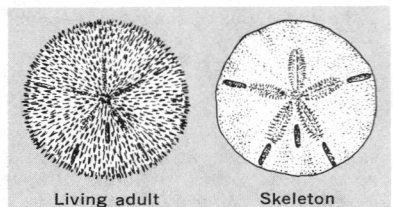
Living adult   Skeleton
Sand dollar

sand·glass (sand′glas′) *n. pl.,* **sand·glass·es.** another word for **hourglass.**

San Di·e·go (san′ dē ā′gō) a port city in southern California, at the Mexican border. Pop. (1970), 696,769.

sand·lot (sand′lot′) *also,* **sand-lot.** *adj.* of or relating to games played by amateurs, as in a vacant lot: *sandlot baseball.*

sand·man (sand′man′) *n. pl.,* **sand·men** (sand′men′). in folklore, a man who is said to make children sleepy by sprinkling sand on their eyes at bedtime.

sand·pa·per (sand′pā′pər) *n.* a strong, heavy paper with a coating of sand or other material, used for smoothing, polishing, or cleaning surfaces. —*v.t.* to smooth, polish, or clean by rubbing with sandpaper.

sand·pip·er (sand′pī′pər) *n.* any of various birds that live along the seashore, having a long, slender bill, long legs, and brown or grayish feathers.

Sandpiper

sand·stone (sand′stōn′) *n.* a sedimentary rock made up mainly of grains of sand, widely used as a building material.

sand·storm (sand′stôrm′) *n.* a storm of high winds that carry sand through the air, commonly occurring in desert areas where loose sand is abundant.

sand·wich (sand′wich) *n. pl.,* **sand·wich·es. 1.** two or more slices of bread with a filling of meat, cheese, or other food. **2.** something like a sandwich: *an ice-cream sandwich.* —*v.t.* to fit, place, or squeeze in tightly: *The book was sandwiched in between two others. He sandwiched four people into the back seat of his car.* [From the fourth Earl of *Sandwich,* 1718–1792, who supposedly thought up the sandwich so that he would not have to leave the gambling table to eat.]

Sandwich Islands, see **Hawaiian Islands.**

sand·y (san′dē) *adj.,* **sand·i·er, sand·i·est. 1.** of, covered with, or like sand: *sandy soil, a sandy road.* **2.** yellowish-red in color: *sandy hair.* —**sand′i·ness,** *n.*

sane (sān) *adj.,* **san·er, san·est. 1.** having a sound and healthy mind; not mentally ill. **2.** having or showing reason or good judgment; sensible; rational: *sane advice.* —**sane′ly,** *adv.* —**sane′ness,** *n.*

San·for·ized (san′fə rīzd′) *adj. Trademark.* (of fabric) preshrunk by a special process before being made into clothing.

San Fran·cis·co (san′ fran sis′kō) a port city in western California, on the Pacific Ocean. Pop. (1970), 715,674.

San Francisco Bay, an inlet of the Pacific Ocean, on the central coast of California.

sang (sang) the past tense of **sing.**

san·guine (sang′gwin) *adj.* **1.** cheerful and optimistic: *a sanguine personality, a sanguine outlook.* **2.** having a red color; ruddy: *a glowing, sanguine complexion.* —**san′-guine·ly,** *adv.*

san·i·tar·i·um (san′ə ter′ē əm) *n. pl.,* **san·i·tar·i·ums** or **san·i·tar·i·a** (san′ə ter′ē ə). **1.** a health resort. **2.** an institution for the care of patients with long-term diseases; sanatorium.

san·i·tar·y (san′ə ter′ē) *adj.* **1.** of or relating to health: *Hospitals must maintain strict sanitary rules.* **2.** free from dirt or germs: *a sanitary swimming pool.* —**san·i·tar·i·ly,** (san′ə ter′ə lē), *adv.*

san·i·ta·tion (san′ə tā′shən) *n.* the protection of public health by keeping a clean and healthy environment, as by removing and disposing of sewage and garbage, controlling the growth of insects and rodents, and keeping the water supply clean.

san·i·tize (san′ə tīz′) *v.t.,* **san·i·tized, san·i·tiz·ing.** to make (something) clean and free of dirt or germs, as by sterilizing.

san·i·ty (san′ə tē) *n.* **1.** a sound and healthy state of mind. **2.** soundness of judgment; reasonableness; sensibleness.

San Joa·quin (san′ wä kēn′) a river in central California, flowing westward to the mouth of the Sacramento River.

San Jo·se (san′ hō zā′) a city in western California. Pop. (1970), 445,779.

San Jo·sé (san′ hō zā′) the capital of Costa Rica, in the central part of the country. Pop. (1970 est.), 205,700.

San Jose scale, a tiny insect found throughout North America, that is destructive to fruit trees and shrubs.

San Juan (san hwän′) the capital of Puerto Rico, a port in the northeastern part of the island. Pop. (1970), 452,749.

sank (sangk) the past tense of **sink.**

San Ma·ri·no (san′ mə rē′nō) a tiny country in southern Europe, near the Adriatic Sea, completely surrounded by Italy. Capital, San Marino. Area, 23 sq. mi. Pop. (1970 est.), 17,726.

San Ma·te·o (san′ mə tā′ō) a city in western California, south of San Francisco. Pop. (1970), 78,991.

sans (sanz) *prep.* without.

San Sal·va·dor (san sal′və dôr′) **1.** the capital and largest city of El Salvador, in the central part of the country. Pop. (1976 est.), 386,600. **2.** an island of the central Bahamas, believed to be the first landing place of Columbus in the New World. Area, 60 sq. mi.

San·skrit (san′skrit) *also,* **San·scrit.** *n.* a language of ancient India, used in literature and religion.

San·ta An·a (san′tə an′ə) a city in southern California, southeast of Los Angeles. Pop. (1970), 156,601.

San·ta An·na, An·to·nio Ló·pez de (sän′tä ä′nä; än tōn′yō lō′pes dä) 1795–1876, the Mexican general who led the army that defeated the Texans at the Alamo in 1836.

San·ta Bar·ba·ra (san′tə bär′bər ə) a city in southern California, on the Pacific Ocean, north of Los Angeles. Pop. (1970), 70,215.

Santa Barbara Islands, an island group off the southern coast of California.

San·ta Cat·a·li·na (san′tə kat′əl ē′nə) one of the Santa Barbara Islands, a resort area noted for its fine beaches and fishing. Also, **Catalina, Catalina Island.**

San·ta Clar·a (san′tə klar′ə) a city in western California. Pop. (1970), 87,717.

San·ta Claus (san′tə klôz′) in American folklore, a jolly old man with a white beard who brings presents to children at Christmas. He wears a red suit and drives a sleigh with eight reindeer.

San·ta Cruz de Te·ne·rife (san′tə krōōz′ də ten′ə rēf′, ten′ə rē′fä) the chief city and port of the Canary Islands. Pop. (1975), 179,613.

San·ta Fe (san′tə fā′) the capital of New Mexico, in the north-central part of the state. Pop. (1970), 41,167.

Santa Fe Trail, an overland trade route between Independence, Missouri and Santa Fe, New Mexico. It was used from 1821 to 1880.

San·ta Is·a·bel (san′tə iz′ə bel′), the former capital of Equatorial Africa. see **Malabo.**

San·ta Mon·i·ca (san′tə mon′i kə) a city in southern California, on the Pacific Ocean, near Los Angeles. Pop. (1970), 88,289.

San·ti·a·go (san′tē ä′gō) *n.* the capital and largest city of Chile, in the central part of the country. Pop. (1970), 510,246.

Santiago de Cu·ba (dä kōō′bä) a port city in southeastern Cuba. Pop. (1970), 276,000.

San·to Do·min·go (san′tō də ming′gō) the capital of the Dominican Republic, on the southern coast of the country, formerly known as Ciudad Trujillo. Pop. (1970), 671,400.

San·tos (sän′tōs) *n.* a port city in southeastern Brazil, on the Atlantic Ocean. Pop. (1970), 341,317.

São Pau·lo (sou pou′loo) the largest city in Brazil, in the southeastern part of the country. Pop. (1975 est.), 7,198,608.

sap¹ (sap) *n.* **1.** a liquid that circulates through a plant and carries water, dissolved minerals, and food from one part of the plant to another. **2.** *Slang.* a person who is foolish or silly. [Old English *sæp.*]

sap² (sap) *v.t.,* **sapped, sap·ping. 1.** to weaken or destroy slowly: *The long illness sapped his strength.* **2.** to weaken by removing the underlying support of (a structure), as by digging under or wearing away the foundation. [Middle French *sapper* to undermine, dig into.]

sa·pi·ence (sā′pē əns) *n.* wisdom.

sa·pi·ent (sā′pē ənt) *adj.* wise; sage. —**sa′pi·ent·ly,** *adv.*

sap·ling (sap′ling) *n.* a young tree.

sap·o·dil·la (sap′ə dil′ə) *n.* **1.** a tall evergreen tree found in tropical America, having a heavy, fine-grained wood, and yielding chicle. **2.** the sweet fruit of this tree, having brownish-yellow flesh and rough, brown skin. It is shaped like an apple and can be eaten.

sa·pon·i·fi·ca·tion (sə pon′ə fi kā′shən) *n.* a changing or being changed into soap.

sa·pon·i·fy (sə pon′ə fī′) *v.,* **sa·pon·i·fied, sa·pon·i·fy·ing.** —*v.t.* to make (a fat) react with an alkali to form soap. —*v.i.* to become changed into soap by this method.

sap·per (sap′ər) *n.* a soldier who lays mines and detects and disarms enemy mines. Sappers also build fortifications and trenches.

sap·phire (saf′īr) *n.* **1.** a precious stone that is transparent and deep blue in color. **2.** a deep blue color. —*adj.* having the color sapphire; deep blue.

Sap·po·ro (sä pō′rō) *n.* a city in northern Japan, on the island of Hokkaido. Pop. (1978 est.), 1,336,702.

sap·py (sap′ē) *adj.,* **sap·pi·er, sap·pi·est. 1.** full of sap; juicy. **2.** *Slang.* silly; foolish. —**sap′pi·ness,** *n.*

sap·ro·phyte (sap′rə fīt′) *n.* a plant, such as the mushroom, that is not green and gets its food from dead or decaying plant or animal matter.

sap·suck·er (sap′suk′ər) *n.* a North American woodpecker that has black or brown feathers and a yellow belly. It feeds on the sap of trees by drilling holes in the tree with its strong, pointed bill.

sap·wood (sap′wood′) *n.* the young, soft wood of a tree or other woody plant found just beneath the bark. It is made up of living cells, through which sap moves upward in the plant.

Sar·a·cen (sar′ə sən) *n.* **1.** a Muslim, especially at the time of the Crusades or during the Middle Ages. **2.** formerly, any Arab.

Sar·a·gos·sa (sar′ə gos′ə) *n.* a city in northeastern Spain. Pop. (1976 est.), 539,021.

Sar·ah (ser′ə) *n.* in the Bible, the wife of Abraham and mother of Isaac.

Sapsucker

Sa·ra·je·vo (sar′ə yä′vō) *n.* a city in central Yugoslavia, where the assassination of the Austrian Archduke Francis Ferdinand took place in 1914, leading to the outbreak of World War I.

sa·ra·pe (sə rä′pē) another spelling of **serape.**

Sa·ra·tov (sä rä′tôf) *n.* a city in the southwestern Soviet Union, on the Volga River. Pop. (1979), 856,000.

Sa·ra·wak (sə rä′wäk) *n.* a state in Malaysia, in northwest Borneo, formerly a British colony.

sar·casm (sär′kaz′əm) *n.* **1.** the use of sharp, bitter, taunting, or scornful remarks or language intended to hurt or make fun of someone or something: *"Please don't trouble yourself,"* Alice said in sarcasm when he made no move *to help her pick up the packages.* **2.** a sharp, bitter, taunting, or scornful remark or language.

sar·cas·tic (sär kas′tik) *adj.* **1.** characterized by sarcasm; mocking: *sarcastic comments.* **2.** given to the use of sarcasm: *a very sarcastic young man.* —**sar·cas′ti·cal·ly,** *adv.*

sar·coph·a·gus (sär kof′ə gəs) *n. pl.,* **sar·coph·a·gi** (sär·kof′ə jī′) or **sar·coph·a·gus·es.** a stone coffin placed above ground. It is often ornamented with sculpture or painting.

---

at; āpe; cär; end; mē; it; īce; hot; ōld; fôrk; wood; fōōl; oil; out; up; turn; sing; thin; this; hw in white; zh in treasure. The symbol ə stands for the sound of **a** in about, **e** in taken, **i** in pencil, **o** in lemon, and **u** in circus.

S

sar·dine (sär dēn′) *n. pl.,* **sar·dines** or **sar·dine.** a food fish that is related to the herring. Sardines are caught while young and small, and are usually packed tightly in oil in flat cans.

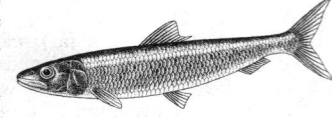

Sardine

Sar·din·i·a (sär din′- ē ə) *n.* an Italian island in the Mediterranean Sea, west of Italy. —**Sar·din′i·an,** *adj., n.*

sar·don·ic (sär don′ik) *adj.* mocking or sneering, often in a sarcastic way: *a sardonic laugh.* —**sar·don′i·cal·ly,** *adv.*

sar·gas·so (sär gas′ō) *n.* a seaweed that floats in large masses in the Gulf Stream and the Sargasso Sea.

Sargasso Sea, an oval-shaped area of the central North Atlantic Ocean, between the West Indies and the Azores.

Sar·gent, John Singer (sär′jənt) 1856–1925, U.S. painter.

sa·ri (sär′ē) *n. pl.,* **sa·ris.** an outer garment worn by women in India and Pakistan. It is made by wrapping a long piece of silk or cotton cloth around the body to form a long skirt, and by bringing one end up in front and over the shoulder to form the top.

Sari

sa·rong (sə rông′, sə rong′) *n.* an outer garment that is worn as a skirt by men and women who live on islands in the Pacific Ocean. It is made by draping a long, rectangular piece of material around the body at the waist.

sar·sa·pa·ril·la (sas′pə ril′ə, sär′sə pə-ril′ə) *n.* **1.** a climbing or trailing vine found in Mexico, Central America, and South America, having prickly stems and large heart-shaped leaves with toothed edges. **2.** the root of this vine, dried and used as a medicine, and as a flavoring for syrups and soft drinks. **3.** a soft drink flavored with this root.

Sar·to, Andrea del (sär′tō) see **Andrea del Sarto.**

sar·to·ri·al (sär tôr′ē əl) *adj.* **1.** of or relating to tailors or their work. **2.** of or relating to clothing or dress, especially men's: *He was dressed in sartorial splendor for the dinner party.* —**sar·to′ri·al·ly,** *adv.*

sash[1] (sash) *n. pl.,* **sash·es.** a broad band of cloth or ribbon, often worn over one shoulder or around the waist as part of a uniform. [Earlier *shash,* from Arabic *shāsh* turban.]

sash[2] (sash) *n. pl.,* **sash·es.** the frame that holds the panes of glass in a window or door. [A form of *chassis.*]

sa·shay (sa shā′) *v.i. Informal.* to walk or move in a noticeably nonchalant or swaggering manner.

Sask., Saskatchewan.

Sas·katch·e·wan (sas kach′ə won′) *n.* a province of Canada, in the western part of the country. Area, 251,700 sq. mi. Pop. (1971), 926,242.

sass (sas) *Informal. n.* back talk; impudence. —*v.t.* to talk impudently or disrespectfully to; talk back to: *He was punished for sassing his father.*

sas·sa·fras (sas′ə fras′) *n. pl.,* **sas·sa·fras·es.** a tree found in North America, whose roots have a bark that is used to make tea and to flavor such things as root beer and tobacco.

sas·sy (sas′ē) *adj.,* **sas·si·er, sas·si·est.** *Informal.* impudent; saucy: *The sassy child talked back to his mother.*

sat (sat) a past tense and past participle of **sit.**

Sat., Saturday.

Sa·tan (sāt′ən) *n.* the Devil.

sa·tan·ic (sā tan′ik) *adj.* of or relating to Satan; very evil or cruel.

satch·el (sach′əl) *n.* a bag or small suitcase for carrying clothing, instruments, books, or other articles. It sometimes has a shoulder strap.

sate (sāt) *v.t.,* **sat·ed, sat·ing. 1.** to fill or satisfy completely: *to sate an appetite.* **2.** to provide with more than enough; glut.

sa·teen (sa tēn′) *n.* a strong cotton fabric woven with a smooth, glossy finish so as to look like satin.

sat·el·lite (sat′əl īt′) *n.* **1.** a heavenly body that revolves in an orbit around another body larger than itself; moon. **2.** an object made to revolve in a particular orbit around a body in space, such as the earth or moon. **3.** a country dominated or controlled by another more powerful country. **4.** a follower or attendant of an important person.

Satellite

sa·tia·ble (sā′shə bəl, sā′shē ə-bəl) *adj.* that can be satiated.

sa·ti·ate (sā′shē āt′) *v.t.,* **sa·ti·at·ed, sa·ti·at·ing. 1.** to provide with more than enough; cloy. **2.** to satisfy completely: *The large dinner satiated the boy's hunger.* —**sa′ti·a′tion,** *n.*

sat·in (sat′in) *n.* a fabric having a smooth, glossy surface, made of silk or various man-made fibers. —*adj.* resembling satin; smooth; glossy: *satin skin.*

sat·in·wood (sat′in wood′) *n.* **1.** any of various kinds of wood having a satiny appearance, used for veneers. **2.** any of the trees having such wood.

sat·in·y (sat′in ē) *adj.* resembling satin in softness, smoothness, or glossiness.

sat·ire (sat′īr) *n.* **1.** the use of humor, irony, or ridicule to attack or make fun of human faults or follies. **2.** a work of literature that attacks or makes fun of human faults or follies by this means.

sa·tir·i·cal (sə tir′i kəl) *adj.* **1.** of, resembling, or characterized by satire. **2.** using satire: *a satirical author.* Also, **sa·tir·ic** (sə tir′ik). —**sa·tir′i·cal·ly,** *adv.*

sat·i·rist (sat′ər ist) *n.* a person who uses satire, especially a writer of satires.

sat·i·rize (sat′ə rīz′) *v.t.,* **sat·i·rized, sat·i·riz·ing.** to attack or make fun of by means of satire.

sat·is·fac·tion (sat′is fak′shən) *n.* **1.** the act of satisfying or the state of being satisfied. **2.** the cause or means of being satisfied. **3.** something that makes up for a wrong, injury, or obligation.

sat·is·fac·to·ry (sat′is fak′tər ē) *adj.* good enough to meet a need or desire; giving satisfaction. —**sat′is·fac′-to·ri·ly,** *adv.* —**sat′is·fac′to·ri·ness,** *n.*

sat·is·fy (sat′is fī′) *v.,* **sat·is·fied, sat·is·fy·ing.** —*v.t.* **1.** to meet the needs or desires of; make contented: *The team's performance in the game didn't satisfy the coach.* **2.** to supply fully with what is needed or desired: *The water satisfied his thirst.* **3.** to fulfill or answer the conditions of: *to satisfy the requirements of a course.* **4.** to pay off: *to satisfy a debt.* **5.** to make up for; redress: *to satisfy a wrong.* **6.** to answer convincingly: *The boy's reply satisfied his father.* —*v.i.* to give satisfaction. —**sat′is·fi′er,** *n.*

sa·trap (sā′trap) *n.* **1.** a governor of a province in the ancient Persian empire. **2.** any official or ruler of lesser rank or position.

sat·u·rate (sach′ə rāt′) *v.t.,* **sat·u·rat·ed, sat·u·rat·ing. 1.** to fill with something to the point where no more can be absorbed, especially to soak thoroughly: *Water saturated the cloth.* **2.** to fill full or to excess: *The smell of* *perfume saturated the room.* **3.** *Chemistry.* to supply (a solvent or solution) with as much of a particular substance as can be dissolved in it.

sat·u·ra·tion (sach′ə rā′shən) *n.* the act of saturating or the state of being saturated.

Sat·ur·day (sat′ər dē, sat′ər dā′) *n.* the seventh day of the week. [Old English *Sæterdæg,* a translation of Latin *Sāturnī diēs* the day of Saturn.]

Sat·urn (sat′ərn) *n.* **1.** *Roman Mythology.* the god of agriculture. In Greek Mythology he was called Cronus. **2.** the second largest planet of the solar system and sixth in order of distance from the sun, having ten moons. Saturn is surrounded by rings that are thought to be made up of millions of tiny ice particles.

Sat·ur·na·li·a (sat′ər nā′lē ə) *n. pl.,* **Sat·ur·na·li·a** or **Sat·ur·na·li·as.** **1.** an ancient Roman festival of Saturn, that began on December 17 and continued for seven days. **2. saturnalia.** any period or occasion of merrymaking and festivity.

sat·ur·nine (sat′ər nīn′) *adj.* having or showing a gloomy or moody nature. [From the former belief that people born under the sign of the planet *Saturn* had a gloomy disposition.] **—sat′ur·nine′ly,** *adv.*

sat·yr (sat′ər, sā′tər) *n. Greek Mythology.* a minor god of the countryside, represented as a man having the horns, tail, and legs of a goat. In Roman mythology it was called a faun.

sauce (sôs) *n.* **1.** a liquid or creamy blend of several ingredients served with food to add to or improve its flavor. **2.** a fruit that has been stewed into a pulp and sweetened: *cranberry sauce.* —*v.t.,* **sauced, sauc·ing.** to prepare or flavor with sauce.

sauce·pan (sôs′pan′) *n.* a small enamel or metal pot with a handle, used for cooking food.

sau·cer (sô′sər) *n.* a small shallow dish, especially one for holding a cup.

sau·cy (sô′sē) *adj.,* **sau·ci·er, sau·ci·est.** bold or rude; impudent. **—sau′ci·ly,** *adv.* **—sau′ci·ness,** *n.*

Satyr

Sa·u·di Arabia (sä ōō′dē) a country in southwestern Asia. Capital, Riyadh. Area, 830,000 sq. mi. Pop. (1976 est.), 7,440,000.

sauer·kraut (sour′krout′) *n.* finely shredded cabbage that has been salted and fermented in its own juice.

Sauk (sôk) *n. pl.,* **Sauks** or **Sauk.** a member of a tribe of North American Indians who formerly lived in what is now Michigan and Wisconsin.

Saul (sôl) *n.* **1.** in the Old Testament, the first king of Israel. **2.** in the New Testament, the Apostle Paul before his conversion to Christianity. Also *(def. 2),* **Saul of Tarsus.**

Sault Ste. Ma·rie Canals (sōō′ sānt mə rē′) two canals linking Lake Superior and Lake Huron. They form part of the border between the United States and Canada.

sau·na (sou′nə, sô′nə) *n.* **1.** a bath resembling a steambath, in which the bather is surrounded by hot, dry air. **2.** a room in which to take such a bath.

saun·ter (sôn′tər) *v.i.* to walk in a slow, relaxed way; stroll. —*n.* a slow, relaxed walk; stroll.

sau·sage (sô′sij) *n.* finely chopped, seasoned meat, such as pork, beef, or veal, made into patties or stuffed in a casing.

sau·té (sô tā′) *v.t.,* **sau·téed, sau·té·ing.** to cook or brown quickly in an open pan using a small amount of very hot

fat. —*n.* food cooked in this manner. —*adj.* cooked or browned quickly in a small amount of very hot fat.

sau·terne (sō turn′) *also,* **Sau·ternes** (sō turn′). *n.* a sweet, white wine.

sav·age (sav′ij) *adj.* **1.** brutal, cruel, or vicious: *savage fighting.* **2.** not civilized: *a savage custom.* **3.** not tamed; wild: *savage beasts.* —*n.* **1.** a person who is not civilized, especially a person belonging to a primitive tribe or group. **2.** a brutal, cruel, or vicious person. **—sav′age·ly,** *adv.* **—sav′age·ness,** *n.*

sav·age·ry (sav′ij rē) *n. pl.,* **sav·age·ries.** **1.** the state or quality of being savage. **2.** savage behavior or actions.

sa·van·na (sə van′ə) *also,* **sa·van·nah.** *n.* a broad, grassy, treeless plain.

Sa·van·nah (sə van′ə) *n.* a port city in southeastern Georgia. Pop. (1970), 118,349.

sa·vant (sa vänt′, sav′ənt) *n.* a person of great learning; scholar.

save[1] (sāv) *v.,* **saved, sav·ing.** —*v.t.* **1.** to free from harm; make safe: *The fireman saved the woman from the burning house.* **2.** to set aside for future use: *Edna saves part of her allowance each week.* **3.** to keep from being lost, spent, or wasted: *She hurried to save time.* **4.** to keep from wear or damage; safeguard; preserve: *Jack wore a raincoat to save his suit during the storm.* **5.** to deliver from sin and its consequences. —*v.i.* **1.** to set aside money, as for future use: *John saved for a new bicycle.* **2.** to avoid expense or waste; economize: *It's difficult to save on groceries.* [Old French *salver, sauver.*] **—sav′er,** *n.*

save[2] (sāv) *prep.* except; but: *No one save the immediate family was invited to the wedding.* [A form of *safe* with the obsolete meaning of reserving, excepting.]

sav·ing (sā′ving) *adj.* **1.** that makes up for everything else; redeeming: *His only saving feature is his honesty.* **2.** thrifty; economical; frugal. —*n.* **1.** the act of a person or thing that saves something: *the saving of time.* **2.** something saved. **3. savings.** money saved, especially in a bank account.

savings account, a bank account for the purpose of saving money, on which interest is paid.

savings bank, a bank whose main purpose is to accept money for lending or investing, and to pay interest on it.

sav·ior (sāv′yər) *also, British,* **sav·iour.** *n.* **1.** a person who saves from harm, danger, or destruction; person who brings salvation. **2. the Savior.** Jesus.

sa·vor (sā′vər) *also, British,* **sa·vour.** *n.* **1.** a particular taste or smell. **2.** the power to arouse interest or excitement. —*v.t.* **1.** to taste or smell with pleasure: *to savor a meal.* **2.** to take great delight in: *She savored the news that her friend had won a scholarship to college.* **3.** to give flavor to; season. **—sa′vor·er,** *n.*

sa·vor·y[1] (sā′vər ē) *also, British,* **sa·vour·y.** *adj.* **1.** agreeable to the taste or smell: *Savory odors came from the kitchen.* **2.** morally acceptable or respectable: *a savory reputation.* **3.** sharp to the taste; pungent. [Old French *savoure.*] **—sa′vor·i·ness,** *n.*

sa·vor·y[2] (sā′vər ē) *n. pl.,* **sa·vor·ies.** a plant having narrow leaves used to flavor food. [Old English *sætherīe.*]

Sa·voy (sə voi′) *n.* a historic region in southeastern France.

at; āpe; cär; end; mē; it; īce; hot; ōld; fôrk; wood; fōōl; oil; out; up; turn; sing; thin; **th**is; hw in white; zh in treasure. The symbol ə stands for the sound of **a** in about, e in taken, i in pencil, o in lemon, and u in circus.

sav·vy (sav′ē) *Slang. v.i.,* **sav·vied, sav·vy·ing.** to know; understand. —*n.* good sense, judgment, or understanding. [A form of Spanish *sabe (Usted)?* do (you) know?]

saw¹ (sô) *n.* **1.** a hand or power tool having a metal blade whose edge is notched with pointed teeth, used for cutting wood, metal, or other hard materials. **2.** a machine having such a tool or tools. —*v.,* **sawed, sawed** or **sawn, saw·ing.** —*v.t.* **1.** to cut with a saw: *Phil sawed the log in half.* **2.** to shape or form by cutting with a saw: *The boys sawed a hole in the ice.* —*v.i.* **1.** to use a saw: *He sawed along the grain of the wood.* **2.** to be cut with a saw: *This wood saws easily.* [Old English *saga.*] —**saw′er,** *n.*

saw² (sô) the past tense of **see¹.**

saw³ (sô) *n.* a traditional and familiar saying. For example: *Too many cooks spoil the broth.* [Old English *sagu* a saying.]

saw·buck (sô′buk′) *n.* **1.** a kind of sawhorse made up of two X-shaped frames. It is used to hold logs while they are being sawed. **2.** *Slang.* a ten-dollar bill.

saw·dust (sô′dust′) *n.* the fine particles that fall from wood or other material as it is being sawed.

saw·fish (sô′fish′) *n. pl.,* **saw·fish** or **saw·fish·es.** a large fish having a long snout with sharp teeth along both edges.

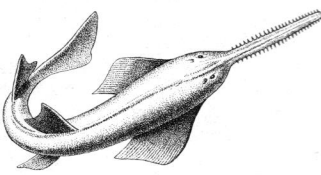

saw·horse (sô′hôrs′) *n.* a frame made up of a plank with two legs at each end. It is used to support boards while they are being sawed.

Sawfish

saw·mill (sô′mil′) *n.* a place where logs are sawed into lumber by machinery.

sawn (sôn) a past participle of **saw¹.**

saw·yer (sô′yər) *n.* a person whose work is sawing wood.

sax (saks) *n. pl.,* **sax·es.** *Informal.* saxophone.

sax·i·frage (sak′sə frij) *n.* any of a large group of plants bearing clusters of white, pink, purple, or yellow flowers.

Sax·on (sak′sən) *n.* **1.** a member or descendant of a Germanic tribe that, along with the Angles and Jutes, conquered Britain in the fifth and sixth centuries A.D. **2.** a person who was born or is living in Saxony. —*adj.* **1.** of or relating to the early Saxons or Anglo-Saxons. **2.** of or relating to Saxony.

Sax·o·ny (sak′sə nē) *n.* a region and former political division of Germany.

sax·o·phone (sak′sə fōn′) *n.* a wind instrument having a single-reed mouthpiece, a curving body made of metal, and a series of keys for changing the pitch of the tones. [From Antoine Joseph *Sax,* 1814–1894, a Belgian instrument maker who invented it.] —**sax′o·phon′ist,** *n.*

say (sā) *v.t.,* **said, say·ing. 1.** to speak or pronounce; utter: *I can't understand what he is saying.* **2.** to make known or express in words; state: *John said that he enjoyed meeting you.* **3.** to state as an opinion; declare: *She couldn't say how much longer the job would take.* **4.** to estimate; suppose; assume: *I would say that he earns $50 a month delivering papers.* **5.** to recite; repeat: *She said grace before lunch.* —*n.* the right or chance to speak: *Give him his say.* —*interj.* used to attract attention, express surprise, or the like: *Say! What was that noise outside?* —**say′er,** *n.*

Saxophone

say·ing (sā′ing) *n.* **1.** a traditional and familiar statement believed to contain truth, wisdom, or common sense. For example: *A stitch in time saves nine.* **2.** something said; statement.

says (sez) the third person singular present indicative of **say.**

say-so (sā′sō′) *n. Informal.* **1.** the authority to decide something: *Fred went ahead with the project on the teacher's say-so.* **2.** a statement that is not supported by any authority: *No one's going to believe such a strange story just on his say-so.*

Sb, the symbol for antimony. [Latin *stibium.*]

S.B., Bachelor of Science.

Sc, the symbol for scandium.

sc. **1.** scale. **2.** scene.

S.C., South Carolina.

scab (skab) *n.* **1.** a crust of dried blood and lymph fluid that forms a protective cover over a sore or wound during healing. **2.** *Informal.* a worker who refuses to join a labor union, especially one who works when the union workers are on strike.

scab·bard (skab′ərd) *n.* a case or sheath for the blade of a sword, bayonet, or other similar weapon.

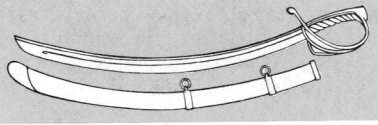

Scabbard with calvary sword

sca·bies (skā′bēz) *n.,pl.* a contagious skin disease producing intense itching. It is caused by mites that burrow under the skin and lay eggs.

scaf·fold (skaf′əld) *n.* **1.** a temporary wooden or metal platform, often suspended from a roof, used to support workmen and materials. **2.** a raised platform on which criminals are executed. **3.** any raised framework, stage, or stand.

scaf·fold·ing (skaf′əl ding) *n.* **1.** a scaffold or a connected series of scaffolds. **2.** the materials used to build a scaffold.

scal·a·wag (skal′ə wag′) *n.* **1.** any white Southerner who helped the Northerners carry out Reconstruction following the Civil War. **2.** a worthless person; rascal.

scald (skôld) *v.t.* **1.** to burn with hot liquid or steam: *The spilled coffee scalded his hand.* **2.** to clean or treat with steam or boiling liquid: *The nurse scalded the medical instruments.* **3.** to heat to a temperature just below the boiling point: *Mother scalded the milk.* —*n.* a burn caused by hot liquid or by steam.

scale¹ (skāl) *n.* **1.** a device for weighing an object by balancing it against another weight or against the force of a spring. **2. scales.** see **balance** *(def. 4).* **3.** a dish, pan, or platform of a balance. —*v.,* **scaled, scal·ing.** —*v.i.* to amount to in weight; weigh. —*v.t.* to weigh (something) in a scale or scales. [Old Norse *skál* a bowl, dish of a balance.]

to tip the scales. a. to weigh: *The boxer tipped the scales at 200 pounds.* **b.** to have a decisive effect: *The lawyer's brilliant, surprising defense tipped the scales in his client's favor.*

scale² (skāl) *n.* **1.** one of the horny, flattened, platelike structures forming all or part of the outer covering of certain animals, such as snakes, lizards, and fish. **2.** any structure resembling this, as on the wings of some insects or on the legs of birds. **3.** a thin, flat, piece or plate, as of armor. —*v.,* **scaled, scal·ing.** —*v.t.* **1.** to remove the scales from: *to scale a fish.* **2.** to remove in thin layers or scales: *to scale the bark off a branch.* —*v.i.* to peel or come off in scales; flake. [Old French *escale* shell, husk.] —**scale′less,** *adj.* —**scale′like′,** *adj.*

scale³ (skāl) *n.* **1.** a series of steps or degrees: *The student thought the grading scale was fair. She ranks high on the social scale.* **2.** the proportion that a plan, map, or model has to what it represents: *The scale of the map is one inch to 200 miles.* **3.** a series of marks made along a line at regularly spaced intervals, used in measuring or calculating: *the scale on a slide rule.* **4.** any instrument marked with such a series of marks. **5.** relative size or extent: *The painter worked on a large scale.* **6.** *Music.* a series of tones that go up or down in pitch according to fixed intervals, especially such a series within an octave: *the scale of C major.* **7.** *Mathematics.* a particular system of numbering: *the decimal scale.* —*v.t.,* **scaled, scal·ing. 1.** to climb up: *to scale a mountain.* **2.** to change or adjust by a fixed proportion or scale: *The two sides scaled down the level of fighting during the peace talks.* **3.** to make according to a scale: *to scale a drawing.* [Latin *scāla* a ladder.]

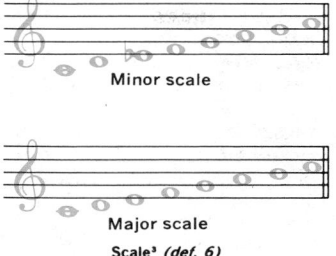

Minor scale

Major scale

Scale³ (def. 6)

scale insect, any of a group of tiny insects that live on plants. The females have no wings.

sca·lene (skā lēn′) *adj.* (of a triangle) having three unequal sides.

scal·lion (skal′yən) *n.* a young onion whose bulb is just beginning to form. Also, **green onion.**

scal·lop (skol′əp, skal′əp) *also,* **scol·lop, es·cal·lop.** *n.* **1.** any of a group of animals that live on the bottom of the sea, having soft bodies enclosed by two circular hinged shells that are ridged and have wavy edges. **2.** a muscle of certain species of this animal, used as food. **3.** one of a series of curves resembling the edge of a scallop shell, forming an ornamental border, as on clothing. —*v.t.* **1.** to shape or ornament with scallops, especially by cutting: *The edges of the tablecloth were scalloped.* **2.** to bake in a casserole with a sauce, often with a topping of bread crumbs: *to scallop potatoes.*

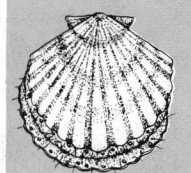

Scallop *(def. 1)*

scalp (skalp) *n.* **1.** the skin that covers the human skull, usually covered with hair. **2.** part of this skin and the attached hair, formerly cut or torn from the head of an enemy by certain North American Indians as a trophy or symbol of victory. —*v.t.* **1.** to cut or tear the scalp from. **2.** *Informal.* to buy and resell (tickets) at a very high profit: *to scalp tickets to a professional basketball game.* —**scalp′er,** *n.*

scal·pel (skal′pəl) *n.* a small, pointed knife with a straight handle and curved cutting edge, used in surgery.

scal·y (skā′lē) *adj.,* **scal·i·er, scal·i·est. 1.** covered with or made up of scales. **2.** resembling scales. **3.** peeling or coming off in scales or flakes; flaking. —**scal′i·ness,** *n.*

scaly anteater, another term for **pangolin.**

scamp (skamp) *n.* **1.** a worthless, dishonest person; rogue. **2.** a mischievous or playful person, especially a youngster.

scam·per (skam′pər) *v.i.* **1.** to run or flee quickly: *The rabbit scampered off into the woods.* **2.** to move about playfully: *The children scampered about the yard.* —*n.* the act of scampering.

scan (skan) *v.,* **scanned, scan·ning.** —*v.t.* **1.** to look at closely and carefully: *Eleanor scanned his face for some* sign that he recognized her. **2.** to search or look over (a wide area) thoroughly, especially by a slow, sweeping movement: *The sailors scanned the horizon for a ship.* **3.** to glance over or go through quickly; skim: *Hank scanned the magazine article.* **4.** to mark off or analyze (verse) according to a metrical pattern. **5.** to trace out closely spaced parallel lines on (a cathode-ray tube or other target). —*v.i.* **1.** to scan verse. **2.** (of verse) to conform to a metrical pattern: *The poem scans easily.* **3.** (of a beam from an electron gun) to trace out closely spaced parallel lines that cover a target, such as the viewing screen of a radar set or some other cathode-ray tube. —*n.* the act of scanning. —**scan′ner,** *n.*

scan·dal (skand′əl) *n.* **1.** something that shocks people or offends their sense of right and wrong, and disgraces those associated or connected with it: *There was a scandal when it was revealed that the mayor had stolen city funds.* **2.** anger or outrage caused by this: *News of the mayor's dishonesty gave rise to a public scandal.* **3.** harmful gossip: *The old woman enjoyed hearing scandal about her neighbors.*

scan·dal·ize (skand′əl īz′) *v.t.,* **scan·dal·ized, scan·dal·iz·ing.** to shock or offend by doing or saying something considered immoral or improper; outrage.

scan·dal·mon·ger (skand′əl mung′gər, skand′əl·mong′gər) *n.* a person who spreads harmful gossip.

scan·dal·ous (skand′əl əs) *adj.* **1.** causing scandal; shocking: *scandalous behavior.* **2.** spreading gossip that harms someone's reputation: *scandalous news.* —**scan′dal·ous·ly,** *adv.* —**scan′dal·ous·ness,** *n.*

Scan·di·na·vi·a (skan′də nā′vē ə) *n.* **1.** a region in northern Europe made up of Norway, Sweden, and Denmark. Iceland and Finland are sometimes also considered part of this area. **2.** a large peninsula of northern Europe occupied by Norway and Sweden.

Scan·di·na·vi·an (skan′də nā′vē ən) *n.* **1.** a person who was born or is living in Scandinavia. **2.** the languages of Scandinavia, including Danish, Norwegian, Icelandic, and Swedish. —*adj.* of or relating to Scandinavia, its people, their language, or their culture.

scan·di·um (skan′dē əm) *n.* a rare, very light, silver-white metal. Symbol: **Sc**

scant (skant) *adj.* **1.** not enough or scarcely enough; meager: *The boys brought only scant food supplies for the camping trip.* **2.** not quite amounting to a specified measure: *a scant six miles, a scant half-hour.* —*v.t.* to furnish a scant amount of; skimp on. —**scant′ly,** *adv.* —**scant′ness,** *n.*

scant·y (skan′tē) *adj.,* **scant·i·er, scant·i·est. 1.** not enough or scarcely enough; meager. **2.** small, as in size; skimpy: *a scanty bathing suit.* —**scant′i·ly,** *adv.* —**scant′i·ness,** *n.*

-scape *combining form* view; scene: *seascape, moonscape.* [From *landscape.*]

scape·goat (skāp′gōt′) *n.* a person or thing made to suffer for or bear the blame for the mistakes or wrongdoings of others.

scap·u·la (skap′yə lə) *n. pl.,* **scap·u·lae** (skap′yə lē) or **scap·u·las.** either of two flat, rectangular bones in the upper part of the back; shoulder blade.

scar (skär) *n.* **1.** any mark or discolored area left on the

at; āpe; cär; end; mē; it; īce; hot; ōld; fôrk; wood; fōōl; oil; out; up; turn; sing; thin; this; hw in white; zh in treasure. The symbol ə stands for the sound of **a** in about, **e** in taken, **i** in pencil, **o** in lemon, and **u** in circus.

skin after tissue that has been damaged or destroyed by injury or disease has healed. **2.** any mark or blemish resembling this. **3.** a lasting effect on the mind produced by a distressing or tragic experience. **4.** *Botany.* a mark showing where something was attached, as where a leaf was attached to a stem. —*v.t.,* **scarred, scar·ring.** to mark with a scar or scars; leave a scar or scars upon.

scar·ab (skar′əb) *n.* **1.** any of a large group of beetles having stocky, oval bodies, especially one of a species of beetles thought of as sacred by the ancient Egyptians. **2.** a gem cut in the shape of this beetle, or a piece of jewelry bearing its image.

scarce (skers) *adj.,* **scarc·er, scarc·est.** difficult to get or find: *Water is scarce in the desert.* —*adv.* scarcely. —**scarce′ness,** *n.*

　to make (oneself) scarce. *Informal.* to go or stay away.

scarce·ly (skers′lē) *adv.* **1.** by a small margin; barely: *I had scarcely come in when the phone rang.* **2.** almost not; hardly: *There was scarcely a person on the street.* **3.** certainly or most probably not: *She could scarcely have gone back to visit them after the way that they treated her.*

scar·ci·ty (sker′sə tē) *n. pl.,* **scar·ci·ties. 1.** an insufficient amount or supply. **2.** the state or quality of being scarce.

scare (sker) *v.,* **scared, scar·ing.** —*v.t.* **1.** to cause to be afraid or alarmed; frighten: *The thunder scared the children.* **2.** to drive or force by frightening: *The dog scared the thief away.* —*v.i.* to become scared: *He doesn't scare easily.* —*n.* **1.** sudden fear or alarm; fright: *The sound of the explosion gave her quite a scare.* **2.** a state of widespread fear or alarm; panic: *There was a bomb scare at the store.*

scare·crow (sker′krō′) *n.* **1.** a crude figure of a man dressed in old clothes, set in a field to frighten crows and other birds away from crops. **2.** a person resembling a scarecrow, especially a very thin or ragged person.

scarf (skärf) *n. pl.,* **scarfs** or **scarves. 1.** a square, oblong, or triangular piece of cloth worn about the neck or head for warmth, protection, or adornment. **2.** a strip of cloth used to cover the top of a piece of furniture, such as a dresser or table.

scar·let (skär′lit) *n.* a bright red or orange-red color. —*adj.* having the color scarlet.

scarlet fever, a highly contagious disease occurring most often in children, marked by a scarlet rash, high fever, and a sore throat.

scarlet tanager, a North American bird. The male is bright red with black wings and tail.

scarp (skärp) *n.* **1.** a cliff or steep slope. **2.** a wall or steep slope at the outer part of a fortification. —*v.t.* to cut or make into a steep slope; form into a scarp.

scarves (skärvz) a plural of **scarf.**

scar·y (sker′ē) *adj.,* **scar·i·er, scar·i·est.** *Informal.* **1.** causing alarm, fear, or uneasiness; frightening: *a scary movie.* **2.** marked by fear: *a scary feeling.* **3.** easily scared; timid.

scat (skat) *v.i.,* **scat·ted, scat·ting.** *Informal.* to go away quickly. ▲ usually used as a command.

scath·ing (skā′thing) *adj.* very severe or harsh: *scathing sarcasm, a scathing rebuke.* —**scath′ing·ly,** *adv.*

scat·ter (skat′ər) *v.t.* **1.** to spread or throw about here and there; strew: *A gust of wind scattered the leaves all over the yard.* **2.** to cause to separate and go off in different directions; disperse: *The gunshot scattered the herd of cattle.* —*v.i.* to separate and go off in different directions: *The crowd scattered when the police arrived.* —**scat′ter·er,** *n.*

scat·ter·brain (skat′ər brān′) *n.* a person who does not think clearly or seriously; silly, flighty, or forgetful person.

scat·ter·brained (skat′ər brānd′) *adj.* silly, flighty, or forgetful.

scat·ter·ing (skat′ər ing) *n.* a small, scattered number or amount.

scatter rug, a small rug used to cover part of a floor. Also, **throw rug.**

scav·en·ger (skav′in jər) *n.* **1.** an animal, such as a vulture or hyena, that feeds on decaying plant or animal matter. **2.** a person who searches through trash or discarded material for things that can be sold or used.

sce·nar·i·o (si ner′ē ō′) *n. pl.,* **sce·nar·i·os. 1.** a script of a motion picture, especially a preliminary script giving an outline of the plot. **2.** a plot outline of any dramatic work.

sce·nar·ist (si ner′ist) *n.* a person who writes scenarios, especially for motion pictures.

scene (sēn) *n.* **1.** the place where an action or event occurs or has occurred: *the scene of a robbery.* **2.** the place and time in which the action of a story, play, or motion picture occurs; setting: *The scene of this novel is Italy during the Renaissance.* **3.** a division of an act of a play, motion picture, or the like: *We left after the first scene of the second act.* **4.** an episode in a story, play, or motion picture. **5.** something presented to the eye; view: *The scene from the window was quite beautiful.* **6.** a display of strong feeling or unpleasant behavior, especially in public: *The little boy made a scene when he couldn't have his way.* **7.** a field of activity or interest: *the political scene.*

　behind the scenes. in private; secretly.

scen·er·y (sē′nər ē) *n. pl.,* **scen·er·ies. 1.** the general appearance or visible features of a place, especially when striking or pleasing: *They drove to the mountains to look at the scenery.* **2.** backdrops or other structures used to create the setting of a play, motion picture, or the like.

sce·nic (sē′nik, sen′ik) *adj.* **1.** of, relating to, or full of natural scenery; picturesque: *a scenic route through the mountains.* **2.** of or relating to stage scenery or effects.

scent (sent) *n.* **1.** a smell, especially an agreeable or delicate one: *the scent of lilacs, the scent of spices.* **2.** a characteristic smell left behind by an animal or man, used in tracking. **3.** the trail or track by which someone or something can be traced or detected: *Some misleading clues threw the police off the scent of the gang.* **4.** the sense of smell. **5.** see **perfume** (def. 1). —*v.t.* **1.** to sense or know by smell: *The dogs scented the rabbit.* **2.** to get a hint or vague idea of: *He was able to scent trouble.* **3.** to make fragrant: *The perfumed soap scented the drawer.*

scep·ter (sep′tər) *also, British,* **scep·tre.** *n.* **1.** a rod or staff carried by a king or queen and serving as a symbol of royal office or power. **2.** royal office or power.

scep·tic (skep′tik) *n.* another spelling of **skeptic.** —**scep′ti·cal,** *adj.*

scep·ti·cism (skep′tə siz′əm) another spelling of **skepticism.**

Scepter

sched·ule (skej′ool) *n.* **1.** a list of the times when certain events are to take place: *a television schedule, a schedule of train departures.* **2.** a plan or group of things to do, or of events to occur at or during a particular time: *Kathy has a busy social schedule.* **3.** the time planned upon or shown, as in a schedule: *The train was running behind schedule because of an accident.* **4.** a written or printed table or list, as of rates or prices: *a schedule of postal rates.* —*v.t.,* **sched·uled, sched·ul·ing. 1.** to place in or on a schedule: *The airline scheduled additional flights because* *of the holidays.* **2.** to plan or arrange for a specified time: *I scheduled an appointment with my dentist for Friday.*

sche·mat·ic (skē matʹik) *adj.* of, relating to, or in the form of a diagram or scheme; diagrammatic: *a schematic drawing.* —**sche·matʹi·cal·ly,** *adv.*

scheme (skēm) *n.* **1.** a program or course of action for doing something; plan: *He has a scheme for remodeling the house.* **2.** an underhanded or secret plan; plot: *The thieves have a scheme for robbing the bank.* **3.** an orderly arrangement of related parts or things; system; design: *Helen chose the color scheme for the decorations in her room.* —*v.,* **schemed, schem·ing.** —*v.t.* to plan (something), especially in an underhanded or secret way; plot. —*v.i.* to make a plan; plot. —**schemʹer,** *n.*

Sche·nec·ta·dy (skə nekʹtə dē) *n.* a city in eastern New York. Pop. (1970), 77,859.

scher·zo (skerʹtsō) *n. pl.,* **scher·zos** or **scher·zi** (skerʹtsē) a playful, lively, or humorous movement or passage in a work of music, such as a symphony.

Schick test (shik) a test used to discover immunity to diphtheria, in which diluted diphtheria toxin is injected just beneath the skin. Reddening of the area that has been injected shows that the person is not immune. [From Béla *Schick,* 1877–1967, U.S. pediatrician, born in Hungary, who developed the test.]

Schil·ler, Jo·hann Frie·drich von (shilʹər; yōʹhän frēʹdrik) 1759–1805, German dramatist and poet.

schism (sizʹəm, skizʹəm) *n.* **1.** a division into opposing groups, especially a division within a church or other religious body. **2.** a sect or group that is formed by such a division.

schis·mat·ic (siz matʹik, skiz matʹik) *adj.* relating to or causing a schism. —*n.* a person who causes or takes part in a schism.

schist (shist) *n.* a rock that is easily split because of its layered structure. It has a high mica content.

schiz·o·phre·ni·a (skitʹsə frēʹnē ə) *n.* any of a group of mental disorders characterized by a severe withdrawal from reality, illogical thought processes, hallucinations, and delusions.

schiz·o·phren·ic (skitʹsə frenʹik) *n.* a person who is suffering from schizophrenia. —*adj.* of, relating to, or characteristic of schizophrenia.

Schles·wig-Hol·stein (shlesʹwig hōlʹstīn) *n.* a state of West Germany, in the northern part of the country, south of Denmark.

schnau·zer (shnouʹzər) *n.* a sturdy, wire-haired dog having small, pointed ears.

schol·ar (skolʹər) *n.* **1.** a person having much knowledge of, or considered to be an authority in, a particular field: *She is a noted Shakespearean scholar.* **2.** a person having much knowledge and an interest in learning and study. **3.** a person holding a scholarship. **4.** a person who attends school; student; pupil.

Schnauzer

schol·ar·ly (skolʹər lē) *adj.* **1.** of, characteristic of, or suited to a scholar: *a scholarly life.* **2.** of, relating to, or based on much knowledge and learning: *a scholarly book.* **3.** having the qualities of a scholar; learned: *a scholarly young man.* —**scholʹar·li·ness,** *n.*

schol·ar·ship (skolʹər ship′) *n.* **1.** a grant of financial aid given to a student to help him continue his studies. **2.** knowledge acquired by study; learning: *The book shows the considerable scholarship of its author.*

scho·las·tic (skə lasʹtik) *adj.* of or relating to schools, scholars, or education: *scholastic standing, a scholastic award.* —**scho·lasʹti·cal·ly,** *adv.*

school[1] (skōōl) *n.* **1.** a place for teaching and learning. **2.** a department or division of a college or university for instruction in a specialized field: *the school of medicine.* **3.** an institution for instruction in a particular field or skill: *an art school, a dancing school.* **4.** the building or group of buildings of a school. **5.** a period or time of instruction at a school: *There is no school today because of the snowstorm.* **6.** the process of being educated at school. **7.** the students, faculty, and other staff members of a school: *The entire school was gathered in the auditorium.* **8.** a group of people following the same methods, styles, or beliefs: *Claude Monet belongs to the impressionist school of painting.* —*v.t.* **1.** to train or teach, as in a school; educate. **2.** to bring under control; discipline: *Doctors must school themselves to be calm during emergencies.* [Old English *scōl.*]

school[2] (skōōl) *n.* a large group of fish or water animals of the same kind swimming together: *a school of tuna, a school of porpoises.* [Dutch *school* troop, crowd.]

school board, a group of persons elected by the citizens of a community to run the public schools of the area.

school·book (skōōlʹbook′) *n.* a book used for study in schools; textbook.

school·boy (skōōlʹboi′) *n.* a boy attending school.

school·girl (skōōlʹgurl′) *n.* a girl attending school.

school·house (skōōlʹhous′) *n. pl.,* **school·hous·es** (skōōlʹhou′ziz). a building used as a school.

school·ing (skōōʹling) *n.* training at school; education: *He has had little schooling.*

school·mas·ter (skōōlʹmas′tər) *n.* a man who teaches in or heads a school. —**schoolʹmis′tress,** *n.*

school·mate (skōōlʹmāt′) *n.* a companion at school.

school·room (skōōlʹrōōm′, skōōlʹroom′) *n.* a room in a school in which classes are held.

school·teach·er (skōōlʹtē′chər) *n.* a person who teaches in a school below the college level.

school·work (skōōlʹwurk′) *n.* lessons or assignments given to a student at school.

school·yard (skōōlʹyärd′) *n.* a yard or playground of a school.

school year, that part of the year during which school is in session, usually from September to June.

schoon·er (skōōʹnər) *n.* **1.** a ship that has two or more masts and fore-and-aft sails. **2.** a large beer glass.

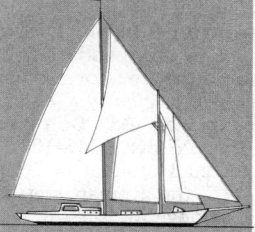

Schooner *(def. 1)*

Scho·pen·hau·er, Arthur (shōʹpən hou′ər) 1788–1860, German philosopher.

Schu·bert, Franz Peter (shōōʹbərt; fränts) 1797–1828, Austrian composer.

Schu·mann, Robert Alexander (shōōʹmän′) 1810–1856, German composer.

schwa (shwä) *n.* a vowel sound occurring in many syllables in English that are pro-

at; āpe; cär; end; mē; it; īce; hot; ōld; fôrk; wood; fōōl; oil; out; up; turn; sing; thin; <u>th</u>is; hw in white; zh in treasure. The symbol ə stands for the sound of **a** in about, **e** in taken, **i** in pencil, **o** in lemon, and **u** in circus.

nounced without any stress, such as the *a* in *ago* or the *o* in *lemon.* **2.** the symbol (ə) representing this sound. Also, **neutral vowel.**

Schwei·tzer, Albert (shwīt′sər) 1875–1965, Alsatian philosopher, theologian, musician, and doctor, noted especially for his humanitarian work in Africa.

sci·at·ic (sī at′ik) *adj.* **1.** of, relating to, or affecting the ischium, or lowest portion of the hipbone. **2.** affecting the hip or the sciatic nerve.

sci·at·i·ca (sī at′i kə) *n.* pain affecting the sciatic nerve and its branches, usually caused by injury or infection.

sciatic nerve, the largest nerve of the body, extending along the back part of the thigh and leg.

sci·ence (sī′əns) *n.* **1.** the body of knowledge and theory dealing with things in nature and the universe, and with the forces that create, shape, and form them. Science is based on facts that are obtained from experiments and careful study. **2.** any particular branch of this body of knowledge, such as physics, chemistry, or biology. **3.** any activity or skill that may be studied like a science: *John maintains that chess is a science, not just a game.*

science fiction, a story based on actual or imaginary happenings or discoveries in science, usually dealing with such subjects as travel in space and life in the future.

sci·en·tif·ic (sī′ən tif′ik) *adj.* **1.** of, relating to, derived from, or used in science: *a scientific theory.* **2.** based on or using the principles and methods of science; systematic; exact: *to take a scientific approach to a problem.*

sci·en·tif·i·cal·ly (sī′ən tif′i kə lē, sī′ən tif′ik lē) *adv.* in a scientific manner.

sci·en·tist (sī′ən tist) *n.* a student of or an expert in science, especially a person who engages in some branch of science as a profession.

scim·i·tar (sim′ə tər) *also,* **scim·i·ter.** *n.* a curved, single-edged sword of Asian origin.

scin·til·la (sin-til′ə) *n.* a very small amount; trace: *There was not a scintilla of truth in his story.*

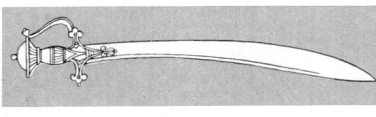
Scimitar

scin·til·late (sint′əl āt′) *v.,* **scin·til·lat·ed, scin·til·lat·ing.** —*v.i.* **1.** to be brilliant: *That author's stories scintillate with wit.* **2.** to give off sparks or flashes of light; sparkle: *The rushing stream scintillated in the morning sun.* —*v.t.* to give off as a flash or flashes. —**scin′til·la′tion,** *n.*

sci·on (sī′ən) *n.* **1.** *also,* **cion.** a bud, or a branch having one or more buds, cut from a plant and used for grafting onto the stock of another plant. **2.** a descendant; heir: *the wealthy scion of a noble family.*

Scip·i·o Af·ri·ca·nus (sip′ē ō′ af′rə kā′nəs) *n.* **1. the Elder.** 234?–183? B.C., the Roman general who defeated Hannibal in 202 B.C. **2. the Younger.** 185?–129? B.C., the Roman statesman and general who destroyed Carthage in 146 B.C.

scis·sor (siz′ər) *v.t.* to cut with scissors. —*n.* see **scissors.**

scis·sors (siz′ərz) *n.,pl.* a cutting instrument having two blades that are fastened together by a bolt and form a double cutting edge when they are closed over each other.

scle·ra (sklēr′ə) *n.* a tough, white membrane covering all of the surface of the eyeball, except for the cornea.

scle·ro·sis (sklə rō′sis) *n. pl.,* **scle·ro·ses** (sklə rō′sēz). the abnormal hardening of a tissue or part of the body, such as the wall of an artery.

scoff (skof, skôf) *v.i.* to express ridicule or contempt; mock; jeer: *He scoffed at his friend's foolish suggestion.* —*n.* a mocking expression. —**scoff′er,** *n.*

scold (skōld) *v.t.* to find fault with; speak sharply to; reprimand: *The mother scolded the child for tracking mud into the house.* —*n.* a person who scolds.

scol·lop (skol′əp) another spelling of **scallop.**

sconce (skons) *n.* a wall bracket or fixture used for holding a candle or other light.

scone (skōn) *n.* a small, often round, biscuit.

scoop (skoōp) *n.* **1.** a utensil shaped like a small shovel, used chiefly for taking up loose material or powdery substances, such as flour or sugar. **2.** a utensil shaped like a deep, rounded cup attached to a handle, used for taking up portions of food, such as ice cream. **3.** a large bucket of a dredge or steam shovel, used for taking up and depositing a load, as of dirt. **4.** the amount taken up in a scoop: *He asked for a scoop of ice cream.* **5.** a dipping or sweeping movement: *The baby picked up the pebbles with a scoop of his hand.* **6.** *Informal.* a news story

Sconce

reported first or exclusively, as by a newspaper or television network. —*v.t.* **1.** to take up or out with a scoop. **2.** to gather with a sweeping motion: *I scooped up my books and left the house.* **3.** *Informal.* to get the better of (another newspaper or reporter) by reporting a news story first or exclusively.

scoop·ful (skoōp′fool′) *n. pl.,* **scoop·fuls.** the amount that a scoop holds: *three scoopfuls of ice cream.*

scoot (skoōt) *v.i. Informal.* to go hurriedly; dart: *The rabbit scooted off into the woods.*

scoot·er (skoō′tər) *n.* **1.** a vehicle having a narrow footboard mounted on two wheels and a handle for steering. It is made to move by pushing one foot against the ground while resting the other foot on the board. **2.** see **motor scooter.**

scope (skōp) *n.* **1.** the range within which something applies or extends; area covered: *The landing of a spacecraft on Mars is within the scope of modern technology. That topic is not within the scope of today's discussion.* **2.** the range of a person's ability to understand or act; grasp: *The article on nuclear physics was beyond his scope.* **3.** opportunity or room for expression, development, or action.

Scooter

-scope *combining form* an instrument for viewing or examining: *microscope.*

scorch (skôrch) *v.t.* **1.** to burn slightly so as to change the appearance or taste of: *The hot iron scorched the tablecloth. The cook scorched the pudding.* **2.** to dry up or wither with heat; parch: *The hot summer sun scorched the grass.* —*n. pl.,* **scorch·es.** a slight burn.

scorch·er (skôr′chər) *n.* **1.** *Informal.* a very hot day. **2.** a person or thing that scorches.

score (skôr) *n.* **1.** a record of points made in a game or contest: *The score after six innings was 5 to 4.* **2.** the number of points made by one side or person in such a game or contest. **3.** a grade or rating on a test or examination: *What was your score on the spelling test?* **4.** a set or group of twenty: *a score of years.* **5. scores.** a large number; very many: *Scores of people flock to the beach every summer.* **6.** a debt, grievance, or wrong to be settled or revenged. **7.** account; ground; basis: *He has no right to brag on that score.* **8.** a notch, line, or other mark.

9. written or printed music. **10.** the music for a motion picture, stage production, or the like. —*v., scored, scoring.* —*v.t.* **1.** to make or gain (points) in a game or contest. **2.** to keep a record of points made in (a game or contest). **3.** to check and give a grade to: *The teacher scored the examination.* **4.** to make a particular grade: *Several students scored 100 percent on the spelling test.* **5.** to make notches, lines, or other marks on. **6.** to criticize severely: *The newspapers scored the mayor for his poor record in office.* **7.** to arrange (music), as for a particular voice or instrument. —*v.i.* **1.** to make or gain a point or points in a game or contest. **2.** to achieve an advantage or success. —**scor′er,** *n.*

score·board (skôr′bôrd′) *n.* a large board on which the score of a game or contest, and often other important information, is shown.

score·card (skôr′kärd′) *n.* a card on which the scores of players in a game or contest are recorded.

score·keep·er (skôr′kē′pər) *n.* a person who keeps the score during a game or contest.

scorn (skôrn) *n.* a feeling of hatred or contempt for someone or something considered low, bad, or vile: *They had nothing but scorn for the dishonest boy.* —*v.t.* **1.** to treat or consider as low, bad, or vile; despise: *to scorn a coward.* **2.** to refuse or reject with contempt: *to scorn an offer.*

scorn·ful (skôrn′fəl) *adj.* showing or feeling scorn; contemptuous. —**scorn′ful·ly,** *adv.* —**scorn′ful·ness,** *n.*

Scor·pi·o (skôr′pē ō′) *n.* **1.** a constellation in the southern sky, thought to resemble a scorpion in shape. **2.** the eighth sign of the zodiac.

scor·pi·on (skôr′pē ən) *n.* any of a group of animals related to the spider, found in temperate and tropical regions, having a long, segmented tail that ends in a poisonous stinger.

Scorpion

Scot (skot) *n.* a person who was born or is living in Scotland.

scotch (skoch) *v.t.* **1.** to put an end to; crush: *The army was sent to scotch the rebellion.* **2.** to injure so as to make harmless.

Scotch (skoch) *n.* **1.** see **Scottish** (*def. 1*). **2.** *also,* **scotch.** a whiskey distilled in Scotland. —*adj.* another term for **Scottish.**

Scotch·man (skoch′mən) *n. pl.,* **Scotch·men** (skoch′mən). another term for **Scotsman.** —**Scotch′wom′an,** *n.*

Scotch terrier, another term for **Scottish terrier.**

scot-free (skot′frē′) *adj.* free from injury, loss, punishment, or other penalty: *The bank robber got off scot-free.*

Scot·land (skot′lənd) *n.* a division of the United Kingdom, north of England. Capital, Edinburgh. Area, 30,411 sq. mi. Pop. (1978 est.), 5,179,400.

Scotland Yard **1.** the police department of London, especially the branch that investigates crime. **2.** its headquarters.

Scots (skots) *adj.* another term for **Scottish.** —*n.* see **Scottish** (*def. 2*).

Scots·man (skots′mən) *n. pl.,* **Scots·men** (skots′mən). see **Scot.** —**Scots′wom′an,** *n.* Also, **Scotchman.**

Scott, Sir Walter (skot) 1771–1832, Scottish author.

Scot·tie (skot′ē) another term for **Scottish terrier.**

Scot·tish (skot′ish) *n.* **1. the Scottish.** the people of Scotland. **2.** the dialect of English spoken in Scotland. —*adj.* of, relating to, or characteristic of Scotland, its people, or their language. ▲ **Scottish, Scots,** and **Scotch** are the adjectives that refer to Scotland. **Scottish** and **Scots** are preferred when referring to the people of Scotland; they

dislike being called *Scotch.* **Scotch** is acceptable when referring to things from Scotland, as in such combinations as *Scotch plaid* and *Scotch whisky.*

Scottish terrier, a small, short-legged dog having a large head, pointed ears, and a rough coat of black, gray, or light tan hair. It is believed to be the oldest breed of dog native to Britain. Also, **Scotch terrier, Scottie.**

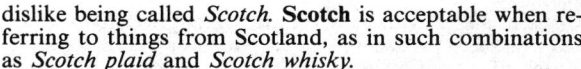
Scottish terrier

scoun·drel (skoun′drəl) *n.* a wicked, base, or dishonest person; villain; rogue. —**scoun′drel·ly,** *adj.*

scour¹ (skour) *v.t.* **1.** to rub (something) vigorously in order to clean, wash, or brighten it: *to scour a pot with a pad of steel wool.* **2.** to remove by rubbing in this manner: *to scour the tarnish off an old silver cup.* **3.** to clean, clear, or wear away, as with flowing water: *The water from melting snow scoured a channel down the mountainside.* —*v.i.* to rub vigorously in order to clean, wash, or brighten. —*n.* the act of scouring. [Middle Dutch *schūren* to clean.]

scour² (skour) *v.t.* to go or move over or through, especially in making a thorough search: *Police scoured the countryside for the escaped convict.* [Possibly of Scandinavian origin.]

scourge (skurj) *n.* **1.** a whip; lash. **2.** a cause of much suffering or destruction: *War has been a scourge of mankind for centuries.* —*v.t.,* **scourged, scourg·ing. 1.** to whip; lash. **2.** to punish or criticize severely. **3.** to cause suffering or destruction to; afflict; ravage.

scout¹ (skout) *n.* **1.** a person or thing sent out to gather and bring back information, such as a soldier, ship, or aircraft sent out during wartime to gather information about the enemy. **2.** a person sent out to find new talent, especially in sports or entertainment. **3.** *also,* **Scout.** a member of the Boy Scouts or Girl Scouts. —*v.i.* to make a search; hunt: *We scouted around to see what we could find to eat.* —*v.t.* to look at or explore in order to obtain information: *The two soldiers went ahead to scout the enemy camp.* [Old French *escoute* a spy, listener.]

scout² (skout) *v.t.* to reject with scorn: *Tim scouted his brother's idea as ridiculous.* [Of Scandinavian origin.]

scout·ing (skou′ting) *also,* **Scout·ing.** *n.* the activities of the Boy Scouts or Girl Scouts.

scout·mas·ter (skout′mas′tər) *n.* the adult leader of a troop of scouts, especially of Boy Scouts.

scow (skou) *n.* a large, flat-bottomed boat with square ends. It is usually pushed and is used chiefly for carrying freight.

scowl (skoul) *n.* an expression of anger or disapproval; a sullen or angry frown. —*v.i.* to have a

Scow

at; āpe; cär; end; mē; it; īce; hot; ōld; fôrk; wood; fōōl; oil; out; up; turn; sing; thin; this; hw in white; zh in treasure. The symbol ə stands for the sound of **a** in about, **e** in taken, **i** in pencil, **o** in lemon, and **u** in circus.

S

look of anger or disapproval; frown angrily: *John scowled at the rude person.* —*v.t.* to express with a scowl: *He scowled his objection to the idea.*

scrab·ble (skrab′əl) *v.i.*, **scrab·bled, scrab·bling. 1.** to scratch or scrape about with hands, feet, or paws: *The dog scrabbled in the dirt for the bone.* **2.** to struggle; strive.

scrag (skrag) *n.* **1.** a thin, scrawny person or animal. **2.** a lean, bony piece of meat, especially of mutton or veal.

scrag·gly (skrag′lē) *adj.*, **scrag·gli·er, scrag·gli·est.** having a ragged, sparse, or rough appearance: *a scraggly beard, a scraggly lawn.*

scrag·gy (skrag′ē) *adj.*, **scrag·gi·er, scrag·gi·est. 1.** thin and bony; scrawny. **2.** rough or jagged in appearance; scraggly. —**scrag′gi·ness,** *n.*

scram (skram) *v.i.*, **scrammed, scram·ming.** *Slang.* to leave quickly or immediately. ▲ usually used as a command.

scram·ble (skram′bəl) *v.*, **scram·bled, scram·bling.** —*v.t.* **1.** to mix together in a confused way; mix up: *to scramble the pieces of a jigsaw puzzle.* **2.** to fry (eggs) with the whites and yolks mixed together. **3.** to alter (a message-carrying wave) so that only a special receiver can reproduce the message. —*v.i.* **1.** to make one's way quickly or frantically: *The hikers scrambled down the rocks along the stream.* **2.** to struggle or compete with others: *Many countries were scrambling for control of the territory.* **3.** to get airplanes into the air on short notice to intercept enemy aircraft. —*n.* **1.** the act of moving or climbing quickly or frantically. **2.** a struggle or competition: *There was a scramble for the best seats in the theater.* —**scram′bler,** *n.*

Scran·ton (skran′tən) *n.* a city in northeastern Pennsylvania. Pop. (1970), 103,564.

scrap¹ (skrap) *n.* **1.** a small piece or fragment; bit: *He wrote her telephone number on a scrap of paper. There wasn't a scrap of evidence against the prisoner.* **2. scraps.** leftover or discarded bits of food. **3.** used or discarded metal that may be used again by melting and refining: *to sell an old car for scrap.* **4.** any material that is left over or discarded as trash, or that can be reprocessed for reuse. —*v.t.*, **scrapped, scrap·ping. 1.** to discard or abandon as useless, worthless, or ineffective: *to scrap an idea.* **2.** to make scrap of: *to scrap an old battleship.* [Old Norse *skrap* trifles, bits.]

scrap² (skrap) *Informal. n.* a noisy quarrel or disagreement. —*v.i.*, **scrapped, scrap·ping.** to take part in a scrap; fight: *The dog and the cat scrapped.* [Possibly from *scrape.*] —**scrap′per,** *n.*

scrap·book (skrap′book′) *n.* a book with blank pages on which pictures, newspaper clippings, or other items may be pasted.

scrape (skrāp) *v.*, **scraped, scrap·ing.** —*v.t.* **1.** to injure or damage the surface of by rubbing against something sharp or rough: *He fell and scraped his knee. Jerry scraped the fender of the car on the wall of the garage.* **2.** to draw, move, or rub (something) roughly or forcefully or with a harsh, grating sound: *The speaker scraped his chair on the floor as he stood up.* **3.** to move or rub roughly or with a harsh, grating sound on or across (something): *The spoon scraped the bottom of the pot.* **4.** to rub (a surface), as with something sharp or abrasive, in order to remove an outer layer or make smooth or clean: *We scraped the dinner plates before we put them in the dishwasher.* **5.** to remove by rubbing in this manner: *to scrape old paint off a wall.* **6.** to collect, gather, or produce with difficulty or serious effort: *to scrape up some money for a trip.* —*v.i.* **1.** to move or rub roughly or with a harsh, grating sound: *The car's broken exhaust pipe scraped along the ground.* **2.** to manage or make one's way barely or with difficulty: *The couple*

scraped by on their small income. —*n.* **1.** a mark made on a surface by scraping. **2.** a harsh, grating sound made by scraping. **3.** the act of moving or rubbing roughly or with a harsh, grating sound. **4.** a difficult, troublesome, or unpleasant situation: *Tom was in a scrape when the ball he threw broke the window.*

scrap·er (skrā′pər) *n.* **1.** any of various tools or devices for cleaning or smoothing a surface, or for removing paint or other matter. **2.** a person or thing that scrapes.

scrap·ple (skrap′əl) *n.* a boiled mixture of ground pork, corn meal or flour, and seasonings, which is chilled until firm and then sliced and fried.

scrap·py¹ (skrap′ē) *adj.*, **scrap·pi·er, scrap·pi·est.** made up of scraps or fragments; fragmentary. [*Scrap¹* + *-y¹*.] —**scrap′pi·ness,** *n.*

scrap·py² (skrap′ē) *adj.*, **scrap·pi·er, scrap·pi·est.** *Informal.* **1.** full of fighting spirit; aggressive: *a scrappy puppy.* **2.** inclined to scrap or quarrel; quarrelsome. [*Scrap²* + *-y¹*.] —**scrap′pi·ly,** *adv.* —**scrap′pi·ness,** *n.*

scratch (skrach) *v.t.* **1.** to cut, mark, or mar with something rough, sharp, or pointed: *The broken glass scratched the table top.* **2.** to scrape, tear, or wound with the nails or claws: *His cat scratched him.* **3.** to rub or scrape in order to relieve itching: *He scratched his back.* **4.** to cause to feel itchy or irritated: *This starched collar scratches my neck.* **5.** to strike out or cancel: *Scratch his name off the list.* **6.** to write or draw by scraping or cutting into a surface: *He scratched his initials on the tree.* **7.** to write hurriedly or carelessly: *to scratch a note.* **8.** to withdraw (an entry) from a race or other competition: *to scratch a horse.* —*v.i.* **1.** to dig, scrape, or wound, as with the nails or claws: *The chickens scratched in the dirt for corn.* **2.** to rub or scrape a part of the body to relieve itching. **3.** to rub with a harsh, grating sound: *We could hear the puppy scratching at the door.* **4.** to become cut, marked, or scraped: *a plastic that scratches easily.* —*n. pl.* **scratch·es. 1.** a mark made by scratching: *a scratch on a table, a scratch on one's leg.* **2.** a harsh, grating sound: *The scratch of the branch against the windowpane startled us.* —*adj.* used for quick, rough, or informal writing or sketching: *scratch paper.*

from scratch. from the beginning; from nothing: *He started his successful business from scratch.*

scratch test, any of various tests to show if a person is allergic to something, made by rubbing a particular substance into small scratches made in the skin.

scratch·y (skrach′ē) *adj.*, **scratch·i·er, scratch·i·est. 1.** that causes itching: *a scratchy wool sweater.* **2.** making a harsh, grating sound: *a scratchy phonograph record.* **3.** not regular or even: *scratchy handwriting.* —**scratch′i·ly,** *adv.* —**scratch′i·ness,** *n.*

scrawl (skrôl) *v.t.* to write or draw (something) hastily or carelessly in a sprawling, irregular way: *to scrawl a note.* —*n.* irregular, sprawling, almost unreadable handwriting. —**scrawl′er,** *n.*

scraw·ny (skrô′nē) *adj.*, **scraw·ni·er, scraw·ni·est.** thin, bony, or undersized; skinny: *a scrawny old mule.* —**scraw′ni·ness,** *n.*

scream (skrēm) *v.i.* **1.** to make a loud, shrill, piercing cry, especially from fright or pain. **2.** to shout or speak loudly or shrilly. —*v.t.* to utter with a loud, shrill, piercing sound: *The drowning man screamed his plea for help.* —*n.* **1.** a loud, shrill, piercing cry or sound: *a scream of terror, the scream of a train whistle.* **2.** *Informal.* a very funny person or thing. —**scream′er,** *n.*

scream·ing (skrē′ming) *adj.* **1.** boldly striking; startling: *a screaming headline, a screaming red color.* **2.** uttering screams. **3.** *Informal.* very funny: *a screaming comedy.* —**scream′ing·ly,** *adv.*

screech (skrēch) *v.i.* to make a shrill, high-pitched sound. —*v.t.* to make or express with a shrill, high-pitched sound: *to screech a warning.* —*n. pl.*, **screech·es.** a shrill, high-pitched sound: *the screech of brakes.*

screech owl, a brown or gray North American owl having tufts of feathers on its forehead and a wavering, whistling call.

screech·y (skrē′chē) *adj.*, **screech·i·er, screech·i·est.** like a screech; shrill: *a screechy voice.*

screen (skrēn) *n.* **1.** mesh or netting, usually of wire and enclosed in a frame: *a window screen, a screen in front of a fireplace.* **2.** a frame or a series of frames hinged together, often used as a room divider or as an ornament. **3.** anything that serves to separate, conceal, or protect. **4.** a surface that reflects light, on which motion pictures or slides may be projected. **5.** a surface on which the image is displayed in a cathode-ray tube, such as that of a television or radar set. **6.** the motion picture industry; motion pictures: *His play was adapted for the screen.* **7.** a sieve used for sifting or grading gravel, sand, and the like. —*v.t.* **1.** to provide with a screen: *He screened the porch to keep out insects.* **2.** to hide or protect with or as if with a screen: *We screened our eyes from the sun with our hands.* **3.** to sift or grade by passing through a screen: *to screen gravel.* **4.** to block, remove, or filter as if by a screen: *The earth's atmosphere screens out much of the sun's radiation.* **5.** to examine carefully or systematically, especially so as to make a selection: *to screen applicants for a job.* **6.** to show (a motion picture) on a screen. —**screen′er,** *n.* —**screen′like′,** *adj.*

Screen *(def. 2)*

screen·play (skrēn′plā′) *n.* a motion picture script.

screen test, a short scene filmed to test a person's ability as a motion-picture actor.

screen·writ·er (skrēn′rī′tər) *n.* a writer of screenplays.

screw (skrōō) *n.* **1.** a fastening device consisting of a tapering rod that is ridged with a spiraling thread and has a head, usually slotted, at one end. It is driven into place by being twisted or turned, as with a screwdriver. **2.** a simple machine, consisting of a cylinder with an inclined plane wound around it, to be fitted into a hole or socket cut with a matching thread. **3.** something like a screw in shape or function. **4.** a twist or turn of a screw. **5.** the propeller of a boat or ship. —*v.t.* **1.** to attach or fasten with a screw or screws: *The workman screwed a lock to the door.* **2.** to insert, attach, or fix (a screw or other threaded or grooved object) in place by a twisting or turning motion: *He screwed a new bulb into the socket. Screw the cap back on the tube of toothpaste.* **3.** to twist out of shape; contort: *She screwed up her mouth with displeasure.* **4.** to call forth or gather with difficulty; muster: *He finally screwed up the courage to ask his boss for a raise.* —*v.i.* **1.** to become attached or fastened by means of a screw or screws: *The towel rack screws to the wall.* **2.** to become inserted, attached, or fixed in place by a twisting or turning motion: *The light bulb screws into the socket.* —**screw′like′,** *adj.*

  to have a screw loose. *Informal.* to be odd, eccentric, or crazy.

  to put the screws on. *Informal.* to exert pressure or force on.

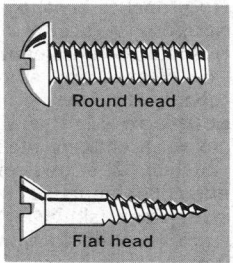

Round head

Flat head

Screws

screw·ball (skrōō′bôl′) *n.* **1.** *Informal.* an odd, eccentric, or crazy person. **2.** *Baseball.* a pitch that breaks in a direction opposite to a curve ball.

screw·driv·er (skrōō′drī′vər) *n.* a tool for turning screws.

screw propeller, a device consisting of a hub with blades mounted at an angle, used to propel certain boats and aircraft.

screw·y (skrōō′ē) *adj.*, **screw·i·er, screw·i·est.** *Informal.* odd; crazy. —**screw′i·ness,** *n.*

scrib·ble (skrib′əl) *v.*, **scrib·bled, scrib·bling.** —*v.t.* to write or draw (something) carelessly or hastily: *He scribbled down the names of all those who were present.* —*v.i.* to make meaningless marks: *to scribble on a pad.* —*n.* writing, drawing, or marks made by scribbling. —**scrib′bler,** *n.*

scribe (skrīb) *n.* **1.** before the invention of printing, a person whose profession was writing down or copying letters, manuscripts, contracts, or other documents. **2.** a public clerk or secretary. **3.** a writer; author. **4.** a teacher who interpreted the Mosaic law among the ancient Hebrews. —*v.t.*, **scribed, scrib·ing.** to mark with a scriber or other pointed instrument.

scrib·er (skrī′bər) *n.* a pointed steel tool for marking on material, such as wood or metal, that is to be cut.

scrim (skrim) *n.* a loosely woven cotton or linen fabric used especially for curtains and bunting.

scrim·mage (skrim′ij) *n.* **1.** *Football.* the play that occurs from the time the ball is snapped back until it is called dead. **2.** a practice session taking the form of a game, as in football and other sports. —*v.i.*, **scrim·maged, scrim·mag·ing.** to participate in a scrimmage.

scrimp (skrimp) *v.i.* to be very sparing or economical: *Sue scrimped and saved for a new dress to wear to the Christmas dance.* —*v.t.* to be very sparing of or with.

scrim·shaw (skrim′shô′) *n.* **1.** the art of carving or engraving designs, often nautical scenes or motifs, on whalebone, ivory, or shell. This work was done especially by sailors during long whaling or other voyages. **2.** articles decorated in this way. —*v.t.* to carve or engrave into scrimshaw. —*v.i.* to make scrimshaw.

scrip (skrip) *n.* **1.** a certificate, token, or the like issued in place of money, to be exchanged for goods or services. **2.** paper money issued for temporary use in times of emergency.

script (skript) *n.* **1.** writing in which the letters are joined together; cursive handwriting. **2.** any of various styles of type resembling this. **3.** a writing system or style: *Babylonian script, Gothic script.* **4.** a typed or written text of a play, motion picture, or radio or television program, that is used by the performers, director, and other members of the production staff.

Scrip·tur·al (skrip′chər əl) *also,* **scrip·tur·al.** *adj.* of, based on, or according to Scripture or any sacred writings.

Scrip·ture (skrip′chər) *n.* **1.** *also,* **the Scriptures.** the books of the Old and New Testaments; the Bible. **2.** *also,* **scripture.** a book or body of writings sacred to a religion.

scriv·en·er (skriv′nər) *n.* *Archaic.* a clerk; scribe.

scrod (skrod) *n.* a young cod.

at; āpe; cär; end; mē; it; īce; hot; ōld; fôrk; wood; fōōl; oil; out; up; turn; sing; thin; this; hw in white; zh in treasure. The symbol ə stands for the sound of **a** in about, **e** in taken, **i** in pencil, **o** in lemon, and **u** in circus.

S

scrof·u·la (skrof′yə lə) *n.* a disorder characterized by swelling and inflammation of the lymph glands, especially those in the neck. It results from infection with tuberculosis.

scrof·u·lous (skrof′yə ləs) *adj.* **1.** of or relating to scrofula. **2.** having scrofula.

scroll (skrōl) *n.* **1.** a roll of parchment, paper, silk, or other material, especially one with writing on it, often wound around a rod or a pair of rods so as to be conveniently used or stored. **2.** a figure or ornamental design resembling a partly unrolled scroll, such as the curved head on a violin. —**scroll′-like′**, *adj.*

scroll saw, a saw having a narrow blade with fine teeth, used to cut curved or intricate patterns in thin wood.

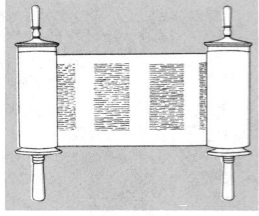

Scroll *(def. 1)*

scroll·work (skrōl′wurk′) *n.* ornamental work consisting chiefly of scroll-like patterns, especially such work cut with a scroll saw.

Scrooge (skrōōj) *also,* **scrooge.** *n.* a nasty, mean-tempered miser. [From Ebenezer *Scrooge,* a mean-tempered miser in Charles Dickens' story *A Christmas Carol.*]

scro·tum (skrō′təm) *n. pl.,* **scro·ta** (skrō′tə) or **scro·tums.** the external sac of skin and muscle that contains the testicles in most male mammals.

scrounge (skrounj) *Slang.* *v.,* **scrounged, scroung·ing.** —*v.t.* **1.** to get, collect, or gather with effort or difficulty or by foraging: *He managed to scrounge up enough money to pay the rent.* **2.** to borrow (something) without intending to return or repay: *to scrounge a meal.* —*v.i.* to search; forage: *I scrounged around in the drawer and found my gloves.*

scrub¹ (skrub) *v.,* **scrubbed, scrub·bing.** —*v.t.* **1.** to rub vigorously in order to wash or clean: *to scrub a floor.* **2.** to remove by such rubbing: *She scrubbed the ink stains off her hands.* **3.** to cleanse (a gas or vapor) of impurities. **4.** *Informal.* to postpone or cancel: *to scrub a missile launch.* —*v.i.* to wash or clean something by hard rubbing. —*n.* the act of scrubbing. [Possibly from Middle Dutch *schrubben.*]

scrub² (skrub) *n.* **1.** low, stunted trees or shrubs. **2.** an undersized person, animal, or thing. **3.** a player who is not a member of the first or regular team. —*adj.* **1.** undersized, stunted, or inferior: *a scrub tree, scrub cows.* **2.** relating to, made up of, or played by players not on the first or regular team. [A form of *shrub.*]

scrub·ber (skrub′ər) *n.* a person or thing that scrubs, especially an apparatus for cleansing gas of impurities.

scrub·by (skrub′ē) *adj.,* **scrub·bi·er, scrub·bi·est.** **1.** undersized, stunted, or inferior: *a scrubby bush.* **2.** covered with or consisting of scrub. **3.** unfair or mean; shabby: *a scrubby trick.* —**scrub′bi·ness,** *n.*

scruff (skruf) *n.* the back of the neck or the skin covering it.

scru·ple (skrōō′pəl) *n.* **1.** a feeling of doubt, hesitancy, or uneasiness of mind that arises from a person's conscience and often restrains or inhibits action: *He has no scruples about telling people exactly what he thinks of them.* **2.** a very small amount or portion. **3.** an apothecaries' weight equal to 20 grains or 1/24 of an ounce. Three scruples are equal to one dram. —*v.i.,* **scru·pled, scru·pling.** to hesitate because of scruples; have scruples.

scru·pu·lous (skrōō′pyə ləs) *adj.* **1.** having or showing a strict regard for what is right: *She is scrupulous about telling the truth.* **2.** very careful of small details; painstaking: *scrupulous neatness, a scrupulous report.* —**scru′pu·lous·ly,** *adv.* —**scru′pu·lous·ness,** *n.*

scru·ti·nize (skrōōt′ən īz′) *v.t.,* **scru·ti·nized, scru·ti·niz·ing.** to look at or examine closely or critically; inspect carefully or minutely: *The immigration officer scrutinized the man's passport.* —**scru′ti·niz′er,** *n.*

scru·ti·ny (skrōōt′ən ē) *n. pl.,* **scru·ti·nies.** close, critical study, examination, or inquiry; careful inspection: *The suspect's movements were under the scrutiny of the police.*

scu·ba (skōō′bə) *n.* a portable, underwater breathing device consisting of one or more cylinders of compressed air that are fastened on a diver's back, and a hose or hoses for transmitting the air to a mouthpiece. —*adj.* of or relating to a scuba or to scuba diving: *a scuba tank, scuba equipment.* [Short for *s*(elf)-*c*(ontained) *u*(nderwater) *b*(reathing) *a*(pparatus).]

scuba diver, a person who engages in scuba diving.

scuba diving, swimming underwater for long periods of time with a scuba.

scud (skud) *v.i.,* **scud·ded, scud·ding.** **1.** to run or move swiftly: *The clouds scudded across the sky.* **2.** *Nautical.* to run before a gale with little or no sail set. —*n.* **1.** the act of scudding or moving swiftly. **2.** light clouds, spray, or rain driven swiftly before the wind.

scuff (skuf) *v.t.* to scratch, mar, or roughen the surface of by scraping or wear: *She scuffed her shoes on the gravel.* —*v.i.* **1.** to walk by dragging the feet; shuffle: *The boy scuffed along to school.* **2.** to become scratched, marred, or roughened by scraping or wear: *This linoleum scuffs easily.* —*n.* the act of scuffing.

scuf·fle (skuf′əl) *n.* a confused, often rough, struggle or fight: *The robber and the policeman had a scuffle.* —*v.i.,* **scuf·fled, scuf·fling.** to struggle or fight at close quarters in a rough, confused manner.

scull (skul) *n.* **1.** an oar used to propel a boat by working it from side to side over the stern. **2.** one of a pair of light oars used together, one on each side of a boat, by a single rower. **3.** a small boat propelled by sculls, especially a light racing boat propelled by one or more rowers. —*v.t., v.i.* to propel (a boat) by a scull or sculls. —**scull′er,** *n.*

scul·ler·y (skul′ər ē) *n. pl.,* **scul·ler·ies.** a place, often a small room adjoining a kitchen, where cooking utensils are cleaned and stored and other dirty, messy kitchen chores are done.

scul·lion (skul′yən) *n. Archaic.* **1.** a servant employed to wash cooking utensils and do dirty, messy work in a kitchen. **2.** a low, contemptible person; wretch.

sculpt (skulpt) *v.t., v.i.* to sculpture: *to sculpt a statue.*

sculp·tor (skulp′tər) *n.* a person who produces sculpture. —**sculp′tress,** *n.*

sculp·tur·al (skulp′chər əl) *adj.* of, relating to, or like sculpture.

sculp·ture (skulp′chər) *n.* **1.** the act or process of making figures or designs, as by carving or chiseling stone or marble, modeling in clay or wax, or casting in bronze or a similar metal. **2.** a figure or design so made. **3.** such figures or designs as a group. —*v.,* **sculp·tured, sculp·tur·ing.** —*v.t.* **1.** to carve or otherwise form (a figure or design) by means of sculpture. **2.** to make a sculpture of. **3.** to ornament or cover with sculpture. —*v.i.* to produce sculpture.

scum (skum) *n.* **1.** a filmy layer that forms on or rises to the surface of a liquid or body of water: *A green scum floated in the fish tank.* **2.** a low, vile, despicable person or persons. —*v.i.,* **scummed, scum·ming.** to become covered with or form scum: *The pond scummed over.*

scum·my (skum′ē) *adj.,* **scum·mi·er, scum·mi·est.** **1.** covered with, containing, or like scum. **2.** low; vile; despicable.

scup (skup) *n. pl.,* **scups** or **scup.** a commercially important food fish found along the eastern coast of the United States.

scup·per (skup′ər) *n.* a hole in the side of a ship that allows water to drain off the deck. [Of uncertain origin.]

scup·per·nong (skup′ər nông′, skup′ər nong′) *n.* a pale-green grape that tastes like a plum, grown in the southeastern United States.

scurf (skurf) *n.* **1.** dead, flaky skin, especially dandruff. **2.** any scaly or flaky matter sticking to a surface.

scur·ril·i·ty (skə ril′ə tē) *n. pl.,* **scur·ril·i·ties. 1.** the quality of being scurrilous. **2.** something that is scurrilous.

scur·ri·lous (skur′ə ləs) *adj.* indecent and coarse; vulgar: *scurrilous language, a scurrilous attack on a person's character.* —**scur′ri·lous·ly,** *adv.* —**scur′ri·lous·ness,** *n.*

scur·ry (skur′ē) *v.i.,* **scur·ried, scur·ry·ing.** to go or move hurriedly: *The deer scurried off into the woods.* —*n. pl.,* **scur·ries.** the act of scurrying.

scur·vy (skur′vē) *n.* a disease caused by a lack of vitamin C in the diet, characterized by spongy and bleeding gums, bleeding under the skin, and extreme weakness. —*adj.,* **scur·vi·er, scur·vi·est.** mean and vile; contemptible; base.

scut (skut) *n.* a short tail, as of a rabbit or deer.

scut·tle¹ (skut′əl) *v.t.,* **scut·tled, scut·tling. 1.** to cause (a boat or ship) to sink by cutting, boring, or uncovering an opening in the bottom, deck, or sides. **2.** to abandon or destroy: *He scuttled his plan to go to college because of a lack of money.* —*n.* **1.** an opening, especially in the deck, side, or compartment of a ship, usually having a movable cover. **2.** a lid or cover for such an opening. [Possibly from middle French *escoutille* a hatchway.]

scut·tle² (skut′əl) *n.* see **coal scuttle.**

scut·tle³ (skut′əl) *v.i.,* **scut·tled, scut·tling.** to go or move with short, rapid steps: *Crabs scuttled across the sand.* —*n.* a short, hurried run. [A form of dialectal English *scuddle.*]

scut·tle·butt (skut′əl but′) *n. Informal.* rumor; gossip.

Scyl·la (sil′ə) *n. Greek Mythology.* a monster having six heads and twelve feet, that lived in a cave on the Strait of Messina, opposite the monster Charybdis. Sailors who were not drowned by Charybdis were snatched from their ships and devoured by Scylla.

  between Scylla and Charybdis. caught between two dangers, neither of which can be avoided without confronting the other.

scythe (sīth) *n.* an implement consisting of a long curved blade attached at an angle to a long bent handle, used for mowing, cutting, or reaping. —*v.t.,* **scythed, scyth·ing.** to mow or cut with a scythe: *to scythe grass.*

Scythe

S. Dak., South Dakota. Also, **S.D.**

Se, the symbol for selenium.

SE, s.e., southeast; southeastern.

sea (sē) *n.* **1.** the continuous body of salt water that covers nearly three-fourths of the earth's surface; the ocean. **2.** a large portion of this, partly enclosed by land, such as the Caribbean Sea or the Aegean Sea. **3.** a large inland body of salt or fresh water, such as the Sea of Galilee or the Caspian Sea. **4.** the condition of the sea's surface, especially with regard to the motion of the waves: *a calm sea, a stormy sea.* **5.** a large, heavy swell or wave: *The ship floundered in rough seas.* **6.** an overwhelming quantity or number: *a sea of troubles.* **7.** see **mare².**

  at sea. a. out on the ocean. **b.** at a loss; in confusion.

sea anemone, any of a group of marine animals that attach themselves to rocks, wharves, and other objects. Sea anemones have numerous, brightly colored tentacles that bear stinging cells and are used to stun prey.

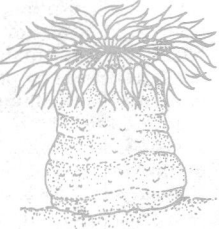

Sea anemone

sea bass (bas) any of a group of saltwater fish that have spiny fins and are important food and game fish.

Sea·bee (sē′bē′) *n.* a member of a U.S. Navy construction battalion that is made up of skilled workers of all trades who build and maintain various installations, such as shipyards and ammunition depots. [A form of *C.B.,* the abbreviation of *C*(onstruction) *B*(attalion).]

sea biscuit, another term for **hardtack.**

sea·board (sē′bôrd′) *n.* land near or bordering on the sea; seacoast: *the Atlantic seaboard.*

sea breeze, a breeze blowing inland from the sea.

sea·coast (sē′kōst′) *n.* land near or bordering on the sea.

sea cow 1. an extinct sea-dwelling mammal, related to the dugong and manatee, with a huge body, front flippers, and a flat, broad tail. **2.** see **dugong. 3.** see **manatee.**

sea cucumber, a cucumber-shaped animal found in coastal waters. It has a flexible body with several tentacles around the mouth that are used to capture food.

sea dog, a sailor, especially an old or experienced one.

sea·far·er (sē′fer′ər) *n.* a person engaged in seafaring, especially a sailor.

sea·far·ing (sē′fer′ing) *adj.* **1.** following the sea as a business or calling: *a seafaring merchant.* **2.** of or relating to the sea or to life or work as a sailor. **3.** traveling on the sea: *a seafaring ship.* Also, **seagoing.** —*n.* **1.** the life or work of a sailor. **2.** travel by sea.

sea·food (sē′fōōd′) *also,* **sea food.** *n.* saltwater fish or shellfish used for food.

sea·girt (sē′gurt′) *adj.* surrounded by the sea.

sea·go·ing (sē′gō′ing) *adj.* **1.** designed, suitable, or used for sea travel. **2.** another word for **seafaring.**

sea green, a medium bluish-green color.

sea gull, see **gull¹.**

sea horse 1. any of various slender fish found in warm and temperate seas, having a head that resembles that of a horse and a tail that is used for clinging to underwater plants. **2.** another term for **walrus. 3.** a mythical sea creature, half fish and half horse.

seal¹ (sēl) *n. pl.,* **seals** or **seal. 1.** any of several sea mammals having a long body, a muscular neck, and limbs that are modified to form flippers. Some seals are hunted for their valuable fur. **2.** the skin or fur of such an animal, especially sealskin. **3.** leather made from the hide of such an animal. —*v.i.* to hunt seals, especially for their fur. [Old English *seolh.*] —**seal′er,** *n.*

Sea horse

at; āpe; cär; end; mē; it; īce; hot; ōld; fôrk; wood; fōōl; oil; out; up; turn; sing; thin; this; hw in white; zh in treasure. The symbol ə stands for the sound of a in about, e in taken, i in pencil, o in lemon, and u in circus.

seal² (sēl) *n.* **1.** the impression of a design, figure, or word stamped on wax, paper, or other soft material to show ownership or authenticity, intended to officially represent a person, institution, or governing body. **2.** the representation of such an impression, or a disk or wafer of wax, paper, or other material bearing such an impression, put on a document to prove authenticity or to close or fasten it tightly. **3.** a stamp, die, ring, or other object engraved with a design, figure, or word, used to make such impressions. **4.** something that fastens firmly, closes completely, or makes airtight or watertight: *the seal on an envelope, the seal on a jar.* **5.** a decorative gummed stamp or sticker. —*v.t.* **1.** to fasten or close firmly, as to make airtight or watertight: *She sealed the envelope.* **2.** to fill or obstruct; stop up: *The painter sealed the cracks in the wall.* **3.** to shut in or confine; enclose tightly: *They sealed the documents in a strongbox.* **4.** to confirm, conclude, or settle: *to seal a bargain with a handshake.* **5.** to put beyond doubt, question, or reversal; decide definitely: *The testimony of the eyewitness sealed the accused man's fate.* **6.** to place a seal on, as to prove authenticity. [Old French *seel.*] —**seal′er,** *n.*

sea legs *Informal.* the ability to walk steadily aboard ship, especially on rough seas.

sea level, the mean level of the surface of the sea, especially halfway between mean high and low water. Land elevations and sea depths are measured as so many feet above or below sea level.

sealing wax, a mixture usually made of shellac and turpentine, which softens when heated but quickly hardens as it cools. It is used to seal letters, packages, and jars.

sea lion, any of various large seals found chiefly in the Pacific Ocean.

seal·skin (sēl′skin′) *n.* the skin or fur of certain seals that are hunted for their pelts.

seam (sēm) *n.* **1.** a line formed by sewing together the edges of two or more pieces of cloth, leather, or similar material: *the seam of a dress.* **2.** a similar line, groove, or ridge formed by joining edges, as of planks or layers of bricks. **3.** any mark resembling a seam. **4.** a thin layer or stratum: *a seam of coal, a seam of rock.* —*v.t.* **1.** to join together by sewing. **2.** to mark with a seam or seams; furrow: *Time had seamed the old sailor's face.* —*v.i.* to become furrowed; crack open. —**seam′less,** *adj.*

Sea lion

sea·man (sē′mən) *n. pl.,* **sea·men** (sē′mən). **1.** a sailor; mariner. **2.** in the U.S. Navy and Coast Guard, an enlisted person of any of the three lowest grades.

sea·man·ship (sē′mən ship′) *n.* skill in and knowledge of managing or sailing a boat or ship.

sea mew, see **mew².**

seam·stress (sēm′stris) *n. pl.,* **seam·stress·es.** a woman who is skilled at sewing, especially one whose occupation is sewing.

seam·y (sē′mē) *adj.,* **seam·i·er, seam·i·est. 1.** dismal, squalid, or degraded; sordid: *the seamy side of life.* **2.** having or showing seams. —**seam′i·ness,** *n.*

sé·ance (sā′äns) *n.* a meeting in which a group of people try to communicate with the spirits of the dead through the help of a medium.

sea otter, a dark brown otter found along the western coast of North America and around offshore islands of the Pacific, having broad hind feet that resemble flippers. It is the largest of all otters and the only one that lives in salt water.

sea·plane (sē′plān′) *n.* an airplane, especially one equipped with floats, that is designed to take off from and land on water. Also, **hy·droplane.**

Seaplane

sea·port (sē′pôrt′) *n.* **1.** a port or harbor for seagoing vessels. **2.** a city or town having such a port or harbor.

sear (sēr) *v.t.* **1.** to burn the surface of; char; scorch: *to sear a steak.* **2.** to dry up or wither: *The hot sun seared the grass.* **3.** to harden or make callous: *The war seared the young soldier's feelings.* —*n.* a mark made by searing or burning. —*adj. Archaic.* dried; sere.

search (surch) *v.t.* **1.** to look through or explore carefully and thoroughly in order to find something: *I've searched all my drawers, but my notebook is still missing. We searched the whole gymnasium for the lost basketball.* **2.** to look into or examine carefully and closely; probe: *She searched her heart and forgave him.* —*v.i.* to look carefully and thoroughly: *He searched through his pockets for his keys.* —*n. pl.,* **search·es.** the act of searching: *They found the lost child after a long search.* —**search′er,** *n.*

search·ing (sur′ching) *adj.* **1.** very observant and penetrating: *a searching glance.* **2.** examining and probing carefully: *searching questions.* —**search′ing·ly,** *adv.*

search·light (surch′līt′) *n.* **1.** a device that projects a strong beam of light. **2.** such a beam of light.

search warrant, a court order authorizing the search of a house or other building for wanted persons or stolen or unlawfully held property.

sea·scape (sē′skāp′) *n.* **1.** a picture or painting showing a view of the sea. **2.** a view of the sea.

sea serpent, any of various legendary sea monsters resembling a snake.

sea·shell (sē′shel′) *n.* the shell of a sea animal, such as an oyster or clam.

sea·shore (sē′shôr′) *n.* land near or bordering on the sea.

sea·sick (sē′sik′) *adj.* nauseated and dizzy as a result of the rolling motion of a boat or ship. —**sea′sick′ness,** *n.*

sea·side (sē′sīd′) *n.* land bordering on the sea; seashore.

sea snake, any of a group of poisonous snakes found in the warm inshore seas of Asia.

sea·son (sē′zən) *n.* **1.** one of the divisions of the year, as determined by the position of the earth in its orbit around the sun. The four seasons, spring, summer, autumn, and winter, are characterized chiefly by differences in weather, temperature, and the number of hours of daylight. **2.** a period or time of the year with reference to the weather conditions that characterize it: *the dry season, the monsoon season.* **3.** any period or time of the year marked by a particular activity or thing: *the football season, the opera season.* **4.** a proper, suitable, or usual time. —*v.t.* **1.** to add seasoning to in order to bring out, heighten, or improve flavor: *to season meat with salt and pepper.* **2.** to add zest or interest to: *The teacher seasoned the lecture with some of his personal experiences.* **3.** to make suitable for use, as by drying or aging: *to season timber.* **4.** to condition or make fit through experience. **5.** to make accustomed: *to season troops to battle.* —*v.i.* to become more suitable for use.

in season. a. available or in the best condition for eating: *Peaches are in season.* **b.** legally permitted to be hunted or caught: *Deer are now in season.*

out of season. not in season.

sea·son·a·ble (sē′zə nə bəl) *adj.* **1.** usual for or in keeping with the time of year: *Seasonable temperatures are expected through Friday.* **2.** done, happening, or coming at the right or proper time; timely. —**sea′son·a·ble·ness,** *n.* —**sea′son·a·bly,** *adv.*

sea·son·al (sē′zən əl) *adj.* affected by, characteristic of, or happening at a certain season or seasons: *Harvesting cherries provides only seasonal employment.* —**sea′son·al·ly,** *adv.*

sea·son·ing (sē′zə ning) *n.* **1.** something used to bring out, heighten, or improve the flavor of food, as a spice, herb, or condiment. **2.** something that adds zest or interest.

seat (sēt) *n.* **1.** something to sit on, such as a chair, stool, or bench. **2.** a place to sit: *Those who arrive late will have to find seats on the floor.* **3.** that part of an object on which one sits: *the seat of a chair.* **4.** that part of the body on which one sits or the part of the clothes covering it: *The seat of his trousers is torn.* **5.** a membership or official position: *a seat in the Senate, a seat on the stock exchange.* **6.** a reserved place for sitting: *We have two seats for the afternoon performance.* **7.** a center or source: *A college is a seat of learning. The capital is the seat of government for the country.* **8.** a manner of sitting, as on horseback. —*v.t.* **1.** to place on or lead to a seat; assign a seat to: *The ushers seated all the wedding guests. She seated the child on a stool.* **2.** to have seats for: *The auditorium seats two hundred people.* **3.** to put a seat in or on.

seat belt, a strap or set of straps that may be buckled to hold a person in the seat of an automobile or airplane in case of a crash or jolt. Also, **safety belt.**

SEATO (sē′tō) Southeast Asia Treaty Organization, a mutual defense agreement between the United States, the United Kingdom, France, Pakistan, Thailand, the Philippines, Australia, and New Zealand, established in 1954.

Se·at·tle (sē at′əl) *n.* a port city in western Washington, on Puget Sound. Pop. (1970), 530,831.

sea urchin, any of a group of sea animals having a shell covered with hard, movable spines.

sea wall, a strong wall or embankment made to prevent waves from wearing away the shoreline or to act as a breakwater.

sea·ward (sē′wərd) *adj.* toward the sea: *a seaward course.* —*adv.* also, **sea·wards.** in the direction of the sea: *The explorers walked seaward.*

sea·way (sē′wā′) *n.* **1.** a route over the sea; shipping lane. **2.** an inland waterway deep and wide enough for ocean-going ships. **3.** the headway of a ship or boat.

sea·weed (sē′wēd′) *n.* any of various plants or algae living in the sea.

sea·wor·thy (sē′wur′thē) *adj.* fit or safe to sail on the sea: *a seaworthy ship.* —**sea′wor′thi·ness,** *n.*

se·ba·ceous (si bā′shəs) *adj.* **1.** of or relating to oil or fat; oily; greasy. **2.** secreting oil or fat.

sebaceous gland, any of the glands of the skin that secrete an oily lubricating fluid to the skin and hair.

sec, secant.

sec. **1.** second. **2.** secondary. **3.** secretary. **4.** section.

se·cant (sē′kant, sē′kənt) *n.* **1.** *Trigonometry.* **a.** (of either acute angle of a right triangle) the ratio of the length of the hypotenuse to the length of the side adjacent to the angle. **b.** a straight line drawn from the center of a circle through one end point of an arc to the tangent drawn from the other end point of the same arc. **2.** *Geometry.* a line inter-

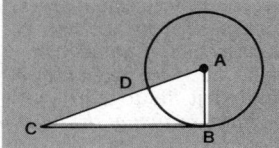

Secant of angle *A = AC/AB*

secting a curve at two or more points. —*adj.* that intersects; intersecting.

se·cede (si sēd′) *v.i.,* **se·ced·ed, se·ced·ing.** to withdraw formally, especially as a group, from an organization, usually to form an alternative organization.

se·ces·sion (si sesh′ən) *n.* **1.** the act or instance of seceding. **2.** *also,* **Secession.** the withdrawal of the eleven Southern states from the Union in 1860 and 1861, resulting in the Civil War.

se·ces·sion·ist (si sesh′ə nist) *n.* **1.** a person who favors or supports secession. **2.** a member of a group that secedes. —*adj.* relating to, favoring, or supporting secession or the beliefs or principles of secessionists.

se·clude (si klood′) *v.t.,* **se·clud·ed, se·clud·ing.** to keep apart or remove from the company of others; isolate: *The writer secluded himself when he was working.*

se·clud·ed (si kloo′did) *adj.* **1.** shut off or screened from view: *The yard was secluded from the street by trees.* **2.** kept apart or removed from others; solitary: *The old man led a secluded life.* —**se·clud′ed·ness,** *n.*

se·clu·sion (si kloo′zhən) *n.* the act of secluding or the state of being secluded.

sec·ond[1] (sek′ənd) *adj.* **1.** (the ordinal of two) next after the first: *Our team finished in second place.* **2.** new or different; another: *a second helping of potatoes, a second chance.* **3.** below the first or best: *Ted is the second pitcher on the baseball team.* **4.** *Music.* of, relating to, or performing a part lower in pitch than or subordinate to another: *second violin, second soprano.* **5.** of or relating to the forward gear next above first or low in a motor vehicle. —*adv.* in the group or position next after the first: *to finish second in a race.* —*n.* **1.** a person or thing that is next after the first: *She was the second to arrive at the party.* **2.** a person who aids or supports another, as in a duel or prize fight. **3.** *also,* **seconds.** goods below the first or best quality: *These towels are seconds.* **4.** the forward gear next above first or low in a motor vehicle. **5.** *Music.* **a.** a note that is a whole step above a given note. D is the second of C. **b.** an interval of one whole step. **c.** a combination of two notes that are separated by this interval. —*v.t.* **1.** to approve or support formally; endorse: *to second a motion to adjourn.* **2.** to give support, encouragement, or assistance to: *They seconded his efforts to have a new hospital built.* [Old French *second.*] —**sec′ond·er,** *n.*

sec·ond[2] (sek′ənd) *n.* **1.** a unit of time equal to 1/60 of a minute or 1/3600 of an hour. **2.** any very short interval of time: *It will take me only a second to put on my coat.* **3.** 1/60 of a minute or 1/3600 of a degree of angular measurement. [French *seconde,* from Medieval Latin *secunda (minuta)* second (minute), referring to a *second* division of an hour into seconds, as distinguished from the first division into minutes.]

Second Advent, another term for **Second Coming.**

sec·ond·ar·y (sek′ən der′ē) *adj.* **1.** coming from or based on something that is original or primary; derived: *He got all his information for his term paper from secondary sources.* **2.** coming below or after the first in order, place, importance, or time: *a secondary fact.* **3.** not main or chief; less important: *a secondary cause.* **4.** of or relating to an electrical coil in which a current is produced by induction

at; āpe; cär; end; mē; it; īce; hot; ōld; fôrk; wood; fool; oil; out; up; turn; sing; thin; **this;** hw in white; zh in treasure. The symbol ə stands for the sound of **a** in about, e in taken, i in pencil, o in lemon, and **u** in circus.

when the current in a primary coil changes. —**sec′ond·ar′-i·ly,** *adv.*

secondary accent **1.** the weaker of the two stresses in any word that has two syllables accented or stressed. The third syllable of *sec′ond·ar′y* has a secondary accent. **2.** the mark (′) showing this accent.

secondary school, a school providing instruction after elementary or grade school, made up of grades seven, eight, or nine through twelve.

secondary sex characteristic, any of the physical features that are characteristic of each sex and usually appear at puberty, such as breast development or beard growth.

sec·ond-best (sek′ənd best′) *adj.* next or inferior to the best.

sec·ond-class (sek′ənd klas′) *adj.* **1.** less than the first or best; inferior: *He is a second-class baseball player.* **2.** of or relating to a class of mail consisting primarily of newspapers and magazines. **3.** of or relating to a form of travel ranking next in price or luxury below first class. —*adv.* by second-class mail or travel accommodations: *The tourist traveled second-class.*

second class **1.** second-class travel accommodations. **2.** second-class mail.

Second Coming, the return of Christ on Judgment Day to judge the living and the dead. Also, **Second Advent.**

sec·ond-guess (sek′ənd ges′) *v.t.* to make judgments about (someone or some decision) after the results of a course of action are known.

sec·ond·hand (sek′ənd hand′) *also,* **sec·ond·hand.** *adj.* **1.** owned, used, or worn by someone else: *a secondhand car.* **2.** not obtained from the original source; derivative; borrowed: *He has only secondhand knowledge of the accident.* **3.** dealing in used goods: *a secondhand furniture store.* —*adv.* in a secondhand manner; indirectly: *We heard the facts secondhand.*

second hand, the hand or pointer of a clock or watch that shows seconds as it moves in a circle.

second lieutenant, an officer of the lowest rank in the U.S. Army, Air Force, or Marine Corps, ranking below a first lieutenant.

sec·ond·ly (sek′ənd lē) *adv.* in the second place.

second nature, a habit or quality acquired by a person, that is so deeply fixed that it seems to be part of his nature.

second person, the form of a pronoun or verb that indicates the person being addressed. In the sentence *You were out when I called, you* and *were* are in the second person.

sec·ond-rate (sek′ənd rāt′) *adj.* not best in some quality or degree; mediocre or inferior: *The team played second-rate baseball and lost the game.*

se·cre·cy (sē′krə sē) *n.* **1.** the state of being secret or being kept secret. **2.** the ability or practice of keeping secrets.

se·cret (sē′krit) *adj.* **1.** known only to oneself or a few; kept from general knowledge: *a secret password, a secret report, a secret plan.* **2.** acting in a hidden way: *a secret agent, a secret organization.* **3.** dependable in keeping to oneself what one knows. —*n.* **1.** something known only to oneself or a few and kept from general knowledge: *to keep a secret.* **2.** a hidden reason or explanation: *the secret of success.* **3.** a cause or process not readily understood or explained; mystery: *the secrets of nature.* —**se′cret·ly,** *adv.*
   in secret. not openly or in public; in private: *She told her best friend the news in secret.*

sec·re·tar·i·al (sek′rə ter′ē əl) *adj.* of or relating to a secretary or a secretary's duties.

sec·re·tar·i·at (sek′rə ter′ē it) *n.* **1.** the administrative department of an organization: *the secretariat of the United*

Nations. **2.** the officials who keep records or perform secretarial duties. **3.** the office or position of a secretary, especially the secretary of a government department.

sec·re·tar·y (sek′rə ter′ē) *n. pl.,* **sec·re·tar·ies.** **1.** a person employed to write letters, keep records, and the like for an individual or company. **2.** an officer of an organization or company responsible for important records and correspondence. **3.** a person who heads an executive department of a government: *the Secretary of Agriculture.* **4.** a piece of furniture having a writing surface, drawers or compartments, and often bookshelves.

secretary bird, a long-legged African bird having a crest of feathers at the back of its head. [From these feathers, which were thought to look like quill pens, such as a secretary of former times might have stuck behind his ear.]

Secretary bird

sec·re·tar·y-gen·er·al (sek′rə ter′ē jen′-ər əl) *n. pl.,* **sec·re·tar·ies-gen·er·al.** the chief administrative officer of a secretariat.

se·crete¹ (si krēt′) *v.t.,* **se·cret·ed, se·cret·ing.** to produce by means of secretion: *Some glands secrete hormones.* [From *secretion.*]

se·crete² (si krēt′) *v.t.,* **se·cret·ed, se·cret·ing.** to put in a hiding place; hide away: *He secreted the documents in a safe.* [A form of obsolete *secret* to hide.]

se·cre·tion (si krē′shən) *n.* **1.** the process by which a particular substance is produced in an organism through some specialized activity of a cell or gland. **2.** the substance so produced. **3.** the act of secreting; hiding.

se·cre·tive (sē′kri tiv, si krē′tiv) *adj.* **1.** of, characterized by, or indicating secrecy or concealment: *a secretive smile.* **2.** another word for **secretory.** —**se′cre·tive·ly,** *adv.* —**se′cre·tive·ness,** *n.*

se·cre·to·ry (si krē′tər ē) *adj.* relating to, producing, or causing secretion.

Secret Service **1.** a division of the U.S. Treasury Department that protects the President and enforces federal laws against counterfeiting U.S. currency and bonds. **2. secret service.** a government department or bureau that makes secret investigations.

secs. **1.** seconds. **2.** sections.

sect (sekt) *n.* **1.** a religious body, especially a small group separated from a large, established church. **2.** any relatively small group having the same principles, beliefs, or opinions.

sect., section.

sec·tar·i·an (sek ter′ē ən) *adj.* **1.** of, relating to, or limited to one small and narrow group: *sectarian ideas.* **2.** of or relating to a religious sect: *a sectarian college.* —*n.* a person who belongs to a religious sect.

sec·tar·i·an·ism (sek ter′ē ə niz′əm) *n.* the practice of being sectarian.

sec·tion (sek′shən) *n.* **1.** a part of something separated or cut off from the rest; portion: *She planted vegetables in one section of the garden.* **2.** a division of something written: *the sports section of a newspaper.* **3.** a part, piece, or unit that fits together with others: *The plumber replaced a leaky section of the pipe.* **4.** a distinctive part of a nation, community, area, or group of people: *the financial section of a city, the violin section of an orchestra.* **5.** a drawing or other representation of something as it would appear if cut through to show its inner structure. **6.** the act of cutting. **7.** a measure of public land equal to one square mile, or 640 acres, and making up 1/36 of a township. —*v.t.* to divide, as by separating or cutting into parts: *He sectioned off the pasture from the rest of the land belonging to the farm.*

sec·tion·al (sek′shən əl) *adj.* **1.** of, coming from, or characteristic of different regions or areas: *sectional interests.* **2.** made up of several sections or parts fitting into one another: *a sectional cabinet.* —**sec′tion·al·ly,** *adv.*

sec·tion·al·ism (sek′shən əl iz′əm) *n.* too great a concern for the local interests of a particular region or area.

sec·tor (sek′tər) *n.* **1.** a particular division or part: *the industrial sector of a country.* **2.** *Geometry.* a plane figure bounded by two radii of a circle and the intercepted arc. **3.** a distinct military area within which a military unit operates and for which it is responsible.

sec·u·lar (sek′yə lər) *adj.* **1.** of or relating to the world outside the church; worldly: *secular education, secular interests.* **2.** (of clergy) living in an outside community, not in a monastery or other religious community: *a secular priest.* —**sec′u·lar·ly,** *adv.*

sec·u·lar·ize (sek′yə lə rīz′) *v.t.,* **sec·u·lar·ized, sec·u·lar·iz·ing.** to make secular; separate from religion or religious institutions. —**sec′u·lar·i·za′tion,** *n.*

se·cure (si kyoor′) *adj.* **1.** not likely to be taken away; certain or guaranteed: *a secure job.* **2.** safe from danger, as of loss or attack: *The cellar was a secure place to be during the hurricane.* **3.** free from worry, care, or fear: *Having life insurance made him feel secure about his family's future.* **4.** not likely to give way; stable: *The house stands on a secure foundation.* —*v.t.,* **se·cured, se·cur·ing. 1.** to get; obtain: *He secured two tickets to the football game.* **2.** to put or fasten firmly: *She secured the door and windows for the night.* **3.** to bring about; effect: *The lawyer secured the prisoner's release by putting up bail.* **4.** to make safe; guard; protect: *The gold shipments were secured against robbers by armed guards.* —**se·cure′ly,** *adv.* —**se·cure′ness,** *n.*

se·cu·ri·ty (si kyoor′ə tē) *n. pl.,* **se·cu·ri·ties. 1.** protection from danger, as of loss or attack: *the security of a fortress.* **2.** freedom from worry, care, or fear: *His savings account gave the old man a feeling of security.* **3.** measures taken to guard against something, such as crime: *That building's security is good.* **4.** *usually,* **securities.** a stock or bond certificate: *He sold his securities to finance his son's education.* **5.** property given as a pledge, as for repayment of a loan. **6.** a person who agrees to be financially responsible for another.

secy. also, **sec′y.** secretary.

se·dan (si dan′) *n.* an automobile with two or four doors and a full-width seat in both the front and the back.

sedan chair, an enclosed chair suspended on poles carried by two men, much used in the seventeenth and eighteenth centuries.

se·date (si dāt′) *adj.* quiet and serious; calm: *a sedate judge.* —*v.t.,* **se·dat·ed, se·dat·ing.** to calm, as with a sedative: *to sedate a patient.* —**se·date′ly,** *adv.* —**se·date′ness,** *n.*

Sedan chair

se·da·tion (si dā′shən) *n.* **1.** the state of being sedated: *The patient is under sedation.* **2.** the act of sedating.

sed·a·tive (sed′ə tiv) *n.* a drug or medicine that lessens nervousness, excitement, or distress. —*adj.* lessening nervousness, excitement, or distress; soothing; calming.

sed·en·tar·y (sed′ən ter′ē) *adj.* **1.** not used to physical exercise, activity, or movement: *a sedentary man.* **2.** requiring little or no physical activity: *Most office jobs are sedentary.* **3.** remaining in one area; not migratory: *sedentary birds.* —**sed′en·tar′i·ness,** *n.*

Se·der (sā′dər) *n.* in Judaism, a religious service and ceremonial feast held during Passover to commemorate the Exodus from Egypt.

sedge (sej) *n.* any of a large group of grassy plants growing in marshes and other wet areas.

sed·i·ment (sed′ə mənt) *n.* **1.** matter that settles to the bottom of a liquid; dregs. **2.** *Geology.* solid matter, such as rocks or earth, deposited by water, ice, or wind.

sed·i·men·tar·y (sed′ə men′tər ē) *adj.* **1.** of or relating to sediment. **2.** formed by the deposit of sediment: *sedimentary rock.*

sed·i·men·ta·tion (sed′ə mən tā′shən) *n.* the act or process of depositing sediment.

se·di·tion (si dish′ən) *n.* a speech or action causing discontent or rebellion against the existing government.

se·di·tious (si dish′əs) *adj.* **1.** taking part in or guilty of sedition. **2.** of, relating to, or containing sedition: *a seditious document, a seditious speech.* —**se·di′tious·ly,** *adv.*

se·duce (si dōōs′, si dyōōs′) *v.t.,* **se·duced, se·duc·ing. 1.** to tempt or persuade to do wrong: *The man was seduced by bribes to give false evidence at the trial.* **2.** to persuade to engage in sexual intercourse. —**se·duc′er,** *n.*

se·duc·tion (si duk′shən) *n.* **1.** the act of seducing or the state of being seduced. **2.** something that seduces.

se·duc·tive (si duk′tiv) *adj.* tending to seduce; alluring; enticing. —**se·duc′tive·ly,** *adv.* —**se·duc′tive·ness,** *n.*

sed·u·lous (sej′ə ləs) *adj.* working industriously; diligent. —**sed′u·lous·ly,** *adv.*

see¹ (sē) *v.,* **saw, seen, see·ing.** —*v.t.* **1.** to become aware of or notice with the eyes; look at: *I cannot see the road signs in this fog.* **2.** to be aware of with the mind; understand: *I do not see why you have to leave so soon.* **3.** to attend as a spectator: *to see a movie.* **4.** to regard; judge; view: *My friend and I see things the same way.* **5.** to find out: *See who is at the door.* **6.** to make sure: *We will see that she leaves on time.* **7.** to go with; accompany; escort: *to see someone to the door.* **8.** to visit or meet: *to see friends, to see a doctor.* **9.** to receive, as for a visit, interview, or examination: *The doctor does not see patients on Thursdays.* **10.** to experience or undergo: *Her brother saw service in the Army.* **11.** to be marked or characterized by: *That corner has seen many car accidents.* **12.** to predict or foresee: *I see many years of trouble ahead.* —*v.i.* **1.** to have or use the power of sight: *A blind man does not see.* **2.** to understand; comprehend. **3.** to judge or discover: *See for yourself.* [Old English *sēon.*]

to see off. to go with (someone) to the departure point: *He saw his friend off at the airport.*

to see out. to continue with to the end; finish.

to see through. a. to continue with to the end. **b.** to watch over in time of difficulty. **c.** to understand the true character or meaning of.

to see to. to attend to; take care of.

see² (sē) *n.* the office or jurisdiction of a bishop. [Old French *sed, sied* the seat or residence of a bishop.]

at; āpe; cär; end; mē; it; īce; hot; ōld; fôrk; wood; fōōl; oil; out; up; turn; sing; thin; this; hw in white; zh in treasure. The symbol ə stands for the sound of a in about, e in taken, i in pencil, o in lemon, and u in circus.

seed (sēd) *n. pl.*, **seeds** or **seed.** **1.** the reproductive body produced by a flowering plant, that contains the developing embryo of a new plant. **2.** any part of a plant from which a new plant will grow, such as a tuber, bulb, or spore. **3.** the origin or beginning from which something larger will grow or develop: *the seeds of rebellion.* **4.** *Archaic.* children, descendants, or offspring. —*v.t.* **1.** to sow (land) with seeds: *to seed a field with alfalfa.* **2.** to remove the seeds from: *to seed a watermelon.* **3.** *Sports.* to place (tournament contestants) so that stronger competitors will not meet each other in the early rounds. **4.** to spray (clouds) with dry ice or other chemical substances in order to produce rain. —*v.i.* to produce seeds. —**seed′like′**, *adj.*

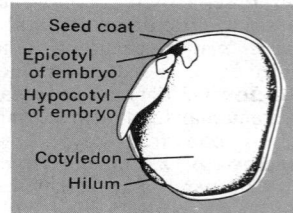

Seed coat
Epicotyl of embryo
Hypocotyl of embryo
Cotyledon
Hilum

Seed

seed·case (sēd′kās′) *n.* the part of a flowering plant that contains the seeds, such as a pod or capsule.

seed coat, the protective outer covering of a seed.

seed·er (sē′dər) *n.* **1.** a person who sows or plants seeds. **2.** a device for sowing seeds. **3.** a device for removing seeds, as from fruit.

seed leaf, the leaf forming part of the embryo in a seed; cotyledon.

seed·ling (sēd′ling) *n.* **1.** any young plant grown from a seed. **2.** a young tree less than three feet high.

seed pearl, a very small pearl.

seed·y (sē′dē) *adj.*, **seed·i·er, seed·i·est.** **1.** not looking fresh, new, or prosperous; shabby: *a seedy restaurant, a seedy old coat.* **2.** having many seeds. —**seed′i·ly**, *adv.* —**seed′i·ness**, *n.*

see·ing (sē′ing) *conj.* in view of the fact; considering: *Seeing that it is late, we should go home.* —*n.* the ability to see; sight. —*adj.* having sight; able to see.

seek (sēk) *v.*, **sought, seek·ing.** —*v.t.* **1.** to go in search of; try to find; look for: *The police are seeking a stolen car.* **2.** to try; attempt: *Every candidate seeks to win.* **3.** to desire or try to get; ask for: *to seek aid.* —*v.i.* to search; make inquiry: *Seek and ye shall find* (Matthew 7:7). —**seek′er**, *n.*

seem (sēm) *v.i.* **1.** to give the feeling of being; appear to be: *The tall, strong boy seemed much older than he really was.* **2.** to be true so far as one can tell: *The child seems happy in his new home. It seems to be about to rain.* **3.** to appear to oneself: *I seem to hear faint footsteps.*

seem·ing (sē′ming) *adj.* that is true, so far as one can tell: *The city has made seeming improvements in garbage collection.* —**seem′ing·ly**, *adv.*

seem·ly (sēm′lē) *adj.*, **seem·li·er, seem·li·est.** suitable, as to a purpose or occasion; proper: *It is not seemly to speak loudly in a church.* —**seem′li·ness**, *n.*

seen (sēn) the past participle of **see**[1].

seep (sēp) *v.i.* to spread or flow slowly, as through openings or pores: *Water seeped from the cracked pipe.*

seep·age (sē′pij) *n.* **1.** the act or process of seeping. **2.** something that seeps.

seer (sēr) *n.* a person who is believed to have the power of foreseeing future events. —**seer′ess**, *n.*

seer·suck·er (sēr′suk′ər) *n.* a lightweight fabric, usually woven with alternating plain and crinkled stripes, and used chiefly for summer clothing and children's wear.

see·saw (sē′sô′) *n.* **1.** a playground device made of a plank supported at the middle so that when a child is seated on either end, one end goes up as the other goes down. Also, **teeter-totter.** **2.** any up-and-down or back-and-forth action or movement: *the seasaw of political power.* —*v.i.* **1.** to move up and down on a seesaw. **2.** to move or act up and down or back and forth.

seethe (sēth) *v.i.*, **seethed, seeth·ing.** **1.** to be very disturbed or agitated: *to seethe with rage.* **2.** to rise, surge, or form bubbles, as if boiling: *The waves seethed around the rocks.*

seg·ment (seg′mənt) *n.* **1.** any of the parts into which a thing is or may be divided; division; section: *the segments of an orange.* **2.** *Geometry.* **a.** a part of a plane figure cut off by a line, such as the part of a circle bounded by an arc and a chord. **b.** the part of a sphere cut off by a plane or by parallel planes. —*v.t.* to divide into segments.

seg·men·tal (seg ment′əl) *adj.* of, relating to, or composed of segments. —**seg·men′tal·ly**, *adv.*

seg·men·ta·tion (seg′mən tā′shən) *n.* **1.** the act or process of dividing into segments. **2.** *Biology.* the division of a cell into many cells, as in a fertilized egg; cleavage.

se·go (sē′gō) *n. pl.*, **se·gos.** **1.** the bell-shaped flower of a plant found in the deserts of the western United States, usually white with pink, purple, or greenish-yellow markings. **2.** the plant that bears this flower.

Sego

seg·re·gate (seg′rə gāt′) *v.*, **seg·re·gat·ed, seg·re·gat·ing.** —*v.t.* **1.** to set apart from others or the rest; isolate: *to segregate a patient with a contagious disease.* **2.** to impose segregation on (a racial group or social facilities): *to segregate schools.* —*v.i.* **1.** to become separate or separated; go apart. **2.** to have or practice racial segregation.

seg·re·ga·tion (seg′rə gā′shən) *n.* **1.** the practice of separating one racial group, especially Negroes, from another or from the rest of society by making them use different schools and social facilities or live in certain areas. **2.** the act of segregating or the state of being segregated.

seg·re·ga·tion·ist (seg′rə gā′shə nist) *n.* a person who practices or supports racial segregation.

sei·gneur (sēn yur′) *n.* a feudal nobleman, especially the lord of a manor.

seine (sān) *n.* a fishing net, especially a long one that hangs vertically in the water, supported by floats on its upper edge and kept taut by weights on the bottom edge. —*v.t., v.i.*, **seined, sein·ing.** to catch (fish) with a seine. —**sein′er**, *n.*

Seine (sān) *n.* a river flowing from eastern France northwestward into the English Channel.

seis·mic (sīz′mik) *adj.* of, caused by, or subject to earthquakes.

seismo- *combining form* of or relating to earthquakes: *seismology.*

seis·mo·graph (sīz′mə graf′) *n.* an instrument that records the location, direction, intensity, and duration of earthquakes and other earth vibrations.

seis·mol·o·gy (sīz mol′ə jē) *n.* the study of earthquakes and other earth vibrations.

seize (sēz) *v.t.*, **seized, seiz·ing.** **1.** to take hold of suddenly and forcibly; grab on to: *The dog seized the bone.* **2.** to take away or get control or possession of by force or authority: *The soldiers seized the fortress.* **3.** to capture or arrest: *The police seized the criminal.* **4.** to take advantage of: *to seize an opportunity.* **5.** to have a sudden and powerful effect on; possess: *Panic seized the crowd when the fire broke out.*
to seize on or **to seize upon.** to take hold of suddenly: *to seize on an idea.*

sei·zure (sē′zhər) *n.* **1.** the act of seizing. **2.** a sudden attack of a disease: *a seizure of epilepsy.*

sel·dom (sel′dəm) *adv.* not often; on few occasions; rarely: *We seldom go to the movies.*

se·lect (si lekt′) *v.t.* to take or pick out from among many; choose: *Select the book you want to read from the library.* —*v.i.* to make a selection; choose. —*adj.* **1.** picked or chosen because of special ability or fitness: *to coach a select group of athletes.* **2.** of high quality; choice: *select apples.* **3.** careful in selecting; discriminating.

se·lec·tion (si lek′shən) *n.* **1.** the act of selecting or the state of being selected. **2.** a person or thing that is selected. **3.** a person or thing that may be selected: *the selections on a menu.* **4.** *Biology.* see **natural selection.**

se·lec·tive (si lek′tiv) *adj.* that selects or is careful in selecting. —**se·lec′tive·ly,** *adv.*

selective service, compulsory military service of persons selected according to age and physical fitness.

se·lec·tiv·i·ty (si lek tiv′ə tē) *n.* the state or quality of being selective.

se·lect·man (se lekt′mən) *n. pl.,* **se·lect·men** (si lekt′-mən). a member of the board that governs a town in most New England states.

se·lec·tor (si lek′tər) *n.* **1.** a person or thing that selects. **2.** a dial, switch, or other device used to control or select different operations of a machine.

Se·le·ne (si lē′nē) *n. Greek Mythology.* the goddess of the moon. In Roman mythology she was called Luna.

se·le·ni·um (si lē′nē əm) *n.* a poisonous, nonmetallic element having chemical properties resembling those of sulfur. Because its electrical conductivity increases with bright light, it is used in photoelectric cells. Symbol: Se

self (self) *n. pl.,* **selves. 1.** one's own person as distinguished from all others. **2.** the qualities or characteristics of a person or thing. **3.** personal interests, welfare, advantage, or the like. —*adj.* of the same material as a garment or article itself: *a self belt.*

self- *prefix* **1.** of or for oneself or itself: *self-confidence, self-conscious.* **2.** by oneself or itself: *self-educated.* **3.** to oneself: *self-addressed.*

●To understand the meaning of a word that begins with **self-** but is not defined in this dictionary, add the words "oneself" or "itself" to the meaning of the basic word. For example, *self-inflicted* means "inflicted by oneself" and *self-regulating* means "regulating itself." For any important *self-* word that has a special meaning, there is an entry in the dictionary.

self-ad·dressed (self′ə drest′) *adj.* addressed to oneself: *a self-addressed envelope.*

self-ap·point·ed (self′ə poin′tid) *adj.* appointed by oneself alone, without the consent or support of others.

self-as·sur·ance (self′ə shoor′əns) *n.* confidence in one's own ability, position, or worth.

self-as·sured (self′ə shoord′) *adj.* having confidence in one's own ability, position, or worth.

self-cen·tered (self′sen′tərd) *adj.* preoccupied with one's own thoughts, interests, or activities to the point of selfishness. —**self′-cen′tered·ness,** *n.*

self-clean·ing (self′klē′ning) *adj.* cleaning itself by mechanical means: *a self-cleaning oven.*

self-con·fi·dent (self′kon′fə dənt) *adj.* having confidence or faith in one's own ability or worth. —**self′-con′fi·dence,** *n.* —**self′-con′fi·dent·ly,** *adv.*

self-con·scious (self′kon′shəs) *adj.* **1.** uncomfortably aware of one's own actions, words, or thoughts, especially in the presence of others; shy and embarrassed. **2.** showing such awareness: *a self-conscious laugh.* —**self′-con′-scious·ly,** *adv.* —**self′-con′scious·ness,** *n.*

self-con·tained (self′kən tānd′) *adj.* **1.** reserved or restrained in behavior. **2.** having all that is necessary in oneself or itself; complete: *a self-contained machine.*

self-con·trol (self′kən trōl′) *n.* control over one's own actions or emotions.

self-de·fense (self′di fens′) *n.* defense or protection of oneself, as against attacks or threats.

self-de·ni·al (self′di nī′əl) *n.* the practice of sacrificing one's own desires and interests for the sake of others.

self-de·ter·mi·na·tion (self′di tur′mə nā′shən) *n.* **1.** the act of making one's own decisions without outside influence. **2.** the right of a people to choose the form of government they shall have.

self-dis·ci·pline (self′dis′ə plin) *n.* stern control or discipline of oneself, one's actions, or one's feelings.

self-ed·u·cat·ed (self′ej′ə kā′tid) *adj.* educated by reading books or studying on one's own, with little or no formal classroom schooling.

self-em·ployed (self′im ploid′) *adj.* earning income from one's own business rather than from an employer.

self-ev·i·dent (self′ev′ə dənt) *adj.* needing no proof or explanation; evident in itself.

self-ex·plan·a·to·ry (self′iks plan′ə tôr′ē) *adj.* needing no extra explanation or details; containing or being its own explanation: *The instructions are self-explanatory.*

self-ex·pres·sion (self′iks presh′ən) *n.* the expression of one's own thoughts, feelings, or true personality.

self-gov·ern·ment (self′guv′ərn mənt) *n.* government or rule of a group by its own members rather than by an outside authority: *Many former colonies in Africa have now achieved self-government.*

self-im·por·tant (self′im pôrt′ənt) *adj.* having an exaggerated opinion of one's own importance. —**self′-im·por′tance,** *n.*

self-im·prove·ment (self′im proōv′mənt) *n.* improvement of oneself through one's own efforts.

self-in·dul·gent (self′in dul′jənt) *adj.* giving in to one's own weaknesses, feelings, or desires. —**self′-in·dul′-gence,** *n.*

self-in·ter·est (self′in′tər ist, self′in′trist) *n.* **1.** personal advantage. **2.** the practice of regarding one's own welfare as more important than the welfare of others.

self·ish (sel′fish) *adj.* concerned for or serving one's own desires and interests above all others: *a selfish person, a selfish attitude.* —**self′ish·ly,** *adv.* —**self′ish·ness,** *n.*

self·less (self′lis) *adj.* having little or no thought for oneself; unselfish. —**self′less·ly,** *adv.* —**self′less·ness,** *n.*

self-made (self′mād′) *adj.* **1.** made by oneself or itself. **2.** rising to wealth or success through one's own efforts: *a self-made man.*

self-pit·y (self′pit′ē) *n.* a feeling of pity for oneself.

self-por·trait (self′pôr′trit) *n.* a portrait of oneself made by oneself.

self-pos·sessed (self′pə zest′) *adj.* in control of oneself; composed.

self-pos·ses·sion (self′pə zesh′ən) *n.* control of oneself; composure.

self-pres·er·va·tion (self′prez′ər vā′shən) *n.* an instinctive desire to protect oneself from injury, death, or danger.

S

self·re·li·ant (self′ri lī′ənt) *adj.* relying on one's own resources or abilities. —**self′-re·li′ance,** *n.*

self·re·spect (self′ri spekt′) *n.* proper regard for or awareness of one's own worth and capabilities as a person.

self·re·spect·ing (self′ri spek′ting) *adj.* having self-respect.

self·right·eous (self′rī′chəs) *adj.* thinking that one's own actions and beliefs are more moral or right than those of others. —**self′-right′eous·ly,** *adv.* —**self′-right′eous·ness,** *n.*

self·sac·ri·fice (self′sak′rə fīs′) *n.* the giving up or ignoring of one's own interests and desires for the sake of duty or the welfare of another. —**self′-sac′ri·fic′ing,** *adj.*

self·same (self′sām′) *adj.* exactly the same; identical.

self·sat·is·fac·tion (self′sat′is fak′shən) *n.* satisfaction with oneself or one's own achievements.

self·sat·is·fied (self′sat′is fīd′) *adj.* feeling or showing satisfaction with oneself or one's achievements.

self·seek·ing (self′sē′king) *adj.* concerned mainly with furthering one's own selfish interests; selfish. —*n.* selfishness.

self·ser·vice (self′sur′vis) *n.* the act or process of serving oneself. —*adj.* that requires self-service: *a self-service store, a self-service elevator.*

self·styled (self′stīld′) *adj.* called or considered so by oneself alone.

self·suf·fi·cient (self′sə fish′ənt) *adj.* capable of providing for oneself without help from others; independent. —**self′-suf·fi′cien·cy,** *n.*

self·sup·port·ing (self′sə pôr′ting) *adj.* supporting or providing for oneself without outside help.

self·taught (self′tôt′) *adj.* taught by oneself without aid from others.

self·will (self′wil′) *n.* insistence on having one's own way; stubbornness; obstinacy.

self·willed (self′wild′) *adj.* stubborn about having one's own way; unmindful of the wishes of others.

self·wind·ing (self′wīn′ding) *adj.* (of a clock or watch) not needing to be wound by hand; wound automatically.

sell (sel) *v.,* **sold, sell·ing.** —*v.t.* **1.** to give in return for money; accept money in payment for: *to sell a car.* **2.** to offer for sale; deal in: *Does this store sell shoes?* **3.** to bring about or promote the sale of: *Advertising sells new products.* **4.** to persuade (someone) to do, approve, or accept something: *Did you sell the bank on giving you a loan to buy a car?* **5.** to convince someone to do, approve, or accept (something) by using persuasive methods. —*v.i.* **1.** to sell goods, property, or the like, especially to engage in selling things for a living. **2.** to be offered for sale or be sold: *This fur coat sells for $1000.* **3.** to gain acceptance or approval: *That idea will never sell.*
  to sell out. a. to dispose of completely by selling: *The store sold out its stock of sweaters.* **b.** *Informal.* to betray: *The spy sold out to the other side by providing secret information.*

sell·er (sel′ər) *n.* **1.** a person who sells. **2.** something that is sold, especially something that is in great demand.

sell·out (sel′out′) *n.* **1.** the act of selling out. **2.** a performance or event for which all tickets have been sold.

sel·vage (sel′vij) *also,* **sel·vedge.** *n.* the narrow, tightly woven edge on a fabric that prevents raveling.

selves (selvz) the plural of **self.**

se·man·tic (si man′tik) *adj.* **1.** of, based on, or concerned with the meanings of words. **2.** of or having to do with semantics. —**se·man′ti·cal·ly,** *adv.*

se·man·tics (si man′tiks) *n., pl.* the branch of linguistics that deals with the meanings of words, especially with regard to their historical development and change. ▲ used with a singular verb.

sem·a·phore (sem′ə fôr′) *n.* **1.** a method of signaling that uses two flags, one held in each hand. Different positions of the arms represent the letters of the alphabet. **2.** an apparatus for signaling, such as a post with movable arms or an arrangement of lights or flags. —*v.i., v.t.,* **sem·a·phored, sem·a·phor·ing.** to signal by semaphore.

Semaphore

sem·blance (sem′bləns) *n.* **1.** outward appearance, often one that is false: *The witness' testimony had a semblance of truth but was actually a complete lie.* **2.** a likeness, image, or copy.

se·men (sē′mən) *n.* a fluid produced by the testes that contains the male reproductive cells.

se·mes·ter (si mes′tər) *n.* one of two terms into which a school or college year is divided.

semi- *prefix* **1.** half: *semicircle.* **2.** in part; partly; not completely: *semiofficial.* **3.** happening twice within a specified time period: *semimonthly.*

sem·i·an·nu·al (sem′ē an′yōō əl) *adj.* happening twice a year, especially at six-month intervals. —**sem′i·an′nu·al·ly,** *adv.*

sem·i·ar·id (sem′ē ar′id) *adj.* of or relating to an area having little rainfall, especially one having an average annual rainfall of less than twenty inches.

sem·i·au·to·mat·ic (sem′ē ô′tə mat′ik) *adj.* **1.** partly automatic. **2.** (of firearms) firing one shot each time the trigger is pulled, without reloading or cocking.

sem·i·cir·cle (sem′ē sur′kəl) *n.* half a circle or something arranged in or resembling half a circle. —**sem′i·cir′cu·lar,** *adj.*

semicircular canal, any of three curved tubes of membrane in the inner ear that help the body maintain balance.

sem·i·co·lon (sem′ē kō′lən) *n.* a mark of punctuation (;) that shows a grammatical separation stronger than that shown by a comma, but not as strong as that shown by a period.

sem·i·con·duc·tor (sem′ē kən duk′tər) *n.* a material, such as germanium or silicon, whose ability to conduct an electric current is greater than that of an insulator, but less than that of a conductor. Semiconductors are used in transistors.

sem·i·fi·nal (sem′ē fīn′əl) *adj.* immediately preceding the final match, as in a tournament. —*n.* a semifinal match.

sem·i·fi·nal·ist (sem′ē fīn′əl ist) *n.* a person who takes part in a semifinal match.

sem·i·month·ly (sem′ē munth′lē) *adj.* appearing or happening twice a month. —*n. pl.,* **sem·i·month·lies.** something that appears or takes place twice a month, such as a magazine. —*adv.* twice a month. ▲ See **bimonthly** for usage note.

sem·i·nal (sem′in əl) *adj.* of, relating to, or containing semen or seed.

sem·i·nar (sem′ə när′) *n.* **1.** a group of advanced students, as at a university, doing independent study or research under supervision. **2.** a meeting in which such a group reports and discusses its findings.

sem·i·nar·y (sem′ə ner′ē) *n. pl.,* **sem·i·nar·ies. 1.** a school that trains students to be priests, ministers, or rabbis. **2.** a school or academy at or beyond the high school level, especially a boarding school for young women.

Sem·i·nole (sem′ə nōl′) *n. pl.,* **Sem·i·noles** or **Sem·i·nole.** a member of a tribe of North American Indians, originally living in Florida. Most of this tribe now lives in Oklahoma.

sem·i·of·fi·cial (sem'ē ə fish'əl) *adj.* having some degree of authority; partly official.

sem·i·pre·cious (sem'ē presh'əs) *adj.* (of gems and minerals) valuable but having less value than precious stones. Garnets, amethysts, and turquoise are semiprecious stones.

Sem·ite (sem'īt) *n.* a member of a group of peoples speaking related Semitic languages, living mainly in the Middle East and parts of Africa. The ancient Hebrews, Phoenicians, and Assyrians were Semites. In modern times, Jews, Arabs, Syrians, and a number of Ethiopians are called Semites.

Se·mit·ic (sə mit'ik) *adj.* of or relating to Semites. —*n.* a language group that includes Hebrew and Arabic.

sem·i·tone (sem'ē tōn') *n.* *Music.* see **half step.**

sem·i·week·ly (sem'ē wēk'lē) *adj.* appearing or happening twice a week: *a semiweekly newspaper.* —*n. pl.,* **sem·i·week·lies.** a publication that is issued twice a week. —*adv.* twice a week. ▲ See **biweekly** for usage note.

Sen. 1. Senate. 2. Senator.

sen·ate (sen'it) *n.* 1. a governing or lawmaking council or assembly. 2. **Senate. a.** the upper house of the legislature of the United States or of most states of the United States. **b.** a similar house in other countries. 3. the ruling body of citizens in ancient Rome. [Going back to Latin *senātus* literally, council of elders, from *senex* old.]

sen·a·tor (sen'ə tər) *also,* **Sen·a·tor.** *n.* a member of a senate.

sen·a·to·ri·al (sen'ə tôr'ē əl) *adj.* of, relating to, or befitting a senator or a senate: *a senatorial debate.*

send (send) *v.t.,* **sent, send·ing.** 1. to cause to go to a certain place or from one place to another: *to send a letter to Boston, to send a spacecraft into orbit.* 2. to cause to go into a certain state or condition: *to send a person into a rage.* 3. to cause to come or be: *The music sent chills up and down my back.* —**send'er,** *n.*
  to send for. a. to ask (someone) to come; summon: *Did you send for the police?* **b.** to ask that something be brought or sent: *We sent for a free booklet.*

send-off (send'ôf') *n.* *Informal.* a demonstration of good will in honor of the start of a journey, new career, or the like.

Sen·e·ca (sen'ə kə) *n.* a member of the largest tribe of the Iroquois confederation of North American Indians, formerly living in western New York State.

Sen·e·ca, Lucius An·nae·us (sen'ə kə; ə nē'əs) 4 B.C.–65 A.D., Roman philosopher and dramatist.

Sen·e·gal (sen'ə gôl') *n.* a country in western Africa, on the Atlantic Ocean. Capital, Dakar. Area, 76,124 sq. mi. Pop. (1971 est.), 4,020,000.

sen·es·chal (sen'ə shəl) *n.* an official in medieval times who was in charge of a royal or noble household.

se·nile (sē'nīl) *adj.* 1. suffering the weakness that often occurs in old age, especially weakness of mental powers. 2. of, having to do with, or caused by old age.

se·nil·i·ty (si nil'ə tē) *n.* 1. the mental and, sometimes, physical weakness of old age. 2. the state of being old.

sen·ior (sēn'yər) *adj.* 1. the older of two. ▲ used after the name of a father whose son has the same name: *Robert Smith, Senior.* 2. of relatively old age: *a senior member of the legal profession.* 3. of higher position or rank, especially after long service or experience: *senior officers of the army, a senior senator.* 4. of or relating to the final year of high school or college. —*n.* 1. a person who is older than another: *My sister is my senior by three years.* 2. a student in the final year of high school or college. 3. a person of higher position or rank.

senior high school, a school attended after junior high school, usually including grades nine or ten through twelve.

sen·ior·i·ty (sēn yôr'ə tē, sēn yor'ə tē) *n.* 1. the state of being more advanced than another or others in age, position, or length of service. 2. special consideration or privileges given a person in a job or office, because of age, position, or length of service.

sen·na (sen'ə) *n.* 1. the dried leaves of any of several tropical plants, used in making a laxative. 2. a plant bearing these leaves.

se·ñor (sen yôr') *n. pl.,* **se·ño·res** (sen yôr'ās). sir; mister. ▲ the Spanish form of respectful or polite address for a man.

se·ño·ra (sen yôr'ə) *n.* madame. ▲ the Spanish form of respectful or polite address for a married woman.

se·ño·ri·ta (sen'yə rē'tə) *n.* miss. ▲ the Spanish form of respectful or polite address for an unmarried girl or woman.

sen·sa·tion (sen sā'shən) *n.* 1. the process of feeling or being aware of things by means of the senses: *the sensation of sight, the sensation of touch.* 2. a feeling or impression arising from some particular condition or set of circumstances: *a sensation of fear. She had a sensation that there was something wrong.* 3. a state of great excitement or interest: *The political scandal caused a nationwide sensation.* 4. a person or thing that causes great excitement or interest: *The young guitarist was a singing sensation.*

sen·sa·tion·al (sen sā'shən əl) *adj.* 1. arousing or intended to arouse great excitement or interest: *a sensational newspaper story.* 2. of or having to do with the senses. 3. *Informal.* outstanding or extraordinary; spectacular: *a sensational play in football.* —**sen·sa'tion·al·ly,** *adv.*

sen·sa·tion·al·ism (sen sā'shən əl iz'əm) *n.* sensational language or writing intended to excite or stimulate an audience or the public.

sense (sens) *n.* 1. any of the special powers by which a living being can be aware of its environment or changes in its own body. Sight, hearing, smell, taste, and touch are the five senses. 2. feeling or awareness; impression: *Having my big brother with me gave me a sense of security.* 3. the ability to appreciate or understand: *He has a good sense of humor.* 4. speech, thought, or action that is reasonable or intelligent. 5. reasonableness; wisdom: *What is the sense of worrying about something that cannot be changed?* 6. judgment; intelligence: *He is a man of good sense.* 7. *also,* **senses.** normal, sound mental ability: *He finally came to his senses.* 8. meaning, as of a word or statement: *There are many different senses of the word run.* —*v.t.,* **sensed, sens·ing.** to be aware or conscious of; feel; understand: *We sensed the tension in the locker room before the final game.*
  in a sense. from one aspect; in one way.
  to make sense. to be reasonable or logical; have an understandable meaning: *This paragraph doesn't make sense as you have written it.*

sense·less (sens'lis) *adj.* 1. lacking wisdom, intelligence, or reason; foolish: *a senseless crime.* 2. unconscious: *The blow knocked him senseless.* 3. meaningless: *senseless political slogans.* —**sense'less·ly,** *adv.* —**sense'less·ness,** *n.*

at; āpe; cär; end; mē; it; īce; hot; ōld; fôrk; wood; fōōl; oil; out; up; turn; sing; thin; this; hw in white; zh in treasure. The symbol ə stands for the sound of **a** in about, **e** in taken, **i** in pencil, **o** in lemon, and **u** in circus.

S

sense organ, any of the organs that receive and are affected by stimuli, such as light, sound, or heat, including the eyes, ears, nose, and taste buds.

sen·si·bil·i·ty (sen′sə bil′ə tē) *n. pl.,* **sen·si·bil·i·ties.** **1.** the power to feel or perceive. **2.** *also,* **sensibilities.** refined or delicate feeling: *The vulgar novel offended her sensibilities.* **3.** sensitiveness in feeling or perception.

sen·si·ble (sen′səl) *adj.* **1.** having, showing, or characterized by good sense or sound judgment; reasonable; wise: *a sensible man, a sensible decision.* **2.** easily perceived, noticed, or detected by the mind or senses. **3.** aware or conscious: *to be sensible of another person's feelings.* —**sen′si·ble·ness,** *n.* —**sen′si·bly,** *adv.*

sen·si·tive (sen′sə tiv) *adj.* **1.** easily or readily affected by: *Her skin is very sensitive to the sun.* **2.** easily damaged, hurt, or irritated: *A baby's skin is very sensitive.* **3.** responsive to outside stimuli: *The film is sensitive to light.* **4.** quick to take offense or be hurt; touchy: *He was very sensitive about his failure to make the team.* **5.** keenly aware of or responsive to other people's feelings, problems, and the like. —**sen′si·tive·ly,** *adv.* —**sen′si·tive·ness,** *n.*

sensitive plant **1.** a shrubby, tropical American plant whose leaflets fold up when touched. **2.** any of various other plants sensitive to touch.

sen·si·tiv·i·ty (sen′sə tiv′ə tē) *n.* the state, condition, or degree of being sensitive: *His own misfortune increased his sensitivity to the hardships of others.*

sen·si·tize (sen′sə tīz′) *v.t.,* **sen·si·tized, sen·si·tiz·ing.** to make sensitive.

sen·sor (sen′sər) *n.* any of various devices used to measure or detect light, radiation, heat, or other stimuli, and to transmit a resulting electrical impulse, as for operating a control.

sen·so·ry (sen′sər ē) *adj.* of, relating to, or conveying sensation: *a sensory nerve.*

sen·su·al (sen′shoo əl) *adj.* **1.** enjoying and seeking the pleasures of the body or senses. **2.** physically pleasing or appealing. **3.** of or relating to stimulation of the body or senses rather than the spirit or intellect. —**sen·su·al·i·ty** (sen′shoo al′ə tē), *n.* —**sen′su·al·ly,** *adv.*

sen·su·ous (sen′shoo əs) *adj.* **1.** of, relating to, or affecting the senses. **2.** enjoying the pleasures of the senses; sensual. —**sen′su·ous·ly,** *adv.* —**sen′su·ous·ness,** *n.*

sent (sent) the past tense and past participle of **send.**

sen·tence (sen′təns) *n.* **1.** a group of words or, sometimes, a single word, that expresses a complete thought. A sentence is a separate grammatical unit, and it usually has a subject and a predicate. *The dog and cat* is not a sentence; *The dog and cat are fighting* is a sentence. **2.** *Law.* **a.** a judgment by a court or judge setting the punishment of a defendant after conviction. **b.** the punishment itself. **3.** *Mathematics.* any statement that expresses a relationship between numbers. A sentence may be true, such as $5 + 3 = 8$, false, such as $6 - 2 = 3$, or neither true nor false, such as $x + 4 > 7$. A **closed sentence** has no unknown quantities, such as $3 + 2 = 5$; an **open sentence** contains at least one variable, such as $3a + 6 = 15$. —*v.t.,* **sen·tenced, sen·tenc·ing.** to set the punishment of: *The judge sentenced the criminal to a term of three years in prison.*

sen·ten·tious (sen ten′shəs) *adj.* **1.** short and meaningful; pithy. **2.** inclined to speak in a pompous or moralizing manner. **3.** tending to use trite phrases or proverbs. —**sen·ten′tious·ly,** *adv.* —**sen·ten′tious·ness,** *n.*

sen·tient (sen′shənt) *adj.* having the power of feeling.

sen·ti·ment (sen′tə mənt) *n.* **1.** a mental attitude or point of view; opinion: *Popular sentiment is against the new tax law.* **2.** an expression of feeling or emotion: *I appreciate the sentiment, but you didn't have to buy me a gift.*

3. refined or tender emotion. **4.** emotion that is exaggerated, overdone, or foolish.

sen·ti·men·tal (sen′tə ment′əl) *adj.* **1.** characterized by or showing emotion or feeling: *a sentimental love song.* **2.** influenced by or inclined to be moved by feeling rather than by reason: *a sentimental person.* **3.** appealing to the emotions: *The candidate made a sentimental plea for support.* **4.** relating to or based on sentiment: *He saved the old photograph for sentimental reasons.* **5.** characterized by exaggerated or foolish emotion. —**sen′ti·men·tal·ly,** *adv.*

sen·ti·men·tal·ism (sen′tə ment′əl iz′əm) *n.* **1.** the quality or state of being sentimental. **2.** the tendency to be influenced by feeling rather than by reason.

sen·ti·men·tal·ist (sen′tə ment′əl ist) *n.* a person who is sentimental.

sen·ti·men·tal·i·ty (sen′tə men tal′ə tē) *n. pl.,* **sen·ti·men·tal·i·ties.** **1.** the quality or state of being sentimental. **2.** the tendency to be influenced by feeling rather than reason. **3.** an expression of exaggerated or excessive emotion.

sen·ti·nel (sent′ən əl) *n.* a person stationed to keep watch and alert others of danger; guard; sentry.

sen·try (sen′trē) *n. pl.,* **sen·tries.** a person, especially a soldier, stationed to keep watch and alert others of danger; guard.

sentry box, a small building or booth for sheltering a sentry at his post.

Seoul (sōl) *n.* the capital and largest city of South Korea, in the northwestern part of the country. Pop. (1970), 5,536,377.

se·pal (sē′pəl) *n.* one of the leaflike divisions of the calyx of a flower, usually green but sometimes, as in the tulip, the same color as the petals.

sep·a·ra·ble (sep′ər ə bəl) *adj.* that can be separated.

sep·a·rate (*v.,* sep′ə rāt′; *adj.,* sep′ər it) *v.,* **sep·a·rat·ed, sep·a·rat·ing.** —*v.t.* **1.** to keep apart; be a barrier between; divide: *A fence separates the garden from the sidewalk.* **2.** to set or place apart: *to separate black socks from white socks, to separate fact from fantasy.* **3.** to divide or sort into individual parts or elements: *to separate a tangle of threads.* —*v.i.* **1.** to come apart; withdraw; part: *At the bell, the fighters separated and returned to their corners.* **2.** (of a married couple) to live apart but without a divorce. —*adj.* **1.** set apart or divided from others: *two separate rooms.* **2.** different; distinct: *Those are separate problems and cannot be handled in the same way.* **3.** single; individual: *each separate item on a list.* —**sep′a·rate·ly,** *adv.*

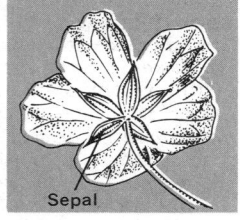

Sepals of a geranium

sep·a·ra·tion (sep′ə rā′shən) *n.* **1.** the act of separating or the state of being separated. **2.** the point at which two or more objects or parts are divided from each other; division. **3.** a condition in which a husband and wife live apart by agreement or by a court order.

sep·a·ra·tist (sep′ər ə tist) *n.* a person who supports or favors separation of his group from a political or religious body.

sep·a·ra·tor (sep′ə rā′tər) *n.* **1.** a person or thing that separates. **2.** an apparatus for separating one thing from another, as cream from milk.

se·pi·a (sē′pē ə) *n.* **1.** a dark brown pigment made from the inky fluid secreted by the cuttlefish. **2.** a dark brown color. —*adj.* having the color sepia; dark brown.

Sept., September.

Sep·tem·ber (sep tem′bər) *n.* the ninth month of the year, having thirty days. [Latin *September,* the seventh month in the early Roman calendar, from *septem* seven.]

sep·tic (sep′tik) *adj.* **1.** of or causing infection. **2.** caused by infection.

sep·ti·ce·mi·a (sep′tə sē′mē ə) *n.* a disease caused by the absorption of certain bacteria and their toxins into the bloodstream; blood poisoning.

septic tank, an underground tank in which sewage is decomposed by the action of bacteria.

sep·tum (sep′təm) *n. pl.,* **sep·ta** (sep′tə). a dividing wall, membrane, or partition in an animal or plant structure, such as the nose.

sep·ul·cher (sep′əl kər) *also, British,* **sep·ul·chre.** *n.* a burial place, especially a vault or tomb.

se·pul·chral (sə pul′krəl) *adj.* **1.** of or relating to a sepulcher or tomb. **2.** of or relating to burial or the dead. **3.** deep, dark, and dismal; funereal.

se·quel (sē′kwəl) *n.* **1.** a literary work that is complete in itself but continues the story of a previous work. **2.** something that follows. **3.** something that comes as a result; consequence.

se·quence (sē′kwəns) *n.* **1.** the coming of one thing after another; succession: *It was a strange sequence of events.* **2.** the order in which things occur or are arranged: *alphabetical sequence.* **3.** a group, collection, or series of connected things: *a sequence of arithmetic exercises.*

se·quent (sē′kwənt) *adj.* that follows in sequence.

se·ques·ter (si kwes′tər) *v.t.* **1.** to withdraw or remove from the world at large; hide away: *The old man sequestered himself in a mountain cabin.* **2.** *Law.* to take and hold (property) until a debt or claim is settled.

se·ques·tra·tion (sē′kwis trā′shən) *n.* **1.** the act of sequestering or the state of being sequestered. **2.** the act or process of taking property into custody until a debt or claim is settled.

se·quin (sē′kwin) *n.* a small, thin disk put on cloth or clothes as decoration.

se·quoi·a (si kwoi′ə) *n.* **1.** a giant evergreen tree of central California and Oregon, that has thick, spongy, reddish-brown bark and sharply pointed leaves. Sequoias are among the oldest and largest of trees. **2.** see **redwood** *(def. 1).*

se·ra (sēr′ə) a plural of **serum.**

se·ragl·io (si ral′yō) *n.* a portion of a Muslim house that has been reserved for women; harem.

se·ra·pe (sə rä′pē) *n. also,* **sa·ra·pe.** an outer garment like a cloak or poncho, often brightly colored, worn chiefly by men in Mexico and in other Latin-American countries.

ser·aph (ser′əf) *n. pl.,* **ser·aphs** or **ser·a·phim** (ser′ə fim′). a member of the highest order of angels. —**se·raph·ic** (si raf′ik), *adj.*

Serb (surb) *n.* **1.** a person who was born or is living in Serbia. **2.** the language of the Serbs; Serbo-Croatian. —*adj.* another word for **Serbian.**

Ser·bi·a (sur′bē ə) *n.* the largest political subdivision of Yugoslavia, in the eastern part of the country. It was formerly an independent country.

Ser·bi·an (sur′bē ən) *adj.* of or relating to Serbia, its people, or their language. —*n.* another word for **Serb.**

Ser·bo-Cro·a·tian (sur′bō krō ā′shən) *n.* a Slavic language spoken mainly by Serbs and Croats in parts of Yugoslavia. —*adj.* of or relating to this language.

sere (sēr) *adj.* withered; dry.

ser·e·nade (ser′ə nād′) *n.* a song or other musical per-

Serape

formance played and sung personally for someone as an expression of love or admiration. —*v.,* **ser·e·nad·ed, ser·e·nad·ing.** —*v.t.* to perform a serenade for (someone). —*v.i.* to sing or play a serenade. —**ser′e·nad′er,** *n.*

ser·en·dip·i·ty (ser′ən dip′ə tē) *n.* the act or ability of making fortunate discoveries by accident.

se·rene (sə rēn′) *adj.* **1.** peaceful; calm; tranquil: *a serene mountain village.* **2.** clear and bright: *a serene sky.* —**se·rene′ly,** *adv.*

se·ren·i·ty (sə ren′ə tē) *n.* the state or quality of being serene; peacefulness.

serf (surf) *n.* **1.** in the Middle Ages, a peasant bound to the land or to the service of the landlord. A serf could neither leave at will nor be forced off the land, and was sold only along with the land. **2.** any slave.

serf·dom (surf′dəm) *n.* **1.** the state or condition of being a serf. **2.** the practice or institution of working the land with serfs.

serge (surj) *n.* any of a group of fabrics woven with slanting ribs, used especially for suits.

ser·geant (sär′jənt) *n.* **1.** in the U.S. Army and Marine Corps, a noncommissioned officer ranking above a corporal. **2.** in the U.S. Air Force, a noncommissioned officer ranking above an airman first class. **3.** a police officer ranking above a patrolman and below a captain or lieutenant.

sergeant at arms *pl.,* **sergeants at arms.** an official charged with preserving order in a legislative assembly or court of law.

sergeant major *pl.,* **sergeants major** or **sergeant majors.** in the U.S. Army and Marine Corps, a noncommissioned officer of the highest grade.

se·ri·al (sēr′ē əl) *n.* a long story broken up into parts that are televised, broadcast, or published one at a time. The end of each part usually leads on to the next part, so that the audience or reader is interested in learning what will happen. —*adj.* **1.** of or relating to a serial: *The novel appeared in the magazine in serial form.* **2.** of, relating to, or arranged in a series. —**se′ri·al·ly,** *adv.*

se·ri·al·ize (sēr′ē ə līz′) *v.t.,* **se·ri·al·ized, se·ri·al·iz·ing.** to televise, broadcast, or publish as a serial.

serial number, a number assigned to a person or thing, as to a member of the armed forces or an automobile engine, for the purpose of identification.

se·ries (sēr′ēz) *n. pl.,* **se·ries.** **1.** a number or group of similar or related things or events coming one after another: *a series of bank robberies, a series of folk concerts, a series of baseball games.* **2.** a set of things that go together to make a whole, often in a certain order: *a series of physical exercises.* **3.** a television program seen each day or each week.

in series. (of electrical devices or circuits) arranged with the positive electrode of one connected to the negative electrode of the next, so that the same current flows through all devices or circuits.

se·ri·ous (sēr′ē əs) *adj.* **1.** of, characterized by, or showing deep and earnest thought; grave; solemn: *The judge gave serious consideration to the case. He is a serious person.* **2.** not joking; in earnest; sincere: *Were you serious when you said that?* **3.** requiring thought or consideration;

at; āpe; cär; end; mē; it; īce; hot; ōld; fôrk;
wood; fool; oil; out; up; turn; sing; thin; this;
hw in white; zh in treasure. The symbol ə
stands for the sound of a in about, e in taken,
i in pencil, o in lemon, and u in circus.

weighty; important: *a serious literary work, a serious problem.* **4.** causing concern or anxiety; dangerous: *a serious illness.* —**se'ri·ous·ly,** *adv.* —**se'ri·ous·ness,** *n.*

ser·mon (sur'mən) *n.* **1.** a public talk delivered by a member of the clergy for the purpose of giving religious or moral instruction. **2.** any long, serious talk dealing with morals, correct behavior, or the like.

Sermon on the Mount, Christ's sermon to His disciples, containing important principles of Christianity, including the Beatitudes.

se·rous (ser'əs) *adj.* **1.** of, relating to, or producing serum. **2.** like serum.

ser·pent (sur'pənt) *n.* **1.** a snake, especially an extremely large or poisonous one. **2.** a monster or creature like a snake, such as a dragon. **3.** a sly or wicked person.

ser·pen·tine (sur'pən tēn', sur'pən tīn') *adj.* **1.** winding about like a snake's body: *a serpentine path through a garden.* **2.** of or resembling a snake or serpent. **3.** sly or wicked. —*n.* a mineral, usually green with a greasy texture, used as a source of magnesium compounds.

ser·rat·ed (ser'ā tid) *adj.* jagged or saw-toothed, as the edges of a saw or of certain leaves: *a knife with a serrated edge.* Also, **ser·rate** (ser'āt).

se·rum (sēr'əm) *n. pl.,* **se·rums** or **se·ra.** **1.** a liquid used to prevent or cure a disease, obtained from the blood of an animal that has been made immune to the disease. **2.** the clear, thin fluid that separates from the blood when a clot forms. **3.** any clear fluid in the body, such as lymph.

serv·ant (sur'vənt) *n.* **1.** a person who is employed in a household to perform certain duties, such as cooking or cleaning. **2.** a person who is dedicated to the service of someone or something, such as a religion, government, or cause: *a servant of God.*

serve (surv) *v.,* **served, serv·ing.** —*v.t.* **1.** to prepare and set (food or drink) on a table or before a person or persons: *My mother serves dinner at six o'clock.* **2.** to set food or drink before (a person or persons): *The waiter did not serve us for a long time.* **3.** to supply regularly or continuously, as with a service or product: *The bakery serves us with fresh bread daily.* **4.** to act as a servant to; attend or wait upon; work for: *The maid served the same family for years.* **5.** to give assistance to: *The salesman asked if he could serve us.* **6.** to honor, obey, or worship: *to serve God.* **7.** to pass (a specified period of time), as in military service, public office, or imprisonment: *He served two terms in the state legislature.* **8.** to be of use or service to; meet the requirements of: *The old trade agreement no longer serves the two countries' needs.* **9.** in tennis, badminton, and other racket games, to put (the ball or shuttlecock) in play. **10.** *Law.* **a.** to present (a court order or writ) to a person. **b.** to present with a court order or writ: *to serve a person with a summons.* —*v.i.* **1.** to set food or drink before a person or persons. **2.** to perform a duty or duties, as of an office: *to serve on a jury, to serve as mayor.* **3.** to be of use; suffice: *The sofa served as a bed.* **4.** to be favorable or suitable. **5.** in tennis, badminton, and other racket games, to put the ball or shuttlecock in play. —*n.* **1.** in tennis, badminton, and other racket games, the act, instance, or manner of serving a ball or shuttlecock. **2.** a player's turn at serving.
  to serve one right. to be just what one deserves: *It served him right to fail the test, since he tried to cheat.*

serv·er (sur'vər) *n.* **1.** a person who serves. **2.** something that is used in serving, as a tray.

ser·vice (sur'vis) *n.* **1.** an act or means of serving or helping; conduct that contributes to the welfare or advantage of another person or persons: *His life was devoted to service to the community.* **2.** a system or means of providing something useful or necessary, especially for the general public: *The postal service is slow in their town.*

3. *usually,* **services.** useful work: *the services of a doctor.* **4.** the repair, maintenance, or replacement of goods that have been sold to customers: *to take a hair dryer back to a store for service.* **5.** the manner of serving food: *The service is very poor in that restaurant.* **6.** a religious ceremony or ritual: *a burial service.* **7.** one of the branches of the armed forces: *He spent three years in the service.* **8.** duty in any such branch. **9.** a branch or department of public employment: *the foreign service.* **10.** the persons employed in this. **11.** a set of things required for table use, such as silver or dishes: *a service for eight.* **12.** in tennis, badminton, and other racket games, the act, instance, or manner of putting the ball or shuttlecock in play. —*v.t.,* **ser·viced, ser·vic·ing.** **1.** to make or keep fit for use: *to service an automobile.* **2.** to supply service to. —*adj.* **1.** of, relating to, or used by those in service: *a service entrance.* **2.** of or relating to the armed forces.

ser·vice·a·ble (sur'vi sə bəl) *adj.* **1.** capable of giving useful service; helpful; beneficial. **2.** wearing well in long or hard use; durable: *a serviceable fabric.* —**ser'vice·a·bil'i·ty,** *n.* —**ser'vice·a·bly,** *adv.*

serv·ice·man (sur'vis man') *n. pl.,* **serv·ice·men** (sur'vis·men'). **1.** a member of the armed forces. **2.** a person whose work is repairing machinery or equipment.

service station, another term for **gas station.**

serv·ice·wom·an (sur'vis woom'ən) *n. pl.* **serv·ice·wom·en** (sur'vis wim'ən). a female member of the armed forces.

ser·vile (sur'vil) *adj.* **1.** acting like a slave; submissive. **2.** of, relating to, or appropriate for a slave or slaves: *servile work.* —**ser'vile·ly,** *adv.*

ser·vil·i·ty (sər vil'ə tē) *n.* the quality or condition of being servile.

serv·ing (sur'ving) *n.* **1.** a portion of food; helping. **2.** the act of a person or thing that serves. —*adj.* used in serving food: *a serving spoon.*

ser·vi·tude (sur'və tōod', sur'və tyōod') *n.* **1.** the condition of being a slave; slavery; bondage. **2.** forced labor as a punishment.

ses·a·me (ses'ə mē) *n.* **1.** a small, oval seed of a tropical plant native to India, used mainly in baked goods and candies. **2.** the plant bearing this seed.

ses·sion (sesh'ən) *n.* **1.** a meeting, as of a court, council, or legislature to carry on business. **2.** a series of such meetings. **3.** the period or term of such a meeting or meetings. **4.** the period or time during which classes are conducted in a school or college. **5.** a meeting held for any purpose or activity: *a recording session.*
  in session. in the process of meeting or being conducted: *Court is now in session.*

set (set) *v.,* **set, set·ting.** —*v.t.* **1.** to place in some location or position; put: *She set the lamp on the table.* **2.** to put in the correct or desired place, position, or condition: *The doctor set the broken bone.* **3.** to arrange (the hair), as with rollers or clips, so as to take on a desired style. **4.** to prepare or arrange for use: *to set a trap, to set the table for a meal.* **5.** to arrange scenery and properties on (a stage) for a presentation. **6.** to adjust or regulate: *to set one's watch.* **7.** to cause to be in a certain condition: *to set a prisoner free, to set a log on fire.* **8.** to cause to be in a firm, settled, or fixed position or condition: *to set one's jaw, to set one's mind on doing something.* **9.** to determine or fix firmly; establish: *Have they set a date for the meeting?* **10.** to place in a certain category or rank: *Most critics set Shakespeare above all other English writers.* **11.** to establish as the highest or greatest level or achievement: *He set a record in the high jump.* **12.** to present or provide for others to follow: *The girl set a good example for her younger sister.* **13.** to cause to take a particular direction;

direct: *The captain set the ship's course for Australia.*
14. to place in a frame or mounting: *to set a diamond.*
15. to adorn or ornament: *to set a crown with jewels.*
16. *Printing.* **a.** to arrange (type) for printing. **b.** to put into type: *to set a manuscript.* **17.** *Music.* to write, adapt, or fit (words) to music: *to set a poem to music.* —*v.i.*
1. to go down below the horizon: *At what time will the sun set today?* **2.** to become firm or hard: *The cement set after a few hours.* **3.** (of a broken bone) to mend properly.
4. to become fast or permanent, as a dye or color.
5. to hang or fit: *That jacket sets well on you.* **6.** (of a hen) to sit on eggs. —*adj.* **1.** fixed or decided beforehand; established: *The repairman charged a set fee.* **2.** fixed in a certain position; rigid: *a set smile.* **3.** stubbornly unchanging; obstinate: *That old man is set in his ways.*
4. determined; intent: *She is set on going.* **5.** ready; prepared: *We are all set to leave on our trip.* —*n.* **1.** the act of setting or the state of being set. **2.** a group of persons or things associated or belonging together: *the younger set, a set of furniture, a chess set.* **3.** *Mathematics.* a collection of numbers, points, objects, or other things that are grouped together or have a certain property in common that distinguishes them from all other things not within the collection: *the set of odd numbers from 0 to 10.*
4. a complete unit of scenery, properties, and structures used for a scene in a play, motion picture, or television program. **5.** a sending or receiving apparatus assembled as a unit for radio, television, telephone, or other communication. **6.** a group of six or more games making up a unit of a match in tennis. **7.** the position or form of the body, or a part of it: *We could tell he was tired by the set of his shoulders.* **8.** the way something fits or hangs, as an article of clothing: *the set of a dress.*

to set about. to begin to do; start.

to set against. a. to cause to be hostile or unfriendly toward. **b.** to balance or compare.

to set aside. a. to place apart or to one side, as for later use; reserve; save. **b.** to discard, dismiss, or reject. **c.** to declare null and void; overrule; annul: *to set aside a verdict.*

to set back. a. to hinder or check. **b.** *Informal.* to cost (a person) a certain sum of money: *My bicycle set me back fifty dollars.*

to set down. a. to record in writing or printing. **b.** to ascribe; attribute.

to set forth. a. to make known; state; declare: *The speaker set forth his ideas on prison reform.* **b.** to start out on a journey.

to set in. to begin to take place: *Winter set in early this year.*

to set off. a. to make more noticeable by contrast: *Dark hair sets off a fair complexion.* **b.** to start out or begin, as on a course or journey. **c.** to explode: *to set off fireworks.* **d.** to cause to begin: *to set off an argument.* **e.** to place apart from others.

to set on or **to set upon.** to attack or urge to attack: *We set the dogs on the burglar.*

to set out. to start out on a journey or course.

to set to. a. to begin; start working. **b.** to start fighting: *The angry boys set to.*

to set up. a. to raise to a position of authority or power. **b.** to assemble, erect, or prepare for use: *to set up a tent.* **c.** to establish; found: *to set up an organization.* **d.** to claim to be: *She sets herself up as an expert on politics and economics.*

set·back (set′bak′) *n.* a defeat or other check to progress.

set·tee (se tē′) *n.* a bench or small sofa with a high back and, usually, arms.

set·ter (set′ər) *n.* **1.** any of several long-haired hunting dogs having drooping ears and a soft, silky coat. A setter is trained to stand in a rigid position and point toward the game being hunted. **2.** a person or thing that sets.

Setter

set theory, a branch of mathematics dealing with sets, their properties, and their relationships.

set·ting (set′ing) *n.* **1.** a thing in which something, such as a jewel, is set. **2.** the place and time of a dramatic or literary work: *The setting of the novel is London during World War II.* **3.** the scenery and other properties for a play. **4.** the surroundings of anything; background; environment: *a cabin in a forest setting.* **5.** music composed for a particular story, poem, or the like. **6.** the number of eggs that a hen sits on for hatching at one time. **7.** the act of a person or thing that sets. **8.** dishes, silverware, and the like used to set one place at a table.

set·tle[1] (set′əl) *v.,* **set·tled, set·tling.** —*v.t.* **1.** to determine or decide; come to agreement about; resolve: *to settle an argument.* **2.** to arrange in an orderly manner; put into order: *I must settle all my affairs before leaving.* **3.** to pay or satisfy: *to settle an account.* **4.** to colonize: *English colonists settled New England.* **5.** to place in a proper or desired position; adjust: *The rider settled his feet in the stirrups.* **6.** to make tranquil or calm; compose: *He took a pill to settle his stomach.* **7.** to cause (a liquid) to become clear. **8.** to cause to sink: *The rain settled the dust.* —*v.i.* **1.** to decide, select, or agree: *She finally settled on the red dress.* **2.** to establish a home or residence: *to settle in a small town.* **3.** to come to rest; alight. **4.** to sink gradually. [Old English *setlan.*]

to settle down. a. to become calm or composed: *After the excitement of the fire drill, it took the class a long time to settle down.* **b.** to direct steady effort and attention: *to settle down to studying.* **c.** to be established in a more regular life, especially as a result of marriage.

set·tle[2] (set′əl) *n.* a long bench or seat for two or more people, with a high back and arms. [Old English *setl* seat.]

set·tle·ment (set′əl mənt) *n.*
1. the act of settling or the state of being settled. **2.** the deciding or determining of something in doubt or debate; decision or agreement: *The strike ended when the two sides reached a settlement.* **3.** a small village or group of houses. **4.** the establishment of people in a new country or region; colonization. **5.** a colony, especially in its earlier stages. **6.** an adjustment or payment, as of claims. **7.** see **settlement house.**

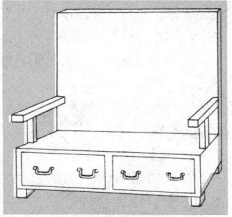
High-backed settle

settlement house, an institution that provides counseling, recreation, food, and other services to the residents of an underprivileged neighborhood.

at; āpe; cär; end; mē; it; īce; hot; ōld; fôrk; wood; fool; oil; out; up; turn; sing; thin; <u>th</u>is; hw in white; zh in treasure. The symbol ə stands for the sound of **a** in about, **e** in taken, **i** in pencil, **o** in lemon, and **u** in circus.

set·tler (set'lər) *n.* a person who settles in a new country or region.

set·up (set'up') *n.* the way in which a thing is arranged or organized; plan or structure of something: *the setup of a business.*

Seu·rat, Georges (soo rä'; zhôrzh) 1859–1891, French painter.

sev·en (sev'ən) *n.* **1.** the cardinal number that is one more than six. **2.** a symbol representing this number, such as 7 or VII. **3.** something having this many units or things, as a playing card. —*adj.* numbering one more than six.

sev·en·fold (sev'ən fōld') *adj.* **1.** seven times as great or as numerous. **2.** having or consisting of seven parts. —*adv.* so as to be seven times greater or more numerous.

seven seas, all the oceans and seas of the world: *The old sailor had sailed the seven seas.*

sev·en·teen (sev'ən tēn') *n.* **1.** the cardinal number that is seven more than ten. **2.** a symbol representing this number, such as 17 or XVII. **3.** something having this many units or things. —*adj.* numbering seven more than ten.

sev·en·teenth (sev'ən tēnth') *adj.* **1.** (the ordinal of seventeen) next after the sixteenth. **2.** being one of seventeen equal parts. —*n.* **1.** something that is next after the sixteenth. **2.** one of seventeen equal parts; 1/17.

sev·enth (sev'ənth) *adj.* **1.** (the ordinal of seven) next after the sixth. **2.** being one of seven equal parts. —*n.* **1.** something that is next after the sixth. **2.** one of seven equal parts; 1/7. **3.** *Music.* **a.** a note that is a total of five whole steps and one half step above a given note. B is the seventh of C. **b.** an interval of five whole steps and one half step. **c.** a combination of two notes that are separated by this interval. —*adv.* in the seventh place.

sev·en·ti·eth (sev'ən tē ith) *adj.* **1.** (the ordinal of seventy) next after the sixty-ninth. **2.** being one of seventy equal parts. —*n.* **1.** something that is next after the sixty-ninth. **2.** one of seventy equal parts; 1/70.

sev·en·ty (sev'ən tē) *n. pl.,* **sev·en·ties. 1.** the cardinal number that is seven times ten. **2.** a symbol representing this number, such as 70 or LXX. —*adj.* numbering seven times ten.

Seven Wonders of the World, the seven most remarkable structures of ancient times, usually listed as the Pyramids of Egypt, the hanging gardens of Babylon, the Colossus of Rhodes, the mausoleum at Halicarnassus, the temple of Diana (Artemis) at Ephesus, the statue of Zeus by Phidias at Olympia, and the Pharos (lighthouse) of Alexandria.

sev·er (sev'ər) *v.t.* **1.** to separate by cutting or breaking; cut apart or off: *Workmen severed dead branches from the tree.* **2.** to end or break off: *to sever diplomatic relations with another country.* —*v.i.* to become separated; be divided into parts. —**sev·er·a·ble,** *adj.*

sev·er·al (sev'ər əl) *adj.* **1.** more than two but not many: *She slept for several hours.* **2.** individual; different: *After the party, the guests went their several ways.* —*n.* more than two but not many; a few: *The police recovered several of the stolen gems.*

sev·er·al·ly (sev'ər ə lē) *adv.* separately; individually.

sev·er·ance (sev'ər əns) *n.* the act of severing or the state of being severed; separation.

se·vere (sə vēr') *adj.,* **se·ver·er, se·ver·est. 1.** very strict or stern; harsh: *severe laws.* **2.** stern or grim in manner or appearance: *a severe face.* **3.** serious; dangerous; grave: *a severe illness, a severe wound.* **4.** plain or simple; without ornament: *a severe dress.* **5.** causing great discomfort; sharp or violent: *severe pain, severe cold.* **6.** difficult; rigorous: *a severe test.* —**se·vere'ly,** *adv.* —**se·vere'ness,** *n.*

se·ver·i·ty (sə ver'ə tē) *n. pl.,* **se·ver·i·ties. 1.** strictness or sternness; harshness: *the severity of a punishment.*

2. seriousness: *the severity of an illness.* **3.** simplicity of style or taste: *severity of dress.* **4.** sharpness or violence: *the severity of a storm.*

Se·ville (sə vil') *n.* a city in southwestern Spain. Pop. (1977 est.), 622,532. Also, *Spanish,* **Se·vil·la** (sā vēl'yä).

sew (sō) *v.,* **sewed, sewed** or **sewn, sew·ing.** —*v.i.* to work with needle and thread or with a sewing machine. —*v.t.* **1.** to fasten, join, or attach with stitches: *to sew a button on a jacket.* **2.** to make or mend by means of a needle and thread or a sewing machine: *to sew a dress.* **3.** to close with stitches: *to sew up a wound.*

sew·age (soo'ij) *n.* the waste matter carried off by sewers and drains.

Sew·ard, William Henry (soo'ərd) 1801–1872, U.S. statesman.

sew·er[1] (soo'ər) *n.* an underground pipe or channel used for carrying off waste water and refuse. [Old French *sewiere* a channel to drain a pond.]

sew·er[2] (sō'ər) *n.* a person or thing that sews. [*Sew* + *-er*[1].]

sew·ing (sō'ing) *n.* **1.** work done with a needle and thread or with a sewing machine. **2.** something to be sewed. **3.** the act of a person who sews.

sewing machine, a mechanical device for sewing fabric and other materials, usually powered by a small electric motor.

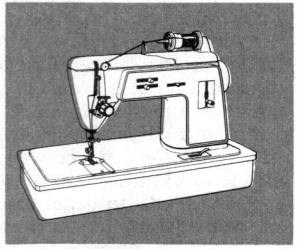

Sewing machine

sewn (sōn) a past participle of **sew.**

sex (seks) *n. pl.,* **sex·es. 1.** either of the two divisions, male or female, into which human beings and most other organisms are divided according to their functions in the process of reproduction. **2.** all the characteristics that determine whether an organism is male or female. **3.** the fact or character of being male or female. **4.** the activities that are part of the process of reproduction.

sex chromosome, either of the two types of chromosomes that determine the sex of an offspring; X chromosome or Y chromosome. A female germ cell always has an X chromosome; a male germ cell may have either an X chromosome or a Y chromosome. A combination of germ cells resulting in a fertilized cell with two X chromosomes produces a female organism; a male results from an X chromosome and Y chromosome combination.

sex·ism (sek'siz'əm) *n.* discrimination based on a person's sex, as in employment or politics. —**sex'ist,** *n., adj.*

sex·tant (seks'tənt) *n.* an instrument used mainly in navigation for measuring the altitude of the sun or a star to determine the position of the observer.

sex·tet (seks·tet') *also,* **sex·tette.** *n.* **1.** a musical composition for six voices or instruments. **2.** a musical group of six performers. **3.** any group or set of six persons or things, such as an ice hockey team.

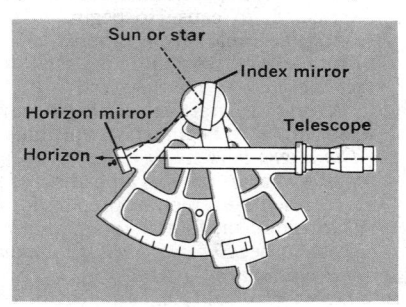

Sextant

sex·ton (seks′tən) *n.* a person employed by a parish to take care of church property whose duties sometimes include ringing the church bell and arranging burials.

sex·u·al (sek′shōō əl) *adj.* **1.** of or relating to sex or the sexes: *sexual instincts, sexual behavior.* **2.** involving the union of male and female germ cells: *sexual reproduction.* —**sex′u·al·ly,** *adv.*

sex·u·al·i·ty (sek′shōō al′ə tē) *n.* **1.** the condition of being distinguished by sex; sexual quality. **2.** a sexual desire or interest.

Sgt., Sergeant.

Sha·ba (shä′bə), see **Katanga.**

shab·by (shab′ē) *adj.,* **shab·bi·er, shab·bi·est. 1.** faded and dingy from wear or exposure: *a shabby coat.* **2.** neglected; run-down: *a shabby house.* **3.** wearing worn and faded clothes; seedy: *a shabby person.* **4.** mean, unfair, or dishonorable: *a shabby act, shabby treatment.* —**shab′-bi·ly,** *adv.* —**shab′bi·ness,** *n.*

shack (shak) *n.* a small, roughly built hut or cabin.

shack·le (shak′əl) *n.* **1.** a metal band fastened around the ankle or wrist of a prisoner, usually one of a pair connected by a chain; fetter. **2.** *usually,* **shackles.** anything that hinders or restrains freedom of action or thought: *the shackles of censorship.* **3.** any of various devices for fastening or coupling. —*v.t.,* **shack·led, shack·ling. 1.** to put a shackle or shackles on; fetter. **2.** to hinder or restrain.

shad (shad) *n. pl.,* **shad** or **shads.** any of several food fish related to herring. They are found in the coastal waters of Europe and North America.

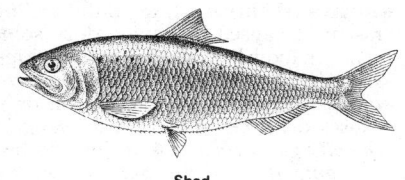

Shad

shade (shād) *n.* **1.** partial darkness caused by something cutting off rays of light, as from the sun: *The old elm tree cast shade on the lawn.* **2.** a place or area sheltered or cut off from light, especially from the sun: *He rested in the shade.* **3.** something that shuts out or reduces light: *Please pull down the shades in the living room. I bought a new shade for the lamp.* **4.** the degree of darkness in color: *The dress was a deep shade of green.* **5.** a dark part or surface, as in a painting. **6.** a small degree or amount; trace: *a shade of doubt.* **7.** a small difference; nuance: *a shade of meaning.* **8.** a spirit; ghost. —*v.,* **shad·ed, shad·ing.** —*v.t.* **1.** to shelter, screen, or protect from glare, heat, or light: *The umbrella shaded us from the hot sun.* **2.** to mark (a drawing, painting, or the like) with various degrees of darkness: *He shaded the figures in the background of the picture.* —*v.i.* to change or vary slightly or by degrees: *The colors in the painting shaded from deep green to bright yellow.*

shad·ing (shā′ding) *n.* **1.** the representing of different degrees of light and dark in a painting, drawing, or the like, to give a feeling of depth or shadow. **2.** a small degree of change or difference. **3.** a shelter from light or heat.

shad·ow (shad′ō) *n.* **1.** a relatively dark area produced when rays of light are blocked by a person or thing: *The thief hid in the shadows of the dark room.* **2.** the dark image or figure cast by a person or thing blocking these light rays: *The shadow of the fruit trees fell long across the fields* (William Faulkner). **3.** a

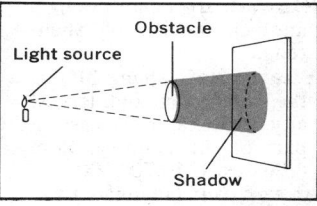

Shadow

darker or shaded portion of a picture. **4.** a ghost; phantom. **5.** something unreal or imaginary. **6.** a faint image or representation: *The event was a shadow of things to come.* **7.** a slight degree or suggestion; faintest trace: *There is not a shadow of a doubt that he is lying.* **8.** a person who follows another closely and secretly, such as a detective. **9.** sadness; gloom; unhappiness. **10. the shadows.** darkness. —*v.t.* **1.** to cast a shadow on or over; cover with a shadow. **2.** to follow closely and secretly: *The detective shadowed the suspect.* **3.** to make gloomy; sadden.

shad·ow·y (shad′ō ē′) *adj.,* **shad·ow·i·er, shad·ow·i·est. 1.** full of shadow or shade; shady: *a shadowy corner.* **2.** like a shadow; dim; unclear: *a shadowy figure.*

shad·y (shā′dē) *adj.,* **shad·i·er, shad·i·est. 1.** sheltered from the sun; full of shade; shaded: *We picnicked in a shady spot under a tree.* **2.** giving shade: *a shady tree.* **3.** *Informal.* of doubtful honesty; disreputable: *a shady business deal.* —**shad′i·ly,** *adv.* —**shad′i·ness,** *n.*

shaft (shaft) *n.* **1.** a long, slender body connected to the head of an arrow or spear. **2.** an arrow or spear. **3.** something aimed like an arrow or spear: *shafts of criticism.* **4.** a ray or beam: *bright shafts of morning light.* **5.** either of the two wooden poles between which a horse or other draft animal is harnessed to pull a carriage or other vehicle. **6.** the long, straight handle of any of various tools or implements, such as a hammer, golf club, or hockey stick. **7.** a bar in a machine that supports rotating parts or transmits motion to other parts. **8.** a deep passage, usually vertical, from ground level to an underground excavation, as in a mine. **9.** a passage like a well, as for an elevator. **10.** the part of a column between the base and capital.

shag (shag) *n.* **1.** rough, matted hair, wool, or the like. **2.** a long, rough nap on cloth, as wool or cotton. **3.** a cloth or article, such as a rug, having such a nap.

shag·bark (shag′bärk′) *n.* **1.** a hickory tree of Canada and the eastern United States, having shaggy gray bark that peels off in long strips. **2.** the wood of this tree, used as timber.

Shagbark

shag·gy (shag′ē) *adj.,* **shag·gi·er,** **shag·gi·est. 1.** covered with or having long, rough hair or wool: *A sheep dog is a shaggy animal.* **2.** long, bushy, and rough: *shaggy eyebrows.* **3.** having a long, rough nap: *a shaggy rug.*

shah (shä) *n.* the title of the hereditary ruler of Iran.

shake (shāk) *v.,* **shook, shak·en, shak·ing.** —*v.t.* **1.** to cause to move quickly to and fro, up and down, or from side to side: *Shake the bottle to mix its contents.* **2.** to throw, bring, or remove with such movements: *The dog shook the water from its back.* **3.** to cause to tremble, vibrate, or quiver: *The earthquake shook the building.* **4.** to weaken or make less firm: *The district attorney could not shake the witness's testimony.* **5.** to move or stir the feelings of; upset; disturb: *The news of the accident shook us all.* **6.** *Informal.* to get rid of or avoid: *The escaped*

at; āpe; cär; end; mē; it; īce; hot; ōld; fôrk; wood; fōōl; oil; out; up; turn; sing; thin; **th**is; hw in white; zh in treasure. The symbol ə stands for the sound of **a** in about, **e** in taken, **i** in pencil, **o** in lemon, and **u** in circus.

convict tried to shake his pursuers. —*v.i.* **1.** to move quickly to and fro, up and down, or from side to side: *The house shakes when the trains go by.* **2.** to tremble; quiver: *The kitten was shaking with fright when we found her.* —*n.* **1.** the act of shaking: *One shake of the stick scared the dog away.* **2. the shakes.** *Informal.* a trembling or shivering, as from fever or chills.

   to shake down. *Slang.* to get money from dishonestly.

   to shake hands. to grasp (another's hand), as in greeting or agreement.

   to shake up. a. to disturb mentally or physically; shock. **b.** to change (something) suddenly and thoroughly.

shak·en (shā′kən) the past participle of **shake.**

shak·er (shā′kər) *n.* **1.** a container having a top with holes, as for sprinkling salt or pepper. **2.** any of various other devices or machines used for shaking: *a cocktail shaker.* **3.** a person who shakes.

Shak·er (shā′kər) *n.* a member of an American religious sect practicing communal living. [Because they used to dance with *shaking* movements at their prayer meetings.]

Shake·speare, William (shāk′spēr) 1564–1616, English poet and dramatist.

Shake·spear·e·an (shāk spēr′ē ən) *also,* **Shake·spear·i·an.** *adj.* of, relating to, or like Shakespeare or his works.

shake-up (shāk′up′) *n.* a sudden, thorough change in organization, as of a business or government.

shak·o (shak′ō) *n. pl.,* **shak·os.** a high, stiff military hat with a visor and, usually, a plume attached in front.

shak·y (shā′kē) *adj.,* **shak·i·er, shak·i·est. 1.** trembling; shaking: *shaky writing.* **2.** liable to break down or give way; unsound: *a shaky bridge.* **3.** not to be depended on: *shaky information.* —**shak′i·ly,** *adv.* —**shak′i·ness,** *n.*

Shako

shale (shāl) *n.* a fine-grained rock, formed from hardened clay in very thin layers that separate easily.

shall (shal) *auxiliary verb* Present tense: *sing.,* first person, **shall;** second, **shall** or *(archaic)* **shalt;** third, **shall;** *pl.,* **shall.** Past tense: *sing.,* first person, **should;** second, **should** or *(archaic)* **shouldest** or **shouldst;** third, **should;** *pl.,* **should. 1.** in the first person, used to express future time: *I shall be glad to help you.* **2.** in the second and third persons, used to express determination, obligation, or compulsion: *She shall do as she is told.* **3.** in all persons, used in direct questions when *shall* is expected in the answer: *Shall he leave tomorrow? Yes, he shall.*

▲ According to the rules of traditional grammar, **shall** is used with the first person to express the simple future tense: *When shall we three meet again* (Shakespeare, *Macbeth*), and **will** is used with the second and third persons: *Some say the world will end in fire* (Robert Frost).

In the same way, it has traditionally been considered correct to use *will* with the first person, and *shall* with the second and third persons, to show determination or obligation: *I will not retreat a single inch and I will be heard* (William Lloyd Garrison). *We here highly resolve . . . that this nation . . . shall have a new birth of freedom* (Abraham Lincoln).

However, this distinction between *shall* and *will* is subtle and somewhat difficult to grasp, and it has never been faithfully observed, even by the best speakers and writers. For example: *We shall never surrender* (Winston Churchill) shows determination, and *Show me a hero and I will write you a tragedy* (F. Scott Fitzgerald) expresses the simple future tense.

In current American usage, *shall* and *will* are used interchangeably, with *will* being much more common. *Shall* is common in British English, but many American speakers feel that it sounds too formal or artificial.

shal·lop (shal′əp) *n.* a small open boat with sails or oars.

shal·lot (shə lot′) *n.* **1.** a small bulb or clove of a plant closely related to the onion, used to flavor foods. **2.** the small plant that grows from this bulb.

shal·low (shal′ō) *adj.* **1.** of little depth; not deep: *a shallow pond.* **2.** lacking depth of thought, reasoning, knowledge, or feeling: *a shallow mind.* —*n.* usually, **shallows.** a shallow area in a body of water. —**shal′low·ly,** *adv.* —**shal′low·ness,** *n.*

shalt (shalt) *Archaic.* the second person singular, present tense of **shall.** ▲ used with *thou.*

sham (sham) *n.* **1.** something false intended to appear genuine or true; fraud; counterfeit: *His friendliness is all sham.* **2.** a person who falsely takes on a certain character for the purpose of deceiving. —*adj.* not real or true; pretended; false: *a sham battle, sham diamonds.* —*v.,* **shammed, sham·ming.** —*v.t.* **1.** to take on the appearance of; feign: *to sham illness.* **2.** to make an imitation of. —*v.i.* to pretend.

sham·ble (sham′bəl) *v.i.,* **sham·bled, sham·bling.** to walk awkwardly or unsteadily; shuffle. —*n.* a shambling walk or gait: *The old horse moved at a shamble.*

sham·bles (sham′bəlz) *n., pl.* **1.** a place or condition of great disorder or confusion: *The burglars left the house in a shambles.* **2.** a scene of slaughter or of great bloodshed.

shame (shām) *n.* **1.** a painful feeling of guilt or embarrassment caused by having done something wrong, indecent, or foolish: *He showed no shame when he was caught stealing.* **2.** dishonor; disgrace: *His arrest brought shame to his entire family.* **3.** a person or thing that brings or causes disgrace: *Widespread corruption was the shame of the city government.* **4.** a thing to be sorry about: *It was a shame that he did not win the race.* —*v.t.,* **shamed, sham·ing. 1.** to cause to feel shame; make ashamed; embarrass. **2.** to bring disgrace upon; dishonor: *His behavior shamed his family.* **3.** to force or drive by shame or fear of shame: *They shamed him into volunteering.*

   for shame. shame on you; how shameful.

   to put to shame. a. to bring disgrace upon; cause to feel ashamed. **b.** to outdo another or others.

shame·faced (shām′fāst′) *adj.* **1.** bashful; shy. **2.** showing shame; ashamed: *a shamefaced look.*

shame·ful (shām′fəl) *adj.* causing shame; disgraceful. —**shame′ful·ly,** *adv.* —**shame′ful·ness,** *n.*

shame·less (shām′lis) *adj.* **1.** having no sense of shame; immodest. **2.** without shame. —**shame′less·ly,** *adv.* —**shame′less·ness,** *n.*

sham·poo (sham pōō′) *v.t.,* **sham·pooed, sham·poo·ing. 1.** to wash (the hair or scalp) with soap and water or a special preparation. **2.** to wash the hair and scalp of. **3.** to clean (upholstery or rugs) with any of various cleaning preparations. —*n. pl.,* **sham·poos. 1.** the act of shampooing. **2.** any special preparation for use in shampooing.

sham·rock (sham′rok′) *n.* a leaf having three leaflets. It is the national emblem of Ireland.

Shan·dong (shän′doong′) another spelling of **Shan·tung.**

Shang·hai (shang hī′) *n.* the chief port and largest city of China, in the eastern part of the country. Pop. (1968 est.), 10,700,000.

shang·hai (shang′hī) *v.t.,* **shang·haied, shang·hai·ing. 1.** to make (someone) uncon-

Wood sorrel   White clover

Shamrocks

scious by drugs, liquor, or a blow in order to force him to serve as a sailor on a ship. **2.** to cause (someone) to do something against his will, especially by trickery or force. [From the earlier practice of acquiring sailors against their will for voyages to *Shanghai*.]

shank (shangk) *n.* **1.** a part of the leg in humans between the knee and the ankle. **2.** a similar part in certain animals and birds. **3.** the entire leg. **4.** a cut of meat from the leg of an animal. **5.** the part of an instrument or tool that connects the working part with a handle or with the part by which it is held or moved.

Shan·non (shan′ən) *n.* a river flowing from north-central Ireland into the Atlantic Ocean.

shan't (shant) shall not.

Shan·tung (shan′tung′) *n.* **1.** a province in northeast China. Area, 55,560 sq. mi. Pop. (1970 est.), 57,000,000. **2.** a peninsula in this province, extending into the Yellow Sea. Also, **Shandong.**

shan·tung (shan′tung′, shan′tung′) *n.* a soft, textured fabric of silk, rayon, or cotton. [From *Shantung*.]

shan·ty¹ (shan′tē) *n. pl.,* **shan·ties.** a crude, flimsily built hut or cabin. [Possibly from Irish *sean toigh* literally, old house.]

shan·ty² (shan′tē) *also,* **shan·tey.** *n. pl.,* **shan·ties.** another spelling of **chantey.**

shape (shāp) *n.* **1.** an outward form or outline; contour; figure: *All circles have the same shape. Melted glass can be molded into many shapes. We saw the hazy shape of a house through the fog.* **2.** condition: *He was in bad shape after the accident.* **3.** good physical condition: *He exercises regularly to keep in shape.* **4.** the outline of a person's body; figure. **5.** a definite, regular, or proper form or arrangement; order: *Let's get the room in shape before the guests arrive.* —*v.,* **shaped, shap·ing.** —*v.t.* **1.** to give form to; fashion; mold: *to shape dough into loaves.* **2.** to adapt in form; adjust; modify: *She shaped the pillows. He shaped his ideas to agree with hers.* **3.** to give definite direction or character to: *to shape one's life.* —*v.i.* to take on a definite form, order, or plan; develop: *Things are shaping up nicely.*
  to take shape. to have or take on a definite form, order, or plan: *Our plans for a vacation are beginnning to take shape.*

shape·less (shāp′lis) *adj.* **1.** without definite or regular shape: *a shapeless mound of earth.* **2.** having no beauty or elegance of form; unshapely; unattractive: *She has a short, shapeless figure.* —**shape′less·ly,** *adv.* —**shape′less·ness,** *n.*

shape·ly (shāp′lē) *adj.,* **shape·li·er, shape·li·est.** having a beautiful or elegant shape; well-formed. —**shape′li·ness,** *n.*

shard (shärd) *n.* a fragment of some brittle material, as of glass or pottery; potsherd.

share¹ (sher) *n.* **1.** the part that is given or belongs to one individual: *I spent my share of the money.* **2.** one of the equal parts into which the ownership of a company or corporation is divided: *He owns fifty shares of an automobile stock.* —*v.,* **shared, shar·ing.** —*v.t.* **1.** to use, enjoy, or take part in together or in common: *to share an apartment, to share someone's happiness.* **2.** to divide into portions and give to others as well as to oneself: *to share one's dinner with friends.* —*v.i.* to have a share; take part: *We all shared in the fun at the party.* [Old English *scearu* a shearing, cutting.]

share² (sher) *n.* another word for **plowshare.**

share·crop·per (sher′krop′ər) *n.* a tenant farmer who farms land for the owner in return for a share of the crops that the land yields.

share·hold·er (sher′hōl′dər) *n.* another word for **stockholder.**

shark¹ (shärk) *n.* any of numerous saltwater fish having skeletons of cartilage rather than bone, with usually gray rough skin, a deeply forked tail, and a large mouth on the underside of the head with several rows of sharp teeth. Sharks eat other

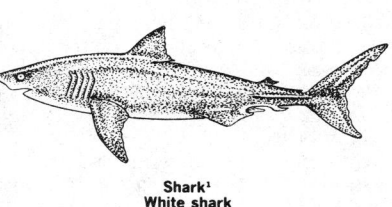
**Shark¹
White shark**

fish and some species will attack human beings. [Of uncertain origin.]

shark² (shärk) *n.* a dishonest person who takes advantage of others; swindler. [Probably from German *Schurke* rogue.]

sharp (shärp) *adj.* **1.** having a fine cutting edge or point; well-suited for cutting or piercing: *a sharp blade, a sharp knife.* **2.** having a pointed end; not rounded or blunt: *The mountain has a sharp peak.* **3.** abrupt or sudden change in direction: *a sharp turn, a sharp curve.* **4.** harsh, biting, or severe: *sharp words.* **5.** keenly affecting the senses or emotions: *sharp pangs of hunger.* **6.** (of food) having a biting taste: *sharp cheese.* **7.** high-pitched; shrill: *a sharp cry of agony.* **8.** clear or distinct, as in outline or contour: *That camera takes sharp pictures.* **9.** having the ability to feel or perceive quickly: *a sharp eye for details.* **10.** shrewd or clever: *to be sharp at cards.* **11.** watchful; alert; vigilant: *Keep a sharp lookout.* **12.** rapid; brisk; energetic: *He walked off at a sharp pace.* **13.** *Slang.* strikingly attractive; stylish: *You really look sharp in that new suit.* **14.** *Music.* **a.** raised a half step in pitch. **b.** above the true and proper pitch; too high. **c.** (of a key) having sharps in the signature. —*adv.* **1.** at the moment specified; promptly; exactly: *We must leave at 1:30 sharp.* **2.** in a sharp manner: *Look sharp or you will miss the turn.* **3.** above the true pitch in music: *to sing sharp.* —*n. Music.* **1.** a note or tone one half step above a given note or tone. **2.** the symbol (♯) which, when placed before a note or on a degree of the staff, shows that the pitch will be raised by a half step. —**sharp′ly,** *adv.* —**sharp′ness,** *n.*

sharp·en (shär′pən) *v.t., v.i.* to make or become sharp or sharper: *to sharpen a pencil.* —**sharp′en·er,** *n.*

sharp·shoot·er (shärp′shōō′tər) *n.* a person who is skilled in shooting, especially with a rifle.

shat·ter (shat′ər) *v.t.* **1.** to break (something, especially a hard or brittle thing) into pieces, as by a sudden blow: *to shatter a glass.* **2.** to destroy completely or damage greatly: *Their lives were shattered by the horrible experience of war.* —*v.i.* to break suddenly into pieces; go to pieces: *The glass shattered when it hit the floor.*

shave (shāv) *v.,* **shaved, shaved** or **shav·en, shav·ing.** —*v.t.* **1.** to remove hair from with a razor: *The barber shaved him carefully.* **2.** to cut (hair) down close to the skin with a razor: *He shaved his beard off.* **3.** to cut down the surface of by removing thin shavings or parings: *The carpenter shaved the edge of the board.* **4.** to cut off in thin slices or parings: *That appliance shaves ice.* **5.** to cut very closely, as a lawn. **6.** to touch slightly or come very near

at; āpe; cär; end; mē; it; īce; hot; ōld; fôrk; wood; fōōl; oil; out; up; turn; sing; thin; this; hw in white; zh in treasure. The symbol ə stands for the sound of a in about, e in taken, i in pencil, o in lemon, and u in circus.

S

835

touching; graze. —*v.i.* to remove hair with a razor. —*n.* the act of shaving.

shav·en (shā′vən) *v.* a past participle of **shave.** —*adj.* **1.** shaved. **2.** closely cut or trimmed, as grass.

shav·er (shā′vər) *n.* **1.** a person who shaves. **2.** any device for shaving. **3.** *Informal.* a youngster; boy.

shav·ing (shā′ving) *n.* **1.** a very thin piece or slice, especially of wood. **2.** the act or process of removing hair or trimming a surface with a razor.

Sha·vu·oth (shə voo′əs) *n.* a Jewish holiday, originally a spring harvest festival, commemorating the giving of the Commandments to Moses. Also, **Pentecost.**

Shaw, George Bernard (shô) 1856–1950, British playwright, born in Ireland.

shawl (shôl) *n.* a square or oblong piece of fabric, usually worn over the shoulders.

Shaw·nee (shô nē′) *n. pl.,* **Shaw·nees** or **Shaw·nee.** a member of a tribe of Algonquian Indians, formerly living in the East, South, and Midwest, now living mainly in Oklahoma.

shay (shā) *n.* a light, two-wheeled carriage; chaise.

she (shē) *pron.* **1.** a female person or animal that has been mentioned or spoken about before: *Jane said that she would be glad to join us.* **2.** something thought of as female: *She is the fastest boat we ever saw.* **3.** any woman or girl: *She who listens learns.* —*n. pl.,* **shes.** a female person or animal.

sheaf (shēf) *n. pl.,* **sheaves. 1.** one of the bundles in which stalks of cereal plants, such as wheat, are bound after reaping. **2.** any bundle of things of the same kind: *a sheaf of papers.*

shear (shēr) *v.t.,* **sheared, sheared** or **shorn, shear·ing. 1.** to clip or cut with shears, scissors, or a similar sharp instrument: *The gardener sheared the lawn too closely.* **2.** to cut the wool or hair from: *to shear sheep.* **3.** to cut off; remove by clipping: *to shear fleece.* —**shear′er,** *n.*

shears (shērz) *n.,pl.* **1.** any of various, usually large, cutting instruments resembling scissors. **2.** large scissors.

sheath (shēth) *n. pl.,* **sheaths** (shēthz). **1.** a case for the blade of a sword, knife, or the like. **2.** any similar covering, such as a membrane covering a muscle. **3.** a tight, close-fitting dress. —*v.t.* to sheathe.

sheathe (shēth) *v.t.,* **sheathed, sheath·ing. 1.** to put into a sheath or scabbard: *to sheathe a sword.* **2.** to enclose or protect in a case or covering: *to sheathe a roof with metal.*

sheath·ing (shē′thing) *n.* **1.** something that covers or protects, such as the first covering of boards on a house or one of the metal plates on the bottom of a ship. **2.** the act of a person who sheathes.

sheave (shēv) *v.t.,* **sheaved, sheav·ing.** to gather and bind into a sheaf or sheaves.

sheaves (shēvz) the plural of **sheaf.**

She·ba (shē′bə) *n.* **1.** an ancient country in southwestern Arabia. **2. Queen of.** in the Old Testament, a queen who visited Solomon to learn for herself if he was really as wise as he was said to be.

shed¹ (shed) *n.* a small structure used for storage or shelter: *a tool shed.* [Old English *scead* shade, shelter.]

shed² (shed) *v.,* **shed, shed·ding.** —*v.t.* **1.** to cause to flow; let fall; let pour: *to shed tears.* **2.** to throw off or lose by natural process: *The snake shed its skin. The trees are beginning to shed their leaves.* **3.** to send out; radiate; exude: *The lilacs shed their fragrance throughout the room.* **4.** to cause to flow off without penetrating: *My new coat sheds rain.* —*v.i.* **1.** to throw off or lose a covering, especially by natural process: *Our dog sheds a lot.* **2.** to fall off or drop: *Leaves shed in the fall.* [Old English *sceādan* to separate, divide.]

she'd (shed) **1.** she had. **2.** she would.

sheen (shēn) *n.* a lustrous brightness; gloss; shininess: *the sheen of a newly polished marble floor.* —**sheen′y,** *adj.*

sheep (shēp) *n. pl.,* **sheep. 1.** any of various cud-chewing animals related to the goat, many of which are widely raised for fleece, meat, milk, and skin. **2.** a person who is timid, meek, or easily led. —**sheep′like′,** *adj.*

Sheep

sheep·cote (shēp′kōt′) *n.* a shed or similar shelter for sheep.

sheep dog also, **sheep·dog** (shēp′dog′). **1.** see **Old English sheepdog. 2.** any dog that has been trained to guard, drive, or tend sheep, such as a collie. Also *(def. 2),* **shepherd dog.**

sheep·fold (shēp′fōld′) *n.* an enclosure for sheep, such as a pen.

sheep·herd·er (shēp′hur′dər) *n.* a person who raises or tends a large number of sheep, especially on open land.

sheep·ish (shē′pish) *adj.* **1.** awkwardly bashful or embarrassed: *a sheepish grin.* **2.** like a sheep; timid or meek. —**sheep′ish·ly,** *adv.* —**sheep′ish·ness,** *n.*

sheep·skin (shēp′skin′) *n.* **1.** the skin of a sheep, especially one prepared with the wool in it, often used for clothing. **2.** leather or parchment made from this skin. **3.** *Informal.* a diploma.

sheer¹ (shēr) *adj.* **1.** very thin and fine; nearly transparent: *a sheer fabric.* **2.** unmixed with anything else: *He grew depressed from the sheer loneliness of his way of living.* **3.** utter; downright: *sheer nonsense, sheer stupidity.* **4.** straight up or straight down; steep: *From the cliff there was a sheer drop of 200 feet.* —*adv.* **1.** completely; quite; altogether. **2.** very steeply up or down. [Possibly from Old English *scīr* bright, shining.] —**sheer′ly,** *adv.* —**sheer′-ness,** *n.*

sheer² (shēr) *v.i.* to turn from a course; swerve: *The ship sheered off to avoid the rocks.* —*v.t.* to cause to turn from a course. —*n.* a moving away of a ship or boat from its course. [Probably from Dutch *scheren* to cut, move aside.]

sheet¹ (shēt) *n.* **1.** a large piece of fabric, usually cotton, used as a bed covering. **2.** any broad, thin, piece or object: *a sheet of clear plastic.* **3.** a single oblong or square piece of paper or parchment for writing or printing on. **4.** a broad, flat expanse or surface: *sheets of flame, a sheet of water.* —*v.t.* **1.** to furnish with a sheet or sheets. **2.** to cover with a sheet: *Snow sheeted the ground.* [Old English *scēte* a large piece of fabric.]

sheet² (shēt) *n.* a rope or chain attached to one or both of the lower ends of a sail, used to adjust or control the sail. [Old English *scēata* the lower corner of a sail.]

sheet·ing (shē′ting) *n.* fabric used for bed sheets.

sheet lightning, lightning appearing as bright, broad flashes, as from within a cloud or beyond the horizon.

sheet metal, metal in thin, flat pieces.

sheet music, music printed on unbound sheets of paper.

Shef·field (shef′ēld′) *n.* a city in northern England. Pop. (1971), 519,703.

sheik (shēk) *also,* **sheikh.** *n.* **1.** the leader of an Arab clan, tribe, or other large group. **2.** a Muslim religious leader, especially the superior of a religious community.

sheik·dom (shēk′dəm) *also,* **sheikh·dom.** *n.* a region governed by a sheik.

shek·el (shek′əl) *n.* **1.** any of various ancient units of weight, especially one used by the Babylonians, Phoenicians, Hebrews, and Assyrians, equal to about half an ounce. **2.** an ancient silver coin of the Hebrews weighing one shekel.

shel·drake (shel′drāk′) *n. pl.,* **shel·drakes** or **shel·drake.**
1. any of several large ducks resembling geese, found in Europe, North Africa, and Asia. **2.** any of various similar ducks, especially the merganser.

shelf (shelf) *n. pl.,* **shelves.**
1. a thin, flat piece of wood, metal, stone, or other material, fastened horizontally to a wall or frame to hold things, such as books or dishes. **2.** anything like a shelf, such as a sandbar, reef, or projecting ledge of rock.

Sheldrake

on the shelf. no longer active or used: *The plan to build a new city hospital is on the shelf for the time being.*

shell (shel) *n.* **1.** a hard or tough outer covering of any of various animals, such as the turtle, lobster, or snail. **2.** the material of which such a covering is made. **3.** any similar covering, as of a seed, fruit, or egg. **4.** something like a shell, such as the framework of a building or a rounded piece of pastry for holding filling. **5.** shyness; reserve: *The friendliness of the boys made the new student come out of his shell.* **6.** a metal projectile fired by cannon and other artillery, designed to explode at or in a target or in the air. **7.** a cartridge for a shotgun or rifle. **8.** a long, light racing boat propelled by oarsmen. —*v.t.* **1.** to remove the shell, husk, or pod of: *to shell peanuts.* **2.** to remove grains from the ear or cob of: *to shell corn.* **3.** to subject to artillery fire; bombard with shells. —**shell′like′,** *adj.*

she'll (shēl) **1.** she shall. **2.** she will.

shel·lac (shə lak′) *n.* **1.** a liquid preparation made of lac dissolved in alcohol, used as a varnish on floors, furniture, or similar surfaces. **2.** the lac itself when not dissolved, used in making certain insulating materials and phonograph records. —*v.t.,* **shel·lacked, shel·lack·ing.** to coat or treat with shellac: *to shellac a floor.*

Shel·ley (shel′ē) **1. Mary Woll·stone·craft** (wool′stən kraft′). 1797–1851, English novelist; the wife of Percy Shelley. **2. Percy Bysshe** (bish). 1792–1822, English poet.

shell·fish (shel′fish′) *n. pl.,* **shell·fish** or **shell·fish·es.** any animal having a shell and living in water, especially a mollusk or crustacean. Shrimps, lobsters, clams, and oysters are shellfish.

shell shock, a nervous or mental disorder resulting from combat in war.

shel·ter (shel′tər) *n.* **1.** something that covers or protects, as from weather, danger, or attack: *The school was turned into a shelter for victims of the earthquake.* **2.** protection; refuge: *We found shelter in an abandoned house during the snowstorm.* —*v.t.* **1.** to provide cover or protection for; shield: *The canopy sheltered us from the rain.* **2.** to take under one's protection. —*v.i.* to find or take shelter.

shelve[1] (shelv) *v.t.,* **shelved, shelv·ing. 1.** to place on a shelf: *to shelve books.* **2.** to put away or aside as done with or not needed: *to shelve a plan.* **3.** to furnish with shelves: *to shelve a wall.* [From **shelves.**]

shelve[2] (shelv) *v.t.,* **shelved, shelv·ing.** to slope gradually. [Of uncertain origin.]

shelves (shelvz) the plural of **shelf.**

shelv·ing (shel′ving) *n.* **1.** material for shelves, such as wood or metal. **2.** shelves as a group: *The library had shelving for ten thousand books.*

Shen·an·do·ah (shen′ən dō′ə) *n.* a river flowing through northern Virginia into the Potomac.

she·nan·i·gan (shi nan′i gən) *usually,* **shenanigans.** *n. Informal.* nonsense or trickery.

She·ol (shē′ol) *n.* in the Old Testament, the dwelling place of the spirits of the dead; underworld.

Shep·ard, Alan Bart·lett (shep′ərd; bärt′lit) 1923—, U.S. astronaut, the first American to make a space flight.

shep·herd (shep′ərd) *n.* **1.** a person who takes care of a flock of sheep. **2.** a spiritual leader; pastor. —*v.t.* **1.** to tend as a shepherd. **2.** to watch over or guide like a shepherd: *The teacher shepherded the children onto the bus.*

shepherd dog, see **sheep dog** *(def. 2).*

shep·herd·ess (shep′ər dis) *n.* a woman or girl who takes care of a flock of sheep.

sher·bet (shur′bit) *n.* a frozen dessert made of fruit juice, water, sweeteners, and small amounts of egg whites or milk.

Sher·i·dan (sher′əd ən) **1. Philip Henry.** 1831–1888, Union general in the Civil War. **2. Richard Brins·ley** (brinz′lē). 1751–1816, British dramatist and statesman, born in Ireland.

sher·iff (sher′if) *n.* the chief law enforcement officer of a county, who is in charge of keeping the peace, serving court orders, maintaining the jails, and other administrative functions.

Sher·lock Holmes (shur′lok) a fictional British detective, noted for his remarkable powers of observation, analysis, and deduction, the main character in mystery stories by Sir Arthur Conan Doyle.

Sher·man, William Te·cum·seh (shur′mən; tə kum′sə) 1820–1891, Union general in the Civil War.

sher·ry (sher′ē) *n. pl.,* **sher·ries.** a strong wine that varies in color from pale amber to dark brown, and in taste from dry to sweet.

Sher·wood Forest (shur′wood′) an ancient royal forest of England, known as the legendary home of Robin Hood.

she's (shēz) **1.** she is. **2.** she has.

Shet·land Islands (shet′lənd) an island group off the northern coast of Scotland, in the Atlantic Ocean.

Shetland pony, a small, hardy pony of a breed that originated in the Shetland Islands. It has a rough coat and a long mane and tail.

Shetland pony

Shetland sheepdog, a dog closely resembling the collie, but smaller.

shew (shō) *n., v.,* **shewed, shewn, shewing.** *Archaic.* another spelling of **show.**

shib·bo·leth (shib′ə lith) *n.* **1.** a catchword, slogan, or custom of a certain group, political party, or class of people, especially one frequently repeated or followed unthinkingly. **2.** any characteristic, as of speech or usage, that distinguishes a group. [Hebrew *shibbōleth* a stream. According to a story in the Bible, this word was used as a password to identify members of an enemy tribe, who were unable to pronounce the *sh* sound at the beginning of the word, saying it as *s* instead.]

S

at; āpe; cär; end; mē; it; īce; hot; ōld; fôrk; wood; fōōl; oil; out; up; turn; sing; thin; this; hw in white; zh in treasure. The symbol ə stands for the sound of **a** in about, **e** in taken, **i** in pencil, **o** in lemon, and **u** in circus.

shied (shīd) the past tense and past participle of **shy²**.

shield (shēld) *n.* **1.** a piece of armor carried on the arm for defense in battle. **2.** a person or thing that defends or protects, as against danger, injury, or distress: *She used the umbrella as a shield against the driving rain.* **3.** something shaped like a shield, such as a policeman's badge. **4.** another word for **escutcheon.** —*v.t.* to shield, protect, or defend: *He shielded his eyes from the glare of the sun with his hand.*

shi·er (shī′ər) a comparative of **shy¹**.

shi·est (shī′ist) a superlative of **shy¹**.

shift (shift) *v.t.* **1.** to move from one person, place, or position to another: *Mother shifted the furniture in the living room.* **2.** to switch or change: *The presidential candidate shifted his position on capital punishment.* **3.** to change (gears) from one arrangement to another, as in driving an automobile. —*v.i.* **1.** to move, as from one place or position to another: *She shifted in her chair.* **2.** to change gears from one arrangement to another, as in driving an automobile. —*n.* **1.** a movement from one person, place, or position to another: *The shift in weight when John changed his seat caused the rowboat to capsize.* **2.** a switch or change, as in attitude: *a shift in policy.* **3.** a group of workers who work during a particular period of time: *The day shift at the factory is just arriving.* **4.** the working time of such a group. **5.** a gearshift, especially in an automobile. **6.** a loosely fitting dress designed to fall with straight lines from the shoulders to the hips.
   to shift for oneself. to get along by oneself.

shift·less (shift′lis) *adj.* lacking in ambition or energy; good-for-nothing; lazy. —**shift′less·ly,** *adv.* —**shift′less·ness,** *n.*

shift·y (shif′tē) *adj.,* **shift·i·er, shift·i·est. 1.** not to be trusted or believed; dishonest; tricky. **2.** showing trickery or dishonesty: *shifty eyes.* —**shift′i·ly,** *adv.* —**shift′i·ness,** *n.*

Shi·ko·ku (shi kō′kōō) *n.* the smallest of the four main islands of Japan, in the southern part of the country.

shil·ling (shil′ing) *n.* a former coin of the United Kingdom, equal to 1/20 of a pound.

shil·ly-shal·ly (shil′ē shal′ē) *v.i.,* **shil·ly-shal·lied, shil·ly-shal·ly·ing. 1.** to be undecided or hesitant. **2.** to waste time; dawdle.

shim·mer (shim′ər) *v.i.* to shine with a faint, wavering light; glimmer. —*n.* a faint, wavering light; glimmer; gleam. —**shim′mer·y,** *adj.*

shim·my (shim′ē) *n. pl.,* **shim·mies. 1.** an unusual shaking or vibration. **2.** a dance characterized by much shaking of the body, popular in the 1920s. —*v.i.,* **shim·mied, shim·my·ing. 1.** to shake; vibrate. **2.** to shake the body, as in dancing the shimmy.

shin (shin) *n.* **1.** the front part of the leg from the knee to the ankle. **2.** a similar part in certain animals and birds. —*v.i.,* **shinned, shin·ning.** to climb by using the hands or arms and the feet or legs in grasping or pulling: *to shin up a tree.*

shin·bone (shin′bōn′) *n.* the inner and thicker of the two bones of the leg, extending from the knee to the ankle; tibia.

shin·dig (shin′dig′) *n. Slang.* a festive or noisy social gathering, as a dance or party.

shine (shīn) *v.,* **shone** or *(v.t.)* **shined, shin·ing.** —*v.i.* **1.** to give out or send out light or brightness: *The sun shone all day.* **2.** to be bright or gleam with reflected light; glow: *The newly waxed floor shone. Her face is shining with happiness.* **3.** to be outstanding; excel: *He shines in math.* —*v.t.* **1.** to put a gloss or polish on: *He shined his shoes.* **2.** to cause to shine: *to shine a flashlight.* —*n.* **1.** light or brightness; radiance. **2.** luster or sheen, as of an object

reflecting light. **3.** fair weather; sunshine: *Let's go on a hike, come rain or shine.* **4.** a polish given to shoes. **5.** *Informal.* a liking; fancy: *to take a shine to someone.*

shin·er (shī′nər) *n.* **1.** a person or thing that shines. **2.** *Informal.* a black eye.

shin·gle¹ (shing′gəl) *n.* **1.** a thin piece of wood or other material, such as asphalt, applied to roofs and outside walls in overlapping rows. **2.** *Informal.* a small signboard, especially outside the office of a doctor or lawyer. **3.** a very short haircut. —*v.t.,* **shin·gled, shin·gling. 1.** to cover with shingles: *to shingle a roof.* **2.** to cut (the hair) very short. [Latin *scindula.*]

shin·gle² (shing′gəl) *n.* loose gravel made up of flattened pebbles and stones, such as that found on beaches. [Of uncertain origin.]

shin·gles (shing′gəlz) *n.,pl.* a virus infection characterized by painful irritation of a group of nerves and the eruption of blisters. ▲ used with a singular verb. [Medieval Latin *cingulus,* from Latin *cingulum* belt; because the blisters often ring the body like a belt.]

shin·ing (shī′ning) *adj.* **1.** sending out or reflecting light; bright. **2.** outstanding; distinguished: *He is a shining example of an honest businessman.* —**shin′ing·ly,** *adv.*

shin·ny¹ (shin′ē) *v.i.,* **shin·nied, shin·ny·ing.** to climb by the use of the hands or arms and the feet or legs in grasping or pulling: *to shinny up a tree.* [From *shin.*]

shin·ny² (shin′ē) *n.* a game resembling hockey, played with a curved stick and a ball or block of wood. [Possibly from *shin ye,* a cry used in the game.]

Shin·to (shin′tō) *n.* **1.** the native religion of Japan, marked by worship of nature, reverence of ancestors and ancient heroes, and the divinity of the emperor. **2.** a person who follows or believes in this religion.

Shin·to·ism (shin′tō iz′əm) *n.* the Shinto religion.

shin·y (shī′nē) *adj.,* **shin·i·er, shin·i·est. 1.** shining; bright. **2.** worn to a glossy smoothness: *The seat of his trousers was shiny from many years of wear.* —**shin′i·ness,** *n.*

ship (ship) *n.* **1.** any large seagoing vessel. **2.** the crew of such a vessel. **3.** an airplane, airship, or spacecraft. **4.** a sailing vessel having three or more masts. —*v.,* **shipped, ship·ping.** —*v.t.* **1.** to send or transport, as by ship, rail, or truck: *We shipped a trunk of clothes home from camp.* **2.** (of a boat or ship) to take on (water) over the side. **3.** to put (an object) in its proper place for use on a boat or ship: *to ship a mast.* —*v.i.* **1.** to go on board a ship; embark. **2.** to leave on a ship, especially as a member of the crew: *He shipped out as a cook.* **3.** (of certain perishable foods) to withstand shipment: *Some fruit does not ship well.* ▲ See **boat** for usage note.

-ship *suffix* (used to form nouns) **1.** the quality, state, or condition of being: *friendship.* **2.** the office, position, or rank of: *ambassadorship.* **3.** the art or skill of being: *horsemanship.*

ship biscuit, another term for **hardtack.**

ship·board (ship′bôrd′) *n.* **on shipboard.** aboard a ship: *Is everything loaded on shipboard?*

ship·build·er (ship′bil′dər) *n.* a person who builds or designs ships.

ship·build·ing (ship′bil′ding) *n.* **1.** the act of building ships. **2.** the art or business of building ships.

ship·load (ship′lōd′) *n.* all that a ship can hold or carry.

ship·mas·ter (ship′mas′tər) *n.* a person in command of a ship.

ship·mate (ship′māt′) *n.* a fellow sailor on a ship.

ship·ment (ship′mənt) *n.* **1.** the act of shipping goods. **2.** something shipped: *a shipment of vegetables.*

ship·per (ship′ər) *n.* a person or company that ships goods.

ship·ping (ship′ing) *n.* **1.** the act or business of sending or transporting goods, as by ship or railroad. **2.** ships as a group, especially those belonging to a particular port, country, or company: *Greek shipping.* **3.** the total tonnage of such ships.

ship·shape (ship′shāp′) *adj.* in good or proper order; neat. —*adv.* in a shipshape manner.

ship·worm (ship′wurm′) *n.* any of a group of animals resembling worms, having long slender bodies and two shells which are used to burrow into wharves or ship timbers.

ship·wreck (ship′rek′) *n.* **1.** the destruction or loss of a ship. **2.** the remains of a wrecked ship; wreckage. **3.** total failure, destruction, or loss: *the shipwreck of one's dreams.* —*v.t.* **1.** to cause (a ship) to be destroyed or lost. **2.** to ruin; destroy. —*v.i.* (of a ship) to be destroyed or lost: *The tanker shipwrecked off the coast of England.*

ship·yard (ship′yärd′) *n.* a place containing docks, workshops, and warehouses where ships can be built, equipped, and repaired.

Shi·raz (shi räz′) *n.* a city in southwestern Iran. Pop. (1966), 269,865.

shire (shīr) *n.* in Great Britain, a county.

shirk (shurk) *v.t.* to avoid or neglect doing (something that should be done): *to shirk one's duties.* —**shirk′er,** *n.*

shirr (shur) *v.t.* **1.** to gather (fabric) by means of a series of parallel threads. **2.** to bake (eggs) in a dish with butter.

shir·ring (shur′ing) *n.* a shirred arrangement of fabric.

shirt (shurt) *n.* **1.** any of various garments for the upper part of the body, usually having a collar, sleeves, and buttons down the front. **2.** an undershirt. —**shirt′like′,** *adj.*

shirt·ing (shur′ting) *n.* fabric used for making shirts or blouses.

shirt·waist (shurt′wāst′) *n.* **1.** a tailored dress having a top that resembles a shirt. **2.** a tailored blouse.

Shirring

shish ke·bab (shish′ kə bob′) *also,* **shish ka·bob, shish ke·bob.** cubes of meat and often onions, tomatoes, or green peppers, broiled on skewers.

Shi·va (shē′və) *n. also,* **Siva.** the Hindu god who personifies the destructive forces of the universe and, with Brahma and Vishnu, forms the Hindu trinity.

shiv·er[1] (shiv′ər) *v.i.* to shake, as with cold or fear; tremble: *She shivered in the cool night air.* —*n.* **1.** the act of shivering. **2.** a shivering sensation: *His ghost story sent shivers up my spine.* [Of uncertain origin.]

shiv·er[2] (shiv′ər) *v.t.* to cause to break into fragments or splinters; shatter. —*v.i.* to break into fragments or splinters; shatter: *The glass shivered when it hit the floor.* —*n.* a small broken bit; fragment. [Middle English *shiveren.*]

shiv·er·y (shiv′ər ē) *adj.* **1.** shivering, as from cold or fear; trembling. **2.** causing shivers: *a shivery tale of horror.* **3.** inclined to shiver, as from cold.

shoal[1] (shōl) *n.* **1.** a sandbank or sandbar seen at low tide. **2.** any area, as in a river or the ocean, where the water is shallow. —*v.i.* to become shallow: *The lake shoals near the shore.* —*v.t.* to make shallow. —*adj.* of little depth; shallow. [Old English *sceald* shallow.]

shoal[2] (shōl) *n.* a school of fish. —*v.i.* (of fish) to collect in a shoal. [Possibly from Old English *scolu* crowd.]

shoat (shōt) *also,* **shote.** *n.* a young pig that has been weaned.

shock[1] (shok) *n.* **1.** a sudden, violent disturbance of the mind or emotions: *He never recovered from the shock of his son's death.* **2.** the cause of this: *The news of the accident came as a shock to us.* **3.** a feeling caused by the passage of an electric current through the body. **4.** a sudden, violent shake, blow, or impact, as of an explosion or earthquake. **5.** a serious weakening of the body or mind caused by a severe physical or emotional injury. Shock is characterized by a weak pulse, cold skin, an ashen complexion, and a great drop in blood pressure. —*v.t.* **1.** to disturb the mind or emotions of: *His crude language shocked us.* **2.** to give an electric shock to. [French *choc* a collision, clash.] —**shock′er,** *n.*

shock[2] (shok) *n.* a bundle, as of wheat or corn, set upright in a field. —*v.t.* to gather into a shock or shocks. [Possibly from Middle Dutch *shocke.*]

shock[3] (shok) *n.* a thick, bushy mass, as of hair. [Possibly from *shock*[2]; from its resemblance to a bundle of wheat.]

shock absorber, a device, as in automobiles, airplanes, or machines, that lessens the jarring or shaking effect of sudden impacts or bumps.

shock·ing (shok′ing) *adj.* **1.** offensive, distasteful, or revolting. **2.** causing horror or surprise: *shocking news.* —**shock′ing·ly,** *adv.*

shock troops, troops specially chosen and trained to make sudden attacks.

shock wave, a disturbance of the atmosphere created by an airplane, rocket, or other body traveling at supersonic speed.

shod (shod) the past tense and past participle of **shoe.**

shod·dy (shod′ē) *adj.,* **shod·di·er, shod·di·est. 1.** poorly made or done; inferior: *a shoddy piece of work.* **2.** mean or nasty: *shoddy treatment.* **3.** worn out; shabby; seedy: *The old rug looks very shoddy.* **4.** made of wool fibers reclaimed from woolen waste or other remnants. —*n. pl.,* **shod·dies. 1.** wool fibers reclaimed from woolen waste or other remnants. **2.** cloth made of such fibers. —**shod′di·ly,** *adv.* —**shod′di·ness,** *n.*

shoe (shoo) *n.* **1.** any of various outer coverings, usually of leather, that protect and support the human foot. **2.** something resembling a shoe in shape, position, or function. **3.** see **horseshoe. 4.** a curved metal piece in a brake that presses against the wheel to slow or stop it. —*v.t.,* **shod, shoe·ing. 1.** to provide with a shoe or shoes. **2.** to provide or protect the end or edge of something with a metal covering.

in someone's shoes. in another person's position or place.

shoe·horn (shoo′hôrn′) *n.* a curved device inserted at the back of a shoe to help slip the heel into the shoe.

shoe·lace (shoo′lās′) *n.* a cord for fastening a shoe.

shoe·mak·er (shoo′mā′kər) *n.* a person who makes or repairs shoes and other footwear.

shoe·string (shoo′string′) *n.* another word for **shoelace.**
on a shoestring. with very little money or resources: *The young artist was living on a shoestring.*

shoe tree, a device put in a shoe to keep its shape when it is not being worn.

shone (shōn) a past tense and past participle of **shine.**

shoo (shoo) *interj.* a sound used to frighten or drive away a person or animal. —*v.,* **shooed, shoo·ing.** —*v.t.* to frighten or drive away by making this sound. —*v.i.* to make such a sound.

shook (shook) the past tense of **shake.**

at; āpe; cär; end; mē; it; īce; hot; ōld; fôrk; wood; fool; oil; out; up; turn; sing; thin; this; hw in white; zh in treasure. The symbol ə stands for the sound of a in about, e in taken, i in pencil, o in lemon, and u in circus.

shoot (shoot) *v.*, **shot, shoot·ing.** —*v.t.* **1.** to wound or kill (a person or animal) with a bullet, arrow, or the like. **2.** to send forth or discharge (a missile) from a weapon, such as a gun or bow: *He shot bullets at the target for practice.* **3.** to cause to discharge or explode: *to shoot a gun, to shoot off fireworks.* **4.** to send forth or direct rapidly or suddenly: *The snake shot out its tongue. He shot a nasty look at her.* **5.** to pass rapidly down, through, or over: *to shoot the rapids of a river.* **6.** to propel (a ball, puck, marble, or other object) toward a target or goal. **7.** to score, as points or a goal, in this way. **8.** to photograph or film, as for television or a motion picture: *They are going to shoot the final scene today.* **9.** to mark with streaks of color: *His black hair was shot with gray.* **10.** to slide into or out of a fastening: *to shoot the bolt of a door.* **11.** to play, as pool or craps. —*v.i.* **1.** to send forth or discharge a bullet, arrow, or other missile from a weapon. **2.** (of a weapon) to send forth a missile in a certain way: *This rifle shoots high.* **3.** to go or move suddenly or rapidly; dart: *He slipped on the ice and his feet shot out from under him.* **4.** to propel a ball, puck, marble, or other object toward a target or goal. **5.** to extend; project: *This piece of land shoots out into the bay.* —*n.* **1.** a new or young growth, as from a bud; sprout. **2.** the part of a plant that bears leaves and buds. —**shoot′er,** *n.*

shooting star, another term for **meteor.**

shop (shop) *n.* **1.** a small store where merchandise is sold at retail: *a dress shop, a pet shop.* **2.** a place where a particular type of work is done: *a barber's shop.* **3.** a place where things are made or repaired: *He took the broken radio to the shop.* —*v.i.*, **shopped, shop·ping.** to visit stores to look at, price, or buy merchandise: *She went shopping in the morning.*

   to talk shop. to talk about matters that relate to one's work.

shop·keep·er (shop′kē′pər) *n.* a person who owns or manages a shop.

shop·lift·er (shop′lif′tər) *n.* a person who steals merchandise from a store while pretending to be a customer.

shop·lift·ing (shop′lif′ting) *n.* the act of stealing merchandise from a store while pretending to be a customer.

shop·per (shop′ər) *n.* a person who visits stores to look at, price, or buy merchandise; customer.

shopping center, a place or area, especially in the suburbs, consisting of a group of stores, shops, and other facilities.

shop·worn (shop′wôrn′) *adj.* **1.** soiled, frayed, or damaged from being displayed or handled in a store. **2.** worn out, as from overuse: *a shopworn phrase.*

shore[1] (shôr) *n.* **1.** the land along the edge of an ocean, lake, or large river. **2.** land: *Those sailors are now stationed on shore.* **3.** also, **shores.** country: *The expatriate eventually returned to his native shore.* [Middle Dutch *schōre.*]

shore[2] (shôr) *v.t.*, **shored, shor·ing.** to support with a timber or beam: *to shore up an unsteady wall.* —*n.* a prop, especially a timber or beam, placed against the side of a structure as a temporary support. [Middle Dutch *schoor* prop.]

shore·line (shôr′līn′) *n.* the outline or contour of a shore.

Shore Patrol, a detail of the U.S. Navy, Coast Guard, or Marine Corps, acting as military police on shore.

shore·ward (shôr′wərd) *adv., adj.* toward the shore.

shorn (shôrn) a past participle of **shear.**

Shores

short (shôrt) *adj.* **1.** having little length; not long: *He has short hair. This dress has a short skirt.* **2.** having relatively little height; not tall: *Harry is a short boy.* **3.** not long in time: *a short wait, a short trip.* **4.** using few words; concise; brief: *a short statement.* **5.** not having enough; lacking: *to be short of funds.* **6.** inadequate in amount: *We had a short supply of food.* **7.** rudely brief or abrupt; curt: *She was very short with me when I spoke to her.* **8.** (of dough or pastry) rich and flaky due to the addition of shortening. **9.** (of vowels) relatively brief in duration, such as the *i* in *bit.* —*adv.* **1.** suddenly; abruptly: *to stop short.* **2.** not quite up to; on the near side of: *The player kicked the ball short of the goal line.* —*n.* **1.** something short. **2.** see **short subject. 3.** see **short circuit. 4. shorts. a.** short pants that reach to or almost to the knee. **b.** men's underpants. —*v.t.* to make a short circuit in. —*v.i.* to have a short circuit. —**short′ness,** *n.*

   for short. as a shortened or shorter form: *Edward is called Ed for short.*

   in short. in summary; briefly.

   short for. as a shortened or shorter form of: *Cab is short for taxicab.*

   short of. less than: *Nothing short of a disaster will prevent our going.*

short·age (shôr′tij) *n.* **1.** too small an amount or supply; lack: *a shortage of funds.* **2.** the amount by which anything is lacking: *The head teller at the bank discovered a shortage of twenty dollars.*

short·bread (shôrt′bred′) *n.* a crumbly, rich cookie made of flour, sugar, and shortening.

short·cake (shôrt′kāk′) *n.* a dessert consisting of a rich biscuit or cake covered or filled with fruit, such as strawberries, and usually topped with whipped cream.

short·change (shôrt′chānj′) *v.t.*, **short·changed, short·chang·ing. 1.** to give less than the proper change to: *The cashier shortchanged me by one dollar.* **2.** to swindle; cheat. —**short′chang′er,** *n.*

short·cir·cuit (shôrt′sur′kit) *v.t.* to cause a short circuit in. —*v.i.* to have a short circuit.

short circuit, an electrical circuit, usually formed accidentally, that has abnormally low resistance, thus resulting in an excessive flow of current through it. A short circuit may blow a fuse or cause a fire. Also, **short.**

short·com·ing (shôrt′kum′ing) *n.* a fault or failure; defect: *The habit of constantly telling lies is his most serious shortcoming.*

short·cut (shôrt′kut′) *also,* **short cut.** *n.* **1.** a way that is shorter than the ordinary way. **2.** any way or means that saves time or effort.

short·en (shôrt′ən) *v.t.* **1.** to make short or shorter. **2.** to make rich or flaky by adding shortening. —*v.i.* to become short or shorter.

short·en·ing (shôrt′ən ing) *n.* **1.** any of various fats, such as butter, lard, or vegetable oil, used in cooking. **2.** the act of a person or thing that shortens.

short·hand (shôrt′hand′) *n.* a method of rapid handwriting in which the words are replaced by symbols, characters, or letters. —*adj.* **1.** using shorthand. **2.** written in shorthand.

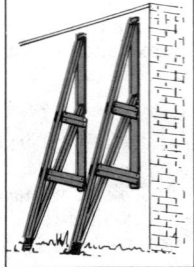

Shorthand for *As we have not heard from you*

short·hand·ed (shôrt′han′did) *adj.* lacking the necessary or usual number of workmen, assistants, or the like: *The football team was shorthanded because of injuries.*

short·horn (shôrt′hôrn′) *n.* one of a breed of beef cattle with short horns, originally bred in northern England.

short-lived (shôrt′līvd′, shôrt′livd′) *adj.* living or lasting only a short time

short·ly (shôrt′lē) *adv.* **1.** in a short time; presently; soon: *The doctor will see you shortly.* **2.** in a few words; briefly. **3.** in a rude or abrupt manner; curtly.

short-range (shôrt′rānj′) *adj.* **1.** not reaching far into the future: *short-range plans.* **2.** capable of firing only a short distance: *short-range guns.*

short shrift, hasty treatment showing little interest, concern, or mercy: *The man gave short shrift to the beggar.*
  to make short shrift of. to take care of quickly.

short·sight·ed (shôrt′sī′tid) *adj.* **1.** not having foresight: *a shortsighted plan.* **2.** nearsighted; myopic. —**short′-sight′ed·ly,** *adv.* —**short′sight′ed·ness,** *n.*

short·stop (shôrt′stop′) *n. Baseball.* **1.** the infield position between second and third base. **2.** a player playing this position.

short story, a work of fiction that has a single theme, a full plot, and a limited number of characters, and is shorter in length than a novel.

short subject, a short film, such as a documentary or cartoon. Also, **short.**

short-tem·pered (shôrt′tem′pərd) *adj.* easily or quickly angered; quick-tempered.

short·wave (shôrt′wāv′) *n.* a radio wave of sixty meters or less.

short-wind·ed (shôrt′win′did) *adj.* suffering from shortness of breath: *The horse was short-winded after the race.*

Sho·sho·ne (shə shō′nē, shō shō′nē) *also,* **Sho·sho·ni.** *n. pl.,* **Sho·sho·nes.** **1.** a member of a tribe of North American Indians living in Idaho, Montana, Nevada, Oregon, Wyoming, and Utah. **2.** the language of this tribe.

Sho·sta·ko·vich, Dmi·tri (shos′tə kō′vich; də mē′trē) 1906–1975, Russian composer.

shot¹ (shot) *n. pl.,* **shots** or *(def. 4)* **shot.** **1.** a discharge of a firearm or other weapon: *Did you hear a shot?* **2.** the act of shooting. **3.** a person who shoots; marksman: *He is a good shot.* **4.** tiny balls of lead or steel that are contained in a cartridge and discharged by a shotgun. **5.** a single ball of lead used as ammunition for a gun or cannon. **6.** the launching of a rocket or missile toward a particular target: *a moon shot.* **7.** an injection given with a needle or syringe; hypodermic. **8.** the distance over which something, such as a missile or sound, can travel; reach; range. **9.** an aim or stroke in certain games: *He took a practice shot at the basket.* **10.** a photograph. **11.** a single piece of motion picture film or magnetic tape recording a continuous action, taken by one camera from one angle. **12.** the heavy metal ball used in the shot put. **13.** *Informal.* a small amount of liquor, often drunk in one gulp. [Old English *sceot.*]

shot² (shot) *v.* the past tense and past participle of **shoot.** —*adj.* **1.** streaked or woven so as to have a mixture of colors: *She wore a scarf of red silk shot with blue.* **2.** *Informal.* completely worn out or ruined: *These shoes are shot.*

shote (shōt) another spelling of **shoat.**

shot·gun (shot′gun′) *n.* a gun designed to fire cartridges that release a quantity of shot when discharged.

shot put, an athletic event in which a shot is thrown for distance.

should (shood) *auxiliary verb* the past tense of **shall.** **1.** used to express an obligation or duty: *You should put a bandage on that cut.* **2.** used to express a condition: *If anyone should call, say that I'll be back in an hour.* **3.** used to express probability or expectation: *He should be here by five o'clock.* **4.** used to lessen the bluntness or directness of a statement: *I should not do that sort of thing if I were you.*

shoul·der (shōl′dər) *n.* **1.** the part on either side of the body from the base of the neck to the upper arm or fore-limb. **2. shoulders.** both shoulders and the part of the back connecting them. **3.** the portion of a garment covering the shoulders: *I ripped my sweater at the shoulder.* **4.** the front quarter of an animal. **5.** an edge or border on either side of a road or highway. **6.** any projecting part or slope: *the shoulder of a hill.* —*v.t.* **1.** to force by pushing with the shoulder or shoulders: *to shoulder one's way through a crowd.* **2.** to take upon oneself, as a burden; assume: *to shoulder the blame, to shoulder responsiblity.* **3.** to place on and support or carry with the shoulder or shoulders: *to shoulder a trunk.* —*v.i.* to push forward or force one's way with the shoulder or shoulders.
  shoulder to shoulder. a. side by side and close together: *to stand shoulder to shoulder.* **b.** in cooperation: *to work shoulder to shoulder.*
  straight from the shoulder. honestly; frankly; candidly.

shoulder blade, either of two flat, triangular bones in the upper part of the back; scapula.

shoulder strap **1.** a strap worn over the shoulder to hold up a garment or to carry a purse, bag, or the like. **2.** an ornamental cloth strip fastened on the shoulder of a uniform, usually to indicate rank.

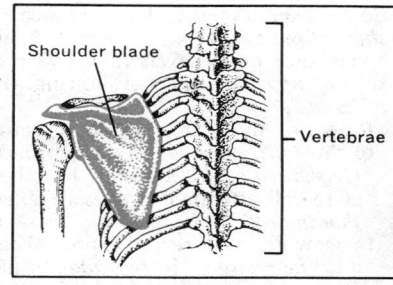

Shoulder blade

Vertebrae

should·n't (shood′ənt) should not: *You shouldn't be afraid of meeting strangers.*

shouldst (shoodst) *Archaic.* the second person singular, past tense, of **shall.** ▲ used with **thou.**

shout (shout) *v.i.* to cry out loudly; yell: *to shout for help.* —*v.t.* to express by a shout: *Shout the alarm!* —*n.* a loud cry or yell. —**shout′er,** *n.*
  to shout down. to silence by shouting: *The crowd shouted down the speaker at the meeting.*

shove (shuv) *v.,* **shoved, shov·ing.** —*v.t.* **1.** to move along by pushing or pressing from behind; push: *Shove the chair closer to the table.* **2.** to push or press roughly: *He shoved the other boy off the sidewalk.* —*v.i.* to push or press roughly. —*n.* a strong push.
  to shove off. a. to push a boat away from the shore. **b.** *Informal.* to leave.

shov·el (shuv′əl) *n.* **1.** a tool with a broad blade attached to a long handle, used for digging up and moving loose material, such as soil, snow, or gravel. **2.** any large power-driven machine for digging up and moving loose material. **3.** a shovelful. —*v.,* **shov·eled, shov·el·ing;** *also, British,* **shov·elled, shov·el·ling.** —*v.t.* **1.** to dig up and move with a shovel: *to shovel dirt.* **2.** to dig or clear with a shovel: *to shovel a path.* **3.** to move or throw in large quantities as if with a shovel: *to shovel food into one's mouth.* —*v.i.* to use a shovel.

shov·el·er (shuv′ə lər) *also, British,* **shov·el·ler.** *n.* **1.** a person or thing that shovels. **2.** any of several freshwater ducks having a broad, flat bill.

at; āpe; cär; end; mē; it; īce; hot; ōld; fôrk; wood; fōol; oil; out; up; turn; sing; thin; this; hw in white; zh in treasure. The symbol ə stands for the sound of **a** in about, **e** in taken, **i** in pencil, **o** in lemon, and **u** in circus.

S

841

shov·el·ful (shuv′əl fool′) *n. pl.,* **shov·el·fuls.** the amount that a shovel can hold.

show (shō) *v.,* **showed, shown** or **showed, show·ing.** —*v.t.* **1.** to bring to sight or view; display: *Please show your tickets at the door. The theater showed the movie last week.* **2.** to make known or clear by one's behavior; reveal: *She showed her anger by throwing a book.* **3.** to point out or lead: *Show him the way to the bus station.* **4.** to register, as on a scale: *The thermometer shows the temperature to be quite high.* **5.** to explain to: *He showed his brother how to change a tire.* **6.** to demonstrate or explain: *I'll show that it can be done.* **7.** to grant or give; bestow: *The judge showed little mercy in his decision.* —*v.i.* **1.** to be in sight or view; appear: *Her dress showed under her coat.* **2.** to be made known: *His anger showed in his face.* —*n.* **1.** something shown; exhibition or display: *an art show, a dog show.* **2.** any entertainment, especially in a theater or on radio or television. **3.** a display meant to attract attention: *a show of wealth.* **4.** appearance; sign: *There was little show of recognition when we met.* **5.** a false or misleading appearance; pretense: *He denied the accusation with a great show of anger.* **6.** the act of showing: *We will vote by a show of hands.*

for show. in order to attract attention; for effect.

to show off. a. to display in a proud or showy manner: *He showed off his new suit.* **b.** to behave in such a way as to call attention to oneself: *The little boy is always showing off.*

to show up. a. to reveal; expose: *You showed him up for what he really is.* **b.** *Informal.* to make an appearance: *We will leave without him if he does not show up soon.*

show bill, a poster advertising a play or other entertainment.

show·boat (shō′bōt′) *n.* a river steamboat having a theater and troupe of performers on board for providing entertainment.

show·case (shō′kās′) *n.* a glass case for displaying and protecting articles, as in a store or museum.

show·down (shō′doun′) *n.* a meeting that forces a matter to a climax or conclusion.

show·er (shou′ər) *n.* **1.** a brief fall of rain. **2.** a fall of anything in large number: *a shower of tears, a shower of sparks.* **3.a.** a bath in which water is sprayed on a person from an overhead nozzle. **b.** a room or apparatus for such a bath. Also, **shower bath. 4.** an abundant or large quantity or supply: *a shower of criticism.* **5.** a party for someone, as a future bride, to which gifts are brought. —*v.i.* **1.** to rain or fall in a shower. **2.** to bathe by taking a shower. —*v.t.* **1.** to wet with water or other liquid; sprinkle; spray. **2.** to cause to fall in a shower: *to shower hail, to shower meteors.* **3.** to give or grant lavishly: *to shower compliments on a person.* —**show′er·y,** *adj.*

shower bath, see **shower** (*defs. 3a, 3b*).

show·ing (shō′ing) *n.* **1.** the act or instance of bringing to view; presentation. **2.** a performance, as in a contest or test: *He made a poor showing in the race.*

show·man (shō′mən) *n. pl.,* **show·men** (shō′mən). **1.** a person who produces, presents, or manages a theatrical show. **2.** a person who acts or presents something in a dramatic or showy way.

show·man·ship (shō′mən ship′) *n.* the skill of a showman.

shown (shōn) a past participle of **show.**

show-off (shō′ôf′) *n.* **1.** a person who shows off; exhibitionist. **2.** the act of showing off.

show·piece (shō′pēs′) *n.* something thought of or shown as a fine example of its kind.

show·room (shō′rōom′, shō′room′) *n.* a room used for the display of merchandise: *a furniture showroom.*

show·y (shō′ē) *adj.,* **show·i·er, show·i·est. 1.** making a striking display: *showy flowers.* **2.** bright or loud in a tasteless way; gaudy; flashy: *a showy dresser.* —**show′i·ly,** *adv.* —**show′i·ness,** *n.*

shrank (shrangk) a past tense of **shrink.**

shrap·nel (shrap′nəl) *n. pl.,* **shrap·nel. 1.** a thin-walled shell filled with small lead fragments or balls that are scattered over a large area when the shell explodes. **2.** scattered fragments from an exploding shell or bomb. [From Henry *Shrapnel,* 1761–1842, a British general who was the inventor of this kind of shell.]

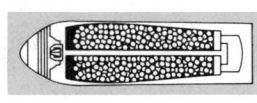

Shrapnel

shred (shred) *n.* **1.** a very small piece or narrow strip torn or cut off: *Shreds of paper covered the floor.* **2.** a small amount; particle; scrap; bit: *There is not a shred of truth in his story.* —*v.t.,* **shred·ded** or **shred, shred·ding.** to tear or cut into shreds: *She shredded cabbage for a salad.*

Shreve·port (shrēv′pôrt′) *n.* a city in northwestern Louisiana. Pop. (1970), 182,064.

shrew (shrōō) *n.* **1.** a very small animal related to the mole, found in nearly all parts of the world, having a long, pointed snout, short, rounded ears, and usually brownish fur. **2.** a bad-tempered, nagging woman.

Shrew

shrewd (shrōōd) *adj.* clever or keen in practical matters; astute: *Mr. Johnson is a shrewd businessman.* —**shrewd′ly,** *adv.* —**shrewd′ness,** *n.*

shrew·ish (shrōō′ish) *adj.* like a shrew; bad-tempered. —**shrew′ish·ly,** *adv.* —**shrew′ish·ness,** *n.*

shriek (shrēk) *n.* a loud, shrill cry or sound: *the shriek of a whistle, shrieks of laughter.* —*v.i.* to make a loud, shrill cry or sound. —*v.t.* to utter with a shriek.

shrift (shrift) *n.* **1.** *Archaic.* a confession made to a priest or the absolution given by a priest. **2.** see **short shrift.**

shrike (shrīk) *n.* a bird of prey having a large head, a strong, hooked beak, and a long tail.

shrill (shril) *adj.* **1.** sharp and high-pitched in sound. **2.** making such a sound: *a shrill whistle.* —*v.i.* to make a shrill sound: *The bagpipes shrilled.* —*v.t.* to utter with a shrill sound. —**shrill′ness,** *n.* —**shrill′ly,** *adv.*

shrimp (shrimp) *n. pl.,* **shrimps** or **shrimp. 1.** any of a number of long-tailed animals related to the lobster, usually found in salt water, and often used as food. **2.** *Slang.* a person who is very short.

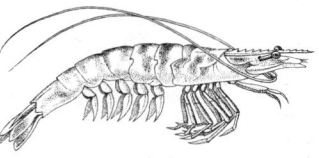

Shrimp

shrine (shrīn) *n.* **1.** a case or other container for sacred relics; reliquary. **2.** the tomb of a saint. **3.** a holy place, or a place set aside for the worship of a god, saint, or other sacred being. **4.** a place or thing revered for its history or past association: *The battlefield at Gettysburg is a national shrine.*

shrink (shringk) *v.,* **shrank** or **shrunk, shrunk** or **shrunk·en, shrink·ing.** —*v.i.* **1.** to become smaller because of heat, cold, or moisture: *Woolen cloth shrinks in hot water.* **2.** to draw back, as in fear, horror, or disgust: *She shrank from the terrible sight.* **3.** to become less; reduce; diminish: *The population of the town has shrunk in recent years.* —*v.t.* to cause to become smaller or less:

The laundry shrank my new blouse. —*n.* the act of shrinking. —**shrink′a·ble,** *adj.* —**shrink′er,** *n.*

shrink·age (shring′kij) *n.* **1.** the act of shrinking. **2.** the amount of shrinking. **3.** a lessening, as in quantity or value; depreciation.

shrive (shrīv) *v.,* **shrove** or **shrived, shriv·en** or **shrived, shriv·ing.** —*v.t.* **1.** to hear the confession of and grant absolution to. **2.** to rid (oneself) of sin by confessing and doing penance. —*v.i.* **1.** to make confession to a priest. **2.** to hear confessions.

shriv·el (shriv′əl) *v.,* **shriv·eled, shriv·el·ing;** *also, British,* **shriv·elled, shriv·el·ling.** —*v.i.* to shrink and become wrinkled or curled up: *The flowers shriveled and died because they were not watered.* —*v.t.* to cause to shrivel: *Exposure to the heat of the sun shriveled the plant.*

shriv·en (shriv′ən) a past participle of **shrive.**

shroud (shroud) *n.* **1.** a cloth or garment used to wrap a dead body for burial. **2.** something that covers or hides: *A shroud of clouds covered the mountain top.* **3.** a rope or wire giving support to a mast on a boat or ship. —*v.t.* **1.** to clothe for burial. **2.** to cover so as to conceal; obscure; veil: *Mist shrouded the harbor. The whole affair was shrouded in secrecy.*

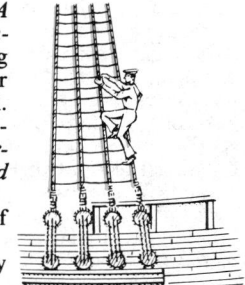

Shrouds *(def. 3)*

shrove (shrōv) a past tense of **shrive.**

Shrove Tuesday, the day before Ash Wednesday.

shrub (shrub) *n.* a woody plant that is smaller than a tree and has many stems that branch at or near the ground.

shrub·ber·y (shrub′ər ē) *n. pl.,* **shrub·ber·ies. 1.** a group of shrubs: *New shrubbery was planted in the park.* **2.** a plot of ground planted with shrubs.

shrub·by (shrub′ē) *adj.,* **shrub·bi·er, shrub·bi·est. 1.** of or resembling a shrub: *a shrubby plant.* **2.** made up of or covered with shrubs.

shrug (shrug) *v.t., v.i.,* **shrugged, shrug·ging.** to raise or draw up (the shoulders), as to show doubt or lack of interest. —*n.* the act of shrugging: *He dismissed the insult with a shrug.*

shrunk (shrungk) a past participle and past tense of **shrink.**

shrunk·en (shrung′kən) *v.* a past participle of **shrink.** —*adj.* shriveled up; made smaller.

shuck (shuk) *n.* **1.** the outer covering of corn or certain nuts. **2.** the shell of an oyster or clam. —*v.t.* **1.** to remove the shucks from. **2.** to take off; remove: *to shuck one's clothes.* —**shuck′er,** *n.*

shud·der (shud′ər) *v.i.* to tremble suddenly, as from horror, disgust, or cold. —*n.* the act of shuddering. —**shud′der·ing·ly,** *adv.*

shuf·fle (shuf′əl) *v.,* **shuf·fled, shuf·fling.** —*v.t.* **1.** to drag (the feet) along the ground or floor. **2.** to mix (playing cards) so as to rearrange them. **3.** to move about or move (something) from one place to another: *to shuffle papers.* —*v.i.* **1.** to walk by dragging the feet: *to shuffle down the street.* **2.** to mix playing cards so as to rearrange them. **3.** to mix or move things about from one place to another. **4.** to move, act, or do something in a clumsy, careless, or hasty manner: *The poor student shuffled through his homework.* —*n.* **1.** the act of shuffling the feet. **2.** the act of shuffling playing cards. **3.** the right or turn to shuffle playing cards. —**shuf′fler,** *n.*

shuf·fle·board (shuf′əl bôrd′) *n.* **1.** a game played by pushing disks with a cue on a smooth level surface marked off in scoring areas. **2.** the marked surface on which this game is played.

shun (shun) *v.t.,* **shunned, shun·ning.** to keep away from; avoid: *The farmer shunned city life for the quiet of the country.* —**shun′ner,** *n.*

shunt (shunt) *v.t.* **1.** to move or turn aside or away. **2.** to switch (a train) from one track to another. **3.** to carry or divert (part of an electric current) by means of a shunt. —*v.i.* to move or turn aside or away. —*n.* **1.** the act of shunting. **2.** a railroad switch. **3.** a conductor joining two points in an electric circuit that provides an electrical bypass for part of the current. —**shunt′er,** *n.*

shush (shush) *interj.* be quiet; hush. —*v.t.* to quiet or silence.

shut (shut) *v.,* **shut, shut·ting.** —*v.t.* **1.** to move (something) into a closed position so as to block an entrance, passageway, or opening: *to shut a window.* **2.** to bring together the parts; fold; close: *to shut an umbrella, to shut a book.* **3.** to confine or enclose: *to shut an animal into a cage.* **4.** to stop the operation of: *to shut a store, to shut down a mine.* **5.** to prevent the passage or flow of: *to shut off water.* —*v.i.* to become shut.

to shut out. *Sports.* to prevent (the opposing team) from scoring in a contest, as in a baseball game.

to shut up. *Informal.* **a.** to quiet or silence (someone). **b.** to become silent.

shut·down (shut′doun′) *n.* the stopping of work, as in a factory.

shut·in (shut′in′) *adj.* confined to a house or hospital. —*n.* a person who is confined to a house or hospital, as by illness.

shut·out (shut′out′) *n. Sports.* **1.** the preventing of the opposing team from scoring. **2.** a game in which one team does not score.

shut·ter (shut′ər) *n.* **1.** a movable panel or screen for a door or window, used to shut out light or to give protection or privacy. **2.** a device that opens and closes the lens opening of a camera. **3.** a person or thing that shuts. —*v.t.* to provide or cover with shutters: *to shutter windows.*

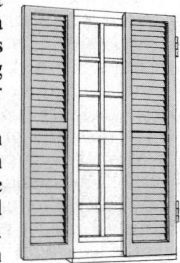

Shutters

shut·tle (shut′əl) *n.* **1.** a device on a loom that carries the yarn back and forth across or through the yarn strung on the loom. **2.** any of various devices that hold and carry thread, as in a sewing machine. **3.** a vehicle in a public transportation system that makes frequent trips back and forth between two points. —*v.,* **shut·tled, shut·tling.** —*v.t.* to move (something) back and forth. —*v.i.* to move back and forth: *The doctor shuttled between the hospital and his office.*

shut·tle·cock (shut′əl kok′) *n.* a cone-shaped object with feathers inserted into a rounded cork or plastic base, used in the game of badminton. Also, **bird.**

shy¹ (shī) *adj.,* **shy·er** or **shi·er, shy·est** or **shi·est. 1.** uncomfortable in the presence of others; bashful; retiring: *The little boy is shy around strangers.* **2.** showing a lack of courage; easily frightened; timid. **3.** cautious or distrustful; wary. **4.** *Informal.* lacking; short: *shy of*

at; āpe; cär; end; mē; it; īce; hot; ōld; fôrk; wood; fŌŌl; oil; out; up; turn; sing; thin; this; hw in white; zh in treasure. The symbol ə stands for the sound of **a** in about, **e** in taken, **i** in pencil, **o** in lemon, and **u** in circus.

S

money. —*v.i.,* **shied, shy·ing. 1.** to move back or aside suddenly, as in fear; start: *The horse shied at the loud noise.* **2.** to draw back, as from caution, dislike, or doubt: *to shy away from something unpleasant.* [Old English *scēoh* timid.] —**shy′ly,** *adv.* —**shy′ness,** *n.*

shy² (shī) *v.t.,* **shied, shy·ing.** to throw (something) with a jerk; fling; toss. —*n. pl.,* **shies.** a quick, jerking throw. [Of uncertain origin.]

Shy·lock (shī′lok′) *n.* **1.** the demanding moneylender in Shakespeare's play *The Merchant of Venice.* **2.** any severe and demanding creditor.

si (sē) *n. Music.* another word for **ti.**

Si, the symbol for silicon.

Si·am (sī am′) *n.* see **Thailand.**

Si·a·mese (sī′ə mēz′) *adj., n. pl.,* **Si·a·mese.** another word for **Thai.**

Siamese cat, a cat of a breed having a long, slender body, a wedge-shaped head, and short hair.

Siamese twins, identical twins who are born joined together. [From *Eng* and *Chang,* 1811–1874, such twins who were born in Siam.]

Si·an (sē′än′) *n.* a city in central China. Pop. (1958) est.), 1,368,000. Also, **Xi'an.**

Si·be·ri·a (sī bēr′ē ə) *n.* a region of the Soviet Union, extending from the Ural Mountains to the Pacific Ocean. —**Si·be′ri·an,** *adj., n.*

Siberian husky, a sturdy dog having a brushlike tail and a soft gray, tan, white, or black coat.

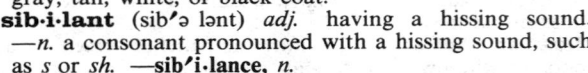

Siamese cat

sib·i·lant (sib′ə lənt) *adj.* having a hissing sound. —*n.* a consonant pronounced with a hissing sound, such as *s* or *sh.* —**sib′i·lance,** *n.*

sib·ling (sib′ling) *n.* a brother or sister.

sib·yl (sib′əl) *n.* **1.** *Greek and Roman Mythology.* any of various women who could predict the future. **2.** any female prophet.

sic¹ (sik) *adv. Latin.* thus; so. ▲ used to show that a word or phrase in a quotation that seems to be an obvious mistake is an exact copy of the original. For example: Her note read "I've taken the dog to the veteran aryan" *(sic).*

sic² (sik) *also,* **sick.** *v.t.,* **sicked** or **sicced, sicking** or **siccing. 1.** to set upon; attack. ▲ used as a command, especially to a dog: *Sic him!* **2.** to cause to attack: *The man sicked his dog on me.* [a form of *seek.*]

Si·chuan (si′chwän′) another spelling of **Szechwan.**

Si·cil·ian (si sil′yən) —*n.* **1.** a person who was born or is living in Sicily. **2.** the dialect of Italian spoken in Sicily. —*adj.* of or relating to Sicily, its people, or their dialect.

Sic·i·ly (sis′ə lē) *n.* an island in the Mediterranean, off the southwestern tip of Italy. It is a part of Italy.

sick¹ (sik) *adj.* **1.** suffering from some disease; having poor health; ill. **2.** suffering from nausea; nauseated. **3.** of or for sick people: *a sick room.* **4.** showing sickness: *He has a sick look.* **5.** completely weary: *John is sick of his job.* **6.** annoyed or disgusted; chagrined: *Gossip about her friends makes her sick.* **7.** gruesome or morbid in some way: *a sick joke.* [Old English *sēoc.*]

sick² (sik) another spelling of **sic².**

sick bay, a hospital or dispensary, especially on a ship.

sick·bed (sik′bed′) *n.* a bed on which a sick person lies.

sick·en (sik′ən) *v.t., v.i.* to make or become sick.

sick·en·ing (sik′ə ning) *adj.* suffering from or causing nausea or disgust. —**sick′en·ing·ly,** *adv.*

sick·ish (sik′ish) *adj.* **1.** somewhat sick. **2.** slightly sickening. —**sick′ish·ly,** *adv.* —**sick′ish·ness,** *n.*

sick·le (sik′əl) *n.* a hand tool made up of a sharp, curved blade attached to a short handle, used for cutting grass, grain, or weeds.

sick·ly (sik′lē) *adj.,* **sick·li·er, sick·li·est. 1.** usually or always sick; in poor health. **2.** of, characteristic of, or causing sickness: *a sickly complexion, a sickly climate.* **3.** suffering from or causing nausea; sickening: *sickly smells.* **4.** faint; feeble; weak: *a sickly smile.* —*adv.* in a sick manner. —**sick′li·ness,** *n.*

sick·ness (sik′nis) *n.* **1.** the state of being sick. **2.** a particular disease or illness. **3.** nausea.

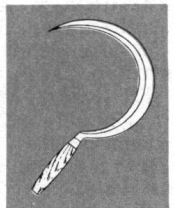

Sickle

side (sīd) *n.* **1.** one of the surfaces or lines that bound an object or figure: *A triangle has three sides.* **2.** either of the two surfaces or lines of an object or figure connecting the front and back, and the top and bottom: *The chair fell on its side. John repainted the sides of his car.* **3.** either of two surfaces of a flat object, such as a piece of paper: *One side of the cloth is smoother than the other.* **4.** either of two parts of a place lying to the right or left of a central line or point: *Put the chairs on the left side of the room.* **5.** any of various parts of a region or place lying beyond a particular, usually central, line or point: *Helen lives on the west side of town.* **6.** either the right or left part of the body of a person or animal. **7.** the area or space next to one's person: *Come stand at my side.* **8.** a region or area separated from another by an object, space, or line: *He has lived on both sides of the Atlantic.* **9.** either of two opposing groups or persons: *Their side won the game. Henry was on his friend's side during the argument.* **10.** an aspect, attitude, or point of view: *Look at all sides of the question.* **11.** a line of descent: *He is my second cousin on my father's side.* —*adj.* **1.** at or near one side: *a side door.* **2.** coming from or directed toward one side. **3.** less important; secondary: *side issues.* —*v.t.,* **sid·ed, sid·ing.** to provide with sides or siding.

on the side. in addition to one's main job or duties.

side by side. next to one another.

to side with. to agree with; support.

side·arm (sīd′ärm′) *adj.* thrown with the arm almost level with the ground: *a sidearm pitch.* —*adv.* with a side-arm motion: *to throw sidearm.*

side arm, a weapon carried on the side, such as a sword or revolver.

side·board (sīd′bôrd′) *n.* a piece of dining-room furniture used especially for storing tableware and linen.

side·burns (sīd′burnz′) *n.,pl.* hair growing down the sides of a man's face, especially when worn as short whiskers with the rest of the beard shaved off. [A form of *burnsides,* from Ambrose *Burnside,* 1824–1881, a Union general in the Civil War, who wore such whiskers.]

side·car (sīd′kär′) *n.* a small one-wheeled car attached to the side of a motorcycle for carrying a passenger.

sid·ed (sī′did) *adj.* having a side or sides. ▲ used in combination: *one-sided.*

side·light (sīd′līt′) *n.* **1.** a light coming from the side. **2.** incidental or additional information or knowledge concerning some subject.

Sideburns

side·line (sīd′līn′) *n.* **1.** either of two lines that mark the side limits of the playing area in certain sports, such as football or basketball. **2.** **sidelines.** the area just beyond these lines. **3.** work additional to one's usual job or duties: *The young lawyer's sideline is coaching basketball.* **4.** a line of goods additional to that regularly sold by a store.

side·long (sīd′lông′) *adj.* directed to the side: *The boy gave her a sidelong glance.* —*adv.* toward the side.

si·de·re·al (sī dēr′ē əl) *adj.* **1.** of or relating to the stars. **2.** determined or measured by means of the stars.

sidereal year, see **year** (*def. 3*).

side·sad·dle (sīd′sad′əl) *n.* a woman's saddle made so that the rider sits with both legs on the same side of the horse. —*adv.* on a sidesaddle.

side·show (sīd′shō′) *n.* a show connected to or part of a larger entertainment or exhibition.

side·step (sīd′step′) *v.*, **side·stepped, side·step·ping.** —*v.t.* to avoid by or as if by stepping aside: *to sidestep a decision.* —*v.i.* **1.** to step to one side. **2.** to avoid a responsibility, decision, or difficulty. —**side′step′per,** *n.*

side·stroke (sīd′strōk′) *n.* a swimming stroke performed while the swimmer lies on his side and extends one arm forward while pushing backward with the other.

side·swipe (sīd′swīp′) *v.t.,* **side·swiped, side·swip·ing.** to strike with a blow along the side, as in passing: *The truck sideswiped a parked car when it skidded.* —*n.* a blow made on or along the side.

side·track (sīd′trak′) *v.t.* **1.** to turn aside from what is most important: *He was sidetracked by the television show and didn't finish his homework.* **2.** to shift (a train) to a siding. —*n.* a railroad siding.

side·walk (sīd′wôk′) *n.* a walk along the side of a street or road for pedestrians.

side·ward (sīd′wərd) *adj.* moving or directed toward one side. —*adv.* also, **sidewards.** toward one side.

side·ways (sīd′wāz′) *also,* **side·way, side·wise** (sīd′-wīz′). *adv.* **1.** toward or from one side. **2.** with one side forward: *He walked sideways through the narrow doorway.* —*adj.* moving or directed toward one side.

sid·ing (sī′ding) *n.* **1.** a short railroad track connected by a switch to a main track. **2.** wood, metal, or other material forming the outside covering of a frame building.

si·dle (sīd′əl) *v.i.,* **si·dled, si·dling.** to move sideways, especially in a sly manner. —*n.* a sideways movement.

siege (sēj) *n.* **1.** the surrounding of a fortified enemy position for a long period of time in order to cut off supplies and force surrender. **2.** any long attempt to overcome something. **3.** a long, distressing or tiring period, as of illness: *a siege of pneumonia.*

Sieg·fried (sēg′frēd′) *n. Germanic Legend.* a hero who killed a dragon and gained a golden treasure.

si·en·na (sē en′ə) *n.* **1.** brown earth used as a yellowish-brown pigment in its natural state (**raw sienna**) or as a reddish-brown pigment after being roasted (**burnt sienna**). **2.** a yellowish-brown or reddish-brown color. —*adj.* having the color sienna; yellowish-brown or reddish-brown.

si·er·ra (sē er′ə) *n.* a chain of rugged hills or mountains with sharp, jagged peaks that look like the teeth of a saw.

Si·er·ra Le·o·ne (sē er′ə lē ō′nē) a country on the western coast of Africa. Capital, Freetown. Area, 27,925 sq. mi. Pop. (1980), 3,474,000.

Si·er·ra Ma·dre (sē er′ə mä′drā) a mountain system in eastern and western Mexico.

Si·er·ra Ne·vad·a (sē er′ə nə vad′ə, sē er′ə nə-vä′də) a mountain range in eastern California.

si·es·ta (sē es′tə) *n.* an afternoon nap or rest, especially one taken during the hottest part of the day in Spain and certain other hot countries.

sieve (siv) *n.* a utensil or device having a bottom made of wire mesh or with holes punched into it, used for sifting or draining. —*v.t.,* **sieved, siev·ing.** to pass (a substance) through a sieve; sift.

sift (sift) *v.t.* **1.** to separate by passing through a sieve: *to sift sand from gravel.* **2.** to remove lumps from or make lighter by passing through a sieve: *to sift flour.* **3.** to sprin-

kle by shaking through a sieve: *to sift sugar over doughnuts.* **4.** to examine closely: *to sift evidence.* —*v.i.* **1.** to sift something. **2.** to fall loosely as if through a sieve: *Dust sifted through the cracks.* —**sift′er,** *n.*

sigh (sī) *v.i.* **1.** to make a long, deep breathing sound, as from sadness, weariness, or relief. **2.** to make a sound like that of a sigh: *The wind sighed in the rafters of the old barn.* **3.** to wish earnestly; yearn; long: *The old man sighed for the days of his youth.* —*v.t.* to express with a sigh. —*n.* the act or sound of sighing. —**sigh′er,** *n.*

sight (sīt) *n.* **1.** the faculty or power of seeing; vision: *His sight improved when he started wearing glasses.* **2.** the act or instance of seeing: *The sight of the strangers frightened the child. He recognized her at first sight.* **3.** the range of one's vision: *Keep the candy out of the children's sight.* **4.** something seen; view: *The sunset was a beautiful sight.* **5.** *usually,* **sights.** something striking or worth seeing: *John enjoyed the sights in New York.* **6.** personal judgment or opinion; regard: *In her sight, Paul can do nothing wrong.* **7.** any of various devices used as an aid in observing or aiming, as on a surveying instrument or firearm: *He adjusted the sight on his rifle.* **8.** *Informal.* something messy or unpleasant to look at: *The room was a sight after the party.* —*v.t.* **1.** to perceive with the eyes; see: *After hiking for hours, we finally sighted a clearing in the forest.* **2.** to aim by means of a sight or sights.

at sight or **on sight.** as soon as seen; immediately: *We bought the house at sight.*

sight·less (sīt′lis) *adj.* unable to see; blind. —**sight′-less·ness,** *n.*

sight·ly (sīt′lē) *adj.,* **sight·li·er, sight·li·est. 1.** pleasing to the eye; comely. **2.** presenting a fine view. —**sight′li-ness,** *n.*

sight·se·er (sīt′sē′ər) *n.* a person who visits places of interest; tourist.

sight·see·ing (sīt′sē′ing) *n.* the act or instance of visiting places of interest. —*adj.* used for or engaged in visiting places of interest: *a sightseeing bus, a sightseeing tour.*

sign (sīn) *n.* **1.** something that stands for, shows, or suggests some state, quality, condition, or feeling: *There were signs of wear on the carpet. His failure to write her a letter is no sign that he has forgotten her.* **2.** a motion, gesture, or action that expresses an idea or gives a command or warning: *His nod was a sign that he agreed with us.* **3.** a lettered plate, board, or the like, bearing a notice or advertisement: *The sign on the door said "Closed for the day."* **4.** something that stands for an object, relationship, idea, or the like; symbol: *The dove is a sign of peace.* **5.** a warning or indication of what is to come; portent; omen. **6.** a trace: *There is no sign of him anywhere.* **7.** one of the twelve divisions of the zodiac: *Jim's sign is Libra.* —*v.t.* **1.** to put one's signature to (something), especially to confirm or show agreement: *If the artist signed the painting, it must be genuine.* **2.** to put as a signature: *She signed her name to the document.* **3.** to hire by means of a contract or other written agreement: *The team signed the star quarterback for the year.* —*v.i.* **1.** to write one's signature: *She signed on the bottom of the page.* **2.** to accept employment or be hired by means of a contract or other written agreement. —**sign′er,** *n.*

at; āpe; cär; end; mē; it; īce; hot; ōld; fôrk; wood; fо̄оl; oil; out; up; turn; sing; thin; **this**; hw in white; zh in treasure. The symbol ə stands for the sound of **a** in about, **e** in taken, **i** in pencil, **o** in lemon, and **u** in circus.

S

to sign off. to cease television or radio transmission for the day.

to sign up. to join an organization or group, especially a branch of military service.

sig·nal (sig′nəl) *n.* **1.** something that serves to warn, direct, inform, or instruct: *The flashing light was a signal that a train was coming.* **2.** an action or happening that serves to bring about or stir up something: *The king's harsh edict was a signal for revolt.* **3.** an electric current that transmits sounds or pictures to receiving equipment. —*v.,* **sig·naled, sig·nal·ing;** *also, British,* **sig·nalled, sig·nal·ling.** —*v.t.* **1.** to make a signal or signals to: *He signaled a passing ship for help.* **2.** to communicate or make known by a signal or signals: *The bugler signaled a retreat.* —*v.i.* to make a signal or signals. —*adj.* **1.** used as a signal: *a signal light.* **2.** remarkable; striking; notable: *a signal event.*

sig·nal·ize (sig′nə līz′) *v.t.,* **sig·nal·ized, sig·nal·iz·ing. 1.** to make notable or striking. **2.** to point out clearly.

sig·nal·ly (sig′nə lē) *adv.* in a signal manner; remarkably; notably.

sig·nal·man (sig′nəl mən, sig′nəl man′) *n. pl.,* **sig·nal·men** (sig′nəl mən, sig′nəl men′). a person whose job is sending signals, as on a railroad or ship, or in the armed forces.

sig·na·ture (sig′nə chər) *n.* **1.** the name of a person, or a mark representing his or her name, written in his or her own handwriting. **2.** a melody, sound effect, or visual effect that identifies a radio or television program. **3.** *Music.* a symbol or group of symbols at the beginning of a staff to indicate pitch or meter.

sign·board (sīn′bôrd′) *n.* a board bearing a notice or advertisement.

sig·net (sig′nit) *n.* **1.** a small seal, especially one used to stamp a document. **2.** an impression made by a signet.

sig·nif·i·cance (sig nif′i kəns) *n.* **1.** the state or quality of having special value or importance: *The fact of his winning the contest has little significance for his friends.* **2.** something that is meant; meaning: *What is the significance of her statement?*

sig·nif·i·cant (sig nif′i kənt) *adj.* **1.** having special value or importance: *a significant event.* **2.** having a meaning; signifying something. **3.** having or expressing a special or hidden meaning; suggestive: *a significant look.* —**sig·nif′i·cant·ly,** *adv.*

sig·ni·fi·ca·tion (sig′nə fi kā′shən) *n.* **1.** something that is meant; meaning: *the signification of a word.* **2.** the act of signifying; communication.

sig·ni·fy (sig′nə fī′) *v.,* **sig·ni·fied, sig·ni·fy·ing.** —*v.t.* **1.** to be a sign, symbol, or indication of; represent; mean: *Her smile signified her happiness.* **2.** to show by signs, speech, or actions: *He signified his disapproval by frowning.* —*v.i.* to be of importance; matter.

sign language, a system of communication in which gestures are used instead of speech. Sign language is used especially by the deaf.

si·gnor (sēn′yôr) *also,* **si·gnior.** *n. pl.,* **si·gnors** or **si·gno·ri** (sēn yôr′ē). mister; sir. ▲ the Italian form of respectful or polite address for a man, usually used before the name.

si·gno·ra (sēn yôr′ə) *n. pl.,* **si·gno·re** (sēn yôr′ā). mistress; lady. ▲ the Italian form of respectful or polite address for a married woman.

si·gno·re (sēn yôr′ā) *n. pl.,* **si·gno·ri** (sēn yôr′ē). mister; sir. ▲ the Italian form of respectful or polite address for a man, used in direct address without the name.

si·gno·ri·na (sēn′yô rē′nə) *n. pl.,* **si·gno·ri·ne** (sēn′yô rē′nā). miss. ▲ the Italian form of respectful or polite address for an unmarried girl or woman.

Sikh (sēk) *n.* a follower of a religion developed about A.D. 1500 that combines elements of both Hinduism and Islam.

Sik·kim (sik′im, si kēm′) *n.* a state of India in the Himalayas of south-central Asia. Capital, Gangtok. Area, 2745 sq. mi. Pop. (1973 est.), 210,000.

si·lage (sī′lij) *n.* green fodder that has been stored in a silo to ferment. Also, **ensilage.**

si·lence (sī′ləns) *n.* **1.** the absence of sound; complete quiet; stillness. **2.** the state of being or keeping silent: *to listen in silence.* —*v.t.,* **si·lenced, si·lenc·ing. 1.** to cause to be or keep silent; bring to silence: *to silence a noisy classroom.* **2.** to put a stop to; suppress: *The dictator tried to silence the critics of his government.*

si·lenc·er (sī′lən sər) *n.* **1.** a person or thing that silences. **2.** a device shaped like a tube and attached to the front of a gun barrel to deaden the sound of the gun being fired.

si·lent (sī′lənt) *adj.* **1.** marked by the absence of sound; completely quiet; still: *We went into the silent forest.* **2.** not speaking or making a sound: *He remained silent during the church service.* **3.** not given to speaking; taciturn: *He was a shy, silent boy.* **4.** not uttered or expressed; unspoken: *There was much silent opposition to the new rules.* **5.** free from activity; inactive: *A silent volcano was located in the center of the island.* **6.** (of a motion picture) having no sound track. **7.** (of a letter) not pronounced in speech, as the *k* in *know* or the *e* in *give.* —**si′lent·ly,** *adv.*

Si·le·sia (si lē′zhə, sī lē′zhə) *n.* a historic region in southwestern Poland and northern Czechoslovakia. —**Si·le′sian,** *adj., n.*

sil·hou·ette (sil′ōō et′) *n.* **1.** the outline of a figure or object filled in with a solid color, usually black. **2.** a dark outline seen against a lighter background. —*v.t.,* **sil·hou·et·ted, sil·hou·et·ting.** to cause to appear in or as if in a silhouette. [From Etienne de *Silhouette,* 1709–1767, a French minister of finance noted for his petty economic policies; probably because silhouettes were cheaper than painted portraits.]

sil·i·ca (sil′i kə) *n.* a hard, transparent mineral that resembles glass, occurring naturally as quartz. It is used in the manufacture of glass and ceramics.

sil·i·cate (sil′ə kit, sil′ə kāt′) *n.* any of various compounds containing silicon, oxygen, metal, and sometimes hydrogen. Window glass and bricks are made of silicates.

sil·i·con (sil′i kən) *n.* a nonmetallic element that exists in its pure state as either brown powder or as dark gray or black crystals. Silicon is the second most abundant element in the earth's crust. Symbol: Si

sil·i·cone (sil′i kōn′) *n.* any of various compounds composed of chains of silicon and oxygen atoms to which organic radicals are attached. Silicones are used as oils, plastics, and synthetic rubbers and in various industrial processes because they are unaffected by extremes of temperature.

silk (silk) *n.* **1.** a soft, shiny fiber spun by silkworms. **2.** a strong, shiny fabric made from these fibers, used for such items as scarves, ties, and blouses. **3.** anything like silk in appearance or texture. —*adj.* of, resembling, or relating to silk.

silk·en (sil′kən) *adj.* **1.** made of silk. **2.** like silk in appearance or texture; silky: *Joan has long, silken black hair.*

silk·worm (silk′wurm′) *n.* the larva, or caterpillar, of a moth originally domesticated in China. The cocoon that it spins is the source of silk thread.

silk·y (sil′kē) *adj.,* **silk·i·er, silk·i·est.** like silk in appearance or texture; smooth, soft, and lustrous. —**silk′i·ly,** *adv.* —**silk′i·ness,** *n.*

sill (sil) *n.* **1.** the part across the bottom of a door or window. **2.** a horizontal beam that forms the foundation of a structure.

sil·ly (sil′ē) *adj.*, **sil·li·er, sil·li·est. 1.** lacking in judgment or common sense; stupid: *a silly person.* **2.** absurd; ridiculous: *a silly notion.* **3.** *Informal.* stunned; dazed, as by a blow: *The blast knocked him silly.* —**sil′li·ness,** *n.*

si·lo (sī′lō) *n. pl.,* **si·los. 1.** a tall, cylindrical tower of metal, concrete, or other material for the storage and fermentation of green fodder. **2.** a deep hole in the ground for storing and launching missiles.

silt (silt) *n.* fine sand, clay, or similar matter carried by water and deposited as sediment. —*v.t.* to fill or choke (something) with silt: *Heavy rains silted the river.* —*v.i.* to become filled or choked with silt. —**silt′y,** *adj.*

Si·lu·ri·an (si loor′ē ən) *n.* the third geological period of the Paleozoic era, during which the first land plants appeared. —*adj.* of, relating to, or characteristic of this period.

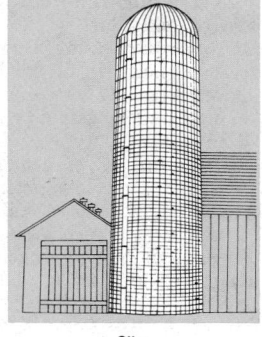

Silo

sil·van (sil′vən) another spelling of **sylvan.**

sil·ver (sil′vər) *n.* **1.** a shiny, white metallic element that is soft and easily shaped, and is the best conductor of heat and electricity of any metal. In the form of alloys, it is used especially in the manufacture of coins, jewelry, and tableware. Symbol: **Ag 2.** this metal used as a commodity or as a standard of currency. **3.** coins, especially those made from silver; change. **4.** articles made of or coated with a thin layer of silver, such as tableware. **5.** the color of silver. —*adj.* **1.** made of or coated with a thin layer of silver: *silver spoons.* **2.** like silver, as in color or shine: *silver paint.* **3.** of or marking the twenty-fifth year or event in a series: *a silver wedding anniversary.* —*v.t.* **1.** to coat with a thin layer of silver. **2.** to give (something) the color or shine of silver: *Age had silvered her hair.* —*v.i.* to become silver or silvery in color.

sil·ver·fish (sil′vər fish′) *n. pl.,* **sil·ver·fish** or **sil·ver·fish·es.** a small white or gray wingless insect. It is a common household pest that feeds on wallpaper, bookbindings, and other starchy materials.

sil·ver·plate (sil′vər plāt′) *v.t.,* **sil·ver·plat·ed, sil·ver·plat·ing.** to coat with a thin layer of silver.

silver plate, articles made of silver or coated with a thin layer of silver, such as tableware.

sil·ver·smith (sil′vər smith′) *n.* a person who makes or repairs articles of silver.

sil·ver·tongued (sil′vər tungd′) *adj.* smooth and effective in speech; eloquent: *a silver-tongued orator.*

sil·ver·ware (sil′vər wer′) *n.* **1.** articles made of silver or coated with a thin layer of silver, especially tableware. **2.** table utensils made of metal other than silver.

sil·ver·y (sil′vər ē) *adj.* **1.** having the shiny whiteness of silver. **2.** having a soft and clear musical sound. **3.** made of or coated with a layer of silver. —**sil′ver·i·ness,** *n.*

sim·i·an (sim′ē ən) *adj.* of, relating to, or resembling an ape or monkey. —*n.* an ape or monkey.

sim·i·lar (sim′ə lər) *adj.* **1.** having or bearing a marked resemblance; alike: *The designs of the two houses were similar.* **2.** *Geometry.* having corresponding angles that are equal, and corresponding sides that are in proportion: *similar triangles.* —**sim′i·lar·ly,** *adv.*

sim·i·lar·i·ty (sim′ə lar′ə tē) *n. pl.,* **sim·i·lar·i·ties. 1.** the quality or state of being similar; likeness. **2.** an instance or point of likeness: *There are many similarities between the two brothers.*

sim·i·le (sim′ə lē) *n.* a figure of speech in which one object or idea is compared with another in order to suggest that they are alike. For example: *His face shone like the sun. Her hands were as cold as ice.*

si·mil·i·tude (si mil′ə tōōd′, si mil′ə tyōōd′) *n.* similarity; likeness.

sim·mer (sim′ər) *v.i.* **1.** (of a liquid or something in a liquid) to cook at, or just below, the boiling point. **2.** to make a murmuring sound, as a liquid does when it begins to boil. **3.** to be on the verge of breaking forth: *to simmer with anger.* —*v.t.* to cook at, or just below, the boiling point. —*n.* the state or process of simmering.

  to simmer down. a. to become calm: *After the argument, Tom simmered down.* **b.** to reduce the amount of liquid by boiling slowly: *She simmered the sauce down for ten minutes.*

Si·mon Peter (sī′mən) see **Peter** *(def. 1).*

si·mo·ny (sī′mə nē, sim′ə nē) *n.* the act or practice of buying or selling sacred things, such as promotions or positions in the church. [From *Simon* Magus, who tried to buy a power given by God to the apostles.]

si·moom (si mōōm′) *also,* **si·moon** (si mōōn′). *n.* a hot, dry, sandy wind of the Arabian and African deserts.

sim·per (sim′pər) *v.i.* to smile in a silly, self-conscious way. —*n.* a silly, self-conscious smile.

sim·ple (sim′pəl) *adj.*, **sim·pler, sim·plest. 1.** easily done, used, or understood: *a simple task, a simple arithmetic problem.* **2.** consisting of only one part or one unit; unmixed: *simple facts, a simple substance.* **3.** with nothing added; mere; pure: *the simple truth.* **4.** without ornament; unadorned; plain: *a simple style of writing, a simple design.* **5.** without pride or sophistication; artless; natural: *a simple and unaffected person.* **6.** straightforward; honest; sincere: *a simple heart, a simple manner.* **7.** without rank; humble or common: *a simple laborer, a simple citizen.* **8.** lacking in judgment or common sense; foolish. —**sim′ple·ness,** *n.*

simple fraction, another term for **common fraction.**

simple machine, one of the basic devices used as an aid in doing work. The lever, the wheel and axle, the inclined plane, the wedge, and the screw are simple machines.

sim·ple·mind·ed (sim′pəl mīn′did) *adj.* **1.** uneducated, foolish, or stupid. **2.** weakminded. **3.** unsophisticated; artless.

simple sentence, a sentence made up of one independent clause without a dependent clause. For example: *He walks quickly.*

sim·ple·ton (sim′pəl tən) *n.* a silly or stupid person; fool.

sim·plic·i·ty (sim plis′ə tē) *n. pl.,* **sim·plic·i·ties. 1.** the state or quality of being simple. **2.** a lack of ornament; plainness: *Her clothes show simplicity and good taste.* **3.** straightforwardness; sincerity. **4.** a lack of common sense; foolishness or stupidity.

sim·pli·fi·ca·tion (sim′plə fi kā′shən) *n.* **1.** the act of simplifying or the state of being simplified. **2.** a result of this.

sim·pli·fy (sim′plə fī′) *v.t.,* **sim·pli·fied, sim·pli·fy·ing.** to make simple: *to simplify an arithmetic problem, to simplify a design.* —**sim′pli·fi′er,** *n.*

S

at; āpe; cär; end; mē; it; īce; hot; ōld; fôrk; wood; fōōl; oil; out; up; turn; sing; thin; **th**is; hw in white; zh in treasure. The symbol ə stands for the sound of **a** in about, **e** in taken, **i** in pencil, **o** in lemon, and **u** in circus.

sim·ply (sim′plē) *adv.* **1.** in a clear, unpretentious, or straightforward manner: *He spoke simply and to the point.* **2.** without ornament; plainly: *The room was decorated simply.* **3.** merely; only: *Answering his call is simply a matter of politeness.* **4.** to the fullest or highest degree; absolutely: *Louise is simply lovely.*

sim·u·late (sim′yə lāt′) *v.t.,* **sim·u·lat·ed, sim·u·lat·ing. 1.** to give the false appearance of; pretend: *to simulate grief.* **2.** to have the appearance of; imitate: *That painted panel simulates marble.* —**sim′u·la′tive,** *adj.* —**sim′u·la′tor,** *n.*

sim·u·la·tion (sim′yə lā′shən) *n.* **1.** the act or process of simulating. **2.** something that simulates; imitation.

si·mul·ta·ne·ous (sī′məl tā′nē əs) *adj.* existing, happening, or done at the same time: *simultaneous events.* —**si′mul·ta′ne·ous·ly,** *adv.*

sin (sin) *n.* **1.** the willful breaking of God's law. **2.** an instance of this. **3.** any offense: *It's a sin to be cruel to animals.* —*v.i.,* **sinned, sin·ning. 1.** to break God's law; commit sin. **2.** to commit an offense of any kind.

sin, sine.

Si·nai (sī′nī) *n.* **1.** a desert area extending southward from the Mediterranean Sea to the northern end of the Red Sea. Also, **Sinai Peninsula. 2. Mount.** in the Old Testament, the mountain on which Moses received the Ten Commandments.

since (sins) *adv.* **1.** from then till now: *John left last week and has been away ever since.* **2.** at some time between then and now: *Ted was sick last month but has since recovered.* —*prep.* **1.** continuously after the time of: *Joyce has been gone since five o'clock.* **2.** during the time following: *There have been many changes in the town since my father's boyhood.* —*conj.* **1.** during the period following the time when: *They haven't seen Gregory since he graduated.* **2.** continuously from the time when: *Betty has lived abroad since she was a young girl.* **3.** in view of the fact that; because: *Since the car isn't working, we'll have to take a bus.*

sin·cere (sin sēr′) *adj.,* **sin·cer·er, sin·cer·est.** without falseness; honest; true: *a sincere wish, a sincere friend.* —**sin·cere′ly,** *adv.*

sin·cer·i·ty (sin ser′ə tē) *n.* the state or quality of being sincere.

sine (sīn) *n.* (of either acute angle of a right triangle) the ratio of the length of the side opposite the angle to the length of the hypotenuse.

si·ne·cure (sī′nə kyoor′, sin′ə kyoor′) *n.* a position or job that demands little or no work or responsibility, especially one with a good salary.

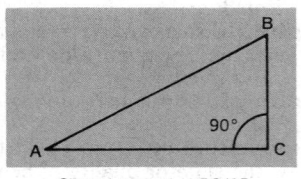

Sine of angle *A* = *BC/AB*

sin·ew (sin′yoō) *n.* **1.** a tendon. **2.** muscular power or strength. **3.** *also,* **sinews.** a source of power or strength.

sin·ew·y (sin′yoō ē) *adj.* **1.** characteristic of or containing sinews; tough; stringy: *a sinewy cut of meat.* **2.** physically strong or powerful; muscular.

sin·ful (sin′fəl) *adj.* full of or marked by sin; wicked; corrupt. —**sin′ful·ly,** *adv.* —**sin′ful·ness,** *n.*

sing (sing) *v.,* **sang** or **sung, sung, sing·ing.** —*v.i.* **1.** to utter words or sounds with musical tones; perform a song: *She sings beautifully.* **2.** to produce musical sounds: *The birds sang in the trees.* **3.** to tell of or praise something in song or verse: *The poet sang of the army's great victory.* **4.** to make a whistling, ringing, or humming sound: *The steam sang as it escaped from the pipe.* —*v.t.* **1.** to utter or perform with musical tones: *The whole class sang a Christmas carol.* **2.** to bring to a particular

state or condition by or with singing: *to sing a child to sleep.* **3.** to recite in a singing voice; intone: *The priest sang a psalm during the church service.* **4.** to proclaim enthusiastically: *She has sung your praises ever since she met you.* —*n.* a gathering of people for the purpose of singing together: *We went to the community sing.*

to sing out. *Informal.* to call or cry out loudly.

sing., singular.

Sin·ga·pore (sing′ə pôr′) *n.* **1.** an island country off the southern tip of the Malay Peninsula. Capital, Singapore. Area, 224 sq. mi. Pop. (1980), 2,427,000. **2.** the capital and largest city of this country. Pop. (1978 est.), 2,334,400.

singe (sinj) *v.t.,* **singed, singe·ing. 1.** to burn slightly: *The hot iron singed her dress.* **2.** to burn the ends or tips of (hair). **3.** to remove feathers or bristles from by burning: *The butcher singed the turkey before putting it out for sale.* —*n.* **1.** the act of singeing. **2.** a slight burn.

sing·er (sing′ər) *n.* **1.** a person who sings, especially a trained or professional vocalist. **2.** a bird that sings.

Sin·gha·lese (sing′gə lēz′) *n. pl.,* **Sin·gha·lese. 1.** a person who was born or is living in Sri Lanka, or Ceylon. **2.** the language spoken in this country. —*adj.* of or relating to Sri Lanka, its people, or their language.

sin·gle (sing′gəl) *adj.* **1.** only one: *A single chair stood against the wall. He tore a single page from his notebook.* **2.** of or designed for the use of one person only: *He asked for a single room at the hotel.* **3.** not married. —*n.* **1.** a single person or thing. **2.** something that is for one person only, such as a hotel room or a ticket. **3.** *Baseball.* a hit that allows the batter to reach first base safely. **4. singles.** a match between two persons, as in tennis. —*v.,* **sin·gled, sin·gling.** —*v.t.* to select or separate from others: *Mary singled out the black cat as her favorite.* —*v.i. Baseball.* to hit a single. —**sin′gle·ness,** *n.*

sin·gle-breast·ed (sing′gəl bres′tid) *adj.* (of clothes, especially coats or jackets) having a row of buttons or other fastenings on one side only.

single file, a line of persons or things one behind another.

sin·gle-hand·ed (sing′gəl han′did) *adj.* without the help or support of anyone. —**sin′gle-hand′ed·ly,** *adv.*

sin·gle-mind·ed (sing′gəl mīn′did) *adj.* having only one aim or purpose. —**sin′gle-mind′ed·ly,** *adv.* —**sin′gle-mind′ed·ness,** *n.*

sin·gle·tree (sing′gəl trē′) *n.* another word for **whiffle-tree.**

sin·gly (sing′glē) *adv.* **1.** one at a time; individually; separately: *to consider each item singly.* **2.** without the aid of another or others; single-handedly.

sing·song (sing′sông′) *n.* **1.** a monotonous rhythm or tone, as in speaking. **2.** verse, song, or speech marked by this. —*adj.* having a monotonous rhythm or tone.

sin·gu·lar (sing′gyə lər) *adj.* **1.** out of the ordinary; unusual or remarkable; extraordinary: *a singular diamond ring, a singular event.* **2.** strange or peculiar; odd: *singular behavior.* **3.** of or relating to a grammatical form showing only one person or thing: *"Am" is a singular verb.* —*n.* the form of a word showing only one person or thing.

sin·gu·lar·i·ty (sing′gyə lar′ə tē) *n. pl.,* **sin·gu·lar·i·ties. 1.** the state or quality of being singular. **2.** something that is singular.

sin·is·ter (sin′is tər) *adj.* **1.** threatening or suggesting evil; ominous: *The dark old house looked sinister at night.* **2.** malicious or evil: *a sinister plot, a sinister laugh.* [Latin *sinister* left; referring to the ancient belief that the left side was unlucky.]

sink (singk) *v.,* **sank** or **sink, sunk** or **sunk·en, sink·ing.** —*v.i.* **1.** to go down below a surface partially or completely: *The wheels of the car sank into the mud. The ship sank after the collision.* **2.** to go down or appear to go down to a lower level, especially gradually: *The water in the pond sank three feet last summer. The sun sank behind the mountain.* **3.** to become less, as in volume, force, degree, or intensity: *The sick man's voice sank to a whisper.* **4.** to become less in value; decline: *His reputation has sunk in our opinion.* **5.** to pass or fall gradually into a certain state or condition: *Bob sank into a deep sleep.* **6.** to penetrate deeply: *The stain sank into the cloth.* —*v.t.* **1.** to cause to go down below a surface: *A sudden storm sank the ship.* **2.** to cause to go down to a lower level. **3.** to make less, as in volume, force, degree, or intensity. **4.** to excavate or dig: *Dad sank a well behind the house.* **5.** to force, lay, or bury in the ground: *The workmen sank a pipeline.* **6.** *Basketball.* to toss (the ball) into the basket. **7.** *Golf.* to putt (the ball) into the hole. —*n.* **1.** a basin of metal or porcelain, usually connected to a water supply, used for washing. **2.** a low area or hollow in a land surface where water collects. —**sink′a·ble,** *adj.*

sink·er (sing′kər) *n.* **1.** a person or thing that sinks. **2.** a weight used to sink a fishing line.

sink·hole (singk′hōl′) *n.* a hole worn straight down in rock, especially limestone, by dripping water.

sin·less (sin′lis) *adj.* free from sin; without sin. —**sin′·less·ly,** *adv.* —**sin′less·ness,** *n.*

sin·ner (sin′ər) *n.* a person who sins.

Sino- *combining form* Chinese: *Sino-Soviet relations.*

sin·u·os·i·ty (sin′yōō os′ə tē) *n. pl.,* **sin·u·os·i·ties.** **1.** the state or quality of being sinuous. **2.** a curve or bend.

sin·u·ous (sin′yōō əs) *adj.* full of curves or bends: *a sinuous line, the sinuous course of a river.* —**sin′u·ous·ly,** *adv.* —**sin′u·ous·ness,** *n.*

si·nus (sī′nəs) *n. pl.,* **si·nus·es.** any of the air-filled cavities connected with the nostrils in the bones of the face.

si·nus·i·tis (sī′nə sī′tis) *n.* the inflammation of a sinus or sinuses.

Si·on (sī′ən) another spelling of **Zion.**

Siou·an (sōō′ən) *n.* **1.** a family of North American Indian languages, including the Sioux, Osage, and Crow. **2.** see **Sioux** *(def. 1).* —*adj.* of or relating to this language family.

Sioux (sōō) *n. pl.,* **Sioux** (sōō, sōōz). **1.** a member of a group of North American Indian tribes that speak a Siouan language, formerly living in Minnesota, North and South Dakota, and Wyoming. **2.** see **Dakota** *(def. 3).* **3.** the Siouan language spoken by these tribes.

Sioux City, a city in western Iowa, on the Missouri River. Pop. (1970), 85,925.

sip (sip) *v.t., v.i.,* **sipped, sip·ping.** to drink a very small amount of (a liquid) at a time; drink little by little: *George sipped the hot coffee.* —*n.* **1.** the amount of liquid sipped at one time. **2.** the act of sipping.

si·phon (sī′fən) *also,* **sy·phon.** *n.* a bent tube with one side longer than the other, used to transfer a liquid from one container to another one at a lower level by means of atmospheric pressure. —*v.t.* to draw off through or as through a siphon. —*v.i.* to pass through a siphon.

sir (sur) *n.* **1.** mister. ▲ a form of respectful or polite address used in place of the name of a man: *May I help you, sir?* **2. Sir.** title and form of address for a knight or baronet.

sire (sīr) *n.* **1.** the male parent of an animal, such as a horse. **2.** a father or forefather. **3. Sire.** ▲ a form of address used in speaking to a king or noble. —*v.t.,* **sired, sir-**

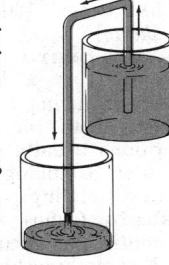

Siphon

ing. to be the male parent of: *Our next-door neighbor's dog sired a litter of puppies.*

si·ren (sī′rən) *n.* **1.** a device for making a loud, shrill sound by the escape of compressed air through a rotating shutter, used as a signal or warning: *an air raid siren, a police siren.* **2. Siren.** *Greek Mythology.* one of several sea nymphs, part bird and part woman, whose singing lured sailors to their destruction. **3.** a charming, but dangerous woman.

Sir·i·us (sir′ē əs) *n.* the brightest star seen in the heavens. Also, **Dog Star.**

sir·loin (sur′loin′) *n.* a cut of beef from the upper part of the loin.

si·roc·co (si rok′ō) *n. pl.,* **si·roc·cos.** **1.** a hot, dry wind blowing northward from North Africa across the Mediterranean Sea and into southern Europe, where it becomes warm and humid. **2.** any hot, oppressive wind.

sir·rah (sir′ə) *n. Archaic.* fellow. ▲ form of address used to show contempt for a man or boy.

sir·up (sir′əp, sur′əp) another spelling of **syrup.**

sis (sis) *n. Informal.* sister.

sis·al (sī′səl, sis′əl) *n.* **1.** a coarse, strong fiber obtained from the leaves of any of several tropical American plants, used to make rope and bags. Also, **sisal hemp. 2.** the plant yielding this fiber.

sis·sy (sis′ē) *n. pl.,* **sis·sies. 1.** a boy or man whose behavior is not manly. **2.** a coward.

sis·ter (sis′tər) *n.* **1.** a girl or woman having the same parents as another person of either sex. **2.** a fellow woman or girl. **3.** a woman who is a fellow member of a church, club, or sorority. **4.** a woman who is a member of a religious order for women; nun.

sis·ter·hood (sis′tər hood′) *n.* **1.** the state or quality of being a sister or sisters; relationship between sisters. **2.** a group of women united by some common aim or interest, or who are bound by vows to a religious organization.

sis·ter-in-law (sis′tər in lô′) *n. pl.,* **sis·ters-in-law. 1.** the sister of one's husband or wife. **2.** the wife of one's brother. **3.** the wife of one's husband's or wife's brother.

sis·ter·ly (sis′tər lē) *adj.* relating to, characteristic of, or befitting a sister; kind; affectionate. —**sis′ter·li·ness,** *n.*

Sis·tine Chapel (sis′tēn) a chapel in the Vatican in Rome, noted for its frescoes by Michelangelo.

Sis·y·phus (sis′ə fəs) *n. Greek Mythology.* a king noted for his craftiness, who was punished in the Underworld by having to push a huge rock to the top of a hill, from which it would roll back down, thus forcing him to begin again.

sit (sit) *v.,* **sat, sit·ting.** —*v.i.* **1.** to be in a position in which the weight of the body rests on the buttocks, while the rest of the body bends at the hips and knees. **2.** to rest on a perch; roost: *The bird sat on a branch.* **3.** (of a chicken) to cover eggs in order to hatch them; brood. **4.** to be placed: *The hut sits in the middle of a forest. Alex left his car sitting alongside the road.* **5.** to hold a particular pose for an artist or photographer; model: *to sit for a portrait.* **6.** to be or remain unused or inactive: *The store sat empty for a year.* **7.** to hold a session: *The legislature sits in the fall.* **8.** to bear down as a burden; weigh: *Old age sits lightly*

at; āpe; cär; end; mē; it; īce; hot; ōld; fôrk; wood; fōōl; oil; out; up; turn; sing; thin; this; hw in white; zh in treasure. The symbol ə stands for the sound of a in about, e in taken, i in pencil, o in lemon, and u in circus.

upon him. **9.** to fit: *The dress sits well on your shoulders.*
—*v.t.* **1.** to cause to sit; seat: *The hostess sat her guests around the table.* **2.** to keep one's seat on (a horse).

> **to sit in on.** to attend or take part in: *A newspaper reporter sat in on the committee meeting.*

> **to sit out.** to take no part in: *We sat out the last waltz.*

si·tar (si tär′) *n.* a stringed musical instrument of India, having a long neck and a rounded body, made from a gourd or hollowed-out wood, played by plucking the strings.

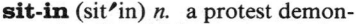

Sitar

sit-down strike (sit′doun′) a strike in which the strikers remain at their jobs but do not work until an agreement is reached.

site (sīt) *n.* **1.** the position or location of a town, city, building, or the like: *The village occupied a mountain site.* **2.** the place where something happened: *Gettysburg is the site of a major battle of the Civil War.*

sit-in (sit′in) *n.* a protest demonstration in which persons sit in a public place and stay there until they are forcibly removed. —*v.i.,* **sat-in, sitting-in.** to take part in a sit-in.

sit·ter (sit′ər) *n.* **1.** a person or thing that sits. **2.** see **baby-sitter.**

sit·ting (sit′ing) *n.* **1.** the act of a person or thing that sits. **2.** the period of time that a person sits for or is occupied with a particular purpose: *She ate the whole box of chocolates in one sitting.*

Sitting Bull, 1834?–1890, Sioux Indian chief.

sitting duck *Informal.* a person or thing that is very vulnerable; easy target.

sitting room, a room used for sitting, as in a home, hotel, or club.

sit·u·ate (sich′ōō āt′) *v.t.,* **sit·u·at·ed, sit·u·at·ing.** to give a position to; place: *to situate a house on top of a mountain.*

sit·u·a·tion (sich′ōō ā′shən) *n.* **1.** a condition or state of affairs: *He found himself in a difficult situation financially. What is the political situation in that country?* **2.** a location; position: *The situation of the barn is at the left of the house.* **3.** the work in which one is engaged or employed. —**sit′u·a′tion·al,** *adj.*

Si·va (sē′və, shē′və) another spelling of **Shiva.**

six (siks) *n. pl.,* **six·es. 1.** the cardinal number that is one more than five. **2.** a symbol representing this number, such as 6 or VI. **3.** something having this many units or things, such as a playing card. —*adj.* numbering one more than five.

six·fold (siks′fōld′) *adj.* **1.** six times as great or numerous. **2.** having or consisting of six parts. —*adv.* so as to be six times greater or more numerous: *The company's profits increased sixfold.*

Six Nations, see **Iroquois.**

six·pence (siks′pəns) *n.* a former coin of the United Kingdom, equal to six pennies.

six·shoot·er (siks′shōō′tər) *n. Informal.* a revolver that can be fired six times without being reloaded.

six·teen (siks′tēn′) *n.* **1.** the cardinal number that is six more than ten. **2.** a symbol representing this number, such as 16 or XVI. **3.** something having this many units or things. —*adj.* numbering six more than ten.

six·teenth (siks′tēnth′) *adj.* **1.** (the ordinal of sixteen) next after the fifteenth. **2.** being one of sixteen equal parts. —*n.* **1.** something that is next after the fifteenth. **2.** one of sixteen equal parts; 1/16.

sixteenth note *Music.* a note having one-sixteenth the time value of a whole note.

sixth (siksth) *adj.* **1.** (the ordinal of six) next after the fifth. **2.** being one of six equal parts. —*n.* **1.** something that is next after the fifth. **2.** one of six equal parts; 1/6. **3.** *Music.* **a.** a note that is a total of four whole steps and one half step above a given note. *A* is the sixth of *C.* **b.** an interval of four whole steps and one half step. **c.** a combination of two notes that are separated by this interval. —*adv.* in the sixth place.

sixth sense, an ability to know or sense things that seemingly exists over and above the five senses; intuition.

six·ti·eth (siks′tē ith) *adj.* **1.** (the ordinal of sixty) next after the fifty-ninth. **2.** being one of sixty equal parts. —*n.* **1.** something that is next after the fifty-ninth. **2.** one of sixty equal parts.

six·ty (siks′tē) *n. pl.,* **six·ties. 1.** the cardinal number that is six times ten. **2.** a symbol representing this number, such as 60 or LX. —*adj.* numbering six times ten.

siz·a·ble (sī′zə bəl) *also,* **size·a·ble.** *adj.* somewhat large: *a sizable house, a sizable donation.*

size¹ (sīz) *n.* **1.** the amount of length, breadth, or height that something has: *the size of a room, the size of a tree.* **2.** greatness of extent; bigness: *The only building of any size in our town is the courthouse.* **3.** amount or number: *the size of an inheritance.* **4.** a measurement for classifying a manufactured article according to size: *What size shoe do you wear?* **5.** *Informal.* the true state of affairs; actual circumstances: *That's the size of it.* —*v.t.,* **sized, siz·ing. 1.** to classify according to size. **2.** to make of a certain or required size: *The jeweler sized the ring to fit her finger.* [Middle English *size.*]

> **to size up.** to make an estimate; form an opinion of: *The congressman sized up the political situation before running for governor.*

size² (sīz) *n.* any of various glues or pastes used to coat or glaze the surface of a fabric or paper. —*v.t.,* **sized, siz·ing.** to treat or coat with size. [Of uncertain origin.]

sized (sīzd) *adj.* having a stated size. ▲ used in combination: *small-sized, full-sized.*

siz·zle (siz′əl) *v.i.,* **siz·zled, siz·zling. 1.** to make a hissing sound, especially when burning or frying. **2.** to be very hot: *It's sizzling outside.* —*n.* a hissing sound: *the sizzle of wet twigs burning.*

Skag·er·ak (skag′ə rak) *n.* a strait between Norway and Denmark, an arm of the North Sea.

skald (skôld) *n.* an ancient Scandinavian poet; bard.

skate¹ (skāt) *n.* **1.** see **ice skate. 2.** see **roller skate.** —*v.i.,* **skat·ed, skat·ing.** to glide or move along on skates. [Dutch *schaats.*] —**skat′er,** *n.*

skate² (skāt) *n. pl.,* **skates** or **skate.** a fish related to the shark and ray, found in warm and temperate seas, having two broad side fins that are shaped like wings. [Old Norse *skata.*]

skate·board (skāt′bôrd′) *n.* a low, flat board having wheels attached to the bottom, ridden usually with the rider balancing himself in a standing position.

Skate²

skein (skān) *n.* **1.** a continuous strand of yarn or thread coiled in a bundle. **2.** something like this: *a skein of hair.*

skel·e·tal (skel′ət əl) *adj.* of, relating to, forming, or like a skeleton.

skel·e·ton (skel′ət ən) *n.* **1.** the framework of bones supporting the body of an animal with a backbone. **2.** a supporting framework or structure, as of a building or ship. **3.** an outline, as of a literary work; sketch. **4.** *Informal.* a very thin or gaunt person or animal.

skeleton key, a key that opens a number of different locks.

skep·tic (skep′tik) *also,* **scep·tic.** *n.* **1.** a person who doubts or questions the truth of beliefs or conclusions accepted by most people. **2.** a person who tends to be doubtful or questioning, especially about the statements of others. **3.** a person who doubts religious beliefs.

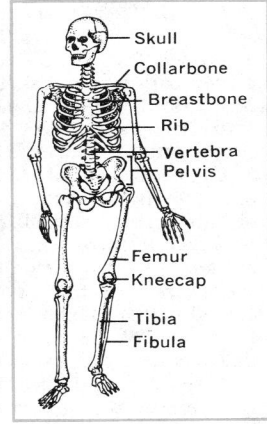
Human skeleton

Skull
Collarbone
Breastbone
Rib
Vertebra
Pelvis
Femur
Kneecap
Tibia
Fibula

skep·ti·cal (skep′ti kəl) *also,* **scep·ti·cal.** *adj.* **1.** characterized by or showing doubt; disbelieving. **2.** of, relating to, or characteristic of skeptics or skepticism. —**skep′ti·cal·ly,** *adv.*

skep·ti·cism (skep′tə siz′əm) *also,* **scep·ti·cism.** *n.* **1.** a doubting or questioning attitude or state of mind. **2.** doubt about religious beliefs.

sketch (skech) *n. pl.,* **sketch·es. 1.** a rough, unfinished, or quick drawing: *The artist made several sketches of the model before starting the painting.* **2.** a short description or plan giving the main features of something; outline. **3.** a brief, informal literary composition. **4.** a short scene or play, as in a revue, musical comedy, or other theatrical program. —*v.t.* to make a sketch of: *Jim sketched the old barn.* —*v.i.* to make a sketch or sketches. —**sketch′er,** *n.*

sketch·book (skech′book′) *n.* a pad or book used for sketching or drawing.

sketch·y (skech′ē) *adj.,* **sketch·i·er, sketch·i·est. 1.** not detailed or finished: *The artist did a sketchy drawing of the model.* **2.** incomplete or fragmentary; imperfect; slight: *The dazed driver could give only a sketchy account of the accident.* —**sketch′i·ly,** *adv.* —**sketch′i·ness,** *n.*

skew (skyoo) *v.i.* to veer away from a straight line; swerve; twist: *The railroad tracks skew to the left after crossing the river.* —*v.t.* **1.** to cause to turn aside from a straight line; set at an angle. **2.** to slant or twist the meaning of; distort: *The witness skewed his testimony.* —*adj.* **1.** having a part that turns aside from a straight line. **2.** not symmetrical. —*n.* a turning from a straight line.

skew·er (skyoo′ər) *n.* a long pin of wood or metal used to hold meat together while cooking. —*v.t.* to fasten or pierce with or as if with a skewer.

ski (skē) *n. pl.,* **skis** or **ski. 1.** one of a pair of long, narrow runners, usually of wood or metal, curving upward at the front and designed to be fastened to a boot for gliding over snow. **2.** see **water ski.** —*v.,* **skied, ski·ing.** —*v.i.* to glide or travel on skis, especially as a sport. —*v.t.* to glide or travel over on skis: *to ski a hill.* —**ski′er,** *n.*

skid (skid) *n.* **1.** the act of sliding or slipping, usually sideways, as over an icy or wet surface. **2.** a device, such as a wedge of wood or metal, placed against the wheel of a vehicle to prevent it from moving. **3.** a plank or frame used as a track on which something heavy may be slid or pushed along. **4.** a runner that is part of the landing gear of certain aircraft. —*v.,* **skid·ded, skid·ding.** —*v.i.* **1.** to slide or slip, usually sideways: *The airplane skidded on the wet runway.* **2.** (of a wheel or a moving vehicle) to slide without turning. —*v.t.* **1.** to prevent (a wheel) from

moving by applying a skid. **2.** to haul, slide, move, or place on a skid or skids.

on the skids. *Slang.* rapidly declining in power, value, quality, or prestige: *The actor's career was on the skids.*

skid row *Slang.* a section of a city where vagrants and derelicts live or gather, made up mostly of cheap rooming houses and bars.

skies (skīz) the plural of **sky.**

skiff (skif) *n.* a small, light boat propelled by motor, sail, or oars.

ski·ing (skē′ing) *n.* the act or sport of gliding or traveling on skis.

ski jump **1.** a steep snow-covered ramp, track, or course ending abruptly above a long, gentle slope, designed for long-distance jumping by skiers. **2.** a jump made by a skier over such a course.

ski lift, an apparatus for carrying skiers up a slope, usually consisting of a motor-operated cable with seats attached.

skill (skil) *n.* **1.** the power or ability to do something, resulting from training, practice, knowledge, or experience; proficiency: *She shows great skill in playing the violin.* **2.** a particular power or ability: *reading skills.*

skilled (skild) *adj.* **1.** having or showing skill or competence; proficient: *a skilled craftsman.* **2.** having or requiring special ability or training: *skilled labor.*

skil·let (skil′it) *n.* a shallow pan with a handle, used for frying; frying pan.

skill·ful (skil′fəl) *also,* British, **skil·ful.** *adj.* having, showing, or involving skill: *a skillful chess player.* —**skill′ful·ly,** *adv.* —**skill′ful·ness,** *n.*

skim (skim) *v.,* **skimmed, skim·ming. 1.** to remove floating matter from (a liquid): *The cook skimmed the soup while it simmered.* **2.** to remove (floating matter) from a liquid. **3.** to glance over or read quickly: *He skimmed the newspaper for a special article.* **4.** to move or glide lightly and swiftly over or across: *to skim across the ice.* **5.** to throw so as to glide or bounce lightly along a surface: *to skim a stone across a lake.* —*v.i.* **1.** to move or glide lightly and swiftly over or across a surface. **2.** to take a quick glance at something. —*adj.* that has been skimmed.

skim·mer (skim′ər) *n.* **1.** a person or thing that skims. **2.** a utensil, especially a shallow ladle having a wire mesh or a flat bowl punched with holes, used to skim liquids. **3.** any of various sea birds that are like gulls, chiefly having black or brown feathers. **4.** a wide-brimmed hat, usually of straw, with a flat crown.

Skimmer (def. 3)

skim milk *also,* **skimmed milk.** milk from which the cream has been removed.

skimp (skimp) *v.i.* to be very sparing or thrifty: *The cook skimped on the meat in the stew.* —*v.t.* **1.** to perform (a task) carelessly, hastily, or with poor material. **2.** to be very sparing or thrifty with: *Don't skimp the gravy on the mashed potatoes.*

skimp·y (skim′pē) *adj.,* **skimp·i·er, skimp·i·est. 1.** less than what is needed; not enough; scanty: *a skimpy supper.*

at; āpe; cär; end; mē; it; īce; hot; ōld; fôrk; wood; fo͞ol; oil; out; up; turn; sing; thin; th̲is; hw in white; zh in treasure. The symbol ə stands for the sound of **a** in about, **e** in taken, **i** in pencil, **o** in lemon, and **u** in circus.

2. very sparing or thrifty: *a skimpy person.* —**skimp′i·ly,** *adv.* —**skimp′i·ness,** *n.*

skin (skin) *n.* **1.** the outer covering of an animal's body. **2.** such an outer covering removed from an animal; pelt or hide. **3.** anything resembling skin in appearance, nature, or function: *the skin of an apple.* **4.** a container made of animal skin, used for holding liquids, especially wine. —*v.t.,* **skinned, skin·ning. 1.** to remove the skin from: *to skin a rabbit.* **2.** to injure the surface of or remove a portion of skin from, especially by scraping.

  by the skin of one's teeth. by a very small amount; barely: *He passed the test by the skin of his teeth.*

  to get under one's skin. *Informal.* to be or become annoying or irritating.

skin-deep (skin′dēp′) *adj.* only on the surface; superficial; shallow: *Beauty is only skin-deep.*

skin-dive (skin′dīv′) *v.i.,* **skin-dived** or **skin-dove** (skin′dōv′), **skin-dived, skin-div·ing.** to engage in skin diving.

skin diver, a person who skin-dives.

skin diving, underwater swimming for extended periods of time, usually with a face mask and flippers, and sometimes with oxygen tanks or a snorkel so that the swimmer can remain under water longer.

skin·flint (skin′flint′) *n.* a very stingy person; miser.

skin·ner (skin′ər) *n.* **1.** a person who deals in animal skins, especially one who removes and treats animal skins and furs. **2.** a driver of mules, horses, or other animals used for hauling loads.

skin·ny (skin′ē) *adj.,* **skin·ni·er, skin·ni·est.** very thin; lean. —**skin′ni·ness,** *n.*

skin·tight (skin′tīt′) *adj.* fitting tightly: *skintight pants.*

skip (skip) *v.,* **skipped, skip·ping.** —*v.i.* **1.** to spring or bound along, hopping lightly on one foot and then on the other: *The children skipped down the path.* **2.** to pass from one point to another, leaving out or paying little attention to what lies between: *to skip over a chapter in a book.* **3.** to bounce along or across a surface; skim. —*v.t.* **1.** to jump or spring lightly over: *to skip rope.* **2.** to leave out or pass over or by: *He skipped the math problems he couldn't do.* **3.** to cause to bounce along or across a surface; skim. **4.** *Informal.* to leave (a place) hurriedly or in secret: *The dishonest bank teller skipped town.* —*n.* **1.** a light springing, bounding, or jumping step. **2.** the act of passing over or leaving out.

skip·per¹ (skip′ər) *n.* the captain of a ship, especially of a small trading, fishing, or pleasure boat. [Middle Dutch *schipper.*]

skip·per² (skip′ər) *n.* **1.** a person or thing that skips. **2.** any of a group of butterflies that fly with quick, darting movements. [*Skip* + *-er¹.*]

skir·mish (skur′mish) *n.* **1.** a brief fight between small groups of persons or small bodies of troops. **2.** any brief or minor conflict. —*v.i.* to take part in a skirmish. —**skir′mish·er,** *n.*

skirt (skurt) *n.* **1.** a woman's or girl's garment that is fastened around the waist or hips and hangs down to varying lengths. **2.** that part of a dress or similar garment that hangs from the waist down. **3.** a rim, edge, or outer margin: *the skirt of a lake.* **4.** one of the flaps hanging from the side of a saddle. —*v.t.* **1.** to lie along or form the border or edge of: *Trees skirted the field.* **2.** to move along the border or edge of; pass around rather than go through: *The highway skirted the town.* **3.** to avoid by refusing to discuss or deal with: *The speaker skirted the controversial question.* —*v.i.* to move along or be near the border or edge of something.

skit (skit) *n.* a short, usually humorous play.

skit·ter (skit′ər) *v.i.* to glide or skim lightly and quickly over a surface. —*v.t.* to cause to skitter.

skit·tish (skit′ish) *adj.* **1.** easily frightened or excited; jumpy: *a skittish horse.* **2.** not dependable; fickle: *a skittish girl.* —**skit′tish·ly,** *adv.* —**skit′tish·ness,** *n.*

skit·tle (skit′əl) *n.* **1.** skittles. a form of ninepins in which a wooden disk or ball is used to knock down the pins. ▲ used with a singular verb. **2.** a pin used in this game.

skoal (skōl) *interj.* to your health. ▲ used as a toast.

skul·dug·ger·y (skul′dug′ər ē) *n.* underhanded or deceitful actions; trickery.

skulk (skulk) *v.i.* **1.** to move in a sneaking or sly way. **2.** to stay out of sight, especially in order to avoid work or danger; hide oneself: *He skulked behind the garage so he would not have to mow the lawn. The cat skulked under the table.* —*n.* a person who skulks. —**skulk′er,** *n.*

skull (skul) *n.* **1.** the bony framework of the head in an animal with a backbone. It consists of the bones that enclose the brain and support the face. **2.** *Informal.* the human head thought of as the seat of thought, intelligence, or understanding: *He couldn't get it through his skull that he was wrong.*

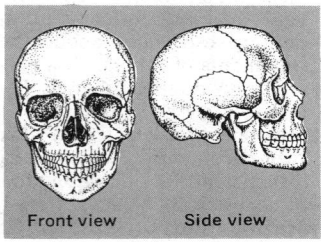

Front view   Side view

Human skull

skull and cross-bones, the representation of a human skull above two crossed bones, a symbol of death once used on the flags of pirate ships, now used chiefly as a warning sign, as on bottles of poison.

skull·cap (skul′kap′) *n.* a close-fitting cap without a brim.

skunk (skungk) *n.* **1.** a black animal with a bushy tail, usually having white stripes along its back. It sprays a liquid with a strong, very unpleasant smell when frightened or attacked. **2.** the fur of this animal. **3.** *Informal.* a mean, hateful person.

skunk cabbage, a weedy marsh plant found in eastern North America, having foul-smelling leaves.

sky (skī) *n. pl.,* **skies. 1.** the upper atmosphere, appearing as a great arch over the earth and having a light-blue color on clear days. **2.** *also,* **skies.** the condition or appearance of the sky: *sunny skies.* **3.** heaven.

sky blue, warm, light blue, like the color of the clear sky.

sky·dive (skī′dīv′) *v.i.,* **sky·dived** or **sky·dove, sky·dived, sky·div·ing.** to engage in skydiving. —**sky′div′er,** *n.*

sky·div·ing (skī′dī′ving) *n.* the act or sport of parachuting from an airplane and falling as far as safely possible before opening the parachute.

sky-high (skī′hī′) *adv.* **1.** to a very high point, level, or degree: *The cost of living rose sky-high.* **2.** into pieces; to bits; apart: *The explosion blew the building sky-high.* —*adj.* very high: *sky-high prices.*

sky·jack (skī′jak′) *v.t. Informal.* to hijack (an airplane), especially a commercial airliner. [*Sky* + (hi)*jack.*] —**sky′jack′er,** *n.*

sky·lark (skī′lärk′) *n.* a lark of Europe, Asia, and northern Africa, having dull brown feathers with black and whitish markings, noted for its melodious song while in flight. —*v.i.* to frolic about; play.

sky·light (skī′līt′) *n.* a window in a roof or ceiling for letting in daylight.

sky·line (skī′līn′) *n.* **1.** the outline of buildings, mountains, or other objects seen against the sky. **2.** the line at which the earth and sky seem to come together; horizon.

sky·rock·et (skī′rok′it) *n.* a small rocket that explodes high in the air, giving off a shower of colored sparks and lights, used chiefly in fireworks displays. —*v.i.* to rise rapidly, suddenly, or greatly: *Apartment rents in the city are skyrocketing.* —*v.t.* to cause to rise rapidly, suddenly, or greatly: *Higher food prices skyrocketed the cost of living.*

sky·scrap·er (skī′skrā′pər) *n.* a very tall building.

sky·ward (skī′wərd) *adv. also,* **sky·wards.** toward or in the direction of the sky: *The rocket flew skyward.* —*adj.* toward the sky: *a skyward glance.*

sky·writ·ing (skī′rī′ting) *n.* **1.** the act or process of forming words or symbols in the sky by releasing a trail of smoke or the like from an airplane. **2.** the words or symbols so formed. —**sky′writ′er,** *n.*

slab (slab) *n.* **1.** a broad, flat, and usually thick piece of some material: *a slab of stone.* **2.** a rough outside piece cut from a log.

slack¹ (slak) *adj.* **1.** not tight or firm; loose: *a slack rope, a slack grip.* **2.** slow in motion; unhurried; sluggish: *Jim walked to school at a slack pace.* **3.** not busy or lively: *The department store's business was slack all afternoon.* **4.** careless or lazy: *He is a slack worker.* —*n.* **1.** the part that is slack or hangs loose: *the slack in a rope.* **2.** a period of little or no activity; lull: *a slack in business.* —*v.t.* to slacken: *Tom slacked the rope.* —*v.i.* to be or become slack: *The wind slacked.* —*adv.* in a slack or loose manner. [Old English *slæc* slow, lazy, careless.] —**slack′ly,** *adv.* —**slack′ness,** *n.*

slack² (slak) *n.* small bits of coal remaining after coal is screened or sifted. [Probably from Middle Dutch *slacke.*]

slack·en (slak′ən) *v.t.* **1.** to make slower: *Jim slackened his pace so that his little brother could catch up.* **2.** to make loose: *to slacken wire.* **3.** to make less; lessen. —*v.i.* **1.** to become slower. **2.** to become loose. **3.** to become less, as in force or intensity: *Phil's interest in poetry slackened after he left school.*

slack·er (slak′ər) *n.* a person who avoids or attempts to avoid work, duty, or responsibility.

slacks (slaks) *n.,pl.* trousers for casual wear.

slag (slag) *n.* waste material left after metal is separated from its ore by smelting.

slain (slān) a past participle of **slay.**

slake (slāk) *v.t.,* **slaked, slak·ing. 1.** to relieve or satisfy; quench: *The cool water slaked the workman's thirst.* **2.** to cause a chemical change in (lime) by treating it with water.

slaked lime, a white compound formed by treating lime with water, used in mortar and cement.

sla·lom (slä′ləm) *n.* a downhill skiing race over a zigzag course that is marked by poles.

slam¹ (slam) *v.,* **slammed, slam·ming.** —*v.t.* **1.** to close forcefully and with a loud noise: *to slam a car door.* **2.** to strike, throw, put, or move (something) with force and a loud noise: *He slammed the phone down.* **3.** *Informal.* to criticize harshly or severely. —*v.i.* **1.** to close with force and a loud noise: *The wind made the door slam.* **2.** to strike or move forcefully and noisily: *The shutters slammed against the side of the house.* —*n.* **1.** a forceful and noisy closing or striking. **2.** the noise made by this. [Probably of Scandinavian origin.]

slam² (slam) *n.* the winning of twelve or all thirteen tricks in a round of bridge; little slam or grand slam. [Of uncertain origin.]

slan·der (slan′dər) *n.* **1.** a false and malicious statement about another that is damaging to his or her reputation or well-being: *The slander destroyed the senator's chance of reelection.* **2.** the uttering or spreading of such a statement. —*v.t.* to utter false and malicious statements about; injure by spreading slander against. —**slan′der·er,** *n.*

slan·der·ous (slan′dər əs) *adj.* **1.** containing slander: *slanderous statements.* **2.** uttering or spreading slander. —**slan′der·ous·ly,** *adv.*

slang (slang) *n.* **1.** a kind of language that expresses ideas in an unconventional, often striking manner. **2.** the vocabulary of a particular group, class, or profession; jargon: *When Dan came home on leave from the Army, he used military slang that we couldn't understand.*

● **Slang** gives our everyday speaking and writing freshness and variety. Modern English slang consists mainly of new words and new meanings of existing words. This is because slang words tend to remain slang for only a relatively short period of time. Eventually they either disappear from use or become a part of the standard English vocabulary.

Many more slang words and phrases disappear from use than become Standard English. If you have ever read a novel, listened to a popular song, or seen a film that is more than twenty-five years old, you have probably noticed some words and expressions that seem strange. Examples of this type of outdated slang are *the bee's knees* and *the cat's pajamas,* meaning "wonderful" or "the best," and *skiddoo,* meaning "go away." Among the words that were slang but are now part of Standard English are *kidnap, skyscraper, jazz, blimp,* and *soap opera.* In a few cases, such as the terms *beat it,* meaning "go away" and *kooky,* meaning "zany," a slang expression has been in our language for a long time but has remained slang.

The way we use slang and the words that we choose to use are often a good indication of social history and general attitudes. Many of the former or current slang terms that have been used to describe money, such as *cabbage, dough,* and *bread,* show that in our society money appears to have the same importance for survival as food does.

Slang comes into our language in various ways. Many slang expressions have come from the *jargon,* or special language, of a particular profession, age group, or region. Among the most important sources of such slang has been the military, because it is composed of a large number of people from all parts of the country and all backgrounds who, temporarily, share a common experience. Other slang terms have come from the secret language of some part of society. While most of the language of criminals is unfamiliar to us, it has provided us with *grand,* meaning "a thousand dollars," among other terms.

The communications media, particularly radio and television, have been responsible for making the spreading of slang more rapid than at any other time in history. They have also been responsible for making the life span of slang terms shorter, because when a slang term becomes common and overused, it loses its fresh and vivid quality and eventually ceases to be used as slang.

The American poet Carl Sandburg described slang as "language which takes off its coat, spits on its hands —and goes to work." But slang is essentially an oral, often spontaneous, form of language, and as such, its fresh simplicity functions well. However, when the ideas to be expressed are subtle or complex, the more precise language of Standard English is required. Slang certainly has a place in our spoken language. It is a colorful supplement to Standard English, but it ought not be considered a replacement for Standard English.

at; āpe; cär; end; mē; it; īce; hot; ōld; fôrk; wood; fōōl; oil; out; up; turn; sing; thin; this; hw in white; zh in treasure. The symbol ə stands for the sound of a in about, e in taken, i in pencil, o in lemon, and u in circus.

slang·y (slang′ē) *adj.*, **slang·i·er**, **slang·i·est. 1.** of the nature of, characterized by, or containing slang. **2.** given to the use of slang: *a slangy writer.* —**slang′i·ness**, *n.*

slant (slant) *v.i.* to have or take a direction that slopes away from the horizontal or vertical, or from a straight line or course: *The barn roof slants toward the ground.* —*v.t.* **1.** to cause to slant: *to slant a ladder against the wall.* **2.** to present in a way that supports a particular opinion or bias, or appeals to a particular interest: *to slant a magazine toward young people.* —*n.* **1.** a slanting direction, line, surface, or plane; inclination; angle: *The picture hung on a slant.* **2.** a point of view; attitude; opinion: *The speech offered a new slant on the problem of crime in the cities.*

slant·wise (slant′wīz′) *adv.* also, **slant·ways** (slant′wāz′). in a slanting direction or position; at a slant. —*adj.* not straight up and down; slanting.

slap (slap) *n.* **1.** a sharp, quick blow, especially with the open hand or with something flat. **2.** the sound made by such a blow. —*v.t.* **1.** to strike with a sharp, quick blow, especially with the open hand or with something flat: *He slapped the fly with a swatter.* **2.** to put or throw noisily, forcefully, or carelessly: *He slapped his books down on the table.* —*v.i.* to strike or beat with a slap: *The waves slapped against the side of the boat.*

slap·dash (slap′dash′) *adj.* hasty and careless: *a slapdash piece of work.* —*adv.* in a hasty and careless manner. —*n.* hasty and careless work or action.

slap·stick (slap′stik′) *n.* comedy characterized by loud, exaggerated, rough action. —*adj.* characterized by or relating to slapstick: *slapstick humor.*

slash (slash) *v.t.* **1.** to cut with a forceful, sweeping stroke or strokes, as with a sharp instrument: *Alice slashed her finger with the kitchen knife.* **2.** to strike with a whip; lash. **3.** to cut slits in (a garment), as to show underlying material of a different color. **4.** to reduce sharply or drastically: *to slash production costs.* **5.** to criticize severely. —*v.i.* to make a forceful, sweeping stroke or strokes with a knife or other sharp instrument. —*n. pl.*, **slash·es. 1.** a forceful, sweeping stroke: *the slash of a whip.* **2.** a cut or gash on the skin or other surface made by such a stroke. **3.** an ornamental slit in a garment. **4.** a sharp or drastic reduction: *a slash in prices.* —**slash′er**, *n.*

slat (slat) *n.* a thin, narrow, flat strip of wood, metal, or other material: *the slats of a Venetian blind.* —*v.t.*, **slat·ted**, **slat·ting.** to provide or make with slats.

slate (slāt) *n.* **1.** a fine-grained, bluish-gray rock that splits easily into thin sheets or layers. **2.** a thin piece of this rock, used especially to make roofing tiles and blackboards. **3.** a small writing tablet, usually held in the hand. **4.** the record of a person's past actions or performance: *That candidate has a clean slate.* **5.** a list of candidates proposed for nomination or election. **6.** a dull, dark, bluish-gray color. —*adj.* having the color slate; bluish-gray. —*v.t.*, **slat·ed**, **slat·ing. 1.** to cover with slate or a substance like slate. **2.** to put on a list of candidates. **3.** to schedule or designate: *The conference was slated for June.*

slat·tern (slat′ərn) *n.* an untidy, slovenly woman or girl.

slat·tern·ly (slat′ərn lē) *adj.* relating to or characteristic of a slattern; slovenly; untidy. —*adv.* in a slovenly manner. —**slat′tern·li·ness**, *n.*

slat·y (slā′tē) *adj.*, **slat·i·er**, **slat·i·est. 1.** of, relating to, containing, or resembling slate. **2.** having the color of slate; bluish-gray.

slaugh·ter (slô′tər) *n.* **1.** the act of killing an animal or animals for food. **2.** brutal or violent killing, especially of a large number of persons; massacre. —*v.t.* **1.** to kill (an animal or animals) for food; butcher. **2.** to kill (persons) in a brutal or violent manner; massacre. —**slaugh′ter·er**, *n.*

slaugh·ter·house (slô′tər hous′) *n. pl.*, **slaugh·ter·hous·es** (slô′tər hou′ziz). a place where animals are butchered for food.

Slav (släv) *n.* a member of a group of peoples speaking related languages and living mainly in eastern, southeastern, and central Europe. Poles, Czechs, Slovaks, Bulgarians, Russians, and Ukrainians are Slavs.

slave (slāv) *n.* **1.** a person who is the property of another person. **2.** a person who is under the control of some influence or person: *a slave to a habit.* **3.** a person who works, or is made to work, hard and long. —*v.i.*, **slaved**, **slav·ing.** to work hard and long: *The writer slaved away at his desk for hours.* —**slave′like′**, *adj.*

slave driver 1. a person who is in charge of slaves at work. **2.** any harsh or exacting employer or taskmaster.

slav·er¹ (slā′vər) *n.* **1.** a person who deals in slaves. **2.** a ship used to transport slaves. [*Slave* + *-er¹.*]

slav·er² (slav′ər) *v.i.* to let saliva run out from the mouth; drool; slobber. —*n.* saliva running out from the mouth. [Of Scandinavian origin.]

slav·er·y (slā′vər ē) *n.* **1.** the institution or practice of owning slaves. **2.** the condition of being a slave. **3.** the condition of being under the control of some influence or person. **4.** hard or exhausting work; drudgery.

Slav·ic (slä′vik) *adj.* of or relating to the Slavs or their languages. —*n.* the group of languages spoken by the Slavs.

slav·ish (slā′vish) *adj.* **1.** of, like, or befitting a slave or slaves. **2.** not original; imitative: *a slavish copy of a great painting.* —**slav′ish·ly**, *adv.* —**slav′ish·ness**, *n.*

slaw (slô) *n.* see **coleslaw**.

slay (slā) *v.t.*, **slew**, **slain**, **slay·ing.** to kill by violent means, as in war. —**slay′er**, *n.*

slea·zy (slē′zē) *adj.*, **slea·zi·er**, **slea·zi·est. 1.** (of cloth) thin or flimsy. **2.** of poor quality; shoddy; cheap: *a sleazy hotel.* —**slea′zi·ness**, *n.*

sled (sled) *n.* **1.** a vehicle on runners that is used to carry people or loads over snow and ice; sledge. **2.** a small, similar vehicle having a wooden frame, used for sport in sliding down snow-covered slopes. —*v.*, **sled·ded**, **sled·ding.** —*v.i.* to ride or be carried on a sled. —*v.t.* to carry on a sled.

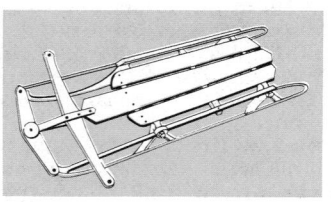

Sled

sled·ding (sled′ing) *n.* **1.** the act of riding on or using a sled. **2.** the condition of the ground for the use of sleds: *The heavy snow made for good sledding.*

hard sledding. difficult conditions affecting the course or progress of any action.

sledge¹ (slej) *n.* a sled or sleigh. —*v.*, **sledged**, **sledg·ing.** —*v.i.* to ride or be carried on a sled or sleigh. —*v.t.* to carry on a sled or sleigh. [Middle Dutch *sleedse* sled.]

sledge² (slej) *n.*, *v.t.*, **sledged**, **sledg·ing.** see **sledgehammer**.

sledge·ham·mer (slej′ham′ər) *n.* a heavy hammer with a long handle, usually held with both hands. —*v.t.* to strike with such a hammer. —*adj.* like a sledgehammer; powerful; smashing: *The boxer gave his opponent a sledgehammer blow.*

sleek (slēk) *adj.* **1.** smooth and glossy: *The cat has sleek black fur.* **2.** having a healthy, well-groomed, or well-fed appearance: *a sleek horse.* **3.** polished in manner or speech: *a sleek politician.* —*v.t.* to make smooth and glossy; polish. —**sleek′ly**, *adv.* —**sleek′ness**, *n.*

sleep (slēp) *n.* **1.** a natural condition of rest occurring in man and other animals at regular intervals, characterized by total or partial unconsciousness and a lack of voluntary movement. **2.** a period of sleep: *I had a good sleep last night.* **3.** any condition of inactivity or lessened consciousness that resembles sleep, such as death or a hypnotic trance. —*v.,* **slept, sleep·ing.** —*v.i.* **1.** to be or fall alseep: *The baby slept peacefully.* **2.** to be in a condition like sleep. —*v.t.* to provide or be able to provide with places for sleeping: *This cabin sleeps six people.*

sleep·er (slē'pər) *n.* **1.** a person or thing that sleeps: *He is a light sleeper.* **2.** an unknown or unimportant person or thing that unexpectedly or suddenly attains success, fame, or importance. **3.** see **sleeping car. 4.** a strong horizontal beam used as a support, especially a railroad tie.

sleeping bag, a long, warmly lined or padded bag, often waterproof, used for sleeping outdoors.

Sleeping bag

sleeping car, a railroad car having sleeping berths for passengers; Pullman.

sleeping sickness, an infectious disease, often fatal, characterized by headaches, high fever, convulsions, and coma. It is most common in tropical Africa and is spread by the bite of the tsetse fly.

sleep·less (slēp'lis) *adj.* **1.** unable to sleep. **2.** without sleep: *a sleepless night.* **3.** always in motion or action. —**sleep'less·ly,** *adv.* —**sleep'less·ness,** *n.*

sleep·walk·ing (slēp'wô'king) *n.* the act or practice of walking about while asleep; somnambulism. —**sleep'walk'er,** *n.*

sleep·y (slē'pē) *adj.,* **sleep·i·er, sleep·i·est. 1.** ready for, in need of, or inclined to sleep; drowsy. **2.** of or characterized by drowsiness: *sleepy eyes.* **3.** characterized by lack of activity; dull; quiet: *a sleepy little village.* —**sleep'i·ly,** *adv.* —**sleep'i·ness,** *n.*

sleep·y·head (slē'pē hed') *n. Informal.* a sleepy person.

sleet (slēt) *n.* frozen or partially frozen rain. —*v.i.* to shower sleet: *It sleeted all day and the roads became very slippery.* —**sleet'y,** *adj.*

sleeve (slēv) *n.* **1.** the part of a garment that covers all or part of the arm. **2.** a tubelike part of a machine that fits over another part. —**sleeve'less,** *adj.*
     up one's sleeve. secretly in reserve for use when needed: *By the look in his eye we knew that he had some trick up his sleeve.*

sleigh (slā) *n.* a vehicle on runners, usually drawn by a horse, used for traveling over snow or ice. —*v.i.* to ride or travel in a sleigh.

sleight (slīt) *n.* **1.** skill or dexterity in doing or making something. **2.** a clever trick or deception.

sleight of hand 1. skill and dexterity in using the hands, especially in performing tricks or feats with the hands. **2.** tricks or feats requiring such skill, such as those performed by a magician or juggler.

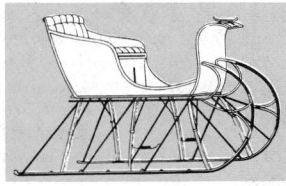
Sleigh

slen·der (slen'dər) *adj.* **1.** thin, especially in an attractive or graceful way: *slender fingers.* **2.** having a small circumference in proportion to height or length: *a slender pole.* **3.** small in size, amount, extent, or degree: *The candidate won the election by a slender margin.* —**slen'der·ly,** *adv.* —**slen'der·ness,** *n.*

slept (slept) the past tense and past participle of **sleep.**

sleuth (slooth) *n.* a detective or investigator. —*v.i.* to act as a detective or investigator.

slew[1] (sloo) the past tense of **slay.**

slew[2] (sloo) another spelling of **slue**[1].

slew[3] (sloo) *n.* see **slough**[1] *(def. 2).*

slew[4] (sloo) *n. Informal.* a large number or group; great amount: *A whole slew of people came to the party.* [Irish Gaelic *sluagh.*]

slice (slīs) *n.* **1.** a thin, flat piece cut from a larger object: *a slice of bread.* **2.** any of various implements having a thin, broad blade, such as a spatula. **3.** *Sports.* **a.** a stroke that causes a ball to curve off to the right, if the player is right-handed, and to the left if he is left-handed. **b.** the course followed by such a ball. —*v.,* **sliced, slic·ing.** —*v.t.* **1.** to cut into slices or pieces: *to slice a cake.* **2.** to remove in the form of a slice or slices: *to slice off a piece of cheese.* **3.** to move through or across like a knife: *The bow of the boat sliced the water.* **4.** *Sports.* to hit (a ball) so that it makes a slice. —*v.i.* **1.** to move or cut like a knife: *The speeding boat sliced through the waves.* **2.** *Sports.* **a.** to hit a ball with a slice. **b.** (of a ball) to curve in a slice. —**slic'er,** *n.*

slick (slik) *adj.* **1.** smooth and glossy; sleek: *slick wet hair.* **2.** smooth and slippery: *The roads were slick with ice.* **3.** cleverly or skillfully thought out, done, or said: *a slick solution to a problem.* **4.** shrewd or sly in thought, action, or speech: *a slick gambler.* **5.** having or showing skill that is only superficial or that lacks any real meaning: *a slick style of writing.* —*n.* **1.** a smooth or slippery area on a surface: *a slick of oil on water.* **2.** *Informal.* a magazine printed on glazed or coated paper. —*v.t. Informal.* **1.** to make sleek, smooth, or glossy. **2.** to make neat, trim, or tidy: *to slick up a messy room.* —**slick'ly,** *adv.* —**slick'ness,** *n.*

slick·er (slik'ər) *n.* **1.** a raincoat made of oilskin, plastic, or a similar material. **2.** *Informal.* a clever, sly person.

slide (slīd) *v.,* **slid** (slid), **slid** or **slid·den** (slid'ən), **slid·ing.** —*v.i.* **1.** to move or pass smoothly along a surface: *The wet bar of soap slid across the floor.* **2.** to shift, fall, or move suddenly from a position, as by loss of balance: *As I crossed the icy walk, my feet slid out from under me.* **3.** to pass or move smoothly, quietly, or gradually: *Ken slid into the seat next to me.* **4.** *Baseball.* to throw oneself along the ground toward a base, usually feet first, in order to avoid being tagged out by a fielder. —*v.t.* **1.** to cause to move or pass smoothly along a surface: *to slide a box along the floor.* **2.** to put or move smoothly, quietly, or gradually: *to slide a note under a door.* —*n.* **1.** the act of sliding: *He took a slide down the hill on his sled.* **2.** a smooth, usually inclined track, channel, or surface for sliding: *The children played on the slide in the playground.* **3.** a small plate of glass on which something is placed for examination under a microscope. **4.** a small, transparent photograph to be magnified and projected on a screen. **5.** the fall of a mass of rock, snow, or other matter down a slope. **6.** such a mass of matter. **7.** a part that operates by sliding, such as the U-shaped section of tubing on a trombone that is pushed in or out to change the pitch of the tones.
     to let slide. to let go by; neglect: *He let his homework slide and failed the course.*

at; āpe; cär; end; mē; it; īce; hot; ōld; fôrk; wood; fōōl; oil; out; up; turn; sing; thin; **th**is; hw in white; zh in treasure. The symbol ə stands for the sound of **a** in about, **e** in taken, **i** in pencil, **o** in lemon, and **u** in circus.

slid·er (slī′dər) *n.* **1.** a person or thing that slides. **2.** *Baseball.* a fast pitch that curves sharply for a short distance.

slide rule, a device having a ruler and a central sliding piece marked with logarithmic scales, used for mathematical calculations.

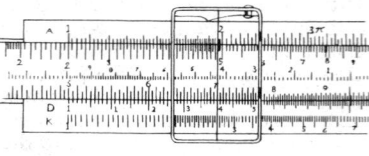

Slide rule

sli·er (slī′ər) a comparative of **sly.**

sli·est (slī′ist) a superlative of **sly.**

slight (slīt) *adj.* **1.** small in quantity, degree, or strength: *There is only a slight possibility that we will win the game.* **2.** of small importance: *a slight problem.* **3.** slender or thin in build or form; delicate: *a slight man.* —*v.t.* **1.** to treat as unimportant or with disrespect; snub or insult: *The girls slighted her by not inviting her to the picnic.* **2.** to do carelessly; neglect: *to slight one's work.* —*n.* disrespectful or insulting treatment. —**slight′ly,** *adv.* —**slight′ness,** *n.*

slight·ing (slī′ting) *adj.* showing disrespect; insulting: *a slighting remark.* —**slight′ing·ly,** *adv.*

sli·ly (slī′lē) *adv.* in a sly manner; slyly.

slim (slim) *adj.,* **slim·mer, slim·mest. 1.** small in thickness in proportion to height or length; slender; thin: *The fashion model had a very slim figure.* **2.** small in amount, degree, or extent: *a slim chance of victory.* —*v.t., v.i.,* **slimmed, slim·ming.** to make or become slim or slender: *She has slimmed down a great deal.* —**slim′ly,** *adv.* —**slim′ness,** *n.*

slime (slīm) *n.* **1.** wet, soft, sticky mud. **2.** any disgusting or filthy substance. **3.** a thin, sticky substance given off by certain animals, such as snails.

slim·y (slī′mē) *adj.,* **slim·i·er, slim·i·est. 1.** covered with slime. **2.** of or like slime. **3.** disgusting or filthy; foul. —**slim′i·ly,** *adv.* —**slim′i·ness,** *n.*

sling (sling) *n.* **1.** a device for hurling stones, usually consisting of a piece of leather with a string fastened to each end. **2.** see **slingshot. 3.** a loop of cloth hanging from the neck to support an injured arm or hand. **4.** a strap for carrying a rifle or other object over the shoulder. **5.** a device, such as a chain or rope formed into a loop, used for raising, lowering, carrying, or hanging heavy objects. **6.** the act of slinging or hurling; throw. —*v.t.,* **slung, sling·ing. 1.** to hurl with or as if with a sling; throw; fling: *to sling a rock.* **2.** to hang with a sling or strap: *A rifle was slung over the hunter's shoulder.* **3.** to hang or throw loosely: *to sling a hammock between two trees.* **4.** to raise, lower, carry, or hang by means of a sling. —**sling′er,** *n.*

sling·shot (sling′shot′) *n.* a Y-shaped piece of wood or metal, with an elastic band fastened to the tips of the prongs, used to shoot stones or other small objects.

slink (slingk) *v.i.,* **slunk, slink·ing.** to move in a quiet or stealthy manner: *The fox slunk closer to his prey.*

slip¹ (slip) *v.,* **slipped** or *(archaic)* **slipt, slip·ping.** —*v.i.* **1.** to lose one's balance or footing; slide suddenly or accidentally: *to slip on a banana peel.* **2.** to move or slide out of place or out of control: *The bottle slipped out of his hands.* **3.** to move or go quietly or stealthily: *The thief slipped out of the apartment without a sound.* **4.** to pass unnoticed: *Another month slipped by.* **5.** to be said or made known unintentionally: *Don't let the truth slip out.* **6.** to decline, fall, or become worse: *Prices on the stock market slipped sharply last year.* **7.** to put on or take off clothing, especially quickly or easily: *She slipped into her pajamas and went to bed.* **8.** to make a mistake: *Dan slipped up on the first question.* —*v.t.* **1.** to cause to move with

a smooth, sliding motion: *to slip a ring off one's finger.* **2.** to put or give quietly or quickly: *Judy slipped me a note during English class.* **3.** to fail to be remembered or noticed by: *Her name has slipped my mind.* **4.** to put on or take off (clothing), especially quickly or easily: *She slipped the sweater on and dashed out the door.* —*n.* **1.** the act of slipping. **2.** a mistake or error. **3.** a woman's undergarment, usually of a light material, such as nylon. **4.** a pillowcase. **5.** a space between wharves or piers where ships can dock. [Middle Dutch *slippen.*]

 to give (someone) the slip. to escape from: *The thief gave the policeman the slip.*

slip² (slip) *n.* **1.** a small shoot or twig cut from a plant, used for grafting or planting. **2.** a long, thin piece or strip of some material. **3.** a small printed piece of paper: *a bank deposit slip.* **4.** a slender or young person: *a mere slip of a girl.* —*v.t.,* **slipped, slip·ping.** to cut a shoot or twig from (a plant) for grafting or planting. [Middle Dutch *slippe* a cutting, strip.]

slip·cov·er (slip′kuv′ər) *n.* a removable cover, usually of cloth, for a piece of furniture, such as a sofa.

slip·knot (slip′not′) *n.* **1.** a knot made so that it will slip along the rope or line around which it is tied. **2.** a knot made so that it can be easily undone by pulling on either of the free ends.

Slipknot *(def. 1)*

slip·on (slip′ôn′, slip′on′) *adj.* (of an article of clothing) easily put on or removed. —*n.* a slip-on article of clothing.

slip·o·ver (slip′ō′vər) *adj.* (of an article of clothing) easily put on or removed by drawing over the head: *a slipover sweater.* —*n.* a slipover article of clothing.

slip·per (slip′ər) *n.* a light, low shoe that is easily slipped on or off the foot, worn chiefly indoors.

slip·per·y (slip′ər ē) *adj.,* **slip·per·i·er, slip·per·i·est. 1.** causing or likely to cause slipping or sliding: *Freezing rain made the roads slippery.* **2.** likely to slip or slide, as from the grasp: *The wet fish was too slippery to hold.* **3.** not to be relied or depended on; tricky. **4.** able to slip away or escape easily: *a slippery thief.* —**slip′per·i·ness,** *n.*

slip·shod (slip′shod′) *adj.* careless or slovenly, as in appearance or workmanship: *He did a slipshod job in building the cabinets.*

slip·stream (slip′strēm′) *n.* a current of air driven back by the revolving propeller of an aircraft.

slipt (slipt) *Archaic.* a past tense of **slip¹.**

slip·up (slip′up′) *n. Informal.* a mistake or error.

slit (slit) *n.* a long, narrow, usually straight cut or opening: *There was a slit up one side of the dress. Sunlight came through the slits in the Venetian blinds.* —*v.t.,* **slit, slit·ting.** to cut or make a slit or slits in.

slith·er (slith′ər) *v.i.* **1.** to move along with a sliding or gliding motion: *The snake slithered under a rock.* **2.** to slip or slide, as on a loose or slippery surface. —*v.t.* to cause to slither or slide.

slith·er·y (slith′ər ē) *adj.* slippery or slick.

sliv·er (sliv′ər) *n.* a slender, often pointed piece that has been broken, cut, or torn off; splinter: *a sliver of wood, a sliver of glass.*

slob (slob) *n. Informal.* a sloppy, dirty, or crude person.

slob·ber (slob′ər) *v.i.* **1.** to let saliva, food, or liquid run or spill from the mouth; slaver. **2.** to speak or write in an overly sentimental way; gush. —*v.t.* to wet or smear with saliva, food, or liquid running from the mouth. —*n.* **1.** saliva, food, or liquid running from the mouth. **2.** overly sentimental speech or writing. —**slob′ber·y,** *adj.*

sloe (slō) *n.* **1.** see **blackthorn. 2.** the fruit of the blackthorn.

slog (slog) *v.,* **slogged, slog·ging.** —*v.i.* **1.** to move with great effort; plod: *to slog through mud.* **2.** to work hard. —*v.t.* to make (one's way) with great effort.

slo·gan (slō′gən) *n.* **1.** a phrase, statement, or motto used by a particular group, such as a club or political party, or by a particular individual, such as a candidate for political office. **2.** a phrase used in advertising or in promoting a particular product, business, or service.

sloop (slōōp) *n.* a fore-and-aft-rigged sailboat with a single mast, a mainsail, and a jib.

Sloop

slop (slop) *n.* **1.** liquid that has been spilled or splashed. **2.** soft, watery mud or snow; slush. **3.** unappetizing or distasteful food or liquid. **4.** *also,* **slops.** waste food used to feed pigs or other animals; swill. **5.** any liquid waste. —*v.,* **slopped, slop·ping.** —*v.i.* **1.** to spill or splash: *The water in the pail slopped all over the floor.* **2.** to walk or move with splashes through mud, slush, or water. —*v.t.* **1.** to cause (a liquid) to spill or splash. **2.** to spill or splash liquid upon. **3.** to feed slop to (animals).

slope (slōp) *v.,* **sloped, slop·ing.** —*v.i.* to lie or move at an angle from the horizontal or vertical; take a slanting direction: *The road slopes toward the river.* —*v.t.* to cause to slope: *The builders sloped the roof of the house.* —*n.* **1.** a stretch of ground that is not flat or level: *The house was built on a slope.* **2.** any slanting line, surface, position, or direction. **3.** the degree or amount of such a slant: *The roof has a steep slope.* **4.** *Mathematics.* **a.** the degree of inclination measured by the tangent of an angle formed by a line and the x-axis. **b.** (of a point on a plane curve) the slope of the line that is tangent to a curve at a point.

slop·py (slop′ē) *adj.,* **slop·pi·er, slop·pi·est. 1.** very wet, muddy, or slushy: *The roads were wet and sloppy.* **2.** spotted or splashed with liquid or slop: *a sloppy floor.* **3.** careless; slipshod: *a sloppy job.* **4.** very untidy; messy: *a sloppy room.* **5.** *Informal.* too sentimental; maudlin. —**slop′pi·ly,** *adv.* —**slop′pi·ness,** *n.*

slosh (slosh) *v.i.* to move clumsily or splash about: *to slosh through mud.* —*v.t.* to stir or splash: *The child sloshed his milk around in his cup.*

slot (slot) *n.* **1.** a narrow, usually straight opening or groove: *A mail box has a slot for letters.* **2.** *Informal.* a place or position, as in a schedule or sequence: *That television program appears in the ten o'clock time slot.* —*v.t.,* **slot·ted, slot·ting.** to make or cut a slot in.

sloth (slôth, slōth) *n.* **1.** dislike of work or exertion; laziness. **2.** any of several tree-dwelling animals of the tropical forests of Central and South America, having long limbs, curved claws, and coarse, shaggy hair. Sloths are the slowest-moving of all mammals.

Sloth

sloth·ful (slôth′fəl, slōth′fəl) *adj.* characterized by sloth; lazy; idle. —**sloth′ful·ly,** *adv.* —**sloth′ful·ness,** *n.*

slot machine, a gambling or vending machine that is worked by putting a coin through a slot.

slouch (slouch) *v.i.* **1.** to sit, stand, or walk in an awkward, drooping posture, or in an overly loose manner. **2.** to hang or bend down; droop. —*n. pl.,* **slouch·es. 1.** a drooping of the head and shoulders while sitting, standing, or walking; awkward or drooping posture. **2.** *Informal.* an awkward, lazy, or untidy person: *Stan's no slouch at tennis.*

slouch hat, a soft, usually felt hat, with a broad brim that turns down easily.

slouch·y (slou′chē) *adj.,* **slouch·i·er, slouch·i·est.** slouching: *She has a slouchy posture.* —**slouch′i·ly,** *adv.* —**slouch′i·ness,** *n.*

slough[1] (*defs. 1, 3* slou; *def. 2* slōō) *n.* **1.** a place full of soft, deep mud. **2.** *also,* **slew, slue.** a swamp, marsh, or bog, especially one that is part of a backwater. **3.** a state of dejection or discouragement. [Old English *slōh.*] —**slough′y,** *adj.*

slough[2] (sluf) *n.* **1.** the outer skin shed by a snake. **2.** anything that has been shed or cast off. —*v.t.* to shed or cast: *to slough off sadness. Dick tried to slough off his bad habit of oversleeping in the morning.* —*v.i.* to be shed or cast off. [Middle English *slughe, slouh.*]

Slo·vak (slō′vak) *n.* **1.** a member of a Slavic people living predominantly in Slovakia and closely related to the Czechs and the Moravians. **2.** the language of these people, belonging to the Slavic family of languages, and closely related to Czech. —*adj.* of or relating to Slovakia, its people, or their language.

Slo·va·ki·a (slō vä′kē ə) *n.* a historic region in eastern Czechoslovakia. —**Slo·va′ki·an,** *adj., n.*

slov·en (sluv′ən) *n.* a person who is untidy or careless, especially in dress or appearance.

Slo·vene (slō′vēn) *n.* **1.** a member of a Slavic people living in Slovenia and closely related to the Serbs and Croats. **2.** the language of these people, belonging to the Slavic family of languages, and closely related to Serb and Croatian. —*adj.* of or relating to Slovenia, its people, or their language.

Slo·ve·ni·a (slō vē′nē ə) *n.* a political subdivision of Yugoslavia, in the northwestern part of the country. —**Slo·ve′ni·an,** *adj., n.*

slov·en·ly (sluv′ən lē) *adj.,* **slov·en·li·er, slov·en·li·est.** untidy or careless, especially in dress or appearance: *He always looks so slovenly when he comes to work.* —*adv.* in a slovenly manner. —**slov′en·li·ness,** *n.*

slow (slō) *adj.* **1.** acting, moving, or happening with little speed; not fast or quick: *a slow reader, slow progress.* **2.** taking a long or longer time than usual: *a slow trip, a slow game.* **3.** indicating a time behind the true time: *My watch is always slow.* **4.** not quick to learn or understand: *a slow student.* **5.** causing a lower speed: *Because of all the rain the day before, the race was run on a slow track.* **6.** not active; sluggish: *Business is slow this season.* **7.** not prompt, hasty, or easily moved: *slow to answer letters, slow to anger.* —*adv.* in a slow manner; slowly: *Drive slow through the town.* —*v.t., v.i.* to make or become slow or slower: *to slow down a car. The car slowed up.* —**slow′ly,** *adv.* —**slow′ness,** *n.*

at; āpe; cär; end; mē; it; īce; hot; ōld; fôrk; wood; fōōl; oil; out; up; turn; sing; thin; this; hw in white; zh in treasure. The symbol ə stands for the sound of **a** in about, **e** in taken, **i** in pencil, **o** in lemon, and **u** in circus.

S

slow·down (slō′doun′) *n.* a deliberate slowing down of the rate of production by workers or management.

slow·ish (slō′ish) *adj.* somewhat slow.

slow·mo·tion (slō′mō′shən) *adj.* of or relating to a motion picture in which the action appears to be taking place at a speed that is much slower than normal.

slow·poke (slō′pōk′) *n. Informal.* a person who moves, works, or acts at a very slow pace.

slow·wit·ted (slō′wit′id) *adj.* slow to understand or learn.

sludge (sluj) *n.* **1.** mud or mire, especially a muddy deposit at the bottom of a body of water. **2.** any muddy or slushy mass or mixture, such as sediment from the treatment of sewage. **3.** broken or half-formed ice, as on the sea. —**sludg′y,** *adj.*

slue¹ (slōō) *also,* **slew.** *v.,* **slued, slu·ing.** —*v.t.* to cause to turn or twist about, especially on a pivot or fixed point: *He slued the steering wheel sharply to the left.* —*v.i.* to turn or twist about; swing around. —*n.* **1.** the act of sluing. **2.** the position attained by sluing. [Of uncertain origin.]

slue² (slōō) *n.* see **slough¹** *(def. 2).*

slug¹ (slug) *n.* **1.** any of several animals closely resembling a snail, but either lacking a shell or having only a partly developed one. **2.** the larva of a moth or certain other insect that looks like a slug.

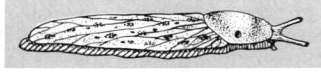
Slug¹ *(def. 1)*

3. a small piece or lump of metal, especially a piece of lead or other metal for firing from a gun. **4.** a piece of metal shaped like, and used in place of, a coin, especially one used illegally, as in a vending machine or pay telephone. **5.** *Printing.* **a.** a strip of metal used to space lines of type. **b.** a line of type cast in one piece, as by a linotype machine. [Probably of Scandinavian origin.]

slug² (slug) *Informal. v.t.,* **slugged, slug·ging.** to strike hard, as with the fist: *The batter slugged the ball over the fence.* —*n.* a heavy blow, as with the fist. [Possibly from *slug¹*.]

slug·gard (slug′ərd) *n.* a person who is lazy or idle. —*adj.* lazy or idle; slothful.

slug·ger (slug′ər) *n.* a person who slugs, especially a hard-hitting baseball player or a prizefighter able to throw hard punches.

slug·gish (slug′ish) *adj.* **1.** having little motion, speed, or activity: *a sluggish river.* **2.** showing a lack of vigor, energy, or alertness: *a sluggish mind.* **3.** not acting or functioning with full or usual energy or efficiency: *My car's engine is sluggish on cold mornings.* —**slug′gish·ly,** *adv.* —**slug′gish·ness,** *n.*

sluice (slōōs) *n.* **1.** an artificial channel for conducting water, having a gate or valve for controlling the rate of flow. **2.** the gate or valve of such a channel. **3.** the water controlled by such a gate or valve. **4.** a long, sloping trough through which water is run, as for separating gold ore or floating logs. —*v.t.,* **sluiced, sluic·ing. 1.** to draw off by means of or through a sluice: *to sluice water.* **2.** to wash (gold) from ore, dirt, or gravel with water running through or from a sluice. **3.** to wash with a rush of water; drench. **4.** to float (logs) in a sluice.

Sluice *(def. 4)*

slum (slum) *n. also,* **slums.** a crowded section of a city, characterized by poverty, run-down housing, and unclean living conditions. —*v.i.,* **slummed, slum·ming.** to visit a slum, as out of curiosity.

slum·ber (slum′bər) *v.i.* **1.** to sleep or doze: *The baby slumbered peacefully.* **2.** to be quiet, calm, or inactive: *The town slumbered under the afternoon sun.* —*v.t.* to pass or spend in sleeping: *to slumber away the day.* —*n.* **1.** a light sleep or doze. **2.** a quiet, calm, or inactive state. —**slum′ber·er,** *n.*

slum·ber·ous (slum′bər əs) *also,* **slum·brous** (slum′brəs). *adj.* **1.** sleepy or drowsy. **2.** causing sleep or drowsiness.

slum·lord (slum′lôrd′) *n.* a landlord of slum housing, especially one who charges unfairly high rents and does not take proper care of his property.

slump (slump) *v.i.* **1.** to fall or sink suddenly or heavily: *The dazed boxer slumped to the floor. The football team slumped badly after its star quarterback was injured.* **2.** to take a drooping posture; slouch: *The boy slumped in his chair during the lecture.* —*n.* **1.** a sharp, sudden decline: *a slump in sales. The baseball player was in a batting slump.* **2.** the act of slumping.

slung (slung) the past tense and past participle of **sling.**

slunk (slungk) the past tense and past participle of **slink.**

slur (slûr) *v.t.,* **slurred, slur·ring. 1.** to pass over hurriedly or carelessly: *In his haste to complete the report, the student slurred over many facts.* **2.** to speak slightingly of; insult: *to slur a person's reputa-*

Slur *(def. 3b)*

tion. **3.** to pronounce indistinctly, as by running sounds together: *to slur one's words.* **4.** *Music.* **a.** to play or sing (two or more tones of different pitch) in a smooth, connected manner. **b.** to mark (a note) with a slur. —*n.* **1.** a slighting or insulting remark. **2.** an indistinct pronunciation of words. **3.** *Music.* **a.** a combination of two or more slurred tones. **b.** a curved mark indicating this.

slurp (slûrp) *Slang. v.t., v.i.* to drink, sip, or eat (something) noisily.

slush (slush) *n.* **1.** partially melted snow or ice. **2.** soft mud; mire. **3.** silly, sentimental speech or writing; drivel. —**slush′i·ness,** *n.* —**slush′y,** *adj.*

slut (slut) *n.* **1.** a sexually immoral woman. **2.** a dirty, slovenly woman.

sly (slī) *adj.,* **sli·er** or **sly·er, sli·est** or **sly·est. 1.** showing or characterized by cleverness, shrewdness, or craftiness: *a sly trick.* **2.** able to deceive or trick; clever; devious: *The sly thief had eluded the police for months.* **3.** mischievous in a playful way: *a sly glance.* —**sly′ly,** *adv.* —**sly′ness,** *n.*

on the sly. in a stealthy way; secretly: *The treasurer was taking club funds on the sly.*

Sm, the symbol for samarium.

smack¹ (smak) *v.t.* **1.** to press together and open (the lips) rapidly so as to make a sharp sound. **2.** to strike or slap sharply, as with the open hand. **3.** to kiss loudly or noisily. —*v.i.* **1.** to smack the lips. **2.** to strike something forcibly and noisily: *The car skidded and smacked into the fence.* —*n.* **1.** a sharp sound made by smacking the lips. **2.** a sharp blow or slap, as with the open hand. **3.** a loud or noisy kiss. —*adv. Informal.* **1.** in a sudden, violent manner: *The boy rode his bicycle smack into a tree.* **2.** squarely or directly: *Judy ran smack into the very person she was trying to avoid.* [Imitative of this sound.]

smack² (smak) *n.* **1.** a slight taste or flavor: *The pudding had a smack of cinnamon.* **2.** a suggestion or trace. —*v.i.* **1.** to have a taste or flavor: *The meat smacks of* garlic. **2.** to have a suggestion or trace: *His actions smack of dishonesty.* [Old English *smæc.*]

smack³ (smak) *n.* a small sailboat, usually fore-and-aft-rigged, used chiefly for fishing. [Dutch *smak.*]

small (smôl) *adj.* **1.** not large or great in size, amount, degree, or number, especially in comparison with others of the same kind: *a small car, a small crowd, a small town.* **2.** not important; trivial: *a small problem.* **3.** carrying on business in a limited way. **4.** soft or weak; low: *The shy girl replied in a small voice.* **5.** mean or selfish: *It was small of him not to pay his share of the cost.* —*n.* a small or narrow part: *the small of the back.* —**small′ness,** *n.*

small arms, firearms, such as pistols or rifles, that can be carried easily and held in the hands when fired.

small capital, a capital letter of slightly smaller size than the regular letter used. THIS SENTENCE IS IN SMALL CAPITALS.

small calorie, see **calorie** *(def. 1).*

small change 1. coins of small value, such as dimes or nickels. **2.** something of small value or importance.

small fry 1. a young or small child or children. **2.** people or things of little or no importance.

small game, small wild animals and birds hunted for sport.

small intestine, the part of the alimentary canal extending from the stomach to the large intestine, consisting of the duodenum, the jejunum, and the ileum.

small·ish (smô′lish) *adj.* somewhat small.

small letter, a letter that is not a capital letter.

small-mind·ed (smôl′mīn′did) *adj.* having or showing a narrow, selfish, or petty outlook; prejudiced. —**small′-mind′ed·ly,** *adv.* —**small′-mind′ed·ness,** *n.*

small·pox (smôl′poks′) *n.* an acute, highly contagious disease caused by a virus and characterized by fever and skin eruptions that often leave pit-shaped permanent scars.

small talk, light conversation about everyday or unimportant matters.

smart (smärt) *adj.* **1.** clever or intelligent; bright: *She is a smart girl.* **2.** neat and trim: *She looked very smart in her school uniform.* **3.** stylish or fashionable: *She bought a smart new dress for the party.* **4.** brisk or vigorous; lively: *The soldiers marched at a smart pace.* —*v.i.* **1.** to cause sharp, stinging pain: *The soap smarted as the nurse washed my cut finger.* **2.** to feel sharp, stinging pain: *My face smarted from the icy cold wind.* **3.** to feel hurt or distress: *The boy smarted from the criticism.* —*n.* a sharp, stinging pain. —**smart′ly,** *adv.* —**smart′ness,** *n.*

smart al·eck (al′ik) *Informal.* a person who is offensively conceited and cocky. —**smart′-al′eck·y,** *adj.*

smart·en (smärt′ən) *v.t., v.i.* to make or become smart or smarter.

smash (smash) *v.t.* **1.** to break (something) into pieces with noise and violence: *The boy smashed the plate with a hammer.* **2.** to strike with a hard blow: *The batter smashed the ball over the fence.* **3.** to destroy, crush, or defeat completely: *His plans to start a small business were smashed by lack of money.* —*v.i.* **1.** to break into pieces: *The plate slipped from my hand and smashed on the floor.* **2.** to move with force or violence; crash: *The cart rolled down the hill and smashed into the side of the house.* —*n. pl.,* **smash·es. 1.** the act of smashing. **2.** the sound of smashing: *the smash of glass.* **3.** a violent collision; smashup. **4.** a complete or crushing defeat or disaster: *the smash of one's hopes.* **5.** *Informal.* a complete success. —*adj. Informal.* completely successful: *The new play is a smash hit.* —**smash′er,** *n.*

smash·ing (smash′ing) *adj. Informal.* extremely good; tremendous: *Her debut as an actress was a smashing success.*

smash·up (smash′up′) *n.* **1.** a violent collision, as of automobiles; crash. **2.** a complete collapse, failure, or defeat.

smat·ter·ing (smat′ər ing) *n.* superficial or very slight knowledge: *He has a smattering of Spanish.*

smear (smēr) *v.t.* **1.** to cover, spread, or make dirty with something wet, sticky, or greasy: *The child smeared the wall with paint.* **2.** to spread or coat with (something wet, sticky, or greasy): *The boy smeared mud all over his clothes.* **3.** to cause to become blurred or indistinct, as by rubbing with the hand: *to smear a signature.* **4.** to damage or harm the reputation of: *The candidate smeared his opponent.* —*v.i.* to be or become smeared: *The wet paint smeared when he touched it.* —*n.* **1.** a mark or stain made by smearing: *There was a smear of dirt on his cheek.* **2.** an attack on a person's reputation; slander. **3.** a small quantity of a substance, such as blood, placed on a slide for examination under a microscope.

smell (smel) *v.,* **smelled** or **smelt, smell·ing.** —*v.t.* **1.** to recognize or become aware of by means of the nose and its nerves; detect the odor of: *Do you smell something burning?* **2.** to test or sample by smelling: *to smell food to see if it is fresh.* **3.** to sense the presence of: *to smell danger.* —*v.i.* **1.** to have or give off an odor: *The kitchen smells of onions.* **2.** to have or give off an unpleasant odor: *Rotten meat smells.* **3.** to use the sense of smell. —*n.* **1.** the sense by means of which odors are recognized or detected. **2.** the quality of a thing or substance that makes it able to be recognized by the sense of smell; odor: *the smell of the sea.* **3.** the act of smelling. **4.** a suggestion, hint, or feeling of something: *The smell of victory was in the air long before the game was over.* —**smell′er,** *n.*

smelling salts, a preparation based on ammonia, inhaled to relieve headaches or faintness.

smell·y (smel′ē) *adj.,* **smell·i·er, smell·i·est.** *Informal.* having or giving off an unpleasant or offensive smell.

smelt¹ (smelt) *v.t.* **1.** to melt (ore) to separate the metal from it. **2.** to refine (metal) in this manner. [Probably from Middle Dutch *smelten* to melt, make liquid.]

smelt² (smelt) *n. pl.,* **smelts** or **smelt.** any of a group of slender, silvery food fish found in cold or temperate waters of the Northern Hemisphere. [Old English *smelt.*]

smelt³ (smelt) a past tense and past participle of **smell.**

smelt·er (smel′tər) *n.* **1.** a person whose work or business is smelting ores or metals. **2.** a place for smelting. **3.** a furnace for smelting.

smid·gen (smij′ən) *n. Informal.* a very small amount; bit.

smi·lax (smī′laks) *n. pl.,* **smi·lax·es.** a climbing African vine having stiff, shiny branches and tiny greenish-white flowers that ripen into small purple berries.

smile (smīl) *n.* an expression of the face formed by an upward turning of the corners of the mouth, showing various feelings, as happiness, amusement, friendliness, sympathy, or contempt. —*v.,* **smiled, smil·ing.** —*v.i.* **1.** to have, show, or give a smile: *The boy smiled with delight when he saw the new baseball glove.*

Smilax

at; āpe; cär; end; mē; it; īce; hot; ōld; fôrk; wood; fōōl; oil; out; up; turn; sing; thin; this; hw in white; zh in treasure. The symbol ə stands for the sound of a in about, e in taken, i in pencil, o in lemon, and u in circus.

S

2. to show approval or favor: *Fortune smiled upon our plans.* —*v.t.* **1.** to express with a smile: *The old man smiled his gratitude for the help we gave him.* **2.** to change or accomplish by smiling: *The mother smiled away the child's fears.* —**smil'er,** *n.* —**smil'ing·ly,** *adv.*

smirch (smurch) *v.t.* **1.** to stain, soil, or discolor with dirt, grime, or a similar substance. **2.** to bring dishonor or disgrace upon: *to smirch a person's reputation.* —*n. pl.,* **smirch·es. 1.** a dirty spot or stain; smudge. **2.** a blot or stain on a person's reputation or honor.

smirk (smurk) *v.i.* to smile in an affected, self-satisfied, or silly manner. —*n.* an affected, self-satisfied, or silly smile.

smite (smīt) *v.t.,* **smote, smit·ten** or **smit** (smit) or **smote, smit·ing. 1.** to strike hard with the hand or with a weapon. **2.** to afflict or attack suddenly and with a disastrous effect: *to be smitten by disease.* **3.** to affect suddenly or strongly with some powerful feeling, such as love, fear, or remorse. —**smit'er,** *n.*

smith (smith) *n.* **1.** a person who makes or repairs metal objects. **2.** see **blacksmith.**

Smith (smith) **1. John.** 1580–1631, English explorer, writer, and early settler of Virginia. **2. Joseph.** 1805–1844, U.S. religious leader. He was the founder of the Mormon Church.

smith·er·eens (smith'ə rēnz') *n., pl. Informal.* little pieces or fragments; bits: *The explosion blew the building to smithereens.*

smith·y (smith'ē) *n. pl.,* **smith·ies. 1.** the workshop of a smith, especially a blacksmith's shop; forge. **2.** a blacksmith.

smit·ten (smit'ən) a past participle of **smite.**

smock (smok) *n.* a loose outer garment, usually resembling a long shirt, worn to protect clothing. —*v.t.* to ornament with smocking.

smock·ing (smok'ing) *n.* a decorative pattern formed by gathering fabric with rows of stitches, often with a honeycomb design.

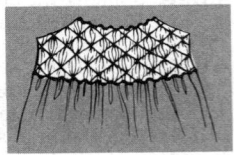
Smocking

smog (smog) *n.* a combination of smoke and fog, found especially in the air over industrial areas. [A blend of *sm*(oke) and (f)*og*.] —**smog'gy,** *adj.*

smoke (smōk) *n.* **1.** a cloud of solid matter in a gas produced by burning something, such as wood or coal. It can be seen because of the carbon particles suspended in it. **2.** anything like this, such as steam or mist. **3.** the act of smoking tobacco. **4.** a cigarette, cigar, or the like. —*v.,* **smoked, smok·ing.** —*v.i.* **1.** to send out or produce smoke: *We could see a chimney smoking in the distance.* **2.** to draw the smoke of a cigarette, cigar, or the like into the mouth, and often the lungs, and then breathe it out. —*v.t.* **1.** to draw in and breathe out the smoke of (a cigarette, cigar, or the like). **2.** to cure or preserve (meat or fish) by exposure to smoke: *to smoke hogs.*

to smoke out. a. to force into the open with smoke: *to smoke out a skunk from under a house.* **b.** to drive or bring out of hiding or secrecy.

smoke·house (smōk'hous') *n. pl.,* **smoke·hous·es** (smōk'hou'ziz). a building where meat or fish is treated with smoke to preserve and flavor it.

smoke·less (smōk'lis) *adj.* having or giving off little or no smoke.

smok·er (smō'kər) *n.* **1.** a person or thing that smokes, especially a person who smokes tobacco. **2.** a railroad car or compartment where smoking is permitted. Also, **smoking car. 3.** an informal social gathering for men.

smoke screen 1. a thick cloud of smoke used to conceal a military force or movement from the enemy. **2.** anything used to conceal or deceive.

smoke·stack (smōk'stak') *n.* a pipe or funnel for the escape of smoke or gases, as on a factory, ship, or locomotive.

smoking car, see **smoker** (*def. 2*).

smok·y (smō'kē) *adj.,* **smok·i·er, smok·i·est. 1.** giving off smoke, especially too much smoke: *a smoky fire, a smoky chimney.* **2.** filled with smoke: *a smoky room, smoky air.* **3.** like smoke, as in color or taste. —**smok'i·ly,** *adv.* —**smok'i·ness,** *n.*

Smoky Mountains, see **Great Smoky Mountains.**

smol·der (smōl'dər) *also,* **smoul·der.** *v.i.* **1.** to burn and smoke with little or no flame: *The coals of the dead fire still smoldered.* **2.** to exist or continue in a hidden or pent-up state: *Resentment against the government smoldered among the people.* **3.** to show hidden or pent-up emotion: *Her eyes smoldered with rage at his accusation.* —*n.* a smoldering fire or the smoke produced by such a fire.

smooth (smōōth) *adj.* **1.** having a surface that is not uneven or rough: *smooth skin, a smooth highway.* **2.** even, easy, or gentle in movement: *The pilot made a smooth landing.* **3.** free from difficulties, obstacles, or trouble: *We made smooth progress on our plans.* **4.** able, skillful, or polished: *a smooth dancer, a smooth talker.* **5.** not harsh in sound or taste: *That radio announcer has a smooth voice.* —*v.t.* **1.** to make smooth, even, or level: *She smoothed the dirt around the plants.* **2.** to free from difficulties or obstacles; make easy: *His father's help smoothed his way to success in business.* **3.** to calm; soothe: *to smooth someone's temper.* —*v.i.* to become smooth. —*adv.* in a smooth manner; smoothly. —**smooth'ly,** *adv.* —**smooth'ness,** *n.*

to smooth over. to make less unpleasant or serious: *She smoothed over the quarrel between the boys.*

smooth·bore (smōōth'bôr') *adj.* (of a firearm) having no spiral grooves cut into the inside of the barrel or bore. —*n.* a firearm having an ungrooved barrel or bore.

smor·gas·bord (smôr'gəs bôrd') *also,* **smör·gås·bord.** *n.* a large assortment of food, such as appetizers, meats, fish, and cheese, usually arranged on a table for each person to serve himself.

smote (smōt) *the* past tense and a past participle of **smite.**

smoth·er (smuth'ər) *v.t.* **1.** to prevent from breathing in air; kill by depriving of air: *The skier was almost smothered by the avalanche of snow.* **2.** to cause (a fire) to go out or die down by covering it so as to cut off oxygen. **3.** to cover thickly: *to smother a steak with onions.* **4.** to conceal or hold back: *to smother a yawn, to smother feelings of jealousy.* —*v.i.* to be prevented from breathing in air. —*n.* something that smothers, such as a dense cloud of smoke or dust.

smoul·der (smōl'dər) another spelling of **smolder.**

smudge (smuj) *v.,* **smudged, smudg·ing.** —*v.t.* **1.** to soil or smear; make dirty: *The boy smudged the white cloth with his grimy hands.* **2.** to fill (a planted area) with dense smoke to drive away insects or protect against frost. —*v.i.* to be or become smudged or smeared: *A charcoal drawing smudges easily.* —*n.* **1.** a mark or stain made by smearing or smudging: *The child's dirty hand left a smudge on the wall.* **2.** a smoky fire built to drive away insects or protect against frost. **3.** the thick smoke produced by such a fire. —**smudg'y,** *adj.*

smudge pot, a pot or similar vessel for burning a fuel to produce smudge.

smug (smug) *adj.,* **smug·ger, smug·gest.** too highly pleased with oneself; self-satisfied; complacent: *a smug young man.* —**smug'ly,** *adv.* —**smug'ness,** *n.*

smug·gle (smug′əl) *v.t.,* **smug·gled, smug·gling. 1.** to take into or out of a country secretly and unlawfully, as goods on which the required duties have not been paid: *She was arrested for smuggling jewels by sewing them into the lining of a coat.* **2.** to bring, take, or transport secretly or stealthily: *to smuggle a weapon to a prisoner in jail.* —*v.i.* to take part in smuggling. —**smug′gler,** *n.*

smut (smut) *n.* **1.** a substance that darkens or soils; soot; dirt. **2.** a spot or stain made by soot or dirt; smudge. **3.** obscene or indecent language or writing. **4.** any of several fungus diseases of plants, commonly affecting cereal grains, such as corn and wheat. It is characterized by the appearance of black, powdery masses or spores. —*v.t.,* **smut·ted, smut·ting.** to mark or stain with smut.

smut·ty (smut′ē) *adj.,* **smut·ti·er, smut·ti·est. 1.** soiled with smut; dirty. **2.** obscene; indecent: *smutty language, a smutty film.* **3.** (of plants) diseased with smut. —**smut′ti·ness,** *n.*

Smyr·na (smur′nə) see **Izmir.**

Sn, the symbol for tin. [Latin *stannum.*]

snack (snak) *n.* a small quantity of food or drink, especially a light meal eaten between regular meals. —*v.i.* to eat a snack.

snack bar, an eating place where snacks are served, especially at a counter.

snaf·fle (snaf′əl) *n.* a slender, jointed horse's bit. Also, **snaf·fle·bit** (snaf′əl bit′). —*v.t.,* **snaf·fled, snaf·fling.** to provide or control with a snaffle.

Snaffle

snag (snag) *n.* **1.** a sharp, jagged, or rough projecting part: *He tore his pants on one of the snags on the barbed wire fence.* **2.** a branch, stump, or trunk of a tree held fast in the bottom of a lake, river, or the like. Snags are a danger to boats. **3.** a tear or hole made by a sharp projection. **4.** an unexpected or hidden obstacle or difficulty: *Their plans for a picnic hit a snag when it began to rain.* —*v.,* **snagged, snag·ging.** —*v.t.* **1.** to catch, tear, or damage on a snag: *Jane snagged her skirt on a nail.* **2.** to hinder; block. **3.** to clear (a lake, river, or the like) of snags. **4.** *Informal.* to catch by quick action: *The outfielder leaped up and snagged the fly ball.* —*v.i.* to be or become caught on or hindered by a snag: *The fishing line snagged as he reeled in his catch.* —**snag′gy,** *adj.*

snag·gle·tooth (snag′əl tōōth′) *n. pl.,* **snag·gle·teeth.** a tooth that sticks out or is broken or irregular. —**snag·gle·toothed** (snag′əl tōōtht′, snag′əl tōōthd′), *adj.*

snail (snāl) *n.* **1.** any of a large group of slow-moving animals found in water and on land. Snails have soft-bodies protected by spirally coiled shells. **2.** a slow-moving or lazy person.

Snail

snake (snāk) *n.* **1.** any of a group of reptiles having long, scaly bodies without legs, arms, or wings. Some snakes have a poisonous bite. **2.** a sly, evil, or unreliable person. **3.** a plumbing tool used to clear clogged drains, made up of a long, very flexible metal wire or rod. —*v.,* **snaked, snak·ing.** —*v.i.* to move, crawl, or curve like a snake: *The river snaked through the hills.* —*v.t.* to drag or pull (something, such as a log): *The lumbermen snaked the newly cut logs through the forest to the river.*

Snake River, a river in the northwestern United States, flowing into the Columbia River.

snake·skin (snāk′skin′) *n.* **1.** the skin of a snake. **2.** leather made from such a skin.

snak·y (snā′kē) *adj.,* **snak·i·er, snak·i·est. 1.** of or relating to a snake or snakes. **2.** having a form or movement like that of a snake; winding; twisting: *a snaky river.* **3.** sly; evil. **4.** overrun or infested with snakes: *a snaky swamp.* —**snak′i·ly,** *adv.* —**snak′i·ness,** *n.*

snap (snap) *v.,* **snapped, snap·ping.** —*v.i.* **1.** to make a sudden, sharp sound: *The dry wood snapped and crackled as it burned.* **2.** to break suddenly, usually with a sharp sound: *The twig snapped when I stepped on it.* **3.** to close or move into place swiftly and with a sharp sound: *The lock snapped shut.* **4.** to give way suddenly under strain or tension: *The strong wind caused the string of the kite to snap.* **5.** to try to bite or seize by closing the jaws suddenly: *The fish snapped at the bait.* **6.** to seize or snatch suddenly or eagerly: *Tom snapped at the opportunity to go to Europe.* **7.** to speak harshly, abruptly, or angrily: *The tired mother snapped at her naughty son.* **8.** to move or act quickly and smartly: *The soldier snapped to attention as the general approached.* —*v.t.* **1.** to break or cut suddenly with a sharp sound: *The big fish snapped the fisherman's line.* **2.** to speak harshly, abruptly, or angrily: *The sergeant snapped a command to the soldiers.* **3.** to cause to make a sudden, sharp sound: *to snap one's fingers.* **4.** to close, fasten, or move into place swiftly and with a sharp sound: *to snap a lock closed.* **5.** to take (a photograph): *Jane snapped pictures of the people at the picnic.* —*n.* **1.** a sharp sound made by breaking: *The stem of the glass broke with a snap.* **2.** the act of snapping or breaking. **3.** a fastener that works with a snapping sound: *Her dress fastened up the back with snaps.* **4.** a sudden snatch or bite: *The fish went after the bait with a snap.* **5.** a brief spell or period, especially of cold weather. **6.** a thin, crisp cookie. **7.** see **snapshot. 8.** *Informal.* something of little or no difficulty: *That spelling test was a snap.* —*adj.* **1.** made or done hastily or with little thought: *a snap judgment, a snap decision.* **2.** *Informal.* of little or no difficulty: *Algebra is a snap course for him.*

to snap out of it. *Informal.* to change from a state or attitude suddenly: *Don't be discouraged; try to snap out of it.*

snap·dra·gon (snap′drag′ən) *n.* **1.** a red, purple, or white flower growing on spikes, widely grown as a garden flower. **2.** the plant bearing this flower.

snap·per (snap′ər) *n.* **1.** a person or thing that snaps. **2.** see **snapping turtle. 3.** any of a large group of brightly colored food and game fish found in warm seas.

snapping turtle, a freshwater turtle found in North and Central America, having powerful jaws.

Snapping turtle

snap·pish (snap′ish) *adj.* **1.** curt, sharp, and ill-tempered in speech or manner; irritable. **2.** inclined to snap or bite, as a dog. —**snap′pish·ly,** *adv.* —**snap′pish·ness,** *n.*

snap·py (snap′ē) *adj.,* **snap·pi·er, snap·pi·est. 1.** *Informal.* lively; brisk: *to walk at a snappy pace.* **2.** *Informal.* smart in appearance; stylish: *a snappy dresser.* **3.** snappish

at; āpe; cär; end; mē; it; īce; hot; ōld; fôrk; wood; fŏŏl; oil; out; up; turn; sing; thin; **this;** hw in white; zh in treasure. The symbol ə stands for the sound of **a** in about, **e** in taken, **i** in pencil, **o** in lemon, and **u** in circus.

in speech or manner; easily annoyed. —**snap′pi·ly,** *adv.*
—**snap′pi·ness,** *n.*

snap·shot (snap′shot′) *n.* an informal photograph, usually taken with a small, inexpensive camera.

snare[1] (sner) *n.* **1.** a trap for catching small animals,
usually consisting of a noose that jerks tight around the
animal when triggered. **2.** anything that tricks or entraps.
—*v.t.,* **snared, snar·ing.** to catch with or as if with a snare:
*The boy snared the chipmunk. The police snared the jewel
thief.* [Old English *sneare.*]

snare[2] (sner) *n.* one of the wires or strings stretched
across the bottom of a snare drum. [Probably from Dutch
snaar cord, string.]

snare drum, a small drum having wires or strings that
are stretched across the lower
head and produce a rattling sound
when the drum is struck.

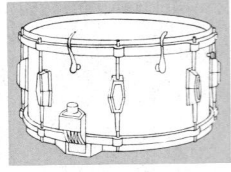

Snare drum

snarl[1] (snärl) *v.i.* **1.** to growl angrily while baring the teeth: *The
dog snarled at the stranger.*
2. to speak angrily: *The grocer
snarled at the clumsy delivery boy.*
—*v.t.* to say with a snarl. —*n.* an
angry growl. [A form of obsolete
snar to growl.] —**snarl′er,** *n.*

snarl[2] (snärl) *n.* **1.** a tangled or knotted mass, as of hair.
2. a confused or disordered state or situation: *Because of
the storm, the airport was in a complete snarl.* —*v.t.*
1. to make tangled or knotted: *The wind and rain had
snarled her hair.* **2.** to make confused or disordered: *The
fierce storm snarled traffic for hours.* —*v.i.* to become
snarled: *The yarn snarled.* [Probably from *snare*[1].]

snatch (snach) *v.t.* to seize or grasp suddenly or quickly:
He snatched the candy from her hand. —*v.i.* to attempt
to seize or grasp something suddenly or quickly: *The thief
snatched at her purse.* —*n. pl.,* **snatch·es. 1.** the act
of snatching. **2.** a brief period of time: *He slept only in
snatches.* **3.** a small amount, part, or portion; bit: *We only
heard snatches of their conversation.* —**snatch′er,** *n.*

sneak (snēk) *v.i.* **1.** to move or go in a quiet, secret, or
cunning manner: *The boy sneaked into the theater by a side
door.* **2.** to behave in a sly or secret manner. —*v.t.* to take
in a sly or secret manner: *The shoplifter sneaked a watch
into her purse.* —*n.* **1.** a person who sneaks, especially a
sly, dishonest person. **2.** the act of sneaking. —*adj.* done,
planned, or acting in a sly or secret manner: *a sneak thief.*

sneak·er (snē′kər) *n.* **1. sneakers.** canvas shoes with soft
rubber soles, worn chiefly for sports. **2.** a person who
sneaks; sneak.

sneak·ing (snē′king) *adj.* **1.** cunning; underhanded.
2. not made known; secret: *I have a sneaking suspicion that
he stole the letter from my desk.* —**sneak′ing·ly,** *adv.*

sneak·y (snē′kē) *adj.,* **sneak·i·er, sneak·i·est. 1.** like or
having the characteristics of a sneak: *He is too sneaky
to be trusted.* **2.** sly, underhanded, or dishonest: *That
was a pretty sneaky trick you pulled!* —**sneak′i·ly,** *adv.*
—**sneak′i·ness,** *n.*

sneer (snēr) *n.* **1.** a facial expression showing hatred or
contempt; scornful look. **2.** a remark that shows hatred
or contempt; scornful comment. —*v.i.* to have or show a
sneer. —*v.t.* to say with a sneer: *She sneered a retort to
his insult.* —**sneer′er,** *n.*

sneeze (snēz) *v.i.,* **sneezed, sneez·ing.** to drive or force
one's breath out through the nose and mouth in a sudden,
violent way. —*n.* the act of sneezing. —**sneez′er,** *n.*
—**sneez′y,** *adj.*

snick·er (snik′ər) *n.* a sly laugh, usually expressing scorn
or disrespect. —*v.i.* to laugh in such a manner. Also,
snigger.

snide (snīd) *adj.,* **snid·er, snid·est.** unkind in a sly or
sarcastic way: *a snide remark.*

sniff (snif) *v.i.* **1.** to take in air through the nose in a short
breath that makes a sound, as in smelling something: *The
kitten sniffed at her food.* **2.** to express disdain or contempt
by sniffing. —*v.t.* **1.** to take in through the nose: *He sniffed
the clean mountain air.* **2.** to smell by sniffing: *She sniffed
the flower.* —*n.* **1.** the act or sound of sniffing. **2.** something sniffed; scent; smell.

snif·fle (snif′əl) *v.i.,* **snif·fled, snif·fling.** to breathe
noisily through the nose, as when crying; sniff repeatedly.
—*n.* **1.** the act or sound of sniffling. **2. the sniffles.** a
condition causing sniffling, such as a head cold.

snig·ger (snig′ər) *n., v.i.* another word for **snicker.**

snip (snip) *v.,* **snipped, snip·ping.** —*v.t.* **1.** to cut with
scissors or shears in short, quick strokes. **2.** to remove
(something) by cutting in this way: *He snipped off several
buds from the rose bush.* —*v.i.* to cut with short, quick
strokes. —*n.* **1.** the act or sound of snipping. **2.** a small
cut made by snipping. **3.** a small piece that is snipped off.

snipe (snīp) *n. pl.,* **snipes** or **snipe.** a long-billed bird that
lives in marshes and bogs. It
usually has brownish feathers
spotted with black and white.
—*v.i.,* **sniped, snip·ing. 1.** to
shoot at a person or persons
from a hidden place. **2.** to hunt
or shoot snipe.

snip·er (snī′pər) *n.* a person
who shoots at another or others from a hidden place.

snip·pet (snip′it) *n.* a small
piece or part; bit; scrap.

Snipe

snip·py (snip′ē) *adj.,* **snip·pi·er, snip·pi·est.** *Informal.*
curt or sharp in a rude or insulting way. Also, **snip·pet·y**
(snip′i tē). —**snip′pi·ness,** *n.*

snitch (snich) *Slang. v.i.* to be an informer; tattle: *Johnny
snitched on his brother.* —*v.t.* to steal; swipe: *He snitched
the watch.* —*n. pl.,* **snitch·es.** a person who snitches; informer; tattletale. Also, **snitch·er** (snich′ər).

sniv·el (sniv′əl) *v.i.,* **sniv·eled, sniv·el·ing;** *also, British,*
sniv·elled, sniv·el·ling. 1. to cry while sniffling. **2.** to have
a running nose. **3.** to complain in a whining manner.
—*n.* the act of sniveling. —**sniv′el·er;** *also, British,* **sniv′-
el·ler,** *n.*

snob (snob) *n.* **1.** a person who admires or tries to imitate
people with wealth or social position, and who looks down
on people whom he considers inferior. **2.** a person who
has little regard or respect for people whom he considers
less intelligent or less gifted than he: *That author is an
intellectual snob.*

snob·ber·y (snob′ər ē) *n. pl.,* **snob·ber·ies.** snobbish
character or conduct.

snob·bish (snob′ish) *adj.* of, relating to, or like a snob:
a snobbish attitude.

snood (snood) *n.* a small net or netlike bag, sometimes
forming part of a hat, worn by women to keep their hair
in place.

snoop (snoop) *Informal. v.i.* to look or go about in a
sneaking, sly way; prowl or pry: *The thief was snooping
around the warehouse.* —*n.* a person who snoops. Also,
snoop·er (snoo′pər).

snoot·y (snoo′tē) *adj.,* **snoot·i·er, snoot·i·est.** *Informal.*
stuck-up or snobbish. —**snoot′i·ly,** *adv.* —**snoot′i·
ness,** *n.*

snooze (snooz) *Informal. v.i.,* **snoozed, snooz·ing.**
to take a short nap; doze. —*n.* a nap; doze.

snore (snôr) *v.i.,* **snored, snor·ing.** to make harsh or noisy
sounds in sleep by breathing through the open mouth or

through the mouth and nose. —*n.* the act or sound of snoring. —**snor′er,** *n.*

snor·kel (snôr′kəl) *n.* **1.** a tubular device in a submarine that can be extended above the surface of the water. It is used to take in fresh air and give off stale air and exhaust fumes. **2.** a tube permitting a person to breath while swimming with the face held underwater. —*v.i.* to swim using a snorkel.

snort (snôrt) *v.i.* **1.** to force air violently and noisily through the nostrils. **2.** to make any similar sound. **3.** to express contempt or anger by snorting. —*v.t.* to utter or express with a snort. —**snort′er,** *n.*

snout (snout) *n.* **1.** the part of an animal's head that projects forward and includes the nose, mouth, and jaws: *Wild boars use their snouts to dig for food.* **2.** something similar to an animal's snout in shape or use.

snow (snō) *n.* **1.** soft, white crystals or flakes of ice formed by the freezing of water vapor in the air. **2.** a fall of snow; snowstorm. **3.** a layer or accumulation of snow. **4.** something that resembles snow. —*v.i.* to fall as snow. —*v.t.* **1.** to cause to fall like snow. **2.** to cover or shut in with or as if with snow: *The farm was snowed in for two days. The post office was snowed under with mail at Christmas.*

snow·ball (snō′bôl′) *n.* **1.** a mass of snow pressed into a ball. **2.** any of several shrubs having large clusters of white flowers resembling such a mass of snow. —*v.t.* to throw snowballs at. —*v.i.* to grow rapidly in size, as a rolling snowball does: *That business has snowballed into a huge industry.*

snow·bank (snō′bangk′) *n.* a large mound or drift of snow.

snow·bird (snō′burd′) *n.* **1.** another word for **junco. 2.** another word for **snow bunting.**

snow·blind (snō′blīnd′) *adj.* affected with snow blindness.

snow blindness, a temporary or partial blindness caused by the sun's glare reflected from snow.

snow·bound (snō′bound′) *adj.* shut in by a heavy fall of snow.

snow bunting, a small finch of cold northern regions, having white feathers with brown or black patches. Also, **snowbird.**

snow·cap (snō′kap′) *n.* a cap or crest of snow, as on a mountain peak. —**snow′-capped′,** *adj.*

snow·drift (snō′drift′) *n.* a heap or mass of snow piled up by the wind.

snow·drop (snō′drop′) *n.* a plant found in Europe and Asia that blooms in the early spring and bears a single white and green flower.

snow·fall (snō′fôl′) *n.* **1.** a fall of snow. **2.** the amount of snow that falls during a given period or in a particular area.

snow·flake (snō′flāk′) *n.* one of the small ice crystals that fall as snow.

snow leopard, a large cat of the mountains of Central Asia, having gray or buff fur marked with black broken rings. Also, **ounce.**

snow line, a line above which a particular area, such as a mountain slope, is always covered with snow.

Snow leopard

snow·man (snō′man′) *n. pl.,* **snow·men** (snō′men′). a figure roughly resembling that of a person, made by shaping a mass of snow.

snow·mo·bile (snō′mō bēl′) *n.* a vehicle for travel on snow, usually having runners or skis.

snow·plow (snō′plou′) *n.* a device or vehicle for clearing away snow, as from a road or sidewalk.

snow·shoe (snō′shoo′) *n.* a light wooden frame strung with a webbing of rawhide, fastened to the foot for walking over deep snow without sinking in.

snowshoe rabbit, a North American rabbit having white fur in winter and brown fur in summer. In winter, its large hind feet, covered with fluffy hairs, enable it to travel over deep snow.

snow·slide (snō′slīd′) *n.* an avalanche of snow.

snow·storm (snō′stôrm′) *n.* a heavy fall of snow with strong winds.

snow·suit (snō′soot′) *n.* a child's outer garment that has a heavy lining for cold weather.

snow·white (snō′hwīt′, snō′wīt′) *adj.* white as snow.

snow·y (snō′ē) *adj.,* **snow·i·er, snow·i·est. 1.** covered with snow: *The snowy houses were barely visible from the road.* **2.** having snow: *snowy weather.* **3.** resembling snow: *snowy blossoms.* —**snow′i·ness,** *n.*

snub (snub) *v.t.,* **snubbed, snub·bing. 1.** to treat with disrespect, scorn, or contempt: *She snubbed him by ignoring his greeting.* **2.** to control or stop (an animal or thing) suddenly by winding an attached rope or line around a post: *Father snubbed the boat to the dock.* —*n.* disrespectful or scornful treatment. —*adj.* (of the nose) short and slightly turned up. —**snub′ber,** *n.*

snub-nosed (snub′nōzd′) *adj.* having a snub nose.

snuff¹ (snuf) *v.t.* **1.** to breathe in through the nose. **2.** to sniff at; smell. —*v.i.* to sniff. —*n.* a preparation of tobacco in powder form taken into the nose by snuffing. [Middle Dutch *snuffen* to sniff.]

up to snuff. *Informal.* in good order or condition: *His work has not been up to snuff lately.*

snuff² (snuf) *v.t.* **1.** to cut or pinch off the burned end of (a candle wick). **2.** to put out: *to snuff out a candle.* **3.** to put an end to suddenly and completely: *Losing the game snuffed out the team's hopes of winning the championship.* —*n.* the burned part of a candle wick. [Of uncertain origin.]

snuff·box (snuf′boks′) *n. pl.,* **snuff·box·es.** a small box for holding snuff.

snuff·ers (snuf′ərz) *n.,pl.* an instrument resembling scissors, used for putting out the flame or removing the burned wick of a candle.

snuf·fle (snuf′əl) *v.,* **snuf·fled, snuf·fling.** —*v.i.* to breathe noisily because of a partly stopped-up nose. —*v.t.* to utter or say in a nasal tone. —*n.* **1.** the act or sound of snuffling. **2.** a nasal tone of voice. —**snuf′fler,** *n.*

snug (snug) *adj.,* **snug·ger, snug·gest. 1.** comfortable and warm; cozy: *a snug bed, a snug cabin.* **2.** fitting closely or tightly: *a snug sweater.* —*adv.* in a snug manner. —**snug′ly,** *adv.* —**snug′ness,** *n.*

snug·gle (snug′əl) *v.,* **snug·gled, snug·gling.** —*v.i.* to draw close, as for warmth, protection, or to show affection: *The bear cub snuggled up against its mother.* —*v.t.* to hold closely and comfortably, as for warmth or protection or to show affection; cuddle: *The young child snuggled the kitten.*

so¹ (sō) *adv.* **1.** in such a manner: *Write the words so.*

at; āpe; cär; end; mē; it; īce; hot; ōld; fôrk; wood; fool; oil; out; up; turn; sing; thin; this; hw in white; zh in treasure. The symbol ə stands for the sound of a in about, e in taken, i in pencil, o in lemon, and u in circus.

2. to such an extent or degree: *It was so cold we stayed indoors.* **3.** very; extremely: *I am so glad.* **4.** very much: *He loved her so.* **5.** for this or that reason; accordingly; therefore: *Tom was tired and so he went home early.* **6.** too; also: *Jim plays on the football team and so does his brother.* **7.** *Informal.* such being the case; as it seems: *So, you didn't like the cake I baked.* —*adj.* in accordance with fact; true: *Say it isn't so.* —*conj.* in order that: *Please turn out the light so I can sleep.* —*pron.* **1.** the same: *Jack is a lazy boy and will always be so.* **2.** more or less: *Lucy will be gone for a month or so.* —*interj.* used to express surprise or displeasure: *So! We meet again.* [Old English *swā.*]

so² (sō) *n.* see **sol.**

So. **1.** South. **2.** Southern.

soak (sōk) *v.t.* **1.** to make very wet; drench: *The sudden, heavy rain soaked him.* **2.** to take in; absorb: *The ground soaked up the heavy rainfall.* **3.** to cause (something) to stay in water or other liquid: *He soaked his sprained ankle to reduce the swelling.* **4.** *Informal.* to charge too much; overcharge: *The garage mechanic soaked us.* —*v.i.* **1.** to become thoroughly wet. **2.** to stay in a liquid: *Mother left the dirty dishes in the sink to soak.* —*n.* the act of soaking or the state of being soaked.

so-and-so (sō′ən sō′) *n. pl.,* **so-and-sos.** someone or something not named.

soap (sōp) *n.* a substance used for washing and cleansing, usually made by treating fats with an alkali. —*v.t.* to rub, cover, or treat with soap.

soap·box (sōp′boks′) *n. pl.,* **soap·box·es. 1.** a box or crate in which soap is packed. **2.** an empty box used as a platform for making a speech, especially on a public street.

soapbox derby, a contest for children in which model racing cars are coasted down a hill.

soap bubble, a bubble formed from soapy water.

soap·stone (sōp′stōn′) *n.* a soft stone having a soapy feel.

soap·suds (sōp′sudz′) *n.,pl.* the suds from soapy water.

soap·y (sō′pē) *adj.,* **soap·i·er, soap·i·est. 1.** containing soap: *soapy water.* **2.** covered with soap: *soapy dishes.* **3.** resembling soap; smooth or slippery. —**soap′i·ly,** *adv.* —**soap′i·ness,** *n.*

soar (sôr) *v.i.* **1.** to fly upward or rise high into the air: *The bird soared overhead.* **2.** to rise to a great height, as a mountain or building. **3.** to go or move upward in position or status; rise sharply: *The price of meat soared.* **4.** to rise above the common or everyday: *The inventor's imagination soared.*

sob (sob) *v.,* **sobbed, sob·bing.** —*v.i.* to cry with short irregular gasps. —*v.t.* **1.** to utter with a sob or sobs: *She sobbed out the sad story.* **2.** to put, bring, or send by sobbing: *The tired child sobbed himself to sleep.* —*n.* the act or sound of sobbing.

so·ber (sō′bər) *adj.* **1.** not drunk. **2.** grave or sedate in character or nature; serious; solemn: *The farmer and his wife lead sober lives.* **3.** not bold or gaudy, as colors or clothes; somber: *The banker wore a sober gray suit.* —*v.t., v.i.* to make or become sober. —**so′ber·ly,** *adv.* —**so′ber·ness,** *n.*

so·bri·e·ty (sə brī′ə tē) *n. pl.,* **so·bri·e·ties. 1.** the state or quality of being sober. **2.** gravity; seriousness; solemnity.

so·bri·quet (sō′brə kā′) *also,* **sou·bri·quet.** *n.* a nickname.

so-called (sō′kôld′) *adj.* called thus, especially wrongly: *My so-called best friend would not help me.*

soc·cer (sok′ər) *n.* a game in which two teams of eleven players each attempt to move a round ball into a goal by kicking it or by striking it with any part of the body except

the hands and arms. [A shortened and changed form of (as)*soc*(iation football); because the game was first played under the rules of the *Football Association* of England.]

so·cia·bil·i·ty (sō′shə bil′ə tē) *n.* the state or quality of being sociable.

so·cia·ble (sō′shə bəl) *adj.* **1.** liking to be with others; fond of company; friendly: *She is a sociable person.* **2.** characterized by companionship and friendly conversation: *The club has a sociable atmosphere.* —*n.* an informal gathering; social. —**so′cia·bly,** *adv.*

so·cial (sō′shəl) *adj.* **1.** of or relating to human beings as a group: *social unrest. The family is a social unit.* **2.** of or relating to fashionable or high society: *one's social position, a social event.* **3.** of, relating to, or furthering companionship or friendly relations: *a social club, a social visit.* **4.** enjoying the company of others; friendly; sociable. **5.** (of animals) living in organized communities, as ants or bees. —*n.* an informal social gathering, as for the members of a church.

social democracy, the principles and beliefs of a social democrat.

social democrat, a member of a political party that favors a gradual, peaceful, and democratic change from capitalism to socialism.

so·cial·ism (sō′shə liz′əm) *n.* **1.** an economic system in which the public owns the basic means of production, such as land and factories, and controls the distribution of food and goods. **2.** the policies or practices of those who favor or support such a system.

so·cial·ist (sō′shə list) *n.* **1.** a person who favors or supports socialism. **2.** *also,* **Socialist.** a member of a Socialist Party. —*adj.* see **socialistic.**

so·cial·is·tic (sō′shə lis′tik) *adj.* **1.** of, relating to, or resembling socialism. **2.** favoring or supporting socialism. —**so′cial·is′ti·cal·ly,** *adv.*

Socialist Party, a political party that favors socialism.

so·cial·ite (sō′shə līt′) *n.* a member of fashionable society; socially prominent person.

so·cial·ize (sō′shə līz′) *v.,* **so·cial·ized, so·cial·iz·ing.** —*v.t.* **1.** to make socialistic: *to socialize medicine, to socialize a country.* **2.** to cause to become sociable. —*v.i.* to take part in social activities; associate with others: *The busy man had little time to socialize.* —**so′cial·i·za′tion,** *n.*

so·cial·ly (sō′shə lē) *adv.* **1.** in a social way: *Do you know him socially?* **2.** as a part of society; with regard to society: *Ruth's parents are socially prominent.* **3.** by or from society.

social science 1. the study of society and the activities and relationship of people and groups within society. **2.** a particular field of study dealing with society, such as sociology, psychology, history, political science, or economics.

social security 1. any system that provides assistance for a person or his family through government programs paid for by taxes. **2.** *also,* **Social Security.** a system of insurance maintained by the U.S. government for making payments to people who are old, retired, unemployed, or handicapped.

social studies, a course of study in an elementary or secondary school that includes geography, history, and political science.

social work, any activity or service that seeks to help people who are old, poor, or handicapped.

social worker, a person who does social work, especially as a profession.

so·ci·e·ty (sə sī′ə tē) *n. pl.,* **so·ci·e·ties. 1.** human beings as a group; all people. **2.** a group of people forming a community and having common interests, traditions, and culture: *Our ancestors lived in an agricultural society.*

3. a group of people gathered together or associated for a common purpose or interest: *John belongs to a literary society.* **4.** the wealthy or aristocratic members of a community; fashionable people as a group. **5.** companionship; company: *The family enjoyed his society and often invited him to dinner.* —*adj.* of or relating to fashionable society: *the society column of a newspaper.*

Society of Friends, a Christian religious group founded by George Fox in England about 1650, having no ritual, clergy, or formal worship service, and opposed to all forms of violence, including war. Its members are commonly called Quakers.

Society of Jesus, the religious order of the Jesuits.

so·ci·o·log·i·cal (sō′sē ə loj′i kəl) *adj.* of or relating to sociology. —**so′ci·o·log′i·cal·ly,** *adv.*

so·ci·ol·o·gist (sō′sē ol′ə jist) *n.* a student of or an expert in sociology.

so·ci·ol·o·gy (sō′sē ol′ə jē) *n.* the science or study of human society, including its history, its different forms, and its institutions.

sock[1] (sok) *n.* a short stocking, especially one reaching above the ankle but below the knee. [Old English *socc* a type of light shoe.]

sock[2] (sok) *Slang. v.t.* to hit or strike hard, especially with the fist. —*n.* a hard blow or punch. [Of uncertain origin.]

sock·et (sok′it) *n.* an opening or hollow part or place into which something fits: *a socket for a light bulb.*

Soc·ra·tes (sok′rə tēz′) 469–399 B.C., Greek philosopher and teacher.

So·crat·ic (sə krat′ik) *adj.* of or relating to Socrates, his philosophy, or his followers.

sod (sod) *n.* **1.** the surface of the ground, especially when covered with grass. **2.** a piece of this grassy surface, usually cut in a square or strip, and held together by roots. —*v.t.,* **sod·ded, sod·ding.** to cover with sod.

so·da (sō′də) *n.* **1.** any of a group of compounds that contain sodium, such as baking soda or washing soda. **2.** see **soda water. 3.** a soft drink made with soda water and flavoring. **4.** a beverage containing soda water, flavoring, and ice cream.

soda fountain, a counter having equipment for preparing and serving soft drinks, sodas, sundaes, ice cream, and the like.

so·dal·i·ty (sō dal′ə tē) *n. pl.,* **so·dal·i·ties.** a society, especially one of the Roman Catholic Church, having religious or charitable aims.

soda pop *Informal.* a soft drink containing soda water and flavoring.

soda water, a bubbling drink consisting of water charged under pressure with carbon dioxide gas. Also, **club soda.**

sod·den (sod′ən) *adj.* **1.** filled with water or moisture; soaked through: *The ground became sodden after the rain.* **2.** damp and heavy: *The cake is sodden because it wasn't baked enough.* —**sod′den·ly,** *adv.* —**sod′den·ness,** *n.*

so·di·um (sō′dē əm) *n.* a very light, soft, silver-white metallic element similar to potassium. Symbol: **Na**

sodium ben·zo·ate (ben′zō āt′) a white powder that is the sodium salt of benzoic acid. It is used chiefly as a food preservative.

sodium bicarbonate, a white, crystalline compound with a slightly salty taste, used especially in cooking as baking soda and in medicine as an antacid. Also, **baking soda, bicarbonate of soda.**

sodium carbonate 1. a white, powdery compound used in making glass, soap, and paper. **2.** a crystalline form of this compound. Also (*def. 2*), **sal soda, washing soda.**

sodium chloride, see **salt** (*def. 1*).

sodium fluoride, a white, poisonous, solid compound, used in the fluoridation of water, as an insecticide, and in rat poisons.

sodium hydroxide, a white, solid compound used in making rayon, soap, and detergents. Also, **caustic soda.**

sodium nitrate, a colorless, crystalline compound used in making explosives and fertilizer.

sodium thi·o·sul·fate (thī′ō sul′fāt) a colorless or white crystalline salt, used in dyeing and in photography to fix negatives. Also, **hyposulfite.**

Sod·om (sod′əm) *n.* in the Old Testament, a city near the Dead Sea that, along with the nearby city of Gomorrah, was destroyed by fire from heaven, because of the wickedness of the people living there.

so·fa (sō′fə) *n.* a long, upholstered seat with a back and arms; couch.

So·fi·a (sō′fē ə) *n.* the capital of Bulgaria, in the western part of the country. Pop. (1969 est.), 868,200.

soft (sôft) *adj.* **1.** easily shaped or worked; readily yielding to the touch; not hard: *soft clay, a soft bed.* **2.** not hard for its kind: *soft wood.* **3.** smooth or fine to the touch; not rough or coarse: *soft skin.* **4.** not loud or harsh; quiet: *a soft voice.* **5.** not glaring, sharp, or harsh to the sight; subdued: *soft lighting.* **6.** mild and agreeable; gentle: *a soft breeze.* **7.** having sympathy; tender; kind: *a soft heart.* **8.** lacking strength; flabby; weak: *soft muscles.* **9.** (of water) free from mineral salts that interfere with the sudsing and cleansing action of soap. **10.** *Phonetics.* **a.** (of *c*) pronounced with the sound of *s,* as in *city.* **b.** (of *g*) pronounced with the sound of *j,* as in *gem.* —*adv.* in a soft manner; gently. —**soft′ly,** *adv.* —**soft′ness,** *n.*

soft·ball (sôft′bôl′) *n.* **1.** a game like baseball but played on a smaller field with a larger and softer ball that is pitched underhand. **2.** the ball used in this game.

soft-boiled (sôft′boild′) *adj.* (of eggs) boiled for only a short time, so that the yolk is still soft.

soft coal, another term for **bituminous coal.**

soft drink, a beverage that contains no alcohol, especially a carbonated beverage.

soft·en (sô′fən) *v.t., v.i.* to make or become soft or softer. —**soft′en·er,** *n.*

soft-heart·ed (sôft′här′tid) *adj.* sympathetic; tender; kind. —**soft′-heart′ed·ness,** *n.*

soft landing, a landing of a spacecraft on the moon or on another body in outer space at a slow speed to keep from damaging the vehicle or its contents.

soft palate, the soft part of the palate at the back of the roof of the mouth.

soft shoulder, the soft earth along the edge of a paved road.

soft-spo·ken (sôft′spō′kən) *adj.* (of persons) speaking with a soft, low voice.

soft·ware (sôft′wer′) *n.* written or printed programs, information, and the like used in a computer, as distinguished from its physical equipment.

soft·wood (sôft′wood′) *n.* **1.** any of a large group of trees bearing cones and having needlelike leaves, such as pines, firs, and spruces. **2.** the wood of such a tree, used chiefly for building. **3.** any soft, light, easily cut wood.

soft·y (sôf′tē) *n. pl.,* **soft·ies.** *Informal.* a weak or overly sentimental person.

---

at; āpe; cär; end; mē; it; īce; hot; ōld; fôrk; wood; fōōl; oil; out; up; turn; sing; thin; this; hw in white; zh in treasure. The symbol ə stands for the sound of **a** in about, **e** in taken, **i** in pencil, **o** in lemon, and **u** in circus.

S

sog·gy (sog′ē) *adj.,* **sog·gi·er, sog·gi·est. 1.** filled with water or moisture; soaked: *soggy ground.* **2.** damp and heavy, as poorly baked bread. —**sog′gi·ness,** *n.*

soil¹ (soil) *n.* **1.** the part of the earth's surface in which plants grow. **2.** a land, country, or region: *to land on foreign soil, a person's native soil.* [Anglo-Norman *soil* land.]

soil² (soil) *v.t.* **1.** to make dirty: *Johnny soiled his jacket.* **2.** to bring disgrace or dishonor to; sully: *Gossip can soil a person's reputation.* —*v.i.* to become soiled or dirty: *White gloves soil easily.* —*n.* a dirty mark or place; spot; stain. [Old French *soillier.*]

soi·ree (swä rā′) *also,* **soi·rée.** *n.* a party or other social gathering taking place in the evening.

so·journ (sō′jurn, sō jurn′) *v.i.* to live in a place for a brief time: *Helen sojourned in Paris during her trip to Europe.* —*n.* a brief stay. —**so′journ·er,** *n.*

sol (sōl) *n. Music.* **1.** the fifth note of the major scale. **2.** the note G. Also, **so.**

Sol (sol) *n.* **1.** *Roman Mythology.* the god of the sun. In Greek mythology he was called Helios. **2.** the sun.

sol·ace (sol′is) *n.* **1.** relief from sorrow or disappointment; comfort: *The widow found solace in her children.* **2.** a person or thing that gives such relief: *Her friends were a solace to her during her grief.* —*v.t.,* **sol·aced, sol·ac·ing.** to relieve from sorrow or disappointment; comfort; console.

so·lar (sō′lər) *adj.* relating to, produced by, or coming from the sun: *solar energy, solar flares.*

solar battery, a device that changes the radiant energy of the sun into electricity.

solar eclipse, the partial or total blocking of the sun's light by the moon as it passes between the sun and earth.

so·lar·i·um (sə ler′ē əm) *n. pl.,* **so·lar·i·a** (sə ler′ē ə). a glass-enclosed room, porch, or balcony where people can sit in the sun, as in a hospital.

solar plex·us (plek′səs) a large network of nerves located just behind the stomach.

solar system, the sun and all the heavenly bodies that revolve around it. It includes the planets and their moons or satellites, as well as asteroids, comets, and meteors.

solar year, see **year** *(def. 2).*

sold (sōld) the past tense and past participle of **sell.**

sol·der (sod′ər) *n.* any metal that can be used when melted for joining metal surfaces or parts. —*v.t.* to join, fasten, or repair with solder. —*v.i.* to perform work with solder. —**sol′der·er,** *n.*

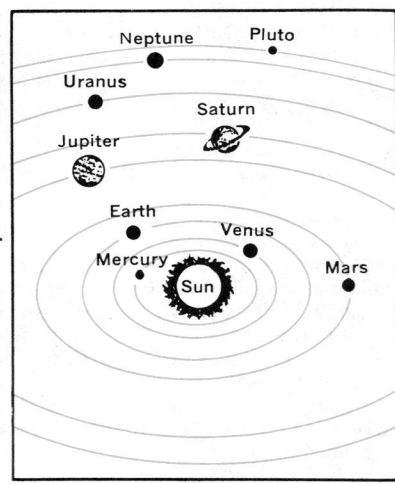

Solar system

sol·dier (sōl′jər) *n.* **1.** a person who serves in an army, especially an enlisted man. **2.** a brave, skilled, or experienced warrior. —*v.i.* to be a soldier; serve in an army. [Old French *soldier* a person who fights for pay, from *soulde* pay, going back to Late Latin *solidus* a Roman gold coin.]

sol·dier·ly (sōl′jər lē) *adj.* relating to or characteristic of a soldier.

soldier of fortune 1. a person who will serve in any army for money, adventure, or pleasure. **2.** any restless, adventurous person.

sol·dier·y (sōl′jər ē) *n.* **1.** soldiers as a group. **2.** military knowledge or training; military science.

sole¹ (sōl) *n.* **1.** the bottom surface of the foot. **2.** the part of a shoe, boot, sock, or other footwear that covers the sole. —*v.t.,* **soled, sol·ing.** to furnish with a sole: *to sole shoes.* [Old French *sole.*]

sole² (sōl) *adj.* **1.** being the only one; only; single: *Jeffrey is the sole heir to the fortune.* **2.** limited or belonging to a single person or group; exclusive: *The film company bought sole rights to the novel.* [Old French *sol* alone.]

sole³ (sōl) *n. pl.,* **soles** or **sole. 1.** any of a group of flatfish found in warm and temperate seas, valued as a food fish. **2.** any of various other flatfish that can be eaten, such as the flounder. [Old French *sole,* from Latin *solea* sole¹; in reference to the flatness of these fish.]

sol·e·cism (sol′ə siz′əm) *n.* **1.** an error in grammar or in the choice of words. **2.** an error in social behavior. [Latin *soloecismus,* going back to *Soloi,* a Greek colony in Asia Minor, where Greek was spoken incorrectly.]

sole·ly (sōl′lē) *adv.* **1.** without any other; by oneself or itself; alone: *He is solely to blame for the accident.* **2.** entirely; exclusively: *to work solely for the good of others.*

sol·emn (sol′əm) *adj.* **1.** serious and earnest; grave; sober: *a solemn man, a solemn mood.* **2.** having much dignity or majesty: *a solemn occasion, a solemn and imposing building.* **3.** having to do with religion or religious observances; sacred. **4.** done with or accompanied by formality or ceremony: *a solemn oath.* —**sol′emn·ly,** *adv.* —**sol′emn·ness,** *n.*

so·lem·ni·ty (sə lem′nə tē) *n. pl.,* **so·lem·ni·ties. 1.** the state or quality of being solemn; seriousness; gravity. **2.** *also,* **solemnities.** a solemn ceremony.

sol·em·nize (sol′əm nīz′) *v.t.,* **sol·em·nized, sol·em·niz·ing. 1.** to celebrate with a formal ceremony or by a ritual: *to solemnize a religious holiday.* **2.** to perform (a ceremony): *to solemnize a marriage.* —**sol′em·ni·za′tion,** *n.*

so·le·noid (sō′lə noid′) *n.* a coil of wire that produces a magnetic field when an electric current is passed through it. The solenoid is the basis for all electromagnets.

so·lic·it (sə lis′it) *v.t.* to seek to obtain; ask for earnestly: *to solicit business, to solicit favors.* —**so·lic′i·ta′tion,** *n.*

so·lic·i·tor (sə lis′ə tər) *n.* **1.** a person who solicits, especially a person who seeks business or trade. **2.** in Great Britain, a lawyer.

so·lic·i·tous (sə lis′ə təs) *adj.* **1.** full of concern: *Mary was solicitous about her aunt's health.* **2.** eager; desirous; anxious. —**so·lic′it·ous·ly,** *adv.* —**so·lic′it·ous·ness,** *n.*

so·lic·i·tude (sə lis′ə tōōd′, sə lis′ə tyōōd′) *n.* the state of being concerned.

sol·id (sol′id) *adj.* **1.** having shape and hardness; not liquid or gaseous: *Melted wax becomes solid when it cools.* **2.** free from empty spaces; completely filled with matter: *These metal bars are solid, not hollow.* **3.** not loose; compact; firm: *The ground is frozen solid.* **4.** of one material, color, or character; unmixed: *The ring is made of solid gold.* **5.** structurally sound or firm: *The building has a solid foundation.* **6.** of sound character; reliable: *Mr. Smith is*

Direction of current

Magnetic field

Solenoid

a solid citizen. **7.** sound; sensible: *He made a solid investment. She supported her opinion with a solid argument.* **8.** united, as in opinion or support; unanimous: *The candidate received solid backing from his political party.* **9.** complete; uninterrupted: *Joe slept for twelve solid hours.* **10.** *Mathematics.* having the three dimensions of length, width, and thickness: *Cubes, spheres, and pyramids are solid figures.* —*n.* **1.** a form of matter having shape and hardness. **2.** *Mathematics.* a figure having length, width, and thickness, as a cube, sphere, or pyramid. —**sol′id·ly,** *adv.* —**sol′id·ness,** *n.*

sol·i·dar·i·ty (sol′ə dar′ə tē) *n.* agreement among the members of a group, as in opinion, objectives, interests, or the like.

solid geometry, a branch of geometry dealing with three-dimensional figures.

so·lid·i·fy (sə lid′ə fī′) *v.t., v.i.,* **so·lid·i·fied, so·lid·i·fy·ing. 1.** to make or become solid: *The heat of the sun solidified the mud into hard clay. The water solidified into ice.* **2.** to make or become firmly united: *The signing of the trade agreement solidified relations between the two countries.* —**so·lid′i·fi·ca′tion,** *n.*

so·lid·i·ty (sə lid′ə tē) *n.* the state or quality of being solid.

sol·id-state (sol′id stāt′) *adj.* **1.** of or relating to the branch of physics that deals with the properties of solids, especially crystals. **2.** of or relating to electronic devices made with transistors or other semiconductors.

so·lil·o·quize (sə lil′ə kwīz′) *v.i.,* **so·lil·o·quized, so·lil·o·quiz·ing.** to talk to oneself.

so·lil·o·quy (sə lil′ə kwē) *n. pl.,* **so·lil·o·quies. 1.** the act of talking to oneself. **2.** a speech in which a character in a play expresses his thoughts to the audience but not to the other characters by speaking as if to himself.

sol·i·taire (sol′ə ter′) *n.* **1.** any of a number of card games for one person. Also, **patience. 2.** a single gem, especially a diamond set by itself in a ring.

sol·i·tar·y (sol′ə ter′ē) *adj.* **1.** living or being alone: *a solitary traveler.* **2.** made, done, or spent alone: *a solitary life.* **3.** not often visited; secluded; lonely: *a solitary cabin.* **4.** single: *Not a solitary person came to visit him.* —*n. pl.,* **sol·i·tar·ies. 1.** a person who chooses to live alone, away from other people; hermit. **2.** *Informal.* see **solitary confinement.** —**sol′i·tar′i·ly,** *adv.* —**sol′i·tar′i·ness,** *n.*

solitary confinement, a punishment in which a prisoner is kept isolated from all other inmates.

sol·i·tude (sol′ə tōōd′, sol′ə tyōōd′) *n.* **1.** the state of being or living alone; loneliness. **2.** a lonely or unvisited place.

so·lo (sō′lō) *n. pl.,* **so·los. 1.** a musical work for a single voice or instrument. **2.** any action done by one person alone, as an airplane flight. —*adj.* **1.** composed, arranged for, or performed by a single voice or instrument. **2.** made or done by one person alone: *a solo flight.* —*v.i.,* **so·loed, so·lo·ing. 1.** to make a flight alone in an airplane, especially for the first time. **2.** to perform alone.

so·lo·ist (sō′lō ist) *n.* a person who performs a solo, especially a musical solo.

Sol·o·mon (sol′ə mən) *n.* **1.** the king of Israel in the tenth century B.C., the son of David. He built the first Temple at Jerusalem and was noted for his wisdom. **2.** any very wise man.

Solomon Islands, an island country in the southwestern Pacific, east of Papua New Guinea. Capital, Honiara. Pop. (1978 est.), 204,000.

So·lon (sō′lən, sō′lon) *n.* **1.** 638?–559? B.C., Athenian lawgiver who was noted for his wisdom. **2.** *also,* **solon.** any wise man, especially a wise lawmaker.

so long *Informal.* good-by.

sol·stice (sol′stis) *n.* either of the two times during the year when the sun appears farthest from the equator. In the Northern Hemisphere, the sun appears farthest north of the equator during the summer solstice, on or about June 21, and farthest south of the equator during the winter solstice, on or about December 22.

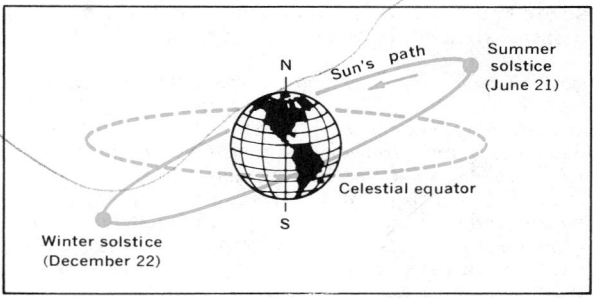

Solstice

sol·u·ble (sol′yə bəl) *adj.* **1.** able to be dissolved in another substance. **2.** able to be solved. —**sol′u·bly,** *adv.*

so·lu·tion (sə lōō′shən) *n.* **1.** the act, process, or method of solving a problem. **2.** an answer to a problem; explanation: *the solution to an arithmetic problem.* **3.** a mixture of two or more substances. Solutions are usually formed by solids, liquids, or gases dissolved in liquids.

solution set *Mathematics.* the set of all the values that satisfy an equation. Also, **truth set.**

solv·a·ble (sol′və bəl) *adj.* able to be solved.

solve (solv) *v.t.,* **solved, solv·ing.** to find the solution to; provide an answer for: *to solve a problem.* —**solv′er,** *n.*

sol·ven·cy (sol′vən sē) *n.* the state of being solvent.

sol·vent (sol′vənt) *adj.* **1.** able to pay all debts: *His business is now solvent.* **2.** having the power to dissolve; causing solution. —*n.* a substance in a solution that dissolves another substance or substances. Solvents are usually liquids.

So·ma·lia (sə mäl′yə) a country in eastern Africa, on the Indian Ocean. Capital, Mogadishu. Area, 246,201 sq. mi. Pop. (1978 est.), 3,450,000.

som·ber (som′bər) *also,* **som·bre.** *adj.* **1.** dark and gloomy: *a somber sky.* **2.** melancholy or depressing: *a somber mood.* —**som′ber·ly,** *adv.* —**som′ber·ness,** *n.*

som·brer·o (som brer′ō) *n. pl.,* **som·brer·os.** a hat with a broad brim, worn especially in Mexico and the southwestern United States.

some (sum) *adj.* **1.** being certain ones not named or known: *Some people don't like spinach. Some birds cannot fly.* **2.** being of a certain number or amount not given: *The accident happened some weeks ago. Please have some potatoes.* **3.** *Informal.* remarkable; striking: *That was some game yesterday!* —*pron.* **1.** certain ones not named or known: *Some of the students like to draw.* **2.** a certain number or amount: *He kept*

Sombrero

at; āpe; cär; end; mē; it; īce; hot; ōld; fôrk; wood; fōōl; oil; out; up; turn; sing; thin; **th**is; hw in white; zh in treasure. The symbol ə stands for the sound of **a** in about, **e** in taken, **i** in pencil, **o** in lemon, and **u** in circus.

some of the candy and gave the rest away. —*adv.* **1.** approximately; about: *The club has some forty members.* **2.** *Informal.* somewhat: *The patient's condition has improved some.*

-some¹ *suffix* (used to form adjectives) characterized by, tending to, or tending to be (what is indicated by the stem): *tiresome, bothersome.* [Old English *-sum.*]

-some² *suffix* used to form nouns indicating a group of a specified number: *threesome, foursome.* [Old English *sum* some.]

-some³ *combining form* body: *chromosome.* [Greek *sōma* body.]

some·bod·y (sum'bod'ē) *pron.* a person who is not named or known; someone: *Somebody has taken my raincoat.* —*n. pl.,* **some·bod·ies.** a person who is important or famous. ▲ **Somebody** and **someone** are both singular. In writing and in formal speech, they are used with a singular pronoun. In conversation, however, these words are often used with a plural pronoun: *Somebody left their* (rather than *his* or *her*) *pencil on my desk.*

some·day (sum'dā') *adv.* at some future time.

some·how (sum'hou') *adv.* in a way not known or stated: *We must get the car fixed somehow.*

some·one (sum'wun') *pron.* a person who is not named or known; somebody: *Someone will have to mail these letters.* ▲ See **somebody** for usage note.

some·place (sum'plās') *adv. Informal.* somewhere: *We'll have dinner someplace near the theater.*

som·er·sault (sum'ər sôlt') *n.* a roll in which the body turns heels over head. —*v.i.* to perform a somersault. Also, **som·er·set** (sum'ər set').

some·thing (sum'thing) *pron.* a certain thing not named or known; some thing: *Something is wrong with the car.* —*n.* an important person or thing: *She thinks she's something since she won the beauty contest.* —*adv.* to some extent; somewhat: *Your house is something like ours.*

some·time (sum'tīm') *adv.* at a time not named or known: *I bought the book sometime last spring. He said he would visit us sometime.* —*adj.* having been formerly; former: *a sometime actress.*

some·times (sum'tīmz') *adv.* now and then; at times: *Sometimes we spend the weekend in the country.*

some·way (sum'wā') *also,* **some·ways.** *adv.* in some way; somehow.

some·what (sum'hwät', sum'wät') *adv.* to some extent; rather: *She was somewhat upset. His work is somewhat better than it was last year.* —*n.* some part, amount, or degree: *That movie was somewhat of a disappointment.*

some·where (sum'hwer', sum'wer') *adv.* **1.** in, at, or to some place not named or known: *He now lives somewhere in California.* **2.** at some time or amount: *The book costs somewhere around ten dollars.* —*n.* a place that is not named or known.

som·nam·bu·lism (som nam'byə liz'əm) *n.* the act or habit of walking about while asleep; sleepwalking.

som·nam·bu·list (som nam'byə list) *n.* a person who walks about while asleep. —**som·nam·bu·lis'tic,** *adj.*

som·no·lence (som'nə ləns) *n.* sleepiness; drowsiness.

som·no·lent (som'nə lənt) *adj.* **1.** sleepy; drowsy. **2.** tending to cause sleep. —**som'no·lent·ly,** *adv.*

son (sun) *n.* **1.** a male child considered in relation to one or both of his parents. **2.** a male descendant: *the sons of Adam.* **3.** a male person regarded as the product of a certain country or place: *a son of Ireland, a son of the soil.* **4.** a familiar term of address to a boy or man from an older person. **5. the Son.** Jesus Christ.

so·nar (sō'när) *n.* an instrument used to detect underwater objects and to determine their location. [Short for *so*(und) *na*(vigation) *r*(anging).]

so·na·ta (sə nä'tə) *n.* a musical composition, often written for the piano. It usually has three or four movements in different rhythms.

song (sông) *n.* **1.** a musical composition for one or more voices. **2.** a poem that can be set to music. **3.** the act or art of singing. **4.** any melodious sound or series of sounds, as the call of a bird.

for a song. at a very low price; very cheaply.

song·bird (sông'burd') *n.* a bird that has a musical call, such as a canary.

song·less (sông'lis) *adj.* having no song; unable to sing: *a songless bird.*

Song of Solomon, a book of the Old Testament, once thought to have been written by Solomon. Also, **Song of Songs.**

song sparrow, a common North American sparrow having brownish feathers marked with dark brown streaks. It is noted for its song.

song·ster (sông'stər) *n.* **1.** a person who sings. **2.** a writer of songs or poems. **3.** a songbird.

song·stress (sông'stris) *n. pl.,* **song·stress·es.** a female singer, especially of popular songs.

song thrush, a European thrush having brown feathers and a yellow and white breast marked with brown spots. Also, **mavis.**

son·ic (son'ik) *adj.* **1.** of, relating to, or using sound: *sonic vibrations.* **2.** of or relating to the speed at which sound travels through the air.

sonic barrier, another term for **sound barrier.**

sonic boom, a loud, explosive noise caused by an aircraft traveling at or above the speed of sound.

son-in-law (sun'in lô') *n. pl.,* **sons-in-law.** the husband of a person's daughter.

son·net (son'it) *n.* a poem that has fourteen lines and a fixed pattern of rhyme.

son·net·eer (son'ə tēr') *n.* a person who writes sonnets.

son·ny (sun'ē) *n.* a young boy.

so·nor·i·ty (sə nôr'ə tē, sə nor'ə tē) *n.* the state or quality of being sonorous.

so·no·rous (sə nôr'əs) *adj.* **1.** making or able to make sound, especially a deep, full, or rich sound. **2.** (of sound) loud, deep, or resonant. —**so·no'rous·ly,** *adv.* —**so·no'rous·ness,** *n.*

soon (sōōn) *adv.* **1.** in the near future; before long; shortly: *Visit us again soon.* **2.** ahead of the expected time; early: *The guests arrived too soon.* **3.** without delay; promptly; quickly: *I'll come as soon as I can.* **4.** readily; willingly: *I would as soon do it now as later.*

soot (soot, sŏōt) *n.* a black, powdery material, composed mostly of carbon. It is formed during the burning of such fuels as wood, coal, or oil. —*v.t.* to soil or cover with soot.

sooth (sōōth) *Archaic. n.* truth; reality. —*adj.* true; real.

soothe (sōō*th*) *v.,* **soothed, sooth·ing.** —*v.t.* **1.** to bring to a quiet or calm state; comfort: *The soft music soothed his nerves.* **2.** to ease or relieve: *The medicine soothed his headache.* —*v.i.* to have a soothing effect. —**sooth'er,** *n.*

sooth·ing (sōō'*th*ing) *adj.* that soothes; calming; quieting: *The mother spoke soothing words to her frightened child.* —**sooth'ing·ly,** *adv.*

sooth·say·er (sōōth'sā'ər) *n.* a person who claims to be able to foretell future events.

sooth·say·ing (sōōth'sā'ing) *n.* **1.** the act or practice of foretelling future events. **2.** an instance of this; prediction; prophecy.

soot·y (soot'ē, sŏō'tē) *adj.,* **soot·i·er, soot·i·est. 1.** covered or soiled with soot: *sooty buildings.* **2.** of, relating to, or making soot: *a sooty layer of dirt.* —**soot'i·ly,** *adv.* —**soot'i·ness,** *n.*

sop (sop) *n.* **1.** a piece of food, such as bread, soaked or dipped in a liquid, such as milk or gravy. **2.** anything given to pacify or quiet, or as a bribe: *He sent her flowers as a sop when she was angry.* —*v.t.,* **sopped, sop·ping. 1.** to soak or dip in a liquid: *to sop bread in milk.* **2.** to take up (water or other liquid) by absorption: *to sop up gravy with bread.* **3.** to wet thoroughly; drench.

soph., sophomore.

soph·ism (sof′iz′əm) *n.* an argument that appears to be true, but is actually false, especially one used to mislead.

soph·ist (sof′ist) *n.* a person who argues in a clever way so that he appears to be right, but who is actually wrong.

so·phis·ti·cate (*v.,* sə fis′tə kāt′; *n.,* sə fis′tə kit, sə fis′tə kāt′) *v.t.,* **so·phis·ti·cat·ed, so·phis·ti·cat·ing. 1.** to cause to have worldly knowledge and experience; make less natural or simple. **2.** to make complicated. —*n.* a sophisticated person.

so·phis·ti·cat·ed (sə fis′tə kā′tid) *adj.* **1.** having worldly knowledge and experience; not naive. **2.** for sophisticated people: *sophisticated entertainment.* **3.** developed to a highly complex level: *sophisticated electronic equipment.*

so·phis·ti·ca·tion (sə fis′tə kā′shən) *n.* **1.** the quality or character of being sophisticated; sophisticated ideas, tastes, or ways. **2.** the act of sophisticating.

soph·ist·ry (sof′is trē) *n. pl.,* **soph·ist·ries. 1.** a way of reasoning that is clever but unsound. **2.** a clever but false argument; sophism.

Soph·o·cles (sof′ə klēz′) 496?–406? B.C., Greek dramatist.

soph·o·more (sof′ə môr′) *n.* a student in the second year of a four-year high school or college.

soph·o·mor·ic (sof′ə môr′ik) *adj.* of, relating to, or characteristic of a sophomore or sophomores.

sop·o·rif·ic (sop′ə rif′ik, sō′pə rif′ik) *adj.* **1.** causing or tending to cause sleep: *a soporific drug.* **2.** sleepy; drowsy. —*n.* something that causes sleep.

sop·ping (sop′ing) *adj.* thoroughly wet; soaked; drenched.

sop·py (sop′ē) *adj.,* **sop·pi·er, sop·pi·est.** soaked through with water or other liquid: *soppy clothes.*

so·pran·o (sə pran′ō) *n. pl.,* **so·pran·os. 1.** the highest singing voice of women and boys. **2.** a singer who has such a voice. **3.** a musical instrument that has a similar range. **4.** a musical part for such a voice or instrument. —*adj.* **1.** able to sing or play soprano: *a soprano voice, a soprano saxophone.* **2.** for a soprano: *a soprano part.*

sor·cer·er (sôr′sər ər) *n.* a person who practices sorcery. —**sor′cer·ess,** *n.*

sor·cer·y (sôr′sər ē) *n. pl.,* **sor·cer·ies.** the use of supernatural powers or magic, especially to do harm to another person; witchcraft.

sor·did (sôr′did) *adj.* **1.** dirty or filthy; foul: *The poor child lived in a sordid slum.* **2.** having a base or degraded character; mean; vile: *The newspaper printed all the sordid details of the crime.* —**sor′did·ly,** *adv.* —**sor′did·ness,** *n.*

sore (sôr) *adj.,* **sor·er, sor·est. 1.** painful or sensitive to the touch, as an injured or diseased part of the body: *John's muscles were sore from exercise.* **2.** feeling physical pain, as from wounds or bruises: *The athlete was sore after the rough game.* **3.** causing sadness, grief, or misery: *The widow is in sore need.* **4.** causing annoyance or anger; annoying: *Jeff's failure on the test is a sore point with him.* **5.** *Informal.* annoyed; angry; offended: *Are you still sore at him for not inviting you to his party?* —*n.* **1.** an area of the body where the skin is broken or bruised and painful or sensitive to the touch. **2.** any source of pain, anger, sorrow, or distress. —**sore′ly,** *adv.* —**sore′ness,** *n.*

sore·head (sôr′hed′) *n. Informal.* a person who is easily angered, annoyed, or offended.

sor·ghum (sôr′gəm) *n.* **1.** any of a group of tall, tropical grasses widely grown for grain, syrup, and fodder. **2.** a syrup made from the juices of this plant.

so·ror·i·ty (sə rôr′ə tē, sə ror′ə tē) *n. pl.,* **so·ror·i·ties.** a social organization of girls or women, especially one having chapters in various colleges.

sor·rel¹ (sôr′əl, sor′əl) *n.* any of a group of plants bearing long branching clusters of small, usually greenish flowers and heart-shaped leaves. The leaves of some kinds of this plant are eaten in salads. [Old French *surele.*]

sor·rel² (sôr′əl, sor′əl) *n.* **1.** a reddish-brown color. **2.** a horse of this color. —*adj.* having the color sorrel; reddish-brown. [Old French *sorel.*]

Sorghum

sor·row (sor′ō) *n.* **1.** sadness, grief, or distress caused by loss, injury, disappointment, or trouble: *The death of his grandmother filled him with sorrow.* **2.** the cause of this: *Her illness is a sorrow to her family.* —*v.i.* to feel or express sorrow; be sad. —**sor′row·er,** *n.*

sor·row·ful (sor′ō fəl) *adj.* **1.** full of sorrow; sad: *A sorrowful crowd watched the funeral procession pass by.* **2.** showing sorrow: *The boy had a sorrowful look on his face.* —**sor′row·ful·ly,** *adv.* —**sor′row·ful·ness,** *n.*

sor·ry (sor′ē) *adj.,* **sor·ri·er, sor·ri·est. 1.** feeling sorrow, pity, sympathy, or regret: *He was sorry to hear of her illness.* **2.** poor in value or quality; worthless: *That was a sorry attempt at a joke.* **3.** causing pity; wretched; miserable: *The boy's new suit was a sorry sight after he fell in the mud.* —**sor′ri·ness,** *n.*

sort (sôrt) *n.* **1.** a group of persons or things that are alike or similar; class; kind; type: *This sort of plant usually grows in sandy soil.* **2.** character; nature: *Remarks of that sort will only make him angry.* **3.** a particular kind of person: *He's not a bad sort.* —*v.t.* to place, arrange, or separate according to kind or type: *to sort mail, to sort socks by color.*

  of sorts. of a poor or average kind: *He is a musician of sorts.*

  out of sorts. feeling slightly ill or peevish.

  sort of. *Informal.* somewhat: *He's been acting sort of strange lately.*

sor·tie (sôr′tē) *n.* **1.** a sudden attack upon the enemy by troops that are hemmed in or surrounded. **2.** a single round trip of an aircraft on a combat mission.

SOS (es′ō′es′) **1.** a radio signal of distress, used especially by ships and airplanes. **2.** any call or signal for help.

so-so (sō′sō′) *adj.* not very good or bad; mediocre: *Skiing conditions were only so-so.* —*adv.* in a mediocre manner; passably.

sot (sot) *n.* a person who habitually drinks too much liquor.

sot·to vo·ce (sot′ō vō′chē) in a low tone of voice, so as not to be overheard. [Italian *sotto voce* literally, under the voice.]

sou (sōō) *n.* a former French coin of small value.

sou·bri·quet (sōō′brə kā′) another spelling of **sobriquet.**

souf·flé (sōō flā′) *n.* a baked dish made light and fluffy

at; āpe; cär; end; mē; it; īce; hot; ōld; fôrk; wood; fōōl; oil; out; up; turn; sing; thin; this; hw in white; zh in treasure. The symbol ə stands for the sound of **a** in about, **e** in taken, **i** in pencil, **o** in lemon, and **u** in circus.

S

by adding beaten egg whites before baking. —*adj.* made light and fluffy by or in cooking.

sough (sou, suf) *v.i.* to make a rushing or sighing sound: *The wind soughed through the branches overhead.* —*n.* a rushing or sighing sound.

sought (sôt) the past tense and past participle of **seek.**

soul (sōl) *n.* **1.** the nonphysical part of humans that is thought to control their thinking, feelings, and actions. Many people believe that the soul separates from the body when a person dies and lives forever. **2.** the emotional part of humans; seat of deep feeling: *Winning the leading role filled her soul with happiness.* **3.** the most important part of anything; that which gives life or spirit: *the soul of wit.* **4.** a person who leads or inspires: *Winston Churchill was the soul of British resistance to Germany in World War II.* **5.** a person who is thought to represent or embody a certain quality; personification: *She is the soul of honesty.* **6.** a person: *Not a soul was about as the night watchman made his rounds.* —*adj. Slang.* relating to, characteristic of, or derived from American blacks or black culture: *soul food, soul music.*

soul·ful (sōl′fəl) *adj.* full of or showing deep feeling: *a soulful gaze, soulful poetry.* —**soul′ful·ly,** *adv.* —**soul′ful·ness,** *n.*

soul·less (sōl′lis) *adj.* having no soul; lacking deep feelings. —**soul′less·ly,** *adv.*

sound¹ (sound) *n.* **1.** vibrations that are carried through the air, water, or another medium, and produce sensation in the ear. **2.** a sensation produced in the ear by such vibrations. **3.** something that is heard: *the sound of music.* **4.** the distance over which a sound may be heard. **5.** one of the noises made by the vocal organs that make up human speech. **6.** a mental impression left by something that is heard or read; implication: *He didn't like the sound of the doctor's report.* **7.** meaningless noise. —*v.i.* **1.** to make or give forth a sound: *The bell sounded.* **2.** to give a certain impression; seem: *His explanation sounds reasonable.* —*v.t.* **1.** to cause to make a sound: *The driver sounded his horn.* **2.** to announce by a sound: *to sound a retreat, to sound a warning.* **3.** to say so it can be heard; pronounce: *to sound a syllable.* **4.** to examine or test by causing to give forth sounds: *The doctor sounded the patient's chest for signs of pneumonia.* [Old French *son.*]

to sound off. *Informal.* **a.** to call out one's name or serial number in a military formation. **b.** to speak in a loud, offensive, or complaining way: *He is always sounding off about getting too much homework.*

sound² (sound) *adj.* **1.** free from damage, defect, or decay: *The house has a sound foundation.* **2.** free from injury or illness; healthy: *a sound mind in a sound body.* **3.** stable or safe; reliable: *a sound investment.* **4.** based on truth, fact, or reason; sensible: *sound reasoning.* **5.** legally valid. **6.** morally good; honest; upright: *a man of sound character.* **7.** (of sleep) deep and unbroken. —*adv.* in a sound manner; soundly: *He is sound asleep.* [Old English *gesund, sund* healthy.] —**sound′ly,** *adv.* —**sound′ness,** *n.*

sound³ (sound) *v.t.* **1.** to measure the depth of (water), as by letting down a line with a weight on the end or by echoing sound off the bottom. **2.** to measure (depth) in this way. **3.** to try to learn the opinions and attitudes of: *He sounded out the other members of the club about the proposal.* —*v.i.* **1.** to measure the depth of water. **2.** (of a whale or fish) to go deep under water; dive swiftly downward. [Old French *sonder.*]

sound⁴ (sound) *n.* **1.** a long, narrow passage of water between larger bodies of water or between the mainland and an island. **2.** a long inlet or arm of the sea. [Old English *sund* the act of swimming, a strait that a person can swim across.]

sound barrier, a sudden sharp increase in resistance which the air presents to an aircraft as its speed nears the speed of sound. Also, **sonic barrier.**

sound·board (sound′bôrd′) *n.* see **sounding board** (*def.* 1).

sound·er¹ (soun′dər) *n.* a person or thing that makes a sound. [*Sound¹* + *-er¹.*]

sound·er² (soun′dər) *n.* a person or thing that measures the depth of water. [*Sound³* + *-er¹.*]

sound·ing¹ (soun′ding) *adj.* **1.** causing or making a sound. **2.** giving forth a deep, full sound; resounding. [*Sound¹* + *-ing².*]

sound·ing² (soun′ding) *n.* **1.** the act of measuring the depth of water, as by letting down a line with a weight on the end. **2.** *also,* **soundings.** the depth of water so measured. **3. soundings.** a place where the water is shallow enough to allow a sounding line to reach bottom. **4.** an investigation of conditions in space or in the atmosphere at a given altitude, usually made with a rocket. [*Sound³* + *-ing¹.*]

sounding board **1.** a thin, resonant board of wood in a musical instrument, as a piano or violin, for increasing the fullness of its tone. Also, **soundboard. 2.** a structure hung behind or over a stage to reflect sound toward the audience. **3.** any means of spreading an idea or opinion: *to use a newspaper column as a sounding board.* **4.** a person or group on whom one tests one's opinions, ideas, or plans: *The executive used his secretary as a sounding board.*

sound·less (sound′lis) *adj.* having or making no sound; silent. —**sound′less·ly,** *adv.*

sound·proof (sound′prōof′) *adj.* not letting sound pass in or out: *a soundproof room.* —*v.t.* to make soundproof: *to soundproof a building.*

sound track **1.** a narrow strip along one edge of a motion-picture film that carries the sound recording. **2.** a recording of the musical score of a play or motion picture.

sound wave, a series of vibrations in the air, a solid, or a liquid, especially one that can be heard by the human ear.

soup (sōop) *n.* a liquid food made by cooking meat, vegetables, fish, or other ingredients in water or a broth.

in the soup. *Slang.* in trouble: *If he gets caught using his father's car without permission, he will really be in the soup.*

to soup up. *Slang.* to increase the power of (a motor, engine, or motor vehicle).

soup·y (sōo′pē) *adj.,* **soup·i·er, soup·i·est.** thick and liquid like soup: *His ice cream became soupy in the hot summer sun.*

sour (sour, sou′ər) *adj.* **1.** having a sharp, acid taste, as lemon or lime juice. **2.** having an acid taste because of fermentation: *The milk is sour.* **3.** distasteful or disagreeable; unpleasant: *a sour odor.* **4.** having or showing an irritable or sullen nature; bad-tempered; peevish: *Her face bore a sour expression.* **5.** (of soil) having too much acid. —*v.t., v.i.* to make or become sour: *The milk soured when it was left in the hot sun.* —**sour′ly,** *adv.* —**sour′ness,** *n.*

source (sôrs) *n.* **1.** a spring, lake, or other body of water that is the place where a river or stream begins. **2.** a place or thing from which something comes, develops, or derives: *The dam is a source of electrical power.* **3.** a person or thing that gives information or evidence, as a book: *The newspapers are a source of information about current events.*

sour·dough (sour′dō′) *n.* **1.** a fermented dough used in making bread. **2.** a prospector or pioneer in western Canada or Alaska.

Sou·sa, John Philip (sōo′zə) 1854–1932, U.S. musical composer and bandmaster.

sou·sa·phone (sōō′zə fōn′) *n.* a large circular tuba with a wide flaring bell that faces forward, used chiefly in brass bands. [From John Philip *Sousa.*]

souse (sous) *v.,* **soused, sous·ing.** —*v.t.* **1.** to put or plunge into water or other liquid. **2.** to make soaking wet; drench: *They were soused by the rain before they could find shelter.* **3.** to soak in vinegar or brine; pickle. —*v.i.* to be or become plunged or soaked in water or other liquid. —*n.* **1.** a pickled food, such as the feet of a pig. **2.** the liquid used in pickling; brine.

south (south) *n.* **1.** the direction to the left as a person faces the sunset. South is one of the four main points of the compass and is located directly opposite north. **2.** *also,* **South.** any region or place lying in this direction. **3. the South.** a region of the United States south of Pennsylvania, the Ohio River, and Missouri, especially the states that fought for the Confederacy in the Civil War. —*adj.* **1.** toward or in the south: *We live on the south side of the street.* **2.** from the south: *a south wind.* —*adv.* toward the south.

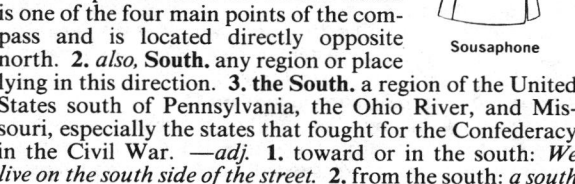
Sousaphone

South Africa, Republic of, a country in southern Africa, on the Atlantic and Indian Oceans, formerly the Union of South Africa. Administrative capital, Pretoria; judicial, Bloemfontein; legislative, Cape Town. Area, 492,359 sq. mi. Pop. (1980), 29,290,000.

South African 1. of or relating to southern Africa. **2.** of or relating to the Republic of South Africa. **3.** a person who was born or is living in the Republic of South Africa.

South African Dutch, see **Afrikaans.**

South America, the fourth largest continent. It is the southern continent in the Western Hemisphere. Area, approx. 6,881,000 sq. mi. Pop. (1980 est.), 245,000,000. —**South American.**

South·amp·ton (south amp′tən) *n.* a port city on the southern coast of England. Pop. (1978 est.), 210,300.

South Bend, a city in northern Indiana. Pop. (1970), 125,580.

south·bound (south′bound′) *adj.* going south: *a southbound train.*

South Carolina, a state in the southeastern United States, on the Atlantic Ocean. Capital, Columbia. Area, 31,055 sq. mi. Pop. (1970), 2,590,516. Abbreviation, **S.C.** —**South Car·o·lin·i·an** (kar′ə lin′ē ən).

● The state of **South Carolina** was once the southern part of the colony of Carolina. King Charles I named the colony *Carolana,* meaning "of Charles." King Charles II later changed the spelling to Carolina when he granted the land to a group of noblemen.

South China Sea, part of the Pacific Ocean, bounded by southeastern China, Vietnam, the Malay Peninsula, Borneo, and the Philippines.

South Da·ko·ta (də kō′tə) a state in the north-central United States. Capital, Pierre. Area, 77,047 sq. mi. Pop. (1970), 665,507. Abbreviations, **S. Dak., S.D.** —**South Dakotan.**

● **South Dakota** was once the southern part of the Dakota Territory. The territory was named for a western branch of the Sioux Indians that lived in this region. The name Dakota means "allied tribes."

south·east (south′ēst′) *n.* **1.** the direction halfway between south and east. **2.** the point of the compass indicating this direction. **3.** a region or place in this direction. **4. the Southeast.** the southeastern part of the United States. —*adj.* **1.** toward or in the southeast; southeastern. **2.** from the southeast: *a southeast wind.* —*adv.* toward the southeast.

Southeast Asia, a region of Asia made up of the countries of Burma, Cambodia, Indonesia, Laos, Malaysia, the Philippines, Singapore, Thailand, and Vietnam.

south·east·er (south′ēs′tər) *n.* a strong wind or storm from the southeast.

south·east·er·ly (south′ēs′tər lē) *adj., adv.* **1.** toward the southeast: *driving in a southeasterly direction.* **2.** from the southeast.

south·east·ern (south′ēs′tərn) *adj.* **1.** toward or in the southeast: *a southeastern town.* **2.** of, relating to, or characteristic of the southeast or Southeast. **3.** from the southeast.

south·east·ward (south′ēst′wərd) *adv. also,* **south·east·wards.** toward the southeast: *We are driving southeastward now.* —*adj.* toward or in the southeast: *Let's hike toward the mountain southeastward of us.* —*n.* a southeastward direction, point, or place.

south·er (sou′thər) *n.* a strong wind from the south.

south·er·ly (su<u>th</u>′ər lē) *adj., adv.* **1.** toward the south: *a southerly direction, to travel southerly.* **2.** from the south: *a southerly breeze.*

south·ern (su<u>th</u>′ərn) *adj.* **1.** toward or in the south: *a room with a southern view.* **2.** *also,* **Southern.** of, relating to, or characteristic of the south or South. **3.** from the south: *a southern wind.*

Southern Cross, a southern constellation having four bright stars in the form of a cross.

south·ern·er (su<u>th</u>′ər nər) *n.* **1.** a person who was born or is living in the south. **2.** *usually,* **Southerner.** a person who was born or is living in the southern part of the United States.

Southern Hemisphere, the half of the earth south of the equator.

Southern lights, another term for **aurora australis.**

south·ern·most (su<u>th</u>′ərn mōst′) *adj.* farthest south.

Southern Rhodesia, see **Zimbabwe.**

Southern Yemen, a country on the southern coast of the Arabian peninsula, bordered on the north by Saudi Arabia and Yemen. Capital, Aden. Its official name is the **People's Democratic Republic of Yemen.** Area, approx. 111,000 sq. mi. Pop. (1975 est.), 1,690,000.

South Island, the larger of the two main islands of New Zealand.

South Korea, a country occupying the southern part of the Korean peninsula. Capital, Seoul. Area, 38,004 sq. mi. Pop. (1980), 37,980,000.

south·land (south′lənd, south′land′) *n. also,* **Southland.** land in the south, such as the southern region of a country.

south·paw (south′pô′) *Informal. n.* a person who is left-handed, especially a left-handed baseball pitcher. —*adj.* left-handed.

South Pole 1. the southernmost point on the earth; southern end of the earth's axis. **2. south pole.** the pole

at; āpe; cär; end; mē; it; īce; hot; ōld; fôrk; wood; fōōl; oil; out; up; turn; sing; thin; <u>th</u>is; hw in white; zh in treasure. The symbol ə stands for the sound of **a** in about, **e** in taken, **i** in pencil, **o** in lemon, and **u** in circus.

of a magnet that points to the south when the magnet swings freely.

South Sea Islands, the islands of the South Pacific; Oceania.

South Seas, the seas south of the equator, especially the South Pacific.

south-south-east (south′south′ēst′) *n.* a point on the compass halfway between south and southeast. —*adj.,* *adv.* toward the south-southeast.

south-south-west (south′south′west′) *n.* a point on the compass halfway between south and southwest. —*adj., adv.* toward the south-southwest.

South Vietnam, see **Vietnam.**

south-ward (south′wərd) *adv.* also, **south-wards.** toward the south: *to travel southward.* —*adj.* toward or in the south. —*n.* a southern direction, point, or place: *The river flows to the southward.*

south-west (south′west′) *n.* **1.** the direction halfway between south and west. **2.** the point of the compass indicating this direction. **3.** a region or place in this direction. **4. the Southwest.** the southwestern part of the United States, especially Oklahoma, Texas, New Mexico, Arizona, and southern California. —*adj.* **1.** toward or in the southwest; southwestern. **2.** from the southwest: *a southwest wind.* —*adv.* toward the southwest: *to sail southwest.*

South-West Africa, also known as **Namibia.** a territory on the southwestern coast of Africa, administered by the Republic of South Africa.

south-west-er (south′wes′tər, sou′wes′tər) *also,* **sou′-west-er.** *n.* **1.** a heavy wind or storm from the southwest. **2.** a waterproof hat with a broad brim that widens in the back to protect the neck in stormy weather, worn especially by sailors.

south-west-er-ly (south′wes′tər lē) *adj., adv.* **1.** toward the southwest. **2.** from the southwest.

south-west-ern (south′wes′tərn) *adj.* **1.** toward or in the southwest. **2.** of, relating to, or characteristic of the southwest or Southwest. **3.** from the southwest.

Southwester

south-west-ward (south′west′wərd) *adv.* also, **southwest-wards.** toward the southwest. —*adj.* toward or in the southwest. —*n.* a southwest direction, point, or place.

sou-ve-nir (sōō′və nēr′, sōō′və nēr′) *n.* something that is kept as a reminder of a person, place, or event; keepsake; memento: *She saved the ticket stub as a souvenir.* [French *souvenir,* from *souvenir* to remember, from Latin *subvenīre* to come up, come to mind.]

sou′west-er (sou′wes′tər) another spelling of **southwester.**

sov-er-eign (sov′rən, sov′ər ən) *n.* **1.** the supreme ruler of a monarchy, such as a king or queen. **2.** a former British gold coin worth one pound. —*adj.* **1.** having supreme power, rank, or authority: *a sovereign ruler.* **2.** not controlled by others; independent: *a sovereign state.* **3.** superior to all others; supreme: *a sovereign right.* **4.** effective or powerful, as a cure or remedy. [Old French *soverain* supreme ruler, supreme, going back to Latin *super.*]

sov-er-eign-ty (sov′rən tē, sov′ər ən tē) *n. pl.,* **sov-er-eign-ties. 1.** supreme authority: *The king holds sovereignty in a monarchy.* **2.** the power of self-government; independence. **3.** a state, community, or other political unit that is politically independent. **4.** the rank, dominion, or authority of a sovereign.

so-vi-et (sō′vē et′) *n.* **1.** a unit of government in the Soviet Union. Soviets are councils that pass laws and govern at local levels, as in cities and towns, and at provincial

and national levels. Members of soviets are elected by the people. **2. the Soviets.** the government or people of the Soviet Union. —*adj.* **1.** relating to a soviet or government by soviets. **2. Soviet.** relating to the Soviet Union.

Soviet Russia 1. another name for the **Soviet Union. 2.** another name for the **Russian Soviet Federated Socialist Republic.**

Soviet Union, the largest country in the world. It extends from eastern Europe to the northeastern coast of Asia and is divided into fifteen republics. Capital, Moscow. Area, 8,599,300 sq. mi. Pop. (1979), 262,442,000. Also, **Union of Soviet Socialist Republics, Russia, Soviet Russia.**

sow[1] (sō) *v.,* **sowed, sown** or **sowed, sow-ing.** —*v.t.* **1.** to spread or scatter (seed) over the ground; plant. **2.** to spread or scatter seed on or upon (land). **3.** to spread; implant: *to sow suspicion.* —*v.i.* to spread or scatter seed over the ground. [Old English *sāwan.*] —**sow′er,** *n.*

sow[2] (sou) *n.* an adult female pig. [Old English *sugu.*]

sow bug (sou) see **wood louse** *(def. 1).*

sown (sōn) a past participle of **sow**[1].

sox (soks) *n.,pl.* another spelling of **socks.**

soy (soi) *n.* **1.** a salty, dark-brown sauce made from fermented soybeans, used especially in Chinese and Japanese cooking. Also, **soy sauce. 2.** see **soybean.**

soy-bean (soi′bēn′) *n.* **1.** the seed of a bushy Asian plant. It is rich in oil and protein and is used for fodder and soil improvement. Oil and meal from the seeds are also used in making many food and chemical products. **2.** the plant bearing this seed.

spa (spä) *n.* **1.** a mineral spring. **2.** a place where such springs exist, especially a resort.

space (spās) *n.* **1.** an unlimited expanse that includes the entire universe. The planet earth and everything and everyone on it exists

Soybean pods

in space. **2.** the region beyond the earth's atmosphere; outer space: *to launch a rocket into space.* **3.** the distance or area between or within points or objects: *a space between buildings.* **4.** a particular area set apart or available for some purpose: *a parking space.* **5.** a period of time: *We worked for the space of an hour.* **6.** any blank or empty place, as between lines in a book. **7.** *Music.* the space between the lines of the staff. —*v.t.,* **spaced, spac-ing. 1.** to arrange with spaces in between; separate by spaces: *The builder spaced the houses far apart.* **2.** to divide into spaces.

space capsule, see **capsule** *(def. 2).*

space-craft (spās′kraft′) *n. pl.,* **space-craft.** any vehicle, manned or unmanned, designed to be orbited around the earth or launched into outer space. Also, **spaceship.**

space flight, a flight into or in outer space.

space-man (spās′man′) *n. pl.,* **space-men** (spās′men′). an astronaut.

space medicine, the branch of medicine that deals with the mental and physical health of astronauts, especially with health problems encountered in space flight.

space platform, another term for **space station.**

space-port (spās′pôrt′) *n.* a place where spacecraft are tested, launched, or maintained.

space probe, an artificial satellite or other spacecraft equipped with instruments designed to collect information about outer space.

space-ship (spās′ship′) *n.* another word for **spacecraft.**

space station, a manned artificial satellite made to orbit the earth and to be used for observation and as a launching site for further space travel. Also, **space platform.**

space suit, a pressurized suit that is made to withstand low air pressure and temperatures, worn by astronauts.

space-time (spās′tīm′) *n.* space thought of as having four dimensions within which any event may be precisely located. Three of these are the ordinary space dimensions, length, breadth, and thickness, and the fourth is time.

spac·ing (spā′sing) *n.* **1.** the act of a person or thing that spaces. **2.** the way spaces are arranged. **3.** a space or spaces, as between printed words.

spa·cious (spā′shəs) *adj.* **1.** having much space: *a house with spacious rooms.* **2.** having a broad range; vast: *spacious skies.* —**spa′cious·ly,** *adv.* —**spa′cious·ness,** *n.*

spade¹ (spād) *n.* a tool used for digging. A spade has a heavy, flat, iron blade that can be pressed into the ground with the foot, and a long handle. —*v.t.,* **spad·ed, spad·ing.** to dig or cut with a spade: *to spade a garden.* [Old English *spadu.*]

　to call a spade a spade. to call something by its right name; speak frankly and truly.

spade² (spād) *n.* **1.** a playing card marked with one or more black figures shaped like this: ♠ **2. spades.** the suit of such playing cards. [Spanish *espada* sword; because a sword was used as a figure on a Spanish playing card.]

spa·dix (spā′diks) *n. pl.,* **spa·dix·es** or **spa·di·ces** (spā′də-sēz). a thick or fleshy spike of tiny flowers, usually enclosed in a spathe.

spa·ghet·ti (spə get′ē) *n.* a white or yellowish starchy food consisting of a mixture of wheat flour and water shaped into long strings and cooked by boiling. It is thinner than macaroni and not hollow.

Spain (spān) *n.* a country in southwestern Europe, south of France. It occupies most of the Iberian Peninsula. Capital, Madrid. Area, 194,884 sq. mi. Pop. (1971 est.), 34,130,000.

spake (spāk) *Archaic.* a past tense of **speak.**

span¹ (span) *n.* **1.** the distance from the tip of the thumb to the tip of the little finger when the hand is fully spread out, considered as nine inches when used as a unit of measure. **2.** the full extent, amount, or reach of anything: *the span of a person's life.* **3.** the distance between two supports, as of an arch, beam, or bridge. **4.** a part or section between two supports. **5.** a short space of time. —*v.t.,* **spanned, span·ning. 1.** to measure by the hand with the thumb and little finger extended. **2.** to extend over or across: *That highway spans the state.* **3.** to provide with something that extends over or across: *to span a river with a bridge.* [Old English *spann.*]

span² (span) *n.* a pair of mules or other draft animals driven together in harness. [Dutch *span.*]

span·gle (spang′gəl) *n.* **1.** a small, thin, often circular piece of glittering metal or plastic used for decoration, especially on clothing. **2.** any small glittering object. —*v.,* **span·gled, span·gling.** —*v.t.* to decorate with or as if with spangles; cause to glitter. —*v.i.* to sparkle with or as if with spangles; glitter.

Span·iard (span′yərd) *n.* a person who was born or is living in Spain.

span·iel (span′yəl) *n.* a small or medium-sized dog of any of various breeds, usually having short legs, long drooping ears, and a silky, wavy coat.

Span·ish (span′ish) *n.* **1.** the people of Spain as a group. **2.** a Romance language spoken in Spain and Spanish America. —*adj.* of or relating to Spain, its people, their language, or their culture.

Spanish America, the countries south of the United States in which the chief language is Spanish, including Mexico, most of the West Indies, Central America except British Honduras, and South America except Brazil and the Guianas.

Span·ish-A·mer·i·can (span′ish ə mer′i kən) *n.* **1.** a person who was born or is living in Spanish America. **2.** a person living in the United States who is of Spanish or Spanish-American descent. —*adj.* **1.** of or relating to Spain and America or to Spain and the United States. **2.** of or relating to Spanish America, its people, their language, or their culture.

Spanish-American War, the war between the United States and Spain in 1898.

Spanish Armada, a fleet sent against England in 1588 by Philip II of Spain. It was defeated by the English and later mostly destroyed by storms. Also, **the Armada.**

Spanish Main 1. formerly, the mainland of Spanish America, especially the northern coast of South America. **2.** the part of the Caribbean Sea through which Spanish merchant ships traveled in colonial times. It was a haunt of pirates.

Spanish moss, a grayish-green flowering plant that grows in long, slender, hanging strands on the branches of certain trees in the southern United States and tropical America.

Spanish Sahara, an overseas possession of Spain, on the northwestern coast of Africa.

Spanish moss

spank (spangk) *v.t.* to strike with the open hand or a flat object, especially on the buttocks, as punishment. —*n.* a blow with the open hand or a flat object.

spank·ing¹ (spang′king) *n.* a series of slaps with the open hand or a flat object, given as punishment. [*Spank* + *-ing¹*.]

spank·ing² (spang′king) *adj.* **1.** very large, great, or fine: *He got a spanking new bicycle for his birthday.* **2.** (of a breeze) brisk and fresh. **3.** moving with a quick, vigorous pace: *a spanking trot.* [Possibly of Scandinavian origin.]

spar¹ (spär) *n.* a pole that holds and stretches out a sail of a ship. A yard, a boom, and a gaff are kinds of spars. —*v.t.,* **sparred, spar·ring.** to furnish (a ship) with spars. [Middle English *sparre.*]

spar² (spär) *v.i.,* **sparred, spar·ring. 1.** to box, especially for practice. **2.** to argue cautiously or in a restrained way, as if to test one's opponent. [Possibly from Old English *sperran* to strike.]

Spar¹

spar³ (spär) *n.* any of various shiny minerals that split

---

at; āpe; cär; end; mē; it; īce; hot; ōld; fôrk; wood; fōol; oil; out; up; turn; sing; thin; this; hw in white; zh in treasure. The symbol ə stands for the sound of a in about, e in taken, i in pencil, o in lemon, and u in circus.

easily into flakes or chips. [Middle Low German *spar* gypsum.]

SPAR (spär) *also,* **Spar.** *n.* a member of the women's reserve of the U.S. Coast Guard. [From Latin *s*(emper) *par*(ātus) always ready (the motto of the U.S. Coast Guard).]

spare (sper) *v.t.,* **spared, spar·ing. 1.** to leave unhurt or uninjured; show mercy to: *The hunter spared the female deer and her young.* **2.** to save or free from pain, sorrow, or trouble; show consideration for: *to spare someone's feelings.* **3.** to do without; give away or give up: *Can you spare a cup of sugar? Could you spare a few minutes to help me with this problem?* **4.** to have left over or in reserve: *We caught the train with only a minute to spare.* **5.** to be sparing of; use in small amounts: *Please give me some more meat, and don't spare the gravy.* —*adj.,* **spar·er, spar·est. 1.** extra or held in reserve; free: *a spare tire, a spare room, spare time.* **2.** not fat; thin; lean: *a man with a spare figure.* **3.** scanty; meager: *a spare meal, a spare diet.* —*n.* **1.** something extra or held in reserve, as a spare tire. **2.** *Bowling.* **a.** the knocking down of all the pins in one frame with two rolls of the ball. **b.** the score so made. —**spare'ly,** *adv.* —**spare'ness,** *n.*

spare·ribs (sper'ribz') *n.,pl.* a cut of pork consisting of the thin end of the ribs with most of the meat trimmed off.

spar·ing (sper'ing) *adj.* careful in spending or using; frugal. —**spar'ing·ly,** *adv.*

spark (spärk) *n.* **1.** a small, hot, glowing particle, as is thrown off from a fire. **2.** a short flash of light produced by a discharge of electricity. **3.** the discharge itself, especially the discharge of a spark plug. **4.** any sparkle or flash of light. **5.** something that moves to action; motivating force: *The assassination of the king was the spark that touched off the war.* **6.** a small amount; trace: *a spark of interest.* —*v.i.* to throw off or produce sparks. —*v.t.* to move into action; activate or incite: *to spark a revolt. The quarterback sparked his team to victory.*

spar·kle (spär'kəl) *v.i.,* **spar·kled, spar·kling. 1.** to shine, as if giving off sparks: *The jewels sparkled. Her eyes sparkled with merriment.* **2.** to give off sparks. **3.** to be brilliant and lively: *His conversation sparkled with wit.* **4.** to bubble, as champagne or soda water. —*n.* **1.** a sparkling appearance or quality: *the sparkle of clear blue ocean waters.* **2.** brilliance or liveliness. **3.** a small spark or glowing particle.

spar·kler (spärk'lər) *n.* **1.** a person or thing that sparkles. **2.** a firework that burns slowly and throws off a brilliant shower of sparks.

spark plug 1. a device that is fitted into the cylinder of an internal-combustion engine and ignites the mixture of fuel and air by means of an electric spark. **2.** *Informal.* a person who inspires or leads some activity or undertaking: *He is the spark plug of the team.*

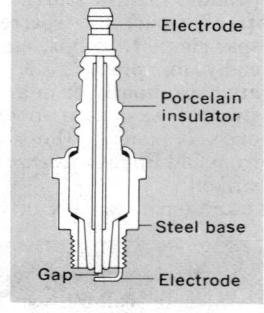

Spark plug

Labels: Electrode, Porcelain insulator, Steel base, Gap, Electrode

spar·row (spar'ō) *n.* any of numerous small, seed-eating birds having a short, thick, cone-shaped bill, a medium-length tail, and mainly brown feathers with a gray or white stomach. —**spar'row·like',** *adj.*

sparrow hawk, a reddish-brown hawk, native to North and Central America. The male has blue wings.

sparse (spärs) *adj.,* **spars·er, spars·est.** thinly spread or distributed; not crowded or dense: *a sparse population, a room with sparse furnishings.* —**sparse'ly,** *adv.* —**sparse'ness,** *n.*

spar·si·ty (spär'sə tē) *n.* an uncrowded condition or lack: *a sparsity of people, a sparsity of movie theaters.*

Spar·ta (spär'tə) *n.* a city-state in ancient Greece, famous for the severely simple way of life of its people and the stern discipline of its soldiers.

Spar·tan (spärt'ən) *adj.* **1.** relating to Sparta, its people, or their culture. **2.** severely simple, stern, or highly disciplined, like the people and life of Sparta. —*n.* **1.** a person who lived in Sparta. **2.** a person who has Spartan characteristics.

spasm (spaz'əm) *n.* **1.** a sudden, involuntary contraction of a muscle or group of muscles. **2.** any sudden, brief burst of energy, activity, or feeling: *a spasm of fear.*

spas·mod·ic (spaz mod'ik) *adj.* **1.** relating to or characterized by a spasm or spasms. **2.** resembling a spasm; sudden, violent, and temporary: *a spasmodic burst of energy.* **3.** happening irregularly; fitful: *His spasmodic attempts to improve his grades were unsuccessful.* —**spas·mod'i·cal·ly,** *adv.*

spas·tic (spas'tik) *adj.* **1.** relating to, characterized by, or suffering from a spasm or spasms. **2.** suffering from spastic paralysis. —*n.* a person who is suffering from spastic paralysis. —**spas'ti·cal·ly,** *adv.*

spastic paralysis, a form of paralysis in which the affected muscles are tense and rigid and the reflexes are abnormal and exaggerated.

spat[1] (spat) *n.* **1.** a petty quarrel; slight argument. **2.** a light slap or slapping sound. —*v.i.,* **spat·ted, spat·ting. 1.** to have a petty argument; quarrel. **2.** to strike with a slapping or splashing sound. [Probably imitative of this sound.]

spat[2] (spat) a past tense and past participle of **spit**[1].

spat[3] (spat) *n. usually,* **spats.** a short covering of cloth or leather worn over the instep of a shoe and the ankle. [Short for earlier *spatterdash* a long legging formerly worn to keep trousers from being spattered.]

spat[4] (spat) *n.* **1.** the spawn of an oyster or similar shellfish. **2.** a young oyster. —*v.i.,* **spat·ted, spat·ting.** (of oysters) to spawn. [Of uncertain origin.]

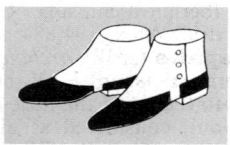

Spats

spate (spāt) *n.* a sudden or strong flood, as of words or emotion: *a spate of hostile feeling.*

spathe (spāth) *n.* a leaf or leaflike part, often large, enclosing a flower cluster or spadix.

spa·tial (spā'shəl) *adj.* **1.** relating to space. **2.** existing or happening in space. —**spa'tial·ly,** *adv.*

spat·ter (spat'ər) *v.t.* **1.** to scatter in drops or small particles: *to spatter paint on a canvas.* **2.** to splash with drops or small particles: *The mud spattered their shoes.* —*v.i.* **1.** to send out or throw off drops or small particles. **2.** to fall or strike in or as if in a shower: *Bullets spattered around the target.* —*n.* **1.** the act of spattering. **2.** the sound made by this: *the spatter of raindrops on a roof.* **3.** a splash or spot of something spattered: *There were spatters of grease on the stove.*

spat·u·la (spach'ə lə) *n.* a small tool with a flat, flexible blade. Spatulas are used for spreading or mixing thick, soft substances, such as paint or cake batter, and for lifting food, such as an egg, from a frying pan.

spav·in (spav'in) *n.* a disease of horses in which a bony growth forms below the hock, causing stiffness and lameness. —**spav'ined,** *adj.*

spawn (spôn) *n.* the eggs of certain animals that live in the water, such as fish or frogs. —*v.t.* **1.** to produce (eggs or offspring). **2.** to give birth to; produce. —*v.i.* to lay eggs.

spay (spā) *v.t.* to remove the ovaries of (an animal).

S.P.C.A., Society for the Prevention of Cruelty to Animals.

S.P.C.C., Society for the Prevention of Cruelty to Children.

speak (spēk) *v.,* **spoke** or *(archaic)* **spake, spo·ken, speak·ing.** —*v.i.* **1.** to utter words; talk: *The baby hasn't learned to speak yet.* **2.** to make known or convey an idea, fact, or feeling: *Will you speak to John about his rude behavior?* **3.** to converse. **4.** to deliver a speech: *The author spoke before a large audience.* —*v.t.* **1.** to give voice to; utter: *She spoke words of sympathy.* **2.** to use or be able to use in speaking: *Michael speaks Spanish fluently.* **3.** to make known or convey; express: *She always speaks the truth.*

so to speak. to say in other words: *What you're saying, so to speak, is that he is a liar.*

to speak for. a. to speak on behalf of; represent: *He spoke for the whole team when he refused the offer.* **b.** to ask for; choose: *The white puppy had already been spoken for, so he had to choose another.*

to speak out or **to speak up. a.** to speak loudly and clearly enough to be understood. **b.** to say what one really believes.

to speak well for. to give a good impression of: *Her manners speak well for her parents.*

speak·er (spē′kər) *n.* **1.** a person who speaks, especially a person who makes a public speech. **2.** *usually,* **Speaker.** the presiding officer in a legislative assembly: *the Speaker of the House.* **3.** see **loudspeaker.**

speak·er·ship (spē′kər ship′) *n.* the position of presiding officer in a legislative assembly.

speak·ing (spē′king) *adj.* **1.** that uses or involves speech: *The senator has a speaking engagement tomorrow.* **2.** expressive, suggestive, or striking: *a speaking likeness.* —*n.* the act or utterance of a person who speaks.

spear (spēr) *n.* **1.** a weapon consisting of a sharp-pointed head attached to a long shaft, used for thrusting or throwing. **2.** a slender stalk, as of grass: *asparagus spears.* —*v.t.* to stab, penetrate, or take hold with or as if with a spear. —*v.i.* (of a plant) to send forth shoots or stems; sprout. —**spear′like′,** *adj.*

spear·head (spēr′hed′) *n.* **1.** a sharp-pointed head of a spear. **2.** a person or group that leads: *The paratroopers were the spearhead of the invasion.* —*v.t.* to lead: *to spearhead an attack.*

spear·man (spēr′mən) *n. pl.,* **spear·men** (spēr′mən). a person who is armed with a spear.

spear·mint (spēr′mint′) *n.* **1.** a fragrant plant that has leaves shaped like the head of a spear. **2.** an aromatic oil from this plant, used as a flavoring.

spe·cial (spesh′əl) *adj.* **1.** out of the ordinary; unusual; exceptional: *She has a special talent for sewing.* **2.** differing from others by some distinguishing quality or character: *She is a special friend of mine.* **3.** made, arranged, or designed for a particular occasion, purpose, or person: *a special broadcast.* —*n.* **1.** something made, designed, or used for a particular occasion or purpose. **2.** a sale at lower prices or something offered at these prices: *a special on winter coats.* —**spe′cial·ly,** *adv.*

special delivery, delivery of mail

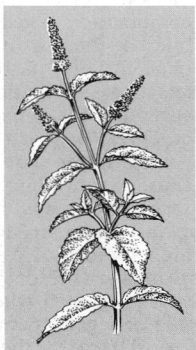
Spearmint

by a special messenger in advance of the regular delivery for an extra fee.

spe·cial·ist (spesh′ə list) *n.* a person who devotes himself to a particular branch of a profession or field of study, especially a doctor who practices a particular branch of medicine: *a heart specialist.*

spe·cial·ize (spesh′ə līz′) *v.,* **spe·cial·ized, spe·cial·iz·ing.** —*v.i.* **1.** to concentrate on a particular product, activity, branch of a profession, or field of study. **2.** *Biology.* to become adapted to a special function or environment. —*v.t.* to adapt or limit to a specific purpose, use, or function.

spe·cial·i·za·tion (spesh′ə lī zā′shən) *n.* the act of specializing or the state of being specialized.

In language, **specialization** means the changing of the definition of a word from a broad, general meaning to a narrow, specific one. Specialization is one of the ways in which our language is constantly changing. Many of the words that we use today originally came from other languages. The meaning that these words had in the language from which they were borrowed is called the *etymological meaning.* The changing from a broad etymological meaning to a narrow modern meaning is one of the ways in which specialization works. The English word *starve* comes from the Old English word *steorfan* which, like the modern German word *sterben* to which it is closely related, meant "to die." Over the years, people forgot the original meaning of this word and began to give it the specialized meaning "to die of hunger."

Specialization also occurs when a group of people give specialized meanings to words that normally have a broader meaning. The word *base* generally refers to the part on which something stands or rests: *The marble statue was placed on a base of granite.* But if you say this word to a soldier he will think of a military headquarters or camp. To a chemist this word would probably mean a chemical compound that reacts with an acid to form a salt. An athlete might think that you were naming one of the four corners of a baseball diamond.

The needs or interests of a particular culture or group of people will often bring about a vocabulary of specialized words. To most of us, the word *horse* is specific enough to describe a certain animal. A person who breeds or raises horses will need to know if we are describing a mare, stallion, gelding, foal, colt, or filly.

If a language contains a number of words that mean exactly the same thing, specialization can eliminate these unnecessary duplications. The English word *deer,* which came from the Old English word *deor,* was originally used to refer to any animal. After the words *animal,* which was borrowed from Latin, and *beast,* which was borrowed from French, came into our language, English contained three words with identical meanings. Eventually, the word *deer* was, by specialization, used to describe only a specific type of animal. The word *beast* has come to refer to any four-legged animal. The word *animal* has remained the most general of these words, and is used to describe any living thing that is not a plant.

---

at; āpe; cär; end; mē; it; īce; hot; ōld; fôrk; wood; fōōl; oil; out; up; turn; sing; thin; this; hw in white; zh in treasure. The symbol ə stands for the sound of a in about, e in taken, i in pencil, o in lemon, and u in circus.

S

spe·cial·ty (spesh′əl tē) *n. pl.*, **spe·cial·ties.** **1.** a particular branch of a profession or field of study that a person devotes or restricts himself to. **2.** a particular product or service that a store or business sells, or something that it does very well: *The restaurant's specialty is Italian food.* **3.** the state of being special or of having a special character or quality.

spe·cie (spē′shē) *n.* coined money; coin.

spe·cies (spē′shēz) *n. pl.*, **spe·cies.** **1.** *Biology.* **a.** a subdivision of a genus in plant and animal classification. Members of a species have certain permanent characteristics in common. **b.** a plant or animal belonging to such a subdivision. **2.** a distinct kind or type; sort: *a strange species of humor.* **3.** **the species.** the human race.

spe·cif·ic (spi sif′ik) *adj.* **1.** explicitly named; definite; precise: *a specific offer, a specific amount.* **2.** belonging exclusively to; peculiar to: *the specific characteristics of a region.* **3.** of or relating to a species of plant or animal. —*n.* **1.** something that has a specific effect or result, such as a medicine used to prevent or treat a particular disease. **2.** *usually,* **specifics.** *Informal.* particulars; details: *Let's discuss the general situation first and then turn to the specifics.*

spe·cif·i·cal·ly (spi sif′ik ə lē, spi sif′ik lē) *adv.* in a specific manner; definitely; explicitly: *Mother specifically said to come right home.*

spec·i·fi·ca·tion (spes′ə fi kā′shən) *n.* **1.** the act of specifying. **2.** an item or article specified, as in a plan or contract. **3.** *usually,* **specifications.** a detailed list and description of the exact materials and methods to be used in building something.

specific gravity, the ratio of the density of a given substance to the density of another substance used as a standard. Water is used as the standard for solids and liquids, and air is used for gases.

specific heat, the amount of heat necessary to raise the temperature of one gram of a given substance by one degree centigrade.

spec·i·fy (spes′ə fī′) *v.t.*, **spec·i·fied, spec·i·fy·ing.** **1.** to mention in a precise and definite way; describe in detail: *John forgot to specify the place where we should meet.* **2.** to set down as a specification: *The architect specified oak for the floors.*

spec·i·men (spes′ə mən) *n.* **1.** a single person or thing considered to be typical of its class or group; example. **2.** a sample, as of blood, taken for medical analysis.

spe·cious (spē′shəs) *adj.* seemingly true, reasonable, or attractive, but actually false: *He used specious arguments to justify his position.* —**spe′cious·ly,** *adv.* —**spe′cious·ness,** *n.*

speck (spek) *n.* **1.** a very small bit; particle: *There was not a speck of dirt anywhere after we finished cleaning.* **2.** a small spot, stain, or mark: *There were specks of paint on the wallpaper.* —*v.t.* to mark with specks; speckle.

speck·le (spek′əl) *n.* a small spot or mark, as on fur or skin. —*v.t.*, **speck·led, speck·ling.** to mark or cover with speckles.

specs (speks) *n., pl. Informal.* **1.** spectacles. **2.** specifications.

spec·ta·cle (spek′tə kəl) *n.* **1.** something seen, especially an impressive or unusual sight: *The sunrise over the valley was a beautiful spectacle.* **2.** a public display or performance, especially on a grand scale. **3.** **spectacles.** a pair of eyeglasses.

spec·tac·u·lar (spek tak′yə lər) *adj.* of, relating to, or resembling a spectacle. —*n.* an elaborate show, such as a long and lavishly made movie. —**spec·tac′u·lar·ly,** *adv.*

spec·ta·tor (spek′tā′tər) *n.* a person who watches but does not take part; member of an audience; observer.

spec·ter (spek′tər) *also, British,* **spec·tre.** *n.* **1.** a visible spirit of a dead person; ghost. **2.** something that threatens or causes fear: *the specter of war.*

spec·tra (spek′trə) a plural of **spectrum.**

spec·tral (spek′trəl) *adj.* **1.** of or resembling a specter; ghostly: *The tree cast spectral shadows on the window.* **2.** of, relating to, or produced by a spectrum.

spec·tre (spek′tər) *British.* another spelling of **specter.**

spec·tro·scope (spek′trə skōp′) *n.* an instrument that separates white light into a spectrum by causing the light to pass through a series of lenses and a prism or through a similar device.

spec·trum (spek′trəm) *n. pl.*, **spec·tra** or **spec·trums.** a band of colors into which white light is separated according to wavelength by being passed through a prism or other material. The colors of the spectrum are red, orange, yellow, green, blue, indigo, and violet.

spec·u·late (spek′yə lāt′) *v.i.*, **spec·u·lat·ed, spec·u·lat·ing.** **1.** to think carefully or seriously about; think of reasons or answers for; conjecture: *She speculated about her friend's reasons for not coming to her party.* **2.** to take risks or gamble on a business opportunity, as by buying or selling stock or real estate in the hope of making a large profit.

spec·u·la·tion (spek′yə lā′shən) *n.* **1.** the act of thinking carefully or seriously about something; conjecture. **2.** a conclusion or opinion reached by conjecture. **3.** the act or practice of speculating in stocks, land, or the like.

spec·u·la·tive (spek′yə lā′tiv) *adj.* **1.** given to serious thinking; thoughtful: *She has a speculative mind.* **2.** theoretical rather than practical: *His ideas are very speculative.* **3.** involving or involved in financial speculation: *speculative stocks.* —**spec′u·la′tive·ly,** *adv.* —**spec′u·la′tive·ness,** *n.*

spec·u·la·tor (spek′yə lā′tər) *n.* a person who speculates, especially in business.

sped (sped) a past tense and past participle of **speed.**

speech (spēch) *n. pl.*, **speech·es.** **1.** the ability to express an idea, thought, or feeling by the use of spoken words. **2.** the act of speaking. **3.** something spoken, especially before an audience: *The candidate's acceptance speech was shown on television.* **4.** a way in which someone speaks: *His speech is very British.* **5.** a particular idiom, dialect, or language: *Southern speech.* **6.** the study of speaking correctly, clearly, and effectively, especially in public.

speech·less (spēch′lis) *adj.* **1.** temporarily unable to speak because of emotion or shock: *We sat speechless with anger listening to his insults.* **2.** that cannot be or is not expressed in words: *She was filled with speechless anxiety.* **3.** not having the power of speech; mute; dumb. —**speech′less·ly,** *adv.* —**speech′less·ness,** *n.*

speed (spēd) *n.* **1.** rapidity or quickness of motion; swiftness: *He ran with all the speed he could muster.* **2.** rate of motion; velocity: *to drive at a safe speed.* **3.** a gear or combination of gears, as in the transmission of an automobile. **4.** the sensitivity of a photographic film, paper, or plate to light. **5.** the amount of light that a camera lens lets through, indicated by its f number. —*v.*, **sped** or **speed·ed, speed·ing.** —*v.i.* **1.** to move or act rapidly or quickly: *He sped through his chores.* **2.** to drive a motor vehicle faster than is safe or legally permitted. —*v.t.* to cause to move rapidly or quickly; give speed to: *She helped speed up the wrapping of the presents.*

speed·boat (spēd′bōt′) *n.* a motorboat built to travel at high speeds.

speed·er (spē′dər) *n.* a person or thing that speeds, especially a person who drives a motor vehicle faster than is safe or legally permitted.

speed limit, the maximum or minimum speed that is legally permitted on a given road.

speed·om·e·ter (spē dom′ə tər) *n.* a device for measuring the speed of a vehicle in miles per hour.

speed·up (spēd′up′) *n.* an increase in speed, output, or work.

speed·way (spēd′wā′) *n.* **1.** a road for driving at high speeds. **2.** a track for motorcycle or automobile races.

speed·well (spēd′wel′) *n.* any of several low-growing plants having small pink, blue, or white flowers.

speed·y (spē′dē) *adj.*, **speed·i·er, speed·i·est. 1.** moving rapidly; swift: *a speedy runner.* **2.** without delay; prompt: *a speedy reply.* —**speed′i·ly,** *adv.* —**speed′i·ness,** *n.*

spell[1] (spel) *v.*, **spelled** or **spelt, spell·ing.** —*v.t.* **1.** to write or name the letters of (a word) in their correct order. **2.** (of letters) to form (a word): *D-o-g spells dog.* **3.** to mean; signify: *His injury spelled defeat for the team.* —*v.i.* to form a word or words by letters. [Old French *espeller* to explain.]

to spell out. to explain clearly or in detail: *He asked her to spell out exactly what she meant by her statement.*

spell[2] (spel) *n.* **1.** a word or phrase having magic power. **2.** a state of enchantment or fascination: *She was caught in the spell of the music.* [Old English *spell* story, saying.]

spell[3] (spel) *n.* **1.** a brief, indefinite period of time: *We sat outside for a spell.* **2.** a period of weather of a specified sort: *a dry spell.* **3.** an attack or bout of something, as an illness: *a dizzy spell.* —*v.t.,* **spelled, spell·ing.** to relieve by taking a turn: *John and his friend spelled each other at the wheel during the trip.* [Old English *spelian* to take the place of.]

spell·bind (spel′bīnd′) *v.t.,* **spell·bound, spell·bind·ing.** to hold under or as if under a spell. —**spell′bind′er,** *n.*

spell·bound (spel′bound′) *adj.* held as if by a spell; entranced; rapt: *The audience was spellbound by the acrobat's performance.*

spell·er (spel′ər) *n.* **1.** a person who spells words. **2.** a textbook used to teach spelling to students.

spell·ing (spel′ing) *n.* **1.** the way a word is spelled; orthography. **2.** the act of a person who spells.

●**Spelling** is the method we use to represent words through the letters of the alphabet. In an ideal system of spelling, each letter of the alphabet would always correspond to one and only one speech sound, and each speech sound would always be represented by one and only one letter. Such a system would be completely *phonetic.* Certain languages, such as Italian and Hungarian, have spelling systems that are close to being phonetic, and therefore relatively easy to learn. In other languages, including English, spelling is often not phonetic and is quite difficult to master. The difficulties we have in spelling in English are partly caused by our language having a larger number of speech sounds than the number of letters of the alphabet with which to represent them. For instance, the letter *u* is used in English to represent a variety of speech sounds, as in the words c*u*be, r*u*le, *u*p, b*u*sy, q*u*ite, b*u*ll, o*u*t, o*u*ght, thro*u*gh, and b*u*ry. The reverse situation, in which a speech sound is represented by various letters and combinations of letters, is another reason that it is difficult to spell English words. The *sh* sound is represented in at least twelve different ways: *sh*ift, mo*ti*on, *s*ure, ti*ss*ue, spe*ci*al, ma*ch*ine, o*ce*an, con*sc*ience, *sch*wa, nau*se*ous, man*si*on, and mi*ss*ion.

The irregularity of English spelling has several historical causes. Although English is a Germanic language, the alphabet that we use comes from Latin. While the alphabet was adequate for Latin, which had a smaller range of speech sounds than English, it is far from adequate for our own language. English sounds that did not have corresponding letters in the Latin alphabet were represented by combining these letters in different ways. Through the use of combinations of letters, Old English spelling was largely phonetic. While spelling remains relatively constant, because it is preserved in written language in books, spoken language continually changes. The changes in Old English, Middle English, and Modern English pronunciation were not accompanied by corresponding changes in spelling, and so the spelling that was once phonetic now very often does not represent speech sounds. Also, the English language has borrowed a great many words from foreign languages. These words often retain their original spelling, although their pronunciation has altered. This process has given us such oddly spelled words as *beauty, tight,* and *psychology.*

The phonetic quality of Old English spelling was the result of the lack of standardization; words were spelled according to the dialect and pronunciation of the writer. The invention of the printing press in the fifteenth century produced a greater degree of standardization which, although it enabled people to read more easily, tended to fix spelling so that it could not change as pronunciation changed.

Attempts were made to standardize English spelling in the eighteenth and nineteenth centuries, particularly by writers of dictionaries. In modern times, the greatest emphasis has been on the reforming and simplifying, rather than standardizing, of spelling. Several new alphabets have been proposed, but they have not had widespread acceptance.

One of the best-known supporters of spelling reform was the English writer George Bernard Shaw who, to point out the irregularity of our spelling, humorously suggested that the word *fish* should be spelled *ghoti,* combining the *gh* from *cough,* the *o* from *women,* and the *ti* from *nation.* Although this spelling looks silly to us, it is not much more illogical than the spelling of many other English words. Because of this basic lack of logic and regularity in English spelling, the only way to learn to spell correctly is to learn those rules of spelling which generally hold true and to memorize the spelling of the great number of words that do not follow the rules. Using your dictionary will help you to remember these spellings and so be able to use written language correctly.

spelling bee, a competition that is won by the person or team spelling the most words correctly.

spelt (spelt) a past tense and past participle of **spell**[1].

spe·lunk·er (spi lung′kər) *n.* a person who explores caves.

Spen·cer, Herbert (spen′sər) 1820–1903, English philosopher.

spend (spend) *v.,* **spent, spend·ing.** —*v.t.* **1.** to pay out (money): *Helen spent ten dollars on a scarf.* **2.** to pass (time) in a specified manner or place: *Charlotte spent a weekend in Vermont.* **3.** to use up or wear out: *Hank spent his energy organizing the rally.* —*v.i.* to pay out or use up money or other possessions. —**spend′er,** *n.*

spend·thrift (spend′thrift′) *n.* a person who spends money foolishly, extravagantly, or wastefully. —*adj.* lavish or wasteful; extravagant.

---

at; āpe; cär; end; mē; it; īce; hot; ōld; fôrk;
wood; fōōl; oil; out; up; turn; sing; thin; <u>th</u>is;
hw in white; zh in treasure. The symbol ə
stands for the sound of **a** in about, **e** in taken,
i in pencil, **o** in lemon, and **u** in circus.

Spen·ser, Edmund (spen′sər) 1552–1599, English poet.

spent (spent) *v.,* the past tense and past participle of **spend.** *—adj.* worn out; exhausted.

sperm (spurm) *n.* **1.** a fluid secreted by the testes, containing the male reproductive cells; semen. **2.** another word for **spermatozoon.**

sper·ma·cet·i (spur′mə set′ē, spur′mə sē′tē) *n.* a white, waxy substance that comes from sperm oil, used to make cosmetics and to waterproof paper and fabrics.

sper·ma·to·phyte (spur mat′ə fīt′) *n.* any plant that produces seeds.

sper·ma·to·zo·on (spur′mə tə zō′ən) *n. pl.,* **sper·ma·to·zo·a** (spur′mə tə zō′ə). a male reproductive cell; male gamete. Also, **sperm.**

sperm oil, a yellow oil derived from the sperm whale, used as a lubricant.

sperm whale, a large-toothed whale having a massive, barrel-shaped head.

spew (spyoo) *v.t.* to cast up, throw out, or discharge; eject; vomit: *The smokestacks of the chemical processing plant spewed forth sooty black smoke.* *—v.i.* to vomit. *—n.* something that is spewed.

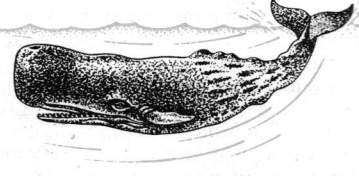

Sperm whale

sp. gr., specific gravity.

sphag·num (sfag′nəm) *n.* any of a group of pale green mosses found growing in bogs and marshes.

sphere (sfēr) *n.* **1.** a round, three-dimensional figure having all the points of its surface at an equal distance from the center. **2.** a body having this shape; ball; globe. **3.** a field, extent, or range of interest, influence, knowledge, or activity: *Anthropology is outside my sphere of knowledge.* **4.** social class, rank, or position. **5.** any of various celestial bodies, such as stars or planets. **6.** see **celestial sphere.**

spher·i·cal (sfer′i kəl) *adj.* **1.** shaped like a sphere; globular. **2.** of or relating to a sphere or spheres. **—spher′·i·cal·ly,** *adv.*

sphe·roid (sfēr′oid) *n.* a three-dimensional figure that resembles a sphere in shape but is not perfectly round.

sphinc·ter (sfingk′tər) *n.* a circular band of muscle that surrounds a passage or opening in the body and contracts or expands to close or open it.

sphinx (sfingks) *n. pl.,* **sphinx·es** or **sphin·ges** (sfin′jēz). **1.** *Egyptian Mythology.* a creature having the head of a human and the body of a lion. **2. the Sphinx.** a large statue of this creature at Giza in Egypt. **3. Sphinx.** *Greek Mythology.* a winged monster having the head of a woman and the body of a lion, who asked a riddle and killed all those who could not guess the answer. **4.** a person who is mysterious and hard to understand.

spice (spīs) *n.* **1.** any of various substances used to season food, such as pepper and cloves. Spices come from plants. **2.** something that adds zest or interest: *Variety's the very spice of life* (William Cowper). *—v.t.,* **spiced, spic·ing. 1.** to season with a spice or spices. **2.** to add zest or interest to: *He spiced his conversation with funny stories.*

spice·bush (spīs′boosh′) *n. pl.,* **spice·bush·es.** a shrub found in swamps in eastern North America, bearing clusters of small yellowish flowers.

Spice Islands, see **Moluccas.**

spick-and-span (spik′ən span′) *also,* **spic-and-span.** *adj.* fresh, neat, and clean: *a spick-and-span house.*

spic·y (spī′sē) *adj.,* **spic·i·er, spic·i·est. 1.** seasoned with spice: *spicy food.* **2.** resembling spice; pungent or fragrant:

The soap has a spicy smell. **3.** slightly improper; risqué: *He told a spicy story.* **—spic′i·ness,** *n.*

spi·der (spī′dər) *n.* any of a group of small animals without backbones, having a body divided into two parts and four pairs of legs. Spiders are able to spin silken threads for making cocoons and webs. **—spi′der·like′,** *adj.*

spider monkey, a monkey of tropical America, having long slender limbs and a long tail that can be used for gripping.

spi·der·y (spī′dər ē) *adj.* resembling a spider or a spider's web; long and thin or delicate: *a spidery handwriting, spidery legs.*

spied (spīd) the past tense and past participle of **spy.**

spies (spīz) *n.* the plural of **spy.** *—v.* the third person singular, present tense of **spy.**

spig·ot (spig′ət) *n.* **1.** another word for **faucet. 2.** a small wooden plug or peg for stopping the opening of a barrel or cask.

spike¹ (spīk) *n.* **1.** a large, heavy nail. **2.** any sharp-pointed object or projection. **3.** one of several sharp-pointed metal projections attached to the sole and heel of a shoe to prevent slipping, worn in golf, baseball, track and field, and other sports. **—v.t.,** **spiked, spik·ing. 1.** to fasten or provide with spikes: *to spike railroad ties together.* **2.** to cut or pierce with a sharp-pointed object. **3.** to stand in the way of or put an end to; block; thwart: *to spike a rumor before it spreads.* [Possibly from Old Norse *spīkr* nail.]

spike² (spīk) *n.* **1.** an ear of grain. **2.** a long cluster of flowers in which the flowers grow along a single stalk. [Latin *spīca* an ear of corn.]

spike·let (spīk′lit) *n.* a small cluster of flowers, as on the spike of a stalk of grass.

spike·nard (spīk′nərd, spīk′närd) *n.* **1.** an East Indian plant having fragrant roots and stems. In ancient times a sweet-smelling ointment was made from this plant. **2.** a woodland herb of eastern North America, having spicy, aromatic roots and clusters of small greenish flowers.

spik·y (spī′kē) *adj.* **1.** having a spike or spikes: *a spiky fence.* **2.** resembling a spike: *spiky thorns.*

spile (spīl) *n.* **1.** a wooden plug for stopping the opening of a barrel or cask. **2.** a small spout for taking sap from a sugar maple. **3.** a strong post driven into the ground as a support; pile. **—v.t.,** **spiled, spil·ing.** to support or stop up with a spile.

spill¹ (spil) *v.,* **spilled** or **spilt, spill·ing.** *—v.t.* **1.** to cause or allow (something) to fall, flow, or run out of a container: *to spill gravy on a cloth, to spill cookies from a box.* **2.** to shed (blood). **3.** *Informal.* to cause to tumble or fall off something. **4.** *Informal.* to reveal; divulge: *to spill a secret.* *—v.i.* to flow or run out: *The water spilled all over the floor. The crowd spilled into the street.* *—n.* **1.** the act of spilling. **2.** the amount spilled. **3.** *Informal.* a tumble or fall. [Old English *spillan* to destroy, kill.]

spill² (spil) *n.* a thin strip of wood or folded piece of paper, used to light a fire. [Possibly from Middle Low German *spile, spille* stalk, spindle.]

spill·way (spil′wā′) *n.* a channel that allows surplus water to run off, as from a reservoir.

spilt (spilt) a past tense and past participle of **spill¹.**

spin (spin) *v.,* **spun, spin·ning.** *—v.t.* **1.** to draw out and twist (fibers) into thread. **2.** to form or make (thread) in this way. **3.** to form (a silken thread, web, or cocoon) from a substance that is secreted from the body and hardens when exposed to air, as spiders and silkworms do. **4.** to cause to turn or revolve rapidly; twirl: *The child was spinning a top.* **5.** to tell: *The old man enjoyed spinning ghost stories.* —*v.i.* **1.** to turn or revolve rapidly; whirl. **2.** to make by spinning, as thread. **3.** to have a sensation of revolving rapidly; feel dizzy: *All that noise made my head spin.* **4.** to go or move rapidly: *The racing car spun over the track.* —*n.* **1.** the act of spinning or the state of being spun: *the spin of a wheel.* **2.** a short ride in a motor vehicle, as for pleasure. **3.** another word for **tailspin.**

spin·ach (spin′ich) *n.* **1.** the dark green leaves of a garden plant, eaten as a vegetable, either cooked or raw. **2.** the plant itself, grown in many temperate regions.

spi·nal (spīn′əl) *adj.* of, relating to, or affecting the spinal column or the spinal cord. —*n.* an anesthetic that is injected in the spine.

spinal column, a series of bones joined in a column that encloses the spinal cord and forms the supporting structure of the body. Also, **spine, backbone.**

spinal cord, a thick band of nerve tissue extending down from the brain through the spinal column. The spinal cord conducts impulses to and from the brain and acts as a center for simple reflexes.

spin·dle (spind′əl) *n.* **1.** a round, tapered stick weighted at one end and turned by hand, used to twist fibers into thread. **2.** any rod that turns or serves as an axis on which something turns, such as a shaft or axle. **3.** a spike set upright in a base for holding papers. **4.** *Biology.* a

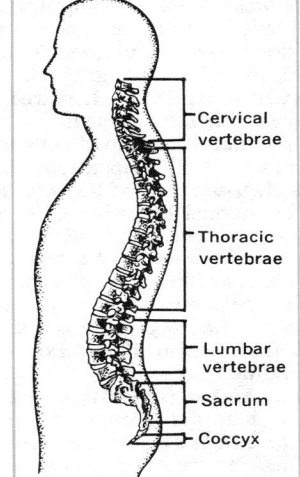

Cervical
vertebrae

Thoracic
vertebrae

Lumbar
vertebrae

Sacrum

Coccyx

Spinal column

mass of fibers formed between the centrioles, along which the chromosomes move during cell division. —*v.,* **spin·dled, spin·dling** —*v.i.* to grow into a long, slender stalk, shape, or body. —*v.t.* **1.** to form into a spindle. **2.** to make holes in (paper) with or as if with a spindle.

spin·dle·leg·ged (spind′əl leg′id, spind′əl legd′) *adj.* having spindlelegs. Also, **spin·dle·shanked** (spind′əl-shangkt′).

spin·dle·legs (spind′əl legz′) *n., pl.* **1.** long, slim legs. **2.** *Informal.* a person with long, slim legs. Also, **spin·dle·shanks** (spind′əl shangks′).

spin·dling (spind′ling) *adj.* tall and slender: *spindling pines.*

spin·dly (spind′lē) *adj.,* **spin·dli·er, spin·dli·est.** having a tall slender shape; spindling.

spin·drift (spin′drift′) *n.* the spray blown from the sea by heavy winds. Also, **spoondrift.**

spine (spīn) *n.* **1.** see **spinal column. 2.** anything resembling or functioning as a backbone, such as the back of a book. **3.** any stiff, pointed projection on a plant or animal, such as a thorn, or the quill of a porcupine.

spine·less (spīn′lis) *adj.* **1.** lacking a spinal column; invertebrate. **2.** of a plant or animal, lacking stiff, pointed projections. **3.** lacking courage or willpower. —**spine′-less·ly,** *adv.* —**spine′less·ness,** *n.*

spin·et (spin′it) *n.* **1.** a stringed keyboard instrument resembling a small harpsichord, having one keyboard and one string for each musical tone. **2.** a small upright piano.

spin·na·ker (spin′ə kər) *n.* a large sail that swells or billows out when filled, used on a yacht or other racing boat when sailing before the wind.

spin·ner·et (spin′ə ret′) *n.* an organ by which various animals without backbones, such as spiders, silkworms, and the like, spin silken threads.

spinning jenny, a hand-operated spinning machine having more than one spindle so that a number of threads can be spun at once.

spinning wheel, a hand-operated spinning machine consisting of a large wheel and a spindle, used to spin fibers into thread.

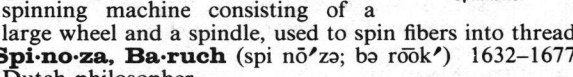

Spinnaker

Spi·no·za, Ba·ruch (spi nō′zə; bə rōōk′) 1632–1677, Dutch philosopher.

spin·ster (spin′stər) *n.* an older woman who has never been married.

spin·y (spī′nē) *adj.,* **spin·i·er, spin·i·est. 1.** having or covered with spines. **2.** resembling a spine or thorn; sharp.

spiny lobster, a sea animal that can be eaten. It is similar to the common lobster, but it has sharp spines on the body and lacks large pincer claws. Also, **rock lobster.**

spi·ra·cle (spī′rə kəl, spir′ə kəl) *n.* an opening for breathing, such as one of the paired openings on the abdomen of an insect or spider or the blowhole of a whale.

spi·ral (spī′rəl) *n.* **1.** a plane curve traced by a point moving around a fixed point while continuously increasing or decreasing its distance from it. **2.** a three-dimensional curve that winds around the surface of a cylinder or cone; helix. **3.** something having the shape or form of a spiral. **4.** a slow, continuous increase or decrease. —*adj.* having the shape or form of a spiral. —*v.i., v.t.,* **spi·raled, spi·ral·ing;** *also, British,* **spi·ralled, spi·ral·ling.** to take or cause to take a spiral form or course. —**spi′ral·ly,** *adv.*

spire[1] (spīr) *n.* **1.** a tall structure that tapers to a point, built on the top of a tower. **2.** any tapering and pointed object or formation. [Old English *spīr* the tapering stalk of a plant.]

spire[2] (spīr) *n.* **1.** a spiral or single twist of a spiral. **2.** the upper portion of a spiral shell. [Latin *spīra.*]

spi·ril·lum (spī ril′əm) *n. pl.,* **spi·ril·la** (spī-ril′ə). any of a group of coiled, rod-shaped bacteria. See **bacteria** for illustration.

spir·it (spir′it) *n.* **1.** the part of humans that is not physical, and is thought to control their thoughts and feelings, and to live forever; soul. **2.** the moral, mental, or emotional part of human nature: *The holy man was concerned with things of the spirit.* **3.** a supernatural being, often thought to haunt living people; specter; ghost. **4.** a person thought to have a certain character or temperament: *a noble spirit, a brave spirit.* **5.** a characteristic quality, mood, or tendency: *The spirit of the age was one of revolution.* **6.** the real meaning or intent: *the spirit of the law.* **7.** liveliness: *She danced with*

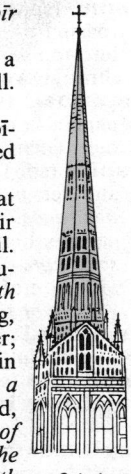

Spire[1]

at; āpe; cär; end; mē; it; īce; hot; ōld; fôrk; wood; fōōl; oil; out; up; turn; sing; thin; **th**is; **hw** in **wh**ite; **zh** in treasure. The symbol ə stands for the sound of **a** in about, **e** in taken, **i** in pencil, **o** in lemon, and **u** in circus.

spirit and grace. **8.** enthusiasm, devotion, and loyalty: *school spirit.* **9. spirits.** a mental state or attitude: *The team members were in good spirits after winning the game.* **10.** *usually,* **spirits.** any distilled alcoholic beverage. —*v.t.* to remove or carry off secretly or mysteriously: *Someone spirited the dog away during the night.*

spir·it·ed (spir′i tid) *adj.* that is full of spirit; lively; vigorous: *a spirited horse.* —**spir′it·ed·ly,** *adv.* —**spir′it·ed·ness,** *n.*

spir·it·less (spir′it lis) *adj.* without enthusiasm or energy; lacking spirit; listless.

spir·i·tu·al (spir′i chōō əl) *adj.* **1.** of or relating to the human soul. **2.** of, relating to, or concerned with things of the spirit. **3.** of, relating to, or concerned with religious matters; sacred. —*n.* a religious folk song or hymn, especially one originated by Negroes in the southern United States. —**spir′i·tu·al·ly,** *adv.*

spir·i·tu·al·ism (spir′i chōō ə liz′əm) *n.* the belief that the dead communicate with the living, especially through a medium.

spir·i·tu·al·ist (spir′i chōō ə list) *n.* a person who believes in or supports spiritualism. —**spir′i·tu·al·is′tic,** *adj.*

spir·i·tu·al·i·ty (spir′i chōō al′ə tē) *n. pl.,* **spir·i·tu·al·i·ties.** devotion to or concern with things of the spirit rather than with material things; state or quality of being spiritual.

spir·i·tu·ous (spir′i chōō əs) *adj.* **1.** containing alcohol. **2.** produced by distillation.

spi·ro·chete (spī′rə kēt′) *n.* any of a large group of bacteria having a slender, spiral shape.

spi·ro·gy·ra (spī′rə jī′rə) *n.* any of various freshwater green algae having spiral chloroplasts.

spirt (spurt) another spelling of **spurt.**

spit¹ (spit) *v.,* **spit** or **spat, spit·ting.** —*v.i.* **1.** to force out saliva from the mouth. **2.** to make a popping or hissing noise, as hot oil or grease. —*v.t.* **1.** to force out from the mouth. **2.** to force out or utter in a violent or noisy manner: *to spit insults.* —*n.* **1.** saliva. **2.** the act of spitting. [Old English *spittan.*] —**spit′ter,** *n.*

spit² (spit) *n.* **1.** a slender, pointed rod on which meat is roasted over a fire. **2.** a narrow point of land extending into the sea. —*v.t.,* **spit·ted, spit·ting.** to pierce or thrust through with a spit. [Old English *spitu* this pointed rod.]

spit·ball (spit′bôl′) *n.* **1.** a wad of folded and chewed paper. **2.** an illegal pitch in baseball, in which the ball is moistened, as with saliva, before being thrown.

spite (spīt) *n.* a feeling of ill will or resentment toward another; malice: *The old woman spread rumors about her next-door neighbors out of spite.* —*v.t.,* **spit·ed, spit·ing.** to irritate, hurt, or humiliate: *She spilled ink on his book to spite him.*

  in spite of. regardless; despite: *The boys went sailing in spite of the bad weather.*

spite·ful (spīt′fəl) *adj.* filled with spite; malicious. —**spite′ful·ly,** *adv.* —**spite′ful·ness,** *n.*

spit·fire (spit′fīr′) *n.* a quick-tempered, fiery person.

spitting image, exact likeness: *Elaine is the spitting image of her mother.*

spit·tle (spit′əl) *n.* saliva; spit.

spit·toon (spi tōōn′) *n.* a receptacle for spit; cuspidor.

spitz (spits) *n. pl.,* **spitz·es.** a small, stocky dog having a pointed muzzle, small, erect ears, a fluffy tail that curls over the back, and a thick white or spotted coat.

splash (splash) *v.t.* **1.** to scatter or throw (a liquid) about: *She accidentally splashed paint on the floor.* **2.** to wet, soil, or stain with a liquid or other substance by scattering or throwing: *He splashed his face with water. A passing car splashed her dress with mud.* **3.** to mark or decorate by or as if by splashing: *The wallpaper was splashed with*

bright colors. —*v.i.* **1.** to cause a liquid to scatter about. **2.** to fall, strike, or move with a splash or splashes: *The diver splashed into the water.* **3.** (of a spacecraft) to land on a body of water. —*n. pl.,* **splash·es. 1.** the act or sound of splashing: *The stone hit the water with a splash.* **2.** an irregular spot or patch, as of color: *The horse had a splash of white on its forehead.* **3.** something that creates a sensation or stir: *The playwright made quite a splash on Broadway with his comedy.* —**splash′er,** *n.*

splash·down (splash′doun′) *n.* the landing of a spacecraft on a body of water.

splash·y (splash′ē) *adj.,* **splash·i·er, splash·i·est. 1.** making a splash or splashes. **2.** full of irregular spots or patches; blotchy; spotty. **3.** creating a sensation or stir; showy.

splat·ter (splat′ər) *v., n.* another word for **spatter.**

splay (splā) *adj.* **1.** spread or spreading out; broad. **2.** awkward or awkwardly formed; clumsy. —*n.* a sloping surface, especially in the opening of a window or door. —*v.t.* **1.** to spread out; extend. **2.** to make slanting; bevel.

spleen (splēn) *n.* **1.** a large, oval organ near the stomach, that serves to produce white blood cells and filter blood. **2.** ill temper; malice; spite.

splen·did (splen′did) *adj.* **1.** having or marked by brilliance or magnificence: *a splendid display of colors, the splendid interior of a palace.* **2.** impressive; illustrious; glorious: *a splendid achievement.* **3.** very good; excellent: *Having a party was a splendid idea.* —**splen′did·ly,** *adv.* —**splen′did·ness,** *n.*

Splay

splen·dor (splen′dər) *n.* **1.** a great display, as of riches or beautiful objects; magnificence; pomp: *People were amazed by the splendor of the king's palace.* **2.** great brightness; brilliance: *The painter tried to recreate on canvas the splendor of the setting sun.*

sple·net·ic (spli net′ik) *adj.* **1.** of or relating to the spleen. **2.** ill-tempered; malicious; spiteful.

splice (splīs) *v.t.,* **spliced, splic·ing. 1.** to unite or join by weaving together the strands of the ends of: *to splice two ropes.* **2.** to join together (film or magnetic tape) at the ends. **3.** to join together (pieces of timber) by overlapping. —*n.* the joint or union made by splicing. —**splic′er,** *n.*

splint (splint) *n.* **1.** a device made of wood, metal, or other material, used to hold in place and protect a fractured, dislocated, or broken bone. **2.** a thin, flexible strip of wood, such as is used in weaving baskets.

splin·ter (splin′tər) *n.* a thin, sharp, usually small piece chipped or broken off from something hard or brittle. —*v.t., v.i.* to break or split into splinters. —**splin′ter·y,** *adj.*

split (split) *v., ***split, split·ting.** —*v.t.* **1.** to break apart or divide lengthwise or in layers: *Jack split logs all afternoon.* **2.** to divide or break up into separate parts or portions: *The three partners split the profits of the business.* **3.** to burst or tear open or apart: *When Tom fell off his bicycle, he split his pants at the seams.* **4.** to divide (the stock of a company) into a larger number of shares. —*v.i.* **1.** to break apart lengthwise or in layers. **2.** to become divided; separate: *The search party split into two groups.* **3.** (of stock) to be or become split. —*n.* **1.** the act of splitting or the state of being split. **2.** a division in a group: *The controversial issue caused a split in the political party.* **3.** *also,* **splits.** a movement or exercise in dancing or calisthenics in which the body slides to the floor with the legs spread apart.

—*adj.* **1.** divided lengthwise or in layers. **2.** broken up; separated. —**split′ter,** *n.*

split infinitive, an infinitive having a word or phrase placed between *to* and the verb. For example: *The end was the option to not work at all* (Russell Baker).

split second, an extremely brief period of time; instant.

split·ting (split′ing) *adj.* very severe: *a splitting headache.*

splotch (sploch) *n. pl.,* **splotch·es.** a large, irregular spot; blot; stain. —*v.t.* to mark or cover with splotches. —**splotch′y,** *adj.*

splurge (splurj) *v.i.,* **splurged, splurg·ing.** to spend money with little or no attention to cost; indulge oneself in spending too much money: *Dan never saves any money because he splurges on clothes.* —*n.* the act or period of spending too much money.

splut·ter (splut′ər) *v.i.* **1.** to speak in a rapid, indistinct way, as when confused, angry, or excited. **2.** to make popping or hissing sounds, as food being fried; sputter. —*v.t.* to utter or express indistinctly: *to splutter an apology.* —*n.* a spluttering noise. —**splut′ter·er,** *n.*

spoil (spoil) *v.,* **spoiled** or **spoilt, spoil·ing.** —*v.t.* **1.** to cause damage or harm to (something): *The spilled coffee spoiled her dress. The fight spoiled the party.* **2.** to weaken or damage the character of: *to spoil a child.* —*v.i.* **1.** to become unfit for use: *The meat spoiled when we left it out of the refrigerator all night.* **2.** to be eager or anxious: *Hank is spoiling for a fight.* —*n. usually,* **spoils. 1.** goods or property seized by force, especially in war; booty; plunder. **2.** jobs or other favors given to supporters of a victorious political party.

spoil·age (spoi′lij) *n.* **1.** the act of spoiling or the state of being spoiled. **2.** something that has spoiled. **3.** the amount that has spoiled.

spoil·er (spoi′lər) *n.* a person or thing that causes spoilage.

spoil·sport (spoil′spôrt′) *n.* a person who spoils the pleasure of others by his behavior or attitude.

spoils system, the system or practice of distributing jobs or other favors to supporters of a victorious political party.

spoilt (spoilt) a past tense and past participle of **spoil.**

Spo·kane (spō kan′) *n.* a city in eastern Washington. Pop. (1970), 170,516.

spoke[1] (spōk) a past tense of **speak.**

spoke[2] (spōk) *n.* **1.** one of the bars or rods that connect the rim of a wheel to its hub. **2.** a rung of a ladder. [Old English *spāca*.]

spo·ken (spō′kən) *v.* the past participle of **speak.** —*adj.* **1.** uttered or expressed in speech; oral. **2.** speaking in a certain way. ▲ used in combination: *a soft-spoken young man.*

● **Spoken language** and **written language** are often quite different. In our own development as children, as well as in the historical development of language, speech comes before writing.

Besides seeming more natural, spoken language can be accompanied by gestures, facial expressions, and, most important, changes in the tone and pitch of the voice that help us to communicate our ideas clearly. The vocabulary of spoken language tends to be less formal than that of written language, often containing a great many colorful idioms and slang terms.

When spoken language acquires the kind of permanent quality that written language has, as when a person speaks into the microphone of a tape recorder, a more formal way of speaking is often adopted. Spoken language also becomes more like written language when gestures and expressions cannot be used to convey meaning, as when a person is speaking on the telephone to someone who obviously cannot see him or her.

In earlier times, written language was considered to be superior to the spoken tongue, and it was felt that the proper standard for language was the written form. Recently, people have begun to reject the formality of written language as the standard for communication. Partly because of the influence of radio and television, spoken language is now beginning to be considered the appropriate language for communication. Most writers and books that teach writing now support the belief that you should try to write in the same natural way that you speak.

---

spoke·shave (spōk′shāv′) *n.* a carpenter's tool having a blade between two handles, used to plane wood.

spokes·man (spōks′mən) *n. pl.,* **spokes·men** (spōks′mən). a person who speaks on behalf of another or others.

spokes·wom·an (spōks′woom′ən) *n. pl.,* **spokes·wom·en** (spōks′wim′ən). a woman who speaks on behalf of another or others.

sponge (spunj) *n.* **1.** any of a large group of water animals that live attached to rocks or other solid objects and have porous bodies that absorb water easily. Sponges are of various sizes, shapes, and colors. **2.** the absorbent skeleton of certain sponges, used for washing or other purposes. **3.** an article made from any of various substances, such as rubber or plastic, resembling this skeleton in structure or use.

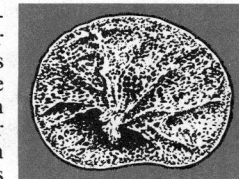

Sponge

4. an absorbent pad, as of gauze or prepared cotton, used in surgery. —*v.,* **sponged, spong·ing.** —*v.t.* **1.** to cleanse or rub with a wet sponge: *The waitress sponged down the table.* **2.** to remove with a sponge: *to sponge crayon marks off a wall.* **3.** to absorb. **4.** *Informal.* to get without paying: *to sponge a cigarette from someone.* —*v.i.* **1.** to absorb liquid, as a sponge. **2.** *Informal.* to live at the expense of another or others: *He sponged off his rich uncle.*

sponge cake, a light cake made with eggs, sugar, flour, and flavoring, but without shortening.

spong·er (spun′jər) *n.* **1.** *Informal.* a person who makes a practice of living at the expense of another or others. **2.** a person or boat that gathers sponges.

spon·gy (spun′jē) *adj.,* **spon·gi·er, spon·gi·est.** of or resembling a sponge; porous; absorbent. —**spon′gi·ness,** *n.*

spon·sor (spon′sər) *n.* **1.** a person who assumes responsibility or support for another person or thing. **2.** a person or organization that finances some event or entertainment, such as a radio or television program. **3.** a person who answers for an infant at baptism, making the required promises and professions of faith; godfather or godmother. —*v.t.* to act as sponsor for.

spon′sor·ship (spon′sər ship′) *n.* the act of sponsoring.

spon·ta·ne·i·ty (spon′tə nē′ə tē) *n.* the fact, quality, or condition of being spontaneous.

spon·ta·ne·ous (spon tā′nē əs) *adj.* **1.** arising from or caused by a natural impulse or desire; not planned or

at; āpe; cär; end; mē; it; īce; hot; ōld; fôrk; wood; fōōl; oil; out; up; turn; sing; thin; this; hw in white; zh in treasure. The symbol ə stands for the sound of **a** in about, **e** in taken, **i** in pencil, **o** in lemon, and **u** in circus.

S

forced: *spontaneous laughter.* **2.** arising or happening without an outside cause; having an internal cause or origin. —**spon·ta′ne·ous·ly,** *adv.*

spontaneous combustion, the bursting into flames of something, such as oily rags, because of the buildup of heat from slow oxidation.

spoof (spoof) *Informal. n.* **1.** a light parody; take off. **2.** a trick or deception; hoax. —*v.t.* **1.** to do a parody or spoof of; satirize lightly. **2.** to trick or deceive.

spook (spook) *Informal. n.* a ghost; specter. —*v.t.* to frighten; scare.

spook·y (spoo′kē) *adj.,* **spook·i·er, spook·i·est.** *Informal.* causing fear or uneasiness; scary: *a spooky old house.*

spool (spool) *n.* **1.** a small piece of wood, plastic, or other material shaped like a cylinder, around which thread, wire, or tape may be wound. **2.** the amount of thread, wire, or tape wound on a spool. —*v.t.* to wind on a spool.

spoon (spoon) *n.* **1.** a wooden, metal, or plastic utensil consisting of a handle with a small, shallow bowl at the end, used in preparing, serving, or eating food. **2.** something resembling this in shape or function. —*v.t.* to lift or transfer with a spoon: *The nurse spooned the soup into the patient's mouth.*

spoon·bill (spoon′bil′) *n.* any of several long-legged wading birds having a long, flat bill with a tip shaped like a spoon.

spoon·drift (spoon′drift′) *n.* another word for **spindrift.**

spoon·ful (spoon′fool′) *n. pl.,* **spoon·fuls.** the amount that can be held by a spoon.

spoor (spoor) *n.* a track or trail, especially of a wild animal.

spo·rad·ic (spə rad′ik) *adj.* **1.** happening from time to time; occasional: *sporadic bursts of gunfire.* **2.** appearing by itself in widely separate places. **3.** (of a disease) occurring in isolated cases; not epidemic. —**spo·rad′i·cal·ly,** *adv.*

spo·ran·gi·um (spə ran′jē əm) *n. pl.,* **spo·ran·gi·a** (spə-ran′jē ə). in certain plants such as ferns, a sac in which spores are produced; spore case.

spore (spôr) *n.* **1.** a tiny reproductive body formed by some plants and microscopic animals. **2.** a hard-covered body that is highly resistant to chemicals, heat, or cold, formed by a bacterium.

spore case, another term for **sporangium.**

spor·ran (spôr′ən, spor′ən) *n.* a large pouch or purse worn from the belt in front of a kilt.

Sporran

sport (spôrt) *n.* **1.** any game that requires physical activity and involves some competition, such as baseball, soccer, bowling, or basketball. **2.** any pastime or activity that provides pleasure or recreation; amusement; diversion. **3.** playfulness or jest; fun: *She said that only in sport and did not mean to hurt your feelings.* **4.** *Informal.* a person with regard to his ability to accept teasing, criticism, or defeat: *Joe is a good sport.* —*v.i.* **1.** to amuse oneself; play; frolic. **2.** to make fun; treat lightly; joke; trifle. —*v.t. Informal.* to display or show off: *Billy sported a new suit.* —*adj. also,*

sports. **1.** of or relating to sports: *a sports event.* **2.** suitable for informal wear: *sport clothes.*

sport·ing (spôr′ting) *adj.* **1.** of, relating to, or suitable for sports: *a sporting event.* **2.** characteristic of a sportsman; fair: *That was very sporting of him.* **3.** of or relating to gambling, especially on a sports event. **4.** *Informal.* involving risk: *a sporting chance.* —**sport′ing·ly,** *adv.*

spor·tive (spôr′tiv) *adj.* frolicsome; playful; lively. —**spor′tive·ly,** *adv.* —**spor′tive·ness,** *n.*

sports car, a small, low automobile capable of high speeds, usually seating two passengers.

sports·cast (spôrts′kast′) *n.* a radio or television broadcast of a sports event. —**sports′cast′er,** *n.*

sports·man (spôrts′mən) *n. pl.,* **sports·men** (spôrts′-mən). **1.** a person who is interested in or engages in sports, especially outdoor sports, such as hunting or fishing. **2.** a person who plays fairly and accepts defeat graciously. —**sports′man·like′,** *adj.*

sports·man·ship (spôrts′mən ship′) *n.* **1.** conduct worthy of a sportsman or sportswoman, such as fair play or the ability to accept defeat graciously. **2.** skill in sports.

sports·wear (spôrts′wer′) *n.* clothing designed for informal wear.

sports·wom·an (spôrts′woom′ən) *n. pl.,* **sports·wom·en** (spôrts′wim′ən). **1.** a woman who is interested in or engages in sports. **2.** a woman who plays fairly and accepts defeat graciously.

sport·y (spôr′tē) *adj.,* **sport·i·er, sport·i·est.** *Informal.* **1.** characteristic of a sportsman or sportswoman; sporting. **2.** loud or flashy, especially in dress.

spot (spot) *n.* **1.** a mark, stain, or blot produced by dirt or other foreign matter: *The mechanic's shirt was covered with spots of grease.* **2.** a flaw or blemish: *a spot on one's reputation.* **3.** a small mark or part differing from the surrounding area, as in color or material: *My dog is white with black spots.* **4.** place; location: *This is a pleasant spot for a picnic.* **5.** *Informal.* a difficult, disagreeable, or embarrassing situation. —*v.,* **spot·ted, spot·ting.** —*v.t.* **1.** to mark with a spot or spots: *The mud spotted the rug.* **2.** to locate or pick out with the eyes; recognize: *We spotted her easily in the crowd.* **3.** to blemish; disgrace: *To spot a person's reputation.* **4.** to place in a particular location. —*v.i.* to become spotted: *This fabric will spot easily.* —*adj.* paid on delivery: *spot cash.*

on the spot. a. at the place indicated: *We were on the spot a long time before the plane arrived.* **b.** at once; immediately: *The salesman demanded payment on the spot.* **c.** *Slang.* in an awkward position.

to hit the spot. *Informal.* to be exactly right or exactly what is needed: *A cold drink hits the spot on a hot day.*

spot-check (spot′chek′) *v.t.* to make a quick examination of samples selected at random.

spot check, a quick check of samples selected at random.

spot·less (spot′lis) *adj.* **1.** absolutely clean; immaculate: *a spotless kitchen.* **2.** having no flaws or blemishes: *a spotless reputation.* —**spot′less·ly,** *adv.* —**spot′less·ness,** *n.*

spot·light (spot′līt′) *n.* **1.** a strong beam of light shone on a particular person, place, or object, as on a performer in a theater. **2.** a lamp projecting such a light. **3.** public attention: *The scientist was in the spotlight after his unexpected discovery.*

spot·ted (spot′id) *adj.* marked or covered with spots.

spot·ty (spot′ē) *adj.,* **spot·ti·er, spot·ti·est.** **1.** marked or covered with spots; spotted. **2.** not regular: *spotty attendance.* —**spot′ti·ly,** *adv.* —**spot′ti·ness,** *n.*

spouse (spous) *n.* a married person; husband or wife.

spout (spout) *v.t.* **1.** to force out (a liquid) in a stream or spray; spurt: *An elephant spouts water from its trunk.*

882

2. *Informal.* to say in a wordy, conceited manner: *He was always spouting advice to other people.* —*v.i.* **1.** to gush or pour out: *Water spouted from the fire hydrant.* **2.** to discharge a liquid continuously or in spurts. **3.** *Informal.* to speak in a wordy, conceited manner: *He spouted off about his award.* —*n.* **1.** a tube or lip projecting from a vessel that channels liquid when it is poured: *the spout of a teapot.* **2.** a faucet, spigot, or the like, through which liquid flows. **3.** a jet or column, as of water. —**spout'er,** *n.*

sprain (sprān) *n.* an injury caused by a violent or sudden wrenching or twisting of the ligaments or tendons around a joint. —*v.t.* to cause a sprain in: *The man tripped and sprained his ankle.*

sprang (sprang) a past tense of **spring.**

sprat (sprat) *n.* **1.** a bluish-green saltwater fish found off the Atlantic coast of Europe, used for food. **2.** any of various related fish, such as a young herring.

sprawl (srôl) *v.i.* **1.** to lie or sit with the body and limbs stretched out in an awkward or careless manner: *The tired boy sprawled on the sofa.* **2.** to spread out in a straggling manner: *Dozens of houses sprawled across the hillside in the suburban community.* —*v.t.* to cause to spread out in an awkward, careless, or straggling manner. —*n.* the act or position of sprawling.

spray¹ (sprā) *n.* **1.** water or other liquid in the form of fine particles or droplets: *the spray from a waterfall.* **2.** anything resembling this: *a spray of powder.* **3.** any of various liquids forced out in a stream of fine particles by an atomizer, pressurized can, or other device: *a spray for killing ants.* **4.** the device holding this liquid. —*v.t.* **1.** to apply spray to (a surface): *He sprayed the wall with paint.* **2.** to apply a spray of: *The woman sprayed perfume on her wrist.* **3.** to discharge a spray in: *to spray a room with disinfectant.* —*v.i.* to scatter or force out spray. [Possibly from Low German *sprei.*] —**spray'er,** *n.*

spray² (sprā) *n.* **1.** a slender branch of a plant with its leaves, flowers, or fruit; sprig. **2.** an ornament, pattern, or design resembling this. [Middle English *spray.*]

spray gun, a device that forces out a spray of a liquid, such as paint or insecticide.

spread (spred) *v.,* **spread, spread·ing.** —*v.t.* **1.** to unfold, open up, or stretch out: *We spread the blanket out on the ground. The bird spread its wings.* **2.** to cover with a thin layer of something: *to spread a roll with jam.* **3.** to put as a thin covering: *to spread butter on toast.* **4.** to distribute or scatter over an area: *The farmer spread fertilizer on the ground.* **5.** to extend over a period of time: *We spread the work over three days.* **6.** to cause to become more widely known: *to spread a rumor.* **7.** to set (a table) for a meal; place food on. —*v.i.* **1.** to be placed, distributed, or scattered over an area; extend: *The rash spread along her arm. The fire spread through the house.* **2.** to be put as a thin covering. **3.** to become more widely known; circulate: *Word spread quickly about the accident.* **4.** to be pushed apart. —*n.* **1.** the act of spreading. **2.** the amount or extent that something opens up or stretches: *the spread of a bird's wings.* **3.** a cloth covering, especially for a bed. **4.** printed material, such as an advertisement, that covers two facing pages or several columns in a magazine or newspaper. **5.** soft food that can be spread, such as butter or cheese. **6.** *Informal.* a lavish display of food; feast. **7.** *Informal.* a ranch or farm. —**spread'er,** *n.*

spree (sprē) *n.* **1.** a period of excessive, unchecked participation in an activity: *a shopping spree.* **2.** lively frolic.

spri·er (sprī'ər) a comparative of **spry.**

spri·est (sprī'ist) a superlative of **spry.**

sprig (sprig) *n.* **1.** a shoot, twig, or branch of a plant with its leaves, flowers, or fruit: *a sprig of parsley.* **2.** a pattern or ornament resembling this.

spright·ly (sprīt'lē) *adj.,* **spright·li·er, spright·li·est.** lively; merry; gay: *a sprightly tune.* —**spright'li·ness,** *n.*

spring (spring) *v.,* **sprang** or **sprung, sprung, spring·ing.** —*v.i.* **1.** to move forward or jump up quickly; leap: *When the general came in, the soldiers sprang to attention.* **2.** to appear or arise suddenly: *A breeze sprang up from the southwest.* **3.** to shift or move by or as if by elastic force: *The rubber band sprang back into shape. The door sprang shut.* **4.** to come into being or grow suddenly or rapidly: *The weeds sprang up everywhere.* **5.** to become warped, cracked, or split: *The wood sprang from the humidity.* —*v.t.* **1.** to cause to work or operate suddenly: *to spring a trap.* **2.** to present or produce suddenly or unexpectedly: *to spring a surprise.* **3.** to cause to warp, crack, or split. **4.** to develop: *The radiator sprang a leak.* —*n.* **1.** the act of springing; leap. **2.** an elastic device, such as a spiral-shaped piece of metal, that recovers its original shape when released after being bent, compressed, or stretched. **3.** the quality of being light, bouncing, or flexible; springiness: *There was no spring in the tired woman's walk.* **4.** a place where underground water flows out of the earth. **5.** the season of the year coming between winter and summer. In the Northern Hemisphere it extends from about March 21 to about June 21. **6.** a source or origin. —*adj.* **1.** of, relating to, or suitable for the season of spring: *spring rain, spring clothing.* **2.** having a spring or springs: *This department store is having a sale on spring mattresses.*

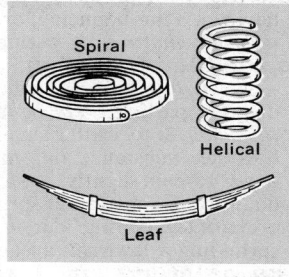

Springs

spring·board (spring'bôrd') *n.* **1.** a flexible board used in tumbling or diving. **2.** something that provides the starting or moving force: *A sharp mind was her springboard to success.*

spring·bok (spring'bok') *n. pl.,* **spring·bok** or **spring·boks.** a small antelope native to the plains of southern Africa, having horns and a tan-and-white coat.

spring fever, a feeling of laziness or listlessness that is commonly associated with the coming of spring.

Spring·field (spring'-fēld') *n.* **1.** the capital of Illinois, in the central part of the state. Pop. (1970), 91,753. **2.** a city in southwestern Massachusetts. Pop. (1970), 163,905. **3.** a city in southwestern Missouri. Pop. (1970), 120,096.

spring·tide (spring'tīd') *n.* another word for **springtime.**

Springbok

at; āpe; cär; end; mē; it; īce; hot; ōld; fôrk; wood; fōōl; oil; out; up; turn; sing; thin; this; hw in white; zh in treasure. The symbol ə stands for the sound of a in about, e in taken, i in pencil, o in lemon, and u in circus.

spring tide, the tide that has the greatest rise and ebb, occurring at or soon after the new or full moon.

spring·time (spring′tīm′) *n.* the season of spring.

spring·y (spring′ē) *adj.,* **spring·i·er, spring·i·est.** having a light, bouncing, or flexible quality: *a springy step, a springy mattress.* —**spring′i·ly,** *adv.* —**spring′i·ness,** *n.*

sprin·kle (spring′kəl) *v.,* **sprin·kled, sprin·kling.** —*v.t.* **1.** to scatter (a liquid or other substance) in small drops or particles: *The baker sprinkled powdered sugar on the cake.* **2.** to scatter small drops or particles of a liquid or other substance on: *to sprinkle flowers with water.* —*v.i.* to rain lightly. —*n.* **1.** a light rain. **2.** a small quantity of something; sprinkling.

sprin·kler (spring′klər) *n.* **1.** any of various devices for sprinkling a lawn. **2.** an outlet of a sprinkler system.

sprinkler system 1. an automatic system for extinguishing fires in buildings. **2.** a system of pipes or hoses for sprinkling a lawn, garden, or other area.

sprin·kling (spring′kling) *n.* a small quantity falling or scattered at random.

sprint (sprint) *n.* a short race at full speed. —*v.i.* to run at full speed, especially for a short distance: *The runners sprinted for sixty yards.* —**sprint′er,** *n.*

sprit (sprit) *n.* a small spar extending diagonally from the mast to the upper corner of a fore-and-aft sail.

sprite (sprīt) *n.* an elf, fairy, or goblin.

sprit·sail (sprit′sāl′, sprit′-səl) *n.* a sail spread and supported by a sprit.

sprock·et (sprok′it) *n.* **1.** any of the projections on the rim of a wheel that are arranged to engage the links of a chain. **2.** a wheel with sprockets. Also, **sprocket wheel.**

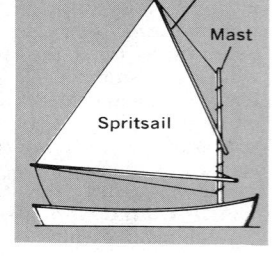

Sprit

sprout (sprout) *v.i.* **1.** to put forth young growth or buds; begin to grow: *The seeds we planted have finally sprouted.* **2.** to develop, grow, or appear suddenly or rapidly: *Many stores have sprouted up near the new housing development.* —*v.t.* to cause to sprout: *The plant sprouted new leaves.* —*n.* a new or young growth on a plant.

spruce[1] (sproos) *n.* **1.** a cone-bearing evergreen tree related to the pine, having short, needle-shaped leaves and drooping cones, found in cold and temperate regions of the Northern Hemisphere. **2.** the wood of this tree, used for construction and paper pulp. [Middle English *Spruce* Prussia; probably because this tree was first found in Prussia.]

spruce[2] (sproos) *v.t., v.i.,* **spruced, spruc·ing.** to make or become neat or trim. —*adj.,* **spruc·er, spruc·est.** having a neat or trim appearance. [Middle English *Spruce* Prussia, possibly from *Spruce* leather, a fine leather from Prussia.] —**spruce′ly,** *adv.* —**spruce′ness,** *n.*

sprung (sprung) a past tense and past participle of **spring.**

spry (sprī) *adj.,* **spry·er** or **spri·er, spry·est** or **spri·est.** lively and nimble: *a spry old gentleman.* —**spry′ly,** *adv.* —**spry′ness,** *n.*

spud (spud) *n.* **1.** a narrow, sharp tool resembling a spade, used for digging up weeds or removing bark from trees. **2.** *Informal.* a potato.

spume (spyoom) *n.* foam; froth. —*v.i.,* **spumed, spuming.** to foam; froth.

spun (spun) the past tense and past participle of **spin.**

spunk (spungk) *n. Informal.* courage, spirit, and determination; pluck.

spunk·y (spung′kē) *adj.,* **spunk·i·er, spunk·i·est.** *Informal.* characterized by or having courage, spirit, and determination; plucky. —**spunk′i·ly,** *adv.* —**spunk′i·ness,** *n.*

spur (spur) *n.* **1.** a pointed device worn on the heel of a horseman's boot, used to urge a horse forward. **2.** something that urges to action: *His wife's encouragement was the spur to his success.* **3.** something that resembles a spur, such as the sharp, hard projection on the leg of a rooster. **4.** a ridge or mountain projecting from the main mountain range. **5.** a short side track of a railroad connected with the main track. —*v.t.,* **spurred, spur·ring. 1.** to urge forward with a spur or spurs. **2.** to urge on; stimulate; incite: *The crowd's cheers spurred the team to victory.*

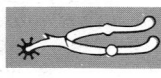

Spur

on the spur of the moment. without planning; on an impulse: *I telephoned her on the spur of the moment.*

spu·ri·ous (spyoor′ē əs) *adj.* not genuine or authentic; false: *a spurious passport, a spurious claim.* —**spu′ri·ous·ly,** *adv.* —**spu′ri·ous·ness,** *n.*

spurn (spurn) *v.t.* to reject with contempt or disdain; scorn: *The athlete spurned all offers to join a professional team.*

spurred (spurd) *adj.* fitted with or having spurs.

spurt (spurt) *also,* **spirt.** *v.i.* **1.** to gush or pour out suddenly or forcibly in a stream; spout: *The water spurted from the broken pipe.* **2.** to make or show a sudden, brief effort: *The car spurted ahead as soon as the traffic light turned green.* —*v.t.* to force out suddenly or forcibly in a stream. —*n.* **1.** a sudden gush, especially of liquid. **2.** a sudden, brief spell, as of activity or effort: *She works in spurts.*

sput·nik (sput′nik, spoot′nik) *n.* any of several man-made earth satellites launched by the Soviet Union. The first was Sputnik I, launched on October 4, 1957.

sput·ter (sput′ər) *v.i.* **1.** to make popping, spitting, or hissing noises: *The motor sputtered and then stopped.* **2.** to utter words or sounds in a confused or hasty manner. **3.** to throw out or spit small bits of food or saliva, as when speaking excitedly. —*v.t.* **1.** to throw out or spit small bits of (food or saliva), as when speaking excitedly. **2.** to utter (words or sounds) in a confused or hasty manner: *The dazed man sputtered nonsense.* —*n.* **1.** the act or noise of sputtering. **2.** confused or hasty speech. —**sput′ter·er,** *n.*

spu·tum (spyoo′təm) *n. pl.,* **spu·ta** (spyoo′tə). saliva; spit.

spy (spī) *n. pl.,* **spies. 1.** a person who is employed by a government to discover secret information about another government. **2.** a person who watches others secretly or who gathers secret information about others. —*v.,* **spied, spy·ing.** —*v.i.* **1.** to act as a spy: *to spy on the enemy.* **2.** to make a search or investigation; pry. —*v.t.* to catch sight of; observe; notice: *We spied a ship on the horizon.*

spy·glass (spī′glas′) *n. pl.,* **spy·glass·es.** a small telescope.

sq., square.

squab (skwob) *n.* a young pigeon.

squab·ble (skwob′əl) *v.i.,* **squab·bled, squab·bling.** to argue noisily, especially over something of little importance: *The children squabbled over who would ride the bicycle first.* —*n.* a petty argument or dispute. —**squab′-bler,** *n.*

squad (skwod) *n.* **1.** a military unit usually composed of ten men and commanded by a noncommissioned officer. **2.** a small group of persons organized for a particular purpose or function: *a baseball squad.*

squad car, another term for **patrol car.**

squad·ron (skwod′rən) *n.* **1.** any of various military units, as of airplanes or ships. **2.** any large organized body or group.

squal·id (skwol′id) *adj.* **1.** having a gloomy, wretched, poverty-stricken appearance: *a squalid beggar, squalid buildings.* **2.** morally bad; sordid: *the squalid details of a scandal.* —**squal′id·ly,** *adv.* —**squal′id·ness,** *n.*

squall¹ (skwôl) *n.* a sudden, strong gust of wind, often accompanied by rain, sleet, or snow. —*v.i.* to blow a squall; storm. [Probably of Scandinavian origin.]

squall² (skwôl) *v.i.* to cry or scream loudly and harshly: *The child squalled when he was spanked.* —*n.* a loud, harsh cry or scream. [Possibly imitative of this sound.]

squall·y (skwô′lē) *adj.,* **squall·i·er, squall·i·est.** marked by squalls; stormy; gusty: *squally seas.*

squal·or (skwol′ər) *n.* the state or condition of being squalid; wretchedness or sordidness.

squa·mous (skwā′məs) *adj.* like or formed of scales.

squan·der (skwon′dər) *v.t.* to spend or use in a wasteful or extravagant manner: *Bob squandered his fortune.*

square (skwer) *n.* **1.** a plane figure having four sides of equal length and four right angles. **2.** something having this shape: *the squares of a checkerboard.* **3.** an open space in a city or town bounded by streets on all sides, often planted with grass, trees, or flowers, and used as a park. **4.** any similar open space, especially one formed by the intersection of several streets. **5.** an L-shaped or T-shaped instrument used for drawing or measuring right angles.

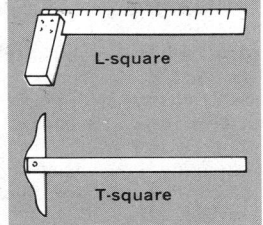

L-square

T-square

Squares *(def. 5)*

6. *Mathematics.* the product of a number multiplied by itself: *Twenty-five is the square of five.* **7.** *Slang.* a conventional and conservative person who does not know or follow the latest trends, fashions, or fads. —*adj.,* **squar·er, squar·est. 1.** having four sides of equal length and four right angles. **2.** resembling a square in form: *a square box.* **3.** designating a system used to measure area in terms of a unit in the form of a square: *We measured the room in square yards.* **4.** of a specified length on each of four sides of a square: *a piece of land one hundred feet square.* **5.** forming a right angle: *a square corner.* **6.** fair or just; honest: *a square deal.* **7.** on equal terms; even: *When he pays me back we'll be square.* **8.** straightforward or direct: *a square denial.* **9.** *Slang.* too conventional or conservative. —*v.,* **squared, squar·ing.** —*v.t.* **1.** to form with four equal sides and four right angles; make or form like a square. **2.** to bring to or as if to the form of a right angle: *to square one's shoulders.* **3.** to mark out or divide into squares. **4.** to cause to agree or conform; adjust: *to square a story with the facts.* **5.** to adjust so as to leave no balance; settle: *to square an account.* **6.** *Mathematics.* to multiply (a number) by itself. —*v.i.* to agree; conform; fit: *His opinions do not square with mine.* —*adv.* so as to be at or form right angles. —**square′ly,** *adv.* —**square′ness,** *n.*

  on the square. a. at right angles. **b.** *Informal.* in a fair or just way; honestly.

  to square off. *Informal.* to prepare to fight.

square dance, a dance performed by groups of four or more couples who are arranged in a square at the beginning of the dance.

square knot, a knot formed by two interlaced loops going in opposite directions.

square meal, a complete or substantial meal.

square measure, a system used to measure area in terms of a unit in the form of a square.

square-rigged (skwer′rigd′) *adj.* having square sails as the principal sails.

square-rig·ger (skwer′rig′ər) *n.* a square-rigged ship.

square root, a number that produces a given number when multiplied by itself: *The square root of 36 is 6.*

Square-rigger

squash¹ (skwosh) *v.t.* **1.** to beat or press into a soft or flat mass; crush: *Michael squashed the flower when he accidentally stepped on it.* **2.** to force or squeeze into a small area; cram; crowd. **3.** to put down or suppress forcibly and completely: *to squash a revolt.* —*v.i.* to be or become crushed. —*n. pl.,* **squash·es. 1.** a crushed or crowded mass. **2.** the act or sound of squashing. **3.** a game played in a walled court with rackets and a rubber ball. [Middle French *esquasser* to crush, crowd.]

squash² (skwosh) *n. pl.,* **squash·es. 1.** the round or oblong fruit of any of a group of plants related to the gourd, cooked and eaten as a vegetable, or used as food for livestock. **2.** a plant bearing this fruit. [Shortened from Algonquian *askutasquash* literally, eaten green.]

Squash²

squash·y (skwosh′ē) *adj.,* **squash·i·er, squash·i·est. 1.** easily squashed: *squashy tomatoes.* **2.** soft and wet.

squat (skwot) *v.i.,* **squat·ted** or **squat, squat·ting. 1.** to crouch or sit with the knees bent and drawn close to or under the body: *Keith squatted down to pet the cat.* **2.** to settle on land without having right or title to it. —*adj.* short and thick; low and broad.

squat·ter (skwot′ər) *n.* **1.** a person or thing that squats. **2.** a person who settles on land to which he or she has no right or title. Squatters are sometimes given title to land after having lived on it for a certain period of time.

squat·ty (skwot′ē) *adj.,* **squat·ti·er, squat·ti·est.** another word for **squat.**

squaw (skwô) *n.* a North American Indian woman or wife.

squawk (skwôk) *v.i.* **1.** to utter a shrill, harsh cry, as a gull or parrot. **2.** *Informal.* to complain or protest loudly or noisily: *He squawked at having to run errands for his older brother.* —*n.* **1.** a shrill, harsh cry, such as that uttered by a gull or parrot. **2.** *Informal.* a loud complaint or protest. —**squawk′er,** *n.*

squeak (skwēk) *n.* a short, thin, high-pitched sound or cry. —*v.i.* **1.** to make or utter a squeak: *The rusty gate squeaked when it was opened.* **2.** to accomplish, get, or earn something by a narrow margin: *He barely squeaked by on the exam.* —**squeak′er,** *n.*

at; āpe; cär; end; mē; it; īce; hot; ōld; fôrk; wood; fōōl; oil; out; up; turn; sing; thin; this; hw in white; zh in treasure. The symbol ə stands for the sound of **a** in about, **e** in taken, **i** in pencil, **o** in lemon, and **u** in circus.

squeak·y (skwē′kē) *adj.*, **squeak·i·er**, **squeak·i·est.** tending to squeak; squeaking: *a squeaky door.*

squeal (skwēl) *v.i.* **1.** to make or utter a loud, shrill cry or sound: *Ann squealed with delight.* **2.** *Slang.* to betray a confidence; turn informer: *The crook squealed on his partner.* —*n.* a loud, shrill cry or sound. —**squeal′er**, *n.*

squeam·ish (skwē′mish) *adj.* **1.** easily sickened or nauseated: *to be squeamish at the sight of blood.* **2.** easily offended or shocked; prudish. —**squeam′ish·ly**, *adv.* —**squeam′ish·ness**, *n.*

squee·gee (skwē′jē) *n.* a T-shaped implement with a rubber or leather edge, used in wiping off or spreading liquid on flat, smooth surfaces, as in washing windows.

squeeze (skwēz) *v.*, **squeezed**, **squeez·ing.** —*v.t.* **1.** to apply strong pressure to (something): *to squeeze a tube of toothpaste.* **2.** to obtain (something) by or as if by applying strong pressure; extract: *to squeeze juice from an orange, to squeeze a contribution from someone.* **3.** to press or hug, as in sympathy or affection: *to squeeze someone's hand.* **4.** to force by pressure; thrust forcibly: *to squeeze a book onto a crowded shelf.* —*v.i.* **1.** to apply pressure. **2.** to be capable of being squeezed; yield to pressure. **3.** to pass or force one's way by squeezing: *to squeeze into a seat.* —*n.* **1.** the act of squeezing; application of pressure: *She gave his hand a gentle squeeze.* **2.** pressure, as of a crowd of people; crush: *There is always a squeeze in the subway during rush hour.* —**squeez′a·ble**, *adj.* —**squeez′er**, *n.*

squelch (skwelch) *v.t.* **1.** to stamp out or eliminate forcibly and completely; crush; quash: *The dictatorship had squelched all opposition.* **2.** *Informal.* to silence or subdue, as with a crushing or sarcastic remark. —*n. Informal.* a crushing or sarcastic remark. —**squelch′er**, *n.*

squib (skwib) *n.* **1.** a short, witty written or spoken attack on someone or something; lampoon. **2.** a small firework that burns with a hissing noise and then explodes. **3.** a broken firecracker that burns but does not explode.

squid (skwid) *n. pl.,* **squids** or **squid.** a sea animal having a round, tubelike body, a pair of fins, and ten arms.

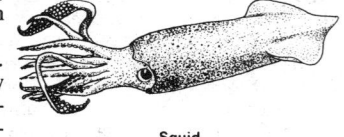
Squid

squire (skwīr) *n.* **1.** an English country gentleman or landowner. **2.** in feudal society, a young nobleman who, in preparation for his own knighthood, attended a knight. **3.** a man who escorts a woman. —*v.t.*, **squired**, **squir·ing.** to escort (a woman).

squirm (skwurm) *v.t.* **1.** to turn or twist the body: *The little boy was bored and began to squirm in his seat.* **2.** to show or feel discomfort, uneasiness, or mental distress: *The lawyer's clever questions made the witness squirm.* —*n.* the act or motion of squirming. —**squirm′y**, *adj.*

squir·rel (skwur′əl) *n.* **1.** an animal related to the mouse, usually having a slender body and a long, bushy tail. Squirrels live in trees and feed chiefly on nuts. **2.** the gray, reddish, or dark-brown fur of this animal.

squirt (skwurt) *v.t.* **1.** to force out (liquid) though a narrow opening in a thin jet or stream: *to squirt oil on a rusty hinge.* **2.** to wet by squirting a liquid: *to squirt someone with a hose.* —*v.i.* **1.** to come out in a thin jet or stream: *The ink squirted from the fountain pen.* **2.** to force out a thin stream of

Squirrel

liquid. —*n.* **1.** the act of squirting. **2.** a thin jet or stream. **3.** something used for squirting liquid, such as a syringe. **4.** *Informal.* a rude, brash young person.

Sr, the symbol for strontium.

Sr., senior.

Sri Lan·ka (srē län′kə) *n.* an island country of southern Asia, in the Indian Ocean, east of the southern tip of India. It was formerly known as Ceylon. Capital, Colombo. Area, 25,332 sq. mi. Pop. (1971 est.), 12,670,000.

St. 1. saint. **2.** street. **3.** strait.

stab (stab) *v.*, **stabbed**, **stab·bing.** —*v.t.* **1.** to pierce or wound with a pointed weapon: *to stab a person with a knife.* **2.** to thrust or drive (a pointed instrument or weapon) into something: *to stab a fork into meat.* **3.** to wound the feelings of. —*v.i.* to thrust with a pointed weapon. —*n.* **1.** a thrust made with a pointed weapon. **2.** a wound or puncture made by stabbing. **3.** a sharp but momentary sensation or feeling; pang: *a stab of pain, a stab of regret.* **4.** *Informal.* an attempt; effort; try: *Even though it was a difficult job, Ethel decided to make a stab at it.* —**stab′ber**, *n.*

sta·bil·i·ty (stə bil′ə tē) *n. pl.,* **sta·bil·i·ties. 1.** the state or condition of being stable. **2.** consistency or steadiness, as of character or purpose. **3.** permanence.

sta·bi·lize (stā′bə līz′) *v.t.*, **sta·bi·lized**, **sta·bi·liz·ing. 1.** to make stable, firm, or steady. **2.** to prevent from changing; keep steady: *The legislator suggested that more severe measures were needed to stabilize prices.* —**sta′bi·li·za′tion**, *n.*

sta·bi·liz·er (stā′bə lī′zər) *n.* **1.** a person or thing that stabilizes. **2.** a gyroscopic device in a ship, airplane, or the like, that keeps it steady in rough water or turbulent air.

sta·ble[1] (stā′bəl) *n.* **1.** a building, especially one with stalls, where horses or cattle are kept and fed. **2.** *also,* **stables.** the race horses belonging to a particular owner or establishment. —*v.t.*, **sta·bled**, **sta·bling.** to put or keep in a stable: *Barbara stabled her horse at Mr. Brown's farm.* [Old French *estable.*]

sta·ble[2] (stā′bəl) *adj.* **1.** not easily moved, shaken, or overthrown; firm: *a stable platform, a stable government.* **2.** reliable, constant, and sure; predictable; steady: *a stable personality.* **3.** continuing without much change; permanent; enduring: *a stable language.* **4.** *Chemistry.* (of chemical compounds) resistant to chemical change; not easily decomposed. [Old French *estable* stable, firm, reliable.] —**sta′bly**, *adv.*

stac·ca·to (stə kä′tō) *adj.* **1.** *Music.* having or produced with breaks between tones; disconnected; abrupt. **2.** composed of or characterized by abrupt and sharp emphasis, sound, or movement: *staccato gunfire.* —*adv.* in a staccato manner.

stack (stak) *n.* **1.** a large, rectangular or cone-shaped pile of hay, straw, or grain. **2.** a pile of things arranged in an orderly way: *a stack of plates, a stack of records.* **3.** a smokestack or chimney. **4.** a rack in which books are arranged above one another on shelves. **5. stacks.** an area in a library in which most of the books are kept. **6.** a number of rifles standing muzzle upward against each other. **7.** *Informal.* a large quantity. —*v.t.* **1.** to gather or arrange in a stack: *to stack books.* **2.** to arrange (playing cards) beforehand so that they will come up in a certain order: *Ken said*

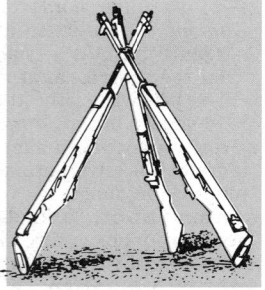
Stack *(def. 6)*

Mike won the game because he had stacked the deck.

sta·di·um (stā′dē əm) *n. pl.,* **sta·di·ums** or **sta·di·a** (stā′dē ə). a large, usually roofless, oval or U-shaped structure surrounding an open area, used for athletic events and other purposes, such as concerts or rallies, and having rows of seats for spectators.

staff (staf) *n. pl.,* **staffs** or *(defs. 1, 5)* **staves. 1.** a stick, rod, or pole, often used as an aid in walking, as a weapon, or as a symbol of authority. **2.** another word for **flagpole. 3.** the entire group or a particular group of permanent employees working in an institution, business, or organiza-

Staff *(def. 5)*

tion: *the staff of a hospital, the nursing staff, the President's advisory staff.* **4.** military personnel with administrative duties who usually do not take part in combat. **5.** *Music.* the five horizontal lines and four spaces on which musical notation is made. —*v.t.* to provide (an office, establishment, military unit, or the like) with officers or employees.

stag (stag) *n.* **1.** a full-grown male deer. **2.** a man who goes to a social gathering unaccompanied by a woman. —*adj.* for or attended by men only: *a stag party.* —*adv.* (of a man) not accompanied by a woman: *When Linda said that she was going to the dance with Barry, Don decided to go stag.*

stage (stāj) *n.* **1.** a raised platform or similar structure in a theater or hall, on which a performance takes place. **2.** the theater as a profession. **3.** a place where some important event takes place; scene of action: *Europe was the stage of World War I.* **4.** a step, period, or degree in a process, progression, or development: *Very few symptoms appeared in the early stages of his disease.* **5.** the distance traveled between two places of rest on a road or journey; part of a journey: *The last stage of our trip took us across the Atlantic Ocean.* **6.** see **stagecoach. 7.** one of the self-propelled sections of a rocket that can be separated from the rest of the vehicle. —*v.t.,* **staged, stag·ing. 1.** to put, arrange, or exhibit on or as if on a stage: *to stage a play.* **2.** to conduct, engage in, or carry on: *The protesters planned to stage a demonstration during the inaugural celebrations.*

stage·coach (stāj′kōch′) *n. pl.,* **stage·coach·es.** a horse-drawn coach that formerly traveled on a regular schedule over a fixed route, carrying passengers, mail, and baggage.

stage·hand (stāj′-hand′) *n.* in the theater, a person who moves scenery, sets up props, controls lighting, and performs certain other duties.

Stagecoach

stage-struck (stāj′struk′) *adj.* fascinated by the theater, especially with the hope of becoming an actor or actress.

stag·ger (stag′ər) *v.i.* **1.** to move unsteadily or with a swaying motion; totter; reel: *The weary man staggered under his heavy load.* **2.** to become confused or overwhelmed; hesitate in purpose or action; waver: *She staggered at the seemingly impossible task.* —*v.t.* **1.** to cause to totter or reel: *The punch staggered the fighter.* **2.** to confuse or overwhelm, as with grief or surprise; shock: *an act of bravery that staggers the imagination.* **3.** to schedule, arrange, or distribute in a continuous or overlapping order: *to stagger traffic lights, to stagger work shifts.* **4.** to arrange

in a zigzag pattern or manner. —*n.* **1.** the act or motion of staggering. **2.** a staggered pattern or arrangement. **3. staggers.** a disease of the central nervous system in cattle and other domestic animals that causes sudden falls and a staggering gait. ▲ used with a singular verb. —**stag′-ger·ing·ly,** *adv.*

stag·ing (stā′jing) *n.* the direction and presentation of a theatrical production or similar entertainment.

stag·nant (stag′nənt) *adj.* **1.** still or motionless, as air or water. **2.** foul from standing still: *stagnant water in a swamp.* **3.** not active, changing, or developing; inactive or dull: *Joan complained that her life in the small town was stagnant.* —**stag′nant·ly,** *adv.*

stag·nate (stag′nāt) *v.i.,* **stag·nat·ed, stag·nat·ing. 1.** to be or become foul from standing still: *The water stagnated in the pond.* **2.** to stop growing, changing, or developing; be or become inactive or dull: *He felt that his mind was stagnating.* —**stag·na′tion,** *n.*

staid (stād) *adj.* conservative or sober in character or style; sedate; serious. —**staid′ly,** *adv.* —**staid′ness,** *n.*

stain (stān) *n.* **1.** a spot or streak produced by foreign matter; mark or discoloration: *an ink stain, grass stains.* **2.** a liquid dye, pigment, or other colored solution used especially in coloring wood. **3.** moral blemish; dishonor: *a stain on one's reputation.* —*v.t.* **1.** to spot or streak with foreign matter: *Spilled coffee stained the carpet.* **2.** to color or treat with a dye, pigment, or other colored solution: *to stain a wooden bookcase.* **3.** to bring dishonor upon; taint; blemish. —*v.i.* **1.** to be or become stained: *This material stains easily.* **2.** to cause a stain: *Be careful when you eat the berries because they stain.* —**stain′er,** *n.*

stain·less (stān′lis) *adj.* having no stains; spotless.

stainless steel, an alloy of steel with large amounts of chromium and nickel, that resists rust and heat, and is strong, durable, and easy to shape. It is used for tableware, cooking and serving utensils, appliances, and structural parts.

stair (ster) *n.* **1.** *usually,* **stairs.** a series or flight of steps for passing from one level or floor to another: *We climbed the stairs to the attic.* **2.** a step or one of a series of steps.

stair·case (ster′kās′) *n.* a flight or a series of flights of stairs with its supporting framework.

stair·way (ster′wā′) *n.* another word for **staircase.**

stake (stāk) *n.* **1.** a stick or post sharpened at one end for driving into the ground, used as a support, boundary mark, or post. **2.** the post to which a person was bound for execution by burning: *Joan of Arc was burned at the stake.* **3.** *also,* **stakes.** something that is risked in a wager or gambling game, such as money. **4.** an emotional or financial interest: *As the star of the play, she has a great stake in its success.* —*v.t.,* **staked, stak·ing. 1.** to mark the boundaries of (land) with or as if with stakes; claim or reserve. **2.** to fasten or tie to a stake; support with a stake. **3.** to gamble or risk: *He staked all his savings on the invention.*

at stake. in question or danger: *The firemen acted quickly because many lives were at stake.*

to pull up stakes. to move on or away; leave: *After years of city life, the family pulled up stakes and moved to the country.*

sta·lac·tite (stə lak′tīt) *n.* a formation resembling an icicle, hanging down from the ceiling of a cave. It is usually composed of calcium carbonate deposited by water seeping through the rock above.

sta·lag·mite (stə lag′mīt) *n.* a formation resembling a cone, built up on the floor of a cave by calcium carbonate dripping from the ceiling.

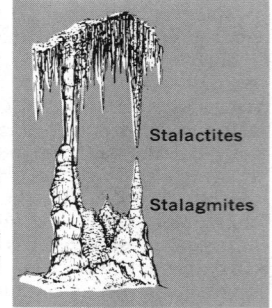

Stalactites

Stalagmites

stale (stāl) *adj.,* **stal·er, stal·est. 1.** no longer fresh: *The old cake was so stale that we could not eat it.* **2.** having lost its novelty or interest: *stale jokes.* **3.** out of condition: *Mark was stale from lack of exercise.* —*v.i.,* **staled, stal·ing.** to become stale. —**stale′ness,** *n.*

stale·mate (stāl′māt′) *n.* **1.** a draw in chess that results when the player whose turn it is cannot make a move without putting his king in check. **2.** any position or situation in which no further action is possible; deadlock; standstill. —*v.t.,* **stale·mat·ed, stal·mat·ing.** to bring to a stalemate; place in a deadlock.

Sta·lin, Joseph (stä′lin) 1879–1953, Soviet revolutionary and from 1924 to 1953 leader of the Soviet Union.

Sta·lin·grad (stä′lin grad′) *n.* see **Volgograd.**

stalk¹ (stôk) *n.* **1.** the main stem of a plant. **2.** the stem of any plant part. **3.** a supporting part. [Possibly from Old English *stela.*]

stalk² (stôk) *v.t.* **1.** to hunt, track, or pursue stealthily: *The lion stalked his prey.* **2.** to move menacingly or stealthily through: *The fugitive stalked the streets.* —*v.i.* to walk in a stiff, determined manner: *The angry man stalked out of the room.* [Old English *bestealcian* to move stealthily.] —**stalk′er,** *n.*

stall (stôl) *n.* **1.** a compartment in a barn or stable for a horse, cow, or other animal. **2.** a booth or counter for setting up wares for sale. **3.** an enclosed seat in the chancel of a church, usually reserved for the clergy. **4.** *Informal.* something used to delay or prevent an action; delaying tactic. —*v.t.* **1.** to delay or prevent from acting: *The store owner stalled the robber until the police arrived.* **2.** to hinder or block the motion or progress of: *The damaged track stalled the train for an hour.* **3.** to cause (an engine, automobile, or the like) to stop running. **4.** to put or keep (an animal) in a stall. —*v.i.* **1.** to make delays; be evasive: *to stall for time.* **2.** to stop running: *The old car's engine stalls frequently on cold days.*

stal·lion (stal′yən) *n.* a male horse, especially one used for breeding.

stal·wart (stôl′wərt) *adj.* **1.** strong or brave: *a stalwart hero.* **2.** firm or unwavering, as in support of a cause; resolute. —*n.* a stalwart person. —**stal′wart·ly,** *adv.* —**stal′wart·ness,** *n.*

sta·men (stā′mən) *n.* the part of a flower that produces pollen. It consists of a slender stalk, called the filament, with an enlarged pollen-bearing tip called the anther.

Stam·ford (stam′fərd) *n.* a city in southwestern Connecticut. Pop. (1970), 108, 798.

stam·i·na (stam′ə nə) *n.* the moral or physical ability to withstand fatigue, disease, or hardship; endurance: *That athlete has stamina.*

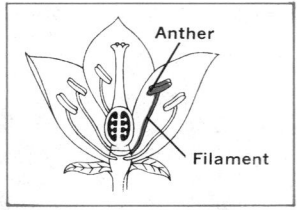

Anther

Filament

Stamen

stam·i·nate (stam′ə nit, stam′ə nāt′) *adj.* **1.** having a stamen or stamens. **2.** having stamens but no pistils.

stam·mer (stam′ər) *v.i.* to speak haltingly, especially by repeating a letter or sound. —*v.t.* to say or utter with a stammer: *She smiled nervously and stammered an excuse for being late.* —*n.* an instance of stammering. —**stam′mer·er,** *n.*

stamp (stamp) *v.t.* **1.** to bring down (the foot or feet) forcefully and heavily: *The spoiled child stamped his foot with rage.* **2.** to strike forcefully with the sole of the foot: *to stamp the ground.* **3.** to put out, stop, or eliminate: *to stamp out a campfire, to stamp out crime.* **4.** to mark (with an impression, design, or the like): *to stamp an initial on stationery.* **5.** to mark (something) with a device that imprints or cuts a design, letters, or the like: *The salesman stamped the bill to show it had been paid.* **6.** to impress deeply; fix: *The canoe trip was forever stamped in his memory.* **7.** to put a postage stamp or other official mark on: *to stamp a letter.* **8.** to pound or crush, as ore. —*v.i.* **1.** to strike the foot forcefully down upon the ground: *He stamped on the floor.* **2.** to walk forcefully with heavy steps: *She stamped out of the room in anger.* —*n.* **1.** a device or tool for impressing or cutting a design, letters, or the like on paper, wax, metal, or another surface. **2.** an impression or design made with such a device. **3.** a postage stamp. **4.** any similar stamped or printed paper issued by a government and placed on something to show that a tax or other charge has been paid. **5.** an official mark or seal: *a royal stamp.* **6.** a distinguishing mark or impression: *The author's work bears the stamp of a vivid imagination.* **7.** a heavy metal block used to crush rock, ore, or the like. **8.** the act of stamping. —**stamp′er,** *n.*

stam·pede (stam pēd′) *n.* **1.** a sudden scattering or headlong flight of frightened animals, such as a herd of cattle or horses. **2.** a sudden scattering or headlong flight of a mob or crowd: *There was a stampede toward the exit when the fire broke out in the movie theater.* —*v.,* **stam·ped·ed, stam·ped·ing.** —*v.i.* to be part of a stampede. —*v.t.* to cause to stampede: *The rustlers stampeded the cattle.*

stance (stans) *n.* **1.** a manner or way of standing, especially the particular position taken by an athlete while playing. **2.** an attitude; viewpoint: *a conservative political stance.*

stanch¹ (stônch, stänch) *also,* **staunch.** *v.t.* **1.** to stop or check the flow of (blood or other liquid). **2.** to stop or check the flow of blood or other liquid from (a wound or other opening). [Old French *estanchier.*] —**stanch′er,** *n.*

stanch² (stônch, stänch) *adj.* another spelling of **staunch¹.** —**stanch′ly,** *adv.* —**stanch′ness,** *n.*

stan·chion (stan′shən) *n.* **1.** an upright pillar or bar used as a support. **2.** a device for restricting the movements of animals, such as cattle, usually consisting of a pair of bars loosely fitting around the neck. —*v.t.* **1.** to provide with or support by stanchions. **2.** to fasten (cattle) with stanchions.

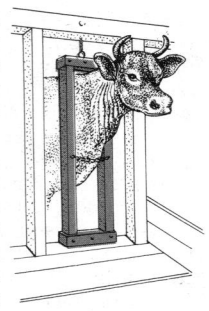

Stanchion

stand (stand) *v.,* **stood, stand·ing.** —*v.i.* **1.** to be in an upright position on one's feet: *We had to stand because there were no seats.* **2.** to rise to one's feet: *The congregation stood to sing the hymn.* **3.** to be or remain upright: *A ladder stood against the side of the barn.* **4.** to have location or position; be situated; lie: *The village stands at the foot of the hill.* **5.** to hold a particular place, as of degree, rank, or class: *Tom stood in first place in the ath-*

letic contest. **6.** to be in a particular state or condition: *The window stood open.* **7.** to remain unchanged or in force; hold good: *The rule against chewing gum in the classroom still stands.* **8.** to take on a certain position, attitude, or opinion: *Mother would not stand for shouting in the house.* **9.** to collect and remain: *Water stood in the gutter.* —*v.t.* **1.** to set in an upright position: *Stand the barrel on its end.* **2.** to put up with; tolerate: *I can't stand all this noise.* **3.** to undergo without damage; withstand: *That cloth has stood the test of time and wear.* **4.** to be subjected to; undergo: *to stand trial.* —*n.* **1.** a position, attitude, or opinion: *What is the President's stand on income taxes?* **2.** determined effort for or against something: *to take a stand against smoking.* **3.** a stop or halt, especially for battle: *The troops made a stand at the entrance to the valley.* **4.** a place where or in which someone or something stands. **5.** a rack or similar structure for placing things: *an umbrella stand.* **6.** a booth, counter, or stall for carrying on a business: *a newspaper stand.* **7.** *also,* **stands.** a raised platform or similar structure, usually having several tiers on which one can sit or stand: *We watched the baseball game from the stands.* **8.** see **witness stand.** **9.** a group of trees or plants: *A stand of trees grew on the hill.*

to stand a chance. to have a chance or likelihood: *Our team doesn't stand a chance of winning.*

to stand by. a. to take the side of; support; defend: *She stood by her friend during the crisis.* **b.** to be or become ready, as for use or action.

to stand for. to represent; symbolize; mean: *Uncle Sam stands for the United States.*

to stand in for. to be a substitute for.

to stand out. a. to jut out; project; protrude. **b.** to be prominent or noticeable: *Robert's red hair made him stand out in a crowd.*

to stand up. a. to rise to or be on one's feet. **b.** to withstand wear, hardship, pressure, or the like; endure; last.

to stand up for. to take the side of; support; defend.

stand·ard (stan′dərd) *n.* **1.** anything accepted or used to set an example or serve as a model: *The army has strict standards of dress and conduct.* **2.** an established measure. **3.** a flag, figure, or other object used as an emblem: *the standard of a regiment.* **4.** an upright support or part: *the standard of a lamp.* —*adj.* **1.** serving or fitted to serve as a standard: *a standard measure of weight.* **2.** having widely accepted excellence or authority: *a standard book on botany.* **3.** widely used; usual: *standard practices.* **4.** conforming to the speech or writing that is generally accepted as correct or preferred: *standard spelling, standard English.*

stand·ard·ize (stan′dər dīz′) *v.t.,* **stand·ard·ized, stand·ard·iz·ing.** to make standard; regulate by a standard: *to standardize machine parts.* —**stand′ard·i·za′tion,** *n.*

standard of living, the average level of goods, services, luxuries, and the like available to a person, group, or country.

standard time, time for any region based on its longitudinal distance from Greenwich, England. The earth is divided into twenty-four time zones. In the continental United States the four standard time zones are Eastern, Central, Mountain, and Pacific.

stand·by (stand′bī′) *n. pl.,* **stand·bys. 1.** a person or thing that can be depended on in an emergency. **2.** a person or thing kept ready to be used as a replacement or substitute.

stand·ee (stan dē′) *n. Informal.* a person who stands because there are no vacant seats, as in a theater, train, or the like.

stand·in (stand′in′) *n.* **1.** a person who takes the place of a motion-picture or television actor or actress while lights, cameras, and other technical equipment are being

set up and adjusted, or during scenes involving dangerous action. **2.** any person who substitutes for another.

stand·ing (stan′ding) *adj.* **1.** upright or on end; straight; erect: *standing corn, a standing collar.* **2.** done from or in an upright position: *a standing ovation.* **3.** continuing in existence, operation, or effect: *a standing rule, a standing committee.* —*n.* **1.** status, grade, or rank, as in a profession or society; reputation: *amateur standing, scholastic standing.* **2.** duration: *a friendship of long standing.*

Stan·dish, Miles (stan′dish; mīlz) 1584?–1656, military leader of the Plymouth Colony.

stand·off·ish (stand′ôf′ish) *adj.* lacking warmth or friendliness; reserved; aloof.

stand·pipe (stand′pīp′) *n.* a large vertical pipe or tower used to store water, usually standing on high ground so as to provide pressure in a water system, such as that in an apartment house or factory.

stand·point (stand′point′) *n.* a position from which things are viewed and judged; point of view.

stand·still (stand′stil′) *n.* a halt; stop: *The strike brought the steel industry to a standstill.*

stank (stangk) a past tense of **stink.**

Stan·ley, Sir Henry Mor·ton (stan′lē; môrt′ən) 1841–1904, English journalist and explorer in Africa.

stan·nic (stan′ik) *adj.* of, relating to, or containing tin, especially in its higher oxidation state of + 4.

stan·nous (stan′əs) *adj.* of, relating to, or containing tin, especially in its lower oxidation state of + 2.

stan·za (stan′zə) *n.* in poetry, a group of lines arranged in any of various patterns according to meter, rhyme, and the like.

sta·pes (stā′pēz) *n. pl.,* **sta·pes** or **sta·pe·des** (stə pē′dēz, stā′pə dēz). the innermost of the three small bones in the middle ear; stirrup.

staph·y·lo·coc·cus (staf′ə-lə kok′əs) *n. pl.,* **staph·y·lo·coc·ci** (staf′ə lə kok′sī). **1.** any of various bacteria that form irregular clusters. **2.** an infection caused by these bacteria.

sta·ple¹ (stā′pəl) *n.* **1.** a small bent piece of thin wire used for fastening together papers, fabrics, or other thin materials. **2.** a U-shaped piece of metal with pointed ends, driven into something for fastening, as to support a hook or to hold wire fencing to a post. —*v.t.,* **stapled, stapling.** to secure, fasten, or attach with a staple or staples. [Old English *stapol* a post, pillar.]

Stapes
Bones of the middle ear

sta·ple² (stā′pəl) *n.* **1.** a basic product in widespread use or demand: *Flour, salt, and sugar are staples.* **2.** a major product grown or manufactured in a country or region: *Rice is a staple of China.* **3.** a basic or major element; substantial part. **4.** raw material. **5.** a textile fiber used in the manufacture of yarn. —*adj.* basic or major: *staple industries.* [Old French *estaple* market.]

at; āpe; cär; end; mē; it; īce; hot; ōld; fôrk; wood; fōōl; oil; out; up; turn; sing; thin; this; hw in white; zh in treasure. The symbol ə stands for the sound of a in about, e in taken, i in pencil, o in lemon, and u in circus.

sta·pler (stā′plər) *n.* a small device for fastening paper and other thin materials together with wire staples.

star (stär) *n.* **1.** any heavenly body that appears as a bright point of light in the night sky. **2.** *Astronomy.* a large, round heavenly body that shines by its own light, as distinguished from planets with their satellites, and comets and meteors. **3.** a geometric figure usually having five or more points radiating from a center. **4.** an asterisk. **5.** a person who is outstanding in some field: *a baseball star.* **6.** an actor, actress, or other performer who plays the lead in a play, motion picture, television program, or the like. —*v.,* **starred, star·ring.** —*v.t.* **1.** to set or ornament with stars. **2.** to mark with an asterisk: *to star a passage in a book.* **3.** to present (a performer) in a leading role: *That movie starred my favorite actor.* —*v.i.* **1.** to perform a leading part: *to star in a play.* **2.** to perform outstandingly: *The pitcher starred in the game.* —*adj.* **1.** most prominent; leading: *a star performer, a star baseball player.* **2.** of or relating to a star or stars. —**star′like′,** *adj.*

star·board (stär′bərd) *n.* the right side of a boat or ship as one faces forward. —*adj.* of, relating to, or on the right side of a boat or ship.

starch (stärch) *n. pl.,* **starch·es. 1.** a white, granular carbohydrate manufactured and stored in all green plants. **2.** any food rich in starch, such as rice, corn, and wheat products. **3.** any of various substances, including natural starch, used for stiffening cloth. —*v.t.* to stiffen with starch: *The laundry starched all Dad's shirts.*

starch·y (stär′chē) *adj.,* **starch·i·er, starch·i·est. 1.** of, resembling, or containing starch: *a starchy diet.* **2.** stiffened with starch: *starchy curtains.* **3.** stiff in manner; formal. —**starch′i·ness,** *n.*

star·dom (stär′dəm) *n.* the state of a star performer: *The actor finally achieved stardom after a long career in the theater.*

stare (ster) *v.,* **stared, star·ing.** —*v.i.* to look intently with the eyes wide open. —*v.t.* to affect in a particular way by staring. —*n.* the act of staring. —**star′er,** *n.*

　to stare down. to make uneasy or embarrassed by staring: *The speaker stared down the heckler and continued with his speech.*

star·fish (stär′fish′) *n. pl.,* **star·fish** or **star·fish·es.** any of a group of flattened, star-shaped sea animals, usually having five tapering arms.

star·gaze (stär′gāz′) *v.i.,* **star·gazed, star·gaz·ing. 1.** to gaze at or study the stars. **2.** to daydream. —**star′gaz·er,** *n.*

Starfish

stark (stärk) *adj.* **1.** absolute or unqualified; complete: *stark tyranny, stark misery.* **2.** harsh, grim, or severe: *stark weather, a stark look.* **3.** barren or desolate; bare: *a stark room, a stark landscape.* **4.** rigid; stiff. —*adv.* absolutely; completely: *stark naked.* —**stark′ly,** *adv.* —**stark′ness,** *n.*

star·let (stär′lit) *n.* in motion pictures, an inexperienced actress or singer who is being given training and publicity by her studio.

star·light (stär′līt′) *n.* the light from a star or stars. —*adj.* another word for **starlit.**

star·ling (stär′ling) *n.* any of various birds found in most parts of the world, usually having a stout body, pointed wings, and a short tail.

Starling

star·lit (stär′lit′) *adj.* lighted by the stars. Also, **starlight.**

Star of David, a six-pointed star, a symbol of Judaism and of the country of Israel.

star·ry (stär′ē) *adj.,* **star·ri·er, star·ri·est. 1.** studded with or lighted by stars. **2.** shining like a star; bright: *Joan's eyes were starry when she received the award.* **3.** shaped in the form of a star.

star·ry-eyed (stär′ē īd′) *adj.* wishful or trusting: *The young girl had a starry-eyed look.*

Stars and Stripes, the flag of the United States, consisting of alternating red and white stripes representing the thirteen original colonies and, in the upper left corner, a blue field with fifty white stars representing the fifty states.

Star of David

Star-Span·gled Banner (stär′spang′gəld) **1.** the national anthem of the United States, the words of which were written by Francis Scott Key during the War of 1812. **2.** the flag of the United States.

start (stärt) *v.i.* **1.** to make a beginning; set out: *Phil has started on his science project.* **2.** to begin; commence: *The movie starts at ten o'clock.* **3.** to make a sudden movement, as from surprise or fear: *Sue started when he tapped her on the shoulder.* **4.** to spring or leap suddenly from a hiding place. **5.** to become loose: *The screws of the pencil sharpener started.* —*v.t.* **1.** to begin (something); commence: *to start a journey.* **2.** to put into action; set in motion: *to start an engine.* **3.** to set up or give rise to; establish or originate: *to start a business, to start a rumor.* **4.** to help (someone) begin something: *His education started him on the road to success.* **5.** to drive from a hiding place; rouse: *The hunting dog started the birds from the bush.* **6.** to cause to loosen. **7.** to enter in a contest: *The owner started his horse in the race.* —*n.* **1.** the beginning, as of a course of action, movement, or journey: *He got an early start on his trip.* **2.** a sudden movement, as from surprise or fear: *He gave a start when I tapped him on the shoulder.* **3.** help for beginning something: *The gift of fifty dollars gave him a good start on a savings account.* **4.** the advantage gained by beginning first, as in a race.

start·er (stär′tər) *n.* **1.** a person who begins something. **2.** the beginning of a process, activity, or series. **3.** a device that starts an engine. **4.** a person whose work is seeing that public conveyances leave on schedule: *a bus starter.* **5.** a person who gives the signal for starting a race. **6.** any of the competitors starting in a race.

star·tle (stärt′əl) *v.,* **star·tled, star·tling.** —*v.t.* to arouse or excite suddenly, as with surprise, fright, or astonishment: *The loud noise startled the baby.* —*v.i.* to become startled. —*n.* sudden surprise, fright, or astonishment.

star·tling (stärt′ling) *adj.* causing sudden surprise, fright, or astonishment: *startling news.* —**star′tling·ly,** *adv.*

star·va·tion (stär vā′shən) *n.* the act of starving or the state of being starved.

starve (stärv) *v.,* **starved, starv·ing.** —*v.i.* **1.** to suffer from or die of hunger: *The women and children of the war-torn country were starving.* **2.** to need or desire greatly: *The orphaned child starved for affection.* **3.** *Informal.* to feel hungry: *I haven't had lunch, and I'm starving.* —*v.t.* **1.** to cause to suffer or die because of hunger. **2.** to bring to a specified condition by starving: *to starve a prisoner into confessing to a crime.*

starve·ling (stärv′ling) *n.* a starving person, animal, or plant. —*adj.* weak from a lack of food; starving; hungry.

stash (stash) *Informal. v.t.* to store or hide for safekeeping or future use. —*n. pl.,* **stash·es.** something stored or hidden.

state (stāt) *n.* **1.** the condition of a person or thing: *The mother was in a state of great anxiety about her lost child. The country was in a state of unrest.* **2.** position, rank, or standing: *What is his state in life?* **3.** *also,* **State.** a body of people living together under one government; nation; commonwealth: *The continent of Africa has many new, independent states.* **4.** *also,* **State.** one of the subdivisions of a nation that has a federal government: *Hawaii is a state of the United States.* **5.** the territory of a state or nation. **6.** *also,* **State.** civil government, authority, or organization: *That diplomat is involved in important affairs of state.* **7.** one of the three conditions, solid, liquid, or gas, in which matter exists. **8. the States.** the United States. —*v.t.,* **stat·ed, stat·ing. 1.** to express or explain fully in words; declare; represent: *to state an opinion, to state a problem.* **2.** to set; fix: *The chairman stated a time for the next meeting.* —*adj.* **1.** *also,* **State.** of or relating to a state: *a state tax, a state highway.* **2.** of or relating to national or state government: *state policy, state affairs.* **3.** of, relating to, or for ceremonious or official occasions; formal: *a state reception.*

state·craft (stāt′kraft′) *n.* the art of conducting state affairs; statesmanship.

state·hood (stāt′hood′) *n.* the condition of being a state, especially a state of the United States.

state·house (stāt′hous′) *also,* **State House.** *n. pl.,* **state·hous·es** (stāt′hou′ziz). a building in which the legislature of a state of the United States meets.

state·less (stāt′lis) *adj.* having no citizenship or nationality: *stateless refugees.*

state·ly (stāt′lē) *adj.,* **state·li·er, state·li·est.** majestic; dignified: *a stately building, a stately old lady.* —**state′·li·ness,** *n.*

state·ment (stāt′mənt) *n.* **1.** the act or manner of stating something: *an accurate statement of the facts.* **2.** something stated: *The suspect made a false statement to the police. The President issued a statement on tax reform to the press.* **3.** a report or summary of financial matters: *a bank statement, a corporation's statement of profit and loss.*

Stat·en Island (stat′ən) an island southwest of Manhattan, forming the borough of Richmond in New York City. Area, 60.9 sq. mi. Pop. (1970), 221,991.

state·room (stāt′rōōm′, stāt′room′) *n.* a private room on a ship or a compartment on a railroad train.

state·side (stāt′sīd′) *also,* **State·side.** *adj.* of or in the continental United States. —*adv.* to, toward, or in the continental United States.

states·man (stāts′mən) *n. pl.,* **states·men** (stāts′mən). a person who shows skill or wisdom in conducting public or national affairs. —**states′man·like,** *adj.*

states·man·ship (stāts′mən ship′) *n.* the skill of a statesman in conducting public or national affairs.

states′ rights 1. rights or powers not delegated to the federal government nor prohibited to the states under the Constitution. **2.** the doctrine that the powers of the U.S. federal government should be shared to a greater degree with the various state governments.

state·wide (stāt′wīd′) *also,* **state-wide.** *adj.* happening throughout a state: *a statewide gas shortage, statewide elections.*

stat·ic (stat′ik) *adj.* **1.** showing little or no growth, change, or movement; that remains the same: *a static population.* **2.** *Mechanics.* of or relating to bodies at rest or to forces in equilibrium. **3.** *Physics.* acting by weight without producing motion: *static pressure.* **4.** of or relating to charges of electricity that have accumulated on a body and do not move about. Static electricity can be produced by combing dry hair with a dry comb. —*n.* electrical charges in the atmosphere, such as those produced by lightning, that may be picked up by a radio receiver and heard as crackling or hissing sounds. —**stat′i·cal·ly,** *adv.*

stat·ics (stat′iks) *n., pl.* the branch of mechanics that deals with bodies at rest or in equilibrium under the action of several forces. ▲ used with a singular verb.

sta·tion (stā′shən) *n.* **1.** a building or place set up as a headquarters for a business, public service, or the like: *a first-aid station.* **2.** a regular stopping place along a route, as of a bus or train line; terminal; depot. **3.** the place in which one stands in the performance of some duty; assigned post. **4.** the social position of an individual. **5.** a place where radio or television programs are recorded and transmitted. **6.** a specific channel used for a broadcast. —*v.t.* to assign to a station; place in a post or position: *That sailor is stationed at Pearl Harbor.*

sta·tion·ar·y (stā′shə ner′ē) *adj.* **1.** having a fixed place or position; permanent: *The desks in the room were stationary.* **2.** not moving: *The elevator was stationary.* **3.** unchanging in character, condition, or quantity.

sta·tion·er (stā′shə nər) *n.* a person who sells stationery.

sta·tion·er·y (stā′shə ner′ē) *n.* **1.** writing paper and envelopes. **2.** materials used in writing, such as pens, pencils, or paper and office supplies.

sta·tion·mas·ter (stā′shən mas′tər) *n.* a person in charge of a railroad station or bus station.

station wagon, an automobile having one or more folding or removable rear seats and a door across the back that can be used for loading and unloading passengers or luggage.

Station wagon

sta·tis·tic (stə tis′tik) *n.* a numerical fact that is collected and used as information about a particular subject.

sta·tis·ti·cal (stə tis′ti kəl) *adj.* of, relating to, consisting of, or based on statistics: *a statistical problem, a statistical analysis.* —**sta·tis′ti·cal·ly,** *adv.*

stat·is·ti·cian (stat′is tish′ən) *n.* a person who is expert in compiling and interpreting statistics.

sta·tis·tics (stə tis′tiks) *n., pl.* **1.** the science of collecting, classifying, and using numerical data as it is related to a particular subject. ▲ used with a singular verb. **2.** the numerical data itself. ▲ used with a plural verb.

sta·tor (stā′tər) *n.* a stationary part in or about which a moving part revolves, as in a motor or dynamo.

stat·u·ar·y (stach′ōō er′ē) *n. pl.,* **stat·u·ar·ies. 1.** statues as a group. **2.** the art of carving statues.

stat·ue (stach′ōō) *n.* a representation, often life-size or larger, of a human or animal figure, carved, cast, or modeled in stone, bronze, clay, or a similar material.

Statue of Liberty, a huge statue of a crowned woman holding a torch aloft. It represents liberty. The Statue of Liberty was given to the United States by France and is located on an island in New York harbor.

stat·u·esque (stach′ōō esk′) *adj.* resembling a statue, as in size, grace, or dignity; stately.

stat·u·ette (stach′ōō et′) *n.* a small statue.

at; āpe; cär; end; mē; it; īce; hot; ōld; fôrk; wood; fōōl; oil; out; up; turn; sing; thin; **th**is; hw in white; zh in treasure. The symbol ə stands for the sound of **a** in about, **e** in taken, **i** in pencil, **o** in lemon, and **u** in circus.

stat·ure (stach′ər) *n.* **1.** the height of a person or animal in a normal standing position: *a woman of average stature.* **2.** level, as of achievement or mental growth; standing: *moral stature.*

sta·tus (stā′təs, stat′əs) *n.* **1.** state; condition: *the status of the nation's economy.* **2.** relative place or rank, especially social or professional standing. **3.** the character or condition of a person or thing as determined by law: *The job applicant refused to answer any questions about his marital status.*

status quo (kwō) the existing or present state of affairs.

stat·ute (stach′ōōt) *n.* **1.** a law enacted by a legislative body. **2.** a written rule or law regulating an organization, such as a university or corporation.

statute mile, another term for **mile.**

stat·u·to·ry (stach′ə tôr′ē) *adj.* of, relating to, set by, or punishable under statute: *a statutory fine, a statutory offense.*

St. Au·gus·tine (ô′gəs tēn′) a city in northeastern Florida, the oldest continuously occupied city in the United States.

staunch[1] (stônch) *also,* **stanch.** *adj.* **1.** loyal and dependable: *a staunch friend.* **2.** strongly built or constructed: *a staunch ship, a staunch argument.* [Old French *estanche* reliable, watertight.] —**staunch′ly,** *adv.* —**staunch′ness,** *n.*

staunch[2] (stônch) another spelling of **stanch**[1].

stave (stāv) *n.* **1.** any long, narrow, flexible strip of wood, such as that which forms the sides of a barrel. **2.** a rod, pole, or staff. **3.** a rung, as of a ladder or chair. **4.** a verse or stanza, as of a poem. **5.** see **staff** (*def.* 5). —*v.,* **staved** *or* **stove, stav·ing.** —*v.t.* **1.** to smash or break a hole in: *A rock stove the hull of the ship.* **2.** to furnish with a stave or staves: *to stave a barrel.* —*v.i.* to be smashed in or punctured.

to stave off. to ward off or prevent: *to stave off a blow.*

staves (stāvz) a plural of **staff.**

Staves of a barrel

stay[1] (stā) *v.,* **stayed, stay·ing.** —*v.i.* **1.** to continue in a specified place or condition: *to stay home, to stay young.* **2.** to live in a place, especially for a short period of time: *They stayed at a hotel while visiting the city.* **3.** to cease movement or activity; stop. **4.** to linger; wait: *We could not stay for the last act.* **5.** *Informal.* to last or endure, as in a race or contest. —*v.t.* **1.** to check or stop, especially temporarily: *He ate an apple to stay his hunger.* **2.** to put off; defer: *The judge stayed the sentence until the following day.* **3.** to remain for the duration of: *to stay the night in a motel.* —*n.* **1.** the act of staying or remaining: *a short stay in town.* **2.** a break or delay of action; stop; halt: *The governor requested a stay on raises for all state employees in an effort to reduce the budget.* **3.** *Law.* a delay in the execution of an order of a court of law. [Probably from Old French *estai-,* a stem of *ester* to stand.]

stay[2] (stā) *n.* **1.** something used to support, strengthen, or sustain; prop; brace. **2.** a piece of plastic or other stiff material, inserted in shirt collars and other garments to give shape and support. **3. stays.** a corset. —*v.t.,* **stayed, stay·ing.** to support, strengthen, or sustain. [Probably from Old French *estayer* to prop, support.]

stay[3] (stā) *n.* **1.** a strong rope, usually of wire, used to support a mast on a boat or ship. **2.** any rope or chain used for a similar purpose. —*v.t.,* **stayed, stay·ing.** to secure or steady with a stay or stays. [Old English *stæg.*]

stay·sail (stā′sāl′, stā′səl) *n.* a sail, usually triangular, that is attached to a stay.

St. Cath·a·rines (kath′ər inz) a city in southeastern Canada, in Ontario. Pop. (1971), 109,636.

St. Croix (kroi) the largest and southernmost of the Virgin Islands. It belongs to the United States.

Ste., Sainte.

stead (sted) *n.* a place or position usually or previously occupied by another: *My brother worked in my stead.*

to stand in good stead. to be of use or service to; be advantageous to.

stead·fast (sted′fast′) *adj.* **1.** not changing; unwavering; faithful: *steadfast loyalty to a cause.* **2.** direct; steady: *a steadfast gaze.* —**stead′fast′ly,** *adv.* —**stead′fast′ness,** *n.*

stead·y (sted′ē) *adj.,* **stead·i·er, stead·i·est. 1.** that is kept at an even rate; regular or uniform: *a steady pace.* **2.** firm or sure in movement or position; not shaking or faltering: *The engraver had a steady hand.* **3.** regular or permanent: *a steady customer, a steady job.* **4.** reliable; dependable: *She is a steady worker.* **5.** not easily upset; calm: *He has steady nerves.* —*v.t., v.i.,* **stead·ied, stead·y·ing.** to make or become steady. —*adv.* in a steady manner; steadily. —**stead′i·ly,** *adv.* —**stead′i·ness,** *n.*

to go steady. to date someone regularly and exclusively.

stead·y-state theory (sted′ē stāt′) the theory about the universe that matter is constantly being created to replace matter that is being destroyed. The universe itself keeps the same basic properties it has always had.

steak (stāk) *n.* a slice of meat or fish cut for cooking by broiling or frying.

steal (stēl) *v.,* **stole, sto·len, steal·ing.** —*v.t.* **1.** to take from another secretly and without right or permission: *The paintings were stolen from the museum.* **2.** to take by surprise or in a tricky way: *to steal an hour off from work.* **3.** to move or place secretly or unobserved: *He stole quietly up the stairs.* **4.** *Baseball.* to gain (the next base) without the help of a hit or error. —*v.i.* **1.** to commit or practice theft. **2.** to move or pass secretly, slowly, or without being seen: *A smile stole over his face.* **3.** *Baseball.* to steal a base. —*n.* **1.** the act of stealing; theft. **2.** *Baseball.* the act of stealing a base. —**steal′er,** *n.*

stealth (stelth) *n.* secret action, procedure, or manner of behavior: *The spy obtained the information by stealth.*

stealth·y (stel′thē) *adj.,* **stealth·i·er, stealth·i·est.** moving or acting in a secret manner. —**stealth′i·ly,** *adv.* —**stealth′i·ness,** *n.*

steam (stēm) *n.* **1.** water in the form of a gas. It is used to provide heat for buildings and to power engines and other machinery. **2.** power, heat, or other energy generated by steam. **3.** a mist formed when water vapor cools: *There was steam on the window above the sink.* **4.** *Informal.* energy; initiative: *He built the bookcase on his own steam.* —*v.t.* to treat with or expose to steam, as in cooking or cleaning: *to steam clams, to steam out the wrinkles in a dress.* —*v.i.* **1.** to give off steam or vapor: *The material steamed from the heat of the iron.* **2.** to rise in the form of or become steam: *The boiling water steamed away.* **3.** to be covered with condensed vapor or mist: *My eyeglasses steamed up in the humid air.* **4.** to move or travel by steam: *The vessel steamed into port.* **5.** *Informal.* to be angry.

to let off steam *or* **to blow off steam.** *Informal.* to release pent-up emotions, energy, or tensions.

steam·boat (stēm′bōt′) *n.* any of various steam-driven boats, used especially in lakes and rivers.

steam engine, an engine using the energy of steam to do mechanical work. The steam expands within a cylinder to drive a piston in a back and forth motion.

steam·er (stē′mər) *n.* **1.** a boat driven by steam; steamship. **2.** a soft-shell clam, usually cooked by steaming. **3.** a special container in which something is steamed, especially a large pot for steaming clams.

steam fitter, a person who installs and repairs steam pipes, fittings, and other heating equipment.

steam·roll·er (stēm′rō′lər) *also,* **steam roller.** *n.* **1.** a vehicle moving on heavy rollers, used in road work, as for leveling freshly laid pavement or smoothing earth. **2.** any force or power that is large and powerful and can overwhelm opposition. —*v.i. Informal.* to move with overwhelming force or organization: *The Presidential campaign steamrollered through the South.* —*v.t.* **1.** to overwhelm or suppress ruthlessly; defeat: *to steamroller opposition.* **2.** to level or smooth with a steamroller.

steam·ship (stēm′ship′) *n.* a large, ocean-going ship propelled by steam power.

steam shovel, a power-driven digging machine having a single large bucket or scoop at the end of a long beam.

steam turbine, a turbine using steam as a source of energy.

Steam shovel

steam·y (stē′mē) *adj.,* **steam·i·er, steam·i·est. 1.** giving off, covered by, or filled with steam. **2.** uncomfortably warm; humid. —**steam′i·ly,** *adv.* —**steam′i·ness,** *n.*

steed (stēd) *n.* a horse, especially a high-spirited riding horse.

steel (stēl) *n.* **1.** any alloy of iron mixed with a small amount of carbon. Other elements, such as manganese, are sometimes added to the alloy to strengthen it. **2.** something made from steel, such as a sword. **3.** a quality characteristic of steel, such as hardness or strength: *to have nerves of steel.* —*adj.* **1.** made of steel. **2.** of or relating to the production of steel: *a steel mill.* **3.** resembling steel. —*v.t.* **1.** to cover with steel, as by edging or plating. **2.** to cause to be strong and hard like steel: *He steeled himself for the bad news.*

steel wool, fine threads of steel matted together, used for polishing or cleaning.

steel·work·er (stēl′wur′kər) *n.* a person who works in a steel mill.

steel·works (stēl′wurks′) *n., pl.* a plant where steel is made.

steel·y (stē′lē) *adj.,* **steel·i·er, steel·i·est. 1.** made of steel. **2.** resembling or suggesting steel: *steely eyes.* —**steel′i·ness,** *n.*

steel·yard (stēl′yärd′, stil′yərd) *n.* a weighing device made up of a bar with the object to be weighed at one end and a movable weight at the other. The weight is slid along the bar until a balance is reached and the correct weight is registered on a scale marked off on the bar.

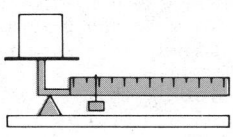
Steelyard

steep¹ (stēp) *adj.* **1.** having a very sharp face or slope: *to climb the steeper side of a mountain, a steep stairway.* **2.** *Informal.* too much or too high; unreasonable: *The lawyer demanded a steep fee from his client.* [Old English *stēap* high, tall, lofty.] —**steep′ly,** *adv.* —**steep′ness,** *n.*

steep² (stēp) *v.t.* **1.** to soak in liquid so as to soften, clean, or extract something, such as flavor: *to steep tea leaves.* **2.** to involve deeply or absorb; saturate: *a house steeped in mystery.* —*v.i.* to undergo soaking in liquid. [Possibly from Old Norse *steypa* to pour out.]

steep·en (stē′pən) *v.t., v.i.* to make or become steeper: *The path steepened as we climbed higher.*

stee·ple (stē′pəl) *n.* a high tower with a spire at the top, built on the roof of a church or other building.

stee·ple·chase (stē′pəl chās′) *n.* a horse race on a course that has hedges, ditches, and other obstacles over which the horses must jump.

stee·ple·jack (stē′pəl jak′) *n.* a man whose work is climbing steeples, towers, and other tall structures to paint them or to make repairs.

steer¹ (stēr) *v.t.* **1.** to guide the course of (a vessel or vehicle) as with a wheel, handle, or the like. **2.** to set and follow (a course): *to steer a course for the West Indies.* **3.** to direct; guide; channel: *The police steered the actress through the crowd in front of the theater.* —*v.i.* **1.** to guide a vessel or vehicle. **2.** to follow or direct one's course: *The captain is steering for the island.* **3.** to be guided, as by a wheel or a person: *The truck does not steer easily.* —*n. Slang.* a piece of advice; suggestion; tip: *His friend gave him a bum steer when he told him to buy that stock.* [Old English *stīeran* to direct, guide.]

to steer clear of. to avoid completely; shun.

steer² (stēr) *n.* a bull, especially one that has been castrated and is raised for beef. [Old English *stēor.*]

steer·age (stēr′ij) *n.* **1.** formerly, the portion of a passenger ship occupied by those passengers paying the cheapest fare. **2.** the act of steering.

steering wheel, a wheel turned by the driver to direct the course of a vehicle or vessel.

steers·man (stērz′mən) *n. pl.,* **steers·men** (stērz′mən). a man who steers a ship; helmsman.

Steeple

steg·o·sau·rus (steg′ə sôr′əs) *n. pl.,* **steg·o·sau·ri** (steg′ə sôr′ī). a large dinosaur that had a spiked tail and two rows of bony plates along its back.

stein (stīn) *n.* a beer mug, usually holding about a pint.

Stein·beck, John (stīn′bek) 1902–1968, U.S. novelist.

Stein·metz, Charles P. (stīn′mets) 1865–1923, U.S. scientist and electrical engineer.

Stegosaurus

stel·lar (stel′ər) *adj.* **1.** of, relating to, or resembling a star or stars. **2.** of or relating to a star performer. **3.** very important or outstanding: *a stellar achievement.*

stem¹ (stem) *n.* **1.** the main supporting part of a plant, from which smaller stalks, leaves, or flowers may grow. **2.** a stalk supporting a leaf, flower, or fruit. **3.** something resembling this in shape or purpose: *the stem of a wine*

at; āpe; cär; end; mē; it; īce; hot; ōld; fôrk; wood; fŏŏl; oil; out; up; turn; sing; thin; this; hw in white; zh in treasure. The symbol ə stands for the sound of **a** in about, **e** in taken, **i** in pencil, **o** in lemon, and **u** in circus.

S

glass, the stem of a pipe. **4.** the part of a word to which affixes and inflectional endings are added to change the meaning of the word. *Swim* is the stem of *swimming, swims,* and *swimmer.* **5.** the bow of a boat or ship. —*v.,* **stemmed, stem·ming.** —*v.t.* to remove the stem of or from: *to stem tobacco, to stem a cluster of grapes.* —*v.i.* to begin, develop, or be descended: *That problem stems from poor living conditions.* [Old English *stemn* the trunk of a tree, stalk of a plant, prow of a ship.]

from stem to stern. from one end to the other; thoroughly: *The house had to be cleaned from stem to stern.*

stem² (stem) *v.t.,* **stemmed, stem·ming. 1.** to stop or restrain by or as if by damming; stanch: *to stem the flood of water from a broken pipe.* **2.** to make progress or headway against. [Old Norse *stemma* to dam up, stop.]

stemmed (stemd) *adj.* **1.** having a stem. ▲ used chiefly in combination: *long-stemmed roses.* **2.** having the stem removed: *stemmed and pitted cherries.*

stench (stench) *n. pl.,* **stench·es.** a very strong and bad odor.

sten·cil (sten′səl) *n.* **1.** a thin sheet, as of metal or paper, in which a pattern is cut. The sheet is put on top of something that is to be decorated, and only the areas that show through the cut out parts are painted or inked. **2.** a printing or design produced by using a stencil. —*v.t.,* **sten·ciled, sten·cil·ing;** *also, British,* **sten·cilled, sten·cil·ling.** to mark or paint with a stencil.

ste·nog·ra·pher (stə nog′rə fər) *n.* a person who is skilled at taking dictation in shorthand and then typing it.

sten·o·graph·ic (sten′ə graf′ik) *adj.* of, relating to, or using stenography.

ste·nog·ra·phy (stə nog′rə fē) *n.* the act, skill, or method of taking shorthand.

sten·to·ri·an (sten tôr′ē ən) *adj.* extremely loud: *to speak in stentorian tones.* [From *Stentor,* a messenger in Greek legend who was said to have a voice as loud as fifty men.]

step (step) *n.* **1.** the movement of raising the foot and putting it down in a new position, as in walking, climbing, dancing, or the like. **2.** the distance covered in one such movement. **3.** any short distance: *The store is only a few steps from our house.* **4.** any place to put the foot in going up or coming down, as a stair or the rung of a ladder. **5. steps.** a flight of stairs. **6.** an action or one of a series of actions leading to a particular goal or result: *The signing of the agreement was a step toward peace.* **7.** a degree or stage in a series: *to bring a project one step nearer to completion.* **8.** the sound made by putting the foot down. **9.** a footprint: *The new snow covered our steps.* **10.** a rhythm or pattern of walking, dancing, marching, or the like: *He was tired and had trouble keeping in step with the other marchers.* **11.** *Music.* an interval corresponding to one degree on the staff or in a scale. —*v.,* **stepped, step·ping.** —*v.i.* **1.** to move by taking a step or steps: *to step to the rear of a bus.* **2.** to put or press the foot: *to step on a piece of broken glass.* —*v.t.* **1.** to put or move (the foot) in taking a step. **2.** to measure by taking steps: *to step off twenty paces.*

step by step. little by little; gradually.

to step down. to resign from a position.

to step on it. to go fast; hurry up.

to step up. to increase; accelerate: *The company had to step up production to fill all the orders.*

to watch one's step. to act or move more carefully.

step·broth·er (step′bruth′ər) *n.* a stepparent's son by a former marriage.

step·child (step′chīld′) *n. pl.,* **step·chil·dren.** a child of one's husband or wife by a former marriage; stepdaughter or stepson.

step·daugh·ter (step′dô′tər) *n.* a daughter of one's husband or wife by a former marriage.

step·fa·ther (step′fä′thər) *n.* the husband of one's mother after the death or divorce of one's father.

step·lad·der (step′lad′ər) *n.* a ladder that stands by itself on four legs and has flat steps instead of rungs.

step·moth·er (step′muth′ər) *n.* the wife of one's father after the death or divorce of one's mother.

step·par·ent (step′per′ənt) *n.* a stepfather or stepmother.

steppe (step) *n.* **1.** any of the vast, grassy plains extending from southeastern Europe into central Siberia. **2.** any vast plain.

step·ping·stone (step′ing stōn′) *also,* **stepping stone.** *n.* **1.** a stone or one of a series of stones on which to step, as in crossing a stream. **2.** an opportunity or means of progressing toward some goal or aim: *The Senate has often been a steppingstone to the Presidency.*

step·sis·ter (step′sis′tər) *n.* a stepparent's daughter by a former marriage.

step·son (step′sun′) *n.* a son of one's husband or wife by a former marriage.

step-up (step′up′) *n.* an increase in intensity, amount, or activity: *a step-up in activity, a step-up in sales.*

-ster *suffix* (used to form nouns) **1.** a person who makes, uses, or is occupied with: *punster, prankster.* **2.** a person who is: *youngster.* **3.** a person who is related or belongs to: *gangster.*

ster·e·o (ster′ē ō′, stēr′ē ō′) *n. pl.,* **ster·e·os. 1.** a stereophonic system of sound reproduction. **2.** stereophonic sound. —*adj.* see **stereophonic.**

ster·e·o·phon·ic (ster′ē ə fon′ik, stēr′ē ə fon′ik) *adj.* of or relating to a system of sound reproduction in which the sound is heard from two or more sources. In stereophonic recording, sounds are picked up by two or more microphones in different locations and reproduced through two or more separate loudspeaker systems, thus giving the effect of natural sound.

ster·e·op·ti·con (ster′ē op′ti kən, stēr′ē op′ti kən) *n.* a slide projector that can project two overlapping pictures at the same time or in quick succession, so as to produce a fading of one into the other.

ster·e·o·scope (ster′ē ə skōp′, stēr′ē ə skōp′) *n.* an optical instrument having two lenses through which each eye views a picture taken from a different angle. This gives the illusion of seeing the picture in three dimensions.

Stereoscope

ster·e·o·scop·ic (ster′ē ə skop′ik, stēr′ē ə skop′ik) *adj.* of, for, or relating to a stereoscope.

ster·e·o·type (ster′ē ə tīp′, stēr′ē ə tīp′) *n.* **1.** a metal plate used in printing, that is cast from a mold of the original composed type. **2.** an oversimplified or conventional image of a certain person, group, issue, or the like. A stereotype is thought to be a typical example of something. A cowboy wearing a white hat and riding a white horse is a stereotype of the hero of Western movies. —*v.t.,* **ster·e·o·typed, ster·e·o·typ·ing. 1.** to make a stereotype of. **2.** to develop a fixed, conventional view of. —**ster′e·o·typ′er,** *n.*

ster·e·o·typed (ster′ē ə tīpt′, stēr′ē ə tīpt′) *adj.* **1.** having or showing no originality or differences; conventional. **2.** printed from stereotype plates.

ster·ile (ster′əl) *adj.* **1.** not able to reproduce; not fertile; barren. **2.** not able to produce or support plants; arid: *a dry and sterile region.* **3.** free from bacteria and dirt: *sterile* *bandages, sterile milk bottles.* **4.** lacking imagination; conventional; stale: *sterile writing.* —**ster′ile·ly,** *adv.*

ste·ril·i·ty (stə ril′ə tē) *n.* the condition of being sterile.

ster·i·li·za·tion (ster′ə li zā′shən) *n.* **1.** the act or process of sterilizing. **2.** the state of being sterilized.

ster·i·lize (ster′ə līz′) *v.t.,* **ster·i·lized, ster·i·liz·ing.** to make sterile. —**ster′i·liz′er,** *n.*

ster·ling (stur′ling) *n.* **1.** a silver alloy containing 92.5 percent pure silver; sterling silver. **2.** something made of sterling silver. **3.** British money. —*adj.* **1.** containing 92.5 percent pure silver. **2.** made of sterling silver. **3.** made up of, relating to, or payable in British money. **4.** very worthy; excellent: *a sterling reputation.*

stern¹ (sturn) *adj.* **1.** severe or strict. **2.** showing extreme displeasure; harsh: *Tom's father spoke in his sternest voice.* **3.** grim or forbidding; gloomy: *a stern look.* **4.** resolute; unwavering: *a stern resolve.* [Old English *stierne* severe, hard.] —**stern′ly,** *adv.* —**stern′ness,** *n.*

stern² (sturn) *n.* the rear part of a boat or ship. [Probably from Old Norse *stjōrn* a steering.]

ster·num (stur′nəm) *n. pl.,* **ster·nums** or **ster·na** (stur′nə). the flat, narrow bone in the center of the chest to which the ribs are joined; breastbone.

stern·wheel·er (sturn′hwē′lər) *n.* a steamboat propelled by a single paddle wheel at the stern.

steth·o·scope (steth′ə skōp′) *n.* an instrument used to listen to sounds made by organs of the body, especially sounds of the lungs and heart.

Stet·tin (shte tēn′) *n.* see Szczecin.

Steu·ben, Baron Frederick William von (stoo′bən, styoo′bən) 1730–1794, Prussian general who aided in the American Revolution.

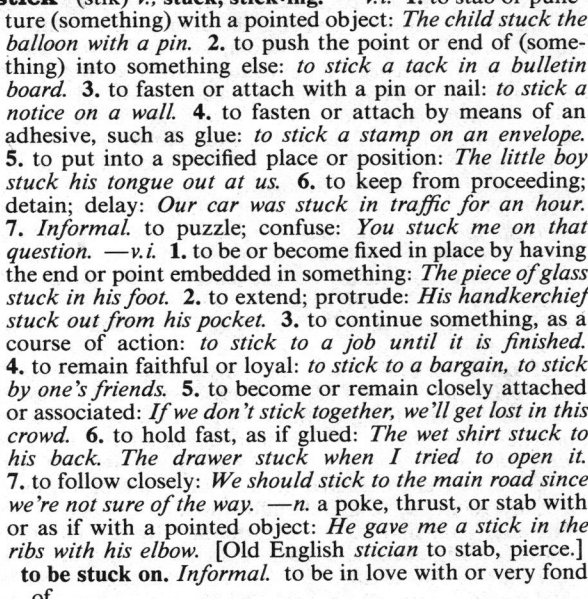

Stethoscope

ste·ve·dore (stē′və dôr′) *n.* a man whose work is loading and unloading cargo from ships.

Ste·ven·son, Robert Louis (stē′vən sən) 1850–1894, Scottish novelist and poet.

stew (stoo, styoo) *v.t.* to cook (food) slowly by simmering. —*v.i.* **1.** to be cooked by slow simmering: *She let the pears stew for half an hour.* **2.** *Informal.* to be angry or worried; fret. —*n.* **1.** food cooked by stewing, especially a mixture of meat and vegetables cooked together. **2.** *Informal.* a state of anger or worry.

stew·ard (stoo′ərd, styoo′ərd) *n.* **1.** a person who manages the property, finances, or affairs of another person. **2.** a man in charge of food and other services, as on a ship, airplane, or train, or for a club or hotel. **3.** any male member of a staff or crew who waits on the passengers of a ship, airplane, or train.

stew·ard·ess (stoo′ər dis, styoo′ər dis) *n. pl.,* **stew·ard·ess·es. 1.** a woman who serves passengers on an airplane. **2.** a female steward.

stew·ard·ship (stoo′ərd ship′, styoo′ərd ship′) *n.* **1.** the position or duties of a steward. **2.** responsibility for wise use or protection: *The speaker talked about the stewardship of our natural resources.*

St. He·le·na (hə lē′nə) a small British island in the south Atlantic Ocean, site of Napoleon Bonaparte's exile from 1815 until his death in 1821.

stick¹ (stik) *n.* **1.** a long thin piece of wood. **2.** anything resembling a stick, especially in shape: *a stick of dynamite.* **3.** an implement used to hit a ball or puck in any of various games: *a hockey stick.* **4.** a lever that controls the up-and-down and side-to-side movement of an airplane. **5. the sticks.** *Informal.* any place that is far from a city or town, especially a place thought of as being very rural. [Old English *sticca.*]

stick² (stik) *v.,* **stuck, stick·ing.** —*v.t.* **1.** to stab or puncture (something) with a pointed object: *The child stuck the balloon with a pin.* **2.** to push the point or end of (something) into something else: *to stick a tack in a bulletin board.* **3.** to fasten or attach with a pin or nail: *to stick a notice on a wall.* **4.** to fasten or attach by means of an adhesive, such as glue: *to stick a stamp on an envelope.* **5.** to put into a specified place or position: *The little boy stuck his tongue out at us.* **6.** to keep from proceeding; detain; delay: *Our car was stuck in traffic for an hour.* **7.** *Informal.* to puzzle; confuse: *You stuck me on that question.* —*v.i.* **1.** to be or become fixed in place by having the end or point embedded in something: *The piece of glass stuck in his foot.* **2.** to extend; protrude: *His handkerchief stuck out from his pocket.* **3.** to continue something, as a course of action: *to stick to a job until it is finished.* **4.** to remain faithful or loyal: *to stick to a bargain, to stick by one's friends.* **5.** to become or remain closely attached or associated: *If we don't stick together, we'll get lost in this crowd.* **6.** to hold fast, as if glued: *The wet shirt stuck to his back. The drawer stuck when I tried to open it.* **7.** to follow closely: *We should stick to the main road since we're not sure of the way.* —*n.* a poke, thrust, or stab with or as if with a pointed object: *He gave me a stick in the ribs with his elbow.* [Old English *stician* to stab, pierce.]

to be stuck on. *Informal.* to be in love with or very fond of.

to stick around. *Informal.* to stay or wait nearby.

to stick out. *Informal.* to be obvious or conspicuous.

to stick up. *Informal.* to rob, especially at gunpoint.

to stick up for. *Informal.* to support or defend.

stick·er (stik′ər) *n.* **1.** a label or other printed paper with glue on the back: *They put a sticker on the car window to show that the car had been inspected.* **2.** a burr, bramble, or the like.

stick·le (stik′əl) *v.i.,* **stick·led, stick·ling.** to argue, hesitate, or raise objections over trifles.

stick·le·back (stik′əl bak′) *n. pl.,* **stick·le·back** or **stick·le·backs.** a fish that has sharp bony spines on the back and bony plates instead of scales on the sides.

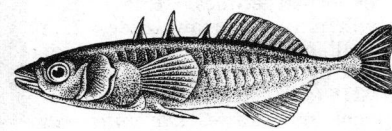

Stickleback

stick·ler (stik′lər) *n.* a person who stubbornly insists that something be done in an exact, strict way: *His aunt was a stickler for neatness.*

stick·pin (stik′pin′) *n.* an ornamental pin worn in a necktie or ascot.

stick·up (stik′up′) *n. Slang.* a robbery, as at gunpoint.

stick·y (stik′ē) *adj.,* **stick·i·er, stick·i·est. 1.** tending to stick or hold fast: *a sticky piece of gum.* **2.** coated or covered with glue or other adhesive: *a sticky poster.* **3.** hot and humid; muggy. **4.** difficult to deal with; touchy. —**stick′i·ly,** *adv.* —**stick′i·ness,** *n.*

sties (stīz) the plural of **sty¹** and **sty².**

stiff (stif) *adj.* **1.** not easily bent; not flexible: *The new leather belt was very stiff.* **2.** unable to move easily without

at; āpe; cär; end; mē; it; īce; hot; ōld; fôrk;
wood; fōōl; oil; out; up; turn; sing; thin; this;
hw in white; zh in treasure. The symbol ə
stands for the sound of **a** in about, **e** in taken,
i in pencil, **o** in lemon, and **u** in circus.

S

pain or difficulty: *My back was stiff after sitting for so many hours.* **3.** not natural, easy, or graceful in manner or movement; formal: *a stiff bow.* **4.** harsh; severe: *The judge gave him a stiff sentence.* **5.** unusually high: *a stiff price.* **6.** that requires great effort to succeed in or overcome; difficult: *stiff competition, a stiff examination in mathematics.* **7.** not liquid or fluid; thick: *Beat the egg whites until they are stiff.* **8.** not working or moving smoothly or easily, as parts of machinery. **9.** having a strong, steady force: *a stiff breeze.* **10.** strong or potent: *a stiff dose of medicine.* —*n. Slang.* **1.** a dead body; corpse. **2.** a very dull, staid, and unresponsive person. **3.** a person: *She's a lucky stiff.* —*adv.* completely or extremely: *to be bored stiff.* —**stiff′ly,** *adv.* —**stiff′ness,** *n.*

stiff·en (stif′ən) *v.t., v.i.* to make or become stiff or stiffer. —**stiff′en·er,** *n.*

stiff-necked (stif′nekt′) *adj.* unyielding; stubborn.

sti·fle (stī′fəl) *v.,* **sti·fled, sti·fling.** —*v.t.* **1.** to prevent or interfere with the growth or progress of: *to stifle someone's creative talent.* **2.** to hold back: *to stifle a yawn, to stifle the urge to laugh.* **3.** to kill by depriving of air. —*v.i.* **1.** to feel smothered because of a lack of air, as in a stuffy room. **2.** to die of suffocation.

stig·ma (stig′mə) *n. pl.,* **stig·ma·ta** (stig mä′tə, stig′mə tə) or **stig·mas.** **1.** a mark of shame or disgrace: *The fact that he had cheated on the test was a stigma that he had to live with.* **2.** a spot on the skin that bleeds. **3.** the part of the pistil of a plant on which pollen is deposited from the anther in pollination. **4. stigmata.** marks or wounds that appear on the same places on a person's body as the five wounds on the crucified body of Jesus.

stig·ma·tize (stig′mə tīz′) *v.t.,* **stig·ma·tized, stig·ma·tiz·ing** to mark as shameful or disgraceful.

stile (stīl) *n.* **1.** a step or series of steps that enable a person to climb over a wall or fence. **2.** see **turnstile.**

sti·let·to (stə let′ō) *n. pl.,* **sti·let·tos** or **sti·let·toes.** **1.** a dagger with a very narrow blade. **2.** a small, pointed instrument used for making eyelets in embroidery.

still¹ (stil) *adj.* **1.** without movement; motionless: *The water was still after the storm.* **2.** without sound; silent: *Be still and listen.* —*v.t.* **1.** to make silent; quiet. **2.** to calm, as fears. —*v.i.* to become still or calm. —*n.* **1.** quiet; silence; calm: *in the still of the night.* **2.** a single photograph, especially one made from a single frame of a motion picture film. —*adv.* **1.** without movement; motionless: *Sit still.* **2.** at or up to the time indicated; as before: *She still lives here.* **3.** in increasing amount or degree; beyond this: *Still greater things were expected from him.* **4.** even then; nevertheless: *Though he dieted, he still could not lose weight.* —*conj.* despite that; yet: *It's raining; still I'd like to go if you don't mind.* [Old English *stille* motionless, silent.] —**still′ness,** *n.*

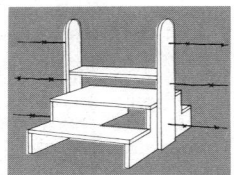

Stile

still² (stil) *n.* **1.** an apparatus for distilling liquids, especially alcoholic liquors. **2.** see **distillery.** [Middle English *stillen.*]

still·born (stil′bôrn′) *adj.* dead at birth.

still life *pl.,* **still lifes.** a painting or photograph of inanimate objects, such as bowls of fruit or flowers.

stilt (stilt) *n. pl.,* **stilts** or (*def. 3*) **stilt.** **1.** one of a pair of long poles, each having a footrest attached at some distance from the bottom end, allowing the wearer to walk with his feet above the ground. Stilts are worn by clowns in circuses to make them seem tall and are also used as

toys by children. **2.** one of the posts used to support a building, pier, or other structure above ground or water. **3.** a water bird that has a slender bill, long, thin legs, and mainly white feathers.

stilt·ed (stil′tid) *adj.* stiffly dignified or formal: *The invitation was written in an old-fashioned, stilted style of writing.*

stim·u·lant (stim′yə lənt) *n.* **1.** a drug, drink, or other substance that speeds up the activity of the mind or body. **2.** anything that moves to action; stimulus.

stim·u·late (stim′yə lāt′) *v.,* **stim·u·lat·ed, stim·u·lat·ing.** —*v.t.* **1.** to move to greater action or effort. **2.** to act as a stimulus or stimulant to (the mind or body). —*v.i.* to act as a stimulus or stimulant. —**stim′u·la′tion,** *n.*

stim·u·lus (stim′yə ləs) *n. pl.,* **stim·u·li** (stim′yə lī′). **1.** something that moves or incites to action or effort. **2.** anything that produces a response in or influences the activity of the mind or body.

sting (sting) *v.,* **stung, sting·ing.** —*v.t.* **1.** to prick painfully with a sharp, usually pointed, organ or object: *The bee stung him on the foot.* **2.** to cause to feel a sharp, smarting pain: *The iodine stung his cut finger.* **3.** to cause to suffer sharp mental or emotional pain: *She was stung by his harsh criticism.* **4.** to goad or incite suddenly and sharply: *Her insult finally stung him into washing the car.* —*v.i.* **1.** to have, use, or wound with a stinger, as certain insects. **2.** to cause or feel sharp physical or mental pain: *Her finger stung where she had cut it.* —*n.* **1.** the act of stinging. **2.** a wound or a smarting, burning sensation resulting from this. **3.** something that causes sharp mental or physical pain: *He felt a sting of regret for what he had said to her.* **4.** see **stinger** (*def. 1*). —**sting′ing·ly,** *adv.*

sting·er (sting′ər) *n.* **1.** a sharp, usually pointed organ with which an insect or animal inflicts a sting. **2.** anything that stings.

sting·ray (sting′rā′) *n.* a large fish having a flat body and a whiplike tail with a poisonous spine.

stin·gy (stin′jē) *adj.,* **stin·gi·er, stin·gi·est.** **1.** not willingly giving or sharing something, such as money; not generous. **2.** barely enough in amount; scanty; meager: *a stingy portion of food.* —**stin′gi·ly,** *adv.* —**stin′gi·ness,** *n.*

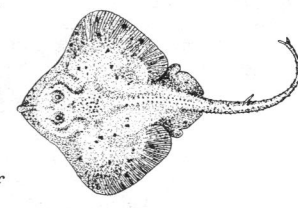

Stingray

stink (stingk) *n.* **1.** a strong, bad smell; disgusting odor. **2.** *Slang.* a great fuss, disturbance, or outcry: *There was quite a stink over who was to blame for the accident.* —*v.,* **stank** or **stunk, stunk, stink·ing.** —*v.i.* **1.** to give off or have a strong, bad smell. **2.** to be extremely offensive or hateful. **3.** *Slang.* to be of an extremely low quality: *That play stinks.* —*v.t.* to cause to stink.

stink·er (stingk′ər) *n.* **1.** a person or thing that stinks. **2.** *Informal.* a nasty, untrustworthy, or disagreeable person.

stint (stint) *v.t.* to limit, as in amount or degree; be stingy with: *to stint one's praise.* —*v.i.* to be stingy or sparing. —*n.* **1.** a share of work or duty to be done: *to serve a two-year stint in the army.* **2.** limitation; restriction: *She spent money on her grandchildren without stint.*

sti·pend (stī′pend) *n.* a fixed or regular pay or allowance, such as one given to a student on a scholarship or fellowship.

stip·ple (stip′əl) *v.t.,* **stip·pled, stip·pling.** **1.** to paint, draw, or engrave by using dots or light, short touches instead of strokes or lines. **2.** to produce slight, gradual changes in shade or color in (something) by painting,

drawing, or engraving in this way. —*n.* also, **stip·pling**
(stip′ling). **1.** the art or technique of producing a painting,
drawing, or engraving by using dots or light, short touches.
2. the effect produced by this technique.

stip·u·late (stip′yə lāt′) *v.t.,* **stip·u·lat·ed, stip·u·lat·ing.**
to demand or specify as a condition of agreement: *The
actor stipulated that he be allowed to have final approval
of the film's script.*

stip·u·la·tion (stip′yə lā′shən) *n.* **1.** the act of stipulat-
ing. **2.** a term or condition of an agreement or contract;
something stipulated.

stip·ule (stip′yōōl) *n.* one of a pair of small leaflike structures found at the base of certain
leaves.

stir (stur) *v.,* **stirred, stir·ring.**
—*v.t.* **1.** to mix (something, such
as a liquid) by a continuous circular movement: *to stir paint.*
2. to urge on or instigate; provoke:
to stir someone to action. **3.** to excite to deep feeling or emotion; affect strongly; move: *His plea for
mercy stirred the jury.* **4.** to rouse or call forth: *She tried
to stir him from his nap.* **5.** to cause to move, especially
slightly: *The breeze stirred the fallen leaves.* —*v.i.* **1.** to
make a slight movement: *The sleeping child didn't stir all
night.* **2.** to move about or begin to move about; be active:
She could hear someone stirring in the kitchen. **3.** to be
roused or called forth. **4.** to be capable of being stirred:
The paste hardened too much to stir. —*n.* **1.** commotion
or excitement; disturbance: *His appearance created quite
a stir.* **2.** a slight or momentary movement. **3.** the act of
stirring, as with a spoon. —**stir′rer,** *n.*

Stipules

stir·ring (stur′ing) *adj.* **1.** inspiring or exciting; thrilling:
a stirring movie. **2.** active; lively. —**stir′ring·ly,** *adv.*

stir·rup (stur′əp, stir′əp) *n.* **1.** one of a pair of metal,
wooden, or leather loops or rings,
flattened at the bottom and suspended from a saddle, used to support a rider's foot in mounting and
riding. **2.** the innermost of the
three bones in the middle ear,
shaped somewhat like a stirrup;
stapes.

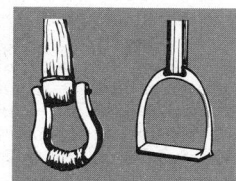
Stirrups

stitch (stich) *n. pl.,* **stitch·es.**
1. one complete movement of a
threaded needle in and out of fab-
ric, as in sewing, or through skin and flesh, as in surgery.
2. a similiar complete movement made with a needle and
yarn or thread, as in knitting. **3.** a single loop or knot of
thread or yarn made by a stitch. **4.** a particular method
of arranging the thread, as in sewing or knitting. **5.** a
sudden, sharp pain, especially in the side or back. **6.** *Informal.* a piece of clothing. **7.** *Informal.* slightest bit: *I didn't
do a stitch of work all day.* —*v.t.* to make, fasten, join, or
mend with stitches: *to stitch up a hole.* —*v.i.* to make
stitches; sew.

St. John, an island of the Virgin Islands. It belongs to
the United States.

St. John's, the capital of Newfoundland, a port on the
southeastern coast. Pop. (1971), 86,290.

St. Lawrence 1. a river in North America flowing from
Lake Ontario northeast into the Gulf of St. Lawrence. It
is the chief outlet of the Great Lakes. **2. Gulf of.** an arm
of the Atlantic Ocean, on the eastern coast of Canada, at
the mouth of the St. Lawrence River.

St. Lawrence Seaway, an inland waterway in east-
central North America connecting the Atlantic Ocean
with the Great Lakes.

St. Lou·is (lōō′is, lōō′ē) a city in eastern Missouri, on
the Mississippi River. Pop. (1970), 622,236.

stoat (stōt) *n.* the ermine, especially when in its brown
summer coat.

stock (stok) *n.* **1.** the total amount of goods that a merchant or commerical establishment keeps on hand for sale:
This store has a large stock of fishing equipment. **2.** a
quantity of something accumulated or held in reserve;
store: *The squirrel was putting away a stock of nuts for the
winter.* **3.** domestic animals raised or kept on a farm or
ranch, such as cattle, sheep, or pigs; livestock. **4.** ancestry
or descent: *a person of Scandinavian stock.* **5.** a family or
other related group of plants or animals. **6.** a liquid in
which meat, poultry, or fish has been boiled, used as a base
for gravies, soups, or sauces. **7.** *Finance.* **a.** the total number of shares that a company or corporation is authorized
to issue. **b.** the number of shares held by an individual
stockholder. **c.** see **stock certificate. 8.** the raw material
from which something is made. **9. stocks.** a wooden frame
with holes for confining a person's ankles and sometimes
his wrists. It was formerly used as a punishment for minor
crimes. **10.** the wooden or metal support or handle of a
gun, to which the barrel and mechanism are attached.
11. a stem of a plant onto which a graft is made. **12.** a tree,
plant, or plant part that furnishes cuttings for grafting.
13. the trunk or main stem of a tree or other plant.
14. the crosspiece below the ring of an anchor. **15.** *Theater.*
a. see **stock company** (*def.* 2). **b.** the repertoire of a stock
company. **16.** any of a group of plants bearing stiff, showy
spikes of broad, petaled flowers. —*v.t.* **1.** to supply or
furnish with stock or a stock: *They stocked the cabin with
enough food for the weekend.* **2.** to have or keep a supply
of, especially for future use or sale: *That hardware store
stocks all kinds of tools.* **3.** to supply with livestock: *to stock
a farm.* **4.** to provide with wild animals, fish, or other
game, especially for private or restricted hunting or fishing:
to stock a lake. —*v.i.* to lay in a stock or supply: *to stock
up for a party.* —*adj.* **1.** regularly kept in stock: *a stock
size.* **2.** commonly or constantly used or brought forward;
commonplace: *a stock phrase.* **3.** employed in handling or
taking care of goods or merchandise: *a stock clerk.*

in stock. on hand for use or sale: *The store does not have
any basketballs in stock at this time.*
out of stock. not on hand for use or sale.
to put stock in or **to take stock in.** to have faith, trust,
or confidence in.
to take stock. a. to make an inventory of the goods one
has on hand for use or sale. **b.** to make an estimate or
examination: *After finishing college he took stock of his
plans for the future.*

stock·ade (sto kād′) *n.* **1.** a defensive barrier made of
strong, usually tall, posts set upright in the ground, usually
forming an enclosure. **2.** any similar barrier or enclosure.
3. a military prison. —*v.t.,* **stock·ad·ed, stock·ad·ing.** to
surround or fortify with a stockade.

stock·bro·ker (stok′brō′kər) *n.* a person who buys and
sells stocks or other securities for others.

stock certificate, a certificate issued by a company or
corporation to a stockholder as evidence of his ownership
of a particular number of shares.

at; āpe; cär; end; mē; it; īce; hot; ōld; fôrk;
wood; fōōl; oil; out; up; turn; sing; thin; this;
hw in white; zh in treasure. The symbol ə
stands for the sound of a in about, e in taken,
i in pencil, o in lemon, and u in circus.

stock company **1.** a company or corporation whose capital is divided into shares. **2.** a theatrical troupe playing regularly at a particular theater in a variety of productions.

stock exchange **1.** a place where stocks and bonds are bought and sold. **2.** an association of stockholders who deal in the buying and selling of stocks and bonds.

stock·hold·er (stok′hōl′dər) *n.* a person who owns stock in a company or corporation; shareholder.

Stock·holm (stok′hōm, stok′hōlm) *n.* the capital and largest city of Sweden, on the western coast of the country. Pop. (1970 est.), 740,500.

stock·ing (stok′ing) *n.* **1.** a close-fitting, knitted covering for the foot and leg, especially one made of nylon or other manufactured fiber and worn by women. **2.** anything resembling this.

stocking cap, a knitted cap, usually having a pointed end that is worn flopped over toward the back.

stock·man (stok′mən) *n. pl.,* **stock·men** (stok′mən). a man who raises livestock.

stock market **1.** a place where stocks and bonds are bought and sold. **2.** the business carried on in such a place.

stock·pile (stok′pīl′) *n.* a supply of foodstuffs, raw materials, or other items accumulated and held in reserve for future use during an emergency or shortage: *a stockpile of uranium.* —*v.,* **stock·piled, stock·pil·ing.** —*v.t.* to accumulate a stockpile of: *to stockpile nuclear weapons.* —*v.i.* to accumulate a stockpile.

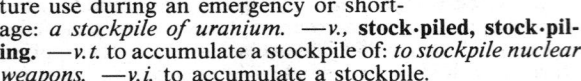

Stocking cap

stock·room (stok′rōōm′, stok′room′) *n.* a room in which stocks of goods are stored.

stock-still (stok′stil′) *adj.* motionless: *to stand stock-still.*

Stock·ton (stok′tən) *n.* a city in central California. Pop. (1970), 107,644.

stock·y (stok′ē) *adj.,* **stock·i·er, stock·i·est.** having a solid, sturdy, and compact build; thickset. —**stock′i·ly,** *adv.* —**stock′i·ness,** *n.*

stock·yard (stok′yärd′) *n.* an enclosure made up of pens and sheds where livestock is kept before being slaughtered or shipped to market.

stodg·y (stoj′ē) *adj.,* **stodg·i·er, stodg·i·est.** **1.** extremely old-fashioned and stuffy: *Jane thought her father was stodgy because he disapproved of women working.* **2.** lacking freshness or interest; commonplace; dull: *a stodgy speech.* **3.** (of food) heavy and thick; indigestible. —**stodg′i·ly,** *adv.* —**stodg′i·ness,** *n.*

sto·gy (stō′gē) *also,* **sto·gie.** *n. pl.,* **sto·gies.** a long, slender, inexpensive cigar.

sto·ic (stō′ik) *n.* a person who is apparently indifferent to or unaffected by pain or pleasure. —*adj. also,* **sto·i·cal** (stō′i kəl). indifferent to or unaffected by pain or pleasure.

stoke (stōk) *v.t.,* **stoked, stok·ing.** **1.** to stir up and feed fuel to (a fire or a furnace). **2.** to tend (a fire or furnace).

stoke·hold (stōk′hōld′) *n.* a room or compartment on a steamship containing the furnaces or boilers.

stoke·hole (stōk′hōl′) *n.* **1.** a hole through which fuel is fed into a furnace. **2.** another word for **stokehold.**

Stoke-on-Trent (stōk′ôn trent′) *n.* a city in west-central England. Pop. (1978), 257,200.

stok·er (stō′kər) *n.* **1.** a man who tends and supplies fuel to a furnace or boiler, as on a steamship or locomotive. **2.** a mechanical device that supplies fuel to a furnace.

STOL (stōl) an airplane that needs only a short distance to take off and land. [Abbreviation of *s*(hort) *t*(ake) *o*(ff) (and) *l*(anding).]

stole¹ (stōl) the past tense of **steal.**

stole² (stōl) *n.* **1.** a woman's long scarf, usually of fur, worn around the shoulders with the ends hanging down in front. **2.** a long narrow strip of silk or other material, worn around the neck by a clergyman during certain religious services. [Old English *stole* a long robe, a long scarf worn by a priest.]

sto·len (stō′lən) the past participle of **steal.**

stol·id (stol′id) *adj.* having or showing little or no emotion; not easily moved or stirred; impassive. —**stol′id·ly,** *adv.*

sto·lid·i·ty (stə lid′ə tē) *n.* the state or condition of being stolid.

sto·lon (stō′lən) *n. Botany.* a stem that trails along the ground and takes root at the tip to form a new plant; runner.

sto·ma (stō′mə) *n. pl.,* **sto·ma·ta** or **sto·mas.** a small opening or pore, especially on a plant leaf, through which gases and water vapor pass in or out.

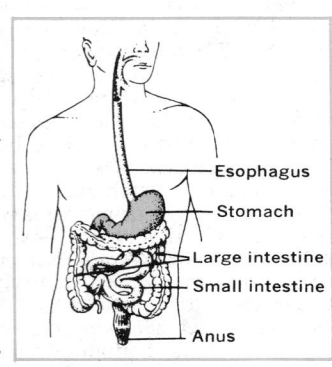

Stole² *(def. 2)*

stom·ach (stum′ək) *n.* **1.** in humans and other animals with backbones, the muscular baglike organ of the alimentary canal that receives swallowed food from the esophagus, lubricates it, mixes it, and begins the digestion of proteins and fats. **2.** a similar part in certain animals without backbones, such as lobsters and insects. **3.** the part of the body containing the stomach; abdomen; belly. **4.** an inclination or liking; desire: *He has no stomach for violence.* —*v.t.* to put up with; tolerate; endure: *I can't stomach Marilyn's rude behavior.*

Stomach

stom·ach·ache (stum′ək āk′) *n.* a pain in or near the region of the stomach.

stom·ach·er (stum′ə kər) *n.* a former ornamental garment covering the stomach and chest, often extending in a V-shape to below the waistline. It was worn especially by women in the sixteenth and seventeenth centuries.

stomach pump, a suction pump with a long flexible tube, used to empty the contents of the stomach, as when a person has swallowed poison.

sto·ma·ta (stō′mə tə, stom′ə tə) a plural of **stoma.**

stomp (stomp) *v.t.* **1.** to tread heavily or violently on or upon: *He stomped the floor in anger.* **2.** to bring down (the foot or feet) forcefully and heavily; stamp: *The little boy stomped his feet on the floor.* —*v.i.* to tread heavily or violently: *She stomped angrily out of the room.*

stone (stōn) *n. pl.,* **stones** or *(def. 8)* **stone.** **1.** a hard, naturally formed mass of mineral matter; rock. **2.** a small fragment or piece of this. **3.** a piece of stone that has been shaped or cut for a particular purpose, as for building, marking a grave, or paving a road. **4.** a precious stone; gem. **5.** anything like a stone, as in shape or hardness: *Too long a sacrifice can make a stone of the heart* (William Butler Yeats). **6.** a hardened mass of matter found in certain organs of the body, such as the gall bladder or kidney. **7.** the hard inner layer enclosing the seed of certain fruits, such as the cherry, peach, or avocado. **8.** a unit of weight of varying value. In Great Britain it is equal to fourteen pounds avoirdupois. —*adj.* **1.** made or built of

898

stone: *a stone house, a stone wall.* **2.** made of stoneware. —*v.t.,* **stoned, ston·ing. 1.** to pelt or kill with stones. **2.** to furnish, fit, pave, or line with stones: *to stone a road.* **3.** to remove the stones from (fruit).

Stone Age, the earliest known stage in the development of civilization, characterized by the use of stone tools and weapons.

stone·blind (stōn′blīnd′) *adj.* completely blind.

stone·cut·ter (stōn′kut′ər) *n.* a person or thing that cuts or carves stone.

stone·deaf (stōn′def′) *adj.* completely deaf.

Stone·henge (stōn′henj′) *n.* a structure in southern England erected by a prehistoric people, consisting mainly of a circular arrangement of giant stone blocks. It is now in ruins.

stone·ma·son (stōn′mā′sən) *n.* a person who cuts stone or builds structures in stone.

stone's throw, a short distance: *His house is just a stone's throw from here.*

stone·ware (stōn′wer′) *n.* pottery made of a mixture of finely ground clay and stone and baked at a very high temperature.

stone·work (stōn′wurk′) *n.* **1.** something made of stone. **2.** the art, process, or technique of working in stone. **3. stoneworks.** a place where stone is cut and prepared. —**stone′work′er,** *n.*

ston·y (stō′nē) *adj.,* **ston·i·er, ston·i·est. 1.** showing no emotion; cold; unfeeling: *a stony stare.* **2.** having or feeling no emotion: *a stony heart.* **3.** full of or covered with stones. **4.** hard as stone. —**ston′i·ly,** *adv.* —**ston′i·ness,** *n.*

stood (stood) the past tense and past participle of **stand.**

stooge (stōōj) *n. Informal.* **1.** an entertainer who assists a comedian, as by feeding lines, heckling from the audience, or serving as the butt of jokes. **2.** anyone who is used or taken advantage of by another; dupe.

stool (stōōl) *n.* **1.** an individual seat supported on legs or a pedestal, usually having no back or arms. **2.** a low backless and armless bench, used as a support for the feet or legs when sitting, or for the knees when kneeling. **3.** waste matter emitted from the bowels.

stool pigeon 1. a pigeon used as a decoy to trap other pigeons. **2.** *Slang.* any person acting as an informer or decoy, especially for the police.

stoop¹ (stōōp) *v.i.* **1.** to bend the body forward and downward, often with the knees bent: *She stooped to pick up the paper she had dropped.* **2.** to stand or walk with the head and shoulders bent forward: *The old lady stoops when she walks.* **3.** to lower or degrade oneself to do or use something: *Jim stooped to cheating in order to pass the examination.* —*v.t.* to bend (one's head or other part of the body) forward. —*n.* **1.** a forward bending of the head and shoulders: *The man walked with a stoop.* **2.** the act of bending forward and downward. [Old English *stūpian* to bend down, bow down.]

stoop² (stōōp) *n.* a structure at the entrance of a building or house, made up of a number of steps leading up to a raised platform. [Dutch *stoep* a threshold, flight of steps.]

stop (stop) *v.,* **stopped, stop·ping.** —*v.t.* **1.** to prevent from moving, operating, acting, or progressing: *to stop a car, to stop a clock, to stop traffic.* **2.** to prevent from continuing; end: *to stop the spread of a fire, to stop an enemy's advance.* **3.** to keep (a person) from carrying out an action; hold

Stoop²

back; restrain: *We couldn't stop him from hitting her.* **4.** to obstruct or close up (a hole, passage, or cavity), as by stuffing something into it or placing something over it: *to stop up a drain.* **5.** to close (a bottle or other vessel) by blocking its mouth with a plug or other stopper: *to stop up a bottle.* **6.** to keep from: *Please stop making so much noise.* **7.** *Music.* to close (a finger hole) or press down on (a string) in order to produce a desired tone. —*v.i.* **1.** to come to an end; discontinue: *The music stopped at midnight.* **2.** to come to a standstill or halt: *She stopped in the middle of her speech and asked if there were any questions.* **3.** to halt during one's journey: *We will stop at this motel for the night.* —*n.* **1.** the act of stopping or the state of being stopped. **2.** a place at which a stop is made: *a bus stop.* **3.** something that stops or hinders. **4.** a punctuation mark. **5.** *Music.* **a.** a graduated set of organ pipes operated by one lever. **b.** a lever operating such a set of pipes. **c.** any mechanical part or device used to stop a string or finger hole. **6.** a device or part of a device that checks or controls movement or action in a mechanism.

stop·gap (stop′gap′) *n.* something devised or used to supply a need temporarily; temporary substitute.

stop·light (stop′līt′) *n.* **1.** another word for **traffic light. 2.** a light on the rear end of a vehicle that lights up when the brakes are applied.

stop·o·ver (stop′ō′vər) *n.* a brief visit or stay, especially overnight, at a place during the course of a journey: *We had a stopover in Paris on our trip to Italy.*

stop·page (stop′ij) *n.* **1.** the act of stopping or the state of being stopped. **2.** something that blocks or obstructs.

stop·per (stop′ər) *n.* **1.** something, such as a cork or plug, used to close or stop up an opening in a bottle or other vessel. **2.** a person or thing that stops or arrests the movement, action, or progress of something. —*v.t.* to close with a stopper.

stop·watch (stop′woch′) *n. pl.,* **stop·watch·es.** a watch having a button that can be pressed to stop the hand or hands instantly, used for making very exact timings of races and contests.

stor·age (stôr′ij) *n.* **1.** the act of storing goods or other items, as in a warehouse. **2.** the state of being stored. **3.** a place for storing goods or other items: *That sofa has been in storage for a year.* **4.** the charge for storing, as in a warehouse. **5.** the part in an electronic computer in which information is stored.

storage battery, a battery that produces an electric current by a chemical reaction and can be recharged by an electric current.

store (stôr) *n.* **1.** a place or establishment in which a variety of goods are kept for sale: *a grocery store, a hardware store, a clothing store.* **2.** a quantity of something put away or held in reserve for future use: *a store of weapons, a store of energy.* **3. stores.** supplies, as of food or equipment. **4.** see **storehouse.** —*v.t.,* **stored, stor·ing. 1.** to put away or hold in reserve for future use: *The squirrel is storing nuts for the winter.* **2.** to put in a warehouse or other place for safekeeping: *to store furniture.* **3.** to provide or furnish; supply.

 in store. in reserve; forthcoming: *There is a surprise in store for you when you get home.*

at; āpe; cär; end; mē; it; īce; hot; ōld; fôrk; wood; fōōl; oil; out; up; turn; sing; thin; this; hw in white; zh in treasure. The symbol ə stands for the sound of a in about, e in taken, i in pencil, o in lemon, and u in circus.

899

to set store by. to regard; value; esteem: *The doctor sets little store by those treatments.*

store·house (stôr′hous′) *n. pl.,* **store·hous·es** (stôr′-hou′ziz). **1.** a place or building where things are stored. **2.** a large supply or source: *My history teacher was a storehouse of information.*

store·keep·er (stôr′kē′pər) *n.* a person who owns or runs a store.

store·room (stôr′rōōm′, stôr′room′) *n.* a room in which things are stored.

sto·rey (stôr′ē) *n. pl.,* **sto·reys.** another spelling of **story²**.

sto·ried¹ (stôr′ēd) *adj.* celebrated or recorded in stories, history, or legend. [*Story¹* + *-ed²*.]

sto·ried² (stôr′ēd) *adj.* having or divided into stories or floors. ▲ usually used in combination: *a six-storied building.* [*Story²* + *-ed²*.]

stork (stôrk) *n. pl.,* **storks** or **stork.** any of various long-legged wading birds having a long neck, a large, strong bill, and, usually, black, white, and gray feathers.

storm (stôrm) *n.* **1.** any disturbed state of the atmosphere, usually accompanied by strong winds and some form of precipitation, such as rain or snow. **2.** a sudden or violent outburst, as of emotion or excitement: *a storm of tears.* **3.** a violent disturbance or upheaval: *The scandal caused a storm in Parliament, resulting in the Prime Minister's resignation.* **4.** a sudden, violent attack, especially on a fortified position: *The enemy took the hill by storm.* **5.** a heavy discharge or shower of objects, such as missiles. —*v.i.* **1.** to rain, snow, sleet, hail, or otherwise precipitate heavily: *It stormed all day Friday.* **2.** to move or rush violently or angrily: *He stormed out of the house.* —*v.t.* to make a sudden, violent attack on: *The rebels stormed the gates of the palace.*

Stork

storm cellar, an underground shelter for use during cyclones, tornadoes, or the like.

storm center **1.** the center of a cyclone, an area of low atmospheric pressure and relative calm. **2.** any focal point or center of trouble, commotion, or controversy.

storm door, an additional door outside an ordinary door, used for protection against storms or other severe weather.

storm petrel, a small bird usually having black or brownish feathers with white markings. According to superstition, its presence indicates an approaching storm. Also, **stormy petrel.**

storm window, an additional window outside an ordinary window, used for protection against storms or other severe weather.

storm·y (stôr′mē) *adj.,* **storm·i·er, storm·i·est. 1.** affected by, characterized by, or subject to storms: *stormy weather, stormy seas.* **2.** characterized by violent or intense emotion or activity: *a stormy session of Congress.* —**storm′i·ly,** *adv.* —**storm′i·ness,** *n.*

sto·ry¹ (stôr′ē) *n. pl.,* **sto·ries. 1.** a narrative or account of an event or series of events that have happened or are supposed to have happened. **2.** a narrative or account, often untrue, intended to entertain the reader or hearer. **3.** an account or statement of the facts of a matter or case: *According to his story, you started the argument.* **4.** *Informal.* a falsehood; lie. [Anglo-Norman *estorie* history, tale.]

sto·ry² (stôr′ē) *also,* **sto·rey.** *n. pl.,* **sto·ries. 1.** one of the horizontal structural divisions of a building, making up the area between two successive floors. **2.** a set of rooms on the same floor level of a building. [Possibly from Medieval Latin *historia* a picture; possibly used originally to refer to painted windows depicting historical events on different floors of a building.]

sto·ry·book (stôr′ē book′) *n.* a book containing a story or stories, especially for children. —*adj.* occurring in or resembling the style of a storybook; romantic: *a storybook marriage.*

sto·ry·tell·er (stôr′ē tel′ər) *n.* a person who tells or writes stories.

stoup (stōōp) *n.* a basin containing holy water at or near the entrance of a church.

stout (stout) *adj.* **1.** having a thick, bulky figure; thickset; fat. **2.** having courage; brave. **3.** having strength and vigor; physically strong; robust. **4.** solid in structure, substance, or material. —*n.* a strong, very dark, heavy ale. —**stout′ly,** *adv.* —**stout′ness,** *n.*

stout-heart·ed (stout′här′tid) *adj.* valiant; brave; courageous: *stout-hearted warriors.* —**stout′-heart′ed·ly,** *adv.* —**stout′-heart′ed·ness,** *n.*

stove¹ (stōv) *n.* **1.** a kitchen appliance used for cooking that runs on gas or electricity and is made up of burners, an oven, and sometimes a storage compartment. **2.** any of various heating or cooking devices that use wood, coal, gas, or electricity. [Probably from Middle Dutch *stove* a heated room.]

stove² (stōv) a past tense and past participle of **stave.**

stove·pipe (stōv′pīp′) *n.* **1.** a pipe, usually of sheet metal, used to carry smoke, fumes, and noxious gases from a stove. **2.** *Informal.* a tall silk hat.

stow (stō) *v.t.* **1.** to put or pack away, especially in a neat, compact manner: *The seamen stowed the cargo and supplies in the ship's hold.* **2.** to fill by packing; load: *We stowed the trunk of the car with our supplies.*

to stow away. to be a stowaway.

stow·a·way (stō′ə wā′) *n.* a person who hides himself on a ship or airplane, especially in order to obtain free passage.

Stowe, Harriet Bee·cher (stō; bē′chər) 1811–1896, U.S. author.

St. Paul, the capital of Minnesota, in the southeastern part of the state. It is located on the Mississippi River, opposite Minneapolis. Pop. (1970), 309,980.

St. Pe·ters·burg (pē′tərz burg′) **1.** see **Leningrad. 2.** a city in west-central Florida on the Gulf of Mexico. Pop. (1970), 216,232.

strad·dle (strad′əl) *v.,* **strad·dled, strad·dling.** —*v.t.* **1.** to sit, stand, or walk with one leg on each side of: *to straddle a fence, to straddle a horse.* **2.** to appear to favor both sides of (an issue). **3.** to spread (the legs) wide apart. —*v.i.* **1.** to sit, stand, or walk with the legs wide apart. **2.** to appear to favor both sides of an issue. **3.** (of the legs) to be wide apart. —*n.* the act of straddling. —**strad′-dler,** *n.*

Strad·i·var·i, An·to·nio (strad′ə vär′ē; än tō′nyō) 1644?–1737, Italian violin maker.

Strad·i·var·i·us (strad′ə ver′ē əs) *n.* a violin, viola, or cello made by Stradivari.

strafe (strāf) *v.t., v.i.,* **strafed, straf·ing.** to attack (troops, ships, or the like) with machine-gun or rocket fire from low-flying aircraft. [From the German expression *Gott strafe England* God punish England, used in World War I.]

strag·gle (strag′əl) *v.i.,* **strag·gled, strag·gling. 1.** to wander or move about in an irregular, rambling manner: *The exhausted hikers straggled into camp.* **2.** to stray from or lag behind the main course or body. —**strag′gler,** *n.*

strag·gly (strag′lē) *adj.,* **strag·gli·er, strag·gli·est.** spread out or scattered in an irregular, rambling manner: *straggly vines.*

straight (strāt) *adj.* **1.** moving in the same direction without a curve, bend, or other irregularity: *a straight line.* **2.** not curly, wavy, or kinky: *straight hair.* **3.** not crooked or stooping; erect: *to stand with a straight back.* **4.** in proper arrangement, order, or condition: *She tried to keep her room straight. I couldn't keep the twins' names straight.* **5.** truthful; frank; candid: *a straight answer.* **6.** without interruption; unbroken; continuous: *She spoke for three hours straight.* **7.** strictly following or supporting the platform, policy, and candidates of a particular political party: *He voted a straight Democratic ticket.* **8.** not mixed, altered, or diluted, as an alcoholic liquor. —*adv.* **1.** in a straight line, course, or manner: *Go straight down Main Street.* **2.** without delay; immediately: *I went straight home after the movie.* —**straight′ly,** *adv.* —**straight′ness,** *n.*
 straight away or **straight off.** without delay; immediately.
straight angle, an angle of 180 degrees.
straight·a·way (strāt′ə wā′) *adv.* at once; immediately. —*adj.* extending in a straight line or course. —*n.* a straight course or part, especially of a race course.
straight·edge (strāt′ej′) *n.* see **ruler** *(def. 2).*
straight·en (strāt′ən) *v.t.* **1.** to make straight: *Straighten your hat.* **2.** to restore to the proper order, arrangement, or condition: *John straightened up his desk.* —*v.i.* to become straight. —**straight′en·er,** *n.*
straight face, a face that shows no emotion.
straight-faced (strāt′fāst′) *adj.* showing no emotion.
straight·for·ward (strāt′fôr′wərd) *adj.* **1.** honest; frank; sincere: *a straightforward answer.* **2.** proceeding or directed straight ahead. —*adv. also,* **straightforwards.** in a straightforward manner or course. —**straight′for′ward·ly,** *adv.* —**straight′for′ward·ness,** *n.*
straight·way (strāt′wā′) *adv.* at once; immediately.
strain¹ (strān) *v.t.* **1.** to draw or pull tight; stretch: *The weight of the cargo strained the ropes.* **2.** to injure or weaken by excessive stretching or overexertion: *to strain a muscle.* **3.** to use or push to the utmost: *She strained her voice to be heard above the noise of the engine.* **4.** to stretch beyond proper, normal, or legitimate limits. **5.** to press or pour through a strainer, sieve, or other filtering device: *to strain freshly squeezed orange juice to remove the pulp.* —*v.i.* **1.** to make violent and continuous effort to do or achieve something; exert oneself to the utmost: *She strained to reach her goal.* **2.** to pull with force: *The horse strained at the rope.* —*n.* **1.** extreme physical force or pressure: *The roof collapsed under the strain of the heavy snow.* **2.** an injury or impairment caused by excessive stretching or overexertion: *muscle strain.* **3.** extreme mental or emotional pressure or tension: *The soldier broke under the strain of combat.* **4.** the act of straining or the state of being strained. [Old French *estraindre* to stretch, wring, press tightly.]
strain² (strān) *n.* **1.** line of descent; ancestry; stock. **2.** a group of animals or plants having distinguishing characteristics and forming a part or subdivision of a larger group. **3.** an inherited or characteristic quality or tendency: *a strain of nobility.* **4.** *also,* **strains.** a musical passage; tune. [Old English *strēon* gain, treasure, stock.]
strained (strānd) *adj.* not natural; forced: *a strained smile.*
strain·er (strā′nər) *n.* **1.** any of various utensils or devices, such as a colander or sieve, through which liquids are passed to separate them from solids. **2.** a person or thing that strains.
strait (strāt) *n.* **1.** a narrow waterway or channel connecting two larger bodies of water. **2.** *also,* **straits.** a position or circumstance of difficulty, distress, or need: *to be in desperate financial straits.*

strait·en (strāt′ən) *v.t.* **1.** to cause to be in need or difficulty, especially for money. **2.** to make narrow or confining.
strait jacket, a canvas garment resembling a jacket, having long sleeves that wrap around the body. It is used to confine the arms of a violent patient or prisoner.
strait-laced (strāt′lāst′) *adj.* excessively strict or rigid in morals or manners; prudish.
strand¹ (strand) *v.t.* **1.** to drive or run (a boat or ship) aground. **2.** to leave in a difficult or helpless position, especially in a strange or isolated place: *The cancellation of our flight stranded us at the airport with very little money.* —*n.* land bordering a body of water; shore or beach. [Old English *strand.*]
strand² (strand) *n.* **1.** one of the threads, wires, or fibers twisted together to form a rope, cord, or other line. **2.** any single thread, hair, or similar structure: *a strand of spaghetti, strands of hair.* **3.** a string of things joined together by twisting, twining, or threading: *a strand of pearls.* [Of uncertain origin.]
strange (strānj) *adj.,* **strang·er, strang·est. 1.** differing from the usual or ordinary; remarkable or odd: *That was a strange thing for her to do.* **2.** not known, seen, or experienced before; unfamiliar: *That part of town is strange to me.* **3.** ill at ease; uncomfortable: *I would feel strange asking him such a favor.* **4.** unaccustomed to or inexperienced in: *Ted is strange to this work, so it will take him a while to do it as fast as Michael.* —**strange′ly,** *adv.* —**strange′ness,** *n.*
stran·ger (strān′jər) *n.* **1.** a person with whom one is not acquainted or familiar. **2.** a foreigner, outsider, or newcomer. **3.** a person who is ignorant of, unacquainted with, or unaccustomed to something specified: *He's no stranger to politics.*
stran·gle (strang′gəl) *v.,* **stran·gled, stran·gling.** —*v.t.* **1.** to kill or attempt to kill by squeezing the throat to stop the breath; throttle. **2.** to suffocate or choke in any manner. **3.** to hold back; stifle: *to strangle a laugh.* —*v.i.* to become strangled. —**stran′gler,** *n.*
stran·gu·la·tion (strang′gyə lā′shən) *n.* the act of strangling or the state of being strangled.
strap (strap) *n.* **1.** a long, narrow, flexible strip of leather, cloth, or other material, often having a buckle or other fastener, used for securing or holding things together or in position. **2.** a narrow metal band used to fasten or hold things together or in position. —*v.t.,* **strapped, strap·ping. 1.** to fasten, secure, or support with a strap: *Henry strapped his pack to his back and started off on a hike.* **2.** to beat with a strap.
strap·ping (strap′ing) *adj. Informal.* tall and sturdy; robust: *a strapping young man.*
Stras·bourg (stras′burg′) *n.* a city in northeastern France, on the Rhine River. Pop. (1968), 249,396.
stra·ta (strā′tə, strat′ə) a plural of **stratum.**
strat·a·gem (strat′ə jəm) *n.* a scheme, trick, or maneuver designed to outwit, deceive, or surprise an enemy or obtain an advantage.
stra·te·gic (strə tē′jik) *adj.* **1.** of or relating to strategy. **2.** important or necessary to strategy, especially military strategy. —**stra·te′gi·cal·ly,** *adv.*

at; āpe; cär; end; mē; it; īce; hot; ōld; fôrk; wood; fo͞ol; oil; out; up; turn; sing; thin; this; hw in white; zh in treasure. The symbol ə stands for the sound of a in about, e in taken, i in pencil, o in lemon, and u in circus.

S

strat·e·gist (strat′ə jist) *n.* a person who is trained or skilled in strategy, especially military strategy.

strat·e·gy (strat′ə jē) *n. pl.,* **strat·e·gies. 1.** the art or science of planning and directing large-scale military operations and campaigns. **2.** the skillful use of planning, as in business or politics. **3.** a plan or device designed to achieve a specific goal or advantage: *What strategy does the company intend to use to sell the new product?*

Strat·ford-on-A·von (strat′fərd ôn ā′vən, strat′fərd on ā′vən) *n.* a town in central England, on the Avon River. It is noted as the birthplace, home, and burial place of William Shakespeare. Also, **Stratford.**

strat·i·fi·ca·tion (strat′ə fi kā′shən) *n.* **1.** the act of stratifying or the state of being stratified. **2.** a stratified structure or formation, as of rock.

strat·i·fy (strat′ə fī′) *v.,* **strat·i·fied, strat·i·fy·ing.** —*v.t.* **1.** to form or arrange in layers or strata. **2.** to divide into groups or classes, as according to common social or economic characteristics: *to stratify society.* —*v.i.* to form strata.

strat·o·sphere (strat′ə sfēr′) *n.* a layer of the atmosphere, above the troposphere and below the mesosphere, extending from about twelve to about thirty-five miles above the earth's surface. Ozone formed in the upper part of this region protects the earth from ultraviolet radiation from the sun.

strat·o·spher·ic (strat′ə sfer′ik) *adj.* of or relating to the stratosphere.

stra·tum (strā′təm, strat′əm) *n. pl.,* **stra·ta** or **stra·tums. 1.** a horizontal layer of material, such as rock or soil, especially one having several parallel layers placed or lying one on top of the other: *The diggers broke through the first stratum of rock.* **2.** a group or class having certain social or economic characteristics in common.

stra·tus (strā′təs, strat′əs) *n. pl.,* **stra·ti** (strā′tī, strat′ī) or **stra·tus.** a low-lying, grayish, watery cloud having a foggy appearance.

Strauss (strous) **1. Jo·hann** (yō′hän). 1804–1849, Austrian composer. **2. Johann.** 1825–1899, his son; Austrian composer. **3. Richard.** 1864–1949, German composer.

Stra·vin·sky, I·gor Feo·do·ro·vich (strə vin′skē; ē′gôr fyô′də rō′vich) 1882–1971, Russian composer.

straw (strô) *n.* **1.** a long slender tube, as of paper or plastic, used for sucking up a liquid. **2.** the dry stalks or stems of any of various grains, such as rye, oats, wheat, or barley, after they have been threshed. Straw is used especially as bedding for livestock and for making hats, baskets, and other woven products. **3.** a single one of such stalks or stems. **4.** something of little value or importance; trifle. —*adj.* **1.** made of straw: *a straw hat.* **2.** resembling straw, as in color.

straw·ber·ry (strô′ber′ē) *n. pl.,* **straw·ber·ries. 1.** a sweet, juicy red fruit of any of a group of plants. **2.** a low-growing plant bearing this fruit, having many slender stalks and grown in temperate regions of the world.

Strawberries

straw poll, an unofficial poll taken to determine the trend of public opinion, as on a particular issue or political candidate.

stray (strā) *v.i.* **1.** to wander from a given course or group or beyond proper limits: *The puppy strayed from the yard.* **2.** to wander or move about idly or without direction; rove. **3.** to turn from a course that is thought to be morally right or good; err. —*adj.* **1.** wandering, lost, or homeless: *a*

stray sheep. **2.** found or occurring randomly or occasionally; scattered or isolated: *There were a few stray hairs on her coat.* **3.** turning from the proper or intended course: *An innocent bystander was hit by a stray bullet.* —*n.* a lost or homeless animal or person.

streak (strēk) *n.* **1.** a long, thin, irregularly shaped mark, line, or band differing in color or texture from the material or surface of which it forms a part: *to have streaks of gray in one's hair.* **2.** a slight trace or tendency: *a streak of genius, a streak of madness.* **3.** a temporary run; brief period: *a streak of bad luck.* —*v.t.* to mark with a streak or streaks; form streaks on or in: *His face was streaked with dirt.* —*v.i.* **1.** to form a streak or streaks. **2.** to become streaked. **3.** to move, run, or go at great speed: *The ambulance streaked down the street.*

streak·y (strē′kē) *adj.,* **streak·i·er, streak·i·est. 1.** marked with, characterized by, or occurring in streaks. **2.** of uneven quality or character; inconsistent: *Rod is a streaky hockey player.* —**streak′i·ly,** *adv.* —**streak′i·ness,** *n.*

stream (strēm) *n.* **1.** a body of running water, especially a small river. **2.** a steady flow or current of any fluid or gas: *a stream of air.* **3.** any continuous, uninterrupted movement: *a stream of people, a stream of words.* —*v.i.* **1.** to flow or issue in a stream: *Tears streamed down her face. Light streamed into the room when I opened the curtains.* **2.** to pour forth a stream: *The runner came off the track streaming with perspiration.* **3.** to move along steadily or smoothly; flow: *The audience streamed out of the auditorium.* **4.** to wave, float, or extend outward: *The banners of the marchers streamed in the wind.* —*v.t.* to pour out, discharge, or emit in a stream: *The cut on his leg streamed blood.*

stream·er (strē′mər) *n.* **1.** a long, narrow flag or banner. **2.** any long, narrow strip of material: *Paper streamers were hanging from the ceiling.*

stream·let (strēm′lit) *n.* a little stream.

stream·line (strēm′līn′) *v.t.,* **stream·lined, stream·lin·ing. 1.** to design or build so that there is the least possible resistance to air or water: *to streamline an automobile.* **2.** to make more modern or efficient: *to streamline the administration of government.* —*adj.* see **streamlined.**

stream·lined (strēm′līnd′) *adj.* **1.** designed or built so as to offer the least possible resistance to air or water. **2.** efficient and modern.

street (strēt) *n.* **1.** a public way in a city or town, usually with sidewalks and buildings on one or both sides: *a tree-lined street, a street of shops.* **2.** the part of such a way for vehicles, not including the sidewalks and buildings: *Be careful crossing the street.* **3.** the people who live, work, or gather in a street: *The whole street went to the meeting of the town council.*

street·car (strēt′kär′) *n.* a public passenger vehicle that operates by electricity and runs on rails in city streets. Also, **trolley, trolley car.**

strength (strength) *n.* **1.** the state or quality of being strong; power, force, or energy: *He lifted heavy weights to build up his strength.* **2.** the power to withstand or resist attack, force, strain, or stress without breaking or yielding: *to test the strength of a rope.* **3.** the degree of concentration, intensity, or effectiveness: *the strength of an electric current, the strength of a drug.* **4.** power, especially military power, derived from numbers of soldiers, equipment, or resources: *The nation's armed forces are not at full strength.* **5.** a person or thing that strengthens; source of power or force.

on the strength of. based or depending on: *He was convicted of robbery on the strength of the witnesses' testimony.*

strength·en (streng'thən) *v.t., v.i.* to make or become strong or stronger. —**strength'en·er,** *n.*

stren·u·ous (stren'yōo əs) *adj.* **1.** requiring or characterized by great effort or exertion: *a strenuous task.* **2.** very active or energetic; vigorous: *strenuous opposition.* —**stren'u·ous·ly,** *adv.* —**stren'u·ous·ness,** *n.*

strep throat (strep) a serious infection of the throat caused by a streptococcus and characterized by fever and the presence of pus in the throat.

strep·to·coc·cus (strep'tə kok'əs) *n. pl.,* **strep·to·coc·ci** (strep'tə kok'sī). any of a group of spherical bacteria that multiply by dividing in one direction only, tending to form chains. Diseases such as scarlet fever, rheumatic fever, and strep throat are caused by various kinds of streptococci.

strep·to·my·cin (strep'tō mī'sin) *n.* a powerful antibiotic prepared from a type of fungus, effective against tuberculosis, typhoid fever, certain types of meningitis, and other bacterial infections.

stress (stres) *n. pl.,* **stress·es.** **1.** mental or emotional strain or pressure: *He became ill from the stress of worry.* **2.** a special meaning, emphasis, or importance attached to something: *Mother always put a lot of stress on good table manners.* **3.** the relative emphasis given to a particular sound, syllable, or word in speech. In the word *employ,* the stress is on the second syllable. **4.** a force or pressure that is applied to something: *the stress of wind on a bridge.* —*v.t.* **1.** to place special meaning, emphasis, or importance on: *The magazine article stressed the need for conservation of natural resources.* **2.** to pronounce (a syllable, word, or words) with a particular stress. **3.** to apply force or pressure to.

stretch (strech) *v.t.* **1.** to straighten or spread out to full length or width: *She got up and stretched her arms and legs.* **2.** to hold out; put forth: *He stretched his hand out to shake mine.* **3.** to cause to reach or extend, as from one place to another or across a given area: *to stretch a clothesline across a yard.* **4.** to strain; pull: *The runner stretched a muscle in his leg.* **5.** to extend beyond proper or natural limits: *to stretch the rules.* **6.** to widen, lengthen, or pull out of shape by force: *to stretch a sweater.* **7.** to cause to last; prolong: *to stretch a visit out for two weeks.* **8.** to exaggerate: *to stretch the truth.* —*v.i.* **1.** to lie down and extend the body to full length: *He stretched out on the bed.* **2.** to straighten or spread out one's body or limbs to full length: *Many people in the audience got up and stretched during the intermission.* **3.** to extend from one place to another or across a given area: *The road stretches for another thirty miles.* **4.** to become widened, lengthened, or pulled out of shape without tearing or breaking: *Rubber stretches.* —*n. pl.,* **stretch·es.** **1.** an unbroken space or area; extent: *The stretch of the river glittered in a still and dazzling splendor* (Joseph Conrad). **2.** an unbroken period of time: *She was out of the country for a stretch of two years.* **3.** the act of stretching or the state of being stretched. **4.** the quality of being elastic; elasticity: *This rubber band has lost its stretch.* **5.** the straight part of a race course. —*adj.* made of material having elastic qualities: *stretch gloves, stretch stockings.*

stretch·er (strech'ər) *n.* **1.** a piece of canvas or similar material stretched across a frame, used for carrying a sick, injured, or dead person. **2.** any of various devices used to stretch, such as the frame on which an artist's canvas is spread. **3.** a person or thing that stretches.

strew (strōo) *v.t.,* **strewed, strewed** or **strewn, strew·ing.** **1.** to spread or throw about at random; scatter: *to strew hay on a barn floor.* **2.** to cover with something spread or thrown about in this way: *The street was strewn with scraps of paper and other litter.* **3.** to be scattered over: *Confetti strewed the floor.*

stri·at·ed (strī'ā'tid) *adj.* marked by or having narrow grooves, bands, or streaks of distinctive color or texture, especially in a parallel arrangement: *striated rock.*

stri·a·tion (strī ā'shən) *n.* the state or condition of being striated: *the striation of crystals.*

strick·en (strik'ən) *v.* a past participle of **strike.** —*adj.* **1.** strongly affected or overwhelmed, as by sorrow, disease, or misfortune: *stricken with grief.* **2.** struck or wounded: *a stricken animal.*

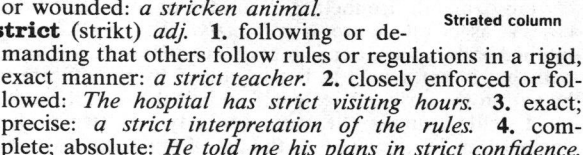

Striated column

strict (strikt) *adj.* **1.** following or demanding that others follow rules or regulations in a rigid, exact manner: *a strict teacher.* **2.** closely enforced or followed: *The hospital has strict visiting hours.* **3.** exact; precise: *a strict interpretation of the rules.* **4.** complete; absolute: *He told me his plans in strict confidence.* —**strict'ly,** *adv.* —**strict'ness,** *n.*

stric·ture (strik'chər) *n.* **1.** unfavorable or severe criticism; censure. **2.** something that limits, confines, or restrains. **3.** an abnormal closing or narrowing of some duct or tube of the body.

stride (strīd) *v.,* **strode, strid·den** (strid'ən), **strid·ing.** —*v.i.* **1.** to walk with long, sweeping steps: *The teacher strode into the room.* **2.** to pass with a single long step: *to stride over a mud puddle.* —*v.t.* **1.** to sit or stand with one leg on each side of; straddle; bestride. **2.** to move over, along, or through with long, sweeping steps. —*n.* **1.** a long, sweeping step. **2.** the distance covered by such a step. **3.** *usually,* **strides.** progress or improvement: *Great strides have been made in medical research.*

to take in one's stride. to adjust to or deal with without difficulty, effort, or hesitation.

stri·dent (strīd'ənt) *adj.* making or having a harsh, shrill, grating sound. —**stri'dence, stri'den·cy,** *n.* —**stri'dent·ly,** *adv.*

strife (strīf) *n.* **1.** bitter conflict, fighting, or trouble. **2.** a contest or struggle between rivals to gain superiority.

strike (strīk) *v.,* **struck, struck** or **strick·en, strik·ing.** —*v.t.* **1.** to give a blow to; hit: *The soldier was court-martialed for striking an officer.* **2.** to deal; inflict: *to strike a blow.* **3.** to come against with force: *The car skidded and struck a tree.* **4.** to cause to come against with force; hit: *She struck her head against the shelf when she fell.* **5.** to set on fire by rubbing or hitting: *to strike a match.* **6.** to erase, cancel, or otherwise remove: *You can strike my name off the list of those coming to the party.* **7.** to make an attack on; assault: *Our troops struck the enemy camp at dawn.* **8.** to give the impression of being; appear to: *She struck me as being very spoiled.* **9.** to assume: *The woman struck a pose for the photographer.* **10.** to give or announce (time) by ringing or otherwise sounding: *The clock struck twelve.* **11.** to find suddenly or unexpectedly; discover: *to strike oil.* **12.** to cause (a feeling or emotion) to penetrate or affect deeply: *The shriek of a woman struck terror into their hearts.* **13.** to stop work at (a factory, company, or the like) until certain demands are met, such as higher pay or better working conditions. **14.** to arrive at or make: *to strike a bargain.* **15.** to come to or fall upon: *The sound*

at; āpe; cär; end; mē; it; īce; hot; ōld; fôrk; wood; fōol; oil; out; up; turn; sing; thin; this; hw in white; zh in treasure. The symbol ə stands for the sound of **a** in about, **e** in taken, **i** in pencil, **o** in lemon, and **u** in circus.

of music struck our ears. **16.** to make or form by pressing or stamping: *to strike coins.* **17.** to lower or take down, as a sail or flag: *The ship struck its sails.* —*v.i.* **1.** to come into violent contact; hit: *His head struck against the door when he slipped.* **2.** to make an attack: *The troops will strike at dawn.* **3.** to stop work until certain demands are met, such as higher pay or better working conditions: *The factory workers will strike tomorrow if a settlement is not reached by midnight.* **4.** to make a sound, as by ringing: *The chimes struck at midnight.* **5.** (of fish) to seize the bait. —*n.* **1.** the act of striking; blow. **2.** a work stoppage until certain demands are met. **3.** a sudden or unexpected discovery, as of oil or ore: *a gold strike.* **4.** *Baseball.* **a.** a pitched ball that a batter swings at and misses. **b.** a pitched ball that is not swung at but is judged by the umpire to be within the strike zone. **c.** a foul ball that is not caught by a fielder, unless the batter already has two strikes against him. **5.** *Bowling.* **a.** the act of knocking down all the pins with the first ball thrown. **b.** a score made in this way. **6.** a seizing of the bait by a fish.

   to strike out. a. to begin, as an undertaking or journey: *We struck out for home at dawn.* **b.** *Baseball.* to put out or be put out by a strikeout.

   to strike up. to begin; start: *The strangers struck up a conversation.*

strike·break·er (strīk′brā′kər) *n.* a person who continues to work during a strike, takes the place of a worker on strike, or supplies workers to take the place of strikers.

strike·out (strīk′out′) *n. Baseball.* an out resulting from three strikes charged against a batter.

strik·er (strī′kər) *n.* **1.** a worker who takes part in a strike. **2.** a person or thing that strikes.

strike zone *Baseball.* an area directly over home plate and between the batter's knees and armpits, through which a pitched ball that is not swung at must pass in order to be judged a strike.

strik·ing (strī′king) *adj.* making a strong impression on the mind or senses; impressive: *There was a striking similarity between the two paintings.* —**strik′ing·ly,** *adv.*

string (string) *n.* **1.** a slender line consisting of twisted or intertwined strands of fiber, wire, or similar material. **2.** anything like this, such as a strip of cloth used for tying parts together: *the strings of an apron.* **3.** a set or number of things joined together by or arranged on a string: *a string of pearls, a string of Christmas tree lights.* **4.** a series or row of persons, things, or events: *a string of traffic signals, a string of robberies.* **5.** *usually,* **strings.** *Informal.* a limitation or condition connected with something: *There were no strings attached to his offer of a loan.* **6.** a thin strand of wire, gut, nylon, or other material used to produce tones in certain musical instruments, such as guitars or pianos. **7. strings.** musical instruments played on such strings with a bow or by plucking, as the violin, viola, and cello, especially when such instruments are considered as a group in an orchestra or ensemble. **8.** a group of players on an athletic team who are ranked together as a unit, usually according to ability: *He plays on the third string of the football team.* **9.** a part of a plant resembling a string: *to pull the strings off green beans.* —*v.t.,* **strung, string·ing. 1.** to put on a string: *to string beads.* **2.** to provide with a string or strings: *to string a violin.* **3.** to cause to reach from one place to another or across a given area: *to string a clothesline across a yard.* **4.** to arrange in a row or series: *We strung the lights on the Christmas tree.* **5.** to remove fibers or strings from: *to string beans.*

   to pull strings. to use one's power or influence in order to get what one wants.

   to string along. *Informal.* **a.** to fool or deceive. **b.** to agree or cooperate.

string bean, a long, green bean, related to the kidney bean, the pod of which is eaten as a vegetable. Also, **green bean.**

stringed instrument, a musical instrument, such as a cello, violin, harp, or guitar, that has strings which produce tones when they are played with a bow or plucked.

strin·gent (strin′jənt) *adj.* **1.** rigidly maintained, enforced, or followed; rigorous: *stringent requirements.* **2.** persuasive or convincing: *a stringent argument.* **3.** characterized by or resulting from a scarcity or lack of available funds. —**strin′gen·cy,** *n.* —**strin′gent·ly,** *adv.*

string·er (string′ər) *n.* **1.** a person or thing that strings. **2.** a long horizontal beam supporting the vertical crosspieces of a framework or structure. **3.** a part-time or local correspondent for a news publication or news service.

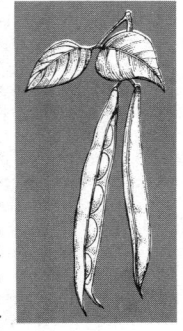

String beans

string·y (string′ē) *adj.,* **string·i·er, string·i·est. 1.** having or consisting of tough fibers: *stringy celery.* **2.** like string; thin: *stringy hair.* **3.** forming strings: *stringy glue.*

strip[1] (strip) *v.,* **stripped** or **stript, strip·ping.** —*v.t.* **1.** to remove or pull off the clothing or other covering from: *The mother stripped her baby before giving him a bath.* **2.** to remove or pull off: *to strip bark from a tree, to strip off one's clothes.* **3.** to take away the rights, honors, or possessions of; divest. **4.** to rob or plunder: *The burglars stripped the house.* **5.** to damage or break the threads or teeth of (a bolt, gear, screw, or the like). —*v.i.* to undress. [Old English *-strīepan* (in the compound *bestrīepan*) to rob, plunder.] —**strip′per,** *n.*

strip[2] (strip) *n.* **1.** a long, narrow piece of something: *a strip of paper, a strip of land.* **2.** see **airstrip. 3.** see **comic strip.** [Probably a form of *stripe*[1].]

stripe[1] (strīp) *n.* **1.** a long, narrow band that is different in color or texture from the material or surface around it: *The cloth had white stripes on a red background.* **2.** any of various strips of cloth worn on the sleeve of a military uniform to indicate rank, length of service, or some other distinction. **3.** a particular kind of character; sort: *a person of a generous stripe.* —*v.t.,* **striped, strip·ing.** to mark with a stripe or stripes. [Possibly from Middle Dutch *strīpe* a long, narrow band, streak.]

stripe[2] (strīp) *n.* a stroke or lash, as with a rod or whip. [Of uncertain origin.]

striped (strīpt, strī′pid) *adj.* having or marked with a stripe or stripes: *a striped material.*

strip·ling (strip′ling) *n.* a youth; lad.

stript (stript) a past tense and past participle of **strip**[1].

strive (strīv) *v.i.,* **strove** or **strived, striv·en** (striv′ən) **striv·ing.** to make a great or strenuous effort.

strode (strōd) the past tense of **stride.**

stroke[1] (strōk) *n.* **1.** the act of striking; blow: *He split the wood with one stroke of the ax.* **2.** an action or event having a powerful or unexpected effect: *a stroke of misfortune.* **3.** a brilliant or inspired act, achievement, or idea: *a stroke of genius.* **4.** the sound produced by striking: *We heard the stroke of the gong.* **5.** time indicated by striking, as of a clock: *They left at the stroke of three.* **6.** a single unbroken or complete movement, as of the hand, an instrument, or something held in the hand: *the stroke of an oar.* **7.** a mark made by a pen, pencil, brush, or other implement: *He finished the drawing with a few strokes of the pen.* **8.** a sudden weakness or paralysis, with or without loss of consciousness, caused by rupture or blockage of blood vessels in the brain; apoplexy. **9.** a combination of repeated arm and leg movements for moving the body through water in swimming. **10.** *Sports.* **a.** the act or instance of striking the ball, as in golf or tennis. **b.** the manner in which this is done. **11.** a beat, as of the heart. **12.** the rower who sets the rhythm for the other oarsmen. —*v.t.,* **stroked, strok·ing.** (of a rower) to set the rhythm for (the other oarsmen). [Middle English *stroke* the act of striking.]

stroke² (strōk) *v.t.,* **stroked, strok·ing.** to rub gently or caressingly with the hand, usually repeatedly and in the same direction: *She stroked the puppy's head.* —*n.* a light, caressing movement of the hand. [Old English *strācian* to rub gently with the hand.]

stroll (strōl) *v.i.* to walk in a leisurely or idle manner: *We strolled through the park.* —*v.t.* to walk along or through in a leisurely or idle manner. —*n.* a leisurely walk.

stroll·er (strō′lər) *n.* **1.** a small baby carriage in which a child sits and is wheeled about. **2.** a person who strolls.

strong (strông) *adj.* **1.** having great muscular power; physically powerful: *strong arms, a strong athlete.* **2.** having good health: *I don't think she's strong enough to go out yet.* **3.** having or using great influence, power, or authority: *a strong ruler, a strong government.* **4.** able to resist or withstand attack, strain, stress, or force: *a strong fort, a strong piece of furniture.* **5.** firm in mind, character, will, or purpose; morally powerful or courageous: *He's strong enough to resist the temptation to cheat.* **6.** persuasive or effective; convincing: *a strong argument.* **7.** having a sharp, bitter, or offensive taste or odor: *a strong cheese, a strong tobacco.* **8.** moving with great force or speed: *strong winds, a strong undertow.* **9.** having a great degree of intensity, force, or power: *a strong smell.* **10.** containing much alcohol. **11.** having a large amount of proper or essential ingredients: *strong tea.* **12.** having a specified numerical force: *an army 10,000 strong.* —*adv.* in a strong manner; vigorously; powerfully. —**strong′ly,** *adv.*

strong·box (strông′boks′) *n. pl.,* **strong·box·es.** a strongly made chest or safe, used for storing money, documents, and other valuables.

strong·hold (strông′hōld′) *n.* **1.** a place fortified against attack or danger. **2.** a place where a particular idea or way of thinking is predominant or strong.

stron·ti·um (stron′shē əm, stron′tē əm) *n.* a soft, silvery metallic element, widely used in compounds for fireworks or flares, and sometimes in alloys. Symbol: **Sr**

strontium 90, a radioactive isotope of strontium with a half-life of twenty-eight years, used in radiotherapy and nuclear batteries. It is found in dangerous amounts in fallout from nuclear explosions.

strop (strop) *n.* a flexible strip of material, such as leather or canvas, used to sharpen razors. —*v.t.,* **stropped, strop·ping.** to sharpen on a strop.

stro·phe (strō′fē) *n.* a group of lines of poetry; stanza.

strove (strōv) a past tense of **strive.**

struck (struk) the past tense and a past participle of **strike.**

struc·tur·al (struk′chər əl) *adj.* **1.** of or relating to structure: *a structural weakness in a building.* **2.** used in or necessary to building or construction: *a structural beam.* —**struc′tur·al·ly,** *adv.*

struc·ture (struk′chər) *n.* **1.** anything that is built or constructed, such as a building or bridge. **2.** the way in which something is built, arranged, or organized: *the structure of a society, the grammatical structure of a language.* **3.** the arrangement or interrelation of the parts or elements that make up a thing: *to study the structure of a cell.* **4.** an organized body or combination of connected and dependent parts or elements: *The brain is a complex structure.* —*v.t.,* **struc·tured, struc·tur·ing.** to build or construct: *to structure a bridge.*

strug·gle (strug′əl) *v.i.,* **strug·gled, strug·gling. 1.** to make a great effort; strive: *He struggled to pass his final examinations.* **2.** to make one's way with great effort: *The children struggled through the heavy snow drifts.* **3.** to fight; battle: *The two dogs struggled for the bone.* —*n.* **1.** a very great or strenuous effort: *It was a struggle for her to understand the arithmetic problem.* **2.** a battle or fight: *The suspected thief gave up without a struggle.*

strum (strum) *v.,* **strummed, strum·ming.** —*v.t.* to play, especially in an idle, monotonous, or unskillful manner: *to strum a banjo, to strum a tune.* —*v.i.* to play a stringed musical instrument, especially in an idle, monotonous, or unskillful manner. —*n.* the act or sound of strumming. —**strum′mer,** *n.*

strum·pet (strum′pit) *n.* a prostitute.

strung (strung) the past tense and past participle of **string.**

strut¹ (strut) *v.i.,* **strut·ted, strut·ting.** to walk in a vain, pompous, or arrogant manner. —*n.* a vain, pompous, or arrogant way of walking. [Old English *strūtian* to stand stiffly, be rigid.] —**strut′ter,** *n.*

strut² (strut) *n.* a bar, brace, or other supporting piece in an architectural framework. —*v.t.,* **strut·ted, strut·ting.** to brace or support with a strut or struts. [Probably from *strut¹*; because this supporting piece is rigid.]

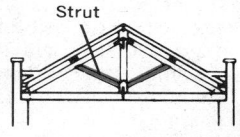

Strut

Strut²

strych·nine (strik′nin, strik′nīn) *n.* a very bitter, colorless drug, used as a rat poison and in medicine as a tonic.

St. Thomas, the westernmost of the Virgin Islands, belonging to the United States.

Stu·art (stoo′ərt, styoo′ərt) *n.* **1.** the royal family that ruled Scotland from 1371 to 1603, and Scotland and England from 1603 to 1714. **2.** a member of this family. **3. Gilbert.** 1755–1828, U.S. painter. **4. James Ew·ell Brown** (yoo′əl). 1833–1864, Confederate general, known as Jeb Stuart. **5. Mary.** see **Mary, Queen of Scots.**

stub (stub) *n.* **1.** a short piece that remains after something has been worn away, removed, cut, or broken off: *a cigar stub, the stub of a pencil.* **2.** the remaining or detachable portion, as of a check, ticket, or bill, that provides a record or receipt of payment. **3.** a short, thick, projecting piece or part. **4.** the stump of a tree trunk or plant stem. —*v.t.,* **stubbed, stub·bing.** to strike (one's toe or foot) accidentally against something: *He stubbed his toe on a chair in the dark.*

stub·ble (stub′əl) *n.* **1.** short stalks of grain and certain other plants left standing in the ground after the crop has been harvested. **2.** anything resembling this, such as a short growth of beard. —**stub′bly,** *adv.*

stub·born (stub′ərn) *adj.* **1.** not giving in to argument, persuasion, or reason; obstinate: *a stubborn person.* **2.** done or carried on in an unyielding, obstinate way: *His stubborn refusal to answer questions angered the lawyer.* **3.** hard to overcome or deal with: *a stubborn cough.* —**stub′born·ly,** *adv.* —**stub′born·ness,** *n.*

stub·by (stub′ē) *adj.,* **stub·bi·er, stub·bi·est. 1.** short and thick: *a stubby tail, stubby toes.* **2.** short, thick, and bristly:

at; āpe; cär; end; mē; it; īce; hot; ōld; fôrk; wood; fōol; oil; out; up; turn; sing; thin; **this**; hw in white; zh in treasure. The symbol ə stands for the sound of **a** in about, **e** in taken, **i** in pencil, **o** in lemon, and **u** in circus.

S

a stubby beard. **3.** covered with or consisting of stubs or stubble: *a stubby field.* —**stub′bi·ness,** *n.*

stuc·co (stuk′ō) *n. pl.,* **stuc·cos** or **stuc·coes. 1.** plaster or cement used for covering outside walls or for ornamenting inside walls. **2.** ornamental work made of stucco. —*v.t.,* **stuc·coed, stuc·co·ing.** to cover or ornament with stucco: *to stucco a wall.*

stuck (stuk) the past tense and past participle of **stick².**

stuck-up (stuk′up′) *adj. Informal.* conceited or snobbish.

stud¹ (stud) *n.* **1.** a nail head, knob, or similar object, usually of metal, fixed to and sticking out from a surface, used especially as an ornament. **2.** an ornamental fastener resembling a button, used on the front of men's formal shirts. **3.** a vertical post, as in the framework of a wall, to which horizontal boards, laths, and the like are nailed. —*v.t.,* **stud·ded, stud·ding. 1.** to set or ornament with studs: *to stud a bracelet with diamonds.* **2.** to be scattered or spread over: *Stars studded the sky.* **3.** to provide with or support by a vertical post or posts. [Old English *studu* post, support.]

stud² (stud) *n.* **1.** a male animal, especially a horse, kept for breeding. **2.** a group of animals, especially horses, selected and raised for breeding. [Old English *stōd.*]

stu·dent (stōōd′ənt, styōōd′ənt) *n.* **1.** a person attending a school, college, or university. **2.** a person devoted to study or investigation of a particular subject: *a student of language.*

stud·ied (stud′ēd) *adj.* carefully planned; deliberate; intentional: *We were surprised by his studied rudeness.* —**stud′ied·ly,** *adv.* —**stud′ied·ness,** *n.*

stu·di·o (stōō′dē ō′, styōō′dē ō′) *n. pl.,* **stu·di·os. 1.** a place where an artist or photographer works. **2.** a place for instruction in and practice of one of the performing arts: *a dance studio.* **3.** a place where motion pictures are filmed. **4.** a place where radio and television programs are performed or recorded.

studio couch, an upholstered couch, usually without arms, that can be used as a bed.

stu·di·ous (stōō′dē əs, styōō′dē əs) *adj.* **1.** given to or fond of study and learning. **2.** showing careful or earnest consideration or attention: *a studious effort to find a summer job.* —**stu′di·ous·ly,** *adv.* —**stu′di·ous·ness,** *n.*

stud·y (stud′ē) *v.,* **stud·ied, stud·y·ing.** —*v.t.* **1.** to apply the mind in order to gain a knowledge of; try to learn: *to study medicine, to study history.* **2.** to look at closely or critically; examine: *to study a map.* **3.** to look or inquire into; investigate: *The mayor appointed a committee to study ways of reducing air pollution.* **4.** to give careful thought and consideration to: *I will study the matter and give you my opinion.* **5.** to try to learn by memorizing: *The actor studied the part before the audition.* —*v.i.* **1.** to apply the mind in order to gain knowledge: *to study for a test.* **2.** to be a student: *He plans to study for the ministry.* —*n. pl.,* **stud·ies. 1.** the act or process of studying: *His many hours of study helped him pass the test.* **2.** a careful or critical examination or investigation. **3.** something that is studied or to be studied; branch of learning. **4.** a room in a house used or set apart for study, reading, writing, or the like. **5.** a sketch, design, or plan for an artistic work, or for some detail or portion of it.

stuff (stuf) *n.* **1.** the substance or material that a thing is made of: *What kind of stuff is in this pillow?* **2.** an indefinite or vague substance or matter: *She went to the cleaners to see if they could get the black stuff off her skirt.* **3.** basic character or qualities: *They thought he would surrender, but being made of sterner stuff, he fought on.* **4.** worthless or useless matter or things: *That closet is full of stuff.* —*v.t.* **1.** to pack or cram full; fill: *to stuff a trunk*

with clothes. **2.** to force or thrust (something) tightly, as into a container: *to stuff papers into an envelope.* **3.** to block or stop up by thrusting something tightly in; plug: *He stuffed his ears with cotton.* **4.** to fill with too much food: *Stop stuffing yourself.* **5.** *Cooking.* to fill (poultry or other food) with stuffing. **6.** to fill the skin of (a dead animal) to restore its natural appearance. **7.** to put fraudulent votes into (a ballot box).

stuffed shirt *Informal.* a person who is extremely pompous or formal and has a great feeling of self-importance.

stuff·ing (stuf′ing) *n.* **1.** something used for filling or packing something: *The stuffing is coming out of the pillow.* **2.** a food mixture, as of seasoned bread crumbs or rice, used to fill poultry or other food.

stuff·y (stuf′ē) *adj.,* **stuff·i·er, stuff·i·est. 1.** lacking fresh air; close: *a stuffy room.* **2.** very strait-laced; formal; pompous: *a stuffy manner.* **3.** stopped up: *a stuffy nose.* **4.** lacking freshness or interest; dull; boring: *a stuffy speech.* —**stuff′i·ly,** *adv.* —**stuff′i·ness,** *n.*

stul·ti·fy (stul′tə fī′) *v.t.,* **stul·ti·fied, stul·ti·fy·ing.** to make useless, weak, or foolish: *Boring teachers stultified his ambition to learn.* —**stul′ti·fi·ca′tion,** *n.*

stum·ble (stum′bəl) *v.i.,* **stum·bled, stum·bling. 1.** to lose one's balance or trip while walking or running: *She stumbled over the cat.* **2.** to move or walk unsteadily or awkwardly: *He stumbled around the dark room until he found the light switch.* **3.** to behave, act, or speak in a clumsy, awkward way: *to stumble over a difficult word, to stumble through a speech.* **4.** to make a mistake or blunder. **5.** to discover accidentally or unexpectedly: *The detective stumbled on an important clue while searching the scene of the crime.* —*n.* **1.** the act of stumbling. **2.** a mistake or blunder; slip. —**stum′bling·ly,** *adv.*

stumbling block, something that stands in the way of or prevents progress; hindrance; obstruction.

stump (stump) *n.* **1.** the lower part of a tree trunk or plant stem remaining in the ground after the main part is cut off. **2.** the part of anything that remains after the main or more important part has been removed, especially the remaining part of an amputated arm or leg. **3.** a place or platform for a political speech. —*v.t.* **1.** *Informal.* to cause to be at a loss; perplex; baffle: *This problem has really stumped me.* **2.** to make political speeches in: *The candidate for senator stumped the southern part of the state.* —*v.i.* **1.** to walk stiffly, heavily, or noisily. **2.** to travel about making political speeches.

stump·y (stum′pē) *adj.,* **stump·i·er, stump·i·est. 1.** short and thick like a stump: *a stumpy tail.* **2.** (of land) abounding with tree stumps. —**stump′i·ness,** *n.*

stun (stun) *v.t.,* **stunned, stun·ning. 1.** to daze or make unconscious, as by a blow. **2.** to overwhelm, shock, or bewilder: *She was stunned by the unexpected news.*

stung (stung) the past tense and past participle of **sting.**

stunk (stungk) a past tense and the past participle of **stink.**

stun·ning (stun′ning) *adj.* **1.** *Informal.* extremely attractive or good-looking: *a stunning person, a stunning dress.* **2.** that stuns, such as a blow or loud noise. —**stun′ning·ly,** *adv.*

stunt¹ (stunt) *v.t.* **1.** to stop or hinder the growth or development of: *You will stunt the tree if you don't give it enough room to grow.* **2.** to check or hinder (growth, development, or progress): *A poor diet stunted the child's growth.* [From dialectal English *stunt* dwarfed in growth.]

stunt² (stunt) *Informal. n.* an act which is done to attract attention, especially one requiring or showing strength, skill, or daring: *She performed dangerous stunts on the high trapeze.* —*v.i.* to perform a stunt or stunts. [Of uncertain origin.]

stu·pe·fac·tion (stoo'pə fak'shən, styoo'pə fak'shən) *n.* **1.** the act of stupefying or the state of being stupefied. **2.** overwhelming astonishment; amazement.

stu·pe·fy (stoo'pə fī', styoo'pə fī') *v.t.*, **stu·pe·fied, stu·pe·fy·ing. 1.** to make stupid, senseless, or inactive; dull the senses of: *The blow stupefied him.* **2.** to amaze or astound; overwhelm: *The daring stunt stupefied the audience.*

stu·pen·dous (stoo pen'dəs, styoo pen'dəs) *adj.* causing amazement or astonishment; overwhelming. —**stu·pen'dous·ly,** *adv.* —**stu·pen'dous·ness,** *n.*

stu·pid (stoo'pid, styoo'pid) *adj.* **1.** lacking ordinary intelligence; slow-witted; dumb. **2.** dull; uninteresting; boring: *That was a stupid movie.* **3.** showing or characterized by a lack of intelligence or common sense: *a stupid answer.* —**stu'pid·ly,** *adv.* —**stu'pid·ness,** *n.*

stu·pid·i·ty (stoo pid'ə tē, styoo pid'ə tē) *n. pl.,* **stu·pid·i·ties. 1.** lack of intelligence or common sense. **2.** a stupid statement, act, or the like.

stu·por (stoo'pər, styoo'pər) *n.* a partly conscious condition; lessening of the power to feel: *She was in a stupor after the operation.*

stur·dy (stur'dē) *adj.,* **stur·di·er, stur·di·est. 1.** having strength; strong; hardy: *sturdy pioneers.* **2.** solidly built. **3.** hard to overcome; not yielding: *The enemy put up a sturdy defense.* —**stur'di·ly,** *adv.* —**stur'di·ness,** *n.*

stur·geon (stur'jən) *n. pl.,* **stur·geons** or **stur·geon.** any of a group of fish found in fresh and salt waters, having rows of bony, pointed scales, and valued as a source of caviar.

Sturgeon

stut·ter (stut'ər) *v.i.* to speak haltingly with frequent, repeated sounds or syllables; stammer. —*v.t.* to utter with a series of repeated sounds or syllables: *He stuttered an apology.* —**stut'ter·er,** *n.* —**stut'ter·ing·ly,** *adv.*

Stutt·gart (stut'gärt) *n.* a city in southwestern West Germany. Pop. (1970), 633,200.

Stuy·ve·sant, Peter (stī'və sənt) 1592–1672, Dutch governor of the colony of New Netherland.

St. Vi·tus' dance (vī'təs) see **Saint Vitus' dance.**

sty[1] (stī) *n. pl.,* **sties. 1.** a pen or enclosure where pigs are kept; pigpen; pigsty. **2.** any filthy place; hovel. [Old English *stī, stig* hall, pigpen.]

sty[2] (stī) *n. pl.,* **sties.** an inflamed swelling on the edge of the eyelid, resembling a small boil. [From earlier *styany,* going back to Old English *stīgend* rising (in the sense of "swelling") + *ēage* eye.]

Styg·i·an (stij'ē ən) *adj.* **1.** of, relating to, or characteristic of the mythological river Styx, or the lower world in which it flows. **2.** like the river Styx; black or gloomy.

style (stīl) *n.* **1.** a particular mode or fashion, especially of dress: *Her coat is in the latest style.* **2.** elegance; tastefulness: *to live in style, to dance with style.* **3.** a particular way of doing or making something: *poetry in the style of Wordsworth, a building in classic Greek style.* **4.** see **stylus** (*def. 1*). **5.** *Botany.* the part of the pistil of a flower, shaped like a stalk, extending from the ovary to the stigma. **6.** special rules, as of spelling, punctuation, or capitalization, followed by a particular author, publisher, or printer. —*v.t.,* **styled, styl·ing. 1.** to design according to a mode or fashion: *to style a fall wardrobe.* **2.** to change in order to conform to an accepted or particular style of printing or writing.

styl·ish (stī'lish) *adj.* according to current or accepted style; fashionable. —**styl'ish·ly,** *adv.* —**styl'ish·ness,** *n.*

styl·ist (stī'list) *n.* **1.** a writer or speaker who is distinguished for the excellence of his style. **2.** a person who designs or advises on styles, as in clothing or furnishings.

sty·lis·tic (stī lis'tik) *adj.* of or relating to style. —**sty·lis'ti·cal·ly,** *adv.*

styl·ize (stī'līz) *v.t.,* **styl·ized, styl·iz·ing.** to make (something, such as an artistic work) follow the rules of a particular style.

sty·lus (stī'ləs) *n. pl.,* **sty·li** (stī'lī) or **sty·lus·es. 1.** an instrument with a pointed or rounded head, used to write on soft materials, such as wax. **2.** a phonograph needle that transforms vibrations from the grooves on a record into an electric current that is amplified and turned into sound.

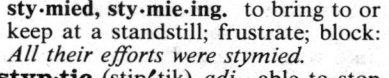

Stylus

sty·mie (stī'mē) *also,* **sty·my.** *v.t.,* **sty·mied, sty·mie·ing.** to bring to or keep at a standstill; frustrate; block: *All their efforts were stymied.*

styp·tic (stip'tik) *adj.* able to stop bleeding by contracting the tissues; astringent. —*n.* any styptic substance, such as alum.

sty·rene (stī'rēn) *n.* a colorless, liquid hydrocarbon, used especially in making plastics and synthetic rubber.

Styx (stiks) *n. Greek Mythology.* the river surrounding Hades, across which Charon ferried the souls of the dead.

sua·sion (swā'zhən) *n.* the act or instance of convincing or urging; persuasion.

suave (swäv) *adj.* having or showing a smooth, polite manner. —**suave'ly,** *adv.* —**suave'ness, suav'i·ty,** *n.*

sub (sub) *Informal. n.* **1.** see **substitute. 2.** see **submarine.** —*v.i.,* **subbed, sub·bing.** to act as a substitute.

sub- *prefix* **1.** under; below; beneath: *submarine.* **2.** nearly; less than: *subtropical.* **3.** used to express a further division or distinction: *subdivide.* **4.** partially; slightly: *subacid.* **5.** lower in position: *subdeacon.* **6.** of minor importance or size: *subcommittee, subhead.*

sub. 1. substitute. **2.** subscription. **3.** suburban.

sub·al·tern (sub ôl'tərn) *n.* **1.** a person of subordinate rank or position; aide. **2.** an officer in the British army, ranking below a captain. —*adj.* having a subordinate rank or position.

sub·a·tom·ic (sub'ə tom'ik) *adj.* of or relating to something smaller than an atom or something happening within an atom.

subatomic particle, any of a number of particles smaller than an atom that are the most basic constituents of nature yet known. Electrons, protons, and neutrons are subatomic particles. Also, **elementary particle.**

sub·com·mit·tee (sub'kə mit'ē) *n.* a committee formed from and acting under a main committee for some special purpose.

sub·con·scious (sub kon'shəs) *adj.* **1.** existing in the mind but only partially perceived by the consciousness: *a subconscious wish.* **2.** not completely conscious. —*n.* the part of the mind that retains experiences and feelings that are difficult to bring back to awareness, often because awareness of them would be painful or produce anxiety. —**sub·con'scious·ly,** *adv.* —**sub·con'scious·ness,** *n.*

at; āpe; cär; end; mē; it; īce; hot; ōld; fôrk; wood; fool; oil; out; up; turn; sing; thin; this; hw in white; zh in treasure. The symbol ə stands for the sound of **a** in about, **e** in taken, **i** in pencil, **o** in lemon, and **u** in circus.

S

sub·con·ti·nent (sub kont′ən ənt) *n.* a large land mass that is smaller than a continent, especially a large section of a continent regarded as a distinct geographical or political unit: *the Indian subcontinent of Asia.*

sub·con·tract (*n.,* sub kon′trakt; *v.,* sub′ken trakt′) *n.* a contract made after another contract, carrying out all or part of the original contract: *Our architect gave a subcontract to a plumber to install all the bathrooms in the house.* —*v.t.* to contract to carry out (all or part of a previous contract).

sub·cu·ta·ne·ous (sub′kyōo tā′nē əs) *adj.* under the surface of the skin. —**sub′cu·ta·ne·ous·ly,** *adv.*

sub·di·vide (sub′di vīd′, sub′di vīd′) *v.,* **sub·di·vid·ed, sub·di·vid·ing.** —*v.t.* to divide or separate (a part of a whole) after a previous division: *to subdivide a tract of land into building lots.* —*v.i.* to be divided again after previous divisions.

sub·di·vi·sion (sub′di vizh′ən, sub′di vizh′ən) *n.* **1.** the act of subdividing or the state of being subdivided. **2.** one of the parts into which a larger part has been divided. **3.** an area of land divided into lots for building homes.

sub·due (səb dōo′, səb dyōo′) *v.t.,* **sub·dued, sub·du·ing. 1.** to bring under control; overcome: *The police subdued the angry crowd.* **2.** to bring into subjection; conquer: *to subdue an enemy.* **3.** to reduce the intensity, strength, or force of; tone down; soften: *The lampshades subdued the light in the room.* —**sub·du′er,** *n.*

sub·fam·i·ly (sub fam′ə lē, sub′fam′ə lē) *n. pl.,* **sub·fam·i·lies.** a subdivision of a family: *a subfamily of plants.*

sub·head (sub′hed′) *n.* **1.** a subordinate heading or title, as in a book, chapter, or article. **2.** one of the subdivisions into which a main heading or title is broken up.

sub·head·ing (sub′hed′ing) *n.* another word for **subhead.**

sub·hu·man (sub hyōo′mən) *adj.* **1.** belonging to or characteristic of any living thing considered to be lower than the human species. **2.** nearly human.

subj. 1. subject. **2.** subjective. **3.** subjunctive.

sub·ject (*n., adj.,* sub′jikt; *v.,* səb jekt′) *n.* **1.** something that is the basis of thought, discussion, or investigation; topic: *The subject under discussion today is the causes of the American Revolution.* **2.** a branch or field of study: *English was my favorite subject in school.* **3.** *Grammar.* a word, phrase, or clause that performs the action of the verb or, if the verb is in the passive voice, receives the action of the verb. In the sentences *He ran fast* and *He was hit, He* is the subject. **4.** a person or thing that is under the authority, control, or influence of another: *The people were loyal subjects of the king.* **5.** a person or thing that undergoes or experiences something: *The scientist used mice as subjects in the experiments. The mayor was the subject of much criticism.* —*adj.* **1.** under the authority, control, or influence of: *The employees are subject to the rules of the company.* **2.** liable; prone: *My sister is subject to all kinds of allergies.* **3.** dependent or conditional upon: *You may go, subject to your father's approval.* —*v.t.* **1.** to bring under influence or control. **2.** to cause to undergo or experience; expose: *to subject a person to ridicule.*

sub·jec·tion (səb jek′shən) *n.* **1.** the act of bringing under the control or influence of another. **2.** the condition of being under the control or influence of another.

sub·jec·tive (səb jek′tiv) *adj.* **1.** of, existing in, or coming from the person who is thinking, based solely on the individual's own feelings, thoughts, and experiences. **2.** in literature and art, based on or expressing the feelings, thoughts, and experiences of the artist or author. **3.** *Grammar.* designating the case of the subject of a verb. —**sub·jec′tive·ly,** *adv.*

sub·jec·tiv·i·ty (sub′jek tiv′ə tē) *n.* the quality, condition, or tendency of viewing things solely in relation to one's own feelings, thoughts, or experiences.

subject matter 1. the main body of facts or ideas under discussion or consideration. **2.** the body of ideas presented in a book, speech, or the like, as distinguished from form or style.

sub·ju·gate (sub′jə gāt′) *v.t.,* **sub·ju·gat·ed, sub·ju·gat·ing.** to bring or have under one's control or dominance; subdue. [Late Latin *subjugātus,* the past participle of *subjugāre* to bring under the yoke; referring to the ancient Roman custom of forcing defeated soldiers to crawl under a yoke to symbolize their defeat.] —**sub′ju·ga′tion,** *n.*

sub·junc·tive (səb jungk′tiv) *n.* **1.** the mood of a verb that indicates an act or state as possible, conditional, contrary to fact, or dependent, rather than as actual. In the sentence *If I were you, I would not go, were* is in the subjunctive. **2.** a verb form in this mood. —*adj.* of or relating to this mood.

sub·king·dom (sub king′dəm, sub′king′dəm) *n.* a subdivision of a kingdom: *an animal subkingdom.*

sub·lease (*n.,* sub′lēs′; *v.,* sub lēs′) *n.* a lease granted by a tenant transferring all or part of his rights under a lease to another person. —*v.t.,* **sub·leased, sub·leas·ing.** to give or obtain a sublease for.

sub·let (sub let′, sub′let′) *v.t.,* **sub·let, sub·let·ting.** to give or obtain a sublease for (some property or business); sublease.

sub·li·mate (*v.,* sub′lə māt′; *n.,* sub′lə mit, sub′lə māt′) *v.t.,* **sub·li·mat·ed, sub·li·mat·ing. 1.** to act upon (something) so as to refine or purify. **2.** to subject (thoughts or impulses) to sublimation. **3.** to sublime (a substance). —*n.* any material resulting when a substance is sublimed.

sub·li·ma·tion (sub′lə mā′shən) *n.* **1.** the act or process of sublimating or subliming. **2.** something that has been sublimated or sublimed.

sub·lime (səb līm′) *adj.* noble or grand in manner, expression, or appearance; lofty: *sublime scenery, a sublime poem.* —*n.* something that is noble or grand in manner, expression, or appearance. —*v.,* **sub·limed, sub·lim·ing.** —*v.t.* to cause (a substance) to change directly from a solid to a gaseous state, or from a gaseous to a solid state, without passing through a liquid state; sublimate. —*v.i.* to change directly from a solid to a gaseous state, or from a gaseous to a solid state, without first becoming a liquid. Mothballs and dry ice sublime.

sub·lim·i·ty (səb lim′ə tē) *n.* the state or quality of being sublime; loftiness; grandeur.

sub·ma·chine gun (sub′mə shēn′) a portable, lightweight, automatic or semiautomatic gun that is designed for shooting from the hip or shoulder.

sub·ma·rine (*n.,* sub′mə rēn′; *adj.,* sub′mə rēn′) *n.* **1.** a ship that can go under water, used as an attack or reconnaissance vessel, or for oceanographic research. **2.** a hero sandwich. —*adj.* below the surface of the sea: *submarine plants.*

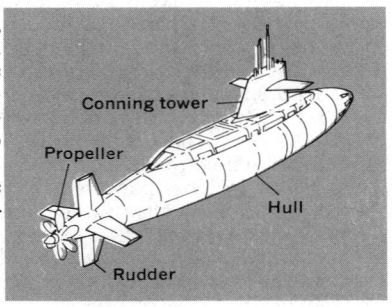

Conning tower
Propeller
Hull
Rudder

Submarine

sub·merge (səb murj′) *v.,* **submerged, sub·merg·ing.** —*v.t.* **1.** to place under or cover with some liquid, especially water:

The flood almost submerged the town. **2.** to overshadow; obscure. —*v.i.* to sink out of sight by going beneath the surface of a liquid: *The submarine submerged quickly.* —**sub·mer′gence,** *n.*

sub·merse (səb murs′) *v.t.,* **sub·mersed, sub·mers·ing.** another word for **submerge.** —**sub·mer·sion** (səb mur′zhən), *n.*

sub·mers·i·ble (səb mur′sə bəl) *adj.* that can be submerged.

sub·mis·sion (səb mish′ən) *n.* **1.** the act of yielding to some power or authority. **2.** humbleness; meekness. **3.** the act of presenting something for consideration or decision.

sub·mis·sive (səb mis′iv) *adj.* tending to yield to power or authority; meek; humble. —**sub·mis′sive·ly,** *adv.* —**sub·mis′sive·ness,** *n.*

sub·mit (səb mit′) *v.,* **sub·mit·ted, sub·mit·ting.** —*v.i.* to yield oneself to some power or authority; give up; surrender: *The robber submitted to the police. The rebels swore never to submit.* —*v.t.* **1.** to present for the consideration or decision of another or others: *Sally submitted her term paper three weeks late.* **2.** to put forward as an opinion or proposition; propose: *I submit that the defendant is not guilty.*

sub·nor·mal (sub nôr′məl) *adj.* less than usual, average, or normal, especially in intelligence. —**sub′nor·mal′i·ty,** *n.* —**sub·nor′mal·ly,** *adv.*

sub·or·bit·al (sub ôr′bit əl) *adj.* (of a missile, spacecraft, space flight, or the like) not making a complete orbit.

sub·or·der (sub′ôr′dər) *n.* a subdivision of an order.

sub·or·di·nate (*adj., n.,* sə bôr′də nit; *v.,* sə bôr′də-nāt′) *adj.* **1.** lower in rank, grade, class, or the like: *a subordinate officer.* **2.** having less importance; dependent; secondary. —*n.* a person or thing that is subordinate. —*v.t.,* **sub·or·di·nat·ed, sub·or·di·nat·ing.** to cause to be, or treat as, subordinate. —**sub·or′di·na′tion,** *n.*

subordinate clause, another term for **dependent clause.**

subordinating conjunction, a conjunction, such as *if* or *when,* that introduces a dependent clause.

sub·orn (sə bôrn′) *v.t.* **1.** to cause (a witness) to give false testimony in a court of law. **2.** to influence (a person) to commit a misdeed, especially bribery. —**sub·or·na·tion** (sub′ôr nā′shən), *n.* —**sub·orn′er,** *n.*

sub·poe·na (sə pē′nə) *also,* **sub·pe·na.** *n.* an official document ordering a person to appear in a court of law; summons. —*v.t.,* **sub·poe·naed, sub·poe·na·ing.** to summon to a court of law by a subpoena.

sub·scribe (səb skrīb′) *v.,* **sub·scribed, sub·scrib·ing.** —*v.i.* **1.** to agree to receive and pay for: *to subscribe to a magazine, to subscribe for theater tickets.* **2.** to promise to give or contribute a definite amount of money: *to subscribe to a hospital drive.* **3.** to sign one's name at the end of something to signify one's approval or agreement: *He subscribed to the petition demanding lower bus fares.* **4.** to give one's assent or approval: *I heartily subscribe to your suggestion.* —*v.t.* to promise to give or pay: *Each member subscribed twenty-five dollars to the charity.* —**sub·scrib′er,** *n.*

sub·script (sub′skript′) *n.* a character, as a number, letter, or symbol, usually of relatively small size, printed or written beneath or on the lower half of a line. In the formula H_2O, 2 is a subscript. —*adj.* printed or written beneath or on the lower half of the line.

sub·scrip·tion (səb skrip′shən) *n.* **1.** the right to receive something, obtained by paying a certain sum of money. **2.** a sum of money given or contributed as to a charity. **3.** a fund raised through the contributions of a number of persons.

sub·sec·tion (sub′sek′shən) *n.* a part or division of a section.

sub·se·quent (sub′sə kwənt) *adj.* coming or happening after or as a result: *Subsequent events proved that she had made a good choice.* —**sub′se·quent·ly,** *adv.*

sub·serve (səb surv′) *v.t.,* **sub·served, sub·serv·ing.** to be important or useful in assisting (someone or something).

sub·ser·vi·ent (səb sur′vē ənt) *adj.* **1.** slavishly submissive or obedient in behavior or attitude. **2.** important or useful in promoting an end or purpose. —**sub·ser′vi·ence,** *n.* —**sub·ser′vi·ent·ly,** *adv.*

sub·set (sub′set′) *n.* Mathematics. a set whose members are all contained within another given set. The subsets of the set {a,b} are {a,b}, {a}, {b}, and {0}.

sub·side (səb sīd′) *v.i.,* **sub·sid·ed, sub·sid·ing.** **1.** to sink to a low or lower level, especially to the normal or usual level: *The flood waters subsided.* **2.** to decrease in volume, activity, or intensity; abate: *After a short time Jerry's anger at her for being late subsided.* —**sub·sid·ence** (səb sīd′əns, sub′səd əns), *n.*

sub·sid·i·ar·y (səb sid′ē er′ē) *adj.* **1.** serving to help, assist, or supplement. **2.** subordinate or secondary. **3.** relating to, consisting of, or depending on a subsidy or subsidies. —*n. pl.,* **sub·sid·i·ar·ies. 1.** a company owned or controlled by another company, usually resulting from the parent company's ownership of all or a majority of the other company's stock. **2.** any subsidiary person or thing.

sub·si·dize (sub′sə dīz′) *v.t.,* **sub·si·dized, sub·si·diz·ing.** to aid or support with a subsidy: *The government subsidizes farmers who agree not to produce certain crops.* —**sub′si·di·za′tion,** *n.* —**sub′si·diz′er,** *n.*

sub·si·dy (sub′sə dē) *n. pl.,* **sub·si·dies.** a contribution, especially of money, often given by a government as a supplement or assistance.

sub·sist (səb sist′) *v.i.* **1.** to maintain existence; support life; exist: *The lost explorers barely managed to subsist on the fruits and berries they could find.* **2.** to exist or continue to exist; remain; abide: *The custom of marriage has subsisted through the ages.*

sub·sist·ence (səb sis′təns) *n.* **1.** the state or condition of supporting life; continued existence. **2.** the means of supporting life; support; livelihood.

sub·soil (sub′soil′) *n.* the layer of soil lying immediately beneath the surface soil.

sub·son·ic (sub son′ik) *adj.* of, relating to, or moving at a speed that is less than that of sound.

sub·spe·cies (sub′spē′shēz, sub spē′shēz) *n. pl.,* **sub·spe·cies.** a subdivision of a species, especially a grouping of plants or animals within a species.

sub·stance (sub′stəns) *n.* **1.** that which a thing consists of; matter; material: *Diamonds and graphite are different forms of the same substance.* **2.** material or matter of a particular kind: *a radioactive substance.* **3.** the real or essential thing or part, especially of something written or spoken: *What was the substance of the speech?* **4.** solid quality; density; body: *This thick soup has substance.* **5.** the quality of being real, rather than imaginary: *There is substance to his accusation.* **6.** material possessions; wealth; means: *a man of substance.*

S

at; āpe; cär; end; mē; it; īce; hot; ōld; fôrk; wood; fōōl; oil; out; up; turn; sing; thin; **this;** hw in white; zh in treasure. The symbol ə stands for the sound of **a** in about, **e** in taken, **i** in pencil, **o** in lemon, and **u** in circus.

sub·stand·ard (sub stan′dərd) *adj.* less than or below the usual or normal standard: *The government tried to eliminate substandard housing.*

sub·stan·tial (səb stan′shəl) *adj.* **1.** of considerable amount or importance; ample: *a substantial profit, a substantial meal.* **2.** firmly or strongly based or constructed: *a substantial house.* **3.** having wealth; wealthy: *a substantial businessman.* **4.** having actual existence or form; not imaginary; real. —**sub·stan·ti·al·i·ty** (səb stan′shē al′ə tē), *n.*

sub·stan·tial·ly (səb stan′shə lē) *adv.* **1.** in the main; essentially: *The newspaper story was substantially accurate.* **2.** actually; really. **3.** strongly or solidly; firmly.

sub·stan·ti·ate (səb stan′shē āt′) *v.t.,* **sub·stan·ti·at·ed, sub·stan·ti·at·ing.** to give factual evidence in order to prove; verify: *Can you substantiate his account of the accident?* —**sub·stan′ti·a′tion,** *n.*

sub·stan·tive (sub′stən tiv) *n. Grammar.* a noun or pronoun, or a group of words used as a noun substitute. —*adj.* **1.** *Grammar.* **a.** used as a noun or noun substitute. **b.** denoting the verb of existence, *to be.* **2.** substantial or solid; real. —**sub′stan·tive·ly,** *adv.*

sub·sta·tion (sub′stā′shən) *n.* a subsidiary station, as of a post office.

sub·sti·tute (sub′stə tōōt′, sub′stə tyōōt′) *n.* a person or thing that acts or is used in the place of another. —*v.,* **sub·sti·tut·ed, sub·sti·tut·ing.** —*v.t.* to put in the place of another: *The coach substituted John for Bill at first base.* —*v.i.* to take the place of another: *She substituted for our regular teacher, who was sick.* —*adj.* taking the place of another: *a substitute teacher.*

sub·sti·tu·tion (sub′stə tōō′shən, sub′stə tyōō′shən) *n.* the act of substituting or the state of being substituted.

sub·stra·tum (sub strā′təm, sub strat′əm) *n. pl.,* **sub·stra·ta** (sub strā′tə, sub strat′ə) or **sub·stra·tums.** **1.** a substance that lies under another, especially a layer of earth beneath the surface layer. **2.** a basis or foundation: *Experiments were the substratum for the scientist's theory.*

sub·ter·fuge (sub′tər fyōoj′) *n.* a device or trick used to conceal one's true purpose or to escape a difficult situation.

sub·ter·ra·ne·an (sub′tə rā′nē ən) *adj.* **1.** being, located, or happening below the surface of the earth; underground: *a subterranean tunnel, subterranean life.* **2.** existing out of sight; done secretly: *a subterranean plot.*

sub·ti·tle (sub′tī′təl) *n.* **1.** a secondary or additional title, as of a book or article. **2.** a word or words printed at the bottom of a motion picture screen, used to translate a foreign language being spoken in a film.

sub·tle (sut′əl) *adj.* **1.** having a faint, delicate quality, so as to be nearly impossible to perceive: *a subtle odor, a subtle laugh.* **2.** capable of seeing or understanding fine distinctions; perceptive: *a subtle mind.* **3.** deceitfully cunning; crafty; sly: *a subtle plan to cheat someone.* **4.** difficult to solve or understand: *a subtle problem.* —**sub′tle·ness,** *n.* —**sub′tly,** *adv.*

sub·tle·ty (sut′əl tē) *n. pl.,* **sub·tle·ties.** **1.** the quality of being subtle. **2.** something that is subtle.

sub·tract (səb trakt′) *v.t.* to take away or deduct (a number) from another number: *If you subtract 3 from 7, you have 4.* —*v.i.* to perform the process of subtraction. —**sub·tract′er,** *n.*

sub·trac·tion (səb trak′shən) *n.* the act or process of figuring the difference between two numbers.

sub·trac·tive (səb trak′tiv) *adj.* of or relating to subtraction.

sub·tra·hend (sub′trə hend′) *n.* the number that is to be subtracted from another. In the equation *11 − 4 = 7, 4* is the subtrahend.

sub·trop·i·cal (sub trop′i kəl) *adj.* of or relating to regions bordering on the tropics; having a nearly tropical climate.

sub·trop·ics (sub trop′iks) *n., pl.* subtropical regions.

sub·urb (sub′urb) *n.* **1.** a residential district close to or on the outer edge of a city. **2. the suburbs.** an area consisting of such districts.

sub·ur·ban (sə bur′bən) *adj.* of, relating to, or characteristic of a suburb.

sub·ur·ban·ite (sə bur′bə nīt′) *n.* a person who lives in the suburbs.

sub·ver·sion (səb vur′zhən) *n.* the act of subverting or the state of being subverted.

sub·ver·sive (səb vur′siv) *adj.* attempting or tending to overthrow, undermine, or destroy: *a subversive speech, subversive activities.* —*n.* a person who attempts to overthrow, undermine, or destroy a belief, or a government or other established institution.

sub·vert (səb vurt′) *v.t.* **1.** to bring about the destruction of; overthrow; destroy: *to subvert a dictatorship.* **2.** to undermine the loyalty, faith, or principles of; corrupt. —**sub·vert′er,** *n.*

sub·way (sub′wā′) *n.* **1.** a railway that runs wholly or partly underground, especially one in a large city. **2.** *British.* an underground passage.

suc·ceed (sək sēd′) *v.i.* **1.** to have the hoped for result; turn out well: *Our plan succeeded.* **2.** to accomplish what is attempted or planned; do well: *He succeeded in fixing the broken radio.* **3.** to come next in the place of the person or thing that came before: *After the death of the king, his son succeeded to the throne.* —*v.t.* to take the place of; come next after: *Mary succeeded Harry as treasurer of the club.*

suc·cess (sək ses′) *n.* **1.** a favorable result or ending: *The success of his first novel made him famous.* **2.** the gaining of wealth, position, or fame: *He has had great success in business.* **3.** a person or thing that succeeds or is successful: *The party was a big success.*

suc·cess·ful (sək ses′fəl) *adj.* having, achieving, or resulting in success: *a successful woman, a successful movie.* —**suc·cess′ful·ly,** *adv.* —**suc·cess′ful·ness,** *n.*

suc·ces·sion (sək sesh′ən) *n.* **1.** a group of people or things following one after another in time or place; sequence; series: *The poor man had a succession of misfortunes.* **2.** the coming of one person or thing after another. **3.** the right of being next in line for an office, rank, or the like that is held by another. **4.** the order or line of persons having such a right: *The young prince is next after his older brother in succession to the throne.*

suc·ces·sive (sək ses′iv) *adj.* coming one after another in an uninterrupted order. —**suc·ces′sive·ly,** *adv.* —**suc·ces′sive·ness,** *n.*

suc·ces·sor (sək ses′ər) *n.* a person or thing that follows or takes the place of another, especially a person who succeeds or is in line to succeed another in some office, rank, or the like.

suc·cinct (sək singkt′) *adj.* expressed in few words; brief and concise; terse: *a succinct style of writing, a succinct remark.* —**suc·cinct′ly,** *adv.* —**suc·cinct′ness,** *n.*

suc·cor (suk′ər) *also, British,* **suc·cour.** *n.* help; assistance; aid. —*v.t.* to give help, assistance, or aid to.

suc·co·tash (suk′ə tash′) *n.* corn kernels and lima beans cooked together.

suc·cour (suk′ər) another spelling of **succor.**

suc·cu·lent (suk′yə lənt) *adj.* full of juice; juicy: *a succulent orange.* —**suc′cu·lence,** *n.*

suc·cumb (sə kum′) *v.i.* **1.** to give way; yield: *She succumbed to the temptation of a second helping of ice cream.* **2.** to die: *to succumb to malaria.*

such (such) *adj.* **1.** of the same kind or degree: *Have you ever heard such a story?* **2.** of that particular kind or degree: *Such an old car was next to useless.* **3.** of a similar kind or degree; like: *She bought lettuce, tomatoes, and such items for a salad.* **4.** of an extreme degree, quantity, or kind: *It was such a surprise.* —*pron.* a person or thing that has already been mentioned: *pies, cakes, and such.*

　as such. a. being of the same or similar kind as already mentioned: *My brother is not really a scholar, as such.* **b.** in itself: *Success, as such, does not always bring happiness.*

　such and such. of indefinite name, location, or the like: *The accident took place on such and such a date.*

　such as. a. of the same or particular kind or degree: *A man such as he will surely succeed.* **b.** for example: *The pet store had dogs, such as dachshunds and poodles.*

suck (suk) *v.t.* **1.** to draw (something) into the mouth with the lips and tongue: *to suck milk through a straw.* **2.** to draw a liquid from (something) with the mouth: *to suck an orange.* **3.** to hold in the mouth and lick: *She sucked a cough drop for her sore throat.* **4.** to draw in or absorb by the use of suction: *The vacuum cleaner sucked the dust up out of the corners of the room.* —*v.i.* to draw milk from a breast or a bottle; suckle. —*n.* the act of sucking.

suck·er (suk'ər) *n.* **1.** a person or thing that sucks. **2.** any of a group of toothless, fresh-water fish having fleshy, sucking lips on the underside of the head. **3.** an organ of any of certain animals, such as squid, barnacles, or certain parasites, used for sucking or for attaching to something by suction. **4.** a shoot growing from the underground stem or root of a plant. **5.** *Informal.* a piece of candy which is held in the mouth and licked, such as a lollipop. **6.** *Slang.* a person who can easily be cheated, fooled, or taken advantage of.

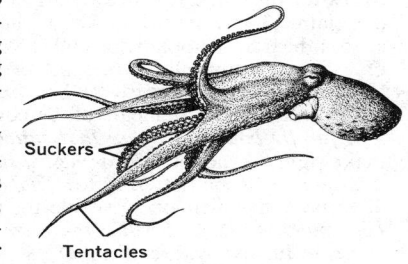

Suckers

Tentacles

Sucker *(def. 3)*

suck·le (suk'əl) *v.*, **suck·led, suck·ling.** —*v.t.* **1.** to give milk to from the breast, udder, or the like. **2.** to bring up; nurture. —*v.i.* to drink milk from the breast, udder, or the like.

suck·ling (suk'ling) *n.* an infant or young animal that is not yet weaned. —*adj.* **1.** young and inexperienced. **2.** not yet weaned: *a suckling pig.*

Su·cre (sōō'krā) *n.* the official capital of Bolivia, in the southern part of the country. Pop. (1970 est.), 84,900.

su·crose (sōō'krōs) *n.* common sugar, a crystalline, organic compound with a sweet taste, obtained especially from sugar beets and sugarcane and used for sweetening foods.

suc·tion (suk'shən) *n.* **1.** a force created by a complete or partial vacuum that draws a gas or liquid into a space from which all or part of the air or liquid has been removed. **2.** the act or instance of drawing a liquid or gas into a space where a partial vacuum has been created. —*adj.* causing, relating to, using, or done by suction: *a suction pump.*

Su·dan (sōō dan') *n.* **1.** a country in northeastern Africa, on the southern border of Egypt, formerly known as the **Anglo-Egyptian Sudan.** Capital, Khartoum. Area, 967,500 sq. mi. Pop. (1971 est.), 16,090,000. **2.** a region extending across Africa from the Atlantic Ocean to Ethiopia and

south from the Sahara Desert to the central and western tropical forests. Much of the Sudan is semiarid grassland.

Su·da·nese (sōō'də nēz') *n. pl.,* **Su·da·nese.** a person who was born or is living in the country or region of Sudan. —*adj.* of, relating to, or characteristic of the country or region of Sudan, or its people.

sud·den (sud'ən) *adj.* **1.** done or happening without warning; unexpected: *The sudden arrival of guests forced her to change her plans.* **2.** quick or abrupt; hasty: *He made a sudden decision. The car came to a sudden stop.* —**sud'den·ness,** *n.*

　all of a sudden. all at once; unexpectedly.

sud·den·ly (sud'ən lē) *adv.* without warning; unexpectedly.

suds (sudz) *n., pl.* **1.** a frothy mass of bubbles that forms on the top of water containing soap. **2.** soapy water: *Wash the sweater in warm suds.* **3.** any foam or froth.

sud·sy (sud'zē) *adj.,* **suds·i·er, suds·i·est.** full of soapsuds.

sue (sōō) *v.,* **sued, su·ing.** —*v.t.* to start a suit against in a court of law. —*v.i.* **1.** to take legal action: *to sue for damages.* **2.** to appeal or plead: *He sued for forgiveness in vain.* —**su'er,** *n.*

suede (swād) *also,* **suède.** *n.* **1.** a soft leather that has a velvety nap. **2.** a fabric made with a short nap on one side to resemble this leather. Also (*def. 2*), **suede cloth.** —*adj.* of, resembling, or made of suede.

su·et (sōō'it) *n.* the hard fat from around the kidneys and loins of cattle and sheep, used in cooking.

Su·ez (sōō ez') *n.* **1.** a port city in northeastern Egypt, at the southern entrance of the Suez Canal. Pop. (1970 est.), 315,000. **2.** see **Suez Canal.**

Suez Canal, a canal in northeastern Egypt connecting the Mediterranean Sea and the Red Sea.

suf·fer (suf'ər) *v.i.* **1.** to have or be subject to pain, sorrow, or distress: *The wounded man suffered. The child suffered from the cruel teasing of her classmates.* **2.** to undergo loss or damage; be hurt: *Lack of studying caused his schoolwork to suffer.* —*v.t.* **1.** to feel or be subject to; undergo: *She suffered embarrassment when speaking before the class.* **2.** to allow or permit: *Suffer the little children to come unto me* (Mark 10:14). **3.** to bear up under; put up with; tolerate: *Our teacher will not suffer noise in the classroom.* —**suf'fer·er,** *n.*

suf·fer·ance (suf'ər əns) *n.* approval or consent given only by failure to prevent.

suf·fer·ing (suf'ər ing) *n.* **1.** the act or instance of undergoing pain, sorrow, or distress. **2.** the condition of a person who suffers.

suf·fice (sə fīs') *v.,* **suf·ficed, suf·fic·ing.** —*v.i.* to be sufficient or enough: *One suitcase will suffice for the trip.* —*v.t.* to be enough for; satisfy: *A light lunch will suffice me.*

suf·fi·cien·cy (sə fish'ən sē) *n. pl.,* **suf·fi·cien·cies.** **1.** an adequate amount or quantity: *a sufficiency of supplies.* **2.** the state or quality of being enough or sufficient; adequacy.

suf·fi·cient (sə fish'ənt) *adj.* as much as is necessary or needed; enough; adequate: *One blanket will provide sufficient warmth.* —**suf·fi'cient·ly,** *adv.*

S

at; āpe; cär; end; mē; it; īce; hot; ōld; fôrk;
wood; fōōl; oil; out; up; turn; sing; thin; **this;**
hw in white; zh in treasure. The symbol ə
stands for the sound of **a** in about, **e** in taken,
i in pencil, **o** in lemon, and **u** in circus.

911

suf·fix (suf′iks) *n. pl.,* **suf·fix·es.** a syllable or syllables added at the end of a word to form another word of different meaning or function, such as *-ness* in *badness, -ly* in *quickly,* and *-er* in *painter.* —*v.t.* to add at the end, especially as a suffix.

suf·fo·cate (suf′ə kāt′) *v.,* **suf·fo·cat·ed, suf·fo·cat·ing.** —*v.t.* **1.** to kill by preventing breathing. **2.** to interrupt or hinder the breathing of: *The small, crowded room was suffocating him.* **3.** to smother; stifle; extinguish: *to suffocate a fire.* —*v.i.* **1.** to die from an interrupted or insufficient supply of air. **2.** to be or become stifled or smothered; choke. —**suf′fo·ca′tion,** *n.*

suf·fra·gan (suf′rə gən) *n.* a bishop who assists another bishop.

suf·frage (suf′rij) *n.* **1.** the right or privilege of voting; franchise. **2.** the act of casting a vote; voting. **3.** a vote, especially in favor of a candidate for office.

suf·fra·gette (suf′rə jet′) *n.* a woman who strongly supports suffrage for women.

suf·fra·gist (suf′rə jist′) *n.* a person who favors extending the right to vote, especially to women.

suf·fuse (sə fyōōz′) *v.t.,* **suf·fused, suf·fus·ing.** to spread through or over, as with a light, color, or emotion: *a room suffused with sunshine, eyes suffused with tears, a face suffused with happiness.* —**suf·fu′sion,** *n.*

sug·ar (shoog′ər) *n.* **1.** any of several white or brown crystalline forms of the organic compound sucrose, obtained mainly from sugarcane and sugar beets, and used for sweetening foods. **2.** any of a group of carbohydrates having a relatively simple molecular structure, including sucrose, glucose, fructose, maltose, and lactose. —*v.t.* **1.** to mix, cover, sprinkle, or sweeten with sugar: *to sugar cookies, to sugar coffee.* **2.** to disguise to make more pleasant; sugar-coat.

sugar beet, a leafy plant whose long, thick, yellow or white roots are a major source of sugar.

sug·ar·cane (shoog′ər kān′) *n.* a tall grass with jointed stems containing a sweet juice that is a major source of sugar.

sug·ar-coat (shoog′ər kōt′) *v.t.* **1.** to cover with sugar: *to sugar-coat a cookie.* **2.** to disguise or soften (something unpleasant) in order to make it more pleasant or acceptable: *to sugar-coat criticism with some kind words.*

sug·ar·loaf (shoog′ər lōf′) *n.* **1.** a cone-shaped, hard mass of refined sugar. **2.** something having the shape of a sugarloaf, such as a hill.

sugar maple, a maple tree of eastern North America, whose sap is the major source of maple syrup.

sug·ar·plum (shoog′ər plum′) *n.* a small, usually round piece of candy.

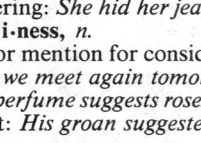
Sugarcane

sug·ar·y (shoog′ər ē) *adj.* **1.** of, consisting of, or like sugar. **2.** sweetly or insincerely flattering: *She hid her jealousy with a sugary smile.* —**sug′ar·i·ness,** *n.*

sug·gest (səg jest′) *v.t.* **1.** to offer or mention for consideration or action; propose: *I suggest we meet again tomorrow.* **2.** to bring or call to mind: *Her perfume suggests roses.* **3.** to express or show indirectly; hint: *His groan suggested his disappointment.*

sug·gest·i·ble (səg jes′tə bəl) *adj.* **1.** easily influenced by suggestion. **2.** able to be suggested. —**sug·ges·ti·bil′i·ty,** *n.*

sug·ges·tion (səg jes′chən) *n.* **1.** the act or instance of suggesting: *We left at his suggestion.* **2.** something that is suggested: *The suggestion of a picnic was popular with everyone.* **3.** the process by which something is brought to

mind through an association or connection with something else: *The cold wind carried a suggestion of the winter to come.* **4.** a very small indication; trace; hint: *There is a suggestion of garlic in the sauce.*

sug·ges·tive (səg jes′tiv) *adj.* **1.** giving a suggestion or hint: *The architecture of the building was suggestive of the classic Greek style.* **2.** tending to bring to mind ideas or actions: *a suggestive talk on ways to raise money for our club.* **3.** tending to suggest something improper or indecent. —**sug·ges′tive·ly,** *adv.* —**sug·ges′tive·ness,** *n.*

su·i·cid·al (sōō′ə sīd′əl) *adj.* **1.** of, relating to, or causing suicide: *suicidal tendencies.* **2.** apt to cause disaster to oneself; ruinous: *He attempted a suicidal climb to the summit of the mountain.* **3.** having a definite inclination to suicide: *a suicidal youth, a suicidal personality.* —**su′i·cid′al·ly,** *adv.*

su·i·cide¹ (sōō′ə sīd′) *n.* **1.** the act or instance of intentionally taking one's own life. **2.** the destruction of one's own interests or aims, as in business or politics. [Latin *suī* of oneself + *-cīdium* a killing.]

su·i·cide² (sōō′ə sīd′) *n.* a person who has intentionally taken his own life. [Latin *suī* of oneself + *-cīda* a killer.]

suit (sōōt) *n.* **1.** a set of garments designed to be worn together, especially a jacket with a matching pair of trousers or skirt. **2.** the act, process, or proceeding in a court of law for the correction of a wrong or for the enforcement of a claim. **3.** any of the four sets of playing cards in a deck; spades, hearts, diamonds, or clubs. **4.** the act or instance of wooing or appealing. **5.** a set of similar or matched things used or intended to be used together. —*v.t.* **1.** to meet the requirements of; be correct or adapted to: *The family bought a house that suited their needs.* **2.** to make right for; adapt: *The orchestra suited its music to the occasion.* **3.** to be flattering to: *That color suits you well.* **4.** to be convenient or agreeable to; please; satisfy: *This book suits my taste. I will come when it suits you.* **5.** *Archaic.* to furnish with clothes; dress. —*v.i.* to be suitable, fitting, or convenient.

 to follow suit. a. to play a card of the same suit as the card led. **b.** to do the same thing as another.

 to suit oneself. to act in the way one wishes.

suit·a·ble (sōō′tə bəl) *adj.* that suits a particular purpose, object, or occasion. —**suit′a·bil′i·ty, suit′a·ble·ness,** *n.* —**suit′a·bly,** *adv.*

suit·case (sōōt′kās′) *n.* a flat, usually rectangular bag used for carrying clothes and other articles when traveling; valise.

suite (swēt; *def. 2 also* sōōt) *n.* **1.** a group of connected rooms considered as a unit, as in a hotel. **2.** a set of matching furniture: *a living room suite.* **3.** any set of similar or matched things, used or intended to be used together. **4.** *Music.* **a.** an instrumental composition made up of a series of dance tunes in the same or related key. **b.** an instrumental composition made up of a series of short movements, often adapted from a longer work.

suit·or (sōō′tər) *n.* **1.** a man who courts or woos a woman. **2.** a person who institutes a lawsuit. **3.** a person who pleads or petitions.

su·ki·ya·ki (sōō′kē yä′kē, skē yä′kē) *n.* a Japanese dish made of thin strips of meat and vegetables sautéed quickly, usually at the dining table.

Suk·koth (sook′əs) *n.* a Jewish holiday in the early fall, giving thanks for the harvest.

sul·fa drug (sul′fə) *also,* **sulpha drug.** any of a group of synthetic drugs used, often with antibiotics, to treat infectious diseases such as pneumonia.

sul·fate (sul′fāt) *also,* **sul·phate.** *n.* a salt of sulfuric acid.

sul·fide (sul′fīd) *also,* **sul·phide.** *n.* a compound obtained when sulfur is heated with another element.

sul·fur (sul′fər) *also,* **sul·phur.** *n.* a yellow nonmetallic element occurring in both free and combined forms. Sulfur is very abundant in nature and is used to make sulfuric acid, to process rubber, and to manufacture insecticides. Symbol: **S**

sulfur dioxide, a colorless gas with a sharp, irritating odor, used to make sulfuric acid, and serving as a bleaching agent, refrigerant, and food preservative.

sul·fu·ric (sul fyoor′ik) *also,* **sul·phu·ric.** *adj.* **1.** of or relating to sulfur. **2.** containing sulfur in its higher valence.

sulfuric acid, a colorless, oily, very reactive liquid compound containing sulfur, hydrogen, and oxygen, used in the manufacture of nearly all chemical products.

sul·fur·ous (sul′fər əs, sul fyoor′əs) *also,* **sul·phur·ous.** *adj.* **1.** of or relating to sulfur. **2.** containing sulfur in its lower valence. **3.** like burning sulfur, as in odor. **4.** of or resembling the fires of hell; infernal.

sulk (sulk) *v.i.* to be silent or withdrawn as a sign of bad humor or anger. —*n.* **1.** the state of sulking: *to be in a sulk.* **2. the sulks.** a display or mood of sulking.

sulk·y (sul′kē) *adj.,* **sulk·i·er, sulk·i·est.** stubbornly silent or withdrawn as a display of bad humor or anger. —*n. pl.,* **sulk·ies.** a light, two-wheeled, one-horse carriage seating one passenger, used especially for harness racing. —**sulk′i·ly,** *adv.* —**sulk′i·ness,** *n.*

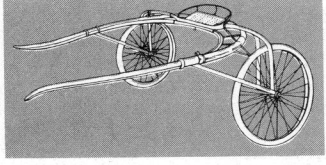

Sulky

sul·len (sul′ən) *adj.* **1.** withdrawn or gloomy because of bad humor or anger; sulky; morose. **2.** dismal or gloomy: *a sullen morning.* —**sul′len·ly,** *adv.* —**sul′len·ness,** *n.*

Sul·li·van, Sir Arthur Seymour (sul′ə vən) 1842–1900, English composer who collaborated with the librettist Sir William S. Gilbert in writing comic operas.

sul·ly (sul′ē) *v.t.,* **sul·lied, sul·ly·ing. 1.** to stain the honor or purity of; defile or disgrace: *The scandal sullied the family name.* **2.** to stain; soil: *The mud had sullied the hem of her long white dress.*

sul·pha drug (sul′fə) see **sulfa drug.**

sul·phate (sul′fāt) another spelling of **sulfate.**

sul·phide (sul′fīd) another spelling of **sulfide.**

sul·phur (sul′fər) another spelling of **sulfur.**

sul·phu·ric (sul fyoor′ik) another spelling of **sulfuric.**

sul·phur·ous (sul′fər əs, sul fyoor′əs) another spelling of **sulfurous.**

sul·tan (sult′ən) *n.* in a Muslim country, a sovereign or ruling monarch. Turkey and Morocco were formerly ruled by sultans.

sul·tan·a (sul tan′ə) *n.* the wife, mother, sister, or daughter of a sultan.

sul·tan·ate (sult′ən āt′) *n.* **1.** a country or other area ruled by a sultan. **2.** the office or reign of a sultan.

sul·try (sul′trē) *adj.,* **sul·tri·er, sul·tri·est.** extremely hot and humid; sweltering: *the sultry tropics.* —**sul′tri·ness,** *n.*

sum (sum) *n.* **1.** a result obtained from addition. **2.** the whole quantity; entirety: *the sum of all our efforts.* **3.** an amount of money: *Large sums were spent on repairs.* **4.** *Informal.* an arithmetic problem, especially a list of numbers to be added. **5.** summary; gist: *That's the sum of it.* —*v.t.,* **summed, sum·ming.** to find the numerical sum of; total.

　to sum up. to tell or present briefly; summarize: *The newscaster summed up the events of the day on the evening broadcast.*

su·mac (shoo′mak, soo′mak) *also,* **su·mach.** *n.* **1.** any of a large group of trees and shrubs having a milky juice that is sometimes poisonous. Poison sumac and poison ivy are sumacs. **2.** the dried leaves of certain of these trees or shrubs, yielding tannin, a substance used in processing leather.

Su·ma·tra (soo mä′trə) *n.* the westernmost island of the Malay Archipelago, in Indonesia. —**Su·ma′tran,** *adj., n.*

Su·mer (soo′mər) *n.* an ancient country in southern Mesopotamia.

Su·me·ri·an (soo mēr′ē ən, soo mer′ē ən) *adj.* of or relating to Sumer, its people, their language, or their culture. —*n.* **1.** a person who lived in Sumer from about 4000 B.C. to 2000 B.C. **2.** the extinct language of Sumer, preserved in inscriptions on rocks and tablets. It is of unknown origin.

sum·ma cum lau·de (sum′ə kum lô′də) with highest honors or praise. ▲ used on diplomas to show graduation with highest honors from a college or university.

sum·mar·i·ly (sə mer′ə lē, sum′ər ə lē) *adv.* in a summary manner; briefly or quickly.

sum·ma·rize (sum′ə rīz′) *v.t.,* **sum·ma·rized, sum·ma·riz·ing.** to make a summary of; state briefly: *to summarize the main points of a speech.*

sum·ma·ry (sum′ər ē) *n. pl.,* **sum·ma·ries.** a short statement or brief account containing the main points of something: *The review gave a summary of the plot of the play.* —*adj.* **1.** containing the main points; concise; brief: *John gave a summary statement of his plan.* **2.** performed rapidly without hesitation or formality: *Stealing caused the employee's summary dismissal.*

sum·ma·tion (sə mā′shən) *n.* **1.** the final part of an argument in which the facts are reviewed and a conclusion is given: *The defense will now give its summation to the jury.* **2.** the act or process of finding the total; addition. **3.** a result of addition; total.

sum·mer (sum′ər) *n.* the season of the year coming between spring and autumn. In the Northern Hemisphere it extends from about June 21 to about September 22. —*adj.* of, relating to, or suitable for summer: *a summer vacation, summer clothes.* —*v.i.* to spend the summer: *We summered at the seashore.*

sum·mer·house (sum′ər hous′) *n. pl.,* **sum·mer·hous·es** (sum′ər hou′ziz). a small, roofed, usually simple building situated in a garden or park, used as a shady retreat in summer.

summer solstice, the time of year, about June 22 in the Northern Hemisphere, when the sun appears the farthest north from the equator.

sum·mer·time (sum′ər tīm′) *n.* the summer season.

sum·mer·y (sum′ər ē) *adj.* like or suitable for summer: *summery weather, a summery dress.*

sum·mit (sum′it) *n.* **1.** the highest part or point; acme. **2.** the highest level, as of government or political authority: *to have a meeting at the summit.* —*adj.* of, for, or concerning the highest level of government or political authority, especially the heads of state: *a summit conference on nuclear disarmament.*

sum·mon (sum′ən) *v.t.* **1.** to send for or request the presence of, especially with authority: *When the burglary was discovered, we summoned the police.* **2.** to order to

S

appear in court by means of a summons; issue a summons to. **3.** to call together; convene; convoke: *to summon a council.* **4.** to bring or urge to action; rouse: *to summon up one's courage.* —**sum'mon·er,** *n.*

sum·mons (sum'ənz) *n. pl.,* **sum·mons·es. 1.** a notice, signal, or command to appear somewhere or to do something. **2.** *Law.* a document notifying someone that he is required to appear in court.

sump (sump) *n.* **1.** a pit or reservoir for collecting liquid, such as water, oil, or sewage. **2.** a pit or well at the bottom of a mining shaft to collect water so that it can be pumped out.

sump·tu·ous (sum'chōō əs) *adj.* costly and magnificent; lavish: *a sumptuous apartment, a sumptuous dinner.* —**sump'tu·ous·ly,** *adv.* —**sump'tu·ous·ness,** *n.*

Sum·ter, Fort (sum'tər) a fort in the harbor of Charleston, South Carolina. On April 12, 1861, the Civil War began when Confederate forces attacked this fort.

sun (sun) *n.* **1.** the star that is the central body of the solar system, around which the earth and other planets revolve and from which they receive light and heat. The sun has an average distance from earth of about 93,000,000 miles, a diameter of about 864,000 miles, and a mass of about 300,000 times that of the earth. **2.** light and heat from the sun; sunshine: *Too much sun at one time can produce a painful burn.* **3.** any star that is the center of a planetary system. —*v.,* **sunned, sun·ning.** —*v.t.* **1.** to expose to the rays of the sun: *We sunned ourselves on the beach.* **2.** to warm or dry in the sun. —*v.i.* to expose oneself to the rays of the sun: *Charlotte sunned on the terrace.*

Sun., Sunday.

sun bath, exposure of the body to the rays of the sun or a sunlamp.

sun·bathe (sun'bā th) *v.i.,* **sun·bathed, sun·bath·ing.** to bask in the sun; take a sun bath: *to sunbathe on the beach.* —**sun'bath·er,** *n.*

sun·beam (sun'bēm') *n.* a beam of sunlight.

sun·bon·net (sun'bon'it) *n.* a woman's bonnet having a broad brim that protects the face and a flap that protects the neck.

sun·burn (sun'burn') *n.* an inflammation of the skin caused by overexposure to the sun or a sunlamp. —*v.,* **sunburned** or **sun·burnt, sun·burn·ing.** —*v.t.* to overexpose to the sun or a sunlamp; affect with sunburn: *Dan sunburned his back at the beach.* —*v.i.* to become affected with sunburn: *She sunburns easily.*

sun·dae (sun'dē, sun'dā) *n.* ice cream served with a topping, such as syrup, nuts, or fruit.

Sun·day (sun'dē, sun'dā) *n.* the first day of the week and the Sabbath for most Christians. [Old English *sunnandæg* literally, sun's day.]

Sunday school 1. a school usually connected with a church and held on Sunday for religious instruction. **2.** the pupils and teachers of such a school.

sun·der (sun'dər) *v.t.* to cause to divide; sever. —*v.i.* to become divided; separate.

Sun·der·land (sun'dər lənd) *n.* a port city in northeastern England, on the North Sea. Pop. (1971), 216,892.

sun·dew (sun'dōō', sun'dyōō') *n.* any of a group of plants having leaves covered with sticky, hairlike structures that trap and digest insects.

sun·di·al (sun'dī'əl) *n.* a device that shows the time of the day by the position and length of a shadow cast on a flat, usually round, surface marked with numbers.

sun·down (sun'doun') *n.* another word for **sunset.**

sun·dries (sun'drēz) *n., pl.* numerous, assorted small items.

sun·dry (sun'drē) *adj.* more than one; several; various: *There were sundry aspects to the problem.*

sun·fish (sun'fish') *n. pl.,* **sun·fish** or **sun·fish·es. 1.** any of several freshwater fish found in North America. **2.** a large fish found in temperate or tropical seas, having a flattened, oval body and weighing up to 2000 pounds.

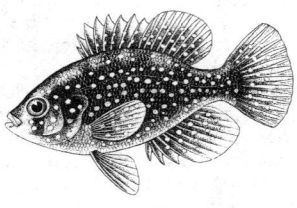

Sunfish

sun·flow·er (sun'flou'ər) *n.* **1.** a large flower of any of several tall plants, having rays of petals surrounding a yellow or purplish-brown disk. **2.** a plant bearing this flower. Sunflowers, which are found chiefly in North America, grow as large as twelve feet high.

sung (sung) a past tense and the past participle of **sing.**

sun·glass·es (sun'glas'iz) *n., pl.* eyeglasses having shaded or tinted lenses to protect the eyes from the sun's glare.

sun god, any god identified with the sun.

sunk (sungk) a past tense and a past participle of **sink.**

sunk·en (sung'kən) *v.* a past participle of **sink.** —*adj.* **1.** having sunk below the surface of the water or ground: *sunken treasure, sunken rock.* **2.** situated below the surrounding area: *a sunken living room.* **3.** abnormally hollow: *sunken cheeks.*

sun·lamp (sun'lamp') *n.* a lamp that gives off ultraviolet radiation, used for tanning the skin.

sun·less (sun'lis) *adj.* without sunlight; dark or gloomy.

sun·light (sun'līt') *n.* the light of the sun.

sun·lit (sun'lit') *adj.* lighted by the sun.

sun·ny (sun'ē) *adj.,* **sun·ni·er, sun·ni·est. 1.** full of or warmed by sunlight: *a sunny room.* **2.** cheerful; happy; bright: *a sunny disposition, a sunny smile.* —**sun'ni·ly,** *adv.* —**sun'ni·ness,** *n.*

sun parlor, a room or porch with glass walls or large windows for letting in sunlight. Also, **sun porch, sun room.**

sun·rise (sun'rīz') *n.* **1.** the apparent rising of the sun above the horizon at the beginning of the day. **2.** the time when the sun rises: *The farmer began his chores before sunrise.* Also, **sunup.**

sun·set (sun'set') *n.* **1.** the apparent descent of the sun below the horizon at the end of the day. **2.** the time when the sun sets. Also, **sundown.**

sun·shade (sun'shād') *n.* something that is used to provide protection from the sun, such as an awning or parasol.

sun·shine (sun'shīn') *n.* **1.** the shining of the sun; direct sunlight. **2.** cheerfulness; happiness; brightness. —**sun'shin'y,** *adj.*

sun·spot (sun'spot') *n.* one of the dark spots that occur in groups on the surface of the sun at regular intervals.

sun·stroke (sun'strōk') *n.* an illness caused by overexposure to the rays of the sun, causing weakness, fever, and sometimes unconsciousness.

sun·up (sun'up') *n.* another word for **sunrise.**

sun·ward (sun'wərd) *also,* **sun·wards.** *adv.* toward the sun. —*adj.* directed toward the sun.

Sun Yat-sen (soon' yät'sen') 1866–1925, Chinese revolutionary leader and statesman.

sup¹ (sup) *v.i.,* **supped, sup·ping.** to eat the evening meal. [Old French *super.*]

sup² (sup) *v.t.,* **supped, sup·ping.** to take (liquid) in small quantities; sip. —*n.* a sip of a liquid. [Old English *sūpan.*]

su·per (sōō'pər) *n. Informal.* **1.** a superintendent in an apartment house. **2.** a performer having a very small part with no lines to say; supernumerary; extra. —*adj. Slang.* very good; excellent.

super- *prefix* **1.** over; above: *superstructure, supersede.* **2.** higher or greater; superior: *superhighway, superpower.* **3.** to an excessive extent or degree: *supersensitive, superabundant.*

su·per·a·bun·dant (soo'pər ə bun'dənt) *adj.* more than is necessary or wanted; too abundant; excessive. —**su'per·a·bun'dance,** *n.*

su·per·an·nu·at·ed (soo'pər an'yoo ā'tid) *adj.* **1.** retired from service with a pension because of age or infirmity. **2.** too old for use or work.

su·perb (soo purb') *adj.* **1.** having nobility or grandeur; magnificent; splendid: *a superb building.* **2.** elegant; rich: *a superb wardrobe.* **3.** of superior quality; very fine: *The actor gave a superb performance on opening night.* —**superb'ly,** *adv.*

su·per·car·go (soo'pər kär'gō) *n. pl.,* **su·per·car·goes** or **su·per·car·gos.** an officer on board a merchant ship who is in charge of the cargo and the business transactions of the voyage.

su·per·charge (soo'pər chärj') *v.t.,* **su·per·charged, su·per·charg·ing.** to increase the power of (an engine) with a supercharger.

su·per·charg·er (soo'pər chär'jər) *n.* a device for increasing the power of an internal-combustion engine by compressing air or a mixture of fuel and air and forcing it into the cylinder at a pressure greater than that of the surrounding atmosphere.

su·per·cil·i·ous (soo'pər sil'ē əs) *adj.* having or showing too much pride or scorn; haughty; arrogant. —**su'per·cil'i·ous·ly,** *adv.* —**su'per·cil'i·ous·ness,** *n.*

su·per·con·duc·tiv·i·ty (soo'pər kon'dək tiv'ə tē) *n. Physics.* the apparent complete loss of all resistance to the passage of an electrical current in certain metals and alloys at temperatures near absolute zero. —**su·per·con·duc·tive** (soo'pər kən duk'tiv), *adj.*

su·per·cool (soo'pər kool') *v.t.* to cool (a liquid) below its freezing point without causing solidification.

su·per·e·rog·a·to·ry (soo'pər i rog'ə tôr'ē) *adj.* **1.** going beyond what is needed or wanted. **2.** not necessary; excessive; superfluous.

su·per·fi·cial (soo'pər fish'əl) *adj.* **1.** of, relating to, or located on the surface: *a superficial wound, a superficial resemblance.* **2.** lacking depth or thoroughness; shallow: *a superficial person, superficial research.* —**su'per·fi'cial·ly,** *adv.*

su·per·fi·ci·al·i·ty (soo'pər fish'ē al'ə tē) *n.* **1.** the state or quality of being superficial. **2.** something superficial.

su·per·fine (soo'pər fīn') *adj.* **1.** extremely fine in quality; of the best kind: *superfine cloth.* **2.** too refined or subtle. **3.** consisting of extremely fine particles or parts: *superfine sugar.*

su·per·flu·i·ty (soo'pər floo'ə tē) *n. pl.,* **su·per·flu·i·ties. 1.** the state of being superfluous. **2.** a greater quantity than is needed or wanted; excess. **3.** something that is superfluous: *John wasted a great deal of his money on expensive superfluities.*

su·per·flu·ous (soo pur'floo əs) *adj.* **1.** more than is needed or wanted. **2.** needless; unnecessary: *a superfluous warning.* —**su·per'flu·ous·ly,** *adv.* —**su·per'flu·ous·ness,** *n.*

su·per·heat (soo'pər hēt') *v.t.* **1.** to heat to an extremely high temperature; overheat. **2.** to raise the temperature of (a liquid) above its normal boiling point without causing vaporization. **3.** to raise the temperature of (vapor or steam) to increase its pressure. —*n.* **1.** the state of being superheated. **2.** the amount by which a vapor is superheated.

su·per·high·way (soo'pər hī'wā') *n.* a highway designed for high speeds, usually having four or more lanes with a center strip separating traffic going in opposite directions.

su·per·hu·man (soo'pər hyoo'mən, soo'pər yoo'mən) *adj.* **1.** beyond what is human; divine: *of superhuman origin.* **2.** beyond the ordinary human ability or power: *a superhuman effort, superhuman strength.* —**su'per·hu'man·ly,** *adv.*

su·per·im·pose (soo'pər im pōz') *v.t.,* **su·per·im·posed, su·per·im·pos·ing.** to place (something) over or on top of something else.

su·per·in·tend (soo'pər in tend') *v.t.* to direct or control the work or operation of; manage. —**su'per·in·tend'ence,** *n.*

su·per·in·tend·en·cy (soo'pər in ten'dən sē) *n. pl.,* **su·per·in·tend·en·cies.** the position, duty, or authority of a superintendent.

su·per·in·tend·ent (soo'pər in ten'dənt) *n.* **1.** a person who directs the work or operation of something, such as a group of workers, an institution, or a business: *a superintendent of police, a superintendent of a school.* **2.** a person who manages and is responsible for the maintenance of an apartment building or office building.

su·pe·ri·or (sə pēr'ē ər) *adj.* **1.** higher or greater than the normal or average in degree or quality; exceptional: *superior talent, a superior individual, a superior piece of writing.* **2.** higher in status, rank, or office: *a superior officer.* **3.** greater in quantity: *The small army surrendered to the superior force.* **4.** haughty; disdainful: *a superior attitude.* **5.** (of an organ or part) higher in place or position; above in relation to another structure. —*n.* **1.** a person who is higher than others, as in status, rank, or office: *John's superior at the office praised his work.* **2.** the head of an abbey, monastery, or other religious community. —**su·pe'ri·or·ly,** *adv.*

Superior, Lake, the largest and northernmost of the Great Lakes, on the border between the United States and Canada.

su·pe·ri·or·i·ty (sə pēr'ē ôr'ə tē, sə pēr'ē or'ə tē) *n.* the state or quality of being superior.

superl., superlative.

su·per·la·tive (sə pur'lə tiv) *adj.* **1.** of the highest degree or quality; going beyond all others; supreme. **2.** *Grammar.* denoting the third or highest degree of quality, quantity, or relation that can be expressed by an adjective or adverb. *Fastest* is the superlative degree of the adjective *fast.* —*n.* **1.** a person or thing that goes beyond all others; highest example. **2.** *Grammar.* **a.** the superlative degree. **b.** a word or group of words that expresses this degree. *Best* is the superlative of *good.* —**su·per'la·tive·ly,** *adv.* —**su·per'la·tive·ness,** *n.*

su·per·man (soo'pər man') *n. pl.,* **su·per·men** (soo'pər men'). a man with more than human strength or intelligence.

su·per·mar·ket (soo'pər mär'kit) *n.* a self-service store, usually large, carrying food and other household items.

su·per·nal (soo purn'əl)) *adj.* **1.** relating to a higher world; heavenly. **2.** of, relating to, or existing in the sky. —**su·per'nal·ly,** *adv.*

---

at; āpe; cär; end; mē; it; īce; hot; ōld; fôrk;
wood; fool; oil; out; up; turn; sing; thin; this;
hw in white; zh in treasure. The symbol ə
stands for the sound of a in about, e in taken,
i in pencil, o in lemon, and u in circus.

su·per·nat·u·ral (sōō′pər nach′ər əl) *adj.* **1.** of or relating to a realm or existence beyond or exceeding the power of the natural world: *supernatural forces.* **2.** of or relating to ghosts or spirits. —*n.* a person or thing that exists beyond the natural world. —**su′per·nat′u·ral·ly,** *adv.*

su·per·nat·u·ral·ism (sōō′pər nach′ər ə liz′əm) *n.* **1.** the state or quality of being supernatural. **2.** a belief in supernatural forces or beings.

su·per·nu·mer·ar·y (sōō′pər nōō′mə rer′ē, sōō′pər nyōō′mə rer′ē) *adj.* greater in number than is usual, expected, or needed; additional; extra. —*n. pl.,* **su·per·nu·mer·ar·ies. 1.** a person or thing that is extra. **2.** a performer in a play or film who has a minor part with no lines to speak.

su·per·pow·er (sōō′pər pou′ər) *n.* one of the powerful nations that dominate world affairs, especially through the possession of nuclear weapons.

su·per·sat·u·rate (sōō′pər sach′ə rāt′) *v.t.,* **su·per·sat·u·rat·ed, su·per·sat·u·rat·ing.** to add to or concentrate in (a solution) more solute than it can normally hold at a given pressure and temperature. If a solution is supersaturated it becomes very unstable.

su·per·script (sōō′pər skript′) *adj.* written above. —*n.* a character or symbol written, printed, or set above and to one side of another. In a^2, the symbol ^{2} is a superscript.

su·per·scrip·tion (sōō′pər skrip′shən) *n.* something written on the top or outside of something, especially an address on a letter or package.

su·per·sede (sōō′pər sēd′) *v.t.,* **su·per·sed·ed, su·per·sed·ing. 1.** to take the place of; replace: *Diesel or electric trains have superseded steam-driven trains.* **2.** to take the job or office of; succeed: *He superseded his uncle as manager of the company.* [Latin *supersedēre* literally, to sit above.] —**su′per·sed′er,** *n.*

su·per·sen·si·tive (sōō′pər sen′sə tiv) *adj.* too sensitive. —**su′per·sen′si·tive·ly,** *adv.* —**su′per·sen′si·tive·ness,** *n.*

su·per·son·ic (sōō′pər son′ik) *adj.* of, relating to, or traveling at a speed greater than the speed of sound in air (762 miles per hour at sea level).

su·per·sti·tion (sōō′pər stish′ən) *n.* **1.** a belief or set of beliefs based on an unreasoning fear of the unknown. **2.** a particular practice based on such a belief or set of beliefs. Throwing rice at weddings to bring good luck is a superstition.

su·per·sti·tious (sōō′pər stish′əs) *adj.* **1.** having superstitions: *a superstitious person.* **2.** of, relating to, or characterized by superstition. —**su′per·sti′tious·ly,** *adv.* —**su′per·sti′tious·ness,** *n.*

su·per·struc·ture (sōō′pər struk′chər) *n.* **1.** the part of a building above the foundation. **2.** the part of a ship, especially a warship, above the main deck.

su·per·tax (sōō′pər taks′) *n. pl.,* **su·per·tax·es.** another word for **surtax.**

su·per·vene (sōō′pər vēn′) *v.i.,* **su·per·vened, su·per·ven·ing.** to take place, especially as something additional or unexpected: *Bad health supervened and kept her from making the trip.*

su·per·vise (sōō′pər vīz′) *v.t.,* **su·per·vised, su·per·vis·ing.** to watch over in order to guide, direct, or control; oversee: *John supervised the workers as they repaired the building.*

su·per·vi·sion (sōō′pər vizh′ən) *n.* **1.** the act or process of supervising. **2.** care or management.

su·per·vi·sor (sōō′pər vī′zər) *n.* a person who supervises.

su·per·vi·so·ry (sōō′pər vī′zər ē) *adj.* of or relating to a supervisor or supervision.

su·pine (sōō pīn′) *adj.* **1.** lying on the back with the face turned upward: *a supine position.* **2.** not caring; apathetic; lazy. —**su·pine′ly,** *adv.* —**su·pine′ness,** *n.*

sup·per (sup′ər) *n.* **1.** the last meal of the day, eaten in the evening. **2.** a social or community event where such a meal is served: *a church supper.*

sup·plant (sə plant′) *v.t.* to take the place of: *The automobile has supplanted the horse as a means of transportation in this country.*

sup·ple (sup′əl) *adj.,* **sup·pler, sup·plest. 1.** easily bent or folded without breaking or cracking; flexible: *the supple branch of a tree. This shirt has a soft, supple collar.* **2.** able to yield or adapt to changes in people, ideas, or surroundings; adaptable: *a supple mind.* —**sup′ple·ly,** *adv.* —**sup′ple·ness,** *n.*

sup·ple·ment (*n.,* sup′lə mənt; *v.,* sup′lə ment′) *n.* something added to improve or complete something else: *Florence takes vitamins as a supplement to her diet.* —*v.t.* to add or form a supplement to.

sup·ple·men·ta·ry (sup′lə men′tər ē) *adj.* serving as a supplement. Also, **sup·ple·men·tal** (sup′lə ment′əl).

supplementary angle, an angle that is added to another angle to make the sum of the two angles 180 degrees.

sup·pli·ant (sup′lē ənt) *n.* a person who supplicates. —*adj.* asking humbly and earnestly; imploring; beseeching; begging. —**sup′pli·ance,** *n.*

sup·pli·cant (sup′lə kənt) *n.* a person who supplicates. —*adj.* asking humbly and earnestly; beseeching; begging.

Supplementary angles

Angle A 135°   Angle B 45°

sup·pli·cate (sup′lə kāt′) *v.,* **sup·pli·cat·ed, sup·pli·cat·ing.** —*v.t.* **1.** to make a humble and earnest request for: *to supplicate mercy.* **2.** to ask humbly and earnestly of; beseech: *to supplicate a king for mercy.* —*v.i.* to make a humble and earnest request, as by prayer. —**sup′pli·ca·tor,** *n.*

sup·pli·ca·tion (sup′lə kā′shən) *n.* **1.** the act of supplicating. **2.** an earnest request or humble prayer: *The woman's supplication for mercy was listened to by the judge.*

sup·pli·ca·to·ry (sup′lə kə tôr′ē) *adj.* making supplication.

sup·pli·er (sə plī′ər) *n.* a person or thing that supplies.

sup·ply[1] (sə plī′) *v.t.,* **sup·plied, sup·ply·ing. 1.** to make available (what is wanted or needed): *The reservoir supplies water to the community. A reference book supplies information.* **2.** to provide (someone) with what is wanted or needed: *He supplied me with the correct answer.* —*n. pl.,* **sup·plies. 1.** the amount needed or available for use; stock; store: *The store has a new supply of pencils.* **2.** *usually,* **supplies.** needed things, such as food, clothing, or equipment, that are set aside and held for use: *The army was cut off from its supplies.* **3.** the quantity of a commodity available for sale at a certain price at a given time. [Old French *soupleier* to fill up, make up, provide with; literally, to fill from below.]

sup·ply[2] (sup′lē) *adv.* in a supple manner. [*Supple* + *-ly*[1].]

sup·port (sə pôrt′) *v.t.* **1.** to hold up; keep from falling: *Brackets support the shelves. That chair won't support your weight.* **2.** to provide for: *to support a family. Scientists doubt that the planet Venus can support life.* **3.** to back; uphold: *The senator did not support either of the candidates.* **4.** to comfort or strengthen: *Her religion supported her after her husband's death.* **5.** to show to be true; verify: *There is no evidence to support his theory.* —*n.* **1.** the act of supporting or the state of being supported. **2.** a person or thing that supports.

sup·port·a·ble (sə pôr′tə bəl) *adj.* that can be supported; bearable; endurable. —**sup·port′a·bly,** *adv.*

sup·port·er (sə pôr′tər) *n.* **1.** a person who supports, especially a person who aids or approves: *Mr. Smith is an ardent supporter of the President.* **2.** something that supports, such as a garter.

sup·pose (sə pōz′) *v.t.,* **sup·posed, sup·pos·ing. 1.** to imagine or take to be possible for the sake of argument: *Just suppose that he doesn't want to go with us.* **2.** to hold as an opinion; believe to be probable: *I suppose that I have enough money to make the trip.* **3.** to expect or require: *The plane is supposed to arrive at nine o'clock.*

sup·posed (sə pōzd′) *adj.* considered to be true, real, or possible, often wrongly: *His supposed good nature is really a cover for a bad temper.* —**sup·pos·ed·ly** (sə pō′zid lē) *adv.*

sup·po·si·tion (sup′ə zish′ən) *n.* **1.** something supposed; assumption. **2.** the act of supposing.

sup·pos·i·to·ry (sə poz′ə tôr′ē) *n. pl.,* **sup·pos·i·to·ries.** a medical substance in solid form, usually in the shape of a cone or cylinder, made to be inserted into the rectum or some other body opening.

sup·press (sə pres′) *v.t.* **1.** to put an end to or to put down by force; crush: *The army suppressed the revolt.* **2.** to hold or keep in; restrain: *She tried to suppress a laugh.* **3.** to prevent or forbid the telling or publishing of; censor: *The government suppressed the news story because it contained secret information.* —**sup·press′i·ble,** *adj.* —**sup·pres′sor;** *also,* **sup·press′er,** *n.*

sup·pres·sion (sə presh′ən) *n.* the act of suppressing or the state of being suppressed.

sup·pres·sive (sə pres′iv) *adj.* tending to suppress.

sup·pu·rate (sup′yə rāt′) *v.i.,* **sup·pu·rat·ed, sup·pu·rat·ing.** to form or give forth pus.

sup·pu·ra·tion (sup′yə rā′shən) *n.* **1.** the formation of pus. **2.** pus.

su·pra·re·nal gland (soo′prə rēn′əl) another term for **adrenal gland.**

su·prem·a·cy (sə prem′ə sē) *n.* the quality or condition of being supreme.

su·preme (sə prēm′) *adj.* **1.** greatest in rank, authority, or power. **2.** greatest in importance, degree, or quality; utmost: *supreme artistry, supreme wisdom, a supreme effort.* **3.** ultimate; final; last: *the supreme sacrifice.* —**su·preme′ly,** *adv.*

Supreme Being, God.

Supreme Court 1. the highest court in the United States, with the power to hear appeals from lower courts and to declare laws unconstitutional. **2.** the highest court in some states of the United States. **3.** the highest court in some other countries, such as Denmark.

Supreme Soviet, the legislature of the Soviet Union, consisting of two houses, one of which is elected according to population and the other elected by the various national groups.

Supt., superintendent.

sur- *prefix* over; above; beyond: *surcharge, surpass.*

sur·cease (sur sēs′) *n. Archaic.* an end: *the surcease of pain.*

sur·charge (*n.,* sur′chärj′; *v.,* sur chärj′, sur′chärj′) *n.* **1.** a charge added to the usual amount: *a tax surcharge.* **2.** an additional mark printed over a postage stamp to raise its value. —*v.t.,* **sur·charged, sur·charg·ing. 1.** to charge an extra amount. **2.** to overcharge. **3.** to print an additional mark on (postage stamps) to raise their value, instead of issuing new stamps.

sur·cin·gle (sur′sing′gəl) *n.* a belt or band around the body of a horse or pack animal to hold down a saddle, blanket, or pack.

sur·coat (sur′kōt′) *n.* an outer coat, especially a short garment worn over armor during the Middle Ages.

Surcoat

surd (surd) *n.* an irrational number that is a root of a positive whole number or the quotient of positive whole numbers. The numbers $\sqrt{3}$ and $\sqrt{3/5}$ are surds.

sure (shoor) *adj.,* **sur·er, sur·est. 1.** firmly believing in something; having or showing no doubt; confident: *I am sure that my answer is right.* **2.** bound to be or happen; inevitable; certain: *That horse is a sure winner. She is sure to be at the party.* **3.** not liable to give way; steady; firm: *He had a sure grip on the bat.* **4.** worthy of trust; dependable: *Jack is a sure friend.* —*adv. Informal.* surely. —**sure′ness,** *n.*

for sure. without doubt.

to make sure. to be certain: *We must make sure that our facts are correct before we make an accusation.*

sure-fire (shoor′fīr′) *adj. Informal.* that cannot fail: *a sure-fire scheme.*

sure-foot·ed (shoor′foot′id) *adj.* not liable to stumble or fall: *a sure-footed horse.* —**sure′-foot′ed·ness,** *n.*

sure·ly (shoor′lē) *adv.* **1.** without doubt; truly; positively: *He will surely be there.* **2.** firmly; steadily.

sure·ty (shoor′ə tē) *n. pl.,* **sure·ties. 1.** security, as against loss or damage. **2.** a person who agrees to be responsible for the debts or actions of another. **3.** the state of being sure; assurance; certainty.

surf (surf) *n.* the swell of the sea or the splash of its waves breaking on the shore or upon a reef. —*v.i.* to ride on the crest of a wave, usually on a surfboard. —**surf′er,** *n.*

sur·face (sur′fis) *n.* **1.** the upper or outer part of a thing: *the earth's surface, the surface of a lake.* **2.** outer appearance: *The problem seemed simple on the surface.* —*adj.* **1.** of, on, or relating to a surface. **2.** without much depth; superficial: *a surface explanation.* —*v.,* **sur·faced, sur·fac·ing.** —*v.i.* to come or rise to the surface: *The submarine surfaced.* —*v.t.* to cover or finish the surface of: *The workmen surfaced the tennis courts with clay.*

surf·board (surf′bôrd′) *n.* a long, flat board used to ride on the crest of a wave. —*v.i.* to engage in surfing.

surf·cast·ing (surf′kas′ting) *n.* the sport of fishing by casting a line into the surf from the shore.

sur·feit (sur′fit) *v.t.* to feed or supply to excess; sate; satiate. —*n.* **1.** an excessive amount or supply. **2.** the act or instance of taking an excessive amount, as of food or drink. **3.** disgust or discomfort caused by this.

surf·ing (sur′fing) *n.* a sport in which a person rides the crest of a wave into the shore, usually on a surfboard.

Surfboard

surge (surj) *v.i.,* **surged, surg·ing. 1.** to move with a

at; āpe; cär; end; mē; it; īce; hot; ōld; fôrk; wood; fōōl; oil; out; up; turn; sing; thin; this; hw in white; zh in treasure. The symbol ə stands for the sound of a in about, e in taken, i in pencil, o in lemon, and u in circus.

violent, heaving motion: *The crowd surged forward to catch a glimpse of the visiting celebrity.* **2.** to increase or rise suddenly: *The crime rate surged during the heat wave.* —*n.* **1.** a heaving motion like that of waves. **2.** a sudden increase or onset: *a surge of electric current.* **3.** a rolling swell or wave.

sur·geon (sur′jən) *n.* a doctor of medicine who specializes in surgery.

Surgeon General *pl.,* **Surgeons General. 1.** the chief medical officer of one of the armed services of the United States. **2.** the chief medical officer of the U.S. Public Health Service.

sur·ger·y (sur′jər ē) *n. pl.,* **sur·ger·ies. 1.** the branch of medicine that deals with the removal or repair of injured or diseased parts of the body. **2.** the removal or repair of injured or diseased parts of the body. **3.** a room or suite of rooms in a hospital where this is done.

sur·gi·cal (sur′ji kəl) *adj.* of, relating to, or used in surgery: *surgical procedures, surgical instruments.* —**sur′gi·cal·ly,** *adv.*

Su·ri·name (soor′ə nam′) *n.* a country on the northeastern coast of South America, formerly known as Dutch or Netherlands Guiana. Capital, Paramaribo. Area, 55,144 sq. mi. Pop. (1978 est.), 445,000.

sur·ly (sur′lē) *adj.,* **sur·li·er, sur·li·est.** ill-tempered and rude; sullen and unfriendly: *a surly person, a surly demand.* —**sur′li·ness,** *n.*

sur·mise (*v.,* sər mīz′; *n.,* sər mīz′, sur′mīz) *v.,* **sur·mised, sur·mis·ing.** —*v.t.* to arrive at an idea or opinion about with little or no evidence; guess: *When we didn't see his coat, we surmised that he had left.* —*v.i.* to guess. —*n.* an idea or opinion based on little or no evidence.

sur·mount (sər mount′) *v.t.* **1.** to overcome; conquer: *to surmount difficulties.* **2.** to climb up or get over: *to surmount a wall.* **3.** to stand, lie, or be above; top; crown: *A dome surmounts the building.* —**sur·mount′a·ble,** *adj.*

sur·name (sur′nām′) *n.* **1.** a last name or family name. **2.** an added name or nickname: *Czar Ivan IV was given the surname "the Terrible."* —*v.t.,* **sur·named, sur·nam·ing.** to give a surname to; call by a surname.

sur·pass (sər pas′) *v.t.* **1.** to go beyond; be better than; excel: *That athlete surpasses the other members of the team in ability.* **2.** to be beyond the range or reach of; exceed. —**sur·pass′a·ble,** *adj.* —**sur·pass′ing·ly,** *adv.*

sur·plice (sur′plis) *n.* a white garment with wide sleeves worn by clergymen and choir members in certain churches.

sur·plus (sur′plus′, sur′pləs) *n.* an amount or quantity above what is used or needed; excess: *a crop surplus, a surplus of dishes.* —*adj.* that is over and above what is used or needed: *surplus army goods.*

Surplice

sur·prise (sər prīz′) *v.t.,* **sur·prised, sur·pris·ing. 1.** to cause to feel sudden wonder or astonishment: *Mr. Smith surprised his children with presents. Johnny surprised his parents by cleaning out the garage.* **2.** to come upon suddenly or unexpectedly; take or catch unawares: *He surprised a thief when he entered the apartment.* **3.** to attack or capture suddenly and without warning: *They surprised the enemy with a night attack.* —*n.* **1.** the state or feeling of being surprised; sudden feeling of wonder. **2.** something that causes this feeling: *The gift was a delightful surprise.* **3.** the act of surprising.

sur·pris·ing (sər prī′zing) *adj.* causing surprise or wonder; unexpected: *The home team experienced a surprising defeat.* —**sur·pris′ing·ly,** *adv.*

sur·re·al·ism (sə rē′ə liz′əm) *n.* a movement in twentieth-century art and literature emphasizing subconscious reality and the importance of dreams and fantasy.

sur·re·al·ist (sə rē′ə list) *n.* an artist or writer whose work is characterized by surrealism. —**sur·re′al·is′tic,** *adj.* —**sur·re′al·is′ti·cal·ly,** *adv.*

sur·ren·der (sə ren′dər) *v.t.* **1.** to give over possession or control of to another or others: *The soldiers surrendered the fort to the enemy.* **2.** to yield (oneself) to an emotion, influence, or course of action: *She surrendered herself to sorrow.* —*v.i.* to give oneself up: *The outlaw surrendered to the sheriff.* —*n.* the act of surrendering.

sur·rep·ti·tious (sur′əp tish′əs) *adj.* **1.** done by secret, sly means: *a surreptitious meeting.* **2.** acting in a secret, sly way: *a surreptitious investigator.* —**sur′rep·ti′tious·ly,** *adv.* —**sur′rep·ti′tious·ness,** *n.*

sur·rey (sur′ē) *n. pl.,* **sur·reys.** a light, four-wheeled carriage with two seats, usually covered with a top. [From *Surrey,* a county in England, where it was first made.]

Surrey

sur·ro·gate (sur′ə gāt′, sur′ə git) *n.* **1.** a person or thing that is substituted for another; substitute. **2.** in some states, a judge having charge of such matters as guardianships and wills.

sur·round (sə round′) *v.t.* to be on all sides of; form a circle around: *A crowd surrounded the movie star's car. He surrounded the pool with a fence.*

sur·round·ings (sə roun′dingz) *n., pl.* the objects, influences, or conditions of a place or way of life: *Tourists sought out the peaceful surroundings of farm villages.*

sur·tax (sur′taks′) *n. pl.,* **sur·tax·es.** an additional or extra tax, especially one added to the normal income tax. Also, **supertax.**

sur·veil·lance (sər vā′ləns) *n.* **1.** a close watch kept over a person, group, or place in order to gather information: *The police have the suspect under constant surveillance.* **2.** a close watch for the purpose of supervision and control: *The new staff members worked under his surveillance.*

sur·vey (*v.,* sər vā′; *n.,* sur′vā, sər vā′) *v.t.* **1.** to view or examine as a whole: *From the tower he surveyed the entire city below.* **2.** to examine or inspect in detail: *The authorities surveyed the damage after the tornado.* **3.** to find the shape, area, and boundaries of (a region or tract of land) by taking measurements. —*v.i.* to survey land. —*n. pl.,* **sur·veys. 1.** a detailed study or examination: *A survey was conducted to find out how many people used the product.* **2.** a general view: *This college course is a survey of American literature.* **3.** the act or process of surveying land.

sur·vey·ing (sər vā′ing) *n.* the act, science, or occupation of making land surveys.

sur·vey·or (sər vā′ər) *n.* a person or thing that surveys, especially a person whose work is surveying land.

sur·viv·al (sər vī′vəl) *n.* **1.** the act of surviving or the state of having survived. **2.** a person or thing that survives, such as a custom or ritual from the past.

sur·vive (sər vīv′) *v.,* **sur·vived, sur·viv·ing.** —*v.t.* **1.** to live longer than; outlive: *He survived his brothers.* **2.** to live or be active through and after: *Two people survived the automobile accident.* —*v.i.* to continue to live or remain active; endure: *Those plants won't survive without sunlight.*

sur·vi·vor (sər vī′vər) *n.* a person or thing that survives.

sus·cep·ti·bil·i·ty (sə sep′tə bil′ə tē) *n. pl.,* **sus·cep·ti-**

bil·i·ties. 1. the quality or condition of being susceptible. **2. susceptibilities.** strong or sensitive feelings.

sus·cep·ti·ble (sə sep′tə bəl) *adj.* **1.** easily affected or influenced by; sensitive or impressionable: *Jane is a susceptible person and easily moved by other people's troubles. My little brother is susceptible to colds.* **2.** able to undergo or experience: *Her research paper is susceptible of improvement.* —**sus·cep′ti·ble·ness,** *n.* —**sus·cep′ti·bly,** *adv.*

sus·pect (*v.,* sə spekt′; *n.,* sus′pekt′; *adj.,* sus′pekt′, sə-spekt′) *v.t.* **1.** to consider true, likely, or possible: *I suspect she has already left for the day.* **2.** to think (someone) guilty with little or no proof: *The police suspected him of the crime.* **3.** to have doubts about; lack confidence in; distrust: *I suspect her sincerity.* —*v.i.* to have suspicions. —*n.* a person who is suspected, especially of having committed a crime. —*adj.* open to or viewed with distrust; suspected: *His motives are suspect.*

sus·pend (sə spend′) *v.t.* **1.** to attach from above so as to hang down: *Dad suspended the swing from a tree branch.* **2.** to hold in place as if attached from above: *Bits of matter were suspended in the water.* **3.** to make no longer effective or binding, especially for a time: *His driver's license was suspended.* **4.** to cause to stop for a time; interrupt: *He suspended payments on the car.* **5.** to keep out or prevent from attending for a time, usually as a punishment: *The principal suspended the boy from school.* —*v.i.* to stop for a time.

sus·pend·ers (sə spen′dərz) *n., pl.* a pair of straps worn over the shoulders and attached to the waistband of trousers or a skirt, usually worn instead of a belt to hold up the garment.

sus·pense (sə spens′) *n.* **1.** a state of being undecided or in doubt: *We were all left in suspense, wondering who had won the contest.* **2.** the worry or tension resulting from this. —**sus·pense′ful,** *adj.*

sus·pen·sion (sə spen′shən) *n.* **1.** the act of suspending or the state of being suspended. **2.** a mixture made up of small solid particles or liquid droplets in a liquid. The particles will separate out if the suspension is allowed to stand. **3.** the state or condition of the particles or droplets in such a mixture: *Dirt particles are held in suspension in muddy water.* **4.** a stopping for a time; interruption.

suspension bridge, a bridge suspended from cables or chains hung between towers.

Suspension bridge

sus·pi·cion (sə spish′ən) *n.* **1.** the act or instance of suspecting something wrong or bad with little or no proof; feeling of distrust or uncertainty. **2.** a feeling or impression: *I have a suspicion that you are right.* **3.** the state or condition of being suspected: *Such an honest man is above suspicion.* **4.** a slight trace or suggestion.

sus·pi·cious (sə spish′əs) *adj.* **1.** tending to arouse suspicion; questionable: *There were a number of suspicious people near the scene of the crime.* **2.** inclined to suspect; distrustful: *The old man is suspicious of strangers.* **3.** expressing or indicating suspicion: *They gave the stranger a suspicious glance.* —**sus·pi′cious·ly,** *adv.* —**sus·pi′cious·ness,** *n.*

Sus·que·han·na (sus′kwə han′ə) *n.* a river flowing through New York, Pennsylvania, and Maryland into Chesapeake Bay.

sus·tain (sə stān′) *v.t.* **1.** to keep up or in effect: *The boy could not sustain interest in the book.* **2.** to keep up the spirits or courage of; keep from despair; comfort: *The poor*

man's religious faith sustained him. **3.** to supply with food, clothing, or other needed things; support: *The supplies will sustain the explorers for a month.* **4.** to keep from sinking or falling; support from below: *These posts are needed to sustain the platform.* **5.** to undergo or experience, as loss or injury: *She sustained a broken arm in the accident.* **6.** to accept or uphold as true or just: *The judge sustained the objection.* **7.** to prove; confirm: *These new facts sustain our earlier opinion.* —**sus·tain′a·ble,** *adj.* —**sus·tain′er,** *n.*

sus·te·nance (sus′tə nəns) *n.* **1.** something that sustains or supports life, especially food. **2.** the act of sustaining or the state of being sustained.

su·ture (sōō′chər) *n.* **1.** the act or method of joining together the edges of a cut or wound by or as if by stitching. **2.** one of the stitches or fastenings of thread, wire, or other material so used. **3.** a line or seam formed in joining two surfaces, such as that of a wound sewed together.

su·ze·rain (sōō′zer in, sōō′zə rān′) *n.* **1.** in feudalism, a lord to whom vassals gave their services in return for the use of a part of his land. **2.** a country that has control of another country, but allows it to have its own government.

su·ze·rain·ty (sōō′zər in tē, sōō′ze rān′tē) *n. pl.,* **su·ze·rain·ties.** the power or position of a suzerain.

Sverd·lovsk (sverd lôfsk′) *n.* a city in the west-central Soviet Union. Pop. (1971 est.), 1,048,000.

SW, S.W., southwest.

swab (swob) *also,* **swob.** *n.* **1.** a small piece of cotton, sponge, or other material, usually wound on a small stick, used to apply medication or cosmetics and to clean certain parts of the body, as the ears. **2.** a mop used on ships to clean decks or other surfaces. —*v.t.,* **swabbed, swab·bing.** to clean, treat, or apply with a swab: *to swab a cut with ointment.*

swad·dle (swod′əl) *v.t.,* **swad·dled, swad·dling. 1.** to wrap or bind with bandages. **2.** to wrap (an infant) in swaddling clothes. —*n.* a band of cloth or bandage used for swaddling.

swaddling clothes, long, narrow bands of cloth formerly wrapped around newborn infants. Also, **swaddling bands.**

swag (swag) *n. Slang.* stolen goods or profits; booty.

swag·ger (swag′ər) *v.i.* **1.** to walk or behave in a bold, rude, or arrogant manner: *He swaggered about, daring the other boy to come out and fight.* **2.** to boast; brag. —*n.* a swaggering movement or manner. —**swag′-ger·er,** *n.*

swagger stick, a short, light cane with metal at each end, carried especially by army officers.

Swa·hi·li (swä hē′lē) *n.* a Bantu language containing words borrowed from Arabic. It is spoken mainly in eastern Africa and the Congo.

swain (swān) *n.* **1.** a lover; suitor. **2.** a country youth. ▲ used especially in literature.

swal·low¹ (swol′ō) *v.t.* **1.** to cause (something, such as food) to pass from the mouth to the stomach. **2.** to take in as if by swallowing: *The darkness swallowed them. The earthquake swallowed up the whole city.* **3.** to take back: *Don swallowed his words.* **4.** to keep from expressing; suppress: *John swallowed his pride and asked for our help.*

at; āpe; cär; end; mē; it; īce; hot; ōld; fôrk; wood; fōōl; oil; out; up; turn; sing; thin; this; hw in white; zh in treasure. The symbol ə stands for the sound of a in about, e in taken, i in pencil, o in lemon, and u in circus.

5. to put up with; accept without protest; tolerate: *He swallowed the insult.* **6.** *Informal.* to accept without question: *She swallowed that lie.* —*v.i.* to perform the act or motion of swallowing. —*n.* **1.** the act of swallowing. **2.** the quantity swallowed at one time: *She took a swallow of tea.* [Old English *swelgan*.] —**swal′low·er**, *n.*

swal·low² (swol′ō) *n.* any of a group of birds having a slender body and a deeply forked tail. [Old English *swealwe*.]

swal·low·tail (swol′ō tāl′) *n.* **1.** a deeply forked tail, such as that of a kite or certain butterflies, resembling the tail of a swallow. **2.** see **swallow-tailed coat.**

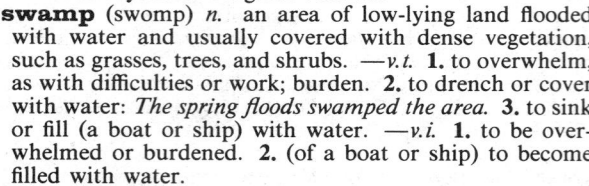
Swallow²

swal·low-tailed coat (swol′ō-tāld′) a man's coat with tails, used for formal wear.

swam (swam) a past tense of **swim.**

swa·mi (swä′mē) *n. pl.,* **swa·mis.** a Hindu mystic or religious teacher.

swamp (swomp) *n.* an area of low-lying land flooded with water and usually covered with dense vegetation, such as grasses, trees, and shrubs. —*v.t.* **1.** to overwhelm, as with difficulties or work; burden. **2.** to drench or cover with water: *The spring floods swamped the area.* **3.** to sink or fill (a boat or ship) with water. —*v.i.* **1.** to be overwhelmed or burdened. **2.** (of a boat or ship) to become filled with water.

swamp·land (swomp′land′) *n.* land covered with swamps.

swamp·y (swom′pē) *adj.,* **swamp·i·er, swamp·i·est.** of or resembling a swamp or swamps.

swan (swon) *n.* any of several graceful, long-necked birds having a broad, flat bill and webbed feet.

swan dive, a dive in which the arms are extended straight out to the side, with the back arched, the arms being brought together in front of the head just before entering the water.

Swan

swank·y (swang′kē) *adj.,* **swank·i·er, swank·i·est.** *Slang.* having much elegance; stylish; posh: *a swanky hotel.* Also, **swank** (swangk). —**swank′i·ly**, *adv.* —**swank′i·ness**, *n.*

swan's-down (swonz′doun′) *n.* **1.** the soft down of a swan. **2.** a fine, thick, soft fabric made from wool or cotton, used for such items as infants' wear.

swan song 1. the song that, according to legend, a swan sings just before it dies. **2.** a final work, as by an artist, musician, or actor at the end of a career or before death.

swap (swop) *also,* **swop.** *v.,* **swapped, swap·ping.** *Informal.* —*v.t.* to exchange (something) for something else; trade: *The boy swapped a pair of skates for a baseball glove.* —*v.i.* to trade: *He wasn't willing to swap.* —**swap′per**, *n.*

sward (swôrd) *n.* land covered with grass; lawn; meadow.

swarm (swôrm) *n.* **1.** a large group of insects or other small animals flying or moving about together. **2.** a group of bees, led by the queen of a hive, that flies off together to start a new colony. **3.** a great number of people or animals: *Swarms of shoppers filled the stores at Christmas time.* —*v.i.* **1.** (of bees) to fly off together to start a new colony. **2.** to come together or move in a large mass or group: *The audience swarmed out of the theater.* **3.** to be filled or overrun; teem: *The river swarmed with alligators.* —*v.t.* to fill with a throng or multitude; crowd.

swarth·y (swôr′thē, swôr′thē) *adj.,* **swarth·i·er, swarth·i·est.** having a dark color or complexion: *swarthy skin.* Also *(archaic),* **swart** (swôrt), **swarth** (swôrth). —**swarth′i·ly**, *adv.* —**swarth′i·ness**, *n.*

swash (swosh) *v.t.* to dash (water or other liquid) about; splash. —*v.i.* to strike or wash with a splash, as waves do. —*n.* the swashing action or sound of water.

swash·buck·ler (swosh′buk′lər) *n.* a bragging, swaggering adventurer or soldier.

swash·buck·ling (swosh′buk′ling) *adj.* like a swashbuckler.

swas·ti·ka (swos′ti kə) *n.* **1.** a symbol or ornament having the shape of a cross with the arms bent in the center at right angles, used in both ancient and modern times. **2.** this symbol, with the arms bent clockwise, used as an emblem of the Nazi party.

swat (swot) *v.,* **swat·ted, swat·ting.** —*v.t.* to hit (someone or something) with a short, sharp blow: *to swat a mosquito.* —*v.i.* to hit someone or something with a short, sharp blow: *He swatted at the fly with a rolled-up newspaper.* —*n.* a short, sharp blow. —**swat′ter**, *n.*

swatch (swoch) *n. pl.,* **swatch·es.** a small sample of a particular cloth or other material.

swath (swoth) *also,* **swathe.** *n.* **1.** the area covered by a single sweep of a scythe or other mowing tool or machine. **2.** a width or strip of grass or other grain cut in one such sweep. **3.** a long broad belt, strip, or path: *a swath of color.* **to cut a wide swath.** to make a big impression: *The speaker cut a wide swath with the audience.*

swathe (swāth) *v.t.,* **swathed, swath·ing.** **1.** to bind or wrap: *to swathe an arm with bandages.* **2.** to surround; enclose. —*n.* a wrapping or binding; bandage.

sway (swā) *v.i.* **1.** to move or swing back and forth or from side to side: *The dancers swayed in time to the music. The trees swayed in the wind.* **2.** to lean or turn to one side: *The car swayed off the road after taking a sharp turn.* —*v.t.* **1.** to cause to move or swing back and forth or from side to side. **2.** to cause to waver or turn aside: *Nothing would sway her in her opinion.* **3.** to cause to be directed or controlled in a certain way; influence: *The speaker swayed the audience with his forceful speech.* —*n.* **1.** the act of swaying. **2.** influence, control, or rule: *The dictator held sway over the entire country.*

sway·back (swā′bak′) *n.* a sagging condition of the back, as of a horse, usually because of overwork.

sway·backed (swā′bakt′) *adj.* having a sagging back.

Swa·zi·land (swä′zē land′) *n.* a country in southeastern Africa. Capital, Mbabane. Area, 6705 sq. mi. Pop. (1971 est.), 420,000.

swear (swer) *v.,* **swore, sworn, swear·ing.** —*v.i.* **1.** to make a solemn statement with an appeal to God or to some other sacred being or object: *The witnesses in the trial had to swear before they could testify.* **2.** to make a solemn promise. **3.** to use profane language. —*v.t.* **1.** to state (something) solemnly with an appeal to God or some other sacred being or object: *The witness swore his oath.* **2.** to promise (something) in a solemn manner: *I swear that I'm telling the truth.* **3.** to cause to take an oath; bind by an oath: *The soldier was sworn to defend his country.*
  to swear by. a. to name (someone or something) when taking an oath. **b.** to place great confidence in.
  to swear in. to bring into office by administering an oath: *The judge swore in the mayor.*
  to swear off. *Informal.* to promise to give up: *John's father has sworn off smoking.*
  to swear out. to get (a warrant for arrest) by making a charge under oath.

swear·word (swer′wurd′) *n.* a profane word used in cursing or swearing.

sweat (swet) *n.* **1.** a clear salty fluid formed by glands beneath the skin and given off through the pores of the skin. **2.** a moisture given off by something or gathered on its surface by condensation. **3.** the act of giving off sweat through the pores of the skin. **4.** *Informal.* an emotional state, such as worry, impatience, or anger: *You needn't get into a sweat over the problem.* —*v.,* **sweat** or **sweat·ed, sweat·ing.** —*v.i.* **1.** to give off sweat through the pores of the skin. **2.** to gather moisture from the surrounding air by condensation: *The glass of ice water sweated in the hot, humid air.* **3.** *Informal.* to work hard; drudge; toil: *Jerry certainly sweated over his project for the science fair.* —*v.t.* **1.** to give off (moisture), as from pores. **2.** to cause to sweat. **3.** to cause to give off moisture. **4.** to get rid of by sweating: *He sweated off several pounds by working in the yard.* **5.** to cause to work hard; overwork: *The foreman at the factory sweated the workmen under him.*
   to sweat out. *Slang.* to wait anxiously or impatiently for: *He sweated out the results of the test.*

sweat·er (swet′ər) *n.* a knitted garment, often of wool, for the upper part of the body.

sweat gland, a small gland beneath the skin that gives off sweat.

sweat shirt, a loose-fitting cotton shirt worn during athletic exercise.

sweat·shop (swet′shop′) *n.* a factory or workshop where workers are employed for long hours, at low wages, or under poor conditions.

sweat·y (swet′ē) *adj.,* **sweat·i·er, sweat·i·est. 1.** covered with, stained with, or smelling of sweat: *sweaty hands, sweaty shoes.* **2.** causing sweat: *sweaty labor.* —**sweat′i·ly,** *adv.* —**sweat′i·ness,** *n.*

Swede (swēd) *n.* a person who was born or is living in Sweden.

Swe·den (swēd′ən) *n.* a country in northern Europe, on the eastern part of the Scandinavian peninsula. Capital, Stockholm. Area, 173,666 sq. mi. Pop. (1971 est.), 8,110,000.

Swed·ish (swē′dish) *n.* **1.** the people of Sweden as a group. **2.** the language of Sweden, a member of the Germanic language family. —*adj.* of or relating to Sweden, its people, their language, or their culture.

sweep (swēp) *v.,* **swept, sweep·ing.** —*v.t.* **1.** to clear or clean with a broom, brush, or the like: *to sweep a floor.* **2.** to remove or collect with a broom, brush, or the like: *to sweep bread crumbs up.* **3.** to pass over or through with a swift, continuous movement: *The sailor's eyes swept the horizon for a sign of land.* **4.** to move, bring, or carry with a swift movement: *The flood swept away everything in its path.* —*v.i.* **1.** to clear or clean a surface with a broom, brush, or the like. **2.** to move or pass along with a swift movement: *The wind swept through the trees.* —*n.* **1.** the act of sweeping. **2.** any swift, sweeping movement: *He removed the papers from the desk with one sweep of his hand.* **3.** a turn, bend, or curve: *the sweep of a dome.* **4.** the reach or range of a sweeping movement: *the sweep of a telescope as it scans the sky.* **5.** a person who sweeps, especially a chimney sweep. **6.** a long oar used to steer or propel a boat or ship. **7.** a victory in every part of a contest, game, or the like. **8. sweeps.** see **sweepstakes.**

sweep·er (swē′pər) *n.* a person or thing that sweeps floors or other surfaces.

sweep·ing (swē′ping) *adj.* **1.** moving, passing, or curving over a wide area: *a sweeping arc.* **2.** covering a wide area: *sweeping reforms.* —*n.* **1. sweepings.** things swept up; trash; rubbish. **2.** the act of a person or thing that sweeps. —**sweep′ing·ly,** *adv.*

sweep·stakes (swēp′stāks′) *also,* **sweep·stake.** *n., pl.* **1.** a lottery in which the winners are determined by the running of a horse race. **2.** a horse race run for this purpose. **3.** any lottery or contest. **4.** any of the prizes awarded in a lottery or similar contest.

sweet (swēt) *adj.* **1.** having a pleasant taste like that of sugar or honey. **2.** pleasing to the senses: *The flower has a sweet fragrance.* **3.** not sour or salted: *sweet cream, sweet butter.* **4.** having or marked by pleasing, agreeable, or kindly qualities: *Beth has a sweet disposition.* —*n.* **1.** a sweet dish, especially a dessert. **2. sweets.** sweet food, such as cake or candy. **3.** a person who is dear; darling. —**sweet′ly,** *adv.* —**sweet′ness,** *n.*

sweet·breads (swēt′bredz′) *n., pl.* the pancreas or thymus gland of an animal, especially a calf or lamb, when used as food.

sweet·bri·er (swēt′brī′ər) *also,* **sweet·bri·ar.** *n.* a rosebush bearing pink flowers and small scarlet fruit. Also, **eglantine.**

sweet corn, a variety of corn with kernels having a high sugar content, grown chiefly in the central United States.

sweet·en (swēt′ən) *v.t., v.i.* to make or become sweet or sweeter.

sweet·en·er (swēt′ən ər) *n.* something that sweetens, such as sugar or saccharin.

sweet·en·ing (swēt′ən ing) *n.* **1.** something that sweetens; sweetener. **2.** the act or process of making something sweet.

sweet flag, a fragrant plant whose root yields an aromatic oil used in liqueurs and perfumes.

sweet·heart (swēt′härt′) *n.* a person who is loved by and loves another: *They've been sweethearts for years.*

sweet·ish (swē′tish) *adj.* somewhat sweet.

sweet marjoram 1. the dried leaves of a fragrant plant, used as a spice. **2.** the plant bearing these leaves, grown as a garden herb.

sweet·meat (swēt′mēt′) *n.* any sweet food, such as candy, cake, or candied or preserved fruit.

sweet pea 1. a fragrant flower growing in a variety of colors. **2.** the plant bearing this flower, having a rough hairy stem and pairs of short oval or oblong leaflets.

sweet pepper 1. a mild-flavored fruit of a pepper plant, usually having a bell shape and eaten in its ripe (red) or unripe (green) state. **2.** the plant bearing this fruit.

sweet potato 1. a fleshy root of a long trailing vine, having soft orange flesh, cooked and eaten as a vegetable. **2.** the vine bearing this root, widely grown in warm areas throughout the world, having violet or pink flowers.

sweet tooth, a fondness for sweets.

sweet william *also,* **sweet William.** a plant widely grown for its red and white flowers with fringed petals.

swell (swel) *v.,* **swelled, swelled** or **swol·len, swell·ing.** —*v.i.* **1.** to increase in size: *The sponge swelled as it absorbed the water.* **2.** to bulge out: *The sails swelled in the breeze.* **3.** to increase in amount, degree, intensity, or force: *Attendance swelled at the evening concerts.* **4.** to rise above the ordinary level: *The heavy rains made the river swell.* **5.** *Informal.* to become filled with pride or other emotion: *His head swelled with pride.* —*v.t.* **1.** to cause to increase in size; enlarge: *The infection swelled his hand.* **2.** to cause to bulge out: *The wind swelled the sails.* **3.** to cause to increase in amount, degree, intensity, or force: *New mem-*

at; āpe; cär; end; mē; it; īce; hot; ōld; fôrk; wood; fo͞ol; oil; out; up; turn; sing; thin; this; hw in white; zh in treasure. The symbol ə stands for the sound of a in about, e in taken, i in pencil, o in lemon, and u in circus.

S

bers swelled the rolls of the club. —*n.* **1.** the act of swelling or the state of being swollen. **2.** a part that is swollen. **3.** a piece of land that rises gradually and evenly above the surrounding level. **4.** an unbroken wave or waves; billow; surge. **5.** *Music.* **a.** a gradual increase immediately followed by a gradual decrease in volume. **b.** the sign (<>) indicating this. **6.** *Informal.* a person of high social position, especially a person who is fashionably dressed. —*adj. Slang.* **1.** excellent; fine. **2.** elegant; stylish.

swell·ing (swel′ing) *n.* **1.** the act or process of increasing, as in size. **2.** an abnormal enlargement of some part of the body.

swel·ter (swel′tər) *v.i.* to sweat or grow tired or weak in great heat; suffer from heat. —*n.* a sweltering condition.

swel·ter·ing (swel′tər ing) *adj.* very hot: *a sweltering day.* —**swel′ter·ing·ly,** *adv.*

swept (swept) the past tense and past participle of **sweep.**

swept-back (swept′bak′) *adj.* (of the wings of an aircraft) extending back to form an acute angle with the main part or body of the aircraft.

swerve (swurv) *v.,* **swerved, swerv·ing.** —*v.i.* to turn aside suddenly: *The car swerved to avoid running into the motorcycle.* —*v.t.* to turn aside: *John swerved his truck.* —*n.* the act of swerving.

swift (swift) *adj.* **1.** moving or able to move with great speed; fleet: *a swift runner.* **2.** happening quickly or without delay: *a swift kick.* —*adv.* fast. —*n.* any of a group of birds resembling swallows, having narrow wings and dark gray, brown, or bluish feathers. —**swift′ly,** *adv.* —**swift′ness,** *n.*

Swift, Jonathan (swift) 1667–1745, English author.

swig (swig) *Informal. n.* a large swallow or gulp. —*v.t.,* **swigged, swig·ging.** to drink in large swallows or gulps. —**swig′ger,** *n.*

swill (swil) *n.* a mixture of liquid and solid food used to feed animals, especially slop fed to swine. —*v.t.* **1.** to drink freely or to excess; guzzle. **2.** to feed (hogs or other animals) with swill.

swim (swim) *v.,* **swam** or **swum, swim·ming.** —*v.i.* **1.** to move along in the water by moving the body or parts of the body. **2.** to float on water or other liquid. **3.** to be covered or flooded with water or other liquid: *The child's eyes swam with tears.* **4.** to have a dizzy feeling; whirl: *All this noise makes my head swim.* —*v.t.* to swim across or through: *Jim tried to swim the lake.* —*n.* the act, period, or distance of swimming: *She took a quick swim before lunch.* —**swim′mer,** *n.*

swim·ming (swim′ing) *n.* the act of a person or thing that swims.

swim·ming·ly (swim′ing lē) *adv.* very well; smoothly: *The two friends get along swimmingly.*

swimming pool, see **pool**[1] *(def. 2).*

swim·suit (swim′soot′) *n.* a garment worn for swimming; bathing suit.

swin·dle (swind′əl) *v.t.,* **swin·dled, swin·dling.** to take away money or property rightfully belonging to (someone) by fraud; defraud of money or property. —*n.* the act of swindling; fraud. —**swin′dler,** *n.*

swine (swīn) *n. pl.,* **swine. 1.** any of a group of animals, such as the pig or boar, having a long snout, cloven hoofs, and thick, bristly skin. **2.** a stupid, crude, or beastly person.

swine·herd (swīn′hurd′) *n.* a person who tends swine.

swing (swing) *v.,* **swung, swing·ing.** —*v.t.* **1.** to cause to move back and forth with a steady motion. **2.** to cause to turn on or as if on a hinge or pivot: *Jack swung the door shut.* **3.** to move or lift in a curved, sweeping motion: *Charlie swung the bat at the ball.* **4.** to cause to turn: *Jim swung his car off the highway onto the dirt road.* **5.** to hang:

He swung the lamp on a hook over the table. **6.** *Informal.* to manage or bring about successfully: *He swung public opinion to his side.* —*v.i.* **1.** to move back and forth with a steady motion: *The child likes to swing on the hammock.* **2.** to turn on or as if on a hinge or pivot: *The gate swung open.* **3.** to move something in a curved, sweeping motion: *The batter swung at the ball and missed.* **4.** to turn: *The car swung onto the road.* —*n.* **1.** the act of swinging: *the swing of a pendulum.* **2.** the distance covered in swinging. **3.** a seat hung by ropes or chains in which a person may move back and forth. **4.** a free, rhythmic movement or gait: *There is a swing in her walk.* **5.** a sweeping blow or stroke: *a swing of an ax.* **6.** a form of jazz developed in the 1930s. —**swing′er,** *n.*

swin·ish (swī′nish) *adj.* like a swine; stupid, crude, or beastly. —**swin′ish·ly,** *adv.* —**swin′ish·ness,** *n.*

swipe (swīp) *n. Informal.* a sweeping stroke or glancing blow: *The cat took a swipe at the ball of yarn.* —*v.t.,* **swiped, swip·ing. 1.** *Informal.* to hit with a sweeping stroke or glancing blow. **2.** *Slang.* to steal; snatch: *to swipe a pocketbook.*

swirl (swurl) *v.i.* to move with a circular, twisting motion; whirl: *A gust of wind made the leaves swirl.* —*v.t.* to cause to whirl; twist. —*n.* **1.** a circular, twisting motion. **2.** something having a twisted shape; curl: *We decorated the cake with chocolate swirls.*

swish (swish) *v.i.* to move with or make a soft, muffled sound; rustle: *Her satin skirt swished as she walked down the hall.* —*v.t.* to cause to swish: *The cow stood silently swishing her tail.* —*n. pl.,* **swish·es.** a swishing movement or sound.

Swiss (swis) *n. pl.,* **Swiss.** a person who was born or is living in Switzerland. —*adj.* of or relating to Switzerland, its people, or their culture.

Swiss cheese, a firm, pale-yellow cheese having many large holes.

switch (swich) *n. pl.,* **switch·es. 1.** a slender rod, twig, or stick used for whipping. **2.** a stroke or lash given with this. **3.** the act of changing, shifting, or turning aside: *Tom made a switch from coffee to tea.* **4.** a device used to open or close an electric circuit. **5.** an apparatus for shifting trains from one track to another. —*v.t.* **1.** to beat, strike, or whip with a switch. **2.** to move or swing suddenly: *The cat switched his tail in anger.* **3.** to change, shift, or turn aside: *Jack switched channels on the television.* **4.** to exchange: *Phil and his friend switched coats.* **5.** to connect or disconnect by means of a switch: *Mary switched the lights on.* **6.** to move (a train) from one track to another; shunt. —*v.i.* to change, shift, or turn aside: *Helen switched to another class.* —**switch′er,** *n.*

switch·blade (swich′blād′) *n.* a pocketknife with a blade that is forced out by a spring when a button on the side of the handle is pressed.

switch·board (swich′bôrd′) *n.* a control panel with switches or openings for plugs, used to connect or disconnect electric circuits, as for telephone lines.

switch hitter, a baseball player who can bat both left-handed and right-handed.

switch·man (swich′mən) *n. pl.,* **switch·men** (swich′-mən). a man in charge of one or more switches on a railroad.

switch·yard (swich′yärd′) *n.* a railroad yard where railroad cars are brought together to form a train, and where trains are switched from one track to another.

Switz·er·land (swit′sər lənd) *n.* a country in central Europe. Capital, Bern. Area, 15,940 sq. mi. Pop. (1971 est.), 6,310,000.

swiv·el (swiv′əl) *n.* **1.** a link or other fastening device that allows attached parts to turn freely. **2.** a base or support placed upon a pivot, on which something, such as a chair or stool, can be turned. —*v.*, **swiv·eled, swiv·el·ing;** *also,* British, **swiv·elled, swiv·el·ling.** —*v.i.* to turn on or as if on a swivel: *Alice swiveled around on the piano stool.* —*v.t.* **1.** to turn (something) on or as if on a swivel: *He swiveled his chair around.* **2.** to secure with a swivel.

swivel chair, a chair whose seat revolves on a swivel.

swol·len (swō′lən) *v.* a past participle of **swell.** —*adj.* made larger by or as if by swelling.

swoon (swōōn) *v.i.* to lose consciousness briefly; faint. —*n.* the act of swooning.

swoop (swōōp) *v.i.* to rush or come down with a sudden, sweeping movement, as a bird diving on its prey: *Outlaws swooped down from the hills to attack the stagecoach.* —*v.t.* to seize or remove suddenly; scoop: *A crane swooped up the junk on the vacant lot.* —*n.* the act of swooping.

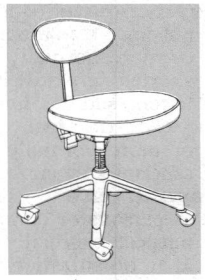

Swivel chair

sword (sôrd) *n.* **1.** a weapon of metal with a hilt and a straight or curved pointed blade, used for thrusting or cutting. **2.** force or the use of force, as in war: *The pen is mightier than the sword* (Edward Bulwer-Lytton). —**sword′like′,** *adj.*

sword·fish (sôrd′fish′) *n. pl.,* **sword·fish** or **sword·fish·es.** a large food and game fish, having a streamlined body without scales and a long, flattened, swordlike snout.

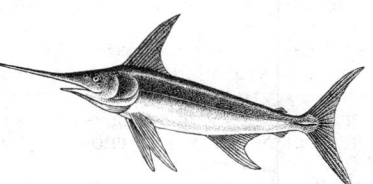

Swordfish

sword·play (sôrd′plā′) *n.* the act or technique of using a sword.

swords·man (sôrdz′mən) *n. pl.,* **swords·men** (sôrdz′-mən). **1.** a person who is armed with a sword, such as a soldier. **2.** a person who is skilled in the use of a sword.

swore (swôr) the past tense of **swear.**

sworn (swôrn) the past participle of **swear.**

swum (swum) the past participle and a past tense of **swim.**

swung (swung) the past tense and past participle of **swing.**

syc·a·more (sik′ə môr′) *n.* **1.** a tree found in eastern North America, having smooth, brown bark that flakes off in thin layers, leaving irregular patches on the trunk. Also, **buttonwood. 2.** a fig tree found in Egypt and Asia Minor, bearing sweet fruit that can be eaten.

syc·o·phant (sik′ə fənt) *n.* a person who flatters powerful or important people as a means of gaining favor or influence. —**syc·o·phan·tic** (sik′ə fan′tik), *adj.*

Syd·ney (sid′nē) *n.* the chief port and largest city of Australia, on the eastern coast of the country. It is the capital of New South Wales. Pop. (1970 est., city and suburbs), 2,780,300.

syl·lab·ic (si lab′ik) *adj.* **1.** of, relating to, or made of a syllable or syllables. **2.** relating to a consonant that forms a separate syllable by itself without the help of a vowel, such as the *l* in *rattle.* —**syl·lab′i·cal·ly,** *adv.*

syl·lab·i·cate (si lab′ə kāt′) *v.t.,* **syl·lab·i·cat·ed, syl·lab·i·cat·ing.** to divide into syllables; syllabify. —**syl·lab·i·ca′tion,** *n.*

syl·lab·i·fy (si lab′ə fī′) *v.t.,* **syl·lab·i·fied, syl·lab·i·fy·ing.** to divide into syllables. —**syl·lab′i·fi·ca′tion,** *n.*

syl·la·ble (sil′ə bəl) *n.* **1.** a word or part of a word pronounced with a single uninterrupted sounding of the voice. The words *bit* and *break* have one syllable; the word *amazement* has three. **2.** a letter or group of letters used in writing and printing to represent this, serving to show where a word may be hyphenated at the end of a line.

syl·la·bus (sil′ə bəs) *n. pl.,* **syl·la·bi** (sil′ə bī′) or **syl·la·bus·es.** a brief summary or outline of something, as in a course of study.

syl·lo·gism (sil′ə jiz′əm) *n.* **1.** a form of reasoning having two statements or premises and a conclusion that is logically drawn from them. If the premises are accepted as true, it must follow that the conclusion is true. For example: All dogs have four legs; a collie is a dog; therefore, a collie has four legs. **2.** reasoning based on deduction; deductive reasoning.

sylph (silf) *n.* **1.** a slender, graceful girl or young woman. **2.** an imaginary being supposed to inhabit the air.

syl·van (sil′vən) *also,* **sil·van.** *adj.* **1.** of, located, or living in a wood or woods: *a sylvan deity.* **2.** formed by or filled with trees; wooded; woody: *a sylvan grove.*

sym·bi·o·sis (sim′bī ō′sis, sim′bē ō′sis) *n. pl.,* **sym·bi·o·ses** (sim′bī ō′sēz, sim′bē ō′sēz). the living together in close, and often helpful, association of two living beings that are not alike. The association between termites and the very tiny animals, or protozoans, that live in their stomachs and intestines is an example of symbiosis. The protozoans break down the cellulose eaten by the termite so that it can be digested, and the termite, in turn, provides all the protozoans' nourishment.

sym·bi·ot·ic (sim′bī ot′ik, sim′bē ot′ik) *adj.* of, relating to, or characterized by symbiosis.

sym·bol (sim′bəl) *n.* **1.** something that stands for or represents something else: *The dove is the symbol of peace. A gold ring is a symbol of marriage.* **2.** a letter or other written figure used to represent something, as in chemistry or mathematics: *C is a symbol for carbon.*

sym·bol·ic (sim bol′ik) *adj.* **1.** serving as a symbol: *The owl is symbolic of wisdom and learning.* **2.** relating to, expressed by, or containing a symbol or symbols: *That poet writes symbolic poetry.* Also, **sym·bol·i·cal** (sim bol′i kəl). —**sym·bol′i·cal·ly,** *adv.*

sym·bol·ism (sim′bə liz′əm) *n.* **1.** the use of symbols, as in art or literature, to represent or express things or ideas. **2.** a system of symbols: *In the symbolism used by the early Christians, the fish represents Christ.*

sym·bol·ist (sim′bə list) *n.* a person who uses or is skilled in the use of symbolism, especially an artist or writer.

sym·bol·ize (sim′bə līz′) *v.,* **sym·bol·ized, sym·bol·iz·ing.** —*v.t.* **1.** to be or serve as a symbol of; represent: *A lily symbolizes purity.* **2.** to represent by a symbol or symbols: *Writing symbolizes the sounds that we make in speaking.* —*v.i.* to use symbols. —**sym′bol·i·za′tion,** *n.*

sym·met·ri·cal (si met′ri kəl) *adj.* having or showing symmetry. See **asymmetrical** for illustration. Also, **sym·met·ric** (si met′rik). —**sym·met′ri·cal·ly,** *adv.*

sym·me·try (sim′ə trē) *n. pl.,* **sym·me·tries. 1.** an arrangement of parts that are alike on either side of a central line, as in the structure of a leaf, or around a central point,

at; āpe; cär; end; mē; it; īce; hot; ōld; fôrk; wood; fōōl; oil; out; up; turn; sing; thin; **this**; hw in white; zh in treasure. The symbol ə stands for the sound of **a** in about, e in taken, i in pencil, o in lemon, and u in circus.

S

as in the structure of a starfish. **2.** beauty, proportion, and harmony of form.

sym·pa·thet·ic (sim′pə thet′ik) *adj.* **1.** feeling or expressing sympathy: *a sympathetic friend, a sympathetic statement.* **2.** in agreement with; in favor of: *He is sympathetic to our plans.* —**sym′pa·thet′i·cal·ly,** *adv.*

sym·pa·thize (sim′pə thīz′) *v.i.,* **sym·pa·thized, sym·pa·thiz·ing. 1.** to feel or express compassion. **2.** to agree with the feelings, ideas, or aims of; be in accord: *I sympathize with his efforts for reform.* —**sym′pa·thiz′ing·ly,** *adv.*

sym·pa·thy (sim′pə thē) *n. pl.,* **sym·pa·thies. 1.** the ability to share the feelings of another or others. **2.** sorrow for the unhappiness or suffering of another or others: *The newspaper story aroused much sympathy for the victims of the hurricane.* **3.** the state or condition of having the same interests or tastes. **4.** agreement; support: *I am in sympathy with what he is doing.*

sym·phon·ic (sim fon′ik) *adj.* of, relating to, or like a symphony or symphony orchestra.

sym·pho·ny (sim′fə nē) *n. pl.,* **sym·pho·nies. 1.** a composition for an orchestra, usually having three or four movements. **2.** see **symphony orchestra. 3.** harmony, as of sounds.

symphony orchestra, a large orchestra for playing symphonies and other similar compositions, usually having string, brass, woodwind, and percussion sections.

sym·po·si·um (sim pō′zē əm) *n. pl.,* **sym·po·si·ums** or **sym·po·si·a** (sim pō′zē ə). **1.** a meeting or conference for the discussion of a particular subject. **2.** a collection of opinions or comments on a particular subject, especially a published group of essays or articles.

symp·tom (simp′təm) *n.* **1.** something that indicates or accompanies a disease or other disorder: *A sore throat and runny nose are often symptoms of a cold.* **2.** anything serving as an indication of something: *The disappearance of fish in a river may be a symptom of water pollution.*

symp·to·mat·ic (simp′tə mat′ik) *adj.* **1.** indicating or accompanying a disease or other disorder: *Repeated coughing may be symptomatic of tuberculosis.* **2.** serving as an indication of something. —**symp′to·mat′i·cal·ly,** *adv.*

syn. 1. synonym. **2.** synonymous.

syn·a·gogue (sin′ə gog′) *n.* **1.** a congregation of Jews. **2.** a building used for their instruction and worship.

syn·apse (sin′aps, si naps′) *n.* the point at which a nerve impulse is transmitted from one nerve cell to another.

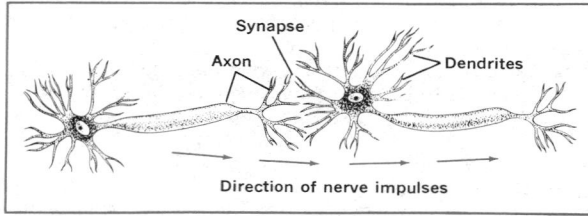

Synapse

syn·chro·nism (sing′krə niz′əm) *n.* the condition or quality of happening at the same time; coincidence.

syn·chro·nize (sing′krə nīz′) *v.,* **syn·chro·nized, syn·chro·niz·ing.** —*v.i.* to happen at the same time; coincide: *The closing of the old store synchronized with the opening of the new shopping center.* —*v.t.* **1.** to cause to happen or operate at the same rate and exactly together: *to synchronize the sound and the action of a motion picture.* **2.** to make (timepieces) agree in keeping or indicating time: *The two boys synchronized their watches.* —**syn′chro·ni·za′tion,** *n.* —**syn′chro·niz′er,** *n.*

syn·chro·nous (sing′krə nəs) *adj.* **1.** happening at the same time. **2.** happening or operating at the same rate of speed. —**syn′chro·nous·ly,** *adv.*

syn·chro·tron (sing′krə tron′) *n.* a machine for accelerating subatomic particles, such as protons, to very high speeds by means of a magnetic field. The magnetic field is made stronger as the speed of the particles increases, so as to hold them in a stable orbit.

syn·co·pate (sing′kə pāt′) *v.t.,* **syn·co·pat·ed, syn·co·pat·ing. 1.** to modify (a passage of music) by stressing one or more normally unaccented beats in a measure. **2.** to shorten (a word) by leaving out one or more sounds or letters, such as *sou′wester* for *southwester.*

syn·co·pa·tion (sing′kə pā′shən) *n.* the stressing of one or more normally unaccented beats in a measure, used especially in jazz.

syn·di·cate (*n.,* sin′di kit; *v.,* sin′di kāt′) *n.* **1.** a group of persons or companies brought together for a business purpose, especially one requiring a large amount of money. **2.** an organization that sells material, such as special articles and photographs, for publication in a number of newspapers or periodicals at the same time. —*v.,* **syn·di·cat·ed, syn·di·cat·ing.** —*v.t.* **1.** to bring together in order to form a syndicate. **2.** to sell (an article, column, comic strip, or the like) for publication in a number of newspapers or periodicals at the same time. —*v.i.* to form a syndicate. —**syn′di·ca′tion,** *n.*

syn·drome (sin′drōm) *n.* a group of symptoms that together are characteristic of a particular disease or disorder.

syn·od (sin′əd) *n.* a council or assembly of church officials. —**syn′od·al,** *adj.*

syn·o·nym (sin′ə nim) *n.* a word that has the same or nearly the same meaning as another word. *Large* is a synonym of *big; leap* is a synonym of *jump.* See **antonym** for further information.

syn·on·y·mous (si non′ə məs) *adj.* being the same or very similar in meaning: *The words "bravery," "valor," "gallantry," and "courage" are synonymous.* —**syn·on′y·mous·ly,** *adv.*

syn·op·sis (si nop′sis) *n. pl.,* **syn·op·ses** (si nop′sēz). a brief statement giving a review or outline of a book, speech, play, or similar work; summary.

syn·tac·tic (sin tak′tik) *adj.* of, relating to, or according to the rules of syntax. Also, **syn·tac·ti·cal** (sin tak′ti kəl). —**syn·tac′ti·cal·ly,** *adv.*

syn·tax (sin′taks) *n.* the way in which words are put together to form sentences and phrases; relationship and arrangement of words in a sentence.

syn·the·sis (sin′thə sis) *n. pl.,* **syn·the·ses** (sin′thə sēz). **1.** the combining of separate parts or elements so as to form a whole. A chemical synthesis is made by combining two or more substances to form a new one. **2.** the whole that is formed in this manner.

syn·the·size (sin′thə sīz′) *v.t.,* **syn·the·sized, syn·the·siz·ing. 1.** to combine so as to form a whole. **2.** to produce by chemical synthesis: *to synthesize rubber.*

syn·thet·ic (sin thet′ik) *adj.* **1.** made artificially by chemical synthesis; not occurring naturally; man-made: *Nylon is a synthetic fiber.* **2.** without genuine emotion; not real: *a synthetic smile.* **3.** of, relating to, or having the nature of a synthesis. Also, **syn·thet·i·cal** (sin thet′i kəl). —*n.* something synthetic: *This fabric is a synthetic.* —**syn·thet′i·cal·ly,** *adv.*

syph·i·lis (sif′ə lis) *n.* a serious, infectious venereal disease. If not treated properly and quickly, the disease progresses by three stages, the first being characterized by a hard sore at the place where a person is first infected, and the second by a skin rash and sores. The third stage, which may develop in one to twenty years after infection, can damage the heart, blood vessels, spinal cord, eyes, or brain.

syph·i·lit·ic (sif'ə lit'ik) *adj.* of, relating to, or affected with syphilis. —*n.* a person who is affected with syphilis.

sy·phon (sī'fən) another spelling of **siphon.**

Syr·a·cuse (sir'ə kyoos') *n.* **1.** a city in central New York. Pop. (1970), 197, 208. **2.** a port city in southeastern Sicily, in ancient times a leading Greek city.

Syr·i·a (sēr'ē ə) *n.* a country in southwestern Asia. Capital, Damascus. Area, 71,498 sq. mi. Pop. (1980 est.), 8,617,000.

Syr·i·an (sēr'ē ən) *n.* a person who was born or is living in Syria. —*adj.* of or relating to Syria, its people, their language, or their culture.

sy·rin·ga (sə ring'gə) *n.* another word for **mock orange.**

sy·ringe (sə rinj') *n.* **1.** a device made up of a nozzle and a rubber bulb for drawing in and then forcing out a liquid in a thin stream. Syringes are used especially for injecting fluids into the body and cleansing wounds. **2.** see **hypodermic syringe.** —*v.t.,* **sy·ringed, sy·ring·ing. 1.** to inject (a liquid) with a syringe. **2.** to cleanse (a wound) with a syringe.

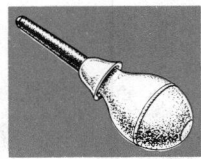

Syringe

syr·inx (sir'ingks) *n. pl.,* **sy·rin·ges** (sə rin'jēz) or **syr·inx·es. 1.** another word for **panpipe. 2.** the vocal organ of birds.

syr·up (sir'əp, sur'əp) *also,* **sir·up.** *n.* a sweet, thick liquid, often made by boiling sugar with water or fruit juice. Some syrups contain medication, as for a cough. —**syr'up·like',** *adj.*

syr·up·y (sir'ə pē, sur'ə pē) *also,* **sir·up·y.** *adj.* of or like syrup.

sys·tem (sis'təm) *n.* **1.** a group of things or parts related or combined in such a way as to form a whole: *a heating system, a system of roads, a public school system.* **2.** a group of organs or parts of the body that have a similar structure and act together to perform a function: *the digestive system.* **3.** the entire body: *His system was greatly weakened by his long illness.* **4.** a set of facts, rules, laws, beliefs, or principles: *a system of philosophy, a system of government.* **5.** an orderly method.

sys·tem·at·ic (sis'tə mat'ik) *adj.* **1.** of, relating to, or done by a system: *a systematic philosophy of life, a systematic study.* **2.** having an orderly method; methodical: *a systematic person.* Also, **sys·tem·at·i·cal** (sis'tə mat'i-kəl). —**sys'tem·at'i·cal·ly,** *adv.*

sys·tem·a·ti·za·tion (sis'tə mə ti zā'shən) *n.* **1.** the act or process of systematizing. **2.** something systematized.

sys·tem·a·tize (sis'tə mə tīz') *v.t.,* **sys·tem·a·tized, sys·tem·a·tiz·ing.** to form into or arrange according to a system. —**sys'tem·a·tiz'er,** *n.*

sys·tem·ic (sis tem'ik) *adj.* **1.** of or relating to a system or systems. **2.** of, relating to, or affecting the body as a whole: *the systemic circulation of the blood.*

sys·to·le (sis'tə lē) *n.* the period of contraction of the heart, during which the blood is forced out of the heart or from one chamber of the heart into another. These periods alternate rhythmically with the diastole, or period of relaxation. —**sys·tol·ic** (sis tol'ik), *adj.*

Szcze·cin (shche tsēn') *n.* a port city in northwestern Poland, formerly known as Stettin. Pop. (1977), 384,100.

Sze·chwan (se'chwän') *n.* a province in southwestern China. Area, 219,700 sq. mi. Pop. (1970 est.), 73,400,000. Also, **Sichuan.**

at; āpe; cär; end; mē; it; īce; hot; ōld; fôrk; wood; fōōl; oil; out; up; turn; sing; thin; this; hw in white; zh in treasure. The symbol ə stands for the sound of a in about, e in taken, i in pencil, o in lemon, and u in circus.

S

1. Egyptian Hieroglyphics	**5. Greek Ninth Century B.C.**
2. Semitic	**6. Etruscan**
3. Phoenician	**7. Latin Fourth Century B.C. Capitals**
4. Early Hebrew	**8. English**

T is the twentieth letter of the English alphabet. The earliest ancestor of **T** was an Egyptian hieroglyphic (1) that probably meant "mark." In the ancient Semitic alphabet, this symbol was adopted for the letter *taw* (2), meaning "mark." The ancient Semitic *taw* and the Phoenician (3) and early Hebrew (4) versions of it were written as a lower case **x** or **t** is written today. *Taw* was the last letter of these early alphabets. The early Greeks borrowed *taw* and called it *tau* (5). *Tau* was adopted, with only slight changes, in the Etruscan alphabet (6). By the fourth century B.C., the Romans (7) were writing their form of *tau* almost exactly the way we write a capital letter **T** today (8).

t, T (tē) *n. pl.,* **t's, T's. 1.** the twentieth letter of the English alphabet. **2.** something having the shape of this letter.
  to a T. perfectly or exactly: *That suit fits you to a T.*
t. 1. teaspoon; teaspoons. **2.** ton; tons.
T. 1. Tuesday. **2.** Territory. **3.** tablespoon.
Ta, the symbol for tantalum.
tab (tab) *n.* **1.** a small flap, strip, or other attachment projecting from an object, used especially as an aid to opening, fastening, or handling: *Pull the tab on the soda can to open it.* **2.** a small extension on a card or the edge of a paper, for use in filing or indexing. **3.** a small ornamental flap or loop on a garment. **4.** *Informal.* a bill to be paid; check: *He picked up the tab for the meal.*
  to keep tabs on or **to keep a tab on.** *Informal.* to watch closely; check up on: *The police kept tabs on the gangster's activities.*
tab·ard (tab′ərd) *n.* a short, loose outer garment resembling a coat, worn by knights over their armor.
Ta·bas·co (tə bas′kō) *n. Trademark.* a hot, pungent sauce made from a kind of red pepper.
tab·by (tab′ē) *n. pl.,* **tab·bies. 1.** a domestic cat having a brown or gray coat with dark stripes. **2.** any domestic cat, especially a female.
tab·er·nac·le (tab′ər nak′əl) *n.* **1.** a place of worship, especially one for a large body of worshipers. **2. Tabernacle. a.** a portable tent containing the Ark of the Covenant, which was used as a place of worship by the Jews during their wanderings from Egypt to Palestine. **b.** a Jewish temple. **3.** in the Roman Catholic and some Anglican churches, a container to hold the consecrated host.
ta·ble (tā′bəl) *n.* **1.** a piece of furniture consisting of a flat, horizontal surface supported by one or more legs. **2.** such

Tabby

a table upon which food is served: *The child left the table before the meal was over.* **3.** the food served at a table or any other place. **4.** the people seated at a table: *The table next to us was very noisy.* **5.** an orderly arrangement of facts or information, usually in a list: *a table of contents in a book, a table of measurements.* **6.** a tableland; plateau. **7.** a thin, flat slab, as of stone or metal, used especially for writing; tablet. —*v.t.,* **ta·bled, ta·bling. 1.** to form into a list; tabulate: *to table population figures.* **2.** to postpone discussion or consideration of: *The committee tabled the proposal to build a new school.*
  to turn the tables. to reverse the situation completely.
  under the table. secretly and illegally: *to pay money under the table to gain a political appointment.*
tab·leau (tab lō′) *n. pl.,* **tab·leaux** (tab lōz′) or **tab·leaus. 1.** a vivid and striking description. **2.** a silent and motionless representation of a scene, painting, or event by a person or persons posed in appropriate costume: *a tableau of George Washington crossing the Delaware.*
ta·ble·cloth (tā′bəl klôth′) *n. pl.,* **ta·ble·cloths** (tā′bəl klôthz′, tā′bəl klôths′). a cloth for covering a table, especially at meals.
ta·ble·land (tā′bəl land′) *n.* an elevated, flat land area; plateau.
ta·ble·spoon (tā′bəl spoon′) *n.* **1.** a spoon, larger than a teaspoon or dessert spoon, used especially for serving and measuring. **2.** the amount one tablespoon will hold. It is a standard cooking measurement equal to three teaspoons, or ½ fluid ounce.
ta·ble·spoon·ful (tā′bəl spoon fool′) *n. pl.,* **ta·ble·spoon·fuls.** the amount a tablespoon holds; tablespoon.
tab·let (tab′lit) *n.* **1.** a number of sheets of writing paper fastened together at one edge; pad. **2.** a small, flat piece of material, such as medicine, soap, or candy. **3.** a thin, flat slab, as of wood or stone, used for writing or drawing. **4.** a slab of stone or metal bearing an inscription.
table tennis, a game similar to tennis, played on a table

with a small plastic ball and wooden paddles. Also, **Ping-Pong.**

ta·ble·ware (tā′bəl wer′) *n.* articles placed on a table for use at meals, such as dishes, glasses, and silverware.

tab·loid (tab′loid) *n.* a newspaper with pages half the size of an ordinary newspaper page, having brief news articles and many pictures, especially one having stories of a sensational nature. —*adj.* condensed or shortened.

ta·boo (tə bōō′, ta bōō′) *also,* **ta·bu.** *n. pl.,* **ta·boos.** **1.** the system or practice of placing a sacred prohibition on certain things or acts. Among certain Polynesian peoples, it is believed that grave danger, misfortune, or death will come directly to anyone who breaks a taboo. **2.** any prohibition or restriction, especially one set by social custom or convention. —*adj.* **1.** prohibited or restricted under a taboo. **2.** prohibited or forbidden for any reason: *During Prohibition the sale of alcoholic beverages was taboo.* —*v.t.,* **ta·booed, ta·boo·ing.** to put under a taboo; ban; prohibit.

ta·bor (tā′bər) *n.* a small drum, especially one formerly used to accompany oneself on a pipe or fife.

Ta·briz (tä brēz′) *n.* a city in northwestern Iran. Pop. (1976), 598,576.

tab·u·lar (tab′yə lər) *adj.* **1.** having a broad, flat surface. **2.** of or arranged in lists or tables.

tab·u·late (tab′yə lāt′) *v.t.,* **tab·u·lat·ed, tab·u·lat·ing.** to arrange in lists or columns; put into a table: *to tabulate statistics.* —**tab′u·la′tion,** *n.*

tab·u·la·tor (tab′yə lā′tər) *n.* **1.** a device on a typewriter used for arranging material in columns. **2.** a machine that tabulates.

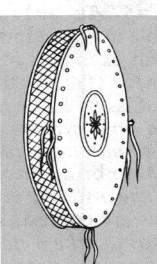

Tabor

ta·chom·e·ter (ta kom′ə tər, tə kom′ə tər) *n.* a device for measuring the speed of rotation of a shaft of an engine.

tac·it (tas′it) *adj.* **1.** not openly expressed but understood or implied: *Her smile was tacit approval of our suggestion.* **2.** without words; unspoken; silent: *a tacit prayer.* —**tac′it·ly,** *adv.*

tac·i·turn (tas′ə turn′) *adj.* not inclined to speak very much; silent or reserved. —**tac′i·tur′ni·ty,** *n.* —**tac′i·turn′ly,** *adv.*

Tac·i·tus (tas′i təs) A.D. 55?–117?, Roman historian.

tack (tak) *n.* **1.** a small nail with a sharp point and a broad, flat head. **2.** a sewing stitch that can be easily removed, used in fastening. **3.** a course of action: *We decided to take a new tack in dealing with the problem.* **4.** *Nautical.* **a.** the direction of a ship with respect to the wind. When the wind is on a ship's starboard or right side, the ship is on a starboard tack. **b.** the change of a ship's direction to take advantage of side winds. **c.** a zigzag course against the wind. **d.** one of a series of movements of a ship in a zigzag course against the wind. **5.** *Nautical.* **a.** a rope holding in place a corner of some sails, as the lower forward corner of a fore-and-aft sail. **b.** a corner so held in place. —*v.t.* **1.** to fasten with a tack or tacks: *She tacked the poster to the wall.* **2.** to sew or fasten with stitches that can be easily removed: *to tack a bow on a dress.* **3.** to add or attach as something extra: *to tack an amendment onto a bill.* **4.** *Nautical.* **a.** to change the course (of a boat or ship) by turning its head to the wind. **b.** to navigate (a boat or ship) against the wind by a series of tacks. —*v.i.* to tack a boat or ship.

tack·le (tak′əl) *n.* **1.** the equipment or gear used for some activity, such as fishing. **2.** a system of ropes and pulleys for hoisting, lowering, or pulling heavy loads, such as those used on a ship to raise, lower, and move the sails.

3. *Football.* **a.** either of the two players who line up between the guard and the end. **b.** the position played by either of these players. **c.** the act of stopping and bringing a ball carrier to the ground. **4.** the act of seizing, stopping, and bringing to the ground. —*v.t.,* **tack·led, tack·ling.** **1.** to deal with; work on: *How do you think we should tackle this problem?* **2.** to seize and force to the ground in order to stop. **3.** *Football.* to bring (a ball carrier) to the ground: *The crowd broke into cheers as our linebacker tackled the opponents' star runner at the five-yard line.* —**tack′ler,** *n.*

tack·y[1] (tak′ē) *adj.,* **tack·i·er, tack·i·est.** sticky: *tacky paint.* [*Tack* to attach + *-y*[1].] —**tack′i·ness,** *n.*

tack·y[2] (tak′ē) *adj.,* **tack·i·er, tack·i·est.** *Informal.* cheap, dowdy, or shabby: *a tacky dress.* [Of uncertain origin.] —**tack′i·ness,** *n.*

ta·co (tä′kō) *n. pl.,* **ta·cos.** a Mexican food consisting of a fried tortilla wrapped around a filling, as of cheese, ground beef, or chicken.

Ta·co·ma (tə kō′mə) *n.* a city in western Washington, on Puget Sound. Pop. (1970), 154,581.

tact (takt) *n.* the ability to deal with people or situations without offending anyone.

tact·ful (takt′fəl) *adj.* having or showing tact: *a tactful person.* —**tact′ful·ly,** *adv.* —**tact′ful·ness,** *n.*

tac·tic (tak′tik) *n.* **1.** a plan of action or any means to achieve a goal. **2.** a method of arranging and using military forces in action. See also **tactics.**

tac·ti·cal (tak′ti kəl) *adj.* **1.** of or relating to tactics, especially military tactics. **2.** characterized by or showing clever planning and maneuvering. —**tac′ti·cal·ly,** *adv.*

tac·ti·cian (tak tish′ən) *n.* a person skilled in tactics.

tac·tics (tak′tiks) *n.,pl.* **1.** the art or science of using and maneuvering military forces and equipment in combat. ▲ used with a singular verb. **2.** such use or maneuvering of military forces. **3.** any methods or devices used to achieve a goal: *campaign tactics.*

tac·tile (tak′til) *adj.* **1.** of or relating to touch: *The skin receives tactile sensations.* **2.** having the sense of touch: *The whiskers of a cat are tactile organs.* **3.** that can be felt by touch; tangible.

tact·less (takt′lis) *adj.* having or showing no tact; lacking diplomacy: *a tactless comment.* —**tact′less·ly,** *adv.* —**tact′less·ness,** *n.*

tad·pole (tad′pōl′) *n.* a frog or toad in the larval stage when it lives in the water and has gills, a slender tail, and no legs. Also, **polliwog.**

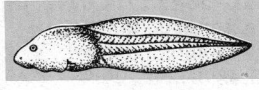

Tadpole

Tae·gu (ta gōō′, tī gōō′) *n.* a city in southeastern South Korea. Pop. (1975), 1,311,078.

taf·fe·ta (taf′ə tə) *n.* a shiny, somewhat stiff fabric, usually woven out of silk or rayon.

taff·rail (taf′rāl′) *n.* a rail around the stern of a ship.

taf·fy (taf′ē) *n. pl.,* **taf·fies.** a chewy candy made of brown sugar or molasses mixed with butter. It is boiled down and then pulled until it holds its shape.

Taft, William Howard (taft) 1857–1930, the twenty-seventh president of the United States, from 1909 to 1913, and the chief justice of the U.S. Supreme Court from 1921 to 1930.

---

at; āpe; cär; end; mē; it; īce; hot; ōld; fôrk; wood; fōōl; oil; out; up; turn; sing; thin; **th**is; hw in white; zh in treasure. The symbol ə stands for the sound of **a** in about, **e** in taken, **i** in pencil, **o** in lemon, and **u** in circus.

tag¹ (tag) *n.* **1.** a piece of paper, plastic, or other material attached to or hanging loosely from something for the purpose of identifying or labeling it: *a name tag, a price tag.* **2.** a part or piece hanging from or loosely attached to something else. **3.** a hard tip or binding on a string, as at the end of a shoelace. **4.** a saying or quotation used in speech or writing for emphasis, ornament, or effect. —*v.,* **tagged, tag·ging.** —*v.t.* to attach an identifying tag to: *to tag a suitcase.* —*v.i.* to follow closely; trail: *The dog tagged along wherever the boys went.* [Probably of Scandinavian origin.]

tag² (tag) *n.* **1.** a game in which one player, usually called "it," chases the other players until he or she touches one. The player who is touched then becomes "it" and must chase the others. **2.** in baseball, the act of putting out a runner by touching him or her with the ball or with the hand holding the ball. —*v.t.,* **tagged, tag·ging.** **1.** to touch or tap, as in the game of tag. **2.** in baseball, to put out (a base runner) by touching him or her with the ball or with the hand holding the ball. [Of uncertain origin.]

Ta·ga·log (tä gä′läg) *n. pl.,* **Ta·ga·logs** or **Ta·ga·log.** **1.** a member of a Malayan people who make up part of the native population of the Philippines. **2.** the language of these people, now the official language of the Philippines.

Ta·hi·ti (tə hē′tē) *n.* a French island in the southern Pacific Ocean.

Ta·hi·tian (tə hē′shən) *n.* **1.** a person who was born or is living in Tahiti. **2.** the language of Tahiti. —*adj.* of or relating to Tahiti, its people, or their language.

Ta·hoe, Lake (tä′hō) a mountain lake in eastern California and western Nevada.

tai·ga (tī′gə) *n.* any of the northernmost forests of cone-bearing trees in North America, Europe, and Asia.

tail (tāl) *n.* **1.** the hindmost part of an animal's body, especially a flexible part that extends beyond the main part of the body. **2.** anything resembling a tail in shape: *the tail of a comet.* **3.** the rear part of an aircraft. **4.** the rear, bottom, or last part of anything: *the tail of a bicycle.* **5. tails.** the reverse side of a coin. **6. tails.** a man's most formal evening wear. —*v.t.* **1.** to provide with a tail. **2.** *Informal.* to follow closely and secretly: *The secret agent tailed the spy.* —*adj.* at or coming from the rear: *the tail feathers of a bird.* —**tail′less,** *adj.* —**tail′like′,** *adj.*
    to turn tail. to run away from danger or trouble.

tail·board (tāl′bôrd′) *n.* another word for **tailgate.**

tail·gate (tāl′gāt′) *n.* a board at the rear of a truck, wagon, station wagon, or other vehicle that can be let down or removed for loading or unloading. —*v.i., v.t.* **tail·gat·ed, tail·gat·ing.** *Informal.* to drive too closely behind another vehicle, so as to be dangerous.

Tailgate

tail·light (tāl′līt′) *n.* a warning light, usually red, at the rear of a vehicle.

tai·lor (tā′lər) *n.* a person who makes, alters, or mends clothing, especially outer garments. —*v.t.* **1.** to make as a tailor: *He tailored the suit to fit perfectly.* **2.** to make, alter, or adapt to meet a special requirement or need: *The reading program was tailored to the needs of young children.* —*v.i.* to work as a tailor.

tai·lor·ing (tā′lər ing) *n.* **1.** the workmanship or skill of a tailor. **2.** the business or occupation of a tailor.

tail·piece (tāl′pēs′) *n.* a part or piece that is the end or that is added on at the end.

tail pipe, a pipe for carrying and discharging the exhaust gases from an engine, as in an automobile.

tail·race (tāl′rās′) *n.* a channel that carries water away from a water wheel.

tail·spin (tāl′spin′) *n.* the rapid, spiraling descent of an airplane, with the nose pointing downward and moving in a smaller circle than the tail.

tail wind, a wind blowing in the same direction that something is moving, such as an aircraft or ship.

taint (tānt) *v.t.* to spoil, blemish, or damage: *The lawyer's reputation was tainted by the scandal.* —*v.i.* to become tainted; spoil. —*n.* a touch of decay or damage: *The meat had a taint.*

Tai·pei (tī′pā′) *also,* **Tai·peh.** *n.* the capital of Taiwan, in the northern part of the island. Pop. (1970 est.), 1,704,800.

Tai·wan (tī′wän′) *n.* an island country in the western Pacific Ocean, east of mainland China. It has been the seat of the Nationalist government of China since 1949. Capital, Taipei. Area, 13,885 sq. mi. Pop. (1970 est.), 14,505,400. Also, **Formosa.**

Taj Ma·hal (täzh′ mə häl′) a mausoleum of white marble in Agra, India, considered to be one of the most beautiful examples of Islamic architecture.

take (tāk) *v.,* **took, tak·en, tak·ing.** —*v.t.* **1.** to get hold of, as with the hand; grasp: *to take a person's hand, to take a book from a shelf.* **2.** to get possession of: *The young woman took control of her father's business after his death.* **3.** to bring into one's possession by force; catch; capture: *The invading army took many prisoners.* **4.** to win or earn, as in a contest: *This painting took first prize.* **5.** to subscribe to: *to take a newspaper.* **6.** to choose; select: *Take a card from the deck.* **7.** to occupy: *Please take a seat near the front.* **8.** to carry with one; bring: *We took two suitcases on the trip.* **9.** to move away; remove: *Take the trash to the town dump.* **10.** to remove by death: *The harsh winter took the lives of many settlers.* **11.** to subtract; deduct: *to take 3 from 5.* **12.** to conduct; lead: *This staircase will take you to an exit.* **13.** to use as a means of transportation: *We took the train home.* **14.** to escort: *Fred took Mary to the party.* **15.** to make use of or find: *The fleeing deer took refuge in the forest.* **16.** to receive into the body, as by swallowing or inhaling: *to take medicine, to take a breath of fresh air.* **17.** to do, perform, or accomplish: *Let's take a walk.* **18.** to undertake or take part in: *to take a test, to take tennis lessons.* **19.** to receive; accept: *Please take my advice.* **20.** to endure; withstand: *Over the years this suitcase has taken a lot of punishment.* **21.** to undergo; suffer: *Our team really took a beating in that game.* **22.** to have a sense of; feel: *He takes pride in his coin collection.* **23.** to need; require: *It takes practice to learn how to play the guitar.* **24.** to please or charm; captivate: *to take one's fancy.* **25.** to record by writing: *The secretary took notes at the meeting.* **26.** to make by photography: *to take someone's picture.* **27.** to determine by some special method: *to take attendance, to take a person's temperature.* **28.** *Grammar.* to be used with in a construction: *A transitive verb takes a direct object.* **29.** *Slang.* to swindle; cheat. —*v.i.* **1.** to be effective; work: *The vaccination did not take.* **2.** (of a seed or plant) to begin to grow. —*n.* **1.** the act of taking. **2.** something that is taken. **3.** the amount or quantity taken. **4.** *Informal.* profit or receipts, as from a show or sporting event. **5.** a portion of a movie, television program, or recording that is photographed or recorded without interruption. ▲ See **bring** for usage note. —**tak′er,** *n.*
    to take after. to resemble in appearance, character, or actions: *The child takes after his father.*
    to take back. to retract: *I take back what I just said.*

to take down. to record in writing: *The reporter took down everything that was said.*

to take for. to suppose to be, especially mistakenly.

to take in. a. to receive; admit: *to take in boarders.* **b.** to reduce in size; make smaller. **c.** to understand. **d.** *Informal.* to deceive; cheat: *to be taken in by a misleading advertisement.* **e.** to include. **f.** *Informal.* to go to see: *to take in a movie.*

to take it. to assume; believe.

to take off. a. to remove: *Take off your hat.* **b.** to rise up in flight: *The airplane took off.*

to take on. a. to hire; employ. **b.** to deal with or handle; undertake: *to take on a new responsibility.*

to take out. a. to get; obtain: *to take out a loan.* **b.** *Informal.* to escort, as on a date.

to take over. to assume ownership, control, or management of: *Sam is taking over his father's business.*

to take to. a. to go to, as for escape. **b.** to form a liking for: *to take to a person.*

to take up. a. to make shorter or smaller: *to take up a hem.* **b.** to begin; undertake: *to take up knitting.* **c.** occupy or consume.

to take up with. *Informal.* to become friendly with.

tak·en (tā′kən) the past participle of **take.**

take·off (tāk′ôf′) *n.* **1.** the act of leaving the ground, especially in beginning an airplane flight. **2.** *Informal.* an imitation, usually humorous or satirical; parody.

take·o·ver (tāk′ō′vər) *n.* the assumption or seizure of ownership, control, responsibility, or authority: *a government take-over of the steel industry.*

tak·ing (tā′king) *adj.* attractive; captivating: *a taking smile.* —*n.* **1.** the act of a person who takes. **2.** *also,* **takings.** something that is taken, especially money or receipts.

talc (talk) *n.* a soft, smooth mineral used in making powders and as an ingredient in ceramics, electrical insulators, paints, and rubber.

tal·cum powder (tal′kəm) a fine powder made of white talc, often medicated, used on the face and body.

tale (tāl) *n.* **1.** a story or account of an event or series of events; narrative: *a tale of life at sea.* **2.** a story that is untrue; falsehood.

tale·bear·er (tāl′ber′ər) *n.* a person who deliberately spreads secrets or rumors. —**tale′bear′ing,** *n.*

tal·ent (tal′ənt) *n.* **1.** a special natural ability or aptitude: *He has musical talent.* **2.** a person or persons having talent: *The movie producer was always looking for new acting talent.* **3.** any of various ancient units of weight and money.

tal·ent·ed (tal′ən tid) *adj.* having, showing, or characterized by talent: *a talented pianist.*

tal·is·man (tal′is mən) *n. pl.,* **tal·is·mans. 1.** an engraved stone, ring, or other object believed to have magic power to keep away evil and bring good fortune. **2.** anything regarded as having magic power.

talk (tôk) *v.i.* **1.** to express ideas or information by means of speech; speak; converse: *Can I talk to you about something?* **2.** to express ideas or information by some other means: *to talk in sign language.* **3.** to consult or confer: *to talk with a doctor.* **4.** to spread rumors; gossip. **5.** *Informal.* to reveal information: *The prisoner refused to talk.* —*v.t.* **1.** to make the subject of one's speech; discuss: *to talk business. Let's talk sense to the American people* (Adlai Stevenson). **2.** to use in speaking: *to talk Spanish.* **3.** to bring, persuade, or cause by speech: *We talked her out of leaving.* —*n.* **1.** an expression of ideas in speech; conversation: *The two friends had a long talk.* **2.** an informal speech or lecture: *The professor gave a talk about Africa.* **3.** a formal discussion; conference: *peace talks.* **4.** rumor or gossip. **5.** the subject of conversation or gossip: *The new*

show *is the talk of New York.* **6.** *Informal.* a particular way of speaking: *baby talk.*

to talk back. to give a rude reply.

to talk down to. to speak to in a condescending manner.

to talk over. to discuss.

talk·a·tive (tô′kə tiv) *adj.* tending to talk a great deal. —**talk′a·tive·ly,** *adv.* —**talk′a·tive·ness,** *n.*

talk·er (tô′kər) *n.* **1.** a person who talks. **2.** a talkative person.

talk·ing-to (tô′king tōō′) *n. pl.,* **talk·ing-tos.** *Informal.* a sharp scolding: *That child needs a good talking-to.*

tall (tôl) *adj.* **1.** of more than average height; not short or low: *a tall man, a tall tree.* **2.** having a specified height: *She is five feet tall.* **3.** unusually large in amount or degree: *a tall price, a tall order.* **4.** *Informal.* exaggerated so as to be unbelievable: *a tall story.* —**tall′ness,** *n.*

Tal·la·has·see (tal′ə has′ē) *n.* the capital of Florida, in the northwestern part of the state. Pop. (1970), 71,897.

tal·low (tal′ō) *n.* the fat from cattle and sheep, used chiefly for making candles, soap, and margarine.

tal·ly (tal′ē) *n. pl.,* **tal·lies. 1.** an account, reckoning, or score. **2.** formerly, a piece of wood with notches that indicated an amount, as of a debt or payment. **3.** anything on which a record or account is kept. —*v.,* **tal·lied, tal·ly·ing.** —*v.t.* to keep or make a count or record: *The grocer tallied up our bill.* —*v.i.* to correspond; agree: *His story of the robbery does not tally with the facts.*

tal·ly·ho (tal′ē hō′) *interj.* a huntsman's shout indicating his sighting of a fox.

Tal·mud (tal′məd) *n.* the collection of Jewish civil and canonical law.

tal·on (tal′ən) *n.* the claw of a bird or other animal, especially of a bird of prey.

ta·lus (tā′ləs) *n. pl.,* **ta·li** (tā′lī). another word for **anklebone.**

tam (tam) *n.* see **tam-o'-shanter.**

ta·ma·le (tə mä′lē) *n.* a Mexican food made of corn meal, chopped meat, and red peppers, rolled up in cornhusks and cooked.

tam·a·rack (tam′ə rak′) *n.* **1.** a North American larch tree valued for its wood. **2.** the wood of this tree, used especially for telephone poles and railroad ties.

tam·a·rind (tam′ə rind′) *n.* **1.** a tropical tree that bears clusters of small, yellow flowers and juicy fruit. **2.** its sharp-tasting fruit, used to make drinks and in foods.

tam·a·risk (tam′ə risk′) *n.* any of a group of shrubs and small trees of western Europe and Asia, having tiny leaves and clusters of pink or white flowers.

tam·bou·rine (tam′bə rēn′) *n.* a shallow, one-headed drum having metal disks loosely mounted in the rim, usually played by shaking or by striking with the knuckles.

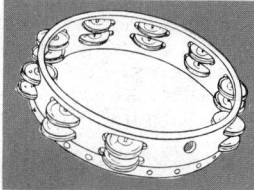

Tambourine

tame (tām) *adj.,* **tam·er, tam·est. 1.** taken by man from a state of native wildness and domesticated. **2.** not ferocious, fearful, or shy; gentle: *The deer was tame enough to let us photograph it.* **3.** not lively, forceful, or exciting; dull:

at; āpe; cär; end; mē; it; īce; hot; ōld; fôrk; wood; fōōl; oil; out; up; turn; sing; thin; this; hw in white; zh in treasure. The symbol ə stands for the sound of a in about, e in taken, i in pencil, o in lemon, and u in circus.

a tame football game. —*v.t.,* **tamed, tam·ing. 1.** to take from a wild state and make tame: *to tame a wild stallion.* **2.** to bring under control; subdue. —**tame′ly,** *adv.* —**tame′ness,** *n.* —**tam′er,** *n.*

tam-o'-shan·ter (tam′ə shan′tər) *n.* a soft, woolen cap of Scottish origin, with a wide, flat, circular crown and a fitted headband, often having a pompom in the center.

tamp (tamp) *v.t.* **1.** to force or pound down by a series of light blows or taps; pack down: *to tamp tobacco into a pipe.* **2.** to pack (a drilled hole) with sand or dirt after an explosive charge has been placed in the hole.

Tam-o'-shanter

Tam·pa (tam′pə) *n.* a port city in western Florida. Pop. (1970), 277,767.

tam·per (tam′pər) *v.i.* **1.** to interfere or meddle, usually with a harmful effect: *Someone has been tampering with the radio.* **2.** to try to influence or corrupt: *to tamper with a jury.* —**tam′per·er,** *n.*

tan (tan) *v.,* **tanned, tan·ning.** —*v.t.* **1.** to make (a hide or skin) into leather by soaking it in tannin or a similar solution. **2.** to make brown by exposure to the sun. **3.** *Informal.* to beat severely. —*v.i.* to become brown by exposure to the sun. —*n.* **1.** a yellowish-brown color. **2.** a brown color given to a person's skin by exposure to the sun. **3.** tannin or a similar tanning agent. **4.** see **tan·bark.** —*adj.,* **tan·ner, tan·nest.** having the color tan.

tan·a·ger (tan′ə jər) *n.* any of various small, brightly colored birds, found chiefly in Central and South America, having a cone-shaped bill.

Ta·na·na·rive (tə nam′ə rēv′) *n.* former name of the capital of Madagascar. See **Antananarivo.**

tan·bark (tan′bärk′) *n.* any bark yielding tannin, as of the oak or hemlock tree. After the tannin has been removed, tanbark is used as a covering, as for circus rings.

tan·dem (tan′dəm) *adv.* one behind the other; in single file: *to march tandem.* —*adj.* arranged or having parts or participants arranged one behind the other: *tandem seats, a tandem bicycle.* —*n.* **1.** a bicycle having two or more seats, one behind the other. **2.** a team of horses harnessed one behind the other. **3.** a two-wheeled carriage drawn by two or more horses so harnessed.

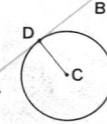

Tandem bicycle

tang (tang) *n.* **1.** a sharp taste, flavor, or odor: *the tang of a crisp, red apple.* **2.** a slight trace or suggestion; hint: *His words had a tang of regret in them.* **3.** the projecting part of a blade, as of a chisel, file, or sword, to which the handle is fitted.

Tan·gan·yi·ka (tan′gən yē′kə) *n.* **1.** a former country in eastern Africa, now part of Tanzania. **2. Lake.** a lake in east-central Africa, the longest freshwater lake in the world.

tan·ge·lo (tan′jə lō′) *n.* a fruit produced by crossing a tangerine and a grapefruit.

tan·gent (tan′jənt) *adj.* **1.** in contact; touching. **2.** *Geometry.* touching a curve or surface at only one point but not intersecting. —*n.* **1.** *Geometry.* a tangent line, curve, or surface. **2.** *Trigonometry.* (of an acute angle of a right triangle) the ratio of the length of the side opposite the acute angle to the length of the side adjacent to the angle. **3.** an abrupt change in thought, discussion, or course of action; digression: *to go off on a tangent.*

Tangent
AB is tangent
at *D*

tan·gen·tial (tan jen′chəl) *adj.* **1.** of or relating to a tangent. **2.** not relevant; digressive. **3.** only slightly connected. —**tan·gen′tial·ly,** *adv.*

tan·ge·rine (tan′jə rēn′) *n.* **1.** a sweet, juicy, reddish-orange citrus fruit having a skin that is easily peeled. **2.** a tree bearing this fruit, widely grown in the United States. **3.** a reddish-orange color. —*adj.* having the color tangerine. [French *Tanger* Tangier, the city from which this fruit was first imported.]

tan·gi·ble (tan′jə bəl) *adj.* **1.** capable of being touched; perceptible to the touch; material: *A book is a tangible object.* **2.** capable of being measured or appraised for value: *A house and its land are tangible assets.* **3.** capable of being understood or grasped by the mind; definite; real: *tangible proof.* —*n., pl.,* **tangibles.** property that can be appraised for value; material assets. —**tan′gi·bil′i·ty,** *n.* —**tan′gi·bly,** *adv.*

Tan·gier (tan jēr′) *n.* a port city in northern Morocco, on the Strait of Gibraltar. Pop. (1970 est.), 170,000.

tan·gle (tang′gəl) *v.,* **tan·gled, tan·gling.** —*v.t.* **1.** to twist together into a disordered mass; snarl: *The wind tangled her hair.* **2.** to catch or involve in something that hampers, obstructs, or confuses: *The fly was tangled in the spider's web. The heavy rain tangled traffic on the highway.* —*v.i.* **1.** to be or become entangled: *The branches tangled as they grew.* **2.** *Informal.* to fight, quarrel, or argue. —*n.* **1.** a jumbled, knotted, or twisted mass: *a tangle of yarn.* **2.** a confused or jumbled condition. **3.** *Informal.* a fight or quarrel; argument: *The girls got into a tangle over whose turn it was to jump rope.*

tan·go (tang′gō) *n. pl.,* **tan·gos. 1.** a ballroom dance of Latin-American origin, characterized by long gliding steps. **2.** the music for such a dance. —*v.i.,* **tan·goed, tan·go·ing.** to dance the tango.

tang·y (tang′ē) *adj.,* **tan·gi·er, tan·gi·est.** having a tang.

tank (tangk) *n.* **1.** a large container for holding a liquid or gas: *an oxygen tank, an oil tank.* **2.** the amount that a tank can hold; tankful: *a tank of gasoline.* **3.** *Military.* a fully enclosed, armored combat vehicle equipped with machine guns and cannon, and moving on two continuous belts of metal treads. —*v.t.* to place, store, or process in a tank.

tank·ard (tang′kərd) *n.* a large drinking cup having a handle and a hinged lid.

tank·er (tang′kər) *n.* a ship, truck, or airplane equipped with tanks for carrying oil or other liquid freight.

tank·ful (tangk′fool′) *n. pl.,* **tank·fuls.** the amount that a tank can hold.

tan·ner (tan′ər) *n.* a person whose work or business is the tanning of hides.

tan·ner·y (tan′ər ē) *n. pl.,* **tan·ner·ies.** a place where hides and skins are tanned and finished as leather.

Tankard

tan·nic acid (tan′ik) a yellowish or brownish mixture of chemical compounds found in the bark and wood of many trees, used in tanning hides and in the preparation of ink, rubber, and medicine.

tan·nin (tan′in) *n.* **1.** another word for **tannic acid. 2.** any of various other substances used to tan hides.

tan·ning (tan′ing) *n.* the art or process of converting hide or skins into leather.

tan·sy (tan′zē) *n. pl.,* **tan·sies.** a strong-smelling plant having yellow flowers and feathery leaves, formerly used in cooking and in medicines.

tan·ta·lize (tant′əl īz′) *v.t.,* **tan·ta·lized, tan·ta·liz·ing.**

to tease or torment by tempting with something that is out of reach. [From *Tantalus,* who was punished by being teased and tormented with things that were out of reach.] —**tan′ta·liz′er,** *n.* —**tan′ta·liz′ing·ly,** *adv.*

tan·ta·lum (tant′əl əm) *n.* a heavy, very hard metallic element with an extremely high melting point, used in alloys for missile and aircraft parts, and for surgical instruments. Symbol: **Ta**

Tan·ta·lus (tant′əl əs) *n. Greek Mythology.* a son of Zeus, who served up his own son as a meal to the gods. He was punished by being immersed in water that moved away as he bent down to drink it, and by being surrounded with delicious fruit that rose up beyond his grasp as he reached up to eat it.

tan·ta·mount (tan′tə mount′) *adj.* having as much importance, value, force, or effect; equivalent: *The man's threat was tantamount to blackmail.*

tan·trum (tan′trəm) *n.* an outburst of bad temper or anger.

Tan·za·ni·a (tan′zə nē′ə) *n.* a country in east-central Africa, formed in 1964 by the merger of the former countries of Tanganyika and Zanzibar. Capital, Dar es Salaam. Area, 362,820 sq. mi. Pop. (1971 est.), 13,630,000.

Tao·ism (tou′iz′əm) *n.* one of the principal religions of China, characterized by a belief in a harmony with nature and one's fellow man.

Tao·ist (tou′ist) *n.* a believer in Taoism. —*adj.* of, relating to, or characteristic of Taoism or Taoists.

tap¹ (tap) *v.,* **tapped, tap·ping.** —*v.t.* **1.** to strike (something) lightly: *The blind man tapped the sidewalk with his cane.* **2.** to strike lightly and usually repeatedly with: *The conductor tapped his baton for attention.* **3.** to make, do, or produce by striking lightly and repeatedly: *to tap out a beat with one's foot.* —*v.i.* to strike with a light blow or blows: *to tap on a desk with a ruler.* —*n.* **1.** a light or gentle blow: *I felt a tap on my shoulder.* **2.** the sound made by such a blow: *the repeated taps of raindrops against a window.* **3.** a piece of metal placed on the heel or sole of a shoe or boot, as for tap-dancing. [Old French *taper* to strike lightly; in imitation of the sound of such a light blow.]

tap² (tap) *n.* **1.** a device consisting of a valve and a handle that opens or closes it, used to turn on or off a flow of liquid, as from a pipe or keg. **2.** a long peg or plug used to close a hole in a cask or other vessel containing liquid. **3.** a place for connecting electrical devices or additional wires to a flow of current. **4.** a tool screwed into an opening or hole to make internal screw threads. —*v.t.,* **tapped, tap·ping. 1.** to pierce (something) in order to draw liquid from: *to tap the trunk of a sugar maple tree for sap.* **2.** to pull out the tap from (a barrel, cask, or other container). **3.** to draw off (liquid) from a source: *to tap the beer in a keg.* **4.** to draw upon or make use of: *We have just begun to tap the vast resources of the oceans.* **5.** to make a connection on in order to draw from (a water, gas, or electric line). **6.** to cut into and connect with secretly, so as to obtain information: *to tap a telephone.* [Old English *tæppa.*]

  on tap. a. (of a beer or liquor) ready to be drawn off and served. **b.** *Informal.* ready for use; available.

tap-dance (tap′dans′) *v.i.,* **tap-danced, tap-danc·ing.** to perform a tap dance. —**tap′danc′er,** *n.*

tap dance, a dance in which the steps and the rhythm are emphasized by loud taps made by the dancer's foot, toe, or heel.

tape (tāp) *n.* **1.** a long, narrow strip of woven fabric, such as that used to bind seams. **2.** any long, narrow strip of metal, plastic, paper, or other material. **3.** magnetic tape on which sound, light, or information has been recorded.

4. a thin strip of string, cloth, or other material stretched across the finishing line of a race. —*v.t.,* **taped, tap·ing. 1.** to fasten, bind, or decorate with tape. **2.** to record on magnetic tape: *to tape an interview, to tape a television program.* **3.** to measure with a tape measure.

tape measure, a long strip of cloth or flexible steel marked with a scale for measuring.

ta·per (tā′pər) *v.t.* to make gradually narrower toward one end: *The tailor tapered the trousers.* —*v.i.* **1.** to become gradually narrower toward one end: *The candle tapers to a point.* **2.** to decrease gradually; diminish: *Sales tapered off after the holidays.* —*n.* **1.** a small or slender candle. **2.** a gradual decrease of thickness or width: *The taper of a spire.*

tape-re·cord (tāp′ri kôrd′) *v.t.* to record on magnetic tape.

tape recorder, a device for recording sound on a tape coated with magnetically sensitive material. Most tape recorders are also equipped to play back the sound recorded.

tape recording 1. the act or process of recording sound on magnetic tape. **2.** a tape on which sound has been recorded.

tap·es·try (tap′is trē) *n. pl.,* **tap·es·tries. 1.** a heavy woven fabric decorated with designs or pictures often showing historical or mythological events. Tapestries are used as wall hangings and to cover floors and furniture. **2.** any of various fabrics made to resemble tapestry, used for such items as upholstery and garments.

tape·worm (tāp′wurm′) *n.* any of a group of flatworms that, in the adult stage, are parasites in the intestines of man and certain other animals.

tap·i·o·ca (tap′ē ō′kə) *n.* a starchy substance obtained from the root of the cassava plant, used in cooking to make pudding and to thicken sauces and soups.

ta·pir (tā′pər) *n.* a large, hoofed animal somewhat like a pig, found in Latin America and southeastern Asia. The tapir has a heavy, rounded body and a short, flexible snout.

Tapir

tap·room (tap′rōōm′, tap′-room′) *n.* a barroom or tavern.

tap·root (tap′rōōt′, tap′-root′) *n.* the main downward-growing root of a plant from which other small, branch roots may develop.

taps (taps) *n., pl.* a bugle call regularly played at the end of the day in military camps to indicate that all lights must be turned off, and also sounded at military funerals and memorial services. ▲ used with a singular verb.

tar¹ (tär) *n.* a thick, dark, sticky substance obtained chiefly by the distillation of coal or wood, used widely to pave roads and as a waterproofing material. —*v.t.,* **tarred, tar·ring.** to smear, coat, or cover with tar: *to tar a highway.* [Old English *teoru, teru.*] —**tar′like′,** *adj.*

  to tar and feather. to pour heated tar over (someone) and then cover with feathers as a punishment.

tar² (tär) *n. Informal.* a sailor. [Short for *tarpaulin,* because tarpaulin formerly meant "a sailor."]

at; āpe; cär; end; mē; it; īce; hot; ōld; fôrk; wood; fōol; oil; out; up; turn; sing; thin; **this**; **hw** in white; **zh** in treasure. The symbol ə stands for the sound of **a** in about, **e** in taken, **i** in pencil, **o** in lemon, and **u** in circus.

T

tar·an·tel·la (tar′ən tel′ə) n. 1. a lively southern Italian dance, usually performed by a single couple. It was once believed to be a cure for the bite of the tarantula. 2. the music for such a dance. [Italian *tarantella* this dance; literally, dance of Taranto, from *Taranto.*]

Ta·ran·to (tə rän′tō) n. a port city in southeastern Italy, on the Ionian Sea. Pop. (1978 est.), 246,828.

ta·ran·tu·la (tə ran′chə lə) n. pl., **ta·ran·tu·las** or **ta·ran·tu·lae** (tə ran′chə lē). any of a group of hairy spiders found chiefly in tropical and semitropical regions. Tarantulas have a bite that is painful but usually not dangerous to man. [Medieval Latin *tarantula,* from *Taranto,* where these spiders are commonly found.]

Tarantula

tar·dy (tär′dē) adj., **tar·di·er, tar·di·est. 1.** coming or happening after the set or appropriate time; late: *The student was punished for being tardy.* 2. moving or happening slowly: *We were tardy in making preparations for the trip.* —**tar′di·ly,** adv. —**tar′di·ness,** n.

tare¹ (ter) n. 1. a kind of vetch grown chiefly as food for livestock. 2. the seed of this plant. 3. in the New Testament, a weed harmful to crops. [Middle English *tare.*]

tare² (ter) n. a deduction made from the total weight of something sold to allow for the weight of the container. [Middle French *tare.*]

tar·get (tär′git) n. 1. an object that is aimed at in shooting practice and competitions. A padded disk marked with circles is a target used in archery. 2. anything that is the object of a military attack: *The white hospital buildings outside the town are not included in the bombing target.* 3. a person or thing that is the object of ridicule, criticism, or abuse: *The candidate's radical views made him an easy target for the opposition.* 4. a person or thing that is the object of an action or effort: *The target of the advertising campaign was the young housewife.*

tar·iff (tar′if) n. 1. a list or system of duties or taxes imposed by a government on imports or exports. 2. a duty or rate of duty so imposed: *a low tariff on cameras.* 3. any list of rates or prices, as at a hotel.

tarn (tärn) n. a small mountain lake or pool.

tar·nish (tär′nish) v.t. 1. to dull the luster of or discolor, as by exposure to air or dirt. 2. to stain or disgrace; sully: *The scandal tarnished the family name.* —v.i. to become dull or discolored, as by exposure to air or dirt: *The silver will tarnish if left uncovered and exposed to the air.* —n. 1. a coating or surface resulting from tarnishing. 2. the loss of luster.

ta·ro (tär′ō) n. pl., **ta·ros. 1.** a tropical plant of Hawaii and other Pacific islands having a starchy root. 2. the root of this plant, used to make poi, or cooked and eaten like a potato.

tar·pau·lin (tär pô′lin) n. waterproofed canvas or other material, such as nylon, used as a protective covering for boats, athletic fields, or other objects exposed to the weather.

tar·pon (tär′pən) n. pl., **tar·pons** or **tar·pon.** a large, silvery game fish found in coastal waters of the Atlantic Ocean and sometimes in fresh water.

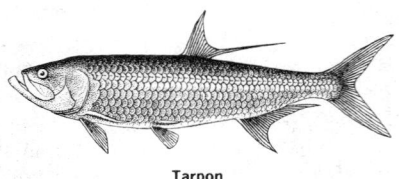
Tarpon

tar·ry¹ (tar′ē) v.i., **tar·ried, tar·ry·ing. 1.** to delay in doing something: *We must not tarry if we want to arrive on time.* 2. to remain in a place; stay: *The tourists tarried a while in Rome before going on to their next stop.* [Middle English *tarien* to irritate, hinder, delay.]

tar·ry² (tär′ē) adj., **tar·ri·er, tar·ri·est.** of, like, or covered with tar: *The tarry surface of the road became soft and sticky in the hot sun.* [*Tar*¹ + -*y*¹.]

tar·sal (tär′səl) adj. of or relating to the tarsus, or ankle.

tar·si·er (tär′sē ā′) n. a tree-dwelling animal native to the East Indies, having large eyes and ears, long fingers and toes, and a long, thin tail.

tar·sus (tär′səs) n. pl., **tar·si** (tär′sī). the ankle, made up of seven small bones in the human being.

Tar·sus (tär′səs) n. a city in south-central Turkey, the birthplace of Saint Paul.

tart¹ (tärt) adj. 1. sharp in taste; not sweet; sour. 2. sharp in tone or meaning; biting: *a tart remark.* [Old English *teart* sharp, severe.] —**tart′ly,** adv. —**tart′ness,** n.

tart² (tärt) n. a pastry shell containing a filling, such as custard or fruit, with or without a top crust. [Old French *tarte.*]

tar·tan (tärt′ən) n. 1. a plaid woolen fabric woven with one of the distinctive patterns of the Scottish Highland clans. 2. the plaid pattern itself. 3. any fabric with a similar design. —adj. of, like, or made of tartan.

tar·tar (tär′tər) n. 1. a brownish deposit on the teeth caused by a combination of food particles and various salts. 2. a substance that collects in wine casks.

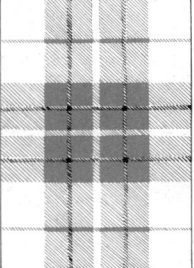
Tartan *(def. 2)*

Tar·tar (tär′tər) n. also, **Ta·tar.** 1. a member of the tribes of Mongols and Turks who overran parts of Asia and Europe during the Middle Ages. 2. a member of a Turkish people descended from them, now living chiefly in parts of the Soviet Union in central and western Asia. 3. the language of these people. —adj. of or relating to the Tartars or their language.

tartar sauce, a sauce made of mayonnaise and chopped pickles, capers, onions, olives, and the like, served especially with seafood.

Tar·ta·rus (tär′tər əs) n. Greek Mythology. 1. a region deep in the underworld where wicked people were punished for their crimes after death. 2. the land of the dead; underworld.

Tash·kent (täsh kent′) n. a city in the south-central Soviet Union, capital of Uzbekistan. Pop. (1979), 1,779,000.

task (task) n. 1. a piece of work to be done, especially one assigned by one person to another. 2. a tiring or burdensome job or duty: *Writing that long report was quite a task.* —v.t. to put a strain on; burden: *His constant complaining tasks my patience.*
to take to task. to scold; reprimand: *The sergeant took the soldier to task for neglecting his duties.*

task force 1. a number of military units brought together under one commander for a particular mission. 2. any group that is formed or brought together to deal with a particular problem.

task·mas·ter (task′mas′tər) n. a person who assigns and closely supervises the carrying out of tasks.

Tas·ma·ni·a (taz mā′nē ə) n. a state of Australia. It is an island south of the mainland. —**Tas·ma′ni·an,** adj., n.

Tass (tas, täs) n. a Soviet news agency run by the government.

tas·sel (tas′əl) *n.* **1.** a hanging ornament made up of a group of threads, cords, or similar materials bound together at one end. **2.** anything resembling this in shape, such as the flower cluster of a corn plant. —*v.,* **tas·seled, tas·sel·ing;** *also, British,* **tas·selled, tas·sel·ling.** —*v.t.* to attach a tassel or tassels to. —*v.i.* (of corn) to put forth tassels.

taste (tāst) *n.* **1.** the sense by which the flavor of something is perceived or distinguished. **2.** a particular sensation perceived by this sense. The four basic tastes are sweet, bitter, sour, and salty. **3.** a small amount eaten or sampled: *May I have a taste of your pie?* **4.** a brief experience of anything; sample: *The preview gave us a taste of what the television series would be like.* **5.** a preference; liking: *That house is not to my taste.* **6.** the ability to recognize and appreciate what is excellent, beautiful, or appropriate: *He has good taste in music.* **7.** the way in which such ability is shown: *She always dresses in good taste.* —*v.,* **tast·ed, tast·ing.** —*v.t.* **1.** to perceive or distinguish the flavor of (something) by means of the sense of taste: *I can taste the garlic in the sauce.* **2.** to take (something) into the mouth in order to test the flavor; sample: *Taste the soup to see if it needs more salt.* **3.** to experience, especially briefly or for the first time: *The dictator tasted power only briefly before being overthrown.* —*v.i.* to have a particular flavor: *The sauce tastes too sweet.*

taste bud, any of a cluster of cells located in the lining of the tongue and mouth, and functioning as organs of taste.

taste·ful (tāst′fəl) *adj.* having or showing a good sense of what is excellent, beautiful, or appropriate: *The young man was a tasteful dresser.* —**taste′ful·ly,** *adv.* —**taste′ful·ness,** *n.*

taste·less (tāst′lis) *adj.* **1.** without flavor; bland: *tasteless food.* **2.** having or showing little or no sense of what is excellent, beautiful, or appropriate: *That was a tasteless remark.* —**taste′less·ly,** *adv.* —**taste′less·ness,** *n.*

tast·er (tās′tər) *n.* a person who tastes, especially one who is employed to judge the quality of tea or wine.

tast·y (tās′tē) *adj.,* **tast·i·er, tast·i·est.** pleasing to the sense of taste; flavorful; savory: *a tasty piece of pie.* —**tast′i·ly,** *adv.* —**tast′i·ness,** *n.*

tat (tat) *v.,* **tat·ted, tat·ting.** —*v.t.* to make by tatting. —*v.i.* to make tatting.

Ta·tar (tä′tər) another spelling of **Tartar.**

tat·ter (tat′ər) *n.* **1.** a torn, ragged piece or shred of something: *The sail was ripped to tatters by the force of the wind.* **2.** **tatters.** torn or ragged clothing; rags. —*v.t.* to tear into pieces or shreds; make ragged.

tat·tered (tat′ərd) *adj.* **1.** hanging or torn in shreds: *a tattered shirt.* **2.** dressed in torn or ragged clothes: *a tattered old man.*

tat·ting (tat′ing) *n.* **1.** the art or process of making a delicate lace by looping and knotting cotton or linen thread with a special shuttle. **2.** the lace made in this way, used for doilies, collars, and trimmings.

tat·tle (tat′əl) *v.,* **tat·tled, tat·tling.** —*v.i.* **1.** to reveal the secrets, activities, or private affairs of another. **2.** to talk idly; chatter. —*v.t.* to tell or reveal by gossiping. —*n.* idle talk or chatter; gossip. —**tat′tler,** *n.*

tat·tle·tale (tat′əl tāl′) *n. Informal.* a person who deliberately reveals secrets; telltale.

Tassels on a corn plant

tat·too[1] (ta tōō′) *n. pl.,* **tat·toos.** **1.** a military signal, as on a bugle, given at night to call soldiers or sailors to return to their quarters. **2.** military exercises given as entertainment. **3.** a rapid, continuous beating or tapping: *the tattoo of rain on a roof.* [Dutch *taptoe.*]

tat·too[2] (ta tōō′) *v.t.,* **tat·tooed, tat·too·ing.** **1.** to mark (the skin) permanently with colored figures or designs, usually by pricking it with a pointed instrument that has been dipped in pigment. **2.** to mark (figures or designs) on the skin in this way. —*n. pl.,* **tat·toos.** a figure or design made by tattooing. [Of Polynesian origin.] —**tat·too′er,** *n.*

taught (tôt) the past tense and past participle of **teach.**

taunt (tônt) *v.t.* **1.** to mock or reproach with insults or scornful language: *The crowd taunted the athlete for his poor performance.* **2.** to get or provoke by taunting: *The children taunted him into diving off the high board.* —*n.* an insulting or scornful remark.

taupe (tōp) *n.* a dark gray color, tinged with brown, purple, or yellow. —*adj.* having the color taupe.

Tau·rus (tôr′əs) *n.* **1.** a constellation in the northern sky, thought to resemble a bull in shape. **2.** the second sign of the zodiac.

taut (tôt) *adj.* **1.** tightly drawn or stretched; not slack or loose: *The acrobats made sure the tightrope was taut.* **2.** showing tension or strain; tight: *My nerves are taut.* **3.** in good condition; orderly; tidy: *The captain keeps a taut ship.* —**taut′ly,** *adv.* —**taut′ness,** *n.*

tau·tog (tô tôg′) *n.* a fish found in Atlantic coastal waters of the United States, used as food.

tau·tol·o·gy (tô tol′ə jē) *n. pl.,* **tau·tol·o·gies.** **1.** the useless repetition of an idea in different words. For example: *The young woman was a widow whose husband was dead.* **2.** a statement that is necessarily true because it includes all possibilities. For example: *Either it will rain tomorrow or it will not.*

tav·ern (tav′ərn) *n.* **1.** a place where alcoholic beverages are sold to be drunk on the premises; bar. **2.** a lodging place or inn.

taw (tô) *n.* **1.** a marble used by a player for shooting in a game of marbles. **2.** the line from which the players shoot in this game.

taw·dry (tô′drē) *adj.,* **taw·dri·er, taw·dri·est.** cheap and gaudy; tasteless; showy. —**taw′dri·ness,** *n.*

taw·ny (tô′nē) *adj.,* **taw·ni·er, taw·ni·est.** brownish-yellow: *The lion has a tawny mane.* —**taw′ni·ness,** *n.*

tax (taks) *n. pl.,* **tax·es.** **1.** money that must be paid by people for the support of the government. **2.** a heavy burden or demand; strain: *The illness was a tax on his strength.* —*v.t.* **1.** to place or impose a tax on: *The government taxes its citizens.* **2.** to make a heavy demand on; strain: *She taxed her brain for hours trying to solve the problem.* **3.** to reprove or accuse: *His friends taxed him for his constant lateness.*

tax·a·ble (tak′sə bəl) *adj.* subject or liable to taxation: *Some of his income is not taxable.*

tax·a·tion (tak sā′shən) *n.* **1.** the act or system of imposing and collecting taxes. **2.** an amount of money raised by taxes.

tax-ex·empt (taks′ig zempt′) *adj.* not subject to taxes.

at; āpe; cär; end; mē; it; īce; hot; ōld; fôrk; wood; fōol; oil; out; up; turn; sing; thin; this; hw in white; zh in treasure. The symbol ə stands for the sound of **a** in about, **e** in taken, **i** in pencil, **o** in lemon, and **u** in circus.

T

tax·i (tak′sē) *n. pl.*, **tax·is** or **tax·ies.** see **taxicab.**
—*v.i.*, **tax·ied, tax·i·ing** or **tax·y·ing. 1.** to ride in a taxicab: *We taxied to the theater.* **2.** (of an aircraft) to move slowly along the ground or over the surface of water: *The airplane taxied out to the runway before taking off.*

tax·i·cab (tak′sē kab′) *n.* an automobile for public hire, usually having a meter that records the fare to be paid.

tax·i·der·mist (tak′si dur′mist) *n.* a person whose work or business is taxidermy.

tax·i·der·my (tak′si dur′mē) *n.* the art of preparing and stuffing the skins of dead animals and mounting them in lifelike positions.

tax·i·me·ter (tak′sē mē′tər) *n.* the meter in a taxicab that shows the fare due.

tax·o·nom·ic (tak′sə nom′ik) *adj.* of, relating to, or according to taxonomy.

tax·on·o·my (tak son′ə mē) *n.* the grouping of animals and plants into categories on the basis of their natural relationships.

tax·pay·er (taks′pā′ər) *n.* a person who pays or is subject to a tax.

Tay·lor, Zach·a·ry (tā′lər; zak′ər ē) 1784–1850, U.S. general, the twelfth president of the United States, from 1849 to 1850.

Tb, the symbol for terbium.

TB, tuberculosis.

Tbi·li·si (tə bi lē′sē′) *n.* a city in the southwestern Soviet Union, capital of the republic of Georgia, formerly known as Tiflis. Pop. (1971 est.), 907,000.

T-bone steak (tē′bōn′) a loin steak containing some tenderloin and a T-shaped bone. Also, **T-bone.**

tbs., tablespoon; tablespoons. Also, **tbsp.**

Tc, the symbol for technetium.

Tchai·kov·sky, Peter Il·yich (chī kôf′skē; il′yich) 1840–1893, Russian composer.

Te, the symbol for tellurium.

tea (tē) *n.* **1.** a drink made from the dried and prepared leaves of an Asian shrub. **2.** the dried leaves used to make this beverage. **3.** the shrub bearing these leaves, having fragrant, drooping, white flowers, grown mainly in China, Japan, and India. **4.** any of similar beverages made from the leaves of various other plants or substances: *sage tea, beef tea.* **5.** *British.* a light meal in the late afternoon, usually consisting of bread and butter, cakes, and similar light food served with tea. **6.** a reception or other social gathering, usually occurring in the afternoon, at which tea and other refreshments are served.

tea bag, a small, porous bag of thin paper or cloth, containing shredded or ground tea leaves for dipping in hot water to make tea.

teach (tēch) *v.*, **taught, teach·ing.** —*v.t.* **1.** to give knowledge to, especially through lessons or formal schooling; instruct: *He taught her to play the piano. She teaches a class of students.* **2.** to give lessons or instruction in: *to teach English literature, to teach swimming.* **3.** to cause or help to learn: *The accident taught her to be more careful.* —*v.i.* to act or be employed as a teacher; give instruction: *My sister teaches at an elementary school.*

teach·a·ble (tē′chə bəl) *adj.* capable of being taught. —**teach′a·bil′i·ty,** *n.*

teach·er (tē′chər) *n.* a person who teaches, especially as an occupation.

teach·ing (tē′ching) *n.* **1.** the act, work, or occupation of a teacher. **2.** *also,* **teachings.** something that is taught: *the teachings of Plato.*

tea·cup (tē′kup′) *n.* **1.** a cup in which tea is served. **2.** see **teacupful.**

tea·cup·ful (tē′kup fool′) *n. pl.*, **tea·cup·fuls.** the amount that a teacup will hold, usually four fluid ounces.

tea·house (tē′hous′) *n. pl.*, **tea·hous·es** (tē′hou′ziz). a public place, especially in China and Japan, where tea and other light refreshments are served.

teak (tēk) *n.* **1.** a hard, yellowish-brown wood used in shipbuilding and in the manufacture of furniture and flooring. Also, **teakwood. 2.** a tree bearing this wood, found in Asia, western Africa, and tropical America. It has large, oval leaves, and small white or bluish flowers.

tea·ket·tle (tē′ket′əl) *n.* a covered kettle with a spout and handle, used to boil water.

teak·wood (tēk′wood′) *n.* see **teak** *(def. 1).*

teal (tēl) *n. pl.*, **teals** or **teal.** any of several small, short-necked ducks that live in rivers or marshes.

Teal

team (tēm) *n.* **1.** a group making up one side in an athletic contest or other competition: *a hockey team, a debating team.* **2.** any group working together in some joint action: *a comedy team, a team of engineers.* **3.** two or more horses or other animals harnessed together, as to pull a wagon or plow. —*v.t.* **1.** to bring or join together in a team: *to team horses.* **2.** to haul or transport by means of a team: *to team logs.* —*v.i.* to work together; form a team: *The children teamed up to collect money for charity.*

team·mate (tēm′māt′) *n.* a fellow member of a team.

team·ster (tēm′stər) *n.* **1.** a person whose work or occupation is driving a truck. **2.** a person whose work or occupation is driving a team of horses or other animals.

team·work (tēm′wurk′) *n.* the cooperative effort or action on the part of a number of people working together, especially to achieve a common goal: *The winning team had great teamwork.*

tea·pot (tē′pot′) *n.* a pot with a lid, spout, and handle, used for making and serving tea.

tear[1] (ter) *v.*, **tore, torn, tear·ing.** —*v.t.* **1.** to pull apart or into pieces: *The workman tore the rag in half. She tore the letter up after reading it.* **2.** to make by tearing: *I accidentally tore a hole in my coat.* **3.** to wound by tearing: *The thorn tore her skin.* **4.** to pull, pluck, or remove by force: *The tornado tore the small tree from the ground.* **5.** to force as if by pulling: *We couldn't tear our eyes away from the movie screen.* **6.** to disrupt, divide, or split into sides: *The country was torn by civil war.* **7.** to distress greatly; torment: *Grief tore her heart.* —*v.i.* **1.** to become torn: *His pants tore when he bent down.* **2.** to move with great haste or energy: *She tore out of the house.* —*n.* **1.** a torn part or place, such as a split or hole: *Let her sew the tear in your sleeve.* **2.** the act of tearing. [Old English *teran* to pull apart, destroy.]

to tear down. to take apart; demolish.

to tear into. *Informal.* to attack vigorously.

tear[2] (tēr) *n.* **1.** a drop of the clear, slightly salty fluid that flows from the eye, as in weeping. **2. tears.** the act of weeping: *She burst into tears when she heard the news.* —*v.i.* to shed tears: *The smoky air made my eyes tear.* [Old English *tēar.*]

tear·drop (tēr′drop′) *n.* a single tear.

tear·ful (tēr′fəl) *adj.* **1.** full of or shedding tears; weeping: *tearful eyes.* **2.** causing tears; sad: *a tearful story.* —**tear′ful·ly,** *adv.* —**tear′ful·ness,** *n.*

tear gas (tēr) any of various gases that irritate the eyes, causing a flow of tears and temporary blindness.

tea·room (tē′rōom′, tē′room′) *n.* a small room or restaurant where beverages and light meals are served.

tease (tēz) *v.*, **teased, teas·ing.** —*v.t.* **1.** to provoke, annoy, or make fun of playfully or mischievously: *He teased* his little sister by hiding her toys. **2.** to fluff (hair) by combing or brushing in strokes from the end of a strand toward the scalp. **3.** to raise a nap on (cloth). **4.** to separate the fibers of in preparation for spinning: *to tease wool.* —*v.i.* to engage in teasing someone. —*n.* **1.** a person who teases. **2.** the act of teasing.

teas·er (tē′zər) *n.* **1.** a person or thing that teases. **2.** *Informal.* something difficult, puzzling, or annoying: *That arithmetic problem was a real teaser.*

tea·spoon (tē′spoon′) *n.* **1.** a spoon that is smaller than a tablespoon or soup spoon, used especially to stir tea or coffee in a cup. **2.** the amount one teaspoon will hold, a standard cooking measurement equivalent to ⅓ of a tablespoon, or 1⅓ fluid drams.

tea·spoon·ful (tē′spoon fool′) *n. pl.,* **tea·spoon·fuls.** the amount that a teaspoon will hold; teaspoon.

teat (tēt) *n.* a small projection on the breast or udder, through which milk is drawn; nipple.

tech. **1.** technical. **2.** technology.

tech·ne·ti·um (tek nē′shē əm) *n.* a silver-gray, radioactive metallic element, the first chemical element to be made artificially. It is not known to occur naturally on earth. Symbol: **Tc**

tech·nic (tek′nik) *n.* a method of procedure; technique.

tech·ni·cal (tek′ni kəl) *adj.* **1.** relating to, involving, or characteristic of some science, art, profession, or other field: *technical training, the technical language of engineering.* **2.** of or relating to engineering, applied science, or the mechanical or industrial arts: *She attended a technical school for two years to qualify as a laboratory assistant.* **3.** of, relating to, or showing technique: *The musician has technical ability but little imagination.* **4.** according to a strict interpretation of rules and principles: *If you really want to be technical, the player should have been disqualified altogether, not just penalized.* —**tech′ni·cal·ly,** *adv.* —**tech′ni·cal·ness,** *n.*

tech·ni·cal·i·ty (tek′ni kal′ə tē) *n. pl.,* **tech·ni·cal·i·ties.** **1.** a point or detail, as of law: *The lawyer won his case on a legal technicality.* **2.** the state or quality of being technical.

tech·ni·cian (tek nish′ən) *n.* **1.** a person who is skilled in some science, art, or profession, especially a person trained to deal with specialized equipment or processes: *a medical technician, a lighting technician.* **2.** a person who is skilled in technique, such as a writer, artist, or musician: *That film director is a good technician but lacks originality.*

Tech·ni·col·or (tek′ni kul′ər) *n. Trademark.* the process of making color motion pictures, in which three single-color films, one in red, one in yellow, and one in blue, are made and then combined into a single developed film with the colors of the original scene.

tech·nique (tek nēk′) *n.* a method or manner of bringing about a desired result in a science, art, sport, or profession: *the techniques of painting. He learned a new technique for serving the ball in tennis.*

tech·no·log·i·cal (tek′nə loj′i kəl) *adj.* of, relating to, or involving technology: *Sending men to the moon is a great technological achievement.* —**tech′no·log′i·cal·ly,** *adv.*

tech·nol·o·gist (tek nol′ə jist) *n.* a person who is skilled in technology.

tech·nol·o·gy (tek nol′ə jē) *n.* **1.** the use of scientific knowledge for practical purposes, especially in the field of industry. **2.** the methods, processes, and devices obtained or resulting from such use. **3.** any use of materials or objects to serve human needs.

ted·dy bear (ted′ē) *also,* **Ted·dy bear.** a toy resembling a small bear, usually stuffed with soft material and covered with furlike fabric. [From *Teddy,* a nickname of President Theodore Roosevelt; from a cartoon in which he was shown sparing the life of a bear cub while hunting.]

Te De·um (tā dā′əm, tē dē′əm) **1.** in the Roman Catholic and Anglican churches, a hymn of praise and thanksgiving sung at morning services or on special occasions. **2.** the music for this hymn. [Latin *Tē Deum (laudāmus)* Thee, God (we praise), the opening words of this hymn.]

te·di·ous (tē′dē əs, tē′jəs) *adj.* causing weariness and boredom because of length, dullness, or the like; boring: *a tedious lesson.* —**te′di·ous·ly,** *adv.* —**te′di·ous·ness,** *n.*

te·di·um (tē′dē əm) *n.* the state of being tedious.

tee (tē) *n.* **1.** a small peg of wood, plastic, or other material, on which a golf ball is placed to be driven at the beginning of each hole. **2.** a small mound of earth or sand used for the same purpose. **3.** a usually raised area from which a player starts each hole on a golf course. —*v.t.,* **teed, tee·ing.** to place (a golf ball) on a tee.

  to tee off. to drive a golf ball from a tee.

teem[1] (tēm) *v.i.* to be at the point of overflowing; be full; abound; swarm: *The creek teemed with trout. By noon the beach was teeming with people.* [Old English *tēman* to produce, bear; from *tēam* race, family.]

teem[2] (tēm) *v.i.* to rain very hard; pour: *It teemed all day Saturday.* [Of Scandinavian origin.]

teen (tēn) *adj.* see **teenage.** —*n.* see **teenager.**

-teen *suffix* (used to form cardinal numbers from thirteen to nineteen) ten more than: *sixteen.*

teen·age (tēn′āj′) *also,* **teen-age, teen·aged, teen-aged.** *adj.* relating to or characteristic of people in their teens.

teen·ag·er (tēn′ā′jər) *also,* **teen-ag·er.** *n.* a person who is between thirteen and nineteen years of age.

teens (tēnz) *n.,pl.* **1.** the years of one's life from thirteen to nineteen. **2.** the numbers thirteen to nineteen.

tee·ny (tē′nē) *adj.,* **tee·ni·er, tee·ni·est.** *Informal.* extremely small; tiny. Also, **teen·sy** (tēn′sē).

tee·pee (tē′pē) another spelling of **tepee.**

tee shirt, another spelling of **T-shirt.**

tee·ter (tē′tər) *v.i.* **1.** to walk or move unsteadily and uncertainly, often with a swaying motion, as if about to fall: *The acrobat teetered on the tightrope.* **2.** to move back and forth in an uncertain way; waver: *The country teetered on the brink of war.* —*n.* a teetering movement.

tee·ter-tot·ter (tē′tər tot′ər) *n.* see **seesaw** *(def. 1).*

teeth (tēth) the plural of **tooth.**

teethe (tēth) *v.i.,* **teethed, teeth·ing.** to grow or develop teeth; cut one's teeth.

tee·to·tal·er (tē′tōt′əl ər) *n.* a person who never drinks alcoholic beverages.

Te·gu·ci·gal·pa (tē gōo′sē gäl′pä) *n.* the capital of Honduras. Pop. (1970 est.), 232,300.

teg·u·ment (teg′yə mənt) *n.* an outer covering.

Te·hran (te′hə rän′) *also,* **Te·he·ran.** *n.* the capital and largest city of Iran, in the north-central part of the country. Pop. (1970 est.), 3,229,000.

tel. **1.** telephone. **2.** telegram. **3.** telegraph.

Tel A·viv (tel′ ə vēv′) a city in west-central Israel, on the Mediterranean Sea, combined with Jaffa in 1950. Official name: **Tel Aviv-Jaffa.** Pop. (1971 est.), 382,900.

tele- *combining form* **1.** at a distance; far: *telepathy.* **2.** of or relating to television: *telethon.*

---

at; āpe; cär; end; mē; it; īce; hot; ōld; fôrk; wood; fōol; oil; out; up; turn; sing; thin; **this;** **hw** in white; **zh** in treasure. The symbol ə stands for the sound of **a** in about, **e** in taken, **i** in pencil, **o** in lemon, and **u** in circus.

T

tel·e·cast (tel′ə kast′) *v.t.,* **tel·e·cast** or **tel·e·cast·ed, tel·e·cast·ing.** to broadcast (a program) by television; televise. —*n.* a program broadcast by television.

tel·e·com·mu·ni·ca·tion (tel′ə kə myōō′nə kā′shən) *also,* **tel·e·com·mu·ni·ca·tions.** *n.* the science or study of sending messages over long distances by electronic means, as by telegraph, television, or telephone.

tel·e·gram (tel′ə gram′) *n.* a message that is sent by telegraph.

tel·e·graph (tel′ə graf′) *n.* the system, process, and equipment used for sending messages over a distance with coded electrical impulses. —*v.t.* **1.** to send (a message) by telegraph. **2.** to send a message to by telegraph.

te·leg·ra·pher (tə leg′rə fər) *n.* a person whose work is sending and receiving messages by telegraph.

tel·e·graph·ic (tel′ə graf′ik) *adj.* of, relating to, or sent by telegraph. Also, **tel·e·graph·i·cal** (tel′ə graf′i kəl). —**tel′e·graph′i·cal·ly,** *adv.*

te·leg·ra·phy (tə leg′rə fē) *n.* the operation or use of telegraphs to send messages.

te·lem·e·ter (tə lem′ə tər) *n.* an electronic instrument for measuring temperature, radiation, or the like, and sending the information to a distant receiving station.

te·lem·e·try (tə lem′ə trē) *n.* the branch of engineering dealing with the measurement of temperature, radiation, or the like, for sending to a distant receiving station.

tel·e·path·ic (tel′ə path′ik) *adj.* of, relating to, or sent by telepathy. —**tel′e·path′i·cal·ly,** *adv.*

te·lep·a·thy (tə lep′ə thē) *n.* the apparent communication of one mind with another directly, without the use of speaking, writing, or gesturing.

tel·e·phone (tel′ə fōn′) *n.* **1.** an electrical system for sending sound or speech over distances. **2.** an instrument used in such a system, equipped with a transmitter, a receiver, and often a dial or buttons for directing calls. —*v.t.,* **tel·e·phoned, tel·e·phon·ing. 1.** to communicate with by telephone: *I will telephone you tomorrow.* **2.** to send by telephone: *to telephone a message.* —*v.i.* to communicate by telephone.

Telephones

tel·e·phon·ic (tel′ə fon′ik) *adj.* of, relating to, or sent by a telephone.

te·leph·o·ny (tə lef′ə nē) *n.* the science or method of sending messages by telephone.

tel·e·pho·to lens (tel′ə fō′tō) a camera lens that enlarges the image of a distant object.

Tel·e·promp·ter (tel′ə promp′tər) *n.* *Trademark.* a television set placed before a speaker or performer on which a magnified script is unrolled line by line.

tel·e·scope (tel′ə skōp′) *n.* an instrument for making distant objects, such as heavenly bodies, appear nearer and larger. The eyepiece contains a magnifying lens or system of lenses. —*v.t.,* **tel·e·scoped, tel·e·scop·ing. 1.** to drive together or into one another like the tubes of certain telescopes: *The collision telescoped the two cars.* **2.** to make shorter or smaller; condense; abridge; compress.

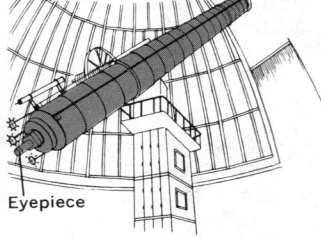
Eyepiece
Telescope

tel·e·scop·ic (tel′ə skop′ik) *adj.* **1.** of, relating to, or characteristic of a telescope: *a telescopic lens.* **2.** seen or obtained by means of a telescope: *a telescopic view of a planet.* **3.** visible only through a telescope: *a telescopic galaxy.* **4.** able to see at a great distance; far-seeing. **5.** consisting of parts capable of sliding into one another, like the tubes of certain telescopes. —**tel′e·scop′i·cal·ly,** *adv.*

tel·e·thon (tel′ə thon′) *n.* a long television program during which callers make pledges to a charity.

Tel·e·type (tel′e tīp′) *n.* *Trademark.* communications equipment by which a message typed on one teletypewriter is sent over an electrical circuit to another teletypewriter, which types out the message. —*v.t.,* **tel·e·typed, tel·e·typ·ing.** to send (a message) by teletypewriter.

tel·e·type·writ·er (tel′ə tīp′rī′tər) *n.* a keyboard machine that looks like an electric typewriter, used for receiving and sending messages over an electrical circuit.

tel·e·vise (tel′ə vīz′) *v.t.,* **tel·e·vised, tel·e·vis·ing.** to send by television: *All the major networks televised the first walk on the moon.*

tel·e·vi·sion (tel′ə vizh′ən) *n.* **1.** a system of sending and receiving images and accompanying sounds by changing them into signals, which are turned back into picture and sound by the receiving set. **2.** a set in which such images are received and reproduced. **3.** the industry, medium, or art of television broadcasting.

tell (tel) *v.,* **told, tell·ing.** —*v.t.* **1.** to give a detailed account of; narrate: *to tell a fairy tale to a child.* **2.** to put or express in written or spoken words: *He promised not to tell a lie.* **3.** to give information to; let know: *Tell us about your vacation.* **4.** to make known, especially something that is confidential; reveal; disclose: *to tell a secret.* **5.** to give an order, command, or direction to: *She told him to be quiet.* **6.** to distinguish; discern; determine: *The jeweler can tell a real diamond from an imitation. Barbara couldn't tell the twins apart.* —*v.i.* **1.** to give an account: *The old sailor told of his many adventures.* **2.** to reveal something secret; report; inform: *If you misbehave, I'll tell.* **3.** to serve as evidence; indicate: *Her frown told of her anger.* **4.** to have or produce an effect: *The strain on him is beginning to tell.*

Tell, William (tel) a legendary hero of Swiss independence who was forced to shoot an apple off his son's head with a bow and arrow.

tell·er (tel′ər) *n.* **1.** a person who relates, narrates, or informs: *Everyone knows that Margo's uncle is a teller of tall stories.* **2.** a person who counts. **3.** a person who is employed in a bank and receives or gives out money over a counter.

tell·ing (tel′ing) *adj.* having the intended or desired effect; striking; forceful: *The boxer gave a telling blow that sent his opponent reeling.* —**tell′ing·ly,** *adv.*

tell·tale (tel′tāl′) *n.* a person who deliberately reveals secrets; tattletale. —*adj.* that reveals what is not intended to be known or seen: *There was a telltale bloodstain on the suspect's coat.*

tel·lu·ri·um (te loor′ē əm) *n.* a lustrous, silver-white element having some metallic properties. It is a semiconductor, and is used in stainless steel and lead alloys. Symbol: Te

te·mer·i·ty (tə mer′ə tē) *n.* too much boldness; rashness: *His temerity led him to challenge the larger boy to a fight.*

temp. **1.** temperature. **2.** temporary.

tem·per (tem′pər) *n.* **1.** a tendency to become angry or irritated: *He has quite a temper and gets mad at the slightest inconvenience.* **2.** an angry state of mind; rage. **3.** a usual frame of mind; temperament: *The child has a sunny temper* and is seldom cross. **4.** control over the emotions; self-control; composure: *to lose one's temper, to keep one's temper.* **5.** the degree of hardness or strength of a substance, especially a metal, given by mixing it with another substance or by treating it in a particular way. —*v.t.* **1.** to lessen the severity or harshness of; moderate; soften: *to temper justice with mercy.* **2.** to bring (a substance) to a proper or desired degree of hardness or strength, by mixing it with another substance or by treating it in a particular way: *to temper steel with heat.*

tem·per·a·ment (tem′pər ə mənt) *n.* the emotional make-up of a person, especially the way a person usually thinks, acts, or responds to other people or to situations: *She has a nervous temperament and becomes upset if anything unexpected happens.*

tem·per·a·men·tal (tem′pər ə ment′əl) *adj.* **1.** showing moodiness, sensitivity, or irritability. **2.** relating to or caused by temperament: *The spoiled child had a temperamental outburst when he could not have his way.* —**tem′per·a·men′tal·ly,** *adv.*

tem·per·ance (tem′pər əns) *n.* **1.** moderation or self-restraint of any kind. **2.** the practice of never drinking alcoholic beverages.

tem·per·ate (tem′pər it) *adj.* **1.** characterized by temperance in behavior. **2.** free from extremes of temperature: *a temperate climate.* —**tem′per·ate·ly,** *adv.* —**tem′per·ate·ness,** *n.*

Temperate Zone, either of the two zones of the earth characterized by a temperate climate with four distinct seasons. One zone lies north of the equator between the Arctic Circle and the Tropic of Cancer, the other south of the equator between the Tropic of Capricorn and the Antarctic Circle.

tem·per·a·ture (tem′pər ə chər) *n.* **1.** the degree of heat or coldness of a body or substance as measured by a thermometer or other graduated scale. **2.** *Informal.* an abnormally high body temperature; fever: *He has a temperature, so he is staying home today.*

tem·pered (tem′pərd) *adj.* **1.** having a particular disposition. ▲ used in combination: *an even-tempered man.* **2.** treated so as to have the desired degree of hardness or strength: *tempered steel.* **3.** changed or softened by the addition of some other substance or quality; lessened.

tem·pest (tem′pist) *n.* **1.** a violent windstorm, usually accompanied by rain, hail, snow, or thunder. **2.** any violent commotion or disturbance; tumult.

tem·pes·tu·ous (tem pes′cho͞o əs) *adj.* characteristic of a tempest; turbulent; violent; stormy: *a tempestuous airplane flight, a tempestuous mob.* —**tem·pes′tu·ous·ly,** *adv.* —**tem·pes′tu·ous·ness,** *n.*

tem·ple¹ (tem′pəl) *n.* **1.** any building dedicated to the worship of a god or gods. **2. Temple.** any of three buildings built one after the other in Jerusalem as the center of Jewish worship. **3.** see **synagogue** *(def. 2).* [Old English *templ, tempel.*]

tem·ple² (tem′pəl) *n.* the flattened part on either side of the forehead, above the cheekbone and in front of the ear. [Old French *temple.*]

tem·po (tem′pō) *n. pl.,* **tem·pos** or **tem·pi** (tem′pē). **1.** *Music.* the relative speed at which a musical composition, movement, or passage is or should be played. **2.** a characteristic pace or speed: *the fast tempo of life in a modern city.*

tem·po·ral¹ (tem′pər əl) *adj.* **1.** of or relating to time. **2.** lasting for a short time; temporary. **3.** of or relating to this life on earth; material; worldly. **4.** not religious; secular; civil; lay: *Charlemagne held both spiritual and temporal power over Western Europe by the year 800.* [Latin *temporālis.*]

tem·po·ral² (tem′pər əl) *adj.* of, relating to, or near the temples. [Late Latin *temporālis.*]

tem·po·rar·y (tem′pə rer′ē) *adj.* lasting, existing, or used for a limited time only; not permanent: *a temporary shelter, a temporary job.* —**tem′po·rar′i·ly,** *adv.*

tem·po·rize (tem′pə rīz′) *v.i.,* **tem·po·rized, tem·po·riz·ing.** **1.** to delay or put off immediate action or decision, so as to avoid arguments or gain time. **2.** to change one's acts or opinions in order to fit the time or circumstances.

tempt (tempt) *v.t.* **1.** to try to persuade (someone) to do something that is sinful, illegal, or foolish: *Hunger tempted the boy to steal.* **2.** to attract strongly; lure: *The unappetizing food didn't tempt her.* **3.** to act in a reckless or bold way toward; provoke; defy: *to tempt fate.*

temp·ta·tion (temp tā′shən) *n.* **1.** the act of tempting or the state of being tempted. **2.** something that tempts.

tempt·er (temp′tər) *n.* a person who tempts.

tempt·ing (temp′ting) *adj.* that tempts or allures; attractive: *a tempting offer.* —**tempt′ing·ly,** *adv.*

tempt·ress (temp′tris) *n. pl.,* **tempt·ress·es.** a woman who tempts.

ten (ten) *n.* **1.** the cardinal number that is one more than nine. **2.** a symbol representing this number, such as 10 or X. **3.** something having this many units or things, such as a playing card. —*adj.* numbering one more than nine.

ten·a·ble (ten′ə bəl) *adj.* that can be held, maintained, or defended: *a tenable fortress, a tenable theory.* —**ten′a·bil′i·ty,** *n.* —**ten′a·bly,** *adv.*

te·na·cious (ti nā′shəs) *adj.* **1.** holding firmly: *a tenacious grip.* **2.** tending to stick to another substance; adhesive: *Tar is tenacious.* **3.** not easily pulled or broken apart: *a tenacious metal.* **4.** stubborn; obstinate. **5.** tending to retain: *a tenacious memory.* —**te·na′cious·ly,** *adv.* —**te·na′cious·ness,** *n.*

te·nac·i·ty (ti nas′ə tē) *n.* the state or quality of being tenacious.

ten·an·cy (ten′ən sē) *n. pl.,* **ten·an·cies.** **1.** the occupancy of property for which rent is paid; state of being a tenant. **2.** the period of time during which a tenant occupies property. **3.** the property occupied by a tenant.

ten·ant (ten′ənt) *n.* **1.** a person who pays rent to occupy or use the property of another, such as land, a house, apartment, or office. **2.** an occupant or inhabitant of any place: *the present tenant of the White House.* —*v.t.* to hold or occupy as a tenant; inhabit.

tenant farmer, a farmer who works land owned by another and pays rent either in cash or with a share of the crops.

ten·ant·ry (ten′ən trē) *n. pl.,* **ten·ant·ries.** **1.** all the tenants of an estate or other property. **2.** the state of being a tenant; tenancy.

Ten Commandments, the ten rules for living and for worshiping that, according to the Old Testament, God presented to Moses on Mount Sinai.

tend¹ (tend) *v.i.* **1.** to be likely or apt: *She tends to overeat. His stories tend to be silly.* **2.** to lead to some state or condition: *Unsanitary living conditions tend to produce disease.* **3.** to move, extend, or be directed in a particular direction: *The path tends toward the left at the river.* [Old French *tendre* to stretch, hold out.]

at; āpe; cär; end; mē; it; īce; hot; ōld; fôrk; wood; fo͞ol; oil; out; up; turn; sing; thin; this; hw in white; zh in treasure. The symbol ə stands for the sound of a in about, e in taken, i in pencil, o in lemon, and u in circus.

tend² (tend) *v.t.* **1.** to take care of the needs of; care for; watch over: *to tend a sick person, to tend a plant.* **2.** to be in charge of or work at; manage or operate: *to tend a machine, to tend a store.* —*v.i. Informal.* to take care of: *Tell her to tend to her own affairs.* [Short for *attend.*]

tend·en·cy (ten′dən sē) *n. pl.,* **tend·en·cies.** a natural or usual inclination: *He has a tendency to get angry if he is criticized. My car's engine has a tendency to stall.*

ten·der¹ (ten′dər) *adj.* **1.** soft or delicate; not tough or hard: *tender beef.* **2.** not hardy, robust, or strong; fragile: *the tender petals of a flower.* **3.** having the delicacy of youth; fresh; immature: *Three is a tender age.* **4.** not rough; light; gentle: *a tender touch.* **5.** showing or characterized by warmth of feeling; kind or loving; affectionate: *tender memories. He gave his wife a tender look.* **6.** very sensitive; easily hurt; sore: *His arm was still tender after the cut healed.* **7.** sensitive to the feelings of others; sympathetic; compassionate: *a tender heart.* **8.** requiring careful, tactful handling or treatment: *a tender subject.* [Old French *tendre.*] —**ten′der·ly,** *adv.* —**ten′der·ness,** *n.*

ten·der² (ten′dər) *v.t.* **1.** to present formally; offer: *to tender one's resignation from a job.* **2.** *Law.* to offer in payment of a debt, claim, or other obligation. —*n.* **1.** a formal offer. **2.** something that is offered, especially money offered in payment of a debt, claim, or other obligation. [Old French *tendre* to hold out, offer.]

ten·der³ (ten′dər) *n.* **1.** a person who cares for, attends to, or manages someone or something. **2.** a small boat or ship that is used to serve a large vessel, as by carrying supplies or passengers between the vessel and the shore. **3.** a railroad car that is attached to the rear of a steam locomotive, used to carry fuel and water. [*Tend²* + *-er¹.*]

Tender³ *(def. 3)*

ten·der·foot (ten′dər foot′) *n. pl.,* **ten·der·foots** or **ten·der·feet** (ten′dər fēt′). **1.** a person who is a newcomer to ranch or frontier life of the West, and is unused to the hardships or rough conditions of such life. **2.** any inexperienced person; novice. **3.** a boy who is in the lowest rank of the Boy Scouts.

ten·der-heart·ed (ten′dər här′tid) *adj.* easily moved to pity, love, or sorrow; compassionate; sympathetic. —**ten′der-heart′ed·ly,** *adv.* —**ten′der-heart′ed·ness,** *n.*

ten·der·iz·er (ten′də rī′zər) *n.* any substance put on meat to make it tender.

ten·der·loin (ten′dər loin′) *n.* the tenderest part of the loin of beef or pork.

ten·don (ten′dən) *n.* a strong cord or band of tissue that attaches a muscle to a bone or other part of the body.

ten·dril (ten′drəl) *n.* **1.** a thin, leafless, often spirally coiling part by which a climbing plant, such as the grape, twines around or clings to a tree trunk, wall, or other object for support. **2.** something resembling this: *wispy tendrils of hair.*

ten·e·ment (ten′ə mənt) *n.* **1.** an apartment building or rooming house that is poorly built or maintained and usually overcrowded, especially one that is located in a slum. **2.** any house or building to live in, especially one that is rented or intended for rent. **3.** a room or set of rooms occupied by a tenant as a separate dwelling.

ten·et (ten′it) *n.* a doctrine, principle, or belief held to be true by an individual or group.

ten·fold (ten′fōld′) *adj.* **1.** ten times as great or numerous. **2.** having or consisting of ten parts. —*adv.* so as to be ten times greater or more numerous.

ten-gal·lon hat (ten′gal′ən) a man's wide-brimmed felt hat with a high crown, worn especially in the southwestern United States.

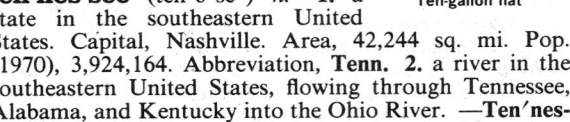

Ten-gallon hat

Tenn., Tennessee.

Ten·nes·see (ten′ə sē′) *n.* **1.** a state in the southeastern United States. Capital, Nashville. Area, 42,244 sq. mi. Pop. (1970), 3,924,164. Abbreviation, **Tenn.** **2.** a river in the southeastern United States, flowing through Tennessee, Alabama, and Kentucky into the Ohio River. —**Ten′nes·se′an,** *adj., n.*

● **Tennessee** comes from the Cherokees' name for their ancient capital. A nearby stream was named for this town, and the name was later given to the Tennessee River. A county of North Carolina that was established in this area took the name Tennessee from the river, and the name was retained when Tennessee became a separate state.

Tennessee Valley Authority, see TVA.

ten·nis (ten′is) *n.* **1.** a racket game in which two or four players hit a light, fabric-covered rubber ball back and forth over a low net stretched across the center of a level, rectangular court of grass, clay, concrete, or other material. **2.** any of several similar and related games.

Ten·ny·son, Alfred, Lord (ten′ə sən) 1809–1892, English poet.

ten·on (ten′ən) *n.* a projecting part on the end of a timber or other piece of wood cut so as to fit into a corresponding hole, or mortise, in another piece to form a joint. —*v.t.* **1.** to cut a tenon in (a piece of wood). **2.** to join (two pieces of wood) with a tenon and mortise joint.

ten·or (ten′ər) *n.* **1.** a general or usual tendency, course, or direction: *the quiet tenor of country life.* **2.** the general meaning or effect of something spoken or written; drift: *The sad tenor of her letter worried him.* **3.** *Music.* **a.** the highest natural adult male voice. **b.** a singer who has such a voice. **c.** a musical instrument that has a similar range. **d.** a musical part for such a voice or instrument. —*adj. Music.* **1.** able to sing or play the tenor: *a tenor voice, a tenor saxophone.* **2.** for the tenor.

ten·pin (ten′pin′) *n.* **1. tenpins.** the game of bowling. ▲ used with a singular verb. **2.** a pin used in this game.

tense¹ (tens) *adj.,* **tens·er, tens·est. 1.** stretched or drawn tight; strained; taut: *tense muscles.* **2.** undergoing or showing mental or emotional strain: *a tense person, a tense look.* **3.** characterized by or causing strain or suspense: *a tense situation, a tense detective story.* —*v.t., v.i.,* **tensed, tens·ing.** to make or become tense. [Latin *tensus,* the past participle of *tendere* to stretch.] —**tense′ly,** *adv.* —**tense′ness,** *n.*

Tenpins

tense² (tens) *n.* **1.** a form of a verb that shows the time of its action or state of being. *He sits* is in the present tense. *He sat* is in the past tense. *He will sit* is in the future tense. **2.** a set of such forms for a particular tense. The present tense of the verb *go* is: *I go, you go, he, she or it goes, we go, you go, they go.* [Old French *tens* time.]

ten·sile (ten′sil) *adj.* **1.** of or relating to tension: *the tensile strain on a rope, the tensile strength of steel.* **2.** that can be stretched: *a tensile metal.*

ten·sion (ten′shən) *n.* **1.** the act of stretching or the state of being stretched. **2.** mental or emotional strain. **3.** any strained state or relationship: *tension between nations.*

ten·sor (ten′sər, ten′sôr) *n.* any muscle that stretches or tenses a part of the body.

tent (tent) *n.* **1.** a collapsible, portable shelter, usually of canvas, supported by one or more poles and fastened by cords attached to pegs in the ground. **2.** anything that resembles this in form or use, such as an oxygen tent. —*v.i.* to live or camp in a tent; encamp.

ten·ta·cle (ten′tə kəl) *n.* **1.** any of various long, slender, flexible growths, growing on the head or about the mouth of certain animals, used for feeling, grasping, and moving. An octopus has eight tentacles. **2.** something resembling a tentacle: *a city held in the tentacles of organized crime.* **3.** *Botany.*

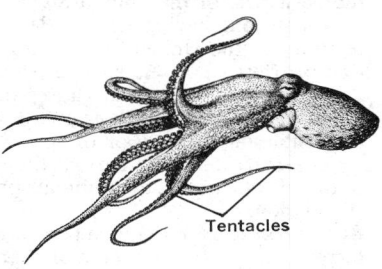
Tentacles

Tentacles of an octopus

a sensitive, hairlike growth on the leaves of some plants.

ten·ta·tive (ten′tə tiv) *adj.* **1.** made, done, or proposed as a trial or experiment; not definite or final: *tentative plans, a tentative outline for a term paper.* **2.** showing hesitancy or uncertainty: *The shy girl gave us a tentative smile.* —**ten′ta·tive·ly,** *adv.* —**ten′ta·tive·ness,** *n.*

ten·ter (ten′tər) *n.* a framework or machine on which cloth is stretched so as to dry evenly without shrinking. —*v.t.* to stretch (cloth) on a tenter.

ten·ter·hook (ten′tər hook′) *n.* a sharp hooked nail used for fastening cloth on a tenter.

on tenterhooks. in a state of suspense or anxiety.

tenth (tenth) *adj.* **1.** (the ordinal of ten) next after the ninth. **2.** being one of ten equal parts. —*n.* **1.** something that is next after the ninth. **2.** one of ten equal parts; ¹/₁₀. —*adv.* in the tenth place.

ten·u·ous (ten′yōō əs) *adj.* **1.** thin or delicate; slender, as a thread. **2.** having little strength, substance, or importance; weak; flimsy: *a tenuous argument.* —**ten′u·ous·ly,** *adv.* —**ten′u·ous·ness,** *n.*

ten·ure (ten′yər) *n.* **1.** the act or right of holding or possessing something, such as property, a title, or office. **2.** the length of time during which something is held: *The tenure of the Presidency is four years.* **3.** the terms under which something is held. **4.** the status of permanent position that is granted to an employee, such as a teacher or civil servant, after specified requirements are fulfilled.

te·pee (tē′pē′) *also,* **tee·pee.** *n.* a cone-shaped tent, usually of animal skins, used by North American Indians, especially the Plains Indians.

tep·id (tep′id) *adj.* moderately or slightly warm; lukewarm: *tepid water.* —**tep′id·ly,** *adv.* —**tep′id·ness,** *n.*

ter·bi·um (tur′bē əm) *n.* a very soft, silver-gray, metallic rare-earth element, used as a laser material. Symbol: **Tb**

term (turm) *n.* **1.** a word or phrase having an exact mean-

Tepee

ing in some particular field: *legal terms, scientific terms.* **2.** any word or phrase used in an exact sense: *"Darling" is a term of affection.* **3.** **terms.** a particular manner of speaking or the kind of language used: *He answered the question in vague terms.* **4.** a definite or limited period of time; time during which something lasts: *the term of a lease, a term of office.* **5.** a division of a school year: *the spring term.* **6.** **terms.** a relationship between people: *to be on good terms with someone.* **7.** **terms.** the conditions according to which something is to be done: *the terms of a peace treaty.* **8.** *Mathematics.* **a.** each of the quantities that make up a fraction or ratio, or form a series or progression. **b.** each of the quantities connected by plus or minus signs in an algebraic expression. —*v.t.* to apply a particular term to; name; designate: *She is termed pretty by everyone.*

to come to terms. to reach an agreement: *The two sides came to terms and the strike was ended.*

ter·ma·gant (tur′mə gənt) *n.* a loud, quarrelsome, scolding woman; shrew. —*adj.* quarrelsome or scolding.

ter·mi·na·ble (tur′mə nə bəl) *adj.* that can be ended: *a terminable contract.* —**ter′mi·na·ble·ness,** *n.*

ter·mi·nal (tur′mən əl) *adj.* **1.** at, forming, or coming at the end, end part, or boundary of something: *a terminal flower on a stem, the terminal payment on a loan.* **2.** ending in death: *a terminal disease.* —*n.* **1.** an end part; end. **2.** the point on an electric circuit where a connection can be made. **3.** a device for making such a connection. **4.** a station at either end of a railroad, bus, air, or other transportation line.

ter·mi·nate (tur′mə nāt′) *v.,* **ter·mi·nat·ed, ter·mi·nat·ing.** —*v.t.* **1.** to bring to an end; put an end to: *to terminate a marriage by divorce.* **2.** to come at the end of; form the conclusion of: *A prayer terminated the services.* **3.** to form the boundary of; bound; limit: *The river terminates his property.* —*v.i.* to come to an end: *The show terminated at eleven o'clock.* —**ter′mi·na′tion** *n.*

ter·mi·nol·o·gy (tur′mə nol′ə jē) *n. pl.,* **ter·mi·nol·o·gies.** the terms or system of terms used in an art, science, trade, or other specialized subject: *legal terminology, the terminology of chemistry.*

ter·mi·nus (tur′mə nəs) *n. pl.,* **ter·mi·ni** (tur′mə nī′) or **ter·mi·nus·es.** **1.** a point or place at which something comes to an end; end or goal. **2.** a station located at either end of a railroad, bus, air, or other transportation line.

ter·mite (tur′mīt) *n.* any of a group of insects that live in colonies, having whitish bodies and dark heads. Termites feed on wood, paper, and other organic material, causing great damage to buildings, furniture, and some crops. Also, **white ant.**

tern (turn) *n.* a web-footed sea bird closely related to the gull, having a slender body, narrow wings, a deeply forked tail, and, usually, white and gray feathers with a black patch on the head.

Tern

terr., territory.

ter·race (ter′is) *n.* **1.** a balcony of a house or apartment building. **2.** an open,

at; āpe; cär; end; mē; it; īce; hot; ōld; fôrk; wood; fōōl; oil; out; up; turn; sing; thin; this; hw in white; zh in treasure. The symbol ə stands for the sound of **a** in about, **e** in taken, **i** in pencil, **o** in lemon, and **u** in circus.

T

usually paved or tiled area next to a house, used for lounging, outdoor cooking or dining, and parties. **3.** a raised,
level platform of earth with a vertical or sloping front or
side, especially one of a series of such levels placed one
above the other. **4.** a group of houses or apartments built
on a raised or sloping area of land. **5.** a street on which
such a row of houses or apartments faces. **6.** the flat roof
of a house, especially an Oriental or Spanish house.
—*v.t.,* **ter·raced, ter·rac·ing.** to form into or provide with
a terrace or terraces: *to terrace a hillside.*

ter·ra cot·ta (ter′ə kot′ə) **1.** a hard, durable, brownish-
orange earthenware used especially for vases, statuettes,
or as a facing for buildings. **2.** something made of this
substance. **3.** a brownish-orange color. —*adj.* **1.** having
the color terra cotta; brownish-orange. **2.** made of terra
cotta: *a terra cotta figurine.*

ter·ra fir·ma (ter′ə fur′mə) solid ground; dry land.

ter·rain (tə rān′, te rān′) *n.* a region or tract of land,
especially with regard to its natural features or suitability
for some special purpose, such as farming: *hilly terrain,
rocky terrain.*

Ter·ra·my·cin (ter′ə mī′sin) *n. Trademark.* an antibiotic derived from a microorganism found in the soil. It is
used against a large number of disease-causing bacteria
and some viruses.

ter·ra·pin (ter′ə pin′) *n.* any of a group of North American turtles found in fresh or partly salt water, especially
the diamondback. The flesh of the terrapin is often eaten
as food.

ter·rar·i·um (tə rer′ē əm) *n. pl.,* **ter·rar·i·ums** or **ter-
rar·i·a** (tə rer′ē ə). a small enclosure or container, often
of glass, used for growing plants or raising small land
animals, such as snakes, turtles, or lizards.

ter·res·tri·al (tə res′trē əl) *adj.* **1.** of, relating to, or
representing the earth: *terrestrial magnetism, a terrestrial
globe.* **2.** relating to or consisting of land, as distinct from
water or air: *the terrestrial areas of the world.* **3.** growing
in the ground or land: *a terrestrial plant.* **4.** living on land,
rather than in the air, water, or trees: *The deer is a terrestrial animal.* **5.** of or relating to this world; worldly;
earthly. —**ter·res′tri·al·ly,** *adv.*

ter·ri·ble (ter′ə bəl) *adj.* **1.** causing terror or awe; dreadful; awful: *The volcano erupted with a terrible roar.*
2. very violent or severe; causing great distress or pain: *a
terrible automobile accident.* **3.** *Informal.* very bad or unpleasant: *terrible weather, terrible food.* **4.** *Informal.* very
great; excessive: *He is a terrible bore.* —**ter′ri·ble·ness,** *n.*
—**ter′ri·bly,** *adv.*

ter·ri·er (ter′ē ər) *n.* any of various lively, rugged, usually small dogs having a
smooth or wiry coat, such as
the fox terrier or Scottish terrier. Terriers were originally
used to hunt animals that burrow in the ground, but are now
kept chiefly as pets.

ter·rif·ic (tə rif′ik) *adj.*
1. *Informal.* unusually great,
intense, or severe: *terrific pain,
a terrific hardship.* **2.** *Slang.*
extremely good; excellent;
wonderful: *That's a terrific
idea.* **3.** causing great fear or dread; terrifying; dreadful.
—**ter·rif′i·cal·ly,** *adv.*

Terrier (fox terrier)

ter·ri·fy (ter′ə fī′) *v.t.,* **ter·ri·fied, ter·ri·fy·ing.** to fill
with terror; frighten or alarm greatly. —**ter′ri·fy′ing·ly,**
adv.

ter·ri·to·ri·al (ter′ə tôr′ē əl) *adj.* **1.** of, relating to, or
belonging to land or territory: *That country made many*

territorial gains during the war. **2.** relating to or restricted
to a particular district or region: *He has territorial rights
to drill for oil in this county.* **3.** *also,* **Territorial.** relating
to a territory of the United States. —**ter′ri·to′ri·al·ly,**
adv.

territorial waters, coastal and inland waters under
the jurisdiction of a state or nation, especially ocean waters
within three miles of shore.

ter·ri·to·ry (ter′ə tôr′ē) *n. pl.,* **ter·ri·to·ries. 1.** any large
area of land; region: *unexplored territory, territory held by
an enemy.* **2.** land and waters under the jurisdiction of a
state, nation, or ruler: *The Yukon is a territory of Canada.*
3. a district or area assigned to a salesman or agent.
4. a field or sphere of action, thought, or interest. **5.** formerly, a part of the United States not having the status
of a state but having its own legislature. Hawaii was a
territory of the United States until 1959.

ter·ror (ter′ər) *n.* **1.** an overpowering or intense fear.
2. a person or thing that causes intense fear: *The cruel
dictator was a terror to the people.* **3.** *Informal.* an annoying
or troublesome person or thing.

ter·ror·ism (ter′ə riz′əm) *n.* the use of terror, violence,
or threats of violence to intimidate or frighten a people into
submission.

ter·ror·ist (ter′ər ist) *n.* a person who believes in or uses
terrorism. —*adj.* relating to or characteristic of terrorism
or terrorists: *terrorist methods.* Also, **ter·ror·is·tic** (ter′ə-
ris′tik).

ter·ror·ize (ter′ə rīz′) *v.t.,* **ter·ror·ized, ter·ror·iz·ing.**
1. to fill with extreme fear; overcome with terror. **2.** to
control, rule, or force through the use of terror: *The ruler
terrorized his subjects into obeying his commands.* —**ter′-
ror·i·za′tion,** *n.*

ter·ry cloth (ter′ē) a fabric having uncut loops on both
sides, especially a highly absorbent cotton cloth, used
chiefly for towels and robes.

terse (turs) *adj.,* **ters·er, ters·est.** brief and to the point;
concise: *a terse reply.* —**terse′ly,** *adv.* —**terse′ness,** *n.*

ter·tian (tur′shən) *adj.* recurring every other day.
—*n.* a tertian fever or ague.

Ter·ti·ar·y (tur′shē er′ē) *n.* the first geological period
of the Cenozoic era, during which high mountain systems,
such as the Alps, Rockies, and Himalayas, were formed
and modern mammals and plants appeared. —*adj.*
1. of, relating to, or characteristic of this period. **2. tertiary.** third in rank, order, or place.

test (test) *n.* **1.** a set of questions, problems or exercises
intended to determine a person's knowledge, skill, or intelligence: *a spelling test.* **2.** any method or means of determining the nature, genuineness, or quality of something:
*a blood test, a swimming test. Their friendship has withstood
the test of time.* **3.** *Chemistry.* a procedure for detecting
the presence of an ingredient in a substance or determining
what the substance is: *a test for carbon dioxide.* —*v.t.*
1. to subject to a test of any kind; give a test to; try: *to test
a class, to test a car, to test a person's loyalty.* **2.** to subject
to a chemical test. —*v.i.* to take or give a test: *to test for
a job, to test for acidity.* —**test′er,** *n.*

Test., Testament.

tes·ta·ment (tes′tə mənt) *n.* **1.** in law, a will, especially
one disposing of personal property. ▲ now used chiefly in
the phrase *last will and testament.* **2. Testament.** either
of the two main divisions of the Bible; Old Testament or
New Testament.

tes·ta·men·ta·ry (tes′tə men′tər ē) *adj.* **1.** relating to
a will or the administration or settlement of a will.
2. given by or contained in a will: *His estate was disposed
of according to his testamentary instructions.* **3.** done in
accordance with a will.

tes·tate (tes′tāt) *adj.* having made or left a legally valid will.

tes·ta·tor (tes′tā tər) *n.* a person who has died and left a legally valid will.

test ban, an agreement among nations not to test nuclear weapons, especially in the atmosphere.

tes·tes (tes′tēz) the plural of **testis.**

tes·ti·cle (tes′ti kəl) *n.* one of the pair of male reproductive glands in man and most other animals, producing sperm and male sex hormones and usually enclosed in the scrotum. Also, **testis.**

tes·ti·fy (tes′tə fī′) *v.,* **tes·ti·fied, tes·ti·fy·ing.** —*v.i.* **1.** to give evidence under oath in a court of law: *He testified against her during the trial.* **2.** to serve as evidence; be proof: *The stolen goods hidden in his home testified to his guilt.* **3.** to bear witness: *I can testify to his honesty.* —*v.t.* to declare under oath in a court of law: *He testified that the defendant was innocent.*

tes·ti·mo·ni·al (tes′tə mō′nē əl) *n.* **1.** a letter or statement affirming the superior character or quality of someone or something; recommendation: *The satisfied customer gave a testimonial for the product.* **2.** something given or done to show respect, admiration, or appreciation: *The retiring employee was given a watch as a testimonial for his years of service.* —*adj.* relating to or being a testimonial: *a testimonial dinner.*

tes·ti·mo·ny (tes′tə mō′nē) *n. pl.,* **tes·ti·mo·nies. 1.** a statement made under oath by a witness in a court of law, usually in answer to questioning by a lawyer. **2.** proof or demonstration; evidence: *Her trembling hands were testimony of her nervousness.* **3.** an open declaration of one's faith.

tes·tis (tes′tis) *n. pl.,* **tes·tes.** another word for **testicle.**

test pilot, a pilot who tests new or experimental aircraft.

test tube, a thin transparent glass tube closed at one end, used in chemical and biological experiments.

tes·ty (tes′tē) *adj.,* **tes·ti·er, tes·ti·est.** showing or characterized by irritability; impatient or cross: *a testy old man.* —**tes′ti·ly,** *adv.* —**tes′ti·ness,** *n.*

Tet (tet) *n.* the lunar new year as celebrated in southeastern Asia, especially Vietnam.

tet·a·nus (tet′ən əs) *n.* an acute, often fatal, disease caused by the toxin of a certain bacillus that usually enters the body through a puncture wound. Tetanus is characterized by violent spasms and stiffness of certain muscles, especially those of the neck and jaw. Also, **lockjaw.**

tête-à-tête (tāt′ə tāt′) *n.* a private or intimate conversation between two people. —*adv.* (of two people) together in private: *to dine tête-à-tête.* —*adj.* for or between two people in private; intimate. [French *tête-à-tête* literally, head to head.]

teth·er (te<u>th</u>′ər) *n.* a rope or chain used to fasten a horse, donkey, or other animal so that it is confined within certain limits. —*v.t.* to fasten or confine with a tether.

  at the end of one's tether. at the end or limit of one's resources, patience, or endurance.

Teu·ton (tōōt′ən, tyōōt′ən) *n.* **1.** a member of an ancient tribe that lived in parts of what is now northern Germany. **2.** a member of any of several groups of northern European peoples, including the Germans, Dutch, Scandinavians, and English. **3.** a person who was born in Germany or who is of German descent.

Teu·ton·ic (tōō ton′ik, tyōō ton′ik) *adj.* **1.** of or relating to the ancient Teutons. **2.** of or relating to any of the Teutons, their languages, or their cultures. **3.** of or relating to Germany or the Germans; German. **4.** of or relating to the Germanic family of languages. —*n.* another word for **Germanic.**

Tex., Texas.

Tex·as (tek′səs) *n.* a state in the south-central United States, bordering Mexico and the Gulf of Mexico. It was once an independent republic. Capital, Austin. Area, 267, 339 sq. mi. Pop. (1970), 11,196,730. Abbreviation, **Tex.** —**Tex′an,** *adj., n.*

● **Texas** comes from an Indian word that means "friends." Spanish explorers thought the word was the name of a tribe and used it for Indians living in the eastern part of present-day Texas. This fact, and later Indian descriptions of an area called "the Great Kingdom of Texas," led Spanish colonists to make Texas the official name of the territory. This name was kept by the independent republic of Texas, and later by the state.

text (tekst) *n.* **1.** the main body of matter on a written or printed page, as distinguished from headings, illustrations, notes, or appendixes. **2.** the original or actual words of a writer or speaker. A text is often changed slightly when it is revised, condensed, or translated. **3.** a short passage or verse from the Bible, quoted or used as the subject of a sermon. **4.** any subject on which one writes or speaks; theme; topic. **5.** see **textbook.**

text·book (tekst′book′) *n.* a book used in the study of a particular subject, especially in a school: *a history textbook, an algebra textbook.*

tex·tile (teks′tīl, teks′til) *n.* **1.** a fabric made by weaving, knitting, or otherwise arranging yarn, thread, or other fibers. **2.** any material that can be made into such a fabric, such as cotton, wool, or nylon. —*adj.* relating to textiles or their manufacture: *the textile industry.*

tex·tu·al (teks′chōō əl) *adj.* relating to, based on, or contained in a text: *This history book has many textual errors.* —**tex′tu·al·ly,** *adv.*

tex·ture (teks′chər) *n.* **1.** the look or feel of a woven fabric resulting from the arrangement, quality, or size of its threads: *Silk has a smooth texture.* **2.** the characteristic arrangement of the parts of anything; composition; structure: *the rough texture of sandpaper.*

-th *suffix* used to form ordinal numbers: *seventh.*

Th, the symbol for thorium.

Thack·er·ay, William Make·peace (thak′ər ē; māk′pēs′) 1811–1863, English novelist.

Thai (tī) *n.* **1.** a person who was born or is living in Thailand. **2.** the official language of Thailand. —*adj.* of or relating to Thailand, its people, or their language. Also, **Siamese.**

Thai·land (tī′land′) *n.* a country in southeastern Asia, formerly known as **Siam.** Capital, Bangkok. Area, 198,500 sq. mi. Pop. (1971 est.), 37,400,000.

thal·a·mus (thal′ə məs) *n. pl.,* **thal·a·mi** (thal′ə mī′). a large oblong mass in the brain, composed largely of gray matter, that relays nerve impulses from one part of the brain to another.

thal·li·um (thal′ē əm) *n.* a soft, bluish-gray, poisonous metallic element that looks like lead. It is used in ant and rat poisons. Symbol: **Tl**

thal·lo·phyte (thal′ə fīt′) *n.* any of a large group of primitive plants, such as algae, fungi, and bacteria, that lack roots, stems, or leaves.

---

at; āpe; cär; end; mē; it; īce; hot; ōld; fôrk; wood; fōōl; oil; out; up; turn; sing; thin; <u>th</u>is; hw in white; zh in treasure. The symbol ə stands for the sound of **a** in about, **e** in taken, **i** in pencil, **o** in lemon, and **u** in circus.

thal·lus (thal′əs) *n. pl.,* **thal·li** (thal′ī) or **thal·lus·es.** a plant not divided into distinct roots, stems, and leaves.

Thames (temz) *n.* a river in southern England, flowing east through London to the North Sea.

than (than; *unstressed* thən) *conj.* **1.** in comparison with: *A cow is bigger than a rabbit. She would rather listen to music than study.* **2.** except; but: *He respects no opinion other than his own.* —*prep.* compared to: *a city than which there is none more beautiful.*

▲ In formal usage, **than** is used as a conjunction in sentences in which things are compared. The word introduced by *than* may be in either the nominative or objective case, depending on how it is used in the sentence: *He is taller than she (is). The story amused him more than (it amused) her.* In informal usage, *than* is sometimes used as a preposition, with the word following *than* being in the objective case: *He spent more money than me.*

thane (thān) *n.* **1.** in English history, a man who held lands from the king in return for military service, especially a member of a class ranking above ordinary freemen but below the nobility. **2.** in Scottish history, a lord or baron, especially the chief of a clan.

thank (thangk) *v.t.* **1.** to express gratitude or appreciation to, as for something given or done; give thanks to: *I thanked him for the gift. Thank you for your help.* **2.** to consider or hold responsible; credit or blame: *He has only himself to thank for failing the test.*

thank·ful (thangk′fəl) *adj.* feeling or expressing thanks; grateful: *Mike was thankful for his father's help with his homework.* —**thank′ful·ly,** *adv.* —**thank′ful·ness,** *n.*

thank·less (thangk′lis) *adj.* **1.** not likely to be rewarded or appreciated: *a thankless task.* **2.** not feeling or showing gratitude; ungrateful: *a spoiled, thankless child.* —**thank′less·ly,** *adv.* —**thank′less·ness,** *n.*

thanks (thangks) *interj.* I thank you: *Thanks for the ride.* —*n.,pl.* **1.** an expression of gratitude: *We gave thanks for our many blessings.* **2.** a feeling of gratitude: *He expressed his thanks for their kindness.*

  thanks to. as a result or consequence of; because of: *Thanks to her efforts, the party was a success.*

thanks·giv·ing (thangks′giv′ing) *n.* **1.** the act of giving thanks. **2.** an expression of thanks, especially a prayer of thanks to God.

Thanksgiving 1. a legal holiday in the United States celebrated on the fourth Thursday in November as a day of thanksgiving and feasting. It observes the memory of the harvest feast celebrated by the Pilgrims in 1621. **2.** a similar holiday celebrated in Canada on the second Monday of October. Also, **Thanksgiving Day.**

Thant, U (thänt; ōō) 1909—, Burmese diplomat, secretary-general of the United Nations from 1961 to 1971.

that (that) *adj. pl.,* **those. 1.** used to indicate a person or thing already mentioned or understood: *That girl won the prize. Who wrote that book?* **2.** used to indicate something that is more distant than or contrasted with another thing: *I prefer this coat to that one. This problem is more difficult than that one.* —*pron. pl.,* **those. 1.** used to indicate a person or thing already mentioned or understood: *That is the man who did it. That was the best movie I have seen this year.* **2.** used to indicate something that is more distant than or contrasted with another thing: *I prefer this dress to that.* **3.** who, whom, or which: *the boy that lives next door, the man that I saw.* ▲ **That** may be used of people, animals, or things; **which** may refer to either animals or things; **who** and **whom** refer only to people. —*conj.* **1.** used to introduce a subordinate clause: *I think that he will accept the job.* **2.** used to show reason or cause: *I'm sorry that you can't come to the party.* **3.** used to show result: *She ate so much that she was ill the next day.*

—*adv.* to such an extent or degree; to that extent; so: *How could she sing that well after only one lesson?*

▲ In formal usage, a distinction is often made between **that** and **which** in relative clauses. **That** is preferred when introducing a restrictive clause: *New York is the only American city that has more than seven million people.* **Which** is preferred when introducing a nonrestrictive clause: *New York, which has more than seven million people, is the largest American city.* However, many good speakers and writers do not follow this distinction, and use *which* interchangeably with *that.* **Which** is used especially when *that* appears elsewhere in the sentence and its double usage might be clumsy or confusing: *. . . that great influence which is one of the few rights of womankind* (Joseph Conrad).

thatch (thach) *n. pl.,* **thatch·es. 1.** straw, reeds, or similar material used to cover a roof. **2.** a roof or roofing of such material. **3.** anything resembling such a covering: *a thick thatch of hair.* —*v.t.* to cover with thatch.

Thatched roof

that'll (that′əl) **1.** that will. **2.** that shall.

that's (thats) that is.

thaw (thô) *v.i.* **1.** to go from a frozen state to a liquid or unfrozen state; become free of frost or ice; melt: *The ice on the road thawed from the heat of the sun.* **2.** to become free of the feeling of being very cold: *The ice skaters thawed out before a large fire.* **3.** (of the weather or temperature) to become warm enough to melt ice or snow. **4.** to grow less stiff and cold in manner; become more friendly: *His aloof manner thawed under her hospitality.* —*v.t.* to cause to thaw: *The sun thawed the snow on the roof.* —*n.* **1.** the act of thawing. **2.** a period of weather warm enough to melt ice and snow: *the spring thaw.* **3.** the act or process of thawing.

the¹ (*before a consonant,* thə; *before a vowel,* thē) *definite article.* **The** refers to a particular person, thing, or group. Some special uses of **the** are: **1.** to indicate a particular one or ones previously mentioned or understood: *Close the door. Give me the book.* **2.** to show that a thing is unique: *the sun, the past, the Amazon River.* **3.** to show that a thing is best known, most important, or greatest: *the place to go for a winter vacation.* **4.** to make a singular noun general: *The lion is found in Africa. He plays the bugle well.* **5.** in place of a possessive pronoun: *A stone hit him on the arm.* **6.** before an adjective to make it function as a noun: *a home for the aged.* **7.** as part of a title: *the Duke of Edinburgh.* [Old English *thē, the.*]

the² (thə, thē) *adv.* to that degree; by that much: *The sooner you finish it the better.* [Old English *thē, thȳ.*]

the·a·ter (thē′ə tər) *also,* **the·a·tre.** *n.* **1.** a building or other place where plays or motion pictures are presented. **2.** a place resembling this, such as a room having rows of seats that is used for surgical demonstrations. **3.** the writing and performing of plays; drama: *the French theater, the modern theater.* **4.** a place where some action takes place; field of operations: *a theater of war.*

the·at·ri·cal (thē at′ri kəl) *adj.* **1.** relating to or characteristic of the theater or actors: *a theatrical performance.* **2.** like a performance on stage; exaggerated; not natural: *a theatrical display of grief.* —*n.* **theatricals.** theatrical performances, especially by amateurs. —**the·at′ri·cal·ly,** *adv.*

Thebes (thēbz) *n.* **1.** an ancient Egyptian city on the Nile River, a former capital of Egypt. **2.** one of the leading city-states of ancient Greece, northwest of Athens. —**The′ban,** *adj., n.*

thee (thē) *pron.* the objective case of **thou.**

theft (theft) *n.* the act or instance of stealing; larceny.

their (ther) *adj.* of or belonging to them: *their house, their work, their friends.*

theirs (therz) *pron.* the one or ones that belong or relate to them: *Our car is new; theirs is old.*

the·ism (thē′iz′əm) *n.* **1.** a belief in one personal God as creator and ruler of the universe. **2.** a belief in the existence of a god or gods.

the·ist (thē′ist) *n.* a person who believes in theism. —**the·is′tic,** *adj.*

them (them; *unstressed* thəm) *pron.* the objective case of **they:** *He met them at the station.*

the·mat·ic (thē mat′ik) *adj.* of or relating to a theme or themes.

theme (thēm) *n.* **1.** the main subject or idea of something: *The theme of the book was courage* **2.** a short essay or written composition: *We were assigned five themes in our English class.* **3.** *Music.* **a.** the principal melody in a musical composition. **b.** a melody on which variations are made.

them·selves (them selvz′, thəm selvz′) *pron.* **1.** the form of **they** or **them** used to give emphasis to the word it goes with: *They had to do the job themselves.* **2.** the form of **them** used to show that the subject and direct object of a verb are the same: *They blamed themselves for the tragedy.* **3.** their normal or average selves: *The players on the losing team were certainly not themselves today.*

then (then) *adv.* **1.** at that time: *He was much thinner then.* **2.** immediately or soon afterward; next: *The play ended and then the curtain went down.* **3.** at another time: *Sometimes the car will run smoothly; then it will stall at every corner.* **4.** in that case; if that is so; therefore: *If you don't want that book, then give it to me.* **5.** in addition; besides: *The price is right, and then I really need a new coat.* —*adj.* being or acting as such at that time; of that time: *The then ambassador to France was present at the conference.* —*n.* that time: *I hope to have it finished before then.*
  now and then. once in a while; occasionally: *Now and then we spend an evening together.*
  then and there. at that very time; immediately: *She decided to stop smoking then and there.*

thence (thens) *adv.* **1.** from that place; from there: *The bank is two blocks thence.* **2.** from that time; after that: *We saw them again a few weeks thence.* **3.** for that reason; consequently; therefore: *He committed a crime, thence he must be punished.*

thence·forth (thens′fôrth′) *adv.* from that time on; after that. Also, **thence·for·ward** (thens′fôr′wərd).

the·oc·ra·cy (thē ok′rə sē) *n. pl.,* **the·oc·ra·cies.** **1.** a government in which God or a god is considered the supreme ruling power. **2.** government by a priesthood or other religious authority. **3.** a country or group ruled in such a way.

the·o·crat·ic (thē′ə krat′ik) *adj.* of or relating to a theocracy.

the·od·o·lite (thē od′əl īt′) *n.* an instrument used in surveying for measuring horizontal and vertical angles.

the·o·lo·gian (thē′ə lō′jən) *n.* an expert in theology.

the·o·log·i·cal (thē′ə loj′i kəl) *adj.* of or relating to theology: *a theological seminary.* —**the′o·log′i·cal·ly,** *adv.*

the·ol·o·gy (thē ol′ə jē) *n. pl.,* **the·ol·o·gies.** **1.** the study of the nature and being of God and His relations to man and the universe. **2.** a particular system of religion or religious beliefs, especially of a Christian church.

the·o·rem (thē′ər əm) *n.* **1.** any statement or proposition that is not self-evident but can be proved to be true. **2.** a statement in mathematics that has been proved or can be proved.

the·o·ret·i·cal (thē′ə ret′i kəl) *adj.* **1.** of or relating to

a theory: *a theoretical explanation.* **2.** not based on fact or experience; hypothetical: *Her knowledge of chess is almost purely theoretical, since she has only played once.* **3.** given to theorizing; speculative. Also, **the·o·ret·ic** (thē′ə ret′ik). —**the′o·ret′i·cal·ly,** *adv.*

the·o·re·ti·cian (thē′ər ə tish′ən) *n.* a person who theorizes, especially a person who specializes in the theory of a science or art rather than in its practical application.

the·o·rist (thē′ər ist) *n.* a person who theorizes.

the·o·rize (thē′ə rīz′) *v.i.,* **the·o·rized, the·o·riz·ing.** to form a theory or theories; speculate: *to theorize about life after death.*

the·o·ry (thē′ər ē) *n. pl.,* **the·o·ries.** **1.** an idea or ideas that explain a group of facts or an event; assumption that has been proved to be true: *Einstein's theory of relativity.* **2.** the rules, facts, or methods of an art, science, or profession rather than the actual practice or application: *He has a good understanding of the theory of football, but he has never played the game.* **3.** an assumption or guess based on some evidence but not proved: *Have you any theory as to what caused the explosion?*

ther·a·peu·tic (ther′ə pyōō′tik) *adj.* of or relating to the treatment or cure of diseases or disorders: *therapeutic medicine, the therapeutic effects of a warm, dry climate.* —**ther′a·peu′ti·cal·ly,** *adv.*

ther·a·peu·tics (ther′ə pyōō′tiks) *n., pl.* a branch of medical science dealing with the treatment of disease. ▲ used with a singular verb.

ther·a·pist (ther′ə pist) *n.* a person who gives therapy, especially a doctor or other person who specializes in a particular kind of therapy: *a physical therapist.*

ther·a·py (ther′ə pē) *n. pl.,* **ther·a·pies.** the treatment of a disease or a physical or mental disorder by any of various methods.

there (ther) *adv.* **1.** at or in that place: *Stay there. Put the box down there.* **2.** to, toward, or into that place: *We walked there after lunch.* **3.** at that point, as in time or action: *There the speaker paused.* **4.** about that matter or issue: *I agree with you there.* **5.** *there* is also used: **a.** to introduce a sentence or clause in which the verb comes before the real subject: *There is no more milk.* The verb may be either singular or plural, depending on the subject: *There is a man at the door. There are thirty-one days in March.* **b.** as a substitute for a name in addressing a person: *Well, hello there.* **c.** to call attention to someone or something: *There is the noon whistle.* —*n.* that place: *Do you know the way home from there?* —*interj.* used to express various emotions, as satisfaction or sympathy: *There, there! Don't worry.*

there·a·bouts (ther′ə bouts′) *also,* **there·a·bout.** *adv.* near that place, time, number, amount, or degree: *He lives in Chicago or thereabouts. It costs ten dollars or thereabouts.*

there·af·ter (ther af′tər) *adv.* from then on; after that; afterward: *The sun shone the first day of their vacation, but it rained every day thereafter.*

there·at (ther at′) *adv.* **1.** at that place or time; there. **2.** because of that.

there·by (ther bī′) *adv.* **1.** by that means: *He finished first in the race, thereby winning the championship for his*

---

at; āpe; cär; end; mē; it; īce; hot; ōld; fôrk;
wood; fōōl; oil; out; up; turn; sing; thin; this;
hw in white; zh in treasure. The symbol ə
stands for the sound of a in about, e in taken,
i in pencil, o in lemon, and u in circus.

school. **2.** in that connection: *Thereby hangs a tale* (Shakespeare, *The Merry Wives of Windsor*).

there·for (t͟her fôr′) *adv.* for or in return for this, that, or it: *He agreed to lend me the money and wrote a check therefor.*

there·fore (t͟her′fôr′) *adv.* for this or that reason; as a result: *He injured his leg and therefore could not run.*

there·from (t͟her frum′, t͟her from′) *adv.* from this, that, or it.

there·in (t͟her in′) *adv.* **1.** in or into that place, time, or thing: *The fire destroyed the warehouse and all the property therein.* **2.** in that particular point or respect; in that matter: *There is no water along that route; therein lies the danger of the expedition.*

there·of (t͟her uv′, t͟her ov′) *adv.* **1.** of that or it: *The new law applies to the town and the residents thereof.* **2.** from that or it.

there·on (t͟her ôn′, t͟her on′) *adv.* **1.** on or upon that or it. **2.** immediately after that; thereupon.

there's (t͟herz) there is.

The·re·sa, Saint (tə rē′sə) 1515–1582, Spanish Carmelite nun, mystic, and writer.

there·to (t͟her to͞o′) *adv.* to that place or thing.

there·to·fore (t͟her′tə fôr′) *adv.* before or until that time; up to then.

there·un·der (t͟her un′dər) *adv.* under or beneath this, that, or it.

there·un·to (t͟her un′to͞o) *adv.* to that place or thing.

there·up·on (t͟her′ə pôn′, t͟her′ə pon′) *adv.* **1.** immediately after that; at once. **2.** as a consequence of that; therefore. **3.** with reference to that; upon that.

there·with (t͟her with′, t͟her wit͟h′) *adv.* **1.** with this, that, or it. **2.** immediately after that; thereupon.

ther·mal (thur′məl) *adj.* of, relating to, or causing heat or warmth: *a thermal unit, thermal baths.* —*n.* a rising current of warm air. —**ther′mal·ly,** *adv.*

thermo- *combining form* heat: *thermoelectricity.*

ther·mo·dy·nam·ic (thur′mō dī nam′ik) *adj.* of or relating to thermodynamics.

ther·mo·dy·nam·ics (thur′mō dī nam′iks) *n.,pl.* the branch of physics that deals with the relationship between heat and other forms of energy, especially mechanical energy, and the conversion of one of these forms into another. ▲ used with a singular verb.

ther·mo·e·lec·tric (thur′mō i lek′trik) *adj.* of or relating to thermoelectricity.

ther·mo·e·lec·tric·i·ty (thur′mō i lek tris′ə tē) *n.* electricity produced by the direct action of heat.

ther·mom·e·ter (thər mom′ə tər) *n.* a device for measuring temperature. The most common thermometer is a thin glass tube containing a column of mercury or colored alcohol that rises or falls as it expands or contracts from changes in temperature.

ther·mo·nu·cle·ar (thur′mō no͞o′klē ər, thur′mō nyo͞o′klē ər) *adj.* **1.** of or relating to the fusion of atomic nuclei at temperatures of millions of degrees, as in the sun or a hydrogen bomb. **2.** of or relating to thermonuclear weapons: *thermonuclear warfare.*

ther·mo·plas·tic (thur′mə plas′tik) *adj.* that becomes soft and pliable when subjected to heat, without any change in its original properties, as certain plastics or resins. —*n.* a thermoplastic substance.

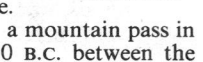

Thermometer

Ther·mop·y·lae (thər mop′ə lē) *n.* a mountain pass in central Greece, site of a battle in 480 B.C. between the Greeks and Persians.

ther·mos bottle (thur′məs) a container in which liquids can be kept hot or cold for many hours, usually consisting of an outer container of metal enclosing one glass bottle within another, with a vacuum between the two bottles to keep the contents from losing or gaining heat. Trademark: **Thermos.**

ther·mo·stat (thur′mə stat′) *n.* an instrument that automatically regulates temperature, as in a furnace, oven, or refrigerator.

the·sau·rus (thə sôr′əs) *n. pl.,* **the·sau·ri** (thə sôr′ī) or **the·sau·rus·es.** **1.** a book that lists words in groups of synonyms and antonyms. **2.** a book that lists words or information about one particular subject: *a thesaurus of music.* **3.** a treasury or storehouse.

these (t͟hēz) the plural of **this.**

The·se·us (thē′sē əs, thē′so͞os) *n. Greek Legend.* a hero and king of Athens who killed the Minotaur and escaped from the Labyrinth with the help of Ariadne.

the·sis (thē′sis) *n. pl.,* **the·ses** (thē′sēz). **1.** a statement or proposition that is presented and then defended, especially in a debate. **2.** an essay or dissertation on a specific topic or theme, especially one presented by a candidate for an academic degree: *a doctoral thesis.*

thes·pi·an (thes′pē ən) also, **Thes·pi·an.** *adj.* of or relating to drama; dramatic. —*n.* an actor or actress. [From *Thespis,* the supposed founder of ancient Greek tragedy.]

Thes·pis (thes′pis) a Greek dramatist of the sixth century B.C.

Thes·sa·lo·ni·ans (thes′ə lō′nē ənz) *n.* either of two books of the New Testament consisting of epistles written by Saint Paul.

Thes·sa·ly (thes′ə lē) *n.* a region in northern Greece, bordering the Aegean Sea. —**Thes·sa·li·an** (the sā′lē ən), *adj., n.*

The·tis (thē′tis) *n. Greek Legend.* a sea nymph who was the mother of Achilles.

thews (tho͞oz) *n., pl.* muscles; sinews.

they (t͟hā) *pron., pl.* nominative, **they;** possessive, **their, theirs;** objective, **them.** **1.** the persons or things mentioned before: *Susan and Bob were late because they missed the train.* **2.** people in general; any persons: *They say that our team will probably win today.*

they'd (t͟hād) **1.** they had. **2.** they would.

they'll (t͟hāl) **1.** they will. **2.** they shall.

they're (t͟her) they are.

they've (t͟hāv) they have.

thi·a·mine (thī′ə min) also, **thi·a·min.** *n.* see **vitamin B₁.**

thick (thik) *adj.* **1.** having relatively great distance from one surface or side to the opposite one; not thin: *a thick piece of wood, a thick steak.* **2.** measured from one side or surface to the other: *That stone wall is three feet thick.* **3.** that does not pour or flow easily: *thick soup.* **4.** growing, being, or happening close together, or having its parts close together: *thick underbrush, a thick beard.* **5.** very noticeable; heavy: *He spoke with a thick German accent.* **6.** mentally dull; stupid. —*adv.* so as to be thick; thickly: *Carve the steak thick.* —*n.* **1.** the thickest part of anything. **2.** a part or place of greatest intensity or activity: *He was in the thick of the fight.* —**thick′ly,** *adv.*

through thick and thin. through the good times and the bad; under any circumstances.

thick·en (thik′ən) *v.t., v.i.* **1.** to make or become thick or thicker. **2.** to make or become more intense or complex, as the plot of a story. —**thick′en·er,** *n.*

thick·en·ing (thik′ə ning) *n.* **1.** something added to a liquid to thicken it. **2.** the act of making or becoming thick. **3.** a thickened place or part.

thick·et (thik′it) *n.* a dense growth, as of shrubs or bushes.

thick·head·ed (thik′hed′id) *adj.* slow to learn or understand; stupid; dull. —**thick′-head′ed·ness**, *n.*

thick·ness (thik′nis) *n. pl.,* **thick·ness·es.** **1.** the state or quality of being thick. **2.** the dimension of a solid between its two opposite surfaces, as distinguished from its length or width. **3.** a layer or sheet, as of paper.

thick·set (thik′set′) *adj.* **1.** having a short, stocky build. **2.** planted, placed, or growing close together.

thick·skinned (thik′skind′) *adj.* **1.** having a thick skin, as certain fruit. **2.** insensitive to criticism, ridicule, or reproach.

thief (thēf) *n. pl.,* **thieves.** a person who steals, especially secretly and without using force.

thieve (thēv) *v.t., v.i.,* **thieved, thiev·ing.** to steal, especially secretly and without using force.

thiev·er·y (thē′vər ē) *n. pl.,* **thiev·er·ies.** the act, instance, or practice of stealing.

thieves (thēvz) the plural of **thief.**

thiev·ish (thē′vish) *adj.* **1.** inclined to stealing. **2.** characteristic of or like a thief; furtive; sly: *a thievish manner.*

thigh (thī) *n.* the part of the leg between the hip and the knee.

thigh·bone (thī′bōn′) *n.* the long bone of the upper leg, extending from the pelvis to the knee; femur.

thim·ble (thim′bəl) *n.* a small metal cap that is worn on the finger tip to protect it when pushing the needle through material in sewing.

Thim·bu (tim′boo) *n.* the capital of Bhutan, in the western part of the country. Pop. (1977 est.), 8,982.

thin (thin) *adj.,* **thin·ner, thin·nest.** **1.** having relatively little distance from one surface or side to the opposite one; not thick: *a thin piece of wood, thin paper.* **2.** not plump or fat; lean: *a long, thin face.* **3.** having little density; flowing or pouring easily; watery: *a thin gravy.* **4.** easily seen through; not convincing; flimsy: *a thin excuse.* **5.** not dense: *thin air.* **6.** having a faint, often shrill sound; weak: *She answered in a small, thin voice.* —*adv.* so as to be thin; thinly: *Slice the ham thin.* —*v.t., v.i.,* **thinned, thin·ning.** to make or become thin or thinner. —**thin′ly**, *adv.* —**thin′ness**, *n.*

thine (thīn) *Archaic. pron.* **1.** belonging to you. **2.** the one or ones belonging to you. —*adj.* thy; your. ▲ used in place of *thy* before a word beginning with a vowel or *h:* *Drink to me only with thine eyes* (Ben Jonson).

thing (thing) *n.* **1.** something that has or can be thought of as having existence: *Two people's love for each other is a thing to be cherished.* **2.** an inanimate object, as distinguished from a living being: *A book is a thing.* **3.** a living being, especially when thought of in terms of pity, affection, or contempt: *The lost child was a sad little thing.* **4.** any act, fact, idea, or statement: *That was a terrible thing to do! She didn't overlook a thing in planning the party. Say the first thing that comes into your mind.* **5. things.** the general state of affairs: *Things have changed since you've been gone.* **6. things.** possessions; belongings: *I put all my things in a box.* **7. the thing.** the latest or proper style or fashion.

think (thingk) *v.,* **thought, think·ing.** —*v.i.* **1.** to use the mind, as in forming opinions or using judgment: *A person should think before making an important decision.* **2.** to have in the mind as an opinion, belief, or attitude: *Mother will always think of him as a child.* **3.** to occupy one's thoughts with something or someone; reflect: *I'll have to think about it before I decide.* **4.** to have in mind the idea of doing something: *We're thinking of going to Europe this summer.* **5.** to call to mind or remember: *She could not think of the incident without smiling.* **6.** to have care or consideration: *He always thinks of himself first.* **7.** to form an image or idea in the mind: *Who thought of the first alphabet?* —*v.t.* **1.** to form or have in the mind as an opinion, belief, or attitude: *She thought we were sisters.* **2.** to hold the opinion that; consider: *I think we should go home.* **3.** to arrive at a decision, conclusion, or answer regarding: *Think it through carefully before you give me your final decision.* —**think′er**, *n.*

think·a·ble (thing′kə bəl) *adj.* that can be thought; conceivable; possible.

thin·ner (thin′ər) *n.* a liquid used to thin a substance: *Turpentine is used as a thinner for some paints.*

thin-skinned (thin′skind′) *adj.* **1.** having a thin skin: *a thin-skinned fruit.* **2.** very sensitive to criticism, ridicule, or reproach; easily hurt or offended.

third (thurd) *adj.* **1.** (the ordinal of three) next after the second. **2.** being one of three equal parts. —*n.* **1.** something that is next after the second. **2.** one of three equal parts; 1/3. **3.** *Music.* **a.** a note that is a total of two whole steps above a given note. E is the third of C. **b.** an interval of two whole steps. **c.** a combination of two notes that are separated by this interval. **4.** the third forward gear, as of an automobile. —*adv.* in the third place.

third-class (thurd′klas′) *adj.* **1.** next or inferior to second-class. **2.** of or relating to a class of mail that includes all printed matter except newspapers and magazines and meets certain governmental limits, as of weight. **3.** of or relating to a class of travel accommodations on a ship or other conveyance, usually the least expensive.

third class **1.** third-class travel accommodations. **2.** third-class mail.

third degree *Informal.* harsh questioning and treatment of a prisoner to obtain information or a confession.

third person, the form of a pronoun or verb that indicates the person or thing spoken of. In the sentence *He realizes his mistake, he, realizes,* and *his* are in the third person.

Third Reich (rīk) Germany under the rule of the Nazis, from 1933 to 1945.

Third World **1.** countries that are not aligned with either the Communist or the non-Communist bloc of nations. **2.** the underdeveloped or emerging countries of the world. **3.** the minorities of a country.

thirst (thurst) *n.* **1.** an uncomfortable feeling of dryness in the mouth and throat caused by a desire or need to drink fluids. **2.** the desire or need to drink: *He has an insatiable thirst.* **3.** a strong or powerful desire; craving: *a thirst for power, a thirst for learning.* —*v.i.* **1.** to want something to drink; be thirsty. **2.** to have a strong desire.

thirst·y (thurs′tē) *adj.,* **thirst·i·er, thirst·i·est.** **1.** feeling the need to drink something. **2.** lacking water or moisture; parched; arid. **3.** having a strong desire: *The dictator was thirsty for power.* —**thirst′i·ly**, *adv.* —**thirst′i·ness**, *n.*

thir·teen (thur′tēn′) *n.* **1.** the cardinal number that is three more than ten. **2.** a symbol representing this number, such as 13 or XIII. —*adj.* numbering three more than ten.

thir·teenth (thur′tēnth′) *adj.* **1.** (the ordinal of thirteen) next after the twelfth. **2.** being one of thirteen equal parts. —*n.* **1.** something that is next after the twelfth. **2.** one of thirteen equal parts; 1/13.

thir·ti·eth (thur′tē ith) *adj.* **1.** (the ordinal of thirty) next after the twenty-ninth. **2.** being one of thirty equal

---

at; āpe; cär; end; mē; it; īce; hot; ōld; fôrk; wood; fŏŏl; oil; out; up; turn; sing; thin; this; hw in white; zh in treasure. The symbol ə stands for the sound of **a** in about, **e** in taken, **i** in pencil, **o** in lemon, and **u** in circus.

T

parts. —*n.* **1.** something that is next after the twenty-ninth. **2.** one of thirty equal parts; 1/30.

thir·ty (thur′tē) *n. pl.,* **thir·ties. 1.** the cardinal number that is three times ten. **2.** a symbol representing this number, such as 30 or XXX. —*adj.* numbering three times ten.

thir·ty-sec·ond note (thur′tē sek′ənd) *Music.* a note having a time value equal to one thirty-second of a whole note.

this (this) *adj. pl.,* **these. 1.** used to indicate a person or thing that is present, nearby, understood, or just mentioned: *This house is ten years old. This cake is delicious.* **2.** used to indicate something that is nearer than or contrasted with another thing: *This dress is cheaper than that one.* —*pron. pl.,* **these. 1.** used to indicate a person or thing that is present, nearby, understood, or just mentioned: *Is this your coat? This is a serious matter.* **2.** used to indicate something that is nearer than or contrasted with another thing: *This is mine; that is hers.* **3.** something about to be said or explained: *This is what I mean.* —*adv.* to this extent or degree; so: *Is it this hot every day?*

this·tle (this′əl) *n.* a prickly plant that has red or purple flowers. —**this′tle·like′,** *adj.*

this·tle·down (this′əl doun′) *n.* the silky down on the flower of a thistle.

thith·er (thith′ər) *adv. Archaic.* to or toward that place; in that direction.

tho (thō) *also,* **tho'.** *conj., adv.* though.

thole (thōl) *n.* a peg or pair of pegs on the upper edge of either side of a boat, used to hold an oar in rowing. Also, **thole·pin** (thōl′pin′).

Thistle

Thom·as (tom′əs) *n.* **1.** one of Christ's Apostles, who refused to believe in the Resurrection unless he could touch Christ's wounds. **2. Dyl·an** (dil′ən). 1914–1953, Welsh poet.

thong (thông, thong) *n.* **1.** a narrow strip of leather or other material, used especially as a fastening. **2.** a sandal that is held to the foot by a pair of thongs that fit between the first two toes. **3.** the lash of a whip.

Thor (thôr) *n. Norse Mythology.* the god of thunder.

tho·rac·ic (thô ras′ik) *adj.* of, relating to, or located in or near the thorax.

tho·rax (thôr′aks) *n. pl.,* **tho·rax·es** or **tho·ra·ces** (thôr′ə sēz′). **1.** in man and certain other animals with backbones, the part of the body extending from the base of the neck to the diaphragm, containing the heart, lungs, and ribs. **2.** the section of an insect's body that contains the wings and legs, extending from the head to the abdomen.

Tho·reau, Henry David (thə rō′) 1817–1862, U.S. writer, philosopher, and naturalist.

tho·ri·um (thôr′ē əm) *n.* a heavy, silver-white, radioactive metallic element used in the manufacture of electronic devices. Symbol: **Th**

thorn (thôrn) *n.* **1.** a short, sharp-pointed growth on a branch or stem, as of a rose. **2.** any of various trees or shrubs bearing thorns.

   thorn in one's side. a cause of annoyance, trouble, or worry.

thorn·y (thôr′nē) *adj.,* **thorn·i·er, thorn·i·est. 1.** full of thorns; spiny; prickly. **2.** difficult or irritating: *a thorny problem.*

thor·ough (thur′ō) *adj.* **1.** done or carried out completely; omitting nothing: *a thorough search, a thorough cleaning.* **2.** extremely accurate and conscientious, especially with regard to details: *She is very thorough in her research.* —**thor′ough·ly,** *adv.* —**thor′ough·ness,** *n.*

thor·ough·bred (thur′ə bred′) *n.* **1.** an animal, such as a horse or dog, that is of pure or unmixed breed or stock. **2. Thoroughbred.** a horse descended from a breed first developed at the end of the eighteenth century by crossing English mares with any one of three specific Arabian stallions. Thoroughbreds are trained chiefly for horse racing. **3.** a person of good breeding and education. —*adj.* **1.** of pure or unmixed breed or stock. **2. Thoroughbred.** relating to or being a Thoroughbred.

thor·ough·fare (thur′ə fer′) *n.* a public road or street that is open at both ends, especially one that is a major route of travel.

thor·ough·go·ing (thur′ə gō′ing) *adj.* thorough; complete: *He is a thoroughgoing liar.*

those (thōz) the plural of **that.**

thou (thou) *pron. Archaic.* the one spoken to; you.

though (thō) *conj.* **1.** in spite of the fact that: *I was late for work, though I got up early.* **2.** but; yet; however: *The meal was good, though it could have been better.* —*adv.* nonetheless; however: *Bill won't help us; you can count on Jim, though.*

thought (thôt) *v.* the past tense and past participle of **think.** —*n.* **1.** the act or process of thinking: *to be lost in thought.* **2.** something that one thinks; idea: *What are your thoughts on the subject?* **3.** the way of thinking or the ideas of a particular group, time, or place: *modern thought, scientific thought.* **4.** careful notice, attention, or consideration: *Please give some thought to the problem.* **5.** something that is intended; aim.

thought·ful (thôt′fəl) *adj.* **1.** expressing, showing, or having a regard for others and their feelings; considerate: *a thoughtful person, a thoughtful gift.* **2.** engaged in or full of thought; meditative: *She had a thoughtful look on her face.* **3.** showing careful attention or consideration: *a thoughtful question.* —**thought′ful·ly,** *adv.* —**thought′ful·ness,** *n.*

thought·less (thôt′lis) *adj.* **1.** having or showing little or no regard for others and their feelings; inconsiderate: *His thoughtless remark hurt her feelings.* **2.** showing a lack of thought; careless. —**thought′less·ly,** *adv.* —**thought′less·ness,** *n.*

thou·sand (thou′zənd) *n.* **1.** the cardinal number that is ten times a hundred. **2.** a symbol representing this number, such as 1000 or M. —*adj.* numbering ten times a hundred.

Thousand Islands, a group of about 1700 small islands in the St. Lawrence River, belonging partly to the United States and partly to Canada.

thou·sandth (thou′zəndth) *adj.* **1.** (the ordinal of thousand) next after the 999th. **2.** being one of a thousand equal parts. —*n.* **1.** something that is next after the 999th. **2.** one of a thousand equal parts; 1/1000.

Thrace (thrās) *n.* an ancient region in the eastern part of the Balkan Peninsula. Once a Roman province, it is now divided among Greece, Bulgaria, and Turkey.

Thra·cian (thrā′shən) *adj.* of or relating to ancient Thrace or its people. —*n.* a person who was born or lived in ancient Thrace.

thrall (thrôl) *n.* **1.** a person who is enslaved; slave; serf. **2.** the condition of being enslaved; slavery.

thrall·dom (thrôl′dəm) *also,* **thral·dom.** *n.* the condition of being enslaved.

thrash (thrash) *v.t.* **1.** to give a beating to. **2.** to defeat completely; overwhelm. **3.** another word for **thresh.** —*v.i.* **1.** to make wild, flailing movements; toss violently: *The animal thrashed about trying to get free from the cage.* **2.** another word for **thresh.**

   to thrash out. to discuss thoroughly and bring to a conclusion.

thrash·er (thrash′ər) *n.* **1.** a person or thing that thrashes. **2.** a North American songbird, closely related to the mockingbird, having a curved bill, a long tail, short wings, and mainly brown feathers.

thrash·ing (thrash′ing) *n.* a severe beating.

Thrasher

thread (thred) *n.* **1.** a very fine, thin cord made of two or more fibers, as of cotton, wool, or silk, twisted together. It is used in sewing and in weaving cloth. **2.** anything resembling thread, as in thinness or length: *A thread of paint dripped down the wall.* **3.** anything that runs through the whole of something and connects its parts: *the thread of a story.* **4.** a spiral ridge running continuously around a screw or nut. —*v.t.* **1.** to pass a thread through: *to thread a needle.* **2.** to string together on or as if on a thread: *to thread beads.* **3.** to pass or proceed through in a winding or twisting manner: *Her hair was threaded with a rope of pearls.* **4.** to make (one's way) in a winding or twisting manner: *He threaded his way through the crowd.* **5.** to cut a thread on, in, or around (a screw or nut). —*v.i.* **1.** to pass or proceed in a winding or twisting manner: *The river threads between the mountains.* **2.** to form a fine thread when dropped from a spoon, as boiling syrup that has reached a certain consistency. —**thread′like′,** *adj.*

thread·bare (thred′ber′) *adj.* **1.** having the nap worn off so the threads show through; worn; shabby: *threadbare upholstery.* **2.** wearing threadbare clothes; seedy. **3.** old and worn out; stale: *a threadbare joke.*

thread·y (thred′ē) *adj.,* **thread·i·er, thread·i·est. 1.** made of or resembling thread. **2.** weak and thin: *a thready voice.* —**thread′i·ness,** *n.*

threat (thret) *n.* **1.** an expression of the intention to inflict punishment, harm, or pain. **2.** a person or thing that is a source of misfortune, danger, or harm: *The murderer was a threat to society.* **3.** a sign or possibility of something that might happen, such as misfortune or danger: *They lived under the threat of war.*

threat·en (thret′ən) *v.t.* **1.** to make a threat against: *The robber threatened Tom's life.* **2.** to be a threat to; endanger: *The drought threatened the farmer's crop.* **3.** to be an indication of: *The dark clouds threaten rain.* **4.** to make a threat of: *He threatened to call the police if they didn't leave his store.* —*v.i.* **1.** to use or utter threats. **2.** to be or pose a threat; menace. —**threat′en·ing·ly,** *adv.*

three (thrē) *n.* **1.** the cardinal number that is one more than two. **2.** a symbol representing this number, such as 3 or III. **3.** something having this many units or things, as a playing card. —*adj.* numbering one more than two.

three-di·men·sion·al (thrē′di men′shən əl) *adj.* **1.** of, relating to, or having three dimensions. **2.** having or giving the illusion of depth.

three-fold (thrē′fōld′) *adj.* **1.** three times as great or numerous. **2.** having or consisting of three parts. —*adv.* so as to be three times greater or more numerous.

three·score (thrē′skôr′) *adj.* three times twenty; sixty.

three·some (thrē′səm) *n.* a group of three persons.

Three Wise Men, another name for the **Magi.**

thren·o·dy (thren′ə dē) *n. pl.,* **thren·o·dies.** a song or poem of lamentation, especially one written for the funeral of an important person.

thresh (thresh) *v.t.* **1.** to separate the grain from (a cereal grass) with a threshing machine or by beating with a flail. **2.** to separate (grain) from straw or chaff in this manner. **3.** to give a beating to; thrash. —*v.i.* **1.** to thresh grain. **2.** to toss violently; thrash.

thresh·er (thresh′ər) *n.* **1.** a person or thing that threshes. **2.** a machine that threshes grain. Also, **threshing machine. 3.** a large shark having a very long tail that it thrashes about in the water in order to drive together schools of small fish which it eats.

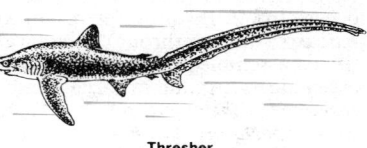

Thresher

thresh·old (thresh′ōld) *n.* **1.** a piece of wood, stone, or metal that forms the bottom of a door frame. **2.** a point of entering or beginning: *The young man was on the threshold of a new career.* **3.** the limit or point below which a stimulus cannot be felt: *to have a high threshold for pain.*

threw (thrōō) the past tense of **throw.**

thrice (thrīs) *adv.* three times.

thrift (thrift) *n.* careful management of money and other resources; frugality.

thrift·less (thrift′lis) *adj.* not thrifty; wasteful.

thrift·y (thrif′tē) *adj.,* **thrift·i·er, thrift·i·est.** very careful in the use and management of money and other resources; avoiding waste or extravagance; frugal. —**thrift′i·ly,** *adv.* —**thrift′i·ness,** *n.*

thrill (thril) *n.* **1.** a pleasurable or exciting feeling or sensation: *She recalled the thrill of seeing her baby take its first steps.* **2.** something that produces such a feeling or sensation: *His first airplane trip was a thrill for him.* —*v.t.* to fill with pleasure or excitement: *The soccer game thrilled the crowd.* —*v.i.* **1.** to have a sudden feeling of pleasure or excitement. **2.** to tremble; quiver. —**thrill′ing·ly,** *adv.*

thrill·er (thril′ər) *n.* **1.** a play, story, book, or the like that causes feelings of excitement or suspense. **2.** a person or thing that thrills.

thrive (thrīv) *v.i.,* **throve** or **thrived, thrived** or **thriv·en** (thriv′ən), **thriv·ing. 1.** to be successful or fortunate: *His new business is thriving.* **2.** to grow very well; be very healthy: *The plant thrived in the sunlight.*

throat (thrōt) *n.* **1.** the area behind and below the mouth, containing the pharynx, the upper part of the esophagus, the larynx, and the upper part of the trachea. **2.** the front of the neck, extending from below the chin to the collarbones. **3.** any narrow opening resembling the throat: *the throat of a bottle.*

throat·y (thrō′tē) *adj.,* **throat·i·er, throat·i·est.** produced deep in the throat; husky: *a throaty laugh.* —**throat′i·ness,** *n.*

throb (throb) *v.i.,* **throbbed, throb·bing. 1.** to beat heavily and fast, as the heart; pound. **2.** to vibrate or sound with a strong, steady rhythm: *The drums throbbed in the night.* —*n.* **1.** the act of throbbing. **2.** a beat or vibration; pulsation: *a heart throb.*

throe (thrō) *n.* **1.** **throes.** a condition of extreme pain, anguish, or struggle: *in the throes of death.* **2.** *also,* **throes.** a violent spasm or pang, especially of pain.

throm·bo·sis (throm bō′sis) *n.* the formation of a clot of blood in a blood vessel or the heart, that stops the flow of blood.

---

at; āpe; cär; end; mē; it; īce; hot; ōld; fôrk; wood; fōōl; oil; out; up; turn; sing; thin; this; hw in white; zh in treasure. The symbol ə stands for the sound of **a** in about, **e** in taken, **i** in pencil, **o** in lemon, and **u** in circus.

T

throne (thrōn) *n.* **1.** a chair on which a sovereign, pope, bishop, or other dignitary sits during state or ceremonial occasions. **2.** royal power or authority; sovereignty.

throng (thrông, throng) *n.* a large number of people or things assembled or crowded together. —*v.i.* to move or assemble in a group or large numbers; crowd: *The people thronged to the county fair.* —*v.t.* **1.** to fill (a place); crowd into: *Spectators thronged the courtroom.* **2.** to crowd around; press in on: *Fans thronged the singer wherever he went.*

throt·tle (throt′əl) *n.* **1.** a valve that controls or regulates the supply of steam in a steam engine or turbine or the supply of fuel vapor in an internal-combustion engine. **2.** a lever or pedal that operates such a valve. —*v.t.,* **throt·tled, throt·tling. 1.** to kill by choking; strangle. **2.** to stop the flow or action of; suppress: *They throttled the rebellion by cutting the lines of supply.* **3.** to reduce or shut off the flow of (steam or fuel vapor) in an engine. **4.** to reduce the speed of (an engine) in this way.

through (thrōō) *prep.* **1.** from the beginning to the end of: *She read through the book in one day.* **2.** in one side or end and out the opposite or other side or end: *to drive a nail through a board.* **3.** in or to various parts or places in: *We plan to travel through Europe this summer.* **4.** in the midst of; among: *She wandered through the trees.* **5.** because of: *He lost his job through constant tardiness.* **6.** by means of: *We got the news through our friend.* **7.** having finished or done with: *Is he through college yet?* —*adv.* **1.** from one side or end to the opposite or other side or end: *The farmer opened the barnyard gate and the cattle went through.* **2.** from beginning to end: *to read a letter through.* **3.** to a conclusion or the end: *to carry a project through.* **4.** along the whole distance; all the way: *The river runs through to the mill.* **5.** throughout; completely: *to be soaked through.* —*adj.* **1.** going or allowing a person to go the whole distance with few or no stops and no changes: *a through train.* **2.** that allows free or unobstructed passage: *a through street.* **3.** having arrived at a point of completion; finished: *Are you through with your homework?* **4.** no longer having relations, dealings, or connections: *Jim's father is through with that political group forever.*

  through and through. completely: *He is a coward through and through.*

through·out (thrōō out′) *prep.* **1.** in every part of; everywhere in: *He is famous throughout the country.* **2.** during the whole time or course of: *She visited me throughout my illness.* —*adv.* **1.** in or to every place or part; everywhere: *He was soaked throughout.* **2.** from beginning to end.

through·way (thrōō wā′) another spelling of **thruway.**

throve (thrōv) a past tense of **thrive.**

throw (thrō) *v.,* **threw, thrown, throw·ing.** —*v.t.* **1.** to send up into or through the air with the hand or hands: *to throw a ball. Please throw me a towel.* **2.** to cause to fall to the ground: *The horse threw its rider. The wrestler threw his opponent.* **3.** to put carelessly or hurriedly: *She threw a coat on and ran out the door.* **4.** to put or place in a specified position, state, or condition: *to throw a crowd into confusion.* **5.** to direct or project; cast: *He threw me a nasty look.* **6.** to move (a lever or switch) so as to connect or disconnect parts of a mechanism. **7.** to lose or shed: *The horse threw a shoe.* **8.** *Informal.* to lose (a game, race, or other contest) on purpose. **9.** *Informal.* to give (a party, dance, or the like). —*v.i.* to send something up into or through the air with the hand or hands. —*n.* **1.** the act of throwing; toss. **2.** the distance that something is or may be thrown. **3.** a scarf, shawl, or coverlet. —**throw′er,** *n.*

  to throw away. a. to dispose of; discard. **b.** to waste;

squander: *He threw away his fortune by gambling.* **c.** to fail to take advantage of: *to throw away an opportunity.*

  to throw in. to add or include as a bonus.

  to throw off. a. to rid or free oneself of. **b.** to give off; emit.

  to throw out. a. to reject; discard. **b.** to offer, as a hint or suggestion. **c.** *Baseball.* to put out (a base runner) by throwing the ball to a defensive player at the base toward which the base runner is running.

  to throw over. to forsake; abandon.

  to throw up. a. *Informal.* to vomit. **b.** to build rapidly. **c.** to give up; abandon.

throw·back (thrō′bak′) *n.* **1.** a reversion to an earlier or ancestral type or character. **2.** an instance of this.

thrown (thrōn) the past participle of **throw.**

throw rug, another term for **scatter rug.**

thru (thrōō) another spelling of **through.**

thrum (thrum) *v.,* **thrummed, thrum·ming.** —*v.t.* to play (a stringed instrument), especially in a monotonous or unskilled manner; strum. —*v.i.* **1.** to drum or tap idly or repeatedly with the fingers: *He thrummed on his notebook.* **2.** to thrum a stringed instrument. —*n.* a monotonous sound produced by thrumming.

thrush (thrush) *n. pl.,* **thrush·es.** any of numerous songbirds, including the robin, bluebird, wood thrush, and nightingale.

thrust (thrust) *v.,* **thrust, thrust·ing.** —*v.t.* **1.** to push or shove suddenly or with force: *He thrust the money into his pocket.* **2.** to stab or pierce: *He thrust the fork into the meat.* **3.** to put forcibly into some

Thrush (wood thrush)

condition, position, or situation: *She thrust herself into our argument.* —*v.i.* **1.** to make a stab or lunge, as with a pointed instrument or weapon: *to thrust with a knife.* **2.** to make or force one's way, as through a crowd. —*n.* **1.** a sudden, forceful push or drive: *The army made a thrust into enemy territory.* **2.** a stab. **3.** the force that pushes a rocket or jet engine forward, created when hot gases rush out through a rear nozzle. **4.** the driving force made by a propeller as it turns.

thru·way (thrōō′wā′) *also,* **through·way.** *n.* a wide, usually divided highway that allows rapid and direct travel between distant places.

Thu·cyd·i·des (thōō sid′ə dēz′) 460?–400? B.C., Greek historian.

thud (thud) *n.* **1.** a dull, heavy sound. **2.** a heavy blow producing such a sound. —*v.i.,* **thud·ded, thud·ding.** to make a thud when falling or striking against something.

thug (thug) *n.* a rough, brutal, and often violent person; ruffian. [Hindi *thag* a cheat, thief; originally referring to a member of a former religious society in northern India that robbed and strangled its victims.]

thu·li·um (thōō′lē əm) *n.* a soft metallic element, one of the rare earths. Symbol: **Tm**

thumb (thum) *n.* **1.** the short, thick finger of the human hand next to the index finger. **2.** a corresponding digit in monkeys and other primates. **3.** the part of a glove or mitten that covers the thumb. —*v.t.* **1.** to turn and glance at the pages of; leaf: *to thumb through a magazine.* **2.** *Informal.* to get by hitchhiking: *to thumb a ride.* —*v.i.* *Informal.* to hitchhike.

  all thumbs. clumsy, as when using the hands.

  thumbs down. a sign or gesture showing disapproval or rejection.

  thumbs up. a sign or gesture showing approval or acceptance.

under the thumb of. completely under the power, control, or influence of.

thumb index, a series of labels or indentations on the outside edges of the pages of a book to mark the different sections.

thumb·nail (thum′nāl′) *n.* the nail of the thumb. —*adj.* very brief, but concise: *She wrote a thumbnail report of what happened.*

thumb·screw (thum′skrōō′) *n.* **1.** a screw made so that it can be turned by the thumb and a finger. **2.** formerly, an instrument of torture used to crush the thumbs.

thumb·tack (thum′tak′) *n.* a tack with a round, flat head, designed to be pressed into a wall, board, or the like by the thumb.

thump (thump) *n.* **1.** a heavy blow, as with a blunt object. **2.** the heavy, hollow sound made by such a blow. —*v.t.* to beat or hit so as to make a heavy, hollow sound: *He thumped his head on the floor when he fell.* —*v.i.* **1.** to produce a thump when falling or striking against something. **2.** to beat heavily and rapidly; throb: *Her heart thumped when they announced the winner.* —**thump′er,** *n.*

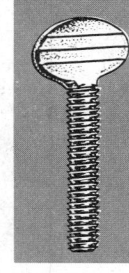

Thumbscrew

thun·der (thun′dər) *n.* **1.** a rumbling or explosive sound made when a lightning discharge heats and expands the air in its path. **2.** any noise resembling thunder: *the thunder of cannons, the thunder of applause.* —*v.i.* **1.** to give forth or produce thunder. **2.** to make a noise resembling thunder: *The freight train thundered through the station.* **3.** to utter loud denunciations or threats. —*v.t.* to speak loudly, especially in a threatening manner; shout.

thun·der·bolt (thun′dər bōlt′) *n.* **1.** a flash of lightning accompanied by a clap of thunder. **2.** something that is sudden, unexpected, and terrible.

thun·der·clap (thun′dər klap′) *n.* **1.** a loud crash or burst of thunder. **2.** something that is sudden, unexpected, and violent.

thun·der·cloud (thun′dər kloud′) *n.* a dark, billowing, electrically charged cloud that produces thunder and lightning.

thun·der·head (thun′dər hed′) *n.* one of the round, swelling cloud masses that often develops into a thundercloud.

thun·der·ous (thun′dər əs) *adj.* producing a noise like thunder: *thunderous applause.* —**thun′der·ous·ly,** *adv.*

thun·der·show·er (thun′dər shou′ər) *n.* a rain shower accompanied by thunder and lightning.

thun·der·storm (thun′dər stôrm′) *n.* a storm accompanied by thunder and lightning, and usually rain.

thun·der·struck (thun′dər struk′) *adj.* stunned or shocked, as with disbelief or surprise; astonished; amazed.

Thurs., Thursday. Also, **Thur.**

Thurs·day (thurz′dē, thurz′dā) *n.* the fifth day of the week. [Old English *Thūresdæg,* influenced by Old Norse *Thōrsdagr* literally, the day of Thor, the god of thunder.]

thus (thus) *adv.* **1.** in this, that, or the following way: *Written thus, the directions are easy to understand.* **2.** as a result; consequently; therefore: *He did not study and thus failed the test.* **3.** to this extent or degree: *We have not heard from them thus far.*

thwack (thwak) *v.t.* to hit hard with something flat; whack. —*n.* a sharp, powerful blow with something flat.

thwart (thwôrt) *v.t.* to prevent from doing or succeeding; oppose successfully: *Nothing will thwart him in his quest for success.* —*n.* a crosswise seat in a boat. —*adj.* lying or extending across something; transverse. —*adv., prep. Archaic.* across; athwart.

thy (thī) *pron. Archaic.* of or belonging to you; your.

thyme (tīm) *n.* a small plant related to the mint. Its leaves are used to season food.

thy·mus (thī′məs) *n.* an endocrine gland, located at the base of the neck. Also, **thymus gland.**

thy·roid (thī′roid) *n.* **1.** see **thyroid gland. 2.** see **thyroid cartilage. 3.** a medicine obtained from the dried thyroid glands of certain animals. —*adj.* of, relating to, or characteristic of the thyroid gland or thyroid cartilage.

thyroid cartilage, the largest cartilage of the larynx, which covers and protects the thyroid gland and forms the Adam's apple.

thyroid gland, an endocrine gland that secretes thyroxin, located in front of and on either side of the trachea.

thy·rox·in (thī rok′sin) *also,* **thy·rox·ine.** *n.* a hormone obtained from the thyroid gland or made synthetically. It is important in regulating the rate at which body cells change food and oxygen into energy and heat.

thy·self (thī self′) *pron. Archaic.* yourself.

ti (tē) *n. Music.* **1.** the seventh note of the major scale. **2.** the note B.

Ti, the symbol for titanium.

Tian·jin (tyän′jin′) another spelling of **Tientsin.**

ti·ar·a (tē ar′ə, tē är′ə) *n.* **1.** an ornament resembling a crown, worn on the head. Tiaras are often decorated with jewels. **2.** the triple crown worn by the pope.

Ti·ber (tī′bər) *n.* a river flowing southward from north-central Italy, through Rome, into the Tyrrhenian Sea.

Ti·be·ri·as, Lake (tī bēr′ē əs) see **Galilee, Sea of.**

Ti·bet (ti bet′) *n.* a mountainous region of southwestern China. It was formerly an independent country.

Ti·bet·an (ti bet′ən) *n.* **1.** a person who was born or is living in Tibet. **2.** the language of Tibet. —*adj.* of or relating to Tibet, its people, or their language.

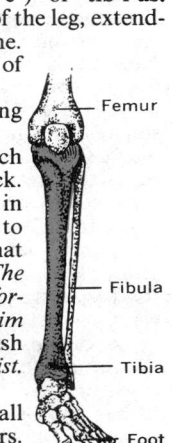

Tiara *(def. 2)*

tib·i·a (tib′ē ə) *n. pl.,* **tib·i·ae** (tib′ē ē′) or **tib·i·as. 1.** the inner and thicker of the two bones of the leg, extending from the knee to the ankle; shinbone. **2.** the corresponding bone in the legs of birds and certain other animals.

tic (tik) *n.* a habitual, involuntary twitching of a muscle, especially in the face.

tick¹ (tik) *n.* **1.** a light, clicking sound, such as that made by a watch or a clock. **2.** a dot, slash, or other mark, often used in checking off items in a series. —*v.i.* **1.** to make a light, clicking sound, such as that made by a clock. **2.** (of time) to pass: *The minutes ticked away as he waited.* **3.** *Informal.* to work; function; go: *What makes him tick?* —*v.t.* to mark or indicate with a slash or other mark: *to tick names off a list.* [Probably imitative of this sound.]

tick² (tik) *n.* **1.** any of a group of very small wingless animals that look like spiders. Ticks attach themselves to the skin of man and animals and suck their blood. Some

— Femur

— Fibula

— Tibia

— Foot

Tibia

---

at; āpe; cär; end; mē; it; īce; hot; ōld; fôrk; wood; fōōl; oil; out; up; turn; sing; thin; this; hw in white; zh in treasure. The symbol ə stands for the sound of **a** in about, **e** in taken, **i** in pencil, **o** in lemon, and **u** in circus.

ticks transmit diseases. **2.** any of various other insects that are parasites of horses, sheep, cattle, and deer. [Middle English *tyke, teke.*]

tick³ (tik) *n.* the cloth covering or case of a mattress or pillow. [Latin *thēca* a case, cover.]

tick·er (tik′ər) *n.* **1.** something that ticks, such as a watch. **2.** a telegraphic instrument that prints stock market reports or news on a paper tape. **3.** *Slang.* the heart.

ticker tape, the paper tape or ribbon on which a ticker prints stock market reports or news.

tick·et (tik′it) *n.* **1.** a card or piece of paper that shows the person who holds it has the right to receive certain services or privileges: *We have to buy our tickets before boarding the train.* **2.** a card, tag, or other piece of paper attached to something to show its price, who owns it, or the like. **3.** a list or group of candidates belonging to a particular political party, to be voted on in an election. **4.** *Informal.* a summons ordering a person to appear in court, especially for a traffic violation: *John got a ticket for speeding.* —*v.t.* **1.** to attach a ticket to: *They ticketed our baggage at the airport.* **2.** to give a legal summons to, especially for a traffic violation: *The policeman ticketed Mr. James for illegal parking.*

tick·ing (tik′ing) *n.* a strong, durable fabric of closely woven cotton or linen, used especially to make covers for mattresses and pillows.

tick·le (tik′əl) *v.,* **tick·led, tick·ling.** —*v.t.* **1.** to touch (a person or a part of the body) so as to produce a tingling sensation, usually causing laughter. **2.** to please, amuse, or excite agreeably; delight: *The smell of food from the kitchen tickled his taste buds. The children were tickled by the clown's antics.* —*v.i.* to feel or produce a tingling sensation. —*n.* **1.** the act of tickling or the state of being tickled. **2.** a tickling sensation: *A tickle in his throat made him cough.* —**tick′ler,** *n.*

tick·lish (tik′lish) *adj.* **1.** sensitive to tickling: *a ticklish person.* **2.** requiring caution, tact, and careful handling; delicate: *Rita is always getting into ticklish situations.* **3.** easily offended; sensitive; touchy. —**tick′lish·ness,** *n.*

Ti·con·der·o·ga (tī′kon də rō′gə) *n.* a village and historic fort on Lake Champlain, in the northeastern part of New York.

tic-tac-toe (tik′tak tō′) *also,* **tick-tack-toe.** *n.* a game played with a diagram having nine squares, in which two players alternately put X's and O's in the squares. The winner is the first person to complete a row of three X's or O's.

tid·al (tīd′əl) *adj.* of, relating to, or affected by tides: *a tidal basin, tidal ebb and flow.*

tidal wave 1. a huge, powerful ocean wave caused by an underwater earthquake. **2.** any great movement or show of strong feeling: *A tidal wave of emotion swept the audience as they listened to the speaker.*

tid·bit (tid′bit) *also,* **tit·bit.** *n.* a small, choice piece, as of food or gossip.

tid·dly·winks (tid′lē winks′) *n.* a game in which the players try to shoot small colored disks into a little cup by snapping them on the edge with a larger disk. ▲ used with a singular verb.

tide (tīd) *n.* **1.** the regular rise and fall of the oceans and other large bodies of water, caused by the gravitational pull of the moon and the sun. High tide occurs at a given place about every twelve hours and twenty-five minutes, with low tide occurring halfway between each high tide. **2.** a general trend or tendency: *The tide of the battle turned against the invaders.* **3.** anything that tends to rise and fall

Tic-tac-toe

or increase and decrease: *A tide of tourists swept through the town every summer.*

to tide over. to aid in getting along during a difficult period or until a specific time: *This money should tide you over until payday.*

to turn the tide. to reverse a condition or situation, especially to a more favorable one.

tide·land (tīd′land′) *n.* land that is covered and then uncovered by the rise and fall of the tides.

tide·wa·ter (tīd′wô′tər) *n.* **1.** a body of water affected by tides. **2.** low-lying coastal land whose waters are affected by tides. **3.** water that floods land at high tide. —*adj.* of, relating to, or situated along a tidewater: *a tidewater estate.*

ti·dings (tī′dingz) *n.,pl.* news; information: *The messenger brought good tidings.*

ti·dy (tī′dē) *adj.,* **ti·di·er, ti·di·est. 1.** clean and neat; well-organized: *His closet was not very tidy. She is a tidy person.* **2.** *Informal.* quite large; considerable: *We managed to save a tidy sum of money.* —*v.t., v.i.,* **ti·died, ti·dy·ing.** to arrange (things or oneself) in a clean and neat manner: *Bob's mother asked him to tidy up his room.* —*n. pl.,* **ti·dies.** a small decorative covering placed over the back or arms of a chair or sofa to keep it from becoming soiled or worn. —**ti′di·ness,** *n.*

tie (tī) *v.,* **tied, ty·ing.** —*v.t.* **1.** to fasten with a rope, string, or similar material: *She tied her hair with a ribbon.* **2.** to fasten with a knot or bow: *to tie a shoe.* **3.** to make a knot or bow in: *to tie one's shoelaces.* **4.** to make (a knot or bow).

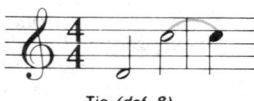

Tie *(def. 8)*

5. to draw together or join closely: *Mutual interests tied us together.* **6.** to restrain or restrict; confine: *A long illness tied him to his bed.* **7.** to equal the score or total of (an opponent). **8.** to equal (a score or total). **9.** *Music.* to unite (notes) by a curved line written above or below two notes of the same pitch. —*v.i.* **1.** to be fastened with a rope, string, or similar material: *This skirt ties in the front.* **2.** to make the same score; be equal: *The two teams tied.* —*n.* **1.** a cord, string, or similar material used to tie things. **2.** anything that unites or joins together: *Ellen believes that the ties of friendship are very strong.* **3.** see **necktie. 4.** an equal score: *The game ended in a tie.* **5.** a competition that ends with an equal score; draw: *The game was a tie.* **6.** a part of a structure, such as a beam or rod, that holds together or strengthens other parts. **7.** one of the crosspieces, usually of wood, to which railroad rails are fastened. **8.** *Music.* a curved line written above or below two notes of the same pitch, indicating that they should be played or sung as one long note.

to tie down. to restrict or confine: *The new baby tied her down.*

to tie in. to connect, especially by being relevant or consistent: *The book Tom read tied in with the term paper he was working on.*

to tie up. a. to fasten with a rope or the like. **b.** to prevent free action or movement: *An accident tied up traffic for an hour.* **c.** to keep in use or to keep busy and not free for anything else: *Her brother ties up the phone every night. Her family's money was tied up in real estate.*

Tien·tsin (tyen′tsin′) *n.* a port city in northeastern China. Pop. (1968 est.), 4,000,000. Also, **Tianjin.**

tier (tēr) *n.* one of a series of layers or rows, as of seats, arranged one above another. —*v.t.* to arrange in tiers.

Tier·ra del Fue·go (tyer′ə del fwā′gō) a group of islands at the southern tip of South America. They are divided between Chile and Argentina.

tie-up (tī′up′) *n.* **1.** a stoppage or slowdown of work, action, or progress: *The accident caused a traffic tie-up at the corner.* **2.** *Informal.* a connection or association.

tiff (tif) *n.* a slight quarrel or spat.

Tif·lis (tif′lis) see **Tbilisi.**

ti·ger (tī′gər) *n.* a large, meat-eating Asian animal of the cat family. It has a yellow coat marked with black or brown stripes. —**ti′ger·like′,** *adj.*

Tiger

tiger beetle, any of a group of brightly colored beetles whose larvae live in sandy soil.

tiger cat 1. any of several tigerlike wildcats, such as the ocelot and serval. **2.** a domestic cat having striped markings, especially a tabby.

ti·ger·ish (tī′gər ish) *adj.* like a tiger in manner or appearance; fierce.

tiger lily, a slender plant that is grown for its showy, trumpet-shaped flowers, which are reddish orange spotted with black.

tiger moth, any of a large group of moths with striped or spotted wings.

tight (tīt) *adj.* **1.** fastened or held firmly; secure: *This window is too tight to open.* **2.** having the parts or units of which it is made close together; compact: *a fabric with a tight weave.* **3.** of such close construction or fit that a liquid or gas cannot pass through. **4.** pulled or stretched as far as possible. **5.** fitting the body closely, especially too closely: *a tight belt.* **6.** having or allowing little time or space to spare: *a tight schedule.* **7.** difficult to deal with or manage: *to be in a tight spot.* **8.** strict; severe: *The government kept tight controls on public utilities.* **9.** *Informal.* not generous, especially with money; stingy. **10.** *Informal.* evenly matched; close: *a tight race.* **11.** *Slang.* intoxicated; drunk. **12.** difficult to get; scarce: *Jobs are tight right now.* —*adv.* in a tight manner; firmly; securely: *The little boy closed the jar tight.* —**tight′ly,** *adv.* —**tight′ness,** *n.*

to sit tight. to hold onto one's position or opinion; take no action.

tight·en (tīt′ən) *v.t., v.i.* to make or become tight or tighter.

tight-fist·ed (tīt′fis′tid) *adj.* stingy; miserly.

tight-lipped (tīt′lipt′) *adj.* **1.** having the lips closed tightly. **2.** quiet or secretive.

tight·rope (tīt′rōp′) *n.* a tightly-stretched wire, cable, or rope placed high above the ground, on which acrobats perform.

tights (tīts) *n.,pl.* a skin-tight garment, usually covering the lower part of the body.

tight·wad (tīt′wod′) *n. Slang.* a stingy person; miser.

ti·gress (tī′gris) *n. pl.,* **ti·gress·es.** a female tiger.

Ti·gris (tī′gris) *n.* a river in southwestern Asia, flowing from eastern Turkey through Iraq, where it joins the Euphrates River to empty into the Persian Gulf. The region watered by this river and the Euphrates River is known as the cradle of civilization.

Ti·jua·na (tē wä′nə, tē′ə wä′nə) *n.* a resort city in northwestern Mexico, at the U.S. border. Pop. (1970), 277,000.

tike (tīk) another spelling of **tyke.**

til·de (til′də) *n.* **1.** in Spanish, a diacritical mark (õ) used over *n* to indicate the pronunciation *ny,* as in *señor* (se-nyôr′). **2.** in Portuguese, the same mark, used over the vowels *a* and *o* to indicate nasal pronunciation.

tile (tīl) *n.* **1.** a thin, often decorated slab, as of baked clay, porcelain, or linoleum, used for covering roofs, floors, or walls. **2.** tiles as a group; tiling. **3.** a piece used in playing various games, as dominoes. **4.** a short pipe, as of clay or concrete, used as a drain. —*v.t.,* **tiled, til·ing.** to cover with tiles.

til·ing (tī′ling) *n.* **1.** tiles as a group. **2.** the act of covering with tiles. **3.** something covered with or made of tiles.

till[1] (til) *prep.* **1.** up to the time of: *Wait till tomorrow before calling.* **2.** before (a specified time): *Grandfather won't arrive till Sunday.* —*conj.* **1.** up to the time when or that: *Wait till you hear from me before writing.* **2.** before: *We didn't see Joe till after the meeting.* [Old English *til* to.] ▲ Till and until may be used interchangeably.

till[2] (til) *v.t.* to prepare and use (land) for raising crops. [Old English *tilian.*] —**till′a·ble,** *adj.*

till[3] (til) *n.* a drawer or other container in which money is kept, as in a store. [Of uncertain origin.]

till·age (til′ij) *n.* **1.** the cultivation of land. **2.** land that is under cultivation. Also, **tilth.**

till·er[1] (til′ər) *n.* a bar or handle used to turn the rudder of a boat. [Old French *telier* a weaver's beam, going back to Latin *tēla* a fabric woven on a loom.]

till·er[2] (til′ər) *n.* a person or thing that tills land. [Till[2] + -er[1].]

tilt (tilt) *v.t.* **1.** to raise one end or side of; put at an angle; tip: *Don't tilt your chair so far back or you will fall over.* **2.** to point or thrust (a lance) in a joust. **3.** to charge (an opponent) in a joust. —*v.i.* **1.** to slope or tip; incline. **2.** to take part in a joust. **3.** to charge or attack in a joust. **4.** to attack in any way: *The young lawyer tilted at injustice.* —*n.* **1.** a sloping position; angle: *The tilt of her head suggested bewilderment.* **2.** a medieval contest between two knights on horseback who were usually armed with long lances; joust. **3.** any fight or confrontation that is like a joust between knights.

full tilt. at full speed: *The car crashed full tilt against the wall.*

tilth (tilth) *n.* another word for **tillage.**

tim·ber (tim′bər) *n.* **1.** wood suitable for building, carpentry, or other forms of construction. **2.** a single piece of wood used in construction; beam. **3.** one of the curved pieces leading from the keel and forming part of the framework of a ship. **4.** trees as a group. **5.** see **timberland.** —*v.t.* to cover, support, or supply with timber: *to timber an underground passage.*

tim·bered (tim′bərd) *adj.* **1.** covered with growing trees; wooded: *a heavily timbered region.* **2.** built or made of timber.

tim·ber·land (tim′bər land′) *n.* land covered with trees, especially trees that are to be cut and used for lumber.

timber line, an imaginary line on mountains and in arctic regions above which or beyond which trees do not grow.

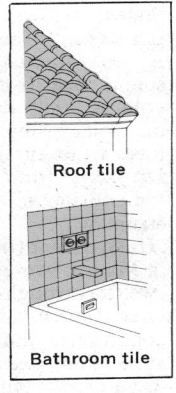

Roof tile

Bathroom tile

Tile

at; āpe; cär; end; mē; it; īce; hot; ōld; fôrk; wood; fōol; oil; out; up; turn; sing; thin; this; hw in white; zh in treasure. The symbol ə stands for the sound of **a** in about, **e** in taken, **i** in pencil, **o** in lemon, and **u** in circus.

timber wolf, a gray wolf of the forest regions of Canada and the northern United States.

Timber wolf

tim·bre (tĭm′bər, tam′bər) *n.* the special quality of sound, apart from pitch and volume, that distinguishes one voice or musical instrument from another.

tim·brel (tĭm′brəl) *n.* a tambourine or similar instrument.

Tim·buk·tu (tĭm′bŭk tōō′) *n.* a town in western Africa, in Mali. It was a great trade and cultural center during the twelfth through fifteenth centuries.

time (tīm) *n.* **1.** an indefinite extent during which events, conditions, and actions happen, exist, or continue in succession: *The changing seasons show the passing of time.* **2.** an exact point in time, especially as shown by a clock or calendar: *What time is it?* **3.** a definite or specific point in time: *The senator has no comment at this time.* **4.** a favorable, right, usual, or appointed point in time: *It's time for lunch.* **5.** a definite or specific part or portion of time: *Summer is the warmest time of the year.* **6.** a portion of time available, necessary, or taken for some purpose: *I have no time to argue with you. The runner's time for the mile was four minutes.* **7.** a system of measuring or determining time: *solar time.* **8.** *also,* **times.** a portion of time in history: *the time of Julius Caesar, medieval times.* **9.** a period of time considered in terms of someone's personal experience: *He had a hard time finding a job.* **10.** one of a number of repeated or recurring actions or instances: *We saw the movie four times.* **11.** a period worked or to be worked by an employee. **12.** the pay received for this period. **13.** *Music.* rhythm, tempo, or meter, especially of a particular kind of musical composition: *waltz time.* —*v.t.,* **timed, tim·ing. 1.** to regulate, adjust, or arrange according to time: *The bomb was timed to go off at midnight.* **2.** to measure or determine the time, duration, or rate of: *to time a runner.* **3.** to choose the time or occasion for: *The President timed his announcement to affect the coming election.* —*adj.* **1.** of or relating to time. **2.** regulated, adjusted, or devised to operate at a certain time: *a time lock.*

  against time. in an attempt to finish within or before a certain time: *The police were working against time in their search for the hidden bomb.*
  at the same time. however; nevertheless.
  at times. sometimes; occasionally.
  behind the times. no longer in fashion; out-of-date.
  for the time being. for the present; for now.
  from time to time. now and then; occasionally.
  in no time. almost instantly; very quickly.
  in time. a. before it is too late: *We got to the station in time to catch the train.* **b.** in the course of time; eventually: *In time, all this will be forgotten.* **c.** in the correct rhythm or tempo: *to clap in time to music.*
  on time. a. at the correct or appointed time: *Did you get to school on time?* **b.** payable in installments over a period of time: *to buy a car on time.*
  time after time or **time and again.** repeatedly.
  to keep time. to record time, as a clock.
  to make time. to move quickly, as in attempting to recover lost time.

time clock, a clock with a mechanism for automatically recording the arrival and departure time of an employee.

time exposure 1. the exposure of a photographic film for a relatively long period of time, often for more than one or two seconds. **2.** a photograph made by such an exposure.

time-hon·ored (tīm′on′ərd) *adj.* revered, respected, or observed because of age or long usage: *a time-honored custom.*

time-keep·er (tīm′kē′pər) *n.* a person or thing that keeps, measures, or records time.

time·less (tīm′lĭs) *adj.* **1.** unaffected by the passage of time; eternal. **2.** referring to or characteristic of no particular time. —**time′less·ly,** *adv.*

time·ly (tīm′lē) *adj.,* **time·li·er, tim·li·est.** happening at a suitable or appropriate time; well-timed. —**time′li·ness,** *n.*

time-out (tīm′out′) *n.* **1.** *Sports.* a short period of time during which play is stopped. **2.** any brief stopping of work or activity; break.

time·piece (tīm′pēs′) *n.* any device that records, measures, or keeps time, especially a watch or clock.

tim·er (tī′mər) *n.* **1.** a person or thing that measures, records, or keeps time. **2.** a device in an internal-combustion engine that causes the spark to be produced in the cylinder at the right instant.

times (tīmz) *prep.* multiplied by: *Two times two equals four.*

time signature *Music.* a sign on a staff, usually expressed as a fraction, showing the meter or rhythm of the music that follows.

Time signature for three-quarter time

time·ta·ble (tīm′tā′bəl) *n.* a list of the times at which a series of events are to be done or happen, especially a schedule showing the arrival and departure times of trains, buses, boats, or airplanes.

time-worn (tīm′wôrn′) *adj.* **1.** showing the effects of time or long use. **2.** used too frequently; trite: *a timeworn joke.*

time zone, any of the twenty-four longitudinal regions of fifteen degrees each into which the earth is divided for measuring standard time from the prime meridian at Greenwich, England.

tim·id (tĭm′ĭd) *adj.* marked by or showing a lack of courage, boldness, or self-confidence; shy. —**ti·mid′i·ty, tim′id·ness,** *n.* —**tim′id·ly,** *adv.*

tim·ing (tī′mĭng) *n.* the act of determining and using the right moment or speed for some action in order to produce the desired effect: *The batter's timing was poor, so he missed the ball when he swung.*

tim·or·ous (tĭm′ər əs) *adj.* marked by or showing a lack of courage, boldness, or self-confidence; timid. —**tim′or·ous·ly,** *adv.* —**tim′or·ous·ness,** *n.*

tim·o·thy (tĭm′ə thē) *n.* a tall stout grass having smooth, hollow stems with clusters of tiny flowers at the tips. It is grown for hay and is sometimes used for grazing.

Tim·o·thy (tĭm′ə thē) *n.* **1.** a disciple of Saint Paul. **2.** either of two books of the New Testament consisting of epistles or letters written to Timothy by Paul.

tim·pa·ni (tĭm′pə nē) *also,* **tym·pa·ni.** *n.,pl. sing.,* **tim·pa·no** (tĭm′pə nō′). kettledrums, especially those played in an orchestra. —**tim′pa·nist,** *n.*

tin (tĭn) *n.* **1.** a soft, silver-white, metallic element that does not easily rust or corrode. It is used especially as a coating on sheet steel for cans. Symbol: **Sn 2.** see **tin plate. 3.** any object made of tin, such as a baking sheet. **4.** *British.* see **can²** *(def. 2).* —*adj.* made of tin. —*v.t.,* **tinned, tin·ning. 1.** to cover, coat, or plate (something) with tin. **2.** *British.* to preserve or pack in tin cans; can: *to tin peaches.*

Timothy

tinc·ture (tingk′chər) *n.* **1.** a solution, usually in alcohol, containing a drug or other medicine. **2.** a small amount; trace; hint. **3.** a tinge of color; tint. —*v.t.*, **tinc·tured, tinc·tur·ing. 1.** to give a tinge of a particular quality or character to. **2.** to tint; stain.

tin·der (tin′dər) *n.* any substance that burns easily, especially something used to start a fire from a spark, such as dry twigs.

tin·der·box (tin′dər boks′) *n. pl.,* **tin·der·box·es. 1.** a box used for holding the materials needed to start a fire, such as flint or coal. **2.** any place or situation that could become a source of strife or trouble.

tine (tīn) *n.* a sharp projecting point or prong, as of a fork.

tin·foil (tin′foil′) *n.* a very thin sheet of tin or other metal, such as aluminum, used as a wrapping.

ting (ting) *n.* a clear, high-pitched, metallic sound, such as that made by a small bell. —*v.i., v.t.* to make or cause to make a clear, high-pitched, metallic sound.

tinge (tinj) *v.t.,* **tinged, tinge·ing** or **ting·ing. 1.** to color slightly; tint; stain. **2.** to affect with a slight trace, touch, or flavor of some other quality or characteristic. —*n.* **1.** a faint trace of color. **2.** a small amount; touch; trace: *There was a tinge of autumn in the air.*

tin·gle (ting′gəl) *v.,* **tin·gled, tin·gling.** —*v.i.* **1.** to have a slight vibrating or stinging sensation, as from sudden excitement, cold, or a slap. **2.** to cause such a sensation. —*v.t.* to cause to tingle. —*n.* a tingling sensation.

tink·er (ting′kər) *n.* **1.** a craftsman, usually one that wanders from place to place, who mends pots, pans, and other metal household utensils. **2.** a person who can do many different kinds of repair work. **3.** an unskillful or clumsy worker; bungler. —*v.i.* **1.** to busy oneself in a trifling or aimless way; putter. **2.** to work in an unskillful or clumsy manner. **3.** to work as a tinker; mend household utensils.

tin·kle (ting′kəl) *v.,* **tin·kled, tin·kling.** —*v.i.* to produce clear, light, ringing sounds. —*v.t.* to cause to tinkle. —*n.* a clear, light, ringing sound.

tin·ner (tin′ər) *n.* **1.** a person who works in a tin mine. **2.** a person who works with or buys and sells tin; tinsmith.

tin·ny (tin′ē) *adj.,* **tin·ni·er, tin·ni·est. 1.** of, relating to, or containing tin. **2.** having a metallic flavor, sound, or quality: *a tinny sound.* —**tin′ni·ness,** *n.*

tin plate, thin sheets of metal, especially iron or steel, coated with tin.

tin·sel (tin′səl) *n.* **1.** very thin strips of glittering metallic material, used for ornamentation, especially on Christmas trees. **2.** anything showy or attractive but having little or no real worth. **3.** a fabric woven with metallic threads, as of silver or gold. —*v.t.,* **tin·seled, tin·sel·ing;** *also, British,* **tin·selled, tin·sel·ling.** to trim with tinsel. —*adj.* **1.** made of, like, or decorated with tinsel. **2.** showy or attractive but having little or no real worth.

tin·smith (tin′smith′) *n.* a person who works with or buys and sells tin or tinware.

tint (tint) *n.* **1.** a shade or variety of a color: *There were tints of red in her hair.* **2.** a delicate, pale color. —*v.t.* to add or give a slight color to: *Anne tinted the Easter eggs.*

Tin·to·ret·to (tin′tə ret′ō) 1518–1594, Italian painter.

tin·type (tin′tīp′) *n.* a photograph made on an iron plate that is coated with tin and treated with a substance that is sensitive to light.

tin·ware (tin′wer′) *n.* articles made of tin plate.

ti·ny (tī′nē) *adj.,* **ti·ni·er, ti·ni·est.** very small or slight.

-tion *suffix* (used to form nouns) **1.** the action or process of: *adoption.* **2.** the state or condition of being: *relaxation.* **3.** the result of: *contamination.*

tip¹ (tip) *n.* **1.** the extreme or outermost point or end of anything: *Jack scuffed the tip of his shoe.* **2.** a small piece or part attached to or forming the end of something: *the tip of a pen.* —*v.t.,* **tipped, tip·ping. 1.** to furnish with a tip. **2.** to cover, decorate, or serve as the tip of. [Middle English *tip, tippe.*]

tip² (tip) *v.,* **tipped, tip·ping.** —*v.t.* **1.** to raise one end or side of. **2.** to cause to fall or tumble; overturn: *I accidentally tipped over the chair.* **3.** to raise or touch (one's hat) in greeting. —*v.i.* **1.** to be in or assume a sloping position or direction; tilt. **2.** to fall or topple: *The ashtray tipped over.* —*n.* an inclined position; tilt. [Middle English *tipen, typen* to overthrow.]

tip³ (tip) *n.* **1.** a gift of money given in return for some service: *Mother gave the doorman a tip for helping her with her packages.* **2.** a piece of useful information, given privately or secretly, especially by an expert: *Father invested in the company on a tip from his stockbroker.* **3.** any useful or helpful hint or suggestion: *The salesman gave me some tips about the care of my new car.* —*v.,* **tipped, tip·ping.** —*v.t.* **1.** to give a gift of money to for some service: *He tipped the waiter.* **2.** to give private or secret information to: *The informer tipped off the police about the plan to rob the bank.* —*v.i.* to give a tip or tips. [Of uncertain origin.] —**tip′per,** *n.*

Tip·per·ar·y (tip′ə rer′ē) *n.* a county in the southern part of the Republic of Ireland.

tip·pet (tip′it) *n.* **1.** a covering that is like a scarf worn about the neck and shoulders with loose ends hanging down in front. **2.** in the Anglican Church, a long black scarf worn over the robe of a clergyman. **3.** formerly, a long, narrow hanging part, as of a hood or sleeve.

tip·ple (tip′əl) *v.t., v.i.,* **tip·pled, tip·pling.** to drink (alcoholic beverages) regularly and frequently in small amounts. —*n.* an alcoholic beverage. —**tip′pler,** *n.*

tip·ster (tip′stər) *n. Informal.* a person who gives or sells private or secret information, especially to people who bet on horse races or the like.

Tippet *(def. 3)*

tip·sy (tip′sē) *adj.,* **tip·si·er, tip·si·est. 1.** slightly drunk. **2.** inclined to tip; unsteady; shaky. —**tip′si·ly,** *adv.* —**tip′si·ness,** *n.*

tip·toe (tip′tō′) *v.i.,* **tip·toed, tip·toe·ing.** to move or walk on the tips of one's toes; walk quietly or stealthily.

tip·top (tip′top′) *Informal. n.* the highest point or part. —*adj.* **1.** located at the highest point. **2.** of the highest quality; first-rate; excellent.

ti·rade (tī rād′, tī′rād) *n.* a long, strongly expressed or very emotional speech, especially one containing abuse or criticism.

Ti·ra·na (ti rä′nə) *also,* **Ti·ra·ne.** *n.* the capital and largest city of Albania, in the central part of the country. Pop. (1970 est.), 171,300.

tire¹ (tīr) *v.,* **tired, tir·ing.** —*v.t.* **1.** to weaken or exhaust the strength or energy of; make weary; fatigue: *Reading in the dim light tired Timothy's eyes.* **2.** to exhaust the attention, interest, or patience of; bore: *The long speech*

at; āpe; cär; end; mē; it; īce; hot; ōld; fôrk; wood; fōōl; oil; out; up; turn; sing; thin; this; hw in white; zh in treasure. The symbol ə stands for the sound of a in about, e in taken, i in pencil, o in lemon, and u in circus.

tired the children. —*v.i.* **1.** to become fatigued or weary: *After his illness he tired more easily.* **2.** to become bored: *The children tired of the new game quickly.* [Old English *tēorian.*]

tire² (tīr) *also, British,* **tyre.** *n.* a band, usually of rubber, either solid or filled with air, around the rim of a wheel. Tires absorb shock and provide traction. [Possibly from *attire;* referring to a covering.]

tired (tīrd) *adj.* worn-out; weary; exhausted. —**tired′ly,** *adv.* —**tired′ness,** *n.*

tire·less (tīr′lis) *adj.* never wearying; untiring: *a tireless worker.* —**tire′less·ly,** *adv.* —**tire′less·ness,** *n.*

tire·some (tīr′səm) *adj.* tedious; boring; tiring. —**tire′some·ly,** *adv.* —**tire′some·ness,** *n.*

ti·ro (tī′rō) *n. pl.,* **ti·ros.** another spelling of **tyro.**

Ti·rol (ti rōl′, tī′rōl) another spelling of **Tyrol.**

'tis (tiz) it is.

tis·sue (tish′ōō) *n.* **1.** in animals and plants, a group of similar cells performing the same function. In the human body there are four basic types of tissue: epithelium, connective tissue, muscle, and the tissue forming the nervous system. **2.** a soft, thin, absorbent piece of paper, usually made up of two layers. It is used especially as a handkerchief. **3.** see **tissue paper. 4.** a woven fabric, usually having a light, gauzy texture. **5.** network; web: *a tissue of lies.*

tissue paper, a very thin, nearly transparent paper, used for wrapping or packing.

tit¹ (tit) *n.* **1.** see **titmouse. 2.** any of various small birds, such as the pipit. [From *titmouse.*]

tit² (tit) *n.* a teat or breast. [Old English *tit.*]

Ti·tan (tīt′ən) *n.* **1.** *Greek Mythology.* any of a race of giants who were the offspring or descendants of Uranus and Gaea. They ruled the world until overthrown by the Olympian gods. **2. titan.** a person who has great size, strength, or power.

Ti·ta·ni·a (ti tā′nē ə) *n. Medieval Legend.* the queen of the fairies.

ti·tan·ic (tī tan′ik) *adj.* **1.** having great size, strength, or power. **2. Titanic.** of, relating to, or like the Titans.

ti·ta·ni·um (tī tā′nē əm) *n.* a light, strong, silver-white metallic element found in the earth's crust and on the moon. It is used especially to make structural parts of aircraft and spacecraft. Symbol: **Ti**

tit·bit (tit′bit′) another spelling of **tidbit.**

tit for tat, something equal given in return; blow for blow.

tithe (tīth) *n.* **1.** one-tenth of a person's yearly income, paid either in labor or money, especially for the support of the church and the clergy. **2.** one-tenth of anything. **3.** any small tax, tribute, or levy. **4.** a very small part. —*v.t.,* **tithed, tith·ing.** **1.** to impose a tax of a tenth on. **2.** to give one-tenth of (one's yearly income), especially for the support of the church and the clergy.

Ti·tian (tish′ən) 1477?–1576, Venetian painter.

tit·il·late (tit′əl āt′) *v.t.,* **tit·il·lat·ed, tit·il·lat·ing. 1.** to excite or stimulate agreeably: *to titillate the imagination.* **2.** to produce a tickling sensation in. —**tit′il·la′tion,** *n.*

tit·lark (tit′lärk′) *n.* see **pipit.**

ti·tle (tīt′əl) *n.* **1.** the name by which a particular thing is identified, known, or referred to, such as a book, painting, or other work of art. **2.** a word or group of words attached to the name of a person or family as an expression of respect, or to show rank, occupation, status, and the like. **3.** a championship: *the heavyweight boxing title.* **4.** *Law.* **a.** a right that a person has to the ownership of property. **b.** something that serves as evidence of such a right, as a deed. **c.** the means by which one gets such a right. **5.** an established or recognized right; just claim. —*v.t.,* **ti·tled, ti·tling.** to give a title to; call.

ti·tled (tīt′əld) *adj.* having a title: *a titled nobleman.*

title page, a page at the beginning of a book, usually containing the title of the book and the names of the author and publisher.

title role, a role or character in a play, motion picture, or other theatrical presentation for which the presentation is named.

tit·mouse (tit′mous′) *n. pl.,* **tit·mice** (tit′mīs′). any of various songbirds. Also, **tit.**

Ti·to (tē′tō) **Marshal,** 1892–1980, the president of Yugoslavia from 1953 to 1980, born Josip Broz.

tit·ter (tit′ər) *v.i.* to laugh in a restrained or nervous way. —*n.* a restrained or nervous laugh.

tit·tle (tit′əl) *n.* **1.** a very small part or amount; tiny quantity. **2.** a small diacritical mark, as over a letter, in writing or printing. The dot over a *j* is a tittle.

Titmouse

tit·tle-tat·tle (tit′əl tat′əl) *v.i.,* **tit·tle-tat·tled, tit·tle-tat·tling.** to talk idly or foolishly; chatter. —*n.* idle or foolish talk.

tit·u·lar (tich′ə lər) *adj.* **1.** having the title or name of an office but not the powers or duties that go with it; nominal: *The former president was the titular leader of the political party.* **2.** of or relating to a title role. —**tit′u·lar·ly,** *adv.*

Ti·tus (tī′təs) *n.* **1.** A.D. 39?–81, the Roman emperor from A.D. 79 to 81. **2.** a Christian convert and disciple of Saint Paul. **3.** the book of the New Testament consisting of an epistle written to Titus by Saint Paul.

tiz·zy (tiz′ē) *n. pl.,* **tiz·zies.** *Slang.* a state of great excitement, agitation, or confusion.

Tl, the symbol for thallium.

Tm, the symbol for thulium.

TNT, a yellow organic compound, widely used as a high explosive.

to (tōō; *unstressed* too, tə) *prep.* **1.** in the direction of; toward: *Turn to the left.* **2.** in the direction of and reaching: *We took the train to Chicago. The tree fell to the ground.* **3.** as far as: *He was wet to the skin.* **4.** on, upon, or against: *Tack the carpet to the floor.* **5.** toward or into a condition of: *The glass was smashed to bits.* **6.** so as to cause or result in: *To our surprise, he agreed with the plan.* **7.** for the purpose of; for: *The police came to our aid.* **8.** until: *The store is open from nine to six.* **9.** before: *It's five minutes to three.* **10.** as compared with: *Our team won by a score of three to one.* **11.** making up; comprising: *There are four cups to a quart.* **12.** belonging with or used with: *Where is the vest to this suit?* **13.** regarding; about; concerning: *That is all there was to it.* **14. To** is also used: **a.** for indicating the receiver of an action: *She gave the letter to him.* **b.** for introducing the infinitive form of a verb: *She began to cry. I learned to swim last summer.* ▲ in this sense *to* is often used alone when the verb is understood from the rest of the statement: *You may go home when you want to.* —*adv.* **1.** forward: *The boat turned to.* **2.** into a shut or closed position: *He slammed the door to.*

toad (tōd) *n.* an animal related to and resembling the frog, having rough, dry bumpy skin and living most of the time on land rather than in water.

toad·stool (tōd′stōōl′) *n.* **1.** any of various mushrooms. **2.** *Informal.* a poisonous mushroom.

toad·y (tō′dē) *n. pl.,* **toad·ies.** a person who flatters another for personal gain; fawning

Toad

person. — *v.i.*, **toad·ied, toad·y·ing.** to be or behave like a toady: *to toady to one's superiors.*

to and fro, forward and backward.

toast¹ (tōst) *n.* sliced bread browned by heat. —*v.t.* **1.** to brown by heating, as in a toaster or over a fire. **2.** to warm thoroughly, as before a fire or heater: *to toast one's feet.* —*v.i.* to become toasted. [Old French *toster* to roast.]

toast² (tōst) *n.* **1.** the act of drinking in honor of or to the health of a person or thing: *There were several toasts to the bride and groom.* **2.** the person or thing that is honored in this way. —*v.t.* to drink to the honor or to the health of. —*v.i.* to propose or drink a toast or toasts. [From *toast*¹; from the former custom of putting spiced toast into liquor that was drunk in toasting a lady.]

toast·er (tōs′tər) *n.* a device, usually electrical, for toasting bread.

toast·mas·ter (tōst′mas′tər) *n.* a person who proposes the toasts and introduces the guests and speakers at a formal dinner or other gathering.

to·bac·co (tə bak′ō) *n. pl.*, **to·bac·cos** or **to·bac·coes. 1.** the prepared leaves of any of various plants, used for smoking, chewing, and as snuff. **2.** any of these plants, having large leaves covered with hairs, and pink, white, or red flowers that are shaped like a funnel. **3.** products prepared from the leaves of these plants, such as cigars, cigarettes, or snuff.

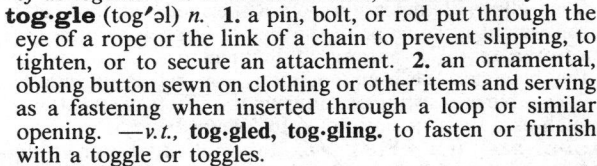

Tobacco leaves

to·bac·co·nist (tə bak′ə nist) *n.* a dealer in tobacco.

To·ba·go (tə bā′gō) *n.* an island of the Lesser Antilles, near Venezuela, forming part of the country of Trinidad and Tobago.

to·bog·gan (tə bog′ən) *n.* a long, flat-bottomed sled without runners, having a curled-up front end. Toboggans are used for coasting on snow or for transporting goods. —*v.i.* **1.** to coast or ride on a toboggan. **2.** to decline or decrease rapidly, as in value.

Toboggan

toc·sin (tok′sin) *n.* **1.** a signal or alarm sounded on a bell. **2.** a bell or other signal that is used to sound an alarm.

to·day (tə dā′) *also*, **to-day.** *n.* the present day, time, or age. —*adv.* **1.** on or during the present day. **2.** at the present time; nowadays; currently: *Fashions today are different from what they were twenty years ago.*

tod·dle (tod′əl) *v.i.*, **tod·dled, tod·dling.** to walk or move with short, unsteady steps, as a child who is just learning to walk. —*n.* the act of toddling.

tod·dler (tod′lər) *n.* a small child, especially one who is just learning to walk.

tod·dy (tod′ē) *n. pl.*, **tod·dies. 1.** a drink made with brandy or other liquor, hot water, spices, sugar, and a slice of lemon. **2.** a drink made from the fermented sap of certain kinds of East Indian palm trees. **3.** the sap of such trees.

to-do (tə dōō′) *n. pl.*, **to-dos.** *Informal.* bustle or fuss; commotion.

toe (tō) *n.* **1.** any of the five end parts of the foot. **2.** the part of a stocking, shoe, or other piece of footwear that covers the toes. **3.** the forward part of a foot or hoof. **4.** anything resembling a toe in shape, position, or function.

— *v.*, **toed, toe·ing.** —*v.t.* **1.** to furnish with a toe or toes. **2.** to drive (a nail) at an angle. **3.** to fasten or attach by nails driven in this way —*v.i.* to turn the toes in a specific direction.

to be on one's toes. to be physically or mentally alert and ready for whatever may happen.

toed (tōd) *adj.* having toes, especially a specific number or kind of toes. ▲ usually used in combination: *a three-toed sloth, square-toed shoes.*

toe·nail (tō′nāl′) *n.* **1.** a nail that grows on a toe. **2.** a nail driven at an angle. —*v.t.* to fasten or attach with nails driven at an angle.

tof·fee (tô′fē, tof′ē) *also*, **tof·fy.** *n.* a hard, chewy candy made of butter, sugar, and often nuts.

tof·fy (tô′fē, tof′ē) *n. pl.*, **tof·fies.** another spelling of **toffee.**

tog (tog) *n.* **togs.** clothes. —*v.t.*, **togged, tog·ging.** to dress or array.

to·ga (tō′gə) *n.* a loose outer garment draped over the entire body, covering the left arm and leaving the right arm bare, worn by male citizens of ancient Rome. The approximate social position of a person could be determined by the color and ornamentation of the toga he wore.

Toga

to·geth·er (tə geth′ər) *adv.* **1.** one with the other; with one another; in company: *The bride and her father walked down the aisle together.* **2.** in or into one gathering, company, mass, or body: *The whole school will meet together next week.* **3.** in or into contact, combination, or association with each other: *Mix the flour and water together.* **4.** in or into agreement, harmony, or cooperation: *Let's try to get together on this problem.* **5.** considered as a whole: *Edward knows more about this than all of us together.* **6.** at the same time; simultaneously.

tog·gle (tog′əl) *n.* **1.** a pin, bolt, or rod put through the eye of a rope or the link of a chain to prevent slipping, to tighten, or to secure an attachment. **2.** an ornamental, oblong button sewn on clothing or other items and serving as a fastening when inserted through a loop or similar opening. —*v.t.*, **tog·gled, tog·gling.** to fasten or furnish with a toggle or toggles.

To·go (tō′gō) *n.* a country in western Africa, on the Gulf of Guinea, between Ghana and Dahomey. Capital, Lomé. Area, 21,580 sq. mi. Pop. (1971 est.), 2,020,000.

toil¹ (toil) *n.* hard and exhausting work or effort. —*v.i.* **1.** to do hard and exhausting work, especially for a considerable length of time: *I toiled wearily in a wretched scrap heap* (Joseph Conrad). **2.** to move with difficulty, weariness, or pain. [Middle English *toilen* to argue, struggle.] —**toil′er,** *n.*

toil² (toil) *n. also,* **toils.** something that ensnares or entangles, as a net: *The bank robber was caught in the toils of the law.* [Middle French *toiles* nets, snares.]

toi·let (toi′lit) *n.* **1.** a fixture consisting of a water-filled basin usually having a lid, a hinged seat, and a flushing device connected to a water tank, used for the elimination

at; āpe; cär; end; mē; it; īce; hot; ōld; fôrk;
wood; fōōl; oil; out; up; turn; sing; thin; this;
hw in white; zh in treasure. The symbol ə
stands for the sound of **a** in about, **e** in taken,
i in pencil, **o** in lemon, and **u** in circus.

T

and disposal of human waste. **2.** a room containing such a fixture; bathroom. **3.** the act or process of washing, dressing, and grooming oneself. **4.** a person's dress; attire. —*adj.* of, relating to, or for the toilet.

toi·let·ry (toi′lit rē) *n. pl.,* **toi·let·ries.** any of various articles, such as soap or cologne, used in grooming oneself.

toilet water, a scented liquid serving as a light perfume, as for use after a bath; cologne.

toil·some (toil′səm) *adj.* requiring hard work; tiresome; laborious.

toil·worn (toil′wôrn′) *adj.* exhausted or worn out by toil or hard work.

to·ken (tō′kən) *n.* **1.** something that serves to indicate or represent some fact, event, object, or feeling; sign; symbol: *This gift is a token of our appreciation.* **2.** something given as an expression of affection or as a memento. **3.** a piece of metal resembling a coin, used as a substitute for money, as in paying for transportation fares. —*adj.* having little or no value, force, or effect: *a token fee, token resistance.*
  by the same token. in an equivalent manner; likewise.

To·ky·o (tō′kē ō′) *n.* the capital and largest city of Japan, in the east-central part of the island of Honshu. Area, 625 sq. mi. Pop. (1970), 8,840,942.

told (tōld) the past tense and past participle of **tell.**
  all told. counting all; in all: *She invited fifty people all told.*

To·le·do (tə lē′dō) *n.* **1.** a port city in northwestern Ohio, on Lake Erie. Pop. (1970), 383,818. **2.** a historic city in central Spain.

tol·er·a·ble (tol′ər ə bəl) *adj.* **1.** that can be endured; bearable. **2.** moderately good; passable: *a tolerable performance.* —**tol′er·a·bly,** *adv.*

tol·er·ance (tol′ər əns) *n.* **1.** the ability or willingness to accept or respect the behavior, customs, opinions, or beliefs of others. **2.** the act of tolerating. **3.** the ability to resist or endure the effects of something, such as a drug or poison, that is given in larger and larger amounts. **4.** the power or ability to endure something, such as pain. **5.** an allowable deviation from a specified standard, as in the weight of coins or in the size of a machine part.

tol·er·ant (tol′ər ənt) *adj.* **1.** inclined to accept or respect the behavior, customs, opinions, or beliefs of others. **2.** capable of resisting or enduring the effects of something, such as a drug or poison. —**tol′er·ant·ly,** *adv.*

tol·er·ate (tol′ə rāt′) *v.t.,* **tol·er·at·ed, tol·er·at·ing. 1.** to allow to exist or be done without prohibiting or interfering. **2.** to suffer or endure; put up with; bear: *How can you tolerate all that noise while you work?* **3.** to develop or have tolerance for (a drug, poison, or the like).

tol·er·a·tion (tol′ə rā′shən) *n.* **1.** the act or practice of tolerating. **2.** recognition of an individual's right to enjoy certain freedoms and privileges, especially freedom of worship.

toll¹ (tōl) *v.i.* (of a bell) to sound with slow, regular strokes; peal. —*v.t.* **1.** to cause (a bell) to sound with slow, regular strokes. **2.** to announce or summon by tolling: *The bells tolled the beginning of the church service.* —*n.* **1.** the act of tolling a bell. **2.** the sound made by a bell being tolled. [Middle English *tollen* to pull, draw.]

toll² (tōl) *n.* **1.** a tax or fixed fee paid for the right or privilege to use something, such as a bridge or highway. **2.** a charge for a particular service rendered, such as the transmission of a long-distance telephone call. **3.** a number of people or things lost, destroyed, or damaged: *The storm took a heavy toll of lives.* [Old English *toll.*]

toll booth, a booth, as at a tollgate, where a toll is collected.

toll·gate (tōl′gāt′) *n.* a gate or other barrier used to block passage until a toll is paid.

Tol·stoy, Leo (tōl′stoi) 1828–1910, Russian novelist.

Tol·tec (tol′tek) *n.* a member of an Indian nation living in Mexico from the eleventh to the thirteenth centuries. —*adj.* of, like, or relating to the Toltecs or their culture.

tol·u·ene (tol′yōō ēn′) *n.* a flammable, aromatic hydrocarbon compound made from petroleum, used in airplane fuel and as a solvent.

tom (tom) *n.* the male of certain animals, especially a cat or turkey.

tom·a·hawk (tom′ə hôk′) *n.* a light ax used as a weapon or tool by North American Indians. —*v.t.* to attack, strike, or kill with a tomahawk.

to·ma·to (tə mā′tō, tə mä′tō) *n. pl.,* **to·ma·toes. 1.** the juicy red, green, or yellow fruit of a plant related to the potato, having a smooth skin and eaten as a vegetable either raw or cooked. **2.** the plant bearing this fruit, having yellow, bell-shaped flowers.

tomb (tōōm) *n.* **1.** a vault or chamber in which a dead body is placed. **2.** any place of burial.

tom·boy (tom′boi′) *n.* a young girl who enjoys activities and interests that are usually considered to be preferred by boys.

tomb·stone (tōōm′stōn′) *n.* a stone placed at the head of a grave, usually inscribed with the dead person's name and dates of birth and death.

tom·cat (tom′kat′) *n.* a male cat.

tome (tōm) *n.* **1.** a book, especially a large, heavy, scholarly one. **2.** one of a set of books containing several volumes.

tom·fool (tom′fōōl′) *adj.* extremely stupid or foolish: *Jumping off the roof was a tomfool thing to do.* —*n.* a person who acts in a stupid or foolish manner.

tom·fool·er·y (tom′fōō′lər ē) *n. pl.,* **tom·fool·er·ies.** foolish or absurd behavior; nonsense.

to·mor·row (tə môr′ō, tə mor′ō) *also,* **to·mor·row.** *n.* **1.** the day after today: *Tomorrow is my birthday.* **2.** some indefinite time in the future: *The world of tomorrow will be very different.* —*adv.* on the day after today: *We are going away tomorrow.*

tom·tit (tom′tit′) *n.* any of various small birds, such as the titmouse and wren.

tom-tom (tom′tom′) *n.* any of various small drums, usually beaten with the hands.

ton (tun) *n.* **1.** a unit of weight equal to 2000 pounds avoirdupois in the United States and Canada. **2.** a unit of weight equal to 2240 pounds avoirdupois in Great Britain. **3.** see **metric ton. 4.** *Informal.* an extremely large quantity of anything: *I have a ton of work to do.*

ton·al (tōn′əl) *adj.* of or relating to tone or tonality.

to·nal·i·ty (tō nal′ə tē) *n. pl.,* **to·nal·i·ties. 1.** *Music.* **a.** the melodic and harmonic relation existing between the tones of a scale or musical system. **b.** a particular scale or system of tones; key. **2.** the arrangement of tones or colors in a painting.

tone (tōn) *n.* **1.** any sound considered with reference to its pitch, quality, duration, or volume. **2.** the quality of sound: *My new radio has good tone.* **3.** *Music.* **a.** a sound having definite pitch and character. **b.** a whole step. **4.** a particular style or manner of speaking or writing: *I knew he was angry by his tone of voice.* **5.** a general or prevailing character, style, or tendency, as of thought or behavior: *The tone of the meeting was serious.* **6.** a degree of tension or firmness, as of muscle. **7.** the effect of the combination of light, shade, and color in a picture: *a silvery tone.* **8.** a tint or shade of a particular color: *The painter used various tones of blue.* —*v.,* **toned, ton·ing.** —*v.t.* **1.** to give a particular tone or quality to, as in sound or color. **2.** to change or correct the color of. —*v.i.* to harmonize in color.

to tone down. to soften or lessen, as in volume, intensity, or severity.

to tone up. to increase or gain, as in strength, intensity, or vitality.

tone arm, the arm of a phonograph that holds the cartridge.

tone-deaf (tōn′def′) *adj.* unable to distinguish differences in musical pitch. —**tone′-deaf′ness,** *n.*

tong (tong, tông) *v.t.* to grasp, hold, or handle with tongs.

Ton·ga (tong′gə) *n.* an island country under British protection, in the southwestern Pacific. It is made up of about 160 small islands. Capital, Nukualofa. Land area, 270 sq. mi. Pop. (1971 est.), 90,000. Also, **Tonga Islands.**

tongs (tongz, tôngz) *n.,pl.* any of various devices for grasping objects, usually having two curved arms connected by a pivot.

tongue (tung) *n.* **1.** a movable organ attached to the floor of the mouth, used for tasting, swallowing, and, in humans, for talking. **2.** an animal's tongue prepared and used as food. **3.** a spoken language or dialect: *His native tongue is French.*

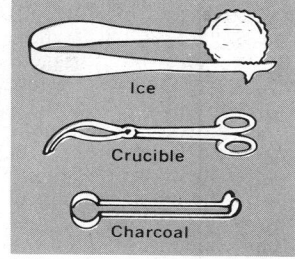

Tongs

4. a manner of speaking, especially in regard to meaning or intent: *a sarcastic tongue.* **5.** the ability to speak; power of speech: *The shy child couldn't find his tongue.* **6.** anything resembling the human tongue in shape, position, or function, such as a tapering jet of flame. **7.** a narrow strip of land projecting into a body of water. **8.** a strip of leather or other material lying under the laces or fastenings of a shoe or boot.

on the tip of one's tongue. about to be remembered or spoken: *The new girl's name is on the tip of my tongue.*

to hold one's tongue. to keep from speaking; be silent.

tongue in cheek. with sarcasm or irony.

tongue-in-cheek (tung′in chēk′) *adj.* sarcastic or insincere: *a tongue-in-cheek remark.*

tongue-tied (tung′tīd′) *adj.* unable to speak or express oneself, as from fear, shyness, or embarrassment.

ton·ic (ton′ik) *n.* **1.** anything that refreshes, invigorates, or strengthens. **2.** a medicine or drug that invigorates or strengthens. **3.** *Music.* a note on which a scale or system of tones is based. **4.** a carbonated beverage containing quinine, used for mixing with liquor, such as gin or vodka. **5.** a liquid preparation for the hair or scalp. —*adj.* **1.** refreshing; bracing; invigorating. **2.** of or relating to tone or tones. **3.** *Music.* of, relating to, or based on a tonic: *a tonic chord.*

to·night (tə nīt′) *also,* **to-night.** *n.* **1.** the night of this day. **2.** the present night; this night. —*adv.* on or during the present or coming night.

Ton·kin, Gulf of (ton′kin′, tong′kin′) a gulf in southeastern Asia, bordered by North Vietnam and China.

ton·nage (tun′ij) *n.* **1.** the carrying capacity of a ship, expressed in tons. **2.** the total amount of shipping, as of a port or nation, in terms of carrying capacity. **3.** a duty, tax, or similar charge levied on ships at so much per ton of cargo. **4.** weight measured in tons, as of goods shipped or produced.

ton·sil (ton′səl) *n.* **1.** either of a pair of oval masses of spongy tissue located on each side of the tongue at the back of the mouth in man. **2.** any of several similar masses of tissue located in the mouth or throat of various animals.

ton·sil·lec·to·my (ton′sə lek′tə mē) *n. pl.,* **ton·sil·lec·to·mies.** the surgical removal of a tonsil or tonsils.

ton·sil·li·tis (ton′sə lī′tis) *n.* inflammation of a tonsil or tonsils.

ton·so·ri·al (ton sôr′ē əl) *adj.* of or relating to a barber or his work.

ton·sure (ton′shər) *n.* **1.** a shaving of a part or all of the head of a man entering the priesthood or a monastic order. **2.** the part of the head so shaven. —*v.t.,* **ton·sured, ton·sur·ing.** to shave the head of.

too (tōō) *adv.* **1.** in addition; besides; also: *Louis is very bright and a good worker, too.* **2.** more than enough: *There were too many people in the room.* **3.** exceedingly; very: *I was not too sorry to see them go.* **4.** *Informal.* indeed. ▲ used for emphasis: *You will too do it!*

Tonsure

took (took) the past tense of **take.**

tool (tōōl) *n.* **1.** any of various devices held in the hand and used in doing work, such as a hammer, wrench, or saw. **2.** a power-driven instrument or machine used to cut and shape machinery parts. **3.** the cutting or shaping part of such an instrument or machine. **4.** a person who is used by another; dupe. **5.** anything used in or necessary to the carrying out of an action, profession, or trade: *Knowledge is a great tool.* —*v.t.* **1.** to work, shape, or mark with a tool. **2.** to provide (a factory or plant) with machinery or tools for production. —*v.i.* to work with a tool or tools.

toot (tōōt) *v.t.* to cause (a horn, whistle, or the like) to sound with a short, quick blast or blasts. —*v.i.* to produce a short, quick blast or blasts. —*n.* **1.** a short, quick blast, such as that produced by a horn. **2.** the act of producing such a sound.

tooth (tōōth) *n. pl.,* **teeth. 1.** in human beings and certain other animals with backbones, one of the hard structures set in the jaws and supported by the gums, used especially for biting and chewing. A human adult has thirty-two permanent teeth. **2.** a similar structure in certain animals without backbones. **3.** something resembling a tooth in shape, position, or use, such as one of the projecting pieces on a comb. —*v.t.* **1.** to furnish with teeth: *to tooth a saw.* **2.** to make jagged, as an edge. —**tooth′like′,** *adj.*

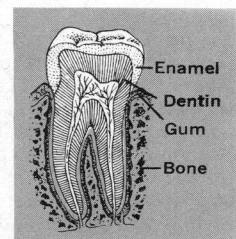

—Enamel
—Dentin
—Gum
—Bone

Tooth

tooth·ache (tōōth′āk′) *n.* a pain in a tooth, the teeth, or the area surrounding the teeth.

tooth·brush (tōōth′brush′) *n. pl.,* **tooth·brush·es.** a small, narrow brush with a long handle, used for cleaning the teeth.

toothed (tōōtht) *adj.* **1.** having teeth, especially of a specific kind or number. ▲ usually used in combination: *a saber-toothed tiger.* **2.** having notches; serrated; jagged: *a toothed leaf.*

tooth·less (tōōth′lis) *adj.* **1.** having no teeth. **2.** without force or effect; ineffectual: *a toothless law.*

---

at; āpe; cär; end; mē; it; īce; hot; ōld; fôrk; wood; fōōl; oil; out; up; turn; sing; thin; **th**is; hw in white; zh in treasure. The symbol ə stands for the sound of **a** in about, **e** in taken, **i** in pencil, **o** in lemon, and **u** in circus.

tooth·paste (tōōth′pāst′) *n.* a paste for cleaning teeth.

tooth·pick (tōōth′pik′) *n.* a small, narrow sliver of wood, plastic, or similar material, used to remove food or other matter from between the teeth.

tooth·some (tōōth′səm) *adj.* **1.** pleasing to the taste; tasty. **2.** attractive; pleasant.

top¹ (top) *n.* **1.** the highest part of anything: *the top of a flagpole, the top of a page.* **2.** the cover or lid of something, or a part forming a cover: *a box top.* **3.** a garment for the upper half of the body, usually part of a two-piece outfit: *a pajama top.* **4.** the part of certain plants that grows above the ground. **5.** the highest or leading position or rank: *to graduate at the top of one's class.* **6.** the highest pitch or degree: *The child was screaming at the top of his voice.* **7.** a platform around the head of a lower mast of a ship, used as a place to stand on for extending the rigging of the topmast. *—adj.* **1.** of or at the top: *the top drawer, the top floor of a building.* **2.** first or highest in rank, position, or quality; foremost: *He is the top man in his field.* **3.** greatest or maximum in degree or amount: *to drive at top speed.* *—v.t.,* **topped, top·ping. 1.** to provide with a top or cover; put a top on. **2.** to serve as, be at, or form the top of: *Cherries topped the cake.* **3.** to reach or go beyond the top of. **4.** to surpass; exceed. **5.** to cut off or remove the top of: *to top a tree before cutting it down.* **6.** to hit (a ball) above the center, as in golf or tennis. [Old English *topp.*]
  to top off. to complete, especially by adding a finishing touch: *to top off a concert with an encore.*

top² (top) *n.* a toy usually having a rounded body that tapers to a point on which it is spun. [Old English *top.*]

to·paz (tō′paz) *n.* a lustrous crystalline mineral, occurring in a variety of colors and used as a gem, especially in the yellow variety.

top·coat (top′kōt′) *n.* a lightweight overcoat.

To·pe·ka (tə pē′kə) *n.* the capital of Kansas, in the northeastern part of the state. Pop. (1970), 125,011.

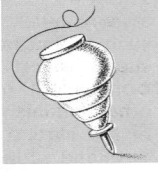

Top²

top·flight (top′flīt′) *adj.* excellent or superior; first-rate.

top·gal·lant (top′gal′ənt, tə gal′ənt) *n.* the mast, sail, rigging, or the like above the topmast. *—adj.* of or relating to the topgallant.

top hat, a man's hat usually made of silk, having a high, cylindrical crown and a small brim. It is worn on formal occasions.

top·heav·y (top′hev′ē) *adj.* too heavy at the top.

top·ic (top′ik) *n.* the subject of a speech, discussion, written composition, or the like.

top·i·cal (top′i kəl) *adj.* **1.** relating to or dealing with matters of current or local interest: *a topical speech, a topical book.* **2.** of, relating to, or belonging to a specific area or place; local. **3.** *Medicine.* relating to, applied to, or affecting a particular part or organ of the body.

Top hat

top·knot (top′not′) *n.* **1.** a knot, tuft, or crest of hair or feathers on the top of the head. **2.** a bow or other ornament worn on the top of the head.

top·mast (top′mast′) *n.* the second section of a mast above the lower mast.

top·most (top′mōst′) *adj.* at the very top; uppermost; highest.

top·notch (top′noch′) *adj. Informal.* first-rate or superior.

to·pog·ra·pher (tə pog′rə fər) *n.* an expert in topography.

top·o·graph·i·cal (top′ə graf′i kəl) *adj.* of, relating to, or involving topography: *a topographical map, a topographical survey.* Also, **top·o·graph·ic** (top′ə graf′ik). **—top′o·graph′i·cal·ly,** *adv.*

to·pog·ra·phy (tə pog′rə fē) *n. pl.,* **to·pog·ra·phies.** the detailed description or drawing of the natural and artificial surface features of a place or area, such as hills, valleys, lakes, roads, and bridges.

top·ping (top′ing) *n.* a sauce, frosting, or other garnish put on food: *a dessert topping.*

top·ple (top′əl) *v.,* **top·pled, top·pling.** *—v.i.* **1.** to fall forward; tumble: *The bookcase toppled over.* **2.** to lean or hang over, as if about to fall. *—v.t.* **1.** to cause to fall or tumble; overturn: *to topple a lamp, to topple a government.*

tops (tops) *adj. Informal.* the very best; first-rate.

top·sail (top′sāl′, top′səl) *n.* **1.** on a square-rigged ship, the square sail next above the lowest sail on a mast. **2.** on a fore-and-aft-rigged ship, the square or triangular sail above the gaff of a lower sail.

top·se·cret (top′sē′krit) *adj.* of, relating to, or containing highly confidential information.

top·side (top′sīd′) *n.* the upper part of a ship's side, especially above the water line. *—adv. also,* **topsides.** to or on the upper portions of a ship; on deck.

top·soil (top′soil′) *n.* the top or upper part of the soil that contains most of the materials essential to plant growth, including minerals and humus.

top·sy·tur·vy (top′sē tur′vē) *adv.* **1.** in reverse of the usual or natural order; upside down. **2.** in or into a state of utter confusion or disorder. *—adj.* **1.** turned upside down. **2.** utterly confused or disordered.

toque (tōk) *n.* **1.** a small, close-fitting woman's hat with a soft crown and either a small, rolled brim or no brim at all. **2.** a small plumed hat with a brim, worn by men and women in the sixteenth century.

To·rah (tôr′ə) *also,* **To·ra.** *n. Judaism.* **1.** the first five books of the Old Testament; Pentateuch. **2.** the hand-written scrolls containing the Pentateuch, used in a synagogue during services. **3.** *also,* **torah.** the whole body of Jewish teaching, thought, and literature.

Toque

torch (tôrch) *n. pl.,* **torch·es. 1.** a flaming light, usually consisting of a stick of wood, or some material soaked in a substance that will burn wound around the end of a stick. **2.** any of various hand-held devices producing a very hot flame, used especially in welding. **3.** something considered to be a source or symbol of enlightenment, inspiration, or guidance: *the torch of liberty.* **4.** *British.* a flashlight.

torch·bear·er (tôrch′ber′ər) *n.* **1.** a person who carries a torch. **2.** a person who is a source of enlightenment, truth, or inspiration.

torch·light (tôrch′līt′) *n.* the light given off by a torch or torches.

tore (tôr) the past tense of **tear¹.**

tor·e·a·dor (tôr′ē ə dôr′) *n.* see **matador.**

to·re·ro (tə rer′ō) *n. pl.,* **to·re·ros.** a matador, especially one who fights on foot.

tor·ment (*v.,* tôr ment′; *n.,* tôr′ment) *v.t.* **1.** to cause (someone) great mental or physical pain or suffering. **2.** to worry, annoy, or aggravate. *—n.* **1.** extreme mental or physical pain or suffering; agony. **2.** the source of such pain or suffering.

tor·men·tor (tôr men′tər) *also,* **tor·ment·er.** *n.* a person or thing that torments.

torn (tôrn) the past participle of **tear¹.**

tor·na·do (tôr nā′dō) *n. pl.,* **tor·na·does** or **tor·na·dos.** a dark column of air shaped like a funnel, extending down from a mass of dark, black clouds and rotating at speeds of up to 500 miles per hour. Tornadoes travel rapidly and suck up and destroy almost everything in their path.

To·ron·to (tə ron′tō) *n.* a city in Canada, in the south-eastern part of the country, on Lake Ontario. Pop. (1971), 698,634.

tor·pe·do (tôr pē′dō) *n. pl.,* **tor·pe·does. 1.** a large, self-driven, underwater missile shaped like a cigar, that can be launched from ships, submarines, or airplanes. Torpedoes are often used for underwater attack against enemy ships. **2.** a small explosive charge placed on a railroad track. It goes off when a train passes over it, and the noise serves as a signal. **3.** a type of firework that explodes when thrown against a hard surface. —*v. t.,* **tor·pe·doed, tor·pe·do·ing.** to damage or sink with or as if with a torpedo.

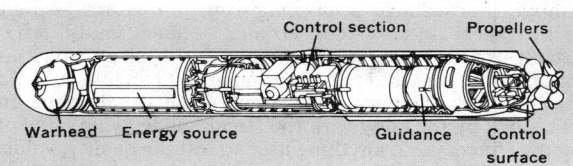

Torpedo

torpedo boat, see **PT boat.**

tor·pid (tôr′pid) *adj.* **1.** sluggish; dull. **2.** dormant, as an animal in hibernation. **3.** lacking the power of motion or feeling; numb. —**tor·pid′i·ty,** *n.* —**tor′pid·ly,** *adv.*

tor·por (tôr′pər) *n.* the state or quality of being torpid.

torque (tôrk) *n.* a force that causes or tends to cause something to turn or twist.

tor·rent (tôr′ənt, tor′ənt) *n.* **1.** a violent, swiftly flowing stream, especially of water. **2.** a violent, overwhelming flow of anything: *a torrent of insults.*

tor·ren·tial (tô ren′chəl) *adj.* of, resembling, or caused by a torrent: *a torrential rainfall.*

tor·rid (tôr′id, tor′id) *adj.* **1.** subjected to or parched by the intense heat of the sun: *the torrid regions of the world.* **2.** intensely hot or burning; scorching: *a torrid climate.* **3.** passionate; ardent: *a torrid love story.* —**tor·rid′i·ty,** *n.*

Torrid Zone, a warm region between the Tropic of Cancer and the Tropic of Capricorn.

tor·sion (tôr′shən) *n.* **1.** the act of twisting or the state of being twisted. **2.** a strain put on an object when one end is twisted in one direction while the other end is held firm or twisted in the opposite direction.

tor·so (tôr′sō) *n. pl.,* **tor·sos. 1.** the trunk of the human body. **2.** a statue of this.

tort (tôrt) *n. Law.* any wrong or injury that does not involve breach of contract and for which the wronged person or party may sue in a civil court.

tor·til·la (tôr tē′yə) *n.* a thin, round, unleavened cake made from water and cornmeal and baked on a griddle.

tor·toise (tôr′təs) *n. pl.,* **tor·tois·es** or **tor·toise.** a turtle that lives on land.

tor·toise-shell (tôr′təs shel′) *adj.* **1.** made of tortoise shell. **2.** having the mottled yellow-and-brown colors of tortoise shell.

tortoise shell 1. the hard, mottled, yellow-and-brown material making up the outer shell of certain turtles. It is used especially to make combs, small decorative objects, and furniture inlay. **2.** any of a group of butterflies with mottled yellow, brown, and black coloration.

tor·tu·ous (tôr′chōō əs) *adj.* **1.** having many twists, turns, or bends; winding: *a tortuous road.* **2.** not direct, straightforward, or frank; devious. —**tor′tu·ous·ly,** *adv.* —**tor′tu·ous·ness,** *n.*

tor·ture (tôr′chər) *v.t.,* **tor·tured, tor·tur·ing. 1.** to subject to severe physical abuse or cruelty: *The enemy tortured the prisoners.* **2.** to cause to suffer extreme mental or physical pain or suffering: *Nightmares of the accident tortured him.* —*n.* **1.** the act of causing severe physical abuse or cruelty. **2.** a source or cause of extreme mental or physical pain or suffering. —**tor′tur·er,** *n.*

tor·tur·ous (tôr′chər əs) *adj.* relating to, characterized by, or causing torture: *a torturous punishment.*

To·ry (tôr′ē) *n. pl.,* **To·ries. 1.** a member of a political party in Great Britain that favored rule by the king and the preservation of the established Anglican Church. Since 1832, it has been known as the Conservative Party. **2.** any colonial American who remained loyal to England at the time of the American Revolution. **3.** *also,* **tory.** any person or group that is conservative in politics. —*adj.* of, relating to, or like a Tory or Tories.

Tos·ca·ni·ni, Ar·tu·ro (tos′kə nē′nē; är toor′ō) 1867–1957, Italian conductor.

toss (tôs) *v.t.* **1.** to throw lightly up into or through the air, especially with the hand or hands: *Please toss me a towel.* **2.** to fling or move back and forth: *The waves tossed the little boat.* **3.** to lift quickly or suddenly: *The horse tossed its head.* **4.** to mix (a salad) lightly, especially so as to coat with a dressing. **5.** to cause to fall to the ground: *The horse tossed its rider.* **6.** to throw (a coin) into the air so as to decide something by the side that lands upward. —*v.i.* **1.** to move about restlessly, especially in one's sleep: *He tossed and turned all night.* **2.** to be flung or moved back and forth. **3.** to throw a coin into the air so as to decide something by the side that lands upward. —*n., pl.* **toss·es. 1.** the act of tossing. **2.** the distance over which something is or can be tossed.

to toss off. a. to do quickly, casually, and easily. **b.** to drink or eat all at once.

toss-up (tôs′up′) *n.* an even chance or possibility: *It's a toss-up whether or not it will rain today.*

tot (tot) *n.* **1.** a small child. **2.** a small amount of something, as an alcoholic beverage.

to·tal (tōt′əl) *adj.* **1.** being, relating to, or making up a whole; full; entire: *I paid the total amount of the bill.* **2.** absolute; complete; utter: *a total disaster, a total lack of respect.* —*n.* the whole amount; sum. —*v.,* **to·taled, to·tal·ing;** *also, British,* **to·talled, to·tal·ling.** —*v.t.* **1.** to compute or find the sum of; add up: *to total a bill.* **2.** to reach to the sum of: *The damage to our home totaled six hundred dollars.* —*v.i.* to amount to: *The bill totals to ten dollars.*

to·tal·i·tar·i·an (tō tal′ə ter′ē ən) *adj.* of or relating to totalitarianism. —*n.* a person who favors or supports totalitarianism.

to·tal·i·tar·i·an·ism (tō tal′ə ter′ē ə niz′əm) *n.* a system of government in which one political party aims at total control over the lives of people, as by using a powerful secret police, restricting meetings and assemblies, and censoring books, newspapers, radio and television broadcasts, and other forms of communication.

to·tal·i·ty (tō tal′ə tē) *n. pl.,* **to·tal·i·ties. 1.** the total amount; whole; sum. **2.** the state of being whole or complete.

at; āpe; cär; end; mē; it; īce; hot; ōld; fôrk; wood; fōōl; oil; out; up; turn; sing; thin; **th**is; hw in white; zh in treasure. The symbol ə stands for the sound of a in about, e in taken, i in pencil, o in lemon, and u in circus.

T

to·tal·ly (tōt′əl ē) *adv.* completely; entirely; wholly.

tote (tōt) *v.t.,* **tot·ed, tot·ing.** *Informal.* to haul or carry: *to tote heavy packages home from the store.* —**tot′er,** *n.*

tote bag, a large handbag used by women, especially to carry small packages and other items.

to·tem (tō′təm) *n.* **1.** among North American Indians, an animal, plant, or other natural object taken as the emblem of a clan or other family group. **2.** a representation of this, especially one carved and painted on poles.

totem pole, a pole consisting of carved and painted representations of totems, erected in front of a dwelling by the American Indians of the northwestern Pacific coast.

Totem pole

tot·ter (tot′ər) *v.i.* **1.** to walk or move with weak or unsteady steps: *The baby tottered across the room.* **2.** to shake or sway as if about to fall or collapse; be unsteady: *The glass tottered on the edge of the table.* —*n.* the act of tottering.

tou·can (tōō′kan) *n.* any of various tropical American birds having a heavy body, a very large beak, and brightly colored feathers.

touch (tuch) *v.t.* **1.** to bring a hand, finger, or other part of the body on or against: *She accidentally touched the hot stove and burned her hand.* **2.** to bring (something) against or into contact with something else: *Tom touched the match to the paper.* **3.** to be against; come into contact with: *His hand touched mine.* **4.** to affect the emotions or feelings of: *The news of his death touched us deeply.* **5.** to have an effect or bearing on; concern: *The new taxes will touch everyone.* **6.** to use or partake of: *The child did not touch any of her dinner.* **7.** to color slightly; tinge: *His hair was touched with gray.* **8.** to injure or mar slightly: *The plants were touched by the frost.* **9.** to compare with; equal: *No one can touch that scientist in his field.* **10.** to arrive at or visit in passing: *I am going ashore when we touch port.* —*v.i.* **1.** to come into or be in contact: *Our hands touched.* **2.** to make a brief stop in passing: *The freighter will touch at New York.* —*n. pl.,* **touch·es.** **1.** the sense by which objects are perceived through direct contact with a part of the body. **2.** the quality of an object as perceived by touching or coming into contact with it: *The soft touch of silk.* **3.** the act of touching: *The balloon burst at the touch of the pin.* **4.** a slight sign or indication: *His work shows a touch of genius.* **5.** a small amount; little bit: *a touch of salt, a touch of rheumatism* **6.** a light stroke, especially one made to change or improve something: *The artist put the final touch to his painting.* **7.** communication or contact: *Have you kept in touch with your friends during the summer?* **8.** a distinctive manner or way of doing something: *The room showed the touch of a decorator.* **9.** the manner of striking or touching the keys of a keyboard instrument or machine, as a piano or typewriter.

to touch down. (of an aircraft) to land.

to touch off. a. to cause to explode; ignite. **b.** to cause to happen: *A misunderstanding touched off the argument.*

to touch on. to deal with or mention briefly or in passing: *The politician's speech hardly touched on the important issues.*

to touch up. to improve by making slight changes: *to touch up a painting.*

touch-and-go (tuch′ən gō′) *adj.* of uncertain outcome: *The ball game was touch-and-go up to the last few seconds.*

touch·back (tuch′bak′) *n.* *Football.* a play in which the ball is declared dead beyond a team's goal line after it has been put there by the opposing team. No points are awarded for a touchback.

touch·down (tuch′doun′) *n.* **1.** *Football.* **a.** a scoring play worth six points, made by being in possession of the ball on or beyond the opponent's goal line. **b.** a score made in this way. **2.** the act of landing an aircraft. **3.** the moment of contact with the ground of a landing aircraft.

touched (tucht) *adj.* **1.** emotionally stirred; moved: *She was touched by the lost child's tears.* **2.** *Informal.* slightly unbalanced mentally.

touch football, a form of football in which a ball carrier is stopped by being touched with one or both hands rather than by being tackled.

touch·ing (tuch′ing) *adj.* stirring or appealing to the emotions or feelings: *a touching scene in a movie.* —*prep.* with respect to; as to; concerning. —**touch′ing·ly,** *adv.*

touch·stone (tuch′stōn′) *n.* **1.** a hard, black stone, as basalt or jasper, used to test the fineness of an alloy of gold or silver, by comparing the color of the streak made on the stone by the alloy with the streak made by an alloy of known fineness. **2.** anything used to test the quality, value, or genuineness of something.

touch·y (tuch′ē) *adj.,* **touch·i·er, touch·i·est.** **1.** easily offended; very sensitive. **2.** requiring caution, tact, and careful handling: *a touchy situation.* —**touch′i·ly,** *adv.* —**touch′i·ness,** *n.*

tough (tuf) *adj.* **1.** able to withstand great pressure or strain without breaking: *Canvas is a tough fabric.* **2.** difficult to cut, tear, or chew: *a tough piece of meat.* **3.** able to endure great strain, hardship, or difficulty: *The pioneers in the West had to be tough.* **4.** harsh; stern: *The traffic laws in this town are tough.* **5.** difficult to do, deal with, or accomplish: *a tough job, a tough question.* **6.** rough; brutal; violent: *a tough neighborhood.* **7.** *Informal.* unhappy or unfortunate: *He's had a tough life.* —*n.* a rough, brutal, and often violent person; ruffian; thug. —**tough′ly,** *adv.* —**tough′ness,** *n.*

tough·en (tuf′ən) *v.t., v.i.* to make or become tough or tougher.

Tou·louse (tōō lōōz′) *n.* a city in southern France. Pop. (1968), 370,796.

Tou·louse-Lau·trec, Hen·ri de (tōō lōōs′ lô trek′; än rē′) 1864–1901, French painter and illustrator.

tou·pee (tōō pā′) *n.* a small wig worn by men to cover baldness.

tour (toor) *n.* **1.** a journey in which many places are visited, usually for short periods of time: *We took a tour of the Greek islands last summer.* **2.** a short journey or trip: *to make a tour of a museum.* **3.** a circuit or journey, as of a theatrical company or speaker, made to a number of places in order to give performances or lectures. **4.** a period of time in which some required task or service is fulfilled: *a tour of duty in the military service.* —*v.t.* to make a tour of or through: *They toured France on their vacation.* —*v.i.* to go on tour.

tour de force (toor′də fôrs′) a feat of unusual strength, skill, or ingenuity.

tour·ism (toor′iz′əm) *n.* **1.** the business of providing services for tourists. **2.** traveling for pleasure.

tour·ist (toor′ist) *n.* a person who travels for pleasure. —*adj.* of or for tourists.

tour·ma·line (toor′mə lin) *n.* a glassy or lustrous mineral containing boron and aluminum, occurring in a variety of colors. Red and green tourmalines are often used as gems.

tour·na·ment (toor′nə mənt, tur′nə mənt) *n.* **1.** a series of contests involving two or more persons or teams:

a chess tournament, a tennis tournament. **2.** a formal medieval combat between two mounted knights armed with lances or other weapons.

tour·ney (toor′nē, tur′nē) *n. pl.,* **tour·neys.** another word for **tournament.**

tour·ni·quet (tur′nə kit) *n.* a device used to stop bleeding by pressing on a blood vessel, especially a strip of cloth or bandage that is tightened by twisting with a stick.

tou·sle (tou′zəl) *v.t.,* **tou·sled, tou·sling.** to put into disorder; make messy; dishevel: *The wind tousled her hair.* —*n.* an untidy, disheveled mass, especially of hair.

tout (tout) *Informal. v.i.* to try to get customers, employment, or support, especially in a brash way: *The campaign manager touted for votes.* —*v.t.* **1.** to praise or publicize in an exaggerated way. **2.** to give or sell information about (a racehorse) to a better. —*n.* a person who touts. —**tout′er,** *n.*

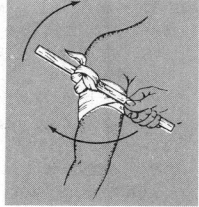
Tourniquet

tow¹ (tō) *v.t.* to pull, drag, or draw behind, especially with a rope, chain, or the like. —*n.* **1.** the act of towing or the state of being towed. **2.** something that is towed. **3.** see **towline.** [Old English *togian* to draw, pull.]

tow² (tō) *n.* coarse, shorter fibers of flax or hemp used to make yarn and twine. [Old English *tow-* spinning.]

to·ward (tôrd, tə wôrd′) *also,* **to·wards.** *prep.* **1.** in the direction of: *The puppy ran toward the house.* **2.** with respect to; concerning; regarding: *What are his feelings toward our plan?* **3.** near in time; shortly before: *The snow stopped toward morning.* **4.** as a help to; in order to get: *He saved his allowance toward a new bicycle.*

tow·boat (tō′bōt′) *n.* another word for **tugboat.**

tow·el (tou′əl) *n.* a piece of absorbent material, especially paper or terry cloth, used for wiping or drying. —*v.t.,* **tow·eled, tow·el·ing;** *also, British,* **tow·elled, tow·el·ling.** to wipe or dry with a towel: *to towel oneself after swimming.*

to throw in the towel. *Informal.* to give up; admit defeat.

tow·er (tou′ər) *n.* a tall but fairly narrow structure, often forming a part of and rising above a church, castle, or other building. —*v.i.* to rise or extend to a great height: *The skyscraper towered above the other buildings.*

tow·er·ing (tou′ər ing) *adj.* **1.** very tall; lofty: *Towering palm trees lined the beach.* **2.** very great; outstanding: *the towering genius of Beethoven.* **3.** very violent or intense: *a towering rage.*

Tower of London, a historic fortress and prison on the north bank of the Thames, in London, England.

tow·head (tō′hed′) *n.* a person having very pale blond hair. —**tow′head′ed,** *adj.*

tow·hee (tou′hē′, tō′hē′) *n.* any of several North American finches resembling a sparrow. Also, **chewink.**

tow·line (tō′līn′) *n.* a rope, chain, or the like used for towing.

town (toun) *n.* **1.** a group of houses and public and private buildings, larger than a village but smaller than a city. **2.** any densely populated place: *New York is an exciting town.* **3.** the people of a town: *The town elected a new mayor.* **4.** the

Tower

business or industrial section of a town or city: *Mother goes into town to shop for groceries twice a week.*

town crier, formerly, a person employed to make public proclamations or announcements in the streets of a town.

town hall, a building that houses the offices of officials of a town or is used for town meetings.

town meeting 1. a meeting of the people who live in a town. **2.** in New England, a meeting of the qualified voters of a town to act upon town business.

town·ship (toun′ship′) *n.* **1.** a division of a county, having some of the powers of municipal government. **2.** in surveys of public land, an area containing thirty-six sections of one square mile each.

towns·man (tounz′mən) *n. pl.,* **towns·men** (tounz′mən). **1.** a person who lives in a town. **2.** a person who lives in one's own town.

towns·peo·ple (tounz′pē′pəl) *n., pl.* the people of a town.

tow·path (tō′path′) *n. pl.,* **tow·paths** (tō′pathz′). a path along the bank of a canal or river used in towing boats.

tow·rope (tō′rōp′) *n.* a rope used in towing, especially a hawser or cable used for towing boats.

tox·e·mi·a (tok sē′mē ə) *also,* **tox·ae·mi·a.** *n.* blood poisoning caused by toxins.

tox·ic (tok′sik) *adj.* **1.** of, relating to, or caused by poison. **2.** poisonous: *a toxic drug.*

tox·ic·i·ty (tok sis′ə tē) *n.* the state or quality of being toxic.

tox·i·col·o·gist (tok′sə kol′ə gist) *n.* a doctor who specializes in toxicology.

tox·i·col·o·gy (tok′sə kol′ə jē) *n.* the branch of medical science that deals with the nature, effects, and detection of poisons and the treatment of poisoning.

tox·in (tok′sin) *n.* any poisonous product of animal or vegetable cells. The toxins produced by harmful bacteria cause the symptoms of many diseases.

toy (toi) *n.* **1.** an object for a child to play with. **2.** something of little or no value or importance. —*v.i.* to play or trifle: *to toy with a pencil. Jane toyed with the idea of going home for Christmas.* —*adj.* **1.** of, like, or used as a toy. **2.** smaller than is usual or standard, as certain breeds of dog.

trace¹ (trās) *n.* **1.** something left behind showing that some person, place, thing, or event has existed or taken place: *The archaeologist found traces of an ancient temple.* **2.** a track made by the passage of someone or something, as a footprint or tire mark. **3.** a very small amount: *I tasted a trace of mint in the drink. There was a trace of sarcasm in his tone.* **4.** a line drawn by a recording instrument, such as an electrocardiograph. —*v.,* **traced, trac·ing.** —*v.t.* **1.** to follow the track, trail, or path of; pursue: *to trace a missing person.* **2.** to follow the course, development, or history of: *to trace the origin of a word.* **3.** to mark out: *to trace a figure in the sand, to trace a route on a map.* **4.** to copy (something) by following lines as seen through a transparent sheet placed over it. —*v.i.* to have its origin; go back in time: *Their friendship traces back to childhood.* [Old French *tracier* to follow a path, mark out.] —**trace′a·ble,** *adj.*

at; āpe; cär; end; mē; it; īce; hot; ōld; fôrk; wood; fōōl; oil; out; up; turn; sing; thin; this; hw in white; zh in treasure. The symbol ə stands for the sound of a in about, e in taken, i in pencil, o in lemon, and u in circus.

trace² (trās) *n.* either of the two straps, ropes, or chains by which the harness of a draft animal is attached to the vehicle it pulls. [Old French *trais,* plural of *trait* a pulling, harness strap.]

trac·er (trā′sər) *n.* **1.** a person or thing that traces. **2.** any of various devices for making tracings of drawings. **3.** an inquiry sent from place to place to locate someone or something that is missing. **4.** an easily detected and located substance, usually a radioisotope, that is put into some system, as the human body, to study the movements and biological or chemical processes inside the system. **5.** a projectile, such as a bullet or shell, treated with a chemical compound that causes its path to be marked by a trail of fire or smoke.

trac·er·y (trā′sər ē) *n. pl.,* **trac·er·ies.** ornamental work forming geometric or curved patterns, used especially in stonework or embroidery.

tra·che·a (trā′kē ə) *n. pl.,* **tra·che·ae** (trā′kē ē′). the tube extending from the larynx to the bronchi. Also, **windpipe.** —**tra′che·al,** *adj.*

Tracery

tra·che·ot·o·my (trā′kē ot′ə mē) *n.* a surgical operation in which an opening is made through the neck into the trachea, usually performed when air cannot flow normally to the lungs because of an obstruction in the throat.

track (trak) *n.* **1.** a mark or set of marks left behind by a person, animal, or object in motion: *There were tire tracks in the snow. The deer's tracks were easy to follow.* **2.** a course along which anything moves; path; route: *the track of a storm, a track through the woods.* **3.** a course of action or way of proceeding: *Your answer is not quite correct, but you are on the right track.* **4.** a rail or set of parallel rails on which a vehicle, such as a railroad car, travels. **5.** a course laid out for racing. **6.** see **track and field.** —*v.t.* **1.** to follow the tracks or scent of: *to track wild game.* **2.** to discover, pursue, or learn by following tracks: *to track down an old friend.* **3.** to observe and record the path of: *to track a hurricane, to track a space vehicle.* **4.** to make marks with (something) carried on one's feet: *to track mud on a carpet.* —**track′er,** *n.*

in one's tracks. *Informal.* exactly where one is at the moment: *The explosion stopped him in his tracks.*

to keep track of. to keep informed about or in contact with: *to keep track of my old friends.*

to lose track of. to fail to keep informed about or in contact with.

track and field, a group of competitive sports events involving running, jumping, walking, and throwing, such as the pole vault, shot put, and hurdles.

track·less (trak′lis) *adj.* **1.** without or unmarked by paths or trails: *a trackless wilderness.* **2.** not running on tracks or rails.

track meet, an athletic contest made up of track and field events.

tract¹ (trakt) *n.* **1.** a stretch or expanse of land; area; region: *a tract of woodland.* **2.** a group of parts or organs in the body that together have a particular function: *the digestive tract, the urinary tract.* [Latin *tractus* a drawing out.]

tract² (trakt) *n.* a booklet or pamphlet, especially one on a religious or political subject. [Latin *tractātus* handling, treatment.]

trac·ta·ble (trak′tə bəl) *adj.* **1.** easily controlled, managed, or influenced; docile: *a tractable horse.* **2.** easily worked or handled; malleable: *a tractable metal.* —**trac′ta·bil′i·ty,** *n.* —**trac′ta·bly,** *adv.*

trac·tion (trak′shən) *n.* **1.** the act of drawing or pulling something, such as a vehicle or load, along a road or other surface. **2.** the state of being drawn or pulled. **3.** the power used for drawing or pulling: *steam traction.* **4.** the friction that causes a body to hold firmly to a surface. A deep tread in tires provides better traction on snow-covered roads.

trac·tor (trak′tər) *n.* **1.** a motor vehicle having rubber tires or treads. It is used especially on farms for hauling heavy loads over rough ground. **2.** a truck having a powerful motor and a driver's cab, used to pull a trailer with a heavy load.

Tractor

trade (trād) *n.* **1.** the business of buying and selling; exchange of goods; commerce: *foreign trade, domestic trade.* **2.** the exchange of one thing for another; swap: *The little boy tried to make a trade of his roller skates for a baseball mitt.* **3.** something that a person does to earn a living, especially a job requiring manual or mechanical skill: *My father is an electrician by trade.* **4.** people or firms engaged in the same business or occupation: *the building trade.* **5.** regular customers; clientele: *That restaurant caters to the theater trade.* **6. trades.** see **trade wind.** —*v.,* **trad·ed, trad·ing.** —*v.i.* **1.** to engage in buying and selling; be in commerce: *He trades in electrical appliances.* **2.** to exchange one thing for another. **3.** to do business; shop: *We trade at the local grocery store.* —*v.t.* **1.** to exchange or swap: *David traded places with his sister so that she could see the parade better.* **2.** to buy and sell.

to trade in. to give in exchange as payment or part payment for something else: *to trade in an old car for a new one.*

to trade on. to take advantage of: *to trade on someone's friendship.*

trade-in (trād′in′) *n.* a used car, appliance, or the like, given or received as payment or part payment for a new one.

trade·mark (trād′märk′) *n.* a mark, picture, or word used by a merchant or manufacturer to identify and distinguish his goods and services from those of his competitors. A trademark is usually registered with the government and cannot be used by anyone else. —*v.t.* **1.** to place a trademark on. **2.** to register as a trademark.

trade name 1. a name, often registered as a trademark, used by a merchant or manufacturer to distinguish his goods or services from those of his competitors. **2.** the name by which an article, service, or the like is commonly known to the trade. **3.** the name under which a firm carries on business.

trad·er (trā′dər) *n.* **1.** a person whose business is buying and selling. **2.** a ship used in trading.

trade school, see **vocational school.**

trades·man (trādz′mən) *n. pl.,* **trades·men** (trādz′mən). a person who carries on trade; shopkeeper.

trade union *also, British,* **trades union. 1.** a labor union made up of workers in a particular trade or craft. **2.** any labor union.

trade wind, either of two winds that blow steadily toward the equator. The trade wind north of the equator comes from the northeast. The trade wind south of the equator comes from the southeast.

trading post, a store or station set up by a trader or trading company in a sparsely settled or frontier region, where the local people can obtain goods, often in exchange for local products.

trading stamp, a stamp given to a customer when he buys something in a store. They can be exchanged in various quantities for merchandise.

tra·di·tion (trə dish′ən) *n.* **1.** the handing down of knowledge, beliefs, customs, or the like from one generation to another. **2.** the knowledge, beliefs, customs, or the like handed down in this way.

tra·di·tion·al (trə dish′ən əl) *adj.* of, coming from, or in accordance with tradition. —**tra·di′tion·al·ly,** *adv.*

● **Traditional grammar** can be described as the set of grammatical rules that have traditionally been taught to students of English in our schools. Traditional grammar is based on the belief that there should be a fixed set of rules governing the English language, and that any expression which breaks these rules is incorrect. Traditional grammarians believe that it is possible for a qualified person to distinguish between good and bad use of the language.

Many distinguished writers and editors endorse traditional grammar. Because they use the English language professionally and have great respect and affection for it, they are deeply concerned about the present state of the language. They feel that English is deteriorating. They say that the language is under attack from people who either do not know, or do not agree with, the traditional rules of grammar. They maintain that unless traditional rules are upheld, the language will eventually become so vague and sloppy that people will have trouble understanding each other.

In recent years, traditional grammar has been sharply criticized by many *linguists,* or language scholars. They state that English is not becoming worse, but simply becoming different. Their studies have led them to the conclusion that all living languages change constantly, and that change in language is in no way harmful. They point out that many common English expressions that today are considered correct by even the strictest traditional grammarian were thought to be very bad at the time they first came into the language. Linguists also believe that it is impossible for language to ever change so fast that people cannot understand each other. They hold that because language is essential to human communication, people would resist any change that was so drastic that it interfered with this communication.

Traditional grammarians believe that speech or writing which follows grammatical rules is clearer and more precise. Linguists argue that ungrammatical English, although it may be considered less acceptable, is certainly not less meaningful. They maintain that the meaning of "She *don't* like school" or "He didn't say *nothing*" is certainly just as clear as the grammatically correct "She *doesn't* like school" or "He didn't say *anything.*"

Many traditional grammarians believe that the discipline of grammar must be mastered by a writer before he can express himself effectively and creatively. On the other hand, linguists contend that writing that follows traditional grammatical rules is not necessarily better or more beautiful than writing that does not. They point out that William Shakespeare, generally considered to be the greatest writer in history, continually breaks the rules of traditional grammar. Many other famous authors, such as Mark Twain and James Joyce, also frequently depart from grammatical rules. Linguists further maintain that the question of whether one style of writing is superior to another really cannot be judged by any artificial standard. F. Scott Fitzgerald, William Faulkner, and Ernest Hemingway, three modern American novelists, each write in

a very different style, and each is considered a highly accomplished writer by critics. Linguists have also shown that even the strongest advocates of traditional rules frequently break them in their own writing, because these rules are often artificial and arbitrary and therefore conflict with the way a person expresses himself naturally.

Linguists would not say that a student should be required to learn no grammar at all. What they do say is that grammatical rules should be based on the way English actually *is* used rather than the way people think it *should* be used. The measure that linguists use for the grammatical status of a word is *Standard English* (English as it is used by the majority of educated people). A linguist will not tell you whether a certain expression is good or bad, but whether or not it is considered acceptable by educated speakers or writers. A linguist is a scientific observer of language, and therefore he does not feel it is his function to express his personal opinions about words. A zoologist, who is a scientific observer of animals, would not say that a deer is a better animal that a wolf, or that he disapproves of the behavior of wolves and likes deer better. He would simply describe the true nature of a wolf, without making personal judgments. In the same way, a linguist describes the true nature of language.

Linguists believe that the purpose of language is to communicate one's thoughts as effectively as possible, and that any rule that makes writing or speaking unclear, awkward, or unnatural should not be followed.

tra·duce (trə dōōs′, trə dyōōs′) *v.t.,* **tra·duced, tra·duc·ing.** to speak falsely or maliciously of; slander. —**tra·duc′er,** *n.*

Tra·fal·gar, Cape (trə fal′gər) a cape in southwestern Spain, on the Atlantic Ocean. It was the site of a naval battle in 1805 in which the fleets of France and Spain were defeated by a British fleet led by Horatio Nelson.

traf·fic (traf′ik) *n.* **1.** automobiles, boats, people, or the like moving along or through an area or route: *There was little traffic on the highway in the early morning hours.* **2.** an exchange of goods, especially for profit; buying and selling; trade. **3.** dealing or bargaining in something illegal or improper: *The police attempted to stop drug traffic in the city.* **4.** the business done by a railroad, steamship, or other transportation line. **5.** the number of passengers or amount of freight transported by such a line. —*v.i.,* **trafficked, traf·fick·ing.** to carry on trade, especially illegally; deal: *The man was arrested for trafficking in stolen goods.* —**traf′fick·er,** *n.*

traffic circle, a circular intersection for two or more roads around which traffic moves in one direction, allowing vehicles to enter or leave any of the roads without disturbing the flow of traffic. Also, **rotary.**

traffic light, a signal, usually with red and green and sometimes amber or yellow lights, that controls the flow of traffic by changing color or by blinking on and off, especially at an intersection. Also, **traffic signal, stoplight.**

tra·ge·di·an (trə jē′dē ən) *n.* an actor who specializes in playing tragic roles.

trag·e·dy (traj′ə dē) *n. pl.,* **trag·e·dies. 1.** a drama in which life is viewed or treated seriously, usually having a

at; āpe; cär; end; mē; it; īce; hot; ōld; fôrk; wood; fōōl; oil; out; up; turn; sing; thin; this; hw in white; zh in treasure. The symbol ə stands for the sound of **a** in about, **e** in taken, **i** in pencil, **o** in lemon, and **u** in circus.

T

sad ending. **2.** any work of literature that is like a dramatic tragedy. **3.** a sad, dreadful, or disastrous event: *The tragedy in the coal mine took the lives of seventeen men.*

trag·ic (traj′ik) *adj.* **1.** of, relating to, or like tragedy, especially dramatic tragedy: *The play had a tragic ending.* **2.** very sad, dreadful, or disastrous: *a tragic accident, a tragic decision.* Also, **trag·i·cal** (traj′i kəl). —**trag′i·cal·ly,** *adv.*

trag·i·com·e·dy (traj′i kom′ə dē) *n. pl.,* **trag·i·com·e·dies.** a drama containing both tragic and comic elements, usually having a happy ending.

trail (trāl) *n.* **1.** a passage or path through a wild or uninhabited region. **2.** a mark, scent, or path made by an animal or person: *The dog lost the fox's trail at the river's edge.* **3.** something that follows along behind: *The car gave off a trail of fumes.* —*v.t.* **1.** to follow behind, especially in a careless or lagging manner: *The children trailed the parade down the street.* **2.** to drag or draw along or behind: *The boys trailed their kites on the ground.* **3.** to follow the track or scent of: *The police trailed the thieves to their hideout.* **4.** to be behind or losing, as in a contest or game. —*v.i.* **1.** to hang down or be drawn behind: *The train of the bride's dress trailed along the floor.* **2.** to move or flow slowly; drift: *The audience trailed in after the intermission.* **3.** to grow over or along the ground or other surface: *Ivy trailed down the side of the building.* **4.** to be losing, as in a contest or game: *Our team trailed in the fifth inning, but went on to win.* **5.** to become less gradually: *Conversation trailed off as the evening wore on.*

trail·blaz·er (trāl′blā′zər) *n.* **1.** a person who marks a trail for others; pathfinder. **2.** a pioneer in any field: *a trailblazer in medicine.*

trail·er (trā′lər) *n.* **1.** a person or thing that trails. **2.** a vehicle without a motor, designed to be pulled by a car, truck, or similar vehicle. It is used for transporting goods or the like. **3.** a similar vehicle equipped to be used as a home.

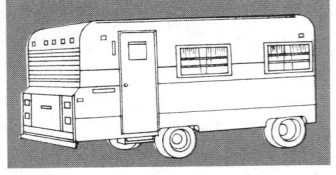

Trailer *(def. 3)*

trailing arbutus, an evergreen vine that grows along the ground in shady areas and bears clusters of small, very fragrant pink or white blossoms.

train (trān) *n.* **1.** a connected line of railroad cars. **2.** a group of people, animals, or vehicles traveling together, especially in a long line or procession: *a wagon train, a mule train.* **3.** a connected series or succession, as of events or ideas: *to follow a train of thought.* **4.** a series of events, circumstances, or conditions coming from or following something: *The hurricane left wrecked boats and flooded homes in its train.* **5.** something that is drawn along behind, especially that part of a dress or robe that trails on the ground behind the wearer. **6.** a group of attendants; following; retinue: *The king was accompanied by a train of servants.* **7.** a series of interconnected mechanical parts for transmitting motion, such as the wheels and pinions of a watch. —*v.t.* **1.** to develop or mold the character, thoughts, and behavior of; bring up; rear: *to train a child to respect the rights of others.* **2.** to make able or skilled by instruction and practice, as in a particular field or profession: *to train a new salesman.* **3.** to prepare physically, as with a regular drill, diet, and exercise: *to train a boxer.* **4.** to instruct (an animal) so as to make it obedient or capable of doing certain tasks or tricks. **5.** to cause to grow or lie in a desired form or direction: *to train one's hair to curl under, to train ivy to grow up a wall.* **6.** to focus or direct; aim: *to train a rifle at a target.*

—*v.i.* to undergo and follow a course of instruction or discipline: *to train for a race, to train for a job. John trained for several years to be an electrician.*

train·ee (trā nē′) *n.* a person who is undergoing training, especially vocational or military training.

train·er (trā′nər) *n.* **1.** a person who trains, especially a person who is responsible for the physical training and conditioning of an athlete, race horse, or the like. **2.** a device used in training.

train·ing (trā′ning) *n.* **1.** the act, process, or method of a person who trains. **2.** the state of being trained.

train·load (trān′lōd′) *n.* the amount that a train can carry.

train·man (trān′mən) *n. pl.,* **train·men** (trān′mən). a person who works for a railroad, such as a brakeman.

traipse (trāps) *v.i.,* **traipsed, traips·ing.** *Informal.* to walk about idly or aimlessly.

trait (trāt) *n.* an aspect or quality, as of a person's character: *The knight possessed bravery, honesty, and other noble traits.*

trai·tor (trā′tər) *n.* **1.** a person who commits treason. **2.** a person who betrays any trust. —**trai′tress,** *n.*

trai·tor·ous (trā′tər əs) *adj.* **1.** of, relating to, or like a traitor. **2.** of, relating to, or like treason. —**trai′tor·ous·ly,** *adv.*

tra·jec·to·ry (trə jek′tər ē) *n. pl.,* **tra·jec·to·ries.** the curved path followed by a bullet, ballistic missile, meteor, or the like, moving through space or the atmosphere.

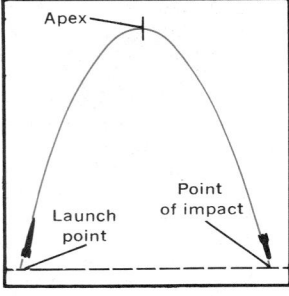

Trajectory

tram (tram) *n. British.* **1.** another word for **streetcar.** **2.** a four-wheeled vehicle that runs on tracks, used to carry coal in a mine.

tram·mel (tram′əl) *n.* **1.** *also,* **trammels.** anything that hinders freedom, action, or progress: *to shake off the trammels of the world and of public opinion* (William Hazlitt). **2.** a shackle for hobbling a horse and training him to amble. **3.** a hook in a fireplace for hanging pots over the fire. **4.** a net for catching birds or fish. —*v.t.,* **tram·meled, tram·mel·ing;** *also, British,* **trammelled, tram·mel·ling.** **1.** to hinder the freedom, action, or progress of; impede. **2.** to entangle in a net; ensnare.

tramp (tramp) *v.i.* **1.** to walk with a firm, heavy step: *He tramped into the house in his overshoes.* **2.** to travel on foot; walk: *Only a fool would tramp across the countryside in this weather.* **3.** to travel or wander as a tramp or vagabond. —*v.t.* **1.** to press or compress by stepping heavily upon; trample: *to tramp the grass.* **2.** to travel over or through on foot: *The hikers tramped the forest.* —*n.* **1.** a person who wanders or travels from place to place, has no permanent home or means of support, and usually begs for food, money, or temporary work. **2.** the sound of a heavy step: *We could hear the tramp of the marching soldiers.* **3.** a long walk; hike. **4.** a cargo ship, especially a steamship, that does not trade regularly between fixed ports, but takes cargo wherever obtainable and for any port. —**tramp′er,** *n.*

tram·ple (tram′pəl) *v.,* **tram·pled, tram·pling.** —*v.t.* **1.** to tread on so heavily as to injure, crush, or destroy: *Do not trample the flowers.* **2.** to treat cruelly or harshly: *When the people began to rebel, the dictator trampled them.* —*v.i.* to tread heavily. —*n.* the act of trampling. —**tram′pler,** *n.*

tram·po·line (tram'pə lēn', tram'pə lēn') *n.* a piece of gymnastic equipment consisting of canvas or net attached by springs to a metal frame on legs, used for acrobatic tumbling.

Trampoline

tram·way (tram'wā') *n. British.* **1.** a streetcar track. **2.** a railway used in a coal mine for hauling loads.

trance (trans) *n.* **1.** a semiconscious state resembling sleep, as that produced by hypnotism. **2.** a dazed or stunned state; stupor. **3.** a state of deep mental absorption or concentration.

tran·quil (trang'kwəl) *adj.* free from disturbance; calm; peaceful: *Grandfather recalled his tranquil childhood. The lake was tranquil.* —**tran'quil·ly,** *adv.*

tran·quil·ize (trang'kwə līz') *v.t., v.i.,* **tran·quil·ized, tran·quil·iz·ing.** to make or become tranquil.

tran·quil·iz·er (trang'kwə lī'zər) *also,* **tran·quil·liz·er.** *n.* any of certain drugs that produce a calming effect by reducing tension, nervous strain, and the like.

tran·quil·li·ty (trang kwil'ə tē) *also,* **tran·quil·i·ty.** *n.* the state or quality of being tranquil.

trans- *prefix* **1.** across; through; over: *transatlantic.* **2.** so as to change completely: *transform.*

trans. **1.** transitive. **2.** transportation. **3.** transactions.

trans·act (tran sakt', tran zakt') *v.t.* to conduct and carry through, especially business affairs: *to transact a sale of real estate.* —*v.i.* to do business. —**trans·ac'tor,** *n.*

trans·ac·tion (tran sak'shən, tran zak'shən) *n.* **1.** the act of transacting or the state of being transacted. **2.** something that is or has been transacted, especially a business deal. **3. transactions.** a published record of the proceedings of a society, club, or the like.

trans·at·lan·tic (trans'ət lan'tik) *adj.* **1.** that crosses the Atlantic Ocean: *a transatlantic telephone call, a transatlantic flight.* **2.** on the opposite side of the Atlantic Ocean.

tran·scend (tran send') *v.t.* **1.** to pass or go beyond the limits of; exceed: *The concept of infinity transcends human understanding.* **2.** to be greater or better than in some respect or quality; surpass: *This painting transcends the artist's earlier works.*

tran·scend·ence (tran sen'dəns) *n.* the act of transcending or the state of being transcendent.

tran·scend·ent (tran sen'dənt) *adj.* **1.** surpassing or excelling others; superior; preeminent. **2.** beyond ordinary or natural limits; transcendental. —**tran·scend'ent·ly,** *adv.*

tran·scen·den·tal (tran'sen dent'əl) *adj.* **1.** superior; transcendent. **2.** beyond or contrary to human experience or to what is natural; supernatural. **3.** *Mathematics.* not capable of being a solution of a rational algebraic equation. Pi is a transcendental number. —**tran'scen·den'tal·ly,** *adv.*

trans·con·ti·nen·tal (trans'kon tə nent'əl) *adj.* **1.** that crosses a continent: *a transcontinental highway.* **2.** on the opposite side of a continent.

tran·scribe (tran skrīb') *v.t.,* **tran·scribed, tran·scrib·ing.** **1.** to make a written or typewritten copy of; rewrite or type: *to transcribe the minutes of the meeting from shorthand notes.* **2.** to arrange or adapt (a musical composition) for a different voice or instrument. **3.** to make a recording of (a radio program or the like) to be broadcast later. —**tran·scrib'er,** *n.*

tran·script (tran'skript') *n.* a written or typewritten copy: *The judge reviewed the transcript of the trial.*

tran·scrip·tion (tran skrip'shən) *n.* **1.** the act of transcribing. **2.** a transcript; copy. **3.** an adaptation or arrangement of a musical composition for another voice or instrument. **4.** a recording, as on magnetic tape, of a radio program or the like to be broadcast later.

tran·sept (tran'sept) *n.* **1.** the part forming the arms of a cross in a church that is built in the shape of a cross. **2.** either side of this part.

trans·fer (*v.,* trans fur', trans'fər; *n.,* trans'fər) *v.,* **transferred, trans·fer·ring.** —*v.t.* **1.** to move or remove from one person, place, or the like to another: *She transferred the bracelet from her right wrist to her left.* **2.** to make over the title or possession of to another: *The man transferred the property to his son.* **3.** to convey (a drawing, design, pattern, or the like) from one surface to another. —*v.i.* **1.** to transfer oneself: *She transferred to a new school.* **2.** to be transferred: *The office will transfer to new quarters.* **3.** to switch from one bus, train, airplane, or the like, to another, usually with little or no extra charge: *to transfer at Chicago.* —*n.* **1.** the act of transferring or the state of being transferred. **2.** something that is transferred, especially a drawing, design, pattern, or the like moved from one surface to another. **3.** a ticket allowing a passenger to continue his journey on another vehicle, usually with little or no extra charge. **4.** the place or means of transferring. —**trans·fer'a·ble,** *adj.*

trans·fer·ence (trans fur'əns) *n.* the act of transferring or the state of being transferred.

transfer RNA, see **RNA.**

trans·fig·u·ra·tion (trans fig'yə rā'shən) *n.* **1.** the act of transfiguring or the state of being transfigured. **2. the Transfiguration. a.** in the New Testament, the miraculous change in the appearance of Christ that took place on a mountain in the presence of the Apostles Peter, James, and John. **b.** the church festival commemorating this event. It falls on August 6.

trans·fig·ure (trans fig'yər) *v.t.,* **trans·fig·ured, trans·fig·ur·ing.** **1.** to change the outward appearance of; change in form or figure. **2.** to give a glorified appearance to; glorify.

trans·fix (trans fiks') *v.t.* **1.** to make motionless, as from awe or fear: *They were transfixed by the sight of the burning building.* **2.** to pierce through with a sharpened instrument; impale: *to transfix a butterfly with a pin.*

trans·form (trans fôrm') *v.t.* **1.** to change in shape, form, or appearance: *A little paint will soon transform this old car.* **2.** to change the character, condition, or nature of: *The chemist transformed the solid into a liquid.* **3.** to change (one form of energy) into another, as mechanical energy into electricity, or electric energy into light or heat. **4.** to change (an electric current) to a higher or lower voltage or to direct or alternating current.

trans·for·ma·tion (trans'fər mā'shən) *n.* the act of transforming or the state of being transformed.

trans·form·er (trans fôr'mər) *n.* **1.** a person or thing that transforms. **2.** a device for transferring electric energy from one alternating current circuit to another, usually with a change in voltage and current.

trans·fuse (trans fyōoz') *v.t.,* **trans·fused, trans·fus·ing.** **1.** to pour (a liquid) from one container into another; transfer by pouring. **2.** to transfer (blood) from one individual to another.

at; āpe; cär; end; mē; it; īce; hot; ōld; fôrk; wood; fōol; oil; out; up; turn; sing; thin; this; hw in white; zh in treasure. The symbol ə stands for the sound of a in about, e in taken, i in pencil, o in lemon, and u in circus.

trans·fu·sion (trans fyōō′zhən) *n.* the act of transfusing, especially the transfer of blood from one individual to another.

trans·gress (trans gres′) *v.i.* to break or violate a law, commandment, or the like; sin. —*v.t.* **1.** to break or violate (a law, commandment, or the like). **2.** to go beyond (a limit or bound): *a restriction that transgresses the rights of the individual.* —**trans·gres′sor,** *n.*

trans·gres·sion (trans gresh′ən) *n.* the act or instance of transgressing, especially the breaking of a law or commandment.

tran·ship (tran ship′) *v.t.* another spelling of **transship.** —**tran·ship′ment,** *n.*

tran·sience (tran′shəns) *n.* the state or quality of being transient. Also, **transiency.**

tran·sient (tran′shənt) *adj.* **1.** being or remaining only for a short time; not lasting or durable; transitory: *transient fame, transient beauty.* **2.** stopping only for a short time; passing through: *a transient hotel guest.* —*n.* a person or thing that is transient, especially a person who passes through a place or stays in it only for a short time: *This boarding house caters to transients.* —**tran′sient·ly,** *adv.*

tran·sis·tor (tran zis′tər) *n.* **1.** a very small electronic device containing semiconductors, which is used instead of vacuum tubes to control and to increase the strength of electric current in television sets, computers, and other electronic equipment. **2.** a radio equipped with transistors.

tran·sis·tor·ize (tran zis′tə rīz′) *v.t.,* **tran·sis·tor·ized, tran·sis·tor·iz·ing.** to equip with transistors.

trans·it (tran′sit, tran′zit) *n.* **1.** the act or instance of passing across or through; movement from one place or point to another: *We were delayed in transit by traffic.* **2.** the act of carrying or the state of being carried from one place or point to another: *The transit of fresh fruit to markets must be done quickly.* **3.** a transition or change. **4.** a telescope used in surveying to measure horizontal and vertical angles. **5.** *Astronomy.* **a.** the passage of a planet directly between the earth and the sun so that it can be seen as a black dot moving across the disk of the sun. **b.** the passage of a celestial body across the celestial meridian. —*v.t.* to pass across or through.

tran·si·tion (tran zish′ən) *n.* **1.** a passage from one state, position, condition, or activity to another: *the transition from childhood to maturity.* **2.** *Music.* **a.** a change of key. **b.** a passage connecting two parts, themes, or the like. —**tran·si′tion·al,** *adj.* —**tran·si′tion·al·ly,** *adv.*

tran·si·tive (tran′sə tiv) *adj.* (of verbs) taking a direct object to complete the action of the sentence. In the sentence *Ted hit the ball, hit* is a transitive verb. —*n.* a verb that is transitive.

tran·si·to·ry (tran′sə tôr′ē) *adj.* lasting for only a short time: *Physical beauty is passing . . . a transitory possession* (Tennessee Williams).

Trans·jor·dan (trans jôrd′ən) *n.* see **Jordan.**

trans·late (trans lāt′) *v.,* **trans·lat·ed, trans·lat·ing.** —*v.t.* **1.** to express in or change into another language: *to translate Shakespeare's plays into German.* **2.** to explain by using other words, terms, or signs: *The scientist's theory cannot be translated into simpler terms.* **3.** to change from one place, form, or condition to another: *to translate dreams into reality.* —*v.i.* **1.** to act as translator: *The guide translated for the tourists.* **2.** to be able to be translated: *Jokes often do not translate well into another language.* —**trans·lat′a·ble,** *adj.*

trans·la·tion (trans lā′shən) *n.* **1.** the act of translating or the state of being translated. **2.** something that is produced as a result of translating, especially a literary work that has been translated from the language in which it was originally written.

trans·la·tor (trans lā′tər) *n.* a person who translates.

trans·lit·er·ate (trans lit′ə rāt′) *v.t.,* **trans·lit·er·at·ed, trans·lit·er·at·ing.** to change (letters or words of one alphabet) into characters of another alphabet that have corresponding sounds. —**trans·lit′er·a′tion,** *n.*

trans·lu·cence (trans lōō′səns) *n.* the state or quality of being translucent. Also, **trans·lu·cen·cy** (trans lōō′sən sē).

trans·lu·cent (trans lōō′sənt) *adj.* allowing light to pass through, but not allowing objects on the other side to be clearly seen. Frosted glass is translucent. —**trans·lu′cent·ly,** *adv.*

trans·mi·grate (trans mī′grāt) *v.i.,* **trans·mi·grat·ed, trans·mi·grat·ing.** (of a soul) to pass to another body at death. —**trans′mi·gra′tion,** *n.*

trans·mis·si·ble (trans mis′ə bəl) *adj.* capable of being transmitted.

trans·mis·sion (trans mish′ən) *n.* **1.** the act of transmitting or the state of being transmitted. Also, **transmittal.** **2.** something that is transmitted, such as a television picture or a telegram. **3.** in an automobile, a series of gears and mechanical devices for transmitting power from the engine to the driving wheels. **4.** the sending out of signals, as in radio or television communication.

trans·mit (trans mit′) *v.t.,* **trans·mit·ted, trans·mit·ting.** **1.** to send or cause to go from one person or place to another: *to transmit freight, to transmit a disease.* **2.** to communicate or convey: *The frown on Father's face transmitted his anger to us.* **3.** to pass on by inheritance or heredity; hand down: *Genes are transmitted from one generation to another by chromosomes.* **4.** to cause (something, such as light, heat, or sound) to pass through a medium: *A tuning fork transmits sound waves through the air.* **5.** (of a medium) to allow (something, such as light, heat, or sound) to pass through: *Water transmits sound.* **6.** to send out (signals, a radio or television program, or the like) on electromagnetic waves.

trans·mit·tal (trans mit′əl) *n.* the act of transmitting or the state of being transmitted.

trans·mit·ter (trans mit′ər) *n.* **1.** a person or thing that transmits. **2.** a device that produces radio or television signals for sending from an antenna. **3.** a device in a telegraph or telephone that changes the message into electrical impulses that can be carried over wires.

trans·mu·ta·tion (trans′myōō tā′shən) *n.* **1.** the act of transmuting or the state of being transmuted. **2.** *Physics.* the conversion of one element into another by a change in its nuclear structure.

trans·mute (trans myōōt′) *v.t.,* **trans·mut·ed, trans·mut·ing.** to change in form, nature, or quality.

trans·o·ce·an·ic (trans′ō shē an′ik) *adj.* **1.** that extends across or crosses an ocean: *a transoceanic voyage.* **2.** on the opposite side of the ocean.

tran·som (tran′səm) *n.* **1.** a window above a door or other window, usually hinged to a horizontal bar. **2.** a horizontal bar that divides a window or separates a door or window from a window above.

tran·son·ic (tran son′ik) *also,* **trans·son·ic.** *adj.* of, relating to, or moving at a speed just above or just below the speed of sound.

trans·pa·cif·ic (trans′pə sif′ik) *adj.* **1.** that extends across or crosses the Pacific Ocean. **2.** on the opposite side of the Pacific Ocean.

trans·par·en·cy (trans per′ən sē, trans par′ən sē) *n. pl.,* **trans·par·en-**

Transom

cies. 1. the state or quality of being transparent: *the transparency of cellophane.* Also, **trans·par·ence** (trans-per′əns, trans par′əns). **2.** something transparent, especially a photographic slide.

trans·par·ent (trans per′ənt, trans par′ənt) *adj.* **1.** allowing light to pass through, so that objects on the other side can be clearly seen. The lenses in a pair of eyeglasses or the panes of a window are transparent. **2.** easily understood or seen through; obvious: *His excuse for not doing his work was a transparent lie.* **3.** frank; open; candid. —**trans·par·ent·ly,** *adv.* —**trans·par·ent·ness,** *n.*

tran·spi·ra·tion (tran′spə rā′shən) *n.* the act or process of transpiring, especially the giving off of waste products in the form of vapor by a living organism.

tran·spire (tran spīr′) *v.,* **tran·spired, tran·spir·ing.** —*v.i.* **1.** to happen; occur: *It was impossible to predict what would transpire at the end of the book.* **2.** to become known; come to light. **3.** to give off waste products in the form of vapor, as through the pores of the skin. —*v.t.* to give off (waste products) in the form of vapor.

trans·plant (*v.,* trans plant′; *n.,* trans′plant) *v.t.* **1.** to remove (a plant) from one place and plant it again in another. **2.** to move from one place to another; transport: *The rancher transplanted the entire herd to a new pasture.* **3.** to transfer (skin, an organ, or the like) from one person or animal to another or from one part of the body to another. —*v.i.* to be capable of being transplanted. —*n.* **1.** something that is transplanted: *The transplant flourished in new soil. The patient received a kidney transplant.* **2.** the act or process of transplanting. —**trans·plant′a·ble,** *adj.* —**trans·plant′er,** *n.*

trans·port (*v.,* trans pôrt′; *n.,* trans′pôrt) *v.t.* **1.** to bring or carry from one place or person to another: *to transport freight by ship.* **2.** to carry away by strong emotion: *The beautiful music transported her.* **3.** to punish (a criminal) by deporting him from his own country. —*n.* **1.** the act of transporting: *The transport of supplies was halted during the labor strike.* **2.** a ship used to carry military personnel. **3.** an airplane used to transport passengers, mail, or freight. **4.** the state or condition of being carried away by strong emotion: *a transport of delight.* —**trans·port′a·ble,** *adj.* —**trans·port′er,** *n.*

trans·por·ta·tion (trans′pər tā′shən) *n.* **1.** the act of transporting or the state of being transported. **2.** a means of transporting: *Do you need transportation to school?* **3.** the cost of transporting, especially for traveling by bus, train, or the like: *Transportation to and from work was thirty cents each way.*

trans·pose (trans pōz′) *v.t.,* **trans·posed, trans·pos·ing. 1.** to reverse the order of; interchange: *The typist accidentally transposed the former President's initials from JFK to KFJ.* **2.** to move (something) from one place or time to another: *The author transposed a medieval story to the twentieth century.* **3.** to write or perform (music) in a key other than the original or given key. **4.** to transfer (an algebraic term) from one side of an equation to the other, changing the plus or minus sign to maintain equality. —**trans·pos′er,** *n.*

trans·po·si·tion (trans′pə zish′ən) *n.* **1.** the act of transposing or the state of being transposed. **2.** something that has been transposed. Also, **trans·po·sal** (trans pō′zəl). —**trans·po·si·tion·al,** *adj.*

trans·ship (trans ship′) *also,* **tran·ship.** *v.t.,* **trans·shipped, trans·ship·ping.** to transfer (cargo) from one ship, train, truck, or the like, to another. —**trans·ship′ment,** *n.*

trans·son·ic (trans son′ik) another spelling of **transonic.**

tran·sub·stan·ti·a·tion (tran′səb stan′shē ā′shən) *n.* **1.** the transformation of one substance into another. **2.** the doctrine that the bread and wine of the Holy Communion service become the body and blood of Christ, although the appearance and taste are unchanged.

Trans·vaal (trans väl′) *n.* a province of the Republic of South Africa, in the northeastern part of the country.

trans·ver·sal (trans vur′səl) *n.* a line that intersects two or more lines.

trans·verse (trans vurs′) *adj.* lying across or in a crosswise direction. —*n.* something that is transverse. —**trans·verse′ly,** *adv.*

Tran·syl·va·ni·a (tran′sil vā′nē ə) *n.* a historic region in central Romania.

trap (trap) *n.* **1.** a device used for catching game or other animals. **2.** any trick to catch a person unawares: *The lawyer's question was a trap that caused the defendant to admit his guilt.* **3.** a bend in a pipe, usually U-shaped or S-shaped, that fills with liquid to form a seal, as to keep air in the pipe or to prevent the return flow of a gas. **4.** a device used to hurl clay pigeons or the like into the air for target shooting. **5.** in certain games, an obstacle or hazard, especially a sand trap in a golf course. —*v.,* **trapped, trap·ping.**

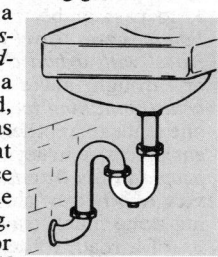

Trap *(def. 3)*

—*v.t.* **1.** to catch in a trap; entrap: *The hunters trapped the bear.* **2.** to furnish or provide with a trap or traps. **3.** to stop and hold (gas, liquid, or the like) with a trap. —*v.i.* to set traps for game; be a trapper.

trap door, a hinged or sliding door in a floor, ceiling, or roof.

tra·peze (tra pēz′, trə pēz′) *n.* a short, swinging horizontal bar suspended from two ropes, used in gymnastics and acrobatics.

tra·pe·zi·um (trə pē′zē əm) *n. pl.,* **tra·pe·zi·ums** or **tra·pe·zi·a** (trə pē′zē ə). a figure having four sides with none of the sides parallel.

trap·e·zoid (trap′ə zoid′) *n.* a figure having four sides with only two sides parallel.

trap·per (trap′ər) *n.* a person who traps wild animals, especially for their fur.

trap·pings (trap′ingz) *n.,pl.* **1.** an ornamented cloth or covering spread over the harness or saddle of a horse. **2.** outer or superficial adornments: *The king wore a purple robe and other trappings of royalty.*

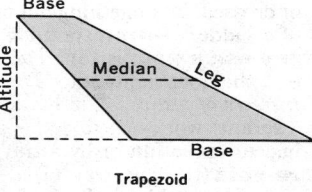

Trapezoid

trap·shoot·ing (trap′shoo′ting) *n.* a sport in which shooters fire shotguns at clay pigeons hurled into the air. —**trap′shoot′er,** *n.*

trash (trash) *n.* **1.** worthless or discarded objects or matter. **2.** worthless or foolish talk, writing, ideas, or the like. **3.** a low, worthless person or persons.

trash·y (trash′ē) *adj.,* **trash·i·er, trash·i·est.** of, like, or

at; āpe; cär; end; mē; it; īce; hot; ōld; fôrk; wood; fo͞ol; oil; out; up; turn; sing; thin; this; hw in white; zh in treasure. The symbol ə stands for the sound of **a** in about, **e** in taken, **i** in pencil, **o** in lemon, and **u** in circus.

containing trash; worthless; inferior: *a trashy movie.*
—**trash′i·ness,** *n.*

trau·ma (trô′mə, trou′mə) *n. pl.,* **trau·ma·ta** (trô′mə tə, trou′mə tə) or **trau·mas. 1.** a severe and painful emotional shock, usually having a lasting effect on the personality. **2.** a bodily wound or injury.

trau·mat·ic (trô mat′ik, trou mat′ik) *adj.* of, relating to, like, or caused by a trauma.

trav·ail (trə vāl′, trav′āl) *n.* **1.** difficult or tiring labor. **2.** intense pain or suffering, especially when caused by great hardship. —*v.i.* to exert oneself; work hard; toil.

trav·el (trav′əl) *v.,* **trav·eled, trav·el·ing;** *also, British,* **trav·elled, trav·el·ling.** —*v.i.* **1.** to go from one place to another; make a journey: *He traveled through Ireland.* **2.** to go from place to place as a traveling salesman. **3.** to pass or be transmitted from one point to another: *Sound waves travel through water.* **4.** to associate with: *to travel with a bad crowd.* —*v.t.* to move or journey over or through; make a tour of: *The candidate traveled the country making speeches.* —*n.* **1.** the act of traveling from one place to another. **2. travels.** a long trip to many different places; journey: *Mr. Richardson met many interesting people in his travels.*

trav·eled (trav′əld) *also, British,* **trav·elled.** *adj.* **1.** having done much traveling, especially to foreign countries. **2.** (of a road, route, or the like) used by many travelers.

trav·el·er (trav′ə lər) *also, British,* **trav·el·ler.** *n.* **1.** a person who travels. **2.** *British.* a traveling salesman.

traveling salesman, a person, usually working for a firm, who travels from place to place selling or taking orders for goods.

trav·e·logue (trav′ə lôg′, trav′ə log′) *also,* **trav·e·log.** *n.* **1.** a lecture describing a trip, as to a foreign country, often illustrated with slides or films. **2.** a motion picture about a particular country or region.

trav·erse (trav′ərs, trə vurs′) *v.,* **trav·ersed, trav·ers·ing.** —*v.t.* **1.** to pass across, over, or through: *The climbers traversed the mountain range.* **2.** to go back and forth over or along; cross and recross. —*v.i.* **1.** to move or go along, across, or back and forth: *The skier traversed down the slope.* **2.** to go or turn from side to side; pivot. —*n.* **1.** the act of traversing or crossing. **2.** a distance traversed or crossed. **3.** something put or lying across, such as a rung of a ladder. —**trav′ers·a·ble,** *adj.* —**trav′ers·er,** *n.*

trav·es·ty (trav′is tē) *n. pl.,* **trav·es·ties. 1.** a distorted or ridiculous imitation: *The jury's unfair verdict was a travesty of justice.* **2.** in literature, a mocking treatment of a serious work or subject. —*v.t.,* **trav·es·tied, trav·es·ty·ing.** to make fun of by a travesty.

tra·vois (trə voi′, trav′oi) *n. pl.,* **tra·vois.** a V-shaped sled formerly used by Indians of the Great Plains, made up of a platform or net supported by two long poles. The front ends of the poles are harnessed to a horse, dog, or other draft animal, and the rear ends of the poles are dragged along the ground.

trawl (trôl) *n.* **1.** a strong net, usually shaped like a bag, towed over the ocean bottom to catch fish. **2.** a long line usually resting near the ocean floor and supported by buoys, having short lines with baited hooks every few feet along its length. It is used to catch fish. —*v.i.* to fish with a trawl.

trawl·er (trô′lər) *n.* **1.** a fishing boat used for trawling. **2.** a person who fishes with a trawl.

tray (trā) *n.* a flat, shallow vessel with a slightly raised rim, used for carrying, storing, or displaying things.

treach·er·ous (trech′ər əs) *adj.* **1.** likely to betray a trust; traitorous; disloyal. **2.** dangerous; hazardous: *Many ships have been sunk on that treacherous reef.* —**treach′er·ous·ly,** *adv.* —**treach′er·ous·ness,** *n.*

treach·er·y (trech′ər ē) *n. pl.,* **treach·er·ies.** the betrayal of a trust.

trea·cle (trē′kəl) *n. British.* another word for **molasses.**

tread (tred) *v.,* **trod, trod·den** or **trod, tread·ing.** —*v.t.* **1.** to walk on, along, or over; step upon. **2.** to press with the feet; trample: *He trod the flowers.* **3.** to form by walking: *The children trod a path across the lawn.* **4.** to put down or oppress; subdue; crush. —*v.i.* **1.** to move on foot; walk or step: *He trod heavily across the room.* **2.** to trample: *He accidentally trod on the flowers.* —*n.* **1.** the act, manner, or sound of treading: *Her father's heavy tread on the stairs awakened her.* **2.** the outer, grooved surface of an automobile tire: *Most of the tread has been worn off this old tire.* **3.** the horizontal part of a step in a staircase. **4.** the part of a wheel that touches the ground or rails. **5.** the part of the sole of a shoe that touches the ground.
to tread water. to keep the head above water while staying in an upright position, usually by moving the feet up and down in a walking motion.

trea·dle (tred′əl) *n.* a lever or pedal worked by the foot to provide motion for operating a machine, such as a potter's wheel. —*v.i.,* **trea·dled, trea·dling.** to work a treadle.

tread·mill (tred′mil′) *n.* **1.** a device turned by animals or persons walking on moving steps attached to a wheel, or treading on an endless sloping belt. It is used to produce motion for doing work. **2.** any monotonous, tiresome routine or activity.

trea·son (trē′zən) *n.* the betrayal of one's country, especially by giving aid to the enemy in wartime.

trea·son·a·ble (trē′zə nə bəl) *adj.* of, relating to, involving, or like treason. Also, **trea·son·ous** (trē′zə nəs).

treas·ure (trezh′ər) *n.* **1.** a store of valuables, such as money or jewels; accumulated riches. **2.** a person or thing that is greatly valued or considered precious: *His grandchildren are his greatest treasure.* —*v.t.,* **treas·ured, treas·ur·ing.** to consider as being of great value; cherish: *Natalie treasured every moment with her friends.*

treas·ur·er (trezh′ər ər) *n.* a person who is entrusted with the care and spending of funds, as of a business, club, or the like.

treas·ure-trove (trezh′ər trōv′) *n.* **1.** *Law.* money, jewels, or other valuables that have been found, and whose owner is not known. **2.** any valuable discovery.

treas·ur·y (trezh′ər ē) *n. pl.,* **treas·ur·ies. 1.** a place where funds, especially public funds, are deposited and stored. **2.** funds, as of a corporation or government. **3. Treasury.** a governmental department that is in charge of the collection of taxes and the management of a country's finances. **4.** a place where treasure is kept. **5.** a person or thing that is thought of as a rich or ample source: *The book is a treasury of information about the Civil War.*

treat (trēt) *v.t.* **1.** to act or behave toward in a particular way: *She treated the children with kindness. The judge treated each defendant fairly.* **2.** to deal with in a particular way: *The teacher treated the subject in great detail.* **3.** to deal with in a speech or writing; discuss: *The article treated the development of space travel.* **4.** to give medical attention to: *The doctor treated the patient's broken leg.* **5.** to subject to a process or application, as for altering or improving: *to treat cloth with a chemical to make it waterproof.* **6.** to pay for or provide the entertainment for; give food, drink, or the like to: *He treated his friend to a good meal.* —*v.i.* **1.** to deal with a subject in speech or writing: *He read a book that treats of military history.* **2.** to pay for another's food, drink, or the like. —*n.* **1.** food, drink, or the like given or paid for by another. **2.** something that gives unexpected or unusual pleasure: *Going to the circus was a treat for Jimmy.* **3.** the act of treating or entertaining. —**treat′er,** *n.*

trea·tise (trē′tis) *n.* a book or other piece of writing dealing in a formal way with some subject: *a treatise on the nature of democratic government.*

treat·ment (trēt′mənt) *n.* **1.** the act, process, or manner of treating. **2.** a course of action or means used to treat something, especially the care and medicine prescribed to treat an illness.

trea·ty (trē′tē) *n. pl.,* **trea·ties.** a formal agreement, especially one between nations: *A peace treaty was signed by all the countries involved in the war.*

tre·ble (treb′əl) *adj.* **1.** three times as much or as many; triple. **2.** of, relating to, or for the highest musical instrument or voice; soprano. —*n.* a soprano voice, part, or instrument. —*v.t.,* **tre·bled, tre·bling.** to make three times as much or as many. —**tre′bly,** *adv.*

treble clef, the clef placed on the second line of the staff, showing that that line corresponds to the note G above middle C. Also, **G clef.** See **clef** for illustration.

tree (trē) *n.* **1.** a plant having a single stem or trunk made up of a solid, permanent, woody tissue, and branches and leaves at some distance above the ground. **2.** any of various bushes, shrubs, or other plants, such as the banana, that are like a tree in size or shape. **3.** any structure or device that is like a tree in shape. **4.** a diagram resembling a tree with its branches. —*v.t.,* **treed, tree·ing.** to chase or force into or up a tree: *The hounds treed a raccoon.* —**tree′less,** *adj.* —**tree′like′,** *adj.*

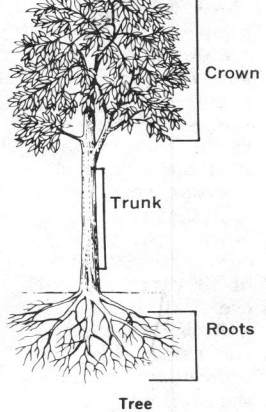

Tree

    up a tree. in an awkward, difficult, or embarrassing position or situation.

tree fern, any of various tropical, treelike ferns that have large fronds and, usually, thick, upright stems.

tree heath, a shrub or small tree found in the Mediterranean region, having fragrant, round, white flowers.

tre·foil (trē′foil′) *n.* **1.** any of several plants related to the pea, having leaves that usually are made up of three oval leaflets. **2.** any of various clovers. **3.** an ornament, used especially in architecture, consisting of three arcs resembling the leaves of a clover.

trek (trek) *v.i.,* **trekked, trek·king.** to travel or journey, especially in a slow, difficult manner. —*n.* a journey, especially one that is slow or difficult.

trel·lis (trel′is) *n. pl.,* **trel·lis·es.** a structure of crossed strips, as of wood, spaced widely apart to support growing vines. —*v.t.* to furnish or support with a trellis.

trel·lis·work (trel′is wurk′) *n.* openwork made from, consisting of, or like a trellis.

trem·a·tode (trem′ə tōd′) *n.* see **fluke**³ *(def. 2).*

trem·ble (trem′bəl) *v.i.,* **trem·bled, trem·bling. 1.** to shake, as with cold, weakness, fear, or anger. **2.** to have a slight, vibrating motion, as from a jarring force: *The ground trembled as the distant volcano erupted.* **3.** to be filled with nervousness or fear. —*n.* the act of trembling. —**trem′bling·ly,** *adv.* —**trem′bly,** *adj.*

Trellis

tre·men·dous (tri men′dəs) *adj.* **1.** of very great size, amount, or intensity: *A tremendous wave capsized the boat. My brother has a tremendous appetite.* **2.** *Informal.* extraordinary or wonderful; astounding: *The landing of men on the moon was a tremendous achievement.* **3.** terrible; dreadful: *Tremendous crimes have been committed in times of war.*

trem·o·lo (trem′ə lō′) *n. pl.,* **trem·o·los.** *Music.* **1.** a trembling or vibrating effect produced by rapidly repeating a single tone or by rapidly alternating two tones. **2.** a device or stop in an organ that is used to produce such an effect.

trem·or (trem′ər) *n.* **1.** a rapid shaking or vibrating movement: *a tremor caused by an earthquake.* **2.** a shaking or trembling, especially of the body or a limb. **3.** a nervous thrill caused by emotion or excitement: *A tremor of anticipation went through the crowd as the game entered the final inning.*

trem·u·lous (trem′yə ləs) *adj.* **1.** marked or affected by trembling; shaking: *His voice was tremulous when he first started his speech.* **2.** lacking firmness or courage; timid; wavering: *a tremulous leader.* —**trem′u·lous·ly,** *adv.* —**trem′u·lous·ness,** *n.*

trench (trench) *n. pl.,* **trench·es. 1.** a long, narrow ditch; deep furrow: *A trench was dug in the field to help irrigate it.* **2.** a long, narrow ditch with the earth piled up in front, used especially to protect soldiers in combat. —*v.t.* to dig a trench or trenches in.

trench·ant (tren′chənt) *adj.* **1.** sharp; cutting; biting: *The writer was well-known for his trenchant wit.* **2.** forceful or effective: *The debater supported his views on the issue with a trenchant argument.* —**trench′an·cy,** *n.* —**trench′ant·ly,** *adv.*

trench coat, a loose-fitting, double-breasted raincoat having a belt around the waist and straps at the shoulders and wrists.

trench·er (tren′chər) *n.* formerly, a wooden platter or board on which food, especially meat, was carved and served.

trench·er·man (tren′chər mən) *n. pl.,* **trench·er·men** (tren′chər mən). a person who eats with a hearty appetite.

trench mouth, an acute inflammation of the mouth and gums, caused by certain bacteria, and marked by painful, bleeding gums.

trend (trend) *n.* a general direction, tendency, or course: *There was a trend in men's fashions toward brighter colors. In that country there has been a conservative trend in politics recently.* —*v.i.* to have or go in a general direction or course; be inclined; tend.

Tren·ton (trent′ən) *n.* the capital of New Jersey, in the western part of the state, on the Delaware River. Pop. (1970), 104,638.

trep·i·da·tion (trep′ə dā′shən) *n.* **1.** nervous or fearful anticipation; anxiety: *The young actress faced her stage debut with trepidation.* **2.** a vibrating motion; trembling; tremor.

tres·pass (tres′pəs, tres′pas′) *v.i.* **1.** *Law.* to unlawfully enter the property of another: *The hunter trespassed on a private estate.* **2.** to encroach or intrude on a person's time,

at; āpe; cär; end; mē; it; īce; hot; ōld; fôrk; wood; fōol; oil; out; up; turn; sing; thin; <u>th</u>is; hw in white; zh in treasure. The symbol ə stands for the sound of **a** in about, **e** in taken, **i** in pencil, **o** in lemon, and **u** in circus.

969

privacy, or the like. **3.** to commit a sin. —*n. pl.*, **tres·pass·es. 1.** a wrong or sin. **2.** *Law.* an illegal act, especially unlawful entry of the property of another. —**tres'·pass·er,** *n.*

tress (tres) *n. pl.*, **tress·es. 1.** a curl, tuft, or strand of human hair. **2.** **tresses.** long hair, especially the hair of a woman or girl when worn long and loose.

tres·tle (tres'əl) *n.* **1.** a short beam or bar supported by four legs, used as support. **2.** a framework used to support a railroad bridge or other raised structure.

trey (trā) *n.* a playing card, die, or domino having three marks.

tri- *combining form* **1.** having or involving three: *triangle, tricycle.* **2.** coming or happening every three: *triweekly.*

Trestle *(def. 2)*

tri·ad (trī'ad) *n.* **1.** a group of three persons or things. **2.** *Music.* a chord of three tones, especially one consisting of a given tone with the third and fifth tones above it.

tri·al (trī'əl) *n.* **1.** an examination of a case in a court of law. **2.** the state of being tried or tested. **3.** a difficult test of one's strength, patience, or faith; hardship. **4.** a source or cause of pain or trouble: *That boy has been a constant trial to his parents.* **5.** the act of making an effort; attempt; try: *Donna learned to cook by trial and error.* —*adj.* of, for, relating to, done as, or used in a trial: *a trial effort, a trial lawyer.*

tri·an·gle (trī'ang'gəl) *n.* **1.** a plane figure with three sides and three angles. **2.** something shaped like a triangle. **3.** a musical instrument made of a metal bar bent into the shape of a triangle, producing a high tone like a bell when struck. **4.** a group of three persons or things.

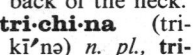
Triangle

tri·an·gu·lar (trī ang'-gyə lər) *adj.* **1.** of, relating to, or resembling a triangle. **2.** of, relating to, or consisting of three persons or things.

tri·an·gu·la·tion (trī ang'gyə lā'shən) *n.* a method used in surveying to determine the relative position of three points on the earth's surface. If one side and two angles of the triangle formed by the points are measured, the remaining sides and angle can be calculated.

Tri·as·sic (trī as'ik) *n.* the earliest geological period of the Mesozoic era, during which there was much volcanic activity and dinosaurs appeared. —*adj.* of, relating to, or characteristic of this period.

trib·al (trī'bəl) *adj.* of, relating to, or characteristic of a tribe or tribes: *a tribal society, tribal customs.* —**trib'al·ly,** *adv.*

tribe (trīb) *n.* **1.** a group of people connected by common ancestry, culture, social customs, and, usually, the same political system: *The ancient Jewish nation was composed of twelve tribes.* **2.** any group or class of people, usually distinguished by a common characteristic, interest, or the like. **3.** a class or group of animals or plants.

tribes·man (trībz'mən) *n. pl.*, **tribes·men** (trībz'mən). a member of a tribe.

trib·u·la·tion (trib'yə lā'shən) *n.* **1.** a condition of severe distress or misery; suffering: *The flood brought much tribulation to the town.* **2.** something that causes such distress or misery.

tri·bu·nal (trī byōōn'əl, tri byōōn'əl) *n.* **1.** a court of justice. **2.** any place of judgment.

trib·une[1] (trib'yōōn) *n.* **1.** an official in ancient Rome appointed to protect the rights and interests of the common people. **2.** a protector or defender of the rights of the public; champion of the people. [Latin *tribunus* originally, the chief of a tribe.]

trib·une[2] (trib'yōōn) *n.* a raised platform, stand, or seat, such as a pulpit. [French *tribune.*]

trib·u·tar·y (trib'yə ter'ē) *n. pl.*, **trib·u·tar·ies. 1.** a river or stream that flows into a larger body of water: *The Tennessee River is a major tributary of the Ohio River.* **2.** a person or group that pays tribute. —*adj.* **1.** flowing into a larger body of water. **2.** subject to paying tribute; taxed.

trib·ute (trib'yōōt) *n.* **1.** anything done, given, or observed as a sign of devotion, gratitude, or respect: *The enthusiastic applause was a tribute to the singer's performance.* **2.** money paid by one ruler or nation to another to show submission or to ensure peace or protection. **3.** any payment given under force.

trice[1] (trīs) *v.t.*, **triced, tric·ing.** to pull up and secure with a rope: *to trice a sail.* [Middle Dutch *trīsen* to hoist.]

trice[2] (trīs) *n.* a very short time; instant; moment: *I'll have that fixed in a trice.* [From *trice*[1], from the phrase *at a trice* at a pull, in an instant.]

tri·ceps (trī'seps) *n. pl.*, **tri·ceps** or **tri·ceps·es.** a muscle at the back of the upper arm that, when contracted, straightens the arm.

tri·cer·a·tops (trī ser'ə tops') *n.* a plant-eating dinosaur that lived in North America and had one long horn over each eye, a shorter horn on the snout, and a bony shield projecting from the skull over the back of the neck.

Triceratops

tri·chi·na (tri·kī'nə) *n. pl.*, **tri·chi·nae** (tri kī'nē). a parasitic roundworm that lives in man and animals. Trichinae enter the human body from infected pork that has not been well-cooked, and the adult worms lodge in the intestines, while the larvae form cysts in the muscles.

trich·i·no·sis (trik'ə nō'sis) *n.* a disease caused by trichinae, characterized by nausea, diarrhea, and stiff and swollen muscles.

trick (trik) *n.* **1.** something done or meant to deceive or cheat: *The misleading advertisement was a trick to draw customers.* **2.** a show of skill or cleverness, especially one meant to amuse: *The boy taught his dog many tricks.* **3.** the particular act or skill of doing something easily and successfully; knack: *She knows the trick of putting others at ease.* **4.** a mischievous act; practical joke; prank: *Harry was always playing tricks on others.* **5.** a habit, trait, or practice; mannerism: *He has the annoying trick of looking away when he is talking to people.* **6.** a group of cards made up of one card played from each player's hand. **7.** such a group of cards considered as a unit of score. —*v.t.* to deceive or cheat with a trick: *The swindler tricked the old lady into giving him her life savings.* —*v.i.* to practice trickery or deception. —*adj.* **1.** relating to or involving a trick or deception. **2.** inclined to give way or collapse: *The accident left him with a trick knee.*

to do the trick. to do what is wanted or needed: *The medicine he took really did the trick.*

trick·er·y (trik′ər ē) *n. pl.,* **trick·er·ies.** the act or instance of deceiving or cheating; deceitful behavior.

trick·le (trik′əl) *v.,* **trick·led, trick·ling.** —*v.i.* **1.** to flow or fall drop by drop or in a thin stream: *The rain trickled down the window. Blood trickled from the cut in his arm.* **2.** to move or go in a very slow, irregular way: *The children trickled into the classroom after recess.* —*v.t.* to cause to trickle. —*n.* **1.** the act of trickling. **2.** a slow stream or movement: *Monday was a slow day at the store, with only a trickle of customers.*

trick·ster (trik′stər) *n.* a person who plays tricks or practices trickery.

trick·y (trik′ē) *adj.,* **trick·i·er, trick·i·est. 1.** given to or marked by tricks or trickery; crafty; wily: *The car salesman gave a tricky sales pitch.* **2.** having unseen or unexpected difficulties; requiring cautious action or handling: *a tricky situation, a tricky question.* —**trick′i·ly,** *adv.* —**trick′i·ness,** *n.*

tri·col·or (trī′kul′ər) *also,* **tri·col·ored.** *adj.* having three colors. —*n.* **1.** a flag having three colors. **2.** *also,* **Tricolor.** the national flag of France, having three equal vertical bands of red, white, and blue.

tri·cot (trē′kō) *n.* **1.** a lightweight, knitted fabric made by hand or machine from wool, nylon, or rayon. **2.** a worsted fabric made of wool.

tri·cus·pid (trī kus′pid) *adj.* having three cusps or points. —*n.* any tooth that has three cusps or points.

tri·cy·cle (trī′si kəl, trī′sik′əl) *n.* a three-wheeled vehicle having two wheels in the back and one in the front, driven by pedals and steered with handlebars. It is usually used by children.

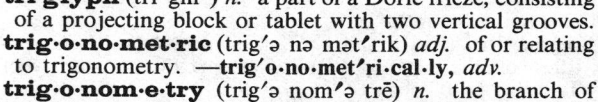

tri·dent (trīd′ənt) *n.* a spear with three prongs.

tried (trīd) *v.* the past tense and past participle of **try.** —*adj.* proved, as by experience or examination; tested.

tri·en·ni·al (trī en′ē əl) *adj.* **1.** lasting or continuing for three years. **2.** done or taking place every three years. —*n.* **1.** an event that takes place every three years. **2.** a third anniversary. —**tri·en′ni·al·ly,** *adv.*

Tricycle

tri·er (trī′ər) *n.* a person or thing that tries.

Tri·este (trē est′) *n.* a port city in northeastern Italy, on the northern coast of the Adriatic Sea. Pop. (1970 est.), 277,133.

tri·fle (trī′fəl) *n.* **1.** something of little or no value or importance; unimportant matter or thing: *There's no sense arguing over trifles.* **2.** a small amount; bit: *He is a trifle annoyed with their careless work.* **3.** a dessert made of sponge cake, having a layer of custard, fruit, or jam, and topped with whipped cream or meringue. —*v.,* **tri·fled, tri·fling.** —*v.i.* **1.** to treat something as having little value or importance; treat lightly: *He has been known to trifle with important business affairs.* **2.** to handle or treat in an idle, careless manner: *He is always trifling with his keys.* —*v.t.* to pass or spend (time, money, or the like) in an idle or foolish way; waste. —**tri′fler,** *n.*

tri·fling (trī′fling) *adj.* having little or no value or importance; unimportant; small. —**tri′fling·ly,** *adv.*

trig·ger (trig′ər) *n.* **1.** a small lever on a gun or other firearm that, when pulled back or pressed with the finger, causes the firearm to discharge. **2.** any similar device, such as a lever that is pressed or pulled to start a process or mechanism. —*v.t.* to start or cause: *Jealousy triggered her angry outburst.*

tri·glyph (trī′glif′) *n.* a part of a Doric frieze, consisting of a projecting block or tablet with two vertical grooves.

trig·o·no·met·ric (trig′ə nə mət′rik) *adj.* of or relating to trigonometry. —**trig′o·no·met′ri·cal·ly,** *adv.*

trig·o·nom·e·try (trig′ə nom′ə trē) *n.* the branch of mathematics dealing with the relations between the sides and angles of triangles, and also with the properties of these relations.

trill (tril) *n.* **1.** a quavering, trembling, usually high-pitched sound: *the chirping trill of a bird.* **2.** *Music.* a rapid alternation of two notes either a whole step or a half step apart. —*v.t.* to sing, play, or utter (something) with a trill. —*v.i.* to sing, play, or utter a trill.

tril·lion (tril′yən) *adj.* **1.** in the United States and France, the cardinal number that is represented by one followed by 12 zeros. **2.** in Great Britain and Germany, the cardinal number that is represented by one followed by 18 zeros. —*adj.* numbering one trillion. —**tril′lionth,** *adj., n.*

tril·li·um (tril′ē əm) *n.* any of a group of plants related to the lily, having leaves in arrangements of three, and bearing flowers with three oval petals.

tri·lo·bate (trī lō′bāt) *adj.* having three lobes, as certain leaves.

tri·lo·bite (trī′lə bīt′) *n.* an extinct sea animal that lived hundreds of millions of years ago, having a segmented body divided into three lobes.

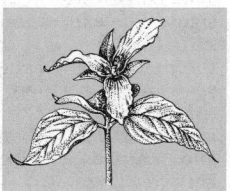

Trillium

tril·o·gy (tril′ə jē) *n. pl.,* **tril·o·gies.** a group of three complete plays, operas, novels, or the like that together make a related series.

trim (trim) *v.t.,* **trimmed, trim·ming. 1.** to make neat and orderly by removing parts, and by cutting: *to trim one's hair, to trim a rose bush.* **2.** to remove (a part or object) in order to make neat or orderly: *to trim the thorns on a rose, to trim unnecessary items off a budget.* **3.** to add ornaments or decorations to; decorate: *to trim a cake, to trim a Christmas tree.* **4.** to balance (a boat or ship) as by arranging the cargo or ballast. **5.** to adjust (yards or sails) for sailing. —*n.* **1.** ornamentation or decoration: *The napkin had a lace trim.* **2.** the state or condition of being fit, ready, or in good order: *The boxer was in trim for the fight.* **3.** the condition of a ship with reference to her fitness for sailing. **4.** woodwork used as a decoration on a building, especially moldings around windows or doors. —*adj.,* **trim·mer, trim·mest.** in good order or condition: *Anne's clothes were always neat and trim.* —*adv.* in a trim manner or way; trimly. —**trim′ly,** *adv.* —**trim′mer,** *n.* —**trim′ness,** *n.*

tri·mes·ter (trī mes′tər) *n.* a period or term made up of three months, especially one of the three terms into which the academic year is sometimes divided.

trim·ming (trim′ing) *n.* **1.** anything used as a decoration or ornament: *The dress had lace trimming on the sleeves.* **2. trimmings.** pieces or parts cut off in trimming something. **3. trimmings.** *Informal.* things that traditionally or usually go with or accompany something: *a birthday party with ice cream, cake, and all the trimmings.*

at; āpe; cär; end; mē; it; īce; hot; ōld; fôrk; wood; fōōl; oil; out; up; turn; sing; thin; **this**; hw in white; zh in treasure. The symbol ə stands for the sound of **a** in about, **e** in taken, **i** in pencil, **o** in lemon, and **u** in circus.

T

tri·month·ly (trī munth′lē) *adj.* done or taking place every three months.

Trin·i·dad (trin′ə dad′) *n.* an island of the Lesser Antilles, off the coast of Venezuela, part of the country of Trinidad and Tobago.

Trinidad and Tobago, a country made up of the West Indian islands of Trinidad and Tobago. Capital, Port-of-Spain. Land area, 1980 sq. mi. Pop. (1971 est.), 1,030,000.

tri·ni·tro·tol·u·ene (trī nī′trō tol′yōō ēn′) *n.* see **TNT.** Also, **tri·ni·tro·tol·u·ol** (trī nī′trō tol′yōō ōl′).

Trin·i·ty (trin′ə tē) *n. pl.,* **Trin·i·ties. 1.** the union of the Father, the Son, and the Holy Ghost as three divine persons, in one divine being. **2. trinity.** any combination or group of three persons or things.

trin·ket (tring′kit) *n.* **1.** any small ornament or fancy article, especially a piece of costume jewelry. **2.** anything of little value or importance; trifle.

tri·no·mi·al (trī nō′mē əl) *adj.* consisting of three terms: *a trinomial equation.* —*n.* a mathematical expression consisting of three terms joined by plus or minus signs. The expression $4x + 7y - 1$ is a trinomial.

tri·o (trē′ō) *n. pl.,* **tri·os. 1.** a musical composition for three voices or instruments. **2.** three musicians performing such a composition. **3.** any group of three persons or things.

tri·ode (trī′ōd) *n.* an electron tube consisting of an anode and a cathode, and a grid that controls the flow of electrons between them.

tri·ox·ide (trī ok′sīd) *n.* an oxide having three atoms of oxygen in each molecule.

trip (trip) *n.* **1.** the act of traveling or going from one place to another, especially over a fairly long distance: *to take a trip to Europe, to go on a camping trip.* **2.** a fall or stumble caused by striking one's foot against an object or by losing one's footing. **3.** a light, quick step. **4.** a spring, catch, or other device that releases a part, as in setting a mechanism in operation. **5.** an error or blunder; slip. —*v.,* **tripped, trip·ping.** —*v.i.* **1.** to strike the foot against something so as to stumble or fall: *to trip over the edge of a rug.* **2.** to make an error or blunder. **3.** to move with quick, light steps; prance. —*v.t.* **1.** to cause to fall or stumble: *The rock tripped him.* **2.** to cause to make a mistake or commit a blunder: *The reporters tried to trip him up with their questions.* **3.** *Machinery.* to operate (a mechanism) by releasing a spring, catch, or other device. **4.** to release (a spring, catch, or other device) in order to set a mechanism in operation.

tri·par·tite (trī pär′tīt) *adj.* **1.** divided into three parts. **2.** having three corresponding parts or copies. **3.** of, relating to, or made by three parties: *a tripartite trade agreement.*

tripe (trīp) *n.* **1.** the walls of the first and second stomachs of certain animals, especially the ox, used as food. **2.** *Informal.* anything of such poor quality as to be useless or worthless.

trip·ham·mer (trip′ham′ər) *n.* a power-driven hammer that is raised by machinery and then tripped by a device and allowed to fall.

tri·ple (trip′əl) *adj.* **1.** consisting of three parts. **2.** three times as much or as many; multiplied by three. —*n.* **1.** a number or amount that is three times as much as another. **2.** *Baseball.* a hit that enables a batter to reach third base safely. —*v.,* **tri·pled, tri·pling.** —*v.t.* to make three times as much or as many. —*v.i.* **1.** to become three times as much or as many: *The population of the town tripled in ten years.* **2.** *Baseball.* to hit a triple.

triple play *Baseball.* a play during which three outs are made.

tri·plet (trip′lit) *n.* **1.** one of three children born at the

same birth. **2.** any set or group of three. **3.** *Music.* a group of three notes of equal time value to be performed in the time of two. **4.** three successive lines of rhyming verse, usually of equal length.

triple time, musical time or rhythm having three beats to the measure, the accent falling on the first beat.

trip·li·cate (*adj., n.,* trip′lə kit; *v.,* trip′lə kāt′) *adj.* three times as much or as many; triple. —*n.* one of three identical things, especially copies of printed matter. —*v.t.,* **trip·li·cat·ed, trip·li·cat·ing.** to multiply by three; triple. —**trip′li·ca′tion,** *n.*

in triplicate. in three identical copies.

tri·ply (trip′lē) *adv.* in a triple degree, amount, or manner.

tri·pod (trī′pod′) *n.* **1.** a three-legged stand for supporting a camera, surveying instrument, or the like. **2.** a pot, stool, table, or similar structure resting on three legs.

Trip·o·li (trip′ə lē) *n.* **1.** a region on the northern coast of Africa, now in western Libya, once a major base for the Barbary pirates. **2.** one of the two capitals of Libya, a port city in the northeastern part of the country, on the Mediterranean Sea. Pop. (1970 est.), 264,000. —**Trip·ol·i·tan** (tripol′ə tən), *adj., n.*

trip·ping (trip′ing) *adj.* moving quickly and lightly: *tripping footsteps.* —**trip′ping·ly,** *adv.*

Tripod

trip·tych (trip′tik) *n.* **1.** a painting or carving consisting of three panels hinged together, especially one that has a religious subject and is used as an altarpiece. **2.** a set of three writing tablets tied or hinged together, used in ancient times.

tri·reme (trī′rēm) *n.* an ancient galley, especially a warship, with three rows of oars, one above the other, on each side.

tri·sect (trī sekt′) *v.t.* to divide into three parts, especially into three equal parts: *to trisect an angle.* —**tri·sec′tion,** *n.*

trite (trīt) *adj.,* **trit·er, trit·est** lacking originality or freshness because of constant repetition. —**trite′ly,** *adv.* —**trite′ness,** *n.*

trit·i·um (trit′ē əm, trish′ē əm) *n.* a radioactive isotope of hydrogen, containing one proton and two neutrons. The fusion of tritium with deuterium releases the explosive force of the hydrogen bomb.

Tri·ton (trīt′ən) *n. Greek Mythology.* a sea god who was half man and half fish.

tri·umph (trī′umf) *n.* **1.** an outstanding success, achievement, or victory: *The discovery of penicillin is a medical triumph of the twentieth century.* **2.** great joy caused by victory or success: *We could see triumph on the winner's face.* **3.** in ancient Rome, a procession and public celebration honoring a victorious commander and his army. —*v.i.* **1.** to achieve a victory; be successful; win: *to triumph over the enemy.* **2.** to rejoice or celebrate because of victory or success.

tri·um·phal (trī um′fəl) *adj.* of, relating to, like, or celebrating a triumph or victory: *triumphal procession.*

tri·um·phant (trī um′fənt) *adj.* **1.** victorious or successful: *Our team was triumphant in the match.* **2.** rejoicing because of victory or success: *The winning team gave a triumphant cheer.* —**tri·um′phant·ly,** *adv.*

tri·um·vir (trī um′vər) *n. pl.,* **tri·um·virs** or **tri·um·vi·ri** (trī um′və rī′). in ancient Rome, one of the members of a triumvirate.

tri·um·vi·rate (trī um′vər it) *n.* **1.** government by three persons, especially in ancient Rome. **2.** the position or term of office of a triumvir. **3.** any group or association of three persons.

triv·et (triv′it) *n.* **1.** a three-legged stand or support used for holding pots over a fire. **2.** a metal or ceramic plate, often having three short legs, placed under hot plates or dishes on a table.

triv·i·a (triv′ē ə) *n.,pl.* unimportant or insignificant facts, matters, or information; trifles.

triv·i·al (triv′ē əl) *adj.* **1.** having little or no importance or significance; trifling: *Don't worry about such a trivial problem.* **2.** commonplace; everyday. —**triv′i·al·ly,** *adv.*

triv·i·al·i·ty (triv′ē al′ə tē) *n. pl.,* **triv·i·al·i·ties. 1.** the quality or state of being trivial. **2.** a thing or matter of little importance or significance; something trivial.

tri·week·ly (trī wēk′lē) *adv.* **1.** every three weeks. **2.** three times a week. —*adj.* **1.** happening or done every three weeks. **2.** happening or done three times a week. —*n. pl.,* **tri·week·lies.** a newspaper, magazine, or the like issued triweekly.

tro·che (trō′kē) *n.* a lozenge containing medicine.

tro·chee (trō′kē) *n.* a metrical foot consisting of two syllables, the first accented, or long, and the second unaccented, or short. For example: *Pe′ ter Pe′ ter pump′ kin eat′ er.*

trod (trod) the past tense and a past participle of **tread.**

trod·den (trod′ən) a past participle of **tread.**

trode (trōd) *Archaic.* a past tense of **tread.**

Tro·jan (trō′jən) *adj.* of or relating to Troy or its people. —*n.* **1.** a person who lived in Troy. **2.** a person who shows great courage, energy, or strength.

Trojan War *Greek Legend.* the war between the Greeks and the Trojans that lasted ten years and ended in the destruction of Troy.

troll[1] (trōl) *v.i.* **1.** to fish with a moving line, usually by trailing the line behind the boat. **2.** to sing in a full, rich voice. —*v.t.* **1.** (of several singers) to sing the parts of (a song) in succession, as in a round. **2.** to sing in a full, rich voice. —*n.* **1.** a song whose parts are sung in succession; round. **2.** a fishing line or lure used for trolling. [Middle French *troller* to wander, possibly from Old High German *trollen* to run with short steps.]

troll[2] (trōl) *n. Scandinavian Folklore.* a dwarf or a giant who lives underground or in a mountain cave. [Old Norse *troll* monster.]

trol·ley (trol′ē) *n. pl.,* **trol·leys. 1.** a small grooved wheel or pulley that moves along an overhead wire to pick up electricity for an electric streetcar, train, or bus. **2.** see **trolley car.**

trolley car, an electric streetcar that gets its current from an overhead wire by means of a trolley.

trol·lop (trol′əp) *n.* a cheap, low, or vulgar woman.

trom·bone (trom bōn′, trom′bōn) *n.* a brass musical instrument consisting of two long, U-shaped tubes, one of which has a flaring end

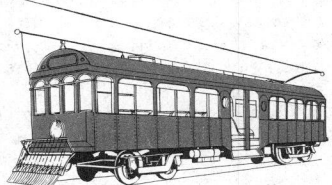

Trolley car

and the other of which may be slid back and forth to change the pitch of the tones. —**trom·bon′ist,** *n.*

troop (trōōp) *n.* **1.** a group of persons: *A troop of students filed into the auditorium.* **2.** formerly, a cavalry unit of the U.S. Army corresponding to an infantry company. **3. troops.** members of the armed forces as a group. **4.** *usually,* **troops.** a flock or swarm. **5.** a unit of Boy or Girl Scouts, usually consisting of several patrols of sixteen to thirty-two members. **6.** another spelling of **troupe.** —*v.i.* to walk or march in a group, especially in orderly fashion: *The game was over, and the players trooped home.*

troop·er (trōō′pər) *n.* **1.** a soldier in a troop of cavalry. **2.** a mounted police officer. **3.** a state police officer. **4.** another spelling of **trouper.**

troop·ship (trōōp′ship′) *n.* a ship used to transport troops.

tro·phy (trō′fē) *n. pl.,* **tro·phies. 1.** a cup, bowl, statuette on a pedestal, or similar object, usually awarded for some achievement, such as winning a sports contest or other competition. **2.** something taken and kept as a reminder or proof of victory or achievement.

trop·ic (trop′ik) *n.* **the tropics. also, the Tropics.** a region of the earth lying between the Tropic of Cancer and the Tropic of Capricorn; Torrid Zone. —*adj.* of or relating to the tropics; tropical.

trop·i·cal (trop′i kəl) *adj.* of, relating to, found in, or characteristic of the tropics: *tropical plants.*

Tropic of Cancer 1. an imaginary line parallel to the equator at latitude 23°27′ north, that marks the northernmost distance from the equator at which the sun appears to be overhead at noon. **2.** the circle of the celestial sphere corresponding to this, parallel to the celestial equator.

Tropic of Capricorn 1. an imaginary line parallel to the equator at latitude 23°27′ south, that marks the southernmost distance from the equator at which the sun appears to be overhead at noon. **2.** the circle of the celestial sphere corresponding to this, parallel to the celestial equator.

tro·pism (trō′piz əm) *n.* the tendency of an animal or plant to turn or grow in response to an outside stimulus. —**tro·pis·tic** (trō pis′tik), *adj.*

trop·o·sphere (trop′ə sfēr′) *n.* the layer of the atmosphere nearest the earth's surface, extending to an altitude of about twelve miles. Most clouds form in the troposphere.

trot (trot) *n.* **1.** the gait of a horse or other four-legged animal, between a walk and a gallop, in which the left hind foot and the right forefoot are lifted together, and then the left forefoot and right hind foot are lifted. **2.** the jogging gait of a human being, between a walk and a run. —*v.,* **trot·ted, trot·ting.** —*v.i.* **1.** to ride or move at a trot: *The horse trotted around the corral.* **2.** to move quickly; hurry: *The little boy trotted to the grocery store.* —*v.t.* to cause to trot.

troth (trôth, trōth) *n.* a promise of faithfulness, as in marriage or betrothal.

Trot·sky, Leon (trot′skē) 1879–1940, Russian revolutionary leader.

trot·ter (trot′ər) *n.* **1.** a horse that trots, especially one bred and trained for trotting races. **2.** a foot, as of a calf, sheep, or pig, used as food.

trou·ba·dour (trōō′bə dôr′) *n.* one of a group of lyric poets who flourished from the eleventh to the thirteenth centuries in southern Europe, especially in France, and were famous for songs about love and chivalry.

trou·ble (trub′əl) *n.* **1.** difficulty, danger, or distress: *The people in the valley will be in trouble if the dam gives way.* **2.** something that causes a problem: *The trouble is that the*

at; āpe; cär; end; mē; it; īce; hot; ōld; fôrk; wood; fōōl; oil; out; up; turn; sing; thin; **this;** hw in white; zh in treasure. The symbol ə stands for the sound of **a** in about, **e** in taken, **i** in pencil, **o** in lemon, and **u** in circus.

T

plan will not work. **3.** extra work or effort; pains: *The hostess went to a lot of trouble to make her guests comfortable.* **4.** a disease or illness; ailment: *kidney trouble.* **5.** a disturbance or disorder; turmoil: *There was trouble at the factory when the workers went out on strike.* —*v.,* **troubled, trou·bling.** —*v.t.* **1.** to put into a state of distress; worry; disturb. **2.** to put (someone) to extra effort; inconvenience: *May I trouble you for a glass of water?* **3.** to cause physical pain; hurt; afflict: *to be troubled by ulcers.* —*v.i.* to take pains; bother.

trou·ble·mak·er (trub′əl mā′kər) *n.* a person or thing that is a cause of trouble.

trou·ble·shoot·er (trub′əl shōō′tər) *n.* a person who specializes in locating and solving troubles, problems, and difficulties.

trou·ble·some (trub′əl səm) *adj.* causing distress, inconvenience, or annoyance: *a troublesome injury, a troublesome person.*

trou·blous (trub′ləs) *adj.* **1.** full of troubles: *troublous times.* **2.** causing trouble; troublesome.

trough (trôf) *n.* **1.** a long, deep, narrow receptacle like a bin, used especially for holding water. **2.** a channel or gutter, as under or along the eaves of a roof, used for carrying water. **3.** a low point, as on a graph. **4.** a long, narrow hollow or depression, as between two mountain ridges or two ocean waves.

trounce (trouns) *v.t.,* **trounced, trounc·ing.** to beat soundly in a contest.

troupe (trōōp) *also,* **troop.** *n.* a group or company, especially of touring actors, singers, or circus performers. —*v.i.,* **trouped, troup·ing.** to go on a tour with such a group.

troup·er (trōō′pər) *also,* **troop·er.** *n.* **1.** a person who faces up to problems or difficulties or goes on in spite of them. **2.** an experienced actor or performer. **3.** a member of a troupe.

trou·sers (trou′zərz) *n.,pl.* a garment for the lower part of the body, reaching from the waist or hips to the ankles, and divided so as to cover each leg separately.

trous·seau (trōō′sō, trōō sō′) *n. pl.,* **trous·seaux** (trōō′sōz, trōō sōz′) *or* **trous·seaus.** all the items brought by a bride to her new home, such as clothing, linen, and silver.

trout (trout) *n. pl.,* **trouts** *or* **trout.** any of a group of freshwater food and game fish related to the salmon, including the lake trout and brook trout.

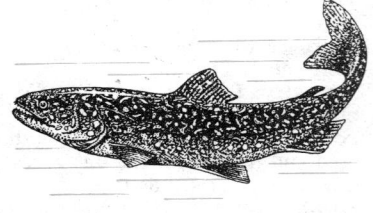

Trout

trow (trō) *v.i. Archaic.* to be of the opinion; suppose; think.

trow·el (trou′əl) *n.* **1.** a hand tool with a flat, rectangular or triangular blade, used for spreading and smoothing plaster or mortar, as in plastering or bricklaying. **2.** a digging tool like a scoop, with a narrow, curved, pointed blade, used in gardening.

Troy (troi) *n.* an ancient city and stronghold in northwestern Asia Minor, near the mouth of the Dardanelles. It was the site of the Trojan War. Also, **Ilium.**

troy weight (troi) a standard system of weights used for gems and precious metals.

tru·an·cy (trōō′ən sē) *n. pl.,* **tru·an·cies.** the act or practice of being truant.

tru·ant (trōō′ənt) *n.* **1.** a student who is absent from school without permission. **2.** a person who shirks or neglects work or duties; idle or lazy person. —*adj.* **1.** of,

relating to, or characteristic of truants: *truant behavior.* **2.** (of a student) being a truant.

truce (trōōs) *n.* a temporary halt to fighting by mutual agreement, often in order to reach a final settlement.

Tru·cial States (trōō′shəl) see **United Arab Emirates.**

truck¹ (truk) *n.* **1.** a motor vehicle designed to carry heavy loads, especially one with a cab in front for the driver, and a trailer or open area in the rear for freight. **2.** a low rectangular frame on four wheels, often motorized, used for moving heavy loads; dolly. **3.** a set of two or more pairs of wheels mounted closely together in a swiveling frame, as on a railroad car or locomotive. —*v.t.* to transport on a truck or trucks: *to truck fresh vegetables to market.* —*v.i.* to drive a truck or engage in trucking. [Probably from Latin *trochus* an iron hoop, from Greek *trochos* wheel.]

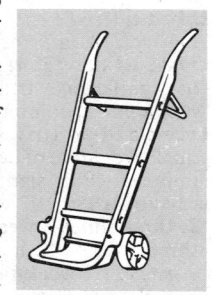

Truck¹ *(def. 2)*

truck² (truk) *n.* **1.** vegetables raised for sale in a market. **2.** *Informal.* dealings: *She will have no truck with her neighbors.* **3.** *Informal.* trash or rubbish. [Old French *troquer* to barter; of uncertain origin.]

truck·er (truk′ər) *n.* **1.** a person or firm owning or operating a trucking business. **2.** a person whose job is driving a truck.

truck farm, a farm on which vegetables are raised for sale in a market.

truck·ing (truk′ing) *n.* the business or process of transporting goods by truck.

truck·le (truk′əl) *v.,* **truck·led, truck·ling.** —*v.i.* **1.** to be subservient or meek: *to truckle to a bully.* **2.** *Archaic.* to move on rollers or casters. —*v.t. Archaic.* to cause to move on rollers or casters.

truckle bed, another term for **trundle bed.**

truc·u·lence (truk′yə ləns) *n.* truculent behavior.

truc·u·lent (truk′yə lənt) *adj.* **1.** savage, fierce, or ferocious. **2.** harsh or scathing: *a truculent speech.* **3.** hostile and belligerent: *He was a truculent young man, always ready for a fight.* —**truc′u·lent·ly,** *adv.*

Tru·deau, Pi·erre El·li·ott (trōō dō′; pē er′ el′ē ət) 1919—, the prime minister of Canada from 1968 to 1979, and since February, 1980.

trudge (truj) *v.,* **trudged, trudg·ing.** —*v.i.* to go on foot in a steady, slow manner; plod: *to trudge up a hill.* —*v.t.* to travel over (a place or distance) in a steady, slow manner: *The soldiers trudged the last mile in the rain.* —*n.* a difficult, tiring walk: *a long trudge back home.*

true (trōō) *adj.,* **tru·er, tru·est.** **1.** that agrees with or correctly represents reality or fact; not false, fictitious, or wrong: *a true story.* **2.** having the proper qualities or characteristics of: *a true gentleman.* **3.** actually being what it seems or is claimed to be; real; genuine: *true gold.* **4.** faithful to someone or something; loyal: *He is true to his old friends.* **5.** conforming closely to an original, standard, or type: *a true copy.* **6.** legitimate; rightful: *the true heir to an estate.* **7.** accurately fitted or placed: *a true door frame.* **8.** determined with reference to the earth's axis rather than the magnetic poles: *true north.* —*adv.* **1.** in a true manner: *to speak true.* **2.** without change from the previous generation: *to breed true.* —*v.t.,* **trued, tru·ing** *or* **true·ing.** to place, adjust, or fit accurately: *True up the window screen.* —**true′ness,** *n.*

to come true. to become real or actual.

true-blue (trōō′blōō′) *adj.* steady in loyalty or faith; staunch: *a true-blue friend.*

truf·fle (truf′əl) *n.* any of a group of mushrooms shaped like a potato and growing underground. Truffles are valued as a food.

tru·ism (trōō′iz′əm) *n.* a statement that is so obviously true that no one would argue with it. For example: *Health is more precious than wealth.*

tru·ly (trōō′lē) *adv.* **1.** in a true manner; sincerely; genuinely: *I am truly sorry that I hurt your feelings.* **2.** in fact; indeed; really: *He is truly the best athlete I know.* **3.** accurately; correctly: *a model truly built from the original ship.*

Tru·man, Harry S (trōō′mən) 1884–1972, the thirty-third president of the United States, from 1945 to 1953.

trump¹ (trump) *n.* **1.** a suit of playing cards that outranks the other suits during the playing of a hand. **2.** any card of this suit. —*v.t.* to play a trump card on (another card or a trick). —*v.i.* to play a trump card. [A form of *triumph.*]

trump² (trump) *v.t.* to make up in order to deceive; fabricate: *to trump up an excuse.* [Possibly from *trump¹.*]

trump·er·y (trum′pər ē) *n. pl.,* **trump·er·ies.** something that appears to be valuable but is really worthless.

trum·pet (trum′pit) *n.* **1.** a brass musical instrument made up of a cylindrical metal tube coiled into a long loop and flaring out at the end, the tones of which are varied by the pressure of the player's lips and

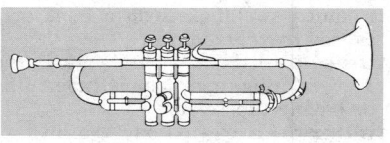

Trumpet

by the use of three valves. **2.** something resembling a trumpet in shape. **3.** a sound like that of a trumpet, such as the cry of an elephant. —*v.i.* **1.** to blow a trumpet. **2.** to make a sound like that of a trumpet. —*v.t.* **1.** to sound or produce on a trumpet. **2.** to announce or proclaim widely and loudly as if with a trumpet; herald. —**trum′pet·er,** *n.*

trumpet creeper, a woody climbing vine bearing clusters of orange and scarlet trumpet-shaped flowers. Also, **trumpet vine.**

trun·cate (trung′kāt) *v.t.,* **trun·cat·ed, trun·cat·ing.** to make smaller by cutting off a part of. —*adj.* having or seeming to have a part or section missing or cut off: *a truncate leaf.* —**trun·ca′tion,** *n.*

trun·cheon (trun′chən) *n.* **1.** a club, especially a long, slender, sturdy one, as used by police. **2.** a staff carried as a symbol of office or authority. —*v.t.* to beat with a truncheon; club.

trun·dle (trund′əl) *v.,* **trun·dled, trun·dling.** —*v.t.* to cause to roll along by pushing: *to trundle a bicycle rather than ride it.* —*v.i.* to move or go on rollers or wheels. —*n.* **1.** a small wheel or caster. **2.** see **trundle bed.**

trundle bed, a low, movable bed that may be pushed under another bed for storage. Also, **truckle bed.**

trunk (trungk) *n.* **1.** the main stem of a tree, as distinguished from its branches. **2.** a large, rectangular box with a hinged lid, used for transporting and storing things. **3.** the baggage compartment of an automobile. **4.** a long flexible snout, especially of an elephant.

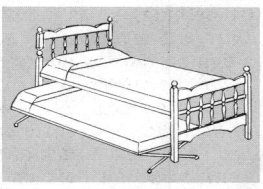

Trundle bed

5. trunks. men's short pants, such as those worn by swimmers, that reach from the waist to the upper thigh. **6.** the main body of a human being or animal, considered apart from the arms, legs, or neck. **7.** see **trunk line.**

trunk line **1.** the main line of a transportation system, as of a railroad. **2.** a line that connects telephone exchanges and carries many calls at once.

truss (trus) *n. pl.,* **truss·es. 1.** a framework of wood or metal, usually consisting of triangular units, used to span an opening or support a heavy load, as of a bridge or roof. **2.** a device, usually consisting of a pad attached to a belt, used for support in cases of hernia. —*v.t.* **1.** to bind or tie; fasten: *She trussed the turkey before cooking it.* **2.** to support or strengthen with a truss or trusses, as a roof or bridge.

trust (trust) *v.t.* **1.** to have faith or confidence in the truthfulness, honesty, ability, reliability, or justice of: *Emily is open and truthful with us because she trusts us.* **2.** to rely upon or believe: *They trusted the weather report when they decided to have a picnic.* **3.** to commit to someone's care; entrust: *to trust a child to a baby sitter.* **4.** to give business credit to: *The grocer trusted me for this week's food.* **5.** to feel sure of; expect with confidence: *I trust that you will get here on time.* —*v.i.* **1.** to have faith or confidence: *to trust in one's own judgment.* **2.** to feel sure: *You are being honest, I trust.* —*n.* **1.** faith or confidence in the truthfulness, honesty, ability, reliability, or justice of someone or something. **2.** keeping or custody; care: *Her niece was left in her trust for the weekend.* **3.** the fact or state of being trusted: *The Presidency is a position of great power and trust.* **4.** a person or thing that is believed or believed in. **5.** an illegal business combination or monopoly of many companies or corporations, that can control the production or distribution of a commodity or service, fix prices, and eliminate competition. **6.** see **trust fund.**

trus·tee (trus tē′) *n.* a person or organization that manages the property or affairs of another person, company, or institution.

trus·tee·ship (trus tē′ship′) *n.* **1.** the office or duties of a trustee. **2.** the administrative authority over a trust territory given to a country by the United Nations. **3.** the territory so administered.

trust·ful (trust′fəl) *adj.* full of trust; trusting. —**trust′ful·ly,** *adv.* —**trust′ful·ness,** *n.*

trust fund, property, such as money, securities, or the like, held by a trustee, usually a bank.

trust·ing (trus′ting) *adj.* full of trust. —**trust′ing·ly,** *adv.*

trust territory, a territory, such as a former colony, that is administered by a country under the supervision of the United Nations.

trust·wor·thy (trust′wur′thē) *adj.* that can be trusted or is worthy of trust. —**trust′wor′thi·ness,** *n.*

trust·y (trus′tē) *adj.,* **trust·i·er, trust·i·est.** that can be trusted or relied on. —*n. pl.,* **trust·ies.** a convict who is given certain duties and special privileges because of good behavior.

truth (trōōth) *n. pl.,* **truths** (trōōthz, trōōths). **1.** something that is true: *to tell the truth.* **2.** the state or quality of being true, accurate, or sincere: *to doubt the truth of a statement.* **3.** an accepted or proven fact, principle, or the like: *a mathematical truth.*

in truth. really; actually.

truth·ful (trōōth′fəl) *adj.* **1.** usually or habitually telling

at; āpe; cär; end; mē; it; īce; hot; ōld; fôrk; wood; fōōl; oil; out; up; turn; sing; thin; this; hw in white; zh in treasure. The symbol ə stands for the sound of **a** in about, **e** in taken, **i** in pencil, **o** in lemon, and **u** in circus.

T

the truth: *a truthful person.* **2.** conforming to truth, fact, or reality: *The book gave a truthful picture of prison life.* —**truth′ful·ly,** *adv.* —**truth′ful·ness,** *n.*

truth set, another term for **solution set.**

try (trī) *v.,* **tried, try·ing.** —*v.t.* **1.** to make an effort to do or accomplish; attempt; undertake: *The two boys tried moving the heavy sofa themselves.* **2.** to test the effect or operation of: *Try out the brakes before you drive down the hill.* **3.** to investigate or examine in a court of law: *to try an accused person, to try a case.* **4.** to attempt to open: *The visitor tried the door, but it was locked.* **5.** to subject to trials or suffering; afflict: *His son's bad behavior sorely tried the old man.* **6.** to subject to strain; tax: *to try someone's patience.* —*v.i.* to make an effort; attempt; undertake. —*n. pl.,* **tries.** an attempt; effort: *The mountain climbers made one more try to reach the top before the end of the day.*

　to try on. to put on (an article of clothing) to test its fit or looks.

　to try out for. to demonstrate one's skill or ability in order to qualify as a member of: *James tried out for the track team.*

try·ing (trī′ing) *adj.* hard to bear or endure with patience; difficult; annoying: *a trying person.*

try·out (trī′out′) *also,* **tryouts.** *n.* a period or session of testing during which people who are trying out, as for parts in a play or positions on a team, are judged for skill or ability.

tryp·sin (trip′sin) *n.* an enzyme in the pancreatic juice that digests proteins.

try square, an L-shaped instrument used in carpentry for laying out and testing right angles.

tryst (trist) *n.* **1.** a prearranged meeting, especially between lovers; rendezvous. **2.** an arrangement to meet at a specified time and place.

tsar (zär) another spelling of **czar.**

tsa·ri·na (zä rē′nə) another spelling of **czarina.**

tset·se fly (tset′sē, tsē′tsē) *also,* **tzet·ze fly.** any of a group of African flies that suck the blood of man and animals. Certain types of tsetse flies transmit sleeping sickness to man and other diseases to animals. Also, **tsetse, tzetze.**

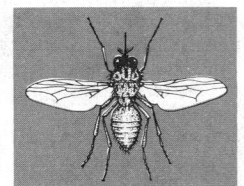

Tsetse fly

T-shirt (tē′shurt′) *also,* **t-shirt, tee shirt.** *n.* **1.** a light, close-fitting undershirt with short sleeves. **2.** an outer shirt resembling this, worn for casual wear or for sports.

Tsi·nan (jē′nän′) *n.* a city in eastern China. Pop. (1958 est.), 882,000. Also, **Chinan, Jinan.**

Tsing·tao (tsing′tou′) *n.* a port city in northeastern China, on the Yellow Sea. Pop. (1958 est.), 1,144,000. Also, **Chingtao, Qingdao.**

tsp., teaspoon.

T square, a tool used by architects and engineers to draw parallel straight lines, made of a long straight piece attached at one end to a short crosspiece that slides along the edge of a drawing board and serves as a guide.

tsu·na·mi (tsoo nä′mē) *n.* a swift, powerful ocean wave caused by an underwater earthquake and causing great destruction to any land area it strikes; tidal wave.

Tu., Tuesday.

tub (tub) *n.* **1.** see **bathtub.** **2.** a large, open container, as for washing clothes. **3.** a round container, often of wood or metal, used for holding butter, honey, fat, or other products. **4.** the amount a tub will hold. **5.** something that is like a tub, especially an old, clumsy boat or ship: *That old tub will never float.*

tu·ba (too′bə, tyoo′bə) *n.* a very large brass musical instrument that produces a deep, mellow tone.

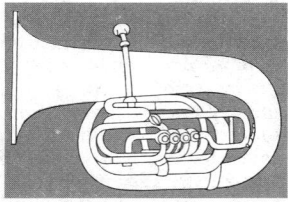

Tuba

tub·by (tub′ē) *adj.,* **tub·bi·er, tub·bi·est.** shaped like a tub; short and broad; fat. —**tub′bi·ness,** *n.*

tube (toob, tyoob) *n.* **1.** a hollow cylinder, as of glass, rubber, or metal, usually used to hold or carry liquids or gases. **2.** anything resembling a tube, as in shape or use, as the bronchial tubes. **3.** a container of soft metal, plastic, or the like, having a cap that screws on, used for packaging toothpaste, shampoo, and other products. **4.** an underground or underwater tunnel through which a train or subway runs. —**tube′like′,** *adj.*

tu·ber (too′bər, tyoo′bər) *n.* the thick, fleshy portion of an underground stem, such as a potato, bearing buds from which new plants grow.

tu·ber·cle (too′bər kəl, tyoo′bər kəl) *n.* **1.** a small, rounded swelling, as on a bone or plant. **2.** a swelling caused by tuberculosis.

tu·ber·cu·lar (too bur′kyə lər, tyoo bur′kyə lər) *adj.* **1.** of, relating to, or having tuberculosis. **2.** of, relating to, or having tubercles.

tu·ber·cu·lin (too bur′kyə lin, tyoo bur′kyə lin) *n.* a liquid prepared from cultures of the bacteria that cause tuberculosis, used in the diagnosis and treatment of the disease.

tu·ber·cu·lo·sis (too bur′kyə lō′sis, tyoo bur′kyə lō′sis) *n.* **1.** an infectious disease caused by a bacterium that may affect any organ of the body, especially the lungs or joints. It is characterized by the formation of tubercles on the affected parts. **2.** tuberculosis of the lungs. Also *(def. 2),* **consumption.**

tu·ber·cu·lous (too bur′kyə ləs, tyoo bur′kyə ləs) *adj.* of, relating to, or having tuberculosis; tubercular.

tube·rose (toob′rōz′, tyoob′rōz′) *n.* a Mexican plant that grows from a tuber, having fragrant, waxy, white flowers.

tu·ber·ous (too′bər əs, tyoo′bər əs) *adj.* **1.** of, like, or bearing a tuber or tubers. **2.** covered with many rounded swellings.

tub·ing (too′bing, tyoo′bing) *n.* **1.** an object or material in the form of a tube: *plastic tubing for a garden hose.* **2.** tubes as a group. **3.** a length or piece of tube.

tu·bu·lar (too′byə lər, tyoo′byə lər) *adj.* **1.** consisting of tubes: *the tubular frame of a modern chair.* **2.** of, relating to, or shaped like a tube: *the tubular body of a worm.*

tu·bule (too′byool, tyoo′byool) *n.* a small tube or tubelike structure.

tuck (tuk) *v.t.* **1.** to push or fold the edge or ends of (something), so as to hold snugly in place: *He tucked his shirt in. She tucked her hair behind her ears.* **2.** to put into a tight or narrow place: *The wasps' nest was tucked underneath the rafters.* **3.** to hide from view or knowledge; store away or conceal: *There were many old things tucked away in the attic.* **4.** to cover snugly: *She tucked her children in bed.* **5.** to sew a tuck or tucks in (material or a garment). —*v.i.* to sew a tuck or tucks in material or a garment. —*n.* a fold sewed in a garment, as to shape or shorten.

tuck·er¹ (tuk′ər) *n.* **1.** formerly, a covering of lace, linen, or other light material worn around the neck and shoulders. **2.** a person or thing that tucks. [*Tuck* + *-er¹.*]

tuck·er² (tuk′ər) *v.t. Informal.* to make tired or weary: *She was tuckered out after the long hike.* [*Tuck* + *-er* repeatedly; because *tuck* formerly meant "to punish."]

Tuc·son (tōō′son) *n.* a city in southeastern Arizona, noted as a health and tourist resort. Pop. (1970), 262,933.

Tu·dor (tōō′dər, tyōō′dər) *n.* **1.** the royal family that ruled England from 1485 to 1603, including Henry VII, Henry VIII, Edward VI, Mary I, and Elizabeth I. **2.** a member of this family. —*adj.* of or relating to a style of architecture that flourished in England during the reign of the Tudor monarchs.

Tues., Tuesday.

Tues·day (tōōz′dē, tōōz′dā, tyōōz′dē, tyōōz′dā) *n.* the third day of the week. [Old English *Tīwesdæg* literally, the day of Tiw, a German god of war.]

tu·fa (tōō′fə, tyōō′fə) *n.* any of various porous rocks formed from material deposited by water.

tuff (tuf) *n.* a rock formed from compressed volcanic ash or dust.

tuf·fet (tuf′it) *n.* a hassock or footstool.

tuft (tuft) *n.* **1.** a dense cluster of flexible fibers, such as feathers, yarn, or hair, bound together or attached at one end and loose and bushy at the other. **2.** a small group or clump, as of trees or bushes. **3.** a cluster of threads sewn through a mattress, pillow, quilt, or the like, to keep the padding in place. —*v.t.* to decorate or provide with a tuft or tufts.

tug (tug) *v.,* **tugged, tug·ging.** —*v.i.* **1.** to give a pull on something: *The child tugged at the man's coat to get his attention.* **2.** to strain to pull or haul: *The horse tugged harder, and finally the log began to move.* —*v.t.* **1.** to give a pull on: *to tug someone's arm.* **2.** to pull or haul with force: *to tug a heavy trunk across a room.* **3.** to tow with a tugboat. —*n.* **1.** a hard pull: *The fisherman felt a tug on the line.* **2.** see **tugboat. 3.** one of the straps of a harness.

tug·boat (tug′bōt′) *n.* a small, powerful boat used to push or tow other boats or ships. Also, **towboat.**

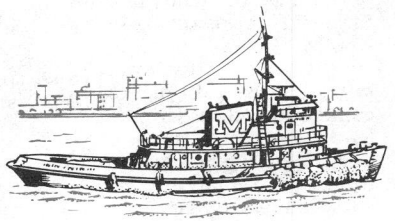
Tugboat

tug of war 1. a game in which two players or teams pull at opposite ends of something, such as a rope, with each trying to force the other either to let go or to be dragged out of place. **2.** any struggle or contest between opposite forces.

tu·i·tion (tōō ish′ən, tyōō ish′ən) *n.* **1.** the amount of money paid by a student for instruction, especially at a college, university, or private school. **2.** teaching; instruction.

tu·lip (tōō′lip, tyōō′lip) *n.* **1.** a cup-shaped flower of any of a group of plants related to the lily. **2.** a plant bearing these flowers, having thick leaves which rise directly from an underground bulb.

tulip tree, a large North American tree having yellowish-green flowers that resemble tulips, and soft wood used to make furniture and other products.

tulle (tōōl) *n.* a fine, stiff net fabric of silk, rayon, or nylon, used in making veils and in dressmaking.

Tul·sa (tul′sə) *n.* a city in northeastern Oklahoma, on the Arkansas River. Pop. (1970), 331,638.

tum·ble (tum′bəl) *v.,* **tum·bled, tum·bling.** —*v.i.* **1.** to fall, especially in an awkward, rolling manner: *The apples tumbled from the overturned cart.* **2.** to roll or toss about: *The clothes tumbled in the dryer.* **3.** to perform acrobatic feats, such as somersaults or handstands. **4.** to go or move in a hurried, disorderly manner: *The children tumbled out the door.* —*v.t.* to cause to tumble

or fall. —*n.* **1.** the act of tumbling; fall. **2.** a state of disorder or confusion; tangle. **3.** a gymnastic feat, such as a somersault.

tum·ble-down (tum′bəl doun′) *adj.* in a dilapidated condition; falling apart: *a tumble-down old barn.*

tum·bler (tum′blər) *n.* **1.** a person who performs gymnastic feats, such as somersaults or leaps; acrobat. **2.** a drinking glass having a flat bottom and no handle. **3.** a rotating drum, especially in an automatic clothes dryer, in which objects are tumbled. **4.** a lever in a lock that must be moved to the correct height by the key in order to release the bolt.

tum·ble·weed (tum′bəl wēd′) *n.* any of several bushy plants of western North America that break off from their roots, usually in autumn, and are blown about by the wind.

Tumbleweed

tum·brel (tum′bril) *also,* **tum·bril.** *n.* **1.** a farmer's cart with a body that can be tilted backward to empty out the load. **2.** a cart used to carry condemned prisoners to be executed, used especially during the French Revolution.

tu·mes·cence (tōō mes′əns, tyōō mes′əns) *n.* **1.** a swollen condition. **2.** a swollen part or organ.

tu·mes·cent (tōō mes′ənt, tyōō mes′ənt) *adj.* swollen or becoming swollen.

tu·mid (tōō′mid, tyōō′mid) *adj.* **1.** abnormally enlarged; swollen. **2.** (of language) pretentious and using big words; pompous.

tum·my (tum′ē) *n. pl.,* **tum·mies.** *Informal.* stomach.

tu·mor (tōō′mər, tyōō′mər) *also, British,* **tu·mour.** *n.* an abnormal growth formed in the body from normal tissue that grows at an abnormally fast rate. —**tu′mor·ous;** *also, British,* **tu′mour·ous,** *adj.*

tu·mult (tōō′məlt, tyōō′məlt) *n.* **1.** a din or commotion; uproar: *The tumult in the crowded room made conversation impossible.* **2.** a very strong disturbance, as of the mind or emotions.

tu·mul·tu·ous (tōō mul′chōō əs, tyōō mul′chōō əs) *adj.* **1.** excited and noisy; disorderly: *a tumultuous meeting.* **2.** disturbed or upset: *tumultuous emotions.* **3.** stormy; turbulent: *tumultuous waves.* —**tu·mul′tu·ous·ly,** *adv.* —**tu·mul′tu·ous·ness,** *n.*

tun (tun) *n.* **1.** a large cask or barrel used for holding liquids, especially wine, ale, or beer. **2.** a liquid measure equal to 252 gallons.

tu·na (tōō′nə) *n. pl.,* **tu·nas** or **tu·na. 1.** any of several large food and game fish related to the mackerel, found in tropical and temperate seas throughout the world. Also, **tunny. 2.** the flesh of the tuna, rich in vitamin A. It is used for food. Also, **tuna fish.**

Tuna

at; āpe; cär; end; mē; it; īce; hot; ōld; fôrk; wood; fōōl; oil; out; up; turn; sing; thin; **th**is; hw in white; zh in treasure. The symbol ə stands for the sound of **a** in about, **e** in taken, **i** in pencil, **o** in lemon, and **u** in circus.

tun·a·ble (tōo′nə bəl, tyōo′nə bəl) *also,* **tune·a·ble.** *adj.* that can be tuned: *a tunable musical instrument.*

tun·dra (tun′drə) *n.* a vast, treeless plain in the northernmost parts of Asia, Europe, and North America, having an arctic or subarctic climate and a layer of permanently frozen soil several inches below the surface.

tune (tōon, tyōon) *n.* **1.** a series of musical notes that make up a melody or theme. **2.** the quality or condition of being at the proper pitch or key: *The old piano is badly out of tune.* **3.** the quality or condition of agreement or accord: *His statement was in tune with what others were saying.* —*v.,* **tuned, tun·ing.** —*v.t.* **1.** to adjust to a standard of pitch; put in tune: *to tune a piano.* **2.** to put (a vehicle or machine) into proper working order, as by lubrication or adjustment of parts: *to tune an engine.* —*v.i.* to bring musical instruments to a standard pitch: *The orchestra was tuning up before the concert.*

   to the tune of. *Informal.* to the sum or extent of: *The repairs cost us to the tune of fifty dollars.*

   to tune in. to adjust a radio or television set so as to receive (a particular station, program, or signal).

   to tune out. to adjust a radio or television set so as to get rid of (interference or the like).

tune·ful (tōon′fəl, tyōon′fəl) *adj.* full of melody; musical. —**tune′ful·ly,** *adv.* —**tune′ful·ness,** *n.*

tune·less (tōon′lis, tyōon′lis) *adj.* having no musical quality. —**tune′less·ly,** *adv.*

tun·er (tōo′nər, tyōo′nər) *n.* **1.** a person or thing that tunes, especially one employed to properly tune musical instruments: *a piano tuner.* **2.** the part of a radio receiver that selects desired radio signals and directs them to an amplifier, where they are converted into sound.

tung·sten (tung′stin) *n.* a grayish, very hard, metallic element, most commonly used in making filaments for electric lamps and electron tubes. Symbol: **W**

tu·nic (tōo′nik, tyōo′nik) *n.* **1.** a garment resembling a long shirt reaching to the knee or below, worn by the ancient Greeks and Romans. **2.** a garment resembling a blouse, often belted and reaching to the hips or below. **3.** a short, close-fitting jacket, often worn as part of a military or police uniform.

tuning fork, a steel instrument with two prongs that vibrates at a constant rate when struck, producing a tone of perfect pitch. It is used in tuning certain musical instruments.

Tu·nis (tōo′nis, tyōo′nis) *n.* **1.** the capital of Tunisia, in the northern part of the country. Pop. (1966), 468,997. **2.** see **Tunisia.**

Tu·ni·sia (tōo nē′zhə, tyōo nē′zhə) *n.* a small country on the northern coast of Africa, on the Mediterranean Sea, formerly known as **Tunis.** Capital, Tunis. Area, 63,379 sq. mi. Pop. (1971 est.), 5,300,000. —**Tu·ni′sian,** *adj., n.*

tun·nel (tun′əl) *n.* a long, narrow, tubelike passageway beneath the ground or water, or under the main part of a structure: *a subway tunnel, a tunnel through the side of a mountain.* —*v.,* **tun·neled, tun·nel·ing;** *also, British,* **tun·nelled, tun·nel·ling.** —*v.i.* to make a passageway under or through something, as by digging: *to tunnel under a wall.* —*v.t.* **1.** to make by tunneling: *The prisoners tunneled an escape route.* **2.** to make a tunnel under, through, or in: *The mole tunneled the lawn.* —**tun′nel·er;** *also, British,* **tun′nel·ler,** *n.*

tun·ny (tun′ē) *n. pl.,* **tun·nies** or **tun·ny.** see **tuna** (*def. 1*).

tu·pe·lo (tōo′pə lō′, tyōo′pə lō′) *n. pl.,* **tu·pe·los. 1.** a tree bearing tiny greenish flowers that ripen into small fruits. **2.** its wood, used to make flooring and crates.

Tunic (def. 3)

tur·ban (tur′bən) *n.* **1.** a head covering worn especially in Arab countries and India, consisting of a long scarf that is wound around the head or around a cap. **2.** any similar headdress, such as a bandanna worn wound around the head by women.

tur·bid (tur′bid) *adj.* **1.** thick with suspended matter; not clear; muddy. **2.** characterized by confusion; muddled; disordered: *turbid emotions.* —**tur·bid′i·ty, tur′bid·ness,** *n.* —**tur′bid·ly,** *adv.*

Turban (def. 1)

tur·bine (tur′bin, tur′bīn) *n.* any of various motors or engines that use the force of a steadily moving stream of gas, vapor, or liquid against slanted blades to turn a rotor. [French *turbine,* from Latin *turbō* whirling motion.]

turbo- *combining form* of, relating to, or operated by a turbine: *turbojet.*

tur·bo·jet (tur′bō jet′) *n.* **1.** a jet propulsion engine in which air is taken in, compressed, mixed with fuel, and then ignited, producing hot, high-pressure gases that turn the turbine that drives the compressor. The hot exhaust provides thrust. **2.** an airplane propelled by such an engine.

tur·bo·prop (tur′bō prop′) *n.* **1.** a turbojet engine in which the power of the exhaust gases is used to drive a propeller. **2.** an airplane that is propelled by such an engine.

tur·bot (tur′bət) *n. pl.,* **tur·bots** or **tur·bot.** a large European flatfish, valued as food.

tur·bu·lence (tur′byə ləns) *n.* the state or quality of being turbulent. Also, **tur·bu·len·cy** (tur′byə lən sē).

tur·bu·lent (tur′byə lənt) *adj.* of, causing, or marked by commotion, disorder, or violence; not calm or smooth; agitated: *turbulent waters, a turbulent period of history.* —**tur′bu·lent·ly,** *adv.*

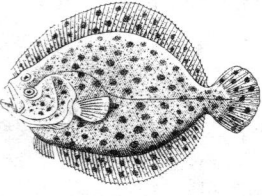

Turbot

tu·reen (tə rēn′) *n.* a deep dish with a cover, used for serving food, especially soup.

turf (turf) *n.* **1.** the surface layer of soil, containing small plants and grasses, their matted roots, and the soil clinging to them. **2.** a separate clump or clumps of this layer, as for replanting. **3.** peat, especially a piece used for fuel. **4.** *Informal.* anything, such as a special status or position or a certain territory, that is jealously guarded and controlled by one person or group. **5. the turf.** the sport of horse racing.

Tur·ge·nev, Ivan Ser·ge·e·vich (toor gā′nyəf; ser-gā′yə vich) 1818–1883, Russian writer.

tur·gid (tur′jid) *adj.* **1.** swollen or distended. **2.** pompous; bombastic: *turgid prose.* —**tur·gid′i·ty, tur′gid·ness,** *n.*

Tu·rin (toor′ən, tyoor′ən) *n.* a city in northwestern Italy, on the Po River. It was important in Roman times. Pop. (1970 est.), 1,190,688.

Turk (turk) *n.* **1.** a person who was born or is living in Turkey. **2.** a person who speaks a Turkic language.

Turk. 1. Turkey. **2.** Turkish.

Tur·ke·stan (tur′ki stan′) *n.* a historic region of central Asia, now divided among the Soviet Union, China, and Afghanistan. It extends from the Caspian Sea to the Gobi desert. It is inhabited mainly by Muslim people who speak Turkic.

tur·key (tur′kē) *n. pl.,* **tur·keys** or **tur·key.** **1.** any of various long-necked birds related to the pheasant, having mainly reddish-brown feathers. Most varieties have been domesticated and are raised for food. **2.** the flesh of a turkey used as food.

Turkey

Tur·key (tur′kē) *n.* a country in western Asia and southeastern Europe. Capital, Ankara. Area, 301, 382 sq. mi. Pop. (1971 est.), 36,160,000.

turkey buzzard, a brownish-black vulture native to North, Central, and South America, having a bare, reddish head.

Tur·kic (tur′kik) *n.* any of various languages spoken by the Turks of Turkey and various Tartar tribes.

Turk·ish (tur′kish) *n.* the language of Turkey. —*adj.* of or relating to Turkey, its people, their language, or culture.

Turkish Empire, another name for **Ottoman Empire.**

Turkish towel *also,* **turkish towel.** a thick towel made of terry cloth.

tur·mer·ic (tur′mər ik) *n.* **1.** a yellow powder with a sharp, bitter taste, obtained from the root of an Asian plant. It is used as a seasoning and as a coloring agent. **2.** the plant yielding this powder, bearing pale-yellow flowers.

tur·moil (tur′moil) *n.* a state or condition of confused agitation or commotion.

turn (turn) *v.i.* **1.** to move around; rotate or revolve: *The earth turns. Once they were free of the mud, the wheels of the car turned easily.* **2.** to move partly around: *The key turned in the lock.* **3.** to change direction; go in a different direction: *The truck turned onto the highway. The river turns south at the bridge.* **4.** to change or reverse to the opposite direction: *Soon our luck will turn for the better.* **5.** to curve or bend: *The corners of the clown's mouth turned down.* **6.** to change in nature or condition: *The leaves turned yellow. The snow turned to rain.* **7.** to become spoiled, rancid, or sour: *The milk turned because we left it out of the refrigerator too long.* **8.** to change position in order to attack or resist: *The lion turned on his trainer and mauled him.* **9.** to take on an attitude of hostility: *His friends turned against him.* **10.** to direct one's effort or attention: *She turned to the job at hand.* **11.** to be or become dizzy or nauseated: *Stanley's stomach turned at the sight of blood.* —*v.t.* **1.** to cause to revolve, as a wheel. **2.** to cause to move partly around: *to turn a doorknob.* **3.** to change the course or direction of: *Rosemary turned the car to the left.* **4.** to cause to curve, curl, or bend: *The seamstress turned the edges of the cloth down.* **5.** to twist or wrench: *to turn one's ankle.* **6.** to reverse; invert: *to turn pancakes on a griddle.* **7.** to go or get around or beyond: *to turn a corner.* **8.** to cause to change; transform: *The hot sun turned the grass brown.* **9.** to make sick; cause nausea or disgust in: *The rich food turned his stomach.* **10.** to direct; aim: *to turn one's energies to completing a job.* **11.** (of age, time, or amount) to be or have passed beyond: *Harry just turned thirty.* **12.** to shape by rotating against a cutting tool, as a lathe: *to turn the legs for a table.* —*n.* **1.** the act of turning. **2.** a change in position or direction: *Make a left turn at the corner.* **3.** the place of changing direction: *a turn in the highway.* **4.** time, occasion, or opportunity that follows another or others in rotation: *It's the catcher's turn to bat.* **5.** an act or deed: *My friend Margaret did me a good turn.* **6.** a change in condition or nature: *The patient took a turn for the worse.*

7. *Informal.* a sudden shock or fright: *The explosion gave me quite a turn!*

at every turn. in every instance; constantly.

by turns. one after another.

in turn. in proper sequence or order.

out of turn. a. not in proper sequence or order. **b.** *Informal.* improperly or impolitely: *Do not speak out of turn.*

to a turn. perfectly: *The dinner was cooked to a turn.*

to take turns. to go in proper or alternating order: *The two boys took turns riding the bicycle.*

to turn down. a. to reject or refuse: *to turn down an invitation.* **b.** to lessen the volume or intensity of: *Please turn down your radio.* **c.** to fold over: *to turn down the blankets on a bed.*

to turn in. *Informal.* to go to bed.

to turn off. a. to cause to stop flowing, such as water, gas, or electricity. **b.** to cause to stop operating: *Turn off the radio when you leave the room.*

to turn on. a. to cause to flow, such as water, gas, or electricity. **b.** to cause to operate: *to turn on a lamp.*

to turn out. a. to produce: *The machine turns out fifty copies per minute.* **b.** to show up; appear: *A large crowd turned out for the football game.* **c.** to have a certain result; end: *How did the movie turn out?* **d.** to put out; extinguish: *to turn out a light.*

to turn over. a. (of an engine) to begin to operate. **b.** to give, transfer, or return: *to turn over a business to one's son.* **c.** to think about; consider carefully: *to turn an idea over in one's mind.*

to turn to. a. to begin to work: *The campers turned to and built a fire.* **b.** to appeal or apply to for help or support: *to turn to a friend.*

to turn up. a. to appear: *The sweater I misplaced turned up at school.* **b.** to discover or search out: *The police turned up new evidence in the case.* **c.** to increase the volume or intensity of: *Turn up the radio if you can't hear it.*

turn·buck·le (turn′buk′əl) *n.* a sleeve or coupling with internal threads that holds together the threaded ends of two rods and can be turned to widen or narrow the gap between the rod ends.

turn·coat (turn′kōt′) *n.* a person who switches to the other side; traitor or renegade.

turn·er (tur′nər) *n.* **1.** a person or thing that turns. **2.** a person who turns or makes things on a lathe.

Tur·ner, Joseph M. W. (tur′nər) 1775–1851, English painter.

turning point, the point at which a decisive or important change takes place; critical point; crisis.

tur·nip (tur′nip) *n.* **1.** the white or yellow root of a plant of the mustard family, cooked and eaten as a vegetable. **2.** the plant bearing this root, having small bright yellow flowers in clusters and soft prickly leaves.

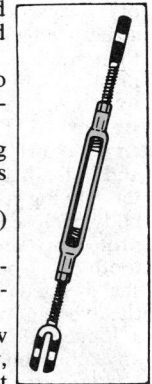

Turnbuckle

turn·key (turn′kē) *n. pl.,* **turn·keys.** a person who has charge of the keys of a prison or jail; jailer.

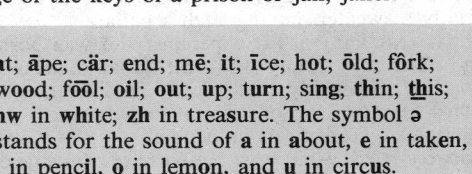

at; āpe; cär; end; mē; it; īce; hot; ōld; fôrk; wood; fool; oil; out; up; turn; sing; thin; this; hw in white; zh in treasure. The symbol ə stands for the sound of **a** in about, **e** in taken, **i** in pencil, **o** in lemon, and **u** in circus.

turn·off (turn′ôf′) *n.* an exit leading off a main road to a side road.

turn·out (turn′out′) *n.* **1.** a gathering of people for some specific occasion: *There was a poor turnout for the football game because of the rainy weather.* **2.** the amount produced; output: *The new machine increased the factory's turnout.* **3.** the act of turning out. **4.** a section of a road that has been widened to enable vehicles to pass or park.

turn·o·ver (turn′ō′vər) *n.* **1.** a small pie made by folding half the crust over a filling and upon the other half. **2.** the number of workers who leave their jobs and are replaced by others during a given period. **3.** the number of times that the stock of goods of a firm is sold and replaced during a given period. **4.** the total amount of business done in a given period: *From a turnover of $5000 for a week, the firm had a profit of $350.*

turn·pike (turn′pīk′) *n.* **1.** a road, especially a large highway, that has, or used to have, a tollgate. **2.** any highway.

turn·stile (turn′stīl′) *n.* a revolving gate or movable bar at an exit or entrance, that lets people pass through one at a time.

turn·ta·ble (turn′tā′bəl) *n.* **1.** a revolving device used to turn things around, especially a circular railroad platform with tracks used to turn locomotives or cars around. **2.** a flat platform on a phonograph that revolves to play records rested upon it.

tur·pen·tine (tur′pən tīn′) *n.* **1.** a thick, sticky substance secreted by certain species of pine trees. **2.** a colorless, combustible liquid obtained by distilling this substance, widely used as a thinner for paints and as a solvent for polishes.

tur·pi·tude (tur′pə tōōd′, tur′pə tyōōd′) *n.* shameful wickedness; depravity; baseness: *moral turpitude.*

tur·quoise (tur′kwoiz, tur′koiz) *n.* **1.** an opaque mineral, usually greenish-blue, having a waxy luster and valued as a gem. **2.** a greenish-blue color. —*adj.* having the color turquoise; greenish-blue.

tur·ret (tur′it) *n.* **1.** a small tower, usually forming part of a larger structure. **2.** an armored, usually revolving, structure used to house antiaircraft guns or cannons and their gunners, as on a ship or tank. **3.** a strong, transparent plastic bubble-shaped structure on a military aircraft, used to protect the gunner.

tur·ret·ed (tur′i tid) *adj.* having a turret or turrets.

tur·tle (turt′əl) *n.* any of a group of reptiles found on land and in fresh and salt water, having a low, wide body enclosed in a hard, protective shell, and a toothless beak with sharp-edged jaws. On the average, turtles have a longer life span than any other animal with a backbone, some living to an age of 130 years.

Turtle

tur·tle·dove (turt′əl duv′) *n.* any of several small wild doves, noted for its soft, cooing call.

tur·tle·neck (turt′əl nek′) *n.* **1.** a high, often turned over, collar that fits snugly around the neck. **2.** a garment, especially a sweater, having such a collar.

Tus·can (tus′kən) *n.* **1.** a person who was born or is living in Tuscany. **2.** any of several Italian dialects spoken in Tuscany, especially that spoken in Florence. **3.** the standard literary form of the Italian language. —*adj.* of or relating to Tuscany or its people.

Tus·ca·ny (tus′kə nē) *n.* a region in north-central Italy.

Tus·ca·ro·ra (tus′kə rôr′ə) *n. pl.*, **Tus·ca·ro·ras** or **Tus·ca·ro·ra.** a member of a tribe of North American Iroquois Indians formerly living in what is now North Carolina, now living in New York.

tusk (tusk) *n.* **1.** a long, pointed, projecting tooth, usually one of a pair, of certain animals, such as elephants, walruses, and wild boars. **2.** any long, pointed, projecting tooth or part that is like a tooth. —*v.t.* to dig up or gore with tusks.

Tusk

Tusks on an elephant

tusk·er (tus′kər) *n.* an animal having well-developed tusks, especially an elephant or wild boar.

tus·sah (tus′ə) *n.* **1.** a coarse brownish or yellowish silk. **2.** an Asiatic silkworm that produces this silk.

tus·sle (tus′əl) *n.* **1.** a disorderly physical fight or struggle; scuffle. **2.** any disorderly conflict or struggle: *The election this fall will be a real tussle.* —*v.i.*, **tus·sled, tus·sling.** to engage in a disorderly physical fight or struggle: *The man tussled with his attacker.*

tus·sock (tus′ək) *n.* a clump, tuft, or matted growth, as of hair or grass.

tut (tut) *interj.* used to express impatience, contempt, annoyance, or rebuke.

Tut·ankh·a·men (tōō′tängk ä′mən) *n.* pharaoh of Egypt in about the middle of the fourteenth century B.C.

tu·te·lage (tōōt′əl ij, tyōōt′əl ij) *n.* **1.** the office or function of a guardian; guardianship. **2.** the act of teaching; instruction. **3.** the state of being under a tutor or guardian.

tu·te·lar·y (tōōt′əl er′ē, tyōōt′əl er′ē) *also,* **tu·te·lar** (tōōt′əl ər, tyōōt′əl ər). *adj.* **1.** having the position of a guardian; protective. **2.** of or relating to a guardian: *tutelary powers.*

tu·tor (tōō′tər, tyōō′tər) *n.* **1.** a teacher or other person who gives private instruction to a student. **2.** *British.* a college official who supervises and advises undergraduate students assigned to him. —*v.t.* to act as a tutor to, especially by giving private instruction. —*v.i.* to act or work as a private instructor.

tu·to·ri·al (tōō tôr′ē əl, tyōō tôr′ē əl) *adj.* of, relating to, or involving a private instructor or instruction: *The school had an afternoon tutorial program.* —*n.* a class or session instructed by a tutor for one student or a small group of students.

tut·ti-frut·ti (tōō′tē frōō′tē) *adj.* containing or made with various candied fruits or fruit flavorings: *tutti-frutti ice cream.*

tu·tu (tōō′tōō) *n.* a very short, full skirt, usually consisting of many layers of sheer fabric, worn by ballerinas.

Tu·tu·i·la (tōō′tōō ē′lä) *n.* the principal island of American Samoa.

tux (tuks) *n. pl.*, **tux·es.** *Informal.* see **tuxedo.**

tux·e·do (tuk sē′dō) *also,* **Tux·e·do.** *n. pl.*, **tux·e·dos.** a man's formal suit, usually dark in color, having a jacket without tails and trousers with a single stripe of satin or similar material along the outer side of each leg. [From *Tuxedo* Park, New York, a wealthy and exclusive community in the nineteenth century, where this suit was popular.]

TV, television.

Tutu

TVA, Tennessee Valley Authority, an independent agency of the U.S. government, established in 1933 for water control and development of resources, especially electrical power, along the Tennessee River and its major tributaries in seven southern states.

twad·dle (twod′əl) *n.* silly or idle talk; prattle. —*v.i.,* **twad·dled, twad·dling.** to talk in a childish or foolish manner. —**twad′dler,** *n.*

twain (twān) *Archaic. adj.* two. —*n.* two; pair: *Oh, East is East, and West is West, and never the twain shall meet* (Rudyard Kipling).

Twain, Mark (twān) 1835–1910, U.S. author and humorist; born Samuel Langhorne Clemens.

twang (twang) *n.* **1.** a sharp, metallic, ringing sound, such as that made by plucking a string on a guitar or other musical instrument. **2.** a sharp, nasal tone of voice. —*v.i.* to make a sharp, metallic, ringing sound: *The wire twanged when it broke.* —*v.t.* to cause to make a sharp, metallic sound.

'twas (twuz, twoz) it was.

tweak (twēk) *v.t.* to pinch and pull sharply with a twisting motion. —*n.* a sharp, twisting pinch.

tweed (twēd) *n.* **1.** a rough fabric, usually made of wool, woven with yarns of two or more colors. **2. tweeds.** clothes made of this fabric.

twee·dle·dum and twee·dle·dee (twēd′əl dum′ ən twēd′əl dē′) two persons or things between which there is almost no difference.

tweet (twēt) *n.* a thin, chirping sound, such as that made by a bird. —*v.i.* to utter a tweet or tweets.

tweet·er (twē′tər) *n.* a loudspeaker designed to reproduce high-frequency sound signals.

tweez·ers (twē′zərs) *n.,pl.* small pincers for plucking out hairs or for picking up tiny objects.

twelfth (twelfth) *adj.* **1.** (the ordinal of twelve) next after the eleventh. **2.** being one of twelve equal parts. —*n.* **1.** something that is next after the eleventh. **2.** one of twelve equal parts; 1/12.

Twelfth night, the evening of, or the night before, the twelfth night after Christmas.

twelve (twelv) *n.* **1.** the cardinal number that is two more than ten. **2.** a symbol representing this number, such as 12 or XII. **3.** something having this many units or things. **4. the Twelve.** the twelve disciples of Jesus chosen by Him to preach His gospel. Also, **the Twelve Apostles.** —*adj.* numbering two more than ten.

twelve·month (twelv′munth′) *n.* a period of twelve months; year.

twen·ti·eth (twen′tē ith) *adj.* **1.** (the ordinal of twenty) next after the nineteenth. **2.** being one of twenty equal parts. —*n.* **1.** something that is next after the nineteenth. **2.** one of twenty equal parts; 1/20.

twen·ty (twen′tē) *n. pl.,* **twen·ties. 1.** the cardinal number that is two times ten. **2.** a symbol representing this number, such as 20 or XX. —*adj.* numbering two times ten.

twen·ty-one (twen′tē wun′) *n.* another word for **blackjack.**

twice (twīs) *adv.* **1.** on two occasions or in two instances; two times. **2.** doubly: *twice as many.*

twice-told (twīs′tōld′) *adj.* **1.** having been told two times. **2.** having been told many times; stale; trite.

twid·dle (twid′əl) *v.,* **twid·dled, twid·dling.** —*v.t.* to turn or twirl (something) idly: *to twiddle a locket on a chain.* —*v.i.* **1.** to play with something in an idle manner. **2.** to be busy about trifles. —*n.* a light, twirling motion, as of the thumbs.

twig (twig) *n.* a small branch or shoot of a tree or other woody plant.

twi·light (twī′līt′) *n.* **1.** a soft, hazy light reflected from the sun just after sunset and, sometimes, just before sunrise. **2.** the period during which this light is seen. **3.** any soft, faint light. **4.** a period or condition marked by the decline of glory, success, achievement, or the like: *the twilight of one's life.* —*adj.* of, relating to, or occurring at twilight.

twill (twil) *n.* **1.** a weave characterized by parallel diagonal ridges. **2.** a strong, durable fabric having such a weave.

twilled (twild) *adj.* woven with parallel diagonal ridges on the surface.

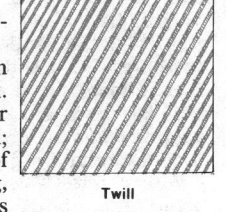
Twill

twin (twin) *n.* **1.** one of two children or animals born at the same birth. **2.** either of two persons, animals, or things that are similar or identical; mate. —*adj.* **1.** being two or one of two born at the same birth. **2.** having, forming, or being one of two things that are similar or identical: *The castle had twin turrets.* —*v.i.,* **twinned, twin·ning.** to give birth to twins.

twine (twīn) *n.* **1.** a strong string or cord made of two or more strands twisted together. **2.** something formed by twisting two or more strands, threads, or the like together. —*v.,* **twined, twin·ing.** —*v.t.* **1.** to twist together. **2.** to form by twisting together. **3.** to wind or coil (something) around something else: *The gardener twined the ivy around the trellis.* **4.** to cover or wrap in this way: *to twine a pole with ribbons.* —*v.i.* to extend, move, or grow in a winding manner or course: *Vines twined over the walls.*

twinge (twinj) *n.* **1.** a sudden, sharp pain: *a twinge of arthritis.* **2.** a sudden, sharp feeling of mental or emotional distress: *a twinge of pity, a twinge of conscience.* —*v.i.,* **twinged, twing·ing.** to feel a twinge.

twin·kle (twing′kəl) *v.i.,* **twin·kled, twin·kling. 1.** to shine with or give flashes of light: *The stars twinkled in the sky.* **2.** (of the eyes) to be bright, as with amusement or pleasure. **3.** to move lightly and quickly. —*n.* **1.** a flicker or flash of light. **2.** brightness of the eyes, as in amusement or pleasure. **3.** a very brief period of time; twinkling.

twin·kling (twing′kling) *n.* **1.** a very brief period of time; moment; instant. **2.** a flicker or flash of light; twinkle.

twirl (twurl) *v.t.* to cause to rotate or spin rapidly. —*v.i.* to rotate or spin rapidly. —*n.* **1.** the act of twirling or the state of being twirled. **2.** something having a curled or spiral shape. —**twirl′er,** *n.*

twist (twist) *v.t.* **1.** to wind (two or more strands, threads, or the like) around each other. **2.** to make or form in this way: *to twist a rope from single strands.* **3.** to rotate or turn: *She twisted the bracelet around her wrist.* **4.** to form into a spiral, as by turning the ends in opposite directions. **5.** to change the natural or usual shape or position of; contort; distort: *He twisted his face into a grimace.* **6.** to injure (a part of the body) in this way; sprain: *John fell and twisted his ankle.* **7.** to change or distort the meaning of: *to twist someone's words.* —*v.i.* **1.** to turn so as to face in a different direction. **2.** to move in or follow a winding course: *The new highway twists through the mountains.* **3.** to become wound or turned: *The thin gold wire twisted easily.* **4.** to become sprained. —*n.* **1.** a curve,

T

bend, or turn: *There is a twist in the road ahead.* **2.** the act of twisting or the state of being twisted. **3.** something having a curled or spiral shape. **4.** an unexpected change in the usual or ordinary: *The movie ended with a surprising twist.* **5.** a thread, cord, or rope made of two or more strands that are twisted together.

twist·er (twis'tər) *n.* **1.** a person or thing that twists. **2.** *Informal.* a tornado.

twit (twit) *v.t.,* **twit·ted, twit·ting.** to tease or taunt, especially by reminding of past errors or embarrassments.

twitch (twich) *v.i.* to move with a sudden, unintentional jerk. —*v.t.* to pull with a sudden tug or jerk. —*n. pl.,* **twitch·es. 1.** a sudden, involuntary muscle contraction. **2.** a sudden, sharp pull or tug; jerk.

twit·ter (twit'ər) *n.* **1.** a series of short, light, chirping sounds made by a bird or birds. **2.** a state or condition of nervous agitation or excitement: *She is always in a twitter before a test.* —*v.i.* to utter a series of light, chirping sounds, as a bird.

twixt (twikst) *also,* **'twixt.** *prep.* between; betwixt.

two (tōō) *n. pl.,* **twos. 1.** the cardinal number that is one more than one. **2.** a symbol representing this number, such as 2 or II. **3.** something having this many units or things, such as a playing card. —*adj.* numbering one more than one.

two bits *Informal.* twenty-five cents; quarter.

two-by-four (tōō'bī fôr') *n.* **1.** a rough piece of lumber that is two inches thick and four inches wide, used especially in building. **2.** a finished piece of lumber that is 1⅝ inches thick and 3⅝ inches wide, used especially in building.

two-faced (tōō'fāst') *adj.* **1.** having two faces or aspects. **2.** deceitful or hypocritical.

two-fist·ed (tōō'fis'tid) *adj.* powerful, strong, or virile.

two·fold (tōō'fōld') *adj.* **1.** two times as great or numerous. **2.** having or consisting of two parts. —*adv.* so as to be two times greater or more numerous.

two-ply (tōō'plī') *adj.* **1.** composed or consisting of two layers, thicknesses, or strands. **2.** consisting of two webs woven into each other: *a two-ply carpet.*

two·some (tōō'səm) *n.* **1.** two persons together; couple. **2.** something played or done by two persons, such as a round of golf played by two people.

two-step (tōō'step') *n.* **1.** a ballroom dance consisting of sliding steps in 2/4 time. **2.** the music for such a dance.

two-time (tōō'tīm') *v.t.,* **two-timed, two-tim·ing.** *Slang.* to be unfaithful to or deceive, especially in love. —**two'-tim'er,** *n.*

two-way (tōō'wā') *adj.* **1.** moving or allowing movement in two directions: *two-way traffic, a two-way street.* **2.** allowing communication in two directions, especially by being able to transmit and receive: *a two-way radio.*

-ty[1] *suffix* multiplied by ten: *sixty, seventy.* [Old English *-tig.*]

-ty[2] *suffix* (used to form nouns) the state, condition, or quality of being: *safety, subtlety.* [Old French *-te,* from Latin *-tas.*]

ty·coon (tī kōōn') *n.* a wealthy, powerful businessman, industrialist, or financier.

ty·ing (tī'ing) the present participle of **tie.**

tyke (tīk) *also,* **tike.** *n.* **1.** *Informal.* a small child, especially one who is mischievous. **2.** a mongrel dog; cur.

Ty·ler, John (tī'lər) 1790–1862, the tenth president of the United States, from 1841 to 1845.

tym·pa·ni (tim'pə nē) *n.,pl. sing.,* **tym·pa·no** (tim'-pə nō'). another spelling of **timpani.**

tym·pan·ic (tim pan'ik) *adj.* **1.** of or relating to the eardrum or the middle ear. **2.** relating to or resembling a drum.

tympanic membrane, a thin membrane that separates the external ear from the middle ear; eardrum.

tym·pa·nist (tim'pə nist) *n.* a member of an orchestra who plays a kettledrum and, usually, other percussion instruments.

tym·pa·num (tim'pə nəm) *n. pl.,* **tym·pa·nums** or **tym·pa·na** (tim'pə nə). **1.** another word for **eardrum. 2.** another word for **middle ear.**

type (tīp) *n.* **1.** a particular kind, class, or group sharing certain common traits or characteristics: *What type of car does he own?* **2.** a person or thing that shows the characteristic qualities of a kind, class, or group; typical or perfect example. **3.** *Printing.* **a.** a rectangular piece or block of metal or wood on one surface of which there is a raised letter, numeral, or other symbol that forms a printing surface. **b.** such pieces or blocks as a group. **4.** a printed or typewritten character or characters: *The book was printed in large type.* **5.** a design or other ornamental figure on either side of a coin or medal. **6.** a blood group. —*v.,* **typed, typ·ing.** —*v.t.* **1.** to write (something) on a typewriter: *to type a letter.* **2.** to identify or determine the type of (a blood sample). **3.** to place in a particular class or group: *Robert typed the stranger as being an Englishman.* —*v.i.* to write on a typewriter.

type·script (tīp'skript') *n.* material that has been typewritten.

type·set·ter (tīp'set'ər) *n.* a person or machine that sets type for printing.

type·set·ting (tīp'set'ing) *n.* the act or process of setting type for printing. —*adj.* used or adapted for setting type: *a typesetting machine.*

type·write (tīp'rīt') *v.,* **type·wrote** (tīp'rōt'), **type·writ·ten** (tīp'rit'ən), **type·writ·ing.** —*v.t.* to write (something) with a typewriter. —*v.i.* to use a typewriter; type.

type·writ·er (tīp'rī'tər) *n.* a machine used to produce clear writing that is like print. It is made up of a set of keys that, when struck, impress letters on paper through an inked ribbon.

type·writ·ing (tīp'rī'ting) *n.* **1.** the act or process of using a typewriter. **2.** something that is done or produced on a typewriter.

Typewriter

ty·phoid (tī'foid) *n.* see **typhoid fever.** —*adj.* of, relating to, like, or typical of typhoid fever.

typhoid fever, an infectious, sometimes fatal, fever characterized by intestinal inflammation and rose-colored spots on the skin. It is caused by a bacillus taken into the body in food or drink.

ty·phoon (tī fōōn') *n.* a severe tropical hurricane occurring in the western Pacific Ocean, usually during the months of July, August, September, and October.

ty·phus (tī'fəs) *n.* any of a group of infectious diseases characterized by severe headache, high fever, and a spotted rash. It is carried by germs carried by fleas or lice.

typ·i·cal (tip'i kəl) *adj.* **1.** conforming to, showing, or indicating the qualities, attributes, or nature characteristic of a particular type: *He is a typical businessman.* **2.** of the nature of or constituting a type. —**typ'i·cal·ly,** *adv.*

typ·i·fy (tip'ə fī') *v.t.,* **typ·i·fied, typ·i·fy·ing. 1.** to have or show the common or usual characteristics of; exemplify. **2.** to serve as a symbol of; represent; symbolize. —**typ'i·fi·ca'tion,** *n.*

typ·ist (tī'pist) *n.* a person who types, especially a person whose job is operating a typewriter.

ty·pog·ra·pher (tī pog'rə fər) *n.* see **printer** *(def. 1).*

ty·po·graph·i·cal (tī'pə graf'i kəl) *adj.* of or relating to typography: *a typographical error.* Also, **ty·po·graph·ic** (tī′pə graf′ik). —**ty′po·graph′i·cal·ly,** *adv.*

ty·pog·ra·phy (tī pog′rə fē) *n.* **1.** the act, art, or process of producing printed matter, especially by means of a printing press. **2.** the arrangement, appearance, or style of printed matter.

ty·ran·ni·cal (ti ran′i kəl) *adj.* of, relating to, or like a tyrant; cruel and unjust. Also, **ty·ran·nic** (ti ran′ik). —**ty·ran′ni·cal·ly,** *adv.*

tyr·an·nize (tir′ə nīz′) *v.,* **tyr·an·nized, tyr·an·niz·ing.** —*v.i.* **1.** to use power in a cruel and unjust way (often with *over*): *The king tyrannized over his people.* **2.** to rule as a tyrant. —*v.t.* to treat or govern tyrannically.

ty·ran·no·saur (ti ran′ə sôr′) *n.* a huge meat-eating dinosaur that once existed in North America. Also, **ty·ran·no·sau·rus** (ti ran′ə sôr′əs).

tyr·an·nous (tir′ə nəs) *adj.* cruel and unjust; tyrannical. —**tyr′an·nous·ly,** *adv.*

tyr·an·ny (tir′ə nē) *n. pl.,* **tyr·an·nies. 1.** the cruel and unjust use of force, power, or authority. **2.** any oppressive or unjustly severe rule or government by one person.

ty·rant (tī′rənt) *n.* **1.** a person who uses power or authority in a cruel and unjust way. **2.** a person who has absolute power and rules or governs in a cruel and unjust way; absolute ruler; despot. **3.** in ancient Greece, an absolute ruler who got his authority illegally.

tyre (tīr) *British.* another spelling of **tire**².

Tyre (tīr) *n.* a principal city of Phoenicia and an important commercial center of the ancient world, on the Mediterranean Sea.

Tyr·i·an (tir′ē ən) *adj.* of or relating to ancient Tyre or its people.

ty·ro (tī′rō) *also,* **ti·ro.** *n. pl.,* **ty·ros.** a person who is just beginning to learn to do something; beginner; novice.

Ty·rol (tir′ol, tī′rōl, ti rōl′) *also,* **Ti·rol.** *n.* a region in western Austria, in the Alps, bordering Italy, Germany, and Switzerland.

Tyr·rhe·ni·an Sea (ti rē′nē ən) the part of the Mediterranean Sea between Italy, Sicily, Sardinia, and Corsica.

tzar (zär) another spelling of **czar**.

tza·ri·na (zä rē′nə) another spelling of **czarina**.

tzet·ze fly (tset′sē, tsēt′sē) another spelling of **tsetse fly**. Also, **tzetze**.

---

at; āpe; cär; end; mē; it; īce; hot; ōld; fôrk; wood; fōōl; oil; out; up; turn; sing; thin; this; hw in white; zh in treasure. The symbol ə stands for the sound of **a** in about, e in taken, i in pencil, o in lemon, and u in circus.

T

1. Semitic	Y	4. Etruscan	V
2. Phoenician	Y	5. Early Latin	V
3. Greek Ninth Century B.C.	Y	6. English	U

U is the twenty-first letter of the English alphabet. It is one of only three letters that we use today that did not come from Latin or from an earlier alphabet. Because the letter **U** developed as a variation of the letter **V**, they can be said to share the same early history. Their earliest ancestor was the ancient Semitic letter *waw* (1), that depicted a hook and stood for the *w* sound, as the *w* in *water*. When the Phoenicians (2) borrowed *waw*, they used it to represent both the consonant sound *w* and the vowel sound *u*, as the *u* in *rude*. The Greeks adopted *waw* and called it *upsilon* (3), writing it as the capital letter **Y** is written today. *Upsilon*, which stood for only the *u* sound, was borrowed by the Etruscans (4) who, like the Phoenicians, used it to represent both the vowel and consonant sounds. The shape of *upsilon* was also altered by the Etruscans, who wrote it as we write the capital letter **V** today. The design and pronunciation of this letter were adopted without change in the Latin alphabet (5). By about 1000 years ago, two forms of this V-shaped letter were being used in writing: **V** at the beginning of a word and a new letter, **U**, in the middle of a word. In following years, the letter **U**, which came to be used exclusively for the vowel sound *u*, was written almost exactly as we write it today (6).

u, U (yōō) *n. pl.,* **u's, U's. 1.** the twenty-first letter of the English alphabet. **2.** something having the shape of this letter.

U, the symbol for uranium.

UAR, United Arab Republic.

u·biq·ui·tous (yōō bik′wə təs) *adj.* being everywhere at once, or seeming to be everywhere at once. —**u·biq′ui·tous·ly,** *adv.* —**u·biq′ui·tous·ness,** *n.*

u·biq·ui·ty (yōō bik′wə tē) *n.* the state of being ubiquitous.

U-boat (yōō′bōt′) *n.* a German submarine, especially one used in World War I or II.

ud·der (ud′ər) *n.* a large sac hanging from the underside of certain female animals, such as cows, containing the milk-producing glands and teats through which milk can be drawn by nursing or milking.

UFO, unidentified flying object.

U·gan·da (yōō gan′də, ōō gan′də) *n.* a country in east-central Africa. Capital, Kampala. Area, 91,134 sq. mi. Pop. (1971 est.), 10,130,000.

ugh (ug, u) *interj.* a grunt or exclamation expressing disgust or horror.

ug·ly (ug′lē) *adj.,* **ug·li·er, ug·li·est. 1.** very unattractive or unpleasant to the eye: *an ugly scar, an ugly painting.* **2.** causing disgust; disagreeable; offensive: *an ugly story, ugly rumors.* **3.** likely to cause trouble or harm; ominous: *an ugly storm.* **4.** bad-tempered: *He was in an ugly mood.* **5.** morally offensive or disgusting: *an ugly prejudice.* —**ug′li·ness,** *n.*

uhf, UHF, ultrahigh frequency.

U.K., United Kingdom.

u·kase (yōō′kās′) *n.* **1.** an official proclamation or decree; edict. **2.** formerly, a decree or order having the force of law, issued by the czar or by the czarist government in Russia.

U·kraine (yōō krān′) *n.* a republic of the Soviet Union, in the southwestern part of the country, on the Black Sea. Official name: **Ukrainian Soviet Socialist Republic.** Area, 232,047 sq. mi. Pop. (1970), 47,126,000.

U·krain·i·an (yōō krā′nē ən) *n.* **1.** a person who was born or is living in the Ukraine. **2.** a Slavic language spoken mostly in the Ukraine. It is closely related to Russian. —*adj.* of or relating to the Ukraine, its people, their language, or their culture.

u·ku·le·le (yōō′kə lā′lē) *n.* a small guitar having four strings.

U·lan Ba·tor (ōō′län bä′tôr) the capital and largest city of the Mongolian People's Republic, in the northeastern part of the country. Pop. (1971 est.), 250,000.

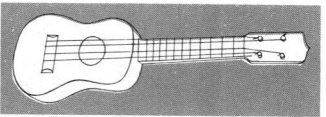

Ukulele

ul·cer (ul′sər) *n.* an open sore on the skin or on a membrane, such as the stomach lining.

ul·cer·ate (ul′sə rāt′) *v.t., v.i.,* **ul·cer·at·ed, ul·cer·at·ing.** to make or become ulcerous.

ul·cer·a·tion (ul′sə rā′shən) *n.* **1.** the act or process of ulcerating or the state of being ulcerated. **2.** an ulcerous condition; ulcer.

ul·cer·ous (ul′sər əs) *adj.* **1.** relating to or like an ulcer or ulcers. **2.** affected with an ulcer or ulcers.

ul·na (ul′nə) *n. pl.,* **ul·nae** (ul′nē) or **ul·nas.** **1.** the larger of the two bones of the forearm, extending from the elbow to the wrist. **2.** a corresponding bone in the forelimb of other animals.

Ul·ster (ul′stər) *n.* a former province of Ireland now comprising all of Northern Ireland and part of the Republic of Ireland.

ul·ster (ul′stər) *n.* a very long, heavy overcoat, often with a belt and a cape. [From *Ulster,* where it was first made.]

ul·te·ri·or (ul tēr′ē ər) *adj.* **1.** beyond what is shown or expressed; hidden: *ulterior motives.* **2.** farther off: *ulterior regions.*

ul·ti·ma (ul′tə mə) *n.* the last syllable of a word.

ul·ti·ma·ta (ul′tə mä′tə) a plural of **ultimatum.**

ul·ti·mate (ul′tə mit) *adj.* **1.** coming at the end; final: *the ultimate cost, the ultimate goal.* **2.** greatest possible: *ultimate courage.* **3.** earliest or farthest possible: *the ultimate origin of life, the ultimate limits.* —*n.* something that is complete or final and cannot be surpassed: *the ultimate in luxury.*

ul·ti·mate·ly (ul′tə mit lē) *adv.* in the end; finally.

ul·ti·ma·tum (ul′tə mä′təm) *n. pl.,* **ul·ti·ma·tums** or **ul·ti·ma·ta.** a final offer, demand, or proposal that implies the threat of punishment, a break in relations, or the use of force if it is rejected.

ul·tra (ul′trə) *adj.* going beyond what is usual or moderate; excessive; extreme. —*n.* a person who has extreme views; extremist.

ultra- *prefix* **1.** beyond what is usual or moderate; excessively; extremely: *ultraconservative.* **2.** on the other side of; beyond: *ultraviolet.* **3.** beyond the range or limits of: *ultrasonic.*

ul·tra·high frequency (ul′trə hī′) a frequency range of radio waves from 300 to 3000 megacycles, used for radio and television broadcasting.

ul·tra·ma·rine (ul′trə mə rēn′) *n.* **1.** a deep-blue color. **2.** a blue coloring matter, originally made from the gem lapis lazuli. —*adj.* having the color ultramarine; deep-blue.

ul·tra·son·ic (ul′trə son′ik) *adj.* of, relating to, or indicating sound waves having a frequency beyond the range or limits of human hearing, usually above 20,000 cycles per second.

ul·tra·vi·o·let (ul′trə vī′ə lit) *adj.* **1.** (of electromagnetic radiation) having wavelengths shorter than those of visible light but longer than those of X rays, ranging from 40 to 4000 angstroms. Ultraviolet rays are present in sunlight. **2.** of, using, or producing ultraviolet radiation.

U·lys·ses (yōō lis′ēz) *n. Greek and Roman Legend.* a king of Ithaca and leader in the Trojan War. Ulysses was forced to wander for ten years after the fall of Troy until the gods finally permitted him to return home. He was called Odysseus by the Greeks.

um·bel (um′bəl) *n.* a flower cluster in which the flower stalks grow out of a common center at the top of the stem.

um·ber (um′bər) *n.* **1.** brown earth, used as a brown pigment. **2.** a brown color. —*adj.* having the color umber.

um·bil·i·cal cord (um bil′i kəl) a cordlike structure that connects the navel of an unborn baby to the placenta of the mother's womb.

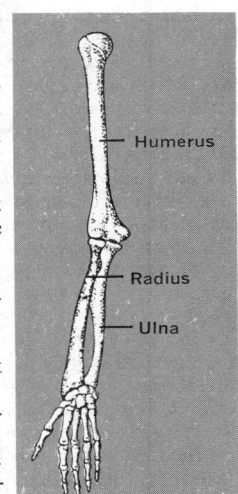

Ulna

um·bra (um′brə) *n. pl.,* **um·brae** (um′brē) or **um·bras.** **1.** *Astronomy.* the cone-shaped shadow cast by the moon in a solar eclipse or by the earth in a lunar eclipse, in the direction away from the sun. **2.** any shaded area or shadow.

um·brage (um′brij) *n.* a feeling of resentment, especially at an imagined insult; offense: *She took umbrage at his joking remark.*

um·brel·la (um brel′ə) *n.* **1.** a device that is made of a circular piece of cloth or other material attached to narrow ribs radiating from a long central rod. It is used to give protection from rain or sun. **2.** something resembling an umbrella in shape or function, such as a group of military aircraft sent up to protect land or sea forces.

umbrella tree, an American magnolia tree having long leaves and spreading branches that cause it to look like an open umbrella.

Um·bri·a (um′brē ə) *n.* a historic region in central Italy.

u·mi·ak (ōō′mē ak′) *n.* a large, open Eskimo boat made of skins stretched over a wooden frame.

um·pire (um′pīr) *n.* an official who rules on plays in certain sports and games, such as baseball. —*v.,* **um·pired, um·pir·ing.** —*v.t.* to act as an umpire of: *to umpire a softball game.* —*v.i.* to act as an umpire.

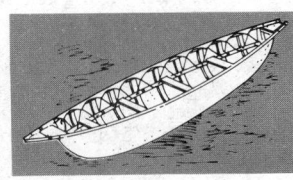

Umiak

un-[1] *prefix* (used to form adjectives, adverbs, and nouns) the opposite of: *uncooked, unbeliever.* [Old English *un-.*]

● To understand the meaning of a word that begins with **un-** but is not defined in this dictionary, add the word *not* to the meaning of the basic word. For example, *unafraid* means "not afraid," *unconvincing* means "not convincing," *untrained* means "not trained," and *unworkable* means "not workable." For any important *un-* word that has a special meaning, there is an entry in the dictionary.

un-[2] *prefix* **1.** (used to form verbs from verbs) **a.** to do the opposite of: *unfasten.* **b.** to make stronger the action of: *unloose.* **2.** (used to form verbs from nouns) **a.** to release, remove, or free from: *unearth.* **b.** to cause to cease to be: *unman.* [Old English *un-, on-, an-.*]

UN, United Nations.

un·a·bashed (un′ə basht′) *adj.* not ashamed, embarrassed, or easily confused. —**un·a·bash·ed·ly** (un′ə bash′-id lē) *adv.*

un·a·bat·ed (un′ə bā′tid) *adj.* at full strength. —**un′a·bat′ed·ly,** *adv.*

un·a·ble (un ā′bəl) *adj.* not having enough power, skills, or qualifications: *I am unable to type.*

un·a·bridged (un′ə brijd′) *adj.* not shortened; complete: *an unabridged edition of a book.*

un·ac·cent·ed (un ak′sen tid) *adj.* not accented. In the word *ago,* the *a* is unaccented.

un·ac·com·pa·nied (un′ə kum′pə nēd′) *adj.* **1.** without a companion or escort; alone: *She went unaccompanied to the theater.* **2.** *Music.* without accompaniment.

at; āpe; cär; end; mē; it; īce; hot; ōld; fôrk; wood; fōōl; oil; out; up; turn; sing; thin; this; hw in white; zh in treasure. The symbol ə stands for the sound of **a** in about, **e** in taken, **i** in pencil, **o** in lemon, and **u** in circus.

un·ac·com·plished (un′ə kom′plisht) *adj.* **1.** not skilled: *He is unaccomplished as a public speaker.* **2.** not completed.

un·ac·count·a·ble (un′ə koun′tə bəl) *adj.* **1.** that cannot be accounted for. **2.** not liable to be called to account. —**un′ac·count′a·bly,** *adv.*

un·ac·cus·tomed (un′ə kus′təmd) *adj.* **1.** not used to: *She is unaccustomed to country life.* **2.** unfamiliar; unusual: *In the emergency he acted with unaccustomed speed.*

un·ac·quaint·ed (un′ə kwān′tid) *adj.* **1.** not known to someone or to each other. **2.** not familiar: *She is unacquainted with the new rules.*

un·a·dorned (un′ə dornd′) *adj.* not decorated; simple; plain.

un·a·dul·ter·at·ed (un′ə dul′tə rā′tid) *adj.* not diluted or mixed; pure: *unadulterated foods.*

un·ad·vis·ed·ly (un′ad vī′zid lē) *adv.* in a rash, thoughtless manner; imprudently.

un·af·fect·ed¹ (un′ə fek′tid) *adj.* not influenced; unmoved: *The judge was unaffected by the defendant's pleas.* [*Un-*¹ + *affected*¹.]

un·af·fect·ed² (un′ə fek′tid) *adj.* genuine; sincere: *unaffected speech, an unaffected manner.* [*Un-*¹ + *affected*².] —**un′af·fect′ed·ly,** *adv.* —**un′af·fect′ed·ness,** *n.*

un·aid·ed (un′ā′did) *adj.* without help or support.

un·al·lied (un′ə līd′) *adj.* not joined by treaty, agreement, or common purpose.

un·al·ter·a·ble (un′ôl′tər ə bəl) *adj.* that cannot be changed: *unalterable plans.* —**un′al·ter·a·bly,** *adv.*

un·al·tered (un′ôl′tərd) *adj.* not changed.

un·A·mer·i·can (un′ə mer′i kən) *adj.* not according to the American character, traditions, or ideals.

u·na·nim·i·ty (yōo′nə nim′ə tē) *n.* the state of being in complete agreement.

u·nan·i·mous (yōo nan′ə məs) *adj.* **1.** in complete agreement: *The club members were unanimous in their support of the project.* **2.** characterized by or showing complete agreement: *The vote was unanimous.* —**u·nan′i·mous·ly,** *adv.* —**u·nan′i·mous·ness,** *n.*

un·an·swer·a·ble (un an′sər ə bəl) *adj.* **1.** that cannot be answered, especially having no known answer. **2.** that cannot be argued against or disproved.

un·ap·proach·a·ble (un′ə prō′chə bəl) *adj.* **1.** difficult to know or deal with; unfriendly: *an unapproachable person.* **2.** that cannot be approached: *The mountain cabin is unapproachable in winter.* —**un′ap·proach′a·ble·ness,** *n.* —**un′ap·proach′a·bly,** *adv.*

un·armed (un ärmd′) *adj.* without weapons.

un·asked (un askt′) *adj.* **1.** without being asked: *They came unasked to the party.* **2.** without being asked for: *unasked advice.*

un·as·sail·a·ble (un′ə sā′lə bəl) *adj.* **1.** that cannot be questioned or denied: *an unassailable argument.* **2.** that cannot be successfully attacked: *an unassailable fortress.*

un·as·sum·ing (un′ə sōo′ming) *adj.* modest in nature or manner; not bold. —**un′as·sum′ing·ly,** *adv.*

un·at·tached (un′ə tacht′) *adj.* **1.** not fastened, joined, or connected. **2.** not engaged or married.

un·at·tend·ed (un′ə ten′did) *adj.* **1.** not accompanied or escorted; alone. **2.** not done or taken care of; neglected: *She left the housework unattended.*

un·a·vail·ing (un′ə vā′ling) *adj.* futile; useless: *Her cries for help were unavailing.* —**un′a·vail′ing·ly,** *adv.*

un·a·void·a·ble (un′ə voi′də bəl) *adj.* that cannot or could not be avoided: *an unavoidable delay, an unavoidable problem.* —**un′a·void′a·bly,** *adv.*

un·a·ware (un′ə wer′) *adj.* not aware: *He was unaware of their dislike for him.*

un·a·wares (un′ə werz′) *adv.* without warning; unexpectedly; suddenly: *The storm caught us unawares.*

un·bal·anced (un bal′ənst) *adj.* **1.** not balanced: *an unbalanced scale.* **2.** not having a sound mind; mentally ill: *an unbalanced person.* **3.** not adjusted so that the debit and credit are equal: *an unbalanced budget.*

un·bar (un bär′) *v.t.,* **un·barred, un·bar·ring.** to remove the bars from; unbolt; open.

un·bear·a·ble (un ber′ə bəl) *adj.* that cannot be endured; intolerable: *unbearable pain, unbearable suspense.* —**un·bear′a·ble·ness,** *n.* —**un·bear′a·bly,** *adv.*

un·beat·a·ble (un bē′tə bəl) *adj.* that cannot be defeated or surpassed: *an unbeatable tennis player.*

un·beat·en (un bēt′ən) *adj.* **1.** never defeated or surpassed: *an unbeaten team.* **2.** not walked over: *an unbeaten path.* **3.** not shaped or mixed by beating: *unbeaten gold, an unbeaten egg.*

un·be·com·ing (un′bi kum′ing) *adj.* **1.** not flattering or attractive: *The color green is unbecoming to her complexion.* **2.** not suitable or appropriate: *He uses unbecoming language.* —**un′be·com′ing·ly,** *adv.*

un·be·knownst (un′bi nōnst′) *also,* **un·be·known** (un′bi nōn′). *adj., adv. Informal.* not known: *Unbeknownst to her friends, she had left the city.*

un·be·lief (un′bi lēf′) *n.* a lack of belief, especially in matters of religion.

un·be·liev·a·ble (un′bi lē′və bəl) *adj.* not to be believed; incredible: *an unbelievable story.* —**un′be·liev′a·bly,** *adv.*

un·be·liev·er (un′bi lē′vər) *n.* **1.** a person who does not believe in a particular religion or in any religion. **2.** a person who doubts; skeptic.

un·be·liev·ing (un′bi lē′ving) *adj.* **1.** doubting; skeptical. **2.** lacking religious belief or beliefs. —**un′be·liev′ing·ly,** *adv.*

un·bend (un bend′) *v.,* **un·bent, un·bend·ing.** —*v.t.* **1.** to straighten (something curved or crooked). **2.** to free from effort or strain: *to unbend one's mind.* **3.** to unfasten, untie, or cast loose: *to unbend a sail.* —*v.i.* **1.** to become free of strain; relax: *She was able to unbend when she went on vacation.* **2.** to become straight or almost straight.

un·bend·ing (un ben′ding) *adj.* **1.** that cannot or will not relax; unyielding: *an unbending will.* **2.** not bending; stiff.

un·bent (un bent′) the past tense and past participle of **unbend.**

un·bi·ased (un bī′əst) *also, British,* **un·bi·assed.** *adj.* free from bias; fair: *an unbiased judge.*

un·bid·den (un bid′ən) *adj.* **1.** not asked or invited: *Several unbidden guests came for dinner.* **2.** not commanded or ordered.

un·bind (un bīnd′) *v.t.,* **un·bound, un·bind·ing.** **1.** to release from bonds; set free. **2.** to remove or undo (something that binds); loose: *to unbind a bandage.*

un·blem·ished (un blem′isht) *adj.* free from flaw or blemish: *an unblemished complexion, an unblemished reputation.*

un·blessed (un blest′) *also,* **un·blest.** *adj.* **1.** not blessed or consecrated. **2.** cursed; evil; unholy.

un·blush·ing (un blush′ing) *adj.* **1.** without shame; shameless; brazen. **2.** not blushing or reddening.

un·bolt (un bōlt′) *v.t.* to open by drawing back bolts.

un·bolt·ed (un bōl′tid) *adj.* not fastened by bolts: *an unbolted door.*

un·born (un bôrn′) *adj.* not yet born: *an unborn child.*

un·bos·om (un booz′əm) *v.t.* **1.** to tell (something burdensome): *He unbosomed his sorrows to a complete stranger.* **2.** to unburden (oneself), as of thoughts, secrets, or feelings.

un·bound (un bound′) *v.* the past tense and past participle of **unbind.** —*adj.* **1.** not tied: *an unbound package.* **2.** without a binding or cover: *an unbound book.*

un·bound·ed (un boun′did) *adj.* having no limits or bounds; boundless; measureless: *unbounded space.*

un·bowed (un boud′) *adj.* not bowed, as by defeat.

un·break·a·ble (un brā′kə bəl) *adj.* that cannot be broken: *unbreakable glass.*

un·bri·dled (un brīd′əld) *adj.* **1.** uncontrolled; ungoverned: *unbridled fury.* **2.** not wearing or fitted with a bridle: *an unbridled pony.*

un·bro·ken (un brō′kən) *adj.* **1.** not torn or broken; whole; intact: *unbroken bones.* **2.** not interrupted; continuous: *an unbroken chain of events.* **3.** not beaten or surpassed: *an unbroken swimming record.* **4.** not used to a harness or rider; untamed: *an unbroken horse.* **5.** not weakened, subdued, or humbled: *Her spirit was unbroken by her poverty.* **6.** not violated; kept: *an unbroken promise.* —**un·bro′ken·ly,** *adv.* —**un·bro′ken·ness,** *n.*

un·buck·le (un buk′əl) *v.t.,* **un·buck·led, un·buck·ling.** to undo or unfasten the buckle or buckles of: *to unbuckle a belt.*

un·bur·den (un burd′ən) *v.t.* **1.** to free or relieve by telling something burdensome: *He unburdened himself to his friend.* **2.** to rid oneself of (something burdensome); reveal: *to unburden one's troubles.*

un·but·ton (un but′ən) *v.t.* to open by unfastening the button or buttons of.

un·called-for (un kôld′fôr′) *adj.* not fit, proper, or necessary; not warranted: *an uncalled-for comment, uncalled-for behavior.*

un·can·ny (un kan′ē) *adj.* **1.** strange and eerie; weird: *There were uncanny sounds in the deserted old house.* **2.** unusually good: *She has an uncanny knack for doing crossword puzzles.* —**un·can′ni·ly,** *adv.* —**un·can′ni·ness,** *n.*

un·cap (un kap′) *v.t.,* **un·capped, un·cap·ping.** to take off the cap of: *He uncapped a bottle of soda.*

un·ceas·ing (un sē′sing) *adj.* without end; continuous: *the unceasing flow of a river, the unceasing noise of traffic.* —**un·ceas′ing·ly,** *adv.*

un·cen·sored (un sen′sərd) *adj.* not censored: *an uncensored book.*

un·cer·e·mo·ni·ous (un′ser ə mō′nē əs) *adj.* **1.** without courtesy; abrupt; curt: *an unceremonious departure.* **2.** characterized by a lack of ceremony; informal. —**un′cer·e·mo′ni·ous·ly,** *adv.* —**un′cer·e·mo′ni·ous·ness,** *n.*

un·cer·tain (un surt′ən) *adj.* **1.** not known, established, or settled for sure; doubtful: *The outcome of the game is still uncertain.* **2.** that cannot be depended on; subject to change; variable: *uncertain weather.* **3.** not clearly defined; vague: *She told him what she thought of him in no uncertain terms.* —**un·cer′tain·ly,** *adv.* —**un·cer′tain·ness,** *n.*

un·cer·tain·ty (un surt′ən tē) *n. pl.,* **un·cer·tain·ties.** **1.** the state or quality of being uncertain. **2.** something that is uncertain.

un·chain (un chān′) *v.t.* to release from a chain or chains; set free.

un·change·a·ble (un chān′jə bəl) *adj.* that does not change or cannot be changed. —**un·change′a·bly,** *adv.*

un·changed (un chānjd′) *adj.* not changed.

un·chang·ing (un chān′jing) *adj.* not changing.

un·charged (un charjd′) *adj.* having no electric charge.

un·char·i·ta·ble (un char′ə tə bəl) *adj.* not generous or forgiving; severe; harsh. —**un·char′i·ta·ble·ness,** *n.* —**un·char′i·ta·bly,** *adv.*

un·chart·ed (un chär′tid) *adj.* not shown on a map or chart; unexplored; unknown: *The explorers discovered several uncharted islands.*

un·chaste (un chāst′) *adj.* not pure, virtuous, or modest; not chaste.

un·checked (un chekt′) *adj.* **1.** not halted or controlled: *the unchecked advance of enemy troops, unchecked anger.* **2.** not verified or corrected: *unchecked test papers.*

un·chris·tian (un kris′chən) *adj.* **1.** not in accord with Christian teachings or ideals: *an unchristian remark.* **2.** not of the Christian religion.

un·cial (un′shəl) *adj.* of or relating to a style of writing having letters similar to, but more rounded than, modern letters. It is found in Greek and Latin manuscripts dating from about the fourth to the ninth centuries A.D.

ABCDEFGHJKL
MNOPQRSTU

Uncial letters

un·civ·il (un siv′əl) *adj.* not polite or courteous; rude: *an uncivil reply.* —**un·civ′il·ly,** *adv.*

un·civ·i·lized (un siv′ə līzd′) *adj.* not civilized; savage: *an uncivilized tribe.*

un·clad (un klad′) *adj.* not clothed or dressed; nude.

un·clasp (un klasp′) *v.t.* **1.** to open or loosen the clasp of: *to unclasp a bracelet.* **2.** to release from a grasp or embrace.

un·clas·si·fied (un klas′ə fīd′) *adj.* not secret: *an unclassified document.*

un·cle (ung′kəl) *n.* **1.** the brother of a person's father or mother. **2.** the husband of a person's aunt.

un·clean (un klēn′) *adj.* **1.** not clean; dirty; foul. **2.** not morally pure: *unclean thoughts.* —**un·clean′ness,** *n.*

un·clean·ly[1] (un klen′lē) *adj.* not cleanly; unclean. [*Un-*[1] + *cleanly*[1].]

un·clean·ly[2] (un klen′lē) *adv.* in an unclean manner. [*Un-*[1] + *cleanly*[2].]

un·clear (un klēr′) *adj.* not clear: *His explanation was unclear.*

un·clench (un klench′) *v.t., v.i.* to open or become opened from a clenched position.

Uncle Sam (sam) **1.** a figure that represents the government or people of the United States. **2.** the government or people of the United States. [From the initials *U.S.,* the abbreviation for United States; supposedly because Samuel Wilson, a government meat inspector, stamped them on U.S. army meat barrels during the War of 1812. These initials were also said to be an abbreviation of his nickname "Uncle Sam."]

un·cloak (un klōk′) *v.t.* **1.** to remove a cloak or cover from. **2.** to reveal; expose.

un·clothed (un klōt͟hd′) *adj.* not clothed; stripped; naked.

un·coil (un koil′) *v.t.* to unwind. —*v.i.* to become unwound.

un·com·fort·a·ble (un kum′fər tə bəl) *adj.* **1.** causing discomfort: *an uncomfortable mattress.* **2.** feeling discomfort: *He was uncomfortable in his tight shoes.* —**un·com′fort·a·ble·ness,** *n.* —**un·com′fort·a·bly,** *adv.*

un·com·mon (un kom′ən) *adj.* rare; unusual: *Rain is uncommon in the desert.* —**un·com′mon·ly,** *adv.* —**un·com′mon·ness,** *n.*

at; āpe; cär; end; mē; it; īce; hot; ōld; fôrk; wood; fo͞ol; oil; out; up; turn; sing; thin; t͟his; hw in white; zh in treasure. The symbol ə stands for the sound of **a** in about, **e** in taken, **i** in pencil, **o** in lemon, and **u** in circus.

U

un·com·mu·ni·ca·tive (un′kə myōō′nə kā′tiv) *adj.* not telling things readily; reticent. —**un′com·mu·ni·ca′-tive·ly**, *adv.* —**un′com·mu′ni·ca′tive·ness**, *n.*

un·com·pli·men·ta·ry (un′kom plə men′tər ē) *adj.* insulting: *an uncomplimentary remark.*

un·com·pro·mis·ing (un kom′prə mī′zing) *adj.* not open to change or compromise; unyielding. —**un′com′-pro·mis′ing·ly**, *adv.*

un·con·cern (un′kən surn′) *n.* **1.** a lack of interest or concern. **2.** freedom from care or anxiety.

un·con·cerned (un′kən surnd′) *adj.* not interested or concerned: *He is unconcerned with your problems.* —**un·con·cern·ed·ly** (un′kən sur′nid lē), *adv.*

un·con·di·tion·al (un′kən dish′ən əl) *adj.* not limited by or subject to a condition or conditions: *unconditional obedience, an unconditional guarantee.* —**un′con·di′tion·al·ly**, *adv.*

un·con·firmed (un′kən furmd′) *adj.* not firmly established or proved: *unconfirmed reports.*

un·con·nec·ted (un′kə nek′tid) *adj.* not joined or fastened together; separate: *The school consists of two unconnected buildings.* —**un′con·nec′ted·ly**, *adv.* —**un′con·nec′ted·ness**, *n.*

un·con·quer·a·ble (un kong′kər ə bəl) *adj.* that cannot be overcome by force: *an unconquerable army.* —**un·con′quer·a·bly**, *adv.*

un·con·scion·a·ble (un kon′shən ə bəl) *adj.* **1.** not influenced, guided, or restrained by conscience; shameful; outrageous: *an unconscionable deed, an unconscionable liar.* **2.** beyond what is reasonable or just; excessive: *an unconscionable price.* —**un·con′scion·a·bly**, *adv.*

un·con·scious (un kon′shəs) *adj.* **1.** temporarily without consciousness: *The driver was unconscious after the accident.* **2.** not knowing; unaware: *The boy seemed unconscious of his sloppy appearance.* **3.** not done on purpose; accidental: *She made an unconscious error. He has an unconscious habit of cracking his knuckles.* —*n.* the part of the mind that contains wishes, fears, and the like that a person is not aware of but that influence his thoughts and behavior. —**un·con′scious·ly**, *adv.* —**un·con′scious-ness**, *n.*

un·con·sti·tu·tion·al (un′kon stə tōō′shən əl, un′kon-stə tyōō′shən əl) *adj.* not in keeping with the constitution of a country, state, or group, especially contrary to the Constitution of the United States. —**un′con·sti·tu′-tion·al·ly**, *adv.*

un·con·sti·tu·tion·al·i·ty (un′kon stə tōō′shə nal′-ə tē, un′kon stə tyōō′shə nal′ə tē) *n.* the state or quality of being unconstitutional.

un·con·trol·la·ble (un′kən trō′lə bəl) *adj.* that cannot be held in check or restrained: *uncontrollable laughter.* —**un′con·trol′la·bly**, *adv.*

un·con·trolled (un′kən trōld′) *adj.* that is not held in check or restrained: *an uncontrolled temper.*

un·con·ven·tion·al (un′kən ven′shən əl) *adj.* not following convention; out of the ordinary: *unconventional clothing.* —**un′con·ven′tion·al·ly**, *adv.*

un·con·ven·tion·al·i·ty (un′kən ven′shə nal′ə tē) *n.* the state or quality of being unconventional.

un·cork (un kôrk′) *v.t.* to draw or remove the cork from.

un·count·ed (un koun′tid) *adj.* **1.** too many to count; innumerable: *Uncounted numbers of people attended the rally.* **2.** not counted.

un·cou·ple (un kup′əl) *v.t.*, **un·cou·pled**, **un·cou·pling.** to disconnect; unfasten: *to uncouple railroad cars.*

un·couth (un kōōth′) *adj.* **1.** lacking culture or refinement; crude: *uncouth manners.* **2.** awkward or clumsy. —**un·couth′ly**, *adv.* —**un·couth′ness**, *n.*

un·cov·er (un kuv′ər) *v.t.* **1.** to lay bare or make known;

bring to light; disclose: *The detective uncovered some new clues.* **2.** to remove the cover or covering from: *She uncovered the dish after she brought it to the table.* **3.** to remove a hat from (one's head) as a sign of respect. —*v.i.* to remove a hat from one's head as a sign of respect.

un·cross (un krôs′) *v.t.* to change from a crossed position: *Jeff uncrossed his legs.*

un·crys·tal·lized (un krist′əl īzd′) *adj.* not crystallized.

unc·tion (ungk′shən) *n.* **1.** the act of anointing as part of a religious or other ritual. **2.** a substance used in anointing, such as oil. **3.** something that soothes or comforts. **4.** exaggerated emotion, as in language.

unc·tu·ous (ungk′chōō əs) *adj.* **1.** characterized by exaggerated emotion; too suave: *an unctuous person, unctuous flattery.* **2.** like oil or ointment; slippery to the touch; greasy. —**unc′tu·ous·ly**, *adv.* —**unc′tu·ous·ness**, *n.*

un·cul·ti·vat·ed (un kul′tə vā′tid) *adj.* **1.** not prepared for growing crops: *uncultivated soil.* **2.** not cultured or refined: *an uncultivated person.*

un·cured (un kyoord′) *adj.* **1.** not made well or healthy: *an uncured patient.* **2.** not prepared for use, as by drying: *uncured tobacco.*

un·curl (un kurl′) *v.t.* to take the curl out of; straighten: *She uncurled her hair.* —*v.i.* to become straightened.

un·cut (un kut′) *adj.* **1.** not cut: *uncut flowers.* **2.** not shortened or edited; unabridged: *an uncut version of a film.* **3.** not changed or shaped by cutting: *an uncut diamond.*

un·dat·ed (un dā′tid) *adj.* not marked with a date.

un·daunt·ed (un dôn′tid) *adj.* not discouraged or frightened; fearless: *Undaunted by the cold, he continued to hike through the snow.* —**un·daunt′ed·ly**, *adv.*

un·de·cid·ed (un′di sī′did) *adj.* **1.** not having one's mind made up: *I am still undecided about what to wear to the dance.* **2.** not yet settled: *The outcome of the election is still undecided.* —**un′de·cid′ed·ly**, *adv.* —**un′de·cid′ed-ness**, *n.*

un·de·clared (un′di klerd′) *adj.* not announced or proclaimed: *an undeclared war.*

un·de·feat·ed (un′di fē′tid) *adj.* not defeated: *the school basketball team was undefeated this season.*

un·de·fined (un′di fīnd′) *adj.* not defined: *an undefined word.*

un·dem·o·crat·ic (un dem′ə krat′ik) *adj.* not agreeing with or supporting the ideals or principles of democracy; not democratic.

un·de·mon·stra·tive (un′di mon′strə tiv) *adj.* not given to showing affection or feeling; reserved. —**un′de-mon′stra·tive·ness**, *n.*

un·de·ni·a·ble (un′di nī′ə bəl) *adj.* that cannot be denied or doubted: *The police had undeniable evidence of his guilt.* —**un′de·ni′a·bly**, *adv.*

un·de·pend·a·ble (un′di pen′də bəl) *adj.* that cannot be depended on; not dependable: *He was undependable and could not be trusted to finish his work.*

un·der (un′dər) *prep.* **1.** in a place down from or lower than; beneath: *He put the paper under a pile of books. Look under the bed.* **2.** below the surface of: *The splinter went under the skin.* **3.** in a position so as to be covered or protected by: *She stood under an umbrella.* **4.** less than: *We drove twenty miles under the speed limit.* **5.** subject to the authority of: *His father served under that general during the war.* **6.** subject to the force or action of: *The metal beam is under great pressure. The fire is under control.* **7.** bound by: *The witness gave his testimony under oath.* **8.** in the process of: *Our new house is under construction.* **9.** according to: *Under the new rules, we can't use the tennis courts for more than one hour.* **10.** because of; considering: *We can't go under the circumstances.* **11.** during the reign or rule of: *Drama in England flourished under Elizabeth I.* **12.** within the particular group or category of: *The article on diamonds was under "precious stones."* —*adv.* in or into a position down from or lower than something: *The raft was sucked under by the whirlpool.* —*adj.* lower in position, rank, degree, or amount: *the under surface of a leaf.*

under- *combining form* **1.** located below: *underpass.* **2.** located beneath the surface of: *underground.* **3.** less than is usual or needed: *underweight, underage.* **4.** lower or inferior, as in rank: *undergraduate.*

un·der·age (un'dər āj') *adj.* not of the usual or legal age.

un·der·arm (un'dər ärm') *adj.* **1.** of, relating to, or used in the armpit; under the arm: *underarm perspiration.* **2.** see **underhand** *(def. 1).* —*n.* the hollow under the arm at the shoulder; armpit. —*adv.* see **underhand** *(def. 1).*

un·der·bid (un'dər bid') *v.t.,* **un·der·bid, un·der·bid·ding.** to bid lower than (a competitor).

un·der·brush (un'dər brush') *n.* a growth of bushes, shrubs, or similar plants beneath the large trees in a forest or woods.

un·der·charge (*v.,* un'dər chärj'; *n.,* un'dər chärj') *v.t.,* **un·der·charged, un·der·charg·ing. 1.** to charge (someone) too small a price. **2.** to supply or load with too small a charge, as a gun. —*n.* too small a charge.

un·der·clothes (un'dər klōz', un'dər klōthz') *n.,pl.* another word for **underwear.**

un·der·cloth·ing (un'dər klō'thing) *n.* another word for **underwear.**

un·der·coat (un'dər kōt') *n.* **1.** a layer of short hairs hidden by the fur on an animal's body. **2.** a layer of varnish, paint, or the like put on a surface before the final coat.

un·der·cov·er (un'dər kuv'ər) *adj.* working or done in secret: *an undercover agent for the government.*

un·der·cur·rent (un'dər kur'ənt) *n.* **1.** a current, as of air or water, under another current or below a surface. **2.** an underlying feeling or emotion: *an undercurrent of annoyance.*

un·der·cut (un'dər kut') *v.t.,* **un·der·cut, un·der·cut·ting. 1.** to sell or work for lower payment than (a competitor). **2.** to cut under or away, as in carving. —*n.* the act or result of cutting under or away.

un·der·de·vel·oped (un'dər di vel'əpt) *adj.* **1.** not completely or properly developed: *underdeveloped muscles.* **2.** behind in growth or development, especially industrial or economic development: *an underdeveloped nation.*

un·der·dog (un'dər dôg') *n.* **1.** a person who is thought most likely to lose, as in a contest or game. **2.** a victim of political or social injustice.

un·der·done (un'dər dun') *adj.* not completely or properly cooked: *an underdone roast.*

un·der·es·ti·mate (*v.,* un'dər es'tə māt'; *n.,* un'dər es'tə mit, un'dər es'tə māt') *v.t.,* **un·der·es·ti·mat·ed, un·der·es·ti·mat·ing. 1.** to estimate at too low an amount: *Dad underestimated the cost of the trip.* **2.** to place too low a value on; have too low an opinion of: *We underestimated the other team's ability.* —*n.* too low an estimate.

un·der·ex·pose (un'dər iks pōz') *v.t.,* **un·der·ex·posed, un·der·ex·pos·ing.** to expose (a photographic film or plate) to too little light, or to light for too short a period of time, to produce a good picture.

un·der·ex·po·sure (un'dər iks pō'zhər) *n.* the act, process, or result of underexposing.

un·der·feed (un'dər fēd') *v.t.,* **un·der·fed** (un'dər fed'), **un·der·feed·ing.** to feed too little.

un·der·foot (un'dər foot') *adv.* **1.** in the way: *My little brother's toys are always underfoot.* **2.** beneath the foot or feet; on the ground: *He wore his boots because it was snowy underfoot.*

un·der·gar·ment (un'dər gär'mənt) *n.* an article of underwear.

un·der·go (un'dər gō') *v.t.,* **un·der·went, un·der·gone** (un'dər gôn', un'dər gon'), **un·der·go·ing. 1.** to pass through; experience: *The neighborhood is undergoing a change.* **2.** to bear up under; endure.

un·der·grad·u·ate (un'dər graj'ōō it) *n.* a college or university student who has not yet received a degree.

un·der·ground (*adj., adv.,* un'dər ground'; *n.,* un'dər ground') *adj.* **1.** below the surface of the earth: *an underground passage.* **2.** hidden; secret: *an underground political movement.* —*n.* **1.** a group working secretly to resist or overthrow the government in power or enemy occupation. **2.** a place or space below the surface of the earth, such as a tunnel. —*adv.* **1.** below the surface of the earth: *The men dug a tunnel underground.* **2.** in or into hiding; in secret: *The robbers plotted underground.*

un·der·growth (un'dər grōth') *n.* a growth of small plants beneath the large trees of a forest; underbrush.

un·der·hand (un'dər hand') *adv.* **1.** with the hand held below the level of the elbow or shoulder: *Harry tossed the ball underhand.* **2.** slyly; secretly. —*adj.* **1.** done with the hand held below the level of the elbow or shoulder: *an underhand pitch.* **2.** another word for **underhanded.**

un·der·hand·ed (un'dər han'did) *adj.* done in a secret, sly manner; deceitful: *an underhanded trick.* —**un'der·hand'ed·ly,** *adv.* —**un'der·hand'ed·ness,** *n.*

un·der·lie (un'dər lī') *v.t.,* **un·der·lay** (un'dər lā'), **un·der·lain** (un'dər lān'), **un·der·ly·ing. 1.** to be located below: *Rocky soil underlies the rich topsoil.* **2.** to be the basis or cause of: *What thoughts underlay his action?*

un·der·line (*v.,* un'dər līn'; *n.,* un'dər līn') *v.t.,* **un·der·lined, un·der·lin·ing. 1.** to draw a line or lines under. **2.** to emphasize; stress: *She underlined the need for caution in working with the chemicals.* —*n.* a line drawn under words for emphasis or to indicate italics.

un·der·ling (un'dər ling) *n.* a person who is lower in rank than another or others and must take orders.

un·der·lip (un'dər lip') *n.* the lower lip.

un·der·ly·ing (un'dər lī'ing) *adj.* **1.** lying below: *an underlying foundation of concrete.* **2.** basic or fundamental: *the underlying principles.*

un·der·mine (un'dər mīn') *v.t.,* **un·der·mined, un·der·min·ing. 1.** to weaken or destroy slowly and secretly: *His poor eating habits have undermined his health.* **2.** to weaken by wearing away at the foundation or base of; erode: *The river undermined the bank.* **3.** to dig a mine or passage under; dig below.

un·der·most (un'dər mōst') *adj., adv.* lowest in place or position; bottom.

un·der·neath (un'dər nēth') *prep.* **1.** in a lower place or position than; on the underside of: *He rolled the ball underneath the chair.* **2.** under the appearance of: *Underneath his gruffness, he's really a nice person.* —*adv.* lower than something; on the underside: *Ann packed the records on top and the books underneath.*

un·der·nour·ish (un'dər nur'ish) *v.t.* to give too little food to. —**un'der·nour'ish·ment,** *n.*

un·der·pants (un'dər pants') *n.,pl.* pants or shorts worn underneath a person's outer clothes.

at; āpe; cär; end; mē; it; īce; hot; ōld; fôrk; wood; fōōl; oil; out; up; turn; sing; thin; this; hw in white; zh in treasure. The symbol ə stands for the sound of a in about, e in taken, i in pencil, o in lemon, and u in circus.

un·der·pass (un'dər pas') *n. pl.,* **un·der·pass·es.** a passage or road that goes underneath a bridge or the like.

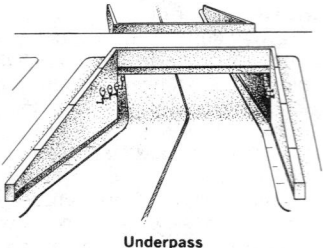
Underpass

un·der·pay (un'dər pā') *v.t.,* **un·der·paid, un·der·pay·ing.** to pay too little or less than deserved.

un·der·pin·ning (un'dər pin'ing) *n.* **1.** the materials or structure used to support or strengthen a building, wall, or the like from below. **2.** anything that supports.

un·der·priv·i·leged (un'dər priv'ə lijd) *adj.* without many advantages and privileges because of poverty: *an underprivileged child.*

un·der·rate (un'dər rāt') *v.t.,* **un·der·rat·ed, un·der·rat·ing.** to rate too low; underestimate: *That player's ability has been underrated by the sportswriters.*

un·der·score (*v.,* un'dər skôr'; *n.,* un'dər skôr') *v.t.,* **un·der·scored, un·der·scor·ing.** to draw a line or lines under; underline. —*n.* a line drawn under a word or words for emphasis or to indicate italics; underline.

un·der·sea (un'dər sē', un'dər sē') *adj.* existing, done, or designed for use beneath the surface of the sea. —*adv. also,* **underseas.** beneath the surface of the sea.

un·der·sec·re·tar·y (un'dər sek'rə ter'ē) *n. pl.,* **un·der·sec·re·tar·ies.** a secretary who ranks directly below the secretary of a government department.

un·der·sell (un'dər sel') *v.t.,* **un·der·sold** (un'dər sōld'), **un·der·sell·ing.** to sell at a lower price than (a competitor).

un·der·shirt (un'dər shurt') *n.* a shirt with short sleeves or no sleeves, worn under a person's outer clothes.

un·der·shot (un'dər shot') *adj.* **1.** (of a water wheel) driven by water passing beneath. **2.** having the lower jaw sticking out beyond the upper jaw.

un·der·side (un'dər sīd') *n.* the bottom side or surface.

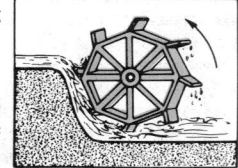
Undershot water wheel

un·der·signed (un'dər sīnd') *adj.* **1.** having signed one's name at the end of a document. **2.** signed at the end of a document: *undersigned names.* —*n.* **the undersigned.** the person or persons who have signed a document.

un·der·sized (un'dər sīzd') *adj.* having less than the normal or usual size: *an undersized cat.*

un·der·skirt (un'dər skurt') *n.* a petticoat worn under a skirt.

un·der·stand (un'dər stand') *v.,* **un·der·stood, un·der·stand·ing.** —*v.t.* **1.** to grasp the meaning of; be clear about: *I don't understand what you mean.* **2.** to be in sympathy or agreement with: *The two sisters understand each other completely.* **3.** to know thoroughly; master: *I don't understand Russian.* **4.** to have as an opinion; assume; conclude: *Am I to understand that you are not going to go with us?* **5.** to take as agreed or settled: *I understand that I can return the tickets before the performance and still get my money back.* —*v.i.* **1.** to grasp the meaning of something: *Even though I've explained it several times, he still doesn't understand.* **2.** to be told or assume: *He is going to Colorado, or so I understand.* **3.** to be sympathetic: *If you are unable to come, I will understand.*

un·der·stand·a·ble (un'dər stan'də bəl) *adj.* that can be understood. —**un'der·stand'a·bly,** *adv.*

un·der·stand·ing (un'dər stan'ding) *n.* **1.** the grasping of the meaning of something: *Paul has a thorough understanding of the situation.* **2.** thorough knowledge or mastery: *Hank's understanding of arithmetic pleased the teacher.* **3.** opinion; conclusion: *It was my understanding that he would bring his camera.* **4.** sympathy or agreement: *Mary shows much understanding when people bring her their problems. They finally reached an understanding after their quarrel.* **5.** the ability to understand; intelligence: *That scientist is a person of superior understanding.* —*adj.* feeling or showing sympathy; sympathetic: *an understanding manner.* —**un'der·stand'ing·ly,** *adv.*

un·der·state (un'dər stāt') *v.t.,* **un·der·stat·ed, un·der·stat·ing.** to tell about or state too weakly or with too little emphasis.

un·der·state·ment (un'dər stāt'mənt) *n.* a statement that tends to make something seem less important or less dramatic than it really is.

un·der·stood (un'dər stood') *v.* the past tense and past participle of **understand.** —*adj.* **1.** agreed or settled upon: *It's understood, then, that we'll meet at four o'clock.* **2.** omitted but implied in a statement: *In the sentence "I'm willing if you are," the word "willing" is understood after "are."*

un·der·stud·y (un'dər stud'ē) *n. pl.,* **un·der·stud·ies.** an actor or singer who learns another's role in order to be a replacement. —*v.,* **un·der·stud·ied, un·der·stud·y·ing.** —*v.t.* **1.** to learn (a role) in order to replace the regular actor or singer. **2.** to act as an understudy to (an actor or singer). —*v.i.* to be an understudy.

un·der·take (un'dər tāk') *v.t.,* **un·der·took, un·der·tak·en, un·der·tak·ing.** **1.** to set about to do: *She undertook the journey on horseback.* **2.** to agree to or accept (something, as a task): *She undertook the patient's care.*

un·der·tak·er (*def. 1* un'dər tā'kər, *def. 2* un'dər tā'kər) *n.* **1.** a person whose job or business is arranging funerals and preparing dead people for burial. **2.** a person who undertakes something, such as a task.

un·der·tak·ing (*def. 1* un'dər tā'king, *def. 2* un'dər tā'king) *n.* **1.** something undertaken, as a task. **2.** the business of an undertaker.

un·der·tone (un'dər tōn') *n.* **1.** a low tone: *The two friends spoke in an undertone during the movie.* **2.** a feeling or emotion that is partly hidden: *We sensed an undertone of anger in her words.* **3.** a soft color or a color seen through other colors: *The painting has an undertone of blue.*

un·der·took (un'dər took') the past tense of **undertake.**

un·der·tow (un'dər tō') *n.* a strong current flowing below the surface of the water, in a direction that is opposite to the direction of the surface current.

un·der·val·ue (un'dər val'yōō) *v.t.,* **un·der·val·ued, un·der·val·u·ing.** to underestimate or underrate.

un·der·wa·ter (un'dər wô'tər) *adj.* lying, used, or performed below the surface of the water: *an underwater plant.* —*adv.* below the surface of the water: *to swim underwater.*

un·der·wear (un'dər wer') *n.* clothing worn under a person's outer clothes, usually next to the skin.

un·der·weight (un'dər wāt') *adj.* weighing too little. —*n.* weight that is below what is normal or desirable.

un·der·went (un'dər went') the past tense of **undergo.**

un·der·world (un'dər wurld') *n.* **1.** the part of society involved in crime, especially organized crime. **2.** *also,* **Underworld.** *Greek and Roman Mythology.* the dwelling place of the dead.

un·der·write (un'dər rīt') *v.,* **un·der·wrote** (un'dər rōt'), **un·der·writ·ten** (un'dər rit'ən), **un·der·writ·ing.** —*v.t.* **1.** to agree to be responsible financially for; support

with money: *to underwrite the production of a play.*
2. to sign (an insurance policy), and thus take on the
obligation to pay for any losses or damage. **3.** to cover with
insurance; insure. **4.** to agree to buy (an issue of stocks
or bonds to be sold to the public) on a specified date and
at a specified price. **5.** to write underneath (something).
—*v.i.* to act as or carry on the business of an underwriter.

un·der·writ·er (un′dər rī′tər) *n.* **1.** a person or company in the insurance business that underwrites insurance.
2. a person or company that underwrites an issue of stocks
or bonds.

un·de·served (un′di zurvd′) *adj.* not deserved: *undeserved punishment.* —**un·de·serv·ed·ly** (un′di zer′-
vid lē), *adv.*

un·de·sir·a·ble (un′di zīr′ə bəl) *adj.* not desirable or
pleasing; objectionable: *an undesirable place to live.*
—*n.* a person thought to be undesirable. —**un′de·sir′a·
bly,** *adv.*

un·de·terred (un′di turd′) *adj.* not discouraged from
doing something: *He was undeterred by the threat of punishment.*

un·de·vel·oped (un′di vel′əpt) *adj.* **1.** not completely
developed: *undeveloped muscles, undeveloped talent.*
2. not developed or fully used: *an undeveloped area, undeveloped resources.*

un·did (un did′) the past tense of **undo.**

un·dies (un′dēz) *n.,pl. Informal.* underwear, especially
women's or children's underpants.

un·dis·cov·ered (un′dis kuv′ərd) *adj.* not discovered:
an undiscovered treasure, undiscovered talent.

un·dis·guised (un′dis gīzd′) *adj.* not hidden; open; obvious: *She looked at him with undisguised dislike.*

un·dis·mayed (un′dis mād′) *adj.* not filled with fear or
discouragement; not dismayed: *The speaker was undis-
mayed by the audience's lack of interest.*

un·dis·put·ed (un′dis pyoō′tid) *adj.* not questioned or
opposed: *He has an undisputed claim to the inheritance.*

un·dis·tin·guished (un′dis ting′gwisht) *adj.* not famous or dignified; not distinguished: *an undistinguished
writer.*

un·dis·turbed (un′dis turbd′) *adj.* not disturbed: *He
was undisturbed by the noise. The storm left the boats in
the harbor undisturbed.*

un·di·vid·ed (un′di vī′did) *adj.* not divided; whole; entire: *an undivided cake, one's undivided attention.*

un·do (un doō′) *v.t.,* **un·did, un·done, un·do·ing. 1.** to
loosen (a fastening); unfasten; untie: *He undid the knot.
He undid his necktie.* **2.** to open or unwrap: *She undid the
package.* **3.** to do away with or reverse (what has been
done): *The fire undid the work of six months. He tried to
undo the harm that he had caused.* **4.** to cause the ruin
or downfall of; destroy: *His foolishness has undone him.*
—**un·do′er,** *n.*

un·do·ing (un doō′ing) *n.* **1.** a doing away with or reversing of what has been done. **2.** ruin or downfall; destruction: *He brought about his own undoing.* **3.** the cause
of ruin or downfall: *Her stubbornness will prove her undoing.* **4.** a loosening or opening.

un·done[1] (un dun′) *adj.* not finished; not done: *He left
the job undone.* [*Un-*[1] + *done.*]

un·done[2] (un dun′) *v.* the past participle of **undo.**
—*adj.* unfastened; untied; open.

un·doubt·ed (un dou′tid) *adj.* accepted as true; not
doubted. —**un·doubt′ed·ly,** *adv.*

un·dreamed-of (un drēmd′uv′) also, **un·dreamt-of** (un-
dremt′uv′). *adj.* not thought possible; unimaginable: *un-
dreamed-of riches.*

un·dress (un dres′) *v.t.* to remove the clothes or covering from: *The child undressed herself and went to bed.*

—*v.i.* to remove one's clothes. —*n.* casual or informal
clothing.

un·due (un doō′, un dyoō′) *adj.* **1.** going beyond what
is necessary; excessive: *She did the work with undue speed.*
2. not just, right, or proper: *He shows undue interest in
other people's business.*

un·du·lant (un′jə lənt) *adj.* moving in waves; having a
wavy outline or form.

un·du·late (*v.,* un′jə lāt′; *adj.,* un′jə lit, un′jə lāt′) *v.,*
un·du·lat·ed, un·du·lat·ing. —*v.i.* **1.** to move in waves or
like a wave: *The corn stalks undulate in the wind.* **2.** to
have a wavy outline, form, or appearance: *The farmer's
land undulates across hills and valleys.* —*v.t.* **1.** to cause
to move in waves or like a wave. **2.** to give a wavy outline,
form, or appearance to. —*adj.* having a wavy outline,
form, or appearance, as a leaf. Also, **un·du·lat·ed** (un′jə-
lā′tid).

un·du·la·tion (un′jə lā′shən) *n.* **1.** a movement in
waves; wavelike motion. **2.** a wavy outline, form, or appearance.

un·du·ly (un doō′lē, un dyoō′lē) *adv.* unnecessarily or
excessively: *unduly concerned, unduly critical.*

un·dy·ing (un dī′ing) *adj.* without end; immortal; eternal: *undying devotion.*

un·earned (un urnd′) *adj.* **1.** not received for work or
service: *unearned income.* **2.** not deserved: *an unearned
scolding.* **3.** not yet earned: *unearned interest on savings.*

un·earth (un urth′) *v.t.* **1.** to dig up out of the earth: *The
dog unearthed his buried bone.* **2.** to bring to light by
searching; discover; reveal: *The detective unearthed several
new clues.*

un·earth·ly (un urth′lē) *adj.* **1.** strange or weird: *an
unearthly shriek.* **2.** not of this world; supernatural: *an
unearthly being.* —**un·earth′li·ness,** *n.*

un·eas·y (un ē′zē) *adj.,* **un·eas·i·er, un·eas·i·est.
1.** lacking ease of mind; worried; anxious: *Dad felt uneasy
about my staying out so late.* **2.** restless; uncomfortable;
tense: *He finally dropped off into an uneasy sleep.* **3.** embarrassed or awkward: *an uneasy laugh, an uneasy silence.*
—**un·eas′i·ly,** *adv.* —**un·eas′i·ness,** *n.*

un·ed·u·cat·ed (un ej′ə kā′tid) *adj.* lacking education,
especially formal education; not educated: *an uneducated
man.*

un·e·mo·tion·al (un′i mō′shə nəl) *adj.* without emotion: *an unemotional person, an unemotional speech.*
—**un′e·mo′tion·al·ly,** *adv.*

un·em·ploy·a·ble (un′em ploi′ə bəl) *adj.* not able to
be employed. —*n.* an unemployable person.

un·em·ployed (un′em ploid′) *adj.* **1.** without a job; out
of work. **2.** not being put to use: *unemployed talents.*
—*n.* **the unemployed.** people out of work.

un·em·ploy·ment (un′em ploi′mənt) *n.* **1.** the state of
being unemployed; lack of employment. **2.** the number of
people who are out of work: *Unemployment has risen this
year.*

un·end·ing (un en′ding) *adj.* that has or seems to have
no end; endless.

un·en·force·a·ble (un′en fôr′sə bəl) *adj.* that cannot
be enforced: *unenforceable laws.*

un·e·qual (un ē′kwəl) *adj.* **1.** not the same: *unequal por-*

U

at; āpe; cär; end; mē; it; īce; hot; ōld; fôrk;
wood; foōl; oil; out; up; turn; sing; thin; this;
hw in white; zh in treasure. The symbol ə
stands for the sound of **a** in about, **e** in taken,
i in pencil, **o** in lemon, and **u** in circus.

tions, *sleeves of unequal length, unequal opportunities.* **2.** not well or equally matched; unfair: *an unequal partnership, an unequal contest.* **3.** lacking the needed strength or ability; not fit or qualified: *He proved unequal to the job.* **4.** not regular or even; uneven: *There was an unequal distribution of heat in the room.* —**un·e′qual·ly,** *adv.*

un·e·qualed (un ē′kwəld) *also, British,* **un·e·qualled.** *adj.* not matched or surpassed; unrivaled: *an unequaled performance.*

un·e·quiv·o·cal (un′i kwiv′ə kəl) *adj.* having a meaning that is clear and easily understood; not equivocal: *an unequivocal denial, an unequivocal statement.* —**un′e·quiv′o·cal·ly,** *adv.*

un·err·ing (un ur′ing, un er′ing) *adj.* **1.** making no mistakes; faultless: *unerring judgment, unerring good taste.* **2.** not going astray or missing the mark: *the unerring flight of a rocket.* —**un·err′ing·ly,** *adv.*

UNESCO (yōō nes′kō) United Nations Educational, Scientific, and Cultural Organization.

un·eth·i·cal (un eth′i kəl) *adj.* not ethical: *The politician was charged with unethical practices.*

un·e·ven (un ē′vən) *adj.* **1.** not straight: *an uneven hem.* **2.** not smooth or flat; jagged: *the uneven surface of a rock.* **3.** not of the same kind or quality throughout: *uneven color.* **4.** (of a number) odd: *The numbers 1, 3, 5, and 7 are uneven.* **5.** not well-matched or balanced; unfair; one-sided: *an uneven game.* —**un·e′ven·ly,** *adv.* —**un·e′ven·ness,** *n.*

un·e·vent·ful (un′i vent′fəl) *adj.* without anything important or exciting happening; routine; ordinary: *an uneventful trip.* —**un′e·vent′ful·ly,** *adv.*

un·ex·am·pled (un′ig zam′pəld) *adj.* without like or equal; unparalleled; unique: *unexampled generosity.*

un·ex·cep·tion·a·ble (un′ik sep′shə nə bəl) *adj.* beyond criticism or reproach: *an unexceptionable man, unexceptionable behavior.* —**un′ex·cep′tion·a·bly,** *adv.*

un·ex·pect·ed (un′iks pek′tid) *adj.* not expected; coming or happening without warning; unforeseen: *an unexpected delay, unexpected kindness.* —**un′ex·pect′ed·ly,** *adv.* —**un′ex·pect′ed·ness,** *n.*

un·fail·ing (un fā′ling) *adj.* **1.** never weakening or changing; constant: *unfailing devotion.* **2.** always certain; trustworthy: *an unfailing cure.* **3.** never running short or stopping: *an unfailing supply of food.* —**un·fail′ing·ly,** *adv.*

un·fair (un fer′) *adj.* **1.** not fair or just: *an unfair criticism.* **2.** not following accepted rules or standards: *unfair business practices.* —**un·fair′ly,** *adv.* —**un·fair′ness,** *n.*

un·faith·ful (un fāth′fəl) *adj.* **1.** not truly loyal or devoted; untrustworthy: *an unfaithful friend.* **2.** not true to marriage vows: *an unfaithful wife.* **3.** not accurate or exact: *an unfaithful translation.* —**un·faith′ful·ly,** *adv.* —**un·faith′ful·ness,** *n.*

un·fa·mil·iar (un′fə mil′yər) *adj.* **1.** not well known or recognizable; strange: *This handwriting is unfamiliar to me.* **2.** not having knowledge of or experience with: *I am unfamiliar with that book.* —**un′fa·mil′iar·ly,** *adv.*

un·fa·mil·i·ar·i·ty (un′fə mil′ē ar′ə tē) *n.* a lack of familiarity.

un·fash·ion·a·ble (un fash′ə nə bəl) *adj.* not in fashion; not stylish. —**un·fash′ion·a·bly,** *adv.*

un·fas·ten (un fas′ən) *v.t.* to detach or undo the fastenings of; open: *to unfasten a dress, to unfasten a suitcase.* —*v.i.* to become opened.

un·fath·om·a·ble (un fath′əm ə bəl) *adj.* **1.** that cannot be measured: *the unfathomable depths of the sea.* **2.** that cannot be fully understood: *unfathomable motives.*

un·fath·omed (un fath′əmd) *adj.* **1.** not measured: *The ship sailed in an unfathomed sea.* **2.** not fully understood: *The mystery has remained unfathomed.*

un·fa·vor·a·ble (un fā′vər ə bəl) *adj.* **1.** not in a person's favor; disadvantageous: *We formed an unfavorable impression of him.* **2.** not approving; critical: *The play received unfavorable reviews.* **3.** denying something desired or requested; negative: *He received an unfavorable reply to his letter.* —**un·fa′vor·a·ble·ness,** *n.* —**un·fa′vor·a·bly,** *adv.*

un·feel·ing (un fē′ling) *adj.* **1.** without sympathy or compassion; hard-hearted; cruel: *an unfeeling man, unfeeling words.* **2.** not able to feel: *unfeeling hands.* —**un·feel′ing·ly,** *adv.* —**un·feel′ing·ness,** *n.*

un·feigned (un fānd′) *adj.* not pretended; genuine; sincere: *unfeigned enthusiasm.* —**un·feign·ed·ly** (un fā′nid lē), *adv.*

un·fet·ter (un fet′ər) *v.t.* to free from chains or bonds; liberate.

un·fin·ished (un fin′isht) *adj.* **1.** not brought to an end; not concluded or completed: *an unfinished speech, an unfinished job.* **2.** not finished, as with paint or varnish; not treated or processed; rough: *unfinished furniture, unfinished fabric.*

un·fit (un fit′) *adj.* **1.** not suited to some end or purpose: *That food is unfit to eat.* **2.** not qualified: *The king was unfit to rule.* **3.** in poor condition; unhealthy. —*v.t.,* **un·fit·ted** or **un·fit, un·fit·ting.** to make unfit. —**un·fit′ness,** *n.*

un·flag·ging (un flag′ing) *adj.* not failing; untiring: *unflagging energy, unflagging spirits.* —**un·flag′ging·ly,** *adv.*

un·fledged (un flejd′) *adj.* **1.** lacking knowledge or experience: *an unfledged poet.* **2.** (of a young bird) without feathers needed for flight.

un·flinch·ing (un flin′ching) *adj.* not drawing back or away from danger, pain, or other hardship. —**un·flinch′ing·ly,** *adv.*

un·fold (un fōld′) *v.t.* **1.** to open or spread out (something folded): *He unfolded the letter. She unfolded the tablecloth.* **2.** to make known gradually: *The general unfolded his plan.* —*v.i.* **1.** to become open or spread out, as the petals of a flower. **2.** to become known gradually: *The story unfolded suspensefully.*

un·forced (un fôrst′) *adj.* **1.** not brought about by force; voluntary. **2.** not done by an effort; not strained; natural: *She had an unforced smile.*

un·fore·seen (un′fôr sēn′) *adj.* not known or guessed beforehand; unexpected: *unforseen difficulties.*

un·for·get·ta·ble (un′fər get′ə bəl) *adj.* not to be forgotten; memorable: *an unforgettable experience.* —**un′for·get′ta·bly,** *adv.*

un·for·giv·a·ble (un′fər giv′ə bəl) *adj.* that cannot be forgiven: *an unforgivable insult.*

un·formed (un fôrmd′) *adj.* **1.** having no definite form; shapeless: *wet, unformed clay.* **2.** not fully developed: *an unformed mind.*

un·for·tu·nate (un fôr′chə nit) *adj.* **1.** having or causing bad luck; unlucky: *an unfortunate man, an unfortunate happening.* **2.** improper or unsuitable: *an unfortunate choice of words.* —*n.* a person who is unfortunate. —**un·for′tu·nate·ly,** *adv.*

un·found·ed (un foun′did) *adj.* without basis in fact or reality; groundless: *an unfounded rumor, unfounded superstitions.*

un·fre·quent·ed (un′fri kwen′tid) *adj.* hardly ever visited: *an unfrequented area of wilderness.*

un·friend·ly (un frend′lē) *adj.,* **un·friend·li·er, un·friend·li·est. 1.** feeling or showing dislike, coldness, or hostility; not friendly: *an unfriendly neighbor, an unfriendly manner.* **2.** not favorable or pleasant: *an unfriendly climate.* —**un·friend′li·ness,** *n.*

un·fruit·ful (un frōōt′fəl) *adj.* **1.** not producing desired

or useful results; unsuccessful: *an unfruitful attempt.*
2. not producing fruit or offspring; barren: *an unfruitful season, an unfruitful marriage.* —**un·fruit′ful·ly,** *adv.* —**un·fruit′ful·ness,** *n.*

un·furl (un furl′) *v.t.* to open or spread out; unroll: *to unfurl a flag.* —*v.i.* to become spread out.

un·fur·nished (un fur′nisht) *adj.* not furnished, as with furniture: *an unfurnished apartment.*

un·gain·ly (un gān′lē) *adj.,* **un·gain·li·er, un·gain·li·est.** not graceful; awkward; clumsy. —**un·gain′li·ness,** *n.*

un·gen·er·ous (un jen′ər əs) *adj.* **1.** not generous; stingy: *an ungenerous person, an ungenerous amount.* **2.** lacking kindness or sympathy: *an ungenerous remark.* —**un·gen′er·ous·ly,** *adv.* —**un·gen′er·ous·ness,** *n.*

un·god·ly (un god′lē) *adj.,* **un·god·li·er, un·god·li·est.** not feeling or showing a reverence for God or religious laws; impious; sinful. —**un·god′li·ness,** *n.*

un·gov·ern·a·ble (un guv′ər nə bəl) *adj.* impossible to control or hold in check; not governable: *an ungovernable mob, an ungovernable temper.* —**un·gov′ern·a·bly,** *adv.*

un·grace·ful (un grās′fəl) *adj.* not graceful; awkward: *ungraceful movements.* —**un·grace′ful·ly,** *adv.* —**un·grace′ful·ness,** *n.*

un·gra·cious (un grā′shəs) *adj.* not kind or courteous; impolite; rude. —**un·gra′cious·ly,** *adv.* —**un·gra′cious·ness,** *n.*

un·gram·mat·i·cal (un′grə mat′i kəl) *adj.* not following the accepted rules or standards of grammar.

un·grate·ful (un grāt′fəl) *adj.* **1.** not thankful for kindness or favors received: *That ungrateful boy did not thank us.* **2.** disagreeable; unpleasant: *Telling him he did not make the team was an ungrateful task.* —**un·grate′ful·ly,** *adv.* —**un·grate′ful·ness,** *n.*

un·ground·ed (un groun′did) *adj.* **1.** without basis in fact or reality: *ungrounded suspicions, ungrounded hopes.* **2.** without knowledge or instruction; not educated: *to be ungrounded in mathematics.*

un·grudg·ing (un gruj′ing) *adj.* without envy or other reservation; wholehearted; unstinting: *He accepted his rival's ungrudging praise for his work.* —**un·grudg′ing·ly,** *adv.*

un·guard·ed (un gär′did) *adj.* **1.** without guard or protection: *an unguarded building.* **2.** without caution; careless: *She revealed the true story in an unguarded moment.* —**un·guard′ed·ly,** *adv.* —**un·guard′ed·ness,** *n.*

un·guent (ung′gwənt) *n.* a salve or ointment.

un·gu·late (ung′gyə lit) *adj.* having hoofs. —*n.* a hoofed animal, such as a cow, horse, or sheep.

un·hal·lowed (un hal′ōd) *adj.* **1.** not made holy: *unhallowed ground.* **2.** sinful; wicked.

un·hand (un hand′) *v.t.* to release from the grasp; let go.

un·hap·py (un hap′ē) *adj.,* **un·hap·pi·er, un·hap·pi·est.** **1.** without happiness or joy; sad: *an unhappy child.* **2.** not fortunate; unlucky: *an unhappy mistake.* **3.** not suitable or appropriate: *an unhappy choice of colors.* —**un·hap′pi·ly,** *adv.* —**un·hap′pi·ness,** *n.*

un·harmed (un härmd′) *adj.* not harmed: *The man managed to escape from the burning building unharmed.*

un·health·ful (un helth′fəl) *adj.* not good for a person's health. —**un·health′ful·ly,** *adv.* —**un·health′ful·ness,** *n.*

un·health·y (un hel′thē) *adj.,* **un·health·i·er, un·health·i·est.** **1.** not in good health, sick; sickly: *an unhealthy person.* **2.** causing poor health: *an unhealthy climate, unhealthy eating habits.* **3.** harmful to a person's morals; unwholesome: *an unhealthy influence.* —**un·health′i·ly,** *adv.* —**un·health′i·ness,** *n.*

un·heard (un hurd′) *adj.* **1.** not heard: *The child's cries went unheard.* **2.** not given a hearing: *an unheard appeal.*

un·heard-of (un hurd′uv′, un hurd′ov′) *adj.* **1.** outrageous; ridiculous: *unheard-of behavior.* **2.** not known or happening before; unknown: *Traveling across the Atlantic Ocean in six hours was unheard-of fifty years ago.*

un·hes·i·tat·ing (un hez′ə tā′ting) *adj.* without hesitation or delay; immediate; prompt: *an unhesitating reply.* —**un·hes′i·tat·ing·ly,** *adv.*

un·hinge (un hinj′) *v.t.,* **un·hinged, un·hing·ing. 1.** to remove from hinges: *The carpenter unhinged the door.* **2.** to throw into confusion or disorder; unsettle; unbalance: *The shock of the accident unhinged his mind.*

un·hitch (un hich′) *v.t.* to set loose; unfasten: *The farmer unhitched the mule from the wagon.*

un·ho·ly (un hō′lē) *adj.,* **un·ho·li·er, un·ho·li·est. 1.** not holy; unhallowed: *unholy ground.* **2.** sinful; wicked; immoral. **3.** *Informal.* dreadful; terrible: *He made an unholy racket when he dropped the box of dishes down the stairs.* —**un·ho′li·ness,** *n.*

un·hook (un hook′) *v.t.* **1.** to remove from a hook: *to unhook a fish.* **2.** to unfasten the hooks of: *to unhook a dress.* —*v.i.* to become unhooked.

un·horse (un hôrs′) *v.t.,* **un·horsed, un·hors·ing.** to throw (a rider) from a horse.

un·hur·ried (un hur′ēd) *adj.* without haste; not hurried: *We ate an unhurried meal.* —**un·hur′ried·ly,** *adv.*

un·hurt (un hurt′) *adj.* not hurt: *He was unhurt by the fall.*

uni- *combining form* only one; single: *unicellular.*

u·ni·cam·er·al (yōō′nə kam′ər əl) *adj.* having or made up of one legislative chamber or house: *The state of Nebraska has a unicameral legislature.*

UNICEF (yōō′nə sef′) United Nations International Children's Emergency Fund.

u·ni·cel·lu·lar (yōō′nə sel′yə lər) *adj.* having or consisting of a single cell: *The ameba is a unicellular animal.*

u·ni·corn (yōō′nə kôrn′) *n.* a legendary animal usually represented in art as a white horse with a long pointed horn in the middle of its forehead.

u·ni·cy·cle (yōō′nə sī′kəl) *n.* a vehicle made up of a single wheel and operated by foot pedals, often having a seat or bar mounted on a shaft. It is used chiefly by acrobats, entertainers, and gymnasts.

u·ni·den·ti·fied (un′ī den′tə fīd′) *adj.* that has not been identified; unknown: *An unidentified man was seen leaving the building.*

u·ni·fi·ca·tion (yōō′nə fi kā′shən) *n.* the act of unifying or the state of being unified.

u·ni·form (yōō′nə fôrm′) *adj.* **1.** without change; always the same; unvarying: *The house is heated at a uniform temperature. The walls of the room are painted a uniform color.* **2.** showing little or no difference: *All the houses in the neighborhood are uniform in design.* —*n.* the special or official clothes worn by the members of a group: *The policemen were in uniform.* —*v.i.* to provide with a uniform. —**u′ni·form′ly,** *adv.* —**u′ni·form′ness,** *n.*

Unicycle

at; āpe; cär; end; mē; it; īce; hot; ōld; fôrk; wood; fōōl; oil; out; up; turn; sing; thin; **th**is; hw in white; zh in treasure. The symbol ə stands for the sound of **a** in about, **e** in taken, **i** in pencil, **o** in lemon, and **u** in circus.

u·ni·form·i·ty (yo͞o′nə fôr′mə tē) *n. pl.,* **u·ni·form·i·ties.** the state, quality, or instance of being uniform.

u·ni·fy (yo͞o′nə fī′) *v.t.,* **u·ni·fied, u·ni·fy·ing.** to combine or make into a whole; cause to be one; unite: *Fear of an enemy invasion unified the people of the small country.* —**u′ni·fi′er,** *n.*

u·ni·lat·er·al (yo͞o′nə lat′ər əl) *adj.* of, affecting, or done by one person or group only: *a unilateral agreement, unilateral disarmament.* —**u′ni·lat′er·al·ly,** *adv.*

un·i·mag·i·na·ble (un′i maj′ə nə bəl) *adj.* that cannot be imagined; hard to imagine: *unimaginable wealth.* —**un′i·mag′i·na·bly,** *adv.*

un·i·mag·i·na·tive (un′i maj′ə nə tiv) *adj.* not having imagination or creativity: *an unimaginative play, an unimaginative writer.* —**un′i·mag′i·na·tive·ly,** *adv.*

un·im·peach·a·ble (un′im pē′chə bəl) *adj.* not to be called into question; above reproach or blame; faultless: *His reputation for honesty is unimpeachable.* —**un′im·peach′a·bly,** *adv.*

un·im·por·tant (un′im pôrt′ənt) *adj.* not having any special value or meaning; not important: *an unimportant incident, an unimportant mistake.* —**un′im·port′ance,** *n.*

un·in·flect·ed (un′in flek′tid) *adj.* not changed or varied: *"Deer" is an uninflected word, because the plural is also "deer."*

un·in·hab·it·ed (un′in hab′i tid) *adj.* not lived in: *The old house has been uninhabited for years.*

un·in·hib·it·ed (un′in hib′i tid) *adj.* lacking or having few inhibitions. —**un′in·hib′i·ted·ly,** *adv.*

un·in·spired (un′in spīrd′) *adj.* not having originality, imagination, or creativity; not inspired; dull: *an uninspired performance.*

un·in·tel·li·gi·ble (un′in tel′ə jə bəl) *adj.* not capable of being made out or understood: *unintelligible handwriting.* —**un′in·tel′li·gi·bil′i·ty,** *n.* —**un′in·tel′li·gi·bly,** *adv.*

un·in·ten·tion·al (un′in ten′shə nəl) *adj.* not done on purpose. —**un′in·ten′tion·al·ly,** *adv.*

un·in·ter·est·ed (un in′tris tid, un in′tə res′tid) *adj.* not interested; unconcerned; indifferent: *He was uninterested in his neighbor's problems.*

▲ **Uninterested** means "not interested." **Disinterested** means "impartial," or "not taking sides in something." *She was uninterested in the hockey game* means that she had no interest in the game. *She was disinterested in the outcome of the hockey game* means that she did not care which team won.

un·in·ter·est·ing (un in′tris ting, un in′tə res′ting) *adj.* not interesting: *She found the book uninteresting.*

un·in·ter·rupt·ed (un′in tə rup′tid) *adj.* without interruption; unbroken; continuous. —**un′in·ter·rupt′ed·ly,** *adv.*

un·in·vit·ed (un′in vī′tid) *adj.* not invited: *an uninvited guest.*

un·in·vit·ing (un′in vī′ting) *adj.* not tempting or attractive: *The stale cake looked uninviting.*

un·ion (yo͞on′yən) *n.* **1.** the act of uniting or the state of being united. **2.** something formed by uniting two or more things. **3.** an association of workers organized to protect and further the interests of its members. **4. the Union. a.** the United States of America. **b.** those states that remained loyal to the Federal government during the Civil War. **5.** the act of marrying or the state of being married marriage. **6.** the emblem on a flag symbolizing unity, such as the three crosses on the British flag or the blue rectangle covered with stars on the U.S. flag. **7.** a coupling device for connecting machinery parts, such as pipes or rods.

un·ion·ism (yo͞on′yə niz′əm) *n.* **1.** the support of or belief in a union or unions or membership in a union, espe-

cially a labor union. **2. Unionism.** loyalty to or support of the Federal government during the Civil War.

un·ion·ist (yo͞on′yə nist) *n.* **1.** a person who belongs to a labor union or believes in unionism. **2. Unionist.** a supporter of the Federal government during the Civil War.

un·ion·ize (yo͞on′yə nīz′) *v.t.,* **un·ion·ized, un·ion·iz·ing. 1.** to organize into a union; cause to join a union: *to unionize workers.* **2.** to put under the rules of a union: *to unionize an industry.* —**un′ion·i·za′tion,** *n.*

union jack 1. *usually,* **Union Jack.** the flag of the United Kingdom. **2.** any flag that consists of the emblem from a national flag.

Union of South Africa, see **South Africa, Republic of.**

Union of Soviet Socialist Republics, another name for the **Soviet Union.**

u·nique (yo͞o nēk′) *adj.* **1.** not having an equal; being unsurpassed. **2.** being the only one of its kind; single; sole. **3.** *Informal.* highly unusual, rare, or noteworthy; remarkable: *a unique experience.* —**u·nique′ly,** *adv.* —**u·nique′ness,** *n.*

▲ **Unique** originally meant "one of a kind," and therefore it could not be logically qualified with words such as *more* or *most: Franklin D. Roosevelt's election to the Presidency for four terms is unique.* However, because there are very few things that are only one of a kind, many people now use *unique* to mean "highly unusual" or "remarkable" with a qualifying adverb: *This situation is completely unique. His style of painting is very unique.*

u·ni·son (yo͞o′nə sən, yo͞o′nə zən) *n.* **1.** complete or perfect agreement. **2.** *Music.* sameness in pitch, as of two or more tones or voices: *The altos and tenors sang in unison.*

u·nit (yo͞o′nit) *n.* **1.** a single person, thing, or group, especially one that is a basic part of a larger group: *a medical unit of an army. Each apartment building contains fifty living units.* **2.** a piece of equipment having a special purpose: *a refrigeration unit.* **3.** any fixed quantity or amount that is considered as a standard of measurement: *An hour is a unit of time.* **4.** *Mathematics.* the smallest whole number; one.

U·ni·tar·i·an (yo͞o′nə ter′ē ən) *n.* **1.** *also,* **unitarian.** a person who does not believe in the Trinity and the divinity of Jesus, but who believes instead that God exists as one being. **2.** a member of a denomination holding these beliefs. —*adj.* of or relating to Unitarians or Unitarianism.

U·ni·tar·i·an·ism (yo͞o′nə ter′ē ə niz′əm) *n.* the beliefs of Unitarians.

u·ni·tar·y (yo͞o′nə ter′ē) *adj.* **1.** of or relating to a unit or units. **2.** like a unit.

u·nite (yo͞o nīt′) *v.,* **u·nit·ed, u·nit·ing.** —*v.t.* to bring or put together: *The two families were united by marriage.* —*v.i.* **1.** to be brought together; join together: *The countries united to form a single nation.* **2.** to join together for a common purpose: *All the people of the country united in battle against the enemy.*

u·nit·ed (yo͞o nī′tid) *adj.* **1.** brought or put together; joined together. **2.** of, formed by, or produced by joint action: *a united effort.* **3.** in agreement or harmony. —**u·nit′ed·ly,** *adv.* —**u·nit′ed·ness,** *n.*

United Arab E·mir·ates (ə mēr′its) a country composed of a group of seven sheikdoms on the east-central coast of the Arabian peninsula. It was formerly known at various times as Trucial States, Trucial Coast, and Trucial Oman. Area, 32,300 sq. mi. Pop. (1978 est.), 244,000.

United Arab Republic, the former name of **Egypt.**

United Kingdom, a country in northwestern Europe, composed of England, Scotland, Wales, and Northern Ireland. Capital, London. Area, 94,214 sq. mi. Pop. (1980), 55,900,000.

United Nations, an international organization, founded in 1945, including as members most of the nations of the world. It seeks to maintain world peace, promote cooperation among nations, and encourage respect for international law. Its headquarters are located in New York City, on Manhattan Island.

United States, a country mainly in North America, comprising fifty states and the District of Columbia. Capital, Washington, D.C. Area, 3,615,202 sq. mi. Pop. (1980 est.), 222,000,000. Also, **America, United States of America.**

unit pricing, a way of pricing foods that shows not only the total price but also the price per pound, quart, or other standard unit of measurement.

u·ni·ty (yōō′nə tē) *n. pl.,* **u·ni·ties. 1.** the state or fact of being one. **2.** the state or quality of being in harmony or agreement. **3.** the arrangement of the parts in a work of art or literature to produce a single design or effect. **4.** *Mathematics.* the number one.

u·ni·valve (yōō′nə valv′) *n.* a mollusk whose shell is made up of a single part, or valve, such as the snail. —*adj.* having a single shell.

u·ni·ver·sal (yōō′nə vur′səl) *adj.* **1.** of or shared by all: *There was universal joy when the war ended.* **2.** existing everywhere or affecting everything: *It is a universal law of science that matter is made up of atoms moving in space.*

U·ni·ver·sal·ist (yōō′nə vur′sə list) *n.* a person who belongs to a denomination that teaches that all mankind will be saved.

u·ni·ver·sal·i·ty (yōō′nə vər sal′ə tē) *n. pl.,* **u·ni·ver·sal·i·ties.** the state or quality of being universal.

universal joint, a joint allowing the parts it connects to move in any direction, especially one that transmits rotary motion from one shaft to another.

Universal joint

u·ni·ver·sal·ly (yōō′nəvur′sə lē) *adv.* in a universal manner; in every instance or place; without exception: *The film was universally acclaimed by audiences and critics alike.*

u·ni·verse (yōō′nə vurs′) *n.* **1.** all that exists, including the earth, the heavens, and all of space; entire physical world. **2.** *Mathematics.* a set that contains all the objects or sets under consideration at any one time. Also *(def. 2),* **universal set.**

u·ni·ver·si·ty (yōō′nə vur′sə tē) *n. pl.,* **u·ni·ver·si·ties.** an institution of higher education, usually including one or more colleges and graduate and professional schools.

un·just (un just′) *adj.* not fair or moral; not just. —**un·just′ly,** *adv.* —**un·just′ness,** *n.*

un·jus·ti·fi·a·ble (un jus′tə fī′ə bəl) *adj.* that cannot be justified. —**un·jus′ti·fi′a·bly,** *adv.*

un·kempt (un kempt′) *adj.* **1.** not combed or groomed: *The boy had shaggy, unkempt hair.* **2.** not neat or clean in appearance: *The house has an unkempt lawn.*

un·kind (un kīnd′) *adj.* not kind; cruel: *an unkind remark.* —**un·kind′ness,** *n.*

un·kind·ly (un kīnd′lē) *adv.* in an unkind manner: *She treated the stranger unkindly.* —*adj.* unkind; cruel.

un·know·a·ble (un nō′ə bəl) *adj.* not able to be known; not knowable.

un·known (un nōn′) *adj.* **1.** not part of a person's knowledge; unfamiliar: *That actor's name is unknown to me.* **2.** not discovered or identified: *an unknown island.* —*n.* a person or thing that is unknown.

un·lace (un lās′) *v.t.,* **un·laced, un·lac·ing.** to undo the laces of.

un·latch (un lach′) *v.t.* to unfasten or open by releasing a latch: *to unlatch a door.* —*v.i.* to become unlatched.

un·law·ful (un lô′fəl) *adj.* against the law; illegal. —**un·law′ful·ly,** *adv.* —**un·law′ful·ness,** *n.*

un·learn (un lurn′) *v.t.,* **un·learned** or **un·learnt** (unlurnt′), **un·learn·ing.** to rid the mind of (something learned); forget.

un·learn·ed *(def. 1* un lur′nid, *def. 2* un lurnd′) *adj.* **1.** not having or showing much knowledge or education: *The unlearned boy did not know the alphabet.* **2.** not gotten by learning or study: *We all have unlearned habits.*

un·leash (un lēsh′) *v.t.* **1.** to let loose from a leash: *to unleash a puppy.* **2.** to let loose: *The hurricane unleashed its fury.*

un·leav·ened (un lev′ənd) *adj.* not leavened, as bread used during Passover.

un·less (un les′) *conj.* except on the condition that; if not: *Unless you return the books that you have, you cannot borrow any more.*

un·let·tered (un let′ərd) *adj.* **1.** not educated; ignorant. **2.** not able to read or write; illiterate.

un·li·censed (un lī′sinst) *adj.* **1.** having no license: *an unlicensed driver.* **2.** done without permission; unauthorized.

un·like (un līk′) *prep.* **1.** different from: *Unlike most of his friends, he enjoys dancing.* **2.** not typical of: *It is unlike him to be rude.* —*adj.* not the same or equal; different: *A deer and a mouse are unlike animals.* —**un·like′ness,** *n.*

un·like·ly (un līk′lē) *adj.,* **un·lik·li·er, un·lik·li·est. 1.** not likely: *It is unlikely that it will rain today.* **2.** not likely to succeed; unpromising: *That is an unlikely scheme.* —**un·like′li·ness,** *n.*

un·lim·it·ed (un lim′ə tid) *adj.* without limits or restrictions: *This pass gives you unlimited use of the pool all summer.*

un·lined (un līnd′) *adj.* without lines: *a sheet of unlined paper.*

un·list·ed (un lis′tid) *adj.* not included on a list; not listed: *My uncle has an unlisted telephone number.*

un·load (un lōd′) *v.t.* **1.** to take off (a load): *The men unloaded freight from the train.* **2.** to remove a load from: *The men unloaded the ship.* **3.** to remove ammunition from (a firearm): *The hunter unloaded his gun.* **4.** to give expression to: *Mary unloaded her troubles to her best friend.* **5.** *Informal.* to get rid of; dispose of: *We unloaded the old furniture at an auction.* —*v.i.* to discharge a load: *The ship unloaded in Boston.*

un·lock (un lok′) *v.t.* **1.** to open or undo the lock of: *Bill unlocked the door with his key.* **2.** to open or release as if by undoing a lock: *The policeman unlocked his grip on the thief's arm.* **3.** to furnish a solution to; disclose: *to unlock a mystery.* —*v.i.* to become unlocked.

un·looked-for (un lookt′fôr′) *adj.* not expected.

un·loose (un lōōs′) *v.t.,* **un·loosed, un·loos·ing. 1.** to let loose; set free; release: *He unloosed the bird from the cage.* **2.** to relax; loosen: *The sailor unloosed his hold on the rope.*

un·loos·en (un lōō′sən) *v.t.* another word for **unloose.**

un·luck·y (un luk′ē) *adj.,* **un·luck·i·er, un·luck·i·est. 1.** not having good luck; unfortunate: *He is an unlucky boy.* **2.** marked by or causing bad luck: *Last year was an unlucky*

at; āpe; cär; end; mē; it; īce; hot; ōld; fôrk; wood; fōōl; oil; out; up; turn; sing; thin; this; hw in white; zh in treasure. The symbol ə stands for the sound of **a** in about, **e** in taken, **i** in pencil, **o** in lemon, and **u** in circus.

season for the team. Some people believe that thirteen is an unlucky number. —**un·luck′i·ly,** *adv.* —**un·luck′i·ness,** *n.*

un·man (un man′) *v.t.,* **un·manned, un·man·ning.** to make less strong or manly; weaken; discourage.

un·man·age·a·ble (un man′i jə bəl) *adj.* that cannot be managed or controlled.

un·manned (un mand′) *adj.* without a crew: *an unmanned spacecraft.*

un·man·ner·ly (un man′ər lē) *adj.* having or showing bad manners; rude. —*adv.* impolitely; rudely. —**un·man′ner·li·ness,** *n.*

un·mar·ried (un mar′ēd) *adv.* not married.

un·mask (un mask′) *v.t.* **1.** to remove a mask or disguise from. **2.** to reveal the true nature of; expose: *The newspaper reporter unmasked the plot.* —*v.i.* to remove one's mask or disguise.

un·mean·ing (un mē′ning) *adj.* **1.** without meaning; senseless: *unmeaning utterances.* **2.** showing no intelligence; vacant: *She had an unmeaning expression on her face.*

un·meet (un mēt′) *adj.* not fit, proper, or suitable.

un·men·tion·a·ble (un men′shə nə bəl) *adj.* not fit for discussion; shameful; embarrassing: *an unmentionable topic.*

un·mer·ci·ful (un mur′si fəl) *adj.* having or showing no mercy; merciless; cruel. —**un·mer′ci·ful·ly,** *adv.* —**un·mer′ci·ful·ness,** *n.*

un·mind·ful (un mīnd′fəl) *adj.* not aware or careful; heedless; forgetful: *He was unmindful of what other people might think.* —**un·mind′ful·ly,** *adv.*

un·mis·tak·a·ble (un′mis tā′kə bəl) *adj.* that cannot be mistaken; obvious; plain: *There was an unmistakable note of anger in her voice.* —**un′mis·tak′a·bly,** *adv.*

un·mit·i·gat·ed (un mit′ə gā′tid) *adj.* **1.** not lessened or softened; not made less intense: *unmitigated cold, unmitigated anger.* **2.** downright; thorough; utter: *an unmitigated liar.*

un·mor·al (un môr′əl, un mor′əl) *adj.* not having or interested in moral standards; amoral. —**un·mor′al·ly,** *adv.*

un·moved (un mōōvd′) *adj.* **1.** not moved. **2.** not affected or disturbed: *She was unmoved by his plea.*

un·named (un nāmd′) *adj.* not named.

un·nat·u·ral (un nach′ər əl) *adj.* **1.** going against or different from the usual in nature; not natural: *The cat grew to an unnatural size.* **2.** shocking to natural feelings; monstrous; inhuman: *unnatural cruelty.* **3.** not genuine; contrived; artificial: *She had an unnatural smile.* —**un·nat′u·ral·ly,** *adv.* —**un·nat′u·ral·ness,** *n.*

un·nec·es·sar·y (un nes′ə ser′ē) *adj.* not needed; needless. —**un·nec′es·sar′i·ly,** *adv.*

un·nerve (un nurv′) *v.t.,* **un·nerved, un·nerv·ing.** to take away the courage or self-control of; make less calm: *The lawyer's questions unnerved the witness.*

un·num·bered (un num′bərd) *adj.* **1.** not marked with a number or numbers: *unnumbered pages.* **2.** countless: *There are unnumbered stars in the sky.*

un·ob·served (un′əb zurvd′) *adj.* **1.** not noticed or perceived: *The man slipped into the house unobserved.* **2.** not followed: *an unobserved law.* **3.** not kept: *an unobserved holiday.*

un·ob·tru·sive (un′əb trōō′siv) *adj.* that does not cause notice or disturbance; inconspicuous. —**un′ob·tru′sive·ly,** *adv.* —**un′ob·tru′sive·ness,** *n.*

un·oc·cu·pied (un ok′yə pīd′) *adj.* **1.** without an occupant; vacant: *an unoccupied apartment.* **2.** not held by troops or enemy forces: *unoccupied territory.* **3.** not busy; unemployed; idle: *an unoccupied person.*

un·of·fi·cial (un′ə fish′əl) *adj.* not official: *an unofficial announcement.* —**un′of·fi′cial·ly,** *adv.*

un·o·pened (un ō′pənd) *adj.* not opened: *an unopened package.*

un·op·posed (un′ə pōzd′) *adj.* not opposed: *The district attorney was unopposed in his campaign for reelection.*

un·or·gan·ized (un ôr′gə nīzd′) *adj.* **1.** not formed into an orderly arrangement or whole; not organized: *The club is still unorganized.* **2.** not unionized: *The workers in that industry are unorganized.*

un·or·tho·dox (un ôr′thə doks′) *adj.* going against accepted beliefs, opinions, customs, or doctrines; not orthodox: *unorthodox teachings, unorthodox behavior.*

un·pack (un pak′) *v.t.* **1.** to empty the contents of: *to unpack a suitcase.* **2.** to remove from a container or packaging: *Dad unpacked the glassware from the box.* **3.** to remove a pack or burden from; unload: *to unpack a mule.* —*v.i.* to unpack something, such as luggage.

un·paid (un pād′) *adj.* **1.** not yet paid: *unpaid wages, an unpaid fine.* **2.** serving without pay; unsalaried: *an unpaid volunteer.*

un·par·al·leled (un par′ə leld′) *adj.* without equal; matchless; unsurpassed: *an unparalleled achievement.*

un·par·don·a·ble (un pärd′ən əb əl) *adj.* that cannot be excused or forgiven: *an unpardonable act of cruelty.*

un·pas·teur·ized (un pas′chə rīzd′) *adj.* not pasteurized: *unpasteurized milk.*

un·pa·tri·ot·ic (un pā′trē ot′ik) *adj.* not showing patriotism; not patriotic.

un·pin (un pin′) *v.t.,* **un·pinned, un·pin·ning. 1.** to remove a pin or pins from. **2.** to open, loose, or unfasten by removing a pin or pins: *The woman unpinned her hair.*

un·pleas·ant (un plez′ənt) *adj.* not pleasing; disagreeable: *an unpleasant odor.* —**un·pleas′ant·ly,** *adv.*

un·pleas·ant·ness (un plez′ənt nis) *n.* **1.** the condition or quality of being unpleasant. **2.** something unpleasant, such as a quarrel.

un·plug (un plug′) *v.t.,* **un·plugged, un·plug·ging. 1.** to remove the plug of (an electrical appliance) from an outlet; disconnect: *She unplugged the toaster.* **2.** to remove a stopper or plug from: *She unplugged the sink.*

un·pol·lut·ed (un′pə lōō′tid) *adj.* not polluted, as by wastes: *The river was still clear and unpolluted.*

un·pop·u·lar (un pop′yə lər) *adj.* not generally liked or accepted; not popular: *She is unpopular at school. He has unpopular opinions.* —**un·pop′u·lar·ly,** *adv.*

un·pop·u·lar·i·ty (un′pop yə lar′ə tē) *n.* the state or condition of being unpopular.

un·prac·ticed (un prak′tist) *also, British,* **un·prac·tised.** *adj.* **1.** lacking experience, practice, or skill: *an unpracticed lawyer.* **2.** not put into practice.

un·prec·e·dent·ed (un pres′ə den′tid) *adj.* not known or done before; without parallel or precedent: *Man's first landing on the moon was an unprecedented event.*

un·pre·dict·a·ble (un′pri dik′tə bəl) *adj.* that cannot be predicted: *The weather is unpredictable at this time of year.* —**un′pre·dict′a·ble·ness,** *n.* —**un′pre·dict′a·bly,** *adv.*

un·prej·u·diced (un prej′ə dist) *adj.* without prejudice; unbiased.

un·pre·med·i·tat·ed (un′prē med′ə tā′tid) *adj.* not planned or thought out beforehand; not premeditated.

un·pre·pared (un′pri perd′) *adj.* **1.** not ready; not prepared: *He was unprepared for the test.* **2.** that has not been prepared beforehand: *The mayor gave an unprepared speech.*

un·pre·pos·sess·ing (un′prē pə zes′ing) *adj.* not making a good impression: *The shy, awkward girl was unprepossessing at first meeting.*

un·pre·ten·tious (un′pri ten′shəs) *adj.* not pretentious; modest; simple. —**un′pre·ten′tious·ly,** *adv.* —**un′pre·ten′tious·ness,** *n.*

un·prin·ci·pled (un prin′sə pəld) *adj.* having or showing a lack of moral principles; unscrupulous: *The unprincipled businessman cheated everyone.*

un·print·a·ble (un prin′tə bəl) *adj.* not fit for publication.

un·pro·fes·sion·al (un′prə fesh′ən əl) *adj.* **1.** going against the standards or rules of a profession: *The doctor was guilty of unprofessional conduct.* **2.** not relating to, characteristic of, or connected with a profession: *an unprofessional opinion, an unprofessional performance.* —**un′pro·fes′sion·al·ly,** *adv.*

un·prof·it·a·ble (un prof′i tə bəl) *adj.* **1.** not useful or rewarding; fruitless: *an unprofitable meeting.* **2.** producing no financial profit: *The investment proved to be unprofitable.* —**un·prof′it·a·bly,** *adv.*

un·qual·i·fied (un kwol′ə fīd′) *adj.* **1.** not having the necessary or proper qualifications; unfit: *Not being a citizen, he is unqualified to vote.* **2.** not limited or restricted: *The writer's first novel was an unqualified success.*

un·quench·a·ble (un kwen′chə bəl) *adj.* **1.** that cannot be satisfied: *an unquenchable thirst.* **2.** that cannot be put out: *an unquenchable fire.*

un·ques·tion·a·ble (un kwes′chə nə bəl) *adj.* beyond doubt or question: *The judge is a person of unquestionable fairness.* —**un·ques′tion·a·bly,** *adv.*

un·ques·tioned (un kwes′chənd) *adj.* not open to or called into question; not doubted.

un·qui·et (un kwī′it) *adj.* **1.** marked by or causing an uneasy feeling; anxious: *unquiet thoughts.* **2.** marked by unrest, disturbance, or disorder: *unquiet times.* —**un·qui′et·ly,** *adv.* —**un·qui′et·ness,** *n.*

un·quote (un kwōt′) *v.i.,* **un·quot·ed, un·quot·ing.** to close or end a quotation.

▲ **Unquote** is used with *quote* in speech to show when another person is being quoted. The words *quote* and *unquote* before and after a statement have the same function as quotation marks do in writing. For example: *He said quote "I had no knowledge of the plan" unquote, but I don't think he's telling the truth.*

un·rav·el (un rav′əl) *v.,* **un·rav·eled, un·rav·el·ing;** *also,* British, **un·rav·elled, un·rav·el·ling.** —*v.t.* **1.** to separate or untangle the threads of: *Mary unraveled the ball of yarn.* **2.** to separate and make clear the parts of; solve; reveal: *We tried to unravel the plot of the story.* —*v.i.* to become unraveled.

un·read (un red′) *adj.* **1.** not yet read: *an unread manuscript.* **2.** having little or no education; ignorant: *an unread person.*

un·read·y (un red′ē) *adj.* not ready.

un·re·al (un rē′əl) *adj.* not real; imaginary; fictitious.

un·re·al·is·tic (un′rē ə lis′tik) *adj.* **1.** not according to reality: *an unrealistic painting.* **2.** not practical: *an unrealistic attitude.*

un·re·al·i·ty (un′rē al′ə tē) *n. pl.,* **un·re·al·i·ties. 1.** the state or quality of being unreal. **2.** an unreal thing, fact, or event; something unreal.

un·rea·son·a·ble (un rē′zə nə bəl, un rēz′nə bəl) *adj.* **1.** not showing or using good sense or judgment; not reasonable: *He is being unreasonable, wanting his own way all the time.* **2.** going beyond what is moderate; excessive: *The prices at that restaurant are unreasonable.* —**un·rea′son·a·ble·ness,** *n.* —**un·rea′son·a·bly,** *adv.*

un·rea·son·ing (un rē′zə ning, un rēz′ning) *adj.* not showing or controlled by reason: *unreasoning anger.* —**un·rea′son·ing·ly,** *adv.*

un·re·cord·ed (un′ri kôr′did) *adj.* not recorded.

un·re·fined (un′ri fīnd′) *adj.* **1.** not made free of impurities: *unrefined petroleum.* **2.** not cultured: *an unrefined person.*

un·re·gen·er·ate (un′ri jen′ər it) *adj.* **1.** not morally or spiritually reborn: *an unregenerate sinner.* **2.** resisting change; stubborn.

un·re·lent·ing (un′ri len′ting) *adj.* **1.** not changing, yielding, or softening, as from pity; harsh: *He is unrelenting in his hatred.* **2.** not lessening or easing, as in intensity, effort, or speed: *That job involves unrelenting pressure.* —**un′re·lent′ing·ly,** *adv.*

un·re·li·a·ble (un′ri lī′ə bəl) *adj.* not to be trusted; untrustworthy: *The unreliable boy never finishes his work.* —**un′re·li·a·bil′i·ty, un′re·li·a·ble·ness,** *n.* —**un′re·li·a·bly,** *adv.*

un·re·mit·ting (un′ri mit′ing) *adj.* never ceasing; constant: *unremitting work.* —**un′re·mit′ting·ly,** *adv.*

un·re·quit·ed (un′ri kwī′tid) *adj.* not returned in kind: *unrequited love.*

un·re·served (un′ri zurvd′) *adj.* **1.** done or given without reservation or restriction; unqualified; full: *unreserved approval.* **2.** free from reserve; candid; open: *an unreserved manner.* —**un·re·serv·ed·ly** (un′ri zur′vid lē) *adv.*

un·rest (un rest′) *n.* restlessness; dissatisfaction; discontent: *political unrest.*

un·re·strained (un′ri strānd′) *adj.* not held in check or under control; not restrained: *The theater was filled with unrestrained laughter.* —**un·re·strain·ed·ly** (un′ri strā′nid lē) *adv.*

un·ripe (un rīp′) *adj.* **1.** not fully developed; immature: *unripe peaches.* **2.** not ready; unprepared: *The young man was unripe for a job involving such responsibilities.* —**un·ripe′ness,** *n.*

un·ri·valed (un rī′vəld) *also,* British, **un·ri·valled.** *adj.* having no rival or equal; matchless; supreme: *unrivaled beauty.*

un·roll (un rōl′) *v.t.* **1.** to open, spread out, or expand (something rolled up): *He unrolled the blanket.* **2.** to unfold; display; reveal. —*v.i.* to become unrolled.

un·ruf·fled (un ruf′əld) *adj.* not ruffled or disturbed: *unruffled waters, an unruffled state of mind.*

un·ruled (un rōold′) *adj.* **1.** not controlled or governed: *an unruled temper.* **2.** not marked with lines: *unruled paper.*

un·ru·ly (un rōo′lē) *adj.,* **un·ru·li·er, un·ru·li·est.** difficult to control or manage: *unruly hair, an unruly mob.* —**un·ru′li·ness,** *n.*

un·sad·dle (un sad′əl) *v.t.,* **un·sad·dled, un·sad·dling. 1.** to remove the saddle from (a horse). **2.** to cause to fall from a horse; unhorse.

un·safe (un sāf′) *adj.* not safe: *Those narrow mountain roads are unsafe.*

un·said (un sed′) *v.* the past tense and past participle of **unsay.** —*adj.* not spoken or expressed: *Some things are better left unsaid.*

un·san·i·tar·y (un san′ə ter′ē) *adj.* not clean or sanitary.

un·sat·is·fac·to·ry (un′sat is fak′tər ē) *adj.* not good enough to meet a need or desire; not satisfactory: *unsatisfactory work.* —**un′sat·is·fac′to·ri·ly,** *adv.*

at; āpe; cär; end; mē; it; īce; hot; ōld; fôrk; wood; fōol; oil; out; up; turn; sing; thin; **th**is; hw in white; zh in treasure. The symbol ə stands for the sound of **a** in about, **e** in taken, **i** in pencil, **o** in lemon, and **u** in circus.

U

un·sat·is·fied (un sat′is fīd′) *adj.* not satisfied: *The boy's thirst was unsatisfied by the drink.*

un·sat·u·rat·ed (un sach′ə rā′tid) *adj.* **1.** *Chemistry.* (of a solution) that can dissolve more of a substance; not saturated. **2.** (of a compound) that can join with other elements without giving up original components.

un·sa·vor·y (un sā′vər ē) also, British, **un·sa·vour·y.** *adj.* **1.** unpleasant to the taste or smell. **2.** morally bad: *an unsavory reputation.* **3.** having no flavor; tasteless. —**un·sa′vor·i·ness,** *n.*

un·say (un sā′) *v.t.,* **un·said, un·say·ing.** to take back or cancel (what has been said).

un·scathed (un skā̱thd′) *adj.* in no way harmed or hurt; uninjured.

un·sci·en·tif·ic (un′sī ən tif′ik) *adj.* not based on or using the principles and methods of science; not scientific. —**un′sci·en·tif′i·cal·ly,** *adv.*

un·scram·ble (un skram′bəl) *v.t.,* **un·scram·bled, un·scram·bling.** to make sense out of or put in order: *He tried to unscramble the mess he found in the desk drawer.*

un·screw (un skrōō′) *v.t.* **1.** to loosen, unfasten, or remove by turning: *He unscrewed the top from the tube of toothpaste.* **2.** to remove the screw or screws from. —*v.i.* to become unscrewed: *The lid of this jar unscrews easily.*

un·scru·pu·lous (un skrōō′pyə ləs) *adj.* showing no regard for what is right or wrong; without scruples: *The unscrupulous businessman cheated his customers.* —**un·scru′pu·lous·ly,** *adv.* —**un·scru′pu·lous·ness,** *n.*

un·seal (un sēl′) *v.t.* **1.** to break or remove the seal of: *to unseal an envelope.* **2.** to free from some constraining influence.

un·search·a·ble (un sur′chə bəl) *adj.* that cannot be searched or explored; mysterious. —**un·search′a·bly,** *adv.*

un·sea·son·a·ble (un sē′zə nə bəl) *adj.* **1.** not characteristic of or right for the season: *Such warm weather is unseasonable for December.* **2.** not done, happening, or coming at the right or proper time: *Midnight is an unseasonable hour to visit someone.* —**un·sea′son·a·ble·ness,** *n.* —**un·sea′son·a·bly,** *adv.*

un·sea·soned (un sē′zənd) *adj.* **1.** not flavored with seasoning: *unseasoned food.* **2.** not disciplined or experienced: *unseasoned soldiers.* **3.** not properly aged: *unseasoned wood.*

un·seat (un sēt′) *v.t.* **1.** to remove from a seat, especially to throw from a saddle: *The horse unseated his rider.* **2.** to remove from an office or position: *to unseat a judge.*

un·seem·ly (un sēm′lē) *adj.,* **un·seem·li·er, un·seem·li·est.** not right or proper for the time or place: *It is unseemly to tell a joke during a funeral service.* —*adv.* in an unseemly manner. —**un·seem′li·ness,** *n.*

un·seen (un sēn′) *adj.* **1.** not noticed or observed: *He came into the room unseen.* **2.** not visible: *an unseen spiritual presence.*

un·self·ish (un sel′fish) *adj.* not selfish; generous: *The unselfish girl shared her toys with her younger sister.* —**un·self′ish·ly,** *adv.* —**un·self′ish·ness,** *n.*

un·set·tle (un set′əl) *v.t.,* **un·set·tled, un·set·tling.** **1.** to trouble or upset; confuse; disturb: *The bad experience unsettled her.* **2.** to change or move; displace; disrupt.

un·set·tled (un set′əld) *adj.* **1.** not peaceful, calm, or orderly; disturbed; disrupted: *Unsettled conditions followed the civil war.* **2.** not determined or decided; unresolved: *an unsettled question.* **3.** not paid or settled: *an unsettled debt.* **4.** not occupied, inhabited, or populated: *an unsettled region of the frontier.*

un·shak·a·ble (un shā′kə bəl) also, **un·shake·a·ble.** *adj.* not easily weakened or shaken; firm: *an unshakable conviction.*

un·shak·en (un shā′kən) *adj.* not shaken: *He has an unshaken faith in his friend's honesty.*

un·sheathe (un shē̱th′) *v.t.,* **un·sheathed, un·sheath·ing.** to draw from a sheath or scabbard; bare: *to unsheathe a sword.*

un·shod (un shod′) *adj.* without shoes: *an unshod horse.*

un·sight·ly (un sīt′lē) *adj.,* **un·sight·li·er, un·sight·li·est.** unpleasant to the sight: *We are not happy about the unsightly litter strewn about the city parks.* —**un·sight′li·ness,** *n.*

un·skilled (un skild′) *adj.* **1.** lacking skill, training, or experience: *an unskilled actor.* **2.** not needing skill or training: *an unskilled job.* **3.** showing a lack of skill: *an unskilled drawing.*

un·skill·ful (un skil′fəl) also, British, **un·skil·ful.** *adj.* not having or showing skill; not skillful; clumsy. —**un·skill′ful·ly,** *adv.* —**un·skill′ful·ness,** *n.*

un·snap (un snap′) *v.t.,* **un·snapped, un·snap·ping.** to undo the snap or snaps of; unfasten.

un·snarl (un snärl′) *v.t.* to free from a snarl or snarls: *She unsnarled her hair by combing it.*

un·so·cia·ble (un sō′shə bəl) *adj.* not liking to be with others; not friendly: *He is an unsociable person and stays by himself.* —**un·so′cia·ble·ness,** *n.* —**un·so′cia·bly,** *adv.*

un·so·phis·ti·cat·ed (un′sə fis′tə kā′tid) *adj.* **1.** not having worldly knowledge and experience; lacking worldliness; naive. **2.** not complex; simple: *an unsophisticated mechanical device.* —**un′so·phis′ti·cat′ed·ly,** *adv.* —**un′so·phis′ti·ca′tion,** *n.*

un·sought (un sôt′) *adj.* not asked for or expected; not sought: *unsought help, an unsought prize.*

un·sound (un sound′) *adj.* **1.** not strong or solid; weak: *The foundation of the house is unsound and may crumble.* **2.** not based on truth, fact, or good judgment; not accurate or sensible: *He gave her unsound advice.* **3.** physically or mentally unhealthy; diseased: *The old man's teeth are unsound.* **4.** not stable or safe; not reliable: *The businessman made an unsound investment.* —**un·sound′ly,** *adv.* —**un·sound′ness,** *n.*

un·spar·ing (un sper′ing) *adj.* **1.** very generous; lavish: *Jim's unsparing efforts made the party a success.* **2.** unmerciful; harsh; severe: *unsparing criticism.* —**un·spar′ing·ly,** *adv.*

un·speak·a·ble (un spē′kə bəl) *adj.* **1.** that cannot be described or expressed in words: *unspeakable pleasure.* **2.** extremely bad or evil: *an unspeakable act, unspeakable behavior.* —**un·speak′a·bly,** *adv.*

un·spoiled (un spoild′) *adj.* not spoiled: *The scenery along that road is unspoiled by billboards or signs.*

un·spo·ken (un spō′kən) *adj.* not described or expressed in words; not spoken: *an unspoken agreement.*

un·sports·man·like (un sports′mən līk′) *adj.* not having or showing the qualities or characteristics worthy of a sportsman, such as fair play and the ability to accept defeat graciously.

un·spot·ted (un spot′id) *adj.* **1.** not marked by spots: *The glassware came out of the dishwasher unspotted.* **2.** without moral fault or defect: *She has an unspotted reputation.*

un·sta·ble (un stā′bəl) *adj.* **1.** not firmly fixed; easily moved; not stable: *an unstable platform, an unstable chair.* **2.** not settled or steady in character; apt to change: *an unstable government.* **3.** emotionally unsettled or troubled: *an unstable person.* **4.** *Chemistry.* readily changed into another compound, element, or isotope. —**un·sta′ble·ness,** *n.* —**un·sta′bly,** *adv.*

un·stead·y (un sted′ē) *adj.* **1.** not firm; shaky: *The ladder is unsteady.* **2.** that is not kept at an even rate: *Food prices have been unsteady.* **3.** changeable in habits or behavior; not reliable: *He is unsteady in his work.* —**un·stead'i·ly**, *adv.* —**un·stead'i·ness**, *n.*

un·stop (un stop') *v.t.,* **un·stopped, un·stop·ping.** **1.** to remove a stopper from: *to unstop a champagne bottle.* **2.** to free from something that blocks: *to unstop a drain.*

un·strap (un strap') *v.t.,* **un·strapped, un·strap·ping.** to remove, unfasten, or loosen the strap or straps of: *to unstrap a trunk.*

un·stressed (un strest') *adj.* not stressed in speech: *an unstressed syllable.*

un·string (un string') *v.t.,* **un·strung, un·string·ing.** **1.** to remove or loosen the string or strings of: *to unstring a violin.* **2.** to remove from a string: *to unstring pearls.* **3.** to upset emotionally; unnerve.

un·stud·ied (un stud'ēd) *adj.* not forced or contrived; natural: *People liked her for her unstudied friendliness.*

un·sub·stan·tial (un'səb stan'shəl) *adj.* **1.** not firm, strong, or solid: *unsubstantial fabric.* **2.** without material substance or form; unreal. —**un'sub·stan'tial·ly**, *adv.*

un·suc·cess·ful (un'sək ses'fəl) *adj.* not meeting with success; not successful: *He was unsuccessful in his attempt to become a novelist.* —**un'suc·cess'ful·ly**, *adv.*

un·suit·a·ble (un sōō'tə bəl) *adj.* not suitable or fit for the time or occasion: *Light clothing is unsuitable for the cold winter months.* —**un·suit'a·bly**, *adv.*

un·suit·ed (un sōō'tid) *adj.* not suited or fit: *A weak man is unsuited for heavy, physical labor.*

un·sul·lied (un sul'ēd) *adj.* not stained or soiled; not sullied: *an unsullied reputation.*

un·sung (un sung') *adj.* **1.** not honored or celebrated: *unsung heroes.* **2.** not sung.

un·sup·port·ed (un'sə pôr'tid) *adj.* **1.** not held up: *an unsupported roof.* **2.** not provided for: *an unsupported family.* **3.** not shown to be true; not verified: *an unsupported statement.*

un·sure (un shoor') *adj.* not sure: *He was unsure of his chances to make the team.*

un·sus·pect·ed (un'səs pek'tid) *adj.* **1.** not under suspicion. **2.** not imagined or thought of: *She discovered that she had an unsuspected talent for writing.*

un·sus·pect·ing (un'səs pek'ting) *adj.* having no suspicion; trusting. —**un'sus·pect'ing·ly**, *adv.*

un·sym·met·ri·cal (un'si met'ri kəl) *adj.* not balanced: *an unsymmetrical design.* —**un'sym·met'ri·cal·ly**, *adv.*

un·sym·pa·thet·ic (un'sim pə thet'ik) *adj.* not feeling or showing sympathy; not sympathetic: *She was unsympathetic to the problems of others.*

un·tan·gle (un tang'gəl) *v.t.,* **un·tan·gled, un·tan·gling.** **1.** to free from a tangle or tangles. **2.** to clear up; explain: *The police tried to untangle the mystery surrounding the murder.*

un·taught (un tôt') *adj.* **1.** not gotten by learning or teaching; natural: *an untaught art, an untaught talent.* **2.** not instructed or educated; ignorant.

un·ten·a·ble (un ten'ə bəl) *adj.* that cannot be supported or defended: *an untenable theory, an untenable position.*

un·thank·ful (un thangk'fəl) *adj.* not grateful or thankful.

un·think·a·ble (un thingk'kə bəl) *adj.* that cannot be thought of or considered: *It is unthinkable that he could have lied.*

un·think·ing (un thingk'king) *adj.* **1.** showing or marked by carelessness or thoughtlessness: *an unthinking remark.* **2.** without the ability to think. —**un·think'ing·ly**, *adv.*

un·thought-of (un thôt'ôf') *adj.* not thought of or imagined.

un·ti·dy (un tī'dē) *adj.,* **un·ti·di·er, un·ti·di·est.** not neat or orderly; messy: *an untidy desk.* —**un·ti'di·ly**, *adv.* —**un·ti'di·ness**, *n.*

un·tie (un tī') *v.,* **un·tied, un·ty·ing.** —*v.t.* **1.** to loosen or undo (something knotted or tied): *to untie a knot.* **2.** to free: *to untie a person's hands.* —*v.i.* to become untied.

un·til (ən til', un til') *prep.* **1.** up to the time of: *Wait until evening before you telephone him.* **2.** before: *Tickets are not available until Wednesday.* —*conj.* **1.** up to the time when: *Wait here until I get back.* **2.** before: *The store couldn't deliver the furniture until the snow melted and the roads were clear.* **3.** to the place, extent, or degree that: *Keep driving straight until you reach the intersection.*

un·time·ly (un tīm'lē) *adj.* **1.** coming or happening before the right or usual time: *an untimely death.* **2.** coming or happening at the wrong time: *an untimely visit.* —*adv.* at a bad time or too soon. —**un·time'li·ness**, *n.*

un·tir·ing (un tīr'ing) *adj.* not tiring; persistent: *untiring patience, untiring efforts.* —**un·tir'ing·ly**, *adv.*

un·to (un'tōō) *prep. Archaic.* to.

un·told (un tōld') *adj.* **1.** too great or too many to be counted or measured: *untold suffering, untold numbers.* **2.** not told: *an untold adventure.*

un·touch·a·ble (un tuch'ə bəl) *adj.* **1.** forbidden to the touch. **2.** beyond criticism. **3.** out of reach. **4.** disagreeable or dangerous to the touch. —*n.* also, **Untouchable.** in India, a member of the lowest caste whose touch was formerly thought to defile members of higher castes.

un·touched (un tucht') *adj.* **1.** not touched. **2.** not used or eaten: *The food remained untouched.* **3.** not moved: *He was untouched by her plea.*

un·to·ward (un tôrd') *adj.* **1.** marked by or causing trouble; unfortunate. **2.** difficult to manage or control; unruly: *an untoward child.*

un·tried (un trīd') *adj.* **1.** not proved or tested, as by experience or use: *an untried worker, an untried machine.* **2.** not brought before a court of law for judgment: *an untried case.*

un·trod (un trod') *adj.* not walked on: *untrod paths.*

un·true (un trōō') *adj.* **1.** not true; incorrect; false: *His remark about her is untrue.* **2.** not faithful or loyal: *He is untrue to his friends.* **3.** not measured correctly; not accurate. —**un'tru'ly**, *adv.*

un·truth (un trōōth') *n.* **1.** something untrue; lie. **2.** the quality or condition of being untrue; falsity.

un·truth·ful (un trōōth'fəl) *adj.* **1.** not truthful; not true: *an untruthful remark.* **2.** given to lying: *an untruthful person.* —**un·truth'ful·ly**, *adv.* —**un·truth'ful·ness**, *n.*

un·tu·tored (un tōō'tərd, un tyōō'tərd) *adj.* not educated; untaught.

un·twine (un twīn') *v.,* **un·twined, un·twin·ing.** —*v.t.* to undo (something twined or tangled). —*v.i.* to become untwined.

un·twist (un twist') *v.t.* to undo (something twisted). —*v.i.* to become untwisted.

un·used (un yōōzd') *adj.* **1.** not in use; not put to use: *an unused shelf in a bookcase.* **2.** never having been used; new; fresh: *an unused postage stamp, an unused toothbrush.* **3.** not accustomed: *He is unused to the quiet of the country.*

---

at; āpe; cär; end; mē; it; īce; hot; ōld; fôrk; wood; fōōl; oil; out; up; turn; sing; thin; this; hw in white; zh in treasure. The symbol ə stands for the sound of **a** in **about**, **e** in **taken**, **i** in **pencil**, **o** in **lemon**, and **u** in **circus.**

U

un·u·su·al (un yōō′zhōō əl) *adj.* not usual, common, or ordinary; rare. —**un·u′su·al·ly,** *adv.* —**un·u′su·al·ness,** *n.*

un·ut·ter·a·ble (un ut′ər ə bəl) *adj.* too deep or great to be put into words: *unutterable joy.*

un·var·nished (un vär′nisht) *adj.* **1.** not covered with varnish. **2.** stated without embellishment; plain; unadorned: *He told the unvarnished truth.*

un·veil (un vāl′) *v.t.* to remove a veil or covering from: *The bride unveiled her face. The sculptor unveiled his new statue.* —*v.i.* to remove a veil.

un·voiced (un voist′) *adj.* **1.** not stated: *an unvoiced objection.* **2.** (of a consonant) spoken without vibration of the vocal cords, such as the *t* sound in *toy.*

un·war·rant·ed (un wär′ən tid) *adj.* without basis; unjustified: *an unwarranted opinion.*

un·war·y (un wer′ē) *adj.* not watchful or careful; careless: *The storekeeper cheated the unwary man.* —**un·war′i·ly,** *adv.* —**un·war′i·ness,** *n.*

un·wel·come (un wel′kəm) *adj.* not received with pleasure; not welcome: *an unwelcome guest.*

un·well (un wel′) *adj.* not well; ill; sick.

un·wept (un wept′) *adj.* **1.** not mourned. **2.** (of tears) not shed.

un·whole·some (un hōl′səm) *adj.* **1.** harmful to the body; unhealthy: *an unwholesome diet.* **2.** harmful to the morals: *unwholesome entertainment.* —**un·whole′some·ly,** *adv.* —**un·whole′some·ness,** *n.*

un·wield·y (un wēl′dē) *adj.* difficult to handle, manage, or use; cumbersome: *an unwieldy package.* —**un·wield′i·ness,** *n.*

un·will·ing (un wil′ing) *adj.* **1.** not wanting to do or be something; not willing; reluctant: *He was unwilling to go with them.* **2.** not done, said, or given readily: *unwilling testimony.* —**un·will′ing·ly,** *adv.* —**un·will′ing·ness,** *n.*

un·wind (un wīnd′) *v.,* **un·wound, un·wind·ing.** —*v.t.* **1.** to undo or reverse the winding of; unroll: *The nurse unwound the bandages.* **2.** to straighten or untangle the twisted parts of. —*v.i.* **1.** to become unrolled or untangled. **2.** to become free from tension; relax: *Dad was able to unwind by reading a good book.*

un·wise (un wīz′) *adj.* showing a lack of wisdom or good sense; not wise; foolish: *It was unwise of him to leave his tools out in the rain.* —**un·wise′ly,** *adv.*

un·wit·ting (un wit′ing) *adj.* not knowing; unaware: *The man was an unwitting accomplice to a crime.* —**un·wit′ting·ly,** *adv.*

un·wont·ed (un wôn′tid, un wōn′tid, un wun′tid) *adj.* not customary; unusual: *He acted with unwonted calm during the fire.* —**un·wont′ed·ly,** *adv.*

un·world·ly (un wurld′lē) *adj.* devoted to spiritual matters instead of to the interests or pleasures of this world. —**un·world′li·ness,** *n.*

un·wor·thy (un wur′thē) *adj.* **1.** not worthy or deserving: *I feel unworthy of such praise.* **2.** not suiting or becoming: *Such cruel remarks were unworthy of him.* —**un·wor′thi·ly,** *adv.* —**un·wor′thi·ness,** *n.*

un·wound (un wound′) the past tense and past participle of **unwind.**

un·wrap (un rap′) *v.,* **un·wrapped, un·wrap·ping.** —*v.t.* to remove a wrapping from; open; undo: *to unwrap a package.* —*v.i.* to become unwrapped.

un·writ·ten (un rit′ən) *adj.* **1.** not written or put in writing: *unwritten testimony.* **2.** accepted by custom; traditional: *an unwritten law.*

un·yield·ing (un yēl′ding) *adj.* not giving way; firm: *She was unyielding in her desire to go home immediately.*

un·yoke (un yōk′) *v.t.,* **un·yoked, un·yok·ing. 1.** to release from a yoke: *to unyoke an ox.* **2.** to separate; part.

up (up) *adv.* **1.** from a lower to a higher place, level, or position: *He climbed up to the top of the ladder. We looked up to see the airplane.* **2.** in, on, or to a higher place: *Mother put the dishes up on the top shelf. They are spending the summer up in the mountains.* **3.** to a higher point or degree: *My weight went up during the summer. Janet turned the sound up on the television.* **4.** above the surface or horizon: *The diver came up for air. The sun came up at five o'clock.* **5.** in or to an upright position: *Sit up straight.* **6.** out of bed: *I got up at seven o'clock.* **7.** in or into a closed state: *Button up your coat. The bird was shut up in a cage.* **8.** in the lead; ahead: *That team is two games up in the pennant race.* **9.** for each side; apiece: *The score is four up.* —*adj.* **1.** going upward: *Take the up escalator.* **2.** at a higher point or degree: *Prices are up again this month.* **3.** risen above the horizon: *The sun is up.* **4.** awake or out of bed: *He won't be up until nine o'clock.* **5.** being presented or considered: *The house is up for sale. The mayor is up for reelection.* **6.** at an end: *Your time is up.* **7.** ahead: *Our team is two games up.* **8.** Baseball. at bat. **9.** *Informal.* going on: *What's up?* —*prep.* to or toward a place higher or farther along: *The spider climbed up the wall. The boys paddled up the river.* —*n.* **1.** an upward movement; ascent: *the ups and downs of prices on the stock market.* **2.** a change for the good; time of good fortune: *the ups and downs of life.* —*v.t.,* **upped, up·ping.** to make higher or larger; increase: *The storekeeper has upped prices on many items during the past year.*

   up against. facing; confronting: *The team is up against great odds.*

   up on. *Informal.* well-informed about: *Clare is up on current events.*

   up to. a. *Informal.* about to do: *What are you up to?* **b.** as far as: *What chapter is the teacher up to in the book?* **c.** capable of; equal to: *Is he up to such an important job?* **d.** dependent upon, as for a decision: *It is up to you to make the change.*

up-and-com·ing (up′ən kum′ing) *adj.* likely to succeed; promising: *an up-and-coming young lawyer.*

up·beat (up′bēt′) *n. Music.* an unaccented beat, especially the last beat of a measure, indicated by an upward movement of the conductor's hand.

up·braid (up brād′) *v.t.* to scold harshly: *The farmer upbraided his sons for not doing their chores.*

up·bring·ing (up′bring′ing) *n.* the care and training received during childhood and youth: *She had a strict upbringing.*

up·coun·try (up′kun′trē) also, **up-coun·try.** *n.* the interior of a region or country. —*adj.* of or coming from the upcountry. —*adv.* toward or in the upcountry.

up·date (up dāt′) *v.t.,* **up·dat·ed, up·dat·ing.** to bring up to date: *The publishers updated the textbook.*

up·draft (up′draft′) *n.* an upward movement of air.

up·end (up end′) *v.t.* to set, stand, or turn on end. —*v.i.* to become upended.

up·grade (up′grād′) *v.t.,* **up·grad·ed, up·grad·ing.** to raise to a higher grade or standard: *The manufacturing firm decided to upgrade its products.* —*n.* an upward slope, as of a hill or road.

   on the upgrade. becoming better; improving: *His marks in history are on the upgrade.*

up·heav·al (up hē′vəl) *n.* **1.** the act of upheaving or the state of being upheaved. **2.** an instance of this. **3.** a violent disturbance or change: *social upheavals.*

up·heave (up hēv′) *v.,* **up·heaved, up·heav·ing.** —*v.t.* to lift or throw up, as by force or pressure from beneath. —*v.i.* to be lifted, thrown, or forced up.

up·held (up held′) the past tense and past participle of **uphold.**

up·hill (up′hil′) *adj.* **1.** going upward on a hill; directed or sloping upward: *We took the uphill path.* **2.** presenting difficulties; hard: *Winning the championship was an uphill battle for the team.* —*adv.* up a hill; upward: *He rode his bicycle uphill.*

up·hold (up hōld′) *v.t.,* **up·held, up·hold·ing. 1.** to support, approve, or agree with: *The students upheld the school rules.* **2.** to keep from falling; hold up: *The posts uphold the porch roof.* —**up·hold′er,** *n.*

up·hol·ster (up hōl′stər) *v.t.* to fit with padding, cushions, or coverings: *to upholster a sofa.*

up·hol·ster·er (up hōl′stər ər) *n.* a person whose work is upholstering furniture.

up·hol·ster·y (up hōl′stər ē) *n. pl.,* **up·hol·ster·ies. 1.** material used in upholstering. **2.** the business or craft of upholstering.

up·keep (up′kēp′) *n.* **1.** the keeping in good condition; maintenance: *Men and money are needed for the upkeep of the city parks.* **2.** the cost of such maintenance: *The upkeep on the estate is very high.*

up·land (up′lənd, up′land′) *n. also,* **uplands.** land that is on a higher level than the land surrounding it. —*adj.* of, relating to, or located on such land.

up·lift (*v.,* up lift′; *n.,* up′lift′) *v.t.* **1.** to raise to a higher moral or social level. **2.** to lift up; elevate. —*n.* **1.** the act, process, or result of lifting up. **2.** a movement to improve the moral or social level of a person, group, or community.

up·most (up′mōst′) *adj.* another word for **uppermost.**

up·on (ə pôn′, ə pon′) *prep.* on.

up·per (up′ər) *adj.* **1.** higher: *the upper story of a house, the upper register of a voice.* **2.** (of places) on higher ground, farther north, or farther inland: *the upper towns of a state.* —*n.* the part of a shoe or boot above the sole.

up·per-case (up′ər kās′) *adj.* of, relating to, or printed in capital letters. —*v.t.,* **up·per-cased, up·per-cas·ing.** to set in or print with capital letters.

upper case, in printing, capital letters.

up·per-class (up′ər klas′) *adj.* of or relating to the upper class.

upper class, the portion of society occupying the highest social and economic position, above the middle class and lower class.

up·per·cut (up′ər kut′) *n.* a blow in boxing directed upwards from beneath, as to an opponent's chin. —*v.t.,* **up·per·cut, up·per·cut·ting.** to strike (an opponent) with an uppercut.

upper hand, a position of control; advantage: *Our team easily gained the upper hand in the last part of the basketball game.*

upper house *also,* **Upper House.** in a legislature having two branches, the smaller and less representative branch, such as the Senate in the U.S. Congress.

up·per·most (up′ər mōst′) *adj.* **1.** highest: *the uppermost floors of a building.* **2.** having the most importance; foremost: *She's always uppermost in his thoughts.* Also, **upmost.** —*adv.* in the highest or most important place, position, or rank.

Upper Vol·ta (vol′tə) a country in western Africa, north of Ghana. Capital, Ouagadougou. Area, 105,869 sq. mi. Pop. (1971 est.), 5,549,000.

up·raise (up rāz′) *v.t.,* **up·raised, up·rais·ing.** to raise or lift up.

up·right (up′rīt′) *adj.* **1.** in a vertical position; straight up; erect: *an upright column.* **2.** having or showing good character and high morals: *an upright person.* —*n.* something in a vertical position, as an upright timber or beam. —*adv.* in a vertical position: *He placed the chair upright.* —**up′right′ly,** *adv.* —**up′right′ness,** *n.*

upright piano, a piano having the strings arranged vertically in a rectangular case.

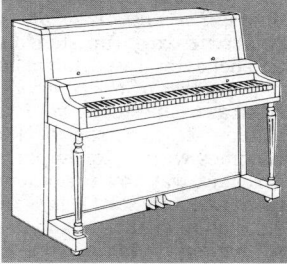

Upright piano

up·rise (up rīz′) *v.i.,* **up·rose, up·ris·en** (up riz′ən), **up·ris·ing. 1.** to arise or get up. **2.** to rise to a higher position, as from below the horizon.

up·ris·ing (up′rī′zing) *n.* a revolt against a government or other authority; rebellion.

up·roar (up′rôr′) *n.* **1.** a state of noisy or confused excitement, disorder, or agitation: *The class was in an uproar.* **2.** the sound of this.

up·roar·i·ous (up rôr′ē əs) *adj.* **1.** making, causing, or marked by an uproar: *The hero was given an uproarious welcome.* **2.** loud, noisy, and unrestrained: *The room filled with uproarious laughter.* **3.** causing hearty laughter; hilarious: *an uproarious comedy.* —**up·roar′i·ous·ly,** *adv.* —**up·roar′i·ous·ness,** *n.*

up·root (up rōot′, up root′) *v.t.* **1.** to tear or pull up by the roots: *The tractor uprooted the bushes.* **2.** to cause to leave familiar surroundings; displace: *The flood uprooted many families.* **3.** to remove or destroy completely; eliminate.

up·rose (up rōz′) the past tense of **uprise.**

up·set (*v., adj.,* up set′; *n.,* up′set′) *v.t.,* **up·set, up·set·ting. 1.** to turn, tip, or knock over; topple; capsize: *I accidentally upset the pitcher of lemonade.* **2.** to throw into confusion or disorder: *The unexpected delay upset his plans.* **3.** to make anxious or uneasy; distress: *News of his sister's accident greatly upset him.* **4.** to make sick: *Eating all that candy will upset your stomach.* **5.** to defeat unexpectedly: *The young tennis player upset the club champion.* —*adj.* **1.** turned, tipped, or knocked over: *The upset glass of water spilled all over me.* **2.** confused or disordered: *an upset train schedule.* **3.** anxious or uneasy; distressed: *I was upset about missing the plane.* **4.** physically disturbed: *She has an upset stomach.* —*n.* **1.** the defeat of an opponent favored to win. **2.** a throwing into confusion or disorder. **3.** anxiety; distress. **4.** physical disturbance: *a stomach upset.* **5.** a turning, tipping, or knocking something over.

up·shot (up′shot′) *n.* the final result; conclusion; outcome.

upside down 1. so that the upper side or part becomes the under or lower side or part: *You are holding the map upside down.* **2.** in or into complete disorder or confusion: *I turned my room upside down looking for the keys.*

up·stage (up′stāj′) *adv.* at or toward the rear of a stage. —*adj.* of or relating to the rear of a stage. —*v.t.,* **up·staged, up·stag·ing. 1.** to draw audience attention away from (another actor) to oneself. **2.** to draw attention to oneself at the expense of (another): *Every time he tried to tell a joke, his brother upstaged him with some funny remark.*

up·stairs (up′sterz′) *adv.* **1.** toward the top of a staircase; up the stairs: *He ran upstairs.* **2.** on or to an upper floor or level: *They are watching television upstairs.*

at; āpe; cär; end; mē; it; īce; hot; ōld; fôrk; wood; fōōl; oil; out; up; turn; sing; thin; **this**; hw in white; zh in treasure. The symbol ə stands for the sound of **a** in about, **e** in taken, **i** in pencil, **o** in lemon, and **u** in circus.

U

—*adj.* of, relating to, or located on an upper floor or floors: *He lives in an upstairs apartment.* —*n.* the upper floor or floors: *The upstairs of the house is not yet finished.*

up·stand·ing (up stan'ding) *adj.* honest in character and behavior; respectable; honorable: *He is a fine, upstanding member of the community.*

up·start (up'stärt') *n.* **1.** a person who is bold and conceited. **2.** a person of humble origins who suddenly becomes wealthy or important and usually behaves in an arrogant way toward others; parvenu.

up·state (up'stāt') *adj.* of or relating to that part of a state lying farther inland or north of a large city: *We took a vacation in upstate New York.* —*adv.* in, to, or toward such a region: *He drove upstate for the weekend.*

up·stream (up'strēm') *adv.* toward or at the source of a stream; against the current: *He decided to fish upstream. The boys rowed upstream.* —*adj.* toward or at a point upstream.

up·surge (up'surj') *n.* a sudden increase or rise: *There was an upsurge of interest in politics in the town around election time.* —*v.i.,* **up·surged, up·surg·ing.** to surge up; increase; rise.

up·swing (up'swing') *n.* **1.** an upward swing or movement. **2.** a marked increase or improvement, as in activity: *Business in that town is on the upswing.*

up·take (up'tāk') *n.* **1.** *Informal.* understanding; comprehension: *He is quick on the uptake.* **2.** a flue or shaft for drawing up air or smoke, as from a mine.

up·tight (up'tīt') *Slang.* tense; nervous; anxious.

up-to-date (up'tə dāt') *adj.* **1.** using or including the latest developments, facts, or information: *We use an up-to-date almanac.* **2.** having or showing the latest style; fashionable; modern: *She wore an up-to-date dress.*

up·town (*adv., n.,* up'toun'; *adj.,* up'toun') *adv.* to, toward, or in the upper or northern part of a town or city: *We have moved uptown.* —*adj.* of, relating to, or in the upper or northern part of a town or city: *uptown traffic, the uptown bus.* —*n.* the upper or northern part of a town or city.

up·turn (up'turn') *n.* an upward turn or trend, especially toward better conditions: *There has been an upturn in his luck lately.*

up·ward (up'wərd) *adv. also,* **up·wards. 1.** from a lower to a higher place or position: *He looked upward.* **2.** toward a higher or greater amount, degree, or rank: *The cost of living has climbed upward.* **3.** toward or into a later time or greater age: *From childhood upward, she had taken piano lessons.* **4.** more; over: *Tickets go for five dollars and upward.* **5.** toward the interior, source, or origin: *The boys followed the river upward.* —*adj.* moving from a lower to a higher place, level, or condition: *an upward trend.* —**up'ward·ly,** *adv.*

upward of or **upwards of.** more than: *There were upwards of fifty people at the party.*

Ur (ur) *n.* a city of ancient Sumer, on the Euphrates River.

U·ral Mountains (yoor'əl) a mountain system in the central Soviet Union. Also, **U·rals** (yoor'əlz).

Ural River, a river rising in the southern Ural Mountains and flowing into the Caspian Sea. Also, **Ural.**

u·ran·i·nite (yoo ran'i nīt') *n.* a rare mineral that is the main ore of uranium. A common variety is pitchblende.

u·ra·ni·um (yoo rā'nē əm) *n.* a heavy, silvery, radioactive metallic element, found in nature in pitchblende. Uranium is important as a source of nuclear energy. Symbol: U

uranium 235 *also,* **uranium-235.** a uranium isotope used as fuel for the chain reaction that releases the energy in a nuclear explosion. It is the only naturally occurring material that undergoes nuclear fission.

uranium 238 *also,* **uranium-238.** a uranium isotope that is the most abundant naturally occurring isotope of uranium.

U·ra·nus (yoor'ə nəs, yoo rā'nəs) *n.* **1.** *Greek Mythology.* the god who was the earliest ruler of the universe and was associated with the sky. He was the father of the Titans. **2.** the third largest planet of the solar system and seventh in order of distance from the sun. It has five known moons.

ur·ban (ur'bən) *adj.* of, in, relating to, or characteristic of a city or city life: *urban expansion, urban problems, an urban population.*

ur·bane (ur bān') *adj.* refined and courteous: *The senator is an urbane, cultured man.* [Latin *urbānus* relating to a city, refined; from *urbs* city; referring to the supposed refinement of city people.] —**ur·bane'ly,** *adv.* —**ur·bane'-ness,** *n.*

ur·ban·i·ty (ur ban'ə tē) *n.* the quality of being urbane.

ur·ban·ize (ur'bə nīz') *v.,* **ur·ban·ized, ur·ban·iz·ing.** —*v.t.* to make urban: *The builders are urbanizing the countryside around the large city.* —*v.i.* to become urban. —**ur'ban·i·za'tion,** *n.*

urban renewal, the planned rehabilitation and reconstruction of deteriorating urban areas, chiefly through the demolition of slums and the building of public housing. It is usually carried out under a government-subsidized program.

ur·chin (ur'chin) *n.* **1.** a small, mischievous boy. **2.** see **sea urchin.**

-ure *suffix* (used to form nouns from verbs) **1.** the act, process, state, or result: *exposure, enclosure.* **2.** a function or a group performing a function: *legislature.*

u·re·a (yoo rē'ə) *n.* a colorless substance that is found in urine and is also made synthetically. It is used in fertilizers and in the manufacture of plastics and explosives.

u·re·ter (yoo rē'tər) *n.* either of two tubes that carry urine from the kidneys to the bladder.

u·re·thra (yoo rē'thrə) *n. pl.,* **u·re·thrae** (yoo rē'thrē) or **u·re·thras.** a duct or canal through which urine is discharged from the bladder.

urge (urj) *v.t.,* **urged, urg·ing. 1.** to try to convince or persuade; plead or reason with: *He urged his friend to try out for the team. We urged her to come with us.* **2.** to drive or force on; influence; spur: *The messenger urged his horse on.* **3.** to speak or argue strongly for; recommend or support earnestly: *The concerned citizens urged prison reform.* —*n.* a strong or driving influence or impulse: *He had a sudden urge for chocolate.*

ur·gen·cy (ur'jən sē) *n.* the quality or condition of being urgent.

ur·gent (ur'jənt) *adj.* **1.** calling for immediate action or attention; compelling; pressing: *The businessman had urgent business to attend to.* **2.** insistent or earnest, as in pleading: *The director of the hospital made an urgent appeal for funds.* —**ur'gent·ly,** *adv.*

u·ri·nal (yoor'ən əl) *n.* **1.** a wall fixture used for urinating. **2.** a container for urine, as one used by a bedridden patient.

u·ri·nal·y·sis (yoor'ə nal'ə sis) *n. pl.,* **u·ri·nal·y·ses** (yoor'ə nal'ə sēz). a chemical or microscopic analysis of urine.

u·ri·nar·y (yoor'ə ner'ē) *adj.* **1.** of or relating to urine. **2.** of, relating to, or involving the organs that produce and discharge urine.

u·ri·nate (yoor'ə nāt') *v.i.,* **u·ri·nat·ed, u·ri·nat·ing.** to discharge urine. —**u'ri·na'tion,** *n.*

u·rine (yoor'in) *n.* a clear, usually yellowish fluid containing waste material that is carried from the kidneys, stored in the bladder, and discharged from the body.

urn (urn) *n.* **1.** a vase with a foot or pedestal, especially one used to hold the ashes of the dead. **2.** a closed vessel having a spigot, used for making, heating, or serving hot drinks: *a coffee urn.*

Ur·sa Major (ur′sə) a constellation in the northern sky, containing the stars of the Big Dipper, thought to resemble a large bear in shape. Also, **Great Bear.**

Ursa Minor, a constellation in the northern sky, containing the bright star Polaris and the stars of the Little Dipper, thought to resemble a small bear in shape. Also, **Little Bear.**

Porcelain urn   Coffee urn
Urns

U·ru·guay (yoor′ə gwā′, oor′ə gwĭ′) *n.* a country on the southeastern coast of South America, between Brazil and Argentina. Capital, Montevideo. Area, 72,172 sq. mi. Pop. (1971 est.), 2,920,000. —**U′ru·guay′an,** *adj., n.*

us (us; *unstressed* əs) *pron.* the objective case of **we.**

U.S., United States.

USA, United States Army.

U.S.A., United States of America.

us·a·ble (yo͞o′zə bəl) *also,* **use·a·ble.** *adj.* capable of being used; fit or convenient for use. —**us·a·bil′i·ty, us′a·ble·ness,** *n.* —**us′a·bly,** *adv.*

USAF, United States Air Force.

us·age (yo͞o′sij, yo͞o′zij) *n.* **1.** the act or manner of using, treating, or handling something; treatment; use: *My shoes get hard usage.* **2.** the customary or usual way in which a language is used, or in which its words and sounds are used. **3.** a customary practice: *That ceremony is a usage that has lasted in the village for centuries.*

● In language, the term **usage** means the way people use words or expressions in speaking or writing. In former times, it was believed that usage should follow the traditionally established rules of grammar. Many of these rules were simply made up by grammarians, or were adapted from Latin grammar, particularly during the eighteenth century. Language scholars of that time believed it was necessary to set and enforce fixed standards for the English language. They criticized people, even great and famous writers, who did not follow these standard rules.

In recent years, scholars have studied the use of language scientifically. They have learned that the traditional rules of grammar do not reflect the way English is actually used, even among the most highly educated and intelligent people. This situation exists because these traditional rules are derived from another language, Latin, and because they are based on artificial and arbitrary judgments rather than on an examination of the English language itself.

Linguists believe strongly that statements about usage should be based on the way language is used, not on the way people feel it should be used. A modern linguist reports facts about usage from studies he has made of how people speak and write. In commenting on a certain word or phrase, he does not say that he thinks it is good or bad. He describes how it is used, by whom it is used, and in what situations it is used. A person who supports the principles of traditional grammar would say flatly that the sentence "He don't live here" is incorrect. A linguist, on the other hand, would not call it incorrect, but would rather state that most educated speakers and writers regard it as incorrect, and do not use it. Therefore, although you may not object to the expression "He don't live here," you will realize from the linguist's evidence that other people do object to it, and that your language will be judged incorrect by them if you use it.

Linguists have described the accepted usage of language as "linguistic etiquette." By this they mean that just as certain actions are considered incorrect or improper by society in general—violations of etiquette—so are certain ways of speaking and writing. People who do not follow accepted rules, whether in their actions or their use of language, are often judged negatively by society. This does not mean that what such people do is wrong in any general or absolute sense, but only that it is human nature to establish certain standards of behavior and to look unfavorably on people who violate these standards. Because of this, most linguists of today would agree with the traditional belief that students should be taught accepted usage. These linguists point out that although no use of language can be "wrong" in theory, this does not really matter as long as people believe that it is wrong. Such a linguist knows that it is an inescapable fact that people are constantly judged by the way they use language. He feels it is unfair to a student not to inform him of the ways in which such judgments are made, whether or not the linguist himself believes that these judgments are scientifically valid or sound.

Thus the popular belief that modern linguists have put an end to the study of usage is not really true. Linguists maintain that judgments about usage can be made, but they should be made on the basis of scientific evidence, not on one man's personal opinion. The hope of linguists is that eventually people will accept the idea that "good" usage is any usage that clearly and effectively conveys the speaker or writer's intended meaning.

USCG, United States Coast Guard.

use (*v.,* yo͞oz; *n.,* yo͞os) *v.t.,* **used, us·ing. 1.** to employ for a particular purpose or end: *May I use your scissors? John used the encyclopedia to check some facts.* **2.** to exhaust the whole or entire supply of: *We used up all the bread at breakfast.* **3.** to take often or by habit: *She uses milk in her tea.* **4.** to act or behave toward; treat: *The general used his prisoners cruelly.* —*n.* **1.** the act of using: *That teacher encourages the use of the dictionary.* **2.** the state or condition of being used: *The classroom is in use until afternoon.* **3.** the quality that makes something suitable for a purpose; usefulness: *What's the use of worrying about it now?* **4.** a need or occasion for using: *Do you have any use for these empty bottles?* **5.** the purpose for which something is used; function: *This tool has many uses.* **6.** the right or privilege to use something: *I have the use of his bicycle for the weekend.* **7.** a manner or way of using: *Show me the proper use of this machine.* **8.** the power or ability to use something: *He lost the use of one eye in the accident.* —**us′er,** *n.*

to have no use for. *Informal.* to dislike: *He has no use for lazy people.*

to make use of. to use; utilize; employ: *How did he make use of his money?*

to put to use. to use to advantage: *That vacant lot could be put to use as a baseball field.*

at; āpe; cär; end; mē; it; īce; hot; ōld; fôrk; wood; fo͞ol; oil; out; up; turn; sing; thin; this; hw in white; zh in treasure. The symbol ə stands for the sound of **a** in about, **e** in taken, **i** in pencil, **o** in lemon, and **u** in circus.

U

used to. a. formerly did: *I used to like her. We used to vacation in the mountains.* **b.** familiar with; accustomed to: *He is not used to country life.*

use·a·ble (yōō′zə bəl) *adj.* another spelling of **usable.** —**use′a·bil′i·ty, use′a·ble·ness,** *n.* —**use′a·bly,** *adv.*

used (yōōzd) *adj.* that has been used by another or others; not new: *used clothing, a used car.*

use·ful (yōōs′fəl) *adj.* serving a good use or purpose; helpful: *How can I make myself useful?* —**use′ful·ly,** *adv.* —**use′ful·ness,** *n.*

use·less (yōōs′lis) *adj.* **1.** serving no purpose; having no use: *The car is useless without a motor.* **2.** not bringing about any result; vain; futile: *It is useless to tell him to drive more carefully.* —**use′less·ly,** *adv.* —**use′less·ness,** *n.*

ush·er (ush′ər) *n.* a person who leads people to their seats, as in a church, theater, or stadium. —*v.t.* **1.** to act as an usher to; conduct; escort: *The waiter ushered the group to a table.* **2.** to mark the beginning or occurrence of: *We ushered the New Year in with a party.* —*v.i.* to act as an usher.

ush·er·ette (ush′ə ret′) *n.* a girl or woman who ushers people to their seats, as in a theater.

USMC, United States Marine Corps.

USN, United States Navy.

USS 1. United States Ship. **2.** United States Senate.

USSR, Union of Soviet Socialist Republics.

u·su·al (yōō′zhōō əl) *adj.* **1.** happening often or regularly; common: *Such heat is usual for July.* **2.** according to custom or habit; customary; expected: *The dentist charged me the usual fee for cleaning my teeth.* —**u′su·al·ly,** *adv.* —**u′su·al·ness,** *n.*

as usual. in the regular or customary way: *The farmer got up at five o'clock, as usual.*

u·su·rer (yōō′zhər ər) *n.* a person who lends money, especially at a very high or unlawful rate of interest.

u·su·ri·ous (yōō zhoor′ē əs) *adj.* **1.** practicing usury: *a usurious lender.* **2.** of, relating to, or characterized by usury: *a usurious contract.* —**u·su′ri·ous·ly,** *adv.* —**u·su′ri·ous·ness,** *n.*

u·surp (yōō surp′, yōō zurp′) *v.t.* to seize and hold without legal right or authority; take possession of by force: *The army usurped control of the government.* —**u·surp′er,** *n.*

u·sur·pa·tion (yōō′sər pā′shən, yōō′zər pā′shən) *n.* the act of usurping.

u·su·ry (yōō′zhər ē) *n. pl.,* **u·su·ries. 1.** the act or practice of lending money at a very high or unlawful rate of interest. **2.** a very high or unlawful rate of interest.

U·tah (yōō′tô, yōō′tä) *n.* a state in the western United States. Capital, Salt Lake City. Area, 84,916 sq. mi. Pop. (1970), 1,059,273. —**U′tah·an,** *adj., n.*

● **Utah** comes from the Spanish pronunciation of the name of a Shoshone tribe that lived in Colorado and Utah. When Congress organized the territory of Utah, they used this name, and the name was later applied to the state.

u·ten·sil (yōō ten′səl) *n.* an article or object that is useful or necessary in doing or making something: *cooking utensils, writing utensils.*

u·ter·us (yōō′tər əs) *n. pl.,* **u·ter·i** (yōō′tə rī′). a hollow muscular organ found in most female mammals, which holds and nourishes the young until birth; womb.

U Thant, see **Thant, U.**

U·ti·ca (yōō′ti kə) *n.* a city in central New York State. Pop. (1970), 91,611.

u·til·i·tar·i·an (yōō til′ə ter′ē ən) *adj.* **1.** of or relating to usefulness. **2.** made for or concerned with usefulness instead of beauty.

u·til·i·ty (yōō til′ə tē) *n. pl.,* **u·til·i·ties. 1.** the state or quality of being useful; usefulness. **2.** a company that provides an important service to the public, as by supplying gas, electricity, or water. Also, **public utility. 3.** the service provided by such a company.

u·ti·lize (yōō′tə līz′) *v.t.,* **u·ti·lized, u·ti·liz·ing.** to take full advantage of; put to good use: *She utilized leftover scraps of the roast to make a hash.* —**u′ti·liz′a·ble,** *adj.* —**u′til·i·za′tion,** *n.* —**u′ti·liz′er,** *n.*

ut·most (ut′mōst′) *adj.* **1.** of the greatest or highest degree or amount: *We have the utmost respect for him. This work is of the utmost importance.* **2.** being or located at the farthest limit or point; most remote. —*n.* the most or greatest possible, as in degree or amount: *The coach did his utmost to form a winning team.* Also, **uttermost.**

u·to·pi·a (yōō tō′pē ə) *also,* **U·to·pi·a.** *n.* **1.** an ideal place or society in which people live together in peace and happiness. **2.** any idealistic plan having the goal of bringing peace and happiness to all people. [Modern Latin *utopia* literally, nowhere; originally referring to an imaginary island in Sir Thomas More's satire *Utopia* (1516) that had an ideal political, economic, and social system.]

u·to·pi·an (yōō tō′pē ən) *also,* **U·to·pi·an.** *adj.* **1.** fine in theory but not possible or practical in reality: *utopian schemes.* **2.** of or like a utopia: *a utopian community, utopian literature.* —*n.* a person who supports or works for impractical or visionary reforms.

u·to·pi·an·ism (yōō tō′pē ə niz′əm) *also,* **U·to·pi·an·ism.** *n.* the beliefs or ideals of a utopian.

U·trecht (yōō′trekt) *n.* a city in the central Netherlands. Pop. (1971 est.), 278,417.

ut·ter[1] (ut′ər) *v.t.* to give voice to; express aloud: *She uttered a sigh.* [Possibly from Middle Dutch *ūteren.*]

ut·ter[2] (ut′ər) *adj.* complete or perfect; total: *The room was in utter darkness. The project was an utter failure.* [Old English *ūtera, ūterra, ūttra* outer.] —**ut′ter·ly,** *adv.*

ut·ter·ance (ut′ər əns) *n.* **1.** something uttered or expressed in words. **2.** the act of uttering: *He gave utterance to his joy.* **3.** the manner of speaking: *Her soft utterance could barely be heard.*

ut·ter·most (ut′ər mōst′) *adj., n.* another word for **utmost.**

u·vu·la (yōō′vyə lə) *n. pl.,* **u·vu·las** or **u·vu·lae** (yōō′vyə lē′). a piece of flesh shaped like a cone that hangs from the soft palate, above and behind the tongue.

Uz·bek·i·stan (ooz bek′i stan′) *n.* a republic of the Soviet Union, in the central part of Asia. Official name: **Uzbek Soviet Socialist Republic.** Area, approx. 173,600 sq. mi. Pop. (1970), 11,960,000.

at; āpe; cär; end; mē; it; īce; hot; ōld; fôrk; wood; fōōl; oil; out; up; turn; sing; thin; this; hw in white; zh in treasure. The symbol ə stands for the sound of a in about, e in taken, i in pencil, o in lemon, and u in circus.

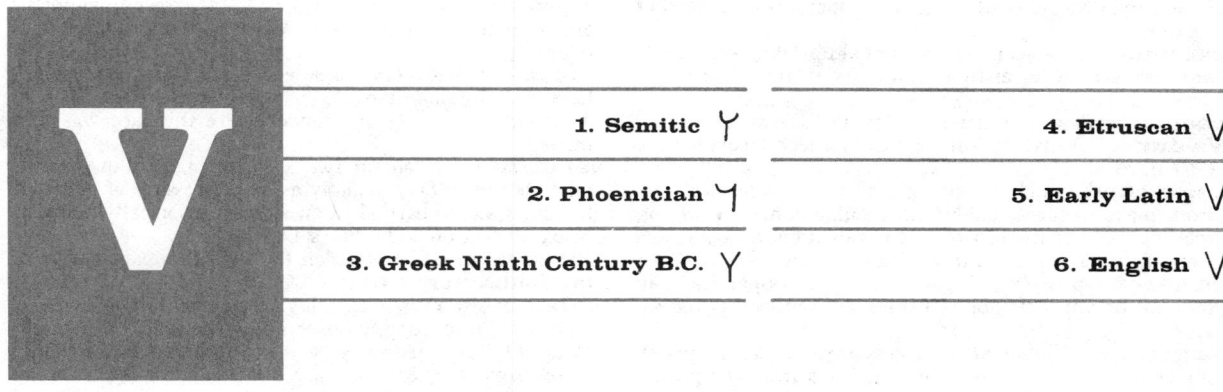

1. Semitic Y	4. Etruscan V
2. Phoenician Y	5. Early Latin V
3. Greek Ninth Century B.C. Y	6. English V

V is the twenty-second letter of the English alphabet. The earliest form of the letter **V** is the ancient Semitic letter *waw* (1) that depicted a hook and stood for the *w* sound, as the *w* in *water*. When the Phoenicians (2) borrowed *waw,* they used it to represent both the consonant sound *w* and the vowel sound *u,* as the *u* in *rude.* The Greeks adopted *waw* and called it *upsilon* (3), writing it as the capital letter Y is written today. *Upsilon,* which stood for only the *u* sound, was borrowed by the Etruscans (4) who, like the Phoenicians, used it to represent both the vowel and consonant sounds. The shape of *upsilon* was also altered by the Etruscans, who gave it the shape we use today. The design and pronunciation of this letter were adopted without change in the Latin alphabet (5). Our modern capital letter **V** (6) is written almost exactly the way the Etruscan and Roman forms of *upsilon* were written. By about 1000 years ago, two forms of this V-shaped letter were being used in writing: **V** at the beginning of a word and a new letter, **U,** in the middle of a word. During the Renaissance, the letter **V** came to be used more and more for the *v* sound, which, although it had not been present in Latin, appeared in the pronunciation of English, French, Italian, and various other European languages.

v, V (vē) *n. pl.,* **v's, V's. 1.** the twenty-second letter of the English alphabet. **2.** something having the shape of this letter. **3.** the Roman numeral for 5.
V, the symbol for vanadium.
v. 1. verb. **2.** verse. **3.** versus.
Va., Virginia.
va·can·cy (vā′kən sē) *n. pl.,* **va·can·cies. 1.** an unoccupied or empty space, especially an apartment or room for rent: *The landlord said that the building had no vacancies.* **2.** an unfilled post, position, or office: *Mr. Carter's retirement left a vacancy in the accounting department.* **3.** the state or condition of being vacant; emptiness.
va·cant (vā′kənt) *adj.* **1.** containing no one or nothing; unoccupied or empty: *a vacant lot, a vacant seat.* **2.** not filled, as a post, position, or office. **3.** lacking or showing a lack of intelligence or awareness: *a vacant mind, a vacant stare.* **4.** free from activity; idle: *vacant hours.* —**va′·cant·ly,** *adv.*
va·cate (vā′kāt) *v.,* **va·cat·ed, va·cat·ing.** —*v.t.* **1.** to cease to occupy; leave empty: *The landlord told him to vacate his apartment.* **2.** to give up (a post, position, or office). —*v.i.* to leave a place or position vacant.
va·ca·tion (vā kā′shən) *n.* a period of rest and freedom from some activity, especially a period of paid free time granted to an employee. —*v.i.* to take or spend a vacation: *Last year they vacationed in Spain.* —**va·ca′tion·er,** *n.*
vac·ci·nate (vak′sə nāt′) *v.t.,* **vac·ci·nat·ed, vac·ci·nat·ing.** to inoculate with a vaccine in order to protect against smallpox or other diseases.
vac·ci·na·tion (vak′sə nā′shən) *n.* **1.** the act or practice of vaccinating. **2.** a scar left by a vaccination.

vac·cine (vak sēn′, vak′sēn) *n.* **1.** the dead or weakened virus or bacteria of certain diseases, prepared and used for inoculation. **2.** the virus that causes cowpox, prepared and used for inoculation against smallpox.
vac·il·late (vas′ə lāt′) *v.i.,* **vac·il·lat·ed, vac·il·lat·ing. 1.** to move to and fro; sway unsteadily; waver. **2.** to waver in mind; be uncertain: *She vacillated between going to the party and staying home.* —**vac′il·la′tion,** *n.*
va·cu·i·ty (va kyōō′ə tē) *n. pl.,* **va·cu·i·ties. 1.** the state or quality of being empty; emptiness. **2.** an empty space; vacuum; void. **3.** emptiness of mind. **4.** something that is foolish or meaningless.
vac·u·ole (vak′yōō ōl′) *n.* a small cavity, usually filled with fluid, in a living organism.
vac·u·ous (vak′yōō əs) *adj.* **1.** containing nothing; empty. **2.** lacking intelligence; foolish. —**vac′u·ous·ly,** *adv.*
vac·u·um (vak′yōō əm, vak′yōōm) *n. pl.,* **vac·u·ums** or *(defs. 1–3)* **vac·u·a** (vak′yōō ə). **1.** a space completely empty of matter. Although a perfect vacuum is possible in theory, it has never been produced in an experiment. **2.** a space from which almost all gas, vapor, and other matter has been removed. **3.** a state of isolation from the reality, events, or influences of the outside world: *to live in a vacuum.* **4.** see **vacuum cleaner.** —*v.t., vi.* to clean with a vacuum cleaner.
vacuum bottle, another term for **thermos bottle.**

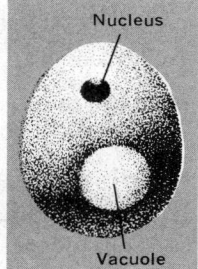

Nucleus

Vacuole

Vacuole

vacuum cleaner, an apparatus for cleaning carpets, floors, upholstery, or the like, that operates by means of suction.

vac·u·um-packed (vak′yo̅o̅ əm pakt′, vak′yo̅o̅m pakt′) *adj.* packed in an airtight container to maintain freshness.

vacuum tube, another term for **electron tube.**

Va·duz (vä′do̅o̅ts) *n.* the capital of Liechtenstein. Pop. (1970), 3790.

vag·a·bond (vag′ə bond′) *n.* a person who wanders from place to place, having no regular home. —*adj.* of, relating to, or characteristic of a vagabond or a vagabond's way of life: *The artist led a vagabond existence.*

va·gar·y (və ger′ē, vā′gər ē) *n. pl.,* **va·gar·ies.** an unusual or unpredictable act, idea, or happening: *the vagaries of life.*

va·gi·na (və jī′nə) *n. pl.,* **va·gi·nas** or **va·gi·nae** (və jī′nē) the canal in female mammals that leads from the genital opening to the uterus.

vag·i·nal (vaj′ən əl, və jīn′əl) *adj.* of or relating to the vagina.

va·gran·cy (vā′grən sē) *n. pl.,* **va·gran·cies.** the state or condition of being a vagrant: *He was arrested for vagrancy.*

va·grant (vā′grənt) *n.* a person who has no regular home or employment and wanders about from place to place; vagabond. —*adj.* **1.** of, relating to, or characteristic of a vagrant or a vagrant's way of life. **2.** wandering from place to place. —**va′grant·ly,** *adv.*

vague (vāg) *adj.,* **va·guer, va·guest. 1.** not definitely or clearly expressed: *She made us a vague promise that she would visit someday.* **2.** not clearly felt or known: *a vague idea. He had a vague feeling of uneasiness.* **3.** not having a definite form or outline; not clear or distinct: *We could only see the vague outline of the building through the fog.* —**vague′ly,** *adv.* —**vague′ness,** *n.*

vain (vān) *adj.* **1.** overly concerned with or proud of one's appearance, abilities, or accomplishments; conceited: *The vain boy spent much time combing his hair.* **2.** not successful or effective: *The mechanic made a vain effort to repair the automobile.* **3.** of no real significance or worth; empty: *One went through the vain motions, but it was mostly a waste of life* (Henry James). —**vain′ly,** *adv.*

  in vain. a. without success; useless: *All attempts at rescue were in vain.* **b.** without proper respect; lightly; irreverently: *to take God's name in vain.*

vain·glo·ri·ous (vān′glôr′ē əs) *adj.* too vain, proud, or boastful. —**vain′glo′ri·ous·ly,** *adv.* —**vain′glo′ri·ous·ness,** *n.*

vain·glo·ry (vān′glôr′ē, vān′glôr′ē) *n.* too much vanity, pride, or boastfulness.

val·ance (val′əns) *n.* **1.** a short drapery or piece of wood or metal hung across the top of a window, as for decoration or to hide curtain fixtures. **2.** a short drapery hanging from a shelf, table, frame of a bed, or the like, often reaching to the floor.

vale (vāl) *n.* a valley or dale.

val·e·dic·to·ri·an (val′ə dik tôr′ē ən) *n.* a student, usually ranking highest in the class, who delivers the valedictory at a graduation exercise.

val·e·dic·to·ry (val′ə dik′tər ē) *n. pl.,* **val·e·dic·to·ries.** a farewell address, especially one delivered at a graduation exercise. —*adj.* of, relating to, or expressing a farewell.

va·lence (vā′ləns) *n.* the combining capacity of an element or radical, determined by the number of electrons that an atom will lose or gain in forming a chemical compound. The sum of the valences of the elements or radicals in the compound must equal zero. For example, sodium has a valence of +1 and chlorine has a valence of −1 in sodium chloride, or common salt (NaCl).

Va·len·ci·a (və len′sē ə, və len′shə) *n.* **1.** a port city in eastern Spain. Pop. (1969 est.), 634,100. **2.** a city in northern Venezuela, southwest of Caracas. Pop. (1970), 648,003.

Va·len·ci·ennes (və len′sē enz′) *n.* a fine lace, usually having a floral design. Also, **Valenciennes lace.** [From *Valenciennes,* a city in France where this lace was first made.]

val·en·tine (val′ən tīn′) *n.* **1.** a greeting card or gift sent on Valentine's Day, usually as an expression of affection for one's sweetheart. **2.** a sweetheart, especially a sweetheart chosen on Valentine's Day.

Val·en·tine, Saint (val′ən tīn′) a Christian martyr of the third century A.D.

Valentine's Day, the day named in honor of Saint Valentine, traditionally observed by the sending of valentines. It falls on February 14. Also, **Saint Valentine's Day.**

va·le·ri·an (və lēr′ē ən) *n.* **1.** a drug having a strong odor, obtained from the roots of a plant, and formerly used to treat nervous conditions. **2.** the plant that produces this drug, having small white or pink flowers.

val·et (val′it, val′ā) *n.* **1.** a man's male servant who performs various personal services for his employer, such as caring for his clothes and helping him dress. **2.** an employee, as of a hotel, who performs similar personal services for guests.

Val·hal·la (val hal′ə) *n. Norse Mythology.* the great hall to which heroes and warriors slain in battle were taken by the Valkyries, so that they could feast at the table of Odin.

val·iant (val′yənt) *adj.* brave; courageous: *a valiant warrior, to put up a valiant fight.* —**val′iant·ly,** *adv.* —**val′iant·ness,** *n.*

val·id (val′id) *adj.* **1.** soundly based on facts or evidence; true: *The experiment proved that the scientist's theory was valid.* **2.** having the desired result; effective: *a valid method of treatment.* **3.** acceptable under the law; legally binding: *a valid driver's license.* —**val′id·ly,** *adv.*

val·i·date (val′i dāt′) *v.t.,* **val·i·dat·ed, val·i·dat·ing. 1.** to make or declare legally valid: *to validate election results.* **2.** to prove to be valid, true, or correct; confirm.

va·lid·i·ty (və lid′ə tē) *n. pl.,* **va·lid·i·ties.** the quality, state, or fact of being valid: *We doubted the validity of his argument.*

va·lise (və lēs′) *n.* a small piece of luggage; suitcase.

Val·kyr·ie (val kēr′ē, val′kēr ē) *n. Norse Mythology.* any of a group of beautiful warrior maidens who were the attendants of Odin, and who took heroes slain in battle to Valhalla.

Val·let·ta (vä let′ə) *n.* the capital of Malta. Pop. (1969), 15,547.

val·ley (val′ē) *n. pl.,* **val·leys. 1.** a region of low land between hills, mountains, or other high land, usually having a river or stream flowing through it. **2.** an area of land drained by a river system; river basin: *the Nile valley.*

Valley Forge, a village in southeastern Pennsylvania, where George Washington and his army camped during the winter of 1777–1778.

val·or (val′ər) *n.* outstanding courage, especially in battle; great bravery.

val·or·ous (val′ər əs) *adj.* having or showing valor; brave; courageous. —**val′or·ous·ly,** *adv.*

Val·pa·rai·so (val′pə rī′zō) *n.* a port city in central Chile. Pop. (1969 est.), 289,500.

val·u·a·ble (val′yo̅o̅ ə bəl, val′yə bəl) *adj.* **1.** having great value; worth much money: *a valuable oil painting, a valuable piece of property.* **2.** of great use, worth, or importance: *valuable advice, a valuable friend.* —*n. usually,* **valuables.** personal property that has value, such as a piece of jewelry.

val·u·a·tion (val′yōō ā′shən) *n.* **1.** the act or process of estimating the value or price of something. **2.** an estimated value or price.

val·ue (val′yōō) *n.* **1.** relative or considered worth, usefulness, importance, or merit: *The museum purchased the old chair for its historical value. Jim places great value on your friendship.* **2.** monetary worth: *The value of land has gone up in recent years.* **3. values.** the principles or standards of a person or group; ideals: *The young man's values kept him from doing what is wrong.* **4.** the exact meaning, as of a word; import. **5.** a numerical quantity: *Find the value of y if $y^2 = 25$.* **6.** *Music.* the relative length of a tone or rest as shown by a note or other symbol. For example, the value of a whole note is twice that of a half note. —*v.t.,* **val·ued, val·u·ing. 1.** to estimate the monetary value of; appraise: *The jeweler valued the necklace at one thousand dollars.* **2.** to consider as having worth, importance, or merit: *He values your friendship.*

val·ued (val′yōōd) *adj.* considered as having worth, importance, or merit; highly regarded; esteemed: *a valued friend, a valued possession.*

val·ue·less (val′yōō lis) *adj.* having no value; worthless.

valve (valv) *n.* **1.** any of various devices used to control the flow of liquids or gases by blocking a passage with a movable part. **2.** the movable part of such a device. **3.** a fold in a membrane lining a hollow organ, that allows a fluid, such as blood, to flow in one direction and prevents it from flowing in the opposite direction: *a heart valve.* **4.** a device in certain brass instruments, such as a trumpet, for changing the pitch of the tone. **5.** one of the pair of hinged shells of an oyster, clam, or similar animal.

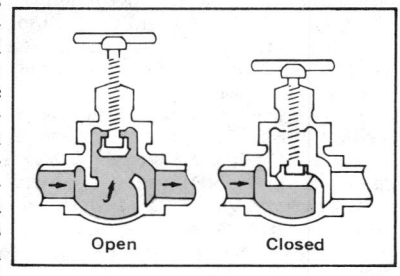
Open   Closed

Valve

va·moose (va mōōs′) *v.i.,* **va·moosed, va·moos·ing.** *Slang.* to leave quickly; go away hastily. [Spanish *vamos* let us go.]

vamp (vamp) *n.* the upper front part of a shoe or boot, covering the instep and sometimes the toes. —*v.t.* **1.** to provide with a vamp; repair with a new vamp. **2.** to patch up; repair.

vam·pire (vam′pīr) *n.* **1.** in folklore, a corpse that leaves its grave at night to suck the blood of sleeping persons. **2.** a person who ruthlessly preys on or takes advantage of others. **3.** see **vampire bat.**

vampire bat 1. any of various bats of Central and South America that feed on blood. **2.** any of various other bats that are mistakenly believed to feed on blood.

van[1] (van) a large, covered truck or other vehicle, used for transporting furniture, goods, or animals. [Short for *caravan.*]

van[2] (van) *n.* see **vanguard.**

va·na·di·um (və nā′dē əm) *n.* a silver-white metallic element used in making steel alloys. Symbol: **V**

Van Al·len radiation belt (van al′ən) a region of intense radiation encircling the earth at high altitudes, consisting of electrons and protons trapped by the earth's magnetic field. Also, **Van Allen belt.** [From James A. *Van Allen,* 1914–, the U.S. physicist who designed the equipment that first detected this region in 1958.]

Van Bu·ren, Martin (van byoor′ən) 1782–1862, the eighth president of the United States, from 1837 to 1841.

Van·cou·ver (van kōō′vər) *n.* **1.** a port city in southwestern British Columbia, Canada. Pop. (1971), 422,278. **2.** an island of British Columbia, Canada, just off the southwestern coast of the mainland.

van·dal (vand′əl) *n.* **1.** a person who willfully damages or destroys public or private property. **2. Vandal.** a member of a Germanic tribe that ravaged Gaul, Spain, and northern Africa in the fourth and fifth centuries A.D., and sacked Rome in A.D. 455.

van·dal·ism (vand′əl iz′əm) *n.* willful damage to or destruction of public or private property.

van·dal·ize (vand′əl īz′) *v.t.,* **van·dal·ized, van·dal·iz·ing.** to damage or destroy (property) willfully.

Van Dyck, Sir Anthony (van dīk′) *also,* **Van·dyke.** 1599–1641, Flemish painter.

Van·dyke (van dīk′) *n.* a short, pointed beard. [From *Van Dyck,* who often painted this kind of beard in his portraits.]

vane (vān) *n.* **1.** a weather vane; weathercock. **2.** a blade or flat or curved part like a blade, as of a windmill or propeller.

Van Gogh, Vincent (van gō′) 1853–1890, Dutch painter.

van·guard (van′gärd′) *n.* **1.** the part of an army that moves ahead of the main force. **2.** the leading or foremost position of a social, political, or other movement.

va·nil·la (və nil′ə) *n.* **1.** a flavoring obtained from the seed pods of a climbing tropical orchid, widely used in candies, ice cream, and cookies. **2.** the seed pod from which this flavoring is obtained. Also, **vanilla bean. 3.** the orchid bearing these pods.

van·ish (van′ish) *v.i.* **1.** to pass from sight, especially suddenly or quickly; disappear: *The airplane vanished in the clouds.* **2.** to cease to exist: *All hope of winning the game vanished when our star player was injured.*

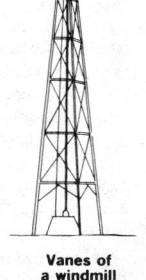
Vanes of a windmill

van·i·ty (van′i tē) *n. pl.,* **van·i·ties. 1.** too much concern with or pride in one's appearance, abilities, deeds, or the like; conceit. **2.** the quality of being worthless: *He finally saw the vanity of attempting to gain revenge.* **3.** see **vanity case.**

vanity case, a woman's small case for carrying cosmetics, toiletries, and other articles.

van·quish (vang′kwish) *v.t.* **1.** to defeat or conquer, as in battle. **2.** to overcome (a feeling): *to vanquish one's fear of heights.* —**van′quish·er,** *n.*

van·tage (van′tij) *n.* **1.** a favorable or superior position. **2.** see **vantage point.**

vantage point, a position that allows a clear or favorable view: *We could see the whole valley from our vantage point on the mountain.*

vap·id (vap′id) *adj.* dull or lifeless; insipid; uninteresting: *He was bored by the vapid conversation.* —**vap′id·ly,** *adv.*

va·por (vā′pər) *n.* **1.** visible particles of matter suspended in the air, such as mist or smoke. **2.** the gaseous state of a substance that is a liquid or a solid under normal conditions of temperature and pressure.

at; āpe; cär; end; mē; it; īce; hot; ōld; fôrk; wood; fōōl; oil; out; up; turn; sing; thin; this; hw in white; zh in treasure. The symbol ə stands for the sound of **a** in about, **e** in taken, **i** in pencil, **o** in lemon, and **u** in circus.

V

va·por·ize (vā′pə rīz′) v., **va·por·ized, va·por·iz·ing.** —v.t. to change (something) into vapor. —v.i. to change into vapor. —**va′por·i·za′tion,** n.

va·por·iz·er (vā′pə rī′zər) n. a device for changing a liquid into a vapor, especially such a device for vaporizing a liquid medicine to be inhaled.

va·por·ous (vā′pər əs) adj. **1.** containing or full of vapor; misty. **2.** like, resembling, or characteristic of vapor.

va·que·ro (vä ker′ō) n. pl., **va·que·ros.** a cowboy, especially of Mexico, South America, or the southwestern United States.

Va·ra·na·si (və rä′nə sē) n. see **Benares.**

var·i·a·ble (ver′ē ə bəl) adj. **1.** likely or liable to change; changeable: variable weather. **2.** that can be changed. —n. **1.** something that varies or is variable. **2.** Mathematics. **a.** a quantity that can have any of a set of values. **b.** a symbol representing such a quantity. —**var′i·a·bil′i·ty, var′i·a·ble·ness,** n. —**var′i·a·bly,** adv.

var·i·ance (ver′ē əns) n. the act or result of varying; difference; disagreement.
at variance. in disagreement: His account of the accident is at variance with the facts.

var·i·ant (ver′ē ənt) adj. different or varying, as from another or others of the same kind: The word "centre" is a variant spelling of "center." —n. something that is variant, such as a different spelling or pronunciation of the same word.

var·i·a·tion (ver′ē ā′shən) n. **1.** the act, fact, or process of varying. **2.** the extent or amount to which something varies: The scientist noted a temperature variation of thirteen degrees. **3.** something that is based on but differs somewhat from another thing: The writer's new play is actually a variation of an earlier play. **4.** Music. the repetition of a theme or tune with changes or additions, as in melody, harmony, rhythm, or key, especially one of a series of such repetitions.

var·i·cel·la (var′ə sel′ə) n. another word for **chicken pox.**

var·i·col·ored (ver′i kul′ərd, var′i kul′ərd) adj. having various colors; variegated.

var·i·cose (var′ə kōs′) adj. abnormally swollen: varicose veins.

var·ied (ver′ēd) adj. **1.** consisting of different or various kinds, items, or parts: a varied menu. **2.** changed; altered.

var·i·e·gat·ed (ver′ē ə gā′tid) adj. **1.** marked or streaked with different colors; varied in color. **2.** having or characterized by variety.

va·ri·e·ty (və rī′ə tē) n. pl., **va·ri·e·ties. 1.** the state or quality of being various or varied; lack of sameness; change or difference: A job that has no variety may soon become boring. **2.** a number or collection of different things: The woman purchased a variety of items at the grocery store. **3.** a different kind or form of something: a new variety of synthetic fabric. **4.** a group of related plants or animals forming a small part of a larger group.

variety show, a show on stage or television with songs, dances, and comedy sketches.

var·i·ous (ver′ē əs) adj. **1.** different from one another; of different kinds: People of various backgrounds applied for the job. **2.** more than one; several; many: We spent the night at various towns on our motor trip. —**var′i·ous·ly,** adv.

var·let (vär′lit) n. Archaic. a scoundrel; knave.

var·mint (vär′mint) n. Informal. a troublesome or objectionable animal or person.

var·nish (vär′nish) n. pl., **var·nish·es. 1.** a liquid preparation usually made up of resins dissolved in alcohol or mixed with an oil, such as linseed oil. Varnish is used to produce a hard, clear coating, as on a wood surface.

2. the glossy coating produced by such a preparation. **3.** an outward show or appearance, especially one that is deceptive; pretense: A varnish of good manners disguised his cruel nature. —v.t. **1.** to apply varnish to; cover with varnish. **2.** to cover with a deceptive appearance.

var·si·ty (vär′sə tē) n. pl., **var·si·ties.** the main team that represents a university, college, or school in an athletic or other competition.

var·y (ver′ē) v., **var·ied, var·y·ing.** —v.t. **1.** to change or make different: A talented actor can vary his manner of speaking. **2.** to give variety to; diversify: to vary one's diet. —v.i. **1.** to be or become changed: My mood varies from day to day. **2.** to be different; differ: The roses in the garden vary in color. **3.** Mathematics. to be subject to change; be variable.

vas·cu·lar (vas′kyə lər) adj. of, composed of, or containing vessels that carry blood, sap, or other animal or plant fluid.

vase (vās, vāz, väz) n. a rounded container that is usually of greater height than width. It is used chiefly for holding flowers or for decoration.

Vas·e·line (vas′ə lēn′) n. Trademark. a yellowish or whitish ointment made from petroleum.

vas·sal (vas′əl) n. **1.** under feudalism, a subject of a lord. Vassals received land and protection from the lord in return for their loyal support and service, especially military service. **2.** a servant; slave. —adj. of, relating to, or characteristic of a vassal.

vas·sal·age (vas′ə lij) n. **1.** the state or condition of being a vassal. **2.** the duties or services required of a vassal. **3.** the land held by a vassal. **4.** servitude; dependence.

vast (vast) adj. very great, as in extent, size, or amount: a vast expanse of land, a vast number of people. —**vast′ly,** adv. —**vast′ness,** n.

vat (vat) n. a large tank or container used for holding liquids.

Vat·i·can (vat′i kən) n. **1.** the official residence of the pope in Vatican City. **2.** the government or authority of the pope.

Vatican City, an independent state ruled by the pope and located within the city of Rome, Italy, having an area of about one-fifth of a square mile.

vaude·ville (vôd′vil, vô′də vil) n. theatrical entertainment popular in the United States in the late nineteenth and early twentieth centuries. A performance usually contained a variety of short acts by singers, jugglers, comedians, and the like.

vault¹ (vôlt) n. **1.** an arched structure of stone, brick, or concrete serving as a roof or ceiling. **2.** something resembling such a structure: the vault of the sky. **3.** an underground compartment or room used as a cellar or storeroom. **4.** a

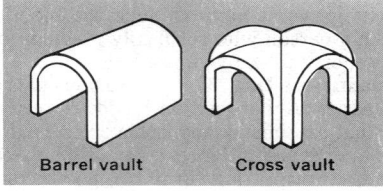

Barrel vault   Cross vault

Vault¹

well-protected or fortified room or compartment, as in a bank, used for the safekeeping of valuables or money. **5.** a burial chamber; tomb. —v.t. **1.** to cover or provide with a vault. **2.** to build in the shape of a vault: The ceiling was vaulted. [Middle French vaulte, volte.]

vault² (vôlt) v.t. to jump over, especially with the aid of the hands or a pole: to vault a fence. —v.i. to jump; spring: to vault over a wall. —n. the act of vaulting; jump; leap. [Old French volter to turn (a horse), leap, going back to Latin volvere to turn around, roll.] —**vault′er,** n.

vaunt (vônt) *v.i.* to boast; brag. —*v.t.* to boast of; brag about: *He vaunted his athletic ability.* —*n.* a boast or brag.

V.C., Vietcong.

VD, venereal disease.

veal (vēl) *n.* the flesh of a calf, used as food.

vec·tor (vek′tər) *n.* a mathematical quantity that has both magnitude and direction, such as velocity. A vector is usually represented by an arrow showing the direction of the force.

veer (vēr) *v.i.* to change in direction or course; shift; turn: *At the bottom of the hill the road veers sharply to the left.* —*v.t.* to change the direction or course of. —*n.* a change in direction or course; swerve.

Ve·ga (vē′gə, vā′gə) *n.* a bright white star, the brightest star in the constellation Lyra.

veg·e·ta·ble (vej′tə bəl, vej′ə tə bəl) *n.* **1.** the part of a plant used as food, eaten cooked or raw. The roots, leaves, flowers, stems, seeds, pods, and fruit of certain plants are eaten as vegetables. **2.** the plant from which such a part comes. **3.** any plant. —*adj.* **1.** of, relating to, or made from plants or parts of plants: *a roadside vegetable stand, vegetable stew.* **2.** like a plant; dull or inactive: *a vegetable existence.*

veg·e·tar·i·an (vej′ə ter′ē ən) *n.* a person who eats only plants and plant products and who eats no meat, fish, or fowl, usually for health or moral reasons. —*adj.* **1.** relating to, supporting, or practicing vegetarianism. **2.** made up entirely of vegetables: *a vegetarian diet.*

veg·e·tar·i·an·ism (vej′ə ter′ē ə niz′əm) *n.* the practices or principles of vegetarians.

veg·e·tate (vej′ə tāt′) *v.i.*, **veg·e·tat·ed, veg·e·tat·ing. 1.** to grow or develop in the way plants do. **2.** to lead a dull or inactive life.

veg·e·ta·tion (vej′ə tā′shən) *n.* **1.** plant life: *a region of lush vegetation.* **2.** the act or process of vegetating.

veg·e·ta·tive (vej′ə tā′tiv) *adj.* **1.** of or relating to plants, plant life, or plant growth. **2.** growing or capable of growing as plants do. **3.** dull or inactive.

ve·he·ment (vē′ə mənt) *adj.* **1.** showing or characterized by intensity of feeling; passionate; ardent: *The workers made vehement demands for higher wages.* **2.** violent; forceful: *a vehement storm.* —**ve′he·mence,** *n.* —**ve′he·ment·ly,** *adv.*

ve·hi·cle (vē′ə kəl) *n.* **1.** a device designed or used for transporting persons or goods. An automobile, sled, or carriage is a vehicle. **2.** the means by which something is expressed, communicated, or achieved: *Poetry is a vehicle of self-expression.* **3.** a liquid with which pigment is mixed to make paint.

ve·hic·u·lar (vē hik′yə lər) *adj.* **1.** of, relating to, or for vehicles: *vehicular traffic.* **2.** serving as a vehicle.

veil (vāl) *n.* **1.** a piece of lightweight fabric, as of lace, silk, or net, worn especially by women over the head and shoulders, or as a covering for the face. **2.** anything that hides or conceals: *a veil of mist, a veil of secrecy.* —*v.t.* to cover, conceal, or disguise with a veil: *She veiled her irritation with a smile.* —**veil′like′,** *adj.*

vein (vān) *n.* **1.** one of the vessels that carry blood from all parts of the body to the heart. **2.** one of the bundles of vascular tissue that form the framework of a leaf. **3.** one of the branching tubular structures that serve to stiffen and strengthen the wing of an insect. **4.** a deposit of a mineral that forms in rock: *a vein of silver.* **5.** a streak

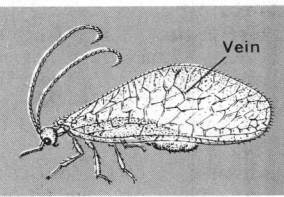

Vein *(def. 3)*

or marking of a different color, as in marble or wood. **6.** a quality, mood, or attitude: *There was a humorous vein in everything he said.* —*v.t.* to provide or mark with veins. —**vein′like′,** *adj.*

veld (velt) *also,* **veldt.** *n.* a region of open grassland in South Africa, having scattered bushes and trees.

vel·lum (vel′əm) *n.* **1.** a fine parchment prepared from calfskin, lambskin, or kidskin, used for writing or for binding fine books. **2.** a paper made to resemble such parchment.

ve·loc·i·pede (vi los′ə pēd′) *n.* **1.** an early form of a bicycle or tricycle. **2.** a child's tricycle.

ve·loc·i·ty (vi los′ə tē) *n. pl.,* **ve·loc·i·ties. 1.** rapidity of motion; speed. **2.** *Physics.* the rate of motion in a particular direction in relation to time. Light has a velocity of about 186,000 miles per second.

ve·lour (vi loor′) *also,* **ve·lours** (vi loor′). *n. pl.,* **ve·lours** (vi loor′, vi loorz′). a soft, thick, closely woven fabric having a finish like velvet, used for clothing, draperies, upholstery, and other items.

vel·vet (vel′vit) *n.* **1.** a fabric made of silk, rayon, nylon, or other fiber, having a smooth, thick pile. **2.** the soft skin that covers the growing antlers of a deer. —*adj.* **1.** made of or covered with velvet. **2.** like velvet in smoothness or softness.

vel·vet·een (vel′və tēn′) *n.* a cotton fabric made with a short, thick pile so that it resembles velvet.

vel·vet·y (vel′və tē) *adj.* **1.** smooth and soft like velvet. **2.** smooth to the taste, as some liquors.

ve·na ca·va (vē′nə kā′və) *n. pl.,* **ve·nae ca·vae** (vē′nē kā′vē). either of the two large veins that return blood to the right atrium of the heart.

ve·nal (vēn′əl) *adj.* **1.** willing to be bribed; open to bribery; corruptible: *a venal policeman.* **2.** that can be gotten or influenced by bribery: *a venal decision by a judge.* **3.** characterized by corruption. —**ve′nal·ly,** *adv.*

ve·nal·i·ty (vē nal′ə tē) *n. pl.,* **ve·nal·i·ties.** the state or instance of being venal.

ve·na·tion (vē nā′shən, və nā′shən) *n.* an arrangement or system of veins, as in a leaf or an insect's wing.

vend (vend) *v.t.* to offer for sale; sell.

ven·det·ta (ven det′ə) *n.* **1.** a feud in which the relatives of a murdered or injured person seek vengeance on the wrongdoer or members of his family. **2.** any bitter feud or dispute in which there is a desire for vengeance.

vending machine, a machine operated by inserting a coin in a slot, used for selling candy, cigarettes, or various other small items.

ven·dor (ven′dər) *also,* **vend·er.** *n.* a person who sells goods: *He bought an apple from a fruit vendor.*

ve·neer (vi nēr′) *n.* **1.** a thin layer of fine wood or other material used in covering a surface or making plywood: *The pine table had a veneer of mahogany.* **2.** an outward appearance, especially one that is deceptive: *She tried to hide her resentment behind a veneer of friendliness.* —*v.t.* **1.** to cover (a surface) with a thin layer of fine wood or other material. **2.** to glue together (layers of wood) to make plywood. **3.** to give an attractive outward appearance to.

ven·er·a·ble (ven′ər ə bəl) *adj.* **1.** deserving respect or

at; āpe; cär; end; mē; it; īce; hot; ōld; fôrk; wood; fo͞ol; oil; out; up; turn; sing; thin; **th**is; hw in white; zh in treasure. The symbol ə stands for the sound of **a** in about, **e** in taken, **i** in pencil, **o** in lemon, and **u** in circus.

V

reverence, as by reason of age, character, or position: *a venerable scholar.* **2.** worthy of respect because of age or historic or religious importance: *the venerable halls of a university.* —**ven·er·a·bly,** *adv.*

ven·er·ate (ven′ə rāt′) *v.t.,* **ven·er·at·ed, ven·er·at·ing.** to regard with deep respect or reverence.

ven·er·a·tion (ven′ə rā′shən) *n.* **1.** the act of venerating or the state of being venerated. **2.** a feeling of deep respect or reverence.

ve·ne·re·al disease (və nēr′ē əl) any of several diseases, such as syphilis and gonorrhea, transmitted by sexual acts with an infected person.

Ve·ne·tian (vi nē′shən) *adj.* of or relating to Venice, its people, or their culture. —*n.* a person who was born or is living in Venice.

Venetian blind, a shade, especially for a window, made of a series of overlapping horizontal slats. The slats can be opened or closed, and the shade can be raised or lowered by means of attached cords.

Ven·e·zue·la (ven′ə zwā′lə, ven′ə zwē′lə) *n.* a country in northern South America, on the Caribbean Sea. Capital, Caracas. Area, 352,144 sq. mi. Pop. (1971 est.), 11,100,000. —**Ven′e·zue′lan,** *adj., n.*

venge·ance (ven′jəns) *n.* the act of causing injury to another person in return for an injury or wrong.

with a vengeance. with great force, intensity, or violence: *The raging wind blew against the shutters with a vengeance.*

Venetian blind

venge·ful (venj′fəl) *adj.* full of or showing a desire for vengeance; seeking revenge: *a vengeful enemy.* —**venge′ful·ly,** *adv.* —**venge′ful·ness,** *n.*

ve·ni·al (vē′nē əl) *adj.* that may be excused or forgiven; not very serious; pardonable: *a venial sin.* —**ve·ni·al·i·ty** (vē′nē al′ə tē), *n.*

Ven·ice (ven′is) *n.* a port city in northeastern Italy, built on 118 small islands in the Adriatic Sea. Pop. (1970 est.), 367,528.

ven·i·son (ven′ə sən, ven′ə zən) *n.* the flesh of a deer, used as food.

ven·om (ven′əm) *n.* **1.** a poison produced by some animals, such as certain snakes or spiders, usually introduced into the body of a victim by a bite or sting. **2.** malice; spite: *His sarcastic comments were filled with venom.*

ven·om·ous (ven′ə məs) *adj.* **1.** able to inflict a poisonous wound, especially by biting or stinging: *a venomous snake.* **2.** containing or full of venom: *a venomous bite.* **3.** malicious; spiteful: *a venomous remark.* —**ven′om·ous·ly,** *adv.* —**ven′om·ous·ness,** *n.*

ve·nous (vē′nəs) *adj.* **1.** of, relating to, or characterized by veins. **2.** of or relating to the blood returning to the heart through the veins. Venous blood contains carbon dioxide but no oxygen.

vent[1] (vent) *n.* **1.** a hole or other small opening for the escape or passage of a gas, liquid, or the like. **2.** a means of escape; outlet; expression: *He gave vent to his fury by shouting.* —*v.t.* **1.** to give expression to: *The man vented his rage on an innocent bystander.* **2.** to provide with a vent or outlet. **3.** to allow to escape through an opening. [French *vent* wind and *évent* hole, opening; both going back to Latin *ventus* wind.]

vent[2] (vent) *n.* a slit in a garment, as at the back of a coat. [Old French *fente* slit.]

ven·ti·late (vent′əl āt′) *v.t.,* **ven·ti·lat·ed, ven·ti·lat·ing. 1.** to let air into; circulate fresh air in: *She ventilated the musty room by opening the windows.* **2.** to bring to public notice; discuss publicly: *to ventilate a political issue.*

ven·ti·la·tion (vent′əl ā′shən) *n.* **1.** the act of ventilating or the state of being ventilated. **2.** a system or means of letting in or circulating fresh air.

ven·ti·la·tor (vent′əl ā′tər) *n.* an apparatus for letting in or circulating fresh air, or for getting rid of foul or stale air.

ven·tral (ven′trəl) *adj.* of or relating to the abdomen or belly; abdominal: *the ventral fins of a fish.*

ven·tri·cle (ven′tri kəl) *n.* either of the two lower chambers or cavities of the heart that receive blood from the auricles and pump it into the arteries.

ven·tril·o·quism (ven tril′ə kwiz′əm) *n.* the art or practice of speaking or producing sounds without moving the lips, so that the sound seems to be coming from some source other than the speaker.

ven·tril·o·quist (ven tril′ə kwist) *n.* a person who practices ventriloquism, especially an entertainer who appears to carry on a conversation with a dummy. [Late Latin *ventriloquus* literally, a person who speaks from his belly; from the former belief that a ventriloquist's voice came from his stomach.]

ven·ture (ven′chər) *n.* an undertaking that involves some risk or danger: *It was a foolhardy business venture that was sure to fail.* —*v.,* **ven·tured, ven·tur·ing.** —*v.t.* **1.** to expose to risk or danger: *He ventured all his savings on his friend's business scheme.* **2.** to run the risk of; brave: *to venture a storm.* **3.** to express at the risk of criticism, objection, or the like: *May I venture a word of advice?* —*v.i.* to do or undertake something despite the risk or danger involved; dare: *The two boys ventured out into the stormy night in search of their lost dog.*

ven·ture·some (ven′chər səm) *adj.* **1.** willing or inclined to take risks; bold; daring: *The venturesome men went into the unexplored cave.* **2.** involving risk or danger; hazardous: *a venturesome journey.*

ven·tur·ous (ven′chər əs) *adj.* **1.** looking for adventure; bold; adventurous. **2.** risky or dangerous; hazardous.

ven·ue (ven′yōō, ven′ōō) *n. Law.* **1.** the place where a crime or other happening that is the cause of legal action takes place. **2.** the county, district, or locality where a jury must be called and where a trial must be held.

Ve·nus (vē′nəs) *n.* **1.** *Roman Mythology.* the goddess of love and beauty. In Greek mythology she was called Aphrodite. **2.** the sixth largest planet of the solar system and second in order of distance from the sun.

Ve·nus's-fly·trap (vē′nə siz flī′trap′) *n.* a plant native to moist, sandy regions of North and South Carolina, having leaves with two lobes that snap shut to trap insects.

ve·ra·cious (və rā′shəs) *adj.* **1.** truthful; honest: *a veracious witness.* **2.** accurate; true: *a veracious account.* —**ve·ra′cious·ly,** *adv.* —**ve·ra′cious·ness,** *n.*

ve·rac·i·ty (və ras′ə tē) *n. pl.,* **ve·rac·i·ties. 1.** truthfulness; honesty. **2.** accuracy; correctness.

Ver·a·cruz (ver′ə krōōz′) *n.* a port city in eastern Mexico, on the Gulf of Mexico. Pop. (1970), 214,000.

ve·ran·da (və ran′də) *also,* **ve·ran·dah.** *n.* an open porch, usually roofed, extending along one or more sides of a house.

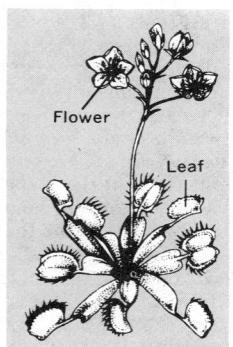

Flower

Leaf

Venus's-flytrap

verb (vurb) *n.* a word belonging to that part of speech that expresses action, existence, or occurrence. Verbs usually form the main element in a predicate. *Be, fly, imagine,* and *spend* are verbs.

ver·bal (vur′bəl) *adj.* **1.** of, relating to, or made up of words: *verbal communication.* **2.** expressed in speech; not written: *a verbal agreement.* **3.** word for word; literal: *a verbal translation.* **4.** *Grammar.* of, relating to, or derived from a verb: *In English "-ed" is a common verbal ending.* —*n. Grammar.* a noun or adjective that is derived from a verb. Gerunds, infinitives, and participles are verbals. —**ver′bal·ly,** *adv.*

ver·bal·ize (vur′bə līz′) *v.,* **ver·bal·ized, ver·bal·iz·ing.** —*v.t.* to express in words: *to verbalize one's feelings.* —*v.i.* to be wordy. —**ver′bal·i·za′tion,** *n.*

ver·ba·tim (vər bā′tim) *adv.* word for word; in exactly the same words: *The newspaper printed the senator's speech verbatim.* —*adj.* word for word: *a verbatim translation.*

ver·be·na (vər bē′nə) *n.* any of a large group of trailing or loosely branching plants having clusters of small flowers.

ver·bi·age (vur′bē ij) *n.* the use of more words than necessary; wordiness.

ver·bose (vər bōs′) *adj.* using more words than necessary; wordy: *a verbose speaker.* —**ver·bose′ly,** *adv.* —**ver·bos·i·ty** (vər bos′ə tē), *n.*

ver·dant (verd′ənt) *adj.* **1.** green with vegetation. **2.** green in color. —**ver′dant·ly,** *adv.*

Verde, Cape (vurd) the westernmost point of Africa, a peninsula on the coast of Senegal.

Ver·di, Giu·sep·pe (ver′dē; jōō zep′pe) 1813–1901, Italian composer of operas.

ver·dict (vur′dikt) *n.* **1.** the decision of a jury in a trial: *The jurors agreed on a verdict of guilty.* **2.** any decision or conclusion on some matter; judgment.

ver·di·gris (ver′də grēs′) *n.* **1.** a poisonous mixture consisting of blue or green crystals that are formed when copper reacts with acetic acid. It is used as a paint pigment and insecticide. **2.** a greenish coating that forms on copper, brass, or bronze objects.

ver·dure (vur′jər) *n.* **1.** the fresh, green color of growing vegetation. **2.** green vegetation.

verge¹ (vurj) *n.* **1.** the edge or border of something. **2.** a point beyond which something happens or begins: *The lost child was on the verge of tears.* —*v.i.,* **verged, verg·ing.** to be on the verge; border: *The man's very strange behavior verged on insanity.* [Old French *verge* rod, from Latin *virga* rod; originally referring to a rod or staff carried as a symbol of authority or office.]

verge² (vurj) *v.i.,* **verged, verg·ing.** to tend; incline; approach. [Latin *vergere* to bend, incline.]

Ver·gil (vur′jəl) another spelling of **Virgil.**

ver·i·fi·a·ble (ver′ə fī′ə bəl) *adj.* that can be verified.

ver·i·fi·ca·tion (ver′ə fi kā′shən) *n.* the act of verifying or the state of being verified.

ver·i·fy (ver′ə fī′) *v.t.,* **ver·i·fied, ver·i·fy·ing. 1.** to prove (something) to be true; confirm: *Several witnesses verified my account of the incident.* **2.** to check or test the accuracy or truth of: *The scientist's tests verified the results of the experiment.*

ver·i·ly (ver′ə lē) *adv. Archaic.* in truth; really.

ver·i·si·mil·i·tude (ver′ə si mil′ə tōōd′, ver′ə si mil′ə-tyōōd′) *n.* the appearance of being true; closeness to truth.

ver·i·ta·ble (ver′i tə bəl) *adj.* true; actual; real. —**ver′i·ta·bly,** *adv.*

ver·i·ty (ver′ə tē) *n. pl.,* **ver·i·ties. 1.** the state or quality of being true, real, or accurate. **2.** a true statement or fact; truth.

Ver·meer, Jan (vər mēr′; yän) 1632–1675, Dutch painter.

ver·mi·cel·li (vur′mə sel′ē) *n.* a pasta made into long, slender threads that are thinner than spaghetti.

ver·mi·form (vur′mə fôrm′) *adj.* shaped like a worm.

vermiform appendix, see **appendix** *(def.1).*

ver·mil·ion (vər mil′yən) *also,* **ver·mil·lion.** *n.* **1.** a bright-red color. **2.** a bright-red pigment. —*adj.* having the color vermilion; bright-red.

ver·min (vur′min) *n. pl.,* **ver·min. 1.** any of various small insects or animals that are harmful, destructive, or troublesome, such as lice, fleas, or rats. **2.** a low or vile person or persons.

Ver·mont (vər mont′) *n.* a state in the northeastern United States. Capital, Montpelier. Area, 9609 sq. mi. Pop. (1970), 444,330. Abbreviation, **Vt.** —**Ver·mont′er,** *n.*

● This area was known by the English as "Green Mountain," and the name **Vermont** was probably suggested by *Verd Mont,* which is the French translation of the English name. The name became popular and was officially adopted for the territory in 1777. It was later retained when the territory became a state.

ver·mouth (vər mōōth′) *n.* a white wine flavored with herbs, used especially in making cocktails.

ver·nac·u·lar (vər nak′yə lər) *n.* **1.** the language native to the people of a certain country or locality. **2.** the common, everyday language of the people. **3.** the vocabulary used by the people of a particular profession or trade. —*adj.* **1.** (of a language or dialect) native to or used by the people of a certain country or locality. **2.** of, in, or using the everyday language of the people: *Mark Twain is a vernacular writer.*

● Although some form of English has been the **vernacular** of England since the Anglo-Saxon invasions in the fifth and sixth centuries A.D., it was at various times considered unsuitable to be used as the language of the court, the nobility, religion, and learning. Because nearly all of the learned men of ancient Britain were part of the church, the vast majority of their writing was done in Latin, the language of the church. The greatest contribution to the development of the vernacular as the language for English writing was made by Alfred the Great, who reigned as king of the West Saxons from A.D. 871 to 899. He was responsible for assigning to various authors who are now unknown the task of writing, in the vernacular, a history of Britain beginning with the Roman invasion in 55 B.C. This work was continued for more than 250 years after his death. His influence on the writers of his time helped to produce the many beautifully decorated manuscripts that were written in English and became famous throughout Europe. English continued to be used in the writing of sermons, moral lessons, lives of the saints, commentaries on the Bible, and various other works. It was the first vernacular to achieve prominence in Western Europe.

The Norman invasion in 1066 brought the French language to Britain. Norman French became the language of the court, the military, and along with Latin, of learning.

at; āpe; cär; end; mē; it; īce; hot; ōld; fôrk; wood; fōōl; oil; out; up; turn; sing; thin; this; hw in white; zh in treasure. The symbol ə stands for the sound of a in about, e in taken, i in pencil, o in lemon, and u in circus.

English survived as the language of the common people. The vernacular did not return to official favor until 1362, when the formal opening of Parliament was conducted, not in French or Latin, but in English. In the same century, another great step was made in the advancement of the vernacular when the religious reformer John Wycliffe supervised the first translation of the Bible into English. The general feeling of writers in England about the vernacular was shared by the great Italian writer Dante, who wrote in his native language, rather than in Latin, in order to reach the widest possible audience.

The revival of interest in Greek and Latin during the fifteenth and sixteenth centuries temporarily reversed the trend toward the universal acceptance of the vernacular. Scholars of that period felt that Greek and Latin were superior to, and more beautiful than, English. The eventual result of this attitude was not the domination of the vernacular by other languages but rather the growth of the vernacular by the addition of many new words from these languages. After that period, the vernaculars of the various Western European countries began to be used in most cultural, political, and intellectual activities. This was caused by two basic factors. First, there was a growing interest in reading and writing among the middle class, partly as a result of the greater amount of written material that the invention of the printing press had made available. Second, the spirit of growing political nationalism caused people to want to use their own language rather than that of another country. The use of the vernacular has persisted until modern times. Although various attempts have been made to create international languages, the vernacular has remained the principal language in all the countries of the Western World.

---

ver·nal (vurn′əl) *adj.* **1.** of, relating to, or happening in spring. **2.** like or suggesting spring; fresh or youthful.

vernal equinox, the equinox that takes place about March 21. It marks the beginning of spring in the Northern Hemisphere.

Verne, Jules (vurn; jŏŏlz) 1828–1905, French novelist.

ver·ni·er (vur′nē ər) *n.* **1.** a short scale that slides along a longer scale and indicates subdivisions of it, used to make very fine measurements. Also, **vernier scale. 2.** a device used to make very fine adjustments in precision instruments. [From Pierre *Vernier,* 1580–1637, the French mathematician who invented this scale.]

Ve·ro·na (və rō′nə) *n.* a city in northeastern Italy. Pop. (1970 est.), 262,014.

Ver·sailles (ver sī′) *n.* a historic city in north-central France, just southwest of Paris. It is the site of the magnificent palace of Louis XIV.

ver·sa·tile (vur′sə til) *adj.* **1.** able to do many different things well: *The young man was a versatile athlete who could play most games with skill.* **2.** having many uses or functions: *a versatile tool.* —**ver′sa·til′i·ty,** *n.*

verse (vurs) *n.* **1.** an arrangement of words according to a particular meter or pattern, often in rhyme; poetry. **2.** a single line of poetry. **3.** a poem. **4.** a section of a poem, song, or similar composition, especially a stanza. **5.** a particular type of poetic structure: *iambic verse.* **6.** one of the short divisions into which the chapters of the Bible are divided.

versed (vurst) *adj.* learned or experienced; knowledgeable; skilled: *The teacher is versed in American history.*

ver·si·fi·ca·tion (vur′sə fi kā′shən) *n.* **1.** the writing of verses. **2.** the art, practice, or theory of writing verses. **3.** a poetic form or style; metrical structure.

ver·si·fy (vur′sə fī′) *v.,* **ver·si·fied, ver·si·fy·ing.** —*v.t.* **1.** to change from prose into verse form. **2.** to tell or describe in verse. —*v.i.* to compose verses. —**ver′si·fi′er,** *n.*

ver·sion (vur′zhən) *n.* **1.** an account or description presented from a particular point of view: *Please tell us your version of the accident.* **2.** a translation from one language into another. **3.** *also,* **Version.** a translation of the Bible or a part of the Bible. **4.** a different or changed form of something: *Congress passed a revised version of the bill.* **5.** an adaptation, as of a literary work: *the movie version of a novel.*

ver·sus (vur′səs) *prep.* **1.** against: *It was the seniors versus the freshmen in the basketball game.* **2.** in contrast to; as an alternative to: *a life of hard work versus one of inactivity.*

ver·te·bra (vur′tə brə) *n. pl.,* **ver·te·brae** (vur′tə brē′) or **ver·te·bras.** any of the small bones that make up the backbone.

ver·te·bral (vur′tə brəl) *adj.* **1.** of, relating to, or of the nature of a vertebra or the vertebrae. **2.** composed of or having vertebrae.

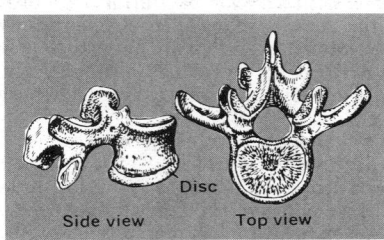
Human vertebra

Side view Top view Disc

ver·te·brate (vur′tə brāt′, vur′tə brit) *adj.* **1.** having a backbone. **2.** of, relating to, or characteristic of animals with backbones. —*n.* any of a large group of animals, including fish, amphibians, reptiles, birds, and mammals, having a backbone, a skeleton of bone or cartilage, and a brain enclosed in a skull.

ver·tex (vur′teks) *n. pl.,* **ver·tex·es** or **ver·ti·ces. 1.** the highest point of something; apex: *the vertex of a mountain.* **2.** *Geometry.* **a.** the point of a triangle, pyramid, or the like, opposite to the base. **b.** the point of intersection of the sides of an angle.

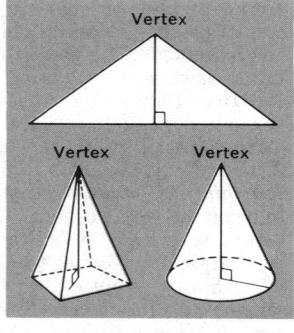
Vertex Vertex Vertex

ver·ti·cal (vur′ti kəl) *adj.* at a right angle to the plane of the horizon; upright; perpendicular. —*n.* something vertical, such as a line or plane. —**ver′ti·cal·ly,** *adv.*

ver·ti·ces (vur′tə sēz′) a plural of **vertex.**

ver·ti·go (vur′tə gō′) *n. pl.,* **ver·ti·goes.** a condition in which a person feels that he or his surroundings are whirling about; dizziness.

verve (vurv) *n.* liveliness or enthusiasm; energy; spirit.

ver·y (ver′ē) *adv.* **1.** in a high degree; to a great extent; extremely: *That boy is very strong for his age. I'm very sorry about our misunderstanding.* **2.** truly; absolutely; exactly: *She is the very best dancer I've ever seen.* —*adj.,* **ver·i·er, ver·i·est. 1.** identical; same: *This is the very textbook we used last term.* **2.** mere: *The very idea of getting up early made him miserable.* **3.** actual: *The thief was caught in the very act.* **4.** exact; precise: *Your gift was the very thing I needed.* **5.** absolute; complete; utter: *Our expenses have been reduced to the very minimum.*

very high frequency, the frequency range of radio waves from 30 to 300 megacycles.

ves·i·cle (ves′i kəl) *n.* any small sac, cavity, or cyst, especially one filled with fluid.

ve·sic·u·lar (vi sik′yə lər) *adj.* of, relating to, or like a vesicle or vesicles.

ves·per (ves′pər) *n.* **1.** the bell that calls people to vespers. **2.** an evening prayer, hymn, or religious service. **3. Vesper.** the planet Venus when it appears as the evening star. —*adj.* **1.** of or relating to evening. **2.** of or relating to vespers.

ves·pers (ves′pərz) *also,* **Ves·pers.** *n., pl.* **1.** the sixth of the seven canonical hours or the service for it. **2.** any religious service that is held in the late afternoon or early evening.

Ves·puc·ci, A·me·ri·go (ve spoo′chē; ä′mə rē′gō) 1454–1512, the Italian explorer after whom America was named.

ves·sel (ves′əl) *n.* **1.** a ship or large boat. **2.** a hollow container, as for liquids. **3.** a duct or tube that carries a body fluid, such as a vein or artery. **4.** a tube in plants for conducting water.

vest (vest) *n.* **1.** a man's short, sleeveless garment, usually buttoning in front and worn under a suit jacket. **2.** a similar garment worn by women. —*v.t.* **1.** to clothe, as with vestments. **2.** to give authority, power, or the like to: *The club president was vested with all the rights and powers of his office.* **3.** to place in the control of: *All power was vested in the king.* —*v.i.* **1.** to clothe oneself, as with vestments. **2.** (of authority, power, or the like) to be or become vested.

Ves·ta (ves′tə) *n. Roman Mythology.* the goddess of the hearth and the hearth fire.

Vest

ves·tal (ves′təl) *n.* **1.** see **vestal virgin.** **2.** a chaste woman; virgin. —*adj.* **1.** of or relating to the goddess Vesta. **2.** of or relating to the vestal virgins. **3.** chaste; pure.

vestal virgin, any of six virgin priestesses who watched over the sacred fire of Vesta in her temple in ancient Rome.

vest·ed (ves′tid) *adj.* **1.** *Law.* not depending on anything; fixed; settled: *a vested right.* **2.** clothed, especially in church vestments.

ves·ti·bule (ves′tə byool′) *n.* **1.** an entrance hall or passage between the outer door and the interior of a building; lobby. **2.** an enclosed space serving as a passage between one railroad passenger car and another. **3.** any small body cavity that leads to another cavity or canal, especially the cavity in the inner ear leading to the cochlea.

ves·tige (ves′tij) *n.* **1.** a trace, sign, or visible evidence of something that no longer exists: *The archaeologist discovered vestiges of an ancient temple.* **2.** *Biology.* a part or organ in a plant or animal that is not fully developed or useful, but once served a useful purpose in an earlier form of the plant or animal.

ves·tig·i·al (ves tij′ē əl) *adj.* of, relating to, or of the nature of a vestige.

vest·ment (vest′mənt) *n.* **1.** any of various garments worn by certain clergymen in the performance of religious services. **2.** a garment, especially an official or ceremonial robe or gown.

ves·try (ves′trē) *n. pl.,* **ves·tries.** **1.** a room in a church where the clergy put on their vestments and where the vestments and other articles used in religious services are kept. **2.** a room in a church or an attached building, used for Sunday school, prayer meetings, and the like. **3.** in parishes of the Anglican churches, a committee that manages the financial affairs of the parish.

ves·try·man (ves′trē mən) *n. pl.,* **ves·try·men** (ves′trē-mən). a member of a vestry.

ves·ture (ves′chər) *n.* **1.** clothing; garments. **2.** something that covers; covering.

Ve·su·vi·us, Mount (vi soo′vē əs) an active volcano in southern Italy, southeast of Naples. A major eruption occurred in A.D. 79, burying the ancient Roman city of Pompeii.

vet¹ (vet) *n. Informal.* a veterinarian.

vet² (vet) *n. Informal.* a veteran.

vetch (vech) *n. pl.,* **vetch·es.** any of a large group of climbing plants related to the pea, grown chiefly for food for cattle and sheep and to enrich the soil.

vet·er·an (vet′ər ən) *n.* **1.** a person who has had a great deal of experience, as in an occupation, office, or position: *The actor was a veteran of stage and screen.* **2.** a person who has served in the armed forces. —*adj.* **1.** having had a great deal of experience, as in an occupation: *a veteran reporter, a veteran professional baseball player.* **2.** having had a great deal of experience in warfare or military matters: *veteran troops.*

Veterans Day, a legal holiday honoring veterans who have fought for the United States, formerly called Armistice Day. It is now celebrated on the fourth Monday in October.

vet·er·i·nar·i·an (vet′ər ə ner′ē ən) *n.* a person trained and licensed to give medical or surgical treatment to animals.

vet·er·i·nar·y (vet′ər ə ner′ē) *adj.* of or relating to the medical or surgical treatment of animals: *veterinary studies.* —*n. pl.,* **vet·er·i·nar·ies.** another word for **veterinarian.**

ve·to (vē′tō) *n. pl.,* **ve·toes.** **1.** the power of a president, governor, or other executive to reject a bill passed by a legislative body. **2.** the use of this power. **3.** any prohibition or refusal of consent by a person in authority. —*v.t.,* **ve·toed, ve·to·ing.** **1.** to reject by a veto: *The President vetoed the bill passed by Congress.* **2.** to refuse to give consent to: *Dad vetoed my idea of using the family car.* [Latin *vetō* I forbid; used by tribunes (officials who protected the rights of the common people in ancient Rome) when they opposed measures of the Senate or acts of their magistrates.] —**ve′to·er,** *n.*

vex (veks) *v.t.* to annoy or irritate: *His constant criticism vexed her.*

vex·a·tion (vek sā′shən) *n.* **1.** the act of vexing or the state of being vexed; annoyance: *There was a look of vexation on the woman's face.* **2.** something that vexes: *This old car has always been a vexation to me.*

vex·a·tious (vek sā′shəs) *adj.* causing or tending to cause vexation; annoying: *a vexatious sales tax, vexatious problems.*

vhf, very high frequency. Also, **VHF**

v.i., intransitive verb.

V.I., Virgin Islands.

vi·a (vī′ə, vē′ə) *prep.* by way of: *Sally drove home via the turnpike.*

vi·a·ble (vī′ə bəl) *adj.* **1.** capable of living: *a viable embryo.* **2.** capable of growing: *a viable seed.* **3.** capable of being used or done; workable; practical: *a viable plan. He suggested a viable alternative to our present method of working.* —**vi′a·bil′i·ty,** *n.*

at; āpe; cär; end; mē; it; īce; hot; ōld; fôrk; wood; fool; oil; out; up; turn; sing; thin; this; hw in white; zh in treasure. The symbol ə stands for the sound of **a** in about, **e** in taken, **i** in pencil, **o** in lemon, and **u** in circus.

V

vi·a·duct (vī′ə dukt′) *n.* a bridge that carries a road or railroad, as over a highway or valley.

vi·al (vī′əl) *also,* **phi·al.** *n.* a small glass bottle for holding a liquid, especially perfume or medicine.

vi·and (vī′ənd) *n.* **1.** an article of food. **2. viands.** choice food; delicacies.

vi·brant (vī′brənt) *adj.* **1.** full of life, energy, and enthusiasm: *a vibrant personality.* **2.** vibrating: *a vibrant string.* **3.** resounding; resonant: *a vibrant sound.* —**vi′bran·cy,** *n.* —**vi′brant·ly,** *adv.*

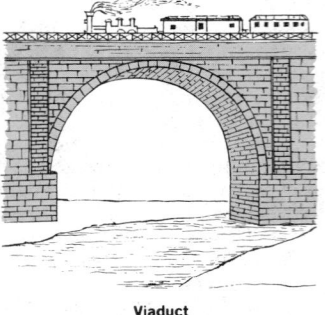

Viaduct

vi·brate (vī′brāt) *v.,* **vi·brat·ed, vi·brat·ing.** —*v.i.* **1.** to move back and forth or up and down rapidly: *The strings of a violin vibrate when plucked.* **2.** to respond or react emotionally; thrill: *The audience vibrated with excitement as the show began.* **3.** (of sounds) to echo; resound: *The explosion vibrated through the tunnel.* —*v.t.* to cause to move back and forth and up and down rapidly: *to vibrate a string.*

vi·bra·tion (vī brā′shən) *n.* **1.** the act of vibrating or the state of being vibrated. **2.** *Physics.* a continuing, periodic, usually rapid motion of the particles of an elastic body or medium back and forth in alternate directions from a central point. **3.** a rapid movement back and forth or up and down; quivering; shaking.

vi·bra·to (vi brä′tō) *n. pl.,* **vi·bra·tos.** *Music.* a trembling effect caused by a fast, very slight variation of the pitch of a musical tone.

vi·bra·tor (vī′brā tər) *n.* something that vibrates, especially an electrical instrument used in massage.

vi·bra·to·ry (vī′brə tôr′ē) *adj.* of, relating to, or producing vibration.

vi·bur·num (vī bur′nəm) *n.* any of a group of shrubs or trees bearing clusters of white or pink flowers.

vic·ar (vik′ər) *n.* **1.** in the Church of England, a parish priest who receives a salary. **2.** in the Protestant Episcopal Church, a clergyman in charge of a chapel in a parish. **3.** any of various Roman Catholic prelates who represent the pope or a bishop. **4.** a person who acts as the representative of another.

vic·ar·age (vik′ər ij) *n.* **1.** the residence of a vicar. **2.** the rank, duties, or salary of a vicar.

vi·car·i·ous (vī ker′ē əs) *adj.* **1.** done or endured for another: *vicarious punishment.* **2.** substituting for or representing another: *a vicarious agent.* **3.** experienced or enjoyed by an imagined sharing in the experience of another: *Her sister's good fortune gave Mary vicarious pleasure.* —**vi·car′i·ous·ly,** *adv.* —**vi·car′i·ous·ness,** *n.*

vice[1] (vīs) *n.* **1.** an immoral or harmful habit or practice: *Lying is his greatest vice.* **2.** immoral conduct; wickedness. [Old French *vice.*]

vice[2] (vīs) *British.* another spelling of **vise.**

vice- *prefix* a person who is subordinate to and acts in place of: *vice-president.*

vice admiral, an officer in the U.S. Navy, ranking below an admiral and above a rear admiral.

vice-pres·i·den·cy (vīs′prez′ə dən sē) *n. pl.,* **vice-pres·i·den·cies.** the office or function of vice-president.

vice-pres·i·dent (vīs′prez′ə dənt) *n.* an officer ranking second to a president and acting in his place when necessary. —**vice′-pres′i·den′tial,** *adj.*

vice·roy (vīs′roi′) *n.* **1.** a governor of a province, kingdom, or colony, ruling as the deputy of a sovereign. **2.** an orange and black butterfly of North America that closely resembles, but is smaller than, the monarch butterfly.

vice ver·sa (vī′sə vur′sə) the opposite or reverse in order or relation; the other way around: *My brother helps me and vice versa.*

Vich·y (vish′ē) *n.* a city in central France, a noted health resort. Vichy served as the capital of France during the German occupation from 1940 to 1944.

vi·chy·ssoise (vish′ē swäz′) *n.* a thick, creamy soup containing potatoes and leeks, usually served chilled.

vi·cin·i·ty (vi sin′ə tē) *n. pl.,* **vi·cin·i·ties.** the area near or surrounding a particular place; neighborhood: *There are several parks in the vicinity of our house.*

vi·cious (vish′əs) *adj.* **1.** marked by wickedness; evil; depraved: *The blackmailers planned a vicious crime.* **2.** full of malice; spiteful: *vicious lies, a vicious attack.* **3.** having an extremely bad disposition; savagely fierce: *a vicious dog.* **4.** intense; severe: *a vicious storm.* —**vi′cious·ly,** *adv.* —**vi′cious·ness,** *n.*

vicious circle, a situation in which the solving of a problem gives rise to another problem, which itself cannot be solved without bringing back the original problem.

vi·cis·si·tude (vi sis′ə tood′, vi sis′ə tyood′) *n. usually,* **vicissitudes.** a change in a situation or condition: *the vicissitudes of a person's life, the vicissitudes of the weather.*

vic·tim (vik′təm) *n.* **1.** a person who is injured, killed, or ruined: *the victim of an automobile accident, a victim of lies and slander.* **2.** a person who is cheated or tricked: *the victim of a swindler.* **3.** a person or animal sacrificed to a god.

vic·tim·ize (vik′tə mīz′) *v.t.,* **vic·tim·ized, vic·tim·iz·ing.** **1.** to make a victim of; inflict harm upon. **2.** to swindle; cheat: *He was victimized by a dishonest salesman.* —**vic′tim·i·za′tion,** *n.*

vic·tor (vik′tər) *n.* a person who wins or conquers, as in a contest, struggle, or armed conflict.

vic·to·ri·a (vik tôr′ē ə) *n.* a low, four-wheeled carriage having a folding top, seats for two passengers, and a raised seat in front for the driver. [From Queen *Victoria.*]

Victoria

Vic·to·ri·a (vik tôr′ē ə) *n.* **1. Queen.** 1819–1901, the queen of England from 1837 to 1901. **2.** a political subdivision of Australia, in the southeastern part of the country. **3. Lake.** a lake in east-central Africa, the largest of the continent. **4.** the capital and commercial center of the colony of Hong Kong. Pop. (1971), 521,612. Also (def. 4), **Hong Kong.**

Vic·to·ri·an (vik tôr′ē ən) *adj.* **1.** of or relating to Queen Victoria or to the period of her reign: *Victorian literature, Victorian architecture.* **2.** of, relating to, or having characteristics associated with English people of Victorian England, such as prudishness or stuffiness: *Victorian social attitudes.* —*n.* a person who lived during the reign of Queen Victoria.

vic·to·ri·ous (vik tôr′ē əs) *adj.* **1.** having achieved a victory, as in a contest or armed conflict: *The victorious army was welcomed home.* **2.** of or relating to victory. —**vic·to′ri·ous·ly,** *adv.* —**vic·to′ri·ous·ness,** *n.*

vic·to·ry (vik′tər ē) *n. pl.,* **vic·to·ries.** the defeat of an opponent or enemy, as in a contest or armed conflict: *The army achieved a great victory.*

Vic·tro·la (vik trō′lə) *n. Trademark.* a phonograph.

vict·ual (vit′əl) *n. usually,* **victuals.** food or provisions. —*v.t.,* **vict·ualed, vict·ual·ing.** to supply with food: *to victual a ship.*

vi·cu·ña (vī kōō′nə, vī kōō′nyə) *n. pl.,* **vi·cu·ñas** or **vi·cu·ña.** **1.** a small South American animal related to the llama, having a slender, graceful body and a long neck. It is highly valued for its silky wool coat. **2.** a fabric made from the wool of this animal.

vid·e·o (vid′ē ō′) *adj.* of or relating to the transmission or reception of television images. —*n.* **1.** the visual part of television. **2.** another word for **television.**

video tape, a magnetic tape used for recording both the picture and sound of a television program.

vie (vī) *v.i.,* **vied, vy·ing.** to be rivals; compete: *The teams vied with one another for first place.*

Vi·en·na (vē en′ə) *n.* the capital and largest city of Austria, in the northeastern part of the country, on the Danube River. Pop. (1977 est.), 1,590,100.

Vi·en·nese (vē′ə nēz′) *n. pl.,* **Vi·en·nese.** a person who was born or is living in Vienna. —*adj.* of, relating to, or characteristic of the city of Vienna or its people.

Vien·tiane (vyen tyän′) *n.* the capital and largest city of Laos, in the western part of the country. Pop. (1974 est.), 174,229.

Vi·et·cong (vē′et kông′, vē′et kong′) *also,* **Viet Cong.** *n.* **1.** the Communist military force formed to wage guerrilla warfare in the former country of South Vietnam. **2.** a member of this group. [Short for Vietnamese *Viet Nam Cong San* Vietnamese Communist.]

Vi·et·minh (vē′et min′) *also,* **Viet Minh.** *n.* the Communist party in Vietnam.

Vi·et·nam (vē′et näm′) *also,* **Viet Nam.** *n.* a country in southeastern Asia, formerly divided into North Vietnam and South Vietnam. Capital, Hanoi. Area, 128,402 sq. mi. Pop. (1980), 52,300,000.

Vi·et·nam·ese (vē et′nä mēz′) *n. pl.,* **Vi·et·nam·ese.** **1.** a person who was born or is living in Vietnam. **2.** the language of Vietnam. —*adj.* of or relating to Vietnam, its people, their language, or their culture.

view (vyōō) *n.* **1.** the act of looking or seeing; sight: *The sailors' first view of land came after many weeks at sea.* **2.** a range of vision: *The airplane soon passed out of view.* **3.** something that is seen or can be seen: *We have a lovely view of the lake from our window.* **4.** a drawing, painting, print, or photograph: *The artist painted several views of the church.* **5.** a particular way of thinking about something; attitude; opinion: *The two friends had different views on smoking.* **6.** intention; aim: *He did his homework early with the view of watching television later.* —*v.t.* **1.** to look at or see: *Many people viewed the museum exhibit.* **2.** to think about; consider: *He viewed his friend's behavior with amusement.*

in view. a. in sight: *We thought we heard footsteps, but there was no one in view.* **b.** under consideration: *Keep the future in view when you make your decision.*

in view of. in consideration of; considering: *In view of the unfavorable weather, we should call off the picnic.*

on view. open to the public; on exhibition: *The new automobile models are on view this week.*

view·er (vyōō′ər) *n.* **1.** a person who views something, especially a person who watches television. **2.** any of several devices used to look at photographic slides or scientific specimens.

view·find·er (vyōō′fīn′dər) *n.* see **finder** *(def. 2).*

view·point (vyōō′point′) *n.* a way of thinking; point of view; mental attitude.

vig·il (vij′əl) *n.* **1.** the act or period of remaining awake to guard or observe something: *The mother kept vigil all night over her sick child.* **2.** a night or day spent in prayer, especially in preparation for a holy day. **3.** the day and night before a solemn feast day, as before Christmas. **4.** *also,* **vigils.** the prayers or religious services held on such a night or day.

vig·i·lance (vij′ə ləns) *n.* alertness; watchfulness.

vig·i·lant (vij′ə lənt) *adj.* alert; watchful: *a vigilant nurse.* —**vig′i·lant·ly,** *adv.*

vig·i·lan·te (vij′ə lan′tē) *n.* a member of a group of persons who, without legal authority, take it upon themselves to punish criminals and maintain order.

vi·gnette (vin yet′) *n.* **1.** a brief literary description or dramatic sketch. **2.** an ornamental design or illustration on the title page of a book or at the beginning or end of a chapter.

vig·or (vig′ər) *n.* **1.** active power or force: *The senator campaigned with great vigor.* **2.** healthy strength: *the vim and vigor of youth.*

vig·or·ous (vig′ər əs) *adj.* full of, characterized by, or done with vigor: *vigorous exercise, a vigorous protest.* —**vig′or·ous·ly,** *adv.*

vi·king (vī′king) *also,* **Vi·king.** *n.* a member of the seafaring raiders from Scandinavia who attacked and plundered the coasts of Europe from the eighth to the eleventh centuries and who made long voyages to the New World.

vile (vīl) *adj.,* **vil·er, vil·est.** **1.** morally base; evil; immoral: *a criminal's vile deeds.* **2.** foul; disgusting; repulsive: *a vile odor, vile language.* **3.** degrading; mean; lowly: *the vile position of a slave.* **4.** very bad; unpleasant: *vile weather.* —**vile′ly,** *adv.* —**vile′ness,** *n.*

vil·i·fy (vil′ə fī′) *v.t.,* **vil·i·fied, vil·i·fy·ing.** to speak or write evil of; slander: *The political candidate vilified his opponent.* —**vil′i·fi·ca′tion,** *n.* —**vil′i·fi′er,** *n.*

vil·la (vil′ə) *n.* a large and luxurious house, especially one located in the country, on the outskirts of a city, or at the seashore.

vil·lage (vil′ij) *n.* **1.** a small community or group of houses, usually smaller than a town. **2.** the inhabitants of a village.

vil·lag·er (vil′i jər) *n.* a person who lives in a village.

vil·lain (vil′ən) *n.* **1.** a wicked, evil, or criminal person. **2.** such a person represented as a character in a novel or play. **3.** another spelling of **villein.** —**vil′lain·ous,** *adj.* —**vil′lain·ous·ly,** *adv.*

vil·lain·y (vil′ə nē) *n. pl.,* **vil·lain·ies.** **1.** the actions or conduct of a villain; extreme wickedness; evil. **2.** a villainous act or deed.

vil·lein (vil′ən) *also,* **vil·lain.** *n.* in feudalism, a peasant attached by rights to his land but owing complete obedience to the lord. A villein was regarded as a freeman in his relations with all persons other than his lord.

vil·lus (vil′əs) *n. pl.,* **vil·li** (vil′ī). any of the small, hairlike projections on the surface of a mucous membrane, especially the membrane of the small intestine, that absorb certain nutrients.

Vil·na (vil′nə) *n.* the Russian name of **Vilnius.**

Vil·ni·us (vil′nē oos) *n.* a city in the western Soviet Union. It is the capital of Lithuania. Pop. (1979), 481,000. Also, *Russian,* **Vilna.**

vim (vim) *n.* energy, strength, or enthusiasm.

Vin·ci, Leonardo da (vin′chē) see **Leonardo da Vinci.**

at; āpe; cär; end; mē; it; īce; hot; ōld; fôrk; wood; fōōl; oil; out; up; turn; sing; thin; this; hw in white; zh in treasure. The symbol ə stands for the sound of a in about, e in taken, i in pencil, o in lemon, and u in circus.

vin·di·cate (vin′də kāt′) *v.t.*, **vin·di·cat·ed, vin·di·cat·ing.** **1.** to clear (someone) of suspicion or charges of wrongdoing: *The testimony of witnesses vindicated the accused man.* **2.** to maintain or defend (a right or claim) against opposition. **3.** to justify: *The success of the play vindicated their support of the young playwright.*

vin·di·ca·tion (vin′də kā′shən) *n.* **1.** the act of vindicating or the state of being vindicated. **2.** something that vindicates.

vin·dic·tive (vin dik′tiv) *adj.* having, showing, or coming from a desire for revenge; vengeful. —**vin·dic′tive·ly,** *adv.* —**vin·dic′tive·ness,** *n.*

vine (vīn) *n.* **1.** a plant with a long, usually slender stem, that grows along the ground or attaches itself to a tree, wall, or other support and grows upward. **2.** a vine on which grapes grow; grapevine.

vin·e·gar (vin′ə gər) *n.* a sour liquid consisting chiefly of acetic acid, made by fermenting cider, wine, malt, or the like. It is used in flavoring or preserving food.

vin·e·gar·y (vin′ə gər ē) *adj.* **1.** of or like vinegar: *a vinegary taste.* **2.** bad-tempered.

vine·yard (vin′yərd) *n.* an area in which grapes are grown.

vin·tage (vin′tij) *n.* **1.** the wine produced from a particular crop of grapes. **2.** a year's crop of grapes. **3.** *Informal.* goods, articles, or items of some particular period or time: *a car of 1930 vintage.* —*adj.* of unusually high quality or merit; choice: *a vintage wine.*

vint·ner (vint′nər) *n.* a person who sells wines and liquors.

vi·nyl (vīn′əl) *n.* any of several flexible, shiny plastics used in floor tiles, raincoats, phonograph records, and many other products.

vi·ol (vī′əl) *n.* any of various stringed musical instruments that are similar to the violin and usually have six strings. Viols were used chiefly in the sixteenth and seventeenth centuries, and were later replaced by violins, violas, and the like.

vi·o·la (vē ō′lə) *n.* a stringed musical instrument of the violin family, slightly larger and lower in pitch than the violin.

vi·o·late (vī′ə lāt′) *v.t.*, **vi·o·lat·ed, vi·o·lat·ing.** **1.** to fail to obey or keep; break: *to violate a law, to violate a peace treaty, to violate a promise.* **2.** to treat disrespectfully; desecrate; defile: *to violate a church by using profane language.* **3.** to break in upon; interrupt; disturb: *to violate someone's privacy.* **4.** to rape. —**vi′o·la′tor,** *n.*

vi·o·la·tion (vī′ə lā′shən) *n.* **1.** the act of violating or the state of being violated: *a violation of a peace treaty.* **2.** an instance of violating: *The driver received a summons for a traffic violation.*

vi·o·lence (vī′ə ləns) *n.* **1.** strong physical force or roughness used to injure or harm: *The criminal used violence in robbing the storekeeper.* **2.** a violent or destructive action: *the violence of a hurricane.* **3.** harm or injury caused by violent action or treatment: *The townspeople suffered violence at the hands of the marauding soldiers.* **4.** intensity of feeling or emotion: *We were shocked by the violence of his outburst.*

vi·o·lent (vī′ə lənt) *adj.* **1.** acting with, characterized by, or resulting from strong physical force or roughness: *The crook met with a violent death.* **2.** caused by or showing intense feeling or emotion; passionate: *He has a violent temper.* **3.** characterized by great intensity or force; severe; extreme: *a violent whirlwind.* —**vi′o·lent·ly,** *adv.*

vi·o·let (vī′ə lit) *n.* **1.** a small purple, white, or rose-colored flower of a plant found in Europe, Africa, and Asia. **2.** the plant bearing this flower. **3.** a bluish-purple color. —*adj.* having the color violet.

vi·o·lin (vī′ə lin′) *n.* a musical instrument having four strings, played with a bow. It is the principal member of a family of stringed instruments that includes the viola and cello.

vi·o·lin·ist (vī′ə lin′ist) *n.* a person who plays the violin.

vi·ol·ist (vē ō′list) *n.* a person who plays the viola.

vi·o·lon·cel·list (vī′ə lən chel′ist) *n.* see **cellist.**

vi·o·lon·cel·lo (vī′ə lən chel′ō) *n. pl.*, **vi·o·lon·cel·los.** see **cello.**

VIP, V.I.P. *Informal.* very important person.

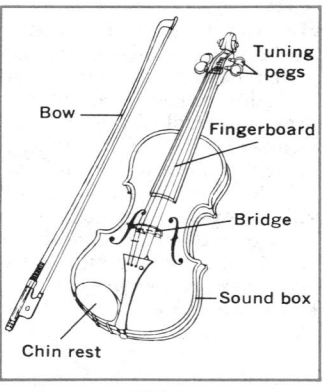

Tuning pegs
Bow
Fingerboard
Bridge
Sound box
Chin rest
Violin

vi·per (vī′pər) *n.* **1.** any of a group of poisonous snakes having a pair of sharp, hollow fangs through which venom is injected. **2.** a spiteful or treacherous person.

vi·per·ous (vī′pər əs) *adj.* **1.** of, like, or relating to a viper or vipers. **2.** spiteful or treacherous.

vi·ra·go (vi rā′gō) *n. pl.*, **vi·ra·goes** or **vi·ra·gos.** a bad-tempered, sharp-tongued woman.

vi·ral (vī′rəl) *adj.* of, relating to, or caused by a virus: *viral pneumonia.*

vir·e·o (vir′ē ō′) *n. pl.*, **vir·e·os.** any of various North American songbirds having green, yellow, brown, or gray feathers.

Vir·gil (vur′jəl) *also,* **Ver·gil.** 70–19 B.C., Roman poet.

vir·gin (vur′jin) *n.* **1.** a person, especially a girl or woman, who has never had sexual intercourse. **2. the Virgin.** the Virgin Mary. —*adj.* **1.** of, relating to, being, or suitable for a virgin. **2.** pure; spotless: *virgin snow.* **3.** not yet used; untouched: *virgin timber.*

vir·gin·al (vur′jən əl) *adj.* of, relating to, or suitable for a virgin.

Vir·gin·ia (vur jin′yə) *n.* a state in the eastern United States. Capital, Richmond. Area, 40,817 sq. mi. Pop. (1970), 4,648,494. Abbreviation, **Va.** —**Vir·gin′ian,** *adj., n.*

● **Virginia** was named by Queen Elizabeth I, who was known as the Virgin Queen because she was unmarried.

Virginia Beach, a resort city in southeastern Virginia, on the Atlantic Ocean. Pop. (1970), 172,106.

Virginia creeper, a North American climbing vine having dull, oval, toothed leaflets and clusters of tiny green flowers. Also, **woodbine.**

Virginia reel, an American folk dance in which partners form two lines facing each other and perform a variety of steps.

Virgin Islands, an island group in the West Indies, divided between the United States and Great Britain.

vir·gin·i·ty (vər jin′ə tē) *n.* the state or condition of being a virgin.

Virgin Mary, Mary, the mother of Jesus.

Virginia creeper

Vir·go (vur′gō) *n.* **1.** a constellation in the northern sky, thought to resemble a young girl holding a spike of wheat. **2.** the sixth sign of the zodiac.

vir·ile (vir′əl) *adj.* **1.** manly; masculine: *The actor had a deep, virile voice.* **2.** vigorous; forceful. **3.** capable of fathering children.

vi·ril·i·ty (vi ril′ə tē) *n.* the state or quality of being virile.

vi·rol·o·gy (vī rol′ə jē) *n.* the branch of microbiology that deals with viruses and the diseases caused by them.

vir·tu·al (vur′chōō əl) *adj.* being so in reality, though not in fact or name: *The king's illness left his eldest son the virtual ruler of the land.*

vir·tu·al·ly (vur′chōō ə lē) *adv.* in almost every way; practically: *Years of war had virtually destroyed the country.*

vir·tue (vur′chōō) *n.* **1.** moral excellence; righteousness; goodness. **2.** a particular type of moral excellence: *Honesty is his greatest virtue.* **3.** any good quality or trait of character: *He has the virtue of being a good listener.* **4.** chastity, especially of a woman. **5.** the power or strength to produce effects: *Innoculations have the virtue of preventing disease.* [Going back to Latin *virtūs* manliness, manhood, from *vir* man.]

  by virtue of. by or through the power or authority of; because of: *By virtue of her position, the judge made the final decision.*

vir·tu·os·i·ty (vur′chōō os′ə tē) *n. pl.,* **vir·tu·os·i·ties.** the skill, style, or art of a virtuoso.

vir·tu·o·so (vur′chōō ō′sō) *n. pl.,* **vir·tu·o·sos** or **vir·tu·o·si** (vur′chōō ō′sē). **1.** a person who is exceptionally skilled in one of the fine arts, especially in music. **2.** a person who is exceptionally skilled in any activity.

vir·tu·ous (vur′chōō əs) *adj.* **1.** characterized by or showing virtue; righteous; good: *a virtuous person, virtuous deeds.* **2.** chaste; pure. —**vir′tu·ous·ly,** *adv.* —**vir′tu·ous·ness,** *n.*

vir·u·lence (vir′yə ləns) *n.* the quality or state of being virulent.

vir·u·lent (vir′yə lənt) *adj.* **1.** extremely poisonous or harmful: *a virulent infection.* **2.** extremely bitter or spiteful; full of hostility and hate: *a virulent speech.* —**vir′u·lent·ly,** *adv.*

vi·rus (vī′rəs) *n. pl.,* **vi·rus·es.** any of a group of microorganisms that are smaller than any known bacteria and can reproduce and grow only in living tissue. Viruses cause many diseases in man, animals, and plants.

vi·sa (vē′zə) *n.* an official endorsement stamped on a person's passport by an official of a country, granting the holder of the passport permission to enter or leave the country.

vis·age (viz′ij) *n.* **1.** the face or facial expression of a person. **2.** the outward aspect or appearance of anything.

vis·cer·a (vis′ər ə) *n., pl.* the soft organs inside the body, such as the heart, stomach, liver, intestines, and kidneys.

vis·cer·al (vis′ər əl) *adj.* **1.** of or relating to the viscera. **2.** arising from or caused by deep emotions or feelings.

vis·cid (vis′id) *adj.* thick and gluey or sticky: *a viscid substance.*

vis·cos·i·ty (vis kos′ə tē) *n. pl.,* **vis·cos·i·ties.** the state or quality of being viscous.

vis·count (vī′kount′) *n.* in Great Britain and certain other countries, a nobleman who ranks just below an earl or count and just above a baron.

vis·count·ess (vī′koun′tis) *n. pl.,* **vis·count·ess·es.** **1.** the wife or widow of a viscount. **2.** a woman who holds a rank equal to that of a viscount in her own right.

vis·cous (vis′kəs) *adj.* (of a liquid) thick and gluey or sticky: *The oil used in the truck's engine was very viscous.*

vise (vīs) *also, British,* **vice.** *n.* a tool with two jaws that are opened and closed by turning a screw. It is used to hold an object firmly in place while it is being worked on.

Vish·nu (vish′nōō) *n.* one of the three chief divinities of Hinduism, believed to be the protector and preserver of mankind. He has been reincarnated many times, especially as Krishna.

Vise

vis·i·bil·i·ty (viz′ə bil′ə tē) *n. pl.,* **vis·i·bil·i·ties.** **1.** the state, condition, or quality of being visible. **2.** the distance that the eye can see when affected by physical conditions, such as light or weather: *Visibility is only a quarter of a mile today because of the fog.*

vis·i·ble (viz′ə bəl) *adj.* **1.** that can be seen; perceptible to the eye: *The house is visible from the road.* **2.** evident; apparent; obvious: *The young man had no visible means of livelihood.* —**vis′i·bly,** *adv.*

Vis·i·goth (viz′ə goth′) *n.* a member of the westernmost branch of the Goths that invaded the Roman Empire in the fourth century A.D. and settled in France and Spain.

vi·sion (vizh′ən) *n.* **1.** the act or power of seeing; sense of sight: *The man's vision weakened as he grew older.* **2.** something that is or has been seen, especially someone or something of great beauty: *The girl was a vision of loveliness in her new gown.* **3.** the ability to plan ahead; foresight: *a ruler of great vision.* **4.** something imagined; mental image: *The young writer had visions of success and fame.* **5.** a conception; view: *He has an unrealistic vision of the world.* **6.** something perceived in a dream, trance, or similar state: *The prophet had a vision of heaven.*

vi·sion·ar·y (vizh′ə ner′ē) *adj.* **1.** of, relating to, or seen in a vision: *the visionary splendors of paradise.* **2.** having visions: *a visionary saint.* **3.** having or characterized by impractical ideas or plans: *The visionary young man thought only of traveling to distant stars.* **4.** that cannot be put into practice; not practicable; unrealistic: *a visionary scheme.* —*n. pl.,* **vi·sion·ar·ies.** **1.** a person who has visions. **2.** a person whose ideas or plans are impractical.

vis·it (viz′it) *v.t.* **1.** to go to see (a person or persons) for social, business, or other reasons: *She visited her aunt last Sunday. Harry visited the dentist.* **2.** to go to (a place) for sightseeing: *The family visited Quebec last summer.* **3.** to stay with as a guest: *They visited friends for the weekend.* **4.** to go or come to see in an official or professional capacity: *The mayor will visit several of the city's jails tomorrow.* **5.** to come upon; afflict; assail: *A plague visited the country.* —*v.i.* **1.** to call on or stay with someone as a guest. **2.** *Informal.* to converse; chat. —*n.* the act or instance of visiting: *She paid a visit to her friend last night.*

vis·it·ant (viz′i tənt) *n.* a visitor, especially one thought to come from the spiritual world.

vis·it·a·tion (viz′i tā′shən) *n.* **1.** the act of visiting, especially an official visit for the purpose of inspection or examination. **2.** a punishment or reward sent by God.

visiting card, another term for **calling card.**

vis·i·tor (viz′i tər) *n.* a person who pays a visit.

---

at; āpe; cär; end; mē; it; īce; hot; ōld; fôrk; wood; fōōl; oil; out; up; turn; sing; thin; this; hw in white; zh in treasure. The symbol ə stands for the sound of **a** in about, **e** in taken, **i** in pencil, **o** in lemon, and **u** in circus.

vi·sor (vī′zər) *also,* **vi·zor.** *n.* **1.** the projecting brim on the front of a cap, designed to shade the eyes from the sun. **2.** in ancient armor, the movable front piece of a helmet that could be lowered to cover the upper part of the face. **3.** a projecting part usually attached above the windshield on the inside of an automobile, designed to shield the eyes from glare.

vis·ta (vis′tə) *n.* **1.** a view, especially one seen through an opening or passage: *a vista of a lake.* **2.** a mental view of a series of events: *new vistas of peace and prosperity.*

VISTA (vis′tə) a U.S. government program that recruits and trains volunteers to teach job skills to the poor. [An abbreviation of *V*(olunteers) *i*(n) *S*(ervice) *t*(o) *A*(merica).]

Vis·tu·la (vis′chə lə) *n.* a river in Poland flowing into the Baltic Sea.

vis·u·al (vizh′oō əl) *adj.* **1.** of, relating to, resulting from, or used in sight: *the visual sense, a visual nerve.* **2.** that can be seen; visible: *visual beauty.* **—vis′u·al·ly,** *adv.*

Visor

Visor (def. 2)

visual aid, any of various devices or materials involving the sense of sight, such as a chart, motion picture, or slide, used to aid or improve learning.

vis·u·al·ize (vizh′oō ə līz′) *v.t.,* **vis·u·al·ized, vis·u·al·iz·ing.** to form a mental image of: *The young mother tried to visualize what her children would look like when grown.* **—vis′u·al·i·za′tion,** *n.*

vi·tal (vīt′əl) *adj.* **1.** of, relating to, or characteristic of life: *vital forces, vital processes.* **2.** necessary to or supporting life: *the vital organs.* **3.** full of life and vigor; energetic: *a vital personality.* **4.** of greatest importance; essential: *His support is vital to the success of our project.* **5.** deadly; fatal: *a vital wound.* **—vi′tal·ly,** *adv.* **—vi′tal·ness,** *n.*

vi·tal·i·ty (vī tal′ə tē) *n. pl.,* **vi·tal·i·ties. 1.** mental or physical vigor or energy: *He is a man of great vitality.* **2.** the power to live or continue living. **3.** the power to endure, continue, or survive: *New industry was necessary to ensure the vitality of the small country.*

vi·tal·ize (vīt′əl īz′) *v.t.,* **vi·tal·ized, vi·tal·iz·ing. 1.** to put vitality or liveliness into. **2.** to give life to. **—vi′tal·i·za′tion,** *n.*

vi·tals (vīt′əlz) *n., pl.* **1.** the parts or organs of the body necessary or vital to life. **2.** the parts or features essential to the operation or existence of something.

vi·ta·min (vī′tə min) *n.* any of a group of organic compounds needed in very small amounts to maintain the health and normal functioning of the body.

vitamin A, any of a group of vitamins necessary for good vision at night, normal development of cells, and healthy skin. It is found in foods of animal origin, such as liver, whole milk, and eggs. A lack of vitamin A causes night blindness.

vitamin B₁, a vitamin necessary for the normal release of energy from carbohydrates. It is found in lean pork, beans, peas, and liver. A lack of vitamin B₁ causes beriberi. Also, **thiamine.**

vitamin B₂, a vitamin necessary for growth. It is found in liver, eggs, milk, and lean meats. Also, **riboflavin, vitamin G.**

vitamin B₆, a vitamin important in the utilization of protein in the body. It is found in whole-grain cereals, yeast, and liver. Also, **pyridoxine.**

vitamin B₁₂, a complex vitamin that contains cobalt and is necessary for the formation of blood cells and for growth. It is found especially in liver.

vitamin B complex, a group of vitamins found in yeast, liver, and other foods, including vitamin B₁ (thiamine), vitamin B₂ (riboflavin), vitamin B₆ (pyridoxine), vitamin B₁₂, vitamin H (biotin), niacin, and folic acid.

vitamin C, a vitamin compound that aids in the formation of connective tissues, increases resistance to infection, and prevents scurvy. It is found in citrus fruits and is made by man. A lack of vitamin C causes scurvy. Also, **ascorbic acid.**

vitamin D, any of several vitamins necessary for normal bone and tooth formation. It is found in fish-liver oils and is manufactured in the body by the action of sunlight on cholesterol. A lack of vitamin D causes rickets.

vitamin E, any of a group of vitamin compounds that may affect the reproductive system. It is found chiefly in green, leafy vegetables, cereal, grains, and certain vegetable oils.

vitamin G, another term for **vitamin B₂.**

vitamin H, a vitamin of the B complex necessary for metabolism and growth. Also, **biotin.**

vitamin K, any of a group of vitamins necessary for the clotting of blood. It is found chiefly in green, leafy vegetables and in tomatoes.

vi·ti·ate (vish′ē āt′) *v.t.,* **vi·ti·at·ed, vi·ti·at·ing. 1.** to impair the quality of; spoil: *The ugly, broken fence vitiated the beauty of the garden.* **2.** to make legally ineffective, such as a contract; invalidate. **—vi·ti·a′tion,** *n.*

vit·re·ous (vit′rē əs) *adj.* **1.** of, relating to, resembling, or of the nature of glass. **2.** made from glass: *vitreous china.* **3.** of or relating to the vitreous humor.

vitreous humor, the transparent, jellylike substance that fills the eyeball behind the lens.

vit·ri·fy (vit′rə fī′) *v.t., v.i.,* **vit·ri·fied, vit·ri·fy·ing.** to change into glass or a glassy substance.

vit·ri·ol (vit′rē əl) *n.* **1.** a sulfate of copper, iron, lead, or zinc. Copper sulfate is blue; iron sulfate is green; lead sulfate and zinc sulfate are white. **2.** another word for **sulfuric acid. 3.** something that is harsh, sharp, or bitter, such as speech or writing.

vit·ri·ol·ic (vit′rē ol′ik) *adj.* **1.** of, like, or derived from vitriol. **2.** very harsh, sharp, or bitter: *vitriolic language.*

vi·tu·per·ate (vī tōō′pə rāt′, vī tyōō′pə rāt′) *v.t.,* **vi·tu·per·at·ed, vi·tu·per·at·ing.** to speak harshly or abusively to or about; berate. **—vi·tu′per·a′tion,** *n.*

vi·tu·per·a·tive (vī tōō′pə rā′tiv, vī tyōō′pə rā′tiv) *adj.* harsh or abusive: *vituperative speech.* **—vi·tu′per·a′tive·ly,** *adv.*

vi·va (vē′və) *interj. Italian, Spanish.* (long) live (a person or thing named). ▲ used as a shout of acclaim.

vi·va·cious (vi vā′shəs, vī vā′shəs) *adj.* full of life; lively or gay; animated: *a vivacious girl, a vivacious personality.* **—vi·va′cious·ly,** *adv.* **—vi·va′cious·ness,** *n.*

vi·vac·i·ty (vi vas′ə tē, vī vas′ə tē) *n.* liveliness or gaiety; animation.

vive (vēv) *interj. French.* (long) live (a person or thing named). ▲ used as a shout of acclaim.

viv·id (viv′id) *adj.* **1.** (of colors) bright or intense; brilliant. **2.** clear and distinct; sharp: *I have a vivid recollection of the accident.* **3.** producing clear or lifelike images in the mind: *The writer gave a vivid description of the battle.* **4.** active; lively: *a vivid imagination.* **—viv′id·ly,** *adv.* **—viv′id·ness,** *n.*

viv·i·fy (viv′ə fī′) *v.t.,* **viv·i·fied, viv·i·fy·ing. 1.** to give life to; animate. **2.** to make vivid: *to vivify a room with bright colors.*

vi·vip·a·rous (vī vip′ər əs) *adj.* bringing forth living young, rather than eggs. Most mammals are viviparous.

viv·i·sect (viv′ə sekt′) *v.t.* to perform vivisection on (a living animal).

viv·i·sec·tion (viv′ə sek′shən) *n.* a surgical operation or other experiment performed on a living animal for the purpose of scientific study.

viv·i·sec·tion·ist (viv′ə sek′shə nist) *n.* a person who practices or supports vivisection.

vix·en (vik′sən) *n.* **1.** a female fox. **2.** an ill-tempered or quarrelsome woman.

viz., namely. [An abbreviation of Latin *vidēlicet*.]

vi·zier (vi zēr′) *also,* **vi·zir.** *n.* in Muslim countries, a high official of the government, especially a minister of state.

vi·zor (vī′zər) another spelling of **visor.**

Vlad·i·vos·tok (vlad′ə vos′tok) *n.* a port city in the southeasternmost part of the Soviet Union, on the Sea of Japan. Pop. (1970), 441,000.

vo·cab·u·lar·y (vō kab′yə ler′ē) *n. pl.,* **vo·cab·u·lar·ies.** **1.** all the words used or understood by a particular person or group, or used in a particular field of knowledge. **2.** a list of words or of words and phrases, usually arranged in alphabetical order and defined or translated. **3.** all the words of a language.

● The English **vocabulary** is one of the largest, if not the largest, of all languages. An unabridged dictionary may contain as many as 500,000 entries. If the words found in scientific, technical, legal, slang, and other specialized dictionaries are added to this number the total would probably be over 750,000. Many language scholars have estimated that the total would actually be nearer to one million words.

There are obviously more words in the English vocabulary than any one person could hope to learn, let alone use. It has been variously estimated that the average educated adult has a vocabulary of between 35,000 and 70,000 words. The variation in the estimates may be caused by the difference between a person's *working vocabulary,* which is made up of the words that he would normally use, and his *recognition vocabulary,* which is made up of those words that he can recognize but would not normally use. One language scholar has estimated that there are only about 20,000 words in full use in our modern English vocabulary. The vocabulary of the King James Bible has been estimated at less than 6,000 words. William Shakespeare's vocabulary has been estimated at somewhere between 16,000 and 25,000 words.

The range of any person's vocabulary depends greatly on his interests, background, profession, and education. By having a good vocabulary, a person can express himself clearly. The only way to develop such a vocabulary is to listen and read carefully. If you come across a word that is unfamiliar to you, looking it up in your dictionary will help you to make it part of your vocabulary. Approximately 65,000 entries have been included in this dictionary, in order to help you build your vocabulary.

vo·cal (vō′kəl) *adj.* **1.** of, relating to, or expressed by the voice. **2.** performed by or intended for the voice: *vocal music.* **3.** readily expressing one's views or opinions in speech: *He was vocal in his criticism.* —**vo′cal·ly,** *adv.*

vocal cords, either of two pairs of membranes in the larynx. The passage of air from the lungs through the lower pair causes them to vibrate, thus producing the sound of the voice.

vo·cal·ic (vō kal′ik) *adj.* **1.** consisting mainly or completely of vowel sounds. **2.** of, relating to, or resembling a vowel sound.

vo·cal·ist (vō′kə list) *n.* a singer.

vo·cal·ize (vō′kə līz′) *v.,* **vo·cal·ized, vo·cal·iz·ing.** —*v.t.* to make vocal; utter or express with the voice: *to vocalize an objection.* —*v.i.* to produce sound with the voice; sing or speak. —**vo′cal·i·za′tion,** *n.*

vo·ca·tion (vō kā′shən) *n.* **1.** an occupation or profession; trade. **2.** a strong desire to pursue a certain career. **3.** the work or career that a person feels called to do or is especially suited for.

vo·ca·tion·al (vō kā′shən əl) *adj.* **1.** of or relating to a vocation or occupation. **2.** of, relating to, or providing training or education in a skill, trade, or occupation, or guidance in choosing an occupation: *a vocational school, a vocational counselor.* —**vo·ca′tion·al·ly,** *adv.*

vo·cif·er·ous (vō sif′ər əs) *adj.* making or characterized by a loud outcry; clamorous: *a vociferous crowd, vociferous objections.* —**vo·cif′er·ous·ly,** *adv.* —**vo·cif′er·ous·ness,** *n.*

vod·ka (vod′kə) *n.* a colorless alcoholic liquor, originally made in Russia, distilled from fermenting grain or potatoes.

vogue (vōg) *n.* **1.** the accepted fashion at a particular time: *Short skirts were in vogue recently.* **2.** popular acceptance or favor; popularity: *Those books had a great vogue several years ago.*

voice (vois) *n.* **1.** sound produced through the mouth, especially sound produced by the vocal organs of a human being, as in speaking or singing. **2.** the ability to produce such sound: *A bad cold caused the singer to lose his voice.* **3.** the quality, condition, or tone of vocal sound: *a soft voice, a high-pitched voice.* **4.** a sound resembling or suggesting vocal utterance: *the voice of the wind, the voice of thunder.* **5.** something likened to human speech: *the voice of conscience.* **6.** the right or privilege of expressing an opinion, view, or choice: *The people must have a voice in city government.* **7.** an expressed opinion, choice, or wish: *A good public official listens to the voice of the people.* **8.** expression: *to give voice to one's feelings.* **9.** any of the vocal or instrumental parts in a musical composition. **10.** a singer. **11.** *Grammar.* a form of a verb that shows whether its subject is active or passive. —*v.t.,* **voiced, voic·ing. 1.** to give utterance to; express: *to voice an opinion, to voice an objection.* **2.** *Phonetics.* to utter (a speech sound) with vibration of the vocal cords.

with one voice. unanimously.

voice box, see **larynx.**

voiced (voist) *adj.* **1.** having a voice. **2.** expressed by the voice. **3.** *Phonetics.* uttered with vibration of the vocal cords: *B is a voiced consonant.*

voice·less (vois′lis) *adj.* **1.** having no voice; mute. **2.** *Phonetics.* not voiced: *P is a voiceless consonant.* —**voice′less·ly,** *adv.*

void (void) *adj.* **1.** having no legal force; not legally valid: *The contract was declared void by the court.* **2.** not occupied by or containing matter; empty: *void space.* **3.** lacking or devoid: *a statement void of meaning.* —*n.* **1.** empty space; vacuum: *the void of outer space.* **2.** a feeling of emptiness or loss: *Working at the hospital helped fill the void after her husband died.* —*v.t.* **1.** to make void or of no effect; cancel: *to void an agreement.* **2.** to empty or discharge. —**void′a·ble,** *adj.*

at; āpe; cär; end; mē; it; īce; hot; ōld; fôrk; wood; fool; oil; out; up; turn; sing; thin; this; hw in white; zh in treasure. The symbol ə stands for the sound of **a** in about, **e** in taken, **i** in pencil, **o** in lemon, and **u** in circus.

voile (voil) *n.* a lightweight, sheer fabric, usually made of cotton or wool, used for curtains, dresses, and other items.

vol., volume.

vol·a·tile (vol′ə til, vol′ət əl) *adj.* **1.** tending to change readily into vapor, especially at ordinary temperatures; evaporating quickly: *Alcohol is a volatile liquid.* **2.** tending to change easily; changeable: *a volatile temperament.* **3.** easily aroused or disturbed; unstable: *a volatile political situation.* —**vol′a·til′i·ty,** *n.*

vol·can·ic (vol kan′ik) *adj.* **1.** of, relating to, or characteristic of a volcano or volcanoes: *a volcanic eruption.* **2.** having or characterized by a volcano or volcanoes. **3.** produced by or discharged from a volcano: *volcanic rock.* **4.** violent; explosive: *She was frightened by his volcanic outburst of anger.*

vol·ca·no (vol kā′nō) *n. pl.,* **vol·ca·noes** or **vol·ca·nos. 1.** an opening in the surface of the earth through which molten rock, gases, and rock fragments are forced out. **2.** a cone-shaped hill or mountain around such an opening, built up by the material forced out. [Italian *volcano,* from Latin *Vulcānus* Vulcan, the god of fire.]

vole (vōl) *n.* any of various gray or brown rodents resembling mice or rats, having a large head, small round ears, and a short tail.

Vole

Vol·ga (vol′gə) *n.* a river in the European part of the Soviet Union, flowing into the Caspian Sea. It is the longest river in Europe.

Vol·go·grad (vol′gə grad′) *n.* a port city in the southwestern Soviet Union, on the Volga River, formerly known as Stalingrad. Pop. (1970 est.), 818,000.

vo·li·tion (vō lish′ən) *n.* an act or power of willing or deciding: *She left the house of her own volition.*

vol·ley (vol′ē) *n. pl.,* **vol·leys. 1.** the discharge of a number of weapons at one time. **2.** the stones, arrows, bullets, or other missiles so discharged. **3.** a burst or outburst of a number of things at once or in rapid succession: *The referee's decision met with a volley of protests.* **4.** *Tennis.* the return of a ball before it touches the ground. **5.** a sequence of hitting a ball back and forth over a net without interruption, as in tennis. —*v.i.,* **vol·leyed, vol·ley·ing. 1.** to be discharged in a volley. **2.** *Tennis.* to return the ball before it touches the ground. **3.** to hit the ball back and forth over the net, as in tennis.

vol·ley·ball (vol′ē bôl′) *n.* **1.** a game in which two teams placed in position on either side of a high net hit a large, light ball back and forth over the net with their hands, without letting it touch the ground. **2.** the ball used in this game.

volt (vōlt) *n.* a unit for measuring the force that makes electrons move in an electric current. One volt causes a current of one ampere to flow through a resistance of one ohm. [From Alessandro *Volta.*]

Vol·ta, A·les·san·dro (vōl′tə; ä′le sän′drō) 1745–1827, Italian physicist.

vol·tage (vōl′tij) *n.* electromotive force expressed in volts.

vol·ta·ic cell (vol tā′ik) a simple unit that produces electricity through the chemical action of two plates or rods of different metals in an electrolyte.

Vol·taire (vol ter′, vōl ter′) 1694–1778, French philosopher and writer.

volt·me·ter (vōlt′mē′tər) *n.* an instrument for measuring the voltage between two points in an electric circuit.

vol·u·ble (vol′yə bəl) *adj.* speaking much and with a smooth, easy flow of words; fluent; talkative. —**vol′u·bil′i·ty,** *n.* —**vol′u·bly,** *adv.*

vol·ume (vol′yōōm) *n.* **1.** a collection of written or printed pages bound together; book. **2.** one of a set or series of related books: *the fourth volume of an encyclopedia.* **3.** a number of issues of a magazine or newspaper, usually all the issues that are published in one year. **4.** the amount of space occupied in three dimensions, measured in cubic units: *the volume of the liquid in a container.* **5.** an amount or quantity: *The volume of business fell off during the summer months.* **6.** the quantity or intensity of sound; loudness: *Please turn down the volume of the radio.*

vol·u·met·ric (vol′yə met′rik) *adj.* of or relating to measurement by volume.

vo·lu·mi·nous (və lōō′mə nəs) *adj.* **1.** of great size or bulk; large: *the voluminous sails of a large ship.* **2.** forming or filling a large volume or many volumes: *the voluminous works of Dickens.* —**vo·lu′mi·nous·ly,** *adv.*

vol·un·tar·y (vol′ən ter′ē) *adj.* **1.** performed, done, or made of one's own free will: *The accused man made a voluntary confession of his crime.* **2.** doing something of one's own free will, often without pay: *voluntary workers in a hospital.* **3.** controlled by the will: *voluntary muscles.* **4.** done on purpose; not accidental: *voluntary manslaughter. He told a voluntary lie.* **5.** supported by private contributions rather than by public funds: *a voluntary hospital.* —**vol·un·tar·i·ly** (vol′ən ter′ə lē), *adv.*

vol·un·teer (vol′ən tēr′) *n.* **1.** a person who offers his services or does something of his own free will, often without pay: *The campaign staff consisted chiefly of volunteers. The lieutenant asked for volunteers for the dangerous mission.* **2.** a person who enters military service of his own free will, rather than as a result of being drafted. —*v.i.* to serve or offer one's services of one's own free will: *Robert volunteered for the army.* —*v.t.* to give or offer readily: *He volunteered an answer to the question.* —*adj.* **1.** of, relating to, or consisting of volunteers: *a volunteer army.* **2.** serving as a volunteer: *a volunteer fireman.*

vo·lup·tu·ar·y (və lup′chōō er′ē) *n. pl.,* **vo·lup·tu·ar·ies.** a person who indulges in sensual or luxurious pleasures.

vo·lup·tu·ous (və lup′chōō əs) *adj.* **1.** having a full and shapely form: *a voluptuous woman.* **2.** giving or characterized by sensual pleasure or luxury. —**vo·lup′tu·ous·ly,** *adv.* —**vo·lup′tu·ous·ness,** *n.*

vom·it (vom′it) *v.i.* **1.** to force out the contents of the stomach through the mouth; throw up. **2.** to be thrown out with force: *Cinder and ash vomited out of the chimney.* —*v.t.* **1.** to force out (the contents of the stomach) through the mouth. **2.** to throw out or discharge in large quantities or with force; spew: *The volcano vomited forth lava.* —*n.* the matter forced out in vomiting.

voo·doo (vōō′dōō) *n. pl.,* **voo·doos. 1.** a set of mysterious religious rites characterized by a belief in sorcery and the power of charms. It originated in West Africa and is still practiced in the West Indies. **2.** a person who practices these rites. —*adj.* of or relating to voodoo.

voo·doo·ism (vōō′dōō iz′əm) *n.* the beliefs and practices of voodoo.

vo·ra·cious (və rā′shəs) *adj.* **1.** eating or craving large amounts of food; ravenous: *a voracious animal, a voracious appetite.* **2.** unable to be satisfied in some activity: *a voracious reader.* —**vo·ra′cious·ly,** *adv.* —**vo·rac′i·ty,** *n.*

vor·tex (vôr′teks) *n. pl.,* **vor·tex·es** or **vor·ti·ces** (vôr′tə sēz′). a whirling mass, as of water or air, moving in a circle or spiral, that sucks nearby objects into its center; whirlpool or whirlwind.

vo·ta·ress (vō′tə ris) *n. pl.,* **vo·ta·ress·es.** a female votary.

vo·ta·ry (vō′tər ē) *n. pl.,* **vo·ta·ries. 1.** a person bound by a vow or vows, especially a monk, nun, or other person in religious life. **2.** a person devoted to a particular pastime, study, or activity; devotee: *He is a votary of tennis.*

vote (vōt) *n.* **1.** the formal expression of a wish or choice, in some matter to be decided: *Each citizen has one vote in the election for President.* **2.** the means by which such a choice is expressed, such as a ballot or show of hands. **3.** a choice or decision so made: *The Senate vote was in favor of the bill.* **4.** the right or privilege of expressing such a choice; suffrage: *The nineteenth amendment to the Constitution gave women the vote.* **5.** the number of votes cast: *The vote was light in the election.* **6.** a group of votes or voters considered together: *the labor vote.* —*v.,* **vot·ed, vot·ing.** —*v.i.* to express one's opinion or choice by a vote; cast a vote: *His father always votes for the Democratic candidate.* —*v.t.* **1.** to support or choose by a vote; cast a vote for: *to vote the Republican ticket.* **2.** to grant or establish by a vote: *Congress voted the necessary funds for the project.* **3.** to declare: *The critics voted the show a success.* —**vot′er,** *n.*
  to vote down. to defeat by voting: *The committee voted down the proposal.*
  to vote in. to elect: *The candidate was voted in by a small margin.*

vo·tive (vō′tiv) *adj.* given, offered, or performed in fulfillment of a vow: *a votive offering.*

vouch (vouch) *v.i.* **1.** to give one's word or assurance: *I can vouch for her honesty.* **2.** to serve as a guarantee: *These papers will vouch for my identity.*

vouch·er (vou′chər) *n.* **1.** a document, such as a canceled check or receipt, that serves as proof of payment. **2.** a person who vouches.

vouch·safe (vouch sāf′) *v.t.,* **vouch·safed, vouch·saf·ing.** to be kind enough to grant; deign: *The king vouchsafed a greeting to the poor farmers.*

vow (vou) *n.* a solemn promise or pledge: *marriage vows. The prince made a vow to avenge his father's murder.* —*v.t.* to promise or pledge solemnly: *to vow revenge, to vow loyalty.* —*v.i.* to make a vow.

vow·el (vou′əl) *n.* **1.** a voiced speech sound produced by not blocking the passage of air through the mouth, and forming a syllable or part of a syllable. **2.** a letter of the alphabet that represents such a sound, such as *a, e, i, o, u* and sometimes *y.* —*adj.* of or relating to a vowel or vowels.

voy·age (voi′ij) *n.* **1.** a journey by water, usually one over the sea or other large body of water. **2.** any long journey: *a voyage to the moon.* —*v.i.,* **voy·aged, voy·ag·ing.** to make a voyage; go on a journey: *The group of explorers voyaged across the ocean.* —**voy′a·ger,** *n.*

V.P., vice-president.

vs., versus.

v.t., transitive verb.

Vt., Vermont.

Vul·can (vul′kən) *n.,* *Roman Mythology.* the god of fire and of metalworking.

vul·can·ite (vul′kə nīt′) *n.* a hard, tough rubber that resembles ebony, used for such items as combs and toys.

vul·can·ize (vul′kə nīz′) *v.t.,* **vul·can·ized, vul·can·iz·ing.** to treat (rubber) with sulfur or other compounds and heat, in order to increase its strength and elasticity. [From *Vulcan.*] —**vul′can·i·za′tion,** *n.*

vul·gar (vul′gər) *adj.* **1.** showing or characterized by a lack of good breeding, refinement, or taste: *a vulgar joke.* **2.** of, relating to, or characteristic of the common people. —**vul′gar·ly,** *adv.*

vul·gar·ism (vul′gə riz′əm) *n.* a word, phrase, or expression that is used mostly by people without education, and is not considered acceptable in standard usage.

vul·gar·i·ty (vul gar′ə tē) *n. pl.,* **vul·gar·i·ties. 1.** the state or quality of being vulgar; lack of good breeding, refinement, or taste. **2.** something that is vulgar, such as an offensive action or expression.

vul·gar·ize (vul′gə rīz′) *v.t.,* **vul·gar·ized, vul·gar·iz·ing. 1.** to make coarse or crude. **2.** to express (something difficult) in a form that the common people can understand; popularize: *The writer of the magazine article vulgarized recent discoveries in astronomy.*

Vulgar Latin, a vernacular form of ancient Latin, the main source of the Romance languages.

Vul·gate (vul′gāt) *n.* the Latin version of the Bible, translated by St. Jerome and completed about A.D. 383. The Vulgate is the official Bible of the Roman Catholic Church and the basis of other translations.

vul·ner·a·ble (vul′nər ə bəl) *adj.* **1.** capable of being physically wounded or damaged; easily hurt: *The athlete's injured knee was his most vulnerable spot.* **2.** capable of being hurt emotionally; sensitive: *The shy boy was very vulnerable to criticism.* **3.** open to attack; not sufficiently protected: *a vulnerable army outpost.* —**vul′ner·a·bil′i·ty,** *n.* —**vul′ner·a·bly,** *adv.*

vul·pine (vul′pīn′) *adj.* of, relating to, or like a fox.

vul·ture (vul′chər) *n.* **1.** any of several large birds having dark, dull feathers and a bald head and neck. Vultures feed chiefly on dead animals. **2.** a greedy, ruthless person.

vul·va (vul′və) *n. pl.,* **vul·vae** (vul′vē) or **vul·vas.** the external parts of the female genital organs.

Vulture

vy·ing (vī′ing) the present participle of **vie.**

---

at; āpe; cär; end; mē; it; īce; hot; ōld; fôrk; wood; fŏŏl; oil; out; up; turn; sing; thin; this; hw in white; zh in treasure. The symbol ə stands for the sound of **a** in about, **e** in taken, **i** in pencil, **o** in lemon, and **u** in circus.

V

1. Semitic Y	4. Etruscan V
2. Phoenician Y	5. Early Latin V
3. Greek Ninth Century B.C. Y	6. English W

W is the twenty-third letter of the English alphabet. It is one of only three letters that we use today that did not come from Latin or from an earlier alphabet. Because **W** developed as a variation of the letter **V,** they can be said to share the same early history. Their earliest ancestor was the ancient Semitic letter *waw* (1), that depicted a hook and stood for the *w* sound, as the *w* in *water.* When the Phoenicians (2) borrowed *waw,* they used it to represent both the consonant sound *w* and the vowel sound *u,* as the *u* in *rude.* The Greeks adapted *waw* and called it *upsilon* (3), writing it as the capital letter **Y** is written today. *Upsilon,* which stood for only the *u* sound, was borrowed by the Etruscans (4) who, like the Phoenicians, used it to represent both the vowel and consonant sounds. The shape of *upsilon* was also altered by the Etruscans, who wrote it as we write the capital letter **V** today. The design and pronunciation of this letter were adopted without change in the Latin alphabet (5). By about 1000 years ago, two forms of this V-shaped letter were being used in writing: **V** at the beginning of a word and a new letter, **U,** in the middle of a word. At about the same time that **U** and **V** became distinct letters, **V** began to be used to stand for only the *v* sound. With this change in the pronunciation of **V,** there was no longer a letter in the alphabet that represented the *w* sound. At first, the problem was solved by writing two **V's** or two **U's.** Norman scribes soon combined these pairs of letters into a new letter that, because of the way it had previously been written, was called "double U." This new letter was written almost exactly the way we write the capital letter **W** today (6).

Because it was not used in Greek or Latin, there are very few scientific or technical words in English that begin with **W.** Most of our words that begin with **W,** such as "water," "wide," "what," and "wheel," come from the everyday words that were used in Old English, a language in which the *w* sound was very common.

w, W (dub′əl yōō′) *n. pl.,* **w's, W's. 1.** the twenty-third letter of the English alphabet. **2.** something having the shape of this letter.

w. 1. week. **2.** width. **3.** weight.

W 1. the symbol for tungsten. [German *Wolfram.*] **2.** West. **3.** Western.

W. 1. Wednesday. **2.** Wales. **3.** Welsh.

Wa·bash (wô′bash) *n.* a river in the north-central United States, flowing from western Ohio into Indiana.

wab·ble (wob′əl) *n., v.t., v.i.,* **wab·bled, wab·bling.** another spelling of **wobble.**

Wac (wak) *n.* a member of the Women's Army Corps.

WAC, Women's Army Corps.

wack·y (wak′ē) *also,* **whack·y.** *adj.,* **wack·i·er, wack·i·est.** *Slang.* strange or crazy, especially in a silly way.

Wa·co (wā′kō) *n.* a city in east-central Texas. Pop. (1970), 95,326.

wad (wod) *n.* **1.** a small, tightly packed mass or lump of soft material: *a wad of cotton, a wad of chewing gum, a wad of paper.* **2.** *Informal.* a tight roll of paper money, especially a large amount of money. —*v.t.,* **wad·ded, wad·ding. 1.** to roll, press, or pack into a wad. **2.** to stuff, pad, or pack with wadding.

wad·ding (wod′ing) *n.* a soft material used for stuffing, padding, or packing.

wad·dle (wod′əl) *v.i.,* **wad·dled, wad·dling.** to walk or move with short steps, swaying the body from side to side: *The duck waddled across the yard.* —*n.* a swaying or rocking walk. —**wad′dler,** *n.*

wade (wād) *v.,* **wad·ed, wad·ing.** —*v.i.* **1.** to walk in or through water, mud, or the like: *We waded across the creek.* **2.** to move or make one's way slowly and with difficulty: *He had to wade through a pile of papers to find the missing letter.* —*v.t.* to walk through or cross by wading: *to wade a brook.* —*n.* the act of wading.

to wade in or **to wade into.** *Informal.* to attack, approach, or begin with energy and enthusiasm.

wad·er (wā′dər) *n.* **1.** a person who wades. **2.** any of various long-legged birds that wade about in shallow water searching for food, such as the crane, heron, or stork. **3. waders.** high, waterproof boots, or a pair of pants having such boots attached, worn especially by fishermen when wading in water.

wa·di (wä′dē) *n. pl.,* **wa·dis. 1.** a ravine in the deserts of Africa or Asia, through which a stream flows after a rainfall. **2.** a stream flowing through such a ravine.

Waf (waf) *n.* a member of the Women's Air Force.
WAF, Women's Air Force.

wa·fer (wā′fər) *n.* **1.** a thin, crisp cookie or cracker, often sweetened and flavored. **2.** a thin disk of unleavened bread given as Holy Communion in the Roman Catholic and other churches. **3.** any thin disk, as of chocolate. **4.** a small, thin disk of paper or dried paste used for sealing letters, fastening documents, or the like.

waf·fle (wof′əl) *n.* a crisp batter cake having a surface patterned with square-shaped indentations, usually cooked in a waffle iron.

waffle iron, a cooking utensil consisting of two hinged metal plates with square-shaped projections, used to make waffles.

waft (waft) *v.i.* to float or be carried through the air or over water: *The smell of freshly brewed coffee wafted through the door.* —*v.t.* to carry lightly and gently through the air or over water. —*n.* **1.** a light breeze; current of air. **2.** something, such as an odor, carried through the air: *a waft of burning leaves.*

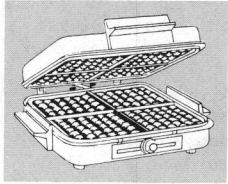

Waffle iron

wag[1] (wag) *v.,* **wagged, wag·ging.** —*v.t.* to cause to move rapidly and repeatedly up and down or from side to side: *The friendly dog wagged its tail at the visitors.* —*v.i.* to move rapidly and repeatedly up and down or from side to side. —*n.* the act of wagging; wagging motion. [Middle English *waggen.*]

wag[2] (wag) *n.* a person who jokes and jests. [Of uncertain origin.]

wage (wāj) *n.* **1.** *usually,* **wages.** payment for work done or services given. **2.** **wages.** something given in return: *For the wages of sin is death* (Romans 6:23). —*v.t.,* **waged, wag·ing.** to carry on or engage in: *to wage a war against crime.*

wage earner, a person who works for wages.

wa·ger (wā′jər) *n.* **1.** an agreement or promise to give or pay something to another person if he is right about something and you are wrong; bet. **2.** something pledged or bet. —*v.t.* to pledge or risk in a wager; bet. —*v.i.* to make a wager; bet. —**wa′ger·er,** *n.*

wag·ger·y (wag′ər ē) *n. pl.,* **wag·ger·ies. 1.** mischievous merrymaking. **2.** a jest or joke.

wag·gish (wag′ish) *adj.* **1.** fond of playing jokes. **2.** of, relating to, or characteristic of a wag or waggery: *The mischievous young boy has a waggish sense of humor.* —**wag′gish·ly,** *adv.* —**wag′gish·ness,** *n.*

wag·gle (wag′əl) *v.t., v.i.,* **wag·gled. wag·gling.** to move or cause to move rapidly and repeatedly up and down or from side to side; wag. —*n.* the act of waggling; waggling motion.

Wag·ner, Richard (väg′nər) 1813–1883, German composer.

wag·on (wag′ən) *n.* **1.** any of various four-wheeled vehicles, usually drawn by a horse or horses, used especially for carrying heavy loads. **2.** a child's low, rectangular, four-wheeled vehicle. **3.** a light truck used for carrying small loads: *a milk wagon, a delivery wagon.* **4.** see **station wagon. 5.** see **patrol wagon.**

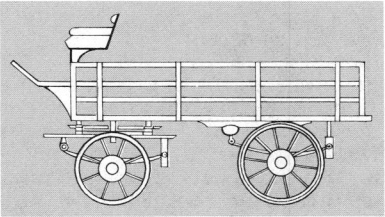

Wagon

on the wagon. *Informal.* no longer drinking alcoholic beverages.

wag·on·er (wag′ə nər) *n.* a person who drives a wagon.

wag·on·load (wag′ən lōd′) *n.* the amount that a wagon carries.

wagon train, a line or group of covered wagons traveling together.

waif (wāf) *n.* **1.** a person having no home, family, or friends, especially a lost child. **2.** anything that is without a home, such as a stray animal.

wail (wāl) *v.i.* **1.** to make a long, mournful cry, especially as an expression of grief or pain: *The baby wailed in her room.* **2.** to make a sound resembling this. —*v.t.* to grieve over; bewail. —*n.* **1.** a long, mournful cry. **2.** any sound resembling this. —**wail′er,** *n.*

wain (wān) *n. Archaic.* a wagon.

wain·scot (wān′skət, wān′skōt) *n.* a wood lining for inside walls, especially a paneled lining on the lower part of a wall. —*v.t.,* **wain·scot·ed, wain·scot·ing;** *also, British,* **wain·scot·ted, wain·scot·ting.** to line with wainscot.

wain·scot·ing (wān′skō′ting) *n.* **1.** another word for **wainscot. 2.** the material used for a wainscot.

waist (wāst) *n.* **1.** the part of the human body between the ribs and the hips. **2.** a garment or part of a garment that covers this part of the body. **3.** the middle, narrow part of anything, such as the middle part of a violin or bell.

waist·band (wāst′band′) *n.* a band of material that encircles the waist, especially one that is attached to the top of a skirt or trousers.

waist·coat (wes′kət, wāst′kōt′) *n.* another word for **vest.**

waist·line (wāst′līn′) *n.* **1.** an imaginary line encircling the narrowest part of the waist. **2.** the part of a garment that encircles this part of the body or falls just above or below it.

wait (wāt) *v.i.* **1.** to remain in a place so as to be ready for something or because something is expected: *Wait until you hear from me before leaving. I had to wait for twenty minutes for the bus this morning.* **2.** to look forward to something: *The wife waited for the day when her husband would be home from the army.* **3.** to be delayed: *Dinner will have to wait until the meat is done.* **4.** to perform the work of a waiter, waitress, or the like. —*v.t.* **1.** to remain in a place so as to be ready for (something): *He waited his turn patiently.* **2.** *Informal.* to put off; delay: *We cannot wait dinner after 8:00.* —*n.* **1.** the act of waiting. **2.** a period of waiting: *There will be a two-hour wait before the next plane.*

to lie in wait. to remain in hiding in order to attack.

to wait on or **to wait upon a.** to serve or help: *There were no clerks to wait on us at the store.* **b.** to visit formally: *The prime minister waited on the queen.*

wait·er (wā′tər) *n.* **1.** a man whose job is serving food and drink, as in a restaurant. **2.** a person who waits.

wait·ing (wā′ting) *n.* the act of a person who waits.

in waiting. in attendance to a king, queen, or other member of a royal family.

waiting list, a list of the names of people who are waiting for something: *There is a long waiting list for apartments in the new building.*

at; āpe; cär; end; mē; it; īce; hot; ōld; fôrk; wood; fōol; oil; out; up; turn; sing; thin; this; hw in white; zh in treasure. The symbol ə stands for the sound of **a** in about, **e** in taken, **i** in pencil, **o** in lemon, and **u** in circus.

waiting room, a room or area provided for the use of people who are waiting, as at an airport or doctor's office.

wait·ress (wā′tris) *n. pl.,* **wait·ress·es.** a woman whose job is serving food and drink, as in a restaurant.

waive (wāv) *v.t.,* **waived, waiv·ing. 1.** to give up voluntarily: *to waive a right, to waive a privilege.* **2.** to put aside for the present; defer: *to waive a question.*

waiv·er (wā′vər) *n.* **1.** the voluntary giving up of something, as a legal right. **2.** a document that states this.

wake¹ (wāk) *v.,* **waked** or **woke, waked** or *(archaic)* **wo·ken, wak·ing.** —*v.i.* **1.** to stop sleeping: *He woke up at the sound of the alarm.* **2.** to become aware, active, or aroused: *He woke to the beauty around him. The townspeople woke to their responsibilities.* **3.** to be or remain awake: *Coffee helps him wake up in the evening.* —*v.t.* **1.** to rouse from sleep: *Be quiet or you'll wake the baby.* **2.** to make active or aroused; stir up: *The news report waked the people to the danger.* —*n.* a watch or vigil over the body of a dead person before burial. [Old English *wacian* to be awake and *wacan* to awake.]

wake² (wāk) *n.* **1.** the track left by a boat, ship, or other object moving through water. **2.** a track or path left by anything that has passed: *the wake of a storm.* [Of Scandinavian origin.]

　in the wake of. following close behind: *The ducklings followed in the wake of their mother.*

wake·ful (wāk′fəl) *adj.* **1.** unable to sleep: *The hurricane blowing outside kept him wakeful.* **2.** without sleep: *The sick child spent a wakeful night.* **3.** watchful; vigilant. —**wake′ful·ness,** *n.*

Wake Island (wāk) a small island in the Pacific Ocean, west of Hawaii, administered by the United States.

wak·en (wā′kən) *v.t.* **1.** to stop from sleeping; wake. **2.** to make active or aroused; stir up: *His book wakened new interest in conservation.* —*v.i.* to stop sleeping: *He wakened when the alarm sounded.*

wale (wāl) *n.* **1.** one of a series of ridges or ribs on the surface of certain fabrics, such as corduroy. **2.** one of several thick planks fastened horizontally to the sides of a boat or ship. **3.** a raised mark on the skin, such as one made by the lash of a whip; welt. —*v.t.,* **waled, wal·ing.** to raise a wale or wales on, as by whipping.

Wales (wālz) *n.* a division of the United Kingdom, west of and bordering England. Area, 8017 sq. mi. Pop. (1971), 2,723,596.

walk (wôk) *v.i.* **1.** to move or proceed at a fairly slow pace, by placing one foot on the ground before lifting the other. **2.** to move or travel on foot for exercise or for pleasure: *We walk after dinner almost every night.* **3.** to move in a way that resembles walking: *The toy duck walked across the floor.* **4.** to behave or live in a particular manner: *to walk in peace.* **5.** *Baseball.* (of a batter) to go to first base as a result of having been pitched four balls. —*v.t.* **1.** to move through, over, or across on foot: *The friends walked the boardwalk after swimming.* **2.** to go with on foot: *I'll walk you to the door.* **3.** to make or help to walk: *to walk a dog, to walk a horse.* **4.** *Baseball.* (of a pitcher) to allow (a batter) to advance to first base by pitching four balls. —*n.* **1.** the act of walking, especially for exercise or for pleasure. **2.** the distance to be walked, often measured in the time required: *The beach is only a ten-minute walk from here.* **3.** a manner of walking: *She has a fast, bouncy walk.* **4.** a place set apart for walking: *The walk was covered with leaves.* **5.** a particular social position or profession: *People from all walks of life live in this neighborhood.* **6.** *Baseball.* the act or fact of allowing a batter to advance to first base by pitching four balls to him.

　to walk off with. a. to win, as a prize. **b.** to steal.

　to walk out. *Informal.* to go on strike: *The workers threatened to walk out on Monday morning.*

　to walk out on. *Informal.* to abandon; desert.

walk·er (wô′kər) *n.* **1.** a person or thing that walks. **2.** something used to help a person walk, especially an enclosed metal framework on wheels.

walk·ie-talk·ie (wô′kē tô′kē) *n. pl.,* **walk·ie-talk·ies.** a small, portable, two-way radio.

walking stick 1. a stick or cane carried in the hand as an aid in walking or hiking. **2.** any of a group of brown or green insects related to the grasshopper, having long legs and a slender body that resembles a stick or twig.

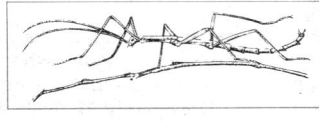

Walking stick

walk-on (wôk′ôn′, wôk′on′) *n.* a very small part in a theatrical presentation.

walk·out (wôk′out′) *n. Informal.* a strike of workers.

walk·o·ver (wôk′ō′vər) *n. Informal.* an easy victory.

walk-up (wôk′up′) *n.* **1.** an apartment or office above the first floor in a building having no elevator. **2.** an apartment house or building having no elevator.

walk·way (wôk′wā′) *n.* a place or passage set apart for walking.

wall (wôl) *n.* **1.** an upright structure of stone, plaster, wood, brick, or similar material, that forms the side of a building or room, or that divides or protects an area. **2.** the side or inner surface of something, such as a part of the body; lining: *the wall of the stomach.* **3.** something that resembles or acts as a wall: *a wall of fire, a wall of anger.* —*v.t.* to form the side of, divide, protect, or block with a wall or walls: *to wall in a courtyard, to wall off a bedroom in an attic, to wall up an old entrance.*

wal·la·by (wol′ə bē) *n. pl.,* **wal·la·bies** or **wal·la·by.** any of various animals that resemble kangaroos and live in Australia and New Zealand.

wall·board (wôl′bôrd′) *n.* a building material made of wood pulp or a similar substance pressed into large sheets, used instead of wood or plaster to cover walls or ceilings.

Wallaby

wal·let (wol′it, wô′lit) *n.* a flat folding case, usually of leather, used for holding money, cards, photographs, and the like.

wall·eye (wôl′ī′) *n.* **1.** an eye that turns outward away from the nose. **2.** an eye whose cornea is opaque or whose iris has little or no color. **3.** a large staring eye, as that of certain fish. **4.** a freshwater fish found in lakes and streams of eastern North America. Walleyes have large, staring eyes, and are caught for food and sport. Also *(def. 4),* **walleyed pike.**

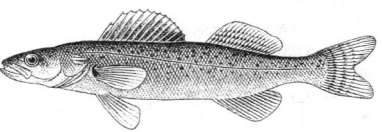

Walleye *(def. 4)*

wall·eyed (wôl′īd′) *adj.* having walleyes.

walleyed pike, see **walleye** *(def. 4).*

wall·flow·er (wôl′flou′ər) *n.* **1.** *Informal.* a person, especially a girl or woman, who does not take part in a dance or party, usually because of shyness or unpopularity. **2.** a plant that bears dense clusters of fragrant yellow or orange flowers.

Wal·loon (wo lōōn′) *n.* **1.** a member of a people living in central and southern Belgium. **2.** the language of this people, a dialect of French.

wal·lop (wol′əp) *Informal. v.t.* **1.** to give a beating to; thrash: *His father walloped him for misbehaving.* **2.** to hit hard; smack; sock: *The batter walloped the ball over the fence.* **3.** to overcome, as in a contest; defeat easily. —*n.* **1.** a forceful blow. **2.** the power to deliver such a blow: *The champion boxer has tremendous wallop in his left fist.*

wal·low (wol′ō) *v.i.* **1.** to toss or roll about in something: *Pigs wallow in mud. The children wallowed in the pile of leaves.* **2.** to take great pleasure; revel: *to wallow in self-pity.* **3.** to have a great amount of something: *He is wallowing in money.* —*n.* **1.** the act of wallowing. **2.** a place where an animal, such as a pig, goes to wallow.

wall·pa·per (wôl′pā′pər) *n.* decorative paper used to cover inside walls. —*v.t.* to put wallpaper on the walls of: *to wallpaper the kitchen.*

Wall Street 1. a street in New York City, near the southern tip of Manhattan, that is the financial center of the United States. **2.** the banks and financiers who control or influence the economy of the United States.

wal·nut (wôl′nut′) *n.* **1.** a sweet, oily nut. **2.** the tree that produces this nut. **3.** the wood of a walnut tree.

wal·rus (wôl′rəs, wol′rəs) *n. pl.,* **wal·rus·es** or **wal·rus.** a large animal that lives in water in the Arctic regions. The walrus resembles but is larger than a seal, and has a thick neck, a pair of long ivory tusks, and a tough hide. Also, **sea horse.**

Walrus

waltz (wôlts) *n., pl.* **waltz·es. 1.** a graceful dance in triple time having an accent on the first beat, performed by couples who whirl and glide across the dance floor. **2.** the music for this dance. —*v.i.* **1.** to dance a waltz. **2.** to move in a lively and confident manner, as if dancing: *She waltzed out of the room.* —*v.t.* to lead in a waltz: *He waltzed her about the dance floor.* —**waltz′er,** *n.*

wam·pum (wom′pəm, wôm′pəm) *n.* **1.** small, polished beads made from shells and strung together or woven into belts, collars, or necklaces. It was used by certain tribes of North American Indians as money. **2.** *Slang.* money. [Short for Algonquian *wampompeag* literally, white strings of money.]

wan (won) *adj.,* **wan·ner, wan·nest. 1.** not having a natural or healthy color; pale: *a wan complexion.* **2.** showing illness or weariness; weak: *a wan smile.* —**wan′ly,** *adv.* —**wan′ness,** *n.*

wand (wond) *n.* **1.** a slender rod, especially a rod used by a magician. **2.** a short staff used as a symbol of office or authority.

wan·der (won′dər) *v.i.* **1.** to go or move about aimlessly; roam: *We wandered all over the countryside.* **2.** to go at a slow, relaxed pace; stroll: *He wandered home.* **3.** to lose one's way or go astray: *The small child wandered off in the store.* **4.** to become easily distracted from the matter at hand: *The speaker wandered off the subject.* —*v.t.* to go or move about aimlessly: *The tramp wandered the streets.* —**wan′der·er,** *n.*

wan·der·lust (won′dər lust′) *n.* a strong urge to travel, especially in a slow, relaxed manner with no fixed destination.

wane (wān) *v.i.,* **waned, wan·ing. 1.** to become less or smaller, as in size, brightness, or strength: *The moon waned. Her love for him waned.* **2.** to become less, as in

power, importance, or influence. **3.** to draw to a close: *The day waned.* —*n.* **1.** the act of waning; becoming smaller or less. **2.** the period of waning.

wan·gle (wang′gəl) *v.,* **wan·gled, wan·gling.** *Informal.* —*v.t.* to bring about or get through cleverness, trickery, or deceit: *He wangled an invitation to the banquet.* —*v.i.* to use cleverness, trickery, or deceit, especially to get something for oneself.

want (wont, wônt) *v.t.* **1.** to have a desire or wish for: *Nancy wants a new dress. Bob wants to go to Europe.* **2.** to have too little of or be without; lack: *She wants experience.* **3.** to need; require: *The stew wants seasoning.* —*v.i.* to be needy or poor. —*n.* **1.** a lack or need: *a want of money.* **2.** the state or condition of being without the necessities of life: *a family in want.* **3.** something that is needed or desired: *He has many wants.*

want ad, a small advertisement found especially in a newspaper, usually offering a job.

want·ing (won′ting, wôn′ting) *adj.* **1.** missing; lacking. **2.** not having something necessary; deficient: *He was wanting in experience.*

wan·ton (wont′ən) *adj.* **1.** showing or resulting from a complete lack of feeling for others; marked by extreme thoughtlessness or ill will: *wanton cruelty, a wanton attack.* **2.** having loose morals; immoral. **3.** not controlled; unruly: *a wanton little boy, a wanton growth of weeds.* —*n.* a person who behaves in an immoral way. —**wan′ton·ly,** *adv.* —**wan′ton·ness,** *n.*

wap·i·ti (wop′i tē) *n. pl.,* **wap·i·tis** or **wap·i·ti.** an elk of North America.

war (wôr) *n.* **1.** an armed conflict between countries or different groups within a country. **2.** any active opposition or struggle; fight: *a war against disease.* **3.** the profession or science of armed conflict. —*v.i.,* **warred, war·ring.** to engage in war; fight. —*adj.* of, relating to, or used in war: *a war dance, war rations.*

War Between the States, another name for the **Civil War.**

war·ble (wôr′bəl) *v.,* **war·bled, war·bling.** —*v.i.* **1.** to sing with quavers or trills, as a bird. **2.** to make a melodic, warbling sound: *The shallow stream warbled as it flowed over the pebbles.* —*v.t.* to sing with quavers or trills: *to warble a tune.* —*n.* a trilling, quavering sound, such as the song of a bird.

war·bler (wôr′blər) *n.* **1.** any of various small songbirds, often having brightly colored feathers. **2.** a person who warbles.

war bonnet, a ceremonial headdress worn by certain North American Indians, especially the Plains Indians. It is usually made of eagle feathers, and each feather represents an act of bravery or other honor earned by the wearer.

Warbler

war crime, any violation of the international laws and customs governing warfare, such as ill-treatment of prisoners or civilians, or unnecessary plunder or destruction of property.

at; āpe; cär; end; mē; it; īce; hot; ōld; fôrk; wood; fōōl; oil; out; up; turn; sing; thin; <u>th</u>is; hw in white; zh in treasure. The symbol ə stands for the sound of **a** in about, **e** in taken, **i** in pencil, **o** in lemon, and **u** in circus.

W

ward (wôrd) *n.* **1.** a room or division of a hospital containing a number of patients: *a children's ward.* **2.** a division of a jail or prison. **3.** a person who is under the care or control of a court or guardian. **4.** an administrative division of a town or city. —*v.t.* to turn back or repel: *to ward off an attack.*

-ward *suffix* in the direction of: *downward, southward.*

ward·en (wôrd′ən) *n.* **1.** a person whose job it is to care for or guard someone or something, especially a person in charge of a prison. **2.** an official who enforces certain laws, as in a game preserve.

ward·er (wôr′dər) *n.* a person who guards; watchman.

ward·robe (wôrd′rōb′) *n.* **1.** a collection of clothing, such as all the clothes belonging to one person. **2.** a piece of furniture or closet for keeping clothes.

-wards a form of the *suffix* -ward.

ware (wer) *n.* **1. wares.** articles for sale: *The shopkeeper displayed his wares.* **2.** a specific kind of manufactured article. ▲ used mainly in combination: *glassware, tableware.* **3.** pots and other objects made of fired clay; pottery: *ceramic ware.*

ware·house (wer′hous′) *n. pl.,* **ware·hous·es** (wer′hou′ziz). a building where merchandise is stored.

war·fare (wôr′fer′) *n.* the act of fighting a war; armed conflict.

war·head (wôr′hed′) *n.* the part in the front of a missile or torpedo that contains the explosive charge.

war·horse (wôr′hôrs′) *n.* **1.** a horse trained for use in battle; charger. **2.** *Informal.* a person who is very experienced, as from having been in many battles or struggles.

war·i·ly (wer′ə lē) *adv.* in a cautious manner; cautiously.

war·i·ness (wer′ē nis) *n.* the state or quality of being cautious.

war·like (wôr′līk′) *adj.* **1.** fond of war; quick to go to war: *a warlike nation.* **2.** threatening war; hostile: *a warlike atmosphere.* **3.** of, relating to, or characteristic of war: *warlike exploits.*

war·lock (wôr′lok′) *n.* a male witch; sorcerer; wizard.

war·lord (wôr′lôrd′) *n.* a strong military leader who controls a territory.

warm (wôrm) *adj.* **1.** having a moderate degree of heat; somewhat hot; not cold: *a warm bath, a warm room.* **2** having a feeling of heat: *He is warm from a fever.* **3.** giving off or holding in heat: *the warm sun, warm clothing.* **4.** full of enthusiasm, kindness, or affection: *warm thanks, a warm person.* **5.** excited or heated; lively: *a warm debate.* **6.** newly made; fresh: *The fox's trail was still warm.* **7.** (of colors) suggesting heat or warmth, as red and yellow. —*v.t.* **1.** to make warm or comfortably heated: *She warmed the bottle for the baby.* **2.** to inspire with affectionate, kindly feelings: *The sight of home warmed their hearts.* —*v.i.* **1.** to become warm. **2.** to become affectionate or kindly toward someone or something: *They warmed to her as they grew to know her better.* —**warm′ly,** *adv.* —**warm′ness,** *n.*

> **to warm up. a.** to make warm, as by heating: *to warm up rolls for dinner.* **b.** to get ready by practicing or exercising: *The runner warmed up before the race.* **c.** to make or become more friendly or enthusiastic: *The timid girl finally warmed up to her new classmates.* **d.** to run (an engine or machine) until it reaches the right condition or temperature for operating.

warm-blood·ed (wôrm′blud′id) *adj.* having blood that stays at almost the same temperature, even though the temperature of the air or other surroundings changes. Birds and mammals are warm-blooded.

warm front, the forward edge of a mass of warm air that is pushing back a mass of cold air.

warm-heart·ed (wôrm′här′tid) *adj.* having or showing enthusiasm, kindness, or affection: *He is a warm-hearted person.* —**warm′-heart′ed·ly,** *adv.* —**warm′-heart′ed·ness,** *n.*

warming pan, a large, covered, long-handled pan that holds hot coals, formerly used to warm beds.

war·mon·ger (wôr′mung′gər, wôr′mong′gər) *n.* a person who favors or tries to bring about war.

warmth (wôrmth) *n.* **1.** the state or quality of being warm: *the warmth of the sun, the warmth of a woolen blanket.* **2.** enthusiasm or excitement; zeal: *The actor was pleased by the warmth of the crowd's applause.* **3.** kindness or affection; friendliness: *the warmth of a person's smile.*

warm-up (wôrm′up′) *n.* **1.** the act of practicing or exercising to get ready for some event: *He watched the warm-up of the pitchers before the baseball game.* **2.** the act of running an engine or machine until it reaches the right temperature or condition for operating.

warn (wôrn) *v.t.* **1.** to put on guard by giving notice beforehand, as of approaching danger; caution: *The radio bulletin warned the townspeople of the storm.* **2.** to give advice to; counsel: *The mother warned her son not to eat too much candy.* **3.** to give notice to; make aware of; signal: *He put out his hand to warn the driver behind him that he was going to stop.* **4.** to notify to keep at a distance: *The notice warned people away from the explosion site.* —*v.i.* to give a warning: *The lighthouse warned of danger ahead.*

warn·ing (wôr′ning) *n.* **1.** notice or advice given beforehand, as of approaching danger: *The darkened sky and heavy wind gave warning of the approaching tornado.* **2.** something that serves to warn: *The sign was a warning to trespassers.* —*adj.* serving to warn: *a warning signal.* —**warn′ing·ly,** *adv.*

War of 1812, the war between the United States and Great Britain lasting from 1812 to 1815.

War of Independence, another name for the **American Revolution.**

warp (wôrp) *v.t.* **1.** to bend, curve, or twist out of shape: *The dampness of the room had warped the books.* **2.** to turn from what is correct or right; twist: *His personal feelings warped his judgment on the matter.* **3.** to move (a ship) by pulling on a line or cable that is fastened to something, such as a dock or anchor. —*v.i.* to be or become bent, curved, or twisted. —*n.* **1.** the state of being bent, curved, or twisted. **2.** threads running lengthwise in a woven fabric. **3.** a line or cable used in moving a ship.

war·path (wôr′path′) *n. pl.,* **war·paths** (wôr′pathz′). the route taken by a group of North American Indians engaged in war.

> **on the warpath. a.** taking part in or getting ready for war. **b.** ready for a fight; angry.

war·plane (wôr′plān′) *n.* an airplane designed and built for use in war.

war·rant (wôr′ənt, wor′ənt) *n.* **1.** something that gives a good reason or justification for: *There is no warrant for his rude remark.* **2.** a document that authorizes something, such as an arrest or the payment of money. —*v.t.* **1.** to approve officially; authorize; sanction: *The law warrants his arrest.* **2.** to give a good reason for: *The facts do not warrant his conclusion.* **3.** to guarantee: *The car dealer warranted the new car for one year.* **4.** to state positively: *I warrant that she's the one who did it.*

warrant officer, an officer of the armed forces who receives a certificate of appointment rather than a commission, and who ranks between a commissioned officer and an enlisted person.

war·ran·ty (wôr′ən tē, wor′ən tē) *n. pl.,* **war·ran·ties.** **1.** a written statement or assurance given by a seller to a buyer that the seller's product is as described or that it will be repaired or replaced if proven defective within a certain period of time; guarantee. **2.** an authorization or justification; warrant.

war·ren (wôr′ən, wor′ən) *n.* **1.** a place where rabbits or other small animals live and breed. **2.** a very crowded place where many people live.

War·ren, Earl (wôr′ən, wor′ən) 1891–1974, the chief justice of the United States Supreme Court from 1953 to 1969.

war·ri·or (wôr′ē ər, wor′ē ər) *n.* a person who fights or who is experienced in fighting battles.

War·saw (wôr′sô) *n.* the capital of Poland, in the east-central part of the country. Pop. (1977 est.), 1,532,100.

war·ship (wôr′ship′) *n.* a ship designed and built for use in war.

wart (wôrt) *n.* **1.** a small, hard lump that grows on the skin, caused by a virus. **2.** a similar growth on a plant. —**wart′like′**, *adj.*

wart hog, an African wild hog having wartlike growths on the sides of its head, two pairs of curved tusks, and a dark coat with bristles and long, coarse hairs.

Wart hog

war·time (wôr′tīm′) *n.* a period of war.

wart·y (wôr′tē) *adj.*, **wart·i·er**, **wart·i·est**. **1.** having or covered with warts. **2.** of or resembling warts.

War·wick (wôr′wik) *n.* a city in eastern Rhode Island. Pop. (1970), 83,694.

war·y (wer′ē) *adj.*, **war·i·er**, **war·i·est**. **1.** always on the alert; watchful: *a wary man.* **2.** characterized by caution; guarded: *a wary reply, a wary expression.* —**war′i·ly**, *adv.*

was (wuz, woz; *unstressed* wəz) the first and third person singular past tense of **be**.

wash (wôsh, wosh) *v.t.* **1.** to make (something) free of dirt, germs, or the like, usually by using soap and water on it: *He washed his face. She washed dishes.* **2.** to remove by using water or soap and water: *Mother washed a gravy stain out of the tablecloth.* **3.** to carry away, wear away, or destroy by the action of water: *The wind and rain turned dreary, washing the silver fish back to sea* (F. Scott Fitzgerald). **4.** to make wet or moist: *The waves washed the deck with salt water. The flowers were washed with dew.* **5.** to cover with a thin coat, as of ink or paint. —*v.i.* **1.** to clean oneself: *He washes before each meal.* **2.** to clean clothes, usually with soap and water. **3.** to be removed by using water or soap and water: *The food stains washed out quickly.* **4.** to undergo washing without damage: *This new fabric washes well.* **5.** to flow over or beat against: *We could hear the waves washing on the rocks.* —*n. pl.,* **wash·es.** **1.** the act of washing or the state of being washed. **2.** the quantity of articles, such as clothes, washed at one time: *She hung the wash on the line this morning.* **3.** a flow or rush of water, or the sound made by this. **4.** a liquid used for a particular purpose: *The doctor gave her a wash for her infected eye.* **5.** a disturbance in the water or air caused by a moving ship or airplane. **6.** a thin coat, as of ink or paint. —*adj.* that can be washed without damage; washable.

  to wash down. a. to clean from top to bottom: *to wash down walls.* **b.** to drink something in order to make swallowing easier: *He washed the pill down with orange juice.*

  to wash (one's) hands of. to refuse to have any more to do with: *She washed her hands of him when she learned that he had lied to her.*

  to wash out. a. to clean the inside of, as with soap and water: *He washed out the bathtub.* **b.** to carry or be carried away by the action of moving water: *The flood washed out the bridge.* **c.** to fail or cause to fail completely: *The economic recession washed out his business.*

  to wash up. a. to wash one's face and hands, as before dinner. **b.** to clean dishes and cooking utensils after a meal: *Mother said we have to wash up before we watch television.* **c.** to ruin or be ruined: *He was washed up as a football player after hurting his knee.*

Wash., Washington.

wash·a·ble (wô′shə bəl, wosh′ə bəl) *adj.* that can be washed without damage, as with soap and water: *a washable sweater.*

wash-and-wear (wôsh′ən wer′, wosh′ən wer′) *adj.* (of a fabric or garment) that requires little or no ironing after washing.

wash·ba·sin (wôsh′bā′sin, wosh′bā′sin) *n.* another word for **washbowl.**

wash·board (wôsh′bôrd′, wosh′bôrd′) *n.* a board with a ridged surface on which clothes are rubbed during washing.

wash·bowl (wôsh′bōl′, wosh′bōl′) *n.* a bowl, basin, or sink used to hold water for washing or shaving. Also, **washbasin, washstand.**

wash·cloth (wôsh′klôth′, wosh′klôth′) *n.* a small cloth used for washing one's body or face. Also, **washrag.**

washed-out (wôsht′out′, wosht′out′) *adj.* **1.** that has faded, as from age or washing. **2.** *Informal.* without strength or energy; exhausted.

washed-up (wôsht′up′, wosht′up′) *adj. Slang.* all through, especially due to failure; finished.

wash·er (wô′shər, wosh′ər) *n.* **1.** a person or thing that washes. **2.** any of various appliances for washing, such as a washing machine. **3.** a flat ring of metal, rubber, or other material, used between a nut and bolt to prevent friction or leakage or to give a tighter fit.

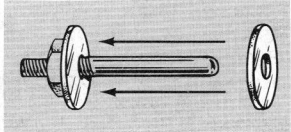
Washer *(def. 3)*

wash·er·wom·an (wô′shər woom′ən, wosh′ər woom′ən) *n. pl.,* **wash·er·wom·en** (wô′shər wim′ən, wosh′ər wim′ən). a woman who is employed to wash clothes; laundress. Also, **washwoman.**

wash·ing (wô′shing, wosh′ing) *n.* **1.** the act of cleaning with water. **2.** the number of articles, such as clothes, washed at one time.

washing machine, an appliance for washing clothes, linen, and the like.

washing soda, see **sodium carbonate** *(def. 2).*

Wash·ing·ton (wô′shing tən, wosh′ing tən) *n.* **1. Book·er T.** (book′ər). 1856–1915, U.S. educator. **2. George.** 1732–1799, general in the American Revolution, and the first president of the United States, from 1789 to 1797. **3. Martha.** 1731–1802, the wife of George Washington. **4.** the capital of the United States, lying between Maryland and northern Virginia, and including the entire District of Columbia. Pop. (1970), 756,510. Also, **Washington, D.C. 5.** a state in the northwestern United States, on the Pacific Ocean. Capital, Olympia. Area, 68,192 sq. mi. Pop. (1970),

at; āpe; cär; end; mē; it; īce; hot; ōld; fôrk; wood; fōōl; oil; out; up; turn; sing; thin; this; hw in white; zh in treasure. The symbol ə stands for the sound of a in about, e in taken, i in pencil, o in lemon, and u in circus.

3,409,169. Abbreviation, **Wash. 6. Mount.** the highest mountain in New England, in northern New Hampshire. —**Wash′ing·to′ni·an,** *adj., n.*

●Congress named the territory of **Washington** after George Washington, and the name was kept when the territory became a state. Washington is the only state to be named for a president.

wash·out (wôsh′out′, wosh′out′) *n.* **1.** the carrying away of something, such as part of a road, by the action of water. **2.** the channel or hole resulting from this. **3.** *Slang.* a failure.

wash·rag (wôsh′rag′, wosh′rag′) *n.* another word for **washcloth.**

wash·room (wôsh′rōōm′, wôsh′room′, wosh′rōōm′, wosh′room′) *n.* a building or room having a toilet and washing facilities; lavatory.

wash·stand (wôsh′stand′, wosh′stand′) *n.* **1.** a piece of furniture, such as a table, for holding a basin and pitcher used for washing. **2.** another word for **washbowl.**

wash·tub (wôsh′tub′, wosh′tub′) *n.* a large tub used for soaking or washing clothes or household linen.

wash·wom·an (wôsh′woom′ən, wosh′woom′ən) *n. pl.,* **wash·wom·en** (wôsh′wim′ən, wosh′wim′ən). another word for **washerwoman.**

was·n't (wuz′ənt, woz′ənt) was not.

wasp (wosp) *n.* any of numerous winged insects that have slender bodies, narrow waists, and can give a painful sting. Most wasps live and work alone, although a few species are social insects and live in colonies.

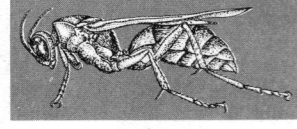

Wasp

WASP (wosp) *n.* an American who is a Protestant Caucasian of English or Northern European descent. [Abbreviation of *w*(hite) *A*(nglo-) *S*(axon) *P*(rotestant).]

wasp·ish (wos′pish) *adj.* **1.** of, resembling, or like a wasp. **2.** quick to become angry; bad-tempered. —**wasp′ish·ly,** *adv.* —**wasp′ish·ness,** *n.*

was·sail (wos′əl) *n.* **1.** an expression used when making a toast, especially to someone's health. **2.** an alcoholic drink usually made of ale or wine with sugar, spices, or roasted apples added. **3.** a festive party where drinks are served and toasts are made. —*v.i.* **1.** to take part in or drink a wassail. **2.** to go from house to house at Christmas singing carols. —*v.t.* to drink to the health of; toast. —**was′sail·er,** *n.*

wast (wost) *Archaic.* the second person singular past tense of **be.**

wast·age (wās′tij) *n.* **1.** loss by use, wear, decay, or the like. **2.** something lost in this way.

waste (wāst) *v.,* **wast·ed, wast·ing.** —*v.t.* **1.** to use or spend in a careless or useless way: *to waste time.* **2.** to use up, wear away, or exhaust: *The long illness had wasted the old man's strength.* **3.** to destroy; ruin: *The advancing army wasted everything in its path.* —*v.i.* to lose energy, strength, health, or the like: *The homeless kitten wasted away from lack of food and care.* —*n.* **1.** the act of wasting or the state of being wasted: *The trip was a waste of time.* **2.** a wild or desolate place where there are few or no living things. **3.** a slow process of wearing away. **4.** worthless material; refuse. **5.** undigested material eliminated from the body. —*adj.* **1.** left over, rejected, or thrown away as worthless: *Sue had a pile of waste material after she finished the dress.* **2.** of, relating to, or for waste: *a waste receptacle.* **3.** having few or no living things; desolate.

to go to waste. to fail to be used properly or at all: *His*

careful planning for the boat trip went to waste when it rained.

to lay waste. to destroy; devastate.

waste·bas·ket (wāst′bas′kit) *n.* a basket or other container used for useless scraps of paper or other trash.

waste·ful (wāst′fəl) *adj.* using or spending in a careless or useless way. —**waste′ful·ly,** *adv.* —**waste′ful·ness,** *n.*

waste·land (wāst′land′) *n.* a barren piece of land or area where there are few or no living things, such as a desert or polar region.

waste·pa·per (wāst′pā′pər) *n.* paper that is no longer useful and has been or is to be thrown away.

wast·er (wās′tər) *n.* a person or thing that wastes, spends, or uses up things in a careless or useless way.

wast·ing (wās′ting) *adj.* that slowly weakens or destroys: *a wasting illness, a wasting drought.*

wast·rel (wās′trəl) *n.* **1.** a wasteful person; spendthrift. **2.** an idle, worthless person; good-for-nothing.

watch (woch) *v.t.* **1.** to look at (someone or something) with attention: *The little boy watched television all afternoon.* **2.** to keep guard over: *The soldier watched the enemy captives.* **3.** to take care of; tend: *The shepherd watched his flock. Can she watch the baby for an hour?* —*v.i.* **1.** to look with attention; observe closely: *Watch carefully while I show you how to hold the golf club.* **2.** to be on the alert; wait expectantly: *She watched for the right moment to make her request.* **3.** to remain awake at night, especially at the bedside of a person who is sick. **4.** to do duty as a guard; keep guard. —*n. pl.,* **watch·es. 1.** the act of watching; close observation. **2.** one or more persons whose work it is to protect or guard someone or something. **3.** the period of time during which a guard is on duty. **4.** the act of remaining awake, especially to take care of someone or something; vigil: *The mother maintained a watch at her sick child's bedside.* **5.** a small device for telling time, usually worn on the wrist. —**watch′er,** *n.*

watch·band (woch′band′) *n.* a band or strap of leather, metal, or the like, used to fasten a watch to the wrist.

watch·dog (woch′dôg′) *n.* **1.** a dog kept to guard a house, property, or the like, and to give warning of the approach of intruders. **2.** any person or thing that serves as a protector or guardian for another or others: *The agency was intended to be a watchdog for consumers against dishonest business practices.*

watch·ful (woch′fəl) *adj.* on the alert; vigilant; wary. —**watch′ful·ly,** *adv.* —**watch′ful·ness,** *n.*

watch·mak·er (woch′mā′kər) *n.* a person who makes, cleans, and repairs watches. —**watch′mak′ing,** *n.*

watch·man (woch′mən) *n. pl.,* **watch·men** (woch′mən). a person whose work it is to guard a building, property, or the like when the owner or tenant is away, especially during the night.

watch·tow·er (woch′tou′ər) *n.* a tower or tall building from which a guard or sentinel keeps watch.

watch·word (woch′wurd′) *n.* **1.** a secret word or phrase that identifies the speaker or allows him or her to pass a guard; password. **2.** a slogan or motto of some group.

wa·ter (wô′tər) *n.* **1.** a liquid compound of hydrogen and oxygen that has no color, odor, or taste in its pure state. It is found over the earth in the form of oceans, lakes, and the like, and it also occurs in a frozen state as ice and a gaseous state as steam and vapor. Water has a freezing point of zero degrees centigrade (32 degrees Fahrenheit) and a boiling point of one hundred degrees centigrade (212 degrees Fahrenheit). Formula: H_2O **2.** *also,* **waters.** any body of water, such as a sea, lake, or river: *We swam in the warm Florida waters.* **3.** any liquid given forth by the body, such as tears, saliva, urine, or the like. **4.** any liquid preparation that contains or resembles water: *toilet water,* *ammonia water.* **5.** a wavy, lustrous sheen on fabric or metal. —*v.t.* **1.** to put water into or upon: *She watered the plants every day. The valley is watered by the melting snow from the mountains.* **2.** to give water to, especially for drinking: *The farmer had to water his cattle every day.* **3.** to dilute or weaken with water: *to water an alcoholic drink.* **4.** to make a wavy, lustrous sheen on (fabric or metal): *to water silk.* —*v.i.* **1.** to get or take in water: *The ship put into port to water. The cattle watered at the river.* **2.** to give forth water from the body, as in the form of tears or saliva: *The smoke made their eyes water. His mouth watered at the thought of dinner.*

in hot water. in trouble, as from misbehaving.

to hold water. to be logical, sound, or true: *The lawyer's argument didn't hold water.*

to throw cold water on. to discourage or forbid: *He threw cold water on our scheme to make money.*

to water down. to make less strong or intense; weaken.

water bird, any bird that lives on or near the water; swimming or wading bird.

wa·ter·borne (wô′tər bôrn′) *adj.* **1.** carried on or by water; floating: *The water-borne flowers drifted in the lake.* **2.** carried by ship or by boat.

wa·ter·buck (wô′tər buk′) *n.* any of several antelopes that live near rivers or marshes in southeastern Africa. A waterbuck has a coat of long, coarse hair that may range from yellowish-brown to nearly black.

water buffalo, a black Asian buffalo having long horns that curve backward. The water buffalo is raised for its milk and is used as a beast of burden.

water bug, any of various insects, such as the cockroach, that live on or near water or in damp places.

Wa·ter·bur·y (wô′tər ber′ē) *n.* a city in western Connecticut. Pop. (1970), 108,033.

water chestnut **1.** the fruit of a plant that lives in water. The water chestnut has a nutlike taste and is widely used in Oriental cooking. **2.** the plant bearing this fruit.

water closet, see **toilet** *(defs. 1, 2).*

wa·ter·col·or (wô′tər kul′ər) *adj.* of, relating to, or made with water colors.

water color **1.** a paint made by mixing pigment with water. **2.** the art or technique of painting with water colors. **3.** a picture or design made with water colors.

water cooler, a device for cooling and dispensing water, often operated by electricity.

wa·ter·course (wô′tər kôrs′) *n.* **1.** any stream of flowing water, such as a river or brook. **2.** a man-made or natural channel of water, such as a canal or riverbed.

wa·ter·craft (wô′tər kraft′) *n.* **1.** skill in sailing boats or in performing water sports. **2.** a boat or ship. **3.** boats or ships as a group.

wa·ter·cress (wô′tər kres′) *n. pl.,* **wa·ter·cress·es.** a plant that grows in water and has sharp-tasting leaves that are used in salads or as a garnish.

wa·ter·fall (wô′tər fôl′) *n.* a flow of water falling from a high place.

wa·ter·fowl (wô′tər foul′) *n. pl.,* **wa·ter·fowls** or **wa·ter·fowl.** a water bird, especially a swimming bird that is hunted as game.

Watercress

wa·ter·front (wô′tər frunt′) *n.* **1.** the part of a city or town that is located beside the harbor of a river or ocean, especially where there are docks and shipping facilities. **2.** land or real estate next to a lake, river, or the like.

water gap, a gorge or valley in a mountain ridge through which a stream flows.

water hole, a hole or hollow place in the ground in which water collects, such as a pond or pool.

watering can, a container used for sprinkling water on plants.

watering place **1.** a place where water may be obtained, as for drinking or for watering cattle. **2.** a resort with mineral springs.

water lily, any of a large group of plants that grow in freshwater ponds and lakes. The leaves and flowers of water lilies float on the surface of the water.

water line, a line where the surface of the water touches the hull of a boat. A stripe is usually painted around the hull to mark this line.

wa·ter·logged (wô′tər lôgd′, wô′tər logd′) *also,* **wa·ter·logged.** *adj.* so full of water that it becomes heavy.

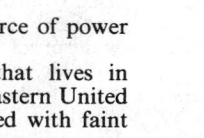
Water lily

Wa·ter·loo (wô′tər loo′) *n.* **1.** a village in central Belgium, the site of the final defeat of Napoleon I on June 18, 1815. **2.** any crushing or final defeat. **3.** a city in east-central Iowa. Pop. (1970), 75,533.

water main, a large, main pipe or pipeline used for supplying water to a particular area.

wa·ter·man (wô′tər mən) *n. pl.,* **wa·ter·men** (wô′tər-mən). a man who works on or with boats.

wa·ter·mark (wô′tər märk′) *n.* **1.** a line or mark that shows how high the water of a river, lake, or ocean tide has risen. **2.** a distinctive mark or design that is impressed on certain kinds of paper, such as stationery, and is visible when the paper is held up to a light. —*v.t.* to impress (paper) with a watermark.

wa·ter·mel·on (wô′tər mel′ən) *n.* **1.** a large, juicy fruit having a thick green rind and watery pulp that is pink, red, or yellow. **2.** the vine bearing this fruit.

water mill, a mill or machine whose source of power is moving water.

water moccasin, a poisonous snake that lives in swamps and other wet regions of the southeastern United States. It has an olive or black body marked with faint crossbars. Also, **cottonmouth.**

water of crystallization, water combined in crystals with another compound. When heated, the water evaporates, causing the crystals to crumble into a powdery substance.

water polo, a water sport played with a large ball by two teams of seven swimmers each. The object is to throw or push the ball into the opponent's goal.

water power, power generated by the force of moving water.

wa·ter·proof (wô′tər proof′) *adj.* that will not let water pass through, especially after having been treated or coated with a substance that prevents water from entering. —*n. British.* a raincoat. —*v.t.* to make waterproof: *to waterproof a garment.*

at; āpe; cär; end; mē; it; īce; hot; ōld; fôrk; wood; fool; oil; out; up; turn; sing; thin; this; hw in white; zh in treasure. The symbol ə stands for the sound of **a** in about, **e** in taken, **i** in pencil, **o** in lemon, and **u** in circus.

water rat **1.** any of various rodents that live on the banks of streams or lakes. **2.** another term for **muskrat.**

wa·ter·re·pel·lent (wô′tər ri pel′ənt) *adj.* having a surface or finish that repels water but is not completely waterproof.

wa·ter·shed (wô′tər shed′) *n.* **1.** a ridge or other high land area separating two different river basins. **2.** the total land area from which water drains into a stream, river, or lake.

wa·ter·ski (wô′tər skē′) *v.i.,* **wa·ter·skied, wa·ter·ski·ing.** to glide over the surface of water on water skis while being pulled by a towline attached to a boat. —**wa′ter·ski′er,** *n.* —**wa′ter·ski′ing,** *n.*

water ski, one of a pair of wooden skis wider and shorter than snow skis, used in water-skiing.

water snake, any of various nonpoisonous snakes living in fresh water.

wa·ter·spout (wô′tər spout′) *n.* **1.** a pipe or nozzle that carries away unneeded water, especially one that runs from the roof down the side of a building to carry off rainwater. **2.** the end of a pipe from which water pours when the pipe is opened. **3.** a tornado occurring over a body of water, appearing as a long, dark funnel extending from the clouds down toward the surface of the water.

water table, the upper surface of a zone in the ground that is completely saturated with water.

wa·ter·tight (wô′tər tīt′) *adj.* **1.** so closely constructed or fitted as to prevent water from passing in or out. **2.** so planned or worded as to be free from error and clearly understood: *He had a watertight alibi.*

water tower **1.** a very large tower used to store a water supply. **2.** formerly, a fire-fighting apparatus for throwing water on the upper stories of tall buildings.

water vapor, water in its gaseous state, but below the boiling point, especially as found in the atmosphere.

wa·ter·way (wô′tər wā′) *n.* **1.** a water route for the passage of ships. **2.** a channel for the passage of water.

water wheel, a wheel turned by the weight or pressure of water falling on it, used to provide power.

water wings, a waterproof device filled with air, worn under the arms to keep the body floating while a person is learning to swim.

wa·ter·works (wô′tər-wurks′) *n., pl.* **1.** the entire system for the distribution of water to a city or town, including reservoirs, buildings, machinery, pipes, and the like. **2.** a building in such a system in which the machinery for pumping water is located.

Water wheel

wa·ter·y (wô′tər ē) *adj.* **1.** of, relating to, or consisting of water: *He explored the watery depths of the ocean.* **2.** full of or saturated with water: *The heavy rain made the ground too watery.* **3.** containing too much water: *a watery gravy.* **4.** pale, as if diluted by water; weak: *watery colors.*

Watt, James (wot) 1736–1819, Scottish engineer and inventor.

watt (wot) *n.* a unit of electrical or mechanical power in the metric system. It is equal to a rate of one joule of work per second. [From James *Watt.*]

watt·age (wot′ij) *n.* **1.** electrical power expressed in watts. **2.** the number of watts of electrical power needed to run an appliance.

watt-hour (wot′our′) *n.* a unit of electrical energy, equal to the work done by one watt acting for one hour, or 3600 joules.

wat·tle (wot′əl) *n.* **1.** a framework or structure made of poles, branches, twigs, or the like woven together, used especially in building walls, fences, or roofs. **2.** the material used to make such a framework or structure. **3.** the fleshy, often brightly colored fold of skin hanging down from the neck or throat of certain fowl, such as turkeys and other animals. —*v.t.,* **wat·tled, wat·tling.** **1.** to build (something) by weaving together twigs, branches, or the like: *to wattle a roof for a grass hut.* **2.** to form into a network or bind together by weaving or interlacing: *to wattle branches to form a roof.* —**wat′tled,** *adj.*

wave (wāv) *v.,* **waved, wav·ing.** —*v.i.* **1.** to sway freely back and forth or up and down; move with a rippling or swaying motion, as stalks of wheat in the wind. **2.** to fall or lie in curves or rows that curve first one way then the other: *Her hair waves beautifully when brushed.* **3.** to gesture by moving the hand or arm up and down, as in a greeting, farewell, or signal: *Robert waved until his friends were out of sight.* —*v.t.* **1.** to cause to move back and forth or up and down: *The people along the road waved their flags as the parade passed by.* **2.** to express or signal by waving something, especially the hand: *Father waved good-by.* **3.** to give a curving form, appearance, or pattern to: *She waved her hair by setting it in curlers.* —*n.* **1.** a curving or rippling movement or swell on the surface of a body of liquid, especially the sea. **2.** anything resembling this in movement or shape: *There were waves in the wallpaper where the glue didn't stick properly.* **3.** the act of waving, especially with the hand or something held in the hand: *He greeted her with a wave of his hand.* **4.** a sudden rush or increase of anything: *Last week we had a terrible heat wave.* **5.** a curve or series of curves, as in the hair. **6.** *Physics.* a vibration or disturbance that travels through a solid, liquid, or gas, such as a sound wave. —**wave′-like′,** *adj.*

Wave (wāv) *n.* a member of the WAVES.

wave·length (wāv′lengkth′, wāv′length′) *n. Physics.* the distance between any two like points of a wave. For example, the distance between the two highest points of a wave is one wave-length.

wave·let (wāv′lit) *n.* a small wave; ripple.

wa·ver (wā′vər) *v.i.* **1.** to move unsteadily up and down or from side to side; sway; totter: *The ladder wavered and fell over.* **2.** to flicker; quiver: *A sign of recognition wavered in his eyes.* **3.** to hesitate or show doubt; be uncertain: *He wavered between spending his money on a vacation or a new car.* **4.** to become unsteady; falter: *His strength never wavers.* —*n.* the act of wavering. —**wa′ver·ing·ly,** *adv.*

WAVES (wāvz) Women's Reserve of the U.S. Navy. [An abbreviation of *W*(omen) *A*(ccepted for) *V*(olunteer) *E*(mergency) *S*(ervice).]

wav·y (wā′vē) *adj.,* **wav·i·er, wav·i·est.** curving in movement or shape; full of waves: *a boy with wavy hair.* —**wav′i·ness,** *n.*

wax¹ (waks) *n. pl.,* **wax·es.** **1.** any of various fatty substances that come from plants or animals, such as beeswax or the wax that forms inside the ear. **2.** any of various natural mineral substances resembling this, such as paraffin. **3.** any of various substances that contain a wax, used to polish furniture, cars, and the like. —*v.t.* to cover, treat, or polish with wax. —*adj.* made of or resembling wax. [Old English *weax* beeswax.] —**wax′like′,** *adj.*

wax² (waks) *v.i.* **1.** to increase gradually, as in size, brightness, or strength: *The moon waxes and wanes.* **2.** to grow or become: *John waxed eloquent about the beauty of the English countryside.* [Old English *weaxan* to grow.]

wax bean, a yellow string bean with a waxy appearance.

waxed paper, another spelling of **wax paper.**

wax·en (wak′sən) *adj.* **1.** made of, covered, or treated with wax: *She worked hard to get a deep waxen shine on her table.* **2.** resembling wax; pale: *The sick boy had a waxen complexion.*

wax myrtle, any of various tall shrubs or trees having fragrant leaves, and small grayish berries coated with a white wax that is used in making candles and soap.

wax paper *also,* **waxed paper.** a paper that is coated with paraffin so that it keeps out moisture, used as a protective wrapping.

wax·wing (waks′wing′) *n.* a small songbird that has a crest on its head, a short, thick bill, and predominantly brown or gray feathers with black, yellow, white, and red markings.

wax·work (waks′wurk′) *n.* **1.** something made of wax, especially a figure or ornament made of wax. **2. waxworks.** a place for showing wax figures of famous persons.

Waxwing

wax·y (wak′sē) *adj.,* **wax·i·er, wax·i·est. 1.** resembling wax, as in texture or appearance: *The plastic flowers looked waxy.* **2.** made of, covered, or treated with wax. **—wax′i·ness,** *n.*

way (wā) *n.* **1.** a course of action or method to be followed in order to do or attain something: *He thought of a way to solve the problem. Being kind to others is a good way to make friends.* **2.** a road, path, or the like, leading from one place to another: *The fallen limb blocked the way. That road is the quickest way to town.* **3.** a direction, as of motion: *The hurricane is heading this way.* **4.** a movement or passage along a particular route or in a particular direction: *John saw her on his way back to school.* **5.** distance: *They walked a long way before finding the house.* **6.** also, **ways.** a usual style of behaving or speaking: *She has very unusual ways.* **7.** a typical or characteristic style of doing something: *She has a special way of smiling.* **8.** something that a person desires to have or do; wish: *He becomes angry if he cannot have his way.* **9.** a particular detail or feature; respect: *In many ways, the plan is a good one.* **10.** space enough to pass: *Make way so that the truck can get by us.* **11.** the course of action that one follows in life. **12.** *Informal.* a condition or state: *Harry is in a bad way financially.* **13.** *Informal.* a neighborhood, region, or area: *Few people visit out our way.* **—adv. 1.** at a distance; far: *We watched the clouds floating way up in the sky.* **2.** to a great degree or point: *The water came way up the beach.*

by the way. with regard to that; incidentally: *By the way, we're leaving at four o'clock.*

by way of. a. by a route that includes; via: *We're going to Florida by way of Tennessee.* **b.** as a means or method of: *He sent her a note by way of an apology.*

in the way. in a position that blocks or slows progress: *Dad can't move the car because the bicycle is in the way.*

out of the way. a. so as not to block or hinder: *Move your toys out of the way of the door.* **b.** in a place that is far away or hard to reach: *Their summer house is out of the way.* **c.** not proper; wrong: *He said nothing out of the way at the party.*

to give way. a. to back down; yield: *He finally gave way after several friends argued with him.* **b.** to break down or collapse: *The bridge gave way under the heavy load.*

to go out of the way or **to go out of one's way.** to do

something that is not easy or convenient: *Her friend went out of his way to help her.*

under way. in progress or motion: *The plane got under way after an hour's delay. The plans for the party were well under way.*

way·far·er (wā′fer′ər) *n.* a traveler, especially a person who travels on foot.

way·far·ing (wā′fer′ing) *adj.* traveling, especially on foot.

way·lay (wā′lā′, wā′lā′) *v.t.,* **way·laid, way·lay·ing. 1.** to lie in wait for in order to seize or attack: *The highwayman waylaid the traveler by the bridge.* **2.** to wait for and stop (a person): *The boy waylaid his friend after school in order to borrow some money.* **—way′lay′er,** *n.*

Wayne, Anthony (wān) 1745–1796, general in the American Revolution, best known as **Mad Anthony Wayne.**

-ways *suffix* used to form adverbs that show direction, position, or manner: *sideways.*

way·side (wā′sīd′) *n.* the land bordering a road or path: *He found his lost wallet lying by the wayside.* **—adj.** of, relating to, or located beside a road or path: *a wayside inn.*

way station, a small station between main stations, as on a railroad.

way·ward (wā′wərd) *adj.* **1.** refusing to do what is right; wrongheaded and disobedient: *a wayward child.* **2.** following no fixed rule or pattern; irregular: *wayward movements.* **—way′ward·ly,** *adv.* **—way′ward·ness,** *n.*

we (wē) *pron., pl.* nominative, **we;** possessive, **our, ours;** objective, **us. 1.** the persons who are speaking or writing: *We won the baseball game. We are glad you can come with us.* **2.** a single person who is speaking or writing officially, such as an author, judge, or king.

weak (wēk) *adj.* **1.** liable to fall, fail, or collapse under strain: *The legs of the chair are weak. The weak bridge swayed under the weight of the trucks.* **2.** not having vigor or strength, as from age, illness, or fatigue: *The invalid is too weak to sit up. She is too weak to lift the chair.* **3.** not having the usual or required ability, power, or authority: *That general is a weak leader.* **4.** not supported by truth, facts, or reason; not sound or convincing: *The lawyer gave a weak argument.* **5.** lacking willpower or strength of character: *He was a weak person who wouldn't stand up for what he believed.* **6.** lacking intensity or power; faint: *The light was too weak to read by. He spoke with a weak voice.* **7.** lacking the full amount; diluted: *She served weak tea.* **8.** lacking in knowledge: *Mary is weak in science.* **9.** *Phonetics.* (of a syllable) having no stress or only light stress. **10.** *Grammar.* (of a verb) forming the past tense and past participle by the addition of a consonant or consonants to the stem, not by the change of a vowel, as in *bake, baked, baked.*

weak·en (wē′kən) *v.t., v.i.* to make or become weak or weaker: *She weakened the tea by adding water. The runner weakened as he neared the finish line.*

weak·fish (wēk′fish′) *n. pl.,* **weak·fish** or **weak·fish·es.** a saltwater fish found in the coastal waters of eastern North America, used for food.

weak·ling (wēk′ling) *n.* a person who is physically, mentally, or morally weak. **—adj.** weak; feeble.

at; āpe; cär; end; mē; it; īce; hot; ōld; fôrk; wood; fōōl; oil; out; up; turn; sing; thin; this; hw in white; zh in treasure. The symbol ə stands for the sound of **a** in about, **e** in taken, **i** in pencil, **o** in lemon, and **u** in circus.

W

weak·ly (wēk′lē) *adv.* in a weak manner. —*adj.*, **weak·li·er, weak·li·est.** not healthy or strong; weak; feeble.

weak-mind·ed (wēk′mīn′did) *adj.* **1.** lacking mental strength or firmness of will: *a weak-minded man.* **2.** feeble-minded.

weak·ness (wēk′nis) *n. pl.,* **weak·ness·es. 1.** the state or quality of being weak. **2.** an example of this; weak point. **3.** a special liking; fondness: *She has a weakness for ice cream.* **4.** something for which one has a special liking.

weal¹ (wēl) *n.* well-being, happiness, or prosperity: *a law passed for the public weal.* [Old English *wela* prosperity.]

weal² (wēl) *n.* a ridge or bump on the skin, as that made by a whip or stick; welt. [A form of *wale.*]

wealth (welth) *n.* **1.** a great quantity of money or valuable possessions; riches. **2.** a great quantity of anything: *That writer has a wealth of new ideas for improving our educational system.*

wealth·y (wel′thē) *adj.,* **wealth·i·er, wealth·i·est.** having wealth.

wean (wēn) *v.t.* **1.** to make (a child or young animal) used to food other than the mother's milk: *He weaned the puppies when they were six weeks old.* **2.** to cause (a person) to give up gradually a habit, practice, or interest: *to wean someone from smoking cigarettes.*

weap·on (wep′ən) *n.* **1.** anything used in a fight to attack or defend, such as a gun or knife. **2.** any means used to gain success in a contest or struggle: *The dictator used censorship as a weapon against those who tried to criticize his policies.*

wear (wer) *v.,* **wore, worn, wear·ing.** —*v.t.* **1.** to carry or have on the body: *to wear clothes, to wear a bracelet.* **2.** to have or show; display: *He wears his hair long. Her face wore a frown.* **3.** to damage or use up, as by scraping or rubbing: *to wear a carpet.* **4.** to cause or make, as by scraping or rubbing: *He wore holes in his socks.* **5.** to bring to a certain condition: *to wear a dress to rags.* —*v.i.* **1.** to last or hold out: *The fabric did not wear well.* **2.** to become damaged through use or age: *These shoes have started to wear.* **3.** to come to a certain condition: *Mary's patience wore thin.* **4.** to pass or advance, especially slowly: *The day wore on.* —*n.* **1.** the act of wearing or the state of being worn: *This suit has had five years of hard wear.* **2.** an article or articles of clothing: *The store sells only women's wear.* **3.** damage caused by use or age: *This rug shows signs of wear.* **4.** lasting quality; durability: *There are several years of wear left in this coat.* —**wear′a·ble,** *adj.* —**wear′er,** *n.*

  to wear down. a. to overcome gradually by continuous effort: *Phil finally wore down his father's resistance to buying him a car.* **b.** to damage or make less, as in size, by wear: *Heavy driving wore down the tread of his tires.*
  to wear off. to become less gradually: *The effects of the aspirin wore off after several hours.*
  to wear out. a. to use until no longer fit or able to be used: *He wore out the batteries of the portable radio.* **b.** to tire or exhaust: *The three-hour hike wore him out.*

wear and tear, damage undergone through use or passage of time.

wear·ing (wer′ing) *adj.* **1.** of, relating to, or made for wear: *Coats and suits are wearing apparel.* **2.** exhausting; tiring: *a wearing experience.*

wea·ri·some (wēr′ē səm) *adj.* causing weariness; tiresome; tedious: *The movie was long and wearisome.* —**wea′ri·some·ly,** *adv.*

wea·ry (wēr′ē) *adj.,* **wea·ri·er, wea·ri·est. 1.** extremely tired, as from hard labor; fatigued: *We were weary after a long day's drive.* **2.** causing or characterized by fatigue; tedious; tiring: *a weary journey.* **3.** having one's interest or patience exhausted: *He grew weary of staying home.*

—*v.,* **wea·ried, wea·ry·ing.** —*v.t.* to exhaust the strength of; make weary; fatigue: *The trip wearied her.* —*v.i.* to become weary: *The child wearied quickly.* —**wea′ri·ly,** *adv.* —**wea′ri·ness,** *n.*

wea·sel (wē′zəl) *n. pl.,* **wea·sels** or **wea·sel.** any of various small meat-eating animals, having a slender body, short legs, a long neck, and a soft, thick, brownish coat.

Weasel

weath·er (weth′ər) *n.* **1.** the condition of the atmosphere at a given time and place: *The weather has been cold and rainy for the past week.* **2.** unpleasant or stormy conditions: *The plane went through much weather during the flight.* —*v.t.* **1.** to expose to the weather, especially in order to dry, bleach, or condition: *to weather lumber.* **2.** to bear up against or overcome; come safely through: *to weather a storm, to weather a crisis.* **3.** to pass or sail to the windward of. —*v.i.* to become changed through exposure to the weather: *The house shingles weathered to a soft grey.* —*adj.* windward.
  under the weather. *Informal.* not well; ailing.

weath·er-beat·en (weth′ər bēt′ən) *adj.* **1.** worn or badly damaged by exposure to the weather: *a weather-beaten old barn.* **2.** seasoned or hardened by exposure to the weather: *The old sailor had a weather-beaten face.*

Weather Bureau, the agency of the U.S. Department of Commerce that studies and forecasts the weather.

weath·er·cock (weth′ər kok′) *n.* a weather vane having the shape of a rooster.

weath·er·glass (weth′ər glas′) *n. pl.,* **weath·er·glass·es.** any of various instruments, such as a barometer, that show the state of the weather.

weath·er·ing (weth′ər ing) *n.* the action of the weather upon something exposed to it.

weath·er·man (weth′ər man′) *n. pl.,* **weath·er·men** (weth′ər men′). a person who studies and forecasts the weather.

weath·er·proof (weth′ər prōōf′) *adj.* capable of resisting the harmful forces of the weather: *Dad bought weatherproof paint for the patio furniture.* —*v.t.* to make weatherproof.

weather station, a station where observations of the weather are made and recorded every day.

weath·er·strip (weth′ər strip′) *v.t.,* **weath·er·stripped, weath·er·strip·ping.** to fit or secure with weather stripping.

weather stripping 1. a narrow strip of metal, felt, or other material put around the openings of a door or window to keep out the wind and cold. Also, **weather strip. 2.** such strips as a group.

weather vane, a device that is moved by the wind and shows the direction in which the wind is blowing.

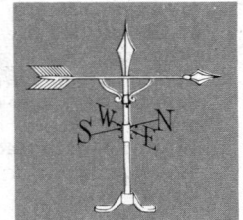

Weather vane

weave (wēv) *v.,* **wove** or *(def. 5)* **weaved, wo·ven, wove** or *(def. 5)* **weaved, weav·ing.** —*v.t.* **1.** to lace together: *to weave yarn into cloth.* **2.** to form or make by lacing together threads, yarn, or strips of straw or other material: *to weave a basket, to weave cloth.* **3.** to spin (a web or cocoon). **4.** to make by putting together different things or parts: *The old man wove stories from his childhood experiences.* **5.** to move or make by

turning and twisting: *to weave one's way through a crowd.*
—*v.i.* to form or make something by weaving. —*n.* a particular method or pattern of weaving: *an open weave.*

weav·er (wē′vər) *n.* a person who weaves or whose work is weaving.

weav·er·bird (wē′vər burd′) *n.* any of a large number of songbirds that often weave nests of grasses and straw.

web (web) *n.* **1.** something woven, especially a whole piece of cloth in the process of being woven or just removed from a loom. **2.** a network of fine threads spun by a spider; cobweb. **3.** any complex structure or network: *a web of streets, a web of lies.* **4.** skin or membrane, especially between the toes of a swimming bird. —*v.t.*, **webbed, web·bing.** to make or join together with a web or webbing: *The craftsman webbed a new seat for the chair.* —**web′-like′,** *adj.*

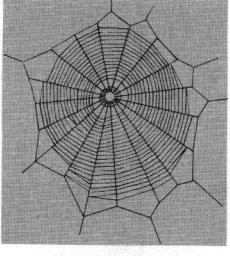

Web *(def. 2)*

webbed (webd) *adj.* having or joined by a web or webbing: *All geese have webbed feet.*

web·bing (web′ing) *n.* **1.** a strong, narrow band of woven fabric, made of cotton, hemp, or other fibers, used for seat belts, harness straps, and other items. **2.** anything forming a web or webs.

web·foot·ed (web′foot′id) *adj.* having the toes joined by a web: *The platypus is a web-footed animal.*

Web·ster (web′stər) **1. Daniel.** 1782–1852, U.S. statesman. **2. Noah.** 1758–1843, U.S. lexicographer and author.

wed (wed) *v.*, **wed·ded, wed·ded** or **wed, wed·ding.** —*v.t.* **1.** to take as one's husband or wife; marry. **2.** to join as husband and wife; unite in wedlock. **3.** to join closely; unite: *to be wed to one's opinion.* —*v.i.* to take a husband or wife; marry.

we'd (wēd) **1.** we had. **2.** we would. **3.** we should.

Wed., Wednesday.

wed·ded (wed′id) *adj.* **1.** in a married state: *a happily wedded couple.* **2.** having to do with marriage: *to live in wedded bliss.* **3.** closely joined: *two groups wedded by a common interest.* **4.** deeply involved; devoted: *a man wedded to his work.*

wed·ding (wed′ing) *n.* **1.** a marriage ceremony. **2.** the anniversary of a marriage: *A golden wedding is a celebration of fifty years of marriage.*

wedge (wej) *n.* **1.** a solid, triangular or tapered piece of wood or metal that can be used to separate, split, or lift objects: *Bill used an iron wedge to split logs into firewood.* **2.** something resembling this in shape: *a wedge of cheese.* **3.** anything that divides in some way: *The struggle over the inheritance drove a wedge between members of the family.* —*v.*, **wedged, wedg·ing.** —*v.t.* **1.** to separate or split by driving a wedge into: *The workman wedged the floor boards apart.* **2.** to fasten or fix in place with a wedge or wedges: *Margaret wedged the door open with a piece of wood.* **3.** to drive, push, or crowd: *He managed to wedge the book into place on the shelf.* —*v.i.* to force one's way: *John wedged into the seat on the train.*

Wedg·wood (wej′wood′) *n. Trademark.* earthenware pottery usually characterized by a blue or green tinted ground and white, raised ornament. [From Josiah *Wedgwood,* 1730–1795, an English potter.]

Wedgwood

wed·lock (wed′lok′) *n.* the state or condition of being married; matrimony.

Wednes·day (wenz′dē, wenz′dā) *n.* the fourth day of the week. [Old English *Wōdnesdæg* literally, Woden's day from *Woden,* the chief god in Teutonic mythology.]

wee (wē) *adj.*, **we·er, we·est. 1.** very small; little: *a wee baby in a cradle.* **2.** early: *in the wee hours of the morning.*

weed[1] (wēd) *n.* a plant that is either useless or harmful and grows where it is not wanted. —*v.t.* **1.** to remove weeds from: *to weed a lawn.* **2.** to remove what is useless or harmful: *to weed out the troublemakers from a group.* —*v.i.* to remove weeds. [Old English *wēod.*]

weed[2] (wēd) *n.* **1. weeds.** the clothes worn by someone in mourning, especially a widow. **2.** a token of mourning, such as a black band worn on the arm. [Old English *wǣd* a garment.]

weed·er (wē′dər) *n.* **1.** a person who weeds. **2.** a tool or device for removing weeds.

weed·y (wē′dē) *adj.*, **weed·i·er, weed·i·est. 1.** full of weeds. **2.** of, relating to, or resembling a weed or weeds.

week (wēk) *n.* **1.** a period of seven days, usually considered to begin with Sunday. **2.** the number of days or hours in a seven-day period devoted to a specific activity: *He works a forty-hour week.* **3.** the part of a seven-day period during which a person works or goes to school: *He doesn't watch television during the week because he has to study.*

week·day (wēk′dā′) *n.* any day of the week except Saturday and Sunday.

week·end (wēk′end′) *n.* the period extending from Friday night or Saturday morning until Sunday night or Monday morning. —*adj.* of, relating to, or happening during a weekend: *Alan looked forward to his weekend golf game.* —*v.i.* to spend a weekend: *to weekend in the country.*

week·ly (wēk′lē) *adj.* **1.** of, for, or relating to a week or weekdays: *She bought a weekly supply of groceries.* **2.** done, happening, or issued once a week: *The children made their weekly telephone call to their grandmother.* —*n. pl.,* **week·lies.** a newspaper, magazine, or the like issued once a week. —*adv.* once each week; every week: *She shopped weekly.*

weep (wēp) *v.*, **wept, weep·ing.** —*v.i.* **1.** to show grief, joy, or other strong emotion by shedding tears: *The sad news made her weep.* **2.** to feel sorrow or grief; mourn. **3.** to drip or leak; ooze: *The sores on his skin wept.* —*v.t.* **1.** to shed or let flow in drops: *to weep salty tears.* **2.** to bring to a particular condition by weeping: *The child wept himself to sleep.* **3.** to weep or mourn for. —**weep′er,** *n.*

weeping willow, a wide-spreading tree having pale-green leaves and greenish branches that droop almost to the ground.

wee·vil (wē′vəl) *n.* any of a group of destructive beetles having a snout or beak. Weevils feed on many crops, such as cotton and grain.

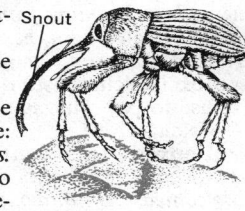

Snout

Weevil

weft (weft) *n.* the crosswise threads in weaving; woof.

weigh (wā) *v.t.* **1.** to measure the weight of, as on a scale or balance: *The grocer weighed the tomatoes. Mother weighed the baby.* **2.** to measure out (an amount of something) according to weight: *The*

at; āpe; cär; end; mē; it; īce; hot; ōld; fôrk; wood; fōol; oil; out; up; turn; sing; thin; this; hw in white; zh in treasure. The symbol ə stands for the sound of a in about, e in taken, i in pencil, o in lemon, and u in circus.

shopkeeper weighed out a pound of coffee. **3.** to think about or examine thoughtfully and carefully: *to weigh the advantages and disadvantages of a plan, to weigh one's words before speaking.* **4.** to lie heavily on; oppress, or burden: *The heavy snowfall weighed down the branches of the trees.* —*v.i.* **1.** to have, amount to, or be equal to a specified weight: *The car weighs 3744 pounds. She weighs exactly the same as her sister.* **2.** to be important; matter: *The boy's good grades weighed heavily in the decision of the scholarship committee.* **3.** to be oppressive or burdensome: *His guilt weighed on his conscience.* —**weigh′er,** *n.*

    to weigh anchor. to raise an anchor from the bottom and start to sail.

    to weigh in. to be weighed, as before a boxing match or other contest: *The champion weighed in at two hundred pounds.*

weight (wāt) *n.* **1.** the amount of heaviness of something: *Her weight is one hundred pounds.* **2.** the quality of any mass or body that results from the pull of gravity upon it: *The weight of helium is less than the weight of air, causing a helium-filled balloon to rise.* **3.** a system of units for expressing weight: *troy weight.* **4.** any unit of weight, such as a ton. **5.** a piece of metal or similar material having a particular weight, used as a standard in weighing. **6.** any heavy thing: *She looked for a weight to keep papers from blowing off her desk.* **7.** a burden or load; pressure: *The weight of his financial problems was ruining his health.* **8.** strong influence; importance: *His opinion carries much weight with his friends.* —*v.t.* **1.** to add weight to; load with additional weight: *The men weighted the cartons with rocks.* **2.** to burden heavily, as with a weight; oppress: *She was weighted down with troubles.*

    to throw one's weight around. *Informal.* to use one's power or authority, especially in an unfair way.

weight·less (wāt′lis) *adj.* **1.** having little or no weight. **2.** (of a body) having no apparent weight due to the absence of the pull of gravity, as in outer space. —**weight′lessness,** *n.*

weight·y (wā′tē) *adj.,* **weight·i·er, weight·i·est. 1.** of great weight; heavy: *a weighty object.* **2.** hard to bear; burdensome: *a weighty responsibility.* **3.** very serious; important: *a weighty decision, a weighty matter.* —**weight′iness,** *n.*

weir (wēr) *n.* **1.** a dam built in a river to raise the level of the water. **2.** a fence of stakes put in a stream or channel to catch fish.

weird (wērd) *adj.* **1.** different from the usual or expected; strange; bizarre; odd: *weird behavior, a weird person.* **2.** suggesting or having to do with the supernatural; difficult to explain or understand; mysterious: *Weird sounds were heard coming from the deserted house.* —**weird′ly,** *adv.* —**weird′ness,** *n.*

Weird Sisters, another name for the **Fates.**

welch (welch, welsh) *also,* **welsh.** *v.i. Informal.* to fail or refuse to pay what is owed, especially after losing a bet. —**welch′er,** *n.*

wel·come (wel′kəm) *v.t.,* **wel·comed, wel·com·ing. 1.** to greet (someone) with pleasure and hospitality: *We welcomed them into our club.* **2.** to receive or accept graciously or with pleasure: *The parents welcomed the news of their daughter's engagement.* —*n.* a glad and friendly greeting; kind or hospitable reception. —*adj.* **1.** received kindly and with pleasure: *a welcome visitor.* **2.** giving pleasure or satisfaction: *a welcome compliment.* **3.** free to use, have, or enjoy: *You are welcome to the telephone.* **4.** under no obligation. ▲ used chiefly in the phrase *you're welcome,* as a response to being thanked for something.

    to wear out one's welcome. to stay too long or visit too often.

weld (weld) *v.t.* **1.** to join (a substance, such as metal or plastic) to another by heating and softening it until it can be hammered and pressed or fused. **2.** to join closely together; unite: *The friends were welded together by their interest in sports.* —*v.i.* to be capable of being welded. —*n.* **1.** the point at which two things are joined by welding. **2.** the act or process of welding or the state of being welded. —**weld′er,** *n.*

wel·fare (wel′fer′) *n.* **1.** the state or condition of being or doing well, as in health or finances: *She inquired about her aunt's welfare when she telephoned.* **2.** financial aid or other assistance given to people in need; relief. It is usually distributed by one or more departments of the government.

welfare state, a state, nation, or government that ensures the well-being of its people by providing such benefits as health and unemployment insurance, guaranteed minimum wages, and subsidized housing.

welfare work, work done by the government, private agencies, and individuals to provide money, food, and services to people in need.

welfare worker, a person who does welfare work, especially as a profession.

wel·kin (wel′kin) *n. Archaic.* the sky; heavens.

well¹ (wel) *adv.,* **bet·ter, best. 1.** in a good or satisfactory way: *Philip plays the violin well. I did not sleep well last night.* **2.** in a thorough or complete way: *Be sure to mix the ingredients well.* **3.** to a considerable extent or degree: *He weighs well over 200 pounds. He walked well ahead of us on the way to town.* **4.** in a close or personal way: *Do you know him well?* **5.** under the circumstances; reasonably: *I can't very well accept your offer.* **6.** clearly; easily; perfectly: *I remember him well.* —*adj.* **1.** in good health; thriving: *Her mother wrote and told her that everyone in the family was well.* **2.** fortunate; good. —*interj.* used to express surprise, doubt, resignation, or to introduce another thought: *Well! How nice to see you. Well, I think it's time to leave now.* [Old English *wel* satisfactorily, thoroughly.]

    as well. a. in addition; also: *He plays the flute, and the guitar and drums as well.* **b.** with the same outcome or effect; equally: *You might as well travel with us as go alone.*

    as well as. a. in addition to; besides: *Her brother as well as her father and mother came to visit.* **b.** to the same extent or degree as: *He swims as well as his older brother.*

well² (wel) *n.* **1.** a hole or pit made in the ground to obtain water or oil. **2.** a natural spring or fountain. **3.** something resembling a well in shape or function: *There was a well for ink in the old desk. An encyclopedia is a well of information.* **4.** an enclosed space in a building, often going through several floors, such as a shaft for stairs or for an elevator. —*v.t.* to spring; rise; fill: *Tears welled in her eyes.* [Old English *wella* a spring of water.]

we'll (wēl) we shall; we will.

well-ad·vised (wel′əd vīzd′) *adj.* showing wisdom and good judgment: *He would be well-advised to do his work more carefully.*

well-ap·point·ed (wel′ə poin′tid) *adj.* properly or excellently furnished or equipped: *The president had a well-appointed office.*

well-a·way (wel′ə wā′) *interj. Archaic.* alas.

well-bal·anced (wel′bal′ənst) *adj.* **1.** nicely or evenly balanced; properly adjusted or regulated: *a well-balanced diet.* **2.** sensible or sane: *a well-balanced personality.*

well-be·haved (wel′bi hāvd′) *adj.* characterized by good conduct or manners: *a well-behaved young boy.*

well-be·ing (wel′bē′ing) *n.* health, happiness, and prosperity; welfare.

well·born (wel′bôrn′) *adj.* born of an aristocratic family.

well-bred (wel′bred′) *adj.* **1.** having or showing good manners or training; polite; tasteful. **2.** (of an animal) coming from good stock or pedigree.

well-de·fined (wel′di fīnd′) *adj.* clear and precise, as in marking or outline: *a girl with well-defined features.*

well-de·vel·oped (wel′di vel′əpt) *adj.* **1.** thought out or done in a thorough or very good way: *a well-developed plan.* **2.** having or showing good physical form: *The wrestler had well-developed arms.*

well-done (wel′dun′) *adj.* **1.** performed well; skillfully done. **2.** (of food) thoroughly cooked.

well-fa·vored (wel′fā′vərd) *adj.* good-looking; handsome.

well-fed (wel′fed′) *adj.* properly or fully nourished.

well-fixed (wel′fikst′) *adj. Informal.* not lacking in money; financially secure.

well-found·ed (wel′foun′did) *adj.* based on solid evidence, good judgment, or sound reasoning: *a well-founded argument.*

well-groomed (wel′grōōmd′) *adj.* carefully and attractively dressed and groomed; neat.

well-ground·ed (wel′groun′did) *adj.* **1.** thoroughly familiar with the fundamental principles of a subject: *well-grounded in mathematics.* **2.** based on sound evidence or reasoning; well-founded.

well-heeled (wel′hēld′) *adj. Informal.* having a lot of money; rich.

well-in·formed (wel′in fôrmd′) *adj.* **1.** having much knowledge and information on a wide variety of subjects. **2.** having correct or much information on a particular subject.

Wel·ling·ton (wel′ing tən) *n.* **1. Duke of.** 1769–1852, English soldier and statesman who defeated Napoleon I at Waterloo. **2.** the capital of New Zealand, on the southwestern tip of North Island. Pop. (1971), 135,515.

well-known (wel′nōn′) *adj.* **1.** famous; renowned: *a well-known movie star.* **2.** generally, widely, or fully known: *well-known facts.*

well-made (wel′mād′) *adj.* that has been made or developed in a careful, skillful, or strong way: *a well-made chair, a well-made plan.*

well-man·nered (wel′man′ərd) *adj.* having or showing good manners; polite.

well-mean·ing (wel′mē′ning) *adj.* **1.** intending to be helpful or good: *a well-meaning person.* **2.** coming or resulting from good intentions: *a well-meaning remark.*

well-nigh (wel′nī′) *adv.* very nearly; almost.

well-off (wel′ôf′) *adj.* **1.** fairly wealthy; financially secure: *His grandparents were very well-off.* **2.** in a position where things are good or going well: *He didn't know when he was well-off, and quit his job.*

well-read (wel′red′) *adj.* knowledgeable through having read many books.

well-round·ed (wel′roun′did) *adj.* **1.** having knowledge or interest in a wide variety of fields or subjects. **2.** made up of a wide variety of fields or subjects: *a well-rounded curriculum.*

Wells, H(erbert) G(eorge) (welz) 1866–1946, English novelist and social philosopher.

well-spo·ken (wel′spō′kən) *adj.* **1.** having educated and refined speech. **2.** said or delivered with style and polish: *a well-spoken rebuttal.*

well-spring (wel′spring′) *n.* **1.** a natural spring; fountainhead. **2.** the source of something, especially an unending source: *The professor seemed to be a wellspring of knowledge.*

well-timed (wel′tīmd′) *adj.* happening or done at the correct or suitable time: *She made a well-timed entrance.*

well-thought-of (wel′thôt′uv′, wel′thôt′ov′) *adj.* having a good reputation; respected: *a well-thought-of mayor.*

well-to-do (wel′tə dōō′) *adj.* having more than enough money; prosperous.

well-wish·er (wel′wish′ər) *n.* a person who wishes good fortune, success, or health, as to another person, a cause, or the like.

well-worn (wel′wôrn′) *adj.* **1.** showing evidence of much use or wear: *a well-worn jacket.* **2.** used too much; trite: *a well-worn phrase.*

welsh (welsh, welch) another spelling of **welch.**

Welsh (welsh, welch) *n.* **1.** a person who was born or is living in Wales. **2.** the language of Wales. —*adj.* of or relating to Wales, its people, their language or culture.

Welsh cor·gi (kôr′gē) a short-legged dog having a foxlike face and a coat of stiff hair.

Welsh·man (welsh′mən, welch′mən) *n. pl.,* **Welsh·men** (welsh′mən, welch′mən). a person who was born or is living in Wales.

Welsh rabbit, melted cheese mixed with beer, ale, or milk, seasoned, and served warm over toast or crackers. Also, **Welsh rarebit.**

welt (welt) *n.* **1.** a strip of material, especially a cord, sewn on an edge or in a seam of a garment or item, such as upholstery, usually for strengthening or decorating. **2.** a strip of leather or other material between the upper part and the sole of a shoe. **3.** a ridge or bump on the skin, such as one made by a stick or whip. —*v.t.* **1.** to put a welt on or in. **2.** *Informal.* to beat so as to raise welts on the skin.

wel·ter (wel′tər) *v.i.* **1.** to roll or toss about; wallow: *The young boys weltered in the muddy pool.* **2.** to be soaked or drenched in some liquid: *The hikers weltered in the rain.* —*n.* **1.** a rolling and tossing motion: *The welter of the waves kept us awake.* **2.** confusion; turmoil.

wel·ter·weight (wel′tər wāt′) *n.* a boxer who weighs between 136 and 147 pounds.

wen (wen) *n.* a benign tumor or cyst on the skin, especially on the scalp.

wench (wench) *n. pl.,* **wench·es. 1.** a girl or young woman. **2.** a female servant. **3.** an immoral woman.

wend (wend) *v.t.,* **wend·ed wend·ing.** to make (one's way); go on (one's way).

went (went) the past tense of **go.**

wept (wept) the past tense and past participle of **weep.**

were (wur) **1.** the plural past tense and the second person singular tense of **be. 2.** the subjunctive of **be:** *If I were you, I wouldn't have done that.*

we're (wēr) we are.

weren't (wurnt, wur′ənt) were not.

were·wolf (wēr′woolf′) *also,* **wer·wolf.** *n. pl.,* **werewolves** (wēr′woolvz′). in European folklore, a human being who sometimes turns into a wolf.

wert (wurt) *v.i. Archaic.* were.

We·ser (vā′zər) *n.* a river in northern West Germany, flowing into the North Sea.

Wes·ley (wes′lē) **1. John.** 1703–1791, English religious leader and the founder of the Methodist Church. **2. Charles.** 1707–1788, his brother; English Protestant reformer.

at; āpe; cär; end; mē; it; īce; hot; ōld; fôrk; wood; fōōl; oil; out; up; turn; sing; thin; <u>th</u>is; hw in white; zh in treasure. The symbol ə stands for the sound of **a** in about, **e** in taken, **i** in pencil, **o** in lemon, and **u** in circus.

Wes·ley·an (wes'lē ən) *n.* a member or disciple of the church founded by John Wesley; Methodist. —*adj.* of or relating to John Wesley or to Methodists or Methodism.

west (west) *n.* **1.** the direction a person faces when he watches the sun set. West is one of the four main points of the compass, located directly opposite east. **2.** *also,* **West.** any region or place lying in this direction. **3. the West. a.** a region of the United States west of the Mississippi River. **b.** the countries of Europe and the Americas as distinguished from those of Asia. —*adj.* **1.** toward or in the west. **2.** from the west: *a west wind.* —*adv.* toward the west.

West Berlin, the part of the city of Berlin belonging to West Germany. It is located in northern East Germany. Pop. (1970), 2,121,000.

west·bound (west'bound') *adj.* going west: *a westbound train.*

west·er·ly (wes'tər lē) *adj., adv.* **1.** toward the west: *The plane took off in a westerly direction.* **2.** from the west: *a westerly wind.*

west·ern (wes'tərn) *adj.* **1.** toward or in the west. **2.** *also,* **Western.** of, relating to, or characteristic of the west or the West. —*n. Informal.* a novel, short story, motion picture, or the like dealing with frontier life in the western United States, especially with the life of cowboys and the early settlers.

Western Australia, the largest state in Australia, occupying about one-third of the continent.

Western Church 1. the part of the Roman Catholic Church that recognizes the supremacy of the pope. **2.** the Roman Catholic, Anglican, and Protestant churches of western Europe and the Americas as a group.

west·ern·er (wes'tər nər) *n.* **1.** a person who was born or is living in the west. **2.** *usually,* **Westerner.** a person who was born or is living in the western United States.

Western Hemisphere, the western half of the earth that includes North and South America.

west·ern·ize (wes'tər nīz') *v.t.,* **west·ern·ized, west·ern·iz·ing.** to cause to adopt certain customs, methods, or characteristics of Europe and the Americas: *American businessmen have westernized manufacturing techniques in some Asian countries.* —**west'ern·i·za'tion,** *n.*

west·ern·most (wes'tərn mōst') *adj.* farthest west.

Western Samoa, an island country in the South Pacific, east of Australia. Capital, Apia. Land area, 1097 sq. mi. Pop. (1971 est.), 148,565.

West Germany, a country in north-central Europe. Capital, Bonn. Area, 95,932. sq. mi. Pop. (1969 est.), 61, 194,600. Official name: **the Federal Republic of Germany.**

West Indian 1. of or relating to the West Indies. **2.** a person who was born or is living in the West Indies.

West Indies, a long chain of islands that reaches from Florida to the coast of Venezuela, separating the Caribbean Sea from the Atlantic Ocean. It comprises the Greater Antilles, the Lesser Antilles, and the Bahamas.

West·ing·house, George (wes'ting hous') 1846–1914, U.S. inventor.

West I·ri·an (ēr'ē än') the western part of New Guinea and its offshore islands, under Indonesian control. It was formerly known as Netherlands New Guinea. Also, **West New Guinea.**

West Malaysia, another name for **Malaya.**

West·min·ster (west'min'stər) *n.* a borough in the central part of Greater London, especially the part containing the court and government buildings.

Westminster Abbey, a Gothic church in London, England. It is the traditional site of coronations and contains the tombs of many English monarchs, statesmen, and national heroes.

West New Guinea, another name for **West Irian.**

West Pakistan, formerly, one of the two provinces of Pakistan. In 1971 the other former province, East Pakistan, became the independent country of Bangladesh, and the country of Pakistan now consists of what was the province of West Pakistan.

West Point 1. the United States Military Academy, a four-year institution providing college-level instruction and officer training for careers in the U.S. Army. **2.** its site, a military reserve on the Hudson River in southeastern New York.

West Virginia, a state in the eastern United States. Capital, Charleston. Area, 24,181 sq. mi. Pop. (1970), 1,744,237. Abbreviation, **W. Va.** —**West Virginian.**

● The name **West Virginia** comes from the fact that this state was once the western part of Virginia. The name Virginia was chosen by Queen Elizabeth I of England, who was called the Virgin Queen because she had never married.

---

west·ward (west'wərd) *adv. also,* **west·wards.** toward the west: *We will be driving westward for several hours.* —*adj.* toward or in the west. —*n.* a westward direction, point, or place.

wet (wet) *adj.,* **wet·ter, wet·test. 1.** covered, soaked, or moist with water or other liquid: *His bathing suit was still wet from his morning swim. The little boy's eyes were wet with tears.* **2.** not yet dry: *A footprint was made in the wet cement.* **3.** marked by rainfall; rainy: *Spring is sometimes a wet season.* **4.** *Informal.* permitting or in favor of the manufacture and sale of alcoholic beverages: *a wet county.* —*v.,* **wet** or **wet·ted, wet·ting.** —*v.t.* to make wet: *Wet the ground before planting.* —*v.i.* to become wet or moist. —*n.* **1.** water or other moisture; wetness. **2.** rainy weather; rain. —**wet'ly,** *adv.* —**wet'ness,** *n.*

wet blanket *Informal.* a person or thing that has a depressing effect, as by discouraging others from having fun.

wet cell, in electricity, a cell having a liquid electrolyte.

weth·er (weth'ər) *n.* a castrated male sheep.

wet suit, a close-fitting, one-piece garment worn for warmth while swimming, especially by skin divers or scuba divers.

we've (wēv) we have.

whack (hwak) *n.* **1.** *Informal.* a sharp, resounding blow. **2.** *Informal.* the sound made by such a blow. **3.** *Slang.* a chance or try at something: *I'll take a whack at fixing the toaster.* —*v.t., v.i. Informal.* to hit or slap with a sharp, resounding blow.

  out of whack. *Informal.* not working properly; broken: *The television set is out of whack.*

whack·y (hwak'ē) *adj.,* **whack·i·er, whack·i·est.** another spelling of **wacky.**

whale[1] (hwāl) *n. pl.,* **whales** or **whale. 1.** any of various large mammals that live in all oceans and certain fresh waters. A whale has a fishlike body, horizontal tail fins, and flippers. Some whales are hunted for their

Whale (blue whale)

oil, flesh, and bone. **2.** *Informal.* something very large or impressive: *There was a whale of a crowd at the game.* —*v.i.,* **whaled, whal·ing.** to hunt whales. [Old English *hwæl.*]

whale² (hwāl) *v.t.,* **whaled, whal·ing.** *Informal.* to beat; thrash. [Of uncertain origin.]

whale·boat (hwāl′bōt′) *n.* a long, narrow rowboat, pointed at both ends, formerly used in whaling.

whale·bone (hwāl′bōn′) *n.* **1.** an elastic, horny material similar to fingernails, forming thin plates that grow in place of teeth in the upper jaw of certain whales. **2.** a thin strip of this material, formerly used for stiffening corsets or other items. Also, **baleen.**

whal·er (hwā′lər) *n.* **1.** a person whose work is whaling. **2.** a ship or boat used in whaling.

whal·ing (hwā′ling) *n.* the act, business, or work of hunting and killing whales for their oil, flesh, and bone.

wharf (hwôrf) *n. pl.,* **wharves** or **wharfs.** a structure built along a shore to be used as a landing place for boats and ships; dock.

wharf·age (hwôr′fij) *n.* **1.** a space at a wharf or the use of a wharf or wharves, as for mooring a ship, loading or unloading cargo, or storing goods. **2.** the charge for using a wharf or wharves. **3.** wharves as a group.

wharves (hwôrvz) a plural of **wharf.**

what (hwut, hwot; *unstressed* hwət) *pron.* **1.** which specific thing or things, action or actions, or the like: *What do you want to do? What is the date of the game?* **2.** that which: *They knew what he was thinking.* **3.** anything that; whatever: *Choose what you want for dinner.* **4.** how much: *What do you think we should charge for our work?* —*adj.* **1.** which one or ones: *What books are missing from the shelf?* **2.** whatever: *Take what food you will need for the picnic.* **3.** how surprising, great, absurd, or the like: *What trouble I had parking the car!* —*adv.* **1.** in what respect; how much: *What does it matter?* **2.** which reason; why: *What did you do that for?* —*interj.* an exclamation used to show surprise, disbelief, anger, or the like.
  what's what. *Informal.* the real state of affairs.
  what with. taking into consideration; because of: *What with the ice and snow, they decided not to drive home.*

what·ev·er (hwət ev′ər) *pron.* **1.** anything that: *Order whatever you want to eat.* **2.** no matter what: *Whatever you say, he still won't do it.* **3.** *Informal.* what: *Whatever is that noise?* —*adj.* **1.** any that: *Take whatever books you want to read.* **2.** of any type, sort, or character; at all.

what·not (hwut′not′, hwot′not′) *n.* a set of open shelves, as for holding ornaments or books.

what's (hwuts, hwots) **1.** what is. **2.** what has.

what·so·ev·er (hwut′sō ev′ər, hwot′sō ev′ər) *pron., adj.* whatever.

wheal (hwēl) *n.* a small ridge or swelling on the skin, as from an insect bite.

wheat (hwēt) *n.* **1.** a cereal grass having a thin, hollow, jointed stem and long, narrow, grasslike leaves. It is a major food source for man and animals. **2.** the tiny grains of this plant, used to make flour and other foods.

wheat·en (hwēt′ən) *adj.* made of wheat.

wheat germ, the embryo of the wheat kernel separated from flour in milling. It is rich in vitamins and is used as a cereal and to enrich other foods.

whee·dle (hwēd′əl) *v.t.,* **whee·dled, whee·dling. 1.** to persuade or try to persuade, as with flattery or the like: *He wheedled his boss into giving him the day off.* **2.** to get by wheedling: *He wheedled the*

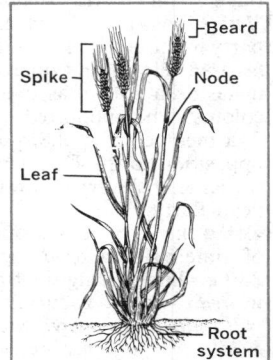
Wheat plant

money that he needed from his mother. —**whee′dler,** *n.* —**whee′dling·ly,** *adv.*

wheel (hwēl) *n.* **1.** a circular frame having a hub connected to the rim by spokes. A wheel can turn on a central axis and is used on vehicles and certain machines. **2.** any of a number of mechanical devices that use a wheel or wheellike part, such as a potter's wheel or spinning wheel. **3.** *usually,* **wheels.** the guiding, controlling, or moving force: *the wheels of business.* **4. wheels.** *Slang.* an automobile, motorcycle, bicycle, or other vehicle. —*v.i.* **1.** to turn on an axis; pivot: *He wheeled around when I called his name.* **2.** to move with a circular motion: *Seagulls wheeled overhead.* **3.** to roll or move along on wheels: *to wheel down the highway.* —*v.t.* **1.** to move or carry on wheels: *to wheel a shopping cart around a supermarket, to wheel a load of cement.* **2.** to cause to turn on an axis. **3.** to provide with wheels.
  at the wheel. a. doing the steering or driving. **b.** in control.

wheel·bar·row (hwēl′bar′ō) *n.* a boxlike device with one or two wheels at the front end and two handles at the back, used to move small loads, as of sand, dirt, bricks, or the like.

wheel·base (hwēl′bās′) *n.* the distance measured in inches between the center of the front wheel and the center of the rear wheel on the same side of an automobile or similar vehicle.

wheel·chair (hwēl′cher′) *also,* **wheel chair.** *n.* a chair mounted on wheels, used especially by invalids.

wheel·house (hwēl′hous′) *n. pl.,* **wheel·hous·es** (hwēl′hou′ziz). a deck of a ship that shelters the steering wheel and the pilot; pilothouse.

wheel·wright (hwēl′rīt′) *n.* a person who makes or repairs wheels, or wheeled vehicles such as carriages and wagons.

wheeze (hwēz) *v.i.,* **wheezed, wheez·ing. 1.** to breathe or utter a hoarse, whistling sound: *He wheezes badly when he has a cold.* **2.** to make a similar whistling sound: *The old bus wheezed when it climbed the hill.* —*n.* the act of wheezing.

wheez·y (hwē′zē) *adj.,* **wheez·i·er, wheez·i·est.** having or making a wheezing sound: *a wheezy cough.* —**wheez′i·ly,** *adv.* —**wheez′i·ness,** *n.*

whelk (hwelk) *n.* any of various large snails that live in salt water and have spiral shells.

whelm (hwelm) *v.t.* to submerge or otherwise overwhelm.

whelp (hwelp) *n.* **1.** the young of certain animals, such as dogs, bears, or lions. **2.** an impudent boy or young man. —*v.i.* to give birth to whelps.

when (hwen) *adv.* at what or which time: *When did he arrive?* —*conj.* **1.** at the time that: *Come when I call you.* **2.** at any time that: *When he is embarrassed his face gets red.* **3.** at what or which time; and then: *The children played until noon, when they had lunch.* **4.** although: *He*

Wheelchair

W

wore only a sweater when he should have worn a heavy coat.
5. considering that: *How can I go when I haven't been invited?* —*pron.* what time; which time: *Since when have you known about that?* —*n.* the time or occasion: *the where and when of an accident.*

whence (hwens) *adv.* from what place or source; from where. —*conj.* from what place, source, or cause: *We did not know whence the messenger came.*

whence·so·ev·er (hwens′sō ev′ər) *adv., conj. Archaic.* from whatever place, source, or cause.

when·e'er (hwen′âr′) *adv., conj. Archaic.* whenever.

when·ev·er (hwen ev′ər) *adv., conj.* at whatever time: *You may come whenever you like.*

when·so·ev·er (hwen′sō ev′ər) *conj., adv.* whenever.

where (hwer) *adv.* **1.** in or at what place: *Where did you put the camera? Where does he live?* **2.** to what place: *Where did Bill go?* **3.** from what place or source: *Where did you get that book?* **4.** in or at which: *This is the restaurant where we will eat.* **5.** in what way or respect; how: *Where can we be of the most help?* —*conj.* **1.** in the place in which; at the place at which: *The car is where you parked it.* **2.** in or at which place: *Let's go inside where we can sit down.* **3.** in the case, condition, circumstances, or respect in which: *She was very protective where her little sister was concerned.* —*n.* the place; scene; locality: *I don't know the when or where of the accident.*

where·a·bouts (hwer′ə bouts′) *adv.* near or in what location: *Whereabouts did you last see him?* —*n., pl.* the location of a person or place: *The police established the whereabouts of the suspect.* ▲ used with a singular or plural verb.

where·as (hwer az′) *conj.* **1.** considering that; since: *The document began "Whereas the finance committee has resolved . . ."* **2.** while; on the contrary: *My friend likes yellow, whereas I prefer green.*

where·at (hwer at′) *Archaic. adv.* at what. —*conj.* whereupon.

where·by (hwer bī′) *conj.* by which or by means of which: *He has a plan to invest his money whereby he will become rich.*

where·fore (hwer′fôr) *adv.* for what reason; why. —*conj.* for which reason; therefore. —*n.* the reason: *Do you know the whys and wherefores of her decision?*

where·from (hwer from′, hwer frum′) *adv., conj. Archaic.* from which; whence.

where·in (hwer in′) *conj.* in which. —*adv.* in what regard; how: *Wherein did we fail?*

where·of (hwer ov′, hwer uv′) *adv., conj.* of what, which, or whom: *Do you know whereof you speak when you say that he is responsible?*

where·on (hwer ôn′, hwer on′) *adv. Archaic.* on what. —*conj.* on which.

where·so·ev·er (hwer′sō ev′ər) *adv., conj. Archaic.* wherever.

where·to (hwer tōō′) *Archaic. conj.* to which or whom. —*adv.* for what purpose.

where·up·on (hwer′ə pôn′, hwer′ə pon′) *conj.* at which time; after which: *They waited for him to finish speaking, whereupon they left.* —*adv. Archaic.* upon what or which.

wher·ev·er (hwer ev′ər) *adv., conj.* in, at, or to whatever place: *Wherever did he buy that suit?*

where·with (hwer with′, hwer with̶′) *adv., conj. Archaic.* with what or which.

where·with·al (hwer′with ôl′) *n.* necessary means or resources, especially money.

wher·ry (hwer′ē) *n. pl.,* **wher·ries.** **1.** a light rowboat used to transport passengers and goods on rivers. **2.** a light rowboat for one person, used for racing.

whet (hwet) *v.t.,* **whet·ted, whet·ting. 1.** to sharpen by grinding, scraping, or rubbing: *The barber whetted his razor on a leather strap.* **2.** to make keen; stimulate: *The article whetted his interest in the subject.* —*n.* the act of whetting.

wheth·er (hweth′ər) *conj.* **1.** used to introduce the first of two choices or alternatives: *You must decide whether to take the train or to go by plane.* **2.** if it be the case that: *Write to us whether you will come to visit next month.* **3.** either: *Whether from bravery or stubbornness, they did not give in.*

  whether or not. in any case; regardless.

whet·stone (hwet′stōn′) *n.* a stone for sharpening knives or tools.

whew (hwyōō) *interj.* an exclamation used to express relief, surprise, dismay, or the like.

whey (hwā) *n.* the watery part of milk that separates from the curd when milk coagulates, as during the process of making cheese.

which (hwich) *pron.* **1.** what one or ones: *Which of the books did you like best?* **2.** any one or ones that; whichever: *Choose which you prefer.* **3.** used in a clause referring to a thing or things mentioned before: *This jacket, which I bought three years ago, still looks new.* **4.** used in place of "that" in a clause providing information that defines or restricts the antecedent: *The team which finishes first will receive the trophy.* ▲ See **that** for usage note. **5.** used after a preposition in defining or restricting a thing or things mentioned before: *The house in which we live is across the street.* **6.** a thing, circumstance, or event that: *You are late, which reminds me that you were late yesterday too.* —*adj.* **1.** what one or ones: *Which girl is your sister? Which highway leads to the football stadium?* **2.** being the thing or things previously mentioned: *He spent four years in France, during which time he learned French.* ▲ See **that** for usage note.

which·ev·er (hwich ev′ər) *pron., adj.* **1.** any one that: *Buy whichever you like best. You can have whichever picture you want.* **2.** no matter which: *Whichever road you follow, the drive to town won't take you more than twenty minutes.*

which·so·ev·er (hwich′sō ev′ər) *pron., adj.* whichever.

whiff (hwif) *n.* **1.** a sudden, light puff, breath, or gust, as of air: *A whiff of smoke rose from the small campfire.* **2.** a slight smell or odor: *A whiff of her perfume lingered in the room after she left.* —*v.t.* **1.** to move with a puff or gust. **2.** to breathe; sniff. —*v.i.* to blow or be carried in a puff or gust.

whif·fle·tree (hwif′əl trē′) *n.* the crossbar to which the traces of a harness are fastened, as in a horse-drawn carriage or plow. Also, **singletree, whippletree.**

Whig (hwig) *n.* **1.** a member of a former British political party in the eighteenth and early nineteenth centuries, that favored reform and opposed the Tory party. Since 1832, it has been known as the Liberal Party. **2.** an American colonist who supported the Revolution against England. **3.** a member of a U.S. political party formed in 1834 in opposition to the Democratic Party. It split in 1852 over the issue of slavery and was later succeeded by the Republican Party.

while (hwīl) *n.* **1.** a period of time, usually a short period of time: *We stopped walking and rested for a while.* **2. the while.** during the time: *She knitted all the while she waited.* —*conj.* **1.** during or in the time that: *Did anyone call while I was away?* **2.** at the same time that; although: *While they are my neighbors, I don't know them well.* —*v.t.,* **whiled, whil·ing.** to pass or spend (time or a period of time) in a leisurely, pleasant manner: *It is nice to while away a warm summer afternoon at the beach.*

whi·lom (whī′ləm) *Archaic. adj.* former. —*adv.* formerly.

whilst (hwīlst) *conj.* while.

whim (hwim) *n.* a sudden or unexpected notion or fanciful idea: *She had a whim to go for a walk in the rain.*

whim·per (hwim′pər) *v.i.* to cry with weak, broken sounds: *The hungry puppy whimpered.* —*v.t.* to utter with a weak, broken crying sound: *The little boy whimpered that he was sorry.* —*n.* a whimpering cry or sound. —**whim′per·er,** *n.* —**whim′per·ing·ly,** *adv.*

whim·sey (hwim′zē) *n. pl.,* **whim·seys.** another spelling of **whimsy.**

whim·si·cal (hwim′zi kəl) *adj.* **1.** full of or characterized by odd or fanciful notions: *They read a whimsical story about a boy who could fly.* **2.** fanciful or odd. —**whim′si·cal·ly,** *adv.*

whim·si·cal·i·ty (hwim′zi kal′ə tē) *n. pl.,* **whim·si·cal·i·ties.** **1.** the quality or state of being whimsical. **2.** a whimsical idea, notion, or action.

whim·sy (hwim′zē) *also,* **whim·sey.** *n. pl.,* **whim·sies.** **1.** an odd or fanciful notion. **2.** odd, curious, or fanciful humor, as in literature.

whine (hwīn) *v.,* **whined, whin·ing.** —*v.i.* **1.** to make a low, plaintive cry or sound, as from pain or peevishness: *The puppies whined because they were hungry.* **2.** to complain in a feeble or childish way. —*v.t.* to say with a low, plaintive cry or sound: *The tired child whined a complaint.* —*n.* the act or sound of whining. —**whin′er,** *n.* —**whin′ing·ly,** *adv.*

whin·ny (hwin′ē) *v.,* **whin·nied, whin·ny·ing.** —*v.i.* to neigh, especially in a low, gentle manner. —*v.t.* to express with such a sound. —*n. pl.,* **whin·nies.** the act or sound of whinnying.

whip (hwip) *v.,* **whipped** or **whipt, whip·ping.** —*v.t.* **1.** to strike with a lash, rod, strap, or the like: *to whip a naughty child.* **2.** to drive, urge, or force with or as if with lashes or blows: *The coach only had a week to whip his team into shape.* **3.** to strike like a whip or lash: *The cold wind whipped Jane's hair.* **4.** to beat (a substance, such as cream or eggs) to a froth or foam. **5.** to move, take, throw, or the like suddenly and rapidly: *to whip a gun out of a holster.* **6.** *Informal.* to defeat, as in a contest or fight. —*v.i.* **1.** to go, come, move, or turn suddenly and rapidly. **2.** to move with a flapping or thrashing motion: *The flag whipped in the wind.* —*n.* **1.** a flexible rod or thong attached to a handle, used especially for driving animals or inflicting punishment. **2.** a whipping or lashing blow, stroke, or motion. **3.** a member of a legislative assembly chosen by his party to be assistant to the party leader and to direct the party's tactics and maintain discipline. **4.** a dessert or other dish made with whipped ingredients, especially cream or eggs. —**whip′like′,** *adj.* —**whip′per,** *n.*

   to whip up. a. to arouse or excite: *The speaker's words whipped up the angry mob.* **b.** to make or prepare quickly: *The boy whipped up a snack from the leftovers from dinner.*

whip·cord (hwip′kôrd′) *n.* **1.** a strong, twisted cord, used for the lashes of whips. **2.** a tough fabric woven with diagonal ribs.

whip hand **1.** the hand in which the whip is held in driving. **2.** a position of control or advantage.

whip·lash (hwip′lash′) *n. pl.,* **whip·lash·es.** **1.** the lash of a whip. **2.** an injury to the neck resulting from a sudden backward or forward movement of the head. Whiplash often results when a person is riding in an automobile that strikes something or is struck.

whip·per·snap·per (hwip′ər snap′ər) *n.* an impudent person, especially a young person.

whip·pet (hwip′it) *n.* a small, slender dog having a short, smooth coat. The whippet is often used for racing.

whip·ple·tree (hwip′əl trē′) *n.* another word for **whiffletree.**

Whippet

whip·poor·will (hwip′ər wil′) *n.* a plump North American bird, having mottled brown, tan, and black feathers. Its call sounds like its name.

whipt (hwipt) a past tense and past participle of **whip.**

whir (hwur) *also,* **whirr.** *v.i., v.t.,* **whirred, whir·ring.** to move or operate with a whizzing or buzzing sound. —*n.* a whizzing or buzzing sound.

whirl (hwurl) *v.i.* **1.** to revolve or turn rapidly: *The blades of the airplane propeller whirled.* **2.** to turn around or aside suddenly or quickly: *The sentry whirled when he heard the noise.* **3.** to move or go swiftly: *The car whirled away from the curb.* **4.** to have a feeling of spinning; feel dizzy or confused: *The dazzling lights made my head whirl.* —*v.t.* **1.** to cause to revolve or turn rapidly; spin: *He grasped the man by the shoulder and whirled him around.* **2.** to move, carry, or drive swiftly, especially in a circular course: *The breeze whirled the leaves around as they fell.* —*n.* **1.** the act of whirling or spinning; whirling movement or motion. **2.** a confused or dizzy condition: *His mind was in a whirl.* **3.** a rapid round of activities or events: *a whirl of parties.* **4.** *Informal.* a short try: *He didn't know how to ice-skate, but he wanted to give it a whirl anyway.* —**whirl′er,** *n.*

whirl·i·gig (hwur′li gig′) *n.* **1.** a toy that whirls or spins about, such as a pinwheel. **2.** see **merry-go-round** *(defs. 1, 2).* **3.** something that moves or seems to move in a whirling motion.

whirl·pool (hwurl′pool′) *n.* a current of water having a swift or violent circular motion, usually occurring in rapidly moving bodies of water; eddy.

whirl·wind (hwurl′wind′) *n.* **1.** a rapidly or violently rotating column of air. **2.** anything resembling a whirlwind, as in swiftness of motion. —*adj.* very swift; hasty: *a whirlwind courtship.*

whirr (hwur) another spelling of **whir.**

whish (hwish) *n. pl.,* **whish·es.** a soft, rushing sound; swish. —*v.i.* to move with such a sound.

whisk (hwisk) *v.t.* **1.** to sweep or brush with swift, light strokes: *She whisked the crumbs off the table.* **2.** to move or cause to move swiftly or abruptly: *A taxicab whisked us to the airport.* **3.** to whip or beat, as eggs. —*v.i.* to move swiftly or lightly: *He whisked out the door.*

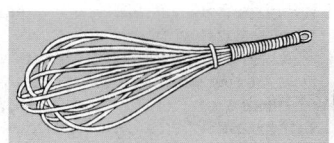
Whisk *(def. 3)*

—*n.* **1.** a quick, light sweeping motion or movement. **2.** see **whisk broom.** **3.** a wire kitchen utensil used especially for whipping cream or eggs.

at; āpe; cär; end; mē; it; īce; hot; ōld; fôrk; wood; fo͞ol; oil; out; up; turn; sing; thin; this; hw in white; zh in treasure. The symbol ə stands for the sound of **a** in about, **e** in taken, **i** in pencil, **o** in lemon, and **u** in circus.

W

whisk broom, a small, short-handled broom used especially for brushing clothes.

whisk·er (hwis′kər) *n.* **1. whiskers.** the hair growing on a man's face; beard or a part of the beard. **2.** a single hair of a beard. **3.** one of the long, stiff hairs growing near the mouth of certain animals, such as dogs, cats, and rats. **4.** *Informal.* a very small margin: *He won the race by a whisker.* —**whisk′ered,** *adj.*

whis·key (hwis′kē) *n. pl.,* **whis·keys.** *n.* **1.** a strong alcoholic liquor distilled from fermenting grain, such as rye, corn, barley, or wheat. **2.** a drink of such liquor. [Short for earlier *usquebaugh* this liquor, from Gaelic *uisgebeatha* literally, water of life.]

whis·ky (hwis′kē) *n. pl.,* **whis·kies.** another spelling of **whiskey.**

whis·per (hwis′pər) *v.i.* **1.** to speak very softly or cautiously, as when telling secrets: *The girls sat in the back of the room whispering. He had a sore throat and could only whisper.* **2.** to make a soft, rustling sound, as leaves blown by a breeze. —*v.t.* to say very softly or secretly: *He whispered the answer to the problem to his friend.* —*n.* **1.** a very soft spoken sound. **2.** something whispered, such as a rumor or secret. **3.** a soft, rustling sound. **4.** a small amount; hint: *There is a whisper of garlic in this sauce.* —**whis′per·er,** *n.*

whist (hwist) *n.* a card game for four players divided into teams of two, played with a full deck of fifty-two cards. It was the forerunner of bridge.

whis·tle (hwis′əl) *v.,* **whis·tled, whis·tling.** —*v.i.* **1.** to make a clear, shrill sound by forcing breath through closed lips or through the teeth. **2.** to produce or send out a sound like this: *The kettle whistled when the water boiled.* **3.** to move with a shrill sound: *A bullet whistled past the soldier's head. The wind whistled through the trees.* —*v.t.* **1.** to produce by whistling: *to whistle a melody.* **2.** to call, signal, or direct by whistling: *The policeman whistled traffic to a halt.* —*n.* **1.** a device designed or used to produce a whistling sound: *a policeman's whistle, a factory whistle.* **2.** a whistling sound. —**whist′ler,** *n.*

Whis·tler, James (hwis′lər) 1834–1903, U.S. painter.

whit (hwit) *n.* a tiny amount; bit: *All that sudden wealth made him not a whit happier.*

white (hwīt) *adj.,* **whit·er, whit·est. 1.** having the lightest of all colors; having the color of fresh snow; opposite of black: *a white shirt.* **2.** light in color: *the white meat of a turkey.* **3.** pale; ashen; pallid: *His face was white with fear.* **4.** silvery or pale gray: *white hair.* **5.** of, relating to, or belonging to a light-skinned people; Caucasian. **6.** not harmful: *white magic.* **7.** snowy: *a white Christmas.* **8.** not written or printed upon; blank. **9.** pure; innocent. —*n.* **1.** the lightest of all colors, reflecting all the visible rays of the spectrum; opposite of black. White is the color of fresh snow. **2.** a white paint, dye, or the like. **3.** something that is white or light-colored, such as the albumen of an egg or the white part of an eyeball. **4.** a member of a light-skinned people; Caucasian. **5.** *also,* **whites.** white clothing or a white uniform. —*v.t.,* **whit·ed, whit·ing.** *Archaic.* to whiten. —**white′ness,** *n.*

white ant, another term for **termite.**

white blood cell, a colorless cell found in the blood, that protects the body against infection by destroying disease germs. Also, **leukocyte, white corpuscle.**

white·cap (hwīt′cap′) *n.* a wave with a crest of white foam.

white-col·lar (hwīt′kol′ər) *adj.* of or relating to workers employed in professional, clerical, or other fields that usually do not involve manual labor. [From the *white* shirts worn by many of these workers.]

white corpuscle, another term for **white blood cell.**

white elephant, something that is expensive or burdensome to keep and, although often rare or unique, is of little value or use to the owner: *Their large old house was a white elephant.* [Originally referring to a rare, white or light-gray Asian elephant which is not required to work in parts of south-eastern Asia because it is regarded as sacred.]

white feather, a sign or symbol of cowardice. [From the superstition that a *white feather* in the tail of a rooster trained for fighting is a sign of a poor fighter.]

white·fish (hwīt′fish′) *n. pl.,* **white·fish** or **white·fish·es.** any of several silvery-white fish related to the salmon, found in freshwater lakes and streams, and used for food.

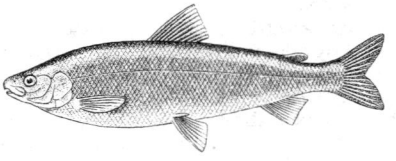

Whitefish

white flag, a white flag, banner, or piece of cloth, used to indicate surrender or truce.

white gold, an alloy of gold and, usually, nickel, used for jewelry. It looks like platinum.

White·hall (hwīt′hôl′) *n.* **1.** a street in London where many offices of the British government are located. **2.** the British government.

white heat 1. an extreme degree of heat at which a substance, such as a metal, glows white. **2.** a condition of extreme emotion, excitement, or activity.

White·horse (hwīt′hôrs′) *n.* a city in northwestern Canada, the capital of the Yukon. Pop. (1971), 11,084.

white-hot (hwīt′hot′) *adj.* **1.** glowing white with heat. **2.** extremely angry or excited.

White House 1. the official residence of the President of the United States, in Washington, D.C. **2.** the executive branch of the U.S. government.

white lie, a lie that is told to be polite or kind, or to conceal a minor mistake or misdeed.

white matter, the part of the brain and spinal cord consisting chiefly of nerve fibers and having a white appearance.

White Mountains, a range of the Appalachian Mountains, located chiefly in northern New Hampshire.

whit·en (hwīt′ən) *v.t., v.i.* to make or become white or whiter: *Bleach whitens clothing.*

White Nile, a river in eastern Africa, flowing northward through Uganda to Khartoum, where it joins the Blue Nile.

white oak 1. any of various oak trees, especially a large oak of eastern North America noted for its strong, heavy wood. **2.** the wood of any of these trees.

white paper, an official government report on a particular subject.

white pepper, a hot, pungent spice that is made from the dried, ground seeds of the berries of the pepper plant.

white pine 1. a tall pine tree of eastern North America, having bluish-green needles and slender cones. **2.** the soft wood of this tree.

White Russia, another name for **Byelorussia.**

white-tailed deer (hwīt′tāld′) a North American deer with a tawny coat and a bushy tail that is white on the underside.

white tie 1. a white bow tie, worn with men's formal evening wear. **2.** men's formal evening wear.

white·wall (hwīt′wôl′) *n.* an automobile tire with a white band on its outer side.

white·wash (hwīt′wôsh′, hwīt′wosh′) *n.* **1.** a white paintlike substance made of a mixture of slaked lime, water, and white chalk. It is used to whiten walls, wood fences, and other surfaces. **2.** the act of covering up something, such as a mistake or wrongdoing. **3.** *Sports.* a defeat in which the loser fails to score any points. —*v.t.* **1.** to coat or cover with whitewash. **2.** to cover up or gloss over (something, as a mistake or wrongdoing). **3.** *Sports.* to defeat (an opponent) without allowing him to score any points.

whith·er (hwith′ər) *adv., conj. Archaic.* to what place; where.

whit·ing[1] (hwī′ting) *n. pl.,* **whit·ings** or **whit·ing.** a silvery fish found in Atlantic coastal waters and used for food. [Dutch *wijting.*]

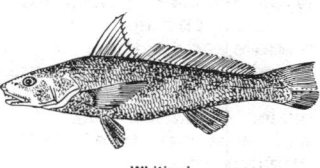

Whiting[1]

whit·ing[2] (hwī′ting) *n.* white chalk, powdered and washed, used especially as a pigment. [*White* + *ing*[1].]

whit·ish (hwī′tish) *adj.* somewhat white: *a whitish bird.*

Whit·man, Walt (hwit′mən) 1819–1892, U.S. poet.

Whit·ney (hwit′nē) *n.* **1.** **E·li** (ē′lī). 1765–1825, U.S. inventor of the cotton gin. **2. Mount.** a mountain of the Sierra Nevada range, in eastern California. It is the highest peak in the United States outside Alaska.

Whit·sun·day (hwit′sun′dē, hwit′sun′dā) *n.* the seventh Sunday after Easter; Pentecost.

Whit·sun·tide (hwit′sən tīd′) *n.* the week beginning with Whitsunday, especially the first three days of this week.

whit·tle (hwit′əl) *v.,* **whit·tled, whit·tling.** —*v.t.* **1.** to cut shavings or small bits or pieces from with a knife: *to whittle wood.* **2.** to make or shape (something) in this way: *Phil whittled a bird from a piece of soap.* **3.** to reduce or diminish gradually: *to whittle down one's expenses.* —*v.i.* to whittle wood or the like. —**whit′tler,** *n.*

whiz (hwiz) *also,* **whizz.** *v.,* **whizzed, whiz·zing.** —*v.i.* **1.** to make a hissing, humming, or buzzing sound, especially while moving swiftly through the air: *The plane whizzed over the roof tops. The automobile whizzed past us.* **2.** to move or go through or by very quickly: *Jean whizzed through her homework.* —*v.t.* to cause to move with a buzzing sound: *Paul whizzed the toy plane across the room.* —*n. pl.,* **whiz·zes. 1.** a whizzing sound or movement. **2.** *Slang.* a person having great skill or ability in some particular field or activity: *Kate is a whiz at crossword puzzles.*

who (hōō) *pron.* possessive, **whose;** objective, **whom. 1.** what or which person or persons: *Who gave you that book?* **2.** that. ▲ used to introduce a relative clause when the preceding noun is a person or persons: *The woman who wrote this play has an excellent sense of humor.* **3.** the person or persons that; whoever: *Who steals my purse steals trash* (Shakespeare, *Othello*).

▲ In formal speech and writing, **who** is used in the nominative case and **whom** in the objective case: *To whom am I speaking? Whom does he suspect of the crime?* However, in speech and informal writing, **who** is often used instead of **whom:** *Who did you call on the phone? Do you know who the committee named as its chairman?* See **that** for an additional usage note.

whoa (hwō, wō) *interj.* stop. ▲ used chiefly as a command to a horse.

who'd (hōōd) **1.** who would. **2.** who had.

who·dun·it (hōō dun′it) *n. Informal.* a mystery story, especially one that centers on the gradual discovery of the criminal's identity.

who·ev·er (hōō ev′ər) *pron.* **1.** any person who; what-

ever person: *Whoever wants to come to the party is welcome.* **2.** no matter who: *Whoever it was that wrote this book, he's very clever.* **3.** what person; who: *Whoever told you such a ridiculous story?*

whole (hōl) *adj.* **1.** made up of the entire amount, quantity, number, or extent: *Did you read the whole book? David has been sick the whole week.* **2.** having all its parts; complete; entire: *A whole deck consists of fifty-two cards.* **3.** not divided into parts or pieces; in one unit: *The whale swallowed the small fish whole.* **4.** not damaged, injured, or broken; intact; sound: *The doll was still whole after having been thrown down the stairs.* **5.** *Mathematics.* not fractional; integral. —*n.* **1.** all the parts or elements that together make up a thing; entire amount, quantity, number, or extent: *She spent the whole of her paycheck on a new dress.* **2.** a combination of parts or elements forming a complete entity or system. —**whole′ness,** *n.*
　on the whole. all things considered; in general.

whole-heart·ed (hōl′här′tid) *adj.* complete, sincere, or enthusiastic: *I will give you my whole-hearted support.* —**whole′-heart′ed·ly,** *adv.* —**whole′-heart′ed·ness,** *n.*

whole note, a musical note having a time value equal to four quarter notes or two half notes.

whole number, a number that tells how many complete things there are. *1, 2, 3,* and *0* are examples of whole numbers; *¾* and other fractions are not whole numbers.

whole·sale (hōl′sāl′) *n.* the selling of goods in large quantities, usually to retailers for resale. —*adj.* **1.** of, relating to, or engaged in the selling of goods in large quantities, usually to retailers for resale. **2.** widespread and complete: *the wholesale slaughter of war.* —*adv.* in a wholesale quantity or at a wholesale price. —*v.,* **wholesaled, whole·sal·ing.** —*v.t.* to sell (goods) at wholesale. —*v.i.* to be sold at wholesale.

whole·sal·er (hōl′sā′lər) *n.* a merchant or dealer in wholesale goods.

whole·some (hōl′səm) *adj.* **1.** good for the health; healthful: *wholesome food.* **2.** of value to the mind or character; worthwhile: *wholesome entertainment.* **3.** showing good health: *a wholesome young girl.* —**whole′some·ness,** *n.*

whole step *Music.* an interval consisting of two adjacent half steps. Also, **whole tone.**

whole-wheat (hōl′hwēt′) *adj.* **1.** made of the entire wheat kernel: *whole-wheat flour.* **2.** made with whole-wheat flour: *whole-wheat bread.*

who'll (hōōl) **1.** who will. **2.** who shall.

whol·ly (hō′lē, hōl′lē) *adv.* entirely; completely: *The company was wholly owned by one family.*

whom (hōōm) *pron.* the objective case of **who.** ▲ See **who** for usage note.

whom·ev·er (hōōm ev′ər) *pron.* the objective case of **whoever.**

whom·so·ev·er (hōōm′sō ev′ər) *pron.* the objective case of **whosoever.**

whoop (hōōp, hwōōp, wōōp) *n.* **1.** a loud cry or shout, as of joy or enthusiasm. **2.** the cry of an owl or certain other birds; hoot. **3.** a loud, gasping sound that follows a fit of coughing in the disease whooping cough. —*v.i.* to utter a whoop or whoops: *Steve whooped for joy when he*

at; āpe; cär; end; mē; it; īce; hot; ōld; fôrk; wood; fōōl; oil; out; up; turn; sing; thin; this; hw in white; zh in treasure. The symbol ə stands for the sound of **a** in about, **e** in taken, **i** in pencil, **o** in lemon, and **u** in circus.

W

won the contest. —*v.t.* **1.** to utter or express with a whoop or whoops: *to whoop one's joy.* **2.** to urge on, drive, or call with whoops or shouts.

whooping cough, a highly contagious, infectious disease, characterized by fits of coughing that end with a loud, gasping sound, or whoop. Whooping cough usually occurs in infants and young children.

whooping crane, a nearly extinct crane having a white body, black-tipped wings, and a red face. It is the tallest of all North American birds.

whop·per (hwop′ər) *n. Informal.* **1.** something very large: *That fish you caught is a whopper!* **2.** a big lie.

whore (hôr) *n.* another word for **prostitute.**

whorl (hwurl, hwôrl) *n.* **1.** *Botany.* a circular arrangement of parts, such as leaves, around the same point on a stem. **2.** *Zoology.* one of the turns of a spiral shell. **3.** any of the circular ridges of a fingerprint. **4.** anything resembling a coil or spiral in form or appearance.

Whorl of a fingerprint

who's (hōōz) **1.** who is. **2.** who has.

whose (hōōz) *pron.* the possessive case of **who** and **which.**

who·so (hōō′sō) *pron.* whoever.

who·so·ev·er (hōō′sō ev′ər) *pron.* whoever.

why (hwī) *adv.* **1.** for what cause, reason, or purpose: *Why are you laughing?* **2.** for which: *The reason why she did it is not known.* —*conj.* **1.** the cause, reason, or purpose for which: *Do you know why she came home early?* **2.** because of which; for which: *I see no reason why you shouldn't go.* —*n. pl.,* **whys.** a cause, reason, or purpose. —*interj.* used to express surprise, hesitation, or other feeling: *Why, look who's here!*

W.I. 1. West Indies. **2.** West Indian.

Wich·i·ta (wich′i tô′) *n.* the largest city in Kansas, in the south-central part of the state. Pop. (1970), 276,554.

Wichita Falls, a city in northern Texas. Pop. (1970), 97,564.

wick (wik) *n.* a cord or thin bundle of fibers, as in an oil lamp, candle, or cigarette lighter, that draws up the fuel to be burned.

wick·ed (wik′id) *adj.* **1.** morally bad; evil. **2.** mischievous; sly: *Patrick is a wicked tease.* **3.** *Informal.* causing or likely to cause harm, trouble, or discomfort: *She had a wicked cold.* —**wick′ed·ly,** *adv.* —**wick′ed·ness,** *n.*

wick·er (wik′ər) *n.* **1.** slender, flexible twigs woven together, used in making baskets, furniture, and the like. **2.** see **wickerwork.** —*adj.* made of or covered with wicker: *a wicker basket.*

wick·er·work (wik′ər wurk′) *n.* something made of wicker.

wick·et (wik′it) *n.* **1.** a small door or gate, especially one that is part of or near a larger one. **2.** a small window or opening. **3.** in cricket, either of the two sets of three stakes that form the targets for the bowler. **4.** in croquet, any of the arches through which the ball must be hit, usually made of wire.

Wickerwork

wick·i·up (wik′ē up′) *n.* a loosely built hut often made of a circular frame of poles covered with brush, used by certain North American Indian tribes.

wide (wīd) *adj.,* **wid·er, wid·est. 1.** extending over or made up of a very large area: *a wide lawn.* **2.** having a greater extent from side to side than is usual: *This coat has* wide lapels. **3.** having a specified extent from side to side: *This room is twelve feet wide.* **4.** great in amount, range, or extent: *This store carries a wide assortment of products.* **5.** fully opened or extended: *The boy's eyes were wide with excitement.* **6.** far or away from a specified point or object: *His arrow was wide of the mark.* —*adv.* **1.** over a large area; extensively: *to travel far and wide.* **2.** to a large or the full extent: *to open a window wide.* **3.** far or away from something aimed at: *The hockey player shot the puck wide and missed the goal.* —**wide′ly,** *adv.* —**wide′-ness,** *n.*

wide-a·wake (wīd′ə wāk′) *adj.* **1.** fully awake. **2.** paying attention to what is happening; alert.

wide-eyed (wīd′īd′) *adj.* with the eyes wide open, as in wonder, disbelief, or surprise.

wid·en (wīd′ən) *v.t., v.i.* to make or become wide or wider: *to widen a road.*

wide·spread (wīd′spred′) *adj.* **1.** occurring, distributed, or prevalent over a wide area or among many people: *a widespread epidemic, a widespread rumor.* **2.** widely extended: *widespread arms.*

widg·eon (wij′ən) *n. pl.,* **widg·eons** or **widg·eon.** any of several freshwater ducks, having mainly brown or gray feathers.

wid·ow (wid′ō) *n.* a woman whose husband is dead, especially one who has not married again. —*v.t.* to cause to become a widow.

wid·ow·er (wid′ō ər) *n.* a man whose wife is dead, especially one who has not married again.

wid·ow·hood (wid′ō hood′) *n.* the state or period of being a widow.

widow's peak, a V-shaped point in a hairline, formed by hair growing down in the middle of the forehead. [From the belief that it indicated that a woman would become a *widow* early in life.]

width (width) *n.* **1.** the measurement of something from side to side; size in terms of wideness; breadth. **2.** a piece of something, especially of cloth, having a certain width: *They needed two widths of curtain material to cover the window.*

width·wise (width′wīz′) *adv.* in the direction of the width; from side to side.

wield (wēld) *v.t.* **1.** to handle or use, as a weapon or tool: *The logger had good experience wielding an axe.* **2.** to exercise, as influence or power: *The judge wielded his authority fairly.* —**wield′er,** *n.*

wie·ner (wē′nər) *n.* another word for **frankfurter.** Also, **wie·ner·wurst** (wē′nər wurst′).

Wies·ba·den (vēs′bäd′ən) *n.* a city in west-central West Germany, noted as a health resort. Pop. (1970), 250,100.

wife (wīf) *n. pl.,* **wives.** a married woman. —**wife′ly,** *adj.*

wig (wig) *n.* a covering for the head made of hair or of a synthetic material resembling hair.

wig·gle (wig′əl) *v.,* **wig·gled, wig·gling.** —*v.i.* to move with short, quick, jerky movements, as from side to side: *His mother told him to stop wiggling and sit still.* —*v.t.* to cause to wiggle: *She wiggled her toes in the sand.* —*n.* the act of wiggling; a wiggling movement. —**wig′gly,** *adj.*

wig·gler (wig′lər) *n.* **1.** a person or thing that wiggles. **2.** a mosquito larva; wriggler.

wight (wīt) *n. Archaic.* a human being; person.

Wight, Isle of (wīt) an island in the English Channel, off the southern coast of England.

wig·wag (wig′wag′) *v.t., v.i.,* **wig·wagged, wig·wag·ging. 1.** to move (something) back and forth. **2.** to send (a message) by waving flags, lights, or the like according to a code. —*n.* **1.** the act or practice of sending messages by waving flags, lights, or the like according to a code. **2.** a message so sent. —**wig′wag′ger,** *n.*

wig·wam (wig′wom, wig′wôm) *n.* a hut used by certain tribes of North American Indians, usually made with an arched framework of poles covered with bark or leaves.

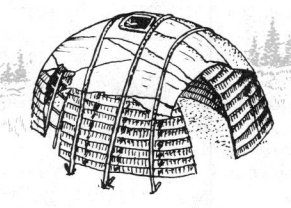

Wigwam

wild (wīld) *adj.* **1.** not brought under the control of man; in a state of nature: *There are still wild horses in that valley.* **2.** growing without the assistance of man: *wild plants.* **3.** unrestrained or disorderly; uncontrolled: *the wild flight of a frightened animal.* **4.** not disciplined; unruly: *wild children, a wild party.* **5.** not neat or orderly in appearance; disheveled: *wild hair.* **6.** characterized by violent or intense activity; turbulent: *the wild sea.* **7.** reckless, crazy, or fantastic: *a wild idea.* **8.** wide of the mark: *a wild shot, a wild throw.* **9.** *Informal.* extremely enthusiastic or excited: *The audience was wild about the new singer.* **10.** (of a card) having any value the player chooses. —*n.* also, **wilds.** an uninhabited or uncultivated place. —*adv.* in a wild manner. —**wild′ly,** *adv.* —**wild′ness,** *n.*
   to run wild. to be free from any form of control or restraint.

wild boar, a wild hog native to Europe, Asia, and North America, having a coarse, gray-brown coat and a pair of short tusks.

wild·cat (wīld′kat′) *n.* **1.** any of various small, wild members of the cat family, including the bobcat and lynx. **2.** an ill-tempered or spiteful person. **3.** an oil well drilled to find out whether there is oil at a given spot. —*adj.* **1.** unsound or reckless: *a wildcat bank, a wildcat scheme.* **2.** unauthorized or illegal: *The union leaders denounced the wildcat strike.* —**wild′cat·ter,** *n.*

Wilde, Oscar (wīld) 1854–1900, Irish playwright, novelist, and essayist.

wil·de·beest (wil′də bēst′) *n. pl.,* **wil·de·beests** or **wil·de·beest.** another word for **gnu.**

Wil·der, Thorn·ton (wīl′dər; thornt′ən) 1897—, U.S. playwright and novelist.

wil·der·ness (wil′dər nis) *n. pl.,* **wil·der·ness·es. 1.** a wild or desolate place where no people live. **2.** a confused or bewildering collection or group of things: *a wilderness of tall buildings.*

wild·fire (wīld′fīr′) *n.* a fire that spreads rapidly and is not easily put out.

wild·flow·er (wild′flou′ər) *also,* **wild flower.** *n.* **1.** any flower of a plant that grows wild, as in a field or woods. **2.** a plant bearing such a flower.

wild·fowl (wīld′foul′) *n. pl.,* **wild·fowl** or **wild·fowls.** a game bird, especially a wild duck or goose.

wild-goose chase (wīld′gōos′) a foolish or hopeless pursuit or endeavor.

wild·life (wīld′līf′) *n.* living things, especially wild animals that live naturally in an area.

wild pitch *Baseball.* a pitch that is thrown beyond the catcher's reach and allows a base runner to advance.

Wild West, the western frontier region of the United States, noted for its rough and lawless conditions during the nineteenth century.

wild·wood (wīld′wood′) *n.* a forest that has not been cut or cultivated and is in its natural state.

wile (wīl) *n.* a trick or stratagem meant to deceive or lure: *She employed her wiles to get the information she needed.* —*v.t.,* **wiled, wil·ing.** to tempt; lure.

wil·i·ness (wī′lē nis) *n.* the state or quality of being wily.

will[1] (wil) Present tense: *sing.,* first person, **will;** second,

will or *(archaic)* **wilt;** third, **will;** *pl.,* **will.** Past tense: *sing.,* first person, **would;** second, **would** or *(archaic)* **wouldst;** third, **would;** *pl.,* **would.** *auxiliary verb* **1.** to be about to; going to: *I will visit you tonight.* **2.** to be willing to: *I will do the job if you promise to help.* **3.** to be obliged or bound to; must: *He will do as he is told.* **4.** to be able to; can: *This chair will not support your weight.* **5.** to be accustomed to: *Sometimes the cat will lie there all afternoon.* —*v.i.* to wish; desire: *Help me move this chair, if you will.* [Old English *willan.*] ▲ See **shall** for usage note.

will[2] (wil) *n.* **1.** the power or capacity of free, conscious choice: *He made the decision of his own free will.* **2.** the ability to determine or control one's actions, especially self-control: *Does he have the will to stop smoking?* **3.** a fixed resolution; purpose: *She survived because of her will to live.* **4.** a preferred course of action; wish: *What is his will in the matter?* **5.** *Law.* a document giving the final settlement of a person's property after he dies. —*v.t.* **1.** to make use of one's power of free choice; exercise the will. **2.** to influence (someone) to do something by using one's will. **3.** to give away (property) by a will: *The man willed his estate to charity.* [Old English *willa.*]
   at will. when or as one wishes.

will·ful (wil′fəl) *also,* **wil·ful.** *adj.* **1.** determined to do as one pleases; obstinate; stubborn: *a willful youngster.* **2.** deliberate; intentional: *a willful waste.* —**will′ful·ly,** *adv.* —**will′ful·ness,** *n.*

Wil·liam I (wil′yəm) 1027?–1087, the king of England from 1066 to 1087. Also, **William the Conqueror.**

Wil·liams (wil′yəmz) **1. Roger.** 1603?–1684, the founder of Rhode Island. **2. Tennessee.** 1914—, U.S. dramatist.

Wil·liams·burg (wil′yəmz burg′) *n.* a historic town in southeastern Virginia.

will·ing (wil′ing) *adj.* **1.** favorably disposed; ready: *willing to work.* **2.** characterized by cheerful readiness: *a willing helper.* **3.** cheerfully given, accepted, or accomplished: *willing service.* —**will′ing·ly,** *adv.* —**will′ing·ness,** *n.*

will-o'-the-wisp (wil′ə thə wisp′) *n.* **1.** a faint light seen at night hovering over marshes. **2.** something deceptive or illusive, such as a hope or goal.

wil·low (wil′ō) *n.* any of a group of trees and shrubs, such as the weeping willow or pussy willow, usually having slender leaves and branches, and tiny flowers growing on furry spikes, called catkins.

wil·low·y (wil′ō ē) *adj.* **1.** graceful and slender. **2.** abounding with willows.

will·pow·er (wil′pou′ər) *n.* the ability to control one's actions; resoluteness of will: *It takes willpower to follow a strict diet.*

wil·ly-nil·ly (wil′ē nil′ē) *adj.* indecisive; vacillating: *a willy-nilly person.* —*adv.* whether one is willing or not; willingly or unwillingly: *You must do it, willy-nilly.*

Wil·ming·ton (wil′ming tən) *n.* the largest city of Delaware, a port in the northeastern part of the state. Pop. (1970), 80,386.

Wil·son (wil′sən) *n.* **1. Harold.** 1916—, the prime minister of Great Britain from 1964 to 1970. **2. (Thomas) Woodrow** (wood′rō). 1865–1924, the twenty-eighth president of the United States, from 1913 to 1921.

W

at; āpe; cär; end; mē; it; īce; hot; ōld; fôrk; wood; fōol; oil; out; up; turn; sing; thin; this; hw in white; zh in treasure. The symbol ə stands for the sound of a in about, e in taken, i in pencil, o in lemon, and u in circus.

wilt¹ (wilt) *v.i.* **1.** to fade or droop; become limp; wither: *The flowers wilted quickly once they were cut.* **2.** to lose energy, strength, or courage: *The girls wilted after walking in the summer heat for an hour.* —*v.t.* to cause to wilt: *The hot, dry weather wilted the flowers.* [A form of dialectal *welk* to wither.]

wilt² (wilt) *Archaic.* the second person singular, present indicative of **will¹**. ▲ used with *thou.*

wil·y (wī′lē) *adj.*, **wil·i·er, wil·i·est.** full of wiles; cunning; crafty.

wim·ple (wim′pəl) *n.* a cloth covering for the head and neck, formerly worn by women out-of-doors, still worn by some nuns.

win (win) *v.*, **won, win·ning.** —*v.i.* **1.** to be victorious over others: *Don is a skilled player who wins often at cards.* **2.** to finish first in a race: *The horse won by a head.* **3.** to succeed in some effort or endeavor: *He won in his efforts to have the rule changed.* —*v.t.* **1.** to be victorious in: *to win a battle, to win a court case.* **2.** to receive in or as if in a contest: *to win a vacation for two, to win ten dollars at the race track.* **3.** to get by effort or merit: *to win respect, to win favor with a teacher.* **4.** to get the good will, favor, or support of; persuade: *The lawyer won over the jury with his moving defense.* **5.** to persuade (someone) to marry or return one's love: *He won her after a long courtship.* **6.** to attain or reach, especially after long effort: *The disabled boat won the shore.* —*n. Informal.* a victory: *The pitcher had a record of ten wins and no losses.*

wince (wins) *v.i.*, **winced, winc·ing.** to draw back or away slightly, as from something painful, dangerous, or unpleasant; flinch: *He winced at the thought of getting the injection.* —*n.* the act of wincing.

winch (winch) *n. pl.*, **winch·es. 1.** a machine for hoisting or pulling, consisting of a drum around which cord or chain is wound. **2.** a crank, handle, or lever by which a revolving machine is turned.

wind¹ (wind) *n.* **1.** air in motion over the surface of the earth; natural movement or current of air: *The wind whistled through the canyon.* **2.** a strong or destructive natural movement of air; gale. **3.** air set in motion artificially, as by a fan or other moving object. **4.** moving air carrying an odor, especially of a person or animal being hunted; scent: *The dogs followed the wind of the fox.* **5.** any compelling force or influence: *the winds of change.* **6.** the ability to breathe; breath: *The blow knocked the wind out of him.* **7.** empty, meaningless talk; chatter. **8.** winds. **a.** wind instruments. **b.** the players of these instruments, making up a section of an orchestra. —*v.t.*, **wind·ed, wind·ing. 1.** to cause to be out of breath, as from physical effort: *Climbing the long flight of stairs winded him.* **2.** to find or follow by scent: *The dogs winded the fox.* **3.** to allow to rest in order to recover breath: *They winded the horses after the long ride uphill.* [Old English *wind* air in motion, breath.]

in the wind. happening or going to happen.

to get wind of. to learn or hear information or hints about: *If he gets wind of the party, the surprise will be ruined.*

wind² (wīnd) *v.*, **wound** or *(archaic)* **wind·ed, wind·ing.** —*v.t.* **1.** to wrap (something) around on itself or on something else: *Jane wound the yarn into a ball. Sue wound the scarf around her neck.* **2.** to cover or entwine, as by wrapping or coiling: *to wind one's hair with ribbons.* **3.** to cause to move or proceed first in one direction and then another: *The policeman wound his car through the city traffic.*

4. to make (one's way) by moving first in one direction and then another. **5.** to adjust or put (a mechanism, such as a clock) into action by turning or coiling some part of it. —*v.i.* **1.** to move in first one direction and then another; go in a crooked or bending course: *The new highway winds around the mountain.* **2.** to twine, turn, or coil around or about something: *The roses wound around the trellis.* **3.** to be capable of being turned or coiled: *The strings on this guitar wind easily.* —*n.* **1.** the act of winding or the state of being wound. **2.** a turn, coil, or twist. [Old English *windan* to turn, twist, move rapidly.]

to wind up. a. to bring to an end; finish: *Let's wind up the work today.* **b.** to come to an end: *The meeting wound up at six o'clock.* **c.** to bring to a state of readiness or excitement; arouse. **d.** (of a baseball pitcher) to make movements with the body or parts of the body in preparation for pitching the ball.

wind·bag (wind′bag′) *n. Informal.* a person who talks much but says little of importance or interest.

wind·break (wind′brāk′) *n.* a structure, such as a fence or growth of trees or shrubs, that serves as a protection from the wind.

wind·break·er (wind′brā′kər) *n. Trademark.* a short jacket made of any of various tightly woven fabrics that resist the passage of air.

wind·burn (wind′burn′) *n.* an irritation of the skin caused by exposure to the wind. —**wind′burned′,** *adj.*

wind·fall (wind′fôl′) *n.* **1.** an unexpected advantage, opportunity, or gain, especially a financial gain. **2.** a fruit that falls from the tree before it is harvested, especially one that is blown down by the wind.

wind·flow·er (wind′flou′ər) *n.* see **anemone** *(def. 1).*

wind·ing (wīn′ding) *n.* **1.** the act of a person or thing that winds. **2.** the state of being wound. **3.** a bend, turn, or curve or a series of these. **4.** something that winds or coils, such as a wire. —*adj.* **1.** full of bends or turns, as a road or stream; rambling: *a winding mountain highway.* **2.** curving about a central core; spiraling: *a winding staircase.*

wind instrument (wind) a musical instrument sounded by air being blown into it, such as the flute, clarinet, trumpet, or tuba.

wind·jam·mer (wind′jam′ər) *n. Informal.* **1.** a merchant sailing ship. **2.** a member of its crew.

wind·lass (wind′ləs) *n. pl.*, **wind·lass·es.** a kind of winch that is turned by a hand crank, used chiefly to lift anchors and buckets in wells.

wind·mill (wind′mil′) *n.* a machine that converts wind power to mechanical power, consisting of a number of vanes or slats radiating from a central axis that is rotated by the wind as it strikes the vanes. Windmills are now used chiefly to pump water.

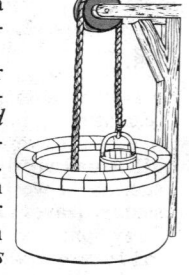

Winch

win·dow (win′dō) *n.* **1.** an opening in the wall or roof of a building, boat, or other structure for admitting light or air, usually fitted with a movable sash and one or more panes of glass. **2.** the framework that holds the panes of glass in a window; sash: *I can't get this window open.* **3.** a windowpane: *We broke the window playing ball.* **4.** anything like a window in shape or use, such as a transparent patch on an

Windmill

envelope through which the address on an enclosure is read.

window box, a long, narrow box on or near a window sill or ledge, used for growing flowering plants.

window dressing 1. the act or art of decorating store windows with attractive merchandise displays. **2.** the displays themselves or the merchandise used to create such displays. **3.** anything that is made to seem or is used to make something else seem more attractive, profitable, or acceptable than it really is.

win·dow·pane (win′dō pān′) *n.* a single pane of glass in a window.

win·dow-shop (win′dō shop′) *v.i.,* **win·dow-shopped, win·dow-shop·ping.** to look at merchandise in store windows or displays without actually buying anything. —**win′dow-shop′per,** *n.*

window sill, the horizontal part across the bottom of a window.

wind·pipe (wind′pīp′) *n.* a tube that extends from the larynx to the bronchi and carries air to and from the lungs; trachea.

wind·row (wind′rō′) *n.* a long row of hay, straw, or grain heaped together to dry.

wind·shield (wind′shēld′) *n.* a transparent screen, usually of glass, attached in front of the occupants of an automobile, motorcycle, or other vehicle to protect against wind.

wind sock (wind) a long, cone-shaped sack hung on a pole or mast, that shows the direction of the wind blowing through it. Also, **wind sleeve.**

Wind·sor (win′zər) *n.* **1. Duke of.** 1894–1972, the son of King George V of England, who was King Edward VIII in 1936 before he abdicated the throne. **2.** the royal house of Great Britain. The name was adopted by George V in 1917. **3.** a city in southern England, southwest of London, on the Thames River. It is the site of Windsor Castle. **4.** a city in southern Ontario, Canada, opposite Detroit, Michigan. Pop. (1971), 199,784.

Windsor Castle, the chief residence of English monarchs since the Norman Conquest, in Windsor, England.

wind·storm (wind′stôrm′) *n.* a storm with high winds but little or no rain or other precipitation.

wind tunnel (wind) a chamber in which air is forced over a scale model of an aircraft or some other object, producing the same effect that would occur if the object itself were moving through the air.

wind-up (wīnd′up′) *n.* **1.** the act of winding up; conclusion; finish: *the wind-up of a political campaign.* **2.** the movements made by a baseball pitcher before pitching the ball.

wind·ward (wind′wərd) *adj.* located on or moving toward the side toward which the wind is blowing. —*n.* the side or direction toward which the wind is blowing. —*adv.* toward the wind.

Wind·ward Islands (wind′wərd) a Caribbean island group forming the southern part of the Lesser Antilles.

wind·y (win′dē) *adj.,* **wind·i·er, wind·i·est. 1.** characterized by or having much wind: *a windy night.* **2.** exposed to or swept by the wind: *a windy beach.* **3.** wordy, boastful, or boring in content or manner: *a windy speech, a windy lecturer.* —**wind′i·ly,** *adv.* —**wind′i·ness,** *n.,*

wine (wīn) *n.* **1.** the fermented juice of grapes, used as an alcoholic beverage. **2.** a fermented juice of other fruits or plants: *blackberry wine.* **3.** a dark purplish-red color, similar to the color of certain wines. —*v.,* **wined, win·ing.** —*v.t.* to furnish with wine. —*v.i.* to drink wine. —*adj.* having the color wine; dark purplish-red.

wine press 1. a machine for pressing the juice from grapes. **2.** a vat in which juice is pressed from grapes.

Wine·sap (wīn′sap′) *n.* a bright red apple with white flesh.

wing (wing) *n.* **1.** a structure that enables a bird, insect, bat, or other flying animal to fly, corresponding to the forelimb in other animals. **2.** the corresponding structure in animals that cannot fly, such as the ostrich or penguin. **3.** anything like a wing in shape or use. **4.** one of the main lifting and supporting surfaces of an airplane. **5.** a structure attached to the side of a house or other larger structure, or considered as a separate section: *to add a new wing to a school.* **6.** the part on either side of a stage that is not seen by the audience. **7.** *Sports.* **a.** either of two positions on either side of the center in ice hockey and certain other goal games. **b.** a player who plays such a position. **8.** a division or faction of an organization representing a particular point of view: *the radical wing of a political party.* **9.** a tactical unit of the U.S. Air Force, together with its supporting units. **10. wings.** an insignia awarded to certain personnel of military aircraft, such as pilots or bombardiers, when they have completed their training. —*v.t.* **1.** to do or accomplish by flight: *The bird winged its way back to the nest.* **2.** to cause to fly as if on wings; give speed to. **3.** to furnish with wings; equip for flight. **4.** to wound, as a bird, in the wing. **5.** *Informal.* to wound slightly: *The bullet winged him in the arm.* —*v.i.* to fly; soar: *The plane winged through the sky.* —**wing′like′,** *adj.*

wing case, one of a pair of hardened fore wings that form a protective covering over the hind wings of certain insects, such as the beetle. Also, **wing cover.**

winged (wingd, wing′id) *adj.* **1.** having wings or a winglike part or parts: *a winged bat.* **2.** moving or passing as if on wings: *winged hours.*

wing·span (wing′span′) *n.* the distance between the fully extended tips of the wings of a bird, insect, or airplane.

wing·spread (wing′spred′) *n.* another word for **wing-span.**

wink (wingk) *v.i.* **1.** to close and open the eyelid of one eye quickly, especially as a sign or signal. **2.** to close and open the eyelids of both eyes quickly. **3.** to shine with flashes of light; twinkle: *The lights of the ship winked in the distance.* —*v.t.* **1.** to close and open (an eye or the eyes) quickly. **2.** to signal or express by winking: *She winked her approval.* —*n.* **1.** the act of winking. **2.** the time required to wink; very short time; instant: *I didn't get a wink of sleep last night.* **3.** a sign or signal conveyed by winking. **4.** a gleam or twinkle.

win·ner (win′ər) *n.* a person or thing that wins: *Who was the winner of the contest?*

win·ning (win′ing) *adj.* **1.** that wins or results in victory or success: *the winning number in a lottery, to score the winning goal in a game.* **2.** charming, pleasing, or attractive: *a winning smile.* —*n.* **1.** the act of a person who wins; victory. **2. winnings.** something that is won, especially money. —**win′ning·ly,** *adv.*

Win·ni·peg (win′ə peg′) *n.* a city in southern Canada, the capital of Manitoba. Pop. (1971), 243,208.

win·now (win′ō) *v.t.* **1.** to expose (grain) to wind or a current of air to blow away the chaff. **2.** to blow away (chaff) in this way. **3.** to separate or remove; sort out: *The*

at; āpe; cär; end; mē; it; īce; hot; ōld; fôrk; wood; fōōl; oil; out; up; turn; sing; thin; this; hw in white; zh in treasure. The symbol ə stands for the sound of a in about, e in taken, i in pencil, o in lemon, and u in circus.

W

lawyer tried to winnow the essential facts from the great mass of evidence. —*v.i.* to separate grain from chaff.

win·some (win′səm) *adj.* attractive or pleasing; charming: *a winsome smile.* —**win′some·ly,** *adv.* —**win′some·ness,** *n.*

Win·ston-Sa·lem (win′stən sā′ləm) *n.* a city in north-central North Carolina. Pop. (1970), 132,913.

win·ter (win′tər) *n.* the season of the year coming between fall and spring. In the Northern Hemisphere it extends from about December 22 to about March 21. —*adj.* of, relating to, or suitable for winter: *winter sports, winter clothes, a winter vacation.* —*v.i.* to spend or pass the winter: *She wintered in Vermont.*

win·ter·green (win′tər grēn′) *n.* **1.** a small evergreen plant of North America, having bright red berries and aromatic leaves. **2.** the oil of this plant, used in medicine or for flavoring. **3.** the flavor of this oil or something having this flavor.

win·ter·ize (win′tə rīz′) *v.t.,* **win·ter·ized, win·ter·iz·ing.** to prepare or make fit for winter weather: *to winterize an automobile.*

winter solstice, the time of year, about December 22 in the Northern Hemisphere, when the sun appears the farthest south from the equator.

win·ter·time (win′tər tīm′) *n.* the winter season.

win·try (win′trē) *adj.,* **win·tri·er, win·tri·est. 1.** of, like, or characteristic of winter: *wintry weather.* **2.** lacking warmth, cheer, or friendliness: *a wintry welcome.* —**win′tri·ness,** *n.*

wipe (wīp) *v.t.,* **wiped, wip·ing. 1.** to rub, usually with something soft, as a towel or mop, in order to clean or dry: *You wash the dishes, and Jan will wipe them.* **2.** to remove by or as if by rubbing: *Sue wiped up the spilled milk. Wipe that grin off your face!* **3.** to rub, move, or apply on or over a surface: *He wiped his shoes on the mat before going in the house.* —*n.* an act or instance of wiping.

> **to wipe out. a.** to kill or destroy completely: *The epidemic wiped out half the town's population.* **b.** to ruin financially: *The stock market crash wiped out many businessmen.*

wip·er (wī′pər) *n.* a person or thing that wipes, especially a device designed or used for wiping: *a windshield wiper.*

wire (wīr) *n.* **1.** metal drawn into a thin strand, thread, or rod. **2.** a length of such metal, used chiefly as a conductor of electricity. It is usually made of copper and surrounded by an insulating covering. **3.** a unit consisting of several strands of wire wound together; cable. **4.** a telegraph. **5.** a telegram. —*adj.* made of or like wire. —*v.,* **wired, wir·ing.** —*v.t.* **1.** to furnish or provide with a network or system of wires: *to wire a house.* **2.** to fasten with a wire or wires: *John wired the parts together.* —*v.i.* to telegraph: *We'd better wire ahead for reservations.*

wire-haired (wīr′herd′) *adj.* having coarse, stiff, or wiry hair: *a wire-haired dog.*

wire·less (wīr′lis) *adj.* **1.** having no wire or wires. **2.** *British.* of or relating to a radio. —*n. pl.,* **wire·less·es. 1.** a wireless telegraph or telephone system. **2.** *British.* a radio.

wire service, a news-gathering agency that supplies news, pictures, and the like to newspapers, magazines, and radio and television stations.

wire·tap (wīr′tap′) *v.,* **wire·tapped, wire·tap·ping.** —*v.i.* to tap a telephone or telegraph wire to obtain information or evidence. —*v.t.* to tap (a telephone or telegraph wire). —*n.* **1.** the act or instance of wiretapping. **2.** a device used in wiretapping.

wire·worm (wīr′wurm′) *n.* the slender, smooth-skinned larva of certain beetles, which destroys the roots and seeds of such crops as cotton, peas, and corn.

wir·ing (wīr′ing) *n.* a network or system of wires, especially for carrying electric current.

wir·y (wīr′ē) *adj.,* **wir·i·er, wir·i·est. 1.** made of or consisting of wire. **2.** like wire; stiff: *wiry hair.* **3.** (of persons or animals) lean and strong: *The young athlete is very wiry.* —**wir′i·ness,** *n.*

Wis., Wisconsin.

Wis·con·sin (wis kon′sən) *n.* a state in the north-central United States, bordering Lake Michigan on the east. Capital, Madison. Area, 56,154 sq. mi. Pop. (1970), 4,417,933. Abbreviation, **Wis.**

> ● **Wisconsin** was named after the Wisconsin River, the principal river in the area. The name is the English version of a French name, which probably came from an Algonquian word meaning "at the big (or the long) river" or, perhaps, "gathering of waters."

wis·dom (wiz′dəm) *n.* **1.** the ability to know or judge what is right, good, and true. **2.** common sense or sound judgment. **3.** knowledge; learning.

wisdom tooth, the last molar tooth on either side of the upper and lower jaws in humans, usually appearing between the ages of seventeen and twenty-five.

wise[1] (wīz) *adj.,* **wis·er, wis·est. 1.** having the ability to know or judge what is right, good, and true. **2.** having or showing common sense or sound judgment; sensible: *That was not a very wise decision.* **3.** having knowledge or information; informed. **4.** *Slang.* rude and bold; smart-alecky; fresh. [Old English *wīs.*] —**wise′ly,** *adv.*

wise[2] (wīz) *n.* a way; manner. ▲ used chiefly in the phrases *in no wise, in this wise, in any wise.* [Old English *wīse.*]

-wise *suffix* (used to form adverbs from nouns or adjectives) in a (specified) manner, direction, or position: *likewise, clockwise.*

wise·a·cre (wīz′ā′kər) *n.* a person who thinks he knows more than he really does.

wise·crack (wīz′krak′) *n.* a short, insulting or sarcastic remark. —*v.i.* to make a wisecrack or wisecracks. —**wise′crack′er,** *n.*

wish (wish) *n. pl.,* **wish·es. 1.** a longing or strong need or desire for something: *John's one wish in life was to be rich.* **2.** an expression of such a need or desire: *Mark went to California against his mother's wishes.* **3.** something that is wished for: *to get one's wish.* —*v.t.* **1.** to have a wish or longing for; desire: *Herb wished he had more money.* **2.** to desire (a person or thing) to be in a particular state or condition: *I wish winter were over.* **3.** to express or have a wish or desire for: *We wish you the best of luck.* **4.** to bid, as a greeting: *to wish someone good morning.* **5.** to impose; force: *I would not wish that task on anyone.* —*v.i.* **1.** to have or feel a wish: *to wish for happiness.* **2.** to make a wish: *to wish upon a star.* —**wish′er,** *n.*

wish·bone (wish′bōn′) *n.* a forked bone in front of the breastbone of most birds. [From the custom in which two people make wishes and then break a dried wishbone in two, with the holder of the longer piece supposedly having his wish come true.]

wish·ful (wish′fəl) *adj.* having, showing, or based on a wish: *a wishful look, wishful thinking.* —**wish′ful·ly,** *adv.* —**wish′ful·ness,** *n.*

wish·y-wash·y (wish′ē wô′shē, wish′ē wosh′ē) *adj. Informal.* **1.** lacking in strength of character or firmness of will: *He is a wishy-washy person who cannot make up his mind.* **2.** thin or watery.

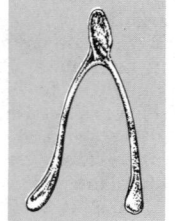

Wishbone

wisp (wisp) *n.* **1.** a small bunch, as of hair. **2.** a small or slight bit, piece, or the like: *a wisp of smoke.* **3.** a person or thing that is small, frail, or delicate: *a wisp of a child.* —**wisp'y,** *adj.*

wist (wist) *Archaic.* the past tense and past participle of **wit².**

wis·te·ri·a (wi stēr'ē ə) *also,* **wis·tar·i·a** (wi ster'ē ə). *n.* a woody vine found in Asia and the United States, bearing long, drooping clusters of white, blue, pink, or purple flowers.

wist·ful (wist'fəl) *adj.* sadly longing; yearning: *The music put her in a wistful mood.* —**wist'ful·ly,** *adv.* —**wist'ful·ness,** *n.*

wit¹ (wit) *n.* **1.** the ability to make clever, amusing, or striking comments about persons, things, or situations. **2.** a person having such ability. **3.** *usually,* **wits. a.** the ability to think and reason; understanding: *to live by one's wits.* **b.** sanity: *to be scared out of one's wits.* [Old English *wit* understanding, intelligence, mind.]

  at one's wits' end. at a loss as to what to do.

  to have one's wits about one or **to keep one's wits about one.** to be or stay calm or alert, as in an emergency: *He kept his wits about him during the fire.*

wit² (wit) *v.t., v.i.,* **wist, wit·ting.** *Archaic.* to be or become aware; know; learn. [Old English *witan* to know.]

  to wit. that is to say; namely.

witch (wich) *n. pl.,* **witch·es. 1.** a person, especially a woman, who practices magic, usually black magic, or is believed to have a pact with the devil; sorceress. **2.** an ugly, ill-natured old woman; hag.

witch·craft (wich'kraft') *n.* the practices or power of a witch; sorcery.

witch doctor, in certain African tribes, a medicine man.

witch·er·y (wich'ər ē) *n. pl.,* **witch·er·ies. 1.** witchcraft; sorcery. **2.** the power to charm; fascination.

witch hazel 1. any of a small group of trees and shrubs found in North America, China, and Japan, having a scaly bark and bearing small clusters of yellow flowers in the fall. **2.** a lotion made from the leaves and bark of a species of witch hazel.

witch hunt *Informal.* an investigation of persons supposedly undertaken to uncover subversion or disloyalty, but actually done to weaken political opposition.

witch·ing (wich'ing) *adj.* **1.** of, relating to, or suitable for witchcraft: *Midnight is the witching hour.* **2.** bewitching; enchanting.

with (with, with) *prep.* **1.** in the company of: *We went with our friends.* **2.** next to; alongside of: *I sat with my mother.* **3.** into: *We mixed chocolate syrup with the milk.* **4.** having as a possession or characteristic: *the girl with the umbrella, the man with a limp.* **5.** by means of; using: *to fish with a pole, to eat with a fork.* **6.** in a manner characterized by: *to dance with grace.* **7.** in addition to: *We had milk with our dinner.* **8.** in the service, employment, or association of: *He is with a large law firm.* **9.** in regard or relation to: *They are pleased with the results of the election.* **10.** in the charge or keeping of: *She left her jewelry with the hotel manager.* **11.** in the opinion of: *It is fine with me if you want to go.* **12.** on account of; because of: *He trembled with fear.* **13.** from: *He hates to part with his old magazines.* **14.** in opposition to; against: *He quarreled with her over money.* **15.** in spite of; notwithstanding: *With all his campaigning, he couldn't get enough votes to win.* **16.** in proportion to: *His anger grew with each insult.* **17.** in support of; on the side of: *Is he with us or against us?*

with- *prefix* **1.** in opposition; against: *withstand.* **2.** back; away: *withdraw, withhold.*

with·al (with ôl', with ôl') *adv.* in addition; besides; also: *His letter was interesting, and instructive withal.*

with·draw (with drô', with drô') *v.,* **with·drew, with·drawn, with·draw·ing.** —*v.t.* **1.** to draw back or away: *The government decided to withdraw troops from the border.* **2.** to take away; remove: *to withdraw a product from the market. He withdrew ten dollars from the bank.* **3.** to take back; retract: *She withdrew her offer of help.* —*v.i.* **1.** to move or go back or away; retire; retreat: *After dinner, the guests withdrew to the living room.* **2.** to remove oneself: *to withdraw from an election, to withdraw from school.*

with·draw·al (with drô'əl, with drô'əl) *n.* the act of withdrawing or the state of being withdrawn.

with·drawn (with drôn', with drôn') *v.* the past participle of **withdraw.** —*adj.* very shy or reserved: *a withdrawn child.*

withe (with, wīth) *n.* a tough flexible twig, usually made of willow, used for binding or tying.

with·er (with'ər) *v.i.* to dry up or shrivel, as from heat or loss of moisture: *The flowers withered soon after they were cut.* —*v.t.* **1.** to cause to dry up or shrivel: *The intense summer heat withered the crops.* **2.** to cause to feel ashamed or embarrassed, as by harsh words or a scornful glance: *to wither someone with an angry look.*

with·ers (with'ərz) *n., pl.* the highest part of the back of a horse or similar animal, between the shoulder blades.

with·hold (with hōld', with hōld') *v.t.,* **with·held** (with-held', with held'), **with·hold·ing. 1.** to refuse to give, grant, or allow: *to withhold judgment, to withhold payment on a check.* **2.** to hold back or check; restrain: *to withhold one's anger.*

withholding tax, the part of an employee's wages or salary taken out by the employer for income tax.

with·in (with in', with in') *prep.* **1.** in or into the inner or interior part or parts of; in the space bounded or enclosed by: *The troops camped within the walls of the fort.* **2.** inside the limits of, as in time, space, amount, or degree: *He promised to return within an hour.* **3.** in the scope, range, or influence of: *That was the worst storm within my memory. That's not within the judge's jurisdiction.* —*adv.* **1.** in or into the inner or interior part or parts; inside. **2.** indoors. —*n.* the inner part or place.

with·out (with out', with out') *prep.* **1.** not having; lacking: *to go without sleep, to be without money.* **2.** so as to neglect or avoid: *She left without saying good-by.* **3.** unaccompanied by: *He went on the trip without his wife.* **4.** at, on, or to the outer or exterior part or parts of; outside of; beyond. —*adv.* **1.** with something absent or lacking: *to go without, to do without.* **2.** on the outer or exterior part or parts; outside. **3.** outdoors. —*n.* the outer part or place.

with·stand (with stand', with stand') *v.t.,* **with·stood** (with stood', with stood'), **with·stand·ing.** to hold out against or oppose successfully: *The house withstood the storm. Henry could not withstand the temptation to eat another piece of cake.*

wit·less (wit'lis) *adj.* lacking intelligence or sense; foolish. —**wit'less·ly,** *adv.* —**wit'less·ness,** *n.*

wit·ness (wit'nis) *n. pl.,* **wit·ness·es. 1.** a person who has personally seen or heard something and can therefore give a first-hand account of it. **2.** a person who testifies in a court of law under oath. **3.** a person who is present at a

at; āpe; cär; end; mē; it; īce; hot; ōld; fôrk; wood; fōōl; oil; out; up; turn; sing; thin; this; hw in white; zh in treasure. The symbol ə stands for the sound of a in about, e in taken, i in pencil, o in lemon, and u in circus.

W

transaction, such as the signing of a contract or will, or at a ceremony, such as a wedding, and can give evidence as to its authenticity. **4.** evidence; testimony. —*v.t.* **1.** to be present to see or hear; observe personally: *to witness an argument.* **2.** to be the time or scene of: *This century has witnessed outstanding scientific achievements.* **3.** to sign (a document) as a witness. **4.** to serve or give as evidence or proof of: *The bruises on the prisoner's body witnessed the cruel treatment he had received.*

   to bear witness. to give or serve as evidence or testimony.

wit·ti·cism (wit′i siz′əm) *n.* a witty saying or remark.

wit·ty (wit′ē) *adj.,* **wit·ti·er, wit·ti·est.** having or characterized by wit; cleverly amusing: *a witty writer, a witty reply.* —**wit′ti·ly,** *adv.* —**wit′ti·ness,** *n.*

wives (wīvz) the plural of **wife.**

wiz·ard (wiz′ərd) *n.* **1.** a person, especially a man, who uses supernatural power to control or influence events, people, or phenomena; male witch; sorcerer. **2.** an extraordinarily clever or skillful person: *a financial wizard.*

wiz·ard·ry (wiz′ərd rē) *n.* **1.** the art or methods of a wizard; witchcraft; sorcery. **2.** great skill or cleverness.

wiz·ened (wiz′ənd) *adj.* dried out; shriveled; withered: *a wizened old man.*

wk. *pl.,* **wks. 1.** week. **2.** work.

wob·ble (wob′əl) *also,* **wab·ble.** *v.i.,* **wob·bled, wob·bling. 1.** to move or sway unsteadily from side to side: *This old chair wobbles. The tire wobbled after the blowout.* **2.** to shake or quaver; tremble: *Tom's voice wobbled when he tried to thank me.* **3.** to be unable to choose between different opinions, feelings, or courses of action; waver. —*n.* an unsteady, swaying movement: *the wobble of a warped phonograph record.*

wob·bly (wob′lē) *also,* **wab·bly.** *adj.* tending to wobble; unsteady; shaky: *This table has wobbly legs.*

Wo·den (wōd′ən) *n. Teutonic Mythology.* the king of the gods. In Norse mythology he was called Odin.

woe (wō) *n.* **1.** great sadness or suffering; sorrow; grief: *a tale of woe.* **2.** great trouble or misfortune; disaster: *economic woes.* —*interj.* alas.

woe·be·gone (wō′bi gôn′, wō′bi gon′) *also,* **wo·be·gone.** *adj.* showing great sorrow or grief; mournful.

woe·ful (wō′fəl) *adj.* **1.** characterized by, expressing, or full of woe; sorrowful; sad: *a woeful look.* **2.** pitiful; deplorable: *woeful inadequacies, woeful merchandise.* —**woe′-ful·ly,** *adv.* —**woe′ful·ness,** *n.*

woke (wōk) a past tense of **wake**[1].

wo·ken (wō′kən) *Archaic.* a past participle of **wake**[1].

wold (wōld) *n.* a high, open tract of rolling land.

wolf (woolf) *n. pl.,* **wolves. 1.** any of various wild animals related to the dog, found chiefly in the cold regions of the Northern Hemisphere, having a pointed muzzle, a bushy tail, and usually gray fur. **2.** the fur of such an animal. **3.** a person who is cruel, greedy, or destructive. —*v.t.* to eat quickly and ravenously: *The hungry little boy wolfed down his food.* —**wolf′like′,** *adj.*

Wolf

   to cry wolf. to raise a false alarm.

   to keep the wolf from the door. to ward off hunger or want.

Wolfe (woolf) **1. James.** 1727–1759, the English general who led the capture of Quebec in 1759. **2. Thomas.** 1900–1938, U.S. novelist.

wolf·hound (woolf′hound′) *n.* any of various large dogs originally bred for hunting wolves, such as the Irish wolfhound.

wolf·ish (wool′fish) *adj.* characteristic of or like a wolf; greedy or cruel. —**wolf′ish·ly,** *adv.* —**wolf′ish·ness,** *n.*

wolf·ram (wool′frəm) *n.* another name for **tungsten.**

Wol·ver·hamp·ton (wool′vər hamp′tən) *n.* a city in west-central England. Pop. (1971), 265,153.

wol·ver·ine (wool′və rēn′) *also,* **wol·ver·ene.** *n.* a meat-eating animal related to the weasel, native to northern regions, having dark-brown fur with pale bands.

Wolverine

wolves (woolvz) the plural of **wolf.**

wom·an (woom′ən) *n. pl.,* **wom·en. 1.** an adult female human being. **2.** adult female human beings as a group; the female part of the human race.

wom·an·hood (woom′ən hood′) *n.* **1.** the state of being an adult female human being: *She has not yet reached womanhood.* **2.** the characteristics or qualities thought to be womanly. **3.** women as a group.

wom·an·ish (woom′ən ish) *adj.* **1.** of, for, or characteristic of a woman. **2.** like a woman; effeminate.

wom·an·kind (woom′ən kīnd′) *n.* women as a group.

wom·an·like (woom′ən līk′) *adj.* having the qualities of or suitable for a woman; womanly.

wom·an·ly (woom′ən lē) *adj.* **1.** having the qualities thought of as characteristic of women. **2.** relating to or suitable for a woman. —**wom′an·li·ness,** *n.*

womb (woom) *n.* a hollow muscular organ found in most female mammals, which holds and nourishes the young until birth; uterus.

wom·bat (wom′bat) *n.* a burrowing animal, native to Australia, that is active at night and has a stocky body and a coarse coat of black or yellowish-brown hair. The female wombat has a pouch for carrying her young after birth.

wom·en (wim′ən) the plural of **woman.**

wom·en·folk (wim′ən fōk′) *also,* **wom·en·folks.** *n., pl.* women as a group, especially all the female members of a family or other group.

women's rights *also,* **woman's rights.** the rights of women to have equal opportunities and privileges with men.

won (wun) a past tense and the past participle of **win.**

won·der (wun′dər) *n.* **1.** something that causes astonishment, curiosity, or admiration: *The Egyptian pyramids are one of the wonders of the ancient world.* **2.** a feeling, attitude, or state caused by this: *We watched with wonder as the sea suddenly became calm.* —*v.i.* **1.** to want to know or learn; be curious or doubtful. **2.** to feel or express admiration and astonishment: *We all wondered at the athlete's strength and endurance.* —*v.t.* to want to know or learn about; be curious or doubtful about: *I wonder what we're having for dinner.* —**won′der·ing·ly,** *adv.*

won·der·ful (wun′dər fəl) *adj.* **1.** causing wonder; astonishing: *a wonderful gift, a wonderful work of art.* **2.** very good; excellent: *We spent a wonderful day in the country last Sunday.* —**won′der·ful·ly,** *adv.* —**won′der·ful·ness,** *n.*

won·der·land (wun′dər land′) *n.* **1.** a wonderful place, region, or scene: *a winter wonderland.* **2.** a wonderful imaginary realm or fantasy world.

won·der·ment (wun′dər mənt) *n.* **1.** the state or emotion of wonder: *The group of tourists stood in wonderment amidst the ancient ruins.* **2.** something that causes wonder.

won·drous (wun′drəs) *adj.* wonderful. —*adv. Archaic.* extraordinarily; wonderfully. —**won′drous·ly,** *adv.* —**won′drous·ness,** *n.*

wont (wōnt, wônt, wunt) *adj.* accustomed; used: *We are* *wont to stay at home on Sundays.* —*n.* a usual practice; habit: *It was his wont to read the paper after work.*

won't (wōnt) will not.

wont·ed (wôn′tid, wôn′tid, wun′tid) *adj.* accustomed; customary: *Dad sat in his wonted place at the head of the table.*

woo (wo͞o) *v.t.* **1.** to seek the love or affection of, especially with the intent to marry; court. **2.** to try to win over: *The corporations wooed college graduates with promises of high salaries.* **3.** to try to obtain or gain; seek: *The politician wooed public support for his plan.* —*v.i.* to seek the love or affection of a person, especially with the intent to marry.

wood (wood) *n.* **1.** the hard material that makes up the greater part of the stems and branches of trees and shrubs, located beneath the bark. **2.** this material, sometimes with the bark still on, cut or prepared for use, as for building, fuel, or paper manufacture; timber; lumber. **3.** *often,* **woods.** a dense growth of trees; forest; grove. **4.** something made of wood, such as a woodwind instrument. **5.** a golf club with a wooden head. —*adj.* **1.** made or consisting of wood; wooden: *a wood bucket.* **2.** made or suitable for using, holding, storing, or cutting wood: *a wood saw.* **3.** living or growing in woods.

  out of the woods. *Informal.* finally clear or free from danger, hazard, or other difficulty.

wood alcohol, another term for **methanol.**

wood·bine (wood′bīn′) *n.* **1.** any of various climbing shrubs or vines, especially the European honeysuckle, bearing flowers that are red or purple on the outside. **2.** another name for **Virginia creeper.**

wood·carv·er (wood′kär′vər) *n.* a person who carves objects out of wood.

wood·carv·ing (wood′kär′ving) *n.* **1.** the art or technique of carving wood. **2.** an object carved of wood.

wood·chuck (wood′chuk′) *n.* a short-legged North American animal having a stocky body and coarse brown or gray fur. Also, **groundhog.**

wood·cock (wood′kok′) *n. pl.,* **wood·cocks** or **wood·cock.** any of several game birds that are native to forests of North America, Europe, and Asia, having a plump body, a long slender bill, and buff, brown, and black feathers.

wood·craft (wood′kraft′) *n.* **1.** skill and knowledge in things relating to the woods and survival in the woods, such as hunting or camping. **2.** the art, process, or skill of working with wood.

Woodchuck

wood·cut (wood′kut′) *n.* **1.** a block of wood engraved so that all the wood is cut away except the design to be printed. **2.** a print or impression that is made from such a block.

wood·cut·ter (wood′kut′ər) *n.* a person whose work is cutting trees or chopping wood.

wood·ed (wood′id) *adj.* having trees or woods: *We had a picnic in a wooded area at the edge of town.*

wood·en (wood′ən) *adj.* **1.** made or consisting of wood: *a wooden pail.* **2.** stiff; clumsy; awkward: *to walk with a wooden gait.* **3.** without warmth or life; lifeless; dull: *He had a wooden expression on his face.* —**wood′en·ly,** *adv.* —**wood′en·ness,** *n.*

wood·land (*n.,* wood′land′, wood′lənd; *adj.,* wood′lənd) *n.* land covered with woods or trees. —*adj.* of, relating to, or living in the woods.

wood louse **1.** any of several small animals that have flat, oval bodies and live in dark, damp places, feeding on

decaying wood, leaves, and other matter. Also, **sow bug.** **2.** any of various small insects living in dark places, as in the woodwork of houses.

wood·man (wood′mən) *n. pl.,* **wood·men** (wood′mən). another spelling of **woodsman.**

wood nymph *Greek Mythology.* a nymph living in or guarding woods and trees.

wood·peck·er (wood′pek′ər) *n.* any of various strong-billed birds that live in forests throughout the world, having stiff, pointed tail feathers and curved nails for clinging to trees. The woodpecker feeds chiefly on insects in trees, which it obtains by drilling holes in bark and wood with its bill.

wood·pile (wood′pīl′) *n.* a pile of wood, especially of wood cut and stacked for use as fuel.

wood pulp, wood reduced to pulp by chemical or mechanical means, used especially for making paper.

wood·shed (wood′shed′) *n.* a shed for storing wood, especially firewood.

woods·man (woodz′mən) *also,* **wood·man.** *n. pl.,* **woods·men** (woodz′mən). **1.** a man, such as a hunter or trapper, who lives or works in the woods and who is skilled in woodcraft. **2.** a woodcutter; lumberjack.

Woodpecker

woods·y (wood′zē) *adj.,* **woods·i·er, woods·i·est.** of, relating to, suitable for, or like the woods: *a woodsy fragrance.*

wood tar, a tar obtained from wood by distillation, used in pitch, medicines, and preservatives.

wood thrush, a thrush found throughout the eastern United States, having brown and white feathers and a reddish head.

wood·wind (wood′wind′) *n.* **1.** any of various instruments, including the flute, oboe, clarinet, and saxophone, consisting of a tube through which a column of air passes, and having holes in the tube which are opened and closed to vary the pitch of the tones produced. **2. woodwinds.** the section of an orchestra consisting of these instruments. —*adj.* of, for, or made up of these instruments: *the woodwind section of an orchestra.*

wood·work (wood′wurk′) *n.* objects or parts made of wood, especially the wooden parts on the inside of a house, such as moldings, doors, and window frames.

wood·work·ing (wood′wur′king) *n.* the art, process, or occupation of making or shaping things of wood.

wood·y (wood′ē) *adj.,* **wood·i·er, wood·i·est. 1.** consisting of or containing wood: *woody plants.* **2.** covered with or full of trees: *a woody island.* **3.** characteristic of or like wood: *a plastic with a woody texture.* —**wood′i·ness,** *n.*

woof (woof, wo͞of) *n.* **1.** the threads that run from side to side in a woven fabric, crossing the lengthwise threads of the warp. **2.** texture, as of a fabric.

woof·er (woof′ər) *n.* a loudspeaker designed to reproduce low-frequency sound signals.

wool (wool) *n.* **1.** the soft, dense, usually curly, hair of sheep and certain other animals, such as the Angora goat, alpaca, or llama, used to make yarn and fabric. **2.** a strong

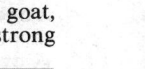

at; āpe; cär; end; mē; it; īce; hot; ōld; fôrk; wood; fo͞ol; oil; out; up; turn; sing; thin; <u>th</u>is; hw in white; zh in treasure. The symbol ə stands for the sound of **a** in about, **e** in taken, **i** in pencil, **o** in lemon, and **u** in circus.

yarn or fabric made from this hair. **3.** any substance resembling the fleece of sheep in texture, such as short, kinky human hair or the furry covering on certain plants. —*adj.* of, relating to, or made of wool: *a wool coat.*

    to pull the wool over (someone's) eyes. to trick or deceive (someone).

wool·en (wool′ən) *also,* **wool·len.** *adj.* **1.** made of wool. **2.** of or relating to wool. —*n. usually,* **woolens.** a cloth or garment made of wool.

wool·gath·er·ing (wool′gath′ər ing) *n.* useless or idle thinking or work, especially daydreaming. —*adj.* given to daydreaming; absent-minded.

wool·len (wool′ən) another spelling of **woolen.**

wool·ly (wool′ē) *also,* **wool·y.** *adj.,* **wool·li·er, wool·li·est. 1.** consisting of or like wool: *a woolly fabric.* **2.** covered with wool or something with a similar texture: *a woolly stuffed animal.* **3.** not clear or well-defined; confused; fuzzy: *woolly thinking.* —*n. pl.,* **wool·lies.** *usually,* **wool·lies.** a garment made of wool, especially a knitted undergarment. —**wool′li·ness,** *n.*

wool·y (wool′ē) *n. pl.,* **wool·ies,** *adj.,* **wool·i·er, wool·i·est.** another spelling of **woolly.** —**wool′i·ness,** *n.*

wooz·y (wōō′zē, wooz′ē) *adj.,* **wooz·i·er, wooz·i·est.** *Informal.* dizzy or dazed. —**wooz′i·ly,** *adv.* —**wooz′i·ness,** *n.*

Worces·ter (woos′tər) *n.* a city in central Massachusetts. Pop. (1970), 176,572.

word (wurd) *n.* **1.** a sound or combination of sounds having meaning and forming a unit of language. **2.** a written or printed character or set of characters representing such a unit. **3.** a short conversation or discussion: *I'd like a word with you before you leave.* **4.** a brief remark or statement: *She gave him a word of advice.* **5.** assurance; promise: *I gave him my word that I would be there.* **6.** information or news; message: *Have you received any word from him?* **7.** a signal or password: *Just give the word and we'll begin.* **8.** a command; order: *His word must be obeyed.* **9. words.** an angry discussion; argument. **10. the Word.** the Bible; Scriptures. —*v.t.* to express in words: *He worded his reply carefully.*

    by word of mouth. by means of spoken language; orally.

    in a word. in short; briefly.

    in so many words. precisely and plainly.

    to eat one's words. to have to take back something that one has said.

    to take the words out of one's mouth. to say exactly what another person was going to say himself.

    word for word. in exactly the same words.

word·book (wurd′book′) *n.* a book containing a list of words, with definitions or explanations, such as a dictionary.

word·ing (wur′ding) *n.* the style or manner of expressing something in words: *The wording of that sentence is confusing.*

word·less (wurd′lis) *adj.* **1.** not using words; silent: *a wordless greeting.* **2.** that cannot be expressed in words: *wordless sorrow.* —**word′less·ly,** *adv.* —**word′less·ness,** *n.*

word of honor, a promise given as a pledge of one's honor.

Words·worth, William (wurdz′wurth′) 1770–1850, English poet.

word·y (wur′dē) *adj.,* **word·i·er, word·i·est.** using or containing too many words: *a wordy author, a wordy essay.* —**word′i·ly,** *adv.* —**word′i·ness,** *n.*

wore (wôr) the past tense of **wear.**

work (wurk) *n.* **1.** physical or mental effort directed toward accomplishing or achieving a definite end or purpose; labor. **2.** what a person does to earn a living; occupation;

trade. **3.** an opportunity for earning a living; employment: *He is looking for work.* **4.** something to be done; undertaking; project: *Each man was assigned work for the week.* **5.** something that is being accomplished or produced, especially as part of one's occupation. **6.** something accomplished or produced; finished product: *a work of sculpture, works of music.* **7.** the way in which something is accomplished or produced; workmanship: *The vase shows careful work.* **8.** a place of employment: *You can call him at work.* **9.** *usually,* **works.** things done; feats; deeds: *She is known for her good works.* **10. works. a.** a place for industrial labor, such as a factory, plant, or mill. ▲ usually used with a singular verb. **b.** the moving parts of a machine or other device, such as a watch. **c.** engineering structures, such as dams, docks, or bridges. **11.** *Physics.* the expenditure of energy in moving mass a given distance, measured by the product of the magnitude of the force and the distance the mass is moved in the direction of the force. —*adj.* of, for, or relating to work: *a work stoppage, work clothes.* —*v.,* **worked** or **wrought, work·ing.** —*v.i.* **1.** to put forth mental or physical effort in order to accomplish a definite end or purpose; labor. **2.** to be employed in some business, occupation, or profession: *He works in a steel mill.* **3.** to perform a function properly; operate: *This typewriter works well.* **4.** to move gradually so as to arrive at a specified state: *The ropes worked loose.* —*v.t.* **1.** to cause to perform a function or work: *to work a machine.* **2.** to carry on one's trade, business, or operation in: *The policeman worked the north side of town.* **3.** to cause to produce or be productive: *The old man still works the farm.* **4.** to do or accomplish; bring about; cause: *This medicine almost works miracles.* **5.** to shape, handle, or process for a particular purpose: *to work copper, to work dough.* **6.** to get or achieve by effort: *We worked our way upstream.* **7.** to solve: *He worked the math problem.* **8.** to act upon the emotions of; excite; rouse: *The speaker worked the crowd into a rage.*

    out of work. without a job; unemployed.

    to make short work of. to do or accomplish quickly.

    to work in. to put in or insert: *Can you work in this sentence at the bottom of the page?*

    to work off. to get rid of; discharge: *to work off an obligation.*

    to work on or **to work upon.** to try to have an influence on; try to persuade.

    to work out. a. to develop or improve: *Work out your ideas before you begin to write.* **b.** to solve: *to work out a problem.* **c.** to come to an end; result: *How did your meeting work out?* **d.** to do exercises or practice: *The boxer worked out at the gym before his big fight.*

work·a·ble (wur′kə bəl) *adj.* **1.** that can be carried out or accomplished: *a workable plan.* **2.** that can be worked: *workable clay.*

work·a·day (wur′kə dā′) *adj.* **1.** commonplace; ordinary: *the workaday world.* **2.** of, relating to, or suitable for workdays.

work·bench (wurk′bench′) *n. pl.,* **work·bench·es.** a table used for working, as by a craftsman or mechanic.

work·book (wurk′book′) *n.* **1.** a book or manual prepared for use by students, containing problems, questions, or exercises based on a particular textbook or relating to a particular course of study. **2.** a book containing a record of work planned or completed.

work·day (wurk′dā′) *n.* **1.** a day on which work is ordinarily done, as distinguished from Sunday or a holiday. **2.** that part of a day in which work is done: *His workday ends at five o'clock.*

work·er (wur′kər) *n.* **1.** a person who works: *He is a fast worker.* **2.** a person who earns a living by working, especially as a laborer. **3.** one of the females in a colony of insects, such as bees, ants, or termites, that cannot reproduce, but perform various services for the colony.

work·horse (wurk′hôrs′) *n.* **1.** a horse used for heavy labor, as distinguished from a horse for racing or riding. **2.** a person who works very hard and tirelessly, especially on very difficult tasks.

work·house (wurk′hous′) *n. pl.,* **work·hous·es** (wurk′-hou′ziz). **1.** a house of correction for petty offenders, who are made to work in gangs repairing roads or railways. **2.** in Great Britain, an institution for sheltering and giving work to poor people.

work·ing (wur′king) *adj.* **1.** that works: *a working telephone.* **2.** engaged in work, especially for a living: *working people.* **3.** that is enough for use: *to have a working knowledge of Russian.* **4.** of, relating to, occupied by, or used for working: *working conditions, working hours.* —*n.* **1.** the manner in which something works; method of operation: *I do not understand the working of this machine.* **2.** *usually,* **workings.** the part of a mine where excavation is being done.

working class, the class of people who do industrial or manual labor and are dependent upon wages for their livelihood.

work·ing·man (wur′king man′) *n. pl.,* **work·ing·men** (wur′king men′). a man who works, especially one who works for a living with his hands or with machines.

working papers, official documents authorizing the employment of aliens or minors.

work·load (wurk′lōd′) *also,* **work load.** *n.* the amount of work assigned to a worker, department, or machine over a specified period of time.

work·man (wurk′mən) *n. pl.,* **work·men** (wurk′mən). a man who works for a living, especially as a craftsman or laborer.

work·man·like (wurk′mən līk′) *adj.* characteristic of or suitable for a good workman; well-executed; skillful: *a workmanlike job.*

work·man·ship (wurk′mən ship′) *n.* **1.** the art or skill of a workman. **2.** the manner in which work is done: *The workmanship of this table is very fine.* **3.** the product of a craftsman's work: *That vase is a fine piece of workmanship.*

work·men's compensation (wurk′mənz) insurance payments provided by law for wage earners who are injured at work.

work·out (wurk′out′) *n.* **1.** a period of practice, exercise, or other physical activity. **2.** a trial or test to determine suitability, fitness, or the like: *He gave the bicycle a workout.*

work·room (wurk′rōōm′, wurk′room′) *n.* a room in which work is done.

work·shop (wurk′shop′) *n.* **1.** a shop or building in which work, especially hand or mechanical work, is done. **2.** a discussion group devoted to a particular subject or field of study: *a workshop in child care, a workshop for poets.*

work·ta·ble (wurk′tā′bəl) *n.* a table used for working, as by a craftsman or seamstress.

world (wurld) *n.* **1.** the earth: *John took a voyage around the world.* **2.** *also,* **World.** a particular part of the earth: *the western world.* **3.** all that exists; the whole of creation; the universe. **4.** all the human inhabitants of the earth as a group; humanity. **5.** all the inhabitants of a community, state, or country; the public in general. **6.** a particular civilization or period of human history: *the world of the Greeks, the Elizabethan world.* **7.** any sphere or area of human concern, pursuit, or activity: *the world of art, the world of fashion.* **8.** a particular group of people sharing

certain interests or activities: *the business world.* **9.** matters, concerns, interests, or pleasures of this life and the people devoted to or associated with them: *She chose to live apart from the world.* **10.** a division of living things: *the plant world.* **11.** any planet or other heavenly body. **12.** any state or condition of existence: *the world of today.* **13.** *Informal.* a large number or quantity; a great deal: *The vacation did her a world of good.*

world·ly (wurld′lē) *adj.,* **world·li·er, world·li·est. 1.** devoted to the matters, concerns, interests, or pleasures of this world. **2.** of or relating to this world; earthly; secular: *worldly pursuits.* **3.** worldly-wise; sophisticated. —**world′li·ness,** *n.*

world·ly-wise (wurld′lē wīz′) *adj.* wise in the ways or affairs of this world.

world power, a country that has considerable influence in or effect upon world affairs.

World Series *also,* **world series.** a series of baseball games played every year between the winning teams in the two major professional leagues after the regular season has ended. It determines the championship of U.S. professional baseball.

world war, a war involving the major powers of the world and extending over a large area.

World War I, a war fought chiefly in Europe, from 1914 to 1918, between England, France, Russia, the United States, and their allies on one side and Germany, Austria-Hungary, and their allies on the other.

World War II, a war fought chiefly in Europe, Asia, and Africa, and in the Atlantic and Pacific Oceans, from 1939 to 1945, between England, France, the Soviet Union, the United States, China, and their allies on one side and Germany, Italy, Japan, and their allies on the other.

world-wea·ry (wurld′wēr′ē) *adj.* tired of the world or of living.

world·wide (wurld′wīd′) *adj.* extending over all the world: *That pianist has achieved worldwide fame.*

worm (wurm) *n.* **1.** any of various long, slender, soft-bodied animals. True worms include the flatworms, roundworms, and annelids. **2.** anything like a worm, as in appearance or movement. **3.** a person who is an object of scorn, disgust, or pity; weak, miserable, or pathetic person. **4. worms.** any of several diseases caused by parasitic worms in the body, especially in the intestines. —*v.i.* to move as a worm does; wriggle: *He wormed through the window.* —*v.t.* **1.** to move or bring about by moving as a worm: *She wormed her way through the mass of people at the door.* **2.** to bring about by stealth or guile: *He wormed his way into her favor.* **3.** to get or achieve by stealth or guile: *Harry wormed the secret out of her.* **4.** to free from worms: *to worm a puppy.* —**worm′like′,** *adj.*

worm-eat·en (wurm′ēt′ən) *adj.* **1.** gnawed or bored by worms; wormy: *worm-eaten vegetables.* **2.** old, worn-out, or out-of-date: *worm-eaten ideas.*

worm gear, a gear that is turned by a revolving shaft with a single spiral thread.

worm·hole (wurm′hōl′) *n.* a hole made by a burrowing worm, as in wood or fruit.

worm·wood (wurm′wood′) *n.* **1.** any of several aromatic plants having small greenish flowers and deeply in-

at; āpe; cär; end; mē; it; īce; hot; ōld; fôrk; wood; fōol; oil; out; up; turn; sing; thin; this; hw in white; zh in treasure. The symbol ə stands for the sound of a in about, e in taken, i in pencil, o in lemon, and u in circus.

dented leaves. **2.** something that is bitter or unpleasant.

worm·y (wur′mē) *adj.*, **worm·i·er, worm·i·est. 1.** containing or full of worms: *a wormy tomato.* **2.** like a worm. —**worm′i·ness,** *n.*

worn (wôrn) *v.* the past participle of **wear.** —*adj.* **1.** damaged by use or wear; threadbare: *His pants were worn at the knees.* **2.** showing the effects of illness, fatigue, or anxiety; exhausted: *He had a worn, weary expression on his face.*

worn-out (wôrn′out′) *adj.* **1.** unfit for use because of long or harmful use or wear: *These shoes are worn-out.* **2.** thoroughly exhausted or fatigued.

wor·ri·some (wur′ē səm) *adj.* **1.** causing worry or anxiety. **2.** given to worry.

wor·ry (wur′ē) *v.*, **wor·ried, wor·ry·ing.** —*v.i.* **1.** to feel anxious or troubled about something: *Mother worries if I am not home by dark.* **2.** to pull or tear at something, as with the teeth: *The puppy worried at the blanket.* —*v.t.* **1.** to cause to feel anxious or troubled; make uneasy: *He worries me when he acts so strangely.* **2.** to bother; pester; annoy. **3.** to bite at, shake, or tear with the teeth: *The dog worried the bone.* —*n. pl.,* **wor·ries. 1.** the act of worrying or the state of being worried; mental uneasiness or distress. **2.** a cause of mental uneasiness or distress; source of anxiety: *She has many worries.* [Old English *wyrgan* to strangle.] —**wor′ri·er,** *n.*

wor·ry·wart (wur′ē wôrt′) *n. Informal.* a person who tends to worry excessively and unnecessarily.

worse (wurs) *adj.* the comparative of **bad** and **ill. 1.** of more inferior quality, condition, ability, or value: *He is a poor student, and his brother is worse.* **2.** more unfavorable, distressing, or unpleasant: *The weather today is even worse than it was yesterday.* **3.** more harmful, damaging, or severe. **4.** in poorer health; less well: *The patient is worse since he took the medicine.* —*adv.* in a worse way or manner: *She sings worse now than before she took lessons.* —*n.* something that is worse.

wors·en (wur′sən) *v.t., v.i.* to make or become worse.

wor·ship (wur′ship) *n.* **1.** respect, honor, or reverence given to God or a god, or to someone or something considered sacred. **2.** the expression of such respect, honor, or reverence, especially religious services consisting of prayers and other acts in honor of God. **3.** a great or intense devotion or regard; adoration. **4.** *British.* a title of honor or respect used in speaking or referring to magistrates and certain other dignitaries, usually preceded by *your* or *his.* —*v.,* **wor·shiped** or **wor·shipped, wor·ship·ing** or **wor·ship·ping.** —*v.t.* **1.** to pay respect, honor, or reverence to: *to worship God.* **2.** to have a great or intense devotion to or regard for; adore. —*v.i.* to take part in worship, especially to attend or take part in a religious service. —**wor′ship·er;** *also,* **wor′ship·per,** *n.*

wor·ship·ful (wur′ship fəl) *adj.* **1.** showing or feeling reverence, respect, or adoration; worshiping. **2.** *British.* deserving of honor or respect; honorable. ▲ used as a title in speaking or referring to persons of rank.

worst (wurst) *adj.* the superlative of **bad** and **ill. 1.** most inferior in quality, condition, ability, or value: *That is the worst book I have ever read.* **2.** most unfavorable, distressing, or unpleasant: *This is the worst news I've heard all day.* **3.** most harmful, damaging, or severe: *That was the worst accident the policeman had ever seen.* —*adv.* in the worst way or manner. —*n.* something that is worst. —*v.t.* to get the better of; defeat: *We worsted them in basketball by ten points.*

if worst comes to worst. if the worst possible thing happens.

in the worst way. *Informal.* very much: *I want to go to the party in the worst way.*

wor·sted (woos′tid, wur′stid) *n.* **1.** a smooth yarn made from long wool fibers that are combed parallel and twisted hard, used in making such fabrics as gabardine. **2.** a tightly woven wool fabric made from such yarn and having a smooth, hard surface. —*adj.* consisting of or made from worsted: *a worsted coat.*

worth (wurth) *prep.* **1.** deserving of; meriting: *That movie is worth seeing.* **2.** having the same value as: *an old coin worth thirty dollars.* **3.** having property or wealth amounting to: *a woman worth sixty thousand dollars.* —*n.* **1.** the quality that makes a person or thing useful, desirable, or important; merit or excellence: *a novel of little worth.* **2.** the value of something in money: *The painting's worth was estimated at half a million dollars.* **3.** the amount of something that can be had for a specific sum: *fifty cents' worth of apples.* **4.** wealth; riches.

worth·less (wurth′lis) *adj.* not having worth or value: *worthless advice, a worthless person.* —**worth′less·ly,** *adv.* —**worth′less·ness,** *n.*

worth·while (wurth′hwīl′) *adj.* having sufficient value or importance to be worth the time, effort, or money spent.

wor·thy (wur′thē) *adj.,* **wor·thi·er, wor·thi·est. 1.** having worth or value: *to contribute to a worthy charity.* **2.** having sufficient worth or value; deserving: *He is a leader worthy of our support.* —*n. pl.,* **wor·thies.** a person of importance, merit, or distinction. —**wor′thi·ly,** *adv.* —**wor′thi·ness,** *n.*

would (wood) *auxiliary verb.* a past tense of **will**[1]. **1.** used to express a condition: *If you would help, we would finish much sooner.* **2.** used to express future time: *We wondered if Don would be on time.* **3.** used to express strong preference or willingness: *She would rather go hungry than beg.* **4.** used to express a choice: *Carol would never have taken the job if it weren't for the money.* **5.** used to express intention or determination: *They promised that they would return before long.* **6.** used to express longing or desire: *Would that I were with her now!* **7.** used to express probability or possibility: *Being late would make her very angry.* **8.** used to express a request: *Would you be kind enough to open the door for me?* **9.** used to express customary or habitual action: *During the summer we would sit on the beach for hours.*

would-be (wood′bē′) *adj.* **1.** desiring or claiming to be: *a would-be artist.* **2.** intended to be: *Police apprehended the would-be killer.*

would·n't (wood′ənt) would not.

wouldst (woodst) *Archaic.* the second person singular past tense of **will**[1]. ▲ used with *thou.*

wound[1] (woond) *n.* **1.** an injury to any part of the body, especially one in which the skin is torn, cut, or pierced. **2.** an injury to the feelings, pride, or the like. —*v.t.* **1.** to injure by tearing, cutting, or piercing the skin: *The police wounded the bank robber.* **2.** to hurt or injure: *His failure to get the job wounded his pride.* [Old English *wund.*]

wound[2] (wound) a past tense and past participle of **wind**[2].

wove (wōv) a past tense and past participle of **weave.**

wo·ven (wō′vən) a past participle of **weave.**

wow (wou) *interj.* used to express surprise, wonder, pleasure, or similar feeling.

wpm, words per minute.

wrack (rak) *n.* **1.** destruction. ▲ used chiefly in the phrase *wrack and ruin.* **2.** seaweed or other sea plants cast ashore.

wraith (rāth) *n.* **1.** the ghost of a person which, when seen while the person is living, is thought to indicate that he will soon die. **2.** a ghost; specter.

wran·gle (rang′gəl) *v.,* **wran·gled, wran·gling.** —*v.i.* to argue or dispute, especially in a noisy or angry manner. —*v.t.* **1.** to bring about, get, or persuade by argument: *I* *wrangled the money he owed me from him.* **2.** in the western United States, to herd, round up, or tend (horses or other livestock). —*n.* a noisy or angry argument; dispute.

wran·gler (rang′glər) *n.* **1.** a person who wrangles. **2.** in the western United States, a person who herds or tends horses or other livestock; cowboy.

wrap (rap) *v.t.,* **wrapped** or **wrapt, wrap·ping. 1.** to fold or place (a covering) around someone or something, as for protection: *to wrap a blanket around a sleeping child.* **2.** to cover in this way: *to wrap a baby in a blanket.* **3.** to cover, especially with paper, and make secure: *to wrap a package, to wrap a present.* **4.** to cover or surround so as to obscure or conceal: *The skyscraper was wrapped in fog.* **5.** to take up completely; engross: *to be wrapped in thought.* **6.** to clasp or fold: *He wrapped his arms around her.* **7.** *Informal.* to bring to an end; conclude: *The detective wrapped up the case in two days.* —*n.* an outer covering or garment, as a shawl.

   under wraps. in concealment or secrecy: *The plan was kept under wraps.*

   wrapped up in. absorbed in or involved in: *to be wrapped up in one's work.*

wrap·per (rap′ər) *n.* **1.** paper or other material in which something is wrapped or enclosed: *a candy wrapper.* **2.** a person or thing that wraps packages, parcels, or the like. **3.** a long, loose dressing gown, robe, or similar garment.

wrap·ping (rap′ing) *n. usually,* **wrappings.** paper or other material designed or used for wrapping packages or other objects.

wrapt (rapt) a past tense and past participle of **wrap.**

wrap-up (rap′up′) *n. Informal.* a brief, summarizing report, as of news.

wrath (rath) *n.* extreme or violent anger; rage: *His rude behavior and language aroused his father's wrath.*

wrath·ful (rath′fəl) *adj.* full of, resulting from, or showing wrath. —**wrath′ful·ly,** *adv.* —**wrath′ful·ness,** *n.*

wreak (rēk) *v.t.* **1.** to inflict or exact: *to wreak havoc, to wreak vengeance.* **2.** to give free expression to; vent: *The man wreaked his anger on the innocent bystander.*

wreath (rēth) *n. pl.,* **wreaths** (rēthz). **1.** a ring of flowers or leaves woven or twined together, worn on the head as a mark of honor or victory, placed on a grave as a memorial, or used as a decoration. **2.** any spiral or curving shape or form resembling this: *Wreaths of smoke rose from the chimney.*

wreathe (rēth) *v.t.,* **wreathed, wreath·ing. 1.** to form or shape into a wreath. **2.** to decorate, encircle, or crown with a wreath or wreaths: *The children wreathed the front door at Christmas.* **3.** to envelop; cover: *Her face was wreathed in smiles.*

wreck (rek) *v.t.* **1.** to cause the physical destruction or ruin of: *to wreck a car in an accident.* **2.** to destroy, ruin, or put an end to: *The scandal nearly wrecked his career. His lateness wrecked my plans for the day.* **3.** to tear down or dismantle, as an old building. —*n.* **1.** the act of wrecking or the state of being wrecked; destruction. **2.** the remains of anything, especially a ship, automobile, or airplane, that has been destroyed, damaged, or disabled. **3.** a person in poor physical or mental condition: *The job interview made him a nervous wreck.* **4.** something in poor or broken-down condition, or in a state of disorder.

wreck·age (rek′ij) *n.* **1.** the remains of anything that has been wrecked; debris. **2.** the act of wrecking or the state of being wrecked.

wreck·er (rek′ər) *n.* **1.** a person or thing that wrecks. **2.** a person whose work is tearing down or demolishing buildings. **3.** a person, vehicle, or piece of equipment used in removing, salvaging, or recovering wrecks. **4.** a person,

boat, or ship employed to recover wrecked or disabled ships or their cargoes.

wren (ren) *n.* any of various songbirds having a slender bill, short rounded wings, a short tail, and brownish feathers that are usually marked with brown, black, or white.

Wren, Sir Christopher (ren) 1632–1723, English architect.

wrench (rench) *n. pl.,* **wrench·es. 1.** a sharp or violent twist, turn, or pull. **2.** an injury or strain, as of the back, caused by a sudden or violent twisting, turning, or jerking motion; sprain. **3.** a sharp, usually sudden, mental or emotional distress or pain. **4.** any of various tools having fixed or movable jaws, used especially for gripping and turning a nut, bolt, or pipe. —*v.t.* **1.** to twist, turn, or pull with a sudden sharp or violent motion: *He wrenched the book out of her hand.* **2.** to injure or strain by twisting or turning suddenly or violently: *Sarah wrenched her back when she fell.*

wrest (rest) *v.t.* **1.** to pull, twist, or take away by force or violence: *The policeman wrested the gun from the thief.* **2.** to seize by force or violence: *The leaders of the army tried to wrest power from the dictator.* **3.** to obtain or extract by great effort: *The farmers wrested a bare existence from the barren land.* **4.** to turn or change from the proper meaning, use, or purpose: *The newspaper reporter wrested the senator's words.*

wres·tle (res′əl) *v.,* **wres·tled, wres·tling.** —*v.i.* **1.** to take part in the sport or activity of wrestling; grapple: *Two boys were wrestling on the ground.* **2.** to struggle or contend, especially in order to gain mastery: *to wrestle with a problem, to wrestle with one's conscience.* —*v.t.* **1.** to take part in wrestling with: *to wrestle a bear.* **2.** to move or force by wrestling: *The policeman wrestled the thief to the ground.* —*n.* **1.** the act or action of wrestling. **2.** a struggle. —**wres′tler,** *n.*

wres·tling (res′ling) *n.* a sport or activity in which two opponents struggle hand to hand, especially in an attempt to throw or force each other to the ground.

wretch (rech) *n. pl.,* **wretch·es. 1.** an unfortunate or unhappy person. **2.** an evil or contemptible person.

wretch·ed (rech′id) *adj.* **1.** very unhappy; deeply distressed: *Ellen sat alone in the corner feeling quite wretched.* **2.** characterized by or causing great unhappiness or discomfort: *to lead a wretched existence, the wretched living conditions in the slums.* **3.** evil or contemptible; despicable. —**wretch′ed·ly,** *adv.* —**wretch′ed·ness,** *n.*

wri·er (rī′ər) the comparative of **wry.**

wri·est (rī′ist) the superlative of **wry.**

wrig·gle (rig′əl) *v.,* **wrig·gled, wrig·gling.** —*v.i.* **1.** to twist or turn from side to side with short, quick movements; squirm: *The bored children were wriggling in their seats.* **2.** to move or proceed with a wriggling motion: *The caterpillar wriggled up the side of the tree.* **3.** to make one's way by tricky or shifty means: *Harry is always wriggling out of trouble.* —*v.t.* **1.** to cause to wriggle. **2.** to bring, get, or make by wriggling: *She wriggled her way into the cave.* —*n.* a wriggling movement or action: *to walk with a wriggle.* —**wrig′gly,** *adj.*

wrig·gler (rig′lər) *n.* **1.** a person or thing that wriggles. **2.** the larva of a mosquito; wiggler.

W

at; āpe; cär; end; mē; it; īce; hot; ōld; fôrk; wood; fool; oil; out; up; turn; sing; thin; this; hw in white; zh in treasure. The symbol ə stands for the sound of a in about, e in taken, i in pencil, o in lemon, and u in circus.

wright (rīt) *n.* a person who makes, constructs, or creates something. ▲ used chiefly in combination: *playwright.*

Wright (rīt) **1. Frank Lloyd.** 1869–1959, U.S. architect. **2. Or·ville** (ôr′vil), 1871–1948, and **Wil·bur** (wil′bər), 1867–1912, U.S. brothers who were the first men to make a successful flight in an airplane.

wring (ring) *v.t.,* **wrung, wring·ing. 1.** to squeeze or twist so as to force out liquid: *to wring wet clothes.* **2.** to force out (liquid) in this way: *to wring water from a wet bathing suit.* **3.** to get by forceful or constant effort: *to wring the truth out of someone.* **4.** to clasp and press or twist (the hands) together. **5.** to twist or squeeze forcefully or violently. **6.** to cause to feel great sadness or pity; torment: *His misery wrung our hearts.* —*n.* the act of wringing; twist or squeeze.

wring·er (ring′ər) *n.* a person or thing that wrings, especially a device or machine for squeezing water out of wet clothes.

wrin·kle (ring′kəl) *n.* **1.** a small fold, ridge, or crease in a normally smooth surface: *Mother ironed out the wrinkles in her dress.* **2.** a small furrow, crease, or line in the skin, as is caused by aging. —*v.,* **wrin·kled, wrin·kling.** —*v.t.* to form or make a wrinkle or wrinkles in: *to wrinkle one's brow.* —*v.i.* to become wrinkled: *This fabric won't wrinkle.*

wrist (rist) *n.* **1.** the joint that connects the hand and arm, or the area surrounding this joint. **2.** the eight small bones that make up this joint; carpus.

wrist·band (rist′band′) *n.* a band, as of a sleeve, that goes around the wrist.

wrist·watch (rist′woch′) *n. pl.,* **wrist·watch·es.** a watch worn on a band or strap around the wrist.

writ[1] (rit) *n.* **1.** a legal document ordering the person or persons named in it to do or not to do something. **2.** something written; writing. [Old English *writ.*]

writ[2] (rit) *Archaic.* a past tense and past participle of **write.**

write (rīt) *v.,* **wrote** or *(archaic)* **writ, writ·ten** or *(archaic)* **writ, writ·ing.** —*v.t.* **1.** to mark or form (letters, words, symbols, or the like) on a surface, as with a pen or pencil. **2.** to form the letters, words, or symbols of: *to write one's name, to write a formula.* **3.** to express, describe, or communicate in or by writing: *to write one's thoughts in a diary.* **4.** to be the author or composer of: *to write short stories.* **5.** to send a letter to: *Please write us when you get home.* **6.** to fill in with the required written information: *to write a check.* **7.** to draw up in legal form: *to write a will.* **8.** to show or indicate plainly: *His guilt was written all over his face.* —*v.i.* **1.** to form letters, words, or symbols on paper or another surface. **2.** to be an author or writer. **3.** to compose or send a letter: *I'll write as soon as I can.* **4.** to produce writing of a certain quality: *Helene writes quite clearly.*

to write down. to put into writing.

to write in. to vote for (a person not listed on a ballot) by inserting his name.

to write off. a. to cancel or remove from an account: *to write off a debt.* **b.** to regard or acknowledge as a loss or failure: *to write off a project.*

to write out. a. to put into writing. **b.** to write in full.

to write up. to describe or set down in writing, especially in a detailed account: *The reporter wrote up the interview and submitted it to the editor.*

write-in (rīt′in′) *n.* a vote cast for a person not listed on a ballot by inserting his name. —*adj.* of or relating to such a vote or votes: *a write-in campaign.*

writ·er (rī′tər) *n.* **1.** a person who writes. **2.** a person whose occupation or profession is writing.

write-up (rīt′up′) *n.* a written account or description.

writhe (rīth) *v.i.,* **writhed, writh·ing. 1.** to move the body with a twisting or turning motion, as in great pain: *The injured man writhed in pain.* **2.** to suffer great mental or emotional distress or discomfort.

writ·ing (rī′ting) *n.* **1.** the act of a person who writes. **2.** handwriting; penmanship: *Her writing is always neat and legible.* **3.** a written form: *I'd like this agreement put in writing.* **4.** something written: *There was writing all over the wall.* **5.** a novel, play, or other literary work: *to study the writings of Aristotle.* **6.** the occupation or profession of a writer or author. **7.** the style, form, or art of literary composition.

● **Writing** is one of man's greatest inventions because it enables us to record language in a visible form and to store vast amounts of information. Man has been writing for only a short time in the total span of human history. The first form of writing known to man was **pictographs.** Pictographs are pictures that are drawn to represent something. If you want to represent the sun in pictographs, you would draw a picture of the sun rather than write the letters "s-u-n." This system is limited to representing things that can be drawn. Because man has always had the need to express ideas and feelings, another system, called **ideographs,** developed. Ideographs are also pictures, but they convey more than just the appearance of an object or animal. A picture of the sun in ideographs can mean "warmth," "light," "day," or any of the other things that we associate with the sun. Chinese writing is the only modern system that is still based on such symbols.

Neither of these methods of writing is "real" writing, because both portray things and ideas rather than language itself. Writing really begins when words that stand for things and ideas are set down. The first system that contained this element of real writing was **logographs.** Logographs are symbols that not only show the appearance of an object but, most importantly, represent the sound of the word used for it. The symbol for the sun in logographs could also be used for the first syllable of "sundae" or the second syllable of "grandson."

The next important advancement was made by altering writing so that it represented sounds only. This was the beginning of true writing. When the sounds represented by symbols are syllables, the system is known as **syllabary.** When the symbols represent individual speech sounds, the system is known as an **alphabet.** Using these methods made writing much easier because the number of symbols needed was much smaller than the number needed for logographs. Although the shapes of the letters have altered and there have been many technological improvements, writing itself has remained unchanged from the time of the first alphabets several thousand years ago until the twentieth century.

writ·ten (rit′ən) a past participle of **write.**

Wroc·law (vrôts′läf) *n.* a city in southwestern Poland. It was known as Breslau when it was a part of eastern Germany before World War II. Pop. (1970), 523,300.

wrong (rông) *adj.* **1.** not correct or accurate; untrue: *His answer to the question was wrong.* **2.** not just, moral, or good: *John felt that it would be wrong to betray his friend's trust.* **3.** not appropriate, suitable, or proper: *Now is the wrong time to ask for a favor.* **4.** not in proper or normal working order; out of order: *There is something wrong with my watch.* **5.** not meant, wanted, or necessary: *Harry made a wrong turn.* **6.** of or relating to the side or surface not meant to be seen: *the wrong side of a fabric.* —*n.* something that is wrong, such as an unjust, immoral, or harmful action: *The ruler committed many wrongs.* —*adv.* in a wrong way or manner. —*v.t.* to treat in an unjust, wrong, or harmful manner; do wrong to. [Old English *wrang* injustice, from Old Norse *rangr* crooked, twisted, unjust.] —**wrong′ly**, *adv.* —**wrong′ness**, *n.*

in the wrong. wrong, mistaken, or at fault: *You were in the wrong in that argument.*

to go wrong. a. to turn out badly or take place incorrectly: *Something went wrong with the experiment.* **b.** to do evil or immoral things. **c.** to make a mistake; err.

wrong·do·er (rông′dōō′ər) *n.* a person who does something wrong.

wrong·do·ing (rông′dōō′ing) *n.* the act of doing something wrong.

wrong·ful (rông′fəl) *adj.* **1.** wrong, unjust, or injurious. **2.** unlawful; illegal. —**wrong′ful·ly,** *adv.* —**wrong′ful·ness,** *n.*

wrong·head·ed (rông′hed′id) *adj.* stubbornly or unreasonably keeping wrong opinions, judgments, or ideas. —**wrong′head′ed·ly,** *adv.*

wrote (rōt) a past tense of **write.**

wroth (rôth) *adj.* angry; wrathful.

wrought (rôt) *v.* a past tense and past participle of **work.** —*adj.* **1.** made or formed: *a skillfully wrought desk.* **2.** (of metals) shaped by hammering.

wrought up. agitated; excited: *Father got all wrought up over the delay.*

wrought iron, an extremely pure form of iron that is tough, easily worked and welded, and relatively resistant to corrosion.

wrung (rung) the past tense and past participle of **wring.**

wry (rī) *adj.,* **wri·er, wri·est. 1.** made by twisting or distorting the features: *a wry smile.* **2.** funny in an ironic, bitter, or perverse way: *a wry sense of humor.* —**wry′ly,** *adv.* —**wry′ness,** *n.*

wt., weight.

Wu·han (wōō′hän′) *n.* a city in east-central China. Pop. (1958 est.), 2,226,000.

Wup·per·tal (voop′ər täl′) *n.* a city in western West Germany. Pop. (1969 est.), 414,700.

wurst (wurst) *n.* a sausage.

W. Va., West Virginia.

Wyc·liffe, John (wi′klif) 1320?–1384, English religious reformer.

Wyo., Wyoming.

Wy·o·ming (wī ō′ming) *n.* a state in the western United States. Capital, Cheyenne. Area, 97,914 sq. mi. Pop. (1970), 332,416. Abbreviation, **Wyo.** —**Wy·o′ming·ite′,** *n.*

● The name **Wyoming** comes from an Algonquian word meaning "at the big plains," "end of the plains," or "on the great plain." It was originally an eastern name for a valley in Pennsylvania, but it described the new western territory well and was adopted by Congress in 1868. The name was kept when the territory became a state.

at; āpe; cär; end; mē; it; īce; hot; ōld; fôrk; wood; fōōl; oil; out; up; turn; sing; thin; this; hw in white; zh in treasure. The symbol ə stands for the sound of **a** in about, **e** in taken, **i** in pencil, **o** in lemon, and **u** in circus.

W

1. Semitic ☩ ✕	4. Etruscan ✕ ☨
2. Greek Ninth Century B.C. ✕	5. Latin Fourth Century B.C. ✕
3. Greek Classical Capitals ✕	6. English ✕

X is the twenty-fourth letter of the English alphabet. The earliest form of **X** was an ancient Semitic letter (1) that was written like a plus sign or like a modern **X**, usually called a "cross sign." When the Greeks (2) borrowed the "cross sign" from the ancient Semitic alphabet, they gave it two different pronunciations: a *ks* sound in the Western Greek alphabet and a *kh* sound in the Eastern Greek alphabet. This letter was adopted, with only slight changes, in the classical Greek (3) and Etruscan (4) alphabets. The Romans (5), who adapted their alphabet from the Western Greek and Etruscan, gave their "cross sign" letter a *ks* pronunciation. By the fourth century B.C., the letter **X** of the Latin alphabet was written almost exactly as we write it today (6). In English, very few words begin with the letter **X**. All of these words, with the exception of new words like "X-ray," came from either Greek, as "xenon" and "xylophone," or from Spanish, as "xebec." One of the most common uses of the letter **X** is in the word "Xmas," in which it stands for the ancient Eastern Greek "cross sign" letter, the first letter in the Greek spelling of "Christ."

x, X (eks) *n. pl.,* **x's, X's. 1.** the twenty-fourth letter of the English alphabet. **2.** something having the shape of this letter. **3.** the Roman numeral for ten. **4.** an unknown person or thing. **5.** *Mathematics.* **a.** a mark used to indicate multiplication: *4 x 10 = 40.* **b.** an unknown quantity or variable: *3x = 6.* **6.** a mark used in place of a signature by a person who cannot write. **7.** a mark used to indicate a particular point or place on a map or diagram.

Xan·thip·pe (zan tip′ē) *n.* **1.** 469?–399 B.C., the wife of Socrates, famous as a scolding, nagging woman. **2.** any scolding, nagging woman; shrew.

Xa·vi·er, Saint Francis (zā′vē ər, zav′ē ər) 1506– 1552, Spanish Jesuit missionary.

x-ax·is (eks′ak′sis) *n. pl.,* **x-ax·es** (eks′ak′sēz). the horizontal axis on a graph, along which the abscissa is measured.

X chromosome, one of a pair of chromosomes that determine sex in nearly all animals and most higher plants. A fertilized egg cell with two X chromosomes produces a female organism. A fertilized egg cell with an X chromosome and a Y chromosome produces a male organism.

Xe, the symbol for xenon.

xe·bec (zē′bek) *n.* a small, three-masted ship, formerly used in the Mediterranean Sea by pirates.

xe·non (zē′non) *n.* a rare, heavy, gaseous chemical element approximately five times heavier than air, used as a light source in neon lights and lasers. Symbol: Xe [Greek *xenon* the strange; because it is a rare element.]

xen·o·pho·bi·a (zen′ə fō′bē ə) *n.* a fear of strangers or of anything strange or foreign.

Xen·o·phon (zen′ə fən) 430?–355? B.C., Greek historian.

Xe·rox (zēr′oks) *n. Trademark.* a process for making photographic copies of printed or pictorial material, in which a positive image of the material to be copied is projected onto an electrically charged surface. Light from the white areas of the material to be copied removes the charge, but the dark areas retain it and attract a black plastic powder which forms the print of the copy. —*v.t. also,* **xe·rox.** to reproduce by this process.

Xerx·es I (zurk′sēz) 519?–465 B.C., king of Persia.

Xi'an (sē′än′) another spelling of **Sian.**

X·mas (kris′məs, eks′məs) *n.* see **Christmas.**

X-ray (eks′rā′) *v.t.* to examine, photograph, or treat with X rays: *to X-ray a broken bone.*

X ray 1. an invisible, high-frequency, shortwave, electromagnetic radiation that can pass through substances which visible light cannot penetrate. It is used in medical diagnosis of internal disorders, such as broken bones, and in treating certain diseases, such as cancer. **2.** a photograph made by means of X rays.

xy·lem (zī′ləm, zī′lem) *n.* the woody tissue of plants that serves to carry water and dissolved nutrients from the roots to the leaves and also helps to support the plant.

xy·lo·phone (zī′lə fōn′) *n.* a musical instrument consisting of a stand on which a row of wooden bars of graduated length is mounted. It is usually sounded by striking the bars with small wooden mallets.

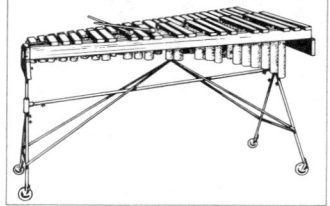

Xylophone

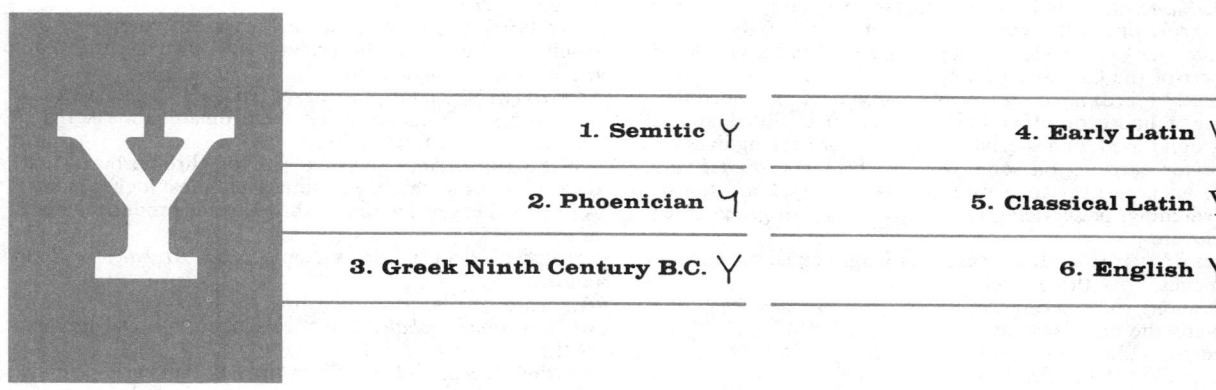

1. Semitic Υ	**4. Early Latin** V
2. Phoenician Y	**5. Classical Latin** Y
3. Greek Ninth Century B.C. Y	**6. English** Y

Y is the twenty-fifth letter of the English alphabet. The letter **Y** has the same early history as the letter **V**, coming from the ancient Semitic letter *waw* (1), that depicted a hook and stood for the *w* sound, as the *w* in *water*. When the Phoenicians (2) borrowed *waw*, they used it to represent both the consonant sound *w* and the vowel sound *u*, as the *u* in *rude*. The ancient Greeks adopted *waw* and called it *upsilon* (3) and gave it its modern form. In the Latin alphabet, *upsilon* was adopted at two different times. In about the sixth or seventh century B.C., *upsilon* was borrowed to form the Latin letter **V** (4) that became the source of our modern letters **U**, **V**, and **W**. About 2000 years ago, *upsilon* was again adopted into the Latin alphabet (5) in order to write words that had been borrowed from the Greek language. This later form of *upsilon* was written almost exactly the way we write the capital letter **Y** today (6).

Unlike the other letters of the alphabet, **Y** commonly functions as both a vowel, as in "funny" and "cry," and a consonant, as in "yesterday" and "young." The letter **Y** was first used as a consonant when it replaced an obsolete Old English letter. Because of this, most of the words we use that begin with **Y** have come from Old English or Middle English. The letter **Y** also replaced the Old English letter *thorn*, which represented a *th* sound and disappeared from the alphabet about 500 years ago. Although the letter **Y** representing a *th* sound is normally no longer used in English, it still appears in old-fashioned spelling, as in "Ye Olde Booke Shoppe."

y, Y (wī) *n. pl.*, **y's, Y's.** **1.** the twenty-fifth letter of the English alphabet. **2.** something having the shape of this letter. **3.** *Mathematics.* an unknown quantity or variable: $4y = 20$.

Y, the symbol for yttrium.

y. **1.** yard. **2.** year.

-y[1] *suffix* (used to form adjectives) **1.** characterized by: *rainy, funny.* **2.** containing; full of: *juicy, sooty.* **3.** inclined to: *itchy, thirsty.* **4.** somewhat: *sugary, powdery, chilly.* **5.** resembling; like: *flowery, icy.* [Old English *-ig.*]

-y[2] *suffix* (used to form nouns) **1.** little: *puppy, kitty.* **2.** dear: *aunty, Bobby.* [Middle English *-y, -i, -ie.*]

-y[3] *suffix* (used to form nouns) state or quality: *jealousy, honesty.* [Latin *-ia,* from Greek *-iā.*]

yacht (yot) *n.* any of various small ships used especially for pleasure trips or racing. —*v.i.* to cruise or race in a yacht.

yak[1] (yak) *n.* a long-haired ox of Tibet and central Asia, having a large hump at the shoulder and curved horns, used as a beast of burden. [Tibetan *gyag.*]

yak[2] (yak) *v.i.*, **yakked, yak·king.** *Slang.* to talk too much or idly; chatter. [Imitative of this sound.]

Yal·ta (yôl′tə) *n.* a re-

Yak[1]

sort city on the Black Sea in the Soviet Union, the site of a conference held by Franklin D. Roosevelt, Winston Churchill, and Joseph Stalin in 1945.

Ya·lu (yä′lōō′) *n.* a river in eastern Asia, flowing between Manchuria and Korea into the Yellow Sea.

yam (yam) *n.* **1.** the root of a trailing tropical vine, used as food. **2.** the vine that bears this root, having large leaves and spikes of small greenish flowers. **3.** a large, reddish sweet potato.

Yang·tze (yäng′tsē′, yang′sē) *n.* the longest river in China, flowing northeastward from Tibet through central China, into the China Sea near Shanghai. Also, **Chang.**

yank (yangk) *Informal. v.t.* to give a sharp, sudden pull to; jerk; tug: *She yanked the dress off the hanger.* —*v.i.* to pull sharply and suddenly: *The little boy yanked at his mother's skirt.* —*n.* a sharp, sudden pull.

Yank (yangk) *n. Informal.* Yankee.

Yan·kee (yang′kē) *n.* **1.** a person who was born or is living in New England. **2.** a person who was born or is living in any of the Northern states. **3.** a person who fought on the side of the Union in the Civil War. **4.** any person who was born or is living in the United States. —*adj.* of or relating to Yankees.

Yankee Doo·dle (dōōd′əl) a song made popular by American soldiers during the Revolutionary War.

Ya·oun·dé (ya ōōn dā′) *n.* the capital of Cameroon, in the south-central part of the country. Pop. (1976), 313,706.

yap (yap) *n.* **1.** a brief, sharp, or shrill bark; yelp. **2.** *Slang.* noisy talk. —*v.i.,* **yapped, yap·ping. 1.** to bark sharply or shrilly; yelp. **2.** *Slang.* to talk noisily.

Yap (yäp) *n.* an island group in the western Pacific Ocean, part of the Caroline Islands.

yard¹ (yärd) *n.* **1.** an area of ground next to or surrounding a house or other building. **2.** an enclosed area of ground used for a special purpose, as for keeping livestock or for carrying on some work or business: *a coal yard.* **3.** an area next to a railroad station, used for storing, switching, or servicing trains. [Old English *geard* an enclosure.]

yard² (yärd) *n.* **1.** a measure of length equal to thirty-six inches, or three feet. **2.** a long rod tapering toward the ends, fastened across a mast to support a sail. [Old English *gierd* a rod, stick, measure.]

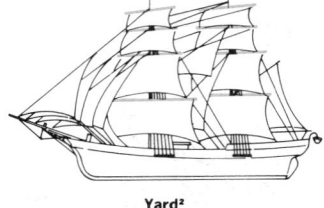

Yard²

yard·age (yär′dij) *n.* the amount or length of something measured in yards: *Our team gained more yardage than theirs did during the football game.*

yard·arm (yärd′ärm′) *n.* either end of a yard supporting a square sail.

yard goods, fabric that is sold by the yard.

yard·mas·ter (yärd′mas′tər) *n.* a person who is in charge of a railroad yard.

yard·stick (yärd′stik′) *n.* **1.** a flat strip of wood or metal one yard long, used in measuring. **2.** any standard used in making a judgment, evaluation, or comparison: *What yardstick does that critic use in judging the quality of a television program?*

yar·mul·ke (yär′məl kə, yä′məl kə) *n.* a skullcap worn by Jewish men and boys, especially during religious services.

yarn (yärn) *n.* **1.** thread spun from natural or man-made fibers, such as cotton, wool, silk, or nylon, used in weaving or knitting. **2.** *Informal.* a long, exaggerated, or made-up story: *The old sailor told many yarns about his days at sea.* —*v.i. Informal.* to tell a yarn or yarns.

yar·row (yar′ō) *n.* any of a large group of plants having finely divided leaves and clusters of small yellow, white, or pink flowers.

yaw (yô) *v.i.* **1.** (of a ship) to turn temporarily and unintentionally from a straight course. **2.** (of an aircraft, spacecraft, or projectile) to turn to the right or left on its vertical axis. —*n.* the act of turning from a straight course.

yawl (yôl) *n.* **1.** a sailboat or small yacht with a large mainmast forward and a smaller mast astern. **2.** a ship's small boat, usually rowed by four or six oarsmen.

yawn (yôn) *v.i.* **1.** to open the mouth wide with a deep breath because of drowsiness, boredom, or weariness. **2.** to be or draw wide open: *The stallion stood against the yawning cavern of the stable door* (William Faulkner). —*v.t.* to say or express with a yawn: *to yawn an answer.* —*n.* the act of

Yawl

yawning: *The tired boy stifled a yawn as the lecturer continued his boring speech.*

yaws (yôz) *n., pl.* a contagious disease occurring in the tropics, characterized by growths and sores on the skin. ▲ used with a singular verb.

y-ax·is (wī′ak′sis) *n. pl.,* **y-ax·es** (wī′ak′sēz). the vertical axis on a graph, along which the ordinate is measured.

Yb, the symbol for ytterbium.

Y chromosome, one of a pair of chromosomes that determine sex in nearly all animals and most higher plants. A fertilized egg cell with a Y chromosome produces a male organism.

y·clept (ē klept′) *also,* **y·cleped.** *adj. Archaic.* called; named.

yd., yard; yards.

ye¹ (yē) *pron. Archaic.* the ones spoken to. [Old English *gē* the ones spoken to.]

ye² (<u>th</u>ē) *Archaic.* the¹. [From the fact that early printers confused an obsolete Old and Middle English character that represented the sound of <u>th</u> with the letter *y.*]

yea (yā) *adv.* **1.** yes: *All those in favor of a school picnic say "yea."* ▲ used in agreeing to or affirming something, especially in voting orally. **2.** *Archaic.* indeed; truly. ▲ used to introduce a sentence or statement. —*n.* an affirmative vote or voter.

year (yēr) *n.* **1.** a period of time consisting of 365 or 366 days, reckoned from January 1 to December 31, and divided into twelve months or fifty-two weeks. Also, **calendar year. 2.** the interval of time between one vernal equinox and the next, equal to 365 days, 5 hours, 48 minutes, and 46 seconds. Also, **solar year. 3.** the interval of time required for the earth to complete one revolution around the sun, measured against the relatively fixed background of the stars, equal to 365 days, 6 hours, 9 minutes, and 9.54 seconds. Also, **sidereal year. 4.** a period of twelve lunar months or 354 days. Also, **lunar year. 5.** any period of twelve months: *He'll have worked here two years as of May 1st.* **6.** a part of a year devoted to a particular activity: *the school year.* **7.** the period of time in which any planet completes one revolution around the sun. **8. years. a.** age, especially old age: *He's getting on in years.* **b.** time, especially a long time: *We've been going there for years.*

year after year. every year.

year by year. with each succeeding year.

year in, year out. every year; continuously.

year·book (yēr′book′) *n.* **1.** a book published every year, usually containing information about or a summary of the events of the previous year. **2.** a book issued by a graduating class of a high school or college, usually containing photographs of the class and information about its activities and achievements.

year·ling (yēr′ling) *n.* an animal that is one year old or in its second year. —*adj.* one year old: *a yearling calf.*

year·long (yēr′lông′) *adj.* lasting for a year.

year·ly (yēr′lē) *adj.* **1.** happening or returning once a year: *He takes a yearly vacation.* **2.** performed during a year; lasting a year: *The communications satellite has just completed its yearly orbit about the earth.* **3.** measured by the year: *a yearly salary.* —*adv.* once a year; annually: *I see my doctor yearly.*

yearn (yurn) *v.i.* **1.** to feel a strong and deep desire: *The old man yearned for the carefree days of his youth.* **2.** to feel deep pity; be moved with compassion: *It made her heart yearn to think of the homeless children.*

yearn·ing (yur′ning) *n.* an earnest or deep desire. —**yearn′ing·ly,** *adv.*

year-round (yēr′round′) *adj., adv.* throughout the year: *a year-round vacation spot. He would like to live here year-round.*

yeast (yēst) *n.* **1.** a substance consisting of very tiny cells of various fungi that cause fermentation in liquids containing sugar. Yeast is used in raising bread, making beer and wine, and in other processes. **2.** a single plant or cell forming this substance. **3.** see **yeast cake. 4.** foam; froth; spume.

yeast cake, yeast compressed with flour or meal into small cakes, used especially in baking and brewing.

Yeats, William Butler (yāts) 1865–1939, Irish poet and dramatist.

yegg (yeg) *n. Slang.* a thief, especially a burglar or safe-cracker.

yell (yel) *v.i.* to cry out loudly, as in pain or anger: *She yelled when the doctor touched her sore arm.* —*v.t.* to say with a yell: *He yelled the answer across the room.* —*n.* **1.** a strong, loud cry, as of pain or anger; scream. **2.** a rhythmic chant or cheer shouted by a group, as at a school or college sports event.

yel·low (yel′ō) *n.* **1.** the color of gold, butter, or ripe lemons. **2.** a paint or dye having this color. **3.** the yolk of an egg. —*adj.* **1.** having the color yellow. **2.** having a yellowish complexion. **3.** *Informal.* not brave; cowardly. —*v.i.* to become yellow: *Mother's wedding dress has yellowed with age.* —*v.t.* to make yellow. —**yel′low·ness,** *n.*

yel·low·bird (yel′ō burd′) *n.* any of various yellow birds, such as the American goldfinch and the yellow warbler.

yellow fever, a contagious, often fatal disease of tropical regions, caused by a virus transmitted by the bite of a mosquito and characterized by high fever, vomiting, jaundice, and hemorrhaging. Also, **yellow jack.**

yel·low·ham·mer (yel′ō ham′ər) *n.* **1.** a finch of Europe and Asia, having black, brown, and yellow feathers and a short cone-shaped bill. **2.** a flicker of North America, having brown feathers with yellow markings on the wings and tail.

yel·low·ish (yel′ō ish) *adj.* somewhat yellow.

yellow jack 1. another term for **yellow fever. 2.** a yellow flag used as a sign of quarantine, as on a ship.

yellow jacket, any of several wasps that have yellow markings.

Yellow River, see Hwang Ho, Huang He.

Yellow Sea, a shallow arm of the Pacific Ocean, between northeastern China and Korea.

Yel·low·stone (yel′ō stōn′) *n.* a river in the northern United States, mainly in Montana, a major tributary of the Missouri River.

Yellow jacket

Yellowstone National Park, a national park in northwestern Wyoming and neighboring sections of Montana and Idaho, noted for its scenery, hot springs, and geysers.

yellow warbler, a small American warbler. The male has yellow feathers with brown streaks.

yelp (yelp) *n.* a short shrill cry, as that made by a dog in pain. —*v.i., v.t.* to make or say with such a cry.

Yem·en (yem′ən) *n.* **1.** a country in the southwestern part of the Arabian peninsula, on the Red Sea. Its official name is the Yemen Arab Republic. Capital, Sana. Area, 75,300 sq. mi. Pop. (1975 est.), 6,700,000. **2. People's Democratic Republic of.** see **Southern Yemen.**

yen¹ (yen) *n. pl.,* **yen.** a monetary unit of Japan. [Japanese *yen.*]

yen² (yen) *Informal. n.* a sharp desire or longing; craving: *He has a yen to travel.* —*v.i.,* **yenned, yen·ning.** to yearn or long. [Chinese *yan* opium, a craving for opium.]

yeo·man (yō′mən) *n. pl.,* **yeo·men** (yō′mən). **1.** a naval petty officer who performs clerical or administrative duties. **2.** in England, a person who owns and farms a small amount of land.

yeo·man·ry (yō′mən rē) *n.* yeomen as a group.

Ye·re·van (ye re vän′) *n.* a city in the southwestern Soviet Union. It is the capital of Armenia. Pop. (1979), 1,019,000.

yes (yes) *adv.* **1.** as you say or ask; it is so. ▲ used to show acceptance, agreement, consent, or affirmation: *Yes, you are right. Yes, you may borrow my book.* **2.** in addition to that; moreover. ▲ used to emphasize a preceding statement by repeating or adding to it: *Andy is a good baseball player, yes, the best on the school team.* —*n. pl.,* **yes·es. 1.** a saying of the word "yes"; positive reply. **2.** an affirmative vote or voter.

ye·shi·va (yə shē′və) *also,* **ye·shi·vah.** *n. pl.,* **ye·shi·vas** or **ye·shi·voth** (yə shē′vōt). **1.** an Orthodox Jewish parochial school. **2.** an Orthodox Jewish institution of higher learning.

yes man *Informal.* a person who always agrees with his superior.

yes·ter·day (yes′tər dē, yes′tər dā′) *n.* **1.** the day before today: *Yesterday was a beautiful day.* **2.** the recent past: *the automobiles of yesterday.* —*adv.* **1.** on the day before today: *I saw him yesterday.* **2.** recently: *It seems that he was a baby only yesterday.*

yes·ter·year (yes′tər yēr′) *n.* **1.** the year before this year; last year. **2.** the past.

yet (yet) *adv.* **1.** at the present time; now: *She is not yet old enough to vote.* **2.** up to the present time; thus far: *Robert has never yet been late for a meeting.* **3.** continuously up to this or that time: *Father rose early and is working yet.* **4.** at some future time; eventually: *The mystery will be solved yet.* **5.** after all the time that has or had gone by: *Aren't you finished eating yet?* **6.** in the time remaining: *There is yet a chance that we will win.* **7.** in addition: *There are three days yet to go until my vacation.* **8.** even; still: *It will be colder yet before spring comes.* **9.** nevertheless; however: *The judge was stern, yet completely fair.* —*conj.* nevertheless; however: *He said he knew the way, yet we soon got lost.*

as yet. up to now: *I have not as yet received the package you sent me.*

yet·i (yet′ē) *n.* another word for the **abominable snowman.**

yew (yōō) *n.* **1.** any of a small group of evergreen trees and shrubs of Europe and Asia, having scaly reddish-brown bark and flattened needle-shaped leaves. **2.** the wood of this tree, used especially in making archery bows.

Yid·dish (yid′ish) *n.* a Germanic language spoken predominantly by Jews in Europe, Israel, and

Yew branch

North and South America. Yiddish, which is written in the Hebrew alphabet, is derived from a dialect of German

at; āpe; cär; end; mē; it; īce; hot; ōld; fôrk; wood; fōōl; oil; out; up; turn; sing; thin; this; hw in white; zh in treasure. The symbol ə stands for the sound of a in about, e in taken, i in pencil, o in lemon, and u in circus.

Y

that was spoken in the Middle Ages, with the addition of many words from Hebrew, and from various Slavic and Romance languages. —*adj.* of or relating to this language.

yield (yēld) *v.t.* **1.** to give forth; produce: *This rich land will yield a large crop. That mine yields silver.* **2.** to give in return, as for an investment: *My bank account yields 5 percent interest per year.* **3.** to give up (something); surrender: *The outnumbered troops yielded the town to the enemy.* **4.** to give or grant: *The driver of the car yielded the right of way to the pedestrians.* —*v.i.* **1.** to give up; surrender; submit: *Our troops refused to yield to the enemy forces.* **2.** to give in; consent: *We yielded to their argument.* **3.** to give way, as to force or pressure: *The lock was old and yielded when we pushed the door.* **4.** to give place, as through inferiority: *He yields to no one in devotion to the cause of human rights.* —*n.* **1.** an amount yielded; product: *The yield of wheat was large this year.* **2.** a return, as from an investment.

yield·ing (yēl'ding) *adj.* tending to yield; submissive; obedient: *The child has a yielding nature.*

yip (yip) *n.* a yelp, especially of a dog. —*v.i.,* **yipped, yipping.** to give a short, sharp cry; yelp.

YMCA, Young Men's Christian Association.

YMHA, Young Men's Hebrew Association.

yo·del (yōd'əl) *v.i.* to sing with frequent alternating changes between the natural voice and a falsetto voice. —*v.t.* to sing (something) with the natural voice and a falsetto voice. —*n.* the act or sound of yodeling. —**yo'del·er,** *n.*

yo·ga (yō'gə) *also,* **Yo·ga.** *n.* a system of mental and physical discipline practiced by Hindus in order to become free of the senses and the external world and reach ultimate reality. It is also practiced by non-Hindus to improve mental and physical health and increase powers of concentration.

yo·ghurt (yō'gərt) another spelling of **yogurt.**

yo·gi (yō'gē) *n. pl.,* **yo·gis.** a person who practices or is a follower of yoga.

yo·gurt (yō'gərt) *also,* **yo·ghurt.** *n.* a fermented, thick food made by adding bacteria to milk.

yoke (yōk) *n. pl., (defs. 1, 3–6)* **yokes** or *(def. 2)* **yoke.** **1.** a wooden frame consisting of a long, curved bar fitted with two hoops by which two work animals are joined together. **2.** a pair of animals, especially oxen, joined together by a yoke. **3.** any of various similar devices, such as a frame carried on the shoulders and designed to carry a pail or other burden at either end.

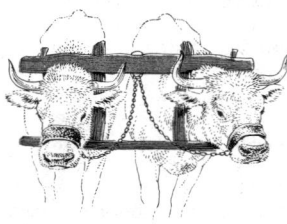

Yoke

4. a force or influence that oppresses or enslaves; burden: *people under the yoke of tyranny.* **5.** something that joins or unites; bond; tie: *the yoke of friendship.* **6.** the top section of a garment, usually consisting of a flat, smooth-fitting piece of fabric, as around the neck and shoulders of a blouse. —*v.t.,* **yoked, yok·ing. 1.** to put a yoke on. **2.** to harness or attach (a work animal) to a yoke. **3.** to join or unite with a yoke. **4.** to join closely: *to be yoked in marriage.*

yoke·fel·low (yōk'fel'ō) *n.* a mate or partner.

yo·kel (yō'kəl) *n.* a country fellow. ▲ usually used to show contempt.

Yo·ko·ha·ma (yō'kə hä'mə) *n.* a port city in east-central Japan, on the island of Honshu. Pop. (1970), 2,238,264.

yolk (yōk) *n.* **1.** the yellow substance of an egg, as distinguished from the albumen, or white part. **2.** the greasy material in unprocessed sheep's wool.

Yom Kip·pur (yom kip'ər) in Judaism, the day of fasting and atonement for sins, observed on the tenth day of the first month of the Jewish calendar. Also, **Day of Atonement.**

yon (yon) *adj., adv. Archaic.* yonder.

yond (yond) *adj., adv. Archaic.* yonder.

yon·der (yon'dər) *adv.* in that place; over there. —*adj.* being at a distance, but within sight: *The cattle are in yonder field.*

Yon·kers (yong'kərz) *n.* a city in southeastern New York, just north of New York City. Pop. (1970), 204,370.

yore (yôr) *adv.* **of yore.** of long ago; in the past: *in days of yore.*

York (yôrk) *n.* the family that ruled England from 1461 to 1485, a branch of the royal house of Plantagenet. Its emblem was a white rose.

York·shire pudding (yôrk'shər) a batter often baked with roasting meat to catch the drippings, frequently served with roast beef.

Yorkshire terrier, a small dog having a coat of long, straight, silky hair that is dark steel-blue and tan.

York·town (yôrk'toun') *n.* a town in southeastern Virginia, the scene in 1781 of the last major encounter of the American Revolution, at which Lord Cornwallis surrendered to George Washington.

Yo·sem·i·te National Park (yō sem'i tē) a large national park in east-central California, noted for its waterfalls and sequoia trees.

you (yōō; *unstressed* yə) *pron.* **1.** the person or persons spoken or written to: *Do you want to go? I'll meet you at six o'clock.* **2.** a person; one; anyone: *You have to be careful when handling dynamite.* ▲ In formal speaking or writing, *one* is preferred to *you* as an indefinite pronoun: *One can never be sure what the future will bring.*

you-all (yōō ôl', yôl) *pron. Informal.* you. ▲ used chiefly in the southern United States in referring to two or more persons.

you'd (yōōd) **1.** you had. **2.** you would.

you'll (yōōl; *unstressed* yool) **1.** you will. **2.** you shall.

young (yung) *adj.,* **young·er** (yung'gər), **young·est** (yung'gist). **1.** having lived or existed for a short time; in the early part of life or growth; not old: *a young boy. A colt is a young horse.* **2.** having or showing the characteristics or look of a young person; fresh; vigorous: *She has a young face for her age.* **3.** of, relating to, or belonging to the early part of life: *He remembered his young years with nostalgia.* **4.** recently begun, formed, or made; in an early stage of progress or development: *a young nation.* **5.** not as old as another with the same name: *Young Mr. Williams is following in his father's footsteps.* **6.** having little experience, skill, or practice: *He was too young in the practice of law to become a partner of the firm.* —*n.* **1.** young people as a group: *That kind of music is popular with the young.* **2.** young offspring, especially of animals: *The lioness fed her young.* —**young'ness,** *n.*

with young. pregnant.

Young, Brig·ham (yung; brig'əm). 1801–1877, U.S. Mormon leader.

young·ish (yung'ish) *adj.* somewhat young.

young·ling (yung'ling) *n.* a young person, animal, or plant.

young·ster (yung'stər) *n.* a young person; child or youth.

Youngs·town (yungz'toun') *n.* a city in northeastern Ohio. Pop. (1970), 139,788.

your (yoor; *unstressed* yər) *adj.* of, belonging, or relating to you: *your sister, your house, your idea.* ▲ **Your** is used in some formal titles: *Your Majesty, Your Excellency, Your Honor.* It is also used informally to refer to people in general: *He is not your typical teacher. Your greatest problem in this city is air pollution.*

you're (yoor, yôr; *unstressed* yər) you are.

yours (yoorz) *pron.* **1.** belonging or relating to you: *This book is yours.* ▲ often used with *of: He is a great admirer of yours.* **2.** the thing or things belonging or relating to you: *His paper was well-written, but yours was even better.*

your·self (yoor self', yər self') *pron. pl.,* **your·selves** (yoor selvz', yər selvz'). **1.** the form of **you** used to give emphasis: *You yourself know that she deserves the credit.* **2.** the form used to refer back to **you** in a sentence: *Be careful of the fire or you will burn yourself.* **3.** your usual or normal self: *You have not been yourself these past few weeks.*

youth (yooth) *n. pl.,* **youths** (yooths, yoothz) or **youth.** **1.** the condition or quality of being young. **2.** the time of life between childhood and adulthood. **3.** an early period in the development or existence of anything. **4.** young people as a group: *Our hope lies in the youth of our nation.* **5.** a young person, especially a young man.

youth·ful (yooth'fəl) *adj.* **1.** still young in years; having youth: *a youthful person.* **2.** characteristic of youth: *youthful energy.* **3.** belonging to or suitable for young people: *a youthful dress.* —**youth'ful·ly,** *adv.* —**youth'ful·ness,** *n.*

you've (yoov; *unstressed* yoov) you have.

yowl (youl) *n.* a long, mournful cry, such as that of a dog; howl; wail. —*v.i.* to make such a cry.

yo-yo (yō'yō) *n. pl.,* **yo-yos.** a toy consisting of two disks connected at their center by a pin around which a string is wound. The yo-yo is lowered and raised by unwinding and rewinding it on the string.

Y·pres (ē'prə) *n.* a historic town in western Belgium, noted for the many battles of World War I that were fought there.

yr. 1. year; years. **2.** your.

yrs. 1. years. **2.** yours.

yt·ter·bi·um (i tur'bē əm) *n.* a soft, silvery metallic element used in alloys and lasers. Symbol: **Yb**

yt·tri·um (it'rē əm) *n.* a dark gray metallic element used especially in iron alloys and in color television tubes. Symbol: **Y**

Yu·ca·tán (yoo'kə tan') *n.* a peninsula in southeastern Mexico and northeastern Central America, between the Gulf of Mexico and the Caribbean Sea.

yuc·ca (yuk'ə) *n.* any of a group of desert plants of the southwestern United States and Latin America, having a woody stem and bearing clusters of white, bell-shaped drooping flowers.

Yucca

Yu·go·slav (yoo'gō släv') *also,* **Ju·go·slav.** *n.* a person who was born or is living in Yugoslavia. —*adj.* of or relating to Yugoslavia or its people.

Yu·go·sla·vi·a (yoo'gō slä'vē ə) *also,* **Ju·go·sla·vi·a.** *n.* a country in southeastern Europe, on the eastern shore of the Adriatic Sea. Capital, Belgrade. Area, 98,766 sq. mi. Pop. (1971), 20,504,516. —**Yu·go·sla'vi·an,** *adj., n.*

Yu·kon (yoo'kon) *n.* **1.** a territory in northwestern Canada. Area, 207,076 sq. mi. Pop. (1971), 18,388. **2.** a river flowing from this territory through central Alaska into the Bering Sea.

Yule (yool) *n.* **1.** another word for **Christmas. 2.** the season of Christmas; Christmastide.

Yule log, a large log burned at Christmas.

Yule·tide (yool'tīd') *n.* the season of Christmas.

YWCA, Young Women's Christian Association.

YWHA, Young Women's Hebrew Association.

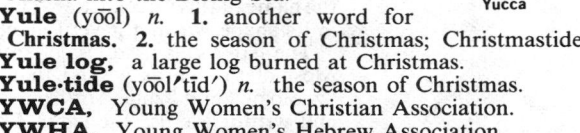

at; āpe; cär; end; mē; it; īce; hot; ōld; fôrk; wood; fool; oil; out; up; turn; sing; thin; this; hw in white; zh in treasure. The symbol ə stands for the sound of a in about, e in taken, i in pencil, o in lemon, and u in circus.

Y

1. Egyptian Hieroglyphics	4. Greek Classical Capitals Z
2. Semitic	5. Latin Fourth Century A.D. Z
3. Phoenician	6. English Z

Z is the twenty-sixth and last latter of the English alphabet. The earliest forms of the letter **Z** were Egyptian hieroglyphics (1) whose meanings are not known. In the ancient Semitic (2) and Phoenician (3) alphabets, these symbols were simplified and became the letter *zayin,* probably meaning "weapon" or "balance." When the Greeks adopted *zayin,* they altered its shape and called it *zeta* (4). *Zed,* which is what **Z** is called in many English-speaking countries, comes from the name of this Greek letter. The Romans (5) borrowed *zeta* and made only the slightest changes in its shape, writing it very much as we write the capital letter **Z** today (6).

The letter **Z** is used less often in the English language than any other letter of the alphabet. Most of the words we use that contain the letter **Z** originally came from Greek, as "zeal," "zoology," and "zone," or from Arabic, as "zero," "zenith," and "azure." In everyday speaking and writing we use the letter **Z** most often in words, such as "familiarize" and "generalize," that have the suffix "-ize" which we borrowed from Greek. **Z** is also used in certain descriptive words that imitate a sound or the sound of an action, as "buzz," "fizz," and "sizzle."

z, Z (zē) *n. pl.,* **z's, Z's. 1.** the twenty-sixth and last letter of the English alphabet. **2.** something having the shape of this letter.

z., Z., zone.

Zach·a·ri·ah (zak'ə rī'ə) *n.* in the New Testament, the father of John the Baptist.

Za·greb (zä'greb) *n.* a city in northwestern Yugoslavia. Pop. (1971), 565,000.

Za·ire (zä ir') *n.* a country in central Africa, formerly known as the Democratic Republic of the Congo. Capital, Kinshasa. Area, 905,967 sq. mi. Pop. (1971 est.), 17,800,000.

Zam·be·zi (zam bē'zē) *n.* a river in southern Africa flowing eastward through Rhodesia and Mozambique, into the Indian Ocean.

Zam·bi·a (zam'bē ə) *n.* a country in south-central Africa, formerly the British protectorate of Northern Rhodesia. Capital, Lusaka. Area, 290,586 sq. mi. Pop. (1971 est.), 4,275,000.

za·ny (zā'nē) *adj.,* **za·ni·er, za·ni·est.** funny in an odd or ridiculous way. —*n. pl.,* **za·nies. 1.** a fool; simpleton. **2.** a clown; buffoon.

Zan·zi·bar (zan'zə bär') *n.* a large island in the Indian Ocean, off the eastern coast of Africa. It is part of Tanzania.

Za·po·rozh·e (zä'pə rozh'ye) *n.* a city in the southwestern Soviet Union, on the Dnieper River, in the Ukraine. Pop. (1970 est.), 658,000.

zeal (zēl) *n.* an intense desire or devotion; earnest enthusiasm: *He did the hard job with zeal.*

Zea·land (zē'lənd) *n.* the largest island of Denmark, on which the city of Copenhagen is situated.

zeal·ot (zel'ət) *n.* a person who shows too much zeal.

zeal·ous (zel'əs) *adj.* filled with or characterized by zeal: *He has a zealous attitude toward his work.* —**zeal'ous·ly,** *adv.* —**zeal'ous·ness,** *n.*

Zeb·e·dee (zeb'ə dē') *n.* in the New Testament, the father of James and John, apostles of Jesus.

ze·bra (zē'brə) *n. pl.,* **ze·bras** or **ze·bra.** any of several wild animals of eastern and southern Africa, related to the horse, having a light-colored coat with black stripes, a short, stiff mane, and a long tail ending in a tuft of hair.

ze·bu (zē'byōō) *n.* a domesticated animal of Asia and Africa, related to the ox, having a large hump over the shoulders.

Zebra

Zech·a·ri·ah (zek'ə rī'ə) *n.* **1.** in the Old Testament, a Hebrew prophet of the sixth century B.C. **2.** a book of the Old Testament attributed to him.

zed (zed) *n. British.* the letter z.

Zen (zen) *n.* **1.** a Japanese Buddhist sect that differs from other Buddhist sects by stressing enlightenment through intuition and contemplation rather than through the scriptures. **2.** the beliefs of this sect.

ze·nith (zē'nith) *n.* **1.** the point in the heavens directly above the place where a person stands. **2.** the highest or greatest point: *This performance was the zenith of the musician's career.*

Ze·no (zē'nō) 336?–262? B.C., Greek philosopher.

Zeph·a·ni·ah (zef'ə nī'ə) *n.* **1.** a Hebrew prophet of the seventh century B.C **2.** a book of the Old Testament believed to have been written by him.

zeph·yr (zef'ər) *n.* **1.** the west wind. **2.** any soft, gentle wind. **3.** any of various lightweight, soft yarns or fabrics.

zep·pe·lin (zep'ə lin) *also,* **Zep·pe·lin.** *n.* a large dirigible having a rigid, cigar-shaped body. [From Count Ferdinand von *Zeppelin,* 1838–1917, the German inventor of this dirigible.]

ze·ro (zēr'ō) *n. pl.,* **ze·ros** or **ze·roes. 1.** the number that leaves any number unchanged when it is added to it; number of members in the empty set. **2.** the symbol representing this number; 0. **3.** a point on a scale, such as a thermometer, from which something is measured: *The temperature is ten degrees above zero.* **4.** a temperature corresponding to zero on the scale of a thermometer. **5.** the total absence of quantity; nothing: *The business lost no money, but its profit was zero.* **6.** the lowest point: *The politician's popularity reached zero after the scandal.* —*adj.* **1.** of, relating to, being, or at zero. **2.** none at all: *That team has had zero victories this season.* —*v.t.,* **ze·roed, ze·ro·ing.** to adjust (an instrument) to a zero point.

   to zero in on. a. to bring a gun or the like into a desired position for aiming and concentrating fire at (something): *The bomber zeroed in on the target.* **b.** to direct attention toward: *to zero in on a problem.*

zero gravity, the condition of a body not subject to any gravitational attraction; weightlessness.

zero hour 1. a set or appointed time, as for the beginning of a military operation. **2.** a time set for the beginning of any important action; critical turning point.

zest (zest) *n.* **1.** keen enjoyment or excitement; relish: *He has a zest for life.* **2.** a pleasant or exciting quality, flavor, or the like: *This spice will add zest to the stew.* [French *zeste* an orange peel or a lemon peel; originally referring to a piece of orange or lemon peel used as a flavoring.]

zest·ful (zest'fəl) *adj.* characterized by zest. —**zest'·ful·ly,** *adv.* —**zest'ful·ness,** *n.*

Zeus (zoos) *n. Greek Mythology.* the supreme god, ruler of the heavens and the earth, whose chief weapon was the thunderbolt. In Roman mythology he was called Jupiter.

Zhou En·lai (jō'en lī') another spelling of **Chou En·lai.**

zig·zag (zig'zag') *adj.* having or moving with a series of short, sharp turns or angles in alternating directions. —*adv.* in a zigzag manner. —*n.* **1.** a zigzag line, course, or pattern. **2.** one of the short turns or angles of a zigzag pattern. —*v.i.,* **zig·zagged, zig·zag·ging.** to form or move in a zigzag: *The road zigzagged through the mountains.*

zil·lion (zil'yən) *n. Informal.* a very large, indefinite number: *I have zillions of things to do before the party.*

Zim·ba·bwe (zim bäb'wē) *n.* a country in south-central Africa, formerly known as Rhodesia. Capital, Salisbury. Area, 150,800 sq. mi. Pop. (1980), 7,396,000.

zinc (zingk) *n.* a grayish-white metallic element with a blue sheen, used to make alloys, such as brass and bronze, to galvanize iron, and in dry-cell batteries. Symbol: **Zn**

zinc oxide, a white, powdery compound, used especially in paints and cosmetics and as an antiseptic.

zing (zing) *n.* **1.** a high-pitched humming or buzzing sound. **2.** *Informal.* vitality; zest; vigor. —*v.i.* to make a high-pitched humming or buzzing sound, especially in moving rapidly: *A bullet zinged through the air.*

zin·ni·a (zin'ē ə) *n.* **1.** the showy flower of any of a small group of plants, growing in all colors except blue and green. **2.** a plant bearing this flower, widely cultivated as a garden plant. [Modern Latin *Zinnia,* from Johann Gottfried *Zinn,* 1727–1759, a German botanist.]

Zi·on (zī'ən) *also,* **Si·on.** *n.* **1.** a hill in Jerusalem on which the royal palace of David and the Temple were built. **2.** the Jewish people or nation; Israel. **3.** the kingdom of heaven. **4.** any place or institution believed to be under God's special protection, especially the church.

Zi·on·ism (zī'ə niz'əm) *n.* a movement to establish a national homeland for Jews in Palestine, resulting in the creation of the state of Israel in 1948 and continuing after that time to support the emigration of Jews and their settlement in Israel.

Zi·on·ist (zī'ə nist) *n.* a person who supports Zionism. —*adj.* of or relating to Zionism or Zionists.

zip (zip) *n.* **1.** a sudden, sharp, hissing sound, as of a flying bullet. **2.** *Informal.* energy; vitality; vim. —*v.i.,* **zipped, zip·ping. 1.** to make or move with a sudden, sharp, hissing sound. **2.** *Informal.* to move or act with energy or speed: *She zipped around the corner to the grocery store to buy some milk.* —*v.t.* to fasten or close with a zipper.

Zip Code, a number having five digits, written directly after the address on a letter, package, or other piece of mail, quickly identifying the U.S. postal delivery area to which it is to be sent. [An abbreviation of *z*(one) *i*(mprovement) *p*(rogram).]

zip·per (zip'ər) *n.* a fastener consisting of two rows of interlocking teeth that may be joined or separated by a sliding device, used especially on clothing and boots.

zip·py (zip'ē) *adj.,* **zip·pi·er, zip·pi·est.** *Informal.* full of energy; lively.

zir·con (zur'kon) *n.* a crystalline mineral used in nuclear reactors and as a semiprecious gem.

zir·co·ni·um (zər kō'nē əm) *n.* a gray, flammable, scaly or powdery metallic element used in explosives, in nuclear reactor chambers, and to bond metals to ceramics. It is the ninth most abundant element in the earth's crust. Symbol: **Zr**

zith·er (zith'ər, zith'ər) *n.* a musical instrument consisting of a shallow, wood sound box over which are stretched thirty to forty-five strings, sounded by plucking the strings with a plectrum and the fingers.

Zn, the symbol for zinc.

zo·di·ac (zō'dē ak') *n.* **1.** an imaginary belt in the heavens extending approximately eight degrees on each side of the path that the sun appears to follow and including the paths of the moon and all the planets except Pluto. The zodiac is divided into twelve parts, called signs, with each part named after a constellation. **2.** a figure or diagram representing

Zither

the zodiac and its signs and symbols, used in astrology.

zo·di·a·cal (zō dī'ə kəl) *adj.* of, relating to, or in the zodiac: *a zodiacal sign.*

Zo·la, É·mile (zō'lə; ā mēl') 1840–1902, French novelist and critic.

zom·bie (zom'bē) *n. pl.,* **zom·bies.** in voodoo belief, a dead person who has been brought back to life and is completely subject to the will of a sorcerer.

zon·al (zōn'əl) *adj.* of, relating to, or marked by a zone or zones.

at; āpe; cär; end; mē; it; īce; hot; ōld; fôrk;
wood; fōōl; oil; out; up; turn; sing; thin; this;
hw in white; zh in treasure. The symbol ə
stands for the sound of **a** in about, **e** in taken,
i in pencil, **o** in lemon, and **u** in circus.

zone (zōn) *n.* **1.** any of the five regions of the earth's surface divided according to the climate found there, comprising two Frigid Zones, two Temperate Zones, and the Torrid Zone. **2.** any region, area, or section that is distinguished from surrounding or adjoining areas by some quality, condition, or use:

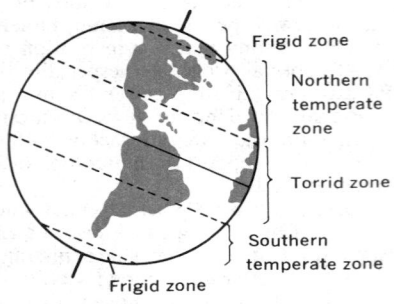

Frigid zone

Northern temperate zone

Torrid zone

Southern temperate zone

Frigid zone

Zone

a war zone. **3.** a section of a city regulated by certain restrictions, especially regarding building: *There were no factories in the residential zone.* **4.** in the U.S. postal system, one of a set of circular areas going outward from a mailing point, by which parcel post charges are determined. **5.** a U.S. postal delivery service area identified by a Zip Code, usually having a central post office. —*v.t.,* **zoned, zon·ing,** to divide into zones: *to zone a city into business and residential areas.*

zon·ing (zō′ning) *n.* a system of districting in cities that regulates the construction and use of buildings in certain areas.

zoo (zōō) *n. pl.,* **zoos.** a park, garden, or similar place where animals are kept for exhibition.

zo·o·log·i·cal (zō′ə loj′i kəl) *adj.* **1.** of or relating to zoology. **2.** of or relating to animals. —**zo′o·log′i·cal·ly,** *adv.*

zoological garden, see **zoo.**

zo·ol·o·gist (zō ol′ə jist) *n.* a student of or an expert in zoology.

zo·ol·o·gy (zō ol′ə jē) *n.* **1.** the science that deals with the origin, development, structure, functioning, and classification of all forms of animal life. **2.** the animal life found in a particular region.

zoom (zōōm) *v.i.* **1.** to move or climb suddenly and swiftly, as in an airplane. **2.** to make or move with a loud, low-pitched humming sound: *The train zoomed by us.* —*v.t.* to cause (an airplane) to zoom. —*n.* the act or sound of zooming.

zoom lens, a single lens, as on a television or motion-picture camera, which allows a change from long-distance shots to close-ups without moving the camera.

Zo·ro·as·ter (zôr′ō as′tər) 628?–551 B.C., Persian religious teacher, the founder of Zoroastrianism.

Zo·ro·as·tri·an (zôr′ō as′trē ən) *adj.* of or relating to Zoroaster or the religion he founded. —*n.* a person who believes in or practices Zoroastrianism.

Zo·ro·as·tri·an·ism (zôr′ō as′trē ə niz′əm) *n.* the religious system founded by Zoroaster, which stresses an ethical way of life and the final triumph of good over evil.

zounds (zoundz) *interj. Archaic.* an oath used to express surprise or anger.

Zr, the symbol for zirconium.

zuc·chi·ni (zōō kē′nē) *n. pl.,* **zuc·chi·ni** or **zuc·chi·nis.** a green, summer squash shaped like a cucumber, eaten as a vegetable.

Zui·der Zee (zī′dər zē′) *also,* **Zuy·der Zee.** a former inlet of the North Sea, on the northern coast of the Netherlands, now closed off by a dike.

Zu·lu (zōō′lōō) *n. pl.,* **Zu·lus** or **Zu·lu.** **1.** a member of any of a group of Bantu tribes in southeastern Africa. **2.** the language of these tribes. —*adj.* of or relating to the Zulus or their language.

Zu·ñi (zōō′nyē) *n. pl.,* **Zu·ñis** or **Zu·ñi.** **1.** a member of a tribe of North American Indians now living in western New Mexico, who dwell in pueblos. **2.** the language of this tribe.

Zu·rich (zoor′ik) *n.* the largest city in Switzerland, in the northern part of the country. Pop. (1970), 422,640.

Zuy·der Zee (zī′dər zē′) another spelling of **Zuider Zee.**

zwie·back (swī′bäk′, zwī′bäk′) *n.* a kind of bread that is often sweetened and flavored, as with cinnamon, baked, and then sliced and toasted until it is crisp and dry.

zy·gote (zī′gōt) *n.* an egg cell that has been fertilized by sperm, before the start of the development of the embryo.

at; āpe; cär; end; mē; it; īce; hot; ōld; fôrk; wood; fōōl; oil; out; up; turn; sing; thin; this; hw in white; zh in treasure. The symbol ə stands for the sound of a in about, e in taken, i in pencil, o in lemon, and u in circus.

CONTENTS

THE WORLD

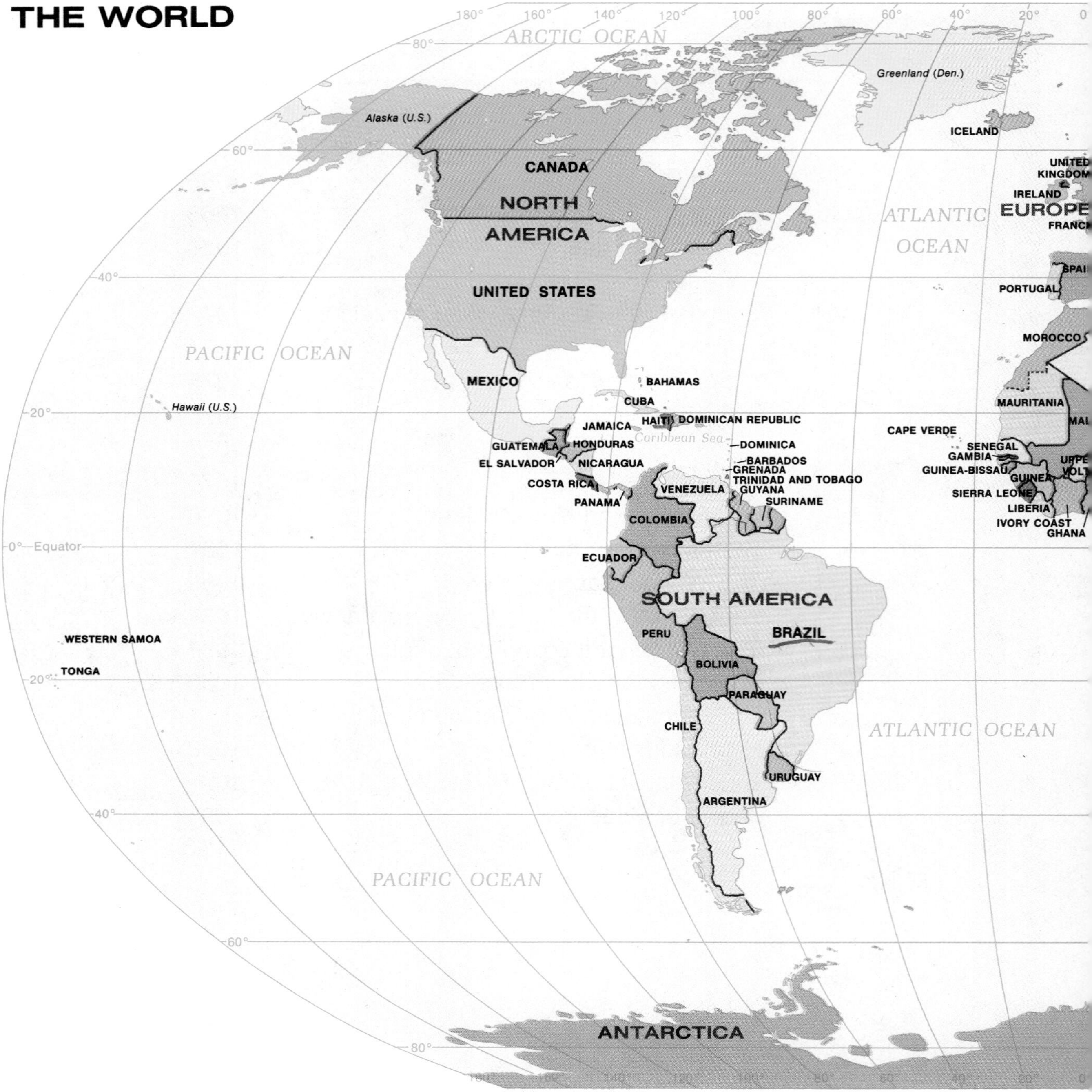

ARCTIC OCEAN

Greenland (Den.)

Alaska (U.S.)

ICELAND

UNITED
KINGDOM

IRELAND

CANADA

ATLANTIC

EUROPE

FRANCE

NORTH

OCEAN

AMERICA

SPAIN

PORTUGAL

PACIFIC OCEAN

UNITED STATES

MOROCCO

MAURITANIA

MEXICO

BAHAMAS

MALI

Hawaii (U.S.)

CUBA

CAPE VERDE

HAITI DOMINICAN REPUBLIC

JAMAICA

SENEGAL

Caribbean Sea

DOMINICA

GAMBIA

UPPE

GUATEMALA HONDURAS

BARBADOS

GUINEA-BISSAU

VOLT

EL SALVADOR NICARAGUA

GRENADA

GUINEA

TRINIDAD AND TOBAGO

SIERRA LEONE

COSTA RICA

VENEZUELA GUYANA

LIBERIA

PANAMA

SURINAME

IVORY COAST

COLOMBIA

GHANA

ECUADOR

SOUTH AMERICA

WESTERN SAMOA

PERU

BRAZIL

TONGA

BOLIVIA

PARAGUAY

CHILE

ATLANTIC OCEAN

URUGUAY

ARGENTINA

PACIFIC OCEAN

ANTARCTICA

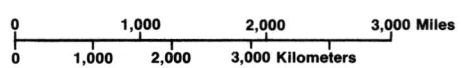

0		1,000		2,000		3,000 Miles

0	1,000	2,000	3,000 Kilometers

Scale true at Equator only

- - - - - - - - **Boundaries: Indefinite, disputed or under treaty**

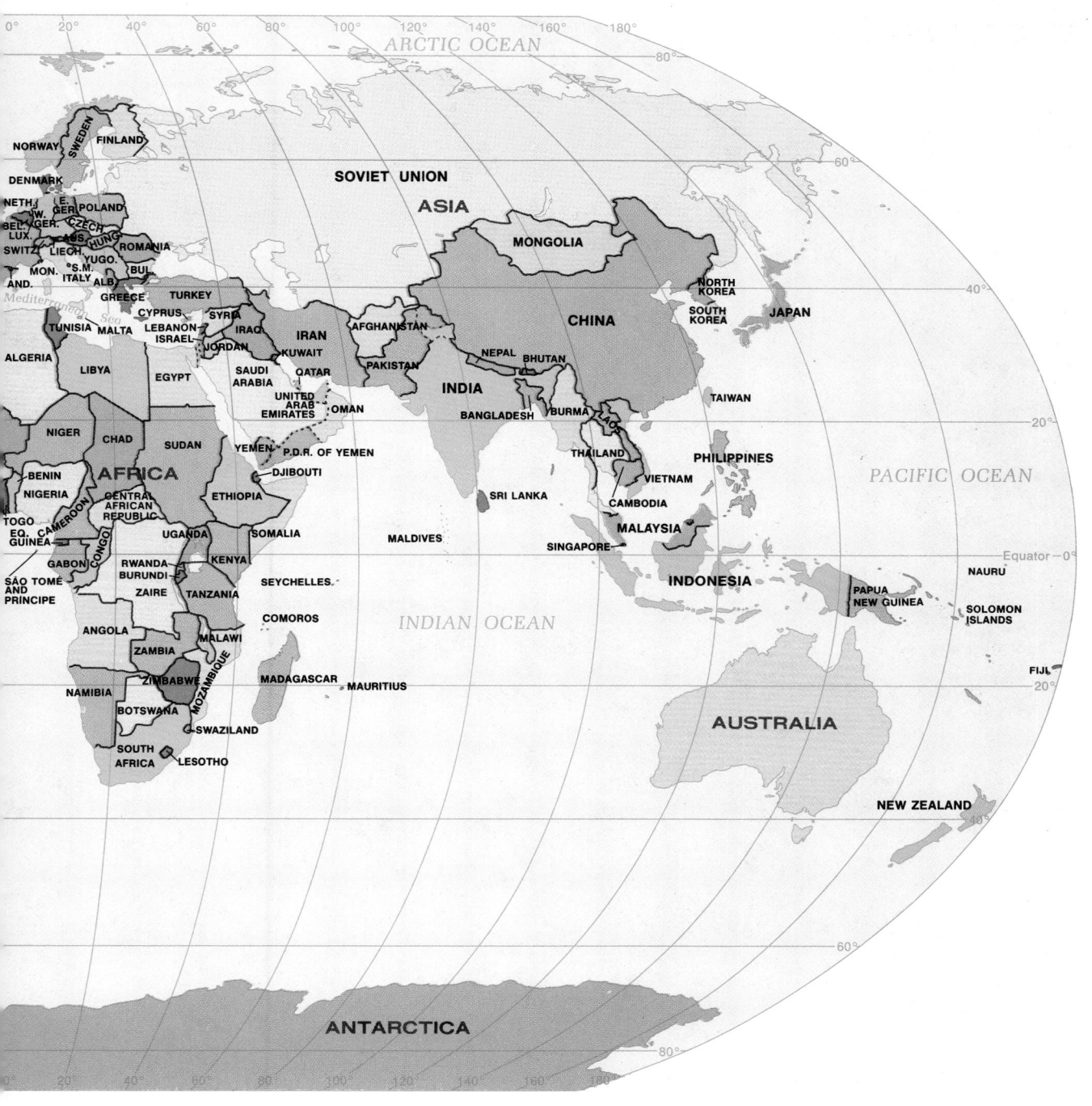

ARCTIC OCEAN

NORWAY
SWEDEN
FINLAND
DENMARK
NETH.
E. GER.
W. GER.
POLAND
BEL.
LUX.
CZECH
SWITZ.
LIECH.
AUS.
HUNG.
MON.
S.M.
YUGO.
ROMANIA
AND.
ITALY
ALB.
BUL.

SOVIET UNION

ASIA

MONGOLIA

NORTH KOREA
SOUTH KOREA
JAPAN

GREECE
TURKEY
CYPRUS
SYRIA
IRAQ
LEBANON
ISRAEL
JORDAN
KUWAIT

IRAN
AFGHANISTAN

CHINA

Mediterranean Sea

TUNISIA
MALTA

TAIWAN

ALGERIA
LIBYA
EGYPT
SAUDI ARABIA
QATAR
UNITED ARAB EMIRATES
OMAN

NEPAL
BHUTAN
PAKISTAN

INDIA

BANGLADESH
BURMA
LAOS

NIGER
CHAD
SUDAN
YEMEN
P.D.R. OF YEMEN

THAILAND

PHILIPPINES

PACIFIC OCEAN

BENIN
NIGERIA
AFRICA
CENTRAL AFRICAN REPUBLIC
ETHIOPIA
DJIBOUTI

SRI LANKA

VIETNAM
CAMBODIA

TOGO
EQ. GUINEA
CAMEROON
CONGO
UGANDA
SOMALIA

MALAYSIA

GABON
RWANDA
BURUNDI
KENYA

SINGAPORE

MALDIVES

INDONESIA

NAURU

Equator — 0°

SÃO TOMÉ AND PRINCIPE
ZAIRE
TANZANIA

SEYCHELLES

PAPUA NEW GUINEA

SOLOMON ISLANDS

ANGOLA
ZAMBIA
MALAWI
COMOROS

INDIAN OCEAN

FIJI

NAMIBIA
ZIMBABWE
MOZAMBIQUE
BOTSWANA
MADAGASCAR
MAURITIUS

AUSTRALIA

SWAZILAND
SOUTH AFRICA
LESOTHO

NEW ZEALAND

ANTARCTICA

ALB.	= ALBANIA	LUX.	= LUXEMBOURG
AND.	= ANDORRA	P.D.R.	= PEOPLE'S DEMOCRATIC REPUBLIC OF YEMEN
AUS.	= AUSTRIA		
BEL.	= BELGIUM	MON.	= MONACO
BUL.	= BULGARIA	NETH.	= NETHERLANDS
CZECH.	= CZECHOSLOVAKIA	S.M.	= SAN MARINO
E.GER.	= EAST GERMANY	SWITZ.	= SWITZERLAND
HUNG.	= HUNGARY	W.GER.	= WEST GERMANY
LIECH.	= LIECHTENSTEIN	YUGO.	= YUGOSLAVIA

THE WORLD
PHYSICAL MAP

180° 160° 140° 120° 100° 80° 60° 40° 20° 0°

ARCTIC OCEAN

Greenland

Iceland

Yukon R.

80°

Great
Slave Lake

60°

British
Isles

Aleutian Islands

NORTH
AMERICA

ROCKY MOUNTAINS

Great
Lakes

St. Lawrence R.

ATLANTIC OCEAN

40°

PACIFIC OCEAN

GREAT
PLAINS

Mississippi R.

APPALACHIAN
MTS.

ATLAS
MTS.

SIERRA MADRE

Gulf of
Mexico

Canary
Islands

Hawaiian
Islands

20°

Bahamas

West Indies

Cape Verde
Islands

Niger R.

Caribbean Sea

Galápagos
Islands

GUIANA
HIGHLANDS

0° Equator

AMAZON
BASIN

Amazon R.

SOUTH AMERICA

MATO
GROSSO

BRAZILIAN HIGHLANDS

20°

ANDES

PACIFIC OCEAN

40°

ATLANTIC OCEAN

PATAGONIA

Falkland Islands

60°

ANTARCTICA

80°

180° 160° 140° 120° 100° 80° 60° 40° 20°

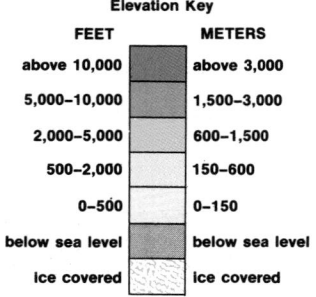

Elevation Key

FEET		METERS
above 10,000		above 3,000
5,000–10,000		1,500–3,000
2,000–5,000		600–1,500
500–2,000		150–600
0–500		0–150
below sea level		below sea level
ice covered		ice covered

1068

ARCTIC OCEAN

Ural Mts.

Volga R.

Ob R.

Irtysh

Yenisey R.

SIBERIA

60°

Sea of Okhotsk

EUROPE

ALPS

Black Sea

CAUCASUS MTS.

Aral Sea

ASIA

Lake Baikal

Amur R.

ALTAI MTS.

TIEN SHAN

TARIM BASIN

KUNLUN MTS.

PLATEAU OF TIBET

GOBI DESERT

Sea of Japan

40°

Honshu

Mediterranean Sea

Caspian Sea

PLATEAU OF IRAN

Tigris R.

Euphrates R.

Persian Gulf

Indus R.

HIMALAYAS

Ganges R.

Taiwan

SAHARA

20°

SAHEL

Arabian Sea

Bay of Bengal

Philippine Islands

PACIFIC OCEAN

AFRICA

ETHIOPIAN HIGHLANDS

Nile R.

South China Sea

ZAIRE BASIN

L. Victoria

Sumatra

Borneo

New Guinea

Equator 0°

INDIAN OCEAN

Solomon Islands

KALAHARI DESERT

Madagascar

20°

DRAKENSBERG

AUSTRALIA

GREAT VICTORIA DESERT

EASTERN HIGHLANDS

Darling R.

North I.

Tasmania

South I.

60°

ANTARCTICA

80°

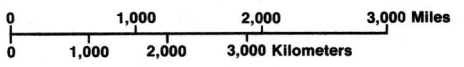

| 0 | 1,000 | 2,000 | 3,000 Miles |
| 0 | 1,000 | 2,000 | 3,000 Kilometers |

Scale true at Equator only

1069

ASIA

ARCTIC OCEAN

ICELAND

Greenland (Denmark)

Chukchi Sea

Bering Sea

Lincoln Sea

Greenland Sea

Alaska (U.S.)

Beaufort Sea

Baffin Bay

Arctic Circle

•Fairbanks

•Anchorage

Gulf of Alaska

Victoria Island

Baffin Island

•Godthåb

Juneau•

Great Bear Lake

•Frobisher Bay

Labrador Sea

•Yellowknife

Great Slave Lake

Hudson Bay

Lake Athabasca

CANADA

•Edmonton

Lake Winnipeg

Newfoundland

Gulf of St. Lawrence

Vancouver Island

•Vancouver

•Seattle

•Winnipeg

•Québec

•Portland

•Minneapolis

Montréal•
Ottawa⊛

•Boston

ATLANTIC OCEAN

•Toronto

Detroit•

•New York

Great Salt Lake

Salt Lake•
City

•Chicago

•Philadelphia

⊛Washington

San Francisco•

UNITED STATES

•St. Louis

Bermuda (U.K.)

Los Angeles•

•Atlanta

•Phoenix

Tropic of Cancer

Ciudad•
Juárez

•Dallas

Houston•

•New Orleans

PACIFIC OCEAN

Miami•

BAHAMAS

Turks and Caicos Is.
(U.K.)

Gulf of Mexico

•Nassau

Virgin Is.
(U.S.) (U.K.)

•Monterey

Havana⊛

CUBA

**DOMINICAN
REPUBLIC**

GUADELOUPE
(Fr.)

MEXICO

HAITI

Puerto
Rico

DOMINICA
Martinique (Fr.)
SAINT LUCIA

•Guadalajara

Port-au-Prince•

Santo
Domingo

(U.S.)

ST. VINCENT

Mexico City⊛

Cayman Is.
(U.K.)

•Kingston

BARBAD
GRENADA

Belmopan•

JAMAICA

Caribbean Sea

Port-of-Spain
TRINIDAD AND
TOBAGO

NORTH AMERICA

Belize (U.K.)

GUATEMALA

Guatemala City⊛

HONDURAS

⊛Tegucigalpa

Netherlands Antilles
(Neth.)

National boundary

San Salvador⊛

NICARAGUA

⊛ National capital

EL SALVADOR

⊛Managua

**SOUTH
AMERICA**

• Other city

San José⊛

•Panamá City

COSTA RICA

PANAMA

0   500   1,000 Miles

Equator

0   500   1,000 Kilometers

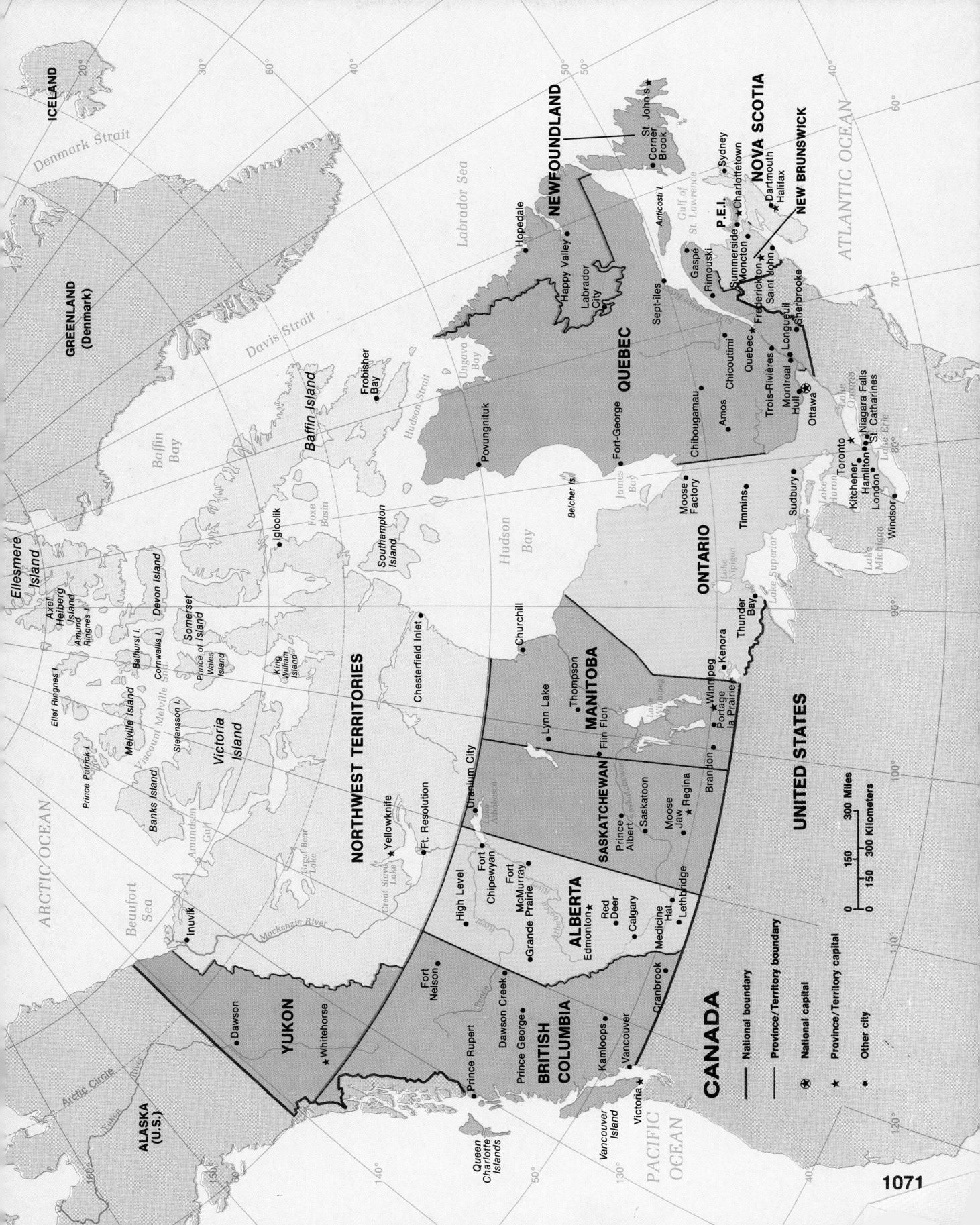

ICELAND

Denmark Strait

GREENLAND
(Denmark)

ARCTIC OCEAN

Ellesmere Island

Axel Heiberg Island

Ellef Ringnes I.
Amund Ringnes I.

Prince Patrick I.

Melville Island

Banks Island

Victoria Island

Beaufort Sea

ALASKA (U.S.)

Dawson

YUKON

Whitehorse

Inuvik

Mackenzie River

Great Bear Lake

Great Slave Lake

Fort Nelson

Dawson Creek

Prince George

BRITISH COLUMBIA

Prince Rupert

Queen Charlotte Islands

Vancouver Island

Kamloops

Vancouver

Victoria

PACIFIC OCEAN

Arctic Circle

Baffin Bay

Devon Island

Somerset Island

Bathurst I.

Cornwallis I.

Prince of Wales Island

King William Island

Stefansson I.

Amundsen Gulf

Igloolik

Southampton Island

Foxe Basin

Baffin Island

Davis Strait

Labrador Sea

Frobisher Bay

Hudson Strait

Ungava Bay

NORTHWEST TERRITORIES

Yellowknife

Ft. Resolution

Uranium City

Chesterfield Inlet

Churchill

Hudson Bay

Belcher Is.

James Bay

Povungnituk

Fort-George

QUEBEC

Hopedale

Happy Valley

Labrador City

NEWFOUNDLAND

St. John's

Corner Brook

Anticosti I.

Gulf of St. Lawrence

Gaspe

Sept-Iles

Rimouski

Chicoutimi

Amos

Chibougamau

Trois-Rivieres

Quebec

Montreal

Hull

Ottawa

Longueuil

Sherbrooke

NOVA SCOTIA

Sydney

Charlottetown

Dartmouth

Halifax

P.E.I.

Summerside

Fredericton

Saint John

Moncton

NEW BRUNSWICK

ATLANTIC OCEAN

High Level

Fort Chipewyan

Fort McMurray

Grande Prairie

ALBERTA

Edmonton

Red Deer

Calgary

Medicine Hat

Lethbridge

Cranbrook

Lynn Lake

Flin Flon

Thompson

MANITOBA

SASKATCHEWAN

Prince Albert

Saskatoon

Moose Jaw

Regina

Brandon

Winnipeg

Portage la Prairie

Kenora

Thunder Bay

Sudbury

Timmins

Moose Factory

ONTARIO

Lake Superior

Lake Nipigon

Lake Huron

Lake Michigan

Lake Ontario

Lake Erie

Toronto

Kitchener

Hamilton

London

Niagara Falls

St. Catharines

Windsor

UNITED STATES

CANADA

National boundary

Province/Territory boundary

★ National capital

★ Province/Territory capital

• Other city

300 Miles

300 Kilometers

150

0

150

0

300

1071

Cape Flattery

Cape Disappointment

Seattle
Spokane
WASHINGTON
Olympia
COLUMBIA
Portland
Salem
OREGON
Eugene

COASTAL RANGES
CASCADE RANGE
KLAMATH MTNS.

PLATEAU
Boise
SNAKE RIVER PLAIN
Snake River
Idaho Falls
IDAHO
Pocatello

LEWIS RANGE
BITTERROOT RANGE
Great Falls
Helena
MONTANA
Billings
ABSAROKA RANGE
ROCKY

BIGHORN MTNS.
WYOMING
Casper
Rock Springs
Cheyenne

Minot
NORTH DAKOTA
Bismarck
Fargo

Lake Oahe
BLACK HILLS
Rapid City
Pierre
SOUTH DAKOTA
BADLANDS
Sioux Falls

SAND HILLS
NEBRASKA
Grand Island
Lincoln

NEVADA
GREAT BASIN
Reno
Carson City
Sacramento
San Francisco

SIERRA NEVADA
CENTRAL LOWLAND

Great Salt Lake
Ogden
Salt Lake City
Provo
UTAH
WASATCH RANGE
UINTA MTNS.

COLORADO PLATEAU
MOUNTAINS
Denver
COLORADO
Colorado Springs
Pueblo
FRONT RANGE
SANGRE DE CRISTO MTNS.

GREAT PLAINS
KANSAS
Wichita

CALIFORNIA
COASTAL RANGES
Las Vegas
MOJAVE DESERT
Santa Cruz I.
Santa Rosa I.
Los Angeles
Santa Catalina I.
San Clemente I.
San Diego

GRAND CANYON
Flagstaff
ARIZONA
Phoenix
Tucson

SAN JUAN MTNS.
Santa Fe
Albuquerque
NEW MEXICO
Las Cruces
El Paso
LLANO ESTACADO

Amarillo
Lawton
OKLAHOMA
Oklahoma City

PACIFIC OCEAN

Ft. Worth
Dallas
TEXAS
EDWARDS PLATEAU
Austin
San Antonio
Colorado River
Rio Grande
Padre Island

MEXICO

HAWAII
Kauai I.
Oahu I.
Honolulu
Molokai I.
Lanai I.
Maui I.
PACIFIC OCEAN
Hawaii I.
Hilo
Kauai Channel
Alenuihaha Channel
0   75   150 Miles
0   75   150 Kilometers

SOVIET UNION
Pt. Barrow
BROOKS RANGE
St. Lawrence I.
Seward Peninsula
Pribilof Is.
Bering Strait
Bering Sea
Nunivak I.
ALASKA
KUSKOKWIM MTNS.
ALASKA RANGE
Fairbanks
Anchorage
Bristol Bay
Gulf of Alaska
Alaska Peninsula
Kodiak Island
Aleutian Islands
Juneau
Alexander Archipelago
PACIFIC OCEAN

0   250   750 Miles
0   250   750 Kilometers

1072

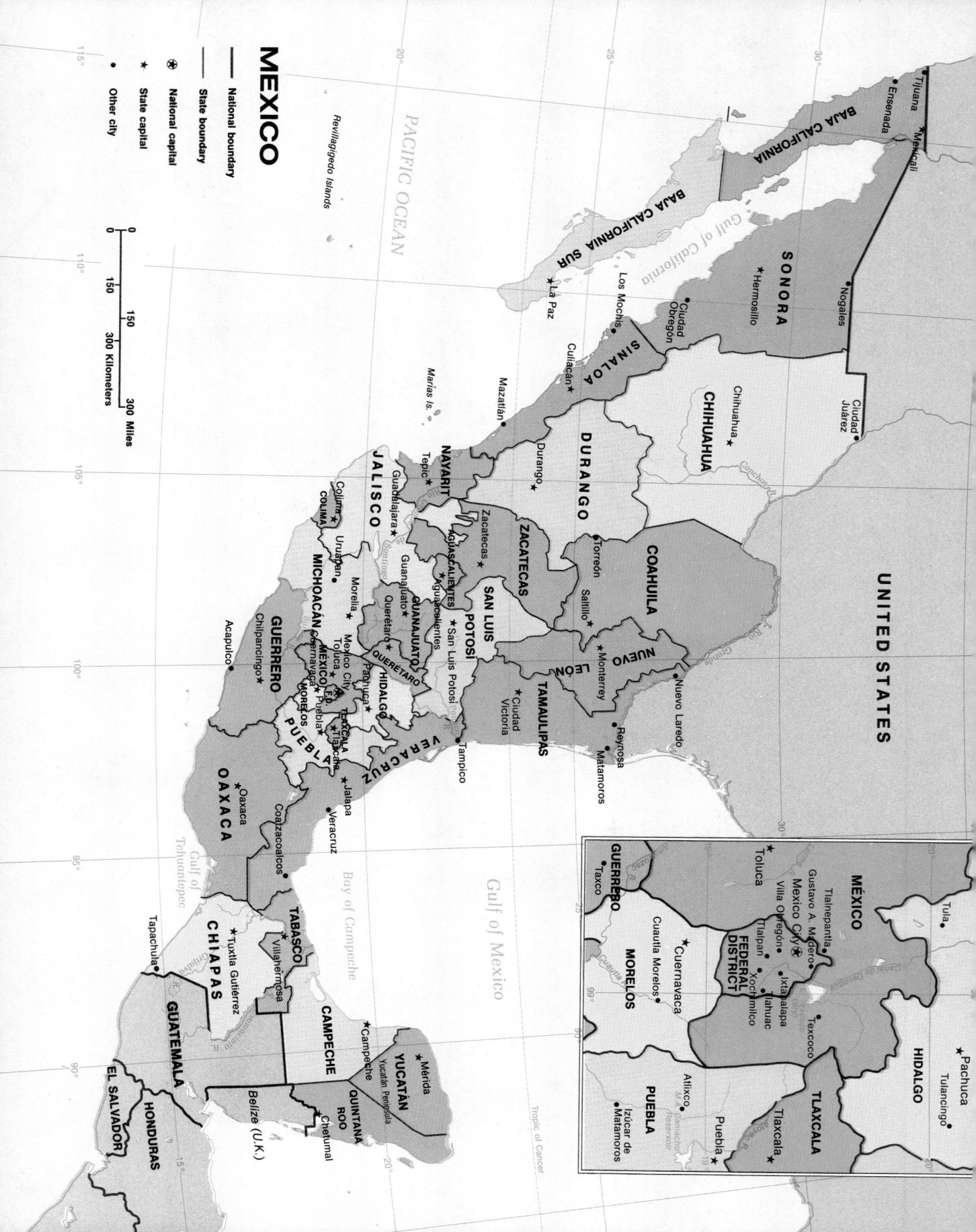

NORTH AMERICA

Caribbean Sea

Barranquilla • *Maracaibo* • *Caracas* G. of Paria

Valencia

Cúcuta

VENEZUELA

Georgetown ✪ *Paramaribo*

GUYANA *Cayenne*

Medellín SURINAME *French Guiana (Fr.)*

Manizales ✪ Bogotá

Cali

COLOMBIA

Malpelo I. (Colombia)

R. Orinoco

R. Negro

Equator

Galápagos Islands (Ecuador)

✪ Quito

ECUADOR

R. Iquitos Solimões (Amazon)

R. Amazon

Marajó I. • Belém

Guayaquil

Manaus

Fortaleza

R. Marañón

Natal

Trujillo

Recife

PERU • Rio Branco

BRAZIL

Maceió

Callao ✪ Lima

Salvador (Bahía)

R. Madeira R. Tapajós R. Xingu R. Tocantins R. São Francisco

Arequipa

La Paz ✪

BOLIVIA

✪ Brasília

Goiânia

Lake Titicaca

• Santa Cruz

✪ Sucre

PACIFIC OCEAN

Tropic of Capricorn

PARAGUAY

• Belo Horizonte

Antofagasta

Concepción

• Juiz de Fora

San Félix I. (Chile) San Ambrosio I. (Chile)

✪ Asunción

Campinas • Rio de Janeiro

São Paulo

Tucumán

Curitiba • Santo André

CHILE

R. Paraguay R. Paraná

Juan Fernández Is. (Chile)

Córdoba

ATLANTIC OCEAN

Pôrto Alegre

Lagoa dos Patos

Viña del Mar *Rosario*

URUGUAY

Valparaíso ✪ Santiago

Buenos Aires ✪ • Montevideo

R. Uruguay

La Plata Rio de la Plata

Concepción

ARGENTINA

• Mar del Plata

R. Colorado

Chiloé I.

R. Negro

Chonos Archipelago

SOUTH AMERICA

——— National boundary

• Comodoro Rivadavia

✪ National capital

Penas Gulf

• Other city

Queen Adelaide Arch.

Falkland Islands (Is Malvinas) (U.K.)

0   250   500 Miles

Strait of Magellan

0   250   500 Kilometers

Punta Arenas

Tierra del Fuego

Hoste I. Cape Horn

Falkland Is. and South Georgia Is. claimed by Argentina

South Georgia (Falkl. Is.)

1075

EUROPE

—— National boundary

✪ National capital

• Other city

AFRICA

0   150   300 Miles

0   150   300 Kilometers

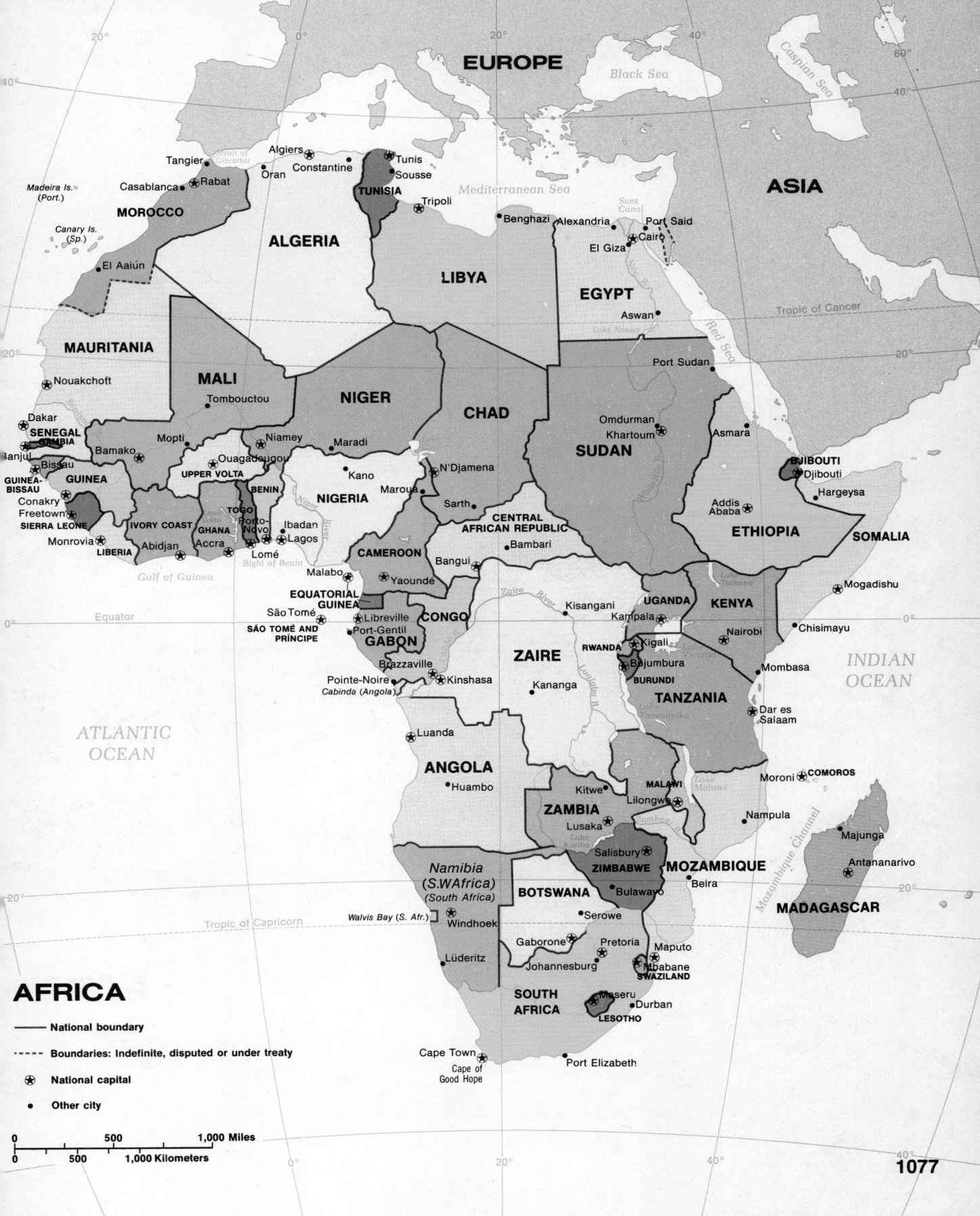

AFRICA

— National boundary

--- Boundaries: Indefinite, disputed or under treaty

⊛ National capital

• Other city

0   500   1,000 Miles
0   500   1,000 Kilometers

1077

ATLANTIC OCEAN

ARCTIC

Franz Josef Is.

North Sea

Barents Sea

•Murmansk

EUROPE

Novaya Zemlya

Baltic Sea

Tallinn•

Vilnius•

•Leningrad

•Arkhangelsk

•Minsk

Yenisey River

Kiev•

⊛Moscow

SOVIET

Kishinev•
•Odessa

•Kharkov

Volga River

•Saratov

Ob River

Black Sea

•Volgograd

Ural R.

•Tomsk

Ankara
⊛

•Astrakan

Omsk•

Novosibirsk•

Irtysh R.

TURKEY

Mediterranean Sea

Nicosia

Euphrates R.

•Tbilisi

CYPRUS ⊛
LEBANON
Beirut•
Jerusalem• SYRIA
⊛ •Damascus
ISRAEL ⊛Amman
JORDAN

•Yerevan

•Baku

Caspian Sea

•Karaganda

Aral Sea

Lake Balkhash

Tropic of Cancer

•Tabriz

IRAQ
•Baghdad ⊛

•Tehran
⊛

Tashkent•

Alma-Ata•
Frunze•

Basra•
KUWAIT ⊛
Kuwait•

•Abadan

IRAN

AFGHANISTAN
⊛
Kabul•

Jammu and Kashmir
⊛

Medina•

Islamabad•

Lahore•

AFRICA

SAUDI
ARABIA

Mecca•
•Riyadh ⊛

BAHRAIN
QATAR
Doha•

Red Sea

Gulf

Str. of Hormuz

PAKISTAN

Delhi•

UNITED ARAB
EMIRATES ⊛

•Abu Dhabi

New
Delhi•

NEPAL
Kathmandu•

Thimbu•

Brahmaputra

Muscat
⊛

Arabian Peninsula

YEMEN ⊛

San'a•

OMAN

Karachi•

BANGLADESH

Ahmadabad•

Calcutta•

P.D.R.
YEMEN

⊛Aden

Gulf of Aden

Bombay•

INDIA

Bay of
Bengal

Socotra
(P.D.R.Yemen)

Arabian Sea

Hyderabad•

Equator

•Madras

Laccadive Is.
(India)

SRI LANKA

-10°

Columbo• ⊛

⊛Male

MALDIVES

INDIAN OCEAN

1078

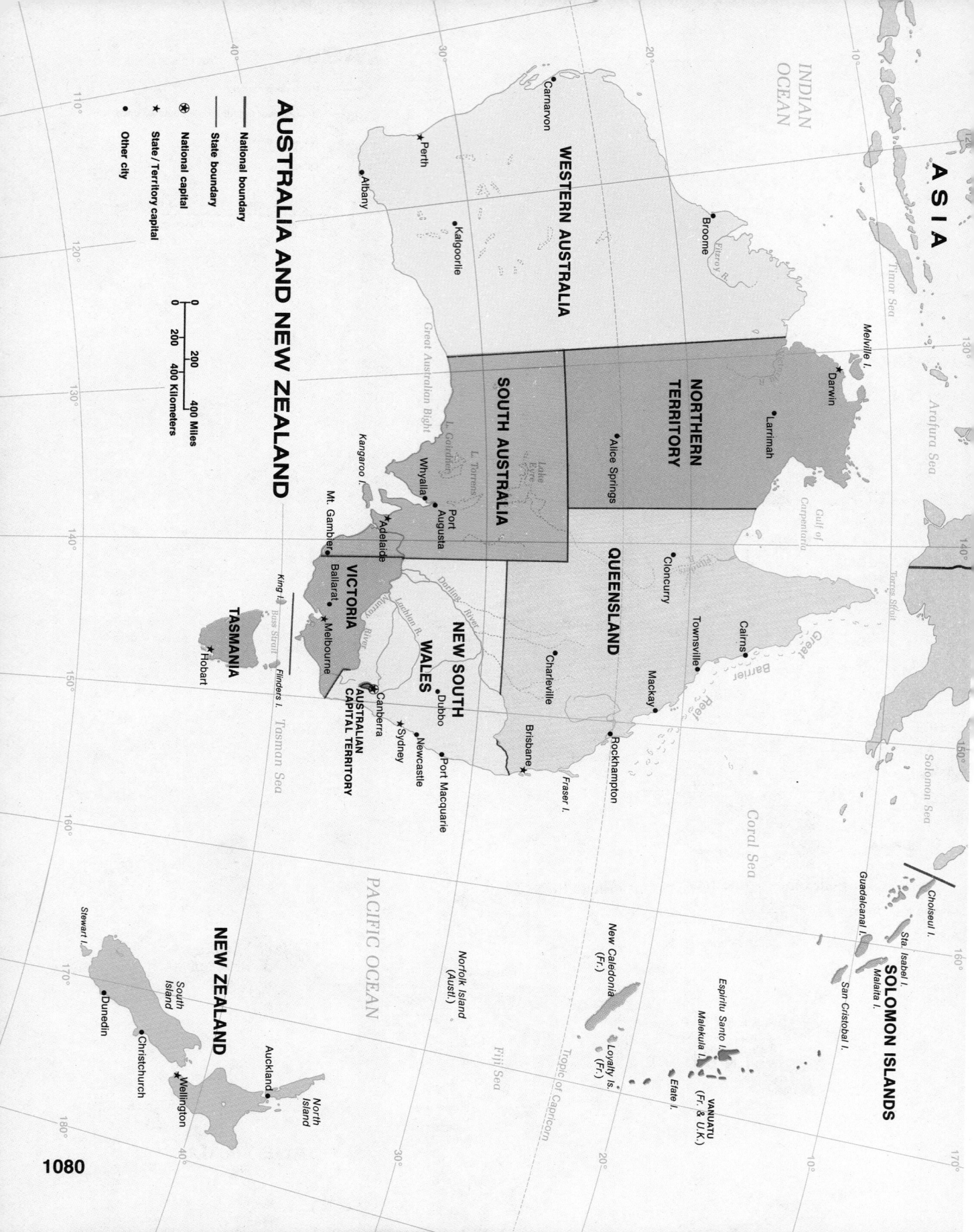

AUSTRALIA AND NEW ZEALAND

— National boundary
— State boundary
⊛ National capital
★ State / Territory capital
• Other city

0 200 400 Miles
0 200 400 Kilometers

INDIAN OCEAN

ASIA

Timor Sea

Arafura Sea

Carnarvon

•Perth

•Albany

•Kalgoorlie

WESTERN AUSTRALIA

Broome

Fitzroy R.

Melville I.

★Darwin

NORTHERN TERRITORY

•Larrimah

•Alice Springs

Gulf of Carpentaria

Torres Strait

Great Australian Bight

L. Gairdner

L. Torrens

Lake Eyre

SOUTH AUSTRALIA

Kangaroo I.

•Whyalla

Port Augusta

★Adelaide

Mt. Gambier•

QUEENSLAND

•Cloncurry

•Townsville

•Cairns

•Mackay

•Charleville

•Rockhampton

Brisbane

Fraser I.

Great Barrier Reef

Coral Sea

Darling River

Murray River

Lachlan R.

NEW SOUTH WALES

•Dubbo

★Canberra

AUSTRALIAN CAPITAL TERRITORY

★Sydney

•Newcastle

•Port Macquarie

VICTORIA

•Ballarat

★Melbourne

King I.

Bass Strait

Flinders I.

TASMANIA

★Hobart

Tasman Sea

PACIFIC OCEAN

Norfolk Island (Austl.)

New Caledonia (Fr.)

Loyalty Is. (Fr.)

Fiji Sea

Tropic of Capricorn

Choiseul I.

Sta. Isabel I.

Malaita I.

San Cristobal I.

SOLOMON ISLANDS

Guadalcanal I.

Solomon Sea

Espiritu Santo I.

Malekula I.

VANUATU (Fr. & U.K.)

Efate I.

NEW ZEALAND

Stewart I.

•Dunedin

•Christchurch

★Wellington

South Island

Auckland•

North Island

110° 120° 130° 140° 150° 160° 170°

STATES OF THE UNITED STATES

Flags of the United States

1775-1777

The Continental Colors

1777

Commonly used

1777

Rarely used

1795

State U.S. Postal Abbreviation		Capital	Admitted to the Union
Alabama	AL	Montgomery	Dec. 14, 1819
Alaska	AK	Juneau	Jan. 3, 1959
Arizona	AZ	Phoenix	Feb. 14, 1912
Arkansas	AR	Little Rock	June 15, 1836
California	CA	Sacramento	Sept. 9, 1850
Colorado	CO	Denver	Aug. 1, 1876
Connecticut*	CT	Hartford	Jan. 9, 1788*
Delaware*	DE	Dover	Dec. 7, 1787*
Florida	FL	Tallahassee	Mar. 3, 1845
Georgia*	GA	Atlanta	Jan. 2, 1788*
Hawaii	HI	Honolulu	Aug. 21, 1959
Idaho	ID	Boise	July 3, 1890
Illinois	IL	Springfield	Dec. 3, 1818
Indiana	IN	Indianapolis	Dec. 11, 1816
Iowa	IA	Des Moines	Dec. 28, 1846
Kansas	KS	Topeka	Jan. 29, 1861
Kentucky	KY	Frankfort	June 1, 1792
Louisiana	LA	Baton Rouge	Apr. 30, 1812
Maine	ME	Augusta	Mar. 15, 1820
Maryland*	MD	Annapolis	Apr. 28, 1788*
Massachusetts*	MS	Boston	Feb. 6, 1788*
Michigan	MI	Lansing	Jan. 26, 1837
Minnesota	MN	St. Paul	May 11, 1858
Mississippi	MS	Jackson	Dec. 10, 1817
Missouri	MO	Jefferson City	Aug. 10, 1821
Montana	MT	Helena	Nov. 8, 1889
Nebraska	NE	Lincoln	Mar. 1, 1867
Nevada	NV	Carson City	Oct. 31, 1864
New Hampshire*	NH	Concord	June 21, 1788*
New Jersey*	NJ	Trenton	Dec. 18, 1787*
New Mexico	NM	Santa Fe	Jan. 6, 1912
New York*	NY	Albany	Jan 26, 1788*
North Carolina*	NC	Raleigh	Nov. 21, 1789*
North Dakota	ND	Bismarck	Nov. 2, 1889
Ohio	OH	Columbus	Mar. 1, 1803
Oklahoma	OK	Oklahoma City	Nov. 16, 1907
Oregon	OR	Salem	Feb. 14, 1859
Pennsylvania*	PA	Harrisburg	Dec. 12, 1787*
Rhode Island*	RI	Providence	May 29, 1790*
South Carolina*	SC	Columbia	May 23, 1788*
South Dakota	SD	Pierre	Nov. 2, 1889
Tennessee	TN	Nashville	June 1, 1796
Texas	TX	Austin	Dec. 29, 1845
Utah	UT	Salt Lake City	Jan. 4, 1896
Vermont	VT	Montpelier	Mar. 4, 1791
Virginia*	VA	Richmond	June 25, 1788*
Washington	WA	Olympia	Nov. 11, 1889
West Virginia	WV	Charleston	June 20, 1863
Wisconsin	WI	Madison	May 29, 1848
Wyoming	WY	Cheyenne	July 10, 1890

*One of the thirteen original states

District of Columbia	DC	Washington	

Outlying Areas of the United States

Areas U.S. Postal Abbreviation		Capital	Date Acquired
Guam		Agana	1898
Puerto Rico		San Juan	1899
Virgin Islands		Charlotte Amalie, St. Thomas Island	1917

1818

1818

Great Star Flag

1861

Civil War Flag

1912-1959

48-Star Flag

Present

50-Star Flag

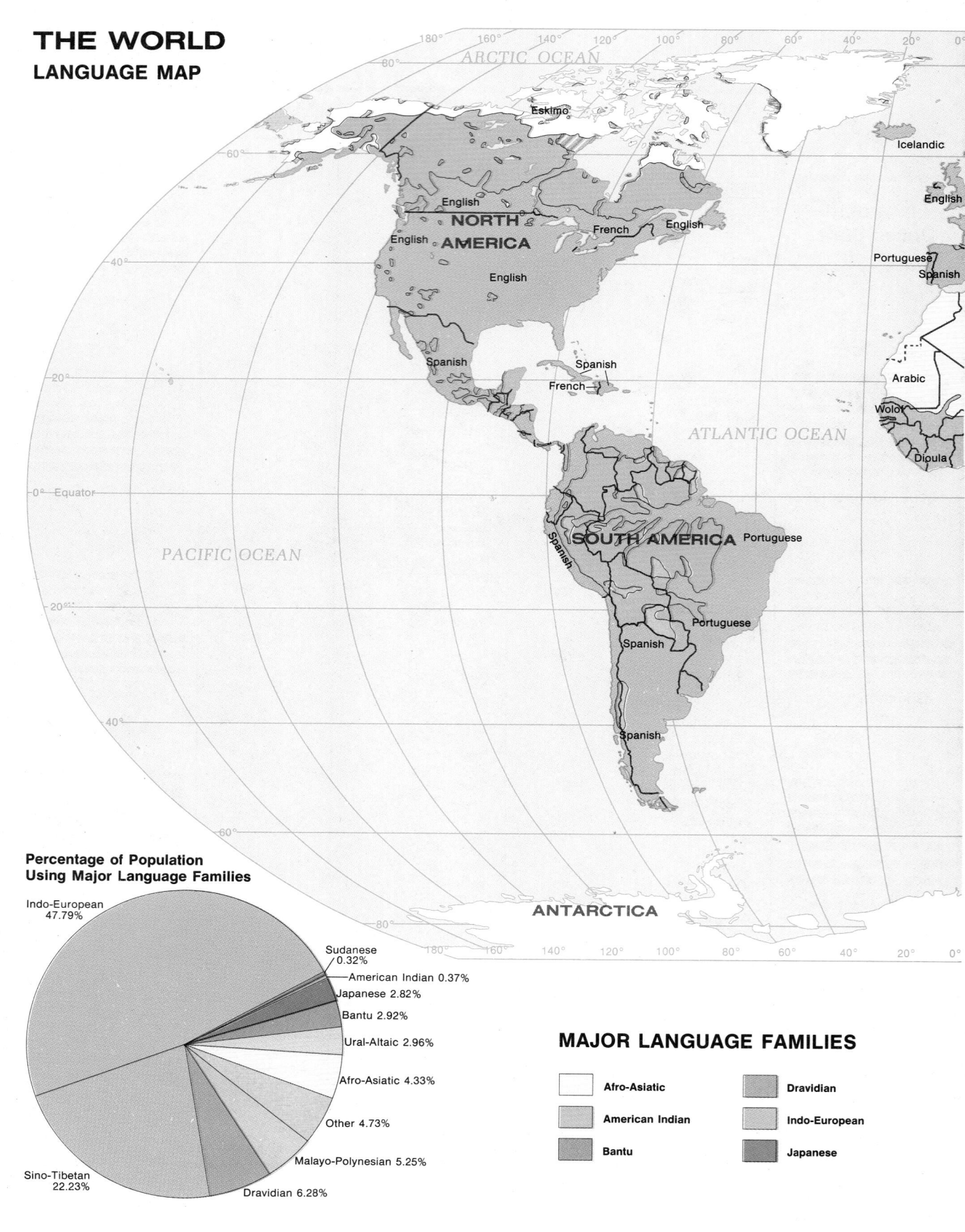

THE WORLD
LANGUAGE MAP

ARCTIC OCEAN

Eskimo

Icelandic

English

English

NORTH
AMERICA

English

French

English

Portuguese

Spanish

English

Spanish

ATLANTIC OCEAN

Arabic

Spanish

French

Wolof

Dioula

Equator

PACIFIC OCEAN

Spanish

SOUTH AMERICA

Portuguese

Portuguese

Spanish

Spanish

ANTARCTICA

**Percentage of Population
Using Major Language Families**

Indo-European
47.79%

Sudanese
0.32%

American Indian 0.37%

Japanese 2.82%

Bantu 2.92%

Ural-Altaic 2.96%

Afro-Asiatic 4.33%

Other 4.73%

Malayo-Polynesian 5.25%

Dravidian 6.28%

Sino-Tibetan
22.23%

MAJOR LANGUAGE FAMILIES

Afro-Asiatic	Dravidian
American Indian	Indo-European
Bantu	Japanese

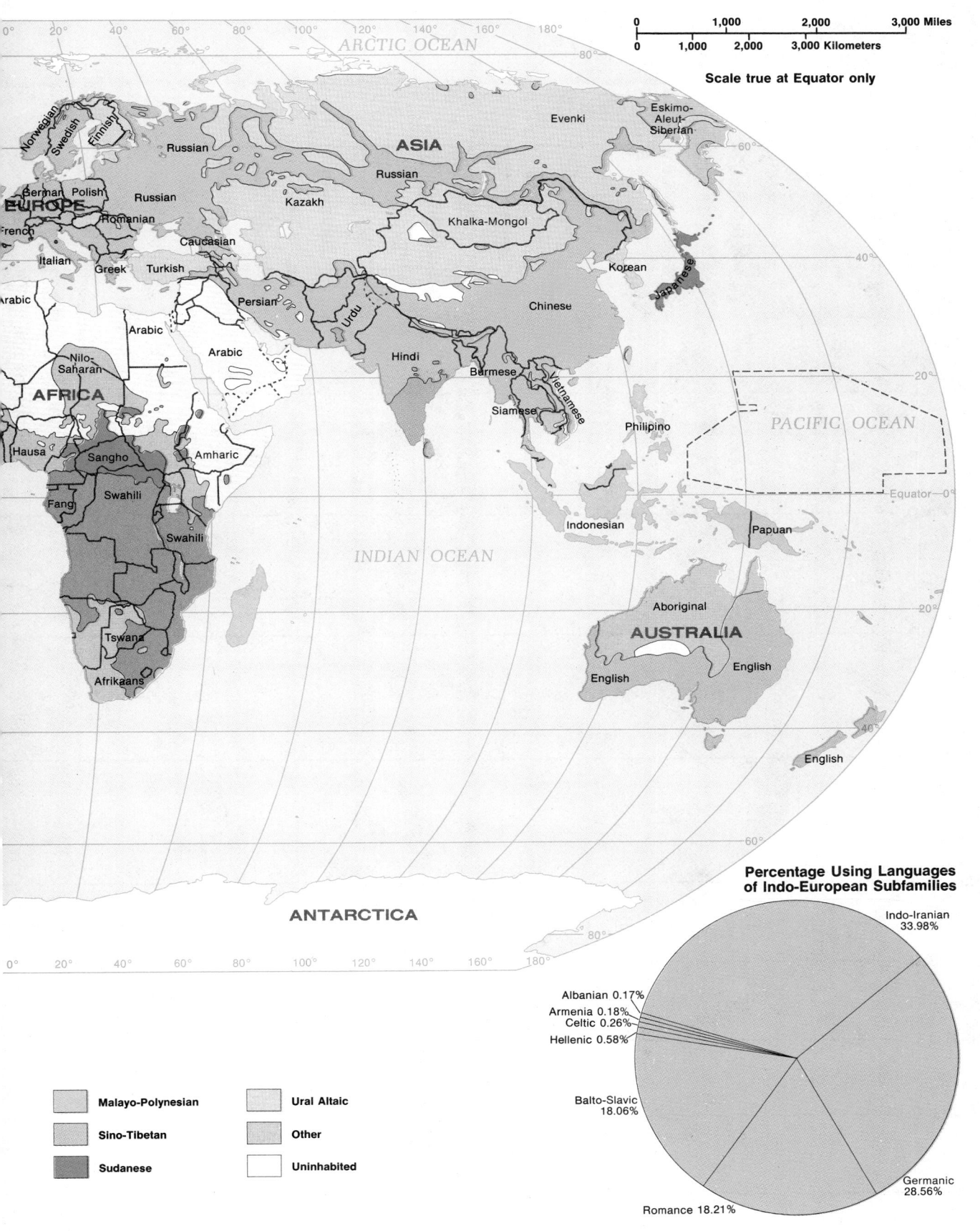

Scale true at Equator only

0 — 1,000 — 2,000 — 3,000 Miles
0 — 1,000 — 2,000 — 3,000 Kilometers

ARCTIC OCEAN

ASIA

Evenki

Eskimo-
Aleut-
Siberian

Russian

Russian

Russian

Kazakh

Khalka-Mongol

Norwegian
Swedish
Finnish

German Polish
EUROPE
French
Romanian
Italian
Greek
Turkish
Caucasian

Korean

Japanese

Arabic

Arabic

Persian

Urdu

Chinese

Arabic

Hindi

Burmese

Vietnamese

Nilo-
Saharan

AFRICA

Amharic

Siamese

Philipino

PACIFIC OCEAN

Hausa

Sangho

Fang

Swahili

Swahili

Indonesian

Papuan

INDIAN OCEAN

Equator — 0°

Tswana

Aboriginal

AUSTRALIA

English

English

Afrikaans

English

ANTARCTICA

English

0° 20° 40° 60° 80° 100° 120° 140° 160° 180°

**Percentage Using Languages
of Indo-European Subfamilies**

Indo-Iranian
33.98%

Albanian 0.17%
Armenia 0.18%
Celtic 0.26%
Hellenic 0.58%

Balto-Slavic
18.06%

Germanic
28.56%

Romance 18.21%

	Malayo-Polynesian		Ural Altaic
	Sino-Tibetan		Other
	Sudanese		Uninhabited

LANGUAGES IN THE

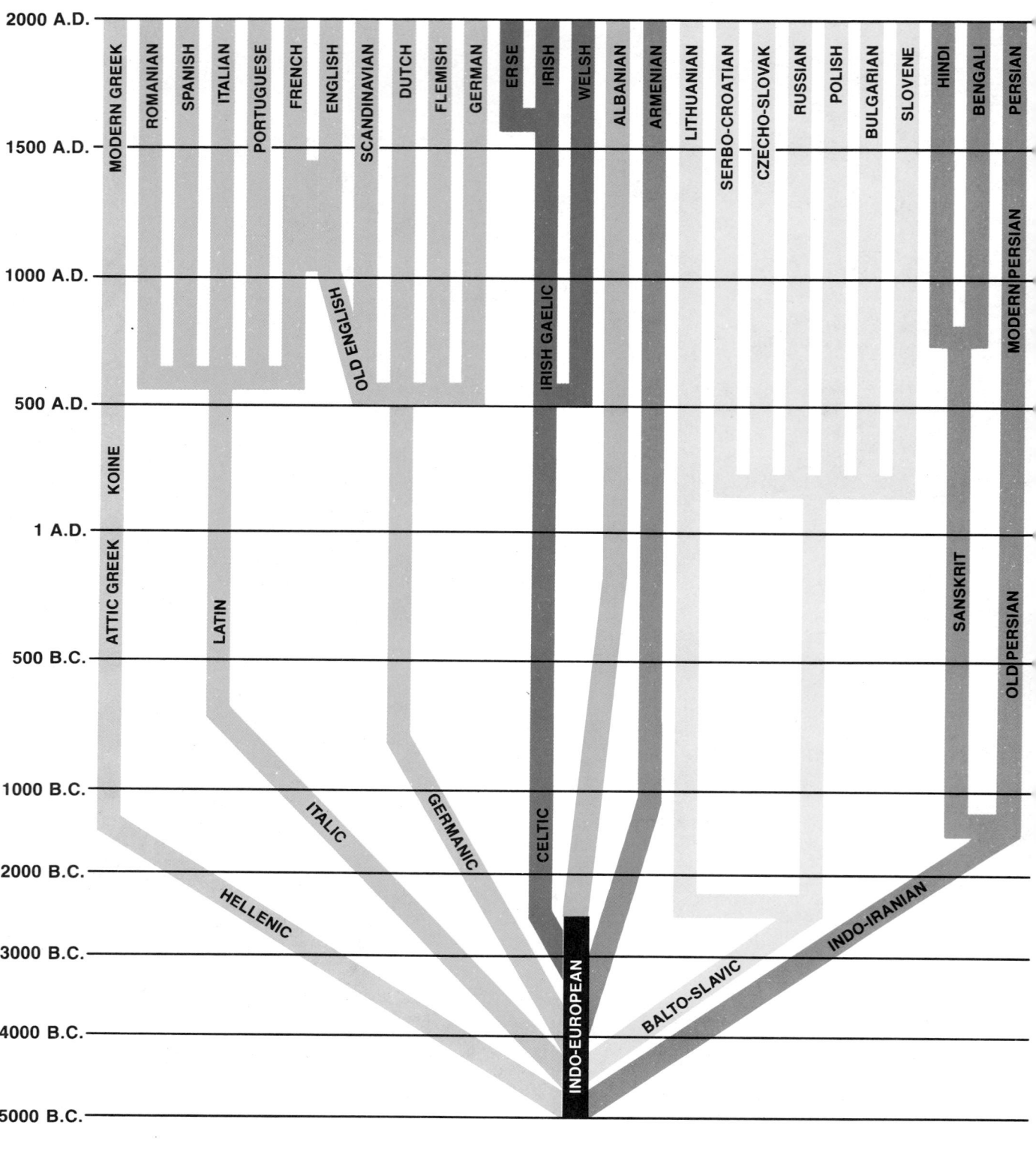

Long ago, only a few languages were spoken. One of them was Indo-European. Experts believe that the people in Central and Northern Europe spoke Indo-European around 5000 B.C. Later, as some of the people moved to other parts of Europe and to India, new languages developed. All these languages are now part of the *Indo-European family.*

Many other language families also exist. However, Indo-European is the most important because almost half the people in the world speak a language belonging to this family.

The History of the English Language

One language in the Indo-European family is English. The chart shows that English is hundreds of years old. However, the English we speak today is not the same as the English of long ago. The language has changed and developed over the years.

Around 500 B.C., people called Celts moved to Britain. They came from central and western Europe. Their language, Celtic, became the language of Britain.

In 43 A.D., Romans arrived in Britain. They spoke a different language, Latin. However, Latin did not affect Celtic much. Only a few Latin words entered the Celtic language. Some examples are *candle, master, port.*

The Romans left Britain in the 400s. Soon after, in 449, Britain was invaded by three Germanic tribes called the Angles, the Saxons, and the Jutes. Because they came from different places, they all spoke different versions of the same language. After they arrived in Britain, they started to speak the same language, *Old English,* which replaced Celtic. Even the name *Britain* was changed to *Angleland. Old English* lasted past the year 1000.

In 1066, French people called Normans conquered England. By 1400, thousands of French words had entered the English language. Examples are *color, dinner, government.* The new language, called *Middle English,* lasted from about 1100 to 1500.

No one knows exactly why, but around 1500, English vowel sounds began to change. For example, the sound of *sweet* changed from *swā′tǝ* to *swēt.* Word spellings, however, stopped changing. With the invention of the printing press, around 1450, people started to use standard spellings for words. The language spoken after 1500 became known as *Modern English.*

Modern English is the English that we use today. The language continues to grow and to incorporate new words constantly, especially words related to science and technology. Examples are *astronaut, bionic, laser.*

LATIN:
CAMP
MASTER
BISHOP

OLD
ENGLISH:
FARMER
SHEEP
CHILD

FRENCH:
ART
JUSTICE
PRESIDENT

INVENTIONS AND INVENTORS

Before 3000 B.C.

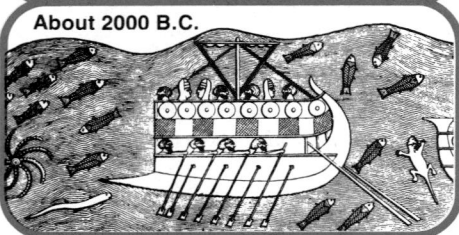

About 2000 B.C.

About 2000 B.C.

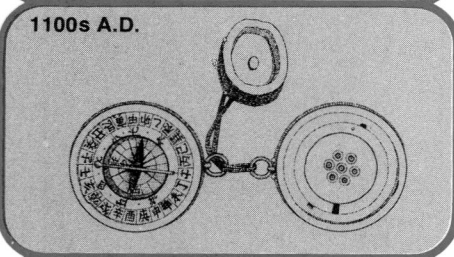

Before 700 B.C.

1100s A.D.

Before 3000 B.C.	Wheel	Textiles
Sledge	Plow	Pottery
3000–2000 B.C.	Written messages	Oil lamps
Copper, silver, iron	Furniture	Dyes
Sailing ship		
2000–1000 B.C.	Glass	Bellows
Alphabet	Iron tools	Weaving loom
Calendar	Pulley	
1000–1 B.C.	Lighthouse	Water-raising device
Coins	Water wheel	Archimedes
Roads	Water pipes	Bridges
	and systems	
1-1000 A.D.	Pump, press	Horseshoe, horsecollar
Paper	Furnace	Crossbow
Ts'ai Lun	Soap	Rubber
Magnetic compass		
1000–1500 A.D.	Spinning wheel	Cannon
Abacus	Coal mining	Blast furnace
Fork	Mechanical clock with	Printing press
Windmill	bells	Johann Gutenberg
Wheelbarrow	Eyeglasses	
1500–1750 A.D.		
Microscope	Early thermometer	Submarine
Zacharias Janssen	Galileo Galilei	Cornelius van Drebbel
Steam engine	Telescope	Barometer
Thomas Savery	Galileo Galilei	Evangelista Torricelli
Adding machine	Microscope	Pendulum clock
Blaise Pascal		

About 1000 A.D.

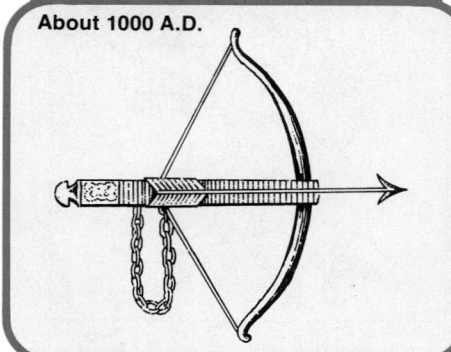

1000-1500 A.D.

1600s A.D.

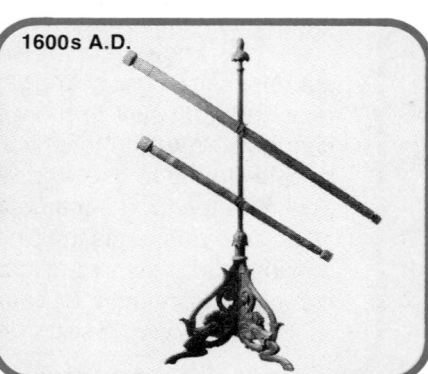

1750–

1769	Improved steam engine James Watt	1895	X-ray machine
1793	Cotton gin Eli Whitney	1896	Motion picture camera Étienne Maray, Thomas Edison, Auguste and Louis Lumière
1804	Railroad locomotive Richard Trevithick	1897	Diesel engine Rudolf Diesel
1807	Steamboat Robert Fulton	1902	Air conditioning
1816	Stethoscope	1903	Airplane Orville and Wilbur Wright
1826	Photography Louis Daguerre	1907	Helicopter Louis and Jacques Bréguet
1840	Electric Telegraph Samuel Morse	1907	Bakelite (plastic) Leo Baekeland
1845	Air-filled tire Robert Thomson	1920s	Television
1846	Sewing machine Elias Howe	1927	Nylon Wallace Carothers
1860	Internal combustion engine Étienne Lenoir	1930	Computer
1867	Dynamite Alfred Nobel	1935	Fluorescent light
1867	Typewriter Christopher Sholes	1938	Photostat copier Chester Carlson
1876	Telephone Alexander Graham Bell	1939	Jet engine aircraft
1879	Incandescent light Thomas Edison	1942	Electronic computer John Mauchly J. Presper Eckert
1885	Gasoline automobile Gottlieb Daimler, Karl Benz	1942	Nuclear reactor
1886	Linotype machine Otto Mergenthaler	1947	Transistor John Bardeen William Shockley Walter Brattain
1887	Electric motor Nikola Tesla	1957	Artificial satellite
1895	Radio Guglielmo Marconi	1960	Laser
		1970	Microprocessor

1804

1807

1826

1895

1903

1920s

1939

1957

PRESIDENTS AND VICE PRESIDENTS

George Washington
1789-1797
Vice President
John Adams

John Adams
1797-1801
Vice President
Thomas Jefferson

Thomas Jefferson
1801-1809
Vice Presidents
Aaron Burr
George Clinton

James Madison
1809-1817
Vice Presidents
George Clinton
Elbridge Gerry

James Monroe
1817-1825
Vice President
Daniel D. Tompkins

John Quincy Adams
1825-1829
Vice President
John C. Calhoun

Andrew Jackson
1829-1837
Vice Presidents
John C. Calhoun
Martin Van Buren

Martin Van Buren
1837-1841
Vice President
Richard M. Johnson

William Henry Harrison*
1841-1841
Vice President
John Tyler

John Tyler
1841-1845

OF THE UNITED STATES

James K. Polk
1845-1849
Vice President
George M. Dallas

Zachary Taylor
1849-1850
Vice President
Millard Fillmore

Millard Fillmore
1850-1853

Franklin Pierce
1853-1857
Vice President
William R. King

James Buchanan
1857-1861
Vice President
John C. Breckinridge

Abraham Lincoln**
1861-1865
Vice Presidents
Hannibal Hamlin
Andrew Johnson

Andrew Johnson
1865-1869

Ulysses S. Grant
1869-1877
Vice Presidents
Schuyler Colfax
Henry Wilson

Rutherford B. Hayes
1877-1881
Vice President
William A. Wheeler

James A. Garfield**
1881-1881
Vice President
Chester A. Arthur

*Died in office   **Assassinated   ***Resigned

Chester A. Arthur
1881-1885

Grover Cleveland
1885-1889, 1893-1897
Vice Presidents
Thomas A. Hendricks
Adlai E. Stevenson

Benjamin Harrison
1889-1893
Vice President
Levi P. Morton

William McKinley**
1897-1901
Vice Presidents
Garret A. Hobart
Theodore Roosevelt

Theodore Roosevelt
1901-1909
Vice President
Charles W. Fairbanks

William Howard Taft
1909-1913
Vice President
James S. Sherman

Woodrow Wilson
1913-1921
Vice President
Thomas R. Marshall

Warren G. Harding*
1921-1923
Vice President
Calvin Coolidge

Calvin Coolidge
1923-1929
Vice President
Charles G. Dawes

Herbert C. Hoover
1929-1933
Vice President
Charles Curtis

Franklin D. Roosevelt*
1933-1945
Vice Presidents
John N. Garner
Henry A. Wallace
Harry S. Truman

Harry S. Truman
1945-1953
Vice President
Alben W. Barkley

Dwight D. Eisenhower
1953-1961
Vice President
Richard M. Nixon

John F. Kennedy**
1961-1963
Vice President
Lyndon B. Johnson

Lyndon B. Johnson
1963-1969
Vice President
Hubert H. Humphrey

Richard M. Nixon***
1969-1974
Vice Presidents
Spiro Agnew
Gerald R. Ford

Gerald R. Ford
1974-1977
Vice President
Nelson A. Rockefeller

James E. Carter
1977-1981
Vice President
Walter F. Mondale

Ronald W. Reagan
1981-
Vice President
George H. W. Bush

*Died in office   **Assassinated   ***Resigned

EVENTS IN UNITED STATES HISTORY

Many tribes of American Indians had been living in North America for thousands of years before European explorers arrived.

1492 Christopher Columbus left Spain, seeking to find a sea route to the Far East, but he landed in San Salvador. Europeans honored him as the discoverer of America.

1565 Spaniards founded St. Augustine on the Atlantic Coast in Florida. It is the oldest city in the U.S.

1607 A group of about a hundred English colonists founded Jamestown, the first permanent British settlement in North America.

1610 Mexicans founded Sante Fe in the area that would later become New Mexico.

1620 The Pilgrims founded Plymouth Colony in Massachusetts. It was the second permanent British settlement in North America.

1733 Georgia became the thirteenth colony. Each colony had its own governing body, but all were under the rule of Britain.

1760 Improvements in land transportation now included the first Conestoga wagons. The Conestoga wagons carried freight and people to new pioneering settlements in the West.

1763 Britain defeated France in the French and Indian War and gained control of a large section of the country. Because the war had cost the British a great deal, they increased taxes on the colonists.

1764-1765 Taxation imposed by King George III and Parliament angered the colonists. Their slogan became "Taxation without representation is tyranny!"

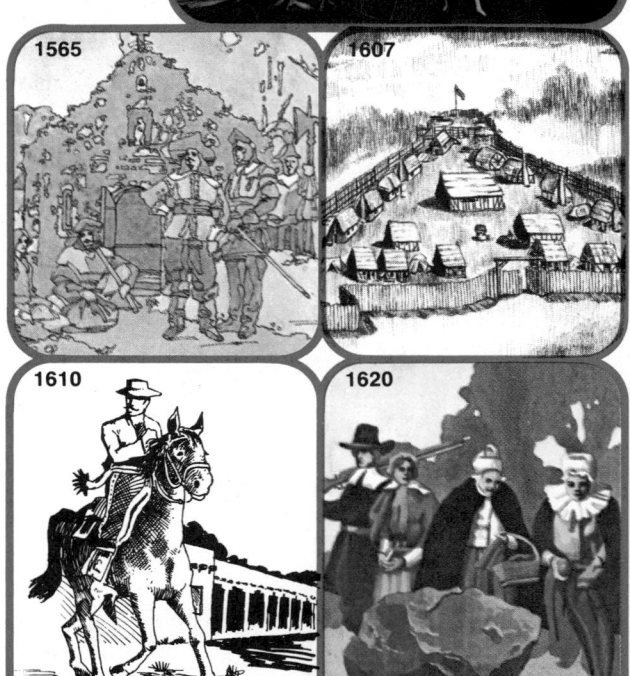

1492

1565

1607

1610

1620

1733

1760

1763

1764-1765

A skull and crossbones on goods protests Taxes

1775

1775 The Revolutionary War between the colonists and Great Britain began at Lexington and Concord.

1776 On July 4, the colonists adopted the Declaration of Independence and formed the United States of America.

1781 The Americans defeated the British at Yorktown, Virginia, in the last major battle of the Revolutionary War.

1787 The Founding Fathers wrote the Constitution.

1793 Eli Whitney invented the cotton gin. His cotton gin made cotton growing profitable and helped to make the new country the world's largest cotton producer.

1776

1781 1787

1793 1800

1800 The federal government moved to Washington, District of Columbia, from its temporary capital in Philadelphia, Pennsylvania.

1803 The Louisiana Purchase doubled the size of the U.S. The government bought the land from France for 15 million dollars and granted money for exploration of the huge new area.

1811 Work began on the Cumberland Road, which linked Cumberland, Maryland, with Vandalia, Illinois. This road was the beginning of the national system of transportation in the U.S.

1812-1815 The United States and Great Britain fought the War of 1812. Many Americans had become angered by British interference in shipping and by the practice of forcing American seamen into service on British ships.

1820 The Missouri Compromise settled disagreements about slavery and specified areas in which slavery was illegal.

1803

1811

1812-1815

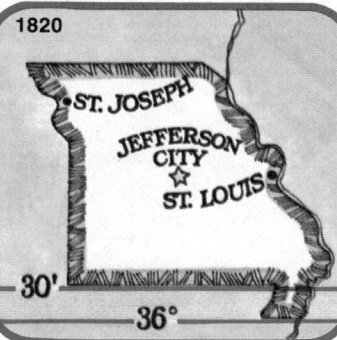
1820

EVENTS IN UNITED STATES HISTORY

1823 The Monroe Doctrine asked Europeans not to interfere in the republics of North and South America and not to form new colonies.

1825 The Erie Canal opened, providing a water route from the Atlantic Ocean to the Great Lakes.

1837 Samuel F. B. Morse demonstrated the first successful telegraph in the U.S. Seven years later, in 1844, he telegraphed his famous message, "What hath God wrought."

1846 Britain yielded the southern part of the Oregon Country to the U.S. after long dispute over boundary lines.

1846-1848 Victory in the Mexican War gave the U.S. new territo in the West. California, Utah, Nevada, and parts of other states were included in that new territory.

1848 Lucretia Mott and Elizabeth Cady Stanton met with a group of women at Seneca Falls, N.Y., to inaugurate the women's rights movement and draw up a declaration asking for full equality for women in all areas of life.

1848 The discovery of gold in California started the Gold Rush. Thousands hurried to establish claims. They were called "forty-niners" because of the date of their arrival.

1853 The U.S. bought additional land from Mexico, setting the nation's present southern border.

1860 Pony express riders began carrying mail from St. Joseph, Missouri, to the Far West. The trip took ten days—twelve days less than the stagecoach Overland Mail.

1860-61 The seven deep South states left the Union in disagreement with the North about slavery and states' rights. They formed the Confederate States of America.

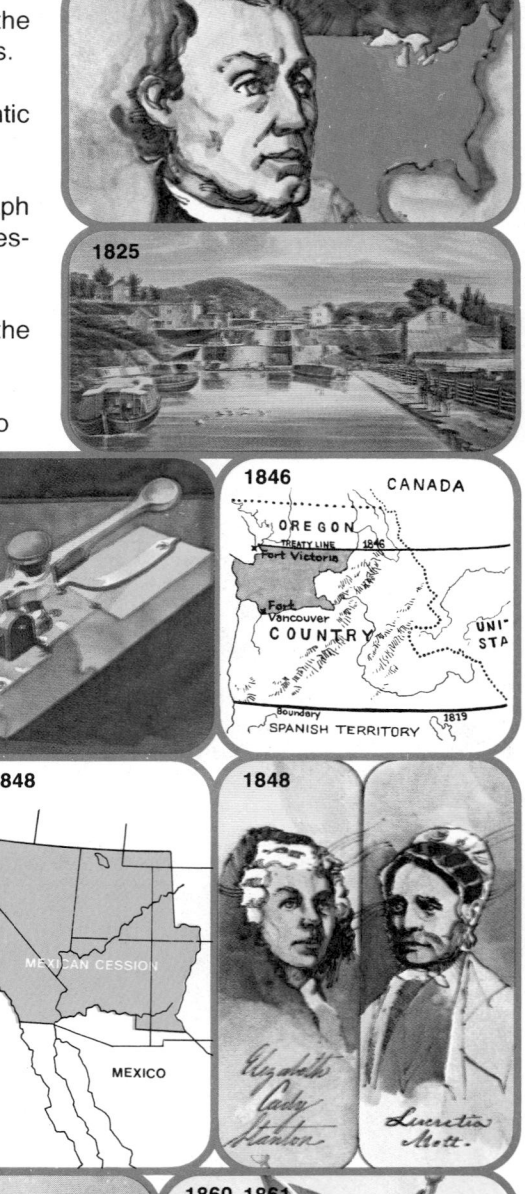

1861 The Civil War began when Confederate troops fired on Fort Sumter in Charleston, South Carolina.

1863 The Emancipation Proclamation was signed by President Abraham Lincoln. The proclamation declared freedom for all slaves in the Confederate-held territory.

1865 General Lee surrendered to General Grant at Appomattox Court House, Virginia.

1865-1870 The Thirteenth Constitutional Amendment outlawed slavery; the Fourteenth gave citizenship to former slaves; the Fifteenth opened voting to all men, regardless of race.

1865-1870

Amendment 13
Proposed on Jan. 31, 1865
Ratified on Dec. 6, 1865.

Amendment 14
Proposed on June 13, 1866
Ratified on July 9, 1868.

Amendment 15
Proposed on Feb. 26, 1869
Ratified on Feb. 3, 1870.

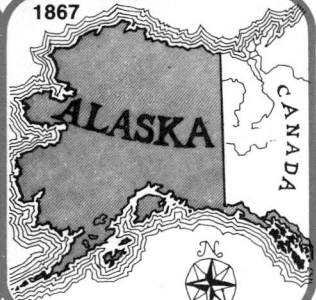

1867 The United States bought Alaska from Russia for a little more than 7 million dollars—less than two cents an acre.

1869 The first transcontinental railroad was completed when tracks joined the Central Pacific and Union Pacific railroads in Utah.

1872 Victoria Claflin Woodhull was the first woman to run for President of the United States. She ran as the candidate for the newly formed Equal Rights Party. The party had the support of many women's voting rights organizations.

1876 Alexander Graham Bell invented the telephone.

1879 Thomas Alva Edison invented the electric light bulb. This and many other inventions grew from research done in his Menlo Park, New Jersey, laboratory.

1886 The American Federation of Labor was formed. It called for better wages and working conditions and for employers to talk and bargain with their workers.

EVENTS IN UNITED STATES HISTORY

1898 The U.S. defeated Spain in the Spanish-American War. Under the terms of the peace treaty, the U.S. received Guam, Puerto Rico, and the Philippines.

1903 The Wright Brothers made the first successful airplane flight.

1909 Henry Ford brought out the Model T. He started the assembly-line way of manufacturing. The assembly line brought parts to workers and speeded production.

1917-1918 The U.S. joined France, Great Britain, Italy, and Russia in the World War I struggle against Germany.

1920 The Nineteenth Amendment to the Constitution gave women the right to vote.

1927 *The Jazz Singer* was the first talking motion picture. It was called a "talkie" but was mainly a silent film with songs.

1927 The first solo transatlantic flight helped to start the Air Age. Charles Lindbergh flew from Garden City, New York, in the U.S. to Paris, France. The 3,600 mile trip took about 33½ hours.

1929 A stock market crash brought financial ruin to thousands and started the Great Depression. It was a period of hardship for many, and it lasted for a decade.

1933 The New Deal program to end the Depression began under President Franklin D. Roosevelt. Many government public work projects provided work and wages for the unemployed.

1941-1945 After the bombing of Pearl Harbor, the U.S. joined Britain, France, and other Allies in World War II. War against Japan, Germany, and Italy was declared.

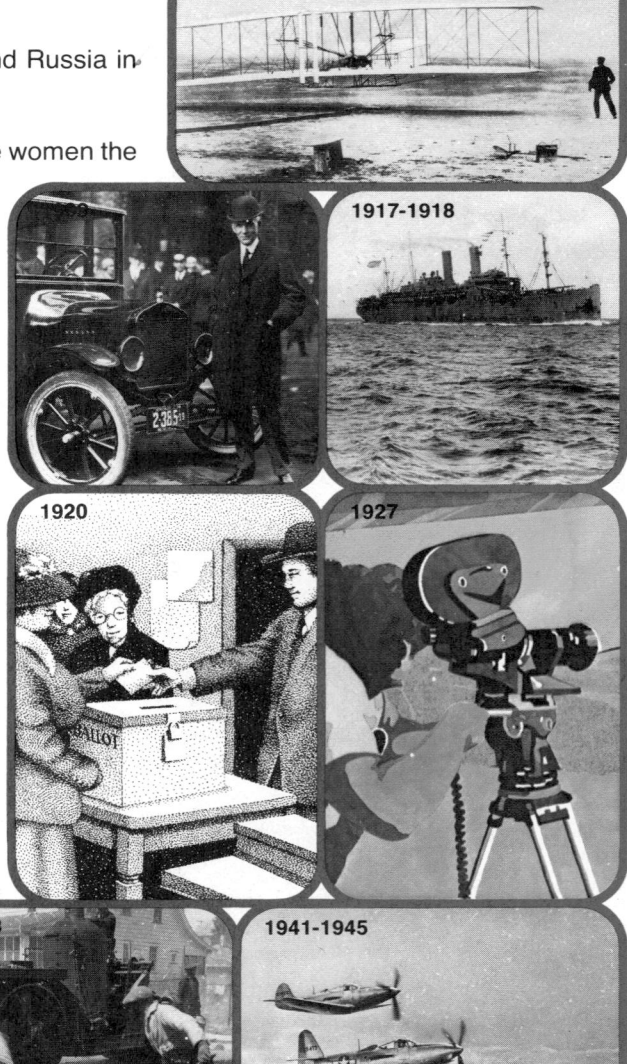

1898

1903

1917-1918

1920

1927

1927

1929
STOCKS COLLAPSE IN 16,
BUT RALLY AT CLOSE
BANKERS OPTIMISTIC,
WORST STOCK CRASH ST
12,894,650-SHARE DAY S
LEADERS CONFER, FIN
STOCK PRICES SLUMP $14,000
IN NATION-WIDE STAMPEDE TO
BANKERS TO SUPPORT MAR

1933

1941-1945

1945 The U.S. became a charter member of the United Nations.

1950s Television became part of millions of Americans' homes.

1950-1953 The U.S. joined with other members of the United Nations in trying to help restore peace in Korea.

1954 The Supreme Court ruled that laws establishing separate schools for blacks and whites were illegal.

1960s Civil rights organizations became very active in demanding civil rights for blacks, Hispanic Americans, American Indians, and other minority groups. Often, whites joined minorities in protests.

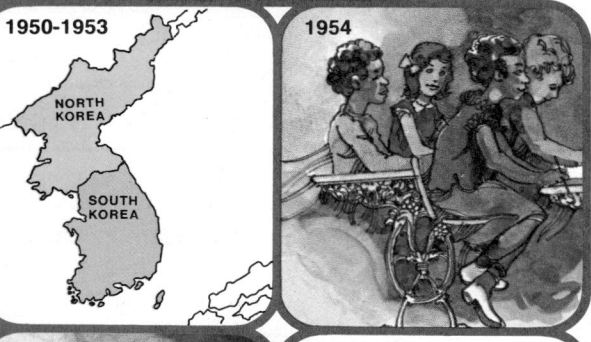

1965-1973 The U.S. supported South Vietnam in its effort to remain independent.

1969 Astronaut Neil A. Armstrong became the first person to walk on the moon. Millions watched on television.

1970s Electronic computers, first developed during the 40s and 50s, began to affect all aspects of everyday life, from complex industrial uses to supermarkets.

1970 The first Earth Day took place to dramatize citizen's concern about growing pollution of the environment. The Environmental Protection Agency was formed to set up and enforce standards.

1976 The United States of America celebrated its bicentennial—the 200th anniversary of the signing of the Declaration of Independence.

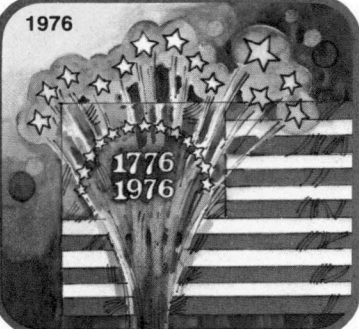

TABLES OF MEASURE

FREQUENTLY USED METRIC UNITS

Length

1 millimeter (mm)	=	.001 meter (m)
1 centimeter (cm)	=	.01 meter
1 meter		
1 kilometer (km)	=	1,000

Prefixes

milli means	.001	deka means	10
centi means	.01	hecto means	100
deci means	.1	kilo means	1000

Area

1 square meter (m²)	=	10,000 square centimeters (cm²)

Volume

1 cubic meter (m³)	=	1,000,000 cubic centimeters (cm³)

Mass

1 milligram (mg)	=	.001 gram (g)
1 kilogram (kg)	=	1,000 grams

Liquid Volume

1 liter (L)	=	1,000 milliliters (mL)

FREQUENTLY USED CUSTOMARY UNITS

Length

1 foot (ft)	=	12 inches (in.)
1 yard (yd)	=	3 feet
1 mile (mi)	=	5,280 feet or 1,760 yards

Area

1 square foot (ft²)	=	144 square inches (in.²)
1 square yard (yd²)	=	9 square feet
1 acre (A)	=	43,560 square feet or 4,840 square yards

Volume

1 cubic foot (ft³)	=	1,728 cubic inches (in.³)
1 cubic yard (yd³)	=	27 cubic feet

Weight

1 pound (lb)	=	16 ounces (oz)
1 ton	=	2,000 pounds

Liquid Volume

1 cup	=	8 fluid ounces (fl oz)
1 pint (pt)	=	2 cups

1 quart (qt)	=	2 pints
1 gallon (gal)	=	4 quarts

TIME UNITS

1 minute (min)	=	60 seconds (sec)
1 hour (hr)	=	60 minutes
1 day (da)	=	24 hours

1 week (wk)	=	7 days
1 year (yr)	=	12 months (mo)

TEMPERATURE SCALES

	Celsius	Fahrenheit
Freezing point of water	0°C	32°F
Boiling point of water	100°C	212°F
Normal body temperature	37°C	98.6°F

INTRODUCTION

The following pages are a supplement to the **Macmillan School Dictionary.** They provide follow-up activities for the lessons contained in the **Guide to the Dictionary** at the front of the book, and they are to be used to reinforce the dictionary skills taught in those lessons. As in the **Guide,** skills are presented in the order that they appear in the entry.

CONTENTS

ALPHABETICAL ORDER

Before you can look up a word, you have to know where it comes in alphabetical order. Here are some exercises to make sure you know how alphabetical order works in a dictionary.

TRY THIS

Read the groups of words below. Write each group in alphabetical order. Number 1 has been done for you.

1. knife   hopscotch
   hopscotch   idea
   lemon   knife
   idea   lemon

2. ocean
   unify
   afire
   envy

3. quote
   poppy
   salad
   roast

4. dynamite
   dampen
   dribble
   delay

5. foul
   funnel
   fraction
   flounder

6. knob
   killjoy
   koala
   kangaroo

7. eat
   ease
   eagle
   each

8. rank
   ranch
   ransack
   range

9. swirl
   swivel
   switch
   swing

10. comet
    comely
    comedy
    comeback

11. paraffin
    parade
    paragraph
    parachute

12. squashy
    square
    squabble
    squat

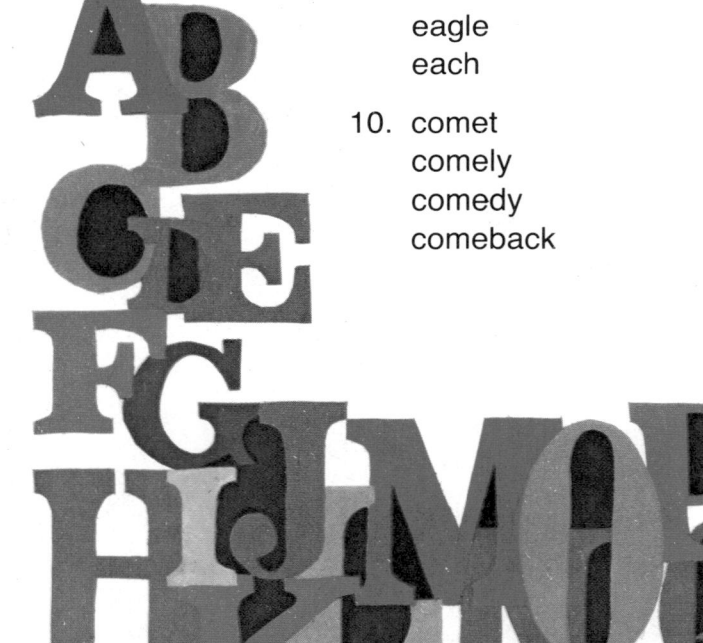

Write the following lists of words in alphabetical order. Skip a line between words. Then think of a word to fill in each blank line. Your word must be in alphabetical order between the word above it and the word below it. Use your dictionary for help. Number 1 has been partly done for you.

1. shovel   sad
   scarf   saxophone
   ski   scarf
   speed   search
   syrup   shovel
   some   ski
   store   smile
   search   some
   sad   speed
   smile   store
               syrup

2. frank
   face
   feather
   fit
   flower
   forest
   fuss
   flame
   frozen
   fancy

3. wrinkle
   wolf
   whale
   wax
   who
   weed
   wander
   wiggle
   worker
   wizard

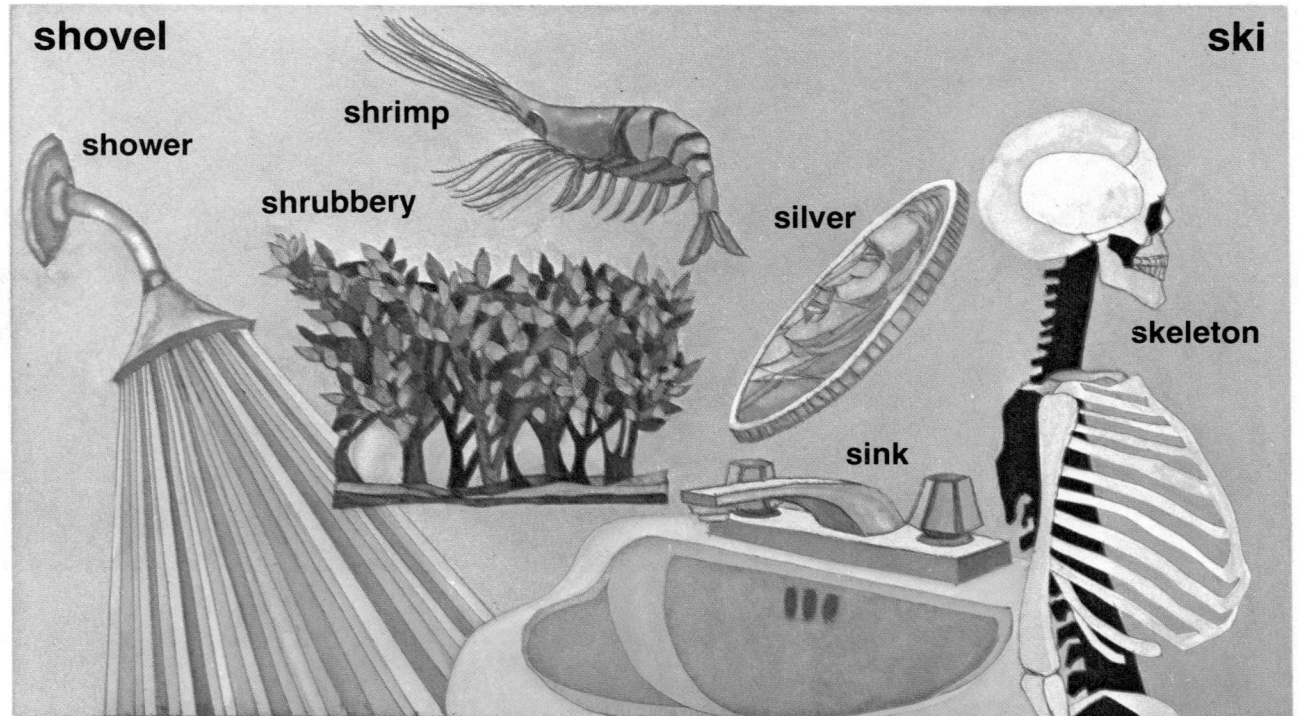

shovel   **ski**

shower

shrimp

shrubbery

silver

skeleton

sink

A helpful hint: Before you go on to the rest of the exercises, look at the **Sample Page** on the inside back cover of your book. It will show you how your dictionary works.

GUIDE WORDS

The **guide words** at the top of each page of the dictionary help you look up a word. They show the first and last words on the page. All the words on a page come between the guide words in alphabetical order.

TRY THIS

Write the words below. Then look up each word in your dictionary. Find the guide words for that page and write them next to the word. Number 1 has been done for you.

1. chain   certainty/chair
4. magazine
7. route
10. windmill
13. visa
16. novel
19. knack

2. disturb
5. orbit
8. sample
11. barnstorm
14. yelp
17. maverick
20. deadlock

3. highway
6. poison
9. thicket
12. uproar
15. zoom
18. jazz
21. academy

cheerleader   cheeseburger   chef   Cherokee

cheerful

Read the groups of words below. Two words in each group are guide words for a page in your dictionary. Two other words in each group belong on the same page as the guide words. One word in each group does not belong at all. Write the guide words. Then write the two words that belong on the same page as the guide words. Number 1 has been done for you.

1. cobweb   cobra/cocoon
    coconut   cobweb
    cobra   coconut
    cocoon
    cod

2. dishrag
    dishful
    disk
    dismal
    disobey

3. least
    leeward
    legacy
    legislator
    left

4. patchwork
    patent
    patrimony
    patriot
    path

5. skinny
    skyscraper
    skyrocket
    skull
    skin

6. stucco
    studio
    stuffing
    stunt[2]
    submarine

7. gravity
    grasp
    gratify
    grassy
    gravy

8. rainbow
    radish
    railroad
    radioactive
    raffle

9. queue
    queer
    quicklime
    queen
    quilt

cherry

chess

ENTRY WORDS

The words listed in your dictionary are called **entry words.** They are printed in large black type to make them easy to find.

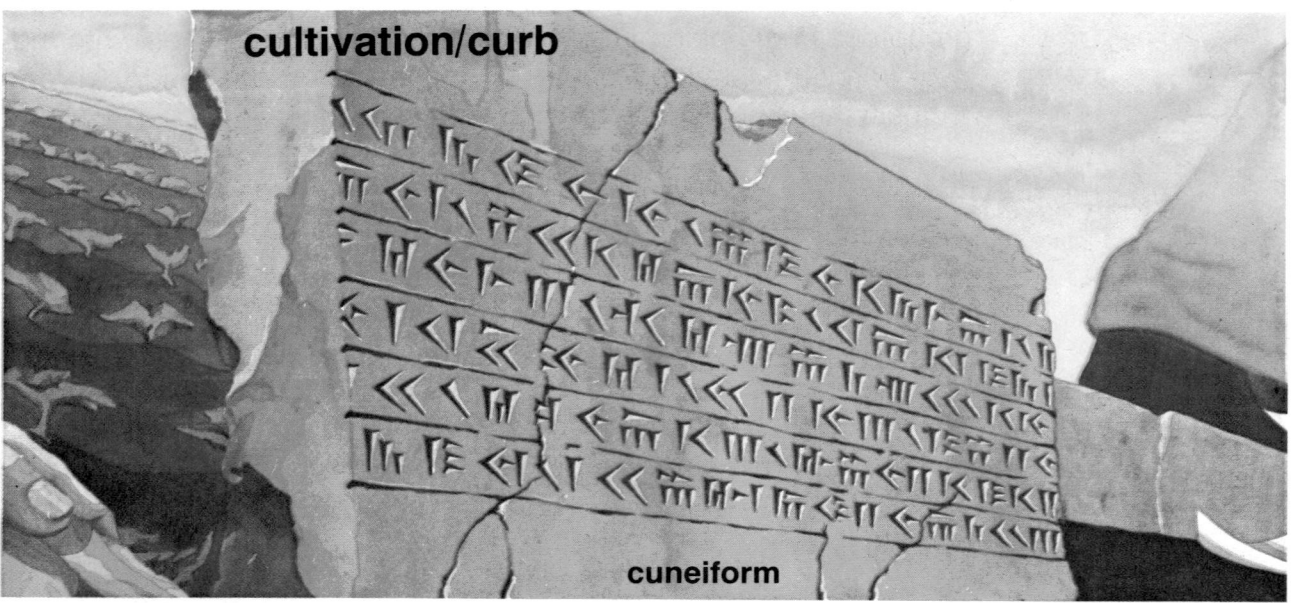

cultivation/curb

cuneiform

TRY THIS

Write the pairs of guide words listed below. Now find the page in your dictionary that has these guide words. Next to the words, write an interesting entry word that you find on the page. Then do the same with the rest of the words. Number 1 shows an example.

1. cultivation/curb   cuneiform
2. designate/destiny
3. emphasize/enamel
4. forgotten/forsake
5. ingot/injure
6. maltreat/mandolin
7. referendum/refugee
8. skeleton/skimpy
9. throne/thumb
10. ward/warranty
11. graceful/grammar
12. hot-blooded/housework
13. joker/joy
14. awe/azure
15. butter/bypass
16. confusion/congruous
17. diligent/dinosaur
18. quiver^2/q.v.
19. uphill/upstairs
20. bind/birdbath
21. imagery/immerse
22. tie-up/timber line
23. juniper/juxtapose
24. loaded/locus

KINDS OF ENTRY WORDS

Not all entries are simple words. Some are phrases made up of two or more words. (These are called **compound entries**.) Some are abbreviations, and some are proper names.

TRY THIS

Turn to pages 468-469 in your dictionary. Match the meanings on the left with the correct entry word from the right-hand column. Write the entry word. Then write whether it is a compound, an abbreviation, or a proper name. Number 1 has been done for you.

1. A metal runner	*ice skate, compound entry*	Ibsen, Henrik
2. Iowa		I
3. The language of Iceland		ice box
4. A ballistic missile		ID
5. The largest city of Nigeria		ice skate
6. Identification		Icelandic
7. Symbol for iodine		ice pick
8. A refrigerator		ICBM
9. A tool used to chip ice		Ia.
10. A frozen dessert		Ibadan
11. A dramatist		ice cream
12. A period of time		ice age

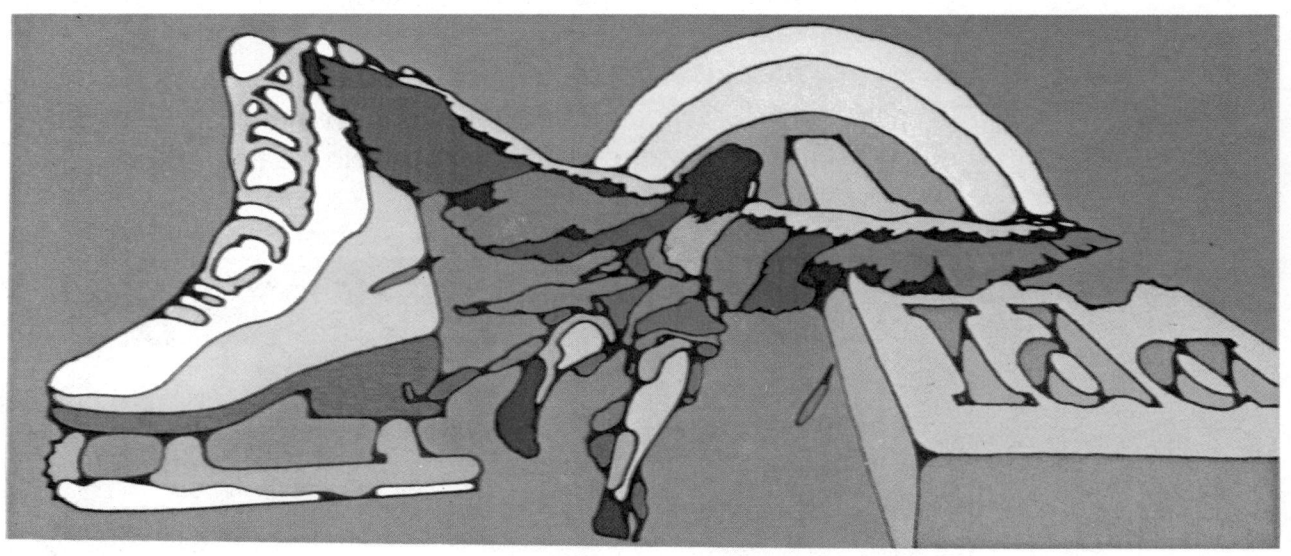

ice skate - compound entry   **Icarus - proper name**   **Ida. - abbreviation**

PREFIXES

Your dictionary has special entries called **prefixes**. A prefix is a letter or a group of letters added to the beginning of a word. Prefixes are used to form new words.

TRY THIS

There is a word with a prefix in each sentence below. The prefix is printed in heavy black letters. Read each sentence. Try to figure out what the prefix means. Then write the prefix. Next to the prefix, write what you think it means. Use your dictionary if you need it. Number 1 has been done for you.

1. Bill had to **re**work the problem because he got the wrong answer.   re, again
2. Ellen bought an **in**expensive coat at last week's sale.
3. The army lost the battle because they were **un**prepared to fight.
4. Jane's **mini**car does not use much gas.
5. The front part of the airplane was reserved for **non**smokers.
6. Charlotte took some **pre**cooked food along on her camping trip.
7. The U.S. flag is **tri**color.
8. The Wilsons have a new **self**-cleaning oven.
9. The townspeople were **fore**warned about the storm.
10. The reporters had a **post**game talk with the winning pitcher.
11. The mystery movie was thrilling, but the cartoon afterward was an **anti**climax.
12. The bracelet is made of **semi**precious stones.
13. The mayor's school policies are very **pro**integration.
14. The **ante**room was crowded with people waiting to get into the doctor's office.

place	able	form
replace	unable	inform
displace	disable	deform

SUFFIXES

Another special kind of entry word is a **suffix**. A suffix is added to the end of a word to form a new word.

fine
fineness
finely

move
mover
movement

real
realize
realism

TRY THIS In each sentence below there is a word with a suffix. The suffix is printed in heavy black letters. Write the suffix. Next to the suffix, write what you think it means. Use your dictionary if you need it. Number 1 has been done for you.

1. Betty is a grace**ful** dancer.   -ful, full of
2. We were pleased by his kind**ness** toward us.
3. Jack tender**ly** petted his dog.
4. The book was written in a clear and understand**able** way.
5. Maria is the best spell**er** in the class.
6. It was child**ish** of him to lose his temper like that.
7. That novel**ist** often writes about the Old West.
8. Thomas Jefferson was noted for his patriot**ism.**
9. Senat**or** Jones gave a speech on television.
10. The watermelons were fresh and juic**y.**
11. The public gardens are especially pleas**ant** in the spring and fall.
12. Persist**ent** practice is needed to develop any skill.
13. There is usually a 10-degree differ**ence** in temperature between city and country.
14. We tried to apolog**ize** for our mistake.
15. You can build resist**ance** to colds by good diet.

BIOGRAPHICAL ENTRIES

One special kind of entry in your dictionary is a **biographical entry.** Biographical entries give information about people.

TRY THIS

Write the numbers 1-15 on a piece of paper. Then look up the biographical entry in each question. Write the answer to each question. Number 1 has been done for you.

1. Who was Jane **Austen**?   An English novelist.
2. What did Edward **Jenner** discover?
3. What did Yuri **Gagarin** do?
4. Who was W. C. **Handy**?
5. What did Enrico **Fermi** do?
6. What was Maria **Montessori** known for?
7. Who was Emily **Dickinson**?
8. Who was **Pocahontas**?
9. Who was Benito **Juárez**?
10. What did Betsy **Ross** do?
11. What organization did Clara **Barton** found?
12. Where was Marco **Polo** born and where did he travel?
13. Who was David **Crockett**?
14. In which areas of science did Louis **Pasteur** work?
15. What did Florence **Nightingale** do?

Pocahontas 1595?-1617

Clara Barton 1821-1912

W. C. Handy 1873-1958

Another special kind of entry is a **geographical entry.** Geographical entries give information about places.

Write the numbers 1-15 on a piece of paper. Then look up the geographical entry in each question. Write the answer to each question. Number 1 has been done for you.

1. What happened at **Lexington,** Massachusetts?
   The first battle of the American Revolution, April 19, 1775.
2. What makes **Hawaii** different from the other states?
3. What is **Oak Ridge** noted for?
4. What are the **Himalayas**?
5. What is the capital of the province of **Quebec**?
6. Is **Boise** the capital of Iowa, Idaho, or Nebraska?
7. What is **Yellowstone National Park** known for?
8. Is **Lower California** a part of the State of California?
9. Where is **Ecuador**?
10. Where is **Guadalcanal**?
11. What is a major activity in **Grand Bank**?
12. What are the former names of **Istanbul**?
13. How could the **Badlands** be described?
14. What characteristics may **Death Valley** have to earn its name?
15. What historic event took place at **Dunkirk**?

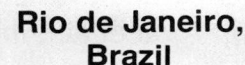

Rio de Janeiro, Brazil

Nile, Egypt

Mount Rushmore, South Dakota

SPELLING

Your dictionary can help you spell words correctly. Check your dictionary whenever you are not sure of the spelling of a word.

TRY THIS In each of the following pairs of words, only one word is spelled correctly. Take a piece of paper and write all the correctly spelled words on it. Use your dictionary to check. Number 1 has been done for you.

1. attendance *attendance*
   attendence

2. business
   bissness

3. moveble
   movable

4. irigate
   irrigate

5. allegience
   allegiance

6. bulletin
   bulettin

7. umbrella
   umbreller

8. goverment
   government

9. grandaughter
   granddaughter

10. committee
    commitee

11. scenery
    scenary

12. wimper
    whimper

13. length
    lenth

14. plummer
    plumber

15. receive
    recieve

16. believe
    beleive

17. strenth
    strength

18. occur
    ocur

19. propel
    propell

20. seperate
    separate

21. sevral
    several

HOMOGRAPHS

Sometimes two or more words in your dictionary have the same spelling. These words are called **homographs.**

palm¹ (päm) *n.* **1.** the inner surface of the hand from the wrist to the base of the fingers. **2.** a measure of length equal to the width of a hand, or about three to four inches. **3.** the part of a glove or mitten covering the palm. —*v.t.* to hold or hide in the palm or hand: *to palm cards.* [Old French *palme, paume.*] **to palm off.** to pass off by deceit or fraud.

palm² (päm) *n.* **1.** any of a group of tropical and subtropical trees or shrubs usually having large, featherlike or fan-shaped leaves growing in a cluster at the top of a tall trunk. **2.** a leaf of such a tree, used as a symbol of victory or success. [Old English *palm,* from Latin *palma* palm tree; originally also palm of the hand; because the flat leaves of this tree were thought to resemble the palm of the hand when the fingers are extended.]

TRY THIS

Look at the words printed in heavy black type. Each of these words has more than one entry in your dictionary. Find the entry word with the meaning that fits the sentence best. Write your answer. Number 1 has been done for you.

1. Which **scale** would you find on a fish?   scale²
2. Which **bank** would you put money in?
3. Which **match** would you light a fire with?
4. Which **mold** might you find on bread?
5. Which **sound** could you swim in?
6. Which **fret** is part of a guitar?
7. Which **mine** would coal be found in?
8. Which **sack** would you carry things in?
9. Which **weed** would you find in a garden?
10. Which **firm** would a lawyer belong to?
11. Which **pick** would you use to break up the ground?
12. Which **pink** has to do with cutting cloth?
13. Which **mole** might be found underground?
14. Which **mat** would you use to frame a picture?

SYLLABLE DIVISION

Entry words in your dictionary are divided into syllables. This syllable division shows you how to break up the word at the end of a line in writing. It also helps in pronouncing the word.

TRY THIS

Look up the following words in your dictionary. Then write them with spaces and dots between the syllables. Use your dictionary to check. Number 1 has been done for you.

1. mosquito mos·qui·to
2. satellite
3. official
4. favorite
5. parachute
6. curtain
7. February
8. responsibility
9. squirrel
10. Minnesota
11. kangaroo
12. umbrella
13. valentine
14. electricity
15. musician
16. amiable
17. anthropological
18. blunderbuss
19. cameraderie
20. elementary
21. experimentation
22. harmonica
23. independent
24. kaleidoscope

Bron·to·sau·rus

PRONUNCIATION

The regular alphabet cannot show all the different sounds in the English language. The reason is simple. Our language has more sounds than it has letters. Also, some letters can be pronounced in more than one way. So pronunciations in your dictionary are written in a special alphabet.

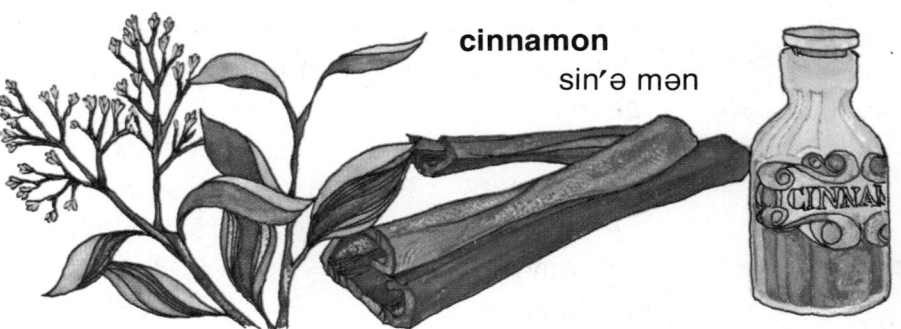

cinnamon
sin′ə mən

TRY THIS

Each word below has two pronunciations under it. One pronunciation is correct, and one pronunciation is not. Write each word. Write the correct pronunciation next to each word. Use your dictionary to check your answers. Number 1 has been done for you.

1. **cinnamon**   sin′ə mən
   sin′a man
   sin′ə mən

2. **furniture**
   fur′nə tur
   fur′ni chər

3. **operation**
   op′ə rā′shən
   op′a rā′shən

4. **father**
   fä′<u>th</u>ər
   fa′thər

5. **coward**
   kow′ərd
   kou′ərd

6. **loathsome**
   lōth′sum
   lō<u>th</u>′səm

7. **woodchuck**
   wood′chuc′
   wood′chuk′

8. **humor**
   hu′mour
   hyōō′mər

9. **honesty**
   on′is tē
   hon′əs tē

10. **pleasure**
    plez′ər
    plezh′ər

11. **careless**
    kār′les
    ker′lis

12. **exhaust**
    eks hôst′
    eg zôst′

13. **blinker**
    bling′kər
    blink′ər

14. **coffee**
    kaw′fe
    kô′fē

15. **peculiar**
    pi kyōōl′yər
    pi kyool′ē ər

INFLECTED FORMS

Many words have more than one form. These forms are called **inflected forms.** Inflected forms show a change in the meaning of the word. They appear in your dictionary just after the entry word and its pronunciation.

TRY THIS Look up the words below in your dictionary. Find their inflected forms. Then write the inflected forms on a piece of paper. Number 1 has been done for you.

1. mystery *mysteries*	2. domino	3. mouse
4. prop	5. sister-in-law	6. spin
7. envy	8. abbreviate	9. draw
10. hungry	11. ill	12. happy
13. potato	14. argue	15. knife
16. moose	17. passerby	18. inquire
19. glum	20. early	21. monkey
22. gratify	23. handkerchief	24. harmonica

noisy　　　　　　　　**noisier**　　　　　　　　**noisiest**

frogs

frog

RUN-ON ENTRIES

At the end of some entries in your dictionary you will see words printed in heavy black type. These are **run-on entries.** The meaning of the run-on entry can be understood from the meaning of the entry word plus the meaning of the suffix.

ski (skē) *n. pl.,* **skis** or **ski. 1.** one of a pair of long, narrow runners, usually of wood or metal, curving upward at the front and designed to be fastened to a boot for gliding over snow. —**ski′er,** *n.*

TRY THIS Write each of these words. Then look up the words in your dictionary. Find the run-on entries at the end of the words. Write them next to the words. Number 1 has been done for you.

1. glad gladly, gladness	2. faint	3. heavy
4. craggy	5. chalk	6. infest
7. know	8. mock	9. improve
10. hawk¹	11. wing	12. undo
13. thread	14. stingy	15. sour
16. parrot	17. pardon	18. glassy
19. crazy	20. shy	21. continue

VARIANTS

Sometimes your dictionary has two different spellings for a word. It may also have two different words that mean exactly the same thing. These are examples of **variants.**

> **plat·y·pus** (plat′ə pəs) *n. pl.,* **plat·y·pus·es** or **plat·y·pi** (plat′ə pī′). an egg-laying mammal found in Australia and Tasmania. It has a flat, wide bill that is very sensitive to touch, webbed feet, and a plump body covered with soft brown fur. Also, **duckbill, duckbilled platypus.**

| duckbill | platypus | duck-billed platypus |

TRY THIS

Look up the following entries in your dictionary. Write each entry word. Then write the variant next to it. Number 1 has been done for you.

1. knicknack   nicknack
2. launching pad
3. Bern
4. blood type
5. syrup
6. caliber
7. cookie
8. lawn bowling
9. caulk
10. termite
11. carat
12. lactose
13. dishcloth
14. disk
15. ladybug
16. gray
17. cagey
18. quartet
19. carom
20. corvette
21. question mark
22. décor
23. dietitian
24. kneecap
25. theater
26. sandbar
27. lodestar
28. reentry
29. hiccup
30. tillage

PARTS OF SPEECH

The words in your dictionary are classified according to their **part of speech.** Knowing a word's part of speech helps you understand its meaning.

n.	noun	*adj.*	adjective
pron.	pronoun	*adv.*	adverb
v.	verb	*prep.*	preposition
v.t.	transitive verb	*conj.*	conjunction
v.i.	intransitive verb	*interj.*	interjection

TRY THIS

Write each of these words. Then look up the word in your dictionary. Next to the word, write its part of speech. Some words can be more than one. Number 1 has been done for you.

1. fossil   n., adj.
2. simply
3. laze
4. necessary
5. spelunker
6. telltale
7. rifle
8. mouthful
9. throughout
10. swagger
11. hose
12. ill
13. however
14. jest
15. mode
16. into
17. far
18. seem
19. ouch
20. mistake

brick *n.* The house was made of brick.
      v.t. They bricked up a window.
      adj. It was a brick house.

DEFINITIONS

The most important single thing in a dictionary entry is the **definition.** The definition gives the meaning of the word.

TRY THIS

Open your dictionary to pages 938-939. Match the meanings on the left with the correct entry word from the box. Write each definition. Next to it, write the correct entry word. Number 1 has been done for you.

1. Thin, leafless part of a plant	tendril	tern
2. Collapsible shelter		tent
3. The tenderest part of beef		tendon
4. A sharp hooked nail		terrace
5. A web-footed sea bird		tepid
6. A muscle that stretches a part of the body		tenderloin
7. A strong band of tissue		tensor
8. Cone-shaped tent, usually of animal skin		tenpins
9. The name of an English poet		tenterhook
10. Slightly warm		tenure
11. The act of possessing something		tenor
12. A natural inclination		Tennyson,
13. A balcony of a house or apartment building		Alfred, Lord
14. The game of bowling		tendency
15. The highest male singing voice		tendril
		tepee

a. b. c. d.

Then look for an illustration of the entry word. Write the letter of the illustration next to the entry word. There are illustrations for four entries.

ILLUSTRATIVE EXAMPLES

Many definitions in your dictionary are followed by examples. The examples show you how the words are actually used. Examples sometimes tell you as much as the definition tells you.

TRY THIS Read the example sentences below. Choose a word from the left to complete each sentence. Write each sentence with the correct word in the blank. Number 1 has been done for you.

sleepy
springboard
glad
overflow
angry
nervous
empty
revise
dangerous
messy
pageant
careful

1. Matt was very ___angry___ when his little brother broke his toy truck.
2. The icy roads made driving very _____ .
3. The actor was _____ before he had to go on stage.
4. Ted threw away the _____ milk carton.
5. Sue was _____ that it stopped raining so she could go out to play.
6. Ellen was _____ because she stayed up late the night before.
7. Ray is a _____ worker who seldom makes a mistake.
8. Betty had to clean her room because it was very _____ .
9. She paused to wave before diving from the _____ .
10. I usually _____ my compositions before I hand them in.
11. We're having a _____ to celebrate the school's fiftieth anniversary.
12. The river will probably _____ its banks because of the spring rains.

"We need the treasurer's _____ before we can spend money for a picnic."

Which words might be used in the blank?

OK   disapproval   approval   agreement   happiness

P21

MULTIPLE MEANINGS

Many words in your dictionary have more than one meaning. Some words have more than twenty different meanings.

mint¹ (mint) *n.* **1.** any of a group of plants, such as the peppermint or spearmint, used as a flavoring or scent. **2.** a piece of candy flavored with mint. [Old English *minte*.] —**mint'y,** *adj.*

mint² (mint) *n.* **1.** a place where money is coined by the government. **2.** *Informal.* a very large amount of money: *Steve spent a mint getting his car repaired.* —*adj.* unused: *in mint condition, a mint stamp.* —*v.t.* **1.** to coin (money). **2.** to create or invent (a phrase or word). [Old English *mynet* a coin.]

TRY THIS

Each sentence below has a key word printed in heavy black type. Find the definition of the word that best fits the sentence. Write the number of the definition on a piece of paper. Number 1 has been done for you.

1. Ed baked a cake with chocolate **frosting.** 1
2. The students had to **dissect** a worm in biology.
3. The prisoner was kept in a **guarded** room.
4. The **fireman** rescued the child from the burning building.
5. Lions are **peculiar** to Africa.
6. The president of that company is a **czar** of the movie business.
7. Several windows at the school were broken by **vandals.**
8. Joan is a clothing **buyer** for a department store.
9. Alex is a **lineman** on the school football team.
10. Karen went to her doctor for a physical **examination.**
11. One **feature** of our program is after-school work experience.
12. The spaghetti sauce was too **hot** for our taste.
13. The **keynote** of the principal's speech was the need for a larger school library.
14. The poster announced the final tennis **match** in June.
15. We went on a tour of a printing **plant.**

SYNONYMS

Many words in your dictionary have the same or almost the same meaning as other words. These words are called **synonyms.**

TRY THIS Write the following entry words. Then find a synonym for each entry word in your dictionary. Write the synonyms next to the entry word. Number 1 has been done for you.

1. clear-headed alert	2. rude 1	3. tuneful
4. spectral 1	5. affectionate	6. gloomy 1
7. build 1	8. verse 1	9. accomplish
10. woe 2	11. gratify	12. generally 1
13. groundwork	14. horde	15. inform
16. lariat	17. lusty	18. mistake
19. possibly 2	20. recuperate	21. commence
22. frank[1]	23. futile	24. commonplace
25. grouchy	26. harm 1	27. indeed

fleet   **swift**

LABELS

Some of the definitions in your dictionary have **labels,** such as *Baseball, Chemistry,* or *Slang.* These labels tell you the way the word is used. For example, the label *Archaic* describes a word that is not commonly used today.

TRY THIS

Read these questions. Find the words in heavy black type in your dictionary. Answer the questions. Write the labels if you wish to.

1. Which meaning of **chemist** is used in Great Britain?
   druggist, British
2. Which meanings of **process** might a lawyer use often?
3. Which meaning of **pill** refers to a person?
4. Which definition of **test** is important in a laboratory?
5. What are the two meanings of **strike** in two different sports?
6. Which meaning of **pause** would be important to a singer?
7. Which meaning of **seed** is not often used today?
8. Which meaning of **horrible** is used in an informal way?
9. Which meaning of **positive** tells about pictures?
10. Which definition of **queen** would a chess player use?
11. Which meanings of **jump** are used in informal speech?
12. Which meanings of **intensive** are used in grammar?
13. Which meaning of **infernal** is used in informal speech?
14. Which noun meaning of **huddle** is used in football?
15. Which meaning of **hold** is used in music?

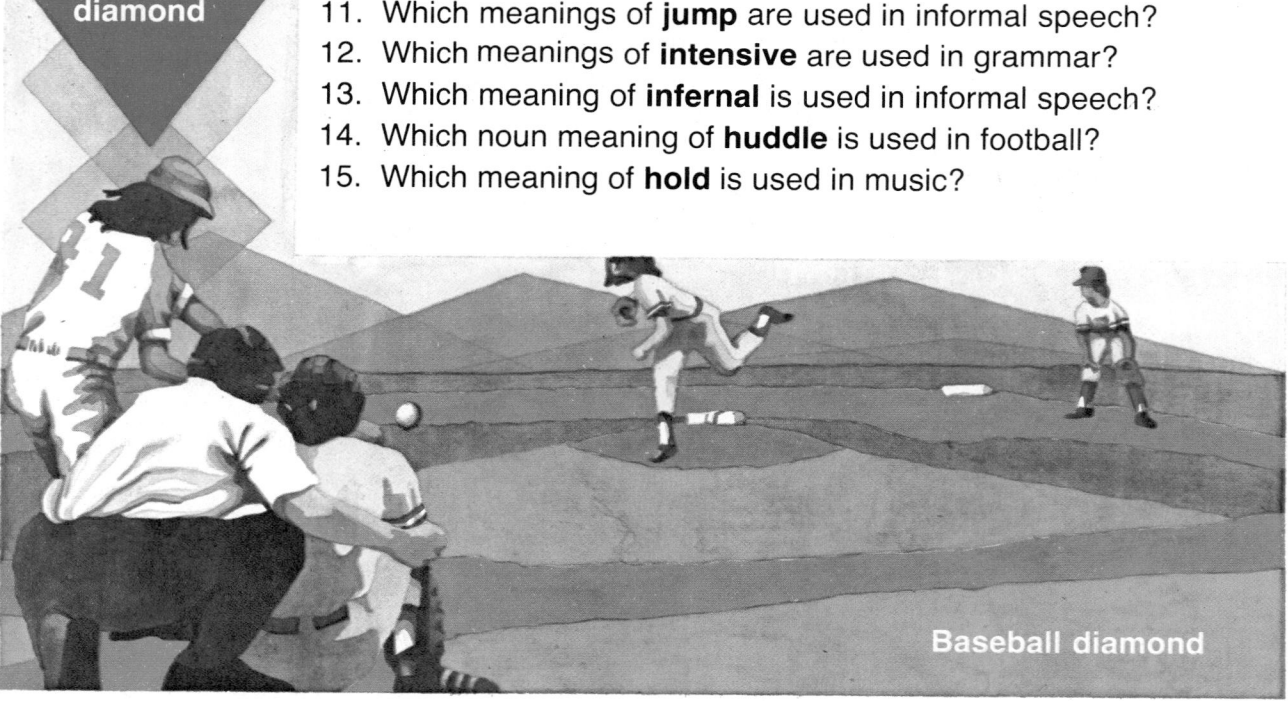

Geometry diamond

Baseball diamond

USAGE NOTES

At the end of some entries in your dictionary you will see a black triangle like this: (▲). This triangle means that a **usage note** follows. A usage note gives you special information about how to use a word correctly.

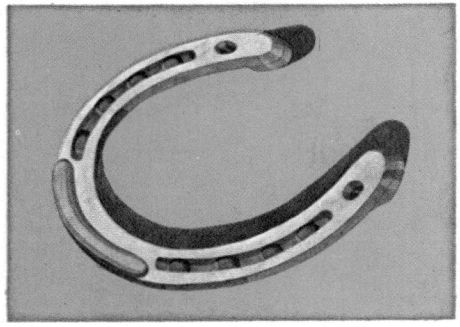

horse·shoe (hôrs′shoo′) *n.* **1.** a U-shaped piece of metal carved to fit the shape of a horse's hoof, attached by means of nails driven into the hard, horny, outer shell of the hoof. **2.** something shaped like a horseshoe. **3. horseshoes.** a game for two or more players in which the object is to pitch a U-shaped piece so that it encircles a stake, normally placed 40 feet away from the pitcher, or lands closest to the stake. ▲ used with a singular verb. —*v.t.*, **horse·shoed, horse·shoe·ing.** to provide with horseshoes.

TRY THIS

Each of the following questions deals with a usage note. The usage note can be found under the word printed in heavy black type. Answer the questions. Write your answers on a piece of paper. Number 1 has been done for you.

1. Here is a **double negative:** "He didn't have no money." Is this considered to be good English today?   No
2. Is it correct to say "Bob and **myself** are going fishing tomorrow"?
3. Which word is right? "The lack of rain will have a bad (**affect,** effect) on the crops."
4. Is **ain't** considered to be good English?
5. If someone says a nice thing to you, is this a "complement" or a "**compliment**"?
6. Which word is correct? "It (**don't,** doesn't) matter what happens now."
7. Which word is right? "Sarah is (disinterested, **uninterested**) in popular music."
8. Would a sailor call a large ocean liner a **"boat"** or a "ship"?
9. Does a lawyer **"persecute"** or "prosecute" a case in court?
10. Which is correct? "**Gymnastics** is a good sport." "**Gymnastics** are a good sport."
11. Which word is right? "We are (all ready, **already**) to go."

ETYMOLOGIES

At the end of some entries in your dictionary you will find information on where the word comes from. This information is called the word's **etymology.**

> **mile** (mīl) *n.* a unit of linear measure equal to 5280 feet or 1760 yards. [Going back to Latin *mīlia pas-suum* literally, a thousand paces.]

TRY THIS

Read the questions below. The answer to each one can be found in an etymology under the word printed in heavy black type. Write your answers. Number 1 has been done for you.

1. Where did the phrase **crocodile tears** come from?
   From the saying that crocodiles moaned to attract people and cried after eating them.
2. Where does the word **radar** come from?
3. How did the **hamburger** get its name?
4. The month of **March** is named after what god?
5. Where does the word **gardenia** come from?
6. How did the **Blackfoot** Indian tribe get its name?
7. What did Roman soldiers use their **salary** for?
8. What man gave his name to the word **boycott**?
9. How did the **Saint Bernard** get its name?
10. Who was **braille** named after?
11. Why would an ancient Roman **candidate** wear a white toga?
12. What did **dachshunds** once hunt?
13. Was a **silhouette** cheaper than a painted portrait?
14. Where was **cheddar** cheese first made?

P26

IDIOMS

Our language has certain words that have a special meaning when they are used together. These special phrases are called **idioms.** An idiom does not mean the same thing as the words in it would mean if they were used alone. For example, "watch your step" does not mean "look at your feet while you're walking."

TRY THIS

Read the sentences below. Then look under the key word printed in heavy black type. Find the idiom in the sentence and write it on a piece of paper. Number 1 has been done for you.

1. The two girls **hit** it off well and became good friends.
   to hit it off
2. Joe racked his **brains** trying to remember the answer.
3. Martha showed her brother how to **hook** up his record player.
4. Andy had to **pass** up a chance to go to the movies because he was sick.
5. Terry is **head** and shoulders above the other players.
6. Dad put his **foot** down and wouldn't let us go out.
7. Jack has his **hands** full caring for his brothers.
8. Robin would never **run** out on a job.
9. The team's performance **speaks** well for the coach.
10. Our principal plans to **step** down next spring.
11. Noisy conversation seems out of **place** in a library.
12. We'll **lead** off the concert with the school song.

LANGUAGE NOTES

At some places in your dictionary you will find a colored circle (●). This circle shows that what follows is a **language note.** Language notes give special information about interesting features of the English language.

TRY THIS

Look at the questions below. Find the answers in the language notes under the key words. They are printed in heavy black type. Write your answers. Number 1 has been done for you.

1. What was the first form of **writing**?   pictographs
2. Where does the name **Texas** come from?
3. Which one letter of the alphabet is used with greater **frequency** than the others?
4. What did the poet Carl Sandburg say about **slang**?
5. What are the five major languages that English **personal names** have come from?
6. How many words are estimated to have been in William Shakespeare's **vocabulary**?
7. Why are people sometimes called **language**-using animals?
8. When was the first real English **dictionary** published?
9. What animal has an American **Indian** name?
10. What is the meaning of the word that **D** comes from?
11. What does the **blend** "telecast" mean?
12. What is an **obsolete** word?

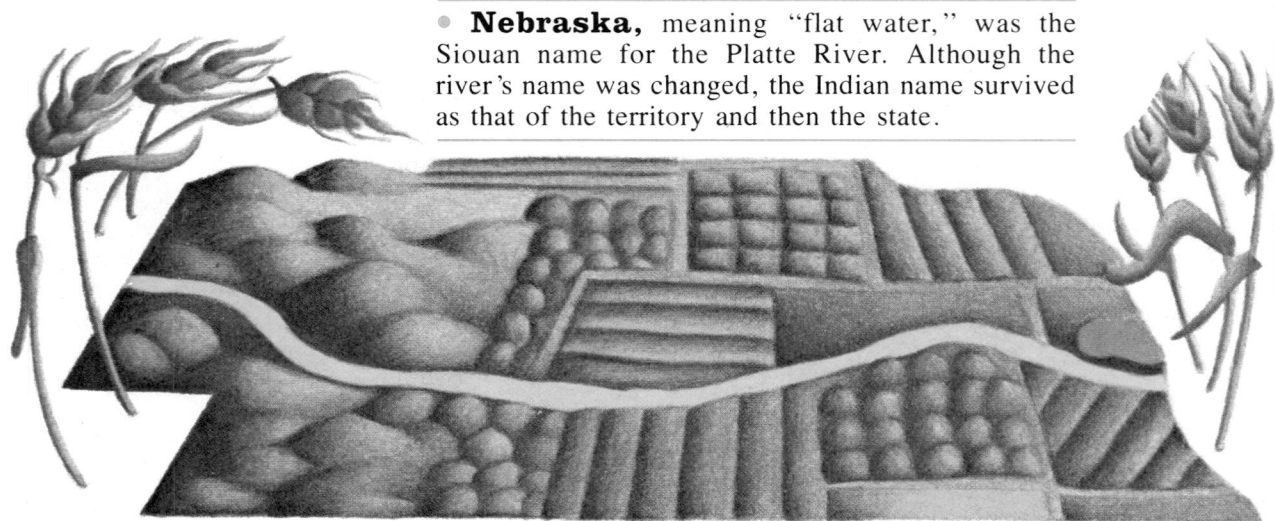

● **Nebraska,** meaning "flat water," was the Siouan name for the Platte River. Although the river's name was changed, the Indian name survived as that of the territory and then the state.

The **illustrations** in your dictionary are not put there to decorate the page. They are meant to give you more information about a word.

mole² (mōl) *n.* an animal that lives in underground burrows. Moles have long claws used for digging, very small eyes, a long, pointed snout, and velvety fur. [Middle English *molle*.]

What color is a ⌐.
⌐

TRY THIS

Read the questions below. Then look up ea⌐ black type. Answer the question by looking at ⌐rd printed in heavy answers. ⌐ture. Write your

1. What is a **rhea**?
2. Which has larger ears, an African or an Indian **eleph**⌐
3. Where would you find a **mizzen**?
4. Where do **peanuts** grow?
5. Where should you sit to paddle a **canoe**?
6. What is a **hammerhead**?
7. How many sides does a **hexagon** have?
8. Who would wear an **obi**?
9. Where in your body would you find a **radius**?
10. Where is the beard on a **wheat** plant?
11. Which is the largest type of **ant**?
12. What are the vertebrae of the **spinal column**?
13. What climate **zone** do you live in?
14. Which sail is set on the **mainmast** of a boat?
15. Where would you wear an **aqualung**?

REVIEW

The exercises in this book cover the skills needed to use your dictionary. Now that you have finished the exercises, this is a good time to go back over what you have learned.

TRY THIS

Look at page 789 of your dictionary. Then read the questions below. Can you find the answers to these questions? Write your answers on a piece of paper.

1. What are the guide words for this page?
2. What is definition 2 of **oil**?
3. Which spelling is correct, **rococo** or **rococoa**?
4. How do you divide **rodeo** into syllables?
5. What is the plural form of **roguery**?
6. There are two entries for the word **roe**. Which one would you find in a food another word for **Rocky Mountain sheep**?
7. Which entry on this page is a geographical entry?
8. What is the pronunciation of **roentgen**?
9. Where does the word **role** come from?
10. Which entry on this page is a biographical entry?
12. What is the variant for **Rocky Mountains**?
13. Which entry is listed as a transitive *and* an intransitive verb?
14. How is **Rocky Mountain spotted fever** transmitted?
15. Which entry from the right-hand column is a compound entry?

Sample page

Main entry — **cache** (kash) *n.* **1.** a hiding place, especially for provisions or treasure. **2.** something hidden or stored in such a place. —*v.t.*, **cached, cach·ing.** to hide or store in a cache.

Syllable division — **ca·jol·er·y** (kə jō′lər ē) *n.* *pl.,* **ca·jol·er·ies.** persuasion by flattery, soothing words, or false promises.

Pronunciation — **Cal·ais** (kal′ā) *n.* a port city on the northern coast of France. It is the continental European city closest to England.

Definition — **cal·i·for·ni·um** (kal′ə fôr′nē ə m) *n.* a man-made radioactive element first produced in 1950. Symbol: **Cf**

cal·la (kal′ə) *n.* any of several plants that bear tiny flowers on a spike inside a showy white or yellow spathe. Also, **calla lily.**

Variants — **cam·o·mile** (kam′ə mīl′) *also,* **cham·o·mile.** *n.* any of several strong-smelling plants found in temperate regions, having flowers that resemble the daisy. The flowers of certain species are dried and used to make tea.

Part of speech — **can·dle·light** (kand′əl līt′) *n.* **1.** the light given by a candle or candles. **2.** twilight; dusk; nightfall.

Inflected forms — **cap·size** (kap′sīz, kap sīz′) *v.,* **cap·sized, cap·siz·ing.** —*v.t.* to cause to overturn: *Rough waves capsized the boat.* —*v.i.* to overturn: *The boat capsized in the hurricane.*

car·go (kär′gō) *n.* *pl.,* **car·goes** or **car·gos.** the goods or merchandise carried by a ship, plane, or vehicle: *The freighter carried a cargo of rice.*

caus·al (kô′zəl) *adj.* of, indicating, or acting as a cause: *There is often a causal relationship between poor study habits and poor grades.* —**caus′al·ly,** *adv.*

Run-on entry —

Subject label — **cen·taur** (sen′tôr) *n.* *Greek Mythology.* one of a race of creatures having the head, arms, and torso of a man, and the body and legs of a horse.

Usage labels — **cheap·skate** (chēp′skāt′) *n.* *Informal.* a stingy person.

chem·ist (kem′ist) *n.* **1.** a person who is a student of or expert in chemistry. **2.** *British.* another word for **druggist.**

civ·ics (siv′iks) *n., pl.* the study of the function, services, and purpose of a government and of the duties, rights, and privileges of citizenship. ▲ used with a singular verb.

Usage note —

civil war 1. a war between two sections or groups within a country. **2.** **Civil War.** in the United States, the war between the North and the South from 1861 to 1865.

Subentry —

Illustration — **clar·i·net** (klar′ə net′) *n.* a musical instrument of the woodwind family, having a single-reed mouthpiece and played by means of finger holes and keys.